Ordnance Survey®

Gazetteer of Great Britain

FOURTH EDITION

All names from the 1:50 000 scale Landranger® maps

First edition published 1987
Second edition published 1989
Third edition published 1992
Fourth edition published 1999 by

ORDNANCE SURVEY
Romsey Road
SOUTHAMPTON
United Kingdom
SO16 4GU

and

MACMILLAN REFERENCE LTD
25 Eccleston Place, London, SW1W 9NF
and Basingstoke

Companies and representatives throughout the world.

http://www.macmillan-reference.co.uk

ISBN 0-333-770293

A catalogue record for this book is available from the British Library.

Compiled by Ordnance Survey

Cover Design by Diana Levy, Macmillan Reference Ltd.

Typeset by Tradespools Ltd, Frome, Somerset.

Printed and bound in the UK by
Antony Rowe Ltd, Chippenham, Wiltshire.

Contents

Figures

The Joy of Maps

As I sit at my window writing this I can look down at the valley below me and see it spread out, farms and fields, river and trees leading northwards to Sedburgh and the beautiful Howgill Fells. In a sense, it is my immediate world that lies below me and I know it from having walked its lanes and footpaths and wandered across its hills.

But my eye only allows me a limited vision. I can only see as far as the high hills that bound my horizon. To know what lies beyond them I turn to the shelf of books and maps that lies behind me and take down the maps. Now I will also be able to reach for this excellent Gazetteer with its wealth of names and information to complement my collection of Ordnance Survey maps. Then I can travel in my mind beyond the bounds of my valley northwards through the Lake district and on into Scotland, or, if I wished, southwards through the Yorkshire Dales National Park through Lancashire to the hills of North Wales.

It is this ability to travel in the imagination that has fascinated me since I was a child. When I appeared on Desert Island Discs I was asked what book apart from The Works of Shakespeare and the Bible I would take with me. I was a bit cheeky and asked for two things, a set of A W Wainwright's walking books and complete set of the 1:50 000 scale Ordnance Survey Landranger maps. Alone on the desert island I could at least travel in my mind through the countryside I loved.

That is one joy I have found in maps. Another comes from being able to use a map to navigate through strange territory. A map, like a book, gives you all the clues you need to find your way through a landscape that is new to you.

The Landranger maps with footpaths and bridleways clearly marked are exactly what you need, as are the 1:25 000 scale Pathfinder®, Explorer™ and Outdoor Leisure™ maps which also include field boundary and fence line detail. If like me you go walking, then all these maps make finding your way around the countryside as easy as reading a book.

Using the map as an aid to navigation also means that you can read the landscape as you go. A look at the map tells you that the hump ahead of you on the rise is a bronze age tumulus or that the old stone stump at the road edge is the remains of a Celtic cross. Patterns of settlement appear on the map, churches and factories and old watermills so that we can learn about the past and present of a landscape as we're travelling through it. The map is our key to understanding the land. In high hills and in remote places the map is sometimes our only lifeline and our only guide; without it we are ignorant and lost.

This gazetteer is a key to unlock the wealth of detail included on Ordnance Survey Landranger maps and to help get more information and pleasure from them. I never tire of looking at maps particularly of areas I have walked or cycled. They tell me what I have seen and spur me on to plan other journeys for the future.

Mike Harding
Former Vice-President, The Ramblers Association

Ordnance Survey

Ordnance Survey is Great Britain's national mapping agency. Founded in 1791, it continues to be responsible for the official surveying and topographic mapping of England, Scotland and Wales – including associated geodetic surveys and scientific work.

Ordnance Survey produces and publishes maps and geographical information both in paper form and as computer data. The largest scale mapping is at 1:1250 scale (about 50 inches to 1 mile), which is so detailed it shows the shapes of individual buildings and follows the kerblines of roads. There are many intermediate scales of published mapping, at progressively smaller scales, right down to individual wall maps or data for every business, administrative, leisure or educational need.

Among the smaller scales of mapping, the 'flagship' is the Landranger map series, with 204 sheets covering the entire country from the Shetland Isles to the Isles of Scilly. It is Britain's most popular map series, with around two million copies sold every year. This Gazetteer, which lists and pinpoints every name included on the entire series of Landranger maps, is part of the Ordnance Survey small-scale product range.

Landranger maps

1:50 000 scale (2 cm to 1 km or 1¼ inches to 1 mile)

Figure 1 shows the layout of sheets and their numbers. Sheet titles are listed on page ix. Each Landranger map covers an area 40 km by 40 km (25 miles by 25 miles).

Information

Ordnance Survey products are available from a wide range of retail outlets worldwide or direct from Ordnance Survey.

Our Customer Information HelpLine provides customers with details of products, services and general information relating to the mapping and geography of Great Britain. The HelpLine operates from 8.30am to 5.00pm Monday to Friday.

Phone:	08456 05 05 05
Fax:	01703 792452
E-mail:	custinfo@ordsvy.gov.uk
World Wide Web:	http:// www.ordsvy.gov.uk

or write to :

Customer Information,
Ordnance Survey,
Romsey Road,
SOUTHAMPTON,
United Kingdom, SO16 4GU

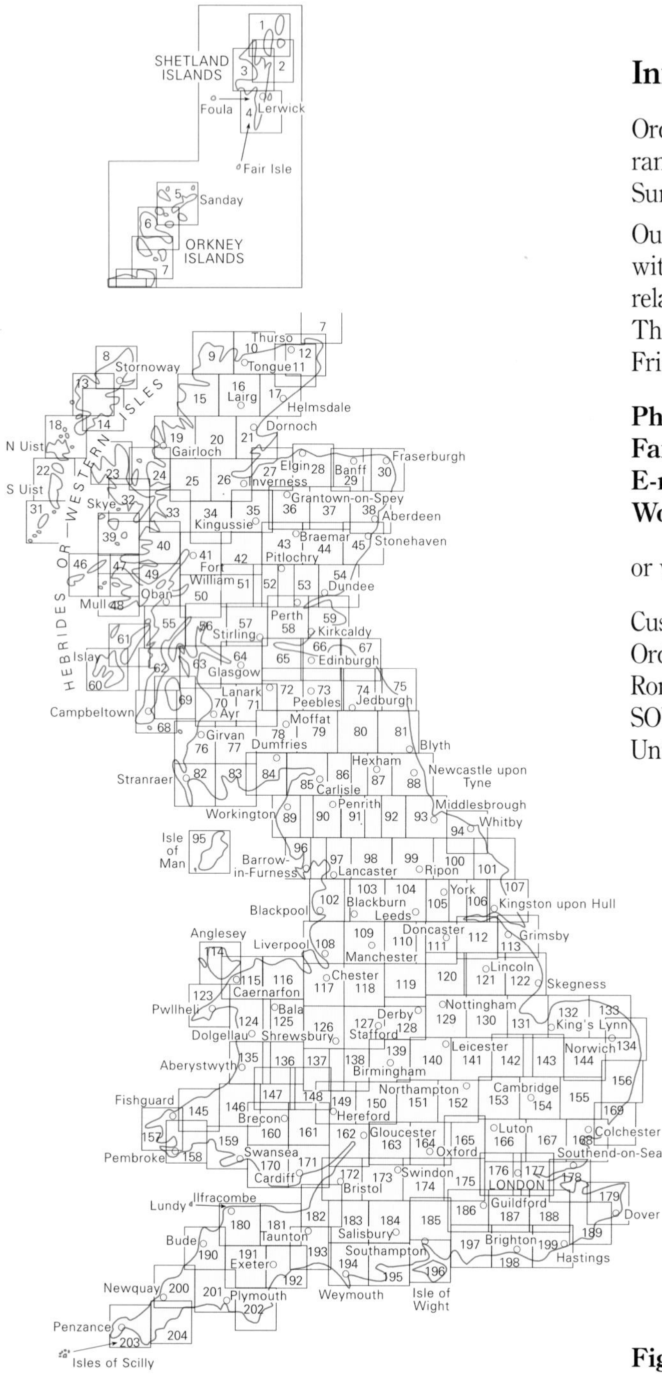

Figure 1. Index to Landranger map series

Landranger Maps

Sheet numbers and names for Figure 1

1 Shetland
Yell, Unst & Fetlar
2 Shetland
Sullom Voe & Whalsay
3 Shetland
North Mainland
4 Shetland
South Mainland
5 Orkney
Northern Isles
6 Orkney
Mainland
7 Orkney
Southern Isles
8 Stornoway & North Lewis
Steornabhagh agus
Ceann a Tuath Leodhais
9 Cape Wrath
Durness & Scourie
10 Strathnaver
Bettyhill & Tongue
11 Thurso & Dunbeath
12 Thurso & Wick
John O'Groats
13 West Lewis & North Harris
Taobh Siar Leòdhais agus
Ceann a Tuath na Haeradh
14 Tarbert & Loch Seaforth
An Tairbeart agus
Loch Shiphoirt
15 Loch Assynt
Lochinver & Kylesku
16 Lairg & Loch Shin
Loch Naver
17 Helmsdale & Strath of Kildonan
18 Sound of Harris & St Kilda
Caolas na Hearadh agus Hiort
19 Gairloch & Ullapool
Loch Maree
20 Beinn Dearg & Loch Broom
Ben Wyvis
21 Dornoch & Alness
Invergordon & Tain
22 Benbecula & South Uist
Beinn na Faoghla agus Uibhist a Deas
23 North Skye
Dunvegan & Portree
24 Raasay & Applecross
Loch Torridon & Plockton
25 Glen Carron & Glen Afric
26 Inverness & Loch Ness
Strathglass
27 Nairn & Forres
River Findhorn
28 Elgin & Dufftown
Buckie & Keith
29 Banff & Huntley
Portsoy & Turriff
30 Fraserburgh
Peterhead & Ellon
31 Barra & South Uist
Vatersay & Eriskay
Barraigh agus Uibhist a Deas
Bhatarsaigh agus Eiriosgaigh
32 South Skye & Cuillin Hills
33 Loch Alsh, Glen Shiel & Loch Hourn
34 Fort Augustus
Glen Albyn & Glen Roy
35 Kingussie & Monadhliath Mountains
36 Grantown & Aviemore
Cairngorm Mountains
37 Strathdon & Alford
38 Aberdeen
Inverurie & Pitmedden
39 Rùm, Eigg & Muck
40 Mallaig & Glenfinnan
Loch Shiel
41 Ben Nevis
Fort William & Glen Coe
42 Glen Garry & Loch Rannoch
43 Braemar & Blair Atholl
44 Ballater & Glen Clova
45 Stonehaven & Banchory
46 Coll & Tiree
47 Tobermory & North Mull
48 Iona & West Mull
Ulva
49 Oban & East Mull
50 Glen Orchy & Loch Etive
51 Loch Tay & Glen Dochart
52 Pitlochry & Crieff
Aberfeldy
53 Blairgowrie & Forest of Alyth
54 Dundee & Montrose
Forfar & Arbroath
55 Lochgilphead & Loch Awe
56 Loch Lomond & Inveraray
57 Stirling & The Trossachs
58 Perth & Alloa
Auchterarder
59 St Andrews
Kirkcaldy & Glenrothes
60 Islay
61 Jura & Colonsay

How to use the gazetteer

This gazetteer comprises some 258 000 names taken from the Landranger map series. The names are listed strictly in alphabetical order across the whole country. They are not subdivided into regions or county blocks. Each name entry contains the following information.

Entry example – Houses of Parliament	C of West	TQ 3097	51° 29.9′	0° 07.2′W	X	176 177
1	2	3	4		5	6

1 Name – The distinctive place/feature name which refers to a specific place or feature, not to a description. For example, London is a distinctive name, Durley Mill is a distinctive name. Mill on its own, however, is descriptive and therefore does not appear in the gazetteer, although many such examples appear on Landranger maps.

2 County or Unitary Authority – The county or unitary authority name (sometimes abbreviated) in which the place or feature lies. A list of abbreviations appears on page xvii.

3 National Grid reference – The National Grid reference comprising two letters and four figures, identifying the location of the named place or feature to within 1.4 kilometres. An explanation of the National Grid reference system is given on page xiv.

4 Latitude and longitude – The latitude and longitude to 0.1 of a minute of the centre point of the National Grid square (1 km x 1 km) in which the named feature lies. A brief explanation of latitude and longitude is given
on page xv.

5 Feature Code –

- A = Antiquity (non Roman)
- F = Forest or other wooded area
- FM = Farm
- H = Hill or mountain
- R = Antiquity (Roman)
- T = City, town, village and so on
- W = Water feature (river, lake and so on)
- X = All other features.

6 Sheet Number – The sheet number(s) of the Landranger map(s) on which the named place or feature appears. Because map sheets overlap, a place or feature can appear on more than one Landranger. Figure 1 (page viii) shows the layout of Landranger maps.

Figure 2. Houses of Parliament, National Grid reference TQ 3079

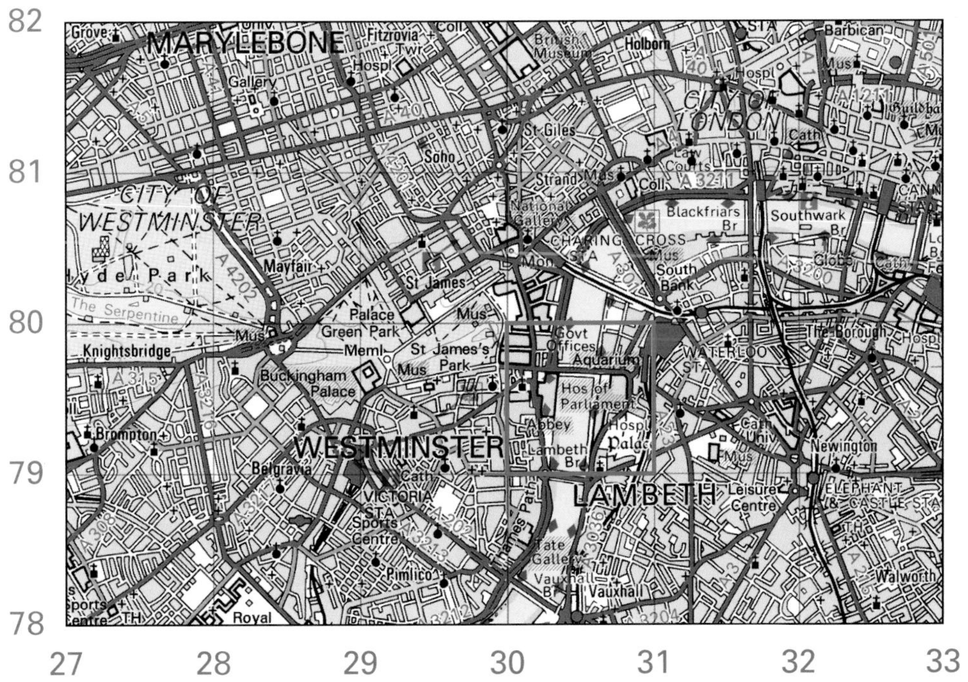

Ordnance Survey National Grid reference system

The National Grid is a reference system of squares overprinted on all Ordnance Survey maps since the 1940s. The system of breaking the country down into squares allows any place in the country to be given a unique reference code.

The squares of the basic grid cover a ground area of 100 km x 100 km ($62\frac{1}{2}$ miles x $62\frac{1}{2}$ miles) and are identified by letters SS, ST, SU and so on (see Figure 3).

These squares are subdivided into smaller units which on Landranger maps cover a ground area of 1 km x 1 km ($\frac{5}{8}$ mile x $\frac{5}{8}$ mile). These smaller squares are identified by the numbers of the grid lines which define their southern and western boundaries. A National Grid reference for a place or feature will always be the same no matter which Ordnance Survey map you use but it is essential always to quote National Grid letters as well as numbers. National Grid references can be given to varying degrees of precision relative to the map scale. In the case of Landranger maps references can be given to two letters and *four* numbers which identifies the south west corner of the grid square in which the particular place or feature lies or to two letters and *six* numbers which pinpoints the location of the place or feature within that grid square.

Each name entry in this gazetteer includes a National Grid reference made up of two letters and four numbers. This reference is for the 1 km x 1 km grid square in which the named place or feature lies. This reference will also apply to other places or features which fall within that square. The following example identifies how these references are constructed.

The Houses of Parliament in London have a National Grid reference – TQ 3079 (see Figure 2).

TQ – These letters identify the 100 km grid square in which the Houses of Parliament fall and appear on Ordnance Survey maps. Figure 3 shows the arrangement of these squares across the country. 100 km squares are subdivided into 1 km squares by grid lines, each line being identified by a two-figure number. These grid lines and numbers also appear on Ordnance Survey maps.

3079 – This four-figure reference pinpoints the south west corner of the 1 km grid square in which the Houses of Parliament are located and is constructed as follows:

30 – Is the reference for one of the grid lines running north/south on the 100 km grid square (see Figure 4). This number can be found in the top and bottom margins of the relevant Ordnance Survey map sheet(s); Landranger 176 or 177 in the case of the Houses of Parliament.

79 – Is the reference of one of the grid lines running east/west across the 100 km grid square (see Figure 4). This number can be found in the left and right hand margins of the relevant Ordnance Survey map sheet(s); Landranger 176 or 177 in the case of the Houses of Parliament.

Figure 3. Diagram showing 100 kilometre grid squares and the letters used to designate them

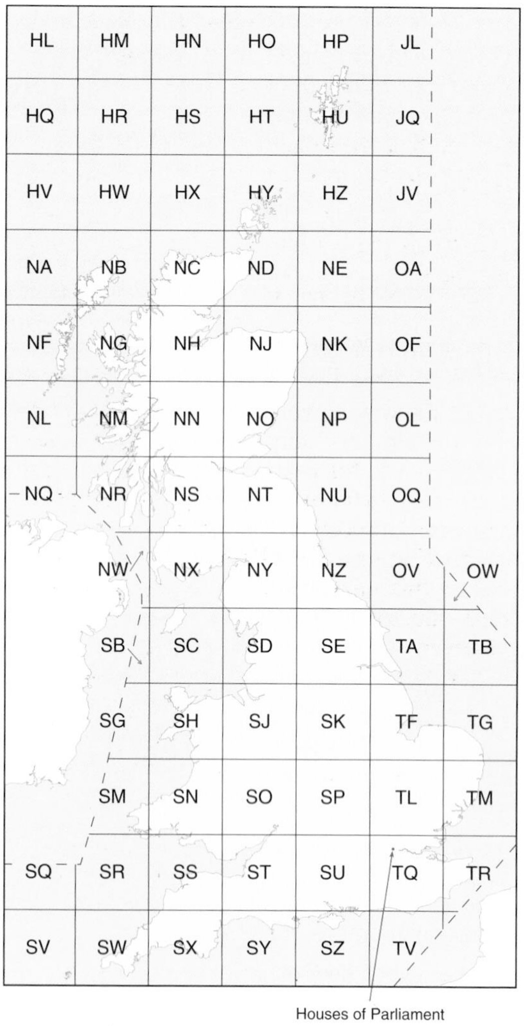

Figure 4. Part of 100 kilometre grid square TQ

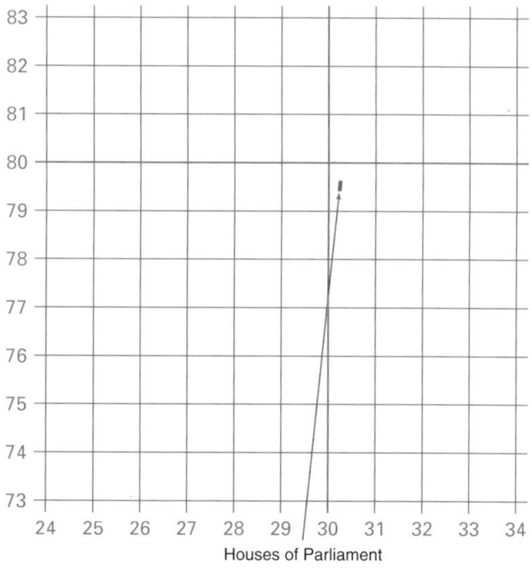

Latitude and longitude

Aside from the National Grid reference system, latitude and longitude will also provide a unique map reference. Latitude and longitude however, unlike National Grid references, are not restricted to Great Britain but can be applied to any place or feature in the world. In this gazetteer however, we are only concerned with latitude and longitude within Great Britain.

Latitude and longitude are imaginary lines which follow the curve of the earth's surface from east to west and from north to south (see Figure 5). In this respect they differ from National Grid lines which refer to a flat surface. Lines of latitude encircle the earth in parallel, the longest of which is the Equator. The Equator is the 'zero' line of latitude to which all others are referenced. All points on the earth's surface are said to be so many degrees, minutes and seconds north or south of the Equator and may be shown on the map as, for example, 31° 11′ 15′′N or 27° 14′ 21′′S.

Lines of longitude all pass through the north and south poles and fan out towards the Equator creating an effect like segments of an orange. The 'zero' line of longitude – or meridian – to which all others are referenced is that which passes through the Greenwich Observatory near London. All points on the earth's surface are said to be so many degrees, minutes and seconds east or west of the Greenwich Meridian and may be shown on the map as, for example, 5° 16′ 26′′E or 23° 07′ 03′′W.

Therefore by giving the reference of the lines of latitude and longitude on which a place or feature lies, its precise location can be identified on a map where the two lines intersect.

Because of the way in which the National Grid references were recorded for this Gazetteer – that is, to the south west corner of the 1 km grid square in which the feature lies – their mathematical conversions to latitude and longitude have been calculated to the centre of the grid square in order to minimise discrepancies between the two systems. The values are given to 0.1 of a minute (′), but the precise latitude and longitude of the named place or feature can be up to 0.6 minutes of latitude and 0.3 minutes of longitude from the Gazetteer position. The letter 'N' after latitude values has been omitted because Great Britain and its offshore islands lie north of the Equator and therefore all latitude references included in this gazetteer may be assumed to be 'N'. Because Great Britain straddles the Greenwich Meridian, longitude values may be east or west of Greenwich and therefore 'E' or 'W' is included with all longitude references in this gazetteer.

Thus, the latitude and longitude references given for the Houses of Parliament are 51° 29.9′ 0° 07.2′W. The intersection of these two lines falls in the centre of National Grid square TQ 3079 (see Figure 6). On the Landranger map, the Houses of Parliament actually lie 5mm from this intersection or approximately 250 metres on the ground. Some names in the gazetteer may be slightly further away from the intersection of their latitude and longitude references quoted but all will be within 16mm on the Landranger map which is equivalent to 800 metres on the ground.

Lines of latitude are marked at intervals of one minute on the black frame line which is printed in the left and right margins of all Landranger maps. They are also annotated with values at five minute intervals (See Figure 7). Lines of longitude are marked at intervals of one minute on the black frame line which is printed in the top and bottom margins of all Landranger maps. They are also annotated with values at five minute intervals (See Figure 7).

The intersection of lines of latitude and longitude are shown on the body of Landranger maps generally at five minute intervals (See Figure 7). By joining up the points of intersection across the face of the map the curve of these imaginary lines as they follow the surface of the earth can be seen.

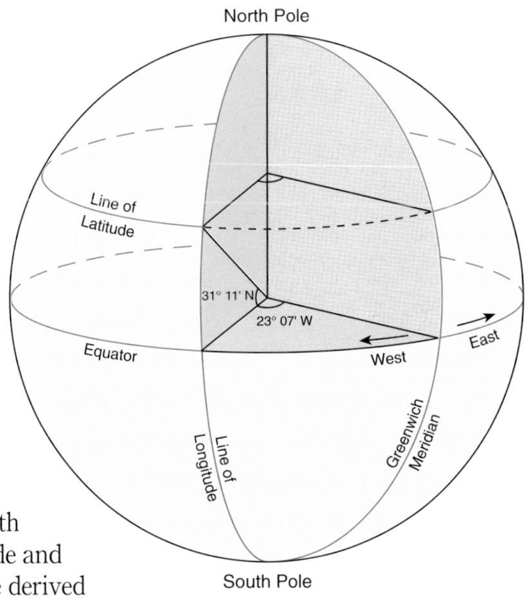

Figure 5. Diagram of the Earth showing how latitude and longitude angles are derived

Figure 6. Latitude and longitude reference for the Houses of Parliament

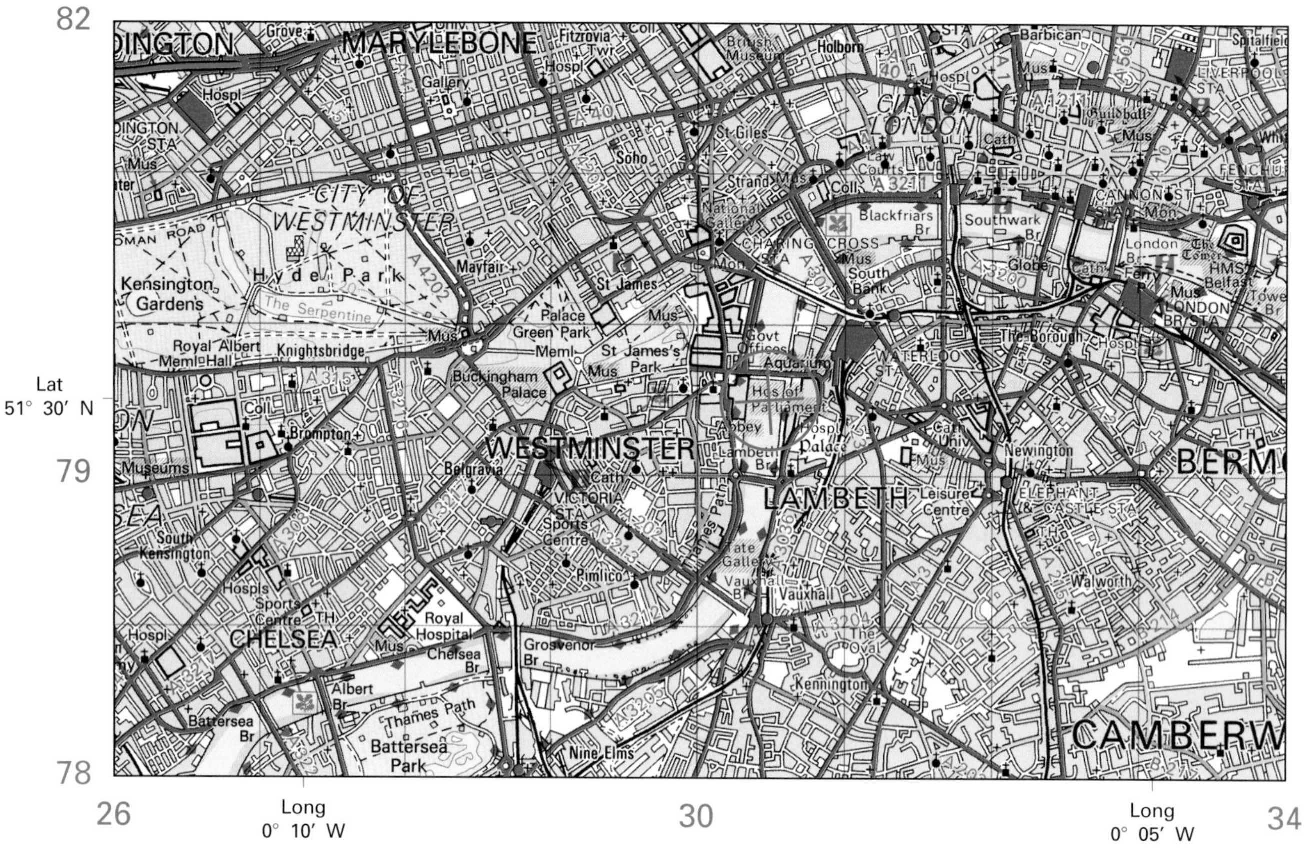

Figure 7. Latitude and longitude intersections and values as shown on Landranger maps

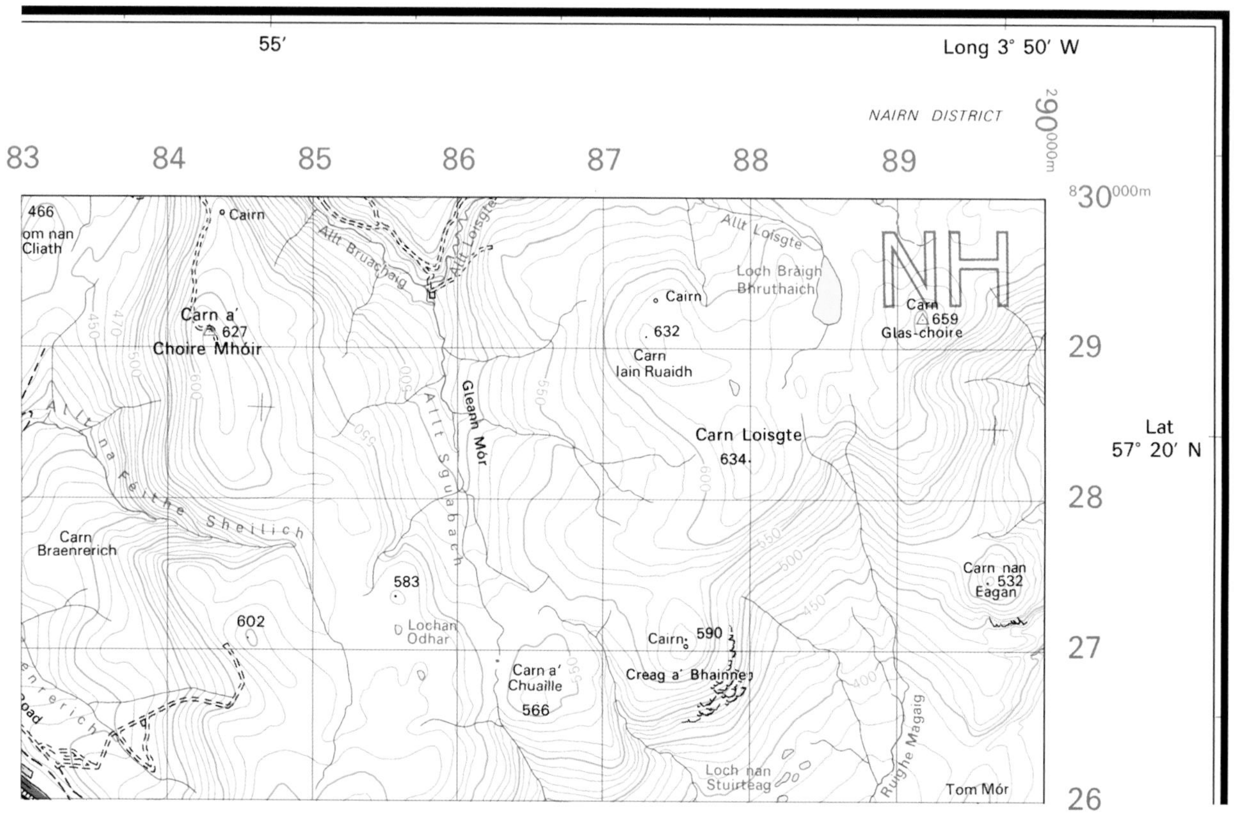

County and Unitary Authority abbreviations

Full Name	Abbreviation
Aberdeenshire	Aberd
Angus	Angus
Argyll and Bute	Arg & Bt
Barking & Dagenham	Bark & Dag
Barnet	Barnet
Barnsley	Barns
Bath and North East Somerset	Bath & NE Somer
Bedfordshire	Beds
Bexley	Bexley
Birmingham	Birm
Blackburn with Darwen	Black w Dar
Blackpool	Blackp
Blaenau Gwent	Blae Gw
Bolton	Bolton
Bournemouth	Bourne
Bracknell Forest	Brackn
Bradford	Brad
Brent	Brent
Bridgend	Brig
Brighton and Hove	Bri & Hov
Bromley	Brom
Buckinghamshire	Bucks
Bury	Bury
Caerphilly	Caer
Calderdale	Cald
Cambridgeshire	Cambs
Camden	Camden
Cardiff	Card
Carmarthenshire	Carm
Ceredigion	Cered
Cheshire	Ches
City of Aberdeen	C of Aber
City of Bristol	C of Bris
City of Derby	C of Derb
City of Dundee	C of Dun
City of Edinburgh	C of Edin
City of Glasgow	C of Glas
City of Kingston upon Hull	K upon H
City of Leicester	C of Leic
City of London	C of Lon
City of Nottingham	C of Nott
City of Peterborough	Peterb
City of Plymouth	C of Plym
City of Portsmouth	C of Port
City of Southampton	C of Soton
City of Stoke-on-Trent	C of Stoke
City of Westminster	C of West
Clackmannan	Clackm
Conwy	Conwy
Cornwall	Corn
Coventry	Cov
Croydon	Croy
Cumbria	Cumbr
Darlington	Darl
Denbighshire	Denb
Derbyshire	Derby
Devon	Devon
Doncaster	Donc
Dorset	Dorset
Dudley	Dudley
Dumfries and Galloway	D & G
Durham	Durham
Ealing	Ealing
East Ayrshire	E Ayr
East Dunbartonshire	E Dunb
East Lothian	E Loth
East Renfrewshire	E Renf
East Riding of Yorkshire	E Yorks
East Sussex	E Susx
Enfield	Enf
Essex	Essex
Falkirk	Falk
Fife	Fife
Flintshire	Flint
Gateshead	Ghead
Gloucestershire	Glos
Greenwich	Gren
Gwynedd	Gwyn
Hackney	Hack
Halton	Halton
Hammersmith & Fulham	Ham & Ful
Hampshire	Hants
Haringey	Hargy
Harrow	Harrow
Hartlepool	Hartpl
Havering	Hav
Herefordshire	Heref
Hertfordshire	Herts
Highland	Highld
Hillingdon	Hill
Hounslow	Houns
Inverclyde	Inverc
Isle of Anglesey	I of Angl
Isle of Man	I of M
Isle of Wight	I of W
Isles of Scilly	I Scilly
Islington	Isling
Kent	Kent
Kingston upon Thames	King
Kirklees	Kirk
Knowsley	Know
Lambeth	Lam
Lancashire	Lancs
Leeds	Leeds

Leicestershire	Leic	Sheffield	Sheff
Lewisham	Lew	Shetland Islands	Shetld
Lincolnshire	Lincs	Shropshire	Shrops
Liverpool	Liv	Slough	Slough
Luton	Luton	Solihull	Sol
Manchester	Man	Somerset	Somer
Medway	Medway	South Ayrshire	S Ayr
Merthyr Tydfil	Merth Tyd	South Gloucestershire	S Glos
Merton	Merton	South Lanarkshire	S Lanak
Middlesborough	Midd	South Tyneside	S Tyne
Midlothian	Midlo	Southend-on-Sea	Sou-on-Sea
Milton Keynes	Mil Key	Southwark	Sthwk
Monmouthshire	Monm	St Helens	St Hel
Moray	Moray	Staffordshire	Staffs
Na h-Eileanan an Iar	N Eil	Stirling	Stir
Neath Port Talbot	Nth Pt Talb	Stockport	Stock
Newcastle upon Tyne	N upon Ty	Stockton on Tees	Stock on T
Newham	Newham	Suffolk	Suff
Newport	Newp	Sunderland	Sund
Norfolk	Norf	Surrey	Surrey
North Ayrshire	N Ayr	Sutton	Sutton
North East Lincolnshire	NE Lincs	Swansea	Swan
North Lanarkshire	N Lanak	Swindon	Swin
North Lincolnshire	N Lincs	Tameside	Tames
North Somerset	N Som	The Vale of Glamorgan	V of Glam
North Tyneside	N Tyne	The Wrekin	Wrekin
North Yorkshire	N Yks	Thurrock	Thurr
Northamptonshire	Northnts	Torbay	Torbay
Northumberland	Northum	Torfaen	Torf
Nottinghamshire	Notts	Tower Hamlets	T Ham
Oldham	Oldham	Trafford	Traf
Orkney Islands	Orkney	Wakefield	Wakf
Oxfordshire	Oxon	Walsall	Wals
Pembrokeshire	Pemb	Waltham Forest	Wal F
Perth and Kinross	Pth & Kin	Wandsworth	Wan
Poole	Poole	Warrington	Warr
Powys	Powys	Warwickshire	Warw
Reading	Read	West Berkshire	W Berks
Redbridge	Redbr	West Dunbartonshire	W Dunb
Redcar & Cleveland	Red & Cl	West Lothian	W Loth
Renfrewshire	Renf	West Sussex	W Susx
Rhondda, Cynon, Taff	Rho Cyn Taf	Wigan	Wigan
Richmond upon Thames	Rich	Wiltshire	Wilts
Rochdale	Roch	Windsor and Maidenhead	Win & Maid
Rotherham	Roth	Wirral	Wirral
Royal Borough of Kensington & Chelsea	Ken & Ch	Wokingham	Wok
Rutland	Rut	Wolverhampton	Wolv
Salford	Salf	Worcestershire	Worcs
Sandwell	Sand	Wrexham	Wrex
Scottish Borders	Scot Bord	York	York
Sefton	Sefton		

GAZETTEER ENTRIES

A

Aalie, The	Shetld	HU3192	60°36·9'	1°25·5'W	X	1
Aaron Crags	Cumbr	NY2210	54°29·0'	3°11·8'W	X	89
Aaron Hill	Cald	SE0123	53°42·4'	1°58·7'W	X	104
Aaron's Hill	Somer	ST7434	51°6·5'	2°21·9'W	X	183
Aaron's Hill	Surrey	SU9543	51°10·9'	0°38·1'W	T	186
Aaron Slack	Cumbr	NY2110	54°29·0'	3°12·7'W	X	89,90
Aaron's Town	Cumbr	NY5360	54°56·2'	2°43·6'W	X	86
Aa Sean Chaisteal	Arg & Bt	NM5549	56°34·4'	5°58·9'W	X	47,48
Aa Skerry	Shetld	HU3142	60°9·9'	1°26·0'W	X	4
Aa Skerry	Shetld	HU3627	60°1·8'	1°20·7'W	X	4
Aaskerry Taing	Shetld	HU3143	60°10·5'	1°26·0'W	X	4
Aastack	Shetld	HP4704	60°43·2'	1°7·8'W	X	1
Aastack	Shetld	HU4596	60°39·0'	1°10·1'W	X	1
Aastack Geo	Shetld	HP4704	60°43·2'	1°7·8'W	X	1
Abbainn Chro Bheinn	Highld	NM4865	56°42·8'	6°6·6'W	W	47
Abbanoy	Renf	NS4062	55°49·7'	4°32·8'W	X	64
Abban Water	Highld	NH6038	57°24·9'	4°19·4'W	W	26
Abbas Combe	Somer	ST7022	51°0·0'	2°25·3'W	T	183
Abbas Hall	Suff	TL9040	52°1·8'	0°46·6'E	A	155
Abberd Brook	Wilts	SU0172	51°27·1'	1°58·7'W	W	173
Abberley	Worcs	SO7467	52°18·3'	2°22·5'W	T	138,150
Abberley Hall	Worcs	SO7466	52°17·7'	2°22·5'W	X	138,150
Abberley Hill	Worcs	SO7667	52°18·3'	2°20·7'W	H	138,150
Abberton	Essex	TM0019	51°50·2'	0°54·6'E	T	168
Abberton	Worcs	SO9953	52°10·8'	2°0·5'W	T	150
Abberton Manor	Essex	TL9919	51°50·3'	0°53·7'E	X	168
Abberton Reservoir	Essex	TL9718	51°49·8'	0°51·9'E	W	168
Abberwick	Northum	NU1213	55°24·9'	1°48·2'W	X	81
Abberwick Mill	Northum	NU1214	55°25·4'	1°48·2'W	X	81
Abberwick Village	Northum	NU1213	55°24·9'	1°48·2'W	A	81
Abbess End	Essex	TL5711	51°46·8'	0°17·0'E	T	167
Abbess Roding	Essex	TL5711	51°46·8'	0°17·0'E	T	167
Abbey	Cumbr	NY1729	54°39·2'	3°16·8'W	X	89,90
Abbey	Devon	ST1410	50°53·2'	3°13·0'W	T	192,193
Abbey	D & G	NX9580	55°6·5'	3°38·3'W	X	78
Abbey	Pth & Kin	NN9522	56°23·0'	3°41·6'W	X	52,53,58
Abbey Bank	Derby	SK1791	53°25·2'	1°44·2'W	X	110
Abbey Barn	Dorset	SY5785	50°40·0'	2°36·1'W	A	194
Abbey Barn Fm	Bucks	SU8791	51°36·9'	0°44·2'W	FM	175
Abbey Brook	Sheff	SK1992	53°25·7'	1°42·4'W	W	110
Abbey Burn	D & G	NX7386	55°9·4'	3°59·2'W	W	77
Abbey Burn	D & G	NX7449	54°49·5'	3°57·3'W	W	83,84
Abbey Burn	Scot Bord	NT8965	55°52·9'	2°10·1'W	W	67
Abbey Burn	S Lanak	NS9253	55°45·8'	3°42·8'W	W	65,72
Abbey Burn Foot	D & G	NX7444	54°46·8'	3°57·1'W	X	83,84
Abbey Chase	Surrey	TQ0567	51°23·8'	0°29·1'W	X	176
Abbey Close	N Yks	NZ2103	54°25·6'	1°40·2'W	X	93
Abbey Cott	Northum	NU1714	55°25·4'	1°43·5'W	X	81
Abbey Cottage	Denb	SJ2044	52°59·5'	3°11·1'W	X	117
Abbey Cowper	Cumbr	NY1550	54°50·5'	3°19·0'W	X	85
Abbey Craig	Stir	NS8195	56°8·2'	3°54·5'W	X	57
Abbeycroft Down	Dorset	ST9505	50°50·9'	2°3·9'W	X	195
Abbey Cwmhir	Powys	SO0571	52°20·0'	3°23·3'W	A	136,147
Abbeycwmhir	Powys	SO0571	52°20·0'	3°23·3'W	T	136,147
Abbeydale	Glos	SO8616	51°50·8'	2°11·8'W	T	162
Abbeydale	Sheff	SK3282	53°20·3'	1°30·8'W	T	110,111
Abbeydale Park	Sheff	SK3180	53°19·2'	1°31·7'W	T	110,111
Abbey Dore	Heref	SO3830	51°58·1'	2°53·8'W	T	149,161
Abbey Fell	D & G	NX9361	54°56·2'	3°39·8'W	H	84
Abbeyfield	Ches	SJ4766	53°11·5'	2°47·2'W	X	117
Abbey Field	Essex	TL9924	51°53·0'	0°53·9'E	T	168
Abbey Field Fm	Norf	TF7012	52°41·0'	0°31·3'E	FM	132,143
Abbeyfields	Ches	SJ7460	53°8·4'	2°22·9'W	X	118
Abbey Flatts	Cumbr	NY0018	54°33·1'	3°32·3'W	X	89
Abbey Fm	Beds	SP9451	52°9·2'	0°37·2'W	FM	153
Abbey Fm	Beds	TL1143	52°4·7'	0°22·4'W	FM	153
Abbey Fm	Cambs	TL1982	52°25·6'	0°14·6'W	FM	142
Abbey Fm	Cambs	TL2180	52°24·5'	0°12·9'W	FM	142
Abbey Fm	Cambs	TL4364	52°15·6'	0°6·1'E	FM	154
Abbey Fm	Cambs	TL4843	52°4·2'	0°10·0'E	FM	154
Abbey Fm	Carm	SN5019	51°51·2'	4°10·3'W	FM	159
Abbey Fm	C of Stoke	SJ9049	53°2·5'	2°8·5'W	FM	118
Abbey Fm	Denb	SJ0277	53°17·1'	3°27·8'W	FM	116
Abbey Fm	Essex	TL5237	52°0·9'	0°13·3'E	FM	154
Abbey Fm	E Yorks	TA0250	53°56·4'	0°26·4'W	FM	106,107
Abbey Fm	Heref	SO2737	52°1·8'	3°3·5'W	FM	161
Abbey Fm	Leic	SK5401	52°36·5'	1°11·8'W	FM	140
Abbey Fm	Lincs	TF0873	53°14·8'	0°22·5'W	FM	121
Abbey Fm	Lincs	TF1170	53°13·2'	0°19·8'W	FM	121
Abbey Fm	Lincs	TF1766	53°10·9'	0°14·5'W	FM	121
Abbey Fm	Lincs	TF2440	52°56·8'	0°8·9'W	FM	131
Abbey Fm	Lincs	TF2893	53°25·3'	0°4·0'W	FM	113
Abbey Fm	Lincs	TF4879	53°17·4'	0°13·6'E	FM	122
Abbey Fm	Lincs	TF5469	53°12·0'	0°18·7'E	FM	122
Abbey Fm	N Lincs	TA1118	53°39·0'	0°18·8'W	FM	113
Abbey Fm	Norf	TF6114	52°42·2'	0°23·4'E	FM	132
Abbey Fm	Norf	TF6600	52°34·6'	0°27·4'E	FM	143
Abbey Fm	Norf	TF6809	52°39·4'	0°29·4'E	FM	143
Abbey Fm	Norf	TF7106	52°37·7'	0°32·0'E	FM	143
Abbey Fm	Norf	TF8539	52°55·2'	0°45·5'E	FM	132
Abbey Fm	Norf	TG0527	52°48·3'	1°2·9'E	FM	133
Abbey Fm	Norf	TG1518	52°43·2'	1°11·4'E	FM	133
Abbey Fm	Norf	TG2133	52°51·2'	1°17·4'E	FM	133
Abbey Fm	Norf	TM0792	52°29·4'	1°3·3'E	FM	144
Abbey Fm	Norf	TM2587	52°26·3'	1°19·0'E	FM	156
Abbey Fm	Notts	SK7340	52°57·4'	0°54·4'W	FM	129
Abbey Fm	N Yks	SE0897	54°22·4'	1°52·2'W	FM	99
Abbey Fm	N Yks	SE8276	54°10·6'	0°44·2'W	FM	100
Abbey Fm	N Yks	SE8980	54°12·7'	0°37·7'W	FM	101
Abbey Fm	Shrops	SJ5740	52°57·6'	2°38·0'W	FM	117
Abbey Fm	Suff	TL9271	52°18·4'	0°49·4'E	FM	144,155
Abbey Fm	Suff	TM1276	52°20·7'	1°7·1'E	FM	144
Abbey Fm	Suff	TM2049	52°6·0'	1°13·1'E	FM	169
Abbey Fm	Suff	TM2477	52°20·9'	1°17·7'E	FM	156
Abbey Fm	Suff	TM2658	52°10·7'	1°18·7'E	FM	156
Abbey Fm	Suff	TM3058	52°10·6'	1°22·2'E	FM	156
Abbey Fm	Suff	TM3186	52°25·6'	1°24·3'E	FM	156
Abbey Fm	Suff	TM3377	52°20·7'	1°25·7'E	FM	156
Abbey Fm	Suff	TM3481	52°22·8'	1°26·7'E	FM	156
Abbey Fm	Suff	TM3957	52°9·8'	1°30·1'E	FM	156
Abbey Fm	Warr	SJ6693	53°26·2'	2°30·3'W	FM	109
Abbey Fm	Warw	SP2171	52°20·4'	1°41·1'W	FM	139
Abbey Fm	Warw	SP4389	52°30·1'	1°21·6'W	FM	140
Abbey Fm	Wrekin	SJ7313	52°43·1'	2°23·6'W	FM	127
Abbey Ford Br	Dorset	ST7323	51°0·6'	2°22·7'W	X	183
Abbey Ford Fm	Leic	SK4318	52°45·7'	1°21·4'W	FM	129
Abbeyford Woods	Devon	SX5997	50°45·6'	3°59·6'W	F	191
Abbey Gate	Devon	SY2997	50°46·3'	3°0·0'W	T	193
Abbey Gate	Kent	TQ7558	51°17·9'	0°31·0'E	T	178,188
Abbey Gate Place	Kent	TQ7553	51°15·2'	0°30·9'E	X	188
Abbey Green	Shrops	SJ5033	52°53·8'	2°44·2'W	T	126
Abbey Green	Staffs	SJ9757	53°6·8'	2°2·3'W	T	118
Abbey Hall Fm	Warw	SP4378	52°24·1'	1°21·7'W	FM	140
Abbey Head	D & G	NX7443	54°46·2'	3°57·1'W	X	83,84
Abbey Heath	Norf	TL8584	52°25·6'	0°43·7'E	F	144
Abbey Hey	Man	SJ8996	53°27·9'	2°9·5'W	T	109
Abbeyhill	C of Edin	NT2774	55°57·5'	3°9·7'W	T	66
Abbey Hill	Devon	ST1410	50°53·2'	3°13·0'W	X	192,193
Abbey Hill	Lincs	TF0764	53°10·0'	0°23·6'W	X	121
Abbey Hill	N Yks	SE1685	54°15·9'	1°44·8'W	X	99
Abbey Hill	Somer	ST2717	50°57·1'	3°2·0'W	X	193
Abbey Hill (Inner)	Scot Bord	NT7561	55°50·7'	2°23·5'W	H	67
Abbey Hill (Outer)	Scot Bord	NT7360	55°50·2'	2°25·4'W	X	67,74
Abbey Hills	Lincs	TF4554	53°4·0'	0°10·3'E	X	122
Abbey Hills (Earthworks)	Lincs	TF4554	53°4·0'	0°10·3'E	A	122
Abbey Ho	Bucks	SP6339	52°3·0'	1°4·5'W	X	152
Abbey Ho	Cumbr	NY1850	54°50·5'	3°16·2'W	X	85
Abbey Ho	Leeds	SE2342	53°52·7'	1°38·6'W	X	104
Abbey Ho	Lincs	TF3588	53°22·5'	0°2·2'E	X	113,122
Abbey Ho	N Yks	NZ9011	54°29·4'	0°36·2'W	X	94
Abbey Ho	Roth	SK5489	53°23·9'	1°10·9'W	X	111,120
Abbey Ho	Scot Bord	NT7562	55°51·3'	2°23·5'W	X	67
Abbey Ho	Suff	TM2165	52°14·5'	1°14·6'E	X	156
Abbey Ho, The	N Yks	SE7972	54°8·5'	0°47·0'W	X	100
Abbey House	Dorset	ST9806	50°51·4'	2°1·3'W	A	195
Abbey House	Notts	SK5948	53°1·8'	1°6·8'W	X	129
Abbey House	Peterb	TF2804	52°37·4'	0°6·1'W	A	142
Abbey Hulton	C of Stoke	SJ9148	53°2·0'	2°7·6'W	T	118
Abbeylands	I of M	SC3679	54°11·1'	4°30·4'W	X	95
Abbeylands	Northum	NU1814	55°25·4'	1°42·5'W	X	81
Abbeylands Fm	W Susx	TQ2319	50°57·7'	0°14·5'W	FM	198
Abbey Mains	E Loth	NT5375	55°58·2'	2°44·7'W	X	66
Abbey Manor	Worcs	SP0345	52°6·4'	1°57·0'W	X	150
Abbey Mead	Surrey	TQ0467	51°23·8'	0°29·9'W	T	176
Abbeymill Fm	E Loth	NT5374	55°57·7'	2°44·7'W	FM	66
Abbey Mills Fm	Northum	NZ1885	55°9·8'	1°42·6'W	FM	81
Abbey Oaks	Suff	TM1144	52°3·5'	1°5·1'E	X	155,169
Abbey Park	Bucks	SP9000	51°41·7'	0°41·5'W	X	165
Abbey Park	C of Leic	SK5805	52°38·6'	1°8·2'W	X	140
Abbey Park	Scot Bord	NT8965	55°52·9'	2°10·1'W	X	67
Abbey Park Fm	Bucks	SU9486	51°34·1'	0°38·2'W	FM	175
Abbey Rigg	Northum	NY8487	55°10·9'	2°14·6'W	H	80
Abbey River	Devon	SS2524	50°59·6'	4°29·2'W	W	190
Abbey St Bathans	Scot Bord	NT7662	55°51·3'	2°22·6'W	T	67
Abbeystead	Lancs	SD5654	53°59·1'	2°39·8'W	T	102
Abbeystead Fell	Lancs	SD5557	54°0·7'	2°40·8'W	X	102
Abbeystead Resr	Lancs	SD5554	53°59·1'	2°40·8'W	W	102
Abbey, The	Bucks	SP8420	51°52·6'	0°46·4'W	X	165
Abbey, The	Bucks	SU8887	51°34·7'	0°43·4'W	X	175
Abbey, The	Cambs	TL5563	52°14·8'	0°16·6'E	X	154
Abbey, The	Hants	SU6737	51°7·9'	1°2·2'W	X	185,186
Abbey, The	Norf	TF9336	52°53·4'	0°52·6'E	X	132
Abbeythune	Angus	NO6647	56°37·1'	2°32·8'W	X	54
Abbeyton	Aberd	NO7678	56°53·8'	2°23·2'W	X	45
Abbey Town	Cumbr	NY1750	54°50·5'	3°17·1'W	T	85
Abbey View Fm	N Yks	SE5636	53°49·3'	1°8·5'W	FM	105
Abbey View Fm	Staffs	SK0639	52°57·1'	1°54·2'W	FM	128
Abbey Village	Lancs	SD6422	53°41·8'	2°32·3'W	T	102,103
Abbey Warren Fm	Lincs	TF1467	53°11·5'	0°17·2'W	FM	121
Abbey Way Ho	Northnts	SP6341	52°4·1'	1°4·5'W	X	152
Abbeywood	Ches	SJ5668	53°12·7'	2°39·1'W	X	117
Abbey Wood	Gren	TQ4678	51°29·2'	0°6·6'E	T	177
Abbey Wood	Kent	TQ8151	51°14·0'	0°36·0'E	F	188
Abbey Wood	Notts	SK5453	53°4·5'	1°11·2'W	F	120
Abbey Wood	Staffs	SK0742	52°58·8'	1°53·3'W	F	119,128
Abbey Wood	Suff	TM3185	52°25·1'	1°24·2'E	F	156
Abbey Wood	Wrekin	SJ7414	52°43·6'	2°22·7'W	F	127
Abbey Yard	D & G	NX7364	54°57·5'	3°58·6'W	T	83,84
Abbey Yard	Norf	TM2585	52°25·2'	1°18·9'E	A	156
Abbot Fm	Norf	TF9738	52°54·4'	0°56·2'E	FM	132
Abbot Hagg Fm	N Yks	SE5784	54°15·2'	1°7·1'W	FM	100
Abbot Hall	Cumbr	SD3975	54°10·3'	2°55·6'W	X	96,97
Abbothill	S Ayr	NS3719	55°26·5'	4°34·2'W	X	70
Abbot Holme	Cumbr	SD6490	54°18·5'	2°32·8'W	X	97
Abbot Park	Cumbr	SD3188	54°17·2'	3°3·2'W	X	96,97
Abbotrule	Scot Bord	NT6012	55°24·3'	2°37·5'W	X	80
Abbots	Essex	TL5635	51°59·7'	0°16·7'E	X	154
Abbot's Bay	Cumbr	NY2519	54°33·9'	3°9·2'W	W	89,90
Abbots Bickington	Devon	SS3813	50°53·9'	4°17·8'W	T	190
Abbots Bromley	Staffs	SK0824	52°49·0'	1°52·5'W	T	128
Abbots Bromley Cycle Way	Staffs	SJ9925	52°49·6'	2°0·5'W	X	127
Abbotsbury	Dorset	SY5785	50°40·0'	2°36·1'W	T	194
Abbotsbury	Herts	TL4037	52°1·1'	0°2·8'E	X	154
Abbotsbury Castle	Dorset	SY5586	50°40·5'	2°37·8'W	A	194
Abbotsbury Castle (fort)	Dorset	SY5586	50°40·5'	2°37·8'W	A	194
Abbotsbury Gardens	Dorset	SY5685	50°40·0'	2°37·0'W	X	194
Abbotsbury Plains	Dorset	SY5885	50°40·0'	2°35·3'W	X	194
Abbotsbury Swannery	Dorset	SY5784	50°39·5'	2°36·1'W	A	194
Abbot's Castle Hill	Staffs	SO8294	52°32·9'	2°15·5'W	X	138
Abbot's Cliff	Kent	TR2738	51°6·0'	1°14·9'E	X	179
Abbot's Close	N Yks	SE4682	54°14·1'	1°17·2'W	X	100
Abbot's Clough Farm	Ches	SJ4972	53°14·8'	2°45·5'W	FM	117
Abbot's Court	Glos	SO8629	51°57·8'	2°11·8'W	A	150
Abbot's Court	Medway	TQ7972	51°25·3'	0°34·9'E	X	178
Abbot's Court Fm	Dorset	SY8697	50°46·6'	2°11·5'W	FM	194
Abbots Deuglie	Pth & Kin	NO1110	56°16·7'	3°25·8'W	X	58
Abbots Down	E Susx	TQ6136	51°6·3'	0°18·4'E	X	188
Abbots Down	Wilts	SU1656	51°18·4'	1°45·8'W	X	173
Abbotsfield	Oxon	SU6579	51°30·6'	1°3·4'W	X	175
Abbotsfield	Somer	ST0727	51°2·3'	3°19·2'W	X	181
Abbotsfield Fm	St Hel	SJ5492	53°25·6'	2°41·1'W	FM	108
Abbot's Fish Ho	Somer	ST4541	51°10·2'	2°46·8'W	A	182
Abbots Fm	Lancs	SD5138	53°50·4'	2°44·3'W	FM	102
Abbot's Fm	Norf	TG2500	52°33·3'	1°19·6'E	FM	134
Abbot's Fm	Suff	TL7561	52°13·4'	0°34·1'E	FM	155
Abbotsford	Scot Bord	NT5034	55°36·1'	2°47·2'W	X	73
Abbotsford	W Susx	TQ3020	50°58·1'	0°8·5'W	T	198
Abbotsford Fm	Devon	ST1510	50°53·2'	3°12·1'W	FM	192,193
Abbot's Hall	Essex	TL7327	51°55·1'	0°31·3'E	X	167
Abbot's Hall	Norf	TG2028	52°48·5'	1°16·3'E	X	133,134
Abbot's Hall	Suff	TL9247	52°5·5'	0°48·6'E	X	155
Abbot's Hall	Suff	TL9358	52°11·4'	0°49·8'E	X	155
Abbot's Hall	Suff	TM0572	52°18·7'	1°0·8'E	X	144,155
Abbot's Hall	Suff	TM1759	52°11·4'	1°10·9'E	X	156
Abbot's Hall Saltings	Essex	TL9713	51°47·1'	0°51·8'E	W	168
Abbotsham	Devon	SS4226	51°0·9'	4°14·8'W	T	180,190
Abbotsham	Devon	SS6608	50°51·6'	3°53·9'W	X	191
Abbotsham Court	Devon	SS4127	51°1·5'	4°15·7'W	X	180
Abbotsham Cross	Devon	SS4225	51°0·4'	4°14·7'W	X	180,190
Abbotshaugh	Aberd	NJ8345	57°30·0'	2°16·6'W	X	29,30
Abbotshay	Herts	TL1917	51°50·6'	0°16·0'W	X	166
Abbot's Hill	Devon	SS5415	50°55·2'	4°4·3'W	X	180
Abbot's Hill	Dorset	ST5309	50°52·9'	2°39·7'W	H	194
Abbot's Hill	Herts	TL0704	51°43·7'	0°26·6'W	X	166
Abbot's Hill Fm	Dorset	ST5508	50°52·4'	2°38·0'W	FM	194
Abbot's Hill Fm	Somer	ST5309	50°52·9'	2°39·7'W	FM	194
Abbot's Ho	N Yks	NZ8400	54°23·6'	0°42·0'W	X	94
Abbotsholme School	Derby	SK1138	52°56·6'	1°49·8'W	X	128
Abbotside Common	N Yks	SD8196	54°21·8'	2°17·1'W	X	98
Abbotside Common	N Yks	SD8893	54°20·2'	2°10·7'W	X	98
Abbotside Fm	Derby	SK0966	53°11·7'	1°51·5'W	FM	119
Abbotside Fm	S Glos	ST6890	51°36·7'	2°27·3'W	FM	162,172
Abbot's Isles	Arg & Bt	NM9534	56°27·5'	5°19·2'W	X	49
Abbotskerswell	Devon	SX8568	50°30·3'	3°36·9'W	T	202
Abbots Langley	Herts	TL0901	51°42·1'	0°25·0'W	T	166
Abbotsleigh	Devon	SX8048	50°19·4'	3°40·8'W	T	202
Abbots Leigh	E Susx	TQ3522	50°59·1'	0°4·2'W	X	198
Abbots Leigh	N Som	ST5473	51°27·5'	2°39·3'W	T	172
Abbots Leigh	W Susx	TQ1013	50°54·6'	0°25·7'W	X	198
Abbotsley	Cambs	TL2256	52°11·6'	0°12·5'W	T	153
Abbotsley Brook	Cambs	TL2457	52°12·1'	0°10·7'W	W	153
Abbot's Lodge	Glos	SO8221	51°53·5'	2°15·3'W	X	162
Abbot's Lodge	Surrey	SU8741	51°9·9'	0°45·0'W	X	186
Abbot's Marsh	Devon	SS6419	50°57·5'	3°55·8'W	X	180
Abbot's Meads	Ches	SJ3967	53°12·0'	2°54·4'W	T	117
Abbots Morton	Worcs	SP0255	52°11·8'	1°57·8'W	T	150
Abbots Moss	Ches	SJ5868	53°12·7'	2°37·3'W	X	117
Abbotsmoss	Scot Bord	NT5133	55°35·5'	2°46·2'W	X	73
Abbots Moss Fm	Cumbr	NY5142	54°46·5'	2°45·3'W	FM	86
Abbot's Oak	Beds	SP9632	51°58·9'	0°35·7'W	X	165
Abbot's Oak	Leic	SK4614	52°43·5'	1°18·7'W	X	129
Abbot's or College Wood	Oxon	SU6580	51°31·1'	1°3·4'W	F	175
Abbots Reading Fm	Cumbr	SD3485	54°15·6'	3°0·4'W	FM	96,97
Abbots Ripton	Cambs	TL2377	52°22·9'	0°11·2'W	T	142
Abbot's Salford	Warw	SP0650	52°9·1'	1°54·3'W	T	150
Abbot's Shrub	Essex	TL8331	51°57·1'	0°40·2'E	F	168
Abbotstone	Hants	SU5634	51°6·4'	1°11·6'W	T	185
Abbotstone Down	Hants	SU5836	51°7·4'	1°9·9'W	F	185
Abbotstone Woods	Hants	SU5936	51°7·4'	1°9·0'W	F	185
Abbot's Wall	Kent	TR3063	51°19·4'	1°18·5'E	A	179
Abbot's Way	Devon	SX6168	50°30·0'	3°57·2'W	X	202
Abbot's Well	Hants	SU1812	50°54·7'	1°44·3'W	W	195
Abbot's Wick Fm	Essex	TL9415	51°48·2'	0°49·2'E	FM	168
Abbot's Wood	E Susx	TQ5607	50°50·7'	0°13·3'E	F	199
Abbotswood	Glos	SP1826	51°56·2'	1°43·9'W	X	163
Abbotswood	Hants	SU3623	51°0·5'	1°28·8'W	T	185
Abbotswood	Surrey	TQ0051	51°15·2'	0°33·6'W	T	186
Abbotswood	Worcs	SO8949	52°8·6'	2°9·2'W	X	150
Abbotswood Fm	Glos	SO8815	51°50·2'	2°10·1'W	FM	162
Abbotswood Fm	Hants	SU3623	51°0·5'	1°28·8'W	FM	185
Abbots Wood Inclosure	Hants	SU8140	51°9·4'	0°50·1'W	F	186
Abbots Worthy	Hants	SU4932	51°5·3'	1°17·6'W	T	185
Abbott Lodge	Cumbr	NY5424	54°36·8'	2°42·3'W	X	90
Abbotts Ann	Hants	SU3243	51°11·3'	1°32·1'W	T	185
Abbott's Barton	Hants	SU4830	51°4·3'	1°18·5'W	A	185
Abbotts Barton Ho	Hants	SU4831	51°4·8'	1°18·5'W	X	185
Abbott's Court	Kent	TR1032	51°3·2'	1°0·2'E	X	189
Abbotts Fm	N Yks	SE7975	54°10·1'	0°47·0'W	FM	100
Abbotts Hall	Essex	TL9614	51°47·6'	0°50·9'E	X	168
Abbott's Hall	Essex	TM1227	51°54·3'	1°5·3'E	X	168,169
Abbott's Hendra	Corn	SX1985	50°38·4'	4°33·2'W	X	201
Abbotts Park	Devon	SS8027	51°2·0'	3°42·3'W	X	181
Abbottswood Fm	Wilts	ST9564	51°22·7'	2°3·9'W	FM	173
Abbott's Wootton Fms	Dorset	SY3796	50°45·8'	2°53·2'W	FM	193
Abcott	Shrops	SO3978	52°24·0'	2°53·4'W	T	137,148
Abden Fm	Fife	NT2687	56°4·5'	3°10·9'W	FM	66
Abdon	Shrops	SO5786	52°28·5'	2°37·6'W	T	137,138
Abdon Burf	Shrops	SO5986	52°28·5'	2°35·8'W	X	137,138
Abdon Liberty	Shrops	SO5886	52°28·5'	2°36·7'W	X	137,138
Abdy	Roth	SK4398	53°28·9'	1°20·7'W	T	111
Abel Cross	Cald	SD9830	53°46·2'	2°1·4'W	A	103
Abel Grange	N Yks	SE4084	54°15·2'	1°22·7'W	X	99
Abel Heath	Norf	TG1727	52°48·0'	1°13·6'E	X	133,134
Abenhall	Glos	SO6717	51°51·3'	2°29·4'W	X	162
Aber	Carm	SN2418	51°50·2'	4°32·9'W	X	158
Aber	Cered	SN4748	52°6·8'	4°13·7'W	X	146
Aber	Gwyn	SH7032	52°52·4'	3°55·5'W	X	124
Aberaeron	Cered	SN4562	52°14·3'	4°15·8'W	T	146
Aberaman	Rho Cyn Taf	SO0101	51°42·2'	3°25·6'W	T	170

Aberangell	Gwyn	SH8410	52°40·8'	3°42·6'W	T	124,125
Aberannell	Powys	SN9151	52°9·0'	3°35·2'W	X	147
Aber Arad	Carm	SN3140	52°2·2'	4°27·4'W	T	145
Aberarder	Highld	NN4787	56°57·2'	4°30·5'W	T	34,42
Aberarder Forest	Highld	NN4788	56°57·7'	4°30·5'W	X	34,42
Aberarder Ho	Highld	NH6225	57°17·9'	4°17·0'W	X	26,35
Aberarder Lodge	Highld	NN5389	56°58·4'	4°24·6'W	X	42
Aberargie	Pth & Kin	NO1615	56°19·5'	3°21·1'W	T	58
Aberarth	Cered	SN4763	52°14·9'	4°14·1'W	T	146
Aberavon	Nth Pt Talb	SS7590	51°35·9'	3°47·9'W	T	170
Aberavon Sands	Nth Pt Talb	SS7390	51°35·9'	3°49·6'W	X	170
Aber Bach	Pemb	SM8835	51°58·6'	5°4·8'W	W	157
Aber Bach	Pemb	SM9938	52°0·5'	4°55·3'W	W	157
Aberbaiden Fm	Nth Pt Talb	SS8584	51°32·8'	3°39·1'W	FM	170
Aber-banc	Cered	SN3541	52°2·8'	4°24·0'W	T	145
Aberbargoed	Caer	SO1500	51°41·8'	3°13·4'W	T	171
Aberbechan	Powys	SO1393	52°31·9'	3°16·6'W	T	136
Aberbechan Dike	Powys	SO1394	52°32·5'	3°16·6'W	X	136
Aberbedw	Cered	SN3449	52°7·1'	4°25·1'W	X	145
Aberbeeg	Blae Gw	SO2102	51°42·9'	3°8·2'W	T	171
Aberbowlan	Carm	SN6938	52°1·7'	3°54·2'W	X	146,160
Aberbran	Powys	SN9829	51°57·2'	3°28·7'W	T	160
Aber Branddu	Carm	SN7045	52°5·5'	3°53·5'W	X	146,147
Aberbrwynen	Cered	SN5976	52°22·1'	4°3·9'W	X	135
Abercairny	Pth & Kin	NN9122	56°22·9'	3°45·5'W	X	52,58
Aber-Camddwr Br	Powys	SO1070	52°19·5'	3°18·8'W	X	136,148
Abercamlais	Powys	SN9629	51°57·2'	3°30·4'W	X	160
Abercanaid	Merth Tyd	SO0503	51°43·3'	3°22·1'W	T	170
Abercarfan	Cered	SN6657	52°11·9'	3°57·2'W	X	146
Abercarn	Caer	ST2194	51°38·6'	3°8·1'W	T	171
Abercastle	Pemb	SM8533	51°57·5'	5°7·4'W	T	157
Abercegin	Gwyn	SH5972	53°13·8'	4°6·3'W	X	114,115
Abercegir	Powys	SH8001	52°35·9'	3°45·9'W	T	135,136
Aberceiro	Cered	SN6286	52°27·5'	4°1·5'W	X	135
Aberchalder	Highld	NH3403	57°5·5'	4°43·9'W	T	34
Aberchalder Burn	Highld	NH5818	57°14·1'	4°20·7'W	W	35
Aberchalder Forest	Highld	NN3499	57°3·4'	4°43·8'W	X	34
Aberchirder	Aberd	NJ6252	57°33·6'	2°37·6'W	T	29
Aberclawdd	Powys	SO0699	52°35·1'	3°22·8'W	X	136
Abercoed	Cered	SN6658	52°12·5'	3°57·3'W	X	146
Abercorn	W Loth	NT0878	55°59·4'	3°28·0'W	T	65
Abercothi Fm	Carm	SN5020	51°51·7'	4°10·3'W	FM	159
Abercothi Ho	Carm	SN5020	51°51·7'	4°10·3'W	X	159
Abercraf	Powys	SN8112	51°47·9'	3°43·2'W	T	160
Abercrai	Powys	SN8928	51°56·6'	3°36·5'W	X	160
Abercregan	Denb	SJ2441	52°57·9'	3°7·5'W	X	117
Abercregan	Nth Pt Talb	SS8596	51°39·3'	3°39·4'W	T	170
Abercrombie	Fife	NO5102	56°12·7'	2°47·0'W	T	59
Abercrychan	Carm	SN7936	52°0·8'	3°45·4'W	X	146,160
Abercwm	Carm	SN5040	52°2·5'	4°10·8'W	X	146
Abercwmboi	Rho Cyn Taf	ST0299	51°41·1'	3°24·7'W	T	170
Abercych	Pemb	SN2440	52°2·1'	4°33·6'W	T	145
Abercyfor	Carm	SN4217	51°50·0'	4°17·2'W	X	159
Abercynafon	Powys	SO0817	51°50·9'	3°19·7'W	X	160
Abercynithon	Powys	SO0250	52°8·6'	3°25·5'W	X	147
Abercynllaith	Powys	SJ2023	52°48·2'	3°10·8'W	X	126
Abercynon	Rho Cyn Taf	ST0895	51°39·0'	3°19·4'W	T	170
Abercynrig	Powys	SO0727	51°56·3'	3°20·8'W	X	160
Abercynrig Mill	Powys	SO0626	51°55·7'	3°21·6'W	X	160
Aber Cysgod	Powys	SJ0326	52°49·6'	3°26·0'W	X	125
Aber-Cywarch	Gwyn	SH8615	52°43·5'	3°40·9'W	T	124,125
Aberdalgie	Pth & Kin	NO0720	56°22·0'	3°29·9'W	T	52,53,58
Aberdare / Aberdar	Rho Cyn Taf	SO0002	51°42·7'	3°26·5'W	T	170
Aberdaron	Gwyn	SH1726	52°48·3'	4°42·5'W	T	123
Aberdaron Bay	Gwyn	SH1725	52°47·7'	4°42·5'W	W	123
Aberdauddwr	Carm	SN4423	51°53·3'	4°15·6'W	X	159
Aberdauddwr	Cered	SN6954	52°10·4'	3°54·5'W	X	146
Aberdaunant	Carm	SN6730	51°57·4'	3°55·7'W	X	146
Aber-ddu	Denb	SJ0956	53°5·9'	3°21·1'W	X	116
Aberdeen	Brad	SE0234	53°48·4'	1°57·8'W	X	104
Aberdeen	C of Aber	NJ9206	57°8·9'	2°7·5'W	T	38
Aberdeen (Dyce) Airport	C of Aber	NJ8712	57°12·2'	2°12·5'W	X	38
Aberdeen Fm	Bolton	SD5911	53°35·9'	2°36·8'W	FM	108
Aberdene Tarn	N Yks	SD9894	54°20·7'	2°1·4'W	W	98
Aberderfel	Gwyn	SH8538	52°55·9'	3°42·3'W	W	124,125
Aberdesach	Gwyn	SH4251	53°2·2'	4°21·0'W	T	115,123
Aberdinas	Pemb	SM7730	51°55·7'	5°14·2'W	W	157
Aberdona Ho	Clackm	NS9495	56°8·4'	3°41·9'W	X	58
Aberdona Mains	Clackm	NS9495	56°8·4'	3°41·9'W	X	58
Aberdour	Fife	NT1985	56°3·3'	3°17·6'W	T	65,66
Aberdour House	Aberd	NJ9064	57°40·2'	2°9·6'W	X	30
Aberdovey Bar,	Gwyn	SN5995	52°32·3'	4°4·3'W	X	135
Aber Draw	Pemb	SM8332	51°56·9'	5°9·1'W	W	157
Aberduhonw	Powys	SO0650	52°8·7'	3°22·0'W	X	147
Aberdulais	Nth Pt Talb	SS7799	51°40·8'	3°46·4'W	T	170
Aber-Dulas-uchaf	Powys	SN9146	52°6·3'	3°35·1'W	X	147
Aberduna Fm	Denb	SJ2062	53°9·2'	3°11·4'W	FM	117
Aberdwr	Cered	SN6859	52°13·0'	3°55·5'W	X	146
Aberdyfi	Gwyn	SN6196	52°32·9'	4°2·6'W	T	135
Aber Dysynni	Gwyn	SH5603	52°36·6'	4°7·2'W	W	135
Aber Eden	Gwyn	SH7224	52°48·1'	3°53·5'W	X	124
Aberedw	Powys	SO0747	52°7·0'	3°21·1'W	T	147
Aberedw Castle	Powys	SO0749	52°8·1'	3°21·1'W	A	147
Aberedw Hill	Powys	SO0851	52°9·2'	3°20·3'W	H	147
Aberedw Rocks	Powys	SO0846	52°6·5'	3°20·2'W	X	147
Abereiddi Bay	Pemb	SM7931	51°56·3'	5°12·5'W	W	157
Abereiddy	Pemb	SM7931	51°56·3'	5°12·5'W	T	157
Aberelwyn	Carm	SN1928	51°55·5'	4°37·6'W	X	145,158
Aberenbwll	Powys	SN8541	52°3·6'	3°40·3'W	X	147,160
Abererch	Gwyn	SH3936	52°54·1'	4°23·2'W	T	123
Aber Falls	Gwyn	SH6669	53°12·3'	4°0·0'W	W	115
Aberfan	Merth Tyd	SO0700	51°41·7'	3°20·3'W	T	170
Aberfeldy	Pth & Kin	NN8549	56°37·4'	3°52·0'W	T	52
Aberfelin	Pemb	SM7023	51°51·7'	5°20·0'W	W	157
Aber Fforest	Pemb	SN0239	52°1·1'	4°52·7'W	W	145,157
Aberffraw	I of Angl	SH3568	53°11·3'	4°27·8'W	T	114
Aberffraw Bay	I of Angl	SH3466	53°10·2'	4°28·6'W	W	114
Aberffrwd	Cered	SN6878	52°23·3'	3°56·0'W	T	135
Aberffrwd	Monm	SO3509	51°46·8'	2°56·1'W	T	161
Aber-Ffrydlan	Powys	SH7702	52°36·4'	3°48·6'W	X	135

Aberford	Leeds	SE4337	53°49·9'	1°20·4'W	T	105
Aberfoyle	Stir	NN5200	56°10·4'	4°22·6'W	T	57
Abergairn	Aberd	NO3597	57°3·8'	3°3·9'W	X	37,44
Abergairn Castle	Aberd	NO3597	57°3·8'	3°3·9'W	A	37,44
Abergarw	Brig	SS9184	51°32·9'	3°33·9'W	T	170
Abergarwed	Nth Pt Talb	SN8102	51°42·5'	3°42·9'W	T	170
Abergavenny Fm	Norf	TF9601	52°34·5'	0°54·0'E	FM	144
Abergavenny / Y Fenni	Monm	SO2914	51°49·4'	3°1·4'W	T	161
Abergefail	Powys	SN8843	52°4·7'	3°37·7'W	X	147,160
Aber Geirch	Gwyn	SH2640	52°56·0'	4°34·9'W	W	123
Abergeldie Castle	Aberd	NO2895	57°2·7'	3°10·7'W	A	37,44
Abergele	Conwy	SH9477	53°17·0'	3°35·0'W	T	116
Abergele Roads	Conwy	SH9279	53°18·1'	3°36·8'W	W	116
Aber-gelli-fâch	Swan	SN6501	51°41·7'	3°56·8'W	X	159
Aber-Giâr	Carm	SN5041	52°3·1'	4°10·9'W	T	146
Aber Glanhirin	Powys	SN8872	52°20·3'	3°38·2'W	X	135,136,147
Aberglaslyn Hall	Gwyn	SH5945	52°59·3'	4°5·6'W	X	115
Aberglasney	Carm	SN5822	51°52·9'	4°3·4'W	X	159
Aber Glesyrch	Powys	SH7706	52°38·5'	3°48·7'W	W	124
Aber-Goleu	Carm	SN5029	51°56·6'	4°10·5'W	X	146
Abergorlech	Carm	SN5833	51°58·9'	4°3·7'W	T	146
Abergrannell	Cered	SN5346	52°5·8'	4°8·4'W	X	146
Abergwdi	Powys	SO0227	51°56·2'	3°25·1'W	X	160
Abergwenlais	Carm	SN7639	52°2·4'	3°48·1'W	X	146,160
Abergwesyn	Powys	SN8552	52°9·5'	3°40·5'W	T	147
Abergwili	Carm	SN4321	51°52·2'	4°16·4'W	T	159
Abergwngu	Cered	SN8773	52°20·8'	3°39·1'W	X	135,136,147
Abergwngu Hill	Cered	SN8674	52°21·4'	3°40·0'W	X	135,136,147
Abergwrog	Cered	SN2843	52°3·8'	4°30·2'W	X	145
Abergwydol	Powys	SH7902	52°36·4'	3°46·8'W	X	135
Abergwynant	Gwyn	SH6717	52°44·3'	3°57·8'W	X	124
Abergwynfi	Nth Pt Talb	SS8996	51°39·3'	3°35·9'W	T	170
Abergwyngregyn	Gwyn	SH6572	53°13·9'	4°0·9'W	T	115
Abergynolwyn	Gwyn	SH6706	52°38·4'	3°57·5'W	T	124
Aberhafesp	Powys	SO0692	52°31·3'	3°22·7'W	X	136
Aberhalen	Carm	SN3340	52°2·2'	4°25·7'W	X	145
Aberhall Fm	Heref	SO5224	51°55·0'	2°41·5'W	FM	162
Aberham	Denb	SJ0865	53°10·7'	3°22·2'W	W	116
Aberhenwen Fawr	Powys	SN8329	51°57·1'	3°41·8'W	X	160
Aberhiriaeth	Powys	SH8406	52°38·6'	3°42·5'W	X	124,125
Aber-Hirnant	Gwyn	SH9532	52°52·8'	3°33·2'W	X	125
Aber Ho	Brig	SS9390	51°36·2'	3°32·3'W	X	170
Aberhoffnant	Cered	SN3940	52°2·3'	4°20·5'W	X	145
Aberhonddu (Brecon)	Powys	SO0428	51°56·8'	3°23·4'W	T	160
Aberhosan	Powys	SN8097	52°33·7'	3°45·8'W	T	135,136
Aberhowy Fm	Powys	SO1619	51°52·0'	3°12·8'W	FM	161
Aberhyddnant	Powys	SN8723	51°53·9'	3°38·1'W	X	160
Aberhydfer	Powys	SN8527	51°56·0'	3°40·0'W	X	160
Aber Isle	W Dunb	NS4188	56°3·8'	4°32·8'W	X	56
Aberithon	Powys	SO0157	52°12·4'	3°26·5'W	X	147
Aberkenfig	Brig	SS8983	51°32·3'	3°35·6'W	T	170
Aberkin	Gwyn	SH4738	52°55·3'	4°16·2'W	X	123
Aberkinsey	Denb	SJ0480	53°18·7'	3°26·0'W	X	116
Aberkirk Fm	Shrops	SO5269	52°19·3'	2°41·9'W	FM	137,138
Aberlady	E Loth	NT4679	56°0·3'	2°51·5'W	T	66
Aberlady Bay	E Loth	NT4580	56°0·8'	2°52·5'W	W	66
Aberlady Mains	E Loth	NT4779	56°0·3'	2°50·6'W	X	66
Aberlady Point	E Loth	NT4580	56°0·8'	2°52·5'W	X	66
Aberlemno	Angus	NO5255	56°41·3'	2°46·6'W	T	54
Aberllerry	Cered	SN6092	52°30·7'	4°3·4'W	T	135
Aber Lledle	Carm	SN4711	51°46·8'	4°12·7'W	X	159
Aberllefenni	Gwyn	SH7709	52°40·1'	3°48·7'W	T	124
Aberlleinau	Carm	SN3439	52°1·7'	4°24·8'W	X	145
Aber-llia	Powys	SN9314	51°49·1'	3°32·8'W	X	160
Aberllolwyn	Cered	SN5877	52°22·6'	4°4·8'W	X	135
Aberlosk	D & G	NT2603	55°19·2'	3°9·5'W	X	79
Aberlosk Burn	D & G	NT2604	55°19·7'	3°9·6'W	W	79
Aberlour Ho	Moray	NJ2743	57°28·5'	3°12·6'W	X	28
Aberlyn	Fife	NT0684	56°2·6'	3°30·1'W	X	65
Abermad	Cered	SN6076	52°22·1'	4°3·0'W	X	135
Abermagwr	Cered	SN6673	52°20·6'	3°57·6'W	T	135
Aber-Magoed	Carm	SN6743	52°4·4'	3°56·0'W	X	146
Aber-marchnant	Powys	SJ0319	52°45·8'	3°25·9'W	X	125
Aber-Marlais Pk	Carm	SN6929	51°56·9'	3°54·0'W	X	146,160
Aber Mawr	Pemb	SM6924	51°52·2'	5°21·0'W	W	157
Aber-mawr	Pemb	SM8834	51°58·1'	5°4·8'W	W	157
Abermenai Point	I of Angl	SH4461	53°7·6'	4°19·5'W	X	114,115
Abermeurig	Cered	SN5656	52°11·2'	4°6·0'W	X	146
Abermithel	Powys	SO1162	52°15·2'	3°17·8'W	X	148
Abermorddu	Flint	SJ3056	53°6·0'	3°2·3'W	T	117
Abermule	Powys	SO1694	52°32·5'	3°13·9'W	T	136
Abernac	Cered	SN6371	52°19·4'	4°0·2'W	X	135
Abernaint	Powys	SJ1221	52°47·0'	3°17·9'W	X	125
Abernant	Carm	SN3323	51°53·1'	4°25·2'W	T	145,159
Abernant	Cered	SN6878	52°23·3'	3°56·0'W	X	135
Abernant	Pemb	SM8328	51°54·7'	5°8·9'W	X	157
Abernant	Powys	SO0746	52°6·5'	3°21·1'W	X	147
Abernant	Powys	SO1797	52°34·1'	3°13·1'W	T	136
Abernant	Rho Cyn Taf	SO0103	51°43·3'	3°25·6'W	X	170
Abernant Fm	Newp	ST3791	51°37·1'	2°54·2'W	FM	171
Abernant Fm	Nth Pt Talb	SN7803	51°43·0'	3°45·6'W	FM	170
Abernant Fm	V of Glam	ST0571	51°26·0'	3°21·6'W	FM	170
Abernant Lake	Powys	SN8946	52°6·3'	3°36·9'W	W	147
Abernefal	Powys	SN9458	52°12·8'	3°32·7'W	X	147
Abernethy	Pth & Kin	NO1816	56°20·0'	3°19·1'W	T	58
Abernethy Bank	Pth & Kin	NO2118	56°21·1'	3°16·3'W	X	58
Abernethy Forest	Highld	NH9918	57°14·8'	3°40·0'W	F	36
Abernethy Glen	Pth & Kin	NO1814	56°18·9'	3°19·1'W	X	58
Abernyte	Pth & Kin	NO2531	56°28·2'	3°12·6'W	T	53
Aber-oer	Wrex	SJ2849	53°2·2'	3°4·0'W	T	117
Aber-Ogwen	Gwyn	SH6172	53°13·9'	4°4·5'W	X	115
Aberogwrn Fm	V of Glam	ST0470	51°25·5'	3°22·5'W	FM	170
Aber-Peithnant	Cered	SN7584	52°26·8'	3°50·0'W	X	135
Aber Pensidan	Pemb	SM9940	52°1·6'	4°55·4'W	W	145,157
Aber Pensidan	Pemb	SN0040	52°1·6'	4°54·5'W	W	145,157
Aber-pergwm Ho	Nth Pt Talb	SN8606	51°44·7'	3°38·7'W	X	160
Aber-pergwm Wood	Nth Pt Talb	SN8506	51°44·7'	3°39·6'W	F	160
Aberporth	Cered	SN2651	52°8·0'	4°32·1'W	T	145
Aber-pwll	Pemb	SM7830	51°55·7'	5°13·4'W	W	157
Aber Rhaeadr	Powys	SJ1324	52°48·6'	3°17·0'W	X	125

Aber Rhigian	Pemb	SN0339	52°1·1'	4°51·9'W	W	145,157
Aber-Rhiwlech	Gwyn	SH9020	52°46·2'	3°37·4'W	X	125
Abersannan	Carm	SN5624	51°54·0'	4°5·2'W	X	159
Aberscross	Highld	NC7600	57°58·6'	4°5·3'W	X	17
Aberscross Hill	Highld	NC7700	57°58·6'	4°4·3'W	H	17
Abersefin	Powys	SN9729	51°57·2'	3°29·5'W	X	160
Abersenni Uchaf	Powys	SN9326	51°55·6'	3°33·0'W	X	160
Abersenny	Powys	SN9226	51°55·6'	3°33·8'W	X	160
Abersky	Highld	NH5926	57°18·4'	4°20·0'W	X	26,35
Abersoch	Gwyn	SH3128	52°49·6'	4°30·1'W	T	123
Aber Step	Pemb	SN0339	52°1·1'	4°51·9'W	W	145,157
Abersychan	Torf	SO2603	51°43·5'	3°3·9'W	T	171
Aber Sychnant	Wrex	SJ2451	53°3·3'	3°7·6'W	W	117
Aber-Tafol	Gwyn	SN6496	52°32·9'	3°59·9'W	X	135
Aber Tairnant	Denb	SJ2255	53°5·4'	3°9·5'W	X	117
Aber Tanat	Shrops	SJ2521	52°47·1'	3°6·3'W	X	126
Abertay	Angus	NO5729	56°27·3'	2°41·4'W	X	54,59
Abertay Sands	Fife	NO5228	56°26·8'	2°46·3'W	X	54,59
Abertegan	Cered	SN4843	52°4·1'	4°12·7'W	X	146
Aberthin	V of Glam	ST0075	51°28·1'	3°26·0'W	T	170
Abertillery or Abertyleri	Blae Gw	SO2104	51°44·0'	3°8·2'W	T	171
Abertridwr	Caer	ST1289	51°35·8'	3°15·8'W	T	171
Abertridwr	Powys	SJ0319	52°45·8'	3°25·9'W	T	125
Abertrinant	Gwyn	SH6305	52°37·8'	4°1·1'W	T	124
Abertyleri or Abertillery	Blae Gw	SO2104	51°44·0'	3°8·2'W	T	171
Abertysswg	Caer	SO1305	51°44·5'	3°15·2'W	T	161
Aberuchill Castle	Pth & Kin	NN7421	56°22·1'	4°1·9'W	X	51,52,57
Aberuthven	Pth & Kin	NN9715	56°19·2'	3°39·5'W	T	58
Aber Village	Powys	SO1021	51°53·1'	3°18·1'W	T	161
Aber-west	Pemb	SM8123	51°52·0'	5°10·5'W	W	157
Aberwheel	Wrex	SJ1836	52°55·2'	3°12·8'W	X	125
Aberyscir	Powys	SN9929	51°57·3'	3°27·8'W	T	160
Aberystwyth	Cered	SN5881	52°24·8'	4°4·9'W	T	135
Aber Yw	Pemb	SM8533	51°57·5'	5°7·4'W	W	157
Abesters	W Susx	SU9229	51°3·4'	0°40·8'W	X	186,197
Abhain a'Bhealaich	Arg & Bt	NM9705	56°11·9'	5°15·9'W	W	55
Abhain a' Ghlinne	Highld	NM3796	56°59·1'	6°19·3'W	W	39
A'Bhainlir	Highld	NG7656	57°32·6'	5°44·1'W	H	24
Abhainn a' Bhàigh	N Eil	NB2502	57°55·6'	6°38·2'W	W	14
Abhainn a' Bhail' Uir	Arg & Bt	NM6627	56°22·9'	5°47·0'W	W	49
Abhainn a' Bhuna	N Eil	NB4351	58°22·6'	6°23·3'W	W	8
Abhainn Achachoish	Arg & Bt	NR8566	55°50·6'	5°25·6'W	W	62
Abhainn a' Chadh' Bhuidhe	Highld	NH1367	57°39·5'	5°7·6'W	W	19
Abhainn a' Chadh Bhuidhe	Highld	NH1467	57°39·5'	5°6·6'W	W	20
Abhainn a' Chaiginn Mhóir	Arg & Bt	NM6126	56°22·2'	5°51·8'W	W	49
Abhainn a' Charra	N Eil	NF7870	57°36·6'	7°23·1'W	W	18
Abhainn a' Chlàir Bhig	N Eil	NB1114	58°1·5'	6°53·2'W	W	13,14
Abhainn Achnacree	Arg & Bt	NM9337	56°29·0'	5°21·3'W	W	49
Abhainn a' Chnocain	Arg & Bt	NR7237	55°34·7'	5°36·6'W	W	68
Abhainn a' Chnocain	Highld	NC2209	58°2·3'	5°0·4'W	W	15
Abhainn a' Chnuic Bhric	Arg & Bt	NR4572	55°52·7'	6°4·2'W	W	60,61
Abhainn a' Chnuic Dhuibh	N Eil	NB1520	58°4·9'	6°49·6'W	W	13,14
Abhainn a' Choilich	Highld	NH0924	57°16·3'	5°9·6'W	W	25,33
Abhainn a' Choire	Arg & Bt	NM6729	56°24·0'	5°46·1'W	W	49
Abhainn a' Choire	Highld	NC3625	58°11·3'	4°46·9'W	W	16
Abhainn a' Choire	N Eil	NG0586	57°46·3'	6°57·2'W	W	14,18
Abhainn a' Choire Bhuig	Highld	NH5685	57°50·1'	4°25·1'W	W	21
Abhainn a Chùirn	Arg & Bt	NR3489	56°1·5'	6°15·7'W	W	61
Abhainn a' Gharbh Choire	Highld	NG8769	57°39·9'	5°33·8'W	W	19,24
Abhainn a' Gharbhrain	Highld	NH2875	57°44·2'	4°52·9'W	W	20
Abhainn a' Ghleann Duirch	Arg & Bt	NR5884	55°59·5'	5°52·4'W	W	61
Abhainn a' Ghlinne	Arg & Bt	NM5020	56°18·6'	6°2·1'W	W	48
Abhainn a' Ghlinne	Arg & Bt	NR3792	56°3·2'	6°13·0'W	W	61
Abhainn a' Ghlinne	Highld	NG2562	57°34·1'	6°35·5'W	W	23
Abhainn a' Ghlinne	N Eil	NB0734	58°12·1'	6°58·8'W	W	13
Abhainn a' Ghlinne Bhig	Highld	NG8515	57°10·8'	5°33·0'W	W	33
Abhainn a' Ghlinne Bhig	Highld	NH3283	57°48·6'	4°49·2'W	W	20
Abhainn a' Ghlinne Dhuibh	Highld	NC2933	58°15·4'	4°54·4'W	X	15
Abhainn a' Ghlinne Dhuibh	N Eil	NB4137	58°15·0'	6°24·4'W	W	8
Abhainn a' Ghlinne Ghil	Highld	NM7250	56°35·5'	5°42·4'W	W	49
Abhainn a' Ghlinne Mheadhonaich	Highld	NG6105	57°4·7'	5°56·2'W	W	32
Abhainn a' Ghlinne Mhóir	Arg & Bt	NM3321	56°18·6'	6°18·6'W	W	48
Abhainn a' Ghlinne Mhóir	Highld	NH4186	57°50·4'	4°40·2'W	W	20
Abhainn a' Ghlinne Ruaidh	N Eil	NB4453	58°23·7'	6°22·4'W	W	8
Abhainn a' Ghlinn Mhòir	N Eil	NB3833	58°12·7'	6°27·2'W	W	8
Abhainn a' Ghuibhais Li	Highld	NH2571	57°42·0'	4°55·7'W	W	20
Abhainn Aimash	N Eil	NF7821	57°10·3'	7°19·2'W	W	31
Abhainn Airigh nan Sidhean	Arg & Bt	NR3371	55°51·8'	6°15·6'W	W	60,61
Abhainn Alligin	Highld	NG8359	57°34·4'	5°37·3'W	W	24
Abhainn a' Lòin	N Eil	NB1220	58°4·8'	6°52·7'W	W	13,14
Abhainn a' Mhuil	N Eil	NB1812	58°0·7'	6°46·0'W	W	13,14
Abhainn a' Mhuilinn	Arg & Bt	NR2668	55°49·9'	6°22·1'W	W	60
Abhainn a' Mhuilinn	N Eil	NF8274	57°38·9'	7°19·4'W	W	18
Abhainn an Acha-leathain	Highld	NG4140	57°22·9'	6°18·1'W	W	23
Abhainn an Daimh-Sgeir	Arg & Bt	NR4467	55°50·0'	6°4·9'W	W	60,61
Abhainn an Easá Mhóir	Arg & Bt	NM4622	56°19·6'	6°6·1'W	W	48
Abhainn an Fhasaigh	Highld	NH0267	57°39·2'	5°18·6'W	W	19
Abhainn an Loch Bhig	Highld	NC2827	58°12·2'	4°55·1'W	W	15
Abhainn an Lòin	Highld	NC3341	58°19·8'	4°50·6'W	W	9
Abhainn an Torrain Duibh	Highld	NH2773	57°43·1'	4°53·8'W	W	20
Abhainn an t-Sratha	N Eil	NB1900	57°54·3'	6°44·1'W	W	14
Abhainn an t-Sratha Bhàin	Arg & Bt	NM6536	56°27·7'	5°48·4'W	W	49
Abhainn an t-Sratha Charnaig	Highld	NH6998	57°57·4'	4°12·4'W	W	21
Abhainn an t-Srathain	Highld	NC2560	58°29·9'	4°59·7'W	W	9
Abhainn an t-Sratha Mhóir	Highld	NG5624	57°14·8'	6°2·2'W	W	32
Abhainn an t-Stath Chuileannaich	Highld	NH4194	57°54·7'	4°40·6'W	W	20
Abhainn an Uisge	N Eil	NG0389	57°47·8'	6°59·5'W	W	18
Abhainn Araig	Arg & Bt	NR4172	55°52·6'	6°8·0'W	W	60,61
Abhainn Arnoil	N Eil	NB3045	58°18·9'	6°36·2'W	W	8
Abhainn Ashik	Highld	NG6924	57°15·2'	5°49·3'W	W	32
Abhainn Bà	Highld	NN3551	56°37·6'	4°40·9'W	W	41
Abhainn Bad na h-Achlaise	Highld	NC1221	58°8·5'	5°11·2'W	W	15
Abhainn Bail' a' Mhuilinn	Arg & Bt	NM4730	56°23·9'	6°5·6'W	W	48

Abhainn Barr Chailleach	Arg & Bt	NM7132	56°25·7′	5°42·4′W	W	49
Abhainn Beinn nan Eun	Highld	NH4473	57°43·4′	4°36·7′W	W	20
Abhainn Beul-ath an Tairbh	Arg & Bt	NM4427	56°22·2′	6°8·3′W	W	48
Abhainn Bhaile Mheadhonaich	Highld	NG3143	57°24·1′	6°28·2′W	W	23
Abhainn Bharabhais	N Eil	NB3746	58°19·7′	6°29·1′W	W	8
Abhainn Bharcasaig	Highld	NG2441	57°22·8′	6°35·1′W	W	23
Abhainn Bheag	Arg & Bt	NR5472	55°53·0′	5°55·6′W	W	61
Abhainn Bheag	Highld	NG7904	57°4·7′	5°38·3′W	W	33
Abhainn Bheag	N Ayr	NR9248	55°41·1′	5°18·1′W	W	62,69
Abhainn Bheagaig	Highld	NM9980	56°52·3′	5°17·4′W	W	40
Abhainn Bheagaig	Highld	NN0079	56°51·8′	5°16·4′W	W	41
Abhainn Bheag an Tunns	Arg & Bt	NR9496	56°7·0′	5°18·4′W	W	55
Abhainn Bhearnach	Arg & Bt	NM6831	56°25·1′	5°45·3′W	W	49
Abhainn Bhearnais	Highld	NH0343	57°26·3′	5°16·5′W	W	25
Abhainn Bhearrarigh	N Eil	NB0515	58°1·8′	6°59·4′W	W	13,14
Abhainn Bhioigadail	N Eil	NB1711	58°0·2′	6°47·0′W	W	13,14
Abhainn Bhogie	Arg & Bt	NR3755	55°43·3′	6°10·9′W	W	60
Abhainn Bhreascleit	N Eil	NB2334	58°12·7′	6°42·5′W	W	8,13
Abhainn Bhuachaig	Highld	NG9143	57°26·0′	5°28·5′W	W	25
Abhainn Bhuidhe	Arg & Bt	NM9600	56°9·2′	5°16·6′W	W	55
Abhainn Bhuirgh	N Eil	NB4255	58°24·7′	6°24·6′W	W	8
Abhainn Bràigh-horrisdale	Highld	NG8169	57°39·7′	5°39·8′W	W	19,24
Abhainn Bruachaig	Highld	NH0562	57°36·6′	5°15·4′W	W	19
Abhainn Bun na Gill	N Eil	NG0898	57°52·8′	6°55·1′W	W	14,18
Abhainn Camas Fhionnairigh	Highld	NG5019	57°11·9′	6°7·9′W	W	32
Abhainn Cam Linne	Arg & Bt	NM9823	56°21·6′	5°15·8′W	W	49
Abhainn Caslavat	N Eil	NB0330	58°9·8′	7°2·5′W	W	13
Abhainn Ceann a' Bhàigh	N Eil	NF7872	57°37·6′	7°23·2′W	W	18
Abhainn Ceann-locha	Highld	NG6916	57°10·9′	5°48·9′W	W	32
Abhainn Ceann Loch Ainort	Highld	NG5325	57°15·2′	6°5·3′W	W	32
Abhainn Ceann Loch Eishort	Highld	NG6817	57°11·4′	5°49·9′W	W	32
Abhainn Ceann-loch-morair	Highld	NM8791	56°57·9′	5°29·8′W	W	33,40
Abhainn Chabharstaidh	N Eil	NB3619	58°5·1′	6°28·3′W	W	14
Abhainn Chaidhsiadair	N Eil	NB5560	58°27·8′	6°11·6′W	W	8
Abhainn Chàrlabhaigh	N Eil	NB2140	58°15·9′	6°45·0′W	W	8,13
Abhainn Chatriona	N Eil	NB1105	57°56·7′	6°52·6′W	W	13,14
Abhainn Cheann Chuisil	N Eil	NB0322	58°5·5′	7°1·9′W	W	13
Abhainn Cheann Loch Ouirn	N Eil	NB3615	58°3·0′	6°28·0′W	W	14
Abhainn Cheothadail	N Eil	NB3012	58°1·2′	6°33·9′W	W	13,14
Abhainn Chia-aig	Highld	NN1891	56°58·7′	4°59·2′W	W	34
Abhainn Chithis	N Eil	NB2313	58°1·5′	6°41·0′W	W	13,14
Abhainn Chithis Bheg	N Eil	NB2412	58°1·0′	6°39·9′W	W	13,14
Abhainn Chlachach	Highld	NM7887	56°55·5′	5°38·4′W	W	40
Abhainn Choishleadar	Highld	NG3449	57°27·5′	6°25·6′W	W	23
Abhainn Chonaig	Highld	NG9722	57°14·9′	5°21·4′W	W	25,33
Abhainn Chòrlabhaidh	N Eil	NB3208	57°59·1′	6°31·6′W	W	13,14
Abhainn Chosaidh	Highld	NG9401	57°3·5′	5°23·4′W	W	33
Abhainn Chragoil	N Eil	NB2809	57°59·5′	6°35·7′W	W	13,14
Abhainn Chrois	N Eil	NB5160	58°27·7′	6°15·7′W	W	8
Abhainn Chromadh an t-Seile	N Eil	NB0726	58°7·8′	6°58·2′W	W	13
Abhainn Chuaig	Highld	NG7156	57°32·4′	5°49·1′W	W	24
Abhainn Chuil	N Eil	NB4540	58°16·7′	6°20·5′W	W	8
Abhainn Cille Mhaire	Highld	NG5418	57°11·5′	6°3·8′W	W	32
Abhainn Cleit Duastal	N Eil	NB1020	58°4·7′	6°54·7′W	W	13,14
Abhainn Coire a' Mhalagain	Highld	NH4484	57°49·4′	4°37·1′W	W	20
Abhainn Coire an Iubhair	Highld	NM9261	56°41·9′	5°23·4′W	W	40
Abhainn Coire an t-Seilich	Highld	NH3393	57°54·0′	4°48·6′W	W	20
Abhainn Coire Mhic Nòbuil	Highld	NG8858	57°34·0′	5°32·2′W	W	24
Abhainn Coire Mhic Nòbuil	Highld	NG9159	57°34·6′	5°29·3′W	W	25
Abhainn Coire na Feòla	Arg & Bt	NM6627	56°22·9′	5°47·0′W	W	49
Abhainn Collam	N Eil	NG0585	57°45·7′	6°57·2′W	W	18
Abhainn Crò Chlach	Highld	NH6307	57°8·3′	4°15·4′W	W	35
Abhainn Cuileig	Highld	NH1776	57°44·5′	5°4·0′W	W	20
Abhainn Cumhang a' Ghlinne	Highld	NG8540	57°24·2′	5°34·3′W	W	24
Abhainn Dalach	Arg & Bt	NN0440	56°30·9′	5°10·7′W	W	50
Abhainn Dearg	Highld	NG8747	57°28·1′	5°32·6′W	W	24
Abhainn Deataidh or Lettie River	Highld	NC6805	58°1·1′	4°13·6′W	W	16
Abhainn Dhail	N Eil	NB5059	58°27·1′	6°16·6′W	W	8
Abhainn Dheabhag	Highld	NH2723	57°16·2′	4°51·7′W	W	25
Abhainn Dhìobadail	N Eil	NB1702	57°55·3′	6°46·3′W	W	14
Abhainn Dhìseig	Arg & Bt	NM5034	56°26·2′	6°2·9′W	W	47,48
Abhainn Dhubh	Highld	NG4361	57°34·2′	6°17·4′W	W	23
Abhainn Dhubh	Highld	NH4963	57°38·2′	4°31·3′W	W	20
Abhainn Dhubh	N Eil	NB2530	58°10·7′	6°40·2′W	W	8,13
Abhainn Dhubh Bheag	N Eil	NB0632	58°11·0′	6°59·7′W	W	13
Abhainn Doire Dhubhaig	Arg & Bt	NM4934	56°26·1′	6°3·9′W	W	47,48
Abhainn Drolla	N Eil	NF7672	57°37·6′	7°25·2′W	W	18
Abhainn Droma	Highld	NH2177	57°45·1′	5°0·0′W	W	20
Abhainn Dubh	Highld	NG7853	57°31·0′	5°42·0′W	W	24
Abhainn Dubh	Highld	NH0757	57°34·0′	5°13·2′W	W	25
Abhainn Dubh	N Eil	NB5458	58°26·7′	6°12·5′W	W	8
Abhainn Dubhag	Highld	NH3396	57°55·6′	4°48·7′W	W	20
Abhainn Dubhan	Arg & Bt	NN0001	56°9·8′	5°12·8′W	W	55
Abhainn Duibhe	Pth & Kin	NN4253	56°38·8′	4°34·2′W	W	42,51
Abhainn Eabhal	N Eil	NB0609	57°58·6′	6°57·9′W	W	13,14
Abhainn Eadarra	N Eil	NB1204	57°56·2′	6°51·5′W	W	13,14
Abhainn Ealaidh	N Eil	NB3319	58°5·0′	6°31·3′W	W	13,14
Abhainn Eallaidh	N Eil	NB3422	58°6·7′	6°30·5′W	W	13,14
Abhainn Eik	N Eil	NF7574	57°38·6′	7°26·4′W	W	18
Abhainn Eilg	Highld	NG8121	57°13·9′	5°37·3′W	W	33
Abhainn Èirearaigh	N Eil	NB3249	58°21·1′	6°34·4′W	W	8
Abhainn Fiachanis	Highld	NM3494	56°57·9′	6°22·1′W	W	39
Abhainn Fionain	Arg & Bt	NM9717	56°18·4′	5°16·4′W	W	55
Abhainn Forse	N Eil	NA9715	58°1·5′	7°7·5′W	W	13
Abhainn Gabhsann bho Thuath	N Eil	NB4658	58°26·5′	6°20·7′W	W	8
Abhainn Gaoithe	Stir	NN3706	56°13·4′	4°37·3′W	W	56
Abhainn Gaorsaic	Highld	NH0224	57°16·1′	5°16·6′W	W	25,33
Abhainn Ghabhsainn bho Dheas	N Eil	NB4457	58°25·8′	6°22·7′W	W	8
Abhainn Ghardail	Highld	NM8355	56°38·5′	5°31·9′W	W	49
Abhainn Ghasacleit	N Eil	NB0522	58°5·6′	6°59·9′W	W	13,14
Abhainn Ghearadha	N Eil	NB5050	58°22·3′	6°16·1′W	W	8
Abhainn Gheatraidh	N Eil	NF7633	57°16·6′	7°22·1′W	W	22
Abhainn Gheurasdail	N Eil	NG1097	57°52·4′	6°53·0′W	W	14
Abhainn Ghil	Arg & Bt	NR2843	55°36·5′	6°18·7′W	W	60
Abhainn Ghlas	Arg & Bt	NR2965	55°48·4′	6°19·1′W	W	60
Abhainn Ghlas	N Eil	NB3427	58°9·4′	6°30·8′W	W	8,13
Abhainn Ghlas	Pth & Kin	NN3737	56°30·1′	4°38·4′W	W	50
Abhainn Ghleann Aoistail	Arg & Bt	NR6186	56°0·7′	5°49·6′W	W	61
Abhainn Ghleann Ouirn	N Eil	NB3416	58°3·5′	6°30·1′W	W	13,14
Abhainn Ghleann Ullibh	Arg & Bt	NR4666	55°49·5′	6°2·9′W	W	60,61
Abhainn Ghriais	N Eil	NB4644	58°18·9′	6°19·7′W	W	8
Abhainn Ghrioda	N Eil	NB3932	58°12·2′	6°26·1′W	W	8
Abhainn Ghriomarstaidh	N Eil	NB2129	58°10·0′	6°44·2′W	W	8,13
Abhainn Ghriòmasdal	N Eil	NG0386	57°46·2′	6°59·2′W	W	18
Abhainn Ghrùgaig	Highld	NG8401	57°3·2′	5°33·2′W	W	33
Abhainn Ghuilbinn	Highld	NN4278	56°52·3′	4°35·1′W	W	42
Abhainn Gil an Tàilleir	N Eil	NG0895	57°51·2′	6°54·9′W	W	14,18
Abhainn Gil Shròmois	N Eil	NB2614	58°2·1′	6°38·1′W	W	13,14
Abhainn Glac an t-Seilich	Highld	NH5382	57°48·5′	4°28·0′W	W	20
Abhainn Glac an t-Seilich	Highld	NH5481	57°48·0′	4°26·9′W	W	21
Abhainn Glas	N Eil	NB5533	58°13·3′	6°9·9′W	W	8
Abhainn Gleann a' Ghàraidh	N Eil	NB1416	58°2·7′	6°50·4′W	W	13,14
Abhainn Gleann Airigh an Domhnall	N Eil	NB2710	58°0·0′	6°36·8′W	W	13,14
Abhainn Gleann Astaile	Arg & Bt	NR4971	55°52·3′	6°0·3′W	W	60,61
Abhainn Gleann Bhalamuis	N Eil	NB2903	57°56·3′	6°34·3′W	W	13,14
Abhainn Gleann Chrionaig	N Eil	NB3006	57°57·9′	6°33·5′W	W	13,14
Abhainn Gleann Claidh	N Eil	NB2407	57°58·3′	6°39·6′W	W	13,14
Abhainn Gleann Iubharnadeal	Arg & Bt	NR4670	55°51·6′	6°3·1′W	W	60,61
Abhainn Gleann Leireag	Highld	NC1531	58°14·0′	5°8·6′W	W	15
Abhainn Gleann na h-Uamha	N Eil	NB2712	58°1·1′	6°36·9′W	W	13,14
Abhainn Gleann nam Fiadh	Highld	NH1625	57°17·0′	5°2·7′W	W	25
Abhainn Gleann na Muic	Highld	NC3813	58°4·9′	4°44·4′W	W	16
Abhainn Gleann na Muice	Highld	NH0477	57°44·7′	5°17·1′W	W	19
Abhainn Gleann Shanndaig	N Eil	NB1417	58°3·3′	6°50·4′W	W	13,14
Abhainn Gremiscaig	Highld	NG4761	57°34·4′	6°13·4′W	W	23
Abhainn Horsa-cleit	N Eil	NG0189	57°47·7′	7°1·5′W	W	18
Abhainn Horsacleit	N Eil	NG1496	57°52·0′	6°48·9′W	W	14
Abhainn Hotarol	N Eil	NB0023	58°5·9′	7°5·1′W	W	13
Abhainn Inbhir Ghuiserein	Highld	NG7604	57°4·6′	5°41·3′W	W	33
Abhainn Iolagro	N Eil	NB2831	58°11·3′	6°37·2′W	W	8,13
Abhainn Lacasaidh	N Eil	NB3022	58°6·5′	6°34·6′W	W	13,14
Abhainn Lacasdail	N Eil	NB3935	58°13·9′	6°26·3′W	W	8
Abhainn Lacasdail	N Eil	NG0997	57°52·3′	6°54·0′W	W	14
Abhainn Langadail	N Eil	NB1411	58°0·0′	6°50·0′W	W	13,14
Abhainn Learg an Uinnsinn	Arg & Bt	NR7463	55°48·7′	5°36·0′W	W	62
Abhainn Leireabhaigh	N Eil	NB4129	58°10·7′	6°23·9′W	W	8
Abhainn Leòsaid	N Eil	NB0509	57°58·6′	6°58·9′W	W	13,14
Abhainn Leum nam Meann	Arg & Bt	NR8660	55°47·4′	5°24·4′W	W	62
Abhainn Lìrein	Arg & Bt	NM6933	56°26·2′	5°44·4′W	W	49
Abhainn Liundale	Arg & Bt	NR5479	55°56·7′	5°56·0′W	W	61
Abhainn Lobhair	Arg & Bt	NM9505	56°11·9′	5°17·8′W	W	55
Abhainn Loch an Nid	Highld	NH0877	57°44·8′	5°13·1′W	W	19
Abhainn Loch an Reithe	N Eil	NB2004	57°56·5′	6°43·4′W	W	13,14
Abhainn Loch a' Sgàil	N Eil	NB1306	57°57·3′	6°50·6′W	W	13,14
Abhainn Loch Fhuaran	Arg & Bt	NM5828	56°23·2′	5°54·8′W	W	48
Abhainn Loch na Fùdarlaich	Arg & Bt	NR5277	55°55·6′	5°57·8′W	W	61
Abhainn Loch na h-Oidhche	Highld	NG8968	57°39·4′	5°31·7′W	W	19
Abhainn Loch na Muilne	N Eil	NB2718	58°4·3′	6°37·3′W	W	13,14
Abhainn Loin	N Eil	NF8168	57°35·6′	7°19·9′W	W	18
Abhainn Lonndabhat	N Eil	NB1900	57°54·3′	6°44·1′W	W	14
Abhainn Lusa	Highld	NG7023	57°14·7′	5°48·3′W	W	33
Abhainn Mhàraig	N Eil	NB1705	57°56·9′	6°46·5′W	W	13,14
Abhainn Mhiabhaig	N Eil	NB1007	57°57·7′	6°53·7′W	W	13,14
Abhainn Mhic'-ill Libhri	Arg & Bt	NR5270	55°51·8′	5°57·4′W	W	61
Abhainn Mhór	Arg & Bt	NM9312	56°15·6′	5°20·1′W	W	55
Abhainn Mhór	Arg & Bt	NR4468	55°50·5′	6°4·9′W	W	60,61
Abhainn Mhór	Arg & Bt	NR7277	55°56·2′	5°38·6′W	W	62
Abhainn Mhór	Arg & Bt	NR7772	55°53·6′	5°33·6′W	W	62
Abhainn Mhór	N Eil	NF0999	57°48·8′	8°34·7′W	W	18
Abhainn Mhór a Ghlinne Ruaidh	N Eil	NB1031	58°10·6′	6°55·5′W	W	13
Abhainn Mhòr Ceann Reasort	N Eil	NB1015	58°2·0′	6°54·3′W	W	13,14
Abhainn Mhungasdail	Highld	NM5754	56°37·2′	5°57·2′W	W	47
Abhainn Mór	Highld	NC2012	58°3·9′	5°2·6′W	W	15
Abhainn na Bà Móire	N Eil	NB2634	58°12·8′	6°39·5′W	W	8,13
Abhainn na Beinne Duibhe	N Eil	NF8272	57°37·8′	7°19·2′W	W	18
Abhainn na Bruaiche Duibhe	Highld	NC5819	58°8·5′	4°24·3′W	W	16
Abhainn na Cist	N Eil	NG0787	57°46·9′	6°55·3′W	W	14,18
Abhainn na Clach Airigh	Highld	NC1420	58°8·1′	5°9·1′W	W	15
Abhainn na Cloich	N Eil	NB5251	58°22·9′	6°14·1′W	W	8
Abhainn na Coinnich	Highld	NM8254	56°37·9′	5°32·8′W	W	49
Abhainn na Coite	Arg & Bt	NR5371	55°52·4′	5°56·5′W	W	61
Abhainn na Corpaich	Arg & Bt	NR5790	56°2·7′	5°53·7′W	W	61
Abhainn na Cùile	Arg & Bt	NR8269	55°52·2′	5°28·6′W	W	62
Abhainn na Fearna	Highld	NM8352	56°36·8′	5°31·7′W	W	49
Abhainn na Frithe	Highld	NC8327	58°13·2′	3°59·0′W	W	17
Abhainn na Fùirneis	Highld	NG9770	57°40·7′	5°23·8′W	W	19
Abhainn na Glasa	Highld	NH4679	57°46·7′	4°34·9′W	W	20
Abhainn na h-Uainaire	Arg & Bt	NR4472	55°52·6′	6°5·1′W	W	60,61
Abhainn na h-Uamha	Arg & Bt	NM5135	56°26·7′	6°2·0′W	W	47,48
Abhainn na h-Uamha	N Eil	NB0626	58°7·8′	6°59·2′W	W	13
Abhainn nam Cnoc	Highld	NG4860	57°33·9′	6°12·4′W	W	23
Abhainn nan Eildean	Highld	NG8400	57°2·7′	5°33·2′W	W	33
Abhainn nan Leac	Highld	NG5219	57°11·9′	6°5·9′W	W	32
Abhainn nan Lub	Highld	NG8350	57°29·6′	5°36·8′W	W	24
Abhainn nan Torr	Arg & Bt	NM4924	56°20·8′	6°3·3′W	W	48
Abhainn na Ruighe Duibhe	Highld	NH3526	57°18·0′	4°43·9′W	W	26
Abhainn Nid	Highld	NH1569	57°40·6′	5°5·7′W	W	20
Abhainn Osgaig	Highld	NC0511	58°3·0′	5°17·8′W	W	15
Abhainn Othagro	N Eil	NB2438	58°14·9′	6°41·8′W	W	8,13
Abhainn Phroaig	Arg & Bt	NR4457	55°44·6′	6°4·3′W	W	60
Abhainn Poiblidh	Highld	NH3096	57°55·5′	4°51·8′W	W	20
Abhainn Rangail	Highld	NM3595	56°58·5′	6°21·2′W	W	39
Abhainn Rath	Highld	NN2668	56°46·5′	4°50·4′W	W	41
Abhainn Righ	Highld	NN0462	56°42·8′	5°11·7′W	W	41
Abhainn Ròg	N Eil	NF7734	57°17·2′	7°21·2′W	W	22
Abhainn Rosgay	N Eil	NF7772	57°37·6′	7°24·2′W	W	18
Abhainn Ruadh	N Eil	NA9923	58°5·9′	7°6·1′W	W	13
Abhainn Ruadh	N Eil	NB2014	58°1·9′	6°44·1′W	W	13,14
Abhainn Scaladail	N Eil	NB1709	57°59·1′	6°46·8′W	W	13,14
Abhainn Sgaladail Mhòir	N Eil	NB2311	58°0·4′	6°40·9′W	W	13,14
Abhainn Sgaladal Beag	N Eil	NB2209	57°59·3′	6°41·8′W	W	13,14
Abhainn Sgathaig	Highld	NM3697	56°59·6′	6°20·3′W	W	39
Abhainn Sgeamhaidh	Highld	NC5716	58°6·9′	4°25·2′W	W	16
Abhainn Sgeireabhat	N Eil	NB2915	58°2·7′	6°35·1′W	W	13,14
Abhainn Sgitheach	Highld	NH5162	57°37·7′	4°29·2′W	W	20
Abhainn Shalachain	Highld	NM6248	56°34·1′	5°52·0′W	W	49
Abhainn Sheileboist	N Eil	NG0695	57°51·1′	6°56·9′W	W	14,18
Abhainn Shiaboist	N Eil	NB2645	58°18·8′	6°40·2′W	W	8
Abhainn Shiadair	N Eil	NB3953	58°23·5′	6°27·5′W	W	8
Abhainn Shira	Arg & Bt	NN2542	56°32·5′	4°50·3′W	W	50
Abhainn Shlatach	Highld	NM8881	56°52·6′	5°28·3′W	W	40
Abhainn Shuaineboist	N Eil	NB5163	58°29·3′	6°15·9′W	W	8
Abhainn Sithidh	Highld	NH0726	57°17·3′	5°11·7′W	W	25,33
Abhainn Smuaisibhig	N Eil	NB2705	57°57·3′	6°36·4′W	W	13,14
Abhainn Srath a' Bhàthaich	Highld	NH3672	57°42·7′	4°44·7′W	W	20
Abhainn Srath Coir' an Easaidh	Highld	NC4241	58°20·0′	4°41·4′W	W	9
Abhainn Srath Mhuilich	Highld	NH1144	57°27·1′	5°8·5′W	W	25
Abhainn Srath na Sealga	Highld	NH0680	57°46·3′	5°15·3′W	W	19
Abhainn Srath na Seilge	Highld	NC6622	58°10·3′	4°16·2′W	W	16
Abhainn Sròn a' Chreagain	Highld	NN0472	56°48·2′	5°12·2′W	W	41
Abhainn Staoin	Arg & Bt	NR4252	55°41·8′	6°5·9′W	W	60
Abhainn Strathainn	Arg & Bt	NR8472	55°53·8′	5°26·9′W	W	62
Abhainn Sùrstabhat	N Eil	NB1524	58°7·1′	6°49·9′W	W	13,14
Abhainn Tamanabhaigh	N Eil	NB0520	58°4·5′	6°59·8′W	W	13,14
Abhainn Teithil	Arg & Bt	NM9842	56°31·9′	5°16·6′W	W	49
Abhainn Thorabridh	N Eil	NB1405	57°56·8′	6°49·6′W	W	13,14
Abhainn Thornaraigh	N Eil	NF7724	57°11·8′	7°20·5′W	W	22
Abhainn Thorraigh	N Eil	NB3648	58°20·7′	6°30·2′W	W	8
Abhainn Thousaidh	N Eil	NB1016	58°2·6′	6°54·4′W	W	13,14
Abhainn Thràil	Highld	NG9153	57°31·4′	5°29·0′W	W	25
Abhainn Tir Chonnuill	Arg & Bt	NM4120	56°18·4′	6°10·8′W	W	48
Abhainn Torascleit	N Eil	NB1701	57°54·8′	6°46·2′W	W	14
Abhainn Torra-mhichaig	Highld	NG5330	57°17·9′	6°5·6′W	W	24,32
Abhainn Uaine	N Eil	NB2709	57°59·5′	6°36·7′W	W	13,14
Abhainn Uisinis	N Eil	NF8534	57°17·5′	7°13·3′W	W	22
Abhainn Uisleitir	N Eil	NB1109	57°58·8′	6°52·9′W	W	13,14
Abhainn Ulladail	N Eil	NB0713	58°0·8′	6°57·2′W	W	13,14
Abhainn Ulladail	N Eil	NB0815	58°1·9′	6°56·4′W	W	13,14
Abhainn Unasta	N Eil	NB1107	57°57·8′	6°52·7′W	W	13,14
Abhainn Ur	Highld	NG8086	57°48·8′	5°41·8′W	W	19
Abhainn Urgha	N Eil	NB1601	57°54·7′	6°47·2′W	W	14
Abham	Devon	SX7764	50°28·0′	3°43·6′W	X	202
A'Bheinn	Arg & Bt	NM8403	56°10·5′	5°28·3′W	X	55
A' Bheinn Bhan	Highld	NM9466	56°44·7′	5°21·7′W	X	40
A Bheirigh	N Eil	NB1743	58°17·3′	6°49·3′W	X	8,13
A'Bheirigh	N Eil	NB1845	58°18·4′	6°48·4′W	X	8
A' Bhog-airigh	Arg & Bt	NM5838	56°28·6′	5°55·3′W	X	47,48
A' Bhrìdeanach	Highld	NM2999	57°0·4′	6°27·4′W	X	39
A' Bhuidheanach	Highld	NN4790	56°58·8′	4°30·6′W	H	34
A' Bhuidheanach	Highld	NN6579	56°53·2′	4°12·5′W	H	42
A' Bhuidheanach Bheag	Pth & Kin	NN6677	56°52·2′	4°11·4′W	H	42
A'Bhuidheanaich	Highld	NH7808	57°9·1′	4°0·5′W	H	35
A' Bhuigneach	Arg & Bt	NM6540	56°29·9′	5°48·6′W	X	49
A' Bhuigneach	Arg & Bt	NM6724	56°21·3′	5°45·8′W	X	49
Abingdon	Oxon	SU4997	51°40·4′	1°17·1′W	T	164
Abingdon Airfield	Oxon	SU4799	51°41·5′	1°18·8′W	X	164
Abingdon Br	Oxon	SU4996	51°39·9′	1°17·1′W	X	164
Abingdon Common	Oxon	SU4796	51°39·9′	1°18·8′W	X	164
Abingdon Lane Down	W Berks	SU4982	51°32·3′	1°17·2′W	X	174
Abingdons Fm	Worcs	SO7759	52°14·0′	2°19·8′W	FM	150
Abinger Bottom	Surrey	TQ1244	51°11·3′	0°23·4′W	X	187
Abinger Common	Surrey	TQ1145	51°11·8′	0°24·3′W	T	187
Abinger Forest	Surrey	TQ1545	51°11·8′	0°20·9′W	F	187
Abinger Hammer	Surrey	TQ0947	51°12·9′	0°26·0′W	T	187
Abington	Northnts	SP7761	52°14·7′	0°51·9′W	T	152
Abington	S Lanak	NS9323	55°29·6′	3°41·2′W	T	71,72
Abington Park Fm	Cambs	TL5246	52°5·7′	0°13·5′E	FM	154
Abington Pigotts	Cambs	TL3044	52°5·0′	0°5·8′W	T	153
Abington Vale	Northnts	SP7861	52°14·7′	0°51·1′W	T	152
Abingworth	W Susx	TQ1016	50°56·2′	0°25·7′W	T	198
Ab Kettleby	Leic	SK7223	52°48·2′	0°55·5′W	T	129
Ablake	Somer	ST4425	51°1·5′	2°47·5′W	X	193
Ab Lench	Worcs	SP0151	52°9·7′	1°58·7′W	T	150
Ablington	Glos	SP1007	51°45·9′	1°50·9′W	T	163
Ablington	Wilts	SU1546	51°13·0′	1°46·7′W	T	184
Ablington Down	Wilts	SU1847	51°13·5′	1°44·1′W	X	184
Ablington Downs	Glos	SP0908	51°46·5′	1°51·8′W	X	163
Ablington Furze	Wilts	SU1848	51°14·1′	1°44·1′W	F	184
Abloads Court	Glos	SO8221	51°53·5′	2°15·3′W	X	162
Abnalls, The	Staffs	SK0910	52°41·5′	1°51·6′W	X	128
Abney	Derby	SK1979	53°18·7′	1°42·5′W	T	119
Abney Clough	Derby	SK2079	53°18·7′	1°41·6′W	X	119
Abney Grange	Derby	SK1978	53°18·2′	1°42·5′W	X	119
Abney Hall	Stock	SJ8589	53°24·1′	2°13·1′W	X	109
Abney Low	Derby	SK2079	53°18·7′	1°41·6′W	H	119
Abneylow	Derby	SK2079	53°18·7′	1°41·6′W	X	119
Abney Moor	Derby	SK1879	53°18·7′	1°43·4′W	X	119
Abney Moor	Derby	SK1980	53°19·2′	1°42·5′W	X	110
Abney Wood	Lincs	SK9836	52°55·0′	0°32·1′W	F	130
Aboon the Brae	E Renf	NS4555	55°46·1′	4°27·8′W	X	64
Abour Hill	N Yks	SE2292	54°19·6′	1°39·3′W	X	99
Above Beck	Lancs	SD6067	54°6·1′	2°36·3′W	X	97

Above Beck Fells	Cumbr	SD2999	54°23·1′	3°5·2′W	H	96,97
Abovemead Fm	Bucks	SP7828	51°56·9′	0°51·5′W	FM	165
Abovetown	Corn	SX1558	50°23·8′	4°35·8′W	X	201
Aboyne	Aberd	NO5298	57°4·5′	2°47·1′W	T	37,44
Aboyne Castle	Aberd	NO5299	57°5·0′	2°47·1′W	X	37,44
Abra Barrow	Hants	SU5047	51°13·4′	1°16·7′W	A	185
Abraham Heights	Lancs	SD4661	54°2·8′	2°49·1′W	T	97
Abraham's Bosom	I of Angl	SH2080	53°17·4′	4°41·6′W	W	114
Abraham's Br	Leic	SP4397	52°34·4′	1°21·5′W	X	140
Abraham's Chair	Tames	SD9802	53°31·1′	2°1·4′W	X	109
Abraham's Fm	Essex	TL8725	51°53·8′	0°43·5′E	FM	168
Abraham's Hut	N Yks	SE7393	54°19·9′	0°52·2′W	X	94,100
Abraham's Hut (Cairn)	N Yks	SE7393	54°19·9′	0°52·2′W	A	94,100
Abraham's Valley	Staffs	SK0020	52°46·9′	1°59·6′W	X	128
Abram	Wigan	SD6001	53°30·5′	2°35·8′W	T	109
Abram's Ward	Shetld	HU2981	60°31·0′	1°27·8′W	X	1,3
Abriachan	Highld	NH5535	57°23·2′	4°24·3′W	T	26
Abridge	Essex	TQ4696	51°38·9′	0°7·0′E	T	167,177
Abronhill	N Lanak	NS7875	55°57·4′	3°56·8′W	T	64
Absalom's Fm	Kent	TQ5652	51°15·0′	0°14·5′E	FM	188
Abshields	Northum	NZ1590	55°12·5′	1°45·4′W	X	81
Abshot	Hants	SU5105	50°50·8′	1°16·1′W	T	196
Absol Park	Essex	TL6619	51°50·9′	0°25·0′E	X	167
Abson	S Glos	ST7074	51°28·1′	2°25·5′W	T	172
Abthorpe	Northnts	SP6446	52°6·7′	1°3·5′W	T	152
Abune the Brae	D & G	NX8771	55°1·5′	3°45·6′W	X	84
Abune-the-hill	Orkney	HY2828	59°8·2′	3°15·0′W	T	6
Aby	Lincs	TF4178	53°17·0′	0°7·3′E	T	122
Aby Grange	Lincs	TF4279	53°17·6′	0°8·2′E	X	122
Aby Green Fm	N Yks	SE6481	54°13·5′	1°0·7′W	FM	100
Aby House Fm	Lincs	TF2343	52°58·4′	0°9·7′W	FM	131
Aby House Fm	Lincs	TF4178	53°17·0′	0°7·3′E	FM	122
Abyssinia	Arg & Bt	NN2511	56°15·8′	4°49·1′W	X	50,56
Abystree	Pemb	SN0716	51°48·8′	4°47·6′W	X	158
Acacia Fm	Suff	TM0638	52°0·4′	1°0·5′E	FM	155
Acacia Hall	Lincs	TF0783	53°20·2′	0°23·2′W	X	121
Acairseid	N Eil	NF7809	57°3·8′	7°18·3′W	X	31
Acairseid an Rubha	Highld	NG5600	57°1·9′	6°0·8′W	X	32,39
Acairseid Eilean a' Chléirich	Highld	NB9202	57°57·8′	5°30·5′W	W	15
Acairseid Folaich	Arg & Bt	NM0745	56°30·6′	6°45·3′W	W	46
Acairseid Lee	N Eil	NF9064	57°33·8′	7°10·6′W	W	18
Acairseid Mhór	Arg & Bt	NM2764	56°41·5′	6°27·1′W	W	46,47
Acairseid Mhór	Arg & Bt	NM3542	56°30·0′	6°17·9′W	W	47,48
Acairseid Mhór	Arg & Bt	NM5155	56°37·5′	6°3·1′W	W	47
Acairseid Mhór	Highld	NG6156	57°32·1′	5°59·1′W	W	24
Acairseid Mhór	N Eil	NF7909	57°3·9′	7°17·3′W	W	31
Acairseid nam Madadh	N Eil	NF9467	57°35·6′	7°6·8′W	W	18
Acairseid Thioram	Highld	NG6157	57°32·7′	5°59·2′W	W	24
Acarsaid	Highld	NM5872	56°46·9′	5°57·2′W	T	39,47
Acarsaid an Duin	Arg & Bt	NM0847	56°31·7′	6°44·5′W	W	46
Acarsaid Falaich	N Eil	NF8537	57°19·1′	7°13·5′W	W	22
Acarseid Mhic Mhurchaidh Oig	Highld	NC1650	58°24·3′	5°8·5′W	W	9
Acaster Hill	N Yks	SE5273	54°9·3′	1°11·8′W	X	100
Acaster Malbis	York	SE5845	53°54·1′	1°6·6′W	T	105
Acaster Selby	N Yks	SE5741	53°52·0′	1°7·6′W	T	105
Accar Las	Denb	SJ0568	53°12·3′	3°24·9′W	X	116
Accerhill Hall	N Yks	SD7663	54°4·0′	2°21·6′W	X	98
Accornlee Hall	Lancs	SD8943	53°53·2′	2°9·6′W	X	103
Accott	Devon	SS6432	51°4·5′	3°56·1′W	X	180
Accraplatts	N Yks	SD8862	54°3·5′	2°10·6′W	X	98
Accre	Denb	SJ1752	53°3·8′	3°13·9′W	X	116
Accrington	Lancs	SD7528	53°45·1′	2°22·3′W	T	103
Accurrach Fm	Arg & Bt	NN1120	56°20·3′	5°3·0′W	FM	50,56
Acha	Arg & Bt	NM1854	56°35·8′	6°35·2′W	T	46
Acha	Arg & Bt	NM7616	56°17·3′	5°36·7′W	X	55
A' Chabag	N Eil	NB4214	58°2·7′	6°21·8′W	X	14
Achabraid	Arg & Bt	NR8381	55°58·6′	5°28·2′W	X	55
Achacha	Arg & Bt	NM9440	56°30·7′	5°20·4′W	X	49
Ach a' Chòis	Arg & Bt	NR9380	55°58·4′	5°18·6′W	X	55
Achachork	Highld	NG4745	57°25·8′	6°12·4′W	T	23
Ach a' Chorrain	Highld	NC3761	58°30·7′	4°47·4′W	H	9
Achadacaie	Arg & Bt	NR8364	55°49·5′	5°27·4′W	X	62
Achadachoun	Arg & Bt	NR9867	55°51·5′	5°13·2′W	X	62
Achaderry	Highld	NN2781	56°53·5′	4°50·0′W	X	34,41
Achadh a' Ghlinne	Highld	NG8610	57°8·1′	5°31·7′W	X	33
Achadh an Eas	Highld	NC6637	58°18·3′	4°16·7′W	X	16
Achadh an t-Seilich	Highld	NG8717	57°11·9′	5°31·1′W	X	33
Achadhantuir	Highld	NC0824	58°10·1′	5°15·4′W	X	15
Achadh Beithe	Arg & Bt	NR7125	55°28·2′	5°37·0′W	X	68
Achadh-Chaorann	Arg & Bt	NR7559	55°46·6′	5°34·8′W	X	62
Achadh Cùl a'Bhàrr	Arg & Bt	NR7676	55°55·8′	5°34·7′W	X	62
Achadh Fada	Arg & Bt	NM6242	56°30·9′	5°51·7′W	X	49
Achadh-Luachrach	Highld	NH2503	57°5·3′	4°52·8′W	X	34
Achadh Luirginn	Arg & Bt	NM6336	56°27·7′	5°50·4′W	X	49
Achadh Mór	Highld	NH4260	57°36·4′	4°38·2′W	X	20
Achadh na Craoibh sgitheich	Highld	NM6944	56°32·1′	5°45·0′W	X	49
Achadh na h-Atha	Arg & Bt	NM5029	56°23·5′	6°2·6′W	X	48
Achadh na h-Innseig	Arg & Bt	NM4928	56°22·9′	6°3·5′W	X	48
Achadh-nan-darach	Highld	NH3105	57°6·6′	4°47·0′W	X	34
Achadh nan Each	Arg & Bt	NM5245	56°32·2′	6°1·6′W	X	47,48
Achadunan	Arg & Bt	NN1913	56°16·8′	4°55·0′W	X	50,56
Achadun Bay	Arg & Bt	NM8039	56°29·8′	5°34·0′W	W	49
Achadun Castle	Arg & Bt	NM8039	56°29·8′	5°34·0′W	A	49
Achaeter	Highld	ND0561	58°31·9′	3°37·4′W	X	11,12
Achafolla	Arg & Bt	NM7410	56°14·0′	5°38·3′W	X	55
Achafour Fm	Arg & Bt	NS1170	55°53·4′	5°0·9′W	FM	63
Achafour Hill	Arg & Bt	NS1270	55°53·4′	4°59·9′W	H	63
Achagavel	Highld	NM7656	56°38·8′	5°38·8′W	X	49
Achaglachgach House	Arg & Bt	NR7962	55°48·3′	5°31·2′W	X	62
Achaglass	Arg & Bt	NR7041	55°36·8′	5°38·7′W	X	62
Achaglass	Arg & Bt	NR7855	55°44·5′	5°31·8′W	X	62
Achaguie	Highld	NG4961	57°34·4′	6°11·4′W	X	23
Achahoish	Arg & Bt	NR7877	55°56·3′	5°32·8′W	T	62
Achahoish Fm	Arg & Bt	NR7877	55°56·3′	5°32·8′W	FM	62
A' Chailleach	Highld	NC2473	58°36·8′	5°1·3′W	X	9
A'Chailleach	Highld	NG3230	57°17·2′	6°26·4′W	X	32
A' Chailleach	Highld	NH1371	57°41·7′	5°7·8′W	H	19

A' Chailleach	Highld	NH6804	57°6·7′	4°10·3′W	H	35
A'Chailleach	Highld	NN1857	56°40·4′	4°57·8′W	X	41
A' Chailleach	N Eil	NB0406	57°57·0′	6°59·7′W	X	13
A' Chairidhe	Arg & Bt	NM1154	56°35·6′	6°42·0′W	X	46
Achairn	Highld	ND3050	58°26·2′	3°11·5′W	X	11,12
Achairn Burn	Highld	ND2849	58°25·7′	3°13·5′W	W	11,12
Achalader	Pth & Kin	NO1245	56°35·6′	3°25·5′W	X	53
Achaleathan	Highld	NG4141	57°23·4′	6°18·2′W	X	23
Achaleven	Arg & Bt	NM9133	56°26·8′	5°23·0′W	T	49
Achalic	Arg & Bt	NM8424	56°21·8′	5°29·4′W	X	49
Achallach	Highld	NC7305	58°1·2′	4°8·5′W	X	16
Achallader	Arg & Bt	NN3244	56°33·7′	4°43·6′W	X	50
Achalone	Highld	ND0363	58°32·9′	3°39·5′W	X	11,12
Achalone	Highld	ND1556	58°29·3′	3°27·0′W	T	11,12
Achamhinish	Arg & Bt	NR6549	55°40·9′	5°43·9′W	X	62
Acha Mòr	N Eil	NB3128	58°9·8′	6°34·0′W	T	8,13
Achamore	Arg & Bt	NM2159	56°38·6′	6°32·6′W	X	46,47
Achamore	Arg & Bt	NR5776	55°55·2′	5°52·9′W	X	61
Achamore	Highld	NH9049	57°31·3′	3°49·7′W	X	27
Achamore Fm	Arg & Bt	NR6447	55°39·8′	5°44·7′W	FM	62
Achamore Ho	Arg & Bt	NR6447	55°39·8′	5°44·7′W	X	62
Achanadriane	Arg & Bt	NR7250	55°41·7′	5°37·2′W	X	62
Acha na Lairig	Arg & Bt	NM8730	56°25·1′	5°26·8′W	X	49
Achanalt	Highld	NH2661	57°36·6′	4°54·3′W	X	20
Achanamara	Arg & Bt	NR7787	56°1·7′	5°34·3′W	T	55
Achanarnich	Arg & Bt	NM7702	56°9·8′	5°35·0′W	X	55
Achanarnich Bay	Arg & Bt	NM7601	56°9·2′	5°36·0′W	W	55
Achanarras	Highld	ND1555	58°28·8′	3°27·0′W	X	11,12
Achanarras Hill	Highld	ND1554	58°28·2′	3°27·0′W	H	11,12
Achandunie	Highld	NH6472	57°43·3′	4°16·5′W	X	21
Achaneich	Highld	NN2481	56°53·5′	4°52·9′W	X	34,41
Achanelid	Arg & Bt	NS0087	56°2·3′	5°12·2′W	T	55
Achanellan Burn	Highld	NC7452	58°26·6′	4°9·0′W	W	10
Achaness Burn	Highld	NC8016	58°7·3′	4°1·8′W	W	17
Ach'an Tobhair	Highld	NN0972	56°48·3′	5°7·2′W	T	41
Achany	Highld	NC5601	57°58·8′	4°25·6′W	X	16
Achany Fm	Highld	NC5601	57°58·8′	4°25·6′W	FM	16
Achany Glen	Highld	NC5702	57°59·3′	4°24·7′W	X	16
A' Chaoirnich	Highld	NN7381	56°54·4′	4°4·7′W	X	42
Achaphubuil	Highld	NN0876	56°50·4′	5°8·4′W	T	41
Achara	Highld	NM9854	56°38·3′	5°17·2′W	X	49
Acharacle	Highld	NM6767	56°44·4′	5°48·2′W	T	40
Acharaskill	Highld	ND1543	58°22·3′	3°26·7′W	X	11,12
Achardale	Highld	ND1156	58°29·3′	3°31·1′W	X	11,12
Achareidh	Highld	NH8656	57°35·0′	3°53·9′W	X	27
Achargary	Highld	NC7254	58°27·6′	4°11·2′W	T	10
Acharn	Angus	NO2876	56°52·4′	3°10·4′W	T	44
Acharn	Arg & Bt	NN1235	56°28·4′	5°2·7′W	X	50
Acharn	Highld	NH5873	57°43·7′	4°22·6′W	X	21
Acharn	Highld	NM7050	56°35·4′	5°44·3′W	X	49
Acharn	Pth & Kin	NN7543	56°34·0′	4°1·6′W	T	51,52
Acharn	Stir	NN5631	56°27·2′	4°19·7′W	X	51
Acharn Burn	Pth & Kin	NN7540	56°32·4′	4°1·5′W	W	51,52
Acharn Point	Pth & Kin	NN7544	56°34·5′	4°1·6′W	X	51,52
Acharole	Highld	ND2151	58°26·7′	3°20·7′W	X	11,12
Acharonich	Arg & Bt	NM4639	56°28·7′	6°7·1′W	X	47,48
Acharonich	Arg & Bt	NM8207	56°12·6′	5°30·5′W	H	55
Acharossan	Arg & Bt	NR9376	55°56·2′	5°18·4′W	X	62
Acharossan Burn	Arg & Bt	NR9477	55°56·8′	5°17·5′W	W	62
A' Charraig	Arg & Bt	NM3651	56°34·9′	6°17·5′W	X	47
A'Charraig	Arg & Bt	NR8467	55°51·1′	5°26·6′W	X	62
Acharry	Highld	NH5649	57°30·8′	4°23·8′W	X	26
Acharry	Highld	NH7089	57°52·6′	4°11·0′W	X	21
Acharry Moor	Highld	NH7091	57°53·6′	4°11·1′W	X	21
Acharry Muir	Highld	NH6991	57°53·6′	4°12·1′W	X	21
A' Chasg	Highld	NC9416	58°7·5′	3°47·5′W	X	17
Achastle	Highld	ND2334	58°17·5′	3°18·3′W	X	11
Achastle-shore	Highld	ND2334	58°17·5′	3°18·3′W	X	11
Achateny	Highld	NM5270	56°45·6′	6°3·0′W	X	39,47
Achateny Water	Highld	NM5269	56°45·1′	6°3·0′W	W	47
Achath	Aberd	NJ7310	57°11·1′	2°26·3′W	X	38
Achatomlinie	Highld	NC6509	58°3·2′	4°16·8′W	X	16
Achavady	Highld	NN2986	56°56·3′	4°48·2′W	X	34,41
Achavaich	Arg & Bt	NM8932	56°26·2′	5°24·9′W	X	49
Achavandra Muir	Highld	NH7793	57°54·8′	4°4·1′W	T	21
Achavanich	Highld	ND1742	58°21·8′	3°24·6′W	X	11,12
Achavarigel	Highld	ND0959	58°30·8′	3°33·2′W	X	11,12
Achavarn	Highld	ND0859	58°30·8′	3°34·3′W	X	11,12
Achavelgin	Highld	NH9150	57°31·9′	3°48·8′W	X	27
Achavoulaig	Arg & Bt	NS0268	55°52·1′	5°9·4′W	X	63
Achavraat	Highld	NH9048	57°30·8′	3°49·7′W	X	27
Achavraid	Arg & Bt	NR7857	55°45·6′	5°31·9′W	X	62
Achavrole	Highld	ND1059	58°30·9′	3°32·2′W	X	11,12
Achavrole	Highld	ND1631	58°15·8′	3°25·4′W	X	11
Achbreck	Moray	NJ2933	57°23·2′	3°10·4′W	X	28
Achbuie	Highld	NH5635	57°23·2′	4°23·3′W	X	26
Achbuiligan Tulloch	Highld	NC9865	58°33·9′	3°44·7′W	A	11
Achcheargary Burn	Highld	NC7154	58°27·6′	4°12·2′W	W	10
Ach Chreagach	Arg & Bt	NR9276	55°56·2′	5°19·4′W	X	62
Achcomhairle	Highld	ND1655	58°28·8′	3°26·0′W	X	11,12
Achculin	Highld	NH5635	57°23·2′	4°23·3′W	X	26
Achddu	Carm	SN4401	51°41·4′	4°15·0′W	T	159
Achdregnie	Moray	NJ2424	57°18·3′	3°15·2′W	X	36
Achduart	Highld	NC0503	57°58·7′	5°17·4′W	X	15
A' Chearc	Highld	NG4311	57°7·3′	6°14·3′W	X	32
A' Chearc	N Eil	NB4928	58°10·4′	6°15·7′W	X	8
Achederson	Highld	NH4650	57°31·1′	4°33·8′W	X	26
Acheilidh	Highld	NC6603	58°0·0′	4°15·6′W	X	16
A'Ch'eir Ghorm	Highld	NC3249	58°24·1′	4°52·0′W	X	9
Acheninver	Highld	NC0405	57°59·7′	5°18·5′W	X	15
Achentoul	Highld	NC8733	58°16·5′	3°55·1′W	X	17
Achentoul Forest	Highld	NC8638	58°19·2′	3°56·3′W	X	17
Achentoul Hill	Highld	NC8933	58°16·6′	3°53·1′W	X	17
Achentoul Lodge	Highld	NC8735	58°17·5′	3°55·2′W	X	17
Acheth	Carm	SN5934	51°59·4′	4°2·8′W	X	146
Acheth	Carm	SN7523	51°53·7′	3°48·6′W	X	160
Achfary	Highld	NC2939	58°18·6′	4°54·7′W	T	15
Achfary Forest	Highld	NC2839	58°18·6′	4°55·7′W	F	15
Achfrish	Highld	NC5612	58°4·7′	4°26·0′W	T	16
Achgarve	Highld	NG8893	57°52·8′	5°34·1′W	T	19

Achianich	Pth & Kin	NN7342	56°33·4′	4°3·5′W	X	51,52
Achie	D & G	NX6178	55°4·9′	4°10·2′W	X	77
Achiemore	Highld	NC3567	58°33·9′	4°49·7′W	X	9
Achiemore	Highld	NC8958	58°30·0′	3°53·8′W	T	10
Achies	Highld	ND1355	58°28·7′	3°29·0′W	X	11,12
A' Chill	Highld	NG2605	57°3·5′	6°30·7′W	T	39
Achiltibuie	Highld	NC0208	58°1·3′	5°20·7′W	T	15
Achimenach	Highld	ND0263	58°32·9′	3°40·6′W	X	11,12
Achina	Highld	NC7060	58°30·8′	4°13·4′W	T	10
Achinael	Highld	NH7597	57°57·0′	4°6·2′W	X	21
Achinahuagh	Highld	NC5864	58°32·7′	4°25·9′W	T	10
Achinavish Hill	Highld	ND0930	58°15·2′	3°32·6′W	H	11,17
Achinchanter	Highld	NH8090	57°53·3′	4°1·0′W	X	21
Achindarroch	Highld	NN0055	56°38·9′	5°15·3′W	T	41
Achindaul	Highld	NN1780	56°52·8′	4°59·7′W	X	34,41
Achindown	Highld	NH8347	57°30·1′	3°56·7′W	X	27
Achinduich	Highld	NC5800	57°58·3′	4°23·6′W	X	16
Achinduin	Arg & Bt	NM8129	56°24·4′	5°32·5′W	X	49
Achingale	Highld	ND2453	58°27·8′	3°17·7′W	X	11,12
Achingills	Highld	ND1562	58°32·5′	3°27·1′W	X	11,12
Achingoul	Highld	ND1054	58°28·2′	3°32·1′W	X	11,12
Achinhoan	Arg & Bt	NR7616	55°23·5′	5°31·8′W	X	68,69
Achinhoan Head	Arg & Bt	NR7617	55°24·0′	5°31·8′W	X	68,69
Achinhoan Hill	Arg & Bt	NR7316	55°23·4′	5°34·6′W	H	68
Achininver	Highld	NC5764	58°32·7′	4°26·9′W	T	10
Achiniyhalavin	Highld	NC5664	58°32·7′	4°28·0′W	X	10
Achinreir	Arg & Bt	NM9540	56°30·7′	5°19·5′W	X	49
Achins	Highld	NC9564	58°33·4′	3°47·8′W	X	11
Achintee	Highld	NG9441	57°25·0′	5°25·4′W	T	25
Achintee Ho	Highld	NN1273	56°48·9′	5°4·4′W	X	41
Achin, The	Highld	NC8029	58°14·3′	4°2·2′W	H	17
Achintraid	Highld	NG8438	57°23·1′	5°35·2′W	T	24
A' Chioch	Arg & Bt	NM5333	56°25·7′	5°59·9′W	X	47,48
A' Chioch	Highld	NC2105	58°0·2′	5°1·3′W	X	15
A' Chioch	Highld	NC5729	58°13·9′	4°25·6′W	X	16
A' Chioch	Highld	NG8144	57°26·3′	5°38·5′W	H	24
A Chioch	Highld	NG9065	57°37·8′	5°30·6′W	X	19
A' Chioch	Highld	NH0509	57°8·1′	5°12·9′W	X	33
A' Chioch	Highld	NH1115	57°11·5′	5°7·2′W	H	34
A' Chioch	Highld	NN7985	56°56·7′	3°58·9′W	H	42
A'Chir	N Ayr	NR9642	55°38·0′	5°14·0′W	X	62,69
A' Chiste Dhubh	Highld	NG8606	57°6·0′	5°31·5′W	X	33
Achkeepster	Highld	ND1651	58°26·6′	3°25·9′W	X	11,12
Achlachan Moss	Highld	ND1453	58°27·7′	3°28·0′W	X	11,12
Achlain	Highld	NH2712	57°10·2′	4°51·2′W	X	34
A' Chlaisir	N Eil	NF0997	57°47·8′	8°34·5′W	W	18
Achlaschoille	Highld	NH6937	57°24·5′	4°10·4′W	X	26
Achleach	Highld	NH5564	57°38·8′	4°25·3′W	X	21
Achleanan	Highld	NM5654	56°37·1′	5°58·2′W	X	47
Achleck	Arg & Bt	NM4145	56°31·8′	6°12·3′W	T	47,48
Achleek	Highld	NM7959	56°40·5′	5°36·0′W	X	49
A' Chlèit	Arg & Bt	NM0342	56°28·8′	6°49·0′W	X	46
A' Chlèit	Arg & Bt	NM4118	56°17·3′	6°10·7′W	X	48
A'Chleit	Arg & Bt	NR6841	55°36·7′	5°40·6′W	X	62
A' Chleit	Highld	NC0220	58°7·7′	5°21·3′W	X	15
A' Chléit	Highld	NC3870	58°35·5′	4°46·8′W	X	9
A'chléit	Highld	NC4462	58°31·4′	4°40·2′W	X	9
A Chleith Mhòr	N Eil	NB4948	58°21·2′	6°16·9′W	X	8
Achleum	Highld	NN8597	57°3·2′	3°53·3′W	X	35,36,43
Achley	Highld	NH7890	57°53·2′	4°3·0′W	X	21
Achlian	Arg & Bt	NN1224	56°22·5′	5°2·2′W	X	50
Achlibster	Highld	ND1152	58°27·1′	3°31·0′W	X	11,12
Achlibster Hill	Highld	ND1051	58°26·5′	3°32·0′W	H	11,12
Achlichnie Fm	Moray	NJ1523	57°17·6′	3°24·2′W	FM	36
Achloa Cottages	Pth & Kin	NN7648	56°36·7′	4°0·8′W	X	51,52
Achlochan	Highld	NC0207	58°0·8′	5°20·6′W	X	15
Achlochrach	Moray	NJ2834	57°23·7′	3°11·4′W	X	28
Achlorachan	Highld	NH3255	57°33·5′	4°48·0′W	X	26
Achluachrach	Highld	NN3081	56°53·6′	4°47·0′W	T	34,41
Achlyness	Highld	NC2452	58°25·5′	5°0·4′W	T	9
Achmelvich	Highld	NC0524	58°10·0′	5°18·4′W	T	15
Achmelvich Bay	Highld	NC0525	58°10·5′	5°18·5′W	W	15
Achmony	Highld	NH5030	57°20·4′	4°29·1′W	X	26
Achmore	Highld	NG8533	57°20·5′	5°33·9′W	T	24
Achmore	Highld	NH0296	57°54·8′	5°20·1′W	T	19
Achmore	Moray	NJ2631	57°22·1′	3°13·4′W	X	37
Achmore	Stir	NN5832	56°27·8′	4°17·8′W	X	51
Achmore Burn	Stir	NN5830	56°26·7′	4°17·8′W	W	51
Achmore Farm	Highld	NC2424	58°10·5′	4°59·1′W	FM	15
Achnaba	Arg & Bt	NM9436	56°28·5′	5°20·2′W	X	49
Achnaba	Arg & Bt	NR9085	56°1·0′	5°21·7′W	X	55
Achnabat	Highld	NC6662	58°31·8′	4°17·6′W	X	10
Achnabat	Highld	NH5930	57°20·6′	4°20·1′W	X	26
Achnabechan	Highld	NH9543	57°28·2′	3°44·6′W	X	27
Achnabobane	Highld	NN1981	56°53·4′	4°57·8′W	X	34,41
Achnabourin	Highld	NC7158	58°29·7′	4°12·3′W	X	10
Achnabreck	Arg & Bt	NR8590	56°3·5′	5°26·8′W	X	55
Achnacairn	Arg & Bt	NM9235	56°27·9′	5°22·1′W	X	49
Achnacarinan	Highld	NC0404	57°59·2′	5°18·5′W	X	15
Achnacarnan	Arg & Bt	NR8363	55°48·9′	5°27·4′W	X	62
Achnacarnin	Highld	NC0432	58°14·3′	5°19·9′W	T	15
Achnacarron	Arg & Bt	NN0522	56°21·3′	5°8·9′W	X	50
Achnacarry	Highld	NN1787	56°56·5′	5°0·0′W	T	34,41
Achnaclach	Arg & Bt	NR6915	55°22·7′	5°38·4′W	X	68
Achnaclaoid	Arg & Bt	NR8060	55°47·3′	5°30·1′W	X	62
Achnaclerach	Highld	NH4065	57°39·1′	4°40·4′W	X	20
Achnacloich	Arg & Bt	NM9534	56°27·5′	5°19·2′W	X	49
Ach-Na-Cloich	Arg & Bt	NS2387	56°2·8′	4°50·1′W	X	56
Achnacloich	Highld	NG5908	57°6·3′	5°58·3′W	T	32,39
Achnacloich	Highld	NH5038	57°24·7′	4°29·4′W	X	26
Achnacly	Highld	ND0359	58°30·8′	3°39·4′W	X	11,12
Achnaclyth	Highld	ND0933	58°16·8′	3°32·6′W	X	11,17
Achnacochine	Highld	NN3080	56°53·1′	4°47·0′W	X	34,41
Achnacon	Highld	NN1156	56°39·7′	5°4·6′W	X	41
Achnacone Ho	Arg & Bt	NM9446	56°33·9′	5°20·7′W	X	49
Achnaconeran	Highld	NH4117	57°13·2′	4°37·5′W	X	34
Achnacraig	Arg & Bt	NM4747	56°33·1′	6°6·6′W	X	47,48
Achnacraobh	Arg & Bt	NN0324	56°22·3′	5°11·0′W	X	50
Achnacree Bay	Arg & Bt	NM9235	56°27·9′	5°22·1′W	X	49
Achnacreebeag	Arg & Bt	NM9336	56°28·5′	5°21·2′W	X	49

Achnacreemore	Arg & Bt	NM9236	56°28·5'	5°22·2'W	X	49
Achnacriche	Highld	NM5553	56°36·6'	5°59·1'W	X	47
Achnacroish	Arg & Bt	NM8540	56°30·4'	5°29·2'W	T	49
Ach na Dàlach Bige	Highld	NG8624	57°15·7'	5°32·5'W	W	33
Achnadrish	Arg & Bt	NM4551	56°35·2'	6°8·7'W	X	47
Achnafad	Arg & Bt	NR7251	55°42·2'	5°37·3'W	X	62
Achnafalnich	Arg & Bt	NN2129	56°25·4'	4°53·7'W	X	50
Achnafauld	Pth & Kin	NN8736	56°30·4'	3°49·7'W	X	52
Achnafauld Burn	Pth & Kin	NN8735	56°29·9'	3°49·7'W	W	52
Achnafoy	Aberd	NO5696	57°3·4'	2°43·1'W	X	37,44
Achnafraschoille	Highld	NN2580	56°53·0'	4°51·9'W	X	34,41
Achnagairn	Highld	NH5544	57°28·1'	4°24·6'W	X	26
Achnagarron	Highld	NC7304	58°0·7'	4°8·5'W	X	16
Achnagarron	Highld	NH6770	57°42·3'	4°13·5'W	X	21
Achnagart	Highld	NH5498	57°57·1'	4°27·6'W	X	21
Achnagoichan	Highld	NH9108	57°9·3'	3°47·7'W	X	36
Achnagoul	Arg & Bt	NN0505	56°12·1'	5°8·2'W	X	56
Achnagoul	Highld	ND1632	58°16·4'	3°25·5'W	X	11
Achnaguie	Pth & Kin	NO0052	56°39·2'	3°37·4'W	X	52,53
Achnaha	Highld	NM4668	56°44·3'	6°8·8'W	T	47
Achnaha	Highld	NM6445	56°32·5'	5°49·9'W	X	49
Achnaha Hill	Highld	NM6446	56°33·1'	5°49·9'W	X	49
Achnahaird	Highld	NC0113	58°4·0'	5°21·9'W	X	15
Achnahaird Bay	Highld	NC0114	58°4·5'	5°22·0'W	W	15
Achnahanat	Highld	NH5198	57°57·0'	4°30·6'W	T	20
Achnahannait	Highld	NG5037	57°21·6'	6°9·0'W	X	23,24,32
Achnahannet	Highld	NH5126	57°18·3'	4°27·9'W	X	26,35
Achnahannet	Highld	NH9727	57°19·6'	3°42·2'W	T	36
Achnahard	Arg & Bt	NM3923	56°19·9'	6°12·9'W	T	48
Achnahatnich Farm	Highld	NH9211	57°10·9'	3°46·7'W	FM	36
Achnahosher	Pth & Kin	NO0154	56°40·3'	3°36·5'W	X	52,53
Achnahuie	Highld	NC7107	58°2·3'	4°10·6'W	X	16
Achnairn	Highld	NC5512	58°4·7'	4°27·1'W	T	16
Achnalea	Highld	NM8560	56°41·2'	5°30·2'W	X	40
Achnaluachrach	Highld	NC6709	58°3·3'	4°14·8'W	X	16
Achnambeithach	Highld	NN1356	56°39·8'	5°2·6'W	X	41
Achnameadhonach	Arg & Bt	NM9830	56°25·4'	5°16·1'W	X	49
Achnamoine	Highld	ND1753	58°27·7'	3°24·9'W	X	11,12
Ach' nan Carragh	Arg & Bt	NM4155	56°37·2'	6°12·9'W	X	47
Achnanclach	Highld	NC6351	58°25·8'	4°20·3'W	X	10
Achnandarach	Highld	NG8031	57°19·3'	5°38·8'W	X	24
Achnanellan	Highld	NM7467	56°44·7'	5°41·3'W	X	40
Achnanellan	Highld	NN0984	56°54·7'	5°7·8'W	X	41
Achnangart Fm	Highld	NG9615	57°11·1'	5°22·1'W	FM	33
Achnasaul	Highld	NN1589	56°57·6'	5°2·1'W	X	34,41
Achnascraw	Moray	NJ2421	57°16·7'	3°15·2'W	X	36
Achnasheen	Highld	NH1658	57°34·7'	5°4·2'W	T	25
Achnashellach Forest	Highld	NH0247	57°28·5'	5°17·7'W	X	25
Achnashellach Lodge	Highld	NH0048	57°29·0'	5°19·7'W	X	25
Achnashellach Sta	Highld	NH0048	57°29·0'	5°19·7'W	X	25
Achnashelloch	Arg & Bt	NR8591	56°4·1'	5°26·8'W	X	55
Achnaslishaig Hill	Arg & Bt	NR6414	55°22·1'	5°43·0'W	H	68
Achnasoul	Highld	NH4852	57°32·2'	4°31·9'W	X	26
Achnatone	Highld	NH9248	57°30·8'	3°47·7'W	X	27
Achnatone Ho	Highld	NH9249	57°31·4'	3°47·7'W	X	27
Achnatra	Arg & Bt	NN1209	56°14·4'	5°1·6'W	X	56
Achnavast	Highld	ND0764	58°33·5'	3°35·4'W	X	11,12
Achneigie	Highld	NH0879	57°45·8'	5°13·2'W	X	19
Achneim	Highld	NH6528	57°19·6'	4°14·1'W	X	26,35
Achneim	Highld	NH8648	57°30·7'	3°53·7'W	X	27
Achness Waterfall	Highld	NC4602	57°59·1'	4°35·8'W	W	16
A' Choich	Aberd	NO0998	57°4·1'	3°29·6'W	X	36,43
A Chòineach Beag	Highld	NG9366	57°38·4'	5°27·6'W	H	19
A' Chòinneach	Moray	NJ0304	57°7·3'	3°35·7'W	H	36
Acholter	Arg & Bt	NS0566	55°51·1'	5°6·5'W	X	63
Achork	Highld	NC7505	58°1·3'	4°6·5'W	X	16
Achormlarie	Highld	NH6994	57°55·2'	4°12·2'W	X	21
Achorn	Highld	ND1330	58°15·3'	3°28·5'W	X	11,17
A'Chorra-bheinn	Highld	NG4748	57°27·4'	6°12·6'W	H	23
A' Chòsag	Highld	NG8570	57°40·4'	5°35·9'W	X	19
Achosnich	Highld	NH7293	57°54·7'	4°9·2'W	X	21
Achosnich	Highld	NM4467	56°43·7'	6°10·7'W	T	47
Achow	Highld	ND2236	58°18·6'	3°19·4'W	X	11
Achpopuli	Highld	NH5334	57°22·6'	4°26·2'W	X	26
A' Chraidhleag	Highld	NH4704	57°6·4'	4°31·1'W	X	34
A' Chràlaig	Highld	NH0914	57°10·9'	5°9·2'W	H	33
Achranich	Highld	NM7047	56°33·8'	5°44·2'W	X	49
A' Chrannag	Arg & Bt	NM4338	56°28·1'	6°9·9'W	H	47,48
A' Chrannag	Arg & Bt	NR7275	55°55·1'	5°38·5'W	X	62
A' Chrannag	Highld	NG8715	57°10·8'	5°31·0'W	X	33
Achray Forest	Stir	NN5204	56°12·6'	4°22·7'W	F	57
Achray Water	Stir	NN4906	56°13·6'	4°25·7'W	W	57
A' Chreag	Arg & Bt	NM1828	56°24·8'	4°56·6'W	X	50
A'Chreag	Highld	NM8460	56°41·2'	5°31·2'W	X	40
A Chreag Mhòr	N Eil	NB1741	58°16·3'	6°49·1'W	H	8,13
Achreamie	Highld	ND0166	58°34·5'	3°41·7'W	T	11,12
Achreregan Hill	Highld	ND0262	58°32·4'	3°40·5'W	X	11,12
Achriabhach	Highld	NN1468	56°46·2'	5°2·2'W	X	41
Achridigill	Highld	NC8862	58°32·2'	3°54·9'W	X	10
Achridigill Loch	Highld	NC8561	58°31·6'	3°58·0'W	W	10
Achriesgill	Highld	NC2554	58°26·6'	4°59·4'W	T	9
Achriesgill Water	Highld	NC2653	58°26·1'	4°58·4'W	W	9
Achrimsdale	Highld	NC9006	58°2·0'	3°51·3'W	T	17
Achrimsdale Hill	Highld	NC7827	58°13·2'	4°4·1'W	X	17
Achrintle Burn	Highld	NC8418	58°8·4'	3°57·7'W	W	17
A Chròic	Arg & Bt	NM2262	56°40·3'	6°31·8'W	X	46,47
A' Chrois	Arg & Bt	NL9647	56°31·3'	6°56·2'W	X	46
A' Chrois	Arg & Bt	NN2807	56°13·7'	4°46·0'W	H	56
A' Chrois	Pth & Kin	NN8142	56°33·6'	3°55·7'W	H	52
A'Chruach	Arg & Bt	NM8901	56°9·6'	5°23·4'W	H	55
A'Chruach	Arg & Bt	NM9021	56°20·3'	5°23·4'W	H	49
A'Chruach	Arg & Bt	NN0534	56°27·7'	5°9·5'W	H	50
A'Chruach	Arg & Bt	NR6110	55°19·8'	5°45·7'W	H	68
A'Chruach	Arg & Bt	NR7124	55°27·6'	5°36·9'W	H	68
A'Chruach	Arg & Bt	NR7631	55°31·5'	5°32·5'W	H	68,69
A'Chruach	Arg & Bt	NR9399	56°8·6'	5°19·5'W	H	55
A'Chruach	Arg & Bt	NR9496	56°7·0'	5°18·4'W	H	55
A'Chruach	Arg & Bt	NR9573	55°54·6'	5°16·4'W	X	62
A' Chruach	Arg & Bt	NS0178	55°57·5'	5°10·8'W	H	63
A' Chruach	Arg & Bt	NS0483	56°0·3'	5°8·2'W	H	56
A' Chruach	Arg & Bt	NS1386	56°2·1'	4°59·7'W	H	56
A' Chruach	Highld	NM7797	57°0·9'	5°39·9'W	H	33,40
A' Chruach	Highld	NM8591	56°57·9'	5°31·7'W	X	33,40
Achruach	Highld	NM9177	56°50·5'	5°25·1'W	H	40
A'Chruach	N Ayr	NR9633	55°33·1'	5°13·6'W	H	68,69
A'Chruach	Pth & Kin	NN3656	56°40·3'	4°40·1'W	X	41
Achscoriclate	Highld	ND0844	58°22·8'	3°33·9'W	X	11,12
Achscrabster	Highld	ND0863	58°33·0'	3°34·4'W	X	11,12
Achtalean	Highld	NG4746	57°26·3'	6°12·5'W	T	23
Achtemarack	Highld	NH4731	57°20·9'	4°32·1'W	X	26
Achterneed	Highld	NH4859	57°36·0'	4°32·1'W	T	26
Achtoty	Highld	NC6762	58°31·8'	4°16·6'W	T	10
Achtriochtan	Highld	NN1557	56°40·4'	5°0·7'W	X	41
Achtuie	Highld	NH5231	57°21·0'	4°27·1'W	X	26
Achu	Highld	NH6791	57°53·6'	4°14·1'W	X	21
A' Chuagach	Highld	NM4788	56°55·1'	6°9·0'W	X	39
Achuan	Highld	NH6295	57°55·6'	4°19·3'W	X	21
Achuaran	Arg & Bt	NM8744	56°32·6'	5°27·4'W	X	49
Achuil	Highld	NH6394	57°55·1'	4°18·3'W	X	21
A' Chùil	Highld	NM9492	56°58·7'	5°22·9'W	X	33,40
Achuirghill	Highld	NC4901	57°58·6'	4°32·7'W	X	16
A' Chùli	Arg & Bt	NM6511	56°14·3'	5°47·1'W	X	55
Achunabust	Highld	NC9964	58°33·4'	3°43·7'W	X	11
Achurch	Northnts	TL0282	52°25·8'	0°29·6'W	T	141
Achuvoldrach	Highld	NC5658	58°29·5'	4°27·7'W	T	10
Achuvoldrach Burn	Highld	NC5458	58°29·4'	4°29·8'W	W	10
Achvaich	Highld	NH7194	57°55·3'	4°10·2'W	X	21
Achvalair	Highld	NM9852	56°37·2'	5°17·1'W	X	49
Achvaneran	Highld	NH6734	57°22·9'	4°12·3'W	X	26
Achvarasdal	Highld	NC9864	58°33·4'	3°44·7'W	X	11
Achvarasdal Burn	Highld	NC9959	58°30·7'	3°43·5'W	W	11
Achvoan	Highld	NC7505	58°1·3'	4°6·5'W	X	16
Achvraid	Highld	NH6438	57°25·0'	4°15·4'W	X	26
Achvraid	Highld	NH6626	57°18·6'	4°13·0'W	X	26,35
Achvraie	Highld	NC0405	57°59·7'	5°18·5'W	X	15
Ackbury Heath	Staffs	SJ8706	52°39·3'	2°11·1'W	X	127,139
Ackender Wood	Hants	SU6938	51°8·5'	1°0·4'W	F	186
Ackenthwaite	Cumbr	SD5081	54°13·6'	2°45·6'W	T	97
Ackergill	Highld	ND3553	58°27·9'	3°6·4'W	T	12
Ackergill Links	Highld	ND3456	58°29·5'	3°7·5'W	X	12
Ackergill Links	Highld	ND3456	58°29·5'	3°7·5'W	X	12
Ackergillshore	Highld	ND3554	58°28·4'	3°6·4'W	X	12
Ackergill Tower	Highld	ND3554	58°28·4'	3°6·4'W	A	12
Ackerley Moor	N Yks	SD9174	54°9·9'	2°7·9'W	X	98
Ackers Crossing	Ches	SJ8458	53°7·4'	2°13·9'W	X	118
Ackers Fm	Traf	SJ7592	53°25·7'	2°22·2'W	FM	109
Ackhill	Powys	SO2865	52°16·9'	3°2·9'W	X	137,148
Ackholt	Kent	TR2451	51°13·1'	1°12·9'E	X	179,189
Ackhurst Hall	Wigan	SD5406	53°33·2'	2°41·3'W	X	108
Ackin Royd	Kirk	SE2508	53°34·3'	1°36·9'W	X	110
Acklam	Midd	NZ4817	54°33·0'	1°15·1'W	T	93
Acklam	N Yks	SE7861	54°2·6'	0°48·1'W	T	100
Acklam Lodge	N Yks	SE7761	54°2·6'	0°49·0'W	X	100
Acklam Wold	N Yks	SE7961	54°2·6'	0°47·2'W	X	100
Acklam Wood	N Yks	SE7762	54°3·1'	0°49·0'W	F	100
Acklands	Somer	SS7339	51°8·4'	3°48·5'W	X	180
Ackland's Moor	Devon	SS1344	51°10·1'	4°40·1'W	H	180
Ackleton	Shrops	SO7798	52°35·0'	2°20·0'W	T	138
Ackley Fm	Powys	SJ2501	52°36·3'	3°6·1'W	FM	126
Ackling Dyke	Dorset	SU0116	50°56·8'	1°58·8'W	X	184
Ackling Dyke (Roman Road)	Dorset	SU0116	50°56·8'	1°58·8'W	R	184
Acklington	Northum	NU2201	55°18·4'	1°38·8'W	T	81
Acklington Park	Northum	NU2002	55°18·9'	1°40·7'W	X	81
Acksea Fm	Shrops	SJ3519	52°46·1'	2°57·4'W	FM	126
Ackthorpe Village	Lincs	TF3089	53°23·1'	0°2·3'W	A	113
Ackthorpe Village	Lincs	TF3089	53°23·1'	0°2·3'W	A	122
Ackton	Wakf	SE4121	53°41·3'	1°22·3'W	T	105
Ack Wood	Powys	SO2365	52°16·9'	3°7·3'W	F	137,148
Ackworth Grange	Wakf	SE4517	53°39·1'	1°18·7'W	X	111
Ackworth Ho	Suff	TM0635	51°58·7'	1°0·4'E	X	155
Ackworth Moor Top	Wakf	SE4316	53°38·6'	1°20·6'W	T	111
Ackworth Park Fm	Wakf	SE4318	53°39·6'	1°20·5'W	FM	111
Ackworth School	Wakf	SE4417	53°39·1'	1°19·6'W	X	111
Ackworthy	Devon	SS2323	50°59·0'	4°30·9'W	X	190
Acland Barton	Devon	SS5932	51°4·4'	4°0·4'W	A	180
Acland Barton	Devon	SS6527	51°1·8'	3°55·1'W	X	180
Acle	Norf	TG4010	52°38·3'	1°33·2'E	T	134
Acle Br	Norf	TG4111	52°38·8'	1°34·2'E	X	134
Acle Marshes	Norf	TG4807	52°36·5'	1°40·2'E	X	134
Acock's Green	Birm	SP1183	52°26·9'	1°49·9'W	T	139
Acol	Kent	TR3067	51°21·5'	1°18·6'E	T	179
Acomb	Northum	NY9366	54°59·6'	2°6·1'W	T	87
Acomb	York	SE5750	53°56·8'	1°7·5'W	T	105
Acomb Fell	Northum	NY9568	55°0·6'	2°4·3'W	X	87
Acomb Fm	Donc	SE6702	53°30·9'	0°59·0'W	FM	111
Acomb Ho	N Yks	SE5874	54°9·6'	0°47·9'W	X	100
Aconbury	Heref	SO5033	51°59·8'	2°43·3'W	A	149
Aconbury Court	Heref	SO5133	51°59·8'	2°42·4'W	X	149
Aconbury Hill	Heref	SO5032	51°59·3'	2°43·3'W	H	149
Acoras Scar	N Yks	SE0571	54°8·3'	1°55·0'W	X	98
Acorn Bank	Cumbr	NY6128	54°39·0'	2°35·8'W	A	91
Acorn Cott	Kent	TR0860	51°18·3'	0°59·4'E	X	179
Acorn Fm	N Yks	SE5561	54°2·8'	1°9·2'W	FM	100
Acorn Lodge	Scot Bord	NT1548	55°43·3'	3°20·8'W	X	72
Acorn Wood	Glos	SO7024	51°55·1'	2°25·8'W	F	162
Acorn Wood	Oxon	SU2186	51°34·6'	1°41·4'W	F	174
Acrau	Conwy	SH9363	53°9·4'	3°35·6'W	X	116
Acre	Lancs	SD7824	53°43·0'	2°19·6'W	X	103
Acre	Oldham	SD9306	53°33·3'	2°5·9'W	T	109
A' Creachan	Highld	NC4964	58°32·5'	4°35·2'W	X	9
Acre Br	Lincs	TF3994	53°25·7'	0°5·9'E	X	113
Acre Burn	D & G	NX6371	55°1·1'	4°8·1'W	W	77
Acredale	Scot Bord	NT9364	55°52·4'	2°6·3'W	X	67
Acrefair	Wrex	SJ2743	52°59·0'	3°4·8'W	T	117
Acre Fen	Cambs	TL3784	52°26·4'	0°1·3'E	X	142,143
Acre Fm	E Yorks	SE7342	53°52·4'	0°53·0'W	FM	105,106
Acre Grain Plantn	N Yks	SE5988	54°17·3'	1°5·2'W	F	100
Acrehead	Cumbr	NY4551	54°51·3'	2°51·0'W	X	86
Acrehead	D & G	NX9873	55°2·7'	3°35·4'W	X	84
Acre Hill Fm	Oxon	SP4210	51°47·5'	1°23·1'W	FM	164
Acre Ho	Lincs	TF1196	53°27·2'	0°19·3'W	X	113
Acre Ho	Lincs	TF4131	52°51·7'	0°6·1'E	X	131
Acre Ho	N Yks	SE5180	54°13·0'	1°12·7'W	X	100
Acreknowe	Scot Bord	NT5010	55°23·1'	2°46·9'W	X	79
Acreknowe Reservoir	Scot Bord	NT4910	55°23·1'	2°47·9'W	W	79
Acreland Fm	Northnts	SP9181	52°25·4'	0°39·3'W	FM	141
Acreland Green	Essex	TL6414	51°48·3'	0°23·1'E	X	167
Acre Lea	Highld	NH8481	57°48·5'	3°56·7'W	X	21
Acres	Cumbr	NY6508	54°28·2'	2°32·0'W	X	91
Acres Down	Hants	SU2708	50°52·5'	1°36·6'W	X	195
Acres Down Ho	Hants	SU2609	50°53·0'	1°37·4'W	X	195
Acres Fm	E Yorks	TA0246	53°54·2'	0°26·4'W	FM	106,107
Acres' Fm	W Berks	SU5870	51°25·8'	1°9·6'W	FM	174
Acresford	Derby	SK2913	52°43·1'	1°33·8'W	X	128
Acres Hall	Leeds	SE2332	53°47·3'	1°38·6'W	X	104
Acres Hill	Somer	ST6234	51°6·5'	2°32·2'W	H	183
Acres Ho	York	SE6047	53°55·2'	1°4·8'W	X	105
Acres Nook	Staffs	SJ8453	53°4·7'	2°13·9'W	T	118
Acrestrype	Aberd	NJ7444	57°29·4'	2°25·6'W	X	29
Acre Valley Ho	E Dunb	NS6175	55°57·1'	4°13·1'W	X	64
Acrewalls	Cumbr	NY0218	54°33·1'	3°30·5'W	X	89
Acrise Place	Kent	TR1942	51°8·3'	1°8·2'E	X	179,189
A' Cruach	Arg & Bt	NM8719	56°19·2'	5°26·2'W	H	55
A'Cruach	Arg & Bt	NM9400	56°9·2'	5°18·6'W	X	55
Acthorpe Fm	Lincs	TF3089	53°23·1'	0°2·3'W	FM	113,122
Acthorpe Top	Lincs	TF3088	53°22·6'	0°2·3'W	X	113,122
Acton	Ches	SJ6353	53°4·6'	2°32·7'W	T	118
Acton	Dorset	SY9878	50°36·3'	2°1·3'W	T	195
Acton	Ealing	TQ2080	51°30·6'	0°15·9'W	T	176
Acton	Kent	TQ9028	51°1·4'	0°42·9'E	X	189
Acton	Northum	NU1802	55°19·0'	1°42·6'W	X	81
Acton	Northum	NY8351	54°51·5'	2°15·5'W	X	86,87
Acton	Northum	NY9852	54°52·0'	2°1·4'W	X	87
Acton	Shrops	SO3184	52°27·2'	3°0·5'W	T	137
Acton	Staffs	SJ8241	52°58·2'	2°15·7'W	T	118
Acton	Suff	TL8944	52°4·0'	0°45·8'E	T	155
Acton	Worcs	SO8467	52°18·3'	2°13·7'W	T	138,150
Acton	Wrex	SJ3451	53°3·4'	2°58·7'W	T	117
Acton Bank	Shrops	SO3185	52°27·8'	3°0·5'W	X	137
Acton Beauchamp	Heref	SO6750	52°9·1'	2°28·5'W	T	149
Acton Br	Staffs	SJ9318	52°45·8'	2°5·8'W	X	127
Acton Bridge	Ches	SJ5975	53°16·5'	2°36·5'W	T	117
Acton Burn	Northum	NY8251	54°51·5'	2°16·4'W	W	86,87
Acton Burn	Northum	NY9753	54°52·6'	2°2·4'W	W	87
Acton Burnell	Shrops	SJ5301	52°36·5'	2°41·2'W	T	126
Acton Burnell Castle	Shrops	SJ5301	52°36·5'	2°41·2'W	A	126
Acton Castle	Corn	SW5528	50°6·3'	5°25·2'W	X	203
Acton Court	Heref	SO6950	52°9·1'	2°26·8'W	X	149
Acton Court	S Glos	ST6784	51°33·5'	2°28·2'W	A	172
Acton Dene	Northum	NU1802	55°19·0'	1°42·6'W	X	81
Acton Fell	Northum	NY9554	54°53·1'	2°4·3'W	X	87
Acton Fm	Ches	SJ8575	53°16·5'	2°13·1'W	FM	118
Acton Fm	Kent	TQ9350	51°13·2'	0°46·2'E	FM	189
Acton Fm	Staffs	SJ8241	52°58·2'	2°15·7'W	FM	118
Acton Grange	Ches	SJ6253	53°4·6'	2°33·6'W	X	118
Acton Green	Heref	SO6950	52°9·1'	2°26·8'W	T	149
Acton Green	Houns	TQ2079	51°30·1'	0°15·9'W	T	176
Acton Hall	Glos	SO6902	51°43·2'	2°26·5'W	X	162
Acton Hall	Worcs	SO8567	52°18·3'	2°12·8'W	X	150
Acton Hill	Staffs	SJ8328	52°51·2'	2°14·7'W	X	127
Acton Hill	Staffs	SJ9419	52°46·4'	2°4·9'W	X	127
Actonhill Fm	Staffs	SJ8241	52°58·2'	2°15·7'W	FM	118
Acton Ho	Northum	NU1902	55°18·9'	1°41·6'W	X	81
Acton Lea	Shrops	SJ5422	52°47·9'	2°40·5'W	X	126
Acton Lodge	S Glos	ST6884	51°33·5'	2°27·3'W	X	172
Acton Mill Fm	Heref	SO7150	52°9·1'	2°25·0'W	FM	149
Acton Moor	Northum	NY8051	54°51·5'	2°18·3'W	X	86,87
Acton Pigott	Shrops	SJ5402	52°37·1'	2°40·4'W	T	126
Acton Place	Suff	TL8845	52°4·5'	0°45·0'E	T	155
Acton Reynald	Shrops	SJ5323	52°48·4'	2°41·4'W	T	126
Acton Round	Shrops	SO6395	52°33·3'	2°32·3'W	T	138
Acton Scott	Shrops	SO4589	52°30·0'	2°48·2'W	T	137,138
Acton's Fm	E Susx	TQ7510	50°52·0'	0°29·6'E	FM	199
Actons Fm	Herts	TL4414	51°48·6'	0°5·7'E	FM	167
Acton Trussell	Staffs	SJ9318	52°45·8'	2°5·8'W	T	127
Acton Turville	S Glos	ST8080	51°31·3'	2°16·9'W	T	173
Adabroc	N Eil	NB5363	58°29·4'	6°13·8'W	T	8
Adam-a-Cove	Cumbr	NY2404	54°25·8'	3°9·9'W	X	89,90
Adambrae	W Loth	NT0465	55°52·4'	3°31·6'W	T	65
Adamcroft	S Ayr	NS4728	55°31·6'	4°25·0'W	X	70
Adam Hill	Bolton	SD6612	53°36·5'	2°30·4'W	X	109
Adamhill	S Ayr	NS4330	55°32·6'	4°28·9'W	X	70
Adams	Lancs	SD8452	53°58·1'	2°14·2'W	X	103
Adam's Chair	D & G	NX8148	54°49·0'	3°50·7'W	X	84
Adam's Cot	Heref	SO6522	51°54·0'	2°30·1'W	X	162
Adam Seat	Cumbr	NY4709	54°28·7'	2°48·7'W	H	90
Adam's Fm	E Susx	TQ7610	50°52·0'	0°30·5'E	FM	199
Adams Gorse Fm	Leic	SK7311	52°41·7'	0°54·8'W	FM	129
Adam's Grave	Wilts	SU1163	51°22·2'	1°50·1'W	X	173
Adam's Grave (Long Barrow)	Wilts	SU1163	51°22·2'	1°50·1'W	A	173
Adam's Green	Dorset	ST5407	50°51·9'	2°38·8'W	T	194
Adam's Hall	N Yks	SE5573	54°9·2'	1°9·1'W	X	100
Adam's Hill	Worcs	SO9279	52°24·8'	2°6·7'W	X	139
Adamson Fm	N Yks	SE6438	53°50·3'	1°1·2'W	FM	105,106
Adamston	Aberd	NJ5637	57°25·5'	2°43·5'W	X	29
Adams Well Fm	Kent	TQ6352	51°14·9'	0°20·5'E	FM	188
Adams Well Fm	Suff	TL9437	52°0·1'	0°50·0'E	FM	155
Adams Wood	Northnts	SP9697	52°34·0'	0°34·6'W	F	141
Adamswood Fm	Worcs	SO6865	52°17·2'	2°27·8'W	FM	138,149
Adamthwaite	Cumbr	SD7099	54°23·4'	2°27·3'W	X	98
Adamton Ho	S Ayr	NS3727	55°30·8'	4°34·5'W	X	70
Adamton Mains	S Ayr	NS3728	55°31·4'	4°34·5'W	X	70
Adbaston	Staffs	SJ7627	52°50·6'	2°21·0'W	T	127
Adbaston Fm	Staffs	SJ7528	52°51·2'	2°21·9'W	FM	127
Adber	Dorset	ST5920	50°58·9'	2°34·7'W	T	183
Adbolton	Notts	SK6038	52°56·4'	1°6·0'W	T	129
Adbury Fm	Hants	SU4862	51°21·5'	1°18·2'W	FM	174
Adbury Ho	Hants	SU4863	51°22·1'	1°18·2'W	X	174

Adbury Park	Hants	SU4862	51°21·5′	1°18·2′W	X	174,174
Adcombe Hill	Somer	ST2217	50°57·1′	3°6·2′W	H	193
Adcote	Shrops	SJ4119	52°46·2′	2°52·1′W	A	126
Adcote Mill	Shrops	SJ4219	52°46·2′	2°51·2′W	X	126
Addah Wood	Rut	SK9617	52°44·8′	0°34·3′W	F	130
Addashaw Fm	Ches	SJ6668	53°12·7′	2°30·1′W	FM	118
Addenbrooke's Hospl	Cambs	TL4655	52°10·7′	0°8·5′E	X	154
Adderbury	Oxon	SP4735	52°0·9′	1°18·5′W	T	151
Adderbury Grounds Fm	Oxon	SP4733	51°59·8′	1°18·5′W	FM	151
Addergill Hill	D & G	NY3590	55°12·3′	3°0·9′W	H	79
Adderley	Shrops	SJ6639	52°57·1′	2°30·0′W	T	127
Adderley	Staffs	SJ9943	52°59·3′	2°0·5′W	X	118
Adderley Green	C of Stoke	SJ9144	52°59·8′	2°7·6′W	T	118
Adderley Green	Staffs	SJ7747	53°1·4′	2°20·2′W	X	118
Adderley Hall Fm	Shrops	SJ6539	52°57·1′	2°30·9′W	FM	127
Adderley Lodge	Shrops	SJ6538	52°56·5′	2°30·8′W	X	127
Adderley Park Sta	Birm	SP0987	52°29·1′	1°51·6′W	X	139
Adder's Green	Staffs	SK0265	53°11·2′	1°57·8′W	X	119
Adder's Moss	Ches	SJ8677	53°17·6′	2°12·2′W	X	118
Adderstone Grange	Northum	NU1430	55°34·1′	1°46·2′W	X	75
Adderstone Hall Fm	Northum	NU1330	55°34·1′	1°47·2′W	FM	75
Adderstone Lowmill	Northum	NU1431	55°34·6′	1°46·2′W	X	75
Adderstone Mains	Northum	NU1331	55°34·6′	1°47·2′W	X	75
Adderstone Rigg	N Yks	SE8790	54°18·1′	0°39·4′W	H	94,101
Adderston Lee	Scot Bord	NT5211	55°23·7′	2°45·0′W	X	79
Adderstonlee Moss	Scot Bord	NT5312	55°24·2′	2°44·1′W	X	79
Adderston Shiels	Scot Bord	NT5109	55°22·6′	2°46·0′W	X	79
Addestone Fm	Wilts	SU0643	51°11·4′	1°54·5′W	FM	184
Addicate	Angus	NO6362	56°45·1′	2°35·9′W	X	45
Addicroft	Corn	SX2972	50°31·6′	4°24·4′W	X	201
Addie Hill	Moray	NJ4459	57°37·3′	2°55·8′W	H	28
Addiewell	W Loth	NS9962	55°50·7′	3°36·3′W	T	65
Addingham	Brad	SE0749	53°56·5′	1°53·2′W	T	104
Addingham High Moor	Brad	SE0747	53°55·4′	1°53·2′W	X	104
Addingham Moorside	Brad	SE0747	53°55·4′	1°53·2′W	T	104
Addingrove Fm	Bucks	SP6611	51°47·9′	1°2·2′W	FM	164,165
Addington	Bucks	SP7428	51°57·0′	0°55·0′W	T	165
Addington	Corn	SX2565	50°27·8′	4°27·6′W	T	201
Addington	Croy	TQ3764	51°21·7′	0°1·5′W	T	177,187
Addington	Kent	TQ6559	51°18·6′	0°22·4′E	T	178,188
Addington	Lancs	SD5268	54°6·6′	2°43·6′W	X	97
Addington Hills	Croy	TQ3564	51°21·8′	0°3·3′W	X	177,187
Addington Manor	Bucks	SP7428	51°57·0′	0°55·0′W	X	165
Addington Palace	Croy	TQ3664	51°21·8′	0°2·4′W	X	177,187
Addinston	Scot Bord	NT5253	55°46·3′	2°45·5′W	T	66,73
Addinston Hill	Scot Bord	NT5154	55°46·9′	2°46·4′W	H	66,73
Addiscombe	Croy	TQ3466	51°22·9′	0°4·1′W	T	176,177
Addiscott	Devon	SX6693	50°43·5′	3°53·5′W	X	191
Addis Fm	Worcs	SO8967	52°18·3′	2°9·3′W	FM	150
Addislade	Devon	SX7164	50°27·9′	3°48·7′W	X	202
Addiston Mains	C of Edin	NT1569	55°54·7′	3°21·1′W	X	65
Addlebrough	N Yks	SD9487	54°17·0′	2°5·1′W	H	98
Addlepits	Pemb	SN0517	51°49·3′	4°49·4′W	X	158
Addlestone	Surrey	TQ0464	51°22·2′	0°30·0′W	T	176,186
Addlestonemoor	Surrey	TQ0465	51°22·7′	0°29·9′W	T	176
Addlethorpe	Lincs	TF5468	53°11·4′	0°18·7′E	T	122
Addlethorpe Grange	N Yks	SE3448	53°55·9′	1°28·5′W	X	104
Addlingham Low Moor	Brad	SE0549	53°56·5′	1°55·0′W	X	104
Addycombe	Northum	NU0502	55°19·0′	1°54·8′W	X	81
Addyfield	Cumbr	SD4089	54°17·8′	2°54·9′W	X	96,97
Addy Ho	Cumbr	NY0700	54°23·5′	3°25·5′W	X	89
Addy's Firs	Glos	ST9193	51°38·4′	2°7·4′W	F	163,173
Adel	Leeds	SE2739	53°51·0′	1°35·0′W	T	104
Adelaide Cottage	Win & Maid	SU9776	51°28·7′	0°35·8′W	X	175,176
Adel Dam	Leeds	SE2741	53°52·1′	1°34·9′W	W	104
Adelphi	Durham	NZ1042	54°46·6′	1°50·2′W	X	88
Aden	Gwyn	SH5164	53°9·4′	4°13·3′W	X	114,115
Aden Cottage	Durham	NZ2543	54°47·1′	1°36·3′W	X	88
Aden Country Park	Aberd	NJ9847	57°31·0′	2°1·5′W	X	30
Adeney	Wrekin	SJ7018	52°45·8′	2°26·3′W	T	127
Ades	E Susx	TQ4019	50°57·4′	0°0·0′W	X	198
Adeyfield	Herts	TL0707	51°45·3′	0°26·6′W	T	166
Adfa	Powys	SJ0501	52°36·2′	3°23·8′W	T	136
Adforton	Heref	SO4071	52°20·3′	2°52·4′W	T	137,148
Adgestone	I of W	SZ5985	50°39·9′	1°9·5′W	T	196
Adhurst St Mary	Hants	SU7624	51°0·8′	0°54·6′W	X	197
Adielinn Plantation	Angus	NO3571	56°49·8′	3°3·5′W	F	44
Adisham	Kent	TR2253	51°14·2′	1°11·2′E	T	179,189
Adisham Court	Kent	TR2254	51°14·7′	1°11·2′E	A	179,189
Adjavin Fm	Devon	SS4225	51°0·4′	4°14·7′W	FM	180,190
Adkin's Wood	Suff	TL8261	52°13·3′	0°40·3′E	F	155
Adlestrop	Glos	SP2427	51°56·7′	1°38·7′W	T	163
Adlestrop Park	Glos	SP2426	51°56·2′	1°38·7′W	X	163
Adley Moor	Heref	SO3774	52°21·9′	2°55·1′W	X	137,148
Adleymoor Common	Heref	SO3774	52°21·9′	2°55·1′W	X	137,148
Adlingfleet	E Yorks	SE8421	53°41·0′	0°43·3′W	T	106,112
Adlingfleet Drain	E Yorks	SE8421	53°41·0′	0°43·3′W	W	106,112
Adlingfleet Grange	E Yorks	SE8119	53°39·9′	0°46·0′W	X	112
Adlington	Ches	SJ9180	53°19·3′	2°7·7′W	T	109
Adlington	Lancs	SD6013	53°37·0′	2°35·9′W	T	109
Adlington Hall	Ches	SJ9080	53°19·3′	2°8·6′W	A	109
Adlington Hall Fm	Lancs	SD5812	53°36·4′	2°37·7′W	FM	108
Adlington Park	Lancs	SD5811	53°35·9′	2°37·7′W	T	108
Admaston	Staffs	SK0523	52°48·5′	1°55·1′W	T	128
Admaston	Wrekin	SJ6312	52°42·5′	2°32·5′W	T	127
Admergill	Lancs	SD8542	53°52·7′	2°13·3′W	X	103
Admergill Pasture	Lancs	SD8643	53°53·2′	2°12·4′W	X	103
Admington	Warw	SP2046	52°7·0′	1°42·1′W	T	151
Admington Grounds	Warw	SP1947	52°7·5′	1°43·0′W	X	151
Admington Lane Fm	Warw	SP1944	52°5·9′	1°43·0′W	FM	151
Admiral Ho	Kent	TQ8457	51°17·2′	0°38·7′E	X	178,188
Admiral Plantn	E Yorks	SE8158	54°0·9′	0°45·4′W	F	106
Admiral's Carr	Suff	TM1675	52°20·1′	1°10·6′E	F	144,156
Admiral's Fm	Essex	TM1122	51°51·6′	1°4·3′E	FM	168,169
Admiral's Fm	Highld	NH6982	57°48·8′	4°11·8′W	FM	21
Admiral's Fm	Norf	TF5624	52°47·7′	0°19·2′E	FM	131
Admirals Gorse	Ches	SJ7143	52°59·3′	2°25·5′W	X	118
Admiral Storr's Tower	E Yorks	TA2833	53°46·9′	0°3·0′W	X	107
Admiral's Wood	Lancs	SD7949	53°56·4′	2°18·8′W	F	103
Admiralty Point	Norf	TF5725	52°48·2′	0°20·1′E	X	131

Admiral Wood	Kent	TQ8558	51°17·7′	0°39·6′E	F	178
Admiston Fm	Dorset	SY7693	50°44·4′	2°20·0′W	FM	194
Adniston	E Loth	NT4272	55°56·5′	2°55·3′W	X	66
Adpar	Cered	SN3041	52°2·7′	4°28·3′W	T	145
Adra-felin	Wrex	SJ4042	52°58·6′	2°53·2′W	X	117
Adsborough	Somer	ST2729	51°3·6′	3°2·1′W	T	193
Adscombe	Somer	ST1837	51°7·8′	3°9·9′W	T	181
Adsdean Ho	W Susx	SU7909	50°52·7′	0°52·2′W	X	197
Adsett	Glos	SO7214	51°49·7′	2°24·0′W	X	162
Adsett Court	Glos	SO7214	51°49·7′	2°24·0′W	X	162
Adstock	Bucks	SP7330	51°58·1′	0°55·8′W	T	152,165
Adstockfields Fm	Bucks	SP7530	51°58·0′	0°54·1′W	FM	152,165
Adstone	Northnts	SP5951	52°9·5′	1°7·9′W	T	152
Adstone	Shrops	SO3994	52°32·7′	2°53·6′W	X	137
Adstone Hill	Shrops	SO3894	52°32·7′	2°54·5′W	H	137
Adstone Ho	Northnts	SP5951	52°9·5′	1°7·9′W	X	152
Adstone Lodge	Northnts	SP5852	52°10·0′	1°8·7′W	X	152
Adstone Lodge	Northnts	SP6050	52°8·9′	1°7·0′W	X	152
Adswood	Stock	SJ8888	53°23·6′	2°10·4′W	T	109
Adventurers' Fen	Cambs	TL4374	52°21·0′	0°6·4′E	X	142,143
Adventurers' Fen	Cambs	TL5569	52°18·1′	0°16·8′E	X	154
Adventurers' Ground Fm	Cambs	TL5564	52°15·4′	0°16·7′E	FM	154
Adventurers' Land	Cambs	TF3602	52°36·2′	0°0·9′E	X	142
Adversane	W Susx	TQ0723	51°0·0′	0°28·1′W	T	197
Advie	Highld	NJ1234	57°23·5′	3°27·4′W	T	28
Adwalton	Leeds	SE2328	53°45·1′	1°38·7′W	T	104
Adwell	Oxon	SU6999	51°41·4′	0°59·7′W	T	165
Adwell Cop	Oxon	SU7099	51°41·4′	0°58·8′W	F	165
Adwell Cop (Mound)	Oxon	SU7099	51°41·4′	0°58·8′W	A	165
Adwell Fm	Oxon	SU7099	51°41·4′	0°58·8′W	FM	165
Adwick Grange	Donc	SE5407	53°33·6′	1°10·7′W	X	111
Adwick Le Street	Donc	SE5307	53°33·7′	1°11·6′W	T	111
Adwick upon Dearne	Donc	SE4701	53°30·5′	1°17·1′W	T	111
Adworthy	Devon	SS7715	50°55·5′	3°44·6′W	X	180
Adwy-dêg	Gwyn	SH6931	52°51·9′	3°56·4′W	X	124
Adwyrwaen	Gwyn	SH5858	53°6·3′	4°6·9′W	X	115
Adwywynt	Powys	SJ0917	52°44·8′	3°20·5′W	X	125
Adziel	Aberd	NJ9453	57°34·3′	2°5·6′W	X	30
Adzor Bank	Heref	SO4847	52°7·4′	2°45·2′W	X	148,149
Ae	D & G	NX9889	55°11·3′	3°35·7′W	T	78
Ae Bridgend	D & G	NY0186	55°9·8′	3°32·8′W	X	78
Aeddren	Conwy	SH9344	52°59·2′	3°35·2′W	X	125
Aelwyd-uchaf	Denb	SJ0974	53°15·6′	3°21·4′W	X	116
Aelybryn	Cered	SN5872	52°19·9′	4°4·6′W	X	135
Ael-y-coryn	Wrex	SJ1633	52°53·5′	3°14·5′W	X	125
Aeron Dale	Cered	SN6260	52°13·5′	4°0·8′W	X	146
Aesha Head	Shetld	HU1460	60°19·7′	1°44·3′W	X	3
Aesica (Roman Fort)	Northum	NY7066	54°59·5′	2°27·7′W	R	86,87
Afallenchwerw	Powys	SN9854	52°10·7′	3°29·1′W	X	147
Afan Argoed Country Park	Nth Pt Talb	SS8194	51°38·2′	3°42·8′W	X	170
Affaland	Devon	SX3298	50°45·7′	4°22·5′W	X	190
Affaland Moor	Devon	SS3100	50°46·7′	4°23·5′W	X	190
Affaland Wood	Corn	SX3198	50°45·7′	4°23·4′W	F	190
Affath	Aberd	NJ8951	57°33·2′	2°10·6′W	X	30
Affeton Barton	Devon	SS7513	50°54·4′	3°46·3′W	X	180
Affeton Moor	Devon	SS7614	50°55·0′	3°45·5′W	X	180
Affetside	Bury	SD7513	53°37·0′	2°22·3′W	T	109
Affleck	Aberd	NJ5540	57°27·1′	2°44·5′W	X	29
Affleck	Aberd	NJ8623	57°18·1′	2°13·5′W	T	38
Affleck	Aberd	NJ9148	57°31·6′	2°8·6′W	X	30
Affleck Castle	Angus	NO4938	56°32·1′	2°49·3′W	A	54
Afflington Fm	Dorset	SY9780	50°37·4′	2°2·2′W	FM	195
Afflochie	Angus	NO4764	56°46·1′	2°51·6′W	X	44
Afforsk	Aberd	NJ7963	57°39·6′	2°20·7′W	X	29,30
Affpuddle	Dorset	SY8093	50°44·4′	2°16·6′W	T	194
Affpuddle Heath	Dorset	SY8092	50°43·9′	2°16·6′W	X	194
Affrick's Fm	Bucks	SU9098	51°40·6′	0°41·5′W	FM	165
Affric Lodge	Highld	NH1822	57°15·4′	5°0·6′W	X	25
Affrusk Fm	Aberd	NO6993	57°1·9′	2°30·2′W	FM	38,45
Afon Aeron	Cered	SN5357	52°11·7′	4°8·7′W	W	146
Afon Afan	Nth Pt Talb	SS8295	51°38·7′	3°41·9′W	W	170
Afon Alaw	I of Angl	SH3483	53°19·3′	4°29·1′W	W	114
Afon Aled	Conwy	SH9260	53°7·8′	3°36·4′W	W	116
Afon Aled	Conwy	SH9567	53°11·6′	3°33·9′W	W	116
Afon Alice	Gwyn	SH6901	52°35·7′	3°55·6′W	W	135
Afon Alun	V of Glam	SS9274	51°27·5′	3°32·9′W	W	170
Afon Alun or River Alyn	Denb	SJ1859	53°7·6′	3°13·1′W	W	116
Afon Alun or River Alyn	Flint	SJ2958	53°7·1′	3°3·2′W	W	117
Afon Alwen	Conwy	SH9056	53°5·6′	3°38·2′W	W	116
Afon Alwen	Conwy	SJ0048	53°1·4′	3°29·1′W	W	116
Afon Alwen	Denb	SJ0343	52°58·8′	3°26·3′W	W	125
Afon Aman	Carm	SN6513	51°48·2′	3°57·1′W	W	159
Afon Amnodd-bwll	Gwyn	SH8037	52°55·3′	3°46·7′W	W	124,125
Afon Anafon	Gwyn	SH6871	53°13·4′	3°58·2′W	W	115
Afon Angell	Gwyn	SH8111	52°41·3′	3°45·2′W	W	124,125
Afon Anghof	Pemb	SN0028	51°55·1′	4°54·1′W	W	145,157,158
Afon Annell	Carm	SN4722	51°52·8′	4°13·0′W	W	159
Afon Annell	Carm	SN6537	52°1·1′	3°57·7′W	W	146
Afon Annell	Carm	SN6942	52°3·9′	3°54·3′W	W	146,160
Afon Arban	Powys	SN8463	52°15·4′	3°41·6′W	W	147
Afon Arddu	Gwyn	SH5857	53°5·7′	4°6·8′W	W	115
Afon Arran	Gwyn	SH7315	52°43·3′	3°52·4′W	W	124
Afon Arth	Cered	SN4862	52°14·4′	4°13·2′W	W	146
Afon Arth	Cered	SN5462	52°14·5′	4°7·9′W	W	146
Afon Artro	Gwyn	SH6128	52°50·1′	4°3·4′W	W	124
Afon Asen	Carm	SN2430	51°56·7′	4°33·3′W	W	145
Afon Babi or Afon Lâs	Gwyn	SH7623	52°47·7′	3°49·9′W	W	124
Afon Bannon	Pemb	SN1635	51°59·2′	4°40·4′W	W	145
Afon Banwy	Powys	SH9612	52°42·0′	3°31·9′W	W	125
Afon Banwy	Powys	SJ0510	52°41·0′	3°23·9′W	W	125
Afon Banwy neu Einion	Powys	SJ1207	52°39·5′	3°17·7′W	X	125
Afon Barddu	Carm	SN3034	51°58·9′	4°28·1′W	W	145
Afon Barlwyd	Gwyn	SH7047	53°0·5′	3°55·9′W	W	115
Afon Bedw	Cered	SN3550	52°7·7′	4°24·2′W	W	145
Afon Beidog	Cered	SN6069	52°18·3′	4°2·8′W	W	135
Afon Bele	Carm	SN3632	51°58·0′	4°22·8′W	W	145
Afon Berthen	Gwyn	SH6464	53°9·6′	4°1·6′W	W	115
Afon Berwyn	Cered	SN7158	52°12·5′	3°52·9′W	W	146,147
Afon Bidno	Powys	SN8782	52°25·7′	3°39·3′W	W	135,136
Afon Biga	Powys	SN8689	52°29·5′	3°40·3′W	W	135,136

Afon Blotweth	Carm	SN5237	52°0·9′	4°9·0′W	W	146
Afon-Bradley Fm	Wrex	SJ2839	52°56·9′	3°3·9′W	FM	126
Afon Braint	I of Angl	SH5069	53°12·1′	4°14·3′W	W	114,115
Afon Brân	Carm	SN7428	51°56·4′	3°49·6′W	W	146,160
Afon Brân	Carm	SN7937	52°1·3′	3°45·4′W	W	146,160
Afon Brân	Cered	SN5462	52°14·5′	4°7·9′W	W	146
Afon Brefi	Cered	SN6754	52°10·3′	3°56·3′W	W	146
Afon Brochan	Powys	SN9383	52°26·3′	3°34·0′W	W	136
Afon Bryn berian	Pemb	SN1135	51°59·1′	4°44·8′W	W	145
Afon Bryn-llin-fawr	Gwyn	SH7830	52°51·5′	3°48·3′W	W	124
Afon Bwlch y Groes	Conwy	SH7451	53°2·7′	3°52·4′W	W	115
Afon Cadair	Gwyn	SH6709	52°40·0′	3°57·6′W	W	124
Afon Cadnant	Conwy	SH8654	53°4·5′	3°41·7′W	W	116
Afon Cadnant	Gwyn	SH4963	53°8·8′	4°15·1′W	W	114,115
Afon Cadnant	I of Angl	SH5675	53°15·4′	4°9·1′W	W	114,115
Afon Cain	Powys	SJ1618	52°45·4′	3°14·3′W	W	125
Afon Cain	Powys	SJ2219	52°46·0′	3°9·0′W	W	126
Afon Caletwr	Conwy	SH8549	53°1·8′	3°42·5′W	W	116
Afon Caletwr	Gwyn	SH9834	52°53·9′	3°30·6′W	W	125
Afon Cammarch	Powys	SN9250	52°8·5′	3°34·3′W	W	147
Afon Camnant	Carm	SN6720	51°52·0′	3°55·5′W	W	159
Afon Cannon	Powys	SH9507	52°39·3′	3°32·7′W	W	125
Afon Caradog	I of Angl	SH3878	53°16·7′	4°25·4′W	W	114
Afon Carno	Powys	SO0192	52°31·3′	3°27·1′W	W	136
Afon Carog	Powys	SN8097	52°33·7′	3°45·8′W	W	135,136
Afon Carrog	Cered	SN5772	52°19·9′	4°5·5′W	W	135
Afon Carrog	Gwyn	SH4657	53°5·5′	4°17·6′W	W	115,123
Afon Caseg	Gwyn	SH6566	53°10·7′	4°0·8′W	W	115
Afon Castell	Cered	SN7881	52°25·0′	3°47·2′W	W	135
Afon Caws	Gwyn	SH8110	52°40·7′	3°45·2′W	W	124,125
Afon Cedig	Powys	SH9924	52°48·5′	3°29·5′W	W	125
Afon Cefni	I of Angl	SH4471	53°13·0′	4°19·8′W	W	114,115
Afon Cegin	Gwyn	SH5767	53°11·1′	4°8·0′W	W	114,115
Afon Ceidiog	Denb	SJ0234	52°53·9′	3°27·0′W	W	125
Afon Ceint	I of Angl	SH4975	53°15·3′	4°15·4′W	W	114,115
Afon Ceiriog or River Ceiriog	Wrex	SJ2438	52°56·3′	3°7·4′W	W	126
Afon Ceirw	Conwy	SH9447	53°0·8′	3°34·4′W	W	116
Afon Ceirw	Conwy	SH9944	52°59·3′	3°29·9′W	W	125
Afon Ceirw	Gwyn	SH7728	52°50·4′	3°49·2′W	W	124
Afon Celynog	Gwyn	SH8020	52°46·1′	3°46·3′W	W	124,125
Afon Cenllusg	Gwyn	SH6465	53°10·1′	4°1·7′W	W	115
Afon Cennen	Carm	SN6418	51°50·9′	3°58·1′W	W	159
Afon Ceri	Cered	SN3247	52°6·0′	4°26·8′W	W	145
Afon Cerist	Gwyn	SH8316	52°44·0′	3°43·6′W	W	124,125
Afon Cerist	Powys	SN9990	52°30·2′	3°28·9′W	W	136
Afon Cerniog	Powys	SN9495	52°32·8′	3°33·4′W	W	136
Afon Cetwr	Cered	SN6692	52°30·8′	3°58·1′W	W	135
Afon Chwiler or River Wheeler	Denb	SJ1070	53°13·4′	3°20·5′W	W	116
Afon Cibi	Monm	SO2817	51°51·1′	3°2·3′W	W	161
Afon Claerddu	Cered	SN8167	52°17·5′	3°44·3′W	W	135,136,147
Afon Claerwen	Cered	SN8268	52°18·1′	3°43·4′W	W	135,136,147
Afon Clarach	Cered	SN6183	52°25·9′	4°2·3′W	W	135
Afon Cledan	Cered	SN5365	52°16·1′	4°8·9′W	X	135
Afon Cledan	Powys	SN9453	52°33·3′	3°34·3′W	W	136
Afon Cleddau	Pemb	SM9432	51°57·1′	4°59·5′W	W	157
Afon Cledwen	Conwy	SH8964	53°9·9′	3°39·2′W	W	116
Afon Clettwr	Cered	SN4543	52°4·1′	4°15·3′W	W	146
Afon Clun	Rho Cyn Taf	ST0582	51°32·0′	3°21·8′W	W	170
Afon Clun-maen	Pemb	SN1434	51°58·6′	4°42·1′W	W	145
Afon Clwyd or River Clwyd	Denb	SJ0967	53°11·8′	3°21·3′W	W	116
Afon Clydach	Carm	SN5333	51°58·8′	4°8·0′W	W	146
Afon Clydach	Carm	SN7221	51°52·6′	3°51·2′W	W	160
Afon Clywedog	Denb	SJ0257	53°6·3′	3°27·4′W	W	116
Afon Clywedog	Denb	SJ0962	53°9·1′	3°21·2′W	W	116
Afon Clywedog	Gwyn	SH7616	52°43·9′	3°49·8′W	W	124
Afon Clywedog	Gwyn	SH8915	52°43·5′	3°38·2′W	W	124,125
Afon Clywedog	Powys	SN8792	52°31·1′	3°39·5′W	W	135,136
Afon Col'-huw	V of Glam	SS9667	51°23·8′	3°29·3′W	W	170
Afon Colwyn	Gwyn	SH5751	53°2·5′	4°7·6′W	W	115
Afon Concwest	Denb	SJ0259	53°7·4′	3°27·5′W	W	116
Afon Conwy	Conwy	SH7873	53°14·6′	3°49·3′W	W	115
Afon Conwy	Conwy	SH8058	53°6·6′	3°47·2′W	W	116
Afon Conwy	Conwy	SH8549	53°1·8′	3°42·5′W	W	116
Afon Corris	Denb	SJ0456	53°5·8′	3°25·6′W	W	116
Afon Corrwg	Nth Pt Talb	SS8899	51°41·0′	3°36·8′W	W	170
Afon Corrwg Fechan	Nth Pt Talb	SN8700	51°41·5′	3°37·7′W	W	170
Afon Cors-y-celyn	Gwyn	SH6451	53°2·6′	4°1·3′W	W	115
Afon Cothi	Carm	SN5122	51°52·8′	4°9·5′W	W	159
Afon Cothi	Carm	SN5326	51°55·0′	4°7·9′W	W	146
Afon Cothi	Carm	SN6134	51°59·5′	4°1·1′W	W	146
Afon Cothi	Carm	SN6944	52°5·0′	3°54·3′W	W	146,160
Afon Cothi	Carm	SN7147	52°6·6′	3°52·6′W	W	146,147
Afon Cownwy	Powys	SJ0018	52°45·3′	3°28·5′W	W	125
Afon Crafnant	Conwy	SH7662	53°8·7′	3°50·8′W	W	115
Afon Crawcwellt	Gwyn	SH6833	52°52·9′	3°57·3′W	W	124
Afon Crawcwellt	Gwyn	SH6929	52°50·8′	3°56·3′W	W	124
Afon Crawnon	Powys	SO1218	51°51·5′	3°16·3′W	X	161
Afon Crewi	Gwyn	SH7800	52°35·3′	3°47·7′W	W	135
Afon Crigyll	I of Angl	SH3274	53°14·4′	4°30·6′W	W	114
Afon Croesor	Gwyn	SH6244	52°58·8′	4°2·9′W	W	124
Afon Crychan	Carm	SN8239	52°2·5′	3°42·8′W	W	160
Afon Crychddwr	Gwyn	SH4750	53°1·8′	4°16·5′W	W	115,123
Afon Cwm	Powys	SH9108	52°39·8′	3°36·3′W	W	125
Afon Cwmau	Pemb	SN0433	51°57·9′	4°50·8′W	W	145,157
Afon Cwmhesgen	Gwyn	SH7930	52°51·5′	3°47·4′W	W	124
Afon Cwm-llechen	Gwyn	SH6721	52°46·5′	3°57·9′W	W	124
Afon Cwm-mynach	Gwyn	SH6821	52°46·5′	3°57·0′W	W	124
Afon Cwmnantcol	Gwyn	SH6226	52°49·1′	4°2·5′W	W	124
Afon Cwm-ochr	Gwyn	SH8221	52°46·7′	3°44·6′W	W	124,125
Afon Cwm-pandy	Gwyn	SH6302	52°36·2′	4°1·0′W	W	135
Afon Cwm-Waun-gron	Carm	SN1814	51°47·9′	4°38·0′W	W	158
Afon Cwm-y-foel	Gwyn	SH6547	53°0·4′	4°0·3′W	W	115
Afon Cŷch	Carm	SN2538	52°1·0′	4°32·6′W	W	145
Afon Cymerig	Gwyn	SH9333	52°53·3′	3°35·0′W	W	125
Afon Cynfal	Gwyn	SH7241	52°57·3′	3°53·9′W	W	124
Afon Cynffig	Brig	SS7883	51°32·2′	3°45·2′W	W	170
Afon Cynffig	Nth Pt Talb	SS8386	51°33·9′	3°40·9′W	W	170
Afon Cynin	Carm	SN2629	51°56·2′	4°31·5′W	W	145,158

Afon Cynon	Rho Cyn Taf	SN9605	51°44·3′	3°30·0′W	W	160
Afon Cynon	Rho Cyn Taf	SO0101	51°42·2′	3°25·6′W	W	170
Afon Cynrig	Powys	SO0625	51°55·2′	3°21·6′W	W	160
Afon Cywarch	Gwyn	SH8617	52°44·6′	3°40·9′W	W	124,125
Afon Cywym	Carm	SN3319	51°50·9′	4°25·1′W	W	159
Afon Cywyn	Carm	SN3328	51°55·8′	4°25·3′W	W	145
Afon Daron	Gwyn	SH1928	52°49·4′	4°40·8′W	W	123
Afon Ddu	Cered	SN6166	52°16·7′	4°1·9′W	W	135
Afon Ddu	Conwy	SH7072	53°14·0′	3°56·5′W	W	115
Afon Ddu	Conwy	SH7168	53°11·9′	3°55·5′W	W	115
Afon Ddu	Conwy	SH7564	53°9·8′	3°51·8′W	W	115
Afon Ddu	Conwy	SH7644	52°59·0′	3°50·4′W	W	124
Afon Ddu	Gwyn	SH4850	53°1·8′	4°15·6′W	W	115,123
Afon-ddu	Gwyn	SH5442	52°57·6′	4°10·0′W	W	124
Afon Denys	Cered	SN5751	52°8·6′	4°5·0′W	W	146
Afon Derfyn	Conwy	SH8562	53°8·8′	3°42·8′W	W	116
Afon Desach	Gwyn	SH4449	53°1·2′	4°19·1′W	W	115,123
Afon Deunant	Conwy	SH9665	53°10·6′	3°33·0′W	W	116
Afon Dewi Fawr	Carm	SN2816	51°49·2′	4°29·3′W	W	158
Afon Dewi Fawr	Carm	SN2819	51°50·8′	4°29·4′W	W	158
Afon Dewi Fawr	Carm	SN2919	51°50·8′	4°28·6′W	W	159
Afon Dewi Fawr	Carm	SN3022	51°52·5′	4°27·8′W	W	145,159
Afon Diliw	Powys	SN8477	52°23·0′	3°41·9′W	W	135,136,147
Afon Dinam	Denb	SJ0134	52°53·9′	3°27·9′W	W	125
Afon Disgynfa	Powys	SJ0629	52°51·3′	3°23·4′W	W	125
Afon Diwaunedd	Conwy	SH6852	53°3·2′	3°57·8′W	W	115
Afon Doethie	Cered	SN7650	52°8·3′	3°48·3′W	W	146,147
Afon Dringarth	Powys	SN9416	51°50·2′	3°31·9′W	W	160
Afon Drws-y-coed	Gwyn	SH5253	53°3·5′	4°12·1′W	W	115
Afon Drywi	Cered	SN4359	52°12·7′	4°17·5′W	W	146
Afon Duad	Carm	SN3730	51°56·9′	4°21·9′W	W	145
Afon Duar	Carm	SN5442	52°3·7′	4°7·4′W	W	146
Afon Dudodyn	Gwyn	SH6160	53°7·4′	4°4·2′W	W	115
Afon Dugoed	Powys	SH9112	52°41·9′	3°36·4′W	W	125
Afon Dulais	Carm	SN4803	51°42·5′	4°11·6′W	W	159
Afon Dulais	Carm	SN6527	51°55·7′	3°57·4′W	W	146
Afon Dulais	Carm	SN7034	51°59·6′	3°53·2′W	W	146,160
Afon Dulas	Carm	SN5523	51°53·4′	4°6·0′W	W	159
Afon Dulas	Carm	SN5827	51°55·6′	4°3·5′W	W	146
Afon Dulas	Cered	SN3147	52°6·0′	4°27·7′W	W	145
Afon Dulas	Cered	SN6153	52°9·7′	4°1·5′W	W	146
Afon Dulas	Pemb	SN2237	52°0·4′	4°35·2′W	W	145
Afon Dulas	Powys	SH7608	52°39·6′	3°49·6′W	W	124
Afon Dulas	Powys	SN7898	52°34·2′	3°47·6′W	W	135
Afon Dulas	Powys	SN8195	52°32·6′	3°44·9′W	W	135,136
Afon Dulas	Powys	SN8843	52°4·7′	3°37·7′W	W	147,160
Afon Dulas	Powys	SN9779	52°24·2′	3°30·4′W	W	136,147
Afon Dulyn	Conwy	SH7367	53°11·3′	3°53·6′W	W	115
Afon Dunant	Carm	SN7338	52°1·8′	3°50·7′W	W	146,160
Afon Dwyfach	Gwyn	SH4742	52°57·5′	4°16·3′W	W	123
Afon Dwyfor	Gwyn	SH4941	52°57·0′	4°14·5′W	W	123
Afon Dwyfor	Gwyn	SH5142	52°57·5′	4°12·7′W	W	124
Afon Dwyfor	Gwyn	SH5348	53°0·8′	4°11·1′W	W	115
Afon Dwynant	Gwyn	SH6317	52°44·2′	4°1·4′W	W	124
Afon Dwyryd	Gwyn	SH6439	52°56·1′	4°1·0′W	W	124
Afon Dyffryn	Gwyn	SH6310	52°40·5′	4°1·2′W	W	124
Afon Dyffryn-gall	Conwy	SH8564	53°9·9′	3°42·8′W	W	116
Afon Dyffryn-gwyn	Gwyn	SN6398	52°34·0′	4°0·9′W	W	135
Afon Dyfi or River Dovey	Gwyn	SH8511	52°41·3′	3°41·7′W	W	124,125
Afon Dyfi or River Dovey	Gwyn	SN7099	52°34·6′	3°54·7′W	W	135
Afon Dyfi or River Dovey	Powys	SH8104	52°37·5′	3°45·1′W	W	135,136
Afon Dyfrdwy	Gwyn	SH8629	52°51·0′	3°41·2′W	W	124,125
Afon Dyfrdwy or River Dee	Ches	SJ4159	53°7·7′	2°52·5′W	W	117
Afon Dyfrdwy or River Dee	Denb	SJ0339	52°56·6′	3°26·2′W	W	125
Afon Dyfrdwy or River Dee	Flint	SJ1683	53°20·5′	3°15·3′W	W	116
Afon Dylif	Gwyn	SH6144	52°58·8′	4°3·8′W	W	124
Afon Dylo	Gwyn	SH8534	52°53·7′	3°42·2′W	W	124,125
Afon Dysynni	Gwyn	SH5903	52°36·6′	4°4·5′W	W	135
Afon Dysynni	Gwyn	SH6407	52°38·9′	4°0·2′W	W	124
Afon Ebwy or Ebbw River	Caer	ST2193	51°38·1′	3°8·1′W	W	171
Afon Eden	Gwyn	SH7226	52°49·2′	3°53·6′W	W	124
Afon Efyrnwy or River Vyrnwy	Powys	SJ0314	52°43·1′	3°25·8′W	W	125
Afon Eidda	Conwy	SH8148	53°1·2′	3°46·0′W	W	116
Afon Eiddew	Powys	SH9424	52°48·4′	3°34·0′W	W	125
Afon Eiddon	Gwyn	SH8023	52°47·7′	3°46·4′W	W	124,125
Afon Einion	Powys	SJ0708	52°39·9′	3°22·1′W	W	125
Afon Eirth	Powys	SJ0426	52°49·6′	3°25·1′W	W	125
Afon Eisingrug	Gwyn	SH6234	52°53·4′	4°2·7′W	W	124
Afon Eitha	Wrex	SJ2944	52°59·6′	3°3·1′W	W	117
Afon Eitha	Wrex	SJ2945	53°0·1′	3°3·1′W	T	117
Afon Elái or Ely River	V of Glam	ST1575	51°28·3′	3°13·0′W	W	171
Afon Elan	Powys	SN8374	52°21·3′	3°42·7′W	W	135,136,147
Afon Elan	Powys	SN8872	52°20·3′	3°38·2′W	W	135,136,147
Afon Erch	Gwyn	SH4037	52°54·6′	4°22·4′W	W	123
Afon Erwent	Gwyn	SH8134	52°53·7′	3°45·7′W	W	124,125
Afon-fach-Pontgarreg	Carm	SN3226	51°54·7′	4°26·2′W	W	145
Afon Fanafas	Carm	SN6544	52°4·9′	3°57·8′W	W	146
Afon Fanagoed	Carm	SN6844	52°5·0′	3°55·2′W	W	146
Afon Fathew	Gwyn	SH6404	52°37·2′	4°0·1′W	W	135
Afon Fawnog	Gwyn	SH7312	52°41·7′	3°52·4′W	W	124
Afon Fawr	Carm	SN3331	51°57·4′	4°25·4′W	W	145
Afon Fechan	Gwyn	SH8928	52°50·5′	3°38·5′W	W	124,125
Afon Feinog	Cered	SN4755	52°10·6′	4°13·9′W	W	146
Afon Felindre	Carm	SN5728	51°56·2′	4°4·4′W	W	146
Afon Fenni	Carm	SN2421	51°51·8′	4°33·0′W	W	145,158
Afon Fflûr	Cered	SN7363	52°15·3′	3°51·2′W	W	146,147
Afon Ffraw	I of Angl	SH3669	53°11·8′	4°26·9′W	W	114
Afon Ffrydlas	Gwyn	SH6367	53°11·2′	4°2·6′W	W	115
Afon Ffynnon-Ddewi	Cered	SN3754	52°9·9′	4°22·6′W	W	145
Afon Foryd	Gwyn	SH4457	53°5·5′	4°19·4′W	W	115,123
Afon Gafel	Pemb	SN1931	51°57·1′	4°37·6′W	W	145
Afon Gafenni	Monm	SO3015	51°50·0′	3°0·6′W	W	161
Afon Gafr	Gwyn	SH6159	53°6·9′	4°4·2′W	W	115
Afon Gain	Gwyn	SH7432	52°52·5′	3°51·9′W	W	124
Afon Gallen	Conwy	SH8766	53°11·0′	3°41·1′W	W	116
Afon Gam	Gwyn	SH6569	53°12·3′	4°0·9′W	W	115
Afon Gam	Gwyn	SH6927	52°49·7′	3°56·3′W	W	124
Afon Gam	Gwyn	SH7542	52°57·9′	3°51·3′W	W	124
Afon Gam	Powys	SH9504	52°37·7′	3°32·7′W	W	136
Afon Gam	Powys	SJ0008	52°39·9′	3°28·3′W	W	125
Afon Gamallt	Gwyn	SH7343	52°58·4′	3°53·1′W	W	124
Afon Gamlan	Gwyn	SH7024	52°48·1′	3°55·3′W	W	124
Afon Garreg-wen	Conwy	SH7167	53°11·3′	3°55·4′W	W	115
Afon Garw	Brig	SS9088	51°35·0′	3°34·9′W	W	170
Afon Gau	Gwyn	SH6828	52°50·2′	3°57·2′W	W	124
Afon Gelyn	Gwyn	SH8342	52°58·0′	3°44·1′W	W	124,125
Afon Giedd	Powys	SN8118	51°51·1′	3°43·3′W	W	160
Afon Gilwydeth	Carm	SN4737	52°0·9′	4°13·4′W	W	146
Afon Glandy	Pemb	SN1528	51°55·4′	4°41·0′W	W	145,158
Afon Glan-rhŷd	Pemb	SM9829	51°55·6′	4°55·9′W	W	157,158
Afon Glasgwm	Conwy	SH7649	53°1·7′	3°50·5′W	W	115
Afon Glaslyn	Gwyn	SH5942	52°57·7′	4°5·6′W	W	124
Afon Glaslyn	Gwyn	SH6553	53°3·7′	4°0·5′W	W	115
Afon Glyn	Gwyn	SH9131	52°52·2′	3°36·8′W	W	125
Afon Goch	Gwyn	SH5659	53°6·8′	4°8·7′W	W	115
Afon Gôch	Gwyn	SH5846	52°59·8′	4°6·5′W	W	115
Afon Goch	Gwyn	SH6148	53°0·9′	4°3·9′W	W	115
Afon Goch	Gwyn	SH6769	53°12·3′	3°59·1′W	W	115
Afon Goch	I of Angl	SH4586	53°21·1′	4°19·3′W	W	114
Afon Goch	Powys	SJ0224	52°48·5′	3°26·8′W	W	125
Afon-goch	Wrex	SJ3045	53°0·1′	3°2·2′W	X	117
Afon Goedol	Gwyn	SH6843	52°58·3′	3°57·5′W	W	124
Afon Gorddinan	Conwy	SH7049	53°1·6′	3°55·9′W	W	115
Afon Gorlech	Carm	SN5636	52°0·5′	4°5·5′W	W	146
Afon Gorsen	Gwyn	SH6150	53°2·0′	4°4·0′W	W	115
Afon Grannell	Cered	SN5248	52°6·9′	4°9·3′W	W	146
Afon Groes	Cered	SN7060	52°13·6′	3°53·8′W	W	146,147
Afon Gronw	Carm	SN2221	51°51·8′	4°34·7′W	W	145,158
Afon Gwaum	Pemb	SN0034	51°58·4′	4°54·3′W	W	145,157
Afon Gwaun	Pemb	SM9935	51°58·9′	4°55·2′W	W	157
Afon Gwenlais	Carm	SN7441	52°3·4′	3°49·9′W	W	146,147,160
Afon Gwesyn	Powys	SN8555	52°11·1′	3°40·5′W	W	147
Afon Gwili	Carm	SN4223	51°53·2′	4°17·4′W	W	159
Afon Gwili	Carm	SN4428	51°56·0′	4°15·8′W	W	146
Afon Gwili	Cered	SN5155	52°10·6′	4°10·4′W	W	146
Afon Gwna	I of Angl	SH4073	53°14·0′	4°23·4′W	W	114,115
Afon Gwngu	Powys	SN8572	52°20·3′	3°40·9′W	W	135,136,147
Afon Gwril	Gwyn	SH6008	52°39·3′	4°3·8′W	W	124
Afon Gwrysgog	Conwy	SH8353	53°3·9′	3°44·4′W	W	116
Afon Gwydderig	Carm	SN8034	51°59·7′	3°44·5′W	W	160
Afon Gwyddon	Carm	SN8342	52°4·1′	3°42·0′W	W	147,160
Afon Gwynon	Carm	SN5418	51°50·7′	4°6·8′W	W	159
Afon Gwyrfai	Gwyn	SH4659	53°6·6′	4°17·6′W	W	115,123
Afon Gwyrfai	Gwyn	SH5358	53°6·2′	4°11·3′W	W	115
Afon Gwyrfai	Gwyn	SH5753	53°3·6′	4°7·6′W	W	115
Afon Gwy / River Wye	Powys	SO1438	52°2·3′	3°14·8′W	W	148,149,161
Afon Gyffin	Conwy	SH7675	53°15·7′	3°51·1′W	W	115
Afon Gyrach	Conwy	SH7374	53°15·1′	3°53·8′W	W	115
Afon Harnog	Gwyn	SH8322	52°47·2′	3°43·7′W	W	124,125
Afon Hen	Gwyn	SH4048	53°0·6′	4°22·7′W	W	115,123
Afon Hengwm	Powys	SN7895	52°32·6′	3°47·5′W	W	135
Afon Hengwm	Powys	SN7989	52°29·4′	3°46·5′W	W	135
Afon Henwy	Gwyn	SH5442	52°57·6′	4°10·0′W	W	124
Afon Hepste	Powys	SN9511	51°47·5′	3°31·0′W	W	160
Afon Hesbin	Denb	SJ1352	53°3·7′	3°17·5′W	W	116
Afon Hesgyn	Gwyn	SH8841	52°57·5′	3°39·6′W	W	124,125
Afon Hirwaun	Cered	SN2646	52°5·3′	4°32·0′W	W	145
Afon Honddu	Monm	SO2926	51°55·9′	3°1·6′W	W	161
Afon Honddu	Powys	SO2434	52°0·2′	3°6·0′W	W	161
Afon Hore	Powys	SN8487	52°28·4′	3°42·1′W	W	135,136
Afon Horon	Gwyn	SH2832	52°51·7′	4°32·9′W	W	123
Afon Hyddgen	Powys	SN7890	52°29·9′	3°47·4′W	W	135
Afon Iaen	Powys	SN9101	52°36·0′	3°36·2′W	W	136
Afon Iwrch	Conwy	SH8355	53°5·0′	3°44·4′W	W	116
Afon Las	Gwyn	SH6258	53°6·3′	4°3·3′W	W	115
Afon Las	Gwyn	SH7440	52°56·8′	3°52·1′W	W	124
Afon Lash	Carm	SN5914	51°48·7′	4°2·3′W	W	159
Afon Lâs or Afon Babi	Gwyn	SH7623	52°47·7′	3°49·9′W	W	124
Afon Leri	Cered	SN6191	52°30·2′	4°2·5′W	W	135
Afon Leri	Cered	SN6688	52°28·7′	3°58·0′W	W	135
Afon Llaethog	Conwy	SH9151	53°3·0′	3°37·2′W	W	116
Afon Llafar	Gwyn	SH6565	53°10·1′	4°0·8′W	W	115
Afon Llafar	Gwyn	SH7337	52°55·2′	3°52·9′W	W	124
Afon Llafar	Gwyn	SH8734	52°53·7′	3°40·4′W	W	124,125
Afon Llan	Swan	SS6399	51°40·6′	3°58·5′W	W	159
Afon Llechach	Carm	SN7825	51°54·9′	3°46·0′W	W	146,160
Afon Llechog	Powys	SH9415	52°43·6′	3°33·8′W	W	125
Afon Llechwedd-mawr	Powys	SN7591	52°30·4′	3°50·1′W	W	135
Afon Lledr	Conwy	SH7352	53°3·3′	3°53·3′W	W	115
Afon Llia	Powys	SN9216	51°50·2′	3°33·7′W	W	160
Afon Llifon	Gwyn	SH4656	53°5·0′	4°17·6′W	W	115,123
Afon Lligwy	I of Angl	SH4784	53°20·1′	4°17·5′W	W	114,115
Afon Lligwy	I of Angl	SH4885	53°20·7′	4°16·6′W	W	114
Afon Llinau	Powys	SH8508	52°39·7′	3°41·6′W	W	124,125
Afon Lliw	Gwyn	SH8331	52°52·1′	3°43·9′W	W	124,125
Afon Lliw	Swan	SN6505	51°43·9′	3°56·9′W	W	159
Afon Lliw	Swan	SS5999	51°40·6′	4°2·0′W	W	159
Afon Lloer	Conwy	SH6661	53°8·0′	3°59·8′W	W	115
Afon Lluestgota	Cered	SN7490	52°29·8′	3°51·0′W	W	135
Afon Llugwy	Conwy	SH6961	53°8·0′	3°57·1′W	W	115
Afon Llugwy	Conwy	SH7059	53°7·0′	3°56·1′W	W	115
Afon Llwyd	Powys	SN8690	52°30·0′	3°40·4′W	W	135,136
Afon Llyfni	Gwyn	SH4852	53°2·9′	4°15·7′W	W	115,123
Afon Llynedno	Gwyn	SH6449	53°1·5′	4°1·3′W	W	115
Afon Llynfi	Powys	SO1228	51°56·9′	3°16·4′W	W	161
Afon Llynfi	Powys	SO1324	51°54·7′	3°15·5′W	W	161
Afon Llynfi	Powys	SO1331	51°58·5′	3°15·6′W	W	161
Afon Llynor	Denb	SJ0537	52°55·6′	3°24·4′W	W	125
Afon Iwrch	Powys	SJ1327	52°50·3′	3°17·1′W	W	125
Afon Lwynor	Carm	SN8144	52°5·1′	3°43·8′W	W	147,160
Afon Machno	Conwy	SH7849	53°1·7′	3°48·7′W	W	115
Afon Maesgwm	Gwyn	SH6444	52°58·8′	4°1·1′W	W	124
Afon Maesgwm	Gwyn	SH7248	53°1·1′	3°54·1′W	W	115
Afon Maes-y-bryn	Conwy	SH7173	53°14·5′	3°55·6′W	W	115
Afon Mamog	Carm	SN3036	52°0·0′	4°28·2′W	W	145
Afon Marchlyn-mawr	Gwyn	SH6063	53°9·0′	4°5·2′W	W	115
Afon Marlais	Carm	SN5132	51°58·2′	4°9·8′W	W	146
Afon Marlais	Carm	SN6137	52°1·1′	4°1·1′W	W	146
Afon Marlais	Carm	SN6831	51°57·9′	3°54·9′W	W	146
Afon Marlais	Carm	SN6929	51°56·9′	3°54·0′W	W	146,160
Afon Marlais	Pemb	SN1515	51°48·4′	4°40·6′W	W	158
Afon Marlas	Carm	SN6117	51°50·3′	4°0·7′W	W	159
Afon Marteg	Powys	SN9975	52°22·1′	3°28·6′W	W	136,147
Afon Mawddach	Gwyn	SH7326	52°49·2′	3°52·7′W	W	124
Afon Medrad	Conwy	SH9644	52°59·2′	3°32·6′W	W	125
Afon Meilwch	Carm	SN7223	51°53·7′	3°51·2′W	W	160
Afon Melau	Gwyn	SH7823	52°47·7′	3°48·2′W	W	124
Afon Melinddwr	Carm	SN5837	52°1·0′	4°3·8′W	W	146
Afon Melindwr	Cered	SN6781	52°24·9′	3°56·9′W	W	135
Afon Mellte	Powys	SN9210	51°46·9′	3°33·5′W	W	160
Afon Meloch	Gwyn	SH9638	52°56·0′	3°32·4′W	W	125
Afon Merch	Gwyn	SH6352	53°3·1′	4°2·2′W	W	115
Afon Merchon	Carm	SN7341	52°3·4′	3°50·7′W	W	146,147,160
Afon Merin	Cered	SN7778	52°23·4′	3°48·1′W	W	135,147
Afon Meurig	Cered	SN7167	52°17·4′	3°53·1′W	W	135,147
Afon Mihartach	Carm	SN7823	51°53·8′	3°46·0′W	W	160
Afon Morlais	Carm	SN4605	51°43·6′	4°13·4′W	W	159
Afon Morlais	Carm	SN5405	51°43·7′	4°6·5′W	W	159
Afon Morwynion	Denb	SJ1346	53°0·5′	3°17·4′W	W	116
Afon Mwyro	Cered	SN7864	52°15·9′	3°46·9′W	W	146,147
Afon Myddyfi	Carm	SN6125	51°54·6′	4°0·9′W	W	146
Afon Mydr	Cered	SN4656	52°11·1′	4°14·8′W	W	146
Afon Myherin	Cered	SN7970	52°19·1′	3°46·1′W	W	135,147
Afon Mynach	Gwyn	SH9040	52°57·0′	3°37·8′W	W	125
Afon Mynys	Carm	SN7235	52°0·2′	3°51·5′W	W	146,160
Afon Nadroedd	Powys	SH9625	52°49·0′	3°32·2′W	W	125
Afon Nant-fach	Gwyn	SH8945	52°59·7′	3°38·8′W	W	116
Afon Nant Peris	Gwyn	SH6356	53°5·3′	4°2·3′W	W	115
Afon Nedd or River Neath	Powys	SN9111	51°47·5′	3°34·4′W	W	160
Afon Nenog	Carm	SN5335	51°59·9′	4°8·1′W	W	146
Afon Nodwydd	I of Angl	SH5279	53°17·5′	4°12·8′W	W	114,115
Afon Nug	Conwy	SH8953	53°4·0′	3°39·0′W	W	116
Afon Nyfer	Pemb	SN0539	52°1·2′	4°50·1′W	W	145
Afon Nyfer	Pemb	SN1436	51°59·7′	4°42·2′W	W	145
Afon Oernant	Conwy	SH7948	53°1·2′	3°47·8′W	W	115
Afon Ogau	Powys	SJ2130	52°51·9′	3°10·0′W	W	126
Afon Ogwen	Gwyn	SH6168	53°11·7′	4°4·4′W	W	115
Afon Pedian	Carm	SN2633	51°58·3′	4°31·6′W	W	145
Afon Peithyll	Cered	SN6382	52°25·4′	4°0·5′W	W	135
Afon Pelenna	Nth Pt Talb	SS8096	51°39·2′	3°43·7′W	W	170
Afon Pennant	Pemb	SN0933	51°58·0′	4°46·4′W	W	145
Afon Penrhos	Gwyn	SH3533	52°52·4′	4°26·7′W	W	123
Afon Pib	Carm	SN4831	51°57·6′	4°12·3′W	W	146
Afon Piliau	Pemb	SN1844	52°4·1′	4°38·9′W	W	145
Afon Porth-llwyd	Conwy	SH7366	53°10·8′	3°53·6′W	W	115
Afon Prysor	Gwyn	SH7235	52°54·1′	3°53·8′W	W	124
Afon Pumryd	Gwyn	SH8919	52°45·7′	3°38·3′W	W	124,125
Afon Pyrddin	Nth Pt Talb	SN8809	51°46·3′	3°37·0′W	W	160
Afon Pysgotwr Fach	Carm	SN7350	52°8·3′	3°50·9′W	W	146,147
Afon Pysgotwr Fawr	Cered	SN7252	52°9·3′	3°51·9′W	W	146,147
Afon Rhaeadr	Powys	SJ1027	52°50·2′	3°19·8′W	W	125
Afon Rhaeadr-bach	Gwyn	SH6669	53°12·3′	4°0·0′W	W	115
Afon Rhaeadr-fawr	Gwyn	SH6671	53°13·4′	4°0·0′W	W	115
Afon Rheidol	Cered	SN7278	52°23·3′	3°52·5′W	W	135,147
Afon Rhiw	Powys	SJ0104	52°37·7′	3°27·4′W	W	136
Afon Rhiw	Powys	SJ0403	52°37·2′	3°24·7′W	W	136
Afon Rhiwlech	Gwyn	SH9121	52°46·8′	3°36·6′W	W	125
Afon Rhiw Saeson	Powys	SH9003	52°37·1′	3°37·1′W	W	136
Afon Rhondda Fach	Rho Cyn Taf	SS9898	51°40·5′	3°28·1′W	W	170
Afon Rhondda Fawr or Rhondda River	Rho Cyn Taf	SS9398	51°40·5′	3°32·5′W	W	170
Afon Rhonwydd	Gwyn	SH7102	52°36·3′	3°53·9′W	W	135
Afon Rhŷd	Gwyn	SH4657	53°5·5′	4°17·6′W	W	115,123
Afon Rhŷd	Gwyn	SH4658	53°6·1′	4°17·6′W	W	115,123
Afon Rhyd-hir	Gwyn	SH3435	52°53·5′	4°27·7′W	W	123
Afon Rhydybennau	Carm	SN1320	51°51·1′	4°42·5′W	W	145,158
Afon Rhyd-y-bil	Pemb	SN1123	51°52·7′	4°44·4′W	W	145,158
Afon Rhydyrhalen	Conwy	SH8148	53°1·2′	3°46·0′W	W	116
Afon Rhymni or Rhymney River	Caer	ST1589	51°35·8′	3°13·2′W	W	171
Afon Rhymni (Rhymney River)	Caer	SO1107	51°45·5′	3°17·0′W	W	161
Afon Rhythallt	Gwyn	SH5563	53°8·9′	4°9·7′W	W	114,115
Afon Ro	Denb	SJ1542	52°58·4′	3°15·5′W	W	125
Afon Roe	Conwy	SH7671	53°13·5′	3°51·0′W	W	115
Afon Saint	Gwyn	SH1627	52°48·8′	4°43·4′W	W	123
Afon Sannan	Carm	SN5526	51°55·1′	4°6·1′W	W	146
Afon Seiont	Gwyn	SH5163	53°8·8′	4°13·3′W	W	114,115
Afon Senni	Powys	SN9223	51°53·9′	3°33·8′W	W	160
Afon Serw	Gwyn	SH8144	52°59·1′	3°46·0′W	W	124,125
Afon Serw	Gwyn	SH7027	52°49·7′	3°55·4′W	W	124
Afon Sien	Carm	SN2526	51°54·5′	4°32·3′W	W	145,158
Afon Soch	Gwyn	SH2431	52°51·1′	4°36·4′W	W	123
Afon Soch	Gwyn	SH2927	52°49·1′	4°31·9′W	W	123
Afon Soden	Cered	SN3954	52°9·9′	4°20·8′W	W	145
Afon Stewy	Cered	SN6584	52°26·5′	3°58·8′W	W	135
Afon Stwlan	Gwyn	SH6744	52°58·9′	3°58·5′W	W	124
Afon Swadde	Carm	SN7323	51°53·7′	3°50·4′W	W	160
Afon Sychlwch	Carm	SN8122	51°53·3′	3°43·4′W	W	160
Afon Syfynwy	Pemb	SN0323	51°52·5′	4°51·3′W	W	145,157,158
Afon Sylgen	Carm	SN3033	51°58·4′	4°28·1′W	W	145
Afon Taf	Carm	SN1622	51°52·2′	4°40·0′W	W	145,158
Afon Taf	Carm	SN2415	51°48·6′	4°32·8′W	W	158
Afon Taf	Pemb	SN2033	51°58·2′	4°36·8′W	W	145
Afon Taf Fawr	Rho Cyn Taf	SO0109	51°46·5′	3°25·7′W	W	160
Afon Tafolog	Conwy	SH7270	53°12·9′	3°54·6′W	W	115
Afon Taf or River Taff	Card	ST1380	51°31·0′	3°14·8′W	W	171
Afon Taihirion	Gwyn	SH7940	52°56·9′	3°47·7′W	W	124
Afon Talog	Carm	SN4537	52°0·8′	4°15·1′W	W	146
Afon Tanat	Powys	SJ0226	52°49·6′	3°26·9′W	W	125
Afon Tanat	Powys	SJ1723	52°48·1′	3°13·5′W	W	125
Afon Tarell	Powys	SO0026	51°55·7′	3°26·9′W	W	160
Afon Tarennig	Cered	SN8182	52°25·6′	3°44·6′W	W	135,136
Afon Tawe or River Tawe	Nth Pt Talb	SN7102	51°42·4′	3°51·6′W	W	170
Afon Teifi	Carm	SN3241	52°2·8′	4°26·6′W	W	145
Afon Teifi	Cered	SN6150	52°8·1′	4°1·5′W	W	146
Afon Teifi	Cered	SN7266	52°16·9′	3°52·2′W	W	135,147
Afon Teigl	Gwyn	SH7243	52°58·4′	3°54·0′W	W	124

Afon Tewgyll	Pemb	SN1331	51°57·0′	4°42·9′W	W	145
Afon Tigen	Carm	SN1926	51°54·4′	4°37·5′W	W	145,158
Afon Trannon	Powys	SN9490	52°30·1′	3°33·3′W	W	136
Afon Treweunydd	Gwyn	SH5754	53°4·1′	4°7·7′W	W	115
Afon Tryal	Cered	SN5868	52°17·7′	4°4·5′W	W	135
Afon Trystion	Denb	SJ0740	52°57·2′	3°22·7′W	W	125
Afon Tryweryn	Gwyn	SH8339	52°56·4′	3°44·1′W	W	124,125
Afon Tryweryn	Gwyn	SH9137	52°55·4′	3°36·9′W	W	125
Afon Twllan	Conwy	SH8953	53°4·0′	3°39·0′W	W	116
Afon Twrch	Carm	SN6446	52°6·0′	3°58·7′W	W	146
Afon Twrch	Carm	SN7715	51°49·4′	3°46·7′W	W	160
Afon Twrch	Gwyn	SH8828	52°50·5′	3°39·4′W	W	124,125
Afon Twrch	Gwyn	SH9024	52°48·4′	3°37·5′W	W	125
Afon Twrch	Powys	SH9714	52°43·1′	3°31·1′W	W	125
Afon Twymyn	Powys	SN8898	52°34·3′	3°38·8′W	W	135,136
Afon Tycerig	Gwyn	SH8423	52°47·8′	3°42·8′W	W	124,125
Afon Tyn-y-rhos	Powys	SH9300	52°35·5′	3°34·4′W	W	136
Afon Tyweli	Carm	SN4238	52°1·3′	4°17·8′W	W	146
Afon Tywi	Carm	SN7538	52°1·8′	3°48·9′W	W	146,160
Afon-wen	Flint	SJ1371	53°14·0′	3°17·8′W	T	116
Afon Wen	Gwyn	SH4437	52°54·7′	4°18·8′W	T	123
Afon Wen	Gwyn	SH4440	52°56·3′	4°18·9′W	W	123
Afon Wen	Gwyn	SH6766	53°10·7′	3°59·0′W	W	115
Afon Wen	Gwyn	SH7424	52°48·2′	3°51·7′W	W	124
Afon Wern	Pemb	SN1229	51°55·9′	4°43·7′W	W	145,158
Afon Wnin	Gwyn	SH7121	52°46·5′	3°54·3′W	W	124
Afon Wnion	Gwyn	SH7518	52°45·0′	3°50·7′W	W	124
Afon Wybrnant	Conwy	SH7651	53°2·8′	3°50·6′W	W	115
Afon Wygyr	I of Angl	SH3991	53°23·7′	4°24·9′W	W	114
Afon Wyre	Cered	SN5970	52°18·8′	4°3·7′W	W	135
Afon Wyre	Cered	SN6374	52°21·1′	4°0·3′W	A	135
Afon Wysg (River Usk)	Monm	SO2714	51°49·4′	3°3·2′W	W	161
Afon Wysg (River Usk)	Powys	SN9329	51°57·2′	3°33·0′W	W	160
Afon y Bedol	Conwy	SH7060	53°7·5′	3°56·2′W	W	115
Afon y Dolau Gwynion	Powys	SJ0122	52°47·4′	3°27·7′W	W	125
Afon Ydw	Carm	SN7631	51°58·1′	3°47·9′W	W	146,160
Afon y Foel	Conwy	SH7646	53°0·1′	3°50·5′W	W	115
Afon y Garth	Flint	SJ1281	53°19·4′	3°18·9′W	W	116
Afon y Glyn	Gwyn	SH5936	52°54·4′	4°5·4′W	W	124
Afon y Llan	Gwyn	SH6168	53°11·7′	4°4·4′W	W	115
Afon y Maes	Denb	SJ1050	53°2·6′	3°20·1′W	W	116
Afon y Maes	Denb	SJ1150	53°2·6′	3°19·2′W	W	116
Afon y Meirchion	Conwy	SJ0269	53°12·8′	3°27·6′W	W	116
Afon Yn-y-groes	Powys	SH9626	52°49·5′	3°32·2′W	W	125
Afon Ysgethin	Gwyn	SH6122	52°46·9′	4°3·3′W	W	124
Afon Ysgir	Powys	SN9932	51°58·9′	3°27·8′W	W	160
Afon Ystrad	Denb	SJ0163	53°9·5′	3°28·4′W	W	116
Afon Ystumiau	Conwy	SH7253	53°3·8′	3°54·2′W	W	115
Afon Ystwyth	Cered	SN7572	52°20·2′	3°49·7′W	W	135,147
Afon y Waun	Powys	SN9716	51°50·2′	3°29·3′W	W	160
Afor Rheidol	Cered	SN7585	52°27·2′	3°50·0′W	W	135
African Violet Centre	Norf	TF5519	52°45·0′	0°18·2′E	X	131
Afton	Devon	SX8462	50°27·0′	3°37·7′W	X	202
Afton	I of W	SZ3486	50°40·6′	1°30·7′W	T	196
Afton Lodge	S Ayr	NS4125	55°29·8′	4°30·6′W	X	70
Afton Manor	I of W	SZ3486	50°40·6′	1°30·7′W	X	196
Afton Reservoir	E Ayr	NS6304	55°18·9′	4°9·1′W	W	77
Afton Water	E Ayr	NS6302	55°17·8′	4°9·0′W	W	77
Afton Water	E Ayr	NS6308	55°21·1′	4°9·2′W	W	71,77
Agar Creek	Norf	TG0244	52°57·5′	1°0·9′E	W	133
Agardsley Park	Staffs	SK1327	52°50·7′	1°48·0′W	X	128
Agar Nook	Leic	SK4514	52°43·5′	1°19·6′W	T	129
Agar's Hill	Northum	NY7758	54°55·2′	2°21·1′W	X	86,87
Agarshill Fell	Northum	NY7558	54°55·2′	2°23·0′W	X	86,87
Agars Plough	Win & Maid	SU9778	51°29·8′	0°35·8′W	X	175,176
Agbrigg	Wakf	SE3419	53°40·2′	1°28·7′W	T	110,111
Agden Bridge	Sheff	SK2493	53°26·2′	1°37·9′W	X	110
Agden Bridge Fm	Warr	SJ7186	53°22·4′	2°25·7′W	FM	109
Agden Brook Fm	Ches	SJ7186	53°22·4′	2°25·7′W	FM	109
Agden Brow	Ches	SJ7185	53°21·9′	2°25·7′W	X	109
Agden Dairy Fm	Ches	SJ5143	52°59·2′	2°43·4′W	FM	117
Agden Fm	Lancs	SD6843	53°53·2′	2°28·8′W	FM	103
Agden Hall	Ches	SJ5144	52°59·7′	2°43·4′W	X	117
Agden Hall	Ches	SJ7185	53°21·9′	2°25·7′W	X	109
Agden Hill Fm	Cambs	TL1266	52°17·1′	0°21·1′W	FM	153
Agden Ho	Ches	SJ5143	52°59·2′	2°43·4′W	X	117
Agdenlane Fm	Warr	SJ7186	53°22·4′	2°25·7′W	FM	109
Agden Resr	Sheff	SK2692	53°25·7′	1°36·1′W	W	110
Agdon Fm	Warw	SP3242	52°4·8′	1°31·6′W	FM	151
Agen Allwedd	Powys	SO1815	51°49·9′	3°11·0′W	X	161
Aggborough	Worcs	SO8375	52°22·6′	2°14·6′W	T	138
Agglestone	Dorset	SZ0282	50°38·5′	1°57·9′W	X	195
Agglethorpe	N Yks	SE0886	54°16·4′	1°52·2′W	T	99
A' Ghairbhe	Highld	NH0259	57°34·9′	5°18·3′W	W	25
A'Ghairbhe	Highld	NH0261	57°36·0′	5°18·4′W	W	19
a' Gheodha	N Eil	NF8580	57°42·2′	7°16·9′W	X	18
A' Ghlaise	Highld	NC3937	58°17·8′	4°44·3′W	H	16
A' Ghlasaird	Highld	NM3980	56°50·6′	6°16·3′W	X	39
A' Ghlas-bheinn	Highld	NH0023	57°15·5′	5°18·5′W	H	25,33
A'Ghlas leac	Highld	NG7833	57°20·3′	5°40·9′W	X	24
A' Ghoil	Highld	NC3471	58°36·0′	4°50·9′W	X	9
A'Ghoil-sgeir	Highld	NC4367	58°34·0′	4°41·5′W	X	9
Agill	N Yks	SE1376	54°11·0′	1°47·6′W	X	99
Agill Ho	N Yks	SE0857	54°0·8′	1°52·3′W	X	104
Agincourt	Win & Maid	SU9368	51°24·4′	0°39·4′W	X	175
Agistment Fm	Devon	SX6097	50°45·6′	3°58·7′W	FM	191
Aglionby	Cumbr	NY4456	54°54·0′	2°52·0′W	T	85
Aglionby Beck	Cumbr	NY6539	54°44·9′	2°32·2′W	W	91
Aglionby Beck	Cumbr	NY6640	54°45·5′	2°31·3′W	W	86
Agmerhurst Fm	E Susx	TQ7014	50°54·2′	0°25·5′E	FM	199
Agneash	I of M	SC4386	54°15·0′	4°24·2′W	T	95
Agnes Gill	Cumbr	SD5699	54°23·3′	2°40·2′W	X	97
Agnes Meadow	Derby	SK2147	53°1·4′	1°40·8′W	X	119,128
Agra Crags	N Yks	SE1581	54°13·7′	1°45·8′W	X	99
Agra Moor	N Yks	SE1482	54°14·3′	1°46·7′W	X	99
Agricultural Coll	Suff	TM1953	52°8·1′	1°12·4′E	X	156
Agricultural Research Council's Field Station	W Berks	SU5180	51°31·2′	1°15·5′W	X	174
Agricultural Show Ground	Somer	ST6339	51°9·2′	2°31·4′W	X	183
Ahmore Strand	N Eil	NF8574	57°39·0′	7°16·4′W	X	18

Aid Moss	Northum	NY9283	55°8·7′	2°7·1′W	X	80
Aifft	Denb	SJ1169	53°12·9′	3°19·6′W	T	116
Aigas Ho	Highld	NH4541	57°26·2′	4°34·5′W	X	26
Aigburth	Liv	SJ3886	53°22·3′	2°55·5′W	T	108
Aiggin Stone	Roch	SD9717	53°39·2′	2°2·3′W	A	109
Aigill Sike	Cumbr	NY6131	54°40·6′	2°35·9′W	W	91
Aiglehill	Cumbr	NY1142	54°46·2′	3°22·6′W	X	85
Aikbank	Cumbr	NY2145	54°47·9′	3°13·3′W	X	85
Aikbank	Cumbr	SD5481	54°13·6′	2°41·9′W	X	97
Aikbank Common	Cumbr	NY4840	54°45·4′	2°48·1′W	X	86
Aikbank Fm	Cumbr	NY0900	54°23·5′	3°23·7′W	FM	89
Aik Bank Fm	Cumbr	NY4740	54°45·4′	2°49·0′W	FM	86
Aik Beck	Cumbr	NY4722	54°35·7′	2°48·8′W	W	90
Aike	E Yorks	TA0445	53°53·7′	0°24·6′W	T	107
Aiken	Cumbr	NY1925	54°37·1′	3°14·8′W	X	89,90
Aiken Beck	Cumbr	NY1826	54°37·6′	3°15·8′W	W	89,90
Aikencleugh	E Ayr	NS6428	55°31·9′	4°8·9′W	X	71
Aiken Crag	Cumbr	NY3914	54°31·3′	2°56·1′W	X	90
Aikendean	Midlo	NT3161	55°50·5′	3°5·7′W	X	66
Aikengall	E Loth	NT7170	55°55·6′	2°27·4′W	X	67
Aikengall Water	E Loth	NT7071	55°56·1′	2°28·4′W	W	67
Aikengill	Lancs	SD6665	54°5·0′	2°30·8′W	X	98
Aikenhead	Aberd	NO6884	56°57·0′	2°31·1′W	X	45
Aikenhead	E Ayr	NS4642	55°39·1′	4°26·4′W	X	70
Aikenhead	Pth & Kin	NO1443	56°34·5′	3°23·5′W	X	53
Aikenshaw	Arg & Bt	NS2387	56°2·8′	4°50·1′W	X	56
Aikenshill	Aberd	NJ9621	57°17·0′	2°3·5′W	X	38
Aikenway	Moray	NJ2949	57°31·8′	3°10·7′W	X	28
Aiker Ness	Orkney	HY3826	59°7·2′	3°4·5′W	H	6
Aikerness	Orkney	HY3826	59°7·2′	3°4·5′W	X	6
Aikerness	Orkney	HY4552	59°21·3′	2°57·6′W	X	5
Aiker Ness	Orkney	HY4651	59°20·8′	2°56·5′W	X	5
Aikers	Orkney	HY5110	58°58·7′	2°50·7′W	X	6
Aikers	Orkney	ND4590	58°47·9′	2°56·6′W	X	7
Aikerskaill	Orkney	HY5804	58°55·5′	2°43·3′W	X	6
Aikeslack	D & G	NX8358	54°54·4′	3°49·1′W	X	84
Aiket	D & G	NY0968	55°0·1′	3°24·9′W	X	85
Aiket Castle	E Ayr	NS3848	55°42·2′	4°34·2′W	A	63
Aiketgate	Cumbr	NY4846	54°48·6′	2°48·1′W	T	86
Aikeyside	E Loth	NT5064	55°52·2′	2°47·5′W	X	66
Aikhead	Cumbr	NY2349	54°50·0′	3°11·5′W	X	85
Aikhead Low Ho	Cumbr	NY2450	54°50·6′	3°10·6′W	X	85
Aikiehill	D & G	NX5860	54°55·1′	4°12·5′W	X	83
Aikin Knott	Cumbr	NY2119	54°33·9′	3°12·9′W	X	89,90
Aikmanhill Fm	S Lanak	NS8335	55°35·9′	3°51·0′W	FM	71,72
Aikrigg	Cumbr	SD6088	54°17·4′	2°36·5′W	X	97
Aikrigg Green	Cumbr	SD5882	54°14·2′	2°38·2′W	X	97
Aikshaw	Cumbr	NY1246	54°48·3′	3°21·7′W	X	85
Aikton	Cumbr	NY2753	54°52·2′	3°7·8′W	T	85
Aikton Ho	Cumbr	NY2753	54°52·2′	3°7·8′W	X	85
Aiky Hill	Fife	NT0092	56°6·9′	3°36·1′W	X	58
Ailanbeg	Highld	NJ0318	57°14·8′	3°36·0′W	X	36
Ailby	Lincs	TF4376	53°15·9′	0°9·1′E	T	122
Ailey	Heref	SO3448	52°7·8′	2°57·5′W	X	148,149
Ailsa Craig	S Ayr	NX0199	55°15·0′	5°7·4′W	X	76
Ailstone	Warw	SP2050	52°9·1′	1°42·1′W	T	151
Ailstone Fm	Warw	SP2151	52°9·6′	1°41·2′W	FM	151
Ailsworth	Peterb	TL1198	52°34·3′	0°21·3′W	T	142
Ailsworth Heath	Peterb	TF1101	52°36·0′	0°21·3′W	X	142
Ailt Bog na Fiodhaig	Highld	NJ0338	57°25·6′	3°36·5′W	W	27
Ailwood Fm	Dorset	SY9981	50°38·0′	2°0·5′W	FM	195
Aimbank	Cumbr	NY5245	54°48·1′	2°44·4′W	X	86
Aimes Green	Essex	TL3902	51°42·2′	0°1·1′E	T	166
Aimster	Highld	ND1163	58°33·0′	3°31·3′W	X	11,12
Ainderby Mires	N Yks	SE2592	54°19·6′	1°36·5′W	X	99
Ainderby Quernhow	N Yks	SE3480	54°13·1′	1°28·3′W	T	99
Ainderby Steeple	N Yks	SE3392	54°19·6′	1°29·1′W	T	99
Aineabhal	N Eil	NB0519	58°4·0′	6°59·7′W	H	13,14
Aine-cleit	N Eil	NG0188	57°47·2′	7°1·4′W	H	18
Aineval	N Eil	NB0931	58°10·6′	6°56·5′W	H	13
Aingers Green	Essex	TM1120	51°50·5′	1°4·2′E	T	168,169
Ain Ho	Cumbr	NY1201	54°24·1′	3°20·9′W	X	89
Ainley Top	Kirk	SE1119	53°40·3′	1°49·6′W	T	110
Ainsdale	Sefton	SD3112	53°36·2′	3°2·2′W	T	108
Ainsdale Hills	Sefton	SD2911	53°35·7′	3°4·0′W	X	108
Ainsdale-on-Sea	Sefton	SD2912	53°36·2′	3°4·0′W	T	108
Ainsdale Sands	Sefton	SD2811	53°35·7′	3°4·9′W	X	108
Ainsey Burn	Northum	NT9115	55°26·0′	2°8·1′W	W	80
Ainshval	Highld	NM3794	56°58·0′	6°19·2′W	H	39
Ainspool Ho Fm	Lancs	SD4743	53°53·1′	2°48·0′W	FM	102
Ainstable	Cumbr	NY5346	54°48·6′	2°43·5′W	T	86
Ainsworth	Bury	SD7610	53°35·4′	2°21·3′W	T	109
Ainsworth Lodge Fm	Bury	SD7709	53°34·9′	2°20·4′W	FM	109
Ainthorpe	N Yks	NZ7008	54°28·0′	0°54·8′W	T	94
Aintree	Sefton	SJ3798	53°28·7′	2°56·5′W	T	108
Aintree Sta	Sefton	SJ3697	53°28·2′	2°57·4′W	X	108
Aintuim	Arg & Bt	NM4351	56°35·1′	6°10·7′W	X	47
Ainville	W Loth	NT1063	55°51·4′	3°25·8′W	X	65
Aiplin	Shetld	HU4751	60°14·7′	1°8·6′W	X	3
Aira Beck	Cumbr	NY3720	54°34·5′	2°58·1′W	W	90
Aira Force	Cumbr	NY3920	54°34·5′	2°56·2′W	W	90
Aira Point	Cumbr	NY4019	54°34·0′	2°55·3′W	X	90
Air Balloon (PH)	Glos	SO9316	51°50·8′	2°5·7′W	X	163
Airbow Point	Fife	NO5913	56°18·7′	2°39·3′W	X	59
Aird	Arg & Bt	NM7600	56°8·7′	5°35·9′W	X	55
Aird	D & G	NX0960	54°54·1′	4°58·3′W	X	82
Aird	Highld	NG7857	57°33·2′	5°42·2′W	H	24
Aird	Highld	NG7874	57°42·3′	5°43·1′W	X	19
Aird	N Eil	NB5635	58°14·4′	6°9·0′W	T	8
Aird	N Eil	NF7654	57°27·9′	7°23·8′W	T	22
Aird a' Bhàigh	N Eil	NB2601	57°55·1′	6°37·2′W	H	14
Aird a' Chaolais	N Eil	NB2034	58°12·6′	6°45·6′W	X	8,13
Aird a' Chaolais	N Eil	NL6197	56°56·7′	7°34·1′W	X	31
Aird a' Chleirich	N Eil	NB4232	58°12·3′	6°23·0′W	X	8
Aird a' Chrainn	Arg & Bt	NM4118	56°17·3′	6°10·7′W	X	48
Aird a' Chrotha	Arg & Bt	NM7331	56°25·3′	5°40·4′W	X	49
Airdachuilinn	Highld	NC2941	58°19·7′	4°54·7′W	X	9
Aird Adhanais	N Eil	NG2294	57°51·2′	6°40·7′W	T	14
Aird a' Ghobhann	N Eil	NB2045	58°18·5′	6°46·4′W	X	8
Aird a Mhachair	N Eil	NF7445	57°23·0′	7°25·1′W	T	22

Aird a' Mhòrain	N Eil	NF8379	57°41·6′	7°18·8′W	H	18
Aird a' Mhulaidh	N Eil	NB1810	57°59·7′	6°45·9′W	T	13,14
Aird an Aiseig	N Eil	NG2197	57°52·8′	6°41·9′W	X	14
Aird an Daraich	Arg & Bt	NM3522	56°19·2′	6°16·7′W	X	48
Aird an Eilein	Arg & Bt	NN0537	56°29·3′	5°9·6′W	X	50
Aird an Fhraoich	N Eil	NF7271	57°36·8′	7°29·1′W	X	18
Aird an Laoigh	N Eil	NF8790	57°47·7′	7°15·6′W	X	18
Aird an Rùnair	N Eil	NF6970	57°36·2′	7°32·1′W	X	18
Aird an Tolmachain	N Eil	NB0904	57°56·1′	6°54·5′W	X	13,14
Aird an Troim	N Eil	NB2316	58°3·1′	6°41·2′W	X	13,14
Aird an t-Sruith	N Eil	NG0087	57°46·6′	7°2·3′W	H	18
Aird a' Phuind	N Eil	NF7974	57°38·8′	7°22·4′W	X	18
Aird Asaig	N Eil	NB1302	57°55·2′	6°50·3′W	T	14
Aird Beitheach	Highld	NM7360	56°40·9′	5°41·9′W	X	40
Aird Bharabhais	N Eil	NB3553	58°23·4′	6°31·6′W	X	8
Aird Bheag	N Eil	NB0319	58°3·9′	7°1·7′W	H	13
Aird Bheag	N Eil	NF9064	57°33·8′	7°10·6′W	X	18
Aird Bheag	N Eil	NG1791	57°49·4′	6°45·5′W	H	14
Aird Bheag Bhràgair	N Eil	NB2750	58°21·5′	6°39·6′W	X	8
Aird Bhearraraidh	N Eil	NB0616	58°2·4′	6°58·5′W	H	13,14
Aird Bianish	N Eil	NB2246	58°19·1′	6°44·4′W	X	8
Aird Br	Aberd	NJ5965	57°40·6′	2°40·8′W	X	29
Aird Brenish	N Eil	NA9727	58°8·0′	7°8·4′W	X	13
Aird Buidhe	N Eil	NF7620	57°9·6′	7°21·1′W	X	31
Aird Buidhe	N Eil	NG1795	57°51·6′	6°45·8′W	X	14
Aird Bun Abhainn Eadarra	N Eil	NB1204	57°56·2′	6°51·5′W	H	13,14
Aird Caol	N Eil	NG0986	57°46·4′	6°53·2′W	X	14
Aird Chaol	N Eil	NB1332	58°11·3′	6°52·5′W	X	13
Aird Chathanais	N Eil	NB1104	57°56·2′	6°52·5′W	H	13,14
Aird Choinnich	N Eil	NF7546	57°23·6′	7°24·2′W	T	22
Aird Chollaim	N Eil	NG1591	57°49·3′	6°47·5′W	H	14
Aird Cumhang	N Eil	NF8347	57°24·4′	7°16·3′W	X	22
Aird da Loch	Highld	NC2532	58°14·8′	4°58·4′W	X	15
Aird Dearg	Arg & Bt	NM4638	56°28·2′	6°7·0′W	X	47,48
Aird Dhail	N Eil	NB4761	58°28·1′	6°19·8′W	T	8
Aird Dhiobadail	N Eil	NB5454	58°24·6′	6°12·2′W	X	8
Aird Dhirecleit	N Eil	NG1697	57°52·6′	6°47·0′W	X	14
Aird Dhubh	Highld	NG9382	57°47·1′	5°28·4′W	X	19
Aird Dhughaill	Arg & Bt	NM3417	56°16·5′	6°17·4′W	X	48
Aird Drollageo	N Eil	NA9920	58°4·3′	7°5·8′W	X	13
Aird Dubh	Arg & Bt	NM3818	56°17·2′	6°13·6′W	X	48
Aird Earshader	N Eil	NB1533	58°11·9′	6°50·6′W	X	13
Airde-chleibhe	N Eil	NG0595	57°51·1′	6°57·9′W	X	14,18
Aird Eilein	Arg & Bt	NN0636	56°28·8′	5°8·6′W	X	50
Airdens	Highld	NH6293	57°54·6′	4°19·3′W	T	21
Airdeny	Arg & Bt	NM9929	56°24·9′	5°15·1′W	X	49
Airde, The	Highld	NC5213	58°5·1′	4°30·1′W	X	16
Aird Fada	Arg & Bt	NM4424	56°20·6′	6°8·1′W	X	48
Aird Fèiltinis	N Eil	NB3924	58°7·9′	6°25·6′W	X	14
Aird Fenish	N Eil	NA9929	58°9·1′	7°6·5′W	X	13
Aird Fhadà	Arg & Bt	NR6443	55°37·7′	5°44·5′W	X	62
Aird Fhada	N Eil	NF8771	57°37·5′	7°14·1′W	X	18
Aird Fm	E Ayr	NS4633	55°34·2′	4°26·1′W	FM	70
Aird Fm	Highld	NJ1131	57°21·9′	3°28·3′W	FM	36
Aird Gaidinis	N Eil	NF7328	57°13·8′	7°24·7′W	X	22
Aird Ghlas	Arg & Bt	NM5321	56°19·3′	5°59·2′W	X	48
Aird Glas	N Eil	NF7873	57°38·2′	7°23·3′W	X	18
Aird Greian	N Eil	NF6504	57°0·6′	7°30·7′W	X	31
Aird Griamanish	N Eil	NA9920	58°4·3′	7°5·8′W	X	13
Aird Grèdanais	N Eil	NB0601	57°54·4′	6°57·3′W	X	14,18
Aird Hill	N Ayr	NS1554	55°44·9′	4°56·4′W	X	63
Aird Hill	N Ayr	NS1759	55°47·6′	4°54·7′W	H	63
Aird Iain	Highld	NM6466	56°43·8′	5°51·0′W	X	40
Airdie Mill	Highld	NH9745	57°29·3′	3°42·6′W	X	27
Airdit	Fife	NO4120	56°22·4′	2°56·9′W	X	54,59
Aird Kilfinichen	Arg & Bt	NM4927	56°22·4′	6°3·5′W	X	48
Aird Laimisiadair	N Eil	NB1742	58°16·8′	6°49·2′W	H	8,13
Airdlin	Aberd	NJ9137	57°25·8′	2°8·5′W	X	30
Aird Linn	D & G	NX8192	55°12·7′	3°51·8′W	W	78
Aird Luing	Arg & Bt	NM7406	56°11·8′	5°38·1′W	X	55
Aird Ma-Ruibhe	N Eil	NF9179	57°41·9′	7°10·8′W	X	18
Aird Mhànais	N Eil	NG1188	57°47·6′	6°51·3′W	X	14
Aird Mheadhonach	N Eil	NB0132	58°10·8′	7°4·7′W	X	13
Aird Mheadhonach	N Eil	NB1945	58°18·5′	6°47·4′W	X	8
Aird Mheadhonach	N Eil	NF1898	57°53·2′	6°45·0′W	X	14
Aird Mhiabhaig	N Eil	NB0805	57°56·6′	6°55·6′W	X	13,14
Aird Mhiabhaig	N Eil	NG1696	57°52·1′	6°46·9′W	X	14
Aird Mhic Caoilt	N Eil	NF7875	57°39·2′	7°23·5′W	X	18
Aird Mhighe	N Eil	NG0887	57°46·9′	6°54·3′W	T	14,18
Aird Mhighe	N Eil	NG1292	57°49·8′	6°50·6′W	T	14
Aird Mhòr	N Eil	NB0317	58°2·8′	7°1·6′W	H	13
Aird Mhor	N Eil	NB1737	58°14·1′	6°48·8′W	X	8,13
Aird Mhòr	N Eil	NB1945	58°18·5′	6°47·4′W	X	8
Aird Mhòr	N Eil	NF7945	57°23·2′	7°20·1′W	T	22
Aird Mhòr	N Eil	NF8259	57°30·8′	7°18·2′W	X	22
Aird Mhòr	N Eil	NF9063	57°33·3′	7°10·5′W	X	18
Aird Mhòr	N Eil	NG0785	57°45·8′	6°55·2′W	X	18
Aird Mhòr	N Eil	NG1289	57°48·1′	6°50·4′W	X	14
Aird Mhòr Bhràgair	N Eil	NB2649	58°20·9′	6°40·5′W	X	8
Aird Molach	Highld	NM7071	56°46·7′	5°45·4′W	H	40
Aird Mór	Arg & Bt	NL9342	56°28·5′	6°58·7′W	X	46
Aird Mór	Arg & Bt	NM3217	56°16·4′	6°19·3′W	H	48
Aird Mór	N Eil	NF9175	57°39·8′	7°10·5′W	X	18
Aird na Craoibhe	N Eil	NF9172	57°38·2′	7°10·2′W	X	18
Aird na Gregaig	N Eil	NF6300	56°58·4′	7°32·4′W	X	31
Aird na h-Eighe	Highld	NH1098	57°56·1′	5°12·1′W	X	19
Aird na h-Iolaire	Arg & Bt	NM4028	56°22·6′	6°12·2′W	X	48
Aird nam Bùth	Highld	NM7283	56°53·2′	5°44·1′W	X	40
Aird nam Fuaran	Highld	NM6687	56°55·2′	5°50·2′W	X	40
Aird nam Madadh	N Eil	NF9467	57°35·6′	7°6·8′W	X	18
Aird na Mòine	N Eil	NB1839	58°15·2′	6°48·0′W	X	8,13
Aird na Mòine	N Eil	NB1937	58°14·2′	6°46·8′W	X	8,13
Aird na Monadh	N Eil	NF7745	57°23·1′	7°22·1′W	T	22
Aird na Muile	N Eil	NF9277	57°40·9′	7°9·6′W	X	18
Aird nan Caorach	Highld	NG9492	57°52·5′	5°28·0′W	X	19
Aird nan Laogh	N Eil	NF8461	57°32·0′	7°16·4′W	X	22
Aird nan Laogh	N Eil	NF9173	57°38·7′	7°10·3′W	X	18
Aird nan Rón	Arg & Bt	NR8673	55°54·4′	5°25·0′W	X	62
Aird nan Ron	N Ayr	NR9024	55°28·1′	5°18·9′W	X	68,69
Aird nan Sruban	N Eil	NF8359	57°30·9′	7°17·2′W	X	22

Aird nan Srùban	N Eil	NF8457	57°29·8′	7°16·1′W	T	22
Aird nan Uan	Highld	NM4080	56°50·6′	6°15·4′W	X	39
Aird Nisabost	N Eil	NG0497	57°52·1′	6°59·1′W	X	18
Aird Nòis	Highld	NN0890	56°57·9′	5°9·0′W	X	33
Aird of Coigach	Highld	NC0711	58°3·0′	5°15·8′W	X	15
Aird of Kinloch	Arg & Bt	NM5228	56°23·0′	6°0·6′W	X	48
Aird of Kinuachdrachd	Arg & Bt	NR7098	56°7·4′	5°41·6′W	X	55,61
Aird of Sleat	Highld	NG5900	57°2·0′	5°57·9′W	T	32,39
Aird Orasay	N Eil	NB1231	58°10·7′	6°53·5′W	X	13
Aird Point	Highld	NG4052	57°29·3′	6°19·9′W	X	23
Aird Point	Highld	NG8688	57°50·1′	5°35·8′W	X	19
Aird Rachdaig	Arg & Bt	NR6397	56°6·7′	5°48·3′W	H	61
Aird Raerinis	N Eil	NB4124	58°8·0′	6°23·5′W	X	14
Aird Reamhar	Arg & Bt	NR2266	55°48·7′	6°25·8′W	X	60
Aird Reamhar	N Eil	NF8472	57°37·9′	7°17·2′W	X	18
Aird Riabhach	N Eil	NG2396	57°52·3′	6°39·8′W	X	14
Airdrie	D & G	NX9658	54°54·6′	3°36·9′W	X	84
Airdrie	Fife	NO5608	56°16·0′	2°42·2′W	X	59
Airdrie	Highld	NH9746	57°29·8′	3°42·7′W	X	27
Airdrie	N Lanak	NS7665	55°52·0′	3°58·5′W	T	64
Airdrieend	S Lanak	NS7639	55°38·0′	3°57·7′W	X	71
Airdrie Hill	D & G	NX9459	54°55·1′	3°38·8′W	H	84
Airdriehill	N Lanak	NS7867	55°53·1′	3°56·6′W	X	64
Aird Ruairidh	N Eil	NF7421	57°10·1′	7°23·2′W	T	31
Aird Rubha Mór	N Eil	NL6997	56°57·0′	7°26·2′W	H	31
Airds	D & G	NX7267	54°59·1′	3°59·6′W	X	83,84
Airds	D & G	NX8148	54°49·0′	3°50·7′W	X	84
Airds	D & G	NX9866	54°58·9′	3°35·2′W	X	84
Airds Bay	Arg & Bt	NM9044	56°32·7′	5°24·5′W	W	49
Airds Bay	Arg & Bt	NN0032	56°26·5′	5°14·2′W	W	50
Airds Bay	D & G	NX5752	54°50·8′	4°13·2′W	W	83
Airds Bay Ho	Arg & Bt	NM9932	56°26·5′	5°15·2′W	X	49
Aird Scàparaid	N Eil	NB2727	58°9·1′	6°37·9′W	X	8,13
Airds Cott	D & G	NX8149	54°49·6′	3°50·7′W	X	84
Aird Sgeiginis	N Eil	NB5462	58°28·9′	6°12·7′W	X	8
Airds Hill	Arg & Bt	NM9245	56°33·3′	5°22·6′W	H	49
Airds Hill	D & G	NX7268	54°59·7′	3°59·6′W	H	83,84
Airds Hill	E Ayr	NS6317	55°25·9′	4°9·5′W	X	71
Aird Shleibhe	N Eil	NG1189	57°48·1′	6°51·4′W	T	14
Airds Ho	Arg & Bt	NM9044	56°32·7′	5°24·5′W	X	49
Airds Ho	D & G	NX6870	55°0·7′	4°3·4′W	X	77,84
Aird Shorragaigh	N Eil	NF8338	57°19·6′	7°15·6′W	X	22
Aird Sleitenish	N Eil	NB0219	58°3·9′	7°2·7′W	X	13
Aird Smeilish	N Eil	NF8668	57°35·8′	7°14·9′W	X	18
Airds Moss	E Ayr	NS6024	55°29·6′	4°12·5′W	X	71
Airds of Kells	D & G	NX6770	55°0·7′	4°4·4′W	X	77,84
Airds Park	Arg & Bt	NM9832	56°26·5′	5°16·2′W	X	49
Airds Point	Arg & Bt	NM9834	56°27·6′	5°16·3′W	X	49
Airds Point	D & G	NX8248	54°49·0′	3°49·8′W	X	84
Airds Point	D & G	NX9966	54°59·0′	3°34·3′W	X	84
Aird Steinis	N Eil	NG1490	57°48·8′	6°48·5′W	X	14
Aird Sticleit	N Eil	NB1300	57°54·1′	6°50·2′W	X	14
Aird Taranaish	N Eil	NB1737	58°14·1′	6°48·8′W	X	8,13
Aird, The	Highld	NG4052	57°29·3′	6°19·9′W	T	23
Aird, The	Highld	NG4375	57°41·7′	6°18·3′W	X	23
Aird, The	Highld	NH5443	57°27·5′	4°25·6′W	X	26
Aird, The	N Eil	NL5780	56°47·4′	7°36·6′W	H	31
Aird Thormaid	N Eil	NF9276	57°40·4′	7°9·5′W	X	18
Aird Thorr-innis	Arg & Bt	NR2167	55°49·2′	6°26·8′W	X	60
Aird Thunga	N Eil	NB4636	58°14·6′	6°19·2′W	T	8
Aird Torranish	N Eil	NB1533	58°11·9′	6°50·6′W	X	13
Airdtorrisdale	Highld	NC6762	58°31·8′	4°16·6′W	T	10
Aird Torrisdale	Highld	NC6763	58°32·4′	4°16·6′W	X	10
Aird Trilleachan	Highld	NN1043	56°32·7′	5°5·0′W	X	50
Aird Tro	N Eil	NA9800	57°53·5′	7°5·3′W	X	18
Aird Uig	N Eil	NB0537	58°13·6′	7°1·0′W	T	13
Aird Vanish	N Eil	NF9999	57°53·0′	7°4·2′W	X	18
Aire and Calder Navigation	E Yorks	SE6318	53°39·5′	1°2·4′W	W	111
Aire and Calder Navigation (Knottingley and Goole Canal)	N Yks	SE5322	53°41·7′	1°11·4′W	W	105
Aire & Calder Navigation	Leeds	SE3728	53°45·1′	1°25·9′W	W	104
Airedale	Brad	SE0345	53°54·3′	1°56·8′W	X	104
Airedale	Wakf	SE4525	53°43·4′	1°18·7′W	T	105
Airedale House Fm	N Yks	SE0346	53°54·8′	1°56·8′W	FM	104
Aire Head	N Yks	SD9062	54°3·5′	2°8·7′W	X	98
Aire Point	Corn	SW3528	50°5·8′	5°42·0′W	X	203
Aire View	N Yks	SD9946	53°54·9′	2°0·5′W	T	103
Aireville Park	N Yks	SD9751	53°57·5′	2°2·3′W	X	103
Airey Hill Fm	Northum	NZ0858	54°55·2′	1°52·1′W	FM	88
Airfield	Midlo	NT3867	55°53·8′	2°59·0′W	X	66
Airfield	Somer	ST5315	50°56·2′	2°39·8′W	X	183
Airfield Camp Netheravon	Wilts	SU1649	51°14·6′	1°45·9′W	X	184
Airfield (disused)	Somer	ST3460	51°20·4′	2°56·5′W	X	182
Airfield Fm	Norf	TM2690	52°27·9′	1°20·0′E	FM	134
Airgiod Bheinn	Pth & Kin	NN9672	56°49·9′	3°41·8′W	H	43
Airgiod-meall	Highld	NH9606	57°8·2′	3°42·6′W	H	36
Airhouse	Scot Bord	NT4853	55°46·3′	2°49·3′W	X	66,73
Airidh a Bhruaich	N Eil	NB2417	58°3·6′	6°40·3′W	T	13,14
Airidh Mhaoraich	Arg & Bt	NM2356	56°37·1′	6°30·5′W	X	46,47
Airidh nam Ban	N Eil	NF7928	57°14·1′	7°18·8′W	X	22
Airie	D & G	NX6178	55°4·9′	4°10·2′W	X	77
Airie	D & G	NX6369	55°0·1′	4°8·1′W	X	83
Airie Bennan	D & G	NX5877	55°4·3′	4°13·0′W	H	77
Airie Burn	D & G	NX6169	55°0·0′	4°10·0′W	W	83
Airie Burn	D & G	NX6170	55°0·6′	4°10·0′W	W	77
Airie Burn	D & G	NX6368	54°59·5′	4°8·1′W	W	83
Airieglasson	D & G	NX2471	55°0·4′	4°44·7′W	X	76
Airie Hill	D & G	NX6268	54°59·5′	4°9·0′W	H	83
Airieland	D & G	NX7557	54°53·8′	3°56·5′W	X	84
Airieland Burn	D & G	NX7656	54°53·3′	3°55·6′W	W	84
Airieland Moor	D & G	NX7656	54°53·3′	3°55·6′W	X	84
Airigh a' Bhealaich	N Eil	NB5358	58°26·7′	6°13·5′W	X	8
Airigh a' Bhreac Laoigh	Arg & Bt	NM4222	56°19·5′	6°9·9′W	X	48
Airigh Achadh dà Mhaoilein	Arg & Bt	NR7773	55°54·2′	5°33·6′W	X	62
Airigh a'Chleirich	Highld	NM7442	56°31·2′	5°40·0′W	X	49
Airigh an t-Srath	N Eil	NB4352	58°23·1′	6°23·3′W	X	8

Airigh an Tuim	N Eil	NB3954	58°24·1′	6°27·6′W	X	8
Airigh Ard	Arg & Bt	NR9296	56°6·9′	5°20·3′W	H	55
Airigh Bhreac	Arg & Bt	NM5244	56°31·6′	6°1·5′W	X	47,48
Airigh Chailleach (Shielings)	Arg & Bt	NN2033	56°27·5′	4°54·8′W	X	50
Airigh Challtuinn	Arg & Bt	NN2035	56°28·6′	4°54·9′W	X	50
Airigh Chlaodhanach	Arg & Bt	NM6627	56°22·9′	5°47·0′W	X	49
Airigh Chreagach	Arg & Bt	NR7665	55°49·8′	5°34·2′W	X	62
Airigh Dhriseach	N Eil	NB3715	58°3·0′	6°27·0′W	X	14
Airigh Dhubh	Arg & Bt	NM5222	56°19·8′	6°0·3′W	X	48
Airigh Dhubh	Arg & Bt	NR3553	55°42·1′	6°12·6′W	X	60
Airigh-drishaig	Highld	NG7636	57°21·8′	5°43·0′W	X	24
Airighean Beinn nan Caorach	N Eil	NB5156	58°25·6′	6°15·4′W	X	8
Airighean Chatuil	N Eil	NB4452	58°23·2′	6°22·3′W	X	8
Airighean Dubha	N Eil	NF9073	57°38·7′	7°11·3′W	X	18
Airighean Loch Bhreitheabhat	N Eil	NB4854	58°24·4′	6°18·4′W	X	8
Airighean Loch Foisneabhat	N Eil	NB4351	58°22·6′	6°23·3′W	X	8
Airighean Molagro	N Eil	NB4352	58°23·1′	6°23·3′W	X	8
Airighean na h-Annaid	N Eil	NG4198	57°54·0′	6°21·8′W	X	14
Airigh Fraoch	Arg & Bt	NM4921	56°19·2′	6°3·1′W	X	48
Airigh Ghlas	Arg & Bt	NR2769	55°50·5′	6°21·2′W	X	60
Airigh Hill	Highld	ND2038	58°19·7′	3°21·5′W	H	11
Airigh Iain Mhic Ailein	N Eil	NB5456	58°25·7′	6°12·3′W	X	8
Airigh Lag nan Cluas	Arg & Bt	NM5031	56°24·6′	6°2·7′W	X	48
Airigh Leathaid	Highld	NC9939	58°19·9′	3°43·0′W	X	11,17
Airigh Liath	Arg & Bt	NR2463	55°47·1′	6°23·7′W	X	60
Airigh-mheadhon	Arg & Bt	NM9747	56°34·5′	5°17·8′W	X	49
Airigh Mhic-caidn	Arg & Bt	NR6490	56°2·9′	5°46·9′W	X	55,61
Airigh Mhic Dhomhnuill	Arg & Bt	NR3673	55°52·9′	6°12·9′W	X	60,61
Airigh Mhic-'ille Mhòire	Arg & Bt	NR4571	55°52·1′	6°4·1′W	X	60,61
Airigh Mhic Ruairidh	N Eil	NF7674	57°38·6′	7°25·4′W	X	18
Airigh na Gaoithe	N Eil	NB5360	58°27·8′	6°13·6′W	X	8
Airigh na Gaoithe	N Eil	NF8267	57°35·1′	7°18·8′W	H	18
Airigh na Glaice	N Eil	NB4957	58°26·0′	6°17·5′W	X	8
Airigh na Maith-innse	Highld	NM3099	57°0·5′	6°26·4′W	X	39
Airigh nam Beist	Arg & Bt	NR4147	55°39·1′	6°6·6′W	X	60
Airigh nan Clach	Arg & Bt	NR3871	55°51·9′	6°10·8′W	X	60,61
Airigh nan Lochan	Arg & Bt	NN0847	56°34·8′	5°7·1′W	W	50
Airigh nan Sidhean	Arg & Bt	NR3671	55°51·8′	6°12·7′W	X	60,61
Airigh na Stainge	Arg & Bt	NM5123	56°20·3′	6°1·3′W	X	48
Airigh Neill	Highld	NG3549	57°27·5′	6°24·6′W	X	23
Airigh Samhraidh	Highld	NG3532	57°18·4′	6°23·6′W	X	32
Airigh Sgallaidh	Arg & Bt	NR1755	55°42·6′	6°29·9′W	X	60
Airigh Shamhraidh	Highld	NM8449	56°35·3′	5°30·6′W	X	49
Airigh Sheileach	Arg & Bt	NR7670	55°52·5′	5°34·4′W	X	62
Airinis	N Eil	NB4230	58°11·3′	6°22·9′W	X	8
Airleywight	Pth & Kin	NO0635	56°30·1′	3°31·2′W	X	52,53
Airlich	Pth & Kin	NN9638	56°31·6′	3°41·0′W	H	52,53
Airlie	Aberd	NJ4901	57°6·1′	2°50·1′W	X	37
Airlie	Aberd	NJ6019	57°15·9′	2°39·3′W	X	37
Airlie	Angus	NO3150	56°38·5′	3°7·1′W	T	53
Airlie Castle	Angus	NO2952	56°39·5′	3°9·0′W	A	53
Airlie Memorial Tower	Angus	NO3761	56°44·4′	3°1·3′W	X	44
Airlies	D & G	NX3651	54°49·9′	4°32·8′W	X	83
Airlig	Arg & Bt	NS2285	56°1·7′	4°51·0′W	H	56
Airlour	D & G	NX3442	54°45·0′	4°34·3′W	X	82
Airman's Corner	Wilts	SU0942	51°10·9′	1°51·9′W	X	184
Airmyn	N Yks	SE7225	53°43·2′	0°54·1′W	T	105,106
Airmyn Grange	E Yorks	SE7023	53°42·2′	0°56·0′W	X	105,106,112
Airneabhal	N Eil	NF7825	57°12·4′	7°19·5′W	H	22
Airne na Sgeire	Arg & Bt	NM2154	56°36·0′	6°32·3′W	X	46,47
Airngarrow	Moray	NJ2440	57°26·9′	3°15·5′W	X	28
Airnistean	N Eil	NB4962	58°28·7′	6°17·9′W	X	8
Airnlee	D & G	NY4177	55°5·3′	2°55·0′W	X	85
Airntully	Pth & Kin	NO0935	56°30·2′	3°28·3′W	T	52,53
Airon	Orkney	HY6544	59°17·1′	2°36·4′W	X	5
Airor	Highld	NG7105	57°5·0′	5°46·3′W	T	33
Airor Burn	Highld	NG7205	57°5·0′	5°45·3′W	W	33
Airor Island	Highld	NG7105	57°5·0′	5°46·3′W	X	33
Airiequhillart	D & G	NX3552	54°50·4′	4°33·7′W	X	83
Air Scar Crags	N Yks	SE0260	54°2·4′	1°57·8′W	X	98
Airth	Falk	NS8987	56°4·0′	3°46·5′W	T	65
Airth Castle	Falk	NS8986	56°3·5′	3°46·5′W	A	65
Airth Mains	Falk	NS8987	56°4·0′	3°46·5′W	X	65
Airthrey Castle	Stir	NS8196	56°8·8′	3°54·5′W	T	57
Airtnoch	E Ayr	NS5043	55°39·7′	4°22·6′W	X	70
Airton	N Yks	SD9059	54°1·9′	2°8·7′W	T	103
Airton Green	N Yks	SD8759	54°1·9′	2°11·5′W	X	103
Airy	Orkney	HY6725	59°6·9′	2°34·1′W	X	5
Airyewn	S Ayr	NX2275	55°2·5′	4°46·7′W	X	76
Airyhassen	D & G	NX3746	54°47·2′	4°31·7′W	X	83
Airyhemming	D & G	NX1759	54°53·8′	4°50·8′W	X	82
Airyhill	D & G	NX7847	54°48·5′	3°53·5′W	X	84
Airy Hill	E Yorks	TA0660	54°1·7′	0°22·5′W	X	101
Airy Hill	N Yks	NZ8909	54°28·4′	0°37·2′W	X	94
Airy Hill Fm	N Yks	TA1177	54°10·8′	0°17·5′W	FM	101
Airy Hill Fm	Red & Cl	NZ6416	54°32·4′	1°0·2′W	FM	94
Airyhillock	Aberd	NJ8125	57°19·2′	2°18·5′W	X	38
Airyholme	N Yks	SE6773	54°9·1′	0°58·0′W	X	100
Airyholme Fm	N Yks	NZ5711	54°29·7′	1°6·8′W	FM	93
Airy Holm Fm	Northum	NZ0453	54°52·6′	1°55·8′W	FM	87
Airylick	D & G	NX3149	54°48·7′	4°37·4′W	X	82
Airyligg	D & G	NX2562	54°55·6′	4°43·4′W	X	82
Airy Muir	Aberd	NO6087	56°58·6′	2°39·0′W	X	45
Airyolland	D & G	NX3047	54°47·6′	4°38·2′W	X	82
Airyolland Moss	D & G	NX1461	54°54·8′	4°53·7′W	X	82
Airy Point	Devon	SS4433	51°4·7′	4°13·2′W	X	180
Ais-an t-Sidhean	Arg & Bt	NN3539	56°31·1′	4°40·5′W	X	50
Aisby	Lincs	SK8792	53°25·3′	0°41·0′W	T	112
Aisby	Lincs	TF0138	52°56·0′	0°29·4′W	T	130
Ais Geo	Orkney	HY6922	59°5·3′	2°32·0′W	X	5
Aisgerbheinn	N Eil	NF7423	57°11·2′	7°22·3′W	H	22
Aisgernis	N Eil	NF7424	57°11·7′	7°23·4′W	T	22
Ais Gill	Cumbr	SD7797	54°22·3′	2°22·7′W	W	98
Aisgill Fm	Cumbr	SD7797	54°22·3′	2°20·8′W	FM	98
Aisgill Moor	Cumbr	SD7696	54°21·8′	2°21·7′W	X	98
Aisgill Moor Cottages	Cumbr	SD7796	54°21·8′	2°20·8′W	X	98

Aish	Devon	SS4408	50°51·3′	4°12·6′W	X	190
Aish	Devon	SS7906	50°50·7′	3°42·7′W	X	191
Aish	Devon	SX6960	50°25·7′	3°50·3′W	T	202
Aish	Devon	SX8458	50°24·9′	3°37·6′W	T	202
Aisholt	Somer	ST1935	51°6·7′	3°9·0′W	T	181
Aisholt Common	Somer	ST1835	51°6·7′	3°9·9′W	X	181
Aisholt Wood	Somer	ST1935	51°6·7′	3°9·0′W	F	181
Aish Ridge	Devon	SX6860	50°25·7′	3°51·1′W	X	202
Aish Tor	Devon	SX7071	50°31·7′	3°49·7′W	X	202
Aiskew	N Yks	SE2788	54°17·5′	1°34·7′W	T	99
Aiskew Fm	N Yks	SE2788	54°17·5′	1°34·7′W	FM	99
Aiskew Grange	N Yks	SE2789	54°18·0′	1°34·7′W	X	99
Aislaby	N Yks	NZ8508	54°27·9′	0°40·9′W	T	94
Aislaby	N Yks	SE7785	54°15·5′	0°48·7′W	T	94,100
Aislaby	Stock on T	NZ4012	54°30·3′	1°22·5′W	T	93
Aislaby Carr	N Yks	SE7784	54°15·0′	0°48·7′W	X	100
Aislaby Grange	Stock on T	NZ3911	54°29·8′	1°23·4′W	X	93
Aislaby Grange	Stock on T	NZ3913	54°30·9′	1°23·4′W	X	93
Aislaby Moor	N Yks	NZ8408	54°27·9′	0°41·8′W	X	94
Aislaby West Fm	Stock on T	NZ3912	54°30·4′	1°23·4′W	FM	93
Aismunderby Village	N Yks	SE3066	54°6·7′	1°32·0′W	A	99
Ais-sgeir	Highld	NG8626	57°16·7′	5°32·6′W	X	33
Aisthorpe	Lincs	SK9480	53°18·7′	0°34·9′W	T	121
Aisthorpe Hall	Lincs	SK9480	53°18·7′	0°34·9′W	X	121
Aitchisons Bank	D & G	NY3270	55°1·4′	3°3·4′W	X	85
Aite Maol	Highld	NG3449	57°27·5′	6°25·6′W	X	23
Aith	Orkney	HY2417	59°2·3′	3°19·0′W	X	6
Aith	Orkney	HY6425	59°6·9′	2°37·2′W	X	5
Aith	Shetld	HU3455	60°16·9′	1°22·6′W	T	3
Aith	Shetld	HU4429	60°2·9′	1°12·1′W	X	4
Aith	Shetld	HU5143	60°10·4′	1°4·4′W	X	4
Aith	Shetld	HU6390	60°35·6′	0°50·5′W	X	1,2
Aithbank	Shetld	HU6489	60°35·0′	0°49·4′W	X	1,2
Aithernie Castle	Fife	NO3703	56°13·2′	3°0·5′W	A	59
Aith Head	Orkney	ND3088	58°46·7′	3°12·2′W	X	7
Aith Hope	Orkney	ND2988	58°46·7′	3°13·2′W	W	7
Aithmuir	Pth & Kin	NO2725	56°25·0′	3°10·5′W	X	53,59
Aithnen	Powys	SJ2022	52°47·6′	3°10·8′W	T	126
Aith Ness	Shetld	HU3359	60°19·1′	1°23·7′W	X	2,3
Aith Ness	Shetld	HU5144	60°10·9′	1°4·3′W	X	4
Aith Ness	Shetld	HU6389	60°35·0′	0°50·5′W	X	1,2
Aithouse Burn	Scot Bord	NT3308	55°21·5′	3°3·0′W	W	79
Aithsdale	Orkney	ND3089	58°47·2′	3°12·2′W	X	7
Aithsetter	Shetld	HU4430	60°3·4′	1°12·1′W	T	4
Aiths Lee	Shetld	HU6489	60°35·0′	0°49·4′W	X	1,2
Aithsness	Shetld	HU3358	60°18·6′	1°23·7′W	X	2,3
Aithsting	Shetld	HU3355	60°16·9′	1°23·7′W	X	3
Aith Voe	Shetld	HU3458	60°18·5′	1°22·6′W	W	2,3
Aith Voe	Shetld	HU4328	60°2·3′	1°13·2′W	W	4
Aith Voe	Shetld	HU5043	60°10·4′	1°5·4′W	W	4
Aith Wick	Shetld	HU4429	60°2·9′	1°12·1′W	W	4
Aitkenhead	Clackm	NS9494	56°7·9′	3°41·9′W	X	58
Aitkenhead	N Lanak	NS7063	55°50·8′	4°4·1′W	X	64
Aitkenhead	S Ayr	NS3408	55°20·5′	4°36·6′W	X	70,76
Aitken Wood	Lancs	SD8240	53°51·6′	2°16·0′W	F	103
Aitnoch	Moray	NH9839	57°26·1′	3°41·5′W	X	27
Attendow	Highld	NJ0238	57°25·6′	3°37·5′W	X	27
Ajalon Ho	N Yks	NZ7204	54°25·8′	0°53·0′W	X	94
Akebank Mill	Cumbr	NY1125	54°37·0′	3°22·3′W	X	89
Akebar Cotts	N Yks	SE1990	54°18·6′	1°42·1′W	X	99
Akebar Fm	N Yks	SE1890	54°18·6′	1°43·0′W	FM	99
Akeld	Northum	NT9529	55°33·5′	2°4·3′W	T	74,75
Akeld Hill	Northum	NT9429	55°33·5′	2°5·3′W	H	74,75
Akeld Steads	Northum	NT9630	55°34·1′	2°3·4′W	X	74,75
Akeley	Bucks	SP7037	52°1·9′	0°58·4′W	T	152
Akeley Wood Fm	Bucks	SP6938	52°2·4′	0°59·2′W	FM	152
Akeley Wood (Sch)	Northnts	SP7438	52°2·4′	0°54·9′W	X	152
Akeley Wood School	Bucks	SP6937	52°1·9′	0°59·3′W	X	152
Akeman Street Fm	Oxon	SP4117	51°51·2′	1°23·9′W	FM	164
Akeman Street (Roman Road)	Bucks	SP8512	51°48·2′	0°45·6′W	R	165
Akeman Street (Roman Road)	Glos	SP1706	51°45·4′	1°44·8′W	R	163
Akeman Street (Roman Road)	Oxon	SP5020	51°52·8′	1°16·0′W	R	164
Akenham	Suff	TM1448	52°5·6′	1°7·8′E	T	169
Akenham Hall	Suff	TM1549	52°6·1′	1°8·8′E	X	169
Akenshawburn	Northum	NY6089	55°11·9′	2°37·3′W	X	80
Akenshaw Burn	Northum	NY6189	55°11·9′	2°36·3′W	W	80
Akermoor Loch	Scot Bord	NT4020	55°28·5′	2°56·5′W	W	73
Akers Geo	Shetld	HU1461	60°20·2′	1°44·3′W	X	3
Akers Houll	Shetld	HP5400	60°41·0′	1°0·2′W	X	1
Akesworth Coppice	Staffs	SJ7736	52°55·5′	2°20·1′W	F	127
Aketil Burn	Highld	NG3245	57°25·2′	6°27·4′W	W	23
Aketon	N Yks	SE3552	53°58·0′	1°27·6′W	X	104
Aketon Lodge	N Yks	SE3452	53°58·0′	1°28·5′W	X	104
Akeygate	Cumbr	NY5923	54°36·3′	2°37·7′W	X	91
Akitt	N Yks	NZ5600	54°23·8′	1°7·8′W	X	93
Akla	Orkney	HY3407	58°57·0′	3°8·3′W	H	6,7
Akran Burn	Highld	NC9062	58°32·2′	3°52·9′W	W	10
Alamein	Aberd	NJ5005	57°8·2′	2°49·1′W	X	37
Alance Bridge	Lancs	SD6215	53°38·1′	2°34·1′W	X	109
Alan Evans Memorial Hostel	Highld	NG5537	57°21·7′	6°4·0′W	X	24,32
Alarip Bay	N Eil	NF8888	57°46·6′	7°14·5′W	W	18
A-la-Ronde	Devon	SY0083	50°38·5′	3°24·5′W	A	192
Alastrean Ho	Aberd	NJ4904	57°7·7′	2°50·1′W	X	37
Alavna Roman Fort	Cumbr	NY0337	54°43·4′	3°29·9′W	R	89
Alavna (Roman Fort)	Cumbr	SD5190	54°18·4′	2°44·8′W	R	97
Albana Wood	Suff	TL8161	52°13·3′	0°39·4′E	F	155
Albans Fm	Kent	TQ6442	51°9·4′	0°21·1′E	FM	188
Albany	Sund	NZ2957	54°54·7′	1°32·4′W	T	88
Albany Burn	S Ayr	NX2792	55°11·8′	4°42·7′W	W	76
Albany Fm	Hants	SU5709	50°52·9′	1°11·0′W	FM	196
Albany Prison	I of W	SZ4890	50°42·7′	1°18·8′W	X	196
Albaston	Corn	SX4270	50°30·7′	4°13·4′W	T	201
Alberbury	Shrops	SJ3614	52°43·4′	2°56·5′W	T	126
Alberbury Castle	Shrops	SJ3514	52°43·4′	2°57·3′W	A	126
Albert Br	Wan	TQ2777	51°28·9′	0°9·9′W	X	176

Albert Br	Win & Maid	SU9875	51°28·2′	0°35·0′W	X	175,176
Albert Dock	Wirral	SJ3485	53°21·7′	2°59·1′W	X	108
Albert Tower	I of M	SC4593	54°18·8′	4°22·5′W	X	95
Albert Town	Pemb	SM9415	51°48·0′	4°58·9′W	T	157,158
Albert Village	Leic	SK3018	52°45·8′	1°32·9′W	T	128
Albie	D & G	NY2477	55°5·1′	3°11·0′W	X	85
Albierig	D & G	NY4180	55°6·9′	2°55·1′W	X	79
Albionhayes	Shrops	SJ4619	52°46·2′	2°47·6′W	X	126
Albion Sands	Pemb	SM7707	51°43·3′	5°13·3′W	X	157
Albourne	W Susx	TQ2616	50°56·0′	0°12·0′W	T	198
Albourne Green	W Susx	TQ2616	50°56·0′	0°12·0′W	T	198
Albourne Place	W Susx	TQ2516	50°56·0′	0°12·9′W	X	198
Albright Hussey	Shrops	SJ5017	52°45·1′	2°44·0′W	A	126
Albrightlee	Shrops	SJ5216	52°44·6′	2°42·3′W	X	126
Albrighton	Shrops	SJ4918	52°45·7′	2°44·9′W	T	126
Albrighton	Shrops	SJ8104	52°38·2′	2°16·4′W	T	127
Albro Castle	Cered	SN1646	52°5·1′	4°40·7′W	T	145
Albrough Fm	Cambs	TL4668	52°17·7′	0°8·9′E	FM	154
Alburgh	Norf	TM2786	52°25·7′	1°20·7′E	T	156
Albury	Herts	TL4324	51°54·0′	0°5·1′E	T	167
Albury	Oxon	SP6505	51°44·6′	1°3·1′W	X	164,165
Albury	Surrey	TQ0547	51°13·0′	0°29·4′W	T	187
Albury Bottom	Surrey	SU9764	51°22·2′	0°36·0′W	X	175,176,186
Albury Downs	Surrey	TQ0448	51°13·5′	0°30·2′W	X	186
Albury End	Herts	TL4223	51°53·5′	0°4·2′E	T	167
Albury Fm	Hants	SU7733	51°5·7′	0°53·6′W	FM	186
Albury Hall	Herts	TL4225	51°54·6′	0°4·3′E	X	167
Albury Heath	Surrey	TQ0646	51°12·4′	0°28·6′W	T	187
Albury Lodge	Herts	TL4323	51°53·5′	0°5·1′E	X	167
Albury Park	Surrey	TQ0647	51°13·0′	0°28·5′W	X	187
Albyfield	Cumbr	NY5452	54°51·9′	2°42·6′W	T	86
Alby Hill	Norf	TG1934	52°51·8′	1°15·6′E	T	133
Albynes, The	Shrops	SO6997	52°34·4′	2°27·0′W	X	138
Albyns	Essex	TQ5096	51°38·8′	0°10·5′E	X	167,177
Albyns Fm	Hav	TQ5283	51°31·8′	0°11·9′E	FM	177
Alcaig	Highld	NH5656	57°34·5′	4°24·0′W	X	26
Alcaig	Highld	NH5657	57°35·1′	4°24·1′W	T	26
Alcar Fm	N Yks	SE5664	54°4·4′	1°8·2′W	FM	100
Alcaston	Shrops	SO4587	52°28·9′	2°48·2′W	T	137,138
Alcester	Dorset	ST8522	51°0·1′	2°12·4′W	T	183
Alcester	Warw	SP0857	52°12·9′	1°52·6′W	T	150
Alcester Lane's End	Birm	SP0780	52°25·3′	1°53·4′W	T	139
Alcester Lodge	Warw	SP0759	52°14·0′	1°53·5′W	X	150
Alcester Park Fm	Warw	SP0559	52°14·0′	1°55·2′W	FM	150
Alcester Warren	Warw	SP0561	52°15·1′	1°55·2′W	X	150
Alchester (Roman Town)	Oxon	SP5720	51°52·8′	1°9·9′W	R	164
Alciston	E Susx	TQ5005	50°49·7′	0°8·2′E	T	199
Alcock's Fm	Glos	SO8632	51°59·4′	2°11·8′W	FM	150
Alcocks Fm	Lancs	SD6066	54°5·5′	2°36·3′W	FM	97
Alcock Tarn	Cumbr	NY3407	54°27·5′	3°0·7′W	W	90
Alcombe	Somer	SS9745	51°11·9′	3°28·1′W	T	181
Alcombe	Wilts	ST8069	51°25·4′	2°16·9′W	T	173
Alcomden Stones	Brad	SD9735	53°48·9′	2°2·3′W	X	103
Alcomden Water	Cald	SD9532	53°47·3′	2°4·1′W	W	103
Alconbury	Cambs	TL1875	52°21·9′	0°15·6′W	T	142
Alconbury Airfield	Cambs	TL2076	52°22·4′	0°13·8′W	X	142
Alconbury Brook	Cambs	TL1280	52°24·6′	0°20·8′W	W	142
Alconbury Brook	Cambs	TL1973	52°20·8′	0°14·8′W	W	153
Alconbury Hill	Cambs	TL1877	52°22·9′	0°15·6′W	X	142
Alconbury Ho	Cambs	TL1975	52°21·8′	0°14·7′W	X	142
Alconbury Weston	Cambs	TL1776	52°22·4′	0°16·5′W	T	142
Alcott Fm	Worcs	SP0573	52°21·5′	1°55·2′W	FM	139
Alcumlow Hall Fm	Ches	SJ8259	53°7·9′	2°15·7′W	FM	118
Aldachuie	Aberd	NJ3115	57°13·5′	3°8·1′W	X	37
Aldandulish	Pth & Kin	NN9069	56°48·2′	3°47·6′W	X	43
Aldboro Moor Fm	N Yks	SE4264	54°4·5′	1°21·1′W	FM	99
Aldboro Point	Essex	TM0518	51°49·6′	0°58·9′E	X	168
Aldborough	Norf	TG1834	52°51·8′	1°14·7′E	T	133
Aldborough	N Yks	SE4066	54°5·5′	1°22·9′W	T	99
Aldborough Grange	N Yks	SE4166	54°5·5′	1°22·0′W	X	99
Aldborough Hall	Norf	TG1635	52°52·4′	1°13·0′E	X	133
Aldborough Hatch	Redbr	TQ4589	51°35·1′	0°6·0′E	T	177
Aldbourne	Wilts	SU2675	51°28·6′	1°37·1′W	T	174
Aldbourne Chase	Wilts	SU2275	51°28·6′	1°40·6′W	X	174
Aldbourne Warren Fm	Wilts	SU2477	51°29·7′	1°38·9′W	FM	174
Aldbrough	E Yorks	TA2438	53°49·6′	0°6·5′W	T	107
Aldbrough Beck	N Yks	NZ1912	54°30·4′	1°42·0′W	W	92
Aldbrough Beck	N Yks	NZ2010	54°29·3′	1°41·1′W	W	93
Aldbrough St John	N Yks	NZ2011	54°29·9′	1°41·1′W	T	93
Aldburgh Hall	N Yks	SE2379	54°12·6′	1°38·4′W	X	99
Aldbury	Herts	SP9612	51°48·1′	0°36·1′W	T	165
Aldbury Common	Herts	SP9712	51°48·1′	0°35·2′W	F	165
Aldby Field Ho	N Yks	SE7059	54°1·6′	0°55·5′W	X	105,106
Aldby Fm	Cumbr	NY4627	54°38·4′	2°49·8′W	FM	90
Aldby Park	N Yks	SE7258	54°1·0′	0°53·7′W	X	105,106
Aldcharmaig	Pth & Kin	NN7959	56°42·7′	3°58·2′W	X	42,51,52
Aldcliffe	Lancs	SD4660	54°2·2′	2°49·1′W	T	97
Aldclune	Pth & Kin	NN8963	56°45·0′	3°48·5′W	T	43
Aldeburgh	Suff	TM4656	52°9·1′	1°36·2′E	T	156
Aldeburgh Bay	Suff	TM4755	52°8·5′	1°37·0′E	W	156
Aldeburgh Marshes	Suff	TM4555	52°8·6′	1°35·2′E	X	156
Aldeby	Norf	TM4593	52°29·0′	1°36·9′E	T	134
Aldeby Ho	Norf	TM4594	52°29·6′	1°37·0′E	X	134
Alden Fm	Lancs	SD7719	53°40·3′	2°20·5′W	FM	109
Alden Fm	Oxon	SU5084	51°33·4′	1°16·3′W	FM	174
Aldenham	Herts	TQ1398	51°40·4′	0°21·6′W	T	166,176
Aldenham Country Park	Herts	TQ1695	51°38·7′	0°19·0′W	X	166,176
Aldenham Park	Shrops	SO6795	52°33·3′	2°28·8′W	A	138
Aldenham Resr	Herts	TQ1695	51°38·7′	0°19·0′W	W	166,176
Aldenham School	Herts	TQ1597	51°39·8′	0°19·8′W	X	166,176
Alden's Fm	Worcs	SO7660	52°14·5′	2°20·7′W	FM	138,150
Alderbarrow	Lancs	SD9138	53°50·5′	2°7·8′W	X	103
Alder Bay	Pth & Kin	NN5067	56°46·5′	4°26·8′W	W	42
Alder Bourne	Bucks	TQ0285	51°33·5′	0°31·3′W	W	176
Alderbourne Fm	Bucks	TQ0185	51°33·5′	0°32·2′W	FM	176
Alderbourne Manor	Bucks	TQ0186	51°34·1′	0°32·2′W	X	176
Alderbrook	E Susx	TQ5229	51°2·6′	0°10·5′E	T	188,199
Alderbrook	Surrey	TQ0642	51°10·3′	0°28·6′W	X	187
Alder Burn	E Ayr	NS6126	55°30·7′	4°11·6′W	W	71
Alder Burn	Pth & Kin	NN4868	56°47·0′	4°28·8′W	W	42

Alder Burn	S Lanak	NS8232	55°34·3′	3°51·9′W	W	71,72
Alderbury	Wilts	SU1826	51°2·2′	1°44·2′W	T	184
Alderbury Fm	Wilts	SU1826	51°2·2′	1°44·2′W	FM	184
Alderbury Ho	Wilts	SU1826	51°2·2′	1°44·2′W	X	184
Aldercar	Derby	SK4447	53°1·3′	1°20·2′W	T	129
Alder Carr	Derby	SK2342	52°58·7′	1°39·0′W	F	119,128
Alder Carr	Norf	TG3429	52°48·7′	1°28·7′E	F	133,134
Alder Carr	Suff	TM0944	52°3·5′	1°3·3′E	F	155,169
Alder Carr	Suff	TM1472	52°18·5′	1°8·8′E	F	144,156
Alder Carr	Suff	TM3357	52°9·9′	1°24·8′E	F	156
Alder Carrs	Norf	TM4392	52°28·5′	1°35·1′E	F	134
Alder Carr Wood	Brad	SE0544	53°53·8′	1°55·0′W	F	104
Aldercar Wood	Notts	SK5251	53°3·5′	1°13·0′W	F	120
Aldercombe Barton	Corn	SS2611	50°52·6′	4°28·0′W	A	190
Alder Coppice	Shrops	SO8196	52°33·9′	2°16·4′W	F	138
Aldercott	Devon	SS3109	50°51·6′	4°23·7′W	X	190
Alderdene Burn	Durham	NZ1547	54°49·3′	1°45·6′W	W	88
Alderden Manor	Kent	TQ7929	51°2·2′	0°33·6′E	X	188,199
Alderfen Broad	Norf	TG3519	52°43·3′	1°29·2′E	W	133,134
Alder Fm	Staffs	SK1101	52°36·6′	1°49·9′W	FM	139
Alderford	Devon	SX4599	50°46·4′	4°11·5′W	X	190
Alderford	Norf	TG1218	52°43·3′	1°8·8′E	T	133
Alderford Common	Norf	TG1218	52°43·3′	1°8·8′E	X	133
Alder Forest	Salf	SJ7599	53°29·5′	2°22·2′W	T	109
Aldergate Wood	Kent	TR0934	51°4·3′	0°59·4′E	F	179,189
Alder Gill Syke	N Yks	SD7065	54°5·0′	2°27·1′W	W	98
Alder Hall	Leic	SK4901	52°36·5′	1°16·2′W	X	140
Alderhill Inclosure	Hants	SU1913	50°55·2′	1°43·4′W	F	195
Alder Ho	Devon	SX4787	50°40·0′	4°9·5′W	X	191
Alder Ho	Lancs	SD7650	53°57·0′	2°21·5′W	X	103
Alderholt	Dorset	SU1212	50°54·7′	1°49·4′W	T	195
Alderholt Common	Dorset	SU1111	50°54·1′	1°50·2′W	X	195
Alderholt Mill Fm	Dorset	SU1114	50°55·8′	1°50·2′W	FM	195
Alderholt Park	Dorset	SU1113	50°55·2′	1°50·2′W	X	195
Alder Hurst	Lancs	SD9136	53°49·5′	2°7·8′W	X	103
Alder Lee	Staffs	SJ9860	53°8·5′	2°1·4′W	X	118
Alderley	Glos	ST7690	51°36·7′	2°20·4′W	T	162,172
Alderley Edge	Ches	SJ8478	53°18·2′	2°14·0′W	T	118
Alderley Edge	Ches	SJ8577	53°17·6′	2°13·1′W	X	118
Alderley Fm	St Hel	SD5000	53°29·9′	2°44·8′W	FM	108
Alderley Lane Fm	Shrops	SJ5429	52°51·6′	2°40·6′W	FM	126
Alderley Park	Ches	SJ8474	53°16·0′	2°14·0′W	X	118
Alderleys, The	Glos	SO7524	51°55·1′	2°21·4′W	X	162
Alderley Wood	Glos	ST7790	51°36·7′	2°19·5′W	F	162,172
Alderman's Barrow	Somer	SS8342	51°10·2′	3°40·0′W	A	181
Alderman's Green	Cov	SP3583	52°26·9′	1°28·7′W	T	140
Alderman's Head Fm	Barns	SE2200	53°30·0′	1°39·7′W	FM	110
Alderman's Hill	Oldham	SE0104	53°32·2′	1°58·7′W	X	110
Alderman's Seat	D & G	NY3270	55°1·4′	3°3·4′W	X	85
Aldermaston Soke	W Berks	SU6163	51°22·0′	1°7·0′W	T	175
Aldermaston Wharf	W Berks	SU6067	51°24·2′	1°7·9′W	T	175
Aldermen's Gorse	E Yorks	TA1048	53°55·2′	0°19·1′W	F	107
Alderminster	Warw	SP2348	52°8·0′	1°39·7′W	T	151
Alderminster Fm	Warw	SP2149	52°8·6′	1°41·2′W	FM	151
Aldermmaston	W Berks	SU5965	51°23·1′	1°8·7′W	T	174
Aldermoor	C of Soton	SU3915	50°56·2′	1°26·3′W	T	196
Alder Moor	Staffs	SK2227	52°50·6′	1°40·0′W	T	128
Alder Moor Copse	Hants	SU7359	51°19·8′	0°56·7′W	F	175,186
Aldermoor Fm	Corn	SX1182	50°36·7′	4°39·9′W	FM	200
Aldernaig Burn	Highld	NH2901	57°4·4′	4°48·8′W	W	34
Aldern Bridge Ho	Hants	SU4963	51°22·1′	1°17·4′W	X	174
Alderney	Poole	SZ0494	50°45·0′	1°56·2′W	T	195
Alder Park	N Yks	NZ8110	54°29·0′	0°44·6′W	X	94
Alder Plantation	Notts	SK6084	53°21·2′	1°5·5′W	F	111,120
Alder Row	Somer	ST7743	51°11·4′	2°19·4′W	T	183
Alders	Staffs	SK0838	52°56·6′	1°52·5′W	X	128
Aldersbrook	Redbr	TQ4087	51°34·1′	0°1·6′E	T	177
Aldersceugh	Cumbr	NY1941	54°45·7′	3°15·1′W	X	85
Alders Coppice	Dorset	ST8310	50°53·6′	2°14·1′W	F	194
Alder's End	Heref	SO6239	52°3·1′	2°32·9′W	T	149
Aldersey Fm	Shrops	SJ5432	52°53·3′	2°40·6′W	FM	126
Aldersey Green	Ches	SJ4656	53°6·2′	2°48·0′W	T	117
Aldersfield Hall	Suff	TL7656	52°10·7′	0°34·8′E	X	155
Alders Fm	Derby	SK1749	53°2·5′	1°44·4′W	FM	119
Alders Fm	Northnts	SP9896	52°33·4′	0°32·9′W	FM	141
Alders Fm	Shrops	SJ5034	52°54·3′	2°44·2′W	FM	126
Aldershawe	Staffs	SK1007	52°39·8′	1°50·7′W	T	139
Aldershot	Hants	SU8650	51°14·8′	0°45·7′W	T	186
Aldershot Fm	Oxon	SP5624	51°54·9′	1°10·8′W	FM	164
Aldersley Fm	Brad	SE1033	53°47·8′	1°50·5′W	FM	104
Aldersley Park	Ches	SJ4556	53°6·1′	2°48·9′W	X	117
Aldersmead	Somer	SS9744	51°11·4′	3°28·1′W	X	181
Aldersnapp Fm	Hants	SU7224	51°0·9′	0°58·0′W	FM	197
Alderson Seat	N Yks	NY8504	54°26·1′	2°13·5′W	X	91,92
Alderstead Fm	Surrey	TQ2954	51°16·5′	0°8·6′W	FM	187
Alderstead Heath	Surrey	TQ3055	51°17·0′	0°7·8′W	X	187
Alders, The	Highld	NH7698	57°57·5′	4°5·3′W	F	21
Alders, The	Shrops	SO5680	52°25·2′	2°38·4′W	X	137,138
Alderston	E Loth	NT4974	55°57·6′	2°48·6′W	X	66
Alderstone Fm	Wilts	SU2424	51°1·1′	1°39·1′W	FM	184
Alderstone House	W Loth	NT0466	55°52·9′	3°31·6′W	A	65
Alderston Mains	E Loth	NT4975	55°58·2′	2°48·6′W	X	66
Alderton	Glos	SP0033	52°0·0′	1°59·6′W	T	150
Alderton	Northnts	SP7446	52°6·7′	0°54·8′W	T	152
Alderton	Shrops	SJ4923	52°48·4′	2°45·0′W	T	126
Alderton	Suff	TM3441	52°1·3′	1°25·0′E	T	169
Alderton	Wilts	ST8382	51°32·4′	2°14·3′W	T	173
Alderton Fields	Glos	SP0032	51°59·4′	1°59·6′W	FM	150
Alderton Grove Fm	Wilts	ST8381	51°31·9′	2°14·3′W	FM	173
Alderton Hall	Shrops	SJ3817	52°45·1′	2°54·7′W	X	126
Alderton Hill	Glos	SP0034	52°0·5′	1°59·6′W	H	150
Alderton Ho	Suff	TM3240	52°0·8′	1°23·2′E	X	169
Alderton Walks	Suff	TM3242	52°1·9′	1°23·3′E	X	169
Alderwasley	Derby	SK3153	53°4·6′	1°31·8′W	T	119
Alderwasley Hall (School)	Derby	SK3253	53°4·6′	1°30·9′W	X	119
Alderybar	Scot Bord	NT4405	55°20·4′	2°52·5′W	X	79
Aldery Cliff	Derby	SK0966	53°11·7′	1°51·5′W	H	119
Aldessan Burn	E Dunb	NS6081	56°0·3′	4°14·3′W	W	64
Aldfield	N Yks	SE2669	54°7·2′	1°35·7′W	T	99
Aldfield Common	Oxon	SU4687	51°35·0′	1°19·8′W	X	174

Aldford	Ches	SJ4159	53°7·7′	2°52·5′W	T	117
Aldford Brook	Ches	SJ4258	53°7·2′	2°51·6′W	W	117
Aldgate	Rut	SK9804	52°37·7′	0°32·7′W	T	141
Aldham	Essex	TL9226	51°54·2′	0°47·9′E	T	168
Aldham	Suff	TM0445	52°4·2′	0°59·0′E	T	155
Aldham Hall	Essex	TL9124	51°53·1′	0°46·9′E	X	168
Aldham Hall	Suff	TM0344	52°3·7′	0°58·1′E	X	155
Aldham Plantn	N Lincs	SE9404	53°31·7′	0°34·5′W	F	112
Aldham Priory	Suff	TM0545	52°4·1′	0°59·9′E	X	155
Aldhams	Essex	TM0930	51°56·0′	1°2·8′E	X	168,169
Aldhow Grange	Lincs	SK8778	53°17·7′	0°41·3′W	X	121
Aldhurst Fm	Surrey	TQ1840	51°9·1′	0°18·4′W	FM	187
Aldie	Aberd	NK0639	57°26·7′	1°53·5′W	X	30
Aldie	Highld	NH7880	57°47·8′	4°2·7′W	X	21
Aldie	Pth & Kin	NN9624	56°24·1′	3°40·7′W	X	52,53,58
Aldie Castle	Pth & Kin	NT0597	56°9·6′	3°31·3′W	A	58
Aldie Water	Highld	NH7579	57°47·3′	4°5·7′W	W	21
Aldingbourne	W Susx	SU9205	50°50·5′	0°41·2′W	T	197
Aldingbourne Ho	W Susx	SU9207	50°51·5′	0°41·2′W	X	197
Aldingbourne Rife	W Susx	SU9201	50°48·3′	0°41·3′W	W	197
Aldingham	Cumbr	SD2871	54°8·0′	3°5·7′W	T	96,97
Aldin Grange	Durham	NZ2442	54°46·6′	1°37·2′W	X	88
Aldington	Kent	TR0636	51°5·4′	0°56·9′E	T	179,189
Aldington	Worcs	SP0644	52°5·9′	1°54·3′W	T	150
Aldington Frith	Kent	TR0436	51°5·4′	0°55·2′E	T	179,189
Aldington Knoll	Kent	TR0735	51°4·8′	0°57·7′E	X	179,189
Aldinna	S Ayr	NX3595	55°13·6′	4°35·2′W	X	77
Aldinna Burn	S Ayr	NX3594	55°13·0′	4°35·2′W	W	77
Aldinna Loch	S Ayr	NX3693	55°12·5′	4°34·2′W	W	77
Aldivalloch	Moray	NJ3626	57°19·5′	3°3·3′W	X	37
Aldmoor Fm	N Yks	SE7865	54°4·7′	0°48·0′W	FM	100
Aldochlay	Arg & Bt	NS3591	56°5·3′	4°38·7′W	X	56
Aldon	Kent	TQ6457	51°17·5′	0°21·5′E	X	188
Aldon	Shrops	SO4379	52°24·6′	2°49·9′W	T	137,148
Aldon	Somer	ST5515	50°56·2′	2°38·0′W	X	183
Aldon Court	Shrops	SO4379	52°24·6′	2°49·9′W	X	137,148
Aldons	S Ayr	NX1989	55°10·0′	4°50·1′W	X	76
Aldons Hill	S Ayr	NX1990	55°10·5′	4°50·1′W	X	76
Aldoth	Cumbr	NY1448	54°49·4′	3°19·9′W	T	85
Aldourie Castle	Highld	NH6037	57°24·4′	4°19·4′W	X	26
Aldous's Corner	Suff	TM3681	52°22·8′	1°28·5′E	X	156
Aldreth	Cambs	TL4473	52°20·4′	0°7·2′E	T	154
Aldrick	I of M	SC1767	54°4·2′	4°47·4′W	W	95
Aldridge	Wals	SK0500	52°36·1′	1°55·2′W	T	139
Aldridgehill Inclosure	Hants	SU2703	50°49·8′	1°36·6′W	F	195
Aldridge Lodge Fm	Wals	SP0599	52°35·6′	1°55·2′W	FM	139
Aldridge's Fm	Suff	TM2773	52°18·7′	1°20·2′E	FM	156
Aldringham	Suff	TM4460	52°11·3′	1°34·6′E	T	156
Aldringham Ho	Suff	TM4461	52°11·8′	1°34·6′E	X	156
Aldrington	Bri & Hov	TQ2705	50°50·1′	0°11·4′W	T	198
Aldro Fm	N Yks	SE8062	54°3·1′	0°46·3′W	FM	100
Aldroughty	Moray	NJ1862	57°38·7′	3°22·0′W	X	28
Aldsworth	Glos	SP1510	51°47·5′	1°46·6′W	T	163
Aldsworth	W Susx	SU7608	50°52·2′	0°54·8′W	X	197
Aldunie	Moray	NJ3626	57°19·5′	3°3·3′W	X	37
Aldwark	Derby	SK2257	53°6·8′	1°39·9′W	T	119
Aldwark	N Yks	SE4663	54°3·9′	1°17·4′W	T	100
Aldwark Br Toll	N Yks	SE4662	54°3·4′	1°17·4′W	X	100
Aldwarke	Roth	SK4494	53°26·7′	1°19·8′W	T	111
Aldwark Moor	N Yks	SE4763	54°3·9′	1°16·5′W	X	100
Aldwark Wood	N Yks	SE4762	54°3·3′	1°16·5′W	F	100
Aldwick	W Susx	SZ9198	50°46·7′	0°42·2′W	T	197
Aldwick Court	N Som	ST4961	51°21·0′	2°43·6′W	X	172,182
Aldwick Court Fm	N Som	ST4960	51°20·4′	2°43·5′W	FM	172,182
Aldwick Grange	E Susx	TQ5332	51°4·2′	0°11·4′E	X	188
Aldwincle	Northnts	TL0081	52°25·3′	0°31·4′W	T	141
Aldwincle Lodge	Northnts	SP9983	52°26·4′	0°32·2′W	X	141
Aldwincle Lodge Fm	Northnts	SP9981	52°25·3′	0°32·2′W	FM	141
Aldworth	W Berks	SU5579	51°30·7′	1°12·1′W	T	174
Aldworth Ho	W Susx	SU9230	51°3·9′	0°40·8′W	X	186
Aleck Low	Derby	SK1759	53°7·9′	1°44·3′W	H	119
Alecock's Grave	Suff	TL9572	52°18·9′	0°52·1′E	X	144,155
Aled Isaf Reservoir	Conwy	SH9159	53°7·3′	3°37·3′W	W	116
Alehouse	Aberd	NJ9323	57°18·1′	2°6·5′W	X	38
Ale House	Scot Bord	NT5325	55°31·2′	2°44·2′W	X	73
Alehouseburn	Aberd	NJ6260	57°38·0′	2°37·7′W	X	29
Ale House Fm	E Susx	TQ6514	50°54·3′	0°21·2′E	FM	199
Alehousehill	Aberd	NJ8950	57°32·7′	2°10·6′W	X	30
Alehousehill	Aberd	NK0430	57°21·9′	1°55·6′W	X	30
Alehousehillock	Aberd	NJ4645	57°29·8′	2°53·6′W	X	28,29
Alemill	Scot Bord	NT9163	55°51·9′	2°8·2′W	X	67
Alemoor Craig	Scot Bord	NT4017	55°26·8′	2°56·5′W	X	79
Alemoor Hill	Scot Bord	NT3915	55°25·8′	2°57·4′W	H	79
Alemoor Reservoir	Scot Bord	NT3914	55°25·2′	2°57·4′W	W	79
Ale Oak	Shrops	SO2284	52°27·1′	3°8·5′W	T	137
Alerigg	Scot Bord	NT5627	55°32·3′	2°41·4′W	X	73
Alethorpe Hall	Norf	TF9431	52°50·7′	0°53·3′E	X	132
Ale Water	Scot Bord	NT3714	55°25·2′	2°59·3′W	W	79
Ale Water	Scot Bord	NT4318	55°27·4′	2°53·6′W	W	79
Ale Water	Scot Bord	NT5224	55°30·7′	2°45·2′W	W	73
Ale Water	Scot Bord	NT6125	55°31·3′	2°36·6′W	W	74
Ale Water	Scot Bord	NT8964	55°52·4′	2°10·1′W	W	67
Alexander Fm	Hants	SU4156	51°18·3′	1°24·3′W	FM	174
Alexander Ho	Kent	TQ5649	51°13·4′	0°14·4′E	X	188
Alexander Ho	W Susx	TQ3536	51°6·7′	0°3·9′W	X	187
Alexander's Fm	Hants	SU6928	51°3·1′	1°0·5′W	FM	186,197
Alexanders Fm	Norf	TG0302	52°34·9′	1°0·2′E	FM	144
Alexanderstone	Powys	SO0730	51°57·9′	3°20·8′W	X	160
Alexandra Palace	Hargy	TQ2990	51°35·9′	0°7·9′W	X	176
Alexandra Park	C of Glas	NS6265	55°51·8′	4°11·9′W	X	64
Alexandria	W Dunb	NS3980	55°59·4′	4°34·4′W	T	63
Alex Fm	Wilts	SU1195	51°39·5′	1°50·1′W	FM	163
Alex Tor	Corn	SX1178	50°34·5′	4°39·8′W	H	200
Aley	Somer	ST1837	51°7·8′	3°9·9′W	T	181
Aley Green	Beds	TL0618	51°51·3′	0°27·3′W	T	166
Alfardisworthy	Devon	SS2911	50°52·6′	4°25·5′W	T	190
Alfington	Devon	SY1198	50°46·7′	3°15·4′W	T	192,193
Alfold	Surrey	TQ0334	51°6·0′	0°31·3′W	T	186
Alfold Bars	W Susx	TQ0333	51°5·4′	0°31·4′W	T	186
Alfold Crossways	Surrey	TQ0435	51°6·5′	0°30·5′W	T	186

Alford	Aberd	NJ5716	57°14·2′	2°42·3′W	T	37
Alford	Lincs	TF4575	53°15·4′	0°10·8′E	T	122
Alford	Somer	ST6032	51°5·4′	2°33·9′W	T	183
Alford Fields	Somer	ST6031	51°4·8′	2°33·9′W	X	183
Alford Fm	Shrops	SJ4623	52°48·4′	2°47·7′W	FM	126
Alford Ho	N Yks	SE5274	54°9·8′	1°11·8′W	X	100
Alford's Mill	Heref	SO6034	52°0·4′	2°34·6′W	X	149
Alford Valley Railway	Aberd	NJ5816	57°14·2′	2°41·3′W	X	37
Alford Well Fm	Somer	ST6031	51°4·8′	2°33·9′W	FM	183
Alfoxton Park Hotel	Somer	ST1441	51°9·9′	3°13·4′W	X	181
Alfred's Castle	Oxon	SU2782	51°32·4′	1°36·2′W	A	174
Alfred's Hall	Glos	SO9703	51°43·8′	2°2·2′W	X	163
Alfred's Hill	Oxon	SU2990	51°36·7′	1°34·5′W	X	164,174
Alfred's Tower	Wilts	ST7435	51°7·1′	2°21·9′W	X	183
Alfred's Well	Worcs	SO9472	52°21·0′	2°4·9′W	T	139
Alfreton	Derby	SK4155	53°5·7′	1°22·9′W	T	120
Alfreton Brook	Derby	SK4156	53°6·2′	1°22·8′W	W	120
Alfreton & Mansfield Parkway Station	Derby	SK4256	53°6·2′	1°22·0′W	X	120
Alfrick	Worcs	SO7453	52°10·7′	2°22·4′W	T	150
Alfrick Pound	Worcs	SO7452	52°10·2′	2°22·4′W	T	150
Alfriston	E Susx	TQ5103	50°48·6′	0°9·0′E	T	199
Algakirk	Lincs	TF2935	52°54·0′	0°4·5′W	T	131
Algare	I of M	SC3581	54°12·1′	4°31·4′W	X	95
Algar Ho	Norf	TM0782	52°24·0′	1°3·0′E	X	144
Algarkirk Fen	Lincs	TF2344	52°59·0′	0°9·7′W	X	131
Algars Manor	S Glos	ST6783	51°32·9′	2°28·2′W	X	172
Algarsthorpe Fm	Norf	TG1408	52°37·9′	1°10·1′E	FM	144
Algeilly Burn	Angus	NO2171	56°49·7′	3°17·2′W	W	44
Algrave Hall Fm	Derby	SK4545	53°0·3′	1°19·4′W	FM	129
Alha Dubh	N Eil	NG0287	57°46·7′	7°0·3′W	W	18
Alhampton	Somer	ST6234	51°6·5′	2°32·2′W	T	183
Alhang	E Ayr	NS6401	55°17·3′	4°8·1′W	H	77
Alicehead	Derby	SK3365	53°11·1′	1°30·0′W	X	119
Alice Holt Forest	Hants	SU8042	51°10·5′	0°50·9′W	F	186
Alice Holt Lodge	Hants	SU8042	51°10·5′	0°50·9′W	X	186
Alicelands	W Susx	TQ1725	51°1·0′	0°19·5′W	X	187,198
Alice's Bower	Pth & Kin	NO1301	56°11·9′	3°23·7′W	X	58
Alice Street Fm	Somer	ST7242	51°10·8′	2°23·6′W	FM	183
Alichmore	Pth & Kin	NN8420	56°21·7′	3°52·2′W	X	52,58
Alichmore	Pth & Kin	NN8520	56°21·8′	3°51·2′W	X	52,58
Alington Hill	Beds	TL1855	52°11·1′	0°16·0′W	X	153
Alin Knowes	Shetld	HU4986	60°33·5′	1°5·9′W	X	1,2,3
Alin Knowes	Shetld	HU5081	60°30·8′	1°4·9′W	X	1,2,3
Alioter	N Eil	NF8972	57°38·1′	7°12·2′W	X	18
Alisary	Highld	NM7479	56°51·1′	5°41·9′W	T	40
Alisary Burn	Highld	NM7479	56°51·1′	5°41·9′W	W	40
Alison Sike	Scot Bord	NT5500	55°17·8′	2°42·1′W	W	80
Alkborough	N Lincs	SE8821	53°40·9′	0°39·6′W	T	106,112
Alkerton	Glos	SO7705	51°44·8′	2°19·6′W	T	162
Alkerton	Oxon	SP3742	52°4·7′	1°27·2′W	T	151
Alkerton Grounds	Oxon	SP3841	52°4·2′	1°26·3′W	X	151
Alkham	Kent	TR2542	51°8·2′	1°13·4′E	T	179
Alkincoats	Lancs	SD8741	53°52·1′	2°11·4′W	X	103
Alkington	Shrops	SJ5238	52°56·5′	2°42·5′W	T	126
Alkington Fm	Glos	ST6998	51°41·0′	2°26·5′W	FM	162
Alkington Grange	Shrops	SJ5238	52°56·5′	2°42·5′W	X	126
Alkin Hill	D & G	NY3096	55°15·4′	3°5·7′W	H	79
Alkmonton	Derby	SK1838	52°56·6′	1°43·5′W	T	128
Alkmonton Old Hall	Derby	SK1937	52°56·0′	1°42·6′W	X	128
Alkmonton Village	Derby	SK1937	52°56·0′	1°42·6′W	A	128
Alkmund Park Fm	Shrops	SJ4815	52°44·0′	2°45·8′W	FM	126
Alkmund Park Pool	Shrops	SJ4716	52°44·6′	2°46·7′W	W	126
Alkrington Garden Village	Roch	SD8704	53°32·2′	2°11·4′W	T	109
Alkrington Hall	Roch	SD8605	53°32·7′	2°12·3′W	X	109
Alksford Fm	E Susx	TQ5236	51°6·4′	0°10·7′E	FM	188
Allabury	Corn	SX2576	50°33·7′	4°27·9′W	A	201
Allacardoch	Moray	NJ4553	57°34·1′	2°54·7′W	X	28,29
Allachlaggan	Moray	NJ3037	57°25·3′	3°9·5′W	X	28
Allachrow	Moray	NJ2546	57°30·1′	3°14·6′W	X	28
Allacott	Devon	SS4307	50°50·7′	4°13·4′W	X	190
Alladale Lodge	Highld	NH4389	57°52·0′	4°38·8′W	X	20
Alladale River	Highld	NH4088	57°51·4′	4°41·3′W	W	20
Allalea	D & G	NY2170	55°1·3′	3°13·7′W	X	85
Allaleckie	Clackm	NS9694	56°7·9′	3°40·0′W	X	58
Allaleigh	Devon	SX8053	50°22·1′	3°40·9′W	T	202
Allalogie	Aberd	NJ4202	57°6·6′	2°57·0′W	X	37
Allaloth	Moray	NJ4059	57°37·3′	2°59·8′W	X	28
Allamichie	Moray	NJ2936	57°24·8′	3°10·5′W	X	28
Allamoor Fm	Notts	SK6157	53°6·6′	1°4·9′W	FM	120
Allan	Highld	NH8177	57°46·3′	3°59·6′W	X	21
Allanaha	Highld	NH8652	57°32·9′	3°53·8′W	X	27
Allanaquoich	Aberd	NO1291	57°0·4′	3°26·5′W	T	43
Allan Bank	Cumbr	NY3307	54°27·5′	3°1·6′W	X	90
Allan Bank	D & G	NX7961	54°56·0′	3°52·9′W	X	84
Allanbank	Highld	NH6252	57°32·5′	4°17·9′W	X	26
Allanbank	N Lanak	NS8457	55°47·8′	3°50·6′W	T	65,72
Allanbank	Scot Bord	NT5247	55°43·1′	2°45·4′W	T	73
Allanbay Park	Brackn	SU8473	51°27·2′	0°47·1′W	X	175
Allander Water	E Dunb	NS5377	55°58·1′	4°20·9′W	W	64
Alland Grange	Kent	TR3166	51°21·0′	1°19·4′E	X	179
Allandoo	D & G	NX0162	54°55·0′	5°5·9′W	X	82
Allanfauld	N Lanak	NS7178	55°58·9′	4°3·6′W	X	64
Allanfearn	Highld	NH7147	57°30·0′	4°8·7′W	X	27
Allangillfoot	D & G	NY2595	55°14·9′	3°10·4′W	X	79
Allanglach	Highld	NH6250	57°31·4′	4°17·8′W	X	26
Allanglachwood	Highld	NH6350	57°31·4′	4°16·8′W	F	26
Allangrange Mains	Highld	NH6251	57°32·0′	4°17·8′W	X	26
Allangrange Park	Highld	NH5552	57°32·4′	4°24·9′W	X	26
Allanhead	E Dunb	NS6180	55°59·8′	4°13·3′W	X	64
Allanhill	Fife	NO5214	56°19·2′	2°46·1′W	X	59
Allan House Fm	Brad	SE0834	53°48·4′	1°52·3′W	FM	104
Allanish	N Eil	NL5987	56°51·2′	7°35·2′W	X	31
Allanmore	Aberd	NO1391	57°0·4′	3°25·5′W	X	43
Allanmore	Highld	NH4930	57°20·4′	4°30·1′W	X	26
Allanreid	Moray	NJ2325	57°18·8′	3°16·2′W	X	36
Allanrowie	Stir	NS5884	56°1·9′	4°16·3′W	X	57,64
Allans	Pth & Kin	NN8317	56°20·1′	3°53·1′W	X	57
Allans	Pth & Kin	NN9016	56°19·7′	3°46·3′W	X	58
Allan's Cairn	D & G	NS6900	55°16·9′	4°3·3′W	X	77

Allan's Fm	Dorset	ST8520	50°59·0′	2°12·4′W	FM	183
Allans Fm	Suff	TM3172	52°18·1′	1°23·7′E	FM	156
Allan's Grange	N Yks	NZ2014	54°31·5′	1°41·0′W	X	93
Allanshaugh	Scot Bord	NT4349	55°44·1′	2°54·0′W	T	73
Allanshaws	Scot Bord	NT4943	55°40·9′	2°48·2′W	T	73
Allanshaw Wood	Midlo	NT3356	55°47·8′	3°3·7′W	F	66,73
Allan Tarn	Cumbr	SD2989	54°17·7′	3°5·0′W	W	96,97
Allantersie	Aberd	NJ4821	57°16·9′	2°51·3′W	X	37
Allanton	D & G	NX7764	54°57·6′	3°54·8′W	X	84
Allanton	D & G	NX9184	55°8·6′	3°42·2′W	X	78
Allanton	E Ayr	NS6037	55°36·6′	4°12·9′W	X	71
Allanton	N Lanak	NS8557	55°47·8′	3°49·6′W	T	65,72
Allanton	Scot Bord	NT8654	55°47·0′	2°13·0′W	T	67,74
Allanton	S Lanak	NS7454	55°46·0′	4°0·1′W	T	64
Allantonplains	E Ayr	NS6137	55°36·7′	4°12·0′W	X	71
Allan Water	Pth & Kin	NN8709	56°15·9′	3°49·0′W	W	58
Allan Water	Scot Bord	NT4707	55°21·5′	2°49·7′W	W	79
Allargue Ho	Aberd	NJ2509	57°10·2′	3°14·0′W	X	37
Allasdale	N Eil	NF6603	57°0·1′	7°29·6′W	T	31
Allaston	Glos	SO6304	51°44·2′	2°31·8′W	T	162
Allathan	Aberd	NJ8448	57°31·6′	2°15·6′W	X	29,30
Allathan	Aberd	NJ9027	57°20·3′	2°9·5′W	X	38
Allathan Ho	Aberd	NJ8447	57°31·0′	2°15·6′W	X	29,30
Allberries	E Yorks	SE7637	53°49·7′	0°50·3′W	X	105,106
Allbrook	Hants	SU4521	50°59·4′	1°21·1′W	T	185
All Cannings	Wilts	SU0761	51°21·1′	1°53·6′W	T	173
All Cannings Br	Wilts	SU0762	51°21·7′	1°53·6′W	X	173
All Cannings Down	Wilts	SU0965	51°23·3′	1°51·9′W	X	173
Allcombe Water	Somer	SS8340	51°9·1′	3°40·0′W	W	181
Allcroft Grange	Kent	TR1560	51°18·1′	1°5·5′E	X	179
All Cùl Airigh Lagain	Highld	NG6919	57°12·5′	5°49·0′W	W	32
Allean Forest	Pth & Kin	NN8561	56°43·8′	3°52·3′W	F	43
Allen Banks	Northum	NY8063	54°57·9′	2°18·3′W	F	86,87
Allenby's Furze	Lincs	TF3086	53°21·5′	0°2·4′W	F	113,122
Allen Crags	Cumbr	NY2308	54°27·9′	3°10·9′W	H	89,90
Allencreich	Aberd	NO5796	57°3·4′	2°42·1′W	X	37,44
Allen Dale	Northum	NY7851	54°51·4′	2°20·1′W	X	86,87
Allendale Common	Northum	NY8245	54°48·2′	2°16·4′W	X	86,87
Allendale Common	Northum	NY8551	54°51·5′	2°13·6′W	H	87
Allendale Town	Northum	NY8355	54°53·6′	2°15·5′W	T	86,87
Allen End	Warw	SP1696	52°33·9′	1°45·4′W	T	139
Allengrove Fm	Wilts	ST8283	51°33·0′	2°15·2′W	FM	173
Allenheads	Northum	NY8545	54°48·2′	2°13·6′W	T	87
Allenheads Park	Northum	NY8544	54°47·7′	2°13·6′W	X	87
Allen Park Fm	Brad	SE0834	53°48·4′	1°52·3′W	FM	104
Allen River	Hants	SU0718	50°57·9′	1°53·6′W	W	184
Allen's Brook	Somer	ST2427	51°2·5′	3°4·7′W	W	193
Allen's Down	Devon	SS9917	50°56·9′	3°25·9′W	X	181
Allen's Fm	Ches	SJ8877	53°17·6′	2°10·4′W	FM	118
Allen's Fm	Essex	TM0525	51°53·4′	0°59·1′E	FM	168
Allen's Fm	E Susx	TQ5724	50°59·9′	0°14·6′E	FM	199
Allen's Fm	Hants	SU1216	50°56·8′	1°49·4′W	FM	184
Allen's Fm	Kent	TQ6153	51°15·4′	0°18·8′E	FM	188
Allens Fm	Lincs	TF1154	53°4·5′	0°20·2′W	FM	121
Allen's Fm	Suff	TM0635	51°58·7′	1°0·4′E	FM	155
Allensford	Durham	NZ0750	54°50·9′	1°53·0′W	T	88
Allen's Green	Herts	TL4516	51°49·7′	0°6·6′E	T	167
Allensgreen	Northum	NY7662	54°57·4′	2°22·1′W	X	86,87
Allenshields	Durham	NY9649	54°50·4′	2°3·3′W	X	87
Allens Hill Fm	Heref	SO4529	51°57·6′	2°47·6′W	FM	149,161
Allensmore	Heref	SO4635	52°0·9′	2°46·8′W	T	149,161
Allen's Rock	Devon	SS5033	51°4·8′	4°8·1′W	X	180
Allensteads	Cumbr	NY5766	54°59·5′	2°39·9′W	X	86
Allens West Sta	Stock on T	NZ4114	54°31·4′	1°21·6′W	X	93
Allenton	C of Derb	SK3732	52°53·3′	1°27·5′W	T	128
Allenwood	Cumbr	NY4955	54°53·5′	2°47·3′W	T	86
Aller	Devon	SS7625	51°0·9′	3°45·7′W	X	180
Aller	Devon	ST0506	50°51·0′	3°20·6′W	T	192
Aller	Devon	SX7483	50°38·2′	3°46·5′W	X	191
Aller	Devon	SX8192	50°43·2′	3°40·8′W	X	191
Aller	Devon	SX8768	50°30·3′	3°35·2′W	T	202
Aller	Dorset	ST7602	50°49·3′	2°20·1′W	T	194
Aller	Somer	ST4029	51°3·7′	2°51·0′W	T	193
Aller Barton	Devon	SS8102	50°48·6′	3°41·0′W	X	191
Aller Barton	Devon	ST0306	50°51·0′	3°22·3′W	X	192
Allerbeck	D & G	NY2473	55°3·0′	3°10·9′W	X	85
Aller Br	Devon	SS7006	50°50·6′	3°50·4′W	X	191
Allerburn Ho	Northum	NU1913	55°24·9′	1°41·6′W	X	81
Allerby	Cumbr	NY0839	54°44·5′	3°25·1′W	T	89
Allercombe	Devon	SY0494	50°44·5′	3°21·3′W	T	192
Allercombe Fm	Devon	ST0910	50°53·2′	3°17·2′W	FM	192
Allercott	Somer	SS9539	51°8·7′	3°29·7′W	X	181
Aller Court Fm	Somer	ST3928	51°3·1′	2°51·8′W	FM	193
Allerdale Ramble	Cumbr	NY0746	54°48·3′	3°26·4′W	X	85
Allerdale Ramble	Cumbr	NY1833	54°41·4′	3°15·9′W	X	89,90
Allerdale Ramble	Cumbr	NY2419	54°33·9′	3°10·1′W	X	89,90
Aller Dean	Northum	NT9847	55°43·2′	2°1·5′W	X	75
Allerdean Grange	Northum	NT9845	55°42·2′	2°1·5′W	X	75
Allerdean Greens	Northum	NT9845	55°42·2′	2°1·5′W	X	75
Allerdean Mill	Northum	NT9847	55°43·2′	2°1·5′W	X	75
Allerdeanmill Burn	Northum	NT9946	55°42·7′	2°0·5′W	W	75
Allerdene	Northum	NU0201	55°18·4′	1°57·7′W	X	81
Aller Down	Devon	SS8204	50°49·6′	3°40·1′W	X	191
Aller Fm	Devon	SS5811	50°53·1′	4°0·7′W	FM	191
Aller Fm	Devon	ST1907	50°51·6′	3°8·7′W	FM	192,193
Aller Fm	Devon	SX9476	50°34·7′	3°29·4′W	FM	192
Aller Fm	Somer	ST0042	51°10·3′	3°25·4′W	FM	181
Allerford	Devon	SX4285	50°38·8′	4°13·6′W	X	201
Allerford	Somer	SS9047	51°12·9′	3°34·1′W	T	181
Allerford	Somer	ST1725	51°1·3′	3°10·6′W	T	181,193
Allergarth	Cumbr	NY5271	55°2·1′	2°44·6′W	X	86
Aller Gill	Durham	NY9738	54°44·5′	2°2·4′W	X	92
Aller Grove	Devon	SY0596	50°45·6′	3°20·4′W	T	192
Aller Hill	Somer	SS9941	51°9·8′	3°26·3′W	H	181
Aller Hill	Somer	ST4029	51°3·7′	2°51·0′W	X	193
Allerhope Burn	Northum	NT9210	55°23·3′	2°7·1′W	W	80
Allerly	Scot Bord	NT5435	55°36·6′	2°43·4′W	X	73
Aller Moor	Somer	ST3828	51°3·1′	2°52·7′W	X	193
Aller Moor	Somer	ST4345	51°12·3′	2°48·6′W	X	182
Allermuir Hill	C of Edin	NT2266	55°53·1′	3°14·4′W	H	66

Alleron	Devon	SX7149	50°19·8′	3°48·4′W	X	202
Aller Park	Devon	SX8769	50°30·8′	3°35·3′W	T	202
Allers Fm	Devon	SS9615	50°55·7′	3°28·4′W	FM	181
Allershaw Burn	S Lanak	NS9611	55°23·2′	3°38·1′W	W	78
Allershaw Lodge	S Lanak	NS9612	55°23·7′	3°38·1′W	X	78
Allerson Loft Marshes	N Yks	SE8780	54°12·7′	0°39·5′W	X	101
Allerston	N Yks	SE8782	54°13·8′	0°39·5′W	T	101
Allerston High Moor	N Yks	SE8795	54°20·8′	0°39·3′W	X	94,101
Allerston Partings	N Yks	SE8883	54°14·3′	0°38·6′W	X	101
Allers Wood	Somer	SS9226	51°1·6′	3°32·0′W	F	181
Allerthorpe	E Yorks	SE7847	53°55·0′	0°48·3′W	T	105,106
Allerthorpe Common	E Yorks	SE7547	53°55·1′	0°51·1′W	F	105,106
Allerthorpe Hall	N Yks	SE3386	54°16·4′	1°29·2′W	A	99
Allerton	Brad	SE1134	53°48·4′	1°49·6′W	T	104
Allerton	Devon	SX7661	50°26·4′	3°44·4′W	X	202
Allerton	Highld	NH7565	57°39·7′	4°5·2′W	X	21,27
Allerton	Liv	SJ4186	53°22·3′	2°52·8′W	T	108
Allerton Bywater	Leeds	SE4227	53°44·5′	1°21·4′W	T	105
Allerton Grange	N Yks	SE4157	54°0·7′	1°22·0′W	X	105
Allerton Head	N Yks	NZ8209	54°28·4′	0°43·7′W	X	94
Allerton Mauleverer	N Yks	SE4158	54°1·2′	1°22·0′W	T	105
Allerton Moor	Somer	ST3950	51°15·0′	2°52·1′W	X	182
Allerton Park	N Yks	SE4158	54°1·2′	1°22·0′W	X	105
Allerton Sta	Liv	SJ4085	53°21·8′	2°53·7′W	X	108
Allerwash	Northum	NY8767	55°0·1′	2°11·8′W	X	87
Allerwash Buildings	Northum	NY8666	54°59·6′	2°12·7′W	X	87
Allerwash Hall	Northum	NY8666	54°59·6′	2°12·7′W	X	87
Aller Wood	Somer	ST4030	51°4·2′	2°51·0′W	F	182
Allerybank	Northum	NY7381	55°7·6′	2°25·0′W	X	80
Allery Burn	Northum	NY7469	55°1·1′	2°24·0′W	W	86,87
Allery or Lyham Burn	Northum	NU0730	55°34·1′	1°52·9′W	W	75
Allesborough Hill	Worcs	SO9346	52°7·0′	2°5·7′W	X	150
Allescholes	Cald	SD9320	53°40·8′	2°5·9′W	X	103
Allesley	Cov	SP2981	52°25·8′	1°34·0′W	T	140
Alleston	Pemb	SN0000	51°40·0′	4°53·1′W	X	158
Allestree	C of Derb	SK3439	52°57·1′	1°29·2′W	T	128
Allestree Park	C of Derb	SK3440	52°57·6′	1°29·2′W	X	119,128
Allet	Corn	SW7948	50°17·7′	5°5·8′W	T	204
Allexton	Leic	SK8100	52°35·7′	0°47·8′W	T	141
Allexton Lodge	Leic	SP8099	52°35·2′	0°48·7′W	X	141
Allexton Wood	Leic	SP8299	52°35·2′	0°47·0′W	F	141
Alleyford	D & G	NX8467	54°59·3′	3°48·4′W	X	84
Allfield	Shrops	SJ5007	52°39·7′	2°44·0′W	X	126
Allfields Fm	W Susx	SU9926	51°1·7′	0°34·9′W	FM	186,197
Allford Brook	Wrekin	SJ6622	52°47·9′	2°29·9′W	W	127
Allfornought	D & G	NY2977	55°5·2′	3°6·3′W	X	85
Allfornought Hill	D & G	NY3078	55°5·7′	3°5·4′W	X	85
Allfreys	W Susx	TQ2222	50°59·3′	0°15·3′W	X	198
Allgood Fm	Northum	NY8574	55°3·9′	2°13·7′W	FM	87
Allgreave	Ches	SJ9766	53°11·7′	2°2·3′W	T	118
Allhallows	Medway	TQ8377	51°28·0′	0°38·5′E	T	178
Allhallows College	Devon	SY2990	50°42·6′	3°0·0′W	X	193
Allhallows Fm	Devon	ST0910	50°53·2′	3°17·2′W	FM	192
All Hallows Fm	Dorset	SU0212	50°54·7′	1°57·9′W	FM	195
All Hallows Hill	Donc	SK5894	53°26·6′	1°7·2′W	X	111
Allhallows Marshes	Medway	TQ8477	51°27·9′	0°39·3′E	X	178
Allhallows-on-Sea	Medway	TQ8378	51°28·5′	0°38·5′E	T	178
Allicky Fm	Cambs	TL5162	52°14·4′	0°13·1′E	FM	154
Alliehar	Aberd	NJ6154	57°34·7′	2°38·7′W	X	29
Allieshaw Rigg	Cumbr	NY5865	54°58·9′	2°39·0′W	H	86
Alligin Shuas	Highld	NG8358	57°33·9′	5°37·2′W	T	24
Allimore Green	Staffs	SJ8519	52°46·3′	2°12·9′W	T	127
Allington	Dorset	SY4693	50°44·3′	2°45·5′W	T	193
Allington	Kent	TQ7457	51°17·4′	0°30·1′E	T	178,188
Allington	Lincs	SK8540	52°57·3′	0°43·7′W	T	130
Allington	Wilts	ST8975	51°28·7′	2°9·1′W	T	173
Allington	Wilts	SU0663	51°22·2′	1°54·4′W	T	173
Allington	Wilts	SU2039	51°9·2′	1°42·5′W	T	184
Allington Bar	Wilts	ST8974	51°28·1′	2°9·1′W	T	173
Allington Castle	Kent	TQ7557	51°17·3′	0°31·0′E	A	178,188
Allington Down	Wilts	SU0866	51°23·8′	1°52·7′W	X	173
Allington Fm	E Susx	TQ3813	50°54·2′	0°1·9′W	FM	198
Allington Fm	Kent	TQ8356	51°16·6′	0°37·8′E	FM	178,188
Allington Hill	Cambs	TL5858	52°12·1′	0°19·1′E	X	154
Allington Manor Fm	Hants	SU4717	50°57·3′	1°19·5′W	FM	185
Allins	Corn	SX1996	50°44·4′	4°33·5′W	X	190
Allin's Week	Devon	SS5218	50°56·8′	4°5·9′W	X	180
Allisdon	Corn	SX2997	50°45·1′	4°25·1′W	X	190
Allisland	Devon	SS4811	50°52·9′	4°9·3′W	X	191
Allison	Devon	SX6796	50°45·1′	3°52·7′W	X	191
Allison Lane End	E Yorks	TA1458	54°0·6′	0°15·2′W	X	107
Allison Wold Fm	N Yks	SE9774	54°9·4′	0°30·5′W	FM	101
Allithorne Wood	Northnts	SP5845	52°6·2′	1°8·8′W	F	152
Allithwaite	Cumbr	SD3876	54°10·8′	2°56·6′W	T	96,97
Allivo Burn	D & G	NX1055	54°51·5′	4°57·2′W	W	82
Allman Well Hill	Sheff	SK2896	53°27·8′	1°33·4′W	H	110
Allmeadows	Ches	SJ9666	53°11·7′	2°3·2′W	X	118
Allnabad	Highld	NC4641	58°20·1′	4°37·3′W	X	9
Allnutt's Fm	Oxon	SP7602	51°42·9′	0°53·6′W	FM	165
Alloa	Clackm	NS8892	56°6·7′	3°47·6′W	T	58
All Oaks Wood	Warw	SP4478	52°24·1′	1°20·8′W	F	140
Alloa Lea	Northum	NY6866	54°59·5′	2°29·6′W	X	86,87
Alloch Dam	E Dunb	NS6477	55°58·3′	4°10·3′W	W	64
Allochie	Aberd	NO8691	57°0·9′	2°13·4′W	X	38,45
Allonby	Cumbr	NY0843	54°46·7′	3°25·4′W	T	85
Allonby Bay	Cumbr	NY0641	54°45·6′	3°27·2′W	W	85
Allostock	Ches	SJ7471	53°14·4′	2°23·0′W	T	118
Allostock Hall	Ches	SJ7271	53°14·4′	2°24·8′W	X	118
Allotment Fm	E Yorks	SE9144	53°53·3′	0°36·5′W	FM	106
Allotment Fm	N Yks	SE5734	53°48·2′	1°7·7′W	FM	105
Allotment Fm	N Yks	SE7495	54°20·9′	0°51·3′W	FM	94,100
Allotment Ho	Durham	NZ0334	54°42·3′	1°56·8′W	X	92
Allotment Ho	Durham	NZ1129	54°39·6′	1°49·3′W	X	92
Allotment Ho	N Yks	SE6692	54°19·4′	0°58·7′W	X	94,100
Allotment, The	N Yks	SD7673	54°9·4′	2°21·6′W	X	98
Allotment, The	Somer	SS8933	51°5·4′	3°34·7′W	X	181
Alloway	S Ayr	NS3318	55°25·9′	4°37·9′W	T	70
Allowenshay	Somer	ST3913	50°55·0′	2°51·7′W	T	193
Allrey	Angus	NO5382	56°55·9′	2°45·9′W	H	44
All Saints	Devon	ST3001	50°48·5′	2°59·2′W	T	193

All Saints Court	N Yks	SE3052	53°58·0′	1°32·1′W	X	104
All Saints South Elmham	Suff	TM3482	52°23·4′	1°26·7′E	T	156
Allscot	Shrops	SO7396	52°33·9′	2°23·5′W	T	138
Allscott	Wrekin	SJ6113	52°43·0′	2°34·2′W	T	127
Allsetts Fm	Worcs	SO7856	52°12·3′	2°18·9′W	FM	150
Allshire	Somer	SS8724	51°0·5′	3°36·3′W	X	181
Allshot's Fm	Essex	TL8220	51°51·2′	0°39·0′E	FM	168
Allsprings	Lancs	SD7333	53°47·8′	2°24·2′W	X	103
Allstone Lee	Derby	SK0477	53°17·6′	1°56·0′W	X	119
All Stretton	Shrops	SO4695	52°33·2′	2°47·4′W	T	137,138
Allt	Carm	SN5502	51°42·1′	4°5·5′W	T	159
Allt	Monm	SO2917	51°51·1′	3°1·5′W	X	161
Allt a' Bhacain	Stir	NN6513	56°17·7′	4°10·4′W	W	57
Allt a' Bhacain-sheilich	Arg & Bt	NM6524	56°21·3′	5°47·8′W	W	49
Allt a' Bhaid Leathain	Highld	NC6320	58°9·1′	4°19·2′W	W	16
Allt a' Bhaid Sgàilich	Highld	NH4581	57°47·8′	4°36·0′W	W	20
Allt a' Bhainne	Highld	NH2802	57°4·9′	4°49·8′W	W	34
Allt a' Bhainne	Highld	NM6996	57°0·1′	5°47·8′W	W	40
Allt a' Bhainne	Highld	NM7096	57°0·1′	5°46·8′W	W	33,40
Allt a' Bhàird	Arg & Bt	NM6323	56°20·7′	5°49·7′W	W	49
Allt a' Bhalachain	Arg & Bt	NN2705	56°12·6′	4°46·9′W	W	56
Allt a' Bhalaich	Highld	NN2656	56°40·1′	4°49·9′W	W	41
Allt a' Bhàthaich	Highld	NC2030	58°13·6′	5°3·4′W	W	15
Allt a' Bhealaich	Arg & Bt	NR8148	55°40·8′	5°28·6′W	W	62,69
Allt a' Bhealaich	Highld	NC2819	58°7·9′	4°54·8′W	W	15
Allt a' Bhealaich	Highld	NG8860	57°35·1′	5°32·3′W	W	19,24
Allt a' Bhealaich	Highld	NH3748	57°29·8′	4°42·7′W	W	26
Allt a' Bhealaich Bhàin	Highld	NG8206	57°5·9′	5°35·5′W	W	33
Allt a' Bhealaich Bhig	Highld	NH2644	57°27·4′	4°53·6′W	W	25
Allt a' Bhealaich Bhric	Highld	NG5431	57°18·5′	6°4·6′W	W	24,32
Allt a' Bhealaich Dhuibh	Highld	NN4973	56°49·7′	4°28·0′W	W	42
Allt a Bhealaich Ghairbh	N Eil	NG0992	57°49·6′	6°53·7′W	W	14
Allt a' Bhealaich Mhóir	Highld	NH4366	57°39·7′	4°37·4′W	W	20
Allt a' Bheithe	Highld	NH2002	57°4·7′	4°57·7′W	W	34
Allt a' Bheithe	Stir	NN7208	56°15·1′	4°3·5′W	W	57
Allt a' Bhioda	Highld	NM6651	56°35·8′	5°48·3′W	W	49
Allt a' Bhiora	Highld	NH2203	57°5·3′	4°55·8′W	W	34
Allt a' Bhiorachain	N Eil	NB3134	58°13·0′	6°34·4′W	W	8,13
Allt a' Bhioraich	N Eil	NB3847	58°20·3′	6°28·1′W	W	8
Allt a' Bhiorain	Highld	NN1046	56°34·3′	5°5·1′W	W	50
Allt a' Bhlair	Arg & Bt	NR7337	55°34·7′	5°35·6′W	W	68
Allt a' Bhlàir Dheirg	Highld	NM7687	56°55·5′	5°40·4′W	W	40
Allt a' Bhlàir Mhòine	Highld	NM5853	56°36·6′	5°56·2′W	W	47
Allt a' Bhodaich	Highld	NH2215	57°11·7′	4°56·3′W	W	34
Allt a' Bhodaich	Highld	NN3386	56°56·4′	4°44·2′W	W	34,41
Allt a' Bhràighe	Highld	NH2182	57°47·8′	5°0·2′W	W	20
Allt a' Bhrathain	N Eil	NB4650	58°22·2′	6°20·1′W	W	8
Allt a' Bhreabadair	Highld	NH8838	57°25·4′	3°51·4′W	W	27
Allt a' Bhreac-dhunain	Arg & Bt	NR4965	55°49·0′	6°0·0′W	W	60,61
Allt a' Bhreadair	Aberd	NJ3404	57°7·6′	3°5·0′W	W	37
Allt a Bhriaghlann	Highld	NM4265	56°42·6′	6°12·5′W	W	47
Allt a' Bhric	Arg & Bt	NM5044	56°31·6′	6°3·5′W	W	47,48
Allt a' Bhuic	Arg & Bt	NR8555	55°44·7′	5°25·1′W	W	62
Allt a' Bhuic	Highld	ND0535	58°17·9′	3°36·8′W	W	11,17
Allt a' Bhuic Mhóir	Highld	NG9026	57°16·8′	5°28·6′W	W	25,33
Allt a' Bhuilg	Highld	NG9617	57°12·2′	5°22·2′W	W	33
Allt a' Bhuird Ruaidh	Highld	NH1957	57°34·3′	5°1·1′W	W	25
Allt a' Bhuiridh	Highld	NM7780	56°51·7′	5°39·0′W	W	40
Allt a' Bhunn	Highld	NC4912	58°4·5′	4°33·1′W	W	16
Allt a' Bhunn	Highld	NC8651	58°26·2′	3°56·7′W	W	10
Allt a' Bhunn Beag	Highld	NC5111	58°4·0′	4°31·1′W	W	16
Allt a' Bhùtha	Highld	NG7488	57°49·7′	5°47·9′W	W	19
Allt Ach' a' Bhàthàich	Highld	NC8114	58°6·2′	4°0·7′W	W	17
Allt Ach' a' Braighe	Highld	NC0506	58°0·3′	5°17·5′W	W	15
Allt Achadh a'Choirce	Arg & Bt	NR7142	55°37·3′	5°37·8′W	W	62
Allt Achadh a' Ghlinne	Highld	NM8997	57°1·2′	5°28·1′W	W	33,40
Allt Achadh Fairidh	Highld	NC2640	58°19·1′	4°57·8′W	W	9
Allt Achadh Fionn a'Bhacain	Arg & Bt	NM9706	56°12·5′	5°15·9′W	W	55
Allt Achadh Forsa	Highld	NM6747	56°33·7′	5°47·1′W	W	49
Allt Achadh Luirginn	Arg & Bt	NM6436	56°27·7′	5°49·4′W	W	49
Allt Achadh na Cuile	Arg & Bt	NM5430	56°24·2′	5°58·8′W	W	48
Allt Achadh na Dalach	Highld	NN1679	56°52·2′	5°0·7′W	W	41
Allt Achadh na Gaodha	Highld	NC9363	58°32·8′	3°49·8′W	W	11
Allt Achadh na Moine	Arg & Bt	NM6638	56°28·8′	5°47·6′W	W	49
Allt Achadh nan Sabhal	Highld	NN1589	56°57·6′	5°2·1′W	W	34,41
Allt Achadh nan Sabhal	Highld	NN1690	56°58·1′	5°1·2′W	W	34
Allt Achadh na Sine	Highld	NH1460	57°35·8′	5°6·3′W	W	20
Allt Achadh na Sìne	Highld	NH1559	57°35·3′	5°5·2′W	W	25
Allt Achadh na Teanga	Highld	NC6507	58°2·2′	4°16·7′W	W	16
Allt Achadh Tom a' Leine	Highld	NC6410	58°3·8′	4°17·8′W	W	16
Allt Achaidh Bhig	Highld	NG3055	57°30·5′	6°30·0′W	W	23
Allt Achaidh Luachraich	Highld	NH2504	57°5·9′	4°52·9′W	W	34
Allt a'Chaigin	Highld	NM8451	56°36·3′	5°30·7′W	W	49
Allt a' Chaime Dhuibh	Pth & Kin	NN5663	56°44·4′	4°20·8′W	W	42
Allt a' Chaimp	N Ayr	NR9440	55°36·9′	5°15·8′W	W	62,69
Allt a' Chairn	Highld	NH1484	57°48·7′	5°7·4′W	W	20
Allt a' Chàise	Highld	NH2810	57°9·2′	4°50·2′W	W	34
Allt a' Chaise	Highld	NM5370	56°45·6′	6°2·0′W	W	39,47
Allt a' Chaise	Pth & Kin	NN8173	56°50·3′	3°56·6′W	W	43
Allt a' Chaiseal Duibh	Highld	NC4448	58°23·8′	4°39·7′W	W	9
Allt a' Chaisil	Highld	NG9722	57°14·9′	5°21·4′W	W	25,33
Allt a' Chaisteil	Highld	NC7257	58°29·2′	4°11·3′W	W	10
Allt a' Chalda Mór	Highld	NC2523	58°9·9′	4°58·0′W	W	15
Allt a' Chamabhreac	Highld	NN3467	56°46·2′	4°42·5′W	W	41
Allt a' Chama' Choire	Pth & Kin	NN6978	56°52·8′	4°8·5′W	W	42
Allt a' Cham-aird	Highld	NG6102	57°3·1′	5°56·0′W	W	32
Allt a Chamais Shalaich	Highld	NM6960	56°40·7′	5°45·8′W	W	40
Allt a' Chàm Dhoire	Highld	NN0586	56°55·7′	5°11·8′W	W	41
Allt a' Cham Lóin Mhóir	Highld	NG7987	57°49·3′	5°42·8′W	W	19
Allt a' Cham-ruidhe	Stir	NN5105	56°13·1′	4°23·7′W	W	57
Allt a' Chamuis Bhàin	Highld	NG9106	57°6·1′	5°26·6′W	W	33
Allt Ach' an t-Srathain	Highld	NC5452	58°26·2′	4°29·6′W	W	10
Allt a' Chaoich	Highld	NG4719	57°11·8′	6°10·8′W	W	32
Allt a' Chaoil-réidhe	Highld	NN5276	56°51·4′	4°25·2′W	W	42
Allt a' Chaol-ghlinne	Highld	NM8984	56°54·2′	5°27·5′W	W	40
Allt a' Chaol Ghlinne	Stir	NN3531	56°26·8′	4°40·2′W	W	50
Allt a' Chaorain	Arg & Bt	NN2324	56°22·8′	4°51·5′W	W	50
Allt a' Chaorainn	Aberd	NN9285	56°56·9′	3°46·1′W	W	43
Allt a' Chaorainn	Arg & Bt	NN2324	56°22·8′	4°51·5′W	W	50
Allt a' Chaorainn	Highld	NH1903	57°5·2′	4°58·8′W	W	34
Allt a' Chaorainn	Highld	NH6902	57°5·7′	4°9·3′W	W	35
Allt a' Chaorainn	Highld	NN1949	56°36·1′	4°56·5′W	W	50
Allt a' Chaorainn	Highld	NN1950	56°36·7′	4°56·5′W	W	41
Allt a' Chaorainn	Highld	NN3684	56°55·4′	4°41·2′W	W	34,41
Allt a' Chaorainn	Highld	NN4693	57°0·4′	4°31·7′W	W	34
Allt a' Chaorainn	Pth & Kin	NN9281	56°54·7′	3°46·0′W	W	43
Allt a' Chaorainn Bhig	Highld	NH0712	57°9·8′	5°11·0′W	W	33
Allt a' Chaorainn Mhóir	Highld	NH0813	57°10·3′	5°10·1′W	W	33
Allt a' Chaoruinn	Highld	NC2703	57°59·2′	4°55·1′W	W	15
Allt a' Chaoruinn	Stir	NN6713	56°17·7′	4°8·5′W	W	57
Allt a' Chapuill	Arg & Bt	NS0279	55°58·1′	5°9·9′W	W	63
Allt a' Chapuill	N Eil	NB2333	58°12·2′	6°42·4′W	W	8,13
Allt a' Charnaich	Highld	NH2352	57°31·7′	4°56·9′W	W	25
Allt a' Charnaich	Highld	NH3602	57°5·1′	4°41·9′W	W	34
Allt a' Chas Bràighe	N Eil	NB0021	58°4·9′	7°4·9′W	W	13
Alltachbeg	Moray	NJ1817	57°14·4′	3°21·1′W	X	36
Allt a'Cheallaich	Highld	NM8455	56°38·5′	5°30·9′W	W	49
Allt a' Chilleine	Pth & Kin	NN7237	56°30·7′	4°4·4′W	W	51,52
Allt a' Chinn Bhric	Highld	NN0095	57°0·4′	5°17·2′W	W	33
Allt a' Chinn Ghairbh	Highld	NC1413	58°4·3′	5°8·7′W	W	15
Allt a' Chinn Mhóir	Highld	NG6414	57°9·6′	5°53·7′W	W	32
Allt a' Chinn Uachdaraich	Highld	NG5929	57°17·5′	5°59·5′W	W	32
Allt a' Chireachain	Pth & Kin	NN7772	56°49·7′	4°0·5′W	W	42
Allt a' Chire Mhóir	Pth & Kin	NN7976	56°51·8′	3°58·6′W	W	42
Allt a' Chlachain	Highld	NH2603	57°5·4′	4°51·8′W	W	34
Allt a' Chlaiginn	Aberd	NO1983	56°56·1′	3°19·4′W	W	43
Allt a' Chlaiginn	Highld	NH1263	57°37·3′	5°8·4′W	W	19
Allt a' Chlaiginn	Highld	NH3989	57°52·0′	4°42·4′W	W	20
Allt a' Chlaiginn	Moray	NJ3230	57°21·6′	3°7·4′W	W	37
Allt a' Chleite Tuath	N Eil	NB1118	58°3·7′	6°53·5′W	W	13,14
Allt a' Chlogaid	Arg & Bt	NM4850	56°34·7′	6°5·8′W	W	47
Allt a' Chloidh	Pth & Kin	NN7136	56°30·2′	4°5·3′W	W	51,52
Allt a' Chnaip	Highld	NN0170	56°47·0′	5°15·0′W	W	41
Allt a' Chnaip Ghiubhais	Highld	NC3519	58°8·0′	4°47·7′W	W	15
Allt Ach' nan Tot	Highld	NC6553	58°26·9′	4°18·3′W	W	10
Allt a' Chnoic	Arg & Bt	NN2613	56°16·9′	4°48·2′W	W	50,56
Allt a' Chobhair	Pth & Kin	NN6245	56°34·9′	4°14·4′W	W	51
Allt a' Choileachain	Moray	NJ2428	57°20·4′	3°15·3′W	W	36
Allt a' Choileachain	Moray	NJ3535	57°24·3′	3°4·4′W	W	28
Allt a' Choilich	Highld	NH5541	57°26·4′	4°24·5′W	W	26
Allt a'Choilich	Highld	NM8046	56°33·5′	5°34·4′W	W	49
Allt a' Choilich	Highld	NN2895	57°1·1′	4°49·5′W	W	34
Allt a' Choin	Highld	NG7018	57°12·0′	5°48·0′W	W	33
Allt a' Choin	Stir	NN4113	56°17·2′	4°33·7′W	W	56
Allt a' Choin Idhir	Highld	NH2668	57°40·4′	4°54·6′W	W	20
Allt a' Choin Idhir	Highld	NH4864	57°38·7′	4°32·3′W	W	20
Allt a' Choir' Aluinn	Highld	NH3350	57°30·8′	4°46·8′W	W	26
Allt a' Choire	Highld	NG3148	57°26·8′	6°28·6′W	W	23
Allt a' Choire	Highld	NG6123	57°14·4′	5°57·2′W	W	32
Allt a' Choire	Highld	NG6421	57°13·4′	5°54·1′W	W	32
Allt a' Choire	Highld	NM4967	56°43·9′	6°5·8′W	W	47
Allt a' Choire	Highld	NM6849	56°34·8′	5°46·2′W	W	49
Allt a' Choire	Highld	NM8885	56°54·7′	5°28·5′W	W	40
Allt a' Choire	Moray	NJ1925	57°18·8′	3°20·2′W	W	36
Allt a Choire àn-t-Seasaich	Highld	NG4128	57°16·4′	6°17·3′W	W	32
Allt a' Choire Bhàin	Arg & Bt	NM6134	56°26·5′	5°52·2′W	W	49
Allt a'Choire Bhàin	Highld	NM8152	56°36·8′	5°33·7′W	W	49
Allt a' Choire Bhig	Highld	NH2068	57°40·2′	5°0·6′W	W	20
Allt a' Choire Bhig	Pth & Kin	NN8074	56°50·8′	3°57·6′W	W	43
Allt a' Choire Bhuidhe	Highld	NG6521	57°13·4′	5°53·1′W	W	32
Allt a' Choire Bhuidhe	Highld	NG7123	57°14·7′	5°47·3′W	W	33
Allt a' Choire Bhuidhe	Highld	NG7822	57°14·4′	5°40·3′W	W	33
Allt a' Choire Bhuidhe	Highld	NH1917	57°12·7′	4°59·4′W	W	34
Allt a' Choire Bhuidhe	Highld	NH2397	57°55·9′	4°58·9′W	W	20
Allt a' Choire Bhuidhe	Highld	NH2710	57°9·2′	4°51·1′W	W	34
Allt a' Choire Bhuidhe	Highld	NH2790	57°52·2′	4°54·5′W	W	20
Allt a' Choire Bhuidhe	Highld	NH5718	57°14·1′	4°21·7′W	W	35
Allt a' Choire Bhuidhe	Highld	NM8380	56°51·9′	5°33·2′W	W	40
Allt a Choire Bhuidhe	Highld	NM9899	57°2·5′	5°19·3′W	W	33,40
Allt a' Choire Bhuidhe	Pth & Kin	NN8062	56°44·3′	3°57·3′W	W	43
Allt a' Choire Chaim	Highld	NN6784	56°56·0′	4°10·7′W	W	42
Allt a' Choire Chàis	Highld	NN6984	56°56·0′	4°8·7′W	W	42
Allt a' Choire Chaoil	Highld	NG9415	57°11·0′	5°24·1′W	W	33
Allt a' Choire Chaoil	Highld	NG9931	57°19·8′	5°19·9′W	W	25
Allt a' Choire Chaoil	Highld	NH0020	57°13·9′	5°18·4′W	W	25,33
Allt a' Choire Charnaich	Pth & Kin	NO0669	56°48·4′	3°31·9′W	W	43
Allt a' Choire Chàrnaig	Highld	NM9185	56°54·8′	5°25·5′W	W	40
Allt a' Choire Chomharsain	Highld	NN4686	56°56·6′	4°31·4′W	W	34,42
Allt a' Choire Chreagaich	Highld	NM4969	56°45·0′	6°5·9′W	W	47
Allt a' Choire Chreagaich	Highld	NN4168	56°46·8′	4°35·7′W	W	42
Allt a' Choire Chruim	Highld	NH1520	57°14·3′	5°3·5′W	W	25
Allt a Choire Dheirg	Highld	NJ0306	57°8·3′	3°35·7′W	W	36
Allt a' Choire Dheirg	Highld	NN1367	56°45·7′	5°3·1′W	W	41
Allt a' Choire Dhomdain	Highld	NG9915	57°11·2′	5°19·1′W	W	33
Allt a' Choire Dhomhain	Highld	NH1528	57°18·6′	5°3·8′W	W	25
Allt a' Choire Dhomhain	Highld	NH1943	57°26·7′	5°0·5′W	W	25
Allt a' Choire Dhuibh	Aberd	NO0192	57°0·8′	3°37·4′W	W	43
Allt a' Choire Dhuibh	Aberd	NO2086	56°57·8′	3°18·5′W	W	44
Allt a' Choire Dhuibh	Highld	NH0134	57°21·4′	5°18·0′W	W	25
Allt a' Choire Dhuibh	Highld	NJ0307	57°8·9′	3°35·7′W	W	36
Allt a' Choire Dhuibh	Highld	NM7767	56°44·7′	5°38·4′W	W	40
Allt a' Choire Dhuibh	Highld	NM8759	56°40·7′	5°28·2′W	W	49
Allt a' Choire Dhuibh	Highld	NM8981	56°52·6′	5°27·3′W	W	40
Allt a' Choire Dhuibh	Highld	NM9389	56°57·0′	5°23·8′W	W	40
Allt a' Choire Dhuibh	Highld	NN3484	56°55·3′	4°43·2′W	W	34,41
Allt a' Choire Dhuibh	Highld	NN5091	56°59·4′	4°27·7′W	W	35
Allt a' Choire Dhuibh	N Eil	NB3005	57°57·4′	6°33·4′W	W	13,14
Allt a' Choire Dhuibh Bhig	Highld	NC2800	57°57·6′	4°54·0′W	W	15
Allt a' Choire Dhuibh Bhig	Highld	NH2899	57°57·1′	4°53·9′W	W	20
Allt a' Choire Dhuibh Mhóir	Highld	NC2700	57°57·6′	4°55·0′W	W	15
Allt a' Choire Dhuibh Mhóir	Highld	NG9458	57°34·2′	5°26·2′W	W	25
Allt a' Choire Dhuibh Mhóir	Highld	NH2799	57°57·1′	4°54·9′W	W	20
Allt a' Choire Fhionnaraich	Highld	NH1544	57°27·2′	5°4·5′W	W	25
Allt a' Choire Fhuadaraich	Stir	NN6019	56°20·8′	4°15·5′W	W	57
Allt a' Choire Ghairbh	Highld	NH2046	57°28·4′	4°59·6′W	W	25
Allt a' Choire Ghlais	Highld	NN0098	57°2·0′	5°17·3′W	W	33
Allt a' Choire Ghlais	Highld	NN2596	57°1·6′	4°52·5′W	W	34
Allt a' Choire Ghlais	Pth & Kin	NN5265	56°45·4′	4°24·8′W	W	42
Allt a' Choire Ghlais	Stir	NN5437	56°30·4′	4°21·9′W	W	51
Allt a' Choire Ghràinde	Highld	NC4240	58°19·5′	4°41·4′W	W	9
Allt a' Choire Ghreadaidh	Highld	NG4223	57°13·8′	6°16·0′W	W	32
Allt a' Choire Ghuirm	Highld	NH1034	57°21·7′	5°9·1′W	W	25
Allt a' Choire Leacaich Mhóir	Highld	NH0606	57°6·5′	5°11·8′W	W	33
Allt a' Choire Mhóir	Aberd	NN9899	57°4·5′	3°40·5′W	W	36,43
Allt a' Choire Mhóir	Highld	NG9630	57°19·2′	5°22·8′W	W	25
Allt a' Choire Mhóir	Highld	NH3187	57°50·7′	4°50·4′W	W	20
Allt a' Choire Mhór	Highld	NH1968	57°40·2′	5°1·6′W	W	20
Allt a' Choire Odhair	Highld	NG8600	57°2·7′	5°31·2′W	W	33
Allt a' Choire Odhair	Highld	NG9111	57°8·8′	5°26·8′W	W	33
Allt a' Choire Odhair	Highld	NH1826	57°17·6′	5°0·8′W	W	25
Allt a' Choire Odhair	Highld	NH2416	57°12·3′	4°54·4′W	W	34
Allt a' Choire Odhair	Highld	NH5005	57°7·0′	4°28·2′W	W	35
Allt a' Choire Odhair-bhig	Highld	NN2258	56°41·1′	4°53·9′W	W	41
Allt a' Choire Odhair Bhig	Highld	NN3865	56°45·2′	4°38·5′W	W	41
Allt a' Choire Odhair Bhig	Pth & Kin	NN5463	56°44·4′	4°22·8′W	W	42
Allt a' Choire Odhair Mhoir	Highld	NH9032	57°22·2′	3°49·3′W	W	27,36
Allt a' Choire Odhair-mhóir	Highld	NN2059	56°41·5′	4°55·9′W	W	41
Allt a' Choire Odhair Mhóir	Highld	NN3764	56°44·6′	4°39·5′W	W	41
Allt a' Choire Odhair Mhóir	Highld	NN3898	57°2·9′	4°39·8′W	W	34
Allt a' Choire Odhar	Highld	NH0436	57°22·6′	5°15·1′W	W	25
Allt a' Choire-rainich	Highld	NH3975	57°44·4′	4°41·8′W	W	20
Allt a' Choire Réidh	Highld	NC0704	57°59·3′	5°15·4′W	W	15
Allt a' Choire Reidh	Highld	NG9309	57°7·8′	5°24·8′W	W	33
Allt a' Choire Réidh	Highld	NH0111	57°9·1′	5°16·9′W	W	33
Allt a' Choire Réidh	Highld	NM9598	57°1·9′	5°22·2′W	W	33,40
Allt a' Choire Reidh	Highld	NM9885	56°55·0′	5°18·7′W	W	40
Allt a' Choire Riabhaich	Highld	NM8151	56°36·2′	5°33·6′W	W	49
Allt a' Choire Riabhaich	Highld	NN0174	56°49·2′	5°15·2′W	W	41
Allt a' Choire Riabhaich	Highld	NN0797	57°1·7′	5°10·4′W	W	33
Allt a' Choire Screamhaich	Highld	NN0188	56°56·7′	5°15·8′W	W	41
Allt a' Choire Sheilach	Highld	NG7404	57°4·6′	5°43·3′W	W	33
Allt a' Choire Uidhre	Pth & Kin	NN5748	56°36·4′	4°19·3′W	W	51
Allt a' Chòis	Highld	NG7838	57°23·0′	5°41·1′W	W	24
Allt a' Chomair	Highld	NH2157	57°34·3′	4°59·1′W	W	25
Allt a' Chòmhlain	Highld	NH0717	57°12·5′	5°11·3′W	W	33
Allt a' Chòmhlain	Highld	NH2218	57°13·4′	4°56·4′W	W	34
Allt a' Chòmhlain	Highld	NN3192	56°59·6′	4°46·5′W	W	34
Alltachonaich	Highld	NM7450	56°35·5′	5°40·4′W	X	49
Allt a' Chonaich	Highld	NM7751	56°36·1′	5°37·5′W	W	49
Allt a' Chonais	Highld	NH0648	57°29·1′	5°13·7′W	W	25
Allt a' Chonnaidh	Arg & Bt	NM6625	56°21·8′	5°46·9′W	W	49
Allt a' Chonnaidh	Arg & Bt	NM7134	56°26·8′	5°42·5′W	W	49
Allt a' Chonnaidh	Arg & Bt	NR5079	55°56·6′	5°59·8′W	W	61
Alltachorain	Highld	NN4795	57°1·5′	4°30·8′W	X	34
Allt a' Choromaig	Arg & Bt	NM9221	56°20·4′	5°21·5′W	W	49
Allt a' Chorra Chnoic	N Eil	NB2420	58°5·2′	6°40·5′W	W	13,14
Allt a' Chòta	Highld	NC4010	58°3·3′	4°42·2′W	W	16
Allt a' Chràisg	Highld	NC5226	58°12·1′	4°30·6′W	W	16
Allt a' Chràisg	Highld	NC6024	58°11·2′	4°22·4′W	W	16
Allt a' Chrannaig	Highld	NN4888	56°57·8′	4°29·5′W	W	34,42
Allt a' Chraois	Highld	NC4338	58°18·4′	4°40·3′W	W	16
Allt a' Chreachail Mhóir	Highld	NH0534	57°21·5′	5°14·1′W	W	25
Allt a' Chreagain Bhuidhe	Highld	NH1442	57°26·1′	5°5·5′W	W	25
Allt a' Chreagain Odhair	Pth & Kin	NN6161	56°43·5′	4°15·8′W	W	42
Allt a' Chreimh	Highld	NC7639	58°19·6′	4°6·6′W	W	17
Allt a' Chròchaiche	Highld	NN0576	56°50·3′	5°11·4′W	W	41
Allt a' Chrochaidh	Pth & Kin	NN9476	56°52·1′	3°43·9′W	W	43
Allt a' Chroin	Stir	NN3917	56°19·3′	4°35·8′W	W	50,56
Allt a' Chroinn	Highld	NH2412	57°10·2′	4°54·2′W	W	34
Allt a'Chroisg	Arg & Bt	NM9607	56°13·0′	5°17·0′W	W	55
Allt a' Chromain	Arg & Bt	NR3870	55°51·4′	6°10·8′W	W	60,61
Allt a' Chrom-alltain	Highld	NN8899	57°4·4′	3°50·4′W	W	35,36,43
Allt a' Chrombaidh	Pth & Kin	NN7969	56°48·1′	3°58·4′W	W	42
Allt a Chrom-uillt	Highld	NH3081	57°47·4′	4°51·1′W	W	20
Allt a' Chruaidh Ghoirtein	Highld	NN5595	57°1·7′	4°22·9′W	W	35
Allt a' Chruinn	Highld	NG9519	57°13·2′	5°23·3′W	W	33
Allt a' Chuaille	Highld	NC1703	57°59·0′	5°5·2′W	W	15
Allt a' Chuil	Highld	NC2856	58°27·8′	4°56·4′W	W	9
Allt a' Chuil	Highld	NC5027	58°12·6′	4°32·7′W	W	16
Allt a' Chùil	Highld	NH7732	57°22·0′	4°2·2′W	W	27
Allt a' Chùil	Pth & Kin	NN8380	56°54·1′	3°54·8′W	W	43
Allt a' Chùil Choirean	Highld	NN2773	56°49·2′	4°49·6′W	W	41
Allt a' Chuilinn	Highld	NC3040	58°19·2′	4°53·7′W	W	9
Allt a' Chuilinn	Stir	NN3520	56°20·9′	4°39·8′W	W	50,56
Allt a' Chuilinn Beag	Highld	NC6527	58°12·9′	4°17·4′W	W	16
Allt a' Chuilinn Mór	Highld	NC6427	58°12·9′	4°18·4′W	W	16
Allt a' Chùirn	Arg & Bt	NN3639	56°31·1′	4°39·5′W	W	50
Allt a' Chùirn	Highld	NG8843	57°25·9′	5°31·4′W	W	24
Allt a' Chuirn	Highld	NH0160	57°35·4′	5°19·3′W	W	19
Allt a' Chuirn	Highld	NM8277	56°50·3′	5°34·0′W	W	40
Allt a' Chùirn Deirg	Highld	NG7545	57°26·6′	5°44·5′W	W	24
Allt a' Chùl Choire	Highld	NN2072	56°48·5′	4°56·5′W	W	41
Allt a' Chumhaing	Highld	NG7940	57°24·1′	5°40·3′W	W	24
Allt a' Chumhainn	Pth & Kin	NN5670	56°48·2′	4°21·0′W	W	42
Allt Acnaidh	Highld	NC3862	58°31·2′	4°46·4′W	W	9
Allt a' Coire Uaine	Highld	NG9215	57°11·0′	5°26·0′W	W	33
Allt a'Deas Muirneag	N Eil	NB4648	58°21·1′	6°20·0′W	W	8
Allt a' Ghabhainn	Arg & Bt	NS1175	55°56·1′	5°1·1′W	W	63
Allt a' Ghairuillt	Highld	NG6017	57°11·1′	5°57·8′W	W	32
Allt a' Ghamhna	Highld	NC2132	58°14·7′	5°2·5′W	W	15
Allt a' Ghamhna	Highld	NN4996	57°2·1′	4°28·8′W	W	34
Allt a' Ghaotharain	Arg & Bt	NR5679	55°56·8′	5°54·0′W	W	61
Allt a' Gharbhain	Highld	NH1781	57°47·1′	5°4·2′W	W	20
Allt a' Gharbh Bhaid	Highld	NH4368	57°40·7′	4°37·5′W	W	20
Allt a' Gharbh-choire	Aberd	NN9598	57°3·9′	3°43·4′W	W	36,43
Allt a' Gharbh-choire	Aberd	NO1679	56°53·9′	3°22·3′W	W	43
Allt a' Gharbh-choire	Highld	NN3974	56°50·0′	4°37·9′W	W	41
Allt a' Gharbh-choire Bhig	Highld	NC4235	58°16·8′	4°41·2′W	W	16
Allt a' Gharbhrain	Highld	NH2777	57°45·2′	4°54·0′W	W	20
Allt a Gheallaidh	Highld	NJ1238	57°25·7′	3°27·5′W	W	28
Allt a' Gheàrr Oir	Highld	NG8016	57°11·2′	5°38·0′W	W	33
Allt a' Ghil	Arg & Bt	NR3167	55°49·5′	6°17·3′W	W	60,61
Allt a Ghille Charaich	Highld	NH5713	57°11·4′	4°21·5′W	W	35
Allt a' Ghiubhais	Highld	NG8745	57°27·0′	5°32·5′W	W	24

Allt a' Ghiubhais	Highld	NH1893	57°53·6'	5°3·8'W	W	20
Allt a' Ghiubhais	Highld	NM8073	56°48·1'	5°35·7'W	W	40
Allt a' Ghiubhais	Highld	NM8681	56°52·5'	5°30·3'W	W	40
Allt a' Ghiubhais	Highld	NN3283	56°54·7'	4°45·1'W	W	34,41
Allt a' Ghiubhais	Highld	NN6185	56°56·4'	4°16·6'W	W	42
Allt a' Ghiubhais Chruinn	Highld	NN0897	57°1·7'	5°9·4'W	W	33
Allt a' Ghlais-choire	Highld	NG4824	57°14·5'	6°10·2'W	W	32
Allt a' Ghlais Choire	Highld	NH2632	57°21·0'	4°53·1'W	W	25
Allt a' Ghlaoidh	Arg & Bt	NR6734	55°32·9'	5°41·2'W	W	68
Allt a' Ghlas-choire	Aberd	NO2588	56°58·9'	3°13·6'W	W	44
Allt a' Ghlas-choire	Highld	NG9829	57°18·7'	5°20·8'W	W	25,33
Allt a' Ghlas-choire	Highld	NH0315	57°11·3'	5°15·1'W	W	33
Allt a' Ghlas Choire	Highld	NN3485	56°55·9'	4°43·2'W	W	34,41
Allt a' Ghlas-choire	Highld	NN3873	56°49·5'	4°38·8'W	W	41
Allt a' Ghlas Choire	Pth & Kin	NN9481	56°54·8'	3°44·0'W	W	43
Allt a' Ghlas-Locha	Highld	NC5032	58°15·3'	4°32·9'W	W	16
Allt a' Ghlasraich	Highld	NC8661	58°31·6'	3°57·0'W	W	10
Allt a' Ghleannain	Highld	NG7424	57°15·3'	5°44·4'W	W	33
Allt a' Ghleannain	Highld	NG9016	57°11·5'	5°28·1'W	W	33
Allt a' Ghléibh	Highld	NH1172	57°42·2'	5°9·8'W	W	19
Allt a' Ghlinne	Highld	NG5805	57°4·6'	5°59·1'W	W	32,39
Allt a' Ghlinne	Highld	NH3500	57°4·0'	4°42·8'W	W	34
Allt a' Ghlinne	Highld	NH3658	57°35·2'	4°44·1'W	W	26
Allt a' Ghlinne	Highld	NH5289	57°52·2'	4°29·2'W	W	20
Allt a' Ghlinne Bhig	Pth & Kin	NO0279	56°53·8'	3°36·1'W	W	43
Allt a' Ghlinne Bhig	Pth & Kin	NO1273	56°50·7'	3°26·1'W	W	43
Allt a' Ghlinne Dhorcha	Highld	NC1817	58°6·5'	5°4·9'W	W	15
Allt a' Ghlinne Dhuibh	Arg & Bt	NM5330	56°24·1'	5°59·7'W	W	48
Allt a' Ghlinne Dhuibh	N Eil	NB0413	58°0·7'	7°0·3'W	W	13
Allt a' Ghlinne Fhada	Highld	NH1717	57°12·7'	5°1·4'W	W	34
Allt a' Ghlinne Mhòir	N Eil	NB3001	57°55·3'	6°33·1'W	W	14
Allt a' Ghlinne Mhóir	Pth & Kin	NO0078	56°53·2'	3°38·0'W	W	43
Allt a' Ghlomaich	Highld	NH0126	57°17·1'	5°17·7'W	W	25,33
Allt a' Ghobhainn	Highld	NH1002	57°4·5'	5°7·6'W	W	34
Allt a' Ghobhair	Highld	NC2664	58°32·0'	4°58·9'W	W	9
Allt a' Ghoirean	Highld	NH2514	57°11·3'	4°53·3'W	W	34
Allt a' Ghoirtean	Highld	NG7713	57°9·5'	5°40·8'W	W	33
Allt a' Ghoirtein	N Eil	NB0110	57°59·0'	7°3·1'W	W	13
Allt a' Ghoirtein-eorna	Highld	NM6266	56°43·8'	5°53·0'W	W	40
Allt a' Ghoirtein Fhearna	Highld	NM6067	56°44·2'	5°55·0'W	W	40
Allt a' Ghoirtein Uaine	Arg & Bt	NM6426	56°22·3'	5°48·9'W	W	49
Allt a' Ghorm-choire	Highld	NC4333	58°15·7'	4°40·1'W	W	16
Allt a' Ghraigh-fhear	Highld	NH0838	57°23·8'	5°11·3'W	W	25
Allt a' Ghuail	Highld	NH3897	57°56·2'	4°43·7'W	W	20
Allt a' Ghuibhais	Highld	NG7968	57°39·1'	5°41·8'W	W	19,24
Allt a' Ghuibhais	Highld	NH1613	57°10·5'	5°2·2'W	W	34
Allt á Guanan	Arg & Bt	NS2399	56°9·3'	4°50·5'W	W	56
Allt Aigeinn	Highld	NG5423	57°14·2'	6°4·1'W	W	32
Allt Ailein	Highld	NN1595	57°0·8'	5°2·4'W	W	34
Allt air Chul	Pth & Kin	NN9474	56°51·0'	3°43·8'W	W	43
Allt Aird Eachaidh	Highld	NN1591	56°58·7'	5°2·2'W	W	34
Allt Airdeasaidh	Highld	NH0487	57°50·0'	5°17·6'W	X	19
Allt Airigh a'Chleirich	Highld	NM7441	56°30·7'	5°39·9'W	W	49
Allt Airigh a' Phuill	Pth & Kin	NN4240	56°31·8'	4°33·7'W	W	51
Allt Airigh Cheiridh	Highld	NH3075	57°44·2'	4°50·9'W	W	20
Allt Airigh-dhamh	Highld	NC8237	58°18·6'	4°0·4'W	W	17
Allt Airigh Meall Beathaig	Highld	NG4634	57°19·8'	6°12·7'W	W	32
Allt Airigh na h-Uamha	N Eil	NB2016	58°2·9'	6°44·3'W	W	13,14
Allt Airigh nan Caisteal	Arg & Bt	NM4128	56°22·7'	6°11·3'W	W	48
Allt Airigh na Saorach	Highld	NG6819	57°12·4'	5°50·0'W	W	32
Allt Airigh na Sròine	Arg & Bt	NR4670	55°51·6'	6°3·1'W	W	60,61
Allt Airigh Os Fid	N Eil	NB1817	58°3·4'	6°46·4'W	W	13,14
Allt Airigh Sgridhe	N Eil	NB3337	58°14·7'	6°32·5'W	W	8,13
Allt Airigh Sheileach	Arg & Bt	NR7671	55°53·1'	5°34·5'W	W	62
Allt Airigh Staic	Arg & Bt	NR8170	55°52·7'	5°29·6'W	W	62
Alltalaird	Highld	NC6330	58°14·5'	4°19·6'W	X	16
Allt a' Mhadaidh	Highld	NH2274	57°43·5'	4°58·9'W	W	20
Allt a' Mhadaidh-ruaidh	Highld	NC6113	58°5·3'	4°21·0'W	W	16
Allt a' Mhàgain	Pth & Kin	NN9465	56°46·1'	3°43·6'W	W	43
Allt a' Mhagharaidh	Highld	NH4777	57°45·7'	4°33·8'W	W	20
Allt á Mhaigh or Moy Burn	Highld	NN4983	56°55·1'	4°28·4'W	W	34,42
Allt a' Mhaim	Arg & Bt	NM5527	56°22·6'	5°57·6'W	W	48
Allt a' Mhàim	Highld	NG4326	57°15·4'	6°15·2'W	W	32
Allt a' Mhaim	Pth & Kin	NN3637	56°30·1'	4°39·4'W	W	50
Allt a' Mhaingir	Highld	NH0000	57°3·1'	5°17·4'W	W	33
Allt a' Mharcaidh	Highld	NH7426	57°18·7'	4°5·1'W	W	35
Allt a' Mharcaidh	Highld	NH8803	57°6·5'	3°50·5'W	W	35,36
Allt a' Mheacain	Highld	NM6147	56°33·5'	5°52·9'W	W	49
Allt a' Mheallain Odhair	Highld	NN5381	56°54·1'	4°24·4'W	W	42
Allt a' Mheanbh-chruidh	Pth & Kin	NN5054	56°39·5'	4°26·4'W	W	42,51
Allt a' Mhèil	Highld	NH0403	57°4·8'	5°13·6'W	W	33
Allt a' Mheinn	Stir	NN6936	56°30·1'	4°7·3'W	W	51
Allt a' Mhiadah	Pth & Kin	NN7312	56°17·3'	4°2·7'W	W	57
Allt a' Mhiadain	Stir	NN7211	56°16·7'	4°3·6'W	W	57
Allt a Mhill Bhuidhe	Arg & Bt	NS1075	55°56·1'	5°2·1'W	W	63
Allt a' Mhill Ghairbh	Highld	NN4597	57°2·5'	4°32·8'W	W	34
Allt a'Mhina	Stir	NN2522	56°21·7'	4°49·5'W	X	50
Allt a' Mhòid	Highld	NC5638	58°18·7'	4°27·0'W	W	16
Allt a' Mhoirneas	Pth & Kin	NN6137	56°30·5'	4°15·1'W	W	51
Allt a' Mhuchaidh	Arg & Bt	NM4830	56°24·0'	6°4·6'W	W	48
Allt a' Mhuilinn	Arg & Bt	NM4145	56°31·8'	6°12·3'W	W	47,48
Allt a Mhuilinn	Arg & Bt	NN2219	56°20·1'	4°52·3'W	W	50,56
Allt a' Mhuilinn	Arg & Bt	NR5167	55°50·2'	5°58·2'W	W	61
Allt a' Mhuilinn	Highld	NC4858	58°29·3'	4°36·0'W	W	9
Allt a' Mhuilinn	Highld	NC5730	58°14·4'	4°25·7'W	W	16
Allt a' Mhuilinn	Highld	NC8313	58°5·7'	3°58·6'W	W	17
Allt a' Mhuilinn	Highld	NC8855	58°28·4'	3°54·7'W	W	10
Allt a' Mhuilinn	Highld	NG5916	57°10·6'	5°58·8'W	W	32
Allt a' Mhuilinn	Highld	NG6305	57°4·8'	5°54·2'W	W	32
Allt a' Mhuilinn	Highld	NG7601	57°3·0'	5°41·1'W	W	33
Allt a' Mhuilinn	Highld	NG8419	57°12·9'	5°34·2'W	W	33
Allt a' Mhuilinn	Highld	NH3913	57°11·0'	4°39·4'W	W	34
Allt a' Mhuilinn	Highld	NH7316	57°13·3'	4°5·7'W	W	35
Allt a' Mhuilinn	Highld	NH7620	57°15·5'	4°2·9'W	W	35
Allt a' Mhuilinn	Highld	NM5949	56°34·5'	5°55·0'W	W	47,48
Allt a' Mhuilinn	Highld	NM7962	56°42·1'	5°36·2'W	W	40
Allt a' Mhuilinn	Highld	NN1574	56°49·5'	5°1·4'W	W	41
Allt a' Mhuilinn	Highld	NN5387	56°57·3'	4°24·6'W	W	42
Allt a' Mhuilinn	Pth & Kin	NN7675	56°51·3'	4°1·8'W	W	42
Allt a' Mhuilinn Duibh	Highld	NC7414	58°6·1'	4°7·8'W	W	16
Allt a' Mhuillnn	Highld	NG6422	57°13·9'	5°54·2'W	W	32
Alltamhuilt	Highld	NC6712	58°4·9'	4°14·9'W	X	16
Allt a' Mhuiseil	Highld	NC4648	58°23·9'	4°37·6'W	W	9
Allt a' Mhula	N Eil	NB0806	57°57·1'	6°55·7'W	W	13,14
Allt a' Mhulinn	Highld	NG8433	57°20·4'	5°34·9'W	W	24
Allt a' Mhullaich	Highld	NM9677	56°50·6'	5°20·2'W	W	40
Alltami	Flint	SJ2665	53°10·9'	3°6·0'W	T	117
Alltanabradhan	Highld	NC0525	58°10·5'	5°18·5'W	X	15
Allt an Abrandern	Arg & Bt	NS0377	55°57·0'	5°8·9'W	W	63
Allt an Achaidh	Highld	NC2307	58°1·3'	4°59·3'W	W	15
Allt an Achaidh Mhóir	Highld	NC5146	58°22·9'	4°32·4'W	W	9
Alltan a' Choin Duibhe	Highld	NC2860	58°29·9'	4°56·6'W	W	9
Alltan an Aghaidh Mhilis	Aberd	NO0699	57°4·6'	3°32·6'W	W	36,43
Allt an Aighe	Highld	NN2961	56°42·8'	4°47·2'W	W	41
Allt an Airich	Arg & Bt	NM6431	56°25·0'	5°49·1'W	W	49
Allt an Amair	Highld	NN0768	56°46·1'	5°9·0'W	W	41
Alltan a Mhullaich	Highld	NC5033	58°15·9'	4°32·9'W	W	16
Allt an Amise	Highld	NH1647	57°28·8'	5°3·7'W	W	25
Allt an Aoinidh Mhóir	Highld	NM6551	56°35·8'	5°49·2'W	W	49
Allt an Aonaich	Highld	NH8421	57°16·2'	3°55·0'W	W	35
Alltan Aonghais	Highld	NC3320	58°8·5'	4°49·7'W	W	15
Allt an Aslaird	Highld	NC4237	58°17·9'	4°41·3'W	W	16
Allt Anavig	Highld	NG7325	57°15·8'	5°45·4'W	W	33
Allt an Ban	Arg & Bt	NR6732	55°31·8'	5°41·1'W	W	68
Alltan Beithe	Highld	NC2219	58°7·7'	5°0·9'W	W	15
Alltan Breac	Highld	NM5267	56°44·0'	6°2·8'W	W	47
Alltan Breac-laraich	Arg & Bt	NR7979	55°57·5'	5°32·0'W	W	62
Alltan Buidhe	Highld	NC5737	58°18·2'	4°25·9'W	W	16
Allt an Daimh	Highld	NG9928	57°18·2'	5°19·7'W	W	25,33
Allt an Daimh	Pth & Kin	NO1469	56°48·5'	3°24·1'W	W	43
Allt an Damhain	Highld	NG7018	57°12·0'	5°48·0'W	W	33
Allt an Daraich	Highld	NG7124	57°15·2'	5°47·3'W	W	33
Allt an Daraich	Highld	NM9281	56°52·7'	5°24·4'W	W	40
Allt an Dèabh	Highld	NM6969	56°45·6'	5°46·3'W	W	40
Allt an Dearg	Aberd	NO2883	56°56·2'	3°10·5'W	W	44
Alltan Dearg	Highld	NC6461	58°31·2'	4°19·6'W	W	10
Allt an Dherue	Highld	NC5345	58°22·4'	4°30·3'W	W	10
Allt an Doire-daraich	Highld	NG7618	57°12·1'	5°42·1'W	W	33
Allt an Doire Dharaich	Highld	NM5367	56°44·0'	6°1·9'W	W	47
Allt an Doire Dharaich	Highld	NM7541	56°30·7'	5°39·0'W	W	49
Allt an Doire-Dharaich	Highld	NM7647	56°34·0'	5°38·3'W	W	49
Allt an Doire Fheàrna	Highld	NH1702	57°4·6'	5°0·7'W	W	34
Allt an Doire Leathain	Highld	NH6219	57°14·7'	4°16·8'W	W	35
Alltan Donn	N Ayr	NR9325	55°28·8'	5°16·1'W	W	68,69
Allt Andoran	Stir	NN3621	56°21·4'	4°38·8'W	W	50,56
Allt an Dorch	Highld	NG9934	57°21·4'	5°20·0'W	W	25
Allt an Doruis	Highld	NJ1021	57°16·5'	3°29·1'W	W	36
Allt an Driùchd	Pth & Kin	NN6830	56°26·9'	4°8·0'W	W	51
Allt an Drochaidean Beaga	Highld	NC5321	58°9·5'	4°29·4'W	W	16
Allt an Droighinn	Highld	NH2455	57°33·3'	4°56·0'W	W	25
Allt an Drollaire	Highld	NG7606	57°5·7'	5°41·4'W	W	33
Alltan Dubh	Arg & Bt	NN0331	56°26·1'	5°11·3'W	W	50
Alltan Dubh	Highld	NC5360	58°30·5'	4°30·9'W	W	10
Alltan Dubh Ceann na Creige	Highld	NC6620	58°9·2'	4°16·1'W	W	16
Allt an Dubh-chadha	Highld	NN7991	56°59·9'	3°59·1'W	W	35
Allt an Dubh-choire	Arg & Bt	NM6837	56°28·3'	5°45·6'W	W	49
Allt an Dubh Choirein	Highld	NM8568	56°45·5'	5°30·6'W	W	40
Allt an Dubh Choirein	Pth & Kin	NN6515	56°18·8'	4°10·5'W	W	57
Allt an Dubh-ghlinne	Aberd	NO0696	57°3·0'	3°32·5'W	W	43
Allt an Dubh-loch	Aberd	NO2283	56°56·2'	3°16·5'W	W	44
Allt an Dubh-loch	Aberd	NO2582	56°55·7'	3°13·5'W	W	44
Allt an Dubh Loch Bhig	Highld	NC4213	58°4·9'	4°40·3'W	W	16
Alltan Dubh Mór	Highld	NH3789	57°51·9'	4°44·4'W	W	20
Allt an Dùin	Highld	NC8124	58°11·6'	4°1·0'W	W	17
Allt an Dùnain	Arg & Bt	NN0524	56°22·3'	5°9·0'W	W	50
Allt an Eachdarra	Highld	NM8094	56°59·4'	5°36·8'W	W	33,40
Allt an Ealaidh	Highld	NC7127	58°13·0'	4°11·3'W	W	16
Allt an Easain Ghil	Highld	NC3647	58°23·1'	4°47·8'W	W	9
Alltan Easain Rabail	Highld	NC2447	58°22·8'	5°0·1'W	W	9
Allt an Eas Bhàin	Highld	NG9723	57°15·4'	5°21·5'W	W	25,33
Allt an Eas Bhàin Mhóir	Highld	NH1536	57°22·9'	5°4·2'W	W	25
Allt an Eas Bhig	Aberd	NO1499	57°4·7'	3°24·7'W	W	36,43
Allt an Eas Bhig	Highld	NH1774	57°43·4'	5°3·9'W	W	20
Allt an Eas Dhuibh	Arg & Bt	NM6140	56°29·7'	5°52·5'W	W	49
Allt an Eas Dhuibh	Highld	NH1531	57°20·2'	5°4·0'W	W	25
Allt an Eas Fors	Arg & Bt	NM4542	56°30·3'	6°8·2'W	W	47,48
Allt an Eas Mhóir	Aberd	NJ1400	57°5·2'	3°24·7'W	W	36
Allt an Eich Dhuibh	Highld	NH4112	57°10·5'	4°37·4'W	W	34
Allt an Eilein Ghuirm	Highld	NH4072	57°42·8'	4°40·7'W	W	20
Allt an Eirean	Arg & Bt	NR4574	55°53·8'	6°4·3'W	W	60,61
Allt an Eireannaich	Arg & Bt	NR5678	55°56·5'	5°54·0'W	W	61
Alltan Eisg	Highld	NG8846	57°27·6'	5°31·6'W	W	24
Allt an Eòin	Highld	NC7114	58°6·0'	4°10·9'W	W	16
Allt an Eòin	Highld	NH2509	57°8·6'	4°53·1'W	W	34
Allt an Eoin Bhinn	Highld	NN2359	56°41·6'	4°53·0'W	W	41
Allt an Erins	Arg & Bt	NR8575	55°55·5'	5°26·0'W	W	62
Alltan Feàrna	Highld	NC5337	58°18·1'	4°30·0'W	W	16
Allt an Fhail	Pth & Kin	NN4349	56°36·7'	4°33·0'W	W	51
Allt an Fhaing	Highld	NG8116	57°11·2'	5°37·0'W	W	33
Allt an Fhaing	Highld	NM7548	56°34·5'	5°39·3'W	W	49
Allt an Fhaing	Highld	NM8459	56°40·6'	5°31·1'W	W	49
Allt an Fhaing	Highld	NM9177	56°50·5'	5°25·1'W	W	40
Allt an Fhaing	Highld	NM9463	56°43·1'	5°21·5'W	W	40
Allt an Fhaing Ghairbh	Arg & Bt	NR2666	55°48·8'	6°22·0'W	W	60
Allt an Fhàsaidh	Highld	NM8362	56°42·2'	5°32·2'W	W	40
Allt an Fheadain	Highld	NH1336	57°22·8'	5°6·2'W	W	25
Allt an Fheadain	Pth & Kin	NN5055	56°40·0'	4°26·4'W	W	42,51
Allt an Fhiona	Highld	NM7676	56°49·6'	5°39·8'W	W	40
Allt an Fhionn	Pth & Kin	NN6826	56°24·7'	4°7·9'W	W	51
Allt an Fhir-eòin	Arg & Bt	NM4220	56°18·4'	6°9·8'W	W	48
Allt an Fhir-eòin	Highld	NH0705	57°6·0'	5°10·7'W	W	33
Allt an Fhithich	Highld	NN0281	56°53·0'	5°14·5'W	W	41
Allt an Fhithich	Highld	NN1495	57°0·8'	5°3·4'W	W	34
Allt an Fhliuch Bhadan	Highld	NH3196	57°55·5'	4°50·8'W	W	20
Allt an Fhraoch-choire	Highld	NH0215	57°11·2'	5°16·1'W	W	33
Allt an Fhraoich-choire	Highld	NH0526	57°17·2'	5°13·7'W	W	25,33
Allt an Fhuadh	Highld	NN0679	56°52·0'	5°10·5'W	W	41
Alltan Glas	Highld	NG9548	57°28·8'	5°24·7'W	W	25
Allt an Iaruinn	Arg & Bt	NN2522	56°21·7'	4°49·5'W	W	50
Allt an Ille Coire	Highld	NM8890	56°57·4'	5°28·7'W	W	33,40
Allt an Ime	Highld	NN4061	56°43·1'	4°36·4'W	W	42
Allt an Inbhir	Highld	NG8822	57°14·6'	5°30·4'W	W	33
Allt an Inbhir	Highld	NN0379	56°51·9'	5°13·5'W	W	41
Allt an Inbhir	Highld	NN2661	56°42·8'	4°50·1'W	W	41
Allt an Inbhire	Highld	NG6119	57°12·2'	5°57·0'W	W	32
Allt an Inbhire	Highld	NM6555	56°37·9'	5°49·5'W	W	49
Alltan Iomhair	Highld	NC3340	58°19·3'	4°50·6'W	W	9
Allt an Iuil	Highld	NH5600	57°4·4'	4°22·1'W	W	35
Allt an Lagain	Highld	NC4059	58°29·7'	4°44·2'W	W	9
Allt an Lagain	Highld	NG7201	57°2·9'	5°45·1'W	W	33
Allt an Lagain	Highld	NN3097	57°2·2'	4°47·6'W	W	34
Allt an Lagain	Highld	NN3662	56°43·5'	4°40·4'W	W	41
Allt an Laghair	Highld	NH2121	57°14·9'	4°57·6'W	W	25
Allt an Laoigh	Arg & Bt	NM4822	56°19·7'	6°4·1'W	W	48
Allt an Laoigh	Highld	NC2222	58°9·3'	5°1·0'W	W	15
Allt an Laoigh	Highld	NC4125	58°11·4'	4°41·8'W	W	16
Allt an Laoigh	Highld	NC4919	58°8·3'	4°33·4'W	W	16
Allt an Lapain	Highld	NH0015	57°11·2'	5°18·1'W	W	33
Alltan Leacach	Highld	NC4311	58°3·9'	4°39·2'W	W	16
Alltan Leacach	Highld	NC5238	58°18·6'	4°31·1'W	W	16
Allt an Learanaich	Highld	ND1333	58°16·9'	3°28·5'W	W	11,17
Allt an Leoghair	Highld	NN0290	56°57·8'	5°15·0'W	W	33
Allt an Leòid Ghaineamhaich	Highld	NG9924	57°16·0'	5°19·5'W	W	25,33
Allt an Leth-ghlinne	Arg & Bt	NM3418	56°17·1'	6°17·4'W	W	48
Allt an Liadain	Highld	NM7043	56°31·6'	5°43·9'W	W	49
Allt an Loch	Aberd	NO1982	56°55·6'	3°19·4'W	W	43
Allt an Lochain Duibh	Highld	NN6399	57°4·0'	4°15·1'W	W	35
Allt an Loch Ghuirm	Highld	NH4732	57°21·4'	4°32·1'W	W	26
Allt an Loch Sgeirich	Highld	NH2472	57°42·5'	4°56·8'W	W	20
Allt an Loin	Arg & Bt	NN1221	56°20·9'	5°2·1'W	W	50,56
Allt an Lòin	Highld	NH4639	57°25·2'	4°33·4'W	W	26
Allt an Lòin	Highld	NM6993	56°58·5'	5°47·6'W	W	40
Allt an Lòin	Highld	NN2178	56°51·8'	4°55·7'W	W	41
Allt an Lòin Bhàin	Highld	NC2258	58°28·7'	5°2·7'W	W	9
Allt an Lòin Bhàin	Highld	NH3594	57°54·6'	4°46·6'W	W	20
Allt an Lòin Chaoil	Highld	NC5461	58°31·0'	4°29·9'W	W	10
Allt an Lòin Duibh	Highld	NC1609	58°2·2'	5°6·5'W	W	15
Allt an Lòin Duibh	Highld	NC2709	58°2·5'	4°55·4'W	W	15
Allt an Lòin Duibh	Highld	NG8322	57°14·5'	5°35·3'W	W	33
Allt an Lòin-fhiodha	Highld	NH0636	57°22·7'	5°13·2'W	W	25
Allt an Lòin Mhóir	Arg & Bt	NM9423	56°21·5'	5°19·6'W	W	49
Allt an Loin Ruaidh	Highld	NG3851	57°28·7'	6°21·8'W	W	23
Allt an Lòin Tharsuinn	Highld	NC7233	58°16·3'	4°10·5'W	W	16
Allt an Lòn Biolaireich	Arg & Bt	NM5044	56°31·6'	6°3·5'W	W	47,48
Allt an Luchda	Highld	NH2291	57°52·6'	4°59·6'W	W	20
Allt an Luib Bhaide	Pth & Kin	NN5365	56°45·5'	4°23·8'W	W	42
Allt an Lùib Ghiubhais	Highld	NH2430	57°19·9'	4°55·0'W	W	25
Alltan Mhic Aoidh	Highld	NN0858	56°40·7'	5°7·6'W	X	41
Alltan Mór	Arg & Bt	NM9608	56°13·5'	5°17·0'W	W	55
Alltan na Beinne	Aberd	NO0896	57°3·0'	3°30·5'W	W	36,43
Alltan na Creige	Highld	NC6157	58°29·0'	4°22·6'W	W	10
Alltan na Criche	Highld	NC2361	58°30·3'	5°1·8'W	W	9
Alltan na Feòla	Highld	NH0850	57°30·2'	5°11·8'W	W	25
Alltan na Fithriach	Highld	NC0232	58°14·2'	5°21·9'W	W	15
Alltan Odhar	Aberd	NO0781	56°54·9'	3°31·2'W	W	43
Alltan Odhar	Highld	NG9547	57°28·3'	5°24·7'W	W	25
Alltan Odhar	Highld	NH0428	57°18·3'	5°14·8'W	W	25,33
Allt an Oir	Arg & Bt	NR4877	55°55·5'	6°1·6'W	W	60,61
Allt an Ràsail	Highld	NC4607	58°1·8'	4°36·0'W	W	16
Allt an Rathain Ruaidh	Highld	NH5517	57°13·5'	4°23·6'W	W	35
Allt an Réidh Choire	Highld	NN4578	56°52·3'	4°32·1'W	W	42
Allt an Réidh-choire	Highld	NN5372	56°49·2'	4°24·1'W	W	42
Allt an Réidhe	Highld	NC7755	58°28·2'	4°6·1'W	W	10
Allt an Reidhean	Highld	NH4007	57°7·8'	4°38·2'W	W	34
Allt an Reidhe Ruaidh	Highld	NC8462	58°32·1'	3°59·1'W	W	10
Allt an Reinidh	Highld	NC3536	58°17·2'	4°48·4'W	W	15
Alltan Riabhach	Highld	NC2242	58°20·1'	5°1·9'W	W	9
Alltan Riabhach	Highld	NC2846	58°22·4'	4°56·0'W	W	9
Alltan Roy	Aberd	NO4791	57°0·7'	2°51·9'W	W	44
Alltan Ruadh	Highld	NC9753	58°27·5'	3°45·4'W	W	11
Allt an Ruadha Dheirg	Highld	NN2762	56°43·3'	4°49·2'W	W	41
Allt an Rubha	Highld	NG3902	57°2·4'	6°17·7'W	W	32,39
Allt an Rubha Ruaidh	Highld	NM5871	56°46·3'	5°57·2'W	W	39,47
Allt an Ruighe	Highld	NG9224	57°15·8'	5°26·5'W	W	25,33
Allt an Ruighe Bhric	Highld	NM6666	56°43·9'	5°49·1'W	W	40
Allt an Ruighe Dhuibh	Highld	NH2427	57°18·2'	4°54·8'W	W	25
Allt an Ruigh Ghil	Pth & Kin	NO0182	56°55·4'	3°37·1'W	W	43
Allt an Rund	Stir	NN2727	56°24·5'	4°47·8'W	W	50
Alltan Seibh	Aberd	NJ2503	57°7·0'	3°13·9'W	W	37
Allt an Sgàilean	Pth & Kin	NN5470	56°48·2'	4°23·0'W	W	42
Allt an Sgùlan	Highld	NG7020	57°13·0'	5°48·1'W	W	33
Allt an Stacain	Arg & Bt	NN1320	56°20·4'	5°1·1'W	W	50,56
Allt an Stalcair	Pth & Kin	NN6873	56°50·0'	4°9·4'W	W	42
Allt an Stuchdain	Highld	NG8322	57°14·5'	5°35·3'W	W	33
Allt an Tàillir	Arg & Bt	NN2122	56°21·6'	4°53·4'W	W	50
Allt an Tairbh	Arg & Bt	NN2536	56°29·3'	4°50·1'W	W	50
Allt an Tairbh	Arg & Bt	NR5588	56°1·6'	5°55·5'W	W	61
Allt an Tairbh	Arg & Bt	NR7430	55°30·9'	5°34·4'W	W	68
Allt an Tairbh	Pth & Kin	NN7516	56°19·5'	4°0·8'W	W	57
Allt an Tiaghaich	Highld	NC1523	58°9·7'	5°8·2'W	W	15
Allt an Tighearna	Highld	NH0446	57°28·0'	5°15·6'W	W	25
Allt an Tireidh	Highld	NC4431	58°14·7'	4°39·0'W	W	16
Allt an Toll-lochain	Highld	NH3390	57°52·4'	4°48·5'W	W	20
Allt an Tomain Odhair	Highld	NG8910	57°8·2'	5°28·8'W	W	33
Allt an Tormain	Arg & Bt	NS1077	55°57·2'	5°2·2'W	W	63
Allt an Torr Eun	Highld	NH6377	57°46·0'	4°17·7'W	W	21
Allt an Torr Fhearna	Highld	NN0575	56°49·8'	5°11·5'W	W	41
Allt an t-Sabhail	Highld	NG6224	57°15·0'	5°56·3'W	W	32
Allt an t-Sagairt	Arg & Bt	NR5373	55°53·5'	5°56·6'W	W	61
Allt an t-Sagairt	Highld	NM7881	56°52·3'	5°38·1'W	W	40
Allt an t-Sailean	Highld	NM6764	56°42·8'	5°48·0'W	W	40
Allt an t-Seachrain	Highld	NG7924	57°15·5'	5°39·4'W	W	33
Allt an t-Seangain	Pth & Kin	NN9739	56°32·2'	3°40·0'W	W	52,53
Allt an t-Seapail	Pth & Kin	NN8471	56°49·2'	3°53·6'W	W	43
Allt an t-Searraich	Arg & Bt	NR5274	55°54·0'	5°57·6'W	W	61
Allt an t-Seilich	Aberd	NO0085	56°57·0'	3°38·2'W	W	43
Allt an t - Sidhein	Arg & Bt	NN1718	56°19·4'	4°57·1'W	W	50,56

Allt an t-Sìdhein	Highld	NN3095	57°1·2′	4°47·6′W	W	34
Allt an t-Sionnaich	Aberd	NO0186	56°57·5′	3°37·2′W	W	43
Allt an t-Sionnaich	Aberd	NO0885	56°57·1′	3°30·3′W	W	43
Allt an t-Sìthein	Highld	NG4932	57°18·8′	6°9·6′W	W	32
Allt an t-Sithein	Highld	NG5725	57°15·3′	6°1·3′W	W	32
Allt an t-Slugain	Aberd	NO1394	57°2·0′	3°25·6′W	W	36,43
Allt an t-Slugain Dhuibh	Highld	NH8518	57°14·6′	3°53·9′W	W	35,36
Allt an t-Slugain Mhóir	Highld	NH8736	57°24·3′	3°52·4′W	W	27
Allt an t-Sluic	Highld	NN6286	56°56·9′	4°15·7′W	W	42
Allt an t-Sluic Bhrodaich	Arg & Bt	NR4674	55°53·8′	6°3·3′W	W	60,61
Allt an t- Sluice	N Ayr	NR9925	55°28·9′	5°10·4′W	W	69
Allt an t-Sluichd	Highld	NM9365	56°44·1′	5°22·6′W	W	40
Allt an t-Sluichd	Moray	NJ1203	57°6·8′	3°26·7′W	W	36
Allt an t-Sluichd Bhig	Moray	NJ1303	57°6·8′	3°25·7′W	W	36
Allt ant-Sluichd Mhoir	Aberd	NJ2717	57°14·5′	3°12·1′W	W	37
Allt an t-Sneachda	Aberd	NO1096	57°3·0′	3°28·6′W	W	36,43
Allt an t-Sneachda	Aberd	NO3387	56°58·4′	3°5·7′W	W	44
Allt an t-Sneachda	Highld	NN1876	56°50·7′	4°58·6′W	W	41
Allt an t-Sniomh	N Eil	NB4438	58°15·6′	6°21·4′W	W	8
Allt an t-Socaich	Arg & Bt	NR8658	55°46·3′	5°24·3′W	W	62
Allt an t-Sratha Bhig	Highld	NG5722	57°13·7′	6°1·1′W	W	32
Allt an t-Srath a Dhuibh	Highld	NC4833	58°15·8′	4°35·0′W	W	16
Allt an t-Srathain	Highld	NC1838	58°17·8′	5°5·9′W	W	15
Allt an t- Srathain	Highld	NC4963	58°32·0′	4°35·1′W	W	9
Allt an t-Srathain	Highld	NG7853	57°31·0′	5°42·0′W	W	24
Allt an t-Srathain	Highld	NH1196	57°55·1′	5°11·0′W	W	19
Allt an t-Srathain Mhóir	Highld	NH2754	57°32·8′	4°53·0′W	W	25
Allt an t-Strathain	Highld	NG7155	57°31·9′	5°49·1′W	W	24
Allt an Tùdair	Highld	NH7918	57°14·5′	3°59·8′W	W	35
Allt an Tuill Bhàin	Highld	NG9156	57°33·0′	5°29·1′W	W	25
Allt an Tuim	Highld	NM9282	56°53·2′	5°24·4′W	W	40
Allt an Tuim Bhric	Pth & Kin	NN6439	56°31·7′	4°12·2′W	W	51
Allt an Tùir	Highld	NC4503	57°59·6′	4°36·9′W	W	16
Allt an Tuirc	Arg & Bt	NR7336	55°34·1′	5°35·6′W	W	68
Allt an Tuirc	Highld	NN6277	56°52·1′	4°15·4′W	W	42
Allt an Tulaich	Highld	NN7691	56°59·9′	4°2·0′W	W	35
Allt an Uchd Bhuidhe	Highld	NG4627	57°16·0′	6°12·3′W	W	32
Allt an Uisge	Aberd	NO3286	56°57·9′	3°6·6′W	W	44
Allt an Ulbhaidh	Highld	NC4825	58°11·5′	4°34·7′W	W	16
Allt an Utha	Highld	NM8783	56°53·6′	5°29·4′W	W	40
Allt Aoil	Highld	ND0528	58°14·1′	3°36·6′W	W	17
Allt a' Phiobaire	Highld	NH0856	57°33·5′	5°12·1′W	W	25
Allt a' Phollain	Highld	NC2207	58°1·3′	5°0·4′W	W	15
Allt a' Phollain Riabhaich	Highld	NC1204	57°59·4′	5°10·3′W	W	15
Allt a' Phris-ghiubhais	Highld	NH9303	57°6·6′	3°45·5′W	W	36
Allt a' Phuill	Highld	NC6453	58°26·9′	4°19·3′W	W	10
Allt Arcabhi	Highld	NN0592	56°58·9′	5°12·1′W	W	33
Allt Ard Chàrna	Highld	NM6357	56°38·9′	5°51·5′W	W	49
Allt Arder	Moray	NJ1542	57°27·9′	3°24·6′W	W	28
Allt Ardnacross	Arg & Bt	NM5349	56°34·3′	6°0·8′W	W	47,48
Allt Ardvorlich	Arg & Bt	NN3111	56°15·9′	4°43·3′W	W	50,56
Allt Arnan	Arg & Bt	NN3018	56°19·7′	4°44·5′W	W	50,56
Alltarnog	Powys	SO0138	52°2·1′	3°26·2′W	X	160
Allt a' Sgàil	N Eil	NB1309	57°58·9′	6°50·9′W	W	13,14
Allt Atharaidh	Arg & Bt	NM5426	56°22·0′	5°58·6′W	W	48
Allt Ath Mhic Mhàirtein	Arg & Bt	NM8505	56°11·6′	5°27·5′W	W	55
Allt Aulich	Pth & Kin	NO0975	56°51·7′	3°29·1′W	W	43
Allt Bac a' Ghaill	N Eil	NB1705	57°56·9′	6°46·5′W	W	13,14
Allt Backlass	Highld	ND0741	58°21·1′	3°34·9′W	W	11,12
Allt Bac nan Laogh	Highld	NN2497	57°2·1′	4°53·6′W	W	34
Allt Bad a' Bhacaidh	Highld	NC4634	58°16·3′	4°37·1′W	W	16
Allt Badain	Highld	NC8150	58°25·6′	4°1·8′W	W	10
Allt Badair Dhonnadh	Highld	NC4002	57°59·0′	4°41·9′W	W	16
Allt Bad a' Mhonaidh	Aberd	NJ1600	57°5·3′	3°22·7′W	W	36
Allt Bad an Fhliuchaidh	Highld	NH2659	57°35·5′	4°54·2′W	W	25
Allt Bad an t-Seabhaig	Highld	NH3768	57°40·6′	4°43·5′W	W	20
Allt Bad Fionnaich	Highld	NH5714	57°11·9′	4°21·6′W	W	35
Allt Bad na h-Achlaise	Highld	NC6405	58°1·1′	4°17·7′W	W	16
Allt Bad nan Clach	Highld	NC5256	58°28·3′	4°31·8′W	W	10
Allt Bad na t-Sagairt	Highld	NC4310	58°3·3′	4°39·2′W	W	16
Allt Badour	Stir	NN4336	56°29·7′	4°32·6′W	W	51
Allt Bad Rabhain	Highld	NC5359	58°29·9′	4°30·9′W	W	10
Allt Bad Ra'fin	Highld	NC6418	58°8·1′	4°18·1′W	W	16
Allt Bad Thearaig	Highld	NC8344	58°22·4′	3°59·5′W	W	10
Allt Bà-finne	N Eil	NF8573	57°38·5′	7°16·3′W	W	18
Allt Bail' a' Ghobhainn	Arg & Bt	NN0710	56°14·9′	5°6·5′W	W	50,56
Allt Bail' a' Mhuilinn	Highld	NH2956	57°34·0′	4°51·1′W	W	25
Allt Bail a' Mhuilinn	Pth & Kin	NN5743	56°33·7′	4°19·2′W	W	51
Allt Bail an t-Soar	Highld	NC6848	58°24·3′	4°15·1′W	W	10
Allt Bail' an Tuim Bhuidhe	Highld	NH2814	57°11·3′	4°50·3′W	W	34
Allt Baile na Creige	Highld	NH3051	57°31·3′	4°49·9′W	W	26
Allt Baile nan Carn	Highld	NH2715	57°11·9′	4°51·4′W	W	34
Allt Ballach	Highld	NH6401	57°5·1′	4°14·2′W	W	35
Allt Bàn	Highld	NG4733	57°19·3′	6°11·7′W	W	32
Allt Bàn	Highld	NG9606	57°6·2′	5°21·6′W	W	33
Allt Bàn	Highld	NH9909	57°9·9′	3°39·7′W	W	36
Allt Bàn	Highld	NN3984	56°55·4′	4°38·3′W	W	34,41
Allt Bàn an Lì-ruighe	Highld	NG9726	57°17·0′	5°21·6′W	W	25,33
Allt Barr Mhin	Arg & Bt	NN2532	56°27·1′	4°49·9′W	W	50
Allt Batavaim	Stir	NN4036	56°29·6′	4°35·5′W	W	51
Allt Beag	Arg & Bt	NM9510	56°14·6′	5°18·1′W	W	55
Allt Beag	Highld	NC7862	58°32·0′	4°5·2′W	W	10
Allt Beag	Highld	NG7444	57°26·1′	5°45·5′W	W	24
Allt Beag	Highld	NH6928	57°19·7′	4°10·1′W	W	26,35
Allt Bealach a' Ghoire	Highld	NN4687	56°57·2′	4°31·5′W	W	34,42
Allt Bealach an Fhuarain	Highld	NC5127	58°12·7′	4°31·7′W	W	16
Allt Bealach Crudhain	Highld	NH0643	57°26·4′	5°13·5′W	W	25
Allt Bealach Easain	Highld	NN2297	57°2·0′	4°55·5′W	W	34
Allt Bealach na h-Eangair	Highld	NM9196	57°0·7′	5°26·1′W	W	33,40
Allt Bealach na h-Imrich	N Eil	NB2817	58°3·8′	6°36·2′W	W	13,14
Allt Bealach na h-Innsig	Arg & Bt	NN0748	56°35·3′	5°8·1′W	W	50
Allt Bealach na h-Oidhche	Highld	NG8414	57°10·2′	5°33·9′W	W	33
Allt Bealach nan Cas	Highld	NG6711	57°8·1′	5°50·6′W	W	32
Allt Bealach Odhar	Highld	NH2208	57°8·0′	4°56·0′W	W	34
Allt Bealach Raonasgail	N Eil	NB0325	58°7·1′	7°2·2′W	W	13
Allt Bealaich Ruaidh	Arg & Bt	NM8900	56°9·0′	5°23·4′W	W	55
Allt Beinn a' Chuirn	Highld	NG8621	57°14·0′	5°32·3′W	W	33
Allt Beinn Chlianaig	Highld	NN2778	56°51·9′	4°49·8′W	W	41
Allt Beinn Deirge	Highld	NG6122	57°13·8′	5°57·1′W	W	32
Allt Beinn Dònuill	Highld	NH2299	57°57·0′	5°0·0′W	W	20
Allt Beinn Eilde	Highld	NN5583	56°55·2′	4°22·5′W	W	42
Allt Beinn Iutharn	Aberd	NO0780	56°54·4′	3°31·2′W	W	43
Allt Beinn Losgarnaich	Pth & Kin	NN8377	56°52·4′	3°54·7′W	W	43
Allt Beith	Highld	NC4046	58°22·7′	4°43·7′W	W	9
Allt Beith a' Mheadhoin	Highld	NC3844	58°21·5′	4°45·7′W	W	9
Allt Beithe	Arg & Bt	NM5535	56°26·9′	5°58·1′W	W	47,48
Allt Beithe	Highld	NC3735	58°16·7′	4°46·3′W	W	16
Allt Beithe	Highld	NG8888	57°50·1′	5°33·8′W	W	19
Alltbeithe	Highld	NH0207	57°6·9′	5°15·8′W	X	33
Alltbeithe	Highld	NH0720	57°14·1′	5°11·4′W	X	25,33
Allt Beithe	Highld	NH1479	57°46·0′	5°7·2′W	W	20
Allt Beithe	Highld	NH3377	57°45·4′	4°47·9′W	W	20
Allt Beithe	Highld	NM6565	56°43·3′	5°50·0′W	W	40
Allt Beitheach	Highld	NM7552	56°36·6′	5°39·5′W	W	49
Allt Beithe Beag	Highld	NN3694	57°0·7′	4°41·6′W	W	34
Allt Beithe Beag	Pth & Kin	NN4551	56°37·8′	4°31·2′W	W	42,51
Allt Beithe Garbh	Highld	NH0621	57°14·6′	5°12·5′W	W	25,33
Allt Beithe Min	Highld	NH0721	57°14·6′	5°11·5′W	W	25,33
Allt Beithe Mór	Highld	NN3794	57°0·8′	4°40·6′W	W	34
Allt Beithe Mór	Pth & Kin	NN4349	56°36·7′	4°33·0′W	W	51
Allt Beochlich	Arg & Bt	NN0315	56°17·5′	5°10·5′W	W	50,55
Allt Beul an Sporain	Highld	NN6179	56°53·2′	4°16·4′W	W	42
Allt Beul-àth nan Sachd	Highld	NG4033	57°19·1′	6°18·6′W	W	32
Allt Bhaic	Pth & Kin	NN8464	56°45·5′	3°53·4′W	W	43
Allt Bhàn	Highld	NN1988	56°57·1′	4°58·1′W	W	34,41
Allt Bharainn	Arg & Bt	NN0649	56°35·8′	5°9·2′W	W	50
Allt Bheadhair	Highld	NJ0411	57°11·0′	3°34·8′W	W	36
Allt Bheargais	Highld	NH3585	57°49·7′	4°46·2′W	W	20
Allt Bheithachan	Moray	NJ1412	57°11·7′	3°24·9′W	W	36
Allt Bheithe	Highld	NN3563	56°44·0′	4°41·4′W	W	41
Allt Bhionasgro	N Eil	NB2545	58°18·7′	6°41·3′W	W	8
Allt Bhlaich Mhóir	Highld	NN0375	56°49·7′	5°13·3′W	W	41
Allt Bhlàraidh	Highld	NH3617	57°13·1′	4°42·5′W	W	34
Allt Bholagair	N Eil	NF7930	57°15·1′	7°18·9′W	W	22
Allt Bhrachain	Pth & Kin	NN6149	56°37·0′	4°15·5′W	W	51
Allt Bhran	Highld	NN7789	56°58·8′	4°1·0′W	W	42
Allt Bhreacnais	Arg & Bt	NN2944	56°33·7′	4°46·5′W	W	50
Allt Bhrodainn	Highld	NN7484	56°56·1′	4°3·8′W	W	42
Allt Bhronn	Aberd	NO0184	56°56·5′	3°37·2′W	W	43
Allt Bhuailteach	Highld	ND1230	58°15·3′	3°29·5′W	W	11,17
Allt Bhuidheanach	Pth & Kin	NN6778	56°52·7′	4°10·5′W	W	42
Allt Bhuinne	Pth & Kin	NN6348	56°36·5′	4°13·5′W	W	51
Allt Bhuruisgidh	Highld	NH2113	57°10·6′	4°57·2′W	W	34
Allt Blaen-hauliw	Carm	SN5336	52°0·4′	4°8·1′W	F	146
Allt Blaravon	Arg & Bt	NN2643	56°33·1′	4°49·4′W	W	50
Allt Blarghour	Arg & Bt	NN0212	56°15·8′	5°11·4′W	W	50,55
Allt Boeth	Carm	SN3139	52°1·7′	4°27·4′W	X	145
Allt Bohenie	Highld	NN3083	56°54·7′	4°47·1′W	W	34,41
Allt Boidheach	Highld	NN3078	56°52·0′	4°46·9′W	W	41
Allt Bolinn	Highld	NH2501	57°4·3′	4°52·7′W	W	34
Allt Bó-Loin	Highld	NN2683	56°54·6′	4°51·0′W	W	34,41
Allt Bò Nighean Mhuirich	N Eil	NB1121	58°5·3′	6°53·8′W	W	13,14
Allt Borgidh Beag	Highld	NC6757	58°29·1′	4°16·4′W	W	10
Allt Braenerich	Highld	NH8326	57°18·8′	3°56·1′W	W	35
Allt Braesgill	Highld	NC4956	58°28·2′	4°34·9′W	W	9
Allt Braglenmore	Arg & Bt	NM9118	56°18·8′	5°22·3′W	W	55
Allt Brander	Arg & Bt	NN0529	56°25·0′	5°9·2′W	W	50
Allt Breabaig	Highld	NH1673	57°42·8′	5°4·9′W	W	20
Allt Breac	Highld	NC9520	58°9·7′	3°46·6′W	W	17
Allt Breac	Highld	NH8538	57°25·3′	3°54·4′W	W	27
Allt Breac	Highld	NJ0632	57°22·4′	3°33·3′W	W	27,36
Allt Breaclaich	Stir	NN6133	56°28·4′	4°14·9′W	W	51
Allt Breac-nic	Stir	NN6012	56°17·0′	4°15·3′W	W	57
Allt Breakachy	Highld	NN6391	56°59·7′	4°14·9′W	W	35
Allt Breineag	Highld	NH4708	57°8·5′	4°31·3′W	W	34
Allt Breisleich	Pth & Kin	NN5642	56°33·1′	4°20·1′W	W	51
Allt Breugach	Highld	NC8646	58°23·5′	3°56·5′W	W	10
Allt Briste	Highld	NC2262	58°30·9′	5°2·9′W	W	9
Allt Briste	Highld	NC2434	58°15·8′	4°59·5′W	W	15
Allt Broighleachan	Arg & Bt	NN2333	56°27·6′	4°51·9′W	W	50
Allt Bruachaig	Highld	NH8430	57°21·0′	3°55·2′W	W	27
Allt Bruachaig	Highld	NH8529	57°20·5′	3°54·2′W	W	35,36
Allt Bruthach an Easain	Highld	NG9976	57°44·0′	5°22·1′W	W	19
Allt Bryn-Llywelyn	Carm	SN5236	52°0·4′	4°9·0′W	F	146
Allt Buidhe	Arg & Bt	NN0244	56°33·0′	5°12·8′W	W	50
Allt Buidhe	Arg & Bt	NR7742	55°37·5′	5°32·1′W	W	62,69
Allt Buidhe	Highld	NM8092	56°58·3′	5°36·7′W	W	33,40
Allt Buidhe Mór	Highld	NM7750	56°35·6′	5°37·5′W	W	49
Allt Bun an Eas	Arg & Bt	NR4576	55°54·8′	6°4·4′W	W	60,61
Allt Bun an Easa	Arg & Bt	NM4322	56°19·5′	6°9·0′W	W	48
Allt Bunbruach	Pth & Kin	NO0159	56°43·0′	3°36·6′W	W	52,53
Allt Bun Chorcabhaig	N Eil	NB2503	57°56·2′	6°38·3′W	W	13,14
Allt Burican	N Ayr	NR9426	55°29·3′	5°15·2′W	W	68,69
Allt Cadha Cleit	N Eil	NB2615	58°2·6′	6°38·1′W	W	13,14
Allt Cadh an Eas	Highld	NG8633	57°20·5′	5°32·9′W	W	24
Allt Cae-dû	Powys	SH9912	52°42·0′	3°29·3′W	H	125
Allt-cae-melyn	Powys	SN7697	52°33·6′	3°49·4′W	X	135
Allt Caile	Pth & Kin	NN4952	56°38·4′	4°27·3′W	W	42,51
Alltcailleach	Aberd	NO3492	57°1·1′	3°4·8′W	X	44
Alltcailleach Forest	Aberd	NO3392	57°1·1′	3°5·8′W	F	44
Allt Caillich	Arg & Bt	NR6735	55°33·4′	5°41·2′W	W	68
Allt Cailliche	Pth & Kin	NN3742	56°32·8′	4°38·6′W	W	50
Allt Caillte	Highld	NG7517	57°11·6′	5°43·0′W	W	33
Allt Cailtidh	Highld	NH6121	57°15·8′	4°17·8′W	W	26,35
Allt Calder	Highld	NH6817	57°13·7′	4°10·7′W	W	35
Allt Calg Choire	Highld	NG8604	57°4·9′	5°31·4′W	W	33
Allt Cam	Highld	NH0828	57°18·4′	5°10·8′W	W	25,33
Allt Càm	Highld	NN2478	56°51·9′	4°52·8′W	W	41
Allt Cam	Highld	NN4477	56°51·8′	4°33·1′W	W	42
Allt Cam	Highld	NN5178	56°52·4′	4°26·2′W	W	42
Allt Camas a' Choirce	Highld	NM7762	56°42·1′	5°38·1′W	W	40
Allt Camas Bhlathain	Highld	NM7667	56°44·7′	5°39·3′W	W	40
Allt Camaslaidh	Pth & Kin	NN4643	56°33·5′	4°29·9′W	W	51
Allt Camas na Croise	Highld	NN0675	56°49·8′	5°10·3′W	W	41
Allt Cam-bàn	Highld	NH0417	57°12·4′	5°14·2′W	W	33
Allt Cam Bàn	Highld	NH5606	57°7·6′	4°22·3′W	W	35
Allt Càm Bhealaich	Highld	NN2093	56°59·8′	4°57·3′W	W	34
Allt Cam Carach	Highld	NM6688	56°55·7′	5°50·3′W	W	40
Allt Cam Carach	Highld	NM6890	56°56·8′	5°48·4′W	W	40
Allt Camghanaidh	Highld	NM9888	56°56·6′	5°18·8′W	W	40
Allt Càm Ghlinne	Highld	NN2452	56°37·9′	4°51·7′W	W	41
Allt Camghouran	Pth & Kin	NN5354	56°39·5′	4°23·4′W	W	42,51
Allt Cam nan Aighean	Highld	NN3067	56°46·1′	4°46·4′W	W	41
Allt Cam nan Cròc	Highld	NH5907	57°8·2′	4°19·3′W	W	35
Allt Caochan an t-Seilich	Pth & Kin	NN5562	56°43·9′	4°21·8′W	W	42
Allt Caoiche	Highld	NH4940	57°25·8′	4°30·4′W	W	26
Allt Caoi-rain	Arg & Bt	NR7765	55°49·9′	5°33·2′W	W	62
Allt Caol	Highld	NC5258	58°29·4′	4°31·9′W	W	10
Allt Caol	Highld	ND1947	58°24·5′	3°22·7′W	W	11,12
Allt Caol	Highld	NM9484	56°54·4′	5°22·5′W	W	40
Allt Caol	Highld	NN4196	57°1·9′	4°36·7′W	W	34
Allt Caonich	Highld	NN0693	56°59·5′	5°11·2′W	W	33
Allt Caoruinn	Highld	NC1821	58°8·7′	5°5·1′W	W	15
Allt Car	Highld	NC4317	58°7·1′	4°39·4′W	W	16
Allt Car Beag	Highld	NC4614	58°5·6′	4°36·3′W	W	16
Allt Carnach	Pth & Kin	NO1569	56°48·5′	3°23·1′W	W	43
Allt Carnaich	Arg & Bt	NM9824	56°22·2′	5°15·8′W	W	49
Allt Carnaig	Stir	NN4520	56°21·1′	4°30·1′W	W	51,57
Allt Carn a' Mhaim	Aberd	NN9996	57°2·9′	3°39·4′W	W	36,43
Allt Carn Chaluim	Arg & Bt	NR8862	55°48·5′	5°22·6′W	W	62
Allt Carn na Ceardaich	Highld	NC3910	58°3·3′	4°43·2′W	W	16
Allt Carn na Fiacail	Highld	NH4223	57°16·5′	4°36·8′W	W	26
Allt Carra-lairige	Pth & Kin	NO1364	56°45·8′	3°24·9′W	W	43
Allt Cas a' Chuirn	Highld	NH2620	57°14·5′	4°52·6′W	W	25
Allt Casgro	N Eil	NB3448	58°20·7′	6°32·3′W	W	8
Allt Casgro	N Eil	NB5459	58°27·3′	6°12·5′W	W	8
Allt Cashlie	Pth & Kin	NN4843	56°33·5′	4°27·9′W	W	51
Allt Catanach	Highld	NJ1019	57°15·4′	3°29·1′W	W	36
Allt Ceann a' Chlàir	Highld	NN0779	56°52·0′	5°9·5′W	W	41
Allt Ceann Locha	Highld	NC3533	58°15·6′	4°48·3′W	W	15
Allt Ceitlein	Highld	NN1647	56°35·0′	4°59·3′W	W	50
Allt Chailleach	Highld	NN2856	56°40·1′	4°48·0′W	W	41
Allt Chaiseagall	Highld	NC5909	58°3·1′	4°22·9′W	W	16
Allt Chàiteag	Highld	ND1146	58°23·9′	3°30·9′W	W	11,12
Allt Chaldar	Pth & Kin	NN4759	56°42·1′	4°29·5′W	W	42,51
Allt Chall	Pth & Kin	NN4340	56°31·8′	4°32·7′W	W	51
Allt Challum	Stir	NN3933	56°28·0′	4°36·4′W	W	50
Allt Chaltuinn	Arg & Bt	NR7546	55°39·6′	5°34·2′W	W	62,69
Allt Chaluim	Arg & Bt	NN2521	56°21·2′	4°49·5′W	W	50,56
Allt Chaluim	Stir	NN4033	56°28·0′	4°35·4′W	W	51
Allt Chamasaidh	Highld	NH1756	57°33·7′	5°3·1′W	W	25
Allt Chaomhain	Arg & Bt	NM4523	56°20·1′	6°7·1′W	W	48
Allt Chaorach	Arg & Bt	NN2643	56°33·1′	4°49·4′W	W	50
Allt Chaorach Beag	Highld	NN3676	56°51·1′	4°40·9′W	W	41
Allt Chaorach Mór	Highld	NN3776	56°51·1′	4°39·9′W	W	41
Alltchaorunn	Highld	NN1950	56°36·7′	4°56·5′W	X	41
Allt Chapull-cloiche	Arg & Bt	NR8764	55°49·6′	5°23·6′W	W	62
Allt Charaidh	Highld	NH2734	57°22·1′	4°52·1′W	W	25
Allt Chàrnan	Highld	NN1351	56°37·1′	5°2·4′W	W	41
Allt Cheanna Mhuir	Highld	NN1092	56°59·1′	5°7·2′W	W	34
Allt Cheathaich	Stir	NN4034	56°28·5′	4°35·4′W	W	51
Allt Chernie	Aberd	NO3690	57°0·1′	3°2·8′W	W	44
Allt Chiorlaich	Pth & Kin	NN4840	56°31·9′	4°27·8′W	W	51
Allt Chnàimhean	Highld	NH0363	57°37·1′	5°17·4′W	W	19
Allt Choille-rais	Highld	NN2076	56°50·7′	4°56·6′W	W	41
Allt Choimhlidh	Highld	NN2376	56°50·8′	4°53·7′W	W	41
Allt Choinneachain	Pth & Kin	NN8227	56°25·5′	3°54·3′W	W	52
Allt Choire a' Bhalachain	Highld	NN1198	57°2·3′	5°6·4′W	W	34
Allt Choire a' Chait	Highld	NH1012	57°9·8′	5°8·1′W	W	34
Allt Choire Chaisil	Highld	NM9489	56°57·0′	5°22·8′W	W	40
Allt Choire Dhuibh	Arg & Bt	NN3434	56°28·4′	4°41·3′W	W	50
Allt Choire Leathanaidh	Pth & Kin	NN6670	56°48·4′	4°11·2′W	W	42
Allt Choire Mhuilinn	Highld	NM5164	56°42·3′	6°3·6′W	W	47
Allt Choire nan Clach	Highld	NG7120	57°13·1′	5°47·1′W	W	33
Allt Choire nan Con	Highld	NC5928	58°13·4′	4°23·6′W	W	16
Allt Choire nan Each	Highld	NM8151	56°36·2′	5°33·6′W	W	49
Allt Choire Odhair	Highld	NJ0624	57°18·1′	3°33·1′W	W	36
Allt Choire Shalachain	Highld	NM8053	56°37·3′	5°34·7′W	W	49
Allt Choire Shaùilegaich	Highld	NH6515	57°12·6′	4°13·7′W	W	35
Allt Cholzie	Aberd	NO3488	56°59·0′	3°4·7′W	W	44
Allt Chomhraig	Highld	NN8197	57°3·2′	3°57·3′W	W	35,43
Allt Chomraidh	Pth & Kin	NN4854	56°39·4′	4°28·3′W	W	42,51
Allt Chonnal	Highld	NN3894	57°0·8′	4°39·6′W	W	34
Allt Chreaga Dubha	Arg & Bt	NM4732	56°25·0′	6°5·7′W	W	48
Allt Chrianaig	N Eil	NB2931	58°11·3′	6°36·2′W	W	8,13
Allt Chriochaidh	Highld	NH8510	57°10·2′	3°53·7′W	W	35,36
Allt Chrioman	Arg & Bt	NM5347	56°33·3′	6°0·7′W	W	47,48
Allt Chriosdain	Moray	NJ1109	57°10·1′	3°27·8′W	W	36
Allt Chuil Bheaga	N Eil	NB3646	58°19·7′	6°30·1′W	W	8
Allt Chuimeanaich	Highld	NN5998	57°3·4′	4°19·0′W	W	35
Allt Chuirn	Highld	NJ0723	57°17·6′	3°32·1′W	W	36
Allt Cille Pheadair	Highld	NC9820	58°9·7′	3°43·5′W	W	17
Allt Cill-fhinn	Pth & Kin	NN8437	56°30·9′	3°52·7′W	W	52
Allt Cinn-locha	Arg & Bt	NR7879	55°57·4′	5°32·9′W	W	62
Allt Clachach	Highld	NH7280	57°47·7′	4°8·7′W	W	21
Allt Clachaig	Highld	NN3882	56°54·3′	4°39·2′W	W	34,41
Allt Clachanlaoigh	Stir	NS4598	56°9·2′	4°29·3′W	W	57
Allt Clach nan Taillear	Aberd	NN9897	57°3·4′	3°40·4′W	W	36,43
Allt Clais an t-Sabhail	Aberd	NN9496	57°2·8′	3°44·4′W	W	36,43
Allt Clais Damh	Highld	NN8385	56°56·7′	3°54·9′W	W	43
Allt Clais Eirigill	Highld	NC5266	58°33·7′	4°32·2′W	W	10
Allt Clais Fhiodha	Pth & Kin	NO0474	56°51·1′	3°34·0′W	W	43
Allt Clais Mhór	Pth & Kin	NO0574	56°51·1′	3°33·0′W	W	43
Allt Clais nam Balgair	Aberd	NO0598	57°4·1′	3°33·6′W	W	36,43
Allt Claonaidh	Highld	NC1205	57°59·9′	5°10·4′W	W	15
Allt Cleiteichean Mhiabhaig	N Eil	NB1716	58°2·8′	6°47·3′W	W	13,14
Allt Cloich Finne	Arg & Bt	NN1938	56°30·2′	4°56·0′W	W	50
Allt Cnoc Airigh an t-Seilich Bhig	Highld	NC6434	58°16·7′	4°18·7′W	W	16
Allt Cnoc an Tighe	Arg & Bt	NN2633	56°27·7′	4°49·0′W	W	50
Allt Cnoc Fhionn	Highld	NG8820	57°13·6′	5°30·3′W	W	33
Allt Cnoc na Cloiche	Highld	NC6831	58°15·1′	4°14·5′W	W	16
Allt Cnoc na Feannaige	Arg & Bt	NM4319	56°17·9′	6°8·8′W	W	48
Allt Cnoc nam Piob	Arg & Bt	NM4920	56°18·6′	6°3·1′W	W	48
Allt Cnoc nan Gall	Highld	NC9242	58°21·5′	3°50·3′W	W	11
Allt Coille Chill' a' Mhoraire	Arg & Bt	NM4447	56°33·0′	6°9·5′W	W	47,48
Allt Coir' a' Chliabhain	Highld	NH3375	57°44·3′	4°47·9′W	W	20
Allt Coir' a' Chruiteir	Highld	NC4034	58°16·2′	4°43·2′W	W	16

Allt Coir' a' Chùndrain	Highld	NH3778	57°46·0'	4°43·9'W	W	20
Allt Coir' a Ghobhainn	Highld	NG4032	57°18·5'	6°18·6'W	W	32
Allt Coir' a' Ghrunnda	Highld	NG4418	57°11·1'	6°13·7'W	W	32
Allt Coir' a' Mhadaidh	Highld	NG4325	57°14·9'	6°15·2'W	W	32
Allt Coir'an Eas	Highld	NC7125	58°12·0'	4°11·2'W	W	16
Allt Coir' an Fheidh	Highld	NC5726	58°12·2'	4°25·5'W	W	16
Allt Coir' an Longairt	Arg & Bt	NN2620	56°20·7'	4°48·5'W	W	50,56
Allt Coire a' Bhàinidh	Highld	NH0347	57°28·5'	5°16·7'W	W	25
Allt Coire a' Bhéin	Highld	NN5194	57°1·0'	4°26·8'W	W	35
Allt Coire a' Bheithe	Highld	NM9286	56°55·4'	5°24·6'W	W	40
Allt Coire a' Bhinnein	Highld	NN2367	56°45·9'	4°53·3'W	W	41
Allt Coire a' Bhric Beag	Highld	NN3365	56°45·1'	4°43·4'W	W	41
Allt Coire a' Bhric Mór	Highld	NN3162	56°43·4'	4°45·3'W	W	41
Allt Coire a' Bhuic	Arg & Bt	NN4147	56°35·5'	4°34·9'W	W	51
Allt Coire Achaladair	Arg & Bt	NN3242	56°32·7'	4°43·5'W	W	50
Allt Coire a' Chaolain	Highld	NN2147	56°35·1'	4°54·4'W	W	50
Allt Coire a' Chaorainn	Highld	NH0007	57°6·9'	5°17·7'W	W	33
Allt Coire a' Chaorainn Mór	Highld	NH5778	57°46·4'	4°23·8'W	W	21
Allt Coire a' Charra	Highld	NH0939	57°24·3'	5°10·3'W	W	25
Allt Coire à Chearcaill	Pth & Kin	NN6749	56°37·1'	4°9·6'W	W	51
Allt Coire a' Chlachair	Highld	NN4679	56°52·9'	4°31·2'W	W	42
Allt Coire a' Chroisg	Pth & Kin	NN7614	56°18·4'	3°59·8'W	W	57
Allt Coire a' Chùil Droma Bhig	Highld	NH0310	57°8·6'	5°14·9'W	W	33
Allt Coire a' Chùil Droma Mhóir	Highld	NH0310	57°8·6'	5°14·9'W	W	33
Allt Coire a' Ghathalach	Arg & Bt	NN3339	56°31·1'	4°42·4'W	W	50
Allt Coire a' Ghiubhais	Pth & Kin	NN4762	56°43·7'	4°29·6'W	W	42
Allt Coireag Searrach	Highld	NH0031	57°19·8'	5°18·9'W	W	25
Allt Coire a' Mhàil	Highld	NN1767	56°45·8'	4°59·2'W	W	41
Allt Coire a' Mhàim	Highld	NH1231	57°20·1'	5°6·9'W	W	25
Allt Coire a' Mhile	Highld	NC6922	58°10·3'	4°13·2'W	W	16
Allt Coire a' Mhór-fhir	Pth & Kin	NN5261	56°43·3'	4°24·7'W	W	42
Allt Coire a' Mhór-fhir	Pth & Kin	NN9839	56°32·2'	3°39·1'W	W	52,53
Allt Coire a' Mhuilinn	Highld	NN1167	56°45·6'	5°5·1'W	W	41
Allt Coire a' Mhuill	Highld	NG9917	57°12·2'	5°19·2'W	W	33
Allt Coire a' Mhusgain	Highld	NN1566	56°45·2'	5°1·1'W	W	41
Allt Coire an Dothaidh	Arg & Bt	NN3039	56°31·0'	4°45·3'W	W	50
Allt Coire an Dubh-chadha	Highld	NN7282	56°55·0'	4°5·7'W	W	42
Allt Coire an Easain	Highld	NN2548	56°35·7'	4°50·6'W	W	50
Allt Coire an Eich	Highld	NH5505	57°7·0'	4°23·2'W	W	35
Allt Coire an Eich	Highld	NM9392	56°58·6'	5°23·9'W	W	33,40
Allt Coire an Eoin	Highld	NN2175	56°50·2'	4°55·6'W	W	41
Allt Coire an Fhàidhe	Pth & Kin	NN6515	56°18·8'	4°10·5'W	W	57
Allt Coire an Laoigh	Pth & Kin	NO0965	56°46·3'	3°28·9'W	W	43
Allt Coire an Lightuinn	Highld	NN1182	56°53·7'	5°5·7'W	W	34,41
Allt Coire an Lochain	Arg & Bt	NN3645	56°34·4'	4°39·7'W	W	50
Allt Coire an Lochain	Highld	NH1228	57°18·5'	5°6·8'W	W	25
Allt Coire an Lochain	Highld	NN1474	56°49·5'	5°2·4'W	W	41
Allt Coire an Ruighe	Highld	NH4724	57°17·1'	4°31·8'W	W	26
Allt Coire an Sgàirne	Highld	NH0020	57°13·9'	5°18·4'W	W	25,33
Allt Coire an Stangain Bhig	Highld	NN0396	57°1·0'	5°14·3'W	W	33
Allt Coire an t-Searraich	Highld	NM9192	56°58·6'	5°25·9'W	W	33,40
Allt Coire an t-Seilich	Aberd	NN9485	56°56·9'	3°44·1'W	W	43
Allt Coire an t-Seilich	Highld	NH5440	57°25·9'	4°25·5'W	W	26
Allt Coire an t-Seilich	Highld	NN2095	57°0·9'	4°57·4'W	W	34
Allt Coire an t-Slugain	Highld	NH0609	57°8·1'	5°11·9'W	W	33
Allt Coire an t-Slugain	Highld	NN4992	56°59·9'	4°28·7'W	W	34
Allt Coire an t-Sneachda	Highld	NH2026	57°17·6'	4°58·8'W	W	25
Allt Coire an t-Sneachda	Highld	NH9805	57°7·7'	3°40·6'W	W	36
Allt Coire an t-Sreatha	Highld	NH6010	57°9·8'	4°18·4'W	W	35
Allt Coire an t-Suidhe	Highld	NM7966	56°44·3'	5°36·4'W	W	40
Allt Coire an Tuim	Highld	NM9483	56°53·8'	5°22·5'W	W	40
Allt Coire an Uinnseinn	Highld	NC3754	58°26·9'	4°47·1'W	W	9
Allt Coire a' Phris	Highld	NC3840	58°19·4'	4°45·5'W	W	9
Allt Coire Ardair	Highld	NN4589	56°58·2'	4°32·5'W	W	34,42
Allt Coire Ardrain	Stir	NN3923	56°22·6'	4°36·0'W	W	50
Allt Coire Attadale	Highld	NG7648	57°28·3'	5°43·7'W	W	24
Allt Coire Beinne Léithe	Highld	NG9852	57°31·1'	5°21·9'W	W	25
Allt Coire Beithe	Highld	NH2528	57°18·8'	4°53·9'W	W	25
Allt Coire Bhànain	Highld	NN4392	56°59·8'	4°34·6'W	W	34
Allt Coire Bhathaich	Highld	NN6583	56°55·4'	4°12·6'W	W	42
Allt Coire Bheachain	Highld	NH4373	57°43·4'	4°37·7'W	W	20
Allt Coire Bhearnaist	Aberd	NO0484	56°56·5'	3°34·2'W	W	43
Allt Coire Bheilg	Pth & Kin	NN7634	56°29·2'	4°0·4'W	W	51,52
Allt Coire Bhenneit	Highld	NH5583	57°49·1'	4°26·0'W	W	21
Allt Coire Bhiocair	Arg & Bt	NN2436	56°29·3'	4°51·1'W	W	50
Allt Coire Bhlàir	Highld	NN8891	57°0·1'	3°50·2'W	W	35,43
Allt Coire Bhran	Highld	NN8086	56°57·2'	3°57·9'W	W	43
Allt Coire Bó Chailein	Highld	NN2599	57°3·2'	4°52·7'W	W	34
Allt Coire Calvie	Highld	NH0439	57°24·2'	5°15·3'W	W	25
Allt Coire Ceirsle	Highld	NN2684	56°55·1'	4°51·1'W	W	34,41
Allt Coire Chailein	Arg & Bt	NN3234	56°28·4'	4°43·2'W	W	50
Allt Coire Chairbe	Highld	NH3145	57°28·1'	4°48·6'W	W	26
Allt Coire Chaoil	Highld	NN8693	57°1·1'	3°52·2'W	W	35,36,43
Allt Coire Chaorach	Arg & Bt	NN1843	56°32·9'	4°57·2'W	W	50
Allt Coire Chaorach	Stir	NN4524	56°23·2'	4°30·2'W	W	51
Allt Coire Cheap	Highld	NN4876	56°51·3'	4°29·1'W	W	42
Allt Coire Cheathaich	Arg & Bt	NS1182	55°59·9'	5°1·4'W	W	56
Allt Coire Cheathaich	Stir	NN4333	56°28·0'	4°32·5'W	W	51
Allt Coire Cheathaich	Stir	NN4622	56°22·2'	4°29·2'W	W	51
Allt Coire Chicheanais	Highld	NM9693	56°59·3'	5°21·0'W	W	33,40
Allt Coire Chlaiginn Mhóir	Highld	NH7211	57°10·6'	4°6·6'W	W	35
Allt Coire Chléirich	Highld	NH8007	57°8·6'	3°58·5'W	W	35
Allt Coire Choille-rais	Highld	NN1785	56°55·5'	5°0·0'W	W	34,41
Allt Coire Choille-rais	Highld	NN4485	56°56·1'	4°33·4'W	W	34,42
Allt Coire Chraoibhe	Highld	NN1584	56°54·9'	5°1·9'W	W	34,41
Allt Coire Chroisg	Stir	NN6018	56°20·3'	4°15·4'W	W	57
Allt Coire Chruitein	Arg & Bt	NN3337	56°30·0'	4°42·3'W	W	50
Allt Coire Chuaich	Highld	NN7086	56°57·1'	4°7·8'W	W	42
Allt Coire Chùirn	Highld	NN6479	56°53·2'	4°13·5'W	W	42
Allt Coire Chultrain	Pth & Kin	NN8331	56°27·7'	3°53·5'W	W	52
Allt Coire Creachainn	Arg & Bt	NN1130	56°25·7'	5°3·5'W	W	50
Allt Coire Cruach Sneachda	Pth & Kin	NN6753	56°39·3'	4°9·7'W	W	42,51
Allt Coire Crubaidh	Highld	NH0653	57°31·8'	5°14·0'W	W	25
Allt Coire Dail Aiteil	Highld	NG9633	57°20·8'	5°23·0'W	W	25
Allt Coire Dhearbhadh	Highld	NN2446	56°34·6'	4°51·5'W	W	50
Allt Coire Dhomhain	Pth & Kin	NN6074	56°50·4'	4°17·3'W	W	42
Allt Coire Dhorrcail	Highld	NG8404	57°4·8'	5°33·4'W	W	33
Allt Coire Dubhaig	Highld	NN6378	56°52·7'	4°14·4'W	W	42
Allt Coire Dubh-beag	Highld	NN3859	56°41·9'	4°38·3'W	W	41
Allt Coire Dubhchraig	Stir	NN3127	56°24·6'	4°43·9'W	W	50
Allt Coire Dubh-mór	Highld	NN3559	56°41·9'	4°41·2'W	W	41
Allt Coire Each	Highld	NG8005	57°5·3'	5°37·4'W	W	33
Allt Coire Eàrra Dheargan	Pth & Kin	NN5059	56°42·2'	4°26·6'W	W	42,51
Allt Coire Easaich	Highld	NH0327	57°17·7'	5°15·7'W	W	25,33
Allt Coire Easain	Highld	NN2471	56°48·1'	4°52·5'W	W	41
Allt Coire Easan	Pth & Kin	NN6169	56°47·8'	4°16·1'W	W	42
Allt Coire Eòghainn	Highld	NH2232	57°20·9'	4°57·0'W	W	25
Allt Coire Eòghainn	Highld	NN1669	56°46·8'	5°0·3'W	W	41
Allt Coire Fhàr	Highld	NN6077	56°52·1'	4°17·3'W	W	42
Allt Coire Fionn	Aberd	NO1578	56°53·4'	3°23·3'W	W	43
Allt Coire Follais	Highld	NH8905	57°7·6'	3°49·6'W	W	35,36
Allt Coire Forsaidh	Highld	NG6020	57°12·7'	5°58·0'W	W	32
Allt Coire Fraoich	Arg & Bt	NM6337	56°28·2'	5°50·4'W	W	49
Allt Coire Gabhail	Highld	NN1655	56°39·3'	4°59·7'W	W	41
Allt Coire Ghaidheil	Highld	NH1021	57°14·7'	5°8·5'W	W	25
Allt Coire Ghiubhasan	Highld	NN2149	56°36·2'	4°54·5'W	W	50
Allt Coire Ghiubhsachain	Highld	NM8876	56°49·9'	5°28·0'W	W	40
Allt Coire Ghlais	Arg & Bt	NN1129	56°25·2'	5°3·4'W	W	50
Allt Coire Giubhsachan	Highld	NN1870	56°47·4'	4°58·3'W	W	41
Allt Coiregrogain	Arg & Bt	NN2808	56°14·3'	4°46·1'W	W	56
Allt Coire Iain	Highld	NN2962	56°43·4'	4°47·2'W	W	41
Allt Coire Iain Oig	Highld	NN5198	57°3·2'	4°26·9'W	W	35
Allt Coire Ionndrainn	Highld	NN2785	56°55·7'	4°50·1'W	W	34,41
Allt Coire Lagain	Pth & Kin	NN9670	56°48·9'	3°41·8'W	W	43
Allt Coire Làgan	Highld	NG4319	57°11·6'	6°14·8'W	W	32
Allt Coire Lair	Arg & Bt	NN2224	56°22·7'	4°52·5'W	W	50
Allt Coire Làir	Highld	NH1211	57°9·3'	5°6·0'W	W	34
Allt Coire Laoigh	Stir	NN2825	56°23·4'	4°46·7'W	W	50
Allt Coire Leachavie	Highld	NH1323	57°15·8'	5°5·6'W	W	25
Allt Coire Legcaich	Arg & Bt	NN0845	56°33·7'	5°7·0'W	W	50
Allt Coire-lochain	Highld	NH0325	57°16·7'	5°15·6'W	W	25,33
Allt Coire Luidhearnaidh	Pth & Kin	NN6272	56°49·4'	4°15·2'W	W	42
Allt Coire Lundie	Highld	NH1511	57°9·4'	5°3·1'W	W	34
Allt Coire Lungard	Highld	NH0931	57°20·0'	5°9·9'W	W	25
Allt Coire Maol Chaluim	Arg & Bt	NN3648	56°36·0'	4°39·8'W	W	50
Allt Coire Mhàlagain	Highld	NG9210	57°8·3'	5°25·8'W	W	33
Allt Coire Mhàlagain	Highld	NG9613	57°10·0'	5°22·0'W	W	33
Allt Coire Mheadhoin	Highld	NH1615	57°11·6'	5°2·3'W	W	34
Allt Coire Mheadhoin	Highld	NN3572	56°48·9'	4°41·7'W	W	41
Allt Coire Mheall Challuim	Highld	NM9058	56°40·3'	5°25·2'W	W	49
Allt Coire Mheasan	Arg & Bt	NS1089	56°3·6'	5°2·7'W	W	56
Allt Coire Mhic Aonghais	Pth & Kin	NN4751	56°37·8'	4°29·2'W	W	42,51
Allt Coire Mhic Fhearchair	Highld	NG9463	57°36·9'	5°26·5'W	W	19
Allt Coire Mhicrail	Highld	NG9306	57°6·2'	5°24·6'W	W	33
Allt Coire Mhic-sith	Pth & Kin	NN6574	56°50·5'	4°12·3'W	W	42
Allt Coire Mhorair	Highld	NN1959	56°41·5'	4°56·9'W	W	41
Allt Coire Mhuilidh	Highld	NH3465	57°38·9'	4°46·4'W	W	20
Allt Coire Mhuillidh	Highld	NH2739	57°24·8'	4°52·4'W	W	25
Allt Coire Misirich	Highld	NH5168	57°40·9'	4°29·5'W	W	20
Allt Coire Mulrooney	Arg & Bt	NN0350	56°36·3'	5°12·1'W	W	41
Allt Coire na Bà	Highld	NN1963	56°43·7'	4°57·1'W	W	41
Allt Coire na Ceardaich	Highld	NN5883	56°55·3'	4°19·5'W	W	42
Allt Coire na Céire	Highld	NH4100	57°4·1'	4°36·9'W	W	34
Allt Coire na Ciche	Highld	NM8895	57°0·1'	5°29·0'W	W	33,40
Allt Coire na Cloiche	Highld	NH0821	57°14·6'	5°10·5'W	W	25,33
Allt Coire na Cloiche	Highld	NH5781	57°48·0'	4°23·9'W	W	21
Allt Coire na Cloiche	Pth & Kin	NN4769	56°47·5'	4°29·8'W	W	42
Allt Coire na Còir	Highld	NN7887	56°57·8'	3°59·9'W	W	42
Allt Coire na Còsaig	Highld	NN4274	56°50·1'	4°34·9'W	W	42
Allt Coire na Creadha	Highld	NH1607	57°7·3'	5°1·9'W	W	34
Allt Coire na Creiche	Highld	NM8561	56°41·7'	5°30·2'W	W	40
Allt Coire na Cruaiche	Highld	NM9198	57°1·8'	5°26·2'W	W	33,40
Allt Coire na Duibhe	Highld	NN2361	56°42·7'	4°53·1'W	W	41
Allt Coire na Faochaige	Highld	NH2141	57°25·7'	4°58·4'W	W	25
Allt Coire na Feàrna	Highld	NC6225	58°11·8'	4°20·4'W	W	16
Allt Coire na Féithe Bige	Pth & Kin	NN5969	56°47·7'	4°18·1'W	W	42
Allt Coire na Gabhalach	Highld	NN2067	56°45·9'	4°56·2'W	W	41
Allt Coire na Garidha	Pth & Kin	NN6069	56°47·8'	4°17·1'W	W	42
Allt Coire na Làrach	Arg & Bt	NN1141	56°31·6'	5°3·9'W	W	50
Allt Coire na Leacaich	Highld	NM9076	56°49·9'	5°26·1'W	W	40
Allt Coire na Longairt	Highld	NN5580	56°53·6'	4°22·4'W	W	42
Allt Coire nam Bràthan	Highld	NH3137	57°23·8'	4°48·3'W	W	26
Allt Coire nam Bruadaran	Highld	NG5225	57°15·2'	6°6·2'W	W	32
Allt Coire nam Eirecheanach	Highld	NH0409	57°8·1'	5°13·9'W	W	33
Allt Coire nam Fear Riabhach	Highld	NH1269	57°40·6'	5°8·7'W	W	19
Allt Coire nam Freumh	Aberd	NJ2703	57°7·0'	3°11·9'W	W	37
Allt Coire nam Frithallt	Highld	NM8859	56°40·7'	5°27·2'W	W	49
Allt Coire nam Fuaran	Arg & Bt	NM6636	56°27·7'	5°47·5'W	W	49
Allt Coire nam Mart	Highld	NN8192	57°0·5'	3°57·1'W	W	35,43
Allt Coire nam Moine	Stir	NN4431	56°27·0'	4°31·4'W	W	51
Allt Coire na Mòine	Highld	NC8002	57°59·7'	4°1·3'W	W	17
Allt Coire nam Plaidean	Highld	NN5582	56°54·7'	4°22·4'W	W	42
Allt Coire nan Aonach	Highld	NH6109	57°9·3'	4°17·4'W	W	35
Allt Coire nan Arr	Highld	NG7943	57°25·7'	5°40·4'W	W	24
Allt Coire nan Cadhan	Highld	NG9047	57°28·1'	5°29·7'W	W	25
Allt Coire nan Capull	Highld	NM8664	56°43·4'	5°29·4'W	W	40
Allt Coire nan Cnàmh	Highld	NG9704	57°5·2'	5°20·6'W	W	33
Allt Coire nan Con	Highld	NM8269	56°46·0'	5°33·6'W	W	40
Allt Coire nan Cuilean	Highld	NG7320	57°13·1'	5°45·1'W	W	33
Allt Coire nan Dearcag	Highld	NN5597	57°2·7'	4°23·0'W	W	35
Allt Coire nan Dearcag	Highld	NN7788	56°58·3'	4°0·9'W	W	42
Allt Coire nan Each	Highld	NH2745	57°28·0'	4°52·6'W	W	25
Allt Coire nan Each	Stir	NN3732	56°27·4'	4°38·3'W	W	50
Allt Coire nan Gabhar	Arg & Bt	NM5336	56°27·3'	6°0·1'W	W	47,48
Allt Coire nan Gall	Highld	NM9288	56°56·5'	5°24·7'W	W	40
Allt Coire nan Gall	Highld	NM9297	57°1·3'	5°25·2'W	W	33,40
Allt Coire nan Gall	Highld	NN4989	56°58·3'	4°28·6'W	W	34,42
Allt Coire nan Gall	Highld	NN4990	56°58·9'	4°28·6'W	W	34
Allt Coire nan Giomach	Pth & Kin	NN4562	56°43·7'	4°31·6'W	W	42
Allt Coire nan Laogh	Highld	NG4518	57°11·2'	6°12·8'W	W	32
Allt Coire nan Laogh	Highld	NH1659	57°35·3'	5°4·2'W	W	25
Allt Coire nan Laogh	Highld	NH1660	57°35·8'	5°4·3'W	W	20
Allt Coire nan Laogh	Highld	NM9699	57°2·5'	5°21·3'W	W	33,40
Allt Coire nan Leac	Highld	NH0806	57°6·6'	5°9·8'W	W	33
Allt Coire nan Saobhaidh	Highld	NN1897	57°2·0'	4°59·5'W	W	34
Allt Coire nan Uth	Highld	NM9394	56°59·7'	5°24·0'W	W	33,40
Allt Coire na Saidhe Duibhe	Highld	NC4835	58°16·9'	4°35·1'W	W	16
Allt Coire na Sgùile	Highld	NH2645	57°28·0'	4°53·6'W	W	25
Allt Coire na Sleaghaich	Highld	NH2945	57°28·0'	4°50·6'W	W	25
Allt Coire na Stri	Highld	NH6308	57°8·8'	4°15·4'W	W	35
Allt Coire Odhair	Arg & Bt	NM9722	56°21·1'	5°16·7'W	W	49
Allt Coire Odhair	Arg & Bt	NN2303	56°11·5'	4°50·7'W	W	56
Allt Coire Odhair	Highld	NN2646	56°34·7'	4°49·5'W	W	50
Allt Coire Peitireach	Highld	NH0303	57°4·8'	5°14·6'W	W	33
Allt Coire Pheiginn	Pth & Kin	NN7251	56°38·3'	4°4·8'W	W	42,51,52
Allt Coire Phìobaire	Highld	NN7495	57°2·0'	4°4·1'W	W	35
Allt Coire Pitridh	Highld	NN4780	56°53·4'	4°30·2'W	W	34,42
Allt Coire Preas nan Seana-char	Highld	NH4280	57°47·2'	4°39·0'W	W	20
Allt Coire Rath	Highld	NN2571	56°48·1'	4°51·5'W	W	41
Allt Coire Rèidh	Highld	NM7458	56°39·8'	5°40·8'W	W	49
Allt Coire Roill	Highld	NG8952	57°30·8'	5°30·9'W	W	24
Allt Coire Ruadh-staca	Highld	NG9661	57°35·8'	5°24·4'W	W	19
Allt Coire Ruairidh	Aberd	NO0799	57°4·6'	3°31·6'W	W	36,43
Allt Coire Ruchain	Highld	NC3103	57°59·3'	4°51·1'W	W	15
Allt Coire Ruchain	Highld	NH4793	57°54·3'	4°34·4'W	W	20
Allt Coire Seilich	Arg & Bt	NM8818	56°18·7'	5°25·2'W	W	55
Allt Coire Seilich	Arg & Bt	NN3346	56°34·8'	4°42·7'W	W	50
Allt Coire Sgamadail	Highld	NG8008	57°6·9'	5°37·6'W	W	33
Allt Coire Sgoireadail	Highld	NG9607	57°6·8'	5°21·7'W	W	33
Allt Coire Sgreumh	Highld	NH1513	57°10·5'	5°3·2'W	W	34
Allt Coire Sgriòdain	Highld	NN1143	56°32·7'	5°4·0'W	W	50
Allt Coire Shaile	Highld	NH1142	57°26·0'	5°8·5'W	W	25
Allt Coire Slat Bheinn	Highld	NG9202	57°4·0'	5°25·4'W	W	33
Allt Coire Taodail	Highld	NG9843	57°26·2'	5°21·5'W	W	25
Allt Coire Tholl Bhruach	Highld	NH0412	57°9·7'	5°14·0'W	W	33
Allt Coire Thorcaill	Highld	NH5883	57°49·1'	4°23·0'W	W	21
Allt Coire Toiteil	Highld	NG9511	57°8·9'	5°22·9'W	W	33
Allt Coire Torr an Asgaill	Highld	NG8003	57°4·2'	5°37·3'W	W	33
Allt Coire Uainean Mór	Highld	NN0667	56°45·5'	5°10·0'W	W	41
Allt Coire Uchdachan	Highld	NN3999	57°3·5'	4°38·8'W	W	34
Allt Coire Uilleim	Highld	NN6582	56°54·8'	4°12·6'W	W	42
Allt Con	Pth & Kin	NN6966	56°46·3'	4°8·2'W	W	42
Allt Conait	Pth & Kin	NN5245	56°34·7'	4°24·1'W	W	51
Allt Connie	Aberd	NO0785	56°57·1'	3°31·3'W	W	43
Allt Coolah	Pth & Kin	NO1274	56°51·2'	3°26·1'W	W	43
Allt Coralan	Arg & Bt	NN3435	56°28·9'	4°41·3'W	X	50
Allt Corrach	Arg & Bt	NS1287	56°2·6'	5°0·7'W	W	56
Allt Coulavie	Highld	NH1322	57°15·3'	5°5·5'W	W	25
Allt Cragach	Pth & Kin	NN7677	56°52·3'	4°1·6'W	W	42
Allt Craobhach	Arg & Bt	NR4060	55°46·1'	6°8·3'W	W	60
Allt Craoinidh	Pth & Kin	NN9173	56°50·4'	3°46·8'W	W	43
Allt Creach	Moray	NJ1851	57°32·8'	3°21·7'W	W	28
Allt Creagach	Highld	NC6034	58°16·6'	4°22·8'W	W	16
Allt Creagach	Highld	NH6412	57°11·0'	4°14·5'W	W	35
Allt Creag a' Chail	Highld	NN3996	57°1·9'	4°38·7'W	W	34
Allt Creag a' Chait	Highld	NH8241	57°26·9'	3°57·5'W	W	27
Allt Creag a' Chromain	Arg & Bt	NM5226	56°21·9'	6°0·5'W	W	48
Allt Creag a' Mhadaidh	Pth & Kin	NN6953	56°39·3'	4°7·8'W	W	42,51
Allt Creagan an Diridh	Highld	NC5334	58°16·5'	4°29·9'W	W	16
Allt Creag an Eighich	Highld	NM7662	56°42·0'	5°39·1'W	W	40
Allt Creag an Leth-choin	Highld	NH9705	57°7·7'	3°41·6'W	W	36
Allt Creagan nam Meann	Highld	NN2749	56°36·3'	4°48·7'W	W	50
Allt Creagan na Seabhaig	Highld	NN4080	56°53·3'	4°37·1'W	W	34,42
Allt Creag Bheithin	Highld	NH7434	57°23·0'	4°5·3'W	W	27
Allt Creag Chomaich	Highld	NH4901	57°4·8'	4°29·0'W	W	34
Allt Creag Chomaich	Highld	NH5002	57°5·3'	4°28·1'W	W	35
Allt Creag Innis nam Bo	Highld	NN1786	56°56·0'	5°0·0'W	W	34,41
Allt Creag na Clibhe	N Eil	NB1714	58°1·8'	6°47·2'W	W	13,14
Allt Creag nan Gobhar	Arg & Bt	NR7871	55°53·1'	5°32·6'W	W	62
Allt Creag Odhar	Highld	NG9988	57°50·4'	5°22·7'W	W	19
Alltcreich	Arg & Bt	NM6839	56°29·4'	5°45·7'W	X	49
Allt Criche	Arg & Bt	NM8525	56°22·4'	5°28·5'W	W	49
Allt Criche	Arg & Bt	NN0335	56°28·2'	5°11·4'W	W	50
Allt Criche	Arg & Bt	NN0432	56°26·6'	5°10·3'W	W	50
Allt Criche	Arg & Bt	NN2003	56°11·4'	4°53·6'W	W	56
Allt Criche	Arg & Bt	NR7239	55°35·7'	5°36·7'W	W	68
Allt Criche	Highld	NN3953	56°38·7'	4°37·1'W	W	41
Allt Criche	Pth & Kin	NN4148	56°36·1'	4°35·0'W	W	51
Allt Criche	Stir	NN3319	56°20·3'	4°41·7'W	W	50,56
Allt Crioch	Stir	NS4398	56°9·2'	4°31·2'W	W	56
Allt Crioch	Stir	NS4499	56°9·7'	4°30·3'W	W	57
Allt Cristie Beag	Aberd	NO0486	56°57·6'	3°34·3'W	W	43
Allt Cristie Mór	Aberd	NO0586	56°57·6'	3°33·3'W	W	43
Allt Crithinn	Highld	NC7522	58°10·4'	4°7·0'W	W	16
Allt Crò-chloich	Pth & Kin	NN5766	56°46·1'	4°19·9'W	W	42
Allt Crò nan Gobhar	N Eil	NG0891	57°49·1'	6°54·6'W	W	14,18
Allt Cruinneachaidh	Highld	NN2898	57°2·7'	4°49·7'W	W	34
Allt Crunachdain	Highld	NN5191	56°59·4'	4°26·7'W	W	35
Allt Cuaich	Highld	NN6786	56°57·0'	4°10·7'W	W	42
Allt Cùil	Highld	NN4196	57°1·9'	4°36·7'W	W	34
Allt Cùil a' Chiarain	Highld	NN0977	56°51·0'	5°7·5'W	W	41
Allt Cùil na Caillich	Highld	NH6805	57°7·3'	4°10·4'W	W	35
Allt Cùl	Aberd	NO1895	57°2·6'	3°20·6'W	W	36,43
Allt Culaibh	Pth & Kin	NN7168	56°47·4'	4°6·3'W	W	42
Allt Cùl a' Mhill	Highld	NM3697	56°59·6'	6°20·3'W	W	39
Allt Cùl an Ruith-chnoic	Highld	NC3101	57°58·2'	4°51·0'W	W	15
Allt Cùl na Coille	Pth & Kin	NO0657	56°42·0'	3°31·7'W	W	52,53
Allt Cumhang	Arg & Bt	NN3533	56°27·9'	4°40·2'W	W	50
Allt Cumh na Coinnich	Moray	NJ0601	57°5·7'	3°32·6'W	W	36
Allt-Cunedda	Carm	SN4008	51°45·1'	4°18·7'W	X	159
Allt Cynhelyg	Powys	SO0247	52°7·0'	3°25·5'W	X	147
Allt Dabhoch	Highld	NG3823	57°13·6'	6°20·0'W	W	32
Allt Dà-ghob	Pth & Kin	NN6945	56°35·0'	4°7·5'W	W	51
Allt Dàidh	Highld	NG3925	57°14·7'	6°19·1'W	W	32
Allt Dail a' Chuirn	Highld	NH2906	57°7·1'	4°49·0'W	W	34
Allt Dail Fàid	Highld	NC4015	58°6·0'	4°42·4'W	W	16
Allt Dail na Mine	Highld	NN0564	56°43·9'	5°10·8'W	W	41
Allt Dail nan Sealg	Highld	NN7892	57°0·4'	4°0·1'W	W	35
Allt Dail Teine	Highld	NC8263	58°32·6'	4°1·2'W	W	10
Allt Daim	Highld	NN1774	56°49·6'	4°59·5'W	W	41
Allt Daimh	Arg & Bt	NN2634	56°28·2'	4°49·0'W	W	50

Allt Daimh	Moray	NJ3227	57°20·0′	3°7·3′W	W	37
Allt Daimheidh	Pth & Kin	NO0367	56°47·3′	3°34·8′W	W	43
Allt Daingean	Highld	NH2404	57°5·9′	4°53·9′W	W	34
Allt Daley	Moray	NJ3149	57°31·8′	3°8·7′W	W	28
Allt Dalharrold	Highld	NC7037	58°18·4′	4°12·6′W	W	16
Allt Dallermaig	Arg & Bt	NM7917	56°17·9′	5°33·9′W	W	55
Allt Damh	Aberd	NJ2606	57°8·6′	3°12·9′W	W	37
Allt Damh Dubh	Pth & Kin	NN8282	56°55·1′	3°55·8′W	W	43
Allt Darach	Arg & Bt	NM4747	56°33·1′	6°6·6′W	W	47,48
Allt Darach	Highld	NG5531	57°18·5′	6°3·6′W	W	24,32
Allt Daraich	Highld	NG4929	57°17·2′	6°9·5′W	W	32
Allt Dderw	Cered	SN6383	52°25·9′	4°0·5′W	X	135
Allt Dderw	Powys	SO1650	52°8·8′	3°13·3′W	H	148
Allt-ddu	Cered	SN3949	52°7·2′	4°20·7′W	H	145
Allt-ddu	Cered	SN7063	52°15·2′	3°53·9′W	X	146,147
Allt-ddu	Cered	SN7197	52°33·6′	3°53·8′W	X	135
Allt-ddu	Conwy	SH9568	53°12·2′	3°33·9′W	X	116
Allt-ddu	Powys	SN8995	52°32·7′	3°37·8′W	H	135,136
Allt Ddu	Powys	SO0223	51°54·1′	3°25·1′W	X	160
Allt Deamhaidh	Highld	NH7014	57°12·2′	4°8·7′W	W	35
Allt Dearcaige	Highld	NJ1213	57°12·2′	3°26·9′W	W	36
Allt Dearg	Aberd	NO1099	57°4·7′	3°28·6′W	W	43
Allt Dearg	Arg & Bt	NM8607	56°12·7′	5°26·6′W	W	55
Allt Dearg	Arg & Bt	NM9318	56°18·8′	5°20·4′W	W	55
Allt Dearg	Highld	NG1847	57°25·8′	6°41·5′W	W	23
Allt Dearg	Highld	NG3845	57°25·5′	6°21·4′W	W	23
Allt Dearg	Highld	NG3849	57°27·6′	6°21·7′W	W	23
Allt Dearg	Highld	NH0450	57°30·1′	5°15·8′W	W	25
Allt Dearg	Highld	NH4661	57°37·0′	4°34·2′W	W	20
Allt Dearg	Highld	NH5036	57°23·6′	4°29·3′W	X	26
Allt Dearg	Highld	NH6580	57°47·6′	4°15·8′W	W	21
Allt Dearg	Highld	NH8143	57°28·0′	3°58·6′W	W	27
Allt Dearg	Highld	NH8347	57°30·1′	3°56·7′W	W	27
Allt Dearg	Highld	NJ0640	57°26·7′	3°33·5′W	W	27
Allt Dearg	Highld	NM8482	56°53·0′	5°32·3′W	W	40
Allt Dearg	Highld	NN3291	56°59·0′	4°45·4′W	W	34
Allt Dearg	Highld	NN3593	57°0·2′	4°42·6′W	W	34
Allt Dearg	Moray	NJ0403	57°6·7′	3°34·7′W	W	36
Allt Dearg	Pth & Kin	NN7577	56°52·3′	4°2·6′W	W	42
Allt Dearg	Stir	NN6130	56°26·8′	4°14·9′W	W	51
Allt Dearg Beag	Highld	NG4727	57°16·1′	6°11·3′W	W	32
Alltdearg Ho	Highld	NG4729	57°17·2′	6°11·4′W	X	32
Allt Dearg Mór	Highld	NG4628	57°16·6′	6°12·4′W	W	32
Allt Deas	Aberd	NO3888	56°59·0′	3°0·8′W	W	44
Allt Derigan	Arg & Bt	NS2696	56°7·8′	4°47·5′W	W	56
Allt Deucheran	Arg & Bt	NR7642	55°37·5′	5°33·0′W	W	62,69
Allt Devanach	Aberd	NJ3605	57°8·1′	3°3·0′W	W	37
Allt Deveron	Moray	NJ3825	57°18·9′	3°1·3′W	W	37
Allt Dhàidh	Stir	NN4221	56°21·6′	4°33·0′W	W	51,56
Allt Dhaidh Beag	Aberd	NN9789	56°59·1′	3°41·2′W	W	43
Allt Dhàidh Mór	Aberd	NN9688	56°58·6′	3°42·2′W	W	43
Allt Dhail Beag	N Eil	NB2344	58°18·1′	6°43·2′W	W	8
Allt Dhepin	N Ayr	NS0126	55°29·5′	5°8·6′W	W	69
Allt Dhoiréann	Arg & Bt	NN1535	56°28·5′	4°59·8′W	W	50
Allt Dhoirrean	Arg & Bt	NN1532	56°26·9′	4°59·6′W	W	50
Allt Dhùin Croisg	Stir	NN5438	56°30·9′	4°21·9′W	W	51
Allt Dhuirinish	Highld	NG7930	57°18·7′	5°39·7′W	W	24
Allt Dihanog	Cered	SN7672	52°20·2′	3°48·8′W	X	135,147
Allt Dinnie	Aberd	NO5295	57°2·9′	2°47·0′W	W	37,44
Allt Diobadail	N Eil	NB5534	58°13·9′	6°9·9′W	W	8
Allt Dionach-caraidh	Highld	NC5542	58°20·8′	4°28·2′W	W	10
Allt Diridh	Pth & Kin	NN8773	56°50·3′	3°50·7′W	W	43
Allt Diubaig	Highld	NG3153	57°29·5′	6°28·9′W	X	23
Allt Dobhrain	Arg & Bt	NM8321	56°20·2′	5°30·2′W	W	49
Allt Dochard	Arg & Bt	NN2044	56°33·5′	4°55·3′W	W	50
Allt Doe	Highld	NH4106	57°7·3′	4°37·1′W	W	34
Allt Dogha	Highld	NN0878	56°51·5′	5°8·5′W	W	41
Allt Doir' an Daimh	Highld	NN1697	57°1·9′	5°1·5′W	W	34
Allt Doire an Sobhrachan	Arg & Bt	NM9405	56°11·8′	5°18·8′W	W	55
Allt Doire Bheithe	Highld	NH0251	57°30·6′	5°17·9′W	W	25
Allt Doire Huan	Highld	NN0999	57°2·8′	5°8·5′W	W	33
Allt Doire na Bainnse	Highld	NM8155	56°38·4′	5°33·8′W	W	49
Allt Doire na Criche	Highld	NG7118	57°12·0′	5°47·0′W	W	33
Allt Doire nan Eun	Pth & Kin	NO0866	56°46·8′	3°29·9′W	W	43
Allt Doire nan Tarbh	Arg & Bt	NN0506	56°12·7′	5°8·2′W	W	56
Allt Dolanog	Powys	SJ0613	52°42·6′	3°23·1′W	H	125
Allt Domhain	Arg & Bt	NR7336	55°34·1′	5°35·6′W	W	68
Allt Domhain	Highld	NC5525	58°11·7′	4°27·5′W	W	16
Allt Domhain	Highld	NH0229	57°18·8′	5°16·8′W	W	25,33
Allt Domhain	Highld	NH5294	57°54·9′	4°29·4′W	W	20
Allt Domhain	Pth & Kin	NN5763	56°44·5′	4°19·8′W	W	42
Allt Domhainn	Highld	NN7783	56°55·6′	4°0·8′W	W	42
Allt Donachain	Arg & Bt	NN1728	56°24·8′	4°57·5′W	W	50
Alltdourie	Aberd	NO1693	57°1·5′	3°22·6′W	X	36,43
Allt Dourie	Aberd	NO1794	57°2·0′	3°21·6′W	W	36,43
Allt Dowrie	Aberd	NO3589	56°59·5′	3°3·7′W	W	44
Allt Dregnie	Moray	NJ2425	57°18·8′	3°15·2′W	W	36
Allt Dregnie	Moray	NJ2526	57°19·4′	3°14·3′W	W	37
Allt Drimneach	Highld	NH3932	57°21·3′	4°40·1′W	W	26
Allt Driseach	N Eil	NB5230	58°11·6′	6°12·7′W	W	8
Allt Dritil	N Eil	NG0591	57°48·9′	6°57·6′W	W	14,18
Allt Droilichean	Pth & Kin	NN6051	56°38·1′	4°16·5′W	W	42,51
Allt Druidh	Highld	NH9406	57°8·2′	3°44·6′W	W	36
Allt Druidhe	Pth & Kin	NN6456	56°40·8′	4°12·7′W	W	42,51
Allt Druim an Reinidh	Highld	NC4842	58°20·7′	4°35·3′W	W	9
Allt Druim na Mòine	Highld	NC5156	58°28·3′	4°32·8′W	W	9
Allt Duasdale Mór	Highld	NC1701	57°57·9′	5°5·1′W	W	15
Allt Dubh	Arg & Bt	NR8377	55°56·5′	5°28·1′W	W	62
Allt Dubh	Arg & Bt	NR9875	55°55·8′	5°13·6′W	W	62
Allt Dubh	Highld	NC8123	58°11·1′	4°1·0′W	W	17
Allt Dubh	Highld	NG4831	57°18·3′	6°10·6′W	W	32
Allt Dubh	Highld	NH0819	57°13·6′	5°10·4′W	W	33
Allt Dubh	Highld	NH2303	57°5·3′	4°54·8′W	W	34
Allt Dubh	Highld	NH8611	57°10·8′	3°52·7′W	W	35,36
Allt Dubh	Highld	NM7898	57°1·4′	5°39·0′W	W	33,40
Allt Dubh	Highld	NN0099	57°2·6′	5°17·4′W	W	33
Allt Dubh	Highld	NN1691	56°58·7′	5°1·2′W	W	34
Allt Dubh	Highld	NN2767	56°46·0′	4°49·4′W	W	41
Allt Dubh	Highld	NN3795	57°1·3′	4°40·7′W	W	34
Allt Dubh	Highld	NN5281	56°54·1′	4°25·4′W	W	42

Allt Dubh	N Ayr	NR9447	55°40·6′	5°16·1′W	W	62,69
Allt Dubh	N Eil	NB1123	58°6·4′	6°53·9′W	W	13,14
Allt Dubh	N Eil	NB4338	58°15·6′	6°22·4′W	W	8
Allt Dubh	Stir	NN3027	56°24·5′	4°44·9′W	W	50
Allt Dubh a'Bhacain	Arg & Bt	NR6996	56°6·3′	5°42·5′W	W	55,61
Allt Dubhach	Highld	NH6863	57°38·5′	4°12·2′W	W	21
Allt Dubhagan	Pth & Kin	NO0765	56°46·3′	3°30·8′W	W	43
Allt Dubhaig	Highld	NM9975	56°49·6′	5°17·2′W	W	40
Allt Dubhaig	Highld	NN3079	56°52·5′	4°46·9′W	W	41
Allt Dubhaig	Pth & Kin	NN6373	56°50·0′	4°14·3′W	W	42
Allt Dubh-beag	Highld	NN3055	56°39·6′	4°46·0′W	W	41
Allt Dubhchlair	Stir	NN5035	56°29·3′	4°25·7′W	W	51
Allt Dubh Cúil na Creige	Highld	NH4808	57°8·5′	4°30·3′W	W	34
Allt Dubh Dhoire Theàrnait	Highld	NM7545	56°32·8′	5°39·2′W	W	49
Allt Dubh Mór	Highld	NC2460	58°29·8′	5°0·7′W	W	9
Allt Dubh-mór	Highld	NN3255	56°39·7′	4°44·0′W	W	41
Allt Dubh nan Searsanach	Highld	NH6312	57°11·0′	4°15·5′W	W	35
Allt Duchairidh	Highld	NH1159	57°35·2′	5°9·2′W	W	25
Allt Dughaill	Highld	NG3239	57°22·0′	6°27·0′W	W	23,32
Allt Duibhleac Riabhach	Highld	NM8558	56°40·1′	5°30·1′W	W	49
Allt Duilleachry	N Ayr	NR9323	55°27·7′	5°16·0′W	W	68,69
Allt Duine	Highld	NH7912	57°11·2′	3°59·7′W	W	35
Allt Duisdale	Highld	NG6712	57°8·7′	5°50·6′W	W	32
Allt Each	Highld	NH8309	57°9·7′	3°55·6′W	W	35
Allt Eachach	Highld	NN3494	57°0·7′	4°43·6′W	W	34
Allt Eachain	Highld	NM7463	56°42·5′	5°41·1′W	W	40
Allt Eaglaiche	Arg & Bt	NM8318	56°18·5′	5°30·0′W	W	55
Allt Ealagan	Pth & Kin	NN8338	56°31·4′	3°53·7′W	W	52
Allt Easach	Arg & Bt	NN0642	56°32·1′	5°8·8′W	W	50
Allt Easach	Arg & Bt	NR7228	55°29·8′	5°36·2′W	W	68
Allt Eas a' Ghaidheil	Highld	NM5669	56°45·2′	5°59·0′W	W	47
Allt Easain	Highld	NM8081	56°52·4′	5°36·2′W	W	40
Allt Eas an Fhèidh	Highld	NM6068	56°44·8′	5°55·1′W	W	40
Allt Eas an Ime	Arg & Bt	NM5230	56°24·1′	6°0·7′W	W	48
Allt Easan Mhic Gorraidh	Highld	NG8422	57°14·5′	5°34·3′W	W	33
Allt Easan Stalcair	Pth & Kin	NN5151	56°37·9′	4°25·3′W	W	42,51
Allt Eas an Taileir	Highld	NM6367	56°44·3′	5°52·1′W	W	40
Allt Easgadill	Highld	NM8059	56°40·5′	5°35·0′W	W	49
Allt Easgaidh	Pth & Kin	NO0776	56°52·2′	3°31·1′W	W	43
Allt Easgainn	Highld	NH5107	57°8·0′	4°27·3′W	W	35
Allt Eas Mór Chùl an Dùin	Highld	NG8115	57°10·7′	5°36·9′W	W	33
Allt Eas na Maoile	Highld	NC3534	58°16·1′	4°48·3′W	W	15
Allt Eas na Maoile	Highld	NC3634	58°16·1′	4°47·3′W	W	16
Allt Eas nam Muc	Highld	NG7823	57°14·9′	5°40·3′W	W	33
Allt Eigheach	Pth & Kin	NN4362	56°43·7′	4°33·5′W	W	42
Allt Eilagadale	Highld	NM5770	56°45·8′	5°58·1′W	W	39,47
Allt Eileag	Highld	NC3007	58°1·4′	4°52·2′W	W	15
Allt Eilidh	Arg & Bt	NN0652	56°37·4′	5°9·3′W	W	41
Allt Eindart	Highld	NN9090	56°59·5′	3°48·2′W	W	43
Allt Eiteachan	Highld	NH5787	57°51·2′	4°24·1′W	W	21
Allt Elrig	Pth & Kin	NO0876	56°52·2′	3°30·1′W	W	43
Allt Enoch	Carm	SN5326	51°55·0′	4°7·9′W	F	146
Allt Eoghainn	Highld	NJ1230	57°21·4′	3°27·3′W	W	36
Allt Eoin Mhóir	Arg & Bt	NR8181	55°58·6′	5°30·2′W	W	55
Allt Essan	Stir	NN4328	56°25·3′	4°32·3′W	W	51
Allt Fada	Highld	NC7550	58°25·5′	4°7·9′W	W	10
Allt Fada	N Eil	NB5460	58°27·8′	6°12·6′W	W	8
Alltfadog	Cered	SN6682	52°25·4′	3°57·8′W	X	135
Allt Faircidh	Highld	NN0275	56°49·7′	5°14·3′W	W	41
Allt Falbea	Arg & Bt	NR7729	55°30·5′	5°31·5′W	W	68,69
Allt Faoileinn	Arg & Bt	NR9977	55°56·9′	5°12·7′W	W	62
Allt Fascadale	Highld	NM5069	56°45·0′	6°4·9′W	W	47
Allt Fathan Glinne	Stir	NN4917	56°19·5′	4°26·1′W	W	57
Allt Fawr	Gwyn	SH3835	52°53·5′	4°24·1′W	X	123
Allt-fawr	Gwyn	SH6847	53°0·5′	3°57·6′W	H	115
Alltfawr	Powys	SJ1313	52°42·7′	3°16·9′W	X	125
Allt Fawr	Powys	SJ1413	52°42·7′	3°16·0′W	X	125
Allt Fawr	Powys	SN9797	52°33·9′	3°30·8′W	H	136
Allt Fearn	Highld	NC6432	58°15·6′	4°18·6′W	W	16
Allt Fearna	Arg & Bt	NM9405	56°11·8′	5°18·8′W	W	55
Allt Fearna	Arg & Bt	NN0306	56°12·6′	5°10·1′W	W	55
Allt Fearna	Arg & Bt	NN1222	56°21·4′	5°2·1′W	W	50
Allt Feàrna	Arg & Bt	NN1825	56°23·2′	4°56·4′W	W	50
Allt Feàrna	Highld	NC7532	58°15·8′	4°7·4′W	W	16
Allt Feàrna	Highld	NG6125	57°15·5′	5°57·3′W	W	32
Allt Fearna	Highld	NH7120	57°15·4′	4°7·9′W	W	35
Allt Fearna	Pth & Kin	NN4756	56°40·5′	4°29·4′W	W	42,51
Allt Fearnach	Pth & Kin	NO0073	56°50·5′	3°37·9′W	W	43
Allt Fearnach	Pth & Kin	NO0466	56°46·8′	3°33·8′W	W	43
Allt Feàrna Mór	Arg & Bt	NR5881	55°57·9′	5°52·2′W	W	61
Allt-fedw	Cered	SN6876	52°22·2′	3°55·9′W	X	135
Allt Féith a' Chatha	Highld	NM8683	56°53·6′	5°30·4′W	W	40
Allt Féith a' Ghiubhais	Highld	NH2531	57°20·4′	4°54·0′W	W	25
Allt Féith a' Ghleannain	Highld	NN2869	56°47·1′	4°48·5′W	W	41
Allt Féith a' Mhadaidh	Highld	NG9837	57°23·0′	5°21·2′W	W	25
Allt Féith a' Mheallain	Highld	NN4271	56°48·5′	4°34·8′W	W	42
Allt Féith a' Mhoraire	Highld	NN3267	56°46·1′	4°44·5′W	W	41
Allt Féith a' Mhoraire	Highld	NN4797	57°2·6′	4°30·9′W	W	34
Allt Féith an t-Seilich	Highld	NN6097	57°2·8′	4°18·0′W	W	35
Allt Féith an t-Seilisdeir	Highld	NH4326	57°18·1′	4°35·9′W	W	26
Allt Feith Bhrunachain	Highld	NN3288	56°57·4′	4°45·3′W	W	34,41
Allt Feith Chiarain	Highld	NN3064	56°44·5′	4°46·3′W	W	41
Allt Féithe Chaillich	Highld	NH0039	57°24·1′	5°19·3′W	W	25
Allt Feith Gharuiareagan	Pth & Kin	NN5567	56°46·6′	4°21·9′W	W	42
Allt Féith Ghuithsachain	Pth & Kin	NN9976	56°52·1′	3°39·0′W	W	43
Allt Féith Làir	Pth & Kin	NO0180	56°54·3′	3°37·1′W	W	43
Allt Féith Mhic Artair	Highld	NM8048	56°34·6′	5°34·5′W	W	49
Allt Féith nam Fearna	Pth & Kin	NN8370	56°48·7′	3°54·5′W	W	43
Allt Féith nan Gaimhne	Highld	NH2159	57°35·4′	4°59·2′W	W	25
Allt Féith nan Sac	Highld	NN2771	56°48·2′	4°49·5′W	W	41
Allt Féith Riabhachain	Highld	NH3529	57°19·6′	4°44·0′W	W	26
Allt Féith Thuill	Highld	NN3772	56°48·9′	4°39·8′W	W	41
Allt Felin-fawr	Pemb	SM6923	51°51·7′	5°20·9′W	X	157
Allt Fhaolain	Highld	NN1552	56°37·7′	5°0·5′W	W	41
Allt Fheannach	Pth & Kin	NN9575	56°51·5′	3°42·9′W	W	43
Allt Fhearchair	Arg & Bt	NM5326	56°22·0′	5°59·5′W	W	48
Allt Fhearghais	Highld	NN3576	56°51·0′	4°41·9′W	W	41
Allt Fhearnagan	Highld	NN8697	57°3·3′	3°52·3′W	W	35,36,43
Allt Fhearnasdail	Highld	NN8399	57°4·3′	3°55·3′W	W	35
Allt Fhiodhan	Highld	NN1057	56°40·2′	5°5·6′W	W	41

Allt Fhionnaich	Highld	NC5547	58°23·5′	4°28·4′W	W	10
Allt Fhuaran	Arg & Bt	NN1925	56°23·2′	4°55·5′W	W	50
Allt Filo	Powys	SO1133	51°59·5′	3°17·4′W	X	161
Allt Fionnach	Highld	NH6615	57°12·6′	4°12·7′W	W	35
Allt Fionna Choire	Highld	NJ0210	57°10·5′	3°36·8′W	W	36
Allt Fionn a' Glinne	Pth & Kin	NN3939	56°31·2′	4°36·6′W	W	50
Allt Fionndairnich	Highld	NH7216	57°13·3′	4°6·7′W	W	35
Allt Fionn-dhail	Highld	NN1498	57°2·4′	5°3·5′W	W	34
Allt Fionn Doire	Highld	NN0284	56°54·6′	5°14·7′W	W	41
Allt Fionndrigh	Highld	NH6601	57°5·1′	4°12·2′W	W	35
Allt Fionn Ghleann	Stir	NN5539	56°31·5′	4°21·0′W	W	51
Allt Fionn Ghlinne	Highld	NN2251	56°37·3′	4°53·6′W	W	41
Allt Fionn Ghlinne	Stir	NN3222	56°21·9′	4°42·7′W	W	50
Allt Fionn-tom Mór	Highld	NH6406	57°7·8′	4°14·3′W	W	35
Allt Fisgro	N Eil	NB4055	58°24·6′	6°26·6′W	W	8
Allt Fm	Carm	SN3908	51°45·1′	4°19·6′W	FM	159
Allt Fm	Monm	ST3896	51°39·8′	2°53·4′W	FM	171
Allt Folais	Highld	NG9572	57°41·7′	5°25·9′W	W	19
Alltforgan	Powys	SH9624	52°48·5′	3°32·2′W	X	125
Allt Forgan	Powys	SO0617	51°50·9′	3°21·5′W	X	160
Allt Forsiescye	Highld	ND0257	58°29·7′	3°40·4′W	W	11,12
Allt Fraoch-choire	Highld	NH0918	57°13·0′	5°9·3′W	W	33
Allt Fraoch Choire	Highld	NH1019	57°13·6′	5°8·4′W	W	34
Allt Fraoch-choire	Highld	NH2019	57°13·8′	4°58·5′W	W	34
Allt Fraoch-choire	Highld	NH2020	57°14·4′	4°58·5′W	W	25
Allt Fraoch-choire	Highld	NH2129	57°19·3′	4°57·9′W	W	25
Allt Fuaranach	Aberd	NJ3108	57°9·7′	3°8·0′W	W	37
Allt Fuaran Mhic Bheathain	Highld	NN4870	56°48·1′	4°28·9′W	W	42
Allt Gaineimh	Moray	NJ1705	57°8·0′	3°21·8′W	W	36
Allt Garaidh Ghualaich	Highld	NN1598	57°2·4′	5°2·5′W	W	34
Allt Garbh	Aberd	NN9791	57°0·2′	3°41·3′W	W	43
Allt Garbh	Arg & Bt	NM9709	56°14·1′	5°16·1′W	W	55
Allt Garbh	Arg & Bt	NN0732	56°26·7′	5°7·4′W	W	50
Allt Garbh	Highld	NC1317	58°6·4′	5°10·0′W	W	15
Allt Garbh	Highld	NC2759	58°29·4′	4°57·6′W	W	9
Allt Garbh	Highld	NG3947	57°26·6′	6°20·5′W	W	23
Allt Garbh	Highld	NG6718	57°11·9′	5°51·0′W	W	32
Allt Garbh	Highld	NH1719	57°13·8′	5°1·4′W	W	34
Allt Garbh	Highld	NH1821	57°14·9′	5°0·5′W	W	25
Allt Garbh	Highld	NH4438	57°24·6′	4°35·4′W	W	26
Allt Garbh	Highld	NM6255	56°37·8′	5°52·4′W	W	49
Allt Garbh	Highld	NN6889	56°58·7′	4°9·9′W	W	42
Allt Garbh	N Ayr	NS0226	55°29·5′	5°7·6′W	W	69
Allt Garbh-airigh	Highld	NH6398	57°57·3′	4°18·4′W	W	21
Allt Garbh Beag	Highld	NC7320	58°9·3′	4°9·0′W	W	16
Allt Garbh-bhruaich	Pth & Kin	NN7069	56°47·9′	4°7·3′W	W	42
Allt Garbh Buidhe	Pth & Kin	NN9981	56°54·8′	3°39·1′W	W	43
Allt Garbh-choire	Highld	NH1836	57°22·9′	5°1·2′W	W	25
Allt Garbh Choirean	Arg & Bt	NN2629	56°25·5′	4°48·8′W	W	50
Allt Garbh-dhalach	Highld	NM4466	56°43·2′	6°10·6′W	W	47
Allt Garbh-Dhoire	Highld	NH2006	57°6·8′	4°57·9′W	W	34
Allt Garbhlach	Highld	NN8695	57°2·2′	3°52·3′W	W	35,36,43
Allt Garbh Mór	Highld	NG5133	57°19·4′	6°7·7′W	W	24,32
Alltgaredig	Carm	SN4230	51°57·0′	4°17·6′W	X	146
Allt Gartain	Highld	NN1752	56°37·7′	4°58·5′W	W	41
Allt Geal	Highld	NC6213	58°5·3′	4°20·0′W	W	16
Allt Geallaidh	Pth & Kin	NN7373	56°50·1′	4°4·4′W	W	42
Allt Geistir	N Eil	NA9926	58°7·5′	7°6·3′W	W	13
Allt Ghabhar	Arg & Bt	NN2243	56°33·0′	4°53·3′W	W	50
Allt Ghallabhaich	Pth & Kin	NN5849	56°36·9′	4°18·4′W	W	51
Allt Ghamhnain	Arg & Bt	NN2835	56°28·8′	4°47·1′W	W	50
Allt Ghaordaidh	Stir	NN5038	56°30·9′	4°25·8′W	W	51
Allt Gharagain	Highld	NH1253	57°32·0′	5°8·0′W	W	25
Allt Gharbh Chaig	Highld	NN7682	56°55·0′	4°1·8′W	W	42
Allt Ghillecaluim	Arg & Bt	NM5731	56°24·8′	5°55·9′W	W	48
Allt Ghiubhais	Highld	NC1404	57°59·4′	5°8·3′W	W	15
Allt Ghiubhais	Highld	NN7394	57°1·4′	4°5·1′W	W	35
Allt Ghiusachan	Arg & Bt	NN1139	56°30·6′	5°3·8′W	W	50
Allt Ghiuthais	Highld	NH8314	57°12·4′	3°55·8′W	W	35
Allt Ghlas	Pth & Kin	NN5364	56°44·9′	4°23·8′W	W	42
Allt Ghleadharan	N Eil	NB2341	58°16·5′	6°43·0′W	W	8,13
Allt Ghleann Aoidhdailean	Highld	NG8714	57°10·3′	5°30·9′W	W	33
Allt Ghleann Sleibhtecoire	Highld	NM6254	56°37·3′	5°52·3′W	W	49
Allt Ghlinne	Arg & Bt	NM9616	56°17·8′	5°17·4′W	W	55
Allt Ghlinn Thaitneich	Pth & Kin	NO0874	56°51·2′	3°30·1′W	W	43
Allt Ghòinean	Pth & Kin	NN6920	56°21·5′	4°6·8′W	W	51,57
Allt Ghormaig	Highld	NH2209	57°8·5′	4°56·1′W	W	34
Allt Ghormailleabhat	N Eil	NB3644	58°18·6′	6°30·0′W	W	8
Allt Ghrunndail	N Eil	NB4257	58°25·8′	6°24·7′W	W	8
Allt Gil' a' Chlàir Mhòir	N Eil	NB1216	58°2·6′	6°52·4′W	W	13,14
Allt Gilbe	Highld	NN4998	57°3·2′	4°28·9′W	W	34
Allt Gilbe	Highld	NN5097	57°2·6′	4°27·9′W	W	35
Allt Gil Bhiogurra	N Eil	NB2608	57°58·9′	6°37·6′W	W	13,14
Allt Gill Lùsga	N Eil	NB1712	58°0·7′	6°47·0′W	W	13,14
Allt Gil Mhic Phaic	N Eil	NB2208	57°58·7′	6°41·7′W	W	13,14
Allt Gil Mhic Phaic	N Eil	NB3409	57°59·7′	6°29·6′W	W	13,14
Allt Gil Oscaro	N Eil	NB2119	58°4·6′	6°43·5′W	W	13,14
Allt Girnaig	Pth & Kin	NN9466	56°46·7′	3°43·6′W	W	43
Allt Giubhais	Highld	NH1006	57°6·6′	5°7·8′W	W	34
Allt Giubhais	Highld	NN1998	57°2·5′	4°58·5′W	W	34
Allt Giubhais Beag	Highld	NH3469	57°41·1′	4°46·6′W	W	20
Allt Glac a' Chuilinn	Highld	NH0507	57°7·0′	5°12·8′W	W	33
Allt Glachavoil	Arg & Bt	NS0277	55°57·0′	5°9·8′W	W	63
Allt Glac na Doimhne	Highld	NH3727	57°18·5′	4°41·9′W	W	26
Allt-glais	Cered	SN5983	52°25·9′	4°4·0′W	X	135
Allt Glas	N Eil	NB1915	58°2·4′	6°45·2′W	W	13,14
Allt Glas	N Eil	NB3118	58°4·4′	6°33·3′W	W	13,14
Allt Glas	N Eil	NB3951	58°22·4′	6°27·4′W	W	8
Allt Glas	Pth & Kin	NN7118	56°20·5′	4°4·8′W	W	57
Allt Glas	Stir	NN4330	56°26·4′	4°32·4′W	W	51
Allt Glas a' Bheòil	Highld	NH6707	57°8·3′	4°11·4′W	W	35
Allt Glas a' Charbaid	Highld	NH6908	57°8·9′	4°9·5′W	W	35
Allt Glas a' Chùil	Highld	NH6608	57°8·9′	4°12·4′W	W	35
Allt Glasahoile	Stir	NN4507	56°14·1′	4°29·6′W	W	57
Allt Glas-choille	Aberd	NJ3103	57°7·0′	3°7·9′W	W	37
Allt Glas-choire	Highld	NN4472	56°49·1′	4°32·9′W	W	42
Allt Glas Choire	Pth & Kin	NN7475	56°51·2′	4°3·5′W	W	42
Allt Glas-Dhoire	Highld	NN2393	56°59·9′	4°54·4′W	W	34
Allt Glas Dhoire	Highld	NN3285	56°55·8′	4°45·2′W	W	34,41

Allt Glas-Dhoire Mór	Highld	NN2392	56°59·4′	4°54·3′W	W	34
Allt Glas Mór	Highld	NH4424	57°17·1′	4°34·8′W	W	26
Allt Glas Toll Beag	Highld	NH3278	57°45·9′	4°49·0′W	W	20
Allt Glas Toll Mor	Highld	NH3176	57°44·8′	4°49·9′W	W	20
Allt Gleadhrach	Highld	NH2850	57°30·7′	4°51·8′W	W	25
Allt Gleann a' Chaolais	Highld	NN1559	56°41·4′	5°0·8′W	W	41
Allt Gleann a' Chlachain	Stir	NN3631	56°26·8′	4°39·2′W	W	50
Allt Gleann a' Choire Dhomhain	Highld	NG9933	57°20·9′	5°20·0′W	W	25
Allt Gleann a' Mhadaidh	Highld	NH2285	57°49·4′	4°59·4′W	W	20
Allt Gleann an t-Srathain	Highld	NC0816	58°5·8′	5°15·0′W	W	15
Allt Gleann Auchreoch	Stir	NN3326	56°24·1′	4°41·9′W	W	50
Allt Gleann Bhisdeal	Arg & Bt	NR4567	55°50·0′	6°3·9′W	W	60,61
Allt Gleann Chaorachain	Highld	NH1084	57°48·6′	5°11·4′W	W	19
Allt Gleann Creag a' Chait	Arg & Bt	NR3854	55°42·8′	6°9·8′W	W	60
Allt Gleann Crotha	Stir	NN5020	56°21·2′	4°25·2′W	W	51,57
Allt Gleann Da-Eig	Pth & Kin	NN5943	56°33·7′	4°17·2′W	W	51
Allt Gleann Gnìomhaidh	Highld	NH0420	57°14·0′	5°14·4′W	W	25,33
Allt Gleann Gniòmhaidh	Highld	NH0619	57°13·5′	5°12·4′W	W	33
Allt Gleann Laoigh	Arg & Bt	NS0686	56°1·9′	5°6·4′W	W	56
Allt Gleann Loch nam Breac	Arg & Bt	NR3955	55°43·3′	6°8·9′W	W	60
Allt Gleann Meadail	Highld	NM8298	57°1·6′	5°35·1′W	W	33,40
Allt Gleann Mhic Caraidh	Arg & Bt	NM4744	56°31·5′	6°6·4′W	W	47,48
Allt Gleann na Giubhsachan	Highld	NN2866	56°45·5′	4°48·4′W	W	41
Allt Gleann na h-Airigh	Arg & Bt	NM9719	56°19·5′	5°16·5′W	W	55
Allt Gleann nan Eun	Highld	NH4308	57°8·4′	4°35·2′W	W	34
Allt Gleann nan Meann	Stir	NN5212	56°16·9′	4°23·0′W	W	57
Allt Gleann Scanasdail	N Eil	NB0924	58°6·8′	6°56·0′W	W	13,14
Allt Gleann Sgathaich	Highld	NH4562	57°37·5′	4°35·3′W	W	20
Allt Gleann Tùlacha	Highld	NG9873	57°42·4′	5°23·0′W	W	19
Allt Gleann Udalain	Highld	NG8528	57°17·8′	5°33·7′W	W	33
Allt Gleann Udalain	Highld	NG8831	57°19·5′	5°30·8′W	W	24
Allt Gleann Unndalain	Highld	NG8702	57°3·9′	5°30·3′W	W	33
Allt Glen Loch	Pth & Kin	NO0071	56°49·4′	3°37·9′W	W	43
Allt Glinne Mhóir	Arg & Bt	NN1905	56°12·5′	4°54·7′W	W	56
Allt Gobhlach	Highld	NC6120	58°9·1′	4°21·2′W	W	16
Alltgobhlach	N Ayr	NR8743	55°38·3′	5°22·6′W	X	62,69
Allt Gobhlach	N Ayr	NR8843	55°38·3′	5°21·7′W	W	62,69
Allt Goch	Cered	SN2452	52°8·5′	4°33·9′W	X	145
Allt-goch	Cered	SN3350	52°7·6′	4°26·0′W	X	145
Alltgoch	Cered	SN4948	52°6·8′	4°11·9′W	X	146
Alltgoch	Cered	SN5367	52°17·1′	4°8·9′W	X	135
Alltgoch	Cered	SN5849	52°7·5′	4°4·1′W	X	146
Alltgoch	Cered	SN6388	52°28·6′	4°0·6′W	X	135
Allt-goch	Conwy	SH7461	53°8·1′	3°52·6′W	X	115
Allt-goch	Gwyn	SH7003	52°36·8′	3°54·8′W	X	135
Allt-gôch	Powys	SJ1217	52°44·8′	3°17·8′W	H	125
Allt Goch	Powys	SJ2025	52°49·2′	3°10·8′W	F	126
Allt Goch	Powys	SJ2125	52°49·2′	3°9·9′W	X	126
Allt Gôch	Powys	SN7999	52°34·8′	3°46·7′W	H	135
Allt Goch	Powys	SN9363	52°15·5′	3°33·7′W	H	147
Allt Goch	Powys	SN9585	52°27·4′	3°32·3′W	X	136
Allt-goch	Powys	SN9772	52°20·4′	3°30·3′W	X	136,147
Alltgochymynydd	Cered	SN7088	52°28·7′	3°54·5′W	X	135
Allt Goibhre	Highld	NH4348	57°30·0′	4°36·7′W	W	26
Allt Goirtein nan Crann	Arg & Bt	NM6140	56°29·7′	5°52·5′W	W	49
Alltgolau	Carm	SN5125	51°54·5′	4°9·6′W	X	146
Allt Gorm	Highld	NG8113	57°9·6′	5°36·8′W	W	33
Allt Gorm	Highld	NH1104	57°5·6′	5°6·7′W	W	34
Allt Gormag	Pth & Kin	NN4360	56°42·6′	4°33·4′W	W	42
Allt Gortain Ruaidh	Arg & Bt	NR7265	55°49·7′	5°38·0′W	W	62
Allt Grannda	Highld	NG8917	57°12·0′	5°29·1′W	W	33
Allt Grannda	Highld	NH0216	57°11·8′	5°16·2′W	W	33
Allt Grigadale	Highld	NM4366	56°43·2′	6°11·6′W	W	47
Allt Grillan	Highld	NG4229	57°17·0′	6°16·4′W	W	32
Allt Gruiniche	Arg & Bt	NN0430	56°25·6′	5°10·3′W	W	50
Allt Grundale	Arg & Bt	NR6289	56°2·3′	5°48·8′W	W	61
Allt Gualainn a' Chàrra Mhóir	Highld	NN4375	56°50·7′	4°34·0′W	W	42
Allt Gualann Dhearcaig	Highld	NN4076	56°51·1′	4°37·0′W	W	42
Allt Guibhais	Highld	NH0563	57°37·2′	5°15·4′W	W	19
Allt Guibhais	Highld	NH0909	57°8·2′	5°8·9′W	W	33
Allt Guibhsachain	Highld	NN0657	56°40·1′	5°9·5′W	W	41
Allt Guin Shuas	Highld	NG6128	57°17·1′	5°57·5′W	W	32
Allt Gwyddgwion	Gwyn	SH6500	52°35·1′	3°59·2′W	X	135
Allt Gymbyd Fm	Denb	SJ2054	53°4·9′	3°11·3′W	FM	117
Allt Hallater	Arg & Bt	NN1339	56°30·6′	5°1·9′W	W	50
Allt Heasgarnich	Pth & Kin	NN4140	56°31·8′	4°34·7′W	W	51
Allt Heiker	N Eil	NF6900	56°58·6′	7°26·5′W	W	31
Allt Horn	Highld	NC3243	58°20·9′	4°51·8′W	W	9
Allt Hostarie	Arg & Bt	NM3946	56°32·3′	6°14·3′W	W	47,48
Allt Iarairidh	Highld	NH3316	57°12·5′	4°45·4′W	W	34
Allt Innis a' Mhuilt	Highld	NH2237	57°23·6′	4°57·3′W	W	25
Allt Innis an Droighinn	Highld	NH2929	57°19·4′	4°49·9′W	W	25
Allt Innis Ceann an Locha	Highld	NC5844	58°22·0′	4°25·2′W	W	10
Allt Innischoarach	Stir	NN4935	56°29·2′	4°26·7′W	W	51
Allt Innis Chòinnich	Highld	NC5463	58°32·1′	4°30·0′W	W	10
Allt Innisdaimh	Stir	NN4635	56°29·2′	4°29·6′W	W	51
Allt Innis na Làrach	Highld	NH2537	57°23·7′	4°54·3′W	W	25
Allt Innis nam Febrag	Highld	NM6262	56°41·6′	5°52·8′W	W	40
Allt Innis Shim	Highld	NN3298	57°2·8′	4°45·7′W	W	34
Allt Iomadaidh	Highld	NJ1019	57°15·4′	3°29·1′W	W	36
Allt Ionndrainn	Highld	NN2783	56°54·6′	4°50·0′W	W	34,41
Allt Isaf	V of Glam	ST0778	51°29·8′	3°20·0′W	X	170
Allt Kinardochy	Pth & Kin	NN7756	56°41·0′	4°0·0′W	W	42,51,52
Allt Kinglass	Arg & Bt	NN3438	56°30·5′	4°41·4′W	W	50
Allt Kinglass	Arg & Bt	NN3538	56°30·6′	4°40·4′W	W	50
Allt Kynachan	Pth & Kin	NN7656	56°41·0′	4°1·0′W	W	42,51,52
Allt Lacasdail	N Eil	NB1802	57°55·4′	6°45·3′W	W	14
Allt Ladaidh	Highld	NN2299	57°3·1′	4°55·6′W	W	34
Allt Laes	V of Glam	ST0777	51°29·3′	3°20·0′W	X	170
Allt Lagan a' Bhainne	Highld	NN3799	57°3·5′	4°40·8′W	W	34
Allt Lagan na Féithe	Highld	NN2458	56°41·1′	4°52·0′W	W	41
Allt Làir	Highld	NH2879	57°46·3′	4°53·1′W	W	20
Allt Làire	Highld	NN3276	56°51·0′	4°44·8′W	W	41
Allt Lairig Eilde	Highld	NN1755	56°39·3′	4°58·7′W	W	41
Allt Lairig Ianachain	Arg & Bt	NN1231	56°26·3′	5°2·5′W	W	50
Allt Lairig Luaidhe	Pth & Kin	NN5242	56°33·1′	4°24·0′W	W	51
Allt Lairig Mhic Bhaidein	Stir	NN3933	56°28·0′	4°36·4′W	W	50
Allt Lairig nan Lunn	Pth & Kin	NN4440	56°31·8′	4°31·7′W	W	51
Allt Laoghain	Pth & Kin	NN5141	56°32·5′	4°25·0′W	W	51
Allt Laoigh	Highld	NH9233	57°22·7′	3°47·3′W	W	27
Allt Laoisich	Pth & Kin	NN5041	56°32·5′	4°25·9′W	W	51
Allt Lathach	Highld	NH7823	57°17·1′	4°1·0′W	W	35
Allt Leac	Highld	NN4098	57°3·0′	4°37·8′W	W	34
Allt Leac a' Bhealaich	Highld	NH1669	57°40·7′	5°4·7′W	W	20
Allt Leacach	Highld	NC2755	58°27·2′	4°57·4′W	W	9
Allt Leacach	Highld	NH1777	57°45·0′	5°4·0′W	W	20
Allt Leacach	Highld	NM6758	56°39·6′	5°47·7′W	W	49
Allt Leacach	Highld	NM7044	56°32·2′	5°44·0′W	W	49
Allt Leacachain	Highld	NH2377	57°45·1′	4°58·0′W	W	20
Allt Leacachan	Stir	NN6127	56°25·1′	4°14·8′W	W	51
Allt Leac Ghiubhais	Pth & Kin	NN5252	56°38·4′	4°24·4′W	W	42,51
Allt Leachdach	Highld	NN2677	56°51·4′	4°50·8′W	W	41
Allt Leac Ladaidh	Highld	NN2398	57°2·6′	4°54·6′W	W	34
Allt Leacoch	Highld	NC6415	58°6·5′	4°18·0′W	W	16
Allt Lean Achaidh	Arg & Bt	NR9681	55°59·0′	5°15·8′W	W	55
Allt Learg Mheuran	Arg & Bt	NN3946	56°35·0′	4°36·8′W	W	50
Allt Leathad an Tobair	Highld	NH0745	57°27·5′	5°12·6′W	W	25
Allt Leathad an Tobair	Highld	NH1135	57°22·2′	5°8·1′W	W	25
Allt Leathad Cartach	Highld	NH3973	57°43·3′	4°41·7′W	W	20
Allt Leathad Doire Ruaidhe	Highld	NC1507	58°1·1′	5°7·5′W	W	15
Allt Leathan	Pth & Kin	NN7156	56°40·9′	4°5·9′W	W	42,51,52
Allt Lebhain	Stir	NN4937	56°30·3′	4°26·8′W	W	51
Allt Leodasclaid or Allt Leodascleit	N Eil	NB4050	58°21·9′	6°26·3′W	W	8
Allt Leth-bheinne	Highld	NH3202	57°5·0′	4°45·9′W	W	34
Allt Leth-shithein	Highld	NG6510	57°7·5′	5°52·5′W	W	32
Allt Lì	Highld	NG8207	57°6·4′	5°35·5′W	W	33
Allt Lian a' Mhaim	Arg & Bt	NM4246	56°32·4′	6°11·4′W	W	47,48
Allt Liath	Highld	NG6231	57°18·7′	5°56·7′W	W	24,32
Allt Liath-choire Mhór	Aberd	NO1698	57°4·2′	3°22·7′W	W	36,43
Allt Liathdoire	Highld	NC1606	58°0·6′	5°6·4′W	W	15
Allt Lice	Highld	NH1740	57°25·1′	5°2·4′W	W	25
Allt Lice Duibhe	Pth & Kin	NN4665	56°45·3′	4°30·7′W	W	42
Allt Ligheach	Highld	NM9477	56°50·6′	5°22·2′W	W	40
Allt Linne a' Bhùirein	Pth & Kin	NO0569	56°48·4′	3°32·9′W	W	43
Allt Linne nan Ribheid	Arg & Bt	NM3220	56°18·1′	6°19·5′W	W	48
Allt Liònogan	Highld	NG8918	57°12·5′	5°29·2′W	W	33
Allt Llwyn-crwn	Carm	SN5344	52°4·7′	4°8·3′W	F	146
Allt Loan	Moray	NJ2432	57°22·6′	3°15·4′W	W	36
Allt Loch a' Chòinich	Highld	NH1516	57°12·1′	5°3·3′W	W	34
Allt Loch a' Choire Bhig	Highld	NH1632	57°20·7′	5°3·0′W	W	25
Allt Loch a' Chràthaich	Highld	NH3718	57°13·7′	4°41·6′W	W	34
Allt Loch a' Ghael	Arg & Bt	NM4146	56°32·3′	6°12·3′W	W	47,48
Allt Loch a' Ghormlaich	Highld	NH2445	57°27·9′	4°55·6′W	W	25
Allt Lochain Buidhe	Highld	NH1380	57°46·5′	5°8·2′W	W	19
Allt Lochain Cruinn	Highld	NG6722	57°14·0′	5°51·2′W	W	32
Allt Lochain Ghaineamhaich	Highld	NN3253	56°38·6′	4°43·9′W	W	41
Allt Lochain na Sàile	Highld	NG7324	57°15·3′	5°45·4′W	W	33
Allt Lochan a' Choinnich	Highld	NM5967	56°44·2′	5°56·0′W	W	47
Allt Lochan an Làir	Arg & Bt	NN0642	56°32·1′	5°8·8′W	W	50
Allt Lochan Dubh nam Breac	Highld	NG6719	57°12·4′	5°51·0′W	W	32
Allt Loch an Dùin	Highld	NN7382	56°55·0′	4°4·7′W	W	42
Allt Loch an Eilein Leithe	N Eil	NB2114	58°1·9′	6°43·1′W	W	13,14
Allt Lochan Feith a' Mhadaidh	Highld	NM7489	56°56·5′	5°42·5′W	W	40
Allt Loch an Fheoir	N Eil	NB4446	58°19·9′	6°21·9′W	W	8
Allt Loch an Fheòir	N Eil	NG0891	57°49·1′	6°54·6′W	W	14,18
Allt Lochan Fhùdair	Highld	NN2097	57°2·0′	4°57·5′W	W	34
Allt Lochan na Crithe	Arg & Bt	NM5051	56°35·3′	6°3·9′W	W	47
Allt Lochan nan Eun	Aberd	NO2187	56°58·3′	3°17·5′W	W	44
Allt Lochan nan Geadas	Stir	NN5930	56°26·7′	4°16·8′W	W	51
Allt Lochan Sgeirich	Highld	NC0310	58°2·4′	5°19·8′W	W	15
Allt Loch an Sgòir	Highld	NG6917	57°11·4′	5°48·9′W	W	32
Allt Loch an Sgòir	Highld	NG7017	57°11·4′	5°47·9′W	W	33
Allt Loch an Tairbh	Highld	NC5632	58°15·5′	4°26·8′W	W	16
Allt Loch an Tairbh	Highld	NG3701	57°1·8′	6°19·6′W	W	32,39
Allt Loch an Tuirc	Highld	NC1025	58°10·6′	5°13·4′W	W	15
Allt Loch an Ulbhaidh	Highld	NC5021	58°9·4′	4°32·5′W	W	16
Allt Loch an Umhlaich	N Eil	NB4448	58°21·0′	6°22·1′W	W	8
Allt Loch Bealach a' Bhùirich	Highld	NC2528	58°12·6′	4°58·2′W	W	15
Allt Loch Calavie	Highld	NH0737	57°23·2′	5°12·2′W	W	25
Allt Loch Carn nan Conbhairean	Highld	NC3617	58°7·0′	4°46·6′W	W	16
Allt Loch Coire na Creige	Highld	NC1521	58°8·6′	5°8·1′W	W	15
Allt Loch Cròcaich	Highld	NC8046	58°23·4′	4°2·7′W	W	10
Allt Loch Gaineamhach	Highld	NG8245	57°26·8′	5°37·5′W	W	24
Allt Loch Innis nan Seangan	Highld	NG9233	57°20·7′	5°26·9′W	W	25
Allt Loch Mhadadh	Highld	ND0035	58°17·8′	3°41·9′W	W	11,17
Allt Loch Mheugaidh	Pth & Kin	NN5260	56°42·8′	4°24·6′W	W	42
Allt Loch na Caillich	Highld	NC5107	58°1·9′	4°30·9′W	W	16
Allt Loch na Caillich	Highld	NH3450	57°30·9′	4°45·8′W	W	26
Allt Loch na Conaire	Arg & Bt	NR6697	56°6·8′	5°45·4′W	W	55,61
Allt Loch na Lap	Highld	NN3970	56°47·9′	4°37·7′W	W	41
Allt Loch nam Breac	Highld	NC8448	58°24·6′	3°58·6′W	W	10
Allt Loch nan Eang	N Eil	NB2007	57°58·1′	6°43·6′W	W	13,14
Allt Loch nan Geadh	N Eil	NB3235	58°13·6′	6°33·4′W	W	8,13
Allt Loch nan Uamh	Highld	NG6208	57°6·3′	5°55·4′W	W	32
Allt Loch Shibhinn	Arg & Bt	NR3165	55°48·5′	6°17·2′W	W	60,61
Allt Loch Tarbhaidh	Highld	NC2854	58°26·7′	4°56·3′W	W	9
Allt Loch Valigan	Pth & Kin	NN9669	56°48·3′	3°41·7′W	W	43
Allt Loin Bheag	Moray	NJ1307	57°9·0′	3°25·8′W	W	36
Allt Loisgle	Highld	NH8829	57°20·5′	3°51·2′W	W	35,36
Allt Loisgte	Highld	NH8630	57°21·0′	3°53·2′W	W	27,36
Allt Lòn a' Chùil	Highld	NC7239	58°19·5′	4°10·7′W	W	16
Allt Lon a' Chuil	Highld	NC7241	58°20·6′	4°10·7′W	W	10
Allt Lòn a' Ghiubhais	Highld	NH5336	57°23·7′	4°26·3′W	W	26
Allt Lòn a' Mhuidhe	Highld	NM8481	56°52·5′	5°32·2′W	W	40
Allt Lòn Bhuidhe	Highld	NG6516	57°10·7′	5°52·8′W	W	32
Allt Lòn Coire nam Feuran	Highld	NC6735	58°17·3′	4°15·6′W	W	16
Allt Lòn Glas Bheinn	Highld	NN1396	57°1·3′	5°4·4′W	W	34
Allt Loraich	Highld	NN3879	56°52·7′	4°39·1′W	W	41
Allt Lorgaidh	Highld	NN8488	56°58·4′	3°54·0′W	W	43
Allt Luachair	Highld	NJ0834	57°23·5′	3°31·4′W	W	27
Allt Luaidhe	Highld	NN4798	57°3·1′	4°30·9′W	W	34
Allt Lub na Criche	Arg & Bt	NM8615	56°17·0′	5°27·0′W	W	55
Allt Lùb nam Meann	Highld	NH1729	57°19·2′	5°1·9′W	W	25
Allt Lùb nan Copag	Highld	NH2147	57°28·9′	4°58·7′W	W	25
Allt Luib Ruairidh	Highld	NN3568	56°46·7′	4°41·6′W	W	41
Allt Luig Mhóir	Highld	NG5212	57°8·2′	6°5·5′W	W	32
Allt Luineag	Highld	NN9295	57°2·3′	3°46·3′W	W	36,43
Allt Lundie	Highld	NH2905	57°6·5′	4°49·0′W	W	34
Allt-lwwyd	Gwyn	SH7928	52°50·4′	3°47·4′W	X	124
Allt-lwyd	Gwyn	SH6107	52°38·8′	4°2·9′W	H	124
Allt Lwyd	Powys	SN9154	52°10·7′	3°35·3′W	X	147
Alltlwyd	Powys	SN9778	52°23·7′	3°30·4′W	X	136,147
Allt Lwyd	Powys	SO0718	51°51·4′	3°20·6′W	H	160
Alltlwyd Home Farm	Cered	SN5268	52°17·7′	4°9·8′W	FM	135
Allt Madagain	Highld	NN6298	57°3·4′	4°16·1′W	W	35
Allt Madaig	Pth & Kin	NN5156	56°40·6′	4°25·5′W	W	42,51
Alltmaen	Cered	SN4049	52°7·2′	4°19·8′W	X	146
Allt Maenderyn	Gwyn	SH6052	53°3·1′	4°4·9′W	X	115
Allt Màiri	Highld	NN2183	56°54·5′	4°55·9′W	W	34,41
Allt Màm a' Ghaill	Highld	NM4867	56°43·9′	6°6·7′W	W	47
Allt Màm Lì	Highld	NG8006	57°5·8′	5°37·5′W	W	33
Allt Màm na Seilg	Highld	NH1004	57°5·5′	5°7·7′W	W	34
Allt Maol Ruainidh	Highld	NN2852	56°38·0′	4°47·8′W	W	41
Allt Maraig	Pth & Kin	NN6767	56°46·8′	4°10·2′W	W	42
Allt Martuin	Highld	NH4838	57°24·7′	4°31·4′W	W	26
Allt Mathaig	Pth & Kin	NN7128	56°25·9′	4°5·1′W	W	51,52
Alltmawr	Powys	SO0746	52°6·5′	3°21·1′W	T	147
Allt Meadhonach	Highld	NC5028	58°13·2′	4°32·7′W	W	16
Allt Meadhonach	Highld	NC7821	58°9·9′	4°4·0′W	W	17
Allt Meall a' Bhealaich	Highld	NN4469	56°47·4′	4°32·8′W	W	42
Allt Meallan Gobhar	Highld	NG8445	57°26·9′	5°35·5′W	W	24
Allt Meall Ardruighe	Highld	NN4480	56°53·4′	4°33·2′W	W	34,42
Allt Meall nan Damh	Stir	NN6532	56°27·9′	4°11·0′W	W	51
Allt Meall na Teanga	Highld	NC5723	58°10·6′	4°25·4′W	W	16
Allt Menach	Pth & Kin	NO0962	56°44·7′	3°28·8′W	W	43
Allt Meran	Pth & Kin	NN3943	56°33·3′	4°36·7′W	W	50
Allt Meurach	Highld	NN0863	56°43·4′	5°7·8′W	W	41
Allt Mhainisteir	Highld	NN5284	56°55·7′	4°25·5′W	W	42
Allt Mhairc	Pth & Kin	NN8874	56°50·9′	3°49·7′W	W	43
Allt Mhàlagain	Highld	NG9713	57°10·0′	5°21·0′W	W	33
Allt Mhaluidh	Arg & Bt	NN1725	56°23·2′	4°57·4′W	W	50
Allt Mharconaich	Highld	NH5410	57°9·7′	4°24·4′W	W	35
Allt Mhartuin	Highld	NH1554	57°32·6′	5°5·0′W	W	25
Allt Mhathain	Highld	NC1631	58°14·0′	5°7·6′W	W	15
Allt Mheuran	Highld	NN1444	56°33·3′	5°1·1′W	W	50
Allt Mhic an Righ	Pth & Kin	NN6980	56°53·8′	4°8·6′W	W	42
Allt Mhic a' Phearsain	Highld	NG8513	57°9·7′	5°32·9′W	W	33
Allt Mhic Bhaidein	Arg & Bt	NN3735	56°29·0′	4°38·4′W	W	50
Allt Mhic Cailein	Highld	NM4769	56°44·9′	6°7·8′W	W	47
Allt Mhic Chiarain	Highld	NM7465	56°43·6′	5°41·2′W	W	40
Allt Mhic Leanain	Highld	NG6125	57°15·5′	5°57·3′W	W	32
Allt Mhic Mhoirein	Highld	NG5227	57°16·2′	6°6·4′W	W	32
Allt Mhic Mhurchaidh Ghèir	Highld	NC2316	58°6·1′	4°59·7′W	W	15
Allt Mhic Slamhaich	Arg & Bt	NM5925	56°21·6′	5°53·7′W	W	48
Allt Mhic Thomais	Pth & Kin	NN4657	56°41·0′	4°30·4′W	W	42,51
Allt Mhoille	Arg & Bt	NN1230	56°25·7′	5°2·5′W	W	50
Allt Mhucaidh (Remony Burn)	Pth & Kin	NN7742	56°33·5′	3°59·6′W	X	51,52
Allt Mhucarnaich	Highld	NH2479	57°46·2′	4°57·1′W	W	20
Allt Mhuic	Highld	NN1293	56°59·7′	5°5·2′W	W	34
Allt Mhuic Bheag	Highld	NN1192	56°59·1′	5°6·2′W	W	34
Allt Mhungasdail	Highld	NG9893	57°53·1′	5°24·0′W	W	19
Allt Mhurlagain	Highld	NN0192	56°58·8′	5°16·0′W	W	33
Allt Mialach	Highld	NH0804	57°5·5′	5°9·7′W	W	33
Allt Mille nan Con	N Eil	NF8136	57°18·4′	7°17·4′W	W	22
Allt Molach	Arg & Bt	NM6231	56°24·9′	5°51·1′W	W	49
Allt Molach	Highld	NH3829	57°19·6′	4°41·0′W	W	26
Allt Molach	N Eil	NB4238	58°15·6′	6°23·4′W	W	8
Allt mo Nionag	Highld	NM8362	56°42·2′	5°32·2′W	W	40
Allt Mór	Arg & Bt	NM3850	56°34·4′	6°15·5′W	W	47
Allt Mór	Arg & Bt	NM5040	56°29·4′	6°3·2′W	W	47,48
Allt Mór	Arg & Bt	NM6239	56°29·2′	5°51·5′W	W	49
Allt Mor	Arg & Bt	NM9208	56°13·4′	5°20·9′W	W	55
Allt Mór	Arg & Bt	NM9511	56°15·1′	5°18·1′W	W	55
Allt Mór	Arg & Bt	NN0217	56°18·5′	5°11·6′W	W	50,55
Allt Mor	Arg & Bt	NR3877	55°55·1′	6°11·2′W	W	60,61
Allt Mòr	Arg & Bt	NR7438	55°35·3′	5°34·7′W	W	68
Allt Mór	Arg & Bt	NR7655	55°44·5′	5°33·7′W	W	62
Allt Mór	Arg & Bt	NR8171	55°53·2′	5°29·7′W	W	62
Allt Mór	Arg & Bt	NR9087	56°2·1′	5°21·8′W	W	55
Allt Mór	Arg & Bt	NR9673	55°54·7′	5°15·4′W	W	62
Allt Mór	Arg & Bt	NS0676	55°56·5′	5°5·9′W	W	63
Allt Mór	Highld	NC1627	58°11·9′	5°7·4′W	W	15
Allt Mór	Highld	NC4901	57°58·6′	4°32·7′W	W	16
Allt Mór	Highld	NG3632	57°18·4′	6°22·6′W	W	32
Allt Mór	Highld	NG3721	57°12·5′	6°20·9′W	W	32
Allt Mór	Highld	NG3740	57°22·7′	6°22·1′W	W	23
Allt Mór	Highld	NG4532	57°18·7′	6°13·6′W	W	32
Allt Mòr	Highld	NG5801	57°2·5′	5°58·9′W	W	32,39
Allt Mór	Highld	NG7221	57°13·6′	5°46·2′W	W	33
Allt Mór	Highld	NG7446	57°27·1′	5°45·6′W	W	24
Allt Mór	Highld	NG7545	57°26·6′	5°44·5′W	W	24
Allt Mór	Highld	NG7681	57°46·0′	5°45·5′W	W	19
Allt Mór	Highld	NG7985	57°48·3′	5°42·7′W	W	19
Allt Mór	Highld	NG8421	57°14·0′	5°34·3′W	W	33
Allt Mór	Highld	NG8516	57°11·3′	5°33·0′W	W	33
Allt Mór	Highld	NG8643	57°25·9′	5°33·4′W	W	24
Allt Mór	Highld	NG9427	57°17·5′	5°24·7′W	W	25,33
Allt Mór	Highld	NH4902	57°5·3′	4°29·1′W	W	34
Allt Mór	Highld	NH5438	57°24·8′	4°25·4′W	W	26
Allt Mor	Highld	NH5704	57°6·5′	4°21·2′W	W	35
Allt Mór	Highld	NH6422	57°16·4′	4°14·9′W	W	26,35
Allt Mór	Highld	NH6436	57°23·9′	4°15·3′W	X	26
Allt Mór	Highld	NH7101	57°5·2′	4°7·3′W	W	35
Allt Mór	Highld	NH7404	57°6·8′	4°4·4′W	W	35
Allt Mór	Highld	NH7416	57°13·3′	4°4·7′W	W	35

Allt Mór	Highld	NH7610	57°10·1′	4°2·6′W	W	35
Allt Mór	Highld	NH9627	57°19·6′	3°43·2′W	W	36
Allt Mór	Highld	NJ0121	57°16·4′	3°38·1′W	W	36
Allt Mór	Highld	NJ0914	57°12·7′	3°29·9′W	W	36
Allt Mór	Highld	NM7043	56°31·6′	5°43·9′W	W	49
Allt Mór	Highld	NN5990	56°59·0′	4°18·8′W	W	35
Allt Mór	Highld	NN8295	57°2·1′	3°56·2′W	W	35,43
Allt Mór	N Ayr	NR9729	55°31·0′	5°12·5′W	W	69
Allt Mòr	N Eil	NB2207	57°58·2′	6°41·6′W	W	13,14
Allt Mór	Pth & Kin	NN6660	56°43·0′	4°10·9′W	W	42
Allt Mór	Pth & Kin	NN7014	56°18·3′	4°5·6′W	W	57
Allt Mór	Pth & Kin	NN7230	56°26·9′	4°4·2′W	W	51,52
Allt Mór	Pth & Kin	NN7453	56°39·4′	4°2·9′W	W	42,51,52
Allt Mór	Pth & Kin	NN7660	56°43·2′	4°1·1′W	W	42
Allt Mór	Pth & Kin	NO1468	56°48·0′	3°24·0′W	W	43
Allt Mòr	Stir	NN3803	56°11·8′	4°36·2′W	W	56
Allt Mór	Stir	NN5513	56°17·5′	4°20·1′W	W	57
Allt Mór an Laoigh	Arg & Bt	NR7232	55°32·0′	5°36·4′W	W	68
Allt Mór Cloined	N Ayr	NR9623	55°27·8′	5°13·2′W	W	68,69
Allt Mór Coire nan Eunachair	Arg & Bt	NM6440	56°29·8′	5°49·6′W	W	49
Allt Mór Dhruideigh	Highld	NG8723	57°15·1′	5°31·4′W	W	33
Allt Mór Doire Mhic-ùin	Highld	NG5229	57°17·3′	6°6·5′W	W	32
Allt Mór Ghalltair	Highld	NG8220	57°13·4′	5°36·2′W	W	33
Allt Mór Gisgil	Highld	NC1741	58°19·4′	5°7·0′W	W	9
Allt Mór na h-Uamha	Highld	NM4097	56°59·7′	6°16·4′W	W	39
Allt Mór na Sròine	Highld	NG4430	57°17·6′	6°14·5′W	W	32
Allt Mór or March Burn	Highld	NJ1122	57°17·1′	3°28·1′W	W	36
Allt Mór Shantaig	Highld	NG7914	57°10·1′	5°38·9′W	W	33
Allt Muic Ruaidh	Arg & Bt	NR8576	55°56·0′	5°26·1′W	W	62
Allt Muigh-bhlàraidh	Highld	NH6582	57°48·7′	4°15·9′W	W	21
Allt Mullach	Highld	NH9813	57°12·0′	3°40·8′W	W	36
Allt Mullardoch	Highld	NH2033	57°21·4′	4°59·1′W	W	25
Allt na Bà	Highld	NC6129	58°13·9′	4°21·6′W	W	16
Allt na Ba Duinne	Highld	NC6623	58°10·8′	4°16·2′W	W	16
Allt na Bainse	Arg & Bt	NR7370	55°52·4′	5°37·3′W	W	62
Allt na Bana-mhorair	Highld	NH4269	57°41·3′	4°38·6′W	W	20
Allt na Baranachd	Highld	NH7905	57°7·5′	3°59·5′W	W	35
Allt na Beinne	Highld	NH6625	57°18·0′	4°13·0′W	W	26,35
Allt na Beinne	Highld	NH7002	57°5·7′	4°8·3′W	W	35
Allt na Beinne	Highld	NH7937	57°24·7′	4°0·4′W	W	27
Allt na Beinne Gairbhe	Highld	NC2023	58°9·8′	5°3·1′W	W	15
Allt na Béiste	Arg & Bt	NR7730	55°31·0′	5°31·5′W	W	68,69
Allt na Bogair	Pth & Kin	NN6055	56°40·2′	4°16·6′W	W	42,51
Allt na Bradan	Moray	NJ3228	57°20·5′	3°7·3′W	W	37
Allt na Bradhan	Highld	NC2128	58°12·5′	5°2·3′W	W	15
Allt na Buaile Duibhe	Highld	NG4218	57°11·1′	6°15·7′W	W	32
Allt na Cailbhe Mór	Highld	NC7637	58°18·5′	4°6·5′W	W	17
Allt na Cailich	Highld	NN0393	56°59·4′	5°14·1′W	W	33
Allt na Caillich	Aberd	NJ2817	57°14·5′	3°11·1′W	W	37
Alltnacaillich	Highld	NC4545	58°22·2′	4°38·5′W	X	9
Allt na Caillich	Highld	NC4746	58°22·8′	4°36·5′W	W	9
Allt na Caillich	Highld	NC6125	58°11·8′	4°21·4′W	W	16
Allt na Caillich	Highld	NH0994	57°53·9′	5°12·9′W	X	19
Allt na Caillich	Highld	NN1576	56°50·6′	5°1·5′W	W	41
Allt na Cailliche	Highld	NC3310	58°3·1′	4°49·3′W	W	15
Allt na Cailliche	Highld	NN2698	57°2·7′	4°51·6′W	W	34
Allt na Caim	Highld	NN3763	56°44·1′	4°39·4′W	W	41
Allt na Caime	Highld	NG9635	57°21·9′	5°23·1′W	W	25
Allt na Caoileig	Highld	NN8196	57°2·6′	3°57·2′W	W	35,43
Allt na Carraige	Highld	NM8351	56°36·3′	5°31·7′W	W	49
Allt na Ceàrdaich	Highld	NG8828	57°17·9′	5°30·7′W	W	33
Allt na Ceàrdaich	Highld	NH5843	57°27·6′	4°21·6′W	W	26
Allt na Ceàrdaich	Highld	NJ0237	57°25·0′	3°37·4′W	W	27
Allt na Ceardaich	Stir	NN5735	56°29·4′	4°18·9′W	W	51
Allt na Cìche	Highld	NH1216	57°12·0′	5°6·3′W	W	34
Allt na Ciste	Highld	NH9907	57°8·8′	3°39·7′W	W	36
Allt na Ciste Duibhe	Highld	NH5897	57°56·6′	4°23·5′W	W	21
Allt na Clach Airigh	Highld	NC1720	58°8·1′	5°6·0′W	W	15
Allt na Claise	Highld	NC1832	58°14·6′	5°5·6′W	W	15
Allt na Claise Brice	Highld	NM7247	56°33·8′	5°42·2′W	W	49
Allt na Claise Càrnaich	Highld	NC2952	58°25·6′	4°55·2′W	W	9
Allt na Claise Móire	Aberd	NO1798	57°4·2′	3°21·7′W	W	36,43
Allt na Claise Móire	Highld	NC4230	58°14·1′	4°41·0′W	W	16
Allt na Claise Móire	Highld	NC9239	58°19·8′	3°50·2′W	W	11,17
Allt na Claise Móire	Highld	NH2358	57°34·9′	4°57·2′W	W	25
Allt na Cléite	Highld	NC8764	58°33·2′	3°56·0′W	W	10
Allt na Cloch	Aberd	NO4392	57°1·2′	2°55·9′W	W	44
Allt na Cloiche	Highld	NM8158	56°40·0′	5°34·0′W	W	49
Allt na Cloiche	Highld	NN7882	56°55·1′	3°59·8′W	W	42
Allt na Codha	Arg & Bt	NM6421	56°19·6′	5°48·6′W	W	49
Allt na Coille Móire	Arg & Bt	NM5030	56°24·0′	6°2·7′W	W	48
Allt na Coille Móire	Highld	NN0380	56°52·4′	5°13·5′W	W	41
Allt na Cois	Highld	NH1743	57°26·7′	5°2·5′W	W	25
Allt na Coite	Arg & Bt	NR2665	55°48·3′	6°21·9′W	W	60
Allt na Cornlaraiche	Highld	NH8109	57°9·6′	3°57·6′W	W	35
Allt na Cosaig	Highld	NG8569	57°39·8′	5°35·8′W	W	19
Allt na Cosaig	Pth & Kin	NN6366	56°46·2′	4°14·0′W	W	42
Allt na Cradh-lice	Highld	NN2758	56°41·2′	4°49·0′W	W	41
Allt na Craidhleig	Highld	NH4904	57°6·4′	4°29·1′W	W	34
Allt na Craidhleig	Highld	NH5004	57°6·4′	4°28·1′W	W	35
Allt na Craige Tarsuinn	Highld	NN3174	56°49·9′	4°45·7′W	W	41
Allt na Crannaich	Arg & Bt	NN3544	56°33·8′	4°40·7′W	W	50
Allt na Craoibhe	Highld	NN7181	56°54·4′	4°6·7′W	W	42
Allt na Craoibhe	N Eil	NB3929	58°10·6′	6°25·9′W	W	8
Allt na Craoibhe-caorainn	Moray	NJ3125	57°18·9′	3°8·3′W	W	37
Allt na Craoibhe-cuilinn	Moray	NJ3123	57°17·8′	3°8·2′W	W	37
Allt na Creadha	Highld	NC7134	58°16·8′	4°11·5′W	W	16
Allt na Creadha	Highld	NG4028	57°16·4′	6°18·3′W	W	32
Allt na Creiche	Arg & Bt	NM3223	56°19·7′	6°19·7′W	W	48
Allt na Creiche	Highld	NC4020	58°8·7′	4°42·6′W	W	16
Allt na Creiche	Highld	NM8358	56°40·1′	5°32·0′W	W	49
Allt na Creige	Arg & Bt	NN1712	56°16·2′	4°56·9′W	W	50,56
Allt na Creige	Highld	NG9078	57°44·8′	5°31·3′W	W	19
Allt na Creige Duibhe	Highld	NH2587	57°50·6′	4°56·4′W	W	20
Allt na Creige Riabhaich	Highld	NC3062	58°31·0′	4°54·6′W	W	9
Allt na Criche	Arg & Bt	NM4227	56°22·2′	6°10·2′W	W	48
Allt na Crìche	Arg & Bt	NM5244	56°31·6′	6°1·5′W	W	47,48
Allt na Criche	Arg & Bt	NR2465	55°48·2′	6°23·8′W	W	60
Allt na Críche	Arg & Bt	NS1380	55°58·9′	4°59·4′W	W	63
Allt na Criche	Highld	NC9150	58°25·8′	3°51·5′W	W	10
Allt na Criche	Highld	NH0729	57°18·9′	5°11·8′W	W	25,33
Allt na Criche	Highld	NH1649	57°29·9′	5°3·8′W	W	25
Allt na Crìche	Highld	NH2611	57°9·7′	4°52·2′W	W	34
Allt na Criche	Highld	NH3446	57°28·7′	4°45·7′W	W	26
Allt na Crìche	Highld	NH3812	57°10·5′	4°40·3′W	W	34
Allt-na-Criche	Highld	NH8710	57°10·3′	3°51·7′W	W	35,36
Allt na Crìche	Highld	NJ1229	57°20·8′	3°27·3′W	W	36
Allt na Crìche	Highld	NM7651	56°36·1′	5°38·5′W	W	49
Allt na Criche	Highld	NM7682	56°52·8′	5°40·1′W	W	40
Allt na Crìche	Highld	NM7844	56°32·4′	5°36·2′W	W	49
Allt na Crìche	Highld	NM7983	56°53·4′	5°37·2′W	W	40
Allt na Criche	Highld	NM9780	56°52·3′	5°19·4′W	W	40
Allt na Crìche	Moray	NJ1529	57°20·9′	3°24·3′W	W	36
Allt na Criche	N Eil	NB1328	58°9·1′	6°52·2′W	W	13
Allt na Criche	Pth & Kin	NN5653	56°39·1′	4°20·5′W	W	42,51
Allt na Crìche	Stir	NN7208	56°15·1′	4°3·5′W	W	57
Allt na Crionaiche Bige	Highld	NC4418	58°7·7′	4°38·5′W	W	16
Allt na Croiche	Arg & Bt	NS0475	55°55·9′	5°7·8′W	W	63
Allt na Croit Rainich	Highld	NN0379	56°51·9′	5°13·5′W	W	41
Allt na-Cruaiche	Highld	NM9277	56°50·5′	5°24·2′W	W	40
Allt na Cruimadh	Highld	NH2330	57°19·8′	4°56·0′W	W	25
Allt na Cubhaige	Highld	NN6192	57°0·2′	4°16·9′W	W	35
Allt na Cuilce	Highld	NN8089	56°58·9′	3°58·0′W	W	43
Allt na Cuile	Stir	NN7211	56°16·7′	4°3·6′W	W	57
Allt na Cuile Riabhaiche	Arg & Bt	NN0619	56°19·7′	5°7·8′W	W	50,56
Allt na Cuinneige	Arg & Bt	NM6423	56°20·7′	5°48·7′W	W	49
Allt na Cuinneige Bige	Highld	NH4882	57°48·4′	4°33·0′W	W	20
Allt na Dail-fearna	Arg & Bt	NN0419	56°19·6′	5°9·8′W	W	50,56
Allt na Dàlach	Highld	NG8423	57°15·1′	5°34·4′W	W	33
Allt na Dìollaid	Highld	NM8280	56°51·9′	5°34·1′W	W	40
Allt na Doire	Highld	NH9611	57°10·9′	3°42·8′W	W	36
Allt na Doire	Highld	NN4692	56°59·9′	4°31·7′W	W	34
Allt na Doire Caoile	Highld	NH2057	57°34·3′	5°0·1′W	W	25
Allt na Doire Cuilinn	Highld	NC2025	58°10·9′	5°3·2′W	W	15
Allt na Doire-daraich	Highld	NH0062	57°36·5′	5°20·4′W	W	19
Allt na Doire Gairbhe	Highld	NH0429	57°18·8′	5°14·8′W	W	25,33
Allt na Doire-giubhais	Highld	NH1062	57°36·7′	5°10·4′W	W	19
Allt na Dubh-chlaise	Highld	NH2513	57°10·7′	4°53·3′W	W	34
Allt na Duinish	Pth & Kin	NN6065	56°45·6′	4°17·0′W	W	42
Allt na Dunaich	Arg & Bt	NR6731	55°31·3′	5°41·0′W	W	68
Allt na Dunaiche	Highld	NG5421	57°13·1′	6°4·0′W	W	32
Allt na Faic	Highld	NC4107	58°1·7′	4°41·1′W	W	16
Allt na Faine	Highld	NH1276	57°44·3′	5°9·0′W	W	19
Allt na Faing	Highld	NH0821	57°14·6′	5°10·5′W	W	25,33
Allt na Faing	Highld	NH1724	57°16·5′	5°1·7′W	W	25
Allt na Faing	Highld	NN2291	56°58·8′	4°55·3′W	W	34
Allt na Fainich	Highld	NH4053	57°32·6′	4°39·9′W	W	26
Allt na Faoilinn Glaise	Arg & Bt	NM6526	56°22·3′	5°47·9′W	W	49
Allt na Faolin	Highld	NG7508	57°6·7′	5°42·5′W	W	33
Allt na Feadaige	Highld	NN2496	57°1·6′	4°53·5′W	W	34
Allt na Fearna	Arg & Bt	NS0680	55°58·7′	5°6·1′W	W	63
Allt na Feárna	Highld	NC2462	58°30·9′	5°0·8′W	W	9
Allt na Feàrna	Highld	NH3509	57°8·8′	4°43·2′W	W	34
Allt na Fearna	Highld	NN7489	56°58·8′	4°3·9′W	W	42
Allt na Fearna Mór	Highld	NC5801	57°58·8′	4°23·6′W	W	16
Allt na Fèinne	Highld	NM7444	56°32·3′	5°40·1′W	W	49
Allt na Feinnich	Highld	NN7490	56°59·3′	4°4·0′W	W	35
Allt na Féith Duibhe	Highld	NH9910	57°10·4′	3°39·8′W	W	36
Allt na Féithe	Highld	NM9793	56°59·3′	5°20·0′W	W	33,40
Allt na Féithe Bàine	Highld	NH0759	57°35·1′	5°13·2′W	W	25
Allt na Féithe Bìane	Highld	NH2236	57°23·0′	4°57·2′W	W	25
Allt na Féithe Buidhe	Highld	NC4641	58°20·1′	4°37·3′W	W	9
Allt na Féithe Buidhe	Highld	NG9332	57°20·2′	5°25·9′W	W	25
Allt na Féithe Buidhe	Highld	NH7000	57°4·6′	4°8·2′W	W	35
Allt na Féithe Riabhaich	Highld	NH1847	57°28·9′	5°1·7′W	W	25
Allt na Féithe Sheilich	Highld	NH8328	57°19·9′	3°56·1′W	W	35
Allt na Féith Riabhach	Highld	NC3626	58°11·8′	4°46·9′W	W	16
Allt na Fiacail	Highld	NH6000	57°4·4′	4°18·1′W	W	35
Allt na Frithe	Highld	NH7728	57°19·8′	4°2·1′W	W	35
Allt na Fuar-ghlaic	Highld	NH7135	57°23·5′	4°8·3′W	W	27
Allt na Gaisge	Pth & Kin	NN7312	56°17·3′	4°2·7′W	W	57
Allt na Gile	Arg & Bt	NR4877	55°55·5′	6°1·6′W	W	60,61
Allt na Gile Mòire	N Eil	NB3309	57°59·7′	6°30·6′W	W	13,14
Allt na Glaic	Highld	NH5038	57°24·7′	4°29·4′W	W	26
Allt na Glaic Móire	Highld	NC2620	58°8·3′	4°56·9′W	W	15
Allt na Glaise	Highld	NC3935	58°16·7′	4°44·3′W	W	16
Allt na Glaise	Pth & Kin	NN5769	56°47·7′	4°20·0′W	W	42
Allt na Glas Bheinne	Highld	NN3793	57°0·2′	4°40·6′W	W	34
Allt na Glùine Móire	Highld	NC4031	58°14·6′	4°43·1′W	W	16
Allt na Graidhe	Highld	NH3307	57°7·7′	4°45·1′W	W	34
Allt-na-guibhsaich	Aberd	NO2985	56°57·3′	3°9·6′W	X	44
Allt na Guile	Highld	NG4132	57°18·6′	6°17·6′W	W	32
Allt na Ha	Moray	NJ1528	57°20·3′	3°24·3′W	W	36
Alltnaha	Moray	NJ1628	57°20·3′	3°23·3′W	X	36
Allt na h-Airbhe	Highld	NC1323	58°9·6′	5°10·2′W	W	15
Allt na h-Airbhe	Highld	NH1193	57°53·5′	5°10·8′W	X	19
Allt na h-Aire	Highld	NC5533	58°16·0′	4°27·8′W	W	16
Allt na h-Aire	Highld	NM8880	56°52·0′	5°28·2′W	W	40
Allt na h-Aireimh	Highld	NC8540	58°20·3′	3°57·4′W	W	10
Allt na h-Airigh	Arg & Bt	NN0313	56°16·4′	5°10·5′W	W	50,55
Allt na h-Airigh	Highld	NH0400	57°3·2′	5°13·5′W	W	33
Allt na h-Airigh	Highld	NM7958	56°40·0′	5°35·9′W	W	49
Allt na h-Airigh	Highld	NM9178	56°51·0′	5°25·2′W	W	40
Allt na h-Airighe	N Ayr	NR8939	55°36·2′	5°20·5′W	W	68,69
Allt na h-Aitennaich	Highld	NH0705	57°6·0′	5°10·7′W	W	33
Allt na h-Annait	Arg & Bt	NN3438	56°30·5′	4°41·4′W	W	50
Allt na Harraw	Highld	NN3892	56°59·7′	4°39·6′W	W	34
Allt na h-Atha duibhe	Highld	NM7566	56°44·1′	5°40·3′W	W	40
Allt na h-Athais	Highld	NH8043	57°27·9′	3°59·6′W	W	27
Allt na h-Eaglaise	Highld	NC8760	58°31·1′	3°55·9′W	W	10
Allt na h-Easaiche	Highld	NM8147	56°34·1′	5°33·4′W	W	49
Allt na Heast	Highld	NG6417	57°11·2′	5°53·9′W	W	32
Allt na h-Eilde	Highld	NN2162	56°43·2′	4°55·1′W	W	41
Allt na h-Eiligeir	Arg & Bt	NM5833	56°25·9′	5°55·1′W	W	47,48
Allt na h-Eilrig	Highld	NN3699	57°3·4′	4°41·8′W	W	34
Allt na h-Eirghe	Highld	NJ0713	57°12·2′	3°31·9′W	W	36
Allt na h-Eiric	Highld	NH1302	57°4·5′	5°4·7′W	W	34
Allt na h-Eirigh	Highld	NG7053	57°30·8′	5°50·0′W	W	24
Allt na h-Eirigh	Highld	NN0476	56°50·3′	5°12·3′W	W	41
Allt na h-Ighine	Highld	NH2181	57°47·2′	5°0·2′W	W	20
Allt na h-Imrich	Highld	NH2326	57°17·7′	4°55·8′W	W	25
Allt na h-Imriche	Highld	NC9345	58°23·1′	3°49·3′W	W	11
Allt na h-Innse Buidhe	Highld	NM8978	56°51·0′	5°27·2′W	W	40
Allt na h-Innse Mór	Highld	NC6514	58°5·9′	4°17·0′W	W	16
Allt na h-Iolaire	Stir	NN5339	56°31·5′	4°22·9′W	W	51
Allt na h-Uamha	Highld	NM4096	56°59·2′	6°16·3′W	W	39
Allt na h-Uamha	Highld	NN4084	56°55·4′	4°37·3′W	W	34,42
Allt na h-Uidhe	Highld	NH2976	57°44·7′	4°51·9′W	W	20
Allt na Kyle	Moray	NJ1714	57°12·8′	3°22·0′W	W	36
Allt na Lairige	Arg & Bt	NN2417	56°19·0′	4°50·3′W	W	50,56
Allt na Lairige	Arg & Bt	NN2617	56°19·1′	4°48·4′W	W	50,56
Allt na Lairige	Highld	NH2387	57°50·5′	4°58·4′W	W	20
Allt na Lairige	Highld	NH7034	57°22·9′	4°9·3′W	W	27
Allt na Lairige	Highld	NN2971	56°48·2′	4°47·6′W	W	41
Allt na Lairige Móire	Highld	NN0964	56°44·0′	5°6·9′W	W	41
Allt na Laoidhre	Highld	NH0025	57°16·6′	5°18·6′W	W	25,33
Allt na Larach	Highld	NN3498	57°2·9′	4°43·7′W	W	34
Allt na Laraiche	Stir	NN2923	56°22·4′	4°45·7′W	W	50
Allt na Leacainn	Highld	NH8743	57°28·1′	3°52·6′W	W	27
Allt na Leacainn Móire	Pth & Kin	NN9766	56°46·7′	3°40·7′W	W	43
Allt na Leth-bheinne	Highld	NG8207	57°6·4′	5°35·5′W	W	33
Allt na Lice Beithe	Highld	NM6152	56°36·2′	5°53·2′W	W	49
Allt na Lòine Mhóir	Highld	NJ0836	57°24·6′	3°31·4′W	W	27
Allt na Loinne Mór	Highld	NH7532	57°21·9′	4°4·2′W	W	27
Allt na Lucha	Highld	NG8830	57°18·9′	5°30·8′W	W	24
Allt na Lùib	Highld	NG9955	57°32·7′	5°21·1′W	W	25
Allt na Lùibe	Highld	NC6608	58°2·7′	4°15·7′W	W	16
Allt na Lùibe Móire	Highld	NC5248	58°24·0′	4°31·5′W	W	10
Allt na Maoile	Arg & Bt	NM9921	56°20·6′	5°14·7′W	W	49
Allt na Maraig	Pth & Kin	NN9375	56°51·5′	3°44·8′W	W	43
Allt nam Bad	Highld	NC4838	58°18·5′	4°35·2′W	W	16
Allt nam Ballach	Highld	NH3954	57°33·1′	4°41·0′W	W	26
Allt nam Beith	Highld	NN5899	57°3·9′	4°20·1′W	W	35
Allt nam Biorag	Highld	NN6490	56°59·1′	4°13·8′W	W	35
Allt nam Breac	Highld	NC2424	58°10·5′	4°59·1′W	W	15
Allt nam Bruach	Highld	NN3178	56°52·0′	4°45·9′W	W	41
Allt nam Clàr	Arg & Bt	NM6236	56°27·6′	5°51·3′W	W	49
Allt na Meacnaish	Highld	NG4317	57°10·6′	6°14·7′W	W	32
Allt na Measarroch	Highld	NG5026	57°15·6′	6°8·3′W	W	32
Allt na Mèinne	Highld	NC7731	58°15·3′	4°5·3′W	W	17
Allt nam Fang	Highld	NN2669	56°47·1′	4°50·4′W	W	41
Allt nam Fiadh	Arg & Bt	NM5230	56°24·1′	6°0·7′W	W	48
Allt nam Fiodhag	Highld	NH3223	57°16·3′	4°46·7′W	W	26
Allt nam Fitheach	Arg & Bt	NR7330	55°30·9′	5°35·3′W	W	68
Allt nam Fitheach	Highld	NG3927	57°15·8′	6°19·3′W	W	32
Allt nam Fraoch-choire	Highld	NG5123	57°14·1′	6°7·1′W	W	32
Allt nam Fuaran	Highld	NN2858	56°41·2′	4°48·0′W	W	41
Allt nam Guibhas	Highld	NN2652	56°37·9′	4°49·8′W	W	41
Allt na Mi-Chomhdhail	Highld	NM5066	56°43·4′	6°4·7′W	W	47
Allt nam Meann	Highld	NC7831	58°15·3′	4°4·3′W	W	17
Allt nam Meirleach	Highld	NN1343	56°32·8′	5°2·1′W	W	50
Allt nam Meur	Highld	NC2508	58°1·9′	4°57·4′W	W	15
Allt nam Moireach	Highld	NH8214	57°12·4′	3°56·7′W	W	35
Allt nam Muc	Arg & Bt	NM9805	56°11·9′	5°14·9′W	W	55
Allt nam Muc	Arg & Bt	NN0407	56°13·2′	5°9·2′W	W	56
Allt nam Mucraidh	Highld	NM6449	56°34·7′	5°50·1′W	W	49
Allt na Mòine	Highld	NC5153	58°26·7′	4°32·7′W	W	9
Allt na Mòine	Highld	NG6953	57°30·8′	5°51·0′W	W	24
Allt na Moine	Highld	NG7567	57°38·5′	5°45·7′W	W	19
Allt na Moine	Pth & Kin	NN8739	56°32·0′	3°49·8′W	W	52
Allt na Moine Bàine	Pth & Kin	NN8570	56°48·7′	3°52·6′W	W	43
Allt na Moine Buidhe	Pth & Kin	NN7161	56°43·6′	4°6·0′W	W	42
Allt nam Paircean	Arg & Bt	NR7164	55°49·2′	5°38·9′W	W	62
Allt nam Peathrain	Highld	NH1910	57°9·0′	4°59·1′W	W	34
Allt na Mucaireachd	Highld	NM7350	56°35·5′	5°41·4′W	W	49
Allt na Muic	Highld	NC8938	58°19·3′	3°53·2′W	W	17
Allt na Muic	Highld	NH2515	57°11·8′	4°53·3′W	W	34
Allt na Muice	Arg & Bt	NR2742	55°36·0′	6°19·6′W	X	60
Allt na Muidhe	Highld	NN1054	56°38·6′	5°5·5′W	W	41
Allt na Muilne	N Eil	NB2229	58°10·0′	6°43·2′W	W	8,13
Allt na Muilne	N Eil	NB5233	58°13·2′	6°12·9′W	W	8
Allt na Muilne	N Eil	NB5248	58°21·3′	6°13·9′W	W	8
Allt nan Achaidhean	Highld	NC7928	58°13·7′	4°3·1′W	W	17
Allt nan Adag	Highld	NH6220	57°15·3′	4°16·8′W	W	26,35
Allt nan Aighean	Aberd	NJ2009	57°10·2′	3°18·9′W	W	36
Allt nan Airighean	Arg & Bt	NR3750	55°40·6′	6°10·6′W	W	60
Allt nan Airighean Ur	N Eil	NB0724	58°6·7′	6°58·0′W	W	13,14
Allt nan Albannach	Highld	NC3833	58°15·6′	4°45·2′W	W	16
Allt nan Cabar	Moray	NJ2113	57°12·3′	3°18·0′W	W	36
Allt nan Cailleach	Highld	NM8064	56°43·2′	5°35·3′W	W	40
Allt nan Càisean	Highld	NH3697	57°56·2′	4°45·7′W	W	20
Allt nan Calaman	N Ayr	NR9734	55°33·7′	5°12·7′W	W	69
Allt nan Calltuinn	Arg & Bt	NR7133	55°32·5′	5°37·4′W	W	68
Allt nan Calman	N Ayr	NR9245	55°39·5′	5°18·0′W	W	62,69
Allt nan Caorach	Highld	NH2692	57°53·3′	4°55·6′W	W	20
Allt nan Caorach	Highld	NH5167	57°40·4′	4°29·4′W	W	20
Allt nan Caorainn	Stir	NN2622	56°21·8′	4°48·6′W	W	50
Allt nan Caorrann	Stir	NN2722	56°21·8′	4°47·6′W	W	50
Allt nan Carnan	Highld	NG8841	57°24·9′	5°31·3′W	W	24
Allt nan Cearcall	Highld	NN4284	56°55·5′	4°35·3′W	W	34,42
Allt nan Clach	Highld	NC7854	58°27·7′	4°5·0′W	W	10
Allt nan Clachan Geala	Highld	NG4825	57°15·0′	6°10·2′W	W	32
Allt nan Clach Aoil	Highld	NC2606	58°0·8′	4°56·3′W	W	15
Allt nan Clach Geala	Aberd	NO0681	56°54·9′	3°32·2′W	W	43
Allt nan Clach Sgoilte	Arg & Bt	NN1736	56°29·1′	4°57·9′W	W	50
Allt nan Clar-lochan	Highld	NH2597	57°55·9′	4°56·9′W	W	20
Allt nan Coileach	Highld	NM6247	56°33·5′	5°51·9′W	W	49
Allt nan Coisiche	Highld	NC0704	57°59·3′	5°15·4′W	W	15
Allt nan Columan	Pth & Kin	NN7928	56°26·0′	3°57·3′W	W	51,52
Allt nan Con	Highld	NG7121	57°13·6′	5°47·2′W	W	33
Allt nan Con-uisge	Highld	NC6116	58°6·9′	4°21·1′W	W	16
Allt nan Corp	Highld	NN2099	57°3·1′	4°57·6′W	W	34
Allt nan Creagan Dubha	Highld	NC4531	58°14·7′	4°38·0′W	W	16
Allt nan Creamh	Arg & Bt	NR6730	55°30·7′	5°41·0′W	W	68
Allt nan Criopag	Highld	NG7117	57°11·5′	5°47·0′W	W	33
Allt nan Cùileach	Highld	NH8803	57°6·5′	3°50·5′W	W	35,36
Allt nan Dearcag	Highld	NH0050	57°30·0′	5°19·8′W	W	25
Allt nan Each	Highld	NC9358	58°30·1′	3°49·7′W	W	11

Allt nan Each	N Eil	NB2217	58°3·6′	6°42·3′W	W	13,14
Allt nan Each	N Eil	NB3226	58°8·8′	6°32·8′W	W	8,13
Allt nan Easan Bàna	Highld	NG8183	57°47·3′	5°40·6′W	W	19
Allt nan Easan Geala	N Eil	NB0125	58°7·0′	7°4·2′W	W	13
Allt nan Eithreag	Highld	NC4846	58°22·8′	4°35·5′W	W	9
Allt nan Gabhar	Highld	NM5265	56°42·9′	6°2·7′W	W	47
Allt nan Gabhar	N Eil	NB3624	58°7·8′	6°28·6′W	W	14
Allt nan Gall	Highld	NC8858	58°30·0′	3°54·8′W	W	10
Allt nan Gamhna	Arg & Bt	NR3959	55°45·5′	6°9·2′W	W	60
Allt nan Gamhuinn	Highld	NJ0814	57°12·7′	3°30·9′W	W	36
Allt nan Gaoirean	Highld	NN1247	56°34·9′	5°3·2′W	W	50
Allt nan Gillean	Arg & Bt	NN0733	56°27·2′	5°7·5′W	W	50
Allt nan Giubhas	Arg & Bt	NN1932	56°27·0′	4°55·8′W	W	50
Allt nan Gleannan	Highld	NG8000	57°2·6′	5°37·1′W	W	33
Allt nan Gleannan	Highld	NN1169	56°46·7′	5°5·2′W	W	41
Allt nan Iomairean	Highld	NM5950	56°35·1′	5°55·0′W	W	47
Allt nan Laogh	Highld	NC7556	58°28·7′	4°8·1′W	W	10
Allt nan Laogh	Highld	NN4086	56°56·5′	4°37·4′W	W	34,42
Allt nan Leac	Highld	NG5918	57°11·6′	5°58·9′W	W	32
Allt nan Leothdean	Arg & Bt	NM5941	56°30·2′	5°54·5′W	W	47,48
Allt nan Leum Easain	Aberd	NO0390	56°59·7′	3°35·3′W	W	43
Allt nan Lochanan Dubha	Highld	NM7945	56°33·0′	5°35·3′W	W	49
Allt nan Iomairean	Highld	NM6050	56°35·1′	5°54·1′W	W	49
Allt nan Losgann	Highld	NN3258	56°41·3′	4°44·1′W	W	41
Allt nan Lùb Bàna	Highld	NC2456	58°27·7′	5°0·5′W	W	9
Allt nan Luch	N Eil	NF8872	57°38·1′	7°13·2′W	W	18
Allt nan Luibean Molach	Highld	NC2301	57°58·1′	4°59·1′W	W	15
Allt nan Luibhean	Highld	NN4091	56°59·2′	4°37·5′W	W	34
Allt nan Lunn	Highld	NM8956	56°39·2′	5°26·1′W	W	49
Allt nan Nathair	Arg & Bt	NR8280	55°58·1′	5°29·2′W	W	55
Allt nan Ramh	Highld	NC2237	58°17·4′	5°1·7′W	W	15
Allt nan Ruadhag	Arg & Bt	NR4668	55°50·6′	6°3·0′W	W	60,61
Allt nan Ruadhag	Highld	NC4737	58°18·0′	4°36·2′W	W	16
Allt nan Sac	Highld	NC8058	58°29·9′	4°3·1′W	W	10
Allt nan Sae	Arg & Bt	NM9804	56°11·4′	5°14·9′W	W	55
Allt nan Sae	Stir	NN3029	56°25·6′	4°45·0′W	W	50
Allt nan Seann Tighean	Arg & Bt	NM6322	56°20·1′	5°49·6′W	W	49
Allt nan Seileach	Highld	NC2798	57°2·7′	4°50·6′W	W	34
Allt nan Seileach	Moray	NJ2117	57°14·5′	3°18·1′W	W	36
Allt nan Sgalag	Highld	NC9054	58°27·9′	3°52·7′W	W	10
Allt nan Sgeith	Highld	NC7904	58°0·8′	4°2·4′W	W	17
Allt nan Slat	Arg & Bt	NN3447	56°35·4′	4°41·8′W	W	50
Allt nan Sliseag	Stir	NN4629	56°25·9′	4°29·4′W	W	51
Allt-nan-sùgh	Highld	NG9029	57°18·5′	5°28·7′W	X	25,33
Allt nan Tiadhan	Arg & Bt	NS0681	55°59·2′	5°6·2′W	W	63
Allt nan Torc	Arg & Bt	NM5052	56°35·9′	6°3·9′W	W	47
Allt nan Torcan	N Eil	NB3228	58°9·8′	6°32·9′W	W	8,13
Allt Nantygwenlli	Gwyn	SH6501	52°35·6′	3°59·2′W	X	135
Allt nan Uamh	Highld	NC2617	58°6·7′	4°56·7′W	W	15
Allt na Pairce	N Ayr	NR9225	55°28·7′	5°17·1′W	W	68,69
Allt na Pairce-fraoich	Highld	NG7324	57°15·3′	5°45·4′W	W	33
Allt na Pairte	Highld	NG6217	57°11·2′	5°55·9′W	W	32
Allt na Plaide	Highld	NG7624	57°15·4′	5°42·4′W	W	33
Allt na Pollaich	Pth & Kin	NO0165	56°46·2′	3°36·7′W	W	43
Allt na Rainich	Highld	NC2661	58°30·4′	4°58·7′W	W	9
Alltnaray	Highld	NN2891	56°59·0′	4°49·4′W	X	34
Allt-na-reigh	Highld	NN1756	56°39·9′	4°58·7′W	X	41
Allt Narrachan	Arg & Bt	NN1037	56°29·5′	5°4·7′W	W	50
Allt na Sàile	Arg & Bt	NM5344	56°31·6′	6°0·5′W	W	47,48
Allt na Sàile Mòire	Highld	NC2847	58°22·9′	4°56·0′W	W	9
Allt na Saobhaidh' Mòire	Highld	NC2229	58°13·1′	5°1·4′W	W	15
Allt na Seabhaig	Arg & Bt	NM9629	56°24·8′	5°18·0′W	W	49
Allt na Sealga	Highld	NM8798	57°1·7′	5°30·1′W	W	33,40
Allt na Seana Gheid	Highld	NG8218	57°12·3′	5°36·1′W	W	33
Allt na Sean-lùibe	Highld	NH0434	57°21·5′	5°15·1′W	W	25
Allt na Searmoin	Arg & Bt	NM5741	56°30·2′	5°56·5′W	W	47,48
Allt na Seilich Bige	Highld	NC6725	58°11·9′	4°15·3′W	W	16
Allt na Seilich Mòire	Highld	NC6825	58°11·9′	4°14·3′W	W	16
Allt na Slabhruidh	Highld	NM8372	56°47·6′	5°32·7′W	W	40
Allt na Slaite	Aberd	NO1085	56°57·1′	3°28·3′W	W	43
Allt na Slanaich	Highld	NH7434	57°23·0′	4°5·3′W	W	27
Allt na Slataich	Highld	NH1401	57°4·0′	5°3·6′W	W	34
Allt na Socaich	Highld	NM7145	56°32·7′	5°43·1′W	W	49
Allt na Sròine	Highld	NC6630	58°14·6′	4°16·5′W	W	16
Allt na Stainge	Pth & Kin	NN7214	56°18·3′	4°3·7′W	W	57
Allt na Suileig	Highld	NC2445	58°21·8′	5°0·0′W	W	9
Alltnasuileig	Highld	NC2545	58°21·8′	4°59·0′W	X	9
Allt na Teanga Duibhe	Highld	NM9276	56°50·0′	5°24·1′W	W	40
Allt na Teangaidh	Arg & Bt	NM4532	56°24·9′	6°7·6′W	W	48
Allt na Teangaidh	Highld	NG5924	57°14·9′	5°59·2′W	W	32
Allt na Teangaidh Baine	Arg & Bt	NM6526	56°22·3′	5°47·9′W	W	49
Allt Nathais	Arg & Bt	NM9832	56°26·5′	5°16·2′W	W	49
Allt Nathrach	Highld	NN1563	56°43·6′	5°1·0′W	W	41
Allt na Trì-dail	Arg & Bt	NR3556	55°43·8′	6°12·8′W	W	60
Allt na Tuaidh	N Ayr	NR9727	55°29·9′	5°12·4′W	W	69
Allt Neacrath	Highld	NH7827	57°19·3′	4°1·1′W	W	35
Allt Nealagro	N Eil	NB0028	58°8·6′	7°5·4′W	W	13
Allt Neurlain	Highld	NN2992	56°59·5′	4°48·4′W	W	34
Allt Niag-àrd	Highld	NG7406	57°5·6′	5°43·4′W	W	33
Allt Nighinn	Arg & Bt	NM9905	56°12·0′	5°14·0′W	W	55
Allt Ockle	Highld	NM5669	56°45·2′	5°59·0′W	W	47
Allt Odhar	Arg & Bt	NN2030	56°25·9′	4°54·7′W	W	50
Allt Odhar	Highld	NH5205	57°7·0′	4°26·2′W	W	35
Allt Odhar	Highld	NH5902	57°5·5′	4°19·2′W	W	35
Allt Odhar	Highld	NH6213	57°11·5′	4°16·6′W	W	35
Allt Odhar	Highld	NH8037	57°24·7′	3°59·4′W	W	27
Allt Odhar	Highld	NN2383	56°54·5′	4°54·0′W	W	34,41
Allt Odhar	Pth & Kin	NN7349	56°37·2′	4°3·7′W	W	51,52
Allt Odhar Beag	Highld	NH6616	57°13·2′	4°12·7′W	W	35
Allt Odhar Mór	Highld	NH6717	57°13·7′	4°11·7′W	W	35
Allt Odhrsgaraidh	Highld	NC4051	58°25·4′	4°43·9′W	W	9
Allt Ohirnie	Arg & Bt	NM6220	56°19·0′	5°50·5′W	W	49
Allt Oigh	Arg & Bt	NR8986	56°1·5′	5°22·7′W	W	55
Allt Ollach	Pth & Kin	NN7013	56°17·8′	4°5·6′W	W	57
Allt Omhain	Arg & Bt	NM6522	56°20·2′	5°47·7′W	W	49
Allt Orain	Arg & Bt	NN2739	56°30·9′	4°48·3′W	W	50
Allt Os a' Faobh	N Eil	NB1918	58°4·0′	6°45·4′W	W	13,14
Allt Osda	Arg & Bt	NR9569	55°52·5′	5°16·2′W	W	62
Allt Osglan	Highld	NG4938	57°22·1′	6°10·0′W	W	23,32
Allt Oss	Stir	NN3023	56°22·4′	4°44·7′W	W	50

Alltour	Highld	NN2281	56°53·4′	4°54·9′W	T	34,41
Allt Overscaig	Highld	NC4124	58°10·8′	4°41·8′W	W	16
Allt Pant-mawr	Powys	SN8582	52°25·7′	3°41·1′W	X	135,136
Allt Penygarreg	Carm	SN5234	51°59·3′	4°8·9′W	F	146
Allt Phocaichain	Highld	NH3211	57°9·8′	4°46·2′W	W	34
Allt Phoineis	Highld	NN7093	57°0·9′	4°8·0′W	W	35
Allt Phort a' Bhàta	Highld	NM5756	56°38·2′	5°57·3′W	W	47
Allt Phouple	Aberd	NJ1601	57°5·8′	3°22·7′W	W	36
Allt Phubuill	Pth & Kin	NN4543	56°33·5′	4°30·9′W	W	51
Allt Poll-airigh	Highld	NH1202	57°4·5′	5°5·6′W	W	34
Allt Poll an Droighinn	Highld	NC2722	58°9·4′	4°55·9′W	W	15
Allt Poll an t-Searraich	Highld	NH4535	57°23·0′	4°34·2′W	W	26
Allt Poll Doire	Highld	NM7151	56°36·0′	5°43·4′W	W	49
Allt Poll Dubh-ghlas	Pth & Kin	NN6468	56°47·3′	4°13·1′W	W	42
Allt Pòll nan Damh	Highld	NC3943	58°21·0′	4°44·6′W	W	9
Allt Port na Cullaidh	Highld	NG5213	57°8·7′	6°5·5′W	W	32
Allt Preas a' Choin	Highld	NJ0811	57°11·1′	3°30·9′W	W	36
Allt Preas Braigh nan Allt	Highld	NC4829	58°13·7′	4°34·8′W	W	16
Allt Preas nam Meirleach	Aberd	NO0093	57°1·3′	3°38·4′W	W	36,43
Allt Raineach	Arg & Bt	NR7566	55°50·3′	5°35·2′W	W	62
Allt Raineachan	Highld	NM8382	56°53·0′	5°33·3′W	W	40
Allt Raon a' Chroisg	Highld	NH1889	57°51·5′	5°3·6′W	W	20
Allt Raonadail	N Eil	NB5144	58°19·1′	6°14·6′W	W	8
Allt Rapach	Highld	NC2302	57°58·6′	4°59·1′W	W	15
Allt Rath a' Bheulain	Highld	NM5167	56°44·0′	6°3·8′W	W	47
Allt Réidhe Ghlais	Highld	NG6919	57°12·5′	5°49·0′W	W	32
Allt Réidhe Ghlais	Highld	NG7019	57°12·5′	5°48·1′W	W	33
Allt Reinain	Arg & Bt	NS1992	56°5·5′	4°54·1′W	W	56
Allt Reireag	Highld	NG5830	57°18·1′	6°0·6′W	W	24,32
Alltreoch	Pth & Kin	NO0956	56°41·5′	3°28·7′W	X	52,53
Allt Reppachie	Aberd	NJ2110	57°10·7′	3°17·9′W	W	36
Allt Rhu	Arg & Bt	NR8362	55°48·4′	5°27·3′W	W	62
Allt Riabhach	Highld	NH2118	57°13·3′	4°57·4′W	W	34
Allt Riabhach	Highld	NH2320	57°14·5′	4°55·5′W	W	25
Allt Riabhach	Highld	NH4190	57°52·5′	4°40·4′W	W	20
Allt Riabhach a' Chinn Tuill	Pth & Kin	NN3355	56°39·7′	4°43·0′W	W	41
Allt Riabhachain	Highld	NH1136	57°22·8′	5°8·2′W	W	25
Allt Riabhach Mór	Pth & Kin	NN3555	56°39·7′	4°41·1′W	W	41
Allt Riabhach na Bioraich	Pth & Kin	NN3655	56°39·7′	4°40·1′W	W	41
Allt Ribhein	Highld	NG3433	57°18·9′	6°24·6′W	W	32
Allt Righ	Arg & Bt	NR7327	55°29·3′	5°35·2′W	W	68
Allt Riobain	Stir	NN4528	56°25·4′	4°30·3′W	W	51
Allt Rioran	Pth & Kin	NN4740	56°31·9′	4°28·8′W	W	51
Allt Rivigill	Highld	NC7346	58°23·3′	4°9·9′W	W	10
Allt Robuic	Arg & Bt	NS0996	56°7·4′	5°3·9′W	W	56
Allt Romain	Arg & Bt	NR8453	55°43·6′	5°26·0′W	X	62
Allt Rostan	Stir	NN3412	56°16·5′	4°40·4′W	W	50,56
Allt Roy	Aberd	NO5095	57°2·9′	2°49·0′W	W	37,44
Allt Ruadh	Arg & Bt	NM5144	56°31·6′	6°2·5′W	W	47,48
Allt Ruadh	Arg & Bt	NR3667	55°49·7′	6°12·5′W	W	60,61
Allt Ruadh	Highld	NG7507	57°6·2′	5°42·5′W	W	33
Allt Ruadh	Highld	NH3115	57°11·9′	4°47·4′W	W	34
Allt Ruadh	Highld	NH8600	57°4·9′	3°52·4′W	W	35,36
Allt Ruadh	N Eil	NB0222	58°5·5′	7°3·0′W	W	13
Allt Ruadh	N Eil	NB3332	58°12·0′	6°32·2′W	W	8,13
Allt Ruadh	N Eil	NF7868	57°35·5′	7°22·9′W	W	18
Allt Ruadh Beag	Highld	NN3583	56°54·8′	4°42·2′W	W	34,41
Allt Ruadh Mór	Highld	NN3583	56°54·8′	4°42·2′W	W	34,41
Allt Ruaidh	Highld	NH8723	57°17·3′	3°52·0′W	W	35,36
Allt Ruairidh	Highld	NG3444	57°24·8′	6°25·3′W	W	23
Allt Ruaraidh	Highld	NN2184	56°55·0′	4°56·0′W	W	34,41
Allt Rubha	Arg & Bt	NR8181	55°58·6′	5°30·2′W	W	55
Allt Rubha na Moine	Highld	NG3803	57°2·9′	6°18·7′W	W	32,39
Allt Rugaidh Bheag	Highld	NC3405	58°0·5′	4°48·1′W	W	15
Allt Rugaidh Mhór	Highld	NC3507	58°1·6′	4°47·2′W	W	15
Alltrugog	Gwyn	SH9533	52°53·3′	3°33·2′W	X	125
Allt Ruighe	Pth & Kin	NN8635	56°29·9′	3°50·7′W	W	52
Allt Ruighe a' Mhadaidh	Pth & Kin	NN5250	56°37·4′	4°24·3′W	W	42,51
Allt Ruighe a' Mhodaidh	Pth & Kin	NN5249	56°36·8′	4°24·2′W	W	51
Allt Ruighe an Eas	Stir	NN6710	56°16·1′	4°8·4′W	W	57
Allt Ruighe an Lagain	Pth & Kin	NO0256	56°41·4′	3°35·6′W	W	52,53
Allt Ruighe an t-Sidhein	Highld	NH5303	57°5·9′	4°25·1′W	W	35
Allt Ruighe an Tuim Dhuibh	Pth & Kin	NN4152	56°38·2′	4°35·1′W	W	42,51
Allt Ruighe Ghiubhas	Pth & Kin	NN5144	56°34·1′	4°25·1′W	W	51
Allt Ruighe Magaig	Highld	NH8826	57°18·9′	3°51·1′W	W	35,36
Allt Ruighe nam Fiadh	Pth & Kin	NN0186	56°55·6′	5°15·8′W	W	41
Allt Ruighe nan Saorach	Pth & Kin	NN6463	56°44·6′	4°13·0′W	W	42
Allt Ruigh Fhearchair	Highld	NH2010	57°9·0′	4°58·1′W	W	34
Allt Ruigh na Braoileig	Highld	NN2972	56°48·7′	4°47·6′W	W	41
Allt Ruigh na Cuileige	Aberd	NJ2703	57°7·0′	3°11·9′W	W	37
Allt Ruigh nan Eas	Pth & Kin	NO0470	56°49·0′	3°33·9′W	W	43
Allt Ruigh na Sealbhaig	Highld	NC6135	58°17·2′	4°21·8′W	W	16
Allt Ruigh na Sròine	Highld	NH9103	57°6·6′	3°47·5′W	W	36
Allt Ruigh Sleigheich	Highld	NG9446	57°27·7′	5°25·6′W	W	25
Allt Ruith an Eas	Stir	NN6610	56°16·1′	4°9·4′W	W	57
Allt Ruithe Bhodail	Highld	NN4794	57°1·0′	4°30·7′W	W	34
Allt Saigh	Highld	NH4020	57°14·8′	4°38·6′W	W	26
Allt Saigh	Highld	NH4319	57°14·4′	4°35·6′W	W	34
Allt Sail an Ruathair	Highld	NC3313	58°4·7′	4°49·4′W	W	15
Allt Sailean an Eòrna	Highld	NM7065	56°43·5′	5°45·1′W	W	40
Allt Salach	N Eil	NB2117	58°3·5′	6°43·3′W	W	13,14
Allt Salach	N Eil	NB2729	58°10·0′	6°38·1′W	W	8,13
Allt Salach	Pth & Kin	NN8238	56°31·4′	3°54·6′W	W	52
Allt Salach-airigh	Highld	NM8395	57°0·0′	5°33·9′W	W	33,40
Allt Samhnachain	Highld	NM7045	56°32·7′	5°44·0′W	W	49
Allt Sanna	Highld	NM4569	56°44·8′	6°9·8′W	W	47
Allt Sasgaig	Highld	NG8720	57°13·5′	5°31·3′W	W	33
Allt Scamodale	Highld	NM8473	56°48·2′	5°31·8′W	W	40
Allt Sealbhach	Highld	NC7649	58°25·0′	4°6·9′W	W	10
Allt Seanabhaile	Highld	NH3927	57°18·6′	4°39·9′W	W	26
Allt Seanghail	Highld	NH3902	57°5·1′	4°38·9′W	W	34
Allt Sgairnich	Highld	NN9096	57°2·8′	3°48·3′W	W	36,43
Allt Sgalagro	N Eil	NB4249	58°21·5′	6°24·2′W	W	8
Allt Sgeiteadh	Highld	NG3622	57°13·0′	6°21·9′W	W	32
Allt Sgialach Coire	Highld	NC3828	58°12·9′	4°45·0′W	W	16
Allt Sgiathaig	Highld	NC2225	58°10·9′	5°1·2′W	W	15
Allt Sgionie	Stir	NN4316	56°18·9′	4°31·9′W	W	56
Allt Sguabach	Highld	NH8528	57°19·9′	3°54·2′W	W	35,36
Allt Sguadaig	Highld	NN3787	56°57·0′	4°40·3′W	W	34,41

Allt Shallainn	Pth & Kin	NN6067	56°46·7′	4°17·0′W	W	42
Allt Shamhnan Insir	Highld	NG3703	57°2·8′	6°19·7′W	W	32,39
Allt Sheargain	Highld	NN1179	56°52·1′	5°5·6′W	W	41
Allt Sheicheachan	Pth & Kin	NN8474	56°50·8′	3°53·7′W	W	43
Alltshellach Ho	Highld	NN0560	56°41·7′	5°10·6′W	X	41
Allt Shios Bhreac-achaidh	Arg & Bt	NM6222	56°20·1′	5°50·6′W	W	49
Allt Shios Chulaibh	Pth & Kin	NN6974	56°50·6′	4°8·4′W	W	42
Allt Shuas Chulaibh	Pth & Kin	NN6875	56°51·1′	4°9·4′W	W	42
Alltsigh	Highld	NH4519	57°14·4′	4°33·6′W	T	34
Allt Siolar	Highld	NH2389	57°51·6′	4°58·5′W	W	20
Allt Slaite Coire	Highld	NM8087	56°55·6′	5°36·5′W	W	40
Allt Slanaidh	Pth & Kin	NN8671	56°49·3′	3°51·6′W	W	43
Allt Slapin	Highld	NG5821	57°13·2′	6°0·1′W	W	32
Allt Sleibh	Pth & Kin	NN6566	56°46·2′	4°12·1′W	W	42
Allt Slochd a' Mhogha	Highld	NG7700	57°2·5′	5°40·1′W	W	33
Allt Slochd Chaimbeil	Aberd	NJ2715	57°13·5′	3°12·1′W	W	37
Allt Slochd Nighinn Bheathain	Highld	NG8902	57°3·9′	5°28·4′W	W	33
Allt Sloc na Creadha	Pth & Kin	NN4952	56°38·4′	4°27·3′W	W	42,51
Allt Slugan a' Choilich	Highld	NM3998	57°0·2′	6°17·5′W	W	39
Allt Smeòrail	Highld	NC8512	58°5·2′	3°56·6′W	W	17
Allt Smoo	Highld	NC4166	58°33·4′	4°43·5′W	W	9
Allt Sniomhach	Highld	NN5692	57°0·1′	4°21·8′W	W	35
Allt Snitut	Highld	ND1144	58°22·8′	3°30·8′W	W	11,12
Allt Socaich	Highld	NN0855	56°39·1′	5°7·5′W	W	41
Allt Socrach	Highld	NH1332	57°20·7′	5°6·0′W	W	25
Allt Sordail	Highld	NM5569	56°45·2′	6°0·0′W	W	47
Allt Sowan Hill	Aberd	NJ3420	57°16·2′	3°5·2′W	H	37
Allt Spioradail	Highld	NH7814	57°12·3′	4°0·7′W	W	35
Allt Srath a' Chomair	Highld	NG8615	57°10·8′	5°32·0′W	W	33
Allt Srath a' Ghlinne	Pth & Kin	NN6717	56°19·9′	4°8·6′W	W	57
Allt Srath Feinne-bheinne	Highld	NC4245	58°22·2′	4°41·6′W	W	9
Allt Srath Lungard	Highld	NG9164	57°37·3′	5°29·5′W	W	19
Allt Srath nan Aisinnin	Highld	NC3331	58°14·4′	4°50·2′W	W	15
Allt Srath nan Sùileag	Highld	NH3291	57°52·9′	4°49·5′W	W	20
Allt Srath Seasgaich	Highld	NC3011	58°3·6′	4°52·4′W	W	15
Allt Srath Shuardail	Highld	NM7345	56°32·8′	5°41·1′W	W	49
Allt Sròn an Duine	Pth & Kin	NN8972	56°49·8′	3°48·7′W	W	43
Allt Sròn Fhearchair	Highld	NH5180	57°47·4′	4°29·9′W	W	20
Allt Sròn na Fearnaig	Highld	NN0590	56°57·9′	5°12·0′W	W	33
Allt Staoine	Highld	ND0222	58°10·8′	3°39·5′W	W	17
Allt Steallaig	Highld	NH7817	57°13·9′	4°0·8′W	W	35
Allt Stionach Coire	Highld	NC6446	58°23·1′	4°19·1′W	W	10
Allt Strath a' Bhàthaich	Highld	NG9049	57°29·2′	5°29·8′W	W	25
Allt Strath Fionan	Pth & Kin	NN7356	56°41·0′	4°3·9′W	W	42,51,52
Allt Strollamus	Highld	NG5925	57°15·4′	5°59·3′W	W	32
Allt Suardal	Highld	NG2954	57°30·0′	6°31·0′W	W	23
Allt Sugach	Arg & Bt	NR2806	56°13·2′	4°46·0′W	W	56
Allt Suil na Curra	Arg & Bt	NN2240	56°31·4′	4°53·2′W	W	50
Allt Sunadale	Arg & Bt	NR7945	55°39·2′	5°30·3′W	W	62,69
Allt Tachair	Highld	NM8195	56°59·9′	5°35·9′W	W	33,40
Allt Taige	Highld	NH1732	57°20·8′	5°2·0′W	W	25
Allt Tairbh	Stir	NN4404	56°12·4′	4°30·5′W	W	57
Allt Tair Ffynnon	Powys	SJ1423	52°48·1′	3°16·1′W	H	125
Allt Tan-coed-cochion	Carm	SN5444	52°4·7′	4°7·4′W	F	146
Allt Tarruinchon	Pth & Kin	NN7956	56°41·1′	3°58·1′W	W	42,51,52
Allt Tarsuinn	Highld	NC2724	58°10·5′	4°56·0′W	W	15
Allt Tarsuinn	Highld	NC3301	57°58·3′	4°48·9′W	W	15
Allt Tarsuinn	Highld	NC4229	58°13·6′	4°40·9′W	W	16
Allt Tarsuinn	Highld	NC6860	58°30·8′	4°15·5′W	W	10
Allt Tarsuinn	Highld	NG6910	57°7·6′	5°48·5′W	W	32
Allt Tarsuinn	Highld	NH2516	57°12·3′	4°53·4′W	W	34
Allt Tarsuinn	Highld	NH3112	57°10·3′	4°47·3′W	W	34
Allt Tarsuinn	Highld	NH7025	57°18·1′	4°9·0′W	W	35
Allt Tarsuinn	Highld	NH9629	57°20·6′	3°43·2′W	W	36
Allt Tarsuinn	Highld	NM9377	56°50·6′	5°23·2′W	W	40
Allt Tarsuinn	Highld	NN1793	56°59·8′	5°0·3′W	W	34
Allt Tarsuinn	Highld	NN3689	56°58·1′	4°41·4′W	W	34,41
Allt Tarsuinn	Highld	NN5989	56°58·5′	4°18·7′W	W	42
Allt Tarsuinn	Pth & Kin	NN4338	56°30·7′	4°32·6′W	W	51
Allt Tarsuinn Mór	Highld	NN5896	57°2·3′	4°20·0′W	W	35
Allt Tasabhaig	Highld	NG6947	57°27·5′	5°50·6′W	W	24
Allt Teanga Bige	Highld	NN3194	57°0·6′	4°46·5′W	W	34
Allt Teanga Brideig	Arg & Bt	NM5631	56°24·8′	5°56·9′W	W	48
Allt Tersie	Moray	NJ3452	57°33·5′	3°5·7′W	W	28
Allt Thailleagro	N Eil	NB3649	58°21·3′	6°30·3′W	W	8
Allt Thuagro	N Eil	NB3946	58°19·8′	6°27·0′W	W	8
Allt Thuill	Highld	NG7417	57°11·5′	5°44·0′W	W	33
Allt Thuill Easaich	Highld	NH0322	57°15·0′	5°15·5′W	W	25,33
Allt Thuilm	N Eil	NG0898	57°52·8′	6°55·1′W	W	14,18
Allt Tigh an Shiorraim	N Ayr	NR9241	55°37·3′	5°17·8′W	W	62,69
Allt Tigh Néill	Highld	NH7397	57°56·9′	4°8·3′W	W	21
Allt Tir Artair	Pth & Kin	NN5836	56°29·9′	4°18·0′W	W	51
Allt Toaig	Arg & Bt	NN2543	56°33·0′	4°50·4′W	W	50
Allt Tokavaig	Highld	NG6010	57°7·4′	5°57·4′W	W	32
Allt Tolaghan	Arg & Bt	NN2540	56°31·4′	4°50·2′W	W	50
Allt Toll a' Chaorachain	Highld	NH0943	57°26·5′	5°10·5′W	W	25
Allt Toll a' Chaorainn	Highld	NH3582	57°48·1′	4°46·1′W	W	20
Allt Toll a' Choin	Highld	NH1443	57°26·6′	5°5·5′W	W	25
Allt Toll a' Ghuibhais	Highld	NG9762	57°36·4′	5°23·4′W	W	19
Allt Tollaidh	Highld	NG8522	57°14·6′	5°33·3′W	W	33
Allt Toll a' Mhadaidh	Highld	NG8759	57°34·5′	5°33·3′W	W	24
Allt Toll a' Mhuic	Highld	NH2340	57°25·2′	4°56·4′W	W	25
Allt Toll Easa	Highld	NH1726	57°17·5′	5°1·8′W	W	25
Allt Toll Sgàile	Highld	NH2442	57°26·3′	4°55·5′W	W	25
Allt Tom a' Chogaidh	Pth & Kin	NN4767	56°46·4′	4°29·8′W	W	42
Allt Tomnabhal	N Eil	NB1706	57°57·5′	6°46·6′W	W	13,14
Allt Tom na h-Innse	Highld	NM5465	56°43·0′	6°0·8′W	W	47
Allt Ton an Eich	Highld	NN5374	56°50·3′	4°24·1′W	W	42
Allt Torr a' Bhacain	Arg & Bt	NM4050	56°34·5′	6°13·5′W	W	47
Allt Torr a' Chall	Highld	NM7349	56°34·9′	5°41·3′W	W	49
Allt Torraidh	N Eil	NB0718	58°3·5′	6°57·6′W	W	13,14
Allt Torr an Tairbh	Highld	NC6046	58°23·1′	4°23·2′W	W	10
Allt Torr na h-Uamha	Arg & Bt	NM5528	56°23·1′	5°57·7′W	W	48
Allt Tòrr na Mòine	Highld	NM5562	56°41·4′	5°59·6′W	W	47
Allt Torr nan Cearc	Highld	NM6167	56°44·3′	5°54·0′W	W	40
Allt Tràigh-leacainn	Arg & Bt	NR7628	55°29·9′	5°32·4′W	W	68,69
Allt Troed-y-rhiw	Carm	SN5235	51°59·9′	4°9·0′W	F	146
Allt Tuileach	Aberd	NJ2108	57°9·6′	3°17·9′W	W	36
Allt Uaine	Arg & Bt	NN2611	56°15·8′	4°48·1′W	W	50,56

Allt Uaine	Highld	NN5788	56°57·9′	4°20·7′W	W	42
Allt Uaine	Highld	NN5796	57°2·2′	4°20·9′W	W	35
Allt Uamha Mhircil	N Eil	NB0428	58°8·8′	7°1·4′W	W	13
Allt Uamha na Muice	Highld	NM4667	56°43·8′	6°8·7′W	W	47
Allt Uamh nam Ban	N Eil	NG0691	57°49·0′	6°56·6′W	W	14,18
Alltuchaf	Powys	SJ0708	52°39·9′	3°22·1′W	X	125
Allt Uchdain Mhoir	Highld	NN1491	56°58·6′	5°3·2′W	W	34
Allt Uchd Rodha	Highld	NH2539	57°24·7′	4°54·4′W	W	25
Allt Udlamain	Highld	NN5673	56°49·8′	4°21·1′W	W	42
Allt Uilleachain	Highld	NC5259	58°29·9′	4°31·9′W	W	10
Allt Uilleim	Highld	NN3085	56°55·8′	4°47·2′W	W	34,41
Allt Uisg' a' Bhrisdidh	Highld	NH2883	57°48·5′	4°53·2′W	W	20
Allt Uisg an t-Sidhein	Highld	NH6018	57°14·1′	4°18·7′W	W	35
Allt Uisgean	Pth & Kin	NN7675	56°51·3′	4°1·6′W	W	42
Allt Uisge na Féithe	Highld	NH0795	57°54·4′	5°15·0′W	W	19
Allt Undalain	Highld	NG9317	57°12·1′	5°25·2′W	W	33
Allt Ur	Highld	NM7370	56°46·2′	5°42·4′W	W	40
Allt Utha	Highld	NG8610	57°8·1′	5°31·7′W	W	33
Alltwalis	Carm	SN4431	51°57·6′	4°15·8′W	T	146
Allt-wen	Cered	SN5779	52°23·7′	4°5·7′W	X	135
Alltwen	Conwy	SH7477	53°16·7′	3°53·0′W	H	115
Allt-wen	Gwyn	SH5540	52°56·5′	4°9·1′W	X	124
Alltwen	Nth Pt Talb	SN7203	51°42·9′	3°50·8′W	T	170
Alltwen Fm	Swan	SS5795	51°38·4′	4°3·6′W	FM	159
Alltwineu	Powys	SN8548	52°7·3′	3°40·4′W	X	147
Alltwnnog	Powys	SO0194	52°32·3′	3°27·2′W	X	136
Allt Wood	Powys	SO2037	52°1·8′	3°9·6′W	F	161
Allt Yairack	Highld	NN4397	57°2·5′	4°34·8′W	W	34
Allt-y-bela	Monm	SO4100	51°42·0′	2°50·8′W	X	171
Alltyblaca	Cered	SN5245	52°5·3′	4°9·2′W	T	146
Alltybrain	Powys	SO0234	52°0·0′	3°25·3′W	X	160
Allt y Bwbach	Carm	SN4528	51°56·0′	4°14·9′W	X	146
Alltybwla	Cered	SN2642	52°3·2′	4°31·9′W	X	145
Alltycadno	Carm	SN4513	51°47·9′	4°14·5′W	X	159
Allt-y-cadno	Cered	SN2646	52°5·4′	4°32·0′W	X	145
Allt y Ceffylau	Gwyn	SH6747	53°0·5′	3°58·5′W	X	115
Allt-y-Celyn	Denb	SJ0751	53°3·1′	3°22·8′W	X	116
Alltycerrig	Powys	SN9935	52°0·5′	3°27·9′W	X	160
Allt y Clych	Powys	SN9756	52°11·8′	3°30·0′W	X	147
Allt y corde	Cered	SN3049	52°7·0′	4°28·6′W	X	145
Allt-y-Coryn	Powys	SO1355	52°11·4′	3°16·0′W	X	148
Allt y Dafarn	Cered	SN7673	52°20·7′	3°48·8′W	X	135,147
Allt y Ddinas	Powys	SN9256	52°11·7′	3°34·4′W	X	147
Allt Yelkie	Highld	NG3860	57°33·5′	6°22·4′W	W	23
Allt y Esgair	Powys	SO1224	51°54·7′	3°16·4′W	X	161
Allt-y-fan	Powys	SN8528	51°56·6′	3°40·0′W	X	160
Allt-y-fanog	Swan	SN6903	51°42·9′	3°53·4′W	X	170
Allt y Fedw	Cered	SN7849	52°7·8′	3°46·5′W	X	146,147
Allt y Ferdre	Carm	SN8033	51°59·2′	3°44·5′W	X	160
Allt-y-ferin Fm	Carm	SN5223	51°53·4′	4°8·7′W	FM	159
Alltyffynnon	Powys	SO0396	52°33·4′	3°25·5′W	X	136
Allt-y-frân	Carm	SN5403	51°42·6′	4°6·4′W	X	159
Allt y Fron	Cered	SN5258	52°12·3′	4°9·6′W	F	146
Allt y Gader	Powys	SJ1417	52°44·9′	3°16·0′W	H	125
Allt y Gaer	Powys	SO0590	52°30·2′	3°23·6′W	X	136
Allt y Genlli	Powys	SN9894	52°32·3′	3°29·8′W	X	136
Allt-y-gest	Powys	SN8952	52°9·5′	3°37·0′W	H	147
Allt-y-Gigfran	Cered	SN7278	52°23·3′	3°52·5′W	X	135,147
Allt-y-goed	Pemb	SN1349	52°6·7′	4°43·5′W	X	145
Allt-y-gog	Carm	SN4721	51°52·2′	4°13·0′W	X	159
Allt-y-gôg	Pemb	SN1428	51°55·4′	4°41·9′W	X	145,158
Alltygraban Fm	Swan	SN6001	51°41·7′	4°1·1′W	FM	159
Allt y Gribin	Powys	SN9623	52°47·9′	3°32·2′W	X	125
Allt-y-gwine	Gwyn	SH8325	52°48·8′	3°43·8′W	X	124,125
Allt y Gwreiddyn	Cered	SN6780	52°24·4′	3°56·9′W	X	135
Allt y Main	Powys	SJ1615	52°43·8′	3°14·2′W	H	125
Allt y Moch	Powys	SO0285	52°27·5′	3°26·1′W	H	136
Alltypistyll	Carm	SN1124	51°53·2′	4°44·4′W	X	145,158
Allt yr Eryr	Powys	SN9523	52°47·9′	3°33·0′W	H	125
Alltyresgob	Cered	SN3342	52°3·3′	4°25·8′W	X	145
Allt yr Hebog	Carm	SN6844	52°5·0′	3°55·2′W	H	146
Allt-y-rheiny	Pemb	SN2042	52°3·1′	4°37·1′W	X	145
Allt yr Hendre	Powys	SO0285	52°27·5′	3°26·1′W	X	136
Alltyrodyn	Cered	SN4444	52°4·6′	4°16·2′W	X	146
Allt-yr-yn	Newp	ST2988	51°35·4′	3°1·1′W	T	171
Allt yr Yn	Pemb	SM9832	51°57·2′	4°56·0′W	X	157
Alltyrynys	Heref	SO3323	51°54·3′	2°58·0′W	X	161
Allum Brook Fm	Ches	SJ7665	53°11·1′	2°21·1′W	FM	118
Allum Green	Hants	SU2707	50°51·9′	1°36·6′W	X	195
Allums	Glos	SO6831	51°58·8′	2°27·6′W	X	149
Allwood Copse	Hants	SU6447	51°13·3′	1°4·6′W	F	185
Allwood Fm	Northnts	SP6148	52°7·8′	1°6·1′W	FM	152
Allwood Fm	Wigan	SJ6998	53°28·9′	2°27·6′W	FM	109
Allwood Green	Suff	TM0472	52°18·7′	1°0·0′E	T	144,155
Alma	Notts	SK4752	53°4·0′	1°17·5′W	T	120
Alma	Shetld	HP6008	60°45·3′	0°53·4′W	X	1
Alma Fm	N Yks	SE0788	54°17·5′	1°53·1′W	FM	99
Alma Fm	N Yks	SE7679	54°12·3′	0°49·7′W	FM	100
Almagill	D & G	NY0975	55°3·9′	3°25·1′W	T	85
Almais Cliff or Little Alms Cliff	N Yks	SE2352	53°58·1′	1°38·5′W	X	104
Alma Lodge	Norf	TF5520	52°45·6′	0°18·2′E	X	131
Alma Park Industrial Estate	Lincs	SK9337	52°55·6′	0°36·6′W	X	130
Alma Wood	Lincs	SK9437	52°55·6′	0°35·7′W	F	130
Almeel Burn	E Dunb	NS5981	56°0·3′	4°15·2′W	W	64
Almeley	Heref	SO3351	52°9·4′	2°58·4′W	T	148,149
Almeley Wooton	Heref	SO3352	52°10·0′	2°58·4′W	T	148,149
Almer	Dorset	SY9198	50°47·1′	2°7·3′W	T	195
Almere	Wrex	SJ4056	53°6·1′	2°53·4′W	X	117
Almholme	Donc	SE5808	53°34·2′	1°7·0′W	T	111
Almington	Staffs	SJ7034	52°54·4′	2°26·4′W	T	127
Alminstone Cross	Devon	SS3420	50°57·6′	4°21·4′W	T	190
Alm'ners Barn Fm	Surrey	TQ0266	51°23·3′	0°31·7′W	FM	176
Almodington	W Susx	SZ8297	50°46·2′	0°49·8′W	X	197
Almond	Falk	NS9576	55°58·2′	3°40·5′W	X	65
Almondbank	Pth & Kin	NO0626	56°25·3′	3°31·0′W	T	52,53,58
Almondbury	Kirk	SE1615	53°38·1′	1°45·1′W	T	110
Almondbury Common	Kirk	SE1714	53°37·6′	1°44·2′W	X	110
Almondell and Calder Wood Country Park	W Loth	NT0868	55°54·0′	3°27·8′W	F	65
Almondhill	C of Edin	NT1275	55°57·9′	3°24·1′W	X	65
Almondsbury	S Glos	ST6084	51°33·4′	2°34·2′W	T	172
Almondvale	W Loth	NT0566	55°52·9′	3°30·7′W	T	65
Almonside	D & G	NY3774	55°3·6′	2°58·8′W	X	85
Almont	S Ayr	NX1887	55°8·9′	4°50·9′W	X	76
Almorness Ho	D & G	NX8253	54°51·7′	3°49·9′W	X	84
Almorness Point	D & G	NX8451	54°50·7′	3°48·0′W	X	84
Almscliff Crag	N Yks	SE2649	53°56·4′	1°35·8′W	X	104
Almsford Br	N Yks	SE3152	53°58·0′	1°31·2′W	X	104
Almshayne Fm	Devon	ST0914	50°55·3′	3°17·3′W	FM	181
Almshoe Bury	Herts	TL2025	51°54·9′	0°14·9′W	X	166
Almshouse Copse	Wilts	SU2867	51°24·3′	1°35·5′W	F	174
Almshouse Fm	Dorset	ST6508	50°52·5′	2°29·5′W	FM	194
Almshouse Green	Essex	TL7533	51°58·3′	0°33·3′E	T	167
Almshouse Green	Suff	TL9353	52°8·7′	0°49·6′E	X	155
Almshouses	Norf	TF8943	52°57·3′	0°49·2′E	X	132
Almsworthy Common	Somer	SS8441	51°9·6′	3°39·2′W	X	181
Alnaboyle	Moray	NJ3740	57°27·0′	3°2·5′W	X	28
Alndyke	Northum	NU2012	55°24·3′	1°40·6′W	X	81
Alne	N Yks	SE4965	54°5·0′	1°14·6′W	T	100
Alne End	Warw	SP1159	52°14·0′	1°49·9′W	T	150
Alne Forest	N Yks	SE5166	54°5·5′	1°12·8′W	X	100
Alne Hills	Warw	SP1160	52°14·5′	1°49·9′W	T	150
Alness	Highld	NH6569	57°41·7′	4°15·4′W	T	21
Alness Bay	Highld	NH6366	57°40·0′	4°17·3′W	W	21
Alnessferry	Highld	NH6665	57°39·6′	4°14·3′W	T	21
Alness Point	Highld	NH6567	57°40·6′	4°15·4′W	X	21
Alness River or River Averon	Highld	NH6273	57°43·8′	4°18·6′W	W	21
Alne Station	N Yks	SE5066	54°5·5′	1°13·7′W	T	100
Alne Wood	Warw	SP1061	52°15·1′	1°50·8′W	F	150
Alney Island	Glos	SO8219	51°52·4′	2°15·3′W	X	162
Alnham	Northum	NT9910	55°23·3′	2°0·5′W	T	81
Alnham Ho	Northum	NT9910	55°23·3′	2°0·5′W	X	81
Alnhammoor	Northum	NT9715	55°26·0′	2°2·4′W	X	81
Alnmouth	Northum	NU2410	55°23·2′	1°36·8′W	T	81
Alnmouth Bay	Northum	NU2510	55°23·2′	1°35·9′W	W	81
Alnmouth Sta	Northum	NU2311	55°23·8′	1°37·8′W	X	81
Alnut's Hospital	Oxon	SU6579	51°30·6′	1°3·4′W	X	175
Alnwick	Northum	NU1813	55°24·9′	1°42·5′W	T	81
Alnwick Abbey	Northum	NU1714	55°25·4′	1°43·5′W	A	81
Alnwick Castle	Northum	NU1813	55°24·9′	1°42·5′W	A	81
Alnwick Fm	Herts	SP8917	51°50·9′	0°42·1′W	FM	165
Alnwick Moor or Aydon Forest (Inner)	Northum	NU1612	55°24·3′	1°44·4′W	X	81
Alnwick Moor or Aydon Forest (Outer)	Northum	NU1410	55°23·3′	1°46·3′W	X	81
Aloe Fm	Norf	TM0888	52°27·2′	1°4·1′E	FM	144
Alperton	Brent	TQ1883	51°32·2′	0°17·5′W	T	176
Alphamstone	Essex	TL8735	51°59·1′	0°43·8′E	T	155
Alpheton	Suff	TL8850	52°7·2′	0°45·2′E	T	155
Alphin	Tames	SE0002	53°31·1′	1°59·6′W	H	110
Alphin Brook	Devon	SX8892	50°43·2′	3°34·8′W	W	192
Alphincombe	Devon	SX8593	50°43·7′	3°37·4′W	X	191
Alphington	Devon	SX9189	50°41·7′	3°32·2′W	T	192
Alphin Pike	Tames	SE0002	53°31·1′	1°59·6′W	X	110
Alpine	I of M	SC3393	54°18·6′	4°33·6′W	X	95
Alpine Br	Powys	SO0963	52°15·7′	3°19·6′W	X	147
Alpington	Norf	TG2901	52°33·7′	1°23·1′E	T	134
Alpity	Aberd	NO7877	56°53·3′	2°21·2′W	X	45
Alport	Derby	SK2264	53°10·6′	1°39·8′W	T	119
Alport	Powys	SO2795	52°33·1′	3°4·2′W	T	137
Alport Castles	Derby	SK1491	53°25·2′	1°47·0′W	X	110
Alport Castles Fm	Derby	SK1391	53°25·2′	1°47·9′W	FM	110
Alport Dale	Derby	SK1392	53°25·7′	1°47·9′W	X	110
Alport Head	Derby	SK1096	53°27·9′	1°50·6′W	X	110
Alport Height	Derby	SK3051	53°3·6′	1°32·7′W	X	119
Alport Moor	Derby	SK1193	53°26·3′	1°49·7′W	X	110
Alpraham	Ches	SJ5859	53°7·8′	2°37·3′W	T	117
Alps Fm	V of Glam	ST1273	51°27·2′	3°15·6′W	FM	171
Alps, The	Cumbr	SD2980	54°12·9′	3°4·9′W	X	96,97
Alren Fm	Corn	SX3673	50°32·3′	4°18·5′W	FM	201
Alresford	Essex	TM0621	51°51·2′	0°59·9′E	T	168
Alresford Creek	Essex	TM0619	51°50·1′	0°59·8′E	W	168
Alresford Grange	Essex	TM0520	51°50·7′	0°59·0′E	X	168
Alresford Hall	Essex	TM0720	51°50·6′	1°0·7′E	X	168,169
Alresford Ho	Hants	SU5833	51°5·8′	1°9·9′W	X	185
Alresford Lodge	Essex	TM0520	51°50·7′	0°59·0′E	X	168
Alrewas	Staffs	SK1614	52°43·6′	1°45·4′W	T	128
Alrewas Hayes	Staffs	SK1314	52°43·6′	1°48·0′W	X	128
Alrick	Angus	NO1962	56°44·8′	3°19·0′W	X	43
Alrick Burn	Angus	NO1861	56°44·3′	3°20·0′W	W	43
Alsager	Ches	SJ7955	53°5·8′	2°18·4′W	T	118
Alsagers Bank	Staffs	SJ8048	53°2·0′	2°17·5′W	T	118
Alsa Lodge	Essex	TL5126	51°54·9′	0°12·1′E	X	167
Alsa Wood	Essex	TL5226	51°54·9′	0°13·0′E	F	167
Alscot	Bucks	SP8004	51°44·0′	0°50·1′W	T	165
Alscot Park	Warw	SP2050	52°9·1′	1°42·1′W	X	151
Alscott Barton	Devon	SS5225	51°0·6′	4°6·2′W	X	180
Alscott Fm	Devon	SS4611	50°52·9′	4°11·0′W	FM	190
Alsia	Corn	SW3925	50°4·3′	5°38·5′W	X	203
Alsop en le Dale	Derby	SK1655	53°5·8′	1°45·3′W	T	119
Alsop Moor Cottages	Derby	SK1656	53°6·3′	1°45·3′W	X	119
Alspath Hall	Sol	SP2682	52°26·4′	1°36·7′W	X	140
Alstead's Fm	Essex	TL7213	51°47·6′	0°30·0′E	FM	167
Alstoe Fm	Rut	SK8911	52°41·6′	0°40·6′W	FM	130
Alston	Corn	SX3875	50°33·4′	4°16·8′W	X	201
Alston	Cumbr	NY7146	54°48·7′	2°26·6′W	T	86,87
Alston	Devon	ST3002	50°49·0′	2°59·2′W	T	193
Alston	Devon	SX4869	50°30·3′	4°8·2′W	X	201
Alston	Devon	SX7772	50°32·3′	3°43·8′W	X	191
Alston	Devon	SX7946	50°18·3′	3°41·6′W	X	202
Alstonby Grange	Cumbr	NY4064	54°58·3′	2°55·8′W	X	85
Alstonby Hall	Cumbr	NY4065	54°58·8′	2°55·8′W	X	85
Alstonby Villa	Cumbr	NY4064	54°58·3′	2°55·8′W	X	85
Alstone	Glos	SO9322	51°54·0′	2°5·7′W	T	163
Alstone	Glos	SO9832	51°59·4′	2°1·4′W	T	150
Alstone	Somer	ST3146	51°12·8′	2°58·9′W	T	182
Alstonefield	Staffs	SK1355	53°5·8′	1°47·9′W	T	119
Alstone Fields Fm	Glos	SO9733	52°0·0′	2°2·2′W	FM	150
Alstone Fm	Staffs	SJ8618	52°45·8′	2°12·0′W	FM	127
Alstone Hall Fm	Staffs	SJ8518	52°45·8′	2°12·9′W	FM	127
Alston Fm	Devon	SX7140	50°15·0′	3°48·2′W	FM	202
Alston Fm	Devon	SX8955	50°23·3′	3°33·3′W	FM	202
Alston Grange	Lancs	SD6136	53°49·4′	2°35·1′W	X	102,103
Alston Hall	Devon	SX5848	50°19·1′	3°59·3′W	X	202
Alston Hall	Lancs	SD6033	53°47·8′	2°36·0′W	X	102,103
Alston Lodge	Lancs	SD6137	53°49·9′	2°35·1′W	X	102,103
Alston Moor	Cumbr	NY7239	54°45·0′	2°25·7′W	X	91
Alston Moor	Cumbr	NY7443	54°47·1′	2°23·8′W	X	86,87
Alston Old Hall	Lancs	SD6133	53°47·8′	2°35·1′W	X	102,103
Alston Resrs	Lancs	SD6036	53°49·4′	2°36·0′W	W	102,103
Alston Sutton	Somer	ST4151	51°15·5′	2°50·3′W	T	182
Alston Wood	Lancs	SD6033	53°47·8′	2°36·0′W	F	102,103
Alswear	Devon	SS7222	50°59·2′	3°49·0′W	T	180
Alswick Hall	Herts	TL3729	51°56·8′	0°0·0′W	X	166
Alt	Oldham	SD9403	53°31·7′	2°5·0′W	T	109
Altagalvash	Arg & Bt	NR9160	55°47·5′	5°19·6′W	X	62
Altaltan	Angus	NO1863	56°45·3′	3°20·0′W	X	43
Alt an Daimh	Arg & Bt	NR2940	55°35·0′	6°17·6′W	W	60
Altandhu	Highld	NB9812	58°3·3′	5°24·9′W	X	15
Altanduin	Highld	NC8026	58°12·7′	4°2·1′W	X	17
Altanour Lodge	Aberd	NO0882	56°55·5′	3°30·2′W	X	43
Altarnun	Corn	SX2281	50°36·3′	4°30·6′W	T	201
Altars of Linnay	Orkney	HY7556	59°23·6′	2°25·9′W	X	5
Altar Stone	D & G	NY2164	54°58·1′	3°13·6′W	X	85
Altarstone	Scot Bord	NT1535	55°36·3′	3°20·5′W	X	72
Altarstones	Fife	NT6599	56°11·2′	2°33·4′W	X	59
Altar, The	Orkney	ND4190	58°47·9′	3°0·8′W	X	7
Altass	Highld	NC4900	57°58·1′	4°32·7′W	T	16
Altbough	Heref	SO5430	51°58·2′	2°39·8′W	T	149
Alt Bridge	Sefton	SD3005	53°32·5′	3°3·0′W	X	108
Altdachie	Aberd	NJ3713	57°12·5′	3°2·1′W	X	37
Altdargue	Aberd	NJ5507	57°9·4′	2°44·2′W	X	37
Altens	C of Aber	NJ9502	57°6·8′	2°4·5′W	T	38
Altens Haven	C of Aber	NJ9602	57°6·8′	2°3·5′W	W	38
Altercannoch	S Ayr	NX2380	55°5·2′	4°46·0′W	X	76
Altersie	Pth & Kin	NN7908	56°15·2′	3°56·7′W	X	57
Alterwall	Highld	ND2865	58°34·3′	3°13·8′W	X	11,12
Altewan	S Ayr	NS2806	55°19·3′	4°42·2′W	X	70,76
Altgaltraig Point	Arg & Bt	NS0373	55°54·8′	5°8·7′W	X	63
Altham	Lancs	SD7732	53°47·3′	2°20·5′W	T	103
Altham Br	Lancs	SD7733	53°47·8′	2°20·5′W	X	103
Alt Hill	Tames	SD9402	53°31·1′	2°5·0′W	T	109
Althorne	Essex	TQ9198	51°39·1′	0°46·1′E	T	168
Althorne	Hants	SU2344	51°11·9′	1°39·9′W	X	184
Althorne Lodge	Essex	TQ9298	51°39·1′	0°46·9′E	X	168
Althorne Sta	Essex	TQ9097	51°38·6′	0°45·2′E	X	168
Althorp	Northnts	SP6865	52°17·0′	0°59·8′W	X	152
Althorpe	N Lincs	SE8309	53°34·5′	0°44·4′W	T	112
Althorpe Sta	N Lincs	SE8310	53°35·0′	0°44·4′W	X	112
Althorp Park	Northnts	SP6865	52°17·0′	0°59·8′W	X	152
Althrey Fm	Wrex	SJ3844	52°59·6′	2°55·0′W	FM	117
Althrey Hall	Wrex	SJ3744	52°59·6′	2°55·9′W	A	117
Althrey Woodhouse	Wrex	SJ3843	52°59·1′	2°55·0′W	X	117
Alticane	S Ayr	NX2086	55°8·4′	4°49·0′W	X	76
Alticry	D & G	NX2749	54°48·6′	4°41·1′W	X	82
Altigabert Burn	S Ayr	NX1177	55°3·3′	4°57·1′W	W	76
Altimeg	S Ayr	NX0976	55°2·8′	4°59·0′W	X	76
Altimeg Hill	S Ayr	NX1076	55°2·8′	4°58·0′W	X	76
Altina Cottage	Pth & Kin	NN9020	56°21·8′	3°46·4′W	X	52,58
Altizourie	S Ayr	NS3706	55°19·5′	4°33·7′W	X	70,77
Altmore	Win & Maid	SU8579	51°30·4′	0°46·1′W	T	175
Altnabreac	Highld	NH4256	57°34·3′	4°38·0′W	X	26
Altnabreac Sta	Highld	ND0045	58°23·2′	3°42·1′W	X	11,12
Altnacardich	Highld	NH5843	57°27·6′	4°21·6′W	X	26
Altnacealgach Hotel	Highld	NC2610	58°3·0′	4°56·4′W	X	15
Altnafeadh	Highld	NN2256	56°40·0′	4°53·8′W	X	41
Altnaglander Cottages	Moray	NJ1628	57°20·3′	3°23·3′W	X	36
Altnaharra	Highld	NC5635	58°17·1′	4°26·9′W	T	16
Altnaharra Lodge	Highld	NC5734	58°16·6′	4°25·8′W	X	16
Altnaharrie Hotel	Highld	NH1193	57°53·5′	5°10·8′W	X	19
Altofts	Wakf	SE3723	53°42·4′	1°26·0′W	T	104
Alton	Aberd	NJ7421	57°17·0′	2°25·4′W	X	38
Alton	Derby	SK3664	53°10·6′	1°27·3′W	T	119
Alton	D & G	NS8501	55°17·6′	3°48·2′W	X	78
Alton	D & G	NT0906	55°20·6′	3°25·7′W	X	78
Alton	D & G	NX1335	54°40·8′	4°53·6′W	X	82
Alton	Hants	SU7139	51°9·0′	0°58·7′W	T	186
Alton	Moray	NJ2142	57°27·9′	3°18·6′W	X	28
Alton	Staffs	SK0742	52°58·8′	1°53·3′W	T	119,128
Alton	Stir	NS8491	56°6·1′	3°51·5′W	X	58
Alton	Wilts	SU1546	51°13·0′	1°46·7′W	T	184
Alton Albany	S Ayr	NX2793	55°12·3′	4°42·7′W	X	76
Alton Albany Fm	S Ayr	NX2793	55°12·3′	4°42·7′W	FM	76
Alton Barnes	Wilts	SU1062	51°21·7′	1°51·0′W	T	173
Alton Burn	E Ayr	NS5039	55°37·5′	4°22·5′W	W	70
Alton Common	Dorset	ST7104	50°50·3′	2°24·3′W	F	194
Alton Common	Staffs	SK0542	52°58·8′	1°55·1′W	X	119,128
Alton Court	Heref	SO4253	52°10·6′	2°50·5′W	X	148,149
Alton Cross	Heref	SO4253	52°10·6′	2°50·5′W	X	148,149
Alton Down	Wilts	SU1146	51°13·0′	1°50·2′W	X	184
Alton Fm	E Dunb	NS6676	55°57·8′	4°8·4′W	FM	64
Alton Grange	Leic	SK3914	52°43·6′	1°24·9′W	X	128
Alton Hall	Derby	SK2750	53°3·0′	1°35·4′W	X	119
Alton Hall Fm	Cov	SP2882	52°26·4′	1°34·9′W	FM	140
Altonhead	N Ayr	NS3842	55°38·9′	4°34·0′W	X	63,70
Altonhill	E Ayr	NS4139	55°37·4′	4°31·1′W	X	70
Altonhill	E Ayr	NS4239	55°37·4′	4°30·1′W	T	70
Alton Hill	Leic	SK3815	52°44·1′	1°25·8′W	X	128
Alton Manor	Derby	SK2851	53°3·6′	1°34·5′W	X	119
Alton Muirside	E Ayr	NS5040	55°38·1′	4°22·5′W	X	70
Alton Pancras	Dorset	ST6902	50°49·2′	2°26·0′W	T	194
Alton Park	Staffs	SK0743	52°59·3′	1°53·3′W	X	119,128
Alton Priors	Wilts	SU1162	51°21·6′	1°50·1′W	T	173
Altonrea	Aberd	NJ4601	57°6·1′	2°53·0′W	X	37
Altons	Aberd	NJ8020	57°16·5′	2°19·4′W	X	38

Altons	Aberd	NJ8241	57°27·8′	2°17·5′W	X	29,30
Altonside	Moray	NJ2957	57°36·1′	3°10·8′W	X	28
Alton Side	Northum	NY8565	54°59·0′	2°13·6′W	X	87
Alton Towers	Staffs	SK0743	52°59·3′	1°53·3′W	X	119,128
Alton Water (Reservoir)	Suff	TM1437	51°59·6′	1°7·4′E	W	169
Altourie	Highld	NH5740	57°25·9′	4°22·5′W	X	26
Altries Ho	Aberd	NO8498	57°4·6′	2°15·4′W	X	38,45
Altrieve	Scot Bord	NT2822	55°29·4′	3°7·9′W	X	73
Altrieve Burn	Scot Bord	NT2822	55°29·4′	3°7·9′W	W	73
Altrieve Lake	Scot Bord	NT2822	55°29·4′	3°7·9′W	W	73
Altrieve Rig	Scot Bord	NT2723	55°30·0′	3°8·9′W	H	73
Altrincham	Traf	SJ7687	53°23·0′	2°21·2′W	T	109
Altrua	Highld	NN2490	56°58·3′	4°53·3′W	X	34
Altry Burn	D & G	NX6799	55°16·3′	4°5·2′W	W	77
Altry Hill	D & G	NS6700	55°16·8′	4°5·2′W	H	77
Altskeith	Stir	NN4602	56°11·4′	4°28·5′W	T	57
Alt, The	D & G	NX3838	54°42·9′	4°30·5′W	H	83
Alt Traighe Leacail	Arg & Bt	NR2744	55°37·0′	6°19·7′W	W	60
Alturlie Point	Highld	NH7149	57°31·0′	4°8·8′W	X	27
Altvounnie	Highld	NJ1238	57°25·7′	3°27·5′W	X	28
Altwynt Fm	Heref	SO5230	51°58·2′	2°41·5′W	FM	149
Altyre	Highld	NH5045	57°28·5′	4°29·6′W	X	26
Altyre Ho	Moray	NJ0254	57°34·2′	3°37·8′W	X	27
Altyre Woods	Moray	NJ0253	57°33·7′	3°37·8′W	F	27
Alum Bay	I of W	SZ3085	50°40·1′	1°34·1′W	W	196
Alum Beck	N Yks	NZ5005	54°26·5′	1°13·3′W	W	93
Alum Chine	Bourne	SZ0790	50°42·8′	1°53·7′W	X	195
Alum Pot	N Yks	SD7775	54°10·5′	2°20·7′W	X	98
Alum Rock	Birm	SP1187	52°29·1′	1°49·9′W	T	139
Alum Waters	Durham	NZ2341	54°46·0′	1°38·1′W	X	88
Alva	Clackm	NS8896	56°8·9′	3°47·7′W	T	58
Alva Burn	Clackm	NS8799	56°10·5′	3°48·8′W	W	58
Alvacott Fm	Corn	SX3195	50°44·0′	4°23·3′W	FM	190
Alva Glen	Clackm	NS8898	56°9·9′	3°47·8′W	X	58
Alvain Burn	E Dunb	NS6181	56°0·4′	4°13·3′W	W	64
Alvanley	Ches	SJ4973	53°15·3′	2°45·5′W	T	117
Alvanley Cliff	Ches	SJ5073	53°15·3′	2°44·6′W	X	117
Alvaston	C of Derb	SK3833	52°53·8′	1°25·7′W	T	128
Alvaston Hall Hotel	Ches	SJ6654	53°5·2′	2°30·1′W	X	118
Alvechurch	Worcs	SP0272	52°21·0′	1°57·8′W	T	139
Alvechurch Lodge Fm	Worcs	SP0372	52°21·0′	1°57·0′W	FM	139
Alvecote	Warw	SK2404	52°38·2′	1°38·3′W	T	139
Alvediston	Wilts	ST9723	51°0·6′	2°2·2′W	T	184
Alveley	Shrops	SO7684	52°27·4′	2°20·8′W	T	138
Alverdiscott	Devon	SS5125	51°0·5′	4°7·1′W	T	180
Alverley Grange	Donc	SK5599	53°29·3′	1°9·9′W	X	111
Alverstoke	Hants	SZ5998	50°46·9′	1°9·4′W	T	196
Alverstone	I of W	SZ5785	50°39·9′	1°11·2′W	T	196
Alverstone Fm	I of W	SZ5292	50°43·7′	1°15·4′W	FM	196
Alverthorpe	Wakf	SE3121	53°41·3′	1°31·4′W	T	104
Alverton	Notts	SK7942	52°58·4′	0°49·0′W	T	129
Alverton Hall Fm	Staffs	SK0941	52°58·2′	1°51·6′W	FM	119,128
Alves	Moray	NJ1362	57°38·6′	3°27·0′W	T	28
Alvescot	Oxon	SP2704	51°44·3′	1°36·1′W	T	163
Alvescot Down	Oxon	SP2707	51°45·9′	1°36·1′W	X	163
Alveston	S Glos	ST6388	51°35·6′	2°31·7′W	T	162,172
Alveston	Warw	SP2356	52°12·3′	1°39·4′W	T	151
Alveston Down	S Glos	ST6288	51°35·6′	2°32·5′W	T	162,172
Alveston Fm	Warw	SP2355	52°11·8′	1°39·4′W	FM	151
Alveston Hill	Warw	SP2254	52°11·3′	1°40·3′W	T	151
Alveston Ho	Warw	SP2356	52°12·3′	1°39·4′W	X	151
Alveston Pastures	Warw	SP2453	52°10·7′	1°38·5′W	X	151
Alves Wood	Moray	NJ1161	57°38·1′	3°29·0′W	F	28
Alvie	Highld	NH8609	57°9·7′	3°52·6′W	T	35,36
Alvie Lodge	Highld	NH8407	57°8·6′	3°54·6′W	X	35
Alvingham	Lincs	TF3691	53°24·1′	0°3·2′E	T	113
Alvingham Mill	Lincs	TF3691	53°24·1′	0°3·2′E	X	113
Alvington	Glos	SO6000	51°42·1′	2°34·3′W	T	162
Alvington	Somer	ST5215	50°56·2′	2°40·6′W	T	183
Alvington Court	Glos	SO6000	51°42·1′	2°34·3′W	X	162
Alvington Manor Fm	I of W	SZ4788	50°41·6′	1°19·7′W	FM	196
Alwalton	Cambs	TL1395	52°32·7′	0°19·6′W	T	142
Alway	Newp	ST3488	51°35·5′	2°56·8′W	T	171
Alwen Reservoir	Conwy	SH9453	53°4·1′	3°34·5′W	W	116
Alwent	Durham	NZ1319	54°34·2′	1°47·5′W	X	92
Alwent Hall	Durham	NZ1418	54°33·7′	1°46·6′W	X	92
Alwent Mill	Durham	NZ1418	54°33·7′	1°46·6′W	X	92
Alweston	Dorset	ST6614	50°55·7′	2°28·6′W	T	194
Alwhat	E Ayr	NS6402	55°17·9′	4°8·1′W	H	77
Alwington	Devon	SS4023	50°59·3′	4°16·4′W	T	180,190
Alwinton	Northum	NT9206	55°21·1′	2°7·1′W	T	80
Alwinton Burn	Northum	NT9108	55°22·2′	2°8·1′W	W	80
Alwoodley	Leeds	SE3040	53°51·6′	1°32·2′W	T	104
Alwoodley Gates	Leeds	SE3140	53°51·6′	1°31·3′W	T	104
Alwoodley Old Hall	Leeds	SE3041	53°52·1′	1°32·2′W	A	104
Alwoodley Park	Leeds	SE2940	53°51·6′	1°33·1′W	T	104
Alwyn Lawn Ho	Bucks	SP7811	51°47·8′	0°51·7′W	X	165
Alyn Waters Country Park	Wrex	SJ3154	53°5·0′	3°1·4′W	X	117
Alyth	Pth & Kin	NO2448	56°37·3′	3°13·9′W	T	53
Alyth Burn	Pth & Kin	NO1954	56°40·5′	3°18·9′W	W	53
Alyth Burn	Pth & Kin	NO2249	56°37·8′	3°15·8′W	W	53
Amadale Ho	Highld	NC7863	58°32·5′	4°5·3′W	X	10
Amadyes	Essex	TL6112	51°47·2′	0°20·5′E	X	167
Amage Fm	Kent	TR0745	51°10·2′	0°58·1′E	FM	179,189
Amalebra	Corn	SW4936	50°10·5′	5°30·6′W	T	203
Amalveor	Corn	SW4837	50°11·0′	5°31·4′W	T	203
Amalveor Downs	Corn	SW4737	50°11·0′	5°32·3′W	X	203
Amalwhidden	Corn	SW4837	50°11·0′	5°31·4′W	X	203
Aman Fach	Carm	SN7415	51°49·4′	3°49·3′W	W	160
Aman Fawr	Carm	SN7515	51°49·4′	3°48·4′W	W	160
Amar River	Highld	NG3638	57°21·6′	6°22·9′W	W	23,32
Amar Srath Ossian	Highld	NN4171	56°48·5′	4°35·8′W	X	42
Amar Stob a' Choin	Stir	NN4116	56°18·8′	4°33·8′W	X	56
Amat	Highld	NC7615	58°6·7′	4°5·8′W	X	17
Amat	Highld	NH3899	57°57·3′	4°43·8′W	X	20
Amat Forest	Highld	NH4589	57°52·1′	4°36·3′W	X	20
Amat Lodge	Highld	NH4790	57°52·7′	4°34·3′W	X	20
Amatnatua	Highld	NH4790	57°52·7′	4°34·3′W	T	20
Amazondean Fm	Midlo	NT1656	55°47·7′	3°19·9′W	FM	65
Am Bacan	Stir	NN6030	56°26·7′	4°15·8′W	H	51

Am Badan	N Ayr	NR9048	55°41·1′	5°20·0′W	X	62,69
Am Bagh-dhùin	Highld	NG3757	57°31·9′	6°23·2′W	W	23
Am Bà Leac	Arg & Bt	NM6537	56°28·3′	5°48·5′W	X	49
Am Balg	Highld	NC1866	58°32·9′	5°7·2′W	X	9
Am Bàrr	Arg & Bt	NM8501	56°9·5′	5°27·3′W	H	55
Am Barr	Arg & Bt	NM9728	56°24·3′	5°17·0′W	X	49
Am Barradhu	Arg & Bt	NL9839	56°27·0′	6°53·7′W	X	46
Am Basteir	Highld	NG4625	57°15·0′	6°12·2′W	X	32
Ambaston	Derby	SK4232	52°53·3′	1°22·1′W	T	129
Ambaston Grange	Derby	SK4331	52°52·7′	1°21·3′W	X	129
Am Bàthach	Highld	NH0713	57°10·3′	5°11·1′W	X	33
Am Bàthaich	Highld	NC3146	58°22·5′	4°52·9′W	X	9
Am Bàthaich	Highld	NG9907	57°6·9′	5°18·7′W	X	33
Am Bàthaich	Highld	NH6714	57°12·1′	4°11·6′W	X	35
Am Beacan	Highld	NG9262	57°36·3′	5°28·4′W	X	19
Am Bealach	Highld	NC3260	58°30·0′	4°52·5′W	X	9
Am Bealach	Highld	NC8959	58°30·6′	3°53·8′W	X	10
Am Beanaidh	Highld	NH9205	57°7·7′	3°46·6′W	W	36
Am Beannan	Highld	NG2204	57°2·9′	6°34·6′W	X	39
Am Beannan	Highld	NG8641	57°24·8′	5°33·3′W	X	24
Am Beannan	Pth & Kin	NN5658	56°41·8′	4°20·6′W	H	42,51
Am Beannan	Pth & Kin	NN6913	56°17·7′	4°6·6′W	H	57
Amberden Hall	Essex	TL5530	51°57·0′	0°15·7′E	X	167
Amberfield	Kent	TQ7950	51°13·5′	0°33·5′E	X	188
Amberfield	Suff	TM2240	52°1·1′	1°14·5′E	X	169
Amber Fm	Lincs	TF2249	53°1·7′	0°10·4′W	FM	131
Ambergate	Derby	SK3551	53°3·5′	1°28·3′W	X	119
Amber Hill	Cumbr	NY7622	54°35·8′	2°21·9′W	X	91
Amber Hill	Derby	SK3262	53°9·5′	1°30·9′W	X	119
Amber Hill	Lincs	TF2346	53°0·1′	0°9·6′W	X	131
Amber Ho	Derby	SK3363	53°10·0′	1°30·0′W	X	119
Amberley	Glos	SO8501	51°42·7′	2°12·6′W	T	162
Amberley	Heref	SO5447	52°7·4′	2°39·9′W	T	149
Amberley	W Susx	TQ0313	50°54·7′	0°31·7′W	T	197
Amberley Court	Monm	SO4813	51°49·0′	2°44·9′W	X	161
Amberley Fm	Derby	SK3753	53°4·6′	1°26·5′W	FM	119
Amberley Fm	W Susx	TQ2639	51°8·4′	0°11·5′W	FM	187
Amberley Mount	W Susx	TQ0412	50°54·1′	0°30·9′W	X	197
Amberley Mount (Tumuli)	W Susx	TQ0412	50°54·1′	0°30·9′W	A	197
Amberley Sta	W Susx	TQ0211	50°53·6′	0°32·6′W	X	197
Amberley Wild Brooks	W Susx	TQ0314	50°55·2′	0°31·7′W	X	197
Amber Manor	Derby	SK3266	53°11·6′	1°30·9′W	X	119
Ambersham Common	W Susx	SU9119	50°58·0′	0°41·9′W	X	197
Amberstone Grange Fm	E Susx	TQ6011	50°52·8′	0°16·9′E	FM	199
Amberwood Inclosure	Hants	SU2013	50°55·2′	1°42·5′W	F	195
Am Biachdaich	Highld	NH1972	57°42·3′	5°1·8′W	X	20
Am Bi-bogha Beag	Highld	NG1938	57°21·0′	6°39·8′W	X	23
Am Bi-bogha Mór	Highld	NG1838	57°21·0′	6°40·8′W	X	23
Am Bidean	Highld	NG3441	57°23·2′	6°25·1′W	X	23
Am Bidein	Highld	NG7508	57°6·7′	5°42·5′W	H	33
Am Binneag	Arg & Bt	NR7162	55°48·1′	5°38·8′W	X	62
Am Binnein	Arg & Bt	NM5230	56°24·1′	6°0·7′W	X	48
Am Binnein	Arg & Bt	NS1285	56°1·5′	5°0·6′W	X	56
Am Binnein	Arg & Bt	NS1990	56°4·4′	4°54·0′W	X	56
Am Binnein	Highld	NN6691	56°59·7′	4°11·9′W	H	35
Am Binnein	N Ayr	NS0042	55°38·1′	5°10·2′W	X	63,69
Am Biod	Highld	NM6457	56°39·0′	5°50·5′W	X	49
Ambion Hill	Leic	SK4000	52°36·0′	1°24·2′W	X	140
Ambion Wood	Leic	SP4099	52°35·5′	1°24·2′W	F	140
Am Bioran	Pth & Kin	NN6922	56°22·6′	4°6·8′W	H	51
Amble	Northum	NU2703	55°19·5′	1°34·0′W	T	81
Amblecote	Dudley	SO8985	52°28·0′	2°9·3′W	T	139
Amblecote	Shrops	SO1885	52°27·6′	3°12·0′W	X	136
Ambler Thorn	Brad	SE0929	53°45·7′	1°51·4′W	T	104
Ambleside	Cumbr	NY3704	54°25·9′	2°57·9′W	T	90
Ambleston	Pemb	SN0025	51°53·5′	4°54·0′W	T	145,157,158
Ambley Fm	Hants	SU3654	51°17·3′	1°28·6′W	FM	185
Ambley Wood	Medway	TQ7965	51°21·6′	0°34·7′E	F	178
Ambling Gate	Durham	NY9440	54°45·5′	2°5·2′W	X	87
Am Bodach	Arg & Bt	NM9616	56°17·8′	5°17·4′W	X	55
Am Bodach	Highld	NC2473	58°36·8′	5°1·3′W	X	9
Am Bodach	Highld	NH6905	57°7·3′	4°9·4′W	X	35
Am Bodach	Highld	NN1658	56°40·9′	4°59·8′W	H	41
Am Bodach	Highld	NN1765	56°44·7′	4°59·1′W	H	41
Am Bodach	Pth & Kin	NN8734	56°29·3′	3°49·7′W	X	52
Am Bog-àirigh	Arg & Bt	NR5674	55°54·1′	5°53·8′W	X	61
Am Braga	N Eil	NB5661	58°28·4′	6°10·6′W	X	8
Ambraigh	Highld	NC1232	58°14·5′	5°11·7′W	X	15
Ambraigh	Highld	NG8703	57°4·4′	5°30·4′W	X	33
Am Breac-leathaid	Highld	NC5247	58°23·5′	4°31·4′W	H	10
Am Brèideanach	Arg & Bt	NM4137	56°27·5′	6°11·8′W	X	47,48
Ambresbury Banks	Essex	TL4300	51°41·1′	0°4·5′E	A	167
Am Brican	Arg & Bt	NM5945	56°32·4′	5°54·8′W	X	47,48
Ambrisbeg	Arg & Bt	NS0659	55°47·4′	5°5·2′W	X	63
Am Briseadh	Highld	NH0676	57°44·2′	5°15·1′W	X	19
Ambrismore	Arg & Bt	NS0658	55°46·8′	5°5·2′W	X	63
Ambro Hill	Leic	SK4125	52°49·5′	1°23·1′W	X	129
Am Broilein	Highld	NM8854	56°38·1′	5°27·0′W	W	49
Ambrosden	Oxon	SP6019	51°52·2′	1°7·3′W	T	164,165
Ambrose Fm	Oxon	SU6688	51°35·4′	1°2·4′W	FM	175
Ambrose Hall	Lancs	SD4935	53°48·8′	2°46·1′W	X	102
Ambrose Hill	Dorset	ST6318	50°57·8′	2°31·2′W	X	183
Am Bru	Arg & Bt	NM3740	56°29·0′	6°15·9′W	W	47,48
Am Buachaille	Arg & Bt	NM3235	56°26·1′	6°20·4′W	X	46,47,48
Am Buachaille	Arg & Bt	NN0507	56°13·2′	5°8·3′W	H	56
Am Buachaille	Highld	NC2065	58°32·4′	5°5·1′W	X	9
Am Buachaille	Highld	NN7494	57°1·5′	4°4·1′W	H	35
Am Bùth	Arg & Bt	NM8323	56°21·2′	5°30·3′W	X	49
Amcotts	N Lincs	SE8514	53°37·2′	0°42·5′W	T	112
Amcotts Grange	N Lincs	SE8313	53°36·7′	0°44·3′W	X	112
Amen Corner	Brackn	SU8468	51°24·5′	0°47·1′W	T	175
Amen Corner	Dorset	SU0010	50°53·6′	1°59·6′W	X	195
Amen Corner	Notts	SK6465	53°10·9′	1°2·1′W	F	120
Amerdale Dub	N Yks	SD9769	54°7·3′	2°2·3′W	W	98
Amerden Ho	Bucks	SU9179	51°30·4′	0°40·9′W	X	175
Amerden Ponds	Bucks	SU9080	51°30·9′	0°41·8′W	X	175
America	Shrops	SJ3716	52°44·5′	2°55·6′W	X	126
America Fm	Essex	TL5308	51°45·2′	0°13·4′E	FM	167
America Fm	Essex	TL8626	51°54·3′	0°42·6′E	FM	168
America Fm	Essex	TQ5997	51°39·2′	0°18·3′E	FM	167,177

America Fm	Leic	SP8294	52°32·5′	0°47·1′W	FM	141
America Fm	Lincs	TF3692	53°24·7′	0°3·2′E	FM	113
America Fm	Lincs	TF5078	53°16·9′	0°15·4′E	FM	122
America Fm	Northnts	TL1090	52°30·0′	0°22·4′W	FM	142
America Fm	Notts	SK4950	53°2·9′	1°15·7′W	FM	120
America Fm	Notts	SK7772	53°14·6′	0°50·4′W	FM	120
America Fm	N Yks	SE0142	53°52·7′	1°58·7′W	FM	104
America Fm	Peterb	TF2300	52°35·3′	0°10·7′W	FM	142
America Fm	Suff	TM0255	52°9·6′	0°57·6′E	FM	155
America Ho	N Yks	NZ7714	54°31·2′	0°48·2′W	X	94
America Lodge	Rut	SK8504	52°37·9′	0°44·2′W	X	141
American Barn	S Glos	ST7984	51°33·5′	2°17·8′W	X	172
American Cemy	Cambs	TL4059	52°12·9′	0°3·4′E	X	154
American Fm	Flint	SJ2160	53°8·1′	3°10·4′W	FM	117
Amersham	Bucks	SU9698	51°40·6′	0°36·3′W	T	165,176
Amersham Common	Bucks	SU9697	51°40·0′	0°36·3′W	T	165,176
Amersham Old Town	Bucks	SU9597	51°40·1′	0°37·2′W	T	165,176
Amersham on the Hill	Bucks	SU9698	51°40·6′	0°36·3′W	T	165,176
Amersidelaw	Northum	NU0627	55°32·4′	1°53·9′W	X	75
Amersidelaw Moor	Northum	NU0827	55°32·4′	1°52·0′W	X	75
Amerston Hall	Hartpl	NZ4230	54°40·0′	1°20·5′W	X	93
Amerston Hill	Hartpl	NZ4330	54°40·0′	1°19·6′W	X	93
Amerton	Staffs	SJ9927	52°50·7′	2°0·5′W	T	127
Amerton Brook	Staffs	SJ9927	52°50·7′	2°0·5′W	W	127
Amery Court	Kent	TR1261	51°18·7′	1°2·9′E	X	179
Amery Wood	Hants	SU7040	51°9·5′	0°59·6′W	F	186
Amesbury	Bath & NE Somer	ST6558	51°19·4′	2°29·8′W	T	172
Amesbury	Wilts	SU1541	51°10·3′	1°46·7′W	T	184
Amesbury Down	Wilts	SU1439	51°9·2′	1°47·6′W	X	184
Amethyst Green	Cumbr	SD0898	54°22·4′	3°24·6′W	X	96
Ameysford	Dorset	SU0702	50°49·3′	1°53·7′W	T	195
Am Falachan	Highld	NM7580	56°51·7′	5°41·0′W	X	40
Am Famhair (Natural Arch)	Highld	NG1855	57°30·1′	6°42·0′W	X	23
Am Fàn	Arg & Bt	NM3919	56°17·8′	6°12·7′W	X	48
Am Faochagach	Highld	NH3079	57°46·4′	4°51·0′W	H	20
Am Faradh	Arg & Bt	NM7714	56°16·2′	5°35·7′W	X	55
Am Fasach	Arg & Bt	NR3565	55°48·6′	6°13·3′W	F	60,61
Am Fàs-allt	Highld	NG9712	57°9·5′	5°20·9′W	X	33
Am Fasarinen	Highld	NG9257	57°33·6′	5°28·2′W	X	25
Am Feadan	Highld	NG5909	57°6·8′	5°58·4′W	X	32,39
Am Feur-loch	Highld	NC4355	58°27·6′	4°41·0′W	W	9
Am Feur-loch	Highld	NG8466	57°38·2′	5°36·7′W	W	19,24
Am Feur-Loch	Highld	NG8572	57°41·5′	5°36·0′W	W	19
Am Fiar-loch	Highld	NH2446	57°28·5′	4°55·6′W	X	25
Am Fireach	Highld	NH0978	57°45·3′	5°12·1′W	X	19
Am Fireach	Highld	NH3957	57°34·7′	4°41·1′W	X	26
Am Fliuch-choire	Highld	NH0848	57°29·2′	5°11·7′W	X	25
Am Fraoch-choire	Highld	NG5124	57°14·6′	6°7·2′W	X	32
Am Fraoch-choire	Highld	NG9911	57°9·0′	5°18·9′W	X	33
Am Fraoch Eilean	Arg & Bt	NR4662	55°47·3′	6°2·7′W	X	60,61
Am Fraoch-eilean	Highld	NM6185	56°53·9′	5°55·0′W	X	40
Am Fraoch-eilean	Highld	NM6783	56°53·1′	5°49·0′W	X	40
Am Fuar-choire	Highld	NG5027	57°16·2′	6°8·4′W	X	32
Am Fuar-mheallan	Highld	NG9557	57°33·7′	5°25·2′W	H	25
A' Mhaighdean	Highld	NH0174	57°43·0′	5°20·0′W	H	19
A' Mhaingir	Highld	NN0099	57°2·6′	5°17·4′W	X	33
A'Mhàlairt	Arg & Bt	NR5772	55°53·0′	5°52·7′W	X	61
A' Mhaoile	Highld	NG6914	57°9·8′	5°48·8′W	H	32
A' Mhaol	Arg & Bt	NM4632	56°25·0′	6°6·7′W	X	48
A' Mhaol Mhòr	Arg & Bt	NM4633	56°25·5′	6°6·7′W	H	47,48
A' Mhaol Odhar	Arg & Bt	NR7679	55°57·4′	5°34·9′W	H	62
A' Mharagach	Highld	NG3403	57°2·7′	6°22·7′W	X	32,39
A' Mharcanach	Highld	NH5410	57°9·7′	4°24·4′W	X	35
A' Mharconaich	Highld	NN6076	56°51·5′	4°17·3′W	H	42
A' Mharconaich	Highld	NN7084	56°56·0′	4°7·7′W	H	42
A' Mheallàch	N Eil	NF7322	57°10·6′	7°24·2′W	X	31
A' Mhoine	Highld	NC5361	58°31·0′	4°30·9′W	X	10
A' Mhuc	Highld	NG9923	57°15·5′	5°19·5′W	H	25,33
A' Mhuing	Highld	NG9415	57°11·0′	5°24·1′W	X	33
Amhuinnsuidhe	N Eil	NB0408	57°58·0′	6°59·9′W	T	13
Amhurst Hill Fm	Kent	TQ6343	51°10·0′	0°20·3′E	FM	188
Amicombe Brook	Devon	SX5784	50°38·5′	4°1·0′W	W	191
Amicombe Hill	Devon	SX5786	50°39·6′	4°1·0′W	H	191
Amiesmill Fm	W Susx	TQ1829	51°3·1′	0°18·6′W	FM	187,198
Amington	Staffs	SK2304	52°38·2′	1°39·2′W	T	139
Amington Hall	Staffs	SK2305	52°38·8′	1°39·2′W	X	139
Amington Hall Fm	Staffs	SK2305	52°38·8′	1°39·2′W	FM	139
Amisfield	D & G	NY0082	55°7·6′	3°33·7′W	T	78
Amisfield Burn	D & G	NY0083	55°8·1′	3°33·7′W	W	78
Amisfield Mains	E Loth	NT5275	55°58·2′	2°45·7′W	X	66
Amisfield Tower	D & G	NX9983	55°8·1′	3°34·6′W	X	78
Amlaird	E Ayr	NS4844	55°40·2′	4°24·6′W	X	70
Amlwch	I of Angl	SH4493	53°24·9′	4°20·4′W	T	114
Amlwch Port	I of Angl	SH4593	53°24·9′	4°19·5′W	T	114
Am Màla	Arg & Bt	NR3271	55°51·7′	6°16·6′W	X	60,61
Am Màm	Arg & Bt	NN2430	56°26·0′	4°50·8′W	X	50
Am Màm	Arg & Bt	NR4257	55°44·5′	6°6·2′W	X	60
Am Màm	Highld	NG4427	57°16·0′	6°14·3′W	H	32
Am Màm	Highld	NG5217	57°10·9′	6°5·8′W	X	32
Am Màm	Highld	NH1230	57°19·6′	5°6·9′W	X	25
Am Màm	Highld	NH5676	57°45·3′	4°24·7′W	X	21
Am Màm	Highld	NN0985	56°55·3′	5°7·8′W	X	41
Am Mam	Stir	NN4521	56°21·6′	4°30·1′W	H	51,57
Ammanford (Rhydaman)	Carm	SN6212	51°47·6′	3°59·7′W	T	159
Am Maoilean	Arg & Bt	NM9639	56°30·2′	5°18·4′W	H	49
Am Maol	Highld	NG4041	57°23·4′	6°19·2′W	H	23
Am Maol	Highld	NM4280	56°50·7′	6°13·4′W	X	39
Am Maol	Highld	NN5694	57°1·1′	4°21·9′W	H	35
Am Maoladh	N Eil	NG1290	57°48·7′	6°50·5′W	X	14
Am Maolan	Arg & Bt	NM6426	56°22·3′	5°48·9′W	X	49
Am Marcach	Highld	NG8976	57°43·7′	5°32·2′W	X	19
Am Meadar	Pth & Kin	NN7078	56°52·8′	4°7·5′W	H	42
Am Meall	Arg & Bt	NR2662	55°46·7′	6°21·8′W	X	60
Am Meall	Arg & Bt	NR4266	55°49·4′	6°6·7′W	X	60,61
Am Meall	Highld	NC5355	58°27·8′	4°30·7′W	X	10
Am Meall	Highld	NG5728	57°16·9′	6°1·5′W	H	32
Am Meall	Highld	NN4686	56°56·6′	4°31·4′W	H	34,42
Am Meall	N Eil	NL6494	56°55·2′	7°30·9′W	H	31
Am Meallan	Highld	NG8633	57°20·5′	5°32·9′W	H	24

Am Meallan	Highld	NH1924	57°16·5'	4°59·7'W	H	25
Ammerdown Ho	Somer	ST7152	51°16·2'	2°24·6'W	X	183
Ammerham	Somer	ST3605	50°50·7'	2°54·2'W	T	193
Am Miadar	Arg & Bt	NR2065	55°48·1'	6°27·7'W	X	60
Am Miadar	Arg & Bt	NR2371	55°51·4'	6°25·2'W	X	60
Am Miodar	Highld	NM6844	56°32·1'	5°45·9'W	X	49
Ammon's Hill	Heref	SO7052	52°10·2'	2°25·9'W	X	149
Am Mullach	Aberd	NO3790	57°0·1'	3°1·8'W	H	44
Amner's Fm	W Berks	SU6769	51°25·2'	1°1·8'W	FM	175
Amnodd-bwll	Gwyn	SH8036	52°54·7'	3°46·7'W	X	124,125
Amnodd-wen	Gwyn	SH8137	52°55·3'	3°45·8'W	X	124,125
Amod	Arg & Bt	NR6412	55°21·0'	5°42·9'W	X	68
Amod	Arg & Bt	NR7038	55°35·1'	5°38·5'W	X	68
Amod Hill	Arg & Bt	NR6311	55°20·4'	5°43·8'W	X	68
Amon's Copse	W Susx	SU8827	51°2·4'	0°44·3'W	F	186,197
Amor Hall	Suff	TM1142	52°2·4'	1°5·0'E	X	155,169
Amotherby	N Yks	SE7473	54°9·1'	0°51·6'W	T	100
Amperley Fm	Shrops	SO5573	52°21·4'	2°39·2'W	FM	137,138
Ampers Wick	Essex	TM1419	51°49·9'	1°6·8'E	X	168,169
Ampfield	Hants	SU4023	51°0·5'	1°25·4'W	T	185
Ampfield Wood	Hants	SU4024	51°1·1'	1°25·4'W	F	185
Ampherlaw	S Lanak	NS9850	55°44·2'	3°37·0'W	X	65,72
Am Plastair	N Eil	NA0502	57°50·2'	8°39·1'W	X	18
Ampleforth	N Yks	SE5878	54°11·9'	1°6·2'W	T	100
Ampleforth Abbey and College	N Yks	SE5978	54°11·9'	1°5·3'W	X	100
Am-ploc	Highld	NG8956	57°33·0'	5°31·1'W	X	24
Am Plodan	Arg & Bt	NR3443	55°36·7'	6°13·0'W	X	60
Ampney Brook	Glos	SP0701	51°42·7'	1°53·5'W	W	163
Ampney Crucis	Glos	SP0601	51°42·7'	1°54·4'W	T	163
Ampney Down Fm	Glos	SP0406	51°45·4'	1°56·1'W	FM	163
Ampney Downs	Glos	SP0406	51°45·4'	1°56·1'W	X	163
Ampneyfield	Glos	SP0603	51°43·8'	1°54·4'W	X	163
Ampney Knowle	Glos	SP0704	51°44·3'	1°53·5'W	X	163
Ampney Park	Glos	SP0602	51°43·2'	1°54·4'W	X	163
Ampney Riding	Glos	SP0703	51°43·8'	1°53·5'W	F	163
Ampney Sheephouse	Glos	SP0504	51°44·3'	1°55·3'W	X	163
Ampney St Mary	Glos	SP0802	51°43·2'	1°52·7'W	T	163
Ampney St Peter	Glos	SP0801	51°42·7'	1°52·7'W	T	163
Am Pollan	Highld	NH0777	57°44·7'	5°14·1'W	X	19
Amport	Hants	SU2944	51°11·9'	1°34·7'W	T	185
Amport Ho	Hants	SU2944	51°11·9'	1°34·7'W	X	185
Am Port Mòr	N Eil	NB1834	58°12·5'	6°47·6'W	W	8,13
Amport Wood	Hants	SU2843	51°11·4'	1°35·6'W	F	184
Am Priosan	Arg & Bt	NM7700	56°8·7'	5°34·9'W	X	55
Ampthill	Beds	TL0337	52°1·5'	0°29·5'W	T	153
Ampthill Grange	Beds	TL0236	52°1·0'	0°30·4'W	X	153
Ampthill Park Ho	Beds	TL0239	52°2·6'	0°30·4'W	X	153
Ampton	Suff	TL8671	52°18·6'	0°44·1'E	T	144,155
Ampton Field	Suff	TL8670	52°18·0'	0°44·1'E	F	144,155
Ampton Park	Suff	TL8670	52°18·0'	0°44·1'E	X	144,155
Ampton Water	Suff	TL8770	52°18·0'	0°45·0'E	W	144,155
Amroth	Pemb	SN1607	51°44·1'	4°39·5'W	T	158
Amroth Castle	Pemb	SN1707	51°44·2'	4°38·6'W	X	158
Amulree	Pth & Kin	NN8936	56°30·4'	3°47·8'W	T	52
Amwell	Herts	TL1613	51°48·4'	0°18·7'W	T	166
Amy Down	Corn	SX3666	50°28·5'	4°18·3'W	X	201
Amy Tree	Corn	SX3666	50°28·5'	4°18·3'W	X	201
Anaboard	Highld	NJ0033	57°22·8'	3°39·3'W	X	27
Anaboard Burn	Highld	NJ0035	57°23·9'	3°39·4'W	W	27
An Acairseid	Highld	NH1491	57°52·5'	5°7·7'W	W	20
An Acairseid	Highld	NM4363	56°41·5'	6°11·4'W	W	47
An Acairseid	N Eil	NF7300	56°58·8'	7°22·5'W	W	31
An Acairseid a Deas	N Eil	NG2195	57°51·7'	6°41·8'W	W	14
An Acairseid a Tuath	N Eil	NG2197	57°52·8'	6°41·9'W	W	14
Ana Cross	N Yks	SE7293	54°19·9'	0°53·1'W	X	94,100
Ana Cross (Tumulus)	N Yks	SE7293	54°19·9'	0°53·1'W	A	94,100
Anagach	Highld	NJ0326	57°19·1'	3°36·2'W	T	36
An Aghaidh Gharbh	Highld	NN2071	56°48·0'	4°56·4'W	X	41
Anaheilt	Highld	NM8162	56°42·2'	5°34·2'W	T	40
An Ailldunn	Highld	NG6030	57°18·1'	5°58·6'W	X	24,32
An Aird	Arg & Bt	NR7083	55°59·3'	5°40·8'W	H	55,61
Anancaun	Highld	NH0263	57°37·1'	5°18·5'W	T	19
An Aodann	Arg & Bt	NN0818	56°19·2'	5°5·8'W	X	50,56
An Ard	Highld	NG8075	57°42·9'	5°41·2'W	X	19
Anaskeog	Arg & Bt	NR8395	56°6·2'	5°28·9'W	X	55
An Càbagach	Highld	NH4692	57°53·7'	4°35·4'W	H	20
An Cabar	Highld	NH1060	57°35·7'	5°10·3'W	H	19
An Cabar	Highld	NH2564	57°38·2'	4°55·4'W	H	20
An Cabar	Highld	NH4566	57°39·7'	4°35·4'W	H	20
An Cabhsair	Highld	NH7516	57°13·3'	4°3·8'W	X	35
An Cairealach	Arg & Bt	NM7330	56°24·7'	5°40·3'W	X	49
An Caisdeal	Highld	NH7102	57°5·7'	4°7·3'W	X	35
An Caisteal	Highld	NC5748	58°24·1'	4°26·3'W	H	10
An Caisteal	Highld	NG8904	57°5·0'	5°28·5'W	H	33
An Caisteal	Stir	NN3719	56°20·4'	4°37·8'W	H	50,56
An Caisteal	Stir	NN4617	56°19·5'	4°29·0'W	X	57
An Cala	Arg & Bt	NM7417	56°17·8'	5°38·7'W	X	55
An Calbh	Arg & Bt	NM2740	56°28·6'	6°25·6'W	X	46,47,48
An Calbh	Highld	NC1536	58°16·7'	5°8·8'W	X	15
An Cam-allt	Highld	NH2729	57°19·4'	4°51·9'W	W	25
An Camas	N Eil	NF8118	57°8·8'	7°16·0'W	W	31
An Camas Aiseig	Highld	NN0164	56°43·8'	5°14·7'W	W	41
An Càmastac	Highld	NG2365	57°35·7'	6°37·7'W	X	23
An Campar Mòr	N Eil	NB5359	58°27·2'	6°13·6'W	X	8
An Caol	Highld	NG6152	57°30·0'	5°58·9'W	X	24
An Caol	Highld	NN1075	56°49·9'	5°6·4'W	X	41
An Caolas	Arg & Bt	NM2920	56°18·0'	6°22·4'W	W	48
An Caol-loch	Highld	NC5544	58°21·9'	4°28·2'W	W	10
An Caorann Beag	Highld	NH0713	57°10·3'	5°11·1'W	X	33
An Caorann Mòr	Highld	NH0813	57°10·3'	5°10·1'W	X	33
An Car	Aberd	NO1290	56°59·8'	3°26·5'W	H	43
An Carn	Arg & Bt	NR3266	55°49·0'	6°16·3'W	X	60,61
An Carn	Arg & Bt	NR3689	56°1·5'	6°13·8'W	X	61
An Carn	Arg & Bt	NR6893	56°4·7'	5°43·3'W	X	55,61
An Carn	Highld	NG7629	57°18·1'	5°42·6'W	X	33
An Càrnach	Highld	NG5519	57°12·0'	6°2·9'W	X	32
An Carnach	Highld	NG8429	57°18·3'	5°34·7'W	X	33
An Càrnais	Arg & Bt	NM6141	56°30·3'	5°52·6'W	X	49
An Carnais	Highld	NH2739	57°24·8'	4°52·4'W	H	25
An Carnan	Arg & Bt	NR2267	55°49·2'	6°25·9'W	X	60
An Càrnan	Highld	NH1067	57°39·4'	5°10·6'W	H	19
An Càrr	Arg & Bt	NS0793	56°5·7'	5°5·7'W	X	56
An Càrr	Arg & Bt	NS0799	56°8·9'	5°6·0'W	H	56
Ancarraig	Highld	NH4925	57°17·7'	4°29·9'W	X	26
An Carraigean	Arg & Bt	NM4625	56°21·2'	6°6·2'W	X	48
Ancaster	Lincs	SK9843	52°58·8'	0°32·0'W	T	130
Ancaster Fm	Cambs	TL4592	52°30·6'	0°8·6'E	FM	143
Ancat Fm	N Yks	SE9686	54°15·9'	0°31·1'W	FM	94,101
An Ceannaich	Highld	NG1350	57°27·2'	6°46·6'W	X	23
An Ceann Geal or Whiten Head	Highld	NC5068	58°34·7'	4°34·3'W	X	9
An Cearcaill	Highld	NG9368	57°39·5'	5°27·7'W	X	19
An Cearcall	Pth & Kin	NN6270	56°48·3'	4°15·2'W	X	42
An Cearcallach	Highld	NN4285	56°56·0'	4°35·3'W	H	34,42
Anceller Ho	Wrekin	SJ7020	52°46·8'	2°26·3'W	X	127
An Ceòthan	N Eil	NF7755	57°28·5'	7°22·9'W	X	22
Anchey Sike	Northum	NY8659	54°55·8'	2°12·7'W	W	87
Ancholme Head	Lincs	SK9685	53°21·4'	0°33·0'W	W	112,121
Anchor	Corn	SW7452	50°19·7'	5°10·2'W	X	204
Anchor	Shrops	SO1785	52°27·6'	3°12·9'W	T	136
Anchorage Cottage	Stir	NS3994	56°7·0'	4°34·9'W	X	56
Anchorage Fm	Lancs	SD4424	53°42·8'	2°50·5'W	FM	102
Anchorage Park	C of Port	SU6703	50°49·6'	1°2·5'W	T	196
Anchorage, The	Highld	NB9907	58°0·7'	5°23·7'W	W	15
Anchorage, The	Moray	NJ1362	57°38·6'	3°27·0'W	X	28
Anchorage, The	Suff	TM4156	52°9·2'	1°31·8'E	X	156
Anchor Corner	Norf	TM0098	52°32·8'	0°57·4'E	T	144
Anchor Fm	N Yks	SE1654	53°59·2'	1°44·9'W	FM	104
Anchoring Hill	Devon	SY0885	50°39·7'	3°17·7'W	X	192
Anchor Inn	E Susx	TQ4416	50°55·8'	0°3·3'E	X	198
Anchor Plain	N Yks	SE6263	54°3·8'	1°2·7'W	X	100
Anchorsholme	Lancs	SD3242	53°52·4'	3°1·6'W	T	102
Anchor Stone	Devon	SX8754	50°22·7'	3°35·0'W	X	202
Anchor Street	Norf	TG3124	52°46·1'	1°25·9'E	T	133,134
An Clachan	Arg & Bt	NR2171	55°51·3'	6°27·1'W	X	60
An Cladach	Arg & Bt	NR4362	55°47·2'	6°5·5'W	X	60,61
An Claigionn	Highld	NH5278	57°46·3'	4°28·8'W	H	20
An Clarsach	Arg & Bt	NM6410	56°13·7'	5°48·0'W	X	55
An Cléireach	Arg & Bt	NM0750	56°33·3'	6°45·7'W	X	46
An Clèireach	Highld	NG3344	57°24·7'	6°26·3'W	H	23
An Cléireach	Highld	NG7713	57°9·5'	5°40·8'W	X	33
Ancliffe Hall	Lancs	SD4865	54°4·9'	2°47·3'W	X	97
An Cliseam	N Eil	NB1507	57°57·9'	6°48·7'W	H	13,14
An Clù-nead	Highld	NC0906	58°0·4'	5°13·5'W	H	15
An Cnap	Arg & Bt	NM0448	56°32·1'	6°48·4'W	X	46
An Cnap	Arg & Bt	NM7910	56°14·1'	5°33·5'W	H	55
An Cnap	Arg & Bt	NN0018	56°19·0'	5°13·6'W	H	50,55
An Cnap	Arg & Bt	NR9965	55°50·4'	5°12·2'W	X	62
An Cnap	Arg & Bt	NR9982	55°59·6'	5°12·9'W	H	55
An Cnap	Highld	NM6964	56°42·9'	5°46·0'W	X	40
An Cnap	Highld	NM7698	57°1·4'	5°41·0'W	X	33,40
An Cnapach	Highld	NH0615	57°11·4'	5°12·2'W	X	33
An Cnoc	N Eil	NB4931	58°12·0'	6°15·8'W	T	8
An Cnoc Buidhe	Highld	NC8827	58°13·3'	3°53·9'W	H	17
Ancoats	Man	SJ8598	53°29·0'	2°13·2'W	T	109
An Coileach	Highld	NG4311	57°7·3'	6°14·3'W	X	32
An Coileach	Highld	NG5230	57°17·9'	6°6·5'W	H	24,32
An Coileach	N Eil	NG0892	57°49·6'	6°54·7'W	H	14,18
An Coileachan	Highld	NH2468	57°40·3'	4°56·6'W	H	20
An Coimhleum	Highld	NC2322	58°9·4'	5°0·0'W	F	15
An Coire	Arg & Bt	NM5438	56°28·5'	5°59·2'W	X	47,48
An Coire	Arg & Bt	NM8114	56°16·3'	5°31·8'W	X	55
An Coire	Arg & Bt	NR1651	55°40·4'	6°30·6'W	X	60
An Coire	Arg & Bt	NR8859	55°46·9'	5°22·4'W	X	62
An Coire	Highld	NM6749	56°34·8'	5°47·2'W	X	49
An Coire	Highld	NM8252	56°36·8'	5°32·7'W	X	49
An Coire	N Eil	NB0112	58°0·1'	7°3·2'W	X	13
An Coireadail	Arg & Bt	NM5830	56°24·3'	5°54·9'W	X	48
An Coroghan	Highld	NG2705	57°3·6'	6°29·7'W	X	39
An Corrach	Highld	NM4485	56°53·4'	6°11·7'W	X	39
An Corran	Highld	NG4868	57°38·2'	6°12·9'W	X	23
An Corran	Highld	NH5972	57°43·2'	4°21·6'W	X	21
An Corran	N Eil	NF7849	57°25·3'	7°21·4'W	X	22
An Corran	N Eil	NF8580	57°42·2'	7°16·9'W	X	18
An Corran	N Eil	NF8986	57°45·6'	7°13·3'W	X	18
An Corr Eilean	Highld	NM5650	56°35·0'	5°58·0'W	X	47
An Corr-eilean	Highld	NM8495	57°0·0'	5°32·9'W	X	33,40
Ancote Hill	Derby	SE0800	53°30·0'	1°52·4'W	X	110
An Cracaiche	Arg & Bt	NM6342	56°30·9'	5°50·7'W	X	49
An Creachal Beag	Highld	NH0633	57°21·0'	5°13·0'W	H	25
An Creachal Mòr	Highld	NH0633	57°21·0'	5°13·0'W	X	25
An Creachan	Arg & Bt	NM8621	56°20·2'	5°27·3'W	H	49
An Creachan	Arg & Bt	NM8915	56°17·1'	5°24·1'W	H	55
An Creachan	Arg & Bt	NN0513	56°16·4'	5°8·5'W	H	50,56
An Creachan	Arg & Bt	NR7669	55°52·0'	5°34·4'W	X	62
An Creachan	Arg & Bt	NR8076	55°55·9'	5°30·9'W	X	62
An Creachan	Arg & Bt	NR8270	55°52·7'	5°28·7'W	X	62
An Creachan	Arg & Bt	NS1085	56°1·5'	5°2·5'W	H	56
An Creagan	Aberd	NO2499	57°4·8'	3°14·8'W	H	36,44
An Creagan	Arg & Bt	NR9787	56°2·2'	5°15·1'W	X	55
Ancre Hill	Monm	SO4913	51°49·0'	2°44·0'W	X	162
An Criathrach	Highld	NG7933	57°20·3'	5°39·9'W	H	24
An Cròcan	Highld	NG3819	57°11·5'	6°19·8'W	X	32
Ancroft	Northum	NU0045	55°42·2'	1°59·6'W	T	75
Ancroft Mill	Northum	NU0144	55°41·6'	1°58·6'W	X	75
Ancroft North Fm	Northum	NT9946	55°42·7'	2°0·5'W	FM	75
Ancroft Northmoor	Northum	NT9645	55°42·2'	2°3·4'W	T	74,75
Ancroft Southmoor	Northum	NT9644	55°41·6'	2°3·4'W	X	74,75
An Crois-sgeir	Arg & Bt	NR1961	55°45·9'	6°28·4'W	X	60
An Crom-allt	Highld	NC6419	58°8·6'	4°18·1'W	W	16
An Cròm-allt	Highld	NC7230	58°14·7'	4°10·4'W	W	16
An Crom-allt	Highld	NH0430	57°19·4'	5°14·9'W	W	25
An Crom-allt	Highld	NH1146	57°28·2'	5°8·6'W	W	25
An Croman	Arg & Bt	NR9699	56°8·7'	5°16·6'W	H	55
An Crosan	Arg & Bt	NM4219	56°17·9'	6°9·8'W	X	48
An Crosan	Arg & Bt	NM4322	56°19·5'	6°9·0'W	X	48
Ancrow Brow	Cumbr	NY4905	54°26·5'	2°46·8'W	H	90
An Cruachan	Arg & Bt	NM5434	56°26·3'	5°59·0'W	X	47,48
An Cruachan	Arg & Bt	NM6900	56°8·5'	5°42·7'W	H	55,61
An Cruachan	Arg & Bt	NS0489	56°3·5'	5°8·4'W	H	56
An Cruachan	Highld	NC4367	58°34·0'	4°41·5'W	X	9
An Cruachan	Highld	NG2442	57°23·3'	6°35·1'W	X	23
An Cruachan	Highld	NG3822	57°13·1'	6°19·9'W	H	32
An Cruachan	Highld	NG6512	57°8·6'	5°52·6'W	H	32
An Cruachan	Highld	NH0935	57°22·2'	5°10·1'W	H	25
An Cruachan	Highld	NH1311	57°9·4'	5°5·1'W	H	34
An Cruachan	Highld	NM4887	56°54·6'	6°7·9'W	X	39
An Cruinn-leum	Highld	NG6848	57°28·0'	5°51·7'W	X	24
Ancrum	Scot Bord	NT6224	55°30·7'	2°35·7'W	T	74
Ancrum Craig	Scot Bord	NT5923	55°30·2'	2°38·5'W	X	73,74
Ancrum Moor	Scot Bord	NT6127	55°32·4'	2°36·6'W	X	74
Ancrum West Mains	Scot Bord	NT6223	55°30·2'	2°35·7'W	X	74
Ancton	W Susx	SU9800	50°47·7'	0°36·2'W	T	197
An Cuaidh	Highld	NG7689	57°50·3'	5°46·0'W	H	19
An Cumhann	N Ayr	NR8831	55°31·9'	5°21·1'W	X	68,69
Ancum Loch	Orkney	HY7654	59°22·6'	2°24·9'W	W	5
Ancumtoun	Orkney	HY7555	59°23·1'	2°25·9'W	T	5
An Curran	Arg & Bt	NR3446	55°38·3'	6°13·2'W	H	60
An Dàm	Arg & Bt	NM8912	56°15·5'	5°24·0'W	W	55
Anderby	Lincs	TF5275	53°15·2'	0°17·1'E	T	122
Anderby Creek	Lincs	TF5476	53°15·7'	0°18·9'E	T	122
Ander Hill	Shetld	HU5241	60°9·3'	1°3·3'W	H	4
Anderitum (Roman Fort)	E Susx	TQ6404	50°49·0'	0°20·1'E	R	199
Andersea	Somer	ST3333	51°5·8'	2°57·0'W	T	182
Andersey Fm	Oxon	SU4290	51°36·7'	1°23·2'W	FM	174
Andersey Island	Oxon	SU5096	51°39·9'	1°16·2'W	X	164
Andersfield	Somer	ST2434	51°6·3'	3°4·7'W	T	182
Andershaw Fm	S Lanak	NS8325	55°30·5'	3°50·7'W	FM	71,72
Anderside Flow	S Lanak	NS6233	55°34·5'	4°10·9'W	X	71
Anderside Hill	S Lanak	NS6133	55°34·5'	4°11·9'W	H	71
Anderson	Dorset	SY8797	50°46·6'	2°10·7'W	T	194
Anderson Manor	Dorset	SY8897	50°46·6'	2°9·8'W	A	194
Anderswick	Orkney	HY3110	58°58·6'	3°11·5'W	X	6
Anderton	Ches	SJ6475	53°16·5'	2°32·0'W	T	118
Anderton	Corn	SS2705	50°49·4'	4°27·0'W	A	190
Anderton	Corn	SX4251	50°20·5'	4°12·9'W	T	201
Anderton	Devon	SX4872	50°31·9'	4°8·3'W	X	191,201
Anderton	Lancs	SD6013	53°37·0'	2°35·9'W	T	109
Anderton Fold	Lancs	SD5139	53°50·9'	2°44·3'W	X	102
Andertons Mill	Lancs	SD5114	53°37·5'	2°44·0'W	T	108
Anderwood Inclosure	Hants	SU2406	50°51·4'	1°39·2'W	F	195
Andet	Aberd	NJ8435	57°24·6'	2°15·5'W	X	29,30
An Diallaid	Highld	NG4322	57°13·3'	6°15·0'W	X	32
An Diollaid	Aberd	NO0797	57°3·5'	3°31·5'W	X	36,43
An Diollaid	Arg & Bt	NM3620	56°18·2'	6°15·6'W	H	48
An Diollaid	Highld	NG8104	57°4·8'	5°36·4'W	X	33
An Diollaid	Highld	NN3366	56°45·6'	4°43·5'W	X	41
An Dirc Mhór	Highld	NN5696	57°2·2'	4°21·9'W	X	35
Andlows Fm	Bucks	SP8800	51°41·7'	0°43·2'W	FM	165
An Doire	Highld	NG8873	57°42·1'	5°33·0'W	X	19
An Doire	Highld	NN4692	56°59·9'	4°31·7'W	H	34
An Doire Loisgte	Highld	NG5931	57°18·6'	5°59·7'W	X	24,32
An Doirionnaich	Highld	NG5600	57°1·9'	6°0·8'W	X	32,39
An Dòirlinn	Arg & Bt	NM8942	56°31·6'	5°25·4'W	W	49
An Dòirlinn	Arg & Bt	NR1864	55°47·5'	6°29·5'W	X	60
An Doirlinn	Arg & Bt	NR7458	55°46·0'	5°35·7'W	X	62
An Dornabac	Highld	NM3597	56°59·6'	6°21·3'W	H	39
An Dorneil	Highld	NG2255	57°30·3'	6°38·0'W	W	23
An Dorus	Highld	NG4423	57°13·8'	6°14·1'W	X	32
Andover	Hants	SU3645	51°12·4'	1°28·7'W	T	185
Andover Down	Hants	SU3945	51°12·4'	1°26·1'W	T	185
Andoversford	Glos	SP0219	51°52·4'	1°57·9'W	T	163
Andover's Gorse	Wilts	ST9789	51°36·2'	2°2·2'W	F	173
Andreas	I of M	SC4199	54°22·0'	4°26·4'W	T	95
Andrew Gannel Hill	Clackm	NN9100	56°11·1'	3°44·0'W	H	58
Andrewhinney Hill	Scot Bord	NT1913	55°24·5'	3°16·3'W	H	79
Andrew Howe	N Yks	NZ8209	54°28·4'	0°43·7'W	A	94
Andrew's Cairn	Scot Bord	NT8068	55°54·5'	2°18·8'W	A	67
Andrews Corner	Glos	SO5505	51°44·7'	2°38·7'W	X	162
Andrews Fm	Cambs	TL4498	52°33·9'	0°7·9'E	FM	142,143
Andrews Fm	Derby	SK0584	53°21·4'	1°55·1'W	FM	110
Andrew's Fm	Devon	ST0505	50°50·4'	3°20·6'W	FM	192
Andrews Fm	Essex	TL6225	51°54·2'	0°21·7'E	FM	167
Andrews Fm	Essex	TQ9198	51°39·1'	0°46·1'E	FM	168
Andrew's Fm	Hants	SU7447	51°13·3'	0°56·0'W	FM	186
Andrew's Fm	W Susx	TQ1634	51°5·8'	0°20·2'W	FM	187
Andrewsford	Aberd	NJ7735	57°24·5'	2°22·5'W	X	29,30
Andrewshayes Fm	Devon	SY2498	50°46·8'	3°4·3'W	FM	192,193
Andrew's Knob	Ches	SJ9579	53°18·7'	2°4·1'W	X	118
Androhal Burn	Pth & Kin	NN7712	56°17·3'	3°58·8'W	W	57
An Dróighneach	Highld	NC7100	57°58·5'	4°10·4'W	H	16
An Druim	Highld	NC4356	58°28·1'	4°41·0'W	X	9
An Druim	Highld	NH0034	57°21·4'	5°19·0'W	X	25
An Dubh Aird	Arg & Bt	NM5836	56°27·5'	5°55·2'W	X	47,48
An Dubh-aird	Highld	NG2350	57°27·6'	6°36·7'W	X	23
An Dubh-aird	Highld	NG7833	57°20·3'	5°40·9'W	X	24
An Dubh Airde	Highld	NG8995	57°53·9'	5°33·2'W	X	19
An Dubh-alltan	Highld	NC6609	58°3·3'	4°15·8'W	W	16
An Dubh-chamas	Highld	NG4615	57°9·6'	6°11·6'W	W	32
An Dubh-laimhrig	Highld	NG4715	57°9·6'	6°10·6'W	X	32
An Dubh-loch	Highld	NC3546	58°22·6'	4°48·8'W	W	9
An Dubh-loch	Highld	NC5560	58°30·5'	4°28·8'W	W	10
An Dubh-loch	Highld	NC6158	58°29·6'	4°22·6'W	W	10
An Dubh Loch	Highld	NG1842	57°23·1'	6°41·1'W	W	23
An Dubh-loch	Highld	NG7350	57°29·3'	5°46·8'W	W	24
An Dubh-lochan	Highld	NC8807	58°2·5'	3°53·4'W	W	17
An Dubh-lochan	Highld	NH4658	57°35·4'	4°34·1'W	W	26
An Dubh-lochan	Highld	NH6228	57°19·6'	4°17·1'W	W	26,35
An Dubh Lochan	Highld	NN3478	56°52·1'	4°42·9'W	W	41
An Dubh-lòn	Highld	NC6832	58°15·7'	4°14·5'W	W	16
An Dubh Sgeir	Arg & Bt	NR3291	56°2·5'	6°17·7'W	X	61
An Dubh-sgeir	Arg & Bt	NR6655	55°44·2'	5°43·2'W	X	62
An Dubh-sgeir	Highld	NC4568	58°34·6'	4°39·5'W	X	9
An Dubh-sgeir	Highld	NG1936	57°19·9'	6°39·7'W	X	23
An Dubh-sgeir	Highld	NG3422	57°13·0'	6°23·9'W	X	32
An Dubh Sgeir	Highld	NG3574	57°40·9'	6°26·3'W	X	23
An Dubh-sgeir a Deas	N Eil	NF8744	57°23·0'	7°12·1'W	X	22
An Dubh-sgeire	Highld	NG4614	57°9·1'	6°11·5'W	X	32
An Dùn	Arg & Bt	NM7936	56°28·1'	5°34·8'W	A	49

An Dùn	Arg & Bt	NM8137	56°28·7′	5°32·9′W	X	49
An Dùn	Arg & Bt	NM9228	56°24·2′	5°21·8′W	X	49
An Dun	Arg & Bt	NN0122	56°21·2′	5°12·8′W	X	50
An Dun	Arg & Bt	NN0901	56°10·1′	5°4·1′W	A	56
An Dùn	Arg & Bt	NR2254	55°42·2′	6°25·1′W	A	60
An Dùn	Arg & Bt	NR4347	55°39·2′	6°4·7′W	X	60
An Dùn	Arg & Bt	NR4750	55°40·9′	6°1·0′W	A	60
An Dun	Highld	NC1601	57°57·9′	5°6·2′W	A	15
An Dùn	Highld	ND1024	58°12·0′	3°31·4′W	X	17
An Dùn	Highld	ND1425	58°12·6′	3°27·3′W	X	17
An Dùn	Highld	NG8075	57°42·9′	5°41·2′W	A	19
An Dùn	Highld	NG8219	57°12·9′	5°36·2′W	X	33
An Dun	Highld	NH5690	57°52·8′	4°25·2′W	X	21
An Dùn	Highld	NM6873	56°47·7′	5°47·5′W	X	40
An Dun	Highld	NN6292	57°0·2′	4°15·9′W	X	35
An Dùn	Highld	NN7180	56°53·9′	4°6·6′W	H	42
An Dùn	Pth & Kin	NO1059	56°43·1′	3°27·8′W	X	53
An Dùnan	Arg & Bt	NM5621	56°19·4′	5°56·3′W	X	48
An Dùnan	Arg & Bt	NM8123	56°21·2′	5°32·2′W	A	49
An Dùnan	Arg & Bt	NR5671	55°52·5′	5°53·6′W	X	61
An Dùnan	Arg & Bt	NR5773	55°53·6′	5°52·8′W	X	61
An Dùnan or Table of Lorn	Highld	NM7343	56°31·7′	5°41·0′W	X	49
An Dùn (Broch)	Arg & Bt	NM8137	56°28·7′	5°32·9′W	A	49
An Dùn (Broch)	Highld	ND1024	58°12·0′	3°31·4′W	A	17
An Dun (Broch)	Highld	NH5690	57°52·8′	4°25·2′W	A	21
An Dùn (Fort)	Arg & Bt	NM9228	56°24·2′	5°21·8′W	A	49
Andurn Point	Devon	SX4949	50°19·5′	4°6·9′W	X	201
Andwell	Hants	SU6952	51°16·0′	1°0·3′W	T	186
Andyke	Hants	SU4242	51°10·8′	1°23·6′W	A	185
An Eag	Highld	NM9495	57°0·3′	5°23·1′W	H	33,40
An Earachd	Highld	NC2940	58°19·2′	4°54·7′W	X	9
AN Eigin	Highld	NH2467	57°39·8′	4°56·6′W	X	20
An Eilid	Highld	NG9494	57°53·5′	5°28·1′W	H	19
An Eiligeir	Arg & Bt	NM7031	56°25·2′	5°43·3′W	X	49
An Eilrig	Highld	NN7797	57°3·1′	4°1·2′W	H	35
An Eilrig	Highld	NN8187	56°57·8′	3°57·0′W	H	43
An Eilrig	Highld	NN8686	56°57·3′	3°52·0′W	H	43
Anelog	Gwyn	SH1527	52°48·8′	4°44·3′W	T	123
An Elric	Highld	NH1517	57°12·6′	5°3·3′W	H	34
Anems Ho	Lancs	SD6574	54°9·9′	2°31·7′W	X	97
Anerley	Brom	TQ3469	51°24·5′	0°4·0′W	T	176,177
Aness	Shetld	HU4428	60°2·3′	1°12·1′W	X	4
An Fhaochag	Highld	NG6903	57°3·9′	5°48·2′W	X	32,33
An Fhaodhail	Arg & Bt	NM0145	56°30·4′	6°51·2′W	W	46
An Fharaid	Highld	NC3969	58°35·0′	4°45·7′W	X	9
An Fharaid Mhór	Highld	NC0524	58°10·0′	5°18·4′W	H	15
Anfield	Liv	SJ3793	53°26·0′	2°56·5′W	T	108
An Fùr	Highld	NG8050	57°29·5′	5°39·8′W	H	24
An Gallanach	Highld	NM4079	56°50·0′	6°15·3′W	H	39
An Gànradh	Arg & Bt	NR3443	55°36·7′	6°13·0′W	X	60
An Garadh	Arg & Bt	NR7690	56°3·3′	5°35·4′W	X	55
An Garadh	Stir	NN4014	56°17·7′	4°34·7′W	H	56
An Garbh-allt	Highld	NC4222	58°9·8′	4°40·7′W	W	16
An Garbh-allt	Highld	NC4852	58°26·1′	4°35·7′W	W	9
An Garbh-allt	Highld	NC5454	58°27·3′	4°29·6′W	W	10
An Garbh-allt	Highld	NC5537	58°18·1′	4°28·0′W	W	16
An Garbh-allt	Highld	NG7628	57°17·5′	5°42·6′W	W	33
An Garbh-allt	Highld	NG8051	57°30·0′	5°39·9′W	W	24
An Garbh-allt	Highld	NM7077	56°49·9′	5°45·8′W	W	40
An Garbh-allt	Highld	NM7871	56°46·9′	5°37·6′W	W	40
An Garbh-allt	Highld	NN9392	57°0·7′	3°45·3′W	W	43
An Garbhanach	Highld	NN1866	56°45·3′	4°58·2′W	H	41
An Garbh-chnoc	Highld	NC5855	58°27·9′	4°25·6′W	H	10
An Garbh Choire	Aberd	NN9598	57°3·9′	3°43·4′W	X	36,43
An Garbh-choire	Highld	NC3245	58°21·9′	4°51·8′W	X	9
An Garbh-choire	Highld	NC4849	58°24·4′	4°35·6′W	X	9
An Garbh-choire	Highld	NG4620	57°12·3′	6°11·9′W	X	32
An Garbh-choire	Highld	NH1434	57°21·8′	5°5·1′W	X	25
An Garbh-eilean	Highld	NC3373	58°37·0′	4°52·0′W	X	9
An Garbh-eilean	Highld	NG8037	57°22·5′	5°39·1′W	X	24
An Garbh-eilean	Highld	NM6783	56°53·1′	5°49·0′W	X	40
An Garbh-leathad	Highld	NH1644	57°27·2′	5°3·6′W	X	25
An Garbh-leitir	Highld	NH1609	57°8·4′	5°2·0′W	X	34
An Garbh-mheall	Highld	NG7252	57°30·3′	5°47·9′W	H	24
Angarrack	Corn	SW5838	50°11·8′	5°23·1′W	T	203
An Garradh	Arg & Bt	NM6020	56°19·0′	5°52·4′W	X	49
Angarrick	Corn	SW7937	50°11·7′	5°5·4′W	T	204
Angas Home	Brom	TQ4459	51°18·9′	0°4·4′E	X	187
An Gead Loch	Highld	NH1038	57°23·8′	5°9·3′W	W	25
An Gearanach	Highld	NN1866	56°45·3′	4°58·2′W	X	41
An Gearna	Arg & Bt	NM5134	56°26·2′	6°1·9′W	X	47,48
An Gearna	Arg & Bt	NM5332	56°25·2′	5°59·9′W	X	48
Angelbank	Shrops	SO5776	52°23·1′	2°37·5′W	T	137,138
Angeldown Fm	Oxon	SU3984	51°33·4′	1°25·9′W	FM	174
Angel Hill	Suff	TM1159	52°11·6′	1°5·6′E	X	155
Angel House Fm	N Yks	SE5734	53°48·2′	1°7·7′W	FM	105
Angelrow Fm	Scot Bord	NT7445	55°42·1′	2°24·4′W	FM	74
Angel's Peak, The or Sgor an Lochain Uaine	Aberd	NN9597	57°3·4′	3°43·4′W	H	36,43
Angel Wells Fm	Lincs	SK9719	52°45·8′	0°33·3′W	FM	130
Angerham	Lancs	SD7040	53°51·6′	2°27·0′W	X	103
Angerholme	Cumbr	SD7798	54°22·9′	2°20·8′W	X	98
Angering Station	W Susx	TQ0602	50°48·7′	0°29·3′W	X	197
Angers Fm	S Glos	ST6485	51°34·0′	2°30·8′W	FM	172
Angersleigh	Somer	ST1919	50°58·1′	3°8·8′W	T	181,193
Angerton	Cumbr	NY2257	54°54·3′	3°12·6′W	T	85
Angerton	Cumbr	SD2184	54°15·0′	3°12·3′W	X	96
Angerton Bank	Cumbr	NY2541	54°45·8′	3°9·5′W	X	85
Angerton Hall	Cumbr	SD2283	54°14·5′	3°11·4′W	X	96
Angerton Hall	Northum	NZ0985	55°9·8′	1°51·1′W	X	81
Angerton Ho	Cumbr	NY2156	54°53·8′	3°13·5′W	X	85
Angerton Marsh	Cumbr	SD2183	54°14·4′	3°12·3′W	W	96
Angertonmoor Cott	Northum	NZ0883	55°8·7′	1°52·0′W	X	81
Angerton North Moor	Northum	NZ0786	55°10·3′	1°53·0′W	X	81
Angerton Steads	Northum	NZ0883	55°8·7′	1°52·0′W	X	81
Angeston Grange	Glos	ST7898	51°41·1′	2°18·7′W	X	162
An Geurachadh	Highld	NN4384	56°55·5′	4°34·3′W	H	34,42
Angiers Fm	Dorset	ST8012	50°54·7′	2°16·7′W	FM	194
An Glais-eilean Meadhonach	N Eil	NF9468	57°36·2′	7°6·9′W	X	18

An Glas-eilean	Arg & Bt	NM2764	56°41·5′	6°27·1′W	X	46,47
An Glas-eilean	Highld	NM6376	56°49·2′	5°52·6′W	X	40
An Glas-eilean	Highld	NM6491	56°57·3′	5°52·4′W	X	40
An Glas-eilean	Highld	NM6682	56°52·5′	5°50·0′W	X	40
An Glas-loch	Highld	NC4931	58°14·8′	4°33·9′W	W	16
An Glas-tholl	Highld	NH1632	57°20·7′	5°3·0′W	X	25
An Glas-tulach	Highld	NG7241	57°24·4′	5°47·3′W	X	24
Angle	Pemb	SM8602	51°40·8′	5°5·3′W	T	157
An Gleann	Arg & Bt	NR1958	55°44·3′	6°28·2′W	X	60
An Gleann	Arg & Bt	NR2743	55°36·5′	6°19·7′W	X	60
An Gleannan	Highld	NH5076	57°45·2′	4°30·8′W	X	20
An Gleannan	Highld	NH8611	57°10·8′	3°52·7′W	X	35,36
An Gleannan	Highld	NM6055	56°37·8′	5°54·3′W	X	49
An Gleann Ur	N Eil	NB4134	58°13·4′	6°24·2′W	T	8
Angle Bay	Pemb	SM8802	51°40·8′	5°3·6′W	W	157,158
Angle Corner Br	Cambs	TL3195	52°32·5′	0°3·7′W	X	142
Angledown Copse	Hants	SU4653	51°16·7′	1°20·0′W	F	185
Angle Fms	Cambs	TL5872	52°19·6′	0°19·5′E	FM	154
Angle Park	Fife	NO2911	56°17·4′	3°8·4′W	X	59
Angle Point	Pemb	SM8703	51°41·4′	5°4·5′W	X	157
Anglers Country Park	Wakf	SE3716	53°38·6′	1°26·0′W	X	110,111
Angler's Crag	Cumbr	NY0915	54°31·6′	3°23·9′W	X	89
Anglers' Retreat	Cered	SN7492	52°30·9′	3°51·0′W	X	135
Anglesey Abbey	Cambs	TL5262	52°14·3′	0°14·0′E	A	154
Anglesey or Ynysmôn	I of Angl	SH4378	53°16·8′	4°20·9′W	X	114,115
Anglesey Show Ground	I of Angl	SH4075	53°15·1′	4°23·5′W	X	114,115
Angles Park	Angus	NO3847	56°36·9′	3°0·2′W	X	54
Angles Way	Norf	TL9581	52°23·8′	0°52·4′E	X	
Angles Way	Norf	TM2683	52°24·1′	1°19·7′E	X	156
Angles Way	Suff	TM0579	52°22·5′	1°1·1′E	X	144
Angles Way	Suff	TM5095	52°30·0′	1°41·4′E	X	134,156
Angle Tarn	Cumbr	NY2407	54°27·4′	3°9·9′W	W	89,90
Angle Tarn	Cumbr	NY4114	54°31·3′	2°54·3′W	W	90
Angletarn Pikes	Cumbr	NY4114	54°31·3′	2°54·3′W	H	90
Angley Fm	Kent	TQ7535	51°5·5′	0°30·3′E	FM	188
Angley Ho	Kent	TQ7736	51°6·0′	0°32·1′E	X	188
Angley Wood	Kent	TQ7636	51°6·0′	0°31·2′E	F	188
Anglezarke Moor	Lancs	SD6317	53°39·1′	2°33·2′W	X	109
Anglezarke Reservoir	Lancs	SD6116	53°38·6′	2°35·0′W	W	109
Angmering	W Susx	TQ0604	50°49·8′	0°29·3′W	T	197
Angmering Park	W Susx	TQ0607	50°51·4′	0°29·3′W	X	197
Angmering Park Fm	W Susx	TQ0607	50°51·4′	0°29·3′W	FM	197
An Gnannan	Highld	NC4347	58°23·3′	4°40·7′W	X	9
An Gobhlach	Arg & Bt	NR7975	55°55·3′	5°31·8′W	H	62
An Gobhlach	Highld	NG6626	57°16·1′	5°52·4′W	X	32
An Gorm-loch	Highld	NC4948	58°23·9′	4°34·5′W	W	9
An Gorm-Loch	Highld	NG9046	57°27·6′	5°29·6′W	W	25
An Gorm-loch	Highld	NH2244	57°27·3′	4°57·6′W	W	25
An Gorm-loch	Highld	NH3746	57°28·8′	4°42·7′W	W	26
An Gorm-lochan	Highld	NH0523	57°15·6′	5°13·5′W	W	25,33
An Grà'dar	Arg & Bt	NM0048	56°32·0′	6°52·3′W	X	46
Angram	N Yks	SD8899	54°23·4′	2°10·7′W	T	98
Angram	N Yks	SE5248	53°55·8′	1°12·1′W	T	105
Angram Common	N Yks	SD8499	54°23·4′	2°14·4′W	X	98
Angram Fm	E Yorks	TA0549	53°55·8′	0°23·6′W	FM	107
Angram Grange	N Yks	SE5176	54°10·9′	1°12·7′W	X	100
Angram Green	Lancs	SD7742	53°52·7′	2°20·6′W	X	103
Angram Hall	N Yks	SE5176	54°10·9′	1°12·7′W	X	100
Angram Low Pasture	N Yks	SE0375	54°10·5′	1°56·8′W	X	98
Angram Reservoir	N Yks	SE0376	54°11·0′	1°56·8′W	W	98
An Grianan	Arg & Bt	NN0747	56°34·8′	5°8·1′W	H	50
An Grianan	Highld	NC2662	58°31·0′	4°58·8′W	H	9
An Grianan	Pth & Kin	NN4842	56°33·0′	4°27·9′W	H	51
An Groban	Highld	NG8374	57°42·5′	5°38·1′W	H	19
An Grosan	Arg & Bt	NM3521	56°18·7′	6°16·7′W	X	48
Angrouse Fm	Corn	SW6719	50°1·8′	5°14·8′W	FM	203
Angrove Fm	Wilts	ST9484	51°33·5′	2°4·8′W	FM	173
Angrove North Fm	N Yks	NZ5410	54°29·2′	1°9·6′W	FM	93
Angrove West Fm	N Yks	NZ5309	54°28·7′	1°10·5′W	FM	93
Angry Brow	Sefton	SD3019	53°40·0′	3°3·2′W	X	108
Angryhaugh	Northum	NT9205	55°20·6′	2°7·1′W	X	80
An Guirean	Highld	NN2275	56°50·2′	4°54·6′W	H	41
An Gurraban	Highld	NG7614	57°10·0′	5°41·8′W	X	33
Angus Fm	E Yorks	SE9456	53°59·7′	0°33·5′W	FM	106
Angus House Fm	Moray	NJ2557	57°36·1′	3°14·8′W	FM	28
Anguswell	Cumbr	NY4766	54°59·4′	2°49·3′W	X	86
Anick	Northum	NY9565	54°59·0′	2°4·3′W	T	87
Anick Grange	Northum	NY9565	54°59·0′	2°4·3′W	X	87
Anie	Stir	NN5810	56°15·9′	4°17·1′W	X	57
Animal Fm	E Yorks	SE6220	53°40·6′	1°3·3′W	FM	105
Animal Land	Corn	SX1759	50°24·4′	4°34·1′W	X	201
An Innis	Highld	NC6365	58°33·4′	4°20·8′W	X	10
An Inntreadh	Highld	NM8254	56°37·9′	5°32·8′W	X	49
An Iola	Arg & Bt	NM9848	56°35·1′	5°16·9′W	W	49
Anjarden	Corn	SW4128	50°6·0′	5°36·9′W	X	203
Ankerbold	Derby	SK3965	53°11·1′	1°24·6′W	X	119
Anker Br	Warw	SP4188	52°29·5′	1°23·4′W	X	140
Ankerdine Hill	Worcs	SO7356	52°12·3′	2°23·3′W	T	150
Ankers Fm	Hants	SU3455	51°17·8′	1°30·4′W	FM	174,185
Ankers Knowl Fm	Ches	SJ9773	53°15·5′	2°2·3′W	FM	118
Ankers Lane Fm	Staffs	SK0057	53°6·9′	1°59·6′W	FM	119
Ankerton	Staffs	SJ8331	52°52·8′	2°14·8′W	X	127
Ankerville	Highld	NH8174	57°44·7′	3°59·5′W	X	21
Ankerville Corner	Highld	NH8274	57°44·7′	3°58·5′W	X	21
Ankness	N Yks	SE6393	54°20·0′	1°1·4′W	X	94,100
Ankridge	Devon	SS6804	50°49·5′	3°52·1′W	X	191
Ankrielaw	Midlo	NT2758	55°48·8′	3°9·5′W	X	66,73
Anlaby	E Yorks	TA0328	53°44·5′	0°25·9′W	T	107
Anlaby Park	K upon H	TA0528	53°44·5′	0°24·1′W	T	107
An Lairig	Highld	NN4977	56°51·9′	4°28·2′W	X	42
An Lairig	Pth & Kin	NO0968	56°47·9′	3°29·0′W	X	43
An Lànach	Arg & Bt	NL9342	56°28·5′	6°58·7′W	X	46
An Laogh	Highld	NC1610	58°2·7′	5°6·6′W	H	15
An Laogh	N Eil	NF7705	57°1·6′	7°19·0′W	X	31
An Laogh	N Eil	NL6994	56°55·4′	7°26·0′W	X	31
An Làpan	Arg & Bt	NM5741	56°30·2′	5°56·5′W	X	47,48
An Leac	Highld	NG4316	57°10·0′	6°14·6′W	X	32
An Leacainn	Highld	NH5741	57°26·5′	4°22·5′W	H	26
An Leacainn Dubh	Highld	NN5191	56°59·4′	4°26·7′W	X	35
An Leacan	Arg & Bt	NS0381	55°59·2′	5°9·0′W	X	55,63

An Leacann	Arg & Bt	NM4129	56°23·2′	6°11·3′W	X	48
An Leacann	Arg & Bt	NR7166	55°50·2′	5°39·0′W	X	62
An Leacann	Arg & Bt	NR8070	55°52·6′	5°30·6′W	X	62
An Lean-chàrn	Highld	NC4252	58°25·9′	4°41·9′W	H	9
An Learg	Arg & Bt	NM6025	56°21·6′	5°52·7′W	X	49
An Leargan	Arg & Bt	NR5065	55°49·1′	5°59·0′W	X	61
An Leathad	Highld	NC1523	58°9·7′	5°8·2′W	X	15
An Leathad	Highld	NH0353	57°31·7′	5°17·0′W	X	25
An Leitir	Highld	NG4536	57°20·9′	6°13·9′W	X	23,32
An Leitir	Highld	NG5032	57°18·9′	6°8·7′W	X	24,32
An Leitir	Highld	NH6803	57°6·2′	4°10·3′W	X	35
An Leth-allt	Highld	NG9224	57°15·8′	5°26·5′W	W	25,33
An Leth-allt	Highld	NH6725	57°18·0′	4°12·0′W	W	26,35
An Leth-allt	Highld	NH8320	57°15·6′	3°55·9′W	W	35
An Leth-allt	Highld	NM7095	56°59·6′	5°46·7′W	W	33,40
An Leth-chreag	Highld	NH1736	57°22·9′	5°2·2′W	X	25
An Leth-chreag	Highld	NH2141	57°25·7′	4°58·4′W	X	25
An Leth-chreag	Highld	NH2149	57°30·0′	4°58·8′W	X	25
An Leth-ghleann	Arg & Bt	NM4641	56°29·8′	6°7·2′W	X	47,48
An Leth-onn	Arg & Bt	NM5328	56°23·0′	5°59·6′W	W	48
Anley Ho	N Yks	SD8162	54°3·5′	2°17·0′W	X	98
An Liathanach	Arg & Bt	NM6725	56°21·9′	5°45·9′W	X	49
An Liathanach	Highld	NH1357	57°34·1′	5°7·1′W	X	25
An Lochain	Pth & Kin	NN9876	56°52·1′	3°39·9′W	W	43
An Lochan Uaine	Highld	NJ0010	57°10·5′	3°38·8′W	W	36
An Lodan	Arg & Bt	NM8704	56°11·1′	5°25·5′W	X	55
An Lònag	Highld	NG3640	57°22·7′	6°23·1′W	X	23
An Lurg	Highld	NJ0409	57°10·0′	3°34·8′W	H	36
Anmer	Norf	TF7429	52°50·1′	0°35·4′E	T	132
Anmer Minque	Norf	TF7528	52°49·5′	0°36·2′E	X	132
Anmore	Hants	SU6711	50°53·9′	1°2·4′W	T	196
Anmore Wood	Pth & Kin	NN8416	56°19·6′	3°52·1′W	F	58
Annabaglish	D & G	NX2958	54°53·5′	4°39·6′W	X	82
Annabaglish Moss	D & G	NX2856	54°52·4′	4°40·4′W	X	82
Annables Fm	Herts	TL1015	51°49·6′	0°23·8′W	FM	166
Annacroich	Pth & Kin	NT1198	56°10·2′	3°25·6′W	X	58
Annait	Highld	NG2652	57°28·8′	6°33·8′W	A	23
Anna Land End	Lancs	SD7453	53°58·6′	2°23·4′W	X	103
Anna Lane Head	Lancs	SD7651	53°57·5′	2°21·5′W	X	103
Annamuick	Aberd	NO7984	56°57·1′	2°20·3′W	X	45
Annan	D & G	NY1966	54°59·2′	3°15·5′W	T	85
Annanbank	D & G	NY1093	55°13·6′	3°24·5′W	X	78
Annanbank Dairy	D & G	NY1094	55°14·2′	3°24·5′W	X	78
Annandale	D & G	NY0994	55°14·2′	3°25·4′W	X	78
Annandale	D & G	NY1583	55°8·3′	3°19·6′W	X	79
Annanhead Hill	D & G	NT0513	55°24·4′	3°29·6′W	H	78
Annanhill	D & G	NY1085	55°9·3′	3°24·3′W	X	78
Annant Hill	D & G	NS9904	55°19·4′	3°35·1′W	H	78
Annapoorna	Durham	NZ1734	54°42·3′	1°43·7′W	X	92
Annas Ghyll	Lancs	SD5564	54°4·4′	2°40·8′W	X	97
Annaside	Cumbr	SD0986	54°15·9′	3°23·4′W	T	96
Annaside Banks	Cumbr	SD0885	54°15·4′	3°24·3′W	X	96
Annaside Beck	N Yks	NY9406	54°27·2′	2°5·1′W	W	91,92
Annat	Arg & Bt	NN0322	56°21·2′	5°10·9′W	T	50
Annat	Highld	NG8954	57°31·9′	5°31·0′W	T	24
Annat	Highld	NN3592	56°59·6′	4°42·5′W	X	34
Annat	Pth & Kin	NN6359	56°42·4′	4°13·8′W	X	42,51
Annat Bay	Highld	NH0397	57°55·4′	5°19·1′W	W	19
Annat Burn	Pth & Kin	NN6360	56°43·0′	4°13·9′W	W	42
Annat Coire	Highld	NN3589	56°58·0′	4°42·4′W	X	34,41
Annat Fm	Highld	NN0877	56°50·9′	5°8·5′W	FM	41
Annathill Fm	N Lanak	NS7271	55°55·2′	4°2·5′W	FM	64
Annatswell	Aberd	NJ5542	57°28·2′	2°44·6′W	X	29
Annat Walls	Cumbr	NY7145	54°48·2′	2°26·6′W	X	86,87
Annavale	S Lanak	NT0338	55°37·8′	3°32·0′W	X	72
Anna Valley	Hants	SU3443	51°11·3′	1°30·4′W	T	185
Annbank	S Ayr	NS4023	55°28·7′	4°31·5′W	T	70
An Nead	Highld	NH1031	57°20·1′	5°8·9′W	X	25
Annedd Wen	Pemb	SN1635	51°59·2′	4°40·4′W	X	145
Anne Hathaway's Cottage	Warw	SP1854	52°11·3′	1°43·8′W	A	151
Annelshope	Scot Bord	NT3016	55°26·2′	3°5·9′W	X	79
Annelshope Hill	Scot Bord	NT3015	55°25·7′	3°5·9′W	H	79
Annery	Devon	SS4522	50°58·8′	4°12·1′W	X	180,190
Annery Kiln	Devon	SS4622	50°58·8′	4°11·3′W	X	180,190
Annesley	Aberd	NJ6201	57°6·2′	2°37·2′W	X	37
Annesley	Notts	SK5053	53°4·5′	1°14·8′W	T	120
Annesley Hall	Notts	SK5052	53°4·0′	1°14·8′W	X	120
Annesley Plantn	Notts	SK5152	53°4·0′	1°13·9′W	F	120
Annesley Woodhouse	Notts	SK4953	53°4·6′	1°15·7′W	T	120
Annesons Corner	Suff	TM4267	52°15·1′	1°33·1′E	X	156
Anne's Well Wood	Staffs	SJ8424	52°49·0′	2°13·8′W	F	127
Annet	I Scilly	SV8608	49°53·6′	6°22·0′W	X	203
Annet	Stir	NN6905	56°13·4′	4°6·3′W	X	57
Annet Burn	Stir	NN6905	56°13·4′	4°6·3′W	W	57
Annet Head	I Scilly	SV8609	49°54·2′	6°22·0′W	X	203
Annet Neck	I Scilly	SV8608	49°53·6′	6°22·0′W	W	203
Annetts Fm	Hants	SU7034	51°6·3′	0°59·6′W	FM	186
Annfield	Aberd	NJ5516	57°14·2′	2°44·3′W	X	37
Annfield	Angus	NO5942	56°34·3′	2°39·6′W	X	54
Annfield	D & G	NX9985	55°9·2′	3°34·7′W	X	78
Annfield	Fife	NO3107	56°15·3′	3°6·4′W	X	59
Annfield	Fife	NO3906	56°14·8′	2°58·6′W	X	59
Annfield	Fife	NT1486	56°3·8′	3°22·4′W	X	65
Annfield	Fife	NT2095	56°8·7′	3°16·8′W	X	58
Annfield	Moray	NJ2343	57°28·5′	3°16·6′W	X	28
Annfield	S Lanak	NS8337	55°37·0′	3°51·0′W	X	71,72
Annfield Fm	Cumbr	NY1330	54°39·7′	3°20·5′W	FM	89
Annfield Ho	Durham	NZ1551	54°51·5′	1°45·6′W	X	88
Annfield Ho	Fife	NT1285	56°3·2′	3°24·3′W	X	65
Annfield Moor	D & G	NX9886	55°9·7′	3°35·6′W	X	78
Annfield Plain	Durham	NZ1751	54°51·5′	1°43·7′W	T	88
Annick Lodge	N Ayr	NS3541	55°38·3′	4°36·9′W	A	70
Annick Water	E Ayr	NS3843	55°39·5′	4°34·1′W	W	63,70
Anniegathel	Angus	NO4162	56°45·0′	2°57·4′W	X	44
Annieshill	N Lanak	NS8066	55°52·6′	3°54·6′W	X	65
Annies Hill	N Lanak	NS8166	55°52·6′	3°53·7′W	X	65
Anniesland	C of Glas	NS5468	55°53·2′	4°19·6′W	T	64
Annieston	S Lanak	NS9936	55°36·7′	3°35·8′W	X	72
Annieswell	Aberd	NJ9445	57°30·0′	2°5·5′W	X	30
Annifirth	Shetld	HU1949	60°13·8′	1°38·9′W	X	3

Annigate	Stock on T	NZ4426	54°37·9'	1°18·7'W	X	93
An Nighe Leathad	Highld	NC3043	58°20·8'	4°53·8'W	X	9
Annikel	Pemb	SM9111	51°45·8'	5°1·3'W	X	157,158
Anningsley Park	Surrey	TQ0262	51°21·1'	0°31·7'W	X	176,186
Annington	W Susx	TQ1809	50°52·3'	0°19·0'W	X	198
Annington Fm	W Susx	TQ1809	50°52·3'	0°19·0'W	FM	198
Annington Hill	W Susx	TQ1709	50°52·3'	0°19·8'W	X	198
Annington Hill Barn	W Susx	TQ1708	50°51·8'	0°19·9'W	X	198
Annishader	Highld	NG4351	57°28·8'	6°16·8'W	T	23
Annis Hill	Somer	ST5625	51°1·6'	2°37·3'W	X	183
Annis Hill	Suff	TM3589	52°27·1'	1°27·9'E	T	156
Anniston	Aberd	NO8072	56°50·6'	2°19·2'W	X	45
Anniston	Angus	NO6748	56°37·6'	2°31·8'W	X	54
Annitsford	N Tyne	NZ2674	55°3·8'	1°35·1'W	T	88
Annochie	Aberd	NJ9342	57°28·3'	2°6·5'W	T	30
Annochie Moss	Aberd	NJ9442	57°28·4'	2°5·5'W	X	30
Annscroft	Shrops	SJ4507	52°39·7'	2°48·4'W	T	126
Ann's Cross on Tumulus	N Yks	NZ8800	54°23·5'	0°38·3'W	A	94
Anns Hill	Cumbr	NY1132	54°40·8'	3°22·4'W	X	89
Ann's Hill	Cumbr	NY5375	55°4·3'	2°43·7'W	X	86
Ann's Hill	Hants	SU5900	50°48·0'	1°9·4'W	T	196
Annsmuir	Fife	NO3111	56°17·4'	3°6·4'W	X	59
Annstead Fm	Northum	NU2230	55°34·0'	1°38·6'W	FM	75
Annwell Place	Derby	SK3418	52°45·7'	1°29·4'W	T	128
Annwood Fm	E Susx	TQ4227	51°1·7'	0°1·9'E	FM	187,198
An Oitir	Arg & Bt	NN0907	56°13·3'	5°4·4'W	X	56
An Oitir	Arg & Bt	NR9794	56°6·0'	5°15·4'W	X	55
An Raon	Highld	NG7478	57°44·4'	5°47·4'W	X	19
An Réidh-choire	Highld	NG8461	57°35·5'	5°36·4'W	X	19,24
An Réidh-choire	Highld	NG8766	57°38·3'	5°33·6'W	X	19
An Réis-choire	Highld	NM8596	57°0·6'	5°32·0'W	X	33,40
An Reithe	Highld	NH1514	57°11·0'	5°3·2'W	H	34
An Reithe	N Eil	NB2002	57°55·4'	6°43·3'W	H	14
An Riabhachan	Highld	NH1234	57°21·7'	5°7·1'W	X	25
An Roinn	Highld	NG5852	57°29·9'	6°1·9'W	X	24
An Romasaig	Highld	NM8291	56°57·8'	5°34·7'W	X	33,40
An Ros	N Ayr	NR9925	55°28·9'	5°10·4'W	X	69
An Ruadh-bruach	Highld	NG8447	57°28·0'	5°35·6'W	X	24
An Ruadh-eilean	Highld	NG6938	57°22·7'	5°50·1'W	X	24,32
An Ruadh-mheallan	Highld	NG8361	57°35·5'	5°37·4'W	H	19,24
An Ruadh-stac	Highld	NG9248	57°28·7'	5°27·7'W	H	25
An Rubha	Arg & Bt	NR3595	56°4·7'	6°15·1'W	X	61
An Ruime	Arg & Bt	NR3171	55°51·7'	6°17·5'W	X	60,61
An Rumach	Arg & Bt	NR3270	55°51·2'	6°16·5'W	X	60,61
An Sagart	Highld	NG8483	57°47·3'	5°37·6'W	X	19
An Sàilean	Arg & Bt	NM5227	56°22·5'	6°0·5'W	W	48
An Sàilean	Arg & Bt	NM8341	56°30·9'	5°31·2'W	W	49
An Sàilean	Arg & Bt	NR5082	55°58·2'	6°0·0'W	W	61
An Samhladh	Arg & Bt	NM8505	56°11·6'	5°27·5'W	X	55
An Saobhadh	Arg & Bt	NR7766	55°50·4'	5°33·3'W	X	62
An Scriodan	N Ayr	NR9452	55°43·3'	5°16·4'W	X	62,69
Ansdell	Lancs	SD3428	53°44·9'	2°59·6'W	T	102
Ansdore	Kent	TR1148	51°11·8'	1°1·6'E	X	179,189
An Sean Chaisteal (Broch)	Arg & Bt	NM5549	56°34·4'	5°58·9'W	A	47,48
An Sean Dun	Arg & Bt	NM4356	56°37·8'	6°11·0'W	A	47
Ansells End	Herts	TL1518	51°51·2'	0°19·4'W	T	166
Ansell's Fm	Essex	TL8735	51°59·1'	0°43·8'E	FM	155
Anser Gallows Fm	Essex	TL6236	52°0·2'	0°22·0'E	FM	154
Anses Wood	Hants	SU2212	50°54·7'	1°40·8'W	F	195
Ansford	Somer	ST6333	51°5·9'	2°31·3'W	T	183
Ansford Br	Somer	ST6333	51°5·9'	2°31·3'W	X	183
Ansford Park Fm	Somer	ST6433	51°5·9'	2°30·5'W	FM	183
An Sgaothach	Highld	NH3988	57°51·4'	4°42·3'W	X	20
An Sgarsoch	Pth & Kin	NN9383	56°55·8'	3°45·0'W	H	43
An Sgor	Highld	NH8536	57°24·3'	3°54·4'W	H	27
An Sgòran	Moray	NJ1126	57°19·2'	3°28·2'W	X	36
An Sgornach	Arg & Bt	NM9822	56°21·1'	5°15·7'W	H	49
An Sgorr	Pth & Kin	NN6450	56°37·6'	4°12·6'W	H	42,51
An Sgorr	Pth & Kin	NN6451	56°38·1'	4°12·6'W	H	42,51
An Sgriodan	Arg & Bt	NM4651	56°35·2'	6°7·8'W	X	47
An Sgriodan	Arg & Bt	NN1933	56°27·5'	4°55·8'W	X	50
An Sgriodhal	Highld	NG8212	57°9·1'	5°35·8'W	X	33
An Sguabach	Highld	NH8310	57°10·2'	3°55·6'W	X	35
An Sguabach	Highld	NN6985	56°56·5'	4°9·2'W	X	42
An Sguiteach	Highld	NG8288	57°50·0'	5°39·9'W	X	19
An Sgùlan	Arg & Bt	NM5425	56°21·5'	5°58·5'W	X	48
An Sgùlan	Highld	NG7219	57°12·6'	5°46·1'W	X	33
An Sgùlan	Pth & Kin	NN5672	56°49·3'	4°21·1'W	H	42
An Sguman	Highld	NG4318	57°11·1'	6°14·7'W	X	32
An Sgùman	Highld	NH1369	57°40·6'	5°7·7'W	H	19
An Sgurr	Highld	NG8538	57°23·2'	5°34·2'W	H	24
An Sgurr	Highld	NM4584	56°52·9'	6°10·7'W	H	39
An Sgurraman	Arg & Bt	NM4527	56°22·3'	6°7·3'W	X	48
An Sgùrran	Highld	NG2143	57°23·8'	6°38·2'W	X	23
An Sidhean	Arg & Bt	NM4548	56°33·5'	6°8·6'W	X	47,48
An Sidhean	Arg & Bt	NM5824	56°21·0'	5°54·6'W	X	48
An Sidhean	Highld	NH1745	57°27·8'	5°2·6'W	H	25
An Sidhean	Highld	NH2439	57°24·7'	4°55·3'W	H	25
An Sidhean	Highld	NH4697	57°56·4'	4°35·6'W	X	20
An Sidhean	Highld	NM9875	56°49·6'	5°18·2'W	H	40
An Sìth	N Eil	NB0413	58°0·7'	7°0·3'W	H	13
An Sithéan	Arg & Bt	NM8314	56°16·4'	5°29·9'W	X	55
An Sleaghach	Highld	NM7643	56°31·8'	5°38·1'W	H	49
Ansley	Warw	SP2991	52°31·2'	1°34·0'W	T	140
Ansley Common	Warw	SP3193	52°32·3'	1°32·2'W	T	140
Ansley Hall	Warw	SP3093	52°32·3'	1°33·1'W	X	140
An Sligearnach	Pth & Kin	NN8482	56°55·1'	3°53·9'W	H	43
An Sligearnach	Pth & Kin	NN9578	56°53·1'	3°42·9'W	H	43
Anslow	Staffs	SK2125	52°49·6'	1°40·9'W	T	128
Anslow Gate	Staffs	SK1924	52°49·0'	1°42·7'W	T	128
An Slugan	Aberd	NO1886	56°57·7'	3°20·5'W	X	43
An Slugan	Highld	NG5825	57°15·4'	6°0·3'W	X	32
An Slugan	Highld	NH9413	57°12·0'	3°44·8'W	X	36
An Snoig	Arg & Bt	NL9343	56°29·0'	6°58·8'W	X	46
An Socach	Aberd	NO0980	56°54·4'	3°29·2'W	H	43
An Socach	Arg & Bt	NR9991	56°4·4'	5°13·3'W	H	55
An Socach	Arg & Bt	NS0587	56°2·4'	5°7·4'W	H	56
An Socach	Highld	NC2658	58°28·8'	4°58·6'W	H	9
An Socach	Highld	NH0823	57°15·7'	5°10·6'W	X	25,33
An Socach	Highld	NH1033	57°21·1'	5°9·0'W	H	25
An Socach	Highld	NH2742	57°26·4'	4°52·5'W	X	25
An Socach	Highld	NH3786	57°50·3'	4°44·3'W	H	20
An Socach	Highld	NH4768	57°40·8'	4°33·5'W	H	20
An Socach	Highld	NH7723	57°17·1'	4°2·0'W	H	35
Anson's Bank	Staffs	SJ9716	52°44·7'	2°2·3'W	X	127
Ansons Fm	Lincs	SK8863	53°9·6'	0°40·6'W	FM	121
An Sopachan	Arg & Bt	NR3768	55°50·3'	6°11·6'W	X	60,61
An Sornach	Highld	NH0921	57°14·7'	5°9·5'W	X	25,33
An Soutar	Highld	NH2535	57°22·6'	4°54·2'W	H	25
An Speireachan	Arg & Bt	NM4856	56°37·9'	6°6·1'W	H	47
An Srachdach	Highld	NM9782	56°53·4'	5°19·5'W	X	40
An Stac	Highld	NC5268	58°34·8'	4°32·2'W	X	10
An Stac	Highld	NG1446	57°25·1'	6°45·4'W	X	23
An Stac	Highld	NG5421	57°13·1'	6°4·0'W	H	32
An Stac	Highld	NM7679	56°51·2'	5°40·0'W	H	40
An Stac	Highld	NM8688	56°56·3'	5°30·6'W	H	40
An Stac	Highld	NN7691	56°59·9'	4°2·0'W	X	35
An Staonach	Highld	NG8248	57°28·5'	5°37·7'W	H	24
An Staonaig	Highld	NH5705	57°7·1'	4°21·2'W	X	35
Ansteadbrook	Surrey	SU9332	51°5·0'	0°39·9'W	T	186
Ansteads Fm	Glos	SO8907	51°45·9'	2°9·2'W	FM	163
An Stèidh	Highld	NG2103	57°2·3'	6°35·5'W	X	39
Anstey	Herts	TL4032	51°58·4'	0°2·7'E	T	167
Anstey	Leic	SK5408	52°40·3'	1°11·7'W	T	140
Anstey Barrow	Devon	SS8728	51°2·7'	3°36·3'W	A	181
Anstey Bury	Herts	TL4131	51°57·8'	0°3·5'E	X	167
Anstey Castle	Herts	TL4032	51°58·4'	0°2·7'E	A	167
Anstey Gate	Devon	SS8329	51°3·1'	3°39·8'W	X	181
Anstey Hall	Cambs	TL4454	52°10·2'	0°6·7'E	X	154
Anstey High Leys	Leic	SK5308	52°40·3'	1°12·6'W	X	140
Anstey's Cove	Torbay	SX9364	50°28·2'	3°30·1'W	W	202
Anstiebury	Surrey	TQ1543	51°10·7'	0°20·9'W	A	187
Anstie Grange	Surrey	TQ1644	51°11·2'	0°20·0'W	X	187
An Stoc-bheinn	Highld	NC6302	57°59·4'	4°18·6'W	H	16
Anston	S Lanak	NT0548	55°43·2'	3°30·3'W	X	72
Anston Brook	Roth	SK5085	53°21·8'	1°14·5'W	W	111,120
Anston Grange Fm	Roth	SK5382	53°20·2'	1°11·8'W	FM	111,120
Anston Stones Wood	Roth	SK5383	53°20·7'	1°11·8'W	F	111,120
Anstool Burn	D & G	NX6562	54°56·3'	4°6·0'W	W	83,84
Anstruther Easter	Fife	NO5703	56°13·3'	2°41·2'W	T	59
Anstruther Wester	Fife	NO5603	56°13·3'	2°42·1'W	T	59
An Struthlag	Arg & Bt	NR7932	55°32·2'	5°29·7'W	X	68,69
An Stùc	Highld	NC3409	58°2·6'	4°48·3'W	H	15
An Stùchd	Arg & Bt	NR7580	55°57·9'	5°35·9'W	H	55
An Stuchd	Pth & Kin	NN3938	56°30·7'	4°36·5'W	H	55
An Stuchd	Stir	NN4414	56°17·8'	4°30·8'W	H	57
An Stùghadh	N Eil	NG0484	57°45·1'	6°58·1'W	X	18
Ansty	Warw	SP3983	52°26·8'	1°25·2'W	T	140
Ansty	Wilts	ST9526	51°2·2'	2°3·9'W	T	184
Ansty	W Susx	TQ2923	50°59·7'	0°9·3'W	T	198
Ansty Coombe	Wilts	ST9526	51°2·2'	2°3·9'W	T	184
Ansty Cross	Dorset	ST7603	50°49·8'	2°20·1'W	T	194
Ansty Hill	Wilts	ST9543	51°11·4'	2°3·9'W	X	184
An Suidhe	Arg & Bt	NN0007	56°13·1'	5°13·1'W	H	55
An Suidhe	Highld	NH3017	57°13·0'	4°48·5'W	H	34
An Suidhe	Highld	NH8107	57°8·6'	3°57·5'W	H	35
An Suidhe	Pth & Kin	NN9256	56°41·3'	3°45·3'W	X	52
Antabreck	Orkney	HY7554	59°22·6'	2°25·9'W	X	5
An t- Aigeach	Highld	NC4565	58°33·0'	4°39·3'W	X	9
An t-Aigeach	Highld	NG1347	57°25·6'	6°46·4'W	X	23
An t-Aigeach	N Eil	NF9364	57°34·0'	7°7·6'W	X	18
An t-Aird	Arg & Bt	NM2621	56°18·4'	6°25·4'W	X	48
An t-Aird	Arg & Bt	NM3523	56°19·8'	6°16·8'W	X	48
An Tàmhanachd	Arg & Bt	NR3867	55°49·8'	6°10·6'W	X	60,61
An Tamhanachd	Arg & Bt	NR4266	55°49·4'	6°6·7'W	X	60,61
Ant-Aonach	Arg & Bt	NM8817	56°18·1'	5°25·2'W	X	55
An t-Aonach	Arg & Bt	NR7966	55°50·5'	5°31·3'W	X	62
An t-Aonach	Highld	NH9906	57°8·3'	3°39·7'W	X	36
An t-Aonach	Highld	NM7481	56°52·2'	5°42·0'W	X	40
An Tarbh	Highld	NG7370	57°40·0'	5°47·9'W	X	19
An t-Ard	Arg & Bt	NM0143	56°29·3'	6°51·0'W	X	46
An t-Each	Highld	NG2706	57°4·1'	6°29·8'W	X	39
An Teallach	Highld	NH0684	57°48·5'	5°15·5'W	H	19
An Teampan	Pth & Kin	NN7965	56°45·9'	3°58·3'W	X	42
An Teampull	Highld	NG6154	57°31·1'	5°59·0'W	A	24
An t-Eilan Meadhoin	Highld	NM7092	56°58·0'	5°46·6'W	X	33,40
Antelope Lodge	N Yks	NZ4911	54°29·8'	1°14·2'W	X	93
Antermony Loch	E Dunb	NS6676	55°57·8'	4°8·4'W	W	64
An t-Eug Allt	Highld	NM6549	56°34·7'	5°49·1'W	W	49
Antfield	Highld	NH6137	57°24·4'	4°18·4'W	X	26
Anthill Common	Hants	SU6412	50°54·5'	1°5·0'W	T	196
Anthills	Norf	TM2583	52°24·1'	1°18·9'E	X	156
Anthony	Corn	SX3954	50°22·1'	4°15·5'W	T	201
Anthony Hill	Cambs	TL4341	52°3·2'	0°5·5'E	X	154
Anthony Hill	Derby	SK0470	53°13·9'	1°56·0'W	H	119
Anthony Ho	N Yks	NZ6703	54°25·3'	0°57·6'W	X	94
Anthonys	Essex	TL5615	51°48·9'	0°16·2'E	X	167
Anthonys	Surrey	TQ0161	51°20·6'	0°32·6'W	X	176,186
Anthony's Cross	Glos	SO7123	51°54·5'	2°24·9'W	T	162
Anthorn	Cumbr	NY1958	54°54·9'	3°15·4'W	T	85
An t-Iasgair	Highld	NG3574	57°40·9'	6°26·3'W	X	23
An t-Inbhir	Arg & Bt	NN0015	56°17·4'	5°13·5'W	W	50,55
Antingham	Norf	TG2533	52°51·1'	1°20·9'E	T	133
Antingham Hall	Norf	TG2532	52°50·5'	1°20·9'E	X	133
Antingham Hill	Norf	TG2632	52°50·5'	1°21·8'E	X	133
An t-Òb	Highld	NG7426	57°16·4'	5°44·5'W	W	33
Antofts	N Yks	SE5882	54°14·1'	1°6·2'W	X	100
An Tom	N Eil	NF7957	57°29·6'	7°21·0'W	X	22
Anton Heights	D & G	NY4197	55°16·1'	2°55·3'W	X	79
Anton Hill	Northum	NY8580	55°7·1'	2°13·7'W	X	80
Antonine Wall	C of Glas	NS5871	55°54·9'	4°15·9'W	R	64
Antonine Wall	Falk	NS8379	55°59·6'	3°52·1'W	R	65
Anton's Gowt	Lincs	TF3047	53°0·5'	0°3·3'W	T	131
Antonshill	Falk	NS8783	56°1·9'	3°48·4'W	T	65
Anton's Hill	Scot Bord	NT7843	55°41·0'	2°20·6'W	X	74
Antonstown Burn	Cumbr	NY5677	55°5·4'	2°40·9'W	W	86
Antony Ho	Corn	SX4156	50°23·2'	4°13·8'W	X	201
Antony Passage	Corn	SX4157	50°23·7'	4°13·9'W	T	201
An Torc or Boar of Badenoch	Pth & Kin	NN6276	56°51·6'	4°15·3'W	H	42
An Torr	Arg & Bt	NM4452	56°35·7'	6°9·8'W	X	47
An Tòrr	Arg & Bt	NN2945	56°34·2'	4°46·6'W	H	50
An Torr	Arg & Bt	NR7876	55°55·8'	5°32·8'W	X	62
An Torr	Arg & Bt	NR7878	55°56·9'	5°32·9'W	H	62
An Torr	Arg & Bt	NR8479	55°57·6'	5°27·2'W	X	62
An Torr	Arg & Bt	NR8887	56°2·0'	5°23·7'W	H	55
An Tòrr	Highld	NG7873	57°41·8'	5°43·1'W	H	19
An Torr	Highld	NH5935	57°23·3'	4°20·3'W	H	26
An Torr	Highld	NH6427	57°19·1'	4°15·0'W	H	26,35
An Torr	Pth & Kin	NN8377	56°52·4'	3°54·7'W	H	43
An Torra Bàn	Highld	NM8463	56°42·8'	5°31·3'W	X	40
An t-Otrach	Highld	NH6512	57°11·0'	4°13·6'W	X	35
Antrobus	Ches	SJ6479	53°18·6'	2°32·0'W	T	118
Antrobus Hall	Ches	SJ6480	53°19·2'	2°32·0'W	X	109
Antrobus Hall	Ches	SJ8078	53°18·2'	2°17·6'W	X	118
Antrobus Ho	Ches	SJ6480	53°19·2'	2°32·0'W	X	109
Antron	Corn	SW6327	50°6·0'	5°18·5'W	X	203
Antron Fm	Corn	SW7633	50°9·5'	5°7·8'W	FM	204
An t-Sàil	Arg & Bt	NR3386	55°59·8'	6°16·5'W	X	61
An t-Sàil	Highld	NC0707	58°0·9'	5°15·6'W	H	15
An t-Sail	Highld	NM9497	57°1·4'	5°23·2'W	H	33,40
An t-Sail Mhor	Highld	NC3448	58°23·6'	4°49·9'W	X	9
An t-Saothair	Highld	NG9191	57°51·8'	5°30·9'W	X	19
An t-Sean Lughard	Highld	NC4441	58°20·1'	4°39·4'W	X	9
An t-Seann Fhrith	Highld	NN1287	56°56·4'	5°5·0'W	X	34,41
An t-Slat-bheinn	Highld	NM7877	56°50·1'	5°37·9'W	H	40
An t-Sleaghach	Arg & Bt	NM6730	56°24·5'	5°46·2'W	X	49
An t-Sleubhaich	Highld	NM8780	56°52·0'	5°29·2'W	H	40
Ant-Sreang	Arg & Bt	NN3001	56°10·5'	4°43·9'W	X	56
An t-Sreang	Highld	NM6750	56°35·3'	5°47·2'W	X	49
An t-Sròn	Aberd	NO2884	56°56·8'	3°10·6'W	H	44
An t-Sròn	Arg & Bt	NL9342	56°28·5'	6°58·7'W	X	46
An t-Sròn	Arg & Bt	NN1910	56°15·1'	4°54·9'W	H	50,56
An t-Sròn	Arg & Bt	NS0683	56°0·3'	5°6·3'W	X	56
An t- Sròn	Highld	NC4458	58°29·2'	4°40·1'W	X	9
An t-Sron	Highld	NC5348	58°24·0'	4°30·4'W	H	10
An t-Sròn	Highld	NC6530	58°14·5'	4°17·5'W	X	16
An t-Sròn	Highld	NG3739	57°22·2'	6°22·0'W	X	23,32
An t-Sròn	Highld	NG5120	57°12·5'	6°6·9'W	H	32
An t-Sron	Highld	NN1355	56°39·2'	5°2·6'W	X	41
An t-Sròn	N Eil	NF7616	57°7·5'	7°20·8'W	X	31
Ant-Sròn	Pth & Kin	NO0359	56°43·0'	3°34·6'W	X	52,53
Ants, The		TF4945	52°59·1'	0°13·6'E	X	131
An t Streang	Arg & Bt	NM9317	56°18·3'	5°20·3'W	X	55
An t-Suil	Arg & Bt	NS0283	56°0·2'	5°10·1'W	X	55
An t-Sùileag	Arg & Bt	NN0181	56°52·9'	5°15·5'W	W	41
Ant t-Sròn	Aberd	NO3084	56°56·8'	3°8·6'W	X	44
An Tudair	Highld	NH1223	57°15·8'	5°6·6'W	H	25
An Tudair Beag	Highld	NH1323	57°15·8'	5°5·6'W	X	25
An Tudan	Arg & Bt	NM6908	56°12·8'	5°43·1'W	X	55
An t-Uiriollach	Highld	NM8399	57°2·1'	5°34·1'W	H	33,40
An Tulachan	Highld	NC3003	57°59·3'	4°52·1'W	X	15
An Tunna	N Ayr	NR9635	55°34·2'	5°13·7'W	H	68,69
An Tunna	N Ayr	NR9747	55°40·7'	5°13·3'W	X	62,69
Antwicks Manor	Oxon	SU3786	51°34·5'	1°27·6'W	X	174
Antye Fm	E Susx	TQ3220	50°58·1'	0°6·8'W	FM	198
An Uamha	Highld	NM6753	56°36·9'	5°47·4'W	X	49
An Uidh	Highld	NH6395	57°55·7'	4°18·3'W	W	21
Anvil Corner	Devon	SS3704	50°49·0'	4°18·5'W	X	190
Anvil Cross	Essex	TL5019	51°51·2'	0°11·1'E	X	167
Anvil Green	Kent	TR1049	51°12·3'	1°0·8'E	T	179,189
Anvilles	W Berks	SU3465	51°23·2'	1°30·3'W	T	174
Anville's Copse	W Berks	SU3464	51°22·7'	1°30·3'W	F	174
Anvill's Fm	Wilts	SU1761	51°21·1'	1°45·0'W	FM	173
Anvil Point	Dorset	SZ0276	50°35·3'	1°57·9'W	X	195
Anvil, The	I of M	SC1966	54°3·7'	4°45·9'W	X	95
Anvil, The	Pemb	SM7508	51°43·8'	5°15·1'W	X	157
Anwick	Lincs	TF1150	53°2·4'	0°20·3'W	T	121
Anwick Fen	Lincs	TF1350	53°2·4'	0°18·5'W	X	121
Anwoth	D & G	NX5856	54°53·0'	4°12·4'W	T	83
Anyon Ho	Lancs	SD5052	53°57·9'	2°45·3'W	X	102
Aobran Allt a' Ghiubhais	Highld	NN0898	57°2·3'	5°9·4'W	W	33
Aodan Grànda	N Eil	NB2205	57°57·1'	6°41·5'W	X	13,14
Aodann an t-Sidhein Mhòir	Highld	NM7386	56°54·8'	5°43·3'W	X	40
Aodann Chléireig	Highld	NM9982	56°53·4'	5°17·5'W	H	40
Aodann Mhór	Highld	NC4069	58°35·0'	4°44·7'W	X	9
Aodann Raineach	Arg & Bt	NN0502	56°10·5'	5°8·0'W	H	56
Aodin	Pth & Kin	NN8751	56°38·5'	3°50·1'W	X	52
Aoineadh Achadh Rainich	Highld	NM7046	56°33·2'	5°44·1'W	X	49
Aoineadh a' Mhaide Ghil	Arg & Bt	NM5521	56°19·3'	5°57·3'W	X	48
Aoineadh Beag	Arg & Bt	NM4619	56°18·0'	6°5·9'W	X	48
Aoineadh Beag	Highld	NM6650	56°35·3'	5°48·2'W	X	49
Aoineadh Beag	Highld	NM6943	56°31·6'	5°44·9'W	X	49
Aoineadh Mhàirtein	Arg & Bt	NM7125	56°22·0'	5°42·0'W	X	49
Aoineadh Mhéinis	Arg & Bt	NM6521	56°19·6'	5°47·5'W	X	49
Aoineadh Mór	Arg & Bt	NM3724	56°20·4'	6°14·9'W	X	48
Aoineadh Mór	Arg & Bt	NM5019	56°18·1'	6°2·0'W	X	48
Aoineadh Mór	Highld	NM6451	56°35·8'	5°50·2'W	X	49
Aoineadh Mór	Highld	NM7242	56°31·1'	5°41·9'W	X	49
Aoineadh nan Gamhna	Arg & Bt	NM5119	56°18·1'	6°1·1'W	X	48
Aoineadh Ros-dail	Arg & Bt	NM4126	56°21·6'	6°11·1'W	X	48
Aoineadh Thapuill	Arg & Bt	NM4129	56°23·2'	6°11·3'W	X	48
Aonach	Highld	NM6273	56°47·5'	5°53·4'W	X	40
Aonach a' Choire Bhuig	Highld	NC4706	58°1·3'	4°34·9'W	X	16
Aonach air Chrith	Highld	NH0508	57°7·6'	5°12·8'W	H	33
Aonachan	Highld	NN2181	56°53·4'	4°55·9'W	T	34,41
Aonach an Nid	Highld	NN1974	56°49·6'	4°57·5'W	X	41
Aonach Baile na Creige	Highld	NG9137	57°22·8'	5°28·1'W	X	25
Aonach Bàn	Pth & Kin	NN7554	56°39·9'	4°1·9'W	X	42,51,52
Aonach Beag	Highld	NG9733	57°20·8'	5°22·0'W	H	25
Aonach Beag	Highld	NM7097	57°0·7'	5°46·8'W	H	33,40
Aonach Beag	Highld	NN1971	56°48·0'	4°57·4'W	H	41
Aonach Beag	Highld	NN4574	56°50·2'	4°32·0'W	H	42
Aonach-bheinn	Arg & Bt	NR4870	55°51·7'	6°1·2'W	H	60,61
Aonach Breac	Arg & Bt	NN0933	56°27·3'	5°5·5'W	X	50
Aonach Buidhe	Highld	NH0532	57°20·5'	5°14·0'W	H	25
Aonach Cas	Highld	NH0733	57°21·1'	5°12·0'W	X	25
Aonach Dubh	Highld	NG9637	57°22·9'	5°23·2'W	X	25
Aonach Dubh	Highld	NH1359	57°35·2'	5°7·2'W	H	25

Aonach Dubh	Highld	NN1555	56°39·3'	5°0·6'W	H	41
Aonach Dubh a' Ghlinne	Highld	NN1153	56°38·1'	5°4·5'W	H	41
Aonach Eagach	Arg & Bt	NN2445	56°34·1'	4°51·4'W	X	50
Aonach Eagach	Highld	NN1558	56°40·9'	5°0·8'W	H	41
Aonach Meadhoin	Highld	NH0413	57°10·2'	5°14·1'W	H	33
Aonach Mór	Highld	NH1423	57°15·9'	5°4·6'W	X	25
Aonach Mór	Highld	NM7197	57°0·7'	5°45·9'W	H	33,40
Aonach Mór	Highld	NN1973	56°49·1'	4°57·5'W	H	41
Aonach Mòr	Highld	NN2148	56°35·6'	4°54·5'W	X	50
Aonach Mór	Highld	NN8094	57°1·6'	3°58·2'W	H	35,43
Aonach na Cloiche Móire	Pth & Kin	NN9076	56°52·0'	3°47·8'W	H	43
Aonach Odhar	Highld	NH4501	57°4·7'	4°33·0'W	H	34
Aonach Odhar	Highld	NH7022	57°16·5'	4°8·9'W	H	35
Aonach Sgoilte	Highld	NG8302	57°3·7'	5°34·3'W	X	33
Aonach Shasuinn	Highld	NH1717	57°12·7'	5°1·4'W	H	34
Aonaig Mhòr	N Eil	NB1507	57°57·9'	6°48·7'W	X	13,14
Aon Garbh	Arg & Bt	NM8037	56°28·7'	5°33·9'W	X	49
Aoradh	Arg & Bt	NR2767	55°49·4'	6°21·1'W	X	60
Apedale	N Yks	SE0194	54°20·7'	1°58·7'W	X	98
Ape Dale	Shrops	SO4889	52°30·0'	2°45·6'W	X	137,138
Apedale	Staffs	SJ8149	53°2·5'	2°16·6'W	T	118
Apedale Beck	N Yks	SE0194	54°20·7'	1°58·7'W	W	98
Apedale Head	N Yks	SE0095	54°21·3'	1°59·6'W	X	98
Aperfield	Brom	TQ4258	51°18·4'	0°2·6'E	T	187
Apes Dale	Worcs	SO9972	52°21·0'	2°0·5'W	T	139
Apes Down	I of W	SZ4587	50°41·1'	1°21·4'W	X	196
Apesdown	I of W	SZ4587	50°41·1'	1°21·4'W	X	196
Apesfield Fm	Beds	SP9331	51°58·4'	0°38·4'W	FM	165
Apesford	Staffs	SK0153	53°4·7'	1°58·7'W	X	119
Apes Hall, The	Cambs	TL5590	52°29·4'	0°17·4'E	X	143
Apethorn	Tames	SJ9493	53°26·3'	2°5·0'W	A	109
Apethorpe	Northnts	TL0295	52°32·8'	0°29·3'W	T	141
Apeton	Staffs	SJ8518	52°45·8'	2°12·9'W	T	127
Aphainn Dheabhag	Highld	NH3027	57°18·4'	4°48·9'W	W	26
A' Phocaid	Highld	NN0907	57°3·3'	5°8·4'W	X	36,43
A' Phoit	Highld	NG8045	57°26·8'	5°39·5'W	H	24
Apley	Lincs	TF1075	53°15·9'	0°20·6'W	T	121
Apley Forge	Shrops	SO7098	52°35·0'	2°26·2'W	T	138
Apley Head Fm	Notts	SK6576	53°16·9'	1°1·1'W	FM	120
Apleyhead Lodge	Notts	SK6477	53°17·4'	1°2·0'W	X	120
Apleyhead Wood	Notts	SK6577	53°17·4'	1°1·1'W	F	120
Apley Park	Shrops	SO7198	52°35·0'	2°25·3'W	X	138
Apley Park Fm	Shrops	SO7199	52°35·5'	2°25·3'W	FM	138
Apley Terrace	Shrops	SO7297	52°34·4'	2°24·4'W	X	138
Aplins Fm	Devon	ST1904	50°50·0'	3°8·6'W	FM	192,193
Apostles Fm	Heref	SO2852	52°9·9'	3°2·8'W	FM	148
Appat	Highld	ND1054	58°28·2'	3°32·1'W	X	11,12
Appat Hill	Highld	ND0954	58°28·2'	3°33·1'W	X	11,12
Apper Beag	Arg & Bt	NM5252	56°35·9'	6°2·0'W	X	47
Apperknowle	Derby	SK3878	53°18·1'	1°25·4'W	T	119
Apperley	Glos	SO8628	51°57·3'	2°11·8'W	T	150
Apperley	Northum	NZ0658	54°55·2'	1°54·0'W	X	87
Apperley Bridge	Brad	SE1937	53°50·0'	1°42·3'W	T	104
Apperley Burn	Northum	NY9355	54°53·6'	2°6·1'W	W	87
Apperley Court	Glos	SO8527	51°56·7'	2°12·7'W	X	162
Apperley Dene	Northum	NZ0558	54°55·2'	1°54·9'W	T	87
Appersett	N Yks	SD8590	54°18·6'	2°13·4'W	T	98
Appersett Pasture	N Yks	SD8490	54°18·6'	2°14·3'W	X	98
Appiehouse	Orkney	HY3411	58°59·1'	3°8·4'W	X	6
Appieteen	Orkney	HY2815	59°1·2'	3°14·8'W	X	6
Appietown	Orkney	HY4119	59°3·5'	3°1·2'W	X	6
Appin	Arg & Bt	NM9346	56°33·9'	5°21·7'W	T	49
Appin	D & G	NX7497	55°15·3'	3°58·5'W	W	77
Appin	E Loth	NT5279	56°0·3'	2°45·7'W	X	66
Appin	Highld	NM9950	56°36·2'	5°16·0'W	X	49
Appin	Highld	NN0153	56°37·9'	5°14·2'W	X	41
Appin Burn	D & G	NX7397	55°15·3'	3°59·5'W	W	77
Appin Burn	D & G	NX7597	55°15·3'	3°57·6'W	W	78
Appin Hill	Arg & Bt	NM9449	56°35·5'	5°20·9'W	H	49
Appin House	Arg & Bt	NM9349	56°35·5'	5°21·8'W	X	49
Appin Lodge	D & G	NX7597	55°15·3'	3°57·6'W	X	78
Appin of Dull	Pth & Kin	NN8048	56°36·8'	3°56·9'W	X	52
Appin Rocks	Arg & Bt	NM8944	56°32·7'	5°25·5'W	X	49
Appleacre Fm	Suff	TL7550	52°7·5'	0°33·8'E	FM	155
Apple Barn	Kent	TR0838	51°6·4'	0°58·7'E	X	179,189
Applebridge Fm	N Yks	NZ5409	54°28·7'	1°9·6'W	FM	93
Applebury Hill Fm	Cumbr	SD3776	54°10·8'	2°57·5'W	FM	96,97
Appleby	D & G	NX4140	54°44·0'	4°27·7'W	X	83
Appleby	N Lincs	SE9514	53°37·1'	0°33·4'W	T	112
Appleby Carrs	N Lincs	SE9613	53°36·5'	0°32·5'W	X	112
Appleby Gate	Northnts	SP8568	52°18·4'	0°44·8'W	X	152
Appleby Ho	Cumbr	NY4467	54°59·9'	2°52·1'W	X	85
Appleby-in-Westmoorland	Cumbr	NY6820	54°34·7'	2°29·3'W	T	91
Appleby Magna	Leic	SK3109	52°40·9'	1°32·1'W	T	128,140
Appleby Parva	Leic	SK3008	52°40·4'	1°33·0'W	T	128,140
Appleby Row	D & G	NX4040	54°44·0'	4°28·7'W	X	83
Applecross	Highld	NG7144	57°26·0'	5°48·5'W	T	24
Applecross Bay	Highld	NG7145	57°26·5'	5°48·5'W	W	24
Applecross Forest	Highld	NG7547	57°27·7'	5°44·6'W	X	24
Applecross Ho	Highld	NG7145	57°26·5'	5°48·5'W	X	24
Appledene	I of M	SC3080	54°11·5'	4°35·9'W	X	95
Appledore	Corn	SX3268	50°29·5'	4°21·7'W	X	201
Appledore	Devon	SS4630	51°3·2'	4°11·5'W	T	180
Appledore	Devon	ST0614	50°55·3'	3°19·9'W	T	181
Appledore	Kent	TQ9529	51°1·9'	0°47·3'E	T	189
Appledore Fm	Devon	SS7401	50°47·9'	3°46·9'W	FM	191
Appledore Fm	Devon	SX6197	50°45·6'	3°57·9'W	FM	191
Appledore Fm	Devon	SY1797	50°46·2'	3°10·2'W	FM	192,193
Appledore Heath	Kent	TQ9530	51°2·4'	0°47·3'E	T	189
Appledore Hill	Devon	SX6197	50°45·6'	3°57·9'W	H	191
Appledore Sta	Kent	TQ9729	51°1·8'	0°49·0'E	X	189
Apple Down	W Susx	SU7915	50°56·0'	0°52·2'W	H	197
Apple Fm	N Som	ST3762	51°21·5'	2°53·9'W	FM	182
Appleford	Oxon	SU5293	51°38·2'	1°14·5'W	T	164,174
Applegarth	Cumbr	NY1750	54°50·5'	3°17·1'W	X	85
Applegarth	Cumbr	SD6284	54°15·3'	2°34·6'W	X	97
Applegarth	N Yks	NZ1201	54°24·5'	1°48·5'W	X	92
Applegarth	N Yks	NZ7403	54°25·3'	0°51·2'W	X	94
Applegarth Manor	N Yks	NZ3903	54°25·5'	1°23·5'W	X	93
Applegarthtown	D & G	NY1084	55°8·8'	3°24·3'W	T	78

Apple Grove Fm	N Yks	NZ5108	54°28·1'	1°12·4'W	FM	93
Applehaigh Fm	Wakf	SE3512	53°36·4'	1°27·8'W	FM	110,111
Applehead	Cumbr	SD1783	54°14·4'	3°16·0'W	X	96
Applehouse Hill	Win & Maid	SU8382	51°32·1'	0°47·8'W	T	175
Applemore	Hants	SU3907	50°51·9'	1°26·4'W	T	196
Apple Orchard Fm	Leic	SP3998	52°34·9'	1°25·1'W	FM	140
Applepie Hill	W Berks	SU5379	51°30·7'	1°13·8'W	X	174
Appleridge Fm	Glos	ST6695	51°39·4'	2°29·1'W	FM	162
Applesham Fm	W Susx	TQ1907	50°51·2'	0°18·2'W	FM	198
Appleshaw	Hants	SU3048	51°14·1'	1°33·8'W	T	185
Appleside Hill	Cumbr	NY5932	54°41·1'	2°37·7'W	H	91
Appleslade Inclosure	Hants	SU1808	50°52·5'	1°44·3'W	F	195
Applethwaite	Cumbr	NY2625	54°37·1'	3°8·3'W	T	89,90
Applethwaite Common	Cumbr	NY4202	54°24·9'	2°53·2'W	X	90
Applethwaite Gill	Cumbr	NY2626	54°37·7'	3°8·4'W	W	89,90
Appleton	Halton	SJ5186	53°22·4'	2°43·8'W	T	108
Appleton	Oxon	SP4401	51°42·6'	1°21·4'W	T	164
Appleton Dale	Notts	SK5853	53°4·5'	1°7·6'W	F	120
Appleton Fm	Kent	TQ8142	51°9·1'	0°35·7'E	FM	188
Appleton Fm	Norf	TF7027	52°49·1'	0°31·8'E	FM	132
Appleton-le-Moors	N Yks	SE7387	54°16·6'	0°52·3'W	T	94,100
Appleton-le-Street	N Yks	SE7373	54°9·1'	0°52·5'W	T	100
Appleton Lower Common	Oxon	SP4200	51°42·1'	1°23·1'W	F	164
Appleton Manor	Kent	TR3447	51°10·7'	1°21·3'E	X	179
Appleton Moss	Warr	SJ6482	53°20·3'	2°32·0'W	X	109
Appleton Park	Warr	SJ6184	53°21·3'	2°34·7'W	T	109
Appleton Resr	Warr	SJ6084	53°21·3'	2°35·7'W	W	109
Appleton Roebuck	N Yks	SE5542	53°52·5'	1°9·4'W	T	105
Appleton Thorn	Warr	SJ6383	53°20·8'	2°32·9'W	T	109
Appleton Upper Common	Oxon	SU4399	51°41·5'	1°22·3'W	F	164
Appleton Wiske	N Yks	NZ3904	54°26·0'	1°23·5'W	T	93
Appletree	Cumbr	NY5965	54°58·9'	2°38·0'W	X	86
Appletree	Northnts	SP4849	52°8·5'	1°17·5'W	X	151
Appletree	Shrops	SO3296	52°33·7'	2°59·8'W	X	137
Appletree Banks	I Scilly	SV8913	49°56·4'	6°19·7'W	X	203
Appletree Eyot	Oxon	SU6874	51°27·9'	1°0·9'W	X	175
Apple Tree Fm	Notts	SK7292	53°25·4'	0°54·6'W	FM	112
Apple Tree Fm	York	SE6353	53°58·4'	1°2·0'W	FM	105,106
Appletreehall	Scot Bord	NT5217	55°26·9'	2°45·1'W	T	79
Appletree Hill	Staffs	SJ8820	52°46·9'	2°10·3'W	X	127
Appletree Ho	N Yks	SE1984	54°15·3'	1°42·1'W	X	99
Appletree Holme	Cumbr	SD2788	54°17·2'	3°6·9'W	X	96,97
Apple Tree Hurst Fm	N Yks	SE5896	54°21·6'	1°6·0'W	FM	100
Appletree Point	I Scilly	SV8814	49°56·9'	6°20·6'W	X	203
Appletree Thwaite	N Yks	SD8997	54°22·3'	2°9·7'W	X	98
Appletreewick	N Yks	SE0560	54°2·4'	1°55·0'W	T	98
Appletreewick Moor	N Yks	SE0664	54°4·6'	1°54·1'W	X	99
Appletreewick Pasture	N Yks	SE0562	54°3·5'	1°55·0'W	X	98
Appletree Worth Beck	Cumbr	SD2593	54°19·9'	3°8·8'W	W	96
Applewithy Rhyne	Somer	ST3151	51°15·5'	2°58·9'W	W	182
Appley	I of W	SZ6092	50°43·7'	1°8·6'W	T	196
Appley	Somer	ST0721	50°59·1'	3°19·1'W	T	181
Appley Bridge	Lancs	SD5209	53°34·8'	2°43·1'W	T	108
Appley Corner	Beds	TL1041	52°3·6'	0°23·3'W	X	153
Applin's Fm	Dorset	ST8415	50°56·3'	2°13·3'W	FM	183
Approach Fm	N Yks	SE6239	53°50·9'	1°3·0'W	FM	105
Apps Hollow	Kent	TQ5052	51°15·1'	0°9·4'E	X	188
Appspond	Herts	TL1105	51°44·2'	0°23·2'W	X	166
Appuldurcombe Ho	I of W	SZ5479	50°36·7'	1°13·8'W	A	196
Apridge Fm	Devon	SX8587	50°40·5'	3°37·3'W	FM	191
Apron Full of Stones	N Yks	SD7078	54°12·1'	2°27·2'W	X	98
Apron Full of Stones (Cairn)	N Yks	SD7078	54°12·1'	2°27·2'W	A	98
Apse Heath	I of W	SZ5683	50°38·9'	1°12·1'W	T	196
Apse Manor Fm	I of W	SZ5681	50°37·8'	1°12·1'W	FM	196
Apsey Green	Suff	TM2763	52°13·3'	1°19·8'E	T	156
Apshill Copse	Wilts	SU2063	51°22·2'	1°42·4'W	F	174
Apsley	Herts	TL0505	51°44·3'	0°28·4'W	T	166
Apsley	Kent	TQ8639	51°7·4'	0°39·9'E	X	189
Apsley Bury Fm	Beds	TL1132	51°58·8'	0°22·6'W	FM	166
Apsley End	Herts	TL1232	51°58·7'	0°21·8'W	T	166
Apsley Fm	Hants	SU4247	51°13·5'	1°23·5'W	FM	185
Apsley Fm	Surrey	TQ4041	51°9·3'	0°0·5'E	FM	187
Apsley Fm	W Susx	TQ1119	50°57·8'	0°24·8'W	FM	198
Apsley Manor Fm	Herts	TL0504	51°43·7'	0°28·4'W	FM	166
Apton Hall Fm	Essex	TQ8892	51°35·9'	0°43·3'E	FM	178
Aptor	Devon	SX8563	50°27·6'	3°36·8'W	X	202
Apuldram	W Susx	SU8403	50°49·5'	0°48·1'W	T	197
Aqualate Mere	Staffs	SJ7720	52°46·9'	2°20·1'W	W	127
Aqualate Park	Staffs	SJ7719	52°46·3'	2°20·1'W	X	127
Aquamoor	Staffs	SJ8314	52°43·6'	2°14·7'W	X	127
Aqueduct	Wrekin	SJ6805	52°38·7'	2°28·0'W	T	127
Aquherton	Aberd	NJ7812	57°12·2'	2°21·4'W	X	38
Aquhorsk	Aberd	NJ8010	57°11·1'	2°19·4'W	X	38
Aquhorthies	Aberd	NO9096	57°3·6'	2°9·4'W	X	38,45
Aquhythie	Aberd	NJ7418	57°15·4'	2°25·4'W	T	38
Aqvae Arnemetiae (Buxton)	Derby	SK0673	53°15·5'	1°54·2'W	R	119
Aqvae Svlis (Bath)	Bath & NE Somer	ST7464	51°22·7'	2°22·0'W	R	172
Arabella	Highld	NH8075	57°45·2'	4°0·5'W	T	21
Ara Burn	S Lanak	NS7338	55°37·4'	4°0·6'W	W	71
Araburn Rig	S Lanak	NS7239	55°37·9'	4°1·6'W	X	71
Ara Clett	Shetld	HU3152	60°15·3'	1°25·9'W	H	3
Araid	Highld	NG7958	57°33·7'	5°41·2'W	X	24
Arail	Blae Gw	SO2103	51°43·4'	3°8·2'W	X	171
Aram Grange	N Yks	SE4074	54°9·9'	1°22·8'W	X	99
Aramstone	Heref	SO5529	51°57·7'	2°38·9'W	X	149
Aran	Powys	SJ1726	52°49·8'	3°13·5'W	X	125
Aran Benllyn	Gwyn	SH8624	52°48·3'	3°41·1'W	H	124,125
Aran Fach	Powys	SJ1725	52°49·2'	3°13·5'W	X	125
Aran Fawddwy	Gwyn	SH8622	52°47·3'	3°41·0'W	H	124,125
Arant Haw	Cumbr	SD6694	54°20·7'	2°31·0'W	H	98
Ararat	Aberd	NO7966	56°47·4'	2°20·2'W	X	45
Arbigland	D & G	NX9857	54°54·1'	3°35·0'W	X	84
Arbikie	Angus	NO6650	56°38·7'	2°32·8'W	X	54
Arbirlot	Angus	NO6040	56°33·3'	2°38·6'W	T	54
Arborfield	Wok	SU7567	51°24·1'	0°54·9'W	T	175
Arborfield Court	Wok	SU7566	51°23·5'	0°54·9'W	X	175
Arborfield Cross	Wok	SU7667	51°24·0'	0°54·1'W	T	175

Arborfield Garrison	Wok	SU7665	51°23·0'	0°54·1'W	T	175
Arbor Low	Derby	SK1663	53°10·1'	1°45·2'W	X	119
Arbor Low (Henge)	Derby	SK1663	53°10·1'	1°45·2'W	A	119
Arbory Hill	S Lanak	NS9423	55°29·6'	3°40·2'W	H	71,72
Arbour	Arg & Bt	NR3897	56°5·9'	6°12·3'W	X	61
Arbour	Lancs	SD5649	53°56·4'	2°39·8'W	X	102
Arboures Fm	Cambs	TL3093	52°31·4'	0°4·6'W	FM	142
Arbour Fm	Lancs	SD6240	53°51·5'	2°34·3'W	FM	102,103
Arbour Ho	Durham	NZ2542	54°46·6'	1°36·3'W	X	88
Arbours, The	Northnts	SP7863	52°15·8'	0°51·0'W	X	152
Arbour, The	Staffs	SJ7137	52°56·0'	2°25·5'W	X	127
Arbourthorne	Sheff	SK3785	53°21·9'	1°26·2'W	T	110,111
Arbour Tree Fm	Sol	SP2073	52°21·5'	1°42·0'W	FM	139
Arbrack	D & G	NX4537	54°42·5'	4°23·9'W	X	83
Arbroath	Angus	NO6441	56°33·8'	2°34·7'W	T	54
Arbrook Common	Surrey	TQ1463	51°21·5'	0°21·4'W	X	176,187
Arbrook Fm	Surrey	TQ1462	51°21·0'	0°21·4'W	FM	176,187
Arbury	Cambs	TL4460	52°13·4'	0°6·9'E	T	154
Arbury	Warr	SJ6192	53°25·6'	2°34·8'W	X	109
Arbury	Warw	SP3389	52°30·1'	1°30·4'W	A	140
Arbury Banks	Herts	TL2638	52°1·8'	0°9·4'W	A	153
Arbury Banks	Northnts	SP4948	52°7·9'	1°16·7'W	A	151
Arbury Hill	Northnts	SP5458	52°13·3'	1°12·2'W	H	152
Arbury Mill Fm	Warw	SP3488	52°29·6'	1°29·6'W	FM	140
Arbury Park	Warw	SP3389	52°30·1'	1°30·4'W	X	140
Arbury Wood	Herts	TL3020	51°52·0'	0°6·3'W	F	166
Arbuthnott	Aberd	NO7975	56°52·2'	2°20·2'W	T	45
Arbuthnott Ho	Aberd	NO7975	56°52·2'	2°20·2'W	X	45
Arcabhi	Highld	NN0592	56°58·9'	5°12·1'W	X	33
Arcadia	Heref	SO3526	51°56·0'	2°56·3'W	X	161
Arcan Mains	Highld	NH5053	57°32·8'	4°29·9'W	X	26
Arcan Muir	Highld	NH4852	57°32·2'	4°31·9'W	X	26
Archaeological Trail	Derby	SK5170	53°13·7'	1°13·8'W	X	120
Archaeological Way	Derby	SK5270	53°13·7'	1°12·9'W	X	120
Archagour	Highld	NH9346	57°29·8'	3°46·7'W	X	27
Archallagan Plantation	I of M	SC3078	54°10·4'	4°35·9'W	F	95
Archan River	Arg & Bt	NN0821	56°20·8'	5°6·0'W	W	50,56
Archballoch	Aberd	NJ5614	57°13·1'	2°43·3'W	X	37
Archbank	D & G	NT0906	55°20·6'	3°25·7'W	X	78
Archdeacon Newton	Darl	NZ2517	54°33·1'	1°36·4'W	T	93
Archenfield	Heref	SO2642	52°4·5'	3°4·4'W	T	148,161
Archerbeck	D & G	NY4177	55°5·3'	2°55·0'W	X	85
Archer Beck	D & G	NY4178	55°5·8'	2°55·0'W	W	85
Archer Cleugh	Northum	NY6396	55°15·7'	2°34·5'W	X	80
Archerfield	E Loth	NT5084	56°3·0'	2°47·7'W	X	66
Archer Hill	Cumbr	NY6504	54°26·1'	2°32·0'W	X	91
Archer Moss	Cumbr	NY6300	54°23·9'	2°33·8'W	X	91
Archer's Drove Fm	Peterb	TF3106	52°38·4'	0°3·4'W	FM	142
Archers Fm	Suff	TL9344	52°3·9'	0°49·3'E	FM	155
Archer's Fm	Wilts	SU0692	51°37·8'	1°54·4'W	FM	163,173
Archers Hall	Cumbr	SD6591	54°19·0'	2°31·9'W	X	97
Archer's Wood	Cambs	TL1780	52°24·6'	0°16·4'W	F	142
Archerton	Devon	SX6379	50°35·9'	3°55·8'W	X	191
Arches	Heref	SO4063	52°16·0'	2°52·4'W	X	137,148
Arches Fm	E Susx	TQ4612	50°53·6'	0°4·9'E	FM	198
Arches Fm	Wilts	ST9286	51°34·6'	2°6·5'W	FM	173
Arches Hall	Herts	TL3920	51°51·9'	0°1·5'E	X	166
Arches Manor	E Susx	TQ4919	50°57·3'	0°7·7'E	X	199
Arches, The	Northnts	SP8254	52°10·9'	0°47·6'W	X	152
Arch Fm	Suff	TL9664	52°14·6'	0°52·7'E	FM	155
Archford Moor	Staffs	SK1158	53°7·4'	1°49·7'W	X	119
Archiebald Gair Head	S Lanak	NS9814	55°24·8'	3°36·2'W	H	78
Archie Grain	D & G	NT2804	55°19·7'	3°7·7'W	W	79
Archie Hill	D & G	NT2906	55°20·8'	3°6·7'W	H	79
Archie's Hill	D & G	NT0510	55°22·7'	3°29·5'W	H	78
Archie's Pike	Cumbr	NY6278	55°5·9'	2°35·3'W	X	86
Archiestown	Moray	NJ2344	57°29·0'	3°16·6'W	T	28
Arch, The	Cered	SN7675	52°21·8'	3°48·9'W	X	135,147
Arch Tor	Devon	SX6378	50°35·4'	3°55·7'W	X	191
Archwood	D & G	NY0988	55°10·9'	3°25·3'W	X	78
Archy's Rigg	Northum	NY7083	55°8·7'	2°27·8'W	X	80
Arclid	Ches	SJ7862	53°9·5'	2°19·3'W	T	118
Arclid Cottage Fm	Ches	SJ7861	53°9·0'	2°19·3'W	FM	118
Arclid Green	Ches	SJ7861	53°9·0'	2°19·3'W	T	118
Arcot Hall	Northum	NZ2475	55°4·4'	1°37·0'W	X	88
Arcow Quarry	N Yks	SD8070	54°7·8'	2°17·9'W	X	98
Arda Beaga	N Eil	NB0009	57°58·4'	7°4·0'W	H	13
Ardachadh	Highld	NC8957	58°29·5'	3°53·8'W	X	10
Ardachearanbeg	Arg & Bt	NS0085	56°1·2'	5°12·1'W	X	55
Ardacheranmor	Arg & Bt	NS0087	56°2·3'	5°12·2'W	X	55
Ardachie	D & G	NX3263	54°56·3'	4°36·9'W	X	82
Ardachie Fell	D & G	NX3264	54°56·8'	4°37·0'W	H	82
Ardachoil	Arg & Bt	NM7030	56°24·6'	5°43·3'W	X	49
Ardachu	Highld	NC6703	58°0·0'	4°14·6'W	T	16
Ardachuple Fm	Arg & Bt	NS0179	55°58·0'	5°10·9'W	FM	63
Ardachuple Lodge	Arg & Bt	NS0180	55°58·6'	5°10·9'W	X	55,63
Ardachy	Arg & Bt	NM3719	56°17·7'	6°14·6'W	X	48
Ardachy	Arg & Bt	NM9535	56°28·0'	5°19·2'W	X	49
Ardachy Lodge	Highld	NH3707	57°7·8'	4°41·1'W	X	34
Ardailly	Arg & Bt	NR6450	55°41·4'	5°44·9'W	X	62
Ardalanish	Arg & Bt	NM3719	56°17·7'	6°14·6'W	T	48
Ardalanish Bay	Arg & Bt	NM3718	56°17·2'	6°14·5'W	W	48
Ardale Beck	Cumbr	NY6534	54°42·2'	2°32·2'W	W	91
Ardale Sch	Thurr	TQ5980	51°30·0'	0°17·8'E	X	177
Ardallie	Aberd	NK0039	57°26·7'	1°59·5'W	T	30
Ardallie Bog	Aberd	NJ9940	57°27·3'	2°0·5'W	X	30
Ardalum Ho	Arg & Bt	NM4340	56°29·2'	6°10·0'W	X	47,48
Arda Móra	N Eil	NB0208	57°58·0'	7°1·9'W	H	13
Ardanaiseig	Arg & Bt	NN0824	56°22·4'	5°6·1'W	T	50
Ardan Breac	Aberd	NJ3806	57°8·7'	3°1·0'W	X	37
Ardaneaskan	Highld	NG8335	57°21·5'	5°36·0'W	T	24
Ard-an-eoin	N Eil	NF8147	57°24·3'	7°18·3'W	X	22
Ardanstur	Arg & Bt	NM8213	56°15·8'	5°30·8'W	X	55
Ardantiobairt	Highld	NM6454	56°37·4'	5°50·4'W	X	49
Ard an Tiobairt	Highld	NM6455	56°37·9'	5°50·4'W	X	49
Ard an Torrain	Highld	NG5849	57°28·3'	6°1·7'W	X	24
Ardantrive	Arg & Bt	NM8430	56°25·0'	5°29·7'W	X	49
Ardantrive Bay	Arg & Bt	NM8430	56°25·0'	5°29·7'W	W	49
Ard an t-Sabhail	Highld	NG3233	57°18·8'	6°26·6'W	X	32
Ardardan	Arg & Bt	NS3378	55°58·2'	4°40·1'W	X	63

Ardarg	Aberd	NJ9735	57°24·6'	2°2·5'W	X	30
Ardargie Mains	Pth & Kin	NO0814	56°18·8'	3°28·8'W	X	58
Ardarroch	Highld	NG8339	57°23·6'	5°36·2'W	T	24
Ardban	Highld	NG6939	57°23·2'	5°50·2'W	X	24,32
Ard Beag	Highld	NG2161	57°33·4'	6°39·4'W	X	23
Ard Beag	Highld	NG2536	57°20·2'	6°33·7'W	H	23
Ardbeg	Arg & Bt	NR4146	55°38·6'	6°6·5'W	T	60
Ardbeg	Arg & Bt	NS0866	55°51·2'	5°3·6'W	T	63
Ardbeg	Arg & Bt	NS1583	56°0·5'	4°57·6'W	X	56
Ardbeg Hill	Arg & Bt	NS0577	55°57·0'	5°7·0'W	X	63
Ardbeg Point	Arg & Bt	NS0678	55°57·6'	5°6·0'W	X	63
Ardbeg Point	Arg & Bt	NS0867	55°51·7'	5°3·6'W	X	63
Ardbennie	Pth & Kin	NN9421	56°22·4'	3°42·5'W	X	52,53,58
Ardbhan Craigs	Arg & Bt	NM8428	56°24·0'	5°29·6'W	X	49
Ard Bheinn	N Ayr	NR9432	55°32·6'	5°15·5'W	H	68,69
Ardblae	Pth & Kin	NO0834	56°29·6'	3°29·2'W	X	52,53
Ardblair	Highld	NH5036	57°23·6'	4°29·3'W	X	26
Ardblair Castle	Pth & Kin	NO1644	56°35·1'	3°21·6'W	A	53
Ardbrecknish Ho	Arg & Bt	NN0621	56°20·8'	5°7·9'W	X	50,56
Ardcanny	Moray	NJ2649	57°31·8'	3°13·7'W	X	28
Ardcanny Wood	Moray	NJ2549	57°31·8'	3°14·7'W	F	28
Ard Caol	Arg & Bt	NR3665	55°48·6'	6°12·4'W	X	60,61
Ard Caol	N Eil	NB2301	57°55·0'	6°40·2'W	X	14
Ard Caol Urgha	N Eil	NG1799	57°53·7'	6°46·1'W	X	14
Ardcarnaig	Stir	NN4518	56°20·0'	4°30·0'W	X	57
Ardcastle Wood	Arg & Bt	NR9491	56°4·3'	5°18·1'W	F	55
Ardchattan Priory	Arg & Bt	NM9734	56°27·5'	5°17·2'W	A	49
Ardchiavaig	Arg & Bt	NM3818	56°17·2'	6°13·6'W	X	48
Ardchoirc	Arg & Bt	NM8227	56°23·4'	5°31·5'W	X	49
Ardchonnel	Arg & Bt	NM9032	56°26·3'	5°23·9'W	X	49
Ardchonnell	Arg & Bt	NM9812	56°15·7'	5°15·3'W	T	55
Ardchrishnish	Arg & Bt	NM4223	56°20·0'	6°10·0'W	X	48
Ardchronie	Highld	NH6188	57°51·9'	4°20·1'W	T	21
Ardchuilk	Highld	NH2638	57°24·2'	4°53·3'W	X	25
Ardchullarie More	Stir	NN5813	56°17·6'	4°17·2'W	T	57
Ardchyle	Stir	NN5229	56°26·1'	4°23·6'W	T	51
Ardchyline Fm	Arg & Bt	NN1106	56°12·8'	5°2·4'W	FM	56
Ardclach	Highld	NH9545	57°29·2'	3°44·6'W	X	27
Ard Clais Shalachar	Highld	NG6851	57°29·7'	5°51·8'W	X	24
Ardconnel	Arg & Bt	NM8931	56°25·7'	5°24·9'W	X	49
Ardconnon	Aberd	NJ7928	57°20·8'	2°20·5'W	X	38
Ard Crags	Cumbr	NY2019	54°33·8'	3°13·8'W	H	89,90
Ardderfin	Carm	SN3215	51°48·7'	4°25·8'W	X	159
Ard-dhubh	Highld	NG7040	57°23·8'	5°49·2'W	X	24
Arddleen	Powys	SJ2515	52°43·9'	3°6·2'W	T	126
Ard Dorch	Highld	NG5728	57°16·9'	6°1·5'W	X	32
Ard Dubh	Highld	NG2759	57°32·6'	6°33·3'W	X	23
Arddwyfaen	Conwy	SH9646	53°0·3'	3°32·6'W	X	116
Ardechive	Highld	NN1490	56°58·1'	5°3·1'W	X	34
Ardeer Mains	N Ayr	NS2742	55°38·7'	4°44·5'W	X	63,70
Ardeley	Herts	TL3027	51°55·8'	0°6·2'W	T	166
Ardeley Bury	Herts	TL3027	51°55·8'	0°6·2'W	X	166
Ardelve	Highld	NG8626	57°16·7'	5°32·6'W	T	33
Ardelve Point	Highld	NG8726	57°16·8'	5°31·6'W	X	33
Arden	Arg & Bt	NS3684	56°1·5'	4°37·5'W	T	56
Arden	C of Glas	NS5459	55°48·4'	4°19·3'W	T	64
Ardencaple Fm	Arg & Bt	NS2884	56°1·3'	4°45·1'W	FM	56
Ardencaple House	Arg & Bt	NM7619	56°18·9'	5°36·9'W	X	55
Ardencote	Warw	SP2065	52°17·2'	1°42·0'W	X	151
Ardendee	D & G	NX6952	54°51·0'	4°2·0'W	X	83,84
Ardendrain	Highld	NH5037	57°24·2'	4°29·3'W	T	26
Arden Fleets	E Yorks	SE9151	53°57·1'	0°36·4'W	X	106
Arden Great Moor	N Yks	SE5092	54°19·5'	1°13·5'W	X	100
Arden Green	Surrey	TQ3945	51°11·5'	0°0·3'W	X	187
Arden Hall	N Yks	SE5190	54°18·4'	1°12·6'W	X	100
Arden Hall	Thurr	TQ6783	51°31·5'	0°24·8'E	X	177,178
Arden Hill Fm	Warw	SP1859	52°14·0'	1°43·8'W	FM	151
Arden Ho	Arg & Bt	NS3684	56°1·5'	4°37·5'W	X	56
Arden Ho	Ches	SJ7683	53°20·8'	2°21·2'W	X	109
Arden Ho	Sol	SP2180	52°25·3'	1°41·1'W	X	139
Ardennish	N Eil	NF9274	57°39·3'	7°9·4'W	X	18
Arden Park	Stock	SJ9191	53°25·2'	2°7·7'W	T	109
Ardenrun	Surrey	TQ3745	51°11·5'	0°2·0'W	X	187
Ardensawah	Corn	SW3723	50°3·2'	5°40·1'W	X	203
Ardens Grafton	Warw	SP1154	52°11·3'	1°49·9'W	T	150
Ardentallen	Arg & Bt	NM8323	56°21·2'	5°30·3'W	T	49
Ardentallen Bay	Arg & Bt	NM8423	56°21·3'	5°29·3'W	W	49
Ardentallen Ho	Arg & Bt	NM8323	56°21·2'	5°30·3'W	X	49
Ardentallen Pt	Arg & Bt	NM8222	56°20·7'	5°31·2'W	X	49
Ardentinny	Arg & Bt	NS1887	56°2·7'	4°54·9'W	T	56
Ardentiny	Arg & Bt	NM8841	56°31·1'	5°26·3'W	X	49
Ardentraive	Arg & Bt	NS0374	55°55·4'	5°8·7'W	X	63
Ardeonaig	Stir	NN6635	56°29·5'	4°10·1'W	T	51
Arderne Hall	Ches	SJ5662	53°9·4'	2°39·1'W	X	117
Ardersier	Highld	NH7855	57°34·4'	4°1·9'W	T	27
Ardery	Highld	NM7562	56°42·0'	5°40·1'W	T	40
Ardessie	Highld	NH0589	57°51·1'	5°16·7'W	T	19
Ardeville	Highld	NH7363	57°38·6'	4°7·2'W	X	21,27
Ardevora	Corn	SW8740	50°13·5'	4°58·8'W	X	204
Ardevora Veor	Corn	SW8740	50°13·5'	4°58·8'W	X	204
Ardfad	Arg & Bt	NM7619	56°18·9'	5°36·9'W	X	55
Ardfad Point	Arg & Bt	NM7719	56°18·9'	5°35·9'W	X	55
Ard Farr	Highld	NC7164	58°33·0'	4°12·5'W	H	10
Ardfenaig	Arg & Bt	NM3423	56°19·7'	6°17·7'W	X	48
Ardfern	Arg & Bt	NM8004	56°10·9'	5°32·3'W	T	55
Ardfernal	Arg & Bt	NR5671	55°52·5'	5°53·6'W	T	61
Ardfillan	D & G	NX2155	54°51·7'	4°46·9'W	X	82
Ardfin	Arg & Bt	NR4763	55°47·9'	6°1·8'W	X	60,61
Ardfork	Aberd	NJ8226	57°19·7'	2°17·5'W	X	38
Ardfour	Aberd	NJ6547	57°31·0'	2°34·6'W	X	29
Ard Gairney	Pth & Kin	NT1098	56°10·2'	3°26·5'W	X	58
Ardgaith	Pth & Kin	NO0331	56°27·9'	3°34·0'W	X	52,53
Ardgaith	Pth & Kin	NO2122	56°23·3'	3°16·3'W	X	53,58
Ardganty	Aberd	NJ9837	57°25·7'	2°1·5'W	X	30
Ardgartan	Arg & Bt	NN2702	56°11·0'	4°46·8'W	T	56
Ardgartan Forest	Arg & Bt	NN2602	56°11·0'	4°47·8'W	F	56
Ardgarth	Angus	NO2837	56°31·4'	3°9·8'W	X	53
Ardgathen	Aberd	NJ5616	57°14·2'	2°43·3'W	X	37
Ardgay	Highld	NH5990	57°52·9'	4°22·2'W	T	21
Ardgayhill	Highld	NH5990	57°52·9'	4°22·2'W	T	21
Ardgeith	Aberd	NJ4010	57°10·9'	2°59·1'W	X	37
Ardgenavan	Arg & Bt	NN1711	56°15·6'	4°56·8'W	X	50,56
Ardgheiltinish	N Eil	NF7104	57°0·8'	7°24·8'W	X	31
Ard Ghunel	Highld	NG7011	57°8·2'	5°47·6'W	X	32,33
Ardgie	Pth & Kin	NN9658	56°42·4'	3°41·5'W	X	52,53
Ardgieth	Moray	NJ1525	57°18·7'	3°24·2'W	X	36
Ardgilzean	Moray	NJ1663	57°39·2'	3°24·0'W	X	28
Ardgilzean	Pth & Kin	NO1129	56°26·9'	3°26·2'W	X	53,58
Ardglassie	Aberd	NK0161	57°38·6'	1°58·5'W	X	30
Ardgour	Highld	NM9367	56°45·2'	5°22·7'W	X	40
Ardgour Ho	Highld	NM9963	56°43·2'	5°16·6'W	X	40
Ardgour Hotel	Highld	NN0163	56°43·2'	5°14·7'W	X	41
Ardgowan	Inverc	NS2073	55°55·2'	4°52·4'W	X	63
Ardgowan Point	Inverc	NS1972	55°54·7'	4°53·3'W	X	63
Ardgowse	Aberd	NJ6011	57°11·5'	2°39·3'W	X	37
Ardgrange	Cered	SN5571	52°19·3'	4°7·3'W	X	135
Ardgye	Moray	NJ1563	57°39·2'	3°25·0'W	X	28
Ardgye Ho	Moray	NJ1562	57°38·7'	3°25·0'W	X	28
Ardhainish	N Eil	NF9275	57°39·8'	7°9·5'W	X	18
Ardharnich	Highld	NH1788	57°50·9'	5°4·5'W	T	20
Ardheisker	N Eil	NF7667	57°34·9'	7°24·8'W	T	18
Ardheslaig	Highld	NG7856	57°32·6'	5°42·1'W	T	24
Ard Hill	Highld	NG8226	57°16·6'	5°36·5'W	H	33
Ardhuncart	Aberd	NJ4717	57°14·7'	2°52·2'W	X	37
Ardhuncart Hill	Aberd	NJ4818	57°15·2'	2°51·3'W	H	37
Ardhuncart Lo	Aberd	NJ4817	57°14·7'	2°51·2'W	X	37
Ard Ialltaig	Highld	NG8073	57°41·8'	5°41·0'W	H	19
Ardichoncherr	Highld	NC7005	58°1·2'	4°11·6'W	X	16
Ardiebrown	Aberd	NJ7117	57°14·8'	2°28·4'W	X	38
Ardiecow	Moray	NJ5361	57°38·4'	2°46·8'W	X	29
Ardie Hill	Fife	NO3522	56°23·4'	3°2·7'W	H	54,59
Ardieknowes	Aberd	NJ8949	57°32·1'	2°10·6'W	X	30
Ardieraar	Aberd	NJ5703	57°7·2'	2°42·2'W	X	37
Ardifuir	Arg & Bt	NR7896	56°6·6'	5°33·8'W	T	55
Ardilistry	Arg & Bt	NR4449	55°40·3'	6°3·8'W	X	60
Ardilistry Bay	Arg & Bt	NR4448	55°39·7'	6°3·8'W	W	60
Ardilistry River	Arg & Bt	NR4349	55°40·2'	6°4·8'W	W	60
Ardimannoch	Moray	NJ4450	57°32·5'	2°55·7'W	X	28
Ard Imersay	Arg & Bt	NR4346	55°38·6'	6°4·6'W	X	60
Ardinamir	Arg & Bt	NM7511	56°14·6'	5°37·4'W	T	55
Ardinamir Bay	Arg & Bt	NM7512	56°15·1'	5°37·5'W	W	55
Ardincaple	Conwy	SH7258	53°6·5'	3°54·3'W	X	115
Ardindrean	Highld	NH1588	57°50·9'	5°6·6'W	T	20
Ardingly	W Susx	TQ3429	51°2·9'	0°4·9'W	T	187,198
Ardingly Resr	W Susx	TQ3229	51°2·9'	0°6·6'W	W	187,198
Ardington	Oxon	SU4388	51°35·6'	1°22·4'W	T	174
Ardington Down	Oxon	SU4385	51°34·0'	1°22·4'W	X	174
Ardington Ho	Oxon	SU4388	51°35·6'	1°22·4'W	X	174
Ardington Wick	Oxon	SU4389	51°36·1'	1°22·4'W	T	174
Ardinn	Aberd	NJ7548	57°31·5'	2°24·6'W	X	29
Ardintigh	Highld	NM7793	56°58·7'	5°39·7'W	X	33,40
Ardintigh Bay	Highld	NM7793	56°58·7'	5°39·7'W	W	33,40
Ardintigh Point	Highld	NM7793	56°58·7'	5°39·7'W	X	33,40
Ardintoul	Highld	NG8324	57°15·6'	5°35·4'W	T	33
Ardintoul Bay	Highld	NG8324	57°15·6'	5°35·4'W	W	33
Ardintoul Point	Highld	NG8324	57°15·6'	5°35·4'W	X	33
Ardioch	Moray	NJ4154	57°34·6'	2°58·7'W	X	28
Ardionra	Arg & Bt	NM2825	56°20·6'	6°23·7'W	X	48
Ardivot	Moray	NJ2267	57°41·4'	3°18·0'W	X	28
Ardjachie	Highld	NH7584	57°50·0'	4°5·8'W	X	21
Ardjachie Point	Highld	NH7585	57°50·5'	4°5·9'W	X	21
Ardkinglas Ho	Arg & Bt	NN1710	56°15·1'	4°56·8'W	X	50,56
Ardlair	Aberd	NJ5528	57°20·7'	2°44·4'W	X	37
Ardlair	Aberd	NO6793	57°1·9'	2°32·2'W	X	38,45
Ardlair	Highld	NG9075	57°43·2'	5°31·1'W	X	19
Ardlair Wood	Aberd	NJ5818	57°15·3'	2°41·3'W	F	37
Ardlamey	Arg & Bt	NR6348	55°40·3'	5°45·7'W	X	62
Ardlamont Bay	Arg & Bt	NR9765	55°50·4'	5°14·1'W	W	62
Ardlamont Ho	Arg & Bt	NR9865	55°50·4'	5°13·1'W	X	62
Ardlamont Point	Arg & Bt	NR9963	55°49·4'	5°12·1'W	X	62
Ardlarach	Arg & Bt	NM7309	56°13·4'	5°39·3'W	X	55
Ardlarach	Arg & Bt	NM8005	56°11·5'	5°32·3'W	X	55
Ardlarach	Arg & Bt	NR2958	55°44·6'	6°18·7'W	X	60
Ardlarach	Highld	NH7681	57°48·4'	4°4·7'W	X	21
Ardlarach	Pth & Kin	NN5358	56°41·7'	4°23·6'W	X	42,51
Ardlaw	Aberd	NK0349	57°32·1'	1°56·5'W	X	30
Ardlawhill	Aberd	NJ8762	57°39·1'	2°12·6'W	T	30
Ardlebank	Pth & Kin	NO1054	56°40·4'	3°27·7'W	X	53
Ardleigh	Essex	TM0529	51°55·5'	0°59·3'E	T	168
Ardleigh Green	Hav	TQ5389	51°35·0'	0°12·9'E	T	177
Ardleigh Heath	Essex	TM0430	51°56·1'	0°58·5'E	T	168
Ardleigh Park	Essex	TM0527	51°54·4'	0°59·2'E	X	168
Ardleigh Reservoir	Essex	TM0328	51°55·0'	0°57·5'E	W	168
Ardleish	Arg & Bt	NN3215	56°18·1'	4°42·5'W	X	50,56
Ardler	Aberd	NJ4216	57°14·1'	2°57·2'W	X	37
Ardler	Pth & Kin	NO2641	56°33·6'	3°11·8'W	T	53
Ardlethen	Aberd	NJ9131	57°22·4'	2°8·5'W	X	30
Ardlewie	Moray	NJ3732	57°22·7'	3°2·4'W	X	37
Ardley	Oxon	SP5427	51°56·6'	1°12·5'W	T	164
Ardley End	Essex	TL5214	51°48·5'	0°12·7'E	T	167
Ardlochan	S Ayr	NS2208	55°20·3'	4°48·0'W	X	70,76
Ardlogie	Aberd	NJ7837	57°25·6'	2°21·5'W	X	29,30
Ardlogie Ho	Fife	NO4021	56°22·9'	2°57·9'W	X	54,59
Ardlui	Arg & Bt	NN3115	56°18·1'	4°43·4'W	T	50,56
Ardlussa	Arg & Bt	NR6487	56°1·3'	5°46·8'W	X	55,61
Ardlussa Bay	Arg & Bt	NR6588	56°1·9'	5°45·9'W	W	55,61
Ardmachron	Aberd	NJ9861	57°38·6'	2°1·5'W	X	30
Ardmachron	Aberd	NK0937	57°25·7'	1°50·6'W	X	30
Ardmaddy Bay	Arg & Bt	NM7815	56°16·8'	5°34·7'W	W	55
Ardmaddy Castle	Arg & Bt	NM7816	56°17·3'	5°34·8'W	X	55
Ardmair	Highld	NH1198	57°56·1'	5°11·1'W	T	19
Ardmaleish	Arg & Bt	NS0769	55°52·8'	5°4·7'W	X	63
Ardmaleish Point	Arg & Bt	NS0769	55°52·8'	5°4·7'W	X	63
Ardmannoch	D & G	NX7373	55°2·4'	3°58·8'W	X	77,84
Ardmannoch Flow	D & G	NX7373	55°2·4'	3°58·8'W	X	77,84
Ardmarnock Bay	Arg & Bt	NR9072	55°54·0'	5°21·1'W	W	62
Ardmarnock House	Arg & Bt	NR9172	55°54·0'	5°20·1'W	X	62
Ardmay	Arg & Bt	NN2802	56°11·0'	4°45·8'W	T	56
Ardmeallie Ho	Aberd	NJ5950	57°32·6'	2°40·6'W	X	29
Ardmeanach	Aberd	NO3594	57°2·2'	3°3·8'W	X	37,44
Ardmedden	Aberd	NJ8032	57°22·9'	2°19·5'W	X	29,30
Ardmenach	Arg & Bt	NM4428	56°22·8'	6°8·4'W	X	48
Ardmenish	Arg & Bt	NR5773	55°53·6'	5°52·8'W	T	61
Ard Mheall	Highld	NM3497	56°59·5'	6°22·3'W	H	39
Ardmhór	N Eil	NF7103	57°0·3'	7°24·7'W	T	31
Ardmiddle Home Fm	Aberd	NJ6849	57°32·1'	2°31·6'W	FM	29
Ardmiddle Mains	Aberd	NJ6947	57°31·0'	2°30·6'W	X	29
Ardmillan Castle	S Ayr	NX1694	55°12·6'	4°53·1'W	X	76
Ardminish	Arg & Bt	NR6448	55°40·3'	5°44·8'W	T	62
Ardminish Bay	Arg & Bt	NR6548	55°40·4'	5°43·8'W	W	62
Ardminish Hill	Arg & Bt	NR7360	55°47·1'	5°36·8'W	H	62
Ardminish Point	Arg & Bt	NR6649	55°40·9'	5°42·9'W	X	62
Ardmolich	Highld	NM7172	56°47·3'	5°44·5'W	T	40
Ardmolich Wood	Highld	NM7071	56°46·7'	5°45·4'W	F	40
Ard Mór	Arg & Bt	NL9947	56°31·4'	6°53·2'W	X	46
Ard Mór	Arg & Bt	NM5743	56°31·2'	5°56·6'W	X	47,48
Ard Mòr	Highld	NG2160	57°32·9'	6°39·4'W	X	23
Ardmore	Aberd	NJ8925	57°19·2'	2°10·5'W	X	38
Ardmore	Arg & Bt	NM4758	56°39·0'	6°7·2'W	X	47
Ardmore	Arg & Bt	NM7927	56°23·3'	5°34·4'W	X	49
Ardmore	Arg & Bt	NR4650	55°40·9'	6°2·0'W	X	60
Ardmore	Arg & Bt	NS3178	55°58·2'	4°42·0'W	X	63
Ardmore	Ches	SJ4669	53°13·2'	2°48·1'W	X	117
Ardmore	Highld	NC2051	58°24·9'	5°4·4'W	X	9
Ardmore	Highld	NG2841	57°23·0'	6°31·1'W	T	23
Ardmore	Highld	NH7086	57°50·9'	4°11·0'W	T	21
Ardmore Bay	Arg & Bt	NM4658	56°39·0'	6°8·2'W	W	47
Ardmore Bay	Highld	NG2260	57°32·9'	6°38·4'W	W	23
Ard More Mangersta	N Eil	NB0032	58°10·8'	7°5·8'W	X	13
Ardmore Point	Arg & Bt	NM4759	56°39·5'	6°7·3'W	X	47
Ardmore Point	Arg & Bt	NR4750	55°40·9'	6°1·0'W	X	60
Ardmore Point	Highld	NC1851	58°24·8'	5°6·5'W	X	9
Ardmore Point	Highld	NC7666	58°34·1'	4°7·4'W	X	10
Ardmore Point	Highld	NG2159	57°32·4'	6°39·3'W	X	23
Ardmore Point	Highld	NH7087	57°51·5'	4°11·0'W	X	21
Ardmucknish Bay	Arg & Bt	NM8937	56°28·9'	5°25·2'W	W	49
Ardmurdo Ho	Aberd	NJ7918	57°15·4'	2°20·4'W	X	38
Ard na Cailc	Highld	NH7486	57°50·9'	4°6·9'W	X	21
Ardnackaig	Arg & Bt	NR7490	56°3·2'	5°37·3'W	X	55
Ardnaclach	Arg & Bt	NM9443	56°32·3'	5°20·6'W	X	49
Ard na Claise Móire	Highld	NG6852	57°30·2'	5°51·9'W	X	24
Ardnacross	Arg & Bt	NM5449	56°34·4'	5°59·9'W	X	47,48
Ardnacross	Arg & Bt	NR7626	55°28·8'	5°32·3'W	X	68,69
Ardnacross Bay	Arg & Bt	NR7624	55°27·8'	5°32·2'W	W	68,69
Ard na Cùile	Arg & Bt	NM8225	56°22·3'	5°31·4'W	X	49
Ardnadam	Arg & Bt	NS1780	55°58·9'	4°55·6'W	T	63
Ardnaff	Highld	NG8835	57°21·6'	5°31·0'W	T	24
Ard na Gailich	Arg & Bt	NN1207	56°13·4'	5°1·5'W	X	56
Ardnagoine	Highld	NB9908	58°1·2'	5°23·7'W	T	15
Ardnagowan	Arg & Bt	NN0904	56°11·7'	5°4·3'W	X	56
Ardnagrask	Highld	NH5149	57°30·7'	4°28·8'W	T	26
Ardnahein	Arg & Bt	NS1993	56°6·0'	4°54·2'W	X	56
Ardnahein	Arg & Bt	NS2093	56°6·0'	4°53·2'W	X	56
Ardnahoe	Arg & Bt	NR4271	55°52·0'	6°7·0'W	X	60,61
Ardnahoe	Arg & Bt	NS0657	55°46·3'	5°5·1'W	X	63
Ardnahoe Loch	Arg & Bt	NR4271	55°52·0'	6°7·0'W	W	60,61
Ardnambuth	Highld	NM7283	56°53·2'	5°44·1'W	X	40
Ardnameacan	Highld	NG7114	57°9·8'	5°46·8'W	X	33
Ardnamoil	S Ayr	NX1776	55°2·9'	4°51·5'W	X	76
Ardnamurach	Highld	NM8293	56°58·9'	5°34·8'W	X	33,40
Ardnamurchan	Highld	NM5267	56°44·0'	6°2·8'W	X	47
Ardnandave Hill	Stir	NN5612	56°17·0'	4°19·1'W	H	57
Ard nan Eireachd	Highld	NG3758	57°32·4'	6°23·2'W	X	23
Ard na Slaite	Arg & Bt	NN1308	56°13·9'	5°0·6'W	X	56
Ardnastang	Highld	NM8061	56°41·6'	5°35·1'W	T	40
Ardnave	Arg & Bt	NR2873	55°52·7'	6°20·5'W	X	60
Ardnave Loch	Arg & Bt	NR2872	55°52·1'	6°20·4'W	W	60
Ardnave Point	Arg & Bt	NR2974	55°53·2'	6°19·6'W	X	60
Ard Neackie	Highld	NC4459	58°29·7'	4°40·1'W	X	9
Ardneidly	Aberd	NJ6715	57°13·7'	2°32·3'W	X	38
Ardneil	N Ayr	NS1848	55°41·7'	4°53·3'W	X	63
Ardneil Bay	N Ayr	NS1848	55°41·7'	4°53·3'W	W	63
Ardness	Highld	NM6645	56°32·6'	5°47·9'W	X	49
Ard Nev	Highld	NM3498	57°0·1'	6°22·4'W	H	39
Ardnish	Highld	NG6723	57°14·6'	5°51·3'W	X	32
Ardnish	Highld	NM7281	56°52·1'	5°44·0'W	X	40
Ardno	Arg & Bt	NN1408	56°14·0'	4°59·6'W	X	56
Ardnoe Point	Arg & Bt	NR7794	56°5·5'	5°34·6'W	X	55
Ardo	Aberd	NJ8539	57°26·7'	2°14·5'W	T	30
Ardoch	Aberd	NJ3200	57°5·4'	3°6·9'W	X	37
Ardoch	Angus	NO5079	56°54·2'	2°48·8'W	X	44
Ardoch	Angus	NO6764	56°46·2'	2°31·9'W	X	45
Ardoch	Arg & Bt	NS3676	55°57·2'	4°37·2'W	T	63
Ardoch	D & G	NS8305	55°19·8'	3°50·2'W	X	71,78
Ardoch	D & G	NX6383	55°7·6'	4°8·5'W	X	77
Ardoch	E Renf	NS5849	55°43·1'	4°15·2'W	X	64
Ardoch	Highld	NH6172	57°43·2'	4°19·6'W	X	21
Ardoch	Highld	NH7164	57°39·1'	4°9·2'W	X	21,27
Ardoch	Moray	NJ0049	57°31·5'	3°39·7'W	X	27
Ardoch	Moray	NJ1251	57°32·7'	3°27·8'W	X	28
Ardoch	Moray	NJ3448	57°31·3'	3°5·7'W	X	28
Ardoch	Moray	NJ5062	57°39·0'	2°49·8'W	X	29
Ardoch	Pth & Kin	NN8409	56°15·8'	3°51·9'W	X	58
Ardoch	Pth & Kin	NN9125	56°24·5'	3°45·5'W	X	52,58
Ardoch	Pth & Kin	NO0937	56°31·2'	3°28·3'W	X	52,53
Ardoch	S Lanak	NS8038	55°37·5'	3°53·9'W	X	71,72
Ardoch	Stir	NN5517	56°19·7'	4°20·3'W	X	57
Ardoch	Stir	NS5479	55°59·2'	4°20·0'W	X	64
Ardoch	W Dunb	NS4186	56°2·7'	4°32·7'W	X	56
Ardoch Burn	E Renf	NS5849	55°43·1'	4°15·2'W	W	64
Ardoch Burn	Stir	NN7504	56°13·0'	4°0·5'W	W	57
Ardoch Fm	Arg & Bt	NS3676	55°57·2'	4°37·2'W	FM	63
Ardoch Hill	D & G	NX6384	55°8·1'	4°8·5'W	H	77
Ardochrig	S Lanak	NS6346	55°41·5'	4°10·3'W	X	64
Ardochrig Hill	S Lanak	NS6246	55°41·5'	4°11·3'W	X	64
Ardochy	Highld	NH4643	57°27·3'	4°33·5'W	X	26
Ardochy	Highld	NH4712	57°10·7'	4°31·4'W	X	34
Ardochy House	Highld	NH2102	57°4·7'	4°56·7'W	X	34
Ardo Ho	Aberd	NJ9221	57°17·0'	2°7·5'W	X	38
Ardonachie	Pth & Kin	NO0734	56°29·6'	3°30·2'W	X	52,53

Ardonald	Aberd	NJ4544	57°29·2'	2°54·6'W	T	28,29
Ardonan	I of M	SC4296	54°20·4'	4°25·4'W	X	95
Ardoon	E Ayr	NS4408	55°20·7'	4°27·2'W	X	70,77
Ardoran	Arg & Bt	NM8424	56°21·8'	5°29·4'W	X	49
Ardormie	Pth & Kin	NO2352	56°39·5'	3°14·9'W	X	53
Ardovie	Angus	NO5956	56°41·9'	2°39·7'W	X	54
Ardow Burn	Arg & Bt	NM4249	56°34·0'	6°11·5'W	W	47,48
Ardownie	Angus	NO4934	56°30·0'	2°49·3'W	X	54
Ardoyne	Aberd	NJ6527	57°20·2'	2°34·4'W	T	38
Ardpatrick Ho	Arg & Bt	NR7559	55°46·6'	5°34·8'W	X	62
Ardpatrick Point	Arg & Bt	NR7357	55°45·4'	5°36·6'W	X	62
Ardpeaton	Arg & Bt	NS2185	56°1·7'	4°51·9'W	T	56
Ardradnaig	Pth & Kin	NN7142	56°33·4'	4°5·5'W	X	51,52
Ardrishaig	Arg & Bt	NR8585	56°0·8'	5°26·5'W	T	55
Ardroag	Highld	NG2743	57°24·0'	6°32·2'W	T	23
Ardroe	Highld	NC0723	58°9·5'	5°16·3'W	X	15
Ardroil	N Eil	NB0432	58°10·9'	7°1·7'W	T	13
Ardross	Fife	NO5000	56°11·7'	2°47·9'W	X	59
Ardross	Highld	NH6174	57°44·3'	4°19·6'W	T	21
Ardrossan	N Ayr	NS2342	55°38·6'	4°48·3'W	T	63,70
Ardross Castle	Highld	NH6174	57°44·3'	4°19·6'W	X	21
Ardross Forest	Highld	NH5178	57°46·3'	4°29·8'W	F	20
Ardroy Sand	Highld	NH6367	57°40·6'	4°17·4'W	X	21
Ards	I of M	SC4589	54°16·6'	4°22·4'W	X	95
Ardscalpsie	Arg & Bt	NS0558	55°46·8'	5°6·1'W	X	63
Ardscalpsie Point	Arg & Bt	NS0457	55°46·3'	5°7·0'W	X	63
Ardshave	Highld	NH7695	57°55·9'	4°5·2'W	X	21
Ardshealach	Highld	NM6867	56°44·5'	5°47·2'W	T	40
Ardsheal Fm	Highld	NM9957	56°40·0'	5°16·4'W	FM	49
Ardsheal Hill	Highld	NM9956	56°39·4'	5°16·3'W	H	49
Ardshellach	Arg & Bt	NM7818	56°18·4'	5°34·9'W	X	55
Ardskenish	Arg & Bt	NR3491	56°2·5'	6°15·8'W	T	61
Ard Skinid	Highld	NC5961	58°31·1'	4°24·8'W	H	10
Ardsley	Barns	SE3805	53°32·7'	1°25·2'W	T	110,111
Ardsley Ho	Derby	SK2238	52°56·6'	1°40·0'W	X	128
Ardsley Resr	Leeds	SE2924	53°42·9'	1°33·2'W	W	104
Ardslignish	Highld	NM5661	56°40·9'	5°58·6'W	X	47
Ards, The	Sol	SP1774	52°22·1'	1°44·6'W	X	139
Ardtalla	Arg & Bt	NR4654	55°43·0'	6°2·2'W	X	60
Ardtalnaig	Pth & Kin	NN7039	56°31·8'	4°6·4'W	T	51,52
Ardtannes	Aberd	NJ7620	57°16·5'	2°23·4'W	X	38
Ardtaraig	Arg & Bt	NS0582	55°59·7'	5°7·2'W	X	56
Ardteatle Cott	Arg & Bt	NN1325	56°23·1'	5°1·3'W	X	50
Ard, The	Arg & Bt	NR3644	55°37·3'	6°11·2'W	X	60
Ard Thurinish	Highld	NM5999	57°1·4'	5°57·8'W	X	32,39
Ard Thùrnais	N Eil	NB0606	57°57·0'	6°57·7'W	X	13,14
Ardtoe	Highld	NM6270	56°45·9'	5°53·2'W	T	40
Ardtoe Island	Highld	NM5271	56°46·1'	6°3·1'W	X	39,47
Ardtornish	Highld	NM7047	56°33·8'	5°44·2'W	X	49
Ardtornish Bay	Highld	NM6942	56°31·1'	5°44·9'W	W	49
Ardtornish Point	Highld	NM6942	56°31·1'	5°44·9'W	X	49
Ardtreck	Highld	NG3334	57°19·4'	6°25·7'W	T	32
Ardtreck Burn	Highld	NG3533	57°18·9'	6°23·6'W	W	32
Ardtreck Point	Highld	NG3336	57°20·4'	6°25·8'W	X	23,32
Ardtrostan	Pth & Kin	NN6723	56°23·1'	4°8·8'W	X	51
Ardtrostan Cott	Pth & Kin	NN6823	56°23·1'	4°7·8'W	X	51
Ardtulichan	Pth & Kin	NN8962	56°44·4'	3°48·4'W	X	43
Ardtun	Arg & Bt	NM3923	56°19·9'	6°12·9'W	T	48
Ardtur	Arg & Bt	NM9146	56°33·8'	5°23·6'W	X	49
Ardtur Ho	Arg & Bt	NM9146	56°33·8'	5°23·6'W	X	49
Arduaine	Arg & Bt	NM8010	56°14·2'	5°32·6'W	T	55
Arduaine Point	Arg & Bt	NM7910	56°14·1'	5°33·5'W	X	55
Ardullie	Highld	NH5863	57°38·3'	4°22·3'W	T	21
Ardullie Lodge	Highld	NH5862	57°37·8'	4°22·2'W	X	21
Ardunie	Pth & Kin	NN9319	56°21·3'	3°43·5'W	X	58
Ardura	Arg & Bt	NM6830	56°24·6'	5°45·2'W	X	49
Ardvannie	Highld	NH6887	57°51·4'	4°13·0'W	T	21
Ardvar	Highld	NC1734	58°15·7'	5°6·7'W	X	15
Ardvasar	Highld	NG6203	57°3·7'	5°55·1'W	T	32
Ardveenish	N Eil	NF7103	57°0·3'	7°24·7'W	T	31
Ardveich	Stir	NN6124	56°23·5'	4°14·7'W	X	51
Ardveich Wood	Stir	NN6324	56°23·6'	4°12·7'W	F	51
Ardvergnish	Arg & Bt	NM5329	56°23·6'	5°59·7'W	X	48
Ardverikie	Highld	NN5087	56°57·3'	4°27·5'W	T	42
Ardverikie Forest	Highld	NN5081	56°54·0'	4°27·3'W	X	42
Ardverlich Cott	Pth & Kin	NN6122	56°22·5'	4°14·6'W	X	51
Ardvorlich	Arg & Bt	NN3212	56°16·5'	4°42·4'W	X	50,56
Ardvorlich	Pth & Kin	NN6322	56°22·5'	4°12·7'W	X	51
Ardvreck Castle	Highld	NC2323	58°9·9'	5°0·1'W	A	15
Ardvuran	N Eil	NF6604	57°0·6'	7°29·7'W	X	31
Ardwall	D & G	NX5854	54°51·9'	4°12·3'W	X	83
Ardwall	D & G	NX9663	54°57·3'	3°37·0'W	X	84
Ardwall Hill	D & G	NX5757	54°53·5'	4°13·4'W	H	83
Ardwall Isle	D & G	NX5749	54°49·2'	4°13·1'W	X	83
Ardwall Mains	D & G	NX9763	54°57·3'	3°36·1'W	X	84
Ardwell	D & G	NX1045	54°46·1'	4°56·8'W	T	82
Ardwell	Moray	NJ3730	57°21·6'	3°2·4'W	X	37
Ardwell	S Ayr	NX1694	55°12·6'	4°53·1'W	X	76
Ardwell Bay	D & G	NX0645	54°46·0'	5°0·5'W	W	82
Ardwell Bay	S Ayr	NX1594	55°12·6'	4°54·0'W	W	76
Ardwell Hill	D & G	NX4765	54°57·6'	4°23·0'W	X	83
Ardwell Ho	D & G	NX1045	54°46·1'	4°56·8'W	X	82
Ardwell Mains	D & G	NX1045	54°46·1'	4°56·8'W	X	82
Ardwell Mill	D & G	NX1048	54°47·7'	4°56·9'W	X	82
Ardwell Point	D & G	NX0644	54°45·5'	5°0·5'W	X	82
Ard Whallin	I of M	SC3583	54°13·2'	4°31·4'W	X	95
Ardwick	Man	SJ8597	53°28·4'	2°13·1'W	T	109
Ardwyn	Carm	SN1422	51°52·2'	4°41·7'W	X	145,158
Ardyne Burn	Arg & Bt	NS1071	55°53·9'	5°1·9'W	W	63
Ardyne Fm	Arg & Bt	NS1168	55°52·3'	5°0·8'W	FM	63
Ardyne Point	Arg & Bt	NS0968	55°52·3'	5°2·7'W	X	63
Arean	Highld	NM6473	56°47·6'	5°51·4'W	T	40
Arecleoch	S Ayr	NX1778	55°4·0'	4°51·5'W	X	76
Arecleoch Forest	S Ayr	NX1780	55°5·1'	4°51·6'W	F	76
Areeming	D & G	NX7874	55°3·0'	3°54·2'W	X	84
Areeming Burn	D & G	NX7874	55°3·0'	3°54·2'W	W	84
Areley Kings	Worcs	SO8070	52°19·9'	2°17·2'W	T	138
Areley Wood	Worcs	SO7871	52°20·4'	2°19·0'W	F	138
Arenig Fach	Gwyn	SH8241	52°57·4'	3°45·0'W	H	124,125
Arenig Fawr	Gwyn	SH8236	52°54·8'	3°44·9'W	H	124,125

Arford	Hants	SU8236	51°7·3'	0°49·3'W	T	186
Arfor Fawr	Cered	SN3352	52°8·7'	4°26·0'W	X	145
Arg	Shetld	HU3044	60°11·0'	1°27·1'W	X	4
Argae	V of Glam	ST1371	51°26·1'	3°14·7'W	X	171
Argal Manor	Corn	SW7632	50°9·0'	5°7·8'W	X	204
Argal Resr	Corn	SW7632	50°9·0'	5°7·8'W	W	204
Argam Dikes	E Yorks	TA1171	54°7·6'	0°17·7'W	A	101
Argam Village	E Yorks	TA1171	54°7·6'	0°17·7'W	A	101
Argaty	Stir	NN7303	56°12·4'	4°2·4'W	X	57
Argent Manor Fm	Suff	TM1435	51°58·6'	1°7·4'E	FM	169
Arger Fen	Suff	TL9335	51°59·0'	0°49·0'E	F	155
Argham	E Yorks	TA1171	54°7·6'	0°17·7'W	X	101
Argill Beck	Cumbr	NY8413	54°31·0'	2°14·4'W	W	91,92
Argill Ho	Cumbr	NY8212	54°30·4'	2°16·3'W	X	91,92
Arglam	E Yorks	SE7835	53°48·6'	0°48·5'W	X	105,106
Arglam Wood	E Yorks	SE7836	53°49·1'	0°48·5'W	F	105,106
Argoed	Caer	SO1700	51°41·8'	3°11·7'W	T	171
Argoed	Cered	SN6070	52°18·9'	4°2·8'W	X	135
Argoed	Cered	SN6758	52°12·5'	3°56·4'W	X	146
Argoed	Pemb	SN0938	52°0·7'	4°46·6'W	X	145
Argoed	Powys	SN9254	52°10·7'	3°34·4'W	X	147
Argoed	Powys	SN9891	52°30·7'	3°29·8'W	X	136
Argoed	Powys	SN9962	52°15·1'	3°28·4'W	X	147
Argoed	Powys	SO0799	52°35·1'	3°22·0'W	X	136
Argoed	Powys	SO0945	52°6·0'	3°19·3'W	X	147
Argoed	Powys	SO2590	52°30·4'	3°5·9'W	T	137
Argoed	Shrops	SJ3220	52°46·6'	3°0·1'W	T	126
Argoed	Shrops	SO3084	52°27·2'	3°1·4'W	T	137
Argoed	V of Glam	SS9979	51°30·3'	3°26·9'W	X	170
Argoed	Wrex	SJ3742	52°58·5'	2°55·9'W	X	117
Argoed-Edwin	Rho Cyn Taf	ST0084	51°33·0'	3°26·1'W	X	170
Argoed-fawr	Cered	SN6588	52°28·6'	3°58·9'W	X	135
Argoed Fm	Carm	SN2641	52°2·6'	4°31·8'W	FM	145
Argoed Fm	Denb	SJ2741	52°57·9'	3°4·8'W	FM	117
Argoed Fm	Flint	SJ2564	53°10·3'	3°6·9'W	FM	117
Argoed Fm	Monm	SO3810	51°47·4'	2°53·5'W	FM	161
Argoed Hall	Flint	SJ2564	53°10·3'	3°6·9'W	X	117
Argoed, The	Monm	SO5208	51°46·4'	2°41·3'W	X	162
Argos Hill	E Susx	TQ5728	51°2·0'	0°14·7'E	T	188,199
Argrennan Ho	D & G	NX7158	54°54·3'	4°0·3'W	X	83,84
Argrennan Mains	D & G	NX7056	54°53·2'	4°1·2'W	X	83,84
Argus Fm	Heref	SO7035	52°1·0'	2°25·8'W	FM	149
Argyll	Arg & Bt	NN0407	56°13·2'	5°9·2'W	X	56
Argyll	Arg & Bt	NN1112	56°16·0'	5°2·7'W	X	50,56
Argyll	Arg & Bt	NR9399	56°8·6'	5°19·5'W	X	55
Argyll Stone, The or Clach Mhic Cailein	Highld	NH9004	57°7·1'	3°48·5'W	X	36
Arhosfa'r Garreg-lwyd	Carm	SN8026	51°55·4'	3°44·3'W	H	160
Arichamish	Arg & Bt	NM9005	56°11·7'	5°22·7'W	X	55
Aricharnach	Highld	NG5527	57°16·3'	6°3·4'W	X	32
Arichastlich	Arg & Bt	NN2534	56°28·2'	4°50·0'W	X	50
Arichonan	Arg & Bt	NR7790	56°3·3'	5°34·4'W	X	55
Aridhglas	Arg & Bt	NM3123	56°19·6'	6°20·6'W	T	48
Arienas Burn	Highld	NM6952	56°36·4'	5°45·4'W	W	49
Arieniskill	Highld	NM7882	56°52·8'	5°38·2'W	X	40
Aries Knowes	D & G	NX4044	54°46·2'	4°28·8'W	X	83
Arifea	Orkney	HY6723	59°5·8'	2°34·1'W	X	5
Arileod	Arg & Bt	NM1654	56°35·8'	6°37·2'W	X	46
Arinabea	Arg & Bt	NN2931	56°26·7'	4°46·0'W	X	50
Arinacrinachd	Highld	NG7458	57°33·6'	5°46·2'W	T	24
Arinafad Beg	Arg & Bt	NR7689	56°2·7'	5°35·4'W	X	55
Arinagour	Arg & Bt	NM2257	56°37·6'	6°31·5'W	T	46,47
Arinagour Fm	Arg & Bt	NM2256	56°37·1'	6°31·5'W	FM	46,47
Arinanuan	Arg & Bt	NR7339	55°35·8'	5°35·7'W	X	68
Arinarach Hill	Arg & Bt	NR7216	55°23·4'	5°35·6'W	H	68
Arinascavach	Arg & Bt	NR7213	55°21·7'	5°35·4'W	X	68
Arinasliseig	Arg & Bt	NM6531	56°25·0'	5°48·2'W	X	49
Arineckaig	Highld	NG9845	57°27·3'	5°21·6'W	X	25
Arinthluic	Arg & Bt	NM2155	56°36·5'	6°32·4'W	X	46,47
Ariogan	Arg & Bt	NM8627	56°23·5'	5°27·6'W	X	49
Arion	Orkney	HY2514	59°0·7'	3°17·9'W	X	6
Arisaig	Highld	NM6586	56°54·6'	5°51·2'W	T	40
Arisaig House	Highld	NM6984	56°53·7'	5°47·1'W	X	40
Aris Dale	Shetld	HU4882	60°31·4'	1°7·0'W	X	1,2,3
Arisdale	Shetld	HU4882	60°31·4'	1°7·0'W	X	1,2,3
Arish Mell	Dorset	SY8580	50°37·4'	2°12·3'W	X	194
Ariundle	Highld	NM8263	56°42·7'	5°33·3'W	T	40
Arivegaig	Highld	NM6567	56°44·4'	5°50·1'W	T	40
Arivoichallum	Arg & Bt	NR3449	55°40·0'	6°13·4'W	X	60
Arivurichardich	Stir	NN6413	56°17·7'	4°11·4'W	X	57
Arkall Fm	Staffs	SK2206	52°39·3'	1°40·1'W	FM	139
Arkendale	Lincs	TF3354	53°4·2'	0°0·5'W	X	122
Arkendale	N Yks	SE3860	54°2·3'	1°24·8'W	T	99
Arkendale Moor	N Yks	SE3860	54°2·3'	1°24·8'W	X	99
Arkendeith	Highld	NH6956	57°34·8'	4°11·0'W	X	26
Arkengarthdale	N Yks	NZ0002	54°25·1'	1°59·6'W	X	92
Arkengarthdale Moor	N Yks	NY9305	54°26·7'	2°6·1'W	X	91,92
Arkesden	Essex	TL4834	51°59·3'	0°9·7'E	T	154
Ark Fm	Wilts	ST9326	51°2·2'	2°5·6'W	FM	184
Ark Hill	Angus	NO3542	56°34·2'	3°3·0'W	H	54
Arkholme	Lancs	SD5871	54°8·2'	2°38·2'W	T	97
Arkland	D & G	NX5559	54°54·5'	4°15·3'W	X	83
Arkland	D & G	NX7773	55°2·4'	3°55·1'W	X	84
Arkland	D & G	NX8097	55°15·4'	3°52·9'W	X	78
Arkland Burn	D & G	NX5659	54°54·6'	4°14·3'W	W	83
Arkland Burn	D & G	NX7898	55°15·9'	3°54·8'W	W	78
Arkland Craig	D & G	NX7998	55°15·9'	3°53·8'W	X	78
Arkland Rig	D & G	NX7898	55°15·9'	3°54·8'W	X	78
Ark Law	Scot Bord	NT2610	55°23·0'	3°9·6'W	H	79
Ark Law	Scot Bord	NT3420	55°28·4'	3°2·2'W	H	73
Arkle	Highld	NC3145	58°21·9'	4°52·9'W	H	9
Arkle Beck	N Yks	NY9804	54°26·1'	2°1·4'W	W	92
Arkleby	Cumbr	NY1439	54°44·6'	3°19·7'W	T	89
Arkleby Ho	Cumbr	NY1339	54°44·6'	3°20·7'W	X	89
Arkleby Mill	Cumbr	NY1440	54°45·1'	3°19·7'W	X	85
Arkleside	N Yks	SE0480	54°13·2'	1°55·9'W	X	98
Arkleside Gill	N Yks	SE0479	54°12·6'	1°55·9'W	W	98
Arkleside Moor	N Yks	SE0579	54°12·6'	1°55·0'W	X	98
Arkleston	Renf	NS5065	55°51·5'	4°23·4'W	X	64
Arkleton	D & G	NY3791	55°12·8'	2°59·0'W	T	79

Arkleton Burn	D & G	NY3891	55°12·8'	2°58·0'W	W	79
Arkleton Cott	D & G	NY4088	55°11·2'	2°56·1'W	X	79
Arkleton Hill	D & G	NY4092	55°13·4'	2°56·2'W	H	79
Arkle Town	N Yks	NZ0002	54°25·1'	1°59·6'W	T	92
Arkley	Barnet	TQ2295	51°38·7'	0°13·8'W	T	166,176
Arkley Hall	Barnet	TQ2295	51°38·7'	0°13·8'W	X	166,176
Arklid Fm	Cumbr	SD2988	54°17·2'	3°5·0'W	FM	96,97
Arklid Intake	Cumbr	SD3189	54°17·8'	3°3·2'W	F	96,97
Arklow Hill	Cumbr	NY7310	54°29·3'	2°24·6'W	X	91
Arklow Hill	N Yks	SE1887	54°16·9'	1°43·0'W	H	99
Arkney Hill	S Lanak	NS8031	55°33·7'	3°53·7'W	X	71,72
Arks	Scot Bord	NT7108	55°22·2'	2°27·0'W	X	80
Arks Edge	Scot Bord	NT7107	55°21·6'	2°27·0'W	X	80
Arksey	Donc	SE5706	53°33·1'	1°8·0'W	T	111
Arksley Fm	Shrops	SO6688	52°29·6'	2°29·6'W	FM	138
Arkstone Common	Heref	SO4335	52°0·9'	2°49·4'W	X	149,161
Arkstone Court	Heref	SO4336	52°1·4'	2°49·4'W	X	149,161
Arkstone Ct	Heref	SO4336	52°1·4'	2°49·4'W	X	149,161
Ark, The	Oxon	SU3987	51°35·1'	1°25·8'W	X	174
Arkwright Cottages	Leic	SP5292	52°31·6'	1°13·6'W	X	140
Arkwright Town	Derby	SK4270	53°13·8'	1°21·8'W	T	120
Arlary	Pth & Kin	NO1305	56°14·0'	3°23·8'W	X	58
Arlaw Banks	Durham	NZ0916	54°32·6'	1°51·2'W	X	92
Arle	Arg & Bt	NM5448	56°33·8'	5°59·8'W	X	47,48
Arle	Glos	SO9223	51°54·6'	2°6·6'W	T	163
Arlebrook	Glos	SO8108	51°46·5'	2°16·1'W	T	162
Arlebury Park	Hants	SU5732	51°5·3'	1°10·8'W	X	185
Arlecdon	Cumbr	NY0419	54°33·7'	3°28·7'W	T	89
Arlecdon Hill	Cumbr	NY0418	54°33·1'	3°28·6'W	X	89
Arlehaven	Stir	NS5380	55°59·7'	4°21·0'W	X	64
Arlescote	Warw	SP3948	52°8·0'	1°25·4'W	T	151
Arlescott Fm	Shrops	SJ6400	52°36·0'	2°31·5'W	FM	127
Arlesey	Beds	TL1935	52°0·3'	0°15·6'W	T	153
Arleston	Wrekin	SJ6610	52°41·4'	2°29·8'W	T	127
Arleston Fm	Derby	SK3429	52°51·7'	1°29·3'W	FM	128
Arleston Hill	Wrekin	SJ6609	52°40·9'	2°29·8'W	X	127
Arleth	Pemb	SN2037	52°0·4'	4°37·0'W	X	145
Arley	Ches	SJ6781	53°19·7'	2°29·3'W	T	109
Arley Brook	Ches	SJ6679	53°18·7'	2°30·2'W	W	118
Arley Brook	Ches	SJ6680	53°19·2'	2°30·2'W	W	109
Arley Brook	Ches	SJ7079	53°18·7'	2°26·6'W	W	118
Arley Green	Ches	SJ6880	53°19·2'	2°28·4'W	T	109
Arley Hall	Ches	SJ6780	53°19·2'	2°29·3'W	A	109
Arley Hall Fm	Warw	SP2790	52°30·7'	1°35·7'W	FM	140
Arley Ho	Worcs	SO7680	52°25·3'	2°20·8'W	X	138
Arley House Fm	Warw	SP2990	52°30·7'	1°34·0'W	FM	140
Arley Moss Fm	Ches	SJ6778	53°18·1'	2°29·3'W	FM	118
Arleyview Fm	Ches	SJ6882	53°20·3'	2°28·4'W	FM	109
Arley Wood	Warw	SP2790	52°30·7'	1°35·7'W	F	140
Arley Wood	Worcs	SO8082	52°26·4'	2°17·3'W	F	138
Arlick	Pth & Kin	NO0746	56°36·1'	3°30·4'W	H	52,53
Arlick Hill	Pth & Kin	NO0605	56°14·0'	3°30·5'W	X	58
Arlick Hill	Pth & Kin	NO0910	56°16·7'	3°27·7'W	H	58
Arliemoor Fm	Devon	SS3605	50°49·5'	4°19·3'W	FM	190
Arlingham	Glos	SO7010	51°47·5'	2°25·7'W	T	162
Arlingham Warth	Glos	SO7112	51°48·6'	2°24·8'W	X	162
Arlington	Devon	SS6140	51°8·8'	3°58·9'W	T	180
Arlington	E Susx	TQ5407	50°50·7'	0°11·6'E	T	199
Arlington	Glos	SP1006	51°45·4'	1°50·9'W	T	163
Arlington Beccott	Devon	SS6141	51°9·3'	3°58·9'W	T	180
Arlington Court	Devon	SS6140	51°8·8'	3°58·9'W	X	180
Arlington Grange Fm	W Berks	SU4771	51°26·4'	1°19·0'W	FM	174
Arlington Reservoir	E Susx	TQ5307	50°50·8'	0°10·8'E	W	199
Arlington Row	Glos	SP1106	51°45·4'	1°50·0'W	A	163
Arllen-Fawr	Powys	SJ0925	52°49·1'	3°20·6'W	X	125
Arllwyd	Conwy	SH9766	53°11·1'	3°32·1'W	X	116
Arlosh Ho	Cumbr	NY2156	54°53·8'	3°13·5'W	X	85
Armadale	Highld	NC7864	58°33·1'	4°5·3'W	T	10
Armadale	W Loth	NS9368	55°53·9'	3°42·2'W	T	65
Armadale Bay	Highld	NC7965	58°33·6'	4°4·3'W	W	10
Armadale Bay	Highld	NG6303	57°3·7'	5°54·1'W	W	32
Armadale Burn	Highld	NC8061	58°31·5'	4°3·2'W	W	10
Armadale Castle	Highld	NG6304	57°4·2'	5°54·1'W	X	32
Armaddy	Arg & Bt	NN0737	56°29·4'	5°7·6'W	X	50
Armaddy Bay	Arg & Bt	NN0738	56°29·9'	5°7·7'W	W	50
Armaside	Cumbr	NY1527	54°38·1'	3°18·6'W	X	89
Armaside Wood	Cumbr	NY7008	54°28·2'	2°27·4'W	F	91
Armathwaite	Cumbr	NY5046	54°48·6'	2°46·3'W	T	86
Armathwaite	N Yks	SE0774	54°9·9'	1°53·1'W	X	99
Armathwaite Gill	N Yks	SE0675	54°10·5'	1°54·1'W	W	99
Armathwaite Hall (Hotel)	Cumbr	NY2032	54°40·9'	3°14·0'W	X	89,90
Armboth	Cumbr	NY3017	54°32·9'	3°4·5'W	X	90
Armboth Fell	Cumbr	NY2915	54°31·8'	3°5·4'W	H	89,90
Armed Knight	Corn	SW3424	50°3·6'	5°42·6'W	X	203
Armer Wood	Devon	SS8727	51°2·1'	3°36·3'W	F	181
Armet Water	Scot Bord	NT4455	55°47·4'	2°53·1'W	W	66,73
Armigers	Essex	TL5928	51°55·9'	0°19·2'E	T	167
Arminghall	Norf	TG2504	52°35·5'	1°19·7'E	T	134
Armishader	Highld	NG5050	57°28·5'	6°9·7'W	X	23,24
Armitage	Staffs	SK0716	52°44·7'	1°53·4'W	T	128
Armitage	Staffs	SK0939	52°57·1'	1°51·6'W	X	128
Armitage Bridge	Kirk	SE1313	53°37·0'	1°47·8'W	T	110
Armitstead	N Yks	SD7864	54°4·5'	2°19·8'W	X	98
Armley	Leeds	SE2733	53°47·8'	1°35·0'W	T	104
Armond Carr	Durham	NZ1039	54°45·0'	1°50·3'W	X	92
Armont Ho	Cumbr	NY1800	54°23·6'	3°15·4'W	X	89,90
Armoor	Somer	SS9434	51°6·0'	3°30·5'W	X	181
Armour Fm	Bucks	SP8006	51°45·0'	0°50·1'W	FM	165
Armours	Essex	TL6313	51°47·7'	0°22·2'E	X	167
Armoury Fm	Essex	TL9727	51°54·6'	0°52·2'E	FM	168
Armrydding	Lancs	SD6742	53°52·6'	2°29·7'W	X	103
Armscote	Warw	SP2444	52°5·9'	1°38·6'W	T	151
Armsdale	Staffs	SJ7632	52°53·3'	2°21·0'W	T	127
Armsey Fm	Essex	TL8539	52°1·3'	0°42·2'E	FM	155
Armshead	Staffs	SJ9348	53°2·0'	2°5·9'W	T	118
Armsheugh	E Ayr	NS4738	55°36·9'	4°25·3'W	X	70
Armston	Northnts	TL0685	52°27·4'	0°26·0'W	T	142
Arms Tor	Devon	SX5386	50°39·5'	4°4·4'W	X	191,201
Armstrong Ho	York	SE6147	53°55·2'	1°3·9'W	X	105
Armswell Fm	Dorset	ST7203	50°49·8'	2°23·5'W	FM	194

Armsworth Hill Fm	Hants	SU6138	51°8·5'	1°7·3'W	FM	185
Armsworth Ho	Hants	SU6037	51°8·0'	1°8·2'W	X	185
Armthorpe	Donc	SE6204	53°32·0'	1°3·5'W	T	111
Army Apprentices College	Glos	ST5591	51°37·2'	2°38·6'W	X	162,172
Arnabol Hill	Highld	NM7584	56°53·8'	5°41·2'W	H	40
Arnaboll	Highld	NC4657	58°28·7'	4°38·0'W	X	9
Arnabost	Arg & Bt	NM2060	56°39·1'	6°33·7'W	X	46,47
Arnaby	Cumbr	SD1884	54°15·0'	3°15·1'W	T	96
Arnage	Aberd	NJ9538	57°26·2'	2°4·5'W	X	30
Arnage Castle	Aberd	NJ9337	57°25·7'	2°6·5'W	A	30
Arnagill Crags	N Yks	SE1577	54°11·6'	1°45·8'W	X	99
Arnagill Moor	N Yks	SE1475	54°10·5'	1°46·7'W	X	99
Arnagill Tower	N Yks	SE1575	54°10·5'	1°45·8'W	X	99
Arnamul	N Eil	NL5482	56°48·3'	7°39·7'W	X	31
Arnaval	Highld	NG3431	57°17·8'	6°24·5'W	H	32
Arna Wood	Lancs	SD4659	54°1·7'	2°49·0'W	X	102
Arnbarrow	Aberd	NO6577	56°53·2'	2°34·0'W	X	45
Arnbarrow Hill	Aberd	NO6577	56°53·2'	2°34·0'W	H	45
Arnbath	Aberd	NJ5765	57°40·6'	2°42·8'W	X	29
Arnbathie	Pth & Kin	NO1725	56°24·9'	3°20·3'W	X	53,58
Arnbeg	Stir	NS6294	56°7·4'	4°12·8'W	X	57
Arnbog	Pth & Kin	NO3146	56°36·3'	3°7·0'W	X	53
Arnburn	Arg & Bt	NS3588	56°3·6'	4°38·6'W	X	56
Arnclerich	Stir	NS6099	56°10·0'	4°14·8'W	X	57
Arncliffe	N Yks	SD9371	54°8·3'	2°6·0'W	T	98
Arncliffe Cote	N Yks	SD9470	54°7·8'	2°5·1'W	X	98
Arncliffe Hall	N Yks	NZ4500	54°23·9'	1°18·0'W	X	93
Arncliffe Wood	N Yks	NZ4600	54°23·8'	1°17·1'W	F	93
Arncliffe Wood	N Yks	SE4599	54°23·3'	1°18·0'W	F	99
Arncroach	Fife	NO5105	56°14·4'	2°47·0'W	T	59
Arndale Beck	Cumbr	SD4289	54°17·8'	2°53·1'W	W	96,97
Arndale Beck	N Yks	NZ0406	54°27·2'	1°55·9'W	W	92
Arndale Head	N Yks	NZ0206	54°27·2'	1°57·7'W	X	92
Arndale Hill	Durham	NZ0206	54°27·2'	1°57·7'W	X	92
Arndale Hole	N Yks	NZ0505	54°26·7'	1°55·0'W	X	92
Arndarroch	D & G	NX6189	55°10·8'	4°10·5'W	X	77
Arndean	Pth & Kin	NS9998	56°10·1'	3°37·2'W	X	58
Arndilly Fm	Moray	NJ2848	57°31·2'	3°11·7'W	FM	28
Arndilly Ho	Moray	NJ2947	57°30·7'	3°10·6'W	X	28
Arndrum	Stir	NS5098	56°9·3'	4°24·5'W	H	57
Arne	Dorset	SY9788	50°41·7'	2°2·2'W	T	195
Arne Bay	Dorset	SY9889	50°42·3'	2°1·3'W	W	195
Arnesby	Leic	SP6192	52°31·6'	1°5·6'W	T	140
Arnesby Lodge	Leic	SP6293	52°32·1'	1°4·8'W	X	140
Arnewood Court	Hants	SZ2896	50°46·0'	1°35·8'W	X	195
Arnewood Ho	Hants	SZ2895	50°45·5'	1°35·8'W	X	195
Arnewood Manor	Hants	SZ2797	50°46·5'	1°36·6'W	X	195
Arnfield	Derby	SK0198	53°29·0'	1°58·7'W	X	110
Arnfield Brook	Derby	SK0399	53°29·5'	1°56·9'W	W	110
Arnfield Flats	Derby	SE0200	53°30·0'	1°57·8'W	X	110
Arnfield Moor	Derby	SK0299	53°29·5'	1°57·8'W	X	110
Arnfield Resr	Derby	SK0197	53°28·4'	1°58·7'W	W	110
Arnford	N Yks	SD8356	54°0·2'	2°15·1'W	X	103
Arnford Wood	N Yks	SD8356	54°0·2'	2°15·1'W	F	103
Arngask	Pth & Kin	NO1310	56°16·7'	3°23·9'W	X	58
Arngask Ho	Pth & Kin	NO1310	56°16·7'	3°23·9'W	X	58
Arngibbon	Stir	NS6094	56°7·4'	4°14·7'W	X	57
Arn Gill	Durham	NZ0724	54°36·9'	1°53·1'W	W	92
Arngill Beck	Durham	NY8521	54°35·3'	2°13·5'W	W	91,92
Arngill Force	Durham	NY8423	54°36·4'	2°14·4'W	W	91,92
Arn Gill Head	N Yks	SD9199	54°23·4'	2°7·9'W	X	98
Arngill Head Brocks	Durham	NY8325	54°37·4'	2°15·4'W	X	91,92
Arngill Ho	Durham	NY8621	54°35·3'	2°12·6'W	X	91,92
Arngomery	Stir	NS6394	56°7·4'	4°11·8'W	X	57
Arnhall	Aberd	NO6169	56°48·9'	2°37·9'W	X	45
Arnhall Castle	Stir	NS7698	56°9·8'	3°59·4'W	A	57
Arnhash	Aberd	NJ8762	57°39·1'	2°12·6'W	X	30
Arnhead	Aberd	NJ7042	57°28·3'	2°29·6'W	X	29
Arn Hill	Oxon	SU4287	51°35·0'	1°23·2'W	X	174
Arn Hill Down	Wilts	ST8746	51°13·0'	2°10·8'W	H	183
Arnicle	Arg & Bt	NR7138	55°35·2'	5°37·6'W	X	68
Arniefoul	Angus	NO4044	56°35·3'	2°58·2'W	X	54
Arnieve	Stir	NS7096	56°8·6'	4°5·1'W	X	57
Arnills Gate	Northnts	SP5569	52°19·2'	1°11·2'W	X	152
Arnimean	S Ayr	NX3080	55°5·4'	4°39·4'W	X	76
Arnipol	Highld	NM7483	56°53·3'	5°42·2'W	X	40
Arnisdale	Highld	NG8410	57°8·1'	5°33·7'W	T	33
Arnisdale Ho	Highld	NG8410	57°8·1'	5°33·7'W	X	33
Arnish	Highld	NG5948	57°27·8'	6°0·6'W	T	24
Arnison Crag	Cumbr	NY3914	54°31·3'	2°56·1'W	X	90
Arnisort	Highld	NG3453	57°29·6'	6°25·9'W	X	23
Arniss Copse	Northnts	SP8654	52°10·9'	0°44·1'W	F	152
Arniston	Midlo	NT3259	55°49·4'	3°4·7'W	X	66,73
Arniston	Midlo	NT3461	55°50·5'	3°2·8'W	T	66
Arniston Mains	Midlo	NT3360	55°50·0'	3°3·7'W	X	66
Arnloss	Falk	NS8771	55°55·4'	3°48·1'W	X	65
Arnmannoch	D & G	NX8560	54°55·5'	3°47·2'W	X	84
Arnmannoch	D & G	NX8875	55°3·7'	3°44·8'W	X	84
Arnol	N Eil	NB3148	58°20·5'	6°35·3'W	T	8
Arnold	E Yorks	TA1241	53°51·4'	0°17·4'W	T	107
Arnold	Notts	SK5945	53°0·2'	1°6·8'W	T	129
Arnold Carr	E Yorks	TA1140	53°50·9'	0°18·3'W	X	107
Arnold Fm	Kent	TQ8152	51°14·5'	0°36·0'E	FM	188
Arnold Grange	E Yorks	TA1141	53°51·4'	0°18·3'W	X	107
Arnold Ho	Cumbr	NY4145	54°48·0'	2°54·6'W	X	85
Arnold Lodge	Notts	SK6047	53°1·3'	1°5·9'W	X	129
Arnolds	Surrey	TQ1742	51°10·1'	0°19·2'W	X	187
Arnolds Down	Pemb	SM9716	51°48·6'	4°56·3'W	X	157,158
Arnold's Fishleigh	Devon	SS5505	50°49·8'	4°3·2'W	X	191
Arnolds Fm	Essex	TQ4997	51°39·3'	0°9·6'E	FM	167,177
Arnold's Fm	Essex	TQ6396	51°38·6'	0°21·7'E	FM	167,177
Arnold's Fm	Warw	SP3749	52°8·5'	1°27·2'W	FM	151
Arnolds Hill	Pemb	SN0115	51°48·1'	4°52·8'W	H	157,158
Arnold's Hill	Wilts	ST8357	51°18·9'	2°14·2'W	X	173
Arnold's Oak Fm	Kent	TQ9755	51°15·8'	0°49·8'E	FM	178
Arnold's Wood	Warw	SP1372	52°21·0'	1°48·1'W	F	139
Arno's Vale	C of Bris	ST6071	51°26·4'	2°34·1'W	T	172
Arnot Boo	Aberd	NO9397	57°4·1'	2°6·5'W	W	38,45
Arnot Burn	Pth & Kin	NO2101	56°12·0'	3°16·0'W	W	58
Arnot Ho	Lancs	SD7745	53°54·3'	2°20·6'W	A	103

Arnot Resr	Pth & Kin	NO2002	56°12·5'	3°16·9'W	W	58
Arnot Tower	Pth & Kin	NO2001	56°11·9'	3°16·9'W	A	58
Arnprior	Stir	NS6194	56°7·4'	4°13·7'W	T	57
Arns	Clackm	NS9190	56°5·7'	3°44·7'W	X	58
Arns	N Lanak	NS8075	55°57·4'	3°54·9'W	X	65
Arns	Pth & Kin	NN9714	56°18·7'	3°39·5'W	X	58
Arnsbrae	Clackm	NS8694	56°7·8'	3°49·6'W	X	58
Arnsgill Ridge	N Yks	SE5296	54°21·7'	1°11·6'W	H	100
Arnsheen	S Ayr	NX2676	55°3·1'	4°43·0'W	X	76
Arnside	Cumbr	NY3301	54°24·3'	3°1·5'W	X	90
Arnside	Cumbr	SD4578	54°11·9'	2°50·2'W	T	97
Arnside Intake	Cumbr	NY3301	54°24·3'	3°1·5'W	H	90
Arnside Knott	Cumbr	SD4577	54°11·4'	2°50·2'W	H	97
Arnside Moss	Cumbr	SD4678	54°11·9'	2°49·2'W	X	97
Arnside Park	Cumbr	SD4477	54°11·4'	2°51·1'W	F	97
Arnside Tower	Cumbr	SD4576	54°10·9'	2°50·1'W	X	97
Arnsow	S Ayr	NS3507	55°20·0'	4°35·6'W	X	70,77
Arntamie	Stir	NN5601	56°11·1'	4°18·8'W	X	57
Arntilly Craig	Aberd	NO5793	57°1·8'	2°42·1'W	H	37,44
Arnton Fell	Scot Bord	NY5295	55°15·1'	2°44·9'W	X	79
Arnvicar	Stir	NS5897	56°8·9'	4°16·7'W	X	57
Arnybogs	Aberd	NJ8638	57°26·2'	2°13·5'W	X	30
Arnyburn	Aberd	NJ7441	57°27·8'	2°25·5'W	X	29
Aros	Arg & Bt	NM5149	56°34·3'	6°2·8'W	X	47,48
Aros	Arg & Bt	NR6821	55°25·9'	5°39·6'W	X	68
Aros Bay	Arg & Bt	NR4652	55°42·0'	6°2·1'W	W	60
Aros Bay	Highld	NG2760	57°33·1'	6°33·4'W	W	23
Aros Castle	Arg & Bt	NM5644	56°31·7'	5°57·6'W	A	47,48
Aros Cott	Arg & Bt	NM5544	56°31·7'	5°58·6'W	X	47,48
Aros Mains	Arg & Bt	NM5645	56°32·3'	5°57·7'W	X	47,48
Aros Moss	Arg & Bt	NR6721	55°25·9'	5°40·5'W	X	68
Aros River	Arg & Bt	NM5345	56°32·2'	6°0·6'W	W	47,48
Arowry	Wrex	SJ4539	52°57·0'	2°48·7'W	T	126
Arpafeelie	Highld	NH6150	57°31·4'	4°18·8'W	T	26
Arpinge	Kent	TR1939	51°6·7'	1°8·1'E	T	179,189
Arpochill Fm	S Lanak	NS6348	55°42·6'	4°10·4'W	FM	64
Arracott	Devon	SX4287	50°39·9'	4°13·8'W	X	190
Arrad Foot	Cumbr	SD3080	54°12·9'	3°4·0'W	T	96,97
Arradoul Ho	Moray	NJ4163	57°39·4'	2°58·9'W	X	28
Arradoul Mains	Moray	NJ4263	57°39·5'	2°57·9'W	X	28
Arragon Ho	I of M	SC3270	54°6·2'	4°33·8'W	X	95
Arragon Moar	I of M	SC3070	54°6·1'	4°35·6'W	X	95
Arragon Veg	I of M	SC3070	54°6·1'	4°35·6'W	X	95
Arrallas	Corn	SW8853	50°20·6'	4°58·4'W	X	200,204
Arram	E Yorks	TA0344	53°53·2'	0°25·6'W	T	107
Arram Carrs	E Yorks	TA0345	53°53·7'	0°25·5'W	X	107
Arram Grange	E Yorks	TA0443	53°52·6'	0°24·7'W	X	107
Arram Hall	E Yorks	TA1649	53°55·7'	0°13·6'W	X	107
Arrandene	Barnet	TQ2292	51°37·0'	0°13·9'W	X	176
Arrarat Hill	S Lanak	NS7729	55°32·6'	3°56·5'W	H	71
Arras	E Yorks	SE9241	53°51·7'	0°35·7'W	X	106
Arras Wold	E Yorks	SE9240	53°51·1'	0°35·7'W	X	106
Arrasy Plantation	I of M	SC2478	54°10·3'	4°41·4'W	F	95
Arrat	Angus	NO6358	56°43·0'	2°35·8'W	X	54
Arrathorne	N Yks	SE2093	54°20·2'	1°41·1'W	T	99
Arrat's Mill	Angus	NO6458	56°43·0'	2°34·8'W	X	54
Arraty Craigs	Fife	NO2207	56°15·2'	3°15·1'W	X	58
Arresgill	D & G	NY3184	55°9·0'	3°4·5'W	X	79
Arresgill Sike	D & G	NY3084	55°9·0'	3°5·5'W	W	79
Arreton	I of W	SZ5486	50°40·5'	1°13·8'W	T	196
Arreton Down	I of W	SZ5487	50°41·0'	1°13·8'W	X	196
Arreton Manor	I of W	SZ5386	50°40·5'	1°14·6'W	A	196
Arrevore	Pth & Kin	NN7813	56°17·9'	3°57·8'W	X	57
Arrevore Burn	Pth & Kin	NN7612	56°17·3'	3°59·8'W	W	57
Arr Fm	Highld	NH9252	57°33·0'	3°47·8'W	FM	27
Ar Riabhach	Stir	NN5130	56°26·6'	4°24·6'W	X	51
Arrieleitrach	Highld	NH3760	57°36·3'	4°43·2'W	X	20
Arrington	Cambs	TL3250	52°8·2'	0°3·9'W	T	153
Arrivain	Arg & Bt	NN2630	56°26·1'	4°48·9'W	X	50
Arrochar	Arg & Bt	NN2904	56°12·1'	4°45·0'W	T	56
Arroch Hill	D & G	NX3684	55°7·6'	4°33·9'W	H	77
Arrochymore	Stir	NS4191	56°5·4'	4°32·9'W	X	56
Arrochymore Point	Stir	NS4091	56°5·4'	4°33·9'W	X	56
Arrotshole	S Lanak	NS6255	55°46·4'	4°11·6'W	X	64
Arrow	Warw	SP0756	52°12·4'	1°53·5'W	T	150
Arrowan	Corn	SW7517	50°0·9'	5°8·1'W	X	204
Arrowan Common	Corn	SW7517	50°0·9'	5°8·1'W	X	204
Arrow Barn	Lancs	SD5065	54°5·0'	2°45·4'W	X	97
Arrow Court	Heref	SO2754	52°11·0'	3°3·7'W	X	148
Arrowe Brook	Wirral	SJ2686	53°22·2'	3°6·3'W	W	108
Arrowe Country Park	Wirral	SJ2686	53°22·2'	3°6·3'W	X	108
Arrowe Hill	Wirral	SJ2787	53°22·7'	3°5·4'W	T	108
Arrowfield Top	Worcs	SP0374	52°22·1'	1°57·0'W	T	139
Arrow Fm	Derby	SK5378	53°18·0'	1°11·9'W	FM	120
Arrow Green	Heref	SO4358	52°13·3'	2°49·7'W	T	148,149
Arrow Valley Lake	Worcs	SP0667	52°18·3'	1°54·3'W	W	150
Arrow Valley Park	Worcs	SP0666	52°17·8'	1°54·3'W	X	150
Arrunden	Kirk	SE1306	53°33·3'	1°47·8'W	T	110
Arsallary	Angus	NO4682	56°55·8'	2°52·8'W	X	44
Arscaig	Highld	NC5014	58°5·6'	4°32·2'W	X	16
Arscott	Devon	SS3505	50°49·5'	4°20·2'W	X	190
Arscott	Devon	SS3800	50°46·9'	4°17·5'W	X	190
Arscott	Shrops	SJ4307	52°39·7'	2°50·2'W	T	126
Arscott Villa	Shrops	SJ4407	52°39·7'	2°49·3'W	X	126
Arshaton Wood	Devon	SS6520	50°58·1'	3°55·0'W	F	180
Artafallie	Highld	NH6249	57°30·9'	4°17·8'W	T	26
Artengill Beck	Cumbr	SD7885	54°15·9'	2°19·8'W	W	98
Artfield	D & G	NX2366	54°57·7'	4°45·5'W	X	82
Artfield Fell	D & G	NX2367	54°58·2'	4°45·5'W	H	82
Artha	Monm	SO4209	51°46·8'	2°50·1'W	X	161
Arthach	Cered	SN3554	52°9·8'	4°24·4'W	X	145
Arthill	Ches	SJ7285	53°21·9'	2°24·8'W	T	109
Arthington	Leeds	SE2744	53°53·7'	1°34·9'W	T	104
Arthington Bank	Leeds	SE2743	53°53·2'	1°34·9'W	X	104
Arthington Hall	Leeds	SE2745	53°54·3'	1°34·9'W	X	104
Arthington Ho	Leeds	SE2545	53°54·3'	1°36·8'W	X	104
Arthington Pastures	Leeds	SE2845	53°54·3'	1°34·0'W	X	104
Arthingworth	Northnts	SP7581	52°25·5'	0°53·4'W	T	141
Arthingworth Lodge	Northnts	SP7481	52°25·6'	0°54·3'W	X	141
Arthingworth Lodge	Northnts	SP7582	52°26·1'	0°53·4'W	X	141

Arthog	Gwyn	SH6414	52°42·6'	4°0·4'W	T	124
Arthrath	Aberd	NJ9636	57°25·1'	2°3·5'W	T	30
Arthurbank	Pth & Kin	NO2542	56°34·1'	3°12·8'W	X	53
Arthurhouse	Aberd	NO7674	56°51·7'	2°23·2'W	X	45
Arthur's Br	Somer	ST6335	51°7·0'	2°31·3'W	X	183
Arthur's Bridge	Moray	NJ2567	57°41·5'	3°15·0'W	X	28
Arthursdale	Leeds	SE3737	53°49·9'	1°25·9'W	T	104
Arthurseat	Aberd	NK0437	57°25·7'	1°55·5'W	X	30
Arthur Seat	Cumbr	NY4978	55°5·9'	2°47·5'W	X	86
Arthurseat Ho	Cumbr	NY5077	55°5·3'	2°46·6'W	X	86
Arthurshiels	S Lanak	NT0041	55°39·4'	3°34·9'W	X	72
Arthur's Pike	Cumbr	NY4620	54°34·6'	2°49·7'W	H	90
Arthur's Point	Moray	NJ4065	57°40·5'	2°59·9'W	X	28
Arthur's Seat	C of Edin	NT2772	55°56·4'	3°9·7'W	X	66
Arthur's Seat	D & G	NT1112	55°23·9'	3°23·9'W	H	78
Arthur's Seat	Surrey	TQ3253	51°15·9'	0°6·1'W	X	187
Arthur's Seat (Fort)	C of Edin	NT2772	55°56·4'	3°9·7'W	A	66
Arthur's Stone	Heref	SO3142	52°4·6'	3°0·0'W	X	148,161
Arthur's Stone	Swan	SS4990	51°35·6'	4°10·4'W	X	159
Arthur's Stone (Burial Chamber)	Heref	SO3142	52°4·6'	3°0·0'W	A	148,161
Arthur's Stone (Burial Chamber)	Swan	SS4990	51°35·6'	4°10·4'W	A	159
Arthurstone	Pth & Kin	NO2642	56°34·1'	3°11·8'W	X	53
Arthurville	Highld	NH7781	57°48·4'	4°3·7'W	X	21
Arthur Wood	Cumbr	SD3799	54°23·2'	2°57·8'W	F	96,97
Artilligan Burn	Arg & Bt	NR8476	55°56·0'	5°27·0'W	W	62
Artilligan Cottage	Arg & Bt	NR8676	55°56·0'	5°25·1'W	X	62
Artington	Surrey	SU9947	51°13·0'	0°34·6'W	T	186
Artiscombe	Devon	SX4474	50°32·9'	4°11·7'W	X	201
Artists Valley or Cwn Einion	Cered	SN7193	52°31·4'	3°53·7'W	X	135
Artlaw	Aberd	NK0750	57°32·7'	1°52·5'W	X	30
Artle Beck	Lancs	SD5463	54°3·9'	2°41·8'W	W	97
Artle Brook Fm	Ches	SJ6749	53°2·5'	2°29·1'W	FM	118
Artle Crag	Cumbr	NY4710	54°29·2'	2°48·7'W	X	90
Artlegarth	Cumbr	NY7202	54°25·0'	2°25·5'W	X	91
Artlegarth Beck	Cumbr	NY7202	54°25·0'	2°25·5'W	W	91
Artnoch	S Ayr	NX2581	55°5·8'	4°44·1'W	X	76
Artrochie	Aberd	NK0031	57°22·4'	1°59·5'W	X	30
Arundel	W Susx	TQ0107	50°51·4'	0°33·5'W	T	197
Arundel Fm	Heref	SO4943	52°5·2'	2°44·3'W	FM	148,149
Arundel Fm	Wilts	SU1940	51°9·8'	1°43·3'W	FM	184
Arundel Grange	N Yks	SE0581	54°13·7'	1°55·0'W	X	98
Arundell Fm	Wilts	ST9223	51°0·6'	2°6·5'W	FM	184
Arundell's Fm	Somer	ST2623	51°0·3'	3°2·9'W	FM	193
Arundel Park	W Susx	TQ0108	50°52·0'	0°33·5'W	X	197
Arun Valley, The	W Susx	TQ0515	50°55·7'	0°30·0'W	X	197
Arva Skerry	Shetld	HT9541	60°9·5'	2°4·9'W	X	4
Arvie	D & G	NX7476	55°4·0'	3°58·0'W	X	77,84
Arvie Burn	D & G	NX6872	55°1·8'	4°3·5'W	W	77,84
Arvie Hill	D & G	NX7376	55°4·0'	3°58·9'W	H	77,84
Arvie Loch	D & G	NX7475	55°3·5'	3°57·9'W	W	77,84
Arvi Taing	Shetld	HU3683	60°32·0'	1°20·1'W	X	1,2,3
Arwallt, The	Monm	SO3318	51°51·6'	2°58·0'W	X	161
Arwick	Orkney	HY3824	59°6·2'	3°4·5'W	X	6
Aryburn	C of Aber	NJ8913	57°12·7'	2°10·5'W	X	38
Aryhoulan	Highld	NN0168	56°45·9'	5°14·9'W	X	41
Asbatch	Shrops	SO5576	52°23·0'	2°39·3'W	X	137,138
Asby	Cumbr	NY0620	54°34·2'	3°26·8'W	T	89
Asby Grange	Cumbr	NY6810	54°29·3'	2°29·2'W	X	91
Asby Hall	Cumbr	NY6813	54°30·9'	2°29·2'W	X	91
Asby Mask	Cumbr	NY7012	54°30·4'	2°27·4'W	X	91
Asby Winderwath Common	Cumbr	NY6510	54°29·3'	2°32·0'W	X	91
Ascleit	N Eil	NB1610	57°59·6'	6°47·9'W	H	13,14
Asc na Gréine	Highld	NC9008	58°3·1'	3°51·4'W	X	17
Ascog	Arg & Bt	NS1063	55°49·6'	5°1·6'W	T	63
Ascog Bay	Arg & Bt	NS1063	55°49·6'	5°1·6'W	W	63
Ascog Point	Arg & Bt	NS1063	55°49·6'	5°1·6'W	X	63
Ascoile	Highld	NC8211	58°4·6'	3°59·6'W	X	17
Ascot	Win & Maid	SU9268	51°24·4'	0°40·2'W	T	175
Ascot Fm	Win & Maid	SU9269	51°25·0'	0°40·2'W	FM	175
Ascot Heath	Win & Maid	SU9269	51°25·0'	0°40·2'W	X	175
Ascot Place	Brackn	SU9171	51°26·1'	0°41·1'W	X	175
Ascott	Bucks	SP8922	51°53·6'	0°42·0'W	X	165
Ascott	Warw	SP3234	52°0·4'	1°31·6'W	T	151
Ascott d' Oyley	Oxon	SP3018	51°51·8'	1°33·5'W	T	164
Ascott Earl	Oxon	SP2918	51°51·8'	1°34·3'W	T	164
Ascott Fm	Oxon	SU6198	51°40·9'	1°6·7'W	FM	164,165
Ascott Ho	Bucks	SP8922	51°53·6'	0°42·0'W	X	165
Ascott Home Fm	Bucks	SP9023	51°54·1'	0°41·1'W	FM	165
Ascott-under-Wychwood	Oxon	SP3018	51°51·8'	1°33·5'W	T	164
Ascreavie	Angus	NO3357	56°42·3'	3°5·2'W	T	53
Ascreavie Hill	Angus	NO3357	56°42·3'	3°5·2'W	H	53
Ascrib Islands	Highld	NG3064	57°35·4'	6°30·6'W	X	23
Ascurry	Angus	NO5446	56°36·5'	2°44·5'W	X	54
Ascurry Mill	Angus	NO5445	56°35·9'	2°44·5'W	X	54
Ascurry Wood	Angus	NO5346	56°36·5'	2°45·5'W	F	54
Asenby	N Yks	SE3975	54°10·4'	1°23·7'W	T	99
Asfordby	Leic	SK7019	52°46·1'	0°57·3'W	T	129
Asfordby Fm	Leic	SK7120	52°46·6'	0°56·4'W	FM	129
Asfordby Hill	Leic	SK7219	52°46·1'	0°55·6'W	T	129
Asgarby	Lincs	TF1145	52°59·7'	0°20·4'W	T	130
Asgarby	Lincs	TF3366	53°10·7'	0°0·2'W	T	122
Asgog	Arg & Bt	NR9468	55°51·9'	5°17·1'W	X	62
Asgog Bay	Arg & Bt	NR9367	55°51·4'	5°18·0'W	W	62
Asgog Loch	Arg & Bt	NR9470	55°53·0'	5°17·2'W	W	62
Asgood Fm	Carm	SN3016	51°49·2'	4°27·6'W	FM	159
Ash	Corn	SX2096	50°44·4'	4°32·7'W	X	190
Ash	Devon	SS8510	50°52·9'	3°37·7'W	X	191
Ash	Devon	SS9119	50°57·8'	3°32·8'W	X	181
Ash	Devon	SX8349	50°20·0'	3°38·3'W	T	202
Ash	Dorset	ST8610	50°53·6'	2°11·6'W	T	194
Ash	Dorset	SY4696	50°45·9'	2°45·6'W	T	193
Ash	Kent	TQ6064	51°21·4'	0°18·3'E	T	177,188
Ash	Kent	TR2958	51°16·7'	1°17·4'E	T	179
Ash	Somer	ST2822	50°59·8'	3°1·2'W	T	193
Ash	Somer	ST4720	50°58·9'	2°44·9'W	T	193

Ash	Surrey	SU8951	51°15·3′	0°43·1′W	T	186
Ash Abbey	Suff	TM3154	52°8·4′	1°23·0′E	X	156
Ashacres	Shrops	SJ5837	52°56·0′	2°37·1′W	X	126
Ashaig	Highld	NG6923	57°14·6′	5°49·3′W	T	32
Ashallow	Aberd	NK0635	57°24·6′	1°53·6′W	X	30
Asham Ho	Somer	ST1522	50°59·7′	3°12·3′W	X	181,193
Ashampstead	W Berks	SU5676	51°29·0′	1°11·2′W	T	174
Ashampstead Common	W Berks	SU5875	51°28·5′	1°9·5′W	F	174
Ashampstead Green	W Berks	SU5677	51°29·6′	1°11·2′W	T	174
Asham Wood	Somer	ST7045	51°12·4′	2°25·4′W	F	183
Ashansworth	Hants	SU4157	51°18·9′	1°24·3′W	T	174
Ashbank	Angus	NO5033	56°29·4′	2°48·3′W	X	54
Ashbank	Kent	TQ8253	51°15·0′	0°36·9′E	T	188
Ash Bank	Staffs	SJ9346	53°0·9′	2°5·9′W	T	118
Ashbank Fm	Ches	SJ6071	53°14·3′	2°35·6′W	FM	118
Ashbank Fm	Ches	SJ8256	53°6·3′	2°15·7′W	FM	118
Ash Barton	Devon	SS5108	50°51·4′	4°6·6′W	X	191
Ash Barton	Devon	SS5137	51°7·0′	4°7·4′W	A	180
Ashbeach Fm	Cambs	TL2588	52°28·8′	0°9·2′W	FM	142
Ashbeck Gill	Cumbr	SD6693	54°20·1′	2°31·0′W	W	98
Ashbeer	Somer	ST0835	51°6·7′	3°18·5′W	T	181
Ashberry Fm	N Yks	SE5784	54°15·2′	1°7·1′W	FM	100
Ashberry Ho	Glos	ST5496	51°39·9′	2°39·5′W	X	162
Ashberry Wood	N Yks	SE5685	54°15·7′	1°8·0′W	F	100
Ashbocking	Suff	TM1654	52°8·7′	1°9·8′E	T	156
Ashbocking Green	Suff	TM1854	52°8·7′	1°11·6′E	X	156
Ashbocking Hall	Suff	TM1654	52°8·7′	1°9·8′E	X	156
Ashbourne	Derby	SK1846	53°0·9′	1°43·5′W	T	119,128
Ash Bourne	E Susx	TQ6713	50°53·8′	0°22·9′E	W	199
Ashbourne Green	Derby	SK1947	53°1·4′	1°42·6′W	X	119,128
Ash Bridge	Shrops	SO6694	52°32·8′	2°29·7′W	X	138
Ashbrittle	Somer	ST0521	50°59·1′	3°20·8′W	T	181
Ash Brook	Ches	SJ6362	53°9·5′	2°32·8′W	W	118
Ash Brook	Devon	SS7703	50°49·0′	3°44·4′W	W	191
Ashbrook	Herts	TL2027	51°55·9′	0°14·9′W	X	166
Ashbrook	Shrops	SO4594	52°32·7′	2°48·3′W	T	137,138
Ash Brook	Staffs	SK0923	52°48·5′	1°51·6′W	W	128
Ashbrook Fm	Beds	SP9844	52°5·4′	0°33·8′W	FM	153
Ashbrook Fm	Ches	SJ6972	53°14·9′	2°27·5′W	FM	118
Ashbrook Fm	Leic	SK6221	52°47·2′	1°4·4′W	FM	129
Ash Bullayne	Devon	SS7704	50°49·6′	3°44·4′W	X	191
Ashburn	Highld	NH5855	57°34·0′	4°22·0′W	X	26
Ashburnham Forge	E Susx	TQ6816	50°55·4′	0°23·8′E	T	199
Ashburnham Place	E Susx	TQ6814	50°54·3′	0°23·8′E	X	199
Ashburton	Devon	SX7570	50°31·2′	3°45·4′W	T	202
Ashburton Down	Devon	SX7672	50°32·3′	3°44·6′W	H	191
Ashbury	Corn	SX2297	50°45·0′	4°31·0′W	A	190
Ashbury	Corn	SX2397	50°45·0′	4°30·2′W	X	190
Ashbury	Devon	SS4217	50°56·1′	4°14·5′W	X	180,190
Ashbury	Devon	SX5098	50°46·0′	4°7·2′W	T	191
Ashbury	Oxon	SU2685	51°34·0′	1°37·1′W	T	174
Ashbury Plantations	Devon	SX5296	50°44·9′	4°5·5′W	X	191
Ashby	N Lincs	SE8908	53°33·9′	0°39·0′W	T	112
Ashby by Partney	Lincs	TF4266	53°10·6′	0°7·9′E	T	122
Ashby cum Fenby	NE Lincs	TA2500	53°29·1′	0°6·6′W	T	113
Ashby Decoy	N Lincs	SE8608	53°33·9′	0°41·7′W	W	112
Ashby de la Launde	Lincs	TF0555	53°5·1′	0°25·5′W	T	121
Ashby-de-la-Zouch	Leic	SK3516	52°44·7′	1°28·5′W	T	128
Ashby-de-la-Zouch Canal	Leic	SK3115	52°44·1′	1°32·0′W	W	128
Ashby-de-la-Zouch Canal	Leic	SP4094	52°32·8′	1°24·2′W	W	140
Ashby Folville	Leic	SK7012	52°42·3′	0°57·4′W	T	129
Ashby Gorse	Northnts	SP5752	52°10·0′	1°9·6′W	F	152
Ashby Grange	Northnts	SP5568	52°18·7′	1°11·2′W	X	152
Ashby Hall	Lincs	TF0555	53°5·1′	0°25·5′W	X	121
Ashby Hall	Norf	TG4115	52°41·0′	1°34·3′E	X	134
Ashby Hill	NE Lincs	TA2400	53°29·2′	0°7·5′W	T	113
Ashby Ho	Leic	SP5387	52°28·9′	1°12·8′W	X	140
Ashby Ho	Lincs	TF3271	53°13·4′	0°1·0′W	X	122
Ashby Ho	Suff	TM4899	52°32·2′	1°39·8′E	X	134
Ashby Lane Fm	Leic	SP5387	52°28·9′	1°12·8′W	FM	140
Ashby Lodge	Leic	SP5489	52°30·0′	1°11·9′W	X	140
Ashby Lodge	Lincs	TF0255	53°5·2′	0°28·2′W	X	121
Ashby Magna	Leic	SP5690	52°30·5′	1°10·1′W	T	140
Ashby Parva	Leic	SP5288	52°29·5′	1°13·6′W	T	140
Ashby Pastures	Leic	SK7012	52°42·8′	0°57·4′W	X	129
Ashby Pastures Fm	Leic	SK7114	52°43·4′	0°56·5′W	FM	129
Ashby Puerorum	Lincs	TF3271	53°13·4′	0°1·0′W	T	122
Ashby's Castle	Powys	SO2118	51°51·5′	3°8·4′W	A	161
Ashby Sitch	Staffs	SK1315	52°44·2′	1°48·0′W	W	128
Ashby St Ledgers	Northnts	SP5768	52°18·7′	1°9·4′W	T	152
Ashby St Mary	Norf	TG3202	52°34·2′	1°25·8′E	T	134
Ashby Warren	Suff	TG4800	52°32·7′	1°39·9′E	F	134
Ash Cabin Flat	Sheff	SK2686	53°22·5′	1°36·1′W	X	110
Ash Carr	Suff	TL8070	52°18·1′	0°38·8′E	X	144,155
Ashchurch	Glos	SO9233	52°0·0′	2°6·6′W	T	150
Ash Cleugh	Northum	NY6461	54°56·8′	2°33·3′W	X	86
Ashclose Fm	Somer	ST6624	51°1·1′	2°28·7′W	FM	183
Ashclyst Fm	Devon	SY0198	50°46·6′	3°23·9′W	FM	192
Ashclyst Forest	Devon	SY0099	50°47·2′	3°24·7′W	F	192
Ashcombe	Devon	SX9179	50°36·3′	3°32·0′W	T	192
Ashcombe	Somer	SS8837	51°7·5′	3°35·6′W	X	181
Ashcombe Bottom	E Susx	TQ3711	50°53·2′	0°2·7′W	X	198
Ashcombe Bottom	Glos	SO9407	51°45·9′	2°4·8′W	F	163
Ashcombe Bottom	Somer	SS7740	51°9·0′	3°45·1′W	X	180
Ashcombe Bottom	Wilts	ST9319	50°58·5′	2°5·6′W	X	184
Ashcombe Fm	Devon	SX5750	50°20·2′	4°0·2′W	FM	202
Ashcombe Fm	Dorset	ST6715	50°56·2′	2°27·8′W	FM	183
Ashcombe Fm	Somer	ST3906	50°51·3′	2°51·6′W	FM	193
Ashcombe Fm	Wilts	ST9320	50°59·0′	2°5·6′W	FM	184
Ashcombe Ho	Bath & NE Somer	ST7469	51°25·4′	2°22·0′W	X	172
Ashcombe Ho	E Susx	TQ3809	50°52·1′	0°1·9′W	X	198
Ashcombe Park	N Som	ST3362	51°21·4′	2°57·3′W	T	182
Ashcombe Park	Staffs	SJ9751	53°3·6′	2°2·3′W	X	118
Ashcombe Tower	Devon	SX9277	50°35·2′	3°31·2′W	X	192
Ashcombe Wood	Surrey	TQ1551	51°15·0′	0°20·7′W	F	187
Ash Common	Surrey	SU9052	51°15·8′	0°42·2′W	X	186
Ash Coppice	Northnts	SP8487	52°28·7′	0°45·4′W	F	141
Ash Coppice	Shrops	SJ6900	52°36·1′	2°27·1′W	F	127

Ash Copse	Glos	SU1398	51°41·1′	1°48·3′W	F	163
Ash Copse	Oxon	SP3819	51°52·3′	1°26·5′W	F	164
Ash Corner	Suff	TM3156	52°9·5′	1°23·0′E	X	156
Ashcott	Somer	ST4337	51°8·0′	2°48·5′W	T	182
Ashcott Corner	Somer	ST4439	51°9·1′	2°47·7′W	T	182
Ashcott Heath	Somer	ST4439	51°9·1′	2°47·7′W	X	182
Ash Covert	Suff	TL8575	52°20·7′	0°43·4′E	F	144
Ash Crags	Cumbr	NY2809	54°28·5′	3°6·2′W	X	89,90
Ashcraig	N Ayr	NS1965	55°50·9′	4°53·0′W	X	63
Ashcroft Fm	Ches	SJ3672	53°14·7′	2°57·1′W	FM	117
Ashcroft Fm	Herts	TL1733	51°59·2′	0°17·4′W	FM	166
Ashcroft Fm	Norf	TG0328	52°48·9′	1°1·1′E	FM	133
Ashcroft Ho	Glos	ST8094	51°38·9′	2°17·0′W	X	162,173
Ashcroft Ho	Worcs	SO7551	52°9·6′	2°21·5′W	X	150
Ashcroft's Fm	Lancs	SD4204	53°32·0′	2°52·1′W	FM	108
Ashcroft's Fm	Lancs	SD4720	53°40·7′	2°47·7′W	FM	102
Ash Cross	Somer	ST2823	51°0·3′	3°1·2′W	X	193
Ashculme	Devon	ST1414	50°55·4′	3°13·0′W	T	181,193
Ashdale	Heref	SO4924	51°55·0′	2°44·1′W	X	162
Ash Dale	N Yks	SE6086	54°16·2′	1°4·3′W	X	94,100
Ashdale	Pemb	SM9809	51°44·8′	4°55·2′W	X	157,158
Ashdale Gill	Cumbr	SD6383	54°14·7′	2°33·7′W	W	97
Ashdale Ho	N Lincs	TA0916	53°38·0′	0°20·7′W	X	112
Ashday Hall	Cald	SE1123	53°42·4′	1°49·6′W	X	104
Ashdon	Essex	TL5842	52°3·5′	0°18·7′E	T	154
Ash Down	E Susx	TQ4330	51°3·3′	0°2·8′E	X	187
Ash Down	E Susx	TQ4630	51°3·3′	0°5·4′E	X	188
Ashdown	Kent	TQ9056	51°16·5′	0°43·8′E	X	178
Ashdown Copse	Wilts	SU2447	51°13·5′	1°39·0′W	F	184
Ashdown Fm	Devon	SY2191	50°43·0′	3°6·8′W	FM	192,193
Ashdown Forest	E Susx	TQ4529	51°2·7′	0°4·5′E	F	188,198
Ashdown Forest Fm	E Susx	TQ4231	51°3·9′	0°2·0′E	FM	187
Ashdown Hill	Kent	TQ9055	51°16·0′	0°43·8′E	X	178
Ashdown Ho	E Susx	TQ4435	51°6·0′	0°3·8′E	X	187
Ashdown Park	Oxon	SU2881	51°31·9′	1°35·4′W	A	174
Ashdown Park (Hotel)	E Susx	TQ4332	51°4·4′	0°2·9′E	X	187
Ash Drain	Cambs	TL3286	52°27·6′	0°3·0′W	W	142
Ashdub	Durham	NY8829	54°39·6′	2°10·7′W	X	91,92
Ashe	Hants	SU5350	51°15·0′	1°14·0′W	T	185
Ashe Hall	Derby	SK2632	52°53·3′	1°36·4′W	X	128
Ashe House	Devon	SY2795	50°45·2′	3°1·7′W	A	193
Ashe Ingen Court	Heref	SO5826	51°56·1′	2°36·3′W	X	162
Ashel Barn	Glos	ST8096	51°40·0′	2°17·0′W	X	162
Asheldham	Essex	TL9701	51°40·6′	0°51·4′E	T	168
Asheldham Brook	Essex	TL9800	51°40·1′	0°52·2′E	W	168
Asheldham Grange	Essex	TL9702	51°41·2′	0°51·4′E	X	168
Ashelford	Devon	SS5840	51°8·7′	4°1·4′W	X	180
Ashen	Devon	SX4367	50°29·1′	4°12·4′W	X	201
Ashen	Essex	TL7442	52°3·2′	0°32·7′E	T	155
Ashen Coppice	Heref	SO6947	52°7·5′	2°26·8′W	F	149
Ashen Copse	Oxon	SP5708	51°46·3′	1°10·0′W	F	164
Ashen Copse	Somer	ST7942	51°10·8′	2°17·6′W	F	183
Ashen Copse Fm	Oxon	SU2593	51°38·3′	1°37·9′W	FM	163,174
Ashen Cross	Somer	ST4927	51°2·6′	2°43·3′W	X	183,193
Ashen Cross Fm	Corn	SX2153	50°21·2′	4°30·6′W	FM	201
Ashenden	E Susx	TQ8316	50°55·1′	0°36·6′E	X	199
Ashenden	Kent	TQ8931	51°3·1′	0°42·2′E	X	189
Ashendene Fm	Herts	TL3006	51°44·5′	0°6·6′W	FM	166
Ash End House Fm	Warw	SP1797	52°34·5′	1°44·5′W	FM	139
Ashendon	Bucks	SP7014	51°49·4′	0°58·7′W	T	165
Ashenfield Fm	Kent	TR0947	51°11·3′	0°59·8′E	FM	179,189
Ashengrove	I of W	SZ4487	50°41·1′	1°22·2′W	X	196
Ashen Hall	Essex	TL7542	52°3·2′	0°33·6′E	X	155
Ashen Ho	Essex	TL7442	52°3·2′	0°32·7′E	X	155
Ashens	Arg & Bt	NR8571	55°53·3′	5°25·8′W	X	62
Ashentree	E Ayr	NS4813	55°23·4′	4°28·3′W	X	70
Ashentree	Stir	NS6998	56°9·7′	4°6·1′W	X	57
Ashentrool	Stir	NN8200	56°10·9′	3°53·6′W	X	57
Ashen Wood	Hants	SU3900	50°48·1′	1°26·4′W	F	196
Ashen Wood Ho	Hants	SU6628	51°3·1′	1°3·1′W	X	185,186
Ashe Park	Hants	SU5449	51°14·5′	1°13·2′W	X	185
Asherfields	Derby	SK3952	53°4·1′	1°24·7′W	X	119
Asheridge	Bucks	SP9304	51°43·8′	0°38·8′W	T	165
Asheridge Fm	Bucks	SP9205	51°44·4′	0°39·7′W	FM	165
Asherne	Devon	SX8446	50°18·4′	3°37·4′W	X	202
Ashes	Cumbr	SD4697	54°22·2′	2°49·5′W	X	97
Ashes	Fife	NS9887	56°4·2′	3°37·9′W	X	65
Ashes	Lancs	SD5640	53°51·5′	2°39·7′W	X	102
Ashes	N Yks	SD7778	54°12·1′	2°20·7′W	X	98
Ashes	N Yks	SE0082	54°14·3′	1°59·6′W	X	98
Ashes	N Yks	SE0985	54°15·9′	1°51·3′W	X	99
Ashes	Shrops	SO4392	52°31·6′	2°50·0′W	X	137
Ashes	Wrex	SJ4437	52°55·9′	2°49·6′W	X	126
Ashes Beck	Cumbr	SD3489	54°17·8′	3°0·4′W	W	96,97
Ashes Fm	Cumbr	SD5691	54°19·0′	2°40·2′W	FM	97
Ashes Fm	Derby	SK1749	53°2·5′	1°44·4′W	FM	119
Ashes Fm	Derby	SK1888	53°23·6′	1°43·4′W	FM	110
Ashes Fm	Dorset	SU0713	50°55·2′	1°53·6′W	FM	195
Ashes Fm	Essex	TL7921	51°51·8′	0°36·4′E	FM	167
Ashes Fm	E Susx	TQ8815	50°54·5′	0°40·8′E	FM	189,199
Ashes Fm	Lancs	SD5937	53°49·9′	2°37·0′W	FM	102
Ashes Fm	Lancs	SD6833	53°47·8′	2°28·7′W	FM	103
Ashes Fm	N Yks	NZ8809	54°28·4′	0°38·1′W	FM	94
Ashes Fm	Staffs	SK0157	53°6·9′	1°58·7′W	FM	119
Ashes Ho	Durham	NY9939	54°45·0′	2°0·5′W	X	92
Ashes Ho	Durham	NZ0636	54°43·4′	1°54·0′W	X	92
Ashes Hollow	Shrops	SO4392	52°31·6′	2°50·0′W	X	137
Ashes Point	Cumbr	SD3279	54°12·4′	3°2·1′W	X	96,97
Ashes, The	Ches	SJ6880	53°19·2′	2°28·4′W	X	109
Ashes, The	Cumbr	NY3942	54°46·4′	2°56·5′W	X	85
Ashes, The	Cumbr	SD4187	54°16·8′	2°54·0′W	X	96,97
Ashes, The	Darl	NZ3409	54°28·8′	1°28·1′W	X	93
Ashes, The	Derby	SK0586	53°22·5′	1°55·1′W	X	110
Ashes, The	Durham	NY9724	54°36·9′	2°2·4′W	X	92
Ashes, The	Lincs	SK8342	52°58·4′	0°45·4′W	X	130
Ashes, The	Norf	TM1191	52°28·8′	1°6·8′E	X	144
Ashes, The	N Yks	NZ1705	54°26·7′	1°43·9′W	X	92
Ashes, The	Staffs	SJ9256	53°6·3′	2°6·8′W	X	118
Ashes, The	Staffs	SJ9354	53°5·2′	2°5·9′W	A	118
Asheston Ho	Pemb	SM8825	51°53·2′	5°4·5′W	X	157

Ashes Wood	E Susx	TQ7217	50°55·8′	0°27·3′E	F	199
Asheton Fm	Essex	TQ5294	51°37·7′	0°12·2′E	FM	167,177
Ashe Warren Ho	Hants	SU5351	51°15·6′	1°14·0′W	X	185
Ashey	I of W	SZ5789	50°42·1′	1°11·2′W	T	196
Ashey Down	I of W	SZ5787	50°41·0′	1°11·2′W	H	196
Ash Fell	Cumbr	NY7304	54°26·1′	2°24·6′W	X	91
Ash Fell	Cumbr	NY7405	54°26·6′	2°23·6′W	H	91
Ash Fell Edge	Cumbr	NY7304	54°26·1′	2°24·6′W	X	91
Ashfield	Arg & Bt	NR7685	56°0·6′	5°35·2′W	T	55
Ashfield	Arg & Bt	NS0863	55°49·6′	5°3·5′W	X	63
Ashfield	Carm	SN6928	51°56·3′	3°54·0′W	T	146,160
Ashfield	Cumbr	NY7304	54°26·1′	2°24·6′W	X	91
Ashfield	Darl	NZ3011	54°29·8′	1°31·8′W	X	93
Ashfield	E Yorks	SE8929	53°45·2′	0°38·6′W	X	106
Ashfield	Hants	SU3619	50°58·4′	1°28·8′W	T	185
Ashfield	Heref	SO5923	51°54·5′	2°35·4′W	T	162
Ashfield	Moray	NJ3364	57°39·9′	3°6·9′W	X	28
Ashfield	Powys	SN9764	52°16·1′	3°30·2′W	X	147
Ashfield	S Ayr	NS3305	55°18·9′	4°37·5′W	X	70,76
Ashfield	Scot Bord	NT7955	55°47·5′	2°19·7′W	X	67,74
Ashfield	Shrops	SJ3125	52°49·3′	3°1·0′W	T	126
Ashfield	Shrops	SO5889	52°30·1′	2°36·7′W	X	137,138
Ashfield	Stir	NN7803	56°12·5′	3°57·6′W	T	57
Ashfield	Suff	TM2062	52°13·0′	1°13·6′E	T	156
Ashfield Barn	Bucks	SU7591	51°37·0′	0°54·6′W	X	175
Ashfield Cott	Arg & Bt	NR7584	56°0·0′	5°36·1′W	X	55
Ashfield Cum Thorpe	Suff	TM2062	52°13·0′	1°13·6′E	T	156
Ashfield Fm	Essex	TL5819	51°51·1′	0°18·0′E	FM	167
Ashfield Green	Suff	TL7655	52°10·1′	0°34·8′E	T	155
Ashfield Green	Suff	TM2673	52°18·7′	1°19·3′E	T	156
Ashfield Hall	Ches	SJ2979	53°18·4′	3°3·5′W	X	117
Ashfield Haugh	Suff	TM0166	52°15·5′	0°57·1′E	X	155
Ashfield Ho	E Loth	NT5779	56°0·4′	2°40·9′W	X	67
Ashfield Ho	Leeds	SE1945	53°54·3′	1°42·2′W	X	104
Ashfield Ho	Lincs	TF0067	53°11·7′	0°29·8′W	X	121
Ashfield Ho	N Yks	SE2565	54°5·1′	1°36·7′W	X	99
Ashfield Ho	W Dunb	NS4084	56°1·6′	4°33·6′W	X	56,64
Ashfield Lodge	Suff	TM2163	52°13·5′	1°14·6′E	X	156
Ashfield Place Fm	Suff	TM2061	52°12·4′	1°13·6′E	FM	156
Ashfields	Donc	SE6612	53°36·3′	0°59·7′W	X	111
Ashfields	Shrops	SJ5839	52°57·0′	2°37·1′W	X	126
Ashfields	Shrops	SJ7026	52°50·1′	2°26·3′W	T	127
Ashflats	Staffs	SJ9219	52°46·4′	2°6·7′W	X	127
Ash Fm	Brackn	SU9073	51°27·2′	0°41·9′W	FM	175
Ash Fm	Bucks	SP8725	51°55·2′	0°43·7′W	FM	165
Ash Fm	Ches	SJ7775	53°16·5′	2°20·3′W	FM	118
Ash Fm	Devon	SS9504	50°49·8′	3°29·1′W	FM	192
Ash Fm	Devon	SX9383	50°38·4′	3°30·4′W	FM	192
Ash Fm	Devon	SY1097	50°46·2′	3°16·2′W	FM	192,193
Ash Fm	E Susx	TQ5602	50°48·0′	0°13·2′E	FM	199
Ash Fm	Glos	SP2124	51°55·1′	1°41·3′W	FM	163
Ash Fm	Heref	SO5664	52°16·6′	2°38·3′W	FM	137,138,149
Ash Fm	Kent	TQ7241	51°8·8′	0°27·9′E	FM	188
Ash Fm	Kent	TQ8742	51°9·0′	0°40·8′E	FM	189
Ash Fm	Norf	TF9305	52°36·7′	0°51·4′E	FM	144
Ash Fm	Norf	TG0123	52°46·3′	0°59·2′E	FM	133
Ash Fm	Somer	SS8447	51°12·9′	3°39·3′W	FM	181
Ash Fm	Suff	TM3382	52°23·4′	1°25·9′E	FM	156
Ash Fm	Suff	TM3578	52°21·2′	1°27·5′E	FM	156
Ash Fm	Suff	TM4889	52°26·8′	1°39·4′E	FM	156
Ash Fm	Traf	SJ7691	53°25·2′	2°21·3′W	FM	109
Ash Fms	Devon	SS4418	50°56·7′	4°12·9′W	FM	180,190
Ashfold	W Susx	TQ2428	51°2·5′	0°13·5′W	X	187,198
Ashfold Crossways	W Susx	TQ2328	51°2·5′	0°14·3′W	T	187,198
Ashfold School	Bucks	SP6713	51°48·9′	1°1·3′W	X	164,165
Ashfold Side	N Yks	SE1266	54°5·6′	1°48·6′W	T	99
Ashfold Side Beck	N Yks	SE0967	54°6·2′	1°51·3′W	W	99
Ashford	Devon	SS5335	51°6·0′	4°5·6′W	T	180
Ashford	Devon	SX6848	50°19·3′	3°50·9′W	T	202
Ashford	Hants	SU1314	50°55·7′	1°48·5′W	T	195
Ashford	Kent	TR0042	51°8·8′	0°52·0′E	T	189
Ashford	Powys	SO1221	51°53·1′	3°16·3′W	X	161
Ashford	Surrey	TQ0671	51°25·9′	0°28·1′W	T	176
Ashford Bowdler	Shrops	SO5170	52°19·8′	2°42·7′W	T	137,138
Ashford Br	Corn	SX2066	50°28·2′	4°31·8′W	X	201
Ashford Carbonell	Shrops	SO5270	52°19·8′	2°41·9′W	T	137,138
Ashford Chace	Hants	SU7426	51°1·9′	0°56·3′W	X	186,197
Ashford Common	Surrey	TQ0870	51°25·3′	0°26·4′W	T	176
Ashford Fm	Somer	ST2339	51°8·9′	3°5·7′W	FM	182
Ashford Fm	Somer	ST3519	50°58·2′	2°55·2′W	FM	193
Ashford Gill Head	N Yks	SE0768	54°6·7′	1°53·2′W	X	99
Ashford Grange	Shrops	SJ5933	52°53·8′	2°36·2′W	X	126
Ashford Hall	Derby	SK2069	53°13·3′	1°41·6′W	X	119
Ashford Hall	Shrops	SO5171	52°20·3′	2°42·8′W	X	137,138
Ashford Hill	Hants	SU5562	51°21·5′	1°12·2′W	T	174
Ashford in the Water	Derby	SK1969	53°13·3′	1°42·5′W	T	119
Ashford Lodge	Essex	TL8232	51°57·6′	0°39·3′E	X	168
Ashford Mill Fm	Oxon	SP3815	51°50·2′	1°26·5′W	FM	164
Ashford Resr	Somer	ST2338	51°8·4′	3°5·7′W	W	182
Ashford Water	Poole	SU1214	50°55·7′	1°49·4′W	W	195
Ashfurlong Hall	Birm	SP1398	52°35·0′	1°48·1′W	X	139
Ashgate	Derby	SK3671	53°14·3′	1°27·2′W	T	119
Ash Gill	Cumbr	NY7640	54°45·5′	2°22·0′W	W	86,87
Ashgill	N Yks	SE0986	54°16·4′	1°51·3′W	X	99
Ashgill	S Lanak	NS7849	55°43·4′	3°56·1′W	T	64
Ash Gill Beck	Cumbr	SD2695	54°21·0′	3°7·9′W	W	96,97
Ashgill Head	Durham	NY8035	54°42·8′	2°18·2′W	X	91,92
Ashgillside	Cumbr	NY7540	54°45·5′	2°22·9′W	X	86,87
Ashgill Side	N Yks	NY8600	54°24·0′	2°12·5′W	X	91,92
Ash Green	Surrey	SU9049	51°14·2′	0°42·3′W	T	186
Ash Green	Warw	SP3385	52°28·0′	1°30·5′W	T	140
Ashgrove	Bath & NE Somer	ST7057	51°18·9′	2°25·4′W	T	172
Ashgrove	Herts	TL3835	52°0·0′	0°1·0′E	X	154
Ash Grove	Monm	SO4015	51°50·1′	2°51·9′W	X	161
Ashgrove	Moray	NJ2262	57°38·7′	3°17·9′W	T	28
Ashgrove	Shrops	SO3894	52°32·7′	2°54·5′W	X	137
Ash Grove	Suff	TL9671	52°18·4′	0°52·9′E	F	144,155
Ash Grove	Wrex	SJ3640	52°57·5′	2°56·8′W	T	117
Ashgrove Fm	Heref	SO5350	52°9·0′	2°40·8′W	FM	149

Ashgrove Fm	Oxon	SP5326	51°56·0'	1°13·4'W	FM	164
Ashgrove Fm	Wilts	ST9118	50°57·9'	2°7·3'W	FM	184
Ashgrove Manor	Shrops	SO5271	52°20·3'	2°41·9'W	X	137,138
Ashgrove or Stevenston Loch	N Ayr	NS2744	55°39·8'	4°44·6'W	W	63,70
Ash Hall	Shrops	SJ5739	52°57·0'	2°38·0'W	A	126
Ash Hall	Staffs	SJ9247	53°1·5'	2°6·8'W	X	118
Ash Hall	V of Glam	ST0178	51°29·8'	3°25·2'W	X	170
Ash Hey	Ches	SJ4370	53°13·7'	2°50·8'W	X	117
Ash Hill	Cumbr	NY5927	54°38·4'	2°37·7'W	X	91
Ash Hill	Devon	SX9173	50°33·0'	3°31·9'W	T	192
Ash Hill	Dorset	SY6593	50°44·4'	2°29·4'W	X	194
Ash Hill	Durham	NY8928	54°39·1'	2°9·8'W	X	91,92
Ash Hill	Glos	SO9302	51°43·2'	2°5·7'W	X	163
Ash Hill	Herts	TL2538	52°1·8'	0°10·3'W	H	153
Ash Hill	Lincs	TF2096	53°27·1'	0°11·2'W	X	113
Ash Hill	Staffs	SK0821	52°47·4'	1°52·5'W	X	128
Ash Hill Fm	Norf	TL6296	52°32·5'	0°23·7'E	FM	143
Ash Hill Ho	Ches	SJ5463	53°10·0'	2°40·9'W	X	117
Ash Hill (Long Barrow)	Lincs	TF2096	53°27·1'	0°11·2'W	A	113
Ash-hining	Cumbr	SD6392	54°19·6'	2°33·7'W	X	97
Ash Ho	Ches	SJ5875	53°16·5'	2°37·4'W	X	117
Ash Ho	Ches	SJ6263	53°10·0'	2°33·7'W	X	118
Ash Ho	Derby	SK2946	53°0·9'	1°33·7'W	X	119,128
Ash Ho	Devon	SS5706	50°50·4'	4°1·5'W	A	191
Ash Ho	N Yks	NZ6400	54°23·7'	1°0·4'W	X	94
Ash Ho	N Yks	SE2198	54°22·9'	1°40·2'W	X	99
Ash Ho	W Susx	SU8523	51°0·2'	0°46·9'W	X	197
Ashholme	Northum	NY6858	54°55·2'	2°29·5'W	X	86,87
Ash Holme	N Yks	SE1746	53°54·8'	1°44·1'W	X	104
Ashholme Common	Northum	NY7056	54°54·1'	2°27·6'W	H	86,87
Ash Holt	Lincs	TA1801	53°29·8'	0°12·9'W	F	113
Ash Holt	Lincs	TF2319	52°45·5'	0°10·2'W	X	131
Ash Holt	Notts	SK6284	53°21·2'	1°3·7'W	F	111,120
Ash House	Cumbr	SD1887	54°16·6'	3°15·1'W	X	96
Ash House Fm	Brad	SE1441	53°52·1'	1°46·8'W	FM	104
Ash House Fm	Ches	SJ5854	53°5·1'	2°37·2'W	FM	117
Ash House Fm	Lincs	TF1365	53°10·4'	0°18·2'W	FM	121
Ashieburn	Scot Bord	NT6025	55°31·3'	2°37·6'W	X	74
Ashie Moor	Highld	NH6031	57°21·1'	4°19·2'W	X	26
Ashiestiel	Scot Bord	NT4235	55°36·6'	2°54·8'W	T	73
Ashiestiel Hill	Scot Bord	NT4134	55°36·0'	2°55·7'W	H	73
Ashilford	Devon	SS9209	50°52·5'	3°31·7'W	X	192
Ashill	Corn	SW6141	50°13·5'	5°20·7'W	X	203
Ashill	Devon	ST0811	50°53·7'	3°18·1'W	T	192
Ashill	Norf	TF8804	52°36·3'	0°47·0'E	T	144
Ashill	Somer	ST3217	50°57·1'	2°57·7'W	T	193
Ashill Common	Norf	TF8905	52°36·8'	0°47·9'E	X	144
Ashill Fm	I of W	SZ4580	50°37·3'	1°21·4'W	FM	196
Ashill Fm	Somer	SS9026	51°1·6'	3°33·7'W	FM	181
Ashill Moor	Devon	ST0810	50°53·2'	3°18·1'W	X	192
Ashingdon	Essex	TQ8693	51°36·5'	0°41·6'E	T	178
Ashington	Northum	NZ2787	55°10·8'	1°34·1'W	T	81
Ashington	Poole	SZ0098	50°47·1'	1°59·6'W	T	195
Ashington	Somer	ST5621	50°59·4'	2°37·2'W	T	183
Ashington	W Susx	TQ1316	50°56·2'	0°23·1'W	T	198
Ashington End	Lincs	TF5266	53°10·4'	0°16·9'E	T	122
Ashington Fm	Northum	NZ2686	55°10·3'	1°35·1'W	FM	81
Ashington Wood	Somer	ST5520	50°58·9'	2°38·1'W	F	183
Ashintully Castle	Pth & Kin	NO1061	56°44·2'	3°27·8'W	X	43
Ashkirk	Scot Bord	NT4722	55°29·6'	2°49·9'W	T	73
Ashkirk Hill	Scot Bord	NT4620	55°28·5'	2°50·8'W	X	73
Ashkirk Loch	Scot Bord	NT4719	55°28·0'	2°49·9'W	W	79
Ashkirktown	Scot Bord	NT4721	55°29·0'	2°49·9'W	X	73
Ashlack Hall	Cumbr	SD2485	54°15·5'	3°9·6'W	A	96
Ashlade Firs	Wilts	SU2267	51°24·3'	1°40·6'W	X	174
Ash Lagoons	E Loth	NT3573	55°57·0'	3°2·0'W	W	66
Ash Lagoons	Notts	SK6980	53°19·0'	0°57·4'W	W	120
Ashland	D & G	NX6754	54°52·0'	4°3·9'W	X	83,84
Ashland	Mil Key	SP8735	52°0·6'	0°43·5'W	X	152
Ashland Hill	Somer	ST4908	50°52·4'	2°43·1'W	H	193,194
Ashlands	Hants	SU6110	50°53·4'	1°7·6'W	X	196
Ashlands	Leic	SK7100	52°35·8'	0°56·7'W	X	141
Ashlands Fm	Staffs	SK2205	52°38·8'	1°40·1'W	FM	139
Ashlar Chair	Brad	SE1244	53°53·8'	1°48·6'W	X	104
Ashlar Ho	Lancs	SD8236	53°49·4'	2°16·0'W	X	103
Ashlawn Ho	Warw	SP5072	52°20·9'	1°15·6'W	X	140
Ashlea Fm	Derby	SK3429	52°51·7'	1°29·3'W	FM	128
Ashlea Grange	Aberd	NJ8120	57°16·5'	2°18·4'W	X	38
Ashleigh	Devon	SX3983	50°37·7'	4°16·2'W	X	201
Ashleigh	Leic	SK7122	52°47·7'	0°56·4'W	X	129
Ashleigh Barton	Devon	SX4762	50°26·5'	4°8·9'W	X	201
Ashleigh Fm	Devon	SX5188	50°40·6'	4°6·2'W	FM	191
Ashleigh Fm	Surrey	SU9363	51°21·7'	0°39·5'W	FM	175,186
Ashleigh Ho	Derby	SK2518	52°45·8'	1°37·4'W	X	128
Ashlett	Hants	SU4603	50°49·7'	1°20·4'W	T	196
Ashlett Creek	Hants	SU4703	50°49·7'	1°19·6'W	W	196
Ash Level	Kent	TR3061	51°18·3'	1°18·4'E	X	179
Ashleworth	Glos	SO8125	51°55·6'	2°16·2'W	T	162
Ashleworth Court	Glos	SO8125	51°55·6'	2°16·2'W	A	162
Ashleworth Quay	Glos	SO8125	51°55·6'	2°16·2'W	X	162
Ashley	Cambs	TL6961	52°13·5'	0°28·9'E	T	154
Ashley	Ches	SJ7784	53°21·4'	2°20·3'W	T	109
Ashley	C of Edin	NT1571	55°55·7'	3°21·2'W	X	65
Ashley	Devon	SS9103	50°49·2'	3°32·5'W	X	192
Ashley	Devon	SS9410	50°53·0'	3°30·0'W	X	192
Ashley	Dorset	SU1304	50°50·4'	1°48·5'W	T	195
Ashley	Glos	ST9394	51°38·9'	2°5·7'W	T	163,173
Ashley	Hants	SU3830	51°4·3'	1°27·1'W	T	185
Ashley	Hants	SU7555	51°17·6'	0°55·1'W	X	175,186
Ashley	Hants	SZ2595	50°45·5'	1°38·3'W	T	195
Ashley	Heref	SO3362	52°15·4'	2°58·5'W	X	137,148,149
Ashley	Highld	NH6350	57°31·4'	4°16·8'W	X	26
Ashley	Kent	TR3048	51°11·3'	1°17·9'E	T	179
Ashley	Northnts	SP7990	52°30·4'	0°49·8'W	T	141
Ashley	Pth & Kin	NO2437	56°31·4'	3°13·7'W	X	53
Ashley	Staffs	SJ7636	52°55·5'	2°21·0'W	T	127
Ashley	Wilts	ST8168	51°24·9'	2°16·0'W	T	173
Ashley Barn	Dorset	SY8195	50°45·5'	2°15·8'W	X	194
Ashley Chase Dairy	Dorset	SY5688	50°41·6'	2°37·0'W	X	194
Ashley Chase Ho	Dorset	SY5687	50°41·1'	2°37·0'W	X	194
Ashley Clinton House	Hants	SZ2693	50°44·4'	1°37·5'W	X	195
Ashley Court	Ches	SJ4646	53°0·8'	2°47·9'W	X	117
Ashley Dale	Staffs	SJ7536	52°55·5'	2°21·9'W	T	127
Ashley Down	C of Bris	ST5975	51°28·6'	2°35·0'W	T	172
Ashley Down	Hants	SU3829	51°3·8'	1°27·1'W	X	185
Ashley Down Fm	Hants	SU6008	50°52·3'	1°8·4'W	FM	196
Ashley Fm	Dorset	SU1306	50°51·4'	1°48·5'W	FM	195
Ashley Fm	Hants	SU6440	51°9·6'	1°4·7'W	FM	185
Ashley Green	Bucks	SP9705	51°44·3'	0°35·3'W	T	165
Ashley Green	Cumbr	NY3503	54°25·3'	2°59·7'W	X	90
Ashley Grove	Cumbr	NX9910	54°28·8'	3°33·1'W	X	89
Ashley Hall	Ches	SJ7684	53°21·4'	2°21·2'W	X	109
Ashley Hall	Lancs	SD5838	53°50·4'	2°37·9'W	X	102
Ashley Heath	Dorset	SU1104	50°50·4'	1°50·2'W	T	195
Ashley Heath	Staffs	SJ7435	52°54·9'	2°22·8'W	T	127
Ashley Heath	Traf	SJ7685	53°21·9'	2°21·2'W	T	109
Ashley Heath Stud	Cambs	TL6763	52°14·6'	0°27·2'E	X	154
Ashley Hill	Wilts	SU1729	51°3·8'	1°45·1'W	H	184
Ashley Hill	Win & Maid	SU8281	51°31·5'	0°48·7'W	H	175
Ashley Hill Forest	Win & Maid	SU8280	51°31·0'	0°48·7'W	F	175
Ashley Ho	Lancs	SD5837	53°49·9'	2°37·9'W	X	102
Ashley Manor Fm	Hants	SZ2594	50°44·9'	1°38·4'W	FM	195
Ashley Moor	Heref	SO4767	52°18·2'	2°46·2'W	T	137,138,148
Ashley or Asholt Wood	Kent	TR1738	51°6·2'	1°6·4'E	F	179,189
Ashley Park	Surrey	TQ1065	51°22·6'	0°24·8'W	T	176
Ashley Park Fm	Hants	SU0915	50°56·3'	1°51·9'W	FM	184
Ashleys	Lancs	SD6367	54°6·1'	2°33·5'W	X	97
Ashley's Copse	Wilts	SU2534	51°6·5'	1°38·2'W	F	184
Ashley Warren Fm	Hants	SU4955	51°17·8'	1°17·4'W	FM	174,185
Ashley Wood	Dorset	ST9205	50°50·9'	2°6·4'W	F	195
Ashley Wood	Hants	SU3931	51°4·8'	1°26·2'W	F	185
Ashley Wood	Suff	TM4483	52°23·7'	1°35·6'E	F	156
Ashley Wood Fm	Wilts	ST9330	51°4·4'	2°5·6'W	FM	184
Ashlings Cottages	Essex	TL5207	51°44·7'	0°12·5'E	X	167
Ashling's Fm	Essex	TL5901	51°41·3'	0°18·4'E	FM	167
Ash Lound	Lincs	SK9070	53°13·4'	0°38·7'W	F	121
Ashludie Fm	Angus	NO5033	56°29·4'	2°48·3'W	FM	54
Ashlyn Fm	Hants	SU5407	50°51·8'	1°13·6'W	FM	196
Ashlyns	Essex	TL5106	51°44·2'	0°11·6'E	X	167
Ashlyn's Hall	Herts	SP9906	51°44·9'	0°33·6'W	X	165
Ash Magna	Shrops	SJ5739	52°57·0'	2°38·0'W	T	126
Ashmanhaugh	Norf	TG3121	52°44·5'	1°25·7'E	T	133,134
Ashman's Fm	Essex	TL8517	51°49·5'	0°41·5'E	FM	168
Ashmans Hall	Suff	TM4189	52°27·0'	1°33·2'E	X	156
Ashmansworthy	Devon	SS3318	50°56·5'	4°22·2'W	T	190
Ashmark	E Ayr	NS6110	55°22·1'	4°11·2'W	X	71
Ashmark Hill	E Ayr	NS6009	55°21·6'	4°12·1'W	X	71,77
Ashmead Brake	Swin	SU1592	51°37·8'	1°46·6'W	F	163,173
Ashmead Green	Glos	ST7699	51°41·6'	2°20·4'W	T	162
Ashmead Ho	Glos	SO7700	51°42·1'	2°19·6'W	X	162
Ash Meadow	Cumbr	SD4578	54°11·9'	2°50·2'W	X	97
Ash Mill	Devon	SS7823	50°59·8'	3°43·9'W	T	180
Ashmill	Devon	SX3995	50°44·2'	4°16·5'W	T	190
Ash Moor	Devon	SS7919	50°57·7'	3°43·0'W	T	180
Ashmoor	Heref	SO2955	52°11·6'	3°1·9'W	X	148
Ashmore	Dorset	ST9117	50°57·4'	2°7·3'W	T	184
Ashmore	Pth & Kin	NO1453	56°39·9'	3°23·7'W	X	53
Ashmore Bottom	Dorset	ST9114	50°55·8'	2°7·3'W	X	195
Ashmore Bottom	Dorset	ST9115	50°56·3'	2°7·3'W	X	184
Ashmore Brook	Staffs	SK0910	52°41·5'	1°51·6'W	X	128
Ashmore Down	Dorset	ST9119	50°58·5'	2°7·3'W	X	184
Ashmore Fm	Bucks	SP6536	52°1·3'	1°2·8'W	FM	152
Ashmore Fm	Bucks	SP7227	51°56·4'	0°56·8'W	FM	165
Ashmore Fm	Dorset	ST9117	50°57·4'	2°7·3'W	FM	184
Ashmore Fm	Pth & Kin	NO1452	56°39·4'	3°23·7'W	FM	53
Ashmore Green	W Berks	SU5069	51°25·3'	1°16·5'W	T	174
Ashmore Ho	Staffs	SJ9160	53°8·5'	2°7·7'W	X	118
Ashmore Ho	Wilts	SU2424	51°1·1'	1°39·1'W	X	184
Ashmore Lake	Wals	SO9699	52°35·6'	2°3·1'W	T	139
Ashmore Park	Wolv	SJ9601	52°36·6'	2°3·1'W	T	127,139
Ashmore's Fm	Worcs	SP0447	52°7·5'	1°56·1'W	FM	150
Ashmore Wood	Dorset	ST9015	50°56·3'	2°8·2'W	F	184
Ash Moss	Cumbr	NY5970	55°1·6'	2°38·1'W	X	86
Ashness Br	Cumbr	NY2719	54°33·9'	3°7·3'W	X	89,90
Ashness Fell	Cumbr	NY2718	54°33·4'	3°7·3'W	X	89,90
Ashness Fm	Cumbr	NY2719	54°33·9'	3°7·3'W	FM	89,90
Ashnott	Lancs	SD6948	53°55·9'	2°27·9'W	X	103
Ashnough Fm	Staffs	SJ8352	53°4·1'	2°14·8'W	FM	118
Asholt or Ashley Wood	Kent	TR1738	51°6·2'	1°6·4'E	F	179,189
Ashop Clough	Derby	SK0990	53°24·6'	1°51·5'W	X	110
Ashop Head	Derby	SK0690	53°24·6'	1°54·2'W	X	110
Ashop Moor	Derby	SK1388	53°23·6'	1°47·9'W	X	110
Ashopton	Derby	SK1986	53°22·5'	1°42·5'W	T	110
Ashorne	Warw	SP3057	52°12·9'	1°33·3'W	T	151
Ashorne Hall	Warw	SP3158	52°13·4'	1°32·4'W	X	151
Ashorne Hill	Warw	SP3058	52°13·4'	1°33·3'W	X	151
Ashorne Hill College	Warw	SP3058	52°13·4'	1°33·3'W	X	151
Ashorne House Fm	Warw	SP3058	52°13·4'	1°33·3'W	FM	151
Ashott Barton	Somer	SS8138	51°8·0'	3°41·7'W	X	181
Ashour Fm	Kent	TQ5443	51°10·7'	0°12·6'E	FM	188
Ashour Wood	Kent	TQ5443	51°10·2'	0°12·6'E	F	188
Ashover	Derby	SK3463	53°10·0'	1°29·1'W	T	119
Ashover Hay	Derby	SK3561	53°8·9'	1°28·2'W	T	119
Ashow	Warw	SP3170	52°19·9'	1°32·3'W	T	140
Ash Park	Cumbr	NY5082	55°8·0'	2°46·6'W	X	79
Ash Parva	Shrops	SJ5739	52°57·0'	2°38·0'W	T	126
Ashperton	Heref	SO6441	52°4·2'	2°31·1'W	T	149
Ashperton Park	Heref	SO6441	52°4·2'	2°31·1'W	F	149
Ash Plantn	Suff	TL7672	52°19·3'	0°35·4'E	F	155
Ashplats Wood	W Susx	TQ4038	51°7·7'	0°0·4'E	F	187
Ashpole Spinney	Leic	SP3697	52°34·4'	1°27·7'W	F	140
Ashprington	Devon	SX8157	50°24·3'	3°40·1'W	T	202
Ash Priors	Somer	ST1529	51°3·5'	3°12·4'W	T	181,193
Ash Priors Common	Somer	ST1528	51°2·9'	3°12·4'W	X	181,193
Ashreigney	Devon	SS6213	50°54·2'	3°57·4'W	T	180
Ashridge	Devon	SS4424	50°59·9'	4°13·0'W	X	180,190
Ashridge	Devon	SS4926	51°1·1'	4°8·8'W	X	180
Ashridge	Devon	SS8206	50°50·7'	3°40·2'W	X	191
Ashridge	Devon	SX6350	50°20·3'	3°55·1'W	X	202
Ashridge	Devon	SX7660	50°25·8'	3°44·4'W	X	202
Ashridge (Coll)	Herts	SP9912	51°48·1'	0°33·5'W	X	165
Ashridge Common	Herts	TL3716	51°49·8'	0°0·3'W	X	166
Ashridge Copse	Hants	SU1014	50°55·8'	1°51·1'W	F	195
Ashridge Court	Devon	SS6603	50°48·9'	3°53·8'W	T	191
Ashridge Fm	Bucks	SP9901	51°42·2'	0°33·6'W	FM	165
Ashridge Fm	Somer	ST4655	51°17·7'	2°46·1'W	FM	172,182
Ashridge Fm	W Berks	SU4978	51°30·2'	1°17·3'W	FM	174
Ashridge Manor	Wok	SU8170	51°25·6'	0°49·7'W	X	175
Ashridge Moor Cross	Devon	SS6703	50°48·9'	3°52·9'W	X	191
Ashridge Park	Herts	SP9812	51°48·1'	0°34·3'W	X	165
Ashridge Wood	W Berks	SU5078	51°30·2'	1°16·4'W	F	174
Ash Row Fm	N Yks	SE5133	53°47·7'	1°13·1'W	FM	105
Ash Slack	Cumbr	SD3289	54°17·8'	3°2·3'W	X	96,97
Ashslack Wood	E Yorks	SE9046	53°54·4'	0°37·4'W	F	106
Ash Spinney	Notts	SK5327	52°50·5'	1°12·4'W	F	129
Ash Spring	Cumbr	SD4894	54°20·6'	2°47·6'W	X	97
Ashstead	Cumbr	NY5502	54°24·9'	2°41·2'W	X	90
Ash Street	Suff	TM0146	52°4·8'	0°56·4'E	T	155
Ashtead	Surrey	TQ1858	51°18·8'	0°18·0'W	T	187
Ashtead Common	Surrey	TQ1759	51°19·3'	0°18·9'W	F	187
Ashtead Park	Surrey	TQ1957	51°18·2'	0°17·2'W	X	187
Ash, The	Cumbr	NY5176	55°4·8'	2°45·6'W	X	86
Ash, The	Northum	NY8177	55°5·5'	2°17·4'W	X	86,87
Ash Thomas	Devon	ST0010	50°53·1'	3°24·9'W	T	192
Ashton	Ches	SJ5069	53°13·2'	2°44·5'W	T	117
Ashton	Corn	SW6028	50°6·5'	5°21·0'W	T	203
Ashton	Corn	SX3868	50°29·6'	4°16·7'W	X	201
Ashton	Hants	SU5419	50°58·3'	1°13·5'W	T	185
Ashton	Heref	SO5164	52°16·6'	2°42·7'W	T	137,138,149
Ashton	Highld	NH7045	57°28·9'	4°9·6'W	X	27
Ashton	Inverc	NS2377	55°57·5'	4°49·7'W	T	63
Ashton	Lancs	SD4043	53°53·0'	2°54·4'W	X	102
Ashton	Northnts	SP7649	52°8·3'	0°53·0'W	T	152
Ashton	Northnts	TL0588	52°29·0'	0°26·8'W	T	142
Ashton	Peterb	TF1005	52°38·1'	0°22·1'W	T	142
Ashton	Powys	SJ1404	52°37·9'	3°15·8'W	X	136
Ashton	Somer	ST4149	51°14·5'	2°50·3'W	T	182
Ashton Brook	Ches	SJ5070	53°13·7'	2°44·5'W	W	117
Ashton Close	Derby	SK1442	52°58·7'	1°47·1'W	X	119,128
Ashton Common	Wilts	ST8958	51°19·5'	2°9·1'W	T	173
Ashton Court	N Som	ST5571	51°26·4'	2°38·5'W	X	172
Ashton Down	Wilts	SU0396	51°40·0'	1°57·0'W	X	163
Ashton Fm	Devon	SS7848	51°13·3'	3°44·4'W	FM	180
Ashton Fm	Dorset	SY6687	50°41·1'	2°28·5'W	FM	194
Ashton Gate	C of Bris	ST5771	51°26·4'	2°36·7'W	T	172
Ashton Green	E Susx	TQ4612	50°53·6'	0°4·9'E	T	198
Ashton Hall	Lancs	SD4657	54°0·6'	2°49·0'W	A	102
Ashton Hayes	Ches	SJ5169	53°13·2'	2°43·6'W	X	117
Ashton Hays	Staffs	SK1014	52°43·7'	1°50·7'W	X	128
Ashton Heath	Ches	SJ5679	53°18·6'	2°39·2'W	T	117
Ashton Hill	Bath & NE Somer	ST6765	51°23·2'	2°28·1'W	X	172
Ashton Hill	N Som	ST5470	51°25·9'	2°39·3'W	H	172
Ashton Hill Plantn	N Som	ST5270	51°25·9'	2°41·0'W	F	172
Ashton House Fm	N Yks	SE4295	54°21·2'	1°20·8'W	FM	99
Ashton-in-Makerfield	Wigan	SJ5799	53°29·4'	2°38·6'W	T	108
Ashton Keynes	Wilts	SU0494	51°38·9'	1°56·1'W	T	163,173
Ashton Lodge Fm	Northnts	SP7750	52°8·8'	0°52·1'W	FM	152
Ashton Meml	Lancs	SD4861	54°2·8'	2°47·2'W	X	97
Ashton Mill Fm	Wilts	ST9256	51°18·4'	2°6·5'W	FM	173
Ashton Park	Lancs	SD5030	53°46·1'	2°45·1'W	X	102
Ashtons	Lancs	SD4808	53°34·2'	2°46·7'W	X	108
Ashtons-cross	Ches	SJ5050	53°2·9'	2°44·3'W	X	117
Ashtons Fm, The	Staffs	SJ8230	52°52·3'	2°15·6'W	FM	127
Ashton under Hill	Worcs	SO9938	52°2·7'	2°0·5'W	T	150
Ashton-Under-Lyne	Tames	SJ9499	53°29·5'	2°5·0'W	T	109
Ashton Upon Mersey	Traf	SJ7892	53°25·7'	2°19·5'W	T	109
Ashton Upthorpe Downs	Oxon	SU5482	51°32·3'	1°12·9'W	X	174
Ashton Vale	C of Bris	ST5670	51°25·9'	2°37·6'W	T	172
Ashton Wold	Northnts	TL0987	52°28·4'	0°23·3'W	F	142
Ashton Wold Fm	Northnts	TL0888	52°29·0'	0°24·2'W	FM	142
Ashton Wold Ho	Northnts	TL0887	52°28·4'	0°24·2'W	X	142
Ashton Wood	Worcs	SO9939	52°3·2'	2°0·5'W	F	150
Ashtown	C of Aber	NJ8610	57°11·1'	2°13·4'W	X	38
Ashtown Fm	Corn	SW5035	50°10·0'	5°29·7'W	FM	203
Ashtown Fm	Devon	SS9524	51°0·6'	3°29·4'W	FM	181
Ashtree	Ghead	NZ1158	54°55·2'	1°49·3'W	X	88
Ash Tree Cave	Derby	SK5176	53°16·9'	1°13·7'W	A	120
Ash Tree Fm	Cambs	TL5573	52°20·2'	0°16·9'E	FM	154
Ash Tree Fm	Ches	SJ6177	53°17·6'	2°34·7'W	FM	118
Ashtree Fm	Ches	SJ6649	53°2·5'	2°30·0'W	FM	118
Ash Tree Fm	Lincs	TF2218	52°45·0'	0°11·1'W	FM	131
Ash Tree Fm	Lincs	TF2550	53°2·2'	0°7·7'W	FM	122
Ashtree Fm	Lincs	TF3116	52°43·8'	0°3·2'W	FM	131
Ash Tree Fm	Lincs	TF3512	52°41·6'	0°0·3'E	FM	131,142
Ash Tree Fm	Norf	TG3906	52°36·2'	1°32·2'E	FM	134
Ashtree Fm	Norf	TG5009	52°37·5'	1°42·0'E	FM	134
Ash Tree Fm	Norf	TM0486	52°26·3'	1°0·5'E	FM	144
Ash Tree Fm	Northnts	SP7270	52°19·6'	0°56·2'W	FM	141
Ash Tree Fm	N Yks	SD8753	53°58·6'	2°11·5'W	FM	103
Ash Tree Fm	N Yks	SE3488	54°17·4'	1°28·2'W	FM	99
Ash Tree Fm	N Yks	SE5718	53°39·6'	1°7·8'W	FM	111
Ashtree Fm	Oxon	SU3397	51°40·5'	1°31·0'W	FM	164
Ash Tree Fm	Somer	ST3446	51°12·8'	2°56·3'W	FM	182
Ashtree Fm	Suff	TM3778	52°21·1'	1°29·2'E	FM	156
Ashtree Fm	Suff	TM4489	52°26·9'	1°35·9'E	FM	156
Ashtrees	Northum	NY8395	55°15·2'	2°15·6'W	X	80
Ashtrees	Scot Bord	NT6413	55°24·8'	2°33·7'W	X	80
Ashurst	E Susx	TQ3615	50°55·3'	0°3·5'W	X	198
Ashurst	Hants	SU3310	50°53·5'	1°31·5'W	T	196
Ashurst	Kent	TQ5138	51°7·5'	0°9·9'E	T	188
Ashurst	Lancs	SD4807	53°33·7'	2°46·7'W	T	108
Ashurst	W Susx	TQ0116	50°56·3'	0°33·4'W	X	197
Ashurst	W Susx	TQ1716	50°56·1'	0°19·7'W	T	198
Ashurst Bridge	Hants	SU3412	50°54·6'	1°30·6'W	T	196
Ashurst Court	Kent	TQ7946	51°11·3'	0°34·1'E	X	188
Ashurst Fm	Warw	SP4385	52°27·9'	1°21·6'W	FM	140
Ashurst Lodge	Hants	SU3308	50°52·5'	1°31·5'W	X	196

Ashurst (New Forest) Station	Hants	SU3310	50°53·5′	1°31·5′W	X	196
Ashurst Place	Kent	TQ5439	51°8·0′	0°12·5′E	X	188
Ashurst Rough	Surrey	TQ1851	51°15·0′	0°18·2′W	F	187
Ashurst's Beacon	Lancs	SD5007	53°33·7′	2°44·9′W	H	108
Ashurst's Hall	Lancs	SD4908	53°34·2′	2°45·8′W	A	108
Ashurst Wood	Hants	SU3309	50°53·0′	1°31·5′W	F	196
Ashurst Wood	Surrey	TQ4136	51°6·6′	0°1·2′E	T	187
Ashvale	Blae Gw	SO1310	51°47·2′	3°15·3′W	T	161
Ash Vale	Surrey	SU8953	51°16·4′	0°43·1′W	T	186
Ashwater	Devon	SX3895	50°44·2′	4°17·4′W	T	190
Ashwater Wood	Devon	SX3894	50°43·6′	4°17·3′W	F	190
Ashway	Somer	SS8631	51°4·3′	3°37·2′W	X	181
Ashway Gap	Oldham	SE0204	53°32·2′	1°57·8′W	X	110
Ashway Rocks	Oldham	SE0204	53°32·2′	1°57·8′W	X	110
Ashway Side	Somer	SS8731	51°4·3′	3°36·4′W	X	181
Ashway Stone	Oldham	SE0304	53°32·2′	1°56·9′W	X	110
Ashwell	Devon	SS5513	50°54·1′	4°3·4′W	X	180
Ashwell	Devon	SX7655	50°23·1′	3°44·3′W	X	202
Ashwell	Devon	SX8974	50°33·5′	3°33·6′W	T	192
Ashwell	Herts	TL2639	52°2·3′	0°9·4′W	T	153
Ashwell	Rut	SK8613	52°42·7′	0°43·2′W	T	130
Ashwell	Somer	SS9339	51°8·7′	3°31·4′W	X	181
Ashwell	Somer	ST3615	50°56·1′	2°54·3′W	T	193
Ashwell End	Herts	TL2540	52°2·9′	0°10·2′W	T	153
Ashwell Grange	Glos	ST5798	51°41·0′	2°36·9′W	X	162
Ashwell Grange	Rut	SK8513	52°42·7′	0°44·1′W	X	130
Ashwell Grove	Glos	ST5699	51°41·5′	2°37·8′W	F	162
Ashwell Hall	Essex	TL7030	51°56·8′	0°28·8′E	X	167
Ashwell Lodge	Glos	SP0409	51°47·0′	1°56·1′W	X	163
Ashwell Moor	Cambs	TL5082	52°25·2′	0°12·7′E	X	143
Ashwell & Morden Sta	Cambs	TL2938	52°1·8′	0°6·8′W	X	153
Ashwells	Essex	TQ5796	51°38·7′	0°16·5′E	X	167,177
Ashwell's Fm	Bucks	TQ0093	51°37·8′	0°32·9′W	FM	176
Ashwellthorpe	Norf	TM1497	52°32·0′	1°9·7′E	T	144
Ashwick	Somer	SS8830	51°3·7′	3°35·5′W	X	181
Ashwick	Somer	ST6348	51°14·0′	2°31·4′W	T	183
Ashwicke Grange	S Glos	ST7871	51°26·5′	2°18·6′W	X	172
Ashwicke Hall (Sch)	S Glos	ST7971	51°26·5′	2°17·7′W	X	172
Ashwicken	Norf	TF7019	52°44·7′	0°31·5′E	T	132
Ash Wood	Cambs	TL1366	52°17·1′	0°20·2′W	F	153
Ash Wood	Devon	SS6214	50°54·8′	3°57·4′W	F	180
Ash Wood	Oxon	SP5118	51°51·7′	1°15·2′W	F	164
Ashwood	Shrops	SJ5840	52°57·6′	2°37·1′W	X	117
Ash Wood	Somer	ST1430	51°4·0′	3°13·3′W	F	181
Ash Wood	Staffs	SJ8224	52°49·0′	2°15·6′W	F	127
Ashwood	Staffs	SO8688	52°29·6′	2°12·0′W	T	139
Ash Wood	Suff	TM4565	52°13·9′	1°35·7′E	F	156
Ashwood Brow Fm	Ches	SJ6380	53°19·2′	2°32·9′W	FM	109
Ashwood Dale	Derby	SK0772	53°14·9′	1°53·3′W	X	119
Ashwoodfield Ho	Staffs	SO8788	52°29·6′	2°11·1′W	X	139
Ashwood Fm	Northnts	SP7851	52°9·3′	0°51·2′W	FM	152
Ashwood Fm	Shrops	SJ5939	52°57·0′	2°36·2′W	FM	126
Ashwood Ho	Ches	SJ4272	53°14·8′	2°51·7′W	X	117
Ashwood Lodge	Norf	TF7112	52°40·9′	0°32·2′E	X	132,143
Ashworth Hall	Roch	SD8413	53°37·0′	2°14·1′W	X	109
Ashworth Moor Resr	Lancs	SD8215	53°38·1′	2°15·9′W	W	109
Ashworthy Fm	S Glos	ST6888	51°35·6′	2°27·3′W	FM	162,172
Ashyard	E Ayr	NS4735	55°35·3′	4°25·2′W	X	70
Ashyards	D & G	NY2475	55°4·1′	3°11·0′W	X	85
Ashyards Gate	D & G	NY2375	55°4·1′	3°11·9′W	X	85
Ashybank	D & G	NT0708	55°21·7′	3°27·6′W	X	78
Ashy Bank	D & G	NT2001	55°18·0′	3°15·2′W	H	79
Ashybank	D & G	NT2201	55°18·1′	3°13·3′W	X	79
Ashy Bank	Durham	NY9539	54°45·0′	2°4·2′W	X	91,92
Ashybank	Scot Bord	NT5417	55°26·9′	2°43·2′W	X	79
Ashy Bog	Northum	NY7595	55°15·2′	2°23·2′W	X	80
Ashy Cleugh	Cumbr	NY5876	55°4·8′	2°39·0′W	X	86
Ashycroft	Cumbr	NY5676	55°4·8′	2°40·9′W	X	86
Ashydoo Church	S Ayr	NX0199	55°15·0′	5°7·4′W	X	76
Ashy Geo	Highld	ND1874	58°39·0′	3°24·3′W	X	7,12
Ashy Geo	Highld	ND3545	58°23·6′	3°6·2′W	X	12
Asick Bottom	N Yks	SE0657	54°0·8′	1°54·1′W	X	104
Askam in Furness	Cumbr	SD2177	54°11·2′	3°12·2′W	T	96
Askam Pier	Cumbr	SD2077	54°11·2′	3°13·1′W	X	96
Aske Beck	N Yks	NZ1803	54°25·6′	1°42·9′W	W	92
Aske Hall	N Yks	NZ1703	54°25·6′	1°43·9′W	A	92
Askelon	Shetld	HU3673	60°26·6′	1°20·2′W	X	2,3
Aske Moor	N Yks	NZ1303	54°25·6′	1°47·6′W	X	92
Aske Moor Fm	N Yks	NZ1503	54°25·6′	1°45·7′W	FM	92
Asker Fm	Arg & Bt	NS3679	55°58·8′	4°37·3′W	FM	63
Asker Hill	Lancs	SD7547	53°55·4′	2°22·4′W	X	103
Askern	Donc	SE5513	53°36·9′	1°9·7′W	T	111
Askernish	N Eil	NF7172	57°38·2′	7°10·2′W	X	18
Askershaw Wood	Northnts	SP8387	52°28·7′	0°46·3′W	F	141
Askerswell	Dorset	SY5292	50°43·8′	2°40·4′W	T	194
Askerswell Down	Dorset	SY5392	50°43·8′	2°39·6′W	X	194
Askerton Castle	Cumbr	NY5569	55°1·1′	2°41·8′W	A	86
Askerton Hill	Notts	SK8046	53°0·6′	0°48·1′W	T	130
Askerton Park	Cumbr	NY5571	55°2·1′	2°41·8′W	X	86
Askett	Bucks	SP8105	51°44·5′	0°49·2′W	T	165
Askew Green	Cumbr	SD4285	54°15·7′	2°53·0′W	X	96,97
Askew Hill	Derby	SK3127	52°50·6′	1°32·0′W	X	128
Askew Hill	Lancs	SD5261	54°2·8′	2°43·6′W	X	97
Askew Rigg Fm	Cumbr	NY3727	54°38·3′	2°58·1′W	FM	90
Askew Spa	Notts	SK5568	53°12·6′	1°10·2′W	W	120
Askham	Cumbr	NY5123	54°36·2′	2°45·1′W	T	90
Askham	Notts	SK7474	53°15·7′	0°53·0′W	T	120
Askham Bogs	York	SE5748	53°55·7′	1°7·5′W	F	105
Askham Bryan	York	SE5548	53°55·8′	1°9·3′W	T	105
Askham Fell	Cumbr	NY4922	54°35·7′	2°46·9′W	X	90
Askham Ho	Cambs	TL3991	52°30·2′	0°3·3′E	X	142,143
Askham Richard	York	SE5348	53°55·8′	1°11·2′W	T	105
Askill	Cumbr	NY1222	54°35·4′	3°21·3′W	X	89
Askill Knott	Cumbr	NY1222	54°35·4′	3°21·3′W	X	89
Askival	Highld	NM3995	56°58·6′	6°17·3′W	H	39
Ask Law	Scot Bord	NT1114	55°25·0′	3°23·9′W	X	78
Asknish	Arg & Bt	NR9391	56°4·3′	5°19·1′W	T	55
Asknish Bay	Arg & Bt	NM7910	56°14·1′	5°33·5′W	W	55
Askomill	Arg & Bt	NR7220	55°25·5′	5°35·8′W	T	68

Askrigg	N Yks	SD9491	54°19·1′	2°5·1′W	T	98
Askrigg Bottoms	N Yks	SD9590	54°18·6′	2°4·2′W	X	98
Askrigg Common	N Yks	SD9493	54°20·2′	2°5·1′W	X	98
Askrigg Hall	Cumbr	NY4237	54°43·7′	2°53·6′W	X	90
Askrigg Pasture	N Yks	SD9392	54°19·7′	2°6·0′W	X	98
Askwith	N Yks	SE1648	53°55·9′	1°45·0′W	T	104
Askwith Moor	N Yks	SE1651	53°57·5′	1°45·0′W	X	104
Aslackby	Lincs	TF0830	52°51·6′	0°23·3′W	T	130
Aslackby Decoy Fm	Lincs	TF1431	52°52·1′	0°18·0′W	FM	130
Aslackby Fen	Lincs	TF1430	52°51·6′	0°18·0′W	X	130
Aslacton	Norf	TM1590	52°28·2′	1°10·3′E	T	144
Asleid Ho	Aberd	NJ8441	57°27·8′	2°15·5′W	X	29,30
Asliesk	Moray	NJ1159	57°37·0′	3°28·9′W	X	28
Aslockton	Notts	SK7440	52°57·4′	0°53·5′W	T	129
Asmall Ho	Lancs	SD3909	53°34·7′	2°54·9′W	X	108
Asney	Somer	ST4636	51°7·5′	2°45·9′W	T	182
Asney Park Fm	Wrex	SJ3643	52°59·1′	2°56·8′W	FM	117
Aspall	Suff	TM1765	52°14·6′	1°11·1′E	T	156
Aspall Ho	Suff	TM1666	52°15·2′	1°10·3′E	X	156
Aspall Wood	Suff	TM1765	52°14·6′	1°11·1′E	F	156
Asparagus Island	Corn	SW6813	49°58·6′	5°13·8′W	X	203
Aspatria	Cumbr	NY1441	54°45·6′	3°19·8′W	T	85
Aspenden	Herts	TL3528	51°56·3′	0°1·8′W	T	166
Aspen Fm	N Lincs	SE9106	53°32·8′	0°37·2′W	FM	112
Aspen Grove	N Yks	SE4783	54°14·7′	1°16·3′W	X	100
Aspenshaw Fm	Derby	SK0188	53°23·6′	1°58·7′W	FM	110
Aspenshaw Hall	Derby	SK0187	53°23·0′	1°58·7′W	X	110
Aspen Wood	Essex	TQ5399	51°40·4′	0°13·2′E	F	167,177
Asperton	Lincs	TF2637	52°55·2′	0°7·1′W	T	131
Asp Ho	N Yks	NZ9107	54°27·3′	0°35·4′W	X	94
Aspinalls	Lancs	SD6936	53°49·4′	2°27·8′W	X	103
Asplands Husk Coppice	Warw	SP0559	52°14·0′	1°55·2′W	F	150
Aspley	C of Nott	SK5342	52°58·6′	1°12·2′W	T	129
Aspley	Staffs	SJ8133	52°53·9′	2°16·5′W	T	127
Aspley Fm	Staffs	SJ9207	52°39·9′	2°6·7′W	FM	127,139
Aspley Guise	Beds	SP9436	52°1·1′	0°37·4′W	T	153
Aspley Hall	Beds	SP9438	52°2·2′	0°37·4′W	X	153
Aspley Heath	Beds	SP9235	52°0·6′	0°39·2′W	T	152
Aspley Heath	Warw	SP0970	52°19·9′	1°51·7′W	T	139
Aspley Manor Fm	Bucks	SP8208	51°46·1′	0°48·3′W	FM	165
Aspley Wood	Beds	SP9335	52°0·6′	0°38·3′W	F	153
Asplins Fm	Cambs	TL3757	52°11·9′	0°0·7′E	FM	154
Asplins Head	Essex	TR0090	51°34·6′	0°53·6′E	X	178
Asps, The	Warw	SP2963	52°16·1′	1°34·1′W	X	151
Aspull	Wigan	SD6108	53°34·3′	2°34·9′W	T	109
Aspult Common	Wigan	SJ6398	53°28·9′	2°33·0′W	T	109
Assart Fm	Northnts	SP7443	52°5·1′	0°54·8′W	FM	152
Assarts Fm	Notts	SK5869	53°13·1′	1°7·5′W	FM	120
Assary	Highld	NM7675	56°49·0′	5°39·8′W	X	40
Assater	Shetld	HU2979	60°29·9′	1°27·8′W	T	3
Asselby	E Yorks	SE7128	53°44·8′	0°55·0′W	T	105,106
Asselby Grange	E Yorks	SE7932	53°46·9′	0°47·6′W	X	105,106
Asselby Island	E Yorks	SE7226	53°43·8′	0°54·1′W	F	105,106
Asselfoot	S Ayr	NX2090	55°10·5′	4°49·2′W	X	76
Asserby	Lincs	TF4977	53°16·4′	0°14·5′E	T	122
Asserby Turn	Lincs	TF4777	53°16·4′	0°12·7′E	T	122
Asserton Fm	Wilts	SU0839	51°9·2′	1°52·7′W	FM	184
Assery	Highld	ND0562	58°32·4′	3°37·4′W	X	11,12
Assich	Highld	NH8147	57°30·1′	3°58·7′W	X	27
Assich Forest	Highld	NH8146	57°29·6′	3°58·7′W	F	27
Assington	Suff	TL9338	52°0·6′	0°49·1′E	T	155
Assington Green	Suff	TL7751	52°8·0′	0°35·6′E	T	155
Assington Ho	Suff	TL9438	52°0·6′	0°50·0′E	X	155
Assington Thicks	Suff	TL9237	52°0·1′	0°48·2′E	F	155
Assley Common	Glos	ST7589	51°36·2′	2°21·3′W	X	162,172
Assloss	E Ayr	NS4440	55°38·0′	4°28·3′W	X	70
Assycombe Hill	Devon	SX6682	50°37·6′	3°53·3′W	H	191
Assynt Ho	Highld	NH5967	57°40·5′	4°21·4′W	X	21
Asta	Shetld	HU4141	60°9·4′	1°15·2′W	X	4
Astbury	Ches	SJ8461	53°9·0′	2°13·9′W	T	118
Astbury Hall	Shrops	SO7289	52°30·1′	2°24·4′W	X	138
Astbury Ho	Ches	SJ3770	53°13·6′	2°56·1′W	X	117
Astbury Mere	Ches	SJ8462	53°9·5′	2°14·0′W	W	118
Astcote	Northnts	SP6753	52°10·5′	1°0·8′W	T	152
Astcote Lodge	Northnts	SP6752	52°10·0′	1°0·8′W	X	152
Asterby	Lincs	TF2679	53°17·8′	0°6·2′W	T	122
Asterby Grange	Lincs	TF2576	53°16·2′	0°7·1′W	X	122
Asterby Ho	Lincs	TF2679	53°17·8′	0°6·2′W	X	122
Asterby Top Fm	Lincs	TF2678	53°17·3′	0°6·2′W	FM	122
Asterleigh Fm	Oxon	SP4022	51°53·9′	1°24·7′W	FM	164
Asterley	Shrops	SJ3707	52°39·7′	2°55·5′W	T	126
Asterton	Shrops	SO3991	52°31·0′	2°53·5′W	T	137
Asterton Prolley Moor	Shrops	SO3992	52°31·6′	2°53·6′W	X	137
Astey Wood	Beds	SP9848	52°7·5′	0°33·7′W	F	153
Asthall	Oxon	SP2811	51°48·0′	1°35·2′W	T	163
Asthall Barrow	Oxon	SP2810	51°47·5′	1°35·2′W	A	163
Asthall Leigh	Oxon	SP3012	51°48·6′	1°33·5′W	T	164
Astle	Ches	SJ8273	53°15·5′	2°15·8′W	T	118
Astle	Highld	NH7391	57°53·7′	4°8·1′W	X	21
Astle Hall	Ches	SJ8173	53°15·5′	2°16·7′W	X	118
Astley	Shrops	SJ5218	52°45·7′	2°42·3′W	T	126
Astley	Shrops	SO7785	52°28·0′	2°19·9′W	X	138
Astley	Warw	SP3189	52°30·1′	1°32·2′W	T	140
Astley	Wigan	SD7000	53°30·0′	2°26·7′W	T	109
Astley	Worcs	SO7867	52°18·3′	2°19·0′W	T	138,150
Astley Abbotts	Shrops	SO7096	52°33·9′	2°26·2′W	T	138
Astley Bridge	Bolton	SD7112	53°36·5′	2°25·9′W	T	109
Astley Bridge Fm	Oxon	SP5918	51°51·7′	1°8·2′W	FM	164
Astley Castle	Warw	SP3189	52°30·1′	1°32·2′W	X	140
Astley Cott	Orkney	HY4917	59°2·5′	2°52·8′W	X	6
Astley Cross	Worcs	SO8069	52°19·4′	2°17·2′W	T	138
Astley Grange	Shrops	SJ5218	52°45·7′	2°42·3′W	X	126
Astley Green	Wigan	SJ7099	53°29·5′	2°26·7′W	T	109
Astley Hall	Lancs	SD5718	53°39·6′	2°38·6′W	A	108
Astley Hall	Worcs	SO7967	52°18·3′	2°18·1′W	X	138,150
Astley Hall Fm	Warw	SP3386	52°28·5′	1°30·4′W	FM	140
Astley Ho	Lancs	SD6141	53°52·1′	2°35·2′W	X	102,103
Astley Lodge	Shrops	SJ5219	52°46·2′	2°42·3′W	X	126
Astley Lodge Fm	Warw	SP3087	52°29·0′	1°33·1′W	FM	140
Astley's Plantation	Cumbr	SD3987	54°16·7′	2°55·8′W	F	96,97

Astmoor	Halton	SJ5383	53°20·8′	2°42·0′W	T	108
Astol	Shrops	SJ7300	52°36·1′	2°23·5′W	X	127
Aston	Birm	SP0889	52°30·2′	1°52·5′W	T	139
Aston	Ches	SJ5578	53°18·1′	2°40·1′W	T	117
Aston	Ches	SJ6146	53°0·8′	2°34·5′W	T	118
Aston	Derby	SK1631	52°52·8′	1°45·3′W	T	128
Aston	Derby	SK1883	53°20·9′	1°43·4′W	T	110
Aston	Flint	SJ3067	53°12·0′	3°2·5′W	T	117
Aston	Heref	SO4662	52°15·5′	2°47·1′W	T	137,138,148
Aston	Heref	SO4671	52°20·3′	2°47·2′W	T	137,138,148
Aston	Herts	TL2722	51°53·2′	0°8·9′W	T	166
Aston	Oxon	SP3403	51°43·7′	1°30·1′W	T	164
Aston	Powys	SO2991	52°31·0′	3°2·4′W	T	137
Aston	Roth	SK4685	53°21·8′	1°18·1′W	T	111,120
Aston	Shrops	SJ5328	52°51·1′	2°41·5′W	T	126
Aston	Shrops	SO8093	52°32·3′	2°17·3′W	T	138
Aston	Staffs	SJ7541	52°58·2′	2°21·9′W	T	118
Aston	Staffs	SJ8923	52°48·5′	2°9·4′W	T	127
Aston	Wok	SU7884	51°33·2′	0°52·1′W	T	175
Aston	Wrekin	SJ6109	52°40·9′	2°34·2′W	X	127
Aston Abbotts	Bucks	SP8420	51°52·6′	0°46·4′W	T	165
Aston Bank	Worcs	SO6270	52°19·8′	2°33·1′W	T	138
Aston Botterell	Shrops	SO6384	52°27·4′	2°32·3′W	T	138
Aston Br	Staffs	SK1631	52°52·8′	1°45·3′W	X	128
Aston Brook	Shrops	SJ3405	52°38·6′	2°58·1′W	W	126
Aston Bury	Herts	TL2721	51°52·6′	0°8·9′W	A	166
Astonbury Wood	Herts	TL2721	51°52·6′	0°8·9′W	F	166
Aston-By-Stone	Staffs	SJ9131	52°52·8′	2°7·6′W	T	127
Aston Cantlow	Warw	SP1359	52°14·0′	1°48·2′W	T	151
Aston Cliff	Staffs	SJ7642	52°58·7′	2°21·0′W	X	118
Aston Clinton	Bucks	SP8712	51°48·2′	0°43·9′W	T	165
Aston Coppice	Shrops	SJ7608	52°40·4′	2°20·9′W	F	127
Aston Court	Worcs	SO6269	52°19·3′	2°33·1′W	X	138
Aston Court Estate	N Som	ST5572	51°26·9′	2°38·5′W	X	172
Aston Court Fm	Worcs	SO9252	52°10·2′	2°6·6′W	FM	150
Aston Crews	Heref	SO6723	51°54·5′	2°28·4′W	T	162
Aston Cross	Glos	SO9433	52°0·0′	2°4·8′W	T	150
Aston Deans	Shrops	SO5187	52°29·0′	2°42·9′W	X	137,138
Aston End	Herts	TL2724	51°54·2′	0°8·8′W	T	166
Aston Eyre	Shrops	SO6594	52°32·8′	2°30·6′W	T	138
Aston Eyre Hall Fm	Shrops	SO6594	52°32·8′	2°30·6′W	FM	138
Aston Fields	Worcs	SO9669	52°19·4′	2°3·1′W	T	139
Aston Firs	Leic	SP4594	52°32·8′	1°19·8′W	F	140
Aston Flamville	Leic	SP4692	52°31·7′	1°18·9′W	T	140
Aston Fm	Glos	SP1421	51°53·5′	1°47·4′W	FM	163
Aston Fm	Glos	ST9099	51°41·6′	2°8·3′W	FM	163
Aston Fm	Shrops	SJ3228	52°51·0′	3°0·2′W	FM	126
Aston Fm	Warw	SP2688	52°29·6′	1°36·6′W	FM	140
Aston Grange	Ches	SJ5677	53°17·5′	2°39·2′W	X	117
Aston Grange	Shrops	SJ5229	52°51·6′	2°42·4′W	X	126
Aston Grove	Glos	SP1218	51°51·9′	1°49·1′W	F	163
Aston Grove	Warw	SP1458	52°13·4′	1°47·3′W	F	151
Aston Hale	Glos	SP2135	52°1·0′	1°41·2′W	X	151
Aston Hall	Ches	SJ6557	53°6·8′	2°31·0′W	X	118
Aston Hall	Powys	SO2991	52°31·0′	3°2·4′W	X	137
Aston Hall	Shrops	SJ3227	52°50·4′	3°0·2′W	X	126
Aston Hall	Shrops	SJ7508	52°40·4′	2°21·8′W	A	127
Aston Hall	Shrops	SO5086	52°28·4′	2°43·8′W	A	137,138
Aston Heath	Derby	SK1732	52°53·3′	1°44·4′W	X	128
Aston Hill	Bucks	SP8810	51°47·1′	0°43·1′W	X	165
Astonhill	Derby	SK2058	53°7·4′	1°41·7′W	X	119
Aston Hill	Powys	SO2990	52°30·4′	3°2·4′W	H	137
Aston Hill	Shrops	SJ3206	52°39·1′	2°59·9′W	H	126
Aston Hill	Shrops	SO6693	52°32·3′	2°29·7′W	X	138
Aston Hill Fm	Derby	SK4029	52°51·7′	1°23·9′W	FM	129
Aston Holdings	Warw	SP1458	52°13·4′	1°47·3′W	X	151
Aston Ingham	Heref	SO6823	51°54·5′	2°27·5′W	T	162
Aston juxta Mondrum	Ches	SJ6456	53°6·2′	2°31·9′W	T	118
Aston le Walls	Northnts	SP4950	52°9·0′	1°16·6′W	T	151
Aston Locks	Shrops	SJ3325	52°49·3′	2°59·3′W	X	126
Aston Lodge	Ches	SJ5578	53°18·1′	2°40·1′W	X	117
Astonlodge Fm	Staffs	SJ9233	52°53·9′	2°6·7′W	FM	127
Aston Magna	Glos	SP1935	52°1·0′	1°43·0′W	T	151
Aston Mills	Heref	SO6622	51°54·0′	2°29·3′W	X	162
Aston Mullins	Bucks	SP7608	51°46·2′	0°53·5′W	X	165
Aston Munslow	Shrops	SO5186	52°28·4′	2°42·9′W	T	137,138
Aston New Fm	Ches	SJ6557	53°6·8′	2°31·0′W	FM	118
Aston on Carrant	Glos	SO9434	52°0·5′	2°4·8′W	T	150
Aston on Clun	Shrops	SO3981	52°25·7′	2°53·4′W	T	137
Aston-on-Trent	Derby	SK4129	52°51·7′	1°23·1′W	T	129
Aston Park	Ches	SJ6778	53°18·1′	2°29·3′W	X	118
Aston Park Stud	Oxon	SU7298	51°40·8′	0°57·1′W	X	165
Aston Pigott	Shrops	SJ3305	52°38·6′	2°59·0′W	T	126
Aston Rogers	Shrops	SJ3406	52°39·1′	2°58·1′W	T	126
Aston Rowant	Oxon	SU7299	51°41·3′	0°57·1′W	T	165
Aston Sandford	Bucks	SP7507	51°45·6′	0°54·4′W	T	165
Aston Somerville	Worcs	SP0438	52°2·7′	1°56·1′W	T	150
Aston Sq	Shrops	SJ3228	52°51·0′	3°0·2′W	T	126
Aston Subedge	Glos	SP1341	52°4·3′	1°48·2′W	T	151
Aston Tirrold	Oxon	SU5585	51°33·9′	1°12·0′W	T	174
Aston Upthorpe	Oxon	SU5586	51°34·4′	1°12·0′W	T	174
Aston Wood	Oxon	SU7397	51°40·3′	0°56·3′W	F	165
Astridge	Pemb	SN1002	51°41·3′	4°44·5′W	X	158
Astrop	Northnts	SP5036	52°1·4′	1°15·9′W	T	151
Astrope	Herts	SP8914	51°49·3′	0°42·1′W	T	165
Astrop Fm	Oxon	SP3008	51°46·4′	1°33·5′W	FM	164
Astrophill Fm	Northnts	SP5138	52°2·5′	1°15·0′W	FM	151
Astrop Ho	Northnts	SP5036	52°1·4′	1°15·9′W	X	151
Astwell Ho	Northnts	SP6044	52°5·7′	1°7·1′W	A	152
Astwell Park Fm	Northnts	SP6243	52°5·1′	1°5·3′W	FM	152
Astwick	Beds	TL2138	52°1·9′	0°13·8′W	T	153
Astwick Manor	Herts	TL2009	51°46·2′	0°15·3′W	X	166
Astwick Village	Northnts	SP5734	52°0·3′	1°9·8′W	A	152
Astwith	Derby	SK4464	53°10·5′	1°20·1′W	T	120
Ast Wood	Heref	SO6738	52°2·6′	2°28·5′W	F	149
Astwood	Mil Key	SP9547	52°7·0′	0°36·4′W	T	153
Astwood	Worcs	SO8657	52°12·9′	2°11·9′W	T	150
Astwood	Worcs	SO9365	52°17·2′	2°5·8′W	T	150
Astwood Bank	Worcs	SP0462	52°15·6′	1°56·1′W	T	150
Astwood Court	Worcs	SP0362	52°15·6′	1°57·0′W	X	150

Astwood Fm	Worcs	SO9465	52°17·2'	2°4·9'W	FM	150
Astwood Fm	Worcs	SP0361	52°15·1'	1°57·0'W	FM	150
Astwood Grange	Mil Key	SP9548	52°7·6'	0°36·3'W	X	153
Astwood Hill Fm	Worcs	SP0262	52°15·6'	1°57·8'W	FM	150
Aswarby	Lincs	TF0639	52°56·5'	0°24·9'W	T	130
Aswarby Thorns	Lincs	TF0741	52°57·6'	0°24·0'W	F	130
Aswardby	Lincs	TF3770	53°12·8'	0°3·5'E	T	122
Aswardby Mill	Lincs	TF3769	53°12·3'	0°3·5'E	X	122
As Wick	Shetld	HU4753	60°15·8'	1°8·5'W	W	3
Aswick	Shetld	HU4753	60°15·8'	1°8·5'W	X	3
Aswick Grange	Lincs	TF3114	52°42·7'	0°3·2'W	X	131
Aswick Skerries	Shetld	HU4852	60°15·2'	1°7·5'W	X	3
Asylum Fm	Warw	SP4171	52°20·4'	1°23·5'W	FM	140
Atcham	Shrops	SJ5409	52°40·8'	2°40·4'W	T	126
Atchen Hill	Worcs	SO8055	52°11·8'	2°17·2'W	X	150
Atchester Wood	Kent	TR1548	51°11·7'	1°5·0'E	F	179,189
Atch Lench	Worcs	SP0350	52°9·1'	1°57·0'W	T	150
Atchley Ho	Shrops	SJ7703	52°37·7'	2°20·0'W	X	127
Atchley Manor	Shrops	SJ7703	52°37·7'	2°20·0'W	X	127
Atcombe Court	Glos	SO8301	51°42·7'	2°14·4'W	X	162
Ath a' Mhàil	N Eil	NB3949	58°21·4'	6°27·2'W	X	8
Athans	Shetld	HP6511	60°46·9'	0°47·9'W	X	1
Ath Cumhang	N Eil	NF8041	57°21·1'	7°18·8'W	X	22
Athelhampton	Dorset	SY7794	50°44·9'	2°19·2'W	T	194
Athelington	Suff	TM2070	52°17·3'	1°13·9'E	T	156
Athelney	Somer	ST3428	51°3·1'	2°56·1'W	T	193
Athelney Hill	Somer	ST3429	51°3·6'	2°56·1'W	X	193
Athelstaneford	E Loth	NT5377	55°59·3'	2°44·8'W	T	66
Athelstaneford Mains	E Loth	NT5477	55°59·3'	2°43·8'W	X	66
Athelstans Wood	Heref	SO5131	51°58·8'	2°42·4'W	F	149
Atherall's Fm	E Susx	TQ4323	50°59·5'	0°2·6'E	FM	198
Atherfield Fm	I of W	SZ4779	50°36·8'	1°19·8'W	FM	196
Atherfield Green	I of W	SZ4679	50°36·8'	1°20·6'W	T	196
Atherfield Point	I of W	SZ4579	50°36·8'	1°21·5'W	X	196
Atherington	Devon	SS5923	50°59·6'	4°0·2'W	T	180
Atherington	W Susx	TQ0000	50°47·7'	0°34·5'W	T	197
Athersley North	Barns	SE3509	53°34·8'	1°27·9'W	T	110,111
Athersley South	Barns	SE3508	53°34·8'	1°27·9'W	T	110,111
Atherstone	Somer	ST3816	50°56·6'	2°52·6'W	T	193
Atherstone	Warw	SP3197	52°34·4'	1°32·2'W	T	140
Atherstone Hill	Somer	ST3816	50°56·6'	2°52·6'W	X	193
Atherstone Hill Fm	Warw	SP1950	52°9·1'	1°42·9'W	FM	151
Atherstone on Stour	Warw	SP2050	52°9·1'	1°42·1'W	T	151
Atherton	Wigan	SD6703	53°31·6'	2°29·5'W	T	109
Atherton Hall	Wigan	SD6601	53°30·5'	2°30·4'W	X	109
Atheston	Pemb	SN0714	51°47·7'	4°47·5'W	X	158
Athill Fm	Corn	SX2885	50°38·6'	4°25·6'W	FM	201
Ath Leitir	Arg & Bt	NM6325	56°21·7'	5°49·8'W	X	49
Athnamulloch	Highld	NH1320	57°14·2'	5°5·5'W	X	25
Atholhill	Aberd	NJ8727	57°20·3'	2°12·5'W	X	38
Atholl	Pth & Kin	NN6871	56°49·0'	4°9·3'W	X	42
Atholl	Pth & Kin	NN8571	56°49·2'	3°52·6'W	X	43
Athron Hall	Pth & Kin	NO0906	56°14·5'	3°27·7'W	X	58
Atkins Fm	Bucks	SP8800	51°41·7'	0°42·2'W	FM	165
Atkinson Ellers	N Yks	SE6896	54°21·5'	0°56·8'W	X	94,100
Atkinson Ground	Cumbr	SD3297	54°22·1'	3°2·4'W	X	96,97
Atkins Wood	E Susx	TQ7017	50°55·9'	0°25·5'E	F	199
Atla Holm	Shetld	HU3636	60°6·7'	1°20·6'W	X	4
Atla Ness	Shetld	HU3636	60°6·7'	1°20·6'W	X	4
Atlantic Corrie	Highld	NM3896	56°59·1'	6°18·3'W	X	39
Atley Field Fm	N Yks	SE4488	54°17·4'	1°19·0'W	FM	99
Atley Fields	N Yks	NZ2902	54°25·0'	1°32·8'W	X	93
Atley Hill	N Yks	NZ2802	54°25·0'	1°33·7'W	X	93
Atley Hill Fm	N Yks	NZ2801	54°24·5'	1°33·7'W	FM	93
Atli's Hill	Shetld	HU5182	60°31·4'	1°3·8'W	X	1,2,3
Atlow	Derby	SK2348	53°2·0'	1°39·0'W	T	119
Atlowtop	Derby	SK2348	53°2·0'	1°39·0'W	X	119
Atlow Winn	Derby	SK2249	53°2·5'	1°39·9'W	X	119
Atners Towers	Hants	SU3636	51°7·6'	1°28·7'W	X	185
Atrim	Dorset	SY4495	50°45·3'	2°47·3'W	T	193
Attadale	Highld	NG9238	57°23·4'	5°27·2'W	T	25
Attadale Forest	Highld	NG9939	57°24·1'	5°20·3'W	X	25
Attadale House	Highld	NG9239	57°23·9'	5°27·3'W	X	25
Attenborough	Notts	SK5134	52°54·3'	1°14·1'W	T	129
Atterbury	Mil Key	SP8939	52°2·8'	0°41·7'W	T	152
Atterby	Lincs	SK9892	53°25·2'	0°31·1'W	T	112
Atterby Beck	Lincs	SK9692	53°25·2'	0°32·9'W	W	112
Atterby Carr	Lincs	TF0093	53°25·7'	0°29·3'W	X	112
Attercliffe	Sheff	SK3788	53°23·5'	1°26·2'W	T	110,111
Atterley	Shrops	SO6497	52°34·4'	2°31·5'W	T	138
Attermire Cave	N Yks	SD8464	54°4·5'	2°14·3'W	A	98
Attermire Scar	N Yks	SD8464	54°4·5'	2°14·3'W	X	98
Atterton	Leic	SP3598	52°35·0'	1°28·6'W	T	140
Attingham	Shrops	SJ5409	52°40·8'	2°40·4'W	X	126
Attinlea	Highld	NJ0517	57°14·3'	3°34·0'W	X	36
Attiquin	S Ayr	NS3208	55°20·5'	4°38·5'W	X	70,76
Attisham	Dorset	ST4001	50°48·6'	2°50·7'W	X	193
Attleboro Fm	Warw	SP1790	52°30·7'	1°44·6'W	FM	139
Attleborough	Norf	TM0495	52°31·1'	1°0·8'E	T	144
Attleborough	Warw	SP3790	52°30·6'	1°26·9'W	T	140
Attleborough Hills	Norf	TM0397	52°32·2'	1°0·0'E	X	144
Attlebridge	Norf	TG1216	52°42·2'	1°8·7'E	T	133
Attlebridge Hall	Norf	TG1315	52°41·7'	1°9·5'E	X	133
Attlebridge Hills	Norf	TG1416	52°42·2'	1°10·5'E	X	133
Attlepin Fm	Glos	SP1540	52°3·7'	1°46·5'W	FM	151
Attleton Green	Suff	TL7454	52°9·6'	0°33·0'E	T	155
Atton	Angus	NO3173	56°50·9'	3°7·4'W	X	44
Attonburn	Scot Bord	NT8122	55°29·7'	2°17·6'W	X	74
Atton Burn	Scot Bord	NT8322	55°29·7'	2°15·7'W	W	74
Atton Burn	Scot Bord	NT8365	55°52·9'	2°15·9'W	W	67
Atton Cott	Scot Bord	NT8364	55°52·4'	2°15·9'W	X	67
Attridge's Fm	Essex	TL6117	51°49·9'	0°20·6'E	FM	167
Attwood Fm	E Susx	TQ6415	50°54·9'	0°20·4'E	FM	199
Atwell Park Fm	Shrops	SJ7512	52°42·5'	2°21·8'W	FM	127
Atwick	E Yorks	TA1950	53°56·2'	0°10·8'W	T	107
Atwick Sands	E Yorks	TA1951	53°56·7'	0°10·8'W	X	107
Atworth	Wilts	ST8665	51°23·3'	2°11·7'W	T	173
Atworthy	Devon	SS3117	50°55·9'	4°23·9'W	X	190
Auberies	Essex	TL8539	52°1·3'	0°42·2'E	X	155
Auberrow	Heref	SO4947	52°7·4'	2°44·3'W	T	148,149

Aubourn	Lincs	SK9262	53°9·1'	0°37·0'W	T	121
Aubrey Ho	Hants	SZ3091	50°43·3'	1°34·1'W	X	196
Aubreys Fm	Glos	SO7533	51°59·9'	2°21·5'W	FM	150
Aubreys, The	Herts	TL0911	51°47·4'	0°24·8'W	A	166
Auburn Fm	E Yorks	TA1662	54°2·7'	0°13·3'W	FM	101
Auburn Hill	N Yks	SE8070	54°7·4'	0°46·1'W	X	100
Auburn Village	E Yorks	TA1662	54°2·7'	0°13·3'W	A	101
Auburys	Heref	SO2733	51°59·7'	3°3·4'W	X	161
Auch	Arg & Bt	NN3235	56°28·9'	4°43·2'W	X	50
Auchaballa	Aberd	NO5694	57°2·4'	2°43·1'W	X	37,44
Auchaber	Aberd	NJ6240	57°27·2'	2°37·5'W	X	29
Auchabhaich	Arg & Bt	NM2825	56°20·6'	6°23·7'W	X	48
Auchabrack	Aberd	NO5490	57°0·2'	2°45·0'W	X	44
Auchabreck	D & G	NX1041	54°43·9'	4°56·6'W	X	82
Auchadaduie	Arg & Bt	NR6936	55°34·0'	5°39·4'W	X	68
Auchadalvorie	Arg & Bt	NR9569	55°52·5'	5°16·2'W	X	62
Auchagallon	N Ayr	NR8934	55°33·5'	5°20·3'W	X	68,69
Auchairn	Aberd	NJ4545	57°29·8'	2°54·6'W	X	28,29
Auchairn	Moray	NJ4153	57°34·1'	2°58·7'W	X	28
Auchairne	S Ayr	NX1081	55°5·5'	4°58·2'W	X	76
Auchaleek	Arg & Bt	NR7022	55°26·5'	5°37·8'W	X	68
Auchalick Bay	Arg & Bt	NR9074	55°55·1'	5°21·2'W	W	62
Auchalick Wood	Arg & Bt	NR9273	55°54·6'	5°19·2'W	F	62
Auchallater	Aberd	NO1588	56°58·8'	3°23·5'W	X	43
Aucha Lochy	Arg & Bt	NR7222	55°26·6'	5°35·9'W	W	68
Auchalochy Burn	Arg & Bt	NR7122	55°26·6'	5°36·8'W	W	68
Auchalton Fm	S Ayr	NS3204	55°18·3'	4°38·4'W	FM	76
Auchameanach Fm	Arg & Bt	NR8856	55°45·3'	5°22·3'W	FM	62
Auchamore	N Ayr	NR8745	55°39·4'	5°22·7'W	X	62,69
Auchanachie	Aberd	NJ4946	57°30·3'	2°50·6'W	X	28,29
Auchanachie	Aberd	NJ5962	57°39·0'	2°40·8'W	X	29
Auchanaskeioch	Arg & Bt	NR9275	55°55·6'	5°19·3'W	X	62
Auchanhandock	Moray	NJ3337	57°25·4'	3°6·5'W	X	28
Auchanland	Aberd	NJ5957	57°36·3'	2°40·7'W	X	29
Auchanruidh	Pth & Kin	NN7963	56°44·8'	3°58·3'W	X	42
Auchans	Renf	NS4366	55°52·0'	4°30·1'W	X	64
Auchans	S Ayr	NS3534	55°34·6'	4°36·6'W	A	70
Auchareoch	N Ayr	NR9924	55°28·4'	5°10·4'W	X	69
Aucharnie	Aberd	NJ6340	57°27·2'	2°36·5'W	X	29
Aucharroch	Angus	NO3256	56°41·7'	3°6·2'W	X	53
Aucharroch Wood	Angus	NO3258	56°42·8'	3°6·2'W	X	53
Aucharua	Arg & Bt	NR7008	55°19·0'	5°37·1'W	X	68
Auchategan	Arg & Bt	NS0085	56°1·2'	5°12·1'W	X	55
Auchattie	Aberd	NO6994	57°2·4'	2°30·2'W	T	38,45
Auchavae	Arg & Bt	NR8657	55°45·8'	5°24·2'W	X	62
Auchavan	Angus	NO1969	56°48·6'	3°19·1'W	X	43
Auchbain	Highld	NH7136	57°24·0'	4°8·3'W	X	27
Auchbreck	Moray	NJ2028	57°20·4'	3°19·3'W	T	36
Auchcairnie	Aberd	NO6875	56°52·2'	2°31·0'W	X	45
Auchedly	Aberd	NJ8933	57°23·5'	2°10·5'W	X	30
Aucheleffan	N Ayr	NR9824	55°28·3'	5°11·3'W	X	69
Auchelie	Aberd	NO0886	56°57·6'	3°30·3'W	X	43
Auchenage	D & G	NX8788	55°10·7'	3°46·0'W	X	78
Auchenage Burn	D & G	NX8689	55°11·2'	3°47·0'W	W	78
Auchenairney	S Ayr	NS3308	55°20·5'	4°37·6'W	X	70,76
Auchenames	Renf	NS3962	55°49·7'	4°33·8'W	X	63
Auchenback	E Renf	NS5058	55°47·8'	4°23·1'W	T	64
Auchenbainzie	D & G	NX8297	55°15·4'	3°51·0'W	T	78
Auchenbainzie Hill	D & G	NX8296	55°14·9'	3°50·9'W	H	78
Auchenbart	E Ayr	NS5736	55°36·1'	4°15·7'W	X	71
Auchenblae	Aberd	NO7278	56°53·8'	2°27·1'W	T	45
Auchenblane	S Ayr	NS2607	55°19·8'	4°44·2'W	X	70,76
Auchenbothie Ho	Inverc	NS3570	55°53·9'	4°37·9'W	X	63
Auchenbothie Mains	Inverc	NS3470	55°53·9'	4°38·9'W	X	63
Auchenbourach	N Ayr	NS3059	55°47·9'	4°42·3'W	X	63
Auchenbowie Ho	Stir	NS7987	56°3·9'	3°56·2'W	X	57
Auchenbrack	D & G	NX7696	55°14·8'	3°56·6'W	X	78
Auchenbreck	Arg & Bt	NR7844	55°38·6'	5°31·2'W	X	62,69
Auchenbreck	Arg & Bt	NS0281	55°59·1'	5°10·0'W	X	55,63
Auchenbreck Burn	Arg & Bt	NS0181	55°59·1'	5°11·0'W	W	55,63
Auchencairn	D & G	NX7951	54°50·6'	3°52·6'W	T	84
Auchencairn	D & G	NX9290	55°11·8'	3°41·4'W	X	78
Auchencairn	D & G	NX9784	55°8·6'	3°36·5'W	T	78
Auchencairn	N Ayr	NS0427	55°30·1'	5°5·8'W	T	69
Auchencairn Bay	D & G	NX8251	54°50·6'	3°49·8'W	W	84
Auchencairn Height	D & G	NX9390	55°11·8'	3°40·4'W	H	78
Auchencairn Ho	D & G	NX8150	54°50·1'	3°50·7'W	X	84
Auchencairn Lane	D & G	NX8151	54°50·6'	3°50·8'W	W	84
Auchencairn Moss	D & G	NX8050	54°50·1'	3°51·7'W	W	84
Auchencar	N Ayr	NR8936	55°34·6'	5°20·4'W	T	68,69
Auchencar Burn	N Ayr	NR9036	55°34·6'	5°19·5'W	W	68,69
Auchencarroch	W Dunb	NS4182	56°0·5'	4°32·6'W	X	56,64
Auchen Castle	D & G	NT0603	55°19·0'	3°28·4'W	A	78
Auchencat Burn	D & G	NT0911	55°23·3'	3°25·8'W	W	78
Auchencheyne	D & G	NX7587	55°9·9'	3°57·3'W	X	78
Auchencleith	Aberd	NJ7626	57°19·7'	2°23·5'W	X	38
Auchenclery	S Ayr	NX1685	55°7·8'	4°52·7'W	X	76
Auchencloich	Renf	NS3663	55°50·2'	4°36·7'W	X	63
Auchencloigh	E Ayr	NS4916	55°25·1'	4°22·7'W	X	70
Auchencloigh	E Ayr	NS5332	55°33·8'	4°19·4'W	X	70
Auchencloigh	N Ayr	NS2954	55°45·2'	4°43·1'W	X	63
Auchencloy Hill	D & G	NX6069	55°0·0'	4°10·9'W	H	83
Auchencloy Monument	D & G	NX6070	55°0·5'	4°10·9'W	X	77
Auchencorth	Midlo	NT1957	55°48·2'	3°17·1'W	X	65,66,72
Auchencorth Moss	Midlo	NT1955	55°47·1'	3°17·1'W	X	65
Auchencorvie	Arg & Bt	NR6716	55°23·2'	5°40·3'W	X	68
Auchencrieff	D & G	NX9879	55°5·9'	3°35·5'W	X	84
Auchencrieve	Aberd	NJ8637	57°25·6'	2°13·5'W	X	30
Auchencrosh	S Ayr	NX0979	55°4·4'	4°59·1'W	X	76
Auchencrosh Hill	S Ayr	NX1078	55°3·9'	4°58·1'W	H	76
Auchencrow	Scot Bord	NT8560	55°50·2'	2°13·9'W	T	67
Auchencrow Mains	Scot Bord	NT8560	55°50·2'	2°13·9'W	X	67
Auchendaff	S Lanak	NS7823	55°29·4'	3°55·4'W	X	71
Auchendaff Hill	S Lanak	NS7723	55°29·4'	3°56·4'W	H	71
Auchendarg	Aberd	NJ9325	57°19·2'	2°6·5'W	X	38
Auchendellan	Aberd	NJ5525	57°19·1'	2°44·4'W	X	37
Auchendennan	Arg & Bt	NS3683	56°1·0'	4°37·4'W	X	56
Auchendennan Muir	Arg & Bt	NS3582	56°0·4'	4°38·3'W	X	56
Auchendinny	Midlo	NT2562	55°51·0'	3°11·4'W	T	66
Auchendinny Ho	Midlo	NT2561	55°50·4'	3°11·4'W	X	66

Auchendinny Mains	Midlo	NT2560	55°49·9'	3°11·4'W	X	66
Auchendolly	D & G	NX7668	54°59·7'	3°55·9'W	X	84
Auchendolly Fm	D & G	NX7669	55°0·3'	3°55·9'W	FM	84
Auchendores Cotts	Inverc	NS3572	55°55·0'	4°38·0'W	X	63
Auchendores Resr	Inverc	NS3572	55°55·0'	4°38·0'W	W	63
Auchendrane	S Ayr	NS3315	55°24·3'	4°37·8'W	X	70
Auchendreich	Aberd	NO8276	56°52·8'	2°17·3'W	X	45
Auchendryne	Aberd	NO1491	57°0·4'	3°24·5'W	T	43
Aucheneck Ho	Stir	NS4883	56°1·2'	4°25·9'W	X	57,64
Auchenfad	D & G	NX8150	54°50·1'	3°50·7'W	X	84
Auchenfad	D & G	NX9469	55°0·5'	3°39·0'W	X	84
Auchenfad Hill	D & G	NX9469	55°0·5'	3°39·0'W	H	84
Auchenfail	S Ayr	NS4726	55°30·5'	4°24·9'W	X	70
Auchenflower	D & G	NX6848	54°48·8'	4°2·8'W	X	83,84
Auchenflower	S Ayr	NX1282	55°6·1'	4°56·4'W	X	76
Auchenfoyle	Inverc	NS3170	55°53·9'	4°41·7'W	X	63
Auchenfraoch	Arg & Bt	NR7842	55°37·5'	5°31·1'W	X	62,69
Auchengaich	Arg & Bt	NS2789	56°4·0'	4°46·3'W	X	56
Auchengaich Burn	Arg & Bt	NS2790	56°4·6'	4°46·3'W	W	56
Auchengaich Hill	Arg & Bt	NS2890	56°4·6'	4°45·4'W	H	56
Auchengairn	S Ayr	NX3397	55°14·6'	4°37·2'W	X	76
Auchengairn Burn	S Ayr	NX3297	55°14·6'	4°38·1'W	W	76
Auchengallie	D & G	NX3348	54°48·2'	4°35·5'W	X	82
Auchengarth	N Ayr	NS1964	55°50·4'	4°53·0'W	X	63
Auchengassel	D & G	NX6455	54°52·5'	4°6·8'W	X	83
Auchengassel	D & G	NX8299	55°16·5'	3°51·0'W	X	78
Auchengate	D & G	NX8162	54°56·6'	3°51·0'W	X	84
Auchengavin	Arg & Bt	NS3492	56°5·8'	4°39·7'W	X	56
Auchengavin Burn	Arg & Bt	NS3492	56°5·8'	4°39·7'W	W	56
Auchengean	Falk	NS8577	55°58·6'	3°50·1'W	X	65
Auchengeith	D & G	NX9590	55°11·8'	3°38·5'W	X	78
Auchengeith Hill	D & G	NX9590	55°11·8'	3°38·5'W	H	78
Auchengibbert	D & G	NX8093	55°13·3'	3°52·8'W	X	78
Auchengibbert	D & G	NX8271	55°1·4'	3°50·3'W	X	84
Auchengibbert Hill	D & G	NX8094	55°13·8'	3°52·8'W	H	78
Auchengillan	Stir	NS5180	55°59·6'	4°22·9'W	X	64
Auchengilloch	S Lanak	NS7035	55°35·7'	4°3·3'W	H	71
Auchenglen	S Lanak	NS8446	55°41·9'	3°50·3'W	X	72
Auchenglen Burn	S Lanak	NS8546	55°41·9'	3°49·3'W	W	72
Auchengool	D & G	NX7349	54°49·4'	3°58·2'W	X	83,84
Auchengowan	Renf	NS3657	55°47·0'	4°36·5'W	X	63
Auchengower	Arg & Bt	NS2184	56°1·2'	4°51·9'W	X	56
Auchengownie	Pth & Kin	NO0912	56°17·8'	3°27·8'W	X	58
Auchengrange	Renf	NS3757	55°47·0'	4°35·5'W	X	63
Auchengray	S Lanak	NS9954	55°46·4'	3°36·2'W	T	65,72
Auchengray Fm	D & G	NX9267	54°59·4'	3°40·9'W	FM	84
Auchengray Hill	D & G	NX9267	54°59·4'	3°40·9'W	H	84
Auchengray Ho	N Lanak	NS8467	55°53·2'	3°50·8'W	X	65
Auchengree	N Lanak	NS6569	55°54·0'	4°9·1'W	X	64
Auchengruith	D & G	NS8209	55°21·9'	3°51·3'W	X	71,78
Auchengyle	D & G	NY2975	55°4·1'	3°6·3'W	X	85
Auchenhain	Renf	NS3257	55°46·9'	4°40·3'W	X	63
Auchenhalrig	Moray	NJ3761	57°38·3'	3°2·9'W	T	28
Auchenhamper	Aberd	NJ6445	57°29·9'	2°35·6'W	X	29
Auchenhard	W Loth	NS9963	55°51·2'	3°36·4'W	X	65
Auchenharvie	N Ayr	NS2541	55°38·1'	4°46·4'W	T	70
Auchenhay	D & G	NX6351	54°50·4'	4°7·6'W	X	83
Auchenhay	D & G	NX7165	54°58·0'	4°0·5'W	X	83,84
Auchenhay	D & G	NX7778	55°5·1'	3°55·2'W	X	84
Auchenhay	D & G	NX8757	54°53·9'	3°45·3'W	X	84
Auchenhay Burn	D & G	NX7778	55°5·1'	3°55·2'W	W	84
Auchenhay Burn	D & G	NX7880	55°6·2'	3°54·3'W	W	78
Auchenhay Hill	D & G	NX6351	54°50·4'	4°7·6'W	H	83
Auchenhay Hill	D & G	NX7879	55°5·7'	3°54·3'W	H	84
Auchenhay Hill	D & G	NX8759	54°55·0'	3°45·4'W	H	84
Auchenheath	S Lanak	NS8043	55°40·2'	3°54·0'W	T	71,72
Auchenhessnane	D & G	NX8096	55°14·9'	3°52·8'W	X	78
Auchenhew	N Ayr	NS0121	55°26·8'	5°8·4'W	T	69
Auchenhew Hill	N Ayr	NS0122	55°27·3'	5°8·4'W	X	69
Auchenhill	D & G	NX8455	54°52·8'	3°48·1'W	X	84
Auchenhove	Aberd	NJ5503	57°7·2'	2°44·1'W	X	37
Auchenhove	N Ayr	NS3055	55°45·8'	4°42·1'W	X	63
Auchenhuive	Aberd	NJ8425	57°19·2'	2°15·5'W	X	38
Auchenibert	Stir	NS5385	56°2·4'	4°21·1'W	X	57
Aucheninnes	D & G	NX8460	54°55·5'	3°48·2'W	X	84
Aucheninnes Moss	D & G	NX8560	54°55·5'	3°47·2'W	X	84
Auchenninnes Plantns	D & G	NX8460	54°55·5'	3°48·2'W	F	84
Auchenkist	N Ayr	NS2844	55°39·8'	4°43·6'W	X	63,70
Auchenknight	D & G	NX8497	55°15·5'	3°49·1'W	X	78
Auchenknight Wood	D & G	NX8398	55°16·0'	3°50·1'W	F	78
Auchen Ladder	D & G	NY0183	55°8·1'	3°32·7'W	X	78
Auchenlaich	Stir	NN6407	56°14·4'	4°11·2'W	X	57
Auchenlarie Burn	D & G	NX5353	54°51·3'	4°17·0'W	W	83
Auchenleck	D & G	NX7751	54°50·6'	3°54·5'W	X	84
Auchenleck Hill	D & G	NX9299	55°16·7'	3°41·6'W	H	78
Auchenleish Fm	Angus	NO2059	56°43·2'	3°18·0'W	FM	53
Auchenlinnhe	W Dunb	NS4185	56°2·1'	4°32·7'W	X	56
Auchenlochan	Arg & Bt	NR9772	55°54·2'	5°14·4'W	T	62
Auchenlochan Fm	Arg & Bt	NR9671	55°53·6'	5°15·3'W	FM	62
Auchenlone Burn	D & G	NS8607	55°20·9'	3°47·4'W	W	71,78
Auchenlongford	E Ayr	NS5928	55°31·8'	4°13·6'W	X	71
Auchenlongford Hill	E Ayr	NS5929	55°32·3'	4°13·6'W	H	71
Auchenlosh	D & G	NX8959	54°55·1'	3°43·5'W	X	84
Auchenlosh Hill	D & G	NX8859	54°55·0'	3°44·4'W	H	84
Auchenmade	N Ayr	NS3448	55°42·1'	4°38·1'W	X	63
Auchenmalg	D & G	NX2352	54°50·1'	4°44·9'W	T	82
Auchenmalg Bay	D & G	NX2351	54°49·6'	4°44·9'W	W	82
Auchenmalg Fm	D & G	NX2352	54°50·1'	4°44·9'W	FM	82
Auchenrath	D & G	NX9784	55°8·6'	3°36·5'W	X	78
Auchenreoch	Angus	NO6065	56°46·7'	2°38·8'W	X	45
Auchenreoch	W Dunb	NS4278	55°58·4'	4°31·5'W	X	64
Auchenreoch Loch	D & G	NX8171	55°1·4'	3°51·3'W	W	84
Auchenreoch Muir	W Dunb	NS4279	55°58·9'	4°31·5'W	X	64
Auchenrivock	D & G	NY3780	55°6·9'	2°58·8'W	X	79
Auchenrivock Flow	D & G	NY3679	55°6·3'	2°59·8'W	X	85
Auchenrivock (Tower)	D & G	NY3780	55°6·9'	2°58·8'W	A	79
Auchenroddan Forest	D & G	NY1288	55°11·0'	3°22·5'W	F	78
Auchenrodden	D & G	NY1289	55°11·5'	3°22·5'W	X	78
Auchenroy	E Ayr	NS4506	55°19·7'	4°26·2'W	X	70,77
Auchenroy Hill	E Ayr	NS4405	55°19·1'	4°27·1'W	H	70

Auchens	D & G	NS8208	55°21·4'	3°51·2'W	X	71,78
Auchensail	Arg & Bt	NS3479	55°58·8'	4°39·2'W	X	63
Auchensale	Renf	NS3764	55°50·8'	4°35·8'W	X	63
Auchensaugh Hill	S Lanak	NS8527	55°31·6'	3°48·9'W	H	71,72
Auchensell Wood	D & G	NS8701	55°17·7'	3°46·3'W	F	78
Auchensheen	D & G	NX8556	54°53·4'	3°47·2'W	X	84
Auchenshinnoch	D & G	NX6590	55°11·4'	4°6·8'W	X	77
Auchenskeith	N Ayr	NS3146	55°40·9'	4°40·8'W	X	63
Auchenskeoch Lodge	D & G	NX9059	54°55·1'	3°42·5'W	X	84
Auchensoul	S Ayr	NX2593	55°12·3'	4°44·6'W	X	76
Auchensoul Burn	S Ayr	NX2593	55°12·3'	4°44·6'W	W	76
Auchensoul Hill	S Ayr	NX2694	55°12·8'	4°43·7'W	H	76
Auchensow Burn	D & G	NS8208	55°21·4'	3°51·2'W	W	71,78
Auchensow Hill	D & G	NS8308	55°21·4'	3°50·3'W	H	71,78
Auchenstroan	D & G	NX7191	55°12·0'	4°1·2'W	X	77
Auchenstroan Craig	D & G	NX6991	55°12·0'	4°3·1'W	H	77
Auchentaggart	D & G	NS8108	55°21·4'	3°52·2'W	X	71,78
Auchentaggart Moor	D & G	NS8110	55°22·4'	3°52·2'W	X	71,78
Auchentarph	Aberd	NJ6928	57°20·7'	2°30·4'W	X	38
Auchenteck Fm	Stir	NN7501	56°11·4'	4°0·4'W	FM	57
Auchenten	Aberd	NK0435	57°24·6'	1°55·5'W	X	30
Auchentibber	S Lanak	NS6654	55°45·9'	4°7·7'W	T	64
Auchentibbert	D & G	NX0649	54°48·2'	5°0·7'W	X	82
Auchentiber	E Ayr	NS4448	55°42·3'	4°28·5'W	X	64
Auchentiber	Inverc	NS3172	55°54·9'	4°41·8'W	X	63
Auchentiber	N Ayr	NS3647	55°41·6'	4°36·1'W	T	63
Auchentiber Moss	N Ayr	NS3547	55°41·6'	4°37·1'W	X	63
Auchentorlie Ho	W Dunb	NS4374	55°56·3'	4°30·4'W	X	64
Auchentullich Namoin	Arg & Bt	NS3586	56°2·6'	4°38·5'W	X	56
Auchentullich Natra	Arg & Bt	NS3586	56°2·6'	4°38·5'W	X	56
Auchentumb	Aberd	NJ9357	57°36·4'	2°6·6'W	X	30
Auchenvennel	Arg & Bt	NS2888	56°3·5'	4°45·3'W	X	56
Auchenvey	D & G	NX7377	55°4·5'	3°58·9'W	X	77,84
Auchenvey Burn	D & G	NX7276	55°4·0'	3°59·8'W	W	77,84
Auchenvey Plantation	D & G	NX7277	55°4·5'	3°59·9'W	F	77,84
Auchenwinsey	N Ayr	NS3342	55°38·8'	4°38·8'W	X	63,70
Auchenwynd	S Ayr	NS3008	55°20·5'	4°40·4'W	X	70,76
Auchenzeoch	Aberd	NO7376	56°52·7'	2°26·1'W	X	45
Aucheoch	Aberd	NJ9250	57°32·7'	2°7·6'W	X	30
Auchernack	Highld	NJ0224	57°18·0'	3°37·1'W	X	36
Auchertyre	Highld	NG8427	57°17·2'	5°34·6'W	T	33
Auchessan	Stir	NN4428	56°25·4'	4°31·3'W	X	51
Auch Gleann	Arg & Bt	NN3436	56°29·5'	4°41·3'W	X	50
Auchgobhal	Pth & Kin	NN8870	56°48·7'	3°49·6'W	X	43
Auchgourish	Highld	NH9315	57°13·1'	3°45·9'W	X	36
Auchgoyle	Arg & Bt	NR9670	55°53·1'	5°15·3'W	X	62
Auchgoyle Bay	Arg & Bt	NR9795	56°6·5'	5°15·4'W	W	55
Auchie Glen	D & G	NX1332	54°39·2'	4°53·5'W	X	82
Auchilhanzie	Pth & Kin	NN8924	56°24·0'	3°47·5'W	X	52,58
Auchinabreck	W Dunb	NS3581	55°59·9'	4°38·3'W	X	63
Auchinairn	C of Glas	NS6169	55°53·9'	4°12·9'W	T	64
Auchinbay	E Ayr	NS4823	55°28·9'	4°23·9'W	X	70
Auchinbo	Aberd	NJ5645	57°29·8'	2°43·6'W	X	29
Auchincally Hill	E Ayr	NS6006	55°19·9'	4°12·0'W	H	71,77
Auchinclech	Aberd	NJ8209	57°10·5'	2°17·4'W	X	38
Auchinclech	Moray	NJ5448	57°31·4'	2°45·6'W	X	29
Auchincloch	Falk	NS7678	55°59·0'	3°58·8'W	X	64
Auchincrieve	Moray	NJ5248	57°31·4'	2°47·6'W	X	29
Auchincross	E Ayr	NS5713	55°23·7'	4°15·0'W	X	71
Auchincruive Agricultural College	S Ayr	NS3823	55°28·7'	4°33·4'W	X	70
Auchinderran	Aberd	NJ6055	57°35·3'	2°39·7'W	X	29
Auchinderran	Moray	NJ4055	57°35·1'	2°59·7'W	T	28
Auchindinnie Hill	Aberd	NJ4533	57°23·3'	2°54·4'W	H	28,29
Auchindoir	Aberd	NJ4824	57°18·5'	2°51·3'W	X	37
Auchindorie	Angus	NO3651	56°39·0'	3°2·2'W	X	54
Auchindown Castle	Moray	NJ3437	57°25·4'	3°5·5'W	A	28
Auchindownie	Fife	NO4205	56°14·3'	2°55·7'W	X	59
Auchindrain	Arg & Bt	NN0303	56°11·0'	5°10·0'W	T	55
Auchindrean	Highld	NH1980	57°46·7'	5°2·2'W	X	20
Auchineden	Stir	NS5080	55°59·6'	4°23·9'W	X	64
Auchineden Fm	Stir	NS5179	55°59·1'	4°22·9'W	FM	64
Auchineden Hill	Stir	NS4980	55°59·6'	4°24·8'W	X	64
Auchinellan	Arg & Bt	NM8602	56°10·0'	5°26·4'W	X	55
Auchingarrich	Pth & Kin	NN7819	56°21·1'	3°58·0'W	X	57
Auchingee	E Ayr	NS5712	55°23·1'	4°15·0'W	X	71
Auchingee Hill	E Ayr	NS4713	55°23·5'	4°24·5'W	X	70
Auchinglen	Pth & Kin	NN9017	56°20·2'	3°46·3'W	X	58
Auchingoul	Aberd	NJ6048	57°31·5'	2°39·6'W	X	29
Auchingree Burn	W Dunb	NS4877	55°58·0'	4°25·7'W	W	64
Auchingyle	Stir	NS4290	56°4·9'	4°31·9'W	X	56
Auchinhandoch	Aberd	NJ4236	57°24·9'	2°57·5'W	X	28
Auchinhove	Aberd	NJ6636	57°25·0'	2°33·5'W	X	29
Auchinhove	Moray	NJ4651	57°33·0'	2°53·7'W	X	28,29
Auchininna	Aberd	NJ6447	57°31·0'	2°35·6'W	X	29
Auchinleck	C of Glas	NS6369	55°53·9'	4°11·0'W	X	64
Auchinleck	D & G	NX4470	55°0·3'	4°25·9'W	X	77
Auchinleck	E Ayr	NS5521	55°27·9'	4°17·2'W	T	71
Auchinleck Burn	E Ayr	NS5621	55°28·0'	4°16·2'W	W	71
Auchinleck Ho	E Ayr	NS5023	55°28·9'	4°22·0'W	A	70
Auchinleck Loch	D & G	NX4672	55°1·4'	4°24·1'W	W	77
Auchinleish	Angus	NO1960	56°43·7'	3°19·0'W	T	43
Auchinleith	Aberd	NJ4623	57°17·9'	2°53·3'W	X	37
Auchinllyinn Spout	Stir	NS7584	56°2·2'	3°59·9'W	W	57,64
Auchinloch	N Lanak	NS6570	55°54·5'	4°9·1'W	T	64
Auchinner	Pth & Kin	NN6915	56°18·8'	4°6·6'W	X	57
Auchinoon	W Loth	NT0961	55°50·3'	3°26·7'W	X	65
Auchinoon Hill	W Loth	NT0962	55°50·8'	3°26·8'W	H	65
Auchinraith	S Lanak	NS6956	55°47·0'	4°4·9'W	T	64
Auchinreoch	E Dunb	NS6776	55°57·8'	4°7·4'W	T	64
Auchinrivoch	N Lanak	NS7479	55°59·5'	4°0·8'W	X	64
Auchinroath	Moray	NJ2651	57°32·8'	3°13·7'W	X	28
Auchinsalt	Stir	NN6401	56°11·2'	4°11·0'W	X	57
Auchinstarry	N Lanak	NS7276	55°57·9'	4°2·6'W	T	64
Auchintae	Moray	NJ3163	57°39·4'	3°8·9'W	X	28
Auchintaple Loch	Angus	NO1964	56°45·9'	3°19·1'W	W	43
Auchintender	Aberd	NJ6335	57°24·5'	2°36·5'W	X	29
Auchintirrie	Arg & Bt	NS0563	55°49·5'	5°6·3'W	X	63
Auchintoul	Aberd	NJ5316	57°14·2'	2°46·3'W	X	37
Auchintoul	Aberd	NJ6706	57°8·9'	2°32·3'W	X	38
Auchintoul	Angus	NO5278	56°53·7'	2°46·8'W	X	44
Auchintoul	Highld	NH5199	57°57·6'	4°30·6'W	X	20
Auchintoul	Highld	NH6869	57°41·8'	4°12·4'W	X	21
Auchintoul	Highld	NH7825	57°18·2'	4°1·0'W	X	35
Auchintoul Moss	Aberd	NJ6153	57°34·2'	2°38·7'W	X	29
Auchinvalley	N Lanak	NS7479	55°59·5'	4°0·8'W	X	64
Auchinvole	E Dunb	NS7176	55°57·8'	4°3·6'W	X	64
Auchinway	E Ayr	NS5318	55°26·3'	4°19·0'W	X	70
Auchinweet	S Ayr	NS4528	55°31·5'	4°26·9'W	X	70
Auchinweet Burn	S Ayr	NS4428	55°31·5'	4°27·8'W	W	70
Auchip	Aberd	NJ5561	57°38·5'	2°44·8'W	X	29
Auchiries	Aberd	NK0837	57°25·7'	1°51·5'W	X	30
Auchivarie	Highld	NN2993	57°0·1'	4°48·5'W	X	34
Auchlane	D & G	NX7458	54°54·3'	3°57·5'W	X	83,84
Auchlane Burn	D & G	NX7358	54°54·3'	3°58·4'W	W	83,84
Auchlannochy Hill	D & G	NX4466	54°58·1'	4°25·8'W	H	83
Auchlany	Pth & Kin	NN7767	56°47·0'	4°0·3'W	X	42
Auchlea	C of Aber	NJ8405	57°8·4'	2°15·4'W	X	38
Auchleach	D & G	NX0071	54°59·9'	5°7·2'W	X	76,82
Auchlean	Highld	NN8597	57°3·2'	3°53·3'W	X	35,36,43
Auchleand	D & G	NX4158	54°53·7'	4°28·3'W	X	83
Auchleand Moor	D & G	NX4058	54°53·7'	4°29·3'W	H	83
Auchlee	Aberd	NK0448	57°31·6'	1°55·5'W	X	30
Auchlee	Aberd	NO8996	57°3·6'	2°10·4'W	X	38,45
Auchleeks House	Pth & Kin	NN7464	56°45·3'	4°3·2'W	X	42
Auchleish	Angus	NO4161	56°44·5'	2°57·4'W	X	44
Auchleskine	Stir	NN5420	56°21·2'	4°21·3'W	X	51,57
Auchlethen	Aberd	NK0436	57°25·1'	1°55·5'W	X	30
Auchleuchrie	Angus	NO4357	56°42·3'	2°55·4'W	X	54
Auchleven	Aberd	NJ6224	57°18·6'	2°37·4'W	T	37
Auchlin	E Ayr	NS4916	55°25·1'	4°22·7'W	X	70
Auchlinn	Aberd	NJ7757	57°36·4'	2°22·6'W	X	29,30
Auchlin Rig	E Ayr	NS5015	55°24·6'	4°21·7'W	X	70
Auchlinsky Hill	Pth & Kin	NN9802	56°12·2'	3°38·2'W	H	58
Auchlishie	Angus	NO3957	56°42·3'	2°59·3'W	X	54
Auchlochan	Moray	NJ0241	57°27·2'	3°37·5'W	X	27
Auchlochan	S Lanak	NS8037	55°37·0'	3°53·9'W	X	71,72
Auchlone Wood	Pth & Kin	NN9221	56°22·4'	3°44·5'W	F	52,58
Auchloon	Aberd	NJ9222	57°17·6'	2°7·5'W	X	38
Auchlossan	Aberd	NJ5702	57°6·7'	2°42·1'W	X	37
Auchloy	Pth & Kin	NN9023	56°23·4'	3°46·5'W	X	52,58
Auchlunachan	Highld	NH1783	57°48·2'	5°4·3'W	X	20
Auchlunies	Aberd	NO8999	57°5·2'	2°10·4'W	X	38,45
Auchlunkart	Moray	NJ3349	57°31·8'	3°6·7'W	X	28
Auchlyne	Stir	NN5129	56°26·0'	4°24·5'W	T	51
Auchlyne East Burn	Stir	NN5131	56°27·1'	4°24·6'W	W	51
Auchlyne West Burn	Stir	NN4930	56°26·5'	4°26·5'W	W	51
Auchmacleddie	Aberd	NJ9257	57°36·4'	2°7·6'W	X	30
Auchmacoy	Aberd	NJ9930	57°21·9'	2°0·5'W	X	30
Auchmadies	Moray	NJ3247	57°30·7'	3°7·6'W	X	28
Auchmair	Moray	NJ3828	57°20·6'	3°1·3'W	X	37
Auchmannoch	E Ayr	NS5430	55°32·8'	4°18·4'W	X	70
Auchmannoch Burn	E Ayr	NS5229	55°32·2'	4°20·3'W	W	70
Auchmannoch Muir	E Ayr	NS5632	55°33·9'	4°16·6'W	X	71
Auchmantle	D & G	NX1562	54°55·4'	4°52·8'W	X	82
Auchmantle Burn	D & G	NX1563	54°55·9'	4°52·8'W	W	82
Auchmar	Aberd	NJ5625	57°19·1'	2°43·4'W	X	37
Auchmar	Stir	NS4491	56°5·4'	4°30·0'W	X	57
Auchmartin	Highld	NH6966	57°40·2'	4°11·3'W	X	21
Auchmaud	Aberd	NK0134	57°24·0'	1°58·5'W	X	30
Auchmeddan	S Lanak	NS8439	55°38·1'	3°50·1'W	X	71,72
Auchmenzie	Aberd	NJ5125	57°19·0'	2°48·4'W	X	37
Auchmill	Aberd	NJ7255	57°35·3'	2°27·6'W	X	29
Auchmillan	E Ayr	NS5129	55°32·2'	4°21·2'W	T	70
Auchmillanhill	E Ayr	NS5229	55°32·2'	4°20·3'W	X	70
Auchmillie	Aberd	NJ5963	57°39·6'	2°40·8'W	X	29
Auchmithie	Angus	NO6744	56°35·5'	2°31·8'W	T	54
Auchmore	Aberd	NJ5965	57°40·6'	2°40·8'W	X	29
Auchmore	Aberd	NJ6705	57°8·3'	2°32·3'W	X	38
Auchmore	Aberd	NK0057	57°36·4'	1°59·5'W	X	30
Auchmore	Highld	NH4950	57°31·2'	4°30·8'W	X	26
Auchmore	Highld	NH6694	57°1·3'	4°12·0'W	X	35
Auchmore	Pth & Kin	NN9635	56°30·0'	3°40·9'W	X	52,53
Auchmore Burn	Pth & Kin	NN9635	56°30·0'	3°40·9'W	W	52,53
Auchmore Wood	Highld	NH4850	57°31·1'	4°31·8'W	F	26
Auchmuirbridge	Fife	NO2101	56°12·0'	3°16·0'W	T	58
Auchmuir Fm	Fife	NO2200	56°11·4'	3°15·0'W	FM	58
Auchmull	Angus	NO5874	56°51·6'	2°40·9'W	X	44
Auchmullen	Aberd	NJ4519	57°15·8'	2°54·3'W	X	37
Auchmunziel	Aberd	NJ8646	57°30·5'	2°13·6'W	X	30
Auchmuty	Fife	NO2700	56°11·5'	3°10·1'W	T	59
Auchnabeich	Pth & Kin	NO0054	56°40·3'	3°37·5'W	X	52,53
Auchnabo	Aberd	NK0332	57°23·0'	1°56·5'W	X	30
Auchnabony	D & G	NX7448	54°48·9'	3°57·2'W	X	83,84
Auchnabreac	Arg & Bt	NN0806	56°12·7'	5°5·3'W	X	56
Auchnacant	Aberd	NJ9626	57°19·7'	2°3·5'W	X	38
Auchnaclach	Aberd	NJ4544	57°29·2'	2°54·6'W	X	28,29
Auchnaclach	Arg & Bt	NR4068	55°50·4'	6°8·7'W	X	60,61
Auchnacloich	Highld	NH9056	57°35·1'	3°49·9'W	X	27
Auchnacloich	Pth & Kin	NN8439	56°32·0'	3°52·7'W	X	52
Auchnacoshan	Arg & Bt	NM9231	56°25·8'	5°22·0'W	X	49
Auchnacraig	W Dunb	NS5073	55°55·9'	4°23·6'W	X	64
Auchnacraig	Arg & Bt	NM7330	56°24·7'	5°40·3'W	X	49
Auchnacree	Angus	NO4663	56°45·6'	2°52·5'W	T	44
Auchnafearn	Highld	NJ0229	57°20·7'	3°37·2'W	X	36
Auchnafree	Pth & Kin	NN8133	56°28·7'	3°55·5'W	X	52
Auchnafree Craig	Pth & Kin	NN8034	56°29·2'	3°56·5'W	H	52
Auchnafree Hill	Pth & Kin	NN8030	56°27·1'	3°56·4'W	H	52
Auchnagain	Moray	NH9847	57°30·4'	3°41·7'W	X	27
Auchnagairn	Highld	NH9847	57°30·4'	3°41·7'W	X	27
Auchnagallin	Highld	NJ0533	57°22·9'	3°34·3'W	X	27
Auchnagarron	Arg & Bt	NS0082	55°59·6'	5°12·0'W	X	55
Auchnagathle	Aberd	NJ6120	57°16·4'	2°38·3'W	X	37
Auchnagatt	Aberd	NJ9341	57°27·8'	2°6·5'W	T	30
Auchnagaul	Highld	NH5668	57°41·0'	4°24·4'W	X	21
Auchnagorth	Aberd	NJ8355	57°35·3'	2°16·6'W	X	29,30
Auchnaha	Arg & Bt	NR9381	55°58·9'	5°18·6'W	X	55
Auchnahanate	Highld	NN2081	56°53·4'	4°56·8'W	X	34,41
Auchnahillin	Highld	NH7438	57°25·2'	4°5·4'W	X	27
Auchnahyle	Moray	NJ1614	57°12·8'	3°23·0'W	X	36
Auchnahyle	Pth & Kin	NN9458	56°42·4'	3°43·4'W	X	52,53
Auchnarie	Aberd	NJ9154	57°34·8'	2°8·6'W	X	30
Auchnarrow	Moray	NJ2123	57°17·7'	3°18·2'W	T	36
Auchnarrowmore	Highld	NJ0532	57°22·4'	3°34·3'W	X	27,36
Auchnasaul	Arg & Bt	NM7919	56°19·0'	5°34·0'W	X	55
Auchnasaul	Highld	NM5751	56°35·5'	5°57·0'W	X	47
Auchnasavil Fm	Arg & Bt	NR7939	55°35·9'	5°30·0'W	FM	68,69
Auchnashag	Aberd	NJ8722	57°17·6'	2°12·5'W	X	38
Auchnashelloch	Pth & Kin	NN7115	56°18·9'	4°4·7'W	X	57
Auchnashelloch Hill	Pth & Kin	NN7014	56°18·3'	4°5·6'W	H	57
Auchnashinn	Aberd	NO5189	56°59·6'	2°47·9'W	H	44
Auchnavaird	Aberd	NJ9440	57°27·3'	2°5·5'W	X	30
Auchneel	D & G	NX0362	54°55·1'	5°4·0'W	X	82
Auchneight	D & G	NX1133	54°39·7'	4°55·4'W	X	82
Auchnerran	Aberd	NJ4103	57°7·1'	2°58·0'W	X	37
Auchness	D & G	NX1044	54°45·6'	4°56·8'W	X	82
Auchness	D & G	NX3943	54°45·6'	4°29·7'W	X	83
Auchness	Moray	NJ1149	57°31·6'	3°28·7'W	X	28
Auchness Moss	D & G	NX3943	54°45·6'	4°29·7'W	X	83
Auchnieve	Aberd	NJ8230	57°21·9'	2°17·5'W	X	29,30
Auchnotroch	S Lanak	NS8243	55°40·2'	3°52·1'W	X	71,72
Auchnotteroch	D & G	NW9960	54°53·9'	5°7·7'W	X	82
Auchoirk Cotts	Arg & Bt	NR9570	55°53·0'	5°16·2'W	X	62
Auchoirk Fm	Arg & Bt	NR9571	55°53·6'	5°16·3'W	FM	62
Auchoish	Arg & Bt	NR8690	56°3·6'	5°25·8'W	X	55
Aucholzie	Aberd	NO3490	57°0·0'	3°4·7'W	X	44
Auchope	Scot Bord	NT8521	55°29·2'	2°13·8'W	X	74
Auchope Cairn	Northum	NT8919	55°28·1'	2°10·0'W	X	80
Auchope Rig	Scot Bord	NT8619	55°28·1'	2°12·9'W	X	80
Auchorachan	Moray	NJ2028	57°20·4'	3°19·3'W	X	36
Auchorrie	Aberd	NJ6605	57°8·3'	2°33·3'W	X	38
Auchorthie	Aberd	NJ9251	57°33·2'	2°7·6'W	X	30
Auchorties	Moray	NJ4348	57°31·4'	2°56·6'W	X	28
Auchoshin	Arg & Bt	NR7083	55°59·3'	5°40·8'W	X	55,61
Auchosnich	Highld	NJ0229	57°20·7'	3°37·2'W	X	36
Auchowrie	Angus	NO5073	56°51·0'	2°48·7'W	X	44
Auchoyle	Highld	NH7573	57°44·0'	4°5·5'W	X	21
Auchrae	D & G	NX6596	55°14·6'	4°7·0'W	X	77
Auchrae Burn	D & G	NX6594	55°13·6'	4°6·9'W	W	77
Auchrae Hill	D & G	NX6595	55°14·1'	4°6·9'W	X	77
Auchrannie	Angus	NO2852	56°39·5'	3°10·0'W	X	53
Auchravie	Aberd	NJ6714	57°13·2'	2°32·3'W	X	38
Auchreach	Stir	NN3527	56°24·6'	4°40·0'W	X	50
Auchren Fm	S Lanak	NS8238	55°37·5'	3°52·0'W	FM	71,72
Auchrennie	Angus	NO5537	56°31·6'	2°43·4'W	X	54
Auchriachan	Moray	NJ1818	57°15·0'	3°21·1'W	X	36
Auchrig	Stir	NN5903	56°12·2'	4°15·9'W	X	57
Auchrobert	S Lanak	NS7638	55°37·4'	3°57·7'W	X	71
Auchrobert Hill	S Lanak	NS7538	55°37·4'	3°58·7'W	H	71
Auchrobert Snout	S Lanak	NS7538	55°37·4'	3°58·7'W	X	71
Auchroisk	Highld	NJ0728	57°20·2'	3°32·2'W	X	36
Auchroisk	Moray	NJ3351	57°32·9'	3°6·7'W	X	28
Auchronie	Aberd	NJ8010	57°11·1'	2°19·4'W	X	38
Auchronie	Angus	NO4480	56°54·7'	2°54·7'W	X	44
Auchronie Hill	Aberd	NJ8009	57°10·5'	2°19·4'W	X	38
Auchrynie	Aberd	NJ9652	57°33·7'	2°3·6'W	X	30
Auchtavan	Aberd	NO2095	57°2·6'	3°18·7'W	X	36,44
Auchtenny	Pth & Kin	NO0610	56°16·6'	3°30·6'W	X	58
Auchter Alyth	Pth & Kin	NO2851	56°39·0'	3°10·0'W	X	53
Auchterarder	Pth & Kin	NN9412	56°17·6'	3°42·3'W	T	58
Auchterarder Ho	Pth & Kin	NN9514	56°18·7'	3°41·4'W	X	58
Auchteraw	Highld	NH3508	57°8·3'	4°43·1'W	X	34
Auchteraw Burn	Highld	NH3409	57°8·8'	4°44·2'W	W	34
Auchteraw Wood	Highld	NH3407	57°7·7'	4°44·1'W	F	34
Auchterblair	Highld	NH9222	57°16·8'	3°47·0'W	X	36
Auchtercairn	Highld	NG8076	57°43·5'	5°41·2'W	T	19
Auchterderran	Fife	NT2195	56°8·7'	3°15·8'W	T	58
Auchterellon Fm	Aberd	NJ9431	57°22·4'	2°5·5'W	FM	30
Auchterflow	Highld	NH6657	57°35·3'	4°14·0'W	X	26
Auchterforfar	Angus	NO4749	56°38·0'	2°51·4'W	X	54
Auchterhead Fm	N Lanak	NS8655	55°46·7'	3°48·6'W	FM	65,72
Auchterhead Muir	N Lanak	NS8954	55°46·3'	3°45·7'W	F	65
Auchterhouse	Angus	NO3337	56°31·5'	3°4·9'W	X	53
Auchterhouse Hill	Angus	NO3539	56°32·6'	3°3·0'W	H	54
Auchtermairnie Fm	Fife	NO3403	56°13·2'	3°3·4'W	FM	59
Auchtermuchty	Fife	NO2311	56°17·4'	3°14·2'W	T	58
Auchtermuchty Common	Fife	NO2413	56°18·5'	3°13·3'W	X	59
Auchterteang	Highld	NH9226	57°19·0'	3°47·1'W	X	36
Auchtertool	Fife	NT2290	56°6·0'	3°14·8'W	T	58
Auchtertool Ho	Fife	NT2190	56°6·0'	3°15·8'W	X	58
Auchtertyre	Angus	NO2841	56°33·6'	3°9·8'W	X	53
Auchtertyre	Moray	NJ1858	57°36·5'	3°21·9'W	X	28
Auchtertyre	Stir	NN3529	56°25·7'	4°40·1'W	X	50
Auchtertyre Hill	Highld	NG8328	57°17·7'	5°35·6'W	H	33
Auchter Water	N Lanak	NS8754	55°46·2'	3°47·6'W	W	65,72
Auchtitench	E Ayr	NS7118	55°26·6'	4°1·9'W	X	71
Auchtitench Hill	E Ayr	NS7118	55°26·6'	4°1·9'W	H	71
Auchtitench Lane	E Ayr	NS7217	55°26·1'	4°0·9'W	W	71
Auchtochter	Aberd	NO7580	56°54·9'	2°24·2'W	X	45
Auchtool	S Lanak	NS8339	55°38·1'	3°51·1'W	X	71,72
Auchtubh	Stir	NN5520	56°21·3'	4°20·4'W	T	51,57
Auchtubhmore Hill	Stir	NN5621	56°21·8'	4°19·4'W	H	51,57
Auchtydonald	Aberd	NK0147	57°31·0'	1°58·5'W	X	30
Auchtydore	Aberd	NK0343	57°28·9'	1°56·5'W	X	30
Auchtygall	Aberd	NK0943	57°28·9'	1°50·5'W	X	30
Auchtygemmell Fm	S Lanak	NS8142	55°39·7'	3°53·1'W	FM	71,72
Auchtygills	Aberd	NJ9754	57°34·8'	2°2·6'W	X	30
Auchvaich	Highld	NH5340	57°25·9'	4°26·4'W	X	26
Auchvochkie	Highld	NJ1435	57°24·1'	3°25·4'W	X	28
Auchyle	Stir	NN5901	56°11·1'	4°15·9'W	X	57
Auckengill	Highld	ND3664	58°33·8'	3°5·5'W	X	12
Auckhorn	Highld	ND3259	58°31·1'	3°9·6'W	X	12
Auckland Fm	Wilts	ST9741	51°10·3'	2°2·2'W	FM	184
Auckland Park	Durham	NZ2228	54°39·0'	1°39·1'W	X	93
Auckland Park	Durham	NZ2230	54°40·1'	1°39·1'W	X	93
Aucklands Fm	N Lincs	SE7303	53°31·4'	0°53·5'W	FM	112
Auckley	Donc	SE6501	53°30·3'	1°0·8'W	T	111
Auckley Common	Donc	SE6501	53°30·3'	1°0·8'W	X	111
Audenshaw	Tames	SJ9297	53°28·4'	2°6·8'W	T	109

Audenshaw Resrs	Tames	SJ9196	53°27·9'	2°7·7'W	W	109
Audit's Br	Heref	SO5025	51°55·5'	2°43·2'W	X	162
Audlands Park	Cumbr	SD5786	54°16·3'	2°39·2'W	X	97
Audleby	Lincs	TA1103	53°31·0'	0°19·1'W	X	113
Audleby Low Covert	Lincs	TA0903	53°31·0'	0°21·0'W	F	112
Audleby Top Fm	Lincs	TA1204	53°31·5'	0°18·2'W	FM	113
Audlem	Ches	SJ6643	52°59·2'	2°30·0'W	T	118
Audley	Staffs	SJ7950	53°3·1'	2°18·4'W	T	118
Audley Brow	Shrops	SJ6335	52°54·9'	2°32·6'W	X	127
Audley End	Essex	TL5237	52°0·9'	0°13·3'E	T	154
Audley End	Essex	TL5238	52°1·4'	0°13·3'E	A	154
Audley End	Essex	TL8137	52°0·3'	0°38·6'E	T	155
Audley End	Norf	TM1482	52°23·9'	1°9·1'E	T	144,156
Audley End	Suff	TL8553	52°8·9'	0°42·6'E	T	155
Audley End Sta	Essex	TL5136	52°0·3'	0°12·4'E	X	154
Audleys Wood	Hants	SU6449	51°14·4'	1°4·6'W	X	185
Audmore	Staffs	SJ8321	52°47·4'	2°14·7'W	X	127
Audmurroch Burn	E Dunb	NS5078	55°58·6'	4°23·8'W	W	64
Auds	Aberd	NJ6564	57°40·1'	2°34·7'W	X	29
Aud, The	Angus	NO3766	56°47·1'	3°1·4'W	X	44
Aughertree	Cumbr	NY2538	54°44·1'	3°9·5'W	T	89,90
Aughertree Fell	Cumbr	NY2637	54°43·6'	3°8·5'W	X	89,90
Aughton	E Yorks	SE7038	53°50·3'	0°55·8'W	T	105,106
Aughton	Lancs	SD3905	53°32·5'	2°54·8'W	T	108
Aughton	Lancs	SD5567	54°6·1'	2°40·9'W	T	97
Aughton	Oxon	SU3789	51°36·1'	1°27·6'W	X	174
Aughton	Roth	SK4586	53°22·4'	1°19·0'W	T	111,120
Aughton	Wilts	SU2356	51°18·4'	1°39·8'W	T	174
Aughton Chase	Lancs	SD3804	53°32·0'	2°55·7'W	X	108
Aughton Common	E Yorks	SE7238	53°50·2'	0°53·9'W	X	105,106
Aughton Down	Wilts	SU2156	51°18·4'	1°41·5'W	X	174
Aughton Fm	Wilts	SU2356	51°18·4'	1°39·8'W	FM	174
Aughton Grange	E Yorks	SE7137	53°49·7'	0°54·9'W	X	105,106
Aughton Park	Lancs	SD4106	53°33·1'	2°53·0'W	T	108
Aughton Ruddings	E Yorks	SE7339	53°50·8'	0°53·0'W	X	105,106
Aughton Ruddings Grange	E Yorks	SE7338	53°50·2'	0°53·0'W	X	105,106
Aughton Spinney	Suff	TL8580	52°23·4'	0°43·5'E	F	144
Augill Beck	Cumbr	NY8114	54°31·5'	2°17·2'W	W	91,92
Augill Castle	Cumbr	NY8013	54°31·0'	2°18·1'W	X	91,92
Augill Ho	Cumbr	NY8114	54°31·5'	2°17·2'W	X	91,92
Augmund Howe	Orkney	HY6737	59°13·4'	2°34·2'W	X	5
Augmund Howe (Cairn)	Orkney	HY6737	59°13·4'	2°34·2'W	A	5
Augurs Hill Copse	Hants	SU3843	51°11·3'	1°27·0'W	F	185
August Hill	Warw	SP2156	52°12·3'	1°41·2'W	X	151
August Pitts Fm	Kent	TQ7043	51°9·9'	0°26·3'E	FM	188
August Rock	Corn	SW7927	50°6·4'	5°5·1'W	X	204
Aukside	Durham	NY9426	54°38·0'	2°5·2'W	T	91,92
Auks, The	Orkney	HY5740	59°14·9'	2°44·7'W	X	5
Auldallan	Angus	NO3158	56°42·8'	3°7·2'W	X	53
Auld Auchindoir	Aberd	NJ4823	57°17·9'	2°51·3'W	X	37
Auldbreck	D & G	NX4640	54°44·1'	4°23·1'W	X	83
Auld Brig o' Doon	S Ayr	NS3217	55°25·3'	4°38·8'W	A	70
Auldby	Cumbr	NY4434	54°42·1'	2°51·7'W	X	90
Auld Byres	E Ayr	NS4219	55°26·6'	4°29·4'W	X	70
Auldcraigoch	E Ayr	NS4504	55°18·6'	4°26·1'W	X	77
Auldcraigoch Hill	S Ayr	NS4404	55°18·6'	4°27·0'W	X	77
Auld Dalbrack	Stir	NN7405	56°13·5'	4°1·5'W	X	57
Auld Darkney	Angus	NO4266	56°47·2'	2°56·5'W	H	44
Auldearn	Highld	NH9155	57°34·6'	3°48·9'W	T	27
Aulden	Heref	SO4654	52°11·1'	2°47·0'W	T	148,149
Auldgirth	D & G	NX9186	55°9·6'	3°42·2'W	T	78
Auldhall	Stir	NS6693	56°6·9'	4°8·9'W	X	57
Auldhame	E Loth	NT5984	56°3·1'	2°39·1'W	X	67
Auldhame	E Loth	NT6084	56°3·1'	2°38·1'W	A	67
Auldhouse	S Lanak	NS6250	55°43·7'	4°11·4'W	T	64
Auldhouseburn	E Ayr	NS7026	55°30·9'	4°3·1'W	X	71
Auldhouse Burn	E Ayr	NS7125	55°30·4'	4°2·1'W	W	71
Auldhousehill Br	D & G	NT0511	55°23·3'	3°29·5'W	X	78
Auldich	Moray	NJ1934	57°23·6'	3°20·4'W	X	28
Auldmuir	N Ayr	NS2649	55°42·5'	4°45·7'W	X	63
Auldmuir Burn	N Ayr	NS2649	55°42·5'	4°45·7'W	W	63
Auldmuir Resr	N Ayr	NS2650	55°43·0'	4°45·8'W	W	63
Auld of Clunie	Pth & Kin	NO1043	56°34·5'	3°27·4'W	X	53
Auldshiels Hill	D & G	NY3990	55°12·3'	2°57·1'W	H	79
Auldton	S Lanak	NS7950	55°44·0'	3°55·2'W	A	64
Auldton Fell	D & G	NT1108	55°21·7'	3°23·8'W	H	78
Auldtonheights	S Lanak	NS8237	55°37·0'	3°52·0'W	X	71,72
Auldtonhill	Aberd	NK0634	57°24·0'	1°53·6'W	X	30
Auldton Hill	D & G	NT1006	55°20·6'	3°24·7'W	X	78
Auldtoun	S Lanak	NS8239	55°38·1'	3°52·0'W	X	71,72
Auldtown	Aberd	NJ4410	57°10·9'	2°55·1'W	X	37
Auldtown	Aberd	NJ4948	57°31·4'	2°50·6'W	X	28,29
Auldtown	Aberd	NJ6347	57°31·0'	2°36·6'W	X	29
Auldtown Hill	Aberd	NJ6550	57°32·6'	2°34·6'W	H	29
Auldtown of Carnousie	Aberd	NJ6550	57°32·6'	2°34·6'W	X	29
Auld Wife's Grave	D & G	NX1364	54°56·4'	4°54·7'W	X	82
Auld Wife's Grave (Chambered Cairn)	D & G	NX1364	54°56·4'	4°54·7'W	A	82
Auldyne	Aberd	NJ4039	57°26·5'	2°59·5'W	X	28
Auldyoch	Aberd	NJ6841	57°27·7'	2°31·5'W	T	29
Aules Hill	Northum	NY6652	54°51·9'	2°31·4'W	X	86
Aulich	Pth & Kin	NN6059	56°42·4'	4°16·8'W	X	42,51
Aulich Burn	Pth & Kin	NN5861	56°43·4'	4°18·8'W	W	42
Aulich Hill	Pth & Kin	NN5959	56°42·3'	4°17·7'W	H	42,51
Aulins Glen	Shetld	HU3047	60°12·6'	1°27·0'W	X	3
Auliston	Highld	NM5457	56°38·7'	6°0·3'W	X	47
Auliston Point	Highld	NM5458	56°39·2'	6°0·4'W	X	47
Ault a' chruinn	Highld	NG9420	57°13·7'	5°24·3'W	X	25,33
Aultahuish	Moray	NJ1449	57°31·6'	3°25·7'W	X	28
Aultahurn	Moray	NJ1448	57°31·1'	3°25·7'W	X	28
Aultanfearn	Highld	NH5875	57°44·8'	4°22·7'W	X	21
Aultanrynie	Highld	NC3436	58°17·1'	4°49·4'W	X	15
Aultbea	Highld	NG8789	57°50·7'	5°34·9'W	T	19
Aultbeg	Moray	NJ2733	57°23·2'	3°12·4'W	X	28
Aultcharn	Highld	NJ0724	57°18·1'	3°32·2'W	X	36
Aultdavie	Aberd	NJ6538	57°26·1'	2°34·5'W	X	29
Aultdearg	Highld	NH2865	57°38·8'	4°52·5'W	X	20
Aultdearg	Moray	NJ3356	57°35·6'	3°6·8'W	X	28
Aultgowrie	Highld	NH4751	57°31·7'	4°32·8'W	X	26
Aultgowrie Br	Highld	NH4750	57°31·1'	4°32·8'W	X	26
Aultgrishan	Highld	NG7485	57°48·1'	5°47·7'W	X	19
Aultguish Inn	Highld	NH3570	57°41·6'	4°45·6'W	X	20
Aulthash	Moray	NJ3755	57°35·1'	3°2·8'W	X	28
Ault Hucknall	Derby	SK4665	53°11·0'	1°18·3'W	T	120
Aultibea	Highld	ND0423	58°11·4'	3°37·5'W	X	17
Aultiphurst	Highld	NC8065	58°33·7'	4°3·3'W	T	10
Aultivullin	Highld	NC8167	58°34·8'	4°2·3'W	T	10
Aultmore	Highld	NJ0121	57°16·4'	3°38·1'W	X	36
Aultmore	Moray	NJ4053	57°34·0'	2°59·7'W	T	28
Aultmore	Moray	NJ4657	57°36·2'	2°53·8'W	X	28,29
Aultmorehill Wood	Moray	NJ4858	57°36·8'	2°51·8'W	F	28,29
Aultmore Lodge	Moray	NJ4959	57°37·3'	2°50·8'W	X	28,29
Aultnagar Lodge Hotel	Highld	NH5898	57°57·2'	4°23·5'W	X	21
Ault-na-goire	Highld	NH5422	57°16·2'	4°24·8'W	X	26,35
Aultnamain Inn	Highld	NH6681	57°48·2'	4°14·8'W	X	21
Aultnancaber	Highld	NH9210	57°10·3'	3°46·7'W	X	36
Aultnapaddock	Aberd	NJ3941	57°27·6'	3°0·5'W	X	28
Aultnaslanach	Highld	NH7534	57°23·0'	4°4·3'W	X	27
Aultnaslat	Highld	NH1301	57°4·0'	5°4·6'W	X	34
Aulton	Aberd	NJ5655	57°35·2'	2°43·7'W	X	29
Aulton	Aberd	NJ6028	57°20·7'	2°39·4'W	X	37
Aulton	Moray	NJ3348	57°31·3'	3°6·7'W	X	28
Aulton Fm	Aberd	NO6995	57°3·0'	2°30·2'W	FM	38,45
Aulton of Ardendraught	Aberd	NK0735	57°24·6'	1°52·6'W	X	30
Aulton of Atherb	Aberd	NJ9149	57°32·1'	2°8·6'W	X	30
Aulton of Coynach Fm	Aberd	NJ9944	57°29·4'	2°0·5'W	FM	30
Aulton of Fochel	Aberd	NJ8232	57°22·9'	2°17·5'W	X	29,30
Aultonrea	Aberd	NO3591	57°0·6'	3°3·8'W	X	44
Aultvaich	Highld	NH5148	57°30·1'	4°28·7'W	T	26
Aultvoulin	Highld	NG7600	57°2·5'	5°41·1'W	X	33
Aultyoun	Highld	NJ1131	57°21·9'	3°28·3'W	X	36
Aumery Park	N Yks	SE6589	54°17·8'	0°59·7'W	X	94,100
Aunby	Lincs	TF0214	52°43·1'	0°29·0'W	T	130
Aundorach	Highld	NH9816	57°13·7'	3°40·9'W	X	36
Aunemouth	Devon	SX6744	50°17·1'	3°51·6'W	X	202
Aune or Avon Head	Devon	SX6569	50°30·5'	3°53·9'W	W	202
Aunhamdale Fm	E Yorks	SE9156	53°59·8'	0°36·3'W	FM	106
Aunk	Devon	ST0400	50°47·7'	3°21·3'W	T	192
Aunsby	Lincs	TF0438	52°56·0'	0°26·8'W	T	130
Aunt's Pool Hill	Hants	SU8252	51°15·9'	0°49·1'W	X	186
Auquhadlie	Aberd	NJ9438	57°26·2'	2°5·5'W	X	30
Auquharney Ho	Aberd	NK0238	57°26·2'	1°57·5'W	X	30
Auquhirie	Aberd	NO8285	56°57·6'	2°17·3'W	X	45
Auquhorthies	Aberd	NJ8329	57°21·3'	2°16·5'W	X	38
Auquorthies	Aberd	NO8889	56°59·8'	2°11·4'W	X	45
Auratote	N Eil	NF7820	57°9·7'	7°19·2'W	T	31
Ausdale	Highld	NH6295	57°55·6'	4°19·3'W	X	21
Ausewell Cross	Devon	SX7372	50°32·3'	3°47·2'W	X	191
Ausewell Rocks	Devon	SX7371	50°31·7'	3°47·1'W	X	202
Ausewell Wood	Devon	SX7271	50°31·7'	3°48·0'W	F	202
Ausgates	Suff	TM5181	52°22·4'	1°41·7'E	F	156
Aushaw	Black w Dar	SD7220	53°40·8'	2°25·0'W	X	103
Ausin Fell Wood	Cumbr	SD3691	54°18·9'	2°58·6'W	F	96,97
Auskerry	Orkney	HY6716	59°2·1'	2°34·0'W	X	5
Aust	I of M	SC4396	54°20·4'	4°24·5'W	X	95
Aust	S Glos	ST5789	51°36·1'	2°36·9'W	T	162,172
Austacre Fm	Lincs	TF1472	53°14·2'	0°17·1'W	FM	121
Austacre Wood	Lincs	TF1471	53°13·7'	0°17·1'W	F	121
Austage End	Herts	TL1625	51°54·9'	0°18·4'W	X	166
Aust Cliff	S Glos	ST5689	51°36·1'	2°37·7'W	X	162,172
Austendike	Lincs	TF2921	52°46·5'	0°4·9'W	T	131
Austen Fen	Lincs	TF3794	53°25·7'	0°4·1'E	T	113
Austens	Bucks	SU9792	51°37·3'	0°35·5'W	X	175,176
Austen's Fm	Kent	TQ6961	51°19·6'	0°25·9'E	FM	177,178,188
Austenwood	Bucks	SU9989	51°35·7'	0°33·9'W	T	175,176
Austerfield	Donc	SK6694	53°26·6'	1°0·0'W	T	111
Austerfield Drain	Donc	SK6796	53°27·6'	0°59·0'W	W	111
Auster Grange	E Yorks	TA1924	53°42·2'	0°11·4'W	X	107,113
Austerlands	Oldham	SD9505	53°32·7'	2°4·1'W	T	109
Auster Lodge	Lincs	TF0619	52°45·7'	0°25·3'W	X	130
Austerson	Ches	SJ6548	53°1·9'	2°30·9'W	FM	118
Austerson Hall	Ches	SJ6547	53°1·4'	2°30·9'W	X	118
Auster Wood	Lincs	TF0719	52°45·7'	0°24·5'W	X	130
Austhorpe	Leeds	SE3733	53°47·8'	1°25·9'W	T	104
Austhorpe Hall	Leeds	SE3634	53°48·3'	1°26·8'W	A	104
Austincroft	Highld	NM7269	56°45·7'	5°43·4'W	X	40
Austins	Devon	SS6015	50°55·3'	3°59·1'W	X	180
Austin's Br	Devon	SX7465	50°28·5'	3°46·2'W	A	202
Australia Fm	Cambs	TL3596	52°32·9'	0°0·1'W	FM	142
Australia Fm	Cambs	TL4772	52°19·8'	0°9·8'E	FM	154
Austrey	Warw	SK2906	52°39·3'	1°33·9'W	T	140
Austrey Ho	Warw	SK3005	52°38·8'	1°33·0'W	X	140
Aust Rock	S Glos	ST5689	51°36·1'	2°37·7'W	X	162,172
Austwick	N Yks	SD7668	54°6·7'	2°21·6'W	T	98
Austwick Beck	N Yks	SD7567	54°6·1'	2°22·5'W	W	98
Austwick Common	N Yks	SD7361	54°2·9'	2°24·3'W	X	98
Austwick Moss	N Yks	SD7666	54°5·6'	2°21·6'W	F	98
Austy Manor	Warw	SP1662	52°15·6'	1°45·5'W	X	151
Austy Wood	Warw	SP1762	52°15·6'	1°44·7'W	F	151
Auterstone	Cumbr	NY4521	54°35·1'	2°50·6'W	X	90
Autherlands	N Yks	SE1277	54°11·6'	1°48·5'W	X	99
Autherley Junction	Wolv	SJ9002	52°37·2'	2°8·5'W	X	127,139
Autherthaws Fm	E Yorks	SE7238	53°50·2'	0°53·9'W	FM	105,106
Authorpe	Lincs	TF4081	53°18·7'	0°6·5'E	T	122
Authorpe Fm	Lincs	SK8144	52°59·5'	0°47·2'W	FM	130
Authorpe Grange	Lincs	TF3880	53°18·2'	0°4·7'E	X	122
Authorpe Row	Lincs	TF5373	53°14·1'	0°18·0'E	T	122
Auton	Devon	SX7242	50°16·1'	3°47·4'W	X	202
Auton Dolwells	Somer	ST1125	51°1·3'	3°15·8'W	X	181,193
Avalon Fm	Somer	ST4638	51°8·6'	2°45·9'W	FM	182
Avarack, The	Corn	SW3735	50°9·6'	5°40·6'W	X	203
Avaries,The	Somer	ST6832	51°5·4'	2°27·0'W	X	183
Avaulds	Aberd	NJ7659	57°37·5'	2°23·6'W	X	29
Avebury	Wilts	SU1069	51°25·4'	1°51·0'W	A	173
Avebury	Wilts	SU1069	51°25·4'	1°51·0'W	T	173
Avebury Down	Wilts	SU1170	51°26·0'	1°50·1'W	X	173
Avebury Manor	Wilts	SU0970	51°26·0'	1°51·8'W	A	173
Avebury Trusloe	Wilts	SU0969	51°25·4'	1°51·8'W	T	173
Aveley	Thurr	TQ5680	51°30·1'	0°15·3'E	T	177
Aveley Marshes	Hav	TQ5379	51°29·6'	0°12·6'E	X	177
Aveley Wood	Suff	TL8650	52°7·2'	0°43·4'E	F	155
Aveline's Hole	N Som	ST4758	51°19·4'	2°45·2'W	A	172,182
Avelshay	Orkney	HY4428	59°8·4'	2°58·2'W	X	5,6
Avely Hall	Suff	TL9439	52°1·2'	0°50·0'E	X	155
Avenbury Court	Heref	SO6552	52°10·1'	2°30·3'W	X	149
Avenel Plantn	Scot Bord	NT5237	55°37·7'	2°45·3'W	F	73
Avenham Hall	Lancs	SD3737	53°49·8'	2°57·0'W	X	102
Avening	Glos	ST8898	51°41·1'	2°10·0'W	T	162
Avening Court	Glos	ST8997	51°40·5'	2°9·2'W	X	163
Avening Green	S Glos	ST7193	51°38·3'	2°24·8'W	T	162,172
Avening Ho	Glos	ST8798	51°41·1'	2°10·9'W	X	162
Avening Park	Glos	ST8797	51°40·5'	2°10·9'W	X	162
Avens House Fm	Red & Cl	NZ6912	54°30·2'	0°55·6'W	FM	94
Avens Wood	Red & Cl	NZ7013	54°30·7'	0°54·7'W	F	94
Avenue Fm	Beds	TL0854	52°10·7'	0°24·8'W	FM	153
Avenue Fm	Cambs	TL3163	52°15·2'	0°4·5'W	FM	153
Avenue Fm	Dorset	ST8525	51°1·7'	2°12·4'W	FM	183
Avenue Fm	E Yorks	SE8537	53°49·6'	0°42·1'W	FM	106
Avenue Fm	Lincs	TF2909	52°40·0'	0°5·1'W	FM	142
Avenue Fm	Lincs	TF4555	53°4·6'	0°10·3'E	FM	122
Avenue Fm	Lincs	TF4624	52°47·9'	0°10·3'E	FM	131
Avenue Fm	Norf	TG3700	52°33·0'	1°30·2'E	FM	134
Avenue Fm	N Yks	SE5740	53°51·4'	1°7·6'W	FM	105
Avenue Fm	Rut	SK9110	52°41·0'	0°38·8'W	FM	130
Avenue Fm	Shrops	SJ6226	52°50·1'	2°33·4'W	FM	127
Avenue Fm	Suff	TL7674	52°20·4'	0°35·4'E	FM	143
Avenue Fm	Wrex	SJ4636	52°55·4'	2°47·8'W	FM	126
Avenue Fm, The	E Yorks	SE9363	54°3·5'	0°34·3'W	FM	101
Avenue Grange	N Yks	SE3984	54°15·3'	1°23·7'W	X	99
Avenuehead	Stir	NS8087	56°3·9'	3°55·2'W	X	57,65
Avenue Head Fm	Northum	NZ3075	55°4·4'	1°31·4'W	FM	88
Avenue Ho	N Yks	SE3756	54°0·2'	1°25·7'W	X	104
Avenue Ho	Warw	SP4272	52°20·9'	1°22·6'W	X	140
Avenue Lodges	Northnts	SP8557	52°12·5'	0°45·0'W	X	152
Avenue, The	E Loth	NT6280	56°0·9'	2°36·1'W	X	67
Avenue, The	Lincs	TF3550	53°2·0'	0°1·2'E	X	122
Avenue, The	Peterb	TF2107	52°39·1'	0°12·3'W	X	142
Avenue, The	Wilts	SU1242	51°10·9'	1°49·3'W	A	184
Avenue Wood	E Yorks	SE9363	54°3·5'	0°34·3'W	F	101
Avenue Wood	Leeds	SE3731	53°46·7'	1°25·9'W	F	104
Avenvogie Cott	Arg & Bt	NR3455	55°43·2'	6°13·7'W	X	60
Avenvogie Fm	Arg & Bt	NR3656	55°43·8'	6°11·9'W	FM	60
Avercombe	Devon	SS7623	50°59·8'	3°45·6'W	X	180
Averham	Notts	SK7654	53°4·9'	0°51·5'W	T	120
Averham Park	Notts	SK7456	53°6·0'	0°53·3'W	A	120
Averhams Plantn	N Yks	SE6760	54°2·1'	0°58·2'W	F	100
Averhill Side	Staffs	SK0659	53°7·9'	1°54·2'W	X	119
Averill Fm	Derby	SK4061	53°8·9'	1°23·7'W	FM	120
Averingdown Fm	Bucks	SU8296	51°39·6'	0°48·5'W	FM	165
Avernish	Highld	NG8426	57°16·7'	5°34·5'W	T	33
Aversley Wood	Cambs	TL1681	52°25·1'	0°17·3'W	F	142
Avery Hill	Gren	TQ4474	51°27·0'	0°4·7'E	T	177
Averys	E Susx	TQ5314	50°54·7'	0°0·7'E	X	198
Aves Ditch	Oxon	SP5123	51°54·4'	1°15·1'W	A	164
Aveton	Devon	SX7250	50°20·4'	3°47·6'W	X	202
Aveton Gifford	Devon	SX6947	50°18·7'	3°50·0'W	T	202
Aviaries, The	Notts	SK6273	53°15·3'	1°3·8'W	X	120
Aviary, The	Ealing	TQ1479	51°30·1'	0°21·1'W	X	176
Aviary, The	Flint	SJ3164	53°10·4'	3°1·5'W	X	117
Avich Falls	Arg & Bt	NM9614	56°16·7'	5°17·3'W	W	55
Aviedale	Orkney	HY4119	59°3·5'	3°1·2'W	X	6
Avielochan	Highld	NH9016	57°13·6'	3°48·9'W	X	36
Aviemore	Highld	NH8912	57°11·4'	3°49·7'W	T	35,36
Aviemore Centre, The	Highld	NH8912	57°11·4'	3°49·7'W	X	35,36
Aville Fm	Somer	SS9743	51°10·9'	3°28·0'W	FM	181
Avil's Fm	Wilts	ST9381	51°31·9'	2°5·7'W	FM	173
Avinagillan	Arg & Bt	NR8367	55°51·1'	5°27·6'W	X	62
Avington	Hants	SU5332	51°5·3'	1°14·2'W	T	185
Avington	W Berks	SU3768	51°24·8'	1°27·7'W	T	174
Avington Manor	W Berks	SU3668	51°24·8'	1°28·6'W	X	174
Avington Manor Fm	Hants	SU5330	51°4·2'	1°14·2'W	FM	185
Avington Park	Hants	SU5332	51°5·3'	1°14·2'W	A	185
Avinlussa	Arg & Bt	NR3558	55°44·8'	6°12·9'W	X	60
Avins Fm	W Susx	TQ3427	51°1·8'	0°5·0'W	FM	187,198
Avishays	Somer	ST3509	50°52·8'	2°55·1'W	A	193
Avisyard	E Ayr	NS6018	55°26·4'	4°12·4'W	X	71
Avisyard Burn	E Ayr	NS6118	55°26·4'	4°11·4'W	W	71
Avisyard Hill	E Ayr	NS6018	55°26·4'	4°12·4'W	H	71
Avoch	Highld	NH7055	57°34·2'	4°10·0'W	T	27
Avoch Bay	Highld	NH7054	57°33·7'	4°9·9'W	W	27
Avochie Ho	Aberd	NJ5346	57°30·4'	2°46·6'W	X	29
Avon	Hants	SZ1498	50°47·1'	1°47·7'W	T	195
Avon	Wilts	ST9576	51°29·2'	2°3·9'W	T	173
Avon Aquatics	Warw	SP2048	52°8·0'	1°42·1'W	X	151
Avonbank	Falk	NS9678	55°59·3'	3°39·6'W	X	65
Avon Br	Wilts	SU1232	51°5·5'	1°49·3'W	X	184
Avonbridge	Falk	NS9172	55°56·0'	3°44·2'W	T	65
Avon Castle	Dorset	SU1303	50°49·8'	1°48·5'W	X	195
Avoncliff	Wilts	ST8059	51°20·0'	2°16·8'W	T	173
Avon Common	Dorset	SZ1398	50°47·1'	1°48·6'W	X	195
Avoncroft Mus	Worcs	SO9568	52°18·8'	2°4·0'W	X	139
Avondale	Leic	SK7116	52°44·5'	0°56·5'W	X	129
Avondale	Shetld	HU2049	60°13·8'	1°37·8'W	X	3
Avondale Ho	Falk	NS9579	55°59·8'	3°40·6'W	X	65
Avon Dam Reservoir	Devon	SX6765	50°28·4'	3°52·1'W	W	202
Avon Dassett	Warw	SP4150	52°9·0'	1°23·6'W	T	151
Avon Fm	Bath & NE Somer	ST6868	51°24·8'	2°27·2'W	FM	172
Avon Gorge	C of Bris	ST5674	51°28·0'	2°37·6'W	X	172
Avon Gorge Nature Reserve	N Som	ST5573	51°27·5'	2°38·5'W	X	172
Avonhead	N Lanak	NS8069	55°54·2'	3°54·7'W	X	65
Avon Head	S Lanak	NS5832	55°33·9'	4°14·7'W	X	71
Avon Head or Aune	Devon	SX6569	50°30·5'	3°53·9'W	W	202
Avon Heath Country Park	Dorset	SU1203	50°49·8'	1°49·4'W	X	195
Avon Ho	Warw	SP4476	52°23·0'	1°20·8'W	X	140
Avonholm	S Lanak	NS7346	55°41·7'	4°0·8'W	X	64
Avon Moss	S Lanak	NS6134	55°35·0'	4°11·9'W	X	71
Avonmouth	C of Bris	ST5277	51°29·6'	2°41·1'W	T	172

Avonside	S Lanak	NS6337	55°36·7'	4°10·1'W	X	71
Avon Tyrrell	Hants	SU1800	50°48·2'	1°44·3'W	X	195
Avon Tyrrell Fm	Hants	SZ1499	50°47·7'	1°47·7'W	FM	195
Avon Valley Country Park	Bath & NE Somer	ST6768	51°24·8'	2°28·1'W	X	172
Avon View Fm	Wilts	ST8661	51°21·1'	2°11·7'W	FM	173
Avon Walkway	Bath & NE Somer	ST6469	51°25·4'	2°30·7'W	X	172
Avon Walkway	N Som	ST5574	51°28·0'	2°38·5'W	X	172
Avon Water	E Ayr	NS6135	55°35·6'	4°11·9'W	W	71
Avon Water	Hants	SZ2599	50°47·6'	1°38·3'W	W	195
Avon Water	Hants	SZ3094	50°44·9'	1°34·1'W	W	196
Avon Water	S Lanak	NS6842	55°39·5'	4°5·5'W	W	71
Avon Water	S Lanak	NS7447	55°42·3'	3°59·9'W	W	64
Avonwick	Devon	SX7158	50°24·7'	3°48·6'W	T	202
Awbridge	Hants	SU3323	51°0·6'	1°31·4'W	T	185
Awbridge Br	Staffs	SO8594	52°32·9'	2°12·9'W	X	139
Awbridge Danes	Hants	SU3123	51°0·6'	1°33·1'W	X	185
Awbridge Ho	Hants	SU3224	51°1·1'	1°32·2'W	X	185
Awbrook	E Susx	TQ3523	50°59·7'	0°4·2'W	X	198
Awelfryn	Carm	SN4223	51°53·2'	4°17·4'W	X	159
Awhirk	D & G	NX0553	54°50·3'	5°1·8'W	X	82
Awhirk	D & G	NX0846	54°46·6'	4°58·7'W	X	82
Awies	D & G	NX1169	54°59·0'	4°56·8'W	X	82
Awkley	S Glos	ST5985	51°34·0'	2°35·1'W	T	172
Awliscombe	Devon	ST1301	50°48·4'	3°13·7'W	T	192,193
Awmack Ho	N Yks	SE4090	54°18·5'	1°22·7'W	X	99
Awnells	Heref	SO6531	51°58·8'	2°30·2'W	X	149
Awre	Glos	SO7008	51°46·4'	2°25·7'W	T	162
Awsland	Devon	SS4711	50°52·9'	4°10·1'W	X	191
Awsworth	Notts	SK4843	52°59·2'	1°16·7'W	T	129
Axbridge	Somer	ST4354	51°17·2'	2°48·7'W	T	182
Axe Edge	Derby	SK0369	53°13·3'	1°56·9'W	X	119
Axe Edge End	Derby	SK0368	53°12·8'	1°56·9'W	X	119
Axe Edge Moor	Derby	SK0270	53°13·9'	1°57·8'W	X	119
Axe Fm	Devon	ST3101	50°48·5'	2°58·4'W	FM	193
Axe Fm	Somer	ST4106	50°51·3'	2°49·9'W	FM	193
Axeland Park	Surrey	TQ2946	51°12·1'	0°8·8'W	X	187
Axen Fm	Dorset	SY4394	50°44·8'	2°48·1'W	FM	193
Axesclose Fm	Somer	ST5118	50°57·8'	2°41·5'W	FM	183
Axe, The	Orkney	ND3088	58°46·7'	3°12·2'W	X	7
Axford	Corn	SX3667	50°29·0'	4°18·3'W	X	201
Axford	Hants	SU6143	51°11·2'	1°7·2'W	T	185
Axford	Wilts	SU2369	51°25·4'	1°39·8'W	T	174
Axford Fm	Wilts	SU2570	51°25·9'	1°38·0'W	FM	174
Axletree Hurn	Lincs	TF4882	53°19·1'	0°13·7'E	X	122
Axletreewell	D & G	NY1976	55°4·6'	3°15·7'W	X	85
Axmansford	Hants	SU5661	51°20·9'	1°11·4'W	T	174
Axmas Fm	W Susx	TQ2136	51°6·9'	0°15·9'W	FM	187
Axminster	Devon	SY2998	50°46·9'	3°0·0'W	T	193
Axmouth	Devon	SY2591	50°43·1'	3°3·4'W	T	192,193
Axna Geo	Orkney	HY2221	59°4·4'	3°21·2'W	X	6
Axna Geo	Orkney	HY5226	59°7·4'	2°49·8'W	X	5,6
Axna Geo	Orkney	HY5334	59°11·7'	2°48·9'W	X	5,6
Axnfell Plantation	I of M	SC4284	54°13·9'	4°25·0'W	F	95
Axnie Geo	Orkney	HY4532	59°10·5'	2°57·2'W	X	5,6
Axon Fm	Devon	ST0815	50°55·9'	3°18·2'W	FM	181
Axstones Spring	Staffs	SJ9562	53°9·5'	2°4·1'W	X	118
Axton	Flint	SJ1080	53°18·8'	3°20·6'W	T	116
Axton Hill	Pemb	SR9398	51°38·8'	4°59·1'W	X	158
Axtown	Devon	SX5167	50°29·3'	4°5·7'W	T	201
Axwell Park	Ghead	NZ1961	54°56·8'	1°41·8'W	T	88
Axworthy	Devon	SX4788	50°40·5'	4°9·5'W	X	191
Aychley Fm	Shrops	SJ6034	52°54·4'	2°35·3'W	FM	127
Aycliff	Kent	TR3040	51°7·0'	1°17·6'E	T	179
Aycliffe	Durham	NZ2822	54°35·8'	1°33·6'W	T	93
Aycliffe School	Durham	NZ2925	54°37·4'	1°32·6'W	X	93
Aycote Fm	Glos	SP0010	51°47·6'	1°59·6'W	FM	163
Aydehurst Fm	Kent	TQ7743	51°9·8'	0°32·3'E	FM	188
Aydon	Northum	NZ0066	54°59·6'	1°59·6'W	T	87
Aydon Castle	Northum	NZ0066	54°59·6'	1°59·6'W	A	87
Aydon Forest or Alnwick Moor (Inner)	Northum	NU1612	55°24·3'	1°44·4'W	X	81
Aydon Forest or Alnwick Moor (Outer)	Northum	NU1410	55°23·3'	1°46·3'W	X	81
Aydon Shields	Northum	NY9256	54°54·2'	2°7·1'W	X	87
Aye Bridge Fm	Wigan	SD6000	53°30·0'	2°35·8'W	FM	109
Aye Gill Pike	Cumbr	SD7288	54°17·5'	2°25·4'W	H	98
Aye Gill Wold	Cumbr	SD7487	54°16·9'	2°23·5'W	X	98
Ayford Fm	S Glos	ST7771	51°26·5'	2°19·5'W	FM	172
Aygill	Cumbr	SD6681	54°13·7'	2°30·9'W	W	98
Ay Gill	Durham	NY9011	54°29·9'	2°8·8'W	W	91,92
Aygill	N Yks	NY8800	54°24·0'	2°10·7'W	X	91,92
Aygill Beck	N Yks	SE0574	54°9·9'	1°55·0'W	W	98
Aygill Pike	N Yks	SE0573	54°9·4'	1°55·0'W	X	98
Ayhope Beck	Durham	NZ0631	54°40·7'	1°54·0'W	W	92
Aykley Heads	Durham	NZ2643	54°47·1'	1°35·3'W	T	88
Aylburton	Glos	SO6101	51°42·6'	2°33·5'W	T	162
Aylburton Common	Glos	SO6002	51°43·2'	2°34·4'W	T	162
Aylburton Warth	Glos	ST6199	51°41·5'	2°33·5'W	X	162
Ayle	Northum	NY7149	54°50·3'	2°26·7'W	T	86,87
Ayle Burn	Northum	NY7149	54°50·3'	2°26·7'W	W	86,87
Ayle Common	Northum	NY7150	54°50·9'	2°26·7'W	H	86,87
Ayleford	Glos	SO6608	51°46·4'	2°29·2'W	X	162
Aylesbeare	Devon	SY0392	50°43·4'	3°22·1'W	T	192
Aylesbeare Common	Devon	SY0590	50°42·3'	3°20·3'W	X	192
Aylesbeare Hill	Devon	SY0592	50°43·4'	3°20·4'W	X	192
Aylesbury	Bucks	SP8113	51°48·8'	0°49·1'W	T	165
Aylesbury Ho (Hotel)	Warw	SP1573	52°21·5'	1°46·4'W	X	139
Aylesbury Ring	Herts	SP8716	51°50·4'	0°43·8'W	X	
Aylesby	NE Lincs	TA2007	53°33·0'	0°10·9'W	T	113
Aylescott	Devon	SS6116	50°55·8'	3°58·3'W	X	180
Aylesford	Kent	TQ7258	51°17·9'	0°28·4'E	T	178,188
Aylesford Brook	Shrops	SJ2701	52°36·4'	3°4·3'W	W	126
Aylesham	Kent	TR2352	51°13·6'	1°12·0'E	T	179,189
Aylesmore	Glos	SO7129	51°57·8'	2°24·9'W	X	149
Aylesmore Ct	Glos	SO5603	51°43·7'	2°37·8'W	X	162
Aylesmore Fm	Warw	SP3042	52°4·8'	1°33·3'W	FM	151
Ayles's Hill	Dorset	ST6100	50°48·1'	2°32·8'W	X	194
Ayleston Cross	Devon	SX6751	50°20·9'	3°51·8'W	X	202

Aylestone	C of Leic	SK5700	52°35·9'	1°9·1'W	T	140
Aylestone Hill	Heref	SO5240	52°3·6'	2°41·6'W	T	149
Aylestone Park	C of Leic	SK5801	52°36·5'	1°8·2'W	T	140
Ayleswade	Kent	TQ8441	51°8·5'	0°38·2'E	X	188
Aylett's Fm	Essex	TL8028	51°55·5'	0°37·5'E	FM	168
Ayleward's Fm	Essex	TL7728	51°55·6'	0°34·9'E	FM	167
Aylmerbank Wood	D & G	NS8207	55°20·8'	3°51·2'W	F	71,78
Aylmer Hall	Norf	TF5514	52°42·3'	0°18·1'E	X	131
Aylmers Fm	Essex	TL4812	51°47·4'	0°9·2'E	FM	167
Aylmerton	Norf	TG1839	52°54·5'	1°14·9'E	T	133
Aylsham	Norf	TG1927	52°48·0'	1°15·3'E	T	133,134
Aylton	Heref	SO6537	52°2·1'	2°30·2'W	T	149
Aylton Court	Heref	SO6536	52°1·5'	2°30·2'W	X	149
Aylworth	Glos	SP1022	51°54·0'	1°50·9'W	X	163
Aymers	Kent	TQ9460	51°18·6'	0°47·4'E	X	178
Aymestrey	Heref	SO4265	52°17·0'	2°50·6'W	T	137,148,149
Aymestrey School	Worcs	SO8154	52°11·3'	2°16·3'W	X	150
Aynho	Northnts	SP5133	51°59·8'	1°15·0'W	T	151
Aynhoe Park Ho	Northnts	SP5132	51°59·3'	1°15·0'W	A	151
Aynho Fields	Northnts	SP5233	51°59·8'	1°14·2'W	X	151
Aynho Wharf	Oxon	SP4932	51°59·3'	1°16·8'W	X	151
Aynsome Manor (Hotel)	Cumbr	SD3879	54°12·4'	2°56·6'W	X	96,97
Ayntree	Shrops	SO4779	52°24·6'	2°46·4'W	X	137,138,148
Ayot Bury	Herts	TL2115	51°49·5'	0°14·3'W	X	166
Ayot Green	Herts	TL2114	51°48·9'	0°14·3'W	T	166
Ayot Greenway	Herts	TL2014	51°48·9'	0°15·2'W	X	166
Ayot Ho	Herts	TL1917	51°50·6'	0°16·0'W	X	166
Ayot Place	Herts	TL2114	51°48·9'	0°14·3'W	X	166
Ayot St Lawrence	Herts	TL1916	51°50·0'	0°16·0'W	T	166
Ayot St Peter	Herts	TL2115	51°49·5'	0°14·3'W	T	166
Ayr	S Ayr	NS3422	55°28·1'	4°37·1'W	T	70
Ayre	Orkney	HY6429	59°9·0'	2°37·3'W	X	5
Ayre Dyke	Shetld	HU3730	60°3·4'	1°19·6'W	X	4
Ayre of Atler	Shetld	HU4561	60°20·1'	1°10·6'W	X	2,3
Ayre of Birrier	Shetld	HU5488	60°34·6'	1°0·4'W	X	1,2
Ayre of Breiwick	Shetld	HU4449	60°13·6'	1°11·8'W	X	3
Ayre of Cara	Orkney	ND4794	58°50·0'	2°54·6'W	X	7
Ayre of Deepdale	Shetld	HU3242	60°9·9'	1°24·9'W	X	4
Ayre of Dury	Shetld	HU4660	60°19·6'	1°9·5'W	X	2,3
Ayre of Skersie	Orkney	HY4427	59°7·8'	2°58·2'W	X	5,6
Ayre of Westermill	Orkney	ND4795	58°50·6'	2°54·6'W	X	7
Ayre Point	Orkney	ND3394	58°50·0'	3°9·2'W	X	7
Ayres	Shetld	HU3457	60°18·0'	1°22·6'W	X	2,3
Ayres End	Herts	TL1512	51°47·9'	0°19·5'W	T	166
Ayres of Selivoe	Shetld	HU2848	60°13·2'	1°29·2'W	T	3
Ayre Sound	Orkney	HY7743	59°16·6'	2°23·7'W	W	5
Ayres Quay	Sund	NZ3957	54°54·6'	1°23·1'W	T	88
Ayres, The	I of M	NX4303	54°24·1'	4°24·7'W	X	95
Ayre,The	Orkney	HY3200	58°53·2'	3°10·3'W	X	6,7
Ayre, The	Orkney	ND2889	58°47·2'	3°14·3'W	X	7
Ayreville	Torbay	SX8460	50°25·9'	3°37·6'W	X	202
Ayrlow Banks	N Yks	SE1793	54°20·2'	1°43·9'W	X	99
Ayrmer Cove	Devon	SX6345	50°17·6'	3°55·0'W	W	202
Aysdale Gate	Red & Cl	NZ6514	54°31·3'	0°59·3'W	X	94
Aysgarth	N Yks	SE0088	54°17·5'	1°59·6'W	T	98
Aysgarth Falls	N Yks	SE0188	54°17·5'	1°58·7'W	W	98
Aysgarth Moor	N Yks	SD9787	54°17·0'	2°2·3'W	X	98
Aysgarth School	N Yks	SE2089	54°18·0'	1°41·1'W	X	99
Aysh	Devon	SX6689	50°41·3'	3°53·4'W	X	191
Ayshford	Devon	ST0415	50°55·8'	3°21·6'W	T	181
Ayside	Cumbr	SD3983	54°14·6'	2°55·7'W	T	96,97
Ayside Pool	Cumbr	SD3882	54°14·0'	2°56·7'W	W	96,97
Ayston	Rut	SK8601	52°36·2'	0°43·4'W	T	141
Aythorpe Roding	Essex	TL5914	51°48·3'	0°18·8'E	T	167
Ayton	Fife	NO3018	56°21·2'	3°7·5'W	X	59
Ayton	Pth & Kin	NO1615	56°19·5'	3°21·1'W	X	58
Ayton	Scot Bord	NT9261	55°50·8'	2°7·2'W	T	67
Ayton	Sund	NZ2855	54°53·6'	1°33·4'W	T	88
Ayton Banks Fm	N Yks	NZ5811	54°29·7'	1°5·8'W	FM	93
Ayton Castle	Scot Bord	NT9261	55°50·8'	2°7·2'W	T	67
Ayton Firs	N Yks	NZ5509	54°28·6'	1°8·7'W	X	93
Ayton Fm	Derby	SK0173	53°24·1'	1°58·7'W	FM	110
Ayton Hill	Fife	NO2919	56°21·7'	3°8·5'W	X	59
Ayton Hill	Scot Bord	NT9263	55°51·9'	2°5·3'W	X	67,74,75
Aytonlaw	Scot Bord	NT9160	55°50·2'	2°8·2'W	X	67
Ayton Mains	Scot Bord	NT9362	55°51·3'	2°6·3'W	X	67
Aytonwood Ho	Scot Bord	NT9162	55°51·3'	2°8·2'W	X	67
Aytounhill	Fife	NO2918	56°21·2'	3°8·5'W	X	59
Ay Wick	Shetld	HU4178	60°29·3'	1°14·7'W	W	2,3
Ay Wick	Shetld	HU5386	60°33·5'	1°1·5'W	W	1,2,3
Ayxa Fm	Lancs	SD6844	53°53·7'	2°28·8'W	FM	103
Azerley	N Yks	SE2574	54°9·9'	1°36·6'W	T	99
Azerley Park	N Yks	SE2574	54°9·9'	1°36·6'W	X	99
Azerley Tower	N Yks	SE2674	54°9·9'	1°35·7'W	X	99
Aztec West	S Glos	ST6082	51°32·4'	2°34·2'W	X	172

B

Baa Berg	Shetld	HU4844	60°10·9'	1°7·6'W	X	4
Baad	Stir	NS7694	56°7·6'	3°59·3'W	X	57
Baadhead	Pth & Kin	NO0012	56°17·7'	3°36·5'W	X	58
Baad Park	W Loth	NT1059	55°49·2'	3°25·7'W	X	65,72
Baad Park	W Loth	NT1060	55°49·7'	3°25·8'W	X	65
Baad Park Burn	W Loth	NT1060	55°49·7'	3°25·8'W	W	65
Baads	C of Aber	NJ8002	57°6·8'	2°19·4'W	X	38
Baads	N Lanak	NS8765	55°52·2'	3°47·9'W	X	65
Baadsmill	W Loth	NT0059	55°49·1'	3°35·3'W	X	65,72
Baad Spring	Stir	NS5396	56°8·3'	4°21·5'W	X	57
Baal Hill	Durham	NZ1839	54°45·0'	1°42·8'W	X	92
Baal Hill Ho	Durham	NZ0738	54°44·5'	1°53·1'W	X	92
Baal Hill Wood	Durham	NZ0639	54°45·0'	1°54·0'W	F	92
Baa-neap	Shetld	HU6791	60°36·1'	0°46·1'W	H	1,2
Baas Hill	Herts	TL3506	51°44·4'	0°2·3'W	X	166
Baas Manor Fm	Herts	TL3506	51°44·4'	0°2·3'W	FM	166
Baas, The	Shetld	HU4079	60°29·8'	1°15·8'W	X	2,3
Baa Taing	Shetld	HU2774	60°27·2'	1°30·1'W	X	3
Babbacombe	Torbay	SX9265	50°28·7'	3°31·0'W	T	202
Babbacombe Bay	Torbay	SX9369	50°30·9'	3°30·2'W	W	202
Babbacombe Cliff	Devon	SS3925	51°0·3'	4°17·3'W	X	190
Babbacombe Fm	Devon	SS4025	51°0·4'	4°16·5'W	FM	180,190
Babbacombe Mouth	Devon	SS3925	51°0·3'	4°17·3'W	W	190
Babbes Fm	Kent	TQ7932	51°3·8'	0°33·7'E	FM	188
Babbet Ness	Fife	NO5914	56°19·3'	2°39·3'W	X	59
Babbington	Corn	SX1562	50°26·0'	4°35·9'W	X	201
Babbington	Devon	SS3307	50°50·5'	4°21·9'W	X	190
Babbington	Notts	SK4943	52°59·2'	1°15·8'W	T	129
Babbington Springs Fm	Notts	SK7870	53°13·5'	0°49·5'W	FM	120,121
Babbinswood	Shrops	SJ3330	52°52·0'	2°59·3'W	T	126
Babbithill	Falk	NS8972	55°56·0'	3°46·2'W	X	65
Babbs Green	Herts	TL3916	51°49·7'	0°1·4'E	T	166
Babcary	Somer	ST5628	51°3·2'	2°37·3'W	T	183
Babcombe	Devon	SX8676	50°34·6'	3°36·2'W	X	191
Babdown Fm	Glos	ST8494	51°38·9'	2°13·5'W	FM	162,173
Babe Hill	Somer	SS8543	51°10·7'	3°38·3'W	X	181
Babel	Carm	SN8335	52°0·3'	3°41·9'W	T	160
Babeleigh Barton	Devon	SS3920	50°57·7'	4°17·2'W	X	190
Babel Green	Suff	TL7348	52°6·4'	0°32·0'E	T	155
Babell	Flint	SJ1573	53°15·1'	3°16·0'W	T	116
Babeny	Devon	SX6775	50°33·8'	3°52·3'W	T	191
Babergh Hall	Suff	TL9044	52°3·9'	0°46·7'E	X	155
Baber's Fm	Dorset	SY3898	50°46·9'	2°52·4'W	FM	193
Baberton Mains	C of Edin	NT1969	55°54·7'	3°17·3'W	X	65,66
Babingley	Norf	TF6726	52°48·6'	0°29·1'E	T	132
Babingley River	Norf	TF6825	52°48·0'	0°29·9'E	W	132
Babington Ho	Somer	ST7051	51°15·7'	2°25·4'W	X	183
Babland Fm	Devon	SX6751	50°20·9'	3°51·8'W	FM	202
Bableigh	Devon	SS5929	51°2·8'	4°0·3'W	X	180
Bablock Hythe	Oxon	SP4304	51°44·2'	1°22·2'W	X	164
Babraham	Cambs	TL5150	52°7·9'	0°12·8'E	T	154
Bà Bridge	Highld	NN2748	56°35·8'	4°48·6'W	X	50
Babshole Fm	Essex	TQ6592	51°36·4'	0°23·4'E	FM	177,178
Babthorpe	N Yks	SE6930	53°45·9'	0°56·8'W	X	105,106
Babworth	Notts	SK6880	53°19·0'	0°58·3'W	T	111,120
Babworth Home Fm	Notts	SK6881	53°19·5'	0°58·3'W	FM	111,120
Babylon	Flint	SJ3260	53°8·2'	3°0·6'W	X	117
Babylon Fm	Kent	TQ8046	51°11·3'	0°34·9'E	FM	188
Babylon Hill	Dorset	ST5816	50°56·7'	2°35·5'W	H	183
Baby's Hill	Moray	NJ2437	57°25·3'	3°15·5'W	X	28
Bac	N Eil	NB4840	58°16·9'	6°17·4'W	T	8
Bac a' Ghaill	N Eil	NB1604	57°56·4'	6°47·5'W	X	13,14
Bac a Mhathachaidh	Highld	NM6259	56°40·0'	5°52·6'W	X	49
Bacan Daraich	Highld	NM7662	56°42·0'	5°39·1'W	X	40
Bac an Eich	Highld	NH2248	57°29·5'	4°57·7'W	H	25
Bac an Leth-choin	Highld	NG7788	57°49·8'	5°44·9'W	H	19
Bac an Lochain	Highld	NM7158	56°39·7'	5°43·8'W	W	49
Bac an Lochain	Highld	NM8255	56°38·4'	5°32·9'W	X	49
Bac an Tailleir-chrubaich	Highld	NH7281	57°48·3'	4°8·8'W	X	21
Baca Ruadh	Highld	NG4757	57°32·2'	6°13·2'W	X	23
Bacastair	Arg & Bt	NR3388	56°0·9'	6°16·6'W	X	61
Bac-a-stoc	N Eil	NF9072	57°38·1'	7°11·2'W	X	18
Bàc Beag	Arg & Bt	NM2337	56°26·9'	6°29·3'W	X	46,47,48
Bàc Chrom	Arg & Bt	NR8098	56°7·7'	5°32·0'W	X	55
Bacchus	Glos	SO8411	51°48·1'	2°13·5'W	X	162
Bac Gobhar	Highld	NM8694	56°59·5'	5°30·9'W	X	33,40
Bach	Heref	SO5460	52°14·4'	2°40·0'W	A	138,149
Bachaethlon	Powys	SO2190	52°30·4'	3°9·4'W	X	137
Bachau	I of Angl	SH4383	53°19·5'	4°21·0'W	T	114,115
Bachawy	Powys	SO1545	52°6·0'	3°14·1'W	W	148
Bachawy	Powys	SO1748	52°7·7'	3°12·4'W	W	148
Bachd Bàn	Pth & Kin	NN7576	56°51·8'	4°2·6'W	X	42
Bachd Buidhe	Moray	NJ2823	57°17·8'	3°11·2'W	X	37
Bachd Mhic an Tosaich	Highld	NG8601	57°3·3'	5°31·3'W	H	33
Bachd na Fribheach	Highld	NH1613	57°10·5'	5°2·2'W	X	34
Bache	Heref	SO5360	52°14·4'	2°40·9'W	X	137,138,149
Bache	Shrops	SO4681	52°25·7'	2°47·3'W	T	137,138
Bache Canol	Denb	SJ2041	52°57·9'	3°11·1'W	X	117
Bache Fm	Powys	SO2262	52°15·3'	3°8·2'W	FM	137,148
Bache Hill	Powys	SO2163	52°15·8'	3°9·1'W	H	137,148
Bache Ho	Ches	SJ6154	53°5·1'	2°34·5'W	X	118
Bacheiddon	Powys	SN8297	52°33·7'	3°44·0'W	X	135,136
Bacheirig	Denb	SJ1557	53°6·4'	3°15·8'W	X	116
Bacheldre	Powys	SO2492	52°31·5'	3°6·8'W	T	137
Bachell Brook	Powys	SO0872	52°20·5'	3°20·6'W	W	136,147
Bachellyn	Gwyn	SH3332	52°51·8'	4°28·4'W	X	123
Bachelors	Kent	TQ9036	51°5·7'	0°43·2'E	X	189
Bachelors	Surrey	TQ0755	51°17·3'	0°27·5'W	X	187
Bachelor's Bump	E Susx	TQ8412	50°52·9'	0°37·3'E	T	199
Bachelors Fm	I of W	SZ5582	50°38·3'	1°12·9'W	FM	196
Bachelor's Hill	Oxon	SU6487	51°34·9'	1°4·2'W	X	175
Bache Mill	Shrops	SO5086	52°28·4'	2°43·8'W	T	137,138
Bache Wood	Heref	SO4147	52°7·3'	2°51·3'W	F	148,149
Bachgen Careg	Nth Pt Talb	SS9098	51°40·4'	3°35·1'W	X	170
Bachie Ganol	Powys	SJ1418	52°45·4'	3°16·1'W	X	125
Bachilton	Pth & Kin	NO0023	56°23·6'	3°36·8'W	X	52,53,58
Bach Island	Arg & Bt	NM7726	56°22·7'	5°36·3'W	X	49
Bachlaig	Arg & Bt	NR4175	55°54·2'	6°8·2'W	X	60,61
Bachnagairn	Angus	NO2579	56°54·0'	3°13·4'W	X	44
Bachsylw	Carm	SN1625	51°53·8'	4°40·1'W	X	145,158
Bachuil	Arg & Bt	NM8643	56°32·1'	5°28·4'W	X	49
Bachwared	Gwyn	SH2925	52°48·0'	4°31·8'W	X	123
Bach Wen	Gwyn	SH4149	53°1·1'	4°21·8'W	X	115,123
Bâch-y-graig	Denb	SJ0771	53°13·9'	3°23·2'W	A	116
Bach-y-gwreiddyn	Swan	SN6000	51°41·1'	4°1·1'W	T	159
Bachymbyd Fawr	Denb	SJ0960	53°8·0'	3°21·2'W	X	116
Bâch-y-rhew	Cered	SN5978	52°23·2'	4°3·9'W	X	135
Bach yr Hilfry	Gwyn	SH5565	53°10·0'	4°9·7'W	X	114,115
Backa	Shetld	HU4587	60°34·1'	1°10·2'W	X	1,2
Backakelday	Orkney	HY4503	58°54·9'	2°56·8'W	X	6,7

Backaland	Orkney	HY5630	59°9·5'	2°45·7'W	T	5,6
Back Allotment	N Yks	SE1553	53°58·6'	1°45·9'W	F	104
Backandsides Fm	Durham	NZ1925	54°37·4'	1°41·9'W	FM	92
Backaquoy	Orkney	ND4384	58°44·7'	2°58·6'W	X	7
Backarass	Orkney	HY4148	59°19·1'	3°1·7'W	X	5
Backaskail Bay	Orkney	HY6438	59°13·9'	2°37·4'W	W	5
Backaskaill	Orkney	HY4850	59°20·3'	2°54·4'W	X	5
Backaskaill	Orkney	HY6439	59°14·4'	2°37·4'W	X	5
Backatown	Orkney	HY3717	59°2·4'	3°5·4'W	X	6
Back Balk	Cumbr	SD6399	54°23·4'	2°33·8'W	X	97
Back Bar	Aberd	NK0759	57°37·5'	1°52·5'W	X	30
Backbarrow	Cumbr	SD3584	54°15·1'	2°59·4'W	T	96,97
Back Bay	D & G	NX3639	54°43·4'	4°32·4'W	W	83
Back Borland	Stir	NS5096	56°8·2'	4°24·4'W	X	57
Backbower	Tames	SJ9593	53°26·3'	2°4·1'W	T	109
Back Br	Wilts	ST9288	51°35·7'	2°6·5'W	X	173
Backbrae	Aberd	NJ6223	57°18·0'	2°37·4'W	X	37
Back Brae	S Lanak	NS9551	55°44·7'	3°39·9'W	X	65,72
Backbraes	D & G	NX4240	54°44·1'	4°26·8'W	X	83
Backbridge Fm	Wilts	ST9288	51°35·7'	2°6·5'W	FM	173
Backburn	Aberd	NJ5334	57°23·9'	2°46·5'W	T	29
Backburn	Aberd	NJ8556	57°35·9'	2°14·6'W	X	30
Backburn	Aberd	NO8591	57°0·8'	2°14·4'W	X	38,45
Backburn	Aberd	NO9194	57°2·5'	2°8·4'W	X	38,45
Back Burn	Cumbr	NY4474	55°3·7'	2°52·2'W	W	85
Back Burn	D & G	NS7807	55°20·8'	3°55·0'W	W	71,78
Back Burn	D & G	NX9056	54°53·5'	3°42·5'W	W	84
Back Burn	D & G	NY1393	55°13·7'	3°21·6'W	W	78
Backburn	D & G	NY1567	54°59·7'	3°19·3'W	X	85
Back Burn	D & G	NY2090	55°12·1'	3°15·0'W	W	79
Back Burn	D & G	NY2282	55°7·8'	3°13·0'W	W	79
Back Burn	D & G	NY3180	55°6·8'	3°4·5'W	W	79
Back Burn	D & G	NY3390	55°12·2'	3°2·7'W	W	79
Back Burn	D & G	NY3485	55°9·5'	3°1·7'W	W	79
Back Burn	E Ayr	NS6629	55°32·4'	4°7·0'W	W	71
Back Burn	E Loth	NT4873	55°57·1'	2°49·5'W	W	66
Back Burn	E Loth	NT7067	55°54·0'	2°28·3'W	W	67
Back Burn	Fife	NO3503	56°13·2'	3°2·4'W	W	59
Back Burn	Moray	NJ2649	57°31·8'	3°13·7'W	W	28
Back Burn	Moray	NJ2726	57°19·4'	3°12·3'W	W	37
Backburn	Moray	NJ4661	57°38·4'	2°53·8'W	X	28,29
Back Burn	Northum	NU0204	55°20·1'	1°57·7'W	W	81
Back Burn	Pth & Kin	NO0208	56°15·5'	3°34·5'W	W	58
Back Burn	Scot Bord	NT1719	55°27·7'	3°18·3'W	W	79
Back Burn	Scot Bord	NT2213	55°24·5'	3°13·5'W	W	79
Back Burn	Scot Bord	NT3515	55°25·7'	3°1·2'W	W	79
Back Burn	Scot Bord	NT4108	55°22·0'	2°55·4'W	W	79
Back Burn	Scot Bord	NT4243	55°40·9'	2°54·9'W	W	73
Back Burn	Scot Bord	NT8417	55°27·0'	2°14·7'W	W	80
Back Burn	S Lanak	NS7136	55°36·3'	4°2·4'W	W	71
Back Burn	S Lanak	NT0215	55°25·4'	3°32·5'W	W	78
Back Burn	S Lanak	NT0426	55°31·4'	3°30·8'W	W	72
Back Burn	S Lanak	NT0944	55°41·1'	3°26·4'W	W	72
Back Burn of Arnbarrow	Aberd	NO6478	56°53·8'	2°35·0'W	W	45
Back Burn of Slickly	Highld	ND3166	58°34·9'	3°10·7'W	W	11,12
Back Burn, The	Pth & Kin	NO0359	56°43·0'	3°34·6'W	W	52,53
Backbury Hill	Heref	SO5838	52°2·6'	2°36·3'W	H	149
Back Dale	Derby	SK0970	53°13·9'	1°51·5'W	X	119
Back Dane	Staffs	SJ9766	53°11·7'	2°2·3'W	X	118
Back Dike	Cumbr	NY6261	54°56·8'	2°35·2'W	W	86
Back Dike	Peterb	TL1396	52°33·2'	0°19·6'W	W	142
Back Dyke	Notts	SK7644	52°59·5'	0°51·7'W	W	129
Backe	Carm	SN2615	51°48·6'	4°31·1'W	T	158
Back Fell	D & G	NX6860	54°55·3'	4°3·2'W	H	83,84
Backfell	D & G	NX6860	54°55·3'	4°3·2'W	X	83,84
Backfield Fm	Aberd	NO7582	56°56·0'	2°24·2'W	FM	45
Backfield of Ladeddie	Fife	NO4313	56°18·6'	2°54·8'W	X	59
Backfields	Fife	NO5705	56°14·4'	2°41·2'W	X	59
Back Fm	Lancs	SD6065	54°5·0'	2°36·3'W	FM	97
Backfolds	Aberd	NK0252	57°33·7'	1°57·5'W	X	30
Backford	Ches	SJ3971	53°14·2'	2°54·4'W	T	117
Backford Cross	Ches	SJ3873	53°15·3'	2°55·4'W	T	117
Back Forest	Staffs	SJ9865	53°11·2'	2°1·4'W	X	118
Back Forest Fm	Staffs	SJ9766	53°11·7'	2°2·3'W	FM	118
Back Gill	N Yks	SD7180	54°13·1'	2°26·3'W	W	98
Back Gill	N Yks	SD9482	54°14·3'	2°5·1'W	W	98
Backgill Burn	Durham	NZ1148	54°49·8'	1°49·3'W	W	88
Back Gill Head	Cumbr	SD7181	54°13·7'	2°26·3'W	X	98
Backglen Burn	S Ayr	NS3809	55°21·2'	4°32·9'W	W	70,77
Back Green	Shetld	HU3516	59°55·9'	1°21·9'W	X	4
Backgreens	Aberd	NJ8229	57°21·3'	2°17·5'W	X	38
Back Gutter	Cumbr	NY8607	54°27·7'	2°12·5'W	W	91,92
Backharn	Highld	NJ0222	57°16·9'	3°37·1'W	X	36
Backhill	Aberd	NJ6205	57°8·3'	2°37·2'W	X	37
Backhill	Aberd	NJ6360	57°38·0'	2°36·7'W	X	29
Backhill	Aberd	NJ7112	57°12·1'	2°28·3'W	X	38
Backhill	Aberd	NJ7319	57°15·9'	2°26·4'W	X	38
Backhill	Aberd	NJ7839	57°26·7'	2°21·5'W	T	29,30
Backhill	Aberd	NJ7947	57°31·0'	2°20·6'W	X	29,30
Backhill	Aberd	NJ8041	57°27·8'	2°19·5'W	X	29,30
Backhill	Aberd	NJ8111	57°11·6'	2°18·4'W	X	38
Backhill	Aberd	NJ8130	57°21·9'	2°18·5'W	X	29,30
Backhill	Aberd	NJ8217	57°14·9'	2°17·4'W	X	38
Backhill	Aberd	NJ8240	57°27·3'	2°17·5'W	X	29,30
Backhill	Aberd	NJ8453	57°34·3'	2°15·6'W	X	29,30
Backhill	Aberd	NJ9116	57°14·3'	2°8·5'W	X	38
Backhill	Aberd	NJ9332	57°23·0'	2°6·5'W	X	30
Backhill	Aberd	NJ9452	57°33·7'	2°5·6'W	X	30
Backhill	Aberd	NJ9828	57°20·8'	2°1·5'W	X	38
Backhill	Aberd	NK0039	57°26·7'	1°59·5'W	X	30
Backhill	Aberd	NO8693	57°1·9'	2°13·4'W	X	38,45
Backhill	C of Aber	NJ8406	57°8·9'	2°15·4'W	X	38
Back Hill	D & G	NY0182	55°7·6'	3°32·7'W	H	78
Backhill	E Loth	NT3769	55°54·9'	3°0·0'W	X	66
Backhill Lenabo	Aberd	NK0241	57°27·8'	1°57·5'W	X	30
Backhill of Barrack	Aberd	NJ8841	57°27·8'	2°11·5'W	X	30
Backhill of Bruntyards	Aberd	NJ7360	57°38·0'	2°26·7'W	X	29
Backhill of Bush (Bothy)	D & G	NX4884	55°7·9'	4°22·6'W	X	77
Backhill of Clackriach	Aberd	NJ9246	57°30·5'	2°7·6'W	T	30
Backhill of Clunie	Aberd	NJ6350	57°32·6'	2°36·6'W	X	29
Backhill of Coldwells	Aberd	NJ9538	57°26·2'	2°4·5'W	X	30
Backhill of Cranbog	C of Aber	NJ9314	57°13·3'	2°6·5'W	X	38
Backhill of Crimond	Aberd	NJ8123	57°18·1'	2°18·5'W	X	38
Backhill of Davah	Aberd	NJ7520	57°16·5'	2°24·4'W	X	38
Backhill of Drachlaw	Aberd	NJ6746	57°30·4'	2°32·6'W	X	29
Backhill of Dudwick	Aberd	NJ9838	57°26·2'	2°1·5'W	X	30
Backhill of Fortrie	Aberd	NJ9640	57°27·3'	2°3·5'W	T	30
Backhill of Garrary	D & G	NX4980	55°5·7'	4°21·6'W	X	77
Backhill of Glack	Aberd	NJ7410	57°11·1'	2°25·4'W	X	38
Back Hill of Glenlee	D & G	NX5779	55°5·3'	4°14·0'W	X	77
Backhill of Gourdas	Aberd	NJ7644	57°29·4'	2°23·6'W	X	29
Backhill of Goval	Aberd	NJ8816	57°14·3'	2°11·5'W	X	38
Backhill of Hatton	Aberd	NJ6842	57°28·3'	2°31·6'W	X	29
Backhill of Ironside	Aberd	NJ8751	57°33·2'	2°12·6'W	X	30
Backhill of Kingoodie	Aberd	NJ8226	57°19·7'	2°17·5'W	X	38
Backhill of Knaven	Aberd	NJ8842	57°28·3'	2°11·5'W	X	30
Backhill of Knockhall	Aberd	NJ9826	57°19·7'	2°1·5'W	X	38
Backhill of Overhill	Aberd	NJ9318	57°15·4'	2°6·5'W	X	38
Backhill of Pitgair	Aberd	NJ7661	57°38·6'	2°23·7'W	X	29
Back Hill of Plaidy	Aberd	NJ7353	57°34·2'	2°26·6'W	X	29
Backhill of Seggat	Aberd	NJ7442	57°28·3'	2°25·6'W	X	29
Backhill of Smiddyburn	Aberd	NJ7333	57°23·5'	2°26·5'W	X	29
Backhill of Thomastown	Aberd	NJ7043	57°28·8'	2°29·6'W	X	29
Backhill of Trustach	Aberd	NO6397	57°4·0'	2°36·2'W	X	37,45
Backhills	Aberd	NJ6139	57°26·6'	2°38·5'W	X	29
Backhills	Pth & Kin	NN9103	56°12·7'	3°45·0'W	X	58
Backieley Croft	Aberd	NJ6154	57°34·7'	2°38·7'W	X	29
Backies	Highld	NC8302	57°59·8'	3°58·3'W	T	17
Backies	Moray	NJ4958	57°36·8'	2°50·8'W	X	28,29
Backies Croft	Aberd	NJ3318	57°15·1'	3°6·2'W	X	37
Backlands	Moray	NJ1469	57°42·4'	3°26·1'W	T	28
Back Lane Fm	Ches	SJ7884	53°21·4'	2°19·4'W	FM	109
Backlane Fm	Derby	SK1078	53°18·2'	1°50·6'W	FM	119
Backlane House Fm	Ches	SJ9470	53°13·9'	2°5·0'W	FM	118
Backlass	Highld	ND0842	58°21·7'	3°33·9'W	X	11,12
Backlass	Highld	ND2054	58°28·3'	3°21·8'W	H	11,12
Backlass Moss	Highld	ND1952	58°27·2'	3°22·8'W	X	11,12
Backlea Plantn	Scot Bord	NT7250	55°44·8'	2°26·3'W	F	67,74
Backley	Aberd	NJ7128	57°20·8'	2°28·5'W	X	38
Backley Bottom	Hants	SU2208	50°52·5'	1°40·9'W	X	195
Backley Inclosure	Hants	SU2207	50°52·0'	1°40·9'W	F	195
Backley Plain	Hants	SU2106	50°51·4'	1°41·7'W	X	195
Backleys	N Yks	SE9290	54°18·1'	0°34·8'W	X	94,101
Backleys Fm	N Yks	SE9290	54°18·1'	0°34·8'W	FM	94,101
Backlink	Highld	ND0866	58°34·6'	3°34·4'W	X	11,12
Back Loch	Scot Bord	NT3515	55°25·7'	3°1·2'W	W	79
Back Mains	Aberd	NJ7610	57°11·1'	2°23·4'W	X	38
Backmill	Aberd	NJ7746	57°30·5'	2°22·6'W	X	29,30
Back Mill	Pth & Kin	NO0535	56°30·1'	3°32·2'W	X	52,53
Backmoor	D & G	NX3550	54°49·3'	4°33·7'W	X	83
Backmoss	Aberd	NJ9142	57°28·3'	2°8·5'W	X	30
Backmuir	Moray	NJ4447	57°30·8'	2°55·6'W	X	28
Backmuir of New Gilston	Fife	NO4308	56°15·9'	2°54·8'W	T	59
Backmuir Wood	Angus	NO3434	56°29·9'	3°3·9'W	F	54
Backney	Heref	SO5827	51°56·6'	2°36·3'W	X	162
Back of Ecton	Staffs	SK1057	53°6·8'	1°50·6'W	X	119
Back of Hill Barn	Lancs	SD6651	53°57·5'	2°30·7'W	X	103
Back of Keppoch	Highld	NM6588	56°55·7'	5°51·3'W	X	40
Back of Moss	W Loth	NS9562	55°50·6'	3°40·2'W	X	65
Back of Ollaberry	Shetld	HU3680	60°30·4'	1°20·2'W	H	1,2,3
Back o' Frank's Hill	Lincs	TF1780	53°18·5'	0°14·2'W	X	121
Back of the Breck	Orkney	HY5904	58°55·5'	2°42·2'W	X	6
Back of the Ness	Orkney	HY4616	59°1·9'	2°56·0'W	X	6
Back o' Hill	E Ayr	NS5019	55°26·8'	4°21·9'W	X	70
Back o' Hill	E Dunb	NS6074	55°56·6'	4°14·1'W	X	64
Back o'th' Brook	Staffs	SK0851	53°3·6'	1°52·4'W	T	119
Back o' th' Edge	Lancs	SD8841	53°52·1'	2°10·5'W	X	103
Back o'th' Hill Fm	Derby	SK1268	53°12·8'	1°48·8'W	FM	119
Back o' th' Hill Fm	N Yks	SE0854	53°59·2'	1°52·3'W	FM	104
Back o' th' Moss Fm	Bury	SD8206	53°33·3'	2°15·9'W	FM	109
Back o' Wall	D & G	NX1858	54°53·3'	4°49·8'W	X	82
Backpark	Aberd	NJ6125	57°19·1'	2°38·4'W	X	37
Back Pasture	N Yks	SD9068	54°6·7'	2°8·8'W	X	98
Back Reach Fm	Cambs	TL3293	52°31·4'	0°2·9'W	FM	142
Backridge	Lancs	SD7142	53°52·6'	2°26·1'W	X	103
Back Rogerton	E Ayr	NS5522	55°28·5'	4°17·2'W	T	71
Back Saddles	Orkney	HY2003	58°54·7'	3°22·9'W	X	7
Back Sand Point	Kent	TR3460	51°17·7'	1°21·8'E	X	179
Back Scar	N Yks	SD8564	54°4·5'	2°13·3'W	X	98
Backshalloch	Moray	NJ3552	57°33·5'	3°4·7'W	X	28
Back Shaw	Brad	SE0639	53°51·1'	1°54·1'W	X	104
Backshiels	S Lanak	NT0640	55°38·9'	3°29·2'W	X	72
Backside	Aberd	NJ4136	57°24·9'	2°58·5'W	X	28
Backside	Aberd	NJ4544	57°29·2'	2°54·6'W	X	28,29
Backside Beck	Cumbr	SD6998	54°22·8'	2°28·2'W	W	98
Backside Burn	Stir	NS6688	56°4·2'	4°8·7'W	W	57
Backside Fell	Durham	NY7931	54°40·7'	2°19·1'W	X	91
Backside of Garden	Stir	NS5995	56°7·9'	4°15·7'W	X	57
Backsides	N Yks	SD8588	54°17·5'	2°13·4'W	X	98
Back Sike	D & G	NT2504	55°19·7'	3°10·5'W	W	79
Back Skerrs	Northum	NU1244	55°41·6'	1°48·1'W	X	75
Back Slack Burn	Highld	NC6743	58°21·6'	4°15·9'W	W	10
Backstane Hill	S Lanak	NS9027	55°31·7'	3°44·1'W	H	71,72
Backstean Gill	N Yks	SE0572	54°8·9'	1°55·0'W	W	98
Backstone Beck	N Yks	SE4804	54°27·2'	2°14·4'W	W	91,92
Backstone Edge	Cumbr	NY7226	54°37·9'	2°25·6'W	X	91
Backstone Edge	N Yks	SE0464	54°4·6'	1°55·9'W	X	98
Backstonegill	Cumbr	SD7187	54°16·9'	2°26·3'W	X	98
Backstone Gill	N Yks	SE0880	54°13·2'	1°52·2'W	W	99
Backstone Gill	N Yks	SE1174	54°9·9'	1°49·5'W	W	99
Backstrath	Aberd	NJ8354	57°34·8'	2°16·6'W	X	29,30
Back Stream	Somer	ST1927	51°2·4'	3°8·9'W	W	181,193
Back Street	Suff	TL7458	52°11·8'	0°33·2'E	T	155
Backstripes	Aberd	NJ4328	57°20·6'	2°56·4'W	X	37
Backs Water	Arg & Bt	NR6922	55°26·5'	5°38·7'W	W	68
Backs Wood	Devon	SS9509	50°52·5'	3°29·2'W	F	192
Backswood Fm	Devon	SS9509	50°52·5'	3°29·2'W	FM	192
Backtack	Aberd	NJ4641	57°27·6'	2°53·5'W	X	28,29
Back Tor	Derby	SK1485	53°21·9'	1°47·0'W	X	110
Back Tor	Derby	SK1990	53°24·6'	1°42·4'W	H	110
Backwaird	Aberd	NJ8321	57°17·0'	2°16·5'W	X	38
Back Warren Plantn	N Yks	SE7960	54°2·0'	0°47·2'W	F	100
Back Water	Angus	NO2558	56°42·7'	3°13·1'W	W	53
Back Water	Oxon	SU5096	51°39·9'	1°16·2'W	W	164
Backwater Reservoir	Angus	NO2559	56°43·3'	3°13·1'W	W	53
Backwater Reservoir	Angus	NO2560	56°43·8'	3°13·1'W	W	44
Backwater Rig	S Lanak	NT0224	55°30·3'	3°32·7'W	H	72
Backway	Devon	SS4507	50°50·7'	4°11·7'W	X	190
Backways Cove	Corn	SX0485	50°38·1'	4°45·9'W	W	200
Backwell	N Som	ST4868	51°24·8'	2°44·5'W	T	172,182
Backwell Common	N Som	ST4869	51°25·3'	2°44·5'W	T	171,172,182
Backwell Green	N Som	ST4969	51°25·3'	2°43·6'W	T	172,182
Backwell Hill	N Som	ST4967	51°24·2'	2°43·6'W	X	172,182
Backwell Hill Ho	N Som	ST4867	51°24·2'	2°44·5'W	X	171,172,182
Backwell Ho	N Som	ST5069	51°25·3'	2°42·8'W	X	172,182
Back Wood	D & G	NS7811	55°22·9'	3°55·1'W	F	71,78
Back Wood	Lincs	TA0901	53°29·9'	0°21·0'W	F	112
Back Wood	Mil Key	SP9133	51°59·5'	0°40·1'W	F	152,165
Backwood Hall	Ches	SJ2779	53°18·4'	3°5·3'W	X	117
Backwood Hill	Aberd	NJ5343	57°28·7'	2°46·6'W	X	29
Backwoodlands Cottage	Pth & Kin	NO0426	56°25·2'	3°32·9'W	X	52,53,58
Back Wood of Rannoch	Pth & Kin	NN5755	56°40·2'	4°19·6'W	F	42,51
Backworth	N Tyne	NZ3072	55°2·7'	1°31·4'W	T	88
Backworth Letch	Northum	NZ0355	54°53·6'	1°56·8'W	X	87
Baclaw	Conwy	SH7774	53°15·2'	3°50·2'W	X	115
Bac Mór or Dutchman's Cap	Arg & Bt	NM2438	56°27·5'	6°28·4'W	X	46,47,48
Bac-nac Laogh	Highld	NN2398	57°2·6'	4°54·6'W	X	34
Bac na Cloiche	Highld	NM8999	57°2·3'	5°28·2'W	X	33,40
Bac na Craoibhe	Pth & Kin	NN4768	56°47·0'	4°29·8'W	H	42
Bac na Creige	Pth & Kin	NN7779	56°53·4'	4°0·7'W	X	42
Bac na Lice	Highld	NC7212	58°5·0'	4°9·8'W	X	16
Bac nam Fòid	Highld	NN0399	57°2·7'	5°14·4'W	X	33
Bac nam Fuaran	Highld	NH4300	57°4·1'	4°34·9'W	H	34
Bac nan Canaichean	Highld	NH0005	57°5·8'	5°17·6'W	X	33
Bacoch's Seat	Arg & Bt	NR7884	56°0·1'	5°33·2'W	X	55
Bacombe Hill	Bucks	SP8507	51°45·5'	0°45·7'W	X	165
Bacombe Warren	Bucks	SP8606	51°45·0'	0°44·9'W	X	165
Bacon End	Essex	TL6018	51°50·5'	0°19·8'E	T	167
Baconend Green	Essex	TL6019	51°51·0'	0°19·8'E	T	167
Bacon Fm	N Yks	SE8378	54°11·7'	0°43·2'W	FM	100
Bacon Fm	Oxon	SP3635	52°1·0'	1°28·1'W	FM	151
Bacon Hall	Shrops	SJ6523	52°48·4'	2°30·8'W	X	127
Bacon Hole	Swan	SS5686	51°33·5'	4°4·3'W	A	159
Bacons	Essex	TL9802	51°41·1'	0°52·3'E	X	168
Bacons	Essex	TM0006	51°43·2'	0°54·1'E	X	168
Bacon Seilich	Arg & Bt	NM6525	56°21·8'	5°47·8'W	X	49
Bacon's End	Sol	SP1787	52°29·1'	1°44·6'W	T	139
Bacons Fm	Essex	TL6824	51°53·6'	0°26·9'E	FM	167
Bacon's Fm	Essex	TL8927	51°54·8'	0°45·3'E	FM	168
Bacons Fm	Essex	TQ6498	51°39·6'	0°22·7'E	FM	167,177
Bacon's Fm	Herts	TL2814	51°48·8'	0°8·2'W	FM	166
Bacon's Ho	Oxon	SP6434	52°0·3'	1°3·7'W	X	152,165
Baconsthorpe	Norf	TG1237	52°53·5'	1°9·5'E	T	133
Bà Cottage	Highld	NN2749	56°36·3'	4°48·7'W	X	50
Bacres	Bucks	SU7787	51°34·8'	0°52·9'W	X	175
Bacton	Heref	SO3632	51°59·2'	2°55·5'W	T	149,161
Bacton	Norf	TG3433	52°50·8'	1°28·9'E	T	133
Bacton	Suff	TM0567	52°16·0'	1°0·7'E	T	155
Bacton Green	Norf	TG3434	52°51·4'	1°29·0'E	T	133
Bacton Green	Suff	TM0365	52°15·0'	0°58·8'E	T	155
Bacton Stud	Heref	SO3732	51°59·2'	2°54·7'W	X	149,161
Bacton Wood	Norf	TG3131	52°49·8'	1°26·2'E	F	133
Bacup	Lancs	SD8622	53°41·9'	2°12·3'W	T	103
Bad a' Bhàcaidh	Highld	NC4535	58°16·8'	4°38·1'W	H	16
Bad a' Bhàthaich	Highld	NH5480	57°47·4'	4°26·9'W	H	21
Bad a' Cheò	Highld	ND1550	58°26·1'	3°26·9'W	X	11,12
Bad a' Chlamhain	Highld	NH4441	57°26·2'	4°35·5'W	H	26
Badachonacher	Highld	NH6973	57°43·9'	4°11·5'W	T	21
Badachonacher Moss	Highld	NH7074	57°44·5'	4°10·6'W	F	21
Bad a' Chreamha	Highld	NG8536	57°22·1'	5°34·1'W	H	24
Badachro	Highld	NG7873	57°41·8'	5°43·1'W	X	19
Badachro Fm	Highld	NG7873	57°41·8'	5°43·1'W	FM	19
Badachro River	Highld	NG7871	57°40·7'	5°42·9'W	W	19
Badachuil	Highld	NH6493	57°54·6'	4°17·3'W	X	21
Bad a' Chuithe	Highld	NC4405	58°0·7'	4°38·0'W	X	16
Badacrain	Highld	NH0396	57°54·9'	5°19·1'W	X	19
Bada Crionard	Angus	NO2266	56°47·0'	3°16·1'W	H	44
Badadarrach	Angus	NO4482	56°55·8'	2°54·8'W	X	44
Badaguish (Outdoor Centre)	Highld	NH9511	57°10·9'	3°43·8'W	X	36
Badahad	Highld	NJ0437	57°25·1'	3°35·4'W	X	27
Badalair	Angus	NO4582	56°55·8'	2°53·8'W	X	44
Badams Court	Glos	ST5493	51°38·3'	2°39·5'W	X	162,172
Bada na Bresoch	Angus	NO2171	56°49·7'	3°17·2'W	X	44
Bad an Achaidh	Highld	ND0823	58°11·4'	3°33·4'W	X	17
Badan Bheag	Highld	NG8749	57°29·1'	5°32·8'W	X	24
Bad an Dobhrain	Highld	NM6575	56°48·7'	5°50·6'W	X	40
Badan Dubh	Highld	NH8200	57°4·8'	3°56·4'W	X	35
Badandun Hill	Angus	NO2067	56°47·5'	3°18·1'W	H	44
Bad an Fhéidh	Highld	NC7001	57°59·0'	4°11·4'W	X	16
Bad an Fheòir	Highld	NC8721	58°10·1'	3°54·8'W	X	17
Bad an Fhithich	N Eil	NB5064	58°29·8'	6°17·0'W	X	8
Bad an Fhithich Mhóir	Highld	NG8815	57°10·9'	5°30·0'W	H	33
Badanloch Forest	Highld	NC7935	58°17·5'	4°3·4'W	X	17
Badanloch Hill	Highld	NC8034	58°17·0'	4°2·3'W	H	17
Badanloch Lodge	Highld	NC7933	58°16·4'	4°3·3'W	X	17
Bad an Lòin	Pth & Kin	NO1270	56°49·0'	3°26·0'W	H	43
Badan Mhugaidh	Highld	NG8554	57°31·8'	5°35·0'W	X	24
Badan Mosach	Highld	NN8696	57°2·7'	3°52·3'W	X	35,36,43
Badantionail	Highld	NG7674	57°42·3'	5°45·1'W	X	19
Bad an t-Seabhaig	Highld	NC4936	58°17·5'	4°34·1'W	X	16
Bad an Tuirc	Pth & Kin	NO0167	56°47·3'	3°36·8'W	H	43
Badarach	Highld	NH5298	57°57·1'	4°29·6'W	X	20
Badavanich	Highld	NH1058	57°34·6'	5°10·2'W	X	25
Badbea	Highld	ND0819	58°9·3'	3°33·3'W	X	17
Badbea	Highld	NH0290	57°51·6'	5°19·8'W	X	19
Bad Beithe	Arg & Bt	NN1018	56°19·2'	5°3·9'W	X	50,56
Badbeithe	Highld	NH6391	57°53·5'	4°18·2'W	X	21

Bad Bheith	Arg & Bt	NR7862	55°48·3'	5°32·1'W	H	62
Bad Bog	Highld	NG9281	57°46·5'	5°29·4'W	X	19
Badbog	Highld	NH6396	57°56·2'	4°18·4'W	X	21
Bad Buidhe	Angus	NO2566	56°47·0'	3°13·2'W	X	44
Badbury	Oxon	SU2694	51°38·9'	1°37·1'W	A	174
Badbury	Somer	ST3520	50°58·8'	2°55·2'W	X	193
Badbury	Swin	SU1980	51°31·3'	1°43·2'W	T	173
Badbury Hill	Oxon	SU2694	51°38·9'	1°37·1'W	H	163,174
Badbury Hill	Warw	SP1163	52°16·1'	1°49·9'W	X	150
Badbury Lane	Northnts	SP5848	52°7·9'	1°8·8'W	X	152
Badbury Rings	Dorset	ST9602	50°49·3'	2°3·0'W	A	195
Badbury Wick	Swin	SU1881	51°31·9'	1°44·0'W	T	173
Badby	Northnts	SP5658	52°13·3'	1°10·4'W	T	152
Badby Down	Northnts	SP5557	52°12·7'	1°11·3'W	X	152
Badby Fields	Northnts	SP5560	52°14·4'	1°11·3'W	X	152
Badby Wood	Northnts	SP5658	52°13·3'	1°10·4'W	F	152
Badcall	Highld	NC2455	58°27·1'	5°0·5'W	T	9
Badcall Bay	Highld	NC1541	58°19·4'	5°9·1'W	W	9
Bad-callda	Highld	NG8155	57°32·2'	5°39·1'W	X	24
Badcaul	Highld	NH0291	57°52·1'	5°19·8'W	T	19
Badcaul	Highld	NH4530	57°20·3'	4°34·1'W	X	26
Badchear	Moray	NJ3532	57°22·7'	3°4·4'W	X	37
Badcocks Fm	Essex	TL6824	51°53·6'	0°26·9'E	FM	167
Badcock's Fm	Essex	TL9021	51°51·5'	0°46·0'E	FM	168
Baddaford	Devon	SX7567	50°29·6'	3°45·4'W	X	202
Baddan	Highld	NH7998	57°57·6'	4°2·2'W	X	21
Baddans	Highld	NH6172	57°43·2'	4°19·6'W	X	21
Bad Dearg	Stir	NN4700	56°10·3'	4°27·4'W	H	57
Baddeley Edge	C of Stoke	SJ9150	53°3·1'	2°7·7'W	T	118
Baddeley Green	C of Stoke	SJ9051	53°3·6'	2°8·5'W	T	118
Badden	Arg & Bt	NR8589	56°3·0'	5°26·7'W	X	55
Badden	Highld	NH5339	57°25·3'	4°26·4'W	X	26
Baddengorm Woods	Highld	NH8923	57°17·3'	3°50·0'W	F	35,36
Baddesley Clinton	Warw	SP2071	52°20·4'	1°42·0'W	A	139
Baddesley Clinton	Warw	SP2072	52°21·0'	1°42·0'W	T	139
Baddesley Common	Hants	SU3920	50°58·9'	1°26·3'W	X	185
Baddesley Common	Warw	SP2797	52°34·4'	1°35·7'W	X	140
Baddesley Ensor	Warw	SP2798	52°35·0'	1°35·7'W	T	140
Baddhu	Highld	NC6007	58°2·1'	4°21·8'W	X	16
Baddidarach	Highld	NC0822	58°9·0'	5°15·3'W	T	15
Baddiley Corner	Ches	SJ6150	53°3·0'	2°34·5'W	X	118
Baddiley Fm	Ches	SJ6151	53°3·5'	2°34·5'W	FM	118
Baddiley Hall	Ches	SJ6050	53°3·0'	2°35·4'W	X	118
Baddiley Hulse	Ches	SJ6049	53°2·4'	2°35·4'W	X	118
Baddiley Mere	Ches	SJ5950	53°3·0'	2°36·3'W	W	117
Baddington Bank Fm	Ches	SJ6349	53°2·5'	2°32·7'W	FM	118
Baddington Fm	Ches	SJ6349	53°2·5'	2°32·7'W	FM	118
Baddinsgill Burn	Scot Bord	NT1156	55°47·6'	3°24·7'W	W	65,72
Baddinsgill Fm	Scot Bord	NT1254	55°46·5'	3°23·7'W	FM	65,72
Baddinsgill Ho	Scot Bord	NT1354	55°46·5'	3°22·8'W	X	65,72
Baddinsgill Resr	Scot Bord	NT1255	55°47·1'	3°23·8'W	W	65,72
Baddoch	Aberd	NO1382	56°55·5'	3°25·3'W	X	43
Baddoch	Highld	NJ0819	57°15·4'	3°31·0'W	H	36
Baddoch Burn	Aberd	NO1179	56°53·9'	3°27·2'W	W	43
Baddock	Highld	NH7956	57°34·9'	4°1·0'W	X	27
Baddow Park	Essex	TL7202	51°41·6'	0°29·7'E	T	167
Badd, The	Arg & Bt	NS1377	55°57·2'	4°59·3'W	X	63
Bad Each	Highld	NH7305	57°7·4'	4°5·4'W	X	35
Bad Each	Highld	NJ0835	57°24·0'	3°31·4'W	X	27
Badeach	Moray	NJ2530	57°21·5'	3°14·3'W	X	37
Baden Burn	Pth & Kin	NO0950	56°38·2'	3°28·6'W	W	52,53
Baden Down Fm	Wilts	SU1652	51°16·2'	1°45·9'W	FM	184
Badenedin	Highld	NJ0421	57°16·4'	3°35·1'W	X	36
Badenerib	Highld	NH5958	57°35·7'	4°21·1'W	X	26
Baden Hall	Staffs	SJ8431	52°52·8'	2°13·9'W	X	127
Badenhall Burn	Aberd	NO5490	57°0·2'	2°45·0'W	W	44
Badenhay Rig	Scot Bord	NT0515	55°25·4'	3°29·6'W	X	78
Badenheath	E Dunb	NS7172	55°55·7'	4°3·4'W	X	64
Baden Hill	S Glos	ST6789	51°36·2'	2°28·2'W	X	162,172
Badenkep	Stir	NS5992	56°6·3'	4°15·6'W	X	57
Badenoch	Highld	NN4985	56°56·2'	4°28·4'W	X	34,42
Badenoch	Highld	NN6291	56°59·6'	4°15·8'W	X	35
Badens	Aberd	NJ5313	57°12·6'	2°46·2'W	X	37
Badenscallie	Highld	NC0306	58°0·2'	5°19·6'W	T	15
Badenscallie Burn	Highld	NC0407	58°0·8'	5°18·6'W	W	15
Baden's Clump	Wilts	SU1853	51°16·8'	1°44·1'W	F	184
Badenscoth	Aberd	NJ6938	57°26·1'	2°30·5'W	T	29
Badenspink	Aberd	NJ5961	57°38·5'	2°40·7'W	X	29
Badentarbat	Highld	NC0110	58°2·3'	5°21·8'W	X	15
Badentarbat Bay	Highld	NC0008	58°1·2'	5°22·7'W	W	15
Badentinan	Moray	NJ2957	57°36·1'	3°10·8'W	X	28
Badentoul	Aberd	NJ5662	57°39·0'	2°43·8'W	X	29
Badentoy Park	Aberd	NO9097	57°4·1'	2°9·4'W	T	38,45
Badentree Hill	Scot Bord	NT0618	55°27·1'	3°28·7'W	H	78
Badenyon	Aberd	NJ3319	57°15·7'	3°6·2'W	X	37
Baderonach Hill	Aberd	NJ4308	57°9·8'	2°56·1'W	H	37
Badfearn	Highld	NG8889	57°50·7'	5°33·9'W	X	19
Bad Féitheanach	Highld	NH7222	57°16·5'	4°6·9'W	X	35
Badgall	Corn	SX2386	50°39·0'	4°29·9'W	T	201
Badgall Downs	Corn	SX2286	50°39·0'	4°30·7'W	X	201
Badge Court	Worcs	SO9069	52°19·4'	2°8·4'W	A	139
Badge Lodge	Northnts	SP7272	52°20·7'	0°56·2'W	X	141
Badgemore Ho	Oxon	SU7483	51°32·7'	0°55·6'W	X	175
Badgeney	Cambs	TL4296	52°32·8'	0°6·1'E	T	142,143
Badger	Shrops	SO7699	52°35·5'	2°20·9'W	T	138
Badgerbank	Ches	SJ8071	53°14·4'	2°17·6'W	X	118
Badgerbank	N Yks	SE3076	54°11·0'	1°32·0'W	X	99
Badger Bank	N Yks	SE7465	54°4·8'	0°51·7'W	X	100
Badger Beck	N Yks	SE1598	54°22·9'	1°45·7'W	W	99
Badgercombe	Devon	SS7830	51°3·6'	3°44·1'W	X	180
Badger Copse	Somer	ST1932	51°5·1'	3°9·0'W	F	181
Badger Dingle	Shrops	SO7699	52°35·5'	2°20·9'W	X	138
Badger Fall	Highld	NH2928	57°18·9'	4°49·9'W	W	25
Badger Farm	Hants	SU4627	51°2·7'	1°20·2'W	FM	185
Badger Fm	Lincs	TF2680	53°18·3'	0°6·1'W	FM	122
Badger Fm	Shrops	SJ7600	52°36·1'	2°20·9'W	FM	127
Badger Gate	Cumbr	SD5680	54°13·1'	2°40·1'W	X	97
Badgergate	Stir	NS7999	56°10·4'	3°56·5'W	X	57
Badger Heath Fm	Shrops	SO7799	52°35·5'	2°20·0'W	FM	138
Badger Hill	Notts	SK5763	53°9·9'	1°8·4'W	X	120
Badger Hills	Lincs	TA1501	53°29·8'	0°15·6'W	X	113
Badger Lane Fm	N Yks	SE2279	54°12·6'	1°39·3'W	FM	99
Badger Lodge	Cered	SN7093	52°31·4'	3°54·6'W	X	135
Badger Moor	Shrops	SO2083	52°26·6'	3°10·2'W	X	137
Badgers Croft	Ches	SJ6683	53°20·8'	2°30·2'W	X	109
Badger's Croft	Staffs	SK0463	53°10·1'	1°56·0'W	X	119
Badger's Cross	Corn	SW4833	50°8·8'	5°31·3'W	X	203
Badger's Cross	Somer	ST4827	51°2·6'	2°44·1'W	X	193
Badger's Cross	Somer	ST6248	51°14·0'	2°32·3'W	X	183
Badger's Hill	Worcs	SP0048	52°8·1'	1°59·6'W	T	150
Badger's Hills	Staffs	SJ9714	52°43·7'	2°2·3'W	H	127
Badger Slade Wood	Staffs	SJ9715	52°44·2'	2°2·3'W	F	127
Badgers Mount	Kent	TQ4962	51°20·5'	0°8·7'E	T	177,188
Badger's Oak	Kent	TQ7533	51°4·4'	0°30·3'E	X	188
Badgers Rake Ho	Ches	SJ3375	53°16·3'	2°59·9'W	X	117
Badger Stone	Brad	SE1146	53°54·8'	1°49·5'W	A	104
Badger Stone	N Yks	NZ6000	54°23·8'	1°4·1'W	X	94
Badger Street	Somer	ST2619	50°58·2'	3°2·9'W	T	193
Badger Way Stoop	N Yks	NZ0607	54°27·7'	1°54·0'W	X	92
Badger Wood	E Yorks	SE9162	54°3·0'	0°36·2'W	F	101
Badger Wood Fm	W Susx	TQ2413	50°54·4'	0°13·8'W	FM	198
Badgeworth	Glos	SO9019	51°52·4'	2°8·3'W	T	163
Badgrinnan	Highld	NH6360	57°36·8'	4°17·1'W	X	21
Badgworth	Somer	ST3952	51°16·1'	2°52·1'W	T	182
Badgworth Court	Somer	ST4052	51°16·1'	2°51·2'W	X	182
Badgworthy Hill	Devon	SS7944	51°11·2'	3°43·5'W	H	180
Badgworthy Lees	Devon	SS7844	51°11·2'	3°44·4'W	X	180
Badgworthy Water	Devon	SS7944	51°11·2'	3°43·5'W	W	180
Badharigo	Highld	ND2339	58°20·2'	3°18·4'W	X	11,12
Badharlick	Corn	SX2686	50°39·1'	4°27·3'W	T	201
Badicaul	Highld	NG7529	57°18·0'	5°43·6'W	T	33
Badiebath Wood	Aberd	NJ8339	57°26·7'	2°16·5'W	F	29,30
Badiemicheal	Moray	NJ1854	57°34·4'	3°21·8'W	X	28
Badievochel	Moray	NJ2422	57°17·2'	3°15·2'W	X	36
Badingair Hill	Aberd	NJ5022	57°17·4'	2°49·3'W	H	37
Badingham	Suff	TM3068	52°15·9'	1°22·6'E	X	156
Badingham Ho	Suff	TM3067	52°15·4'	1°22·6'E	X	156
Badinluchie	Highld	NH2760	57°36·1'	4°53·2'W	X	20
Badintagairt	Highld	NC4210	58°3·3'	4°40·2'W	X	16
Badivow	Stir	NS5193	56°6·6'	4°23·3'W	X	57
Badlake Fm	Devon	SS8527	51°2·1'	3°38·0'W	FM	181
Badland Fm	Powys	SO2363	52°15·8'	3°7·3'W	FM	137,148
Badlesmere	Kent	TR0053	51°14·7'	0°52·3'E	T	189
Badlesmere Court	Kent	TR0155	51°15·7'	0°53·3'E	X	178
Badley Green Fm	Suff	TM0555	52°9·5'	1°0·2'E	FM	155
Badley Hall	Essex	TM0728	51°54·9'	1°1·0'E	X	168,169
Badley Hall	Essex	TM0926	51°53·8'	1°2·7'E	X	168,169
Badley Hall Fm	Suff	TM0655	52°9·5'	1°1·1'E	FM	155
Badley Hill	Suff	TM0756	52°10·0'	1°2·0'E	X	155
Badleys	Suff	TL9142	52°2·8'	0°47·5'E	X	155
Badley Wood Common	Heref	SO6957	52°12·9'	2°26·8'W	X	149
Badlieu	Scot Bord	NT0519	55°27·6'	3°29·7'W	X	78
Badlieu Burn	Scot Bord	NT0418	55°27·1'	3°30·6'W	W	78
Badlieu Rig	Scot Bord	NT0417	55°26·5'	3°30·6'W	H	78
Badlingham Manor	Cambs	TL6770	52°18·4'	0°27·4'E	X	154
Badlipster	Highld	ND2449	58°25·6'	3°17·6'W	X	11,12
Badliss Hall	Essex	TM0629	51°55·5'	1°0·2'E	X	168
Bad Lònanach	Highld	NC2345	58°21·7'	5°1·1'W	X	9
Badluarach	Highld	NG9994	57°53·7'	5°23·0'W	T	19
Badminston Common	Hants	SU4501	50°48·6'	1°21·3'W	X	196
Badminston Fm	Hants	SU4602	50°49·2'	1°20·4'W	FM	196
Badminton	S Glos	ST8082	51°32·4'	2°16·9'W	T	173
Badminton Down	S Glos	ST8185	51°34·0'	2°16·1'W	X	173
Badminton Ho	S Glos	ST8082	51°32·4'	2°16·9'W	A	173
Badminton Park	S Glos	ST8083	51°33·0'	2°16·9'W	X	173
Badmondisfield Hall	Suff	TL7457	52°11·3'	0°33·1'E	X	155
Bad na Bàighe Forest	Highld	NC2346	58°22·3'	5°1·1'W	F	9
Badnaban	Highld	NC0720	58°7·9'	5°16·2'W	T	15
Badnabay	Highld	NC2146	58°22·2'	5°3·2'W	X	9
Bad na Beinne	Aberd	NJ3808	57°9·8'	3°1·1'W	X	37
Bad na Curra	Arg & Bt	NR8475	55°55·4'	5°27·0'W	X	62
Badnafrave	Moray	NJ2015	57°13·4'	3°19·0'W	X	36
Badnage	Heref	SO4546	52°6·8'	2°47·8'W	X	148,149
Badnage Wood	Heref	SO4546	52°6·8'	2°47·8'W	F	148,149
Badnagie	Highld	ND1531	58°15·8'	3°26·5'W	T	11,17
Badnagoach	Aberd	NJ3808	57°9·8'	3°1·1'W	X	37
Bad na Gualainn	Arg & Bt	NN3846	56°34·9'	4°37·8'W	X	50
Badnagyle	Highld	NC0611	58°3·0'	5°16·8'W	X	15
Bad na h-Earba	Highld	NC7524	58°11·5'	4°7·1'W	X	16
Badnaheen	Highld	NC9944	58°22·6'	3°43·1'W	X	11
Bad nam Beith	Arg & Bt	NR8894	56°5·8'	5°24·1'W	H	55
Badnambiast	Pth & Kin	NN7173	56°50·1'	4°6·4'W	X	42
Bad nam Bò	Highld	NC9952	58°26·9'	3°43·4'W	X	11
Bad nan Ceann fionn	Highld	NM7459	56°40·4'	5°40·9'W	X	49
Bad nan Glac	Highld	ND1130	58°15·2'	3°30·5'W	X	11,17
Bad nan Nathraichean	Highld	NG2660	57°33·1'	6°34·4'W	X	23
Badnellan	Highld	NC8804	58°0·9'	3°53·3'W	X	17
Badninish	Highld	NH7694	57°55·4'	4°5·1'W	T	21
Badnocks Fm	Essex	TL9501	51°40·7'	0°49·6'E	FM	168
Badnonan	Highld	NH9134	57°23·3'	3°48·3'W	X	27
Badnyrieves	Aberd	NJ9145	57°30·0'	2°8·6'W	X	30
Bad Ochainaich	Stir	NS4692	56°6·0'	4°28·1'W	H	57
Badochurn	Aberd	NJ2408	57°9·7'	3°14·9'W	X	36
Badour	Stir	NN4335	56°29·1'	4°32·5'W	X	51
Badrain	Highld	NH6259	57°36·3'	4°18·1'W	X	26
Badrallach	Highld	NH0691	57°52·2'	5°15·8'W	T	19
Badrinsary	Highld	ND1124	58°12·0'	3°30·4'W	X	17
Badryrie	Highld	ND2043	58°22·3'	3°21·6'W	X	11,12
Badsaddle Fm	Northnts	SP8372	52°20·6'	0°46·5'W	FM	141
Badsaddle Wood	Northnts	SP8372	52°20·6'	0°46·5'W	F	141
Badsell Manor Fm	Kent	TQ6544	51°10·5'	0°22·0'E	FM	188
Badsell Park Fm	Kent	TQ6543	51°10·0'	0°22·0'E	FM	188
Badsey	Worcs	SP0743	52°5·4'	1°53·5'W	T	150
Badsey Brook	Worcs	SP0641	52°4·3'	1°54·4'W	W	150
Badsey Field	Worcs	SP0843	52°5·4'	1°52·6'W	X	150
Badshalloch	W Dunb	NS4587	56°3·3'	4°28·9'W	T	57
Badshot Fm	Surrey	SU8648	51°13·1'	0°45·7'W	FM	186
Badshot Lea	Surrey	SU8648	51°13·7'	0°45·7'W	T	186
Badslake	Devon	SS4716	50°55·6'	4°10·2'W	X	180
Bad Step, The	Highld	NG4919	57°11·8'	6°8·9'W	X	32
Badsworth	Wakf	SE4614	53°37·5'	1°17·9'W	T	111
Badvoon	Highld	NH5888	57°51·8'	4°23·1'W	X	21
Badwell Ash	Suff	TL9969	52°17·2'	0°55·5'E	T	155
Badwell Green	Suff	TM0169	52°17·2'	0°57·2'E	T	155
Badworthy	Devon	SX6861	50°26·3'	3°51·2'W	T	202
Badworthy Fm	Devon	SS4312	50°53·4'	4°13·6'W	FM	180,190
Badyen Fm	Arg & Bt	NS3379	55°58·8'	4°40·2'W	FM	63
Badyo	Pth & Kin	NN9861	56°44·0'	3°39·6'W	X	43
Bae Colwyn or Colwyn Bay	Conwy	SH8678	53°17·4'	3°42·2'W	T	116
Baela	Shetld	HU6291	60°36·1'	0°51·6'W	X	1,2
Baemore	Highld	NH4130	57°20·2'	4°38·0'W	X	26
Baerlochan	D & G	NX6654	54°52·0'	4°4·9'W	X	83,84
Bae'r Nant	Gwyn	SH1222	52°46·0'	4°46·8'W	W	123
Bae y Rhigol	Gwyn	SH1122	52°46·0'	4°47·7'W	W	123
Baffham Fm	N Yks	SE7959	54°1·5'	0°47·2'W	FM	105,106
Baffins	C of Port	SU6601	50°48·5'	1°3·4'W	T	196
Bagbear	Devon	SS4815	50°55·1'	4°9·4'W	X	180
Bagbeare	Devon	SS3909	50°51·7'	4°16·9'W	X	190
Bagber	Dorset	ST7513	50°55·2'	2°21·0'W	T	194
Bagber Br	Dorset	ST7615	50°56·3'	2°20·1'W	X	183
Bagber Common	Dorset	ST7614	50°55·7'	2°20·1'W	X	194
Bagber Fm	Dorset	SY8099	50°47·6'	2°16·6'W	FM	194
Bagbie	D & G	NX4955	54°52·3'	4°20·8'W	X	83
Bagborough	Devon	SS7804	50°49·6'	3°43·6'W	X	191
Bagborough Fms	Somer	ST6239	51°9·2'	2°32·2'W	FM	183
Bagborough Hill	Somer	ST1634	51°6·2'	3°11·6'W	X	181
Bagborough Ho	Somer	ST1633	51°5·6'	3°11·6'W	X	181
Bagbury	Corn	SS2105	50°49·3'	4°32·1'W	X	190
Bagbury	Powys	SO3193	52°32·1'	3°0·6'W	X	137
Bagby	N Yks	SE4680	54°13·1'	1°17·3'W	T	100
Bagby Grange	N Yks	SE4580	54°13·1'	1°18·2'W	T	99
Bagdale Fm	N Yks	NZ5204	54°26·0'	1°11·5'W	FM	93
Bagden Fm	Surrey	TQ1451	51°15·0'	0°21·6'W	FM	187
Bagden Hall	Kirk	SE2409	53°34·9'	1°37·8'W	X	110
Bage	Heref	SO2656	52°12·1'	3°4·6'W	X	148
Bage Fm, The	Heref	SO4139	52°3·0'	2°51·2'W	FM	149,161
Bag Enderby	Lincs	TF3472	53°13·9'	0°0·9'E	T	122
Bagendon	Glos	SP0106	51°45·4'	1°58·7'W	T	163
Bagendon Downs	Glos	SP0006	51°45·4'	1°59·6'W	X	163
Bagfield Copse	Wilts	SU2321	50°59·5'	1°40·0'W	F	184
Baggarah	Cumbr	NY5863	54°57·8'	2°38·9'W	X	86
Baggarett's Fm	Essex	TL8731	51°57·0'	0°43·7'E	FM	168
Baggeridge Country Park	Staffs	SO8992	52°31·8'	2°9·3'W	X	139
Baggeridge Wood Fm	Staffs	SO8993	52°32·3'	2°9·3'W	FM	139
Baggerton	Angus	NO4653	56°40·2'	2°52·4'W	X	54
Bagger Wood	Barns	SE3002	53°31·1'	1°32·4'W	F	110,111
Bagginswood	Shrops	SO6881	52°25·8'	2°27·8'W	T	138
Baggrave Hall	Leic	SK6908	52°40·2'	0°58·4'W	X	141
Baggrave Village	Leic	SK6908	52°40·2'	0°58·4'W	A	141
Baggra Yeat	Cumbr	NY2636	54°43·1'	3°8·5'W	X	89,90
Baggridge Fms	Bath & NE Somer	ST7456	51°18·4'	2°22·0'W	FM	172
Baggrow	Cumbr	NY1741	54°45·7'	3°17·0'W	T	85
Baggy Moor	Shrops	SJ3927	52°50·5'	2°53·9'W	X	126
Baggy Point	Devon	SS4140	51°8·5'	4°16·0'W	X	180
Bàgh	N Eil	NB3809	57°59·8'	6°25·6'W	W	14
Bàgh a' Bhiorain	N Eil	NF9062	57°32·8'	7°10·5'W	W	22
Bàgh a' Bhràoige	N Eil	NF8747	57°24·6'	7°12·3'W	W	22
Bàgh Achadh dà Mhaoilein	Arg & Bt	NR7372	55°53·5'	5°37·4'W	W	62
Bàgh a' Chnoic Mhaoileanaich	Arg & Bt	NM3019	56°17·5'	6°21·4'W	W	48
Bàgh a' Chotain	N Eil	NF9886	57°46·0'	7°4·3'W	W	18
Bàgh a' Deas	N Eil	NL6393	56°54·6'	7°31·8'W	W	31
Bàgh a' Ghallanaich	Highld	NM4080	56°50·6'	6°15·4'W	W	39
Bàgh a' Ghlinne	N Eil	NG1898	57°53·2'	6°45·0'W	W	14
Bàgh a' Ghlinn-mhòir	N Eil	NF8125	57°12·5'	7°16·6'W	W	22
Bàgh Aird a' Mhulaidh	N Eil	NB1910	57°59·7'	6°44·9'W	W	13,14
Bàgh Aird nam Madadh	Suff	NF9367	57°35·6'	7°7·8'W	W	18
Bagham	Kent	TR0753	51°14·5'	0°58·3'E	T	179,189
Bàgh a' Mhuilinn	Highld	NG6405	57°4·8'	5°53·2'W	W	32
Bàgh an Dà Dhoruis	Arg & Bt	NR4178	55°55·8'	6°8·4'W	W	60,61
Bàgh an Dubh Ard	Highld	NG6214	57°9·6'	5°55·7'W	W	32
Bàgh an Duine	Highld	NC2034	58°15·7'	5°3·6'W	W	15
Bàgh an Eireannach	N Eil	NF9056	57°29·6'	7°10·0'W	W	22
Bàgh an Iollaich	Arg & Bt	NM4335	56°26·5'	6°9·7'W	W	47,48
Bàgh an Tailleir	Arg & Bt	NR8480	55°58·1'	5°27·2'W	W	55
Bàgh an Tigh-Stòir	Arg & Bt	NM7907	56°12·5'	5°33·4'W	W	55
Bàgh an Trailleich	Arg & Bt	NM2161	56°39·7'	6°32·8'W	W	46,47
Bàgh an t-Srathain	Highld	NC0721	58°8·4'	5°16·2'W	W	15
Bàgh an t-Srathaidh	Highld	NG7832	57°19·7'	5°40·8'W	W	24
Bàgh a' Phòllain	Highld	NC1858	58°28·6'	5°6·8'W	W	9
Bàgh a Tuath	N Eil	NB5532	58°12·8'	6°9·8'W	W	8
Bàgh a Tuath	N Eil	NF7446	57°23·5'	7°25·2'W	W	22
Bàgh a Tuath	N Eil	NF8540	57°20·8'	7°13·8'W	W	22
Baghay Fm	Somer	ST1224	51°0·8'	3°14·9'W	FM	181,193
Bàgh Bàn	Arg & Bt	NM7703	56°10·3'	5°35·1'W	W	55
Bàgh Bàn	N Eil	NL6187	56°51·3'	7°33·3'W	W	31
Bàgh Bàn	N Eil	NL6492	56°54·1'	7°30·7'W	W	31
Bàgh Beag	N Eil	NL6598	56°57·4'	7°30·2'W	W	31
Bàgh Bhiogadail	N Eil	NB1911	58°0·2'	6°44·9'W	W	13,14
Bàgh Bholuim	N Eil	NF8228	57°14·2'	7°15·8'W	W	22
Bàgh Blaaskie	N Eil	NF7276	57°39·5'	7°29·6'W	W	18
Bàgh Buic	Arg & Bt	NR9170	55°52·9'	5°20·1'W	W	62
Bàgh Carragraich	N Eil	NG1998	57°53·2'	6°44·0'W	W	14
Bàgh Ceann na Muice	N Eil	NG2294	57°51·2'	6°40·7'W	W	14
Bàgh Chàirminis	N Eil	NG0284	57°45·1'	7°0·1'W	W	18
Bàgh Chaise	N Eil	NF9773	57°39·0'	7°4·3'W	W	18
Bàgh Chalbha	Highld	NC1637	58°17·3'	5°7·8'W	W	15
Bàgh Chlann Alasdair	N Eil	NF8539	57°20·2'	7°13·7'W	W	22
Bàgh Chlann Neill	N Eil	NB1340	58°15·6'	6°53·1'W	W	13
Bàgh Chlann Neill	N Eil	NG4398	57°54·1'	6°19·8'W	W	14
Bàgh Chliasmoil	N Eil	NB0706	57°57·1'	6°56·7'W	W	13,14
Bàgh Choradail	N Eil	NF8330	57°15·3'	7°15·0'W	W	22
Bàgh Ciarach	N Eil	NB2502	57°55·6'	6°38·2'W	W	14
Bàgh Clach an Dobhrain	Arg & Bt	NM7937	56°28·7'	5°34·9'W	W	49
Bàgh Clann-Nèil	N Eil	NF8855	57°28·9'	7°11·9'W	W	22
Bàgh Cnoc nan Gobhàr	N Eil	NF8056	57°29·1'	7°20·0'W	W	22

Bàgh Dail nan Ceann	Arg & Bt	NM7704	56°10·8′	5°35·1′W	W	55
Bàgh Dhail Mòr	N Eil	NB2145	58°18·6′	6°45·3′W	W	8
Bàgh Diracleit	N Eil	NG1598	57°53·1′	6°48·0′W	W	14
Bàgh Dùnan Ruadh	Highld	NG7819	57°12·7′	5°40·1′W	W	33
Bàgh Dùn Mhuilig	Arg & Bt	NM7701	56°9·2′	5°35·0′W	W	55
Bàgh Fearnoch	Arg & Bt	NS0176	55°56·4′	5°10·7′W	W	63
Bàgh Feisdlum	Arg & Bt	NM2558	56°38·2′	6°28·7′W	W	46,47
Bàgh Feith a'Chaorainn	Arg & Bt	NR6598	56°7·3′	5°46·4′W	W	55,61
Bàgh Gleann a'Mhaoil	Arg & Bt	NM7103	56°10·1′	5°40·9′W	W	55
Bàgh Gleann nam Muc	Arg & Bt	NM6800	56°8·4′	5°43·6′W	W	55,61
Bàgh Gleann Righ Mòr	Arg & Bt	NR5282	55°58·3′	5°58·0′W	W	61
Bàgh Gleann Speireig	Arg & Bt	NR6396	56°6·1′	5°48·2′W	W	61
Bàgh Hirivagh	N Eil	NF7103	57°0·3′	7°24·7′W	W	31
Bàgh Huilavagh	N Eil	NF7103	57°0·3′	7°24·7′W	W	31
Baghill Sta	Wakd	SE4621	53°41·2′	1°17·8′W	X	105
Bàgh Inbhir h-Aibhne	Arg & Bt	NM3125	56°20·7′	6°20·8′W	W	48
Bàgh Lachlainn	Arg & Bt	NM7511	56°14·6′	5°37·4′W	W	55
Bàgh Lamasaigh	N Eil	NF8432	57°16·4′	7°14·1′W	W	22
Bàgh Leathann	Highld	NC1638	58°17·8′	5°7·9′W	W	15
Bàgh Loch an Ròin	Highld	NC1954	58°26·5′	5°5·6′W	W	9
Bàgh Loch Sian	Highld	NC4462	58°31·4′	4°40·2′W	W	9
Bàgh Mile-Feala	N Eil	NF8634	57°17·6′	7°12·3′W	W	22
Bàgh Mòr	N Eil	NF7914	57°6·6′	7°17·7′W	W	31
Bàgh Mòr	N Eil	NF8259	57°30·8′	7°18·2′W	W	22
Bàgh Mòr	N Eil	NF8756	57°29·4′	7°13·0′W	T	22
Bàgh Mòr	N Eil	NF8756	57°29·4′	7°13·0′W	W	22
Bàgh Mòraig	N Eil	NF9158	57°30·7′	7°9·2′W	W	22
Bàgh na Bèiste	N Eil	NB5532	58°12·8′	6°9·8′W	W	8
Bàgh na Caiplich	N Eil	NF9056	57°29·6′	7°10·0′W	W	22
Bàgh na Cille	Arg & Bt	NM7700	56°8·7′	5°34·9′W	W	55
Bàgh na Coille	Arg & Bt	NM2762	56°40·5′	6°27·0′W	W	46,47
Bàgh na Creige Loisgte	N Eil	NF8244	57°22·8′	7°17·0′W	W	22
Baghna Dalach	Arg & Bt	NM8113	56°15·8′	5°31·7′W	W	55
Bàgh nà Dalach	Arg & Bt	NN0638	56°29·9′	5°8·7′W	W	50
Bàgh na Doide	Arg & Bt	NR6976	55°55·6′	5°41·4′W	W	61,62
Bàgh na Dòirlinne	Arg & Bt	NR6554	55°43·6′	5°44·1′W	W	62
Bàgh na h-Aird	Arg & Bt	NM7405	56°11·3′	5°38·1′W	W	55
Bàgh na h-Aoineig	N Eil	NL5583	56°48·9′	7°38·8′W	W	31
Bàgh na h-Uain	N Eil	NF8745	57°23·5′	7°12·2′W	W	22
Bàgh na h-Uamha	Highld	NM4297	56°59·8′	6°14·4′W	W	39
Bagh Nam Faoilean	N Eil	NF8344	57°22·8′	7°16·1′W	W	22
Bàgh nam Fiadh	N Eil	NF7841	57°21·0′	7°20·8′W	W	22
Bàgh na Muice	N Eil	NF8653	57°27·8′	7°13·8′W	W	22
Bàgh nan Clach	N Eil	NF6908	57°2·9′	7°27·1′W	W	31
Bàgh nan Craobhag	N Eil	NF7776	57°39·7′	7°24·5′W	W	18
Bàgh nan Gunnaichean	Highld	NG4573	57°40·7′	6°16·2′W	W	23
Bàgh nan Toll	N Eil	NF8340	57°20·7′	7°15·7′W	W	22
Bàgh Niabhag	N Eil	NF8552	57°27·2′	7°14·7′W	W	22
Bag House Fm	Derby	SK0377	53°17·6′	1°56·9′W	FM	119
Bàgh Phabail Iarach	N Eil	NB5230	58°11·6′	6°12·7′W	W	8
Bàgh Phabail Uarach	N Eil	NB5331	58°12·2′	6°11·8′W	W	8
Bàgh Phort Bholair	N Eil	NB5636	58°15·0′	6°9·0′W	W	8
Bàgh Rubha Mhoil Ruaidh	Highld	NG3903	57°2·9′	6°17·8′W	W	32,39
Bàgh Scaraloid	N Eil	NF8551	57°26·7′	7°14·6′W	W	22
Bàgh Scotbheinn	N Eil	NF8655	57°28·9′	7°13·9′W	W	22
Bàgh Sean-ghairt	Arg & Bt	NR7371	55°53·0′	5°37·3′W	W	62
Bàgh Sheigra	Highld	NC1859	58°29·1′	5°6·8′W	W	9
Bàgh Sheisiadair	N Eil	NB5534	58°13·9′	6°9·9′W	W	8
Bàgh Shiùrabhagh	N Eil	NF8351	57°26·6′	7°16·6′W	W	22
Bàgh Shuardail	N Eil	NB4831	58°12·0′	6°16·9′W	W	8
Bàgh Siar	N Eil	NL6295	56°55·6′	7°32·9′W	W	31
Bàgh Steinigie	N Eil	NG0193	57°49·9′	7°1·8′W	W	18
Bàgh Stiùchleit	N Eil	NB1200	57°54·1′	6°51·2′W	W	14
Bàgh Thacanais	N Eil	NF6262	57°31·6′	7°38·4′W	W	22
Bàgh Theilisnis	N Eil	NB1004	57°56·1′	6°53·5′W	W	13,14
Bàgh Tholmair	N Eil	NF8342	57°21·7′	7°15·9′W	W	22
Bàgh Thuilm	N Eil	NB4530	58°11·4′	6°19·9′W	W	8
Bàgh Tigh-an-Droighinn	Arg & Bt	NR8579	55°57·6′	5°26·2′W	W	62
Bàgh Tir Chille	Arg & Bt	NM3218	56°17·0′	6°19·4′W	W	48
Bàgh Uamh Dhadhaidh	Highld	NC4564	58°32·5′	4°39·3′W	W	9
Bàgh Uamh Mhór Beinn Nan Capull	Arg & Bt	NR6799	56°7·9′	5°44·5′W	W	55,61
Bàgh Uamh nan Giall	Arg & Bt	NR6698	56°7·3′	5°45·4′W	W	55,61
Bàgh uisinis	N Eil	NF8533	57°17·0′	7°13·2′W	W	22
Bàgh Urgha	N Eil	NG1899	57°53·7′	6°45·1′W	W	14
Bàgh Urgha Beag	N Eil	NG1799	57°53·7′	6°46·1′W	W	14
Bagillt	Flint	SJ2275	53°16·2′	3°9·8′W	T	117
Bagillt Bank	Flint	SJ2376	53°16·8′	3°8·9′W	X	117
Baginton	Warw	SP3474	52°22·0′	1°29·6′W	T	140
Bagi Stack	Shetld	HP4705	60°43·8′	1°7·8′W	X	1
Baglan	Nth Pt Talb	SS7592	51°37·0′	3°47·9′W	T	170
Baglan Bay	Nth Pt Talb	SS7192	51°37·0′	3°51·4′W	W	170
Baglan Fm	Pemb	SN0309	51°44·9′	4°50·8′W	FM	157,158
Bagley	Leeds	SE2235	53°48·9′	1°39·5′W	T	104
Bagley	Shrops	SJ4027	52°50·5′	2°53·0′W	T	126
Bagley	Somer	ST4545	51°12·3′	2°46·9′W	T	182
Bagley Fm	Donc	SK5991	53°25·0′	1°6·3′W	FM	111
Bagley Fm	N Yks	NZ3105	54°26·6′	1°30·9′W	FM	93
Bagley Green	Somer	ST1219	50°58·1′	3°14·8′W	T	181,193
Bagley Hill Fm	Devon	ST3100	50°48·0′	2°58·4′W	FM	193
Bagley Marsh	Shrops	SJ3928	52°51·0′	2°53·9′W	T	126
Bagley's Rough	Shrops	SJ7000	52°36·1′	2°26·2′W	F	127
Bagley's Rough	Shrops	SO7099	52°35·5′	2°26·2′W	F	138
Bagley Wood	Oxon	SP5102	51°43·1′	1°15·3′W	F	164
Bagman's Fm	Dorset	SU0408	50°52·5′	1°56·2′W	FM	195
Bag Mere	Ches	SJ7964	53°10·6′	2°18·4′W	W	118
Bagmere Bank Fm	Ches	SJ7964	53°10·6′	2°18·4′W	FM	118
Bagmere Fm	Ches	SJ7964	53°10·6′	2°18·4′W	FM	118
Bagmoor Common	Surrey	SU9242	51°10·4′	0°40·6′W	F	186
Bagmoor Fm	N Lincs	SE9016	53°38·2′	0°37·9′W	FM	112
Bagmoors	S Lanak	NS9543	55°40·4′	3°39·7′W	X	72
Bagmore	Devon	SS9905	50°50·4′	3°25·7′W	X	192
Bagmore	Hants	SU6644	51°11·7′	1°2·9′W	T	185,186
Bagnall	C of Stoke	SJ9250	53°3·1′	2°6·8′W	T	118
Bagnall	Staffs	SK1514	52°43·6′	1°46·3′W	X	128
Bagnell Fm	Somer	ST4814	50°55·6′	2°44·0′W	FM	193
Bagnol	I of Angl	SH2678	53°16·5′	4°36·2′W	X	114
Bagnor	W Berks	SU4569	51°25·3′	1°20·8′W	T	174
Bagnum Fm	Hants	SU1702	50°49·3′	1°45·1′W	FM	195
Bagot Forest	Staffs	SK0727	52°50·7′	1°53·4′W	F	128
Bagot Forest	Staffs	SK1028	52°51·2′	1°50·7′W	F	128
Bagot's Bromley	Staffs	SK0626	52°50·1′	1°54·3′W	X	128
Bagot's Park	Staffs	SK0927	52°50·7′	1°51·6′W	X	128
Bagpark	Devon	SX7278	50°35·5′	3°48·1′W	X	191
Bagpath	Glos	SO8502	51°43·2′	2°12·6′W	T	162
Bagpath	Glos	ST8094	51°38·9′	2°17·0′W	T	162,173
Bagpiper's Tump	Heref	SO5736	52°1·5′	2°37·2′W	H	149
Bagrae	Aberd	NJ6857	57°36·4′	2°31·7′W	X	29
Bagraw	Northum	NY8596	55°15·7′	2°13·7′W	X	80
Bagraw Fm	Northum	NY8963	54°57·9′	2°9·9′W	FM	87
Bagraw Ford	Scot Bord	NY6099	55°17·3′	2°37·4′W	X	80
Bagshaw	Derby	SK0781	53°19·8′	1°53·3′W	T	110
Bagshot	Surrey	SU9163	51°21·8′	0°41·2′W	T	175,186
Bagshot	Wilts	SU3165	51°23·2′	1°32·9′W	T	174
Bagshot Heath	Surrey	SU8963	51°21·8′	0°42·9′W	X	175,186
Bagshot Heath	Surrey	SU9161	51°20·7′	0°41·2′W	T	175,186
Bagshot Park	Surrey	SU9063	51°21·8′	0°42·0′W	X	175,186
Bagslate Moor	Roch	SD8613	53°37·0′	2°12·3′W	T	109
Bagstone	Corn	SX1462	50°25·9′	4°36·8′W	X	200
Bagstone	S Glos	ST6887	51°35·1′	2°27·3′W	T	172
Bagthorpe	Norf	TF7932	52°51·6′	0°39·9′E	T	132
Bagthorpe	Notts	SK4751	53°3·5′	1°17·5′W	T	120
Bagthorpe Fm	Derby	SK3271	53°14·3′	1°30·8′W	FM	119
Bagton	Devon	SX7041	50°15·5′	3°49·1′W	X	202
Bag Tor	Devon	SX7675	50°33·9′	3°44·7′W	X	191
Bagtor Ho	Devon	SX7675	50°33·9′	3°44·7′W	X	191
Baguley	Man	SJ8189	53°24·1′	2°16·7′W	T	109
Baguley Fold	Ches	SJ8076	53°17·1′	2°17·6′W	X	118
Baguley Hall	Man	SJ8188	53°23·6′	2°16·7′W	A	109
Bagwell Fm	Dorset	SY6281	50°37·9′	2°31·9′W	FM	194
Bagwich	I of W	SZ5182	50°38·4′	1°16·3′W	X	196
Bagwith Ho	N Yks	SE1974	54°9·9′	1°42·1′W	X	99
Bagworth	Leic	SK4408	52°40·3′	1°20·6′W	T	140
Bagworth Heath	Leic	SK4407	52°39·8′	1°20·6′W	X	140
Bagworth Park	Leic	SK4508	52°40·3′	1°19·7′W	X	140
Bagwyllydiart	Heref	SO4426	51°56·0′	2°48·5′W	T	161
Baharm House	Moray	NJ3449	57°31·8′	3°5·7′W	X	28
Ba' Hill	Aberd	NJ5337	57°25·5′	2°46·6′W	H	29
Baiden Fm	Brig	SS8785	51°33·4′	3°37·4′W	FM	170
Baidlandhill	N Ayr	NS2651	55°43·5′	4°45·8′W	X	63
Baidland Hill	S Ayr	NS2522	55°27·9′	4°45·7′W	X	70
Baiglie	Pth & Kin	NO1515	56°19·4′	3°22·0′W	X	58
Baikie	Angus	NO3149	56°37·9′	3°7·0′W	X	53
Baikiehill	Aberd	NJ6936	57°25·1′	2°30·5′W	X	29
Baikiehowe	Aberd	NJ7632	57°22·9′	2°23·5′W	X	29
Baikies	Angus	NO4263	56°45·6′	2°56·5′W	X	44
Baila	Shetld	HP5704	60°43·2′	0°56·8′W	X	1
Bail-a'-Mhinister	Highld	NG8154	57°31·7′	5°39·0′W	X	24
Bailanfhraoich	Highld	NH5691	57°53·4′	4°25·3′W	X	21
Bailanloan	Pth & Kin	NN8666	56°46·6′	3°51·5′W	T	43
Bail-ard	N Eil	NF7974	57°38·8′	7°22·4′W	X	18
Bailbrook	Bath & NE Somer	ST7667	51°24·3′	2°20·3′W	T	172
Baildon	Brad	SE1539	53°51·1′	1°45·9′W	T	104
Baildon Green	Brad	SE1438	53°50·5′	1°46·8′W	T	104
Baildon Moor	Brad	SE1440	53°51·6′	1°46·8′W	X	104
Baile	N Eil	NF9381	57°43·1′	7°8·9′W	X	18
Bailea	Powys	SN8530	51°57·6′	3°40·0′W	X	160
Bailea	Powys	SN9428	51°56·7′	3°32·1′W	X	160
Bailea	Powys	SO0424	51°54·6′	3°23·3′W	X	160
Bailea Fm	Powys	SN9224	51°54·5′	3°33·8′W	FM	160
Baile Ailein	N Eil	NB2920	58°5·4′	6°35·4′W	T	13,14
Baile an Òr	Highld	NC9121	58°10·1′	3°50·7′W	X	17
Baile an Teampaill	N Eil	NB1942	58°16·9′	6°47·2′W	X	8,13
Baile an Truiseil	N Eil	NB3753	58°23·5′	6°29·6′W	T	8
Bailebeag	Highld	NH5018	57°14·0′	4°28·6′W	X	35
Baile Boidheach	Arg & Bt	NR7473	55°54·1′	5°36·5′W	T	62
Bailefuil	Stir	NN5519	56°20·7′	4°20·3′W	X	57
Baile Geamhraidh	Highld	NM6255	56°37·8′	5°52·4′W	X	49
Baile Gharbhaidh	N Eil	NF7646	57°23·6′	7°23·2′W	T	22
Baile Glas	N Eil	NF8457	57°29·8′	7°16·1′W	T	22
Baileguish	Highld	NN8298	57°3·7′	3°56·3′W	X	35,43
Baile Mhanaich	N Eil	NF7755	57°28·5′	7°22·9′W	T	22
Baile Mór	Arg & Bt	NM2824	56°20·1′	6°23·6′W	T	48
Baile na Bruaich	Pth & Kin	NN8967	56°47·2′	3°48·6′W	X	43
Baile na Cille	Highld	NC0834	58°15·4′	5°15·9′W	X	15
Bailenacille	N Eil	NF8886	57°45·6′	7°14·3′W	X	18
Baile nan Cailleach	N Eil	NF7753	57°27·4′	7°22·7′W	T	22
Baileouchdarach	Arg & Bt	NM8743	56°32·1′	5°27·4′W	X	49
Baile Phail	N Eil	NB4116	58°3·7′	6°23·0′W	X	14
Baile Tharbhach	Arg & Bt	NR3667	55°49·7′	6°12·5′W	X	60,61
Bailetonach	Highld	NM6373	56°47·6′	5°52·4′W	T	40
Bailey	Cered	SN2443	52°3·7′	4°33·7′W	X	145
Bailey	Cumbr	NY5179	55°6·4′	2°45·7′W	X	86
Bailey	Devon	SX8896	50°45·4′	3°34·9′W	X	192
Bailey	Heref	SO6321	51°53·4′	2°31·9′W	X	162
Bailey	Powys	SO1649	52°8·2′	3°13·2′W	X	148
Bailey-bedw	Powys	SO0968	52°18·4′	3°19·7′W	X	136,147
Bailey Bedw	Powys	SO1644	52°5·5′	3°13·2′W	X	148,161
Bailey Bog	Powys	SO0375	52°22·1′	3°25·1′W	X	136,147
Baileybrook	Heref	SO6220	51°52·9′	2°32·7′W	X	162
Bailey Brook	Shrops	SJ6132	52°53·3′	2°34·4′W	W	127
Bailey Einon	Powys	SO0761	52°14·6′	3°21·3′W	X	147
Bailey Flat	Derby	SK0873	53°15·5′	1°52·4′W	X	119
Bailey Fm	Powys	SO2171	52°20·1′	3°9·2′W	FM	137,148
Bailey Fold	Brad	SE1034	53°48·4′	1°50·5′W	X	104
Bailey Gate	Norf	TF8115	52°42·4′	0°41·2′E	X	132
Bailey Glace	Monm	SO4708	51°46·3′	2°45·7′W	X	161
Bailey Green	Hants	SU6627	51°2·5′	1°3·1′W	T	185,186
Bailey Hall	Lancs	SD6737	53°49·9′	2°29·7′W	X	103
Baileyhaulwen	Powys	SN9973	52°21·0′	3°28·6′W	X	136,147
Bailey Head	Cumbr	NY5180	55°7·0′	2°45·7′W	X	79
Bailey Hey	Lancs	SD5743	53°53·1′	2°38·8′W	X	102
Bailey Hill	Essex	TL7039	52°1·6′	0°29·1′E	X	154
Bailey Hill	Powys	SO0375	52°22·1′	3°25·1′W	H	136,147
Bailey Hill	Powys	SO2372	52°20·7′	3°7·4′W	X	137,148
Bailey Hill	Sheff	SK2692	53°25·7′	1°36·1′W	A	110
Bailey Hill	Wilts	SU2879	51°30·8′	1°35·4′W	X	174
Bailey Hill Fm	Wilts	SU2878	51°30·2′	1°35·4′W	FM	174
Bailey Hills	Essex	TL4723	51°53·4′	0°8·6′E	X	167
Bailey Ho	Lancs	SD6738	53°50·5′	2°29·7′W	X	103
Bailey Home Fm	Carm	SN7223	51°53·7′	3°51·2′W	FM	160
Bailey-mawr	Powys	SO1263	52°15·7′	3°17·0′W	X	148
Bailey Mill	Cumbr	NY5178	55°5·9′	2°45·6′W	X	86
Bailey Pit Fm	Monm	SO4812	51°48·5′	2°44·9′W	FM	161
Baileypool Br	Suff	TL9368	52°16·8′	0°50·2′E	X	155
Bailey Ridding	Ches	SJ8972	53°14·9′	2°9·5′W	X	118
Bailey Ridge Fms	Dorset	ST6309	50°53·0′	2°31·2′W	FM	194
Baileys	Essex	TL6413	51°47·7′	0°23·1′E	X	167
Bailey's Close	Derby	SK2038	52°56·6′	1°41·7′W	X	128
Bailey's Down	Hants	SU3827	51°2·7′	1°27·1′W	X	185
Bailey's Fm	Ches	SJ9881	53°19·8′	2°1·4′W	FM	109
Bailey's Fm	Herts	TL1521	51°52·8′	0°19·4′W	FM	166
Bailey's Hard	Hants	SU3901	50°48·7′	1°26·4′W	X	196
Bailey's Whins	N Yks	SE2547	53°55·4′	1°36·7′W	F	104
Baileytown	Cumbr	NY4371	55°2·1′	2°53·1′W	X	85
Bailey Water	Cumbr	NY5179	55°6·4′	2°45·7′W	W	86
Bail Fell	D & G	NX9360	54°55·6′	3°39·8′W	H	84
Bail Green	Durham	NY9623	54°36·4′	2°3·3′W	X	91,92
Bail Hill	D & G	NS7614	55°24·5′	3°57·1′W	H	71,78
Bail Hill	D & G	NS8611	55°23·0′	3°47·5′W	H	71,78
Bail Hill	D & G	NX7295	55°14·2′	4°0·3′W	H	77
Bail Hill	Durham	NY9622	54°35·8′	2°3·3′W	X	91,92
Bail Hill	Durham	NY9722	54°35·8′	2°2·4′W	X	92
Bail Hill	Durham	NZ0321	54°35·3′	1°56·8′W	X	92
Bailie Burn	Scot Bord	NT3822	55°29·5′	2°58·4′W	W	73
Bailie Fea	Orkney	ND2696	58°51·0′	3°16·5′W	X	6,7
Bailiehill	D & G	NY2590	55°12·2′	3°10·3′W	X	79
Bailie Ho	Dorset	SY9499	50°47·7′	2°4·7′W	X	195
Bailielands	Pth & Kin	NN9615	56°19·2′	3°40·4′W	X	58
Bailiesward	Aberd	NJ4737	57°25·5′	2°52·5′W	X	28,29
Bailiff Bridge	Cald	SE1424	53°43·0′	1°46·9′W	T	104
Bailiff Ground	Cumbr	SD2280	54°12·8′	3°11·3′W	X	96
Bailiff's Letch	Northum	NZ2193	55°14·1′	1°39·8′W	W	81
Bailing Hill Fm	W Susx	TQ1532	51°4·8′	0°21·1′W	FM	187
Bail' Iochdrach	N Eil	NF8159	57°30·8′	7°19·2′W	T	22
Baillie	Highld	ND0465	58°34·0′	3°38·5′W	X	11,12
Baillie Hill	Highld	ND0464	58°33·5′	3°38·5′W	X	11,12
Baillie Hill	Orkney	HY3519	59°3·4′	3°7·5′W	X	6
Baillieknowe	Scot Bord	NT7138	55°38·3′	2°27·2′W	X	74
Baillies	Angus	NO4882	56°55·8′	2°50·8′W	X	44
Bailieshall	S Lanak	NS8435	55°35·9′	3°50·0′W	X	71,72
Bailliesland Fm	Moray	NJ2565	57°40·4′	3°15·0′W	FM	28
Bailieston	C of Glas	NS6763	55°50·8′	4°7·0′W	T	64
Baillieston	N Ayr	NS3055	55°45·8′	4°42·1′W	X	63
Bailliewhirr	D & G	NX4242	54°45·1′	4°26·9′W	X	83
Bailrigg	Lancs	SD4858	54°1·2′	2°47·2′W	T	102
Bail Uachdraich	N Eil	NF8160	57°31·3′	7°19·3′W	X	22
Bail' Ur Tholastaidh	N Eil	NB5348	58°21·3′	6°12·9′W	T	8
Bail Wood	E Yorks	TA2536	53°48·6′	0°5·7′W	F	107
Baily Bach	Powys	SO0139	52°2·7′	3°26·2′W	X	160
Baily Brith	Powys	SO0139	52°2·7′	3°26·2′W	X	160
Baily Glas Uchaf	Nth Pt Talb	SN7011	51°47·2′	3°52·7′W	X	160
Bailyhelig	Powys	SO0327	51°56·2′	3°24·3′W	X	160
Baily Mawr	Carm	SN2220	51°51·3′	4°34·7′W	X	145,158
Bain	Orkney	HY2517	59°2·3′	3°17·9′W	X	6
Bain	Orkney	HY2520	59°3·9′	3°18·0′W	X	6
Bainbridge	N Yks	SD9390	54°18·6′	2°6·0′W	T	98
Bainbridge Fm	Kent	TR0131	51°2·8′	0°52·4′E	FM	189
Bainbridge Gate	Cumbr	NY5325	54°37·3′	2°43·3′W	X	90
Bainbridge High Pasture	N Yks	SD9188	54°17·5′	2°7·9′W	X	98
Bainbridge Ings	N Yks	SD8889	54°18·0′	2°10·6′W	X	98
Bainbridge Low Pasture	N Yks	SD9189	54°18·0′	2°7·9′W	X	98
Baincraig	Fife	NO2312	56°17·9′	3°14·2′W	X	58
Baines Cragg	Lancs	SD5461	54°2·8′	2°41·7′W	X	97
Bainesse	N Yks	SE2497	54°22·3′	1°37·4′W	X	99
Baing	S Ayr	NS4001	55°16·9′	4°30·7′W	X	77
Baing Burn	S Ayr	NS4002	55°17·4′	4°30·8′W	W	77
Baing Loch	S Ayr	NS4102	55°17·4′	4°29·8′W	W	77
Bainley Hill Fm	Dorset	ST7727	51°2·7′	2°19·3′W	FM	183
Bainloch Hill	D & G	NX8957	54°54·0′	3°43·4′W	H	84
Bainly Bottom	Dorset	ST7727	51°2·7′	2°19·3′W	X	183
Bainsbank Fm	Cumbr	SD6184	54°15·3′	2°35·5′W	FM	97
Bain's Burn	S Lanak	NS7621	55°28·3′	3°57·3′W	W	71
Bainsford	Falk	NS8882	56°1·3′	3°47·4′W	T	65
Bainshole	Aberd	NJ6035	57°24·5′	2°39·5′W	T	29
Bain's Knowe	S Lanak	NS7822	55°28·9′	3°55·4′W	X	71
Bainstree Cross	Heref	SO4456	52°12·2′	2°48·8′W	X	148,149
Bainton	E Yorks	SE9652	53°57·5′	0°31·8′W	T	106
Bainton	Oxon	SP5826	51°56·0′	1°9·0′W	T	164
Bainton	Peterb	TF0906	52°38·7′	0°22·9′W	T	142
Bainton Balk Fm	E Yorks	SE9651	53°57·0′	0°31·8′W	FM	106
Bainton Burrows	E Yorks	SE9550	53°56·5′	0°32·7′W	X	106
Bainton Heights	E Yorks	SE9453	53°58·1′	0°33·6′W	X	106
Baintown	Fife	NO3503	56°13·2′	3°2·4′W	T	59
Bainwood Head	N Yks	SE7190	54°18·3′	0°54·1′W	X	94,100
Baird's Covert	Scot Bord	NT7958	55°49·1′	2°19·7′W	F	67,74
Bairnkine	Scot Bord	NT6515	55°25·9′	2°32·8′W	T	80
Baitings Pasture	Cald	SE0019	53°40·3′	1°59·6′W	X	110
Baitings Resr	Cald	SE0018	53°39·8′	1°59·6′W	W	110
Bait Island or St Mary's	N Tyne	NZ3575	55°4·3′	1°26·7′W	X	88
Baitlaw Fm	S Lanak	NT0240	55°38·9′	3°33·0′W	FM	72
Baitlaws	S Lanak	NS9830	55°33·4′	3°36·6′W	X	72
Baits Bite Lock	Cambs	TL4862	52°14·4′	0°10·5′E	X	154
Baitsrand	Northum	NT9554	55°47·0′	2°4·3′W	X	67,74,75
Baittens	Scot Bord	NT6823	55°30·2′	2°30·0′W	X	74
Bake	Corn	SX3258	50°24·1′	4°21·5′W	X	201
Bakebare	Moray	NJ3639	57°26·5′	3°3·5′W	X	28
Bake Barn	Wilts	ST9234	51°6·5′	2°6·5′W	X	184
Bake Fm	Corn	SX1854	50°21·7′	4°33·2′W	FM	201
Bake Fm	Wilts	SU1127	51°2·8′	1°50·2′W	FM	184
Bakerhill	Highld	NH5357	57°35·0′	4°27·1′W	X	26
Bake Rings	Corn	SX1854	50°21·7′	4°33·2′W	A	201
Baker's Br	Lincs	TF2842	52°57·8′	0°5·2′W	X	131
Baker's Br	Lincs	TF3645	52°59·3′	0°2·0′E	X	131
Baker's Brake	Devon	SY0687	50°40·7′	3°19·4′W	F	192
Baker's Cross	Dorset	SY3795	50°45·3′	2°53·2′W	X	193
Baker's Cross	Kent	TQ7835	51°5·4′	0°32·9′E	T	188
Bakers End	Herts	TL3916	51°49·7′	0°1·4′E	T	166
Baker's Fm	Essex	TL7530	51°56·7′	0°33·2′E	FM	167

Baker's Fm	Glos	SO9104	51°44·3'	2°7·4'W	FM	163
Baker's Fm	Hants	SU6457	51°18·7'	1°4·5'W	FM	175
Baker's Fm	Herts	TL1009	51°46·4'	0°23·9'W	FM	166
Bakers Fm	Herts	TL4614	51°48·6'	0°7·5'E	FM	167
Baker's Fm	Mil Key	SP8846	52°6·5'	0°42·5'W	FM	152
Baker's Fm	Somer	ST1812	50°54·3'	3°9·6'W	FM	181,193
Bakers Fm	W Susx	SZ8596	50°45·7'	0°47·3'W	FM	197
Baker's Fm	W Susx	TQ1323	50°59·9'	0°23·0'W	FM	198
Baker's Hall	Essex	TL8933	51°58·0'	0°45·5'E	X	168
Baker's Hanging	Dorset	SU1306	50°51·4'	1°48·5'W	X	195
Baker's Hill	Glos	SO5811	51°48·0'	2°36·2'W	T	162
Baker's Hill	Glos	SP1642	52°4·8'	1°45·6'W	X	151
Baker's Hill	Shrops	SJ2531	52°52·5'	3°6·5'W	H	126
Baker's Island	Hants	SU6903	50°49·6'	1°0·8'W	X	197
Bakers Mead	Devon	SY2498	50°46·8'	3°4·3'W	X	192,193
Baker's Mill	Dorset	ST4604	50°50·2'	2°45·6'W	X	193
Bakerstead	Cumbr	NY1502	54°24·6'	3°18·2'W	X	89
Baker Street	Thurr	TQ6381	51°30·5'	0°21·3'E	T	177
Baker's Wood	Bucks	TQ0287	51°34·6'	0°31·3'W	T	176
Baker's Wood	Surrey	TQ3440	51°8·8'	0°4·7'W	F	187
Baker Way	Ches	SJ4865	53°11·0'	2°46·3'W	X	117
Bakesdown	Corn	SS2400	50°46·6'	4°29·4'W	T	190
Bakesdown	Devon	SX7192	50°43·0'	3°49·3'W	X	191
Bakestall	Cumbr	NY2630	54°39·8'	3°8·4'W	X	89,90
Bakestonedale Moor	Ches	SJ9579	53°18·7'	2°4·1'W	X	118
Bakestone Moor	Derby	SK5276	53°16·9'	1°12·8'W	T	120
Bake, The	Wilts	ST9935	51°7·1'	2°0·5'W	X	184
Bakethin Reservoir	Northum	NY6391	55°13·0'	2°34·5'W	W	80
Bakewell	Derby	SK2168	53°12·8'	1°40·7'W	T	119
Bake Wood	Corn	SX3057	50°23·5'	4°23·1'W	F	201
Baki Ber	Orkney	HY5907	58°57·2'	2°42·3'W	X	6
Bakiebutts	C of Aber	NJ8314	57°13·2'	2°16·4'W	X	38
Bakie Skerry	Orkney	HY4441	59°15·4'	2°58·4'W	X	5
Bakingstone Hill	Orkney	ND2593	58°49·3'	3°17·4'W	H	7
Bakka	Shetld	HU1751	60°14·8'	1°41·1'W	X	3
Bakkasetter	Shetld	HU3715	59°55·4'	1°19·8'W	X	4
Bakka Skeo	Shetld	HU6299	60°40·4'	0°51·4'W	X	1
Bak, The	Shetld	HU2742	60°10·0'	1°30·3'W	X	4
Bala	Gwyn	SH9236	52°54·9'	3°36·0'W	T	125
Balaam's Heath	Shrops	SO5488	52°29·5'	2°40·3'W	X	137,138
Bala Brook	Devon	SX6762	50°26·8'	3°52·0'W	W	202
Balachailloch	Aberd	NJ3809	57°10·3'	3°1·1'W	X	37
Balach Rocks	Arg & Bt	NR3177	55°54·9'	6°17·9'W	X	60,61
Balachroick	Highld	NH8400	57°4·8'	3°54·4'W	X	35
Balachuirn	Highld	NG5540	57°23·3'	6°4·2'W	X	24
Balaclava	Orkney	HY4817	59°2·5'	2°53·9'W	X	6
Balaclava Bay	Dorset	SY6974	50°34·1'	2°25·9'W	W	194
Balaclava Fm	Norf	TF5523	52°47·2'	0°18·3'E	FM	131
Balado	Pth & Kin	NO0902	56°12·4'	3°27·6'W	X	58
Balado Ho	Pth & Kin	NO0802	56°12·4'	3°28·5'W	X	58
Balado Home Fm	Pth & Kin	NO0802	56°12·4'	3°28·5'W	FM	58
Balafark	Stir	NS6190	56°5·2'	4°13·6'W	X	57
Balagowan	Arg & Bt	NS1381	55°59·4'	4°59·4'W	X	63
Balak Fm	Wilts	SU2974	51°28·1'	1°34·6'W	FM	174
Bala Lake or Llyn Tegid	Gwyn	SH9033	52°53·2'	3°37·7'W	W	125
Bala Lake Railway or Rheilffordd Llyn Tegid	Gwyn	SH9133	52°53·2'	3°36·8'W	X	125
Balaldie	Highld	NH8779	57°47·4'	3°53·6'W	X	21
Balance Hill	Staffs	SK0832	52°53·4'	1°52·5'W	T	128
Balandro	Aberd	NO7967	56°47·9'	2°20·2'W	X	45
Balaneasie	Pth & Kin	NN9071	56°49·3'	3°47·7'W	X	43
Balanreich	Aberd	NO3496	57°3·3'	3°4·8'W	X	37,44
Balanton	Stir	NN5200	56°10·4'	4°22·6'W	X	57
Balantoul Burn	Highld	NH3611	57°9·9'	4°42·3'W	W	34
Balantrath	Highld	ND1430	58°15·3'	3°27·5'W	X	11,17
Balantsionnach	Highld	ND1252	58°27·1'	3°30·0'W	X	11,12
Balantyre Wood	Arg & Bt	NN0811	56°15·4'	5°5·5'W	F	50,56
Balarchibald	Pth & Kin	NN9453	56°39·7'	3°43·3'W	X	52,53
Balas	V of Glam	ST1274	51°27·7'	3°15·6'W	X	171
Balass	Fife	NO3914	56°19·1'	2°58·7'W	X	59
Balaton Lodge	Suff	TL6464	52°15·2'	0°24·6'E	X	154
Balavil	Highld	NH5453	57°32·9'	4°25·9'W	X	26
Balavil	Highld	NH7902	57°5·8'	3°59·4'W	T	35
Balavil Ho	Highld	NH5453	57°32·9'	4°25·9'W	X	26
Balavoulin	Highld	NG8419	57°12·9'	5°34·2'W	X	33
Balavoulin	Pth & Kin	NN8761	56°43·9'	3°50·4'W	X	43
Balavreed	Highld	ND1042	58°21·7'	3°31·8'W	X	11,12
Balavulich	Highld	NH5050	57°31·2'	4°29·8'W	X	26
Bal-bach	Monm	SO2726	51°55·9'	3°3·3'W	X	161
Balbaird	Fife	NO4305	56°14·3'	2°54·7'W	X	59
Balbedie	Fife	NT1999	56°10·9'	3°17·9'W	X	58
Balbeg	Highld	ND1653	58°27·7'	3°25·9'W	X	11,12
Balbeg	Highld	NH4531	57°20·9'	4°34·1'W	T	26
Balbeg	Highld	NH4924	57°17·2'	4°29·9'W	X	26
Balbeg	S Ayr	NS3802	55°17·4'	4°32·6'W	X	77
Balbeg Burn	S Ayr	NS3602	55°17·3'	4°34·5'W	W	77
Balbeggie	Pth & Kin	NO1629	56°27·0'	3°21·3'W	T	53,58
Balbegno Castle	Aberd	NO6373	56°51·1'	2°35·9'W	A	45
Balbeuchley Ho	Angus	NO3637	56°31·5'	3°2·0'W	X	54
Balbie Fm	Fife	NT2388	56°5·0'	3°13·8'W	FM	66
Balbinny	Angus	NO5256	56°41·9'	2°46·6'W	X	54
Balbirnie	Angus	NO2948	56°37·4'	3°9·0'W	X	53
Balbirnie Burns	Fife	NO2802	56°12·6'	3°9·2'W	X	59
Balbirnie Ho	Fife	NO2902	56°12·6'	3°8·2'W	X	59
Balbirnie Mill	Angus	NO6358	56°43·0'	2°35·8'W	X	54
Balbithan	Aberd	NJ7917	57°14·9'	2°20·4'W	X	38
Balbithan Ho	Aberd	NJ8118	57°15·4'	2°18·4'W	X	38
Balbithan Island	Aberd	NJ7916	57°14·3'	2°20·4'W	X	38
Balblair	Aberd	NJ7006	57°8·9'	2°29·3'W	T	38
Balblair	Highld	NH5045	57°28·5'	4°29·6'W	T	26
Balblair	Highld	NH5894	57°55·0'	4°23·4'W	X	21
Balblair	Highld	NH7066	57°40·2'	4°10·3'W	T	21,27
Balblair	Highld	NH7084	57°49·9'	4°10·9'W	X	21
Balblair	Highld	NH8051	57°32·3'	3°59·8'W	X	27
Balblair	Highld	NH8097	57°57·0'	4°1·2'W	X	21
Balblair	Highld	NH8277	57°46·3'	3°58·6'W	X	21
Balblair	Highld	NH8755	57°34·5'	3°52·9'W	X	27
Balblair Ho	Highld	NH5345	57°28·6'	4°26·6'W	X	26
Balblair Wood	Highld	NH5044	57°28·0'	4°29·6'W	F	26
Balblair Wood	Highld	NH5994	57°55·1'	4°22·3'W	F	21
Balblair Wood	Highld	NH8097	57°57·0'	4°1·2'W	F	21
Balblythe	Aberd	NO6391	57°0·8'	2°36·1'W	X	45
Balboughty	Pth & Kin	NO1227	56°25·9'	3°25·2'W	X	53,58
Balbougie	Fife	NT1484	56°2·7'	3°22·4'W	X	65
Balbridie	Aberd	NO7395	57°3·0'	2°26·2'W	X	38,45
Balbridie Plantn	Aberd	NO7395	57°3·0'	2°26·2'W	F	38,45
Balbrogie	Pth & Kin	NO2442	56°34·1'	3°13·8'W	X	53
Balbrydie	Angus	NO3654	56°40·7'	3°2·2'W	X	54
Balbuthie	Fife	NO5002	56°12·7'	2°47·9'W	T	59
Balby	Donc	SE5501	53°30·4'	1°9·8'W	T	111
Balby Carr Fm	Donc	SE5800	53°29·8'	1°7·1'W	FM	111
Balcairn	Aberd	NJ7828	57°20·8'	2°21·5'W	X	38
Balcalk	Angus	NO3939	56°32·6'	2°59·1'W	X	54
Balcamie	S Ayr	NS2701	55°16·6'	4°43·0'W	X	76
Balcanquhal	Fife	NO1609	56°16·2'	3°20·9'W	X	58
Balcarres Ho	Fife	NO4704	56°13·8'	2°50·9'W	A	59
Balcarres Mains	Fife	NO4804	56°13·8'	2°49·9'W	X	59
Balcarres Ward	Fife	NO4607	56°15·4'	2°51·9'W	X	59
Balcarry	D & G	NX2055	54°51·7'	4°47·9'W	X	82
Balcarse	Highld	NH5645	57°28·6'	4°23·6'W	X	26
Balcary Bay	D & G	NX8249	54°49·6'	3°49·8'W	W	84
Balcary Fishery	D & G	NX8250	54°50·1'	3°49·8'W	W	84
Balcary Hill	D & G	NX8249	54°49·6'	3°49·8'W	H	84
Balcary Point	D & G	NX8249	54°49·6'	3°49·8'W	X	84
Balcaskie Ho	Fife	NO5203	56°13·3'	2°46·0'W	X	59
Balcastle Fm	N Lanak	NS7078	55°58·9'	4°4·6'W	FM	64
Balcastle Ho	Falk	NS8572	55°55·9'	3°50·0'W	X	65
Balcathie	Angus	NO6039	56°32·7'	2°38·6'W	T	54
Balchalum	Pth & Kin	NO2325	56°24·9'	3°14·4'W	X	53,58
Balchandy	Pth & Kin	NN9655	56°40·8'	3°41·4'W	X	52,53
Balcharn	Highld	NC5906	58°1·5'	4°22·8'W	X	16
Balcherry	Highld	NH8282	57°49·0'	3°58·7'W	X	21
Balchers	Aberd	NJ7158	57°36·9'	2°28·7'W	X	29
Balchimmy	Aberd	NJ5111	57°11·5'	2°48·2'W	X	37
Balchladich	Highld	NC0330	58°13·2'	5°20·8'W	T	15
Balchladich Bay	Highld	NC0230	58°13·1'	5°21·8'W	W	15
Balchraggan	Highld	NH5030	57°20·4'	4°29·1'W	X	26
Balchraggan	Highld	NH5343	57°27·5'	4°26·6'W	T	26
Balchraggan	Highld	NH5425	57°17·8'	4°24·9'W	X	26,35
Balchraggan	Highld	NH5634	57°22·7'	4°23·2'W	T	26
Balchrick	Highld	NC1959	58°29·2'	5°5·8'W	T	9
Balchriston	S Ayr	NS2411	55°21·9'	4°46·2'W	X	70
Balchrochan	Pth & Kin	NO0759	56°43·1'	3°30·7'W	X	52,53
Balchroich	Pth & Kin	NN7749	56°37·3'	3°59·8'W	X	51,52
Balchrystie	Fife	NO4503	56°13·2'	2°52·8'W	X	59
Balchuirn	Highld	NH5425	57°17·8'	4°24·9'W	X	26,35
Balcladaich	Highld	NH2926	57°17·8'	4°49·8'W	X	25
Balcladich	Highld	ND1529	58°14·8'	3°26·4'W	X	11,17
Balclaggan	Highld	NC7304	58°0·7'	4°8·5'W	X	16
Balcletchie	S Ayr	NX2496	55°13·9'	4°45·6'W	X	76
Balcnock	Arg & Bt	NS3090	56°4·6'	4°43·5'W	X	56
Balcombe	W Susx	TQ3130	51°3·5'	0°7·5'W	T	187
Balcombe Forest	W Susx	TQ2932	51°4·6'	0°9·1'W	F	187
Balcombe Ho	W Susx	TQ3030	51°3·5'	0°8·3'W	X	187
Balcombe Lane	W Susx	TQ3132	51°4·6'	0°7·4'W	T	187
Balcombe Place	W Susx	TQ3229	51°2·9'	0°6·6'W	X	187,198
Balcomie	Fife	NO6209	56°16·6'	2°36·4'W	X	59
Balconie Point	Highld	NH6265	57°39·5'	4°18·3'W	X	21
Balconnel	Angus	NO5263	56°45·6'	2°46·7'W	X	44
Balcormo	Fife	NO4105	56°14·3'	2°56·7'W	X	59
Balcormo Fm	Fife	NO5104	56°13·8'	2°47·0'W	FM	59
Balcormo Mains	Fife	NO4005	56°14·3'	2°57·6'W	X	59
Balcorrach	E Dunb	NS6178	55°58·7'	4°13·2'W	X	64
Balcraggie Lodge	Highld	ND1430	58°15·3'	3°27·5'W	X	11,17
Balcraig	Pth & Kin	NO1525	56°24·8'	3°22·2'W	X	53,58
Balcraig Moor	D & G	NX3745	54°46·7'	4°31·6'W	X	83
Balcray Plantn	D & G	NX4538	54°43·0'	4°24·0'W	F	83
Balcreuchan Burn	S Ayr	NX1187	55°8·7'	4°57·5'W	W	76
Balcreuchan Port	S Ayr	NX0987	55°8·7'	4°59·4'W	W	76
Balculchaich	Highld	NH8749	57°31·3'	3°52·7'W	X	27
Balcurvie	Fife	NO3400	56°11·5'	3°3·4'W	T	59
Balcurvie Ho	Fife	NO3401	56°12·1'	3°3·4'W	X	59
Baldardo	Angus	NO5053	56°40·2'	2°48·5'W	X	54
Baldarroch	Aberd	NO7496	57°3·5'	2°25·3'W	X	38,45
Baldarroch	Pth & Kin	NO1038	56°31·8'	3°27·3'W	X	53
Baldarroch Fm	Pth & Kin	NO1138	56°31·8'	3°26·4'W	FM	53
Baldastard	Fife	NO4106	56°14·8'	2°56·7'W	X	59
Baldastard Mains	Fife	NO4107	56°15·4'	2°56·7'W	X	59
Baldcar Head	N Yks	SE1279	54°12·6'	1°48·5'W	X	99
Balder Beck	Durham	NY8716	54°32·6'	2°11·6'W	W	91,92
Balderfield	Notts	SK8349	53°2·1'	0°45·3'W	X	130
Balder Grange	Durham	NZ0019	54°34·2'	1°59·6'W	X	92
Balder Head	Durham	NY9018	54°33·7'	2°8·9'W	X	91,92
Balderhead Reservoir	Durham	NY9118	54°33·7'	2°7·9'W	W	91,92
Baldernock	E Dunb	NS5775	55°57·1'	4°17·0'W	X	64
Baldersbury Hill	Northum	NT9553	55°46·5'	2°4·3'W	X	67,74,75
Baldersby	N Yks	SE3578	54°12·0'	1°27·4'W	T	99
Baldersby Park	N Yks	SE3876	54°10·9'	1°24·6'W	X	99
Baldersby St James	N Yks	SE3676	54°11·0'	1°26·5'W	T	99
Baldersdale	Durham	NY9418	54°33·7'	2°5·1'W	X	91,92
Balderston	Falk	NS9978	55°59·3'	3°36·7'W	X	65
Balderstone	Lancs	SD6332	53°47·2'	2°33·3'W	T	102,103
Balderstone	Roch	SD9011	53°36·0'	2°8·7'W	T	109
Balderstone Hall	Lancs	SD6133	53°47·8'	2°35·1'W	X	102,103
Balderstones	Lancs	SD5555	53°59·6'	2°40·8'W	X	102
Balderston Plantn	Scot Bord	NY4797	55°16·1'	2°49·6'W	F	79
Balderton	Ches	SJ3762	53°9·3'	2°56·1'W	T	117
Balderton	Notts	SK8151	53°3·2'	0°47·1'W	T	121
Balderton Grange	Notts	SK8048	53°1·6'	0°48·0'W	X	130
Balderton Hall	Shrops	SJ4823	52°48·4'	2°45·9'W	X	126
Baldfields Fm	Derby	SK2533	52°53·9'	1°37·3'W	FM	128
Bald Hill	Devon	SY1292	50°43·5'	3°14·4'W	X	192,193
Bald Hill	Oxon	SU7296	51°39·7'	0°57·1'W	X	165
Bald Hill	Pth & Kin	NN9303	56°12·7'	3°43·1'W	X	58
Baldhill	Scot Bord	NT3211	55°23·5'	3°4·0'W	X	79
Bald Hill	Scot Bord	NT3310	55°23·0'	3°3·0'W	H	79
Bald Hill's Fm	Derby	SK2511	52°42·0'	1°37·4'W	FM	128
Baldhoon	I of M	SC4184	54°13·9'	4°25·9'W	T	95
Baldhorns Park	W Susx	TQ2036	51°6·9'	0°16·7'W	X	187
Bald Howe	Cumbr	NY4023	54°36·2'	2°55·3'W	X	90
Baldhu	Corn	SW7742	50°14·4'	5°7·3'W	T	204
Baldingstone	Bury	SD8014	53°37·6'	2°17·7'W	T	109
Baldinnie	Fife	NO4211	56°17·5'	2°55·8'W	T	59
Baldinnies	Pth & Kin	NO0216	56°19·8'	3°34·7'W	X	58
Baldinny	Pth & Kin	NO2438	56°31·9'	3°13·7'W	X	53
Baldmire	Cumbr	SD1381	54°13·3'	3°19·6'W	X	96
Baldock	Herts	TL2433	51°59·1'	0°11·3'W	T	166
Baldock	Herts	TL2434	51°59·7'	0°11·2'W	T	153
Baldon Brook	Oxon	SU5798	51°40·9'	1°10·1'W	W	164
Baldon Hill	Oxon	SU5485	51°33·9'	1°12·9'W	X	174
Baldon Ho	Oxon	SU5699	51°41·4'	1°11·0'W	X	164
Baldon Row	Oxon	SP5600	51°42·0'	1°11·0'W	T	164
Baldoon	Highld	NH6275	57°44·9'	4°18·7'W	X	21
Baldoon Mains	D & G	NX4253	54°51·1'	4°27·2'W	X	83
Baldoon Sands	D & G	NX4552	54°50·6'	4°24·4'W	X	83
Baldoukie	Angus	NO4658	56°42·9'	2°52·5'W	X	54
Baldovan Ho	Angus	NO3934	56°29·9'	2°59·0'W	X	54
Baldovie	Angus	NO3254	56°40·6'	3°6·1'W	X	53
Baldovie	C of Dun	NO4533	56°29·4'	2°53·1'W	T	54
Baldow	E Dunb	NS6177	55°58·2'	4°13·2'W	X	64
Baldow	Highld	NH8306	57°8·1'	3°55·5'W	X	35
Baldowrie	Pth & Kin	NO2639	56°32·5'	3°11·8'W	X	53
Baldragon	C of Dun	NO3734	56°29·9'	3°1·0'W	X	54
Baldrence	N Yks	SE5171	54°8·2'	1°12·7'W	X	100
Baldrine	I of M	SC4281	54°12·3'	4°24·9'W	T	95
Baldromma	I of M	SC4279	54°11·2'	4°24·9'W	X	95
Baldromma Beg	I of M	SC4891	54°17·8'	4°19·7'W	X	95
Baldromma Fm	I of M	SC4295	54°19·8'	4°25·4'W	FM	95
Baldruim Wood	Highld	NH7287	57°51·5'	4°9·0'W	F	21
Baldslow	E Susx	TQ7913	50°53·5'	0°33·1'E	T	199
Balduff Hill	Pth & Kin	NO2253	56°40·0'	3°15·9'W	H	53
Baldwin	I of M	SC3581	54°12·1'	4°31·4'W	T	95
Baldwinholme	Cumbr	NY3351	54°51·2'	3°2·2'W	T	85
Baldwin River	I of M	SC3581	54°12·1'	4°31·4'W	W	95
Baldwin's Fm	Essex	TL8725	51°53·8'	0°43·5'E	FM	168
Baldwin's Fm	E Susx	TQ7220	50°57·4'	0°27·3'E	FM	199
Baldwins Fm	Thurr	TQ5783	51°31·7'	0°16·2'E	FM	177
Baldwin's Gate	Staffs	SJ7939	52°57·1'	2°18·4'W	T	127
Baldwins Hill	W Susx	TQ3839	51°8·2'	0°1·3'W	T	187
Baldwin's Wood	Herts	TQ0199	51°41·1'	0°31·9'W	F	166,176
Baldyquash	Aberd	NJ7033	57°23·4'	2°29·5'W	X	29
Baldyvin	Aberd	NJ5917	57°14·8'	2°40·3'W	X	37
Bale	Norf	TG0136	52°53·3'	0°59·7'E	T	133
Balearn	Aberd	NK0254	57°34·8'	1°57·5'W	X	30
Baleave	Pth & Kin	NO1101	56°11·9'	3°25·6'W	X	58
Baledgarno	Pth & Kin	NO2730	56°27·6'	3°10·6'W	X	53
Baledmund	Pth & Kin	NN9459	56°42·9'	3°43·5'W	X	52,53
Baledmund	Pth & Kin	NO0051	56°38·7'	3°37·4'W	X	52,53
Bale Hall	Norf	TG0037	52°53·8'	0°58·8'E	A	133
Bale Hill	Cumbr	NY7715	54°32·0'	2°20·9'W	X	91
Balehill Ho	Durham	NY9549	54°50·4'	2°4·2'W	X	87
Baleloch	N Eil	NF7273	57°37·9'	7°29·3'W	X	18
Balelone	N Eil	NF7273	57°37·9'	7°29·3'W	X	18
Balemartine	Arg & Bt	NL9841	56°28·1'	6°53·8'W	T	46
Balemore	N Eil	NF7367	57°34·7'	7°27·8'W	T	18
Balendoch	Pth & Kin	NO2847	56°36·8'	3°9·9'W	X	53
Bale New Plantn	N Yks	SD8849	53°56·5'	2°10·6'W	F	103
Balephetrish	Arg & Bt	NM0046	56°30·9'	6°52·2'W	T	46
Balephetrish Bay	Arg & Bt	NM0047	56°31·4'	6°52·3'W	W	46
Balephetrish Hill	Arg & Bt	NM0147	56°31·5'	6°51·3'W	H	46
Balephuil	Arg & Bt	NL9540	56°27·5'	6°56·6'W	T	46
Balephuil Bay	Arg & Bt	NL9440	56°27·4'	6°57·6'W	W	46
Balerno	C of Edin	NT1666	55°53·0'	3°20·1'W	T	65,66
Baleromindubh Glac Mhór	Arg & Bt	NR3892	56°3·2'	6°12·0'W	T	61
Balerominmore	Arg & Bt	NR3891	56°2·7'	6°12·0'W	X	61
Bale's Ash	Devon	SS6019	50°57·4'	3°59·2'W	X	180
Baleshare	N Eil	NF7863	57°32·8'	7°22·5'W	X	18
Baleshare or Baile Sear	N Eil	NF7860	57°31·2'	7°22·3'W	X	22
Bales Ho	N Yks	SE1682	54°14·2'	1°44·9'W	X	99
Bales Plantn	N Yks	SE1681	54°13·7'	1°44·9'W	F	99
Balevulin	Arg & Bt	NM4829	56°23·4'	6°4·5'W	X	48
Balevullin	Arg & Bt	NL9546	56°30·7'	6°57·1'W	T	46
Bale Water	Somer	SS7539	51°8·4'	3°46·8'W	W	180
Baley Fm	Aberd	NJ6062	57°39·0'	2°39·8'W	FM	29
Baley Hill	Derby	SK1454	53°5·2'	1°47·1'W	X	119
Balfarg	Fife	NO2803	56°13·1'	3°9·2'W	X	59
Balfeith	Aberd	NO7576	56°52·7'	2°24·2'W	X	45
Balfiddy	Aberd	NO6193	57°1·8'	2°38·1'W	X	37,45
Balfield	Angus	NO5468	56°48·3'	2°44·7'W	T	44
Balfluig Castle	Aberd	NJ5815	57°13·7'	2°41·3'W	A	37
Balforbes	Aberd	NJ6116	57°14·2'	2°38·3'W	X	37
Balfour	Aberd	NO5596	57°3·4'	2°44·1'W	X	37,44
Balfour	Aberd	NO7896	57°3·5'	2°21·3'W	X	38,45
Balfour	Angus	NO5364	56°46·2'	2°45·7'W	X	44
Balfour	Fife	NO3200	56°11·5'	3°5·3'W	A	59
Balfour	Orkney	HY4716	59°1·9'	2°54·9'W	T	6
Balfour Castle	Angus	NO3354	56°40·6'	3°5·2'W	A	53
Balfour Castle	Orkney	HY4716	59°1·9'	2°54·9'W	X	6
Balfour Mains	Angus	NO3354	56°40·6'	3°5·2'W	X	53
Balfour Mains	Fife	NT3299	56°11·0'	3°5·3'W	X	59
Balfour Mains	Orkney	HY4717	59°2·5'	2°54·9'W	X	6
Balfour's Wood	Dorset	ST8916	50°56·8'	2°9·0'W	F	184
Balfreish	Highld	NH7947	57°30·1'	4°0·7'W	X	27
Balfron	Stir	NS5488	56°4·0'	4°20·3'W	T	57
Balfron Station	Stir	NS5289	56°4·5'	4°22·2'W	T	57
Balfunning Ho	Stir	NS5189	56°4·5'	4°23·2'W	X	57
Balgaidh Burn	Arg & Bt	NS1476	55°56·7'	4°58·3'W	W	63
Balgair Muir	Stir	NS6090	56°5·2'	4°14·6'W	X	57
Balgarrock	Angus	NO5157	56°42·4'	2°47·6'W	X	54
Balgarthno	C of Dun	NO3431	56°28·2'	3°3·8'W	X	54
Balgarvie	Pth & Kin	NO1426	56°25·4'	3°23·2'W	X	53,58
Balgate	Highld	NH5041	57°26·3'	4°29·5'W	X	26
Balgaveny	Aberd	NJ6540	57°27·2'	2°34·5'W	T	29
Balgaverie	S Ayr	NX2397	55°14·4'	4°46·6'W	X	76
Balgavies House	Angus	NO5451	56°39·2'	2°44·6'W	X	54
Balgavies Loch	Angus	NO5350	56°38·6'	2°45·5'W	W	54
Balgay	Pth & Kin	NO2727	56°26·0'	3°10·6'W	X	53,59
Balgay Hill	C of Dun	NO3731	56°28·3'	3°0·9'W	H	54
Balgeddie	Fife	NO2502	56°12·5'	3°12·1'W	X	59
Balgerran	D & G	NX7468	54°59·7'	3°57·7'W	X	83,84

Balgersho	Pth & Kin	NO2238	56°31·9'	3°15·6'W	X	53
Balgholan Craig	Pth & Kin	NN9963	56°45·1'	3°38·7'W	X	43
Balgibbon	Stir	NN6407	56°14·4'	4°11·2'W	X	57
Balgillie Resr	Fife	NO2303	56°13·1'	3°14·1'W	W	58
Balglass Burn	Stir	NS5886	56°3·0'	4°16·4'W	W	57
Balglassie	Angus	NO5357	56°42·4'	2°45·6'W	X	54
Balgonar	Fife	NT0293	56°7·4'	3°34·1'W	T	58
Balgone Barns	E Loth	NT5582	56°2·0'	2°42·9'W	X	66
Balgone Ho	E Loth	NT5682	56°2·0'	2°41·9'W	X	67
Balgonie	Pth & Kin	NO1917	56°20·6'	3°18·2'W	X	58
Balgonie Cott	Fife	NO3000	56°11·5'	3°7·2'W	X	59
Balgonie South Parks	Fife	NT3199	56°11·0'	3°6·3'W	X	59
Balgornie	W Loth	NS9365	55°52·2'	3°42·2'W	X	65
Balgothrie	Fife	NO2304	56°13·6'	3°14·1'W	X	58
Balgove	Aberd	NJ8133	57°23·5'	2°18·5'W	X	29,30
Balgove	Fife	NO4817	56°20·8'	2°50·0'W	X	59
Balgove	Pth & Kin	NO2437	56°31·4'	3°13·7'W	X	53
Balgowan	D & G	NX1143	54°45·0'	4°55·8'W	X	82
Balgowan	Highld	NN6394	57°1·3'	4°14·9'W	T	35
Balgowan	N Ayr	NR9129	55°30·9'	5°18·2'W	X	68,69
Balgowan	Pth & Kin	NN9755	56°40·8'	3°40·4'W	X	52,53
Balgowan	Pth & Kin	NN9922	56°23·0'	3°37·7'W	X	52,58
Balgowan Home Farm	Pth & Kin	NN9823	56°23·6'	3°38·7'W	FM	52,53,58
Balgowan Point	D & G	NX1242	54°44·5'	4°54·8'W	X	82
Balgown	D & G	NX0069	54°58·8'	5°7·1'W	X	82
Balgown	Highld	NG3438	57°21·6'	6°24·9'W	T	23,32
Balgown	Highld	NG3868	57°37·8'	6°22·9'W	T	23
Balgownie	Angus	NO3546	56°36·3'	3°3·1'W	X	54
Balgownie Links	C of Aber	NJ9512	57°12·2'	2°4·5'W	X	38
Balgownie Mains	Fife	NS9888	56°4·7'	3°37·9'W	X	65
Balgownie Muir Plantation	Angus	NO3545	56°35·8'	3°3·1'W	F	54
Balgown Moss	D & G	NX0068	54°58·2'	5°7·1'W	X	82
Balgracie	D & G	NW9860	54°53·9'	5°8·6'W	X	82
Balgray	N Ayr	NS2953	55°44·7'	4°43·0'W	X	63
Balgray	Pth & Kin	NO1730	56°27·5'	3°20·4'W	X	53
Balgray	S Lanak	NS8824	55°30·1'	3°46·0'W	X	71,72
Balgrayhill	D & G	NY1586	55°9·9'	3°19·6'W	X	79
Balgray Ho	D & G	NY1486	55°9·9'	3°20·6'W	X	78
Balgray Home Fm	D & G	NY1486	55°9·9'	3°20·6'W	FM	78
Balgray Mill	E Ayr	NS4545	55°40·7'	4°27·5'W	X	64
Balgray Resr	E Renf	NS5157	55°47·3'	4°22·1'W	W	64
Balgreddan	D & G	NX7251	54°50·5'	3°59·2'W	X	83,84
Balgreddan Burn	D & G	NX7252	54°51·0'	3°59·2'W	W	83,84
Balgreen	Aberd	NJ7458	57°36·9'	2°25·7'W	X	29
Balgreen	E Ayr	NS3814	55°23·8'	4°33·1'W	X	70
Balgreen	Moray	NJ2070	57°43·0'	3°20·1'W	X	28
Balgreen	Renf	NS3560	55°48·6'	4°37·5'W	X	63
Balgreen	W Loth	NT0563	55°51·3'	3°30·6'W	X	65
Balgreggan	D & G	NX0850	54°48·7'	4°58·9'W	X	82
Balgreggan	S Ayr	NS3504	55°18·4'	4°35·5'W	X	77
Balgreggie Fm	Fife	NT2296	56°9·3'	3°14·9'W	FM	58
Balgrennie	Aberd	NJ4005	57°8·2'	2°59·0'W	X	37
Balgriebank	Fife	NO3504	56°13·7'	3°2·5'W	X	59
Balgrochan	E Dunb	NS6174	55°56·6'	4°13·1'W	X	64
Balgrochan	E Dunb	NS6278	55°58·8'	4°12·3'W	T	64
Balgrummo	Fife	NO3703	56°13·2'	3°0·5'W	X	59
Balgunearie	Highld	NH6149	57°30·9'	4°18·8'W	T	26
Balgunloune	Highld	NH6248	57°30·3'	4°17·7'W	T	26
Balgy	Highld	NG8454	57°31·7'	5°36·0'W	X	24
Balhalach	Aberd	NO3396	57°3·3'	3°5·8'W	X	37,44
Balhaldie	Stir	NN8105	56°13·6'	3°54·7'W	X	57
Balhalgardy	Aberd	NJ7623	57°18·1'	2°23·4'W	T	38
Balhall Lodge	Angus	NO5164	56°46·2'	2°47·7'W	X	44
Balham	Wan	TQ2873	51°26·7'	0°9·1'W	T	176
Balham Hill	Somer	ST4614	50°55·6'	2°45·7'W	X	193
Balham House Fm	Suff	TM1152	52°7·8'	1°5·4'E	FM	155
Balhamie Hill	S Ayr	NX1386	55°8·2'	4°55·6'W	H	76
Balhams Farm Ho	Oxon	SU7389	51°35·9'	0°56·4'W	X	175
Balham's Wood	Oxon	SU7489	51°35·9'	0°55·5'W	F	175
Balharvie Moss	Fife	NO2106	56°14·7'	3°16·0'W	X	58
Balhary	Pth & Kin	NO2646	56°36·3'	3°11·9'W	X	53
Balhearty	Clackm	NS9395	56°8·4'	3°42·9'W	X	58
Balhelvie	Fife	NO3021	56°22·8'	3°7·6'W	X	53,59
Balhennie	Aberd	NJ4004	57°7·6'	2°59·0'W	X	37
Balhepburn	Pth & Kin	NO1720	56°22·2'	3°20·2'W	X	53,58
Balhill	Pth & Kin	NO1830	56°27·6'	3°19·4'W	X	53
Balholmie	Pth & Kin	NO1436	56°30·7'	3°23·4'W	X	53
Balhomais	Pth & Kin	NN8249	56°37·3'	3°54·9'W	X	52
Balhomish	Pth & Kin	NO0140	56°32·8'	3°36·2'W	X	52,53
Balhouffie	Fife	NO5506	56°14·9'	2°43·1'W	X	59
Balhousie	Angus	NO5736	56°31·1'	2°41·5'W	X	54
Balhousie	Fife	NO4206	56°14·8'	2°55·7'W	X	59
Balhungie	Angus	NO5134	56°30·0'	2°47·3'W	X	54
Baliasta	Shetld	HP6009	60°45·8'	0°53·4'W	T	1
Balig	D & G	NX7146	54°47·8'	4°0·0'W	X	83,84
Balig	S Ayr	NS3017	55°25·3'	4°40·7'W	X	70
Balig Fm	S Ayr	NX0983	55°6·5'	4°59·2'W	FM	76
Balig Hill	D & G	NX7145	54°47·3'	3°59·9'W	H	83,84
Baligill	Highld	NC8565	58°33·7'	3°58·1'W	X	10
Baligill Burn	Highld	NC8564	58°33·2'	3°58·1'W	W	10
Baligortan	Arg & Bt	NM3841	56°29·6'	6°15·0'W	X	47,48
Baligrundle	Arg & Bt	NM8340	56°30·4'	5°31·1'W	T	49
Balimeanach	Pth & Kin	NN6322	56°22·5'	4°12·7'W	X	51
Balimore	Arg & Bt	NR7074	55°54·5'	5°40·4'W	T	61,62
Balinakill	Arg & Bt	NR7756	55°45·0'	5°32·8'W	X	62
Balindore	Arg & Bt	NM9830	56°25·4'	5°16·1'W	X	49
Balindrum	Highld	NH8477	57°46·3'	3°56·5'W	X	21
Balinoe	Arg & Bt	NL9742	56°28·6'	6°54·8'W	T	46
Balinoe	Arg & Bt	NM8724	56°21·9'	5°26·5'W	X	49
Balinoe	Highld	NH5893	57°54·5'	4°23·3'W	X	21
Balinroich	Highld	NH8176	57°45·7'	3°59·5'W	X	21
Balintombuie	Highld	NH2812	57°10·3'	4°50·2'W	X	34
Balintore	Angus	NO2859	56°43·3'	3°10·1'W	T	53
Balintore	Highld	NH8675	57°45·3'	3°54·5'W	T	21
Balintore Castle	Angus	NO2859	56°43·3'	3°10·1'W	X	53
Balintore Fm	Highld	NH8676	57°45·8'	3°54·5'W	FM	21
Balintraid	Highld	NH7370	57°42·4'	4°7·4'W	T	21
Balintraid Pier	Highld	NH7471	57°42·9'	4°6·4'W	X	21
Balintuim	Aberd	NO1589	56°59·3'	3°23·5'W	X	43
Balintyre	Pth & Kin	NN6847	56°36·0'	4°8·6'W	X	51

Baliscate	Arg & Bt	NM5054	56°36·9'	6°4·0'W	X	47
Baljean	I of M	SC4284	54°13·9'	4°25·0'W	X	95
Balkaithly	Fife	NO5411	56°17·6'	2°44·1'W	X	59
Balkeachy	S Ayr	NX1893	55°12·1'	4°51·2'W	X	76
Balkeerie	Angus	NO3244	56°35·2'	3°6·0'W	T	53
Balkello	Angus	NO3637	56°31·5'	3°2·0'W	X	54
Balkemback	Angus	NO3938	56°32·1'	2°59·1'W	X	54
Balkenna Isle	S Ayr	NS1904	55°18·1'	4°50·6'W	X	76
Balker	D & G	NX1063	54°55·8'	4°57·5'W	X	82
Balker Moor	D & G	NX1164	54°56·3'	4°56·6'W	X	82
Balker Wood	D & G	NX1063	54°55·8'	4°57·5'W	F	82
Balk Field	Notts	SK7181	53°19·5'	0°55·6'W	T	120
Balk Grange	N Yks	SE4779	54°12·5'	1°16·3'W	X	100
Balkholme	E Yorks	SE7827	53°44·3'	0°48·6'W	T	105,106
Balkholme Common	E Yorks	SE7928	53°44·8'	0°47·7'W	X	105,106
Balkiellie	Angus	NO7054	56°40·9'	2°28·9'W	T	54
Balkissock	S Ayr	NX1381	55°5·5'	4°55·4'W	X	76
Balkissock Hill	S Ayr	NX1380	55°5·0'	4°55·4'W	X	76
Balk, The	Corn	SW7112	49°58·1'	5°11·2'W	X	203
Balk Wood Fm	N Yks	SE4881	54°13·6'	1°15·4'W	FM	100
Ball	Corn	SX0073	50°31·6'	4°48·9'W	T	200
Ball	Shrops	SJ3026	52°49·9'	3°1·9'W	T	126
Balla	N Eil	NF7811	57°4·9'	7°18·5'W	T	31
Ballabane	I of M	NX4201	54°23·1'	4°25·6'W	X	95
Ballabeg	I of M	SC2470	54°6·0'	4°41·1'W	T	95
Ballabeg	I of M	SC2671	54°6·6'	4°39·3'W	X	95
Ballabeg	I of M	SC4098	54°21·4'	4°27·3'W	X	95
Ballabeg	I of M	SC4282	54°12·8'	4°25·0'W	T	95
Ballabeg	Stir	NN6001	56°11·1'	4°14·9'W	X	57
Ballabeg Sta	I of M	SC2569	54°5·5'	4°40·1'W	X	95
Ballabrooie	I of M	SC2681	54°12·0'	4°39·6'W	X	95
Ballabunt	I of M	SC3376	54°9·4'	4°33·0'W	X	95
Ballacain	I of M	SC2177	54°9·7'	4°44·1'W	X	95
Ballacain	I of M	SC3597	54°20·8'	4°31·9'W	X	95
Ballacaley	I of M	SC3793	54°18·6'	4°29·9'W	X	95
Ballacallin	I of M	SC2481	54°11·9'	4°41·5'W	X	95
Ballacallin Mooar	I of M	SC3176	54°9·4'	4°34·9'W	X	95
Ballacannell	I of M	SC2272	54°7·0'	4°43·0'W	X	95
Ballacannell	I of M	SC2573	54°7·6'	4°40·3'W	X	95
Ballacannell	I of M	SC4382	54°12·8'	4°24·0'W	T	95
Ballacarnane Beg	I of M	SC3088	54°15·8'	4°36·2'W	T	95
Ballacarrooin	I of M	SC4082	54°12·8'	4°26·8'W	X	95
Ballacashin	I of M	SC3781	54°12·2'	4°29·5'W	X	95
Ballachallan	Pth & Kin	NN9951	56°38·7'	3°38·4'W	X	52,53
Ballachar	Highld	NH6128	57°19·5'	4°18·1'W	X	26,35
Ballacharney	I of M	SC2779	54°10·9'	4°38·6'W	X	95
Ballacharry	I of M	SC2873	54°7·7'	4°37·5'W	X	95
Ballach Cottage	Highld	NC8837	58°18·7'	3°54·2'W	X	17
Ballachladdich	Highld	NH5964	57°38·9'	4°21·3'W	X	21
Ballachlaggan	Aberd	NO2293	57°1·6'	3°16·6'W	X	36,44
Ballachlaven	Arg & Bt	NR3767	55°49·7'	6°11·5'W	X	60,61
Ballachly	Highld	ND1530	58°15·3'	3°26·4'W	X	11,17
Ballachly	Highld	ND1944	58°22·9'	3°22·6'W	X	11,12
Ballachnecore	Highld	NH4856	57°34·4'	4°32·0'W	X	26
Ballachraggan	Highld	NH6468	57°41·1'	4°16·4'W	X	21
Ballachraggan	Moray	NJ1349	57°31·6'	3°26·7'W	X	28
Ballachraggan	Pth & Kin	NN9338	56°31·6'	3°43·9'W	X	52
Ballachraggan	Pth & Kin	NN9953	56°39·7'	3°38·3'W	X	52,53
Ballachraggan	Pth & Kin	NO1259	56°43·1'	3°25·8'W	X	53
Ballachraggan	Stir	NN6706	56°13·9'	4°8·3'W	X	57
Ballachrask	Highld	NH4944	57°27·9'	4°30·6'W	X	26
Ballachrine	I of M	SC3070	54°6·1'	4°35·6'W	X	95
Ballachrink	I of M	SC2371	54°6·5'	4°42·0'W	X	95
Ballachrink	I of M	SC2379	54°10·8'	4°42·3'W	X	95
Ballachrink	I of M	SC2782	54°12·5'	4°38·8'W	X	95
Ballachrink	I of M	SC2972	54°7·2'	4°36·6'W	X	95
Ballachrink	I of M	SC3076	54°9·4'	4°35·8'W	X	95
Ballachrink	I of M	SC3580	54°11·6'	4°31·3'W	X	95
Ballachrink	I of M	SC3682	54°12·7'	4°30·5'W	X	95
Ballachrink	I of M	SC3979	54°11·1'	4°27·6'W	X	95
Ballachrink	I of M	SC3999	54°21·9'	4°28·2'W	X	95
Ballachrink	I of M	SC4499	54°22·0'	4°23·7'W	T	95
Ballachrink Fm	I of M	SC3171	54°6·7'	4°34·7'W	FM	95
Ballachristory	I of M	SC3899	54°21·9'	4°29·2'W	X	95
Ballachroan	Highld	NH7300	57°4·7'	4°5·3'W	X	35
Ballachrochin	Highld	NH8436	57°24·2'	3°55·4'W	X	27
Ballachrosk	Aberd	NO3498	57°4·4'	3°4·9'W	X	37,44
Ballachuan Fm	Arg & Bt	NM7514	56°16·2'	5°37·6'W	FM	55
Ballachuan Loch	Arg & Bt	NM7615	56°16·7'	5°36·7'W	W	55
Ballachule	Highld	NJ0927	57°19·7'	3°30·2'W	X	36
Ballachulish	Highld	NN0858	56°40·7'	5°7·6'W	T	41
Ballachulish Ho	Highld	NN0459	56°41·2'	5°11·6'W	X	41
Ballachurry	I of M	SC2069	54°5·4'	4°44·7'W	X	95
Ballachurry	I of M	SC3172	54°7·2'	4°34·7'W	X	95
Ballachurry	I of M	SC4096	54°20·3'	4°27·3'W	X	95
Ballachurry Fm	I of M	SC4197	54°20·9'	4°26·4'W	FM	95
Ballaclague	I of M	SC2470	54°6·0'	4°41·1'W	X	95
Ballacleator	I of M	SC3997	54°20·8'	4°28·2'W	X	95
Ballaclucas	I of M	NX3800	54°22·4'	4°29·2'W	X	95
Ballacoar	I of M	SC4182	54°12·8'	4°25·9'W	X	95
Ballacoine	I of M	SC3288	54°15·9'	4°34·4'W	X	95
Ballacomish	I of M	SC2471	54°6·5'	4°41·1'W	X	95
Ballacondra	I of M	NX4502	54°23·6'	4°22·8'W	X	95
Ballaconley	I of M	NX3800	54°22·4'	4°29·2'W	X	95
Ballacooiley	I of M	SC3394	54°19·1'	4°33·6'W	X	95
Ballacoraige	I of M	SC3495	54°19·7'	4°32·7'W	X	95
Ballacorey	I of M	SC4398	54°21·5'	4°24·5'W	X	95
Ballacorkish	I of M	SC2270	54°6·0'	4°42·9'W	X	95
Ballacorris	I of M	SC3073	54°7·7'	4°35·7'W	X	95
Ballacosnahan	I of M	SC2581	54°11·9'	4°40·6'W	X	95
Ballacotch Manor	I of M	SC3377	54°9·9'	4°33·1'W	X	95
Ballacottier River	I of M	SC3980	54°11·7'	4°27·7'W	W	95
Ballacottier	I of M	NX4500	54°22·6'	4°22·8'W	X	95
Ballacottier	I of M	SC2578	54°10·3'	4°40·4'W	X	95
Ballacottier	I of M	SC4497	54°20·9'	4°23·6'W	X	95
Ballacowin	I of M	SC4184	54°13·9'	4°25·9'W	X	95
Ballacoyne	I of M	SC3780	54°11·6'	4°29·5'W	X	95
Ballacraine	I of M	SC2881	54°12·0'	4°37·8'W	X	95
Ballacrebbin	I of M	SC4196	54°20·4'	4°26·3'W	X	95
Ballacreetch	I of M	SC3779	54°11·1'	4°29·5'W	X	95

Ballacregga	I of M	SC3472	54°7·3'	4°32·0'W	X	95
Ballacregga Fm	I of M	NX4302	54°23·6'	4°24·7'W	FM	95
Ballacreggan	I of M	SC4380	54°11·8'	4°24·0'W	X	95
Ballacreggan	I of M	SC4691	54°17·7'	4°21·6'W	X	95
Ballacreggan Fm	I of M	SC3573	54°7·8'	4°31·1'W	FM	95
Ballacroak	I of M	SC3073	54°7·7'	4°35·7'W	X	95
Ballacross Fm	I of M	SC2683	54°13·0'	4°39·7'W	FM	95
Ballacubbon	I of M	SC3375	54°8·9'	4°33·0'W	X	95
Ballacuberagh Plantation	I of M	SC3793	54°18·6'	4°29·9'W	F	95
Ballacurnkeil	I of M	SC3393	54°18·6'	4°33·6'W	X	95
Ballacurn Mooar	I of M	SC3492	54°18·0'	4°32·6'W	X	95
Ballacutchal	I of M	SC3275	54°8·9'	4°33·9'W	X	95
Balladda Fm	I of M	SC2177	54°9·7'	4°44·1'W	FM	95
Balladen	Lancs	SD8021	53°41·3'	2°17·8'W	T	103
Balladoole	I of M	SC2468	54°4·9'	4°41·0'W	X	95
Balladoole Fm	I of M	SC4497	54°20·9'	4°23·6'W	FM	95
Balladoole Ho	I of M	SC2468	54°4·9'	4°41·0'W	X	95
Balladoyle	Cumbr	NY1251	54°51·0'	3°21·8'W	X	85
Balladrum	Aberd	NO7694	57°2·4'	2°23·3'W	X	38,45
Balladfadda	I of M	SC2572	54°7·1'	4°40·2'W	X	95
Ballafageen	I of M	SC3291	54°17·5'	4°34·5'W	X	95
Ballafayle-e-Callow	I of M	SC4789	54°16·7'	4°20·6'W	X	95
Ballafesson	I of M	SC2070	54°5·9'	4°44·8'W	X	95
Ballafodda	I of M	SC2471	54°6·5'	4°41·1'W	X	95
Ballafreer	I of M	SC3478	54°10·5'	4°32·2'W	X	95
Ballafurt	I of M	SC3170	54°6·1'	4°34·7'W	X	95
Ballagan	W Dunb	NS4083	56°1·1'	4°33·6'W	X	56,64
Ballagan Burn	Stir	NS5780	55°59·8'	4°17·1'W	W	64
Ballagan Fm	Stir	NS5879	55°59·2'	4°16·1'W	FM	64
Ballagan Ho	Stir	NS5779	55°59·2'	4°17·1'W	X	64
Ballagarey Fm	I of M	SC2973	54°7·7'	4°36·6'W	FM	95
Ballagarmin	I of M	SC2370	54°6·0'	4°42·0'W	X	95
Ballagarraghyn	I of M	SC2981	54°12·0'	4°36·9'W	X	95
Ballagarrett	I of M	NX4201	54°23·1'	4°25·6'W	X	95
Ballagawne	I of M	SC2169	54°5·4'	4°43·8'W	T	95
Ballagawne	I of M	SC2371	54°6·5'	4°42·0'W	X	95
Ballagawne	I of M	SC3089	54°16·4'	4°36·2'W	X	95
Ballageeil	I of M	SC2986	54°14·7'	4°37·0'W	X	95
Ballageich Hill	E Renf	NS5350	55°43·5'	4°20·0'W	H	64
Ballaggan	D & G	NS8301	55°17·6'	3°50·1'W	X	78
Ballaggan	Highld	NH5324	57°17·2'	4°25·9'W	X	26,35
Ballaggan	Highld	NH7543	57°27·9'	4°4·6'W	X	27
Ballaggan	Highld	NH7952	57°32·8'	4°0·8'W	X	27
Ballaghaie	I of M	NX3700	54°22·4'	4°30·1'W	X	95
Ballaghaue	I of M	SC4199	54°22·0'	4°26·4'W	X	95
Ballaghennie	I of M	NX4302	54°23·6'	4°24·7'W	X	95
Ballagick	I of M	SC3173	54°7·8'	4°34·8'W	X	95
Ballagill	I of M	SC2778	54°10·4'	4°38·6'W	X	95
Ballagilley	I of M	SC4591	54°17·7'	4°22·5'W	X	95
Ballaglass	I of M	SC4690	54°17·2'	4°21·5'W	X	95
Ballaglass Glen	I of M	SC4689	54°16·7'	4°21·5'W	X	95
Ballagloney	I of M	SC2070	54°5·9'	4°44·8'W	X	95
Ballaglonney	I of M	SC3072	54°7·2'	4°35·7'W	X	95
Ballaglonney	I of M	SC3275	54°8·9'	4°33·9'W	X	95
Ballaglonney Fm	I of M	SC2672	54°7·1'	4°39·3'W	FM	95
Ballagrawe	I of M	SC3481	54°12·1'	4°32·3'W	X	95
Ballagunnell	I of M	NX3800	54°22·4'	4°29·2'W	X	95
Ballagyr	I of M	SC2684	54°13·6'	4°39·7'W	X	95
Ballaharry	I of M	SC3280	54°11·5'	4°34·1'W	X	95
Ballaheannagh Gdns	I of M	SC4283	54°13·4'	4°25·0'W	X	95
Ballahick	I of M	SC2869	54°5·5'	4°37·4'W	X	95
Ballahig	I of M	SC2780	54°11·4'	4°38·7'W	X	95
Ballahimmin	I of M	SC3185	54°14·2'	4°35·2'W	X	95
Ballahott	I of M	SC2770	54°6·1'	4°38·3'W	X	95
Ballahowin	I of M	SC3175	54°8·8'	4°34·8'W	X	95
Ballaig	Pth & Kin	NN8023	56°23·3'	3°56·2'W	X	52
Ballaimish	I of M	SC3891	54°17·6'	4°28·9'W	X	95
Ballaird	D & G	NX3654	54°51·5'	4°32·9'W	X	83
Ballaird	S Ayr	NX2084	55°7·3'	4°48·9'W	X	76
Ballaird Loch	D & G	NX3553	54°50·9'	4°33·8'W	W	83
Ballajeraie	I of M	SC3073	54°7·7'	4°35·7'W	X	95
Ballajora	I of M	SC4790	54°17·2'	4°20·6'W	T	95
Ballakaighen	I of M	SC2568	54°4·9'	4°40·1'W	X	95
Ballakaighen	I of M	SC2985	54°14·2'	4°37·0'W	X	95
Ballakaighen Fm	I of M	SC2568	54°4·9'	4°40·1'W	FM	95
Ballakaighin	I of M	SC2986	54°14·7'	4°37·0'W	X	95
Ballakelly	I of M	SC3271	54°6·7'	4°33·8'W	X	95
Ballakelly	I of M	SC3479	54°11·0'	4°32·2'W	X	95
Ballakelly	I of M	SC3999	54°21·9'	4°28·2'W	X	95
Ballakerka Plantation	I of M	SC3892	54°18·1'	4°29·0'W	F	95
Ballakew	I of M	SC3073	54°7·7'	4°35·7'W	X	95
Ballakewin	I of M	SC2771	54°6·6'	4°38·4'W	X	95
Ballakilley	I of M	NX4401	54°23·1'	4°23·7'W	X	95
Ballakilley	I of M	SC2873	54°7·7'	4°37·5'W	X	95
Ballakilley	I of M	SC4891	54°17·8'	4°19·7'W	X	95
Ballakilleyclieu Fm	I of M	SC3288	54°15·9'	4°34·4'W	FM	95
Ballakilley Fm	I of M	SC4379	54°11·2'	4°24·0'W	FM	95
Ballakillingan	I of M	SC4294	54°19·3'	4°25·3'W	X	95
Ballakillowey	I of M	SC2170	54°5·9'	4°43·8'W	X	95
Ballakilmartin	I of M	SC4079	54°11·2'	4°26·7'W	X	95
Ballakilmurray Fm	I of M	SC2783	54°13·1'	4°38·8'W	FM	95
Ballakilpheric	I of M	SC2271	54°6·5'	4°43·0'W	X	95
Ballakinnag	I of M	NX4102	54°23·6'	4°26·5'W	X	95
Ballakissack	I of M	SC3172	54°7·2'	4°34·7'W	X	95
Ballaleece	I of M	SC2782	54°12·5'	4°38·8'W	X	95
Ballaleigh	I of M	SC3189	54°16·4'	4°35·3'W	T	95
Ballalheaney	I of M	SC4298	54°21·4'	4°25·5'W	X	95
Ballalhen	I of M	NX3802	54°23·5'	4°29·3'W	X	95
Ballalhergy	I of M	SC4496	54°20·4'	4°23·6'W	X	95
Ballalonna	I of M	SC3289	54°16·4'	4°34·4'W	X	95
Ballalough	I of M	SC2683	54°13·0'	4°39·7'W	X	95
Ballalough	I of M	SC3481	54°12·1'	4°32·3'W	X	95
Ballamaddrell	I of M	SC2570	54°6·0'	4°40·2'W	X	95
Ballamanaugh	I of M	SC3893	54°18·7'	4°29·0'W	X	95
Ballaman Hill	Scot Bord	NT0915	55°25·5'	3°25·8'W	H	78
Ballamas Geo	Shetld	HU6670	60°24·8'	0°47·6'W	X	2
Ballameanagh	I of M	SC3797	54°20·8'	4°30·0'W	X	95
Ballamenagh	I of M	SC3186	54°14·8'	4°35·2'W	X	95
Ballamenagh	I of M	SC3680	54°11·6'	4°30·4'W	X	95
Ballamenaugh Beg	I of M	SC4280	54°11·7'	4°24·9'W	X	95

Ballamenoch	Stir	NS5793	56°6·8'	4°17·5'W	X	57
Ballamillaghyn	I of M	SC3578	54°10·5'	4°31·3'W	X	95
Ballamin Fm	I of M	NX4402	54°23·6'	4°23·8'W	FM	95
Ballamoar	I of M	SC2482	54°12·5'	4°41·5'W	X	95
Ballamoar	I of M	SC4484	54°13·9'	4°23·2'W	X	95
Ballamoar Beg Fm	I of M	SC3796	54°20·3'	4°30·0'W	FM	95
Ballamoar Castle	I of M	SC3697	54°20·8'	4°31·0'W	X	95
Ballamodda Fm	I of M	SC3581	54°12·1'	4°31·4'W	FM	95
Ballamodha	I of M	SC2773	54°7·7'	4°38·4'W	T	95
Ballamodha Mooar	I of M	SC2773	54°7·7'	4°38·4'W	X	95
Ballamona	I of M	SC2878	54°10·4'	4°37·7'W	X	95
Ballamona	I of M	SC3076	54°9·4'	4°35·8'W	X	95
Ballamona	I of M	SC3473	54°7·8'	4°32·0'W	X	95
Ballamona	I of M	SC4095	54°19·8'	4°27·2'W	X	95
Ballamona Beg Fm	I of M	SC3495	54°19·7'	4°32·7'W	FM	95
Ballamona Mooar	I of M	SC3496	54°20·2'	4°32·8'W	X	95
Ballamooar	I of M	SC3593	54°18·6'	4°31·8'W	X	95
Ballanank	I of M	SC2872	54°7·2'	4°37·5'W	X	95
Ballanard	I of M	SC3778	54°10·6'	4°29·4'W	X	95
Ballanass	I of M	SC2779	54°10·9'	4°38·6'W	X	95
Ballanayre	I of M	SC2886	54°14·7'	4°38·0'W	X	95
Ballanayre Strand	I of M	SC2786	54°14·7'	4°38·9'W	X	95
Ballands Castle	Somer	ST7531	51°4·9'	2°21·0'W	A	183
Ballanea Fm	I of M	SC3188	54°15·8'	4°35·3'W	FM	95
Ballangrew	Stir	NS6198	56°9·5'	4°13·8'W	X	57
Ballanicholas	I of M	SC3076	54°9·4'	4°35·8'W	X	95
Ballan Moor	Monm	ST4889	51°36·1'	2°44·7'W	X	171,172
Ballantager	Fife	NO3013	56°18·5'	3°7·4'W	X	59
Ballantnes Fm	Cambs	TL3078	52°23·3'	0°5·0'W	FM	142
Ballantrae	S Ayr	NX0882	55°6·0'	5°0·1'W	T	76
Ballantrae Bay	S Ayr	NX0783	55°6·5'	5°1·1'W	W	76
Ballanucater	Stir	NN6302	56°11·7'	4°12·0'W	X	57
Ballaoates	I of M	SC2880	54°11·5'	4°37·8'W	X	95
Ballaoates	I of M	SC3679	54°11·1'	4°30·4'W	X	95
Ballaquaggan	I of M	SC2970	54°6·1'	4°36·5'W	X	95
Ballaquane	I of M	NX4100	54°22·5'	4°26·5'W	X	95
Ballaquane	I of M	SC2279	54°10·8'	4°43·2'W	X	95
Ballaquark Fm	I of M	NX4501	54°23·1'	4°22·8'W	FM	95
Ballaquiggin Fm	I of M	SC3271	54°6·7'	4°33·8'W	FM	95
Ballaquine	I of M	SC2988	54°15·8'	4°37·1'W	X	95
Ballaquine	I of M	SC3481	54°12·1'	4°32·3'W	X	95
Ballaquine	I of M	SC4084	54°13·9'	4°26·9'W	X	95
Ballaquinnea Beg	I of M	SC3377	54°9·9'	4°33·1'W	X	95
Ballaquinnea Mooar	I of M	SC3378	54°10·5'	4°33·1'W	X	95
Ballaquinney	I of M	SC2472	54°7·1'	4°41·2'W	X	95
Ballaragh	I of M	SC4585	54°14·5'	4°22·3'W	T	95
Ballarat House	Orkney	HY3016	59°1·8'	3°12·7'W	X	6
Ballard	Arg & Bt	NM1655	56°36·3'	6°37·2'W	X	46
Ballard Cliff	Dorset	SZ0481	50°38·0'	1°56·2'W	X	195
Ballard Down	Dorset	SZ0381	50°38·0'	1°57·1'W	X	195
Ballard Point	Dorset	SZ0481	50°38·0'	1°56·2'W	X	195
Ballard Point	I Scilly	SV8713	49°56·3'	6°21·4'W	X	203
Ballard's Ash	Wilts	SU0684	51°33·5'	1°54·4'W	T	173
Ballard's Fm	Worcs	SP0140	52°3·7'	1°58·7'W	FM	150
Ballards Gore	Essex	TQ9092	51°35·9'	0°45·0'E	T	178
Ballard's Green	Warw	SP2791	52°31·2'	1°35·7'W	T	140
Ballarhenny	I of M	SC3291	54°17·5'	4°34·5'W	X	95
Ballarie	N Ayr	NR9449	55°41·7'	5°16·2'W	X	62,69
Ballarobin	I of M	SC2573	54°7·6'	4°40·3'W	X	95
Ballarock	I of M	SC2171	54°6·5'	4°43·9'W	X	95
Ballasaig	I of M	SC4691	54°17·7'	4°21·6'W	X	95
Ballasalla	I of M	SC2870	54°6·1'	4°37·4'W	T	95
Ballasalla	I of M	SC3497	54°20·7'	4°32·8'W	X	95
Ballasayle	I of M	SC3184	54°13·7'	4°35·1'W	X	95
Ballaseyre	I of M	SC4298	54°21·4'	4°25·5'W	X	95
Ballaseyre	I of M	SC4299	54°22·0'	4°25·5'W	X	95
Ballas Fm	Brig	SS8380	51°30·6'	3°40·8'W	FM	170
Ballashamrock	I of M	SC3473	54°7·8'	4°32·0'W	X	95
Ballaskeig Beg	I of M	SC4789	54°16·7'	4°20·6'W	X	95
Ballaskeig Mooar	I of M	SC4789	54°16·7'	4°20·6'W	X	95
Ballaskelly	I of M	SC3880	54°11·7'	4°28·6'W	X	95
Ballaskerroo	I of M	SC4282	54°12·8'	4°25·0'W	X	95
Ballaskyr	I of M	SC3187	54°15·3'	4°35·2'W	X	95
Ballaslig	I of M	SC3573	54°7·8'	4°31·1'W	X	95
Ballaslig	I of M	SC4399	54°22·0'	4°24·6'W	X	95
Ballasloe	I of M	SC4690	54°17·2'	4°21·5'W	X	95
Ballaspet	I of M	SC2681	54°12·0'	4°39·6'W	X	95
Ballaspit	I of M	SC2681	54°12·0'	4°39·6'W	X	95
Ballaspur	I of M	SC2882	54°12·5'	4°37·8'W	X	95
Ballastowell	I of M	SC3576	54°9·4'	4°31·2'W	X	95
Ballast Quay Fm	Essex	TM0420	51°50·7'	0°58·1'E	FM	168
Ballast Quay Fm	Essex	TM0421	51°51·2'	0°58·1'E	FM	168
Ballat	Stir	NS5291	56°5·6'	4°22·3'W	X	57
Ballateare	I of M	SC3497	54°20·7'	4°32·8'W	X	95
Ballater	Aberd	NO3695	57°2·8'	3°2·8'W	T	37,44
Ballaterach	Aberd	NO4296	57°3·3'	2°56·9'W	X	37,44
Ballaterson	I of M	SC2483	54°13·0'	4°41·5'W	X	95
Ballaterson	I of M	SC4892	54°18·3'	4°19·8'W	T	95
Ballaterson Beg	I of M	SC3594	54°19·1'	4°31·8'W	X	95
Ballathie	Pth & Kin	NO1437	56°31·3'	3°23·4'W	X	53
Ballathie House Hotel	Pth & Kin	NO1436	56°30·7'	3°23·4'W	X	53
Ballatrollag	I of M	SC2671	54°6·6'	4°39·3'W	X	95
Ballaugh	I of M	SC3493	54°18·6'	4°32·7'W	T	95
Ballaugh Bridge	I of M	SC3493	54°18·6'	4°32·7'W	X	95
Ballaugh Plantation	I of M	SC3591	54°17·5'	4°31·7'W	F	95
Ballaughton	I of M	SC3676	54°9·5'	4°30·3'W	X	95
Ballavagher	I of M	SC3475	54°8·9'	4°32·1'W	X	95
Ballavair	I of M	SC4499	54°22·0'	4°23·7'W	X	95
Ballavaish	I of M	SC2884	54°13·6'	4°37·9'W	X	95
Ballavale	I of M	SC3172	54°7·2'	4°34·7'W	X	95
Ballavar	I of M	SC3071	54°6·7'	4°35·6'W	X	95
Ballavarane	I of M	SC4279	54°11·2'	4°24·9'W	X	95
Ballavarkish	I of M	NX4600	54°22·6'	4°21·8'W	X	95
Ballavarran	I of M	SC3697	54°20·8'	4°31·0'W	X	95
Ballavarry	I of M	SC4098	54°21·4'	4°27·3'W	X	95
Ballavarteen	I of M	SC4397	54°20·9'	4°24·5'W	X	95
Ballavartyn	I of M	SC3273	54°7·8'	4°33·9'W	X	95
Ballavarvane	I of M	SC3074	54°8·3'	4°35·7'W	X	95
Ballaveare	I of M	SC3473	54°7·8'	4°32·0'W	X	95
Ballavell	I of M	SC2671	54°6·6'	4°39·3'W	X	95
Ballavelt	I of M	SC4690	54°17·2'	4°21·5'W	X	95
Ballavitchel Fm	I of M	SC3280	54°11·5'	4°34·1'W	FM	95
Ballavoddan	I of M	SC4198	54°21·4'	4°26·4'W	X	95
Ballavolley	I of M	SC3694	54°19·2'	4°30·9'W	X	95
Ballavoulen	Highld	NH5774	57°44·2'	4°23·7'W	X	21
Ballavoulin	Highld	NH5967	57°40·5'	4°21·4'W	X	21
Ballawattleworth Fm	I of M	SC2583	54°13·0'	4°40·6'W	FM	95
Ballawhane	I of M	NX3901	54°23·0'	4°28·3'W	X	95
Ballawilleykilley	I of M	SC3379	54°11·0'	4°33·1'W	X	95
Balla Wray	Cumbr	SD3799	54°23·2'	2°57·8'W	X	96,97
Ballawyllin	I of M	SC3682	54°12·7'	4°30·5'W	X	95
Ballawyllin Fm	I of M	SC2582	54°12·5'	4°40·6'W	FM	95
Ballayockey	I of M	SC4296	54°20·4'	4°25·4'W	X	95
Ball Bank House Fm	Staffs	SK0665	53°11·2'	1°54·2'W	FM	119
Ballcorach	Moray	NJ1526	57°19·3'	3°24·2'W	X	36
Ball Covert	Somer	ST2032	51°5·1'	3°8·1'W	F	182
Ballcross Fm	Derby	SK2269	53°13·3'	1°39·8'W	FM	119
Ball Down	Wilts	SU0450	51°15·2'	1°56·2'W	X	184
Ballechin	Pth & Kin	NN9353	56°39·7'	3°44·3'W	X	52
Ballechin Wood	Pth & Kin	NN9454	56°40·2'	3°43·3'W	F	52,53
Ballees Fm	N Ayr	NS2249	55°42·4'	4°49·5'W	FM	63
Balleich	Stir	NN5100	56°10·4'	4°23·6'W	X	57
Balleigh	Highld	NH7084	57°49·9'	4°10·9'W	T	21
Ballelby	I of M	SC2278	54°10·3'	4°43·2'W	T	95
Ballellin	I of M	SC4587	54°15·6'	4°22·4'W	X	95
Ballencleuch Law	S Lanak	NS9304	55°19·4'	3°40·7'W	H	78
Ballencrieff	E Loth	NT4878	55°59·8'	2°49·6'W	T	66
Ballencrieff House	E Loth	NT4878	55°59·8'	2°49·6'W	A	66
Ballencrieff Mains	E Loth	NT4778	55°59·8'	2°50·5'W	X	66
Ballencrieff Toll	W Loth	NS9770	55°55·0'	3°38·4'W	T	65
Ballencrief Mains	W Loth	NS9770	55°55·0'	3°38·4'W	X	65
Ballendall	Pth & Kin	NN7906	56°14·1'	3°56·7'W	X	57
Ballendrick Ho	Pth & Kin	NO1117	56°20·5'	3°25·9'W	X	58
Ballenkirk	Fife	NO3204	56°13·7'	3°5·4'W	X	59
Ballenlish	Moray	NJ1526	57°19·3'	3°24·2'W	X	36
Ballentink	Highld	ND1531	58°15·8'	3°26·5'W	X	11,17
Ballentoul	Pth & Kin	NN8865	56°46·0'	3°49·5'W	T	43
Balleny Fm	C of Edin	NT1765	55°52·5'	3°19·2'W	FM	65,66
Ballevoulin	Arg & Bt	NS2988	56°3·5'	4°44·3'W	X	56
Ballfield Plantn	Fife	NT2396	56°9·3'	3°13·9'W	F	58
Ballfields	Staffs	SK0053	53°4·7'	1°59·6'W	X	119
Ball Fm	Somer	ST7330	51°4·4'	2°22·7'W	FM	183
Ball Gate	Devon	SX6761	50°26·3'	3°52·0'W	X	202
Ball Green	C of Stoke	SJ8952	53°4·1'	2°9·4'W	T	118
Ball Hall	Cumbr	SD2291	54°18·8'	3°11·5'W	X	96
Ball Hall Fm	E Yorks	SE7243	53°52·9'	0°53·9'W	FM	105,106
Ballharn Hill	Highld	ND2444	58°22·9'	3°17·5'W	X	11,12
Ball Haye Green	Staffs	SJ9857	53°6·9'	2°1·4'W	T	118
Ballhill	Devon	SS2624	50°59·6'	4°28·4'W	T	190
Ball Hill	Devon	SS4727	51°1·6'	4°10·5'W	X	180
Ball Hill	Devon	SX7655	50°23·1'	3°44·3'W	X	202
Ball Hill	Devon	SY1696	50°45·7'	3°11·1'W	X	192,193
Ball Hill	Devon	SY2095	50°45·2'	3°7·7'W	X	192,193
Ball Hill	Dorset	ST7203	50°49·8'	2°23·5'W	H	194
Ball Hill	Hants	SU4263	51°22·1'	1°23·4'W	T	174
Ball Hill	Orkney	ND4289	58°47·3'	2°59·7'W	X	7
Ball Hill	Somer	ST3737	51°8·0'	2°53·6'W	H	182
Ball Hill Fm	Devon	SX6295	50°44·5'	3°57·0'W	FM	191
Ballianlay	Arg & Bt	NS0462	55°48·9'	5°7·3'W	X	63
Balliargey	I of M	SC3680	54°11·6'	4°30·4'W	X	95
Ballibeg	Arg & Bt	NR8885	56°0·9'	5°23·6'W	X	55
Ballicherry	Highld	NH7064	57°39·1'	4°10·2'W	X	21,27
Ballidon	Derby	SK2054	53°5·2'	1°41·7'W	T	119
Ballidonmoor	Derby	SK2155	53°5·7'	1°40·8'W	X	119
Balliefurth Fm	Highld	NJ0123	57°17·5'	3°38·1'W	FM	36
Balliekine	N Ayr	NR8739	55°36·1'	5°22·4'W	X	68,69
Ballieknowe	D & G	NY0170	55°1·1'	3°32·5'W	X	84
Balliemeanoch	Arg & Bt	NN0116	56°17·9'	5°12·5'W	X	50,55
Balliemeanoch	Arg & Bt	NN1000	56°9·5'	5°3·1'W	X	56
Balliemore	Arg & Bt	NM8228	56°23·9'	5°31·5'W	X	49
Balliemore	Arg & Bt	NS0584	56°0·8'	5°7·3'W	X	56
Balliemore	Arg & Bt	NS1099	56°9·0'	5°3·1'W	X	56
Balliemore	Highld	NH6040	57°26·0'	4°19·5'W	X	26
Balliemore	Highld	NJ0021	57°16·4'	3°39·0'W	X	36
Balliemore Burn	Arg & Bt	NS0584	56°0·8'	5°7·3'W	W	56
Balliemullich	Moray	NJ2339	57°26·3'	3°16·5'W	X	28
Ballieston	S Ayr	NS3929	55°31·9'	4°32·6'W	X	70
Ballieward	Highld	NJ0231	57°21·8'	3°37·3'W	X	27,36
Ballifeary	Highld	NH6644	57°28·3'	4°13·6'W	T	26
Ballig	I of M	SC2882	54°12·5'	4°37·8'W	X	95
Ballig	I of M	SC3086	54°14·7'	4°36·1'W	X	95
Ballig	I of M	SC4588	54°16·1'	4°22·4'W	X	95
Ballig Fm	I of M	SC4079	54°11·2'	4°26·7'W	FM	95
Balligmorrie	S Ayr	NX2290	55°10·6'	4°47·3'W	X	76
Balligmorrie Burn	S Ayr	NX2290	55°10·6'	4°47·3'W	W	76
Ballikillet	N Ayr	NS1755	55°45·5'	4°54·6'W	X	63
Ballikinrain	Stir	NS5787	56°3·5'	4°17·4'W	X	57
Ballikinrain Burn	Stir	NS5585	56°2·4'	4°19·2'W	W	57
Ballikinrain Castle	Stir	NS5687	56°3·5'	4°18·3'W	X	57
Ballikinrain Muir	Stir	NS5785	56°2·5'	4°17·3'W	X	57
Ballilesk	Clackm	NO0001	56°11·7'	3°36·3'W	X	58
Ballimeanoch	Arg & Bt	NM4455	56°37·3'	6°9·9'W	X	47
Ballimenach	Arg & Bt	NR7518	55°24·5'	5°32·8'W	X	68,69
Ballimenach Hill	Arg & Bt	NR7517	55°24·0'	5°32·8'W	X	68,69
Ballimony	Arg & Bt	NR1955	55°42·7'	6°28·0'W	X	60
Ballimore	Arg & Bt	NN0525	56°22·9'	5°9·1'W	T	50
Ballimore	Arg & Bt	NR8785	56°0·9'	5°24·6'W	X	55
Ballimore	Arg & Bt	NR9283	56°0·0'	5°19·7'W	T	55
Ballimore	Stir	NN5217	56°19·6'	4°23·2'W	X	57
Ballinaby	Arg & Bt	NR2267	55°49·2'	6°25·9'W	X	60
Ballinbreich	Fife	NO2720	56°22·3'	3°10·5'W	X	53,59
Ballinbreich Castle	Fife	NO2720	56°22·3'	3°10·5'W	A	53,59
Ballindalloch	Highld	NH5520	57°15·1'	4°23·7'W	X	26,35
Ballindalloch	Pth & Kin	NN7426	56°24·8'	4°2·1'W	X	51,52
Ballindalloch	Stir	NS5488	56°4·0'	4°20·3'W	X	57
Ballindalloch Castle	Moray	NJ1736	57°24·7'	3°22·4'W	A	28
Ballindalloch Muir	Stir	NS5789	56°4·6'	4°17·4'W	X	57
Ballindarroch	Highld	NH6139	57°25·5'	4°18·4'W	X	26
Ballindean	Fife	NO3622	56°23·4'	3°1·8'W	X	54,59
Ballindean	Pth & Kin	NO2529	56°27·1'	3°12·6'W	X	53,59
Ballindean House	Pth & Kin	NO2629	56°27·1'	3°11·6'W	X	53,59
Ballindore	Highld	NH9442	57°27·6'	3°45·6'W	X	27
Ballindoun	Highld	NH5243	57°27·5'	4°27·6'W	X	26
Ballingall	Pth & Kin	NO1004	56°13·5'	3°26·6'W	X	58
Ballingdon	Suff	TL8640	52°1·9'	0°43·1'E	T	155
Ballingdon Bottom	Herts	TL0314	51°49·1'	0°29·9'W	T	166
Ballingdon Grove	Essex	TL8740	52°1·8'	0°44·0'E	X	155
Ballingdon Grove	Suff	TL8640	52°1·9'	0°43·1'E	X	155
Ballinger Bottom	Bucks	SP9103	51°43·3'	0°40·6'W	T	165
Ballinger Bottom (South)	Bucks	SP9102	51°42·8'	0°40·6'W	T	165
Ballinger Common	Bucks	SP9103	51°43·3'	0°40·6'W	T	165
Ballingham	Heref	SO5731	51°58·8'	2°37·2'W	T	149
Ballingham Hill	Heref	SO5732	51°59·3'	2°37·2'W	T	149
Ballingrew	Stir	NS6999	56°10·2'	4°6·2'W	X	57
Ballingry	Fife	NT1797	56°9·8'	3°19·7'W	T	58
Ballingry Fm	Fife	NT1798	56°10·3'	3°19·8'W	FM	58
Ballington Grange Fm	Staffs	SJ9955	53°5·8'	2°0·5'W	FM	118
Ballington Manor	Wilts	SU0237	51°8·2'	1°57·9'W	X	184
Ballinlagg Fm	Highld	NJ0632	57°22·4'	3°33·3'W	FM	27,36
Ballinlick	Pth & Kin	NN9740	56°32·7'	3°40·1'W	X	52,53
Ballinloan	Pth & Kin	NN5947	56°35·9'	4°17·3'W	X	51
Ballinloan	Pth & Kin	NN9652	56°39·2'	3°41·3'W	X	52,53
Ballinloan	Pth & Kin	NN9740	56°32·7'	3°40·1'W	X	52,53
Ballinloan Burn	Pth & Kin	NN9542	56°33·8'	3°42·1'W	W	52,53
Ballinluig	Highld	NH8610	57°10·3'	3°52·7'W	X	35,36
Ballinluig	Highld	NJ0524	57°18·1'	3°34·1'W	X	36
Ballinluig	Pth & Kin	NN9457	56°41·8'	3°43·4'W	T	52,53
Ballinluig	Pth & Kin	NN9752	56°39·2'	3°40·4'W	T	52,53
Ballinluig	Pth & Kin	NO0957	56°42·0'	3°28·7'W	X	52,53
Ballinluig	Stir	NN5319	56°20·7'	4°22·3'W	X	57
Ballinluig Island	Pth & Kin	NN9753	56°39·7'	3°40·4'W	X	52,53
Ballinnie	D & G	NX7390	55°11·5'	3°59·7'W	X	77
Ballinnie Burn	D & G	NX7290	55°11·5'	4°0·2'W	W	77
Ballinreach	Highld	NC9208	58°3·1'	3°49·3'W	X	17
Ballinreich	Highld	NH8154	57°33·9'	3°58·9'W	X	27
Ballinreigh	Pth & Kin	NN9137	56°31·0'	3°45·8'W	X	52
Ballinshoe	Angus	NO4153	56°40·2'	2°57·3'W	X	54
Ballinshoe Smithy	Angus	NO4152	56°39·6'	2°57·3'W	X	54
Ballintean	Highld	NH8401	57°5·4'	3°54·4'W	X	35
Ballintober	Aberd	NO3694	57°2·2'	3°2·8'W	X	37,44
Ballintomb	Highld	NJ0024	57°18·0'	3°39·1'W	X	36
Ballintomb Burn	Moray	NJ2144	57°29·0'	3°18·6'W	W	28
Ballinton	Stir	NS6898	56°9·6'	4°7·1'W	X	57
Ballintua	Highld	NJ0525	57°18·6'	3°34·2'W	X	36
Ballintuim	Highld	NJ0617	57°14·3'	3°33·0'W	X	36
Ballintuim	Pth & Kin	NO1054	56°40·4'	3°27·7'W	T	53
Ballitarsin	Arg & Bt	NR3561	55°46·4'	6°13·1'W	X	60
Balliveolan	Arg & Bt	NM8442	56°31·5'	5°30·3'W	T	49
Ballivicar	Arg & Bt	NR3446	55°38·3'	6°13·2'W	X	60
Ballmishag	Highld	NN5894	57°1·2'	4°19·9'W	X	35
Ballnahowe	I of M	SC1968	54°4·8'	4°45·6'W	X	95
Ballnalargy	I of M	SC2279	54°10·8'	4°43·2'W	X	95
Ballnaselich	Highld	NM7967	56°44·8'	5°36·4'W	X	40
Ballnellan Burn	Moray	NJ1326	57°19·2'	3°26·2'W	W	36
Ball Oaks	Devon	SX8393	50°43·7'	3°39·1'W	X	191
Balloan	Highld	NC5905	58°1·0'	4°22·7'W	T	16
Balloan	Highld	NH5858	57°35·6'	4°22·1'W	X	26
Balloan	Highld	NH6732	57°21·8'	4°12·2'W	X	26
Balloan	Highld	NH6742	57°27·2'	4°12·5'W	X	26
Balloan	Highld	NH7890	57°53·2'	4°3·0'W	X	21
Balloan	Highld	NH8550	57°31·8'	3°54·8'W	X	27
Balloch	Angus	NO1664	56°45·9'	3°22·0'W	X	43
Balloch	Angus	NO3557	56°42·3'	3°3·2'W	X	54
Balloch	Arg & Bt	NR6718	55°24·3'	5°40·4'W	X	68
Balloch	Highld	NC3261	58°30·6'	4°52·5'W	X	9
Balloch	Highld	NH7346	57°29·5'	4°6·7'W	T	27
Balloch	N Lanak	NS7374	55°56·8'	4°1·6'W	T	64
Balloch	Pth & Kin	NO2649	56°37·9'	3°11·9'W	X	53
Balloch	W Dunb	NS3982	56°0·5'	4°34·5'W	T	56
Ballochallan	Stir	NN6505	56°13·4'	4°10·2'W	X	57
Ballochan	Aberd	NO5290	57°0·2'	2°47·0'W	T	44
Ballochargie	Pth & Kin	NN8318	56°20·7'	3°53·1'W	X	57
Ballocharush Burn	D & G	NX3773	55°1·7'	4°32·6'W	W	77
Ballochbeatties	S Ayr	NX4195	55°13·7'	4°29·6'W	X	77
Ballochbroe	S Ayr	NS3108	55°20·5'	4°39·5'W	X	70,76
Ballochbuie Forest	Aberd	NO1990	56°59·9'	3°19·5'W	F	43
Ballochbuie Forest	Aberd	NO2090	56°59·9'	3°18·6'W	F	44
Balloch Burn	D & G	NX4958	54°53·9'	4°20·9'W	W	83
Balloch Burn	S Ayr	NX3394	55°13·0'	4°37·1'W	W	76
Balloch Castle	W Dunb	NS3983	56°1·0'	4°34·5'W	X	56
Ballochduie	Aberd	NJ3419	57°15·7'	3°5·2'W	X	37
Ballochearn	Stir	NS5888	56°4·1'	4°16·4'W	T	57
Ballochford	Moray	NJ3633	57°23·2'	3°3·4'W	X	28
Ballochgair	Arg & Bt	NR7727	55°29·4'	5°31·4'W	X	68,69
Ballochgoy	Arg & Bt	NS0864	55°50·1'	5°3·5'W	T	63
Balloch Hill	S Ayr	NX3294	55°13·0'	4°38·0'W	X	76
Balloch Ho	Pth & Kin	NO2649	56°37·9'	3°11·9'W	X	53
Balloch Lane	S Ayr	NX4294	55°13·2'	4°28·6'W	W	77
Ballochleam	Stir	NS6592	56°6·4'	4°9·8'W	X	57
Ballochling Loch	E Ayr	NX4594	55°13·2'	4°25·8'W	W	77
Ballochmartin	N Ayr	NS1757	55°46·6'	4°54·6'W	X	63
Ballochmartin Bay	N Ayr	NS1856	55°46·0'	4°53·6'W	W	63
Balloch More	Moray	NJ3235	57°24·3'	3°7·4'W	X	28
Ballochmorrie	S Ayr	NX2184	55°7·3'	4°48·0'W	X	76
Ballochmorrie Fm	S Ayr	NX2184	55°7·3'	4°48·0'W	FM	76
Ballochmyle Hospital	E Ayr	NS5126	55°30·6'	4°21·1'W	X	70
Ballochnafraesan	Arg & Bt	NR6319	55°24·7'	5°44·2'W	X	68
Ballochneck	Stir	NN6501	56°11·2'	4°10·1'W	X	57
Ballochneck	Stir	NS5593	56°6·7'	4°19·5'W	X	57
Ballochney	N Lanak	NS7967	55°53·1'	3°55·6'W	X	64
Ballochniel	S Ayr	NS2206	55°19·2'	4°47·9'W	X	70,76
Balloch Plantation	Aberd	NO1994	57°2·1'	3°19·6'W	F	36,43
Balloch Plantation	S Ayr	NX3695	55°13·6'	4°34·3'W	F	77
Ballochrae Burn	D & G	NX3160	54°54·6'	4°37·8'W	W	82
Ballochroy	Arg & Bt	NR7252	55°42·7'	5°37·3'W	X	62
Ballochroy Burn	Arg & Bt	NR7451	55°42·2'	5°35·4'W	W	62
Ballochroy Glen	Arg & Bt	NR7451	55°42·2'	5°35·4'W	X	62
Ballochruin	Stir	NS5288	56°4·0'	4°22·2'W	X	57
Balloch, The	Aberd	NJ4748	57°31·4'	2°52·6'W	X	28,29
Balloch, The	Pth & Kin	NN8319	56°21·2'	3°53·2'W	X	57

Balloch, The	Pth & Kin	NN8419	56°21·2′	3°52·2′W	X	58
Balloch Wood	Moray	NJ4649	57°31·9′	2°53·7′W	F	28,29
Ballochy	Angus	NO6562	56°45·2′	2°33·9′W	X	45
Ballochyle	Arg & Bt	NS1382	55°59·9′	4°59·5′W	X	56
Ballochyle Hill	Arg & Bt	NS1383	56°0·5′	4°59·5′W	H	56
Ball o' Ditton	Halton	SJ4986	53°22·3′	2°45·6′W	T	108
Ballogie	Aberd	NO5795	57°2·9′	2°42·1′W	T	37,44
Ballogie Ho	Aberd	NO5795	57°2·9′	2°42·1′W	X	37,44
Balloleys	Pth & Kin	NO2332	56°28·7′	3°14·6′W	X	53
Ballom Hill	Worcs	SO9857	52°12·9′	2°1·4′W	X	150
Ballomill	Fife	NO3210	56°16·9′	3°5·5′W	X	59
Ballone	Highld	ND1552	58°27·1′	3°26·9′W	X	11,12
Ballone	Highld	NH5538	57°24·8′	4°24·4′W	X	26
Ballone	Highld	NH6853	57°33·1′	4°11·9′W	X	26
Ballone Cas	Highld	NH9283	57°49·7′	3°48·6′W	A	21
Balloon Barn Fm	Suff	TL8472	52°19·1′	0°42·4′E	FM	144,155
Ballo Reservoir	Fife	NO2204	56°13·6′	3°15·0′W	W	58
Ballourie	Highld	NH8307	57°8·6′	3°55·6′W	X	35
Ballowfield	N Yks	SD9989	54°18·0′	2°0·5′W	X	98
Ballownie	Angus	NO6164	56°46·2′	2°37·8′W	X	45
Ball Rock	Devon	SX7635	50°12·4′	3°43·9′W	X	202
Balls	Devon	SS5413	50°54·1′	4°4·2′W	X	180
Ballsaddle Rock	Devon	SX7936	50°12·9′	3°41·4′W	X	202
Balls Corner	Devon	SS6416	50°55·9′	3°55·7′W	X	180
Balls Cotts	Hants	SU3944	51°11·9′	1°26·1′W	X	185
Balls Cross	Devon	SS7731	51°4·1′	3°45·0′W	X	180
Ball's Cross	Heref	SO3628	51°57·0′	2°55·5′W	X	149,161
Balls Cross	W Susx	SU9826	51°1·7′	0°35·8′W	T	186,197
Balls Fm	Devon	SY2896	50°45·8′	3°0·9′W	FM	193
Balls Fm	Somer	ST2834	51°6·3′	3°1·3′W	FM	182
Ball's Fm	Suff	TM1859	52°11·4′	1°11·8′E	FM	156
Ballsgate Common	Heref	SO4166	52°17·6′	2°51·5′W	X	137,148,149
Balls Green	Essex	TM0923	51°52·2′	1°2·6′E	T	168,169
Balls Green	E Susx	TQ4936	51°6·5′	0°8·1′E	T	188
Ball's Green	Glos	ST8699	51°41·6′	2°11·8′W	T	162
Balls Green	W Susx	TQ1023	51°0·0′	0°25·6′W	T	198
Ball's Hall	Wrex	SJ3658	53°7·2′	2°57·0′W	X	117
Balls Hill	Sand	SO9993	52°32·3′	2°0·5′W	T	139
Balls Pond Fm	Herts	TL0602	51°42·6′	0°27·6′W	FM	166
Balls Wood	Herts	TL3410	51°46·6′	0°3·1′W	F	166
Balluderon Hill	Angus	NO3639	56°32·6′	3°2·0′W	X	54
Ballumbie	C of Dun	NO4433	56°29·4′	2°54·1′W	X	54
Ballure	Arg & Bt	NR7149	55°41·1′	5°38·1′W	X	62
Ballure Plantation	I of M	SC4592	54°18·3′	4°22·5′W	F	95
Balluskie	S Ayr	NX2382	55°6·3′	4°46·0′W	X	76
Ball Wood	N Som	ST4564	51°22·6′	2°47·0′W	F	172,182
Ballyack Ho	Wilts	SU3460	51°20·5′	1°30·3′W	X	174
Ballyalnach	Pth & Kin	NN9453	56°39·7′	3°43·3′W	X	52,53
Ballyardley Hill	Northum	NY8598	55°16·8′	2°13·7′W	H	80
Ballyaurgan	Arg & Bt	NR7574	55°54·6′	5°35·6′W	X	62
Ballybrennan	Arg & Bt	NR6813	55°21·6′	5°39·2′W	X	68
Ballycaul	Arg & Bt	NS0463	55°49·5′	5°7·3′W	X	63
Ballychatrigan	Arg & Bt	NR3241	55°35·6′	6°14·8′W	X	60
Ballycoach	S Ayr	NS3611	55°22·2′	4°34·8′W	X	70
Ballycurrie	Arg & Bt	NS0461	55°48·4′	5°7·2′W	X	63
Ballygowan Farm	Arg & Bt	NM8928	56°24·1′	5°24·7′W	FM	49
Ballygown	Arg & Bt	NM4343	56°30·8′	6°10·2′W	T	47,48
Ballygown Bay	Arg & Bt	NM4343	56°30·8′	6°10·2′W	W	47,48
Ballygrant	Arg & Bt	NR3966	55°49·3′	6°9·6′W	T	60,61
Ballygrant Burn	Arg & Bt	NR3865	55°48·7′	6°10·5′W	W	60,61
Ballygreggan	Arg & Bt	NR6619	55°24·8′	5°41·4′W	X	68
Ballygroggan	Arg & Bt	NR6219	55°24·7′	5°45·2′W	X	68
Ballyhaugh	Arg & Bt	NM1758	56°38·0′	6°36·5′W	X	46
Ballymeanach	Arg & Bt	NR1753	55°41·5′	6°29·8′W	X	60
Ballymeanoch	Arg & Bt	NR8396	56°6·7′	5°29·0′W	T	55
Ballymeanochglen	N Ayr	NS0222	55°27·4′	5°7·5′W	X	69
Ballymenach	Arg & Bt	NR7422	55°26·6′	5°34·0′W	X	68
Ballymenach	Arg & Bt	NR7522	55°26·7′	5°33·0′W	X	68,69
Ballymenoch	Arg & Bt	NS3086	56°2·5′	4°43·3′W	X	56
Ballymichael Glen	N Ayr	NR9331	55°32·0′	5°16·4′W	X	68,69
Ballyoukan Ho	Pth & Kin	NN9656	56°41·3′	3°41·4′W	X	52,53
Ballywilline	Arg & Bt	NR7122	55°26·6′	5°36·8′W	X	68
Ballywilline Hill	Arg & Bt	NR7123	55°27·1′	5°36·9′W	H	68
Balmacaan Forest	Highld	NH4226	57°18·1′	4°36·9′W	X	26
Balmacara	Highld	NG8127	57°17·1′	5°37·6′W	T	33
Balmacara Bay	Highld	NG8027	57°17·1′	5°38·6′W	W	33
Balmacara Burn	Highld	NG8128	57°17·7′	5°37·6′W	W	33
Balmacara Ho	Highld	NG8027	57°17·1′	5°38·6′W	X	33
Balmacara Square	Highld	NG8028	57°17·6′	5°38·6′W	T	33
Balmacassie	Aberd	NJ9731	57°22·4′	2°2·5′W	X	30
Balmachie	Angus	NO5436	56°31·1′	2°44·4′W	X	54
Balmachree	Highld	NH7347	57°30·0′	4°6·7′W	X	27
Balmachreuchie	Pth & Kin	NO1053	56°39·9′	3°27·7′W	X	53
Balmaclellan	D & G	NX6579	55°5·5′	4°6·5′W	T	77,84
Balmacnaughton	Pth & Kin	NN7643	56°34·0′	4°0·6′W	X	51,52
Balmacneil	Pth & Kin	NN9750	56°38·1′	3°40·3′W	T	52,53
Balmacolly	Pth & Kin	NO0534	56°29·6′	3°32·1′W	X	52,53
Balmacqueen	Highld	NG4474	57°41·2′	6°17·2′W	T	23
Balmacron	Pth & Kin	NO2844	56°35·2′	3°9·9′W	X	53
Balmadies House	Angus	NO5549	56°38·1′	2°43·6′W	X	54
Balmadity	Angus	NO5062	56°45·1′	2°48·6′W	X	44
Balmae	D & G	NX6844	54°46·7′	4°2·7′W	X	83,84
Balmae Burn	D & G	NX6844	54°46·7′	4°2·7′W	W	83,84
Balmae Ha'en	D & G	NX6744	54°46·7′	4°3·6′W	X	83,84
Balmaghie Ho	D & G	NX7163	54°57·0′	4°0·4′W	X	83,84
Balma Glaster	Highld	NN2896	57°1·6′	4°49·6′W	X	34
Balmaha	Stir	NS4290	56°4·9′	4°31·9′W	T	56
Balmain	Fife	NO4105	56°14·3′	2°56·7′W	X	59
Balmain Fm	Aberd	NO6472	56°50·5′	2°35·0′W	FM	45
Balmains	Pth & Kin	NO1437	56°31·3′	3°23·4′W	X	53
Balmakewan	Aberd	NO6666	56°47·3′	2°32·9′W	X	45
Balmakin	Fife	NO4804	56°13·8′	2°49·9′W	X	59
Balmalcolm	Fife	NO3208	56°15·8′	3°5·4′W	T	59
Balmalcolm	Pth & Kin	NO2132	56°28·7′	3°16·5′W	X	53
Balmalcolm Fm	Fife	NO3108	56°15·8′	3°6·4′W	FM	59
Balmalloch	N Lanak	NS7078	55°58·9′	4°4·6′W	T	64
Balmalloch	S Ayr	NX2684	55°7·4′	4°43·3′W	X	76
Balmangan	D & G	NX6545	54°47·2′	4°5·5′W	X	83,84
Balmangan	D & G	NX7548	54°48·9′	3°56·3′W	X	84
Balmangan Bar	D & G	NX6545	54°47·2′	4°5·5′W	X	83,84

Balmanno Castle	Pth & Kin	NO1415	56°19·4′	3°23·0′W	A	58
Balmannocks	Aberd	NJ6206	57°8·9′	2°37·2′W	X	37
Balmanno Hill	Pth & Kin	NO1414	56°18·9′	3°23·0′W	H	58
Balmanno Ho	Aberd	NO6966	56°47·3′	2°30·0′W	X	45
Balmartin	N Eil	NF7273	57°37·9′	7°29·3′W	T	18
Balmashanner	Angus	NO4649	56°38·0′	2°52·4′W	T	54
Balmaud	Aberd	NJ7557	57°36·4′	2°24·6′W	X	29
Balmavicar	Arg & Bt	NR5909	55°19·2′	5°47·5′W	X	68
Bâl-Mawr	Monm	SO2627	51°56·4′	3°4·2′W	H	161
Balmblair	Pth & Kin	NO0728	56°26·4′	3°30·1′W	X	52,53,58
Balmeadow	Fife	NO2917	56°20·7′	3°8·5′W	X	59
Balmeadow Hill	Fife	NO2917	56°20·7′	3°8·5′W	H	59
Balmeadowside	Fife	NO3118	56°21·2′	3°6·6′W	X	59
Balmeanach	Arg & Bt	NM4433	56°25·4′	6°8·6′W	X	47,48
Balmeanach	Arg & Bt	NM6541	56°30·4′	5°48·7′W	X	49
Balmeanach	Highld	NG3243	57°24·2′	6°27·2′W	T	23
Balmeanach	Highld	NG4058	57°32·5′	6°20·2′W	X	23
Balmeanach	Highld	NG4668	57°38·1′	6°14·9′W	T	23
Balmeanach	Highld	NG5234	57°20·0′	6°6·8′W	T	24,32
Balmeanach	Highld	NG5540	57°23·3′	6°4·2′W	X	24
Balmeanach	Highld	NH5959	57°36·2′	4°21·1′W	X	26
Balmeanach Bay	Highld	NG5334	57°20·0′	6°5·8′W	W	24,32
Balmeanoch	Highld	NH5874	57°44·3′	4°22·6′W	X	21
Balmedie	Aberd	NJ9617	57°14·9′	2°3·5′W	T	38
Balmedie Fm	Aberd	NJ9517	57°14·9′	2°4·5′W	FM	38
Balmenach	Aberd	NO3697	57°3·8′	3°2·9′W	X	37,44
Balmenoch	Pth & Kin	NN6147	56°35·9′	4°15·4′W	W	51
Balmenoch Burn	Stir	NS6487	56°3·6′	4°10·6′W	W	57
Balmer	Shrops	SJ4434	52°54·3′	2°49·6′W	T	126
Balmer Down	E Susx	TQ3610	50°52·6′	0°3·6′W	X	198
Balmer Fm	E Susx	TQ3509	50°52·1′	0°4·5′W	FM	198
Balmer Heath	Shrops	SJ4434	52°54·3′	2°49·6′W	T	126
Balmerino	Fife	NO3524	56°24·5′	3°2·8′W	T	54,59
Balmer Lawn	Hants	SU3003	50°49·8′	1°34·1′W	X	196
Balmerlawn	Hants	SU3003	50°49·8′	1°34·1′W	T	196
Balmesh	D & G	NX1859	54°53·8′	4°49·9′W	X	82
Balmichael	N Ayr	NR9231	55°32·0′	5°17·3′W	T	68,69
Balminnoch	D & G	NX2765	54°57·2′	4°41·7′W	X	82
Balminnoch	S Ayr	NS3705	55°19·0′	4°33·7′W	X	70,77
Balminnoch	S Ayr	NX4087	55°9·3′	4°30·2′W	X	77
Balminnoch Loch	S Ayr	NX4187	55°9·4′	4°29·3′W	W	77
Balmitchell	Falk	NS8873	55°56·5′	3°47·2′W	X	65
Balmonth	Fife	NO5306	56°14·9′	2°45·1′W	X	59
Balmoral	Scot Bord	NT4836	55°37·1′	2°49·1′W	T	73
Balmoral Castle	Aberd	NO2595	57°2·7′	3°13·7′W	X	37,44
Balmoral Forest	Aberd	NO2487	56°58·3′	3°14·6′W	X	44
Balmore	Aberd	NO2194	57°2·1′	3°17·6′W	X	36,44
Balmore	E Dunb	NS6073	55°56·0′	4°14·0′W	T	64
Balmore	Highld	ND0067	58°35·0′	3°42·7′W	T	11,12
Balmore	Highld	NG2841	57°23·0′	6°31·1′W	T	23
Balmore	Highld	NH3533	57°21·7′	4°44·1′W	X	26
Balmore	Highld	NH5635	57°23·2′	4°23·3′W	X	26
Balmore	Highld	NH6239	57°25·5′	4°17·4′W	X	26
Balmore	Highld	NH8845	57°29·1′	3°51·6′W	X	27
Balmore	Pth & Kin	NN7059	56°42·5′	4°7·0′W	X	42,51,52
Balmore	Pth & Kin	NN8250	56°37·9′	3°55·0′W	X	52
Balmore Forest	Highld	NH3234	57°22·2′	4°47·2′W	X	26
Balmore Haughs	E Dunb	NS5973	55°56·0′	4°15·0′W	X	64
Balmore of Leys	Highld	NH6640	57°26·1′	4°13·5′W	X	26
Balmore Wood	Bucks	SP7123	51°54·3′	0°57·7′W	F	165
Balmory	Arg & Bt	NS1062	55°49·1′	5°1·5′W	X	63
Balmossie	C of Dun	NO4733	56°29·4′	2°51·2′W	X	54
Balmossie Mill	C of Dun	NO4732	56°28·9′	2°51·2′W	X	54
Balmuchy	Highld	NH8678	57°46·9′	3°54·6′W	X	21
Balmuckety	Angus	NO4052	56°39·6′	2°58·3′W	X	54
Balmuick	Pth & Kin	NN7624	56°23·8′	4°0·1′W	X	51,52
Balmuir	Angus	NO4034	56°29·9′	2°58·0′W	X	54
Balmuir	Angus	NO4137	56°31·5′	2°57·1′W	X	54
Balmuir	W Loth	NS9471	55°55·5′	3°41·3′W	X	65
Balmule	Fife	NT1091	56°6·5′	3°26·4′W	X	58
Balmule Fm	Fife	NT2088	56°4·9′	3°16·7′W	FM	66
Balmullie	Angus	NO6448	56°37·6′	2°34·8′W	X	54
Balmullo	Fife	NO4220	56°22·4′	2°55·9′W	T	54,59
Balmungie	Highld	NH7359	57°36·5′	4°7·1′W	X	27
Balmungo	Fife	NO5214	56°19·2′	2°46·1′W	X	59
Balmurrie	D & G	NX2066	54°57·6′	4°48·3′W	X	82
Balmurrie Fell	D & G	NX2167	54°58·2′	4°47·4′W	H	82
Balmuto	Fife	NT2289	56°5·5′	3°14·8′W	X	66
Balmydown	Angus	NO3835	56°30·4′	3°0·0′W	X	54
Balmyle	Pth & Kin	NO1055	56°40·9′	3°27·7′W	X	53
Balmyle	Pth & Kin	NO2744	56°35·2′	3°10·9′W	X	53
Balmyre	Pth & Kin	NO2126	56°25·4′	3°16·4′W	X	53,58
Balnaan	Highld	NH9724	57°18·0′	3°42·1′W	X	36
Balnab	D & G	NX4639	54°43·6′	4°23·1′W	X	83
Balnabeen	Highld	NH5856	57°34·6′	4°22·0′W	X	26
Balnabeeran	Highld	NH5625	57°17·8′	4°22·9′W	X	26,35
Balnabeggan	Pth & Kin	NN9152	56°39·1′	3°46·2′W	X	52
Balnabein	Pth & Kin	NN9152	56°39·1′	3°46·2′W	X	52
Bal-na-biggan	Pth & Kin	NO1153	56°39·9′	3°26·7′W	X	53
Balnabodach	N Eil	NF7101	56°59·2′	7°24·6′W	T	31
Balnabodach	Pth & Kin	NN8160	56°43·3′	3°56·2′W	X	43,52
Balnaboth	Aberd	NO6092	57°1·3′	2°39·1′W	X	45
Balnaboth	Angus	NO3166	56°47·1′	3°7·3′W	T	44
Balnaboth Craig	Angus	NO3267	56°47·6′	3°6·3′W	H	44
Balnabraid Glen	Arg & Bt	NR7415	55°22·9′	5°33·6′W	X	68
Balnabreich	Moray	NJ3450	57°32·4′	3°5·7′W	X	28
Balnabriech	Angus	NO5458	56°42·9′	2°44·6′W	X	54
Balnabruach	Highld	NH9084	57°50·2′	3°50·7′W	T	21
Balnabruaich	Highld	NH7969	57°41·9′	4°1·3′W	X	21,27
Balnabruich	Highld	ND1529	58°14·8′	3°26·4′W	T	11,17
Balnabruich	Highld	NH5491	57°53·3′	4°27·3′W	X	21
Balnabual	Highld	NH7749	57°31·1′	4°2·8′W	X	27
Balnacake	Angus	NO5557	56°42·4′	2°43·7′W	X	54
Balnacarn	Highld	NH2713	57°10·8′	4°51·3′W	X	34
Balnaclash	Highld	NJ0531	57°21·8′	3°34·3′W	X	27,36
Balnacoil	Aberd	NO5198	57°4·5′	2°48·0′W	X	37,44
Balnacoil	Highld	NC8011	58°4·6′	4°1·6′W	T	17
Balnacoil Hill	Highld	NC8111	58°4·6′	4°0·6′W	X	17
Balnacoil Lodge	Highld	NC8011	58°4·6′	4°1·6′W	X	17
Balnacoole	N Ayr	NR9130	55°31·4′	5°18·2′W	X	68,69

Balnacoul	Moray	NJ3146	57°30·2′	3°8·6′W	X	28
Balnacoul Castle	Pth & Kin	NN7326	56°24·8′	4°3·1′W	H	51,52
Balnacoul Wood	Moray	NJ3159	57°37·2′	3°8·8′W	F	28
Balnacra	Highld	NG9846	57°27·8′	5°21·6′W	T	25
Balnacraig	Aberd	NJ4700	57°5·5′	2°52·0′W	X	37
Balnacraig	Aberd	NJ6003	57°7·2′	2°39·2′W	X	37
Balnacraig	Highld	NH2953	57°32·4′	4°50·9′W	X	25
Balnacraig	Highld	NH5230	57°20·5′	4°27·1′W	X	26
Balnacraig	Highld	NH5876	57°45·3′	4°22·7′W	X	21
Balnacraig	Highld	NH6471	57°42·8′	4°16·5′W	X	21
Balnacraig	Highld	NH8203	57°6·4′	3°56·4′W	X	35
Balnacraig	Pth & Kin	NN7447	56°36·1′	4°2·7′W	X	51,52
Balnacraig	Pth & Kin	NN9359	56°42·9′	3°44·4′W	X	52
Balnacraig Ho	Aberd	NO5898	57°4·5′	2°41·1′W	X	37,44
Balnacree	Pth & Kin	NN9657	56°41·8′	3°41·4′W	X	52,53
Balnacroft	Aberd	NO2894	57°2·1′	3°10·7′W	X	37,44
Balnacroft	Pth & Kin	NN8266	56°46·5′	3°55·4′W	X	43
Balnacroft	Pth & Kin	NN8951	56°38·5′	3°48·2′W	X	52
Balnacruie	Highld	NH9524	57°17·9′	3°44·1′W	X	36
Balnacruie	Highld	NH9722	57°16·9′	3°42·1′W	X	36
Balnadelson	Highld	NC6006	58°1·5′	4°21·8′W	T	16
Balnaferry	Moray	NJ0357	57°35·8′	3°36·9′W	X	27
Balnafettach	Highld	NJ0828	57°20·3′	3°31·2′W	X	36
Balnafoich	Highld	NH5932	57°21·7′	4°20·2′W	X	26
Balnafoich	Highld	NH6835	57°23·4′	4°11·3′W	X	26
Balnafoich	Highld	NH9521	57°16·3′	3°44·0′W	X	36
Balnafroig	Highld	NH6238	57°24·9′	4°17·4′W	X	26
Balnagaig Fm	Highld	NH6342	57°27·1′	4°16·5′W	FM	26
Balnagall	Highld	NH8381	57°48·5′	3°57·7′W	X	21
Balnagarline	Highld	NH5525	57°17·8′	4°23·9′W	X	26,35
Balnagarrow	Angus	NO3757	56°42·3′	3°1·3′W	X	54
Balnagask	C of Aber	NJ9604	57°7·9′	2°3·5′W	T	38
Balnageith	Moray	NJ0257	57°35·8′	3°37·9′W	X	27
Balnaglack	Highld	NH7450	57°31·6′	4°5·8′W	X	27
Balnaglaic	Highld	NH4431	57°20·8′	4°35·1′W	X	26
Balnagleck	Arg & Bt	NR6725	55°28·1′	5°40·7′W	X	68
Balnagordonach	Highld	NH8026	57°18·8′	3°59·1′W	X	35
Balnagore Holdings	Highld	NH8277	57°46·3′	3°58·6′W	X	21
Balnagowan	Aberd	NJ5100	57°5·6′	2°48·1′W	X	37
Balnagowan Hill	Aberd	NJ5000	57°5·6′	2°49·1′W	H	37
Balnagower Cottage	Aberd	NO1593	57°1·5′	3°23·6′W	X	36,43
Balnagown	Arg & Bt	NM8541	56°31·0′	5°29·2′W	X	49
Balnagown	Highld	NH5349	57°30·7′	4°26·8′W	X	26
Balnagown Castle	Highld	NH7675	57°45·1′	4°4·6′W	A	21
Balnagown River	Highld	NH7475	57°45·1′	4°6·6′W	W	21
Balnagrantach	Highld	NH4931	57°20·9′	4°30·1′W	X	26
Balnaguard	Pth & Kin	NN9451	56°38·6′	3°43·3′W	T	52,53
Balnaguard Burn	Pth & Kin	NN9350	56°38·0′	3°44·2′W	W	52
Balnagubs	Aberd	NO8694	57°2·5′	2°13·4′W	X	38,45
Balnaguie	Highld	NH6354	57°33·6′	4°16·9′W	X	26
Balnaguisich	Highld	NH6771	57°42·8′	4°13·5′W	X	21
Balnaha	Highld	NH8880	57°48·0′	3°52·6′W	X	21
Balnahanaid	Pth & Kin	NN6247	56°35·9′	4°14·4′W	X	51
Balnahard	Aberd	NO6093	57°1·8′	2°39·1′W	X	37,45
Balnahard	Arg & Bt	NM4534	56°26·0′	6°7·7′W	T	47,48
Balnahard	Arg & Bt	NR4199	56°7·1′	6°9·6′W	T	61
Balnahard Wood	Aberd	NO6094	57°2·4′	2°39·1′W	F	37,45
Balnahow	I of M	SC3371	54°6·7′	4°32·9′W	X	95
Balnain	Highld	NH4430	57°20·3′	4°35·1′W	T	26
Balnain	Highld	NH5254	57°33·4′	4°28·0′W	X	26
Balnairn	Pth & Kin	NN7857	56°41·6′	3°59·1′W	X	42,51,52
Balnakailly	Arg & Bt	NS0173	55°54·8′	5°10·6′W	X	63
Balnakailly Bay	Arg & Bt	NS0174	55°55·3′	5°10·7′W	W	63
Balnakailly Burn	Arg & Bt	NS0272	55°54·3′	5°9·6′W	W	63
Balnakeil	Highld	NC3968	58°34·5′	4°45·6′W	T	9
Balnakeil Bay	Highld	NC3869	58°35·0′	4°46·7′W	W	9
Balnakeil Craft Village	Highld	NC3967	58°33·9′	4°45·6′W	T	9
Balnakeil Forge	Cumbr	NY0334	54°41·8′	3°29·9′W	X	89
Balnakeilly	Pth & Kin	NN9459	56°42·9′	3°43·5′W	X	52,53
Balnakelly	Aberd	NJ5011	57°11·5′	2°49·2′W	X	37
Balnakiel Ho	Scot Bord	NT4637	55°37·7′	2°51·0′W	X	73
Balnakilly	Pth & Kin	NO0760	56°43·6′	3°30·7′W	T	43
Balnaknock	Highld	NG4262	57°34·7′	6°18·5′W	T	23
Balnakyle	Highld	NH6454	57°33·6′	4°15·9′W	X	26
Balnakyle	Moray	NJ2340	57°26·9′	3°16·5′W	X	28
Balnalick	Highld	NH4331	57°20·8′	4°36·1′W	X	26
Balnallan	Highld	NJ1031	57°21·9′	3°29·3′W	X	36
Balnalon	Moray	NJ1425	57°18·7′	3°25·2′W	X	36
Balnalurigin	Highld	NH4430	57°20·3′	4°35·1′W	X	26
Balnamennoch	Angus	NO1963	56°45·4′	3°19·0′W	X	43
Balnamoan	Pth & Kin	NN9952	56°39·2′	3°38·4′W	X	52,53
Balnamoon	Aberd	NJ8955	57°35·4′	2°10·6′W	T	30
Balnamoon	Angus	NO5563	56°45·6′	2°43·7′W	T	44
Balnamoon	Moray	NJ4855	57°35·2′	2°51·7′W	X	28,29
Balnamoonhill	Moray	NJ4856	57°35·7′	2°51·7′W	X	28,29
Balnamoon's Cave	Angus	NO3983	56°56·3′	2°59·7′W	X	44
Balnamuir	Pth & Kin	NN9651	56°38·6′	3°41·3′W	X	52,53
Balnansteuartach	Pth & Kin	NN8465	56°46·0′	3°53·4′W	X	43
Balnapaling	Highld	NH7969	57°41·9′	4°1·3′W	T	21,27
Balnapolaig	Highld	NH7891	57°53·8′	4°3·0′W	X	21
Balnarge	Highld	NH5668	57°41·0′	4°24·4′W	X	21
Balnaroid	Highld	NH8550	57°31·8′	3°54·8′W	X	27
Balnasctiten	Highld	NN8499	57°4·3′	3°54·3′W	X	35,43
Balnasmurich	Highld	ND1955	58°28·8′	3°22·9′W	X	11,12
Balnastraid	Aberd	NJ4402	57°6·6′	2°55·0′W	X	37
Balnastraid	Highld	NH9324	57°17·9′	3°46·1′W	X	36
Balnasuim	Pth & Kin	NN6638	56°31·2′	4°10·2′W	X	51
Balnaut	Aberd	NO2494	57°2·1′	3°14·7′W	X	36,44
Balne	N Yks	SE5819	53°40·1′	1°6·9′W	T	111
Balnearn	Pth & Kin	NN7043	56°33·9′	4°6·5′W	X	51,52
Balneath Manor	E Susx	TQ3917	50°56·4′	0°0·9′W	X	198
Balneath Wood	E Susx	TQ4017	50°56·3′	0°0·1′W	F	198
Balneaves Cottage	Angus	NO6049	56°38·1′	2°38·7′W	X	54
Balne Beck	Wakf	SE3122	53°41·9′	1°31·4′W	W	104
Balne Croft	E Yorks	SE6318	53°39·5′	1°2·4′W	X	111
Balneden	Moray	NJ1322	57°17·1′	3°26·1′W	X	36
Balne Hall	N Yks	SE6118	53°39·5′	1°4·2′W	X	111
Balneil	D & G	NX1763	54°55·9′	4°51·0′W	X	82
Balnellan	Moray	NJ3245	57°29·7′	3°7·6′W	X	28
Balne Lodge	N Yks	SE6218	53°39·5′	1°3·3′W	X	111

Balne Moor	N Yks	SE5819	53°40·1′	1°6·9′W	X	111
Balne Moor Cross Roads	N Yks	SE5619	53°40·1′	1°8·7′W	X	111
Balnespick	Highld	NH8303	57°6·4′	3°55·4′W	X	35
Balnethill	Pth & Kin	NO1703	56°13·0′	3°19·9′W	X	58
Balniel	Fife	NO4705	56°14·3′	2°50·9′W	X	59
Balnillo	Angus	NO6560	56°44·1′	2°33·9′W	X	45
Balno	Aberd	NJ3200	57°5·4′	3°6·9′W	X	37
Balno	Highld	NH4851	57°31·7′	4°31·8′W	X	26
Balno	Highld	NJ0318	57°14·8′	3°36·0′W	X	36
Balnoe	Aberd	NO2193	57°1·5′	3°17·6′W	X	36,44
Balnoe	Highld	NH5621	57°15·7′	4°22·8′W	X	26,35
Balnoon	Aberd	NJ6244	57°29·3′	2°37·6′W	X	29
Balnowlart	S Ayr	NX1183	55°6·6′	4°57·4′W	X	76
Balnreich	Pth & Kin	NN6437	56°30·6′	4°12·2′W	X	51
Balnuarin	Highld	NH7544	57°28·4′	4°4·6′W	X	27
Balnught	Highld	NH8840	57°26·5′	3°51·5′W	X	27
Balnuick	Highld	NH9825	57°18·5′	3°41·1′W	X	36
Balnuith	Angus	NO3937	56°31·5′	2°59·0′W	X	54
Balog	I of Angl	SH4792	53°24·4′	4°17·7′W	X	114
Balole	Arg & Bt	NR3566	55°49·1′	6°13·4′W	X	60,61
Balone	Fife	NO4815	56°19·7′	2°50·0′W	X	59
Balormie	Moray	NJ2167	57°41·4′	3°19·0′W	X	28
Balornock	C of Glas	NS6268	55°53·4′	4°12·0′W	T	64
Balphadrig	Highld	NH6443	57°27·7′	4°15·6′W	X	26
Balquhadly	Angus	NO4762	56°45·1′	2°51·6′W	X	44
Balquhain	W Dunb	NS4484	56°1·7′	4°29·8′W	X	57,64
Balquhain Castle	Aberd	NJ7323	57°18·1′	2°26·4′W	A	38
Balquhain Mains	Aberd	NJ7323	57°18·1′	2°26·4′W	X	38
Balquhandy	Pth & Kin	NO0311	56°17·1′	3°33·6′W	X	58
Balquhandy Burn	Pth & Kin	NO0312	56°17·7′	3°33·6′W	W	58
Balquhandy Hill	Pth & Kin	NO0311	56°17·1′	3°33·6′W	X	58
Balquharn	Aberd	NJ5618	57°15·3′	2°43·3′W	X	37
Balquharn	Angus	NO4862	56°45·1′	2°50·6′W	X	44
Balquharn	Clackm	NS8697	56°9·4′	3°49·7′W	X	58
Balquharn	Pth & Kin	NO0335	56°30·1′	3°34·1′W	X	52,53
Balquharn Burn	Clackm	NS8699	56°10·5′	3°49·7′W	W	58
Balquharrage	E Dunb	NS6375	55°57·2′	4°11·2′W	X	64
Balquhatstone Ho	Falk	NS8572	55°55·9′	3°50·0′W	X	65
Balquhidder	Stir	NN5320	56°21·2′	4°22·3′W	T	51,57
Balquhindachy	Aberd	NJ7648	57°31·6′	2°23·6′W	X	29
Balquhindachy	Aberd	NJ8542	57°28·3′	2°14·5′W	X	30
Balquholly	Aberd	NJ7145	57°29·9′	2°28·6′W	X	29
Balrailan	Highld	NH5856	57°34·6′	4°22·0′W	X	26
Balranaich	Moray	NJ1425	57°18·7′	3°25·2′W	X	36
Balranald	N Eil	NF7270	57°36·3′	7°29·1′W	T	18
Balrazzie	S Ayr	NX1381	55°5·5′	4°55·4′W	X	76
Balrazzie Fells	S Ayr	NX1380	55°5·0′	4°55·4′W	X	76
Balreavie	Fife	NO2606	56°14·7′	3°11·2′W	X	59
Balrennie	Angus	NO5867	56°47·8′	2°40·8′W	X	44
Balrishallich	Highld	NH6375	57°44·9′	4°17·6′W	X	21
Balrobbie Fm	Pth & Kin	NN9062	56°44·5′	3°47·5′W	FM	43
Balrobert	Highld	NH6539	57°25·5′	4°14·4′W	X	26
Balronald Wood	Aberd	NJ4006	57°8·7′	2°59·0′W	F	37
Balrossie School	Inverc	NS3469	55°53·4′	4°38·8′W	X	63
Balrownie	Aberd	NO7491	57°0·8′	2°25·2′W	X	38,45
Balrownie	Angus	NO5664	56°46·2′	2°42·7′W	X	44
Balruddery Fm	Angus	NO3032	56°28·8′	3°7·7′W	FM	53
Balruddie	Clackm	NO0101	56°11·7′	3°35·3′W	X	58
Balruddrie	Clackm	NO 021	56°14·5′	7°58·0′W	X	58
Balruddrie	Clackm	NO0201	56°11·7′	3°34·3′W	X	
Balsaggart	S Ayr	NS3204	55°18·3′	4°38·4′W	X	76
Balsall	Sol	SP2376	52°23·1′	1°39·3′W	T	139
Balsall Common	Sol	SP2377	52°23·7′	1°39·3′W	T	139
Balsall Heath	Birm	SP0784	52°27·5′	1°53·4′W	T	139
Balsall Lodge Fm	Sol	SP2175	52°22·6′	1°41·1′W	FM	139
Balsalloch	S Ayr	NX1188	55°9·3′	4°57·6′W	X	76
Balsalloch Hill	S Ayr	NX1288	55°9·3′	4°56·6′W	H	76
Balsall Street	Sol	SP2276	52°23·1′	1°40·2′W	T	139
Balsam	Cambs	TL5850	52°7·8′	0°18·9′E	T	154
Balsamfield Ho	Norf	TF5518	52°44·5′	0°18·2′E	X	131
Balsams	Herts	TL4021	51°52·4′	0°2·4′E	X	167
Balsam's Fm	W Susx	SU7907	50°51·7′	0°52·3′W	FM	197
Balsarroch	D & G	NW9969	54°58·8′	5°8·0′W	A	82
Balscalloch	D & G	NX0072	55°0·4′	5°7·2′W	X	76,82
Balscote	Oxon	SP3941	52°4·2′	1°25·5′W	T	151
Balscote Mill	Oxon	SP3940	52°3·7′	1°25·5′W	X	151
Balsdean Fm	Bri & Hov	TQ3704	50°49·4′	0°2·9′W	FM	198
Balsdon Fm	W Berks	SU3665	51°23·2′	1°28·6′W	FM	174
Balsdon Hall Fm	Suff	TL8948	52°6·1′	0°46·0′E	FM	155
Balsham Wood	Cambs	TL5849	52°7·2′	0°18·9′E	F	154
Balshando	Angus	NO2836	56°30·9′	3°9·8′W	X	53
Balshando Hill	Angus	NO2735	56°30·3′	3°10·7′W	H	53
Balsier	D & G	NX4346	54°47·3′	4°26·1′W	X	83
Balsillie	Fife	NO2402	56°12·5′	3°13·1′W	X	59
Balskaig Hill	S Ayr	NX3094	55°12·9′	4°39·9′W	X	76
Balspardon	Highld	NH8052	57°32·8′	3°59·8′W	X	27
Balsporran Cottages	Highld	NN6279	56°53·2′	4°15·4′W	X	42
Balstack	D & G	NY1882	55°7·8′	3°16·7′W	X	79
Balstard	Angus	NO3556	56°41·7′	3°3·2′W	X	54
Balstone	Devon	SX4768	50°29·7′	4°9·1′W	X	201
Balstone Fm	Hants	SU5655	51°17·7′	1°11·4′W	FM	174,185
Balstonia	Thurr	TQ6983	51°31·5′	0°26·6′E	T	177,178
Balstout	Angus	NO6854	56°40·9′	2°30·9′W	X	54
Balta	Shetld	HP6607	60°44·7′	0°46·9′W	X	1
Baltasound	Shetld	HP6208	60°45·3′	0°51·2′W	T	1
Balta Sound	Shetld	HP6508	60°45·2′	0°47·9′W	W	1
Baltasound (Ordale) Airstrip	Shetld	HP6207	60°44·7′	0°51·3′W	X	1
Balterley	Staffs	SJ7650	53°3·0′	2°21·1′W	T	118
Balterley Green	Staffs	SJ7650	53°3·0′	2°21·1′W	T	118
Balterley Heath	Staffs	SJ7450	53°3·0′	2°22·9′W	T	118
Baltersan	D & G	NX4261	54°55·4′	4°27·5′W	X	83
Baltersan Cross	D & G	NX4262	54°55·9′	4°27·5′W	X	83
Baltersan Mains	S Ayr	NS2809	55°21·0′	4°42·3′W	X	70,76
Balthangie	Aberd	NJ8351	57°33·2′	2°16·6′W	T	29,30
Balthangie Cottage	Aberd	NJ8450	57°32·6′	2°15·6′W	X	29,30
Balthangie Mains	Aberd	NJ8350	57°32·6′	2°16·6′W	X	29,30
Balthayock Ho	Pth & Kin	NO1723	56°23·8′	3°20·2′W	X	53,58
Balthayock Wood	Pth & Kin	NO1823	56°23·8′	3°19·3′W	F	53,58
Baltic Fm	Wilts	SU0466	51°23·8′	1°56·2′W	FM	173
Baltier	D & G	NX4642	54°45·2′	4°23·2′W	X	83
Baltilly	Fife	NO3911	56°17·5′	2°58·7′W	T	59
Baltimore	Aberd	NJ3816	57°14·1′	3°1·2′W	X	37
Baltington	Dorset	SY8780	50°37·4′	2°10·6′W	X	194
Baltonsborough	Somer	ST5434	51°6·4′	2°39·0′W	T	182,183
Baluachraig	Arg & Bt	NR8397	56°7·2′	5°29·0′W	X	55
Baluain	Pth & Kin	NN8366	56°46·5′	3°54·4′W	X	43
Baluain Wood	Pth & Kin	NN8366	56°46·5′	3°54·4′W	F	43
Balulive	Arg & Bt	NR4069	55°50·9′	6°8·8′W	X	60,61
Balunton Hill	D & G	NX3481	55°6·0′	4°35·7′W	H	76
Balure	Arg & Bt	NM6727	56°22·9′	5°46·0′W	X	49
Balure	Arg & Bt	NM8643	56°32·1′	5°28·4′W	X	49
Balure	Arg & Bt	NM8738	56°29·4′	5°27·1′W	X	49
Balure	Arg & Bt	NM9041	56°31·1′	5°24·4′W	X	49
Balure	Arg & Bt	NN0132	56°26·6′	5°13·3′W	X	50
Balure	Arg & Bt	NR7168	55°51·3′	5°39·1′W	X	62
Balure	Arg & Bt	NR7886	56°1·2′	5°33·3′W	X	55
Baluss	Aberd	NK0047	57°31·0′	1°59·5′W	X	30
Balvack	Aberd	NJ6813	57°12·7′	2°31·3′W	X	38
Balvaird	Highld	NH5351	57°31·8′	4°26·8′W	X	26
Balvaird	Pth & Kin	NO1712	56°17·8′	3°20·0′W	X	58
Balvaird	S Ayr	NS2408	55°20·3′	4°46·1′W	X	70,76
Balvaird Castle	Pth & Kin	NO1611	56°17·3′	3°21·0′W	A	58
Balvaird Mains	Highld	NH5351	57°31·8′	4°26·8′W	X	26
Balvalachlan	Stir	NN6306	56°13·9′	4°12·2′W	X	57
Balvalaich	Highld	NC9418	58°8·6′	3°47·6′W	X	17
Balvalley Moss	Moray	NJ3725	57°18·9′	3°2·3′W	X	37
Balvarran	Pth & Kin	NO0762	56°44·7′	3°30·8′W	X	43
Balvattan	Highld	NH9622	57°16·9′	3°43·0′W	X	36
Balvattie	Highld	NH5449	57°30·7′	4°25·8′W	X	26
Balvenie	Moray	NJ3242	57°28·1′	3°7·6′W	T	28
Balvenie Castle	Moray	NJ3240	57°27·0′	3°7·5′W	A	28
Balvicar	Arg & Bt	NM7616	56°17·3′	5°36·7′W	T	55
Balvicar Bay	Arg & Bt	NM7717	56°17·8′	5°35·8′W	W	55
Balvicar Fm	Arg & Bt	NM7615	56°16·7′	5°36·7′W	FM	55
Balvidoch	Pth & Kin	NO0944	56°35·0′	3°28·4′W	X	52,53
Balvlair	Moray	NJ0148	57°30·9′	3°38·7′W	X	27
Balvonie	Highld	NH7239	57°25·7′	4°7·4′W	X	27
Balvonie of Inshes	Highld	NH6943	57°27·8′	4°10·6′W	X	26
Balvonie of Leys	Highld	NH6639	57°25·6′	4°13·4′W	X	26
Balvorist	Stir	NN6707	56°14·5′	4°8·3′W	X	57
Balvoulin	Highld	NH6328	57°19·6′	4°16·1′W	X	26,35
Balvraid	Highld	NG8416	57°11·3′	5°34·0′W	X	33
Balvraid	Highld	NH5051	57°31·7′	4°29·8′W	T	26
Balvraid	Highld	NH7243	57°27·8′	4°7·6′W	X	27
Balvraid	Highld	NH8231	57°21·5′	3°57·2′W	X	27
Balvraid Lodge	Highld	NH8331	57°21·5′	3°56·2′W	X	27
Balvraid Steading	Highld	NH7795	57°55·9′	4°4·2′W	X	21
Balvraid Wood	Highld	NH7794	57°55·4′	4°4·1′W	F	21
Balwaistie	S Lanak	NT0439	55°38·4′	3°31·1′W	X	72
Balwearie	Aberd	NJ5510	57°11·0′	2°44·2′W	X	37
Balwearie	Aberd	NO6898	57°4·6′	2°31·2′W	X	38,45
Balwearie	Fife	NT2590	56°6·1′	3°11·9′W	X	59
Balwest	Corn	SW5930	50°7·5′	5°21·9′W	T	203
Balwharrie	Pth & Kin	NN8717	56°20·2′	3°49·2′W	X	58
Balwherrie	D & G	NX0165	54°56·7′	5°6·0′W	X	82
Balwhyme	Pth & Kin	NO2350	56°38·4′	3°14·9′W	X	53
Balwyllo	Angus	NO6559	56°43·5′	2°33·9′W	X	54
Balzeordie	Angus	NO5564	56°46·2′	2°43·7′W	X	44
Bamber Bridge	Lancs	SD5626	53°44·0′	2°39·6′W	T	102
Bambers	Lancs	SD7349	53°56·4′	2°24·3′W	X	103
Bamber's Br	Lincs	TF4982	53°19·1′	0°14·6′E	X	122
Bamber's Green	Essex	TL5723	51°53·2′	0°17·3′E	T	167
Bamburgh	Northum	NU1734	55°36·2′	1°43·4′W	T	75
Bamburgh Castle	Northum	NU1835	55°36·7′	1°42·4′W	A	75
Bambury Hill Fm	Wilts	ST9690	51°36·8′	2°3·1′W	FM	163,173
Bame Wood	Devon	SX4863	50°27·1′	4°8·1′W	F	201
Bamff	Pth & Kin	NO2251	56°38·9′	3°15·9′W	X	53
Bamflatt	Scot Bord	NT0736	55°36·8′	3°28·2′W	X	72
Bamford	Derby	SK2083	53°20·8′	1°41·6′W	T	110
Bamford	Roch	SD8613	53°37·0′	2°12·3′W	T	109
Bamford Edge	Derby	SK2084	53°21·4′	1°41·6′W	X	110
Bamford Hall	Roch	SD8512	53°36·5′	2°13·2′W	X	109
Bamford Moor	Derby	SK2185	53°21·9′	1°40·7′W	X	110
Bamford Sta	Derby	SK2082	53°20·3′	1°41·6′W	X	110
Bamfurlong	Glos	SO9021	51°53·5′	2°8·3′W	T	163
Bamfurlong	Wigan	SD5901	53°30·5′	2°36·7′W	T	108
Bamham	Corn	SX3484	50°38·2′	4°20·5′W	X	201
Bampfylde Hill	Devon	SS7231	51°4·1′	3°49·2′W	X	180
Bampton	Cumbr	NY5118	54°33·5′	2°45·0′W	T	90
Bampton	Devon	SS9522	50°59·5′	3°29·4′W	T	181
Bampton	Oxon	SP3103	51°43·7′	1°32·7′W	T	164
Bampton Beck	Cumbr	NY2654	54°52·8′	3°8·8′W	W	85
Bampton Common	Cumbr	NY4716	54°32·4′	2°48·7′W	X	90
Bampton Down	Devon	SS9921	50°59·0′	3°26·0′W	X	181
Bampton Grange	Cumbr	NY5218	54°33·5′	2°44·1′W	T	90
Bampton Heath Fm	Oxon	SP3204	51°44·3′	1°31·8′W	FM	164
Bamson	Devon	SS8311	50°53·4′	3°39·4′W	X	191
Banachmore	Highld	ND1355	58°28·7′	3°29·0′W	X	11,12
Banaltrum Mhór	Arg & Bt	NR3055	55°43·1′	6°17·5′W	X	60
Bàn Beag	N Eil	NA9721	58°4·7′	7°7·9′W	X	13
Ban Brook	Warw	SP0652	52°10·2′	1°54·3′W	W	150
Banbury	Devon	SX4188	50°40·4′	4°14·6′W	X	190
Banbury	Oxon	SP4540	52°3·6′	1°20·2′W	T	151
Banbury	Shrops	SO6084	52°27·4′	2°34·9′W	X	138
Banbury Hill	Dorset	ST7811	50°54·1′	2°18·4′W	H	194
Banbury Hill Fm	Oxon	SP3620	51°52·9′	1°28·2′W	FM	164
Banbury Hill (Fort)	Dorset	ST7811	50°54·1′	2°18·4′W	A	194
Banbury Lane	Northnts	SP6552	52°10·0′	1°2·6′W	X	152
Banbury Resr	Enf	TQ3691	51°36·3′	0°1·8′W	W	177
Banbury Stone	Worcs	SO9540	52°3·7′	2°4·0′W	X	150
Bancar	Denb	SJ1166	53°11·3′	3°19·5′W	X	116
Banc Beili-Tew	Carm	SN6134	51°59·5′	4°1·1′W	H	146
Banc Blaendyffryn	Carm	SN7240	52°2·9′	3°51·6′W	X	146,147,160
Banc Blaen Magwr	Cered	SN6976	52°22·2′	3°55·1′W	X	135
Banc Blodeuyn	Carm	SN4935	51°59·8′	4°11·6′W	X	146
Banc Bronderwgoed	Powys	SN8798	52°34·3′	3°39·6′W	H	135,136
Banc Bronffin	Carm	SN6941	52°3·4′	3°54·2′W	X	146,160
Bancbryn	Carm	SN6810	51°46·6′	3°54·4′W	X	159
Banc Bwlchygarreg	Cered	SN7294	52°32·0′	3°52·8′W	H	135
Banc Cefngarreg	Carm	SN8238	52°1·9′	3°42·8′W	H	160
Banc Cefnperfedd	Powys	SO0984	52°27·0′	3°19·9′W	X	136
Banc Cerrig-fendigaid	Cered	SN8474	52°21·3′	3°41·8′W	X	135,136,147
Banc Creignant Mawr	Cered	SN7382	52°25·5′	3°51·7′W	H	135
Banc Creigol	Powys	SN9858	52°12·9′	3°29·2′W	H	147
Banc Cwmhelen	Carm	SN6811	51°47·2′	3°54·4′W	X	159
Banc Darren-fawr	Swan	SN6505	51°43·9′	3°56·9′W	X	159
Banc Dolhelfa	Powys	SN9274	52°21·4′	3°34·8′W	X	136,147
Banc Dolwen	Cered	SN7978	52°23·4′	3°46·3′W	X	135,147
Banc Du	Carm	SN5137	52°0·9′	4°9·9′W	X	146
Banc Du	Carm	SN5440	52°2·6′	4°7·3′W	X	146
Banc Du	Pemb	SN0734	51°58·5′	4°48·2′W	H	145
Banc Du	Powys	SN8656	52°11·7′	3°39·7′W	X	147
Banc Du	Powys	SN9083	52°26·3′	3°36·7′W	X	136
Banc Du	Powys	SO0479	52°24·3′	3°24·3′W	X	136,147
Bancffosfelen	Carm	SN4811	51°46·9′	4°11·8′W	T	159
Banc Fm	Carm	SN5635	51°59·9′	4°5·5′W	FM	146
Banc Gelli-las	Powys	SN9870	52°19·4′	3°29·4′W	X	136,147
Banc Gorddwr	Powys	SO1183	52°26·5′	3°18·2′W	H	136
Banc Gwyn	Powys	SO0071	52°19·9′	3°27·7′W	X	136,147
Banc Hir	Cered	SN8073	52°20·8′	3°45·3′W	X	135,136,147
Banchor	Highld	NH9140	57°26·5′	3°48·5′W	X	27
Banchor Mains Farm	Highld	NN7098	57°3·5′	4°8·2′W	FM	35
Banchoruan	Highld	NH7522	57°16·6′	4°3·9′W	X	35
Banchory	Aberd	NO6995	57°3·0′	2°30·2′W	T	38,45
Banchory	Fife	NT2688	56°5·0′	3°10·9′W	X	66
Banchory-Devenick	Aberd	NJ9102	57°6·8′	2°8·5′W	T	38
Banc Llechwedd-mawr	Powys	SN7789	52°29·3′	3°48·3′W	H	135
Banc Llety Ifan Hen	Cered	SN7185	52°27·1′	3°53·5′W	X	135
Banc Lluestnewydd	Powys	SN7989	52°29·4′	3°46·5′W	H	135
Banc Llwyd Mawr	Cered	SN8276	52°22·4′	3°43·6′W	X	135,136,147
Bancllyn	Cered	SN6066	52°16·7′	4°2·7′W	X	135
Banc Maestir-mawr	Swan	SN6605	51°43·9′	3°56·0′W	X	159
Banc Maes-yr-haidd	Carm	SN6943	52°4·4′	3°54·3′W	H	146,160
Banc Mawr	Cered	SN7260	52°13·6′	3°52·1′W	X	146,147
Banc Mawr	Cered	SN7971	52°19·7′	3°46·1′W	H	135,147
Banc Melyn	Carm	SN5440	52°2·6′	4°7·3′W	H	146
Banc Myheryn	Cered	SN7976	52°22·4′	3°46·2′W	X	135,147
Banc Mynyddgorddu	Cered	SN6686	52°27·6′	3°57·9′W	H	135
Banc Nant-rhys	Cered	SN8279	52°24·0′	3°43·7′W	X	135,136,147
Banc Nantycreuau	Cered	SN7979	52°24·0′	3°46·3′W	X	135,147
Bancombe Hill	Somer	ST4729	51°3·7′	2°45·0′W	X	193
Banc Paderau	Powys	SN8752	52°9·5′	3°38·7′W	X	147
Banc Paderau (Cairn)	Powys	SN8752	52°9·5′	3°38·7′W	A	147
Bancroft	Mil Key	SP8340	52°3·4′	0°47·0′W	X	152
Bancroft	Staffs	SK1117	52°45·3′	1°49·8′W	X	128
Bancroft Lodge	Rut	SK8501	52°36·2′	0°44·3′W	X	141
Banc Tan-yr-allt	Cered	SN6958	52°12·5′	3°54·6′W	X	146
Banc Trawsnant	Cered	SN7083	52°26·0′	3°54·3′W	H	135
Banc Ty-canol	Pemb	SN0332	51°57·3′	4°51·6′W	H	145,157
Banc Wernwgan	Carm	SN6818	51°50·9′	3°54·6′W	X	159
Banc y Bont	Cered	SN7476	52°22·3′	3°50·7′W	H	135,147
Bancycapel	Carm	SN4215	51°48·9′	4°17·1′W	T	159
Banc y Celyn	Powys	SO0446	52°6·5′	3°23·7′W	H	147
Banc y Cwm	Powys	SN9647	52°6·9′	3°30·7′W	X	147
Banc y Cwn	Powys	SN8496	52°33·2′	3°42·3′W	X	135,136
Banc-y-Daren	Carm	SN5329	51°56·6′	4°7·9′W	H	146
Banc-y-Darren	Cered	SN6782	52°25·4′	3°57·0′W	T	135
Banc y Ddau Fryn	Carm	SN7244	52°5·0′	3°51·7′W	X	146,147,160
Banc y Defaid	Powys	SN8772	52°20·3′	3°39·1′W	X	135,136,147
Bancyfelin	Carm	SN3218	51°50·4′	4°25·9′W	T	159
Bancyfford	Carm	SN4037	52°0·7′	4°19·5′W	T	146
Banc-y-ffordd	Carm	SN4137	52°0·8′	4°18·6′W	X	146
Banc y Garth	Carm	SN7147	52°6·6′	3°52·6′W	H	146,147
Bancyglyn	Carm	SN5936	52°0·5′	4°2·9′W	X	146
Banc y Gorlan	Powys	SH9203	52°37·1′	3°35·3′W	X	136
Banc y Graig	Carm	SN6944	52°5·0′	3°54·3′W	X	146,160
Banc y Groes	Powys	SN8888	52°28·9′	3°38·6′W	H	135,136
Banc-y-Gwyngoed	Cered	SN6855	52°10·9′	3°55·4′W	H	146
Bancylan	Carm	SN6731	51°57·9′	3°55·8′W	X	146
Bancyllain	Carm	SN2320	51°51·3′	4°33·8′W	X	145,158
Banc-y-llyn	Cered	SN8065	52°16·4′	3°45·1′W	X	135,136,147
Banc y Merddwr	Gwyn	SH8335	52°54·2′	3°44·0′W	X	124,125
Banc y Moelfre	Cered	SN5349	52°7·4′	4°8·4′W	H	146
Bancyn-ffald	Pemb	SM6922	51°51·2′	5°20·9′W	X	157
Banc yr Adarn	Cered	SN7877	52°22·9′	3°47·2′W	X	135,147
Banc yr Esgair	Carm	SN7041	52°3·4′	3°53·4′W	X	146,147,160
Banc yr Wyn	Cered	SN7490	52°29·8′	3°51·0′W	X	135
Banc yr Wyn	Cered	SN8173	52°20·8′	3°44·4′W	X	135,136,147
Banc-y-Warren	Cered	SN2047	52°5·8′	4°37·3′W	X	145
Bandeath Industrial Estate	Stir	NS8592	56°6·7′	3°50·5′W	X	58
Bandeen	Aberd	NJ5710	57°11·0′	2°42·2′W	X	37
Bandirran	Fife	NO4010	56°17·0′	2°57·7′W	X	59
Bandirran	Pth & Kin	NO2030	56°27·6′	3°17·4′W	X	53
Bandley	Aberd	NJ6017	57°14·8′	2°39·3′W	X	37
Bandley Wood	Cumbr	NY6719	54°34·2′	2°30·2′W	F	91
Bandoch	Angus	NO6449	56°38·1′	2°34·8′W	X	54
Bandodle	Aberd	NJ6506	57°8·9′	2°34·3′W	X	38
Bandominie	Falk	NS7977	55°58·5′	3°55·9′W	X	64
Bandon	Fife	NO2704	56°13·6′	3°10·2′W	X	59
Bandonhill	Sutton	TQ2964	51°21·8′	0°8·4′W	T	176,187
Bandons Fm	Herts	TL4033	51°58·9′	0°2·7′E	FM	167
Bandrake Head	Cumbr	SD3187	54°16·7′	3°3·2′W	T	96,97
Bandrum	Fife	NT0391	56°6·4′	3°33·1′W	X	58
Bandry	Arg & Bt	NS3590	56°4·7′	4°38·6′W	X	56
Bands	N Yks	SD8689	54°18·0′	2°12·5′W	X	98
Bandshed Moss	Aberd	NJ7513	57°12·7′	2°24·4′W	X	38
Bands, The	Durham	NY8927	54°38·5′	2°9·8′W	X	91,92
Band, The	Cumbr	NY2605	54°26·4′	3°8·0′W	X	89,90
Bane Carreg-feol-gam	Carm	SN7123	51°53·7′	3°52·1′W	F	160
Bane Du	Pemb	SN0630	51°56·3′	4°48·9′W	X	145
Bàn Eileanan	Arg & Bt	NM6741	56°30·5′	5°46·8′W	X	49
Bane's Fm	Suff	TM3077	52°20·8′	1°23·0′E	FM	156
Banff	Aberd	NJ6864	57°40·1′	2°31·7′W	T	29
Banff	Aberd	NO7973	56°51·1′	2°20·2′W	X	45
Banff Bay	Aberd	NJ6964	57°40·1′	2°30·7′W	W	29
Banff Hill	Aberd	NO7872	56°50·6′	2°21·2′W	X	45
Bangel Wood	S Glos	ST7987	51°35·1′	2°17·8′W	F	172
Banger House Fm	N Yks	SE1660	54°2·4′	1°44·9′W	FM	99
Bangeston Hall	Pemb	SM9903	51°41·6′	4°54·1′W	X	157,158

Bangle Fm	Somer	ST7246	51°13·0′	2°23·7′W	FM	183
Bangley Fm	Staffs	SK1702	52°37·2′	1°44·5′W	FM	139
Bangley Park	Staffs	SJ9414	52°43·7′	2°4·9′W	X	127
Bangly Hill	E Loth	NT4875	55°58·2′	2°49·5′W	X	66
Bangor	Gwyn	SH5771	53°13·3′	4°8·1′W	T	114,115
Bangor Flats	Gwyn	SH5973	53°14·4′	4°6·4′W	X	114,115
Bangor-is-y-coed or Bangor on Dee	Wrex	SJ3945	53°0·2′	2°54·1′W	T	117
Bangor on dee or Bangor-is-y-coed	Wrex	SJ3945	53°0·2′	2°54·1′W	T	117
Bangor Race Course	Wrex	SJ3744	52°59·6′	2°55·9′W	X	117
Bangors	Corn	SX2099	50°46·0′	4°32·8′W	T	190
Bangor's Green	Lancs	SD3709	53°34·7′	2°56·7′W	X	108
Bangor Teifi	Cered	SN3840	52°2·3′	4°21·3′W	T	145
Bangour Village Hospital	W Loth	NT0271	55°55·6′	3°33·7′W	X	65
Bangrove Wood	Suff	TL9372	52°19·0′	0°50·3′E	F	144,155
Bangup Barn	Glos	SP1219	51°52·4′	1°49·1′W	X	163
Banhadla	Powys	SJ1624	52°48·7′	3°14·4′W	X	125
Banhadlog Hall	Powys	SN9780	52°24·7′	3°30·5′W	X	136
Banham	Norf	TM0688	52°27·3′	1°2·3′E	T	144
Banham Hall	Norf	TM0689	52°27·8′	1°2·4′E	A	144
Banham Moor	Norf	TM0488	52°27·3′	1°0·6′E	X	144
Banham's Fm	Norf	TL7094	52°31·3′	0°30·7′E	FM	143
Banhaw Wood	Northnts	SP9887	52°28·6′	0°33·0′W	F	141
Banheath	Pth & Kin	NN9007	56°14·8′	3°46·1′W	X	58
Baniorlach	N Ayr	NR9135	55°34·1′	5°18·5′W	X	68,69
Banishiel Rig	Scot Bord	NT6353	55°46·4′	2°35·0′W	X	67,74
Banister Hey	Lancs	SD5442	53°52·6′	2°41·6′W	X	102
Banisters Fm	Wok	SU7763	51°21·9′	0°53·2′W	FM	175,186
Bank	Cumbr	NY1425	54°37·0′	3°19·5′W	X	89
Bank	Cumbr	NY3821	54°35·1′	2°57·1′W	X	90
Bank	Hants	SU2807	50°51·9′	1°35·7′W	T	195
Bank	Powys	SJ2512	52°42·3′	3°6·2′W	X	126
Bank	Powys	SO2262	52°15·3′	3°8·2′W	X	137,148
Bank	Shrops	SO2798	52°34·7′	3°4·2′W	X	137
Bank	S Lanak	NT0019	55°27·5′	3°34·5′W	H	78
Bankben	D & G	NX6361	54°55·7′	4°7·9′W	H	83
Bankbrae	Inverc	NS3565	55°51·3′	4°37·7′W	X	63
Bank Brow	Red & Cl	NZ7518	54°33·3′	0°50·0′W	X	94
Bankburn	Orkney	ND4492	58°49·0′	2°57·7′W	X	7
Bankburnfoot	D & G	NY2692	55°13·3′	3°9·4′W	X	79
Bank Close Fm	N Yks	SE3893	54°20·1′	1°24·5′W	FM	99
Bank Cottage	D & G	NS7006	55°20·1′	4°2·5′W	X	71,77
Bankdale Farm	Cumbr	NY4148	54°49·7′	2°54·7′W	FM	85
Bankdale Park	Cumbr	NY4148	54°49·7′	2°54·7′W	X	85
Bankdam Fm	Durham	NZ3638	54°44·4′	1°26·0′W	FM	93
Bankell	E Dunb	NS5775	55°57·1′	4°17·0′W	X	64
Bank End	Brad	SE0450	53°57·0′	1°55·9′W	X	104
Bank End	Cumbr	NY0438	54°43·9′	3°29·0′W	T	89
Bankend	Cumbr	NY0717	54°32·6′	3°25·8′W	X	89
Bankend	Cumbr	NY2753	54°52·2′	3°7·8′W	X	85
Bankend	Cumbr	NY3150	54°50·7′	3°4·0′W	X	85
Bankend	Cumbr	NY3538	54°44·2′	3°0·1′W	X	90
Bankend	Cumbr	NY3660	54°56·1′	2°59·5′W	X	85
Bank End	Cumbr	NY5177	55°5·4′	2°45·6′W	X	86
Bank End	Cumbr	SD1988	54°17·1′	3°14·2′W	T	96
Bank End	Cumbr	SD2385	54°15·5′	3°10·5′W	X	96
Bank End	Cumbr	SD2692	54°19·3′	3°7·8′W	X	96,97
Bankend	D & G	NT0801	55°17·9′	3°26·5′W	X	78
Bankend	D & G	NY0268	55°0·1′	3°31·5′W	T	84
Bank End	Lancs	SD6763	54°4·0′	2°29·8′W	X	98
Bank End	Lancs	SD8441	53°52·1′	2°14·2′W	X	103
Bank End	Leeds	SE2843	53°53·2′	1°34·0′W	X	104
Bankend	Scot Bord	NT7463	55°51·8′	2°24·5′W	X	67
Bankend	S Lanak	NS6436	55°36·2′	4°9·1′W	X	71
Bankend	S Lanak	NS8033	55°34·8′	3°53·8′W	X	71,72
Bank End	Staffs	SJ9554	53°5·2′	2°4·1′W	X	118
Bank End Fm	Lancs	SD4452	53°57·9′	2°50·8′W	FM	102
Bankend Hill	D & G	NY0268	55°0·1′	3°31·5′W	H	84
Bankend Rig	S Lanak	NS6433	55°34·6′	4°9·0′W	H	71
Bankfield	D & G	NX1957	54°52·8′	4°48·9′W	X	82
Bank Field	Red & Cl	NZ5716	54°32·4′	1°6·7′W	X	93
Bankfield	S Lanak	NS6847	55°42·2′	4°5·6′W	X	64
Bankfield Fm	Lancs	SD3839	53°50·9′	2°56·1′W	FM	102
Bankfield Grange	W Susx	TQ2221	50°58·8′	0°15·3′W	X	198
Bankfield (Inn)	Cumbr	SD1480	54°12·8′	3°18·7′W	X	96
Bank Fm	Bucks	SP9305	51°44·4′	0°38·8′W	FM	165
Bank Fm	Cambs	TL3195	52°32·5′	0°3·7′W	FM	142
Bank Fm	Cambs	TL3488	52°28·6′	0°1·2′W	FM	142
Bank Fm	Cambs	TL5168	52°17·6′	0°13·3′E	FM	154
Bank Fm	Ches	SJ4744	52°59·7′	2°47·0′W	FM	117
Bank Fm	Ches	SJ5645	53°0·3′	2°38·9′W	FM	117
Bank Fm	Ches	SJ6153	53°4·6′	2°34·5′W	FM	118
Bank Fm	Ches	SJ6867	53°12·2′	2°28·3′W	FM	118
Bank Fm	Ches	SJ6875	53°16·5′	2°28·4′W	FM	118
Bank Fm	Ches	SJ7658	53°7·4′	2°21·1′W	FM	118
Bank Fm	Ches	SJ7868	53°12·8′	2°19·4′W	FM	118
Bank Fm	Ches	SJ8054	53°5·2′	2°17·5′W	FM	118
Bank Fm	Ches	SJ8156	53°6·3′	2°16·6′W	FM	118
Bank Fm	Ches	SJ8468	53°12·8′	2°14·0′W	FM	118
Bank Fm	Ches	SJ8560	53°8·5′	2°13·0′W	FM	118
Bank Fm	Ches	SJ8766	53°11·7′	2°11·3′W	FM	118
Bank Fm	Denb	SJ2040	52°57·3′	3°11·0′W	FM	117
Bank Fm	Flint	SJ3162	53°9·3′	3°1·5′W	FM	117
Bank Fm	Flint	SJ3767	53°12·0′	2°56·2′W	FM	117
Bank Fm	Glos	SP0136	52°1·6′	1°58·7′W	FM	150
Bank Fm	Heref	SO3058	52°13·2′	3°1·1′W	FM	148
Bank Fm	Heref	SO3134	52°0·2′	2°59·9′W	FM	161
Bank Fm	Heref	SO7546	52°6·9′	2°21·5′W	FM	150
Bank Fm	Kent	TQ6245	51°11·1′	0°19·5′E	FM	188
Bank Fm	Kent	TR0537	51°6·0′	0°56·1′E	FM	179,189
Bank Fm	Lancs	SD3641	53°51·9′	2°58·0′W	FM	102
Bank Fm	Lancs	SD5347	53°55·3′	2°42·5′W	FM	102
Bank Fm	Leic	SP3399	52°35·5′	1°30·4′W	FM	140
Bank Fm	Lincs	TF1958	53°6·6′	0°12·9′W	FM	122
Bank Fm	Lincs	TF3249	53°1·6′	0°1·5′W	FM	131
Bank Fm	Lincs	TF3751	53°2·6′	0°3·0′E	FM	122
Bank Fm	Norf	TF5915	52°42·8′	0°21·6′E	FM	131
Bank Fm	Norf	TL5494	52°31·6′	0°16·6′E	FM	143
Bank Fm	Norf	TL6190	52°29·3′	0°22·7′E	FM	143

Bank Fm	Notts	SK6147	53°1·2′	1°5·0′W	FM	129
Bank Fm	Notts	SK6430	52°52·1′	1°2·5′W	FM	129
Bank Fm	Powys	SJ1603	52°37·3′	3°14·1′W	FM	136
Bank Fm	Powys	SJ2318	52°45·5′	3°8·1′W	FM	126
Bank Fm	Powys	SJ2330	52°52·0′	3°8·2′W	FM	126
Bank Fm	Shrops	SJ3213	52°42·9′	3°0·0′W	FM	126
Bank Fm	Shrops	SJ3503	52°37·5′	2°57·2′W	FM	126
Bank Fm	Shrops	SJ3803	52°37·5′	2°54·6′W	FM	126
Bank Fm	Shrops	SJ5633	52°53·8′	2°38·8′W	FM	126
Bank Fm	Shrops	SJ5942	52°58·7′	2°36·2′W	FM	117
Bank Fm	Shrops	SO5778	52°24·1′	2°37·5′W	FM	137,138
Bank Fm	Shrops	SO5868	52°18·7′	2°36·6′W	FM	137,138
Bank Fm	Suff	TL6476	52°21·7′	0°24·9′E	FM	143
Bank Fm	Wakf	SE2614	53°37·6′	1°36·0′W	FM	110
Bank Fm	Worcs	SO6162	52°15·5′	2°33·9′W	FM	138,149
Bank Fm	Worcs	SO6267	52°18·2′	2°33·0′W	FM	138,149
Bank Fm	Worcs	SO7763	52°16·1′	2°19·8′W	FM	138,150
Bank Fm	Wrex	SJ3357	53°6·6′	2°59·6′W	FM	117
Bank Fm	Wrex	SJ4840	52°57·5′	2°46·0′W	FM	117
Bank Fold	Black w Dar	SD7124	53°42·9′	2°26·0′W	T	103
Bankfold	Pth & Kin	NN9709	56°16·0′	3°39·3′W	X	58
Bankfoot	Angus	NO6543	56°34·9′	2°33·7′W	X	54
Bankfoot	Cumbr	NY7246	54°48·7′	2°25·7′W	X	86,87
Bankfoot	D & G	NX9384	55°8·6′	3°40·3′W	X	78
Bank Foot	Durham	NY9243	54°47·2′	2°7·0′W	X	87
Bankfoot	Inverc	NS2173	55°55·3′	4°51·4′W	X	63
Bankfoot	Northum	NY6664	54°58·4′	2°31·4′W	X	86
Bank Foot	Northum	NY9565	54°59·0′	2°4·3′W	X	87
Bankfoot	Northum	NZ0778	55°6·0′	1°53·0′W	X	88
Bank Foot	N Yks	NZ5906	54°27·0′	1°5·0′W	X	93
Bank Foot	N Yks	SE0043	53°53·2′	1°59·6′W	X	104
Bankfoot	Pth & Kin	NO0635	56°30·1′	3°31·2′W	T	52,53
Bank Foot Fm	Leeds	SE2744	53°53·7′	1°34·9′W	FM	104
Bankglen	E Ayr	NS5912	55°23·2′	4°13·1′W	T	71
Bank Green	Derby	SK3076	53°17·0′	1°32·6′W	X	119
Bank Green Grove	Cered	SN5156	52°11·2′	4°10·4′W	X	146
Bank Ground	Cumbr	SD3196	54°21·5′	3°3·3′W	X	96,97
Bank Hall	Cumbr	NY6433	54°41·7′	2°33·1′W	X	91
Bank Hall	Derby	SK0578	53°18·2′	1°55·1′W	X	119
Bank Hall	Lancs	SD4620	53°40·7′	2°48·6′W	A	102
Bank Hall	Lancs	SD4620	53°40·7′	2°48·6′W	X	102
Bank Hall	Lancs	SD5234	53°48·2′	2°43·3′W	X	102
Bankhall	Stir	NS8490	56°5·6′	3°51·4′W	X	58
Bankhead	Aberd	NJ5025	57°19·0′	2°49·4′W	X	37
Bankhead	Aberd	NJ5326	57°19·6′	2°46·4′W	X	37
Bankhead	Aberd	NJ5606	57°8·8′	2°43·2′W	X	37
Bankhead	Aberd	NJ5845	57°29·9′	2°41·6′W	X	29
Bankhead	Aberd	NJ6061	57°38·5′	2°39·7′W	X	29
Bankhead	Aberd	NJ6117	57°14·8′	2°38·3′W	X	37
Bankhead	Aberd	NJ6508	57°9·9′	2°34·3′W	X	38
Bankhead	Aberd	NJ7040	57°27·2′	2°29·5′W	X	29
Bankhead	Aberd	NJ8222	57°17·6′	2°17·5′W	X	38
Bankhead	Aberd	NJ8235	57°24·6′	2°17·5′W	X	29,30
Bankhead	Aberd	NJ8764	57°40·2′	2°12·6′W	X	30
Bankhead	Aberd	NO7378	56°53·8′	2°26·1′W	X	45
Bankhead	Aberd	NO7591	57°0·8′	2°24·2′W	X	38,45
Bankhead	Aberd	NO8180	56°54·9′	2°18·3′W	X	45
Bankhead	Angus	NO4639	56°32·7′	2°52·2′W	T	54
Bankhead	Angus	NO4846	56°36·4′	2°50·4′W	X	54
Bankhead	Angus	NO5043	56°34·8′	2°48·4′W	X	54
Bankhead	Angus	NO5864	56°46·2′	2°40·8′W	X	44
Bankhead	Angus	NO6042	56°34·4′	2°38·6′W	X	54
Bankhead	C of Aber	NJ8809	57°10·6′	2°11·5′W	T	38
Bank Head	Cumbr	NY1834	54°41·9′	3°15·9′W	X	89,90
Bankhead	Cumbr	NY2149	54°50·0′	3°13·4′W	X	85
Bank Head	Cumbr	NY4858	54°55·1′	2°48·2′W	X	86
Bankhead	Cumbr	NY5476	55°4·8′	2°42·8′W	X	86
Bank Head	Cumbr	NY6313	54°30·9′	2°33·9′W	X	91
Bank Head	Cumbr	SD4992	54°19·5′	2°46·6′W	X	97
Bankhead	D & G	NS7412	55°23·4′	3°58·9′W	X	71
Bankhead	D & G	NX0767	54°57·9′	5°0·5′W	X	82
Bankhead	D & G	NX7648	54°48·9′	3°55·4′W	X	84
Bankhead	D & G	NX8488	55°10·6′	3°48·9′W	X	78
Bankhead	D & G	NX9384	55°8·6′	3°40·3′W	X	78
Bankhead	D & G	NY0580	55°6·6′	3°28·9′W	X	78
Bankhead	D & G	NY4580	55°6·9′	2°51·3′W	X	79
Bankhead	E Ayr	NS4937	55°36·4′	4°23·4′W	X	70
Bankhead	E Loth	NT3972	55°56·5′	2°58·2′W	X	66
Bankhead	E Loth	NT4763	55°51·7′	2°50·4′W	X	66
Bankhead	E Loth	NT5880	56°0·9′	2°40·0′W	X	67
Bankhead	Falk	NS8080	56°0·1′	3°55·0′W	T	65
Bankhead	Fife	NO4009	56°16·4′	2°57·7′W	X	59
Bankhead	Fife	NO4410	56°17·0′	2°53·8′W	X	59
Bankhead	Fife	NO5805	56°14·4′	2°40·2′W	X	59
Bankhead	Fife	NT2089	56°5·5′	3°16·7′W	X	66
Bankhead	Highld	NH9283	57°49·7′	3°48·6′W	X	21
Bankhead	Moray	NH9658	57°36·3′	3°44·0′W	X	27
Bankhead	Moray	NJ5151	57°33·0′	2°48·7′W	X	29
Bankhead	N Ayr	NS1961	55°48·8′	4°52·9′W	X	63
Bankhead	N Ayr	NS2747	55°41·4′	4°44·7′W	X	63
Bankhead	N Ayr	NS3449	55°42·6′	4°38·1′W	X	63
Bankhead	Northum	NU0305	55°20·6′	1°56·7′W	X	81
Bankhead	Northum	NY7764	54°58·5′	2°21·1′W	X	86,87
Bankhead	Northum	NY8479	55°6·6′	2°14·6′W	X	86,87
Bankhead	Orkney	HY2719	59°3·4′	3°15·9′W	X	6
Bankhead	Pth & Kin	NO0401	56°11·8′	3°32·4′W	X	58
Bankhead	Pth & Kin	NO0418	56°20·9′	3°32·8′W	X	58
Bankhead	Pth & Kin	NO2650	56°38·4′	3°11·9′W	X	53
Bank Head	Scot Bord	NT0824	55°30·3′	3°27·0′W	H	72
Bankhead	Scot Bord	NT7727	55°32·4′	2°21·4′W	X	74
Bankhead	Scot Bord	NT7742	55°40·5′	2°21·5′W	X	74
Bankhead	S Lanak	NS6060	55°49·0′	4°13·6′W	X	64
Bankhead	S Lanak	NS8842	55°39·8′	3°46·4′W	T	71,72
Bankhead	S Lanak	NS9844	55°41·0′	3°36·9′W	X	72
Bankhead	Stir	NS7199	56°10·2′	4°4·2′W	X	57
Bankhead	W Loth	NT0272	55°56·1′	3°33·7′W	X	65
Bankhead Burn	D & G	NY2693	55°13·8′	3°9·4′W	W	79
Bankhead Fm	Ches	SJ4955	53°5·6′	2°45·3′W	FM	117

Bankhead Fm	Fife	NO3803	56°13·2′	2°59·5′W	FM	59
Bankhead Fm	Fife	NT0385	56°3·1′	3°33·0′W	FM	65
Bankhead Fm	Fife	NT1685	56°3·3′	3°20·5′W	FM	65,66
Bankhead Fm	N Lanak	NS7162	55°50·3′	4°3·2′W	FM	64
Bankhead Fm	N Yks	SE4192	54°19·6′	1°21·8′W	FM	99
Bankhead Glen	D & G	NY0483	55°8·2′	3°29·9′W	X	78
Bank Head Hill	D & G	NY2693	55°13·8′	3°9·4′W	H	79
Bankhead Ho	C of Edin	NT1566	55°53·0′	3°21·1′W	X	65
Bankhead Moss	N Ayr	NS3450	55°43·2′	4°38·1′W	X	63
Bankhead of Balcurvie	Fife	NO3300	56°11·5′	3°4·3′W	X	59
Bankhead of Kinloch	Pth & Kin	NO2543	56°34·6′	3°12·8′W	X	53
Bankhead of Raith	Fife	NT2392	56°7·1′	3°13·9′W	X	58
Bankhead of Tinwald	D & G	NY0483	55°8·2′	3°29·9′W	X	78
Bank Heads	N Yks	SD9697	54°22·4′	2°3·3′W	X	98
Bank Hey	Black w Dar	SD6930	53°46·2′	2°27·8′W	T	103
Bank Hill	Aberd	NO8191	57°0·8′	2°18·3′W	H	38,45
Bank Hill	Clackm	NS9599	56°10·6′	3°41·0′W	X	58
Bank Hill	D & G	NS7007	55°20·6′	4°2·6′W	H	71,77
Bank Hill	Powys	SJ1402	52°36·8′	3°15·8′W	H	136
Bank Hill	Scot Bord	NT7222	55°29·7′	2°26·2′W	H	74
Bank Ho	Ches	SJ8160	53°8·4′	2°16·6′W	X	118
Bank Ho	Cumbr	NY0847	54°48·8′	3°25·5′W	X	85
Bank Ho	Cumbr	NY2257	54°54·3′	3°12·6′W	X	85
Bank Ho	Cumbr	NY3054	54°52·8′	3°5·0′W	X	85
Bank Ho	Cumbr	NY3733	54°41·5′	2°58·2′W	X	90
Bank Ho	Cumbr	NY4845	54°48·1′	2°48·1′W	X	86
Bank Ho	Cumbr	SD1785	54°15·5′	3°16·0′W	X	96
Bank Ho	Cumbr	SD5497	54°22·2′	2°42·1′W	X	97
Bank Ho	Derby	SK1658	53°7·4′	1°45·2′W	X	119
Bank Ho	Derby	SK4674	53°15·9′	1°18·2′W	X	120
Bank Ho	Donc	SE6617	53°39·0′	0°59·7′W	X	111
Bank Ho	E Yorks	SE7357	54°0·5′	0°52·8′W	X	105,106
Bank Ho	E Yorks	SE7723	53°42·1′	0°49·6′W	X	105,106,112
Bank Ho	Lancs	SD3641	53°51·9′	2°58·0′W	X	102
Bank Ho	Lancs	SD6577	54°11·5′	2°31·8′W	X	97
Bank Ho	Lancs	SD8137	53°50·0′	2°16·9′W	X	103
Bank Ho	Lincs	TF2436	52°54·7′	0°9·0′W	X	131
Bank Ho	Lincs	TF2532	52°52·5′	0°8·2′W	X	131
Bank Ho	Lincs	TF5160	53°7·2′	0°15·8′E	X	122
Bank Ho	Lincs	TF5475	53°15·2′	0°18·9′E	X	122
Bank Ho	Northum	NU2005	55°20·6′	1°40·6′W	X	81
Bank Ho	N Yks	NZ5500	54°23·8′	1°8·8′W	X	93
Bank Ho	N Yks	SD6774	54°9·9′	2°29·9′W	X	98
Bank Ho	Pemb	SM8130	51°55·8′	5°10·7′W	X	157
Bank Ho	Shrops	SJ5235	52°54·9′	2°42·4′W	X	126
Bank Ho	Shrops	SJ5638	52°56·5′	2°38·9′W	X	126
Bank Ho	Shrops	SO6377	52°23·6′	2°32·2′W	X	138
Bank Ho	Staffs	SK0663	53°10·1′	1°54·2′W	X	119
Bank Ho	Wrex	SJ4541	52°58·1′	2°48·7′W	X	117
Bankhouse	Scot Bord	NT4347	55°43·0′	2°54·0′W	X	73
Bank House Fm	Brad	SE0344	53°53·8′	1°56·8′W	FM	104
Bankhouse Fm	Ches	SJ5352	53°4·0′	2°41·7′W	FM	117
Bank House Fm	Ches	SJ5851	53°3·5′	2°37·2′W	FM	117
Bankhouse Fm	Ches	SJ7954	53°5·2′	2°18·4′W	FM	118
Bank House Fm	Cumbr	NY0704	54°25·6′	3°25·6′W	FM	89
Bank House Fm	Cumbr	NY3923	54°36·2′	2°56·2′W	FM	90
Bank House Fm	Donc	SE7210	53°35·1′	0°54·3′W	FM	112
Bank House Fm	Lancs	SD4575	54°10·3′	2°50·1′W	FM	97
Bank House Fm	Lancs	SD5766	54°5·5′	2°39·0′W	FM	97
Bank House Fm	Leeds	SE2942	53°52·6′	1°33·1′W	FM	104
Bank House Fm	Lincs	TF1720	52°46·1′	0°15·5′W	FM	130
Bank House Fm	Lincs	TF3230	52°51·3′	0°2·0′W	FM	131
Bank House Fm	Lincs	TF3249	53°1·6′	0°1·5′W	FM	131
Bank House Fm	Lincs	TF3648	53°1·0′	0°2·0′E	FM	131
Bank House Fm	N Yks	NZ8407	54°27·3′	0°41·8′W	FM	94
Bank House Fm	N Yks	SE6233	53°47·6′	1°3·1′W	FM	105
Bank House Fm	Shrops	SJ5137	52°55·9′	2°43·3′W	FM	126
Bankhouse Fm	Shrops	SJ6539	52°57·1′	2°30·9′W	FM	127
Bank House Fm	Shrops	SJ6820	52°46·8′	2°28·1′W	FM	127
Bank House Fm	Shrops	SO5882	52°26·3′	2°36·7′W	FM	137,138
Bank House Fm	Shrops	SO8091	52°31·2′	2°17·3′W	FM	138
Bank House Moor	Cumbr	SD2480	54°12·9′	3°9·5′W	H	96
Bank Houses	Lancs	SD4353	53°58·4′	2°51·7′W	T	102
Banking, The	Aberd	NJ7833	57°23·5′	2°21·5′W	X	29,30
Bankland	Somer	ST3129	51°3·6′	2°58·7′W	T	193
Bankland Br	Somer	ST3229	51°3·6′	2°57·8′W	X	193
Bankland Fm	Devon	SS6705	50°50·0′	3°52·9′W	FM	191
Banklands	Norf	TF5822	52°46·6′	0°21·0′E	X	131
Bank Lane	Bury	SD7917	53°39·2′	2°18·7′W	T	109
Banklug	E Renf	NS4456	55°46·6′	4°28·8′W	X	64
Bank Moor	Cumbr	NY6412	54°30·4′	2°32·9′W	X	91
Bank Newton	N Yks	SD9153	53°58·6′	2°7·8′W	T	103
Banknock	Falk	NS7879	55°59·6′	3°56·9′W	T	64
Banknock	Falk	NS7980	56°0·1′	3°56·0′W	T	64
Bank of Gallery	Angus	NO6663	56°45·7′	2°32·9′W	X	45
Bank of Roseisle	Moray	NJ1466	57°40·8′	3°26·1′W	X	28
Bank Plantn	D & G	NY0378	55°5·5′	3°30·8′W	F	84
Bankrugg	E Loth	NT5067	55°53·9′	2°47·5′W	X	66
Banks	Aberd	NJ4945	57°29·8′	2°50·6′W	X	28,29
Banks	Aberd	NJ8036	57°25·1′	2°19·5′W	X	29,30
Banks	Cumbr	NY5664	54°58·4′	2°40·8′W	T	86
Banks	Cumbr	NY7201	54°24·5′	2°25·5′W	X	91
Banks	Cumbr	SD7086	54°16·4′	2°27·2′W	X	98
Banks	D & G	NX6948	54°48·8′	4°1·9′W	T	83,84
Banks	D & G	NY0067	54°59·5′	3°33·4′W	X	84
Banks	D & G	NY1882	55°7·8′	3°16·7′W	X	79
Banks	Highld	ND2353	58°27·8′	3°18·7′W	X	11,12
Banks	Inverc	NS2275	55°56·4′	4°50·6′W	X	63
Banks	Lancs	SD3920	53°40·6′	2°55·0′W	T	102
Banks	N Yks	SE0552	53°58·1′	1°55·0′W	X	104
Banks	Orkney	HY2528	59°8·2′	3°18·2′W	X	6
Banks	Orkney	HY2723	59°5·5′	3°16·0′W	X	6
Banks	Orkney	HY4022	59°5·1′	3°2·3′W	X	5,6
Banks	Orkney	HY4430	59°9·5′	2°58·3′W	X	5,6
Banks	Orkney	HY4547	59°18·6′	2°57·5′W	X	5
Banks	Orkney	HY5100	58°53·3′	2°50·5′W	X	6,7
Banks	Orkney	HY6523	59°5·8′	2°36·2′W	X	5
Banks	Orkney	ND3692	58°48·9′	3°6·0′W	X	7
Banks	Orkney	ND4583	58°44·1′	2°56·5′W	X	7

Banks Brows	Cumbr	SD7085	54°15·8′	2°27·2′W	X	98
Banks Cott	D & G	NX9866	54°58·9′	3°35·2′W	X	84
Banks Fee	Glos	SP1728	51°57·2′	1°44·8′W	X	163
Banks Fee Fm	Glos	SP1628	51°57·2′	1°45·6′W	FM	163
Banks Fm	Cumbr	NY3538	54°44·2′	3°0·1′W	FM	90
Banks Fm	Cumbr	NY7246	54°48·7′	2°25·7′W	FM	86,87
Banks Fm	Derby	SK4359	53°7·8′	1°21·0′W	FM	120
Banks Fm	D & G	NX8858	54°54·5′	3°44·4′W	FM	84
Banks Fm	Donc	SE6717	53°39·0′	0°58·8′W	FM	111
Banks Fm	E Susx	TQ4316	50°55·8′	0°2·5′E	FM	198
Banks Fm	N Yks	SE2648	53°55·9′	1°35·8′W	FM	104
Banks Fm	N Yks	SE5472	54°8·7′	1°10·0′W	FM	100
Banks Fm	Staffs	SK0938	52°56·6′	1°51·6′W	FM	128
Banks Fm	Staffs	SK1044	52°59·8′	1°50·7′W	FM	119,128
Banks Gate	Cumbr	NY8414	54°31·5′	2°14·4′W	X	91,92
Bank's Green	Worcs	SO9967	52°18·3′	2°0·5′W	T	150
Banks Hall	Barns	SE2806	53°33·2′	1°34·2′W	X	110
Bankshead	Cumbr	NY5864	54°58·4′	2°38·9′W	X	86
Banks Head	Orkney	ND4683	58°44·1′	2°55·5′W	X	7
Banks Head	Shetld	HU1755	60°17·0′	1°41·1′W	X	3
Bankshead	Shrops	SO3089	52°29·9′	3°1·5′W	T	137
Banks Hill	D & G	NX8858	54°54·5′	3°44·4′W	H	84
Bankshill	D & G	NY1981	55°7·3′	3°15·8′W	T	79
Banks Ho	Cumbr	NY5664	54°58·4′	2°40·8′W	X	86
Bankside	Cumbr	SD1583	54°14·4′	3°17·8′W	X	96
Bank Side	Cumbr	SD7485	54°15·8′	2°23·5′W	X	98
Bankside	D & G	NY1475	55°4·0′	3°20·4′W	X	85
Bank Side	Donc	SE6716	53°38·4′	0°58·8′W	X	111
Bankside	Falk	NS8981	56°0·8′	3°46·4′W	T	65
Bankside	Fife	NO2719	56°21·7′	3°10·4′W	X	59
Bank Side	Leeds	SE2843	53°53·2′	1°34·0′W	X	104
Bankside Brook	Ches	SJ6260	53°8·4′	2°33·7′W	W	118
Bankside Fm	Ches	SJ6362	53°9·5′	2°32·8′W	FM	118
Bankside Fm	E Yorks	SE7619	53°40·0′	0°50·6′W	FM	112
Bankside Fm	N Yks	NZ6010	54°29·1′	1°4·0′W	FM	94
Banksideyett	D & G	NY1375	55°4·0′	3°21·3′W	X	85
Bank Slack	N Yks	SE2154	53°59·1′	1°40·4′W	A	104
Banks Marsh	Lancs	SD3924	53°42·8′	2°55·0′W	W	102
Banks of Dee	D & G	NX6568	54°59·6′	4°6·2′W	X	83,84
Banks of Finnercy	Aberd	NJ7503	57°7·3′	2°24·3′W	X	38
Banks of Ladgarth	Orkney	HY5322	59°5·2′	2°48·7′W	X	5,6
Banks of Runabout	Orkney	HY4819	59°3·6′	2°53·9′W	X	6
Banks of Strichen	Aberd	NJ9654	57°34·8′	2°3·6′W	X	30
Banks of the Lees	Shetld	HU4444	60°10·9′	1°11·9′W	X	4
Banks of Yarphey	Orkney	HY5436	59°12·8′	2°47·9′W	X	5
Banks Plantn	N Yks	SE2585	54°15·8′	1°36·6′W	F	99
Banks Sands	Lancs	SD3624	53°42·8′	2°57·8′W	X	102
Banks, The	E Susx	TQ7220	50°57·4′	0°27·3′E	X	199
Banks, The	Norf	TM0279	52°22·5′	0°58·5′E	X	144
Banks, The	N Yks	SE3895	54°21·2′	1°24·5′W	X	99
Banks, The	Powys	SO0656	52°11·9′	3°22·1′W	X	147
Bank Stile	Powys	SO0672	52°20·5′	3°22·4′W	X	136,147
Bank Street	Worcs	SO6362	52°15·5′	2°32·1′W	T	138,149
Bankswell	D & G	NW9968	54°58·2′	5°8·0′W	X	82
Bank, The	Ches	SJ4446	53°0·7′	2°49·7′W	X	117
Bank,The	Cumbr	NY6214	54°31·4′	2°34·8′W	X	91
Bank, The	Scot Bord	NT0919	55°27·6′	3°25·9′W	H	78
Bank, The	Scot Bord	NT8617	55°27·0′	2°12·8′W	X	80
Bank, The	S Lanak	NT0426	55°31·4′	3°30·8′W	H	72
Bank, The	S Lanak	NT0945	55°41·7′	3°26·4′W	X	72
Bank, The	Wrex	SJ4843	52°59·2′	2°46·1′W	X	117
Bankton	E Loth	NT3973	55°57·0′	2°58·2′W	X	66
Bankton	W Susx	TQ3437	51°7·2′	0°4·7′W	X	187
Bankton Park	Fife	NO3008	56°15·8′	3°7·4′W	X	59
Bank Top	Bolton	SD7212	53°36·5′	2°25·0′W	T	109
Bank Top	Brad	SE0937	53°50·0′	1°51·4′W	X	104
Bank Top	Brad	SE1836	53°49·4′	1°43·2′W	T	104
Bank Top	Cald	SE1024	53°43·0′	1°50·5′W	T	104
Bank Top	Ches	SJ7853	53°4·7′	2°19·3′W	X	118
Banktop	Ches	SJ9370	53°13·9′	2°5·9′W	X	118
Banktop	Ches	SJ9869	53°13·3′	2°1·4′W	X	118
Bank Top	C of Stoke	SJ8751	53°3·6′	2°11·2′W	T	118
Banktop	Derby	SK1337	52°56·1′	1°48·0′W	X	128
Bank Top	Derby	SK1849	53°2·5′	1°43·5′W	X	119
Bank Top	Lancs	SD5107	53°33·7′	2°44·0′W	T	108
Bank Top	Lancs	SD6636	53°49·4′	2°30·6′W	X	103
Bank Top	Lancs	SD7646	53°54·8′	2°21·5′W	X	103
Bank Top	Lancs	SD8325	53°43·5′	2°15·0′W	X	103
Bank Top	Leeds	SE2743	53°53·2′	1°34·9′W	X	104
Banktop	Northum	NU1310	55°23·3′	1°47·3′W	X	81
Banktop	Northum	NY6565	54°59·0′	2°32·4′W	X	86
Bank Top	Northum	NZ3174	55°3·8′	1°30·4′W	X	88
Bank Top	N upon Ty	NZ1466	54°59·5′	1°46·4′W	T	88
Bank Top	N Yks	SE0362	54°3·5′	1°56·8′W	X	98
Bank Top	N Yks	SE4193	54°20·1′	1°21·7′W	X	99
Bank Top	N Yks	SE7295	54°21·0′	0°53·1′W	X	94,100
Bank Top	Shrops	SJ7342	52°58·7′	2°23·7′W	X	118
Banktop	Staffs	SJ9746	53°0·9′	2°2·3′W	X	118
Bank Top	Staffs	SK0246	53°0·9′	1°57·8′W	X	119,128
Banktop	Staffs	SK1159	53°7·9′	1°49·7′W	X	119
Bank Top Fm	Cald	SD9127	53°44·6′	2°7·8′W	FM	103
Bank Top Fm	Derby	SK1261	53°9·0′	1°48·8′W	FM	119
Banktop Fm	Derby	SK2151	53°3·6′	1°40·8′W	FM	119
Bank Top Fm	N Yks	SE4191	54°19·0′	1°21·8′W	FM	99
Bank Top Fm	Red & Cl	NZ5819	54°34·0′	1°5·8′W	FM	93
Banktop Fm	Staffs	SK0230	52°52·3′	1°57·8′W	FM	128
Banktop Hey	Derby	SK1593	53°26·3′	1°46·0′W	X	110
Banktop Wood	Staffs	SK1328	52°51·2′	1°48·0′W	F	128
Bank Wood	Cumbr	NY5544	54°47·6′	2°41·6′W	F	86
Bankwood	Cumbr	NY7319	54°34·2′	2°24·6′W	X	91
Bank Wood	D & G	NS8115	55°25·1′	3°52·4′W	F	71,78
Bank Wood	N Yks	SE6574	54°9·7′	0°59·9′W	F	100
Bank Wood	N Yks	SE7267	54°5·9′	0°53·5′W	F	100
Bank Wood	Wakf	SE2613	53°37·0′	1°36·0′W	F	110
Bankwood Fm	Notts	SK6650	53°2·8′	1°0·5′W	FM	120
Bân Lôn	Arg & Bt	NM9820	56°20·0′	5°15·6′W	X	49
Bannachra	Arg & Bt	NS3484	56°1·5′	4°39·4′W	X	56
Bannachra Muir	Arg & Bt	NS3383	56°0·9′	4°40·3′W	X	56
Bannadon	Devon	SX4794	50°43·8′	4°9·7′W	X	191
Banna Fell	Cumbr	NY1017	54°32·7′	3°23·1′W	H	89
Bannafield	Fife	NO5211	56°17·6′	2°46·1′W	X	59
Bannall's Fm	Worcs	SO6463	52°16·1′	2°31·3′W	FM	138,149
Banna Minn	Shetld	HU3630	60°3·5′	1°20·7′W	W	4
Bannamoor	Northum	NU1218	55°27·6′	1°48·2′W	X	81
Bannam's Wood	Warw	SP1164	52°16·7′	1°49·9′W	F	150
Bannans	Highld	NH7663	57°38·7′	4°4·2′W	X	21,27
Banna (Roman Fort)	Cumbr	NY6166	54°59·5′	2°36·1′W	R	86
Bannaty	Fife	NO1608	56°15·7′	3°20·9′W	X	58
Bannaty Mill	Fife	NO1708	56°15·7′	3°20·0′W	X	58
Bannatyne House	Angus	NO2841	56°33·6′	3°9·8′W	X	53
Bannau Duon	Cered	SN4254	52°9·9′	4°18·2′W	X	146
Bannau Sir Gaer	Carm	SN8121	51°52·7′	3°43·3′W	H	160
Bannel Head	Cumbr	SD4995	54°21·1′	2°46·7′W	X	97
Bannerbank Fm	E Renf	NS4952	55°44·5′	4°23·9′W	FM	64
Bannerdale	Cumbr	NY3429	54°39·4′	3°1·0′W	X	90
Bannerdale	Cumbr	NY4215	54°31·9′	2°53·4′W	X	90
Bannerdale Beck	Cumbr	NY4215	54°31·9′	2°53·4′W	W	90
Bannerdale Crags	Cumbr	NY3329	54°39·3′	3°1·9′W	X	90
Banner Down	Bath & NE Somer	ST7968	51°24·9′	2°17·7′W	X	172
Bannerfield Ho	Scot Bord	NT4629	55°33·4′	2°50·9′W	X	73
Bannerhill Fm	Warw	SP2669	52°19·3′	1°36·7′W	FM	151
Bannerley Pool	Warw	SP2186	52°28·5′	1°41·0′W	W	139
Banner Rigg	Cumbr	SD4299	54°23·2′	2°53·2′W	X	96,97
Bannerrigg Fm	Cumbr	SD4298	54°22·7′	2°53·2′W	FM	96,97
Banners Fm	Lancs	SD4941	53°52·0′	2°46·1′W	FM	102
Banners Gate	Birm	SP0895	52°33·4′	1°52·5′W	T	139
Bannest Hill	Cumbr	NY3534	54°42·1′	3°0·1′W	X	90
Bannial Flat Fm	N Yks	NZ8610	54°28·9′	0°39·9′W	FM	94
Banningham	Norf	TG2129	52°49·0′	1°17·2′E	T	133,134
Banniscue Wood	N Yks	SE5590	54°18·4′	1°8·9′W	F	100
Bannisdale	Cumbr	NY5103	54°25·5′	2°44·9′W	X	90
Bannisdale Beck	Cumbr	NY5203	54°25·5′	2°44·0′W	W	90
Bannisdale Fell	Cumbr	NY5005	54°26·5′	2°45·8′W	X	90
Bannisdale Head	Cumbr	NY5104	54°26·0′	2°44·9′W	X	90
Banniskirk Ho	Highld	ND1657	58°29·9′	3°26·0′W	X	11,12
Banniskirk Mains	Highld	ND1657	58°29·9′	3°26·0′W	X	11,12
Banniskirk Moss	Highld	ND1658	58°30·4′	3°26·0′W	X	11,12
Bannister Green	Essex	TL6920	51°51·4′	0°27·6′E	T	167
Bannister's Coppice	Shrops	SJ6103	52°37·6′	2°34·2′W	F	127
Bannister's Hollies	Staffs	SK1821	52°47·4′	1°43·6′W	F	128
Bannoch	N Ayr	NS3144	55°39·9′	4°40·8′W	X	63,70
Bannock Burn	Highld	NC8633	58°16·5′	3°56·1′W	W	17
Bannock Burn	Stir	NS7790	56°5·5′	3°58·2′W	W	57
Bannockburn	Stir	NS8090	56°5·5′	3°55·3′W	T	57
Bannockburn Ho	Stir	NS8088	56°4·4′	3°55·2′W	X	57,65
Bannock Hill	Aberd	NO6076	56°52·7′	2°38·9′W	H	45
Bannock Hole	Shetld	HU4421	59°58·6′	1°12·2′W	X	4
Banno Crags	Northum	NY8272	55°2·8′	2°16·5′W	X	86,87
Banns	Corn	SW7048	50°17·5′	5°13·4′W	T	203
Banns Fm	Corn	SW3926	50°4·8′	5°38·5′W	FM	203
Bannut Tree Fm	Worcs	SO7579	52°24·7′	2°21·7′W	FM	138
Banqueting Fm	Staffs	SJ7424	52°49·0′	2°22·7′W	FM	127
Ban Rubha	Arg & Bt	NM7106	56°11·8′	5°41·0′W	X	55
Banses Wood	Heref	SO4133	51°59·8′	2°51·2′W	F	149,161
Banstead	Surrey	TQ2559	51°19·2′	0°12·0′W	T	187
Banstead Downs	Surrey	TQ2561	51°20·3′	0°11·9′W	X	176,187
Banstead Heath	Surrey	TQ2354	51°16·5′	0°13·8′W	F	187
Banstead Place	Surrey	TQ2659	51°19·2′	0°11·1′W	X	187
Banstead's Fm	Cambs	TL7055	52°10·2′	0°29·6′E	FM	154
Banstead Wood	Surrey	TQ2657	51°18·1′	0°11·2′W	F	187
Bantam Grove	Leeds	SE2727	53°44·6′	1°35·0′W	T	104
Bantaskin	Falk	NS8779	55°59·7′	3°48·3′W	T	65
Banteith	Aberd	NJ7109	57°10·5′	2°28·3′W	X	38
Banterwick Fm	W Berks	SU5077	51°29·6′	1°16·4′W	FM	174
Bantham	Devon	SX6643	50°16·5′	3°52·5′W	T	202
Banthorpe Lodge	Lincs	TF0611	52°41·4′	0°25·5′W	X	130,142
Banton	Monm	ST5199	51°41·5′	2°42·1′W	X	162
Banton	N Lanak	NS7579	55°59·5′	3°59·8′W	T	64
Banton Ho	Lancs	SD4957	54°0·6′	2°46·3′W	X	102
Banton Loch	N Lanak	NS7378	55°58·9′	4°1·7′W	W	64
Bantons	Lancs	SD5152	53°58·0′	2°44·4′W	X	102
Bantony	E Susx	TQ7424	50°59·6′	0°29·2′E	X	199
Bantrach	Moray	NJ0245	57°29·3′	3°37·6′W	X	27
Bant's Carn	I Scilly	SV9012	49°55·9′	6°18·8′W	A	203
Banvie Burn	Pth & Kin	NN8568	56°47·6′	3°52·5′W	W	43
Banwell	N Som	ST3959	51°19·8′	2°52·1′W	T	182
Banwell Castle	N Som	ST4058	51°19·3′	2°51·3′W	X	172,182
Banwell Hill	N Som	ST3958	51°19·3′	2°52·1′W	H	182
Banwen	Nth Pt Talb	SN8509	51°46·3′	3°39·6′W	X	160
Banwen Fm	Nth Pt Talb	SN7401	51°41·9′	3°49·0′W	FM	170
Banwen Gŵyn	Powys	SN8019	51°51·6′	3°44·2′W	X	160
Banwen Gwythwch	Carm	SN6717	51°50·4′	3°55·4′W	X	159
Banwen Pyrddin	Nth Pt Talb	SN8509	51°46·3′	3°39·6′W	X	160
Banwen Torybetel	Nth Pt Talb	SS8299	51°40·9′	3°42·0′W	X	170
Banyard's Green	Suff	TM3072	52°18·1′	1°22·8′E	X	156
Banyards Hall	Norf	TM1392	52°29·3′	1°8·6′E	X	144
Banyer Hall	Norf	TF4907	52°38·6′	0°12·5′E	X	143
Baobh-bhacan Duoba	Highld	NH0244	57°26·9′	5°17·5′W	X	25
Baosbheinn	Highld	NG8666	57°38·3′	5°34·6′W	H	19,24
Bapchild	Kent	TQ9262	51°19·7′	0°45·8′E	T	178
Baptist End	Dudley	SO9488	52°29·6′	2°4·9′W	T	139
Baptiston	Stir	NS5283	56°1·3′	4°22·0′W	X	57,64
Bapton	Wilts	ST9938	51°8·7′	2°0·5′W	T	184
Bara	E Loth	NT5669	55°55·0′	2°41·8′W	X	67
Barabhas	N Eil	NB3649	58°21·3′	6°30·3′W	T	8
Barabhas Iarach	N Eil	NB3549	58°21·2′	6°31·3′W	T	8
Baracaldine Forest	Arg & Bt	NM9740	56°30·8′	5°17·5′W	F	49
Barach	Gwyn	SH2729	52°50·1′	4°33·7′W	X	123
Barachander	Arg & Bt	NN0325	56°22·8′	5°11·0′W	X	50
Barachandroman	Arg & Bt	NM6525	56°21·8′	5°47·8′W	X	49
Baradychwallt	Nth Pt Talb	SS7896	51°39·3′	3°45·4′W	X	170
Bara Fm	E Loth	NT5669	55°55·0′	2°41·8′W	FM	67
Barafundle Bay	Pemb	SR9994	51°36·8′	4°54·2′W	W	158
Baramill Plantn	Scot Bord	NT7756	55°48·1′	2°21·6′W	F	67,74
Baramore	Highld	NM6474	56°48·1′	5°51·5′W	T	40
Baranlongart Burn	Arg & Bt	NR7876	55°55·8′	5°32·8′W	W	62
Baraset	Warw	SP2355	52°11·8′	1°39·4′W	X	151
Baraskomill	Arg & Bt	NR7421	55°26·1′	5°33·9′W	X	68
Barassie	S Ayr	NS3232	55°33·4′	4°39·4′W	T	70
Barassie	S Ayr	NS3333	55°34·0′	4°38·5′W	X	70
Barassie Sands	S Ayr	NS3233	55°34·0′	4°39·4′W	X	70
Baravaig	Highld	NG6909	57°7·1′	5°48·5′W	X	32
Baravalla	Arg & Bt	NR8366	55°50·6′	5°27·5′W	X	62
Baravullin	Arg & Bt	NM8940	56°30·5′	5°25·3′W	T	49
Bara Wood	E Loth	NT5669	55°55·0′	2°41·8′W	F	67
Barbachlaw	E Loth	NT3671	55°55·9′	3°1·0′W	X	66
Barbadoes	Stir	NS5496	56°8·3′	4°20·5′W	X	57
Barbadoes Green	Monm	SO5201	51°42·6′	2°41·3′W	X	162
Barbadoes Hill	Monm	SO5200	51°42·0′	2°41·3′W	X	162
Barbae	S Ayr	NX2186	55°8·4′	4°48·1′W	X	76
Barbae	S Ayr	NX2294	55°12·7′	4°47·4′W	X	76
Barbae Dounie	Arg & Bt	NR7591	56°3·8′	5°36·4′W	X	55
Barbae Hill	S Ayr	NX2285	55°7·9′	4°47·1′W	X	76
Barbain	D & G	NX7872	55°1·9′	3°54·1′W	X	84
Barbarafield	Fife	NO3711	56°17·5′	3°0·6′W	X	59
Barbaraville	Highld	NH7472	57°43·5′	4°6·5′W	T	21
Barbaryball	Devon	SX4185	50°38·8′	4°14·6′W	X	201
Barbary Fm	Kent	TQ9761	51°19·1′	0°50·0′E	FM	178
Barbauchlaw	W Loth	NS9369	55°54·4′	3°42·3′W	T	65
Barbauchlaw Burn	W Loth	NS9168	55°53·8′	3°44·2′W	W	65
Barbay Hill	N Ayr	NS1756	55°46·0′	4°54·6′W	H	63
Barbellie Wood	S Ayr	NS3804	55°18·5′	4°32·7′W	F	77
Barben Beck	N Yks	SE0462	54°3·5′	1°55·9′W	W	98
Barber Booth	Derby	SK1184	53°21·4′	1°49·7′W	T	110
Barberfield	E Loth	NT4871	55°56·0′	2°49·5′W	X	66
Barberfields Fm	Sheff	SK2982	53°20·3′	1°33·5′W	FM	110
Barber Green	Cumbr	SD3982	54°14·1′	2°55·7′W	T	96,97
Barber's Coppice	Sol	SP1880	52°25·3′	1°43·7′W	F	139
Barber's Court Fm	S Glos	ST7088	51°35·6′	2°25·6′W	FM	162,172
Barbers Fm	Cambs	TF4212	52°41·5′	0°6·5′E	FM	131,142,143
Barbers Fm	Suff	TM2877	52°20·8′	1°21·3′E	FM	156
Barbershall	D & G	NX7269	55°0·2′	3°59·6′W	X	83,84
Barber's Hill	Lincs	TF0214	52°43·1′	0°29·0′W	X	130
Barber's Hill or Geriant	Denb	SJ2042	52°58·4′	3°11·1′W	H	117
Barbers Lodge Fm	Herts	TL2705	51°44·0′	0°9·3′W	FM	166
Barber's Moor	Lancs	SD4919	53°40·1′	2°45·9′W	T	108
Barber's Point	Suff	TM4356	52°9·1′	1°33·5′E	X	156
Barberswells	Angus	NO3049	56°37·9′	3°8·0′W	X	53
Barbeth	D & G	NX0165	54°56·7′	5°6·0′W	X	82
Barbeth	D & G	NX9665	54°58·4′	3°37·1′W	X	84
Barbeth	E Dunb	NS7072	55°55·7′	4°4·4′W	X	64
Barbethill	Aberd	NJ6555	57°35·3′	2°34·7′W	X	29
Barbey	D & G	NX6454	54°52·0′	4°6·7′W	X	83
Barbey	D & G	NX8569	55°0·4′	3°47·5′W	X	84
Barbeys Hill	E Ayr	NS5507	55°20·4′	4°16·7′W	X	71,77
Barbhas Uarach	N Eil	NB3650	58°21·8′	6°30·4′W	T	8
Barbican	C of Plym	SX4854	50°22·2′	4°7·9′W	T	201
Barbieston	S Ayr	NS4317	55°25·6′	4°28·4′W	T	70
Barboigh	E Ayr	NS5230	55°32·7′	4°20·3′W	X	70
Barbon	Cumbr	SD6282	54°14·2′	2°34·6′W	T	97
Barbon Beck	Cumbr	SD6482	54°14·2′	2°32·7′W	W	97
Barbondale	Cumbr	SD6582	54°14·2′	2°31·8′W	X	97
Barbondale	Cumbr	SD6683	54°14·7′	2°30·9′W	X	98
Barbon High Fell	Cumbr	SD6783	54°14·7′	2°30·0′W	X	98
Barbon Low Fell	Cumbr	SD6481	54°13·7′	2°32·7′W	X	97
Barbon Manor	Cumbr	SD6382	54°14·2′	2°33·6′W	X	97
Barbon Park	Cumbr	SD6483	54°14·7′	2°32·7′W	X	97
Barbot Hall	Roth	SK4294	53°26·7′	1°21·6′W	X	111
Barbour	Arg & Bt	NS2184	56°1·2′	4°51·9′W	X	56
Barbourne	Worcs	SO8457	52°12·9′	2°13·7′W	T	150
Barbra Taing	Shetld	HU4775	60°27·6′	1°8·2′W	X	2,3
Barbreack	Arg & Bt	NR7185	56°0·5′	5°40·0′W	T	55
Barbreck	Arg & Bt	NN0422	56°21·2′	5°9·9′W	X	50
Barbreck Ho	Arg & Bt	NM8306	56°12·1′	5°29·5′W	X	55
Barbreck River	Arg & Bt	NM8307	56°12·6′	5°29·5′W	W	55
Barbrethan	S Ayr	NS3307	55°20·0′	4°37·5′W	X	70,76
Barbridge	Ches	SJ6156	53°6·2′	2°34·5′W	T	118
Bar Bridge Fm	Lincs	TF3554	53°4·2′	0°1·3′E	FM	122
Barbridge Junction	Ches	SJ6157	53°6·8′	2°34·6′W	X	118
Bar Brook	Derby	SK2774	53°16·0′	1°35·3′W	W	119
Barbrook	Devon	SS7045	51°11·6′	3°51·2′W	T	180
Barbrook	Devon	SS7147	51°12·7′	3°50·4′W	T	180
Barbrook Resr	Derby	SK2777	53°17·6′	1°35·3′W	W	119
Barbuchany	D & G	NX4064	54°57·0′	4°29·5′W	X	83
Barbuie	D & G	NX7791	55°12·1′	3°55·5′W	X	78
Barbuie Burn	D & G	NX8581	55°6·9′	3°47·8′W	W	78
Barbuie Fm	D & G	NX8581	55°6·9′	3°47·8′W	FM	78
Barburgh Mill	D & G	NX9088	55°10·7′	3°43·2′W	X	78
Barbury Castle	Swin	SU1476	51°29·2′	1°47·5′W	A	173
Barbury Castle Country Park	Swin	SU1576	51°29·2′	1°46·6′W	X	173
Barbury Castle Fm	Wilts	SU1575	51°28·7′	1°46·7′W	FM	173
Barbury Hill	Wilts	SU1476	51°29·2′	1°47·5′W	H	173
Barbush	D & G	NX9572	55°2·1′	3°38·2′W	X	84
Barby	Northnts	SP5470	52°19·8′	1°12·1′W	T	140
Barby Hill	Northnts	SP5369	52°19·2′	1°12·9′W	X	152
Barby Lodge Fm	Northnts	SP5372	52°20·8′	1°12·9′W	FM	140
Barby Nortoft	Northnts	SP5572	52°20·8′	1°11·2′W	T	140
Barby Wood Fm	Northnts	SP5270	52°19·8′	1°13·8′W	FM	140
Barcafley Burn	D & G	NX8758	54°54·5′	3°45·3′W	W	84
Barcaldine	Arg & Bt	NM9641	56°31·3′	5°18·5′W	T	49
Barcaldine Castle	Arg & Bt	NM9040	56°30·6′	5°24·3′W	A	49
Barcapel	E Renf	NS5457	55°47·3′	4°19·3′W	X	64
Barcaple	D & G	NX6757	54°53·7′	4°4·0′W	X	83,84
Barcasdail	N Eil	NB3740	58°16·5′	6°28·7′W	X	8
Barcelona	Corn	SX2153	50°21·2′	4°30·6′W	T	201
Barch	Pemb	SM8823	51°52·2′	5°4·4′W	X	157
Barchain	D & G	NX8058	54°54·4′	3°51·9′W	X	84
Barchain Hill	D & G	NX8058	54°54·4′	3°51·9′W	H	84
Barcham Fm	Cambs	TL4985	52°26·8′	0°11·9′E	FM	143
Barcham Fm	Cambs	TL5876	52°21·8′	0°19·6′E	FM	143
Barcheskie	D & G	NX7345	54°47·3′	3°58·1′W	X	83,84
Barcheston	Warw	SP2639	52°3·2′	1°36·9′W	T	151
Barcheston Ground Fm	Warw	SP2840	52°3·7′	1°35·1′W	FM	151
Barchlewan	S Ayr	NX1590	55°10·4′	4°53·9′W	X	76
Barclaugh	S Ayr	NS3921	55°27·6′	4°32·0′W	X	70
Barclaugh	S Ayr	NS4020	55°27·1′	4°31·4′W	X	70
Barclay	Carm	SN4701	51°41·5′	4°12·4′W	X	159
Barclay	S Ayr	NS3208	55°20·5′	4°38·5′W	X	70,76

Barclayfield	Pth & Kin	NO1614	56°18·9'	3°21·0'W	X	58
Barclayhill Ho	Pth & Kin	NO1229	56°27·0'	3°25·2'W	X	53,58
Barclays Gill Syke	N Yks	SD7062	54°3·4'	2°27·1'W	W	98
Barclodiad y Gawres	I of Angl	SH3270	53°12·3'	4°30·5'W	X	114
Barclodiad y Gawres (Chambered Cairn)	I of Angl	SH3270	53°12·3'	4°30·5'W	A	114
Barclose	Cumbr	NY4462	54°57·2'	2°52·0'W	T	85
Barclosh	D & G	NX8562	54°56·6'	3°47·3'W	X	84
Barclosh Hill	D & G	NX8562	54°56·6'	3°47·3'W	H	84
Barcloy	D & G	NX7451	54°50·5'	3°57·3'W	X	83,84
Barcloy Hill	D & G	NX7552	54°51·1'	3°56·4'W	H	84
Barcloy Hill	D & G	NX8552	54°51·2'	3°47·1'W	H	84
Barcloy Hill	D & G	NX8755	54°52·9'	3°45·3'W	H	84
Barcombe	E Susx	TQ4114	50°54·7'	0°0·7'E	T	198
Barcombe	Somer	SS7934	51°5·8'	3°43·3'W	X	180
Barcombe Cross	E Susx	TQ4215	50°55·2'	0°1·6'E	T	198
Barcombe Down	Devon	SS7531	51°4·1'	3°46·7'W	H	180
Barcombe Fm	Dorset	ST7003	50°49·8'	2°25·2'W	FM	194
Barcombe Ho	E Susx	TQ4314	50°54·7'	0°2·4'E	X	198
Barcosh	N Ayr	NS3351	55°43·7'	4°39·1'W	X	63
Barcote Barn	Oxon	SU3296	51°39·9'	1°31·8'W	X	164
Barcote Hill	Oxon	SU3197	51°40·5'	1°32·7'W	X	164
Barcote Manor	Oxon	SU3197	51°40·5'	1°32·7'W	X	164
Barcraigs Resr	Renf	NS3857	55°47·0'	4°34·6'W	W	63
Barcroft	Brad	SE0437	53°50·0'	1°55·9'W	T	104
Barcroft	Lancs	SD8630	53°46·2'	2°12·3'W	A	103
Barcully	S Ayr	NS3104	55°18·3'	4°39·3'W	X	76
Bard	Shetld	HU5136	60°6·6'	1°4·5'W	X	4
Bardachan	Highld	NC7008	58°2·8'	4°11·7'W	X	16
Bardale Beck	N Yks	SD8785	54°15·9'	2°11·6'W	W	98
Bardale Head	N Yks	SD8684	54°15·3'	2°12·5'W	X	98
Bardaravine	Arg & Bt	NR8464	55°49·5'	5°26·5'W	X	62
Bardaravine River	Arg & Bt	NR8564	55°49·5'	5°25·5'W	W	62
Bardarroch Fm	D & G	NX7772	55°1·9'	3°55·0'W	FM	84
Bardarroch Fm	E Ayr	NS4718	55°26·2'	4°24·7'W	FM	70
Bardarroch Hill	D & G	NX7772	55°1·9'	3°55·0'W	H	84
Barden	N Yks	SE1493	54°20·2'	1°46·7'W	X	99
Barden Beck	N Yks	SE0257	54°0·8'	1°57·8'W	W	104
Barden Br	N Yks	SE0557	54°0·8'	1°55·0'W	X	104
Barden Broad Park	N Yks	SE0357	54°0·8'	1°56·8'W	X	104
Barden Fell	N Yks	SE0858	54°1·3'	1°52·3'W	X	104
Barden Fell	N Yks	SE1496	54°21·8'	1°46·7'W	X	99
Barden Furnace Fm	Kent	TQ5442	51°9·6'	0°12·5'E	FM	188
Barden Moor	N Yks	SE0257	54°0·8'	1°57·8'W	X	104
Barden Moor	N Yks	SE1495	54°21·3'	1°46·7'W	X	99
Bardennoch	D & G	NX5791	55°11·8'	4°14·4'W	X	77
Bardennoch	D & G	NX7791	55°12·1'	3°55·5'W	X	78
Bardennoch Hill	D & G	NX5691	55°11·8'	4°15·3'W	H	77
Bardennoch Hill	D & G	NX7892	55°12·7'	3°54·6'W	H	78
Barden Old Hall	N Yks	SE1493	54°20·2'	1°46·7'W	A	99
Barden Park	Kent	TQ5746	51°11·7'	0°15·2'E	T	188
Barden Scale	N Yks	SE0556	54°0·2'	1°55·0'W	X	104
Barden Tower	N Yks	SE0557	54°0·8'	1°55·0'W	A	104
Bardfield End Green	Essex	TL6230	51°56·9'	0°21·8'E	T	167
Bardfield Saling	Essex	TL6826	51°54·7'	0°26·9'E	T	167
Bard Head	Shetld	HU5135	60°6·0'	1°4·5'W	X	4
Bard Hill	Norf	TG0743	52°56·9'	1°5·3'E	X	133
Bardingley	Kent	TQ7945	51°10·8'	0°34·1'E	X	188
Bardister	Shetld	HU2350	60°14·3'	1°34·6'W	X	3
Bardister	Shetld	HU3577	60°28·8'	1°21·3'W	X	2,3
Bardley Court	Shrops	SO6980	52°25·3'	2°27·0'W	X	138
Bardmony	Pth & Kin	NO2445	56°35·7'	3°13·8'W	X	53
Bardmony Ho	Pth & Kin	NO2545	56°35·7'	3°12·8'W	X	53
Bardnabeinne	Highld	NH7190	57°53·1'	4°10·1'W	X	21
Bardnaclavan	Highld	ND0765	58°34·1'	3°35·5'W	X	11,12
Bardnaheigh	Highld	ND0364	58°33·5'	3°39·5'W	X	11,12
Bardnahoich	Highld	ND1356	58°29·3'	3°29·1'W	X	11,12
Bardner Wood	N Yks	SE2655	53°59·7'	1°35·8'W	F	104
Bardney	Lincs	TF1169	53°12·6'	0°19·9'W	T	121
Bardney Common	Lincs	TF1269	53°12·6'	0°19·0'W	X	121
Bardney Dairies	Lincs	TF1473	53°14·7'	0°17·1'W	X	121
Bardney Lock	Lincs	TF1070	53°13·2'	0°20·7'W	X	121
Bardogs Fm	Kent	TQ4651	51°14·6'	0°5·9'E	FM	188
Bardolfeston Village	Dorset	SY7694	50°44·9'	2°20·0'W	A	194
Bardolf Manor	Dorset	SY7695	50°45·5'	2°20·0'W	X	194
Bardolphs	Herts	TL3119	51°51·5'	0°5·5'W	X	166
Bardon	Leic	SK4512	52°42·5'	1°19·6'W	T	129
Bardon	Moray	NJ2054	57°34·4'	3°19·8'W	X	28
Bardon	Somer	ST0540	51°9·3'	3°21·1'W	X	181
Bardon Drive Fm	Leic	SK4712	52°42·5'	1°17·9'W	FM	129
Bardon Fm	Herts	TL3314	51°48·8'	0°3·8'W	FM	166
Bardon Hall	Leic	SK4612	52°42·5'	1°18·7'W	X	129
Bardon Hill	Leic	SK4613	52°43·0'	1°18·7'W	H	129
Bardon Mill	Northum	NY7864	54°58·5'	2°20·2'W	T	86,87
Bardonside	Moray	NJ2154	57°34·4'	3°18·8'W	X	28
Bardowie	E Dunb	NS5873	55°56·0'	4°15·9'W	T	64
Bardowie Cas	E Dunb	NS5773	55°56·0'	4°16·9'W	A	64
Bardowie Loch	E Dunb	NS5773	55°56·0'	4°16·9'W	W	64
Bardown	E Susx	TQ6629	51°2·4'	0°22·5'E	T	188,199
Bardrainney	Inverc	NS3373	55°55·5'	4°39·9'W	T	63
Bardrill	Pth & Kin	NN9108	56°15·4'	3°45·1'W	X	58
Bardrishaig	Arg & Bt	NM7412	56°15·1'	5°38·5'W	X	55
Bardristane	D & G	NX5352	54°50·7'	4°16·9'W	X	83
Bardrochat	S Ayr	NX1585	55°7·7'	4°53·7'W	X	76
Bardrochwood	D & G	NX4665	54°57·6'	4°23·9'W	X	83
Bardrochwood Moor	D & G	NX4864	54°57·1'	4°22·0'W	X	83
Bardsea	Cumbr	SD3074	54°9·7'	3°3·9'W	T	96,97
Bardsey	Leeds	SE3643	53°53·2'	1°26·7'W	T	104
Bardsey Green	Cumbr	SD2974	54°9·7'	3°4·8'W	X	96,97
Bardsey Island or Ynys Enlli	Gwyn	SH1221	52°45·5'	4°46·8'W	X	123
Bardsey Sound	Gwyn	SH1323	52°46·6'	4°45·9'W	W	123
Bards Hall	Essex	TL6613	51°47·7'	0°24·8'E	X	167
Bardsley	Oldham	SD9301	53°30·6'	2°5·9'W	T	109
Bardsley House	Oldham	SD9201	53°30·6'	2°6·8'W	A	109
Bard Sound	Shetld	HU4723	59°59·6'	1°9·0'W	W	4
Bardspark	Aberd	NO8384	56°57·1'	2°16·3'W	X	45
Bardwell	Suff	TL9473	52°19·5'	0°51·2'E	T	144,155
Bardwell Manor	Suff	TL9372	52°19·0'	0°50·3'E	X	144,155

Bardwell Windmill	Suff	TL9473	52°19·5'	0°51·2'E	X	144,155
Bar Dyke	Sheff	SK2494	53°26·8'	1°37·9'W	A	110
Bare	Lancs	SD4564	54°4·4'	2°50·0'W	T	97
Barean Loch	D & G	NX8655	54°52·9'	3°46·2'W	W	84
Bare Ash	Somer	ST2535	51°6·8'	3°3·9'W	T	182
Bareback Knowe	Scot Bord	NT3542	55°40·3'	3°1·6'W	H	73
Barebrecks	Orkney	HY3607	58°57·0'	3°6·3'W	X	6,7
Barebrecks	Orkney	HY3816	59°1·9'	3°4·3'W	X	6
Barecroft Common	Monm	ST4186	51°34·4'	2°50·7'W	X	171,172
Bareden Down	Dorset	ST8815	50°56·3'	2°9·9'W	X	183
Barefield	Arg & Bt	NS1057	55°46·4'	5°1·3'W	X	63
Barefolds	Aberd	NJ4340	57°27·1'	2°56·5'W	X	28
Barefoot Ho	Hants	SU6560	51°20·4'	1°3·6'W	X	175,186
Barefoots Fm	Hants	SU7528	51°3·0'	0°55·4'W	FM	186,197
Baregains Fm	Heref	SO6738	52°2·6'	2°28·5'W	FM	149
Bare Geo	Orkney	HY4049	59°19·7'	3°2·8'W	X	5
Bare Hill	Brad	SD9739	53°51·1'	2°2·3'W	X	103
Bare Hill	Cambs	TL3871	52°19·4'	0°1·9'E	X	154
Barehill Fm	Northnts	SP5559	52°13·8'	1°11·3'W	FM	152
Barehillock	Aberd	NJ4606	57°8·8'	2°53·1'W	X	37
Bare Ho	N Yks	SE0066	54°5·6'	1°59·6'W	X	98
Bareholme Moss	Derby	SE0601	53°30·6'	1°54·2'W	H	110
Barelands Fm	E Susx	TQ6035	51°5·7'	0°17·5'E	FM	188
Bare Lane Sta	Lancs	SD4564	54°4·4'	2°50·0'W	X	97
Bareleg Hill	Staffs	SK0264	53°10·6'	1°57·8'W	X	119
Bareleigh	Herts	TL2723	51°53·7'	0°8·9'W	X	166
Bareless	Northum	NT8738	55°38·4'	2°12·0'W	T	74
Barend	D & G	NX6973	55°2·3'	4°2·6'W	X	77,84
Barend	D & G	NX7064	54°57·5'	4°1·4'W	X	83,84
Barend	D & G	NX7548	54°48·9'	3°56·3'W	X	84
Barend	D & G	NX8855	54°52·9'	3°44·3'W	T	84
Bar End	Hants	SU4828	51°3·2'	1°18·5'W	T	185
Barend Burn	D & G	NX7074	55°2·9'	4°1·7'W	W	77,84
Barend Hill	D & G	NX6971	55°1·2'	4°2·5'W	H	77,84
Barend Hill	D & G	NX7448	54°48·9'	3°57·2'W	H	83,84
Barend Lane	D & G	NX7063	54°56·9'	4°1·4'W	W	83,84
Bareness	D & G	NX9257	54°54·0'	3°40·6'W	X	84
Barepot	Cumbr	NY0129	54°39·0'	3°31·6'W	T	89
Bareppa	Corn	SW7829	50°7·4'	5°6·0'W	T	204
Baretilt Fm	Kent	TQ7633	51°4·4'	0°31·1'E	FM	188
Barevan	Highld	NH5050	57°31·2'	4°29·8'W	X	26
Barf	Cumbr	NY2126	54°37·6'	3°13·0'W	H	89,90
Barfad	Arg & Bt	NM7903	56°10·4'	5°33·2'W	X	55
Barfad	Arg & Bt	NR8669	55°52·3'	5°24·8'W	X	62
Barfad	D & G	NX3266	54°57·9'	4°37·0'W	X	82
Barfad Fell	D & G	NX3265	54°57·3'	4°37·0'W	X	82
Barfad Loch	D & G	NX3266	54°57·9'	4°37·0'W	W	82
Barf End	N Yks	SD9598	54°22·9'	2°4·2'W	X	98
Barfen Fm	Lincs	TF4484	53°20·2'	0°10·2'E	FM	122
Barff Fm	Lincs	TF0190	53°24·1'	0°28·4'W	FM	112
Barff Fm	Lincs	TF0666	53°11·1'	0°24·4'W	FM	121
Barff Fm	Lincs	TF0961	53°8·3'	0°21·8'W	FM	121
Barff Hill Fm	E Yorks	TA0447	53°54·8'	0°24·6'W	FM	107
Barff Ho	E Yorks	TA1047	53°54·7'	0°19·1'W	X	107
Barf Fm	N Yks	TA1075	54°9·8'	0°18·5'W	FM	101
Barf Ho	N Yks	NZ2805	54°26·6'	1°33·7'W	X	93
Barfield	Cumbr	SD1087	54°16·5'	3°22·5'W	X	96
Barfield Ho	Lincs	TF0475	53°15·9'	0°26·0'W	X	121
Barfield Tarn	Cumbr	SD1086	54°16·0'	3°22·5'W	W	96
Barfil	D & G	NX8472	55°2·0'	3°48·5'W	X	84
Barfil Hill	D & G	NX8473	55°2·5'	3°48·5'W	X	84
Barfillan	Renf	NS3968	55°53·0'	4°34·0'W	X	63
Barflat	Aberd	NJ5025	57°19·0'	2°49·4'W	X	37
Bar Fm	Cambs	TL3865	52°16·2'	0°1·7'E	FM	154
Bar Fm	E Yorks	SE7649	53°56·1'	0°50·1'W	FM	105,106
Bar Fm	E Yorks	SE8239	53°50·7'	0°44·8'W	FM	106
Bar Fm	Lincs	TF2217	52°44·4'	0°11·2'W	FM	131
Bar Fm	N Yks	SE7669	54°6·9'	0°49·8'W	FM	100
Barfold	W Susx	SU9231	51°4·5'	0°40·8'W	X	186
Barfoot Br	Traf	SJ7993	53°26·2'	2°18·6'W	X	109
Barford	Hants	SU8537	51°7·8'	0°46·7'W	T	186
Barford	Norf	TG1107	52°37·4'	1°7·5'E	T	144
Barford	Warw	SP2760	52°14·5'	1°35·9'W	T	151
Barford Br	Northnts	SP8682	52°26·0'	0°43·7'W	X	141
Barford Bridge	Beds	TL1351	52°9·0'	0°20·5'W	A	153
Barford Down	Wilts	SU0532	51°5·5'	1°55·3'W	X	184
Barford Down	Wilts	SU2022	51°0·1'	1°42·5'W	X	184
Barford Down Fm	Wilts	SU1922	51°0·1'	1°43·4'W	FM	184
Barford Fm	Dorset	ST9600	50°48·2'	2°3·0'W	FM	195
Barford Fms	Hants	SU2617	50°57·3'	1°37·4'W	FM	184
Barford Ho	Somer	ST2335	51°6·8'	3°5·6'W	A	182
Barford House Fm	Leic	SP6590	52°30·5'	1°2·1'W	FM	141
Barford Park Fm	Wilts	SU1822	51°0·1'	1°44·2'W	FM	184
Barfords	Suff	TL8655	52°9·9'	0°43·6'E	X	155
Barford St John	Oxon	SP4333	51°59·9'	1°22·0'W	T	151
Barford St Martin	Wilts	SU0531	51°4·9'	1°55·3'W	T	184
Barford St Michael	Oxon	SP4332	51°59·3'	1°22·0'W	T	151
Barford Wood	Warw	SP2862	52°15·6'	1°35·0'W	F	151
Barforth Grange	Durham	NZ1615	54°32·0'	1°44·7'W	X	92
Barforth Hall	Durham	NZ1616	54°32·6'	1°44·7'W	X	92
Barfrestone	Kent	TR2650	51°12·5'	1°14·5'E	T	179
Barfs Hill	N Yks	SE5666	54°5·5'	1°8·2'W	X	100
Bargain Hill	S Ayr	NX1988	55°9·4'	4°50·0'W	H	76
Bargains Hill	Kent	TQ9260	51°18·6'	0°45·7'E	X	178
Bargain Wood	Monm	SO5203	51°43·7'	2°41·3'W	F	162
Bargaly	D & G	NX4666	54°58·1'	4°23·9'W	X	83
Bargaly Farm House	D & G	NX4666	54°58·1'	4°23·9'W	X	83
Bargaly Glen	D & G	NX4667	54°58·7'	4°24·0'W	X	83
Bargane Hill	Inverc	NS2173	55°55·3'	4°51·4'W	H	63
Bargany	S Ayr	NS2400	55°16·0'	4°45·8'W	A	76
Bargany Mains	S Ayr	NS2401	55°16·6'	4°45·8'W	X	76
Bar Gap	Durham	NY9610	54°29·4'	2°3·3'W	X	91,92
Bargarran	Renf	NS4671	55°54·7'	4°27·4'W	T	64
Bargate	Derby	SK3646	53°0·8'	1°27·4'W	T	119,128
Bargate	Kent	TQ8436	51°5·8'	0°38·1'E	X	188
Bargate Fm	Suff	TL6774	52°20·5'	0°27·5'E	FM	143
Bargate Hill	Lincs	TF1046	53°0·2'	0°21·2'W	X	130
Bargatton	D & G	NX6863	54°56·9'	4°3·2'W	X	83,84
Bargatton Hill	D & G	NX6962	54°56·4'	4°2·3'W	H	83,84
Bargatton Loch	D & G	NX6961	54°55·8'	4°2·2'W	W	83,84

Bargeddie	N Lanak	NS7063	55°50·8'	4°4·1'W	T	64
Barge Fm	Bucks	SU9080	51°30·9'	0°41·8'W	FM	175
Bargehouse Point	Arg & Bt	NS0571	55°53·8'	5°6·7'W	X	63
Bargenoch	S Ayr	NS4117	55°25·5'	4°30·3'W	X	70
Bargh Ho	N Yks	SD8168	54°6·7'	2°17·0'W	X	98
Barglachan	E Ayr	NS5722	55°28·5'	4°15·3'W	X	71
Barglass	Aberd	NJ4102	57°6·6'	2°58·0'W	X	37
Barglass	D & G	NX4151	54°50·0'	4°28·1'W	X	83
Bargod or Bargoed	Caer	ST1499	51°41·2'	3°14·3'W	T	171
Bargod Taf	Merth Tyd	SO0802	51°42·8'	3°19·5'W	W	170
Bargod Taf	Merth Tyd	ST1098	51°40·7'	3°17·7'W	W	171
Bargoed	Cered	SN3846	52°5·6'	4°21·5'W	X	145
Bargoed	Cered	SN4359	52°12·7'	4°17·5'W	X	146
Bargoed or Bargod	Caer	ST1499	51°41·2'	3°14·3'W	T	171
Bargower	E Ayr	NS4832	55°33·7'	4°24·2'W	X	70
Bargrennan	D & G	NX3576	55°3·3'	4°34·6'W	T	77
Bargrennan Burn	D & G	NX3479	55°4·9'	4°35·6'W	W	76
Bargrennan Cott	D & G	NX3378	55°4·4'	4°36·5'W	X	76
Bargrove	Kent	TR1736	51°5·2'	1°6·3'E	X	179,189
Bargrug	D & G	NX8663	54°57·2'	3°46·4'W	X	84
Bargrug Cott	D & G	NX8662	54°56·6'	3°46·4'W	X	84
Barguillean Farm	Arg & Bt	NM9828	56°24·3'	5°16·0'W	FM	49
Barham	Cambs	TL1375	52°21·9'	0°20·0'W	T	142
Barham	Fife	NO3112	56°18·0'	3°6·5'W	X	59
Barham	Kent	TR2050	51°12·6'	1°9·4'E	T	179,189
Barham	Suff	TM1451	52°7·2'	1°8·0'E	T	156
Barham Ct	Kent	TQ7053	51°15·3'	0°26·6'E	A	188
Barham Downs	Kent	TR1953	51°14·3'	1°8·6'E	X	179,189
Barham Downs	Kent	TR2151	51°13·1'	1°10·3'E	X	179,189
Barham Green	Suff	TM1451	52°7·2'	1°8·0'E	X	156
Barham Hall	Cambs	TL5746	52°5·6'	0°17·9'E	X	154
Barham Hill	Somer	SS7045	51°11·6'	3°51·2'W	H	180
Barham Ho	E Susx	TQ5317	50°56·2'	0°11·0'E	X	199
Barham's Mill Fm	Kent	TQ8746	51°11·2'	0°40·9'E	FM	189
Barhapple	D & G	NX3060	54°54·6'	4°38·7'W	X	82
Barhapple Loch	D & G	NX2559	54°54·0'	4°43·3'W	W	82
Barharrow	D & G	NX6152	54°50·9'	4°9·5'W	T	83
Barhaskine	D & G	NX2653	54°50·7'	4°42·2'W	X	82
Barhaugh Burn	Northum	NY7052	54°52·0'	2°27·6'W	W	86,87
Barhaugh Common	Northum	NY7152	54°52·0'	2°26·7'W	X	86,87
Bar Hill	Cambs	TL3863	52°15·1'	0°1·7'E	T	154
Bar Hill	D & G	NX5849	54°49·2'	4°12·2'W	H	83
Bar Hill	D & G	NX6054	54°51·9'	4°10·5'W	H	83
Bar Hill	D & G	NX6954	54°52·1'	4°2·1'W	H	83,84
Bar Hill	D & G	NX7348	54°48·9'	3°58·2'W	H	83,84
Barhill	D & G	NX8361	54°56·1'	3°49·1'W	X	84
Bar Hill	E Dunb	NS7076	55°57·8'	4°4·5'W	H	64
Bar Hill	Staffs	SJ7643	52°59·3'	2°21·0'W	T	118
Barhill Fm	Ches	SJ5246	53°0·8'	2°42·5'W	FM	117
Barhill Fm	D & G	NX1044	54°45·6'	4°56·8'W	FM	82
Bar Hill House Fm	Staffs	SJ7643	52°59·3'	2°21·0'W	FM	118
Bar Hill (Roman Fort)	E Dunb	NS7076	55°57·8'	4°4·5'W	R	64
Barhill Wood	D & G	NX6850	54°49·9'	4°2·9'W	F	83,84
Barhill Wood	D & G	NX7953	54°51·7'	3°52·7'W	F	84
Barhoise Burn	D & G	NX3362	54°55·7'	4°36·0'W	W	82
Barhoise Farm	D & G	NX3361	54°55·2'	4°35·9'W	FM	82
Barholm	D & G	NX5253	54°51·2'	4°17·9'W	X	83
Barholm	Lincs	TF0910	52°40·8'	0°22·9'W	T	130,142
Barholme Fm	Lincs	TF2132	52°52·5'	0°11·7'W	FM	131
Barholm Hill	D & G	NX5354	54°51·8'	4°17·0'W	H	83
Barholm Mains	D & G	NX4759	54°54·4'	4°22·8'W	X	83
Barhough Hall (Study Centre)	Northum	NY6951	54°51·4'	2°28·5'W	X	86,87
Barhouse	Glos	SO7714	51°49·7'	2°19·6'W	X	162
Barjarg	S Ayr	NX3277	55°3·8'	4°37·4'W	X	76
Barjarg Hill	S Ayr	NX3178	55°4·3'	4°38·4'W	H	76
Barjarg Moor	D & G	NX8590	55°11·7'	3°48·0'W	X	78
Barjarg Tower	D & G	NX8790	55°11·7'	3°46·1'W	X	78
Barkbeth	Cumbr	NY2431	54°40·3'	3°10·3'W	X	89,90
Barkbethdale	Cumbr	NY2430	54°39·8'	3°10·3'W	X	89,90
Barkbooth	Cumbr	SD4190	54°18·4'	2°54·0'W	X	96,97
Barkby	Leic	SK6309	52°40·7'	1°3·7'W	T	140
Barkby Holt	Leic	SK6709	52°40·7'	1°0·1'W	F	141
Barkby Holt Fm	Leic	SK6609	52°40·7'	1°1·0'W	FM	141
Barkby Lodge	Leic	SK6210	52°41·3'	1°4·6'W	X	129
Barkby Thorpe	Leic	SK6309	52°40·7'	1°3·7'W	T	140
Barker	N Yks	SD9785	54°15·9'	2°2·3'W	X	98
Barkerfield	Lancs	SD7842	53°52·7'	2°19·7'W	X	103
Barker Hill	Notts	SK6746	53°0·7'	0°59·7'W	X	129
Barker Ho	Northum	NY9158	54°55·2'	2°8·0'W	X	87
Barker Knott Fm	Cumbr	SD4094	54°20·5'	2°55·0'W	FM	96,97
Barker Plantn	N Yks	SE6296	54°21·6'	1°2·3'W	F	94,100
Barker Scar	Cumbr	SD3378	54°11·9'	3°1·2'W	X	96,97
Barker's Crags	N Yks	NZ5200	54°23·8'	1°11·5'W	X	93
Barkers Fm	Cambs	TL4644	52°4·7'	0°8·2'E	FM	154
Barker's Fm	Essex	TM1624	51°52·6'	1°8·7'E	FM	168,169
Barker's Fm	Norf	TL9790	52°28·6'	0°54·5'E	FM	144
Barkers Green	Shrops	SJ5228	52°51·1'	2°42·4'W	T	126
Barkers Hill	Wilts	ST9025	51°1·7'	2°8·2'W	T	184
Barkers Holt	N Lincs	SE8818	53°39·3'	0°39·7'W	F	112
Barker Slack	N Yks	SE7291	54°18·8'	0°53·2'W	X	94,100
Barker's Plantn	Leeds	SE3743	53°53·2'	1°25·8'W	F	104
Barker's Square	Shrops	SJ5813	52°43·0'	2°36·9'W	X	126
Barker Stakes	N Yks	SE7881	54°13·4'	0°47·8'W	X	100
Barkers Yard	Lincs	TF3054	53°4·3'	0°3·2'W	X	122
Barkestone-le-Vale	Leic	SK7834	52°54·1'	0°50·0'W	T	129
Barkestone Wood	Leic	SK7932	52°53·0'	0°49·2'W	F	129
Barkeval	Highld	NM3797	56°59·6'	6°19·4'W	H	39
Bark Fm	Lincs	TF2760	53°7·6'	0°5·7'W	FM	122
Barkfold Manor	W Susx	TQ0226	51°1·7'	0°32·3'W	X	186,197
Barkham	Somer	SS7833	51°5·2'	3°44·1'W	X	180
Barkham	Wok	SU7867	51°24·0'	0°52·3'W	T	175
Barkham Manor	Wok	SU7867	51°24·0'	0°52·3'W	X	175
Barkham Manor Vineyard	E Susx	TQ4321	50°58·5'	0°2·6'E	X	198
Barkham Square	Wok	SU7867	51°23·5'	0°52·3'W	X	175
Bark Hill	Shetld	HT9539	60°8·4'	2°4·9'W	H	4
Bark Ho	Ches	SJ6368	53°12·7'	2°32·8'W	X	118
Barkhouse	Cumbr	NY1931	54°40·3'	3°14·9'W	X	89,90
Bark Houses	N Yks	SD7968	54°6·7'	2°18·9'W	X	98
Bark House Wood	Cumbr	SD3792	54°19·4'	2°57·7'W	F	96,97

Barkin	Cumbr	SD6685	54°15·8'	2°30·9'W	X	98
Barkin Beck	Cumbr	SD6684	54°15·3'	2°30·9'W	W	98
Barking	Bark & Dag	TQ4484	51°32·4'	0°5·0'E	T	177
Barking	Suff	TM0753	52°8·4'	1°1·9'E	T	155
Barkin Gate	Lancs	SD6064	54°4·5'	2°36·3'W	X	97
Barking Creek	Newham	TQ4482	51°31·3'	0°4·9'E	W	177
Barkingdon Manor	Devon	SX7765	50°28·5'	3°43·6'W	X	202
Barking Reach	Gren	TQ4681	51°30·8'	0°6·6'E	W	177
Barkingside	Redbr	TQ4489	51°35·1'	0°5·1'E	T	177
Barking Tye	Suff	TM0652	52°7·9'	1°1·0'E	T	155
Barkin Ho	Cumbr	SD5785	54°15·8'	2°39·2'W	X	97
Barkin Isles	N Eil	NB4023	58°7·4'	6°24·5'W	X	14
Barkisland	Cald	SE0519	53°40·3'	1°55·0'W	T	110
Barkla Shop	Corn	SW7350	50°18·6'	5°10·9'W	T	204
Barklye	E Susx	TQ6123	50°59·3'	0°18·0'E	X	199
Bark Plantn	N Yks	SD9464	54°4·6'	2°5·1'W	F	98
Barksore	Kent	TQ8667	51°22·5'	0°40·7'E	X	178
Barksore Marshes	Kent	TQ8768	51°23·0'	0°41·6'E	W	178
Bark Stack	Shetld	HU3894	60°37·9'	1°17·8'W	X	1,2
Barkston	Lincs	SK9341	52°57·7'	0°36·5'W	T	130
Barkston Ash	N Yks	SE4936	53°49·3'	1°14·9'W	T	105
Barkston Gorse Fm	Lincs	SK9143	52°58·8'	0°38·3'W	FM	130
Barkston Granges	Lincs	SK9241	52°57·7'	0°37·4'W	X	130
Barkston Heath	Lincs	SK9541	52°57·7'	0°34·7'W	X	130
Barkway	Herts	TL3835	52°0·0'	0°1·0'E	T	154
Barkway Equestrian Centre	Herts	TL3834	51°59·5'	0°1·0'E	X	154
Barkway Hill	Herts	TL3936	52°0·5'	0°1·9'E	X	154
Barlae	D & G	NX2760	54°54·5'	4°41·5'W	X	82
Barlae	D & G	NX3953	54°51·0'	4°30·0'W	X	83
Barlae Hill	D & G	NX5888	55°10·2'	4°13·3'W	X	77
Barlae Hill	D & G	NX7857	54°53·8'	3°53·7'W	H	84
Barlae Hill	D & G	NX9072	55°2·1'	3°42·8'W	H	84
Barlaes	D & G	NX6385	55°8·7'	4°8·5'W	X	77
Barlaes Cott	D & G	NX6185	55°8·6'	4°10·4'W	X	77
Barlaes Hill	D & G	NX6285	55°8·7'	4°9·5'W	H	77
Barlaes Plantation	D & G	NX6284	55°8·1'	4°9·5'W	F	77
Barlake	Somer	ST6549	51°14·6'	2°29·7'W	T	183
Barlake Fm	Somer	ST6649	51°14·6'	2°28·8'W	FM	183
Barlam Beck	E Yorks	SE7357	54°0·5'	0°52·8'W	W	105,106
Barlanark	C of Glas	NS6664	55°51·3'	4°8·0'W	T	64
Barland	Powys	SO2862	52°15·3'	3°2·9'W	T	137,148
Barland Common	Swan	SS5889	51°35·2'	4°2·6'W	T	159
Barland Fields	Notts	SK6729	52°51·5'	0°59·9'W	X	129
Barlaston	Staffs	SJ8938	52°56·6'	2°9·4'W	T	127
Barlaston Common	Staffs	SJ9239	52°57·1'	2°6·7'W	X	127
Barlauchlan	D & G	NX3961	54°55·3'	4°30·3'W	X	83
Barlaugh	S Ayr	NS3309	55°21·1'	4°37·6'W	X	70,76
Barlavington	W Susx	SU9716	50°56·3'	0°36·8'W	T	197
Barlavington Down	W Susx	SU9615	50°55·8'	0°37·6'W	H	197
Barlay	D & G	NX6877	55°4·4'	4°3·6'W	X	77,84
Barlay	D & G	NX9466	54°58·9'	3°39·0'W	X	84
Barlay Burn	D & G	NX6258	54°54·1'	4°8·7'W	W	83
Barlay Burn	D & G	NX6878	55°5·0'	4°3·6'W	W	77,84
Barlay Hill	D & G	NX7078	55°5·0'	4°1·8'W	X	77,84
Barlay Hill	D & G	NX9467	54°59·4'	3°39·0'W	H	84
Barlborough	Derby	SK4777	53°17·5'	1°17·3'W	T	120
Barlborough Common	Derby	SK4776	53°17·0'	1°17·3'W	X	120
Barlborough Hall	Derby	SK4778	53°18·0'	1°17·3'W	X	120
Barlborough Low Common	Derby	SK4677	53°17·5'	1°18·2'W	X	120
Barlby	N Yks	SE6334	53°48·1'	1°2·2'W	T	105,106
Barlea	Arg & Bt	NR6636	55°33·9'	5°42·2'W	X	68
Barledziew	D & G	NX4245	54°46·8'	4°27·0'W	X	83
Barleighford Fm	Ches	SJ9464	53°10·6'	2°5·0'W	FM	118
Barleith	E Ayr	NS4535	55°35·3'	4°27·1'W	X	70
Barlennan	D & G	NX3260	54°54·6'	4°36·8'W	X	82
Barlestone	Leic	SK4205	52°38·7'	1°22·4'W	T	140
Barlewan	S Ayr	NS3108	55°20·5'	4°39·5'W	X	70,76
Barley	Herts	TL4038	52°1·6'	0°2·8'E	T	154
Barley	Lancs	SD8240	53°51·6'	2°16·0'W	T	103
Barley Bank	Lancs	SD6565	54°5·0'	2°31·7'W	X	97
Barley Bay	Devon	SS2327	51°1·1'	4°31·0'W	W	190
Barleybeans	Herts	TL1519	51°51·7'	0°19·4'W	X	166
Barley Burn	Scot Bord	NY4799	55°17·2'	2°49·6'W	W	79
Barley Carr Tongue	N Yks	SE9296	54°21·3'	0°34·6'W	X	94,101
Barleycastle Fm	Warr	SJ6583	53°20·8'	2°31·1'W	FM	109
Barley Close	Lincs	TF2845	52°59·5'	0°5·2'W	X	131
Barleyclose Fm	S Glos	ST7278	51°30·2'	2°23·8'W	FM	172
Barleycombe	Devon	SX7159	50°25·2'	3°48·6'W	X	202
Barleycombe Lodge	N Som	ST3857	51°18·8'	2°53·0'W	X	182
Barleycroft End	Herts	TL4327	51°55·6'	0°5·2'E	T	167
Barleycroft Fm	Wilts	SU0643	51°11·4'	1°54·5'W	FM	184
Barley Down Ho	Hants	SU5529	51°3·7'	1°12·5'W	X	185
Barley End	Bucks	SP9614	51°49·2'	0°36·0'W	T	165
Barley Fields	Oxon	SP6331	51°58·7'	1°4·6'W	X	152,165
Barley Green	Lancs	SD8140	53°51·6'	2°16·9'W	T	103
Barley Green	Suff	TM2474	52°19·3'	1°17·6'E	X	156
Barley Green	Suff	TM2573	52°18·8'	1°18·5'E	X	156
Barley Hall	Durham	NZ1752	54°52·0'	1°43·7'W	X	88
Barley Hill	Northum	NT8834	55°36·2'	2°11·0'W	H	74
Barleyhill	Northum	NZ0254	54°53·1'	1°57·7'W	X	87
Barley Hill	Somer	ST3112	50°54·4'	2°58·5'W	X	193
Barley Hill Fm	Oxon	SP3222	51°54·0'	1°31·7'W	FM	164
Barleyhill Fm	Wilts	ST9660	51°20·6'	2°3·1'W	FM	173
Barleyholme Wood	Notts	SK7344	52°59·5'	0°54·3'W	F	129
Barley Knapp Fm	Heref	SO3239	52°3·0'	2°59·1'W	FM	161
Barleylands	Essex	TQ6992	51°36·3'	0°26·8'E	X	177,178
Barley Mill	E Loth	NT4566	55°53·3'	2°52·3'W	X	66
Barleymill Bank	Northum	NT9240	55°39·5'	2°7·2'W	X	74,75
Barley Moor	Lancs	SD7940	53°51·6'	2°18·7'W	X	103
Barley Mount	Carm	SN5220	51°51·8'	4°8·6'W	X	159
Barley Mow	Ghead	NZ2754	54°53·0'	1°34·3'W	T	88
Barley Mow Fm	Northnts	SP5733	51°59·8'	1°9·8'W	FM	152
Barleypark Fm	Oxon	SP3406	51°45·3'	1°30·1'W	FM	164
Barleypark Wood	Oxon	SP3406	51°45·3'	1°30·1'W	F	164
Barley Pound	Hants	SU7946	51°12·7'	0°51·7'W	A	186
Barley Ridge	S Glos	ST7887	51°35·1'	2°18·7'W	X	172
Barleyside	Falk	NS8676	55°58·1'	3°49·1'W	X	65
Barleythorpe	Rut	SK8409	52°40·6'	0°45·1'W	T	141
Barley Wood	N Som	ST4863	51°22·1'	2°44·4'W	F	172,182
Barleywood Fm	Hants	SU7236	51°7·4'	0°57·9'W	FM	186
Barlia Hill	Arg & Bt	NR9972	55°54·2'	5°12·5'W	H	62
Bar-liath	Arg & Bt	NR9694	56°6·0'	5°16·4'W	X	55
Barling	Essex	TQ9389	51°34·2'	0°47·5'E	T	178
Barling Fm	Kent	TQ8348	51°12·3'	0°37·6'E	FM	188
Barling Green Fm	Kent	TQ8545	51°10·7'	0°39·2'E	FM	189
Barling Hall Fm	Essex	TQ9389	51°34·2'	0°47·5'E	FM	178
Barling Marsh	Essex	TQ9390	51°34·8'	0°47·5'E	X	178
Barling Ness	Essex	TQ9491	51°35·3'	0°48·4'E	X	178
Barlings	Lincs	TF0774	53°15·4'	0°23·4'W	T	121
Barlings Eau	Lincs	TF0579	53°18·1'	0°25·1'W	W	121
Barlings Eau	Lincs	TF0973	53°14·8'	0°21·6'W	W	121
Barlings Hall	Lincs	TF0874	53°15·4'	0°22·5'W	X	121
Barlings Park	Lincs	TF0674	53°15·4'	0°24·3'W	F	121
Barlocco	D & G	NX5948	54°48·7'	4°11·2'W	X	83
Barlocco	D & G	NX7847	54°48·4'	3°53·5'W	X	84
Barlocco Bay	D & G	NX7946	54°47·9'	3°52·5'W	W	84
Barlocco Heugh	D & G	NX7846	54°47·9'	3°53·4'W	X	84
Barlocco Isle	D & G	NX5748	54°48·6'	4°13·1'W	X	83
Barlochan	D & G	NX8157	54°53·9'	3°50·9'W	X	84
Barlochan Hill	D & G	NX8157	54°53·9'	3°50·9'W	H	84
Barlockhart	D & G	NX2156	54°52·3'	4°47·0'W	X	82
Barlockhart Fell	D & G	NX2056	54°52·3'	4°47·9'W	H	82
Barlockhart Loch	D & G	NX2056	54°52·3'	4°47·9'W	W	82
Barlockhart Moor	D & G	NX2156	54°52·2'	4°47·0'W	X	82
Barlogan Fm	Renf	NS3767	55°52·4'	4°35·9'W	FM	63
Barlosh	E Ayr	NS4818	55°26·2'	4°23·7'W	X	70
Barlow	Derby	SK3474	53°16·0'	1°29·0'W	T	119
Barlow	Ghead	NZ1560	54°56·3'	1°45·5'W	T	88
Barlow	N Yks	SE6428	53°44·9'	1°1·4'W	T	105,106
Barlow Brook	Derby	SK3575	53°16·5'	1°28·1'W	W	119
Barlow Burn	Ghead	NZ1561	54°56·9'	1°45·5'W	W	88
Barlowfold	Ches	SJ9185	53°21·9'	2°7·7'W	X	109
Barlow Grange	Derby	SK3173	53°15·4'	1°31·7'W	X	119
Barlow Grange	N Yks	SE6330	53°46·0'	1°2·2'W	X	105,106
Barlow Home Fm	Shrops	SO3883	52°26·7'	2°54·3'W	FM	137
Barlow House Fm	Ches	SJ8280	53°19·2'	2°15·8'W	FM	109
Barlow House Fm	Ches	SJ9483	53°20·9'	2°5·0'W	FM	109
Barlow Lees	Derby	SK3376	53°17·0'	1°29·9'W	X	119
Barlow Lodge	N Yks	SE6229	53°45·5'	1°3·2'W	X	105
Barlow Moor	Man	SJ8292	53°25·7'	2°15·8'W	T	109
Barlow Woodseats	Derby	SK3175	53°16·5'	1°31·7'W	A	119
Barluack	Moray	NJ2652	57°33·4'	3°13·7'W	X	28
Barluith	D & G	NY0578	55°5·5'	3°28·9'W	X	85
Barluka	D & G	NX6554	54°52·0'	4°5·8'W	X	83,84
Barlure	D & G	NX1766	54°57·6'	4°51·1'W	X	82
Barlynch Fm	Somer	SS9228	51°2·7'	3°32·1'W	FM	181
Barlynch Wood	Somer	SS9328	51°2·7'	3°31·2'W	F	181
Barm	Orkney	HY3616	59°1·8'	3°6·4'W	X	6
Barmaddy	Arg & Bt	NM9512	56°15·6'	5°18·2'W	X	55
Barmagachan	D & G	NX6149	54°49·2'	4°9·4'W	X	83
Barmark	D & G	NX7478	55°5·1'	3°58·0'W	X	77,84
Barmark Hill	D & G	NX7479	55°5·6'	3°58·0'W	H	77,84
Barmbyfield Ho	E Yorks	SE7850	53°56·7'	0°48·3'W	X	105,106
Barmby Grange	E Yorks	SE7932	53°46·9'	0°47·6'W	X	105,106
Barmby Marsh	E Yorks	SE7029	53°45·4'	0°55·9'W	X	105,106
Barmby Moor	E Yorks	SE7748	53°55·6'	0°49·2'W	T	105,106
Barmby on the Marsh	E Yorks	SE6828	53°44·9'	0°57·7'W	T	105,106
Barmeal	D & G	NX3841	54°44·5'	4°30·6'W	X	83
Barmekin Hill	Aberd	NJ7207	57°9·4'	2°27·3'W	H	38
Barmekin of Echt	Aberd	NJ7207	57°9·4'	2°27·3'W	X	38
Barmer	Norf	TF8133	52°52·1'	0°41·8'E	T	132
Bar Mere	Ches	SJ5347	53°1·3'	2°41·6'W	W	117
Barmere Ho	Ches	SJ5447	53°1·3'	2°40·7'W	X	117
Barmickhill	E Ayr	NS5218	55°26·3'	4°19·9'W	X	70
Barming Heath	Kent	TQ7255	51°16·3'	0°28·3'E	T	178,188
Barmings	Barns	SE1700	53°30·0'	1°44·2'W	X	110
Barming Sta	Kent	TQ7256	51°16·9'	0°28·4'E	X	178,188
Barmkyn, The	Aberd	NJ5920	57°16·4'	2°40·3'W	X	37
Barmkyn, The (Fort)	Aberd	NJ5919	57°15·8'	2°40·3'W	A	37
Barmody Wood	S Ayr	NS3107	55°19·9'	4°39·4'W	F	70,76
Barmoffity	D & G	NX7870	55°0·8'	3°54·1'W	X	84
Barmollack	Arg & Bt	NR8043	55°38·1'	5°29·3'W	X	62,69
Barmolloch	Arg & Bt	NR8799	56°8·4'	5°25·3'W	X	55
Barmondsway Village	Durham	NZ3434	54°42·2'	1°27·9'W	A	93
Barmoor	Derby	SK0879	53°18·7'	1°52·4'W	X	119
Bar Moor	Ghead	NZ1464	54°58·5'	1°46·5'W	T	88
Bar Moor	Northum	NT9938	55°38·4'	2°0·5'W	X	75
Barmoor	N Yks	SE7090	54°18·3'	0°55·0'W	X	94,100
Barmoor Castle	Northum	NT9939	55°38·9'	2°0·5'W	X	75
Barmoor Clough	Derby	SK0780	53°19·3'	1°53·3'W	X	110
Barmoor Fm	Northum	NZ2184	55°9·2'	1°39·8'W	FM	81
Barmoor Hill	Northum	NT9940	55°39·5'	2°0·5'W	X	75
Barmoorhill Fm	S Ayr	NS4428	55°31·5'	4°27·8'W	FM	70
Barmoor Lane End	Northum	NU0039	55°38·9'	1°59·6'W	X	75
Barmoor Ridge	Northum	NT9639	55°38·9'	2°3·4'W	X	74,75
Barmoor South Moor	Northum	NT9838	55°38·4'	2°1·5'W	X	75
Barmore	Arg & Bt	NS0660	55°47·9'	5°5·3'W	X	63
Barmore	D & G	NX0553	54°50·3'	5°1·8'W	X	82
Barmore	D & G	NX2861	54°55·1'	4°40·6'W	X	82
Barmore Hill	D & G	NX0552	54°49·7'	5°1·7'W	H	82
Barmore Island	Arg & Bt	NR8771	55°53·4'	5°23·9'W	X	62
Barmore Red Ho	Northum	NU0037	55°37·8'	1°59·6'W	X	75
Barmore Wood	Arg & Bt	NN0505	56°12·1'	5°8·2'W	F	56
Barmore Wood	Arg & Bt	NS0761	55°48·5'	5°4·4'W	F	63
Barmouth	Gwyn	SH6115	52°43·1'	4°3·1'W	T	124
Barmouth Bay		SH5913	52°42·0'	4°4·8'W	W	124
Barmouth Bridge	Gwyn	SH6215	52°43·1'	4°2·2'W	X	124
Barmpton	Darl	NZ3118	54°33·6'	1°30·8'W	T	93
Barmston	E Yorks	TA1659	54°1·1'	0°13·4'W	T	107
Barmston	Sund	NZ3156	54°54·1'	1°30·6'W	T	88
Barmston Main Drain	E Yorks	TA1658	54°0·5'	0°13·4'W	W	107
Barmston Sands	E Yorks	TA1759	54°1·1'	0°12·4'W	X	107
Barmuckity	Moray	NJ2461	57°38·2'	3°15·9'W	X	28
Barmuir	S Ayr	NS4428	55°31·5'	4°27·8'W	X	70
Barmullan Burn	D & G	NX3748	54°48·3'	4°31·7'W	W	83
Barmulloch	C of Glas	NS6268	55°53·4'	4°12·0'W	T	64
Barmurrie	D & G	NX6779	55°5·5'	4°4·6'W	X	77,84
Barnabuck	Arg & Bt	NM8028	56°23·8'	5°33·5'W	X	49
Barnaby Fm	Suff	TM4188	52°26·4'	1°33·2'E	FM	156
Barnaby Grange	Red & Cl	NZ5715	54°31·9'	1°6·7'W	X	93
Barnaby Green	Suff	TM4779	52°21·4'	1°38·1'E	T	156
Barnaby's Fm	Suff	TM1668	52°16·3'	1°10·4'E	FM	156
Barnaby Side	Red & Cl	NZ5716	54°32·4'	1°6·7'W	X	93
Barnaby's Sands	Lancs	SD3445	53°54·1'	2°59·9'W	X	102
Barnacabber	Arg & Bt	NS1788	56°3·3'	4°55·9'W	X	56
Barnacarry	Arg & Bt	NM8826	56°23·0'	5°25·6'W	X	49
Barnacarry	Arg & Bt	NS0094	56°6·1'	5°12·5'W	X	55
Barnack	Peterb	TF0704	52°37·6'	0°24·7'W	T	142
Barnacle	Warw	SP3884	52°27·4'	1°26·0'W	T	140
Barnacle Rock	N Eil	NL5785	56°50·0'	7°37·0'W	X	31
Barnacott	Corn	SS2409	50°51·5'	4°29·7'W	X	190
Barnacott Fm	Devon	SS6534	51°5·6'	3°55·3'W	FM	180
Barnacre Lo	Lancs	SD5146	53°54·7'	2°44·3'W	X	102
Barnacre Resrs	Lancs	SD5247	53°55·3'	2°43·4'W	W	102
Barnacres	N Yks	NZ2002	54°25·0'	1°41·1'W	X	93
Barnafield	Shetld	HU3482	60°31·5'	1°22·3'W	T	1,2,3
Barnagad	Arg & Bt	NR7887	56°1·7'	5°33·3'W	X	55
Barnagad Burn	Arg & Bt	NR7986	56°1·2'	5°32·3'W	W	55
Barnagh	I of M	SC3291	54°17·5'	4°34·5'W	X	95
Barnahill	E Ayr	NS3742	55°38·9'	4°35·0'W	H	70
Barnakill Fm	Arg & Bt	NR8191	56°4·0'	5°30·7'W	FM	55
Barnaline	Arg & Bt	NM9613	56°16·2'	5°17·2'W	X	55
Barnaline Lodge	Arg & Bt	NM9713	56°16·2'	5°16·3'W	X	55
Barnamuc	Arg & Bt	NN0449	56°35·8'	5°11·1'W	X	50
Barn and Fourth Reach Fm	Cambs	TL2791	52°30·4'	0°7·3'W	FM	142
Barnard Castle	Durham	NZ0516	54°32·6'	1°54·9'W	T	92
Barnard Gate	Oxon	SP4010	51°47·5'	1°24·8'W	T	164
Barnardiston	Suff	TL7148	52°6·5'	0°30·2'E	T	154
Barnardiston Hall (Sch)	Suff	TL7150	52°7·5'	0°30·3'E	X	154
Barnard's Fm	Essex	TL5733	51°58·6'	0°17·6'E	FM	167
Barnard's Fm	Essex	TM1622	51°51·5'	1°8·6'E	FM	168,169
Barnard's Fm	Essex	TQ7599	51°40·0'	0°32·2'E	FM	167
Barnard's Fm	Norf	TG1004	52°35·8'	1°5·5'E	FM	144
Barnard's Green	Worcs	SO7845	52°6·4'	2°18·9'W	T	150
Barnards Hill	Pemb	SM9126	51°53·8'	5°1·9'W	X	157,158
Barnard's Well Mountain	Pemb	SN0529	51°55·8'	4°49·8'W	H	145,158
Barnardtown	Newp	ST3188	51°35·4'	2°59·4'W	T	171
Barna sgeir	Arg & Bt	NL9748	56°31·8'	6°55·2'W	X	46
Barnashaig	Arg & Bt	NR7286	56°1·0'	5°39·1'W	X	55
Barnauld	Arg & Bt	NS0760	55°47·9'	5°4·3'W	X	63
Barnayarry	Arg & Bt	NM7817	56°17·9'	5°34·8'W	X	55
Barnbackle	D & G	NX8672	55°2·0'	3°46·6'W	X	84
Barnbackle Hill	D & G	NX8773	55°2·6'	3°45·7'W	H	84
Barnbarroch	D & G	NX3951	54°49·9'	4°30·0'W	X	83
Barnbarroch	D & G	NX8456	54°53·4'	3°48·1'W	X	84
Barnbarroch Fm	D & G	NX8457	54°53·9'	3°48·1'W	FM	84
Barnbeth	Renf	NS3664	55°50·7'	4°36·7'W	X	63
Barnboard	D & G	NX7161	54°55·9'	4°0·4'W	X	83,84
Barn Bottom	Wilts	ST9451	51°15·7'	2°4·8'W	X	184
Barnbougle Castle	C of Edin	NT1678	55°59·5'	3°20·4'W	X	65,66
Barnbow Carr	Leeds	SE3936	53°49·4'	1°24·0'W	T	104
Barnbow Common	Leeds	SE3934	53°48·3'	1°24·1'W	X	104
Barnbow Wood	Leeds	SE3835	53°48·8'	1°25·0'W	F	104
Barnbrock Fm	Renf	NS3564	55°50·7'	4°37·7'W	FM	63
Barnburgh	Donc	SE4803	53°31·5'	1°16·1'W	T	111
Barnburgh Grange	Donc	SE4901	53°30·4'	1°15·3'W	X	111
Barnby	Suff	TM4789	52°26·8'	1°38·5'E	T	134,156
Barnby Broad	Suff	TM4790	52°27·3'	1°38·5'E	W	134
Barnby Dun	Donc	SE6109	53°34·7'	1°4·3'W	T	111
Barnby Fox Covert	Notts	SK6683	53°20·6'	1°0·1'W	F	111,120
Barnby Hall	Barns	SE2908	53°34·3'	1°33·3'W	X	110
Barnby Ho	N Yks	SE7260	54°2·1'	0°53·6'W	X	100
Barnby Howe	N Yks	NZ8313	54°30·6'	0°42·7'W	X	94
Barnby in the Willows	Notts	SK8552	53°3·7'	0°43·5'W	T	121
Barnby Manor	Notts	SK8654	53°4·8'	0°42·6'W	X	121
Barnby Manor Fm	Notts	SK8653	53°4·3'	0°42·6'W	FM	121
Barnby Moor	Notts	SK6684	53°21·2'	1°0·1'W	T	111,120
Barnby Sleights	N Yks	NZ8211	54°29·5'	0°43·6'W	X	94
Barnby Tofts	N Yks	NZ8213	54°30·6'	0°43·6'W	X	94
Barncailzie Hall	D & G	NX8070	55°0·9'	3°52·2'W	X	84
Barncaughla	D & G	NX4468	54°59·2'	4°25·9'W	X	83
Barnchalloch	D & G	NX0653	54°50·3'	5°0·8'W	X	82
Barncleugh	D & G	NX9076	55°4·2'	3°42·9'W	X	84
Barnclose Fm	N Yks	SE5687	54°16·8'	1°8·0'W	FM	100
Barncluith	S Lanak	NS7254	55°46·0'	4°2·0'W	T	64
Barncombe Bottom	Glos	SP0014	51°49·7'	1°59·6'W	F	163
Barn Common	Norf	TM0490	52°28·4'	1°0·6'E	X	144
Barncorkrie	D & G	NX0935	54°40·7'	4°57·3'W	X	82
Barncorkrie Moor	D & G	NX0936	54°41·2'	4°57·4'W	X	82
Barncorse Knowe	Scot Bord	NT0815	55°25·5'	3°26·8'W	H	78
Barn Croft	Hants	SU4161	51°21·0'	1°24·3'W	X	174
Barncrosh	D & G	NX7059	54°54·8'	4°1·3'W	X	83,84
Barnden Fm	Kent	TQ8641	51°8·5'	0°39·9'E	FM	189
Barndennoch	D & G	NX8988	55°10·7'	3°44·2'W	X	78
Barndon Fm	Oxon	SP5316	51°50·6'	1°13·4'W	FM	164
Barn Down	Devon	SS5519	50°57·4'	4°3·5'W	X	180
Barndromin	Arg & Bt	NM8423	56°21·3'	5°29·3'W	X	49
Barnean	D & G	NX3763	54°56·4'	4°32·2'W	X	83
Barnearnie	D & G	NX3159	54°54·1'	4°37·7'W	X	82
Barne Barton	C of Plym	SX4457	50°23·8'	4°11·3'W	T	201
Barnecourt	Devon	SX7583	50°38·2'	3°45·7'W	X	191
Barnehurst	Bexley	TQ5075	51°27·5'	0°9·9'E	T	177
Barneight	D & G	NX3264	54°56·8'	4°37·0'W	X	82
Barneight	E Ayr	NS5030	55°32·7'	4°22·2'W	X	70
Barneighthill	E Ayr	NS5030	55°32·7'	4°22·2'W	X	70
Barneil	S Ayr	NS2100	55°16·0'	4°48·6'W	X	76
Barneil	S Ayr	NS3608	55°20·6'	4°34·7'W	X	70,77
Barnellan	E Dunb	NS5874	55°56·5'	4°16·0'W	X	64
Barn Elms Fm	W Berks	SU6073	51°27·4'	1°7·8'W	FM	175
Barnes	Rich	TQ2276	51°28·4'	0°14·2'W	T	176
Barnes Br	Rich	TQ2176	51°28·4'	0°15·1'W	X	176
Barnes Castle	E Loth	NT5276	55°58·7'	2°45·7'W	A	66
Barnes Common	Houns	TQ2275	51°27·9'	0°14·2'W	X	176
Barnes Cray	Bexley	TQ5275	51°27·4'	0°11·7'E	T	177
Barnes Cross	Dorset	ST6911	50°54·1'	2°26·1'W	X	194
Barnes Fm	Derby	SK3379	53°18·7'	1°29·9'W	FM	119
Barnes Fm	Essex	TQ9099	51°39·7'	0°45·2'E	FM	168
Barnes Fm	Herts	TL0603	51°43·2'	0°27·5'W	FM	166
Barnes Hall	Sheff	SK3395	53°27·3'	1°29·8'W	T	110,111

Barnes High	I of W	SZ4380	50°37·3'	1°23·1'W	X	196
Barnes Loch	Scot Bord	NT4808	55°22·0'	2°48·8'W	W	79
Barnes Lodge	Herts	TL0603	51°43·2'	0°27·5'W	X	166
Barnes Street	Kent	TQ6448	51°12·7'	0°21·3'E	T	188
Barnes Surges	Devon	SY1693	50°44·1'	3°11·0'W	X	192,193
Barnes, The	Cumbr	NY5562	54°57·3'	2°41·7'W	X	86
Barnes, The	Northum	NY8477	55°5·5'	2°14·6'W	X	86,87
Barneston Manor	Dorset	SY9381	50°37·9'	2°5·6'W	A	195
Barne's Wood	E Susx	TQ7620	50°57·4'	0°30·8'E	F	199
Barnet	Barnet	TQ2495	51°38·6'	0°12·1'W	T	166,176
Barnetby le Wold	N Lincs	TA0509	53°34·3'	0°24·4'W	T	112
Barnetby Sta	N Lincs	TA0509	53°34·3'	0°24·4'W	X	112
Barnetby Wold Fm	N Lincs	TA0808	53°33·7'	0°21·8'W	FM	112
Barnet Gate	Barnet	TQ2195	51°38·7'	0°14·7'W	T	166,176
Barnetrigg	Cumbr	NY3347	54°49·1'	3°2·1'W	X	85
Barnet Side	Hants	SU7128	51°3·0'	0°58·8'W	X	186,197
Barnett Brook	Ches	SJ6143	52°59·2'	2°34·5'W	W	118
Barnett Brook	Ches	SJ6244	52°59·8'	2°33·6'W	T	118
Barnettbrook	Worcs	SO8876	52°23·2'	2°10·2'W	T	139
Barnett Fm	Surrey	TQ0144	51°11·4'	0°32·9'W	FM	186
Barnett Hill	Surrey	TQ0245	51°11·9'	0°32·0'W	X	186
Barnett Hill	Worcs	SO8877	52°23·7'	2°10·2'W	H	139
Barnett Ho	Bucks	SP8315	51°49·9'	0°47·3'W	X	165
Barnett's Fm	W Susx	SU9419	50°58·0'	0°39·3'W	FM	197
Barnetts Wood Fm	Hants	SU6233	51°5·8'	1°6·5'W	FM	185
Barnett Wood	Heref	SO3968	52°18·6'	2°53·3'W	F	137,148
Bar Newydd	Gwyn	SH5627	52°49·5'	4°7·8'W	X	124
Barney	Norf	TF9932	52°51·1'	0°57·7'E	T	132
Barney Beck	N Yks	SE0099	54°23·4'	1°59·6'W	W	98
Barney Mains	E Loth	NT5276	55°58·7'	2°45·7'W	X	66
Barney Water	D & G	NX6171	55°1·1'	4°10·0'W	X	77
Barnfield	Essex	TL6316	51°49·4'	0°22·3'E	X	167
Barnfield	Kent	TQ9247	51°11·6'	0°45·3'E	T	189
Barnfield	Surrey	TQ0135	51°6·5'	0°33·0'W	X	186
Barnfield	W Susx	TQ2323	50°59·8'	0°14·4'W	X	198
Barnfield Fm	Cambs	TL3575	52°21·6'	0°0·6'W	FM	142
Barnfield Fm	Heref	SO5660	52°14·4'	2°38·3'W	FM	137,138,149
Barnfields	Glos	SP0504	51°44·3'	1°55·3'W	X	163
Barnfields	Heref	SO4542	52°4·7'	2°47·8'W	T	148,149,161
Barnfields	Staffs	SJ9755	53°5·8'	2°2·3'W	T	118
Barnfields	Staffs	SK0046	53°0·9'	1°59·6'W	X	119,128
Barnfield Wood	N Yks	NZ5903	54°25·4'	1°5·0'W	F	93
Barn Fm	Ches	SJ3173	53°15·2'	3°1·6'W	FM	117
Barn Fm	Cumbr	SD4795	54°21·1'	2°48·5'W	FM	97
Barn Fm	Derby	SK2419	52°46·3'	1°38·3'W	FM	128
Barn Fm	Derby	SK2462	53°9·5'	1°38·1'W	FM	119
Barn Fm	Devon	SX8099	50°46·9'	3°41·8'W	FM	191
Barn Fm	Essex	TM1430	51°55·9'	1°7·2'E	FM	168,169
Barn Fm	E Susx	TQ9621	50°57·5'	0°47·8'E	FM	189
Barn Fm	Glos	SO9026	51°56·2'	2°8·3'W	FM	163
Barn Fm	Hants	SU5311	50°54·0'	1°14·4'W	FM	196
Barn Fm	Heref	SO4068	52°18·6'	2°52·4'W	FM	137,148
Barn Fm	Leic	SK5923	52°48·3'	1°7·1'W	FM	129
Barn Fm	Leic	SK6718	52°45·6'	1°0·0'W	FM	129
Barn Fm	Leic	SP3396	52°33·9'	1°30·4'W	FM	140
Barn Fm	Leic	SP3499	52°35·5'	1°29·5'W	FM	140
Barn Fm	Leic	SP4297	52°34·4'	1°22·4'W	FM	140
Barn Fm	Leic	SP7199	52°35·3'	0°56·7'W	FM	141
Barn Fm	Lincs	SK9458	53°6·9'	0°35·3'W	FM	121
Barn Fm	Lincs	SK9863	53°9·5'	0°31·6'W	FM	121
Barn Fm	Lincs	TF1028	52°50·5'	0°21·6'W	FM	130
Barn Fm	Lincs	TF1379	53°18·0'	0°17·9'W	FM	121
Barn Fm	Newp	ST3687	51°34·9'	2°55·0'W	FM	171
Barn Fm	Norf	TG4811	52°38·6'	1°40·4'E	FM	134
Barn Fm	Notts	SK5322	52°47·8'	1°12·4'W	FM	129
Barn Fm	Notts	SK5932	52°53·2'	1°7·0'W	FM	129
Barn Fm	Notts	SK6146	53°0·7'	1°5·0'W	FM	129
Barn Fm	Notts	SK6731	52°52·6'	0°59·9'W	FM	129
Barn Fm	Pemb	SM9212	51°46·3'	5°0·5'W	FM	157,158
Barn Fm	Staffs	SK1124	52°49·0'	1°49·8'W	FM	128
Barn Fm	Warw	SP4766	52°17·6'	1°18·3'W	FM	151
Barnford	S Ayr	NS3513	55°23·2'	4°35·9'W	X	70
Barn Gill	Lancs	SD7254	53°59·1'	2°25·2'W	W	103
Barngill Ho	Cumbr	NX9922	54°35·2'	3°33·4'W	X	89
Barnglies	D & G	NY3277	55°5·2'	3°3·5'W	X	85
Barnglieshead	D & G	NY3278	55°5·8'	3°3·5'W	X	85
Barn Grounds Fm	Warw	SP3244	52°5·8'	1°31·6'W	FM	151
Barn Hall Fm	Essex	TL9214	51°47·7'	0°47·5'E	FM	168
Barnhall Fm	Worcs	SO8461	52°15·1'	2°13·7'W	FM	138,150
Barnham	Suff	TL8779	52°22·9'	0°45·3'E	T	144
Barnham	W Susx	SU9604	50°49·9'	0°37·8'W	T	197
Barnham Broom	Norf	TG0707	52°37·5'	1°3·9'E	T	144
Barnham Carr	Suff	TL8979	52°22·8'	0°47·0'E	F	144
Barnham Court	W Susx	SU9503	50°49·4'	0°38·7'W	A	197
Barnhamcross Common	Norf	TL8681	52°23·9'	0°44·4'E	X	144
Barnham Heath	Suff	TL8879	52°22·8'	0°46·1'E	X	144
Barnharrow	D & G	NX2966	54°57·8'	4°39·8'W	X	82
Barnhead	Angus	NO6657	56°42·5'	2°32·9'W	T	54
Barn Heugh	D & G	NX5947	54°48·1'	4°11·2'W	X	83
Barnhill	Aberd	NO7371	56°50·0'	2°26·1'W	X	45
Barnhill	Arg & Bt	NR7097	56°6·9'	5°41·5'W	X	55,61
Barn Hill	Brent	TQ1987	51°34·4'	0°16·6'W	H	176
Barnhill	Ches	SJ4854	53°5·1'	2°46·2'W	T	117
Barnhill	C of Dun	NO4731	56°28·3'	2°51·2'W	T	54
Barnhill	D & G	NX9477	55°4·8'	3°39·2'W	X	84
Barn Hill	Essex	TQ3897	51°39·5'	0°0·1'E	X	166,177
Barn Hill	E Yorks	SE7328	53°44·8'	0°53·2'W	X	105,106
Barn Hill	Kent	TQ7251	51°14·2'	0°28·2'E	X	188
Barnhill	Moray	NJ1457	57°36·0'	3°25·9'W	X	28
Barnhill	Moray	NJ5650	57°32·5'	2°43·6'W	X	29
Barnhill	Northum	NU2103	55°19·5'	1°39·7'W	X	81
Barnhill	Northum	NZ0380	55°7·1'	1°56·7'W	X	81
Barnhill	Pth & Kin	NO1222	56°23·2'	3°25·1'W	T	53,58
Barnhill	Renf	NS4567	55°52·5'	4°28·2'W	X	64
Barnhill	S Lanak	NS6757	55°47·5'	4°6·8'W	X	64
Barn Hill	Warw	SP3458	52°13·4'	1°29·7'W	X	151
Barnhill	W Dunb	NS4275	55°56·8'	4°31·4'W	X	64
Barn Hill	Wrex	SJ3050	53°2·8'	3°2·2'W	X	117
Barnhill Bay	Fife	NT1884	56°2·8'	3°18·5'W	W	65,66
Barnhill Fm	Bucks	SP7934	52°0·2'	0°50·6'W	FM	152,165
Barnhill Fm	Ches	SJ4855	53°5·6'	2°46·2'W	FM	117
Barnhill Fm	Glos	ST8095	51°39·4'	2°17·0'W	FM	162
Barnhill Fm	Pth & Kin	NT0196	56°9·0'	3°35·2'W	FM	58
Barnhill Hall	E Yorks	SE7328	53°44·8'	0°53·2'W	X	105,106
Barnhillies	D & G	NX6676	55°3·9'	4°5·5'W	X	77,84
Barnhill Plantation	Glos	SO6010	51°47·5'	2°34·4'W	F	162
Barnhills	D & G	NW9871	54°59·8'	5°9·1'W	X	76,82
Barnhills Fm	Scot Bord	NT5921	55°29·1'	2°38·5'W	FM	73,74
Barnhills Moor Plantn	Scot Bord	NT5822	55°29·7'	2°39·5'W	F	73,74
Barnhill Springs	D & G	NT0803	55°19·0'	3°26·6'W	X	78
Barnhorne Manor	E Susx	TQ7007	50°50·5'	0°25·3'E	X	199
Barnhorn Manor	E Susx	TQ6907	50°50·5'	0°24·4'E	X	199
Barnhourie	D & G	NX9150	54°50·2'	3°41·4'W	X	84
Barnhouse	Orkney	HY3012	58°59·6'	3°12·6'W	X	6
Barnhouse	Orkney	HY3111	58°59·1'	3°11·5'W	X	6
Barnhouse Fm	Ches	SJ4871	53°14·3'	2°46·3'W	FM	117
Barnhouse Fm	W Susx	TQ1221	50°58·9'	0°23·9'W	FM	198
Barnhurst Fm	Kent	TQ9241	51°8·4'	0°45·1'E	FM	189
Barningham	Durham	NZ0810	54°29·4'	1°52·2'W	T	92
Barningham	Suff	TL9676	52°21·0'	0°53·1'E	T	144
Barningham Green	Norf	TG1233	52°51·4'	1°9·3'E	T	133
Barningham Hall	Norf	TG1435	52°52·4'	1°11·2'E	A	133
Barningham Moor	Durham	NZ0608	54°28·3'	1°54·0'W	X	92
Barningham Park	Durham	NZ0809	54°28·8'	1°52·2'W	X	92
Barningham Park	Durham	NZ0810	54°29·4'	1°52·2'W	X	92
Barningham Park	Suff	TL9477	52°21·6'	0°51·4'E	X	144
Barnkin of Craigs	D & G	NY0072	55°2·2'	3°33·5'W	X	84
Barnkirk Point	D & G	NY1964	54°58·1'	3°15·5'W	X	85
Barnlake	Pemb	SM9705	51°42·7'	4°55·9'W	X	157,158
Barnland Fm	Kent	TR0171	51°24·4'	0°53·8'E	FM	178
Barnley Beck	N Yks	SE1082	54°14·3'	1°50·4'W	W	99
Barnley Moss	N Yks	SE0981	54°13·7'	1°51·3'W	X	99
Barnlongart Ho	Arg & Bt	NR7776	55°55·8'	5°33·8'W	X	62
Barnluasgan	Arg & Bt	NR7891	56°3·9'	5°33·5'W	T	55
Barnlunich	Arg & Bt	NM8307	56°12·6'	5°29·5'W	X	55
Barnmoor Green	Warw	SP1864	52°16·7'	1°43·8'W	T	151
Barnmuir	D & G	NX9191	55°12·3'	3°42·3'W	X	78
Barnmuir Hill	D & G	NX9191	55°12·3'	3°42·3'W	H	78
Barnoldby le Beck	NE Lincs	TA2303	53°30·8'	0°8·3'W	T	113
Barnoldswick	Lancs	SD8746	53°54·8'	2°11·5'W	T	103
Barnoldswick	N Yks	SD6671	54°8·3'	2°30·8'W	T	98
Barn Park Fm	Devon	ST2104	50°50·0'	3°6·9'W	FM	192,193
Barn Park Fm	Devon	ST2105	50°50·6'	3°6·9'W	FM	192
Barn Plantation	Norf	TG1940	52°55·0'	1°15·9'E	F	133
Barn Pool	Corn	SX4552	50°21·1'	4°10·4'W	W	201
Barnpool	Devon	SS6517	50°56·4'	3°54·9'W	X	180
Barnridge Copse	Wilts	SU2429	51°3·8'	1°39·1'W	F	184
Barn Rocks	W Susx	SZ9097	50°46·2'	0°43·0'W	X	197
Barns	Aberd	NJ4013	57°12·5'	2°59·1'W	X	37
Barns	Aberd	NO7494	57°2·4'	2°25·3'W	X	38,45
Barns	Cumbr	NY4174	55°3·7'	2°55·0'W	X	85
Barns	Cumbr	NY5267	55°0·0'	2°44·6'W	X	86
Barns	D & G	NY0996	55°15·2'	3°25·5'W	X	78
Barns	Falk	NS8870	55°54·9'	3°47·1'W	X	65
Barns	Pth & Kin	NN9310	56°16·5'	3°43·2'W	X	58
Barns	Scot Bord	NT2139	55°38·5'	3°14·9'W	T	73
Barns	Scot Bord	NT5009	55°22·6'	2°46·9'W	X	79
Barnsallie	D & G	NX2155	54°51·7'	4°46·9'W	X	82
Barnsallie Fell	D & G	NX2255	54°51·7'	4°46·0'W	X	82
Barnsbury	Isling	TQ3084	51°32·6'	0°7·1'W	T	176,177
Barn Scar	Cumbr	SD0498	54°22·4'	3°28·2'W	X	96
Barnscar	Cumbr	SD1395	54°20·8'	3°19·9'W	X	96
Barns Cliff	N Yks	SE9394	54°20·2'	0°33·8'W	X	94,101
Barns Close	Devon	SS9307	50°51·4'	3°30·8'W	X	192
Barnsdale	Angus	NO4253	56°40·2'	2°56·3'W	X	54
Barnsdale	Cumbr	SD5196	54°21·7'	2°44·8'W	X	97
Barnsdale	Donc	SE5114	53°37·4'	1°13·3'W	X	111
Barnsdale	Rut	SK9009	52°40·5'	0°39·7'W	T	141
Barnsdale Avenue	Rut	SK9109	52°40·5'	0°38·8'W	X	141
Barnsdale Avenue	Rut	SK9110	52°41·0'	0°38·8'W	X	130
Barnsdale Bar	Donc	SE5113	53°36·9'	1°13·3'W	X	111
Barnsdale Wood	Rut	SK9108	52°40·0'	0°38·9'W	F	141
Barnsden	E Susx	TQ4728	51°2·2'	0°6·2'E	X	188,198
Barnsfarm Hill	W Susx	TQ1012	50°54·0'	0°25·8'W	X	198
Barnsfield Heath	Dorset	SU1100	50°48·2'	1°50·2'W	X	195
Barns Fm	Lincs	SK9848	53°1·5'	0°31·9'W	FM	130
Barns Fm	Northum	NZ1090	55°12·5'	1°50·1'W	FM	81
Barns Fm	Red & Cl	NZ6418	54°33·4'	1°0·2'W	FM	94
Barns Fm	Red & Cl	NZ6720	54°34·5'	0°57·4'W	FM	94
Barns Fm	Shrops	SO3890	52°30·5'	2°54·4'W	FM	137
Barns Fm	Wrekin	SJ6219	52°46·3'	2°33·4'W	FM	127
Barns Fm	W Susx	TQ1012	50°54·0'	0°25·8'W	FM	198
Barnsfold Fm	Derby	SK0386	53°22·5'	1°56·9'W	FM	110
Barns Fold Fm	Lancs	SD5741	53°52·1'	2°38·8'W	FM	102
Barns Fold Resrs	Lancs	SD5741	53°52·1'	2°38·8'W	W	102
Barnsgate	E Susx	TQ4828	51°2·2'	0°7·0'E	X	188,198
Barns Green	W Susx	TQ1227	51°2·1'	0°23·8'W	T	187,198
Barnshake	Inverc	NS3266	55°51·7'	4°40·6'W	X	63
Barnshalloch	D & G	NX6775	55°3·4'	4°4·5'W	X	77,84
Barnshangan	D & G	NX1865	54°57·0'	4°50·1'W	X	82
Barnshaw Hall Fm	Ches	SJ7771	53°14·4'	2°20·3'W	FM	118
Barnshayes	Devon	SY0397	50°46·1'	3°22·2'W	X	192
Barnshean Loch	S Ayr	NS3711	55°22·2'	4°33·9'W	W	70
Barns Heath Fm	Leic	SK3210	52°41·4'	1°31·2'W	FM	128
Barn Shelley	Devon	SS7504	50°49·6'	3°46·1'W	X	191
Barnside	Kirk	SE1705	53°32·7'	1°44·2'W	T	110
Barnside	Lancs	SD9341	53°52·2'	2°6·0'W	X	103
Barnside	Scot Bord	NT7461	55°50·7'	2°24·5'W	X	67
Barnside Fm	Sheff	SK2398	53°28·9'	1°38·8'W	FM	110
Barnside Hill	Scot Bord	NT7462	55°51·3'	2°24·5'W	X	67
Barnside Moor	Sheff	SK2298	53°28·9'	1°39·7'W	X	110
Barnskew	Cumbr	NY6218	54°33·6'	2°34·8'W	X	91
Barnslands Fm	Shrops	SO6674	52°22·0'	2°29·6'W	FM	138
Barns Lane Bottom	Lancs	SD5841	53°52·1'	2°37·9'W	X	102
Barns Law	Fife	NO5911	56°17·6'	2°39·3'W	X	59
Barnslee	Fife	NO3001	56°12·0'	3°7·3'W	X	59
Barns Lee	Staffs	SJ9360	53°8·5'	2°5·9'W	X	118
Barnsley	Barns	SE3406	53°33·2'	1°28·8'W	T	110,111
Barnsley	Glos	SP0705	51°44·9'	1°53·5'W	T	163
Barnsley	Shrops	SO7593	52°32·3'	2°21·7'W	T	138
Barnsley Fm	Dorset	ST9903	50°49·8'	2°0·5'W	FM	195
Barnsley Fm	I of W	SZ6090	50°42·6'	1°8·6'W	FM	196
Barnsley Park	Glos	SP0806	51°45·4'	1°52·7'W	A	163
Barnsley Wold	Glos	SP0607	51°45·9'	1°54·4'W	X	163
Barnsmuir	Fife	NO5906	56°14·9'	2°39·3'W	X	59
Barnsnap	W Susx	TQ2231	51°4·1'	0°15·1'W	X	187
Barnsnaught	D & G	NY0495	55°14·6'	3°30·2'W	X	78
Barns Ness	E Loth	NT7277	55°59·4'	2°26·5'W	X	67
Barns of Airlie	Angus	NO3151	56°39·0'	3°7·1'W	X	53
Barns of Ayre	Orkney	HY5804	58°55·5'	2°43·3'W	X	6
Barns of Bynack	Moray	NJ0405	57°7·8'	3°34·7'W	X	36
Barns of Craig	Angus	NO7055	56°41·4'	2°28·9'W	X	54
Barns of Wedderburn	Angus	NO4334	56°29·9'	2°55·1'W	X	54
Barnsole	Kent	TR2756	51°15·7'	1°15·6'E	T	179
Barnsoul	D & G	NX8777	55°4·7'	3°45·8'W	X	84
Barn Stane	Shetld	HU5439	60°8·2'	1°1·2'W	X	4
Barnstaple	Devon	SS5633	51°4·9'	4°3·0'W	T	180
Barnstaple or Bideford Bay		SS3526	51°0·8'	4°20·8'W	W	190
Barnstaple or Bideford Bay	Devon	SS4133	51°4·7'	4°15·8'W	W	180
Barnston	Essex	TL6419	51°51·0'	0°23·3'E	T	167
Barnston	Wirral	SJ2883	53°20·6'	3°4·5'W	T	108
Barnstone	Notts	SK7335	52°54·7'	0°54·5'W	T	129
Barnstone Fm	Heref	SO5853	52°10·7'	2°36·5'W	FM	149
Barnstone Lodge	Notts	SK7434	52°54·1'	0°53·6'W	X	129
Barnston Fm	Devon	SX7749	50°19·9'	3°43·3'W	FM	202
Barnston Lodge	Essex	TL6519	51°50·9'	0°24·1'E	X	167
Barnswood	Staffs	SJ9460	53°8·5'	2°5·0'W	X	118
Barnsworthy Fm	Somer	ST1741	51°10·0'	3°10·8'W	FM	181
Barnt Green	Worcs	SP0073	52°21·5'	1°59·6'W	T	139
Barn, The	Shrops	SO4878	52°24·1'	2°45·5'W	X	137,138,148
Barntimpen	D & G	NY0596	55°15·2'	3°29·2'W	X	78
Barnton	Aberd	NJ7803	57°7·3'	2°21·3'W	X	38
Barnton	Angus	NO3255	56°41·2'	3°6·2'W	X	53
Barnton	Ches	SJ6375	53°16·5'	2°32·9'W	T	118
Barnton	C of Edin	NT1975	55°57·9'	3°17·4'W	T	65,66
Barnton Cut	Ches	SJ6374	53°15·9'	2°32·9'W	W	118
Barntown	Devon	SS6106	50°50·4'	3°58·1'W	X	191
Barnultoch	D & G	NX0856	54°52·0'	4°59·1'W	X	82
Barnvannoch	D & G	NX1373	55°1·2'	4°55·1'W	X	76
Barnwalls	D & G	NX6576	55°3·9'	4°6·4'W	X	77,84
Barnweil	S Ayr	NS4130	55°32·5'	4°30·8'W	X	70
Barnwell	Bucks	SP6424	51°54·9'	1°3·8'W	X	164,165
Barnwell	Northnts	TL0484	52°26·9'	0°27·8'W	T	141
Barnwell Country Park	Northnts	TL0387	52°28·5'	0°28·6'W	X	141
Barnwell Lodge Fm	Northnts	TL0483	52°26·3'	0°27·8'W	FM	141
Barnwell Wold	Northnts	TL0781	52°25·2'	0°25·2'W	F	142
Barn Wood	Bucks	SU7993	51°38·0'	0°51·1'W	F	175
Barnwood	Glos	SO8518	51°51·9'	2°12·7'W	T	162
Barny	Angus	NO2563	56°45·4'	3°13·1'W	X	44
Barnyards	Aberd	NJ7305	57°8·4'	2°26·3'W	X	38
Barnyards	Aberd	NJ7551	57°33·2'	2°24·6'W	X	29
Barnyards	Aberd	NK0045	57°30·0'	1°59·5'W	X	30
Barnyards	Angus	NO4757	56°42·4'	2°51·5'W	X	54
Barnyards	Fife	NO4802	56°12·7'	2°49·9'W	T	59
Barnyards	Highld	NH5346	57°29·1'	4°26·7'W	X	26
Barnyards	Moray	NJ3053	57°34·0'	3°9·7'W	X	28
Barnyards of Badenyouchers	Aberd	NJ5357	57°36·3'	2°46·7'W	X	29
Barnyards of Findlater	Aberd	NJ5366	57°41·1'	2°46·8'W	X	29
Barnyhill	Pth & Kin	NO2442	56°34·1'	3°13·8'W	X	53
Barochan	Renf	NS4069	55°53·5'	4°33·1'W	X	64
Barochan Ho	Renf	NS4168	55°53·0'	4°32·1'W	X	64
Barochan Moss	Renf	NS4268	55°53·0'	4°31·1'W	F	64
Barochreal	Arg & Bt	NM8320	56°19·6'	5°30·1'W	X	49
Bar of Barlay	D & G	NX6058	54°54·1'	4°10·6'W	H	83
Barone Hill	Arg & Bt	NS0663	55°49·5'	5°5·4'W	H	63
Baron Hill	Conwy	SH8672	53°14·2'	3°42·1'W	X	116
Baron Hill	I of Angl	SH5976	53°16·0'	4°6·4'W	X	114,115
Baron's Cairn	C of Aber	NJ9503	57°7·3'	2°4·5'W	A	38
Barons' Cross	Heref	SO4758	52°13·3'	2°46·2'W	T	148,149
Baronsdown	Somer	SS9329	51°3·3'	3°31·2'W	X	181
Baron's Folly	Scot Bord	NT6326	55°31·8'	2°34·7'W	X	74
Baron's Grange	E Susx	TQ9024	50°59·3'	0°42·8'E	X	189
Baron's Hill	Angus	NO3256	56°41·7'	3°6·2'W	H	53
Baron's Hill Fm	Devon	SX7057	50°24·1'	3°49·4'W	FM	202
Baronsmill	Aberd	NJ5959	57°37·4'	2°40·7'W	X	29
Baron's Place	Kent	TQ6554	51°15·9'	0°22·3'E	X	188
Barons Point	Arg & Bt	NS2280	55°59·1'	4°50·8'W	X	63
Baron's Wood	Devon	SS6903	50°48·9'	3°51·2'W	X	191
Baron Wood	Cumbr	NY5143	54°47·0'	2°45·3'W	F	86
Baronwood Fm	Cumbr	NY5143	54°47·0'	2°45·3'W	FM	86
Baronwood Park	Cumbr	NY5241	54°45·9'	2°44·3'W	X	86
Barony	I of M	SC4687	54°15·6'	4°21·4'W	X	95
Barony Agricultural College	D & G	NY0287	55°10·3'	3°31·9'W	X	78
Barony Colliery	E Ayr	NS5221	55°27·9'	4°20·0'W	X	70
Barony Hill	I of M	SC4687	54°15·6'	4°21·4'W	H	95
Barony Hill	S Ayr	NS3101	55°16·7'	4°39·2'W	X	76
Barony Moss	S Ayr	NS3200	55°16·2'	4°38·2'W	X	76
Barony, The	Orkney	HY2527	59°7·7'	3°18·1'W	T	6
Barpark Corner	Devon	ST1616	50°56·5'	3°11·4'W	X	181,193
Bar Pasture Fm	Peterb	TF2502	52°36·3'	0°8·8'W	FM	142
Barpham Hill	W Susx	TQ0609	50°52·5'	0°29·2'W	H	197
Bar Point	D & G	NX6545	54°47·2'	4°5·5'W	X	83,84
Bar Point	I Scilly	SV9112	49°55·9'	6°18·0'W	X	203
Barquhar	D & G	NX8874	55°3·1'	3°44·8'W	X	84
Barquharrie	E Ayr	NS5019	55°26·8'	4°21·9'W	X	70
Barquhey	S Ayr	NS4121	55°27·7'	4°30·5'W	X	70
Barquhill	D & G	NX3555	54°52·0'	4°33·8'W	X	83
Barr	Arg & Bt	NR3960	55°46·0'	6°9·2'W	X	60
Barr	Arg & Bt	NR9695	56°6·5'	5°16·4'W	X	55
Barr	D & G	NS7609	55°21·8'	3°56·9'W	X	71,78
Barr	D & G	NX8292	55°12·7'	3°50·8'W	X	78
Barr	D & G	NX8974	55°3·1'	3°43·8'W	X	84
Barr	Highld	NM6155	56°37·8'	5°53·4'W	X	49
Barr	N Ayr	NS2065	55°50·9'	4°52·1'W	X	63

Barr	S Ayr	NX2794	55°12·9′	4°42·7′W	T	76
Barr	Somer	ST1924	51°0·8′	3°8·9′W	T	181,193
Barra	N Eil	NF6801	56°59·1′	7°27·5′W	X	31
Barraby	D & G	NX9093	55°13·4′	3°43·3′W	X	78
Barra Castle	Aberd	NJ7925	57°19·2′	2°20·5′W	X	38
Bàrr a Chaistealain	Arg & Bt	NN1626	56°23·7′	4°58·4′W	X	50
Barrachan	D & G	NX3649	54°48·8′	4°32·7′W	T	83
Barrachan	D & G	NX3657	54°53·1′	4°33·0′W	X	83
Barrachan Home Fm	D & G	NX3650	54°49·3′	4°32·7′W	FM	83
Barrachnie	C of Glas	NS6664	55°51·3′	4°8·0′W	T	64
Barrachuile	Arg & Bt	NR8895	56°6·3′	5°24·1′W	X	55
Barrackan	Arg & Bt	NM7803	56°10·3′	5°34·1′W	X	55
Barrack Fm	Kent	TQ9131	51°3·0′	0°43·9′E	FM	189
Barrack Hill	Newp	ST3089	51°36·0′	3°0·3′W	T	171
Barracks	Cumbr	NY4769	55°1·0′	2°49·3′W	X	86
Barracks	W Loth	NT0267	55°53·4′	3°33·6′W	X	65
Barracks Fm	Notts	SK5651	53°3·4′	1°9·5′W	FM	120
Barracks Fm	Oxon	SU6185	51°33·9′	1°6·8′W	FM	175
Barracks, The	Glos	SO6309	51°46·9′	2°31·8′W	X	162
Barracks, The	Notts	SK6482	53°20·1′	1°1·9′W	X	111,120
Barracks, The	W Berks	SU4681	51°31·8′	1°19·8′W	X	174
Barrack Wood	Essex	TQ5991	51°35·9′	0°18·1′E	F	177
Barra Cottage	Aberd	NJ8125	57°19·2′	2°18·5′W	X	38
Barraer	D & G	NX3861	54°55·3′	4°31·2′W	X	83
Barraer Fell	D & G	NX3761	54°55·3′	4°32·2′W	H	83
Barrage	Arg & Bt	NN0428	56°24·5′	5°10·2′W	X	50
Barraglom	N Eil	NB1634	58°12·5′	6°49·6′W	T	13
Barra Head	N Eil	NL5579	56°46·7′	7°38·5′W	X	31
Barrahormid	Arg & Bt	NR7183	55°59·4′	5°39·9′W	T	55
Bàrr Aille	Arg & Bt	NM7917	56°17·9′	5°33·9′W	H	55
Barra-mhail	N Eil	NF8364	57°33·6′	7°17·6′W	W	18
Barran	Arg & Bt	NM8825	56°22·4′	5°25·5′W	T	49
Barran	Arg & Bt	NN1624	56°22·6′	4°58·3′W	X	50
Barrananaoil	Arg & Bt	NM8207	56°12·6′	5°30·5′W	X	55
Barran Caltum	Arg & Bt	NM8930	56°25·2′	5°24·8′W	X	49
Barrance	E Renf	NS5655	55°46·3′	4°17·3′W	X	64
Barrance Hill	E Renf	NS5153	55°45·1′	4°22·0′W	X	64
Bàrr an Daimh	Arg & Bt	NM8303	56°10·5′	5°29·3′W	X	55
Barran Dubh	Arg & Bt	NN0433	56°27·2′	5°10·4′W	X	50
Bàrr an Eich	Arg & Bt	NS0297	56°7·7′	5°10·7′W	H	55
Barran Fuar	Arg & Bt	NR8794	56°5·7′	5°25·0′W	H	55
Barrangary	Renf	NS3469	55°53·6′	4°29·2′W	X	64
Bàrr an Longairt	Arg & Bt	NS0196	56°7·2′	5°11·6′W	H	55
Barranrioch	Arg & Bt	NM8929	56°24·6′	5°24·8′W	X	49
Barrapol	Arg & Bt	NL9542	56°28·5′	6°56·8′W	T	46
Barrard's Hall	Suff	TM0246	52°4·8′	0°57·3′E	X	155
Barras	Cumbr	NY8412	54°30·4′	2°14·4′W	T	91,92
Barras	I of Angl	SH4765	53°9·9′	4°16·9′W	X	114,115
Barrascrofts	D & G	NY4079	55°6·4′	2°56·0′W	X	85
Barras End	N Yks	NY9801	54°24·5′	2°1·4′W	X	92
Barrasford	Northum	NY9173	55°3·3′	2°8·0′W	T	87
Barrasford Green	Northum	NY9273	55°3·3′	2°7·1′W	X	87
Barrasford Park	Northum	NY9276	55°5·0′	2°7·1′W	X	87
Barrasgate	D & G	NY1566	54°59·1′	3°19·3′W	X	85
Barras Hill	Durham	NZ2447	54°49·3′	1°37·2′W	X	88
Barras Nose	Corn	SX0589	50°40·3′	4°45·2′W	X	200
Barraston Fm	E Dunb	NS6075	55°57·1′	4°14·1′W	FM	64
Barras Top	Cumbr	NY5664	54°58·4′	2°40·8′W	X	86
Barravourich	Arg & Bt	NN3345	56°34·3′	4°42·6′W	X	50
Barravullin	Arg & Bt	NM8207	56°12·6′	5°30·5′W	X	55
Barr Bàn	Arg & Bt	NR7892	56°4·4′	5°33·6′W	H	55
Barr Beacon	Wals	SP0697	52°34·5′	1°54·3′W	X	139
Barr Burn	D & G	NS7408	55°21·2′	3°58·8′W	W	71,77
Barr Burn	D & G	NS7609	55°21·8′	3°56·9′W	W	71,78
Barr Burn	D & G	NT2205	55°20·2′	3°13·4′W	W	79
Barr Burn	D & G	NX3346	54°47·1′	4°35·4′W	W	82
Barr Burn	D & G	NX7981	55°6·8′	3°53·4′W	W	78
Barr Castle	Renf	NS3458	55°47·5′	4°38·4′W	A	63
Barr Common	Wals	SP0599	52°35·6′	1°55·2′W	T	139
Barr Dubh	Arg & Bt	NM8229	56°24·4′	5°31·6′W	H	49
Barr Dubh	Arg & Bt	NN2126	56°23·8′	4°53·6′W	X	50
Barr Dubh	Arg & Bt	NR7460	55°47·1′	5°35·8′W	X	62
Barr Dubh	Pth & Kin	NN8019	56°21·1′	3°56·1′W	X	57
Barre	Pemb	SN1414	51°47·9′	4°41·5′W	X	158
Barregarrow	I of M	SC3287	54°15·3′	4°34·3′W	T	95
Barrel Fm	Heref	SO6822	51°54·0′	2°27·5′W	FM	162
Barrel Hill	Heref	SO6231	51°58·8′	2°32·8′W	X	149
Barrel Hill	Notts	SK7865	53°10·8′	0°49·6′W	X	120,121
Barrel Hill Fm	Warw	SP2847	52°7·5′	1°35·1′W	FM	151
Barrel Law	Scot Bord	NT4118	55°27·4′	2°55·5′W	H	79
Barrel Obe	N Eil	NA9909	57°58·4′	7°5·0′W	W	13
Barrel of Butter	Orkney	HY3500	58°53·2′	3°7·2′W	X	6,7
Barrelwell	Angus	NO5660	56°44·0′	2°42·7′W	X	44
Barremman	Arg & Bt	NS2485	56°1·8′	4°49·0′W	X	56
Barrent Point Scar	Cumbr	SD2665	54°4·8′	3°7·4′W	X	96,97
Barrenthwaite Hall	Cumbr	NY8513	54°31·0′	2°13·5′W	X	91,92
Barrets Green	Ches	SJ5859	53°7·8′	2°37·3′W	T	117
Barretts	Shrops	SO2286	52°28·2′	3°8·5′W	X	137
Barrett's Br	Cambs	TF4209	52°39·8′	0°6·4′E	X	142,143
Barretts Hall	Essex	TL8033	51°58·2′	0°37·6′E	X	168
Barrett's Hall	Essex	TL8034	51°58·7′	0°37·7′E	X	155
Barretts Hill Fm	Pemb	SM9208	51°44·2′	5°0·4′W	FM	157,158
Barrett's Hill Wood	Heref	SO3738	52°2·4′	2°54·7′W	F	149,161
Barrett's Mill	Shrops	SO5269	52°19·3′	2°41·9′W	X	137,138
Barrett's Zawn	Corn	SX0281	50°35·9′	4°47·5′W	W	200
Barr Fm	Lincs	TF1655	53°5·0′	0°15·7′W	FM	121
Barr Fm	Lincs	TF2372	53°14·1′	0°9·0′W	FM	122
Barr Ganuisg	Arg & Bt	NR9280	55°58·3′	5°19·6′W	H	55
Barr Glen	Arg & Bt	NR6937	55°34·6′	5°39·4′W	X	68
Barr Green Fm	Stock	SJ8882	53°20·3′	2°10·4′W	FM	109
Barr Hall	Derby	SK2118	52°45·8′	1°40·9′W	X	128
Barr Hall	Essex	TL7435	51°59·4′	0°32·5′E	X	155
Barrhead	E Renf	NS5058	55°47·8′	4°23·1′W	T	64
Barr Hill	Arg & Bt	NR8670	55°52·8′	5°24·8′W	H	62
Barr Hill	Arg & Bt	NS0952	55°43·7′	5°2·1′W	X	63,69
Barr Hill	D & G	NX3247	54°47·6′	4°36·4′W	H	82
Barr Hill	D & G	NX7881	55°6·8′	3°54·3′W	H	78
Barr Hill	D & G	NX8169	55°0·3′	3°51·2′W	H	84
Barr Hill	D & G	NX8391	55°12·2′	3°49·9′W	H	78
Barrhill	D & G	NX9086	55°9·6′	3°43·2′W	X	78
Barrhill	E Dunb	NS6376	55°57·7′	4°11·2′W	X	64
Barr Hill	E Renf	NS4755	55°46·1′	4°25·9′W	X	64
Barrhill	N Ayr	NS3256	55°46·3′	4°40·3′W	X	63
Barrhill	S Ayr	NS3416	55°24·8′	4°36·9′W	X	70
Barrhill	S Ayr	NS4527	55°31·0′	4°26·9′W	X	70
Barrhill	S Ayr	NX2382	55°6·3′	4°46·0′W	T	76
Barrhill Fm	D & G	NX4164	54°57·0′	4°28·5′W	FM	83
Barricane Beach	Devon	SS4544	51°10·7′	4°12·7′W	X	180
Barrichbeyan	Arg & Bt	NM8007	56°12·5′	5°32·4′W	X	55
Barrier Bank	Notts	SK6994	53°26·5′	0°57·3′W	X	111
Barrier Bank	Notts	SK7094	53°26·5′	0°56·4′W	X	112
Barrington	Cambs	TL3949	52°7·5′	0°2·2′E	T	154
Barrington	Fife	NO2108	56°15·7′	3°16·1′W	X	58
Barrington	Somer	ST3818	50°57·7′	2°52·6′W	T	193
Barrington Bushes	Glos	SP2116	51°50·8′	1°41·3′W	F	163
Barrington Court	Somer	ST3918	50°57·7′	2°51·7′W	A	193
Barrington Downs Fm	Glos	SP1809	51°47·0′	1°44·0′W	FM	163
Barrington Hall	Essex	TL5417	51°50·0′	0°14·5′E	X	167
Barrington Hill	Somer	ST2917	50°57·1′	3°0·3′W	H	193
Barrington Ho	Lincs	TF3521	52°46·4′	0°0·5′E	X	131
Barrington Park	Glos	SP2013	51°49·1′	1°42·2′W	X	163
Barrington's Fm	Thurr	TQ6581	51°30·5′	0°23·1′E	FM	177,178
Bàrr Iola	Arg & Bt	NR9382	55°59·4′	5°18·7′W	H	55
Bàrr Iolaich	Arg & Bt	NR9469	55°52·5′	5°17·1′W	X	62
Barri or Barry	V of Glam	ST1168	51°24·5′	3°16·4′W	T	171
Barripper	Corn	SW6338	50°11·9′	5°18·9′W	T	203
Barrisdale	Highld	NG8704	57°4·9′	5°30·4′W	X	33
Barrisdale Bay	Highld	NG8605	57°5·4′	5°31·5′W	W	33
Barrisdale Forest	Highld	NG9102	57°4·0′	5°26·4′W	X	33
Barris Hill	Pemb	SM9522	51°51·8′	4°58·3′W	X	157,158
Barritshayes	Devon	SY2195	50°45·2′	3°6·8′W	X	192,193
Barritts Fm	Essex	TL9931	51°56·7′	0°54·1′E	FM	168
Bàrr Kilmhealaird	Arg & Bt	NM8613	56°15·9′	5°26·9′W	H	55
Bàrr Liath	Arg & Bt	NM9011	56°15·0′	5°22·9′W	H	55
Barr Liath	Arg & Bt	NR9773	55°54·7′	5°14·4′W	X	62
Barr Loch	D & G	NX7779	55°5·7′	3°55·2′W	W	84
Barr Loch	Renf	NS3557	55°46·9′	4°37·4′W	W	63
Barrmains	Arg & Bt	NR6634	55°32·9′	5°42·1′W	X	68
Barr Meadhonach	Arg & Bt	NM7429	56°24·2′	5°39·3′W	X	49
Barrmill	N Ayr	NS3651	55°43·7′	4°36·3′W	T	63
Barr Moor	D & G	NS7408	55°21·2′	3°58·8′W	X	71,77
Barrmoor Cotts	D & G	NS7509	55°21·8′	3°57·9′W	X	71,78
Bàrr Mór	Arg & Bt	NM7515	56°16·7′	5°37·6′W	H	55
Bàrr Mór	Arg & Bt	NM7803	56°10·3′	5°34·1′W	H	55
Bàrr Mór	Arg & Bt	NM8138	56°29·3′	5°33·0′W	H	49
Bàrr Mór	Arg & Bt	NM9130	56°25·2′	5°22·9′W	H	49
Bàrr Mór	Arg & Bt	NM9444	56°32·8′	5°20·6′W	H	49
Bàrr Mór	Arg & Bt	NN0500	56°9·4′	5°8·0′W	H	56
Bàrr Mór	Arg & Bt	NN1312	56°16·1′	5°0·7′W	H	50,56
Bàrr Mór	Arg & Bt	NR7760	55°47·2′	5°33·0′W	X	62
Bàrr Mor	Arg & Bt	NR7787	56°1·7′	5°34·3′W	H	55
Bàrr Mór	Arg & Bt	NR7992	56°4·4′	5°32·6′W	X	55
Bàrr Mór	Arg & Bt	NR8096	56°6·6′	5°31·8′W	H	55
Bàrr Mór	Arg & Bt	NR8164	55°49·4′	5°29·3′W	H	62
Bàrr Mór	Arg & Bt	NR8499	56°8·3′	5°28·2′W	H	55
Bàrr Mór	Arg & Bt	NS0197	56°7·8′	5°11·7′W	X	55
Barr Muir	E Ayr	NS5833	55°34·5′	4°14·7′W	X	71
Barrnacarry	Arg & Bt	NM8122	56°20·6′	5°32·2′W	X	49
Barrnacarry Bay	Arg & Bt	NM8122	56°20·6′	5°32·2′W	W	49
Bàrr na Cour	Arg & Bt	NR7761	55°47·7′	5°33·0′W	X	62
Bàrr na criche	Arg & Bt	NR7660	55°47·1′	5°33·9′W	X	62
Bàrr na Gile	Arg & Bt	NM8229	56°24·4′	5°31·6′W	H	49
Bàrr na h-Earba	Arg & Bt	NN1324	56°22·5′	5°1·3′W	X	50
Bàrr-nam-boc Bay	Arg & Bt	NM7928	56°23·8′	5°34·4′W	W	49
Bàrr nam Muc	Arg & Bt	NM7333	56°26·3′	5°40·5′W	X	49
Bàrr nan Cadhag	Arg & Bt	NM8229	56°24·4′	5°31·6′W	H	49
Bàrr nan Cnoc	Arg & Bt	NR8666	55°50·6′	5°24·7′W	X	62
Bàrr nan Damh	Arg & Bt	NN0820	56°20·3′	5°5·9′W	X	50,56
Bàrr nan Damh	Arg & Bt	NR9370	55°53·0′	5°18·1′W	X	62
Bàrr nan Damh	Arg & Bt	NS0297	56°7·7′	5°10·7′W	H	55
Bàrr nan Gall	Arg & Bt	NR8267	55°51·1′	5°28·5′W	X	62
Bàrr na Saille	Arg & Bt	NR8496	56°6·7′	5°28·0′W	H	55
Barrock	Highld	ND2571	58°37·5′	3°17·0′W	T	7,12
Barrock End	Cumbr	NY4747	54°49·2′	2°49·1′W	X	86
Barrock Fell	Cumbr	NY4647	54°49·2′	2°50·0′W	H	86
Barrock-Gill	Cumbr	NY4646	54°48·6′	2°50·0′W	X	86
Barrock Ho	Highld	ND2862	58°32·7′	3°13·7′W	X	11,12
Barrock Park	Cumbr	NY4546	54°48·6′	2°50·9′W	X	86
Barrock Side	Cumbr	NY4547	54°49·1′	2°50·9′W	X	86
Barrockstown	Cumbr	NY3964	54°58·3′	2°56·7′W	X	85
Barrodger	Renf	NS3556	55°46·4′	4°37·4′W	X	63
Barr of Spottes	D & G	NX8168	54°59·8′	3°51·2′W	X	84
Barrogill Mains Fm	Highld	ND2973	58°38·6′	3°12·9′W	FM	7,12
Barron House	Northum	NY6467	55°0·0′	2°33·3′W	X	86
Barron's Fm	Lincs	TF1811	52°41·3′	0°14·8′W	FM	130,142
Barron's Pike	Cumbr	NY5975	55°4·3′	2°38·1′W	X	86
Barron's Pike (Roman Signal Stn)	Cumbr	NY5975	55°4·3′	2°38·1′W	R	86
Barroose Fm	I of M	SC4281	54°12·3′	4°24·9′W	FM	95
Barrow	Cumbr	NY2221	54°34·9′	3°12·0′W	H	89,90
Barrow	Glos	SO8824	51°55·1′	2°10·1′W	T	162
Barrow	Lancs	SD7338	53°50·5′	2°24·2′W	T	103
Barrow	Northum	NT9106	55°21·1′	2°8·1′W	X	80
Barrow	Roth	SK3798	53°28·9′	1°26·1′W	T	110,111
Barrow	Rut	SK8915	52°43·8′	0°40·5′W	T	130
Barrow	Shrops	SJ6500	52°36·0′	2°30·6′W	T	127
Barrow	Shrops	SO6599	52°35·5′	2°30·6′W	T	138
Barrow	Somer	ST5541	51°10·2′	2°38·2′W	T	182,183
Barrow	Suff	TL7663	52°14·4′	0°35·1′E	T	155
Barroway Burn	Fife	NO2211	56°17·4′	3°15·2′W	W	58
Barroway Drove	Norf	TF5603	52°36·4′	0°18·6′E	T	143
Barrow Bay	Cumbr	NY2620	54°34·4′	3°8·3′W	W	89,90
Barrow Beck	Cumbr	NY3729	54°39·4′	2°58·2′W	W	90
Barrow Bridge	Bolton	SD6811	53°35·9′	2°28·6′W	T	109
Barrow Burn	Northum	NT8610	55°23·3′	2°12·8′W	W	80
Barrow Burn	Northum	NT8711	55°23·8′	2°11·9′W	W	80
Barrow Burn	Northum	NT9004	55°20·0′	2°9·0′W	W	80
Barrowbush Hill	Oxon	SU3091	51°37·3′	1°33·6′W	X	164,174
Barrowby	Lincs	SK8836	52°55·1′	0°41·1′W	T	130
Barrowby	N Yks	SE3348	53°55·9′	1°29·4′W	X	104
Barrowby Grange	N Yks	SE3347	53°55·3′	1°29·4′W	X	104
Barrowby Hall	Leeds	SE3833	53°47·8′	1°25·0′W	X	104
Barrowby Lodge	Lincs	SK8835	52°54·5′	0°41·1′W	X	130
Barrowcliff	N Yks	TA0289	54°17·4′	0°25·6′W	T	101
Barrowcliffe Fm	Leic	SK6712	52°42·3′	1°0·1′W	FM	129
Barrow Clough	Derby	SK1497	53°28·4′	1°46·9′W	X	110
Barrow Clump Buildings	Suff	TL8277	52°21·9′	0°40·8′E	X	144
Barrow Common	Norf	TF7943	52°57·5′	0°40·3′E	X	132
Barrow Common	N Som	ST5467	51°24·2′	2°39·3′W	T	172,182
Barrow Court	N Som	ST5168	51°24·8′	2°41·9′W	X	172,182
Barrow Court	Somer	ST6228	51°3·2′	2°32·1′W	X	183
Barrowden	Rut	SK9400	52°35·6′	0°36·3′W	T	141
Barrow Elm Fm	Glos	SP1604	51°44·3′	1°45·7′W	FM	163
Barrowfield	Cumbr	SD4890	54°18·4′	2°47·5′W	X	97
Barrow Field	Suff	TL7665	52°15·5′	0°35·1′E	X	155
Barrowfield Wood	Cumbr	SD4892	54°19·5′	2°47·6′W	F	97
Barrow Fm	Essex	TL6202	51°41·8′	0°21·0′E	FM	167
Barrow Fm	Somer	ST7342	51°10·8′	2°22·8′W	FM	183
Barrow Fm	Wilts	ST9275	51°28·7′	2°6·5′W	FM	173
Barrow Fms	Heref	SO7149	52°8·5′	2°25·0′W	FM	149
Barrowford	Lancs	SD8539	53°51·1′	2°13·3′W	T	103
Barrowford Lock Ho	Lancs	SD8640	53°51·6′	2°12·4′W	X	103
Barrow Gdns	Lancs	SD7439	53°51·0′	2°23·3′W	X	103
Barrow Grange	N Lincs	TA0619	53°39·6′	0°23·3′W	X	112
Barrow Green	Kent	TQ9563	51°20·2′	0°48·4′E	T	178
Barrow Green Court	Surrey	TQ3753	51°15·8′	0°1·8′W	X	187
Barrow Green Fm	Surrey	TQ3752	51°15·3′	0°1·8′W	FM	187
Barrow Green Fm	Surrey	TQ4045	51°11·4′	0°0·6′E	FM	187
Barrow Gurney	N Som	ST5367	51°24·2′	2°40·2′W	T	172,182
Barrow Hall	N Lincs	TA0620	53°40·2′	0°23·3′W	X	107,112
Barrow Hall Fm	Essex	TQ9288	51°33·7′	0°46·6′E	FM	178
Barrow Hann	N Lincs	TA0822	53°41·2′	0°21·5′W	T	107,112
Barrow Haven	N Lincs	TA0622	53°41·3′	0°23·3′W	X	107,112
Barrow Heath	Suff	TL7765	52°15·5′	0°36·0′E	X	155
Barrow Hill	Bath & NE Somer	ST6460	51°20·5′	2°30·6′W	H	172
Barrow Hill	Ches	SJ4669	53°13·2′	2°48·1′W	X	117
Barrow-hill	Derby	SK3529	52°51·7′	1°28·4′W	X	128
Barrow Hill	Derby	SK4175	53°16·5′	1°22·7′W	T	120
Barrow Hill	Dorset	SY9596	50°46·0′	2°3·9′W	T	195
Barrow Hill	Dudley	SO9189	52°30·2′	2°7·6′W	H	139
Barrow Hill	Essex	TM0214	51°47·5′	0°56·1′E	X	168
Barrow Hill	Glos	SO7310	51°47·5′	2°23·1′W	X	162
Barrow Hill	Glos	SO8226	51°56·2′	2°15·3′W	H	162
Barrow Hill	Hants	SU3114	50°55·7′	1°33·1′W	X	196
Barrow Hill	Hants	SU3541	51°10·3′	1°29·6′W	X	185
Barrow Hill	Hants	SU7022	50°59·8′	0°59·8′W	H	197
Barrow Hill	Herts	TL4116	51°49·7′	0°3·2′E	A	167
Barrow Hill	Kent	TQ7174	51°26·6′	0°28·0′E	X	178
Barrowhill	Kent	TR1037	51°5·8′	1°0·4′E	T	179,189
Barrow Hill	Leic	SK5819	52°46·2′	1°8·0′W	X	129
Barrow Hill	Norf	TL8482	52°24·5′	0°42·7′E	X	144
Barrow Hill	Northnts	SP5646	52°6·8′	1°10·5′W	X	152
Barrow Hill	Northum	NT9004	55°20·0′	2°9·0′W	H	80
Barrow Hill	N Som	ST5167	51°24·2′	2°41·9′W	X	172,182
Barrow Hill	Oxon	SP6033	51°59·8′	1°7·2′W	X	152,165
Barrow Hill	Poole	SY9997	50°46·6′	2°0·5′W	X	195
Barrow Hill	Somer	ST7450	51°15·1′	2°22·0′W	H	183
Barrowhill	Staffs	SK1040	52°57·7′	1°50·7′W	X	119,128
Barrow Hill	Suff	TL8945	52°4·5′	0°45·9′E	X	155
Barrow Hill	Suff	TM0438	52°0·4′	0°58·7′E	X	155
Barrow Hill	Wilts	ST9923	51°0·6′	2°0·5′W	H	184
Barrow Hill	Worcs	SO9175	52°22·6′	2°7·5′W	X	139
Barrow Hill Fm	Leic	SK4119	52°46·3′	1°23·1′W	FM	129
Barrow Hill Fm	Lincs	TF0541	52°57·6′	0°25·8′W	FM	130
Barrow Hills	Notts	SK6792	53°25·5′	0°59·1′W	X	111
Barrowhills	Surrey	SU9965	51°22·8′	0°34·3′W	X	175,176
Barrow Hill (Tumulus)	Hants	SU7022	50°59·8′	0°59·8′W	A	197
Barrow Hill (Tumulus)	Oxon	SP6033	51°59·8′	1°7·2′W	A	152,165
Barrow Hollin	Cumbr	SD4084	54°15·1′	2°54·8′W	X	96,97
Barrow-In-Furness	Cumbr	SD1969	54°6·9′	3°13·9′W	T	96
Barrow Island	Cumbr	SD1968	54°6·3′	3°13·9′W	X	96
Barrowland Fm	Dorset	SY5496	50°45·9′	2°38·8′W	FM	194
Barrow Lane Fm	Somer	ST7232	51°5·4′	2°23·6′W	FM	183
Barrow Law	Northum	NT8611	55°23·8′	2°12·8′W	H	80
Barrowling	Cumbr	NY4645	54°48·1′	2°50·0′W	X	86
Barrow Ling	Lincs	TA0101	53°30·0′	0°28·2′W	X	112
Barrow Mere	N Lincs	TA0521	53°40·7′	0°24·2′W	X	107,112
Barrow Mill	Cumbr	NY4543	54°47·0′	2°50·9′W	X	86
Barrow Mill	Northum	NT9106	55°21·1′	2°8·1′W	X	80
Barrowmoor	Cumbr	NY6620	54°34·7′	2°31·1′W	X	91
Barrow Moor	Hants	SU2507	50°51·9′	1°38·3′W	F	195
Barrow Moor	Staffs	SK0564	53°10·6′	1°55·1′W	X	119
Barrowmore Estate	Ches	SJ4769	53°13·2′	2°47·2′W	T	117
Barrow Nook	Lancs	SD4402	53°30·9′	2°50·3′W	T	108
Barrow Plantn	Wilts	SU2251	51°15·7′	1°40·7′W	F	184
Barrow Scar	Northum	NT9005	55°20·6′	2°9·0′W	X	80
Barrowsgate	Aberd	NO7899	57°5·1′	2°21·3′W	X	38,45
Barrows Green	Ches	SJ6958	53°7·3′	2°27·4′W	T	118
Barrows Green	Cumbr	SD5288	54°17·4′	2°43·8′W	T	97
Barrow's Green	Halton	SJ5287	53°22·9′	2°42·9′W	T	108
Barrows Green	Notts	SK4552	53°4·0′	1°19·3′W	T	120
Barrow's Hams	Somer	ST4548	51°13·9′	2°46·9′W	X	182
Barrows Hill	Kent	TQ9272	51°25·1′	0°46·1′E	X	178
Barrows Hill	Somer	ST4812	50°54·5′	2°44·0′W	X	193
Barrows House Fm	N Yks	SE7278	54°11·8′	0°53·4′W	FM	100
Barrowsland Fm	Kent	TQ9130	51°2·5′	0°43·9′E	FM	189
Barrows, The	Rut	SP8997	52°34·0′	0°40·8′W	H	141
Barrow Stones	Derby	SK1396	53°27·9′	1°47·8′W	X	110
Barrow Street	Wilts	ST8330	51°4·4′	2°14·2′W	T	183
Barrow upon Humber	N Lincs	TA0720	53°40·2′	0°22·4′W	T	107,112
Barrow upon Soar	Leic	SK5717	52°45·1′	1°8·9′W	T	129
Barrow upon Trent	Derby	SK3528	52°51·1′	1°28·4′W	T	128
Barrow Vale	Bath & NE Somer	ST6460	51°20·5′	2°30·6′W	T	172
Barrow Vale	N Lincs	TA0519	53°39·7′	0°24·2′W	X	112
Barrow Wake	Glos	SO9215	51°50·2′	2°6·6′W	T	163
Barrow Wold Fm	N Lincs	TA0518	53°39·1′	0°24·3′W	FM	112
Barrow Wood	N Som	ST5368	51°24·8′	2°40·2′W	F	172,182
Bàrr Phort	Arg & Bt	NM9610	56°14·6′	5°17·1′W	X	55

Barr Point	Arg & Bt	NS0853	55°44·2'	5°3·1'W	X	63
Barr Point	D & G	NX3145	54°46·5'	4°37·2'W	X	82
Barr Reamhar	Arg & Bt	NR7659	55°46·6'	5°33·9'W	X	62
Barr River	Arg & Bt	NR4062	55°47·1'	6°8·4'W	W	60,61
Barr River	Highld	NM6155	56°37·8'	5°53·4'W	W	49
Barrs	Arg & Bt	NN0739	56°30·5'	5°7·7'W	X	50
Barr Sailleach	Arg & Bt	NM8200	56°8·8'	5°30·1'W	H	55
Barr Salachaidh	Pth & Kin	NO0965	56°46·3'	3°28·9'W	H	43
Barr's Court	S Glos	ST6572	51°27·0'	2°29·8'W	X	172
Barrshouse	E Ayr	NS5525	55°30·1'	4°17·3'W	X	71
Barrsyard	D & G	NX8162	54°56·6'	3°51·0'W	X	84
Barr, The	Arg & Bt	NR8494	56°5·7'	5°27·9'W	X	55
Barr, The	D & G	NX8153	54°51·7'	3°50·8'W	X	84
Barr, The	D & G	NY0082	55°7·6'	3°33·7'W	X	78
Barr Thormaid	Arg & Bt	NR7183	55°59·4'	5°39·9'W	H	55
Barrule Beg	I of M	SC2776	54°9·3'	4°38·5'W	X	95
Barr Water	Arg & Bt	NR7037	55°34·6'	5°38·5'W	W	68
Barr Water	Arg & Bt	NR7441	55°36·9'	5°34·9'W	W	62
Barr Wood	Stir	NS7987	56°3·9'	3°56·2'W	F	57
Barry	Angus	NO5334	56°30·0'	2°45·4'W	T	54
Barry Bank Fm	N Yks	NZ8010	54°29·0'	0°45·5'W	FM	94
Barry Buddon Camp	Angus	NO5132	56°28·9'	2°47·3'W	X	54
Barrycott Lodge	Norf	TF5212	52°41·3'	0°15·3'E	X	131,143
Barry Dock	V of Glam	ST1168	51°24·5'	3°16·4'W	T	171
Barry Hill	Aberd	NJ5654	57°34·7'	2°43·7'W	H	29
Barry Hill	Pth & Kin	NO2650	56°38·4'	3°11·9'W	H	53
Barry Island	V of Glam	ST1166	51°23·4'	3°16·4'W	T	171
Barry Island Fm	Pemb	SM8131	51°56·3'	5°10·8'W	FM	157
Barry Links	Angus	NO5432	56°28·9'	2°44·4'W	X	54
Barry or Barri	V of Glam	ST1168	51°24·5'	3°16·4'W	T	171
Barry Sands	Angus	NO5430	56°27·8'	2°44·3'W	X	54
Barry's Wood	Ches	SJ5970	53°13·8'	2°36·4'W	F	117
Barsale Fm	Norf	TF6400	52°34·6'	0°25·6'E	FM	143
Barsalloch Fm	D & G	NX4558	54°53·8'	4°24·6'W	FM	83
Barsalloch Point	D & G	NX3441	54°44·4'	4°34·3'W	X	83
Bar Sand	Lincs	TF4643	52°58·1'	0°10·9'E	X	131
Barsby	Leic	SK6911	52°41·8'	0°58·3'W	T	129
Barsby Lodge	Leic	SK6711	52°41·8'	1°0·1'W	X	129
Barscarrow	D & G	NX0847	54°47·1'	4°58·7'W	X	82
Barscobe Castle	D & G	NX6580	55°6·0'	4°6·5'W	A	77
Barscobe Hill	D & G	NX6780	55°6·0'	4°4·6'W	X	77
Barscobe Loch	D & G	NX6681	55°6·6'	4°5·6'W	W	77
Barscraigh	D & G	NX8657	54°53·9'	3°46·2'W	X	84
Barscraigh Hill	D & G	NX8657	54°53·9'	3°46·2'W	H	84
Barscube	Renf	NS3970	55°54·0'	4°34·1'W	X	63
Barscube Hill	Renf	NS3871	55°54·5'	4°35·1'W	H	63
Barsey Fm	Cambs	TL6345	52°5·0'	0°23·1'E	FM	154
Barsey Walk Fm	Lincs	TF2170	53°13·0'	0°10·9'W	FM	122
Bars Geo	Shetld	HU5145	60°11·4'	1°4·3'W	X	4
Barsham	Suff	TM3989	52°27·0'	1°31·4'E	T	134
Barsham	Suff	TM3989	52°27·0'	1°31·4'E	T	156
Barsham Hill	Suff	TM4089	52°27·0'	1°32·3'E	X	156
Barsham Marshes	Suff	TM4090	52°27·5'	1°32·4'E	X	134
Barshare	E Ayr	NS5719	55°26·9'	4°15·2'W	T	71
Barshill	D & G	NY0183	55°8·1'	3°32·7'W	X	78
Barskelly	S Ayr	NS3406	55°19·5'	4°36·6'W	X	70,76
Barskeoch	D & G	NX3663	54°56·3'	4°33·2'W	X	83
Barskeoch Fell	D & G	NX2962	54°55·7'	4°39·7'W	H	82
Barskeoch Hill	D & G	NX5883	55°7·5'	4°13·2'W	X	77
Barskeoch Hill	D & G	NX8161	54°56·0'	3°51·0'W	H	84
Barskeoch Mains	D & G	NX6083	55°7·6'	4°11·3'W	X	77
Barskimming	E Ayr	NS4825	55°30·0'	4°23·9'W	X	70
Barskimming Mains	E Ayr	NS4824	55°29·4'	4°23·9'W	X	70
Barsloisnoch	Arg & Bt	NR8195	56°6·1'	5°30·8'W	T	55
Barsneb	N Yks	SE2864	54°4·5'	1°33·9'W	X	99
Barsneb Wood	N Yks	SE2763	54°4·0'	1°34·8'W	F	99
Barsolis Hill	D & G	NX7569	55°0·2'	3°56·8'W	H	84
Barsolus	D & G	NX1056	54°52·0'	4°57·2'W	X	82
Bars o' Strem Ness	Shetld	HT9741	60°9·5'	2°2·7'W	X	4
Barstable	Essex	TQ7188	51°34·1'	0°28·4'E	T	178
Barstibly	D & G	NX7057	54°53·7'	4°1·2'W	X	83,84
Barstobrick	D & G	NX6960	54°55·3'	4°2·2'W	X	83,84
Barston	Sol	SP2078	52°24·2'	1°42·0'W	T	139
Barston Park Fm	Sol	SP2077	52°23·7'	1°42·0'W	FM	139
Barstow Hall Fm	N Yks	SE3493	54°20·1'	1°28·2'W	FM	99
Barswick	Orkney	ND4385	58°45·2'	2°58·6'W	X	7
Barswick	Orkney	ND4386	58°45·7'	2°58·6'W	W	7
Bartaggart Hill	D & G	NX6878	55°5·0'	4°3·6'W	X	77,84
Bar Taing	Orkney	ND4396	58°51·1'	2°58·8'W	X	6,7
Barteliver	Corn	SW9247	50°17·4'	4°54·8'W	X	204
Barter's Hill Fm	Oxon	SP3021	51°53·4'	1°33·4'W	FM	164
Bartestree	Heref	SO5641	52°4·2'	2°38·1'W	T	149
Barth	Cumbr	SD6988	54°17·4'	2°28·2'W	X	98
Bart Hall	Essex	TL8829	51°55·9'	0°44·5'E	X	168
Bar, The	Angus	NO6440	56°33·3'	2°34·7'W	X	54
Bar, The	Cered	SN5780	52°24·2'	4°5·7'W	X	135
Bar, The	Devon	SX7337	50°13·4'	3°46·4'W	X	202
Bar, The	Gwyn	SH4160	53°7·1'	4°22·1'W	X	114,115
Bar, The	Gwyn	SH6014	52°42·6'	4°3·9'W	X	124
Bar, The	Highld	NH9260	57°37·3'	3°48·0'W	X	21,27
Bar, The	W Susx	TQ1623	50°59·9'	0°20·4'W	X	198
Barth Head	Orkney	ND4285	58°45·2'	2°59·7'W	X	7
Barthol Chapel	Aberd	NJ8134	57°24·0'	2°18·5'W	T	29,30
Bartholomew Green	Essex	TL7221	51°51·9'	0°30·3'E	T	167
Bartholomew's Hills	Norf	TF8113	52°41·3'	0°41·1'E	X	132
Barthomley	Ches	SJ7652	53°4·1'	2°21·1'W	T	118
Barthorpe	N Yks	SE7659	54°1·5'	0°50·0'W	X	105,106
Barthorpe Grange	N Yks	SE7759	54°1·5'	0°49·1'W	X	105,106
Bartie Fm	Shrops	SJ3438	52°56·4'	2°58·5'W	FM	126
Bartiestown	Cumbr	NY4772	55°2·6'	2°49·3'W	X	86
Bartindale Fm	N Yks	TA1073	54°8·7'	0°18·5'W	FM	101
Bartindale Plantn	N Yks	TA1173	54°8·7'	0°17·6'W	F	101
Bartindale Row	N Yks	TA0975	54°9·8'	0°19·4'W	X	101
Bartindale Village	N Yks	TA1173	54°8·7'	0°17·6'W	A	101
Bartine Castle	Corn	SW3929	50°6·5'	5°38·7'W	A	203
Bartinney Downs	Corn	SW3929	50°6·5'	5°38·7'W	H	203
Bartle Hall (Hotel)	Lancs	SD4833	53°47·7'	2°47·0'W	X	102
Bartlehill	Scot Bord	NT7740	55°39·4'	2°21·5'W	X	74
Bartle's Hill	Cumbr	NY4977	55°5·3'	2°47·5'W	H	86
Bartlett Creek	Medway	TQ8269	51°23·7'	0°37·4'E	W	178
Bartlett Fm	Kent	TQ9739	51°7·2'	0°49·3'E	FM	189
Bartletts	Kent	TR2567	51°21·7'	1°14·3'E	X	179
Bartlett's Fm	Essex	TL7127	51°55·1'	0°29·6'E	FM	167
Bartlett's Fm	Essex	TQ7798	51°39·4'	0°33·9'E	FM	167
Bartlett's Green Fm	I of W	SZ6090	50°42·6'	1°8·6'W	FM	196
Bartlewood Fm	Derby	SK4237	52°56·0'	1°22·1'W	FM	129
Bartley	Hants	SU3013	50°55·2'	1°34·0'W	T	196
Bartley Grange	Hants	SU3113	50°55·2'	1°33·2'W	X	196
Bartley Green	Birm	SP0182	52°26·4'	1°58·7'W	T	139
Bartley Heath	Hants	SU7253	51°16·5'	0°57·7'W	X	186
Bartley Lodge	Hants	SU2913	50°55·2'	1°34·9'W	X	196
Bartley Manor	Hants	SU3012	50°54·6'	1°34·0'W	X	196
Bartley Resr	Birm	SP0081	52°25·9'	1°59·6'W	W	139
Bartley Water	Hants	SU3412	50°54·6'	1°30·6'W	W	196
Bartlow	Cambs	TL5845	52°5·1'	0°18·8'E	T	154
Bartlow Hills	Cambs	TL5844	52°4·5'	0°18·7'E	X	154
Bartlow Hills (Tumuli)	Essex	TL5844	52°4·5'	0°18·7'E	R	154
Bartom's Hill	Dorset	SY9395	50°45·5'	2°5·6'W	X	195
Barton	Cambs	TL4055	52°10·8'	0°3·3'E	T	154
Barton	Ches	SJ4454	53°5·1'	2°49·8'W	T	117
Barton	Cumbr	NY4826	54°37·8'	2°47·9'W	X	90
Barton	Devon	SS4805	50°49·7'	4°9·1'W	X	191
Barton	Devon	SS7423	50°59·8'	3°47·4'W	X	180
Barton	Devon	SS9115	50°55·7'	3°32·7'W	X	181
Barton	Devon	SX8694	50°44·3'	3°36·6'W	X	191
Barton	Devon	SY2199	50°47·3'	3°6·9'W	A	192,193
Barton	Devon	SY2597	50°46·3'	3°3·4'W	A	192,193
Barton	Glos	SO8417	51°51·3'	2°13·5'W	T	162
Barton	Glos	SP0925	51°55·6'	1°51·8'W	T	163
Barton	Heref	SO2957	52°12·6'	3°2·0'W	X	148
Barton	I of W	SZ5089	50°42·1'	1°17·1'W	T	196
Barton	Lancs	SD3509	53°34·7'	2°58·5'W	T	108
Barton	Lancs	SD5137	53°49·9'	2°44·3'W	T	102
Barton	N Som	ST3956	51°18·2'	2°52·1'W	T	182
Barton	N Yks	NZ2308	54°28·3'	1°38·3'W	T	93
Barton	Oxon	SP5507	51°45·8'	1°11·8'W	T	164
Barton	Staffs	SJ8718	52°45·8'	2°11·2'W	X	127
Barton	Torbay	SX9067	50°29·8'	3°32·7'W	T	202
Barton	Warw	SP1051	52°9·7'	1°50·8'W	T	150
Barton Abbey	Oxon	SP4524	51°55·0'	1°20·3'W	T	164
Barton Aerodrome	Salf	SJ7497	53°28·4'	2°23·1'W	X	109
Barton Bendish	Norf	TF7105	52°37·2'	0°32·0'E	T	143
Barton Bendish Fen	Norf	TF7103	52°36·1'	0°31·9'E	X	143
Barton Bottom	Suff	TL8668	52°16·9'	0°44·0'E	X	155
Barton Br	N Yks	SE7163	54°3·7'	0°54·5'W	X	100
Barton Broad	Norf	TG3621	52°44·3'	1°30·2'E	W	133,134
Barton Brook	Lancs	SD5237	53°49·9'	2°43·3'W	W	102
Bartonbury	Devon	SS7303	50°49·0'	3°47·8'W	X	191
Barton Cliff	N Lincs	TA0022	53°41·3'	0°28·7'W	X	106,107,112
Barton Copse	Hants	SU6238	51°8·5'	1°6·4'W	F	185
Barton Copse	Wilts	SU1769	51°25·4'	1°44·9'W	F	173
Barton Court	Devon	SS6140	51°8·8'	3°58·9'W	X	180
Barton Court	Heref	SO7440	52°3·7'	2°22·4'W	T	150
Barton Court	W Berks	SU3867	51°24·3'	1°26·8'W	X	174
Barton Cross	Devon	SS6427	51°1·8'	3°56·0'W	X	180
Barton Cross	Devon	SS7231	51°4·3'	3°49·2'W	X	180
Barton Down	Wilts	SU1670	51°26·0'	1°45·8'W	X	173
Barton End	Glos	ST8497	51°40·5'	2°13·5'W	T	162
Barton Farm Country Park	Wilts	ST8160	51°20·6'	2°16·0'W	X	173
Barton Fell	Cumbr	NY4621	54°35·1'	2°49·7'W	X	90
Barton Field Fm	N Lincs	TA0219	53°39·7'	0°27·0'W	FM	112
Bartonfields	Derby	SK2135	52°55·0'	1°40·9'W	X	128
Barton Fm	Corn	SW6927	50°6·1'	5°13·5'W	FM	203
Barton Fm	Hants	SU4731	51°4·8'	1°19·4'W	FM	185
Barton Fm	S Glos	ST6970	51°25·9'	2°26·4'W	FM	172
Barton Fm	Somer	ST2738	51°8·4'	3°2·2'W	FM	182
Barton Fm	Warw	SP1150	52°9·1'	1°50·0'W	FM	150
Barton Fm	Warw	SP2447	52°7·5'	1°38·6'W	FM	151
Barton Fm,The	Devon	SS4730	51°3·2'	4°10·6'W	FM	180
Barton Fold Fm	Bolton	SD6408	53°34·3'	2°32·2'W	FM	109
Barton Gate	Devon	SS2905	50°49·4'	4°25·3'W	X	190
Barton Gate	Devon	SS6841	51°9·4'	3°52·9'W	T	180
Bartongate	Oxon	SP4426	51°56·1'	1°21·2'W	X	164
Barton Gate	Staffs	SK1719	52°46·3'	1°44·5'W	T	128
Barton Grange	N Lincs	TA0120	53°40·2'	0°27·9'W	X	106,107,112
Barton Grange	N Yks	NZ2408	54°28·3'	1°37·4'W	X	93
Barton Grange	Salf	SJ7296	53°27·8'	2°24·9'W	X	109
Barton Grange	Somer	ST2219	50°58·1'	3°6·3'W	X	193
Barton Green	Staffs	SK1818	52°45·8'	1°43·6'W	T	128
Barton Grounds Fm	Bucks	SP6229	51°57·6'	1°5·5'W	FM	164,165
Barton Hall	Cumbr	NY4725	54°37·3'	2°48·8'W	X	90
Barton Hall	Derby	SK2034	52°54·4'	1°41·8'W	X	128
Barton Hall	Essex	TQ9191	51°35·3'	0°45·8'E	X	178
Barton Hall	Lancs	SD5236	53°49·3'	2°43·3'W	X	102
Barton Hartshorn	Bucks	SP6431	51°58·7'	1°3·7'W	T	152,165
Barton Heights	N Yks	SE7273	54°9·1'	0°53·4'W	X	100
Barton Hill	C of Bris	ST6072	51°27·0'	2°34·1'W	T	172
Barton Hill	Devon	SS9816	50°56·3'	3°26·7'W	H	181
Barton Hill	Dorset	ST9211	50°54·1'	2°6·4'W	X	195
Barton Hill	N Yks	SE7064	54°4·3'	0°55·4'W	T	100
Barton Hill	Oxon	SP3839	52°3·1'	1°26·4'W	H	151
Barton Hill	Warw	SP2631	51°58·8'	1°36·9'W	X	151
Bartonhill Cutting	Beds	TL0729	51°57·2'	0°26·2'W	X	166
Barton Hill Fm	Beds	TL0928	51°56·6'	0°24·5'W	FM	166
Barton Hill Fm	Bucks	SP6329	51°57·6'	1°4·6'W	FM	164,165
Barton Hill Fm	N Lincs	TA0220	53°40·2'	0°26·9'W	FM	106,107,112
Barton Hill Ho	N Yks	SE7064	54°4·3'	0°55·4'W	X	100
Barton Hills	Beds	TL0929	51°57·2'	0°24·4'W	X	166
Barton Ho	Cumbr	NY4825	54°37·3'	2°47·9'W	X	90
Barton Ho	Devon	SX8366	50°29·2'	3°38·6'W	X	202
Barton Ho	Lancs	SD5336	53°49·3'	2°42·4'W	X	102
Barton Holt	Lincs	TF4217	52°44·1'	0°6·6'E	X	131
Barton House	Devon	SS7807	50°51·2'	3°43·6'W	X	191
Barton Howle	N Yks	NZ8008	54°27·9'	0°45·5'W	X	94
Barton in Fabis	Notts	SK5232	52°53·2'	1°13·2'W	T	129
Barton in the Beans	Leic	SK3906	52°39·3'	1°25·0'W	T	140
Barton-le-Clay	Beds	TL0831	51°58·2'	0°25·3'W	T	166
Barton-le-Street	N Yks	SE7274	54°9·6'	0°53·4'W	T	100
Barton-le-Willows	N Yks	SE7163	54°3·7'	0°54·5'W	T	100
Barton Leys	Norf	TF6904	52°36·7'	0°30·2'E	F	143
Barton Leys Fm	Oxon	SP4423	51°54·5'	1°21·2'W	FM	164
Barton Locks	Salf	SJ7496	53°27·8'	2°23·1'W	X	109
Barton Lodge	Brackn	SU9273	51°27·1'	0°40·2'W	X	175
Barton Lodge	N Lincs	TA0419	53°39·7'	0°25·2'W	X	112
Barton Lodge	Notts	SK5232	52°53·2'	1°13·2'W	X	129
Barton Lodge	Oxon	SP4524	51°55·0'	1°20·3'W	X	164
Barton Lower Fm	Somer	ST5433	51°5·9'	2°39·0'W	FM	182,183
Barton Manor	I of W	SZ5294	50°44·8'	1°15·4'W	X	196
Bartonmere Ho	Suff	TL9166	52°15·8'	0°48·3'E	X	155
Barton Mills	Suff	TL7173	52°19·9'	0°31·0'E	T	154
Barton Moor	Notts	SK5431	52°52·7'	1°11·5'W	X	129
Barton Moor	N Yks	SE7376	54°10·7'	0°52·5'W	X	100
Barton Moor Ho	N Yks	SE7063	54°3·7'	0°55·4'W	X	100
Barton Moss	Salf	SJ7397	53°28·4'	2°24·0'W	X	109
Bartonmoss Fm	Salf	SJ7296	53°27·8'	2°24·9'W	FM	109
Barton Old Hall Fm	Lancs	SD5338	53°50·4'	2°42·4'W	FM	102
Barton on Sea	Hants	SZ2393	50°44·4'	1°40·1'W	T	195
Barton-on-the-Heath	Warw	SP2532	51°59·4'	1°37·8'W	T	151
Barton Park	Cumbr	NY4622	54°35·7'	2°49·7'W	F	90
Bartonpark	Derby	SK1935	52°55·0'	1°42·6'W	X	128
Barton Park	Staffs	SK1718	52°45·8'	1°44·5'W	X	128
Barton Pines	Torbay	SX8461	50°26·5'	3°37·6'W	X	202
Barton Place	Devon	SX9195	50°44·9'	3°32·3'W	X	192
Barton's Corner	I of W	SZ4189	50°42·2'	1°24·8'W	X	196
Bartons Cottage	Rich	TQ1470	51°25·3'	0°21·2'W	X	176
Barton Seagrave	Northnts	SP8977	52°23·3'	0°41·1'W	T	141
Bartons Fm	Cumbr	NY4340	54°45·4'	2°52·7'W	FM	85
Bartonsham	Heref	SO5139	52°3·1'	2°42·5'W	T	149
Barton's House	D & G	NY0177	55°4·9'	3°32·6'W	X	84
Barton Shrub	Suff	TL8965	52°15·3'	0°46·5'E	F	155
Barton's Point	Kent	TQ9474	51°26·1'	0°47·9'E	X	178
Barton Stacey	Hants	SU4341	51°10·2'	1°22·7'W	T	185
Barton St David	Somer	ST5432	51°5·4'	2°39·0'W	T	182,183
Barton Stud	Suff	TL8766	52°15·8'	0°44·8'E	X	155
Barton, The	Devon	SS2905	50°49·4'	4°25·3'W	X	190
Barton, The	Devon	SS6530	51°3·4'	3°55·2'W	X	180
Barton, The	Devon	SS6600	50°47·3'	3°53·7'W	A	191
Barton, The	Devon	SS8508	50°51·8'	3°37·7'W	X	191
Barton, The	Devon	SX9088	50°41·1'	3°33·0'W	X	192
Barton Town	Devon	SS6840	51°8·9'	3°52·9'W	T	180
Barton Turf	Norf	TG3522	52°44·9'	1°29·3'E	T	133,134
Barton Turn	Staffs	SK2018	52°45·8'	1°41·8'W	T	128
Barton-under-Needwood	Staffs	SK1818	52°45·8'	1°43·6'W	T	128
Barton-Upon-Humber	N Lincs	TA0322	53°41·3'	0°26·0'W	T	107,112
Barton Upon Irwell	Salf	SJ7697	53°28·4'	2°21·3'W	T	109
Barton Vale	N Lincs	TA0520	53°40·2'	0°24·2'W	X	107,112
Barton Waterside	N Lincs	TA0223	53°41·8'	0°26·9'W	T	106,107,112
Barton Wood	Devon	SS7448	51°13·3'	3°47·9'W	F	180
Barton Wood	I of W	SZ5294	50°44·8'	1°15·4'W	F	196
Bartridge	Devon	SS6022	50°59·1'	3°59·3'W	X	180
Bartridge Common	Devon	SS5226	51°1·1'	4°6·2'W	X	180
Bartrostan	D & G	NX3859	54°54·2'	4°31·2'W	X	83
Bartrostan Burn	D & G	NX3759	54°54·2'	4°32·1'W	W	83
Barturk	E Ayr	NS4922	55°28·4'	4°22·9'W	X	70
Bartwood	Heref	SO6321	51°53·4'	2°31·9'W	X	162
Barugh	Barns	SE3108	53°34·3'	1°31·5'W	T	110,111
Barugh	Cumbr	NY2246	54°48·4'	3°12·4'W	X	85
Barugh Br	N Yks	SE7479	54°12·3'	0°51·5'W	X	100
Barugh Cottages	Cumbr	NY5444	54°47·6'	2°42·5'W	X	86
Barugh Fm	N Yks	SE3374	54°9·9'	1°29·3'W	FM	99
Barugh Green	Barns	SE3107	53°33·8'	1°31·5'W	T	110,111
Barugh Ho	Cumbr	NY6305	54°26·6'	2°33·8'W	X	91
Barughsyke	Cumbr	NY2246	54°48·4'	3°12·4'W	X	85
Barugh, The	N Yks	SE4976	54°10·9'	1°14·5'W	X	100
Barvalgans	D & G	NX2973	55°1·6'	4°40·1'W	X	76
Barvennan	D & G	NX3860	54°54·8'	4°31·2'W	X	83
Barvennan Moss	D & G	NX3760	54°54·7'	4°32·1'W	X	83
Barvernochan	D & G	NX3852	54°50·5'	4°30·9'W	X	83
Barvick Burn	Pth & Kin	NN8327	56°25·5'	3°53·4'W	W	52
Barville Fm	Kent	TR3050	51°12·4'	1°18·0'E	FM	179
Barvin Hill	Herts	TL2900	51°41·3'	0°7·6'W	X	166
Barvin Park	Herts	TL2801	51°41·8'	0°8·5'W	X	166
Barward	E Ayr	NS4836	55°35·9'	4°24·3'W	X	70
Barway	Cambs	TL5475	52°21·3'	0°16·1'E	T	143
Barway Fm	Cambs	TL3689	52°29·1'	0°0·6'E	FM	142
Barwell	King	TQ1763	51°21·5'	0°18·8'W	T	176,187
Barwell	Leic	SP4497	52°34·4'	1°20·6'W	T	140
Barwell Fields Fm	Leic	SP4498	52°34·9'	1°20·6'W	FM	140
Barwhanny	D & G	NX4149	54°48·9'	4°28·0'W	X	83
Barwheys	E Ayr	NS5029	55°32·2'	4°22·2'W	X	70
Barwheys	S Ayr	NS3310	55°21·6'	4°37·6'W	X	70
Barwheys	S Ayr	NS3924	55°29·3'	4°32·5'W	X	70
Barwhillanty	D & G	NX7270	55°0·7'	3°59·7'W	X	77,84
Barwhinnock	D & G	NX6554	54°52·0'	4°5·8'W	X	83,84
Barwhin Point	S Ayr	NS2109	55°20·8'	4°49·0'W	X	70,76
Barwhirran	D & G	NX4061	54°55·3'	4°29·4'W	X	83
Barwhirran Croft	D & G	NX4161	54°55·4'	4°28·4'W	X	83
Barwick	Corn	SW9445	50°16·4'	4°53·1'W	X	204
Barwick	Devon	SS5907	50°51·0'	3°59·8'W	T	191
Barwick	Herts	TL3819	51°51·4'	0°0·6'E	T	166
Barwick	Somer	ST5613	50°55·1'	2°37·2'W	T	194
Barwick	Stock on T	NZ4314	54°31·4'	1°19·7'W	X	93
Barwick Hall	Cumbr	SD6283	54°14·7'	2°34·6'W	X	97
Barwick Hall Fm	Norf	TF8135	52°53·1'	0°41·8'E	FM	132
Barwick Ho	Norf	TF8035	52°53·2'	0°40·9'E	X	132
Barwick Ho	Somer	ST5614	50°55·7'	2°37·2'W	X	194
Barwick in Elmet	Leeds	SE3937	53°49·9'	1°24·0'W	T	104
Barwinnock	D & G	NX3843	54°45·6'	4°30·6'W	X	83
Barwinnock	S Ayr	NX3077	55°3·8'	4°39·3'W	X	76
Barwise Hall	Cumbr	NY6517	54°33·1'	2°32·0'W	A	91
Barwythe Hall	Beds	TL0214	51°49·1'	0°30·8'W	X	166
Baryerrock	D & G	NX3950	54°49·4'	4°29·9'W	X	83
Basan Hill	Dorset	SY7696	50°46·0'	2°20·0'W	X	194
Baschurch	Shrops	SJ4221	52°47·2'	2°51·2'W	T	126
Bascodyke	Cumbr	NY5245	54°48·1'	2°44·4'W	X	86
Bascodyke Foot	Cumbr	NY5245	54°48·1'	2°44·4'W	X	86
Bascodyke Head	Cumbr	NY5245	54°48·1'	2°44·4'W	X	86
Bascote	Warw	SP4063	52°16·1'	1°24·4'W	T	151
Bascote Heath	Warw	SP3962	52°15·5'	1°25·3'W	T	151
Bascote Lodge Fm	Warw	SP3963	52°16·1'	1°25·3'W	FM	151

Base Brown	Cumbr	NY2211	54°29·5'	3°11·8'W	H	89,90
Basefield Wood	Cambs	TL6557	52°11·4'	0°25·2'E	F	154
Base Green	Suff	TM0163	52°13·9'	0°57·0'E	T	155
Basford	Shrops	SO3985	52°27·8'	2°53·5'W	T	137
Basford	Staffs	SJ8546	53°0·9'	2°13·0'W	T	118
Basford Grange	Staffs	SJ9952	53°4·2'	2°0·5'W	X	118
Basford Green	Staffs	SJ9951	53°3·6'	2°0·5'W	T	118
Basford Hall	Ches	SJ7152	53°4·1'	2°25·6'W	X	118
Basford Hall	Staffs	SJ9851	53°3·6'	2°1·4'W	X	118
Bashall Brook	Lancs	SD7142	53°52·6'	2°26·1'W	W	103
Bashall Eaves	Lancs	SD6943	53°53·2'	2°27·9'W	T	103
Bashall Hall	Lancs	SD7142	53°52·6'	2°26·1'W	A	103
Bashall Town	Lancs	SD7142	53°52·6'	2°26·1'W	X	103
Bashfield Fm	Lancs	SD8944	53°53·8'	2°9·6'W	FM	103
Bashley	Hants	SZ2497	50°46·6'	1°39·2'W	T	195
Bashley Manor Fm	Hants	SZ2396	50°46·0'	1°40·0'W	FM	195
Bashley Park	Hants	SZ2497	50°46·6'	1°39·2'W	T	195
Bashurst	W Susx	TQ1229	51°3·2'	0°23·7'W	X	187,198
Basildon	Essex	TQ7389	51°34·6'	0°30·2'E	T	178
Basildon Park	W Berks	SU6078	51°30·1'	1°7·7'W	X	175
Basil Fm	Corn	SX1984	50°37·9'	4°33·2'W	FM	201
Basill	Corn	SX2084	50°37·9'	4°32·3'W	A	201
Basin Br	Leic	SP3996	52°33·9'	1°25·1'W	X	140
Basin Fm	Norf	TF5004	52°37·0'	0°13·3'E	FM	143
Basing Fm	Kent	TQ4340	51°8·7'	0°3·1'E	FM	187
Basing Ho	Hants	SU6652	51°16·0'	1°2·8'W	A	185,186
Basing Home Fm	Hants	SU6728	51°3·1'	1°2·3'W	FM	185,186
Basing Park	Hants	SU6828	51°3·1'	1°1·4'W	X	185,186
Basingstoke	Hants	SU6352	51°16·0'	1°5·4'W	T	185
Basingstoke Canal	Surrey	SU8955	51°17·5'	0°43·0'W	W	175,186
Basin Howe	N Yks	SE9286	54°15·9'	0°34·8'W	A	94,101
Basin Howe	N Yks	SE9286	54°15·9'	0°34·8'W	X	94,101
Basin, The	Northum	NU1242	55°40·5'	1°48·1'W	W	75
Basin, The	Orkney	HY5318	59°3·1'	2°48·7'W	W	6
Basin, The	Pemb	SM7108	51°43·7'	5°18·6'W	W	157
Baskell Fm	Cumbr	SD1993	54°19·8'	3°14·3'W	FM	96
Basket	S Lanak	NS6655	55°46·4'	4°7·7'W	X	64
Baskets Fm	Somer	ST7426	51°2·2'	2°21·9'W	FM	183
Basket's Gate	Heref	SO4563	52°16·0'	2°48·0'W	X	137,138,148
Baskeybay	Cambs	TL6278	52°22·8'	0°23·2'E	X	143
Baslow	Derby	SK2572	53°14·9'	1°37·1'W	T	119
Baslow Edge	Derby	SK2674	53°16·0'	1°36·2'W	X	119
Baslow Hall	Derby	SK2573	53°15·4'	1°37·1'W	X	119
Bason	Devon	SS4107	50°50·7'	4°15·1'W	X	190
Bason Bridge	Somer	ST3445	51°12·3'	2°56·3'W	T	182
Bason Crag	Cumbr	NY4614	54°31·4'	2°49·6'W	X	90
Basore Point	Corn	SW5329	50°6·8'	5°26·9'W	X	203
Bassage Fm	Worcs	SO8669	52°19·4'	2°11·9'W	FM	139
Bassaleg	Newp	ST2786	51°34·3'	3°2·8'W	T	171
Bassardsbank	Shrops	SO6571	52°20·4'	2°30·4'W	X	138
Bass Burn	D & G	NX7996	55°14·9'	3°53·8'W	W	78
Bassen Beck	Cumbr	NY3944	54°47·5'	2°56·5'W	W	85
Bassendean	Scot Bord	NT6245	55°42·1'	2°35·8'W	X	74
Bassendeanhill	Scot Bord	NT6246	55°42·6'	2°35·9'W	X	74
Bassendean Ho	Scot Bord	NT6245	55°42·1'	2°35·8'W	X	74
Bassenfell Manor	Cumbr	NY2132	54°40·9'	3°12·7'W	X	89,90
Bassenhally Fm	Cambs	TL2898	52°34·1'	0°6·3'W	FM	142
Bassenhally Moor	Peterb	TF2900	52°35·2'	0°5·3'W	X	142
Bassenthwaite	Cumbr	NY2332	54°40·9'	3°11·2'W	T	89,90
Bassenthwaite Common	Cumbr	NY2529	54°39·3'	3°9·3'W	X	89,90
Bassenthwaite Lake	Cumbr	NY2129	54°39·2'	3°13·0'W	W	89,90
Basses Fm	Lincs	TF3860	53°7·4'	0°4·1'E	FM	122
Basset Down Fm	Wilts	SU1180	51°31·4'	1°50·1'W	FM	173
Basset Manor	Oxon	SU6783	51°32·7'	1°1·6'W	A	175
Basset's Cove	Corn	SW6344	50°15·1'	5°19·1'W	W	203
Basset's Cross	Devon	SS5503	50°48·7'	4°3·1'W	A	191
Basset's Fm	Hants	SU5447	51°13·4'	1°13·2'W	FM	185
Bassett	C of Soton	SU4116	50°56·7'	1°24·6'W	T	185
Bassett	Sheff	SK2884	53°21·4'	1°34·3'W	T	110
Bassett Court	Glos	ST7395	51°39·4'	2°23·0'W	X	162
Bassett Dockem	Glos	SO9700	51°42·2'	2°2·2'W	X	163
Bassett Fm	Derby	SK4439	52°57·0'	1°20·3'W	FM	129
Bassett Fm	Leic	SP4899	52°35·4'	1°17·1'W	FM	140
Bassett Green	C of Soton	SU4216	50°56·7'	1°23·7'W	T	185
Bassett Ho	N Yks	SE8473	54°9·0'	0°42·4'W	X	100
Bassetts	E Susx	TQ6030	51°3·0'	0°17·4'E	X	188
Bassetts	Kent	TQ4941	51°9·2'	0°8·2'E	X	188
Bassett's Fm	Essex	TL6105	51°43·5'	0°20·3'E	FM	167
Bassett's Fm	Essex	TL7808	51°44·8'	0°35·1'E	FM	167
Bassett's Fm	Suff	TL8846	52°5·0'	0°45·0'E	FM	155
Bassetts Lodge Fm	Northnts	SP7177	52°23·4'	0°57·0'W	FM	141
Bassett's Manor	E Susx	TQ4637	51°7·0'	0°5·6'E	X	188
Bassett's Moor	Wilts	ST9770	51°26·0'	2°2·2'W	F	173
Bassett's Ridge	Devon	SS5134	51°5·4'	4°7·3'W	X	180
Bassett Wood Fm	Derby	SK1751	53°3·6'	1°44·4'W	FM	119
Basset Wood	Oxon	SU6783	51°32·7'	1°1·6'W	F	175
Bassies	Angus	NO2973	56°50·8'	3°9·4'W	X	44
Bassie Sound	Shetld	HU4119	59°57·5'	1°15·5'W	W	4
Bassingbourn	Cambs	TL3343	52°4·4'	0°3·2'W	T	154
Bassingbourn Manor Fm	Cambs	TL6370	52°18·5'	0°23·9'E	FM	154
Bassingfield	Notts	SK6237	52°55·8'	1°4·3'W	T	129
Bassingham	Lincs	SK9159	53°7·5'	0°38·0'W	T	121
Bassingham Fen	Lincs	SK9358	53°6·9'	0°36·2'W	X	121
Bassingham Grange	Lincs	SK9260	53°8·0'	0°37·1'W	X	121
Bassingthorpe	Lincs	SK9628	52°50·7'	0°34·1'W	T	130
Bassington	Northum	NU1416	55°26·5'	1°46·3'W	X	81
Bassleton Wood	Stock on T	NZ4415	54°31·9'	1°18·8'W	F	93
Bassmead Fm	Beds	TL1361	52°14·4'	0°20·3'W	FM	153
Bassnimoor Fm	Peterb	TF3100	52°35·2'	0°3·6'W	FM	142
Bass Point	Corn	SW7111	49°57·6'	5°11·2'W	X	203
Bass Pool	Cumbr	SD2363	54°3·7'	3°10·2'W	W	96
Bass Rock	E Loth	NT6087	56°4·7'	2°38·1'W	X	67
Bassus Green	Herts	TL3025	51°54·7'	0°6·2'W	T	166
Bass Wood	Lincs	SK8488	53°23·2'	0°43·8'W	F	112,121
Bassymoor	E Yorks	TA1548	53°55·2'	0°14·5'W	X	107
Basta	Shetld	HU5294	60°37·8'	1°2·5'W	T	1,2
Basta Ness	Shetld	HU5393	60°37·3'	1°1·4'W	X	1,2
Bastard, The	Arg & Bt	NR7512	55°21·3'	5°32·5'W	H	68
Basta Voe	Shetld	HU5296	60°38·9'	1°2·4'W	W	1
Basted	Kent	TQ6055	51°16·5'	0°18·0'E	T	188
Bastifell	Cumbr	NY8207	54°27·7'	2°16·2'W	X	91,92
Basting's Hall	Suff	TM2057	52°10·3'	1°13·4'E	X	156
Bastion	Fife	NO2912	56°18·0'	3°8·4'W	X	59
Bastion Hill	Surrey	SU9153	51°16·4'	0°41·3'W	X	186
Bastleford	Pemb	SM9409	51°44·8'	4°58·7'W	X	157,158
Bastleridge	Scot Bord	NT9359	55°49·7'	2°6·3'W	X	67,74,75
Baston	Lincs	TF1114	52°43·0'	0°21·0'W	T	130
Baston Burn	Stir	NS7393	56°7·0'	4°2·1'W	W	57
Baston Fen	Lincs	TF1415	52°43·5'	0°18·3'W	X	130
Bastonford	Worcs	SO8150	52°9·1'	2°16·3'W	T	150
Baston Manor	Brom	TQ4064	51°21·7'	0°1·0'E	X	177,187
Bastow Wood	N Yks	SD9965	54°5·1'	2°0·5'W	F	98
Bastreet Downs	Corn	SX2476	50°33·7'	4°28·7'W	X	201
Bastwick	Norf	TG4217	52°42·0'	1°35·3'E	T	134
Baswich	Staffs	SJ9422	52°48·0'	2°4·9'W	T	127
Baswick Landing	E Yorks	TA0747	53°54·7'	0°21·8'W	X	107
Baswick Seer	E Yorks	TA0747	53°54·7'	0°21·8'W	X	107
Bàtachain Bàna	Arg & Bt	NR3447	55°38·9'	6°13·2'W	X	60
Bàt a' Charchel	Stir	NS4992	56°6·1'	4°25·2'W	H	57
Batailshiel Haugh	Northum	NT8810	55°23·3'	2°10·9'W	X	80
Ba Taing	Shetld	HU5490	60°35·7'	1°0·3'W	X	1,2
Batavaime	Stir	NN4234	56°28·6'	4°33·5'W	X	51
Bat & Ball (PH)	Hants	SU6716	50°56·6'	1°2·4'W	X	185
Batch	Somer	ST3255	51°17·6'	2°58·1'W	T	182
Batchacre Hall	Staffs	SJ7525	52°49·6'	2°21·9'W	X	127
Batchacre Park	Staffs	SJ7526	52°50·1'	2°21·9'W	X	127
Batch Brook	Shrops	SO6280	52°25·2'	2°33·1'W	W	138
Batchcott	Shrops	SO4970	52°19·8'	2°44·5'W	T	137,138,148
Batchelor's Br	Worcs	SO7350	52°9·1'	2°23·3'W	X	150
Batchelor's Fm	Surrey	TQ4248	51°13·0'	0°2·4'E	FM	187
Batchelor's Hall	E Susx	TQ4516	50°55·7'	0°4·2'E	X	198
Batchen	Moray	NJ1861	57°38·2'	3°21·9'W	X	28
Batches, The	Heref	SO5458	52°13·3'	2°40·0'W	X	149
Batchfields	Heref	SO6549	52°8·5'	2°30·3'W	T	149
Batch Fm	Glos	SO8811	51°48·1'	2°10·0'W	FM	162
Batch Fm	Somer	ST4942	51°10·7'	2°43·4'W	FM	182,183
Batch Fm	Somer	ST6547	51°13·5'	2°29·7'W	FM	183
Batch Fm	Somer	ST7051	51°15·7'	2°25·4'W	FM	183
Batchley	Heref	SO6057	52°12·8'	2°34·7'W	X	149
Batchley	Worcs	SP0267	52°18·3'	1°57·8'W	T	150
Batchley Fm	Hants	SZ2995	50°45·5'	1°34·9'W	FM	196
Batchmere's Fm	W Susx	SZ8298	50°46·8'	0°49·8'W	FM	197
Batch, The	Heref	SO3751	52°9·5'	2°54·9'W	X	148,149
Batch,The	N Som	ST4866	51°23·7'	2°44·5'W	X	171,172,182
Batch, The	Shrops	SO4495	52°33·2'	2°49·2'W	X	137
Batch, The	Shrops	SO6885	52°28·0'	2°27·9'W	A	138
Batch, The	Somer	ST5250	51°15·1'	2°40·9'W	X	182,183
Batch Wood	Herts	TL1309	51°46·3'	0°21·3'W	F	166
Batchwood Hall	Herts	TL1308	51°45·8'	0°21·4'W	X	166
Batchworth	Herts	TQ0694	51°38·3'	0°27·7'W	T	166,176
Batchworth Heath	Herts	TQ0792	51°37·2'	0°26·9'W	T	176
Batchy Hill	Heref	SO3936	52°1·4'	2°52·9'W	X	149,161
Batcombe	Dorset	ST6104	50°50·3'	2°32·8'W	T	194
Batcombe	Somer	ST6939	51°9·2'	2°26·2'W	T	183
Batcombe Fm	Somer	ST4751	51°15·6'	2°45·2'W	FM	182
Batcombe Hill	Dorset	ST6103	50°49·7'	2°32·8'W	H	194
Batcombe Vale	Somer	ST6837	51°8·1'	2°27·1'W	X	183
Bate Heath	Ches	SJ6879	53°18·7'	2°28·4'W	T	118
Bateinghope Burn	Northum	NT6904	55°20·0'	2°28·9'W	W	80
Bateman Fold	Cumbr	SD4394	54°20·5'	2°52·2'W	X	97
Bateman Ho	Notts	SK6345	53°0·2'	1°3·3'W	X	129
Bateman's	E Susx	TQ6623	50°59·2'	0°22·3'E	A	199
Bateman's Green	Worcs	SP0776	52°23·2'	1°53·4'W	T	139
Bateman's Hill	Pemb	SN0104	51°42·2'	4°52·4'W	T	157,158
Bate Mill	Ches	SJ8072	53°14·9'	2°17·6'W	X	118
Batemoor	Sheff	SK3580	53°19·2'	1°28·1'W	T	110,111
Batenbush	Cumbr	NY3771	55°2·0'	2°58·7'W	X	85
Bates Fm	Northnts	SP5360	52°14·4'	1°13·0'W	FM	152
Bates Fm	Staffs	SJ7838	52°56·6'	2°19·2'W	FM	127
Bates Fm	Warr	SJ6593	53°26·2'	2°31·2'W	FM	109
Bate's Lodge	Cambs	TL1192	52°31·1'	0°21·4'W	X	142
Bates Moor Fm	Norf	TG0425	52°47·3'	1°1·9'E	FM	133
Bateson's Fm	Lancs	SD6024	53°42·9'	2°36·0'W	FM	102,103
Bates Wharf Br	Leic	SK3705	52°38·7'	1°26·8'W	X	140
Batey Shield	Northum	NY6560	54°56·3'	2°32·2'W	X	86
Batford	Herts	TL1415	51°49·5'	0°20·4'W	T	166
Bath	Bath & NE Somer	ST7464	51°22·7'	2°22·0'W	T	172
Bath	Fife	NS9790	56°5·8'	3°38·9'W	X	58
Bàthach-bàn Cott	Arg & Bt	NN1609	56°14·5'	4°57·7'W	X	56
Bathafarn Fm	Denb	SJ1457	53°6·4'	3°16·7'W	FM	116
Bathafarn Hall	Denb	SJ1457	53°6·4'	3°16·7'W	X	116
Batham Gate (Roman Road)	Derby	SK1077	53°17·6'	1°50·6'W	R	119
Batham Gate (Roman Road)	Derby	SK1681	53°19·8'	1°45·2'W	R	110
Bathampton	Bath & NE Somer	ST7766	51°23·8'	2°19·4'W	T	172
Bathampton Down	Bath & NE Somer	ST7765	51°23·2'	2°19·4'W	H	172
Bathampton Ho	Wilts	SU0138	51°8·7'	1°58·8'W	X	184
Bath Copse	Warw	SP3255	52°11·8'	1°31·5'W	F	151
Bathealton	Somer	ST0724	51°0·7'	3°19·2'W	T	181
Bathealton Court	Somer	ST0724	51°0·7'	3°19·2'W	X	181
Batheaston	Bath & NE Somer	ST7867	51°24·3'	2°18·6'W	T	172
Bathe Hill	Cambs	TL3274	52°21·1'	0°3·3'W	X	142
Batherm Bridge	Devon	ST0025	51°1·2'	3°25·2'W	X	181
Batherton Dairy Ho	Ches	SJ6550	53°3·0'	2°30·9'W	X	118
Batherton Hall	Ches	SJ6549	53°2·5'	2°30·9'W	X	118
Bathesland Water	Pemb	SM8620	51°50·5'	5°6·0'W	W	157
Bath Fm	Lancs	SD4208	53°34·2'	2°52·1'W	FM	108
Bath Fm	Staffs	SJ8507	52°39·9'	2°12·9'W	FM	127,139
Bathford	Bath & NE Somer	ST7966	51°23·8'	2°17·7'W	T	172
Bathford Hill	Bath & NE Somer	ST7965	51°23·3'	2°17·7'W	X	172
Bathgate	W Loth	NS9769	55°54·4'	3°38·4'W	T	65
Bathgate Hills	W Loth	NS9870	55°55·0'	3°37·5'W	X	65
Bath Hill	Warw	SP2952	52°10·2'	1°34·2'W	X	151
Bath Hills	Norf	TM3191	52°28·3'	1°24·5'E	X	134
Bath Hotel and Shearsby Spa	Leic	SP6290	52°30·5'	1°4·8'W	X	140
Bath House Fm	Ches	SJ5655	53°5·7'	2°39·0'W	FM	117
Bath House Fm	Somer	ST2822	50°59·8'	3°1·2'W	FM	193
Bathingbourne	I of W	SZ5483	50°38·9'	1°13·8'W	X	196
Bathley	Notts	SK7759	53°7·6'	0°50·5'W	T	120
Bathleyhill Fm	Notts	SK7660	53°8·1'	0°51·4'W	FM	120
Bath Moor Plantation	Fife	NS9791	56°6·3'	3°38·9'W	F	58
Bathpool	Corn	SX2874	50°32·7'	4°25·3'W	T	201
Bathpool	Somer	ST2526	51°1·9'	3°3·8'W	T	193
Bath Side	Essex	TM2532	51°56·7'	1°16·8'E	T	169
Bathurst Fm	E Susx	TQ6217	50°56·0'	0°18·7'E	FM	199
Bath Vale	Ches	SJ8763	53°10·1'	2°11·3'W	T	118
Bathville	W Loth	NS9367	55°53·3'	3°42·2'W	T	65
Bathway	Somer	ST5952	51°16·2'	2°34·9'W	T	182,183
Bathwick	Bath & NE Somer	ST7565	51°23·2'	2°21·2'W	T	172
Bath Wood	Durham	NZ1221	54°35·3'	1°48·4'W	F	92
Batingau	Denb	SJ0658	53°6·9'	3°23·9'W	X	116
Batlers Green	Herts	TQ1598	51°40·4'	0°19·8'W	T	166,176
Batley	Kirk	SE2424	53°43·0'	1°37·8'W	T	104
Batley Carr	Kirk	SE2323	53°42·4'	1°38·7'W	T	104
Batley Fm	Derby	SK4964	53°10·5'	1°15·6'W	FM	120
Batney Fm	Devon	SS7518	50°57·1'	3°46·4'W	FM	180
Batrudding Fm	N Yks	SE5742	53°52·5'	1°7·6'W	FM	105
Bat's Castle	Somer	SS9842	51°10·3'	3°27·2'W	X	181
Bat's Castle (Settlement)	Somer	SS9842	51°10·3'	3°27·2'W	A	181
Batsford	Glos	SP1833	51°59·9'	1°43·9'W	T	151
Batsford Park	Glos	SP1833	51°59·9'	1°43·9'W	X	151
Bat's Head	Dorset	SY7980	50°37·4'	2°17·4'W	X	194
Bat's Hogsty	Hants	SU8451	51°15·3'	0°47·4'W	A	186
Batslays	V of Glam	ST0067	51°23·8'	3°25·9'W	X	170
Batsom Fm	Somer	SS8434	51°5·9'	3°39·0'W	FM	181
Batson	Devon	SX7339	50°14·5'	3°46·5'W	T	202
Batsworthy	Devon	SS8219	50°57·7'	3°40·4'W	T	181
Batsworthy Cross	Devon	SS8120	50°58·3'	3°41·3'W	X	181
Battans of Brabster	Highld	ND3267	58°35·4'	3°9·7'W	X	12
Battarain Plantn	Notts	SK5871	53°14·2'	1°7·5'W	F	120
Battel Hall	Kent	TQ8253	51°15·0'	0°36·9'E	A	188
Battenhurst Fm	E Susx	TQ6727	51°1·3'	0°23·3'E	FM	188,199
Battens Fm	Devon	ST0213	50°54·7'	3°23·3'W	FM	181
Batten's Fm	Devon	ST1512	50°54·3'	3°12·2'W	FM	181,193
Battens Fm	Devon	ST2404	50°50·1'	3°4·4'W	FM	192,193
Batten's Green	Somer	ST2918	50°57·7'	3°0·3'W	T	193
Battenton Green	Worcs	SO8365	52°17·2'	2°14·6'W	T	138,150
Batteries Fm	Kent	TQ9461	51°19·1'	0°47·4'E	FM	178
Battern Cliffs	Corn	SX3254	50°22·0'	4°21·4'W	X	201
Battersby	N Yks	NZ5907	54°27·5'	1°5·0'W	T	93
Battersby Junction	N Yks	NZ5807	54°27·5'	1°5·9'W	X	93
Battersby Moor	N Yks	NZ6006	54°27·0'	1°4·1'W	X	94
Battersby Plantation	N Yks	NZ6007	54°27·5'	1°4·0'W	F	94
Battersby Plantn	N Yks	NZ5905	54°26·5'	1°5·0'W	F	93
Battersea	Wan	TQ2876	51°28·3'	0°9·0'W	T	176
Battersea Br	Wan	TQ2777	51°28·9'	0°9·9'W	X	176
Battersea Park	Wan	TQ2777	51°28·9'	0°9·9'W	X	176
Battersea Reach	Wan	TQ2676	51°28·4'	0°10·8'W	W	176
Battery Bank	Dorset	SY8588	50°41·7'	2°12·4'W	A	194
Battery Bank	Dorset	SY8887	50°41·2'	2°9·8'W	A	194
Battery Hill	Wilts	SU2034	51°6·5'	1°42·5'W	H	184
Battery Point	Devon	SS1244	51°10·1'	4°41·0'W	X	180
Battery Point	N Som	ST4677	51°29·6'	2°46·3'W	X	171,172
Battery, The	Cumbr	NY1937	54°43·5'	3°15·0'W	X	89,90
Battery, The	D & G	NX6846	54°47·7'	4°2·8'W	A	83,84
Battin's Fm	Somer	ST0632	51°5·0'	3°20·1'W	FM	181
Battisborough Cross	Devon	SX5948	50°19·1'	3°58·5'W	X	202
Battisborough Ho	Devon	SX6047	50°18·6'	3°57·6'W	X	202
Battisborough Island	Devon	SX6047	50°18·1'	3°57·6'W	X	202
Battisford	Suff	TM0554	52°9·0'	1°0·2'E	T	155
Battisford Tye	Suff	TM0254	52°9·1'	0°57·6'E	T	155
Battishill Fm	Devon	SX5085	50°39·0'	4°6·9'W	FM	191,201
Battle	E Susx	TQ7416	50°55·3'	0°28·9'E	T	199
Battle	Powys	SO0030	51°57·8'	3°26·9'W	T	160
Battle Barn Fm	E Susx	TQ7816	50°55·2'	0°32·3'E	FM	199
Battlebarrow Ho	Cumbr	NY6820	54°34·7'	2°29·3'W	X	91
Battleborough	Somer	ST3450	51°15·0'	2°56·4'W	X	182
Battle Br	Glos	SP1639	52°3·2'	1°45·6'W	X	151
Battle Bridge	Northum	NU1112	55°24·4'	1°49·1'W	X	81
Battlebury	Somer	ST5244	51°11·8'	2°40·8'W	X	182,183
Battleby	Pth & Kin	NO0829	56°26·9'	3°29·1'W	X	52,53,58
Battledene Fm	Glos	SP1739	52°3·2'	1°44·7'W	FM	151
Battledore Hill	Norf	TF9642	52°56·6'	0°55·4'E	X	132
Battledown	Glos	SO9621	51°53·5'	2°3·1'W	T	163
Battledown Cross	Devon	SS4509	50°51·8'	4°11·8'W	T	190
Battledown Fm	Glos	SO9204	51°44·3'	2°6·6'W	FM	163
Battledown Fm	Hants	SU5950	51°15·0'	1°8·9'W	FM	185
Battledykes	Angus	NO4555	56°41·3'	2°53·4'W	X	54
Battle End	Powys	SO0031	51°58·3'	3°27·0'W	X	160
Battle Fawr	Powys	SO0032	51°58·9'	3°27·0'W	X	160
Battlefield	C of Glas	NS5861	55°49·5'	4°15·6'W	T	64
Battlefield	Highld	NH6040	57°26·0'	4°19·5'W	X	26
Battlefield	Shrops	SJ5116	52°44·6'	2°43·1'W	T	126
Battlefield Brook	Worcs	SO9471	52°20·5'	2°4·9'W	W	139
Battlefield Line, The	Leic	SK3805	52°38·7'	1°25·9'W	X	140
Battlefields	S Glos	ST7270	51°25·9'	2°23·8'W	X	172
Battle Flat	Leic	SK4411	52°41·9'	1°20·5'W	X	129
Battleflat Lodge Fm	Leic	SK4410	52°41·4'	1°20·5'W	FM	129
Battle Ford	Devon	SX7945	50°17·8'	3°41·6'W	X	202
Battle Gate	Cambs	TL3461	52°14·1'	0°1·9'W	X	154
Battle Hill	Aberd	NJ5439	57°26·6'	2°45·5'W	H	29
Battlehill	D & G	NY2165	54°58·7'	3°13·6'W	X	85
Battle Hill	Durham	NY9816	54°32·6'	2°1·4'W	X	92
Battle Hill	Northum	NY9591	55°13·0'	2°4·3'W	H	81
Battle Hill	N Tyne	NZ3068	55°0·6'	1°31·4'W	T	88
Battle Hill	Powys	SO0134	52°0·0'	3°26·1'W	H	160
Battlehillock	Aberd	NJ4620	57°16·3'	2°53·3'W	X	37
Battlehurst Fm	W Susx	TQ0123	51°0·1'	0°33·2'W	FM	197
Battle Lake	Wilts	SU0688	51°35·7'	1°54·4'W	W	173
Battlelake Fm	Wilts	SU0687	51°35·1'	1°54·4'W	FM	173
Battle Moor	Northum	NT9145	55°42·2'	2°8·2'W	X	74,75

Battle Moss	Highld	ND3143	58°22·5'	3°10·3'W	X	11,12
Battle of Britain Memorial Flight	Lincs	TF2157	53°6·0'	0°11·2'W	X	122
Battle Plain	Dorset	SY9084	50°39·6'	2°8·1'W	X	195
Battle Ring	Corn	SX3180	50°36·0'	4°22·9'W	A	201
Battlesbridge	Essex	TQ7794	51°37·2'	0°33·8'E	T	167,178
Battlesbury	Wilts	ST8945	51°12·5'	2°9·1'W	A	184
Battlesbury Hill	Wilts	ST8945	51°12·5'	2°9·1'W	H	184
Battlescombe	Glos	SO9106	51°45·4'	2°7·4'W	T	163
Battlesden	Beds	SP9628	51°56·8'	0°35·8'W	T	165
Battlesden Park	Beds	SP9529	51°57·3'	0°36·7'W	X	165
Battlesea Green	Suff	TM2275	52°19·9'	1°15·9'E	T	156
Battles Hall	Essex	TQ4995	51°38·3'	0°9·6'E	X	167,177
Battlestead Hill	Staffs	SK2122	52°47·9'	1°40·9'W	X	128
Battle Stone	Northum	NT9230	55°34·1'	2°7·2'W	A	74,75
Battleswick Fm	Essex	TM0222	51°51·8'	0°56·4'E	FM	168
Battle's Wood	Essex	TL4728	51°56·1'	0°8·7'E	F	167
Battleton	Somer	SS9127	51°2·2'	3°32·9'W	T	181
Battleton Holt	Warw	SP3548	52°8·0'	1°28·9'W	X	151
Battle Wood	E Susx	TQ7419	50°56·9'	0°29·0'E	F	199
Battlies Green	Suff	TL8964	52°14·7'	0°46·5'E	T	155
Battlies Ho	Suff	TL9064	52°14·7'	0°47·4'E	X	155
Batton	Devon	SX8039	50°14·6'	3°40·6'W	X	202
Battram	Leic	SK4209	52°40·9'	1°22·3'W	T	140
Battramsley	Hants	SZ3099	50°47·6'	1°34·1'W	T	196
Battramsley Cross	Hants	SZ3198	50°47·1'	1°33·2'W	T	196
Batts	Scot Bord	NT7119	55°28·1'	2°27·1'W	X	80
Batt's Brook	Devon	SX8587	50°40·5'	3°37·3'W	W	191
Batt's Brook	Hants	SU7627	51°2·5'	0°54·6'W	W	186,197
Batt's Corner	Hants	SU8141	51°10·0'	0°50·1'W	T	186
Batt's Fm	Essex	TL9402	51°41·2'	0°48·8'E	FM	168
Batt's Fm	Somer	ST7137	51°8·1'	2°24·5'W	FM	183
Batt's Fm	Suff	TM0866	52°15·4'	1°3·3'E	FM	155
Batts Fm	Surrey	TQ3458	51°18·5'	0°4·3'W	FM	187
Batts Hall	Sol	SP1876	52°23·1'	1°43·7'W	X	139
Batts, The	N Yks	SE2099	54°23·4'	1°41·1'W	X	99
Batt's Wood	E Susx	TQ6327	51°1·4'	0°19·8'E	F	188,199
Battyeford	Kirk	SE1920	53°40·8'	1°42·3'W	T	104
Batty Hill	Lancs	SD4652	53°57·9'	2°49·0'W	X	102
Batty Ho	Lancs	SD9147	53°55·4'	2°7·8'W	X	103
Batty Nick	N Yks	SE0770	54°7·8'	1°53·2'W	W	99
Batty's Corner	E Yorks	TA3027	53°43·6'	0°1·4'W	X	107
Batworthy	Devon	SX6686	50°39·7'	3°53·4'W	X	191
Batworthy	Devon	SX7185	50°39·2'	3°49·1'W	T	191
Bauble's Barrow	Glos	SP1414	51°49·7'	1°47·4'W	A	163
Bauchland	Pth & Kin	NO1529	56°27·0'	3°22·3'W	X	53,58
Bauchlaw	Aberd	NJ6762	57°39·1'	2°32·7'W	X	29
Bauchle Hill	D & G	NY3589	55°11·7'	3°0·8'W	H	79
Baucott Fm	Shrops	SO5387	52°29·0'	2°41·1'W	FM	137,138
Baudnacauner	Aberd	NO5588	56°59·1'	2°44·0'W	H	44
Bauds	Moray	NJ1752	57°33·3'	3°22·8'W	X	28
Bauds of Cullen	Moray	NJ4766	57°41·1'	2°52·9'W	X	28,29
Bauds Wood	Moray	NJ4766	57°41·1'	2°52·9'W	F	28,29
Baudygaun	Aberd	NJ6307	57°9·4'	2°36·2'W	X	37
Baudy Meg	Aberd	NO4993	57°1·8'	2°50·0'W	H	37,44
Baugh	Arg & Bt	NM0243	56°29·3'	6°50·0'W	T	46
Baugh Cott	Arg & Bt	NM0144	56°29·8'	6°51·1'W	X	46
Baugh Fell	Cumbr	SD7393	54°20·2'	2°24·5'W	H	98
Baughton	Worcs	SO8741	52°4·3'	2°11·0'W	T	150
Baughton Hill	Worcs	SO8941	52°4·3'	2°9·2'W	X	150
Baughurst	Hants	SU5860	51°20·4'	1°9·6'W	T	174
Baughurst Ho	Hants	SU5759	51°19·9'	1°10·5'W	X	174
Bauks Hill	Wilts	SU2853	51°16·8'	1°35·5'W	X	184
Baulker Fm	E Yorks	SE8041	53°51·8'	0°46·6'W	FM	106
Baulker Fm	Notts	SK6155	53°5·6'	1°4·9'W	FM	120
Baulk Head	Corn	SW6521	50°2·8'	5°16·6'W	X	203
Baulk Hill	Pth & Kin	NO0709	56°16·1'	3°29·7'W	X	58
Baulking	Oxon	SU3190	51°36·7'	1°32·7'W	T	164,174
Baulking Grange Fm	Oxon	SU3390	51°36·7'	1°31·0'W	FM	164,174
Baulking Hill	Oxon	SU3291	51°37·2'	1°31·9'W	X	164,174
Baulk of Struie	Pth & Kin	NO0709	56°16·1'	3°29·7'W	X	58
Baulk, The	Oxon	SU6578	51°30·1'	1°3·4'W	X	175
Baumber	Lincs	TF2174	53°15·2'	0°10·8'W	T	122
Baumber Top Yard	Lincs	TF2175	53°15·7'	0°10·7'W	X	122
Bauminich	Highld	NJ1120	57°16·0'	3°28·1'W	X	36
Baunton	Glos	SP0204	51°44·3'	1°57·9'W	T	163
Baunton Downs	Glos	SP0306	51°45·4'	1°57·0'W	X	163
Baurch	D & G	NY2865	54°58·7'	3°7·1'W	X	85
Bausley Hill	Powys	SJ3214	52°43·4'	3°0·0'W	X	126
Bausley Ho	Powys	SJ3315	52°44·0'	2°59·1'W	X	126
Bavelaw Burn	C of Edin	NT1462	55°50·9'	3°22·0'W	W	65
Bavelaw Castle	C of Edin	NT1662	55°50·9'	3°20·1'W	A	65,66
Bavelaw Mill Fm	C of Edin	NT1562	55°50·9'	3°21·0'W	FM	65
Baveney Brook	Shrops	SO7077	52°23·7'	2°26·1'W	W	138
Baveney Wood	Shrops	SO6979	52°24·7'	2°26·9'W	X	138
Baverstock	Wilts	SU0231	51°4·9'	1°57·9'W	T	184
Bavinge Fm	Kent	TR1046	51°10·7'	1°0·7'E	FM	179,189
Bavington Hall	Northum	NY9978	55°6·0'	2°0·5'W	X	87
Bavington Hill Head	Northum	NY9979	55°6·5'	2°0·5'W	X	87
Bavington Mount	Northum	NY9878	55°6·0'	2°1·5'W	X	87
Bawburgh	Norf	TG1508	52°37·9'	1°11·0'E	T	144
Bawburgh Hill	Norf	TG1507	52°37·3'	1°11·0'E	X	144
Bawcombe	Devon	SX3782	50°37·1'	4°17·9'W	X	201
Bawd Bod	Aberd	NO7085	56°57·6'	2°29·1'W	X	45
Bawdenhayes	Devon	SS8203	50°49·1'	3°40·1'W	X	191
Bawden Rocks or Man & his man	Corn	SW7053	50°20·2'	5°13·6'W	X	203
Bawdens	Corn	SX0061	50°25·1'	4°48·6'W	X	200
Bawdeswell	Norf	TG0420	52°44·6'	1°1·7'E	T	133
Bawdeswell Heath	Norf	TG0320	52°44·6'	1°0·9'E	X	133
Bawd Hall	Cumbr	NY2119	54°33·9'	3°12·9'W	X	89,90
Bawdoe Fm	Corn	SX1359	50°24·3'	4°37·5'W	FM	200
Bawdon Casle Fm	Leic	SK4914	52°43·5'	1°16·1'W	FM	129
Bawdon Lodge	Leic	SK4915	52°44·1'	1°16·1'W	X	129
Bawdrip	Somer	ST3439	51°9·0'	2°56·2'W	T	182
Bawdrip Level	Somer	ST3539	51°9·0'	2°55·4'W	X	182
Bawdsey	Suff	TM3440	52°0·8'	1°25·0'E	T	169
Bawdsey Hall	Suff	TM3439	52°0·2'	1°25·0'E	X	169
Bawdsey Manor	Suff	TM3337	51°59·2'	1°24·0'E	X	169
Bawdy Craig	Aberd	NO8192	57°1·4'	2°18·3'W	H	38,45
Bawdy Moss	W Loth	NT0755	55°47·0'	3°28·5'W	X	65,72
Bawhelps	Angus	NO2272	56°50·2'	3°16·3'W	H	44
Bawk Ho	Ches	SJ6163	53°10·0'	2°34·6'W	X	118
Bawmier	Lancs	SD8946	53°54·8'	2°9·6'W	X	103
Bawnhead	D & G	NS6200	55°16·7'	4°9·9'W	X	77
Bawsey	Norf	TF6819	52°44·8'	0°29·7'E	T	132
Bawsgate Fm	Ches	SJ6268	53°12·7'	2°33·7'W	FM	118
Bawshen	I of M	SC3281	54°12·1'	4°34·1'W	X	95
Bawthorpe Hall	Lancs	SD8034	53°48·4'	2°17·8'W	A	103
Bawtry	Donc	SK6593	53°26·0'	1°0·9'W	T	111
Bawtry Forest	Donc	SK6395	53°27·1'	1°2·7'W	F	111
Bax	Kent	TQ9463	51°20·2'	0°47·5'E	X	178
Baxby Manor	N Yks	SE5175	54°10·3'	1°12·7'W	A	100
Baxenden	Lancs	SD7726	53°44·0'	2°20·5'W	T	103
Baxter Hall	N Yks	SE6727	53°44·3'	0°58·6'W	X	105,106
Baxterhill	Notts	SK4962	53°9·4'	1°15·6'W	X	120
Baxter Ho	N Yks	SD9548	53°55·9'	2°4·2'W	X	103
Baxterknowe	Pth & Kin	NO1017	56°20·5'	3°26·9'W	X	58
Baxterley	Warw	SP2797	52°34·4'	1°35·7'W	T	140
Baxter's Bank	Powys	SO0567	52°17·8'	3°23·2'W	H	136,147
Baxter's Fm	Devon	ST2008	50°52·2'	3°7·8'W	FM	192,193
Baxter's Green	Suff	TL7558	52°11·8'	0°34·0'E	T	155
Baxters Ho	Shrops	SJ5906	52°39·3'	2°36·0'W	A	126
Baxter Square Fm	Lincs	TF2185	53°21·1'	0°10·5'W	FM	122
Baxtersyke	E Loth	NT5565	55°52·8'	2°42·7'W	X	66
Baxter Wood	Durham	NZ2542	54°46·6'	1°36·3'W	F	88
Baxton Fell	Lancs	SD6756	54°0·2'	2°29·8'W	H	103
Baxtonhowe	N Yks	SE6872	54°8·6'	0°57·1'W	X	100
Baxton's Grange	N Yks	SE6085	54°15·7'	1°4·3'W	X	94,100
Baxton's Wood	N Yks	SE6089	54°17·8'	1°4·3'W	F	94,100
Baxworthy Cross	Devon	SS2822	50°58·5'	4°26·6'W	X	190
Bay	Dorset	ST8126	51°2·2'	2°15·6'W	T	183
Bay	Highld	NG2653	57°29·3'	6°33·9'W	T	23
Bay	Orkney	HY6424	59°6·3'	2°37·2'W	X	5
Bayard Barn	Dorset	SY6786	50°40·6'	2°27·6'W	X	194
Bayard Hill	Dorset	SY6685	50°40·1'	2°28·5'W	X	194
Bayardo Fm	Wilts	SU1665	51°23·3'	1°45·8'W	FM	173
Bay Br	Wilts	SU1870	51°26·0'	1°44·1'W	X	173
Baybridge	Hants	SU5223	51°0·5'	1°15·1'W	T	185
Baybridge	Northum	NY9550	54°50·9'	2°4·2'W	T	87
Bay Bridge	W Susx	TQ1620	50°58·3'	0°20·5'W	X	198
Baybridge Ho	Hants	SU5223	51°0·5'	1°15·1'W	X	185
Baybrooks	Kent	TQ7142	51°9·3'	0°27·1'E	X	188
Baycliff	Cumbr	SD2872	54°8·6'	3°5·7'W	T	96,97
Baycliffe Fm	Wilts	ST8139	51°9·2'	2°15·9'W	FM	183
Baydale Beck	Darl	NZ2514	54°31·5'	1°36·4'W	W	93
Baydale Fm	Darl	NZ2613	54°30·9'	1°35·5'W	FM	93
Bay Dillyn	Pemb	SM7022	51°51·2'	5°20·0'W	W	157
Baydon	Wilts	SU2877	51°29·7'	1°35·4'W	T	174
Baydon Hole	W Berks	SU2978	51°30·2'	1°34·5'W	X	174
Baydon Manor	Wilts	SU2875	51°28·6'	1°35·4'W	X	174
Baydon Wood	Wilts	SU2976	51°29·2'	1°34·5'W	F	174
Bayfield	Highld	NH6652	57°32·6'	4°13·9'W	X	26
Bayfield Brecks	Norf	TG0640	52°55·3'	1°4·3'E	X	133
Bayfield Hall	Norf	TG0440	52°55·3'	1°2·5'E	X	133
Bayfield Ho	Highld	NH8072	57°43·6'	4°0·4'W	X	21
Bayfield Loch	Highld	NH8271	57°43·1'	3°58·4'W	W	21
Bayfields Fm	Hants	SU8237	51°7·8'	0°49·3'W	FM	186
Bay Fine	I of M	SC1868	54°4·8'	4°46·5'W	W	95
Bay Fm	Highld	NH6753	57°33·1'	4°12·9'W	FM	26
Bayford	Herts	TL3008	51°45·6'	0°6·6'W	T	166
Bayford	Kent	TQ8469	51°23·6'	0°39·1'E	X	178
Bayford	Somer	ST7229	51°3·8'	2°23·6'W	T	183
Bayfordbury	Herts	TL3110	51°46·6'	0°5·7'W	X	166
Bayfordbury Park Fm	Herts	TL3110	51°46·6'	0°5·7'W	FM	166
Bayford Ct	Kent	TQ9163	51°20·3'	0°44·9'E	X	178
Bayford Hall	Herts	TL3009	51°46·1'	0°6·6'W	X	166
Bayford Ho	Herts	TL3007	51°45·0'	0°6·6'W	A	166
Bayford Lodge	Somer	ST7229	51°3·8'	2°23·6'W	X	183
Bayford Wood	Herts	TL3008	51°45·6'	0°6·6'W	F	166
Bay Gate	Lancs	SD7549	53°56·4'	2°22·4'W	T	103
Bay Hall	Lincs	TF3946	52°59·8'	0°4·7'E	X	131
Bayham Abbey	E Susx	TQ6436	51°6·2'	0°20·9'E	X	188
Bayham Abbey	Kent	TQ6536	51°6·2'	0°21·8'E	A	188
Bayham Lake	E Susx	TQ6336	51°6·2'	0°20·1'E	W	188
Bay Head	Highld	NH6552	57°32·5'	4°14·9'W	X	26
Bayhead	N Eil	NF7468	57°35·3'	7°26·9'W	T	18
Bayhead	N Eil	NG0685	57°45·8'	6°56·2'W	T	18
Bayherivagh	N Eil	NF7002	56°59·7'	7°25·6'W	T	31
Bay Hevda	Shetld	HU2485	60°33·1'	1°33·2'W	X	3
Bay Horse	Lancs	SD4953	53°58·5'	2°46·2'W	T	102
Bay Hunadu	N Eil	NL5784	56°49·5'	7°37·0'W	W	31
Bayhurst Wood Country Park	Hill	TQ0688	51°35·1'	0°27·8'W	F	176
Bayker's Fm	Essex	TL7732	51°57·7'	0°35·0'E	FM	167
Bayldon	Northum	NY7465	54°59·0'	2°23·9'W	X	86,87
Bayle Hill Fm	Cumbr	NY7245	54°48·2'	2°25·7'W	FM	86,87
Bayles	Cumbr	NY7044	54°47·6'	2°27·6'W	T	86,87
Bayleys	Essex	TL6620	51°51·5'	0°25·0'E	X	167
Bayley's Corner	Shrops	SO7398	52°35·0'	2°23·5'W	X	138
Bayley's Hill	Kent	TQ5151	51°14·5'	0°10·2'E	T	188
Baylham	Suff	TM1051	52°7·3'	1°4·5'E	T	155
Baylham Common	Suff	TM1051	52°7·3'	1°4·5'E	X	155
Baylham Hall	Suff	TM0951	52°7·3'	1°3·6'E	A	155
Bayliau	Cered	SN6048	52°7·0'	4°2·3'W	X	146
Baylisden	Kent	TQ9141	51°8·4'	0°44·2'E	X	189
Baylis Green	Worcs	SP0870	52°19·9'	1°52·6'W	T	139
Bayliss' Fm	Glos	SO8028	51°57·2'	2°17·1'W	FM	150
Baylis's Hill	Worcs	SP1245	52°6·4'	1°49·1'W	X	150
Baylis Wood	E Yorks	SE8243	53°52·8'	0°44·7'W	F	106
Baynards	Surrey	TQ0735	51°6·5'	0°27·9'W	X	187
Baynard's Green	Oxon	SP5429	51°57·6'	1°12·4'W	T	164
Baynard's Park	Surrey	TQ0836	51°7·0'	0°27·0'W	X	187
Bay Ness Fm	N Yks	NZ9406	54°26·7'	0°32·6'W	FM	94
Baynhall	Worcs	SO8547	52°7·5'	2°12·8'W	T	150
Baynhall Fm	Worcs	SO9853	52°10·8'	2°1·4'W	FM	150
Baynham Fm	Kent	TR0023	50°58·5'	0°51·3'E	FM	189
Baynham Hall	Powys	SO2351	52°9·4'	3°7·1'W	X	148
Baynhams	Heref	SO5717	51°51·2'	2°37·1'W	X	162
Baynham's Fm	Heref	SO6839	52°3·1'	2°27·6'W	FM	149
Bay ny Carrickey	I of M	SC2268	54°4·9'	4°42·9'W	W	95
Bay of Ayre	Orkney	HY4701	58°53·8'	2°54·7'W	W	6,7
Bay of Backaland	Orkney	HY5730	59°9·5'	2°44·6'W	W	5,6
Bay of Berstane	Orkney	HY4710	58°58·7'	2°54·8'W	W	6
Bay of Bomasty	Orkney	HY6123	59°5·8'	2°40·4'W	W	5
Bay of Brenwell	Shetld	HU2257	60°18·1'	1°35·6'W	W	3
Bay of Brough	Orkney	HY4547	59°18·6'	2°57·5'W	W	5
Bay of Brough	Orkney	HY6541	59°15·5'	2°36·3'W	W	5
Bay of Brough	Shetld	HP5404	60°43·2'	1°0·1'W	W	1
Bay of Burland	Orkney	HY5050	59°20·3'	2°52·2'W	W	5
Bay of Carness	Orkney	HY4613	59°0·3'	2°55·9'W	W	6
Bay of Carrick	Orkney	HY5638	59°13·8'	2°45·8'W	W	5
Bay of Clachtoll	Highld	NC0327	58°11·5'	5°20·6'W	W	15
Bay of Cleat	Orkney	HY4647	59°18·6'	2°56·4'W	W	5
Bay of Cornquoy	Orkney	ND5199	58°52·8'	2°50·5'W	W	6,7
Bay of Creekland	Orkney	HY2304	58°55·2'	3°19·8'W	W	6,7
Bay of Crook	Orkney	HY5218	59°3·0'	2°49·7'W	W	6
Bay of Cruden	Aberd	NK0934	57°24·0'	1°50·6'W	W	30
Bay of Cubbigeo	Orkney	HY4743	59°16·5'	2°55·3'W	W	5
Bay of Culkein	Highld	NC0433	58°14·8'	5°19·9'W	W	15
Bay of Cullen	Aberd	NJ7264	57°40·2'	2°27·7'W	W	29
Bay of Cuppa	Shetld	HU5242	60°9·8'	1°3·3'W	W	4
Bay of Deepdale	Orkney	HY4404	58°55·4'	2°57·9'W	W	6,7
Bay of Deepdale	Shetld	HU1754	60°16·5'	1°41·1'W	W	3
Bay of Doomy	Orkney	HY5534	59°11·7'	2°46·8'W	W	5,6
Bay of Firth	Orkney	HY3814	59°0·8'	3°4·3'W	W	6
Bay of Fladdabister	Shetld	HU4332	60°4·5'	1°13·1'W	W	4
Bay of Franks	Orkney	HY6428	59°8·5'	2°37·3'W	W	5
Bay of Furrowend	Orkney	HY4719	59°3·5'	2°55·0'W	W	6
Bay of Garth	Shetld	HU2158	60°18·6'	1°36·7'W	W	3
Bay of Greentoft	Orkney	HY5628	59°8·5'	2°45·7'W	W	5,6
Bay of Ham	Orkney	HY4432	59°10·5'	2°58·3'W	W	5,6
Bay of Havey	Orkney	HY4846	59°18·1'	2°54·3'W	W	5
Bay of Heogan	Shetld	HU4743	60°10·4'	1°8·7'W	W	4
Bay of Hinderayre	Orkney	HY4219	59°3·5'	3°0·2'W	W	6
Bay of Holland	Orkney	HY6422	59°5·3'	2°37·2'W	W	5
Bay of Houseby	Orkney	HY6821	59°4·7'	2°33·0'W	W	5
Bay of Houton	Orkney	HY3103	58°54·8'	3°11·4'W	W	6,7
Bay of Icevay	Orkney	HY5633	59°11·2'	2°45·7'W	W	5,6
Bay of Ireland	Orkney	HY2809	58°58·0'	3°14·6'W	W	6,7
Bay of Isbister	Orkney	HY4017	59°2·4'	3°2·3'W	W	6
Bay of Keisgaig	Highld	NC2469	58°34·7'	5°1·1'W	W	9
Bay of Kirbist	Orkney	HY4243	59°16·4'	3°0·6'W	W	5
Bay of Kirkwall	Orkney	HY4413	59°0·3'	2°58·0'W	W	6
Bay of Laing	Highld	NM4688	56°55·1'	6°10·0'W	W	39
Bay of Linton	Orkney	HY5318	59°3·1'	2°48·7'W	W	6
Bay of Lochielair	Aberd	NJ9267	57°41·8'	2°7·6'W	W	30
Bay of London	Orkney	HY5634	59°11·7'	2°45·7'W	W	5,6
Bay of Lopness	Orkney	HY7443	59°16·6'	2°26·9'W	W	5
Bay of Moclett	Orkney	HY4949	59°19·7'	2°53·3'W	W	5
Bay of Myre	Orkney	HY3203	58°54·8'	3°10·4'W	W	6,7
Bay of Navershaw	Orkney	HY2609	58°58·0'	3°16·7'W	W	6,7
Bay of Newark	Orkney	HY5535	59°12·2'	2°46·8'W	W	5,6
Bay of Newark	Orkney	HY7039	59°14·5'	2°31·1'W	W	5
Bay of Noup	Orkney	HY4149	59°19·7'	3°1·7'W	W	5
Bay of Okraquoy	Shetld	HU4331	60°3·9'	1°12·1'W	W	4
Bay of Ollaberry	Shetld	HU3680	60°30·4'	1°20·2'W	W	1,2,3
Bay of Pierowall	Orkney	HY4448	59°19·1'	2°58·5'W	W	5
Bay of Puldrite	Orkney	HY4218	59°3·0'	3°0·2'W	W	6
Bay of Quendale	Shetld	HU3712	59°53·8'	1°19·8'W	W	4
Bay of Quoys	Orkney	HY2403	58°54·7'	3°18·7'W	W	6,7
Bay of Ryasgeo	Orkney	HY7554	59°22·6'	2°25·9'W	W	5
Bay of Sandber	Orkney	HY4600	58°53·3'	2°55·7'W	W	6,7
Bay of Sandgarth	Orkney	HY5115	59°1·4'	2°50·7'W	W	6
Bay of Sandoyne	Orkney	HY4601	58°53·8'	2°55·7'W	W	6,7
Bay of Sandquoy	Orkney	HY7345	59°17·7'	2°28·0'W	W	5
Bay of Sandside	Orkney	HY2605	58°55·8'	3°16·6'W	W	6,7
Bay of Sannick	Highld	ND3973	58°38·7'	3°2·8'W	W	7,12
Bay of Scousburgh	Shetld	HU3718	59°57·0'	1°19·8'W	W	4
Bay of Semolie	Orkney	HY5201	58°53·9'	2°49·5'W	X	6,7
Bay of Sjaivar	Orkney	HY7855	59°23·1'	2°22·7'W	W	5
Bay of Skaill	Orkney	HY2319	59°3·3'	3°20·1'W	W	6
Bay of Skaill	Orkney	HY4551	59°20·8'	2°57·5'W	W	5
Bay of Skaill	Orkney	HY4629	59°8·9'	2°56·2'W	W	5,6
Bay of Sowerdie	Orkney	HY7646	59°18·3'	2°24·8'W	W	5
Bay of Stoer	Highld	NC0328	58°12·1'	5°20·7'W	W	15
Bay of Stove	Orkney	HY6134	59°11·7'	2°40·5'W	W	5
Bay of Suckquoy	Orkney	HY5204	58°55·5'	2°49·5'W	W	6,7
Bay of Swandro	Orkney	HY3729	59°8·9'	3°5·6'W	W	6
Bay of Swartmill	Orkney	HY4746	59°18·1'	2°55·4'W	W	5
Bay of Swordly	Highld	NC7363	58°32·5'	4°10·4'W	W	10
Bay of Tafts	Orkney	HY4941	59°15·4'	2°53·2'W	W	5
Bay of the Tongue	Orkney	HY2004	58°55·2'	3°22·9'W	W	7
Bay of Tresness	Orkney	HY6938	59°13·9'	2°32·1'W	W	5
Bay of Tuquoy	Orkney	HY4644	59°17·0'	2°56·4'W	W	5
Bay of Ulsta	Shetld	HU4679	60°29·8'	1°9·3'W	W	2,3
Bay of Vady	Orkney	HY4628	59°8·4'	2°56·1'W	W	5,6
Bay of Westness	Orkney	HY3828	59°8·3'	3°4·5'W	W	6
Bay of Weyland	Orkney	HY4512	58°59·8'	2°57·0'W	W	6
Bay of Wheevi	Orkney	HY7643	59°16·6'	2°24·8'W	W	5
Bay of Whelkmulli	Orkney	HY4225	59°6·7'	3°0·3'W	W	5,6
Bay of Whinnifirt	Shetld	HU5382	60°31·4'	1°1·6'W	W	1,2,3
Bay of Work	Orkney	HY4813	59°0·3'	2°53·8'W	W	6
Baypark	Corn	SX1494	50°43·2'	4°37·7'W	X	190
Bay River	Highld	NG2752	57°28·8'	6°32·8'W	W	23
Baysbrown	Cumbr	NY3104	54°25·9'	3°3·4'W	X	90
Bay Scalan	N Eil	NF9670	57°37·3'	7°5·1'W	W	18
Baysdale	N Yks	NZ6307	54°27·5'	1°1·3'W	X	94
Baysdale Abbey	N Yks	NZ6206	54°27·0'	1°2·2'W	X	94
Baysdale Beck	N Yks	NZ6407	54°27·5'	1°0·3'W	W	94
Baysdale Moor	N Yks	NZ6204	54°25·9'	1°2·2'W	X	94
Baysgarth Fm	N Lincs	TA1418	53°39·0'	0°16·1'W	FM	113
Baysham	Heref	SO5727	51°56·6'	2°37·1'W	T	162
Bay Sletta	N Eil	NL5584	56°49·4'	7°38·9'W	W	31
Bays Loch	N Eil	NF9281	57°43·1'	7°9·9'W	W	18
Bay Spanish	N Eil	NF8864	57°33·8'	7°12·6'W	W	18
Bay Stacka	I of M	SC1866	54°3·7'	4°46·4'W	W	95
Baystone Bank	Cumbr	SD1785	54°15·5'	3°16·0'W	X	96
Baystone Bank Resr	Cumbr	SD1785	54°15·5'	3°16·0'W	W	96
Baystones	Cumbr	NY4005	54°26·5'	2°55·1'W	H	90

Bayston Fm	Shrops	SJ4908	52°40·3′	2°44·9′W	FM	126
Bayston Hill	Shrops	SJ4708	52°40·3′	2°46·6′W	T	126
Bayswater	C of West	TQ2580	51°30·5′	0°11·5′W	T	176
Bays Water	Shetld	HU3367	60°23·4′	1°23·6′W	W	2,3
Bayswater Brook	Oxon	SP5408	51°46·3′	1°12·6′W	W	164
Bays Wood	S Glos	ST7386	51°34·6′	2°23·0′W	F	172
Bay, The	Kent	TR0371	51°24·3′	0°55·5′E	W	178,179
Bay, The	Kent	TR3471	51°23·6′	1°22·2′E	W	179
Baythorne End	Essex	TL7242	52°3·2′	0°30·9′E	T	154
Baythorne Lodge	Suff	TL7145	52°4·8′	0°30·1′E	X	154
Baythorne Park	Essex	TL7242	52°3·2′	0°30·9′E	X	154
Baythorpe	Lincs	TF2441	52°57·4′	0°8·8′W	T	131
Bayton	Worcs	SO6973	52°21·5′	2°26·9′W	T	138
Bayton Common	Worcs	SO7172	52°21·0′	2°25·1′W	T	138
Baytree	Lincs	TF2824	52°48·1′	0°5·7′W	X	131
Baytree Fm	Ches	SJ8559	53°7·9′	2°13·0′W	FM	118
Baytree Fm	Essex	TL7923	51°52·8′	0°36·4′E	FM	167
Baytree, The	Shrops	SO6385	52°27·9′	2°32·3′W	X	138
Bay View	Kent	TR0170	51°23·8′	0°53·8′E	T	178
Bayvil Fm	Pemb	SN1040	52°1·8′	4°45·8′W	FM	145
Bayworth	Oxon	SP5001	51°42·6′	1°16·2′W	T	164
Bazeland	Oxon	SP2602	51°43·2′	1°37·0′W	X	163
Bazeley Copse	Hants	SU5037	51°8·0′	1°16·7′W	F	185
Bazeley Fm	Somer	ST0919	50°58·0′	3°17·4′W	FM	181
Bazil Point	Lancs	SD4356	54°0·1′	2°51·8′W	X	102
Bazley's Plantn	Corn	SX0965	50°27·5′	4°41·1′W	F	200
Bazon Hill	Dorset	ST6403	50°49·8′	2°30·3′W	X	194
Bea	Orkney	HY2728	59°8·2′	3°16·1′W	X	6
Beach	Arg & Bt	NM4623	56°20·1′	6°6·1′W	X	48
Beach	Arg & Bt	NS2097	56°8·2′	4°53·4′W	X	56
Beach	Highld	NM7653	56°37·2′	5°38·6′W	X	49
Beach	S Glos	ST7070	51°25·9′	2°25·5′W	T	172
Beachampton	Bucks	SP7736	52°1·3′	0°52·3′W	T	152
Beachampton Grove	Bucks	SP7836	52°1·2′	0°51·4′W	F	152
Beacham's Fm	Suff	TL9636	51°59·5′	0°51·7′E	FM	155
Beachamwell	Norf	TF7505	52°37·1′	0°35·5′E	T	143
Beachamwell Fen	Norf	TF7403	52°36·0′	0°34·6′E	X	143
Beachamwell Warren	Norf	TF7507	52°38·2′	0°35·6′E	X	143
Beachan	Highld	NH6834	57°22·9′	4°11·3′W	X	26
Beachans	Moray	NJ0246	57°29·9′	3°37·7′W	X	27
Beacharr	Arg & Bt	NR6943	55°37·8′	5°39·7′W	X	62
Beachbank Fm	Lincs	TF2328	52°50·4′	0°10·0′W	FM	131
Beachborough	Kent	TR1638	51°6·3′	1°5·5′E	X	179,189
Beachcomber Ho	Northum	NU0644	55°41·6′	1°53·8′W	X	75
Beachcroft Towse, The	W Susx	TQ3836	51°6·6′	0°1·3′W	X	187
Beach Ditch	Cambs	TL4767	52°17·1′	0°9·7′E	X	154
Beachendon Fm	Bucks	SP7513	51°48·9′	0°54·3′W	FM	165
Beachern Wood	Hants	SU2802	50°49·2′	1°35·8′W	F	195
Beachet Wood	Essex	TL4900	51°41·0′	0°9·7′E	F	167
Beachfarm Marshes	Suff	TM5284	52°24·0′	1°42·7′E	X	156
Beach Fm	S Glos	ST7170	51°25·9′	2°24·6′W	FM	172
Beach Fm	Shrops	SO3594	52°32·6′	2°57·1′W	FM	137
Beach Fm	Suff	TM5383	52°23·4′	1°43·5′E	FM	156
Beach Hay	Worcs	SO7174	52°22·0′	2°25·2′W	T	138
Beach-hill	Ches	SJ6373	53°15·4′	2°32·9′W	X	118
Beach Hill Park	Essex	TQ4099	51°40·6′	0°1·9′E	X	167,177
Beach Ho	Shetld	HP5402	60°42·1′	1°0·1′W	X	1
Beachin Cotts	Ches	SJ4456	53°6·1′	2°49·8′W	X	117
Beachlands	E Susx	TQ6604	50°48·9′	0°21·8′E	T	199
Beachley	Glos	ST5591	51°37·2′	2°38·6′W	T	162,172
Beachley Point	Glos	ST5490	51°36·7′	2°39·5′W	X	162,172
Beachmenach	Arg & Bt	NR6842	55°37·2′	5°40·6′W	X	62
Beach Park	N Ayr	NS3137	55°36·1′	4°40·6′W	X	70
Beach River	Arg & Bt	NM4722	56°19·6′	6°5·1′W	W	48
Beach's Barn	Wilts	SU1851	51°15·7′	1°44·1′W	X	184
Beach's Plantation	Wilts	SU1850	51°15·2′	1°44·1′W	F	184
Beach, The	Norf	TG5307	52°36·3′	1°44·6′E	X	134
Beachy Head	E Susx	TV5895	50°44·2′	0°14·7′E	X	199
Beacom Houses	Stock	SJ9692	53°25·7′	2°3·2′W	X	109
Beacon	Corn	SW6539	50°12·5′	5°17·2′W	T	203
Beacon	Corn	SW9668	50°28·8′	4°52·2′W	X	200
Beacon	Devon	SS6915	50°55·4′	3°51·5′W	X	180
Beacon	Devon	ST1705	50°50·5′	3°10·4′W	T	192,193
Beacon	Devon	ST2308	50°52·2′	3°5·3′W	T	192,193
Beacon Alley	I of W	SZ5181	50°37·8′	1°16·4′W	X	196
Beacon Ash	Glos	ST5599	51°41·5′	2°38·7′W	X	162
Beacon Bank	Staffs	SJ9731	52°52·8′	2°2·3′W	X	127
Beacon Batch	Somer	ST4857	51°18·8′	2°44·4′W	H	172,182
Beacon Batch (Tumuli)	Somer	ST4857	51°18·8′	2°44·4′W	A	172,182
Beacon Castle	Devon	SS6646	51°12·1′	3°54·7′W	X	180
Beacon (Cesarewitch) Course	Cambs	TL5962	52°14·2′	0°20·1′E	X	154
Beacon Cove	Corn	SW8466	50°27·5′	5°2·2′W	X	200
Beacon Cross	Corn	SW9845	50°16·5′	4°49·7′W	X	204
Beacon Cross	Devon	SS7903	50°49·1′	3°42·7′W	X	191
Beacon Cross	Devon	SX6499	50°46·7′	3°55·4′W	X	191
Beacon Cross	Devon	SY0798	50°46·7′	3°18·8′W	X	192
Beacon Down	E Susx	TQ5521	50°58·3′	0°12·9′E	T	199
Beacon End	Essex	TL9524	51°53·0′	0°50·4′E	T	168
Beacon Farm	N Yks	NZ8907	54°27·3′	0°37·2′W	FM	94
Beacon Fell	Lancs	SD5642	53°52·6′	2°39·7′W	H	102
Beaconfield Fm	Bath & NE Somer	ST5556	51°18·3′	2°38·3′W	FM	172,182
Beaconfield Fm	E Yorks	TA3021	53°40·4′	0°1·5′W	FM	107,113
Beaconfield Fm	Notts	SK8254	53°4·8′	0°46·1′W	FM	121
Beacon Fm	Bucks	SU8289	51°35·9′	0°48·6′W	FM	175
Beacon Fm	Cambs	TL1361	52°14·4′	0°20·3′W	FM	153
Beacon Fm	E Yorks	SE8238	53°50·1′	0°44·8′W	FM	106
Beacon Fm	E Yorks	SE9653	53°58·1′	0°31·8′W	FM	106
Beacon Fm	E Yorks	TA2269	54°6·4′	0°7·6′W	FM	101
Beacon Fm	Glos	SO9201	51°42·7′	2°6·6′W	FM	163
Beacon Fm	Kent	TQ9634	51°4·5′	0°48·3′E	FM	189
Beacon Fm	N Yks	SE9992	54°19·1′	0°28·3′W	FM	94,101
Beacon Fm	Somer	ST6345	51°12·4′	2°31·4′W	FM	183
Beacon Fm	Staffs	SJ9424	52°49·0′	2°4·9′W	FM	127
Beacon Fm	Suff	TM4181	52°22·7′	1°32·9′E	FM	156
Beacon Fm	Wals	SP0597	52°34·5′	1°55·2′W	FM	139
Beacon Fm	W Berks	SU3367	51°24·3′	1°31·1′W	FM	174
Beacon Fm	Wilts	SU3058	51°19·4′	1°33·8′W	FM	174
Beacon Guest	N Yks	SE5696	54°21·6′	1°7·9′W	X	100

Beacon Hall	W Susx	TQ2726	51°1·4′	0°11·0′W	X	187,198
Beacon Hill	Bath & NE Somer	ST7566	51°23·8′	2°21·2′W	T	172
Beacon Hill	Bri & Hov	TQ3602	50°48·3′	0°3·8′W	X	198
Beacon Hill	Bucks	SP6424	51°54·9′	1°3·8′W	X	164,165
Beacon Hill	Bucks	SP8306	51°45·0′	0°47·5′W	H	165
Beacon Hill	Bucks	SP9616	51°50·3′	0°36·0′W	H	165
Beacon Hill	Bucks	SU9093	51°37·9′	0°41·6′W	T	175
Beacon Hill	Cald	SE0418	53°39·7′	1°56·0′W	H	110
Beacon Hill	Cald	SE1025	53°43·5′	1°50·5′W	H	104
Beacon Hill	Corn	SX1259	50°24·3′	4°38·4′W	H	200
Beacon Hill	Cumbr	NY5231	54°40·6′	2°44·2′W	H	90
Beacon Hill	Cumbr	NY6309	54°28·7′	2°33·8′W	H	91
Beacon Hill	Cumbr	SD2170	54°7·4′	3°12·1′W	T	96
Beacon Hill	Cumbr	SD2671	54°8·0′	3°7·5′W	H	96,97
Beacon Hill	Devon	SS1344	51°10·1′	4°40·1′W	H	180
Beacon Hill	Devon	ST0719	50°58·0′	3°19·1′W	H	181
Beacon Hill	Devon	ST2009	50°52·7′	3°7·8′W	X	192,193
Beacon Hill	Devon	ST2402	50°49·0′	3°4·3′W	H	192,193
Beacon Hill	Devon	ST2903	50°49·6′	3°0·1′W	X	193
Beacon Hill	Devon	SX5746	50°18·0′	4°0·1′W	X	202
Beacon Hill	Devon	SX8067	50°29·7′	3°41·1′W	H	202
Beacon Hill	Devon	SX9595	50°44·9′	3°28·9′W	X	192
Beacon Hill	Devon	SY1191	50°42·9′	3°15·3′W	H	192,193
Beacon Hill	D & G	NY0579	55°6·0′	3°28·9′W	H	85
Beacon Hill	Dorset	SY7393	50°44·4′	2°22·6′W	X	194
Beacon Hill	Dorset	SY9095	50°45·5′	2°8·1′W	X	195
Beacon Hill	Dorset	SY9794	50°45·0′	2°2·2′W	T	195
Beacon Hill	Durham	NZ4345	54°48·1′	1°19·4′W	H	88
Beacon Hill	Essex	TL8512	51°46·8′	0°41·3′E	T	168
Beacon Hill	Essex	TQ5598	51°39·8′	0°14·9′E	X	167,177
Beacon Hill	Essex	TQ8994	51°37·0′	0°44·2′E	X	168,178
Beacon Hill	E Susx	TQ4701	50°47·6′	0°5·5′E	X	198
Beacon Hill	E Yorks	TA2269	54°6·4′	0°7·6′W	X	101
Beacon Hill	E Yorks	TA2736	53°48·5′	0°3·9′W	X	107
Beacon Hill	E Yorks	TA3422	53°40·9′	0°2·1′E	X	107,113
Beacon Hill	Hants	SU4029	51°3·8′	1°25·4′W	X	185
Beacon Hill	Hants	SU4557	51°18·8′	1°20·9′W	H	174
Beacon Hill	Hants	SU6022	50°59·9′	1°8·3′W	H	185
Beacon Hill	Hants	SU8250	51°14·8′	0°49·1′W	H	186
Beacon Hill	Hartpl	NZ4432	54°41·1′	1°18·6′W	X	93
Beacon Hill	Heref	SO6945	52°6·4′	2°26·8′W	X	149
Beacon Hill	Kent	TQ8232	51°3·7′	0°36·2′E	T	188
Beacon Hill	Kent	TQ9861	51°19·0′	0°50·9′E	X	178
Beacon Hill	Kent	TR0153	51°14·7′	0°53·2′E	X	189
Beacon Hill	Lancs	SD7548	53°55·9′	2°22·4′W	H	103
Beacon Hill	Leic	SK5114	52°45·3′	1°14·6′W	H	129
Beacon Hill	Leic	SK8139	52°56·8′	0°47·3′W	X	130
Beacon Hill	Lincs	SK9263	53°9·6′	0°37·0′W	X	121
Beacon Hill	Lincs	SK9821	52°46·9′	0°32·4′W	X	130
Beacon Hill	Lincs	TF0932	52°52·7′	0°22·4′W	X	130
Beacon Hill	Lincs	TF0943	52°58·6′	0°22·2′W	X	130
Beacon Hill	Lincs	TF2279	53°17·9′	0°9·8′W	X	122
Beacon Hill	Lincs	TF3798	53°27·9′	0°4·2′E	X	113
Beacon Hill	Medway	TQ7571	51°24·9′	0°31·4′E	X	178
Beacon Hill	Monm	SO5105	51°44·7′	2°42·2′W	H	162
Beacon Hill	N Lincs	TA0220	53°40·2′	0°26·9′W	X	106,107,112
Beacon Hill	Norf	TF7342	52°57·1′	0°34·9′E	X	132
Beacon Hill	Norf	TF8341	52°56·3′	0°43·8′E	X	132
Beacon Hill	Norf	TF9026	52°48·1′	0°49·5′E	X	132
Beacon Hill	Norf	TG1841	52°55·6′	1°15·0′E	X	133
Beacon Hill	Norf	TG2838	52°53·7′	1°23·8′E	X	133
Beacon Hill	Norf	TM0090	52°28·5′	0°57·1′E	X	144
Beacon Hill	Norf	TM2482	52°23·6′	1°17·9′E	X	156
Beacon Hill	Norf	TM4098	52°31·8′	1°32·7′E	X	134
Beacon Hill	Northum	NU1807	55°21·6′	1°42·5′W	H	81
Beacon Hill	Northum	NY7659	54°55·8′	2°22·0′W	X	86,87
Beacon Hill	Northum	NZ1491	55°13·0′	1°46·4′W	H	81
Beaconhill	Northum	NZ2576	55°4·9′	1°36·1′W	T	88
Beacon Hill	Notts	SK7490	53°24·3′	0°52·8′W	A	112
Beacon Hill	Notts	SK8153	53°4·3′	0°47·1′W	T	121
Beacon Hill	N Yks	NZ7309	54°28·5′	0°52·0′W	X	94
Beacon Hill	N Yks	NZ9209	54°28·3′	0°34·4′W	X	94
Beacon Hill	N Yks	TA1080	54°12·5′	0°18·4′W	X	101
Beacon Hill	N Yks	TA1474	54°9·2′	0°14·8′W	X	101
Beacon Hill	Oxon	SU7297	51°40·3′	0°57·1′W	X	165
Beacon Hill	Powys	SO1876	52°22·8′	3°11·9′W	X	136,148
Beacon Hill	Roth	SK5190	53°24·5′	1°13·6′W	X	111
Beacon Hill	Somer	ST1241	51°9·9′	3°15·1′W	H	181
Beacon Hill	Somer	ST3615	50°56·1′	2°54·3′W	X	193
Beacon Hill	Somer	ST6345	51°12·4′	2°31·4′W	H	183
Beacon Hill	Staffs	SJ8913	52°43·1′	2°9·4′W	X	127
Beacon Hill	Staffs	SJ9425	52°49·6′	2°4·9′W	H	127
Beacon Hill	Staffs	SK2427	52°50·6′	1°38·1′W	X	128
Beacon Hill	Suff	TM1273	52°19·1′	1°7·0′E	A	144,155
Beacon Hill	Suff	TM2347	52°4·8′	1°15·7′E	T	169
Beacon Hill	Surrey	SU8736	51°7·2′	0°45·0′W	T	186
Beacon Hill	Thurr	TQ5678	51°29·0′	0°15·2′E	X	177
Beacon Hill	Torbay	SX8562	50°27·1′	3°36·8′W	H	202
Beacon Hill	Warw	SP4860	52°14·4′	1°17·4′W	H	151
Beacon Hill	Wilts	ST9130	51°4·4′	2°7·3′W	H	184
Beacon Hill	Wilts	ST9965	51°23·3′	2°0·5′W	X	173
Beacon Hill	Wilts	SU0176	51°29·2′	1°58·7′W	X	173
Beacon Hill	Wilts	SU2044	51°11·9′	1°42·4′W	H	184
Beacon Hill	Worcs	SO9875	52°22·6′	2°1·4′W	H	139
Beacon Hill	W Susx	SU8018	50°57·6′	0°51·3′W	H	197
Beacon Hill	W Susx	TQ2233	51°5·2′	0°15·1′W	X	187
Beacon Hill Barn	Mil Key	SP9446	52°6·5′	0°37·2′W	X	153
Beaconhill Brook	Shrops	SO6394	52°32·8′	2°32·3′W	W	138
Beacon Hill Fm	Cumbr	NY4044	54°47·5′	2°55·6′W	FM	85
Beacon Hill Fm	Durham	NZ3828	54°39·0′	1°24·2′W	FM	93
Beacon Hill Fm	Essex	TL9605	51°42·8′	0°50·6′E	FM	168
Beacon Hill Fm	Wilts	SU1942	51°10·8′	1°43·3′W	FM	184
Beacon Hill (Fort)	Bucks	SP9616	51°50·3′	0°36·0′W	A	165
Beacon Hill (Fort)	Hants	SU4557	51°18·8′	1°20·9′W	A	174
Beacon Hill (Fort)	W Susx	SU8018	50°57·6′	0°51·3′W	A	197
Beacon Hill Ho	N Yks	SE0951	53°57·5′	1°51·4′W	X	104
Beacon Hill Services	Suff	TM1054	52°8·9′	1°4·6′E	X	155
Beacon Ho	N Yks	SE5979	54°12·4′	1°5·3′W	X	100
Beacon Ho	Staffs	SJ8759	53°7·9′	2°11·3′W	X	118

Beacon Howes	N Yks	NZ9701	54°24·0′	0°29·9′W	A	94
Beacon Hut	Corn	SW6930	50°7·7′	5°13·6′W	A	203
Beacon Knap	Dorset	SY5188	50°41·6′	2°41·2′W	H	194
Beaconland	E Susx	TQ6119	50°57·1′	0°17·9′E	X	199
Beacon Lane Fm	Somer	ST1417	50°57·0′	3°13·1′W	FM	181,193
Beacon Lodge	Powys	SO1874	52°21·7′	3°11·9′W	X	136,148
Beacon Lough	Ghead	NZ2759	54°55·7′	1°34·3′W	T	88
Beacon or Big End	Lancs	SD8041	53°52·1′	2°17·8′W	X	103
Beacon Park	Lancs	SD5006	53°33·1′	2°44·9′W	X	108
Beacon Plain	Devon	SX6659	50°25·2′	3°52·8′W	X	202
Beacon Plantation	Leeds	SE4431	53°46·6′	1°19·5′W	F	105
Beacon Plantn	N Yks	NZ1402	54°25·0′	1°46·6′W	F	92
Beacon Point	Devon	SS5348	51°13·0′	4°5·9′W	X	180
Beacon Point	Devon	SX6145	50°17·5′	3°56·7′W	X	202
Beacon Point	Devon	SX6740	50°14·9′	3°51·6′W	X	202
Beacon Point	Durham	NZ4445	54°48·1′	1°18·5′W	X	88
Beacon Point	Northum	NZ3189	55°11·9′	1°30·3′W	X	81
Beacon Rigg	Northum	NY8359	54°55·8′	2°15·5′W	X	86,87
Beacon Ring	Powys	SJ2605	52°38·5′	3°5·2′W	X	126
Beacon Ring (Fort)	Powys	SJ2605	52°38·5′	3°5·2′W	A	126
Beacon Sand	Glos	ST5796	51°39·9′	2°36·9′W	X	162
Beacon's Bottom	Bucks	SU7895	51°39·1′	0°52·0′W	T	165
Beacons Down	V of Glam	SS8875	51°28·0′	3°36·4′W	X	170
Beaconsfield	Bucks	SU9390	51°36·3′	0°39·0′W	T	175
Beaconsfield	Bucks	SU9589	51°35·7′	0°37·3′W	T	175,176
Beaconsfield Fm	Oxon	SP4027	51°56·6′	1°24·7′W	FM	164
Beaconside	Cumbr	NY4044	54°47·5′	2°55·6′W	X	85
Beaconside	Staffs	SJ9324	52°49·0′	2°5·8′W	T	127
Beacons Resr	Powys	SN9818	51°51·3′	3°28·5′W	W	160
Beacons, The	Brig	SS8479	51°30·1′	3°39·9′W	X	170
Beacons, The	Conwy	SH7779	53°17·9′	3°50·3′W	X	115
Beacons, The	Rho Cyn Taf	ST0183	51°32·5′	3°25·3′W	A	170
Beacons, The	Wirral	SJ2781	53°19·5′	3°5·4′W	X	108
Beacon Tarn	Cumbr	SD2790	54°18·3′	3°6·9′W	W	96,97
Beacon, The	Corn	SW4129	50°6·5′	5°37·4′W	X	203
Beacon, The	Corn	SW8466	50°27·5′	5°2·2′W	X	200
Beacon, The	Corn	SX0666	50°27·9′	4°43·6′W	H	200
Beacon, The	Corn	SX1895	50°43·8′	4°34·4′W	X	190
Beacon, The	Corn	SX1979	50°35·2′	4°33·0′W	H	201
Beacon, The	Corn	SX3554	50°22·0′	4°18·8′W	H	201
Beacon, The	Cumbr	NX9618	54°33·0′	3°36·1′W	X	89
Beacon, The	Cumbr	NY5771	55°2·1′	2°39·9′W	H	86
Beacon, The	Devon	SS6649	51°13·7′	3°54·8′W	X	180
Beacon, The	Devon	SX4679	50°35·7′	4°10·2′W	X	201
Beacon, The	Devon	SY2597	50°46·3′	3°3·4′W	A	192,193
Beacon The	E Susx	TQ7821	50°57·9′	0°32·5′E	X	199
Beacon, The	Northum	NT9500	55°17·9′	2°4·3′W	H	81
Beacon, The	Somer	ST6323	51°0·5′	2°31·3′W	X	183
Beacon, The	Surrey	SU8836	51°7·2′	0°44·2′W	X	186
Beacon, The	Swan	SS4288	51°34·4′	4°16·4′W	X	159
Beacon, The (Tumulus)	Corn	SX1895	50°43·8′	4°34·4′W	A	190
Beacon View Fm	Leic	SK5517	52°45·1′	1°10·7′W	FM	129
Beacrabhaic	N Eil	NG1190	57°48·6′	6°51·5′W	X	14
Beadaig	Highld	NC6437	58°18·3′	4°18·8′W	H	16
Beadale Wood	N Yks	SE7786	54°16·1′	0°48·6′W	F	94,100
Beadies	Shetld	HU4021	59°58·6′	1°16·5′W	X	4
Beadlam	N Yks	SE6584	54°15·1′	0°59·7′W	T	100
Beadlam Grange	N Yks	SE6484	54°15·1′	1°0·6′W	X	100
Beadlam Rigg	N Yks	SE6388	54°17·3′	1°1·5′W	H	94,100
Beadle's Hall	Essex	TL6711	51°46·6′	0°25·6′E	X	167
Beadlow	Beds	TL1038	52°2·0′	0°23·4′W	T	153
Bead na Cloiche Glaise	Highld	NG2661	57°33·6′	6°34·4′W	X	23
Beadnell	Northum	NU2329	55°33·5′	1°37·7′W	T	75
Beadnell Bay	Northum	NU2327	55°32·4′	1°37·7′W	W	75
Beadnell Harbour	Northum	NU2328	55°33·0′	1°37·7′W	W	75
Beadnell Haven	Northum	NU2329	55°33·5′	1°37·7′W	W	75
Beadon Fm	Devon	SX8181	50°37·2′	3°40·6′W	FM	191
Beadshallock Hill	Aberd	NJ4911	57°11·5′	2°50·2′W	H	37
Beafield	Orkney	HY6840	59°15·0′	2°33·2′W	X	5
Beaford	Devon	SS5514	50°54·7′	4°3·4′W	T	180
Beaford Br	Devon	SS5414	50°54·7′	4°4·2′W	X	180
Beaford Brook	Devon	SS5515	50°55·2′	4°3·4′W	W	180
Beaford Moor	Devon	SS5714	50°54·7′	4°1·7′W	X	180
Beagle	Corn	SW7557	50°22·4′	5°9·5′W	X	200
Beagles Point	Corn	SW7616	50°0·4′	5°7·2′W	X	204
Beagletodn Downs	Corn	SW4738	50°11·5′	5°32·3′W	X	203
Beak Fm	Essex	TL9030	51°56·4′	0°46·2′E	FM	168
Beak Hills	N Yks	NZ5402	54°24·9′	1°9·7′W	X	93
Beaks Fm	E Susx	TQ4318	50°56·8′	0°2·5′E	FM	198
Beal	Northum	NU0642	55°40·5′	1°53·8′W	T	75
Beal	N Yks	SE5325	53°43·4′	1°11·4′W	T	105
Bealach	Highld	NM9851	56°36·7′	5°17·1′W	X	49
Bealach a' Bharnish	Highld	NN3986	56°56·5′	4°38·3′W	X	34,41
Bealach a Bhàsteir	Highld	NG4625	57°15·0′	6°12·2′W	X	32
Bealach a' Bhòta	Highld	NM7288	56°55·9′	5°44·4′W	X	40
Bealach a' Bhràigh Bhig	Highld	NM3499	57°0·6′	6°22·4′W	X	39
Bealach a' Chaolais	N Eil	NF8122	57°10·9′	7°16·3′W	X	31
Bealach a' Chaolais	N Eil	NF8123	57°11·5′	7°16·4′W	X	22
Bealach a' Chaòl-reidh	Highld	NG4649	57°27·9′	6°13·7′W	H	23
Bealacha' Chasain	Highld	NG9014	57°10·4′	5°28·0′W	X	33
Bealach a' Chlaib	Highld	NG3334	57°19·4′	6°25·7′W	X	32
Bealach a'Choin Ghlas	Arg & Bt	NM7107	56°12·3′	5°41·1′W	W	55
Bealach a' Chòinich	Highld	NH0614	57°10·8′	5°12·1′W	X	33
Bealach a' Choire	Highld	NG8831	57°19·5′	5°30·8′W	X	24
Bealach a'Choire Bhain	Highld	NM7952	56°36·7′	5°35·6′W	X	49
Bealach a' Choire Bhuidhe	Highld	NM8378	56°50·8′	5°33·1′W	X	40
Bealach a' Choire Ghairbh	Highld	NG9348	57°28·8′	5°26·7′W	X	25
Bealach a' Choire Mhòir	Highld	NM8076	56°49·7′	5°35·9′W	X	40
Bealach a' Choire Odhair	Highld	NG8205	57°5·3′	5°35·4′W	X	33
Bealach a' Chòmhla	Highld	NG8860	57°35·1′	5°32·3′W	X	19,24
Bealach a' Chonnaidh	Highld	NC3749	58°24·2′	4°46·9′W	X	9
Bealach a' Chonnaidh	Stir	NN5116	56°19·0′	4°24·1′W	X	57
Bealach a' Chonnaidh	Highld	NC2028	58°12·5′	5°3·3′W	X	15
Bealach a' Chuirn	Highld	NG4854	57°30·6′	6°12·0′W	X	23
Bealach a Chùirn	Highld	NG9774	57°42·9′	5°24·0′W	X	19
Bealach a' Gharbh-choire	Highld	NG4520	57°12·3′	6°12·9′W	X	32
Bealach a' Ghlas-chnoic	Highld	NG8944	57°26·5′	5°30·5′W	X	24
Bealach a' Ghlas-chnoic	Highld	NG9044	57°26·5′	5°29·5′W	X	25
Bealach a' Ghlinne	Highld	NG6321	57°13·4′	5°55·1′W	X	32
Bealach a' Ghlinne	Highld	NM6149	56°34·6′	5°53·0′W	X	49

Bealach Airneabhail	N Eil	NF7826	57°13·0′	7°19·6′W	X	22
Bealach Alltan Ruairidh	Highld	NG9838	57°23·5′	5°21·2′W	X	25
Bealach Amadal	Highld	NG4561	57°34·3′	6°15·4′W	X	23
Bealach a' Mhaim	Arg & Bt	NN2507	56°13·7′	4°48·9′W	X	56
Bealach a' Mhàim	Highld	NG4426	57°15·4′	6°14·2′W	X	32
Bealach a' Mhàma	Highld	NM7485	56°54·3′	5°42·3′W	X	40
Bealach a' Mheim	Stir	NN3612	56°16·6′	4°38·5′W	X	50,56
Bealach a'Mhonmhuir	Highld	NM8457	56°39·6′	5°31·0′W	X	49
Bealach a Mhòramhain	Highld	NG4562	57°34·8′	6°15·5′W	H	23
Bealach an Amais	Highld	NH1518	57°13·2′	5°3·4′W	X	34
Bealach an Daimh	Arg & Bt	NS0890	56°4·1′	5°4·6′W	X	56
Bealachandrain	Arg & Bt	NR9983	56°0·1′	5°13·0′W	T	55
Bealach an Dubh-bhràigh	Highld	NM3199	57°0·5′	6°25·4′W	X	39
Bealach an Dubh Choirein	Pth & Kin	NN6218	56°20·3′	4°13·5′W	X	57
Bealach an Easain	Highld	NN1994	57°0·4′	4°58·4′W	X	34
Bealach an Easain	N Eil	NF8120	57°9·9′	7°16·2′W	X	31
Bealach an Easain Duibh	Arg & Bt	NN2308	56°14·2′	4°50·9′W	X	56
Bealach an Fhalaisg Dhuibh	Highld	NM7878	56°50·7′	5°38·0′W	X	40
Bealach an Fhiodha	Highld	NG7405	57°5·1′	5°43·3′W	X	33
Bealach an Fhiona	Highld	NM7678	56°50·6′	5°39·9′W	X	40
Bealach an Fhir-bhogha	N Ayr	NR9541	55°37·4′	5°14·9′W	X	62,69
Bealach an Fhuarain	Highld	NM3794	56°58·0′	6°19·2′W	X	39
Bealach an Ionalaidh	N Eil	NG0692	57°49·5′	6°56·7′W	X	14,18
Bealach an Lapain	Highld	NH0014	57°10·7′	5°18·1′W	X	33
Bealach an Locha	Highld	NG4330	57°17·6′	6°15·5′W	X	32
Bealach an Lochain	Arg & Bt	NN1400	56°9·6′	4°59·3′W	X	56
Bealach an Oir	Highld	NM3895	56°58·6′	6°18·3′W	X	39
Bealach an Sgàirne	Highld	NH0121	57°14·5′	5°17·4′W	X	25,33
Bealach an Sgoltaidh	Highld	NH0641	57°25·3′	5°13·4′W	X	25
Bealach an Sgriodain	Highld	NM8773	56°48·2′	5°28·9′W	X	40
Bealach an Tarabairt	Arg & Bt	NM6612	56°14·8′	5°46·2′W	X	55
Bealach an Torc-choire	Highld	NM8399	57°2·1′	5°34·1′W	X	33,40
Bealach an t- Sionnaich	Arg & Bt	NS1891	56°4·9′	4°55·0′W	X	56
Bealach Aoidhdailean	Highld	NG8812	57°9·3′	5°29·9′W	X	33
Bealach a' Phollaidh	Highld	NC2537	58°17·5′	4°58·7′W	X	15
Bealach Arnasdail	Highld	NG8512	57°9·2′	5°32·8′W	X	33
Bealachasan	Highld	NG8917	57°12·0′	5°29·1′W	X	33
Bealach Bairc-mheall	Highld	NM3897	56°59·7′	6°18·4′W	X	39
Bealach Bàn	Highld	NG5907	57°5·7′	5°58·3′W	X	32,39
Bealach Bàn	Highld	NG8206	57°5·9′	5°35·5′W	X	33
Bealach Bàn	Highld	NG9451	57°30·4′	5°25·9′W	X	25
Bealach Ban	Highld	NH2368	57°40·3′	4°57·6′W	X	20
Bealach Bàn	Highld	NM6758	56°39·6′	5°47·7′W	X	49
Bealach Beag	Highld	NG4953	57°30·1′	6°10·9′W	X	23
Bealach Beag	Highld	NH1127	57°17·9′	5°7·8′W	X	25
Bealach Beag	Highld	NH4263	57°38·0′	4°38·3′W	X	20
Bealach Beithe	Highld	NN5172	56°49·2′	4°26·0′W	X	42
Bealach Bharcasaig	Highld	NG2241	57°22·7′	6°37·1′W	X	23
Bealach Bhasteir	Highld	NG4625	57°15·0′	6°12·2′W	X	32
Bealach Bhearnais	Highld	NH0644	57°27·0′	5°13·5′W	X	25
Bealach Bholla	Highld	NH1133	57°21·2′	5°8·0′W	X	25
Bealach Biudhe	Highld	NM8096	57°0·4′	5°36·9′W	X	33,40
Bealach Breabag	Highld	NN5069	56°47·6′	4°26·9′W	X	42
Bealach Breac	Highld	NM7580	56°51·7′	5°41·0′W	H	40
Bealach Brittle	Highld	NG3923	57°13·7′	6°19·0′W	X	32
Bealach Buidhe	Aberd	NO1783	56°56·1′	3°21·4′W	X	43
Bealach Buidhe	Arg & Bt	NM3519	56°17·6′	6°16·5′W	X	48
Bealach Buidhe	Highld	NG2755	57°30·4′	6°33·0′W	X	23
Bealach Carach	Highld	NM6675	56°48·7′	5°49·6′W	X	40
Bealach Carn na h-Urchaire	Highld	NN1694	57°0·3′	5°1·3′W	X	34
Bealach Carra Dhomhnuill Ghuirm	N Eil	NF7932	57°16·2′	7°19·1′W	X	22
Bealach Chaiplin	Highld	NG4560	57°33·8′	6°15·4′W	X	23
Bealach Choinnich	Highld	NC2914	58°5·2′	4°53·6′W	X	15
Bealach Choire a' Chait	Highld	NH1114	57°10·9′	5°7·2′W	X	34
Bealach Choire a' Ghuirein	Highld	NN1894	57°0·3′	4°59·4′W	X	34
Bealach Choire nam Muc	Highld	NM9566	56°44·7′	5°20·7′W	X	40
Bealach Clais nan Ceap	Highld	NC5949	58°24·7′	4°24·3′W	X	10
Bealach Clith	Highld	NM4985	56°53·6′	6°6·8′W	X	39
Bealach Clithe	Highld	NM4787	56°54·6′	6°8·9′W	X	39
Bealach Cnoc na h-Uidhe	Highld	NC2566	58°33·1′	5°0·0′W	X	9
Bealach Coir' a' Choin	Highld	NC2764	58°32·1′	4°57·8′W	X	9
Bealach Coire a' Chuidhe	Highld	NC2765	58°32·6′	4°57·9′W	X	9
Bealach Coire an Laoigh	Stir	NN4215	56°18·3′	4°32·8′W	X	56
Bealach Coire Dhorrcail	Highld	NG8303	57°4·3′	5°34·3′W	X	33
Bealach Coire Ghàidheil	Highld	NH0924	57°16·3′	5°9·6′W	X	25,33
Bealach Coire Laoghan	Arg & Bt	NN2145	56°34·0′	4°54·4′W	X	50
Bealach Coire Mhàlagain	Highld	NG9412	57°9·4′	5°23·9′W	X	33
Bealach Coire na Banachdich	Highld	NG4421	57°12·8′	6°13·9′W	X	32
Bealach Coire na Circe	Highld	NG4427	57°16·0′	6°14·3′W	X	32
Bealach Coire nan Cearc	Highld	NM9385	56°54·9′	5°23·6′W	H	40
Bealach Coire Sgreamhach	Highld	NG5922	57°13·8′	5°59·1′W	X	32
Bealach Corrach	Arg & Bt	NR4356	55°44·0′	6°5·2′W	X	60
Bealach Crosgard	N Eil	NF8129	57°14·7′	7°16·9′W	X	22
Bealach Crudhain	Highld	NH0644	57°27·0′	5°13·5′W	X	25
Bealach Cumhang	Highld	NG5045	57°25·9′	6°9·4′W	X	23,24
Bealach Cumhann	Arg & Bt	NN1339	56°30·6′	5°1·9′W	X	50
Bealach Cumhann	Highld	NN4671	56°48·6′	4°30·9′W	X	42
Bealach Dearg	Aberd	NO1798	57°4·2′	3°21·7′W	X	36,43
Bealach Driseach	Stir	NN4918	56°20·1′	4°26·1′W	X	57
Bealach Dubh	Highld	NN4873	56°49·7′	4°29·0′W	X	42
Bealach Duibh Leac	Highld	NG9611	57°8·9′	5°21·9′W	X	33
Bealach Eadar dà Bheinn	Highld	NG3924	57°14·2′	6°19·1′W	X	32
Bealach-eadar-dha Beinn	Stir	NN4323	56°22·7′	4°32·1′W	X	51
Bealach Easach	Highld	NC5825	58°11·7′	4°24·5′W	X	16
Bealach Eas nan Cabar	Arg & Bt	NN2037	56°29·7′	4°55·0′W	X	50
Bealach Eòrabhat	N Eil	NG1094	57°50·8′	6°52·8′W	X	14
Bealach Féith na Gamhna	Highld	NH2419	57°13·9′	4°54·5′W	X	34
Bealach Fhionnghaill	Highld	NN1352	56°37·6′	5°2·5′W	X	41
Bealach Fuar-chathaidh	Highld	NN2248	56°35·7′	4°53·5′W	X	50
Bealach Gaothach	Arg & Bt	NR7782	55°59·0′	5°34·1′W	X	55
Bealach Gaothach	Arg & Bt	NS1475	55°56·2′	4°58·2′W	X	63
Bealach Gaoth' Near	Arg & Bt	NR4178	55°55·8′	6°8·4′W	X	60,61
Bealach Gaoth' Niar	Arg & Bt	NR4077	55°55·2′	6°9·3′W	X	60,61
Bealach Garbh	Highld	NG5704	57°4·0′	6°0·1′W	X	32,39
Beaiach Garbh	N Eil	NB1603	57°55·8′	6°47·4′W	X	13,14
Bealach Garbh	N Eil	NG0893	57°50·1′	6°54·7′W	X	14,18
Bealach Ghlas Leathaid	Stir	NN3733	56°27·9′	4°38·3′W	X	50
Bealach Gorm	Highld	NH0971	57°41·6′	5°11·8′W	X	19
Bealach Hartaval	Highld	NG4655	57°31·1′	6°14·1′W	X	23
Bealach Horn	Highld	NC3346	58°22·5′	4°50·9′W	X	9
Bealach Ille Coire	Highld	NM8699	57°2·2′	5°31·2′W	X	33,40
Bealach Iochdarach	Highld	NG4173	57°40·6′	6°20·2′W	X	23
Bealach Leireag	Highld	NC1928	58°12·5′	5°4·4′W	X	15
Bealach Luachrach	Highld	NG8222	57°14·5′	5°36·3′W	X	33
Bealach Luib nam Feadag	Highld	NH0334	57°21·5′	5°16·0′W	X	25
Bealach Maari	N Eil	NF8673	57°38·5′	7°15·3′W	X	18
Bealach Mhèinnidh	Highld	NG9673	57°42·3′	5°25·0′W	X	19
Bealach Mhic Bheathain	Highld	NG9830	57°19·2′	5°20·8′W	X	25
Bealach Mhic Néill	Highld	NM3899	57°0·7′	6°18·5′W	X	39
Bealach Mór	Arg & Bt	NM8304	56°11·0′	5°29·4′W	X	55
Bealach Mór	Arg & Bt	NN0123	56°21·7′	5°12·8′W	H	50
Bealach Mór	Highld	NC1518	58°7·0′	5°8·0′W	H	15
Bealach Mór	Highld	NC3860	58°30·2′	4°46·3′W	X	9
Bealach Mór	Highld	NG4135	57°20·2′	6°17·8′W	X	32
Bealach Mór	Highld	NG4539	57°22·5′	6°14·1′W	X	23,32
Bealach Mór	Highld	NG4851	57°29·0′	6°11·8′W	X	23
Bealach Mór	Highld	NG8232	57°19·9′	5°36·8′W	X	24
Bealach Mór	Highld	NH4365	57°39·1′	4°37·4′W	X	20
Bealach Mosgaraidh	Highld	NG5128	57°16·8′	6°7·4′W	X	32
Bealach na Bá	Highld	NG7841	57°24·6′	5°41·3′W	X	24
Bealach na Beinne	N Eil	NF9076	57°40·3′	7°11·5′W	X	18
Bealach na Beinne Brice	Highld	NG4428	57°16·5′	6°14·4′W	X	32
Bealach na Béiste	Highld	NG5323	57°14·1′	6°5·1′W	X	32
Bealach na Ceardaich	Highld	NG5704	57°4·0′	6°0·1′W	X	32,39
Bealach na Ciste	N Eil	NG0792	57°49·6′	6°55·7′W	X	14,18
Bealach na Cloiche Duibhe	Highld	NH1734	57°21·8′	5°2·1′W	X	25
Bealach na Creige Duibhe	Highld	NC4632	58°15·3′	4°37·0′W	X	16
Bealach na Creige Riabhaich	Highld	NC4951	58°25·5′	4°34·7′W	X	9
Bealach na Croiche	Highld	NG3625	57°14·6′	6°22·1′W	X	32
Bealach na Croise	Highld	NH0671	57°41·5′	5°14·8′W	X	19
Bealach na Cruinn-leum	Highld	NG7318	57°12·1′	5°45·0′W	X	33
Bealach na Féithe	Highld	NC3741	58°19·9′	4°46·6′W	X	9
Bealach na Gaoithe	Highld	NG8258	57°33·8′	5°38·2′W	X	24
Bealach na Gaoithe	Highld	NM6875	56°48·8′	5°47·6′W	X	40
Bealach na h-Airigh Mhùrain	Highld	NG3820	57°12·0′	6°19·8′W	X	32
Bealach na h-Eangair	Highld	NM9097	57°1·2′	5°27·1′W	X	33,40
Bealach na h-Eige	Highld	NH1327	57°18·0′	5°5·8′W	X	25
Bealach na h- Imrich	Highld	NC3650	58°24·7′	4°48·0′W	X	9
Bealach na h-Imrich	Highld	NH1070	57°41·0′	5°10·8′W	X	19
Bealach na h-Imriche	Stir	NN4811	56°16·3′	4°26·8′W	H	57
Bealach na h-Uamha	N Eil	NB1511	58°0·1′	6°49·0′W	X	13,14
Bealach na Leacaich	Highld	NG4659	57°33·3′	6°14·3′W	X	23
Bealach na Lice	Highld	NG9350	57°29·8′	5°26·8′W	X	25
Bealach na Lice	Highld	NM7876	56°49·6′	5°37·9′W	X	40
Bealach nam Bo	Stir	NN4707	56°14·1′	4°27·7′W	X	57
Bealach nam Fiann	Highld	NC2738	58°18·1′	4°56·7′W	X	15
Bealach nam Meirleach	Highld	NC4136	58°17·3′	4°42·3′W	X	16
Bealach nam Mulachag	Highld	NG7622	57°14·3′	5°42·3′W	X	33
Bealach na Mòine	Arg & Bt	NR7691	56°3·8′	5°35·5′W	H	55
Bealach na Muic	Highld	NC7021	58°9·8′	4°12·1′W	X	16
Bealach nan Arr	Highld	NG7844	57°26·2′	5°41·5′W	X	24
Bealach nan Cabar	Stir	NN6016	56°19·2′	4°15·4′W	X	57
Bealach nan Cabrach	Arg & Bt	NN1622	56°21·5′	4°58·3′W	X	50
Bealach nan Coisichean	Highld	NG4365	57°36·4′	6°17·7′W	X	23
Bealach nan Coisichean	Highld	NM6873	56°47·7′	5°47·5′W	X	40
Bealach nan Corp	Stir	NN3615	56°18·2′	4°38·6′W	H	50,56
Bealach nan Daoine	Highld	NM8693	56°59·0′	5°30·9′W	X	33,40
Bealach nan Each	Highld	NM5168	56°44·5′	6°3·9′W	X	47
Bealach na Nighinn	Arg & Bt	NM8225	56°22·3′	5°31·4′W	X	49
Bealach nan Lice	Highld	NG4624	57°14·4′	6°12·1′W	X	32
Bealach nan Sac	Arg & Bt	NS0790	56°4·1′	5°5·6′W	X	56
Bealach nan Sac	Highld	NG9572	57°41·7′	5°25·9′W	X	19
Bealach nan Sac	Highld	NM7593	56°58·7′	5°41·7′W	X	33,40
Bealach nan Sgòr	Pth & Kin	NN4467	56°46·4′	4°32·7′W	X	42
Bealach na Sgairde	Highld	NG5129	57°17·3′	6°7·5′W	X	32
Bealach na Srèine	Arg & Bt	NS1177	55°57·2′	5°1·2′W	X	63
Bealach na Sròine	Highld	NH0024	57°16·0′	5°18·6′W	X	25,33
Bealach Odhar	Highld	NH0472	57°42·0′	5°16·9′W	X	19
Bealach Ràtagain	Highld	NG8919	57°13·1′	5°29·2′W	X	33
Bealach Ruadh	Highld	NM4567	56°43·8′	6°9·7′W	X	47
Bealach Ruadh	Pth & Kin	NN6721	56°22·0′	4°8·7′W	X	51,57
Bealach Sheabhal	N Eil	NF7726	57°12·9′	7°20·6′W	X	22
Bealach Sheiliosdail	N Eil	NF8132	57°16·3′	7°17·1′W	X	22
Bealach Sloc an Eich	Highld	NM6557	56°39·0′	5°49·6′W	X	49
Bealach Toll Easa	Highld	NH1727	57°18·1′	5°1·8′W	X	25
Bealach Uachdarach	Highld	NG4173	57°40·6′	6°20·2′W	X	23
Bealach Udal	Highld	NG7520	57°13·2′	5°43·2′W	X	33
Bealach Uige	Highld	NG4464	57°35·9′	6°16·6′W	X	23
Bealbury	Corn	SX3766	50°28·5′	4°17·5′W	T	201
Beald Fm	Cambs	TL5180	52°24·1′	0°13·6′E	FM	143
Beale Fm	Kent	TQ7342	51°9·3′	0°28·8′E	FM	188
Beal Hill	Highld	ND2955	58°28·9′	3°12·6′W	X	11,12
Beal Hill	Pth & Kin	NO2027	56°26·0′	3°17·4′W	H	53,58
Beal Ho	N Yks	SE3986	54°16·3′	1°23·6′W	X	99
Beal House Fm	W Susx	TQ0027	51°2·2′	0°34·0′W	FM	186,197
Bealings Hall	Suff	TM2349	52°5·9′	1°15·8′E	X	169
Bealings Ho	Suff	TM2448	52°5·3′	1°16·6′E	X	169
Bea Loch	Orkney	HY6540	59°15·0′	2°36·3′W	W	5
Beal Point	Northum	NU0843	55°41·1′	1°51·9′W	X	75
Beals	Corn	SX3676	50°33·9′	4°18·6′W	X	201
Beal Sands	Northum	NU0842	55°40·5′	1°51·9′W	X	75
Beal's Green	Kent	TQ7631	51°3·3′	0°31·1′E	T	188
Bealsmill	Corn	SX3576	50°33·9′	4°19·4′W	T	201
Bealy Court	Devon	SS7415	50°55·5′	3°47·2′W	X	180
Beam	Falk	NS8376	55°58·0′	3°52·0′W	X	65
Beam Br	N Som	ST4662	51°21·5′	2°46·1′W	X	172,182
Beambridge	Shrops	SO3881	52°25·6′	2°54·3′W	X	137
Beambridge	Shrops	SO5388	52°29·5′	2°41·1′W	T	137,138
Beam Bridge	Somer	ST1019	50°58·0′	3°16·5′W	T	181,193
Beam Brook	Surrey	TQ2041	51°9·6′	0°16·6′W	W	187
Beamer	Fife	NT1280	56°0·5′	3°24·2′W	X	65
Beamer Hill	N Yks	SE8461	54°2·5′	0°42·6′W	X	100
Beam Hill	Staffs	SK2326	52°50·1′	1°39·1′W	T	128
Beam Ho	Devon	SS4720	50°57·8′	4°10·3′W	X	180
Beam Ho	Shrops	SJ4018	52°45·6′	2°52·9′W	X	126
Beamhurst	Staffs	SK0536	52°55·5′	1°55·1′W	T	128
Beamhurst Lane	Staffs	SK0635	52°55·0′	1°54·2′W	T	128
Beaminster	Dorset	ST4701	50°48·6′	2°44·8′W	T	193
Beaminster Down	Dorset	ST4903	50°49·7′	2°43·1′W	H	193,194
Beamish	Durham	NZ2253	54°52·5′	1°39·0′W	T	88
Beamish Burn	Durham	NZ2054	54°53·1′	1°40·9′W	X	88
Beamish East Moor	Ghead	NZ2255	54°53·6′	1°39·0′W	X	88
Beamish Fm	Shrops	SJ8204	52°38·2′	2°15·6′W	FM	127
Beamish Hall	Durham	NZ2154	54°53·1′	1°39·9′W	X	88
Beamish Open Air Museum	Durham	NZ2154	54°53·1′	1°39·9′W	X	88
Beamond End	Bucks	SU9196	51°39·6′	0°40·7′W	T	165
Beamond Wood	Bucks	SU9197	51°40·1′	0°40·7′W	F	165
Beam River	Bark & Dag	TQ5185	51°32·8′	0°11·1′E	W	177
Beamsley	N Yks	SE0752	53°58·1′	1°53·2′W	T	104
Beamsley Beacon or Howber Hill	N Yks	SE0952	53°58·1′	1°51·4′W	H	104
Beamsley Moor	N Yks	SE1053	53°58·6′	1°50·4′W	X	104
Beamsworthy	Devon	SX4797	50°45·4′	4°9·8′W	X	191
Beam, The	S Lanak	NS8524	55°30·0′	3°48·8′W	H	71,72
Beamwham	Northum	NY8168	55°0·6′	2°17·4′W	X	86,87
Bean	D & G	NX0654	54°50·8′	5°0·9′W	X	82
Bean	Kent	TQ5872	51°25·7′	0°16·8′E	T	177
Beanacre	Wilts	ST9065	51°23·3′	2°8·2′W	T	173
Beanaidh Bheag	Highld	NH9402	57°6·1′	3°44·5′W	W	36
Beananach	Stir	NN5619	56°20·7′	4°19·4′W	X	57
Beananach Wood	Highld	NH8821	57°16·2′	3°51·0′W	F	35,36
Bean Burn	Northum	NY7565	54°59·0′	2°23·0′W	W	86,87
Beancroft Fm	Beds	SP9842	52°4·3′	0°33·8′W	FM	153
Beancross	Falk	NS9179	55°59·8′	3°44·4′W	T	65
Bea Ness	Orkney	HY6538	59°13·9′	2°36·3′W	X	5
Beanfield Fm	Leic	SK3508	52°40·4′	1°28·5′W	FM	128,140
Beanford Fm	E Susx	TQ7716	50°55·2′	0°31·5′E	FM	199
Beanford Fm	Notts	SK6151	53°3·4′	1°5·0′W	FM	120
Beanhall Mill Fm	Worcs	SP0060	52°14·5′	1°59·6′W	FM	150
Bean Hill	D & G	NX0554	54°50·8′	5°1·8′W	H	82
Beanhill	Glos	SO5901	51°42·6′	2°35·2′W	X	162
Beanhill	Mil Key	SP8636	52°1·2′	0°44·4′W	T	152
Bean Hill	Somer	ST7341	51°10·3′	2°22·8′W	X	183
Beanhill Fm	Wilts	ST9779	51°30·8′	2°2·2′W	FM	173
Beanit Fm	Sol	SP2575	52°22·6′	1°37·6′W	FM	140
Beanlands Park	Cumbr	NY4860	54°56·2′	2°48·3′W	X	86
Beanley	Northum	NU0818	55°27·6′	1°52·0′W	T	81
Beanley Moor	Northum	NU1018	55°27·6′	1°50·1′W	X	81
Beanley Plantation	Northum	NU0917	55°27·1′	1°51·0′W	F	81
Beannain Beaga	Highld	NN4591	56°59·3′	4°32·6′W	H	34
Beannan	Arg & Bt	NS1795	56°7·0′	4°56·2′W	X	56
Beannan a' Deas	N Eil	NB0529	58°9·3′	7°0·4′W	H	13
Beannan Beag	N Eil	NB2910	58°0·1′	6°34·7′W	X	13,14
Beannan Beaga	Highld	NC1102	57°58·3′	5°11·3′W	X	15
Beannan Breaca	Highld	NM4486	56°53·9′	6°11·8′W	X	39
Beannan Dubh	Arg & Bt	NR4165	55°48·8′	6°7·6′W	X	60,61
Beannan Mòr	N Eil	NB2809	57°59·5′	6°35·7′W	H	13,14
Beannan nan Stoc	Arg & Bt	NR9999	56°8·7′	5°13·7′W	H	55
Beannie	Pth & Kin	NN8211	56°16·9′	3°53·9′W	X	57
Beansburn	E Ayr	NS4339	55°37·4′	4°29·2′W	T	70
Beanscroft	E Ayr	NS4741	55°38·6′	4°25·4′W	X	70
Beans Hill	C of Aber	NJ8403	57°7·3′	2°15·4′W	H	38
Beans Land Fm	Somer	ST7143	51°11·4′	2°24·5′W	FM	183
Beanston	E Loth	NT5476	55°58·7′	2°43·8′W	X	66
Beanston Mains	E Loth	NT5576	55°58·7′	2°42·8′W	X	66
Beanthwaite	Cumbr	SD2484	54°15·0′	3°9·6′W	T	96
Beanthwaite End	Cumbr	SD5896	54°21·7′	2°38·4′W	X	97
Beanwood Fm	S Glos	ST7079	51°30·8′	2°25·5′W	FM	172
Beaper Fm	I of W	SZ6089	50°42·1′	1°8·6′W	FM	196
Beaple's Barton	Devon	SS8122	50°59·3′	3°41·4′W	X	181
Beaple's Hill	Devon	SS8221	50°58·8′	3°40·5′W	X	181
Beaple's Moor	Devon	SS8121	50°58·8′	3°41·3′W	X	181
Beaquoy	Orkney	HY3022	59°5·0′	3°12·8′W	T	6
Beaquoy Fm	Orkney	HY3021	59°4·5′	3°12·8′W	FM	6
Beara	Devon	SS4222	50°58·8′	4°14·7′W	X	180,190
Beara	Devon	SS4724	50°59·9′	4°10·4′W	X	180
Beara	Devon	SS5618	50°56·8′	4°2·6′W	X	180
Beara	Devon	SS5728	51°2·3′	4°2·0′W	X	180
Beara	Devon	SS6438	51°7·7′	3°56·2′W	X	180
Beara	Devon	SS6919	50°57·6′	3°51·5′W	X	180
Beara	Devon	SS7017	50°56·5′	3°50·6′W	X	180
Beara	Devon	SS7035	51°6·2′	3°51·0′W	X	180
Beara	Devon	SS7219	50°57·6′	3°49·0′W	X	180
Beara	Devon	SX3886	50°39·3′	4°17·1′W	X	201
Beara	Devon	SX7866	50°29·1′	3°42·8′W	X	202
Beara Charter Barton	Devon	SS5238	51°7·6′	4°6·5′W	X	180
Beara Common	Devon	SX7061	50°26·3′	3°49·5′W	X	202
Beara Court	Devon	SS4604	50°49·1′	4°10·8′W	X	190
Beara Down	Devon	SS5239	51°8·1′	4°6·5′W	X	180
Beara Down	Devon	SX5087	50°40·0′	4°7·0′W	H	191
Beara Fm	Corn	SX1760	50°24·9′	4°34·2′W	FM	201
Beara Fm	Devon	SS5347	51°12·4′	4°5·9′W	FM	180
Bearah Fm	Devon	SS4219	50°57·2′	4°14·6′W	FM	180,190
Beara Hill Head	Devon	SS7135	51°6·2′	3°50·2′W	X	180
Bearah Tor	Corn	SX2574	50°32·6′	4°27·8′W	X	201
Beara Moor	Devon	SS5619	50°57·4′	4°2·6′W	X	180
Bearasay	N Eil	NB1242	58°16·6′	6°54·3′W	X	13
Bear Br	Bucks	SP6436	52°1·4′	1°3·6′W	X	152
Bear Craig	D & G	NT1905	55°20·2′	3°16·2′W	H	79
Bearcroft	D & G	NX9579	55°5·9′	3°38·3′W	X	84
Bear Cross	Bourne	SZ0596	50°46·0′	1°55·4′W	T	195
Bearda	Staffs	SJ9664	53°10·6′	2°3·2′W	X	118
Beard Hall Fm	Derby	SK0084	53°21·4′	1°59·6′W	FM	110
Beard Hill	Somer	ST6240	51°9·7′	2°32·2′W	T	183
Beardly Batch	Somer	ST6241	51°10·3′	2°32·2′W	T	183
Beard Mill Fm	Oxon	SP3905	51°44·8′	1°25·7′W	FM	164
Beardon	Corn	SX3093	50°42·9′	4°24·1′W	X	190
Beardon	Devon	SX5184	50°38·4′	4°6·1′W	X	191,201
Beardon Hill	Devon	SX8583	50°38·4′	3°37·2′W	H	191
Beardon Plantn	Corn	SX2994	50°43·5′	4°25·0′W	F	190
Beardown Fm	Devon	SX6075	50°33·7′	3°58·2′W	FM	191

Beardown Hill	Devon	SX6076	50°34·3′	3°58·2′W	H	191
Beardown Man	Devon	SX5979	50°35·9′	3°59·2′W	A	191
Beardown Plantn	Devon	SX3395	50°44·1′	4°21·6′W	F	190
Beardown Tors	Devon	SX6077	50°34·8′	3°58·3′W	H	191
Beard's Fm	E Susx	TQ6314	50°54·4′	0°19·5′E	FM	199
Beard's Hall Fm	Kent	TR2343	51°8·8′	1°11·7′E	FM	179,189
Beardshaw Head	Lancs	SD9038	53°50·5′	2°8·7′W	X	103
Beard Stane	Moray	NJ4024	57°18·4′	2°59·3′W	X	37
Beardwood	Black w Dar	SD6629	53°45·6′	2°30·5′W	T	103
Beardwood Fm	Derby	SK0184	53°21·4′	1°58·7′W	FM	110
Beare	Devon	SS9800	50°47·7′	3°26·5′W	T	192
Beare	Devon	SX8299	50°47·0′	3°40·1′W	X	191
Beare Green	Surrey	TQ1743	51°10·7′	0°19·2′W	T	187
Bearehurst	Surrey	TQ1542	51°10·2′	0°20·9′W	X	187
Bearfauld	Angus	NO3760	56°43·9′	3°1·3′W	X	44
Bearfauld	Angus	NO6542	56°34·4′	2°33·7′W	X	54
Bearford Burn	E Loth	NT5473	55°57·1′	2°43·8′W	W	66
Bear Grove	Wok	SU8179	51°30·5′	0°49·6′W	F	175
Bearhill	Aberd	NK0949	57°32·1′	1°50·5′W	X	30
Bearhill Fm	E Dunb	NS6372	55°55·6′	4°11·1′W	FM	64
Bearholm	D & G	NT0901	55°17·9′	3°25·6′W	X	78
Bearhurst Fm	Ches	SJ8672	53°14·9′	2°12·2′W	FM	118
Bearhurst Fm	E Susx	TQ6727	51°1·3′	0°23·3′E	FM	188,199
Bearl	Northum	NZ0564	54°58·5′	1°54·9′W	X	87
Bearley	Warw	SP1860	52°14·5′	1°43·8′W	T	151
Bearley Brook	Somer	ST4922	50°59·9′	2°43·2′W	W	183,193
Bearley Cross	Warw	SP1660	52°14·5′	1°45·5′W	T	151
Bearley Fm	Somer	ST4922	50°59·9′	2°43·2′W	FM	183,193
Bearman's Fm	Essex	TL6602	51°41·8′	0°24·5′E	FM	167
Bearn a' Chlaidheimh	Highld	NH7377	57°46·1′	4°7·6′W	X	21
Bearneas	Highld	NH0242	57°25·8′	5°17·4′W	X	25
Bearnie	Aberd	NJ9634	57°24·0′	2°3·5′W	X	30
Bearn Iorach an Toa	N Eil	NB5344	58°19·2′	6°12·6′W	X	8
Bearnock	Highld	NH4130	57°20·2′	4°38·0′W	X	26
Bearnus	Arg & Bt	NM3941	56°29·6′	6°14·0′W	X	47,48
Bearpark	Durham	NZ2343	54°47·1′	1°38·1′W	T	88
Bear Park	N Yks	SE0088	54°17·5′	1°59·6′W	X	98
Bear Place	Wok	SU8179	51°30·5′	0°49·6′W	X	175
Bearragan	N Eil	NB0507	57°57·5′	6°58·8′W	H	13,14
Bear & Ragged Staff (PH)	Hants	SU3325	51°1·6′	1°31·4′W	X	185
Bearraich	Arg & Bt	NM4127	56°22·1′	6°11·2′W	H	48
Bearran	N Eil	NF8651	57°26·7′	7°13·6′W	X	22
Bearranan	N Eil	NF9176	57°40·3′	7°10·5′W	X	18
Bearreraig Bay	Highld	NG5153	57°30·2′	6°8·9′W	W	23,24
Bearsbridge	Northum	NY7857	54°54·7′	2°20·2′W	T	86,87
Bearsbrook	Staffs	SK0133	52°53·9′	1°58·7′W	X	128
Bearscombe	Devon	SX7544	50°17·2′	3°44·9′W	X	202
Bearscombe	Devon	SX7553	50°22·1′	3°45·1′W	X	202
Bear's Copse	Northnts	SP7343	52°5·1′	0°55·7′W	F	152
Bear's Croft Fm	Cambs	TL2569	52°18·5′	0°9·6′W	FM	153
Bearsden	E Dunb	NS5172	55°55·3′	4°22·6′W	T	64
Bear's Downs	Corn	SW8968	50°28·7′	4°58·1′W	X	200
Bearse Common	Glos	SO5705	51°44·8′	2°37·0′W	X	162
Bearse Fm	Glos	SO5705	51°44·8′	2°37·0′W	FM	162
Bearsett	N Yks	SD8691	54°19·1′	2°12·5′W	X	98
Bear's Grove	Norf	TG2915	52°41·3′	1°23·7′E	F	133,134
Bears Hall	Essex	TL5637	52°0·8′	0°16·8′E	X	154
Bearshank Wood	Northnts	SP9986	52°28·0′	0°32·2′W	F	141
Bears Hay Fm	Staffs	SK1511	52°42·0′	1°46·3′W	FM	128
Bear's Head	Northum	NU0151	55°45·4′	1°58·6′W	X	75
Bear's Head Fm	Ches	SJ8059	53°7·9′	2°17·5′W	FM	118
Bearside	Stir	NS7891	56°6·0′	3°57·2′W	X	57
Bear's Rails	Win & Maid	SU9773	51°27·1′	0°35·8′W	X	175,176
Bear's Rails (Moat)	Win & Maid	SU9773	51°27·1′	0°35·8′W	A	175,176
Bearsted	Kent	TQ7955	51°16·2′	0°34·4′E	T	178,188
Bears, The	Corn	SW5328	50°6·3′	5°26·9′W	X	203
Bearstone	Shrops	SJ7239	52°57·1′	2°24·6′W	T	127
Bearstone Mill	Shrops	SJ7239	52°57·1′	2°24·6′W	X	127
Bear's Wood	Heref	SO5837	52°2·0′	2°36·3′W	F	149
Bearswood Common	Heref	SO7349	52°8·6′	2°23·3′W	X	150
Beart an Fhir	Arg & Bt	NM2562	56°40·4′	6°28·9′W	X	46,47
Bearwalls	Devon	SX5284	50°38·5′	4°5·2′W	X	191,201
Bearwardcote Fm	Derby	SK2833	52°53·9′	1°34·6′W	FM	128
Bearwardcote Hall	Derby	SK2734	52°54·4′	1°35·5′W	X	128
Bearwood	Birm	SP0286	52°28·6′	1°57·8′W	T	139
Bear Wood	Corn	SX1165	50°27·5′	4°39·4′W	F	200
Bearwood	Heref	SO3856	52°12·2′	2°54·0′W	T	148,149
Bear Wood	Oxon	SU6983	51°32·7′	0°59·9′W	F	175
Bearwood	Poole	SZ0597	50°46·6′	1°55·4′W	T	195
Bearwood College	Wok	SU7769	51°25·1′	0°53·2′W	X	175
Bear Wood Lake	Wok	SU7768	51°24·6′	0°53·2′W	W	175
Beary Mountain	I of M	SC3183	54°13·1′	4°35·1′W	H	95
Beary, The	I of M	SC2883	54°13·1′	4°37·9′W	X	95
Beasdale Burn	Highld	NM7285	56°54·3′	5°44·2′W	W	40
Beasley	Somer	SS9540	51°9·2′	3°29·7′W	X	181
Beasley	Staffs	SJ8349	53°2·5′	2°14·8′W	T	118
Beasley Bank	Staffs	SJ7337	52°56·0′	2°23·7′W	X	127
Beasley Fm	Somer	SS9126	51°1·6′	3°32·9′W	FM	181
Beast Cliff	N Yks	TA0099	54°22·8′	0°27·2′W	X	101
Beasthorpe House Fm	Lincs	TF0396	53°27·3′	0°26·5′W	FM	112
Beastock Rig	D & G	NY0994	55°14·2′	3°25·4′W	X	78
Beaston	Devon	SX7966	50°29·1′	3°42·0′W	A	202
Beath Bleachfield	Fife	NT1590	56°6·0′	3°21·5′W	X	58
Beatland Corner	Devon	SX5462	50°26·6′	4°3·0′W	X	201
Beatons Fm	Cambs	TL3597	52°33·5′	0°0·1′W	FM	142
Beatrice Webb House	Surrey	TQ1144	51°11·3′	0°24·3′W	X	187
Beatrix	Lancs	SD6651	53°57·5′	2°30·7′W	X	103
Beatrix Fell	Lancs	SD6653	53°58·6′	2°30·7′W	X	103
Beatshach	Moray	NJ2737	57°25·3′	3°12·5′W	X	28
Beattie Lodge	Aberd	NO7170	56°49·5′	2°28·1′W	X	45
Beattie's Cairn	Angus	NO5064	56°46·2′	2°48·6′W	X	44
Beatties Cott	Aberd	NJ8000	57°5·7′	2°19·4′W	X	38
Beattock	D & G	NT0702	55°18·5′	3°27·5′W	T	78
Beattock Hill	D & G	NT0602	55°18·4′	3°28·4′W	H	78
Beattock Summit	S Lanak	NS9915	55°25·4′	3°35·3′W	X	78
Beaucastle	Worcs	SO7674	52°22·0′	2°20·8′W	X	138
Beauchamp	Devon	SS9315	50°55·7′	3°31·0′W	X	181
Beauchamp Barn	Notts	SK6964	53°10·4′	0°57·7′W	X	120
Beauchamp Court	Warw	SP0858	52°13·4′	1°52·6′W	X	150
Beauchamp Court	Worcs	SO8450	52°9·1′	2°13·6′W	X	150
Beauchamp Grange	Leic	SP6992	52°31·5′	0°58·6′W	X	141
Beauchamp Ho	Glos	SO7818	51°51·8′	2°18·8′W	X	162
Beauchamp Ho	Wilts	ST9125	51°1·7′	2°7·3′W	X	184
Beauchamp Roding	Essex	TL5810	51°46·2′	0°17·8′E	T	167
Beauchamps	Essex	TL7617	51°49·7′	0°33·6′E	X	167
Beauchamps	Essex	TQ9088	51°33·8′	0°44·9′E	X	178
Beauchamps	Herts	TL3831	51°57·8′	0°0·9′E	X	166
Beauchief	Sheff	SK3381	53°19·7′	1°29·9′W	T	110,111
Beauclerc	Northum	NZ0061	54°56·9′	1°59·6′W	T	87
Beaudesert	Warw	SP1566	52°17·8′	1°46·4′W	T	151
Beaudesert Old Park	Staffs	SK0313	52°43·1′	1°56·9′W	X	128
Beaudesert Park	Warw	SP1466	52°17·8′	1°47·3′W	X	151
Beaufoe Manor	Lincs	SK9963	53°9·5′	0°30·8′W	X	121
Beaufort	Blae Gw	SO1611	51°47·7′	3°12·7′W	T	161
Beaufort Castle	Highld	NH5043	57°27·4′	4°29·6′W	X	26
Beaufront Castle	Northum	NY9665	54°59·0′	2°3·3′W	X	87
Beaufront Hill Head	Northum	NY9666	54°59·6′	2°3·3′W	X	87
Beaufront Red Ho	Northum	NY9765	54°59·0′	2°2·4′W	X	87
Beaufront Wood Head Fm	Northum	NY9566	54°59·6′	2°4·3′W	FM	87
Beaulieu	Hants	SU3802	50°49·2′	1°27·2′W	T	196
Beaulieu-fawr	Carm	SN4318	51°50·6′	4°16·4′W	X	159
Beaulieu Hall	Northnts	TL0985	52°27·4′	0°23·3′W	A	142
Beaulieu Heath	Hants	SU3905	50°50·8′	1°26·4′W	X	196
Beaulieu Heath	Hants	SZ3599	50°47·6′	1°29·8′W	X	196
Beaulieu River	Hants	SU3805	50°50·8′	1°27·2′W	W	196
Beaulieu Road Sta	Hants	SU3406	50°51·4′	1°30·6′W	X	196
Beaulieu Wood	Dorset	ST7006	50°51·4′	2°25·2′W	T	194
Beauly	Highld	NH5246	57°29·1′	4°27·7′W	T	26
Beauly Firth	Highld	NH6247	57°29·8′	4°17·7′W	W	26
Beaumanor Hall	Leic	SK5315	52°44·0′	1°12·5′W	X	129
Beaumans	E Susx	TQ6732	51°4·0′	0°23·4′E	X	188
Beaumaris	I of Angl	SH6076	53°16·0′	4°5·5′W	T	114,115
Beaumont	Cumbr	NY3459	54°55·5′	3°1·4′W	T	85
Beaumont	Devon	SX9898	50°46·6′	3°26·4′W	X	192
Beaumont	Essex	TM1725	51°53·1′	1°9·6′E	T	168,169
Beaumont	Win & Maid	SU9973	51°27·1′	0°34·1′W	T	175,176
Beaumont Castle	Oxon	SP6134	52°0·3′	1°6·3′W	A	152,165
Beaumont Cote	Lancs	SD4966	54°5·5′	2°46·4′W	X	97
Beaumontcote Fm	N Lincs	TA0317	53°38·6′	0°26·1′W	FM	112
Beaumont Gate Fm	Lancs	SD4764	54°4·4′	2°48·2′W	FM	97
Beaumont Grange	Lancs	SD4865	54°4·9′	2°47·3′W	X	97
Beaumont Hall	Essex	TM1724	51°52·6′	1°9·6′E	X	168,169
Beaumont Hall	Herts	TL1110	51°46·9′	0°23·1′W	X	166
Beaumont Hall	Suff	TM2033	51°57·3′	1°12·5′E	X	169
Beaumont Hill	Darl	NZ2918	54°33·6′	1°32·7′W	T	93
Beaumont Hill Fm	Warw	SP1171	52°20·5′	1°49·9′W	FM	139
Beaumont Ho	Northum	NY9572	55°2·8′	2°4·3′W	X	87
Beaumont Leys	C of Leic	SK5608	52°40·2′	1°9·9′W	T	140
Beaumont Manor	Herts	TL3305	51°43·9′	0°4·0′W	X	166
Beaumont Otes	Essex	TL6809	51°45·5′	0°26·5′E	X	167
Beaumont Quay	Essex	TM1924	51°52·5′	1°11·3′E	X	168,169
Beaumont's Hall	Suff	TL9467	52°16·2′	0°51·0′E	X	155
Beaumont Wood	Lincs	SK9521	52°46·9′	0°35·1′W	F	130
Beauport Park	E Susx	TQ7814	50°54·1′	0°32·3′E	X	199
Beauport Park Hotel	E Susx	TQ7813	50°53·6′	0°32·3′E	X	199
Beaupre Hall Fm	Norf	TF5104	52°37·0′	0°14·2′E	FM	143
Beaurepaire Fm	Hants	SU6257	51°18·8′	1°6·2′W	FM	175
Beaurepaire Ho	Hants	SU6358	51°19·3′	1°5·4′W	X	175
Beausale	Warw	SP2370	52°19·9′	1°39·3′W	T	139
Beausale Ho	Warw	SP2469	52°19·3′	1°38·5′W	X	139,151
Beauthorn	Cumbr	NY4422	54°35·7′	2°51·6′W	X	90
Beautiport Fm	Devon	SY0292	50°43·4′	3°22·9′W	FM	192
Beauty Hill	Aberd	NJ9020	57°16·5′	2°9·5′W	H	38
Beauvale	Notts	SK4846	53°0·8′	1°16·7′W	T	129
Beauvale	Notts	SK5248	53°1·8′	1°13·1′W	T	129
Beauvale Ho	Notts	SK4849	53°2·4′	1°16·6′W	X	129
Beauvale Manor Fm	Notts	SK4948	53°1·9′	1°15·8′W	FM	129
Beauvale Priory	Notts	SK4948	53°1·9′	1°15·8′W	A	129
Beauville Fm	V of Glam	ST1372	51°26·7′	3°14·7′W	FM	171
Beauworth	Hants	SU5725	51°1·5′	1°10·8′W	T	185
Beaux Aires Fm	Kent	TQ8260	51°18·8′	0°37·1′E	FM	178,188
Beavan's Hill	Heref	SO6724	51°55·0′	2°28·4′W	T	162
Beaver	Lancs	SD9237	53°50·0′	2°6·9′W	X	103
Beaver Dyke Resrs	N Yks	SE2254	53°59·1′	1°39·5′W	W	104
Beaver Grove	Conwy	SH9061	53°8·3′	3°38·3′W	X	116
Beaver's Croft	Derby	SK1692	53°25·7′	1°45·1′W	X	110
Beaver's Hill	Pemb	SN0500	51°40·1′	4°48·8′W	X	158
Beavor Grange	Devon	SY3297	50°46·3′	2°57·5′W	X	193
Beaw Field	Shetld	HU5081	60°30·8′	1°4·9′W	X	1,2,3
Beaworthy	Devon	SX4599	50°46·4′	4°11·5′W	T	190
Beazley End	Essex	TL7429	51°56·2′	0°32·3′E	T	167
Bebington	Wirral	SJ3383	53°20·6′	3°0·0′W	T	108
Beboran	Orkney	HY3017	59°2·3′	3°12·7′W	X	6
Bebside	Northum	NZ2881	55°7·6′	1°33·2′W	T	81
Bebside Hall	Northum	NZ2781	55°7·6′	1°34·2′W	X	81
Becca Banks	Leeds	SE4238	53°50·4′	1°21·3′W	A	105
Becca Hall	Leeds	SE4138	53°50·4′	1°22·2′W	X	105
Becca Home Fm	Leeds	SE4138	53°50·4′	1°22·2′W	FM	105
Beccles	Suff	TM4290	52°27·5′	1°34·1′E	T	134
Beccles Common	Suff	TM4390	52°27·5′	1°35·0′E	X	134
Beccles Marshes	Suff	TM4391	52°28·0′	1°35·1′E	X	134
Becconsall	Lancs	SD4422	53°41·7′	2°50·5′W	T	102
Beccott	Devon	SS5942	51°9·8′	4°0·6′W	X	180
Bechan Brook	Powys	SO0798	52°34·6′	3°21·9′W	W	136
Bechan Brook	Powys	SO1097	52°34·0′	3°19·3′W	X	136
Beck	Cumbr	NY0719	54°33·7′	3°25·9′W	X	89
Becka Brook	Devon	SX7680	50°36·6′	3°44·8′W	W	191
Beckadon	Devon	SX4076	50°33·9′	4°15·2′W	X	201
Becka Falls	Devon	SX7580	50°36·6′	3°45·6′W	W	191
Beckaford Fm	Devon	SX7679	50°36·1′	3°44·8′W	FM	191
Beckbank	Cumbr	NY5435	54°42·7′	2°42·4′W	X	90
Beckbottom	Cumbr	NY2745	54°47·9′	3°7·7′W	X	85
Beck Bottom	Cumbr	SD2984	54°15·1′	3°5·0′W	T	96,97
Beck Bottom	Wakf	SE3023	53°42·4′	1°32·3′W	T	104
Beckbottom Fm	N Yks	SE2449	53°56·4′	1°37·6′W	FM	104
Beck Brook	Wrekin	SJ7717	52°45·2′	2°20·0′W	W	127
Beck Brook Fm	Cambs	TL4061	52°14·0′	0°3·4′E	FM	154
Beckbrow	Cumbr	NY2157	54°54·3′	3°13·5′W	X	85
Beckbrow	Cumbr	NY5247	54°49·2′	2°44·4′W	X	86
Beck Burn	Cumbr	NY3571	55°2·0′	3°0·6′W	W	85
Beck Burn	D & G	NX9356	54°53·5′	3°39·7′W	W	84
Beckbury	Glos	SP0629	51°57·8′	1°54·4′W	A	150,163
Beckbury	Shrops	SJ7601	52°36·6′	2°20·9′W	T	127
Beckces	Cumbr	NY4127	54°38·3′	2°54·4′W	T	90
Beckcote Fm	Cumbr	NY0507	54°27·2′	3°27·5′W	FM	89
Beck Cottages	Cumbr	NY4443	54°47·0′	2°51·8′W	X	85
Beck Dyke	Notts	SK7444	52°59·5′	0°53·4′W	W	129
Beckenham	Brom	TQ3769	51°24·4′	0°1·4′W	T	177
Beckenham Palace Park	Lew	TQ3870	51°25·0′	0°0·5′W	X	
Becken Howe	N Yks	SE9095	54°20·8′	0°36·5′W	A	94,101
Beckering	Lincs	TF1280	53°18·5′	0°18·7′W	X	121
Beckerings Park	Beds	SP9936	52°1·0′	0°33·0′W	X	153
Beckermet	Cumbr	NY0106	54°26·6′	3°31·2′W	T	89
Beckermonds	N Yks	SD8780	54°13·2′	2°11·5′W	T	98
Beckermonds Scar	N Yks	SD8580	54°13·2′	2°13·4′W	X	98
Beckerthwaite Beck	Lancs	SD5773	54°9·3′	2°39·1′W	X	97
Beckery	Somer	ST4838	51°8·6′	2°44·2′W	T	182
Becket Barn Fm	Kent	TQ9626	51°0·2′	0°48·0′E	FM	189
Becket's Barn	W Susx	SZ8897	50°46·2′	0°44·7′W	A	197
Becket's Down	Hants	SU5742	51°10·7′	1°10·7′W	X	185
Beckett	Devon	SX4196	50°44·7′	4°14·8′W	X	190
Beckett End	Norf	TL7798	52°33·3′	0°37·1′E	T	144
Beckett Park	Leeds	SE2636	53°49·4′	1°35·9′W	X	104
Becketts Corner	Bucks	SP6841	52°4·0′	1°0·1′W	X	152
Beckett's Fm	Glos	SO8826	51°56·2′	2°10·1′W	FM	162
Beckett's Fm	Kent	TQ5146	51°11·8′	0°10·1′E	FM	188
Beckett's Fm	Norf	TG1137	52°53·6′	1°8·6′E	FM	133
Beckett's Wood	Ches	SJ5478	53°18·1′	2°41·0′W	F	117
Beckfield Cross	I of W	SZ4881	50°37·8′	1°18·9′W	X	196
Beckfield Fm	Herts	TL3233	51°59·0′	0°4·3′W	FM	166
Beckfield Fm	N Yks	SE4528	53°45·0′	1°18·6′W	FM	105
Beckfield Ho	N Yks	SE5673	54°9·2′	1°8·1′W	X	100
Beck Fm	Cambs	TL4465	52°16·1′	0°7·0′E	FM	154
Beck Fm	Cumbr	NY1948	54°49·5′	3°15·2′W	FM	85
Beck Fm	Cumbr	NY5244	54°47·6′	2°44·4′W	FM	86
Beck Fm	Hants	SZ3797	50°46·5′	1°28·1′W	FM	196
Beck Fm	Lincs	SK8442	52°58·4′	0°44·5′W	FM	130
Beck Fm	Lincs	SK9992	53°25·2′	0°30·2′W	FM	112
Beck Fm	Lincs	TF1828	52°50·4′	0°14·5′W	FM	130
Beck Fm	Norf	TG1719	52°43·7′	1°13·2′E	FM	133,134
Beck Fm	Norf	TG2416	52°41·9′	1°19·3′E	FM	133,134
Beck Fm	N Yks	SE6042	53°52·5′	1°4·8′W	FM	105
Beck Fm	York	SE6644	53°53·5′	0°59·3′W	FM	105,106
Beck Fm, The	Cumbr	NY5063	54°57·8′	2°46·4′W	FM	86
Beck Foot	Brad	SE1038	53°50·5′	1°50·5′W	T	104
Beckfoot	Cumbr	NY0949	54°49·9′	3°24·6′W	T	85
Beckfoot	Cumbr	NY1016	54°32·1′	3°23·0′W	X	89
Beckfoot	Cumbr	NY1600	54°23·6′	3°17·2′W	X	89
Beckfoot	Cumbr	NY5020	54°34·6′	2°46·0′W	X	90
Beckfoot	Cumbr	NY7611	54°29·9′	2°21·8′W	X	91
Beckfoot	Cumbr	SD1989	54°17·7′	3°14·3′W	X	96
Beck Foot	Cumbr	SD6196	54°21·7′	2°35·6′W	T	97
Beck Foot	Cumbr	SD6295	54°21·2′	2°34·7′W	X	97
Beckfoot	D & G	NY2165	54°58·7′	3°13·6′W	X	85
Beckfoot	Lancs	SD7753	53°58·6′	2°20·6′W	X	103
Beckfoot Fm	Cumbr	SD6181	54°13·6′	2°35·5′W	FM	97
Beck Foot Fm	N Yks	SE1348	53°55·9′	1°47·7′W	FM	104
Beckford	Hants	SU6310	50°53·4′	1°5·9′W	X	196
Beckford	Worcs	SO9735	52°1·0′	2°2·2′W	T	150
Beckford Br	Devon	ST2601	50°48·5′	3°2·6′W	A	192,193
Beckford Hill	Worcs	SO9838	52°2·7′	2°1·4′W	X	150
Beckford's Twr	Bath & NE Somer	ST7367	51°24·3′	2°22·9′W	X	172,172
Beckhall	D & G	NY3475	55°4·2′	3°1·6′W	X	85
Beck Hall	Norf	TG0220	52°44·6′	1°0·0′E	X	133
Beckham	Somer	SS8041	51°9·6′	3°42·6′W	X	181
Beckhampton	Wilts	SU0868	51°24·9′	1°52·7′W	T	173
Beckhampton Penning	Wilts	SU0967	51°24·3′	1°51·8′W	X	173
Beckhampton Village	W Berks	SU3378	51°30·2′	1°31·1′W	A	174
Beck Head	Cumbr	NY5710	54°29·3′	2°39·4′W	X	91
Beck Head	Cumbr	SD4484	54°15·2′	2°51·2′W	T	97
Beckhead Crag	Cumbr	NY5783	55°8·6′	2°40·0′W	X	80
Beck Hill	N Yks	NZ2601	54°24·5′	1°35·5′W	X	93
Beck Hill	Warw	SP4868	52°18·7′	1°17·4′W	X	151
Beckhithe	Norf	TG1506	52°36·8′	1°11·0′E	X	144
Beck Ho	Cumbr	NY4247	54°49·1′	2°53·7′W	X	85
Beck Ho	Cumbr	SD6187	54°16·9′	2°35·5′W	X	97
Beck Ho	Cumbr	SD6396	54°21·7′	2°33·7′W	X	97
Beck Ho	Lancs	SD7745	53°54·3′	2°20·6′W	X	103
Beck Ho	N Yks	NZ2410	54°29·3′	1°37·3′W	X	93
Beck Ho	N Yks	NZ5705	54°26·5′	1°6·8′W	X	93
Beck Ho	N Yks	SD8556	54°0·2′	2°13·3′W	X	103
Beck Ho	N Yks	SE8272	54°8·5′	0°44·3′W	X	100
Beck Hole	N Yks	NZ8202	54°24·6′	0°43·8′W	W	94
Beckhouse	Cumbr	NY1629	54°39·2′	3°17·7′W	X	89
Beck House Fm	Lincs	TF1684	53°20·6′	0°15·0′W	FM	121
Beckhouse Fm	N Yks	SE7489	54°17·7′	0°51·4′W	FM	94,100
Beck Houses	Cumbr	SD5896	54°21·7′	2°38·4′W	T	97
Beckingham	Lincs	SK8753	53°4·3′	0°41·7′W	T	121
Beckingham	Notts	SK7790	53°24·3′	0°50·1′W	T	112
Beckingham Hall	Essex	TL9011	51°46·1′	0°45·6′E	X	168
Beckingham Hall	Essex	TL9320	51°50·9′	0°48·5′E	X	168
Beckingham Place Park	Brom	TQ3770	51°25·0′	0°1·4′W	X	177
Beckingham Wood	Notts	SK7589	53°23·8′	0°51·9′W	F	112,120
Beckington	Somer	ST8051	51°15·7′	2°16·8′W	T	183
Beckjay	Shrops	SO3977	52°23·5′	2°53·4′W	T	137,148
Beckland Bay	Devon	SS2826	51°0·7′	4°26·7′W	W	190
Beckland Fm	Devon	SS2726	51°0·7′	4°27·6′W	FM	190
Becklands	Cumbr	NY3661	54°56·6′	2°59·5′W	X	85
Becklees	Cumbr	NY3571	55°2·0′	3°0·6′W	X	85
Beckley	Durham	NZ1956	54°54·1′	1°41·8′W	X	88
Beckley	E Susx	TQ8523	50°58·8′	0°38·5′E	T	189,199
Beckley	Hants	SZ2296	50°46·0′	1°40·9′W	T	195
Beckley	Oxon	SP5610	51°47·4′	1°10·9′W	T	164
Beckley Fm	Hants	SZ2196	50°46·0′	1°41·7′W	FM	195
Beckley Furnace	E Susx	TQ8321	50°57·8′	0°36·8′E	T	199
Beckley Hill	Kent	TQ7074	51°26·6′	0°27·2′E	X	178
Beckley Park	Oxon	SP5711	51°47·9′	1°10·0′W	A	164
Beckley Woods	E Susx	TQ8521	50°57·7′	0°38·5′E	F	189,199

Beck Lodge	Suff	TL7077	52°22·1′	0°30·2′E	X	143
Beck Meetings	N Yks	NY8203	54°25·6′	2°16·2′W	W	91,92
Beck Mill	Cumbr	NY5933	54°41·7′	2°37·7′W	X	91
Beckney Fm	Essex	TQ8495	51°37·6′	0°39·9′E	FM	168
Becknor Manor	Worcs	SO9461	52°15·1′	2°4·9′W	X	150
Beck Plantn	E Yorks	SE7858	54°1·0′	0°48·2′W	F	105,106
Beck Row	Suff	TL6977	52°22·1′	0°29·3′E	T	143
Becks	D & G	NY3484	55°9·0′	3°1·7′W	X	79
Beck Scar	Cumbr	NY0849	54°49·9′	3°25·5′W	X	85
Becks Drain	E Yorks	SE9744	53°53·2′	0°31·0′W	W	106
Becks Fm	N Yks	SE7761	54°2·6′	0°49·0′W	FM	100
Beck's Fm	Worcs	SO9463	52°16·1′	2°4·9′W	FM	150
Beck's Green	Suff	TM3884	52°24·4′	1°30·4′E	X	156
Beckside	Cumbr	NY0123	54°35·8′	3°31·5′W	X	89
Beckside	Cumbr	NY3571	55°2·0′	3°0·6′W	X	85
Beckside	Cumbr	NY3629	54°39·4′	2°59·1′W	X	90
Beckside	Cumbr	NY4128	54°38·9′	2°54·4′W	X	90
Beckside	Cumbr	SD1584	54°14·9′	3°17·9′W	X	96
Beck Side	Cumbr	SD2382	54°13·9′	3°10·5′W	T	96
Beck Side	Cumbr	SD2880	54°12·9′	3°5·8′W	X	96,97
Beck Side	Cumbr	SD3780	54°13·0′	2°57·5′W	T	96,97
Beckside	Cumbr	SD4595	54°21·1′	2°50·4′W	X	97
Beckside	Cumbr	SD4693	54°20·0′	2°49·4′W	X	97
Beckside	Cumbr	SD5588	54°17·4′	2°41·1′W	X	97
Beckside	Cumbr	SD6188	54°17·4′	2°35·5′W	T	97
Beckside	Cumbr	SD6290	54°18·5′	2°34·6′W	X	97
Beck Side	Cumbr	SD6995	54°21·2′	2°28·2′W	X	98
Beck Side	Durham	NZ0622	54°35·8′	1°54·0′W	X	92
Beck Side	N Yks	SD7994	54°20·7′	2°19·0′W	X	98
Beckside Fm	Cumbr	SD3185	54°15·6′	3°3·1′W	FM	96,97
Beckside Fm	Durham	NZ1130	54°40·1′	1°49·3′W	FM	92
Beckside Hall	Cumbr	SD6388	54°17·4′	2°33·7′W	X	97
Becksland	Thurr	TQ6679	51°29·4′	0°23·9′E	X	177,178
Becksteddle Fm	Hants	SU6930	51°4·1′	1°0·5′W	FM	186
Beckstonegate	Cumbr	NY5863	54°57·8′	2°38·9′W	X	86
Beckstones	Cumbr	NY4014	54°31·3′	2°55·2′W	X	90
Beckstones	Cumbr	NY7004	54°26·1′	2°27·3′W	X	91
Beckstones	Cumbr	SD1890	54°18·2′	3°15·2′W	X	96
Beck Stones	Cumbr	SD2585	54°15·6′	3°8·7′W	X	96
Beckstones Plantation	Cumbr	NY2125	54°37·1′	3°13·0′W	F	89,90
Becksyke Fm	N Yks	SE6432	53°47·1′	1°1·3′W	FM	105,106
Beck, The	Cumbr	NY3572	55°2·5′	3°0·6′W	X	85
Beck, The	Cumbr	NY5682	55°8·1′	2°41·0′W	W	80
Beck, The	Cumbr	SD1680	54°12·8′	3°16·9′W	X	96
Beck, The	E Yorks	SE7445	53°54·0′	0°52·0′W	W	105,106
Beck, The	Lincs	SK9351	53°3·1′	0°36·3′W	W	121
Beck, The	Lincs	TF1245	52°59·7′	0°19·5′W	W	130
Beck, The	Lincs	TF4366	53°10·5′	0°8·8′E	W	122
Beck, The	N Lincs	TA0622	53°41·3′	0°23·3′W	W	107,112
Beck, The	Notts	SK7161	53°8·7′	0°55·9′W	W	120
Beck, The	Notts	SK7862	53°9·2′	0°49·6′W	W	120,121
Beck, The	Suff	TM3284	52°24·5′	1°25·1′E	W	156
Beck, The	Worcs	SO7450	52°9·1′	2°22·4′W	H	150
Beckthorns	Cumbr	NY3220	54°34·5′	3°2·7′W	X	90
Beckton	D & G	NY1282	55°7·7′	3°22·4′W	X	78
Beckton	Newham	TQ4381	51°30·8′	0°4·0′E	T	177
Beckwith	N Yks	SE2852	53°58·0′	1°34·0′W	T	104
Beckwith Ho	N Yks	SE2852	53°58·0′	1°34·0′W	X	104
Beckwithshaw	N Yks	SE2652	53°58·0′	1°35·8′W	T	104
Beck Wood	Cumbr	SD1580	54°12·8′	3°17·8′W	F	96
Beck Wythop	Cumbr	NY2128	54°38·7′	3°13·0′W	X	89,90
Becontree	Bark & Dag	TQ4885	51°32·9′	0°8·5′E	T	177
Bectonhall	D & G	NY3072	55°2·5′	3°5·3′W	X	85
Beda Fell	Cumbr	NY4216	54°32·4′	2°53·4′W	X	90
Bedafell Knott	Cumbr	NY4216	54°32·4′	2°53·4′W	X	90
Beda Head	Cumbr	NY4217	54°32·9′	2°53·4′W	H	90
Bedale	N Yks	SE2688	54°17·5′	1°35·6′W	T	99
Bedale Beck	N Yks	SE2888	54°17·5′	1°33·8′W	X	99
Bedale Grange	N Yks	SE9684	54°14·8′	0°31·2′W	X	101
Bedales	W Susx	TQ3623	50°59·6′	0°3·3′W	X	198
Bedales Sch	Hants	SU7425	51°1·4′	0°56·3′W	X	186,197
Bedale Wood Fm	N Yks	SE2487	54°16·9′	1°37·5′W	FM	99
Bedborough Fm	Dorset	SU0501	50°48·7′	1°55·4′W	FM	195
Bedburn	Durham	NZ1031	54°40·7′	1°50·3′W	T	92
Bedburn Beck	Durham	NZ1031	54°40·7′	1°50·3′W	W	92
Bedchester	Dorset	ST8517	50°57·4′	2°12·4′W	T	183
Bedcow	E Dunb	NS6872	55°55·6′	4°6·3′W	X	64
Bedda Cleuch	Scot Bord	NY4788	55°11·3′	2°49·5′W	X	79
Bedda Hill	Scot Bord	NY4687	55°10·7′	2°50·4′W	H	79
Beddau	Rho Cyn Taf	ST0585	51°33·6′	3°21·8′W	T	170
Beddau'r Cewri	Powys	SJ0216	52°44·2′	3°26·7′W	A	125
Beddau'r Derwyddon	Carm	SN6618	51°50·9′	3°56·3′W	X	159
Beddau'r Derwyddon (Pillow Mounds)	Carm	SN6618	51°50·9′	3°56·3′W	A	159
Bedd Branwen	I of Angl	SH3684	53°19·9′	4°27·4′W	A	114
Bedd Crynddyn	Powys	SJ0528	52°50·7′	3°24·2′W	A	125
Beddgelert	Gwyn	SH5948	53°0·9′	4°5·7′W	T	115
Beddgelert Forest	Gwyn	SH5554	53°4·1′	4°9·4′W	F	115
Beddgelert Forest	Gwyn	SH5649	53°1·4′	4°8·4′W	F	115
Beddgeraint	Cered	SN3146	52°5·4′	4°27·6′W	X	145
Bedd Gwyl Illtyd	Powys	SN9726	51°55·6′	3°29·5′W	A	160
Beddingham	E Susx	TQ4407	50°50·9′	0°3·1′E	T	198
Beddingham Hill	E Susx	TQ4506	50°50·3′	0°4·0′E	X	198
Bedding Hill Moor	Lancs	SD9236	53°49·5′	2°6·9′W	X	103
Beddington	Sutton	TQ3065	51°22·4′	0°7·5′W	T	176,177
Beddington Corner	Sutton	TQ2866	51°22·9′	0°9·2′W	T	176
Beddington Park	Sutton	TQ2965	51°22·4′	0°8·4′W	X	176
Beddlestead Fm	Surrey	TQ3957	51°17·9′	0°0·0′E	FM	187
Beddlestone Fm	Kent	TR0743	51°9·1′	0°58·0′E	FM	179,189
Beddmanarch Bay	I of Angl	SH2780	53°17·6′	4°35·3′W	W	114
Bedd Morris	Pemb	SN0336	51°59·5′	4°51·8′W	X	145,157
Bedd Taliesin	Cered	SN6791	52°30·3′	3°57·2′W	A	135
Beddugre	Powys	SO1069	52°18·9′	3°18·8′W	X	136,148
Beddugre Hill	Powys	SO0870	52°19·5′	3°20·6′W	H	136,147
Bedd-y-cawr	Denb	SJ0171	53°13·9′	3°28·0′W	X	116
Bedd-y-coedwr	Gwyn	SH7428	52°50·3′	3°51·8′W	X	124
Beddyrafanc (Chambered Cairn)	Pemb	SN1034	51°58·6′	4°45·6′W	A	145
Bede Ho	Rut	SP8797	52°34·1′	0°42·6′W	A	141
Bedelands Fm	W Susx	TQ3220	50°58·1′	0°6·8′W	FM	198
Bedersaig	N Eil	NA9911	57°59·4′	7°5·2′W	T	13
Bede's Well	S Tyne	NZ3164	54°58·4′	1°30·5′W	A	88
Bedfield	Suff	TM2266	52°15·1′	1°15·5′E	T	156
Bedfield Little Green	Suff	TM2365	52°14·5′	1°16·4′E	X	156
Bedford	Beds	TL0549	52°8·0′	0°27·6′W	T	153
Bedford	Wigan	SJ6799	53°29·4′	2°29·4′W	T	109
Bedford Br	Devon	SX5070	50°30·9′	4°6·6′W	X	201
Bedford Fm	Suff	TL6783	52°25·4′	0°27·8′E	FM	143
Bedford Fm	Surrey	SU9038	51°8·3′	0°42·4′W	FM	186
Bedford Gap	Cambs	TL5553	52°9·4′	0°16·4′E	X	154
Bedford Grange	N Yks	SE7979	54°12·3′	0°46·9′W	X	100
Bedford Level (Middle Level)	Cambs	TL3590	52°29·7′	0°0·3′W	X	142
Bedford Level (North Level)	Peterb	TF2504	52°37·4′	0°8·8′W	X	142
Bedford Level (South Level)	Cambs	TL5681	52°24·5′	0°18·0′E	X	143
Bedford Moss	Wigan	SJ6997	53°28·4′	2°27·6′W	X	109
Bedford Park	Ealing	TQ2179	51°30·0′	0°15·0′W	T	176
Bedford Purlieus	Peterb	TL0499	52°35·0′	0°27·5′W	F	141
Bedfords	Essex	TL6120	51°51·5′	0°20·7′E	X	167
Bedfords	Essex	TL6313	51°47·7′	0°22·2′E	X	167
Bedfords Park	Hav	TQ5192	51°36·6′	0°11·2′E	X	177
Bedgebury Cross	Kent	TQ7134	51°5·0′	0°26·9′E	T	188
Bedgebury Forest	Kent	TQ7333	51°4·4′	0°28·6′E	F	188
Bedgebury Park Sch	Kent	TQ7234	51°5·0′	0°27·7′E	X	188
Bedgebury Pinetum	Kent	TQ7233	51°4·5′	0°27·7′E	X	188
Bedgrove	Bucks	SP8412	51°48·2′	0°46·5′W	T	165
Bedham	W Susx	TQ0121	50°59·0′	0°33·3′W	T	197
Bedhampton	Hants	SU7006	50°51·2′	0°59·9′W	T	197
Bedingfield	Suff	TM1868	52°16·2′	1°12·1′E	T	156
Bedingfield Green	Suff	TM1866	52°15·2′	1°12·0′E	X	156
Bedingfield Hall	Suff	TM1967	52°15·7′	1°13·0′E	X	156
Bedingfield Ho	Suff	TM1767	52°15·7′	1°11·2′E	X	156
Bedingham Green	Norf	TM2892	52°28·9′	1°21·9′E	T	134
Bedingham Hall Fm	Norf	TM2993	52°29·4′	1°22·8′E	FM	134
Bedlam	Cald	SE0032	53°47·3′	1°59·6′W	X	104
Bedlam	Cambs	TL4696	52°32·8′	0°9·6′E	X	143
Bedlam	Dorset	SY8593	50°44·4′	2°12·4′W	X	194
Bedlam	Lancs	SD7526	53°44·0′	2°22·3′W	X	103
Bedlam	Mil Key	SP9046	52°6·5′	0°40·7′W	X	152
Bedlam	N Yks	SE2661	54°2·9′	1°35·8′W	T	99
Bedlam	Shrops	SO5877	52°23·6′	2°36·6′W	X	137,138
Bedlam	Somer	ST7549	51°14·6′	2°21·1′W	T	183
Bedlam Bottom	Hants	SU6246	51°12·8′	1°6·4′W	X	185
Bedlam Br	Cambs	TL4694	52°31·7′	0°9·5′E	X	143
Bedlam Corner Fm	Cambs	TL4596	52°32·8′	0°8·7′E	FM	143
Bedlam Fm	Cambs	TL4564	52°15·5′	0°7·9′E	FM	154
Bedlam Fm	Cambs	TL4573	52°20·4′	0°8·1′E	FM	154
Bedlam Fm	Cambs	TL4695	52°32·2′	0°9·6′E	FM	143
Bedlam Green Fm	Somer	ST7333	51°6·0′	2°22·8′W	FM	183
Bedlam Hill	NE Lincs	TA2302	53°30·3′	0°8·3′W	X	113
Bedlam Lane	Kent	TQ8845	51°10·6′	0°41·8′E	X	189
Bedlams Bottom	Kent	TQ8868	51°23·0′	0°42·5′E	X	178
Bedlam Street	W Susx	TQ2715	50°55·5′	0°11·2′W	T	198
Bedlands Gate	Cumbr	NY5619	54°34·1′	2°40·4′W	X	90
Bedlar's Green	Essex	TL5220	51°51·7′	0°12·8′E	T	167
Bedlay Cas	N Lanak	NS6970	55°54·6′	4°5·3′W	A	64
Bedlington	Northum	NZ2681	55°7·6′	1°35·1′W	T	81
Bedlingtonlane Fm	Northum	NZ2581	55°7·6′	1°36·0′W	FM	81
Bedlington Station	Northum	NZ2782	55°8·1′	1°34·2′W	T	81
Bedlinog	Merth Tyd	SO0901	51°42·3′	3°18·6′W	T	171
Bedlormie	W Loth	NS8767	55°53·2′	3°48·0′W	A	65
Bedlormie Ho	W Loth	NS8867	55°53·2′	3°47·0′W	X	65
Bedlwyn	Caer	SO1404	51°43·9′	3°14·3′W	X	171
Bedlwyn Fm	Flint	SJ2355	53°5·4′	3°8·6′W	FM	117
Bedmill Fm	Dorset	ST6015	50°56·2′	2°33·8′W	FM	183
Bedminster	C of Bris	ST5871	51°26·4′	2°35·9′W	T	172
Bedminster Down	C of Bris	ST5769	51°25·3′	2°36·7′W	T	172,182
Bedmond	Herts	TL0903	51°43·1′	0°24·9′W	T	166
Bedmonton	Kent	TQ8758	51°17·6′	0°41·3′E	X	178
Bednall	Staffs	SJ9517	52°45·3′	2°4·0′W	T	127
Bednall Head	Staffs	SJ9617	52°45·3′	2°3·2′W	T	127
Bedol	Flint	SJ2274	53°15·7′	3°9·8′W	X	117
Bedport	Devon	SS6217	50°56·4′	3°57·5′W	X	180
Bedran	Powys	SJ1428	52°50·8′	3°16·2′W	X	125
Bedran	Powys	SO1788	52°29·3′	3°12·9′W	H	136
Bedrule	Scot Bord	NT6018	55°27·5′	2°37·5′W	T	80
Bedrule Mill	Scot Bord	NT5918	55°27·5′	2°38·5′W	X	80
Bedruthan Steps	Corn	SW8469	50°29·1′	5°2·3′W	X	200
Bedshiel	Scot Bord	NT6851	55°45·3′	2°30·2′W	X	67,74
Bedstone	Shrops	SO3675	52°22·4′	2°56·0′W	T	137,148
Bedstone Hill	Shrops	SO3575	52°22·4′	2°56·9′W	H	137,148
Bedw	Powys	SN9886	52°28·0′	3°29·7′W	X	136
Bedw	Powys	SO0645	52°6·0′	3°21·9′W	X	147
Bedwas	Caer	ST1789	51°35·9′	3°11·5′W	T	171
Bedwell	Herts	TL2424	51°54·3′	0°11·5′W	T	166
Bedwell	Wrex	SJ3646	53°0·7′	2°56·8′W	T	117
Bedwell Hey Fm	Cambs	TL5277	52°22·4′	0°14·4′E	FM	143
Bedwell Lodge Fm	Herts	TL2707	51°45·1′	0°9·2′W	FM	166
Bedwell Park	Herts	TL2707	51°45·1′	0°9·2′W	X	166
Bedwellpark Fm	Herts	TL2808	51°45·6′	0°8·3′W	FM	166
Bedwellty	Caer	SO1600	51°41·8′	3°12·5′W	T	171
Bedwellty Pits	Blae Gw	SO1506	51°45·0′	3°13·5′W	T	161
Bedw-hir	Powys	SO0543	52°4·9′	3°22·8′W	X	147,160
Bedw-Hirion	Carm	SN4534	51°59·2′	4°15·0′W	X	146
Bedwindle Fm	Corn	SX1362	50°25·9′	4°37·6′W	FM	200
Bedwin Sands	Monm	ST4783	51°32·8′	2°45·5′W	X	171,172
Bedwlwyn	Powys	SN9225	51°55·0′	3°33·8′W	X	160
Bedwlwyn	Wrex	SJ2236	52°55·2′	3°9·2′W	T	126
Bedworth	Warw	SP3586	52°28·5′	1°28·7′W	T	140
Bedworth Heath	Warw	SP3486	52°28·5′	1°29·6′W	T	140
Bedworth Woodlands	Warw	SP3487	52°29·0′	1°29·6′W	T	140
Bedwyn	Conwy	SH9167	53°11·6′	3°37·5′W	X	116
Bedwyn Brail	Wilts	SU2862	51°21·6′	1°35·5′W	F	174
Bedwyn Common	Wilts	SU2565	51°23·2′	1°38·1′W	X	174
Bedwyn Dyke	Wilts	SU2864	51°22·7′	1°35·5′W	A	174
Bedwyn Dyke	Wilts	SU2964	51°22·7′	1°34·6′W	A	174
Bedwyn Sta	Wilts	SU2864	51°22·7′	1°35·5′W	X	174
Beeby	Leic	SK6608	52°40·2′	1°1·0′W	T	141
Beeby Grange	Leic	SK6608	52°40·2′	1°1·0′W	X	141
Beeby House Fm	Leic	SK6609	52°40·7′	1°1·0′W	FM	141
Beeby Spring Grange	Leic	SK6708	52°40·2′	1°0·1′W	X	141
Beech	Hants	SU6938	51°8·5′	1°0·4′W	T	186
Beech	Staffs	SJ8538	52°56·6′	2°13·0′W	T	127
Beecham Fm	Warw	SP2250	52°9·1′	1°40·3′W	FM	151
Beechbank	Aberd	NJ5664	57°40·1′	2°43·8′W	X	29
Beech Barrow	Hants	SU3231	51°4·9′	1°32·2′W	A	185
Beech Bed Inclosure	Hants	SU2206	50°51·4′	1°40·9′W	F	195
Beechburn Beck	Durham	NZ1632	54°41·2′	1°44·7′W	W	92
Beechburn Fm	Durham	NZ1731	54°40·7′	1°43·8′W	FM	92
Beechbush	D & G	NY1773	55°2·9′	3°17·5′W	X	85
Beechcliff	Staffs	SJ8538	52°56·6′	2°13·0′W	T	127
Beechcliffe	Brad	SE0542	53°52·7′	1°55·0′W	T	104
Beechcombe Fm	Devon	SX4886	50°39·5′	4°8·7′W	FM	191,201
Beech Copse	S Glos	ST7782	51°32·4′	2°19·5′W	F	172
Beech Copse	Somer	ST2130	51°4·1′	3°7·3′W	F	182
Beech Court	Kent	TQ9950	51°13·1′	0°51·4′E	X	189
Beech Court Fm	V of Glam	SS9076	51°28·6′	3°34·6′W	FM	170
Beechcroft Fm	Kent	TR0426	51°0·1′	0°54·8′E	FM	189
Beechcroft Fm	Norf	TG2434	52°51·6′	1°20·1′E	FM	133
Beechcroft Fm	Northnts	SP5153	52°10·6′	1°14·9′W	FM	151
Beechdown Wood	E Susx	TQ7116	50°55·3′	0°26·4′E	F	199
Beechenbank Wood	Heref	SO4165	52°17·0′	2°51·5′W	F	137,148,149
Beechen Cliff	Bath & NE Somer	ST7564	51°22·7′	2°21·2′W	T	172
Beechengrove Wood	Herts	TQ0497	51°40·0′	0°29·4′W	F	166,176
Beechenhill	Staffs	SK1252	53°4·1′	1°48·8′W	X	119
Beechen Wood	E Susx	TQ5132	51°4·3′	0°9·7′E	F	188
Beechen Wood	Kent	TQ5164	51°21·5′	0°10·5′E	F	177,188
Beechenwood Fm	Kent	TQ4542	51°9·8′	0°4·8′E	FM	188
Beeches	Herts	TL4430	51°57·2′	0°6·1′E	A	167
Beeches	Wrex	SJ4045	53°0·2′	2°53·2′W	X	117
Beeches Fm	Essex	TQ7994	51°37·2′	0°35·5′E	FM	167,178
Beeches Fm	E Susx	TQ4520	50°57·9′	0°4·3′E	FM	198
Beeches Fm	E Susx	TQ4537	51°7·1′	0°4·7′E	FM	188
Beeches Fm	Flint	SJ3466	53°11·5′	2°58·9′W	FM	117
Beeches Fm	Hants	SU4334	51°6·5′	1°22·8′W	FM	185
Beeches Fm	Kent	TQ5867	51°23·0′	0°16·6′E	FM	177
Beeches Fm	Kent	TQ7829	51°2·2′	0°32·7′E	FM	188,199
Beeches Fm	Kent	TR2951	51°13·0′	1°17·1′E	FM	179
Beeches Fm	Leic	SP5695	52°33·2′	1°10·0′W	FM	140
Beeches Fm	Lincs	TF5570	53°12·5′	0°19·7′E	FM	122
Beeches Fm	Northnts	SP5557	52°12·7′	1°11·3′W	FM	152
Beeches Fm	Somer	ST2316	50°56·5′	3°5·4′W	FM	193
Beeches Fm	Surrey	TQ4341	51°9·2′	0°3·1′E	FM	187
Beeches, The	Devon	SS5541	51°9·2′	4°4·0′W	X	180
Beeches, The	Lincs	TF1875	53°15·8′	0°13·4′W	X	122
Beeches, The	Lincs	TF3154	53°4·3′	0°2·3′W	X	122
Beeches,The	Lincs	TF4522	52°46·8′	0°9·4′E	X	131
Beeches, The	Norf	TL9789	52°28·0′	0°54·4′E	X	144
Beeches, The	Norf	TM2084	52°24·8′	1°14·5′E	X	156
Beeches, The	N Yks	SE9770	54°7·2′	0°30·5′W	X	101
Beeches, The	Oxon	SP4725	51°55·5′	1°18·6′W	X	164
Beeches, The	Shrops	SJ2803	52°37·4′	3°3·4′W	X	126
Beeches, The	Shrops	SJ3239	52°56·9′	3°0·3′W	X	126
Beeches, The	Shrops	SJ5339	52°57·0′	2°41·6′W	X	126
Beeches, The	Staffs	SO8493	52°32·3′	2°13·8′W	X	138
Beeches, The	Warw	SP1272	52°21·0′	1°49·0′W	X	139
Beeches Way	Brackn	SU8765	51°22·9′	0°44·6′W	X	175,176
Beech Farm Ho	E Susx	TQ7719	50°56·8′	0°31·6′E	X	199
Beechfield	Surrey	TQ3240	51°8·9′	0°6·4′W	X	187
Beechfield	W Susx	TQ0022	50°59·5′	0°34·1′W	X	197
Beechfield Cott	Aberd	NJ8018	57°15·4′	2°19·4′W	X	38
Beechfield Ho	Shrops	SJ4111	52°41·8′	2°52·0′W	X	126
Beechfield Ho	Wilts	ST9065	51°23·3′	2°8·2′W	X	173
Beech Fm	Ches	SJ7976	53°17·1′	2°18·5′W	FM	118
Beech Fm	Ches	SJ8684	53°21·4′	2°12·2′W	FM	109
Beech Fm	Dorset	SY7486	50°40·6′	2°21·7′W	FM	194
Beech Fm	E Susx	TQ7224	50°59·6′	0°27·5′E	FM	199
Beech Fm	E Susx	TQ7316	50°55·3′	0°28·1′E	FM	199
Beech Fm	Hants	SU2835	51°7·0′	1°35·6′W	FM	184
Beech Fm	Herts	TL1909	51°46·2′	0°16·1′W	FM	166
Beech Fm	Monm	SO3201	51°42·5′	2°58·7′W	FM	171
Beech Fm	Norf	TM2393	52°29·6′	1°17·5′E	FM	134
Beech Fm	Norf	TM4893	52°28·9′	1°39·6′E	FM	134
Beech Fm	Notts	SK6484	53°21·2′	1°1·9′W	FM	111,120
Beech Fm	N Yks	SE7158	54°1·0′	0°54·6′W	FM	105,106
Beech Fm	Oxon	SU6282	51°32·2′	1°6·0′W	FM	175
Beech Fm	Oxon	SU6378	51°30·1′	1°5·1′W	FM	175
Beech Fm	Surrey	TQ3857	51°17·9′	0°0·8′W	FM	187
Beech Fm	W Susx	TQ2925	51°0·8′	0°9·3′W	FM	187,198
Beech Green Park	E Susx	TQ4838	51°7·6′	0°7·3′E	X	188
Beechgrove	D & G	NY2165	54°58·7′	3°13·6′W	X	85
Beechgrove	Fife	NO3513	56°18·6′	3°2·6′W	X	59
Beech Grove	Lancs	SD4135	53°48·7′	2°53·4′W	X	102
Beech Grove	Leeds	SE3540	53°51·5′	1°27·7′W	X	104
Beech Grove	N Lincs	TA0521	53°40·7′	0°24·2′W	X	107,112
Beech Grove	Staffs	SJ8226	52°50·1′	2°15·6′W	X	127
Beechgrove Fm	Bucks	SU7799	51°41·3′	0°52·8′W	FM	165
Beechgrove Fm	C of Edin	NT1365	55°52·5′	3°23·0′W	FM	65
Beech Grove Fm	Durham	NZ2250	54°50·9′	1°39·0′W	FM	88
Beech Hall	Ches	SJ9174	53°16·0′	2°7·7′W	X	118
Beech Hanger Copse	Hants	SU4255	51°17·8′	1°23·5′W	F	174,185
Beech Hill	Cumbr	NY1124	54°36·4′	3°22·3′W	X	89
Beech Hill	Cumbr	NY1139	54°44·5′	3°22·5′W	X	89
Beechhill	Cumbr	NY1545	54°47·8′	3°18·9′W	X	85
Beech Hill	Cumbr	NY5002	54°24·9′	2°45·8′W	X	90
Beech Hill	Devon	SS7808	50°51·8′	3°43·6′W	X	191
Beech Hill	E Loth	NT5470	55°55·5′	2°43·7′W	X	66
Beech Hill	Herts	TL1125	51°55·0′	0°22·8′W	X	166
Beech Hill	Monm	SO3701	51°42·5′	2°54·3′W	X	171
Beech Hill	Monm	SO4022	51°53·8′	2°51·9′W	X	161
Beech Hill	N Yks	SE4296	54°21·7′	1°20·8′W	X	99
Beech Hill	W Berks	SU6964	51°22·5′	1°0·1′W	T	175,186
Beech Hill	Wigan	SD5607	53°33·7′	2°39·4′W	T	108
Beechhill Fm	Derby	SK2846	53°0·9′	1°34·6′W	FM	119,128
Beech Hill Fm	E Susx	TQ6216	50°55·5′	0°18·7′E	FM	199
Beech Hill Fm	Notts	SK7099	53°29·2′	0°56·3′W	FM	112
Beech Hill Ho	W Berks	SU7064	51°22·5′	0°59·3′W	X	175,186

Beech Hill Hotel	Cumbr	SD3892	54°19·4'	2°56·8'W	X	96,97
Beech Hill Wood	Notts	SK6463	53°9·9'	1°2·2'W	F	120
Beech Ho	Ches	SJ6364	53°10·6'	2°32·8'W	X	118
Beech Ho	Hants	SZ2097	50°46·6'	1°42·6'W	X	195
Beech Ho	Lancs	SD3949	53°56·3'	2°55·3'W	X	102
Beech Ho Fm	Staffs	SJ8537	52°56·1'	2°13·0'W	FM	127
Beech Ho Stud	Cambs	TL6762	52°14·1'	0°27·1'E	X	154
Beech House Fm	Ches	SJ7275	53°16·5'	2°24·8'W	FM	118
Beech House Fm	E Susx	TQ7425	51°0·1'	0°29·2'E	FM	188,199
Beech House Fm	Lincs	TF2549	53°1·7'	0°7·8'W	FM	131
Beech House Fm	Northnts	SP7643	52°5·0'	0°53·1'W	FM	152
Beech Hyde	Herts	TL1108	51°45·8'	0°23·1'W	X	166
Beech Hyde Fm	Herts	TL1813	51°48·4'	0°16·9'W	FM	166
Beechingstoke	Wilts	SU0859	51°20·0'	1°52·7'W	T	173
Beechland	E Susx	TQ4120	50°58·0'	0°0·9'E	X	198
Beechlane Fm	Ches	SJ5764	53°10·5'	2°38·2'W	FM	117
Beech Lane Fm	S Glos	ST8087	51°35·1'	2°16·9'W	FM	173
Beech Lanes	Birm	SP0185	52°28·0'	1°58·7'W	T	139
Beechmeadow Fm	Glos	SO7503	51°43·7'	2°21·3'W	FM	162
Beechmoor Fm	Bucks	SP8120	51°52·6'	0°49·0'W	FM	165
Beechpike	Glos	SO9610	51°47·6'	2°3·1'W	X	163
Beech Tree	Worcs	SO8680	52°25·3'	2°12·0'W	X	139
Beech Tree Fm	Kent	TQ9531	51°2·9'	0°47·3'E	FM	189
Beechtree Fm	Lincs	TF2718	52°44·9'	0°6·7'W	FM	131
Beech Tree Fm	Suff	TM0175	52°20·4'	0°57·4'E	FM	144
Beech Tree Fm	Suff	TM5088	52°26·2'	1°41·1'E	FM	156
Beech Tree Ho	N Yks	SE6977	54°11·3'	0°56·1'W	X	100
Beech Wood	Ches	SJ8575	53°16·5'	2°13·1'W	F	118
Beechwood	Devon	SX4379	50°35·6'	4°12·7'W	X	201
Beechwood	Devon	SX5757	50°24·0'	4°0·4'W	X	202
Beechwood	D & G	NY3170	55°1·4'	3°4·3'W	X	85
Beechwood	Halton	SJ5380	53°19·1'	2°41·9'W	T	108
Beechwood	Highld	NH6944	57°28·3'	4°10·6'W	T	26
Beechwood	Leeds	SE3436	53°49·4'	1°28·6'W	X	104
Beechwood	Leeds	SE3437	53°49·9'	1°28·6'W	X	104
Beechwood	Newp	ST3388	51°35·4'	2°57·6'W	T	171
Beech Wood	N Yks	SE5981	54°13·5'	1°5·3'W	F	100
Beechwood	Oxon	SU7094	51°38·7'	0°58·9'W	X	175
Beechwood	Scot Bord	NT4527	55°32·3'	2°51·9'W	X	73
Beechwood	Sol	SP2676	52°23·1'	1°36·7'W	T	140
Beech Wood	W Berks	SU5376	51°29·1'	1°13·8'W	F	174
Beechwood	W Susx	TQ2133	51°5·2'	0°15·9'W	X	187
Beechwood Fm	Norf	TL5097	52°33·2'	0°13·2'E	FM	143
Beech Wood Fm	Notts	SK6580	53°19·0'	1°1·0'W	FM	111,120
Beechwood Fm	Oxon	SU6788	51°32·2'	1°1·6'W	FM	175
Beechwood Fm	Devon	SS6020	50°58·0'	3°59·2'W	X	180
Beechwood Ho	E Susx	TQ3814	50°54·8'	0°1·8'W	X	198
Beechwood Ho	E Yorks	SE7354	53°58·9'	0°52·8'W	X	105,106
Beechwood Ho	Hants	SU2912	50°54·6'	1°34·9'W	X	196
Beechwood Ho	Herts	TL0414	51°49·1'	0°29·1'W	A	166
Beechy Dean Copse	Wilts	SU1930	51°4·4'	1°43·3'W	F	184
Beechy House Fm	Lincs	TF0689	53°23·5'	0°24·0'W	FM	112,121
Bee Cott	Pth & Kin	NO0539	56°32·3'	3°32·2'W	X	52,53
Bee Cottage Fm	Durham	NZ0645	54°48·2'	1°54·0'W	FM	87
Beecraigs	W Loth	NT0073	55°56·6'	3°35·6'W	X	65
Beecraigs Country Park	W Loth	NT0073	55°56·6'	3°35·6'W	F	65
Beecroft	Beds	TL0022	51°53·5'	0°32·4'W	T	166
Beecroft	N Yks	SD8156	54°0·2'	2°17·0'W	X	103
Beecroft Hall	N Yks	SD7972	54°8·8'	2°18·9'W	X	98
Beecroft Moor Plantn	N Yks	SE1753	53°58·6'	1°44·0'W	F	104
Bee Dale	N Yks	SE9586	54°15·9'	0°32·1'W	X	94,101
Beedale Beck	N Yks	SE9684	54°14·8'	0°31·2'W	W	101
Beedale Beck	N Yks	SE9685	54°15·3'	0°31·2'W	W	94,101
Beeding Hill	W Susx	TQ2109	50°52·3'	0°16·4'W	X	198
Beedinglee	W Susx	TQ2126	51°1·5'	0°16·1'W	X	187,198
Beedings	W Susx	TQ0720	50°58·4'	0°28·2'W	X	197
Beedingwood House	W Susx	TQ2132	51°4·7'	0°16·0'W	X	187
Beedon	W Berks	SU4878	51°30·2'	1°18·1'W	T	174
Beedon Common	W Berks	SU4776	51°29·1'	1°19·0'W	X	174
Beedon Hill	W Berks	SU4877	51°29·6'	1°18·1'W	T	174
Beedon Ho	W Berks	SU4877	51°29·6'	1°18·1'W	X	174
Beedon Manor	W Berks	SU4878	51°30·2'	1°18·1'W	X	174
Bee Edge	Scot Bord	NT8964	55°52·4'	2°10·1'W	X	67
Beef Barrel, The	D & G	NX0273	55°1·0'	5°5·4'W	X	76,82
Beef Neck	I Scilly	SV8916	49°58·0'	6°19·9'W	W	203
Beeford	E Yorks	TA1254	53°58·4'	0°17·1'W	T	107
Beeford Grange	E Yorks	TA1355	53°59·0'	0°16·2'W	X	107
Beef Stand	Northum	NT8213	55°24·9'	2°16·6'W	H	80
Beefstand Hill	Northum	NT8214	55°25·4'	2°16·6'W	H	80
Beehive Fm	Ches	SJ6569	53°13·3'	2°31·0'W	FM	118
Beehive Fm	Somer	ST2714	50°55·5'	3°1·9'W	FM	193
Beehive Hut	Devon	SX6381	50°37·0'	3°55·8'W	A	191
Beek's Fm	S Glos	ST7671	51°26·5'	2°20·3'W	FM	172
Beeleigh Abbey	Essex	TL8307	51°44·1'	0°39·4'E	A	168
Beeleigh Fms	Essex	TL8307	51°44·1'	0°39·4'E	FM	168
Beeleigh Grange Fm	Essex	TL8307	51°44·1'	0°39·4'E	FM	168
Beeley	Derby	SK2667	53°12·2'	1°36·2'W	T	119
Beeley Hilltop	Derby	SK2668	53°12·7'	1°36·2'W	A	119
Beeley Lodge	Derby	SK2668	53°12·7'	1°36·2'W	X	119
Beeley Moor	Derby	SK2967	53°12·2'	1°33·5'W	X	119
Beeley Plantn	Derby	SK2767	53°12·2'	1°35·3'W	F	119
Beeley Wood	Sheff	SK3192	53°25·7'	1°31·6'W	F	110,111
Bee Low	Derby	SK0979	53°18·7'	1°51·5'W	H	119
Bee Low	Derby	SK1964	53°10·6'	1°42·5'W	A	119
Beelow Hill	Staffs	SK0644	52°59·8'	1°54·2'W	H	119,128
Beelsby	NE Lincs	TA2001	53°29·8'	0°11·0'W	T	113
Bee Ness Jetty	Medway	TQ8472	51°25·2'	0°39·2'E	X	178
Beenham	W Berks	SU5868	51°24·7'	1°9·6'W	T	174
Beenham Grange	W Berks	SU5967	51°24·2'	1°8·7'W	X	174
Beenham Hill	W Berks	SU5968	51°24·7'	1°8·7'W	X	174
Beenham Ho	W Berks	SU6069	51°25·2'	1°7·8'W	X	175
Beenham's Heath	Win & Maid	SU8475	51°28·3'	0°47·0'W	T	175
Beenham Stocks	W Berks	SU5968	51°24·7'	1°8·7'W	X	174
Beenleigh	Devon	SX7556	50°23·7'	3°45·1'W	X	202
Beenleigh	Devon	SX7956	50°23·7'	3°41·8'W	X	202
Beeny	Corn	SX1192	50°42·1'	4°40·2'W	T	190
Beeny Cliff	Corn	SX1092	50°42·0'	4°41·1'W	X	190
Beeny Sisters	Corn	SX1093	50°42·6'	4°41·1'W	X	190
Beepark Copse	Corn	SX2787	50°39·7'	4°26·5'W	F	190
Beer	Devon	SS5804	50°49·3'	4°0·6'W	X	191

Beer	Devon	SX6395	50°44·5'	3°56·1'W	X	191
Beer	Devon	SY2289	50°42·0'	3°5·9'W	T	192
Beer	Somer	ST4031	51°4·7'	2°51·0'W	T	182
Beera	Devon	SS6513	50°54·3'	3°54·8'W	X	180
Beera Fm	Devon	SX4076	50°33·9'	4°15·2'W	FM	201
Beer Beck	Durham	NY9922	54°35·8'	2°0·5'W	W	92
Beer Crocombe	Somer	ST3220	50°58·8'	2°57·7'W	T	193
Beer Door	Somer	ST4031	51°4·7'	2°51·0'W	X	182
Beer Down	Somer	ST0118	50°57·4'	3°24·2'W	X	181
Beer Down Fm	Devon	ST0117	50°56·9'	3°24·2'W	FM	181
Beere Fm	Devon	SS8227	51°2·1'	3°40·6'W	FM	181
Beere Manor Fm	Somer	ST2441	51°10·0'	3°4·8'W	FM	182
Beer Fm	Devon	SS8411	50°53·4'	3°38·6'W	FM	191
Beer Fm	Devon	ST1003	50°49·4'	3°16·3'W	FM	192,193
Beer Fm	Somer	SS8926	51°1·6'	3°34·6'W	FM	181
Beer Furlong Buildings	Glos	SP1906	51°45·4'	1°43·1'W	X	163
Beer Hackett	Dorset	ST5911	50°54·1'	2°34·6'W	T	194
Beerhall Fm	Devon	ST3501	50°48·5'	2°55·0'W	FM	193
Beer Head	Devon	SY2287	50°40·9'	3°5·9'W	X	192
Beerhill	Devon	SS6302	50°48·3'	3°56·3'W	X	191
Beerhouse Fm	Norf	TG1425	52°47·0'	1°10·8'E	FM	133
Beer Mill Fm	Somer	ST3220	50°58·8'	2°57·7'W	FM	193
Beer Moors	Somer	SS8826	51°1·6'	3°35·4'W	X	181
Beer Roads	Devon	SY2388	50°41·4'	3°5·0'W	W	192
Beers	Devon	SS7502	50°48·5'	3°46·1'W	X	191
Beerway Fm	Somer	ST4238	51°8·5'	2°49·4'W	FM	182
Beesands	Devon	SX8140	50°15·1'	3°39·8'W	T	202
Beesby	Lincs	TF4680	53°18·0'	0°11·9'E	T	122
Beesby	NE Lincs	TF2696	53°27·0'	0°5·7'W	X	113
Beesby Grange	Lincs	TF4680	53°18·0'	0°11·9'E	X	122
Beesby Top	NE Lincs	TF2596	53°27·0'	0°6·6'W	X	113
Beesby Village	NE Lincs	TF2696	53°27·0'	0°5·7'W	A	113
Beesfield Fm	Kent	TQ5566	51°22·5'	0°14·0'E	FM	177
Bee Skerries	Orkney	HY6824	59°6·4'	2°33·0'W	X	5
Beesknowe	E Loth	NT6276	55°58·8'	2°36·1'W	X	67
Beeslack	Midlo	NT2461	55°50·4'	3°12·4'W	T	66
Beesley's Fm	Lancs	SD5138	53°50·4'	2°44·3'W	FM	102
Beeson	Devon	SX8140	50°15·1'	3°39·8'W	T	202
Beesonend Fm	Herts	TL1311	51°47·4'	0°21·3'W	FM	166
Beesons, The	Cambs	TL4578	52°23·1'	0°8·2'E	X	143
Beesthorpe Hall	Notts	SK7260	53°8·2'	0°55·0'W	X	120
Beeston	Beds	TL1648	52°7·3'	0°17·9'W	T	153
Beeston	Ches	SJ5458	53°7·3'	2°40·8'W	T	117
Beeston	Leeds	SE2830	53°46·2'	1°34·1'W	T	104
Beeston	Norf	TF9015	52°42·2'	0°49·1'E	T	132
Beeston	Notts	SK5236	52°55·4'	1°13·2'W	T	129
Beeston Canal	C of Nott	SK5536	52°55·4'	1°10·5'W	W	129
Bee Stone Fm	N Yks	SE6893	54°19·9'	0°56·8'W	FM	94,100
Beeston Gate Fm	Ches	SJ5558	53°7·3'	2°39·9'W	FM	117
Beeston Hall	Norf	TG3321	52°44·4'	1°27·5'E	X	133,134
Beeston Hall Fm	Ches	SJ5459	53°7·8'	2°40·8'W	FM	117
Beeston Hill	Leeds	SE2931	53°46·7'	1°33·2'W	T	104
Beeston Leasoes Fm	Beds	TL1347	52°6·8'	0°20·6'W	FM	153
Beeston Moss	Ches	SJ5558	53°7·3'	2°39·9'W	X	117
Beeston Park	Norf	TG2513	52°40·3'	1°20·1'E	X	133,134
Beeston Park Side	Leeds	SE2929	53°45·6'	1°33·2'W	T	104
Beeston Plantation	Donc	SK5899	53°29·3'	1°7·1'W	F	111
Beeston Regis	Norf	TG1642	52°56·1'	1°13·3'E	T	133
Beeston Royds	Leeds	SE2630	53°46·2'	1°35·9'W	T	104
Beestons	E Susx	TQ6016	50°55·5'	0°17·0'E	X	199
Beeston's Fm	Suff	TM1749	52°6·0'	1°10·5'E	FM	169
Beeston St Lawrence	Norf	TG3221	52°44·4'	1°26·6'E	T	133,134
Beeston Tor	Staffs	SK1054	53°5·2'	1°50·6'W	X	119
Beeswing	D & G	NX8969	55°0·4'	3°43·7'W	T	84
Beet Fm	Derby	SK0583	53°20·9'	1°55·1'W	FM	110
Beetham	Cumbr	SD4979	54°12·5'	2°46·5'W	T	97
Beetham	Somer	ST2712	50°54·4'	3°1·9'W	T	193
Beetham Bank	Cumbr	SD5197	54°22·2'	2°44·8'W	X	97
Beetley	Norf	TF9717	52°43·1'	0°55·4'E	T	132
Beetley Hall	Norf	TF9718	52°43·7'	0°55·5'E	X	132
Beetor Fm	Devon	SX7184	50°38·7'	3°49·1'W	FM	191
Beet, The	Derby	SK0374	53°16·0'	1°56·9'W	X	119
Beetylands Park	D & G	NY1468	55°0·2'	3°20·2'W	X	85
Beever's Br	E Yorks	SE6619	53°40·0'	0°59·7'W	X	111
Beezley Falls	N Yks	SD7074	54°9·9'	2°27·2'W	W	98
Beezleys	N Yks	SD7074	54°9·9'	2°27·2'W	X	98
Beezling Fen	Cambs	TL3688	52°28·6'	0°0·6'E	X	142
Beffcote	Staffs	SJ8019	52°46·3'	2°17·4'W	T	127
Began	Card	ST2283	51°32·7'	3°7·1'W	T	171
Begbie	E Loth	NT4970	55°55·5'	2°48·5'W	X	66
Begbie Wood	E Loth	NT4970	55°55·5'	2°48·5'W	F	66
Begbroke	Oxon	SP4713	51°49·1'	1°18·7'W	T	164
Begbroke Hill	Oxon	SP4713	51°49·1'	1°18·7'W	X	164
Begbroke Wood	Oxon	SP4613	51°49·1'	1°19·6'W	F	164
Begburn	Aberd	NJ5457	57°36·3'	2°45·7'W	X	29
Begdale	Cambs	TF4506	52°38·2'	0°9·0'E	T	143
Begelly	Pemb	SN1107	51°44·0'	4°44·3'W	T	158
Beggar Bogg	Northum	NY7968	55°0·6'	2°19·3'W	X	86,87
Beggarbush Hill	Oxon	SU6390	51°36·5'	1°5·0'W	X	164,175
Beggar Hall	N Yks	SE4857	54°0·6'	1°15·6'W	X	105
Beggar Hill	Essex	TL6301	51°41·3'	0°21·9'E	T	167
Beggar Hill	Lincs	SE8902	53°30·7'	0°39·1'W	X	112
Beggarhill Brook Fm	Shrops	SO6397	52°34·4'	2°32·4'W	FM	138
Beggarington Hill	Kirk	SE2724	53°42·9'	1°35·0'W	T	104
Beggarington Hill	Leeds	SE2724	53°42·9'	1°35·0'W	H	104
Beggarmire Wood	N Yks	SE1792	54°19·6'	1°44·2'W	F	99
Beggars Ash	Heref	SO7039	52°3·2'	2°25·9'W	T	149
Beggars' Barn Fm	Kent	TQ5244	51°10·7'	0°10·9'E	FM	188
Beggar's Bridge Fm	Cambs	TL3296	52°33·0'	0°3·4'W	FM	142
Beggar's Bush	Devon	SX8979	50°36·2'	3°33·7'W	X	192
Beggars Bush	E Susx	TQ6031	51°3·6'	0°17·4'E	X	188
Beggar's Bush	Powys	SO2664	52°16·4'	3°4·7'W	X	137,148
Beggars Bush	W Susx	TQ1607	50°51·3'	0°20·7'W	T	198
Beggars Bush	W Susx	TQ1715	50°55·6'	0°19·7'W	X	198
Beggar's Cap	E Loth	NT6283	56°2·6'	2°36·2'W	X	67
Beggar's Hall	Essex	TL5220	51°51·7'	0°12·8'E	X	167
Beggar's Knoll	Wilts	ST8850	51°15·2'	2°9·9'W	X	183
Beggars Pound	V of Glam	ST0168	51°24·4'	3°25·0'W	T	170
Beggars Reach	Pemb	SN0008	51°44·3'	4°53·4'W	W	157,158
Beggearn Huish	Somer	ST0439	51°8·8'	3°22·0'W	T	181

Begg Fm, The	Fife	NT2595	56°8·8'	3°12·0'W	FM	59
Beggshill	Aberd	NJ5938	57°26·1'	2°40·5'W	X	29
Begin Hill	Cumbr	NY7106	54°27·2'	2°26·4'W	X	91
Begley Fm	Surrey	SU9037	51°7·7'	0°42·4'W	FM	186
Begoade	I of M	SC4080	54°11·7'	4°26·7'W	X	95
Begrow	Moray	NJ1668	57°41·9'	3°24·1'W	X	28
Begrums	Essex	TQ6397	51°39·1'	0°21·8'E	X	167,177
Begsley	C of Aber	NJ8313	57°12·7'	2°16·4'W	X	38
Beguildy	Powys	SO1979	52°24·4'	3°11·0'W	T	136,148
Begwary	Beds	TL1257	52°12·2'	0°21·3'W	X	153
Begwary Brook	Beds	TL1256	52°11·7'	0°21·3'W	W	153
Begwns, The	Powys	SO1544	52°5·5'	3°14·0'W	H	148,161
Behinties	Aberd	NJ5410	57°11·0'	2°45·2'W	X	37
Behrens Whin	N Yks	SE7680	54°12·8'	0°49·7'W	F	100
Beich Burn	Stir	NN6227	56°25·2'	4°13·8'W	W	51
Beidig	N Eil	NB0310	57°59·1'	7°1·0'W	H	13
Beidiog Isa	Conwy	SH9264	53°10·0'	3°36·5'W	X	116
Beidiog Ucha	Conwy	SH9163	53°9·4'	3°37·4'W	X	116
Beidleston	C of Aber	NJ8515	57°13·8'	2°14·5'W	X	38
Beighterton House Fm	Staffs	SJ8011	52°42·0'	2°17·4'W	FM	127
Beighton	Norf	TG3807	52°36·7'	1°31·3'E	T	134
Beighton	Sheff	SK4483	53°20·8'	1°19·9'W	T	111,120
Beightonfields Priory	Derby	SK4576	53°17·0'	1°19·1'W	X	120
Beighton Hill	Derby	SK2951	53°3·6'	1°33·6'W	T	119
Beighton Marshes	Norf	TG4606	52°36·0'	1°38·4'E	X	134
Beighton's Gorse	Lincs	SK9248	53°1·5'	0°37·3'W	F	130
Beilby Wood	Leeds	SE4046	53°54·8'	1°23·0'W	F	105
Beili	Carm	SN3827	51°55·3'	4°21·0'W	X	145
Beili	Cered	SN3352	52°8·7'	4°26·0'W	X	145
Beili	Powys	SN8883	52°26·3'	3°38·5'W	X	135,136
Beili	Powys	SO0460	52°14·0'	3°23·9'W	X	147
Beiliau	Monm	SO3814	51°49·5'	2°53·6'W	X	161
Beiliau	Powys	SO1518	51°51·5'	3°13·7'W	X	161
Beilibedw	Carm	SN4940	52°2·5'	4°11·7'W	X	146
Beili Bedw	Carm	SN5832	51°58·3'	4°3·6'W	X	146
Beili-bedw	Carm	SN7423	51°53·7'	3°49·5'W	X	160
Beili-bedw	Powys	SN9128	51°56·6'	3°34·8'W	X	160
Beilibedw Mawn Pool	Powys	SO1656	52°12·0'	3°13·4'W	W	148
Beili-coch	Carm	SN5746	52°5·9'	4°4·9'W	X	146
Beili-Ficer	Carm	SN6336	52°0·6'	3°59·4'W	X	146
Beili glas	Carm	SN4527	51°55·4'	4°14·9'W	X	146
Beili-glâs	Carm	SN5419	51°51·3'	4°6·8'W	X	159
Beili-glâs	Carm	SN7830	51°57·5'	3°46·1'W	X	146,160
Beili-glas	Monm	SO3010	51°47·3'	3°0·5'W	T	161
Beili-Griffith	Powys	SO0338	52°2·2'	3°24·5'W	X	160
Beiligwern	Powys	SN9024	51°54·5'	3°35·6'W	X	160
Beili-Neuadd	Powys	SN9969	52°18·8'	3°28·5'W	X	136,147
Beilsbeck Fm	E Yorks	SE8638	53°50·1'	0°41·2'W	FM	106
Bein Domhnuill	Pth & Kin	NN6419	56°20·9'	4°11·6'W	H	57
Beinglas	Stir	NN3218	56°19·7'	4°42·6'W	X	50,56
Bein Inn	Pth & Kin	NO1613	56°18·4'	3°21·0'W	X	58
Beinn a' Bha' ach Ard	Highld	NH3643	57°27·1'	4°43·5'W	H	26
Beinn a' Bhacaidh	Highld	NH4311	57°10·0'	4°35·3'W	H	34
Beinn a' Bhaile	N Eil	NF7169	57°35·7'	7°30·0'W	X	18
Beinn a' Bhàillidh	Highld	NM6474	56°48·1'	5°51·5'W	H	40
Beinn a Bhainne	Arg & Bt	NM6222	56°20·1'	5°50·6'W	H	49
Beinn a' Bhathaich	Highld	NH5728	57°19·5'	4°22·0'W	H	26,35
Beinn a' Bhearnais	Arg & Bt	NM3519	56°17·6'	6°16·5'W	H	48
Beinn a' Bhearraidh	Highld	NM7090	56°56·9'	5°46·5'W	H	33,40
Beinn a' Bheithir	Highld	NN0455	56°39·0'	5°11·4'W	H	41
Beinn a' Bheurlaich	Highld	NH7336	57°24·1'	4°6·4'W	H	27
Beinn a' Bhoth	N Eil	NB1316	58°2·7'	6°51·4'W	H	13,14
Beinn a' Bhragaidh	Highld	NC8101	57°59·2'	4°0·3'W	H	17
Beinn a' Bhràghad	Highld	NG4125	57°14·8'	6°17·2'W	H	32
Beinn a' Bhric	Highld	NH3465	57°38·9'	4°46·4'W	H	20
Beinn a' Bhric	Highld	NN3164	56°44·5'	4°45·3'W	H	41
Beinn a' Bhuchanaich	Highld	NH7640	57°26·3'	4°3·5'W	H	27
Beinn a'Bhuic	Stir	NN5638	56°31·0'	4°20·0'W	H	51
Beinn A' Bhuird	Aberd	NO0898	57°4·1'	3°30·6'W	H	36,43
Beinn a' Bhuiridh	Arg & Bt	NN0928	56°24·6'	5°5·3'W	H	50
Beinn a' Bhuna	N Eil	NB3330	58°11·0'	6°32·1'W	X	8,13
Beinn a' Bhùtha	Highld	NC2934	58°16·0'	4°54·4'W	H	15
Beinn Acha' Bhràghad	Highld	NH6523	57°16·9'	4°13·9'W	H	26,35
Beinn a' Chairein	Highld	NH2931	57°20·5'	4°50·0'W	H	25
Beinn a' Chàisgein Beag	Highld	NG9682	57°47·1'	5°25·4'W	H	19
Beinn a' Chàisgein Mór	Highld	NG9878	57°45·0'	5°23·2'W	H	19
Beinn a Chaisil	Highld	NM7847	56°34·0'	5°36·4'W	H	49
Beinn a' Chaisteil	Arg & Bt	NN3436	56°29·5'	4°41·5'W	H	50
Beinn a' Chaisteil	Highld	NH3680	57°47·0'	4°45·0'W	H	20
Beinn a' Chait	Highld	NG3643	57°24·3'	6°23·3'W	H	23
Beinn a' Chait	Highld	NG8248	57°28·5'	5°37·7'W	X	24
Beinn a' Chait	Pth & Kin	NN8674	56°50·9'	3°51·7'W	H	43
Beinn Achaladair	Arg & Bt	NN3442	56°32·7'	4°41·6'W	H	50
Beinn a' Chamais Dhrisich	Highld	NM7683	56°53·3'	5°40·2'W	X	40
Beinn a' Chaoinich	Highld	NG8518	57°12·4'	5°33·1'W	H	33
Beinn a' Chaol-airigh	Arg & Bt	NM3518	56°17·1'	6°16·5'W	H	48
Beinn a' Chaolais	Arg & Bt	NR4873	55°53·3'	6°1·4'W	H	60,61
Beinn a' Chaolais	N Eil	NF9078	57°41·4'	7°11·7'W	H	18
Beinn a' Chaolais	N Eil	NG2199	57°53·9'	6°42·1'W	H	14
Beinn a' Chaorainn	Highld	NM7964	56°43·2'	5°34·5'W	H	40
Beinn a' Chaorainn	Highld	NM8377	56°50·3'	5°33·0'W	H	40
Beinn a' Chaorainn	Highld	NN3885	56°55·9'	4°39·3'W	H	34,41
Beinn a' Chaorainn	Moray	NJ0401	57°5·7'	3°34·6'W	H	36
Beinn a' Chaorainn Bheag	Aberd	NJ0501	57°5·7'	3°33·6'W	H	36
Beinn a' Chapuill	Highld	NG2042	57°23·2'	6°39·1'W	H	23
Beinn a' Chapuill	Highld	NG2648	57°26·6'	6°33·6'W	H	23
Beinn a' Chapuill	Highld	NG4353	57°29·9'	6°16·9'W	H	23
Beinn a' Chapuill	Highld	NG5743	57°25·0'	6°2·3'W	H	24
Beinn a' Chapuill	Highld	NG8215	57°10·7'	5°36·0'W	H	33
Beinn a' Charnain	N Eil	NB1528	58°9·2'	6°50·2'W	H	13
Beinn a' Charnain	N Eil	NF7504	57°1·0'	7°20·9'W	H	31
Beinn a' Charnain	N Eil	NF8856	57°29·5'	7°12·0'W	H	22
Beinn a' Charnain	N Eil	NF8988	57°46·7'	7°13·5'W	H	18
Beinn a' Charra	N Eil	NF7731	57°15·6'	7°21·0'W	H	22
Beinn a' Charra	N Eil	NF7869	57°36·0'	7°23·0'W	X	18
Beinn a' Chearcaill	Highld	NG3547	57°26·4'	6°24·5'W	H	23
Beinn a' Chearcaill	Highld	NG4650	57°28·4'	6°13·7'W	H	23
Beinn a' Chearcaill	Highld	NG9363	57°36·8'	5°27·5'W	H	19
Beinn a' Chlachain	Highld	NG7148	57°28·1'	5°48·7'W	X	24
Beinn a' Chlachair	Highld	NN4778	56°52·4'	4°30·2'W	H	42

Beinn a' Chlaidheimh	Highld	NH0677	57°44·7'	5°15·1'W	H	19
Beinn a' Chlaonaidh	Highld	NH4245	57°28·3'	4°37·6'W	H	26
Beinn a' Chleibh	Arg & Bt	NN2525	56°23·4'	4°49·6'W	H	50
Beinn a Chlèirich	Highld	NG3345	57°25·3'	6°26·4'W	H	23
Beinn a' Chliabhain	N Ayr	NR9740	55°36·9'	5°13·0'W	X	62,69
Beinn Ach' nam Bard	Highld	NG4350	57°28·3'	6°16·7'W	H	23
Beinn a' Chochuill	Arg & Bt	NN1132	56°26·8'	5°3·5'W	H	50
Beinn a' Choin	Arg & Bt	NN3513	56°17·1'	4°39·5'W	H	50,56
Beinn a' Chraisg	Highld	NC2359	58°29·3'	5°1·7'W	H	9
Beinn a' Chràsgain	Highld	NN6098	57°3·4'	4°18·0'W	H	35
Beinn a' Chreachain	Pth & Kin	NN3744	56°33·8'	4°38·7'W	H	50
Beinn a' Chroin	Stir	NN3918	56°19·9'	4°35·8'W	H	50,56
Beinn a' Chruachain	Pth & Kin	NO0469	56°48·4'	3°33·9'W	H	43
Beinn a' Chruinnich	Moray	NJ2313	57°12·3'	3°16·0'W	H	36
Beinn a' Chrùlaiste	Highld	NN2456	56°40·0'	4°51·9'W	H	41
Beinn a' Chuailein	N Eil	NB1924	58°7·2'	6°45·9'W	H	13,14
Beinn a' Chuallaich	Pth & Kin	NN6861	56°43·6'	4°9·0'W	H	42
Beinn a' Chùirn	Arg & Bt	NN2137	56°29·7'	4°54·0'W	H	50
Beinn a' Chùirn	Arg & Bt	NN3541	56°32·2'	4°40·5'W	H	50
Beinn a' Chùirn	Arg & Bt	NR3569	55°50·7'	6°13·6'W	X	60,61
Beinn a' Chuirn	Highld	NG8621	57°14·0'	5°32·3'W	H	33
Beinn a' Chumhainn	Highld	NN4671	56°48·6'	4°30·9'W	H	42
Beinn a' Deas	N Eil	NB0823	58°6·2'	6°56·9'W	H	13,14
Beinn a' Deas	N Eil	NF8533	57°17·0'	7°13·2'W	H	22
Beinn a' Ghlinne Bhig	Highld	NG3945	57°25·5'	6°20·4'W	H	23
Beinn a' Ghlinne Mhóir	Arg & Bt	NM3420	56°18·1'	6°17·6'W	H	48
Beinn a' Ghlo	Pth & Kin	NN9673	56°50·5'	3°41·8'W	X	43
Beinn a' Ghobhainn	Highld	NG2463	57°34·6'	6°36·6'W	H	23
Beinn a' Ghràig	Arg & Bt	NM5437	56°27·9'	5°59·2'W	H	47,48
Beinn a' Ghrianain	Highld	NC2834	58°15·9'	4°55·5'W	H	15
Beinn a' Ghuilbein	Highld	NH4263	57°38·0'	4°38·3'W	H	20
Beinn Ailein	N Eil	NF7926	57°13·0'	7°18·6'W	H	22
Beinn Aird da Loch	Highld	NC2731	58°14·3'	4°56·3'W	H	15
Beinn Airein	Highld	NM4079	56°50·0'	6°15·3'W	H	39
Beinn Airigh a' Bhràghad	N Eil	NB4755	58°24·9'	6°19·5'W	H	8
Beinn Airigh Charr	Highld	NG9376	57°43·8'	5°28·1'W	H	19
Beinn Akie	Highld	NC3364	58°32·2'	4°51·6'W	X	9
Beinn Alligin	Highld	NG8660	57°35·0'	5°34·3'W	H	19,24
Beinn a' Mhadaidh	Highld	NC7641	58°20·7'	4°6·6'W	H	10
Beinn a' Mhadaidh	Highld	NG3841	57°23·3'	6°21·1'W	H	23
Beinn a' Mhanaich	Arg & Bt	NS2694	56°6·7'	4°47·5'W	H	56
Beinn a' Mheadhoin	Arg & Bt	NM5831	56°24·8'	5°55·0'W	H	48
Beinn a' Mheadhoin	Highld	NG6117	57°11·2'	5°56·9'W	H	32
Beinn a' Mheadhoin	Highld	NG9128	57°18·0'	5°27·7'W	H	25,33
Beinn a' Mheadhoin	Highld	NH2125	57°17·1'	4°57·7'W	H	25
Beinn a' Mhonicag	Highld	NN2885	56°55·7'	4°49·1'W	H	34,41
Beinn a' Mhuil	N Eil	NB1913	58°1·3'	6°45·1'W	H	13,14
Beinn a' Mhuilinn	N Eil	NF7526	57°12·8'	7°22·6'W	H	22
Beinn a' Mhùinidh	Highld	NH0366	57°38·7'	5°17·6'W	H	19
Beinn an Achaidh Mhóir	Highld	NM6692	56°57·9'	5°50·5'W	H	40
Beinn an Albannaich	Highld	NM7664	56°43·1'	5°39·2'W	H	40
Beinn an Amair	Highld	NC3665	58°32·8'	4°48·6'W	H	9
Beinn an Aoinidh	Arg & Bt	NM4819	56°18·0'	6°4·0'W	X	48
Beinn an Aonaich Mhóir	Highld	NN0562	56°42·8'	5°10·7'W	H	41
Beinn an Dòthaidh	Arg & Bt	NN3240	56°31·6'	4°43·4'W	H	50
Beinn an Dubhaich	Highld	NG5919	57°12·2'	5°59·0'W	H	32
Beinn an Duibhe	Highld	NC3470	58°35·4'	4°50·9'W	H	9
Beinn an Duibh Leathaid	Highld	NG6811	57°8·1'	5°49·6'W	H	32
Beinn an Eoin	Highld	NC1006	58°0·4'	5°12·5'W	H	15
Beinn an Eòin	Highld	NC3808	58°2·2'	4°44·2'W	H	16
Beinn an Eòin	Highld	NG3820	57°12·0'	6°19·8'W	H	32
Beinn an Eòin	Highld	NG8965	57°37·8'	5°31·6'W	H	19,24
Beinn an Eòin	Highld	NH2409	57°8·6'	4°54·1'W	H	34
Beinn an Eòin Bheag	Highld	NC3705	58°0·5'	4°45·1'W	H	16
Beinn an Fhaireachaidh	N Eil	NF9671	57°37·8'	7°5·1'W	H	18
Beinn an Fhògharaidh	Stir	NN4703	56°12·0'	4°27·5'W	H	57
Beinn an Fhraoich	Highld	NG2047	57°25·9'	6°39·5'W	H	23
Beinn an Fhuarain	Highld	NC2615	58°5·7'	4°56·6'W	H	15
Beinn an Fhudair	Highld	NJ0522	57°17·0'	3°34·1'W	H	36
Beinn an Fhurain	Highld	NC2921	58°9·0'	4°53·9'W	H	15
Beinn an Iomaire	Highld	NH1616	57°12·1'	5°2·3'W	H	34
Beinn an Laoigh	Highld	NG4460	57°33·7'	6°16·4'W	H	23
Beinn an Leathaid	Highld	NM5167	56°44·0'	6°3·8'W	H	47
Beinn an Loch	Highld	NG1941	57°22·6'	6°40·0'W	H	23
Beinn an Loch	Highld	NG3946	57°26·0'	6°20·5'W	H	23
Beinn an Lochain	Arg & Bt	NM3947	56°32·8'	6°14·3'W	H	47,48
Beinn an Lochain	Arg & Bt	NM4633	56°25·5'	6°6·7'W	X	47,48
Beinn an Lochain	Arg & Bt	NM5124	56°20·8'	6°1·3'W	X	48
Beinn an Lochain	Arg & Bt	NN2107	56°13·6'	4°52·8'W	H	56
Beinn an Lochain	Highld	NG4652	57°29·5'	6°13·9'W	H	23
Beinnan Lochan	Highld	NG2243	57°23·8'	6°37·2'W	X	23
Beinn an Oir	Arg & Bt	NR4974	55°53·9'	6°0·5'W	H	60,61
Beinn-an Righ	Highld	NG4453	57°30·0'	6°15·9'W	H	23
Beinn an Rosail Beag	Highld	NC4304	58°0·1'	4°38·9'W	X	16
Beinn an Rubha Riabhaich	Highld	NH4352	57°32·1'	4°36·9'W	H	26
Beinn an Sguirr or Score Horan	Highld	NG2859	57°32·6'	6°32·3'W	X	23
Beinn an Tòib	N Eil	NG0285	57°45·6'	7°0·2'W	H	18
Beinn an t-Sagairt	N Eil	NF8856	57°29·5'	7°12·0'W	H	22
Beinn an t-Samhainn	Highld	NM8174	56°48·6'	5°34·8'W	H	40
Beinn an t- Seilich	Arg & Bt	NN2007	56°13·5'	4°53·8'W	H	56
Beinn an t-Sidhein	Arg & Bt	NN1819	56°20·0'	4°56·2'W	H	50,56
Beinn an t-Sidhein	Highld	NH2315	57°11·8'	4°55·3'W	H	34
Beinn an t-Sidhein	Stir	NN5417	56°19·6'	4°21·2'W	H	57
Beinn an t-Sneachda	Highld	NM9880	56°52·3'	5°18·4'W	H	40
Beinn an t-Socaich	Highld	NH0521	57°14·6'	5°13·4'W	H	25,33
Beinn an t-Sratha	Highld	NH1990	57°52·0'	5°2·6'W	H	20
Beinn an t-Sruthain	Highld	NM6048	56°34·0'	5°53·9'W	H	49
Beinn an Tuim	Highld	NM9283	56°53·8'	5°24·5'W	H	40
Beinn an Tuirc	Arg & Bt	NR7536	55°34·2'	5°33·7'W	H	68,69
Beinn an Uain	Highld	NH7735	57°23·6'	4°2·3'W	H	27
Beinn an Uisge	Highld	NG1944	57°24·2'	6°40·3'W	H	23
Beinn Aoidhdailean	Highld	NG8814	57°10·3'	5°30·0'W	H	33
Beinn a' Sga	Highld	NG4269	57°38·5'	6°18·9'W	H	23
Beinn a' Sgà	Highld	NG4356	57°31·5'	6°17·1'W	H	23
Beinn a' Sgridhe	N Eil	NB3438	58°15·3'	6°31·6'W	H	8,13
Beinn a' Sgùmain	Highld	NG2855	57°30·5'	6°32·0'W	H	23
Beinn a' Sgurain	N Eil	NB1823	58°6·6'	6°46·8'W	H	13,14
Beinn a' Theine	Arg & Bt	NR6007	55°18·2'	5°46·4'W	H	68
Beinn a Tuath	Arg & Bt	NR3896	56°5·4'	6°12·3'W	X	61

Beinn a' Tuath	N Eil	NB0923	58°6·3'	6°55·9'W	H	13,14
Beinn a Tuath	N Eil	NF8746	57°24·1'	7°12·2'W	H	22
Beinn Bhac-ghlais	Highld	NG2240	57°22·2'	6°37·0'W	H	23
Beinn Bhalgairean	Arg & Bt	NN2024	56°22·7'	4°54·5'W	H	50
Beinn Bhàn	Arg & Bt	NM8122	56°20·6'	5°32·2'W	H	49
Beinn Bhàn	Arg & Bt	NR3956	55°43·9'	6°9·0'W	X	60
Beinn Bhàn	Arg & Bt	NR8599	56°8·4'	5°27·2'W	H	55
Beinn Bhàn	Highld	NG8045	57°26·8'	5°39·5'W	H	24
Beinn Bhàn	Highld	NH2817	57°13·0'	4°50·4'W	H	34
Beinn Bhàn	Highld	NM6648	56°34·2'	5°48·1'W	H	49
Beinn Bhan	Highld	NM7356	56°38·7'	5°41·7'W	H	49
Beinn Bhàn	Highld	NN0566	56°45·0'	5°10·9'W	H	41
Beinn Bhàn	Highld	NN0657	56°40·1'	5°9·5'W	X	41
Beinn Bhàn	Highld	NN1385	56°55·4'	5°3·9'W	H	34,41
Beinn Bhàn	Highld	NN2575	56°50·3'	4°51·7'W	X	41
Beinn Bhàn	Highld	NN3296	57°1·7'	4°45·6'W	H	34
Beinn Bhan	Stir	NN3901	56°10·7'	4°35·2'W	H	56
Beinn Bharabhais	N Eil	NB3638	58°15·4'	6°29·5'W	H	8
Beinn Bharra-dail	Arg & Bt	NR3862	55°47·1'	6°10·3'W	H	60,61
Beinn Bharrain	N Ayr	NR9042	55°37·8'	5°19·7'W	H	62,69
Beinn Bheag	Arg & Bt	NM5438	56°28·5'	5°59·2'W	X	47,48
Beinn Bheag	Arg & Bt	NM5827	56°22·7'	5°54·7'W	X	48
Beinn Bheag	Arg & Bt	NM6335	56°27·1'	5°50·3'W	H	49
Beinn Bheag	Arg & Bt	NM6734	56°26·7'	5°46·4'W	X	49
Beinn Bheag	Arg & Bt	NN0542	56°32·0'	5°9·8'W	H	50
Beinn Bheag	Arg & Bt	NN3132	56°27·3'	4°44·1'W	H	50
Beinn Bheag	Arg & Bt	NR8184	56°0·2'	5°30·3'W	H	55
Beinn Bheag	Arg & Bt	NS1293	56°5·8'	5°0·9'W	H	56
Beinn Bheag	Highld	NG1950	57°27·5'	6°40·7'W	H	23
Beinn Bheag	Highld	NG3144	57°24·7'	6°28·3'W	H	23
Beinn Bheag	Highld	NG3232	57°18·3'	6°26·5'W	H	32
Beinn Bheag	Highld	NG3959	57°33·0'	6°21·3'W	X	23
Beinn Bheag	Highld	NG7420	57°13·2'	5°44·1'W	H	33
Beinn Bheag	Highld	NG8653	57°31·3'	5°34·0'W	X	24
Beinn Bheag	Highld	NH0700	57°3·3'	5°10·5'W	H	33
Beinn Bheag	Highld	NH0871	57°41·5'	5°12·8'W	H	19
Beinn Bheag	Highld	NH1037	57°23·3'	5°9·2'W	H	25
Beinn Bheag	Highld	NM7782	56°52·8'	5°39·2'W	H	40
Beinn Bheag	Highld	NM9063	56°42·9'	5°25·4'W	X	40
Beinn Bheag	Highld	NN2258	56°41·1'	4°53·9'W	H	41
Beinn Bheag	N Eil	NB0700	57°53·9'	6°56·3'W	X	14,18
Beinn Bheag	N Eil	NF8117	57°8·2'	7°16·0'W	H	31
Beinn Bheag	Pth & Kin	NN9470	56°48·8'	3°43·7'W	H	43
Beinn Bheag Deas	N Eil	NF7828	57°14·0'	7°19·8'W	H	22
Beinn Bheag Tuath	N Eil	NF7830	57°15·1'	7°19·9'W	H	22
Beinn Bhearnach	Arg & Bt	NM6534	56°26·6'	5°48·3'W	H	49
Beinn Bhearnach	Arg & Bt	NM6632	56°25·6'	5°47·2'W	H	49
Beinn Bhearnach	N Eil	NB3438	58°15·3'	6°31·6'W	H	8,13
Beinn Bheigier	Arg & Bt	NR4356	55°44·0'	6°5·2'W	H	60
Beinn Bheòil	Highld	NN5171	56°48·7'	4°26·0'W	H	42
Beinn Bheula	Arg & Bt	NS1598	56°8·6'	4°58·2'W	H	56
Beinn Bhiorach	Arg & Bt	NR3344	55°37·2'	6°14·0'W	H	60
Beinn Bhiorach	N Ayr	NR9346	55°40·1'	5°17·1'W	H	62,69
Beinn Bhiorgaig	Arg & Bt	NR6998	56°7·4'	5°42·6'W	H	55,61
Beinn Bhòidheach	Arg & Bt	NN1922	56°21·6'	4°55·3'W	H	50
Beinn Bhoidheach	Highld	NG5135	57°20·5'	6°7·8'W	X	24,32
Beinn Bhoidheach	Pth & Kin	NN5665	56°45·5'	4°20·9'W	H	42
Beinn Bhragair	N Eil	NB2643	58°17·7'	6°40·1'W	H	8
Beinn Bhràghd	Highld	NG6712	57°8·7'	5°50·6'W	H	32
Beinn Bhreac	Aberd	NO0597	57°3·5'	3°33·5'W	H	36,43
Beinn Bhreac	Arg & Bt	NM9940	56°30·8'	5°15·6'W	H	49
Beinn Bhreac	Arg & Bt	NN0210	56°14·7'	5°11·3'W	H	50,55
Beinn Bhreac	Arg & Bt	NN2021	56°21·1'	4°54·3'W	H	50,56
Beinn Bhreac	Arg & Bt	NN3200	56°10·0'	4°41·9'W	H	56
Beinn Bhreac	Arg & Bt	NR3571	55°51·8'	6°13·7'W	H	60,61
Beinn Bhreac	Arg & Bt	NR3797	56°5·9'	6°13·3'W	H	61
Beinn Bhreac	Arg & Bt	NR3848	55°39·5'	6°9·5'W	H	60
Beinn Bhreac	Arg & Bt	NR3953	55°42·3'	6°8·8'W	X	60
Beinn Bhreac	Arg & Bt	NR4198	56°6·5'	6°9·5'W	H	61
Beinn Bhreac	Arg & Bt	NR4261	55°46·7'	6°6·4'W	X	60
Beinn Bhreac	Arg & Bt	NR5377	55°55·6'	5°56·8'W	H	61
Beinn Bhreac	Arg & Bt	NR5990	56°2·8'	5°51·8'W	H	61
Beinn Bhreac	Arg & Bt	NR6108	55°18·7'	5°45·6'W	H	68
Beinn Bhreac	Arg & Bt	NR7538	55°35·3'	5°33·8'W	H	68,69
Beinn Bhreac	Arg & Bt	NR7667	55°50·9'	5°34·3'W	X	62
Beinn Bhreac	Arg & Bt	NR7770	55°52·6'	5°33·5'W	X	62
Beinn Bhreac	Arg & Bt	NR7947	55°40·2'	5°30·4'W	X	62,69
Beinn Bhreac	Arg & Bt	NR9877	55°56·9'	5°13·7'W	H	62
Beinn Bhreac	Arg & Bt	NS0576	55°56·5'	5°6·9'W	H	63
Beinn Bhreac	Arg & Bt	NS1694	56°6·5'	4°57·1'W	H	56
Beinn Bhreac	Arg & Bt	NS2695	56°7·2'	4°47·5'W	H	56
Beinn Bhreac	Highld	NC6056	58°28·5'	4°23·6'W	H	10
Beinn Bhreac	Highld	NG2553	57°29·3'	6°34·9'W	H	23
Beinn Bhreac	Highld	NG3426	57°15·1'	6°24·2'W	H	32
Beinn Bhreac	Highld	NG4328	57°16·5'	6°15·4'W	H	32
Beinn Bhreac	Highld	NG4615	57°9·6'	6°11·6'W	H	32
Beinn Bhreac	Highld	NG7116	57°10·9'	5°46·9'W	H	33
Beinn Bhreac	Highld	NG7502	57°3·5'	5°42·2'W	H	33
Beinn Bhreac	Highld	NG8363	57°36·6'	5°37·5'W	H	19,24
Beinn Bhreac	Highld	NG9624	57°15·9'	5°22·5'W	H	25,33
Beinn Bhreac	Highld	NH2192	57°53·2'	5°0·7'W	H	20
Beinn Bhreac	Highld	NH2916	57°12·4'	4°49·4'W	H	34
Beinn Bhreac	Highld	NH7029	57°20·2'	4°9·1'W	H	35
Beinn Bhreac	Highld	NH7093	57°54·7'	4°11·2'W	H	21
Beinn Bhreac	Highld	NH7405	57°7·4'	4°4·4'W	H	35
Beinn Bhreac	Highld	NH7527	57°19·2'	4°4·1'W	H	35
Beinn Bhreac	Highld	NH7837	57°24·7'	4°1·4'W	H	27
Beinn Bhreac	Highld	NM5868	56°44·7'	5°57·0'W	H	47
Beinn Bhreac	Highld	NM6871	56°46·6'	5°47·4'W	H	40
Beinn Bhreac	Highld	NN2499	57°3·2'	4°53·7'W	H	34
Beinn Bhreac	N Ayr	NR9044	55°38·9'	5°19·8'W	H	62,69
Beinn Bhreac	N Ayr	NR9445	55°39·5'	5°16·1'W	H	62,69
Beinn Bhreac	N Ayr	NR9531	55°32·0'	5°14·5'W	H	68,69
Beinn Bhreac	N Eil	NB4012	58°1·5'	6°23·7'W	H	14
Beinn Bhreac	N Eil	NF9076	57°40·3'	7°11·5'W	H	18
Beinn Bhreac	Pth & Kin	NN7340	56°32·4'	4°3·5'W	H	51,52
Beinn Bhreac	Pth & Kin	NN8682	56°55·2'	3°51·9'W	H	43
Beinn Bhreac	Stir	NN4505	56°13·0'	4°29·5'W	H	57
Beinn Bhreac	Stir	NN4714	56°17·9'	4°27·9'W	H	57
Beinn Bhreac	Stir	NN5033	56°28·2'	4°25·7'W	H	51

Beinn Bhreac	Stir	NN6013	56°17·6'	4°15·3'W	H	57
Beinn Bhreac	Stir	NS4296	56°8·1'	4°32·1'W	H	56
Beinn Bhreac-bheag	Arg & Bt	NN0109	56°14·2'	5°12·2'W	H	55
Beinn Bhreac Bheag	Highld	NH6718	57°14·3'	4°11·8'W	H	35
Beinn Bhreac-liath	Arg & Bt	NN3034	56°28·3'	4°45·1'W	H	50
Beinn Bhreac Mhór	Highld	NH6719	57°14·8'	4°11·8'W	H	35
Beinn Bhrotain	Aberd	NN9592	57°0·7'	3°43·3'W	H	43
Beinn Bhùgan	Arg & Bt	NM4523	56°20·1'	6°7·1'W	H	48
Beinn Bhuide	Highld	NG9623	57°15·4'	5°22·5'W	H	25,33
Beinn Bhuidhe	Arg & Bt	NM3749	56°33·8'	6°16·4'W	H	47,48
Beinn Bhuidhe	Arg & Bt	NM4346	56°32·4'	6°10·4'W	X	47,48
Beinn Bhuidhe	Arg & Bt	NM4643	56°30·9'	6°7·3'W	H	47,48
Beinn Bhuidhe	Arg & Bt	NM5841	56°30·2'	5°55·5'W	X	47,48
Beinn Bhuidhe	Arg & Bt	NM5939	56°29·1'	5°54·4'W	X	47,48
Beinn Bhuidhe	Arg & Bt	NN2018	56°19·5'	4°54·2'W	H	50,56
Beinn Bhuidhe	Highld	NG1743	57°23·6'	6°42·2'W	H	23
Beinn Bhuidhe	Highld	NG2443	57°23·9'	6°35·2'W	H	23
Beinn Bhuidhe	Highld	NG2464	57°35·2'	6°36·6'W	X	23
Beinn Bhuidhe	Highld	NG2856	57°31·0'	6°32·1'W	H	23
Beinn Bhuidhe	Highld	NG3630	57°17·3'	6°22·4'W	H	32
Beinn Bhuidhe	Highld	NG3927	57°15·8'	6°19·3'W	H	32
Beinn Bhuidhe	Highld	NG6017	57°11·1'	5°57·8'W	H	32
Beinn Bhuidhe	Highld	NG7721	57°13·8'	5°41·2'W	H	33
Beinn Bhuidhe	Highld	NG8511	57°8·6'	5°32·8'W	H	33
Beinn Bhuidhe	Highld	NG8804	57°5·0'	5°29·4'W	X	33
Beinn Bhuidhe	Highld	NG9618	57°12·7'	5°22·2'W	H	33
Beinn Bhuidhe	Highld	NG9821	57°14·4'	5°20·4'W	H	25,33
Beinn Bhuidhe	Highld	NH6221	57°15·8'	4°16·8'W	H	26,35
Beinn Bhuidhe	Highld	NH7004	57°6·8'	4°8·3'W	X	35
Beinn Bhuidhe	Highld	NM4367	56°43·7'	6°11·6'W	H	47
Beinn Bhuidhe	Highld	NM4989	56°55·7'	6°7·1'W	X	39
Beinn Bhuidhe	Highld	NM5662	56°41·4'	5°58·6'W	H	47
Beinn Bhuidhe	Highld	NM6053	56°36·7'	5°54·2'W	H	49
Beinn Bhuidhe	Highld	NM8296	57°0·5'	5°35·0'W	H	33,40
Beinn Bhuidhe	Highld	NM8376	56°49·8'	5°33·0'W	H	40
Beinn Bhuidhe	Highld	NN7698	57°3·6'	4°2·2'W	H	35
Beinn Bhuidhe Bheag	Highld	NH7942	57°27·4'	4°0·5'W	X	27
Beinn-bhuidhe Ho	Arg & Bt	NN1313	56°16·6'	5°0·8'W	X	50,56
Beinn Bhuidhe Mhór	Highld	NH7840	57°26·3'	4°1·5'W	H	27
Beinn Bhuidhe na Coille Móire	Arg & Bt	NM4842	56°30·4'	6°5·3'W	H	47,48
Beinn Bhùraich	Highld	NH5815	57°12·5'	4°20·6'W	H	35
Beinn Bhùraich	Highld	NH6826	57°18·6'	4°11·0'W	H	26,35
Beinn Buidhe na Creige	Highld	NG3625	57°14·6'	6°22·1'W	H	32
Beinn Capuill	Arg & Bt	NR9775	55°55·8'	5°14·5'W	H	62
Beinn Casgro	N Eil	NB4126	58°9·1'	6°23·7'W	T	8
Beinn Ceadraiseal	N Eil	NB3223	58°7·2'	6°32·6'W	H	13,14
Beinn Ceannabeinne	Highld	NC4264	58°32·4'	4°42·4'W	H	9
Beinn Ceann a' Mhara	Arg & Bt	NL9341	56°27·9'	6°58·6'W	H	46
Beinn Ceitlein	Highld	NN1749	56°36·1'	4°58·4'W	H	50
Beinn Chabhair	Stir	NN3617	56°19·3'	4°38·7'W	H	50,56
Beinn Chailein	N Eil	NB3537	58°14·8'	6°30·5'W	H	8
Beinn Chàirn	Highld	NG5930	57°18·1'	5°59·6'W	H	24,32
Beinn Chàisgidle	Arg & Bt	NM6033	56°26·0'	5°53·1'W	H	49
Beinn Chàiteag	Highld	ND1347	58°24·4'	3°28·9'W	X	11,12
Beinn Cham	Arg & Bt	NR3467	55°49·6'	6°14·4'W	X	60,61
Beinn Chaorach	Arg & Bt	NM8110	56°14·2'	5°31·6'W	H	55
Beinn Chaorach	Arg & Bt	NS2892	56°5·6'	4°45·5'W	H	56
Beinn Chaorach	Highld	NM7483	56°53·3'	5°42·2'W	H	40
Beinn Chaorach	Highld	NN1545	56°33·9'	5°0·2'W	H	50
Beinn Chaorach	Highld	NN2950	56°36·9'	4°46·7'W	H	41
Beinn Chaorach	Stir	NN3532	56°27·3'	4°40·2'W	H	50
Beinn Chapull	Arg & Bt	NM9319	56°19·4'	5°20·4'W	H	55
Beinn Chàrnach	Highld	NG1547	57°25·7'	6°44·4'W	H	23
Beinn Charnach Bheag	Highld	NG2757	57°31·5'	6°33·2'W	H	23
Beinn Chàrsaig	Arg & Bt	NM5522	56°19·9'	5°57·4'W	H	48
Beinn Chas	Arg & Bt	NN1916	56°18·4'	4°55·1'W	H	50,56
Beinn Cheathaich	Stir	NN4432	56°27·5'	4°31·5'W	H	51
Beinn Chladan	Arg & Bt	NM3223	56°19·7'	6°19·7'W	H	48
Beinn Chlaonleud	Highld	NM7453	56°37·1'	5°40·6'W	H	49
Beinn Chleiteir	N Eil	NB2919	58°4·9'	6°35·4'W	H	13,14
Beinn Chlianaig	Highld	NN2978	56°52·0'	4°47·9'W	H	41
Beinn Choarach	N Ayr	NR9137	55°35·2'	5°18·5'W	H	68,69
Beinn Choinnich	N Eil	NB2843	58°17·8'	6°38·1'W	H	8
Beinn Cholarich	Arg & Bt	NM3418	56°17·1'	6°17·4'W	H	48
Beinn Chorranach	Arg & Bt	NN2509	56°14·7'	4°49·0'W	H	56
Beinn Chraoibh	Highld	NN1492	56°59·2'	5°3·2'W	H	34
Beinn Chreagach	Arg & Bt	NM4040	56°29·1'	6°12·9'W	H	47,48
Beinn Chreagach	Arg & Bt	NM4520	56°18·5'	6°6·9'W	H	48
Beinn Chreagach	Arg & Bt	NM4634	56°26·0'	6°6·8'W	X	47,48
Beinn Chreagach	Arg & Bt	NM4852	56°35·8'	6°5·9'W	X	47
Beinn Chreagach	Arg & Bt	NM5121	56°19·2'	6°1·2'W	H	48
Beinn Chreagach	Arg & Bt	NM5149	56°34·3'	6°2·8'W	X	47,48
Beinn Chreagach	Arg & Bt	NM6737	56°28·3'	5°46·5'W	X	49
Beinn Chreagach	Highld	NG2045	57°24·8'	6°39·3'W	H	23
Beinn Chreagach	Highld	NG2853	57°29·4'	6°31·9'W	H	23
Beinn Chreagach	Highld	NH4199	57°57·4'	4°40·8'W	H	20
Beinn Chreagach Bheag	Arg & Bt	NM6239	56°29·2'	5°51·5'W	X	49
Beinn Chreagach Mhór	Arg & Bt	NM6339	56°29·3'	5°50·5'W	H	49
Beinn Chrianaig	N Eil	NB2932	58°11·9'	6°36·3'W	H	8,13
Beinn Chuirn	Stir	NN2829	56°25·6'	4°46·9'W	H	50
Beinn Chùl-achaidh	Arg & Bt	NM4121	56°18·9'	6°10·9'W	X	48
Beinn Chuldail	Highld	NC7961	58°31·5'	4°4·2'W	H	10
Beinn Churalain	Arg & Bt	NM9846	56°34·0'	5°16·8'W	H	49
Beinn Chùrlaich	Arg & Bt	NR3257	55°44·2'	6°15·7'W	X	60
Beinn Clachach	Highld	NG8710	57°8·2'	5°30·7'W	H	33
Beinn Clach an Fheadain	Highld	NH6383	57°49·2'	4°17·9'W	H	21
Beinn Coire nan Eunachair	Arg & Bt	NM6340	56°29·8'	5°50·6'W	X	49
Beinn Coire nan Gall	Highld	NM7979	56°51·3'	5°37·0'W	H	40
Beinn Conchra	Highld	NG8829	57°18·4'	5°30·7'W	H	33
Beinn Coraraidh	N Eil	NF7528	57°13·9'	7°22·7'W	H	22
Beinn Corradail	N Eil	NF8132	57°16·3'	7°17·1'W	H	22
Beinn Damh	Highld	NG8850	57°29·7'	5°31·8'W	H	24
Beinn Damhain	Arg & Bt	NN2817	56°19·1'	4°46·4'W	H	50,56
Beinn Dearg	Arg & Bt	NM9521	56°20·5'	5°18·6'W	H	49
Beinn Dearg	Arg & Bt	NN0204	56°11·5'	5°11·0'W	H	55
Beinn Dearg	Highld	NC2765	58°32·6'	4°57·9'W	H	9
Beinn Dearg	Highld	NG5127	57°16·2'	6°7·4'W	X	32
Beinn Dearg	Highld	NG8960	57°35·1'	5°31·3'W	H	19,24

Beinn Dearg	Highld	NH1499	57°56·8′	5°8·1′W	H	20
Beinn Dearg	Highld	NH2581	57°47·3′	4°56·2′W	H	20
Beinn Dearg	Highld	NH2868	57°40·4′	4°52·6′W	H	20
Beinn Dearg	Pth & Kin	NN6049	56°37·0′	4°16·4′W	H	51
Beinn Dearg	Pth & Kin	NN6919	56°21·0′	4°6·7′W	X	57
Beinn Dearg	Pth & Kin	NN7248	56°36·6′	4°4·7′W	H	51,52
Beinn Dearg	Pth & Kin	NN8577	56°52·5′	3°52·8′W	H	43
Beinn Dearg	Stir	NN5803	56°12·2′	4°16·9′W	H	57
Beinn Dearg Bad Chailleach	Highld	NG9187	57°49·7′	5°30·7′W	H	19
Beinn Dearg Bheag	Highld	NG5921	57°13·2′	5°59·1′W	H	32
Beinn Dearg Bheag	Highld	NH0181	57°46·7′	5°20·3′W	H	19
Beinn Dearg Mheadhonach	Highld	NG5127	57°16·2′	6°7·4′W	H	32
Beinn Dearg Mhór	Highld	NG5228	57°16·8′	6°6·4′W	H	32
Beinn Dearg Mhór	Highld	NG5822	57°13·7′	6°0·1′W	H	32
Beinn Dearg Mhór	Highld	NG8692	57°52·2′	5°36·0′W	H	19
Beinn Dearg Mór	Highld	NH0379	57°45·7′	5°18·2′W	H	19
Beinn Dhail	N Eil	NB5056	58°25·5′	6°16·4′W	H	8
Beinn Dhorain	Highld	NC9215	58°6·9′	3°49·5′W	H	17
Beinn Dhrinisiadair	N Eil	NG1794	57°51·0′	6°45·7′W	H	14
Beinn Dhubh	Arg & Bt	NN2711	56°15·9′	4°47·2′W	H	50,56
Beinn Direach	Highld	NC4038	58°18·4′	4°43·4′W	H	16
Beinn Doimhne	N Eil	NB3407	57°58·6′	6°29·5′W	X	13,14
Beinn Domhnaill	Highld	NH6896	57°56·3′	4°13·3′W	H	21
Beinn Domhnuill	Pth & Kin	NN6419	56°20·9′	4°11·6′W	H	57
Beinn Donachain	Arg & Bt	NN1931	56°26·4′	4°55·7′W	H	50
Beinn Donn	Arg & Bt	NM9647	56°34·5′	5°18·8′W	H	49
Beinn Dònuill	Highld	NH1998	57°56·3′	5°3·0′W	H	20
Beinn Dòrain	Arg & Bt	NN3237	56°30·0′	4°43·3′W	H	50
Beinn Dronaig	Highld	NH0237	57°23·1′	5°17·2′W	H	25
Beinn Dubh	Arg & Bt	NN2628	56°25·0′	4°48·8′W	H	50
Beinn Dubh	Arg & Bt	NR4263	55°47·7′	6°6·5′W	H	60,61
Beinn Dubh	Arg & Bt	NS3395	56°7·4′	4°40·8′W	H	56
Beinn Dubh	Highld	NG3636	57°20·5′	6°22·8′W	H	23,32
Beinn Dubh	Highld	NG7117	57°11·5′	5°47·0′W	X	33
Beinn Dubh	Highld	NH1739	57°24·5′	5°2·3′W	H	25
Beinn Dubh	Highld	NH7032	57°21·9′	4°9·2′W	H	27
Beinn Dubh	Highld	NM6047	56°33·5′	5°53·9′W	H	49
Beinn Dubh	N Eil	NB0800	57°53·9′	6°55·2′W	H	14,18
Beinn Dubh	Stir	NN4004	56°12·4′	4°34·3′W	H	56
Beinn Dubh a' Bhealaich	Highld	NG7318	57°12·1′	5°45·0′W	H	33
Beinn Dubhain	Arg & Bt	NS1497	56°8·0′	4°59·1′W	H	56
Beinn Dubhain	Highld	NC9320	58°9·6′	3°48·6′W	H	17
Beinn Dubh Airigh	Arg & Bt	NM9503	56°10·8′	5°17·7′W	H	55
Beinn Dubh an Iaruinn	Highld	NH1738	57°24·0′	5°2·3′W	H	25
Beinn Dubhcharaidh	Highld	NH5819	57°14·6′	4°20·7′W	H	35
Beinn Dubhchraig	Stir	NN3025	56°23·5′	4°44·8′W	H	50
Beinn Dubh Shollais	N Eil	NF8273	57°38·3′	7°19·3′W	H	18
Beinn Ducteach	Arg & Bt	NN3415	56°18·2′	4°40·5′W	H	50,56
Beinn Duill	Arg & Bt	NM3447	56°32·6′	6°19·2′W	H	47,48
Beinn Duirinnis	Arg & Bt	NN0234	56°27·7′	5°12·4′W	H	50
Beinn Each	Stir	NN6015	56°18·7′	4°15·3′W	H	57
Beinn Eagagach	Pth & Kin	NN8556	56°41·2′	3°52·2′W	H	52
Beinnean Dearga	Highld	NG3829	57°16·9′	6°20·4′W	H	32
Beinn Edra	Highld	NG4562	57°34·8′	6°15·5′W	H	23
Beinn Eibhinn	Highld	NN4473	56°49·6′	4°32·9′W	H	42
Beinn Eibhne	Arg & Bt	NR3790	56°2·1′	6°12·9′W	H	61
Beinn Eich	Arg & Bt	NS3094	56°6·8′	4°43·6′W	H	56
Beinn Eighe	Highld	NG9659	57°34·8′	5°24·3′W	H	25
Beinn Eighe	Highld	NG9660	57°35·3′	5°24·3′W	H	19
Beinn Eighe National Nature Reserve	Highld	NG9959	57°34·8′	5°21·3′W	X	25
Beinn Eighe National Nature Reserve	Highld	NG9963	57°37·0′	5°21·5′W	X	19
Beinn Eilde	Highld	NN5685	56°56·3′	4°21·6′W	H	42
Beinn Eilideach	Highld	NH1692	57°53·0′	5°5·7′W	H	20
Beinn Eineig	N Eil	NB2128	58°9·4′	6°44·1′W	H	8,13
Beinn Eirisalain	Highld	NG3252	57°29·0′	6°27·8′W	H	23
Beinn Eisgein	N Eil	NB3312	58°1·3′	6°30·8′W	H	13,14
Beinn Enaiglair	Highld	NH2280	57°46·7′	4°59·1′W	H	20
Beinn Eolasary	Arg & Bt	NM3840	56°29·0′	6°14·9′W	H	47,48
Beinn Eun	Highld	NH1926	57°17·6′	4°59·8′W	X	25
Beinn Eunaich	Arg & Bt	NN1332	56°26·8′	5°1·6′W	H	50
Beinneun Forest	Highld	NH2208	57°8·0′	4°56·0′W	X	34
Beinn Feusag	N Eil	NB2742	58°17·2′	6°39·0′W	H	8,13
Beinn Fhada	Arg & Bt	NM5235	56°26·8′	6°1·0′W	H	47,48
Beinn Fhada	Arg & Bt	NM6329	56°23·9′	5°50·0′W	H	49
Beinn Fhada	Highld	NG8523	57°15·1′	5°33·4′W	H	33
Beinn Fhada	Highld	NN1654	56°38·8′	4°59·6′W	H	41
Beinn Fhada or Ben Attow	Highld	NH0219	57°13·4′	5°16·3′W	H	33
Beinn Fhionnlaidh	Arg & Bt	NN0949	56°35·9′	5°6·2′W	H	50
Beinn Fhionnlaidh	Highld	NH1128	57°18·5′	5°7·8′W	H	25
Beinn Fhuar	Highld	NG4260	57°33·7′	6°18·4′W	X	23
Beinn fo Thuath	N Eil	NA9814	58°1·0′	7°6·4′W	H	13
Beinn Freiceadain	Highld	ND0555	58°28·6′	3°37·3′W	H	11,12
Beinn Fuath	Pth & Kin	NN6821	56°22·0′	4°7·8′W	H	51,57
Beinn Gàire	Highld	NM7874	56°48·5′	5°37·8′W	H	40
Beinn Gharbh	Highld	NC2122	58°9·3′	5°2·0′W	H	15
Beinn Gharbh	Highld	NM8887	56°55·8′	5°28·6′W	H	40
Beinn Gharbh	Highld	NM9288	56°56·5′	5°24·7′W	H	40
Beinn Gharbh	Pth & Kin	NN8579	56°53·5′	3°52·8′W	H	43
Beinn Gheur	Highld	NM6670	56°46·0′	5°49·3′W	H	40
Beinn Ghibeach	Arg & Bt	NR3466	55°49·1′	6°14·4′W	X	60,61
Beinn Ghibheach	Arg & Bt	NR3672	55°52·4′	6°12·8′W	X	60,61
Beinn Ghille-choimnich	Highld	NG2048	57°26·4′	6°39·5′W	H	23
Beinn Ghlas	Arg & Bt	NM9525	56°22·6′	5°18·8′W	H	49
Beinn Ghlas	Arg & Bt	NN1318	56°19·3′	5°1·0′W	H	50,56
Beinn Ghlas	Arg & Bt	NR9899	56°8·7′	5°14·7′W	H	55
Beinn Ghlas	Pth & Kin	NN6240	56°32·2′	4°14·2′W	H	51
Beinn Ghobhlach	Highld	NH0594	57°53·8′	5°16·9′W	H	19
Beinn Ghormaig	Highld	NM6557	56°39·0′	5°49·6′W	H	49
Beinn Ghòt	N Eil	NF8634	57°17·6′	7°12·3′W	H	22
Beinn Ghott	Arg & Bt	NM0345	56°30·5′	6°49·2′W	H	46
Beinn Ghreineabhal	N Eil	NB2534	58°12·8′	6°40·5′W	H	8,13
Beinn Ghuilbin	Highld	NH8917	57°14·1′	3°49·9′W	H	35,36
Beinn Ghuilean	Arg & Bt	NR7217	55°23·9′	5°35·6′W	H	68
Beinn Giubhais	Highld	NH1396	57°55·1′	5°9·0′W	H	19
Beinn Glas-choire	Highld	ND0338	58°19·5′	3°38·9′W	H	11,17
Beinn Greidaig	N Eil	NB3633	58°12·7′	6°29·2′W	X	8
Beinn Heasgarnich	Pth & Kin	NN4138	56°30·7′	4°34·6′W	H	51
Beinn Hough	Arg & Bt	NL9446	56°30·6′	6°58·0′W	H	46
Beinn Iaruinn	Highld	NN2990	56°58·4′	4°48·3′W	H	34
Beinn Ime	Arg & Bt	NN2508	56°14·2′	4°49·0′W	H	56
Beinn Iobhair	N Eil	NB2916	58°3·3′	6°35·2′W	H	13,14
Beinn Iosbhal	N Eil	NB0918	58°3·6′	6°55·6′W	H	13,14
Beinn Ithearlan	Highld	NM6657	56°39·0′	5°48·6′W	H	49
Beinn Iutharn Bheag	Aberd	NO0679	56°53·8′	3°32·1′W	H	43
Beinn Iutharn Mhór	Pth & Kin	NO0479	56°53·8′	3°34·1′W	H	43
Beinn Iadain	Highld	NM6956	56°38·6′	5°45·6′W	H	49
Beinn Lagan	Arg & Bt	NS1199	56°9·0′	5°2·1′W	H	56
Beinn Làir	Highld	NG9873	57°42·4′	5°23·0′W	H	19
Beinn Laoigh	Arg & Bt	NM9601	56°9·7′	5°16·7′W	H	55
Beinn Larachan	Arg & Bt	NN1835	56°28·6′	4°56·9′W	H	50
Beinn Leabhainn	Stir	NN5728	56°25·6′	4°18·7′W	H	51
Beinn Leacach	Highld	NG5217	57°10·9′	6°5·8′W	H	32
Beinn Leamhain	Highld	NM9562	56°42·5′	5°20·5′W	H	40
Beinn Leathaig	Arg & Bt	NR3345	55°37·8′	6°14·1′W	X	60
Beinn Leòid	Highld	NC3229	58°13·3′	4°51·2′W	H	15
Beinn Liath	Pth & Kin	NN7926	56°24·9′	3°57·2′W	X	51,52
Beinn Liath	Pth & Kin	NN8940	56°32·6′	3°47·9′W	H	52
Beinn Liathanach	Arg & Bt	NM3524	56°20·3′	6°16·8′W	H	48
Beinn Liath Bheag	Highld	NG9852	57°31·1′	5°21·9′W	H	25
Beinn Liath Bheag	Highld	NH2473	57°43·0′	4°56·8′W	H	20
Beinn Liath Bheag	Highld	NH3169	57°41·0′	4°49·6′W	H	20
Beinn Liath Mhór	Highld	NG9751	57°30·5′	5°22·9′W	H	25
Beinn Liath Mhór a' Ghiubhais Li	Highld	NH2871	57°42·0′	4°52·7′W	H	20
Beinn Liath Mhór Fannaich	Highld	NH2172	57°42·4′	4°59·8′W	H	20
Beinn Lice	Highld	NC3235	58°16·6′	4°51·4′W	H	15
Beinn Lighe	Arg & Bt	NM4122	56°19·4′	6°10·9′W	H	48
Beinn Lite	N Eil	NB3537	58°14·8′	6°30·5′W	H	8
Beinn Lochain	Arg & Bt	NN1600	56°9·7′	4°57·3′W	H	56
Beinn Lochain	Arg & Bt	NS2996	56°7·8′	4°44·6′W	H	56
Beinn Lochain	N Ayr	NR9037	55°35·1′	5°19·5′W	H	68,69
Beinn Loch a' Mhuilinn	Highld	NG6229	57°17·6′	5°56·6′W	H	32
Beinn Loinne	Highld	NH1507	57°7·3′	5°2·9′W	H	34
Beinn Lora	Arg & Bt	NM9137	56°29·0′	5°23·2′W	H	49
Beinn Losgarnaich	Pth & Kin	NN8377	56°52·4′	3°54·7′W	H	43
Beinn Luibhean	Arg & Bt	NN2407	56°13·6′	4°49·9′W	H	56
Beinn Lunndaidh	Highld	NC7901	57°59·2′	4°2·3′W	H	17
Beinn Lurachan	Arg & Bt	NN1633	56°27·5′	4°58·7′W	H	50
Beinn MacDuibh or Ben Macdui	Aberd	NN9999	57°4·5′	3°39·5′W	H	36,43
Beinn Maol Chaluim	Highld	NN1352	56°37·6′	5°2·5′W	H	41
Beinn Mhanach	Pth & Kin	NN3741	56°32·2′	4°38·6′W	H	50
Beinn Mhaol	Pth & Kin	NN9371	56°49·4′	3°44·7′W	H	43
Beinn Mhaol Stacaiseal	N Eil	NB3035	58°13·5′	6°35·5′W	H	8,13
Beinn Mhartainn	N Eil	NF6602	56°59·6′	7°29·6′W	H	31
Beinn Mheadhanach	N Eil	NB0923	58°6·3′	6°55·9′W	H	13,14
Beinn Mheadhanach	N Eil	NB2913	58°1·7′	6°34·9′W	H	13,14
Beinn Mheadhoin	Highld	NH2547	57°29·0′	4°54·7′W	H	25
Beinn Mheadhoin	Highld	NH4811	57°10·1′	4°30·4′W	H	34
Beinn Mheadhoin	Highld	NH5516	57°13·0′	4°23·6′W	H	35
Beinn Mheadhoin	Highld	NH6021	57°15·8′	4°18·8′W	H	26,35
Beinn Mheadhoin	Highld	NM7951	56°36·2′	5°35·6′W	H	49
Beinn Mheadhoin	Highld	NM8769	56°46·1′	5°28·7′W	X	40
Beinn Mheadhoin	Highld	NN1592	56°59·2′	5°2·2′W	H	34
Beinn Mheadhoin	Moray	NJ0201	57°5·6′	3°36·6′W	H	36
Beinn Mheadhon	Arg & Bt	NM6537	56°28·3′	5°48·5′W	H	49
Beinn Mheadhon	Arg & Bt	NN0306	56°12·6′	5°10·1′W	H	55
Beinn Mheadhonach	Arg & Bt	NN0136	56°28·7′	5°13·4′W	H	50
Beinn Mheadhonach	Arg & Bt	NN0643	56°32·6′	5°8·9′W	H	50
Beinn Mheadhonach	Highld	NG2854	57°29·9′	6°32·0′W	H	23
Beinn Mheadhonach	Highld	NG4037	57°21·2′	6°18·9′W	H	23,32
Beinn Mheadhonach	Highld	NG4749	57°27·9′	6°12·7′W	H	23
Beinn Mheadhonach	N Eil	NB4850	58°22·2′	6°18·1′W	H	8
Beinn Mheadhonach	Pth & Kin	NN8875	56°51·4′	3°49·8′W	H	43
Beinn Mheadhonach	Stir	NN4413	56°17·3′	4°30·8′W	H	57
Beinn Mhealaich	Highld	NC9614	58°6·4′	3°45·4′W	H	17
Beinn Mhearsamail	Arg & Bt	NR4972	55°52·8′	6°0·4′W	H	60,61
Beinn Mhialairigh	Highld	NG8012	57°9·0′	5°37·8′W	H	33
Beinn Mhic Cèdidh	Highld	NM8278	56°50·8′	5°34·0′W	H	40
Beinn Mhic Chasgaig	Highld	NN2150	56°36·7′	4°54·6′W	X	41
Beinn Mhic-Mhonaidh	Arg & Bt	NN2034	56°28·1′	4°54·9′W	H	50
Beinn Mhic na Céisich	Arg & Bt	NN0149	56°35·7′	5°14·0′W	H	50
Beinn Mhic Uilleim	Highld	NG2352	57°28·7′	6°36·8′W	H	23
Beinn Mhocaidh	Highld	NG6614	57°9·7′	5°51·7′W	H	32
Beinn Mholach	N Eil	NB3535	58°13·7′	6°30·4′W	H	8
Beinn Mholach	N Eil	NB3538	58°15·3′	6°30·6′W	H	8
Beinn Mholach	Pth & Kin	NN5865	56°45·6′	4°18·9′W	H	42
Beinn Mhór	Arg & Bt	NM7921	56°20·0′	5°34·1′W	H	49
Beinn Mhór	Arg & Bt	NR2940	55°35·0′	6°17·6′W	H	60
Beinn Mhór	Arg & Bt	NS1090	56°4·2′	5°2·7′W	H	56
Beinn Mhór	Highld	NH3225	57°17·3′	4°46·8′W	H	26
Beinn Mhór	Highld	NH9928	57°20·1′	3°40·2′W	H	36
Beinn Mhòr	N Eil	NB2509	57°59·4′	6°38·7′W	H	13,14
Beinn-Mhór	N Eil	NB4224	58°8·0′	6°22·5′W	H	14
Beinn Mhòr	N Eil	NF8031	57°15·7′	7°18·0′W	H	22
Beinn Mhór	N Eil	NF8976	57°40·2′	7°12·5′W	H	18
Beinn Mòine	Highld	NG4154	57°30·4′	6°19·0′W	H	23
Beinn Mòlurgainn	Arg & Bt	NN0140	56°30·9′	5°13·6′W	H	50
Beinn Mothal	N Eil	NB1723	58°6·6′	6°47·8′W	H	13,14
Beinn na Bile	N Eil	NF9571	57°37·8′	7°6·1′W	H	18
Beinn na Boineid	Highld	NG2339	57°21·7′	6°35·9′W	H	23
Beinn na Boineide	Highld	NG2952	57°28·9′	6°30·8′W	H	23
Beinn na Caillich	Arg & Bt	NR4459	55°45·7′	6°4·4′W	H	60
Beinn na Caillich	Highld	NG6023	57°14·4′	5°58·2′W	H	32
Beinn na Caillich	Highld	NG7722	57°14·3′	5°41·3′W	H	33
Beinn na Caillich	Highld	NG7906	57°5·8′	5°38·4′W	H	33
Beinn na Caillich	Highld	NN1362	56°43·0′	5°2·9′W	H	41
Beinn na Caillich Beag	Arg & Bt	NR4559	55°45·7′	6°3·5′W	H	60
Beinn na Cille	Arg & Bt	NM4148	56°33·4′	6°12·5′W	H	47,48
Beinn na Cille	Arg & Bt	NR4268	55°50·4′	6°6·8′W	X	60,61
Beinn na Cille	Highld	NM8554	56°38·0′	5°29·9′W	H	49
Beinn na Cille	Highld	NN0066	56°44·8′	5°15·8′W	H	41
Beinn na Cloich	N Eil	NB2444	58°18·1′	6°42·2′W	H	8
Beinn na Cloiche	Highld	NG3641	57°23·2′	6°23·1′W	H	23
Beinn na Cloiche	Highld	NN2865	56°45·0′	4°48·3′W	H	41
Beinn na Cloiche	N Eil	NB3947	58°20·3′	6°27·1′W	X	8
Beinn na Cloiche Moire	Highld	NM7683	56°53·3′	5°40·2′W	X	40
Beinn na Coille	N Eil	NF8461	57°32·0′	7°16·4′W	H	22
Beinn na Còinnich	Highld	NG1546	57°25·2′	6°44·4′W	H	23
Beinn na Còinnich	Highld	NG2043	57°23·7′	6°39·2′W	H	23
Beinn na Corrafidheag	Highld	NG1646	57°25·2′	6°43·4′W	H	23
Beinn na Crèiche	Highld	NG2048	57°26·4′	6°39·5′W	H	23
Beinn na Crò	Highld	NG5624	57°14·8′	6°2·2′W	H	32
Beinn na Croise	Arg & Bt	NM5525	56°21·5′	5°57·5′W	H	48
Beinn na Cuinneig	Highld	NG3526	57°15·1′	6°23·2′W	X	32
Beinn na Doire Léithe	Arg & Bt	NR4566	55°49·5′	6°3·8′W	H	60,61
Beinn na Drise	Arg & Bt	NM4742	56°30·4′	6°6·3′W	H	47,48
Beinn na Duatharach	Arg & Bt	NM6036	56°27·6′	5°53·3′W	H	49
Beinn na Faire	Arg & Bt	NR6017	55°23·6′	5°47·0′W	H	68
Beinn na Feusaige	Highld	NH0954	57°32·4′	5°11·0′W	H	25
Beinn na Gainimh	Pth & Kin	NN8334	56°29·3′	3°53·6′W	H	52
Beinn na Gaoithe	Highld	NG4428	57°16·5′	6°14·4′W	H	32
Beinn na Glas-choille	Highld	NC5229	58°13·8′	4°30·7′W	H	16
Beinn na Greine	Highld	NG4541	57°23·5′	6°14·2′W	H	23
Beinn na Gucaig	Highld	NN0665	56°44·4′	5°9·9′W	H	41
Beinn na h-Aire	N Eil	NF8169	57°36·2′	7°20·0′W	X	18
Beinn na h-Aire	N Eil	NF8435	57°18·0′	7°14·4′W	H	22
Beinn na h-Aire	N Eil	NF9058	57°30·6′	7°10·2′W	H	22
Beinn na h-Aire	N Eil	NG0485	57°45·7′	6°58·2′W	X	18
Beinn na h-Eaglaise	Highld	NG8512	57°9·2′	5°32·8′W	H	33
Beinn na h-Eaglaise	Highld	NG9052	57°30·8′	5°29·9′W	H	25
Beinn na Heraibh	Arg & Bt	NR3570	55°51·3′	6°13·6′W	X	60,61
Beinn na h-Imeilte	Highld	NM4567	56°43·8′	6°9·7′W	H	47
Beinn na h-Iolaire	Arg & Bt	NM4531	56°24·4′	6°7·6′W	H	48
Beinn na h-Iolaire	Highld	NG6050	57°28·9′	5°59·8′W	H	24
Beinn na h-Iolaire	Highld	NH7834	57°23·1′	4°1·3′W	H	27
Beinn na h-Uamha	Arg & Bt	NM5840	56°29·7′	5°55·5′W	H	47,48
Beinn na h-Uamha	Highld	NM6753	56°36·9′	5°47·4′W	H	49
Beinn na h-Uamha	Highld	NM9166	56°44·6′	5°24·6′W	H	40
Beinn na h-Uamha	N Eil	NB2711	58°0·5′	6°36·8′W	H	13,14
Beinn na h-Uidhe	N Eil	NB0200	57°53·7′	7°1·3′W	H	18
Beinn na h-Urchrach	Highld	NM5363	56°41·9′	6°1·6′W	H	47
Beinn na Lap	Highld	NN3769	56°47·3′	4°39·7′W	H	41
Beinn na Leac	Highld	NG5937	57°21·8′	6°0·0′W	H	24,32
Beinn na Lice	Arg & Bt	NR6008	55°18·7′	5°46·5′W	H	68
Beinn nam Bad Mór	Highld	NC9955	58°28·6′	3°43·4′W	H	11
Beinn nam Ban	Highld	NH1090	57°51·8′	5°11·7′W	H	19
Beinn nam Beathrach	Highld	NM7557	56°39·3′	5°39·8′W	H	49
Beinn nam Bò	Highld	NC7858	58°29·9′	4°5·1′W	H	10
Beinn nam Feannag	Arg & Bt	NM5626	56°22·1′	5°56·6′W	H	48
Beinn nam Fitheach	Arg & Bt	NR3470	55°51·2′	6°14·6′W	X	60,61
Beinn nam Fitheach	Arg & Bt	NR4096	56°5·4′	6°10·4′W	H	61
Beinn nam Fitheach	Highld	NH4146	57°28·8′	4°38·7′W	H	26
Beinn nam Fuaran	Arg & Bt	NN3638	56°30·6′	4°39·5′W	H	50
Beinn nam Meann	Arg & Bt	NM6638	56°28·8′	5°47·6′W	X	49
Beinn na Moine	Highld	NG2539	57°21·8′	6°33·9′W	H	23
Beinn na Mòine	Highld	NG4450	57°28·3′	6°15·7′W	H	23
Beinn na Moine	N Eil	NF6500	56°58·4′	7°30·4′W	H	31
Beinn na Mointeich	Highld	NG2658	57°32·0′	6°34·2′W	H	23
Beinn na Mointich Leathainn	Highld	NM5666	56°43·6′	5°58·9′W	X	47
Beinn na Muice	Highld	NH2140	57°25·2′	4°58·4′W	H	25
Beinn nan Aighenan	Arg & Bt	NN1440	56°31·2′	5°1·0′W	H	50
Beinn nan Braclaich	Highld	NG3440	57°22·6′	6°25·1′W	H	23
Beinn nan Cabag	Highld	NH3566	57°39·5′	4°45·5′W	H	20
Beinn nan Cabar	Highld	NM7686	56°54·9′	5°40·3′W	H	40
Beinn nan Cailleach	Highld	NH7232	57°21·9′	4°7·2′W	H	27
Beinn nan Caorach	Arg & Bt	NR3694	56°4·2′	6°14·1′W	H	61
Beinn nan Caorach	Highld	NC0805	57°59·8′	5°14·5′W	H	15
Beinn nan Caorach	Highld	NG6229	57°17·6′	5°56·6′W	H	32
Beinn nan Caorach	Highld	NG8712	57°9·2′	5°30·8′W	H	33
Beinn nan Caorach	Highld	NM7486	56°54·9′	5°42·3′W	H	40
Beinn nan Càorach	N Eil	NB3949	58°21·4′	6°27·2′W	H	8
Beinn nan Caorach	N Eil	NF8129	57°14·7′	7°16·9′W	H	22
Beinn nan Capull	Arg & Bt	NR6899	56°7·9′	5°43·6′W	H	55,61
Beinn nan Capull	Highld	NG4935	57°20·4′	6°9·8′W	H	32
Beinn nan Carn	Arg & Bt	NM5042	56°30·5′	6°3·3′W	H	47,48
Beinn nan Càrn	Highld	NG6318	57°11·8′	5°54·9′W	H	32
Beinn nan Carnan	N Eil	NL6898	56°57·5′	7°27·3′W	H	31
Beinn nan Clach	Stir	NN4229	56°25·9′	4°33·3′W	X	51
Beinn nan Clach-corra	Arg & Bt	NM4247	56°32·9′	6°11·4′W	H	47,48
Beinn nan Cnaimhseag	Highld	NC2717	58°6·8′	4°55·7′W	H	15
Beinn nan Codhan	Highld	NM4463	56°41·6′	6°10·4′W	H	47
Beinn nan Coireag	Highld	ND1225	58°12·6′	3°29·4′W	H	17
Beinn nan Creagan	Highld	NH7844	57°28·5′	4°1·6′W	X	27
Beinn nan Cuithean	Highld	NG3129	57°16·6′	6°27·3′W	X	32
Beinn nan Dearcag	Arg & Bt	NM4253	56°36·1′	6°11·8′W	H	47
Beinn nan Druidhneach	N Eil	NF8955	57°29·0′	7°10·9′W	H	22
Beinn nan Dubh-lochan	Highld	NG3132	57°18·2′	6°27·5′W	H	32
Beinn nan Each	Highld	NN2768	56°46·5′	4°49·4′W	H	41
Beinn nan Eachan	Stir	NN5738	56°31·0′	4°19·0′W	H	51
Beinn nan Eun	Highld	NH4475	57°44·5′	4°36·8′W	H	20
Beinn nan Gabhar	Arg & Bt	NM3424	56°20·3′	6°17·8′W	H	48
Beinn nan Gabhar	Arg & Bt	NM5436	56°27·4′	5°59·1′W	H	47,48
Beinn nan Gearran	Highld	NH7380	57°47·8′	4°7·7′W	X	21
Beinn nan Gobhar	Arg & Bt	NM5331	56°24·7′	5°59·8′W	X	48
Beinn nan Gobhar	Arg & Bt	NM5824	56°21·0′	5°54·6′W	H	48
Beinn nan Gudairean	Arg & Bt	NR3894	56°4·3′	6°12·2′W	H	61
Beinn nan Imirean	Stir	NN4130	56°26·4′	4°34·3′W	H	51
Beinn nan Leac	N Eil	NG1298	57°53·0′	6°51·1′W	H	14
Beinn nan Lochan	Highld	NG3836	57°20·6′	6°20·8′W	X	23,32
Beinn nan Losgann	Highld	NM5365	56°42·9′	6°1·7′W	H	47
Beinn nan Lus	Arg & Bt	NM5940	56°29·7′	5°54·5′W	H	47,48
Beinn nan Lus	Arg & Bt	NN1337	56°29·5′	5°1·8′W	H	50
Beinn nan Oighreag	Pth & Kin	NN5441	56°32·6′	4°22·0′W	H	51
Beinn nan Oighrean	Highld	NH6182	57°48·6′	4°19·9′W	X	21
Beinn nan Ord	Highld	NM4464	56°42·1′	6°10·5′W	H	47
Beinn nan Ramh	Highld	NH1366	57°39·0′	5°7·6′W	H	19
Beinn nan Sparra	Highld	NH2524	57°16·7′	4°53·7′W	H	25
Beinn nan Stac	Highld	NM3994	56°58·1′	6°17·2′W	H	39
Beinn nan Surrag	N Eil	NB3131	58°11·4′	6°34·2′W	H	8,13
Beinn Narnain	Arg & Bt	NN2706	56°13·2′	4°47·0′W	H	56
Beinn na Seamraig	Highld	NG7217	57°11·5′	5°46·0′W	H	33
Beinn na Seilg	Highld	NM4564	56°42·1′	6°9·5′W	H	47
Beinn na Sgiathaig	Arg & Bt	NM3850	56°34·4′	6°15·5′W	X	47

Beinn na Socaich	Highld	NN2373	56°49·2'	4°53·6'W	X	41
Beinn na Srèine	Arg & Bt	NM4530	56°23·9'	6°7·5'W	H	48
Beinn na Srōine	Arg & Bt	NM6723	56°20·8'	5°45·8'W	H	49
Beinn na Srōine	Arg & Bt	NN2328	56°24·9'	4°51·7'W	H	50
Beinn na Teanga	N Eil	NB1502	57°55·2'	6°48·3'W	H	14
Beinn na Tobha	N Eil	NF8128	57°14·2'	7°16·8'W	H	22
Beinn Nuis	N Ayr	NR9539	55°36·3'	5°14·8'W	X	68,69
Beinn Odhar	Highld	NH6002	57°5·5'	4°18·2'W	X	35
Beinn Odhar	Pth & Kin	NN7112	56°17·2'	4°4·6'W	H	57
Beinn Odhar	Stir	NN3333	56°27·8'	4°42·2'W	H	50
Beinn Odhar Bheag	Highld	NM8477	56°50·3'	5°32·0'W	H	40
Beinn Odhar Mhor	Highld	NM8579	56°51·4'	5°31·1'W	H	40
Beinn Oronsay	Arg & Bt	NR3589	56°1·5'	6°14·7'W	H	61
Beinn Phabail	N Eil	NB5030	58°11·5'	6°14·8'W	X	8
Beinn Pharlagain	Pth & Kin	NN4462	56°43·7'	4°32·5'W	H	42
Beinn Phlacaig	Arg & Bt	NN0235	56°28·2'	5°12·4'W	H	50
Beinn Poll an Tobair	Highld	NC0727	58°11·6'	5°16·5'W	H	15
Beinn Raimh	Highld	NG8431	57°19·4'	5°34·8'W	H	24
Beinn Ràtha	Highld	NC9561	58°31·7'	3°47·7'W	H	11
Beinn Rathacleit	N Eil	NB2642	58°17·1'	6°40·0'W	H	8,13
Beinn Rèidh	Highld	NC2121	58°8·8'	5°2·0'W	H	15
Beinn Reireag Bheag	Highld	NG5831	57°18·6'	6°0·6'W	H	24,32
Beinn Reithe	Arg & Bt	NS2298	56°8·7'	4°51·5'W	H	56
Beinn Resipol	Highld	NM7665	56°43·6'	5°39·2'W	H	40
Beinn Reudle	Arg & Bt	NM3646	56°32·2'	6°17·2'W	H	47,48
Beinn Riabhach	Highld	NN1171	56°47·8'	5°5·2'W	X	41
Beinn Riabhach	N Eil	NB2832	58°11·8'	6°37·3'W	X	8,13
Beinn Riabhach	N Eil	NF7474	57°38·5'	7°27·4'W	H	18
Beinn Rifa-gil	Highld	NC7448	58°24·4'	4°8·9'W	H	10
Beinn-ri-Oitir	N Eil	NF7822	57°10·8'	7°19·3'W	H	31
Beinn Rodagrich	N Eil	NF8954	57°28·4'	7°10·8'W	H	22
Beinn Roineach	Arg & Bt	NR2469	55°50·4'	6°24·1'W	X	60
Beinn Rosail	Highld	NC4106	58°1·2'	4°41·0'W	H	16
Beinn Rosail	Highld	NC7040	58°20·0'	4°12·7'W	H	10
Beinn Ruadh	Arg & Bt	NS1371	55°54·0'	4°59·0'W	H	63
Beinn Ruadh	Arg & Bt	NS1588	56°3·2'	4°57·8'W	H	56
Beinn Ruadh	Highld	NC8459	58°30·5'	3°59·0'W	H	10
Beinn Ruadh	Highld	NC9263	58°32·8'	3°50·9'W	H	11
Beinn Ruigh Choinnich	N Eil	NF8019	57°9·3'	7°17·1'W	H	31
Beinn Ruighe Raonuill	Highld	NM8266	56°44·3'	5°33·4'W	H	40
Beinn Ruisg	Arg & Bt	NS3291	56°5·2'	4°41·6'W	H	56
Beinn Scalabhat	N Eil	NF8334	57°17·5'	7°15·3'W	X	22
Beinn Scarastaigh	N Eil	NB1931	58°11·0'	6°46·4'W	H	8,13
Beinn Scorabhaig	N Eil	NG2395	57°51·8'	6°39·8'W	H	14
Beinn Scorabhig bho Dheas	N Eil	NG2394	57°51·2'	6°39·7'W	X	14
Beinn Sgaillinish	Arg & Bt	NR6184	55°59·6'	5°49·5'W	H	61
Beinn Sgeireach	Highld	NC4511	58°3·9'	4°37·2'W	H	16
Beinn Sgiath	Highld	NN5698	57°3·3'	4°22·0'W	H	35
Beinn Sgluich	Arg & Bt	NM9651	56°36·7'	5°19·0'W	H	49
Beinn Sgreamhaidh	Highld	NC4415	58°6·1'	4°38·3'W	H	16
Beinn Sgritheall	Highld	NG8312	57°9·1'	5°34·8'W	H	33
Beinn Sgulaird	Arg & Bt	NN0445	56°33·6'	5°10·9'W	H	50
Beinn Sgùmain	Highld	NG3651	57°28·6'	6°23·8'W	H	23
Beinn Sgurrach	Highld	NH5014	57°11·8'	4°28·5'W	H	35
Beinn Sheileboist	N Eil	NG0596	57°51·6'	6°58·0'W	X	14,18
Beinn Sheilg	Highld	NG3938	57°21·7'	6°20·0'W	H	23,32
Beinn Sheunta	N Eil	NB4453	58°23·7'	6°22·4'W	H	8
Beinn Shiantaidh	Arg & Bt	NR5174	55°53·9'	5°58·6'W	H	61
Beinn Shlèibhe	N Eil	NF9283	57°44·1'	7°10·1'W	H	18
Beinn Sholum	Arg & Bt	NR3949	55°40·1'	6°8·6'W	H	60
Beinn Shurabhat	N Eil	NF7823	57°11·3'	7°19·4'W	H	22
Beinn Sitheag	Arg & Bt	NR9272	55°54·0'	5°19·2'W	H	62
Beinn Smeòrail	Highld	NC8611	58°4·7'	3°55·5'W	H	17
Beinn Spionnaidh	Highld	NC3657	58°28·5'	4°48·3'W	H	9
Beinn Staic	Highld	NG3923	57°13·7'	6°19·0'W	H	32
Beinn Stumanadh	Highld	NC6449	58°24·8'	4°19·2'W	H	10
Beinn Suidhe	Arg & Bt	NN2140	56°31·3'	4°54·1'W	H	50
Beinn Tairbeirt	N Eil	NF8039	57°20·0'	7°18·6'W	H	22
Beinn Talaidh	Arg & Bt	NM6234	56°26·5'	5°51·2'W	H	49
Beinn Tarsuinn	Arg & Bt	NR5476	55°55·1'	5°55·8'W	H	61
Beinn Tarsuinn	Highld	NC1105	57°59·9'	5°11·4'W	H	15
Beinn Tarsuinn	Highld	NH0372	57°41·9'	5°17·9'W	H	19
Beinn Tarsuinn	N Ayr	NR9227	55°29·8'	5°17·1'W	H	68,69
Beinn Tarsuinn	N Ayr	NR9244	55°39·0'	5°17·9'W	H	62,69
Beinn Tarsuinn	N Ayr	NR9337	55°35·2'	5°16·6'W	H	68,69
Beinn Tarsuinn	N Ayr	NR9541	55°37·4'	5°14·9'W	H	62,69
Beinn Tart a' Mhill	Arg & Bt	NR2156	55°43·3'	6°26·2'W	H	60
Beinn Teallach	Highld	NN3685	56°55·9'	4°41·3'W	H	34,41
Beinn Tharsuinn	Arg & Bt	NN1601	56°10·2'	4°57·4'W	H	56
Beinn Tharsuinn	Arg & Bt	NS2991	56°5·1'	4°44·5'W	H	56
Beinn Tharsuinn	Highld	NH0543	57°26·4'	5°14·5'W	X	25
Beinn Tharsuinn	Highld	NH4182	57°48·2'	4°40·1'W	H	20
Beinn Tharsuinn	Highld	NH6079	57°47·0'	4°20·8'W	H	21
Beinn Tharsuinn	N Eil	NB2000	57°54·4'	6°43·1'W	H	14
Beinn Tharsuinn	N Eil	NG0387	57°46·7'	6°59·3'W	H	18
Beinn Tharsuinn Chaol	Highld	NG9973	57°42·4'	5°22·0'W	X	19
Beinn Thearabeirt	N Eil	NB5346	58°20·2'	6°12·7'W	X	8
Beinn Thorsiadair	N Eil	NB2442	58°17·1'	6°42·1'W	H	8,13
Beinn Thrasda	Arg & Bt	NR4177	55°55·2'	6°8·3'W	H	60,61
Beinn Thuaithealain	Highld	NG3637	57°21·1'	6°22·9'W	H	23,32
Beinn Thulabaigh	N Eil	NB3634	58°13·2'	6°29·3'W	H	8
Beinn Thùlagabhal	N Eil	NB3141	58°16·8'	6°34·9'W	H	8,13
Beinn Thunicaraidh	Arg & Bt	NM6636	56°27·7'	5°47·5'W	H	49
Beinn Tighe	Arg & Bt	NG2506	57°4·0'	6°31·8'W	H	39
Beinn Tighe	Highld	NM4486	56°53·9'	6°11·8'W	H	39
Beinn Toaig	Arg & Bt	NN2645	56°34·1'	4°49·5'W	X	50
Beinn Totaig	Highld	NG4036	57°20·7'	6°18·8'W	H	23,32
Beinn Trilleachan	Arg & Bt	NN0843	56°32·6'	5°6·9'W	H	50
Beinn Tuath	Highld	NG4353	57°29·9'	6°16·9'W	H	23
Beinn Tulaichean	Stir	NN4119	56°20·5'	4°33·9'W	H	56
Beinn Uamha	Stir	NN3806	56°13·4'	4°36·3'W	H	56
Beinn Uan	Highld	NH7743	57°27·9'	4°2·6'W	H	27
Beinn Udlaidh	Arg & Bt	NN2733	56°27·7'	4°48·0'W	H	50
Beinn Udlamain	Highld	NN5773	56°49·9'	4°20·2'W	H	42
Beinn Uidhe	Highld	NC2825	58°11·1'	4°55·1'W	H	15
Beinn Uilleim	Highld	NG3748	57°27·0'	6°22·6'W	H	23
Beinn Uird	Stir	NS3998	56°9·1'	4°35·1'W	H	56
Beinn Ulbhaidh	Highld	NH4496	57°55·8'	4°37·6'W	H	20
Beinn Uraraidh	Arg & Bt	NR4054	55°42·8'	6°7·9'W	H	60

Beinn-y-Phott	I of M	SC3886	54°14·9'	4°28·8'W	H	95
Beins Law	Pth & Kin	NO1812	56°17·9'	3°19·1'W	X	58
Beirghe	N Eil	NB5464	58°30·0'	6°12·9'W	X	8
Beirhope	Scot Bord	NT7519	55°28·1'	2°23·3'W	X	80
Beirnfels	Suff	TM4563	52°12·9'	1°35·6'E	X	156
Beitarsaig	N Eil	NA9911	57°59·4'	7°5·2'W	W	13
Beith	N Ayr	NS3453	55°44·8'	4°38·2'W	T	63
Beith Og	Highld	NN2890	56°58·4'	4°49·3'W	H	34
Bejowan	Corn	SW8560	50°24·3'	5°1·2'W	X	200
Beke Hall	Essex	TQ7891	51°35·6'	0°34·6'E	X	178
Bekesbourne	Kent	TR1955	51°15·3'	1°8·7'E	T	179
Bekesbourne Hill	Kent	TR1856	51°15·9'	1°7·9'E	T	179
Bekka Hill	Shetld	HU3448	60°13·2'	1°22·7'W	H	3
Belach Stocleit	N Eil	NG1194	57°50·8'	6°51·8'W	X	14
Belah	Cumbr	NY3957	54°54·5'	2°56·7'W	T	85
Belahbridge Ho	Cumbr	NY7912	54°30·4'	2°19·0'W	X	91
Belan	Powys	SJ0012	52°42·0'	3°28·4'W	X	125
Belan	Powys	SJ0506	52°38·8'	3°23·9'W	X	125
Belan	Powys	SJ1120	52°46·5'	3°18·8'W	X	125
Belan	Powys	SJ1500	52°35·7'	3°14·9'W	X	136
Belan	Powys	SJ2004	52°37·9'	3°10·5'W	T	126
Belan Bank	Shrops	SJ2805	52°38·5'	3°3·4'W	X	126
Belan Bank	Shrops	SJ3419	52°46·1'	2°58·3'W	X	126
Belan Bank (Motte & Bailey)	Shrops	SJ3419	52°46·1'	2°58·3'W	A	126
Belan-ddu	Powys	SJ0301	52°36·1'	3°25·5'W	X	136
Belan-deg	Powys	SJ0902	52°36·7'	3°20·2'W	X	136
Belan Hall	Powys	SJ0006	52°38·8'	3°28·3'W	X	125
Belan Locks	Powys	SJ2105	52°38·5'	3°9·7'W	X	126
Belan Place	Wrex	SJ3041	52°58·0'	3°2·1'W	X	117
Belas Knap (Long Barrow)	Glos	SP0225	51°55·6'	1°57·9'W	A	163
Belaugh	Norf	TG2818	52°42·9'	1°23·0'E	T	133,134
Belaugh Broad	Norf	TG2917	52°42·4'	1°23·8'E	W	133,134
Belaugh Green	Norf	TG2919	52°43·4'	1°23·9'E	X	133,134
Belbroughton	Worcs	SO9176	52°23·2'	2°7·5'W	T	139
Belby Hall	E Yorks	SE7728	53°44·8'	0°49·5'W	X	105,106
Belchalwell	Dorset	ST7909	50°53·0'	2°17·5'W	T	194
Belchalwell Street	Dorset	ST7909	50°53·0'	2°17·5'W	T	194
Belchamber's Fm	W Susx	TQ0127	51°2·2'	0°33·2'W	FM	186,197
Belchamp Brook	Essex	TL8340	52°1·9'	0°40·5'E	W	155
Belchamp Otten	Essex	TL8041	52°2·5'	0°37·9'E	T	155
Belchamps	Essex	TQ8491	51°35·5'	0°39·8'E	X	178
Belchamp St Paul	Essex	TL7942	52°3·1'	0°37·0'E	T	155
Belchamp Walter	Essex	TL8140	52°2·0'	0°38·7'E	T	155
Belcherrie	Moray	NJ4034	57°23·8'	2°59·4'W	X	28
Belchers	Essex	TL4105	51°43·8'	0°2·9'E	X	167
Belcher's Bar	Leic	SK4008	52°40·3'	1°24·1'W	T	140
Belcher's Fm	Oxon	SP6101	51°42·5'	1°6·6'W	FM	164,165
Belcher's Fm	Oxon	SU6198	51°40·9'	1°6·7'W	FM	164,165
Belcher's Lodge	Leic	SP8196	52°33·6'	0°47·9'W	X	141
Belchester	Scot Bord	NT7943	55°41·1'	2°19·6'W	X	74
Belchford	Lincs	TF2975	53°15·6'	0°3·6'W	T	122
Belchford Hill	Lincs	TF3076	53°16·1'	0°2·6'W	X	122
Belcombe	Somer	ST2812	50°54·4'	3°1·1'W	X	193
Belcombe Court	Wilts	ST8160	51°20·6'	2°16·0'W	A	173
Belcot Fm	Kent	TQ8932	51°3·6'	0°42·2'E	FM	189
Belcumber Hall	Essex	TL6735	51°59·5'	0°26·3'E	X	154
Beldcraig Wood	D & G	NT1001	55°17·9'	3°24·6'W	F	78
Beld Hill	Pth & Kin	NN9811	56°17·1'	3°38·4'W	H	58
Beldin Gill	N Yks	SE0879	54°12·6'	1°52·2'W	W	99
Beld Knowe	S Lanak	NT0008	55°21·6'	3°34·2'W	H	78
Beldon	N Yks	SD9894	54°20·7'	2°1·4'W	X	98
Beldon Beck	N Yks	SD9893	54°20·2'	2°1·4'W	W	98
Beldon Bottom	N Yks	SD9794	54°20·7'	2°2·3'W	X	98
Beldon Brook	Kirk	SE1914	53°37·6'	1°42·4'W	W	110
Beldon Burn	Durham	NY9249	54°50·4'	2°7·0'W	W	87
Beldon Peat Moor	N Yks	SD9892	54°19·7'	2°1·4'W	X	98
Beldon Shields	Northum	NY9249	54°50·4'	2°7·0'W	X	87
Beldoo Hill	Cumbr	NY8913	54°31·0'	2°9·8'W	H	91,92
Beldoo Moss	Cumbr	NY8813	54°31·0'	2°10·7'W	X	91,92
Beldorney Castle	Aberd	NJ4237	57°25·4'	2°57·5'W	A	28
Bele Brook	Powys	SJ2614	52°43·4'	3°5·3'W	W	126
Beley	Fife	NO5310	56°17·1'	2°45·1'W	X	59
Beleybridge	Fife	NO5410	56°17·1'	2°44·1'W	X	59
Belfast Fm	I of M	SC4198	54°21·4'	4°26·4'W	FM	95
Belfatton	Aberd	NK0155	57°35·4'	1°58·5'W	T	30
Belfield	Roch	SD9113	53°37·0'	2°7·8'W	T	109
Belfield Ho	Devon	SX9698	50°46·6'	3°28·1'W	X	192
Belfit Hill	Derby	SK3766	53°11·6'	1°26·4'W	X	119
Belfont	Powys	SN8725	51°55·0'	3°38·2'W	X	160
Belford	Northum	NU1033	55°35·7'	1°50·0'W	T	75
Belford	N Yks	SE2072	54°8·8'	1°41·2'W	X	99
Belford	Scot Bord	NT8120	55°28·7'	2°17·6'W	X	74
Belford Burn	Northum	NU1133	55°35·7'	1°49·1'W	W	75
Belford Mains	Northum	NU0932	55°35·1'	1°51·0'W	X	75
Belford Moor	Northum	NU0732	55°35·1'	1°52·9'W	X	75
Belford Station	Northum	NU1233	55°35·7'	1°48·1'W	X	75
Belfry, The (Hotel)	Warw	SP1895	52°33·4'	1°43·7'W	X	139
Belgar Fm	Kent	TQ8933	51°4·1'	0°42·3'E	FM	189
Belgar Fm	Kent	TR0522	50°57·9'	0°55·6'E	FM	189
Belgate Fm	Heref	SO3863	52°15·9'	2°54·1'W	FM	137,148,149
Belgaverie	D & G	NX2369	54°59·3'	4°45·6'W	X	82
Belgic Oppidum	Herts	TL1813	51°48·4'	0°16·9'W	A	166
Belgrano	Conwy	SH9578	53°17·6'	3°34·1'W	T	116
Belgrave	Ches	SJ3861	53°8·8'	2°55·2'W	T	117
Belgrave	C of Leic	SK5906	52°39·1'	1°7·3'W	T	140
Belgrave	Lancs	SD8621	53°41·4'	2°12·3'W	T	103
Belgrave	Staffs	SK2202	52°37·2'	1°40·1'W	T	139
Belgrave Avenue	Ches	SJ3961	53°8·8'	2°54·3'W	X	117
Belgrave Fm	Ches	SJ3861	53°8·8'	2°55·2'W	FM	117
Belgrave Moat Fm	Ches	SJ3960	53°8·3'	2°54·3'W	FM	117
Belgravia	C of West	TQ2879	51°30·0'	0°9·0'W	T	176
Belgraystone	E Renf	NS5056	55°46·7'	4°23·1'W	X	64
Belgrove Fm	Suff	TM4885	52°24·6'	1°39·2'E	FM	156
Belgrove Ho	Devon	SX4376	50°34·0'	4°12·6'W	X	201
Belhamage	S Ayr	NX2184	55°7·3'	4°48·0'W	X	76
Belhamie	S Ayr	NX1385	55°7·7'	4°55·6'W	X	76
Belham Wood	Peterb	TF1502	52°36·4'	0°17·7'W	F	142
Belhangie	Aberd	NO6196	57°3·5'	2°38·1'W	X	37,45
Belhaven	E Loth	NT6678	55°59·9'	2°32·3'W	T	67

Belhaven Bay	E Loth	NT6578	55°59·9'	2°33·2'W	W	67
Belhelvie	Aberd	NJ9417	57°14·9'	2°5·5'W	T	38
Belhelvie Lodge	Aberd	NJ9417	57°14·9'	2°5·5'W	X	38
Belhie	Pth & Kin	NN9716	56°19·8'	3°39·5'W	X	58
Belhinnie	Aberd	NJ4627	57°20·1'	2°53·4'W	X	37
Belhuish Ho	Dorset	SY8282	50°38·5'	2°14·9'W	X	194
Belhus Park	Thurr	TQ5781	51°30·6'	0°16·1'E	X	177
Belhus Woods Country Park	Hav	TQ5782	51°31·1'	0°16·2'E	F	177
Belig	Highld	NG5424	57°14·7'	6°4·2'W	H	32
Belivat	Highld	NH9447	57°30·3'	3°45·7'W	X	27
Bellabeg	Aberd	NJ3513	57°12·4'	3°4·1'W	T	37
Bellabeg	Aberd	NJ4103	57°7·1'	2°58·0'W	X	37
Belladrum Burn	Highld	NH5139	57°25·3'	4°28·4'W	X	26
Belladrum Home Fm	Highld	NH5241	57°26·4'	4°27·5'W	FM	26
Bellafax Grange	N Yks	SE8078	54°11·7'	0°46·0'W	X	100
Bella Fm	N Yks	SE8664	54°4·1'	0°40·7'W	FM	101
Bellahill	Angus	NO5355	56°41·3'	2°45·6'W	X	54
Bellahouston	C of Glas	NS5563	55°50·6'	4°18·5'W	T	64
Bellahouston Park	C of Glas	NS5463	55°50·5'	4°19·5'W	X	64
Bellair	Dorset	SY3793	50°44·2'	2°53·2'W	X	193
Bellamarsh Barton	Devon	SX8577	50°35·1'	3°37·1'W	X	191
Bellamore	Heref	SO3940	52°3·5'	2°53·0'W	X	148,149,161
Bellamore	S Ayr	NX2386	55°8·5'	4°46·2'W	X	76
Bellamour	Northum	NZ1496	55°15·7'	1°46·4'W	X	81
Bellams Fm	Cambs	TL3053	52°9·8'	0°5·6'W	FM	153
Bellamy's Br	Cambs	TF4008	52°39·3'	0°4·6'E	X	142,143
Bellan	Flint	SJ2165	53°10·8'	3°10·5'W	X	117
Belland	Devon	SX3596	50°44·6'	4°19·9'W	X	190
Bellandy	Moray	NJ2832	57°22·6'	3°11·4'W	X	37
Bellan Ho	Powys	SJ3215	52°43·9'	3°0·0'W	X	126
Bellanoch	Arg & Bt	NR8092	56°4·5'	5°31·7'W	T	55
Bellanrigg	Scot Bord	NT2338	55°38·0'	3°13·0'W	T	73
Bella or Knight Close	N Yks	SD8986	54°16·4'	2°9·7'W	X	98
Bellaport Home Fm	Shrops	SJ6940	52°57·6'	2°27·3'W	FM	118
Bellaport Lodge	Shrops	SJ7039	52°57·1'	2°26·4'W	X	127
Bellaport Old Hall	Shrops	SJ7040	52°57·6'	2°26·4'W	X	118
Bellart How Moss	Cumbr	SD4583	54°14·6'	2°50·2'W	X	97
Bellasis	Surrey	TQ1952	51°15·5'	0°17·3'W	X	187
Bellasis Bridge	Northum	NZ1977	55°5·5'	1°41·7'W	X	88
Bellasis Fm	Northum	NZ1978	55°6·0'	1°41·7'W	FM	88
Bellasize	Corn	SX1365	50°27·5'	4°37·7'W	X	200
Bellasize	E Yorks	SE8227	53°44·2'	0°45·0'W	T	106
Bellasize Grange	E Yorks	SE8227	53°44·2'	0°45·0'W	X	106
Bellaty	Angus	NO2359	56°43·2'	3°15·0'W	X	53
Bellaty Lodge	Angus	NO2358	56°42·7'	3°15·0'W	X	53
Bella Wood	Donc	SE4704	53°32·1'	1°17·0'W	F	111
Bellbank	Cumbr	NY5273	55°3·2'	2°44·7'W	X	86
Bell Bar	Herts	TL2505	51°44·0'	0°11·0'W	T	166
Bell Bay	N Ayr	NS1657	55°46·5'	4°55·6'W	W	63
Bellbeaver Rigg	Cumbr	NY7635	54°42·8'	2°21·9'W	H	91
Bell Bottom	N Yks	SE6972	54°8·6'	0°56·2'W	F	100
Bellbrae	Fife	NO3713	56°18·6'	3°0·7'W	T	59
Bellbridge	Cumbr	NY3643	54°46·9'	2°59·3'W	X	85
Bell Brook	Shrops	SJ5809	52°40·9'	2°36·9'W	W	126
Bell Burn	Durham	NZ2131	54°40·7'	1°40·0'W	W	93
Bell Busk	N Yks	SD9056	54°0·2'	2°8·7'W	T	103
Bellcairn	Arg & Bt	NS2183	56°0·7'	4°51·8'W	X	56
Bell Common	Essex	TL4401	51°41·6'	0°5·4'E	T	167
Bell Coppice	Shrops	SO7175	52°22·6'	2°25·2'W	F	138
Bellcrag Flow	Northum	NY7772	55°2·8'	2°21·2'W	X	86,87
Bell Crags	Cumbr	NY2914	54°31·2'	3°5·4'W	X	89,90
Bell Crags	Northum	NY7773	55°3·3'	2°21·2'W	X	86,87
Bell Craig	Scot Bord	NT1812	55°24·0'	3°17·3'W	H	79
Bellcraig Fm	Fife	NO2200	56°11·4'	3°15·0'W	FM	58
Bell Dean	Brad	SE0933	53°47·8'	1°51·4'W	X	104
Bell Dip Fm	Leic	SK7009	52°40·7'	0°57·5'W	FM	141
Belleair	Ches	SJ5476	53°17·0'	2°41·0'W	X	117
Belleau	Lincs	TF4078	53°17·1'	0°6·4'E	T	122
Belleau Br	Lincs	TF4077	53°16·5'	0°6·4'E	X	122
Belle Eau Park	Notts	SK6659	53°7·7'	1°0·4'W	T	120
Belle Eisle Fm	Powys	SJ3013	52°42·8'	3°1·8'W	FM	126
Belle Grange	Cumbr	SD3898	54°22·7'	2°56·9'W	X	96,97
Belle Grange Bay	Cumbr	SD3898	54°22·7'	2°56·9'W	W	96,97
Belle Green	Barns	SE3909	53°34·8'	1°24·2'W	T	110,111
Bellehatch Park	Oxon	SU7480	51°31·1'	0°55·6'W	X	175
Belleheiglash	Moray	NJ1837	57°25·2'	3°21·5'W	X	28
Belle Isle	Cumbr	SD3996	54°21·7'	2°55·9'W	X	96,97
Belle Isle	Kent	TR2566	51°21·1'	1°14·3'E	X	179
Belle Isle	Leeds	SE3129	53°45·6'	1°31·4'W	T	104
Belle Isle	Leic	SK6116	52°44·5'	1°5·4'W	X	129
Belleisle	N Yks	NZ1501	54°24·5'	1°45·7'W	X	92
Belle Isle Fm	Oxon	SP3535	52°1·0'	1°29·0'W	FM	151
Belleisle Park	S Ayr	NS3319	55°26·4'	4°38·0'W	X	70
Bellemere Fm	Leic	SK7626	52°49·8'	0°51·9'W	FM	129
Bell End	Worcs	SO9477	52°23·7'	2°4·9'W	T	139
Bellendean Burn	Scot Bord	NT3514	55°25·2'	3°1·2'W	W	79
Bellendean Rig	Scot Bord	NT3715	55°25·7'	2°59·3'W	H	79
Bellendean Shank	Scot Bord	NT3614	55°25·2'	3°0·2'W	X	79
Bellenden	Devon	SX9195	50°44·9'	3°32·3'W	X	192
Belle Port	Highld	NH6769	57°41·7'	4°13·4'W	X	21
Bellerby	N Yks	SE1192	54°19·7'	1°49·4'W	T	99
Bellerby Beck	N Yks	SE1392	54°19·6'	1°47·6'W	W	99
Bellerby Camp	N Yks	SE0992	54°19·7'	1°51·3'W	X	99
Bellerby Moor	N Yks	SE0993	54°20·2'	1°51·3'W	X	99
Bellerby Ranges	N Yks	SE0994	54°20·7'	1°51·3'W	X	99
Belles Knott	Cumbr	NY2908	54°28·0'	3°5·3'W	X	89,90
Belle Vale	Dudley	SO9584	52°27·5'	2°4·0'W	T	139
Belle Vale	Liv	SJ4288	53°23·4'	2°51·9'W	T	108
Bellever	Devon	SX6577	50°34·9'	3°54·0'W	T	191
Bellever Tor	Devon	SX6476	50°34·3'	3°54·9'W	H	191
Bellevue	Cered	SN6273	52°20·5'	4°1·1'W	X	135
Bellevue	Ches	SJ4948	53°1·9'	2°45·2'W	X	117
Belle Vue	Cumbr	NY1131	54°40·2'	3°22·4'W	T	89
Belle Vue	Cumbr	NY3755	54°53·4'	2°58·5'W	T	85
Belle Vue	Cumbr	SD5981	54°13·6'	2°37·3'W	X	97
Belle Vue	Devon	SX8175	50°34·0'	3°40·4'W	X	191
Bellevue	D & G	NX8592	55°12·8'	3°48·0'W	X	78
Belle Vue	Donc	SE5902	53°30·9'	1°6·2'W	T	111
Belle Vue	Durham	NY9740	54°45·5'	2°2·4'W	X	87

Bellevue	Highld	NH5448	57°30·2′	4°25·7′W	X	26
Belle Vue	Lancs	SD4242	53°52·5′	2°52·5′W	X	102
Belle Vue	Man	SJ8796	53°27·9′	2°11·3′W	T	109
Bellevue	Orkney	HY6544	59°17·1′	2°36·4′W	X	5
Bellevue	Pth & Kin	NN8921	56°22·4′	3°47·4′W	X	52,58
Belle Vue	Shrops	SJ4911	52°41·9′	2°44·9′W	T	126
Belle Vue	Shrops	SJ4929	52°51·6′	2°45·0′W	X	126
Belle Vue	Wakf	SE3419	53°40·2′	1°28·7′W	T	110,111
Bellevue	Worcs	SO9774	52°22·1′	2°2·2′W	T	139
Belle Vue Fm	Ches	SJ4467	53°12·1′	2°49·9′W	FM	117
Belle Vue Fm	N Lincs	SE9104	53°31·7′	0°37·2′W	FM	112
Belle Vue Fm	N Yks	NZ4404	54°26·0′	1°18·9′W	FM	93
Belle Vue Fm	N Yks	SD6667	54°6·1′	2°30·8′W	FM	98
Belle Vue Fm	N Yks	SE9567	54°5·6′	0°32·4′W	FM	101
Bellevue Hill	Leic	SK5021	52°47·3′	1°15·1′W	X	129
Bellevue Plantation	Devon	SY1397	50°46·2′	3°13·6′W	F	192,193
Bellevue Plantation	Hants	SU5344	51°11·8′	1°14·1′W	F	185
Belle Vue Villa	S Tyne	NZ3660	54°56·2′	1°25·9′W	X	88
Bellfield	Aberd	NO8577	56°53·3′	2°14·3′W	X	45
Bellfield	C of Aber	NJ8706	57°8·9′	2°12·4′W	X	38
Bellfield	E Ayr	NS4335	55°35·3′	4°29·0′W	T	70
Bellfield	Fife	NO2210	56°16·8′	3°15·1′W	X	58
Bellfield	Fife	NO3101	56°12·1′	3°6·3′W	X	59
Bellfield	Highld	NH6448	57°30·4′	4°15·7′W	X	26
Bellfield	Pth & Kin	NO0602	56°12·3′	3°30·5′W	X	58
Bellfield	S Lanak	NS8234	55°35·4′	3°51·9′W	X	71,72
Bellfield	S Lanak	NS9620	55°28·0′	3°38·3′W	X	72
Bellfield Fm	D & G	NX9482	55°7·5′	3°39·3′W	FM	78
Bellfield Fm	Kent	TR0632	51°3·2′	0°56·8′E	FM	189
Bellfield Fm	warr	SJ6084	53°21·3′	2°35·7′W	FM	109
Bellfields	Surrey	SU9951	51°15·2′	0°34·5′W	T	186
Bellflask	N Yks	SE2977	54°11·5′	1°32·9′W	X	99
Bell Fm	Beds	TL0146	52°6·4′	0°31·1′W	FM	153
Bell Fm	Beds	TL1255	52°11·1′	0°21·3′W	FM	153
Bell Fm	Bucks	SU9982	51°31·9′	0°34·0′W	FM	175,176
Bell Fm	Ches	SJ8765	53°11·2′	2°11·3′W	FM	118
Bell Fm	E Yorks	SE7537	53°49·7′	0°51·2′W	FM	105,106
Bell Fm	Herts	TL4034	51°59·4′	0°2·7′E	FM	154
Bell Fm	Lancs	SD5565	54°5·0′	2°40·9′W	FM	97
Bell Fm	N Lincs	SK9297	53°27·9′	0°36·4′W	FM	112
Bell Fm	Wilts	ST9190	51°36·8′	2°7·4′W	FM	163,173
Bell Fm	Wilts	ST9767	51°24·4′	2°2·2′W	FM	173
Bell Fold	Lancs	SD4936	53°49·3′	2°46·1′W	X	102
Bell Fold Fm	Lancs	SD5137	53°49·9′	2°44·3′W	FM	102
Bellgate	Cumbr	SD6380	54°13·1′	2°33·6′W	X	97
Bell Green	Cov	SP3681	52°25·8′	1°27·8′W	T	140
Bell Green	Lew	TQ3672	51°26·1′	0°2·2′W	T	177
Bell Ground	Barns	SK3599	53°29·4′	1°27·9′W	F	110,111
Bell Grove	Cumbr	NY4523	54°36·2′	2°50·7′W	X	90
Bell Hall	Worcs	SO9377	52°23·7′	2°5·8′W	X	139
Bell Hall	York	SE6043	53°53·0′	1°4·8′W	A	105
Bell Heath	Worcs	SO9577	52°23·7′	2°4·0′W	T	139
Bell Hill	Cumbr	SD4793	54°20·0′	2°48·5′W	H	97
Bell Hill	Dorset	ST7908	50°52·5′	2°17·5′W	H	194
Bell Hill	Hants	SU7424	51°0·9′	0°56·3′W	T	197
Bell Hill	Norf	TG4601	52°33·3′	1°38·1′E	X	134
Bell Hill	Northum	NT8410	55°23·3′	2°14·7′W	H	80
Bell Hill	Scot Bord	NT4928	55°32·8′	2°48·1′W	H	73
Bell Hill	Scot Bord	NT8366	55°53·5′	2°15·9′W	X	67
Bell Hill	Scot Bord	NT9168	55°54·6′	2°8·2′W	X	67
Bell Hill	Scot Bord	NY5397	55°16·1′	2°44·0′W	H	79
Bell Hill (Battery)	Norf	TG4601	52°33·3′	1°38·1′E	A	134
Bell Hill Fm	Cumbr	SD0898	54°22·4′	3°24·6′W	FM	96
Bellhill Fm	Lancs	SD5561	54°2·8′	2°40·8′W	FM	97
Bell Hill Fm	N Yks	SE9899	54°22·9′	0°29·0′W	FM	94,101
Bell Ho	Cumbr	NX9714	54°30·9′	3°35·0′W	X	89
Bell Ho	Cumbr	NY5247	54°49·2′	2°44·4′W	X	86
Bell Ho	Durham	NZ1219	54°34·2′	1°48·4′W	X	92
Bellholm	D & G	NX9682	55°7·5′	3°37·4′W	X	78
Bellhouse Fm	Essex	TL9423	51°52·5′	0°49·5′E	FM	168
Bellhouse Fm	Lincs	TF0942	52°58·1′	0°22·2′W	FM	130
Bell House Moor	Cald	SD9924	53°43·0′	2°0·5′W	X	103
Bellhurst	E Susx	TQ7227	51°1·2′	0°27·5′E	X	188,199
Bellhurst	Lancs	SD6166	54°5·6′	2°35·4′W	X	97
Bellhurst Fm	Staffs	SJ8411	52°42·0′	2°13·8′W	FM	127
Bellhurst Fms	E Susx	TQ8625	50°59·9′	0°39·4′E	FM	189,199
Belliehill	Angus	NO5663	56°45·6′	2°44·7′W	X	44
Bellimore-on-Tig	S Ayr	NX1482	55°6·1′	4°54·5′W	X	76
Bellingburn	Northum	NY6890	55°12·4′	2°29·7′W	X	80
Belling Burn	Northum	NY6990	55°12·4′	2°28·8′W	W	80
Bellingburn Head	Northum	NY6991	55°13·0′	2°28·8′W	X	80
Bellingdon	Bucks	SP9405	51°44·4′	0°37·9′W	T	165
Bellingdon Fm	Bucks	SP9405	51°44·4′	0°37·9′W	FM	165
Bellingham	Lew	TQ3771	51°25·5′	0°1·4′W	T	177
Bellingham	Northum	NY8383	55°8·7′	2°15·6′W	T	80
Belling Hill	Scot Bord	NT6412	55°24·3′	2°33·7′W	H	80
Belling Rigg	Northum	NY7890	55°12·5′	2°20·3′W	H	80
Bellington Fm	Derby	SK4231	52°52·7′	1°22·2′W	FM	129
Bellington Fm	Worcs	SO8876	52°23·2′	2°10·2′W	FM	139
Bellington Hill	Derby	SK4231	52°52·7′	1°22·2′W	X	129
Bellion	Northum	NZ0889	55°12·0′	1°52·0′W	X	81
Bellion Edge	Northum	NY9792	55°13·6′	2°2·4′W	X	81
Bellisle	E Ayr	NS4835	55°35·4′	4°24·3′W	X	70
Bellister Castle	Northum	NY7063	54°57·9′	2°27·7′W	X	86,87
Belliston	Fife	NO5005	56°14·3′	2°48·0′W	X	59
Bellitaw	Scot Bord	NT6943	55°41·0′	2°29·1′W	X	74
Bellknowes	Fife	NT0884	56°2·7′	3°28·2′W	X	65
Bellmaco	Norf	TL6196	52°32·5′	0°22·9′E	X	143
Bellmanear Fm	N Yks	SE8468	54°6·3′	0°42·5′W	FM	100
Bellman Ground	Cumbr	SD4094	54°20·5′	2°55·0′W	X	96,97
Bellman's Cross	Somer	ST7320	50°59·0′	2°22·7′W	X	183
Bellman's Cross	Worcs	SO7881	52°25·8′	2°19·0′W	X	138
Bellman's Head	Aberd	NO8785	56°57·6′	2°12·4′W	X	45
Bellmarsh Ho	Ches	SJ7971	53°14·4′	2°18·5′W	X	118
Bellmire Hill	N Yks	SE7266	54°5·3′	0°53·5′W	X	100
Bellmont	Cumbr	NY4145	54°48·0′	2°54·6′W	X	85
Bellmoor Fm	Somer	ST3312	50°54·4′	2°56·8′W	FM	193
Bellmoor Plantn	N Yks	SE4584	54°15·2′	1°18·1′W	F	99
Bell Mount	Cumbr	NY4929	54°39·5′	2°47·0′W	X	90
Bellmount	Lincs	SK9438	52°56·1′	0°35·7′W	X	130

Bellmount	Norf	TF5421	52°46·1′	0°17·4′E	T	131
Bellmount	Stock on T	NZ4013	54°30·9′	1°22·5′W	X	93
Bellmuir	Aberd	NJ8736	57°25·1′	2°12·5′W	X	30
Belloch	Arg & Bt	NR6737	55°34·5′	5°41·3′W	X	68
Bellochantuy	Arg & Bt	NR6632	55°31·8′	5°42·0′W	T	68
Bellochantuy Bay	Arg & Bt	NR6532	55°31·8′	5°43·0′W	W	68
Bell o' th' Hill	Ches	SJ5245	53°0·3′	2°42·5′W	T	117
Bell o' th' Hill Fm	Ches	SJ5244	52°59·7′	2°42·5′W	FM	117
Bellour	Pth & Kin	NN9825	56°24·6′	3°38·7′W	X	52,53,58
Bellowal	Corn	SW4326	50°4·9′	5°35·2′W	X	203
Bellow End	Cumbr	SD7190	54°18·5′	2°26·3′W	X	98
Bellows Cross	Dorset	SU0613	50°55·2′	1°54·5′W	X	195
Bellows Mill	Beds	SP9819	51°51·9′	0°34·2′W	X	165
Bellows, The	Corn	SW6813	49°58·6′	5°13·8′W	X	203
Bellow Water	E Ayr	NS6123	55°29·1′	4°11·6′W	W	71
Bell Rib	Cumbr	NY1707	54°27·3′	3°16·4′W	X	89,90
Bellridden	D & G	NY1069	55°0·7′	3°24·0′W	X	85
Bellridge	Northum	NZ0476	55°5·0′	1°55·8′W	X	87
Bellrigg	D & G	NX7358	54°54·3′	3°58·4′W	X	83,84
Bell Rock	Fife	NT1984	56°2·8′	3°17·6′W	X	65,66
Bell Rock	S Ayr	NS3324	55°29·1′	4°38·1′W	X	70
Bell Rock	Torbay	SX9267	50°29·8′	3°31·0′W	X	202
Bell Rush	N Yks	SE4085	54°15·8′	1°22·7′W	X	99
Bellsbank	E Ayr	NS4704	55°18·6′	4°24·2′W	T	77
Bellsbank	S Ayr	NS3819	55°26·5′	4°33·2′W	X	70
Bellsbank Plantation	E Ayr	NS4803	55°18·1′	4°23·2′W	F	77
Bell's Br	Lancs	SD4746	53°54·7′	2°48·0′W	X	102
Bell's Br	Lincs	TF3718	52°44·8′	0°2·2′E	X	131
Bell's Braes	Northum	NY6871	55°2·2′	2°29·6′W	X	86,87
Bell's Bridge	Durham	NY8542	54°46·6′	2°13·6′W	X	87
Bells Burn	Scot Bord	NT8355	55°47·5′	2°15·8′W	W	67,74
Bells Burn	Scot Bord	NY5993	55°14·0′	2°38·3′W	W	80
Bellsburnfoot	Northum	NY6195	55°15·1′	2°36·4′W	X	80
Bellscamphie	Aberd	NK0133	57°23·5′	1°58·5′W	X	30
Bell's Castle	Worcs	SO9538	52°2·7′	2°4·0′W	X	150
Bell's Close	N upon Ty	NZ1964	54°58·5′	1°41·8′W	T	88
Bell's Copse	Beds	SP9233	51°59·5′	0°39·2′W	F	152,165
Bell's Copse	Hants	SU7010	50°53·3′	0°59·9′W	F	197
Bell's Corner	Suff	TL9937	52°0·0′	0°54·3′E	T	155
Bellscraigs	S Lanak	NT0242	55°40·0′	3°33·0′W	X	72
Bells Creek	Kent	TQ9867	51°22·3′	0°51·1′E	W	178
Bellscroft	S Lanak	NS7741	55°39·1′	3°56·8′W	X	71
Bell's Cross	Suff	TM0859	52°11·6′	1°3·0′E	X	155
Bell's Cross	Suff	TM1552	52°7·7′	1°8·9′E	X	156
Bell's Flow	D & G	NY3176	55°4·7′	3°4·4′W	X	85
Bells Fm	Kent	TQ6549	51°13·2′	0°22·2′E	FM	188
Bell's Fm	W Susx	TQ2427	51°2·0′	0°13·5′W	FM	187,198
Bell's Forstal	Kent	TQ9953	51°14·7′	0°51·5′E	X	189
Bellsgrove Loch	Highld	NM8465	56°43·9′	5°31·4′W	W	40
Bellsgrove Lodge	Highld	NM8365	56°43·8′	5°32·4′W	X	40
Bellshiel	Northum	NY8199	55°17·3′	2°17·5′W	X	80
Bellshiel	Scot Bord	NT8149	55°44·3′	2°17·7′W	X	74
Bellshiel Burn	Northum	NT8000	55°17·9′	2°18·5′W	W	80
Bellshiel Law	Northum	NT8101	55°18·4′	2°17·5′W	H	80
Bell's Hill	Durham	NY9644	54°47·7′	2°3·3′W	X	87
Bell's Hill	Midlo	NT2064	55°52·0′	3°16·3′W	H	66
Bellshill	N Lanak	NS7259	55°48·7′	4°2·1′W	T	64
Bellshill	Northum	NU1230	55°34·1′	1°48·1′W	X	75
Bellshill	Pth & Kin	NN9610	56°16·5′	3°40·3′W	X	58
Bell's Ho	Durham	NZ1542	54°46·6′	1°45·6′W	X	88
Bellside	N Lanak	NS8058	55°48·3′	3°54·4′W	T	65,72
Bell Sike	Durham	NY9825	54°37·5′	2°1·4′W	W	92
Bell Sike	Scot Bord	NT2927	55°32·1′	3°7·1′W	W	73
Bellsland Fm	E Ayr	NS4241	55°38·5′	4°30·2′W	FM	70
Bells Mains	Midlo	NT3460	55°50·0′	3°2·8′W	X	66
Bells Moor	Northum	NY6095	55°15·1′	2°37·3′W	X	80
Bellsmyre	W Dunb	NS4076	55°57·3′	4°33·3′W	T	64
Bellspool	Scot Bord	NT1635	55°36·3′	3°19·6′W	T	72
Bellsprings	D & G	NY2067	54°59·7′	3°14·6′W	X	85
Bellsquarry	W Loth	NT0465	55°52·4′	3°31·6′W	T	65
Bellstane	D & G	NX8399	55°16·5′	3°50·1′W	X	78
Bell Stane	N Ayr	NS1947	55°41·2′	4°52·3′W	X	63
Bellstane	N Lanak	NS7570	55°54·7′	3°59·5′W	X	64
Bell Stone	Dorset	SY5395	50°45·4′	2°39·6′W	X	194
Bellstown	D & G	NY2674	55°3·5′	3°9·1′W	X	85
Bell's Valley	Northum	NT9527	55°32·5′	2°4·3′W	X	74,75
Bell's Valley	Northum	NT9527	55°32·5′	2°4·3′W	X	74,75
Bell's Wood	N Yks	NZ3609	54°28·7′	1°26·2′W	F	93
Bells Yew Green	E Susx	TQ6036	51°6·3′	0°17·5′E	T	188
Bell Sykes	Lancs	SD7252	53°58·0′	2°25·2′W	X	103
Bell, The	Cumbr	SD2897	54°22·1′	3°6·1′W	H	96,97
Bell, The	Northum	NT9028	55°33·0′	2°9·1′W	H	74,75
Bell, The	Scot Bord	NT1150	55°44·4′	3°24·6′W	X	65,72
Bell, The	Scot Bord	NT6763	55°51·8′	2°31·2′W	F	67
Bellton Wood	Highld	NH6355	57°34·1′	4°17·0′W	F	26
Bell Tor	Devon	SX7377	50°35·0′	3°47·8′W	X	191
Belltrees	Renf	NS3758	55°47·5′	4°35·6′W	X	63
Belluton	Bath & NE Somer	ST6164	51°22·7′	2°33·2′W	T	172
Bell Water Drain	Lincs	TF4058	53°6·3′	0°5·9′E	W	122
Bellwater Fm	Lincs	TF4259	53°6·8′	0°7·7′E	FM	122
Bell Wood	Aberd	NO5498	57°4·5′	2°45·1′W	F	37,44
Bellwood	Midlo	NT2362	55°51·0′	3°13·4′W	X	66
Bellwood Hall	N Yks	SE3168	54°6·7′	1°31·1′W	X	99
Bellybought Hill	D & G	NX9099	55°16·6′	3°43·5′W	H	78
Bellyclone	Pth & Kin	NN9320	56°21·9′	3°43·5′W	X	52,58
Bellyeoman	Fife	NT1088	56°4·8′	3°26·3′W	T	65
Bellymack	D & G	NX6964	54°57·5′	4°2·3′W	X	83,84
Bellyside Hill	Northum	NT9022	55°29·8′	2°9·1′W	X	74,75
Belmaduthy	Highld	NH6456	57°34·7′	4°16·0′W	X	26
Belmanshaws	Scot Bord	NT4020	55°28·5′	2°56·5′W	H	73
Belmesthorpe	Rut	TF0410	52°40·9′	0°27·3′W	T	130
Belmesthorpe Grange	Rut	TF0409	52°40·4′	0°27·3′W	X	141
Belmont	Barnet	TQ2293	51°37·6′	0°13·9′W	X	176
Belmont	Black w Dar	SD6716	53°38·6′	2°29·5′W	T	109
Belmont	Conwy	SH7964	53°9·8′	3°48·2′W	X	115
Belmont	Derby	SK3470	53°13·8′	1°29·0′W	X	119
Belmont	Durham	NY9726	54°38·0′	2°2·4′W	X	92
Belmont	Durham	NZ3043	54°47·1′	1°31·6′W	T	88

Belmont	E Susx	TQ5216	50°55·6′	0°10·2′E	X	199
Belmont	E Susx	TQ8310	50°51·9′	0°36·4′E	T	199
Belmont	Harrow	TQ1690	51°36·0′	0°19·1′W	T	176
Belmont	Kent	TQ9856	51°16·3′	0°50·7′E	X	178
Belmont	N Yks	SE2094	54°20·7′	1°41·1′W	X	99
Belmont	Oxon	SU3988	51°35·6′	1°25·8′W	T	174
Belmont	Pemb	SM8714	51°47·3′	5°4·9′W	X	157
Belmont	S Ayr	NS3420	55°27·0′	4°37·1′W	T	70
Belmont	Scot Bord	NT7240	55°39·4′	2°26·3′W	X	74
Belmont	Shetld	HP5600	60°41·0′	0°58·0′W	T	1
Belmont	Stock	SJ8687	53°23·0′	2°12·2′W	X	109
Belmont	Sutton	TQ2562	51°20·8′	0°11·9′W	T	176,187
Belmont Abbey	Heref	SO4838	52°2·5′	2°45·1′W	X	149,161
Belmont Castle	Pth & Kin	NO2843	56°34·7′	3°9·9′W	X	53
Belmont Dairy Fm	Ches	SJ6578	53°18·1′	2°31·1′W	FM	118
Belmont Fm	Kent	TQ9442	51°8·9′	0°46·8′E	FM	189
Belmont Fm	Red & Cl	NZ6115	54°31·8′	1°3·0′W	FM	94
Belmont Hall	Ches	SJ6578	53°18·1′	2°31·1′W	X	118
Belmont Hall	Staffs	SK0049	53°2·5′	1°59·6′W	X	119
Belmont Ho	Lincs	TF2183	53°20·0′	0°10·6′W	X	122
Belmont Ho	N Som	ST5170	51°25·8′	2°41·9′W	X	172
Belmont Hotel	Heref	SO4738	52°2·5′	2°46·0′W	X	149,161
Belmont Resr	Black w Dar	SD6716	53°38·6′	2°29·5′W	W	109
Belmont Ring	Norf	TF7425	52°47·9′	0°35·3′E	F	132
Belmoredean	W Susx	TQ1923	50°59·9′	0°17·9′W	X	198
Belmore Fm	Shrops	SO4096	52°33·8′	2°52·7′W	FM	137
Belmore Ho	Hants	SU5521	50°59·4′	1°12·6′W	X	185
Belmot Fm	Staffs	SK1925	52°49·6′	1°42·7′W	FM	128
Belmount	Cumbr	SD3599	54°23·2′	2°59·6′W	X	96,97
Belmount	Durham	NY9747	54°49·3′	2°2·4′W	X	87
Belmount	Lancs	SD4664	54°4·4′	2°49·1′W	X	97
Belnaboth	Aberd	NJ3715	57°13·5′	3°2·1′W	X	37
Belnaboth	Aberd	NJ4312	57°12·0′	2°56·1′W	X	37
Belnabothie	Aberd	NJ4440	57°27·1′	2°55·5′W	X	28
Belnacraig	Aberd	NJ3716	57°14·1′	3°2·2′W	T	37
Belnagarrow	Moray	NJ3247	57°30·7′	3°7·6′W	X	28
Belnagauld	Aberd	NJ3510	57°10·8′	3°4·1′W	X	37
Belnaglach	Moray	NJ1645	57°29·5′	3°23·6′W	X	28
Belnaglack	Aberd	NJ3816	57°14·1′	3°1·2′W	X	37
Belnagone	Moray	NJ1645	57°29·5′	3°23·6′W	X	28
Belnahua	Arg & Bt	NM7112	56°15·0′	5°41·3′W	X	55
Belney Fm	Hants	SU6409	50°52·8′	1°5·0′W	FM	196
Belniden	Aberd	NJ3109	57°10·3′	3°8·0′W	X	37
Belnie	Lincs	TF2530	52°51·4′	0°8·2′W	T	131
Belnoe	Moray	NJ2220	57°16·1′	3°17·1′W	X	36
Belnollo	Pth & Kin	NN9023	56°23·4′	3°46·5′W	X	52,58
Belno of Achnascraw	Moray	NJ2521	57°16·7′	3°14·2′W	X	37
Belossack	Corn	SW6922	50°3·4′	5°13·3′W	X	203
Below Beck Fells	Cumbr	SD2798	54°22·6′	3°7·0′W	X	96,97
Belowda	Corn	SW9661	50°25·0′	4°51·9′W	T	200
Belowda Beacon	Corn	SW9762	50°25·6′	4°51·1′W	H	200
Belowda Beacon (Tumulus)	Corn	SW9762	50°25·6′	4°51·1′W	A	200
Belper	Derby	SK3547	53°1·4′	1°28·3′W	T	119,128
Belper Lane End	Derby	SK3349	53°2·5′	1°30·1′W	T	119
Belph	Derby	SK5475	53°16·4′	1°11·0′W	T	120
Belridding	D & G	NY0479	55°6·0′	3°29·8′W	X	84
Belrorie	Aberd	NO4796	57°3·4′	2°52·0′W	X	37,44
Belrorie Hill	Aberd	NO4897	57°3·9′	2°51·0′W	H	37,44
Belsars Field	Cambs	TL4269	52°18·3′	0°5·4′E	X	154
Belsar's Hill	Cambs	TL4270	52°18·8′	0°5·4′E	X	154
Belsar's Hill (Fort)	Cambs	TL4270	52°18·8′	0°5·4′E	A	154
Belsay	Northum	NZ1078	55°6·0′	1°50·2′W	T	88
Belsay Barns	Northum	NZ0577	55°5·5′	1°54·9′W	X	87
Belsay Castle	Northum	NZ0878	55°6·0′	1°52·0′W	A	88
Belsay Dene Ho	Northum	NZ0678	55°6·0′	1°53·9′W	X	87
Belscamphie	Aberd	NJ9118	57°15·4′	2°8·5′W	X	38
Belses Mill Fm	Scot Bord	NT5826	55°31·8′	2°39·5′W	FM	73,74
Belses Moor	Scot Bord	NT5723	55°30·2′	2°40·4′W	X	73,74
Belsford	Devon	SX7659	50°25·3′	3°44·4′W	T	202
Belshand Knowe	D & G	NY1291	55°12·6′	3°22·5′W	X	78
Belshaw's Knowe	Scot Bord	NT8316	55°26·5′	2°15·7′W	X	80
Belsize	Herts	TL0300	51°41·6′	0°30·2′W	T	166
Belsize Fm	Peterb	TF1301	52°35·9′	0°19·5′W	FM	142
Belskavie	Aberd	NJ8100	57°5·7′	2°18·4′W	X	38
Belsom Fm	E Yorks	SE7650	53°56·7′	0°50·1′W	FM	105,106
Belstane	Pth & Kin	NO0335	56°30·1′	3°34·1′W	X	52,53
Belstane	W Loth	NT1064	55°51·9′	3°25·8′W	X	65
Belstane Place	S Lanak	NS8452	55°45·1′	3°50·5′W	X	65,72
Belstane Town Fm	S Lanak	NS8551	55°44·6′	3°49·5′W	FM	65,72
Belstead	Suff	TM1341	52°1·8′	1°6·7′E	T	169
Belstead Brook	Suff	TM1341	52°1·8′	1°6·7′E	W	169
Belstead Hall	Essex	TL7210	51°46·0′	0°30·0′E	X	167
Belstead Hall	Suff	TM1241	52°1·8′	1°5·8′E	X	155,169
Belsteads	Essex	TL7211	51°46·5′	0°30·0′E	X	167
Belston	S Ayr	NS3820	55°27·1′	4°33·3′W	T	70
Belstone	Devon	SX6193	50°43·4′	3°57·8′W	T	191
Belstone Cleave	Devon	SX6293	50°43·5′	3°56·9′W	X	191
Belstone Common	Devon	SX6192	50°42·9′	3°57·8′W	X	191
Belstone Corner	Devon	SX6298	50°46·1′	3°57·0′W	T	191
Belstone Tor	Devon	SX6192	50°42·9′	3°57·8′W	H	191
Belston Loch	E Ayr	NS4716	55°25·1′	4°24·6′W	W	70
Belswardyne Hall	Shrops	SJ6003	52°37·6′	2°35·1′W	X	127
Belsyde	W Loth	NS9775	55°57·7′	3°38·6′W	X	65
Belt Ash Coppice	Cumbr	SD3896	54°21·6′	2°56·8′W	F	96,97
Beltcraigs	Aberd	NO7095	57°3·0′	2°29·2′W	X	38,45
Beltcraigs	Aberd	NO8995	57°3·0′	2°10·4′W	X	38,45
Beltedstane	D & G	NY2370	55°1·4′	3°11·8′W	X	85
Belt Fm	Lincs	SK8390	53°24·3′	0°44·7′W	FM	112
Belthorn	Lancs	SD7124	53°42·9′	2°26·0′W	T	103
Belt Howe	Cumbr	NY5802	54°24·9′	2°38·4′W	H	91
Beltie Burn	Aberd	NJ6103	57°7·2′	2°38·2′W	W	37
Beltinge	Kent	TR1968	51°22·3′	1°9·2′E	T	179
Beltingham	Northum	NY7863	54°57·9′	2°20·2′W	T	86,87
Beltingham Burn	Northum	NY7863	54°57·9′	2°20·2′W	W	86,87
Belt Knowe	D & G	NT2202	55°18·6′	3°13·3′W	X	79
Belt Knowe	E Ayr	NS7528	55°32·0′	3°58·4′W	H	71
Beltoft	N Lincs	SE8006	53°32·9′	0°47·1′W	T	112
Beltoft Grange	N Lincs	SE8208	53°34·0′	0°45·3′W	X	112

Belton	Leic	SK4420	52°46·8′	1°20·5′W	T	129
Belton	Lincs	SK9239	52°56·7′	0°37·4′W	T	130
Belton	N Lincs	SE7806	53°32·9′	0°49·0′W	T	112
Belton	Norf	TG4802	52°33·8′	1°40·0′E	T	134
Belton	Shrops	SJ5240	52°57·6′	2°42·5′W	X	117
Belton Ashes	Lincs	SK9539	52°56·6′	0°34·8′W	X	130
Belton Common	Norf	TG4702	52°33·8′	1°39·1′E	X	134
Beltondod	Scot Bord	NT6567	55°53·9′	2°33·1′W	X	67
Belton Fm	Lincs	TF2633	52°53·0′	0°7·2′W	FM	131
Beltonford	E Loth	NT6477	55°59·3′	2°34·2′W	X	67
Belton Grange	N Lincs	SE7710	53°35·1′	0°49·8′W	X	112
Beltonhill	D & G	NX9075	55°3·7′	3°42·9′W	X	84
Belton Ho	Lincs	SK9239	52°56·7′	0°37·4′W	A	130
Belton-in-Rutland	Rut	SK8101	52°36·3′	0°47·8′W	T	141
Belton Marshes	Norf	TG4603	52°34·4′	1°38·2′E	X	134
Belton Park	Lincs	SK9338	52°56·1′	0°36·6′W	X	130
Belton's Hill	Cambs	TL1273	52°20·8′	0°20·9′W	X	153
Belton Wood	Norf	TG4901	52°33·2′	1°40·8′E	F	134
Bel Tor	Devon	SX6972	50°32·2′	3°50·5′W	H	191
Belt Plantns	N Yks	NZ8904	54°25·7′	0°37·3′W	F	94
Beltring	Kent	TQ6747	51°12·1′	0°23·8′E	T	188
Beltring Ho	Kent	TQ6746	51°11·6′	0°23·8′E	X	188
Belts of Collonach	Aberd	NO6893	57°1·9′	2°31·2′W	X	38,45
Belts, The	Cambs	TL3352	52°9·2′	0°3·0′W	F	154
Belt, The	Norf	TF8840	52°55·7′	0°48·2′E	F	132
Belt, The	N Yks	SE2582	54°14·2′	1°36·6′W	F	99
Belt, The	Somer	ST1043	51°11·0′	3°16·9′W	F	181
Belt, The	Suff	TM2947	52°4·7′	1°20·9′E	X	169
Belt, The	Wilts	SU2146	51°13·0′	1°41·6′W	F	184
Beluncle Fm	Medway	TQ7973	51°25·9′	0°34·9′E	FM	178
Belvedere	Bexley	TQ4978	51°29·1′	0°9·2′E	T	177
Belvedere	W Loth	NS9669	55°54·4′	3°39·4′W	T	65
Belvedere Wood	Norf	TL7688	52°27·9′	0°35·9′E	F	143
Belvidere	Aberd	NJ7636	57°25·1′	2°23·5′W	X	29
Belvidere	D & G	NX0855	54°51·4′	4°59·1′W	X	82
Belvidere	Lancs	SD5253	53°58·5′	2°43·5′W	X	102
Belvidere Ho	Kent	TQ7056	51°16·9′	0°26·7′E	X	178,188
Belvide Reservoir	Staffs	SJ8610	52°41·5′	2°12·0′W	W	127
Belvidere Wood	E Loth	NT7571	55°56·1′	2°23·6′W	F	67
Belville	Scot Bord	NT7943	55°41·1′	2°19·6′W	X	74
Belvoir	Leic	SK8233	52°53·5′	0°46·5′W	T	130
Belvoir Castle	Leic	SK8133	52°53·5′	0°47·4′W	A	130
Belvoir Fm	Leic	SK8134	52°54·1′	0°47·3′W	FM	130
Belwade	Aberd	NO5598	57°4·5′	2°44·1′W	X	37,44
Belwood Fm	N Lincs	SE7907	53°33·5′	0°48·0′W	FM	112
Belzies	D & G	NY0584	55°8·7′	3°29·0′W	X	78
Bemborough Fm	Glos	SP1027	51°56·7′	1°50·9′W	FM	163
Bembridge	I of W	SZ6487	50°41·0′	1°5·3′W	T	196
Bembridge Airport	I of W	SZ6387	50°41·0′	1°6·1′W	X	196
Bembridge Down	I of W	SZ6286	50°40·4′	1°7·0′W	H	196
Bembridge Fm	I of W	SZ6386	50°40·4′	1°6·1′W	FM	196
Bembridge Fort	I of W	SZ6286	50°40·4′	1°7·0′W	A	196
Bembridge Harbour	I of W	SZ6388	50°41·5′	1°6·1′W	W	196
Bembridge Ledge	I of W	SZ6687	50°41·0′	1°3·6′W	X	196
Bembridge Point	I of W	SZ6488	50°41·5′	1°5·2′W	X	196
Bembridge School	I of W	SZ6486	50°40·4′	1°5·3′W	X	196
Bembridge Trail	I of W	SZ5786	50°40·5′	1°11·2′W	X	196
Bemersley Green	C of Stoke	SJ8854	53°5·2′	2°10·3′W	X	118
Bemersyde	Scot Bord	NT5933	55°35·6′	2°38·6′W	T	73,74
Bemersyde Hill	Scot Bord	NT5934	55°36·1′	2°38·6′W	H	73,74
Bemersyde House	Scot Bord	NT5933	55°35·6′	2°38·6′W	A	73,74
Bemersyde Moss	Scot Bord	NT6134	55°36·1′	2°36·7′W	W	74
Bemerton	Wilts	SU1230	51°4·4′	1°49·3′W	T	184
Bemerton Heath	Wilts	SU1231	51°4·9′	1°49·3′W	T	184
Bempton	E Yorks	TA1972	54°8·0′	0°10·3′W	T	101
Bempton Cliffs	E Yorks	TA2073	54°8·6′	0°9·4′W	X	101
Bempton Grange	E Yorks	TA1973	54°8·6′	0°10·3′W	X	101
Bemuchlye	Highld	NH8253	57°33·4′	3°57·9′W	X	27
Benachally	Pth & Kin	NO0649	56°37·7′	3°31·5′W	H	52,53
Ben-a-chielt	Highld	ND1937	58°19·1′	3°22·5′W	H	11
Benacre	Suff	TM5184	52°24·0′	1°41·8′E	T	156
Benacre Broad	Suff	TM5282	52°22·9′	1°42·6′E	W	156
Benacre Ness	Suff	TM5383	52°23·4′	1°43·5′E	X	156
Benacre Park	Suff	TM5084	52°24·0′	1°40·9′E	X	156
Benacres Plantns	Northum	NZ1371	55°2·2′	1°47·4′W	F	88
Benacre Wood	Suff	TM4984	52°24·1′	1°40·0′E	F	156
Ben Aden	Highld	NM8998	57°1·8′	5°28·2′W	H	33,40
Ben Aigan	Moray	NJ3048	57°31·3′	3°9·7′W	H	28
Benailsa	D & G	NX4273	55°1·8′	4°27·9′W	X	77
Ben Aketil	Highld	NG3246	57°25·8′	6°27·4′W	H	23
Ben Alder	Highld	NN4971	56°48·6′	4°28·0′W	H	42
Benalder Cottage	Highld	NN4967	56°46·5′	4°27·8′W	X	42
Ben Alder Forest	Highld	NN5275	56°50·8′	4°25·1′W	X	42
Ben Alder Lodge	Highld	NN5778	56°52·5′	4°20·3′W	X	42
Ben Alisky	Highld	ND0438	58°19·5′	3°37·9′W	H	11,17
Benallack	Corn	SW9056	50°22·2′	4°56·8′W	X	200
Ben Allarnish	Highld	NG1843	57°23·7′	6°41·2′W	H	23
Benalt	E Ayr	NS6718	55°26·5′	4°5·7′W	X	71
Benan	S Ayr	NX2491	55°11·2′	4°45·4′W	X	76
Benan Ardifuir	Arg & Bt	NR7897	56°7·1′	5°33·8′W	H	55
Benan Hill	D & G	NX8886	55°9·6′	3°45·0′W	H	78
Benan Hill	S Ayr	NX2393	55°12·2′	4°46·5′W	H	76
Ben An or Binnein	Stir	NN5008	56°14·7′	4°24·8′W	H	57
Benaquhallie	Aberd	NJ6008	57°9·9′	2°39·2′W	H	37
Benar	Conwy	SH7351	53°2·7′	3°53·3′W	X	115
Benar	Conwy	SH7951	53°2·8′	3°47·9′W	X	115
Ben Armine	Highld	NC6927	58°13·0′	4°13·3′W	X	16
Ben Armine Forest	Highld	NC6721	58°9·7′	4°15·2′W	X	16
Ben Armine Lodge	Highld	NC7019	58°8·7′	4°12·0′W	X	16
Ben Arnaboll	Highld	NC4558	58°29·2′	4°39·1′W	H	9
Benarth Fm	Heref	SO4229	51°57·6′	2°50·3′W	FM	149,161
Benarth Hall	Conwy	SH7876	53°16·3′	3°49·4′W	X	115
Ben Arthur	Arg & Bt	NN2505	56°12·6′	4°48·9′W	H	56
Benarty Hill	Fife	NT1597	56°9·7′	3°21·7′W	H	58
Benarty Ho	Fife	NT1596	56°9·2′	3°21·7′W	X	58
Benarty Wood	Fife	NT1697	56°9·8′	3°20·7′W	F	58
Ben Aslak	Highld	NG7519	57°12·7′	5°43·1′W	H	33
Ben Attow or Beinn Fhada	Highld	NH0219	57°13·4′	5°16·3′W	H	33
Ben Aulasary	N Eil	NF8070	57°36·6′	7°21·1′W	H	18
Ben Auskaird	Highld	NC2040	58°19·0′	5°3·9′W	H	9

Benavie	Highld	NN1177	56°51·0′	5°5·5′W	T	41
Ben Avon	Aberd	NJ1301	57°5·8′	3°25·7′W	X	36
Benaw	S Ayr	NX1578	55°4·0′	4°53·4′W	H	76
Benawhirn	S Ayr	NX1178	55°3·9′	4°57·2′W	X	76
Benawhirter	S Ayr	NX1279	55°4·4′	4°56·3′W	X	76
Benbain	E Ayr	NS5008	55°20·8′	4°21·5′W	X	70,77
Benbain	E Ayr	NS5009	55°21·4′	4°21·5′W	H	70,77
Benbecula Airport	N Eil	NF7956	57°29·1′	7°21·0′W	X	22
Benbecula (Beinn na Faoghla)	N Eil	NF8151	57°26·5′	7°18·6′W	X	22
Benbeoch	E Ayr	NS4908	55°20·8′	4°22·5′W	H	70,77
Ben Blandy	Highld	NC6260	58°30·6′	4°21·6′W	H	10
Benbole	Corn	SX0374	50°32·2′	4°46·4′W	X	200
Benbole	Corn	SX0581	50°36·0′	4°45·0′W	X	200
Ben Bowie	Arg & Bt	NS3382	56°0·4′	4°40·3′W	H	56
Benbow Pond	W Susx	SU9122	50°59·6′	0°41·8′W	W	197
Benbrack	D & G	NS5300	55°16·6′	4°18·4′W	H	77
Benbrack	D & G	NX5580	55°5·8′	4°15·9′W	H	77
Benbrack	D & G	NX6075	55°3·2′	4°11·1′W	X	77
Benbrack	D & G	NX6797	55°15·2′	4°5·1′W	H	77
Benbrack	E Ayr	NS5205	55°19·3′	4°19·5′W	H	70,77
Benbrack Burn	D & G	NX6795	55°14·1′	4°5·1′W	W	77
Benbrack Burn	E Ayr	NS5205	55°19·3′	4°19·5′W	W	70,77
Benbrake Hill	D & G	NX2274	55°2·0′	4°46·7′W	H	76
Benbraniachan	E Ayr	NS4808	55°20·8′	4°23·4′W	H	70,77
Ben Breaclete	N Eil	NB1431	58°10·8′	6°51·4′W	H	13
Ben Brogaskil	Highld	NG4161	57°34·2′	6°19·4′W	H	23
Ben Brook	Devon	SS9625	51°1·1′	3°28·6′W	W	181
Ben Buck	Clackm	NN8901	56°11·6′	3°46·9′W	X	58
Ben Buie	Arg & Bt	NM6027	56°22·7′	5°52·8′W	H	49
Benbuie	D & G	NX7196	55°14·7′	4°1·3′W	X	77
Benbuie Burn	D & G	NX7196	55°14·7′	4°1·3′W	W	77
Bencallen	S Ayr	NX3494	55°13·0′	4°36·1′W	X	76
Bences Barton	Devon	ST0119	50°58·0′	3°24·2′W	X	181
Bench	Dorset	SY6286	50°40·6′	2°31·9′W	X	194
Ben Challum	Stir	NN3832	56°27·4′	4°37·3′W	H	50
Bench Barn Fm	Suff	TL7545	52°4·8′	0°33·6′E	FM	155
Bench Hill	Kent	TQ9532	51°3·5′	0°47·4′E	X	189
Benchil Burn	Pth & Kin	NO0933	56°29·1′	3°28·2′W	W	52,53
Benchill	Man	SJ8288	53°23·6′	2°15·8′W	T	109
Ben Chonzie	Pth & Kin	NN7730	56°27·0′	3°59·3′W	H	51,52
Ben Chracaig	Highld	NG4943	57°24·7′	6°10·3′W	H	23
Bench, The	Pemb	SM7508	51°43·8′	5°15·1′W	X	157
Bench Tor	Devon	SX6871	50°31·7′	3°51·4′W	X	202
Ben Clach	Pth & Kin	NN7515	56°18·9′	4°0·8′W	H	57
Ben Cladville	Arg & Bt	NR1854	55°42·1′	6°28·9′W	H	60
Ben Cleat	Highld	NG5215	57°9·8′	6°5·6′W	H	32
Ben Cleuch	Clackm	NN9000	56°11·1′	3°45·9′W	H	58
Ben Cliad	N Eil	NF6704	57°0·7′	7°28·7′W	H	31
Bencloich Mains	E Dunb	NS6378	55°58·8′	4°11·3′W	X	64
Bencombe	Glos	ST7997	51°40·5′	2°17·8′W	T	162
Bencombe Fm	Bucks	SU8588	51°35·3′	0°46·0′W	FM	175
Ben Connan	Highld	NG1940	57°22·1′	6°40·0′W	H	23
Ben Corkeval	Highld	NG1844	57°24·2′	6°41·2′W	H	23
Ben Cragg	Cumbr	SD2881	54°13·4′	3°5·8′W	X	96,97
Ben Crakavaig	N Eil	NF7810	57°4·4′	7°18·4′W	H	31
Bencroft Grange	Northnts	SP9763	52°15·6′	0°34·3′W	X	153
Bencroft Hill	Wilts	ST9673	51°27·6′	2°3·1′W	X	173
Bencroft Wood	Herts	TL3206	51°44·5′	0°4·9′W	F	166
Ben Cruachan	Arg & Bt	NN0630	56°25·6′	5°8·3′W	H	50
Ben Cuidad	Highld	NG2239	57°21·7′	6°36·9′W	H	23
Ben Cuier	N Eil	NL6394	56°55·1′	7°31·9′W	H	31
Ben Culeshader	Highld	NG4641	57°23·6′	6°13·2′W	H	23
Bencummin	S Ayr	NX1483	55°6·6′	4°54·5′W	X	76
Bendalls Fm	Derby	SK3324	52°49·0′	1°30·2′W	FM	128
Bendalls Fm	Suff	TM0965	52°14·8′	1°4·1′E	FM	155
Bendameer Ho	Fife	NT2186	56°3·9′	3°15·7′W	X	66
Ben-Damph Forest	Highld	NG8853	57°31·3′	5°32·0′W	F	24
Ben-Damph Forest	Highld	NG9053	57°31·4′	5°30·0′W	X	25
Bendauch	C of Aber	NJ8314	57°13·2′	2°16·4′W	X	38
Bendeallt	Highld	NH5570	57°42·1′	4°25·5′W	H	21
Ben Dearg	Highld	NG4750	57°28·4′	6°12·7′W	H	23
Benderloch	Arg & Bt	NM9038	56°29·5′	5°24·2′W	T	49
Benderloch	Arg & Bt	NM9238	56°29·5′	5°22·3′W	X	49
Bendgate	N Yks	SD8457	54°0·8′	2°14·2′W	X	103
Bendigo	Orkney	HY4407	58°57·1′	2°57·9′W	X	6,7
Bendike Ho	Lincs	TF2529	52°50·9′	0°8·2′W	X	131
Bendings	Aberd	NO8281	56°55·5′	2°17·3′W	X	45
Bendish	Herts	TL1621	51°52·8′	0°18·5′W	T	166
Ben Diubaig	Highld	NG3155	57°30·6′	6°29·0′W	H	23
Bendles, The	Shrops	SJ6526	52°50·1′	2°30·8′W	X	127
Ben Donich	Arg & Bt	NN2104	56°12·0′	4°52·7′W	H	56
Bendor	Northum	NT9629	55°33·5′	2°3·4′W	X	74,75
Bendoran Cottage	Arg & Bt	NM3621	56°18·7′	6°15·7′W	X	48
Ben Dorrery	Highld	ND0655	58°28·7′	3°36·2′W	H	11,12
Ben Dreavie	Highld	NC2639	58°18·6′	4°57·7′W	H	15
Bendrick Rock	V of Glam	ST1366	51°23·4′	3°14·6′W	X	171
Bendrigg	Cumbr	SD5890	54°18·5′	2°38·3′W	X	97
Bendrigg Lodge	Cumbr	SD5889	54°17·9′	2°38·3′W	X	97
Bendronaig Lodge	Highld	NH0138	57°23·6′	5°18·2′W	X	25
Ben Drovinish	N Eil	NB1531	58°10·8′	6°50·4′W	H	13
Ben Duagrich	Highld	NG3938	57°21·7′	6°20·0′W	H	23,32
Bendysh Hall	Essex	TL6039	52°1·8′	0°20·3′E	X	154
Ben Earb	Pth & Kin	NO0769	56°48·5′	3°30·9′W	H	43
Beneath-a-burn	Shetld	HU4134	60°5·6′	1°15·3′W	X	4
Benedict Otes	Essex	TL6406	51°43·9′	0°22·9′E	X	167
Ben Effrey	Pth & Kin	NN9811	56°17·1′	3°38·4′W	X	58
Beneknowle	Devon	SX7157	50°24·2′	3°48·5′W	X	202
Benelip Sound	Shetld	HU6669	60°24·2′	0°47·6′W	W	2
Ben End	Cumbr	SD6997	54°22·3′	2°28·2′W	X	98
Benenden	Kent	TQ8032	51°3·8′	0°34·5′E	T	188
Benenden School	Kent	TQ8033	51°4·3′	0°34·6′E	X	188
Ben Eoligarry	N Eil	NF7007	57°2·4′	7°26·0′W	H	31
Benera	D & G	NX4372	55°1·3′	4°26·9′W	X	77
Beneraird	D & G	NX1378	55°3·9′	4°55·3′W	H	76
Ben Erival	N Eil	NF6904	57°0·8′	7°26·8′W	H	31
Ben Ernakater	N Eil	NF7771	57°37·1′	7°24·2′W	H	18
Ben Ettow	Highld	NG1752	57°28·5′	6°42·8′W	H	23
Ben Ever	Clackm	NN8900	56°11·0′	3°46·9′W	H	58
Benfadyeon	D & G	NX6160	54°55·2′	4°9·7′W	X	83

Ben Feall	Arg & Bt	NM1454	56°35·7′	6°39·1′W	H	46
Benfield	D & G	NX3764	54°56·9′	4°32·3′W	X	83
Benfield	Stock	SJ9691	53°25·2′	2°3·2′W	X	109
Benfieldside	Durham	NZ0952	54°52·0′	1°51·2′W	T	88
Benfleet Creek	Essex	TQ7885	51°32·4′	0°34·4′E	W	178
Ben Forsan	Highld	NG1548	57°26·2′	6°44·5′W	H	23
Ben Fuailaval	N Eil	NB1631	58°10·9′	6°49·4′W	H	13
Bengairn	D & G	NX7754	54°52·2′	3°54·6′W	H	84
Bengairn Ho	D & G	NX7852	54°51·1′	3°53·6′W	X	84
Bengairn Loch	D & G	NX7852	54°51·1′	3°53·6′W	W	84
Bengal	Northnts	SP6649	52°8·4′	1°1·7′W	X	152
Bengal	Pemb	SM9532	51°57·2′	4°58·6′W	T	157
Bengall	D & G	NY1178	55°5·6′	3°23·2′W	X	85
Bengallhill	D & G	NY1077	55°5·0′	3°24·2′W	X	85
Ben Garrisdale	Arg & Bt	NR6394	56°5·1′	5°48·1′W	H	61
Bengarth	Cumbr	NY1104	54°25·7′	3°21·9′W	X	89
Ben Gaskin	Highld	NG4739	57°22·5′	6°12·1′W	H	23,32
Bengate	Norf	TG3027	52°47·7′	1°25·1′E	T	133,134
Ben Geary	Highld	NG2561	57°33·6′	6°35·4′W	H	23
Bengengie Hill	Clackm	NN8600	56°11·0′	3°49·8′W	H	58
Bengeo	Herts	TL3213	51°48·2′	0°4·7′W	T	166
Bengeo Temple Fm	Herts	TL3317	51°50·4′	0°3·8′W	FM	166
Benges Wood	W Susx	SU9312	50°54·2′	0°40·3′W	F	197
Bengeworth	Worcs	SP0443	52°5·4′	1°56·1′W	T	150
Ben Glas	Stir	NN3419	56°20·3′	4°40·7′W	H	50,56
Ben Glas Burn	Arg & Bt	NN3317	56°19·2′	4°41·6′W	W	50,56
Benglog	Gwyn	SH8023	52°47·7′	3°46·4′W	X	124,125
Ben Gorm	Highld	NG4265	57°36·3′	6°18·7′W	H	23
Ben Grasco	Highld	NG4343	57°24·5′	6°16·3′W	H	23
Bengray	D & G	NX6359	54°54·7′	4°7·8′W	H	83
Ben Griam Beg	Highld	NC8341	58°20·8′	3°59·5′W	H	10
Ben Griam Mór	Highld	NC8038	58°19·1′	4°2·4′W	H	17
Bengrove	Glos	SO9732	51°59·4′	2°2·2′W	T	150
Bengrove Fm	Glos	SO8322	51°54·0′	2°14·4′W	FM	162
Bengrove Fm	Somer	ST5935	51°7·0′	2°34·8′W	FM	182,183
Ben Gulabin	Pth & Kin	NO1072	56°50·1′	3°28·1′W	H	43
Ben Gullipen	Stir	NN5904	56°12·7′	4°16·0′W	H	57
Ben Gunnary	N Eil	NF6901	56°59·2′	7°26·5′W	H	31
Bengyl	I of Angl	SH4469	53°12·0′	4°19·7′W	X	114,115
Ben Hacklett	N Eil	NF9571	57°37·8′	7°6·1′W	H	18
Ben Halistra	Highld	NG2560	57°33·1′	6°35·4′W	H	23
Benhall	Glos	SO9221	51°53·5′	2°6·6′W	T	163
Benhall Green	Suff	TM3861	52°12·0′	1°29·4′E	T	156
Benhall Lodge	Suff	TM3760	52°11·5′	1°28·5′E	X	156
Benhall Place	Suff	TM3561	52°12·0′	1°26·7′E	X	156
Benhall Street	Suff	TM3561	52°12·0′	1°26·7′E	T	156
Ben Halton	Pth & Kin	NN7120	56°21·5′	4°4·8′W	H	51,52,57
Benham Fm	W Berks	SU4169	51°25·3′	1°24·2′W	FM	174
Benham Grange	W Berks	SU4168	51°24·8′	1°24·2′W	X	174
Benham Marsh Fm	W Berks	SU4267	51°24·3′	1°23·4′W	FM	174
Benham Park	W Berks	SU4367	51°24·3′	1°22·5′W	X	174
Benhams	Bucks	SU7586	51°34·3′	0°54·7′W	X	175
Benhams Fm	Hants	SU7731	51°4·6′	0°53·7′W	FM	186
Benham's Fm	W Berks	SU6466	51°23·6′	1°4·4′W	FM	175
Ben Harrald	Highld	NC5131	58°14·8′	4°31·8′W	X	16
Ben Hee	Highld	NC4233	58°15·7′	4°41·1′W	H	16
Ben Heilam	Highld	NC4661	58°30·9′	4°38·1′W	H	9
Ben Hiant	Highld	NM5363	56°41·9′	6°1·6′W	H	47
Ben Hiel	Highld	NC5950	58°25·2′	4°24·4′W	H	10
Benhilton	Sutton	TQ2665	51°22·4′	0°11·0′W	T	176
Ben Hogh	Arg & Bt	NM1858	56°38·0′	6°35·5′W	H	46
Benholm	Aberd	NO8069	56°49·0′	2°19·2′W	T	45
Ben Hope	Highld	NC4750	58°25·0′	4°36·7′W	H	9
Ben Horn	Highld	NC8006	58°1·9′	4°1·5′W	H	17
Ben Horneval	Highld	NG2849	57°27·3′	6°31·6′W	H	23
Ben Hutig	Highld	NC5365	58°33·2′	4°31·1′W	H	10
Ben Hynish	Arg & Bt	NL9639	56°27·0′	6°55·6′W	H	46
Beniar	Conwy	SH9668	53°12·2′	3°33·0′W	X	116
Ben Idrigill	Highld	NG2338	57°21·2′	6°35·9′W	H	23
Benigarth	Shetld	HU3691	60°36·3′	1°20·0′W	X	1,2
Beningbrough	N Yks	SE5257	54°0·6′	1°12·0′W	T	105
Beningbrough Grange	N Yks	SE5358	54°1·2′	1°11·0′W	X	105
Beningbrough Hall	N Yks	SE5158	54°1·2′	1°12·9′W	X	105
Beningbrough Park	N Yks	SE5158	54°1·2′	1°12·9′W	X	105
Benington	Herts	TL3023	51°53·7′	0°6·2′W	T	166
Benington	Lincs	TF3946	52°59·8′	0°4·7′E	T	131
Benington Br	Lincs	TF3750	53°2·0′	0°3·0′E	X	122
Benington Ho	Herts	TL3122	51°53·1′	0°5·4′W	X	166
Benington Park	Herts	TL3023	51°53·7′	0°6·2′W	X	166
Benington Sea End	Lincs	TF4046	52°59·8′	0°5·6′E	T	131
Beninner	D & G	NX6096	55°14·6′	4°11·7′W	H	77
Beninner Gairy	D & G	NX6097	55°15·1′	4°11·7′W	X	77
Ben Inverveigh	Arg & Bt	NN2738	56°30·4′	4°48·2′W	H	50
Beni Taing	Shetld	HU4022	59°59·1′	1°16·5′W	X	4
Benjafield Fm	Dorset	ST8028	51°3·3′	2°16·7′W	FM	183
Benjamin's Hurst	Suff	TL7976	52°21·4′	0°38·1′E	X	144
Benjamy	Somer	SS7343	51°10·6′	3°48·6′W	X	180
Benjarg Wood	D & G	NX6257	54°53·6′	4°8·7′W	F	83
Ben John	D & G	NX5454	54°51·8′	4°16·1′W	H	83
Benkhill Ho	N Yks	SE2687	54°16·9′	1°35·6′W	X	99
Ben Killilan	Highld	NG9731	57°19·7′	5°21·9′W	H	25
Ben Klibreck	Highld	NC5930	58°14·4′	4°23·6′W	H	16
Benknowle Fm	Hartpl	NZ4431	54°40·6′	1°18·6′W	FM	93
Ben Knowle Hill	Somer	ST5144	51°11·8′	2°41·7′W	H	182,183
Benkshill	Northum	NY7169	55°1·1′	2°26·8′W	X	86,87
Benks Hills	Northum	NY7068	55°0·6′	2°27·7′W	X	86,87
Ben Laga	Highld	NM6462	56°41·7′	5°50·8′W	H	40
Benlan	Carm	SN7138	52°1·8′	3°52·4′W	X	146,160
Ben Lane Fm	Lancs	SD4502	53°31·0′	2°49·4′W	FM	108
Ben Langass	N Eil	NF8465	57°34·1′	7°16·7′W	H	18
Ben Lawers	Pth & Kin	NN6341	56°32·7′	4°13·3′W	H	51
Ben Ledi	Stir	NN5609	56°15·4′	4°19·0′W	H	57
Ben Lee	Highld	NG5033	57°19·4′	6°8·7′W	H	24,32
Benley Cross	Devon	SS7315	50°55·5′	3°48·0′W	X	180
Benlister	N Ayr	NS0130	55°31·6′	5°8·7′W	X	69
Benlister Burn	N Ayr	NS0030	55°31·6′	5°9·7′W	W	69
Benlister Glen	N Ayr	NR9931	55°32·1′	5°10·7′W	X	69
Benllech	I of Angl	SH5182	53°19·1′	4°13·8′W	T	114,115
Benllech Sand	I of Angl	SH5282	53°19·1′	4°12·9′W	X	114,115
Benloch Burn	D & G	NX5694	55°13·4′	4°15·4′W	W	77

Ben Lomond	Stir	NN3602	56°11·2′	4°38·1′W	H	56
Ben Loyal	Highld	NC5748	58°24·1′	4°26·3′W	H	10
Ben Lui	Stir	NN2626	56°23·9′	4°48·7′W	H	50
Ben Luskentyre	N Eil	NG0999	57°53·4′	6°54·2′W	H	14
Ben Macdui or Beinn MacDuibh	Aberd	NN9999	57°4·5′	3°39·5′W	H	36,43
Ben Main	Moray	NJ3535	57°24·3′	3°4·4′W	H	28
Ben Meabost	Highld	NG5315	57°9·8′	6°4·7′W	H	32
Benmeal	D & G	NX5668	54°59·4′	4°14·6′W	H	83
Benmeal Burn	D & G	NX5667	54°58·9′	4°14·6′W	W	83
Ben Meggernie	Pth & Kin	NN5547	56°35·8′	4°21·3′W	H	51
Ben Miavaig	N Eil	NB0734	58°12·1′	6°58·8′W	H	13
Ben Mocacleit	N Eil	NB1627	58°8·7′	6°49·1′W	H	13
Ben More	Arg & Bt	NM5233	56°25·7′	6°0·9′W	H	47,48
Benmore	Arg & Bt	NS1385	56°1·5′	4°59·6′W	T	56
Benmore	D & G	NX3984	55°7·7′	4°31·1′W	H	77
Ben More	Stir	NN4324	56°23·2′	4°32·1′W	H	51
Ben More Assynt	Highld	NC3120	58°8·5′	4°51·8′W	H	15
Benmore Burn	Stir	NN4124	56°23·2′	4°34·1′W	W	51
Ben Môre Coigach	Highld	NC0904	57°59·3′	5°13·4′W	H	15
Benmore Farm	Stir	NN4125	56°23·7′	4°34·1′W	FM	51
Benmore Forest	Highld	NC3216	58°6·3′	4°50·6′W	X	15
Benmore Glen	Stir	NN4124	56°23·2′	4°34·1′W	X	51
Benmore Home Fm	Arg & Bt	NS1386	56°2·1′	4°59·7′W	FM	56
Benmore Lodge	Arg & Bt	NM5538	56°28·5′	5°58·3′W	X	47,48
Benmore Lodge	Highld	NC3211	58°3·6′	4°50·4′W	X	15
Bennachie	Aberd	NJ6522	57°17·5′	2°34·4′W	H	38
Bennachie Forest	Aberd	NJ6821	57°17·0′	2°31·4′W	F	38
Bennacott	Corn	SX2992	50°42·4′	4°24·9′W	T	190
Bennah	Devon	SX8384	50°38·9′	3°38·9′W	T	191
Bennallack	Corn	SW9249	50°18·5′	4°54·9′W	X	204
Bennals	S Ayr	NS4026	55°30·4′	4°31·6′W	X	70
Bennan	D & G	NX4082	55°6·6′	4°30·1′W	X	77
Bennan	D & G	NX5075	55°3·1′	4°20·5′W	X	77
Bennan	D & G	NX5679	55°5·3′	4°14·9′W	H	77
Bennan	D & G	NX5691	55°11·8′	4°15·3′W	X	77
Bennan	D & G	NX6690	55°11·4′	4°5·9′W	H	77
Bennan	D & G	NX6988	55°10·4′	4°3·0′W	H	77
Bennan	D & G	NX7894	55°13·8′	3°54·7′W	X	78
Bennan	D & G	NX7994	55°13·8′	3°53·7′W	H	78
Bennan	D & G	NX8277	55°4·7′	3°50·5′W	H	84
Bennan	S Ayr	NS3704	55°18·4′	4°33·7′W	X	77
Bennanbrack	D & G	NX4477	55°4·0′	4°26·2′W	X	77
Bennan Burn	S Ayr	NX2492	55°11·7′	4°45·5′W	W	76
Bennan Cott	D & G	NX6571	55°1·2′	4°6·3′W	X	77,84
Bennane Head	S Ayr	NX0986	55°8·1′	4°59·4′W	X	76
Bennane Lea	S Ayr	NX0985	55°7·6′	4°59·3′W	X	76
Bennan Fm	E Renf	NS5151	55°44·0′	4°21·9′W	FM	64
Bennan Head	N Ayr	NR9920	55°26·2′	5°10·2′W	X	69
Bennan Hill	D & G	NX1577	55°3·4′	4°53·4′W	X	76
Bennan Hill	D & G	NX2948	54°48·1′	4°39·2′W	H	82
Bennan Hill	D & G	NX4575	55°3·0′	4°25·1′W	H	77
Bennan Hill	D & G	NX5386	55°9·0′	4°18·0′W	H	77
Bennan Hill	D & G	NX6264	54°57·3′	4°8·9′W	X	83
Bennan Hill	D & G	NX6468	54°59·5′	4°7·1′W	H	83
Bennan Hill	D & G	NX6472	55°1·7′	4°7·2′W	H	77
Bennan Hill	E Renf	NS5250	55°43·5′	4°21·0′W	H	64
Bennan Hill	S Ayr	NS3703	55°17·9′	4°33·6′W	H	77
Bennan Loch	E Renf	NS5250	55°43·5′	4°21·0′W	W	64
Bennan Moss	D & G	NX6471	55°1·2′	4°7·2′W	X	77
Bennan Plantation	D & G	NX3264	54°56·8′	4°37·0′W	F	82
Bennar-fawr	Gwyn	SH5822	52°46·9′	4°5·9′W	X	124
Ben na Scute	N Eil	NL6298	56°57·2′	7°33·2′W	H	31
Bennathie	Pth & Kin	NO2041	56°33·5′	3°17·6′W	X	53
Bennecarrigan	N Ayr	NR9423	55°27·7′	5°15·1′W	T	68,69
Bennecarrigan Fm	N Ayr	NR9422	55°27·2′	5°15·0′W	FM	68,69
Benneeve	D & G	NX7183	55°7·7′	4°1·0′W	H	77
Bennel Fm	Cambs	TL3756	52°11·3′	0°0·6′E	FM	154
Bennel Hill	D & G	NX8958	54°54·5′	3°43·5′W	H	84
Bennethead	Cumbr	NY4423	54°36·2′	2°51·6′W	X	90
Bennet Hill	Moray	NJ1167	57°41·3′	3°29·1′W	X	28
Bennetland	E Yorks	SE8228	53°44·8′	0°45·0′W	T	106
Bennet's Burn	E Loth	NT6473	55°57·2′	2°34·2′W	W	67
Bennetsfield	Highld	NH6753	57°33·1′	4°12·9′W	X	26
Bennetston Hall (Hotel)	Derby	SK0879	53°18·7′	1°52·4′W	X	119
Bennet's Wood	W Berks	SU5878	51°30·1′	1°9·5′W	F	174
Bennett End	Bucks	SU7896	51°39·7′	0°51·9′W	T	165
Bennetts	Corn	SX2698	50°45·6′	4°27·6′W	X	190
Bennett's Cross	Devon	SX6781	50°37·0′	3°52·4′W	A	191
Bennett's Cross	Devon	SX7857	50°24·2′	3°42·6′W	X	202
Bennetts End	Herts	TL0605	51°44·2′	0°27·5′W	T	166
Bennettsfield	Northum	NY8595	55°15·2′	2°13·7′W	X	80
Bennett's Fm	Essex	TL8032	51°57·7′	0°37·6′E	FM	168
Bennetts Fm	Kent	TQ7143	51°9·9′	0°27·1′E	FM	188
Bennett's Fm	Suff	TM1761	52°12·5′	1°11·0′E	FM	156
Bennetts Fm	W Susx	TQ1217	50°56·7′	0°24·0′W	FM	198
Bennettshayes Fm	Devon	ST1103	50°49·4′	3°15·4′W	FM	192,193
Bennettshill	Ches	SJ9566	53°11·7′	2°4·1′W	X	118
Bennett's Hill Fm	Dorset	SY4890	50°42·7′	2°43·8′W	FM	193
Bennett's Hill Fm	Worcs	SP0645	52°6·4′	1°54·3′W	FM	150
Bennett, The	Pemb	SN0540	52°1·7′	4°50·2′W	X	145
Ben Nevis	Highld	NN1671	56°47·9′	5°0·3′W	H	41
Ben Newe	Aberd	NJ3814	57°13·0′	3°1·1′W	H	37
Benn Hills Fm	Leic	SK3001	52°36·6′	1°33·0′W	FM	140
Benni Cuml	Orkney	HY6721	59°4·7′	2°34·1′W	A	5
Bennieloan	D & G	NX6890	55°11·5′	4°4·0′W	X	77
Benniguinea	D & G	NX5676	55°3·7′	4°14·9′W	H	77
Benningham Grange	Suff	TM1670	52°17·4′	1°10·4′E	X	144,156
Benningham Hall	Suff	TM1670	52°17·4′	1°10·4′E	X	144,156
Benningholme Grange	E Yorks	TA1138	53°49·8′	0°18·4′W	X	107
Benningholme Hall	E Yorks	TA1238	53°49·8′	0°17·5′W	X	107
Bennington Fen	Lincs	SK8147	53°1·1′	0°47·1′W	X	130
Bennison Ho	N Yks	NZ9008	54°27·8′	0°36·3′W	X	94
Benniworth	Lincs	TF2081	53°19·0′	0°11·5′W	T	122
Benniworth Grange	Lincs	TF2180	53°18·4′	0°10·6′W	X	122
Benniworth Ho	Lincs	TF2283	53°20·0′	0°9·7′W	X	122
Benniworth Moor Fm	Lincs	TF1980	53°18·4′	0°12·4′W	FM	122
Benniworth Walk Fm	Lincs	TF2281	53°18·9′	0°9·7′W	FM	122
Benn, The	Cumbr	NY3019	54°33·9′	3°4·5′W	X	90
Bennybeg	Pth & Kin	NN8618	56°20·7′	3°50·2′W	X	58

Bennybeg Pond	Pth & Kin	NN8618	56°20·7′	3°50·2′W	W	58
Benny Bent	N Yks	SE1462	54°3·5′	1°46·8′W	X	99
Bennyfold Fm	W Susx	TQ0024	51°0·6′	0°34·1′W	FM	197
Bennygray	Angus	NO5283	56°56·4′	2°46·9′W	H	44
Benny Mill	Corn	SW8457	50°22·6′	5°1·9′W	X	200
Benoak	Corn	SX2360	50°25·0′	4°29·1′W	X	201
Ben Obe	N Eil	NF7002	56°59·7′	7°25·6′W	H	31
Ben Orosay	N Eil	NL6397	56°56·7′	7°32·1′W	H	31
Ben Orosay	N Eil	NL6797	56°56·9′	7°28·2′W	H	31
Benorth	Corn	SX1169	50°29·7′	4°39·5′W	X	200
Ben Oss	Stir	NN2825	56°23·4′	4°46·7′W	H	50
Ben Our	Stir	NN6120	56°21·4′	4°14·5′W	H	51,57
Benover	Kent	TQ7048	51°12·6′	0°26·4′E	T	188
Benquhat Hill	E Ayr	NS4610	55°21·8′	4°25·4′W	X	70
Ben Raah	N Eil	NB0301	57°54·2′	7°0·4′W	H	18
Ben Reid	Angus	NO3175	56°51·9′	3°7·5′W	X	44
Ben Reoch	Arg & Bt	NN3101	56°10·6′	4°42·9′W	H	56
Ben Rhydding	Brad	SE1347	53°55·4′	1°47·7′W	T	104
Benridge	Durham	NZ4637	54°43·8′	1°16·7′W	X	93
Benridge Hagg	Northum	NZ1687	55°10·9′	1°44·5′W	X	81
Benridge Hall	Northum	NZ1475	55°4·4′	1°46·4′W	X	88
Benridge Moor	Northum	NZ1688	55°11·4′	1°44·5′W	X	81
Benrig	Scot Bord	NT6030	55°34·0′	2°37·6′W	X	74
Ben Rinnes	Moray	NJ2435	57°24·2′	3°15·4′W	H	28
Benrinnes Wood	Moray	NJ2735	57°24·2′	3°12·4′W	F	28
Ben Risary	N Eil	NF7672	57°37·6′	7°25·2′W	H	18
Ben Roishader	Highld	NG3948	57°27·1′	6°20·6′W	H	23
Ben Rulibreck	N Eil	NL6294	56°55·1′	7°32·9′W	H	31
Ben Salachill	Pth & Kin	NN9444	56°34·8′	3°43·1′W	H	52,53
Ben Sca	Highld	NG3347	57°26·4′	6°26·5′W	H	23
Ben Scaalan	Highld	NG3326	57°15·1′	6°25·1′W	X	32
Ben Scaapar	N Eil	NF9570	57°37·3′	7°6·1′W	H	18
Benscliffe Wood	Leic	SK5112	52°42·4′	1°14·3′W	F	129
Ben Scolpaig	N Eil	NF7376	57°39·6′	7°28·6′W	H	18
Benscravie	Angus	NO4062	56°45·0′	2°58·4′W	H	44
Ben Screavie	Highld	NC3039	58°18·7′	4°53·6′W	H	15
Ben Scrien	N Eil	NF7911	57°4·9′	7°17·5′W	H	31
Ben Scudaig	Highld	NG3541	57°23·2′	6°24·1′W	H	23
Ben Scurrival	N Eil	NF6908	57°2·9′	7°27·1′W	H	31
Bense Bridge Fm	N Yks	NZ5207	54°27·6′	1°11·4′W	FM	93
Bensel	Angus	NO4652	56°39·7′	2°52·4′W	X	54
Bensfield	Falk	NS8884	56°2·4′	3°47·4′W	X	65
Bensgreen Fm	Hants	SU7127	51°2·5′	0°58·8′W	FM	186,197
Bensham	Ghead	NZ2462	54°57·4′	1°37·1′W	T	88
Benshaw Hill	Scot Bord	NT0929	55°33·0′	3°26·1′W	H	72
Benshayes Fm	Devon	SS9322	50°59·5′	3°31·1′W	FM	181
Ben Shee	Pth & Kin	NN9053	56°12·7′	3°41·1′W	H	58
Ben Sheildaig	Highld	NG8351	57°30·1′	5°36·9′W	H	24
Benshinnie	D & G	NX7173	55°2·3′	4°0·7′W	X	77,84
Ben Skievie	Pth & Kin	NO0064	56°45·7′	3°37·7′W	H	43
Benskins	E Susx	TQ8116	50°55·1′	0°34·9′E	X	199
Ben Skriaig	Highld	NG1653	57°29·0′	6°43·9′W	H	23
Benslie	N Ayr	NS3343	55°39·4′	4°38·8′W	T	63,70
Benson	Oxon	SU6191	51°37·1′	1°6·7′W	T	164,175
Benson Airfield	Oxon	SU6291	51°37·1′	1°5·9′W	X	164,175
Benson Hall	Cumbr	SD5394	54°20·6′	2°43·0′W	X	97
Benson Knott	Cumbr	SD5494	54°20·6′	2°42·0′W	H	97
Bensons	Lancs	SD4143	53°53·0′	2°53·4′W	X	102
Benson's Brook	Shrops	SO5877	52°23·6′	2°36·6′W	W	137,138
Benson's Fell	Northum	NY9262	54°57·4′	2°7·1′W	X	87
Benson's Fen	Cambs	TL4188	52°28·5′	0°5·0′E	X	142,143
Benson's Fm	Cambs	TL4188	52°28·5′	0°5·0′E	FM	142,143
Benson's Fm	Essex	TQ6990	51°35·2′	0°26·8′E	FM	177,178
Benson's Fm	W Susx	TQ2033	51°5·3′	0°16·8′W	FM	187
Benson's Hill	W Susx	TQ2632	51°4·6′	0°11·7′W	X	187
Benson's Ho	Lancs	SD5336	53°49·3′	2°42·4′W	X	102
Ben Stack	Highld	NC2642	58°20·2′	4°57·9′W	H	9
Ben Stack	N Eil	NF7909	57°3·9′	7°17·3′W	H	31
Ben Starav	Highld	NN1242	56°32·2′	5°3·0′W	H	50
Benstead Marshes	Suff	TM3691	52°28·2′	1°28·9′E	X	134
Benston	E Ayr	NS3915	55°24·4′	4°32·1′W	X	70
Benston	S Ayr	NS4324	55°29·3′	4°28·7′W	X	70
Benston	Shetld	HU4653	60°15·8′	1°9·6′W	T	3
Benston Fm	E Ayr	NS5815	55°24·8′	4°14·2′W	FM	71
Benstonhall	Orkney	HY5536	59°12·8′	2°46·8′W	X	5
Benstor Ho	Derby	SK1676	53°17·1′	1°45·2′W	X	119
Ben Strome	Highld	NC2436	58°16·9′	4°59·6′W	H	15
Ben Suardal	Highld	NG6320	57°12·8′	5°55·0′W	H	32
Bent	Aberd	NO6972	56°50·6′	2°30·0′W	X	45
Bent	E Ayr	NS4917	55°25·7′	4°22·7′W	X	70
Bent	E Ayr	NS5033	55°34·3′	4°22·3′W	X	70
Bent	N Yks	SD9944	53°53·8′	2°0·5′W	X	103
Bent	Renf	NS4359	55°48·2′	4°29·9′W	X	64
Bent	S Lanak	NS7842	55°39·6′	3°55·9′W	X	71
Bent	W Dunb	NS4386	56°2·7′	4°30·8′W	X	56
Bentall's Fm	Essex	TL8232	51°57·6′	0°39·3′E	FM	168
Ben Tangaval	N Eil	NL6399	56°57·8′	7°32·3′W	H	31
Ben Tarvie	Highld	NH7495	57°55·9′	4°7·2′W	H	21
Ben Tee	Highld	NN2497	57°2·3′	4°53·6′W	H	34
Bentend	N Lanak	NS7383	56°1·6′	4°1·8′W	X	57,64
Bent End Fm	Staffs	SJ9663	53°10·1′	2°3·2′W	FM	118
Benter	Somer	ST6449	51°14·6′	2°30·6′W	T	183
Bentfield	S Ayr	NS3424	55°29·2′	4°37·2′W	X	70
Bentfield Bury	Essex	TL4925	51°54·4′	0°10·4′E	T	167
Bentfield Green	Essex	TL5025	51°54·4′	0°11·2′E	T	167
Bent Fm	Ches	SJ8362	53°9·5′	2°14·8′W	FM	118
Bent Fm	Derby	SK1852	53°4·1′	1°43·5′W	FM	119
Bent Fm	Hants	SU6313	50°55·0′	1°5·8′W	FM	196
Bentfoot	N Lanak	NS8564	55°51·6′	3°49·8′W	X	65
Bent Gate	Lancs	SD7921	53°41·3′	2°18·7′W	T	103
Bentgate	Roch	SD9311	53°36·0′	2°5·9′W	T	109
Bent Geo	Orkney	ND4897	58°51·7′	2°53·6′W	X	6,7
Benthall	Shrops	SJ3913	52°42·9′	2°53·8′W	X	126
Benthall	Shrops	SJ6602	52°37·1′	2°29·7′W	T	127
Bent Hall	S Lanak	NS6250	55°43·7′	4°11·4′W	X	64
Benthall Edge	Shrops	SJ6503	52°37·7′	2°30·6′W	X	127
Benthall Edge Wood	Shrops	SJ6603	52°37·7′	2°29·7′W	F	127
Bentham	Glos	SO9116	51°50·8′	2°7·4′W	T	163
Bentham Ho	Wilts	SU0989	51°36·2′	1°51·8′W	X	173
Bentham Moor	N Yks	SD6571	54°8·3′	2°31·7′W	X	97

Bentha Plantn	Lancs	SD8750	53°57·0′	2°11·5′W	F	103
Bent Haw Scar	Cumbr	SD1766	54°5·2′	3°15·7′W	X	96
Benthead	D & G	NX9195	55°14·5′	3°42·4′W	X	78
Benthead	Fife	NT0992	56°7·0′	3°27·4′W	X	58
Benthead	N Ayr	NS3346	55°41·0′	4°38·9′W	X	63
Benthead	S Lanak	NT0054	55°46·4′	3°35·2′W	X	65,72
Benthead	Staffs	SK0061	53°9·0′	1°59·6′W	X	119
Benthill	Derby	SK3454	53°5·2′	1°29·1′W	X	119
Benthill Fm	Bucks	SP7032	51°59·2′	0°58·4′W	FM	152,165
Bent Hill Fm	N Yks	SE1054	53°59·2′	1°50·4′W	FM	104
Bent Hills	Sheff	SK2893	53°26·2′	1°34·3′W	X	110
Benthills Wood	N Som	ST3758	51°19·3′	2°53·9′W	F	182
Bent Ho	Derby	SK2133	52°53·9′	1°40·9′W	X	128
Bent Ho	Lancs	SD7757	54°0·8′	2°20·6′W	X	103
Bent Ho	Northum	NY7785	55°9·8′	2°21·2′W	X	80
Benthoul	C of Aber	NJ8003	57°7·3′	2°19·4′W	T	38
Bent House Fm	Durham	NZ2941	54°46·0′	1°32·5′W	FM	88
Benthouse Fm	Staffs	SK0038	52°56·6′	1°59·6′W	FM	128
Bent Houses	Cumbr	NY0927	54°38·0′	3°24·2′W	X	89
Ben Thrush	Pth & Kin	NN9805	56°13·9′	3°38·3′W	H	58
Ben Tianavaig	Highld	NG5140	57°23·2′	6°8·1′W	H	23,24
Bentick	Pth & Kin	NN8008	56°15·2′	3°55·8′W	X	57
Bentie Knowe	Pth & Kin	NN9502	56°12·2′	3°41·1′W	X	58
Bentilee	C of Stoke	SJ9146	53°0·9′	2°7·6′W	T	118
Bentilee	Staffs	SK1023	52°48·5′	1°50·7′W	X	128
Bentilee Park	Staffs	SK1122	52°48·0′	1°49·8′W	X	128
Bentilee Wood	Staffs	SJ8143	52°59·3′	2°16·6′W	F	118
Bentinck Fm	Norf	TF5622	52°46·6′	0°19·2′E	FM	131
Ben Tirran	Angus	NO3674	56°51·4′	3°2·5′W	X	44
Bent Laithe	Lancs	SD9042	53°52·7′	2°8·7′W	X	103
Bentlass	Pemb	SM9601	51°40·5′	4°56·6′W	T	157,158
Bentlawnt	Shrops	SJ3301	52°36·4′	2°59·0′W	T	126
Bentleigh Fm	Wilts	SU2132	51°5·4′	1°41·6′W	FM	184
Bentley	Donc	SE5605	53°32·6′	1°8·9′W	T	111
Bentley	Essex	TQ5696	51°38·7′	0°15·7′E	T	167,177
Bentley	E Yorks	TA0135	53°48·3′	0°27·6′W	T	106,107
Bentley	Hants	SU7844	51°11·6′	0°52·6′W	T	186
Bentley	Suff	TM1136	51°59·2′	1°4·8′E	X	155,169
Bentley	Wals	SO9898	52°35·0′	2°1·4′W	T	139
Bentley	Warw	SP2895	52°33·4′	1°34·8′W	T	140
Bentley Br	Derby	SK3161	53°9·0′	1°31·8′W	X	119
Bentley Brook	Derby	SK1739	52°57·1′	1°44·4′W	W	128
Bentley Brook	Staffs	SK0113	52°43·1′	1°58·7′W	W	128
Bentley Close Fm	Durham	NZ0825	54°37·4′	1°52·1′W	FM	92
Bentley Common	Donc	SE5805	53°32·5′	1°7·1′W	X	111
Bentley Common	Warw	SP2896	52°33·9′	1°34·8′W	T	140
Bentley Fields Open Fm	Derby	SK1838	52°56·6′	1°43·5′W	FM	128
Bentley Fm	Derby	SK3779	53°18·6′	1°26·3′W	FM	119
Bentley Fm	E Susx	TQ4815	50°55·2′	0°6·7′E	FM	198
Bentley Fm	Lincs	TA0006	53°32·7′	0°29·0′W	FM	112
Bentley Fm	Shrops	SJ4728	52°51·1′	2°46·8′W	FM	126
Bentley Fm	Warw	SK2804	52°38·2′	1°34·8′W	FM	140
Bentley Fm	Worcs	SO8162	52°15·6′	2°16·3′W	FM	138,150
Bentley Fms	Hants	SU3129	51°3·8′	1°33·1′W	FM	185
Bentley Ford Fm	Shrops	SO5099	52°35·4′	2°43·9′W	FM	137,138
Bentley Green Fm	Hants	SU7843	51°11·1′	0°52·6′W	FM	186
Bentley Hall	Bury	SD7611	53°35·9′	2°21·3′W	X	109
Bentley Hall	Derby	SK1738	52°56·6′	1°44·4′W	A	128
Bentley Hall	Derby	SK1750	53°3·1′	1°44·4′W	X	119
Bentley Hall	Hants	SU7942	51°10·5′	0°51·8′W	X	186
Bentleyhall Fm	Derby	SK3779	53°18·6′	1°26·3′W	FM	119
Bentley Hall Fm	Staffs	SK0818	52°45·8′	1°52·5′W	FM	128
Bentley Heath	Herts	TQ2499	51°40·8′	0°12·0′W	T	166,176
Bentley Heath	Sol	SP1675	52°22·6′	1°45·5′W	T	139
Bentley Ho	Worcs	SO9966	52°17·8′	2°0·5′W	X	150
Bentleyhurst Fm	Ches	SJ7180	53°19·2′	2°25·7′W	FM	109
Bentley Long Wood	Suff	TM1039	52°0·8′	1°4·0′E	F	155,169
Bentley Manor	Essex	TM1225	51°53·2′	1°5·2′E	X	168,169
Bentley Manor	Sol	SP1574	52°22·1′	1°46·4′W	X	139
Bentley Manor	Suff	TM1239	52°0·8′	1°5·8′E	X	155,169
Bentley Old Hall	Suff	TM1139	52°0·8′	1°4·9′E	X	155,169
Bentley Park	Suff	TM1138	52°0·2′	1°4·8′E	X	155,169
Bentley Park Wood	Warw	SP2895	52°33·4′	1°34·8′W	F	140
Bentley Priory	Harrow	TQ1593	51°37·7′	0°19·9′W	X	176
Bentley Rise	Donc	SE5604	53°32·0′	1°8·9′W	T	111
Bentley's Fm	Ches	SJ6280	53°19·2′	2°33·8′W	FM	109
Bentley's Fm	Warw	SP2487	52°29·1′	1°38·4′W	FM	139
Bentley's Fm	Wrex	SJ3447	53°1·2′	2°58·6′W	FM	117
Bentley Sta	Hants	SU7943	51°11·1′	0°51·8′W	X	186
Bentley Wood	E Susx	TQ4816	50°55·7′	0°6·8′E	F	198
Bentley Wood	E Susx	TQ5016	50°55·7′	0°8·5′E	F	199
Bentley Wood	Wilts	SU2530	51°4·4′	1°38·2′W	F	184
Ben Toirlean	Highld	NG3239	57°22·0′	6°27·0′W	H	23,32
Benton	Arg & Bt	NR7310	55°20·2′	5°34·3′W	X	68
Benton	Devon	SS6536	51°6·7′	3°55·3′W	T	180
Benton Castle	Pemb	SN0006	51°43·3′	4°53·4′W	A	157,158
Benton Close	N Yks	SD8295	54°21·3′	2°16·2′W	X	98
Benton Green	Sol	SP2579	52°24·7′	1°37·5′W	T	140
Ben Tongue	Highld	NC6058	58°29·5′	4°23·6′W	H	10
Benton Hall	Essex	TL8213	51°47·4′	0°38·7′E	X	168
Bentons	Suff	TL9950	52°7·0′	0°54·8′E	X	155
Bentons Place Fm	W Susx	TQ1319	50°57·8′	0°23·1′W	FM	198
Benton Square	N Tyne	NZ2970	55°1·7′	1°32·4′W	X	88
Benton Wood	Pemb	SN0007	51°43·8′	4°53·4′W	F	157,158
Ben Totaig	Highld	NG1949	57°26·9′	6°40·6′W	H	23
Ben Tote	Highld	NG4150	57°28·2′	6°18·7′W	H	23
Bentpath	D & G	NY3190	55°12·2′	3°4·6′W	T	79
Bentries Fm	Suff	TM2858	52°10·6′	1°20·5′E	FM	156
Bent Rig	S Lanak	NS9828	55°32·4′	3°36·5′W	H	72
Bents	Aberd	NO8297	57°4·1′	2°17·4′W	X	38,45
Bents	D & G	NX8664	54°57·7′	3°46·4′W	X	84
Bents	D & G	NY0387	55°10·3′	3°30·9′W	X	78
Bents	N Yks	SD8698	54°22·9′	2°12·5′W	X	98
Bents	N Yks	SD9598	54°22·9′	2°4·2′W	X	98
Bents	S Ayr	NX2183	55°6·8′	4°48·0′W	X	76
Bents	S Lanak	NS6947	55°42·2′	4°4·6′W	X	64
Bents	W Loth	NS9762	55°50·7′	3°38·3′W	T	65
Bents	W Loth	NT0562	55°50·8′	3°30·6′W	X	65
Bents Cottages	Cumbr	NY4341	54°45·9′	2°52·7′W	X	85
Bents Farm	D & G	NX4367	54°58·6′	4°26·8′W	FM	83

Bents Fm	Cumbr	NY3663	54°57·7'	2°59·5'W	FM	85
Bents Fm	Cumbr	NY7006	54°27·2'	2°27·3'W	FM	91
Bent's Fm	N Yks	SE1464	54°4·5'	1°46·7'W	FM	99
Bents Fm, The	Fife	NT0592	56°6·9'	3°31·2'W	FM	58
Bents Head	Brad	SE0836	53°49·5'	1°52·3'W	T	104
Bents Head	Durham	NY8439	54°45·0'	2°14·5'W	X	91,92
Bents Ho	N Yks	SD9796	54°21·8'	2°2·4'W	X	98
Bents Ho	N Yks	SE1871	54°8·3'	1°43·1'W	X	99
Bents Ho	Sheff	SK2289	53°24·1'	1°39·7'W	X	110
Bents, The	Angus	NO5552	56°39·7'	2°43·6'W	X	54
Bents, The	Fife	NT2686	56°3·9'	3°10·9'W	X	66
Bents, The	S Tyne	NZ3767	55°0·0'	1°24·9'W	X	88
Bents Wood	E Loth	NT5267	55°53·9'	2°45·6'W	F	66
Bent, The	Derby	SK2133	52°53·9'	1°40·9'W	X	128
Bent, The	Derby	SK3052	53°4·1'	1°32·7'W	X	119
Bent, The	Derby	SK3649	53°2·5'	1°27·4'W	X	119
Bent, The	Staffs	SK0762	53°9·5'	1°53·3'W	X	119
Bent, The	Traf	SJ7089	53°24·1'	2°26·7'W	X	109
Bentudor	D & G	NX7554	54°52·2'	3°56·4'W	H	84
Bentwaters Airfield	Suff	TM3553	52°7·7'	1°26·4'E	X	156
Bentwichen	Devon	SS7333	51°5·2'	3°48·4'W	T	180
Bentworth	Hants	SU6640	51°9·6'	1°3·0'W	T	185,186
Bentworth Hall	Hants	SU6639	51°9·0'	1°3·0'W	X	185,186
Bentworth Lodge	Hants	SU6840	51°9·5'	1°1·3'W	X	185,186
Benty Cowan Hill	E Ayr	NS5708	55°21·0'	4°14·9'W	H	71,77
Benty Grange	Derby	SK1464	53°10·6'	1°47·0'W	X	119
Benty Gutter	N Yks	SD8598	54°22·9'	2°13·4'W	W	98
Bentyhall	E Loth	NT5464	55°52·3'	2°43·7'W	X	66
Benty Hill	Cumbr	NY6643	54°47·1'	2°31·3'W	X	86
Benty Hill	Cumbr	NY6743	54°47·1'	2°30·4'W	H	86,87
Benty Hill (Cairn)	Cumbr	NY6743	54°47·1'	2°30·4'W	A	86,87
Benty Howe	Cumbr	NY4613	54°30·8'	2°49·6'W	X	90
Benty Roads	Angus	NO3376	56°52·5'	3°5·5'W	H	44
Ben Uarie	Highld	NC9216	58°7·5'	3°49·5'W	H	17
Benuff Burn	S Lanak	NS9409	55°22·1'	3°39·9'W	W	71,78
Benuick	Corn	SW9273	50°31·4'	4°55·7'W	X	200
Ben Uigshader	Highld	NG3649	57°27·5'	6°23·7'W	H	23
Ben Vane	Arg & Bt	NN2709	56°14·8'	4°47·1'W	H	56
Benvane	Stir	NN5313	56°17·5'	4°22·1'W	H	57
Ben Vanisary	N Eil	NF7473	57°38·0'	7°27·3'W	H	18
Ben Vaslain	N Eil	NF6904	57°0·8'	7°26·8'W	H	31
Ben Vatten	Highld	NG2944	57°24·6'	6°30·3'W	H	23
Ben Venue	Stir	NN4706	56°13·6'	4°27·6'W	H	57
Ben Verrisey	N Eil	NF6802	56°59·6'	7°27·6'W	H	31
Ben Vic Askill	Highld	NG2847	57°26·2'	6°31·5'W	H	23
Benvie	Angus	NO3231	56°28·2'	3°5·8'W	T	53
Benville	Dorset	ST5403	50°49·7'	2°38·8'W	T	194
Benville Br	Dorset	ST5503	50°49·7'	2°38·0'W	X	194
Benville Manor	Dorset	ST5303	50°49·7'	2°39·7'W	A	194
Ben Volovaig	Highld	NG4376	57°42·3'	6°18·4'W	H	23
Ben Vorlich	Arg & Bt	NN2912	56°16·4'	4°45·3'W	H	50,56
Ben Vorlich	Pth & Kin	NN6318	56°20·3'	4°12·5'W	H	57
Ben Vrackie	Pth & Kin	NN9563	56°45·1'	3°42·6'W	H	43
Ben Vratabreck	Highld	NG1645	57°24·7'	6°43·3'W	H	23
Ben Vuirich	Pth & Kin	NN9970	56°48·9'	3°38·8'W	H	43
Benwell	N upon Ty	NZ2164	54°58·5'	1°39·9'W	T	88
Benwells	Aberd	NJ9447	57°31·0'	2°5·6'W	X	30
Benwick	Cambs	TL3490	52°29·7'	0°1·2'W	T	142
Benwick Mere	Cambs	TL3488	52°28·6'	0°1·2'W	X	142
Ben Wyvis	Highld	NH4668	57°40·8'	4°34·5'W	H	20
Benyellary	D & G	NX4183	55°7·2'	4°29·2'W	H	77
Benyon's Inclosure	Hants	SU6263	51°22·0'	1°6·2'W	F	175
Benziaroth	Orkney	HY3614	59°0·8'	3°6·4'W	X	6
Benziecott	Orkney	HY4939	59°14·3'	2°53·1'W	X	5
Benzien Craig	D & G	NS7206	55°20·1'	4°0·6'W	X	71,77
Beobridge	Shrops	SO7991	52°31·2'	2°18·2'W	T	138
Beoch	D & G	NX0865	54°56·8'	4°59·5'W	X	82
Beoch	D & G	NX3271	55°0·6'	4°37·2'W	X	76
Beoch	D & G	NX6860	54°55·3'	4°3·2'W	X	83,84
Beoch	E Ayr	NS4700	55°16·5'	4°24·1'W	X	77
Beoch	S Ayr	NS2914	55°23·7'	4°41·6'W	X	70
Beoch Burn	D & G	NX0965	54°56·8'	4°58·5'W	W	82
Beoch Burn	D & G	NX3172	55°1·1'	4°38·2'W	W	76
Beoch Hill	D & G	NX0967	54°57·9'	4°58·6'W	H	82
Beoch Lane	E Ayr	NS5211	55°22·5'	4°19·7'W	W	70
Beoch Moor	D & G	NX6861	54°55·8'	4°3·2'W	X	83,84
Beolary	Highld	NG8620	57°13·5'	5°32·2'W	X	33
Beoley	Worcs	SP0669	52°19·4'	1°54·3'W	T	139
Beoley Hall	Worcs	SP0670	52°19·9'	1°54·3'W	X	139
Beolka	Shetld	HU4328	60°2·3'	1°13·2'W	X	4
Beoraidbeg	Highld	NM6793	56°58·4'	5°49·6'W	T	40
Beoraidbeg Hill	Highld	NM6794	56°59·0'	5°49·6'W	H	40
Beorgs of Collafirth	Shetld	HU3484	60°32·6'	1°22·3'W	X	1,2,3
Beorgs of Housetter	Shetld	HU3585	60°33·1'	1°21·2'W	H	1,2,3
Beorgs of Skelberry	Shetld	HU3588	60°34·7'	1°21·2'W	H	1,2
Beorgs of Uyea	Shetld	HU3389	60°35·3'	1°23·4'W	H	1,2
Beosetter	Shetld	HU4944	60°10·9'	1°6·5'W	X	4
Bephillick	Corn	SX2259	50°24·5'	4°29·9'W	X	201
Bepton	W Susx	SU8518	50°57·5'	0°47·0'W	T	197
Bepton Down	W Susx	SU8517	50°57·0'	0°47·0'W	X	197
Bera Bach	Gwyn	SH6767	53°11·3'	3°59·0'W	H	115
Berain	Conwy	SJ0069	53°12·8'	3°29·4'W	A	116
Bera Mawr	Gwyn	SH6768	53°11·8'	3°59·1'W	H	115
Berber Hill	Devon	SX9284	50°39·0'	3°31·3'W	X	192
Berclees	D & G	NY2975	55°4·1'	3°6·3'W	X	85
Bercoed-uchaf	Cered	SN3939	52°1·8'	4°20·4'W	X	145
Ber Dale	Shetld	HU2776	60°28·3'	1°30·0'W	X	3
Berden	Essex	TL4629	51°56·6'	0°7·8'E	T	167
Berden Hall	Essex	TL4629	51°56·6'	0°7·8'E	A	167
Berden Priory Fm	Essex	TL4630	51°57·2'	0°7·9'E	FM	167
Berea	Pemb	SM7929	51°55·2'	5°12·4'W	X	157
Bere Alston	Devon	SX4466	50°28·6'	4°11·5'W	T	201
Bere Chapel	Dorset	ST3905	50°50·7'	2°51·6'W	X	193
Berechurch	Essex	TL9922	51°51·9'	0°53·8'E	T	168
Bere Court	W Berks	SU6175	51°28·5'	1°6·9'W	X	175
Bere Down	Dorset	SY8497	50°46·6'	2°13·2'W	X	194
Bere Ferrers	Devon	SX4563	50°27·0'	4°10·6'W	T	201
Bere Fm	Dorset	ST3705	50°50·7'	2°53·3'W	FM	193
Bere Fm	Dorset	SY9493	50°44·4'	2°4·7'W	FM	195
Bere Fm	Hants	SU5909	50°52·9'	1°9·3'W	FM	196

Bere Fm	Hants	SU6014	50°55·6'	1°8·4'W	FM	196
Bere Fm	Hants	SU6225	51°1·5'	1°6·6'W	FM	185
Bere Fm	Kent	TR3343	51°8·5'	1°20·3'E	FM	179
Berefold	Aberd	NJ9735	57°24·6'	2°2·5'W	T	30
Bereforstal Fm	Kent	TR1742	51°8·4'	1°6·5'E	FM	179,189
Bere Heath	Dorset	SY8590	50°42·8'	2°12·4'W	X	194
Bere Heath	Dorset	SY8692	50°43·9'	2°11·5'W	X	194
Bere Hill Fm	Hants	SU3744	51°11·9'	1°27·8'W	FM	185
Berehill Fm	Hants	SU4649	51°14·5'	1°20·1'W	FM	185
Bereleigh Ho	Hants	SU6723	51°0·4'	1°2·3'W	X	185
Bere Mills Fm	Somer	ST3412	50°54·5'	2°55·9'W	FM	193
Berepper	Corn	SW6522	50°3·3'	5°16·6'W	T	203
Bere Regis	Dorset	SY8495	50°45·5'	2°13·2'W	T	194
Beresford Dale	Staffs	SK1259	53°7·9'	1°48·8'W	X	119
Bereton Fm	Heref	SO4055	52°11·6'	2°52·3'W	FM	148,149
Bere Wood	Dorset	SY8695	50°45·5'	2°11·5'W	F	194
Berewyk Hall	Essex	TL8830	51°56·4'	0°44·5'E	X	168
Berfern	Inverc	NS2071	55°54·2'	4°52·3'W	X	63
Ber Field	Shetld	HU3649	60°13·7'	1°20·5'W	H	3
Bergamoor	Lincs	TF1764	53°9·8'	0°14·6'W	X	121
Bergerie	Hants	SZ3997	50°46·5'	1°26·4'W	X	196
Berges Island	Swan	SS4496	51°38·7'	4°14·9'W	X	159
Bergh Apton	Norf	TG3001	52°33·7'	1°24·0'E	T	134
Berghersh House Fm	Suff	TM1752	52°7·6'	1°10·6'E	FM	156
Berghers Hill	Bucks	SU9187	51°34·7'	0°40·8'W	T	175
Berghill	Shrops	SJ3530	52°52·1'	2°57·5'W	X	126
Berghill Cotts	Shrops	SJ3530	52°52·1'	2°57·5'W	X	126
Ber Gill	N Yks	SD8577	54°11·6'	2°13·4'W	X	98
Berg, The	Shetld	HU4122	59°59·1'	1°15·4'W	X	4
Berhill	Somer	ST4436	51°7·5'	2°47·6'W	T	182
Berhills Fm	Wilts	ST9562	51°21·7'	2°3·9'W	FM	173
Bericote Wood	Warw	SP3269	52°19·3'	1°31·4'W	F	151
Berie	N Eil	NB1035	58°12·8'	6°55·8'W	X	13
Berinsfield	Oxon	SU5796	51°39·8'	1°10·2'W	T	164
Berins Hill	Oxon	SU6584	51°33·3'	1°3·4'W	X	175
Berinshill Wood	Oxon	SU6585	51°33·8'	1°3·3'W	F	175
Berk	I of M	SC3189	54°16·4'	4°35·3'W	X	95
Berkeley	Glos	ST6899	51°41·6'	2°27·4'W	T	162
Berkeley Fm	Wilts	ST7935	51°7·1'	2°17·6'W	FM	183
Berkeley Heath	Glos	ST6999	51°41·6'	2°26·5'W	T	162
Berkeley Pill	Glos	ST6699	51°41·6'	2°29·1'W	W	162
Berkeley Road	Glos	SO7100	51°42·1'	2°24·8'W	T	162
Berkeley Towers	Ches	SJ6953	53°4·6'	2°27·4'W	X	118
Berkesdon Green	Herts	TL3327	51°55·8'	0°3·5'W	X	166
Berkhamsted	Herts	SP9808	51°46·0'	0°34·4'W	T	165
Berkhamsted Common	Herts	SP9911	51°47·6'	0°33·5'W	F	165
Berkley	Somer	ST8149	51°14·6'	2°15·9'W	T	183
Berkley Down	Somer	ST7948	51°14·1'	2°17·7'W	T	183
Berkley Marsh	Somer	ST8049	51°14·6'	2°16·8'W	T	183
Berkswell	Sol	SP2479	52°24·7'	1°38·4'W	T	139
Berkswell Sta	Sol	SP2477	52°23·7'	1°38·4'W	X	139
Berlea Fm	Leic	SK7023	52°48·2'	0°57·3'W	FM	129
Berllan	Pemb	SN1239	52°1·3'	4°44·0'W	X	145
Berllan	Powys	SO0626	51°55·7'	3°21·6'W	X	160
Berllan-ber	Powys	SO0150	52°8·6'	3°26·4'W	X	147
Berllandawel	Carm	SN1727	51°54·9'	4°39·3'W	X	145,158
Berllan-dêg	Cered	SN5258	52°12·3'	4°9·6'W	X	146
Berllan-deg	Monm	ST3594	51°38·7'	2°56·0'W	A	171
Berllan-deg	Powys	SH8202	52°36·4'	3°44·2'W	X	135,136
Berllan-deri	Monm	SO3906	51°45·2'	2°52·6'W	X	161
Bermondsey	Sthwk	TQ3379	51°29·9'	0°4·6'W	T	176,177
Bermuda	Scot Bord	NT5553	55°46·3'	2°42·6'W	X	66,73
Bermuda	Warw	SP3589	52°30·1'	1°28·7'W	T	140
Bernards Heath	Herts	TL1508	51°45·8'	0°19·6'W	T	166
Bernard's Smithy	Fife	NT1987	56°4·4'	3°17·6'W	X	65,66
Bernard's Well	Pemb	SN0528	51°55·2'	4°49·8'W	X	145,158
Bernard Wharf	Lancs	SD3451	53°57·3'	2°59·9'W	X	102
Berne Fm	Dorset	SY3894	50°44·8'	2°52·3'W	FM	193
Bernera	Arg & Bt	NM1957	56°37·5'	6°34·4'W	X	46
Bernera Barracks	Highld	NG8119	57°12·8'	5°37·2'W	X	33
Bernera Bay	Arg & Bt	NM7939	56°29·7'	5°35·0'W	W	49
Bernera Fm	Highld	NG8020	57°13·3'	5°38·2'W	FM	33
Bernera Island	Arg & Bt	NM7939	56°29·7'	5°35·0'W	X	49
Berneray	N Eil	NF9181	57°43·0'	7°10·9'W	X	18
Berneray	N Eil	NL5580	56°47·3'	7°38·6'W	X	31
Berner's Cross	Devon	SS6309	50°52·1'	3°56·4'W	T	191
Bernersfield Fm	Suff	TL7874	52°20·3'	0°37·2'E	FM	144
Berners Hall	Essex	TL6010	51°46·2'	0°19·5'E	X	167
Berner's Heath	Suff	TL7976	52°21·4'	0°38·1'E	X	144
Berner's Hill	E Susx	TQ7030	51°2·9'	0°25·9'E	T	188
Berners Roding	Essex	TL6009	51°45·6'	0°19·5'E	T	167
Berney Arms Mill	Norf	TG4604	52°34·9'	1°38·3'E	A	134
Berney Arms Reach	Norf	TG4604	52°34·9'	1°38·3'E	W	134
Berney Arms Sta	Norf	TG4605	52°35·4'	1°38·3'E	X	134
Bernice	Arg & Bt	NS1391	56°4·8'	4°59·9'W	X	56
Bernice Glen	Arg & Bt	NS1291	56°4·8'	5°0·8'W	X	56
Bernisdale	Highld	NG4050	57°28·2'	6°19·7'W	T	23
Bernithan Court	Heref	SO5421	51°53·4'	2°39·7'W	A	162
Bernwood Fm	Bucks	SP7324	51°54·8'	0°55·9'W	FM	165
Ber of Twitha	Orkney	HY3200	58°53·2'	3°10·3'W	X	6,7
Berrach	Carm	SN5819	51°51·3'	4°3·3'W	X	159
Berrag	I of M	SC3797	54°20·8'	4°30·0'W	X	95
Berralaft	Shetld	HU1754	60°16·5'	1°41·1'W	X	3
Berra Runies	Shetld	HU3150	60°14·3'	1°25·9'W	X	3
Berrarunies Loch	Shetld	HU3250	60°14·2'	1°24·8'W	W	3
Berra Tor	Devon	SX4769	50°30·3'	4°9·1'W	X	201
Berrick Prior	Oxon	SU6294	51°38·7'	1°5·8'W	T	164,175
Berrick Salome	Oxon	SU6294	51°38·7'	1°5·8'W	T	164,175
Berridon	Devon	SS3114	50°54·3'	4°23·8'W	X	190
Berriedale	Highld	ND1222	58°10·9'	3°29·3'W	T	17
Berrie Dale	Orkney	HY1901	58°53·6'	3°23·9'W	X	7
Berriedale	Orkney	HY4549	59°19·7'	2°57·5'W	X	5
Berriedale	Orkney	ND4693	58°49·5'	2°55·4'W	X	7
Berriedale Water	Highld	ND0130	58°15·1'	3°40·7'W	W	11,17
Berrier	Cumbr	NY4029	54°39·4'	2°55·5'W	T	90
Berrier End	Cumbr	NY4129	54°39·4'	2°54·5'W	X	90
Berrier Hill	Cumbr	NY4030	54°39·9'	2°55·4'W	H	90
Berries Head	Lancs	SD4753	53°58·5'	2°48·1'W	X	102
Berrieswalls	N Lanak	NS8066	55°52·6'	3°54·6'W	X	65
Berriew	Powys	SJ1800	52°35·7'	3°12·2'W	T	136

Berriewood Stud Fm	Shrops	SJ5004	52°38·1'	2°43·9'W	FM	126
Berrington	Devon	SX3897	50°45·2'	4°17·4'W	X	190
Berrington	Heref	SO5767	52°18·2'	2°37·4'W	T	137,138,149
Berrington	Northum	NU0043	55°41·1'	1°59·6'W	T	75
Berrington	Shrops	SJ5206	52°39·2'	2°42·2'W	T	126
Berrington Backhill	Northum	NU0043	55°41·1'	1°59·6'W	X	75
Berrington Burn	Northum	NT9742	55°40·5'	2°2·4'W	X	75
Berrington Green	Heref	SO5766	52°17·7'	2°37·4'W	T	137,138,149
Berrington Hall	Heref	SO5063	52°16·0'	2°43·6'W	X	137,138,149
Berrington Hall	Shrops	SJ5207	52°39·8'	2°42·2'W	X	126
Berrington Ho	Northum	NU0043	55°41·1'	1°59·6'W	X	75
Berringtonlaw	Northum	NT9843	55°41·1'	2°1·5'W	X	75
Berrington Lough	Northum	NT9743	55°41·1'	2°2·4'W	X	75
Berrington Pool	Heref	SO5063	52°16·0'	2°43·6'W	W	137,138,149
Berrington Pool	Shrops	SJ5207	52°39·8'	2°42·2'W	W	126
Berriowbridge	Corn	SX2775	50°33·2'	4°26·2'W	T	201
Berrisbrook	Carm	SN7137	52°1·2'	3°52·4'W	X	146,160
Berristall Hall	Ches	SJ9478	53°18·2'	2°5·0'W	X	118
Berrow	Somer	ST2952	51°16·0'	3°0·7'W	T	182
Berrow	Worcs	SO7934	52°0·5'	2°18·0'W	T	150
Berrow Flats	Somer	ST2854	51°17·1'	3°1·6'W	X	182
Berrow Fm	Worcs	SO7458	52°13·4'	2°22·4'W	FM	150
Berrow Green	Worcs	SO7458	52°13·4'	2°22·4'W	T	150
Berrow Hill	Worcs	SO7458	52°13·4'	2°22·4'W	H	150
Berrow Hill	Worcs	SO9962	52°15·6'	2°0·5'W	H	150
Berrowhill Fm	Worcs	SP0062	52°15·6'	1°59·6'W	FM	150
Berrow Hill (Fort)	Worcs	SO7458	52°13·4'	2°22·4'W	A	150
Berrow Manor	Somer	ST2952	51°16·0'	3°0·7'W	X	182
Berrowsfield Fm	Worcs	SO9957	52°12·9'	2°0·5'W	FM	150
Berrow's Fm	Glos	SO7331	51°58·8'	2°23·2'W	FM	150
Berry	Devon	SS2325	51°0·1'	4°31·0'W	X	190
Berry	Devon	SS4310	50°52·3'	4°13·5'W	X	190
Berry	Devon	SS9716	50°56·3'	3°27·6'W	X	181
Berry	Shetld	HU4040	60°8·8'	1°16·3'W	X	4
Berry	Swan	SS4787	51°33·9'	4°12·1'W	T	159
Berry Bank	Durham	NZ0051	54°51·5'	1°59·6'W	X	87
Berrybank	Scot Bord	NT8860	55°50·2'	2°11·1'W	X	67
Berry Bank Fm	Ches	SJ9868	53°12·8'	2°1·4'W	FM	118
Berry Barton	Devon	SX8090	50°42·1'	3°41·6'W	X	191
Berry Barton	Devon	SY1888	50°41·4'	3°9·3'W	X	192
Berry Beeches	Hants	SU2106	50°51·4'	1°41·7'W	X	195
Berrybrae	Aberd	NJ5729	57°21·2'	2°42·4'W	X	37
Berrybrae	Aberd	NJ7535	57°24·5'	2°24·5'W	X	29
Berrybrae	Aberd	NK0256	57°35·9'	1°57·5'W	X	30
Berrybrae	Pth & Kin	NO1243	56°34·5'	3°25·5'W	X	53
Berry Brow	Kirk	SE1314	53°37·6'	1°47·8'W	T	110
Berry Burn	Arg & Bt	NS1575	55°56·2'	4°57·3'W	W	63
Berryburn	Moray	NJ0545	57°29·4'	3°34·6'W	X	27
Berryburn	Northum	NU0144	55°41·6'	1°58·6'W	X	75
Berry Bush	Pemb	SM8627	51°54·3'	5°6·3'W	X	157
Berrybush	Scot Bord	NT2719	55°27·8'	3°8·8'W	X	79
Berrybush Burn	Scot Bord	NT2618	55°27·3'	3°9·8'W	W	79
Berrybushes Wood	Herts	TL0600	51°41·6'	0°27·6'W	F	166
Berry Cairn	Angus	NO5167	56°47·8'	2°47·7'W	H	44
Berry Camp	Devon	SY1888	50°41·4'	3°9·3'W	A	192
Berry Camp	Devon	SY1888	50°41·4'	3°9·3'W	A	192,193
Berry Castle	Devon	SS4922	50°58·9'	4°8·7'W	A	180
Berry Castle	Devon	SS8009	50°52·3'	3°41·9'W	X	191
Berry Castle	Somer	SS8544	51°11·3'	3°38·4'W	A	181
Berry Castle Lodge	Devon	SX8361	50°26·5'	3°38·5'W	X	202
Berry Castle (Settlement)	Devon	SS8317	50°56·7'	3°39·5'W	A	181
Berry Clough	Derby	SK0272	53°14·9'	1°57·8'W	X	119
Berry Court	Kent	TQ8943	51°9·5'	0°42·6'E	X	189
Berry Court Fm	Hants	SU3035	51°7·0'	1°33·9'W	FM	185
Berry Court Fm	Medway	TQ7475	51°27·1'	0°30·6'E	FM	178
Berry Cross	Devon	SS4714	50°54·5'	4°10·2'W	T	180
Berryden Fm	Aberd	NK0743	57°28·9'	1°52·5'W	FM	30
Berry Down	Corn	SX1968	50°29·3'	4°32·7'W	X	201
Berry Down	Corn	SX3755	50°22·6'	4°17·2'W	H	201
Berry Down	Devon	SS5643	51°10·3'	4°3·2'W	H	180
Berrydown	Devon	SX6687	50°40·3'	3°53·4'W	X	191
Berrydown Court	Hants	SU5249	51°14·5'	1°14·9'W	X	185
Berry Down Cross	Devon	SS5743	51°10·3'	4°2·4'W	T	180
Berrydown Fm	Hants	SU4027	51°2·7'	1°25·4'W	FM	185
Berrydown Fm	Hants	SU5249	51°14·5'	1°14·9'W	FM	185
Berrydown Fm	Hants	SU6243	51°11·2'	1°6·4'W	FM	185
Berrydown Plantation	Devon	SX6198	50°46·1'	3°57·9'W	F	191
Berrydrum	Aberd	NJ5556	57°35·8'	2°44·7'W	X	29
Berrydyke	Pth & Kin	NN8511	56°16·9'	3°51·0'W	X	58
Berry Edge Fm	Durham	NZ1052	54°52·0'	1°50·2'W	FM	88
Berryfauld	Angus	NO6242	56°34·4'	2°36·7'W	X	54
Berryfell Fm	Scot Bord	NT5207	55°21·5'	2°45·0'W	FM	79
Berryfell Hill	Scot Bord	NT5307	55°21·5'	2°44·1'W	H	79
Berryfield	Kent	TQ9972	51°24·9'	0°52·1'E	X	178
Berryfield	Wilts	ST8962	51°21·7'	2°9·1'W	T	173
Berryfield Fm	Oxon	SP3332	51°59·4'	1°30·8'W	FM	151
Berryfield Fm	Warw	SP2245	52°6·4'	1°40·3'W	FM	151
Berryfield Ho	Bucks	SP7916	51°50·5'	0°50·8'W	X	165
Berryfield Ho	Highld	NH5845	57°28·6'	4°21·6'W	X	26
Berry Fields	Northnts	SP5363	52°16·0'	1°13·0'W	X	152
Berryfields Fm	Bucks	SP7816	51°50·5'	0°51·7'W	FM	165
Berryfields Fm	Wals	SP0499	52°35·6'	1°56·1'W	FM	139
Berry Fm	Beds	TL0043	52°4·8'	0°32·0'W	FM	153
Berry Fm	Corn	SX3160	50°25·2'	4°22·4'W	FM	201
Berry Fm	Devon	SS3809	50°51·7'	4°17·7'W	FM	190
Berry Fm	Devon	SS5010	50°52·4'	4°7·5'W	FM	191
Berry Fm	Devon	ST0125	51°1·2'	3°24·3'W	FM	181
Berry Fm	Dorset	ST7311	50°54·1'	2°22·7'W	FM	194
Berrygate Hill	E Yorks	TA2324	53°42·1'	0°7·8'W	T	107,113
Berry Grain	D & G	NS9300	55°17·2'	3°40·7'W	W	78
Berry Hall	Norf	TF9437	52°54·0'	0°53·5'E	A	132
Berry Hall	Norf	TG3523	52°45·4'	1°29·4'E	X	133,134
Berry Hall	Sol	SP1679	52°24·8'	1°45·5'W	A	139
Berry Head	Torbay	SX9456	50°23·9'	3°29·1'W	X	202
Berry Head Common	Torbay	SX9456	50°23·9'	3°29·1'W	X	202
Berry Head Country Park	Torbay	SX9456	50°23·9'	3°29·1'W	X	202
Berry Hill	Aberd	NJ7101	57°6·2'	2°28·3'W	H	38
Berryhill	Aberd	NJ8108	57°10·0'	2°18·4'W	X	38
Berryhill	Aberd	NK0946	57°30·5'	1°50·5'W	X	30
Berryhill	Angus	NO3133	56°29·3'	3°6·8'W	X	53

Berry Hill	Bourne	SZ1096	50°46·0'	1°51·1'W	X	195
Berry Hill	Bucks	SU9081	51°31·5'	0°41·8'W	X	175
Berryhill	C of Aber	NJ9512	57°12·2'	2°4·5'W	X	38
Berry Hill	C of Stoke	SJ9046	53°0·9'	2°8·5'W	T	118
Berry Hill	Corn	SX3758	50°24·2'	4°17·3'W	H	201
Berry Hill	Cumbr	NY5269	55°1·0'	2°44·6'W	X	86
Berry Hill	Cumbr	NY6472	55°2·7'	2°33·4'W	X	86
Berry Hill	Devon	SS6737	51°7·2'	3°53·6'W	H	180
Berryhill	E Ayr	NS4840	55°38·0'	4°24·4'W	X	70
Berryhill	E Ayr	NS5622	55°28·5'	4°16·3'W	X	71
Berry Hill	E Loth	NT6971	55°56·1'	2°29·3'W	X	67
Berryhill	Fife	NO2515	56°19·5'	3°12·3'W	X	59
Berry Hill	Glos	SO5712	51°48·5'	2°37·0'W	T	162
Berry Hill	Highld	ND2365	58°34·2'	3°19·0'W	X	11,12
Berryhill	Highld	NH5691	57°53·4'	4°25·3'W	X	21
Berry Hill	I of W	SZ4882	50°38·4'	1°18·9'W	X	196
Berry Hill	N Ayr	NS2469	55°53·2'	4°48·4'W	X	63
Berryhill	N Lanak	NS7380	56°0·0'	4°1·7'W	X	64
Berryhill	Northum	NT9340	55°39·5'	2°6·2'W	X	74,75
Berryhill	Northum	NZ1390	55°12·5'	1°47·3'W	X	81
Berry Hill	Notts	SK5459	53°7·8'	1°11·2'W	X	120
Berry Hill	Notts	SK6736	52°55·3'	0°59·8'W	X	129
Berryhill	Orkney	HY4108	58°57·6'	3°1·1'W	X	6,7
Berry Hill	Pemb	SN0640	52°1·7'	4°49·3'W	T	145
Berry Hill	Pth & Kin	NN8805	56°13·7'	3°48·0'W	X	58
Berry Hill	Pth & Kin	NN9504	56°13·2'	3°41·2'W	X	58
Berryhill	Pth & Kin	NO0234	56°29·5'	3°35·1'W	X	52,53
Berry Hill	Pth & Kin	NO0235	56°30·1'	3°35·1'W	H	52,53
Berry Hill	Pth & Kin	NO1112	56°17·8'	3°25·8'W	H	58
Berryhill	Pth & Kin	NO1131	56°28·0'	3°26·2'W	X	53
Berryhill	Scot Bord	NT7235	55°36·7'	2°26·2'W	X	74
Berry Hill	Staffs	SJ7939	52°57·1'	2°18·4'W	X	127
Berryhill	Stir	NS7590	56°5·4'	4°0·1'W	X	57
Berry Hill	Worcs	SO8964	52°16·7'	2°9·3'W	T	150
Berryhill Cott	Scot Bord	NT8863	55°51·8'	2°18·7'W	X	67
Berry Hill Fm	Staffs	SJ9238	52°56·6'	2°6·7'W	FM	127
Berryhill Fm	Warw	SP4654	52°11·2'	1°19·2'W	FM	151
Berryhill Ho	Aberd	NO9095	57°3·0'	2°9·4'W	X	38,45
Berryhillock	Aberd	NO7668	56°48·4'	2°23·1'W	X	45
Berry Hillock	Angus	NO3744	56°35·3'	3°1·1'W	H	54
Berryhillock	Angus	NO3744	56°35·3'	3°1·1'W	X	54
Berryhillock	Moray	NJ5054	57°34·7'	2°49·7'W	X	29
Berryhillock	Moray	NJ5060	57°37·9'	2°49·8'W	T	29
Berryhillock	Pth & Kin	NO1841	56°33·5'	3°19·6'W	X	53
Berry Hills	Northum	NY9683	55°8·7'	2°3·3'W	H	81
Berryhills	N Yks	SE3180	54°13·1'	1°31·1'W	X	99
Berry Hills	Scot Bord	NT8018	55°27·6'	2°18·5'W	H	80
Berry Ho	Lancs	SD4215	53°37·9'	2°52·2'W	X	108
Berry Ho	N Yks	SE1399	54°23·4'	1°47·6'W	X	99
Berry Holes	D & G	NS8302	55°18·1'	3°50·1'W	X	78
Berry Holme	Cumbr	SD4988	54°17·4'	2°46·6'W	X	97
Berryknowe	Pth & Kin	NO1112	56°17·8'	3°25·8'W	X	58
Berry Knowe	Shetld	HP5807	60°44·8'	0°55·7'W	X	1
Berryknowe Burn	Scot Bord	NT2619	55°27·8'	3°9·8'W	W	79
Berryland	D & G	NX8981	55°6·9'	3°44·0'W	X	78
Berrylands	King	TQ1967	51°23·6'	0°17·0'W	T	176
Berrylane Fm	Worcs	SO9169	52°19·4'	2°7·5'W	FM	139
Berry Law	Fife	NT0687	56°4·3'	3°30·2'W	X	65
Berryley	Aberd	NK0640	57°27·3'	1°53·5'W	X	30
Berryley	Moray	NH9956	57°35·2'	3°40·9'W	X	27
Berryleys	Aberd	NJ5361	57°38·4'	2°46·8'W	X	29
Berryleys	Moray	NJ3141	57°27·5'	3°8·5'W	X	28
Berryleys Fm	Moray	NJ4652	57°33·6'	2°53·7'W	FM	28,29
Berry Lochs	Orkney	ND2490	58°47·7'	3°18·4'W	W	7
Berryl's Point	Corn	SW8467	50°28·0'	5°2·3'W	X	200
Berrymill Cottage	Shrops	SO4384	52°27·3'	2°49·9'W	X	137
Berry Moor	Barns	SE2903	53°31·6'	1°33·3'W	T	110
Berrymoor Edge	Northum	NY7297	55°16·2'	2°26·0'W	H	80
Berrymoss	Aberd	NK0539	57°26·7'	1°54·5'W	X	30
Berry Moss	S Lanak	NS7136	55°36·3'	4°2·4'W	X	71
Berry Mound	Worcs	SP0977	52°23·7'	1°51·7'W	X	139
Berry Mound (Fort)	Worcs	SP0977	52°23·7'	1°51·7'W	A	139
Berrymuir Head	Aberd	NO9294	57°2·5'	2°7·5'W	X	38,45
Berrynarbor	Devon	SS5646	51°11·9'	4°3·3'W	T	180
Berry Park	Devon	SS2217	50°55·7'	4°31·6'W	X	190
Berry Pomeroy	Devon	SX8261	50°26·5'	3°39·3'W	T	202
Berry Pound	Devon	SX7180	50°36·6'	3°49·0'W	A	191
Berry Rig	D & G	NS9301	55°17·7'	3°40·7'W	X	78
Berry Ring	Staffs	SJ8821	52°47·4'	2°10·3'W	A	127
Berrysbridge	Devon	SS9201	50°48·1'	3°31·6'W	T	192
Berryscaur	D & G	NY1590	55°12·1'	3°19·7'W	X	79
Berry's Green	Brom	TQ4359	51°19·0'	0°3·5'E	T	187
Berry Sike	Cumbr	NY6372	55°2·7'	2°34·3'W	W	86
Berryslacks	Aberd	NK0135	57°24·6'	1°58·5'W	X	30
Berry Slade	Pemb	SR8896	51°37·6'	5°3·4'W	X	158
Berrysloch	Aberd	NO5994	57°2·4'	2°40·1'W	X	37,44
Berry's Maple	Kent	TQ6063	51°20·8'	0°18·2'E	X	177,188
Berrystall Lodge	Derby	SK1579	53°18·7'	1°46·1'W	X	119
Berrystead	Beds	SP9833	51°59·4'	0°34·0'W	X	165
Berrystone Rock	Devon	SX7658	50°24·8'	3°44·3'W	X	202
Berry, The	Orkney	ND2390	58°47·7'	3°19·5'W	X	7
Berry, The	Orkney	ND2490	58°47·7'	3°18·4'W	H	7
Berryton	Aberd	NJ6859	57°37·4'	2°31·7'W	X	29
Berry Top	Aberd	NO8696	57°3·5'	2°13·4'W	H	38,45
Berrytop Fm	Aberd	NO8695	57°3·0'	2°13·4'W	FM	38,45
Berry Tower	Corn	SX0767	50°28·5'	4°42·8'W	A	200
Berrywell	Scot Bord	NT7953	55°46·4'	2°19·6'W	X	67,74
Berry Wood	Hants	SU2105	50°50·9'	1°41·7'W	F	195
Berrywood	Shrops	SJ3528	52°51·0'	2°57·5'W	X	126
Berry Wormington	Glos	SP0533	52°0·0'	1°55·2'W	X	150
Bersa Hill	Shetld	HU4138	60°7·7'	1°15·2'W	H	4
Berscar	D & G	NX8989	55°11·2'	3°44·2'W	X	78
Bersets, The	Shetld	HP6305	60°43·7'	0°50·2'W	X	1
Bersham	Wrex	SJ3049	53°2·3'	3°2·2'W	T	117
Berstane	Orkney	HY4610	58°58·7'	2°55·9'W	X	6
Berst Ness	Orkney	HY4441	59°15·4'	2°58·4'W	X	5
Berston	Orkney	ND4792	58°49·0'	2°54·6'W	X	7
Berth	Denb	SJ1360	53°8·0'	3°17·6'W	X	116
Berth	Powys	SN9872	52°20·4'	3°29·4'W	X	136,147
Berthabley	Powys	SO0069	52°18·8'	3°27·6'W	X	136,147
Bertha Loch	Pth & Kin	NO0727	56°25·8'	3°30·0'W	W	52,53,58
Berthapark	Pth & Kin	NO0926	56°25·3'	3°28·1'W	X	52,53,58
Berthaur	Gwyn	SH2034	52°52·6'	4°40·1'W	X	123
Berth Bach	Denb	SJ0670	53°13·4'	3°24·1'W	X	116
Berth-ddu	Conwy	SH8060	53°7·7'	3°47·2'W	X	116
Berth-ddu	Denb	SJ0644	52°59·3'	3°23·6'W	X	125
Berth-ddu	Flint	SJ2069	53°13·0'	3°11·5'W	T	117
Berth-ddu	Gwyn	SH4351	53°2·2'	4°20·1'W	X	115,123
Berth-ddu	Gwyn	SH7033	52°53·0'	3°55·5'W	X	124
Berthddu	Powys	SN8645	52°5·7'	3°39·5'W	X	147
Berth-ddû	Powys	SN9132	51°58·8'	3°34·8'W	X	160
Berthddu	Powys	SO0185	52°27·5'	3°27·0'W	X	136
Berthdomled	Cered	SN6469	52°18·4'	3°59·3'W	X	135
Berthele	Cered	SN5553	52°9·6'	4°6·8'W	X	146
Berthengam	Flint	SJ1179	53°18·3'	3°19·7'W	T	116
Berthen-gron	Denb	SJ1451	53°3·2'	3°16·6'W	X	116
Bertheos	Conwy	SH7151	53°2·7'	3°55·1'W	X	115
Berth-Fawr	Powys	SJ0610	52°41·0'	3°23·0'W	X	125
Berth-glyd Fm	Monm	SO3817	51°51·1'	2°53·6'W	FM	161
Berthgoed	Cered	SN7665	52°16·4'	3°48·6'W	X	135,147
Berth Hill	Staffs	SJ7839	52°57·1'	2°19·2'W	A	127
Berth Hill	Worcs	SO8030	51°58·3'	2°17·1'W	X	150
Berth Ho	Shrops	SO3397	52°34·2'	2°58·9'W	X	137
Berthin Brook	Monm	SO3401	51°42·5'	2°56·9'W	W	171
Berth-lafar	Gwyn	SH9436	52°54·9'	3°34·2'W	X	125
Berth-las	Powys	SH9003	52°37·1'	3°37·1'W	X	136
Berthlwyd	Carm	SN2319	51°50·7'	4°33·8'W	X	158
Berthlwyd	Carm	SN2828	51°55·7'	4°29·7'W	X	145,158
Berthlwyd	Carm	SN3320	51°51·5'	4°25·1'W	X	145,159
Berthlwyd	Carm	SN3421	51°52·0'	4°24·3'W	X	145,159
Berthlwyd	Carm	SN3618	51°50·4'	4°22·4'W	X	159
Berthlwyd	Cered	SN4056	52°11·0'	4°20·0'W	X	146
Berthlwyd	Cered	SN5550	52°8·0'	4°6·7'W	X	146
Berthlwyd	Cered	SN6373	52°20·5'	4°0·3'W	X	135
Berth-lwyd	Gwyn	SH2732	52°51·7'	4°33·8'W	X	123
Berth-Lwyd	Gwyn	SH6248	53°0·9'	4°3·0'W	A	115
Berthlwyd	Gwyn	SH7318	52°44·9'	3°52·5'W	X	124
Berthlwyd	Powys	SJ1629	52°51·4'	3°14·5'W	X	125
Berthlwyd	Rho Cyn Taf	ST0788	51°35·2'	3°20·2'W	X	170
Berthlŵyd	Swan	SS5696	51°38·9'	4°4·5'W	X	159
Berth-lwyd Coppice	Powys	SN9684	52°26·9'	3°31·4'W	F	136
Berthlwyd Fawr	Cered	SN5855	52°10·7'	4°4·2'W	X	146
Berthlwyd Fm	Powys	SN9113	51°48·5'	3°34·5'W	FM	160
Bertholau Graig	Newp	ST3993	51°38·2'	2°52·5'W	X	171
Bertholey Ho	Monm	ST3994	51°38·7'	2°52·5'W	X	171
Berth Pool	Shrops	SJ4223	52°48·3'	2°51·2'W	W	126
Berth-Rhys	Cered	SN5674	52°21·0'	4°6·5'W	X	135
Berth, The	Shrops	SJ4223	52°48·3'	2°51·2'W	A	126
Berthyfedwen	Cered	SN3441	52°2·8'	4°24·9'W	X	145
Bertie Lodge	Lincs	TF3628	52°50·2'	0°1·5'E	X	131
Bertram Hill	Northum	NY6751	54°51·4'	2°30·4'W	X	86,87
Bertram Ho	N Yks	NZ2104	54°26·1'	1°40·2'W	X	93
Bertram Ho	S Lanak	NT0047	55°42·6'	3°35·1'W	X	72
Bervie	Aberd	NJ7509	57°10·5'	2°24·4'W	X	38
Bervie Bay	Aberd	NO8372	56°50·6'	2°16·3'W	W	45
Bervie Brow	Aberd	NO8473	56°51·1'	2°15·3'W	H	45
Bervie Water	Aberd	NO7777	56°53·3'	2°22·2'W	W	45
Berw-ddu	Rho Cyn Taf	SN9602	51°42·7'	3°29·9'W	X	170
Berwick	Aberd	NJ8318	57°15·4'	2°16·5'W	X	38
Berwick	Carm	SS5498	51°39·9'	4°6·3'W	X	159
Berwick	Dorset	SY5289	50°42·2'	2°40·4'W	X	194
Berwick	Essex	TL5100	51°40·9'	0°11·4'E	X	167
Berwick	E Susx	TQ5105	50°49·7'	0°9·0'E	T	199
Berwick	Kent	TR1235	51°4·7'	1°2·0'E	T	179,189
Berwick	N Yks	SE0552	53°58·1'	1°55·0'W	X	104
Berwick	S Glos	ST5580	51°31·3'	2°38·5'W	T	172
Berwick Bassett	Wilts	SU0973	51°27·6'	1°51·8'W	T	173
Berwick Bassett Clump	Wilts	SU1273	51°27·6'	1°49·2'W	F	173
Berwick Court	E Susx	TQ5204	50°49·2'	0°9·9'E	X	199
Berwick Down	Wilts	ST9419	50°58·5'	2°4·7'W	X	184
Berwick Down	Wilts	SU0440	51°9·8'	1°56·2'W	X	184
Berwick Grove	Shrops	SJ5310	52°41·4'	2°41·3'W	X	126
Berwick Hall	Essex	TL5712	51°47·3'	0°17·0'E	X	167
Berwick Hall	Essex	TL7337	52°0·5'	0°31·6'E	X	155
Berwick Hill	Northum	NZ1775	55°4·4'	1°43·6'W	T	88
Berwick Hill Low Ho	Northum	NZ1776	55°4·9'	1°43·6'W	X	88
Berwick Hills	Midd	NZ5118	54°33·5'	1°12·3'W	T	93
Berwick Ho	Shrops	SJ4714	52°43·5'	2°46·7'W	X	126
Berwick Intake Fm	N Yks	SE0451	53°57·5'	1°55·9'W	FM	104
Berwick Lodge	S Glos	ST5680	51°31·3'	2°37·7'W	X	172
Berwick Manor	Hav	TQ5483	51°31·7'	0°13·6'E	X	177
Berwick Place	Essex	TL7711	51°46·4'	0°34·3'E	X	167
Berwick Ponds Fm	Hav	TQ5483	51°31·7'	0°13·6'E	FM	177
Berwick Sta	E Susx	TQ5206	50°50·2'	0°9·9'E	X	199
Berwick St James	Wilts	SU0739	51°9·2'	1°53·6'W	T	184
Berwick St John	Wilts	ST9422	51°0·1'	2°4·7'W	T	184
Berwick St Leonard	Wilts	ST9233	51°6·0'	2°6·5'W	T	184
Berwick-Upon-Tweed	Northum	NT9952	55°45·9'	2°0·5'W	T	75
Berwick Wharf	Shrops	SJ5410	52°41·9'	2°40·4'W	T	126
Berw-uchaf	I of Angl	SH4671	53°13·1'	4°18·0'W	X	114,115
Berwyn	Denb	SJ0633	52°53·4'	3°23·4'W	H	125
Berwyn	Denb	SJ0633	52°53·4'	3°23·4'W	H	125
Berwyn	Denb	SJ1943	52°58·9'	3°12·0'W	T	125
Berwyn	Powys	SJ2022	52°47·6'	3°10·8'W	H	126
Berwyn Ho	Shrops	SJ3418	52°45·6'	2°58·3'W	X	126
Beryl	Somer	ST5646	51°12·9'	2°37·4'W	X	182,183
Bescaby	Leic	SK8226	52°49·8'	0°46·6'W	T	130
Bescar	Lancs	SD3913	53°36·8'	2°54·9'W	T	108
Bescar Lane Sta	Lancs	SD3914	53°37·4'	2°54·9'W	X	108
Bescot	Wals	SP0096	52°33·9'	1°59·6'W	T	139
Besdarra	N Eil	NF9382	57°43·6'	7°9·0'W	X	18
Besford	Shrops	SJ5524	52°48·9'	2°39·7'W	T	126
Besford	Worcs	SO9144	52°5·9'	2°7·5'W	T	150
Besford Bridge	Worcs	SO9246	52°7·0'	2°6·6'W	X	150
Besford Court	Worcs	SO9145	52°6·4'	2°7·5'W	X	150
Besford Wood	Shrops	SJ5425	52°49·5'	2°40·6'W	F	126
Beslow	Shrops	SJ5708	52°40·3'	2°37·8'W	X	126
Beslyns	Essex	TL6631	51°57·4'	0°25·4'E	X	167
Besom Barn (Hotel)	Northum	NU1202	55°19·0'	1°48·2'W	X	81
Besom Fleet	Essex	TM0012	51°46·5'	0°54·3'E	W	168
Besom Fm	Shrops	SO6082	52°26·3'	2°34·9'W	FM	138
Besom Hill	Oldham	SD9508	53°34·4'	2°4·1'W	X	109
Besom Hill Resr	Oldham	SD9508	53°34·4'	2°4·1'W	W	109
Besore	Corn	SW7944	50°15·5'	5°5·7'W	X	204
Besowsa	Corn	SW9054	50°21·1'	4°56·8'W	X	200
Bessacarr	Donc	SE6101	53°30·4'	1°4·4'W	T	111
Bessack Rock	Corn	SW5741	50°13·4'	5°24·0'W	X	203
Bess Bagley	Leic	SK4813	52°43·0'	1°17·0'W	X	129
Bessborough Reservoir	Surrey	TQ1268	51°24·2'	0°23·0'W	W	176
Bessells	Dorset	ST8513	50°55·2'	2°12·4'W	X	194
Bessel Moor	N Ayr	NS2462	55°49·4'	4°48·1'W	X	63
Bessels Green	Kent	TQ5055	51°16·7'	0°9·4'E	T	188
Bessels Leigh	Oxon	SP4501	51°42·6'	1°20·5'W	T	164
Bessels Leigh (Sch)	Oxon	SP4501	51°42·6'	1°20·5'W	X	164
Besses o' th' Barn	Bury	SD8105	53°32·7'	2°16·8'W	T	109
Besshill Fm	Devon	SS6340	51°8·8'	3°57·1'W	FM	180
Bessie's Cairn	Angus	NO1974	56°51·3'	3°19·2'W	X	43
Bessiewalla	D & G	NX8782	55°7·4'	3°45·9'W	X	78
Bessie Yon	D & G	NX3938	54°42·9'	4°29·5'W	X	83
Bessingby	E Yorks	TA1565	54°4·3'	0°14·1'W	T	101
Bessingdale Plantn	E Yorks	SE9160	54°1·9'	0°36·2'W	F	101
Bessingham	Norf	TG1636	52°52·9'	1°13·0'E	T	133
Bessyboot	Cumbr	NY2512	54°30·1'	3°9·1'W	X	89,90
Bessy's Cove	Corn	SW5527	50°5·8'	5°25·2'W	W	203
Best Beech Hill	E Susx	TQ6131	51°3·6'	0°18·2'E	T	188
Bestbrook Fm	Powys	SO2362	52°15·3'	3°7·3'W	FM	137,148
Besthorpe	Norf	TM0695	52°31·1'	1°2·6'E	T	144
Besthorpe	Notts	SK8264	53°10·2'	0°46·0'W	T	121
Bestwood	C of Nott	SK5645	53°0·2'	1°9·5'W	T	129
Bestwood Lodge	C of Nott	SK5646	53°0·7'	1°9·5'W	X	129
Bestwood Village	Notts	SK5547	53°1·3'	1°10·4'W	T	129
Beswick	E Yorks	TA0148	53°55·3'	0°27·3'W	T	106,107
Beswick	Man	SJ8697	53°28·4'	2°12·2'W	T	109
Beswick Rush Plantn	E Yorks	TA0348	53°55·3'	0°25·5'W	F	107
Betchcott	Shrops	SO4398	52°34·8'	2°50·1'W	T	137
Betchcott Hills	Shrops	SO4298	52°34·8'	2°51·0'W	H	137
Betchcott Hollow	Shrops	SO4498	52°34·9'	2°49·2'W	X	137
Betchton Fm	Ches	SJ7957	53°6·8'	2°18·4'W	FM	118
Betchton Heath	Ches	SJ7760	53°8·4'	2°20·2'W	T	118
Betchton Ho	Ches	SJ7959	53°7·9'	2°18·4'W	X	118
Betchworth	Surrey	TQ2150	51°14·4'	0°15·6'W	T	187
Betchworth Castle	Surrey	TQ1950	51°14·4'	0°17·3'W	A	187
Betchworth Ho	Surrey	TQ2149	51°13·9'	0°15·6'W	X	187
Betchworth Park	Surrey	TQ1849	51°13·9'	0°18·2'W	X	187
Betchworth Sta	Surrey	TQ2151	51°14·9'	0°15·6'W	X	187
Bethania	Cered	SN5763	52°15·0'	4°5·3'W	T	146
Bethania	Gwyn	SH6250	53°2·0'	4°3·1'W	T	115
Bethania	Gwyn	SH7045	52°59·4'	3°55·8'W	T	115
Bethany	Corn	SX3259	50°24·6'	4°21·5'W	T	201
Bethasda	Gwyn	SH6266	53°10·6'	4°3·5'W	X	115
Bethecar Moor	Cumbr	SD3090	54°18·3'	3°4·1'W	X	96,97
Bethel	Corn	SX0352	50°20·3'	4°45·7'W	T	200,204
Bethel	Gwyn	SH5265	53°9·9'	4°12·4'W	T	114,115
Bethel	Gwyn	SH9839	52°56·6'	3°30·7'W	T	125
Bethel	I of Angl	SH3970	53°12·4'	4°24·2'W	T	114
Bethel	Powys	SJ1021	52°47·0'	3°19·7'W	X	125
Bethel Fm	Norf	TM1981	52°23·2'	1°13·5'E	FM	156
Bethel Fm	Norf	TM2996	52°31·0'	1°22·9'E	FM	134
Bethelnie	Aberd	NJ7830	57°21·9'	2°21·5'W	X	29,30
Bethel Row	Kent	TQ9954	51°15·2'	0°51·5'E	X	189
Bethern	S Lanak	NS6149	55°43·1'	4°12·3'W	X	64
Bethersden	Kent	TQ9240	51°7·8'	0°45·0'E	T	189
Bethesda	Gwyn	SH4656	53°5·0'	4°17·6'W	T	115,123
Bethesda	Pemb	SN0917	51°49·4'	4°45·9'W	T	158
Bethgeth	Conwy	SH9072	53°14·3'	3°38·5'W	X	116
Bethlehem	Carm	SN6825	51°54·7'	3°54·8'W	T	146
Bethlem Fm	Lincs	TF4358	53°6·2'	0°8·6'E	FM	122
Bethlin	Aberd	NJ6807	57°9·4'	2°31·3'W	X	38
Bethlin Burn	Aberd	NJ7008	57°10·0'	2°29·3'W	W	38
Bethnal Green	T Ham	TQ3482	51°31·5'	0°3·7'W	T	176,177
Bethwines Fm	W Susx	SU8305	50°50·5'	0°48·9'W	FM	197
Bethwins Fm	Surrey	SU9534	51°6·1'	0°38·2'W	FM	186
Betlands	Swan	SS4589	51°35·0'	4°13·8'W	X	159
Betley	Staffs	SJ7548	53°2·0'	2°22·0'W	T	118
Betley Common	Staffs	SJ7448	53°2·0'	2°22·9'W	T	118
Betley Mere	Ches	SJ7447	53°1·4'	2°22·9'W	W	118
Betlow Fm	Herts	SP8917	51°50·9'	0°42·1'W	FM	165
Betsham	Kent	TQ6071	51°25·1'	0°18·5'E	T	177
Betsoms Fm	Kent	TQ4455	51°16·8'	0°4·3'E	FM	187
Betsom's Hill	Kent	TQ4355	51°16·8'	0°3·4'E	X	187
Bettenham Manor	Kent	TQ8139	51°7·5'	0°35·6'E	X	188
Bettenhill	Derby	SK0395	53°27·3'	1°56·9'W	X	110
Betterton Down	Oxon	SU4284	51°33·4'	1°23·3'W	X	174
Betterton Fm	Oxon	SU4386	51°34·5'	1°22·4'W	FM	174
Betterton Ho	Oxon	SU4386	51°34·5'	1°22·4'W	X	174
Betteshanger	Kent	TR3152	51°13·4'	1°18·9'E	T	179
Betteshanger Colliery	Kent	TR3353	51°13·9'	1°20·7'E	X	179
Bettfield Fm	Derby	SK0882	53°20·3'	1°52·4'W	FM	110
Betting-uchaf	Nth Pt Talb	SN7409	51°46·2'	3°49·5'W	X	160
Bettinson's Br	Lincs	TF2354	53°4·4'	0°9·4'W	X	122
Bettiscombe	Dorset	ST3900	50°48·0'	2°51·6'W	T	193
Bettiscombe Manor Ho	Dorset	ST4000	50°48·0'	2°50·7'W	A	193
Bettisfield	Wrex	SJ4635	52°54·8'	2°47·8'W	T	126
Bettisfield Hall Fm	Wrex	SJ4636	52°55·4'	2°47·8'W	FM	126
Bettisfield Park	Wrex	SJ4537	52°55·9'	2°48·7'W	X	126
Betton	Shrops	SJ3102	52°36·9'	3°0·7'W	X	126
Betton	Shrops	SJ6936	52°55·5'	2°27·3'W	T	127
Betton Abbots	Shrops	SJ5107	52°39·8'	2°43·1'W	X	126
Betton Alkmere	Shrops	SJ5009	52°40·8'	2°44·0'W	X	126
Betton Coppice	Shrops	SJ5008	52°40·3'	2°44·0'W	F	126
Betton Fm	N Yks	TA0085	54°15·3'	0°27·5'W	FM	101
Betton Hall Fm	Shrops	SJ6937	52°56·0'	2°27·3'W	FM	127
Betton Moss	Shrops	SJ6836	52°55·5'	2°28·2'W	F	127
Betton Pool	Shrops	SJ5107	52°39·8'	2°43·1'W	W	126
Betton Strange	Shrops	SJ5009	52°40·8'	2°44·0'W	T	126
Betton Wood	Shrops	SJ6737	52°56·0'	2°29·1'W	X	127
Bett's Fm	Essex	TL6925	51°54·1'	0°27·8'E	FM	167
Bettws	Carm	SN4026	51°54·8'	4°19·2'W	X	146
Bettws	I of Angl	SH5081	53°18·5'	4°14·7'W	X	114,115
Bettws	Monm	SO2919	51°52·1'	3°1·5'W	T	161

Bettws	Monm	SO3807	51°45·7′	2°53·5′W	X	161
Bettws	Newp	ST2990	51°36·5′	3°1·1′W	T	171
Bettws	Powys	SO1156	52°11·9′	3°17·7′W	X	148
Bettws Bach	Gwyn	SH4641	52°56·9′	4°17·1′W	X	123
Bettws Cedewain	Powys	SO1296	52°33·5′	3°17·5′W	T	136
Bettws Dingle	Powys	SO2246	52°6·6′	3°7·9′W	X	148
Bettws Gwerfil Goch	Denb	SJ0346	53°0·4′	3°26·3′W	T	116
Bettws Hill	Powys	SO0895	52°32·9′	3°21·0′W	X	136
Bettws Newydd	Monm	SO3605	51°44·6′	2°55·2′W	T	161
Bettws-y-crwyn	Shrops	SO2081	52°25·5′	3°10·2′W	T	137
Bettyfield	Scot Bord	NT6534	55°36·2′	2°32·9′W	X	74
Bettyhill	Highld	NC7061	58°31·3′	4°13·5′W	T	10
Bettyknowes	D & G	NX8573	55°2·5′	3°47·6′W	X	84
Betty's Close Fm	Stock on T	NZ4313	54°30·9′	1°19·7′W	FM	93
Betty's Grave	Glos	SP1002	51°43·2′	1°50·9′W	X	163
Bettywharran	Angus	NO4467	56°47·7′	2°54·6′W	X	44
Between Guards	Cumbr	NY0905	54°26·2′	3°23·8′W	X	89
Betws	Brig	SS8986	51°34·0′	3°35·7′W	T	170
Betws	Carm	SN6311	51°47·1′	3°58·8′W	T	159
Betws	Gwyn	SJ0142	52°58·2′	3°28·0′W	X	125
Betws	I of Angl	SH3993	53°24·8′	4°24·9′W	X	114
Betws Bledrws	Cered	SN5952	52°9·1′	4°3·3′W	T	146
Betws Fawr	Gwyn	SH4639	52°55·8′	4°17·1′W	X	123
Betws Garmon	Gwyn	SH5456	53°5·1′	4°10·4′W	T	115
Betws Ifan	Cered	SN3047	52°6·0′	4°28·5′W	T	145
Betws-y-Coed	Conwy	SH7956	53°5·5′	3°48·0′W	T	115
Betws-yn-Rhos	Conwy	SH8974	53°15·3′	3°39·4′W	T	116
Beuchan	D & G	NX8691	55°12·3′	3°47·1′W	X	78
Beuchanhill Plantation	D & G	NX8590	55°11·7′	3°48·0′W	F	78
Beuchen Moor	D & G	NX8491	55°12·2′	3°48·9′W	X	78
Beudiau	Cered	SN5549	52°7·5′	4°6·7′W	X	146
Beudyhir	Powys	SJ0302	52°36·7′	3°25·6′W	X	136
Beudy-mawr	Gwyn	SH3133	52°52·3′	4°30·3′W	X	123
Beufre Fm	Hants	SU3801	50°48·7′	1°27·3′W	FM	196
Beugh Burn	W Loth	NT0671	55°55·6′	3°29·8′W	W	65
Beukley	Northum	NY9870	55°1·7′	2°1·4′W	X	87
Beul a' Bhealaich	N Eil	NF6800	56°58·6′	7°27·4′W	X	31
Beul a' Chasain	Highld	NH4909	57°9·1′	4°29·3′W	X	34
Beulah	Cered	SN2846	52°5·4′	4°30·2′W	T	145
Beulah	Powys	SN9251	52°9·0′	3°34·3′W	T	147
Beulah Fm	Lincs	TF4390	53°23·5′	0°9·4′E	FM	113
Beulah Hall	Suff	TM4789	52°26·8′	1°38·5′E	X	156
Beul an Toim	N Eil	NF7957	57°29·6′	7°21·0′W	W	22
Beul Choire nan Each	Highld	NM8050	56°35·7′	5°34·6′W	X	49
Beul Làma Sgorr	Highld	NG2606	57°4·1′	6°30·8′W	X	39
Beul Leathad	Arg & Bt	NR6997	56°6·9′	5°42·5′W	H	55,61
Beul na Bearnadh	N Eil	NG1297	57°52·4′	6°51·0′W	X	14
Beum a' Chlaidheimh	Highld	NH9330	57°21·1′	3°46·2′W	X	27,36
Bevans Fm	Suff	TL8355	52°10·0′	0°41·0′E	FM	155
Bevendean	Bri & Hov	TQ3406	50°50·5′	0°5·4′W	T	198
Bevenden	Kent	TQ9539	51°7·2′	0°47·6′E	X	189
Bever Batch	Devon	SY3297	50°46·3′	2°57·5′W	F	193
Bevercotes	Notts	SK6972	53°14·7′	0°57·6′W	X	120
Bevercotes Park	Notts	SK6971	53°14·1′	0°57·6′W	X	120
Bevere	Worcs	SO8459	52°14·0′	2°13·7′W	T	150
Bevere Island	Worcs	SO8359	52°14·0′	2°14·5′W	X	150
Beveriche Manor Fm	Suff	TM4068	52°15·7′	1°31·4′E	FM	156
Beveridge Park	Fife	NT2790	56°6·1′	3°10·0′W	X	59
Beverley	E Yorks	TA0440	53°51·0′	0°24·7′W	T	107
Beverley 20	E Yorks	SE9932	53°46·7′	0°29·4′W	X	106
Beverley 20	E Yorks	TA0034	53°47·8′	0°28·5′W	X	106,107
Beverley 20	E Yorks	TA0138	53°49·9′	0°27·5′W	X	106,107
Beverley and Barmston Drain	E Yorks	TA0545	53°53·7′	0°23·7′W	W	107
Beverley Brook	Rich	TQ2173	51°26·8′	0°15·1′W	W	176
Beverley Clump	E Yorks	SE9432	53°46·8′	0°34·0′W	X	106
Beverley Parks Crossing	E Yorks	TA0437	53°49·4′	0°24·8′W	X	107
Beverley Spring	Notts	SK7378	53°17·9′	0°53·9′W	F	120
Beverley Wood	N Yks	NZ3506	54°27·1′	1°27·2′W	F	93
Bevern Stream	E Susx	TQ4116	50°55·8′	0°0·8′E	X	198
Beversbrook Fm	Wilts	SU0073	51°27·6′	1°59·6′W	FM	173
Beverston	Glos	ST8693	51°38·4′	2°11·7′W	T	162,173
Beverton Pond	Somer	ST0134	51°6·0′	3°24·5′W	W	181
Bevexe-fâch	Swan	SS5994	51°37·9′	4°1·8′W	X	159
Bevexe-fawr	Swan	SS5994	51°37·9′	4°1·8′W	X	159
Bevills	Essex	TL9034	51°58·5′	0°46·4′E	A	155
Bevill's Hill	Corn	SS2601	50°47·2′	4°27·7′W	X	190
Bevill's Leam	Cambs	TL2893	52°31·4′	0°6·4′W	W	142
Bevill's Wood	Cambs	TL2079	52°24·0′	0°13·8′W	X	142
Bevingdon Ho	Essex	TL8142	52°3·0′	0°38·8′E	A	155
Bevingford	E Susx	TQ4824	51°0·0′	0°6·9′E	X	198
Bevington	Glos	ST6596	51°39·9′	2°30·0′W	T	162
Bevington Waste	Worcs	SP0353	52°10·8′	1°57·0′W	X	150
Bevis Fm	Oxon	SP3718	51°51·8′	1°27·4′W	FM	164
Bevis Hall	Cambs	TF4306	52°38·2′	0°7·2′E	X	142,143
Bevis's Thumb	W Susx	SU7815	50°56·0′	0°53·0′W	X	197
Bevis's Thumb (Long Barrow)	W Susx	SU7815	50°56·0′	0°53·0′W	A	197
Bevla	Shetld	HU3043	60°10·5′	1°27·1′W	X	4
Bevos Fm	Brig	SS8678	51°29·6′	3°38·1′W	FM	170
Bewaldeth	Cumbr	NY2134	54°41·9′	3°13·1′W	T	89,90
Bewan	Orkney	HY7855	59°23·1′	2°22·7′W	X	5
Bewbarrow Crag	Cumbr	NY5114	54°31·4′	2°45·0′W	H	90
Bewbush	W Susx	TQ2435	51°6·3′	0°13·3′W	T	187
Bew Castle	Cumbr	NY5674	55°3·8′	2°40·9′W	A	86
Bewcastle	Cumbr	NY5674	55°3·8′	2°40·9′W	T	86
Bewcastle Fells	Cumbr	NY5681	55°7·5′	2°41·0′W	X	80
Bewdley	Durham	NY9639	54°45·0′	2°3·3′W	X	91,92
Bewdley	Worcs	SO7875	52°22·6′	2°19·0′W	T	138
Bewerley	N Yks	SE1564	54°4·5′	1°45·8′W	T	99
Bewerley Moor	N Yks	SE1164	54°4·6′	1°49·5′W	X	99
Bewholme	E Yorks	TA1650	53°56·2′	0°13·6′W	T	107
Bewick Br	Northum	NU0522	55°29·8′	1°54·8′W	X	75
Bewick Folly	Northum	NU0622	55°29·8′	1°53·9′W	X	75
Bewick Hall	E Yorks	TA2339	53°50·2′	0°7·4′W	X	107
Bewick Moor	Northum	NU0922	55°29·8′	1°51·0′W	X	75
Bewl Bridge Fm	Kent	TQ6834	51°5·1′	0°24·3′E	FM	188
Bewley Common	Wilts	ST9368	51°24·9′	2°5·7′W	T	173
Bewley Court	Wilts	ST9268	51°24·9′	2°6·5′W	A	173
Bewley Down	Devon	ST2806	50°51·2′	3°1·0′W	X	193
Bewley Fm	Kent	TQ5955	51°16·5′	0°17·2′E	FM	188
Bewley Fm	Wilts	SU2665	51°23·2′	1°37·2′W	FM	174
Bewley Hill	Stock on T	NZ3617	54°33·1′	1°26·2′W	X	93
Bewlie	Scot Bord	NT5625	55°31·3′	2°41·4′W	T	73
Bewliehill	Scot Bord	NT5626	55°31·8′	2°41·4′W	X	73
Bewlie Mains	Scot Bord	NT5525	55°31·3′	2°42·3′W	T	73
Bewl Water	E Susx	TQ6733	51°4·5′	0°23·4′E	W	188
Bewsey	Warr	SJ5989	53°24·0′	2°36·6′W	T	108
Bewshaugh	Northum	NY6192	55°13·5′	2°36·4′W	X	80
Bewsley Fm	Devon	SS7703	50°49·0′	3°44·4′W	FM	191
Bexfield	Norf	TG0225	52°47·3′	1°0·1′E	T	133
Bexhill	E Susx	TQ7308	50°51·0′	0°27·8′E	T	199
Bexhill Down	E Susx	TQ7308	50°51·0′	0°27·8′E	X	199
Bexley	Bexley	TQ4675	51°27·5′	0°6·5′E	T	177
Bexleyheath	Bexley	TQ4875	51°27·5′	0°8·2′E	T	177
Bexleyhill	W Susx	SU9125	51°1·3′	0°41·8′W	T	186,197
Bexleyhill Common	W Susx	SU9124	51°0·7′	0°41·8′W	F	197
Bexley Woods	Bexley	TQ4873	51°26·4′	0°8·2′E	F	177
Bexon	Kent	TQ8959	51°18·1′	0°43·1′E	T	178
Bexton Hall	Ches	SJ7477	53°17·6′	2°23·0′W	A	118
Bexwell	Norf	TF6303	52°36·2′	0°24·8′E	T	143
Beyond-the-Burn	D & G	NY0672	55°2·3′	3°27·8′W	X	85
Beyond The Moss	Cumbr	NY4576	55°4·8′	2°51·3′W	X	86
Beyond-the-Wood	Cumbr	NY4376	55°4·8′	2°53·1′W	X	85
Beyton	Suff	TL9363	52°14·1′	0°50·0′E	T	155
Beyton Green	Suff	TL9363	52°14·1′	0°50·0′E	T	155
Beyton Ho	Suff	TL9362	52°13·6′	0°50·0′E	X	155
Beytonsdale	Derby	SK1179	53°18·7′	1°49·7′W	X	119
Bezurrel	Corn	SW5936	50°10·7′	5°22·2′W	X	203
Bezza Ho	Lancs	SD5931	53°46·7′	2°36·9′W	X	102
Bhalamus	N Eil	NB2901	57°55·2′	6°34·1′W	X	14
Bhatarsaidh	N Eil	NB4023	58°7·4′	6°24·5′W	X	14
Bhatasgeir	N Eil	NB4839	58°16·3′	6°17·4′W	X	8
Bhlàraidh	Highld	NH3816	57°12·6′	4°40·5′W	X	34
Bhlàraidh Reservoir	Highld	NH3518	57°13·6′	4°43·5′W	W	34
Bhoiseabhal	N Eil	NG0487	57°46·8′	6°58·3′W	H	18
Bhómasdal	N Eil	NG0389	57°47·8′	6°59·5′W	X	18
Bhonic	Aberd	NO1996	57°3·1′	3°19·7′W	H	43
Bhran Cottage	Highld	NN7591	56°59·9′	4°3·0′W	X	35
Bhreaca	Arg & Bt	NM3121	56°18·6′	6°20·5′W	X	48
Bial a' Chaolais	N Eil	NF7365	57°33·7′	7°27·7′W	W	18
Biallaid	Highld	NN7098	57°3·5′	4°8·2′W	X	35
Biallidbeg	Highld	NN6997	57°3·0′	4°9·1′W	X	35
Biargar	Shetld	HU3635	60°6·1′	1°20·7′W	X	4
Bias Scar	Red & Cl	NZ7619	54°33·9′	0°49·1′W	X	94
Bias Wood	Devon	SS6721	50°58·6′	3°53·3′W	F	180
Bibaloe Beg	I of M	SC4179	54°11·2′	4°25·8′W	X	95
Bibaloe-moar	I of M	SC4078	54°10·6′	4°26·7′W	X	95
Bibbear Fm	Devon	SS4316	50°55·6′	4°13·7′W	FM	180,190
Bibberne Fm	Dorset	ST7417	50°57·3′	2°21·8′W	FM	183
Bibbill Fm	E Yorks	SE7542	53°52·4′	0°51·1′W	FM	105,106
Bibbington	Derby	SK0877	53°17·6′	1°52·4′W	X	119
Bibblon Hill	E Ayr	NS6632	55°34·1′	4°7·1′W	H	71
Bibbsworth Hall Fm	Herts	TL1816	51°50·0′	0°16·8′W	FM	166
Bib Knowl	Roch	SD9313	53°37·1′	2°5·9′W	H	109
Biblins, The	Heref	SO5414	51°49·6′	2°39·7′W	X	162
Bibstone	S Glos	ST6991	51°37·3′	2°26·5′W	T	162,172
Bibsworth Fm	Worcs	SP1038	52°2·7′	1°50·9′W	FM	150
Bibury	Glos	SP1106	51°45·4′	1°50·0′W	T	163
Bibury Court (Hotel)	Glos	SP1106	51°45·4′	1°50·0′W	A	163
Bibury Fm	Glos	SP1207	51°45·9′	1°49·2′W	FM	163
Bica Common	Monm	ST4494	51°38·8′	2°48·2′W	X	171,172
Bicester	Oxon	SP5822	51°53·8′	1°9·0′W	T	164
Bickaton	Devon	SX7966	50°29·1′	3°42·0′W	X	202
Bickell Cross	Devon	SS6027	51°1·8′	3°59·4′W	X	180
Bickenbridge	Devon	SS4944	51°10·8′	4°9·2′W	X	180
Bickenhall	Somer	ST2818	50°57·7′	3°1·1′W	T	193
Bickenhall Fm	Somer	ST2819	50°58·2′	3°1·1′W	FM	193
Bickenhall Plain	Somer	ST2918	50°57·7′	3°0·3′W	X	193
Bickenhill	Sol	SP1882	52°26·4′	1°43·7′W	T	139
Bickenhill Plantations	Sol	SP1984	52°27·5′	1°42·8′W	F	139
Bicker	Lincs	TF2237	52°55·2′	0°10·7′W	T	131
Bicker Bar	Lincs	TF2338	52°55·8′	0°9·8′W	T	131
Bicker Fen	Lincs	TF1939	52°56·3′	0°13·3′W	X	130
Bicker Fen	Lincs	TF2039	52°56·3′	0°12·5′W	X	131
Bicker Friest	Lincs	TF2137	52°55·2′	0°11·6′W	X	131
Bicker Gauntlet	Lincs	TF2139	52°56·3′	0°11·6′W	T	131
Bicker Haven	Lincs	TF2533	52°53·0′	0°8·1′W	X	131
Bickershaw	Wigan	SD6202	53°31·0′	2°34·0′W	T	109
Bickerstaffe	Lancs	SD4404	53°32·0′	2°50·3′W	T	108
Bickerstaffe Moss	Lancs	SD4302	53°30·9′	2°51·2′W	X	108
Bickerston Br	Norf	TG0808	52°38·0′	1°4·8′E	X	144
Bickerston Fm	Norf	TG0809	52°38·6′	1°4·9′E	FM	144
Bickerton	Ches	SJ5052	53°4·0′	2°44·4′W	T	117
Bickerton	Devon	SX8138	50°14·0′	3°39·7′W	T	202
Bickerton	Northum	NT9900	55°17·9′	2°0·5′W	X	81
Bickerton	N Yks	SE4550	53°56·9′	1°18·4′W	T	105
Bickerton Burn	W Loth	NS9563	55°51·2′	3°40·2′W	W	65
Bickerton Court	Heref	SO6530	51°58·3′	2°30·2′W	X	149
Bickerton Hall	W Loth	NS9563	55°51·2′	3°40·2′W	X	65
Bickerton Hill	Ches	SJ5052	53°4·0′	2°44·4′W	H	117
Bickethall	E Ayr	NS3845	55°40·5′	4°34·1′W	X	63
Bickfield Fm	Bath & NE Somer	ST5458	51°19·4′	2°39·2′W	FM	172,182
Bickford	Staffs	SJ8814	52°43·6′	2°10·3′W	T	127
Bickford Grange	Staffs	SJ8813	52°43·1′	2°10·3′W	X	127
Bickham	Devon	SX4965	50°28·2′	4°7·3′W	X	201
Bickham	Somer	SS9541	51°9·8′	3°29·7′W	T	181
Bickham Barton	Devon	SS8620	50°58·3′	3°37·0′W	X	181
Bickham Br	Devon	SX7255	50°23·1′	3°47·7′W	X	202
Bickham Ho	Devon	SX9184	50°39·0′	3°32·1′W	X	192
Bickham Moor	Devon	SS8621	50°58·9′	3°37·1′W	X	181
Bickingcott	Devon	SS7728	51°2·5′	3°44·9′W	T	180
Bickington	Devon	SS5332	51°4·3′	4°5·5′W	T	180
Bickington	Devon	SX7972	50°32·4′	3°42·1′W	T	191
Bickle Fm	Devon	SS6028	51°2·3′	3°59·4′W	FM	180
Bickleigh	Devon	SS9407	50°51·4′	3°30·0′W	T	192
Bickleigh	Devon	SX5262	50°26·6′	4°4·7′W	T	201
Bickleigh	Devon	SX7854	50°22·6′	3°42·6′W	X	202
Bickleigh Castle	Devon	SS9306	50°50·9′	3°30·8′W	X	192
Bickleigh Mill	Devon	SS9307	50°51·4′	3°30·8′W	X	192
Bickleigh Vale	Devon	SX5261	50°26·0′	4°4·7′W	X	201
Bickleigh Wood	Devon	SS9418	50°57·3′	3°30·2′W	F	181
Bickleton	Devon	SS5031	51°3·8′	4°8·1′W	T	180
Bickley	Brom	TQ4269	51°24·4′	0°2·9′E	T	177
Bickley	N Yks	SE9191	54°18·6′	0°35·7′W	X	94,101
Bickley	Worcs	SO6371	52°20·4′	2°32·2′W	T	138
Bickley Brook	Ches	SJ5248	53°1·9′	2°42·5′W	W	117
Bickley Coppice	Shrops	SJ4416	52°44·6′	2°49·4′W	F	126
Bickley Cotts	Somer	ST1225	51°1·3′	3°14·9′W	X	181,193
Bickley Fm	Somer	ST1324	51°0·8′	3°14·0′W	FM	181,193
Bickley Gate Fm	N Yks	SE9191	54°18·6′	0°35·7′W	FM	94,101
Bickley Hall Fm	Ches	SJ5247	53°1·3′	2°42·5′W	FM	117
Bickley Moss	Ches	SJ5449	53°2·4′	2°40·8′W	T	117
Bickley's Rough	Shrops	SJ8001	52°36·6′	2°17·3′W	X	127
Bickley Town	Ches	SJ5348	53°1·9′	2°41·6′W	T	117
Bickleywood	Ches	SJ5247	53°1·3′	2°42·5′W	T	117
Bickmarsh	Worcs	SP1049	52°8·6′	1°50·8′W	T	150
Bickmarsh Hall	Worcs	SP1049	52°8·6′	1°50·8′W	X	150
Bickmarsh Lodge	Worcs	SP1147	52°7·5′	1°50·0′W	X	150
Bicknacre	Essex	TL7802	51°41·5′	0°34·9′E	T	167
Bicknell's Br	Somer	ST4226	51°2·1′	2°49·2′W	X	193
Bicknoller	Somer	ST1139	51°8·8′	3°16·0′W	T	181
Bicknoller Hill	Somer	ST1139	51°8·8′	3°16·0′W	X	181
Bicknoller Post	Somer	ST1240	51°9·4′	3°15·1′W	X	181
Bicknor	Kent	TQ8658	51°17·7′	0°40·5′E	T	178
Bicknor Ct	Glos	SO5715	51°50·2′	2°37·1′W	X	162
Bicknor Fm	Devon	SS7427	51°2·0′	3°47·4′W	FM	180
Bickramside	Fife	NT0190	56°5·8′	3°35·0′W	X	58
Bickton	Hants	SU1412	50°54·7′	1°47·7′W	T	195
Bicton	Corn	SX3962	50°26·4′	4°15·7′W	X	201
Bicton	Heref	SO4663	52°16·0′	2°47·1′W	T	137,138,148
Bicton	Pemb	SM8407	51°43·4′	5°7·3′W	T	157
Bicton	Shrops	SJ4415	52°44·0′	2°49·4′W	T	126
Bicton	Shrops	SO2882	52°26·1′	3°3·1′W	T	137
Bicton Common	Devon	SY0386	50°40·2′	3°22·0′W	X	192
Bicton Heath	Shrops	SJ4513	52°43·0′	2°48·5′W	T	126
Bicton Hill	Shrops	SO2185	52°27·7′	3°9·4′W	X	137
Bicton Ho	Shrops	SJ4414	52°43·5′	2°49·4′W	X	126
Bicton House (Agricultural College)	Devon	SY0786	50°40·2′	3°18·6′W	X	192
Bicton Manor	Corn	SX3169	50°30·0′	4°22·6′W	X	201
Bicton Park	Devon	SY0785	50°39·7′	3°18·6′W	X	192
Bicton Wood	Corn	SX3169	50°30·0′	4°22·6′W	F	201
Bidbeare	Devon	SS6605	50°50·0′	3°53·8′W	X	191
Bidborough	Kent	TQ5643	51°10·1′	0°14·3′E	T	188
Bidcombe Hill	Wilts	ST8339	51°9·2′	2°14·2′W	H	183
Biddacott	Devon	SS6225	51°0·7′	3°57·7′W	X	180
Bidden	Hants	SU7049	51°14·4′	0°59·4′W	T	186
Biddenden	Kent	TQ8438	51°6·9′	0°38·1′E	T	188
Biddenden Green	Kent	TQ8843	51°9·5′	0°41·7′E	T	189
Biddenfield	Hants	SU5512	50°54·5′	1°12·7′W	X	196
Bidden Grange Fm	Hants	SU7049	51°14·4′	0°59·4′W	FM	186
Biddenham	Beds	TL0250	52°8·6′	0°30·2′W	T	153
Biddesden Ho	Wilts	SU2950	51°15·1′	1°34·7′W	X	185
Biddestone	Wilts	ST8673	51°27·6′	2°11·7′W	T	173
Biddick	Sund	NZ3055	54°53·6′	1°31·5′W	T	88
Biddick Hall	Durham	NZ3152	54°52·0′	1°30·6′W	A	88
Biddick Hall	S Tyne	NZ3563	54°57·9′	1°26·8′W	T	88
Biddisham	Somer	ST3853	51°16·6′	2°52·9′W	T	182
Biddlesden	Bucks	SP6339	52°3·0′	1°4·5′W	T	152
Biddlesden Ho	Bucks	SP6339	52°3·0′	1°4·5′W	X	152
Biddlesden Park	Bucks	SP6239	52°3·0′	1°5·4′W	X	152
Biddle's Fm	Worcs	SO7837	52°2·1′	2°18·8′W	FM	150
Biddlesgate Fm	Dorset	SU0714	50°55·8′	1°53·6′W	FM	195
Biddlestone	Heref	SO5423	51°54·5′	2°39·7′W	X	162
Biddlestone	Northum	NT9508	55°22·2′	2°4·3′W	X	81
Biddlestone Burn	Northum	NT9509	55°22·7′	2°4·3′W	W	81
Biddlestone Edge	Northum	NT9507	55°21·7′	2°4·3′W	X	81
Biddlestone Home Fm	Northum	NT9508	55°22·2′	2°4·3′W	FM	81
Biddle Stones	Northum	NT9508	55°22·2′	2°4·3′W	A	81
Biddlestone Town Foot	Northum	NT9608	55°22·2′	2°3·4′W	X	81
Biddrie	Aberd	NO7567	56°47·9′	2°24·1′W	X	45
Biddulph	Staffs	SJ8857	53°6·8′	2°10·4′W	T	118
Biddulph Common	Staffs	SJ9061	53°9·0′	2°8·6′W	X	118
Biddulph Moor	Staffs	SJ9058	53°7·4′	2°8·6′W	T	118
Biddulph Old Hall	Staffs	SJ8960	53°8·5′	2°9·5′W	X	118
Biddulph Park	Staffs	SJ9061	53°9·0′	2°8·6′W	X	118
Bidean an Eòinn Deirg	Highld	NH1044	57°27·1′	5°9·5′W	H	25
Bidean Mhic Iain Ghlais	Highld	NM9995	57°0·4′	5°18·1′W	X	33,40
Bidean nam Bian	Highld	NN1454	56°38·7′	5°1·6′W	H	41
Bideford	Devon	SS4426	51°1·0′	4°13·1′W	T	180,190
Bideford Bar	Devon	SS4333	51°4·7′	4°14·1′W	W	180
Bideford or Barnstaple Bay		SS3526	51°0·8′	4°20·8′W	W	190
Bideford or Barnstaple Bay	Devon	SS4133	51°4·7′	4°15·8′W	W	180
Bidein a' Chabair	Highld	NM8893	56°59·0′	5°28·9′W	X	33,40
Bidein a' Choire Sheasgaich	Highld	NH0441	57°25·3′	5°15·4′W	H	25
Bidein a' Ghlas Thuill	Highld	NH0684	57°48·5′	5°15·5′W	H	19
Bideinan	N Eil	NF9988	57°47·1′	7°3·4′W	H	18
Bidein an Fhithich	Highld	NG5214	57°9·3′	6°5·6′W	H	32
Bidein Boidheach	Highld	NM4486	56°53·9′	6°11·8′W	X	39
Bidein Clann Raonaild	Highld	NH0559	57°35·0′	5°15·2′W	H	25
Bidein Druim nan Ramh	Highld	NG4524	57°14·4′	6°13·1′W	X	32
Bidein na h-Iolaire	Arg & Bt	NM7008	56°12·8′	5°42·1′W	H	55
Bidfield Fm	Glos	SO9010	51°47·5′	2°8·3′W	FM	163
Bidford-on-Avon	Warw	SP1051	52°9·7′	1°50·8′W	T	150
Bidhein Bad na h-Iolaire	Highld	NN1170	56°47·3′	5°5·2′W	H	41
Bidhouse Burn	S Lanak	NS9913	55°24·3′	3°35·3′W	W	78
Bidhouse Grains	S Lanak	NT0013	55°24·3′	3°34·3′W	W	78
Bidhouse Knowe	S Lanak	NT0113	55°24·3′	3°33·4′W	H	78
Bidigi	N Eil	NB0408	57°58·0′	6°59·9′W	H	13
Bidigidh	N Eil	NB0809	57°58·7′	6°55·9′W	H	13,14
Bidlake	Devon	SX4988	50°40·6′	4°7·9′W	T	191
Bidlake Fm	Dorset	SY4496	50°45·9′	2°47·3′W	FM	193
Bidney Fm	Heref	SO4156	52°12·2′	2°51·4′W	FM	148,149

Bidoan nan Cailleach	Highld	NG3738	57°21·7′	6°21·9′W	X	23,32
Bidston	Wirral	SJ2890	53°24·4′	3°4·6′W	T	108
Bidston Hill	Wirral	SJ2889	53°23·8′	3°4·6′W	T	108
Bidston Moss	Wirral	SJ2991	53°24·9′	3°3·7′W	X	108
Bidston Sta	Wirral	SJ2890	53°24·4′	3°4·6′W	X	108
Bidwell	Beds	TL0124	51°54·6′	0°31·5′W	T	166
Bidwell	Devon	SS9303	50°49·2′	3°30·8′W	X	192
Bidwell Barton	Devon	SX9098	50°46·5′	3°33·2′W	X	192
Bidwell Brook	Devon	SX7661	50°26·4′	3°44·4′W	W	202
Bidwell Fm	Devon	ST2007	50°51·7′	3°7·8′W	FM	192,193
Biel	E Loth	NT6375	55°58·2′	2°35·1′W	X	67
Bielby	E Yorks	SE7843	53°52·9′	0°48·4′W	T	105,106
Bielby Beck	E Yorks	SE7944	53°53·4′	0°47·5′W	W	105,106
Bielby Field	E Yorks	SE8044	53°53·4′	0°46·5′W	X	106
Bieldside	C of Aber	NJ8802	57°6·8′	2°11·4′W	T	38
Bield, The	Cumbr	NY3103	54°25·3′	3°3·4′W	X	90
Bield,The	Scot Bord	NT6942	55°40·5′	2°29·1′W	X	74
Bieldy Pike	Northum	NU0704	55°20·0′	1°52·9′W	X	81
Bielgrange	E Loth	NT6175	55°58·2′	2°37·1′W	X	67
Bielhill	E Loth	NT6376	55°58·8′	2°35·1′W	X	67
Bielmill	E Loth	NT6275	55°58·2′	2°36·1′W	X	67
Biel of Duncansby	Highld	ND3870	58°37·1′	3°3·6′W	X	7,12
Biel Water	E Loth	NT6476	55°58·8′	2°34·2′W	W	67
Bienne na Gréine	Highld	NG7522	57°14·3′	5°43·3′W	H	33
Bienn nam Bad Beag	Highld	ND0154	58°28·0′	3°41·4′W	H	11,12
Biergate Fm	Lincs	TF3696	53°26·8′	0°3·3′E	FM	113
Bierley	Brad	SE1830	53°46·2′	1°43·2′W	T	104
Bierley	I of W	SZ5178	50°36·2′	1°16·4′W	T	196
Bierton	Bucks	SP8315	51°49·9′	0°47·3′W	T	165
Biffie	Aberd	NJ9747	57°31·0′	2°2·5′W	X	30
Bigadon Ho	Devon	SX7465	50°28·5′	3°46·2′W	X	202
Big Airds Hill	D & G	NX8148	54°49·0′	3°50·7′W	H	84
Big Annie	Lincs	TF4930	52°51·0′	0°13·2′E	X	131
Big Audle	Highld	NH7770	57°42·4′	4°3·4′W	W	21
Big Balcraig	D & G	NX3843	54°45·6′	4°30·6′W	X	83
Big Barns	Highld	NC8601	57°59·3′	3°55·2′W	X	17
Big Brae	Moray	NJ1603	57°6·9′	3°22·8′W	X	36
Bigbreck	Orkney	HY2624	59°6·1′	3°17·0′W	X	6
Bigbrook	Devon	SS7820	50°58·2′	3°43·9′W	X	180
Big Burn	D & G	NS6808	55°21·2′	4°4·5′W	W	71,77
Big Burn	Highld	NG8926	57°16·8′	5°29·6′W	W	33
Big Burn	Highld	NH6069	57°41·6′	4°20·5′W	W	21
Big Burn	Highld	NH6539	57°25·5′	4°14·4′W	W	26
Bigbury	Devon	SX6646	50°18·2′	3°52·5′W	T	202
Bigbury	Kent	TR1157	51°16·6′	1°1·9′E	A	179
Bigbury Bay		SX6442	50°16·0′	3°54·1′W	W	202
Bigbury Court	Devon	SX6646	50°18·2′	3°52·5′W	X	202
Bigbury Fm	I of W	SZ5683	50°38·9′	1°12·1′W	FM	196
Bigbury-on-Sea	Devon	SX6544	50°17·1′	3°53·3′W	T	202
Bigby	Lincs	TA0507	53°33·2′	0°24·5′W	T	112
Bigby Top	Lincs	TA0707	53°33·2′	0°22·7′W	X	112
Big Covert	Northnts	SP8772	52°20·6′	0°43·0′W	F	141
Big Craig	D & G	NX9689	55°11·3′	3°37·6′W	H	78
Big Craigenlee	D & G	NX1971	55°0·3′	4°49·4′W	X	76
Big Croft	Cumbr	NY0318	54°33·1′	3°29·6′W	X	89
Big Dod	Scot Bord	NT0620	55°28·1′	3°28·8′W	H	72
Big End or Beacon	Lancs	SD8041	53°52·1′	2°17·8′W	X	103
Bigenor Fm	W Susx	SU9918	50°57·4′	0°35·0′W	FM	197
Bigert Mire	Cumbr	SD1792	54°19·3′	3°16·1′W	X	96
Big Fell	S Ayr	NX1380	55°5·0′	4°55·4′W	H	76
Big Forest	Powys	SJ1610	52°41·1′	3°14·2′W	F	125
Bigfrith	Win & Maid	SU8584	51°33·1′	0°46·0′W	T	175
Bigga	Shetld	HU4479	60°29·8′	1°11·4′W	X	2,3
Big Gairy	D & G	NX4970	55°0·4′	4°21·2′W	X	77
Biggal	I Scilly	SV8512	49°55·7′	6°23·0′W	X	203
Biggal	I Scilly	SV9413	49°56·6′	6°15·6′W	X	203
Biggal of Gorregan	I Scilly	SV8406	49°52·5′	6°23·6′W	X	203
Big Gap	Norf	TF9245	52°58·3′	0°52·0′E	X	132
Biggar	Cumbr	SD1966	54°5·3′	3°13·9′W	T	96
Biggar	S Lanak	NT0437	55°37·3′	3°31·0′W	T	72
Biggar Bank	Cumbr	SD1866	54°5·3′	3°14·8′W	X	96
Biggar Common	S Lanak	NT0039	55°38·3′	3°34·9′W	X	72
Biggar Common	S Lanak	NT0139	55°38·3′	3°33·9′W	X	72
Biggards	Cumbr	NY3238	54°44·2′	3°2·9′W	X	90
Biggar Park	S Lanak	NT0337	55°37·3′	3°32·0′W	X	72
Biggar Road	N Lanak	NS7860	55°49·3′	3°56·4′W	T	64
Biggar Sands	Cumbr	SD1966	54°5·3′	3°13·9′W	X	96
Biggarshiels	S Lanak	NT0540	55°38·9′	3°30·1′W	X	72
Biggarshiels Fm	S Lanak	NT0440	55°38·9′	3°31·1′W	FM	72
Biggarshiels Mains	S Lanak	NT0441	55°39·4′	3°31·1′W	X	72
Biggarts	D & G	NY0799	55°16·8′	3°27·4′W	X	78
Big Garvery Burn	Highld	ND0023	58°11·3′	3°41·6′W	W	17
Big Garvoun	Moray	NJ1408	57°9·5′	3°24·9′W	H	36
Biggar Water	Scot Bord	NT0936	55°36·8′	3°26·2′W	W	72
Biggenden	Kent	TQ6743	51°9·9′	0°23·7′E	X	188
Biggen House Fm	Durham	NZ1845	54°48·2′	1°42·8′W	FM	88
Big Geo of Stromness	Shetld	HU2965	60°22·3′	1°27·9′W	X	3
Biggersbank	Cumbr	SD5598	54°22·8′	2°41·1′W	X	97
Bigges Fm	W Susx	TQ2827	51°1·9′	0°10·1′W	FM	187,198
Bigges' Pillar	Northum	NU1207	55°21·7′	1°48·2′W	X	81
Biggin	Derby	SK1559	53°7·9′	1°46·1′W	T	119
Biggin	Derby	SK2648	53°2·0′	1°36·3′W	T	119
Biggin	N Yks	SE5434	53°48·2′	1°10·4′W	T	105
Biggin	Thurr	TQ6577	51°28·3′	0°22·9′E	T	177,178
Biggin Abbey	Cambs	TL4861	52°13·9′	0°10·4′E	A	154
Biggin Dale	Derby	SK1457	53°6·8′	1°47·0′W	X	119
Biggin Fm	Derby	SK4462	53°9·4′	1°20·1′W	FM	120
Biggin Fm	Leeds	SE3442	53°52·6′	1°28·6′W	FM	104
Bigging	Orkney	HY2822	59°5·0′	3°14·9′W	X	6
Bigging	Orkney	HY2917	59°2·3′	3°13·7′W	X	6
Bigging	Orkney	HY3612	58°59·7′	3°6·3′W	X	6
Biggin Grange	Derby	SK1459	53°7·9′	1°47·0′W	X	119
Biggin Grange	Northnts	TL0288	52°29·1′	0°29·5′W	X	141
Biggin Grange	N Yks	SE2174	54°9·9′	1°40·3′W	X	99
Biggings	Orkney	HY2910	58°58·5′	3°13·6′W	X	6
Biggings	Orkney	HY3014	59°0·7′	3°12·6′W	X	6
Biggings	Orkney	HY4450	59°20·2′	2°58·6′W	X	5
Biggings	Orkney	HY4702	58°54·4′	2°54·7′W	X	6,7
Biggings	Orkney	HY5403	58°55·0′	2°47·4′W	X	6,7
Biggings	Shetld	HT9637	60°7·3′	2°3·8′W	X	4
Biggings	Shetld	HU1760	60°19·7′	1°41·0′W	T	3
Biggings	Shetld	HU3455	60°16·9′	1°22·6′W	X	3
Biggin Hall	Northnts	TL0189	52°29·6′	0°30·3′W	X	141
Biggin Hill	Brom	TQ4159	51°19·0′	0°1·8′E	T	187
Biggin Hill Airport	Brom	TQ4160	51°19·5′	0°1·8′E	X	177,187
Biggin House Fm	N Yks	NZ8009	54°28·4′	0°45·5′W	FM	94
Biggin Manor	Herts	TL3833	51°58·9′	0°1·0′E	X	166
Bigginmoor Fm	Derby	SK1658	53°7·4′	1°45·2′W	FM	119
Biggins	Durham	NZ0435	54°42·8′	1°55·9′W	X	92
Biggins	Highld	ND3255	58°28·9′	3°9·5′W	X	12
Biggins	Stir	NN7600	56°10·8′	3°59·4′W	X	57
Biggins Fm	Cambs	TL4788	52°28·4′	0°10·3′E	FM	143
Biggins Fm	Essex	TQ9192	51°35·9′	0°45·9′E	FM	178
Biggin's Fm	Herts	TL3919	51°51·4′	0°1·5′E	FM	166
Biggleswade	Beds	TL1944	52°5·1′	0°15·4′W	T	153
Biggleswade Common	Beds	TL1947	52°6·7′	0°15·3′W	X	153
Biggleswade (Old Warden) Aerodrome	Beds	TL1544	52°5·2′	0°18·9′W	X	153
Big Harcar	Northum	NU2338	55°38·3′	1°37·6′W	X	75
Big Hill	D & G	NT1203	55°19·0′	3°22·8′W	H	78
Big Hill	Northnts	SP5561	52°14·9′	1°11·3′W	H	152
Big Hill	N Yks	SD7661	54°2·9′	2°21·6′W	H	98
Big Hill of Glenmount	E Ayr	NS4500	55°16·4′	4°26·0′W	H	77
Big Hill of the Baing	S Ayr	NS4102	55°17·4′	4°29·8′W	H	77
Big Hind Heath	Ches	SJ7459	53°7·9′	2°22·9′W	X	118
Bigholm	N Ayr	NS3654	55°45·4′	4°36·5′W	X	63
Big Holm	Shetld	HU6288	60°34·5′	0°51·6′W	X	1,2
Bigholms	D & G	NY3181	55°7·4′	3°4·5′W	X	79
Bigholms Burn	D & G	NY3181	55°7·4′	3°4·5′W	W	79
Bighouse	Highld	NC8964	58°33·3′	3°54·0′W	X	10
Bighouse Hill	Highld	NC8857	58°29·5′	3°54·8′W	H	10
Bight a Doubleyou	Devon	SS3224	50°59·7′	4°23·3′W	W	190
Bight of Aith	Orkney	HY6423	59°5·8′	2°37·2′W	W	5
Bight of Baywest	Orkney	HY6124	59°6·3′	2°40·4′W	W	5
Bight of Bellister	Shetld	HU4860	60°19·5′	1°7·4′W	W	2,3
Bight of Brimness	Shetld	HU4648	60°13·1′	1°9·7′W	W	3
Bight of Cudda	Shetld	HU5364	60°21·7′	1°1·9′W	W	2,3
Bight of Doonatown	Orkney	HY6223	59°5·8′	2°39·3′W	W	5
Bight of Haggrister	Shetld	HU3469	60°24·5′	1°22·5′W	W	2,3
Bight of Ham	Shetld	HU4939	60°8·2′	1°6·6′W	W	4
Bight of Lotheran	Orkney	HY7743	59°16·6′	2°23·7′W	W	5
Bight of Matpow	Orkney	HY6425	59°6·9′	2°37·2′W	W	5
Bight of Milldale	Orkney	HY5735	59°12·2′	2°44·7′W	W	5,6
Bight of Mousland	Orkney	HY2112	58°59·5′	3°22·0′W	W	6
Bight of Niddister	Shetld	HU2875	60°27·7′	1°29·0′W	W	3
Bight of Quoyolie	Orkney	HY4850	59°20·3′	2°54·4′W	W	5
Bight of Sandbister	Orkney	HY5236	59°12·7′	2°50·0′W	W	5
Bight of Scarma	Orkney	HY6521	59°4·7′	2°36·2′W	W	5
Bight of Stackaback	Orkney	HY6629	59°9·1′	2°35·2′W	W	5
Bight of Stavaness	Shetld	HU4960	60°19·5′	1°6·3′W	W	2,3
Bight of Stonyquoy	Orkney	HY5739	59°14·4′	2°44·7′W	W	5
Bight of the Graand	Orkney	HY5739	59°14·4′	2°44·7′W	W	5
Bight of the Sandy Geos	Shetld	HU3529	60°2·9′	1°21·8′W	W	4
Bight of Vatsland	Shetld	HU4645	60°11·5′	1°9·7′W	W	4
Bight of Warwick	Shetld	HU3461	60°20·2′	1°22·6′W	W	2,3
Bighton	Hants	SU6134	51°6·4′	1°7·3′W	T	185
Bighton Bottom Fm	Hants	SU6132	51°5·3′	1°7·4′W	FM	185
Bighton Ho	Hants	SU6235	51°6·9′	1°6·5′W	X	185
Bighton Manor	Hants	SU6034	51°6·4′	1°8·2′W	X	185
Big Hunt Hill	Stir	NN8401	56°11·5′	3°51·7′W	H	58
Big Kiln	Shetld	HU3518	59°57·0′	1°21·9′W	X	4
Big Knock	Scot Bord	NT1017	55°26·6′	3°24·9′W	H	78
Big Knowe	D & G	NX9794	55°14·0′	3°36·7′W	X	78
Big Knowe	Pth & Kin	NO0511	56°17·2′	3°31·6′W	X	58
Bigknowle	E Susx	TQ6224	50°59·8′	0°18·9′E	X	199
Bigland	Orkney	HY4332	59°10·5′	2°59·3′W	X	5,6
Bigland Hall	Cumbr	SD3583	54°14·6′	2°59·4′W	X	96,97
Biglands	Cumbr	NY2553	54°52·3′	3°9·7′W	T	85
Biglands	Cumbr	SD5597	54°22·2′	2°41·1′W	X	97
Bigland Scar	Cumbr	SD3578	54°11·9′	2°59·4′W	X	96,97
Biglands Ho	Cumbr	NY2061	54°56·5′	3°14·5′W	X	85
Bigland Tarn	Cumbr	SD3582	54°14·0′	2°59·4′W	W	96,97
Biglawburn	Scot Bord	NT9363	55°51·9′	2°6·3′W	X	67
Biglies Fm	N Ayr	NS2051	55°43·4′	4°51·5′W	FM	63
Biglis Fm	V of Glam	ST1469	51°25·0′	3°13·8′W	FM	171
Big Low	Ches	SJ9577	53°17·6′	2°4·1′W	X	118
Big Mancot	Flint	SJ3167	53°12·0′	3°1·6′W	T	117
Bigmarsh Fm	Bucks	SP6808	51°46·2′	1°0·5′W	FM	164,165
Big Meaul	D & G	NS5600	55°16·6′	4°15·6′W	X	77
Big Meowl	S Ayr	NX4191	55°11·5′	4°29·4′W	X	77
Big Mere	Ches	SJ5545	53°0·3′	2°39·8′W	W	117
Big Milldown	D & G	NX1867	54°58·1′	4°50·2′W	X	82
Big Moor	Derby	SK2776	53°17·1′	1°35·3′W	X	119
Bigmore Fm	Bucks	SU7894	51°38·6′	0°52·0′W	FM	175
Big Morton Hill	D & G	NX7389	55°11·0′	3°59·2′W	H	77
Bignall End	Staffs	SJ8051	53°3·6′	2°17·5′W	T	118
Bignall Hill	Staffs	SJ8250	53°3·1′	2°15·7′W	X	118
Bignell Ho	Oxon	SP5522	51°53·9′	1°11·6′W	X	164
Bignell Park Fm	Oxon	SP5522	51°53·9′	1°11·6′W	FM	164
Bignell's Corner	Herts	TL2200	51°41·4′	0°13·7′W	X	166
Bignell Wood	Hants	SU2813	50°55·2′	1°35·7′W	F	195
Big-nev Geo	Shetld	HU3092	60°36·9′	1°26·6′W	X	1
Bigni	Cered	SN2051	52°7·9′	4°37·4′W	X	145
Bignor	W Susx	SU9814	50°55·3′	0°36·0′W	T	197
Bignor Fm	W Susx	TQ0729	51°3·2′	0°28·0′W	FM	187,197
Bignor Hill	W Susx	SU9813	50°54·7′	0°36·0′W	H	197
Bignor Mill	W Susx	SU9814	50°55·3′	0°36·0′W	X	197
Bignorpark	W Susx	SU9915	50°55·8′	0°35·1′W	X	197
Bignor Park Cott	W Susx	SU9916	50°56·3′	0°35·1′W	X	197
Bigods	Essex	TL6224	51°53·7′	0°21·7′E	T	167
Bigod's Hill	Norf	TM3992	52°28·6′	1°31·6′E	X	134
Bigod's Wood	Essex	TL6225	51°54·2′	0°21·7′E	F	167
Bigore Head	Orkney	ND4689	58°47·4′	2°55·6′W	X	7
Big Park	Arg & Bt	NM9343	56°32·3′	5°21·5′W	X	49
Bigpark	S Ayr	NX0880	55°4·9′	5°0·1′W	X	76
Bigpath Fm	Hants	SU5420	50°58·8′	1°13·5′W	FM	185
Big Picket Rock	Devon	SY1085	50°39·7′	3°16·0′W	X	192
Big Plantation	D & G	NX0759	54°53·6′	5°0·1′W	F	82
Big Pool	Shrops	SJ6338	52°56·5′	2°32·6′W	W	127
Bigport Fm	Devon	SX7989	50°41·5′	3°42·4′W	FM	191
Bigram's Fm	Cambs	TL1168	52°18·2′	0°21·9′W	FM	153
Bigrigg	Cumbr	NY0013	54°30·4′	3°32·2′W	T	89
Big Rob's Cove	Aberd	NO8473	56°51·1′	2°15·3′W	W	45
Big Sand	Highld	NG7579	57°44·9′	5°46·4′W	T	19
Bigsburn Hill	Hants	SU1607	50°52·0′	1°46·0′W	X	195
Bigsby's Corner	Suff	TM3861	52°12·0′	1°29·4′E	X	156
Big Scare	D & G	NX2533	54°40·0′	4°42·4′W	X	82
Big Smagill	S Lanak	NT0028	55°32·4′	3°34·6′W	W	72
Big Stirk	Highld	NM5357	56°38·6′	6°1·3′W	X	47
Big Stoke	Somer	ST4950	51°15·0′	2°43·5′W	F	182,183
Big Strushel Burn	D & G	NT1803	55°19·1′	3°17·1′W	W	79
Bigsweir Br	Monm	SO5305	51°44·7′	2°40·5′W	A	162
Bigsweir Ho	Glos	SO5304	51°44·2′	2°40·4′W	X	162
Bigswell	Orkney	HY3210	58°58·6′	3°10·5′W	X	6
Big Tithe Fm	Notts	SK6052	53°3·9′	1°5·9′W	FM	120
Bigton	Shetld	HU3721	59°58·6′	1°19·7′W	T	4
Bigton Wick	Shetld	HU3721	59°58·6′	1°19·7′W	W	4
Big Water of Fleet	D & G	NX5564	54°57·2′	4°15·4′W	W	83
Big Water of Fleet Viaduct	D & G	NX5564	54°57·2′	4°15·4′W	X	83
Big West End Fm	Hants	SU6417	50°57·2′	1°4·9′W	FM	185
Big Windgate Burn	S Lanak	NS9212	55°23·7′	3°41·9′W	W	71,78
Big Wood	Brackn	SU8368	51°24·5′	0°48·0′W	F	175
Big Wood	Ches	SJ6780	53°19·2′	2°29·3′W	F	109
Big Wood	Ches	SJ8673	53°15·5′	2°12·2′W	F	118
Big Wood	Devon	SY0897	50°46·2′	3°17·9′W	F	192
Big Wood	Devon	SY1292	50°43·5′	3°14·4′W	F	192,193
Big Wood	Fife	NT0191	56°6·3′	3°35·1′W	F	58
Big Wood	Heref	SO4232	51°59·2′	2°50·3′W	F	149,161
Big Wood	Leic	SK8431	52°52·4′	0°44·7′W	F	130
Big Wood	Lincs	SK9186	53°22·0′	0°37·5′W	F	112,121
Big Wood	Lincs	TA0800	53°29·4′	0°21·9′W	F	112
Big Wood	Norf	TF7629	52°50·0′	0°37·2′E	F	132
Big Wood	Norf	TF7914	52°41·9′	0°39·3′E	F	132
Big Wood	Norf	TL9784	52°25·3′	0°54·2′E	F	144
Big Wood	Norf	TM2089	52°27·5′	1°14·7′E	F	156
Big Wood	N Yks	SE4085	54°15·8′	1°22·7′W	F	99
Big Wood	N Yks	SE4696	54°21·7′	1°17·1′W	F	100
Big Wood	Pth & Kin	NN7363	56°44·7′	4°4·1′W	F	42
Big Wood	Scot Bord	NT4725	55°31·2′	2°49·9′W	F	73
Big Wood	Scot Bord	NT6529	55°33·5′	2°32·9′W	F	74
Big Wood	Shrops	SJ5203	52°37·6′	2°42·1′W	F	126
Big Wood	Shrops	SO5289	52°30·0′	2°42·0′W	F	137,138
Big Wood	Shrops	SO6085	52°27·9′	2°34·9′W	F	138
Big Wood	Staffs	SJ8323	52°48·5′	2°14·7′W	F	127
Big Wood	Staffs	SJ8406	52°39·3′	2°13·8′W	F	127
Big Wood	Staffs	SK0033	52°53·9′	1°59·6′W	F	128
Big Wood	Stir	NS5998	56°9·5′	4°15·8′W	F	57
Big Wood	Suff	TM0774	52°19·7′	1°2·7′E	F	144
Big Wood	Suff	TM4372	52°17·8′	1°34·2′E	F	156
Bigws	Pemb	SN0226	51°54·1′	4°52·3′W	X	145,157,158
Bigyn	Carm	SN4403	51°42·5′	4°15·1′W	X	159
Bilascleiter	N Eil	NB5557	58°26·2′	6°11·4′W	X	8
Bilberry	Corn	SX0260	50°24·6′	4°46·8′W	T	200
Bilberryhill	Devon	SX7266	50°29·0′	3°47·9′W	X	202
Bilberry Knoll	Derby	SK3057	53°6·8′	1°32·7′W	H	119
Bilberry Wood	Flint	SJ3164	53°10·4′	3°1·5′W	F	117
Bilbo	Aberd	NJ6639	57°26·7′	2°33·5′W	X	29
Bilbo	Aberd	NJ7529	57°21·3′	2°24·5′W	X	38
Bilbo	Aberd	NK0656	57°35·9′	1°53·5′W	X	30
Bilbo	Aberd	NK0733	57°23·5′	1°52·6′W	X	30
Bilborough	C of Nott	SK5241	52°58·1′	1°13·1′W	T	129
Bilbrook	Somer	ST0341	51°9·8′	3°22·9′W	T	181
Bilbrook	Staffs	SJ8803	52°37·7′	2°10·2′W	T	127,139
Bilbrook Sta	Staffs	SJ8702	52°37·2′	2°11·1′W	X	127,139
Bilbrough	N Yks	SE5346	53°54·7′	1°11·2′W	T	105
Bilbrough Whin	N Yks	SE5145	53°54·2′	1°13·0′W	F	105
Bilbster	Highld	ND2852	58°27·3′	3°13·6′W	T	11,12
Bilbster Mains	Highld	ND2853	58°27·8′	3°13·6′W	T	11,12
Bilbury	Heref	SO4968	52°18·7′	2°44·5′W	X	137,138,148
Bilbury Fm	Wilts	SU0136	51°7·6′	1°58·8′W	FM	184
Bilbury Rings	Wilts	SU0136	51°7·6′	1°58·8′W	A	184
Bilbut Fm	Glos	SO6719	51°52·4′	2°28·4′W	FM	162
Bilby	Notts	SK6383	53°20·6′	1°2·8′W	T	111,120
Bildershaw	Durham	NZ2024	54°36·9′	1°41·0′W	T	93
Bildeston	Suff	TL9949	52°6·4′	0°54·8′E	T	155
Bile Buidhe	Highld	NJ0711	57°11·1′	3°31·9′W	H	36
Bile Gharbh	Arg & Bt	NN0813	56°16·5′	5°5·6′W	X	50,56
Bilfield	Heref	SO5957	52°12·8′	2°35·6′W	X	149
Bilham Fm	Kent	TR0239	51°7·1′	0°53·6′E	FM	189
Bilham Grange	Donc	SE4906	53°33·1′	1°15·2′W	X	111
Bilham Grange	Kirk	SE2610	53°35·4′	1°36·0′W	X	110
Bilham House Fm	Donc	SE4806	53°33·1′	1°16·1′W	FM	111
Bilhaugh	Notts	SK6368	53°12·6′	1°3·0′W	F	120
Bilks Hill	E Yorks	SE9430	53°45·7′	0°34·0′W	X	106
Billa Barra	Leic	SK4611	52°41·9′	1°18·8′W	X	129
Billacombe	C of Plym	SX5254	50°22·3′	4°4·5′W	T	201
Billacombe	Devon	SX4282	50°37·2′	4°13·6′W	X	201
Billacott	Corn	SX2590	50°41·2′	4°28·3′W	T	190
Billany Fm	Devon	SX7762	50°26·9′	3°43·6′W	FM	202
Billeaford Hall	Suff	TM4360	52°11·3′	1°33·7′E	X	156
Biller Howe	N Yks	NZ9000	54°23·5′	0°36·4′W	X	94
Biller Howe	N Yks	NZ9101	54°24·0′	0°35·5′W	X	94
Biller Howe Dale	N Yks	NZ9101	54°24·0′	0°35·5′W	X	94
Billericay	Essex	TQ6794	51°37·4′	0°25·2′E	T	167,177,178
Billerley	Northum	NY8379	55°6·6′	2°15·6′W	X	86,87
Billerwell	Scot Bord	NT5915	55°25·9′	2°38·4′W	X	80
Billesdon	Leic	SK7102	52°36·9′	0°56·7′W	T	141
Billesdon Brook	Leic	SK7002	52°36·9′	0°57·6′W	W	141
Billesdon Coplow	Leic	SK7004	52°38·0′	0°57·5′W	F	141
Billesdon Lodge	Leic	SK7203	52°37·4′	0°55·8′W	XM	141
Billesley	Birm	SP0980	52°25·3′	1°51·7′W	T	139
Billesley	Warw	SP1456	52°12·4′	1°47·3′W	T	151
Billesley Common	Birm	SP0880	52°25·3′	1°52·5′W	T	139
Billets Fm	Essex	TL9616	51°48·7′	0°51·0′E	FM	168
Bill Fm	Pemb	SM9626	51°54·0′	4°57·5′W	FM	157,158
Billhay Fm	Wilts	ST8928	51°3·3′	2°9·0′W	FM	184
Bill Hill Park	Wok	SU8071	51°26·2′	0°50·6′W	X	175
Billhole	Devon	SS3311	50°52·7′	4°22·1′W	X	190
Billhole Fm	Devon	SS7811	50°53·4′	3°43·7′W	FM	191
Billholm	D & G	NY2792	55°13·3′	3°8·4′W	X	79

Billholm Burn	D & G	NY2793	55°13·8'	3°8·4'W	W	79
Billhope	Scot Bord	NY4497	55°16·1'	2°52·4'W	X	79
Billhope Burn	Scot Bord	NY4498	55°16·6'	2°52·5'W	W	79
Billia Cletts	Shetld	HU3623	59°59·7'	1°20·8'W	X	4
Billia Croo	Orkney	HY2210	58°58·5'	3°20·9'W	W	6
Billia Field	Shetld	HU3786	60°33·6'	1°19·0'W	H	1,2,3
Billia Skerry	Shetld	HU3785	60°33·1'	1°19·0'W	X	1,2,3
Billia Skerry	Shetld	HU6568	60°23·7'	0°48·7'W	X	2
Billie Castle	Scot Bord	NT8559	55°49·7'	2°13·9'W	A	67,74
Billiemains	Scot Bord	NT8558	55°49·2'	2°13·9'W	X	67,74
Billiemire Burn	Scot Bord	NT8759	55°49·7'	2°12·0'W	W	67,74
Billies	D & G	NX7257	54°53·7'	3°59·3'W	X	83,84
Billincoat Fm	Cumbr	SD2272	54°8·5'	3°11·2'W	FM	96
Billingbear	Brackn	SU8372	51°26·7'	0°47·9'W	X	175
Billingbear Park	Win & Maid	SU8272	51°26·7'	0°48·8'W	X	175
Billingborough	Lincs	TF1134	52°53·8'	0°20·6'W	T	130
Billingborough Fen	Lincs	TF1433	52°53·2'	0°17·9'W	X	130
Billing Brook	Cambs	TL1293	52°31·6'	0°20·5'W	W	142
Billinge	St Hel	SD5300	53°29·9'	2°42·1'W	T	108
Billinge Head Fm	Ches	SJ9577	53°17·6'	2°4·1'W	FM	118
Billinge Hill	Black w Dar	SD6528	53°45·1'	2°31·4'W	H	102,103
Billinge Hill	St Hel	SD5201	53°30·5'	2°43·0'W	H	108
Billinger Barns	N Yks	SD8267	54°6·2'	2°16·1'W	X	98
Billinges	Lancs	SD4104	53°32·0'	2°53·0'W	X	108
Billinge Scarr	Black w Dar	SD6529	53°45·6'	2°31·4'W	X	102,103
Billingford	Norf	TG0120	52°44·6'	0°59·1'E	T	133
Billingford	Norf	TM1678	52°21·7'	1°10·7'E	T	144,156
Billingford Common	Norf	TG0119	52°44·1'	0°59·0'E	X	133
Billingford Wood	Norf	TM1780	52°22·7'	1°11·7'E	F	156
Billingham	Stock on T	NZ4623	54°36·2'	1°16·9'W	T	93
Billingham Beck	Stock on T	NZ4423	54°36·3'	1°18·7'W	W	93
Billingham Fm	E Susx	TQ8619	50°56·6'	0°39·3'E	FM	189,199
Billingham Manor	I of W	SZ4881	50°37·8'	1°18·9'W	X	196
Billinghay	Lincs	TF1554	53°4·5'	0°16·6'W	T	121
Billinghay Dales	Lincs	TF1754	53°4·5'	0°14·8'W	X	121
Billinghay Dales	Lincs	TF1854	53°4·4'	0°13·9'W	X	122
Billinghay Fen	Lincs	TF1556	53°5·6'	0°16·6'W	X	121
Billinghay Hurn	Lincs	TF1756	53°5·5'	0°14·8'W	X	121
Billinghay Skirth	Lincs	TF1755	53°5·0'	0°14·8'W	W	121
Billinghay Skirth	Lincs	TF1855	53°5·0'	0°13·9'W	W	122
Billingley	Barns	SE4304	53°32·1'	1°20·7'W	T	111
Billingley Green	Barns	SE4404	53°32·1'	1°19·8'W	X	111
Billingsbourne	Essex	TQ4694	51°37·8'	0°7·0'E	X	167,177
Billing Shield	Durham	NY9538	54°44·5'	2°4·2'W	X	91,92
Billings Hill	E Yorks	TA1451	53°56·8'	0°15·4'W	X	107
Billingshurst	W Susx	TQ0825	51°1·1'	0°27·2'W	T	187,197
Billingside Wood	Durham	NZ1353	54°52·5'	1°47·4'W	F	88
Billingsley	Shrops	SO7085	52°28·0'	2°26·1'W	T	138
Billingsley Hall Fm	Shrops	SO7185	52°28·0'	2°25·2'W	FM	138
Billingsmoor	Devon	SS9706	50°50·9'	3°27·4'W	X	192
Billings Ring	Shrops	SO3687	52°28·9'	2°56·1'W	A	137
Billington	Beds	SP9422	51°53·5'	0°37·6'W	T	165
Billington	Lancs	SD7235	53°48·9'	2°25·1'W	T	103
Billington	Staffs	SJ8820	52°46·9'	2°10·3'W	T	127
Billington Manor	Beds	SP9422	51°53·5'	0°37·6'W	X	165
Billingtons	Lancs	SD6138	53°50·5'	2°35·1'W	X	102,103
Billins	Flint	SJ1972	53°14·6'	3°12·4'W	X	116
Billinside Moor	N Yks	SD9083	54°14·8'	2°8·8'W	X	98
Billister	Shetld	HU4860	60°19·5'	1°7·4'W	X	2,3
Bill Law	Northum	NU0134	55°36·2'	1°58·6'W	X	75
Billockby	Norf	TG4213	52°39·9'	1°35·1'E	T	134
Bill of Portland	Dorset	SY6768	50°30·9'	2°27·5'W	X	194
Billow Fm	Glos	SO7101	51°42·7'	2°24·8'W	FM	162
Billown	I of M	SC2669	54°5·5'	4°39·2'W	X	95
Billow Ness	Fife	NO5602	56°12·8'	2°42·1'W	X	59
Bill Quay	Ghead	NZ2962	54°57·4'	1°32·4'W	T	88
Billscleuch Moor	D & G	NT0912	55°23·9'	3°25·8'W	X	78
Billsmoorfoot	Northum	NY9497	55°16·3'	2°5·2'W	X	80
Billsmoor Park	Northum	NY9496	55°15·7'	2°5·2'W	X	80
Bill's Wood	Sol	SP1178	52°24·2'	1°49·9'W	F	139
Bill, The	Cambs	TL2886	52°27·6'	0°6·6'W	X	142
Billups' Siding Fm	Cambs	TL3782	52°25·4'	0°1·3'E	FM	142,143
Billyards Fm	Lincs	SK9188	53°23·1'	0°37·5'W	FM	112,121
Billy Fm	Somer	ST0829	51°3·4'	3°18·4'W	FM	181
Billylaw	Northum	NT9849	55°44·3'	2°1·5'W	X	75
Billy Mill	N Tyne	NZ3369	55°1·1'	1°28·6'W	T	88
Billy Row	Durham	NZ1637	54°43·9'	1°44·7'W	T	92
Bilmarsh	Shrops	SJ4925	52°49·4'	2°45·0'W	T	126
Bilsborrow	Lancs	SD5139	53°50·9'	2°44·3'W	T	102
Bilsby	Lincs	TF4776	53°15·9'	0°12·7'E	T	122
Bilsby Field	Lincs	TF4675	53°15·3'	0°11·7'E	X	122
Bilsdale	N Yks	SE5692	54°19·5'	1°7·9'W	X	100
Bilsdale Beck	N Yks	NZ5601	54°24·3'	1°7·8'W	W	93
Bilsdale East Moor	N Yks	SE5996	54°21·6'	1°5·1'W	X	100
Bilsdale Hall	N Yks	NZ5600	54°23·8'	1°7·8'W	X	93
Bilsdale West Moor	N Yks	NZ5201	54°24·3'	1°11·5'W	X	93
Bilsdale West Moor	N Yks	SE5595	54°21·1'	1°8·8'W	X	100
Bilsdean	E Loth	NT7672	55°56·7'	2°22·6'W	X	67
Bilsdean Creek	Scot Bord	NT7772	55°56·7'	2°21·7'W	W	67
Bilsdens Fm	Essex	TL5304	51°43·1'	0°13·3'E	FM	167
Bilsdon	Devon	SX8291	50°42·6'	3°39·9'W	T	191
Bilsey Hill	Norf	TG0142	52°56·5'	0°59·9'E	X	133
Bilsford	Devon	SS4018	50°56·6'	4°16·3'W	X	180,190
Bilsham	W Susx	SU9702	50°48·8'	0°37·0'W	T	197
Bilsham Fm	S Glos	ST5787	51°35·0'	2°36·8'W	FM	172
Bilshay Fm	Dorset	SY4594	50°44·8'	2°46·4'W	FM	193
Bilsington	Kent	TR0434	51°4·4'	0°55·1'E	T	179,189
Bilson Green	Glos	SO6514	51°49·6'	2°30·1'W	T	162
Bilsthorpe	Notts	SK6460	53°8·2'	1°2·2'W	T	120
Bilsthorpe Moor	Notts	SK6559	53°7·7'	1°1·3'W	T	120
Bilston	Midlo	NT2664	55°52·1'	3°10·5'W	T	66
Bilston	Wolv	SO9497	52°34·5'	2°4·9'W	T	139
Bilston Brook Fm	Staffs	SK0912	52°42·6'	1°51·6'W	FM	128
Bilston Burn	Midlo	NT2764	55°52·1'	3°9·6'W	W	66
Bilstone	Leic	SK3605	52°38·7'	1°27·7'W	T	140
Bilting	Kent	TR0549	51°12·4'	0°56·5'E	T	179,189
Bilton	E Yorks	TA1633	53°47·1'	0°13·9'W	T	107
Bilton	Northum	NU2210	55°23·3'	1°38·7'W	T	81
Bilton	N Yks	SE3057	54°0·7'	1°32·1'W	T	104
Bilton	Warw	SP4873	52°21·4'	1°17·3'W	T	140
Bilton Banks	N Yks	SE3258	54°1·3'	1°30·3'W	X	104
Bilton Barns	Northum	NU2210	55°23·3'	1°38·7'W	X	81
Bilton Dene	N Yks	SE3257	54°0·7'	1°30·3'W	X	104
Bilton Fields	Warw	SP4972	52°20·9'	1°16·4'W	X	140
Bilton Grange	N Yks	SE4751	53°57·4'	1°16·6'W	X	105
Bilton Grange (Sch)	Warw	SP4971	52°20·3'	1°16·4'W	X	140
Bilton Haggs	N Yks	SE4649	53°56·3'	1°17·5'W	T	105
Bilton Hall	N Yks	SE3357	54°0·7'	1°29·4'W	X	104
Bilton in Ainst	N Yks	SE4750	53°56·9'	1°16·6'W	T	105
Bilton Ings	N Yks	SE0056	54°0·2'	1°59·6'W	X	104
Bilton Mill	Northum	NU2212	55°24·3'	1°38·7'W	X	81
Biltons FM	Lincs	SK8563	53°9·7'	0°43·3'W	FM	
Biltons Fm	Notts	SK8563	53°9·7'	0°43·3'W	FM	121
Bimbister	Orkney	HY3216	59°1·8'	3°10·6'W	T	6
Bimmerhill	Northum	NY8086	55°10·3'	2°18·4'W	X	80
Binbrook	Lincs	TF2193	53°25·4'	0°10·3'W	T	113
Binbrook Airfield	Lincs	TF1996	53°27·1'	0°12·1'W	X	113
Binbrook Grange	Lincs	TF2192	53°24·9'	0°10·4'W	X	113
Binbrook Hall	Lincs	TF2494	53°25·9'	0°7·6'W	X	113
Binbrook Hill Fm	Lincs	TF2291	53°24·3'	0°9·5'W	FM	113
Binbrook Top	Lincs	TF1993	53°25·5'	0°12·1'W	X	113
Binbrook Walk Ho	Lincs	TF2492	53°24·8'	0°7·6'W	X	113
Bin Burn	E Dunb	NS6582	56°1·0'	4°9·5'W	W	57,64
Binchester	Durham	NZ2031	54°40·7'	1°41·0'W	X	93
Binchester Blocks	Durham	NZ2232	54°41·2'	1°39·1'W	T	93
Binchester Crag Fm	Durham	NZ2132	54°41·2'	1°40·0'W	FM	93
Binchurn Fm	Pemb	SM8431	51°56·4'	5°8·2'W	FM	157
Bincknoll Castle	Wilts	SU1079	51°30·8'	1°51·0'W	A	173
Bincknoll Fm	Wilts	SU1079	51°30·8'	1°51·0'W	FM	173
Bincknoll Wood	Wilts	SU1078	51°30·3'	1°51·0'W	F	173
Bincombe	Dorset	SY6884	50°39·5'	2°26·8'W	T	194
Bin Combe	Somer	SS9041	51°9·7'	3°34·0'W	X	181
Bin Combe	Somer	ST1739	51°8·9'	3°10·8'W	X	181
Bincombe	Somer	ST1839	51°8·9'	3°10·0'W	T	181
Bincombe	Somer	ST4309	50°52·9'	2°48·2'W	X	193
Bincombe Hill	Dorset	SY6884	50°39·5'	2°26·8'W	X	194
Bincombe Wood	Wilts	ST9282	51°32·4'	2°6·5'W	F	173
Bindal	Highld	NH9284	57°50·2'	3°48·7'W	T	21
Bindal Muir	Highld	NH9385	57°50·8'	3°47·7'W	X	21
Bind Barrow	Dorset	SY4988	50°41·6'	2°42·9'W	A	193,194
Binderton Ho	W Susx	SU8410	50°53·2'	0°48·0'W	A	197
Bindloss Fm	Cumbr	SD6378	54°12·0'	2°33·6'W	FM	97
Bindon	Devon	SY2790	50°42·5'	3°1·7'W	A	193
Bindon	Somer	ST1024	51°0·7'	3°16·6'W	T	181,193
Bindon Abbey	Dorset	SY8586	50°40·6'	2°12·4'W	A	194
Bindon Hill	Dorset	SY8380	50°37·4'	2°14·0'W	H	194
Bin Down	Corn	SX2757	50°23·5'	4°25·7'W	X	201
Bind, The	Shrops	SO7283	52°26·9'	2°24·3'W	X	138
Bine	D & G	NW9968	54°58·2'	5°8·0'W	X	82
Bine Cotts, The	Shrops	SO6689	52°30·1'	2°29·7'W	X	138
Bine Fm	Shrops	SO7789	52°30·1'	2°19·9'W	FM	138
Binegar	Somer	ST6149	51°14·6'	2°33·1'W	T	183
Binegar Fm	Dorset	ST8419	50°58·4'	2°13·3'W	FM	183
Bineham Fm	Somer	ST4925	51°1·6'	2°43·2'W	FM	183,193
Bine Hill	Somer	ST3823	51°0·4'	2°52·6'W	X	193
Bines Green	W Susx	TQ1817	50°56·6'	0°18·8'W	T	198
Binfield	Brackn	SU8471	51°26·1'	0°47·1'W	T	175
Binfield Fm	I of W	SZ5191	50°43·2'	1°16·3'W	FM	196
Binfield Heath	Oxon	SU7478	51°30·0'	0°55·6'W	T	175
Binfield Lodge	Brackn	SU8473	51°27·2'	0°47·1'W	X	175
Binfield Manor	Brackn	SU8571	51°26·1'	0°46·2'W	X	175
Binfield Park Hospl	Brackn	SU8471	51°26·1'	0°47·1'W	X	175
Bin Forest, The	Aberd	NJ5243	57°28·7'	2°47·6'W	F	29
Bing	D & G	NX4250	54°49·4'	4°27·1'W	X	83
Binga Fea	Orkney	ND2892	58°48·8'	3°14·3'W	H	7
Bingfield	Northum	NY9772	55°2·8'	2°2·4'W	T	87
Bingfield Combe	Northum	NY9872	55°2·8'	2°1·5'W	X	87
Bingfield East Quarter	Northum	NY9874	55°3·9'	2°1·5'W	X	87
Bingfield Eastside	Northum	NY9873	55°3·3'	2°1·5'W	X	87
Bingham	C of Edin	NT3072	55°56·4'	3°6·8'W	T	66
Bingham	Notts	SK7039	52°56·9'	0°57·1'W	T	129
Bingham Lodge	Lincs	TF3932	52°52·3'	0°4·3'E	X	131
Bingham's Fm	Dorset	SY4796	50°45·9'	2°44·7'W	FM	193
Binghams Fm	Lincs	TF2294	53°26·0'	0°9·4'W	FM	113
Bingham's Melcombe	Dorset	ST7702	50°49·3'	2°19·2'W	A	194
Binghill	C of Aber	NJ8502	57°6·8'	2°14·4'W	X	38
Bingletts Wood	E Susx	TQ6221	50°58·2'	0°18·8'E	F	199
Bingley	Brad	SE1139	53°51·1'	1°49·6'W	T	104
Bingley	Denb	SJ0956	53°5·9'	3°21·1'W	X	116
Bingley Moor	Brad	SE1142	53°52·7'	1°49·5'W	X	104
Bings Heath	Shrops	SJ5418	52°45·7'	2°40·5'W	T	126
Binhall	Aberd	NJ4945	57°29·8'	2°50·6'W	X	28,29
Binham	Norf	TF9839	52°54·9'	0°57·1'E	T	132
Binham Fm	Somer	ST0342	51°10·4'	3°22·9'W	FM	181
Binham Moor	Somer	ST3949	51°14·5'	2°52·0'W	X	182
Binhamy	Corn	SS2205	50°49·3'	4°31·3'W	X	190
Binkleys Fm	N Yks	SE9691	54°18·5'	0°31·0'W	FM	94,101
Bink Moss	Durham	NY8724	54°36·9'	2°11·7'W	H	91,92
Binks	Scot Bord	NT4004	55°19·8'	2°56·3'W	X	79
Binks Hill	Scot Bord	NT4103	55°19·3'	2°55·4'W	H	79
Binks Ho	Durham	NY8232	54°41·2'	2°16·3'W	X	91,92
Binks, The	C of Edin	NT1978	55°59·5'	3°17·5'W	X	65,66
Binky Burn	Northum	NY6684	55°9·2'	2°31·6'W	W	80
Binley	Cov	SP3777	52°23·6'	1°27·0'W	T	140
Binley	Hants	SU4253	51°16·7'	1°23·5'W	T	185
Binley Fm	Glos	ST8197	51°40·5'	2°16·1'W	FM	162
Binley Woods	Warw	SP3977	52°23·6'	1°25·2'W	T	140
Binn	Pth & Kin	NO1713	56°18·4'	3°20·0'W	X	58
Binn	Pth & Kin	NT1496	56°9·2'	3°22·6'W	X	58
Binnal	Shrops	SO7096	52°33·9'	2°26·2'W	X	138
Binnamore	Devon	SX6861	50°26·3'	3°51·2'W	X	202
Binna Ness	Shetld	HU3742	60°9·9'	1°19·5'W	X	4
Binnaquoy	Orkney	HY3514	59°0·8'	3°7·4'W	X	6
Binn Burn	Pth & Kin	NO1712	56°17·8'	3°20·0'W	W	58
Binneag a'Bhacain	Arg & Bt	NR6996	56°6·3'	5°42·5'W	H	55,61
Binnean nan Gobhar	Stir	NS4196	56°8·1'	4°33·1'W	H	56
Binneford	Devon	SS8307	50°51·3'	3°39·4'W	X	191
Binneford	Devon	SX7596	50°45·2'	3°45·9'W	X	191
Binneford Water	Devon	SS8309	50°52·4'	3°39·4'W	W	191
Binnegar	Dorset	SY8787	50°41·2'	2°10·7'W	T	194
Binnegar Fm	Dorset	SY8888	50°41·7'	2°9·8'W	FM	194
Binnegar Hall	Dorset	SY8887	50°41·2'	2°9·8'W	X	194
Binnegar Plain	Dorset	SY8787	50°41·2'	2°10·7'W	X	194
Binnein an Fhidhleir	Arg & Bt	NN2110	56°15·2'	4°52·9'W	H	50,56
Binnein Ban	Arg & Bt	NR9471	55°53·5'	5°17·2'W	X	62
Binnein Beag	Highld	NN2267	56°45·9'	4°54·3'W	H	41
Binnein Brander	Arg & Bt	NN0528	56°24·5'	5°9·2'W	X	50
Binnein Fithich	Arg & Bt	NR6014	55°21·9'	5°46·8'W	X	68
Binnein Furachail	Arg & Bt	NM7411	56°14·5'	5°38·4'W	X	55
Binnein Ghorrie	Arg & Bt	NM4819	56°18·0'	6°4·0'W	X	48
Binnein Liath	Arg & Bt	NR5590	56°2·7'	5°55·6'W	X	61
Binnein Mór	Arg & Bt	NR9975	55°55·8'	5°12·6'W	X	62
Binnein Mór	Highld	NN2166	56°45·3'	4°55·2'W	H	41
Binnein Mór	Highld	NN6496	57°2·4'	4°14·0'W	H	35
Binnein na h- Uaimh	N Ayr	NR9433	55°33·1'	5°15·5'W	X	68,69
Binnein or Ben An	Stir	NN5008	56°14·7'	4°24·8'W	H	57
Binnein Riabhach	Arg & Bt	NR3696	56°5·3'	6°14·2'W	H	61
Binnein Shios	Highld	NN4985	56°56·2'	4°28·4'W	H	34,42
Binnein Shuas	Highld	NN4682	56°54·5'	4°31·3'W	H	34,42
Binnel Bay	I of W	SZ5175	50°34·6'	1°16·4'W	W	196
Binnel Point	I of W	SZ5275	50°34·6'	1°15·6'W	X	196
Binnend	Fife	NT2387	56°4·4'	3°13·8'W	X	66
Binner Downs	Corn	SW6133	50°9·2'	5°20·4'W	X	203
Binnerton Manor	Corn	SW6033	50°9·1'	5°21·2'W	X	203
Binney Bank	Cumbr	NY5753	54°52·4'	2°39·8'W	F	86
Binney Fm	Medway	TQ8477	51°27·9'	0°39·3'E	FM	178
Binn Hill	Moray	NJ3065	57°40·4'	3°10·0'W	H	28
Binn Hill	Pth & Kin	NO1713	56°18·4'	3°20·0'W	H	58
Binniehill	Falk	NS8572	55°55·9'	3°50·0'W	T	65
Binnilidh Bheag	Highld	NH3215	57°12·0'	4°46·4'W	H	34
Binnilidh Mhór	Highld	NH3316	57°12·5'	4°45·4'W	H	34
Binnimoor Fen	Cambs	TL4497	52°33·3'	0°7·8'E	X	142,143
Binnington	N Yks	SE9978	54°11·5'	0°28·5'W	X	101
Binnington Carr	N Yks	SE9979	54°12·0'	0°28·5'W	X	101
Binnington Wold Fm	N Yks	TA0077	54°11·0'	0°27·6'W	FM	101
Binning Wood	E Loth	NT6080	56°0·9'	2°38·1'W	F	67
Binn Moor	Kirk	SE0510	53°35·4'	1°55·1'W	X	110
Binns	Angus	NO2933	56°29·3'	3°8·7'W	X	53
Binns	Derby	SE0902	53°31·1'	1°51·4'W	X	110
Binns	Moray	NJ3164	57°39·9'	3°8·9'W	X	28
Binns Fm	Staffs	SK1011	52°42·0'	1°50·7'W	FM	128
Binns Mill	W Loth	NT0678	55°59·4'	3°30·0'W	X	65
Binns Moss	Derby	SE0802	53°31·1'	1°52·4'W	X	110
Binns, The	W Loth	NT0578	55°59·4'	3°30·9'W	A	65
Binn, The	Fife	NT2387	56°4·4'	3°13·8'W	X	66
Binn, The	Pth & Kin	NO1522	56°23·2'	3°22·2'W	X	53,58
Binn Wall, The	S Glos	ST5385	51°34·0'	2°40·3'W	X	172
Binn Wood	Pth & Kin	NO1613	56°18·4'	3°21·0'W	F	58
Binn Wood	Pth & Kin	NT1497	56°9·7'	3°22·6'W	F	58
Binny Cotts	Kent	TQ9364	51°20·8'	0°46·7'E	X	178
Binny Craig	W Loth	NT0473	55°56·7'	3°31·8'W	X	65
Binny Ho	W Loth	NT0573	55°56·7'	3°30·8'W	X	65
Bin of Cullen	Moray	NJ4764	57°40·0'	2°52·8'W	H	28,29
Binscarth	Orkney	HY3414	59°0·7'	3°8·5'W	X	6
Binscombe	Surrey	SU9645	51°12·0'	0°37·2'W	T	186
Binsdale Fm	E Yorks	TA1268	54°6·0'	0°16·8'W	FM	101
Binsey	Cumbr	NY2235	54°42·5'	3°12·2'W	H	89,90
Binsey	Oxon	SP4907	51°45·8'	1°17·0'W	T	164
Binside	Aberd	NJ4943	57°28·7'	2°50·6'W	X	28,29
Binsness	Moray	NJ0362	57°38·5'	3°37·0'W	X	27
Binsoe	N Yks	SE2579	54°12·6'	1°36·6'W	T	99
Binstead	Hants	SU7741	51°10·0'	0°53·5'W	T	186
Binstead	I of W	SZ5792	50°43·7'	1°11·2'W	T	196
Binstead Place	Hants	SU7841	51°10·0'	0°52·7'W	X	186
Binsted	W Susx	SU9806	50°50·9'	0°36·1'W	T	197
Binsted Wood	W Susx	SU9906	50°50·9'	0°35·2'W	F	197
Binswood	Hants	SU7637	51°7·9'	0°54·4'W	F	186
Bin, The	Aberd	NJ5043	57°28·7'	2°49·6'W	H	29
Binton	Warw	SP1454	52°11·3'	1°47·3'W	T	151
Binton Brook	Warw	SP1554	52°11·3'	1°46·4'W	W	151
Binton Fm	Surrey	SU8846	51°12·6'	0°44·0'W	FM	186
Binton Hill	Warw	SP1453	52°10·7'	1°47·3'W	X	151
Binton Hill Fm	Warw	SP1454	52°11·3'	1°47·3'W	FM	151
Bintree	Norf	TG0123	52°46·3'	0°59·2'E	T	133
Bintree Hills	Norf	TF9922	52°45·8'	0°57·4'E	X	132
Bintree Mill	Norf	TF9924	52°46·8'	0°57·4'E	X	132
Bintree Woods	Norf	TG0022	52°45·7'	0°58·3'E	F	133
Bint's Fm	Oxon	SU7477	51°29·5'	0°55·7'W	FM	175
Binwell Fm	Bucks	SP7119	51°52·1'	0°57·7'W	FM	165
Binweston	Shrops	SJ3004	52°38·0'	3°1·7'W	A	126
Binworthy Barton	Devon	SS4213	50°53·9'	4°14·4'W	X	180,190
Binzian	Pth & Kin	NO0715	56°19·4'	3°29·8'W	X	58
Binzian Burn	Pth & Kin	NO0612	56°17·7'	3°30·7'W	W	58
Binzian Mill	Pth & Kin	NO0714	56°18·8'	3°29·8'W	X	58
Bioda Buidhe	Highld	NG4366	57°36·9'	6°17·7'W	H	23
Biod a' Choltraiche	Highld	NG2565	57°35·7'	6°35·7'W	X	23
Biod a' Ghoill	Highld	NG2759	57°32·6'	6°33·3'W	X	23
Biod an Athair	Highld	NG1555	57°30·0'	6°45·0'W	H	23
Biod an Fhithich	Highld	NG9127	57°17·4'	5°27·6'W	H	25,33
Biod an Fhithich	Highld	NG9514	57°10·5'	5°23·0'W	H	33
Biod Bàn	Highld	NG1349	57°26·7'	6°46·6'W	X	23
Biod Bàn	Highld	NG8120	57°13·4'	5°37·2'W	H	33
Biod Eag	Highld	NC7740	58°20·1'	4°5·6'W	X	10
Biod Mór	Highld	NG3727	57°15·7'	6°21·2'W	H	32
Biod na Fionaich	Highld	NG3624	57°14·1'	6°22·0'W	X	32
Biod nan Laogh	Highld	NG3058	57°32·2'	6°30·2'W	X	23
Biod nan Sgarbh	Arg & Bt	NR3576	55°54·5'	6°14·0'W	X	60,61
Biod Ruadh	Highld	NG3128	57°16·1'	6°27·3'W	H	32
Biod Sgiath na Corra-gribhich	Highld	NG2266	57°36·2'	6°38·8'W	X	23
Biorach	Highld	NH0669	57°40·4'	5°14·7'W	H	19
Bioran Beag	Pth & Kin	NN6923	56°23·1'	4°6·9'W	X	51
Bior eilean	N Eil	NF7665	57°33·8'	7°24·7'W	X	18
Birbrook	Devon	SS5725	51°0·6'	4°1·9'W	X	180
Birch	Devon	SS6232	51°4·5'	3°57·8'W	X	180
Birch	Devon	SS6435	51°6·1'	3°56·3'W	X	180
Birch	Essex	TL9419	51°50·4'	0°49·4'E	T	168
Birch	Roch	SD8507	53°33·8'	2°13·2'W	T	109

Birch Acre	Worcs	SP0773	52°21·5'	1°53·4'W	T	139
Birchall	Heref	SO6538	52°2·6'	2°30·2'W	T	149
Birchall	Herts	TL2711	51°47·2'	0°9·1'W	X	166
Birchall	Staffs	SJ9854	53°5·2'	2°1·4'W	T	118
Birchall Brook	Ches	SJ6944	52°59·8'	2°27·3'W	W	118
Birchallmoss Fm	Ches	SJ6745	53°0·3'	2°29·1'W	FM	118
Bircham	Devon	SS6516	50°55·9'	3°54·9'W	X	180
Bircham Common	Norf	TF7831	52°51·1'	0°39·0'E	X	132
Bircham Heath	Norf	TF7629	52°50·0'	0°37·2'E	X	132
Bircham Newton	Norf	TF7633	52°52·2'	0°37·3'E	T	132
Bircham Newton Training Centre	Norf	TF7934	52°52·6'	0°40·0'E	X	132
Bircham Tofts	Norf	TF7732	52°51·6'	0°38·2'E	T	132
Birchan Coppice	Worcs	SO8174	52°22·1'	2°16·3'W	T	138
Birchanger	Essex	TL5122	51°52·8'	0°12·0'E	T	167
Birchanger	Somer	SS8646	51°12·3'	3°37·5'W	X	181
Birchanger Cross	Devon	SX7775	50°33·9'	3°43·8'W	X	191
Birchanger Fm	Somer	ST0637	51°7·7'	3°20·2'W	FM	181
Birchanger Fm	Wilts	ST8952	51°16·3'	2°9·1'W	FM	184
Birchanger Green Services	Essex	TL5121	51°52·3'	0°12·0'E	X	167
Birch Bank	Cumbr	SD2687	54°16·6'	3°7·8'W	X	96,97
Birch Bank	Lancs	SD6149	53°56·4'	2°35·2'W	X	102,103
Birchbank	Moray	NJ2944	57°29·1'	3°10·6'W	X	28
Birch Bank Fm	Ches	SJ4566	53°11·5'	2°49·0'W	FM	117
Birch Berrow	Worcs	SO7364	52°16·6'	2°23·3'W	T	138,150
Birch Brook	Essex	TM0122	51°51·8'	0°55·6'E	W	168
Birchburn	N Ayr	NR9129	55°30·9'	5°18·2'W	T	68,69
Birch Carr	N Yks	NZ2706	54°27·2'	1°34·6'W	F	93
Birchcleave Ho	Devon	SX4970	50°30·9'	4°7·4'W	X	201
Birch Cleuch	D & G	NY4089	55°11·2'	2°56·1'W	X	79
Birch Close	Brad	SE1341	53°52·1'	1°47·7'W	X	104
Birch Close	Dorset	ST8803	50°49·8'	2°9·8'W	X	194
Birch Coppice	Shrops	SO5198	52°34·9'	2°43·0'W	F	137,138
Birch Copse	Northnts	SP7042	52°4·5'	0°58·3'W	F	152
Birch Copse	Wilts	SU2466	51°23·8'	1°38·9'W	F	174
Birch Craig	Cumbr	NY5962	54°57·3'	2°38·0'W	X	86
Birch Cross	Staffs	SK1230	52°52·3'	1°48·9'W	T	128
Birchdale Ho	N Yks	NZ7714	54°31·2'	0°48·2'W	X	94
Birchden	E Susx	TQ5336	51°6·4'	0°11·5'E	T	188
Birchdown	Devon	SS9522	50°59·5'	3°29·4'W	X	181
Birchen	Highld	NH7692	57°54·3'	4°5·1'W	T	21
Birchen Bank Moss	Derby	SK1098	53°29·0'	1°50·5'W	X	110
Birchencliff	Ches	SJ9480	53°19·3'	2°5·0'W	X	109
Birchencliffe	Kirk	SE1118	53°39·7'	1°49·6'W	T	110
Birchen Coppice	Shrops	SO5688	52°29·5'	2°38·5'W	F	137,138
Birchen Coppice Fm	Worcs	SO8173	52°21·5'	2°16·3'W	FM	138
Birchend	Heref	SO6644	52°5·8'	2°29·4'W	T	149
Birchendale	Staffs	SK0538	52°56·6'	1°55·1'W	T	128
Birchen Edge	Derby	SK2772	53°14·9'	1°35·3'W	X	119
Birchenfields Fm	Flint	SJ3667	53°12·0'	2°57·1'W	FM	117
Birchen Lee	Lancs	SD6244	53°53·7'	2°34·3'W	X	102,103
Birchen Oak	Devon	SS9808	50°52·0'	3°26·6'W	X	192
Birchenough	Stock	SJ9888	53°23·6'	2°1·4'W	X	109
Birchenough Hill	Ches	SJ9967	53°12·3'	2°0·5'W	H	118
Birchen Park	Shrops	SO7080	52°25·3'	2°26·1'W	F	138
Birchensale	Worcs	SP0268	52°18·8'	1°57·8'W	X	139
Birchen Spring	Bucks	SU9592	51°37·4'	0°37·3'W	F	175,176
Birchen Tree	Cumbr	SD7486	54°16·4'	2°23·5'W	X	98
Birchen Wood	Glos	SO5411	51°48·0'	2°39·6'W	F	162
Birchenwood Fm	E Susx	TQ7029	51°2·3'	0°25·9'E	FM	188,199
Bircher	Heref	SO4765	52°17·1'	2°46·2'W	T	137,138,148
Bircher Common	Heref	SO4666	52°17·6'	2°47·1'W	X	137,138,148
Birches	Heref	SO2953	52°10·5'	3°1·9'W	X	148
Birches	Monm	SO3823	51°54·4'	2°53·7'W	X	161
Birches Copse	Dorset	SU0610	50°53·6'	1°54·5'W	F	195
Birches Fm	E Susx	TQ4517	50°56·3'	0°4·2'E	FM	198
Birches Fm	Shrops	SO6289	52°30·1'	2°33·2'W	FM	138
Birches Fm	Tames	SJ9592	53°25·7'	2°4·1'W	FM	109
Birches Green	Birm	SP1190	52°30·7'	1°49·9'W	T	139
Birches Hall	Ches	SJ7037	52°56·1'	2°26·6'W	X	118
Birches Head	C of Stoke	SJ8948	53°2·0'	2°9·4'W	T	118
Birches, The	Heref	SO2538	52°2·4'	3°5·2'W	X	161
Birches, The	Heref	SO3662	52°15·4'	2°55·9'W	F	137,148,149
Birches, The	Heref	SO5362	52°15·5'	2°40·9'W	X	138,149
Birches, The	Heref	SO6061	52°15·0'	2°34·8'W	X	138,149
Birches, The	Kent	TQ5363	51°21·0'	0°12·2'E	F	177,188
Birches, The	Shrops	SO6178	52°24·2'	2°34·0'W	X	138
Birches, The	Suff	TM4052	52°7·1'	1°30·7'E	F	156
Birches, The	Worcs	SO8981	52°25·8'	2°9·3'W	X	139
Birches Wood	Surrey	TQ1538	51°8·0'	0°21·0'W	F	187
Birche, The	Worcs	SO7363	52°16·1'	2°23·3'W	T	138,150
Birchett's Green	E Susx	TQ6631	51°3·5'	0°22·5'E	T	188
Birchett Wood	Kent	TQ9835	51°5·0'	0°50·0'E	F	189
Birchfield	Birm	SP0790	52°30·7'	1°53·4'W	T	139
Birchfield	Cumbr	SD6095	54°21·2'	2°36·5'W	X	97
Birchfield	Derby	SK1884	53°21·4'	1°43·4'W	X	110
Birchfield	Highld	NH4999	57°57·5'	4°32·7'W	X	20
Birchfield	Highld	NH9920	57°15·8'	3°40·0'W	X	36
Birchfield	Moray	NJ1614	57°12·8'	3°23·0'W	X	36
Birchfield	Shrops	SJ8204	52°38·2'	2°15·6'W	X	127
Birchfield Fm	Beds	TL1253	52°10·1'	0°21·3'W	FM	153
Birchfield Fm	Kent	TQ4854	51°16·2'	0°7·7'E	FM	188
Birchfield Fm	Norf	TF5600	52°34·8'	0°18·5'E	FM	143
Birchfield Gate	Northum	NY6864	54°58·4'	2°29·6'W	X	86,87
Birchfield Ho	I of W	SZ5086	50°40·5'	1°17·2'W	X	196
Birchfield House Fm	N Yks	SE2160	54°2·4'	1°40·3'W	FM	99
Birch Fm	Ches	SJ7373	53°15·4'	2°23·9'W	FM	118
Birch Fm	Devon	SS7005	50°50·0'	3°50·4'W	FM	191
Birch Fm	Northnts	TL0175	52°22·1'	0°30·6'W	FM	141
Birch Fm	Salf	SJ7297	53°28·4'	2°24·9'W	FM	109
Birch Fm	Shrops	SO7380	52°25·3'	2°23·4'W	FM	138
Birch Fm	Suff	TM1256	52°9·9'	1°6·4'E	FM	155
Birch Fm	Traf	SJ7290	53°24·6'	2°24·9'W	FM	109
Birch Fm	W Berks	SU5273	51°27·4'	1°14·7'W	FM	174
Birch Fm	W Susx	TQ3734	51°5·6'	0°2·2'W	FM	187
Birchfold	Aberd	NJ6402	57°6·7'	2°35·2'W	X	37
Birchfold Copse	W Susx	SU9830	51°3·9'	0°35·7'W	F	186
Birch Green	Essex	TL9418	51°49·8'	0°49·3'E	T	168
Birch Green	Herts	TL2911	51°47·2'	0°7·4'W	T	166
Birch Green	Lancs	SD4906	53°33·1'	2°45·8'W	T	108
Birch Green	Worcs	SO8545	52°6·4'	2°12·7'W	T	150
Birchgrove	Card	ST1680	51°31·0'	3°12·2'W	T	171
Birch-grove	Cered	SN6673	52°20·6'	3°57·6'W	X	135
Birchgrove	Swan	SS7098	51°40·2'	3°52·4'W	T	170
Birchgrove	W Susx	TQ4029	51°2·8'	0°0·2'E	T	187,198
Birch Grove Ho	W Susx	TQ4030	51°3·4'	0°0·2'E	X	187
Birchgrove Pool	Shrops	SJ4323	52°48·3'	2°50·3'W	W	126
Birch Hagg Ho	N Yks	SE6891	54°18·8'	0°56·9'W	X	94,100
Birch Hagg Plantn	N Yks	SE6892	54°19·4'	0°56·8'W	F	94,100
Birch Hall	Essex	TL9520	51°50·9'	0°50·3'E	X	168
Birch Hall	Essex	TM2122	51°51·4'	1°13·0'E	X	169
Birch Hall	Essex	TQ4499	51°40·5'	0°5·4'E	X	167,177
Birch Hall	Shrops	SJ4033	52°53·7'	2°53·1'W	X	126
Birch Hall	Staffs	SJ9725	52°49·6'	2°2·3'W	X	127
Birch Hall	Surrey	SU9363	51°21·7'	0°39·5'W	X	175,186
Birch Hall	Worcs	SO7769	52°19·4'	2°19·8'W	X	138
Birchhall Corner	Essex	TM0430	51°56·1'	0°58·5'E	T	168
Birch Hall Cott	N Yks	SE9292	54°19·2'	0°34·7'W	X	94,101
Birch Head	Cumbr	NY5560	54°56·2'	2°41·7'W	X	86
Birch Head	Staffs	SK0650	53°3·1'	1°54·2'W	X	119
Birch Heath	Ches	SJ5461	53°8·9'	2°40·9'W	T	117
Birch Heath Fm	Ches	SJ4565	53°11·0'	2°49·0'W	FM	117
Birch Hill	Brackn	SU8766	51°23·4'	0°44·6'W	T	175
Birch Hill	Cered	SN6259	52°13·0'	4°0·8'W	X	146
Birch Hill	Ches	SJ5273	53°15·4'	2°42·8'W	X	117
Birch Hill	Ches	SJ5367	53°12·1'	2°41·8'W	X	117
Birch Hill	Devon	ST2409	50°52·8'	3°4·4'W	X	192,193
Birch Hill	Dorset	ST5919	50°58·4'	2°34·7'W	X	183
Birch Hill	Heref	SO4536	52°1·4'	2°47·7'W	X	149,161
Birch Hill	I of M	SC3978	54°10·6'	4°27·6'W	X	95
Birch Hill	Leic	SK4713	52°43·0'	1°17·8'W	X	129
Birch Hill	N Yks	NZ5212	54°30·3'	1°11·4'W	X	93
Birch Hill	S Glos	ST7685	51°34·0'	2°20·4'W	X	172
Birch Hill	Shrops	SO6673	52°21·5'	2°29·6'W	H	138
Birch Hill Fm	N Yks	NZ7513	54°30·6'	0°50·1'W	FM	94
Birch Ho	Derby	SK2342	52°58·7'	1°39·0'W	X	119,128
Birch Ho	N Yks	NZ8304	54°25·7'	0°42·8'W	X	94
Birch Ho	N Yks	SE6378	54°11·9'	1°1·6'W	X	100
Birch Ho	Powys	SJ0900	52°35·7'	3°20·2'W	X	136
Birch Hoe Fm	Essex	TM2020	51°50·3'	1°12·0'E	FM	169
Birch Holt	Essex	TL9118	51°49·9'	0°46·7'E	X	168
Birch Holt	Lincs	SK9474	53°15·5'	0°35·0'W	F	121
Birch Holt Fm	Lincs	SK8660	53°8·0'	0°42·5'W	FM	121
Birch House Fm	N Yks	SE3062	54°3·4'	1°32·1'W	FM	99
Birch House Fm	Suff	TM0841	52°1·9'	1°2·3'E	FM	155,169
Birchill	Devon	ST3003	50°49·6'	2°59·3'W	T	193
Birchill Bank Wood	Derby	SK2271	53°14·4'	1°39·8'W	F	119
Birchill Fm	Devon	SS4616	50°55·6'	4°11·1'W	FM	180,190
Birchills	Derby	SK2132	52°53·3'	1°40·9'W	X	128
Birchills	Wals	SP0099	52°35·6'	1°59·6'W	T	139
Birchills Fm	Derby	SK2270	53°13·8'	1°39·8'W	FM	119
Birchin Clough	Derby	SK1191	53°25·2'	1°49·7'W	X	110
Birchingrove Fm	Surrey	TQ1951	51°15·0'	0°17·3'W	FM	187
Birchington	Kent	TR3069	51°22·6'	1°18·7'E	T	179
Birchin Hat	Derby	SK1491	53°25·2'	1°47·0'W	X	110
Birchinhill Fm	Suff	TL6679	52°23·3'	0°26·8'E	FM	143
Birchinlee	Derby	SK1691	53°25·2'	1°45·1'W	X	110
Birchinlee Pasture	Derby	SK1591	53°25·2'	1°46·0'W	X	110
Birchinley Hall	Roch	SD9313	53°37·1'	2°5·9'W	A	109
Birch Island	D & G	NX6170	55°0·6'	4°10·0'W	X	77
Birchitt	Derby	SK3579	53°18·6'	1°28·1'W	X	119
Birchlands Fm	Hants	SU3808	50°52·4'	1°27·2'W	FM	196
Birchley Fm	Shrops	SO8098	52°35·0'	2°17·3'W	FM	138
Birchley Fm	Warw	SP4178	52°24·1'	1°23·4'W	FM	140
Birchley Fm	Worcs	SO5964	52°16·6'	2°35·7'W	FM	137,138,149
Birchley Hall	St Hel	SJ5299	53°29·4'	2°43·0'W	A	108
Birchley Hall Fm	Warw	SP2784	52°27·4'	1°35·8'W	FM	140
Birchley Hays Wood	Warw	SP2684	52°27·4'	1°36·6'W	F	140
Birchley Heath	Warw	SP2894	52°32·8'	1°34·8'W	T	140
Birchley Ho	Kent	TQ8437	51°6·4'	0°38·1'E	X	188
Birchleys	Essex	TL8433	51°58·1'	0°41·1'E	X	168
Birchley Wood	Warw	SP4178	52°24·1'	1°23·4'W	F	140
Birch Linn	D & G	NX3376	55°3·3'	4°36·4'W	W	76
Birchmoor	Warw	SK2501	52°36·6'	1°37·4'W	T	140
Birchmoor Fm	Beds	SP9434	52°0·0'	0°37·4'W	FM	153,165
Birchmoor Green	Beds	SP9433	51°59·5'	0°37·5'W	T	165
Birch Moors, The	Wrekin	SJ7019	52°46·3'	2°26·3'W	X	127
Birchmore Fm	I of W	SZ5185	50°40·0'	1°16·3'W	FM	196
Birch Oak Fm	Devon	ST2509	50°52·8'	3°3·6'W	FM	192,193
Bircholt Court	Kent	TR0741	51°8·1'	0°57·9'E	X	179,189
Bircholt Forstal	Kent	TR0841	51°8·0'	0°58·8'E	T	179,189
Birchope	Shrops	SO3795	52°33·2'	2°55·4'W	X	137
Birchover	Derby	SK2362	53°9·5'	1°39·0'W	T	119
Birch Park	Shrops	SJ4023	52°48·3'	2°53·0'W	X	126
Birch Pits	Ches	SJ5147	53°1·3'	2°43·4'W	X	117
Birch Plantn	N Yks	SE8678	54°11·7'	0°40·5'W	F	101
Birch Service Station	Roch	SD8407	53°33·8'	2°14·1'W	X	109
Birchshow Rocks	N Yks	SD7862	54°3·5'	2°19·7'W	X	98
Birch Spinney	Northnts	SP8076	52°22·8'	0°49·1'W	F	141
Birch Spring	Essex	TL6202	51°41·8'	0°21·0'E	F	167
Birch Spring Fm	Lincs	SK8970	53°13·4'	0°39·6'W	FM	121
Birch Springs	N Yks	NZ2706	54°27·2'	1°34·6'W	X	93
Birchtimber Hill	Cumbr	NY4474	55°3·7'	2°52·2'W	X	85
Birch Tor	Devon	SX6881	50°37·1'	3°51·6'W	H	191
Birch Tree Fm	Cambs	TL3293	52°31·4'	0°2·9'W	FM	142
Birchtree Fm	Shrops	SJ5031	52°52·7'	2°44·2'W	FM	126
Birch Trees Fm	Staffs	SJ9359	53°7·9'	2°5·9'W	FM	118
Birch Vale	Derby	SK0286	53°22·5'	1°57·8'W	T	110
Birchview	Moray	NJ1838	57°25·8'	3°21·5'W	X	28
Birch Wood	Beds	TL1117	51°50·7'	0°22·9'W	F	166
Birch Wood	Derby	SK2735	52°54·9'	1°35·5'W	F	128
Birch Wood	Devon	SX4671	50°31·3'	4°10·0'W	F	201
Birch Wood	Essex	TM0330	51°56·1'	0°57·6'E	F	168
Birch Wood	Glos	SO6314	51°49·6'	2°31·8'W	F	162
Birch Wood	Heref	SO6132	51°59·3'	2°33·7'W	F	149
Birchwood	Heref	SO7550	52°9·1'	2°21·5'W	F	150
Birch Wood	Herts	TL1105	51°44·2'	0°23·2'W	F	166
Birchwood	Herts	TL2209	51°46·2'	0°13·5'W	T	166
Birch Wood	Lincs	SK8491	53°24·8'	0°43·8'W	F	112
Birchwood	Lincs	SK9369	53°12·8'	0°36·0'W	T	121
Birch Wood	Lincs	TF1367	53°11·5'	0°18·1'W	F	121
Birchwood	N Yks	NZ8400	54°23·6'	0°42·0'W	X	94
Birch Wood	N Yks	SE1963	54°4·0'	1°42·2'W	F	99
Birch Wood	N Yks	SE5791	54°18·9'	1°7·0'W	F	100
Birchwood	Somer	ST2414	50°55·5'	3°4·5'W	T	193
Birch Wood	Staffs	SK1124	52°49·0'	1°49·8'W	F	128
Birch Wood	Warr	SJ5885	53°21·9'	2°37·5'W	F	108
Birchwood	Warr	SJ6491	53°25·1'	2°32·1'W	T	109
Birch Wood	Worcs	SO8081	52°25·8'	2°17·3'W	F	138
Birchwood Common	Heref	SO7450	52°9·1'	2°22·4'W	X	150
Birchwood Fm	Kent	TQ8436	51°5·8'	0°38·1'E	FM	188
Birchwood Fm	Lincs	SK9074	53°15·6'	0°38·6'W	FM	121
Birchwood Hall	Northum	NU1427	55°32·4'	1°46·3'W	X	75
Birchwood Ho	Bath & NE Somer	ST6363	51°22·1'	2°31·5'W	X	172
Birchwood Ho	Surrey	TQ3556	51°17·5'	0°3·4'W	X	187
Birchwood House Fm	Hants	SU3022	51°0·0'	1°34·0'W	FM	185
Birchwood Lodge	Highld	NC9818	58°8·6'	3°43·5'W	X	17
Birchwoodmoor	Derby	SK1440	52°57·7'	1°47·1'W	X	119,128
Birchwood Park	Derby	SK1540	52°57·7'	1°46·2'W	X	119,128
Birchwood Park	Staffs	SK0033	52°53·9'	1°59·6'W	X	128
Birchwood Sta	Warr	SJ6590	53°24·6'	2°31·2'W	X	109
Birchy Cross Fm	Warw	SP1271	52°20·5'	1°49·0'W	FM	139
Birchyfield	Heref	SO6453	52°10·7'	2°31·2'W	X	149
Birchy Hill	Hants	SZ2898	50°47·1'	1°35·8'W	T	195
Birchy Lake	Devon	SX6292	50°42·9'	3°56·9'W	X	191
Bircotes	Notts	SK6391	53°25·0'	1°2·7'W	T	111
Birdale Ho	Cumbr	NY3742	54°46·4'	2°58·3'W	X	85
Birdbrook	Essex	TL7041	52°2·7'	0°29·1'E	T	154
Birdbush	Wilts	ST9123	51°0·6'	2°7·3'W	T	184
Birdcombe Court	N Som	ST4771	51°26·4'	2°45·4'W	X	171,172
Bird Dyke	Cumbr	NY0921	54°34·8'	3°24·1'W	X	89
Bird Fall	Highld	NH3509	57°8·8'	4°43·2'W	W	34
Bird Farm	Oxon	SU6485	51°33·8'	1°4·2'W	FM	175
Birdfield	Arg & Bt	NR9694	56°6·0'	5°16·4'W	T	55
Birdfield	Derby	SK3982	53°20·2'	1°24·4'W	X	110,111
Birdfield Wood	Arg & Bt	NR9594	56°5·9'	5°17·3'W	F	55
Birdforth	N Yks	SE4875	54°10·4'	1°15·5'W	T	100
Birdforth Beck	N Yks	SE4775	54°10·4'	1°16·4'W	W	100
Bird Green	Essex	TL4533	51°58·8'	0°7·1'E	T	167
Birdgreen Fm	Essex	TL7434	51°58·9'	0°32·4'E	FM	155
Birdham	W Susx	SU8200	50°47·9'	0°49·8'W	T	197
Birdham Pool	W Susx	SU8201	50°48·4'	0°49·8'W	W	197
Bird Hill	Herts	TL2632	51°58·6'	0°9·5'W	X	166
Bird Ho	Cumbr	NY2037	54°43·5'	3°14·1'W	X	89,90
Birdholme	Derby	SK3869	53°13·2'	1°25·4'W	T	119
Birdholme Fm	Derby	SK3868	53°12·7'	1°25·5'W	FM	119
Birdhope	Northum	NY8198	55°16·8'	2°17·5'W	X	80
Birdhow	Cumbr	NY2001	54°24·1'	3°13·5'W	X	89,90
Bird-in-eye Fm	E Susx	TQ4820	50°57·8'	0°6·8'E	FM	198
Birdingbury	Warw	SP4368	52°18·7'	1°21·8'W	T	151
Birdingbury Fields Fm	Warw	SP4366	52°17·7'	1°21·8'W	FM	151
Bird in Hand	Glos	SO8308	51°46·5'	2°14·4'W	X	162
Birdlestanes	D & G	NY2596	55°15·4'	3°10·4'W	A	79
Birdlip	Cered	SN3946	52°5·6'	4°20·6'W	X	145
Birdlip	Glos	SO9214	51°49·7'	2°6·6'W	T	163
Birdlip Hill	Glos	SO9214	51°49·7'	2°6·6'W	H	163
Birdlymes Fm	Wilts	SU1837	51°8·2'	1°44·2'W	FM	184
Bird Obsy	Shetld	HZ2272	59°32·3'	1°36·2'W	T	4
Birdoswald	Cumbr	NY6166	54°59·5'	2°36·1'W	X	86
Birdsall	N Yks	SE8165	54°4·7'	0°45·3'W	T	100
Birdsall Brow	N Yks	SE8263	54°3·6'	0°44·4'W	X	100
Birdsall Grange	N Yks	SE8165	54°4·7'	0°45·3'W	X	100
Birdsall Ho	N Yks	SE8164	54°4·2'	0°45·3'W	X	100
Birdsall Ings Ho	N Yks	SE8465	54°4·7'	0°42·5'W	X	100
Birdsbush Fm	S Glos	ST7286	51°34·6'	2°23·9'W	FM	172
Bird's Drove Fm	Lincs	TF2329	52°50·9'	0°10·0'W	FM	131
Birds Edge	Kirk	SE2007	53°33·8'	1°41·5'W	T	110
Birdsend	Glos	SO7521	51°53·5'	2°21·4'W	X	162
Birds End	Suff	TL7760	52°12·8'	0°35·9'E	T	155
Bird's Fm	Cambs	TL4055	52°10·8'	0°3·3'E	FM	154
Bird's Fm	Essex	TL7413	51°47·5'	0°31·8'E	FM	167
Bird's Fm	Somer	ST2925	51°1·4'	3°0·4'W	FM	193
Birds Fm	Suff	TL9353	52°8·7'	0°49·6'E	FM	155
Birds Green	Essex	TL5808	51°45·1'	0°17·7'E	T	167
Birdsgreen	Shrops	SO7684	52°27·4'	2°20·8'W	T	138
Bird's Hill	Cumbr	NY3947	54°49·1'	2°56·5'W	X	85
Birds Hill	Leic	SK3211	52°42·0'	1°31·2'W	X	128
Bird's Hill	Somer	ST0636	51°7·2'	3°20·2'W	X	181
Birdshill Fm	Carm	SN6022	51°53·0'	4°1·7'W	FM	159
Birds Hurst	Suff	TL8181	52°24·0'	0°40·0'E	F	144
Birds Kitchen	Kent	TR0422	50°57·9'	0°54·7'E	X	189
Birdsley Fm	Staffs	SK2008	52°40·4'	1°41·9'W	FM	128
Birdslint	Moray	NJ4554	57°34·6'	2°54·7'W	X	28,29
Bird's Marsh	Wilts	ST9175	51°28·7'	2°7·4'W	F	173
Birdsmill Ho	W Loth	NT1071	55°55·7'	3°26·0'W	X	65
Birdsmoorgate	Dorset	ST3900	50°48·0'	2°51·6'W	T	193
Bird's Nest Fm	Derby	SK4130	52°52·2'	1°23·0'W	FM	129
Birds Park Fm	Cumbr	SD5393	54°20·1'	2°43·0'W	FM	97
Bird's Pastures Fm	Cambs	TL3460	52°13·5'	0°1·9'W	FM	154
Birds Rock	Cered	SN3760	52°13·1'	4°22·8'W	X	145
Birds' Rock or Craig yr Aderyn	Gwyn	SH6406	52°38·3'	4°0·2'W	H	124
Birdston	E Dunb	NS6575	55°57·2'	4°9·3'W	T	64
Bird Street	Suff	TM0052	52°8·0'	0°55·7'E	T	155
Bird's Wood	Ches	SJ5778	53°18·1'	2°38·3'W	F	117
Birdwell	Barns	SE3401	53°30·5'	1°28·8'W	T	110,111
Birdwell Fm	N Yks	SE3149	53°56·4'	1°31·2'W	FM	104
Birdwood	Glos	SO7418	51°51·8'	2°22·3'W	T	162
Birehope Burn	Scot Bord	NT3943	55°40·9'	2°57·8'W	W	73
Birgham	Scot Bord	NT7939	55°38·9'	2°19·6'W	T	74
Birgham Wood	Scot Bord	NT7940	55°39·4'	2°19·6'W	F	74
Birgidale Crieff	Arg & Bt	NS0759	55°47·4'	5°4·3'W	X	63
Birgidale Crieff Butts	Arg & Bt	NS0758	55°46·9'	5°4·2'W	X	63
Birgidale Knock	Arg & Bt	NS0759	55°47·4'	5°4·3'W	X	63
Birka Carr	N Yks	SE2368	54°6·7'	1°38·5'W	X	99
Birkacre	Lancs	SD5715	53°38·0'	2°38·6'W	T	108
Birka Lees	Shetld	HU4695	60°38·4'	1°9·0'W	X	1,2

Birka Vird	Shetld	HU3174	60°27·2'	1°25·7'W	H	3
Birka Water	Shetld	HU3187	60°34·2'	1°25·6'W	W	1
Birk Bank	Cumbr	NY1226	54°37·5'	3°21·4'W	X	89
Birk Bank	N Yks	SE5586	54°16·2'	1°8·9'W	X	100
Birk Beck	Cumbr	NY5808	54°28·2'	2°38·5'W	W	91
Birkbeck Fells Common	Cumbr	NY5707	54°27·6'	2°39·4'W	X	91
Birkbeck Wood	N Yks	SD9499	54°23·4'	2°5·1'W	F	98
Birk Burn	D & G	NS7012	55°23·3'	4°2·7'W	W	71
Birk Burn	D & G	NS7309	55°21·8'	3°59·8'W	W	71,77
Birk Burn	D & G	NS7410	55°22·3'	3°58·9'W	W	71
Birk Burn	E Ayr	NS5345	55°40·8'	4°19·8'W	W	64
Birk Bush	Cumbr	NY5373	55°3·2'	2°43·7'W	X	86
Birkbush	D & G	NX8680	55°6·3'	3°46·8'W	X	78
Birkby	Cumbr	NY0537	54°43·4'	3°28·1'W	T	89
Birkby	Kirk	SE1318	53°39·7'	1°47·8'W	T	110
Birkby	N Yks	NZ3302	54°25·0'	1°29·1'W	T	93
Birkby Brow Wood	Leeds	SE2426	53°44·0'	1°37·8'W	F	104
Birkby Cottages	N Yks	NZ3301	54°24·4'	1°29·1'W	X	93
Birkby Fell	Cumbr	SD1496	54°21·4'	3°19·0'W	X	96
Birkby Fm	N Yks	NZ3303	54°25·5'	1°29·1'W	FM	93
Birkby Gate Fm	N Yks	NZ3501	54°24·4'	1°27·2'W	FM	93
Birkby Grange	Leeds	SE3539	53°51·0'	1°27·7'W	X	104
Birkby Grange	N Yks	NZ3401	54°24·4'	1°28·2'W	X	93
Birkby Hall	Cumbr	SD3777	54°11·3'	2°57·5'W	X	96,97
Birkby Hill	Leeds	SE3539	53°51·0'	1°27·7'W	H	104
Birkby Lodge	Cumbr	NY0638	54°43·9'	3°27·2'W	X	89
Birkby Manor	N Yks	NZ3302	54°25·0'	1°29·1'W	X	93
Birkby Nab	N Yks	SE2872	54°8·8'	1°33·9'W	X	99
Birkcleugh	S Lanak	NS8520	55°27·9'	3°48·7'W	X	71,72
Birk Cleugh Hill	Scot Bord	NT6665	55°52·9'	2°32·2'W	X	67
Birk Crag	Cumbr	NY3113	54°30·7'	3°3·5'W	X	90
Birk Crag	Cumbr	NY4321	54°35·1'	2°52·5'W	H	90
Birk Crag	N Yks	SE2854	53°59·1'	1°34·0'W	X	104
Birk Craigs	Scot Bord	NT1016	55°26·0'	3°24·9'W	H	78
Birkdale	Cumbr	NY8027	54°38·5'	2°18·2'W	X	91,92
Birk Dale	N Yks	NY8202	54°25·0'	2°16·2'W	X	91,92
Birkdale	N Yks	NY8501	54°24·5'	2°13·4'W	X	91,92
Birkdale	Sefton	SD3315	53°37·9'	3°0·4'W	T	108
Birkdale Beck	N Yks	NY8302	54°25·0'	2°15·3'W	W	91,92
Birkdale Common	N Yks	NY8302	54°25·0'	2°15·3'W	X	91,92
Birkdale Fm	N Yks	SE6869	54°7·0'	0°57·2'W	FM	100
Birkdale Hills	Sefton	SD3013	53°36·8'	3°3·1'W	X	108
Birkdale Sands	Sefton	SD3015	53°37·9'	3°3·1'W	X	108
Birkdale Tarn	N Yks	NY8501	54°24·5'	2°13·4'W	W	91,92
Birk Dault	Cumbr	SD3483	54°14·6'	3°0·3'W	X	96,97
Birkenbog	Aberd	NJ5365	57°40·6'	2°46·8'W	X	29
Birkenbower	Aberd	NJ4621	57°16·8'	2°53·3'W	X	37
Birken Burn	N Lanak	NS6880	55°59·9'	4°6·6'W	W	64
Birkenburn	Pth & Kin	NO0245	56°35·5'	3°35·3'W	X	52,53
Birken Burn	Stir	NS5983	56°1·4'	4°15·3'W	W	57,64
Birkenburn Reservoir	N Lanak	NS6780	55°59·9'	4°7·5'W	W	64
Birkenbush	Angus	NO4554	56°40·7'	2°53·4'W	X	54
Birkenbush	Moray	NJ2741	57°27·5'	3°12·5'W	X	28
Birkenbush	Moray	NJ4262	57°38·9'	2°57·8'W	X	28
Birkenhead	Renf	NS4466	55°52·0'	4°29·1'W	X	64
Birkenhead	S Lanak	NS7736	55°36·4'	3°56·7'W	X	71
Birkenhead	S Lanak	NS8846	55°41·9'	3°46·5'W	X	72
Birkenhead	Wirral	SJ3088	53°23·3'	3°2·7'W	T	108
Birkenhead Burn	S Lanak	NS7636	55°36·4'	3°57·7'W	W	71
Birkenhead Park	Wirral	SJ3089	53°23·8'	3°2·8'W	X	108
Birkenhill	Aberd	NJ5436	57°25·0'	2°45·5'W	X	29
Birkenhill	Aberd	NO5995	57°2·9'	2°40·1'W	X	37,44
Birkenhill Croft	Moray	NJ2260	57°37·7'	3°17·9'W	X	28
Birkenhills	Aberd	NJ7445	57°29·9'	2°25·6'W	X	29
Birkenshaw	Kirk	SE2028	53°45·1'	1°41·4'W	T	104
Birkenshaw	N Lanak	NS6962	55°50·3'	4°5·1'W	T	64
Birkenshaw	S Lanak	NS7649	55°43·4'	3°58·0'W	T	64
Birkenshaw	W Loth	NS9369	55°54·3'	3°42·3'W	X	65
Birkenshaw Bottoms	Kirk	SE2127	53°44·6'	1°40·5'W	T	104
Birkenside	Northum	NZ0352	54°52·0'	1°56·8'W	X	87
Birkenside	Scot Bord	NT5642	55°40·4'	2°41·5'W	T	73
Birkenside	Scot Bord	NT6816	55°26·5'	2°29·9'W	X	80
Birkenwood	Stir	NS6895	56°8·0'	4°7·0'W	X	57
Birker Beck	Cumbr	SD1799	54°23·0'	3°16·3'W	W	96
Birker Fell	Cumbr	NY2100	54°23·6'	3°12·6'W	X	89,90
Birker Fell	Cumbr	SD1797	54°22·0'	3°16·2'W	X	96
Birker Force	Cumbr	SD1899	54°23·0'	3°15·3'W	W	96
Birkerthwaite	Cumbr	SD1798	54°22·5'	3°16·2'W	X	96
Birker Houses	Cumbr	SD4193	54°20·0'	2°54·0'W	X	96,97
Birkett	Lancs	SD6849	53°56·4'	2°28·8'W	X	103
Birkett Bank	Cumbr	NY3123	54°36·1'	3°3·7'W	X	90
Birkett Beck	Cumbr	NY8008	54°28·3'	2°18·1'W	W	91,92
Birkett Common	Cumbr	NY7703	54°25·6'	2°20·9'W	H	91
Birkett Fell	Cumbr	NY3620	54°34·5'	2°59·0'W	X	90
Birkett Fell	Lancs	SD6748	53°55·9'	2°29·7'W	H	103
Birkett Field	Cumbr	NY3425	54°37·2'	3°0·9'W	X	90
Birket, The	Wirral	SJ2691	53°24·9'	3°6·4'W	W	108
Birkett Mire	Cumbr	NY3124	54°36·6'	3°3·7'W	T	90
Birketts Fm	Surrey	TQ1242	51°10·2'	0°23·5'W	FM	187
Birk Fell	Cumbr	NY2901	54°24·2'	3°5·2'W	X	89,90
Birk Fell	Cumbr	NY4018	54°33·5'	2°55·2'W	H	90
Birk Field	Cumbr	SD4899	54°23·3'	2°47·6'W	X	97
Birkford	Aberd	NJ3509	57°10·3'	3°4·0'W	X	37
Birk Gill	N Yks	SE1381	54°13·7'	1°47·6'W	W	99
Birkgill Moss	Cumbr	NY6602	54°25·0'	2°31·0'W	W	91
Birk Gill Wood	N Yks	SE1381	54°13·7'	1°47·6'W	F	99
Birk Hagg	Cumbr	SD5391	54°19·0'	2°42·9'W	X	97
Birkhall	Aberd	NO3493	57°1·7'	3°4·8'W	X	37,44
Birkhall	Aberd	NO5897	57°4·0'	2°41·1'W	X	37,44
Birkhall	D & G	NX9480	55°6·4'	3°39·3'W	X	78
Birk Hall	Durham	NZ0512	54°30·4'	1°54·9'W	X	92
Birkham Wood	N Yks	SE3555	53°59·6'	1°27·6'W	F	104
Birk Hat	Durham	NY9318	54°33·7'	2°6·1'W	X	91,92
Birkhaw	Cumbr	SD6394	54°20·7'	2°33·7'W	X	97
Birkhead	N Ayr	NS2549	55°42·4'	4°46·7'W	X	63
Birk Head	N Yks	NZ8210	54°29·0'	0°43·6'W	X	94
Birk Hill	Aberd	NJ4010	57°10·9'	2°59·1'W	H	37
Birkhill	Aberd	NJ5916	57°14·2'	2°40·3'W	X	37
Birkhill	Aberd	NJ9113	57°12·7'	2°8·5'W	X	38
Birkhill	Angus	NO2059	56°43·2'	3°18·0'W	X	53

Birkhill	Angus	NO3534	56°29·9'	3°2·9'W	T	54
Birkhill	Angus	NO6444	56°35·4'	2°34·7'W	X	54
Birkhill	Clackm	NS9393	56°7·3'	3°42·8'W	X	58
Birk Hill	Cumbr	NY4753	54°52·4'	2°49·1'W	X	86
Birk Hill	D & G	NS7200	55°16·9'	4°0·5'W	X	77
Birkhill	D & G	NT2015	55°25·6'	3°15·4'W	X	79
Birkhill	D & G	NX7893	55°13·2'	3°54·6'W	X	78
Birkhill	D & G	NY2666	54°59·2'	3°9·0'W	X	85
Birkhill	Falk	NS9678	55°59·3'	3°39·6'W	X	65
Birk Hill	Northum	NY7876	55°4·9'	2°20·2'W	X	86,87
Birkhill	Northum	NY8595	55°15·2'	2°13·7'W	X	80
Birk Hill	Notts	SK6587	53°22·8'	1°1·0'W	X	111,120
Birkhill	Scot Bord	NT5642	55°40·4'	2°41·5'W	T	73
Birkhill Clay Mine	Falk	NS9679	55°59·8'	3°39·6'W	X	65
Birkhill Fm	S Lanak	NS8346	55°41·9'	3°51·3'W	FM	72
Birkhill Fm	S Lanak	NS8539	55°38·1'	3°49·2'W	FM	71,72
Birkhill Ho	Fife	NO3323	56°23·9'	3°4·7'W	X	53,59
Birkhill Wood	E Yorks	TA0335	53°48·3'	0°25·7'W	F	107
Birk Ho	Durham	NZ0513	54°31·0'	1°54·9'W	X	92
Birk Ho	N Yks	SE7156	53°59·9'	0°54·6'W	X	105,106
Birk Ho Fm	Kirk	SE2009	53°34·9'	1°41·5'W	FM	110
Birkholme	E Yorks	TA1829	53°44·9'	0°12·2'W	X	107
Birkholme	Lincs	SK9723	52°48·0'	0°33·3'W	T	130
Birkhot	Durham	NZ0447	54°49·3'	1°55·8'W	X	87
Birkhouse	Cald	SE1524	53°43·0'	1°45·9'W	T	104
Birkhouse Moor	Cumbr	NY3616	54°32·4'	2°58·9'W	X	90
Birkhurst	Cumbr	NY5863	54°57·8'	2°38·9'W	X	86
Birkiebrae	Scot Bord	NT3906	55°20·9'	2°57·3'W	X	79
Birkie Rig	D & G	NY0494	55°14·1'	3°30·1'W	X	78
Birkin	N Yks	SE5326	53°43·9'	1°11·4'W	T	105
Birkin Brook	Ches	SJ7682	53°20·3'	2°21·2'W	W	109
Birkindale Burn	Scot Bord	NT3120	55°28·4'	3°5·1'W	W	73
Birkindale Knowe	Scot Bord	NT3021	55°28·9'	3°6·0'W	X	73
Birkin Fm	Ches	SJ7684	53°21·4'	2°21·2'W	FM	109
Birkin Ho	Dorset	SY7191	50°43·3'	2°24·3'W	X	194
Birkitt Hill	Herts	TL1427	51°56·0'	0°20·1'W	X	166
Birk Knot	Cumbr	NY6000	54°23·9'	2°36·5'W	X	91
Birk Knott	Cumbr	SD2990	54°18·3'	3°5·1'W	X	96,97
Birk Knott	N Yks	SD7263	54°4·0'	2°25·3'W	X	98
Birkland Barrow	Lancs	SD5269	54°7·1'	2°43·6'W	X	97
Birklands	Notts	SK6067	53°12·0'	1°5·7'W	F	120
Birk Lane Drain	E Yorks	SE7137	53°49·7'	0°54·9'W	W	105,106
Birk Lodge	Donc	SK5095	53°27·2'	1°14·4'W	X	111
Birk Moss	Cumbr	NY0715	54°31·6'	3°25·8'W	X	89
Birk Moss	Cumbr	NY3035	54°42·6'	3°4·8'W	X	90
Birk Moss	Cumbr	SD4393	54°20·0'	2°52·2'W	X	97
Birk Nab Fm	N Yks	SE6290	54°18·4'	1°2·4'W	FM	94,100
Birk Park	N Yks	SE0099	54°23·4'	1°59·6'W	X	98
Birkrigg	Cumbr	NY2219	54°33·9'	3°12·0'W	X	89,90
Birk Rigg	Cumbr	NY4702	54°24·9'	2°48·6'W	H	90
Birk Rigg	Cumbr	NY7800	54°23·9'	2°19·9'W	X	91
Birkrigg	Cumbr	SD7290	54°18·5'	2°25·4'W	X	98
Birk Rigg	Cumbr	SD7586	54°16·4'	2°22·6'W	X	98
Birkrigg Common	Cumbr	SD2874	54°9·7'	3°5·7'W	X	96,97
Birkrigg Fm	N Yks	SD8491	54°19·1'	2°14·3'W	FM	98
Birkrigg Park	Cumbr	SD5487	54°16·8'	2°42·0'W	X	97
Birk Rigg Side	N Yks	SD9286	54°16·4'	2°7·0'W	X	98
Birk Row	Cumbr	SD2987	54°16·7'	3°5·0'W	X	96,97
Birks	Cumbr	NY3814	54°31·3'	2°57·1'W	H	90
Birks	Cumbr	NY5736	54°43·3'	2°39·6'W	X	91
Birks	Cumbr	NY7215	54°32·0'	2°25·5'W	X	91
Birks	Cumbr	SD2399	54°23·1'	3°10·7'W	X	96
Birks	Cumbr	SD5693	54°20·1'	2°40·2'W	X	97
Birks	Cumbr	SD6591	54°19·0'	2°31·9'W	T	97
Birks	Cumbr	SD6994	54°20·7'	2°28·2'W	X	98
Birks	Lancs	SD6139	53°51·0'	2°35·2'W	X	102,103
Birks	Leeds	SE2626	53°44·0'	1°35·9'W	T	104
Birks	Northum	NY7884	55°9·2'	2°20·3'W	X	80
Birks	Northum	NY9461	54°56·9'	2°5·2'W	X	87
Birks	Northum	NZ1296	55°15·7'	1°48·2'W	X	81
Birks	Scot Bord	NT2933	55°35·4'	3°7·2'W	X	73
Birks	S Lanak	NS8151	55°44·5'	3°53·3'W	X	65,72
Birks Brow	Cumbr	SD4191	54°18·9'	2°54·0'W	X	96,97
Birks Burn	Aberd	NJ6620	57°16·4'	2°33·4'W	W	38
Birkscairn Hill	Scot Bord	NT2733	55°35·4'	3°9·1'W	H	73
Birks Crag	Cumbr	NY4612	54°30·3'	2°49·6'W	H	90
Birks Fell	N Yks	SD9276	54°11·0'	2°6·9'W	X	98
Birks Fm	Cumbr	NY0215	54°31·5'	3°30·4'W	FM	89
Birks Fm	Derby	SK2976	53°17·0'	1°33·5'W	FM	119
Birks Fm	Lancs	SD3629	53°45·5'	2°57·8'W	FM	102
Birk's Fm	Lancs	SD4244	53°53·6'	2°52·5'W	FM	102
Birks Fm	Lancs	SD5246	53°54·7'	2°43·4'W	FM	102
Birks Fm	Lancs	SD6366	54°5·6'	2°33·5'W	FM	97
Birkshaw	D & G	NX8585	55°9·0'	3°47·8'W	X	78
Birkshaw	D & G	NY1277	55°5·0'	3°22·3'W	X	85
Birkshaw	Northum	NY7765	54°59·0'	2°21·1'W	T	86,87
Birkshaw Forest	D & G	NY1177	55°5·0'	3°23·2'W	F	85
Birks Head	Cumbr	NY6725	54°37·4'	2°30·2'W	X	91
Birks Head	Cumbr	NY7214	54°31·5'	2°25·5'W	X	91
Birks Hill	Cumbr	NY3743	54°46·9'	2°58·3'W	X	85
Birks Hill	Scot Bord	NT2833	55°35·4'	3°8·1'W	H	73
Birk Side	Cumbr	NY3313	54°30·7'	3°1·7'W	X	90
Birkside	Northum	NY9450	54°50·9'	2°5·2'W	X	87
Birkside Fell	Northum	NY9451	54°51·5'	2°5·2'W	X	87
Birkside Law	Scot Bord	NT1327	55°32·0'	3°22·3'W	H	72
Birks Moor	Northum	NY7684	55°9·2'	2°22·2'W	X	80
Birks of Aberfeldy	Pth & Kin	NN8547	56°36·3'	3°52·0'W	X	52
Birks Plantn	E Loth	NT6071	55°56·1'	2°38·0'W	F	67
Birks Tarn	N Yks	SD9275	54°10·5'	2°6·9'W	W	98
Birks,The	Aberd	NJ7261	57°38·5'	2°27·7'W	X	29
Birks, The	Aberd	NJ7402	57°6·8'	2°25·3'W	X	38
Birks Wood	Cumbr	SD2093	54°19·8'	3°13·4'W	F	96
Birks Wood	D & G	NX4954	54°51·7'	4°20·7'W	F	83
Birks Wood	N Yks	SD9376	54°11·0'	2°6·0'W	F	98
Birkthwaite	Cumbr	NY4347	54°49·1'	2°52·8'W	X	85
Birkwith Allotment	N Yks	SD8377	54°11·6'	2°15·2'W	X	98
Birkwith Cave	N Yks	SD8076	54°11·0'	2°18·0'W	X	98
Birkwith Moor	N Yks	SD8177	54°11·6'	2°17·1'W	X	98
Birkwood	Aberd	NO7195	57°3·0'	2°28·2'W	X	38,45
Birkwood	S Lanak	NS7942	55°39·6'	3°55·0'W	X	71

Birkwood Burn	S Lanak	NS7840	55°38·6'	3°55·9'W	W	71
Birkwood Fm	Wakf	SE3523	53°42·4'	1°27·8'W	FM	104
Birkwood Fm	Wakf	SE3818	53°39·7'	1°25·1'W	FM	110,111
Birkwood Hall	Lincs	TF2659	53°7·0'	0°6·6'W	X	122
Birkwood Hospital	S Lanak	NS8139	55°38·1'	3°53·0'W	X	71,72
Birkwood Mains	S Lanak	NS8039	55°38·0'	3°53·9'W	X	71,72
Birkwray	Cumbr	SD3599	54°23·2'	2°59·6'W	X	96,97
Birkyburn	Northum	NY9789	55°12·0'	2°2·4'W	X	81
Birky Grain	Northum	NY6680	55°7·0'	2°31·6'W	W	80
Birky Shank	Cumbr	NY6675	55°4·3'	2°31·5'W	X	86
Birley	Aberd	NJ6200	57°5·6'	2°37·2'W	X	37
Birley	Derby	SK3173	53°15·4'	1°31·7'W	X	119
Birley	Heref	SO4553	52°10·6'	2°47·9'W	T	148,149
Birley Carr	Sheff	SK3392	53°25·7'	1°29·8'W	T	110,111
Birley Edge	Sheff	SK3392	53°25·7'	1°29·8'W	T	110,111
Birley Fm	Derby	SK2282	53°20·3'	1°39·8'W	FM	110
Birley Fm	Derby	SK4479	53°18·6'	1°20·0'W	FM	120
Birley Fold	Lancs	SD6531	53°46·7'	2°31·5'W	X	102,103
Birleyhay	Derby	SK3980	53°19·2'	1°24·5'W	T	110,111
Birley Hill	Heref	SO4551	52°9·5'	2°47·8'W	H	148,149
Birley Stone, The	Sheff	SK3293	53°26·2'	1°30·7'W	A	110,111
Birling	Kent	TQ6860	51°19·1'	0°25·0'E	T	177,178,188
Birling	Northum	NU2406	55°21·1'	1°36·9'W	X	81
Birling Ashes	Kent	TQ6859	51°18·5'	0°25·0'E	X	178,188
Birling Carrs	Northum	NU2507	55°21·6'	1°35·9'W	X	81
Birling Fm	E Susx	TV5596	50°44·8'	0°12·2'E	FM	199
Birling Gap	E Susx	TV5596	50°44·8'	0°12·2'E	T	199
Birlingham	Worcs	SO9343	52°5·4'	2°5·7'W	T	150
Birling Ho	Kent	TQ7956	51°16·7'	0°34·4'E	X	178,188
Birling Lodge	Kent	TQ6760	51°19·1'	0°24·2'E	X	177,178,188
Birling Place	Kent	TQ6761	51°19·6'	0°24·2'E	X	177,178,188
Birmingham	Birm	SP0987	52°29·1'	1°51·6'W	T	139
Birmingham & Fazeley Canal	Warw	SP2097	52°34·5'	1°41·9'W	W	139
Birmingham International Airport	Sol	SP1683	52°26·9'	1°45·5'W	X	139
Birmingham International Sta	Sol	SP1883	52°26·9'	1°43·7'W	X	139
Birnam	Pth & Kin	NO0341	56°33·3'	3°34·2'W	T	52,53
Birnam Hill	Pth & Kin	NO0340	56°32·8'	3°34·2'W	X	52,53
Birnam Wood	Pth & Kin	NO0439	56°32·3'	3°33·2'W	F	52,53
Birnbeck Island	N Som	ST3062	51°21·4'	2°59·9'W	X	182
Birney Hall	Northum	NZ1469	55°1·2'	1°46·4'W	X	88
Birney Hill	Northum	NY9481	55°7·6'	2°5·2'W	H	80
Birneyknowe	Scot Bord	NT5411	55°23·7'	2°43·1'W	X	79
Birnie Brae	Scot Bord	NT1909	55°22·4'	3°16·3'W	H	79
Birnie Brae	Scot Bord	NT8620	55°28·7'	2°12·9'W	X	74
Birnie Craig	Fife	NO5402	56°12·8'	2°44·1'W	X	59
Birniehall	S Lanak	NS9052	55°45·2'	3°44·7'W	X	65,72
Birnie Hill	Aberd	NO6679	56°54·3'	2°33·0'W	X	45
Birniehill	Pth & Kin	NO1207	56°15·1'	3°24·8'W	X	58
Birniehill	S Ayr	NS2408	55°20·3'	4°46·1'W	X	70,76
Birniehill	S Lanak	NS6453	55°45·3'	4°9·6'W	T	64
Birniehill Wood	Aberd	NO7974	56°51·7'	2°20·2'W	F	45
Birnieknowe	E Ayr	NS5722	55°28·5'	4°15·3'W	X	71
Birnie Knowe	Scot Bord	NT3216	55°26·2'	3°4·1'W	X	79
Birnieknowes	E Loth	NT7572	55°56·7'	2°23·6'W	X	67
Birnie Rocks	C of Edin	NT2177	55°59·0'	3°15·5'W	X	66
Birnock	S Lanak	NS9725	55°30·7'	3°37·4'W	X	72
Birnock Burn	S Lanak	NT0025	55°30·8'	3°34·6'W	W	72
Birnock Cloves	D & G	NT1210	55°22·8'	3°22·9'W	X	78
Birnock Water	D & G	NT1008	55°21·7'	3°24·8'W	W	78
Birns	Angus	NO5042	56°34·3'	2°48·4'W	X	54
Birns	Fife	NO2911	56°17·4'	3°8·4'W	X	59
Birns Water	E Loth	NT4964	55°52·2'	2°48·5'W	W	66
Birny Fell	Scot Bord	NY4790	55°12·3'	2°49·5'W	X	79
Birny Gill	D & G	NT1400	55°17·4'	3°20·8'W	W	78
Birny Gill	D & G	NT1500	55°17·5'	3°19·9'W	W	79
Birny Hill	D & G	NS5403	55°18·2'	4°17·6'W	H	77
Birny Hill	D & G	NY2883	55°8·4'	3°7·3'W	X	79
Birny Hills	W Dunb	NS4976	55°57·5'	4°24·7'W	X	64
Birny Knowe	E Loth	NT7069	55°55·0'	2°28·4'W	X	67
Birny Rig	D & G	NS8202	55°18·1'	3°51·1'W	H	78
Birrens Hill	D & G	NY2481	55°7·3'	3°11·1'W	X	79
Birren Sike	D & G	NY3992	55°13·4'	2°57·1'W	W	79
Birrier	Shetld	HP4705	60°43·8'	1°7·8'W	X	1
Birrier	Shetld	HU4391	60°36·3'	1°12·4'W	X	1,2
Birrier	Shetld	HU5488	60°34·6'	1°0·4'W	X	1,2
Birrier Geo	Shetld	HU6394	60°37·7'	0°50·4'W	X	1,2
Birrier (Settlement)	Shetld	HU4391	60°36·3'	1°12·4'W	A	1,2
Birries Houlla Komba	Shetld	HU4786	60°33·6'	1°8·1'W	X	1,2,3
Birsay	Orkney	HY2825	59°6·6'	3°15·0'W	X	6
Birsay Bay	Orkney	HY2327	59°7·6'	3°20·2'W	W	6
Birsca	D & G	NY2284	55°8·9'	3°13·0'W	X	79
Birse	Aberd	NO5597	57°4·0'	2°44·1'W	T	37,44
Birsebeg	Aberd	NO5397	57°4·0'	2°46·1'W	X	37,44
Birse Castle	Aberd	NO5190	57°0·2'	2°47·9'W	X	44
Birselasie	Aberd	NJ6406	57°8·9'	2°35·2'W	X	37
Birsemohr Fm	Aberd	NO5397	57°4·0'	2°46·1'W	FM	37,44
Birsemore	Aberd	NO5297	57°4·0'	2°47·0'W	T	37,44
Birsemore Hill	Aberd	NO5296	57°3·4'	2°47·0'W	H	37,44
Birse Shades	Angus	NO4469	56°48·8'	2°54·6'W	X	44
Birseslees	Scot Bord	NT5727	55°32·3'	2°40·4'W	X	73,74
Birset	D & G	NY0774	55°3·4'	3°26·9'W	X	85
Birshaw Burn	S Lanak	NS8729	55°32·8'	3°47·0'W	W	71,72
Birshaw Rig	S Lanak	NS8729	55°32·8'	3°47·0'W	X	71,72
Birsi Geo	Orkney	ND3188	58°46·7'	3°11·1'W	X	7
Birs Labis	Orkney	ND5399	58°52·8'	2°48·4'W	X	6,7
Birsley Wood	Northum	NU1109	55°22·7'	1°49·2'W	F	81
Birsley Woodside	Northum	NU1009	55°22·7'	1°50·1'W	X	81
Birstall	Kirk	SE2226	53°44·0'	1°39·6'W	T	104
Birstall	Leic	SK5909	52°40·8'	1°7·2'W	T	140
Birstall Smithies	Kirk	SE2225	53°43·5'	1°39·6'W	T	104
Birstwith	N Yks	SE2359	54°1·8'	1°38·5'W	T	104
Birstwith Hall	N Yks	SE2458	54°1·3'	1°37·6'W	X	104
Birswick	D & G	NX9190	55°11·8'	3°42·3'W	X	78
Birt Hill	Lincs	TF1569	53°12·6'	0°16·3'W	X	121
Birthorpe	Lincs	TF1033	52°53·2'	0°21·5'W	T	130
Birthplace of General Roy	S Lanak	NS8249	55°43·5'	3°52·3'W	X	72
Birthplace of Mungo Park	Scot Bord	NT4229	55°33·3'	2°54·7'W	X	73

Birthwaite Hall	Barns	SE3010	53°35·4′	1°32·4′W	X	110,111
Birthwood	S Lanak	NT0230	55°33·5′	3°32·8′W	X	72
Birtle	Roch	SD8313	53°37·0′	2°15·0′W	T	109
Birtlebog	N Ayr	NS2854	55°45·2′	4°44·0′W	X	63
Birtles Fm	Ches	SJ7683	53°20·8′	2°21·2′W	FM	109
Birtles Hall	Ches	SJ8574	53°16·0′	2°13·1′W	X	118
Birtley	Ghead	NZ2756	54°54·1′	1°34·3′W	T	88
Birtley	Heref	SO3669	52°19·2′	2°55·9′W	T	137,148
Birtley	Northum	NY8778	55°6·0′	2°11·8′W	T	87
Birtley	Shrops	SO4790	52°30·6′	2°46·5′W	T	137,138
Birtley Green	Surrey	TQ0143	51°10·9′	0°32·9′W	T	186
Birtley Ho	Surrey	TQ0143	51°10·9′	0°32·9′W	X	186
Birtley Shields	Northum	NY8779	55°6·6′	2°11·8′W	X	87
Birts Hill	Somer	ST5108	50°52·4′	2°41·4′W	H	194
Birtsmorton	Worcs	SO8035	52°1·0′	2°17·1′W	T	150
Birtsmorton Court	Worcs	SO8035	52°1·0′	2°17·1′W	A	150
Birts Street	Worcs	SO7836	52°1·6′	2°18·8′W	T	150
Biruaslum	N Eil	NL6096	56°56·1′	7°35·0′W	X	31
Bisbrooke	Rut	SP8899	52°35·1′	0°41·7′W	T	141
Bisbrooke Hall	Rut	SK8900	52°35·7′	0°40·8′W	X	141
Biscathorpe	Lincs	TF2284	53°20·6′	0°9·6′W	T	122
Biscathorpe Ho	Lincs	TF2284	53°20·6′	0°9·6′W	X	122
Biscathorpe Village	Lincs	TF2284	53°20·6′	0°9·6′W	A	122
Biscombe	Somer	ST1713	50°54·9′	3°10·5′W	T	181,193
Biscot	Luton	TL0822	51°53·4′	0°25·4′W	T	166
Biscovey	Corn	SX0653	50°20·8′	4°43·2′W	T	200,204
Biscovillack Fm	Corn	SW9954	50°21·3′	4°49·2′W	FM	200
Bisgarth	Orkney	HY3924	59°6·2′	3°3·4′W	X	6
Bis Geos	Orkney	HY4147	59°18·6′	3°1·7′W	X	5
Bisham	Win & Maid	SU8585	51°33·7′	0°46·0′W	T	175
Bishampton	Worcs	SO9851	52°9·7′	2°1·4′W	T	150
Bishampton Bank	Worcs	SP0049	52°8·6′	1°59·6′W	F	150
Bishampton Fields Fm	Worcs	SP0050	52°9·1′	1°59·6′W	FM	150
Bish Mill	Devon	SS7425	51°0·9′	3°47·4′W	T	180
Bishon Common	Heref	SO4243	52°5·2′	2°50·4′W	T	148,149,161
Bishop Ashbury's Cottage	Sand	SP0393	52°32·3′	1°56·9′W	X	139
Bishop Ashbury's Cottage	Sand	SP0394	52°32·9′	1°56·9′W	X	139
Bishop Auckland	Durham	NZ1928	54°39·0′	1°41·9′W	T	92
Bishop Auckland	Durham	NZ2028	54°39·0′	1°41·0′W	T	93
Bishop Br	Lincs	SK9573	53°15·0′	0°34·2′W	X	121
Bishopbrae	W Loth	NS9771	55°55·5′	3°38·5′W	X	65
Bishop Brandon Walk	Durham	NZ1933	54°41·7′	1°41·9′W	X	92
Bishopbridge	Lincs	TF0391	53°24·6′	0°26·6′W	T	112
Bishopbriggs	E Dunb	NS6170	55°54·3′	4°13·0′W	T	64
Bishop Burn	D & G	NX0861	54°54·7′	4°59·3′W	W	82
Bishop Burn	D & G	NX4060	54°54·8′	4°29·3′W	W	83
Bishop Burton	E Yorks	SE9839	53°50·5′	0°30·2′W	T	106
Bishop Burton Wold	E Yorks	SE9739	53°50·5′	0°31·1′W	X	106
Bishopcourt Glen	I of M	SC3392	54°18·0′	4°33·6′W	X	95
Bishop Croft	Moray	NJ1739	57°26·3′	3°22·5′W	X	28
Bishopdale	N Yks	SD9885	54°15·9′	2°1·4′W	X	98
Bishopdale Beck	N Yks	SE0188	54°17·5′	1°58·7′W	W	98
Bishopdale Edge	N Yks	SD9782	54°14·3′	2°2·3′W	X	98
Bishopdale Gavel	N Yks	SD9580	54°13·2′	2°4·2′W	X	98
Bishopdale Head	N Yks	SD9580	54°13·2′	2°4·2′W	X	98
Bishopdown	Wilts	SU1531	51°4·9′	1°46·8′W	T	184
Bishop Dyke	N Yks	SE5133	53°47·7′	1°13·1′W	W	105
Bishoper Fm	Wilts	ST9390	51°36·8′	2°5·7′W	FM	163,173
Bishopfield Fm	Notts	SK6488	53°23·3′	1°1·9′W	FM	111,120
Bishop Field (Hotel)	Northum	NY8256	54°54·2′	2°16·4′W	X	86,87
Bishop Forest Hill	D & G	NX8479	55°5·8′	3°48·6′W	H	84
Bishop Hagg Wood	N Yks	SE7386	54°16·1′	0°52·3′W	F	94,100
Bishophall	Pth & Kin	NO1338	56°31·8′	3°24·4′W	X	53
Bishop Hill	Cumbr	NY6158	54°55·2′	2°36·1′W	X	86
Bishop Hill	Pth & Kin	NO1804	56°13·5′	3°18·9′W	X	58
Bishop Ho	N Yks	SE4671	54°8·2′	1°17·3′W	X	100
Bishop Kinkell	Highld	NH5453	57°32·9′	4°25·9′W	T	26
Bishop Lands	Cambs	TF3404	52°37·3′	0°0·8′W	X	142
Bishop Lands Fm	Cambs	TF3405	52°37·8′	0°0·8′W	FM	142
Bishop Loch	C of Glas	NS6866	55°52·4′	4°6·1′W	W	64
Bishop Lough	Cumbr	NY3547	54°49·1′	3°0·3′W	X	85
Bishop Middleham	Durham	NZ3331	54°40·6′	1°28·9′W	T	93
Bishopmill	Moray	NJ2163	57°39·3′	3°19·0′W	T	28
Bishop Monkton	N Yks	SE3266	54°5·6′	1°30·2′W	T	99
Bishop Norton	Lincs	SK9892	53°25·2′	0°31·1′W	T	112
Bishop Oak	Durham	NZ0639	54°45·0′	1°54·0′W	X	92
Bishop Ooze	Medway	TQ8370	51°24·2′	0°38·3′E	X	178
Bishop Park	Oldham	SD9608	53°34·4′	2°3·2′W	X	109
Bishop Rock	I Scilly	SV8006	49°52·4′	6°26·9′W	X	203
Bishops and Clerks	Pemb	SM6724	51°52·2′	5°22·7′W	X	157
Bishop's Barn	Wilts	SU3260	51°20·5′	1°32·0′W	X	174
Bishop's Barton	Somer	ST0720	50°58·5′	3°19·1′W	X	181
Bishop's Bog	Scot Bord	NT7840	55°39·4′	2°20·5′W	X	74
Bishopsbourne	Kent	TR1852	51°13·8′	1°7·7′E	T	179,189
Bishops Bowl Lakes	Warw	SP3859	52°13·9′	1°26·2′W	W	151
Bishop's Br	Pemb	SN0607	51°43·9′	4°48·2′W	X	158
Bishop's Br	Pth & Kin	NN8715	56°19·1′	3°49·2′W	X	58
Bishop's Canning Down	Wilts	SU0566	51°23·8′	1°55·3′W	H	173
Bishops Cannings	Wilts	SU0364	51°22·7′	1°57·0′W	T	173
Bishop's Castle	Shrops	SO3288	52°29·4′	2°59·7′W	T	137
Bishop's Caundle	Dorset	ST6913	50°55·2′	2°26·1′W	T	194
Bishop's Cleeve	Glos	SO9527	51°56·7′	2°4·0′W	T	163
Bishop's Close	Durham	NZ2433	54°41·7′	1°37·2′W	X	93
Bishops Court	C of Aber	NJ8405	57°8·4′	2°15·4′W	X	38
Bishops Court	C of Aber	NJ8406	57°8·9′	2°15·4′W	X	38
Bishop's Court	Devon	SX9891	50°42·8′	3°26·3′W	X	192
Bishop's Court	Devon	SY0893	50°44·0′	3°17·8′W	X	192
Bishop's Court	I of M	SC3292	54°18·0′	4°34·5′W	T	95
Bishop's Court	Oxon	SU5794	51°38·7′	1°10·2′W	X	164,174
Bishops Court Dairy	Dorset	ST9302	50°49·3′	2°5·6′W	X	195
Bishopsdale Fm	Kent	TQ8434	51°4·8′	0°38·0′E	FM	188
Bishop's Down	Dorset	ST6712	50°54·6′	2°27·8′W	T	194
Bishopsdown Fm	Wilts	SU1532	51°5·5′	1°46·8′W	FM	184
Bishopsdown Stud Fm	Hants	SU5618	50°57·8′	1°11·8′W	FM	185
Bishop's Dyke	Cumbr	NY3751	54°51·2′	2°58·5′W	A	85
Bishop's Dyke	Hants	SU3404	50°50·3′	1°30·6′W	A	196
Bishopsfauld	Pth & Kin	NN7719	56°21·1′	3°59·0′W	X	57
Bishop's Fm	Cambs	TL4954	52°10·1′	0°11·1′E	FM	154
Bishop's Fm	Kent	TQ7748	51°12·4′	0°32·4′E	FM	188
Bishop's Fm	Lincs	TF3352	53°3·2′	0°0·5′W	FM	122

Bishops Fm	Warw	SP1165	52°17·2′	1°49·9′W	FM	150
Bishops Frome	Heref	SO6648	52°8·0′	2°29·4′W	T	149
Bishopsgarth	Stock on T	NZ4120	54°34·7′	1°21·5′W	T	93
Bishopsgate	Surrey	SU9871	51°26·0′	0°35·0′W	T	175,176
Bishop's Glen	Arg & Bt	NS1576	55°56·7′	4°57·3′W	X	63
Bishop's Gorse Fm	Warw	SP3454	52°11·2′	1°29·8′W	FM	151
Bishop's Grange	Durham	NZ2746	54°48·7′	1°34·4′W	X	88
Bishops Green	Essex	TL6217	51°49·9′	0°21·5′E	T	167
Bishop's Green	W Berks	SU5063	51°22·1′	1°16·5′W	T	174
Bishop's Hall	Essex	TQ4795	51°38·3′	0°7·9′E	X	167,177
Bishopshall	Lincs	TF0322	52°47·4′	0°28·0′W	F	130
Bishop's Hall Fm	Essex	TL7316	51°49·2′	0°31·0′E	FM	167
Bishopshayne Fm	Devon	ST1302	50°48·9′	3°13·7′W	FM	192,193
Bishop's Hill	Hants	SU5158	51°19·4′	1°15·7′W	X	174
Bishop's Hill	Highld	ND1963	58°33·1′	3°23·0′W	X	11,12
Bishop's Hill	Staffs	SK1525	52°49·6′	1°46·2′W	X	128
Bishop's Hill	Suff	TL7675	52°20·9′	0°35·4′E	X	143
Bishop's Hill Wood	S Glos	ST7387	51°35·1′	2°23·0′W	F	172
Bishops Ho	Lancs	SD6551	53°57·5′	2°31·6′W	X	102,103
Bishops Ho	Shrops	SJ4238	52°56·4′	2°51·4′W	X	126
Bishop's Hull	Somer	ST2024	51°0·8′	3°8·0′W	T	193
Bishopside	Northum	NY8158	54°55·2′	2°17·4′W	X	86,87
Bishop's Itchington	Warw	SP3957	52°12·8′	1°25·4′W	T	151
Bishop's Land	Cambs	TL4888	52°28·4′	0°11·1′E	X	143
Bishopsland Fm	Oxon	SU7278	51°30·0′	0°57·4′W	FM	175
Bishopsleigh	Devon	SS7709	50°52·3′	3°44·5′W	X	191
Bishops' Loch	Aberd	NJ9114	57°13·3′	2°8·5′W	W	38
Bishops Lydeard	Somer	ST1629	51°3·5′	3°11·5′W	T	181,193
Bishop's Meadow	Powys	SO0530	51°57·9′	3°22·6′W	X	160
Bishop's Meads	Devon	SX6665	50°28·4′	3°52·9′W	X	202
Bishop's Moat	Essex	TQ4895	51°38·3′	0°8·7′E	A	167,177
Bishop's Moat	Shrops	SO2989	52°29·9′	3°2·4′W	X	137
Bishopsmore	Hants	SU5814	50°55·6′	1°10·1′W	X	196
Bishop's Norton	Glos	SO8424	51°55·1′	2°13·6′W	T	162
Bishop's Nympton	Devon	SS7523	50°59·8′	3°46·5′W	T	180
Bishop's Offley	Staffs	SJ7729	52°51·7′	2°20·1′W	T	127
Bishop's Palace	Carm	SN4320	51°51·6′	4°16·4′W	X	159
Bishop's Palace	Hants	SU5517	50°57·2′	1°12·6′W	A	185
Bishop's Palace	Herts	TL2310	51°46·7′	0°12·6′W	X	166
Bishop's Palace	Suff	TM3083	52°24·0′	1°23·3′E	A	156
Bishops Park	Herts	TL4720	51°51·8′	0°8·5′E	X	167
Bishop Spit	Medway	TQ8471	51°24·7′	0°39·1′E	X	178
Bishop's Place	W Susx	TQ2615	50°55·5′	0°12·0′W	X	198
Bishop's Quay	Corn	SW7225	50°5·1′	5°10·9′W	T	204
Bishops Rock	Corn	SX3677	50°34·4′	4°18·6′W	X	201
Bishop's Seat	Arg & Bt	NS1377	55°57·2′	4°59·3′W	H	63
Bishop's Stortford	Herts	TL4921	51°52·3′	0°10·3′E	T	167
Bishop's Sutton	Hants	SU6031	51°4·7′	1°8·2′W	T	185
Bishop's Tachbrook	Warw	SP3161	52°15·0′	1°32·4′W	T	151
Bishop's Tawton	Devon	SS5630	51°3·3′	4°2·9′W	T	180
Bishopsteignton	Devon	SX9073	50°33·0′	3°32·8′W	T	192
Bishopstoke	Hants	SU4619	50°58·3′	1°20·3′W	T	185
Bishopston	Aberd	NO8998	57°4·6′	2°10·4′W	X	38,45
Bishopston	C of Aber	NJ8411	57°11·6′	2°15·4′W	X	38
Bishopston	C of Bris	ST5875	51°28·6′	2°35·9′W	T	172
Bishopston	Swan	SS5788	51°34·6′	4°3·4′W	T	159
Bishopstone	Bucks	SP8010	51°47·2′	0°50·0′W	T	165
Bishopstone	E Susx	TQ4701	50°47·6′	0°5·5′E	T	198
Bishopstone	Heref	SO4143	52°5·2′	2°51·3′W	T	148,149,161
Bishopstone	Kent	TR2068	51°22·3′	1°10·1′E	T	179
Bishopstone	Swin	SU2483	51°33·0′	1°38·8′W	T	174
Bishopstone	Wilts	SU0725	51°1·7′	1°53·6′W	T	184
Bishopstone Sta	E Susx	TV4699	50°46·6′	0°4·6′E	X	198
Bishopstrow	Wilts	ST8943	51°11·4′	2°9·1′W	T	184
Bishopstrow Down	Wilts	ST9146	51°13·0′	2°7·3′W	X	184
Bishopstrow Ho (Hotel)	Wilts	ST8944	51°11·9′	2°9·1′W	X	184
Bishop Sutton	Bath & NE Somer	ST5859	51°19·9′	2°35·8′W	T	172,182
Bishop's Waltham	Hants	SU5517	50°57·2′	1°12·6′W	T	185
Bishop's Well Plantn	Scot Bord	NT8058	55°49·1′	2°18·7′W	F	67,74
Bishop's Wood	Corn	SX0069	50°29·4′	4°48·8′W	F	200
Bishop's Wood	Heref	SO5919	51°52·3′	2°35·3′W	F	162
Bishop's Wood	Herts	TQ0691	51°36·7′	0°27·8′W	F	176
Bishop's Wood	Kent	TR0037	51°6·1′	0°51·8′E	F	189
Bishopswood	Somer	ST2512	50°54·4′	3°3·6′W	T	193
Bishop's Wood	Staffs	SJ7531	52°52·8′	2°21·9′W	F	127
Bishop's Wood	Staffs	SJ7533	52°53·9′	2°21·9′W	F	127
Bishops Wood	Staffs	SJ8309	52°40·9′	2°14·7′W	T	127
Bishop's Wood	Swan	SS5987	51°34·1′	4°1·7′W	F	159
Bishop's Wood	Worcs	SO8368	52°18·8′	2°14·6′W	F	138
Bishopswood Fm	Oxon	SU6980	51°31·1′	0°59·9′W	FM	175
Bishopsworth	C of Bris	ST5768	51°24·8′	2°36·7′W	T	172,182
Bishop, The	Cumbr	NY2126	54°37·6′	3°13·0′W	X	89,90
Bishop Thornton	N Yks	SE2663	54°4·0′	1°35·7′W	T	99
Bishopthorpe	N Lincs	SE9022	53°41·4′	0°37·8′W	X	106,112
Bishopthorpe	York	SE5947	53°55·2′	1°5·7′W	T	105
Bishopthorpe Fm	Lincs	TA3103	53°30·7′	0°1·1′W	FM	113
Bishopton	Darl	NZ3621	54°35·2′	1°26·2′W	T	93
Bishopton	D & G	NX4341	54°44·6′	4°25·9′W	T	83
Bishopton	D & G	NX6650	54°49·9′	4°4·7′W	X	83,84
Bishopton	N Yks	SE2971	54°8·3′	1°32·9′W	T	99
Bishopton	Renf	NS4371	55°54·6′	4°30·3′W	T	64
Bishopton	Warw	SP1956	52°12·3′	1°42·9′W	T	151
Bishopton Beck	Darl	NZ3622	54°35·8′	1°26·1′W	W	93
Bishopton Hill	Warw	SP1757	52°12·9′	1°44·7′W	X	151
Bishopton Sta	Renf	NS4370	55°54·1′	4°30·2′W	X	64
Bishopwearmouth	Sund	NZ3956	54°54·1′	1°23·1′W	T	88
Bishop Wilton	E Yorks	SE7955	53°59·3′	0°47·3′W	T	105,106
Bishop Wilton Beck	E Yorks	SE7953	53°58·3′	0°47·3′W	W	105,106
Bishop Wilton Wold	E Yorks	SE8055	53°59·3′	0°46·4′W	X	106
Bishop Wilton Wold	E Yorks	SE8155	53°59·3′	0°45·5′W	X	106
Bishop Wood	N Yks	SE5533	53°47·7′	1°9·5′W	F	105
Bishop Woods	Cumbr	SD3794	54°20·5′	2°57·7′W	F	96,97
Bishpool	Newp	ST3488	51°35·5′	2°56·8′W	T	171
Bishpool Fm	Somer	ST1934	51°6·2′	3°9·0′W	FM	181
Bishton	Newp	ST3987	51°35·0′	2°52·4′W	T	171
Bishton	Staffs	SK0220	52°47·1′	1°57·8′W	T	128
Bishton Fm	Staffs	SK0221	52°47·4′	1°57·8′W	FM	128
Bishton Manor	Shrops	SJ8001	52°36·6′	2°17·3′W	A	127
Bisley	Glos	SO9006	51°45·4′	2°8·3′W	T	163

Bisley	Surrey	SU9559	51°19·6′	0°37·8′W	T	175,186
Bisley Camp	Surrey	SU9357	51°18·5′	0°39·6′W	X	175,186
Bisley Common	Surrey	SU9458	51°19·0′	0°38·7′W	X	175,186
Bisley Ranges	Surrey	SU9358	51°19·0′	0°39·5′W	X	175,186
Bispham	Blackp	SD3040	53°51·3′	3°3·4′W	T	102
Bispham Green	Lancs	SD4813	53°36·9′	2°46·8′W	T	108
Bispham Hall	Wigan	SD5202	53°31·0′	2°43·0′W	A	108
Biss Bottom	Wilts	ST8648	51°14·1′	2°11·6′W	X	183
Biss Brook	Wilts	ST8552	51°16·3′	2°12·5′W	W	183
Bissell Wood	Worcs	SO8677	52°23·7′	2°11·9′W	F	139
Bissethill	Aberd	NK0740	57°27·3′	1°52·5′W	X	30
Bisset Moss	Aberd	NJ6137	57°25·6′	2°38·5′W	X	29
Bisset's Hill	Aberd	NO8482	56°56·0′	2°15·3′W	X	45
Biss Fm	Wilts	ST8756	51°18·4′	2°10·8′W	FM	173
Bissoe	Corn	SW7741	50°13·9′	5°7·2′W	T	204
Bissom	Corn	SW7934	50°10·1′	5°5·3′W	T	204
Biss Wood	Wilts	ST8756	51°18·4′	2°10·8′W	F	173
Bisterne	Hants	SU1401	50°48·7′	1°47·7′W	T	195
Bisterne Close	Hants	SU2202	50°49·3′	1°40·9′W	T	195
Bisterne Common	Hants	SU1801	50°48·7′	1°44·3′W	X	195
Bisterne Manor	Hants	SU1500	50°48·2′	1°46·8′W	X	195
Bistock	Kent	TQ9358	51°17·5′	0°46·5′E	X	178
Bitchagreen	N Yks	SE6796	54°21·5′	0°57·7′W	X	94,100
Bitch Burn	E Ayr	NS5706	55°19·9′	4°14·8′W	W	71,77
Bitch Craig	Scot Bord	NT1926	55°31·5′	3°16·6′W	H	72
Bitches, The	Pemb	SM7023	51°51·7′	5°20·0′W	X	157
Bitchet Common	Kent	TQ5653	51°15·5′	0°14·5′E	F	188
Bitchet Green	Kent	TQ5754	51°16·0′	0°15·4′E	T	188
Bitchfield	Lincs	SK9828	52°50·7′	0°32·3′W	T	130
Bitchfield	Northum	NZ0977	55°5·5′	1°51·1′W	X	88
Biteabout Fm	Northum	NU0036	55°37·3′	1°59·6′W	FM	75
Biteford	Devon	SS3018	50°56·4′	4°24·8′W	X	190
Bite, The	Corn	SX0348	50°18·2′	4°45·6′W	X	204
Bitham Fm	Oxon	SU4286	51°34·5′	1°23·2′W	FM	174
Bitham Hall	Warw	SP4150	52°9·0′	1°24·5′W	X	151
Bitham Hill	Warw	SP4050	52°9·0′	1°24·5′W	X	151
Bith-bheinn	Arg & Bt	NM5834	56°26·4′	5°55·1′W	X	47,48
Bitheasdail	N Eil	NB1000	57°54·0′	6°53·2′W	X	14
Bithefin Moor	Devon	SS6314	50°54·8′	3°56·6′W	X	180
Bithnie	Aberd	NJ5117	57°14·7′	2°48·3′W	X	37
Bittadon	Devon	SS5441	51°9·2′	4°4·9′W	T	180
Bittaford	Devon	SX6657	50°24·1′	3°52·8′W	T	202
Bittell Fm	Worcs	SP0274	52°22·1′	1°57·8′W	FM	139
Bittens Fm	Corn	SX2689	50°40·7′	4°27·4′W	FM	190
Bittens, The	Shetld	HU1756	60°17·5′	1°41·1′W	X	3
Bittering	Norf	TF9317	52°43·2′	0°51·9′E	T	132
Bitterley	Shrops	SO5677	52°23·6′	2°38·4′W	T	137,138
Bitterley Hyde	Heref	SO5751	52°9·6′	2°37·3′W	X	149
Bitterly Court	Shrops	SO5777	52°23·6′	2°37·5′W	X	137,138
Bitterne	C of Soton	SU4513	50°55·1′	1°21·2′W	T	196
Bitterne Park	C of Soton	SU4414	50°55·7′	1°22·0′W	T	196
Bitterscote	Staffs	SK2003	52°37·7′	1°41·9′W	T	139
Bittesby Ho	Leic	SP5085	52°27·9′	1°15·4′W	X	140
Bittesby Village	Leic	SP5085	52°27·9′	1°15·4′W	A	140
Bittescombe Hill	Somer	ST0127	51°2·3′	3°24·3′W	X	181
Bittescombe Manor	Somer	ST0129	51°3·3′	3°24·4′W	X	181
Bitteswell	Leic	SP5385	52°27·9′	1°12·8′W	T	140
Bitteswell Hall	Leic	SP5387	52°28·9′	1°12·8′W	X	140
Bitteswell Lodge	Leic	SP5286	52°28·4′	1°13·7′W	X	140
Bittia Fm	Monm	ST3599	51°41·4′	2°56·0′W	FM	171
Bittlesea Fm	Wilts	ST9979	51°30·8′	2°0·5′W	FM	173
Bittles Fm	Hants	SU6413	50°55·0′	1°5·0′W	FM	196
Bittles Green	Dorset	ST8524	51°1·1′	2°12·4′W	T	183
Bittlestone Height	D & G	NY3890	55°12·3′	2°58·0′W	H	79
Bitton	S Glos	ST6869	51°25·4′	2°27·2′W	T	172
Bitton Hill	S Glos	ST6770	51°25·9′	2°28·1′W	X	172
Bitworthy	Devon	SS3422	50°58·6′	4°21·5′W	X	190
Biulacraig	N Eil	NL5582	56°48·3′	7°38·8′W	X	31
Bivelham Fm	E Susx	TQ6326	51°0·8′	0°19·8′E	FM	188,199
Bivelham Forge Fm	E Susx	TQ6426	51°0·8′	0°20·7′E	FM	188,199
Bix	Oxon	SU7285	51°33·8′	0°57·3′W	T	175
Bix Fm	S Glos	ST7585	51°34·0′	2°21·3′W	FM	172
Bix Hall	Oxon	SU7285	51°33·8′	0°57·3′W	X	175
Bixley Fm	Norf	TM1298	52°32·5′	1°8·0′E	FM	144
Bix Manor Fm	Oxon	SU7284	51°33·2′	0°57·3′W	FM	175
Bixmoor Wood	Oxon	SU6586	51°34·4′	1°3·3′W	F	175
Bixter	Shetld	HU3352	60°15·3′	1°23·7′W	T	3
Bixter Voe	Shetld	HU3251	60°14·8′	1°24·8′W	W	3
Bizzle Burn	Northum	NT8922	55°29·7′	2°10·0′W	W	74
Bizzle Crags	Northum	NT8921	55°29·2′	2°10·0′W	X	74
Blaber River	I of M	SC3183	54°13·1′	4°35·1′W	W	95
Blabers Hall Fm	Warw	SP2586	52°28·5′	1°37·5′W	FM	140
Blà Bheinn	Highld	NG5221	57°13·0′	6°6·0′W	H	32
Blable Ho	Corn	SW9470	50°29·9′	4°53·9′W	X	200
Blaby	Leic	SP5697	52°34·3′	1°10·0′W	T	140
Blaby Hill	Leic	SP5897	52°34·3′	1°8·2′W	X	140
Blachford	Devon	SX6159	50°25·1′	3°57·0′W	X	202
Blachrie	Aberd	NJ7744	57°29·4′	2°22·6′W	X	29,30
Blackabroom	Devon	SX5187	50°40·1′	4°6·1′W	X	191
Blackaburn	Northum	NY7778	55°6·0′	2°21·2′W	F	86,87
Blackaburn	Northum	NY7977	55°5·5′	2°19·3′W	X	86,87
Blacka Burn	Northum	NY8077	55°5·5′	2°18·4′W	W	86,87
Blackaburn Lough	Northum	NY7679	55°6·5′	2°22·1′W	W	86,87
Black - acre	Corn	SW9461	50°25·0′	4°53·6′W	X	200
Blackacre	D & G	NY0490	55°11·9′	3°30·1′W	X	78
Blackacre Fm	Wilts	ST8462	51°21·6′	2°13·4′W	FM	173
Blackacre Hill	Suff	TM1149	52°6·2′	1°5·3′E	X	155,169
Blackacres Fm	Oxon	SU3692	51°37·8′	1°28·4′W	FM	164,174
Blackadder Bank	Scot Bord	NT8652	55°45·9′	2°13·0′W	X	67,74
Blackadder Mains	Scot Bord	NT8452	55°45·9′	2°14·9′W	X	67,74
Blackadder Mount	Scot Bord	NT8553	55°46·5′	2°13·9′W	X	67,74
Blackadder Water	Scot Bord	NT6551	55°45·3′	2°33·0′W	W	67,74
Blackadder Water	Scot Bord	NT6948	55°43·7′	2°29·2′W	W	74
Blackadder Water	Scot Bord	NT8152	55°45·9′	2°17·7′W	W	67,74
Blackadder West	Scot Bord	NT8452	55°45·9′	2°14·9′W	X	67,74
Blackaddie Br	D & G	NS7709	55°21·8′	3°56·0′W	X	71,78
Blackadon	Corn	SX1877	50°34·1′	4°33·8′W	X	201
Blackadon Tor	Devon	SX7173	50°32·8′	3°48·9′W	H	191
Blacka Hill	Sheff	SK2880	53°19·2′	1°34·4′W	X	110
Blackaldern	Pemb	SN1114	51°47·8′	4°44·1′W	X	158

Blackalder Wood	Devon	SX8296	50°45·3′	3°40·0′W	X	191
Blackaller Fm	Devon	ST1315	50°55·9′	3°13·9′W	FM	181,193
Blackaller's Cove	Torbay	SX9268	50°30·3′	3°31·0′W	W	202
Blackamoor Wood	Ches	SJ5577	53°17·5′	2°40·1′W	F	117
Black Andrew Wood	Scot Bord	NT4029	55°33·3′	2°56·6′W	F	73
Black Ashop Moor	Derby	SK0890	53°24·6′	1°52·4′W	X	110
Blackaterry Point	Devon	SX5846	50°18·0′	3°59·3′W	X	202
Blackaton Brook	Devon	SX6691	50°42·4′	3°53·5′W	W	191
Blackaton Cross	Devon	SX5763	50°27·2′	4°0·5′W	A	202
Blackaton Down	Devon	SX7078	50°35·5′	3°49·8′W	H	191
Blackaton Fm	Corn	SX2580	50°35·8′	4°28·0′W	FM	201
Blackaton Manor	Devon	SX6977	50°34·9′	3°50·6′W	X	191
Black-a-ven Brook	Devon	SX5990	50°41·8′	3°59·4′W	W	191
Black Averham Fm	N Yks	SE6760	54°2·1′	0°58·2′W	FM	100
Blackawall	Orkney	ND3594	58°50·0′	3°7·1′W	X	7
Blackawton	Devon	SX8050	50°20·5′	3°40·8′W	T	202
Black Ball	Devon	SS8130	51°3·7′	3°41·5′W	X	181
Black Ball	Somer	SS9842	51°10·3′	3°27·2′W	X	181
Blackball Firs	Wilts	SU0947	51°13·6′	1°51·9′W	F	184
Black Ball Hill	Somer	ST1339	51°8·9′	3°14·2′W	X	181
Black Band	Cumbr	NY7240	54°45·5′	2°25·7′W	H	86,87
Black Band	Durham	NY8125	54°37·4′	2°17·2′W	X	91,92
Black Bank	Cambs	TL5385	52°26·7′	0°15·5′E	T	143
Black Bank	Northum	NT9241	55°40·0′	2°7·2′W	X	74,75
Black Bank	N Yks	SD7664	54°4·5′	2°21·6′W	X	98
Black Bank	N Yks	SD8697	54°22·3′	2°12·5′W	X	98
Blackbank	Pth & Kin	NO2127	56°26·0′	3°16·4′W	X	53,58
Black Bank	Shetld	HU2152	60°15·4′	1°36·7′W	H	3
Black Bank	Shrops	SO2387	52°28·8′	3°7·6′W	X	137
Black Bank	Staffs	SJ8147	53°1·4′	2°16·6′W	X	118
Blackbank	Staffs	SK0164	53°10·6′	1°58·7′W	X	119
Blackbank	Staffs	SK0366	53°11·7′	1°56·9′W	X	119
Black Bank	Warw	SP3586	52°28·5′	1°28·7′W	T	140
Black Bank Fm	N Lincs	SE8503	53°31·2′	0°42·7′W	FM	112
Black Bank Ho	Durham	NZ1135	54°42·8′	1°49·3′W	X	92
Blackbank Plantation	D & G	NS8303	55°18·7′	3°50·2′W	F	78
Black Banks	Darl	NZ2912	54°30·4′	1°32·7′W	T	93
Blackbanks	Moray	NJ1753	57°33·8′	3°22·8′W	X	28
Black Banks	Moray	NJ2635	57°24·2′	3°13·4′W	X	28
Black Bank Wood	D & G	NX6080	55°5·9′	4°11·2′W	F	77
Blackbank Wood	Staffs	SK0349	53°2·5′	1°56·9′W	F	119
Black Barn	Kent	TQ8928	51°1·4′	0°42·1′E	X	189
Black Barn	Lincs	TF4328	52°50·1′	0°7·8′E	T	131
Blackbarn	N Ayr	NS3157	55°46·9′	4°41·3′W	X	63
Black Barn	Shrops	SJ5506	52°39·2′	2°39·5′W	X	126
Black Barn Fm	Bucks	SP7606	51°45·1′	0°53·5′W	FM	165
Black Barn Fm	Oxon	SU6286	51°34·4′	1°5·9′W	FM	175
Black Barn Fm	Shrops	SO5895	52°33·3′	2°36·8′W	FM	137,138
Black Barony	Scot Bord	NT2347	55°42·9′	3°13·1′W	X	73
Black Barrow	Dorset	SY8683	50°39·0′	2°11·5′W	X	194
Black Barrow	Hants	SU1810	50°53·6′	1°44·3′W	X	195
Black Barrow	Somer	SS8344	51°11·2′	3°40·1′W	A	181
Blackbaulk	Aberd	NJ4518	57°15·2′	2°54·2′W	X	37
Black Bay	Arg & Bt	NR7726	55°28·9′	5°31·3′W	W	68,69
Blackbeck	Cumbr	NY0206	54°26·6′	3°30·3′W	T	89
Black Beck	Cumbr	NY0211	54°29·3′	3°30·4′W	W	89
Black Beck	Cumbr	NY1710	54°29·0′	3°16·4′W	W	89,90
Black Beck	Cumbr	SD1395	54°20·8′	3°19·9′W	W	96
Black Beck	Cumbr	SD1886	54°16·0′	3°15·1′W	W	96
Black Beck	Cumbr	SD3385	54°15·6′	3°1·3′W	W	96,97
Black Beck	Cumbr	SD3597	54°22·1′	2°59·6′W	W	96,97
Black Beck	Cumbr	SD3683	54°14·6′	2°58·5′W	W	96,97
Black Beck	Durham	NY8717	54°33·1′	2°11·6′W	W	91,92
Black Beck	Durham	NY9113	54°31·0′	2°7·9′W	W	91,92
Black Beck	Durham	NZ0517	54°33·1′	1°54·9′W	W	92
Black Beck	N Yks	NZ6105	54°26·4′	1°3·1′W	W	94
Black Beck	N Yks	SE1093	54°20·2′	1°50·4′W	X	99
Black Beck	N Yks	SE9292	54°19·2′	0°34·7′W	W	94,101
Black Beck Hole	Brad	SE0946	53°54·8′	1°51·4′W	X	104
Blackbeck Knotts	Cumbr	NY1509	54°28·4′	3°18·3′W	X	89
Blackbeck Tarn	Cumbr	NY2012	54°30·1′	3°13·7′W	W	89,90
Blackbellie Hill	D & G	NX8057	54°53·9′	3°51·8′W	H	84
Black Belt	Suff	TL7566	52°16·1′	0°34·3′E	F	155
Black Benwee Hill	D & G	NX4573	55°1·9′	4°25·1′W	H	77
Blackberry Farm Animal Centre	Bucks	SP7618	51°51·6′	0°53·4′W	X	165
Blackberry Fm	Devon	SY0686	50°40·2′	3°19·4′W	FM	192
Blackberry Fm	Leic	SK4111	52°41·9′	1°23·2′W	FM	129
Blackberry Fm	N Yks	NZ3703	54°25·5′	1°25·4′W	FM	93
Blackberry Fox Covert	Northnts	SP8669	52°19·0′	0°43·9′W	F	152
Blackberry Hill	Bath & NE Somer	ST6360	51°20·5′	2°31·5′W	H	172
Blackberry Hill	Leic	SK8132	52°53·0′	0°47·4′W	X	130
Blackberry Hill	Notts	SK6333	52°53·7′	1°3·4′W	X	129
Blackberry Hill	Notts	SK7539	52°56·8′	0°52·6′W	X	129
Blackberry Hill or Blackbow Hill	Shrops	SJ3924	52°48·8′	2°53·9′W	X	126
Blackberry Knowe	S Ayr	NX3194	55°12·9′	4°39·0′W	X	76
Black Binks	Angus	NO2565	56°46·5′	3°13·2′W	H	44
Black Birches	Shrops	SJ5021	52°47·3′	2°44·1′W	X	126
Blackbird Hill Fm	Lincs	SK8092	53°25·4′	0°47·4′W	FM	112
Blackbird Hill Fm	Northnts	SP5348	52°7·9′	1°13·1′W	FM	152
Blackbirds	Essex	TL9804	51°42·2′	0°52·3′E	X	168
Blackbirds Fm	Herts	TQ1499	51°40·9′	0°20·7′W	FM	166,176
Blackbird's Nest	Leic	SK5115	52°44·0′	1°14·3′W	X	129
Black Birn	S Lanak	NT0553	55°45·9′	3°30·4′W	X	65,72
Blackblair	Aberd	NJ5641	57°27·7′	2°43·5′W	X	29
Blackblakehope	Northum	NY7599	55°17·3′	2°23·2′W	X	80
Blackboath	Angus	NO5546	56°36·5′	2°43·5′W	X	54
Blackbog	Aberd	NJ7337	57°25·6′	2°26·5′W	X	29
Blackbog	S Lanak	NS7151	55°44·4′	4°2·8′W	X	64
Blackbog Burn	Northum	NY8880	55°7·1′	2°10·9′W	W	80
Blackborough	Devon	ST0909	50°52·6′	3°17·2′W	T	192
Blackborough	Norf	TF6714	52°42·1′	0°28·7′E	T	132
Blackborough End	Norf	TF6614	52°42·1′	0°27·8′E	T	132
Blackborough Ho	Devon	ST0909	50°52·6′	3°17·2′W	X	192
Blackbottle Rock	Corn	SX1350	50°19·5′	4°37·3′W	X	200
Black Bourn, The	Suff	TL9272	52°19·0′	0°49·4′E	W	144,155
Black Bourton	Oxon	SP2804	51°44·3′	1°35·3′W	T	163
Black Bourton Brook	Oxon	SP2901	51°42·7′	1°34·4′W	W	164
Blackbow Hill or Blackberry Hill	Shrops	SJ3924	52°48·8′	2°53·9′W	X	126
Blackboys	E Susx	TQ5220	50°57·8′	0°10·3′E	T	199
Black Br	Cambs	TL2771	52°19·6′	0°7·8′W	X	153
Black Br	Pemb	SM9106	51°43·1′	5°1·2′W	X	157,158
Blackbraes	Aberd	NJ8918	57°15·4′	2°10·5′W	X	38
Blackbraes	Falk	NS9075	55°57·6′	3°45·3′W	X	65
Black Braes	Northum	NT8314	55°25·4′	2°15·7′W	H	80
Black Braes	Orkney	HY2211	58°59·0′	3°20·9′W	X	6
Blackbraes	Orkney	HY3105	58°55·9′	3°11·4′W	X	6,7
Blackbreast	D & G	NX7552	54°51·1′	3°56·4′W	H	84
Black Bridge	Aberd	NJ5719	57°15·8′	2°42·3′W	X	37
Black Bridge	Highld	NH3770	57°41·7′	4°43·6′W	X	20
Black Bridge	N Yks	NZ3200	54°23·9′	1°30·0′W	X	93
Blackbridge Brook	I of W	SZ5590	50°42·6′	1°12·9′W	W	196
Black Bridge Burn	D & G	NX7262	54°56·4′	3°59·5′W	W	83,84
Blackbridge Fm	Northnts	SP9076	52°22·7′	0°40·3′W	FM	141
Blackbriggs	Aberd	NJ8437	57°25·6′	2°15·5′W	X	29,30
Blackbriggs	Aberd	NJ9442	57°28·4′	2°5·5′W	X	30
Blackbriggs	D & G	NX6349	54°49·3′	4°7·5′W	X	83
Blackbriggs	E Ayr	NS5329	55°32·2′	4°19·3′W	X	70
Black Brook	Cald	SE0517	53°39·2′	1°55·0′W	W	110
Blackbrook	Derby	SK0780	53°19·3′	1°53·3′W	T	110
Black Brook	Derby	SK2743	52°59·3′	1°35·3′W	W	119,128
Blackbrook	Derby	SK3347	53°1·4′	1°30·1′W	T	119,128
Black Brook	Flint	SJ2960	53°8·2′	3°3·3′W	W	117
Blackbrook	Flint	SJ3061	53°8·7′	3°2·4′W	X	117
Black Brook	Lancs	SD3712	53°36·3′	2°56·7′W	W	108
Black Brook	Lancs	SD6755	53°59·6′	2°29·8′W	W	103
Black Brook	Leic	SK4720	52°46·8′	1°17·8′W	W	129
Black Brook	Powys	SO0167	52°17·8′	3°26·7′W	W	136,147
Black Brook	Powys	SO1861	52°14·7′	3°11·7′W	W	148
Blackbrook	Staffs	SJ7639	52°57·1′	2°21·0′W	T	127
Black Brook	Staffs	SJ9965	53°11·2′	2°0·5′W	W	118
Black Brook	Staffs	SK0064	53°10·6′	1°59·6′W	W	119
Black Brook	Staffs	SK0451	53°3·6′	1°56·0′W	X	119
Black Brook	Staffs	SK0557	53°6·8′	1°55·1′W	X	119
Black Brook	Staffs	SK1403	52°37·7′	1°47·2′W	W	139
Blackbrook	St Hel	SJ5496	53°27·8′	2°41·2′W	T	108
Blackbrook	Surrey	TQ1846	51°12·3′	0°18·3′W	T	187
Black Brook	Wrekin	SJ7020	52°46·8′	2°26·3′W	W	127
Black Brook	Wrex	SJ3144	52°59·6′	3°1·3′W	W	117
Blackbrook Fm	Derby	SK2645	53°0·3′	1°36·3′W	FM	119,128
Blackbrook Fm	Kent	TQ8826	51°0·4′	0°41·2′E	FM	189,199
Blackbrook Fm	Leic	SK4518	52°45·7′	1°19·6′W	FM	129
Blackbrook Fm	Northum	NZ1898	55°16·8′	1°42·6′W	FM	81
Blackbrook Fm	W Susx	SU9924	51°0·6′	0°34·9′W	FM	197
Blackbrook Head	Devon	SX5877	50°34·8′	4°0·0′W	W	191
Blackbrook Ho	Monm	SO4220	51°52·8′	2°50·2′W	X	161
Blackbrook Resr	Leic	SK4617	52°45·2′	1°18·7′W	W	129
Blackbrook River	Devon	SX5875	50°33·7′	3°59·9′W	W	191
Blackbrook Wood	E Susx	TQ3417	50°56·4′	0°5·2′W	F	198
Blackbroom	Devon	SX4793	50°43·2′	4°9·7′W	X	191
Blackbrough Hill	Scot Bord	NT8017	55°27·0′	2°18·5′W	H	80
Black Brow	Cumbr	NY3153	54°52·3′	3°4·1′W	X	85
Black Brow	Cumbr	NY3810	54°29·1′	2°57·0′W	H	90
Black Brow	N Yks	NZ8504	54°25·7′	0°41·0′W	H	94
Black Brow Fm	Traf	SJ7489	53°24·1′	2°23·1′W	FM	109
Black Bull	Scot Bord	NT8470	55°55·6′	2°14·9′W	X	67
Black Bull Fm	Durham	NZ1016	54°32·6′	1°50·3′W	FM	92
Black Bull Fm	Lincs	SK9321	52°46·9′	0°36·9′W	FM	130
Black Buoy Sand	Lincs	TF4139	52°56·0′	0°6·3′E	X	131
Black Burn	Aberd	NJ6735	57°24·5′	2°32·5′W	W	29
Blackburn	Aberd	NJ7154	57°34·8′	2°28·6′W	X	29
Blackburn	Aberd	NJ8212	57°12·2′	2°17·4′W	T	38
Black Burn	Aberd	NJ8743	57°28·9′	2°12·5′W	W	30
Black Burn	Aberd	NO2880	56°54·6′	3°10·5′W	W	44
Black Burn	Aberd	NO3988	56°59·0′	2°59·8′W	W	44
Black Burn	Aberd	NO6467	56°47·8′	2°34·9′W	W	45
Black Burn	Aberd	NO6872	56°50·6′	2°31·0′W	W	45
Black Burn	Angus	NO5382	56°55·9′	2°45·9′W	W	44
Blackburn	Black w Dar	SD6827	53°44·5′	2°28·7′W	T	103
Black Burn	Cumbr	NY6258	54°55·2′	2°35·1′W	W	86
Black Burn	Cumbr	NY6937	54°43·9′	2°28·5′W	W	91
Black Burn	Cumbr	NY6942	54°46·6′	2°28·5′W	W	86,87
Black Burn	D & G	NS8104	55°19·2′	3°52·1′W	W	78
Black Burn	D & G	NS8315	55°25·2′	3°50·5′W	W	71,78
Black Burn	D & G	NX2768	54°58·8′	4°41·8′W	W	82
Black Burn	D & G	NX3577	55°3·9′	4°34·6′W	W	77
Black Burn	D & G	NX3585	55°8·2′	4°34·9′W	W	77
Black Burn	D & G	NX3841	54°44·5′	4°30·6′W	W	83
Black Burn	D & G	NX3977	55°3·9′	4°30·8′W	W	77
Black Burn	D & G	NX4072	55°1·3′	4°29·7′W	W	77
Black Burn	D & G	NX5583	55°7·5′	4°16·0′W	W	77
Black Burn	D & G	NX6293	55°13·0′	4°9·7′W	W	77
Black Burn	D & G	NY0790	55°12·0′	3°27·2′W	W	78
Blackburn	D & G	NY0791	55°12·5′	3°27·3′W	X	78
Black Burn	D & G	NY2393	55°13·8′	3°12·2′W	W	79
Black Burn	D & G	NY3198	55°16·5′	3°4·7′W	W	79
Black Burn	Durham	NY9934	54°42·3′	2°0·5′W	W	92
Black Burn	Durham	NZ0040	54°45·5′	1°59·6′W	W	87
Blackburn	Durham	NZ1945	54°48·2′	1°41·8′W	X	88
Black Burn	E Ayr	NS5008	55°20·8′	4°21·5′W	W	70,77
Black Burn	E Ayr	NS6617	55°26·0′	4°6·6′W	W	71
Black Burn	Falk	NT0579	55°59·9′	3°31·0′W	W	65
Black Burn	Highld	NH3702	57°5·1′	4°40·9′W	W	34
Blackburn	Highld	NH3802	57°5·1′	4°39·9′W	X	34
Black Burn	Midlo	NT2257	55°48·3′	3°14·2′W	W	66,73
Black Burn	Midlo	NT3154	55°46·7′	3°5·6′W	W	66,73
Black Burn	Moray	NJ1558	57°36·5′	3°24·9′W	W	28
Blackburn	Moray	NJ2958	57°36·6′	3°10·8′W	T	28
Black Burn	Northum	NT8303	55°19·5′	2°15·6′W	W	80
Black Burn	Northum	NU0801	55°18·4′	1°52·0′W	W	81
Black Burn	Northum	NU1221	55°29·2′	1°48·2′W	W	75
Black Burn	Northum	NY6558	54°55·2′	2°32·3′W	W	86
Black Burn	Northum	NY7792	55°13·6′	2°21·3′W	W	80
Black Burn	Northum	NY9188	55°11·4′	2°8·1′W	W	80
Black Burn	Northum	NY9858	54°55·2′	2°1·4′W	X	87
Blackburn	N Yks	SD8799	54°23·4′	2°11·6′W	X	98
Blackburn	Pth & Kin	NN9314	56°18·6′	3°43·3′W	X	58
Blackburn	Roth	SK3892	53°25·6′	1°25·3′W	T	110,111
Black Burn	S Ayr	NX3795	55°13·6′	4°33·3′W	W	77
Blackburn	Scot Bord	NT5150	55°44·7′	2°46·4′W	X	66,73
Black Burn	Scot Bord	NT6406	55°21·1′	2°33·6′W	W	80
Blackburn	Scot Bord	NT7766	55°53·4′	2°21·6′W	X	67
Blackburn	Scot Bord	NT8958	55°49·2′	2°10·1′W	X	67,74
Black Burn	Scot Bord	NY4689	55°11·8′	2°50·5′W	W	79
Blackburn	Scot Bord	NY4788	55°11·3′	2°49·5′W	X	79
Black Burn	S Lanak	NS6746	55°41·6′	4°6·5′W	W	64
Blackburn	S Lanak	NS6846	55°41·6′	4°5·6′W	X	64
Black Burn	S Lanak	NS8526	55°31·1′	3°48·9′W	W	71,72
Black Burn	S Lanak	NS8825	55°30·6′	3°46·0′W	W	71,72
Blackburn	S Lanak	NS8825	55°30·6′	3°46·0′W	X	71,72
Black Burn	W Dunb	NS4378	55°58·4′	4°30·5′W	W	64
Blackburn	W Loth	NS9865	55°52·3′	3°37·4′W	T	65
Black Burn	W Loth	NT0560	55°49·7′	3°30·6′W	W	65
Blackburn Bank	Cumbr	NY6942	54°46·6′	2°28·5′W	X	86,87
Blackburn Common	Northum	NY7992	55°13·6′	2°19·4′W	X	80
Blackburn Hall	Beds	TL0458	52°12·9′	0°28·3′W	X	153
Blackburn Head	Cumbr	NY6155	54°53·5′	2°36·1′W	X	86
Black Burn Head	D & G	NY3398	55°16·5′	3°2·8′W	H	79
Blackburnhead	Northum	NY7794	55°14·6′	2°21·3′W	X	80
Blackburn Ho	Scot Bord	NT7966	55°53·5′	2°19·7′W	X	67
Blackburn Ho	W Loth	NT0065	55°52·3′	3°35·5′W	X	65
Blackburn Lake	Northum	NU0801	55°18·4′	1°52·0′W	W	81
Blackburn Mains	W Loth	NS9864	55°51·8′	3°37·3′W	X	65
Blackburn Mill	Scot Bord	NT7665	55°52·9′	2°22·6′W	X	67
Blackburn Moss	Aberd	NO7990	57°0·3′	2°20·3′W	X	38,45
Blackburn Rig	Scot Bord	NT6505	55°20·5′	2°32·7′W	X	80
Blackburn Rig	Scot Bord	NT7866	55°53·4′	2°20·7′W	X	67
Blackburnrig Wood	Scot Bord	NT7865	55°52·9′	2°20·7′W	F	67
Blackburn Rocks		NS3221	55°27·5′	4°39·0′W	X	70
Blackbury	Heref	SO5838	52°2·6′	2°36·3′W	A	149
Blackbury Camp (Fort)	Devon	SY1892	50°43·5′	3°9·3′W	A	192,193
Blackbury Castle	Devon	SY1892	50°43·5′	3°9·3′W	A	192,193
Black Bush	Cambs	TL2593	52°31·5′	0°9·0′W	X	142
Black Bush	Carm	SN4624	51°53·8′	4°13·9′W	X	159
Black Bush	E Yorks	TA1939	53°50·3′	0°11·1′W	X	107
Black Bush	Hants	SU1903	50°49·8′	1°43·4′W	X	195
Blackbush Down	Dorset	SU0415	50°56·3′	1°56·2′W	X	184
Blackbushe Airport	Hants	SU8059	51°19·7′	0°50·7′W	X	175,186
Blackbushe Fm	Hants	SU8057	51°18·6′	0°50·7′W	FM	175,186
Blackbush Fm	Heref	SO3833	51°59·8′	2°53·8′W	FM	149,161
Black Bush Plain	Hants	SU2515	50°56·3′	1°38·3′W	X	184
Blackbush Wood	Kent	TQ7335	51°5·5′	0°28·6′E	F	188
Black Butten	Shetld	HU3084	60°32·6′	1°26·7′W	X	1,3
Blackbutts	Aberd	NO8892	57°1·4′	2°11·4′W	X	38,45
Blackbyres	E Renf	NS5060	55°48·9′	4°23·2′W	X	64
Blackbyres	S Ayr	NS3214	55°23·7′	4°38·7′W	X	70
Black Cairn	Aberd	NJ6833	57°23·4′	2°31·5′W	A	29
Black Cairn	D & G	NX2452	54°50·2′	4°44·0′W	X	82
Black Callerton	N upon Ty	NZ1769	55°1·2′	1°43·6′W	T	88
Blackcap	E Susx	TQ3712	50°53·7′	0°2·7′W	X	198
Blackcap Fm	E Susx	TQ4605	50°49·8′	0°4·8′E	FM	198
Blackcap Hill	E Susx	TQ4604	50°49·3′	0°4·8′E	X	198
Black Carn	Corn	SW3622	50°2·6′	5°40·9′W	X	203
Black Carr	Brad	SE0831	53°46·8′	1°52·3′W	X	104
Black Carr	Brad	SE2032	53°47·3′	1°41·4′W	F	104
Black Carr	Norf	TL9785	52°25·9′	0°54·3′E	X	144
Black Carr	Norf	TM0995	52°31·0′	1°5·2′E	T	144
Black Carr	Suff	TL9080	52°23·3′	0°47·9′E	F	144
Black Carr Fm	Derby	SK2545	53°0·3′	1°37·2′W	FM	119,128
Black Carr Plantation	Donc	SE6301	53°30·4′	1°2·6′W	F	111
Black Carts	Northum	NY8871	55°2·2′	2°10·8′W	X	87
Black Cart Water	Renf	NS3960	55°48·6′	4°33·7′W	W	63
Black Cart Water	Renf	NS4464	55°50·9′	4°29·1′W	W	64
Black Castle	E Loth	NT5766	55°53·4′	2°40·8′W	X	67
Blackcastle	Highld	NH8254	57°33·9′	3°57·9′W	X	27
Blackcastle	Midlo	NT4159	55°49·5′	2°56·1′W	T	66,73
Blackcastle	S Lanak	NT0253	55°45·9′	3°33·3′W	X	65,72
Black Castle (Fort)	E Loth	NT5766	55°53·4′	2°40·8′W	A	67
Blackcastle Hill	E Loth	NT7171	55°56·1′	2°27·4′W	H	67
Blackcastle Hill	Scot Bord	NT4821	55°29·1′	2°48·9′W	H	73
Blackcat	Essex	TL5509	51°45·7′	0°15·2′E	X	167
Black Cave	N Ayr	NR9920	55°26·2′	5°10·2′W	A	69
Black Cave	Pemb	SM8700	51°39·7′	5°4·4′W	X	157
Blackchambers	Aberd	NJ7911	57°11·6′	2°20·4′W	X	38
Blackchapel	Essex	TL6617	51°49·8′	0°24·9′E	A	167
Blackchester	Northum	NU0010	55°23·3′	1°59·6′W	X	81
Blackchester	Scot Bord	NT5050	55°44·7′	2°47·4′W	X	66,73
Black Chew Head	Oldham	SE0502	53°31·1′	1°55·1′W	X	110
Black Chirnells	Northum	NU0303	55°19·5′	1°56·7′W	X	81
Blackchub	D & G	NX8592	55°12·8′	3°48·0′W	X	78
Blackchurch Rock	Devon	SS2926	51°0·7′	4°25·9′W	X	190
Black Clauchrie	S Ayr	NX2984	55°7·5′	4°40·5′W	X	76
Black Cleuch	Northum	NT6905	55°20·5′	2°28·9′W	X	80
Black Cleuch	Scot Bord	NT1115	55°25·5′	3°23·9′W	X	78
Black Cleuch	Scot Bord	NT2529	55°33·2′	3°10·9′W	X	73
Blackcleuch	Scot Bord	NT3702	55°18·7′	2°59·1′W	X	79
Black Cleuch	Scot Bord	NT5100	55°17·8′	2°45·9′W	X	79
Black Cleuch	Scot Bord	NT5503	55°19·4′	2°42·1′W	X	80
Blackcleuch Burn	S Lanak	NT0219	55°27·6′	3°32·6′W	W	78
Blackcleuch Burn	S Lanak	NT0220	55°28·1′	3°32·6′W	W	72
Blackcleuch Rig	Scot Bord	NT3704	55°19·8′	2°59·2′W	H	79
Blackcleugh	D & G	NY2675	55°4·1′	3°9·1′W	X	85
Black Cleugh	Northum	NY6780	55°7·0′	2°30·6′W	X	80
Black Cleugh	Northum	NY7562	54°57·4′	2°23·0′W	X	86,87
Black Cleugh	Northum	NY7948	54°49·8′	2°19·2′W	X	86,87
Blackcleugh Burn	Northum	NY6683	55°8·7′	2°31·6′W	W	80
Blackcleugh Burn	Northum	NY7051	54°51·4′	2°27·6′W	W	86,87
Blackcleugh Rig	Scot Bord	NT7062	55°51·3′	2°28·3′W	X	67
Blackcleugh Rigg	Northum	NY7461	54°56·8′	2°23·9′W	X	86,87
Black Cliff	Corn	SW5538	50°11·7′	5°25·6′W	X	203
Black Cliff	Monm	ST5398	51°41·0′	2°40·4′W	X	162
Black Cliff	Pemb	SM8519	51°49·9′	5°6·8′W	X	157
Blackcliffe Hill	Notts	SK6032	52°53·2′	1°6·1′W	X	129
Blackcliffe Hill Plantation	Notts	SK6671	53°14·2′	1°0·3′W	F	120
Black Clough	Cald	SD9733	53°47·8′	2°2·3′W	X	103
Blackclough	Derby	SK0169	53°13·3′	1°58·7′W	X	119

Black Clough	Derby	SK1393	53°26·3'	1°47·8'W	X	110
Black Clough	Lancs	SD6052	53°58·0'	2°36·2'W	X	102,103
Black Combe	Cumbr	SD1386	54°16·0'	3°19·7'W	H	96
Black Corner	W Susx	TQ2939	51°8·4'	0°9·0'W	T	187
Blackcorrie Burn	Highld	NN5399	57°3·8'	4°25·0'W	W	35
Black Corries	Highld	NN3657	56°40·8'	4°40·2'W	X	41
Black Corries Lodge	Highld	NN2955	56°39·6'	4°46·9'W	X	41
Black Country Museum	Dudley	SO9491	52°31·2'	2°4·9'W	X	139
Black Cove	D & G	NY4092	55°13·4'	2°56·2'W	X	79
Black Covert	Glos	SO9100	51°42·2'	2°7·4'W	F	163
Black Crag	Cumbr	NY1219	54°33·8'	3°21·2'W	X	89
Black Crag	Cumbr	NY2303	54°25·2'	3°10·8'W	X	89,90
Black Crag	Cumbr	NY2418	54°33·3'	3°10·1'W	X	89,90
Black Crag	Cumbr	NY2703	54°25·3'	3°7·1'W	X	89,90
Black Crag	Cumbr	NY3718	54°33·4'	2°58·0'W	X	90
Black Crag	Cumbr	NY3814	54°31·3'	2°57·1'W	X	90
Black Crag	Cumbr	NY4117	54°32·9'	2°54·3'W	X	90
Black Crag	Northum	NY8190	55°12·5'	2°17·5'W	H	80
Black Crag	N Yks	SE1059	54°1·9'	1°50·4'W	X	104
Black Crags	Cumbr	NY2508	54°28·0'	3°9·0'W	X	89,90
Black Crags	Cumbr	SD1383	54°14·4'	3°19·7'W	X	96
Black Crags	Northum	NY7382	55°8·1'	2°25·0'W	X	80
Black Crag Wham	N Yks	SE0959	54°1·9'	1°51·3'W	W	104
Black Craig	Aberd	NO4390	57°0·1'	2°55·8'W	H	44
Black Craig	Aberd	NO4394	57°2·3'	2°55·9'W	H	37,44
Black Craig	Aberd	NO4994	57°2·3'	2°50·0'W	H	37,44
Black Craig	Angus	NO7254	56°40·9'	2°27·0'W	X	54
Black Craig	Arg & Bt	NS1079	55°58·2'	5°2·2'W	X	63
Black Craig	Arg & Bt	NS1176	55°56·7'	5°1·2'W	H	63
Black Craig	D & G	NT1311	55°23·4'	3°22·0'W	X	78
Black Craig	D & G	NX4178	55°4·5'	4°29·0'W	X	77
Blackcraig	D & G	NX4464	54°57·0'	4°25·7'W	X	83
Black Craig	D & G	NX5095	55°13·8'	4°21·1'W	H	77
Blackcraig	D & G	NX6449	54°49·3'	4°6·6'W	H	83
Blackcraig	D & G	NX7180	55°6·1'	4°0·9'W	X	77
Blackcraig	E Ayr	NS6308	55°21·1'	4°9·2'W	X	71,77
Black Craig	Fife	NO3119	56°21·8'	3°6·6'W	X	59
Black Craig	Fife	NO3321	56°22·8'	3°4·7'W	H	53,59
Black Craig	Highld	NN5792	57°0·1'	4°20·8'W	X	35
Black Craig	Orkney	HY2211	58°59·0'	3°20·9'W	X	6
Black Craig	Orkney	HY5227	59°7·9'	2°49·8'W	X	5,6
Blackcraig	Pth & Kin	NO1152	56°39·3'	3°26·7'W	X	53
Black Craig	Scot Bord	NT5021	55°29·1'	2°47·0'W	X	73
Black Craig	Stir	NS6892	56°6·4'	4°6·9'W	X	57
Blackcraig	W Loth	NT0271	55°55·6'	3°33·7'W	X	65
Blackcraig Burn	Arg & Bt	NS1180	55°58·8'	5°1·3'W	W	63
Black Craig Burn	Arg & Bt	NS1275	55°56·1'	5°0·2'W	W	63
Blackcraig Castle	Pth & Kin	NO1053	56°39·9'	3°27·7'W	X	53
Blackcraig Forest	Pth & Kin	NO1051	56°38·8'	3°27·6'W	F	53
Blackcraig Hill	D & G	NS7401	55°17·5'	3°58·6'W	H	77
Blackcraig Hill	D & G	NX7082	55°7·2'	4°1·9'W	H	77
Blackcraig Hill	D & G	NX7098	55°15·8'	4°2·3'W	H	77
Blackcraig Hill	D & G	NX9288	55°10·7'	3°41·3'W	H	78
Blackcraig Hill	E Ayr	NS6406	55°20·0'	4°8·2'W	H	71,77
Blackcraig Hill	Pth & Kin	NO0952	56°39·3'	3°28·6'W	H	52,53
Black Craig of Dee or Cairnsmore	D & G	NX5875	55°3·2'	4°13·0'W	H	77
Blackcraigs	Angus	NO5380	56°54·8'	2°45·9'W	X	44
Black Craigs	D & G	NX9855	54°53·0'	3°35·0'W	X	84
Black Craigs	Pth & Kin	NO0810	56°16·7'	3°28·7'W	X	58
Blackcraigs	Pth & Kin	NO1627	56°25·9'	3°21·3'W	X	53,58
Black Crane Cleuch	Scot Bord	NY5892	55°13·5'	2°39·2'W	X	80
Black Crofts	Arg & Bt	NM9234	56°27·4'	5°22·1'W	T	49
Black Cross	Corn	SW9060	50°24·4'	4°57·0'W	T	200
Black Culphin	Aberd	NJ5959	57°37·4'	2°40·7'W	X	29
Blackdale Fm	N Yks	SE7083	54°10·3'	1°2·6'W	FM	100
Black Dam	Hants	SU6451	51°15·5'	1°4·6'W	T	185
Blackdam	Moray	NJ3160	57°37·7'	3°8·9'W	X	28
Blackdams	Aberd	NJ7502	57°6·8'	2°24·3'W	X	38
Black Darren	Heref	SO2929	51°57·5'	3°1·6'W	X	161
Blackdean Curr	Scot Bord	NT8422	55°29·7'	2°14·8'W	H	74
Blackden	Angus	NO5455	56°41·3'	2°44·6'W	X	54
Blackden Brook	Derby	SK1288	53°23·6'	1°48·8'W	W	110
Blackden Edge	Derby	SK1388	53°23·6'	1°47·9'W	X	110
Blackden Hall	Ches	SJ7870	53°13·8'	2°19·4'W	X	118
Blackden Heath	Ches	SJ7871	53°14·4'	2°19·4'W	T	118
Blackden Manor	Ches	SJ7869	53°13·3'	2°19·4'W	X	118
Blackden Moor	Derby	SK1188	53°23·6'	1°49·7'W	X	110
Blackden Rind	Derby	SK1188	53°23·6'	1°49·7'W	W	110
Black Devon	Clackm	NS9693	56°7·4'	3°39·9'W	W	58
Black Dike	E Yorks	SE7650	53°56·7'	0°50·1'W	W	105,106
Black Dike	E Yorks	SE8039	53°50·7'	0°46·6'W	W	106
Black Dike	Lincs	TF3693	53°25·2'	0°3·2'E	W	113
Black Dike or Gutter	N Yks	SE1674	54°9·9'	1°44·9'W	W	99
Black Dike Plantn	N Yks	SE6758	54°1·1'	0°58·2'W	F	105,106
Blackdikes	Angus	NO6164	56°46·2'	2°37·8'W	X	45
Black Ditch	D & G	NX4444	54°46·3'	4°25·1'W	W	83
Blackditch	Oxon	SP4105	51°44·8'	1°24·0'W	T	164
Black Ditch	Somer	ST3343	51°11·2'	2°57·1'W	W	182
Black Ditch	W Berks	SU4671	51°26·4'	1°19·9'W	A	174
Black Ditch	W Susx	TQ0504	50°49·8'	0°30·2'W	W	197
Blackditch Cross	Devon	SS7106	50°50·6'	3°49·6'W	X	191
Black Ditches	Suff	TL7672	52°19·3'	0°35·4'E	A	155
Black Ditches	Suff	TL7768	52°17·1'	0°36·1'E	A	155
Blackditch Fm	Oxon	SP7204	51°44·0'	0°57·0'W	FM	165
Black Ditch Level	Norf	TF5512	52°41·2'	0°18·0'E	X	131,143
Black Dod	S Lanak	NT0319	55°27·6'	3°31·6'W	H	78
Blackdog	Aberd	NJ9514	57°13·3'	2°4·5'W	T	38
Black Dog	Devon	SS8009	50°52·3'	3°41·9'W	T	191
Blackdog Burn	C of Aber	NJ9414	57°13·3'	2°5·5'W	W	38
Black Dog Fm	Wilts	ST8348	51°14·1'	2°14·2'W	FM	183
Black Dog Fm	Wilts	ST9955	51°17·9'	2°0·5'W	FM	173
Blackdog Links	Aberd	NJ9614	57°13·3'	2°3·5'W	X	38
Blackdog Rock	Aberd	NJ9613	57°12·7'	2°3·5'W	X	38
Black Dog Woods	Wilts	ST8249	51°14·6'	2°15·1'W	F	183
Blackdon Hill	E Susx	TQ5532	51°4·2'	0°13·1'E	X	188
Black Down	Corn	SX2259	50°24·5'	4°29·9'W	X	201
Black Down	Devon	ST0907	50°51·6'	3°17·2'W	F	192
Blackdown	Devon	SX5079	50°35·7'	4°6·8'W	X	191,201
Black Down	Devon	SX5182	50°37·4'	4°6·0'W	X	191,201

Black Down	Devon	SX5891	50°42·3'	4°0·3'W	X	191
Black Down	Devon	SX7953	50°22·1'	3°41·7'W	X	202
Black Down	Devon	SX8496	50°45·4'	3°38·3'W	X	191
Blackdown	Dorset	ST3903	50°49·6'	2°51·6'W	T	193
Black Down	Dorset	SY5890	50°42·7'	2°35·3'W	X	194
Black Down	Dorset	SY6087	50°41·1'	2°33·6'W	X	194
Black Down	Dorset	SZ0282	50°38·5'	1°57·9'W	X	195
Black Down	Hants	SU3506	50°51·4'	1°29·8'W	X	196
Blackdown	Hants	SU5322	50°59·9'	1°14·3'W	T	185
Black Down	Northum	NY9586	55°10·3'	2°4·3'W	X	81
Black Down	Somer	ST4757	51°18·8'	2°45·2'W	X	172,182
Blackdown	Warw	SP3168	52°18·8'	1°32·3'W	T	151
Blackdown	W Susx	SU9129	51°3·4'	0°41·7'W	X	186,197
Black Down	W Susx	SU9130	51°4·0'	0°41·7'W	X	186
Black Down Common	Devon	ST1116	50°56·4'	3°15·6'W	X	181,193
Blackdown Fm	Northnts	SP5155	52°11·7'	1°14·8'W	FM	151
Blackdown Fm	Northnts	SP6076	52°23·0'	1°6·7'W	FM	140
Blackdown Fm	W Susx	SU9228	51°2·9'	0°40·9'W	FM	186,197
Blackdown Hill	Dorset	ST3903	50°49·6'	2°51·6'W	H	193
Black Down Hills	Devon	ST1616	50°56·5'	3°11·4'W	H	181,193
Blackdown Manor	Warw	SP3069	52°19·3'	1°33·2'W	X	151
Blackdown Plantation	Devon	SX8097	50°45·8'	3°41·7'W	F	191
Blackdown Rings	Devon	SX7252	50°21·5'	3°47·6'W	A	202
Blackdowns	Glos	SP2038	52°2·6'	1°42·1'W	X	151
Blackdown Wood	Devon	SX4184	50°38·3'	4°14·5'W	F	201
Black Down Wood	Somer	ST0639	51°8·8'	3°20·2'W	F	181
Black Drove Fm	Lincs	TF1516	52°44·0'	0°17·4'W	FM	130
Black Dub	Cumbr	NY1044	54°47·2'	3°23·6'W	W	85
Black Dub	Cumbr	NY5352	54°51·9'	2°43·5'W	X	86
Blackdub	Stir	NS5796	56°8·7'	4°0·3'W	X	57
Black Dunghill	Devon	SX5877	50°34·8'	4°0·0'W	H	191
Black Dwarf's Cottage	Scot Bord	NT2137	55°37·5'	3°14·8'W	X	73
Blackdyke	Cumbr	NY1452	54°51·6'	3°20·0'W	T	85
Blackdyke	Cumbr	NY3762	54°57·2'	2°58·6'W	X	85
Blackdyke	E Ayr	NS5328	55°31·7'	4°19·3'W	X	70
Black Dyke	Highld	NH4752	57°32·2'	4°32·9'W	X	26
Black Dyke	Lincs	SK9995	53°26·8'	0°30·2'W	X	112
Blackdyke Fm	Norf	TL6988	52°28·1'	0°29·7'E	FM	143
Black Dyke Moor	N Yks	NZ7510	54°29·0'	0°50·1'W	X	94
Blackdykes	Angus	NO2454	56°40·6'	3°14·0'W	X	53
Blackdykes	E Loth	NT5883	56°2·5'	2°40·0'W	T	67
Black Edge	Derby	SK0676	53°17·1'	1°54·2'W	X	119
Black Edge	D & G	NY2092	55°13·2'	3°15·0'W	H	79
Black Edge	D & G	NY4288	55°11·2'	2°54·2'W	X	79
Black Edge	N Yks	SE0269	54°7·3'	1°57·7'W	X	98
Blackedge Fm	Derby	SK0776	53°17·1'	1°53·3'W	FM	119
Blackedge Point	Essex	TQ9391	51°35·3'	0°47·6'E	X	178
Black Eldrick	D & G	NX7354	54°52·1'	3°58·3'W	H	83,84
Blackend Spinney	Bucks	SP8625	51°55·2'	0°44·6'W	F	165
Blackenhall Fm	Derby	SK2516	52°44·7'	1°37·4'W	FM	128
Blacker	Barns	SE3309	53°34·8'	1°29·7'W	T	110,111
Blacker Hill	Barns	SE3602	53°31·0'	1°27·0'W	T	110,111
Blackerne	D & G	NX7864	54°57·6'	3°53·9'W	X	84
Blacker's Hill	Somer	ST6350	51°15·1'	2°31·4'W	X	183
Blackers Hole	Dorset	SZ0076	50°35·3'	1°59·6'W	X	195
Blackerstone	Scot Bord	NT7761	55°50·8'	2°21·6'W	X	67
Blackerton	Devon	SS8524	51°0·5'	3°38·0'W	X	181
Black Esk	D & G	NY2193	55°13·7'	3°14·1'W	W	79
Black Esk Reservoir	D & G	NY2096	55°15·4'	3°15·1'W	W	79
Blacket Ho	D & G	NY2474	55°3·5'	3°11·0'W	X	85
Blacketlees	D & G	NY1868	55°0·2'	3°16·5'W	X	85
Blacketts	Kent	TQ9465	51°21·3'	0°47·6'E	T	178
Blacketty Water	Inverc	NS3167	55°52·3'	4°41·6'W	W	63
Blacketyside Fm	Fife	NO3802	56°12·6'	2°59·5'W	FM	59
Blackfan Wood	Herts	TL3107	51°45·0'	0°5·7'W	F	166
Black Farland	Arg & Bt	NR9872	55°54·2'	5°13·4'W	X	62
Blackfauldhead	E Ayr	NS5122	55°28·4'	4°21·0'W	X	70
Blackfaulds	Clackm	NS9095	56°8·4'	3°45·8'W	X	58
Blackfaulds	Fife	NO4311	56°17·5'	2°54·8'W	X	59
Blackfaulds	Pth & Kin	NO1431	56°28·1'	3°23·3'W	X	53
Blackfaulds	W Loth	NS9172	55°56·0'	3°44·2'W	X	65
Black Fell	Cumbr	NY3402	54°24·8'	3°0·6'W	H	90
Black Fell	Cumbr	NY6444	54°47·6'	2°33·2'W	H	86
Black Fell	D & G	NT0511	55°23·3'	3°29·5'W	H	78
Black Fell	Lancs	SD5460	54°2·3'	2°41·7'W	X	97
Black Fell	N Ayr	NS2666	55°51·6'	4°46·4'W	X	63
Black Fell	Northum	NY6093	55°14·0'	2°37·3'W	H	80
Black Fell	Northum	NY7073	55°3·3'	2°27·7'W	X	86,87
Black Fell	S Ayr	NS3501	55°16·8'	4°35·4'W	X	77
Blackfell	Sund	NZ2956	54°54·1'	1°32·4'W	T	88
Blackfell Crags	N Yks	SE0074	54°10·0'	1°59·6'W	X	98
Black Fell Moss	Cumbr	SD8099	54°23·4'	2°18·1'W	X	98
Blackfen	Bexley	TQ4574	51°27·0'	0°5·6'E	T	177
Black Fen	Leeds	SE4140	53°51·5'	1°22·2'W	F	105
Blackfield	Hants	SU4401	50°48·6'	1°22·1'W	T	196
Black Field	Wilts	SU2169	51°25·4'	1°41·5'W	X	174
Blackfield Green	Worcs	SO7855	52°11·8'	2°18·9'W	X	150
Blackfield Loch	N Ayr	NS2167	55°52·0'	4°51·2'W	W	63
Blackfields Fm	Bucks	SP7636	52°1·3'	0°53·1'W	FM	152
Black Flatts Fm	Staffs	SK0619	52°46·4'	1°54·3'W	FM	128
Blackfleet Broad	Norf	TG4421	52°44·1'	1°37·3'E	W	134
Blackfold	Highld	NH5840	57°26·0'	4°21·5'W	T	26
Blackfold	Moray	NJ3955	57°35·1'	3°0·8'W	X	28
Blackfolds	Aberd	NJ5940	57°27·2'	2°40·5'W	X	29
Blackfolds	Moray	NJ2643	57°28·5'	3°13·6'W	X	28
Black Force	Cumbr	SD6499	54°23·4'	2°32·8'W	W	97
Blackford	Cumbr	NY3962	54°57·2'	2°56·7'W	T	85
Blackford	D & G	NX8167	54°59·3'	3°51·2'W	X	84
Blackford	D & G	NY1380	55°6·2'	3°21·4'W	T	78
Blackford	Highld	NH7848	57°30·6'	4°1·7'W	X	27
Blackford	Pth & Kin	NN8908	56°15·4'	3°47·1'W	T	58
Blackford	Shrops	SO2598	52°34·7'	3°6·0'W	X	137
Blackford	Shrops	SO5982	52°26·3'	2°35·8'W	T	137,138
Blackford	Somer	SS9245	51°11·9'	3°32·4'W	T	181
Blackford	Somer	ST4147	51°13·4'	2°50·3'W	T	182
Blackford	Somer	ST6526	51°2·2'	2°29·6'W	T	183
Blackford	W Dunb	NS4585	56°2·2'	4°28·8'W	X	57
Blackford Br	Notts	SK7544	52°59·5'	0°52·6'W	X	129
Blackford Bridge	Bury	SD8007	53°33·8'	2°17·7'W	T	109
Blackford Burn	D & G	NX7851	54°50·6'	3°53·6'W	W	84

Blackfordby	Leic	SK3217	52°45·2'	1°31·1'W	T	128
Blackfordby Ho	Leic	SK3218	52°45·8'	1°31·1'W	X	128
Blackford Fm	E Susx	TQ6014	50°54·4'	0°16·9'E	FM	199
Blackford Fm	Swin	SU1695	51°39·4'	1°45·7'W	FM	163
Blackford Hall	Norf	TG2501	52°33·8'	1°19·6'E	X	134
Blackford Hill	C of Edin	NT2570	55°55·3'	3°11·6'W	H	66
Blackford Mill Fm	Warw	SP1565	52°17·2'	1°46·4'W	FM	151
Blackford Moor	Somer	ST3948	51°13·9'	2°52·0'W	X	182
Blackfords	Staffs	SJ9811	52°42·0'	2°1·4'W	T	127
Black Forest Lodge	Devon	SX9481	50°37·4'	3°29·5'W	X	192
Blackfoss Beck	E Yorks	SE7247	53°55·1'	0°53·8'W	W	105,106
Blackfriars	E Susx	TQ7615	50°54·7'	0°30·6'E	X	199
Blackfriars	Glos	SO8218	51°51·9'	2°15·3'W	X	162
Blackfriars Br	Lam	TQ3180	51°30·5'	0°6·3'W	X	176,177
Black Gairy	D & G	NX4281	55°6·1'	4°28·2'W	X	77
Black Gairy	D & G	NX4285	55°8·3'	4°28·3'W	X	77
Black Gairy	D & G	NX4583	55°7·3'	4°25·4'W	X	77
Black Gairy Hill	D & G	NX4174	55°2·4'	4°28·9'W	X	77
Blackgang	I of W	SZ4876	50°35·1'	1°18·9'W	T	196
Blackgang Chine	I of W	SZ4876	50°35·1'	1°18·9'W	X	196
Blackgannoch	D & G	NS7517	55°26·1'	3°58·1'W	X	71,78
Blackgannoch Cleuch	D & G	NS7716	55°25·6'	3°56·2'W	X	71,78
Black Garpel	E Ayr	NX4490	55°11·0'	4°26·6'W	W	77
Blackgate	Angus	NO4852	56°39·7'	2°50·5'W	X	54
Black Gate	Powys	SO1085	52°27·6'	3°19·1'W	X	136
Blackgate Rig	Scot Bord	NY4490	55°12·3'	2°52·4'W	X	79
Black Geo	Orkney	ND4784	58°44·7'	2°54·5'W	X	7
Black Geo	Orkney	ND5298	58°52·3'	2°49·5'W	X	6,7
Black Geo	Shetld	HU3826	60°1·3'	1°18·6'W	X	4
Black Goit	Aberd	NO6077	56°53·2'	2°38·9'W	X	45
Black Grain	D & G	NY0470	55°1·2'	3°29·7'W	W	84
Black Grain	D & G	NY4186	55°10·1'	2°55·1'W	W	79
Black Grain	Scot Bord	NT2214	55°25·1'	3°13·5'W	W	79
Black Grain	Scot Bord	NY4586	55°10·2'	2°51·4'W	W	79
Black Grain Plantn	D & G	NY0469	55°0·6'	3°29·6'W	F	84
Blackgrain Rig	Scot Bord	NT3328	55°32·7'	3°3·3'W	H	73
Blackgrain Shoulder	D & G	NS9103	55°18·8'	3°42·6'W	X	78
Blackgraves Copse	Shrops	SO7478	52°24·2'	2°22·5'W	F	138
Blackgreaves Fm	Warw	SP1994	52°32·8'	1°42·8'W	FM	139
Blackgreves Fm	Worcs	SP0675	52°22·6'	1°54·3'W	FM	139
Blackground Plantn	Norf	TF8219	52°44·5'	0°42·2'E	F	132
Black Grounds	Essex	TQ9686	51°32·6'	0°50·0'E	X	178
Blackground, The	Norf	TF7728	52°49·5'	0°38·0'E	F	132
Blackgrove Farm Ho	Bucks	SP7619	51°52·1'	0°53·4'W	X	165
Blackgrove Fm	Surrey	TQ3746	51°12·0'	0°2·0'W	FM	187
Blackguard Sand	Norf	TF5934	52°53·0'	0°22·2'E	X	131
Black Gutter Bottom	Hants	SU2016	50°56·8'	1°42·5'W	X	184
Black Gutter or Dike	N Yks	SE1674	54°9·9'	1°44·9'W	W	99
Blackhafields Plantn	Beds	TL0037	52°1·6'	0°32·2'W	F	153
Black Hag	Scot Bord	NT8623	55°30·3'	2°12·9'W	H	74
Blackhaggs Rigg	Northum	NT8724	55°30·8'	2°11·9'W	H	74
Black Hags	Durham	NY9045	54°48·2'	2°8·9'W	X	87
Black Hales Fm	Sol	SP2574	52°22·0'	1°37·6'W	FM	140
Blackhall	Aberd	NO6795	57°3·0'	2°32·2'W	X	38,45
Blackhall	Angus	NO5462	56°45·1'	2°44·7'W	X	44
Blackhall	Cambs	TL3494	52°31·9'	0°1·1'W	X	142
Blackhall	C of Aber	NJ7901	57°6·2'	2°20·3'W	X	38
Blackhall	C of Edin	NT2174	55°57·4'	3°15·5'W	T	66
Black Hall	Cumbr	NY2301	54°24·2'	3°10·8'W	X	89,90
Black Hall	Devon	SX7157	50°24·2'	3°48·5'W	X	202
Blackhall	D & G	NX7871	55°1·4'	3°54·1'W	X	84
Blackhall	D & G	NY3996	55°15·5'	2°57·2'W	X	79
Black Hall	Durham	NZ1334	54°42·3'	1°47·5'W	X	92
Black Hall	Essex	TL5818	51°50·5'	0°18·0'E	X	167
Blackhall	Fife	NT0984	56°2·7'	3°27·2'W	X	65
Black Hall	Heref	SO4662	52°15·5'	2°47·1'W	X	137,138,148
Blackhall	Herts	TL4331	51°57·8'	0°5·3'E	X	167
Blackhall	Kent	TQ5455	51°16·6'	0°12·9'E	X	188
Blackhall	Moray	NJ2748	57°31·2'	3°12·7'W	X	28
Black Hall	Northum	NY9358	54°55·2'	2°6·1'W	X	87
Blackhall	Orkney	HY4612	58°59·8'	2°55·9'W	X	6
Black Hall	Powys	SO1588	52°29·2'	3°14·7'W	X	136
Blackhall	Renf	NS4963	55°50·5'	4°24·3'W	T	64
Black Hall	Shrops	SO2476	52°22·8'	3°6·6'W	X	137,148
Blackhall	S Lanak	NS8439	55°38·1'	3°50·1'W	X	71,72
Black Hall	V of Glam	SS9074	51°27·5'	3°34·6'W	X	170
Blackhall	W Loth	NT0562	55°50·8'	3°30·6'W	X	65
Blackhall Colliery	Durham	NZ4539	54°44·9'	1°17·6'W	T	93
Blackhall Cott	Glos	ST6798	51°41·0'	2°28·2'W	X	162
Blackhall Fm	Devon	SX6594	50°44·0'	3°54·4'W	FM	191
Black Hall Fm	Norf	TM1296	52°31·5'	1°7·9'E	FM	144
Blackhall Fm	Pth & Kin	NO1456	56°41·5'	3°23·8'W	FM	53
Blackhall Forest	Aberd	NO6695	57°2·9'	2°33·2'W	F	38,45
Blackhall Hill	D & G	NY4095	55°15·0'	2°56·2'W	H	79
Blackhall Hill	Scot Bord	NT7811	55°23·8'	2°20·4'W	H	80
Blackhall Mill	Ghead	NZ1156	54°54·2'	1°49·3'W	T	88
Blackhall Park	Cumbr	NY4149	54°50·2'	2°54·7'W	X	85
Blackhall Plantations	Northum	NY8662	54°57·4'	2°12·7'W	F	87
Blackhall Rocks	Durham	NZ4638	54°44·3'	1°16·7'W	T	93
Black Halls	Durham	NZ4738	54°44·3'	1°15·8'W	X	93
Black Halls	Northum	NT7910	55°23·3'	2°19·5'W	X	80
Blackhalls	Northum	NY9785	55°9·8'	2°2·4'W	X	81
Blackhall Wood	Cumbr	NY3851	54°51·2'	2°57·5'W	X	85
Black Ham	Cambs	TL2191	52°30·4'	0°12·6'W	W	142
Blackham	E Susx	TQ5039	51°8·1'	0°9·0'E	T	188
Blackhamar	Orkney	HY3831	59°9·9'	3°4·6'W	X	6
Black Hambleton	N Yks	SE4894	54°20·6'	1°15·3'W	H	100
Blackham Court	E Susx	TQ5037	51°7·0'	0°9·0'E	X	188
Black Hameldon	Lancs	SD9129	53°45·7'	2°7·8'W	H	103
Black Hamilton	Durham	NZ1736	54°43·4'	1°43·7'W	X	92
Blackhamsley Ho	Hants	SU2800	50°48·2'	1°35·8'W	X	195
Black Harbour	Arg & Bt	NR9072	55°54·0'	5°21·1'W	X	62
Blackhaugh	Angus	NO4671	56°49·7'	2°52·6'W	X	44
Blackhaugh	Pth & Kin	NO1040	56°32·9'	3°27·4'W	X	53
Blackhaugh	Scot Bord	NT4238	55°38·2'	2°54·8'W	X	73
Black Hayes	Wrekin	SJ6508	52°40·4'	2°30·7'W	F	127
Blackhayes Fm	Devon	ST2306	50°51·1'	3°5·3'W	FM	192,193
Blackhazel Beck	Cumbr	NY3130	54°39·9'	3°3·8'W	W	90
Black Head	Corn	SW7716	50°0·4'	5°6·4'W	X	204
Black Head	Corn	SX0347	50°17·6'	4°45·6'W	X	204

Blackhead	Devon	SS7450	51°14·4'	3°47·9'W	X	180
Black Head	Devon	SY0882	50°38·1'	3°17·7'W	X	192
Black Head	D & G	NW9856	54°51·7'	5°8·4'W	X	82
Black Head	Dorset	SY7281	50°37·9'	2°23·4'W	X	194
Black Head	I of M	SC1865	54°3·2'	4°46·4'W	H	95
Black Head	Torbay	SX9464	50°28·2'	3°29·2'W	X	202
Blackhead of Breigeo	Shetld	HU2179	60°29·9'	1°36·6'W	X	3
Black Heath	Dorset	SY8993	50°44·4'	2°9·0'W	X	195
Blackheath	Essex	TM0021	51°51·3'	0°54·7'E	T	168
Blackheath	Highld	ND0768	58°35·7'	3°35·5'W	X	11,12
Blackheath	Lew	TQ3976	51°28·2'	0°0·5'E	T	177
Blackheath	Sand	SO9786	52°28·6'	2°2·3'W	T	139
Black Heath	Staffs	SK0449	53°2·5'	1°56·0'W	X	119
Black Heath	Suff	TM4257	52°9·7'	1°32·7'E	X	156
Blackheath	Suff	TM4275	52°19·4'	1°33·5'E	X	156
Blackheath	Surrey	TQ0346	51°12·5'	0°31·1'W	X	186
Black Heath	Wilts	SU0651	51°15·7'	1°54·5'W	X	184
Blackheath Clump	Oxon	SP2515	51°50·2'	1°37·8'W	F	163
Blackheath Covert	Staffs	SJ9524	52°49·0'	2°4·0'W	F	127
Blackheath Down	Hants	SU0717	50°57·4'	1°53·6'W	X	184
Blackheath Fm	Devon	SX9485	50°39·5'	3°29·6'W	FM	192
Blackheath Park	Gren	TQ4075	51°27·6'	0°1·3'E	T	177
Black Heath Wood	Suff	TM4158	52°10·3'	1°31·9'E	F	156
Black Heddon	Northum	NU0340	55°39·5'	1°56·7'W	X	75
Black Heddon	Northum	NZ0776	55°5·0'	1°53·0'W	T	88
Blackheddon Br	Northum	NZ0874	55°3·9'	1°52·1'W	X	88
Blackheddon Burn	Northum	NZ0675	55°4·4'	1°53·9'W	W	87
Blackheddon Burn	Northum	NZ0775	55°4·4'	1°53·0'W	W	88
Black Hedley	Northum	NZ0551	54°51·5'	1°54·9'W	X	87
Black Height	Scot Bord	NY4487	55°10·7'	2°52·3'W	H	79
Black Hey Fm	Leeds	SE2032	53°47·3'	1°41·4'W	FM	104
Blackhill	Aberd	NJ4642	57°28·2'	2°53·6'W	X	28,29
Black Hill	Aberd	NJ5219	57°15·8'	2°47·3'W	H	37
Black Hill	Aberd	NJ6208	57°9·9'	2°37·2'W	H	37
Black Hill	Aberd	NJ6321	57°16·9'	2°36·4'W	H	37
Black Hill	Aberd	NJ6711	57°11·6'	2°32·3'W	H	37
Blackhill	Aberd	NK0431	57°22·4'	1°55·6'W	X	30
Blackhill	Aberd	NK0755	57°35·4'	1°52·5'W	T	30
Black Hill	Aberd	NO3182	56°55·7'	3°7·6'W	H	44
Black Hill	Aberd	NO7078	56°53·8'	2°29·1'W	X	45
Black Hill	Angus	NO2056	56°41·6'	3°17·9'W	H	53
Blackhill	Angus	NO3248	56°37·4'	3°6·0'W	X	53
Black Hill	Angus	NO4063	56°45·5'	2°58·4'W	H	44
Black Hill	Angus	NO4575	56°52·0'	2°53·7'W	H	44
Black Hill	Angus	NO5471	56°49·9'	2°44·8'W	H	44
Black Hill	Arg & Bt	NR6916	55°23·3'	5°38·4'W	X	68
Black Hill	Brad	SE0441	53°52·2'	1°55·9'W	T	104
Black Hill	Ches	SJ9882	53°20·3'	2°1·4'W	H	109
Blackhill	C of Glas	NS5770	55°54·4'	4°16·8'W	X	64
Black Hill	Cumbr	NY5784	55°9·2'	2°40·1'W	H	80
Black Hill	Cumbr	NY7944	54°47·7'	2°19·2'W	X	86,87
Black Hill	Derby	SK2764	53°10·6'	1°35·4'W	X	119
Black Hill	Devon	SX6084	50°38·6'	3°58·4'W	H	191
Black Hill	Devon	SX7679	50°36·1'	3°44·8'W	H	191
Black Hill	Devon	SY0285	50°39·6'	3°22·8'W	H	192
Black Hill	D & G	NS7107	55°20·7'	4°1·6'W	H	71,77
Black Hill	D & G	NS7714	55°24·5'	3°56·1'W	H	71,78
Black Hill	D & G	NS8612	55°23·6'	3°47·6'W	H	71,78
Black Hill	D & G	NS8905	55°19·8'	3°44·6'W	H	71,78
Black Hill	D & G	NT1500	55°17·5'	3°19·9'W	H	79
Blackhill	D & G	NX2058	54°53·3'	4°48·0'W	X	82
Black Hill	D & G	NX6363	54°56·8'	4°7·9'W	H	83
Black Hill	D & G	NX6898	55°15·8'	4°4·2'W	X	77
Blackhill	D & G	NX6946	54°47·8'	4°1·8'W	X	83,84
Black Hill	Dorset	ST6700	50°48·1'	2°27·7'W	X	194
Black Hill	Dorset	SY7486	50°40·6'	2°21·7'W	X	194
Black Hill	Dorset	SY8394	50°45·0'	2°14·1'W	X	194
Black Hill	Dorset	SY9491	50°43·3'	2°4·7'W	X	195
Black Hill	Durham	NY8741	54°46·1'	2°11·7'W	H	87
Black Hill	Durham	NY9019	54°34·2'	2°8·9'W	H	91,92
Black Hill	Durham	NY9032	54°41·2'	2°8·9'W	X	91,92
Black Hill	Durham	NY9135	54°42·8'	2°8·0'W	H	91,92
Black Hill	Durham	NY9846	54°48·8'	2°1·4'W	X	87
Black Hill	Durham	NZ0330	54°40·1'	1°56·8'W	H	92
Blackhill	Durham	NZ0951	54°51·5'	1°51·2'W	T	88
Black Hill	E Ayr	NS5413	55°23·6'	4°17·9'W	X	70
Black Hill	E Ayr	NS5843	55°39·8'	4°15·0'W	X	71
Black Hill	E Ayr	NS6204	55°18·9'	4°10·0'W	H	77
Black Hill	E Ayr	NS6610	55°22·2'	4°6·4'W	X	71
Black Hill	E Ayr	NS6918	55°26·6'	4°3·8'W	H	71
Black Hill	E Ayr	NS7029	55°32·5'	4°3·2'W	H	71
Black Hill	E Renf	NS4851	55°44·0'	4°24·8'W	X	64
Blackhill	Falk	NS8077	55°58·5'	3°54·9'W	X	65
Black Hill	Fife	NO2207	56°15·2'	3°15·1'W	X	58
Black Hill	Hants	SU1022	51°0·1'	1°51·1'W	X	184
Blackhill	Hants	SU3018	50°57·9'	1°34·0'W	T	185
Black Hill	Heref	SO2734	52°0·2'	3°3·4'W	H	161
Black Hill	Highld	ND3057	58°30·0'	3°11·6'W	X	11,12
Black Hill	Highld	ND3868	58°36·0'	3°3·5'W	X	12
Blackhill	Highld	NG3450	57°28·0'	6°25·7'W	T	23
Black Hill	Highld	NH5763	57°38·3'	4°23·3'W	X	21
Blackhill	Highld	NH5763	57°38·3'	4°23·3'W	X	21
Blackhill	Highld	NH7148	57°30·5'	4°8·7'W	X	27
Blackhill	Highld	NH8273	57°44·1'	3°58·4'W	X	21
Blackhill	I of M	SC2871	54°6·6'	4°37·5'W	X	95
Black Hill	Kirk	SE0704	53°32·2'	1°53·3'W	H	110
Black Hill	Lancs	SD7561	54°2·9'	2°22·5'W	X	98
Black Hill	Lancs	SD7660	54°2·4'	2°21·6'W	X	98
Black Hill	Leeds	SE2742	53°52·7'	1°34·9'W	X	104
Black Hill	Leic	SK5013	52°43·0'	1°15·2'W	X	129
Black Hill	Lincs	TF3373	53°14·5'	0°0·0'W	X	122
Black Hill	Midlo	NT1863	55°51·4'	3°18·2'W	H	65,66
Black Hill	Moray	NJ3532	57°22·7'	3°4·4'W	H	37
Black Hill	Moray	NJ4030	57°21·7'	2°59·4'W	H	37
Black Hill	Moray	NJ4659	57°37·3'	2°53·8'W	H	28,29
Black Hill	Moray	NJ4757	57°36·3'	2°52·8'W	X	28,29
Black Hill	N Ayr	NS2153	55°44·5'	4°50·7'W	X	63
Black Hill	N Lanak	NS6781	56°0·5'	4°7·5'W	X	64
Blackhill	N Lanak	NS8172	55°55·8'	3°53·8'W	X	65
Black Hill	N Lanak	NS8265	55°52·1'	3°52·7'W	H	65
Black Hill	Northum	NY6552	54°51·9'	2°32·3'W	H	86
Black Hill	Northum	NY6747	54°49·3'	2°30·4'W	X	86,87
Black Hill	Northum	NY8052	54°52·0'	2°18·3'W	H	86,87
Black Hill	Northum	NY8195	55°15·2'	2°17·5'W	H	80
Black Hill	Northum	NY9097	55°16·3'	2°9·0'W	X	80
Black Hill	Northum	NY9297	55°16·3'	2°7·1'W	X	80
Black Hill	Northum	NY9767	55°0·1'	2°2·4'W	X	87
Blackhill	Northum	NZ0077	55°5·5'	1°59·6'W	X	87
Black Hill	Notts	SK6160	53°8·3'	1°4·9'W	F	120
Black Hill	N Som	ST4173	51°27·4'	2°50·6'W	X	171,172
Black Hill	N Yks	NY8104	54°26·1'	2°17·2'W	X	91,92
Black Hill	N Yks	SD8498	54°22·9'	2°14·4'W	X	98
Black Hill	N Yks	SD8666	54°5·6'	2°12·4'W	H	98
Black Hill	N Yks	SD9199	54°23·4'	2°7·9'W	X	98
Black Hill	N Yks	SE0862	54°3·5'	1°52·2'W	X	99
Black Hill	N Yks	SE1155	53°59·7'	1°49·5'W	X	104
Black Hill	N Yks	SE2170	54°7·8'	1°40·3'W	X	99
Blackhill	Orkney	HY4211	58°59·2'	3°0·1'W	X	6
Black Hill	Pemb	SM9612	51°46·4'	4°57·0'W	X	157,158
Black Hill	Powys	SO1752	52°9·8'	3°12·4'W	H	148
Black Hill	Powys	SO2469	52°19·1'	3°6·5'W	H	137,148
Blackhill	Pth & Kin	NN8752	56°39·0'	3°50·1'W	X	52
Black Hill	Pth & Kin	NN9604	56°13·3'	3°40·2'W	H	58
Black Hill	Pth & Kin	NN9909	56°16·0'	3°37·4'W	H	58
Blackhill	Pth & Kin	NO0331	56°27·9'	3°34·0'W	X	52,53
Black Hill	Pth & Kin	NO0607	56°15·0'	3°30·6'W	X	58
Black Hill	Pth & Kin	NO0744	56°35·0'	3°30·4'W	X	52,53
Black Hill	Pth & Kin	NO1671	56°49·6'	3°22·1'W	H	43
Black Hill	Pth & Kin	NO2231	56°28·1'	3°15·5'W	H	53
Black Hill	S Ayr	NS4104	55°18·5'	4°29·9'W	H	77
Black Hill	S Ayr	NX3796	55°14·1'	4°33·4'W	X	77
Black Hill	Scot Bord	NT5837	55°37·7'	2°39·6'W	H	73,74
Black Hill	Scot Bord	NT6006	55°21·0'	2°37·4'W	H	80
Black Hill	Scot Bord	NT6459	55°49·6'	2°34·0'W	X	67,74
Black Hill	Scot Bord	NT7356	55°48·0'	2°25·4'W	H	67,74
Black Hill	Scot Bord	NT8323	55°30·3'	2°15·7'W	H	74
Blackhill	Scot Bord	NT8863	55°51·9'	2°11·1'W	X	67
Black Hill	Shetld	HU3166	60°22·9'	1°25·8'W	H	3
Black Hill	Shetld	HU3744	60°11·0'	1°19·5'W	H	4
Black Hill	Shrops	SO3278	52°24·0'	2°59·6'W	H	137,148
Black Hill	S Lanak	NS7633	55°34·7'	3°57·6'W	H	71
Black Hill	S Lanak	NS7839	55°38·0'	3°55·8'W	H	71
Blackhill	S Lanak	NS8244	55°40·8'	3°52·2'W	X	71,72
Black Hill	S Lanak	NS8919	55°27·4'	3°44·9'W	X	71,78
Black Hill	S Lanak	NS9024	55°30·1'	3°44·1'W	H	71,72
Black Hill	S Lanak	NS9136	55°36·6'	3°43·4'W	H	71,72
Black Hill	S Lanak	NS9155	55°46·8'	3°43·8'W	X	65,72
Blackhill	S Lanak	NS9651	55°44·7'	3°39·0'W	X	65,72
Black Hill	Somer	SS8144	51°11·2'	3°41·8'W	X	181
Black Hill	Somer	SS9840	51°9·2'	3°27·1'W	X	181
Black Hill	Somer	ST1438	51°8·3'	3°13·4'W	X	181
Black Hill	Stir	NN8303	56°12·6'	3°52·7'W	H	57
Black Hill	Suff	TL8874	52°20·1'	0°46·0'E	X	144
Black Hill	Wakf	SE3519	53°40·2'	1°27·8'W	H	110,111
Black Hill	Warw	SP2359	52°14·0'	1°39·4'W	X	151
Blackhill	W Loth	NS9661	55°50·1'	3°39·2'W	X	65
Black Hill	W Loth	NT0758	55°48·6'	3°28·6'W	X	65,72
Black Hill Clump	Notts	SK6079	53°18·5'	1°5·6'W	F	120
Blackhill Croft	D & G	NX3662	54°55·8'	4°33·1'W	X	83
Black Hill End	Derby	SE0701	53°30·6'	1°53·3'W	X	110
Blackhill Fm	Aberd	NK0843	57°28·9'	1°51·5'W	FM	30
Blackhill Fm	Ches	SJ7477	53°17·6'	2°23·0'W	FM	118
Blackhill Fm	Heref	SO2932	51°59·2'	3°1·6'W	FM	161
Black Hill Fm	Lancs	SD4345	53°54·1'	2°51·6'W	FM	102
Blackhill Fm	Leeds	SE2742	53°52·7'	1°34·9'W	FM	104
Blackhill Fm	Northum	NY8876	55°4·9'	2°10·9'W	FM	87
Blackhill Fm	Northum	NY9061	54°56·9'	2°8·9'W	FM	87
Blackhill Fm	N Yks	NZ1707	54°27·7'	1°43·8'W	FM	92
Black Hill Fm	Warw	SP2359	52°14·0'	1°39·4'W	FM	151
Blackhill Ho	N Yks	SE2076	54°11·0'	1°41·2'W	X	99
Blackhillie	Aberd	NJ9325	57°19·2'	2°6·5'W	X	38
Blackhill Moss	D & G	NS9101	55°17·7'	3°42·6'W	X	78
Black Hill Moss	N Yks	SD8494	54°20·7'	2°14·3'W	X	98
Black Hillock	Aberd	NJ2402	57°6·4'	3°14·8'W	H	36
Blackhillock	Aberd	NJ3915	57°13·6'	3°0·2'W	X	37
Black Hillock	Aberd	NJ5623	57°18·0'	2°43·4'W	H	37
Blackhillock	Aberd	NJ8142	57°28·3'	2°18·5'W	X	29,30
Blackhillock	Aberd	NJ8956	57°35·9'	2°10·6'W	X	30
Blackhillock	Moray	NJ0853	57°33·7'	3°31·8'W	X	27
Blackhillock	Moray	NJ0858	57°36·4'	3°31·9'W	X	27
Blackhillock	Moray	NJ2044	57°29·0'	3°19·6'W	X	28
Blackhillock	Moray	NJ3342	57°28·1'	3°6·6'W	X	28
Black Hillock	Moray	NJ3729	57°21·1'	3°2·4'W	X	37
Blackhillock	Moray	NJ4348	57°31·4'	2°56·6'W	T	28
Blackhillocks	Moray	NJ8264	57°40·2'	2°17·6'W	X	29,30
Black Hill of Garleffin	S Ayr	NX3499	55°15·7'	4°36·3'W	H	76
Black Hill of Kippen	Pth & Kin	NO0011	56°17·1'	3°36·5'W	X	58
Black Hill of Knockgardner	S Ayr	NS3502	55°17·3'	4°35·5'W	H	77
Black Hill of Mark	Aberd	NO3281	56°55·2'	3°6·6'W	H	44
Black Hill of Orchars	D & G	NX5570	55°0·5'	4°15·6'W	X	77
Black Hill or Gawky Hill	S Lanak	NT0432	55°34·6'	3°30·9'W	H	72
Blackhill Plantation	Pth & Kin	NT0897	56°9·7'	3°28·4'W	F	58
Black Hill (Roman Signal Station)	Pth & Kin	NO1738	56°31·9'	3°20·5'W	R	53
Blackhills	Aberd	NJ5107	57°9·3'	2°48·1'W	X	37
Blackhills	Aberd	NJ6157	57°36·3'	2°38·7'W	X	29
Blackhills	Aberd	NJ9261	57°38·6'	2°7·6'W	X	30
Blackhills	Aberd	NK0156	57°35·9'	1°58·5'W	X	30
Blackhills	Aberd	NK0452	57°33·7'	1°55·5'W	X	30
Blackhills	Aberd	NK1139	57°26·7'	1°48·5'W	X	30
Blackhills	Aberd	NO8990	57°0·3'	2°10·4'W	X	38,45
Blackhills	Angus	NO5380	56°54·8'	2°45·9'W	X	44
Black Hills	Brad	SE0937	53°50·0'	1°51·4'W	X	104
Blackhills	D & G	NX7574	55°2·9'	3°57·0'W	X	84
Blackhills	D & G	NY2168	55°0·3'	3°13·7'W	X	85
Blackhills	Highld	NH9454	57°34·1'	3°45·9'W	X	27
Blackhills	Moray	NJ0654	57°34·2'	3°33·8'W	X	27
Blackhills	Moray	NJ1553	57°33·8'	3°24·8'W	X	28
Blackhills	Moray	NJ2758	57°36·6'	3°12·8'W	X	28
Black Hills	Notts	SK5553	53°4·5'	1°10·3'W	F	120
Blackhills	Pth & Kin	NO2047	56°36·7'	3°17·8'W	X	53
Blackhills	Swan	SS5891	51°36·2'	4°2·6'W	T	159
Black Hill (Settlement)	Dorset	ST6700	50°48·1'	2°27·7'W	A	194
Blackhills Fm	Lincs	TF0983	53°20·2'	0°21·4'W	FM	121
Black Hills Fm	Notts	SK6366	53°11·5'	1°3·0'W	FM	120
Blackhills Ho	Moray	NJ2758	57°36·6'	3°12·8'W	X	28
Blackhills of Cairnrobin	Aberd	NO9399	57°5·2'	2°6·5'W	X	38,45
Black Hill, The	Shetld	HU4937	60°7·1'	1°6·6'W	H	4
Black Hill Top Fm	Durham	NZ0930	54°40·1'	1°51·2'W	FM	92
Black Hill (Tumulus)	Suff	TL8874	52°20·1'	0°46·0'E	A	144
Blackhill Wood	Moray	NJ4049	57°31·9'	2°59·7'W	F	28
Blackhill Wood	N Yks	SE7088	54°17·2'	0°55·1'W	F	94,100
Black Ho	Cambs	TL4959	52°12·8'	0°11·3'E	X	154
Black Ho	Cumbr	NY2354	54°52·7'	3°11·6'W	X	85
Black Ho	Cumbr	NY4674	55°3·7'	2°50·3'W	X	86
Black Ho	Cumbr	NY7145	54°48·2'	2°26·6'W	X	86,87
Black Ho	E Loth	NT5073	55°57·1'	2°47·6'W	X	66
Black Ho	Lancs	SD7254	53°59·1'	2°25·2'W	X	103
Black Ho	N Eil	NB3149	58°21·1'	6°35·4'W	X	8
Black Ho	Northum	NY9362	54°57·4'	2°6·1'W	X	87
Black Ho	N Yks	SE2462	54°3·4'	1°37·6'W	X	99
Blackhoe Cottages	Shrops	SJ5140	52°57·5'	2°43·4'W	X	117
Black Hoe Plantn	N Lincs	SE9205	53°32·3'	0°36·3'W	F	112
Blackhole	Aberd	NO6091	57°0·8'	2°39·1'W	X	45
Black Hole	Northum	NU2619	55°28·1'	1°34·9'W	W	81
Blackhole Gut	Swan	SS4485	51°32·8'	4°14·6'W	X	159
Black Holm	Orkney	HY5902	58°54·5'	2°42·2'W	X	6
Black Holm	Shetld	HZ1970	59°31·2'	1°39·4'W	X	4
Black Holt	Lincs	TF2457	53°6·0'	0°8·5'W	F	122
Black Hope	D & G	NT1312	55°23·9'	3°22·0'W	X	78
Blackhope	Scot Bord	NT3351	55°45·1'	3°3·6'W	X	66,73
Blackhope	Scot Bord	NY5995	55°15·1'	2°38·3'W	X	80
Blackhope Burn	D & G	NT1311	55°23·4'	3°22·0'W	W	78
Blackhopebyre	Scot Bord	NT3444	55°41·4'	3°2·6'W	X	73
Blackhopebyre Burn	Scot Bord	NT3544	55°41·4'	3°1·6'W	W	73
Blackhope Hill	Scot Bord	NT4535	55°36·6'	2°52·0'W	H	73
Blackhope Scar	Midlo	NT3148	55°43·5'	3°5·5'W	H	73
Blackhope Water	Scot Bord	NT3351	55°45·1'	3°3·6'W	W	66,73
Blackhorse	Devon	SX9793	50°43·9'	3°27·2'W	T	192
Blackhorse	S Glos	ST6677	51°29·7'	2°29·0'W	T	172
Black Horse Br	Lincs	TF4260	53°7·3'	0°7·7'E	X	122
Black Horse Drove	Cambs	TL5991	52°29·9'	0°20·9'E	T	143
Blackhorse Fm	Herts	TL2434	51°59·7'	0°11·2'W	FM	153
Black Horse Fm	Leeds	SE4338	53°50·4'	1°20·4'W	FM	105
Black Horse Fm	Lincs	TF1663	53°9·3'	0°15·5'W	FM	121
Black Horse Fm	Suff	TL7657	52°11·2'	0°34·9'E	FM	155
Blackhorse Hill	E Susx	TQ7714	50°54·1'	0°31·4'E	X	199
Blackhouse	Aberd	NJ8644	57°29·4'	2°13·6'W	X	30
Blackhouse	Aberd	NK1246	57°30·5'	1°47·5'W	T	30
Blackhouse	Scot Bord	NT2827	55°32·1'	3°8·0'W	X	73
Blackhouse	Scot Bord	NT8260	55°50·2'	2°16·8'W	X	67
Blackhouse	Stir	NN5995	56°7·9'	4°15·7'W	X	57
Blackhouse	Stir	NS6396	56°8·5'	4°11·9'W	X	57
Blackhouse Fm	E Renf	NS5352	55°44·6'	4°20·1'W	FM	64
Black House Fm	E Susx	TQ9420	50°57·0'	0°46·1'E	FM	189
Black House Fm	Glos	SO7122	51°54·0'	2°24·9'W	FM	162
Black House Fm	Hants	SU6025	51°1·5'	1°8·3'W	FM	185
Black House Fm	Heref	SO4528	51°57·1'	2°47·6'W	FM	149,161
Black House Fm	Lincs	TF1319	52°45·6'	0°19·1'W	FM	130
Black House Fm	Lincs	TF3350	53°2·1'	0°0·6'W	FM	122
Black House Fm	Lincs	TF5366	53°10·4'	0°17·8'E	FM	122
Black House Fm	Lincs	TF5377	53°16·3'	0°18·1'E	FM	122
Black House Fm	Powys	SO1848	52°7·7'	3°11·5'W	FM	148
Black House Fm	Wilts	ST8330	51°4·4'	2°14·2'W	FM	183
Blackhouse Heights	Scot Bord	NT2229	55°33·2'	3°13·8'W	H	73
Blackhouse Moor	N Ayr	NS2064	55°50·4'	4°52·0'W	X	63
Blackhouse Plantns	Cumbr	NY5064	54°58·3'	2°46·4'W	F	86
Blackhouse Wood	Kent	TR0737	51°5·9'	0°57·8'E	F	179,189
Black How	Cumbr	NY0213	54°30·4'	3°30·4'W	X	89
Black How	Cumbr	NY0401	54°24·0'	3°28·3'W	X	89
Black Howe	N Yks	NY8602	54°25·0'	2°12·5'W	X	91,92
Black Howe	N Yks	SE8090	54°18·2'	0°45·8'W	A	94,100
Black Howes	Red & Cl	NZ6612	54°30·2'	0°58·4'W	A	94
Blackhurst	Ches	SJ5950	53°3·0'	2°36·3'W	X	117
Blackhurst	Kent	TQ6140	51°8·4'	0°18·5'E	X	188
Blackhurst	Shrops	SO5098	52°34·9'	2°43·9'W	X	137,138
Blackhurst Fm	Ches	SJ6140	52°57·6'	2°34·4'W	FM	118
Blackhurst Fm	Wrex	SJ4633	52°53·7'	2°47·8'W	FM	126
Black Hurworth	Durham	NZ4134	54°42·2'	1°21·4'W	X	93
Black Hut	I of M	SC4088	54°16·0'	4°27·0'W	X	95
Blackiemuir	Aberd	NO6971	56°50·0'	2°30·0'W	X	45
Blackingstone Rock	Devon	SX7885	50°39·3'	3°43·2'W	X	191
Black Intake	N Yks	SE5799	54°23·2'	1°6·9'W	X	100
Blackird Leys	Oxon	SP5503	51°43·6'	1°11·8'W	T	164
Black Island	D & G	NX3485	55°8·1'	4°35·8'W	X	76
Black Island	Stir	NN4011	56°16·1'	4°34·6'W	X	56
Black Islands	Arg & Bt	NN0924	56°22·4'	5°5·1'W	X	50
Black Islands	Highld	NG7529	57°18·0'	5°43·6'W	X	33
Black Islands	N Eil	NF7202	56°59·8'	7°23·7'W	X	31
Blackisle	Highld	ND2152	58°27·2'	3°20·7'W	X	11,12
Black Isle	Highld	NH6457	57°35·2'	4°16·0'W	X	26
Black Isle	Highld	NH7057	57°35·3'	4°10·0'W	X	27
Blackitt's Fm	Lincs	TF2734	52°53·5'	0°6·3'W	FM	131
Black Jack	Angus	NO7053	56°40·3'	2°28·9'W	X	54
Blackjack	Lincs	TF2639	52°56·2'	0°7·1'W	T	131
Blackjack Fm	Lincs	TF2639	52°56·2'	0°7·1'W	FM	131
Black Jane Fm	Ches	SJ5980	53°19·2'	2°36·5'W	FM	108
Black Jane Fm	Oxon	SP4231	51°58·8'	1°22·9'W	FM	151
Blackkip	Northum	NT7904	55°20·0'	2°19·4'W	H	80
Black Knoll	Shrops	SO3988	52°29·4'	2°53·5'W	X	137
Black Knors	Cumbr	NY5379	55°6·4'	2°43·8'W	X	86
Black Knowe	Cumbr	NY5882	55°8·1'	2°39·1'W	H	80
Black Knowe	D & G	NT2807	55°21·4'	3°7·7'W	H	79
Black Knowe	D & G	NY3187	55°10·6'	3°4·6'W	H	79
Black Knowe	D & G	NY3386	55°10·1'	3°2·7'W	H	79
Black Knowe	Northum	NT8208	55°22·2'	2°16·6'W	H	80
Black Knowe	Northum	NY5891	55°12·9'	2°39·2'W	H	80
Black Knowe	Northum	NY6481	55°7·6'	2°33·4'W	H	80
Black Knowe	Orkney	HY3619	59°3·5'	3°6·5'W	X	6
Black Knowe	Scot Bord	NT2211	55°23·5'	3°13·5'W	H	79

Black Knowe	Scot Bord	NT3140	55°39·2′	3°5·4′W	H	73
Black Knowe	Scot Bord	NY5487	55°10·8′	2°42·9′W	H	79
Black Knowe Covert	Scot Bord	NT7831	55°34·6′	2°20·5′W	F	74
Black Knowe Head	Scot Bord	NT1911	55°23·4′	3°16·3′W	H	79
Black Knowe Head	Scot Bord	NT3122	55°29·5′	3°5·1′W	H	73
Black Knowe Head	Scot Bord	NT3826	55°31·7′	2°58·5′W	H	73
Black Knowe (Tumulus)	Orkney	HY3619	59°3·5′	3°6·5′W	A	6
Black Knowl	Hants	SU2903	50°49·8′	1°34·9′W	X	196
Black Ladies	Staffs	SJ8409	52°40·9′	2°13·8′W	A	127
Black Laggan	D & G	NX4677	55°4·1′	4°24·3′W	X	77
Black Laggan Burn	D & G	NX4776	55°3·5′	4°23·3′W	W	77
Black Laggan Ward	D & G	NX4778	55°4·6′	4°23·4′W	X	77
Blacklains Fm	Glos	SO9213	51°49·2′	2°6·6′W	FM	163
Black Lake	Sand	SO9992	52°31·8′	2°0·5′W	T	139
Black Lake	Surrey	SU8644	51°11·6′	0°45·8′W	W	186
Blacklake Fm	Devon	SY1192	50°43·5′	3°15·3′W	FM	192,193
Blackland	Devon	SX8046	50°18·3′	3°40·7′W	X	202
Blackland	Wilts	SU0168	51°24·9′	1°58·7′W	T	173
Blackland Fm	Bucks	SP8225	51°55·3′	0°48·1′W	FM	165
Blackland Fm	E Susx	TQ3833	51°5·0′	0°1·4′W	FM	187
Blackland Fm	V of Glam	ST0772	51°26·6′	3°19·9′W	FM	170
Blackland Park	Wilts	SU0169	51°25·4′	1°58·7′W	X	173
Blackland Plantation	Dorset	ST9308	50°52·5′	2°5·6′W	F	195
Blacklands	Bath & NE Somer	ST5864	51°22·6′	2°35·8′W	X	172,182
Blacklands	Beds	TL0857	52°12·3′	0°24·8′W	X	153
Blacklands	Devon	SS7719	50°57·7′	3°44·7′W	X	180
Blacklands	Essex	TL5122	51°52·8′	0°12·0′E	X	167
Blacklands	E Susx	TQ7613	50°53·6′	0°30·5′E	X	199
Blacklands	E Susx	TQ8110	50°51·9′	0°34·7′E	T	199
Blacklands	Heref	SO6342	52°4·7′	2°32·0′W	T	149
Blacklands	N Lanak	NS6770	55°54·5′	4°7·2′W	X	64
Blacklands	N Lanak	NS7266	55°52·5′	4°2·3′W	X	64
Blacklands	Somer	SS8336	51°6·9′	3°39·9′W	X	181
Blacklands	Surrey	SU9243	51°11·0′	0°40·6′W	X	186
Blacklands Copse	W Berks	SU5468	51°24·7′	1°13·0′W	F	174
Blackland's Fm	Hants	SU6854	51°17·1′	1°1·1′W	FM	185,186
Blacklands Fm	I of W	SZ5289	50°42·1′	1°15·4′W	FM	196
Blacklands Fm	Warw	SP3249	52°8·5′	1°31·5′W	FM	151
Blacklands Hall	Suff	TL8146	52°5·2′	0°38·9′E	X	155
Blackland Wood	Wilts	SU0168	51°24·9′	1°58·7′W	F	173
Black Lane	Bury	SD7708	53°34·3′	2°20·4′W	T	109
Black Lane Ends	Lancs	SD9243	53°53·2′	2°6·9′W	X	103
Blacklane Fm	Cambs	TF3911	52°41·0′	0°3·8′E	FM	131,142,143
Blacklatch Burn	Aberd	NJ5209	57°10·4′	2°47·2′W	W	37
Black Law	Aberd	NJ6354	57°34·7′	2°36·7′W	H	29
Blacklaw	Aberd	NJ6355	57°35·3′	2°36·7′W	T	29
Black Law	D & G	NS7319	55°27·2′	4°0·1′W	H	71
Blacklaw	D & G	NT0408	55°21·7′	3°30·4′W	X	78
Black Law	E Ayr	NS4650	55°43·4′	4°26·7′W	X	64
Black Law	N Ayr	NS2759	55°47·9′	4°45·2′W	H	63
Black Law	Northum	NY8073	55°3·3′	2°18·4′W	X	86,87
Black Law	Pth & Kin	NO0207	56°15·0′	3°34·5′W	X	58
Blacklaw	Pth & Kin	NO2245	56°35·7′	3°15·8′W	X	53
Black Law	Scot Bord	NT2127	55°32·1′	3°14·7′W	H	73
Black Law	Scot Bord	NT3042	55°40·2′	3°6·3′W	H	73
Black Law	Scot Bord	NT4039	55°38·7′	2°56·8′W	H	73
Black Law	Scot Bord	NT6118	55°27·5′	2°36·6′W	H	80
Black Law	Scot Bord	NT7064	55°52·3′	2°28·3′W	X	67
Black Law	S Lanak	NS8953	55°45·7′	3°45·7′W	X	65,72
Black Law	S Lanak	NT0752	55°45·4′	3°28·5′W	H	65,72
Blacklaw Cott	E Ayr	NS4649	55°42·9′	4°26·6′W	X	64
Blacklaw Hill	Angus	NO2834	56°29·8′	3°9·7′W	H	53
Blacklaw Hill	D & G	NT0507	55°21·1′	3°29·5′W	X	78
Blacklawhill	E Ayr	NS4649	55°42·9′	4°26·6′W	X	64
Blacklaw Moss	N Ayr	NS2659	55°47·8′	4°46·1′W	X	63
Blacklaw Moss	S Lanak	NS9248	55°43·1′	3°42·7′W	X	72
Blacklaws	Fife	NO5606	56°14·9′	2°42·2′W	X	59
Blacklaws	W Loth	NS9563	55°51·2′	3°40·2′W	X	65
Blacklaw Twr	D & G	NT0506	55°20·6′	3°29·4′W	A	78
Blackleach	Lancs	SD4734	53°48·2′	2°47·9′W	T	102
Blackleach	Lancs	SD7232	53°47·3′	2°25·1′W	X	103
Black Leach	N Yks	SD7860	54°2·4′	2°19·7′W	X	98
Blackleach Brook	Derby	SK2972	53°14·9′	1°33·5′W	W	119
Black Leases Fm	Cumbr	NY6327	54°38·5′	2°34·0′W	FM	91
Black Leech	Brad	SE0035	53°48·9′	1°59·6′W	X	104
Blacklees Fm	Staffs	SJ9606	52°39·3′	2°3·1′W	FM	127,139
Blackler	Devon	SX7766	50°29·1′	3°43·7′W	X	202
Blackley	Cald	SE1019	53°40·3′	1°50·5′W	T	110
Blackley	Devon	SX4505	50°49·7′	4°11·7′W	X	190
Blackley	Man	SD8602	53°31·1′	2°12·3′W	T	109
Blackley Clough	Derby	SK1588	53°23·6′	1°46·1′W	X	110
Blackley Down	Devon	SY1993	50°44·1′	3°8·5′W	X	192,193
Blackley Hey	Derby	SK1488	53°23·6′	1°47·0′W	X	110
Blackley Hurst Hall	St Hel	SJ5399	53°29·4′	2°42·1′W	X	108
Black Leys	Oxon	SP5217	51°51·2′	1°14·3′W	F	164
Blackley's Fm	Essex	TL7220	51°51·3′	0°30·3′E	FM	167
Black Ling	Cumbr	NX9909	54°28·2′	3°33·1′W	X	89
Black Linn	D & G	NX3778	55°4·8′	4°32·8′W	W	77
Black Linn	D & G	NY0089	55°11·4′	3°33·8′W	W	78
Blacklinn Burn	Northum	NY7590	55°12·5′	2°23·1′W	W	80
Black Linn Resr	W Dunb	NS4477	55°57·9′	4°29·5′W	W	64
Black Lion Fm	Shrops	SJ3203	52°37·5′	2°51·0′W	FM	126
Blackloanhead	Aberd	NJ6258	57°36·9′	2°37·7′W	X	29
Black Loch	Aberd	NO4689	56°59·6′	2°52·9′W	W	44
Black Loch	Arg & Bt	NR7117	55°23·9′	5°36·6′W	W	68
Black Loch	Arg & Bt	NR7324	55°27·7′	5°35·0′W	W	68
Black Loch	D & G	NX1161	54°54·7′	4°56·5′W	W	82
Black Loch	D & G	NX2765	54°57·2′	4°41·7′W	W	82
Black Loch	D & G	NX2850	54°49·2′	4°40·2′W	W	82
Black Loch	D & G	NX3054	54°51·4′	4°38·5′W	W	82
Black Loch	D & G	NX3175	55°2·7′	4°38·3′W	W	76
Black Loch	D & G	NX3256	54°52·5′	4°36·7′W	W	82
Black Loch	D & G	NX4675	55°3·0′	4°24·2′W	W	77
Black Loch	D & G	NX4972	55°1·4′	4°21·3′W	W	77
Blackloch	D & G	NX5956	54°53·0′	4°11·5′W	X	83
Black Loch	D & G	NX7871	55°1·4′	3°54·1′W	W	84
Black Loch	D & G	NX9987	55°10·3′	3°34·7′W	W	78
Black Loch	E Ayr	NS4402	55°17·5′	4°27·0′W	W	77
Black Loch	E Loth	NT6673	55°57·2′	2°32·2′W	W	67
Black Loch	E Renf	NS4951	55°44·0′	4°23·9′W	W	64
Black Loch	Falk	NS8669	55°54·3′	3°49·0′W	W	65
Black Loch	Fife	NO2614	56°19·0′	3°11·3′W	W	59
Black Loch	Fife	NT0791	56°6·4′	3°29·3′W	W	58
Black Loch	Highld	ND0854	58°28·1′	3°34·2′W	X	11,12
Black Loch	Highld	ND1873	58°38·5′	3°24·3′W	W	7,12
Black Loch	Highld	ND2074	58°39·1′	3°22·2′W	W	7,12
Black Loch	Highld	ND3163	58°33·2′	3°10·7′W	W	11,12
Black Loch	Highld	ND3770	58°37·1′	3°4·6′W	W	7,12
Black Loch	Highld	ND3770	58°37·1′	3°4·6′W	W	12
Black Loch	Highld	NJ0639	57°26·2′	3°33·5′W	W	27
Black Loch	Moray	NH9855	57°34·7′	3°41·9′W	W	27
Black Loch	Orkney	HY4805	58°56·0′	2°53·7′W	W	6,7
Blackloch	Pth & Kin	NO1243	56°34·5′	3°25·5′W	X	53
Black Loch	Pth & Kin	NO1742	56°34·0′	3°20·6′W	W	53
Black Loch	Pth & Kin	NT0796	56°9·1′	3°29·4′W	W	58
Black Loch	S Ayr	NX1983	55°6·8′	4°49·8′W	W	76
Black Loch	S Ayr	NX2476	55°3·1′	4°44·9′W	W	76
Black Loch	S Ayr	NX2684	55°7·4′	4°43·3′W	W	76
Black Loch	Shetld	HP5906	60°44·2′	0°54·6′W	W	1
Black Loch	Shetld	HU4249	60°13·7′	1°14·0′W	W	3
Black Loch	W Dunb	NS4976	55°57·5′	4°24·7′W	W	64
Black Loch Moss	S Lanak	NS6233	55°34·5′	4°10·9′W	X	71
Black Lochs	Arg & Bt	NM9231	56°25·8′	5°22·0′W	W	49
Black Lochs of Kilquhockadale	D & G	NX2769	54°59·4′	4°41·8′W	W	82
Black Lock	E Ayr	NS5916	55°25·3′	4°13·2′W	W	71
Black Lodge	Northnts	TL0272	52°20·4′	0°29·8′W	X	141,153
Blacklorg Hill	E Ayr	NS6504	55°18·9′	4°7·2′W	H	77
Blacklot	Northum	NY8348	54°49·8′	2°15·5′W	X	86,87
Black Lough	Northum	NU1308	55°22·2′	1°47·3′W	W	81
Black Low	Northum	NU0841	55°40·0′	1°51·9′W	W	75
Blacklunans	Pth & Kin	NO1460	56°43·7′	3°23·9′W	T	43
Black Lyne	Cumbr	NY5075	55°4·3′	2°46·6′W	W	86
Blacklyne Common	Cumbr	NY5682	55°8·1′	2°41·0′W	X	80
Blacklyne Ho	Cumbr	NY5481	55°7·5′	2°42·9′W	X	79
Black Maller	Pth & Kin	NN9509	56°16·0′	3°41·3′W	H	58
Blackman's Law	Northum	NY7498	55°16·8′	2°24·1′W	H	80
Blackmanstone Bridge	Kent	TR0729	51°1·6′	0°57·5′E	X	189
Blackmanston Fm	Dorset	SY9180	50°37·4′	2°7·3′W	FM	195
Black Mares Rock, The	Highld	NG8738	57°23·2′	5°32·2′W	X	24
Blackmark	D & G	NX6591	55°11·9′	4°6·8′W	X	77
Blackmark	D & G	NX7185	55°8·8′	4°1·0′W	X	77
Black Mark	D & G	NX7583	55°7·8′	3°57·2′W	X	78
Blackmark Burn	D & G	NX7085	55°8·8′	4°2·0′W	W	77
Black Marsh	Shrops	SO3299	52°35·3′	2°59·6′W	X	137
Blackmarsh Fm	Dorset	ST6417	50°57·3′	2°30·4′W	FM	183
Blackmarstone	Heref	SO5039	52°3·1′	2°43·4′W	T	149
Black Martin Hill	Warw	SP2747	52°7·5′	1°35·9′W	X	151
Black Meldon	Scot Bord	NT2042	55°40·1′	3°15·9′W	H	73
Blackmere Fm	Beds	SP9762	52°15·1′	0°34·3′W	FM	153
Blackmiddens	Aberd	NJ4225	57°19·0′	2°57·3′W	X	37
Black Middens	N Tyne	NZ3768	55°1·6′	1°24·9′W	X	88
Blackmill	Aberd	NJ4506	57°8·8′	2°54·1′W	X	37
Blackmill	Brig	SS9386	51°34·0′	3°32·2′W	T	170
Blackmill	Highld	NH8503	57°6·5′	3°53·5′W	X	35,36
Black Mill	Norf	TM4795	52°30·0′	1°38·8′E	X	134
Black Mill Bay	Arg & Bt	NM7308	56°12·9′	5°39·2′W	W	55
Black Mill Fm	Kent	TQ8244	51°10·2′	0°36·6′E	FM	188
Blackmill Loch	Arg & Bt	NR9495	56°6·5′	5°18·3′W	W	55
Blackminster	Worcs	SP0744	52°5·9′	1°53·5′W	T	150
Blackmire	Cumbr	SD7687	54°16·9′	2°21·7′W	X	98
Blackmire	Moray	NJ1050	57°32·1′	3°29·7′W	X	28
Blackmire Burn	S Lanak	NS8124	55°30·0′	3°52·6′W	W	71,72
Blackmires	N Yks	NZ6804	54°25·9′	0°56·7′W	X	94
Blackmires Fm	Lincs	SK8650	53°2·7′	0°42·6′W	FM	121
Blackmire's Fm	Northnts	SP6443	52°5·1′	1°3·6′W	FM	152
Black Mixen	Pemb	SN0106	51°43·3′	4°52·5′W	X	157,158
Black Mixen	Powys	SO1964	52°16·3′	3°10·8′W	H	148
Black Moor	Barns	SE2701	53°30·5′	1°35·2′W	X	110
Blackmoor	Bath & NE Somer	ST5563	51°22·1′	2°38·4′W	T	172,182
Black Moor	Brad	SE0435	53°48·9′	1°55·9′W	X	104
Black Moor	Cald	SD9231	53°46·8′	2°6·9′W	X	103
Black Moor	Derby	SK0691	53°25·2′	1°54·2′W	X	110
Black Moor	Devon	SX6398	50°46·2′	3°56·2′W	X	191
Blackmoor	Devon	SX7368	50°30·1′	3°47·1′W	X	202
Blackmoor	Hants	SU7733	51°5·7′	0°53·6′W	T	186
Blackmoor	Kirk	SE0812	53°36·5′	1°52·3′W	X	110
Black Moor	Lancs	SD4714	53°37·4′	2°47·7′W	T	108
Black Moor	Leeds	SE2939	53°51·0′	1°33·1′W	T	104
Blackmoor	N Som	ST4661	51°21·0′	2°46·1′W	T	172,182
Black Moor	N Yks	NY8903	54°25·6′	2°9·8′W	X	91,92
Black Moor	N Yks	SE5198	54°22·7′	1°12·5′W	X	100
Black Moor	Pemb	SN1309	51°45·2′	4°42·2′W	X	158
Blackmoor	Somer	ST1618	50°57·6′	3°11·4′W	X	181,193
Blackmoor	Wigan	SD6900	53°30·0′	2°27·6′W	T	109
Blackmoor Br	Lincs	SK9462	53°9·0′	0°35·3′W	X	121
Blackmoor Copse	Wilts	SU2329	51°3·8′	1°39·9′W	F	184
Blackmoor Fm	Heref	SO3934	52°0·3′	2°52·9′W	FM	149,161
Blackmoor Fm	Lincs	SK9169	53°12·9′	0°37·8′W	FM	121
Blackmoor Fm	Lincs	SK9462	53°9·0′	0°35·3′W	FM	121
Blackmoor Fm	Norf	TF9707	52°37·7′	0°55·1′E	FM	144
Blackmoor Fm	Somer	ST4008	50°52·3′	2°50·8′W	FM	193
Blackmoor Fm	Suff	TM4883	52°23·5′	1°39·1′E	FM	156
Blackmoor Fm	Surrey	TQ0956	51°17·8′	0°25·8′W	FM	187
Blackmoorfoot	Kirk	SE0913	53°37·0′	1°51·4′W	T	110
Blackmoorfoot Resr	Kirk	SE0912	53°36·5′	1°51·4′W	W	110
Blackmoor Gate	Devon	SS6443	51°10·4′	3°56·3′W	T	180
Blackmoor Hill	Pemb	SN1116	51°48·9′	4°44·1′W	X	158
Blackmoorhill Fm	Bucks	SP7025	51°55·4′	0°58·5′W	FM	165
Blackmoor Ho	Hants	SU7732	51°5·2′	0°53·6′W	X	186
Black Moor Plantn	Durham	NZ4128	54°39·0′	1°21·5′W	F	93
Black Moor Rigg	N Yks	SE7698	54°22·5′	0°49·4′W	X	94,100
Blackmoor Vale	Dorset	ST7113	50°55·2′	2°24·4′W	X	194
Blackmoor Wood	Oxon	SU7293	51°38·1′	0°57·2′W	F	175
Black Moray Plantn	D & G	NX6849	54°49·4′	4°2·9′W	F	83,84
Blackmore	Essex	TL6001	51°41·3′	0°19·3′E	T	167
Blackmore	Shrops	SJ3109	52°40·7′	3°0·8′W	T	126
Blackmore Down	Wilts	SU2651	51°15·7′	1°37·3′W	X	184
Blackmore End	Essex	TL7330	51°56·7′	0°31·4′E	T	167
Blackmore End	Herts	TL1616	51°50·1′	0°18·6′W	T	166
Blackmore End	Worcs	SO8144	52°5·9′	2°16·2′W	T	150
Blackmore Fm	Oxon	SU7180	51°31·1′	0°58·2′W	FM	175
Blackmore Fm	Somer	ST2438	51°8·4′	3°4·8′W	A	182
Blackmore Fm	Wilts	ST9264	51°22·7′	2°6·5′W	FM	173
Blackmore Ford Br	Dorset	ST6709	50°53·0′	2°27·8′W	X	194
Blackmore Park Fm	Worcs	SO7943	52°5·3′	2°18·0′W	FM	150
Blackmore Thick Fm	Northnts	SP9893	52°31·8′	0°32·9′W	FM	141
Black Moss	Aberd	NJ4601	57°6·1′	2°53·0′W	X	37
Black Moss	Aberd	NJ7400	57°5·7′	2°25·3′W	X	38
Black Moss	Aberd	NO4193	57°1·7′	2°57·9′W	X	37,44
Black Moss	Cumbr	NY0310	54°28·8′	3°29·4′W	X	89
Black MOSS	Cumbr	NY5875	55°4·3′	2°39·0′W	X	86
Black Moss	Cumbr	SD2288	54°17·1′	3°11·5′W	X	96
Blackmoss	Cumbr	SD4398	54°22·7′	2°52·2′W	X	97
Black Moss	Cumbr	SD7298	54°22·8′	2°25·4′W	X	98
Black Moss	Derby	SK1198	53°29·0′	1°49·6′W	X	110
Black Moss	Kirk	SE0408	53°34·4′	1°56·0′W	X	110
Black Moss	Lancs	SD7452	53°58·0′	2°23·4′W	X	103
Blackmoss	S Lanak	NS6746	55°41·6′	4°6·5′W	X	64
Blackmoss Fm	Lancs	SD6040	53°51·5′	2°36·1′W	FM	102,103
Blackmoss Ho (Hotel)	Lancs	SD6039	53°51·0′	2°36·1′W	X	102,103
Black Moss of Evrigert	Orkney	HY3621	59°4·5′	3°6·5′W	X	6
Blackmoss Plantn	D & G	NY1479	55°6·1′	3°20·4′W	F	85
Blackmoss Pool	Cumbr	NY4847	54°49·2′	2°48·1′W	W	86
Black Moss Resr	Oldham	SE0308	53°34·4′	1°56·9′W	W	110
Black Moss Resrs	Lancs	SD8241	53°52·1′	2°16·0′W	W	103
Black Moss Tarn	Cumbr	SD5497	54°22·2′	2°42·1′W	W	97
Black Mount	Arg & Bt	NN2842	56°32·6′	4°47·4′W	X	50
Black Mount	Highld	NH8624	57°17·8′	3°53·1′W	X	35,36
Black Mount	Highld	NN2947	56°35·3′	4°46·6′W	H	50
Black Mount	S Lanak	NT0746	55°42·2′	3°28·4′W	H	72
Black Mountain	Powys	SO1677	52°23·3′	3°13·7′W	H	136,148
Black Mountain	Shrops	SO1983	52°26·6′	3°11·1′W	H	136
Blackmountain Fm	Shrops	SO2182	52°26·1′	3°9·3′W	FM	137
Black Mountains, The (Y Mynydd Du)	Carm	SN7417	51°50·5′	3°49·3′W	H	160
Black Mountains, The / Y Mynyddoedd Duon	Powys	SO2427	51°56·4′	3°5·9′W	H	161
Black Muir	Fife	NO0688	56°4·8′	3°30·2′W	T	65
Blackmuir	Moray	NJ3743	57°28·6′	3°2·6′W	X	28
Blackmuir Wood	Highld	NH4857	57°34·9′	4°32·1′W	F	26
Blackmyre	Aberd	NK0752	57°33·7′	1°52·5′W	X	30
Blackmyre	D & G	NX4957	54°53·3′	4°20·8′W	X	83
Blackmyre Moor	D & G	NX5057	54°53·4′	4°19·9′W	X	83
Black Nab	N Yks	NZ9210	54°28·9′	0°34·4′W	X	94
Blackness	Aberd	NJ8624	57°18·6′	2°13·5′W	X	38
Blackness	Aberd	NO6992	57°1·3′	2°30·2′W	X	38,45
Blackness	Angus	NO4678	56°53·7′	2°52·7′W	X	44
Blackness	E Susx	TQ5230	51°3·2′	0°10·5′E	T	188
Blackness	Falk	NT0580	56°0·5′	3°31·0′W	T	65
Blackness	Highld	ND2937	58°19·2′	3°12·2′W	X	11
Blackness Bay	Falk	NT0580	56°0·5′	3°31·0′W	W	65
Blackness Castle	Falk	NT0580	56°0·5′	3°31·0′W	A	65
Blackness Ho	Falk	NT0479	55°59·9′	3°31·9′W	X	65
Blackness Rock	Devon	SX8555	50°23·3′	3°36·7′W	X	202
Blacknest	Hants	SU7941	51°10·0′	0°51·8′W	T	186
Blacknest	Win & Maid	SU9568	51°24·4′	0°37·7′W	T	175,176
Blacknest Fm	Surrey	SU9935	51°6·6′	0°34·8′W	FM	186
Blacknest Fm	W Berks	SU5663	51°22·0′	1°11·3′W	FM	174
Blacknest Ho	D & G	NX8995	55°14·5′	3°44·3′W	X	78
Black Neuk	S Ayr	NX1695	55°13·2′	4°53·1′W	X	76
Black Nev	Orkney	ND1898	58°52·0′	3°24·8′W	X	7
Blackney	Dorset	SY4299	50°47·5′	2°49·0′W	T	193
Blackney Hill	Kent	TR2556	51°15·7′	1°13·9′E	X	179
Blacknoll	Dorset	SY8086	50°40·6′	2°16·6′W	X	194
Blacknor	Dorset	SY6771	50°32·5′	2°27·6′W	X	194
Black Nore	N Som	ST4476	51°29·0′	2°48·0′W	X	171,172
Blacknor Park	Devon	SX4880	50°36·2′	4°8·5′W	X	191,201
Black Notley	Essex	TL7620	51°51·3′	0°33·7′E	T	167
Blacknowes	Pth & Kin	NT1398	56°10·3′	3°23·6′W	X	58
Blacknuck	Pemb	SN0727	51°54·7′	4°48·0′W	X	145,158
Blacko	Lancs	SD8541	53°52·1′	2°13·3′W	T	103
Black-oak	Carm	SN3135	51°59·5′	4°27·3′W	X	145
Blackoe	Shrops	SJ5139	52°57·0′	2°43·4′W	T	126
Blacko Foot	Lancs	SD8441	53°52·1′	2°14·2′W	X	103
Blacko Hill Side	Lancs	SD8642	53°52·7′	2°12·4′W	X	103
Black o' Muir	Stir	NS8189	56°5·0′	3°54·3′W	X	57,65
Black Pan	I of W	SZ5883	50°38·9′	1°10·4′W	X	196
Blackpark	Arg & Bt	NR2963	55°47·3′	6°18·9′W	X	60
Blackpark	D & G	NW9961	54°54·5′	5°7·7′W	X	82
Blackpark	D & G	NX3757	54°53·1′	4°32·0′W	X	83
Blackpark	D & G	NX3864	54°56·9′	4°31·3′W	X	83
Blackpark	D & G	NX7562	54°56·5′	3°56·7′W	X	84
Blackpark	D & G	NX8172	55°2·0′	3°51·3′W	X	84
Blackpark	D & G	NX9181	55°6·9′	3°42·1′W	X	78
Blackpark	Highld	ND2755	58°28·9′	3°14·6′W	X	11,12
Blackpark	Highld	ND2864	58°33·8′	3°13·8′W	X	11,12
Black Park	Highld	NG6423	57°14·5′	5°54·2′W	T	32
Blackpark	Highld	NH5139	57°25·3′	4°28·4′W	X	26
Blackpark	Highld	NH6345	57°28·7′	4°16·6′W	X	26
Blackpark	Highld	NH6783	57°49·3′	4°13·9′W	X	21
Blackpark	Highld	NH7244	57°28·4′	4°7·6′W	X	27
Blackpark	Highld	NH8954	57°34·0′	3°50·9′W	X	27
Blackpark	Highld	NH9009	57°9·8′	3°48·7′W	X	36
Black Park	Norf	TG2016	52°42·0′	1°15·8′E	F	133,134
Black Park	Shrops	SJ5642	52°58·7′	2°38·9′W	X	117
Black Park	Stir	NN7202	56°11·9′	4°3·3′W	F	57
Black Park	Wrex	SJ3040	52°57·4′	3°2·1′W	T	117
Black Park Country Park	Bucks	TQ0183	51°32·4′	0°32·2′W	F	176
Blackpark Fm	Shrops	SJ5743	52°59·2′	2°38·0′W	FM	117
Blackpark Lake	Bucks	TQ0083	51°32·4′	0°33·1′W	W	176
Blackpark Lodge	N Yks	SE7590	54°18·2′	0°50·4′W	X	94,100
Blackpark Lodge	Pth & Kin	NO0430	56°27·4′	3°33·0′W	X	52,53
Black Park (Nature Reserve)	Shetld	HU5397	60°39·4′	1°1·3′W	X	1
Black Pasture	N Yks	SD9686	54°16·4′	2°3·3′W	X	98
Blackpatch Hill	W Susx	TQ0909	50°52·4′	0°26·7′W	H	198
Black Peak	Cambs	TL4044	52°4·8′	0°3·0′E	X	154

Black Pill	Swan	SS6190	51°35·7′	4°0·0′W	T	159
Black Pit	Glos	SP2126	51°56·2′	1°41·3′W	X	163
Blackpit Fm	Bucks	SP6740	52°3·5′	1°1·0′W	FM	152
Blackpits	Shrops	SJ5404	52°38·1′	2°40·4′W	F	126
Blackpits Barn	Northnts	SP5842	52°4·6′	1°8·8′W	X	152
Blackpits Copse	Glos	SP1710	51°47·5′	1°44·8′W	F	163
Blackpitts Gate	Somer	ST5641	51°9·5′	3°46·0′W	X	180
Blackpit Wood	Kent	TQ8747	51°11·7′	0°41·0′E	F	189
Black Plantation	N Yks	NZ1504	54°26·1′	1°45·7′W	F	92
Black Plantation	Staffs	SJ9228	52°51·2′	2°6·7′W	F	127
Black Plantn	E Yorks	SE7353	53°58·3′	0°52·8′W	F	105,106
Black Plantn	E Yorks	SE7936	53°49·1′	0°47·6′W	F	105,106
Black Plantn	Norf	TL9285	52°26·0′	0°49·9′E	F	144
Black Plantn	Northum	NU1809	55°22·7′	1°42·5′W	F	81
Black Plantn	N Yks	SE2985	54°15·8′	1°32·9′W	F	99
Black Plantn	N Yks	SE5977	54°11·4′	1°5·3′W	F	100
Black Plantn	N Yks	SE7570	54°7·5′	0°50·7′W	F	100
Black Plantn	N Yks	SE8971	54°7·9′	0°37·9′W	F	101
Black Plantn	York	SE6647	53°55·1′	0°59·3′W	F	105,106
Black Point	Arg & Bt	NR7104	55°16·9′	5°35·9′W	X	68
Black Point	Essex	TQ9196	51°38·0′	0°46·0′E	X	168
Black Point	Hants	SZ7599	50°47·4′	0°55·8′W	X	197
Black Point	Pemb	SM8515	51°47·8′	5°6·7′W	X	157
Black Point	Somer	ST2858	51°19·2′	3°1·6′W	X	182
Blackpole	Heref	SO4962	52°15·5′	2°44·4′W	X	137,138,148
Black Pole	Lancs	SD4836	53°49·3′	2°47·0′W	T	102
Blackpole	Worcs	SO8657	52°12·9′	2°11·9′W	T	150
Black Pond	Surrey	TQ1262	51°21·0′	0°23·1′W	W	176,187
Blackpool	Aberd	NJ6213	57°12·6′	2°37·3′W	X	37
Blackpool	Aberd	NJ8144	57°29·4′	2°18·6′W	X	29,30
Blackpool	Blackp	SD3136	53°49·2′	3°2·5′W	T	102
Blackpool	Devon	SX5654	50°22·3′	4°1·1′W	T	202
Black Pool	Devon	SX6558	50°24·6′	3°53·6′W	W	202
Blackpool	Devon	SX8174	50°33·5′	3°40·4′W	T	191
Blackpool	Devon	SX8547	50°18·9′	3°36·5′W	T	202
Blackpool	Northum	NZ1393	55°14·1′	1°47·3′W	X	81
Blackpool	Pemb	SN0614	51°47·7′	4°48·4′W	T	158
Black Pool	Powys	SO1270	52°19·5′	3°17·1′W	X	136,148
Blackpool Airport	Lancs	SD3131	53°46·5′	3°2·4′W	X	102
Blackpool Br	Glos	SO6508	51°46·4′	2°30·0′W	A	162
Blackpool Corner	Devon	SY3398	50°46·9′	2°56·6′W	T	193
Blackpool Gate	Cumbr	NY5377	55°5·4′	2°43·8′W	X	86
Black Post	Kent	TQ8755	51°16·0′	0°41·2′E	X	178
Black Pot	N Yks	SD9094	54°20·7′	2°8·8′W	X	98
Blackpots	Aberd	NJ9541	57°27·8′	2°4·5′W	X	30
Black Pots	Brad	SE0746	53°54·8′	1°53·2′W	X	104
Black Pots	Cumbr	NY0913	54°30·5′	3°23·9′W	X	89
Blackpotts	Scot Bord	NT9067	55°54·0′	2°9·2′W	X	67
Black Pows	Orkney	ND2693	58°49·4′	3°16·4′W	X	7
Black Preston	Cumbr	NY5876	55°4·8′	2°39·0′W	X	86
Blackquarter	D & G	NX3666	54°58·0′	4°33·3′W	X	83
Blackrabbit Warren	Norf	TL9193	52°30·3′	0°49·3′E	F	144
Black Rake	N Yks	SD7882	54°14·2′	2°19·8′W	X	98
Blackraw	W Loth	NT0865	55°52·4′	3°27·8′W	X	65
Black Rhadley Hill	Shrops	SO3495	52°33·2′	2°58·0′W	H	137
Black Ridge	Devon	SX5985	50°39·1′	3°59·3′W	H	191
Blackridge	W Loth	NS8967	55°53·3′	3°46·0′W	T	65
Black Ridge Brook	Devon	SX5884	50°38·5′	4°0·1′W	W	191
Blackridge Fm	N Lanak	NS8163	55°51·0′	3°53·6′W	FM	65
Black Rig	D & G	NS7001	55°17·4′	4°2·4′W	H	77
Black Rig	D & G	NS7803	55°18·6′	3°54·9′W	X	78
Blackrig	D & G	NY0681	55°7·1′	3°28·0′W	X	78
Blackrig	Falk	NS9175	55°57·6′	3°44·3′W	X	65
Black Rig	Scot Bord	NT1920	55°28·3′	3°16·4′W	H	72
Black Rig	Scot Bord	NT2025	55°31·0′	3°15·6′W	H	73
Black Rig	Scot Bord	NT2325	55°31·0′	3°12·7′W	H	73
Black Rig	Scot Bord	NT3413	55°24·6′	3°2·1′W	H	79
Black Rig	Scot Bord	NT3414	55°25·2′	3°2·1′W	X	79
Black Rig	Scot Bord	NT3531	55°34·4′	3°1·4′W	X	73
Black Rig	Scot Bord	NT3719	55°27·9′	2°59·4′W	X	79
Black Rig	Scot Bord	NT5000	55°17·7′	2°46·8′W	X	79
Black Rig	Scot Bord	NY4582	55°8·0′	2°51·3′W	H	79
Blackrig Burn	Scot Bord	NT7353	55°46·4′	2°25·4′W	W	67,74
Blackrigg	Aberd	NJ9159	57°37·5′	2°8·6′W	X	30
Blackrigg	Cumbr	NY3662	54°57·2′	2°59·5′W	X	85
Blackrigg	Cumbr	NY4470	55°1·5′	2°52·1′W	X	85
Black Rigg	Cumbr	NY4981	55°7·5′	2°47·6′W	H	79
Black Rigg	Cumbr	NY6162	54°57·3′	2°36·1′W	X	86
Black Rigg	Northum	NY6769	55°1·1′	2°30·5′W	H	86,87
Black Rigg	Northum	NY7574	55°3·8′	2°23·1′W	X	86,87
Black Rigg	N Yks	SE7896	54°21·5′	0°47·6′W	X	94,100
Blackrigg Foot	Cumbr	NY6176	55°4·9′	2°36·2′W	X	86
Black Rigging	Angus	NO2073	56°50·8′	3°18·2′W	X	44
Black Rigg Moss	Fife	NT0894	56°8·0′	3°28·4′W	X	58
Black Riggs	Cumbr	NY8712	54°30·4′	2°11·6′W	X	91,92
Blackrig Plantn	Scot Bord	NT6626	55°31·8′	2°31·9′W	H	74
Blackrig Plantn	Scot Bord	NT7253	55°46·4′	2°26·3′W	F	67,74
Black Roads	Moray	NJ1846	57°30·1′	3°21·6′W	X	28
Black Robin Beck	N Yks	SE2478	54°12·1′	1°37·5′W	X	99
Black Robin Fm	E Susx	TV5897	50°45·3′	0°14·8′E	FM	199
Black Robins Fm	Surrey	TQ4148	51°13·1′	0°1·5′E	FM	187
Blackrock	Arg & Bt	NR3063	55°47·4′	6°18·0′W	T	60
Black Rock	Arg & Bt	NR7304	55°16·9′	5°34·0′W	X	68
Black Rock	Arg & Bt	NR7894	56°5·5′	5°33·7′W	X	55
Blackrock	Bath & NE Somer	ST6265	51°23·2′	2°32·4′W	T	172
Black Rock	Bri & Hov	TQ3303	50°48·9′	0°6·3′W	T	198
Black Rock	Corn	SS1901	50°47·1′	4°33·7′W	X	190
Black Rock	Corn	SW6634	50°9·8′	5°16·2′W	T	203
Black Rock	Corn	SW7215	49°59·7′	5°10·5′W	X	204
Black Rock	Corn	SW8331	50°8·6′	5°1·9′W	X	204
Black Rock	Corn	SX1979	50°35·2′	4°33·0′W	X	201
Black Rock	Corn	SX3956	50°23·1′	4°15·5′W	X	201
Black Rock	Derby	SK2955	53°5·7′	1°33·6′W	X	119
Black Rock	Devon	SS1343	51°9·5′	4°40·1′W	X	180
Black Rock	Devon	SS4441	51°9·1′	4°13·5′W	X	180
Black Rock	Glos	SO6500	51°42·1′	2°30·0′W	X	162
Black Rock	Highld	NC3113	58°4·7′	4°51·5′W	X	15
Black Rock	Highld	NN0467	56°45·5′	5°11·9′W	X	41
Blackrock	Monm	SO2112	51°48·3′	3°8·4′W	T	161
Black Rock	Monm	ST5188	51°35·6′	2°42·1′W	X	162,172
Black Rock	N Som	ST3058	51°19·2′	2°59·9′W	X	182
Black Rock	Orkney	HY6942	59°16·1′	2°32·1′W	X	5
Black Rock	Orkney	ND4897	58°51·7′	2°53·6′W	X	6,7
Black Rock	Somer	ST1043	51°11·0′	3°16·9′W	X	181
Black Rock	Somer	ST4854	51°17·2′	2°44·4′W	X	182
Blackrock Cottage	Highld	NN2653	56°38·5′	4°49·8′W	X	41
Black Rock Gorge	Highld	NH5866	57°40·0′	4°22·4′W	X	21
Black Rocks		NS3229	55°31·8′	4°39·3′W	X	70
Black Rocks	Brig	SS8476	51°28·5′	3°39·8′W	X	170
Black Rocks	C of Edin	NT2777	55°59·1′	3°9·8′W	X	66
Black Rocks	Derby	SK2154	53°5·2′	1°40·8′W	X	119
Black Rocks	E Loth	NT4884	56°3·0′	2°49·7′W	X	66
Black Rocks	Fife	NT2485	56°3·4′	3°12·8′W	X	66
Black Rocks	I of M	SC2268	54°4·9′	4°42·9′W	X	95
Black Rocks	I Scilly	SV8614	49°56·9′	6°22·3′W	X	203
Black Rocks	N Yks	TA0486	54°15·8′	0°23·8′W	X	101
Black Rocks	V of Glam	SS8674	51°27·4′	3°38·1′W	X	170
Black Rock Sands	Gwyn	SH5336	52°53·3′	4°10·7′W	X	124
Blackrod	Wigan	SD6110	53°35·4′	2°34·9′W	T	109
Blackroot Pool	Birm	SP1097	52°34·5′	1°50·7′W	W	139
Black Row	S Ayr	NX3695	55°13·6′	4°34·3′W	X	77
Blackrow Fm	Dorset	ST7211	50°54·1′	2°23·5′W	FM	194
Blackrow Plantn	Norf	TG1818	52°43·2′	1°14·1′E	F	133,134
Black Sail Hut	Cumbr	NY1912	54°30·1′	3°14·6′W	X	89,90
Black Sail Pass	Cumbr	NY1811	54°29·5′	3°15·5′W	X	89,90
Black Sails	Cumbr	NY2800	54°23·7′	3°6·1′W	H	89,90
Black Sark	D & G	NY3270	55°1·4′	3°3·4′W	W	85
Blacksboat	Moray	NJ1838	57°25·8′	3°21·5′W	X	28
Black's Bog	D & G	NT2203	55°19·1′	3°13·3′W	X	79
Black Scar	Carm	SN3110	51°46·0′	4°26·6′W	X	159
Black Scar	Cumbr	SD2064	54°4·2′	3°12·9′W	X	96
Black Scar	N Yks	SE0486	54°16·4′	1°55·9′W	X	98
Black Scar	Pemb	SM7922	51°51·4′	5°12·2′W	X	157
Black Scars	Cumbr	SD3276	54°10·8′	3°2·1′W	X	96,97
Black Score	Highld	ND3865	58°34·4′	3°3·5′W	X	12
Black Screed	Notts	SK6084	53°21·2′	1°5·5′W	F	111,120
Blackseat Hill	Northum	NY9422	55°29·8′	2°5·3′W	H	74,75
Blacks Fm	Lincs	TF4056	53°5·2′	0°5·8′E	FM	122
Black Shank	Angus	NO3875	56°52·0′	3°0·6′W	X	44
Black Share	N Yks	SE4599	54°23·3′	1°18·0′W	X	99
Blackshaw	D & G	NY0465	54°58·5′	3°29·6′W	X	84
Blackshaw Bank	D & G	NY0462	54°56·9′	3°29·5′W	X	84
Blackshaw Bank	D & G	NY0662	54°56·9′	3°27·6′W	X	85
Blackshaw Clough	Derby	SK0596	53°27·9′	1°55·1′W	X	110
Blackshaw Fm	Derby	SK0288	53°23·6′	1°57·8′W	FM	110
Blackshaw Fm	Derby	SK0496	53°27·9′	1°56·0′W	FM	110
Blackshaw Fm	N Ayr	NS2349	55°42·4′	4°48·6′W	FM	63
Blackshaw Head	Cald	SD9527	53°44·6′	2°4·1′W	T	103
Blackshaw Heys Fm	Ches	SJ7882	53°20·3′	2°19·4′W	FM	109
Blackshaw Hill	N Ayr	NS2248	55°41·8′	4°49·5′W	H	63
Blackshaw Moor	Staffs	SK0059	53°7·9′	1°59·6′W	T	119
Blackshawmoor Resrs	Staffs	SK0160	53°8·5′	1°58·7′W	W	119
Blackshaws	Cumbr	NY6373	55°3·3′	2°34·3′W	X	86
Blackshaws Hill	Cumbr	NY6375	55°4·3′	2°34·3′W	X	86
Blackshaws Sike	Cumbr	NY6474	55°3·8′	2°33·4′W	W	86
Blacksheil Burn	Aberd	NO2288	56°58·9′	3°16·5′W	W	44
Blackshiels	Midlo	NT4360	55°50·0′	2°54·2′W	X	66
Black Shiver Moss	N Yks	SD7375	54°10·4′	2°24·4′W	X	98
Black Shore		TF5531	52°51·5′	0°18·5′E	X	131
Black Shoulder	D & G	NS6704	55°19·0′	4°5·3′W	X	77
Black Shoulder	D & G	NX5996	55°14·5′	4°12·6′W	X	77
Blackshouse	S Lanak	NS9439	55°38·2′	3°40·6′W	X	71,72
Blackside	E Ayr	NS5728	55°31·7′	4°15·5′W	X	71
Blackside	E Ayr	NS5830	55°32·8′	4°14·6′W	H	71
Blackside	E Ayr	NS7029	55°32·5′	4°3·2′W	X	71
Black Side	N Yks	SD7989	54°18·0′	2°18·9′W	X	98
Blacksidend	E Ayr	NS5729	55°32·3′	4°15·5′W	X	71
Blacksidend	E Ayr	NS5829	55°32·3′	4°14·6′W	X	71
Black Side of Tarnbrook Fell	Lancs	SD6056	54°0·2′	2°36·2′W	X	102,103
Blackside Pasture	N Yks	SD7180	54°13·1′	2°26·3′W	X	98
Black Sike	Cumbr	SD2194	54°20·4′	3°12·5′W	W	96
Black Sike	Durham	NY9327	54°38·5′	2°5·4′W	W	91,92
Black Sike	Northum	NY7491	55°13·0′	2°24·1′W	W	80
Black Sike	Northum	NY8751	54°51·5′	2°11·7′W	W	87
Black Sike	N Yks	SE1156	54°0·2′	1°49·5′W	W	104
Black Sike	Scot Bord	NT3430	55°33·8′	3°2·4′W	W	73
Black Sike	Scot Bord	NY4386	55°10·2′	2°53·3′W	W	79
Black Skerry	Shetld	HU3169	60°24·5′	1°25·7′W	X	3
Black Skerry	Shetld	HU3526	60°1·3′	1°21·8′W	X	4
Black Skerry	Shetld	HU3838	60°7·8′	1°18·5′W	X	4
Black Skerry	Shetld	HU5385	60°33·0′	1°1·5′W	X	1,2,3
Black Skerry of Ramnageo	Shetld	HU3070	60°25·0′	1°26·8′W	X	3
Blackslack	Aberd	NJ9953	57°34·3′	2°0·5′W	X	30
Blackslade	Devon	SX7275	50°33·9′	3°48·1′W	X	191
Blackslade Down	Devon	SX7375	50°33·9′	3°47·2′W	H	191
Black Slough Fm	Staffs	SK1213	52°43·1′	1°48·9′W	FM	128
Blacksmill Burn	Scot Bord	NT7057	55°48·6′	2°28·3′W	W	67,74
Blacksmill Hill	Scot Bord	NT7154	55°47·0′	2°27·3′W	X	67,74
Blacksmith's Corner	Suff	TM1340	52°1·3′	1°6·7′E	T	169
Blacksmith's Green	Suff	TM1465	52°14·7′	1°8·5′E	T	156
Black's Moor Hill	Somer	ST4826	51°2·1′	2°44·1′W	X	193
Blacksnape	Black w Dar	SD7121	53°41·3′	2°25·9′W	T	103
Blacks Ness	Shetld	HU4039	60°8·3′	1°16·3′W	X	4
Black Snib	Cumbr	NY4267	54°59·9′	2°54·0′W	F	85
Black Snout	D & G	NX9199	55°16·6′	3°42·5′W	X	78
Blacksole Field	Kent	TQ6059	51°18·7′	0°18·1′E	X	188
Black's Plantn	D & G	NX4240	54°44·1′	4°26·8′W	F	83
Black's Plantn	N Yks	SD8362	54°3·5′	2°15·2′W	F	98
Black Spout	Pth & Kin	NN9557	56°41·8′	3°42·4′W	W	52,53
Black Spring Fm	Lincs	SK9921	52°46·9′	0°31·5′W	FM	130
Black Squares	Stock on T	NZ4027	54°38·4′	1°22·4′W	F	93
Blackstand	Highld	NH7161	57°37·5′	4°9·1′W	X	21,27
Black Stane	Shetld	HU2760	60°19·7′	1°30·2′W	X	3
Blackstan Hill	D & G	NY2584	55°8·9′	3°10·2′W	H	79
Black Stank	Aberd	NK0531	57°22·4′	1°54·6′W	W	30
Black Stank	D & G	NX0758	54°53·0′	5°0·1′W	W	82
Blackstank	Moray	NJ2737	57°25·3′	3°12·5′W	X	28
Black Stantling	Cumbr	NY5979	55°6·5′	2°38·1′W	H	86
Blacksticks	Lancs	SD5942	53°52·6′	2°37·0′W	X	102
Black Stitchel	Northum	NY9098	55°16·8′	2°9·0′W	H	80
Blackstock	Aberd	NJ6609	57°10·5′	2°33·3′W	X	38
Blackstockarton Moor	D & G	NX7255	54°52·7′	3°59·3′W	X	83,84
Blackstock Fm	E Susx	TQ5913	50°53·9′	0°16·1′E	FM	199
Blackston	E Ayr	NS5621	55°28·0′	4°16·2′W	X	71
Blackston	Falk	NS9273	55°56·5′	3°43·3′W	X	65
Blackstone	Aberd	NJ9635	57°24·6′	2°3·5′W	X	30
Black Stone	Devon	SX8336	50°13·0′	3°38·0′W	X	202
Blackstone	D & G	NX7789	55°11·1′	3°55·5′W	X	78
Blackstone	N Ayr	NS2549	55°42·4′	4°46·7′W	X	63
Blackstone	Worcs	SO7974	52°22·1′	2°18·1′W	T	138
Blackstone	W Susx	TQ2416	50°56·0′	0°13·7′W	T	198
Blackstone Bay	Arg & Bt	NS0098	56°8·2′	5°12·7′W	W	55
Blackstone Edge	Roch	SD9716	53°38·7′	2°2·3′W	X	109
Blackstone Edge Fold	Roch	SD9616	53°38·7′	2°3·2′W	X	109
Blackstone Edge Reservoir	Roch	SD9718	53°39·8′	2°2·3′W	W	109
Blackstone Gate Fm	W Susx	TQ2417	50°56·6′	0°13·7′W	FM	198
Blackstone Mains	Renf	NS4666	55°52·0′	4°27·2′W	X	64
Blackstone Point	Cumbr	SD4377	54°11·4′	2°52·0′W	X	97
Blackstone Point	Devon	SS6048	51°13·1′	3°59·9′W	X	180
Blackstone Point	Devon	SX5346	50°18·0′	4°3·5′W	X	201
Blackstone Point	Devon	SX8849	50°20·1′	3°34·0′W	X	202
Blackstone Rocks	C of Bris	ST3870	51°25·8′	2°53·1′W	X	182
Blackstone Rocks	Devon	SX5148	50°19·0′	4°5·2′W	X	201
Blackstone Rocks	N Som	ST3870	51°25·8′	2°53·1′W	X	171,182
Black Stones	N Yks	SE4053	53°58·5′	1°23·0′W	X	105
Black Stones	Pemb	SM7408	51°43·8′	5°16·0′W	X	157
Blackstone's Low	Derby	SK2055	53°5·7′	1°41·7′W	A	119
Blackstoun	Renf	NS4566	55°52·0′	4°28·2′W	X	64
Black Strand	D & G	NX4463	54°56·5′	4°25·7′W	W	83
Black Street	Suff	TM5186	52°25·1′	1°41·9′E	T	156
Black Stripe	Moray	NJ1550	57°32·2′	3°24·7′W	W	28
Blacksyke	Cumbr	NY7215	54°32·0′	2°25·5′W	X	91
Black Sykes	Cumbr	NY4637	54°43·8′	2°49·9′W	X	90
Blacktail Spit	Essex	TR0486	51°32·4′	0°56·9′E	X	178
Black Taing	Orkney	HY3917	59°2·4′	3°3·3′W	X	6
Black Tar	Pemb	SM9909	51°44·9′	4°54·3′W	T	157,158
Blacktar Point	Pemb	SM9909	51°44·9′	4°54·3′W	X	157,158
Black Tewthwaite	Cumbr	NY8714	54°31·5′	2°11·6′W	X	91,92
Blackthird	W Dunb	NS3481	55°59·9′	4°39·3′W	X	63
Blackthorn	Oxon	SP6219	51°52·2′	1°5·6′W	T	164,165
Blackthorn Copse	Hants	SU2613	50°55·2′	1°37·4′W	F	195
Blackthorn Fm	Norf	TM1381	52°23·4′	1°8·2′E	FM	144,156
Blackthorn Hill	Lincs	SK9282	53°19·8′	0°36·7′W	X	121
Blackthorn Hill	Oxon	SP6121	51°53·3′	1°6·4′W	X	164,165
Blackthorn Lodge	Northnts	SP9587	52°28·6′	0°35·7′W	X	141
Blackthorpe	Suff	TL9063	52°14·2′	0°47·4′E	T	155
Blacktoft	E Yorks	SE8424	53°42·6′	0°43·2′W	T	106,112
Blacktoft Channel	E Yorks	SE8423	53°42·0′	0°43·2′W	W	106,112
Blacktoft Grange	E Yorks	SE8331	53°46·4′	0°44·0′W	X	106
Blacktoft Ho	E Yorks	SE8325	53°43·1′	0°44·1′W	X	106
Blacktoft Sands	E Yorks	SE8423	53°42·0′	0°43·2′W	X	106,112
Blackton	Durham	NY9317	54°33·1′	2°6·1′W	X	91,92
Blackton	Shetld	HU2847	60°12·6′	1°29·2′W	X	3
Blackton Beck	Durham	NZ0025	54°37·5′	1°59·6′W	W	92
Blackton Fm	V of Glam	ST0768	51°24·4′	3°19·8′W	FM	170
Blacktongue	N Lanak	NS7870	55°54·7′	3°56·7′W	X	64
Blackton Head	Durham	NZ0125	54°37·5′	1°58·6′W	X	92
Blackton Resr	Durham	NY9418	54°33·7′	2°5·1′W	W	91,92
Blacktop	C of Aber	NJ8604	57°7·9′	2°13·4′W	T	38
Black Top	D & G	NX7192	55°12·6′	4°1·2′W	X	77
Blacktop Hill	S Ayr	NS2615	55°24·1′	4°44·4′W	H	70
Black Tor	Derby	SE0600	53°30·0′	1°54·2′W	X	110
Black Tor	Derby	SK2757	53°6·8′	1°35·4′W	X	119
Black Tor	Devon	SX5689	50°41·2′	4°1·9′W	X	191
Black Tor	Devon	SX5771	50°31·5′	4°0·7′W	H	202
Black Tor	Devon	SX6863	50°27·4′	3°51·2′W	X	202
Blacktor Downs	Corn	SX1573	50°31·9′	4°36·3′W	X	201
Black Torrington	Devon	SS4605	50°49·7′	4°10·8′W	T	190
Blacktown	Highld	NH7443	57°27·9′	4°5·6′W	X	27
Blacktown	Newp	ST2681	51°31·6′	3°3·6′W	T	171
Black Vein	Caer	ST2291	51°37·0′	3°7·2′W	T	171
Black Ven	Dorset	SY3593	50°44·2′	2°54·9′W	X	193
Blackven Common	Dorset	ST8319	50°58·4′	2°14·1′W	X	183
Black Ven Fm	E Susx	TQ4425	51°0·6′	0°3·6′E	FM	187,198
Black Venn Fm	Dorset	ST8223	51°0·6′	2°15·0′W	FM	183
Black Walks	Suff	TM4254	52°8·1′	1°32·6′E	X	156
Blackwall	Derby	SK2549	53°2·5′	1°37·2′W	T	119
Blackwall	T Ham	TQ3880	51°30·3′	0°0·3′W	T	177
Blackwall Bridge	Essex	TL6608	51°45·0′	0°24·7′E	X	167
Blackwall Fm	Kent	TR0443	51°9·2′	0°55·4′E	FM	179,189
Black Wall Nook	N Lincs	SE9102	53°30·6′	0°37·3′W	X	112
Blackwall Reach	T Ham	TQ3879	51°29·8′	0°0·3′W	W	177
Blackwalls	Fife	NO4511	56°17·6′	2°52·9′W	X	59
Black Walter	Northum	NU0708	55°22·2′	1°52·9′W	X	81
Black Ward	Shetld	HU2351	60°14·8′	1°34·6′W	X	3
Blackwardine	Heref	SO5356	52°12·3′	2°40·9′W	X	149
Black Wars	Cumbr	NY2604	54°25·8′	3°8·0′W	X	89,90
Blackwater	Corn	SW7346	50°16·5′	5°10·8′W	T	204
Black Water	D & G	NX6288	55°10·3′	4°9·6′W	W	77
Black Water	D & G	NX6788	55°10·4′	4°4·9′W	W	77
Blackwater	Dorset	SZ1395	50°45·5′	1°48·6′W	T	195
Black Water	E Ayr	NS5112	55°23·0′	4°20·7′W	W	70
Black Water	Hants	SU2704	50°50·3′	1°36·6′W	W	195
Blackwater	Hants	SU8559	51°19·7′	0°46·4′W	T	175,186
Black Water	Highld	NC7117	58°7·7′	4°11·0′W	W	16
Black Water	Highld	NC7815	58°6·7′	4°3·8′W	W	17
Black Water	Highld	NH4066	57°39·6′	4°40·4′W	W	20
Black Water	Highld	NH4457	57°34·8′	4°36·1′W	W	26
Black Water	Highld	NH4691	57°53·2′	4°35·4′W	W	20
Black Water	Highld	NH5776	57°45·3′	4°23·7′W	W	21
Black Water	Highld	NM7253	56°37·1′	5°42·5′W	W	49
Black Water	Highld	NN3861	56°43·0′	4°38·4′W	W	41
Blackwater	Inverc	NS3267	55°52·3′	4°40·7′W	X	63
Blackwater	I of W	SZ5086	50°40·5′	1°17·2′W	T	196
Black Water	Moray	NJ3428	57°20·5′	3°5·3′W	W	37
Black Water	Norf	TF9619	52°44·2′	0°54·6′E	W	132

Black Water	Norf	TG0829	52°49·3′	1°5·6′E	W	133
Blackwater	Norf	TG0920	52°44·5′	1°6·2′E	T	133
Blackwater	Norf	TL9481	52°23·8′	0°51·5′E	X	144
Black Water	Pth & Kin	NO1455	56°41·0′	3°23·8′W	W	53
Black Water	Shetld	HU2278	60°29·4′	1°35·5′W	W	3
Black Water	Shetld	HU4657	60°17·9′	1°9·6′W	W	2,3
Blackwater	Somer	ST2615	50°56·0′	3°2·8′W	T	193
Black Water	Stir	NN5306	56°13·7′	4°21·8′W	W	57
Blackwater Br	Norf	TG0830	52°49·9′	1°5·7′E	X	133
Blackwater Corner	Norf	TG2326	52°47·4′	1°18·8′E	X	133,134
Blackwater Fm	Essex	TL8703	51°41·9′	0°42·8′E	FM	168
Blackwaterfoot	N Ayr	NR8928	55°30·3′	5°20·0′W	T	68,69
Blackwater Forest	Moray	NJ3126	57°19·4′	3°8·3′W	X	37
Blackwater Lodge	Moray	NJ3328	57°20·5′	3°6·3′W	X	37
Black Water of Dee or River Dee	D & G	NX5574	55°2·6′	4°15·7′W	W	77
Black Water of Dee or River Dee	D & G	NX6569	55°0·1′	4°6·2′W	W	83,84
Black Water or Uisge Dubh	Highld	NH0038	57°23·6′	5°19·2′W	W	25
Blackwater Reservoir	Highld	NN3059	56°41·8′	4°46·1′W	W	41
Blackwater River	Hants	SU8360	51°20·2′	0°48·1′W	W	175,186
Blackwater River	Norf	TG0104	52°36·0′	0°58·5′E	W	144
Blackwater River	Somer	ST3601	50°48·5′	2°54·1′W	W	193
Blackwaters	Staffs	SJ7732	52°53·3′	2°20·1′W	X	127
Blackwater Wood	Oxon	SP5811	51°47·9′	1°9·1′W	F	164
Blackway	Heref	SO6445	52°6·4′	2°31·1′W	X	149
Blackweir	Card	ST1777	51°29·4′	3°11·3′W	T	171
Blackwell	Cumbr	NY4053	54°52·3′	2°55·7′W	T	85
Blackwell	Cumbr	SD4094	54°20·5′	2°55·0′W	X	96,97
Blackwell	Darl	NZ2712	54°30·4′	1°34·6′W	T	93
Blackwell	Derby	SK1272	53°14·9′	1°48·8′W	T	119
Blackwell	Derby	SK4358	53°7·3′	1°21·0′W	T	120
Blackwell	Somer	ST0026	51°1·7′	3°25·2′W	T	181
Blackwell	Warw	SP2443	52°5·3′	1°38·6′W	T	151
Blackwell	Worcs	SO9872	52°21·0′	2°1·4′W	T	139
Blackwell	W Susx	TQ3939	51°8·2′	0°0·4′W	T	187
Blackwell Br	N Yks	NZ2712	54°30·4′	1°34·6′W	X	93
Blackwell Common	Hants	SU4301	50°48·6′	1°23·0′W	X	196
Blackwell Court	Worcs	SO9971	52°20·5′	2°0·5′W	X	139
Blackwell Fm	Cambs	TL0870	52°19·3′	0°24·5′W	FM	153
Blackwell Fm	Surrey	SU9649	51°14·2′	0°37·1′W	FM	186
Blackwell Hall	Bucks	SU9899	51°41·1′	0°34·5′W	X	165,176
Blackwell Lodge	Leic	SK8430	52°51·9′	0°44·7′W	X	130
Blackwell Parks	Devon	SX7151	50°20·9′	3°48·4′W	X	202
Blackwells End Green	Glos	SO7825	51°55·6′	2°18·8′W	X	162
Black Wood	Angus	NO5538	56°32·2′	2°43·5′W	F	54
Black Wood	Ches	SJ3761	53°8·8′	2°56·1′W	F	117
Black Wood	Darl	NZ3409	54°28·8′	1°28·1′W	F	93
Black Wood	D & G	NX9087	55°10·2′	3°43·2′W	F	78
Blackwood	D & G	NX9087	55°10·2′	3°43·2′W	X	78
Blackwood	E Ayr	NS4840	55°38·0′	4°24·4′W	X	70
Blackwood	E Ayr	NS6413	55°23·8′	4°8·4′W	X	71
Black Wood	E Loth	NT5767	55°53·9′	2°40·8′W	F	67
Black Wood	E Loth	NT6069	55°55·0′	2°38·0′W	F	67
Black Wood	E Yorks	SE9561	54°2·4′	0°32·5′W	F	101
Black Wood	Fife	NO3923	56°24·0′	2°58·9′W	F	54,59
Black Wood	Hants	SU5342	51°10·7′	1°14·1′W	F	185
Black Wood	Hants	SU7157	51°18·7′	0°58·5′W	F	175,186
Blackwood	Highld	NG9543	57°26·1′	5°24·5′W	F	25
Black Wood	Highld	NH5241	57°26·4′	4°27·5′W	F	26
Black Wood	Highld	NH7088	57°52·0′	4°11·0′W	F	21
Black Wood	Highld	NN5791	56°59·5′	4°20·8′W	F	35
Black Wood	Lancs	SD5665	54°5·0′	2°39·9′W	F	97
Blackwood	Leeds	SE3239	53°51·0′	1°30·4′W	X	104
Black Wood	N Yks	SD6471	54°8·3′	2°32·6′W	F	97
Black Wood	N Yks	SE5467	54°6·0′	1°10·0′W	F	100
Black Wood	Powys	SO1598	52°34·6′	3°14·9′W	F	136
Blackwood	S Lanak	NS7943	55°40·2′	3°55·0′W	T	71
Black Wood	Suff	TL7854	52°9·6′	0°36·5′E	F	155
Blackwood	Warr	SJ6290	53°24·6′	2°33·9′W	T	109
Blackwood	Wrex	SJ4040	52°57·5′	2°53·2′W	X	117
Blackwood Br	D & G	NX9187	55°10·2′	3°42·2′W	X	78
Blackwood Common	Cald	SE0117	53°39·2′	1°58·7′W	X	110
Blackwood Common	Cald	SE0124	53°43·0′	1°58·7′W	X	104
Blackwood Cottage	Pth & Kin	NN5656	56°40·7′	4°20·6′W	X	42,51
Blackwood End	Lancs	SD5057	54°0·6′	2°45·4′W	X	102
Blackwood Hall	N Yks	SE6736	53°49·2′	0°58·5′W	X	105,106
Blackwood Hill	E Renf	NS5448	55°42·5′	4°19·0′W	H	64
Blackwood Hill	Scot Bord	NY5296	55°15·6′	2°44·9′W	H	79
Blackwood Hill	S Lanak	NS8130	55°33·2′	3°52·8′W	X	71,72
Blackwood Hill	Staffs	SJ9255	53°5·8′	2°6·8′W	X	118
Blackwood Ho	S Lanak	NS7743	55°40·2′	3°56·9′W	X	71
Blackwood Ho	Staffs	SJ9257	53°6·8′	2°6·8′W	X	118
Blackwood House Fm	N Yks	SE6736	53°49·2′	0°58·5′W	FM	105,106
Blackwood or Coed Duon	Caer	ST1797	51°40·2′	3°11·6′W	T	171
Blackwoodridge	D & G	NY2476	55°4·6′	3°11·0′W	X	85
Blackwoods Ho Fm	N Yks	SE5566	54°5·5′	1°9·1′W	FM	100
Blackwool Law	Northum	NY8098	55°16·8′	2°18·5′W	H	80
Blackworthy	Devon	SS4900	50°47·0′	4°8·1′W	X	191
Blackworthy Hill	Somer	ST6232	51°5·4′	2°32·2′W	X	183
Black Yatt	Powys	SO1856	52°12·0′	3°11·6′W	X	148
Blackyduds	Aberd	NJ6803	57°7·3′	2°31·3′W	H	38
Black Yeats	Cumbr	SD5483	54°14·7′	2°41·9′W	X	97
Blackyett	D & G	NY2571	55°1·9′	3°10·0′W	X	85
Blacky More	Northnts	SP7556	52°12·1′	0°53·8′W	X	152
Blaco Hill	Notts	SK6988	53°23·3′	0°57·3′W	X	111,120
Blacon	Ches	SJ3867	53°12·0′	2°55·3′W	T	117
Blacon Fm	Warw	SP2262	52°15·6′	1°40·3′W	FM	151
Blacow House Fm	Lancs	SD5237	53°49·9′	2°43·7′W	FM	102
Bladbean	Kent	TR1747	51°11·1′	1°6·7′E	T	179,189
Bladdering Cleugh	E Loth	NT6969	55°55·0′	2°29·3′W	X	67
Bladeley Hill	Dorset	ST6804	50°50·3′	2°26·9′W	X	194
Blade Moss	Cumbr	SD2682	54°13·9′	3°7·7′W	X	96,97
Blades	N Yks	SD7993	54°20·2′	2°19·0′W	X	98
Blades	N Yks	SD9898	54°22·9′	2°1·4′W	T	98
Blades Fm	N Yks	SE5468	54°6·5′	1°10·0′W	FM	100
Blades, The	Shetld	HU2981	60°31·0′	1°27·8′W	X	1,3
Bladnoch	D & G	NX4254	54°51·6′	4°27·3′W	T	83
Bladon	Oxon	SP4414	51°49·6′	1°21·3′W	T	164

Bladon Castle	Derby	SK2625	52°49·6′	1°36·4′W	X	128
Bladon Heath	Oxon	SP4513	51°49·1′	1°20·4′W	F	164
Bladon House School	Derby	SK2624	52°49·0′	1°36·4′W	X	128
Blaebeck	D & G	NT0907	55°21·2′	3°25·7′W	X	78
Blaeberry Burn	Durham	NY9234	54°42·3′	2°7·0′W	W	91,92
Blaeberry Burn	Northum	NY7655	54°53·6′	2°22·0′W	W	86,87
Blaeberry Burn	S Lanak	NS7335	55°35·8′	4°0·5′W	W	71
Blaeberry Hill	D & G	NT2004	55°19·7′	3°15·2′W	H	79
Blaeberry Hill	D & G	NT2801	55°18·1′	3°7·6′W	H	79
Blaeberry Hill	D & G	NY1290	55°12·0′	3°22·5′W	X	78
Blaeberry Hill	W Loth	NS9564	55°51·7′	3°40·2′W	X	65
Blaeberry Isle	E Ayr	NX4491	55°11·6′	4°26·6′W	X	77
Blaefaulds	Falk	NS7981	56°0·7′	3°56·0′W	X	64
Blae Loch	N Ayr	NS2455	55°45·6′	4°47·9′W	W	63
Blaelochhead	N Ayr	NS3953	55°44·9′	4°33·5′W	X	63
Blaeloch Hill	N Ayr	NS2455	55°45·6′	4°47·9′W	H	63
Blaemount Rig	Scot Bord	NY5185	55°9·7′	2°45·7′W	H	79
Blaen	Heref	SO2733	51°59·7′	3°3·4′W	X	161
Blaenachddu	Carm	SN2937	52°0·5′	4°29·1′W	X	145
Blaenafon	Carm	SN1324	51°53·2′	4°42·7′W	X	145,158
Blaenafon	Carm	SN3832	51°58·0′	4°21·1′W	X	145
Blaenafon	Cered	SN3748	52°6·6′	4°22·4′W	X	145
Blaenannerch	Cered	SN2449	52°6·9′	4°33·8′W	T	145
Blaenant	Cered	SN3242	52°3·3′	4°26·6′W	X	145
Blaenant	Nth Pt Talb	SN7503	51°42·9′	3°48·2′W	X	170
Blaenant Cadno	Carm	SN6409	51°46·0′	3°57·9′W	X	159
Blaenau	Carm	SN4815	51°49·0′	4°11·9′W	X	159
Blaenau	Carm	SN5510	51°46·4′	4°5·7′W	X	159
Blaenau	Carm	SN6014	51°48·7′	4°1·5′W	T	159
Blaenau	Carm	SN7924	51°54·3′	3°45·1′W	X	160
Blaenau	Denb	SH9961	53°8·4′	3°30·2′W	X	116
Blaenau	Flint	SJ2455	53°5·5′	3°7·7′W	T	117
Blaenau	Gwyn	SH7922	52°47·2′	3°47·3′W	X	124
Blaenau	Heref	SO2639	52°2·9′	3°4·4′W	X	161
Blaenau	Heref	SO2937	52°1·8′	3°1·7′W	X	161
Blaenau	Powys	SO2423	51°54·3′	3°5·9′W	X	161
Blaenau Dolwyddelan	Conwy	SH7051	53°2·7′	3°55·9′W	T	115
Blaenau-draw	Powys	SO1726	51°55·8′	3°12·0′W	X	161
Blaenau Ffestiniog	Gwyn	SH7045	52°59·4′	3°55·8′W	T	115
Blaenaufforest	Carm	SN6145	52°5·4′	4°1·3′W	X	146
Blaenau-fry	Powys	SO1926	51°55·8′	3°10·3′W	X	161
Blaenau-gwenog	Cered	SN4751	52°8·4′	4°13·8′W	X	146
Blaenau-Gwent	Blae Gw	SO2104	51°44·0′	3°8·2′W	T	171
Blaenau Isaf	Powys	SN8425	51°54·8′	3°40·8′W	X	160
Blaenau-Isaf	Powys	SO2034	52°0·2′	3°9·5′W	X	161
Blaenau Uchaf	Powys	SN8325	51°54·9′	3°41·7′W	X	160
Blaenau-Uchaf	Powys	SO1831	51°58·5′	3°11·2′W	X	161
Blaenau Uchaf	Wrex	SJ2540	52°57·4′	3°6·6′W	X	117
Blaenavon	Torf	SO2509	51°46·7′	3°4·8′W	T	161
Blaenawey	Monm	SO2919	51°52·1′	3°1·5′W	X	161
Blaen Bache	Denb	SJ1940	52°57·3′	3°11·9′W	X	125
Blaenbargod	Carm	SN3734	51°59·1′	4°22·0′W	X	145
Blaenbarre	Cered	SN3649	52°7·1′	4°23·3′W	X	145
Blaen Bedw	Cered	SN4259	52°12·6′	4°18·4′W	X	146
Blaenbedw Fach	Cered	SN3651	52°8·2′	4°23·4′W	X	145
Blaenbedw Fawr	Cered	SN3651	52°8·2′	4°23·4′W	T	145
Blaenbedw Isaf	Cered	SN3650	52°7·7′	4°23·4′W	X	145
Blaenblodau	Carm	SN4637	52°0·8′	4°14·3′W	X	146
Blaenborthyn	Cered	SN4641	52°3·0′	4°14·4′W	X	146
Blaenbowi	Carm	SN3235	51°59·5′	4°26·4′W	X	145
Blaen Bran	Carm	SN3335	51°59·5′	4°25·6′W	X	145
Blaen Bran Resrs	Torf	ST2697	51°40·3′	3°3·8′W	W	171
Blaenbrefi	Cered	SN7155	52°10·9′	3°52·8′W	W	146,147
Blaenbryn	Carm	SN3426	51°54·7′	4°24·4′W	X	145
Blaenbrynich	Powys	SN9523	51°54·0′	3°31·2′W	X	160
Blaen-bwch	Powys	SO2332	51°59·1′	3°6·9′W	X	161
Blaen Bwch Fm	Powys	SO0145	52°5·9′	3°26·3′W	FM	147
Blaen-bydernyn	Cered	SN5543	52°4·2′	4°6·5′W	X	146
Blaenbythigion	Powys	SN8882	52°25·7′	3°38·4′W	X	135,136
Blaencaerau	Nth Pt Talb	SS8694	51°38·2′	3°38·5′W	T	170
Blaen Camarch	Powys	SN8757	52°12·2′	3°38·8′W	X	147
Blaencamlais	Powys	SN9525	51°55·1′	3°31·2′W	X	160
Blaencanaid	Rho Cyn Taf	SO0204	51°43·8′	3°24·8′W	X	170
Blaen-car	Powys	SN8418	51°51·2′	3°40·7′W	X	160
Blaencarno	Caer	SO0908	51°46·0′	3°18·7′W	X	161
Blaencarreg	Carm	SN5444	52°4·7′	4°7·4′W	X	146
Blaencarreg	Cered	SN5772	52°19·9′	4°5·5′W	X	135
Blaencastell	Cered	SN5859	52°12·9′	4°4·3′W	X	146
Blaencathal	Cered	SN4546	52°5·7′	4°15·4′W	X	146
Blaencediw	Carm	SN2020	51°51·2′	4°36·4′W	X	145,158
Blaencefel	Cered	SN4245	52°5·1′	4°18·0′W	X	146
Blaen-Ceiment	Carm	SN5841	52°3·2′	4°3·9′W	X	146
Blaencelyn	Cered	SN3554	52°9·8′	4°24·4′W	T	145
Blaencennen Fm	Carm	SN6919	51°51·5′	3°53·7′W	FM	160
Blaencerde	Powys	SO2151	52°9·3′	3°8·9′W	X	148
Blaencerdinfach	Cered	SN3748	52°6·6′	4°22·4′W	X	145
Blaencerniog	Powys	SN9494	52°32·3′	3°33·4′W	X	136
Blaen-Ceulan	Cered	SN7190	52°29·8′	3°53·6′W	X	135
Blaencilgoed Fm	Pemb	SN1410	51°45·8′	4°41·3′W	FM	158
Blaenclettwr	Cered	SN4453	52°9·4′	4°16·4′W	X	146
Blaenclydach	Carm	SN7519	51°51·6′	3°48·5′W	X	160
Blaenclydach	Powys	SN8831	51°58·2′	3°37·4′W	X	160
Blaen Clydach	Rho Cyn Taf	SS9893	51°37·8′	3°28·0′W	T	170
Blaenclydwyn	Brig	SS9186	51°34·0′	3°34·0′W	X	170
Blaenclyn	Powys	SN9624	51°54·5′	3°30·3′W	X	160
Blaencoed	Monm	SO3516	51°50·6′	2°56·2′W	X	161
Blaencorse	Carm	SN2417	51°49·7′	4°32·9′W	X	158
Blaen-Cothi	Carm	SN6948	52°7·1′	3°54·3′W	X	146
Blaen Cownwy	Powys	SH9419	52°45·7′	3°33·9′W	X	125
Blaen Cownwy	Powys	SH9818	52°45·2′	3°30·3′W	X	125
Blaencrai	Powys	SN8822	51°53·4′	3°37·3′W	X	160
Blaen Cregan	Nth Pt Talb	SS8599	51°40·9′	3°39·4′W	W	170
Blaen-cribor	Cered	SN4048	52°6·7′	4°19·8′W	X	146
Blaencrymlyn	Brig	SS9385	51°33·5′	3°32·2′W	X	170
Blaencwm	Carm	SN4137	52°0·8′	4°18·6′W	X	146
Blaencwm	Carm	SN4625	51°54·4′	4°13·9′W	X	146
Blaencwm	Carm	SN5438	52°1·5′	4°7·3′W	X	146
Blaencwm	Carm	SN5729	51°56·7′	4°4·4′W	X	146
Blaencwm	Carm	SN6034	51°59·4′	4°1·9′W	X	146
Blaen Cwm	Gwyn	SH9940	52°57·1′	3°29·8′W	X	125

Blaencwm	Powys	SO2136	52°1·2′	3°8·7′W	X	161
Blaencwm	Rho Cyn Taf	SS9298	51°40·5′	3°33·3′W	T	170
Blaen Cwm Banw	Powys	SO0722	51°53·6′	3°20·7′W	X	160
Blaen-cwmcerwyn	Brig	SS8390	51°36·0′	3°41·0′W	X	170
Blaen Cwmcleisfer	Powys	SO1316	51°50·4′	3°15·4′W	X	161
Blaen Cwmdû	Brig	SS8792	51°37·2′	3°37·5′W	X	170
Blaen-cwm-llawenog	Wrex	SJ1034	52°54·0′	3°19·9′W	X	125
Blaen Cwm-Magwr	Cered	SN7076	52°22·2′	3°54·2′W	X	135,147
Blaencwmmau	Carm	SN2022	51°52·3′	4°36·5′W	X	145,158
Blaen-cwm-mynach	Gwyn	SH6822	52°47·0′	3°57·0′W	X	124
Blaencwmpridd	Cered	SN3852	52°8·8′	4°21·7′W	X	145
Blaencwrt	Cered	SN5048	52°6·8′	4°11·0′W	X	146
Blaencynllaith	Carm	SN3528	51°55·8′	4°23·6′W	X	145
Blaencynnen	Carm	SN3722	51°52·6′	4°21·7′W	X	145,159
Blaencywarch	Gwyn	SH8518	52°45·1′	3°41·8′W	X	124,125
Blaen-ddôl	Gwyn	SH7042	52°57·8′	3°55·7′W	X	124
Blaendigedi	Powys	SO2236	52°1·3′	3°7·8′W	X	161
Blaen-Dinam	Denb	SJ0235	52°54·5′	3°27·0′W	X	125
Blaendoithie	Cered	SN7453	52°9·9′	3°50·1′W	X	146,147
Blaenduad	Carm	SN4033	51°58·6′	4°19·4′W	F	146
Blaen Dyar	Monm	SO2312	51°48·3′	3°6·6′W	X	161
Blaen-dyffryn	Carm	SN7140	52°2·8′	3°52·5′W	X	146,147,160
Blaendyffryn	Cered	SN7081	52°24·9′	3°54·3′W	X	135
Blaendyffryn	Pemb	SN1328	51°55·4′	4°42·8′W	X	145,158
Blaendyffryn Fm	Cered	SN3941	52°2·9′	4°20·5′W	FM	145
Blaendyflin	Carm	SN2127	51°55·0′	4°35·8′W	X	145,158
Blaendyfod	Carm	SN3127	51°55·2′	4°27·1′W	X	145
Blaendyryn	Powys	SN9336	52°1·0′	3°33·2′W	X	160
Blaen Edw	Powys	SO1459	52°13·6′	3°15·2′W	X	148
Blaen Edw Bank	Powys	SO1459	52°13·6′	3°15·2′W	X	148
Blaen-egel-fawr	Nth Pt Talb	SN7209	51°46·1′	3°50·9′W	X	160
Blaen Eidda Isaf	Conwy	SH8249	53°1·8′	3°45·2′W	X	116
Blaen Eidda Uchaf	Conwy	SH8148	53°1·2′	3°46·0′W	X	116
Blaeneifed	Cered	SN2445	52°4·8′	4°33·7′W	X	145
Blaeneinion	Cered	SN7193	52°31·4′	3°53·7′W	X	135
Blaeneinon	Carm	SN4645	52°5·2′	4°14·5′W	X	146
Blaenfallen	Cered	SN5559	52°12·9′	4°7·0′W	X	146
Blaenfflyman	Cered	SN1950	52°7·4′	4°38·2′W	X	145
Blaenffos	Carm	SN3137	52°0·6′	4°27·4′W	X	145
Blaenffos	Pemb	SN1937	52°0·4′	4°37·8′W	T	145
Blaenfirnant	Powys	SO0545	52°6·0′	3°22·8′W	X	147
Blaengafren	Pemb	SN1539	52°1·4′	4°41·4′W	X	145
Blaengarw	Brig	SS8994	51°38·3′	3°35·9′W	X	170
Blaengarw	Brig	SS9092	51°37·2′	3°34·9′W	T	170
Blaengavenny	Monm	SO3119	51°52·2′	2°59·7′W	X	161
Blaengelli	Carm	SN2524	51°53·5′	4°32·2′W	X	145,158
Blaengeuffordd	Cered	SN6480	52°24·3′	3°59·6′W	X	135
Blaengilfach	Pemb	SN2632	51°57·8′	4°31·6′W	X	145
Blaenglanhanog	Powys	SN9599	52°35·0′	3°32·6′W	X	136
Blaen-Glasffrwd	Cered	SN7663	52°15·3′	3°48·6′W	X	146,147
Blaen Glaswen	Powys	SJ0430	52°51·8′	3°25·2′W	X	125
Blaen Gloddfa-fawr	Merth Tyd	SO0314	51°49·2′	3°24·1′W	X	160
Blaenglowonfach	Cered	SN4051	52°8·3′	4°19·9′W	X	146
Blaenglyn	Powys	SN9722	51°53·5′	3°29·4′W	X	160
Blaenglynolwyn	Powys	SN9860	52°14·0′	3°29·2′W	X	147
Blaengofer	Carm	SN3425	51°54·2′	4°24·4′W	X	145
Blaengofiarth	Carm	SN6139	52°2·2′	4°1·2′W	X	146
Blaengorffen	Cered	SN7262	52°14·7′	3°52·1′W	X	146,147
Blaengorlech	Carm	SN5438	52°1·5′	4°7·3′W	X	146
Blaen-gors	Pemb	SN1632	51°57·6′	4°40·3′W	X	145
Blaengwaithnoah	Pemb	SN1412	51°46·8′	4°41·4′W	X	158
Blaengwawr	Rho Cyn Taf	SO0001	51°42·2′	3°26·4′W	X	170
Blaengweche	Carm	SN6317	51°50·3′	3°58·9′W	X	159
Blaen-Gwenddwr	Powys	SO0445	52°5·9′	3°23·7′W	X	147
Blaengwen Fm	Carm	SN4533	51°58·7′	4°15·0′W	FM	146
Blaengwenllan Cross	Cered	SN3344	52°4·4′	4°25·8′W	X	145
Blaengwnfel	Powys	SN9056	52°11·7′	3°36·2′W	X	147
Blaengwrach	Nth Pt Talb	SN8605	51°44·2′	3°38·7′W	T	160
Blaengwy	Powys	SN9735	52°0·5′	3°29·6′W	X	160
Blaengwyddon	Carm	SN3039	52°1·6′	4°28·3′W	X	145
Blaengwynfi	Nth Pt Talb	SS8996	51°39·3′	3°35·9′W	T	170
Blaengyfre	Carm	SN4333	51°58·6′	4°16·8′W	X	146
Blaenhalen	Carm	SN3339	52°1·7′	4°25·7′W	X	145
Blaen Henllan	Powys	SO1045	52°6·0′	3°18·4′W	X	148
Blaenhenwysg	Rho Cyn Taf	ST0591	51°36·8′	3°21·9′W	X	170
Blaenhiraeth	Carm	SN5404	51°43·2′	4°6·4′W	X	159
Blaenhirbant-uchaf	Cered	SN4746	52°5·7′	4°13·6′W	X	146
Blaen Hirnant	Powys	SJ0322	52°47·5′	3°25·9′W	X	125
Blaenhow	Powys	SO0945	52°6·0′	3°19·3′W	X	147
Blaenige	Carm	SN3726	51°54·8′	4°21·8′W	X	145
Blaen Irfon	Powys	SN8361	52°14·3′	3°42·4′W	W	147
Blaenisfael	Carm	SN4617	51°50·1′	4°13·7′W	X	159
Blaenllaethdy	Pemb	SN0924	51°53·2′	4°46·1′W	X	145,158
Blaenllan	Cered	SN3544	52°4·4′	4°24·1′W	X	145
Blaenllechach	Carm	SN7826	51°55·4′	3°46·1′W	X	146,160
Blaenllechau	Rho Cyn Taf	SS9997	51°40·0′	3°27·2′W	T	170
Blaen Llia	Powys	SN9316	51°50·2′	3°32·8′W	F	160
Blaen Lliedi	Carm	SN5008	51°45·3′	4°10·0′W	X	159
Blaen-Lliw	Gwyn	SH8033	52°53·1′	3°46·6′W	X	124,125
Blaen-lliwe	Carm	SN1818	51°50·1′	4°38·1′W	X	158
Blaenlliw Isaf	Gwyn	SH8033	52°53·1′	3°46·6′W	X	124,125
Blaen Lluest	Cered	SN5261	52°13·9′	4°9·6′W	X	146
Blaenllundeg	Powys	SO1543	52°5·0′	3°14·0′W	X	148,161
Blaenllwydarth	Pemb	SN0926	51°54·2′	4°46·2′W	X	145,158
Blaenllwynau	Merth Tyd	SO1002	51°42·8′	3°17·8′W	X	171
Blaen-Llyn	Pemb	SM8729	51°55·4′	5°5·5′W	X	157
Blaenllynfell	Carm	SN7618	51°51·0′	3°47·6′W	W	160
Blaen-Llynnant	Carm	SN6921	51°52·6′	3°53·8′W	X	160
Blaen Llynor	Denb	SJ0836	52°55·1′	3°21·7′W	X	125
Blaen-Marchnant	Cered	SN7770	52°19·1′	3°47·9′W	X	135,147
Blaenmarlais	Carm	SN6734	51°59·6′	3°55·8′W	X	146
Blaenmeini	Pemb	SN0642	52°2·8′	4°49·4′W	X	145
Blaenmelyn	Torf	SO2406	51°45·1′	3°5·7′W	X	161
Blaen-mergi	Pemb	SN1740	52°1·9′	4°39·7′W	X	145
Blaenmilo Fm	Powys	SO0949	52°8·1′	3°19·4′W	FM	147
Blaenmilo-uchaf	Powys	SO0950	52°8·7′	3°19·4′W	X	147
Blaen-moelfre	Cered	SN5349	52°7·4′	4°8·4′W	X	146
Blaen-myddfai	Swan	SN6504	51°43·3′	3°56·9′W	X	159
Blaen-Myherin	Cered	SN8079	52°24·0′	3°45·4′W	X	135,136,147
Blaen Nanmor	Gwyn	SH6348	53°1·0′	4°2·1′W	X	115

Blaennant	Carm	SN6533	51°59·0'	3°57·6'W	X	146
Blaen-nant	Nth Pt Talb	SN7311	51°47·2'	3°50·1'W	X	160
Blaen-nant-ddu	Swan	SN6305	51°43·9'	3°58·6'W	X	159
Blaen-nant Fm	Powys	SO0724	51°54·6'	3°20·7'W	FM	160
Blaennantgwyn	Carm	SN3633	51°58·5'	4°22·9'W	X	145
Blaen-nant-gwyn	Carm	SN4935	51°59·8'	4°11·6'W	X	146
Blaennanthir	Carm	SN3132	51°57·9'	4°27·2'W	X	145
Blaennanthrys	Carm	SN4136	52°0·2'	4°18·6'W	X	146
Blaen-nant-wen	Merth Tyd	SO1001	51°42·3'	3°17·8'W	X	171
Blaen Nant-y-bedd	Powys	SO2327	51°56·4'	3°6·8'W	X	161
Blaen-nant-y-groes	Rho Cyn Taf	SO0202	51°42·7'	3°24·7'W	X	170
Blaen-nant-y-mab	Carm	SN5423	51°53·4'	4°6·9'W	X	159
Blaen-nedd-Isaf	Powys	SN9114	51°49·1'	3°34·5'W	X	160
Blaen Ochran	Monm	SO2908	51°46·2'	3°1·3'W	X	161
Blaen Onnau	Powys	SO1516	51°50·4'	3°13·6'W	X	161
Blaenos	Carm	SN7534	51°59·7'	3°48·8'W	X	146,160
Blaenpalis	Pemb	SN0431	51°56·8'	4°50·7'W	X	145,157
Blaenpant	Carm	SN2328	51°55·6'	4°34·1'W	X	145,158
Blaenpant	Carm	SN2824	51°53·5'	4°29·6'W	X	145,158
Blaen-pant	Carm	SN3131	51°57·4'	4°27·2'W	X	145
Blaen-pant	Cered	SN2544	52°4·2'	4°32·8'W	T	145
Blaenpant	Cered	SN4946	52°5·7'	4°11·9'W	X	146
Blaen-pant	Powys	SN7798	52°34·2'	3°48·5'W	X	135
Blaenparsel	Cered	SN3228	51°55·8'	4°26·2'W	X	145
Blaen Pathiog	Powys	SN9282	52°25·8'	3°34·9'W	X	136
Blaenpedol	Carm	SN7017	51°50·4'	3°52·8'W	X	160
Blaen-Peithnant	Cered	SN7684	52°26·6'	3°49·1'W	X	135
Blaenpennal	Cered	SN6264	52°15·7'	4°0·9'W	T	146
Blaen pennant	Gwyn	SH9021	52°46·8'	3°37·4'W	X	125
Blaenpentre	Cered	SN7274	52°21·2'	3°52·4'W	X	135,147
Blaenpibwr	Carm	SN4918	51°50·7'	4°11·1'W	X	159
Blaenpibydd Fm	Pemb	SN2832	51°57·8'	4°29·8'W	FM	145
Blaenpistyll	Cered	SN2347	52°5·8'	4°34·7'W	X	145
Blaenpistyll	Pemb	SN2436	51°59·9'	4°33·4'W	X	145
Blaenplwyf	Cered	SN2151	52°7·9'	4°36·5'W	X	145
Blaenplwyf	Cered	SN5775	52°21·5'	4°5·6'W	T	135
Blaen-plwyf-isaf	Cered	SN5949	52°7·5'	4°3·2'W	X	146
Blaenplwyf Isaf	Powys	SH8409	52°40·2'	3°42·5'W	X	124,125
Blaenporth	Cered	SN2648	52°6·4'	4°32·1'W	T	145
Blaenrheon	Powys	SN9827	51°56·2'	3°28·6'W	X	160
Blaen Rhestr	Powys	SN8469	52°18·7'	3°41·7'W	X	135,136,147
Blaen Rhisglog Plantation	Carm	SN6947	52°6·6'	3°54·4'W	F	146
Blaen-rhiwarth	Powys	SJ0229	52°51·2'	3°26·9'W	X	125
Blaen Rhiwlas Uchaf	Wrex	SJ1832	52°53·0'	3°12·7'W	X	125
Blaen Rhiwnant	Powys	SN8558	52°12·7'	3°40·6'W	X	147
Blaenrhondda	Rho Cyn Taf	SS9299	51°41·0'	3°33·3'W	T	170
Blaen-Rhymney	Caer	SO1010	51°47·1'	3°17·9'W	X	161
Blaensaith Fawr	Cered	SN2749	52°7·0'	4°31·2'W	X	145
Blaen-Sannan	Carm	SN5529	51°56·7'	4°6·2'W	X	146
Blaen-sawd	Pemb	SN0925	51°53·7'	4°46·2'W	X	145,158
Blaensawdde	Carm	SN7823	51°53·8'	3°46·0'W	X	160
Blaen-Senni	Powys	SN9321	51°52·9'	3°32·9'W	X	160
Blaensiedi Fawr	Carm	SN4035	51°59·7'	4°19·4'W	X	146
Blaensylgen	Carm	SN3132	51°57·9'	4°27·2'W	X	145
Blaensylltyn	Cered	SN3044	52°4·3'	4°28·4'W	X	145
Blaen-Tafolog	Powys	SH8909	52°40·3'	3°38·1'W	X	124,125
Blaentillery Fm	Blae Gw	SO2208	51°46·2'	3°7·4'W	FM	161
Blaen-tîr	Cered	SN3854	52°9·9'	4°21·7'W	X	145
Blaentrafle	Carm	SN2326	51°54·5'	4°34·0'W	X	145,158
Blaen-Twrch	Carm	SN6849	52°7·7'	3°55·3'W	X	146
Blaenwaun	Carm	SN2013	51°47·4'	4°36·2'W	X	158
Blaenwaun	Carm	SN2327	51°55·0'	4°34·0'W	T	145,158
Blaenwaun	Carm	SN6032	51°58·4'	4°1·9'W	X	146
Blaenwaun	Cered	SN3049	52°7·0'	4°28·6'W	X	145
Blaen Waun	Cered	SN3449	52°7·1'	4°25·1'W	X	145
Blaen-waun	Cered	SN3953	52°9·4'	4°20·8'W	T	145
Blaen-waun	Cered	SN5261	52°13·9'	4°9·6'W	X	146
Blaen-waun-ganol	Cered	SN5048	52°6·8'	4°11·0'W	X	146
Blaenwenen	Cered	SN2447	52°5·8'	4°33·8'W	X	145
Blaen-wern	Carm	SN5542	52°3·7'	4°6·5'W	X	146
Blaenwern	Cered	SN3446	52°5·5'	4°25·0'W	X	145
Blaenwern	Cered	SN4256	52°11·0'	4°18·3'W	X	146
Blaenwern	Cered	SN6253	52°9·7'	4°0·7'W	X	146
Blaen-wern	Pemb	SN0327	51°54·6'	4°51·5'W	X	145,157,158
Blaenwernddu	Carm	SN1719	51°50·6'	4°39·0'W	X	158
Blaen-y-cae	Gwyn	SH6931	52°51·9'	3°56·4'W	X	124
Blaen-y-clawdd-du	Powys	SN8775	52°21·9'	3°39·2'W	H	135,136,147
Blaenycoed	Carm	SN2618	51°50·3'	4°31·1'W	X	158
Blaen-y-coed	Carm	SN3427	51°55·2'	4°24·4'W	X	145
Blaen-y-coed	Conwy	SH8145	52°59·6'	3°46·0'W	X	116
Blaen-y-cwm	Blae Gw	SO1311	51°47·7'	3°15·3'W	T	161
Blaen-y-cwm	Carm	SN3037	52°0·6'	4°28·2'W	X	145
Blaen-y-cwm	Carm	SN7035	52°0·1'	3°53·2'W	X	146,160
Blaenycwm	Cered	SN8275	52°21·9'	3°43·6'W	X	135,136,147
Blaen-y-cwm	Conwy	SH8847	53°0·8'	3°39·8'W	X	116
Blaen-y-cwm	Denb	SJ0232	52°52·8'	3°27·0'W	X	125
Blaen-y-cwm	Flint	SJ1467	53°11·8'	3°16·8'W	X	116
Blaen-y-cwm	Gwyn	SH7121	52°46·5'	3°54·3'W	X	124
Blaen-y-cwm	Gwyn	SH7738	52°55·8'	3°49·4'W	X	124
Blaen y Cwm	Gwyn	SH8413	52°42·4'	3°42·6'W	X	124,125
Blaen-y-cwm	Gwyn	SH8435	52°54·2'	3°43·1'W	X	124,125
Blaen-y-cwm	Gwyn	SH9024	52°48·4'	3°37·5'W	X	125
Blaen-y-cwm	Monm	SO2528	51°57·0'	3°5·1'W	X	161
Blaen-y-cwm	Powys	SH9107	52°39·2'	3°36·3'W	X	125
Blaen y Cwm	Powys	SJ0127	52°50·1'	3°27·8'W	X	125
Blaen-y-cwm	Powys	SJ0820	52°46·4'	3°21·4'W	X	125
Blaen-y-cwm	Powys	SJ0932	52°52·9'	3°20·7'W	X	125
Blaen-y-cwm	Powys	SN9296	52°33·3'	3°35·2'W	X	136
Blaen-y-cwm	Powys	SN9463	52°15·5'	3°32·8'W	X	147
Blaen-y-cwm	Powys	SN9898	52°34·5'	3°29·9'W	X	136
Blaen-y-cwm	Powys	SO1625	51°55·3'	3°12·9'W	X	161
Blaen-y-cwm	Powys	SO2057	52°12·6'	3°9·9'W	X	148
Blaen-y-cwm	Powys	SO2470	52°19·6'	3°6·5'W	X	137,148
Blaen-y-cwm	Torf	SO2401	51°42·4'	3°5·6'W	X	171
Blaen-y-cwm	Torf	ST2593	51°38·1'	3°4·6'W	X	171
Blaen-y-cwm	V of Glam	SS9070	51°25·3'	3°34·5'W	X	170
Blaen-y-cwm	Wrex	SJ1437	52°55·7'	3°16·4'W	X	125
Blaen y Cylchau	Carm	SN7518	51°51·0'	3°48·5'W	X	160
Blaen-y-dre	Denb	SJ0335	52°54·5'	3°26·1'W	X	125
Blaen-Ydw	Carm	SN7931	51°58·1'	3°45·3'W	X	146,160
Blaen-y-glyn	Denb	SJ0538	52°56·1'	3°24·4'W	X	125
Blaen-y-glyn	Gwyn	SH7626	52°49·3'	3°50·0'W	X	124
Blaen-y-nant	Conwy	SH7360	53°7·6'	3°53·5'W	X	115
Blaen-y-nant	Conwy	SH9768	53°12·2'	3°32·1'W	X	116
Blaen-y-nant	Denb	SJ1659	53°7·5'	3°14·9'W	X	116
Blaen-y-nant	Gwyn	SH6460	53°7·4'	4°1·5'W	X	115
Blaen-yr-esgair	Cered	SN5260	52°13·3'	4°9·6'W	X	146
Blaen-yr-esgair	Cered	SN6565	52°16·2'	3°58·3'W	X	135
Blaen-yr-henbant	Powys	SO2522	51°53·7'	3°5·0'W	X	161
Blaen-yr-olchfa-fawr	Swan	SN6604	51°43·4'	3°56·0'W	X	159
Blaenythan	Cered	SN3944	52°4·5'	4°20·6'W	X	145
Blaen-y-wergloedd	Conwy	SH9163	53°9·4'	3°37·4'W	X	116
Blaewanders	Pth & Kin	NN9721	56°22·5'	3°39·6'W	X	52,53,58
Blaeweneirch	Carm	SN1920	51°51·2'	4°37·3'W	X	145,158
Blagaton	Devon	SX4197	50°45·3'	4°14·9'W	X	190
Blagden Copse	Hants	SU3652	51°16·2'	1°28·6'W	F	185
Blagden Ho	Hants	SU3552	51°16·2'	1°29·5'W	X	185
Blagdon	Corn	SX2094	50°43·3'	4°32·6'W	X	190
Blagdon	Devon	SS3121	50°58·1'	4°24·0'W	X	190
Blagdon	Devon	SX5295	50°44·4'	4°5·5'W	X	191
Blagdon	N Som	ST5058	51°19·4'	2°42·7'W	T	172,182
Blagdon	Somer	SS9139	51°8·6'	3°33·1'W	X	181
Blagdon	Torbay	SX8561	50°26·5'	3°36·8'W	T	202
Blagdonburn	Northum	NZ0596	55°15·7'	1°54·8'W	X	81
Blagdon Burn	Northum	NZ1488	55°11·4'	1°46·4'W	W	81
Blagdon Fm	Devon	SS2327	51°1·1'	4°31·0'W	FM	190
Blagdon Fm	Dorset	SU0517	50°57·4'	1°55·3'W	FM	184
Blagdon Fm	Somer	SS9734	51°6·0'	3°27·9'W	FM	181
Blagdon Hall	Northum	NZ2177	55°5·5'	1°39·8'W	X	88
Blagdon Hill	Dorset	ST4303	50°49·7'	2°48·2'W	H	193
Blagdon Hill	Dorset	SU0517	50°57·4'	1°55·3'W	X	184
Blagdon Hill	Somer	SS9733	51°5·5'	3°27·9'W	H	181
Blagdon Hill	Somer	ST2118	50°57·6'	3°7·1'W	T	193
Blagdon Hill Fm	Somer	ST5057	51°18·8'	2°42·7'W	FM	172,182
Blagdon Lake	Devon	SX3796	50°44·7'	4°18·2'W	W	190
Blagdon Lake	N Som	ST5159	51°19·9'	2°41·8'W	W	172,182
Blagdon Manor	Devon	SX3696	50°44·7'	4°19·1'W	X	190
Blagdon Manor Fm	Corn	SX2997	50°45·1'	4°25·1'W	FM	190
Blagdonmoor Wharf	Devon	SS3605	50°49·5'	4°19·3'W	X	190
Blagdon Park	Northum	NZ2176	55°4·9'	1°39·8'W	X	88
Blagdon Wood	Devon	SX3696	50°44·7'	4°19·1'W	F	190
Blagill	Cumbr	NY7347	54°49·3'	2°24·8'W	T	86,87
Blagillhead	Cumbr	NY7448	54°49·8'	2°23·9'W	X	86,87
Blagrave Fm	Read	SU6976	51°29·0'	1°0·0'W	FM	175
Blagrove	Devon	SS7716	50°56·1'	3°44·6'W	X	180
Blagrove Fm	Devon	SX4594	50°43·7'	4°11·4'W	FM	190
Blagrove Fm	Oxon	SP4800	51°42·0'	1°17·9'W	FM	164
Blagrove Fm	Somer	ST5036	51°7·5'	2°42·5'W	FM	182,183
Blagrove's Fm	Somer	ST1425	51°1·3'	3°13·2'W	FM	181,193
Blaguegate	Lancs	SD4506	53°33·1'	2°49·4'W	T	108
Blaich	Highld	NN0376	56°50·3'	5°13·3'W	T	41
Blaiket Mains	D & G	NX8267	54°59·3'	3°50·2'W	X	84
Blaikiewell Fm	Aberd	NO8698	57°4·6'	2°13·4'W	FM	38,45
Blaik Law	E Loth	NT6671	55°56·1'	2°32·2'W	H	67
Blain	Highld	NM6769	56°45·5'	5°48·3'W	T	40
Blaina	Blae Gw	SO1908	51°46·1'	3°10·0'W	T	161
Blair	Aberd	NJ7123	57°18·1'	2°28·4'W	X	38
Blair	Aberd	NJ8426	57°19·7'	2°15·5'W	X	38
Blair	E Ayr	NS4847	55°41·8'	4°24·7'W	X	64
Blair	Fife	NT0289	56°5·3'	3°34·1'W	X	65
Blair	Fife	NT3194	56°8·3'	3°6·2'W	T	59
Blair	N Ayr	NS3047	55°41·5'	4°41·8'W	A	63
Blair	S Ayr	NS2302	55°17·1'	4°46·8'W	X	76
Blair	S Ayr	NS3202	55°17·3'	4°38·3'W	X	76
Blair	S Lanak	NS8246	55°41·5'	3°52·2'W	X	72
Blair	Stir	NS4093	56°6·4'	4°33·9'W	X	56
Blairadam	Pth & Kin	NT1295	56°8·6'	3°24·5'W	X	58
Blairanboich	Arg & Bt	NS1169	55°52·9'	5°0·9'W	X	63
Blairannaich	Arg & Bt	NN3206	56°13·3'	4°42·1'W	X	56
Blair Ardoch	N Ayr	NS3045	55°40·4'	4°41·8'W	X	63
Blair Atholl	Pth & Kin	NN8765	56°46·0'	3°50·5'W	T	43
Blairbeg	Highld	NH5029	57°19·9'	4°29·0'W	X	26,35
Blairbeg	N Ayr	NS0231	55°32·2'	5°7·8'W	T	69
Blairbell	Pth & Kin	NO0219	56°21·4'	3°34·7'W	X	58
Blairbowie	Aberd	NJ7222	57°17·5'	2°27·4'W	X	38
Blairbowie	S Ayr	NS3211	55°22·1'	4°38·6'W	X	70
Blairbuie	Arg & Bt	NS1174	55°55·6'	5°1·1'W	X	63
Blairbuie	Highld	NB9714	58°4·4'	5°26·1'W	X	15
Blairbuie	Pth & Kin	NN8160	56°43·3'	3°56·2'W	X	43,52
Blairbuies Burn	D & G	NX4766	54°58·2'	4°23·0'W	W	83
Blairbuies Hill	D & G	NX4867	54°58·7'	4°22·1'W	X	83
Blairburn	Fife	NS9885	56°3·1'	3°37·8'W	T	65
Blair Burn	Stir	NS4193	56°6·5'	4°33·0'W	W	56
Blairbuy	D & G	NX3641	54°44·5'	4°32·4'W	X	83
Blair Castle	Fife	NS9685	56°3·1'	3°39·7'W	X	65
Blair Castle	Pth & Kin	NN8666	56°46·6'	3°51·5'W	A	43
Blaircessnock	Stir	NS6099	56°10·0'	4°14·8'W	X	57
Blairchroisk	Pth & Kin	NN9854	56°40·3'	3°39·4'W	X	52,53
Blaircochrane	Scot Bord	NT2154	55°46·6'	3°15·1'W	X	66,73
Blaircreich	Stir	NN4317	56°19·4'	4°31·9'W	X	56
Blair Croft	Aberd	NJ8526	57°19·7'	2°14·5'W	X	38
Blairdaff	Aberd	NJ6917	57°14·8'	2°30·4'W	X	38
Blairdenon Hill	Clackm	NN8601	56°11·5'	3°49·8'W	H	58
Blairderry	D & G	NX2662	54°55·6'	4°42·5'W	X	82
Blairderry Moss	D & G	NX2661	54°55·1'	4°42·5'W	X	82
Blairdhu	Highld	NH5750	57°31·3'	4°22·8'W	X	26
Blair Drummond	Stir	NS7398	56°9·7'	4°2·3'W	T	57
Blairdrummond Moss	Stir	NS7297	56°9·2'	4°3·2'W	X	57
Blairduff	Aberd	NJ5225	57°19·0'	2°47·4'W	X	37
Blairenbathie	Fife	NT1194	56°8·1'	3°25·5'W	X	58
Blairennich	W Dunb	NS4285	56°2·2'	4°31·7'W	X	56
Blairfad	Stir	NS4990	56°5·0'	4°25·2'W	X	57
Blairfettie	Pth & Kin	NN7564	56°45·3'	4°2·2'W	X	42
Blairfield	Angus	NO3534	56°29·9'	3°2·9'W	X	54
Blairfield	Pth & Kin	NO1406	56°14·6'	3°22·8'W	X	58
Blairfindy	Moray	NJ2027	57°19·9'	3°19·3'W	X	36
Blairfindy Lodge (Hotel)	Moray	NJ1928	57°20·4'	3°20·3'W	X	36
Blair Fm	S Ayr	NX2481	55°5·8'	4°45·1'W	FM	76
Blairfoid	Highld	NH6858	57°35·8'	4°12·1'W	X	26
Blairfowl	Aberd	NJ8038	57°26·2'	2°19·5'W	X	29,30
Blairgar	Stir	NS5382	56°0·8'	4°21·0'W	X	57,64
Blairglas	Arg & Bt	NS3486	56°2·5'	4°39·5'W	X	56
Blairglass	Aberd	NO2599	57°4·8'	3°13·8'W	X	37,44
Blairgorm	Highld	NJ0320	57°15·9'	3°36·0'W	X	36
Blairgowrie	Pth & Kin	NO1745	56°35·6'	3°20·7'W	T	53
Blairhall	Angus	NO3131	56°28·2'	3°6·8'W	X	53
Blairhall	Fife	NS9987	56°4·2'	3°36·9'W	X	65
Blairhall	Fife	NT0089	56°5·3'	3°36·0'W	T	65
Blairhall	Pth & Kin	NO1128	56°26·4'	3°26·2'W	X	53,58
Blairhall Mains	Fife	NS9887	56°4·2'	3°37·9'W	X	65
Blairhead	Aberd	NJ6501	57°6·2'	2°34·2'W	X	38
Blairhead	Pth & Kin	NO1407	56°15·1'	3°22·8'W	X	58
Blairhill	Clackm	NT0099	56°10·6'	3°36·2'W	X	58
Blair Hill	Devon	SX8666	50°29·2'	3°36·0'W	X	202
Blairhill	N Lanak	NS7265	55°51·9'	4°2·3'W	T	64
Blairhill	S Lanak	NS8724	55°30·1'	3°46·9'W	X	71,72
Blair Ho	Fife	NT0289	56°5·3'	3°34·1'W	X	65
Blair Ho	Stir	NN5106	56°13·7'	4°23·8'W	X	57
Blairhoyle	Stir	NN6101	56°11·1'	4°13·9'W	X	57
Blairhullichan	Stir	NN4401	56°10·8'	4°30·4'W	X	57
Blair Hur	Moray	NJ1644	57°29·0'	3°23·6'W	X	28
Blairindinny	Aberd	NJ5128	57°20·7'	2°48·4'W	X	37
Blairingone	Pth & Kin	NS9896	56°9·0'	3°38·1'W	T	58
Blairinnie	D & G	NX7269	55°0·2'	3°59·6'W	X	83,84
Blairinnie Hill	D & G	NX7369	55°0·2'	3°58·7'W	X	83,84
Blairish	Pth & Kin	NN7648	56°36·7'	4°0·8'W	X	51,52
Blairkibboch Burn	E Ayr	NS5530	55°32·8'	4°17·5'W	W	71
Blairkip	E Ayr	NS5429	55°32·2'	4°18·4'W	X	70
Blairland	N Ayr	NS2948	55°42·0'	4°42·8'W	T	63
Blairlick Hill	Moray	NJ3822	57°17·3'	3°1·3'W	H	37
Blairlinn	N Lanak	NS7572	55°55·7'	3°59·6'W	T	64
Blairlinnans	W Dunb	NS4085	56°2·1'	4°33·6'W	X	56
Blairlogie	Stir	NS8296	56°8·8'	3°53·5'W	T	57
Blairlomond	Arg & Bt	NS1999	56°9·2'	4°54·4'W	X	56
Blairlusk	W Dunb	NS4184	56°1·6'	4°32·6'W	X	56,64
Blairmack	D & G	NT0103	55°18·9'	3°33·2'W	X	78
Blair Mains	Fife	NS9686	56°3·6'	3°39·8'W	X	65
Blairmains	N Lanak	NS8664	55°51·6'	3°48·8'W	X	65
Blair Mains	Stir	NS8296	56°8·8'	3°53·5'W	X	57
Blair Mill	Fife	NT1596	56°9·2'	3°21·7'W	X	58
Blair Mill	N Ayr	NS3247	55°41·5'	4°39·9'W	X	63
Blairmore	Aberd	NJ4339	57°26·5'	2°56·5'W	X	28
Blairmore	Arg & Bt	NS1981	55°59·5'	4°53·7'W	T	63
Blairmore	Arg & Bt	NS1982	56°0·1'	4°53·7'W	T	56
Blairmore	Arg & Bt	NS1983	56°0·6'	4°53·8'W	X	56
Blairmore	Highld	NC1959	58°29·2'	5°5·8'W	X	9
Blairmore	Highld	NC7404	58°0·7'	4°7·5'W	X	16
Blairmore	Highld	NH5136	57°23·7'	4°28·3'W	X	26
Blairmore	Highld	NH8651	57°32·3'	3°53·8'W	X	27
Blairmore	Pth & Kin	NN7318	56°20·5'	4°2·8'W	X	57
Blairmore	Pth & Kin	NN8110	56°16·3'	3°54·9'W	X	57
Blairmore	Pth & Kin	NN9324	56°24·0'	3°43·6'W	X	52,58
Blairmore Hill	Arg & Bt	NS1784	56°1·1'	4°55·7'W	H	56
Blair More Hill	D & G	NX0069	54°58·8'	5°7·1'W	H	82
Blairmuckhill	N Lanak	NS8965	55°52·2'	3°46·0'W	X	65
Blairmuckhole	N Lanak	NS8864	55°51·6'	3°46·9'W	X	65
Blair Muir	Angus	NO5765	56°46·7'	2°41·8'W	X	44
Blairmuir Wood	Pth & Kin	NO1432	56°28·6'	3°23·3'W	F	53
Blairmulloch	E Ayr	NS5528	55°31·7'	4°17·4'W	X	71
Blairnabard	Stir	NS5097	56°8·8'	4°24·4'W	X	57
Blairnadergid	Highld	NH8650	57°31·8'	3°53·8'W	X	27
Blairnafade	Highld	NH8451	57°32·3'	3°55·8'W	X	27
Blairnairn	Arg & Bt	NS2988	56°3·5'	4°44·3'W	X	56
Blairnamarrow	Moray	NJ2015	57°13·4'	3°19·0'W	X	36
Blairnathort	Pth & Kin	NO1306	56°14·6'	3°23·8'W	X	58
Blairnha'	Moray	NJ1954	57°34·4'	3°20·8'W	X	28
Blairnile	Arg & Bt	NS3486	56°2·5'	4°39·5'W	X	56
Blairninich	Highld	NH4959	57°36·0'	4°31·1'W	T	26
Blairno	Angus	NO5367	56°47·8'	2°45·7'W	X	44
Blairnyle	W Dunb	NS4183	56°1·1'	4°32·6'W	X	56,64
Blairoch	D & G	NX7096	55°14·7'	4°2·3'W	X	77
Blairoer	Stir	NS4987	56°3·4'	4°25·1'W	X	57
Blairordens	Aberd	NJ5107	57°9·3'	2°48·1'W	X	37
Blairour	Highld	NN2282	56°54·0'	4°54·9'W	X	34,41
Blairpark	N Ayr	NS2457	55°46·7'	4°47·9'W	X	63
Blair Point	Fife	NT3193	56°7·7'	3°6·2'W	X	59
Blairquhan	S Ayr	NS3605	55°19·0'	4°34·6'W	X	70,77
Blairquhanan	W Dunb	NS4283	56°1·1'	4°31·6'W	X	56,64
Blairquhomrie	W Dunb	NS4282	56°0·6'	4°31·6'W	X	56,64
Blairquhomrie Muir	W Dunb	NS4381	56°0·0'	4°30·6'W	X	64
Blairquhosh	Stir	NS5282	56°0·7'	4°22·0'W	X	57,64
Blairs	Aberd	NJ7616	57°14·3'	2°23·4'W	X	38
Blairs	Aberd	NO8386	56°58·2'	2°16·3'W	X	45
Blairs	D & G	NX4661	54°55·5'	4°23·8'W	X	83
Blairs	Falk	NS8585	56°2·9'	3°50·3'W	X	65
Blairs	Pth & Kin	NN9620	56°21·9'	3°40·6'W	X	52,53,58
Blairs College	Aberd	NJ8800	57°5·7'	2°11·4'W	X	38
Blair's Ferry	Arg & Bt	NR9869	55°52·6'	5°13·3'W	X	62
Blairsgreen	Fife	NT0290	56°5·8'	3°34·1'W	X	58
Blairs Hill	D & G	NX4762	54°56·0'	4°22·9'W	H	83
Blairshinnoch	Aberd	NJ6362	57°39·0'	2°36·7'W	X	29
Blairshinnoch	D & G	NX3646	54°47·2'	4°32·6'W	X	83
Blairshinnoch	D & G	NX8868	54°59·9'	3°44·6'W	X	84
Blairshinnoch Hill	D & G	NX8669	55°0·4'	3°46·5'W	H	84
Blairs Home Fm	Moray	NJ0255	57°34·7'	3°37·9'W	FM	27
Blairskaith	E Dunb	NS5975	55°57·1'	4°15·1'W	T	64
Blairskaith Muir	E Dunb	NS5976	55°57·6'	4°15·1'W	X	64
Blairs of Dumbarrow	Angus	NO5448	56°37·6'	2°44·5'W	X	54
Blairston Mains	S Ayr	NS3316	55°24·8'	4°37·9'W	X	70
Blairstruie	Pth & Kin	NO1313	56°18·3'	3°23·9'W	X	58
Blair, The	Aberd	NJ8420	57°16·5'	2°15·5'W	X	38
Blair, The	Angus	NO5770	56°49·4'	2°41·8'W	H	44
Blairton	Aberd	NJ9618	57°15·4'	2°3·5'W	X	38
Blairton Links	Aberd	NJ9718	57°15·4'	2°2·5'W	X	38
Blairtummock	E Dunb	NS5879	55°59·2'	4°16·1'W	X	64
Blairuachdar	Pth & Kin	NN8767	56°47·1'	3°50·5'W	X	43
Blairuachdar Wood	Pth & Kin	NN8768	56°47·7'	3°50·6'W	F	43
Blairuskinmore	Stir	NN4303	56°11·9'	4°31·2'W	X	56
Blairvadach	Arg & Bt	NS2685	56°1·8'	4°47·1'W	X	56
Blairvaich	Stir	NS4599	56°9·8'	4°29·3'W	X	57

Blairvockie	Stir	NS3796	56°8·0'	4°36·9'W	X	56
Blairydryne	Aberd	NO7492	57°1·4'	2°25·2'W	X	38,45
Blairyfeddon	Angus	NO4454	56°40·7'	2°54·4'W	X	54
Blairythan Smithy	Aberd	NJ9723	57°18·1'	2°2·5'W	X	38
Blairy Wood	Scot Bord	NT2931	55°34·3'	3°7·1'W	F	73
Blaisdon	Glos	SO7016	51°50·7'	2°25·7'W	T	162
Blaisdon Wood	Glos	SO6917	51°51·3'	2°26·6'W	F	162
Blaise Fm	Kent	TQ6556	51°17·0'	0°22·4'E	FM	178,188
Blaise Hamlet	C of Bris	ST5578	51°30·2'	2°38·5'W	T	172
Blaithwaite	N Yks	SD7864	54°4·5'	2°19·8'W	X	98
Blaithwaite Ho	Cumbr	NY2144	54°47·3'	3°13·3'W	X	85
Blaize Bailey	Glos	SO6611	51°48·0'	2°29·2'W	F	162
Blakeamaya Pasture	N Yks	SD7080	54°13·1'	2°27·2'W	X	98
Blakebank	Cumbr	SD4591	54°18·9'	2°50·3'W	X	97
Blakebeck	Cumbr	NY3627	54°38·3'	2°59·1'W	X	90
Blake Brook	Derby	SK2874	53°16·0'	1°34·4'W	W	119
Blake Brook	Staffs	SK0862	53°9·5'	1°52·4'W	W	119
Blakebrook	Worcs	SO8176	52°23·1'	2°16·4'W	T	138
Blakedale	E Yorks	TA0160	54°1·8'	0°27·1'W	X	101
Blake Dean	Cald	SD9531	53°46·8'	2°4·1'W	X	103
Blakedean	Scot Bord	NT8222	55°29·7'	2°16·7'W	X	74
Blakeden Fm	Ches	SJ6266	53°11·6'	2°33·7'W	FM	118
Blakedown	Worcs	SO8778	52°24·2'	2°11·1'W	T	139
Blake End	Essex	TL7022	51°52·5'	0°28·6'E	T	167
Blake Fell	Cumbr	NY1119	54°33·8'	3°22·2'W	H	89
Blake Hall	Essex	TL4705	51°43·7'	0°8·1'E	X	167
Blake Hall	Essex	TL5305	51°43·6'	0°13·3'E	X	167
Blake Hall	Lancs	SD5338	53°50·4'	2°42·4'W	X	102
Blake Hall Fm	Shrops	SJ7444	52°59·8'	2°22·8'W	FM	118
Blakehill Fm	Wilts	SU0891	51°37·3'	1°52·7'W	FM	163,173
Blakehill Fm	Wilts	SU0891	51°37·3'	1°52·7'W	FM	173
Blake Hills Fm	Cumbr	NY3628	54°38·8'	2°59·1'W	FM	90
Blake Ho	Derby	SK1844	52°59·8'	1°43·5'W	X	119,128
Blake Holme	Cumbr	SD3889	54°17·8'	2°56·7'W	X	96,97
Blake Holme Plantation	Cumbr	SD3989	54°17·8'	2°55·8'W	F	96,97
Blakehope	Northum	NY8594	55°14·6'	2°13·7'W	X	80
Blakehope Burn	Northum	NY7599	55°17·3'	2°23·2'W	W	80
Blakehopeburnhaugh	Northum	NT7800	55°17·9'	2°20·4'W	X	80
Blakehope Fell	Northum	NY8494	55°14·6'	2°14·7'W	H	80
Blakehope Head	Scot Bord	NT1030	55°33·6'	3°25·2'W	H	72
Blakehope Nick	Northum	NY7198	55°16·8'	2°27·0'W	X	80
Blakehouse Burn	S Lanak	NS9614	55°24·8'	3°38·1'W	W	78
Blake House Fm	Ches	SJ8371	53°14·4'	2°14·9'W	FM	118
Blake House Fm	Essex	TL7023	51°53·0'	0°28·6'E	FM	167
Blakehurst	W Susx	TQ0406	50°50·9'	0°31·0'W	X	197
Blakelands	Mil Key	SP8642	52°4·4'	0°44·3'W	T	152
Blakelands	Staffs	SO8291	52°31·2'	2°15·5'W	X	138
Blake Law	Northum	NT8536	55°37·3'	2°13·9'W	X	74
Blakelaw	Northum	NY8484	55°9·3'	2°14·6'W	X	80
Blakelaw	Northum	NY9286	55°10·3'	2°7·1'W	X	80
Blakelaw	N upon Ty	NZ2166	54°59·5'	1°39·9'W	T	88
Blakelaw	Scot Bord	NT7730	55°34·0'	2°21·4'W	X	74
Blakelaw Covert	Scot Bord	NT7730	55°34·0'	2°21·4'W	F	74
Blakeley	Durham	NZ1020	54°34·8'	1°50·3'W	X	92
Blakeley	Staffs	SO8692	52°31·8'	2°12·0'W	T	139
Blakeley Field	Durham	NY8341	54°46·1'	2°15·4'W	X	86,87
Blakeley Fm	Ches	SJ8081	53°19·8'	2°17·6'W	FM	109
Blakeley Fm	Staffs	SK0447	53°1·5'	1°56·0'W	FM	119,128
Blakeley Hill	Durham	NZ4135	54°42·7'	1°21·4'W	X	93
Blakeleyhill	Shrops	SJ5724	52°49·0'	2°37·9'W	X	126
Blakeley Lane	Staffs	SJ9747	53°1·5'	2°2·3'W	T	118
Blakeley Lodge	Derby	SK2630	52°52·2'	1°36·4'W	X	128
Blakeley Moss	Cumbr	NY0613	54°30·5'	3°26·7'W	X	89
Blakeley Raise	Cumbr	NY0613	54°30·5'	3°26·7'W	H	89
Blakeley Resr	Kirk	SE0509	53°34·9'	1°55·1'W	W	110
Blakelow	Ches	SJ6851	53°3·6'	2°28·2'W	T	118
Blake Low	Derby	SK2260	53°8·4'	1°39·9'W	X	119
Blakelow	Staffs	SJ8635	52°55·0'	2°12·1'W	X	127
Blakelow	Staffs	SJ9736	52°55·5'	2°2·3'W	X	127
Blakelow	Staffs	SK0352	53°4·2'	1°56·9'W	X	119
Blake Low	Staffs	SK1146	53°0·9'	1°49·8'W	X	119,128
Blakelow Hill	Derby	SK3360	53°8·4'	1°30·0'W	X	119
Blakely Hall Fm	Durham	NZ1532	54°41·2'	1°45·6'W	FM	92
Blakeman's Crag	Scot Bord	NT7123	55°30·2'	2°27·1'W	X	74
Blakeman's Law	Northum	NY8795	55°15·2'	2°11·8'W	H	80
Blake Mere	Derby	SK2558	53°7·4'	1°37·2'W	W	119
Blakemere	Heref	SO3640	52°3·5'	2°55·6'W	T	148,149,161
Blake Mere	Shrops	SJ4133	52°53·7'	2°52·2'W	W	126
Blake Mere	Shrops	SJ5542	52°58·6'	2°39·8'W	W	117
Blakemere Hill Wood	Heref	SO3639	52°3·0'	2°55·6'W	F	149,161
Blake Mire	Cumbr	SD7093	54°20·1'	2°27·3'W	W	98
Blake Mire	Cumbr	SD7792	54°19·6'	2°20·8'W	X	98
Blake Moor	Cald	SD9821	53°41·4'	2°1·4'W	X	103
Blake Moor	Derby	SK0596	53°27·9'	1°55·1'W	X	110
Blakemoor	Shrops	SO4288	52°29·4'	2°50·9'W	X	137
Blakemoorflat	Shrops	SJ3700	52°35·9'	2°55·4'W	X	126
Blakemoor Fm	Northum	NZ2894	55°14·6'	1°33·1'W	FM	81
Blakemoorgate	Shrops	SJ3701	52°36·4'	2°55·4'W	X	126
Blakemore	Devon	SX7660	50°25·8'	3°44·4'W	X	202
Blakemore Fm	Worcs	SO7272	52°21·0'	2°24·3'W	FM	138
Blakemore Hill	Heref	SO4734	52°0·4'	2°45·9'W	X	149,161
Blakemore Ho	Staffs	SJ7822	52°47·9'	2°19·2'W	X	127
Blake Muir	Scot Bord	NT3030	55°33·8'	3°6·2'W	H	73
Blakenall Heath	Wals	SK0001	52°36·6'	1°59·6'W	T	139
Blakeney	Glos	SO6606	51°45·3'	2°29·2'W	T	162
Blakeney	Norf	TG0243	52°57·0'	1°0·8'E	T	133
Blakeney Channel	Norf	TG0145	52°58·1'	1°0·0'E	W	133
Blakeney Eye	Norf	TG0445	52°58·0'	1°2·7'E	X	133
Blakeney Fm	Norf	TL8785	52°26·1'	0°45·5'E	FM	144
Blakeney Harbour	Norf	TF9846	52°58·7'	0°57·4'E	W	132
Blakeney Hill	Glos	SO6607	51°45·9'	2°29·2'W	X	162
Blakeneyhill Woods	Glos	SO6508	51°46·4'	2°30·0'W	F	162
Blakeney Pit	Norf	TG0045	52°58·1'	0°59·1'E	W	133
Blakeney Point	Norf	TG0046	52°58·7'	0°59·1'E	X	133
Blakeney Walk	Glos	SO6509	51°47·0'	2°30·1'W	F	162
Blakenhall	Ches	SJ7247	53°1·4'	2°24·6'W	T	118
Blakenhall	Wolv	SO9197	52°34·5'	2°7·6'W	T	139
Blakenhall Fm	Leic	SP5284	52°27·3'	1°13·7'W	FM	140
Blakenhall Moss	Ches	SJ7248	53°2·0'	2°24·6'W	F	118
Blakenhall Park	Staffs	SK1718	52°45·8'	1°44·5'W	X	128
Blakeridge Wood	Shrops	SO3086	52°28·3'	3°1·4'W	F	137
Blake Rigg	Cumbr	NY2804	54°25·8'	3°6·3'W	X	89,90
Blake Rigg	Cumbr	SD7284	54°15·3'	2°25·4'W	X	98
Blakerstone Moor	Scot Bord	NT7663	55°51·8'	2°22·6'W	X	67
Blakes	Essex	TL5101	51°41·5'	0°11·5'E	X	167
Blakes	I of W	SZ4383	50°38·9'	1°23·1'W	X	196
Blake's Copse	Wilts	SU2572	51°27·0'	1°38·0'W	F	174
Blakes Fm	Somer	ST6446	51°13·0'	2°30·5'W	FM	183
Blakes Fm	W Susx	TQ1815	50°55·6'	0°18·9'W	FM	198
Blakeshall	Worcs	SO8381	52°25·8'	2°14·6'W	T	138
Blakeshall Common	Worcs	SO8281	52°25·8'	2°15·5'W	X	138
Blakeshay Wood	Leic	SK5111	52°41·9'	1°14·3'W	F	129
Blake's Hill	Worcs	SP0339	52°3·2'	1°57·0'W	H	150
Blakeshouse	Aberd	NJ7858	57°36·9'	2°21·6'W	X	29,30
Blakes Keiro	Corn	SW9675	50°32·6'	4°52·4'W	X	200
Blake's Lane Fm	Surrey	TQ0651	51°15·1'	0°28·5'W	FM	187
Blakesley	Northnts	SP6250	52°8·9'	1°5·2'W	T	152
Blake Stiles	N Yks	SE5271	54°8·2'	1°11·8'W	X	100
Blakestonedale Fm	Ches	SJ9679	53°18·7'	2°3·2'W	FM	118
Blake Street Sta	Birm	SK1000	52°36·1'	1°50·7'W	X	139
Blakesware Manor	Herts	TL4016	51°49·7'	0°2·3'E	X	167
Blake's Wood	Essex	TL7706	51°43·7'	0°34·2'E	F	167
Blakethwaite	N Yks	NY9303	54°25·6'	2°6·1'W	X	91,92
Blakeway	Shrops	SJ6524	52°49·0'	2°30·8'W	X	127
Blakeway Coppice	Shrops	SO5998	52°34·9'	2°35·9'W	F	137,138
Blakeway Fm	Shrops	SO5999	52°35·5'	2°35·9'W	FM	137,138
Blakeway Fm	Somer	ST4344	51°11·8'	2°48·6'W	FM	182
Blakewell	Devon	SS5535	51°6·0'	4°3·9'W	X	180
Blakewell	Devon	SS6124	51°0·2'	3°58·5'W	X	180
Blakewell	Devon	SS6930	51°3·5'	3°51·8'W	X	180
Blakey Gill	N Yks	SE6798	54°22·6'	0°57·7'W	W	94,100
Blakey Hall	Lancs	SD8740	53°51·6'	2°11·4'W	X	103
Blakey Hey	Lancs	SD6128	53°45·1'	2°35·1'W	X	102,103
Blakey Howe	N Yks	SE6799	54°23·2'	0°57·7'W	A	94,100
Blakey Ridge	N Yks	SE6897	54°22·1'	0°56·8'W	X	94,100
Blakey Topping	N Yks	SE8793	54°19·7'	0°39·3'W	H	94,101
Blak Moat	Oxon	SP3207	51°45·9'	1°31·8'W	A	164
Blamire Fm	E Yorks	SE8143	53°52·8'	0°45·7'W	FM	106
Blamphayne Fm	Devon	SY2096	50°45·7'	3°7·7'W	FM	192,193
Blamster's Fm	Essex	TL8030	51°56·6'	0°37·5'E	FM	168
Blamster's Hall	Essex	TL6126	51°54·8'	0°20·8'E	X	167
Blance	E Loth	NT4868	55°54·4'	2°49·5'W	X	66
Blanch Burn	Northum	NZ0195	55°15·2'	1°58·6'W	W	81
Blanch Dale Plantn	E Yorks	SE8851	53°57·1'	0°39·1'W	F	106
Blanchdown Wood	Devon	SX4273	50°32·4'	4°13·4'W	F	201
Blanche Fm	Herts	TL2100	51°41·4'	0°14·6'W	FM	166
Blanche's Fm	W Susx	TQ1919	50°57·7'	0°17·9'W	FM	198
Blanches Geo	Shetld	HU3775	60°27·7'	1°19·1'W	X	2,3
Blanch Fell	Lancs	SD5760	54°2·3'	2°39·0'W	X	97
Blanch Fm	E Yorks	SE8953	53°58·2'	0°38·2'W	FM	106
Blanchland	Northum	NY9650	54°50·9'	2°3·3'W	T	87
Blanchland Moor	Northum	NY9553	54°52·6'	2°4·2'W	X	87
Blanchworth	Glos	ST7198	51°41·0'	2°24·8'W	X	162
Bland	Cumbr	SD6595	54°21·2'	2°31·9'W	X	97
Bland Close	N Yks	SE2968	54°6·7'	1°33·0'W	X	99
Blandford Camp	Dorset	ST9208	50°52·5'	2°6·4'W	T	195
Blandford Forest	Dorset	ST8309	50°53·0'	2°14·1'W	F	194
Blandford Forum	Dorset	ST8806	50°51·4'	2°9·8'W	T	194
Blandford St Mary	Dorset	ST8805	50°50·9'	2°9·8'W	T	194
Bland Hill	N Yks	SE2053	53°58·6'	1°41·3'W	T	104
Bland Ho	Cumbr	NY6308	54°28·2'	2°33·8'W	X	91
Blandred Fm	Kent	TR2043	51°8·9'	1°9·1'E	FM	179,189
Blands	Cumbr	NY5621	54°35·2'	2°40·4'W	X	90
Blands	Cumbr	SD7486	54°16·4'	2°23·5'W	X	98
Blandsgill	Cumbr	SD6395	54°21·2'	2°33·7'W	X	97
Blands Wath	Cumbr	NY7612	54°30·4'	2°21·8'W	X	91
Blandy	Highld	NC6259	58°30·1'	4°21·6'W	T	10
Blandy's Fm	Oxon	SU3786	51°34·5'	1°27·6'W	FM	174
Blanefield	S Ayr	NS2507	55°19·8'	4°45·1'W	X	70,76
Blanefield	Stir	NS5579	55°59·2'	4°19·0'W	T	64
Blanerne	Scot Bord	NT8356	55°48·1'	2°15·8'W	T	67,74
Blaneswell	Stir	NS5183	56°1·3'	4°23·0'W	X	57,64
Blane Water	Stir	NS5184	56°1·8'	4°23·0'W	W	57,64
Blank Bank	Staffs	SJ8147	53°1·4'	2°16·6'W	T	118
Blankets	Aberd	NJ8026	57°19·7'	2°19·5'W	X	38
Blankets Fm	Thurr	TQ6285	51°32·7'	0°20·6'E	FM	177
Blankney	Lincs	TF0660	53°7·8'	0°24·5'W	T	121
Blankney Dales	Lincs	TF1563	53°9·3'	0°16·4'W	X	121
Blankney Fen	Lincs	TF1262	53°8·8'	0°19·1'W	X	121
Blankney Grange	Lincs	TF0459	53°7·3'	0°26·3'W	X	121
Blankney Heath	Lincs	TF0359	53°7·3'	0°27·2'W	X	121
Blankney Park	Lincs	TF0660	53°7·8'	0°24·5'W	X	121
Blankney Wood	Lincs	TF1062	53°8·9'	0°20·9'W	F	121
Blanksmill Br	Devon	SX7241	50°15·5'	3°47·4'W	X	202
Blannicombe	Devon	SY1597	50°46·2'	3°11·9'W	T	192,193
Blansby Park	N Yks	SE8187	54°16·0'	0°44·9'W	X	94,100
Blansby Park Fm	N Yks	SE8286	54°16·0'	0°44·0'W	FM	94,100
Blanster	Orkney	ND4492	58°49·0'	2°57·7'W	X	7
Blantrothy	Monm	SO3721	51°53·3'	2°54·5'W	X	161
Blantyre	S Lanak	NS6857	55°47·6'	4°5·9'W	T	64
Blantyre Ho	Kent	TQ7540	51°8·2'	0°30·5'E	X	188
Blantyre Muir	S Lanak	NS6652	55°44·8'	4°7·7'W	X	64
Blantyre Park	S Lanak	NS6855	55°46·5'	4°5·8'W	X	64
Blanyoy	Monm	SO3024	51°54·8'	3°0·7'W	X	161
Blanyvaird Loch	D & G	NX3076	55°3·2'	4°39·3'W	W	76
Blaoch Choire	Highld	NC3640	58°19·3'	4°47·5'W	X	9
Blàr Achaidh	Pth & Kin	NO0666	56°46·8'	3°31·9'W	H	43
Blàr a' Chaorainn	Highld	NN1066	56°45·1'	5°6·0'W	X	41
Blàr a' Chath	Highld	NH9286	57°51·3'	3°48·7'W	X	21
Blàr a' Ghille Dhomhnaich	Highld	ND0022	58°10·8'	3°41·6'W	H	17
Blàran	Arg & Bt	NM8517	56°18·1'	5°28·1'W	X	55
Blàr an Domblais	N Eil	NB5155	58°25·0'	6°15·4'W	X	8
Blàr an Fhraoich	Highld	ND1741	58°21·2'	3°24·6'W	X	11,12
Blàr an Liana Mhóir	Highld	NN7393	57°0·9'	4°5·0'W	X	35
Blàr an Lochain	Highld	NN2088	56°57·2'	4°57·1'W	X	34,41
Blàr an Lóin Duibh	Highld	NG8680	57°45·8'	5°35·4'W	X	19
Blarantibert	Arg & Bt	NR8091	56°3·9'	5°31·6'W	X	55
Blàr Beinn Tighe	Highld	NG2506	57°4·0'	6°31·8'W	X	39
Blàr-Bhuidhe	Highld	NH6734	57°22·9'	4°12·3'W	X	26
Blàr Buidhe	Arg & Bt	NR4169	55°50·9'	6°7·8'W	X	60,61
Blàr Buidhe	Arg & Bt	NR4877	55°55·5'	6°1·6'W	X	60,61
Blàr Buidhe	Arg & Bt	NS1074	55°55·6'	5°2·0'W	X	63
Blàr Buidhe	Highld	NC6901	57°59·0'	4°12·5'W	X	16
Blàr Buidhe	Highld	NC9521	58°10·2'	3°46·6'W	X	17
Blarbuie	Arg & Bt	NR8789	56°3·0'	5°24·8'W	T	55
Blarbuie	Highld	NC5613	58°5·2'	4°26·1'W	X	16
Blarchaorain	Arg & Bt	NN1424	56°22·6'	5°0·3'W	X	50
Blarchasgaig	Arg & Bt	NM9345	56°33·3'	5°21·6'W	X	49
Blar Cnoc na Gaoith	Highld	ND0061	58°31·8'	3°42·6'W	X	11,12
Blarcreen	Arg & Bt	NM9935	56°28·1'	5°15·3'W	X	49
Blarcreen Burn	Arg & Bt	NN0135	56°28·2'	5°13·4'W	W	50
Blàr Dearg	Highld	ND0453	58°27·5'	3°38·2'W	X	11,12
Blàr Dubh	Arg & Bt	NM3819	56°17·7'	6°13·6'W	X	48
Blàr Dubh	Highld	NC7962	58°32·0'	4°4·2'W	X	10
Blàr Dubh	Highld	NM4787	56°54·6'	6°8·9'W	X	39
Blaree Burn	D & G	NX5090	55°11·1'	4°20·9'W	W	77
Blarene Burn	E Ayr	NS5909	55°21·5'	4°13·0'W	W	71,77
Blarene Hill	E Ayr	NS5809	55°21·5'	4°14·0'W	X	71,77
Blàr Garvary	Highld	NH5886	57°50·7'	4°23·1'W	F	21
Blàr Geal	Highld	ND1051	58°26·5'	3°32·0'W	X	11,12
Blarghour	Arg & Bt	NM9913	56°16·3'	5°14·3'W	X	55
Blargie	Highld	NN6094	57°1·2'	4°17·9'W	X	35
Blargie Craig	Highld	NN5995	57°1·7'	4°18·9'W	X	35
Blarich	Highld	NC6904	58°0·6'	4°12·6'W	X	16
Blarloch Mór	Highld	NC2849	58°24·0'	4°56·1'W	W	9
Blarmachfoldach	Highld	NN0969	56°46·7'	5°7·1'W	T	41
Blàr Mór	Arg & Bt	NM3822	56°19·3'	6°13·8'W	X	48
Blàr Mór	Arg & Bt	NM5942	56°30·8'	5°54·6'W	X	47,48
Blàr Mór	Highld	NC8533	58°16·5'	3°57·2'W	X	17
Blàr Mór	Highld	NC9054	58°27·9'	3°52·7'W	X	10
Blàr Mór	Highld	NH8825	57°18·4'	3°51·1'W	X	35,36
Blàr Mór	Highld	NJ0532	57°22·4'	3°34·3'W	X	27,36
Blàr Mór	Highld	NM4280	56°50·7'	6°13·4'W	X	39
Blàr Mór	Highld	NM4790	56°56·2'	6°9·1'W	X	39
Blàr Mór	Highld	NM4886	56°54·1'	6°7·9'W	X	39
Blàr Mór	Highld	NN1276	56°50·5'	5°4·5'W	X	41
Blarmore	Highld	NC9963	58°32·9'	3°43·6'W	X	11
Blàr na Caillich Buidhe	Highld	NM6890	56°56·8'	5°48·4'W	X	40
Blàr na Cóinnich	Arg & Bt	NM3820	56°18·3'	6°13·7'W	X	48
Blàr na Fola	N Eil	NB3844	58°18·7'	6°27·9'W	X	8
Blarnalearoch	Highld	NH1490	57°51·9'	5°7·7'W	T	20
Blàr nam Faoileag	Highld	ND1344	58°22·8'	3°28·8'W	X	11,12
Blàr nam Faoileag	N Eil	NB3850	58°21·9'	6°28·3'W	X	8
Blàr nam Faoileag	N Eil	NB4143	58°18·2'	6°24·8'W	X	8
Blàr nam Faoileag	N Eil	NB4752	58°23·3'	6°19·3'W	X	8
Blàr nam Fear Móra	Highld	NC1425	58°10·7'	5°9·3'W	X	15
Blàr nam Fiadh	Highld	NH8353	57°33·4'	3°56·9'W	X	27
Blàr nam Fiadhag	Highld	NC2520	58°8·3'	4°57·9'W	H	15
Blàr nan Coileach	Highld	NC7116	58°7·1'	4°10·9'W	X	16
Blàr nan Con	Arg & Bt	NR8268	55°51·6'	5°28·6'W	X	62
Blàr-nan-laogh	Arg & Bt	NM9948	56°35·1'	5°15·9'W	X	49
Blàr nan Lian	Highld	NC5662	58°31·6'	4°27·9'W	X	10
Blàr nan Lombaidean	N Eil	NB4050	58°21·9'	6°26·3'W	X	8
Blàr nan Stearnag	N Eil	NB4355	58°24·7'	6°23·5'W	X	8
Blàr nan Sùil Gorma	Highld	NC6408	58°2·7'	4°17·8'W	X	16
Blàr nan Uan	Arg & Bt	NM6440	56°29·8'	5°49·6'W	X	49
Blarnavaid	Stir	NS4888	56°3·9'	4°26·0'W	X	57
Blarnish Burn	Moray	NJ1342	57°27·9'	3°26·6'W	W	28
Blàr Odhar	Highld	NN2182	56°54·0'	4°55·9'W	X	34,41
Blarourie	Aberd	NO7089	56°59·7'	2°29·2'W	H	45
Blàr Shinndanais	N Eil	NB4554	58°24·3'	6°21·4'W	X	8
Blarstainge	Arg & Bt	NN3217	56°19·2'	4°42·5'W	X	50,56
Blàr Uilleim	Highld	NC8330	58°14·9'	3°59·1'W	X	17
Blaruskinbeg	Stir	NN4302	56°11·3'	4°31·4'W	X	56
Blary	Arg & Bt	NR6937	55°34·6'	5°39·4'W	X	68
Blary Hill	Arg & Bt	NR7136	55°34·1'	5°37·5'W	H	68
Blasford Hill	Essex	TL7011	51°46·5'	0°28·2'E	T	167
Blashaval	N Eil	NF8970	57°37·0'	7°12·1'W	T	18
Blashaval	N Eil	NF8971	57°37·6'	7°12·1'W	H	18
Blashenwell Fm	Dorset	SY9580	50°37·4'	2°3·9'W	FM	195
Blashford	Hants	SU1506	50°51·4'	1°46·8'W	T	195
Blashford Fm	Hants	SU1407	50°52·0'	1°47·7'W	FM	195
Blasterfield Fm	Cumbr	NY6311	54°29·8'	2°33·9'W	FM	91
Blaster Hole	Orkney	HY6202	58°54·5'	2°39·1'W	X	6
Blasthill	Arg & Bt	NR7108	55°19·0'	5°36·1'W	X	68
Blaston	Leic	SP8095	52°33·1'	0°48·8'W	T	141
Blaston Lodge	Leic	SP8196	52°33·6'	0°47·9'W	X	141
Blatridge Hill	Devon	SS7324	51°0·3'	3°48·2'W	H	180
Blatchborough	Devon	SS2814	50°54·2'	4°26·4'W	X	190
Blatchbridge	Somer	ST7745	51°12·5'	2°19·4'W	T	183
Blatches	Essex	TL6622	51°52·5'	0°25·1'E	X	167
Blatches Fm	Essex	TQ8489	51°34·4'	0°39·7'E	FM	178
Blatchford	Devon	SX5191	50°42·2'	4°6·2'W	X	191
Blatchford	Devon	SX8572	50°32·4'	3°37·0'W	X	191
Blatchworthy	Devon	SS8817	50°56·7'	3°35·3'W	X	181
Blates Mill	D & G	NX6766	54°58·5'	4°4·3'W	X	83,84
Blath Bhalg	Pth & Kin	NO0161	56°44·1'	3°36·6'W	H	43
Blatherwycke	Northnts	SP9795	52°32·9'	0°33·8'W	T	141
Blatherwycke Lake	Northnts	SP9796	52°33·4'	0°33·7'W	W	141
Blatobvlgivm (Roman Fort)	D & G	NY2175	55°4·0'	3°13·8'W	R	85
Blawath Beck	N Yks	SE8197	54°22·0'	0°44·8'W	W	94,100
Blawdty	Gwyn	SH2027	52°48·9'	4°39·9'W	X	123
Blawearie	Northum	NU0639	55°38·9'	1°53·8'W	X	75
Blawearie	Northum	NU0822	55°29·8'	1°52·0'W	X	75
Blawearie	Scot Bord	NT4416	55°26·3'	2°52·7'W	X	79
Blawearie	Scot Bord	NT5917	55°27·0'	2°38·5'W	X	80
Blawhorn Moss	W Loth	NS8868	55°53·8'	3°47·0'W	X	65
Blawith	Cumbr	SD2888	54°17·2'	3°5·9'W	T	96,97
Blawith Fells	Cumbr	SD2790	54°18·3'	3°6·9'W	X	96,97
Blawith Knott	Cumbr	SD2688	54°17·2'	3°7·8'W	H	96,97
Blawith Point	Cumbr	SD4178	54°11·9'	2°53·8'W	X	96,97
Blawplain	D & G	NX8693	55°13·3'	3°47·1'W	X	78
Blawquhairn Fm	D & G	NX6283	55°7·6'	4°9·4'W	FM	77
Blaxhall	Suff	TM3657	52°9·9'	1°27·5'E	T	156
Blaxhall Common or Blaxhall Heath	Suff	TM3856	52°9·3'	1°29·2'E	X	156
Blaxhall Hall	Suff	TM3557	52°9·9'	1°26·6'E	X	156
Blaxland Fm	Kent	TR1663	51°19·7'	1°6·4'E	FM	179
Blaxter Cottages	Northum	NY9390	55°12·5'	2°6·2'W	X	80
Blaxter Lough	Northum	NY9389	55°12·0'	2°6·2'W	W	80

Blaxton	Devon	SX4762	50°26·5′	4°8·9′W	X	201
Blaxton	Donc	SE6700	53°29·8′	0°59·0′W	T	111
Blaxton Common	Donc	SE6801	53°30·3′	0°58·1′W	X	111
Blaxton Wood	Devon	SX4663	50°27·0′	4°9·8′W	F	201
Blaydike Moss	N Yks	SD8576	54°11·0′	2°13·4′W	X	98
Blaydon	Ghead	NZ1762	54°57·4′	1°43·6′W	T	88
Blaydon Burn	Ghead	NZ1662	54°57·4′	1°44·6′W	T	88
Blaydon Haughs	Ghead	NZ1963	54°57·9′	1°41·8′W	T	88
Blayshaw Crags	N Yks	SE0972	54°8·9′	1°51·3′W	X	99
Blayshaw Gill	N Yks	SE0871	54°8·3′	1°52·2′W	W	99
Blaythorne	Oxon	SP3121	51°53·4′	1°32·6′W	X	164
Blaze	Ches	SJ9767	53°12·2′	2°2·3′W	X	118
Blaze Fell	Cumbr	NY4943	54°47·0′	2°47·2′W	H	86
Blazefield	N Yks	SE1265	54°5·1′	1°48·6′W	X	99
Blazefield	N Yks	SE1765	54°5·1′	1°44·0′W	X	99
Blaze Hill	D & G	NY1394	55°14·2′	3°21·7′W	H	78
Blaze Moss	Lancs	SD6152	53°58·0′	2°35·3′W	X	102,103
Blea Barf	N Yks	SD9596	54°21·8′	2°4·2′W	H	98
Blea Beck	Durham	NY8626	54°38·0′	2°12·6′W	W	91,92
Blea Beck	N Yks	SE0367	54°6·2′	1°56·8′W	W	98
Blea Beck Dams	N Yks	SE0466	54°5·6′	1°55·9′W	W	98
Bleabeck Force	Durham	NY8727	54°38·5′	2°11·7′W	W	91,92
Bleabeck Grains	Durham	NY8625	54°37·4′	2°12·6′W	W	91,92
Bleaberry Beck	Cumbr	NY8407	54°27·7′	2°14·4′W	W	91,92
Bleaberry Fell	Cumbr	NY2819	54°33·9′	3°6·4′W	X	89,90
Bleaberry Gill	Cumbr	NY1111	54°29·4′	3°22·0′W	W	89
Bleaberry Haws	Cumbr	SD2694	54°20·4′	3°7·9′W	X	96,97
Bleaberry Head	N Yks	SD8598	54°22·9′	2°13·4′W	X	98
Bleaberry Hill	Cumbr	NY5140	54°45·4′	2°45·3′W	H	86
Bleaberryrigg	Cumbr	NY4369	55°1·0′	2°53·1′W	X	85
Bleaberry Tarn	Cumbr	NY1615	54°31·6′	3°17·5′W	W	89
Bleachery, The	Durham	NZ4337	54°43·8′	1°19·5′W	X	93
Bleachfield	Arg & Bt	NR6820	55°25·4′	5°39·5′W	X	68
Bleachfield	Highld	ND1166	58°34·6′	3°31·4′W	X	11,12
Bleach Fm	E Yorks	SE7256	53°59·9′	0°53·7′W	FM	105,106
Bleach Fm	Norf	TM2387	52°26·3′	1°17·3′E	FM	156
Bleach Fm	Suff	TM3779	52°21·7′	1°29·3′E	FM	156
Bleach Green	Cumbr	NX9819	54°33·6′	3°34·2′W	T	89
Bleach Green	Suff	TM2377	52°21·0′	1°16·9′E	T	156
Bleach House Fm	N Yks	SE3365	54°5·0′	1°29·3′W	FM	99
Bleach Mill Fm	N Yks	NZ5909	54°28·6′	1°4·9′W	FM	93
Bleack Hall	Beds	TL2140	52°2·9′	0°13·7′W	X	153
Blea Crag	Cumbr	NY2610	54°29·0′	3°8·1′W	X	89,90
Blea Crag	Cumbr	NY3007	54°27·5′	3°4·4′W	X	90
Bleadale Moss	Lancs	SD6048	53°55·8′	2°36·1′W	X	102,103
Bleadale Nab	Lancs	SD6049	53°56·4′	2°36·1′W	X	102,103
Bleadale Ridge	Lancs	SD6049	53°56·4′	2°36·1′W	X	102,103
Bleadale Water	Lancs	SD6049	53°56·4′	2°36·1′W	W	102,103
Bleadney	Somer	ST4845	51°12·3′	2°44·3′W	T	182
Bleadon	N Som	ST3456	51°18·2′	2°56·4′W	T	182
Bleadon Hill	N Som	ST3557	51°18·7′	2°55·6′W	H	182
Bleadon Level	N Som	ST3256	51°18·2′	2°58·1′W	X	182
Bleaflatt	Cumbr	NY7303	54°25·5′	2°24·5′W	X	91
Bleagate	Cumbr	NY7143	54°47·1′	2°26·6′W	X	86,87
Blea Gills	Cumbr	SD7082	54°14·2′	2°27·2′W	X	98
Bleagill Sike	Durham	NY9130	54°40·1′	2°7·9′W	W	91,92
Blea Gill Waterfall	N Yks	SE0466	54°5·6′	1°55·9′W	W	98
Blea Hill Beck	N Yks	NZ8900	54°23·5′	0°37·3′W	W	94
Blea Hill Howe	N Yks	NZ9000	54°23·5′	0°36·4′W	A	94
Blea Hill Rigg	N Yks	NZ9000	54°23·5′	0°36·4′W	X	94
Bleak Acre	Heref	SO6049	52°8·5′	2°34·7′W	T	149
Bleak Bank	N Yks	SD7271	54°8·3′	2°25·3′W	X	98
Bleak Br	Somer	ST3044	51°11·7′	2°59·7′W	X	182
Bleak Burn	Scot Bord	NT3524	55°30·6′	3°1·3′W	W	73
Bleak Down	I of W	SZ5181	50°37·8′	1°16·4′W	X	196
Bleakedgate Moor	Roch	SD9713	53°37·1′	2°2·3′W	X	109
Bleakfield	S Lanak	NS9829	55°32·9′	3°36·6′W	X	72
Bleak Hall	Mil Key	SP8536	52°1·2′	0°45·3′W	T	152
Bleak Hall	Suff	TM0747	52°5·2′	1°1·7′E	X	155,169
Bleak Hey Nook	Oldham	SE0009	53°34·9′	1°59·6′W	T	110
Bleak Hill	Hants	SU1311	50°54·1′	1°48·5′W	T	195
Bleak Hills	Leic	SK7224	52°48·8′	0°55·5′W	X	129
Bleak Ho	Cumbr	NY0217	54°32·6′	3°30·5′W	X	89
Bleak Ho	Cumbr	NY5031	54°40·5′	2°46·1′W	X	90
Bleak Ho	Derby	SK3072	53°14·9′	1°32·6′W	X	119
Bleak Ho	Derby	SK3724	52°49·0′	1°26·7′W	X	128
Bleak Ho	Devon	SX5586	50°39·6′	4°2·7′W	X	191
Bleak Ho	Leic	SK4525	52°49·5′	1°19·5′W	X	129
Bleak Ho	Leic	SP6999	52°35·3′	0°58·5′W	X	141
Bleak Ho	Lincs	SK9245	52°59·9′	0°37·3′W	X	130
Bleak Ho	Lincs	TF4987	53°21·8′	0°14·8′E	X	113,122
Bleak House	Kent	TR3967	51°21·3′	1°26·4′E	X	179
Bleak House	Lincs	SK9649	53°2·0′	0°33·7′W	X	130
Bleak House Fm	E Yorks	TA3019	53°39·3′	0°1·6′W	FM	113
Bleak House Fm	Lincs	TF1111	52°41·3′	0°21·1′W	FM	130,142
Bleak House Fm	Lincs	TF4529	52°50·6′	0°9·6′E	FM	131
Bleak House Fm	Lincs	TF4921	52°46·2′	0°12·9′E	FM	131
Bleak House Fm	Notts	SK8352	53°3·8′	0°45·3′W	FM	121
Bleak How	Cumbr	NY2712	54°30·1′	3°7·2′W	X	89,90
Bleak Knoll	Derby	SK1879	53°18·7′	1°43·4′W	H	119
Bleak Law	Durham	NY8032	54°41·2′	2°18·2′W	X	91,92
Bleak Law	E Loth	NT5361	55°50·6′	2°44·6′W	X	66
Bleak Law	E Loth	NT5763	55°51·7′	2°40·8′W	H	67
Bleak Law	E Loth	NT6166	55°53·4′	2°37·0′W	H	67
Bleak Law	Northum	NT9410	55°23·3′	2°5·3′W	X	80
Bleaklaw	Northum	NY8475	55°4·4′	2°14·6′W	X	86,87
Bleak Law	Scot Bord	NT3716	55°26·3′	2°59·3′W	H	79
Bleak Law	S Lanak	NT0651	55°44·9′	3°29·4′W	H	65,72
Bleaklow	Derby	SK0996	53°27·9′	1°51·5′W	X	110
Bleaklow	Derby	SK2173	53°15·5′	1°40·7′W	X	119
Bleaklow Head	Derby	SK0996	53°27·9′	1°51·5′W	H	110
Bleaklow Hill	Derby	SK1096	53°27·9′	1°50·6′W	H	110
Bleaklow Meadows	Derby	SK1097	53°28·4′	1°50·6′W	X	110
Bleaklow Stones	Derby	SK1196	53°27·9′	1°49·6′W	X	110
Blea Moor	N Yks	SD7682	54°14·2′	2°21·7′W	H	98
Blea Moor Moss	Cumbr	SD7882	54°14·2′	2°19·8′W	X	98
Blea Moss	Cumbr	NY5212	54°30·3′	2°44·1′W	X	90
Blean	Kent	TR1260	51°18·2′	1°2·9′E	T	179
Bleangate	Kent	TR1664	51°20·3′	1°6·5′E	X	179
Blean High Pasture	N Yks	SD9386	54°16·4′	2°6·0′W	X	98

Blean West Pasture	N Yks	SD9286	54°16·4′	2°7·0′W	X	98
Blean Wood	Kent	TR0860	51°18·3′	0°59·4′E	F	179
Bleara Lowe	Lancs	SD9245	53°54·3′	2°6·9′W	A	103
Bleara Moor	Lancs	SD9245	53°54·3′	2°6·9′W	X	103
Bleara Side	Lancs	SD9244	53°53·8′	2°6·9′W	X	103
Blea Rigg	Cumbr	NY2908	54°28·0′	3°5·3′W	X	89,90
Blea Rock	Cumbr	NY2611	54°29·6′	3°8·1′W	X	89,90
Bleasby	Lincs	TF1384	53°20·7′	0°17·7′W	T	121
Bleasby	Notts	SK7149	53°2·2′	0°56·1′W	T	129
Bleasby Field	Lincs	TF1284	53°20·7′	0°18·6′W	X	121
Bleasby Moor	Lincs	TF1283	53°20·2′	0°18·7′W	T	121
Bleasdale	Lancs	SD5745	53°54·2′	2°38·9′W	T	102
Bleasdale Circle	Lancs	SD5746	53°54·7′	2°38·9′W	A	102
Bleasdale Moors	Lancs	SD5648	53°55·8′	2°39·8′W	X	102
Bleasdale Tower	Lancs	SD5546	53°54·7′	2°40·7′W	X	102
Blease Fell	Cumbr	NY3026	54°37·7′	3°4·6′W	X	90
Blease Fell	Cumbr	NY6200	54°23·9′	2°34·7′W	H	91
Blease Fm	Cumbr	NY3125	54°37·2′	3°3·7′W	FM	90
Blease Gill	Cumbr	NY3125	54°37·2′	3°3·7′W	W	90
Blease Hall	Cumbr	SD5489	54°17·9′	2°42·0′W	X	97
Blease Hill	Cumbr	SD5983	54°14·7′	2°37·3′W	X	97
Blease Hill	Cumbr	SD6182	54°14·2′	2°35·5′W	X	97
Blea Tarn	Cumbr	NY1601	54°24·1′	3°17·2′W	W	89
Blea Tarn	Cumbr	NY2904	54°25·8′	3°5·2′W	W	89,90
Blea Tarn	Cumbr	NY2914	54°31·2′	3°5·4′W	W	89,90
Bleatarn	Cumbr	NY4661	54°56·7′	2°50·2′W	X	86
Bleatarn	Cumbr	NY7313	54°30·9′	2°24·6′W	T	91
Bleatarn Gill	Cumbr	NY2815	54°31·8′	3°6·3′W	W	89,90
Bleatarn Ho	Cumbr	NY2904	54°25·8′	3°5·2′W	X	89,90
Blea Tarn Resr	Lancs	SD4958	54°1·2′	2°46·3′W	W	102
Bleathgill	Cumbr	NY8512	54°30·4′	2°13·5′W	X	91,92
Bleathwaite Crag	Cumbr	NY4409	54°28·6′	2°51·4′W	X	90
Bleathwaite Pasture	Cumbr	SD2895	54°21·0′	3°6·0′W	X	96,97
Bleathwood Common	Heref	SO5570	52°19·8′	2°39·2′W	X	137,138
Bleathwood Manor Fm	Heref	SO5669	52°19·3′	2°38·3′W	FM	137,138
Bleaton Hill	Pth & Kin	NO1260	56°43·7′	3°25·8′W	H	43
Bleaval	N Eil	NG0291	57°48·8′	7°0·6′W	H	18
Blea Water	Cumbr	NY4410	54°29·2′	2°51·4′W	W	90
Bleawath	Cumbr	NY0502	54°24·5′	3°27·4′W	X	89
Blea Wyke Point	N Yks	NZ9901	54°23·9′	0°28·1′W	X	94
Blebocraigs	Fife	NO4215	56°19·7′	2°55·8′W	X	59
Blebo Ho	Fife	NO4214	56°19·1′	2°55·8′W	X	59
Blebo Mains	Fife	NO4214	56°19·1′	2°55·8′W	X	59
Bleddfa	Powys	SO2068	52°18·5′	3°10·0′W	T	137,148
Bledington	Glos	SP2422	51°54·0′	1°38·7′W	T	163
Bledington Grounds	Glos	SP2324	51°55·1′	1°39·5′W	X	163
Bledington Heath	Glos	SP2424	51°55·1′	1°38·7′W	X	163
Bledisloe	Glos	SO9800	51°42·2′	2°1·3′W	X	163
Bledisloe Fm	Glos	SO6808	51°46·4′	2°27·4′W	FM	162
Bledlow	Bucks	SP7702	51°42·9′	0°52·7′W	T	165
Bledlow Cross	Oxon	SP7600	51°41·8′	0°53·6′W	X	165
Bledlow Great Wood	Bucks	SP7700	51°41·8′	0°52·8′W	F	165
Bledlow Ridge	Bucks	SU7898	51°40·8′	0°51·9′W	X	165
Bledlow Ridge	Bucks	SU7997	51°40·2′	0°51·1′W	T	165
Bleet	Wilts	ST8958	51°19·5′	2°9·1′W	T	173
Bleet Fm	Dorset	ST7924	51°1·1′	2°17·6′W	FM	183
Blegbie	E Loth	NT4761	55°50·6′	2°50·3′W	X	66
Blegbie Hill	E Loth	NT4860	55°50·1′	2°49·4′W	X	66
Blegbury	Devon	SS2326	51°0·6′	4°31·0′W	T	190
Blelack	Aberd	NJ5504	57°7·7′	2°44·1′W	X	37
Blelack Fm	Aberd	NJ4403	57°7·1′	2°55·0′W	FM	37
Blelack Hill	Aberd	NJ5505	57°8·3′	2°44·2′W	H	37
Blelham Tarn	Cumbr	NY3600	54°23·7′	2°58·7′W	W	90
Blencarn	Cumbr	NY6331	54°40·6′	2°34·0′W	T	91
Blencarn Beck	Cumbr	NY6231	54°40·6′	2°34·9′W	W	91
Blencathra Centre	Cumbr	NY3025	54°37·2′	3°4·6′W	X	90
Blencathra or Saddleback	Cumbr	NY3227	54°38·3′	3°2·8′W	H	90
Blencogo	Cumbr	NY1947	54°48·9′	3°15·2′W	T	85
Blencow Hall	Cumbr	NY4432	54°41·0′	2°51·7′W	A	90
Blendewing	Scot Bord	NT0734	55°35·7′	3°28·1′W	X	72
Blendworth	Hants	SU7113	50°55·0′	0°59·0′W	T	197
Blendworth Common	Hants	SU7011	50°53·9′	0°59·9′W	X	197
Blengdale	Cumbr	NY0805	54°26·2′	3°24·7′W	X	89
Blengdale Forest	Cumbr	NY0906	54°26·7′	3°23·8′W	F	89
Bleng Fell	Cumbr	NY0705	54°26·2′	3°25·6′W	H	89
Blenheim	C of Nott	SK5246	53°0·8′	1°13·1′W	X	129
Blenheim	Oxon	SP2716	51°50·7′	1°36·1′W	X	163
Blenheim	Oxon	SP5702	51°43·1′	1°10·1′W	T	164
Blenheim	Oxon	SP5705	51°44·7′	1°10·1′W	T	164
Blenheim	Sol	SP2473	52°21·5′	1°38·5′W	X	139
Blenheim Fm	Oxon	SP3639	52°3·1′	1°28·1′W	FM	151
Blenheim Fm	Oxon	SU6388	51°35·5′	1°5·0′W	FM	175
Blenheim Ho	Lincs	TF2822	52°47·1′	0°5·7′W	X	131
Blenheim Palace	Oxon	SP4416	51°50·7′	1°21·3′W	A	164
Blenkinsopp Castle	Northum	NY6664	54°58·4′	2°31·4′W	A	86
Blenkinsopp Common	Northum	NY6563	54°57·9′	2°32·4′W	X	86
Blenkinsopp Hall	Northum	NY6864	54°58·4′	2°29·6′W	T	86,87
Blenley Lodge	Northnts	SP8556	52°12·0′	0°45·0′W	X	152
Blenman's Fm	Hants	SU2815	50°56·3′	1°35·7′W	FM	184
Blennerhasset	Cumbr	NY1741	54°45·7′	3°17·0′W	T	85
Blennerhazel	Cumbr	NY0603	54°25·1′	3°26·5′W	X	89
Blererno	Aberd	NO7783	56°56·5′	2°22·2′W	X	45
Bleriot Meml	Kent	TR3242	51°8·0′	1°19·4′E	X	179
Blerrick	Corn	SX3853	50°21·5′	4°16·3′W	X	201
Blervie Castle	Moray	NJ0757	57°35·9′	3°32·9′W	X	27
Blervie House	Moray	NJ0655	57°34·8′	3°33·9′W	X	27
Blestivm (Monmouth)	Monm	SO5012	51°48·5′	2°43·1′W	R	162
Bletadith	Orkney	HY3226	59°7·2′	3°10·8′W	X	6
Bletch Brook	Derby	SK1853	53°4·7′	1°43·5′W	W	119
Bletchenden	Kent	TQ8343	51°9·6′	0°37·4′E	X	188
Bletchingdon	Oxon	SP5017	51°51·2′	1°16·0′W	T	164
Bletchingdon Park	Oxon	SP5018	51°51·7′	1°16·0′W	X	164
Bletchingley	Surrey	TQ3350	51°14·2′	0°5·3′W	T	187
Bletchingley Fm	Kent	TQ7741	51°8·7′	0°32·2′E	FM	188
Bletchinglye Fm	E Susx	TQ5730	51°3·1′	0°14·8′E	FM	188
Bletchley	Mil Key	SP8634	52°0·1′	0°44·4′W	T	152,165
Bletchley	Shrops	SJ6233	52°53·8′	2°33·5′W	T	127
Bletchley Leys Fm	Bucks	SP8232	51°59·1′	0°48·0′W	FM	152,165
Bletchley Manor	Shrops	SJ6233	52°53·8′	2°33·5′W	X	127
Bletherston	Pemb	SN0621	51°51·5′	4°48·6′W	T	145,158

Bletsoe	Beds	TL0258	52°12·9′	0°30·0′W	T	153
Blett	Orkney	HY5738	59°13·9′	2°44·7′W	X	5
Blett	Shetld	HU3917	59°56·4′	1°17·6′W	X	4
Blett	Shetld	HU4229	60°2·9′	1°14·3′W	X	4
Blewburton Hill	Oxon	SU5486	51°34·4′	1°12·9′W	X	174
Blewburton Hill (fort)	Oxon	SU5486	51°34·4′	1°12·9′W	A	174
Blewbury	Oxon	SU5385	51°33·9′	1°13·7′W	T	174
Blewbury Down	Oxon	SU5182	51°32·3′	1°15·5′W	X	174
Blewgyd	Carm	SN2816	51°49·2′	4°29·3′W	X	158
Blibberhill	Angus	NO5556	56°41·9′	2°43·6′W	X	54
Bliby	Kent	TR0237	51°6·0′	0°53·5′E	T	189
Blickling	Norf	TG1728	52°48·6′	1°13·6′E	T	133,134
Blidworth	Notts	SK5956	53°6·1′	1°6·7′W	T	120
Blidworth Bottoms	Notts	SK5954	53°5·0′	1°6·7′W	T	120
Blidworth Dale	Notts	SK5753	53°4·5′	1°8·5′W	T	120
Blidworth Lodge	Notts	SK5853	53°4·5′	1°7·6′W	X	120
Bligg	Shetld	HP4905	60°43·8′	1°5·6′W	X	1
Blights Fm	Devon	SS9423	51°0·0′	3°30·3′W	FM	181
Blind Beck	Durham	NY9318	54°33·7′	2°6·1′W	X	91,92
Blind Beck	N Yks	SD8073	54°9·4′	2°18·0′W	W	98
Blindburn	Aberd	NJ9435	57°24·6′	2°5·5′W	X	30
Blindburn	E Ayr	NS5527	55°31·2′	4°17·4′W	X	71
Blindburn	Northum	NT8210	55°23·3′	2°16·6′W	X	80
Blind Burn	Northum	NT8211	55°23·8′	2°16·6′W	W	80
Blindburn	Northum	NY8678	55°6·0′	2°12·7′W	X	87
Blindcrake	Cumbr	NY1434	54°41·9′	3°19·6′W	T	89
Blind End Copse	Hants	SU4843	51°11·3′	1°18·4′W	F	185
Blinder Ho	Derby	SK1168	53°12·8′	1°49·7′W	X	119
Blind Fiddler, The	Corn	SW4128	50°6·0′	5°36·9′W	X	203
Blind Fiddler, The (Standing Stone)	Corn	SW4128	50°6·0′	5°36·9′W	A	203
Blind Foot Fm	St Hel	SJ4698	53°28·8′	2°48·4′W	FM	108
Blindgill Moss	Durham	NY8421	54°35·3′	2°14·4′W	X	91,92
Blindgrooms	Kent	TQ9838	51°6·6′	0°50·1′E	X	189
Blind Hall Fm	Sol	SP2479	52°24·7′	1°38·4′W	FM	139
Blindhaugh Burn	Scot Bord	NT4221	55°29·0′	2°54·6′W	W	73
Blindhillbush	D & G	NY1589	55°11·5′	3°19·7′W	X	79
Blindhouse	Kent	TR1239	51°6·9′	1°2·1′E	X	179,189
Blindhurst	Lancs	SD5844	53°53·7′	2°37·9′W	X	102
Blindhurst	Lancs	SD6114	53°37·5′	2°35·0′W	X	109
Blindhurst Fell	Lancs	SD5945	53°54·2′	2°37·0′W	X	102
Blind Knights	Essex	TL9719	51°50·3′	0°52·0′E	A	168
Blindley Heath	Surrey	TQ3645	51°11·5′	0°2·8′W	T	187
Blind Lochs	D & G	NY0683	55°8·2′	3°28·0′W	W	78
Blindman's Bay	Arg & Bt	NR9965	55°50·4′	5°12·2′W	W	62
Blindmills	Aberd	NJ7339	57°26·7′	2°26·5′W	X	29
Blindmoor	Somer	ST2614	50°55·5′	3°2·8′W	T	193
Blind Pill Rhyne	Somer	ST3651	51°15·5′	2°54·6′W	W	182
Blind Side	N Yks	SE5485	54°15·7′	1°9·8′W	F	100
Blind Sike	Northum	NY6778	55°6·0′	2°30·6′W	W	86,87
Blindstones	Oldham	SE0401	53°30·6′	1°56·0′W	X	110
Blind Tarn	Cumbr	SD2696	54°21·5′	3°7·9′W	W	96,97
Blindtarn Gill	Cumbr	NY3208	54°28·0′	3°2·5′W	W	90
Blindwell	Devon	SS8031	51°4·2′	3°42·4′W	X	181
Blind Well	Lincs	TF0820	52°46·2′	0°23·5′W	W	130
Blindwell	Pth & Kin	NO1610	56°16·8′	3°21·0′W	X	58
Blindwell Fm	Somer	SS9927	51°2·2′	3°26·1′W	FM	181
Blindwells	Angus	NO5942	56°34·3′	2°39·6′W	X	54
Blindwells	Fife	NO4103	56°13·2′	2°56·6′W	X	59
Blindwells	Pth & Kin	NO1231	56°28·0′	3°25·3′W	X	53
Blingery	Highld	ND3049	58°25·7′	3°11·4′W	X	11,12
Blingery Hill	Highld	ND2948	58°25·1′	3°12·5′W	X	11,12
Blingsby Gate	Derby	SK4564	53°10·5′	1°19·2′W	X	120
Blinkbonnie	Pth & Kin	NO0940	56°32·8′	3°28·4′W	X	52,53
Blinkbonny	C of Edin	NT1867	55°53·6′	3°18·2′W	X	65,66
Blinkbonny	Fife	NO2718	56°21·2′	3°10·4′W	T	59
Blinkbonny	Fife	NO4404	56°13·8′	2°53·8′W	X	59
Blinkbonny	Fife	NO5104	56°13·8′	2°47·0′W	X	59
Blinkbonny	Moray	NH9756	57°35·2′	3°42·9′W	X	27
Blinkbonny	Northum	NT9036	55°37·3′	2°9·1′W	X	74,75
Blinkbonny	Orkney	HY4108	58°57·6′	3°1·1′W	X	6,7
Blinkbonny	Orkney	HY6723	59°5·8′	2°34·1′W	X	5
Blinkbonny	Scot Bord	NT2151	55°45·0′	3°15·1′W	X	66,73
Blinkbonny	Scot Bord	NT6738	55°38·3′	2°31·0′W	X	74
Blinkbonny	Scot Bord	NT9356	55°48·1′	2°6·3′W	X	67,74,75
Blinkbonny	Scot Bord	NY4985	55°9·7′	2°47·6′W	X	79
Blinkbonny Burn	E Loth	NT5262	55°51·2′	2°45·6′W	W	66
Blinkbonny Height	Scot Bord	NY5084	55°9·1′	2°46·6′W	H	79
Blinkbonny Ho	E Loth	NT4772	55°56·5′	2°50·5′W	X	66
Blinkbonny Lodge	Fife	NO2717	56°20·6′	3°10·4′W	X	59
Blinkbonny Wood	E Loth	NT5364	55°52·3′	2°44·6′W	F	66
Blinkeerie	Fife	NS9789	56°5·2′	3°38·9′W	X	65
Blinsham	Devon	SS5116	50°55·7′	4°6·8′W	X	180
Blishmire Close	N Yks	SD8472	54°8·9′	2°14·3′W	X	98
Blishmire Ho	N Yks	SD8572	54°8·9′	2°13·4′W	X	98
Blisland	Corn	SX1073	50°31·8′	4°40·5′W	T	200
Blissford	Hants	SU1713	50°55·2′	1°45·1′W	T	195
Bliss Gate	Worcs	SO7472	52°21·0′	2°22·5′W	T	138
Blists Hill	Wrekin	SJ6903	52°37·7′	2°27·1′W	T	127
Blisworth	Northnts	SP7253	52°10·5′	0°56·4′W	T	152
Blisworth Hill	Northnts	SP7252	52°9·9′	0°56·4′W	X	152
Blisworth Hill Fm	Northnts	SP7351	52°9·4′	0°55·6′W	FM	152
Blisworth Lodge	Northnts	SP7353	52°10·5′	0°55·6′W	X	152
Blithbury	Staffs	SK0820	52°46·9′	1°52·5′W	T	128
Blithfield Hall	Staffs	SK0423	52°48·5′	1°56·0′W	A	128
Blithfield Reservoir	Staffs	SK0523	52°48·5′	1°55·1′W	W	128
Blithford Fm	Staffs	SK0821	52°47·4′	1°52·5′W	FM	128
Blitterlees	Cumbr	NY1052	54°51·5′	3°23·7′W	T	85
Blixe's Fm	Essex	TL7517	51°49·7′	0°32·8′E	FM	167
Bloakhillhead	E Ayr	NS3846	55°41·1′	4°34·2′W	X	63
Bloak Moss	E Ayr	NS3645	55°40·5′	4°36·0′W	X	63
Bloan Fm	Cumbr	NY8112	54°30·4′	2°17·2′W	FM	91,92
Blobrick	Shetld	HT9440	60°8·9′	2°6·0′W	X	4
Blochairn	E Dunb	NS5875	55°57·1′	4°16·0′W	X	64
Bloch Burn	D & G	NY3381	55°7·4′	3°2·6′W	W	79
Bloch Fm	D & G	NY3281	55°7·4′	3°3·5′W	FM	79
Bloch Hill	D & G	NY3482	55°7·9′	3°1·7′W	H	79
Blocka Hall	Suff	TM4799	52°32·2′	1°38·9′E	X	134
Block Eary	I of M	SC3989	54°16·5′	4°27·9′W	X	95

Block Fen	Cambs	TL4289	52°29·1'	0°5·9'E	X	142,143
Block Fen	Cambs	TL4383	52°25·8'	0°6·6'E	X	142,143
Blockfield Wood	Surrey	TQ4140	51°8·7'	0°1·3'E	F	187
Block Fm	Cambs	TL6070	52°18·5'	0°21·2'E	FM	154
Block Fm	Essex	TM1626	51°53·7'	1°8·8'E	FM	168,169
Block Fm	Suff	TL8956	52°10·4'	0°46·2'E	FM	155
Blockhouse	Aberd	NJ8224	57°18·6'	2°17·5'W	X	38
Blockhouse Fm	Somer	ST1423	51°0·2'	3°13·2'W	FM	181,193
Blockhouses	Corn	SX1251	50°20·0'	4°38·1'W	A	200
Blockley	Glos	SP1634	52°0·5'	1°45·6'W	T	151
Blockmoor Fen	Cambs	TL4181	52°24·8'	0°4·8'E	X	142,143
Blockmoor Fen	Cambs	TL5675	52°21·3'	0°17·8'E	X	143
Blockmoor Fm	Cambs	TL4280	52°24·2'	0°5·6'E	FM	142,143
Block Moors	Cambs	TL4782	52°25·2'	0°10·1'E	X	143
Block Wood	Powys	SO1586	52°28·2'	3°14·7'W	F	136
Blodeuen	Carm	SN4736	52°0·3'	4°13·4'W	X	146
Blodnant	Conwy	SH9846	53°0·3'	3°30·8'W	X	116
Blodwel Hall	Shrops	SJ2622	52°47·7'	3°5·4'W	X	126
Blodwel Rock	Shrops	SJ2622	52°47·7'	3°5·4'W	X	126
Bloe Greet	Lancs	SD6958	54°1·3'	2°28·0'W	X	103
Blofield	Norf	TG3309	52°37·9'	1°27·0'E	T	134
Blofield Corner	Norf	TG3111	52°39·1'	1°25·3'E	X	133,134
Blofield Heath	Norf	TG3211	52°39·0'	1°26·2'E	T	133,134
Bloie Geo	Orkney	ND4092	58°48·9'	3°1·8'W	X	7
Blois Fm	Essex	TL6841	52°2·7'	0°27·4'E	FM	154
Blois Hall	Essex	TL7434	51°58·9'	0°32·4'E	X	155
Blois Hall Fm	N Yks	SE3472	54°8·8'	1°28·4'W	FM	99
Blomvyle Hall	Suff	TM3059	52°11·1'	1°22·3'E	X	156
Blonks Fm	W Susx	TQ1319	50°57·8'	0°23·1'W	FM	198
Blo' Norton	Norf	TM0179	52°22·6'	0°57·6'E	T	144
Blo Norton Ho	Norf	TM0179	52°22·6'	0°57·6'E	X	144
Bloodgate Hill	Norf	TF8535	52°53·1'	0°45·4'E	X	132
Blood Hall	Suff	TM1864	52°14·1'	1°12·0'E	X	156
Blood Hill	Norf	TL8487	52°27·2'	0°42·9'E	X	144
Blood Hills	Norf	TG4718	52°42·4'	1°39·8'E	X	134
Blood Hill (Tumulus)	Norf	TL8487	52°27·2'	0°42·9'E	A	144
Bloodhope Burn	D & G	NT2307	55°21·3'	3°12·4'W	W	79
Bloodhope Head	D & G	NT2209	55°22·4'	3°13·4'W	X	79
Bloodman's Corner	Suff	TM5199	52°32·1'	1°42·5'E	T	134
Bloodmire Moss	D & G	NX8174	55°3·0'	3°51·3'W	X	84
Bloodmoor Hill	Suff	TM5289	52°26·7'	1°42·9'E	X	156
Blood Moss	D & G	NX2171	55°0·3'	4°47·5'W	X	76
Blood Moss	D & G	NX8860	54°55·6'	3°44·4'W	X	84
Blood Moss	Highld	ND2237	58°19·1'	3°19·4'W	X	11
Blood Moss	Inverc	NS2169	55°53·1'	4°51·3'W	X	63
Bloodoaks Fm	Hants	SU2616	50°56·8'	1°37·4'W	FM	184
Bloodstone Hill	Highld	NG3100	57°1·0'	6°25·5'W	H	32,39
Bloody Acre	S Glos	ST6991	51°37·3'	2°26·5'W	X	162,172
Bloody Acre (Fort)	S Glos	ST6991	51°37·3'	2°26·5'W	A	162,172
Bloody Bay	Arg & Bt	NM4858	56°39·0'	6°6·2'W	W	47
Bloody Beck	N Yks	SE9397	54°21·8'	0°33·7'W	W	94,101
Bloody Bush	Northum	NY5790	55°12·4'	2°40·1'W	X	80
Bloodybush Edge	Northum	NT9014	55°25·4'	2°9·0'W	H	80
Bloody Gill	D & G	NY0297	55°15·7'	3°32·1'W	W	78
Bloody Inches	Pth & Kin	NO1438	56°31·8'	3°23·4'W	X	53
Bloodylaws	Scot Bord	NT7216	55°26·5'	2°26·1'W	X	80
Bloodylaws Hill	Scot Bord	NT7217	55°27·0'	2°26·1'W	H	80
Bloodymire	Aberd	NJ7263	57°39·6'	2°27·7'W	X	29
Bloody Mires	D & G	NX5388	55°10·1'	4°18·0'W	W	77
Bloody Moss	Highld	ND1156	58°29·3'	3°31·1'W	X	11,12
Bloody Moss	Highld	ND2072	58°38·0'	3°22·2'W	X	7,12
Bloody Moss	Northum	NT9002	55°19·0'	2°9·0'W	W	80
Bloody Oaks	Rut	SK9611	52°41·5'	0°33·4'W	F	130
Bloody Pool	Devon	SX7062	50°26·8'	3°49·5'W	X	202
Bloodyquoys	Highld	ND1958	58°30·4'	3°22·9'W	X	11,12
Bloody Stone	Highld	NG4823	57°14·0'	6°10·1'W	X	32
Bloody Tuaks	Orkney	HY4245	59°17·5'	3°0·6'W	X	5
Bloody Vale	N Yks	SD9595	54°21·3'	2°4·2'W	X	98
Bloomer Hill	N Yks	SE0147	53°55·4'	1°58·7'W	X	104
Bloomer's Fm	Dorset	ST8228	51°3·3'	2°15·0'W	FM	183
Bloomfield	Bath & NE Somer	ST6659	51°20·0'	2°28·9'W	T	172
Bloomfield	Bath & NE Somer	ST7463	51°22·2'	2°22·0'W	T	172
Bloomfield	D & G	NX9878	55°5·4'	3°35·5'W	X	84
Bloomfield	Fife	NO2116	56°20·0'	3°16·2'W	X	58
Bloomfield	Fife	NO4721	56°23·0'	2°51·1'W	X	54,59
Bloomfield	Moray	NJ4767	57°41·6'	2°52·9'W	X	28,29
Bloomfield	Orkney	HY4109	58°58·1'	3°1·1'W	X	6,7
Bloomfield	Pth & Kin	NO2117	56°20·6'	3°16·2'W	X	58
Bloomfield	Sand	SO9593	52°32·3'	2°4·0'W	T	139
Bloomfield	Scot Bord	NT5824	55°30·7'	2°39·5'W	X	73,74
Bloomfield Fm	Bucks	SP9405	51°44·4'	0°37·9'W	FM	165
Bloomfield Hatch	W Berks	SU6865	51°23·0'	1°1·0'W	X	175
Bloomfield's Covert	Suff	TM3962	52°12·5'	1°30·3'E	F	156
Bloomfields Fm	Suff	TL7156	52°10·8'	0°30·5'E	FM	154
Bloom Fm	Bucks	SU8689	51°35·8'	0°45·1'W	FM	175
Bloomhill Fm	E Yorks	SE8032	53°46·9'	0°46·7'W	FM	106
Bloomridge	E Ayr	NS3845	55°40·5'	4°34·1'W	X	63
Bloomsbank Fm	S Ayr	NS3721	55°27·6'	4°34·2'W	FM	70
Bloomsbury	Camden	TQ3082	51°31·5'	0°7·2'W	T	176,177
Bloomsbury	Shrops	SJ7714	52°43·6'	2°20·0'W	X	127
Bloom's Fm	Essex	TL7535	51°59·4'	0°33·3'E	FM	155
Blooms Gorse Fm	Notts	SK6262	53°9·3'	1°4·0'W	FM	120
Blooms Hall	Suff	TL8550	52°7·3'	0°42·5'E	X	155
Bloom's Hall	Suff	TM3381	52°22·9'	1°25·8'E	X	156
Bloomsholm	S Lanak	NS6741	55°38·9'	4°6·4'W	X	71
Bloom Wood	Bucks	SU8789	51°35·8'	0°44·2'W	F	175
Bloors Place	Medway	TQ8167	51°22·6'	0°36·4'E	X	178
Bloors Wharf	Medway	TQ8167	51°22·6'	0°36·4'E	X	178
Blore	Staffs	SJ7234	52°54·4'	2°24·6'W	T	127
Blore	Staffs	SK1349	53°2·5'	1°48·0'W	T	119
Bloreheath	Staffs	SJ7135	52°54·9'	2°25·5'W	T	127
Bloreheath (1459)	Staffs	SJ7135	52°54·9'	2°25·5'W	A	127
Blorenge	Monm	SO2611	51°47·8'	3°4·0'W	H	161
Blorepipe	Staffs	SJ7730	52°52·3'	2°20·1'W	X	127
Blosses	Suff	TM1656	52°9·3'	1°9·9'E	X	156
Blossom	Orkney	HY4950	59°20·3'	2°53·3'W	X	5
Blossomfield	Sol	SP1378	52°24·2'	1°48·1'W	T	139
Blossom Fm	Worcs	SO8561	52°15·1'	2°12·8'W	FM	150

Blossom Hill	Northum	NY9063	54°57·9'	2°8·9'W	X	87
Blossomwood Fm	Essex	TM0424	51°52·9'	0°58·2'E	FM	168
Blosta	Shetld	HU4429	60°2·9'	1°12·1'W	X	4
Blotchnie Fiold	Orkney	HY4128	59°8·4'	3°1·4'W	H	5,6
Blotting Raise	Cumbr	NY5949	54°50·3'	2°37·9'W	H	86
Blotweth	Carm	SN5236	52°0·4'	4°9·0'W	X	146
Blouk Field	Shetld	HU1853	60°15·9'	1°40·0'W	H	3
Blounce	Hants	SU7145	51°12·2'	0°58·6'W	X	186
Blountfield	D & G	NY0675	55°3·9'	3°27·9'W	X	85
Blount's	Bucks	SU8387	51°34·8'	0°47·7'W	X	175
Blounts Fm	Essex	TQ8292	51°36·1'	0°38·1'E	FM	178
Blount's Fm	Herts	TL4517	51°50·2'	0°6·7'E	FM	167
Blount's Green	Staffs	SK0732	52°53·4'	1°53·4'W	T	128
Blouth, The	Corn	SW9238	50°12·6'	4°54·5'W	X	204
Blovid	Shetld	HU4119	59°57·5'	1°15·5'W	X	4
Blower's Brook	Leic	SK3912	52°42·5'	1°25·0'W	W	128
Blower's Common	Suff	TM4375	52°19·4'	1°34·4'E	X	156
Blow Gill	N Yks	SE5394	54°20·6'	1°10·7'W	W	100
Blow Hole	Swan	SS3887	51°33·8'	4°19·8'W	X	159
Blow Houses	N Yks	SE2990	54°18·5'	1°32·8'W	X	99
Blowick	Cumbr	NY3917	54°32·9'	2°56·2'W	X	90
Blowick	Sefton	SD3516	53°38·4'	2°58·6'W	T	108
Blo Wick	Shetld	HU3671	60°25·5'	1°20·3'W	W	2,3
Blowinghouse	Corn	SW7451	50°19·2'	5°10·1'W	T	204
Blowing Stone	Oxon	SU3287	51°35·1'	1°31·9'W	X	174
Blowingstone Hill	Oxon	SU3286	51°34·5'	1°31·9'W	X	174
Bloworth Slack	N Yks	SE6299	54°23·2'	1°2·3'W	W	94,100
Bloworth Wood	N Yks	SE6299	54°23·2'	1°2·3'W	F	94,100
Blow's Fm	Essex	TL6306	51°44·0'	0°22·0'E	FM	167
Blows Moss	Orkney	ND4585	58°45·2'	2°56·6'W	X	7
Blow Tarn	N Yks	SE0961	54°2·9'	1°51·3'W	W	99
Blowty	Powys	SJ0111	52°41·5'	3°27·5'W	X	125
Blowup Nose	Aberd	NO9498	57°4·6'	2°5·5'W	X	38,45
Blox Hall	Suff	TL9752	52°8·1'	0°53·1'E	X	155
Bloxham	Oxon	SP4335	52°0·9'	1°22·0'W	T	151
Bloxham Barn Fm	Warw	SP3553	52°10·7'	1°28·9'W	FM	151
Bloxham Br	Oxon	SP4633	51°59·8'	1°19·4'W	X	151
Bloxham Grove	Oxon	SP4536	52°1·5'	1°20·3'W	X	151
Bloxham Lodge	Wilts	SU2663	51°22·2'	1°37·2'W	X	174
Bloxholm	Lincs	TF0653	53°4·1'	0°24·7'W	X	121
Bloxwich	Wals	SJ9902	52°37·2'	2°0·5'W	T	127,139
Bloxworth	Dorset	SY8894	50°45·0'	2°9·8'W	T	194
Bloxworth Down	Dorset	SY8796	50°46·0'	2°10·7'W	X	194
Bloxworth Heath	Dorset	SY8892	50°43·9'	2°9·8'W	X	194
Bloxworth Ho	Dorset	SY8794	50°45·0'	2°10·7'W	X	194
Blubberhouses	N Yks	SE1655	53°59·7'	1°44·9'W	T	104
Blubberhouses Moor	N Yks	SE1354	53°59·2'	1°47·7'W	X	104
Blubbersdale	Orkney	HY3720	59°4·0'	3°5·4'W	X	6
Blucks Ho	Shrops	SO6889	52°30·1'	2°27·9'W	X	138
Blucks Pool	Pemb	SR8897	51°38·2'	5°3·4'W	W	158
Blue Anchor	Corn	SW9157	50°22·8'	4°56·0'W	T	200
Blue Anchor	Somer	ST0243	51°10·9'	3°23·7'W	T	181
Blue Anchor	Swan	SS5495	51°38·3'	4°6·2'W	T	159
Blue Anchor Bay	Somer	ST0145	51°12·0'	3°24·6'W	W	181
Blue Bache Fm	Ches	SJ6043	52°59·2'	2°35·3'W	FM	118
Blue Back	Lincs	TF4536	52°54·3'	0°9·8'E	X	131
Blue Barn	N Yks	NZ4607	54°27·6'	1°17·0'W	X	93
Blue Barn	Oxon	SP4006	51°45·3'	1°24·8'W	X	164
Blue Barn Fm	Kent	TQ7438	51°7·1'	0°29·6'E	FM	188
Blue Barn Fm	Notts	SK5371	53°14·2'	1°11·9'W	FM	120
Blue Barn Fm	Oxon	SP4627	51°56·6'	1°19·5'W	FM	164
Blue Barns Fm	Essex	TM0230	51°56·1'	0°56·7'E	FM	168
Bluebauds	Moray	NJ3749	57°31·9'	3°2·7'W	X	28
Blue Beck	N Yks	NZ8004	54°25·7'	0°45·6'W	X	94
Blue Bell	Lancs	SD9040	53°51·6'	2°8·7'W	X	103
Bluebell	Shrops	SJ5910	52°41·4'	2°36·0'W	T	126
Bluebell Fm	Ches	SJ7479	53°18·7'	2°23·0'W	FM	118
Bluebell Fm	Monm	ST4295	51°39·3'	2°49·9'W	FM	171
Blue Bell Fm	Peterb	TF2708	52°39·5'	0°6·9'W	FM	142
Bluebell Fm	Worcs	SO8641	52°4·3'	2°11·9'W	FM	150
Blue Bell Hill	Kent	TQ7462	51°20·0'	0°30·3'E	T	178,188
Bluebell Lakes	Northnts	TL0592	52°31·2'	0°26·7'W	W	142
Bluebell Railway	W Susx	TQ3729	51°2·9'	0°2·3'W	X	187,198
Bluebell Railway	W Susx	TQ3730	51°3·4'	0°2·3'W	X	187
Blue Ben	Somer	ST1143	51°11·0'	3°16·0'W	X	181
Blueberry Fm	Kent	TQ4759	51°18·9'	0°7·0'E	FM	188
Blueberry Lodge	Northnts	SP7375	52°22·3'	0°55·3'W	X	141
Blue Boar Fm	Ches	SJ9776	53°17·1'	2°2·3'W	FM	118
Bluebeots Burn	E Ayr	NS5213	55°23·6'	4°19·8'W	W	70
Blue Br	Lincs	TF4357	53°5·7'	0°8·5'E	X	122
Blue Br	N Yks	SE5362	54°3·3'	1°11·0'W	X	100
Bluebrae Plant	Fife	NO2407	56°15·2'	3°13·2'W	F	59
Blue Bridge	Mil Key	SP8240	52°3·4'	0°47·8'W	X	152
Bluebridge	N Yks	SD8590	54°18·6'	2°13·4'W	X	98
Bluebridge Ho	Essex	TL8229	51°56·0'	0°39·2'E	X	168
Blueburn	Northum	NZ0495	55°15·2'	1°55·8'W	X	81
Blueburn Knowe	Northum	NZ0395	55°15·2'	1°56·7'W	X	81
Bluebutts Fm	Lancs	SD7051	53°57·5'	2°27·0'W	FM	103
Blue Cairn	Aberd	NJ4402	57°6·6'	2°55·0'W	X	37
Blue Cairn	Angus	NO4776	56°52·6'	2°51·7'W	X	44
Blue Cairn	Angus	NO4979	56°54·2'	2°49·8'W	A	44
Blue Cairn	D & G	NT1010	55°22·8'	3°24·8'W	H	78
Blue Cairn	D & G	NY0198	55°16·2'	3°33·1'W	A	78
Blue Cairn	Moray	NJ3136	57°24·8'	3°8·5'W	X	28
Bluecairn	Scot Bord	NT5341	55°39·9'	2°44·4'W	T	73
Blue Cairn Hill	D & G	NT2309	55°22·4'	3°12·5'W	X	79
Bluecaster	Cumbr	SD7196	54°21·8'	2°26·4'W	H	98
Bluecaster Side	Cumbr	SD7096	54°21·8'	2°27·3'W	X	98
Blue Coat Fm	N Yks	SE6964	54°4·3'	0°56·3'W	FM	100
Blue Covert	Northnts	SP7678	52°23·9'	0°52·6'W	F	141
Blue Craigs	Pth & Kin	NN8229	56°26·6'	3°54·4'W	X	52
Blue Dial	Cumbr	NY0740	54°45·0'	3°26·3'W	X	85
Bluefield Fm	Northnts	TL0396	52°33·4'	0°28·4'W	FM	141
Bluefolds	Moray	NJ2232	57°22·6'	3°17·4'W	X	36
Blue Gate	Somer	SS7537	51°7·4'	3°46·8'W	X	180
Bluegate Fm	Beds	SP9623	51°54·1'	0°35·9'W	FM	165
Bluegate Fm	Suff	TM1439	52°0·7'	1°7·5'E	FM	169
Bluegate Hall	Essex	TL6829	51°56·3'	0°27·0'E	X	167
Blue Gates	Essex	TM0722	51°51·7'	1°0·8'E	X	168,169
Blue Geo	Orkney	HY6340	59°15·0'	2°38·4'W	X	5

Blue Geo	Shetld	HU5144	60°10·9'	1°4·3'W	X	4
Bluegrass	Cumbr	NY8314	54°31·5'	2°15·3'W	X	91,92
Blue Hall Fm	E Yorks	TA2635	53°48·0'	0°4·8'W	FM	107
Blue Hayes	Devon	SX9995	50°45·0'	3°25·5'W	X	192
Blue Head	Highld	NH8066	57°40·3'	4°0·3'W	X	21,27
Blue Head	Shetld	HU3191	60°36·3'	1°25·5'W	X	1
Blue Hemmel	Northum	NY7475	55°4·4'	2°24·0'W	X	86,87
Bluehemmel Sike	Northum	NY7374	55°3·8'	2°24·9'W	W	86,87
Blue Hill	Aberd	NJ9200	57°5·7'	2°7·5'W	H	38
Bluehill	D & G	NX7851	54°50·6'	3°53·6'W	X	84
Blue Hill	Herts	TL2920	51°52·0'	0°7·2'W	T	166
Blue Hill	Moray	NJ2942	57°28·0'	3°10·6'W	X	28
Blue Hill	Notts	SK6834	52°54·2'	0°58·9'W	X	129
Blue Hills	Corn	SW7251	50°19·1'	5°11·8'W	X	204
Blue Hills	Staffs	SK0162	53°9·5'	1°58·7'W	X	119
Blue Ho	Durham	NZ2630	54°40·1'	1°35·4'W	X	93
Blue Ho	Hartpl	NZ4729	54°39·5'	1°15·9'W	X	93
Blue Ho	Red & Cl	NZ7116	54°32·3'	0°53·7'W	X	94
Blue Ho	Suff	TM2773	52°18·7'	1°20·2'E	X	156
Blue Ho Fm	Northum	NZ2482	55°8·2'	1°37·0'W	FM	81
Bluehouse	Arg & Bt	NR3362	55°46·9'	6°15·1'W	X	60,61
Blue House	Hartpl	NZ4726	54°37·9'	1°15·9'W	X	93
Bluehouse	Kent	TR1537	51°5·7'	1°4·6'E	X	179,189
Blue House Fm	Essex	TL6111	51°46·7'	0°20·4'E	FM	167
Bluehouse Fm	Essex	TM1530	51°55·8'	1°8·0'E	FM	168,169
Blue House Fm	Essex	TQ9188	51°33·7'	0°45·7'E	FM	178
Blue House Fm	Hants	SU7257	51°18·7'	0°57·6'W	FM	175,186
Blue House Fm	Kent	TQ7546	51°11·4'	0°30·7'E	FM	188
Blue House Fm	Kent	TQ9924	50°59·1'	0°50·5'E	FM	189
Blue House Fm	Kent	TR0026	51°0·1'	0°51·4'E	FM	189
Blue House Fm	S Tyne	NZ3860	54°56·2'	1°24·0'W	FM	88
Blue House Fm	Thurr	TQ6387	51°33·7'	0°21·5'E	FM	177
Bluehouse Fm	Thurr	TQ6880	51°29·9'	0°25·6'E	FM	177,178
Blue Houses	Scot Bord	NT7340	55°39·4'	2°25·3'W	X	74
Bluejibs	Shetld	HP6616	60°49·5'	0°46·7'W	X	1
Blue John Cavern	Derby	SK1383	53°20·9'	1°47·9'W	X	110
Blue Lagoon Park	Mil Key	SP8632	51°59·0'	0°44·5'W	X	152,165
Blue Lins Brook	Powys	SO0482	52°25·9'	3°24·3'W	W	136
Blue Lodge	S Glos	ST6974	51°28·1'	2°26·4'W	X	172
Blue Lodge Fm	Derby	SK4371	53°14·3'	1°20·9'W	FM	120
Blue Man-i'-th'-Moss	N Yks	SE7699	54°23·1'	0°49·4'W	X	94,100
Blue Man-i'-th'-Moss (Standing Stone)	N Yks	SE7699	54°23·1'	0°49·4'W	A	94,100
Bluemill	Aberd	NJ4112	57°12·0'	2°58·1'W	X	37
Blue Mills	Essex	TL8313	51°47·4'	0°39·6'E	X	168
Blue Moor	Lancs	SD4638	53°50·4'	2°48·8'W	X	102
Blue Mull	Shetld	HP5504	60°43·2'	0°59·0'W	X	1
Bluemull Sound	Shetld	HP5502	60°42·1'	0°59·0'W	W	1
Blue Pigeons	Kent	TR3456	51°15·5'	1°21·6'E	X	179
Blue Point	I of M	NX3902	54°23·5'	4°28·4'W	X	95
Blue Pool	Dorset	SY9383	50°39·0'	2°5·6'W	W	195
Bluepool Corner	Swan	SS4093	51°37·0'	4°18·3'W	X	159
Blue Post	Devon	SX7359	50°25·3'	3°46·9'W	X	202
Bluepump Fm	Norf	TM0880	52°22·9'	1°3·8'E	FM	144
Blue Row	Essex	TM0214	51°47·5'	0°56·1'E	X	168
Blue Scar	N Yks	SD9370	54°7·8'	2°6·0'W	X	98
Blue Scar	N Yks	SD9891	54°19·1'	2°1·4'W	X	98
Bluescudda Kame	Shetld	HP5915	60°49·1'	0°54·4'W	X	1
Blueslate Fm	Ches	SJ7768	53°12·8'	2°20·3'W	FM	118
Blue Slates Fm	E Yorks	SE7340	53°51·3'	0°53·0'W	FM	105,106
Bluestone	Ches	SJ6353	53°4·6'	2°32·7'W	X	118
Blue Stone	Fife	NO6310	56°17·1'	2°35·4'W	X	59
Bluestone Edge	Northum	NT8602	55°19·0'	2°12·8'W	H	80
Bluestone Fm	Lincs	TF7141	52°56·6'	0°33·1'E	FM	132
Bluestone Fm	Norf	TF8536	52°53·6'	0°45·4'E	FM	132
Blue Stone Fm, The	Shrops	SO6178	52°24·2'	2°34·0'W	FM	138
Bluestone Grange	Durham	NZ0519	54°34·2'	1°54·9'W	X	92
Bluestone Heath Road	Lincs	TF3376	53°16·1'	0°0·1'E	X	122
Bluestone Plantn	Norf	TG1326	52°47·6'	1°10·0'E	F	133
Blue Stones	D & G	NS6200	55°16·7'	4°9·9'W	X	77
Bluethwaite Hill	Cumbr	NY7026	54°37·9'	2°27·5'W	X	91
Blue Tile Fm	Norf	TG0724	52°46·7'	1°4·6'E	FM	133
Blue Tile Fm	Suff	TM4182	52°23·2'	1°32·9'E	FM	156
Blueton	Pth & Kin	NN8507	56°14·8'	3°50·9'W	X	58
Bluetown	Kent	TQ9158	51°17·6'	0°44·8'E	T	178
Blue Town	Kent	TQ9175	51°26·7'	0°45·3'E	T	178
Blue Vein	Wilts	ST8367	51°24·3'	2°14·3'W	T	173
Blue Violet	Devon	SX7398	50°46·3'	3°47·7'W	X	191
Bluewath Beck	N Yks	SE7599	54°23·1'	0°50·3'W	W	94,100
Bluey's Fm	Bucks	SU8289	51°35·9'	0°48·6'W	FM	175
Blughasary	Highld	NC1301	57°57·8'	5°9·2'W	X	15
Blundel Brook	Lancs	SD5434	53°48·3'	2°41·5'W	W	102
Blundell Fm	Shrops	SO6783	52°26·9'	2°28·7'W	FM	138
Blundells	Bucks	SU7391	51°37·0'	0°56·3'W	X	175
Blundellsands	Sefton	SJ3099	53°29·2'	3°2·9'W	T	108
Blunderfield	Cumbr	NY5643	54°47·0'	2°40·6'W	X	86
Blundeston	Suff	TM5197	52°31·0'	1°42·4'E	T	134
Blundeston Marshes	Suff	TM5095	52°30·0'	1°41·4'E	X	134
Blundies	Staffs	SO8287	52°29·1'	2°15·5'W	T	138
Blunham	Beds	TL1551	52°8·9'	0°18·8'W	T	153
Blunham Grange	Beds	TL1452	52°9·5'	0°19·6'W	X	153
Blunk	Shetld	HU3452	60°15·3'	1°22·6'W	X	3
Blunsdon Abbey	Swin	SU1389	51°36·2'	1°48·3'W	X	173
Blunsdon Hill	Swin	SU1390	51°36·8'	1°48·3'W	X	163,173
Blunsdon St Andrew	Swin	SU1389	51°36·2'	1°48·3'W	T	173
Blunt Ho	Durham	NY9626	54°38·0'	2°3·3'W	X	91,92
Blunthie Well	Northum	NT9933	55°35·7'	2°0·5'W	W	75
Bluntington	Worcs	SO8974	52°22·1'	2°9·3'W	T	139
Bluntisham	Cambs	TL3674	52°21·1'	0°0·2'E	T	142
Blunts	Corn	SX3463	50°26·8'	4°19·9'W	T	201
Blunts	Essex	TL6516	51°49·3'	0°24·0'E	X	167
Blunt's Corner	Norf	TF8939	52°55·1'	0°49·1'E	X	132
Blunt's Fm	Cambs	TL4486	52°27·4'	0°7·6'E	FM	142,143
Blunt's Fm	Essex	TL6331	51°57·4'	0°22·7'E	FM	167
Blunts Fm	Essex	TQ4699	51°40·5'	0°7·1'E	FM	167,177
Blunt's Green	Warw	SP1368	52°18·8'	1°48·2'W	T	139,151
Blunt's Hall	Essex	TL8014	51°48·0'	0°37·0'E	X	168
Bluntshay	Dorset	SY4197	50°46·4'	2°49·8'W	T	193
Bluntsmoor Fm	Dorset	ST4506	50°51·3'	2°46·5'W	FM	193
Blunts Wall	Essex	TQ6594	51°37·5'	0°23·4'E	X	167,177,178

Blurton	C of Stoke	SJ8942	52°58·8′	2°9·4′W	T	118
Blurton Grange Fm	Staffs	SJ9041	52°58·2′	2°8·5′W	FM	118
Bluther Burn	Fife	NS9690	56°5·7′	3°39·9′W	W	58
Bluther Burn	Fife	NS9988	56°4·7′	3°36·9′W	W	65
Bluthers Geo	Orkney	HY6824	59°6·4′	2°33·0′W	X	5
Blwch-côch	Gwyn	SH7415	52°43·3′	3°51·5′W	X	124
Blwch Main	Powys	SH8209	52°40·2′	3°44·3′W	X	124,125
Blyborough	Lincs	SK9394	53°26·3′	0°35·6′W	T	112
Blyborough Covert	Lincs	SK9094	53°26·3′	0°38·3′W	F	112
Blyborough Grange	Lincs	SK9594	53°26·3′	0°33·8′W	X	112
Blyborough Hall	Lincs	SK9394	53°26·3′	0°35·6′W	X	112
Blye Water	Moray	NJ2621	57°16·7′	3°13·2′W	W	37
Blyford	Suff	TM4276	52°19·9′	1°33·5′E	T	156
Blyford Wood	Suff	TM4278	52°21·0′	1°33·6′E	F	156
Blymhill	Staffs	SJ8012	52°42·6′	2°17·4′W	T	127
Blymhill Common	Staffs	SJ7812	52°42·6′	2°19·1′W	X	127
Blymhill Lawns	Staffs	SJ8111	52°42·0′	2°16·5′W	T	127
Blymhill Marsh	Staffs	SJ8012	52°42·6′	2°17·4′W	X	127
Blynfield Fm	Dorset	ST8321	50°59·5′	2°14·1′W	FM	183
Blyth	Northum	NZ3081	55°7·6′	1°31·3′W	T	81
Blyth	Notts	SK6287	53°22·8′	1°3·7′W	T	111,120
Blyth	Scot Bord	NT1345	55°41·7′	3°22·6′W	T	72
Blyth Bank	Scot Bord	NT1446	55°42·2′	3°21·7′W	X	72
Blyth Br	Warw	SP2189	52°30·1′	1°41·0′W	X	139
Blyth Bridge	Scot Bord	NT1345	55°41·7′	3°22·6′W	T	72
Blythburgh	Suff	TM4575	52°19·3′	1°36·1′E	T	156
Blythbury Fm	Shrops	SJ7208	52°40·4′	2°24·4′W	FM	127
Blyth Corner	Notts	SK6473	53°15·2′	1°2·0′W	F	120
Blythe	Scot Bord	NT5849	55°44·2′	2°39·7′W	T	73,74
Blythe Bridge	Staffs	SJ9541	52°58·2′	2°4·1′W	T	118
Blythe Edge	Scot Bord	NT6056	55°48·0′	2°37·8′W	X	67,74
Blythe Fm	Gwyn	SH4457	53°5·5′	4°19·4′W	FM	115,123
Blythe Hall	Lancs	SD4310	53°35·3′	2°51·3′W	X	108
Blythe Hall	Sol	SP1577	52°23·7′	1°46·4′W	X	139
Blythe Ho	Sol	SP2178	52°24·2′	1°41·1′W	X	139
Blythe Ho	Staffs	SJ9937	52°56·1′	2°0·5′W	X	127
Blythe Marsh	Staffs	SJ9641	52°58·2′	2°3·2′W	T	118
Blythemo	Orkney	HY3424	59°6·1′	3°8·6′W	X	6
Blythemor	Orkney	HY3722	59°5·1′	3°5·5′W	X	6
Blyth End	Warw	SP2190	52°30·7′	1°41·0′W	T	139
Blythe Rig	Scot Bord	NT5756	55°48·0′	2°40·7′W	X	67,73,74
Blythe Sands	Medway	TQ7580	51°29·7′	0°31·7′E	X	178
Blythe's Tower	Fife	NT2299	56°10·9′	3°15·0′W	X	58
Blythe Water	Scot Bord	NT5748	55°43·7′	2°40·6′W	W	73,74
Blyth Hall	Warw	SP2090	52°30·7′	1°41·9′W	A	139
Blyth Law Hill	Notts	SK6484	53°21·2′	1°1·9′W	X	111,120
Blyth Muir	Scot Bord	NT1347	55°42·8′	3°22·6′W	H	72
Blythot	Shetld	HU3580	60°30·4′	1°21·3′W	X	1,2,3
Blythswood	Renf	NS5068	55°53·2′	4°23·5′W	T	64
Blyton	Lincs	SK8594	53°26·4′	0°42·8′W	T	112
Blyton Grange	Lincs	SK8696	53°27·5′	0°41·9′W	X	112
BMln Fm	Bucks	SU7496	51°39·7′	0°55·4′W	FM	165
BMockmore Fm	Bucks	SU7585	51°33·8′	0°54·7′W	FM	175
Boadhole	Cumbr	SD1987	54°16·6′	3°14·2′W	X	96
Boadie Geo	Shetld	HU4755	60°16·9′	1°8·5′W	X	3
Boadle Ground	Cumbr	SD0898	54°22·4′	3°24·6′W	X	96
Boag	N Ayr	NS2953	55°44·7′	4°43·0′W	X	63
Boag Fm	S Lanak	NS7342	55°39·6′	4°0·7′W	FM	71
Boagside Fm	N Ayr	NS2960	55°48·4′	4°43·3′W	FM	63
Boagstown	Falk	NS8973	55°56·5′	3°46·2′W	X	65
Boakley Fm	Wilts	ST9188	51°35·7′	2°7·4′W	FM	173
Boak Port	D & G	NX0173	55°1·0′	5°6·3′W	W	76,82
Boal	Angus	NO5051	56°39·1′	2°48·5′W	X	54
Boame's Fm	W Berks	SU4464	51°22·6′	1°21·7′W	FM	174
Boarbank Hall	Cumbr	SD3776	54°10·8′	2°57·5′W	X	96,97
Boar Cleuch Flow	Scot Bord	NT2024	55°30·4′	3°15·6′W	X	73
Boarded Barn	Ches	SJ8258	53°7·4′	2°15·7′W	X	118
Boarded Barn Fm	Warr	SJ5793	53°26·2′	2°38·4′W	FM	108
Boarded Barns Fm	Essex	TL5604	51°43·0′	0°15·9′E	FM	167
Boarded Ho	Powys	SO2790	52°30·4′	3°4·1′W	X	137
Boarden Fm	Kent	TQ8044	51°10·2′	0°34·9′E	FM	188
Boardenhouse Fm	Cambs	TL3590	52°29·7′	0°0·3′W	FM	142
Boardhouse	Orkney	HY2527	59°7·7′	3°18·1′W	X	6
Boardhouse	Orkney	HY3216	59°1·8′	3°10·6′W	X	6
Boardinghouse Fm	Cambs	TL3894	52°31·8′	0°2·5′E	FM	142,143
Boards	Stir	NS5479	55°59·2′	4°20·0′W	X	64
Boardy Green	Suff	TM2557	52°10·1′	1°17·8′E	X	156
Boaredale Head	Cumbr	NY4117	54°32·9′	2°54·3′W	X	90
Boar Flat	Tames	SK0199	53°29·5′	1°58·7′W	X	110
Boarfold	Derby	SJ9892	53°25·7′	2°1·4′W	X	109
Boarhill	Kent	TQ4851	51°14·6′	0°7·6′E	X	188
Boar Hill	Notts	SK4856	53°6·2′	1°16·6′W	X	120
Boarhills	Fife	NO5614	56°19·2′	2°42·2′W	T	59
Boarhunt	Hants	SU6008	50°52·3′	1°8·4′W	T	196
Boar Knoll	Hants	SU2540	51°9·8′	1°38·2′W	H	184
Boarley Fm	Kent	TQ7659	51°18·4′	0°31·9′E	FM	178,188
Boar of Badenoch or An Torc	Pth & Kin	NN6276	56°51·6′	4°15·3′W	H	42
Boarpit Rough	Shrops	SJ5322	52°47·9′	2°41·4′W	F	126
Boarsbarrow Hill	Dorset	SY4993	50°44·3′	2°43·0′W	H	193,194
Boarscroft	Herts	SP8717	51°50·9′	0°43·8′W	X	165
Boar's Den	Lancs	SD5111	53°35·8′	2°44·0′W	X	108
Boarsden	Lancs	SD6750	53°56·9′	2°29·8′W	X	103
Boar's Den (Tumulus)	Lancs	SD5111	53°35·8′	2°44·0′W	A	108
Boarsgreave	Lancs	SD8420	53°40·8′	2°14·1′W	T	103
Boars Green Fm	Surrey	TQ2854	51°16·5′	0°9·5′W	FM	187
Boarsgrove	Staffs	SK0462	53°9·5′	1°56·0′W	X	119
Boarshead	E Susx	TQ5332	51°4·2′	0°11·4′E	T	188
Boar's Head	Wigan	SD5708	53°34·3′	2°38·5′W	T	108
Boar's Head Fm	Northnts	SP9993	52°31·8′	0°32·0′W	FM	141
Boar's Head Rock	Moray	NJ2867	57°41·5′	3°12·0′W	X	28
Boars Hill	Oxon	SP4802	51°43·1′	1°17·9′W	T	164
Boar's Hill Fm	Heref	SO4331	51°58·7′	2°49·4′W	FM	149,161
Boars Hole Fm	W Berks	SU5271	51°26·4′	1°14·7′W	FM	174
Boarsney Fm	E Susx	TQ7526	51°0·6′	0°30·1′E	FM	188,199
Boars of Duncansby	Highld	ND3775	58°39·8′	3°4·7′W	W	7,12
Boarstall	Bucks	SP6214	51°49·5′	1°5·6′W	T	164,165
Boarstall Wood	Bucks	SP6212	51°48·4′	1°5·6′W	F	164,165
Boar Stone	Highld	NH6541	57°26·6′	4°14·5′W	A	26
Boar, The	Orkney	HY5142	59°16·0′	2°51·1′W	X	5
Boarzell	E Susx	TQ7229	51°2·3′	0°27·6′E	X	188,199
Boarzell Wood	E Susx	TQ7129	51°2·3′	0°26·7′E	F	188,199
Boasley	Devon	SX4992	50°42·7′	4°8·0′W	X	191
Boasley Cross	Devon	SX5093	50°43·3′	4°7·1′W	T	191
Boat Bay	Highld	NC1015	58°5·3′	5°12·9′W	W	15
Boat Cave	Arg & Bt	NM3235	56°26·1′	6°20·4′W	X	46,47,48
Boatcroft	D & G	NX7359	54°54·8′	3°58·4′W	X	83,84
Boat Croft	D & G	NX7364	54°57·5′	3°58·6′W	X	83,84
Boatcroft	D & G	NX8890	55°11·7′	3°45·1′W	X	78
Boath	Highld	NH5773	57°43·7′	4°23·6′W	X	21
Boath Hill	Angus	NO5645	56°35·9′	2°42·5′W	H	54
Boath Ho	Highld	NH9155	57°34·6′	3°48·9′W	X	27
Boathouse Br	C of Edin	NT1474	55°57·3′	3°22·2′W	X	65
Boathouse Covert	Suff	TM5283	52°23·4′	1°42·6′E	F	156
Boathouse Creek	Norf	TF6630	52°50·7′	0°28·3′E	W	132
Boathouse Fm	E Susx	TQ4516	50°55·7′	0°4·2′E	FM	198
Boathouse Plantn	Northum	NT8439	55°38·9′	2°14·8′W	F	74
Boat How	Cumbr	NY0810	54°28·9′	3°24·8′W	X	89
Boat How	Cumbr	NY1703	54°25·2′	3°16·3′W	H	89,90
Boat How	Cumbr	NY1911	54°29·5′	3°14·6′W	X	89,90
Boathow Crag	Cumbr	NY1013	54°30·5′	3°23·0′W	X	89
Boathvic	Highld	NH5674	57°44·2′	4°24·7′W	X	21
Boating Dike	N Lincs	SE7410	53°35·1′	0°52·5′W	W	112
Boat Knowe	D & G	NX6280	55°6·0′	4°9·3′W	X	77
Boatlands	Pth & Kin	NO0839	56°32·3′	3°29·3′W	X	52,53
Boatleys	Aberd	NJ7216	57°14·3′	2°27·4′W	X	38
Boat Mere Fm	Lincs	TF4527	52°49·5′	0°9·5′E	FM	131
Boatmill	Pth & Kin	NO0919	56°21·5′	3°27·9′W	X	58
Boat Museum	Ches	SJ4077	53°17·4′	2°53·6′W	X	117
Boat o' Brig	Moray	NJ3251	57°32·9′	3°7·7′W	X	28
Boat of Balliefurth	Highld	NJ0124	57°18·0′	3°38·1′W	X	36
Boat of Cromdale	Highld	NJ0629	57°20·8′	3°33·3′W	X	36
Boat of Garten	Highld	NH9418	57°14·7′	3°44·9′W	T	36
Boat of Hatton	Aberd	NJ8315	57°13·8′	2°16·4′W	X	38
Boat of Muiresk	Aberd	NJ7050	57°32·6′	2°29·6′W	X	29
Boatrick Ho	Medway	TQ7277	51°28·2′	0°29·0′E	X	178
Boatrig	D & G	NX9285	55°9·1′	3°41·3′W	X	78
Boats Hall	Suff	TM3170	52°17·0′	1°23·6′E	X	156
Boatside Fm	Powys	SO2243	52°5·0′	3°7·9′W	FM	148,161
Boats Noost	Shetld	HU4118	59°57·0′	1°15·5′W	X	4
Boatsroom Voe	Shetld	HU4971	60°25·5′	1°6·1′W	W	2,3
Bobberstone Fm	I of W	SZ5582	50°38·3′	1°12·9′W	FM	196
Bobbing	Kent	TQ8865	51°21·4′	0°42·4′E	T	178
Bobbing Court	Kent	TQ8864	51°20·9′	0°42·4′E	X	178
Bobbington	Staffs	SO8090	52°30·7′	2°17·3′W	T	138
Bobbington Hall	Staffs	SO8089	52°30·2′	2°17·3′W	X	138
Bobbingworth	Essex	TL5305	51°43·6′	0°13·3′E	T	167
Bobbin Mill	Cumbr	SD3788	54°17·3′	2°57·6′W	X	96,97
Bobble Barn	Glos	SP1920	51°52·9′	1°43·0′W	X	163
Bobbolds Fm	W Susx	SU8325	51°1·3′	0°48·6′W	FM	186,197
Bobby Hill	Suff	TM0074	52°19·9′	0°56·5′E	T	144
Bobgins Burn	Durham	NZ1956	54°54·1′	1°41·8′W	W	88
Bob Hall's Sand	Norf	TF9146	52°58·9′	0°51·1′E	X	132
Bò Bheanachan	N Eil	NF7502	56°59·9′	7°20·7′W	X	31
Boblainy	Highld	NH4939	57°25·2′	4°30·4′W	X	26
Boblainy Forest	Highld	NH4837	57°24·1′	4°31·3′W	F	26
Boblow	Essex	TL6540	52°2·3′	0°24·7′E	X	154
Bob Scar	N Yks	SE0192	54°19·7′	1°58·7′W	X	98
Bo Burn	Aberd	NO7198	57°4·6′	2°28·2′W	W	38,45
Bobus	Kirk	SE0309	53°34·9′	1°56·9′W	X	110
Boc a' Chro' Bhric	Highld	NG3456	57°31·2′	6°26·1′W	X	23
Bocaddon	Corn	SX1758	50°23·8′	4°34·1′W	T	201
Boc Beag	Highld	NG9024	57°15·8′	5°28·5′W	H	25,33
Boced	Denb	SJ0358	53°6·9′	3°26·6′W	X	116
Boch-ailean	Highld	ND1020	58°9·8′	3°31·3′W	X	17
Bochastle	Stir	NN6107	56°14·4′	4°14·1′W	X	57
Bochastle Hill	Stir	NN5908	56°14·9′	4°16·1′W	H	57
Bochdag	N Eil	NB0401	57°54·3′	6°59·4′W	X	18
Bochel	Moray	NJ2322	57°17·2′	3°16·2′W	X	36
Bochel, The	Moray	NJ2323	57°17·7′	3°16·2′W	H	36
Bochonie	Pth & Kin	NN7863	56°44·8′	3°59·2′W	X	42
Bochruben	Highld	NH5727	57°18·9′	4°22·0′W	X	26,35
Bochym Manor	Corn	SW6820	50°2·3′	5°14·0′W	A	203
Bochym Manor	Corn	SW6920	50°2·4′	5°13·2′W	A	203
Boch y Rhaeadr	Gwyn	SH8439	52°56·4′	3°43·2′W	X	124,125
Bockan	Orkney	HY2814	59°0·7′	3°14·7′W	X	6
Bockendon Grange	Warw	SP2775	52°22·6′	1°35·8′W	X	140
Bockenfield	Northum	NZ1797	55°16·3′	1°43·5′W	A	81
Bockerly Hill	Wilts	ST8935	51°7·1′	2°9·0′W	H	184
Bocketts Fm	Surrey	TQ1554	51°16·6′	0°20·7′W	FM	187
Bockhampton Down	W Berks	SU3481	51°31·8′	1°30·2′W	X	174
Bockhanger	Kent	TR0144	51°9·8′	0°52·9′E	T	189
Bockhill Fm	Kent	TR3745	51°9·5′	1°23·8′E	FM	179
Bocking	Essex	TL7523	51°52·9′	0°33·0′E	T	167
Bocking Churchstreet	Essex	TL7625	51°54·0′	0°33·9′E	T	167
Bockingfold	Kent	TQ7044	51°10·4′	0°26·3′E	X	188
Bockingfold Fm	Kent	TQ7339	51°7·7′	0°28·7′E	FM	188
Bocking Hall	Essex	TM0314	51°47·5′	0°57·0′E	X	168
Bocking Hall	Suff	TM1758	52°10·9′	1°10·9′E	X	156
Bockingham Hall Fm	Essex	TL9321	51°51·5′	0°48·6′E	FM	168
Bocking's Elm	Essex	TM1516	51°48·3′	1°7·5′E	T	168,169
Bockleton	Worcs	SO5961	52°15·0′	2°35·6′W	T	137,138,149
Bockleton Brook	Shrops	SO5781	52°25·8′	2°37·5′W	W	137,138
Bockleton Court	Shrops	SO5783	52°26·8′	2°37·6′W	X	137,138
Bockmer End	Bucks	SU8186	51°34·3′	0°49·5′W	T	175
Bockmer Ho	Bucks	SU8086	51°34·3′	0°50·3′W	X	175
Boclair	E Dunb	NS5672	55°55·4′	4°17·8′W	X	64
Boc Mór	Highld	NG9125	57°16·3′	5°27·5′W	H	25,33
Bocombe	Devon	SS3821	50°58·2′	4°18·1′W	T	190
Boconnion	Corn	SX0669	50°29·6′	4°43·7′W	X	200
Boconnoc	Corn	SX1460	50°24·9′	4°36·7′W	X	200
Bodach Beag	Highld	NH3588	57°51·3′	4°46·4′W	H	20
Bodach Dearg	Highld	NC5068	58°34·7′	4°34·3′W	X	9
Bodach Mór	Highld	NH3689	57°51·9′	4°45·4′W	H	20
Bodachra	C of Aber	NJ9113	57°12·7′	2°8·5′W	X	38
Bodach, The	Moray	NJ1630	57°21·4′	3°23·3′W	X	36
Bodafon Isaf	I of Angl	SH4787	53°21·7′	4°17·5′W	X	114
Bodafon-y-glyn	I of Angl	SH4685	53°20·6′	4°18·4′W	X	114
Bodaioch Hall	Powys	SN9790	52°30·1′	3°30·6′W	X	136
Bodandere Hill	Angus	NO3061	56°44·4′	3°8·2′W	X	44
Bodanna	Corn	SW8857	50°22·7′	4°58·5′W	X	200
Bodannon	Corn	SX0080	50°35·4′	4°49·2′W	X	200
Bodanwydog	Denb	SJ1750	53°2·7′	3°13·9′W	X	116
Bodawen	Gwyn	SH5639	52°56·0′	4°8·2′W	X	124
Bodbrane	Corn	SX2359	50°24·5′	4°29·1′W	X	201
Bodbury Hill	Shrops	SO4494	52°32·7′	2°49·1′W	X	137
Bodbury Ring	Shrops	SO4494	52°32·7′	2°49·1′W	A	137
Bodcoll	Cered	SN7576	52°22·3′	3°49·8′W	X	135,147
Bodcott Fm	Heref	SO3343	52°5·1′	2°58·3′W	FM	148,149,161
Boddam	Aberd	NK1342	57°28·3′	1°46·5′W	T	30
Boddam	Aberd	NO6093	57°1·8′	2°39·1′W	X	37,45
Boddam	Shetld	HU3915	59°55·4′	1°17·7′W	T	4
Bod Deiniol	I of Angl	SH3785	53°20·5′	4°26·5′W	X	114
Bodden	Somer	ST6344	51°11·9′	2°31·4′W	T	183
Boddin	Angus	NO7153	56°40·3′	2°27·9′W	T	54
Boddington	Glos	SO8925	51°55·6′	2°9·2′W	T	163
Boddington Hill	Bucks	SP8707	51°45·5′	0°44·0′W	X	165
Boddington Resr	Northnts	SP4952	52°10·1′	1°16·6′W	W	151
Boddin Harbour	Angus	NO7153	56°40·3′	2°27·9′W	W	54
Boddin Point	Angus	NO7153	56°40·3′	2°27·9′W	X	54
Boddle Moss	Northum	NY9997	55°16·3′	2°0·5′W	X	81
Boddomend	Aberd	NJ5500	57°5·6′	2°44·1′W	X	37
Bodedern	I of Angl	SH3380	53°17·7′	4°29·9′W	T	114
Bod Ednyfed	I of Angl	SH4592	53°24·4′	4°19·5′W	X	114
Bodegri	I of Angl	SH3489	53°22·6′	4°29·3′W	X	114
Bodegroes	Gwyn	SH3535	52°53·5′	4°26·8′W	A	123
Bodeilian	Gwyn	SH3440	52°56·2′	4°27·8′W	X	123
Bodeilias	Gwyn	SH3141	52°56·6′	4°30·5′W	X	123
Bodeilio	I of Angl	SH4977	53°16·4′	4°15·5′W	A	114,115
Bodeiliog-isaf	Denb	SJ0264	53°10·1′	3°27·6′W	X	116
Bodeiliog-Uchaf	Conwy	SJ0164	53°10·1′	3°28·5′W	X	116
Bod Elith	Gwyn	SH9839	52°56·6′	3°30·7′W	X	125
Bodella	Corn	SW9456	50°22·3′	4°53·4′W	X	200
Bodellick	Corn	SW9573	50°31·5′	4°53·2′W	T	200
Bodelva	Corn	SX0554	50°21·5′	4°44·1′W	T	200
Bodelwa	I of Angl	SH3470	53°12·3′	4°28·7′W	X	114
Bodelwyddan	Denb	SJ0075	53°16·0′	3°29·6′W	T	116
Bodelwyddan Castle	Denb	SH9974	53°15·4′	3°30·4′W	X	116
Bodelwyddan Park	Denb	SJ0074	53°15·5′	3°29·5′W	X	116
Bodelwyn	I of Angl	SH3790	53°23·1′	4°26·6′W	X	114
Boden	Orkney	HY5055	59°23·0′	2°52·3′W	X	5
Boden Hall	Ches	SJ8158	53°7·4′	2°16·6′W	X	118
Bodenham	Heref	SO5351	52°9·6′	2°40·8′W	T	149
Bodenham	Wilts	SU1626	51°2·2′	1°45·9′W	T	184
Bodenham Bank	Heref	SO6432	51°59·4′	2°31·1′W	T	149
Bodenham Moor	Heref	SO5450	52°9·0′	2°39·9′W	T	149
Bodennog	I of Angl	SH3475	53°15·0′	4°28·9′W	X	114
Bodermid	Gwyn	SH1525	52°47·7′	4°44·2′W	X	123
Boderwennack	Corn	SW6830	50°7·7′	5°14·4′W	X	203
Bodesbeck	D & G	NT1509	55°22·3′	3°20·0′W	X	79
Bodesbeck Burn	D & G	NT1609	55°22·3′	3°19·1′W	W	79
Bodesbeck Law	D & G	NT1610	55°22·9′	3°19·1′W	H	79
Bodesi	Conwy	SH6760	53°7·5′	3°58·9′W	X	115
Bodewran	I of Angl	SH4177	53°16·2′	4°22·7′W	X	114,115
Bodewryd	I of Angl	SH3990	53°23·2′	4°24·8′W	T	114
Bodfach Hall	Powys	SJ1320	52°46·5′	3°17·0′W	X	125
Bodfan	Gwyn	SH4455	53°4·4′	4°19·3′W	X	115,123
Bodfan	Gwyn	SH6018	52°44·7′	4°4·0′W	X	124
Bodfardden-ddu	I of Angl	SH3185	53°20·3′	4°31·9′W	X	114
Bodfardden-wen	I of Angl	SH3184	53°19·8′	4°31·9′W	X	114
Bodfari	Denb	SJ0970	53°13·4′	3°21·4′W	T	116
Bodfeddan	I of Angl	SH3675	53°15·0′	4°27·1′W	X	114
Bodfeillion	I of Angl	SH3878	53°16·7′	4°25·4′W	X	114
Bodfeirig	I of Angl	SH3468	53°11·2′	4°28·7′W	X	114
Bodffordd	I of Angl	SH4276	53°15·7′	4°21·7′W	T	114,115
Bodgadle	Gwyn	SH3135	52°53·4′	4°30·3′W	X	123
Bodgaeaf	Gwyn	SH2231	52°51·1′	4°38·2′W	X	123
Bodgarad	Gwyn	SH5058	53°6·1′	4°14·0′W	X	115
Bodgate	Corn	SX2890	50°41·3′	4°25·7′W	X	190
Bodgedwydd	I of Angl	SH3671	53°12·9′	4°27·0′W	X	114
Bodgers Fm	Norf	TF5606	52°38·0′	0°18·7′E	FM	143
Bodgylched	I of Angl	SH5876	53°16·0′	4°7·3′W	X	114,115
Bodgynda	I of Angl	SH4781	53°18·5′	4°17·4′W	X	114,115
Bodha Hunish	Highld	NG4176	57°42·2′	6°20·4′W	X	23
Bodham	Norf	TG1240	52°55·2′	1°9·6′E	T	133
Bodham Common	Norf	TG1139	52°54·6′	1°8·7′E	X	133
Bodham Hill	Norf	TG1338	52°54·1′	1°10·4′E	X	133
Bodha Ruadh	Highld	NG4475	57°41·8′	6°17·3′W	X	23
Bodha Trodday	Highld	NG4478	57°43·4′	6°17·5′W	X	23
Bod-hedd	I of Angl	SH3389	53°22·5′	4°30·2′W	X	114
Bodhenlli	I of Angl	SH4273	53°14·1′	4°21·6′W	X	114,115
Bodheulog	Denb	SJ0441	52°57·7′	3°25·4′W	X	125
Bodhunod	I of Angl	SH4193	53°24·8′	4°23·1′W	X	114
Bod Hyfryd	Conwy	SH7867	53°11·4′	3°49·2′W	X	115
Bodiam	E Susx	TQ7825	51°0·0′	0°32·6′E	T	188,199
Bodiam Br	E Susx	TQ7825	51°0·0′	0°32·6′E	X	188,199
Bodicote	Oxon	SP4637	52°2·0′	1°19·4′W	T	151
Bodicote Mill Ho	Oxon	SP4537	52°2·0′	1°20·2′W	X	151
Bod Idris (Hotel)	Denb	SJ2053	53°4·3′	3°11·2′W	X	117
Bodiebae	Moray	NJ3924	57°18·4′	3°0·3′W	X	37
Bodiechell	Aberd	NJ7944	57°29·4′	2°20·6′W	X	29,30
Bodieve	Corn	SW9973	50°31·6′	4°49·8′W	T	200
Bodigga Cliff	Corn	SX2754	50°21·9′	4°25·6′W	X	201
Bodiggo	Corn	SX0458	50°23·6′	4°45·1′W	T	200
Bodilan	Gwyn	SH6508	52°39·4′	3°59·4′W	X	124
Bodilly	Corn	SW6632	50°8·8′	5°16·1′W	T	203
Bodimans	W Susx	TQ1527	51°2·1′	0°21·2′W	X	187,198
Bodinglee	S Lanak	NS8930	55°33·3′	3°45·1′W	X	71,72
Bodinglee Law	S Lanak	NS8829	55°32·8′	3°46·1′W	X	71,72
Bodington Hall	Leeds	SE2738	53°50·5′	1°35·0′W	X	104
Bodiniel	Corn	SX0568	50°29·0′	4°44·6′W	X	200
Bodinnick	Corn	SX1352	50°20·5′	4°37·3′W	T	200
Bodior	I of Angl	SH2876	53°15·4′	4°34·3′W	X	114
Bod-isaf	Gwyn	SH1526	52°48·2′	4°44·3′W	X	123
Bodithiel Fm	Corn	SX1764	50°27·1′	4°34·3′W	FM	201
Bodkin	Brad	SE0134	53°48·4′	1°58·7′W	X	104
Bodkin Fm	Kent	TR1466	51°21·4′	1°4·8′E	FM	179
Bodkin Fm	Leic	SK4816	52°44·6′	1°16·9′W	FM	129
Bodkin Hazel Wood	S Glos	ST7884	51°33·5′	2°18·7′W	F	172
Bodkin Wood	S Glos	ST7885	51°34·0′	2°18·7′W	F	172

Bodlas	Gwyn	SH2833	52°52·3'	4°32·9'W	X	123
Bodlasan Fawr	I of Angl	SH2982	53°18·7'	4°33·6'W	X	114
Bodlasan Groes	I of Angl	SH2982	53°18·7'	4°33·6'W	X	114
Bodle Street Green	E Susx	TQ6514	50°54·3'	0°21·2'E	T	199
Bodlew	I of Angl	SH4869	53°12·0'	4°16·1'W	X	114,115
Bodley	Devon	SS6645	51°11·5'	3°54·7'W	T	180
Bodlith	Powys	SJ2129	52°51·4'	3°10·0'W	X	126
Bodlondeb	Conwy	SH7877	53°16·8'	3°49·4'W	X	115
Bodlondeb	Conwy	SH8371	53°13·6'	3°44·8'W	X	116
Bodlondeb	Gwyn	SH2831	52°51·2'	4°32·9'W	X	123
Bodlonfa	Denb	SJ0876	53°16·6'	3°22·4'W	X	116
Bodmin	Corn	SX0667	50°28·5'	4°43·7'W	T	200
Bodmin Airfield	Corn	SX1170	50°30·2'	4°39·5'W	X	200
Bodmin Moor	Corn	SX1976	50°33·6'	4°33·0'W	X	201
Bodmin Parkway Sta	Corn	SX1164	50°27·0'	4°39·4'W	X	200
Bodmin Steam Rly	Corn	SX0865	50°27·4'	4°41·9'W	X	200
Bodmin & Wenford Rly	Corn	SX0765	50°27·4'	4°42·8'W	X	200
Bodmiscombe	Devon	ST1009	50°52·6'	3°16·4'W	T	192,193
Bodnamoor	Moray	NJ1753	57°33·8'	3°22·8'W	X	28
Bodnant	Conwy	SH8072	53°14·1'	3°47·5'W	X	116
Bodnant Bach	Conwy	SH8072	53°14·1'	3°47·5'W	X	116
Bodnant Gardens	Conwy	SH7972	53°14·1'	3°48·4'W	X	115
Bodnant Ucha	Conwy	SH8072	53°14·1'	3°47·5'W	X	116
Bodnasparet	Angus	NO2269	56°48·6'	3°16·2'W	H	44
Bodnastalker	Moray	NJ1653	57°33·8'	3°23·8'W	X	28
Bodneithior	I of Angl	SH4485	53°20·6'	4°20·2'W	X	114
Bodnets, The	Staffs	SK1703	52°37·7'	1°44·5'W	X	139
Bodney	Norf	TL8398	52°33·2'	0°42·4'E	T	144
Bodney Camp	Norf	TL8598	52°33·1'	0°44·1'E	X	144
Bodney Fm	Suff	TL8572	52°19·1'	0°43·3'E	FM	144,155
Bodney Warren	Norf	TL8497	52°32·6'	0°43·2'E	X	144
Bodnithoedd	Gwyn	SH2531	52°51·1'	4°35·5'W	X	123
Bodorgan	I of Angl	SH3867	53°10·8'	4°25·0'W	X	114
Bodorgan Sta	I of Angl	SH3870	53°12·4'	4°25·1'W	X	114
Bodoryn Fawr	Conwy	SH9776	53°16·5'	3°32·3'W	X	116
Bodowen	Gwyn	SH5805	52°37·7'	4°5·5'W	X	124
Bodowen	I of Angl	SH3866	53°10·2'	4°25·0'W	X	114
Bodowyr	I of Angl	SH3279	53°17·1'	4°30·8'W	X	114
Bodowyr	I of Angl	SH4668	53°11·5'	4°17·9'W	X	114,115
Bodowyr-isaf	I of Angl	SH4669	53°12·0'	4°17·9'W	X	114,115
Bodrach	Conwy	SH8562	53°8·8'	3°42·8'W	X	116
Bodran	Powys	SJ1119	52°45·9'	3°18·7'W	X	125
Bodrane	Corn	SX2061	50°25·5'	4°31·7'W	X	201
Bodrawl Fm	Corn	SX1962	50°26·0'	4°32·5'W	FM	201
Bodrean	Corn	SW8447	50°17·2'	5°1·6'W	X	204
Bodrhyddan Hall	Denb	SJ0478	53°17·7'	3°26·0'W	A	116
Bodrida	I of Angl	SH4667	53°10·9'	4°17·9'W	X	114,115
Bodrifty	Corn	SW4435	50°9·8'	5°34·7'W	X	203
Bodrigan	Corn	SX0773	50°31·7'	4°43·0'W	X	200
Bodrochwyn	Conwy	SH9372	53°14·3'	3°35·8'W	X	116
Bodrugan Barton	Corn	SX0143	50°15·4'	4°47·1'W	X	204
Bodrwyn	I of Angl	SH4173	53°14·1'	4°22·5'W	X	114,115
Bodsberry Hill	S Lanak	NS9616	55°25·9'	3°38·2'W	H	78
Bodsey Br	Cambs	TL2987	52°28·2'	0°5·7'W	X	142
Bodsey House	Cambs	TL2987	52°28·2'	0°5·7'W	A	142
Bodsham	Kent	TR1045	51°10·2'	1°0·6'E	T	179,189
Bodstone Barton	Devon	SS5744	51°10·9'	4°2·4'W	X	180
Bodsuran	I of Angl	SH3781	53°18·3'	4°26·4'W	X	114
Bodtacho Ddu	Gwyn	SH3039	52°55·5'	4°31·3'W	X	123
Bod Talog	Gwyn	SN6099	52°34·5'	4°3·6'W	X	135
Bodtalog	Powys	SN8675	52°21·9'	3°40·1'W	X	135,136,147
Bodtegir	Conwy	SJ0048	53°1·4'	3°29·1'W	X	116
Boduan	Gwyn	SH3237	52°54·5'	4°29·5'W	T	123
Boduel	Corn	SX2263	50°26·6'	4°30·0'W	T	201
Bodulgate	Corn	SX0781	50°36·0'	4°43·3'W	X	200
Bodvell Hall	Gwyn	SH3436	52°54·0'	4°27·7'W	X	123
Bodwannick	Corn	SX0365	50°27·3'	4°46·1'W	X	200
Bodwarren Fm	I of Angl	SH2281	53°18·0'	4°39·9'W	FM	114
Bodway	Corn	SX2962	50°26·2'	4°24·1'W	X	201
Bodwen	Corn	SX0360	50°24·6'	4°46·0'W	T	200
Bodwen	Corn	SX0771	50°30·7'	4°43·0'W	X	200
Bodwen Fm	Corn	SX0660	50°24·7'	4°43·5'W	FM	200
Bodweni	Gwyn	SH9636	52°54·9'	3°32·4'W	X	125
Bodwi	Gwyn	SH2929	52°50·1'	4°31·9'W	X	123
Bodwigiad	Rho Cyn Taf	SN9508	51°45·9'	3°30·9'W	X	160
Bodwina	I of Angl	SH4076	53°15·7'	4°23·5'W	X	114,115
Bodwrdda	Gwyn	SH1827	52°48·8'	4°41·6'W	A	123
Bodwrdin	I of Angl	SH3971	53°12·9'	4°24·3'W	X	114
Bodwrog	I of Angl	SH3977	53°16·2'	4°24·5'W	X	114
Bodwyddog	Gwyn	SH2127	52°48·9'	4°39·0'W	X	123
Bodwylan	Gwyn	SH6009	52°39·9'	4°3·8'W	X	124
Bodwyn	Gwyn	SH4960	53°7·2'	4°15·0'W	X	114,115
Bodwyn	I of Angl	SH3288	53°22·0'	4°31·1'W	X	114
Bodychain	Gwyn	SH4649	53°1·2'	4°17·4'W	X	115,123
Bodychell	Aberd	NJ9562	57°39·1'	2°4·6'W	X	30
Bodychen	I of Angl	SH3879	53°17·2'	4°25·4'W	A	114
Bodyddon	Powys	SJ1121	52°47·0'	3°18·8'W	X	125
Bodymoor Green Fm	Warw	SP2294	52°32·8'	1°40·1'W	FM	139
Bodymoor Heath	Warw	SP2096	52°33·9'	1°41·9'W	T	139
Bodynfoel	Powys	SJ1720	52°46·5'	3°13·4'W	X	125
Bodynfoel	Powys	SJ1821	52°47·1'	3°12·5'W	X	125
Bodynfoel Wood	Powys	SJ1821	52°47·1'	3°12·5'W	F	125
Bodynlliw	Denb	SJ0347	53°0·9'	3°26·4'W	X	116
Bod-Ynys	Denb	SJ1061	53°8·6'	3°20·3'W	X	116
Bodysgallen (Hotel)	Conwy	SH7979	53°17·9'	3°48·5'W	A	115
Bodysgaw Isa	Conwy	SH9971	53°13·8'	3°30·4'W	X	116
Bodyst	Carm	SN6612	51°47·7'	3°56·2'W	X	159
Bodystead	N Yks	SD9193	54°20·2'	2°7·9'W	X	98
Boehill	Devon	ST0315	50°55·8'	3°22·4'W	X	181
Boelie	Shetld	HP6018	60°50·7'	0°53·3'W	X	1
Boethuog	Gwyn	SH7522	52°47·1'	3°50·8'W	X	124
Boey's Pike	Glos	SO6514	51°49·6'	2°30·1'W	X	162
Bofarnel	Corn	SX1063	50°26·4'	4°40·2'W	T	200
Bofarnel Downs	Corn	SX1163	50°26·4'	4°39·3'W	X	200
Bog	Aberd	NJ6134	57°23·9'	2°38·5'W	X	29
Bog	Aberd	NJ8318	57°15·4'	2°16·5'W	X	38
Bog	Cered	SN7569	52°18·5'	3°49·6'W	X	135,147
Bog	Cumbr	NY1347	54°48·9'	3°20·8'W	X	85
Bog	Moray	NJ4354	57°34·6'	2°56·7'W	X	28
Bog a' Bhreacaich	Highld	NH5362	57°37·7'	4°27·2'W	X	20

Bogach	N Eil	NF7102	56°59·8'	7°24·7'W	T	31
Bogach Druim Reallasger	N Eil	NF8566	57°34·7'	7°15·8'W	X	18
Bogach Flisaval	N Eil	NF8869	57°36·4'	7°13·0'W	X	18
Bogach Loch Fada	N Eil	NF8871	57°37·5'	7°13·1'W	X	18
Bogach Loch nan Eun	N Eil	NF8468	57°35·7'	7°16·9'W	X	18
Bogach Maari	N Eil	NF8571	57°37·4'	7°16·1'W	X	18
Bogach Mhic-fhearghuis	N Eil	NF8271	57°37·3'	7°19·2'W	X	18
Bogach nan Sgadan	N Eil	NF8068	57°35·6'	7°20·9'W	X	18
Bogairdy	Aberd	NJ4835	57°24·4'	2°51·5'W	X	28,29
Bogallan	Highld	NH6350	57°31·4'	4°16·8'W	T	26
Bogallan Wood	Highld	NH6450	57°31·4'	4°15·8'W	F	26
Bogallie	Moray	NJ3943	57°28·6'	3°0·6'W	X	28
Boganclogh Lodge	Aberd	NJ4329	57°21·1'	2°56·4'W	X	37
Bogangreen	Scot Bord	NT9066	55°53·5'	2°9·2'W	X	67
Bogany Point	Arg & Bt	NS1065	55°50·7'	5°1·7'W	X	63
Bogany Wood	Arg & Bt	NS0964	55°50·1'	5°2·6'W	F	63
Bogardo	Angus	NO5056	56°41·8'	2°48·5'W	X	54
Bogarn	Aberd	NO6590	57°0·2'	2°34·1'W	X	38,45
Bogarrow	Moray	NJ1929	57°20·9'	3°20·3'W	X	36
Bogay Hall	Sol	SP1779	52°24·8'	1°44·6'W	A	139
Bogbain	Highld	NH7041	57°26·7'	4°9·5'W	X	27
Bogbain	Highld	NH8079	57°47·3'	4°0·6'W	X	21
Bogbank	Scot Bord	NT8565	55°52·9'	2°13·9'W	X	67
Bogbrae	Aberd	NK0234	57°24·0'	1°57·5'W	X	30
Bogbrae Croft	Aberd	NK0335	57°24·6'	1°56·5'W	X	30
Bogbraidy	Aberd	NJ5318	57°15·3'	2°46·3'W	X	37
Bogbuie	Highld	NH5855	57°34·0'	4°22·0'W	X	26
Bogbuie Wood	Highld	NH6257	57°35·2'	4°18·0'W	F	26
Bogburn	Aberd	NO7181	56°55·4'	2°28·1'W	X	45
Bog Burn	Angus	NO4558	56°42·9'	2°53·5'W	W	54
Bog Burn	Pth & Kin	NT1199	56°10·8'	3°25·6'W	W	58
Bog Burn	W Loth	NT0260	55°49·7'	3°33·4'W	W	65
Bogburn Fm	Highld	NH5955	57°34·0'	4°21·0'W	FM	26
Bogcup	Aberd	NJ6142	57°28·3'	2°38·6'W	X	29
Bogdavie	Aberd	NJ7736	57°25·1'	2°22·5'W	X	29,30
Bogden Fm	Kent	TQ7646	51°11·4'	0°31·5'E	FM	188
Bogee Common	Corn	SW9168	50°28·7'	4°56·4'W	X	200
Bogee Fm	Corn	SW9069	50°29·2'	4°57·3'W	FM	200
Bogenchapel	Aberd	NJ6104	57°7·8'	2°38·2'W	X	37
Bogend	Aberd	NJ5227	57°20·1'	2°47·4'W	X	37
Bogend	Aberd	NJ5410	57°11·0'	2°45·2'W	X	37
Bogend	Aberd	NJ5721	57°16·9'	2°42·3'W	X	37
Bogend	E Ayr	NS5232	55°33·8'	4°20·4'W	X	70
Bogend	E Ayr	NS5324	55°29·5'	4°19·2'W	X	70
Bogend	Falk	NS8585	56°2·9'	3°50·3'W	X	65
Bogend	Northum	NT9755	55°47·5'	2°2·4'W	X	75
Bogend	Notts	SK4946	53°0·8'	1°15·8'W	T	129
Bogend	S Ayr	NS3925	55°29·8'	4°32·5'W	X	70
Bogend	S Ayr	NS3932	55°33·6'	4°32·7'W	T	70
Bogend	Scot Bord	NT7949	55°44·3'	2°19·6'W	X	74
Bogend Fm	Moray	NJ4463	57°39·5'	2°55·8'W	FM	28
Bogend Fm	N Lanak	NS8866	55°52·7'	3°47·0'W	FM	65
Bogendinnie	Aberd	NJ7411	57°11·6'	2°25·4'W	X	38
Bogendollo	Aberd	NO6576	56°52·7'	2°34·0'W	X	45
Bogeney	Moray	NJ0243	57°28·3'	3°37·6'W	X	27
Bogengarrie	Aberd	NK0139	57°26·7'	1°58·5'W	X	30
Bogengarrie	Aberd	NK0140	57°27·3'	1°58·5'W	X	30
Bogenhilt	Aberd	NJ6552	57°33·7'	2°34·6'W	X	29
Bogenjohn	Aberd	NJ9352	57°33·7'	2°6·6'W	X	30
Bogenlea	Aberd	NJ8252	57°33·7'	2°17·6'W	X	29,30
Bogenraith	Aberd	NO8096	57°3·5'	2°19·3'W	X	38,45
Bogensourie	Aberd	NJ9457	57°36·4'	2°5·6'W	X	30
Bogenspro	Aberd	NJ5645	57°29·8'	2°43·6'W	X	29
Bogentory	Aberd	NJ7509	57°10·5'	2°24·4'W	X	38
Bogfechel	Aberd	NJ8525	57°19·2'	2°14·5'W	X	38
Bogfern	Aberd	NJ5207	57°9·3'	2°47·2'W	X	37
Bogfields	Aberd	NJ5208	57°9·9'	2°47·2'W	X	37
Bog Fm	Kent	TQ8665	51°21·4'	0°40·7'E	FM	178
Bogfold	Aberd	NJ7612	57°12·1'	2°23·4'W	X	38
Bogfold	Aberd	NJ8558	57°37·0'	2°14·6'W	X	30
Bogfond	Aberd	NO8396	57°3·5'	2°16·4'W	X	38,45
Bogfoot	D & G	NX8373	55°2·5'	3°49·4'W	X	84
Bogfoot	D & G	NX9159	54°55·1'	3°41·6'W	X	84
Bogforlea	Aberd	NJ3912	57°11·9'	3°0·1'W	X	37
Bogforran	Aberd	NO7392	57°1·4'	2°26·2'W	X	38,45
Bogforth	Aberd	NJ4741	57°27·6'	2°52·5'W	X	28,29
Bogfur	Aberd	NJ7618	57°15·4'	2°23·4'W	X	38
Bogg	D & G	NS8011	55°23·0'	3°53·2'W	X	71,78
Bogg	D & G	NX8494	55°13·8'	3°49·0'W	X	78
Boggart Hole Clough	Man	SD8602	53°31·1'	2°12·3'W	X	109
Boggarts Roaring Holes	N Yks	SD7272	54°8·8'	2°25·3'W	X	98
Bogg Hall	N Yks	SE5572	54°8·7'	1°9·1'W	X	100
Bogg Hall	N Yks	SE7186	54°16·1'	0°54·2'W	X	94,100
Bogg Hall	N Yks	SE9878	54°11·5'	0°29·5'W	X	101
Bogg Ho	Durham	NY9924	54°36·9'	2°0·5'W	X	92
Boggie	Angus	NO5061	56°44·5'	2°48·6'W	X	44
Boggiefern	Aberd	NO5496	57°3·4'	2°45·1'W	X	37,44
Boggierow	Aberd	NJ5765	57°40·6'	2°42·8'W	X	29
Boggieshalloch	Aberd	NJ5521	57°16·9'	2°44·3'W	X	37
Boggieshalloch	Aberd	NJ7348	57°31·5'	2°26·6'W	X	29
Boggiewell	Highld	NH7058	57°35·9'	4°10·0'W	X	27
Boggle Ho	N Yks	NZ8303	54°25·2'	0°42·8'W	X	94
Boggle Hole	N Yks	NZ9504	54°25·6'	0°31·7'W	X	94
Boggs Fm	E Loth	NT4570	55°55·4'	2°52·4'W	FM	66
Boggs, The	Cumbr	NY3963	54°57·7'	2°56·7'W	X	85
Bogha an t-Sasunnaich	Highld	NG7226	57°16·3'	5°46·5'W	X	33
Bogha Beag	Highld	NG7326	57°16·4'	5°45·5'W	X	33
Bogh a' Bhasa Moil	N Eil	NB0316	58°2·3'	7°1·5'W	X	13
Bogha Bhuilg	Highld	NM5552	56°36·0'	5°59·0'W	X	47
Bogha Caol Ard	Highld	NM4762	56°41·1'	6°7·4'W	X	47
Boghachan Móra	Arg & Bt	NR2673	55°52·6'	6°22·4'W	X	60
Boghachan Ruadha	Arg & Bt	NM4434	56°26·0'	6°8·7'W	X	47,48
Bogh a'Chuirn	Arg & Bt	NR6893	56°4·7'	5°43·3'W	X	55,61
Bogh' a' Churaich	Highld	NM4385	56°53·4'	6°12·7'W	X	39
Bogha-cloiche	Highld	NN7486	56°57·1'	4°3·8'W	H	42
Bogha Còrr	N Eil	HW6131	59°2·6'	6°10·0'W	X	8
Bogha Crom	Arg & Bt	NM4434	56°26·0'	6°8·7'W	X	47,48
Bogha Daraich	Highld	NG5710	57°7·3'	6°0·4'W	X	32
Bogha Dearg	Arg & Bt	NM1752	56°34·7'	6°36·1'W	X	46
Bogha Dearg	Highld	NM6694	56°58·9'	5°50·6'W	X	40

Bogha Dubh	N Eil	NB1038	58°14·4'	6°56·0'W	X	13
Bogha Eilean nan Geodh	Arg & Bt	NM5254	56°37·0'	6°2·1'W	X	47
Bogha Garbh-àird	Arg & Bt	NM8636	56°28·3'	5°28·0'W	X	49
Bogha Ghuthalum	Arg & Bt	NL9649	56°32·3'	6°56·3'W	X	46
Bogha Leathan	Arg & Bt	NM4434	56°26·0'	6°8·7'W	X	47,48
Boghall	Aberd	NO6675	56°52·2'	2°33·0'W	X	45
Boghall	Aberd	NO7775	56°52·2'	2°22·2'W	X	45
Boghall	Angus	NO4939	56°32·7'	2°49·3'W	X	54
Boghall	Clackm	NS9797	56°9·5'	3°39·1'W	X	58
Bog Hall	Cumbr	NY2643	54°46·8'	3°8·6'W	X	85
Boghall	D & G	NX6971	55°1·2'	4°2·5'W	X	77,84
Bog Hall	D & G	NX9485	55°9·1'	3°39·4'W	X	78
Boghall	E Dunb	NS5774	55°56·5'	4°16·9'W	X	64
Boghall	Fife	NO5813	56°18·7'	2°40·3'W	X	59
Bog Hall	Kirk	SE1819	53°40·3'	1°43·2'W	X	110
Boghall	Midlo	NT2465	55°52·6'	3°12·4'W	T	66
Bog Hall	N Ayr	NS3654	55°45·4'	4°36·4'W	X	63
Boghall	Northum	NZ0478	55°6·0'	1°55·8'W	X	87
Bog Hall	N Yks	SE7270	54°7·5'	0°53·5'W	X	100
Boghall	Pth & Kin	NO0413	56°18·2'	3°32·6'W	X	58
Boghall	Pth & Kin	NO1727	56°25·9'	3°20·3'W	X	53,58
Boghall	Scot Bord	NY5391	55°12·9'	2°43·9'W	X	79
Bog Hall	Shrops	SJ6727	52°50·6'	2°29·0'W	X	127
Boghall	S Lanak	NS9449	55°43·6'	3°40·8'W	X	72
Boghall	Stir	NS6899	56°10·2'	4°7·1'W	X	57
Boghall	W Loth	NS9968	55°53·9'	3°36·5'W	T	65
Boghall	W Loth	NT0177	55°58·8'	3°34·8'W	X	65
Boghall Burn	Fife	NO4206	56°14·8'	2°55·7'W	W	59
Boghall Burn	Midlo	NT2465	55°52·6'	3°12·4'W	W	66
Boghall Burn	Scot Bord	NY5391	55°12·9'	2°43·9'W	W	79
Bog Hall Fm	Durham	NZ3425	54°37·4'	1°28·0'W	FM	93
Boghall Fm	S Lanak	NT0337	55°37·3'	3°32·0'W	FM	72
Boghall Hill	Pth & Kin	NO0413	56°18·2'	3°32·6'W	X	58
Bogha Lurcain	Highld	NM6844	56°32·1'	5°45·9'W	X	49
Bogha Mairi	N Eil	NF8482	57°43·3'	7°18·0'W	X	18
Bogha Mhic Gill'-Iosa	Highld	NM4882	56°51·9'	6°7·6'W	X	39
Bogha Mór	Arg & Bt	NL9838	56°26·5'	6°53·6'W	X	46
Bogha Mór	Arg & Bt	NM2665	56°42·0'	6°28·1'W	X	46,47
Bogha Mór	Arg & Bt	NM4024	56°20·5'	6°12·0'W	X	48
Bogha na Brice-nis	Highld	NM4690	56°56·2'	6°10·1'W	X	39
Bogha na Fionn-aird	Highld	NM4178	56°49·5'	6°14·3'W	X	39
Bogha nam Meann	Highld	NC0733	58°14·9'	5°16·8'W	X	15
Bogha nam Gabhar	Arg & Bt	NM6124	56°21·1'	5°51·7'W	X	49
Bogha na Sgeirean Móra	N Eil	NF7304	57°0·9'	7°22·8'W	X	31
Bogha na Sruthlaig	Arg & Bt	NM5254	56°37·0'	6°2·1'W	X	47
Bogh an Fhéidh	N Eil	NF9056	57°29·6'	7°10·0'W	X	22
Boghannan Lisgear	N Eil	HW8133	59°7·9'	5°49·2'W	X	8
Bogh' an Sgùlain	Arg & Bt	NM4124	56°20·5'	6°11·0'W	X	48
Bogh' an Taillir	Arg & Bt	NM7226	56°22·5'	5°41·1'W	X	49
Bogha Ruadh	Arg & Bt	NM2942	56°29·8'	6°23·8'W	X	46,47,48
Bogha Ruadh	Highld	NM4278	56°49·6'	6°13·3'W	X	39
Bogha Ruadh	Highld	NM7842	56°31·3'	5°36·1'W	X	49
Bogha Ruadh	N Eil	NB3610	58°0·3'	6°27·7'W	X	14
Bogharvey	Aberd	NJ6451	57°33·1'	2°35·6'W	X	29
Bogha Sgiobagair	Arg & Bt	NL9348	56°31·7'	6°59·1'W	X	46
Bogha Thangaraidh	Highld	NM4689	56°55·6'	6°10·0'W	X	39
Boghead	Aberd	NJ4440	57°27·1'	2°55·5'W	X	28
Boghead	Aberd	NJ4822	57°17·4'	2°51·3'W	X	37
Boghead	Aberd	NJ5003	57°7·2'	2°49·1'W	X	37
Boghead	Aberd	NJ5227	57°20·1'	2°47·4'W	X	37
Boghead	Aberd	NJ5445	57°29·8'	2°45·6'W	X	29
Boghead	Aberd	NJ5639	57°26·6'	2°43·5'W	X	29
Boghead	Aberd	NJ6013	57°12·6'	2°39·3'W	X	37
Boghead	Aberd	NJ6038	57°26·1'	2°39·5'W	X	29
Boghead	Aberd	NJ6246	57°30·4'	2°37·6'W	X	29
Boghead	Aberd	NJ6259	57°37·4'	2°37·7'W	X	29
Boghead	Aberd	NJ6323	57°18·0'	2°36·4'W	X	37
Boghead	Aberd	NJ6331	57°22·3'	2°36·5'W	X	29,37
Boghead	Aberd	NJ6553	57°34·2'	2°34·6'W	X	29
Boghead	Aberd	NJ7119	57°15·9'	2°28·4'W	X	38
Boghead	Aberd	NJ7123	57°18·1'	2°28·4'W	X	38
Boghead	Aberd	NJ7262	57°39·1'	2°27·7'W	X	29
Boghead	Aberd	NJ8013	57°12·7'	2°19·4'W	X	38
Boghead	Aberd	NJ8048	57°31·6'	2°19·6'W	X	29,30
Boghead	Aberd	NJ8343	57°28·9'	2°16·6'W	X	29,30
Boghead	Aberd	NJ8917	57°14·9'	2°10·5'W	X	38
Boghead	Aberd	NJ9465	57°40·7'	2°5·6'W	X	30
Boghead	Aberd	NJ9735	57°24·6'	2°2·5'W	X	30
Boghead	Aberd	NK0049	57°32·1'	1°59·5'W	X	30
Boghead	Aberd	NK0253	57°34·3'	1°57·5'W	X	30
Boghead	Aberd	NO4799	57°5·0'	2°52·0'W	X	37,44
Boghead	Aberd	NO6192	57°1·3'	2°38·1'W	X	45
Boghead	Aberd	NO6893	57°1·9'	2°31·2'W	X	38,45
Boghead	Aberd	NO7867	56°47·9'	2°21·2'W	X	45
Boghead	Angus	NO6846	56°36·5'	2°30·8'W	X	54
Boghead	D & G	NY0474	55°3·3'	3°29·7'W	X	84
Boghead	E Ayr	NS5130	55°32·7'	4°21·3'W	X	70
Boghead	E Ayr	NS6324	55°29·7'	4°9·7'W	X	71
Boghead	E Dunb	NS6471	55°55·0'	4°10·1'W	X	64
Boghead	Moray	NJ3640	57°27·0'	3°3·5'W	X	28
Boghead	Moray	NJ3932	57°22·7'	3°0·4'W	X	37
Boghead	Northum	NY7360	54°56·3'	2°24·9'W	X	86,87
Boghead	Renf	NS4665	55°51·5'	4°27·2'W	X	64
Boghead	S Ayr	NS4329	55°32·0'	4°28·8'W	X	70
Boghead	S Lanak	NS6950	55°43·8'	4°4·7'W	X	64
Boghead	S Lanak	NS7741	55°39·1'	3°56·8'W	X	71
Boghead	S Lanak	NS9420	55°28·0'	3°40·2'W	X	71,72
Boghead Burn	E Ayr	NS6423	55°29·2'	4°8·7'W	W	71
Boghead Fm	Aberd	NJ6954	57°34·8'	2°30·6'W	FM	29
Boghead Hill	Aberd	NJ6346	57°30·4'	2°36·6'W	H	29
Boghead Lane	E Ayr	NS6324	55°29·7'	4°9·7'W	W	71
Bogheadly	Aberd	NO8188	56°59·2'	2°18·3'W	X	45
Boghead of Cobairdy	Aberd	NJ5644	57°29·3'	2°43·6'W	X	29
Boghead of Laithers	Aberd	NJ6845	57°29·9'	2°31·6'W	X	29
Boghead of Orrock	Aberd	NJ9620	57°16·5'	2°3·5'W	X	38
Bogheads	Highld	NH9256	57°35·1'	3°47·9'W	X	27
Boghill	S Lanak	NS8239	55°38·1'	3°52·0'W	X	71,72
Bog Hill	S Lanak	NT0414	55°24·9'	3°30·6'W	H	78
Bog Ho	Cumbr	NY2324	54°36·6'	3°11·1'W	X	89,90
Bog Ho	Northum	NZ0570	55°1·7'	1°54·9'W	X	87

Bog Ho	Northum	NZ2077	55°5·5′	1°40·8′W	X	88
Bog Ho	N Yks	SD8590	54°18·6′	2°13·4′W	X	98
Bog Ho	N Yks	SE6593	54°19·9′	0°59·6′W	X	94,100
Bogh' Oitir	Highld	NM6489	56°56·2′	5°52·3′W	X	40
Boghole Fm	Highld	NH9655	57°34·6′	3°43·9′W	FM	27
Boghouse	Aberd	NJ8730	57°21·9′	2°12·5′W	X	30
Boghouse	Scot Bord	NT6237	55°37·8′	2°35·8′W	X	74
Boghouse	S Lanak	NS8723	55°29·5′	3°46·9′W	X	71,72
Bogiesavoch	Aberd	NJ9543	57°28·9′	2°4·5′W	X	30
Bogieshiel	Aberd	NO5694	57°2·4′	2°43·1′W	X	37,44
Bogieshiel Lodge	Aberd	NO5695	57°2·9′	2°43·1′W	X	37,44
Bogincaber	Aberd	NO7482	56°56·0′	2°25·2′W	X	45
Bogindhu	Aberd	NJ6907	57°9·4′	2°30·3′W	X	38
Bogindollo	Angus	NO4655	56°41·3′	2°52·4′W	X	54
Boginduie	Moray	NJ2640	57°26·9′	3°13·5′W	X	28
Bogingore	Aberd	NO4399	57°5·0′	2°56·0′W	X	37,44
Boginthort	Aberd	NJ6217	57°14·8′	2°37·3′W	X	37
Bogjurgan	Aberd	NO7584	56°57·1′	2°24·2′W	X	45
Bogknowe	D & G	NX9059	54°55·1′	3°42·5′W	X	84
Boglach Mhòr	Arg & Bt	NM5624	56°21·0′	5°56·5′W	X	48
Boglach nan Tarbh	Arg & Bt	NM6824	56°21·3′	5°44·9′W	X	49
Boglach nan Tarbh	Arg & Bt	NR4073	55°53·1′	6°9·0′W	X	60,61
Boglairoch	W Dunb	NS4675	55°56·9′	4°27·5′W	X	64
Boglashin	Highld	NH5227	57°18·8′	4°27·0′W	X	26,35
Bogle	Kent	TQ9461	51°19·1′	0°47·4′E	A	178
Boglea	N Lanak	NS7771	55°55·2′	3°57·7′W	X	64
Boglea	Pth & Kin	NO2344	56°35·2′	3°14·8′W	X	53
Bogle Burn	Northum	NZ0666	54°59·6′	1°53·9′W	W	87
Bogle Burn	Scot Bord	NT5733	55°35·6′	2°40·5′W	W	73,74
Bogle Crag	Cumbr	SD3393	54°19·9′	3°1·4′W	X	96,97
Bogle Ho	Durham	NZ0824	54°36·9′	1°52·1′W	X	92
Bogle Hos	Northum	NU0538	55°38·4′	1°54·8′W	X	75
Bogleys	Fife	NT2995	56°8·8′	3°8·1′W	X	59
Bogligarths Geo	Shetld	HP5707	60°44·8′	0°56·8′W	X	1
Boglily	Fife	NT2591	56°6·6′	3°11·9′W	X	59
Bog Loch	Aberd	NO6397	57°4·0′	2°36·2′W	W	37,45
Bogloch Fm	Aberd	NJ5603	57°7·2′	2°43·1′W	FM	37
Bog Lodge	Rich	TQ1973	51°26·8′	0°16·9′W	X	176
Bogmarsh	Heref	SO5434	52°0·4′	2°39·8′W	X	149
Bogmill	Aberd	NJ7021	57°17·0′	2°29·4′W	X	38
Bogmill	Aberd	NO6573	56°51·1′	2°34·0′W	X	45
Bogmiln Fm	Pth & Kin	NO2825	56°25·0′	3°9·6′W	FM	53,59
Bogmire Gill	N Yks	SE6092	54°19·4′	1°4·2′W	W	94,100
Bogmoon	Aberd	NJ4843	57°28·7′	2°51·6′W	X	28,29
Bogmoor	Moray	NJ3562	57°38·9′	3°4·9′W	T	28
Bog Moor	Staffs	SJ9616	52°44·7′	2°3·2′W	X	127
Bogmore	Aberd	NJ4423	57°17·9′	2°55·3′W	X	37
Bogmore	Aberd	NJ6415	57°13·7′	2°35·3′W	X	37
Bogmore	Aberd	NO6090	57°0·2′	2°39·1′W	X	45
Bog Moss	Durham	NY9309	54°28·8′	2°6·1′W	X	91,92
Bogmuchals	Aberd	NJ5559	57°37·4′	2°44·7′W	X	29
Bogmuir	Aberd	NO6571	56°50·0′	2°34·0′W	X	45
Bognacruie	Highld	NJ0415	57°13·2′	3°34·9′W	X	36
Bognafuaran	Highld	NH8954	57°34·0′	3°50·9′W	X	27
Bog na Gaoithe	Highld	ND1548	58°25·0′	3°26·8′W	X	11,12
Bog nam Biast	Highld	NH5061	57°37·1′	4°30·2′W	X	20
Bognie	Moray	NJ1055	57°34·8′	3°29·8′W	X	28
Bogniebrae	Aberd	NJ5945	57°29·9′	2°40·6′W	T	29
Bognor Common	W Susx	TQ0021	50°59·0′	0°34·1′W	F	197
Bognor Regis	W Susx	SZ9399	50°47·2′	0°40·5′W	T	197
Bognor Rocks	W Susx	SZ9298	50°46·7′	0°41·3′W	X	197
Bog of Artamford	Aberd	NJ8948	57°31·6′	2°10·6′W	X	30
Bog of Cawdor	Highld	NH8450	57°31·8′	3°55·8′W	X	27
Bog of Cullicudden	Highld	NH6564	57°39·0′	4°15·3′W	X	21
Bog o' Fearn	Moray	NJ2757	57°36·1′	3°12·8′W	X	28
Bog of Findon	Highld	NH6261	57°37·3′	4°18·2′W	X	21
Bog of Luchray	Aberd	NO6283	56°56·5′	2°37·0′W	X	45
Bog of Minnonie	Aberd	NJ7861	57°38·6′	2°21·7′W	W	29,30
Bog of Pitkennedy	Angus	NO5353	56°40·2′	2°45·6′W	X	54
Bog of Saughs	Aberd	NO6785	56°57·6′	2°32·1′W	X	45
Bog of Shannon Wood	Highld	NH6856	57°34·8′	4°12·0′W	F	26
Bog of Surtan	Orkney	HY3422	59°5·1′	3°8·6′W	X	6
Bogower	Aberd	NJ6345	57°29·9′	2°36·6′W	X	29
Bogpark Burn	Scot Bord	NT6951	55°45·3′	2°29·2′W	W	67,74
Bog Plantn	Leeds	SE2844	53°53·7′	1°34·0′W	F	104
Bog Pond	Cered	SN7282	52°25·5′	3°52·6′W	W	135
Bogra	D & G	NY3275	55°4·1′	3°3·5′W	X	85
Bogra Ho	D & G	NX7055	54°52·6′	4°1·1′W	X	83,84
Bograxie	Aberd	NJ7019	57°15·9′	2°29·4′W	T	38
Bogridge Fm	N Yks	SE2547	53°55·4′	1°36·7′W	FM	104
Bogrie	D & G	NX8184	55°8·4′	3°51·6′W	X	78
Bogrie	D & G	NY3276	55°4·7′	3°3·5′W	X	85
Bogrie Burn	D & G	NX8085	55°8·9′	3°52·6′W	W	78
Bogrie Hill	D & G	NX7885	55°8·9′	3°54·4′W	H	78
Bogrie Lane	D & G	NX8975	55°3·7′	3°43·8′W	W	84
Bogrie Moor	D & G	NX7985	55°8·9′	3°53·5′W	X	78
Bogrie Wood	D & G	NX8498	55°16·0′	3°49·1′W	F	78
Bogriffie	Aberd	NJ8417	57°14·9′	2°15·5′W	X	38
Bogrough	D & G	NX8493	55°13·3′	3°49·0′W	X	78
Bogroy	Highld	NH9023	57°17·3′	3°49·0′W	X	36
Bogroy	Moray	NJ2342	57°28·0′	3°16·6′W	X	28
Bogs	Aberd	NJ5823	57°18·0′	2°41·4′W	X	37
Bogs Bank	Scot Bord	NT1550	55°44·4′	3°20·8′W	T	65,72
Bogs Burn	D & G	NS8012	55°23·5′	3°53·2′W	W	71,78
Bog Shaw	D & G	NY0394	55°14·1′	3°31·1′W	H	78
Bog Shield	Northum	NY8979	55°6·2′	2°9·9′W	X	87
Bogs Ho	N Yks	SE3470	54°7·7′	1°28·4′W	X	99
Bogshole Fm	Kent	TR1164	51°20·4′	1°2·2′E	FM	179
Bogside	Aberd	NJ5410	57°11·0′	2°45·2′W	X	37
Bogside	Aberd	NJ5736	57°25·0′	2°42·5′W	X	29
Bogside	Aberd	NJ7047	57°31·0′	2°29·6′W	X	29
Bogside	Aberd	NJ7158	57°36·9′	2°28·7′W	X	29
Bogside	Aberd	NJ7846	57°30·5′	2°21·6′W	X	29,30
Bogside	Aberd	NJ8135	57°24·6′	2°18·5′W	X	29,30
Bogside	Aberd	NO6170	56°49·4′	2°37·9′W	X	45
Bogside	Angus	NO3961	56°44·5′	2°59·4′W	X	44
Bogside	Angus	NO4452	56°39·6′	2°54·4′W	X	54
Bogside	C of Glas	NS6468	55°53·4′	4°10·0′W	X	64
Bogside	Cumbr	NY5574	55°3·8′	2°41·8′W	X	86
Bogside	D & G	NX0354	54°50·8′	5°3·7′W	X	82

Bogside	D & G	NY0473	55°2·8′	3°29·7′W	X	84
Bogside	E Renf	NS5553	55°45·2′	4°18·2′W	X	64
Bogside	Fife	NO3303	56°13·1′	3°4·4′W	X	59
Bogside	Fife	NS9690	56°5·7′	3°39·9′W	X	58
Bogside	Inverc	NS2172	55°54·7′	4°51·4′W	X	63
Bogside	Moray	NJ2538	57°25·8′	3°14·5′W	X	28
Bogside	Moray	NJ4564	57°40·0′	2°54·9′W	X	28,29
Bogside	N Lanak	NS7177	55°58·4′	4°3·6′W	X	64
Bogside	N Lanak	NS8071	55°55·3′	3°54·8′W	X	65
Bogside	N Lanak	NS8354	55°46·2′	3°51·5′W	T	65,72
Bogside	Renf	NS3672	55°55·0′	4°37·0′W	X	63
Bogside	S Ayr	NS2811	55°22·0′	4°42·4′W	X	70
Bogside	S Ayr	NS4218	55°26·1′	4°29·4′W	X	70
Bogside	S Lanak	NS7544	55°40·7′	3°58·8′W	X	71
Bogside	S Lanak	NS7849	55°43·4′	3°56·1′W	X	64
Bogside	S Lanak	NS8240	55°38·6′	3°52·1′W	X	71,72
Bogside	S Lanak	NS8552	55°45·1′	3°49·5′W	X	65,72
Bogside	Stir	NS6286	56°3·1′	4°12·5′W	X	57
Bogside Flats	N Ayr	NS3039	55°37·2′	4°41·5′W	X	70
Bogside Ho	S Ayr	NS3827	55°30·9′	4°33·5′W	X	70
Bogside of Boath	Highld	NH9256	57°35·1′	3°47·9′W	X	27
Bogside Race Course	N Ayr	NS3039	55°37·2′	4°41·5′W	X	70
Bogside Wood	Aberd	NJ7058	57°36·9′	2°29·7′W	F	29
Bogskeathy	C of Aber	NJ8704	57°7·9′	2°12·4′W	X	38
Bogs of Blervie	Moray	NJ0757	57°35·9′	3°32·9′W	X	27
Bogs of Coullie	Aberd	NJ7116	57°14·3′	2°28·4′W	X	38
Bogs of Laithers	Aberd	NJ6847	57°31·0′	2°31·6′W	X	29
Bogs of Noth	Aberd	NJ5131	57°22·3′	2°48·4′W	X	29,37
Bogs of Plaidy	Aberd	NJ7253	57°34·2′	2°27·6′W	X	29
Bogs Plantn	N Yks	SE2784	54°15·3′	1°34·7′W	F	99
Bogs, The	Staffs	SJ7738	52°56·6′	2°20·1′W	F	127
Bogston	Aberd	NJ3909	57°10·3′	3°0·1′W	X	37
Bogston	N Ayr	NS3551	55°43·7′	4°37·2′W	X	63
Bogston Sta	Inverc	NS3074	55°56·0′	4°42·8′W	X	63
Bogtama	Aberd	NJ7440	57°27·2′	2°25·5′W	X	29
Bog, The	Durham	NY9510	54°29·4′	2°4·2′W	X	91,92
Bog, The	E Yorks	TA2728	53°44·2′	0°4·1′W	F	107
Bog, The	Northum	NY6854	54°53·0′	2°29·5′W	X	86,87
Bog, The	Powys	SO0157	52°12·4′	3°26·5′W	W	147
Bog, The	Shrops	SO3597	52°34·3′	2°57·1′W	T	137
Bog, The	Shrops	SO7597	52°34·5′	2°21·7′W	W	138
Bogthorn	Brad	SE0439	53°51·1′	1°55·9′W	T	104
Bogton	Aberd	NJ5757	57°36·3′	2°42·7′W	X	29
Bogton	Aberd	NJ6140	57°27·2′	2°38·5′W	X	29
Bogton	Aberd	NJ6751	57°33·1′	2°32·6′W	T	29
Bogton	Aberd	NO7383	56°56·5′	2°26·2′W	X	45
Bogton	Angus	NO5570	56°49·4′	2°43·8′W	X	44
Bogton	E Dunb	NS6273	55°56·1′	4°12·1′W	X	64
Bogton	Falk	NS8481	56°0·7′	3°51·2′W	X	65
Bogton	Moray	NJ2760	57°37·7′	3°12·9′W	X	28
Bogton	S Lanak	NS5953	55°45·2′	4°14·4′W	X	64
Bogton Fm	Aberd	NO8199	57°5·2′	2°18·4′W	FM	38,45
Bogtonlea	Pth & Kin	NO0415	56°19·3′	3°32·7′W	X	58
Bogton Loch	E Ayr	NS4605	55°19·2′	4°25·2′W	W	70,77
Bogton of Balhall	Angus	NO5063	56°45·6′	2°48·6′W	X	44
Bogtown	Aberd	NJ5665	57°40·5′	2°43·8′W	X	29
Bogtown	Devon	SX4997	50°45·4′	4°8·1′W	X	191
Bogue	D & G	NX6481	55°6·5′	4°7·5′W	X	77
Bogue Fell	D & G	NX6482	55°7·1′	4°7·5′W	X	77
Bogue Moor	D & G	NX6482	55°7·1′	4°7·5′W	X	77
Bogues	D & G	NY1672	55°2·4′	3°18·4′W	X	85
Boguille	N Ayr	NR9427	55°29·9′	5°15·3′W	X	68,69
Boguillie	N Ayr	NR9748	55°41·2′	5°13·3′W	X	62,69
Bog Wood	D & G	NX3876	55°3·4′	4°31·8′W	F	77
Bog Wood	Donc	SK6195	53°27·1′	1°4·5′W	F	111
Bogwood	E Ayr	NS4827	55°31·0′	4°24·0′W	X	70
Bohago	Corn	SW9346	50°16·9′	4°54·0′W	X	204
Bohally	Pth & Kin	NN7859	56°42·7′	3°59·1′W	X	42,51,52
Bohally Wood	Pth & Kin	NN7859	56°42·7′	3°59·1′W	F	42,51,52
Boheadlag	Pth & Kin	NN9150	56°38·0′	3°46·2′W	X	52
Bohemia	E Susx	TQ8010	50°51·9′	0°33·9′E	T	199
Bohemia	N Yks	SE5662	54°3·3′	1°8·3′W	X	100
Bohemia	Wilts	SU2019	50°58·4′	1°42·5′W	T	184
Bohemia Corner	I of W	SZ5183	50°38·9′	1°16·3′W	X	196
Bohenie	Highld	NN2982	56°54·1′	4°48·0′W	T	34,41
Bohenuil Trodday	Highld	NG4378	57°43·4′	6°18·5′W	X	23
Bohetherick	Corn	SX4167	50°29·1′	4°14·1′W	T	201
Bohomy Hill	E Loth	NT5065	55°52·8′	2°47·5′W	X	66
Bohortha	Corn	SW8632	50°9·2′	4°59·4′W	T	204
Bohune Down	Wilts	SU1655	51°17·9′	1°45·8′W	X	173
Bohuns Hall	Essex	TL9509	51°45·0′	0°49·9′E	X	168
Bohunt	Hants	SU8330	51°4·0′	0°48·5′W	X	186
Bohuntine	Highld	NN2883	56°54·6′	4°49·0′W	T	34,41
Bohuntine Hill	Highld	NN2885	56°55·7′	4°49·1′W	H	34,41
Bohuntinville	Highld	NN2882	56°54·1′	4°49·0′W	X	34,41
Boig	Aberd	NJ4707	57°9·3′	2°52·1′W	X	37
Boiley Fm	Derby	SK4479	53°18·6′	1°20·0′W	FM	120
Boiling Well	Shrops	SO4294	52°32·7′	2°50·9′W	W	137
Boiling Wells Fm	Lincs	TF0445	52°59·8′	0°26·6′W	FM	130
Boinna Skerry	Shetld	HU1861	60°20·2′	1°39·9′W	X	3
Bois Hall	Essex	TQ5598	51°39·8′	0°14·9′E	X	167,177
Bois Ho	Corn	SX1774	50°32·5′	4°34·6′W	X	201
Bois Mill	Bucks	SU9899	51°41·1′	0°34·5′W	X	165,176
Bojea Fm	Corn	SX0154	50°21·4′	4°47·5′W	FM	200
Bojewans Carn	Corn	SW4326	50°4·9′	5°35·2′W	X	203
Bojewyan	Corn	SW3934	50°9·2′	5°38·9′W	T	203
Bojuthnoe	Corn	SW4132	50°8·1′	5°37·1′W	X	203
Bokelly	Corn	SX0477	50°33·8′	4°45·7′W	X	200
Bokenham Fm	Norf	TF9209	52°38·9′	0°50·7′E	FM	144
Bokenna Cross	Corn	SX2166	50°28·2′	4°31·0′W	X	201
Bokenna Wood	Corn	SX2066	50°28·2′	4°31·8′W	F	201
Bokenver Wood	Corn	SX2856	50°23·0′	4°24·8′W	F	201
Bokerley Ditch	Dorset	SU0419	50°58·5′	1°56·2′W	R	184
Bokerley Down	Dorset	SU0418	50°57·9′	1°56·2′W	X	184
Bokes Fm	Kent	TQ7329	51°2·3′	0°28·4′E	FM	188,199
Bokiddick	Corn	SX0562	50°25·8′	4°44·4′W	T	200
Bokiddick Downs	Corn	SX0461	50°25·2′	4°45·2′W	X	200
Bolahaul	Carm	SN4218	51°50·5′	4°17·2′W	T	159
Bolam	Durham	NZ1922	54°35·8′	1°41·9′W	T	92
Bolam	Northum	NZ0982	55°8·2′	1°51·1′W	T	81

Bolam Grange	Durham	NZ2021	54°35·3′	1°41·0′W	X	93
Bolam Lake	Northum	NZ0881	55°7·6′	1°52·0′W	W	81
Bolam Low Ho	Northum	NZ0881	55°7·6′	1°52·0′W	X	81
Bolam West Houses	Northum	NZ0682	55°8·2′	1°53·9′W	T	81
Bolas Heath	Wrekin	SJ6721	52°47·4′	2°29·0′W	T	127
Bolas Ho	Wrekin	SJ6521	52°47·4′	2°30·7′W	X	127
Bolatherick	Corn	SX1176	50°33·4′	4°39·7′W	X	200
Bolaval Scarasta	N Eil	NG0091	57°48·7′	7°2·6′W	H	18
Bolberry	Devon	SX6939	50°14·4′	3°49·9′W	T	202
Bolberry Down	Devon	SX6838	50°13·9′	3°50·7′W	X	202
Bolbro	Powys	SO1795	52°33·0′	3°13·0′W	X	136
Bold	St Hel	SJ5492	53°25·6′	2°41·1′W	X	108
Bold Burn	Scot Bord	NT3735	55°36·5′	2°59·6′W	W	73
Bolderford Br	Hants	SU2904	50°50·3′	1°34·9′W	X	196
Bolder Hall	Ches	SJ9882	53°20·3′	2°1·4′W	X	109
Bolder Mere	Surrey	TQ0758	51°18·9′	0°27·5′W	W	187
Boldershaw	Staffs	SK1345	53°0·4′	1°48·0′W	X	119,128
Bolderwood Cottage	Hants	SU2408	50°52·5′	1°39·1′W	X	195
Bolderwood Fm	Hants	SU2308	50°52·5′	1°40·0′W	FM	195
Bolderwood Grounds	Hants	SU2407	50°51·9′	1°39·2′W	F	195
Bolderwood Ornamental Drive	Hants	SU2506	50°51·4′	1°38·3′W	X	195
Boldford Bridge	Devon	SX3688	50°40·4′	4°18·9′W	X	190
Bold Heath	St Hel	SJ5389	53°24·0′	2°42·0′W	T	108
Bolding Hatch	Essex	TL6210	51°46·1′	0°21·3′E	X	167
Boldings, The	Shrops	SO7197	52°34·4′	2°25·3′W	X	138
Boldmere	Birm	SP1194	52°32·9′	1°49·9′W	T	139
Boldon Colliery	S Tyne	NZ3461	54°56·8′	1°27·7′W	T	88
Boldon North Br	S Tyne	NZ3662	54°57·3′	1°25·8′W	X	88
Boldow	Moray	NJ1740	57°26·8′	3°22·5′W	X	28
Boldre	Hants	SZ3298	50°47·1′	1°32·4′W	T	196
Boldre Grange	Hants	SZ3198	50°47·1′	1°33·2′W	X	196
Boldrewood Fm	Kent	TQ8852	51°14·4′	0°42·0′E	FM	189
Boldridge Fm	Glos	ST9292	51°37·8′	2°6·5′W	FM	163,173
Bold Rig	Scot Bord	NT3634	55°36·0′	3°0·5′W	H	73
Boldron	Durham	NZ0314	54°31·5′	1°56·8′W	T	92
Boldshaves	Kent	TQ9135	51°5·2′	0°44·0′E	X	189
Boldstart Fm	W Berks	SU3277	51°29·7′	1°32·0′W	FM	174
Bold, The	Shrops	SO6484	52°27·4′	2°31·4′W	X	138
Boldventure	Devon	SX4495	50°44·3′	4°12·3′W	X	190
Bold Venture Farm	Lancs	SD7530	53°46·2′	2°22·3′W	FM	103
Bole	Notts	SK7987	53°22·7′	0°48·3′W	T	112,120,121
Bolealler Ho	Devon	ST0204	50°49·9′	3°23·1′W	X	192
Bolebroke Castle	E Susx	TQ4737	51°7·0′	0°6·4′E	A	188
Bole Edge Plantation	Sheff	SK2291	53°25·2′	1°39·7′W	F	110
Bole Fields	Notts	SK7787	53°22·7′	0°50·1′W	X	112,120
Bolehall	Staffs	SK2103	52°37·7′	1°41·0′W	T	139
Bole Hill	Derby	SK0584	53°21·4′	1°55·1′W	H	110
Bole Hill	Derby	SK1075	53°16·6′	1°50·6′W	H	119
Bole Hill	Derby	SK1867	53°12·2′	1°43·4′W	H	119
Bole Hill	Derby	SK2179	53°18·7′	1°40·7′W	X	119
Bole Hill	Derby	SK2284	53°21·4′	1°39·8′W	X	110
Bole Hill	Derby	SK2579	53°18·7′	1°37·1′W	X	119
Bolehill	Derby	SK2955	53°5·7′	1°33·6′W	T	119
Bolehill	Derby	SK3374	53°16·0′	1°29·9′W	T	119
Bole Hill	Derby	SK3666	53°11·6′	1°27·3′W	X	119
Bolehill	Derby	SK4078	53°18·1′	1°23·6′W	T	120
Bolehill	Derby	SK4170	53°13·8′	1°22·7′W	T	120
Bole Hill	Sheff	SK2979	53°18·7′	1°33·5′W	X	119
Bole Hill	Sheff	SK2980	53°19·2′	1°33·5′W	X	110
Bolehill	Sheff	SK3582	53°20·3′	1°28·1′W	T	110,111
Bole Hill Fm	Derby	SK1867	53°12·2′	1°43·4′W	FM	119
Bolehyde Manor	Wilts	ST8975	51°28·7′	2°9·1′W	X	173
Boleigh	Corn	SW4324	50°3·9′	5°35·1′W	X	203
Bole Ings	Notts	SK8087	53°22·7′	0°47·4′W	X	112,121
Bolenowe	Corn	SW6737	50°11·5′	5°15·5′W	T	203
Bolesbridge	Corn	SX2989	50°40·8′	4°24·8′W	X	190
Bolesbridge Water	Corn	SX2889	50°40·8′	4°25·7′W	W	190
Boleside	Scot Bord	NT4933	55°35·5′	2°48·1′W	T	73
Boleskine Ho	Highld	NH5022	57°16·1′	4°28·8′W	X	26,35
Bolesworth Castle	Ches	SJ4956	53°6·2′	2°45·3′W	X	117
Boley Park	Staffs	SK1309	52°41·4′	1°48·1′W	T	128
Bolfornought	Stir	NS8293	56°7·2′	3°53·4′W	X	57
Bolfracks	Pth & Kin	NN8248	56°36·8′	3°54·9′W	X	52
Bolfracks Hill	Pth & Kin	NN8247	56°36·3′	3°54·9′W	X	52
Bolgoed	Powys	SO0027	51°56·2′	3°26·9′W	X	160
Bolgoed	Swan	SN6002	51°42·2′	4°1·2′W	X	159
Bolgoed Fm	V of Glam	ST0479	51°30·3′	3°22·6′W	FM	170
Bolham	Devon	SS9514	50°55·2′	3°29·2′W	T	181
Bolham	Notts	SK7082	53°20·1′	0°56·5′W	T	120
Bolham Hall	Notts	SK7083	53°20·6′	0°56·5′W	X	120
Bolham Hill	Devon	ST1612	50°54·3′	3°11·3′W	X	181,193
Bolham Ho	Somer	ST2541	51°10·0′	3°4·0′W	X	182
Bolham River	Devon	ST1711	50°53·8′	3°10·4′W	W	192,193
Bolham Water	Devon	ST1612	50°54·3′	3°11·3′W	X	181,193
Bolholt	Bury	SD7811	53°35·9′	2°19·5′W	T	109
Bolinge Hill Fm	Hants	SU7321	50°59·3′	0°57·2′W	FM	197
Bolingey	Corn	SW7653	50°20·3′	5°8·5′W	T	200,204
Bolingey	Corn	SW8866	50°27·6′	4°58·8′W	X	200
Bolinn Hill	Highld	NH2501	57°4·3′	4°52·7′W	H	34
Bolitho	Corn	SW6634	50°9·8′	5°16·2′W	T	203
Bolitho	Corn	SX2563	50°26·7′	4°27·5′W	X	201
Bolivia Mount	I of M	SC4496	54°20·4′	4°23·6′W	X	95
Bolla Hill	Shetld	HU4687	60°34·1′	1°9·1′W	H	1,2
Bolland	Devon	SX5098	50°46·0′	4°7·2′W	X	191
Bolland's Hall	Staffs	SK0656	53°6·3′	1°54·2′W	X	119
Bol Las	Nth Pt Talb	SS8498	51°40·4′	3°40·3′W	X	170
Bolldow	Moray	NJ1936	57°24·7′	3°20·4′W	X	28
Bolle Hall	Lincs	TF2437	52°55·2′	0°8·9′W	X	131
Bolletten	Moray	NJ2220	57°16·1′	3°17·1′W	X	36
Bollihope	Durham	NZ0034	54°42·3′	1°59·6′W	T	92
Bollihope Burn	Durham	NY9634	54°42·3′	2°3·3′W	W	91,92
Bollihope Burn	Durham	NZ0135	54°42·8′	1°58·6′W	W	92
Bollihope Carrs	Durham	NY9635	54°42·8′	2°3·3′W	X	91,92
Bollihope Common	Durham	NY9834	54°42·3′	2°1·4′W	X	92
Bollihope Ho	Durham	NZ0135	54°42·8′	1°58·6′W	X	92
Bollihope Shield	Durham	NY9935	54°42·8′	2°0·5′W	X	92
Bollingham Ho	Heref	SO3052	52°9·9′	3°1·0′W	X	148
Bollington	Ches	SJ9377	53°17·6′	2°5·9′W	T	118
Bollington Cross	Ches	SJ9277	53°17·6′	2°6·8′W	T	118

Bollington Grange	Ches	SJ8474	53°16·0′	2°14·0′W	X	118
Bollington Hall	Essex	TL5027	51°55·5′	0°11·3′E	X	167
Bollinhey Fm	Ches	SJ8484	53°21·4′	2°14·0′W	FM	109
Bollin House Fm	Ches	SJ8082	53°20·3′	2°17·6′W	FM	109
Bollin Point	Warr	SJ6888	53°23·5′	2°28·5′W	X	109
Bollitree Castle	Heref	SO6324	51°55·0′	2°31·9′W	X	162
Boll-o-Bere	C of Edin	NT1365	55°52·5′	3°23·0′W	X	65
Bollow	Glos	SO7413	51°49·1′	2°22·2′W	X	162
Bollow Fm	Somer	ST7944	51°11·9′	2°17·6′W	FM	183
Boll, The	Clackm	NS8896	56°8·9′	3°47·7′W	X	58
Bolney	W Susx	TQ2623	50°59·8′	0°11·9′W	T	198
Bolney Ct (Sch)	W Susx	TQ2722	50°59·2′	0°11·0′W	X	198
Bolnhurst	Beds	TL0859	52°13·3′	0°24·7′W	T	153
Bolnore	W Susx	TQ3223	50°59·7′	0°6·7′W	T	198
Boloquoy	Orkney	HY6239	59°14·4′	2°39·5′W	X	5
Bolsa	Arg & Bt	NR3877	55°55·1′	6°11·2′W	X	60,61
Bolsay	Arg & Bt	NR2257	55°43·9′	6°25·3′W	X	60
Bolshan	Angus	NO6152	56°39·7′	2°37·7′W	X	54
Bolshayne	Devon	SY2393	50°44·1′	3°5·1′W	X	192,193
Bolsover	Derby	SK4770	53°13·7′	1°17·3′W	T	120
Bolsover Moor	Derby	SK4971	53°14·3′	1°15·5′W	X	120
Bolster Moor	Kirk	SE0815	53°38·1′	1°52·3′W	X	110
Bolsterstone	Sheff	SK2796	53°27·8′	1°35·2′W	T	110
Bolstone	Heref	SO5532	51°59·3′	2°38·9′W	T	149
Boltachan	Pth & Kin	NN8549	56°37·4′	3°52·0′W	X	52
Bolt Burn	E Ayr	NS6207	55°20·5′	4°10·1′W	W	71,77
Boltby	N Yks	SE4986	54°16·3′	1°14·4′W	T	100
Boltby Forest	N Yks	SE4888	54°17·4′	1°15·3′W	F	100
Boltby Scar	N Yks	SE5086	54°16·3′	1°13·5′W	X	100
Boltcraig Hill	E Ayr	NS6207	55°20·5′	4°10·1′W	X	71,77
Bolt Edge	Derby	SK0779	53°18·7′	1°53·3′W	X	119
Bolter End	Bucks	SU7992	51°37·5′	0°51·1′W	T	175
Bolter's Bridge	Somer	ST6033	51°5·9′	2°33·9′W	A	183
Boltgate	N Lincs	SE8117	53°38·8′	0°46·1′W	X	112
Bolt Hall	Essex	TQ8994	51°37·0′	0°44·2′E	X	168,178
Bolt Head	Devon	SX7235	50°12·3′	3°47·2′W	X	202
Bolt How	Cumbr	NY0700	54°23·5′	3°25·5′W	X	89
Bolting Holme Fm	Notts	SK8462	53°9·1′	0°43·3′W	FM	121
Bolton	Bolton	SD7108	53°34·3′	2°25·9′W	T	109
Bolton	Brad	SE1635	53°48·9′	1°45·0′W	T	104
Bolton	Cumbr	NY6323	54°36·3′	2°33·9′W	T	91
Bolton	E Loth	NT5070	55°55·5′	2°47·6′W	T	66
Bolton	E Yorks	SE7752	53°57·7′	0°49·2′W	T	105,106
Bolton	Heref	SO3553	52°10·5′	2°56·6′W	X	148,149
Bolton	Northum	NU1013	55°24·9′	1°50·1′W	T	81
Bolton Abbey	N Yks	SE0753	53°58·6′	1°53·2′W	T	104
Bolton Abbey Station	N Yks	SE0653	53°58·6′	1°54·1′W	X	104
Bolton Bridge	N Yks	SE0653	53°58·6′	1°54·1′W	T	104
Bolton-by-Bowland	Lancs	SD7849	53°56·4′	2°19·7′W	T	103
Bolton Close Plantn	Lancs	SD8049	53°56·4′	2°17·9′W	F	103
Bolton Fell	Cumbr	NY4868	55°0·5′	2°48·4′W	X	86
Boltonfellend	Cumbr	NY4768	55°0·5′	2°49·3′W	T	86
Bolton Fold	Lancs	SD6035	53°48·8′	2°36·0′W	X	102,103
Bolton Garths	Durham	NZ1723	54°36·4′	1°43·8′W	X	92
Boltongate	Cumbr	NY2240	54°45·2′	3°12·3′W	T	85
Boltongate	Staffs	SJ9344	52°59·8′	2°5·9′W	X	118
Bolton Gill Plantn	N Yks	SE0493	54°20·2′	1°55·9′W	F	98
Bolton Grange	N Yks	SE5440	53°51·4′	1°10·3′W	X	105
Bolton Green	Lancs	SD5517	53°39·1′	2°40·4′W	T	108
Bolton Hall	Cumbr	NY0802	54°24·6′	3°24·6′W	X	89
Bolton Hall	E Yorks	SE7551	53°57·2′	0°51·0′W	X	105,106
Bolton Hall	Lancs	SD6227	53°44·5′	2°34·2′W	X	102,103
Bolton Hall	Lancs	SD6734	53°48·3′	2°29·7′W	R	103
Bolton Hall	N Yks	SE0754	53°59·2′	1°53·2′W	A	104
Bolton Hall	N Yks	SE0789	54°18·0′	1°53·1′W	X	99
Bolton Hall Fm	Lancs	SD7848	53°55·9′	2°19·7′W	FM	103
Bolton Haw End	N Yks	SE0365	54°5·1′	1°56·8′W	X	98
Bolton Heads	Cumbr	SD2573	54°9·1′	3°8·5′W	X	96
Bolton Hill	Durham	NZ0821	54°35·3′	1°52·1′W	X	92
Boltonhill	Pemb	SM9211	51°45·8′	5°0·5′W	X	157,158
Bolton Hill Fm	E Yorks	SE7651	53°57·2′	0°50·1′W	FM	105,106
Bolton Holmes	Lancs	SD4869	54°7·1′	2°47·3′W	X	97
Bolton Houses	Lancs	SD4433	53°47·7′	2°50·6′W	T	102
Bolton-le-Sands	Lancs	SD4868	54°6·6′	2°47·3′W	T	97
Bolton Lodge	Cumbr	NY6421	54°35·2′	2°33·0′W	X	91
Bolton Lodge	N Yks	SE5240	53°51·5′	1°12·1′W	X	105
Bolton Low Houses	Cumbr	NY2344	54°47·3′	3°11·4′W	T	85
Bolton Mill	Northum	NU1113	55°24·9′	1°49·1′W	X	81
Bolton Muir Wood	E Loth	NT5068	55°54·4′	2°47·5′W	F	66
Bolton New Houses	Cumbr	NY2444	54°47·4′	3°10·5′W	T	85
Bolton-on-Swale	N Yks	SE2599	54°23·4′	1°36·5′W	T	99
Bolton Park	Cumbr	NY2641	54°45·8′	3°8·6′W	X	85
Bolton Park	Lancs	SD7848	53°55·9′	2°19·7′W	X	103
Bolton Park	N Yks	SE0855	53°59·7′	1°52·3′W	X	104
Bolton Park Fm	N Yks	SE0855	53°59·7′	1°52·3′W	FM	104
Bolton Parks	N Yks	SE0292	54°19·7′	1°57·7′W	X	98
Bolton Park Wood	Darl	NZ3409	54°28·8′	1°28·1′W	F	93
Bolton Peel	Lancs	SD7748	53°55·9′	2°20·6′W	X	103
Bolton Percy	N Yks	SE5341	53°52·0′	1°11·2′W	T	105
Bolton's Barrow	Dorset	SY8696	50°46·0′	2°11·5′W	A	194
Boltons Park	Herts	TL2502	51°42·4′	0°11·1′W	X	166
Bolton Town End	Lancs	SD4867	54°6·0′	2°47·3′W	T	97
Bolton Upon Dearne	Barns	SE4502	53°31·0′	1°18·9′W	T	111
Bolton Wood	Cumbr	NY1004	54°25·7′	3°22·8′W	F	89
Bolton Woodhall	Northum	NU1114	55°25·4′	1°49·1′W	X	81
Bolton Wood Lane	Cumbr	NY2544	54°47·4′	3°9·6′W	T	85
Bolton Woods	Brad	SE1535	53°48·9′	1°45·9′W	T	104
Bolts	Somer	ST2332	51°5·2′	3°5·6′W	X	182
Bolt's Burn	Durham	NY9547	54°49·3′	2°4·2′W	W	87
Bolt's Cross	Oxon	SU7182	51°32·2′	0°58·2′W	X	175
Bolts Fm	Devon	SS7701	50°48·0′	3°44·3′W	FM	191
Bolts Fm	Essex	TQ9189	51°34·3′	0°45·8′E	FM	178
Boltshope	Durham	NY9446	54°48·8′	2°5·2′W	X	87
Boltshope Park	Durham	NY9447	54°49·3′	2°5·2′W	T	87
Bolts Law	Durham	NY9445	54°48·2′	2°5·2′W	H	87
Bolts Law	Northum	NY6981	55°7·6′	2°28·7′W	H	80
Bolt's Walls	Durham	NY9443	54°47·2′	2°5·2′W	X	87
Bolt Tail	Devon	SX6639	50°14·4′	3°52·4′W	X	202
Bolt Wood	Leic	SP8296	52°33·6′	0°47·0′W	F	141
Bolvean	Highld	NG2643	57°24·0′	6°33·2′W	X	23
Bolventor	Corn	SX1876	50°33·6′	4°33·8′W	T	201
Bolwick Hall	Norf	TG1924	52°46·4′	1°15·2′E	X	133,134
Bolyell	Angus	NO1865	56°46·4′	3°20·1′W	X	43
Bo'mains Fm	Falk	NS9979	55°59·9′	3°36·7′W	FM	65
Bomakelloch	Moray	NJ4145	57°29·7′	2°58·6′W	X	28
Bomarsund	Northum	NZ2784	55°9·2′	1°34·1′W	T	81
Bomber	Lancs	SD8348	53°55·9′	2°15·1′W	X	103
Bombers Fm	Brom	TQ4457	51°17·9′	0°4·3′E	FM	187
Bombers Fm	Surrey	TQ4147	51°12·5′	0°1·5′E	FM	187
Bombie	D & G	NX7150	54°49·9′	4°0·1′W	X	83,84
Bombie Glen	D & G	NX7150	54°49·9′	4°0·1′W	X	83,84
Bombie Hill	D & G	NX7149	54°49·4′	4°0·1′W	H	83,84
Bombie Hill	D & G	NY3287	55°10·6′	3°3·6′W	H	79
Bombo Burn	N Ayr	NS3149	55°42·6′	4°41·0′W	W	63
Bomby	Cumbr	NY5217	54°33·0′	2°44·1′W	T	90
Bomere Fm	Shrops	SJ4719	52°46·2′	2°46·7′W	FM	126
Bomere Heath	Shrops	SJ4719	52°46·2′	2°46·7′W	T	126
Bomere Pool	Shrops	SJ4908	52°40·3′	2°44·9′W	W	126
Bomere Wood	Shrops	SJ5007	52°39·7′	2°44·0′W	F	126
Bommertown	Devon	SS8126	51°1·5′	3°41·4′W	X	181
Bonallack Barton	Corn	SW7126	50°5·6′	5°11·7′W	X	203
Bonaly	C of Edin	NT2168	55°54·2′	3°15·4′W	T	66
Bonaly Country Park	C of Edin	NT2066	55°53·1′	3°16·3′W	X	66
Bonaly Resr	C of Edin	NT2066	55°53·1′	3°16·3′W	W	66
Bonaly Tower	C of Edin	NT2167	55°53·6′	3°15·4′W	X	66
Bonar Bridge	Highld	NH6191	57°53·5′	4°20·2′W	T	21
Bonas Hill Fm	Northum	NZ1478	55°6·0′	1°46·4′W	FM	88
Bonaveh	Arg & Bt	NR3995	56°4·9′	6°11·3′W	X	61
Bonawe	Arg & Bt	NN0033	56°27·1′	5°14·3′W	T	50
Bonawe Furnace	Arg & Bt	NN0131	56°26·0′	5°13·2′W	X	50
Bonber	N Yks	SD8956	54°0·2′	2°9·7′W	X	103
Bonbusk	Notts	SK5373	53°15·3′	1°11·9′W	X	120
Bonby	N Lincs	TA0015	53°37·6′	0°28·9′W	T	112
Bonby Carrs	N Lincs	SE9814	53°37·0′	0°30·7′W	X	112
Bonby Lodge	N Lincs	TA0216	53°38·1′	0°27·0′W	X	112
Bonby Top Fm	N Lincs	TA0115	53°37·5′	0°28·0′W	FM	112
Bonc	Wrex	SJ1637	52°55·7′	3°14·6′W	X	125
Boncath	Pemb	SN2038	52°0·9′	4°37·0′W	T	145
Bonc Fadog	I of Angl	SH4578	53°16·8′	4°19·1′W	X	114,115
Bonchester Bridge	Scot Bord	NT5811	55°23·7′	2°39·4′W	T	80
Bonchester Hill	Scot Bord	NT5911	55°23·7′	2°38·4′W	H	80
Bonchurch	I of W	SZ5777	50°35·6′	1°11·3′W	T	196
Bonc Twni	I of Angl	SH3766	53°10·2′	4°25·9′W	X	114
Boncyn Celyn	Powys	SJ0318	52°45·3′	3°25·8′W	H	125
Boncyn y Beddau	Powys	SO1098	52°34·6′	3°19·3′W	X	136
Boncyn y Waen-grogen	Denb	SJ1654	53°4·8′	3°14·8′W	X	116
Bond Ash Hill Fm	York	SE5748	53°55·7′	1°7·5′W	FM	105
Bond Beck	Lancs	SD7654	53°59·1′	2°21·5′W	W	103
Bondend	Glos	SO8615	51°50·2′	2°11·8′W	T	162
Bond End	Staffs	SK1418	52°45·8′	1°47·1′W	T	128
Bond Hall	Suff	TM1638	52°0·1′	1°9·2′E	X	169
Bondhay Common	Derby	SK5178	53°18·0′	1°13·7′W	X	120
Bondi Carrs	Northum	NU2801	55°18·4′	1°33·1′W	X	81
Bond Ings	N Yks	SE5032	53°47·2′	1°14·1′W	X	105
Bondleigh	Devon	SS6504	50°49·4′	3°54·6′W	T	191
Bondman Hays	Leic	SK4907	52°39·7′	1°16·1′W	T	140
Bonds	Lancs	SD4944	53°53·6′	2°46·1′W	T	102
Bond's Corner	Suff	TM2152	52°7·5′	1°14·1′E	X	156
Bond's Covert	Staffs	SJ8225	52°49·6′	2°15·6′W	F	127
Bond's Fm	Cambs	TL4991	52°30·0′	0°12·1′E	FM	143
Bond's Fm	Lancs	SD4248	53°55·7′	2°52·6′W	FM	102
Bond's Fm	Suff	TM2167	52°15·6′	1°14·7′E	FM	156
Bond's Green	Heref	SO3554	52°11·1′	2°56·6′W	X	148,149
Bondwood Fm	Derby	SK3223	52°48·5′	1°31·1′W	FM	128
Bone	Corn	SW4632	50°8·3′	5°32·9′W	X	203
Bonehayne	Devon	SY2194	50°44·6′	3°6·8′W	X	192,193
Bonehill	Devon	SX7277	50°35·0′	3°48·1′W	T	191
Bone Hill	Herts	TL1204	51°43·6′	0°21·6′W	X	166
Bonehill	Staffs	SK1902	52°37·2′	1°42·8′W	T	139
Bonehill Down	Devon	SX7377	50°35·0′	3°47·3′W	H	191
Bonehill Fm	Derby	SK2934	52°54·4′	1°33·7′W	FM	128
Bone Hill Fm	Lancs	SD4346	53°54·7′	2°51·6′W	FM	102
Bonehill Fm	Staffs	SK1903	52°37·7′	1°42·8′W	FM	139
Bonemill Br	Shrops	SJ7706	52°39·3′	2°20·0′W	X	127
Bonemills Fm	Peterb	TF0401	52°36·0′	0°27·5′W	FM	141
Bonerbo	Fife	NO5407	56°15·5′	2°44·1′W	X	59
Bonerick	D & G	NX9076	55°4·2′	3°42·9′W	X	84
Bone's Barn	Norf	TF7700	52°34·4′	0°37·1′E	X	144
Bone's Belt	Norf	TF8743	52°57·3′	0°47·4′E	F	132
Bone's Fm	Lincs	TF0944	52°59·2′	0°22·2′W	FM	130
Bones Plantation	D & G	NX0946	54°46·6′	4°57·8′W	F	82
Bo'ness	Falk	NS9981	56°0·9′	3°36·8′W	T	65
Bo'ness & Kinneil Rly	Falk	NS9981	56°0·9′	3°36·8′W	X	65
Bonfail	Moray	NJ4138	57°26·0′	2°58·5′W	X	28
Bonfield	Fife	NO4516	56°20·2′	2°52·9′W	X	59
Bonfield Fm	E Yorks	TA1547	53°54·6′	0°14·5′W	FM	107
Bonfield Ghyll	N Yks	SE6094	54°20·5′	1°4·2′W	X	94,100
Bonfield Gill	N Yks	SE6192	54°19·4′	1°3·3′W	W	94,100
Bonfire Hall	Cumbr	SD4793	54°20·0′	2°48·5′W	X	97
Bonfire Hill	Dorset	SU1213	50°55·2′	1°49·4′W	X	195
Bonfire Hill	Worcs	SO6467	52°18·2′	2°31·3′W	X	138,149
Bonham	Wilts	ST7733	51°6·0′	2°19·3′W	X	183
Bonhams	Hants	SU5810	50°53·4′	1°10·1′W	X	196
Bonham's Fm	Hants	SU7441	51°10·0′	0°56·1′W	FM	186
Bonhard	Angus	NO5940	56°33·3′	2°39·6′W	X	54
Bonhard	Angus	NO5968	56°48·4′	2°39·8′W	X	44
Bonhard Ho	Pth & Kin	NO1425	56°24·8′	3°23·2′W	X	53,58
Bonharry	Aberd	NO5973	56°51·1′	2°39·9′W	X	44
Bonhill	W Dunb	NS4079	55°58·9′	4°33·4′W	T	64
Bonhill Top	Devon	SS6848	51°13·2′	3°53·0′W	X	180
Bonhunt	Essex	TL5133	51°58·7′	0°12·3′E	X	167
Bonibrik	Shetld	HT9636	60°6·8′	2°3·8′W	X	4
Bonidale	Shetld	HU5064	60°21·7′	1°5·1′W	X	2,3
Boningale	Shrops	SJ8102	52°37·2′	2°16·4′W	X	127
Boningale Manor	Shrops	SJ8202	52°37·2′	2°15·5′W	X	127
Bonis Hall	Ches	SJ9079	53°18·7′	2°8·6′W	X	118
Bonjedward	Scot Bord	NT6523	55°30·2′	2°32·8′W	X	74
Bonjedward Ho	Scot Bord	NT6522	55°29·7′	2°32·8′W	X	74
Bonkle	N Lanak	NS8356	55°47·2′	3°51·5′W	T	65,72
Bonkyl Lodge	Scot Bord	NT7957	55°48·6′	2°19·7′W	X	67,74
Bonlee Hill	Aberd	NJ4007	57°9·3′	2°59·1′W	H	37
Bonnanhill	S Lanak	NS7242	55°39·5′	4°1·6′W	X	71
Bonnavoulin	Highld	NM5653	56°36·6′	5°58·1′W	T	47
Bonner Hill	Notts	SK6148	53°1·8′	1°5·0′W	X	129
Bonners	Herts	TL0716	51°50·2′	0°26·4′W	X	166
Bonners Fm	Suff	TM3678	52°21·2′	1°28·3′E	FM	156
Bonners Leaze Fm	Somer	ST3611	50°53·9′	2°54·2′W	FM	193
Bonnethill	Moray	NJ4553	57°34·1′	2°54·7′W	X	28,29
Bonnet Knowe	Shetld	HU3968	60°23·9′	1°17·0′W	X	2,3
Bonnet Plantn	Scot Bord	NT5548	55°43·7′	2°42·6′W	F	73
Bonnetts	Surrey	TQ1637	51°7·5′	0°20·2′W	A	187
Bonnie Doune	Aberd	NK0364	57°40·2′	1°56·5′W	X	30
Bonnie Hill Fm	N Yks	NZ5705	54°26·5′	1°6·8′W	FM	93
Bonnieton	E Ayr	NS5435	55°35·5′	4°18·6′W	X	70
Bonning Gate	Cumbr	SD4895	54°21·1′	2°47·6′W	T	97
Bonnington	C of Edin	NT1169	55°54·6′	3°25·0′W	T	65
Bonnington	E Loth	NT5583	56°2·5′	2°42·9′W	X	66
Bonnington	Kent	TR0535	51°4·9′	0°56·0′E	T	179,189
Bonnington	Pth & Kin	NO1847	56°36·7′	3°19·7′W	X	53
Bonnington	Scot Bord	NT2538	55°38·0′	3°11·0′W	T	73
Bonnington Fm	Kent	TR2553	51°14·1′	1°13·8′E	FM	179
Bonnington Ho	C of Edin	NT1169	55°54·6′	3°25·0′W	X	65
Bonnington Linn	S Lanak	NS8840	55°38·7′	3°46·3′W	W	71,72
Bonnington Mains	C of Edin	NT1269	55°54·6′	3°24·0′W	X	65
Bonnington Mains	S Lanak	NS8941	55°39·2′	3°45·4′W	X	71,72
Bonningtons	Herts	TL4013	51°48·1′	0°2·2′E	X	167
Bonnington Smiddy	Angus	NO5739	56°32·7′	2°41·5′W	T	54
Bonn Knowes	Shetld	HU2546	60°12·1′	1°32·4′W	X	4
Bonnybank	Fife	NO3503	56°13·2′	3°2·4′W	T	59
Bonny Blacks	Lancs	SD8446	53°54·8′	2°14·2′W	X	103
Bonny Braes	D & G	NX0669	54°58·9′	5°1·5′W	X	82
Bonnybridge	Falk	NS8280	56°0·2′	3°53·1′W	T	65
Bonny Burn	D & G	NX4074	55°2·3′	4°29·8′W	W	77
Bonny Cross	Devon	SS9524	51°0·6′	3°29·4′W	X	181
Bonnyfield	Falk	NS8180	56°0·1′	3°54·1′W	X	65
Bonnyfleeces	Aberd	NO5881	56°55·4′	2°40·9′W	H	44
Bonny Fm	Cumbr	NX9920	54°34·2′	3°33·3′W	FM	89
Bonnygate	Cumbr	NY7411	54°29·9′	2°23·7′W	X	91
Bonnygate Fm	N Yks	SE6172	54°8·7′	1°3·6′W	FM	100
Bonny Grove Fm	Midd	NZ5213	54°30·8′	1°11·4′W	FM	93
Bonnyhill	Cumbr	NY1133	54°41·3′	3°22·4′W	X	89
Bonnyhill Fm	Falk	NS8478	55°59·1′	3°51·1′W	FM	65
Bonnykelly	Aberd	NJ8553	57°34·3′	2°14·6′W	T	30
Bonny Lands	Heref	SO2839	52°2·9′	3°2·6′W	X	161
Bonnyleigh Hill	Somer	ST7950	51°15·2′	2°17·7′W	H	183
Bonnyrigg and Lasswade	Midlo	NT3065	55°52·6′	3°6·7′W	T	66
Bonnyrigg Hall	Northum	NY7669	55°1·1′	2°22·1′W	X	86,87
Bonnyside	Aberd	NJ5300	57°5·6′	2°46·1′W	X	37
Bonnyton	Aberd	NJ6730	57°21·8′	2°32·5′W	T	29
Bonnyton	Aberd	NJ7463	57°39·6′	2°25·7′W	X	29
Bonnyton	Aberd	NJ8927	57°20·3′	2°10·5′W	X	38
Bonnyton	Angus	NO3338	56°32·0′	3°4·9′W	T	53
Bonnyton	Angus	NO4542	56°34·3′	2°53·3′W	X	54
Bonnyton	Angus	NO6655	56°41·4′	2°32·9′W	T	54
Bonnyton	E Ayr	NS4138	55°36·8′	4°31·0′W	T	70
Bonnyton	E Ayr	NS4515	55°24·5′	4°26·5′W	X	70
Bonnyton	E Renf	NS5553	55°45·2′	4°18·2′W	X	64
Bonnyton	Fife	NO4106	56°14·8′	2°56·7′W	X	59
Bonnyton	Fife	NT0689	56°5·3′	3°30·2′W	X	65
Bonnytonhill	Aberd	NJ8964	57°40·2′	2°10·6′W	X	30
Bonnyton Ho	Angus	NO5839	56°32·7′	2°40·5′W	X	54
Bonnyton Moor	E Renf	NS5452	55°44·6′	4°19·1′W	X	64
Bonnytoun Fm	W Loth	NT0078	55°59·3′	3°35·7′W	FM	65
Bonnytounside	Falk	NS9978	55°59·3′	3°36·7′W	X	65
Bonnytown	Fife	NO5412	56°18·1′	2°44·2′W	X	59
Bonnyview	Pth & Kin	NN9818	56°20·9′	3°38·6′W	X	58
Bonny Water	Falk	NS8280	56°0·2′	3°53·1′W	W	65
Bonny Wood	Suff	TM0751	52°7·3′	1°1·8′E	F	155
Bonsall	Derby	SK2758	53°7·3′	1°35·4′W	T	119
Bonsall Lane Fm	Derby	SK2559	53°7·9′	1°37·2′W	FM	119
Bonsall Mines	Derby	SK2657	53°6·8′	1°36·3′W	A	119
Bonsall Moor	Derby	SK2559	53°7·9′	1°37·2′W	X	119
Bonscale	Cumbr	NY4520	54°34·6′	2°50·6′W	X	90
Bonscale Pike	Cumbr	NY4520	54°34·6′	2°50·6′W	H	90
Bonscombe	Dorset	SY4892	50°43·8′	2°43·8′W	X	193
Bonsdale Fm	Lincs	SK8936	53°26·4′	0°40·1′W	FM	112
Bonsey's Fm	Surrey	TQ0161	51°20·6′	0°32·6′W	FM	176,186
Bons Fm	Essex	TQ5096	51°38·6′	0°10·5′E	FM	167,177
Bonshaw	E Ayr	NS3744	55°40·0′	4°35·1′W	X	63,70
Bonshawside	D & G	NY2372	55°2·4′	3°11·9′W	X	85
Bonshaw Tower	D & G	NY2472	55°2·5′	3°10·9′W	A	85
Bonskeid Ho	Pth & Kin	NN8961	56°43·9′	3°48·4′W	X	43
Bonsley Common	Dorset	ST8208	50°52·5′	2°15·0′W	F	194
Bonson	Somer	ST2240	51°9·5′	3°6·5′W	T	182
Bonson Wood Fm	Somer	ST2241	51°10·0′	3°6·6′W	FM	182
Bont	Monm	SO3819	51°52·2′	2°53·6′W	X	161
Bont	Powys	SO2422	51°53·7′	3°5·9′W	X	161
Bontddu	Gwyn	SH6618	52°44·8′	3°58·7′W	T	124
Bont Dolgadfan	Powys	SH8800	52°35·4′	3°38·8′W	T	135,136
Bont-faen	I of Angl	SH3768	53°11·3′	4°26·0′W	X	114
Bont Fawr	Carm	SN7125	51°54·8′	3°52·1′W	T	146,160
Bont Fechan	Gwyn	SH4637	52°54·7′	4°17·0′W	X	123
Bont Fm	Carm	SN4206	51°44·1′	4°16·9′W	FM	159
Bont Fm	I of Angl	SH4168	53°11·4′	4°22·4′W	FM	114,115
Bont-garreg	Conwy	SH9064	53°10·0′	3°38·3′W	X	116
Bont-Garreg	Denb	SJ0961	53°8·5′	3°21·2′W	X	116
Bont-goch or Elerch	Cered	SN6886	52°27·6′	3°56·2′W	T	135
Bonthorne Fm	Staffs	SK1817	52°45·3′	1°43·6′W	FM	128
Bonthorpe	Lincs	TF4872	53°13·7′	0°13·4′E	T	122
Bontnewydd	Cered	SN6165	52°16·2′	4°1·8′W	X	135
Bont-newydd	Conwy	SH7567	53°11·4′	3°51·8′W	X	115
Bont-newydd	Conwy	SJ0170	53°13·3′	3°28·6′W	T	116
Bontnewydd	Gwyn	SH4859	53°6·6′	4°15·8′W	T	115,123
Bont Newydd	Gwyn	SH6672	53°13·9′	4°0·1′W	A	115
Bont Newydd	Gwyn	SH7140	52°56·8′	3°54·8′W	X	124
Bont Newydd	Gwyn	SH7720	52°46·1′	3°49·0′W	X	124
Bont-newydd	Powys	SN9885	52°27·4′	3°29·7′W	X	136
Bontuchel	Denb	SJ0857	53°6·4′	3°22·1′W	T	116
Bont-y-Gwyddel	Conwy	SH9571	53°13·8′	3°34·0′W	X	116
Bonvilles Fm	Essex	TQ7790	51°35·1′	0°33·7′E	FM	178

Bonvils	Dorset	SY9676	50°35·3'	2°3·0'W	X	195
Bonvilston	V of Glam	ST0674	51°27·7'	3°20·8'W	T	170
Bonw	I of Angl	SH3190	53°23·0'	4°32·1'W	X	114
Bonwm	Denb	SJ1043	52°58·9'	3°20·0'W	X	125
Bonwycks Place	W Susx	TQ2337	51°7·4'	0°14·2'W	X	187
Bonxa Hill	Shetld	HU3927	60°1·8'	1°17·5'W	H	4
Bonyalva	Corn	SX3059	50°24·6'	4°23·2'W	X	201
Bon-y-maen	Swan	SS6895	51°38·5'	3°54·1'W	T	159
Bon-yr-on	Denb	SJ0646	53°0·4'	3°23·7'W	X	116
Bonython Manor	Corn	SW6921	50°2·9'	5°13·2'W	X	203
Bonython Plantns	Corn	SW6920	50°2·4'	5°13·2'W	F	203
Booby Dingle	Heref	SO3036	52°1·3'	3°0·8'W	X	161
Booby's Bay	Corn	SW8575	50°32·4'	5°1·7'W	W	200
Boode	Devon	SS5038	51°7·5'	4°8·2'W	T	180
Boode Fm	Devon	SS5423	50°59·5'	4°4·4'W	FM	180
Booden Fm	Staffs	SJ8619	52°46·3'	2°12·0'W	FM	127
Boohay	Devon	SX8952	50°21·7'	3°33·3'W	X	202
Booilushag	I of M	SC4890	54°17·2'	4°19·7'W	X	95
Bookan	Orkney	HY2814	59°0·7'	3°14·7'W	X	6
Booker	Bucks	SU8391	51°36·9'	0°47·7'W	T	175
Booker Common	Bucks	SU8391	51°36·9'	0°47·7'W	F	175
Bookers	Lancs	SD7245	53°54·3'	2°25·2'W	X	103
Booker's Fm	W Susx	TQ2523	50°59·8'	0°12·7'W	FM	198
Bookers Lee	Surrey	TQ0436	51°7·1'	0°30·5'W	X	186
Bookham	Dorset	ST7004	50°50·3'	2°25·2'W	T	194
Bookham Lodge	Surrey	TQ1257	51°18·3'	0°23·2'W	X	187
Book Hurst	Surrey	TQ0739	51°8·6'	0°27·8'W	F	187
Bookilber Barn	N Yks	SD8559	54°1·9'	2°13·3'W	X	103
Bookil Gill Beck	N Yks	SD8460	54°2·4'	2°14·2'W	W	98
Books, The	Devon	SX6741	50°15·5'	3°51·6'W	X	202
Booley	Shrops	SJ5725	52°49·5'	2°37·9'W	X	126
Booleybank	Shrops	SJ5725	52°49·5'	2°37·9'W	T	126
Booley Ho	Shrops	SJ5725	52°49·5'	2°37·9'W	X	126
Boolroad	Aberd	NJ8530	57°21·9'	2°14·5'W	X	30
Boomer	Somer	ST2732	51°5·2'	3°2·2'W	X	182
Boon	Scot Bord	NT5745	55°42·0'	2°40·6'W	T	73,74
Boonatown	Orkney	HY6524	59°6·4'	2°36·2'W	X	5
Boondatoon	Orkney	HY5311	58°59·3'	2°48·6'W	X	6
Boondreigh Burn	Scot Bord	NT5951	55°45·3'	2°38·8'W	W	66,73
Boondreigh Burn	Scot Bord	NT6052	55°45·8'	2°37·8'W	W	67,74
Boondreigh Water	Scot Bord	NT5646	55°42·6'	2°41·6'W	W	73
Boon Hill	Cumbr	NY5558	54°55·1'	2°41·7'W	X	86
Boon Hill	Scot Bord	NT5746	55°42·6'	2°40·6'W	H	73,74
Boon Hill	Staffs	SJ8050	53°3·1'	2°17·5'W	T	118
Boonhill Common	N Yks	SE6690	54°18·3'	0°58·7'W	X	94,100
Boon Hills Wood	Notts	SK5369	53°13·2'	1°12·0'W	F	120
Boonies Cottage	D & G	NY3089	55°11·7'	3°5·5'W	X	79
Boonraw Burn	Scot Bord	NT5017	55°26·9'	2°47·0'W	W	79
Boon's Fm	Cambs	TL4687	52°27·9'	0°9·4'E	FM	143
Boon's Fm	Essex	TL7827	51°55·0'	0°35·7'E	FM	167
Boon's Fm	Somer	ST2720	50°58·7'	3°2·0'W	FM	193
Boon's Heath	Norf	TM4692	52°28·4'	1°37·7'E	X	134
Boonshill	E Susx	TQ9323	50°58·7'	0°45·4'E	X	189
Boonslie	E Loth	NT6670	55°55·6'	2°32·2'W	X	67
Boonslie Shank	E Loth	NT6671	55°56·1'	2°32·2'W	X	67
Boons Park	Kent	TQ4749	51°13·5'	0°6·7'E	X	188
Boon Wood	Cumbr	NY0021	54°34·7'	3°32·4'W	X	89
Boonwood	Cumbr	NY0604	54°25·6'	3°26·5'W	X	89
Boon Wood	N Yks	SE7563	54°3·7'	0°50·8'W	F	100
Boon Woods	N Yks	SE6586	54°16·2'	0°59·7'W	X	94,100
Boor	Highld	NG8481	57°46·3'	5°37·5'W	X	19
Boor Hill	Highld	NG8381	57°46·2'	5°38·5'W	H	19
Boorley Green	Hants	SU5014	50°55·6'	1°16·9'W	T	196
Boor Rocks	Highld	NG8482	57°46·8'	5°37·5'W	X	19
Boosbeck	Red & Cl	NZ6617	54°32·9'	0°58·4'W	T	94
Boose's Green	Essex	TL8430	51°56·5'	0°41·0'E	T	168
Boosley Grange	Staffs	SK0662	53°9·5'	1°54·2'W	X	119
Boostagill	N Yks	SD7859	54°1·8'	2°19·7'W	X	103
Booston Wood	Ches	SJ3878	53°18·0'	2°55·4'W	X	117
Boot	Cumbr	NY1701	54°24·1'	3°16·3'W	T	89,90
Boot Fm	W Berks	SU5663	51°22·0'	1°11·3'W	FM	174
Booth	Cald	SE0427	53°44·6'	1°55·9'W	T	104
Booth	Orkney	ND3389	58°47·3'	3°9·1'W	X	7
Booth	Staffs	SK0427	52°50·7'	1°56·0'W	T	128
Boot Hall	Staffs	SJ9457	53°6·8'	2°5·0'W	X	118
Bootham Stray	York	SE5954	53°59·0'	1°5·6'W	X	105
Boothay Fm	Derby	SK1839	52°57·1'	1°43·5'W	FM	128
Booth Bank	Ches	SJ7285	53°21·9'	2°24·8'W	T	109
Booth Bank	Kirk	SE0613	53°37·1'	1°54·1'W	X	110
Boothbed Fm	Ches	SJ7571	53°14·4'	2°22·1'W	FM	118
Booth Bridge	N Yks	SD9147	53°55·0'	2°7·8'W	T	103
Boothby	Cumbr	NY5562	54°57·3'	2°41·7'W	X	86
Boothby Graffoe	Lincs	SK9859	53°7·4'	0°31·7'W	T	121
Boothby Graffoe Heath	Lincs	SK9959	53°7·4'	0°30·8'W	X	121
Boothby Graffoe Low Fields	Lincs	SK9658	53°6·9'	0°33·5'W	X	121
Boothby Grange	Lincs	TF4868	53°11·5'	0°13·2'E	X	122
Boothby Great Wood	Lincs	SK9531	52°52·3'	0°34·9'W	F	130
Boothby Hall	Lincs	TF4868	53°11·5'	0°13·2'E	X	122
Boothby Little Wood	Lincs	SK9731	52°52·3'	0°33·1'W	F	130
Boothby Pagnell	Lincs	SK9730	52°51·8'	0°33·1'W	T	130
Boothen	C of Stoke	SJ8744	52°59·8'	2°11·2'W	T	118
Boothferry	E Yorks	SE7326	53°43·8'	0°53·2'W	T	105,106
Boothferry Br	E Yorks	SE7326	53°43·8'	0°53·2'W	X	105,106
Booth Fm	Derby	SK0568	53°12·8'	1°55·1'W	FM	119
Booth Fm, The	Staffs	SK0045	53°0·4'	1°59·6'W	FM	119,128
Boothgate	Derby	SK3749	53°2·5'	1°26·5'W	T	119
Booth Green	Ches	SJ9281	53°19·8'	2°6·8'W	T	109
Booth Ho	Brad	SE0534	53°48·4'	1°55·0'W	X	104
Booth Holme	Cumbr	SD1991	54°18·7'	3°14·3'W	X	96
Booth House Fm	N Lincs	SE9219	53°39·8'	0°36·0'W	FM	112
Boothlands Fm	Surrey	TQ2140	51°9·0'	0°15·8'W	FM	187
Booth of Toft	Shetld	HU4376	60°28·2'	1°12·6'W	T	2,3
Boothorpe	Leic	SK3117	52°45·2'	1°32·0'W	X	128
Boothouse Fm	Ches	SJ5862	53°9·5'	2°37·3'W	FM	117
Boothroyd	Kirk	SE2321	53°41·3'	1°38·7'W	T	104
Boothroyd Fm	Cald	SD9630	53°46·2'	2°3·2'W	FM	103
Boothroyd Wood	Kirk	SE1812	53°36·5'	1°43·3'W	F	110
Booths	Shetld	HP6414	60°48·5'	0°48·9'W	X	1
Booths Burn	D & G	NY2287	55°10·5'	3°13·1'W	W	79

Boothsdale	Ches	SJ5367	53°12·1'	2°41·8'W	T	117
Booth's Fm	Notts	SK7945	53°0·0'	0°49·0'W	FM	129
Booth's Fm	Warr	SJ6484	53°21·3'	2°32·0'W	FM	109
Booths Hall	Ches	SJ7677	53°17·6'	2°21·2'W	X	118
Booth's Hall	Staffs	SK0148	53°2·0'	1°58·7'W	X	119
Booths Mere	Ches	SJ7678	53°18·1'	2°21·2'W	W	118
Boothstown	Salf	SD7200	53°30·0'	2°24·9'W	T	109
Boothtown	Cald	SE0826	53°44·1'	1°52·3'W	T	104
Boothville	Northnts	SP7864	52°16·3'	0°51·0'W	T	152
Boothwaite Nook	Cumbr	SD2186	54°16·1'	3°12·4'W	X	96
Booth Wood	Cald	SE0316	53°38·7'	1°56·9'W	T	110
Booth Wood Resr	Cald	SE0216	53°38·7'	1°57·8'W	W	110
Bootle	Cumbr	SD1088	54°17·0'	3°22·5'W	T	96
Bootle	Sefton	SJ3394	53°26·6'	3°0·1'W	T	108
Bootle Fell	Cumbr	SD1388	54°17·1'	3°19·8'W	X	96
Bootle Sta	Cumbr	SD0989	54°17·6'	3°23·5'W	X	96
Bootle Stone	Cumbr	SD1570	54°7·4'	3°17·6'W	X	96
Boot of Mickle Fell	Durham	NY8124	54°36·9'	2°17·2'W	X	91,92
Booton	Norf	TG1122	52°45·5'	1°8·0'E	T	133
Booton Hall	Norf	TG1122	52°45·5'	1°8·0'E	X	133
Boot's Br	Cambs	TL4491	52°30·1'	0°7·7'E	X	142,143
Boots Fm	Warw	SP4371	52°20·4'	1°21·7'W	FM	140
Boots Green	Ches	SJ7572	53°14·9'	2°22·1'W	T	118
Boot Street	Suff	TM2248	52°5·4'	1°14·8'E	T	169
Booze	N Yks	NZ0102	54°25·1'	1°58·7'W	T	92
Booze Moor	N Yks	NZ0204	54°26·1'	1°57·7'W	X	92
Booze Wood	Durham	NY9819	54°34·2'	2°1·4'W	X	92
Bopeep Fm	E Susx	TQ4905	50°49·7'	0°7·3'E	FM	199
Bo-Peep Fm	Oxon	SP4834	52°0·4'	1°17·6'W	FM	151
Boquhan	Stir	NS5387	56°3·5'	4°21·2'W	T	57
Boquhan	Stir	NS6794	56°7·5'	4°7·9'W	X	57
Boquhan Burn	Stir	NS6489	56°4·7'	4°10·7'W	W	57
Boquhan Burn	Stir	NS6693	56°6·9'	4°8·9'W	W	57
Boquhan Glen	Stir	NS5486	56°2·9'	4°20·2'W	X	57
Boquhan Home Fm	Stir	NS6795	56°8·0'	4°8·0'W	FM	57
Boquhan Old Ho	Stir	NS5487	56°3·5'	4°20·2'W	X	57
Boquhapple	Stir	NN6500	56°10·7'	4°10·0'W	T	57
Boquio	Corn	SW6733	50°9·3'	5°15·3'W	T	203
Bora Chnoc	Highld	NG8918	57°12·5'	5°29·2'W	H	33
Boram Home Fm	Glos	SP1933	51°59·9'	1°43·0'W	FM	151
Boraston	Shrops	SO6169	52°19·3'	2°33·9'W	T	138
Boraston Dale	Shrops	SO6170	52°19·8'	2°33·9'W	T	138
Boray	Orkney	HY4421	59°4·6'	2°58·1'W	X	5,6
Borbg	N Eil	NF7650	57°25·7'	7°23·5'W	X	22
Borbles Hall	Lancs	SD5054	53°59·0'	2°45·3'W	X	102
Borcombe Fm	Devon	SY1991	50°43·0'	3°8·5'W	FM	192,193
Bord a Dubh	Arg & Bt	NR7231	55°31·4'	5°36·3'W	X	68
Bordadubh Water	Arg & Bt	NR7331	55°31·5'	5°35·4'W	W	68
Bordean Ho	Hants	SU6924	51°0·9'	1°0·6'W	X	197
Bordeaux Fms	Essex	TL5141	52°3·0'	0°12·5'E	FM	154
Borde Hill	W Susx	TQ3226	51°1·3'	0°6·7'W	X	187,198
Borden	Kent	TQ8862	51°19·8'	0°42·3'E	T	178
Borden	W Susx	SU8224	51°0·8'	0°49·5'W	T	197
Borden Hill	Kent	TQ8561	51°19·3'	0°39·7'E	X	178
Borden Wood	W Susx	SU8325	51°1·3'	0°48·6'W	F	186,197
Border	Angus	NO6048	56°37·6'	2°38·7'W	X	54
Border	Cumbr	NY1654	54°52·7'	3°18·1'W	T	85
Border	Somer	ST7337	51°8·1'	2°22·8'W	X	183
Border End	Cumbr	NY2202	54°24·7'	3°11·7'W	X	89,90
Border Fm	Wrex	SJ3953	53°4·5'	2°54·2'W	FM	117
Border Ho	Ches	SJ3866	53°11·5'	2°55·3'W	X	117
Border Range	Cumbr	NY2855	54°53·3'	3°6·9'W	X	85
Borderrigg	Cumbr	NY5775	55°4·3'	2°40·0'W	X	86
Borders	E Susx	TQ6925	51°0·2'	0°24·9'E	X	188,199
Borderside	Aberd	NJ8346	57°30·5'	2°16·6'W	X	29,30
Borderside	Cumbr	SD4190	54°18·4'	2°54·0'W	X	96,97
Border Side	Lancs	SD5854	53°59·1'	2°38·0'W	X	102
Borders Wood	Notts	SK6632	52°53·1'	1°0·7'W	F	129
Border View Fm	Derby	SK3379	53°18·7'	1°29·9'W	FM	119
Bordesley	Birm	SP0886	52°28·5'	1°52·5'W	T	139
Bordesley Green	Birm	SP1086	52°28·5'	1°50·8'W	T	139
Bordesley Hall	Worcs	SP0470	52°19·9'	1°56·1'W	X	139
Bordesley Park Fm	Worcs	SP0469	52°19·4'	1°56·1'W	FM	139
Bordeville	Lincs	TF0308	52°39·8'	0°28·2'W	X	141
Bordie	Fife	NS9586	56°3·6'	3°40·7'W	X	65
Bordi Knowe	Shetld	HP5804	60°43·2'	0°55·7'W	X	1
Bordlands	Scot Bord	NT1546	55°42·3'	3°20·7'W	T	72
Bordley	N Yks	SD9464	54°4·6'	2°5·1'W	T	98
Bordley Beck	N Yks	SD9463	54°4·0'	2°5·1'W	W	98
Bordley Hall	N Yks	SD9463	54°4·0'	2°5·1'W	X	98
Bòrd Mòr	Arg & Bt	NR7533	55°32·6'	5°33·6'W	H	68,69
Bordon	Hants	SU7935	51°6·8'	0°51·9'W	T	186
Bordon Hill	Warw	SP1754	52°11·3'	1°44·7'W	H	151
Bordriggs	Cumbr	SD2287	54°16·6'	3°11·5'W	X	96
Borea	Corn	SW4935	50°10·0'	5°30·5'W	X	203
Boreas Hill	E Yorks	TA1825	53°42·7'	0°12·3'W	X	107,113
Boreatton Ho	Shrops	SJ4122	52°47·8'	2°52·1'W	X	126
Boreatton Moss	Shrops	SJ4122	52°47·8'	2°52·1'W	F	126
Boreatton Park	Shrops	SJ4023	52°48·3'	2°53·0'W	X	126
Boredale	Cumbr	NY4217	54°32·9'	2°53·4'W	X	90
Boredale Beck	Cumbr	NY4217	54°32·9'	2°53·4'W	W	90
Boredale House	Cumbr	NY4015	54°31·9'	2°55·2'W	X	90
Boreham	Essex	TL7509	51°45·4'	0°32·5'E	T	167
Boreham	Wilts	ST8944	51°11·9'	2°9·9'W	T	183
Boreham Down	Wilts	ST9047	51°13·6'	2°8·2'W	X	184
Boreham Hall	Essex	TL7508	51°44·8'	0°32·5'E	X	167
Boreham House	Essex	TL7409	51°45·4'	0°31·7'E	A	167
Boreham Street	E Susx	TQ6611	50°52·7'	0°22·0'E	T	199
Borehamwood	Herts	TQ1997	51°39·8'	0°16·4'W	T	166,176
Boreham Wood	Wilts	SU1365	51°23·3'	1°48·4'W	F	173
Borehouse Manor Fm	Suff	TL9541	52°2·2'	0°51·0'E	FM	155
Bo-Rèidh	N Eil	NG0385	57°45·6'	6°59·2'W	X	18
Boreland	D & G	NX3558	54°53·6'	4°33·9'W	X	83
Boreland	D & G	NX3967	54°58·6'	4°30·5'W	X	83
Boreland	D & G	NX7263	54°57·0'	3°59·5'W	X	83,84
Boreland	D & G	NX8486	55°9·5'	3°48·8'W	X	78
Boreland	D & G	NX8779	55°5·8'	3°45·8'W	X	84
Boreland	D & G	NX9970	55°1·1'	3°34·4'W	X	84
Boreland	D & G	NY0695	55°14·7'	3°28·3'W	X	78
Boreland	D & G	NY1791	55°12·6'	3°17·8'W	T	79

Boreland	E Ayr	NS4013	55°23·3'	4°31·1'W	X	70
Boreland	Fife	NT3094	56°8·3'	3°7·1'W	T	59
Boreland	Pth & Kin	NN7144	56°34·5'	4°5·5'W	X	51,52
Boreland	Pth & Kin	NN8517	56°20·1'	3°51·2'W	X	58
Boreland	Pth & Kin	NN8809	56°15·9'	3°48·1'W	X	58
Boreland	Pth & Kin	NO2136	56°30·8'	3°16·6'W	X	53
Boreland	Pth & Kin	NT0898	56°10·2'	3°28·5'W	X	58
Boreland	S Ayr	NX2781	55°5·9'	4°42·3'W	X	76
Boreland	Scot Bord	NT2548	55°43·4'	3°11·2'W	X	73
Boreland	S Lanak	NS8340	55°38·6'	3°51·1'W	X	71,72
Boreland Bar	D & G	NX6450	54°49·8'	4°6·6'W	X	83
Boreland Burn	D & G	NX5951	54°50·3'	4°11·3'W	W	83
Boreland Burn	D & G	NX9260	54°55·6'	3°40·7'W	W	84
Boreland Burn	D & G	NY1891	55°12·6'	3°16·9'W	W	79
Boreland Fell	D & G	NX3459	54°54·1'	4°34·9'W	H	82
Boreland Fm	D & G	NX6953	54°51·5'	4°2·0'W	FM	83,84
Boreland Hill	D & G	NX9460	54°55·7'	3°38·8'W	H	84
Boreland Hill	Wilts	SU1137	51°8·2'	1°50·2'W	H	184
Boreland Hill Cottage	D & G	NX9260	54°55·6'	3°40·7'W	X	84
Boreland Ho	D & G	NY1791	55°12·6'	3°17·8'W	X	79
Boreland Ho	Stir	NN5534	56°28·8'	4°20·8'W	X	51
Boreland Motte	D & G	NX6970	55°0·7'	4°2·5'W	A	77,84
Boreland of Anwoth	D & G	NX5855	54°52·4'	4°12·4'W	X	83
Boreland of Borgue	D & G	NX6451	54°50·4'	4°6·6'W	X	83
Boreland of Colvend	D & G	NX8753	54°51·8'	3°45·2'W	X	84
Boreland-of-Dryfe	D & G	NY1791	55°12·6'	3°17·8'W	X	79
Boreland of Girthon	D & G	NX5851	54°50·3'	4°12·2'W	X	83
Boreland of Kelton	D & G	NX7857	54°53·8'	3°53·7'W	X	84
Boreland of Longcastle	D & G	NX3847	54°47·8'	4°30·8'W	X	83
Boreland of Parton	D & G	NX6980	55°6·1'	4°2·8'W	X	77
Boreland of Southwick	D & G	NX9260	54°55·6'	3°40·7'W	X	84
Boreley	Worcs	SO8265	52°17·2'	2°15·4'W	T	138,150
Boreley Ho	Worcs	SO8264	52°16·7'	2°15·4'W	X	138,150
Borelick	Pth & Kin	NN9539	56°32·1'	3°42·0'W	X	52,53
Borenich	Pth & Kin	NN8360	56°43·3'	3°54·3'W	X	43,52
Bore Place	Kent	TQ5049	51°13·5'	0°9·3'E	X	188
Boreraig	Highld	NG6116	57°10·6'	5°56·8'W	X	32
Boreray	N Eil	NA1505	57°52·4'	8°29·3'W	X	18
Boreray	N Eil	NF8581	57°42·8'	7°16·9'W	X	18
Boresford Fm	Heref	SO3469	52°19·1'	2°57·7'W	FM	137,148
Bore Stane	C of Edin	NT1459	55°49·3'	3°21·9'W	X	65,72
Boreston	Devon	SX7653	50°22·1'	3°44·2'W	X	202
Borestone	Stir	NS7990	56°5·5'	3°56·2'W	T	57
Borestone Cottage	Pth & Kin	NN9718	56°20·8'	3°39·5'W	X	58
Bore, The	Orkney	HY4956	59°23·5'	2°53·4'W	W	5
Boreton	Shrops	SJ5106	52°39·2'	2°43·1'W	X	126
Boretree Tarn	Cumbr	SD3587	54°16·7'	2°59·5'W	W	96,97
Borewell Fm	Northum	NU0149	55°44·3'	1°58·6'W	FM	75
Borfa-hafed	Powys	SO0597	52°34·0'	3°23·7'W	X	136
Borfa-wen	Powys	SO1689	52°29·8'	3°13·8'W	X	136
Borgadalemore Point	Arg & Bt	NR6305	55°17·2'	5°43·5'W	X	68
Borgadale Water	Arg & Bt	NR6107	55°18·2'	5°45·5'W	W	68
Borgan	D & G	NX3674	55°2·3'	4°33·6'W	X	77
Borgh	N Eil	NB4156	58°25·2'	6°25·7'W	T	8
Borghastan	N Eil	NB1942	58°16·9'	6°47·2'W	T	8,13
Borgie	Highld	NC6759	58°30·2'	4°16·5'W	T	10
Borgie	Highld	ND2654	58°28·3'	3°15·6'W	X	11,12
Borgie Br	Highld	NC6658	58°29·6'	4°17·5'W	X	10
Borgie Forest	Highld	NC6654	58°27·5'	4°17·3'W	F	10
Borgie Ho	Highld	ND1967	58°35·3'	3°23·1'W	X	11,12
Borgie Mains	Highld	ND1964	58°33·7'	3°23·1'W	X	11,12
Borg, The	Highld	NC8951	58°26·3'	3°53·6'W	X	10
Borgue	D & G	NX6348	54°48·7'	4°7·5'W	T	83
Borgue	Highld	ND1325	58°12·6'	3°28·4'W	T	17
Borgue Ho	D & G	NX6348	54°48·7'	4°7·5'W	X	83
Borgue Langwell	Highld	ND1021	58°10·4'	3°31·3'W	X	17
Borgue Loch	Highld	ND1227	58°13·6'	3°29·4'W	W	17
Borgue Old House	D & G	NX6348	54°48·7'	4°7·5'W	A	83
Borichill Mór	Arg & Bt	NR3164	55°47·9'	6°17·1'W	X	60,61
Boringdon Camp	Devon	SX5459	50°25·0'	4°2·9'W	A	201
Boringdon Hall (Hotel)	C of Plym	SX5357	50°23·9'	4°3·7'W	X	201
Borland	E Ayr	NS3949	55°42·7'	4°33·3'W	X	63
Borland	E Ayr	NS4440	55°38·0'	4°28·3'W	X	70
Borland	E Ayr	NS5817	55°25·8'	4°14·2'W	X	71
Borland	E Renf	NS5652	55°44·7'	4°17·2'W	X	64
Borland	Pth & Kin	NN9804	56°13·3'	3°38·3'W	X	58
Borland	Pth & Kin	NO0859	56°43·1'	3°29·7'W	X	52,53
Borland	Pth & Kin	NO1560	56°43·7'	3°22·9'W	X	43
Borland	S Lanak	NT0646	55°42·2'	3°29·3'W	X	72
Borland Burn	E Renf	NS5652	55°44·7'	4°17·2'W	W	64
Borland Fm	Stir	NS5196	56°8·3'	4°23·4'W	FM	57
Borland Glen	Pth & Kin	NN9906	56°14·4'	3°37·3'W	X	58
Borland Ho	Stir	NS5196	56°8·3'	4°23·4'W	X	57
Borland Mains	E Ayr	NS5918	55°26·4'	4°13·3'W	X	71
Borlase	Corn	SW9566	50°27·7'	4°52·9'W	X	200
Borlasevath	Corn	SW9466	50°27·7'	4°53·8'W	X	200
Borlase Wood	Corn	SW8540	50°13·5'	5°0·5'W	F	204
Borle Brook	Shrops	SO7087	52°29·0'	2°26·1'W	W	138
Borley	Essex	TL8442	52°3·0'	0°41·4'E	T	155
Borley Green	Essex	TL8342	52°3·0'	0°40·5'E	T	155
Borley Green	Herts	TL4230	51°57·2'	0°4·4'E	X	167
Borley Green	Suff	TL9960	52°12·4'	0°55·1'E	T	155
Borley Hall	Essex	TL8542	52°3·0'	0°42·3'E	X	155
Borley Wood	Cambs	TL5848	52°6·7'	0°18·8'E	F	154
Borlick	Pth & Kin	NN8549	56°37·4'	3°52·0'W	X	52
Borlick	Pth & Kin	NN8649	56°37·4'	3°51·0'W	X	52
Borlum	Highld	NH3808	57°8·3'	4°40·2'W	X	34
Borlum	Highld	NH5129	57°19·9'	4°28·0'W	X	26,35
Borlum	Highld	NH6240	57°26·0'	4°17·5'W	X	26
Borlum Br	Highld	NH5129	57°19·9'	4°28·0'W	X	26,35
Borlum Hill	Highld	NH4008	57°8·4'	4°38·2'W	H	34
Borlum Ho	Highld	NC9764	58°33·4'	3°45·7'W	X	11
Bornacott	Devon	SS7132	51°4·6'	3°50·1'W	X	180
Bornais	N Eil	NF7329	57°14·4'	7°24·8'W	T	22
Borneskeitaig	Highld	NG3771	57°39·4'	6°24·1'W	T	23
Borness	D & G	NX6145	54°47·1'	4°9·3'W	T	83
Borness Bar	D & G	NX6245	54°47·1'	4°8·3'W	X	83
Borness Batteries	D & G	NX6244	54°46·6'	4°8·3'W	X	83
Borness Batteries (Fort)	D & G	NX6244	54°46·6'	4°8·3'W	A	83
Borness Point	D & G	NX6144	54°46·6'	4°9·2'W	X	83

Borocourt Hospital	Oxon	SU6882	51°32·2'	1°0·8'W	X	175
Borosdale	N Eil	NG0383	57°44·6'	6°59·0'W	X	18
Borosdale Point	N Eil	NF9886	57°46·0'	7°4·3'W	X	18
Borough	Devon	SS2602	50°47·7'	4°27·8'W	X	190
Borough	Devon	SX4181	50°36·7'	4°14·5'W	X	201
Borough	Devon	SX7447	50°18·8'	3°45·8'W	X	202
Borough	Devon	SX7837	50°13·5'	3°42·2'W	X	202
Borough	I Scilly	SV8914	49°56·9'	6°19·8'W	T	203
Boroughbridge	N Yks	SE3966	54°5·5'	1°23·8'W	T	99
Borough Court	Hants	SU7355	51°17·6'	0°56·8'W	X	175,186
Borough Cross	Devon	SS4744	51°10·7'	4°11·0'W	X	180
Borough Fen	Norf	TL7499	52°33·9'	0°34·4'E	X	143
Borough Fields	Derby	SK2116	52°44·7'	1°40·9'W	X	128
Borough Fm	Bucks	SP8530	51°57·9'	0°45·4'W	FM	152,165
Borough Fm	Devon	SS4844	51°10·7'	4°10·1'W	FM	180
Borough Fm	Devon	SS5324	51°0·0'	4°5·3'W	FM	180
Borough Fm	Devon	SS9922	50°59·5'	3°26·0'W	FM	181
Borough Fm	Devon	SX6049	50°19·7'	3°57·6'W	FM	202
Borough Fm	Hants	SU5038	51°8·6'	1°16·7'W	FM	185
Borough Fm	Somer	ST3025	51°1·4'	2°59·5'W	FM	193
Borough Fm	Surrey	SU9241	51°9·9'	0°40·7'W	FM	186
Borough Fm	W Susx	TQ0620	50°58·4'	0°29·0'W	FM	197
Borough Green	Kent	TQ6057	51°17·6'	0°18·1'E	T	188
Borough Green Fm	N Yks	NZ5809	54°28·6'	1°5·9'W	FM	93
Borough Head	Pemb	SM8312	51°46·1'	5°8·3'W	X	157
Borough Hill	Derby	SK2117	52°45·2'	1°40·9'W	X	128
Borough Hill	Northnts	SP5862	52°15·4'	1°8·6'W	X	152
Borough Hill	Warw	SP2740	52°3·7'	1°36·0'W	X	151
Borough Hill	W Berks	SU4372	51°27·0'	1°22·5'W	X	174
Borough Holme	Derby	SK2016	52°44·7'	1°41·8'W	X	128
Borough Marsh	Wok	SU7777	51°29·4'	0°53·1'W	T	175
Borough Park	Staffs	SK2105	52°38·8'	1°41·0'W	T	139
Borough Post	Somer	ST3124	51°0·9'	2°58·6'W	T	193
Borough's Oak Fm	Kent	TQ6749	51°13·2'	0°23·9'E	FM	188
Borough,The	Dorset	ST7011	50°54·1'	2°25·2'W	T	194
Borough Valley	Devon	SS4845	51°11·3'	4°10·1'W	X	180
Boro Wood	Devon	SX7571	50°31·8'	3°45·4'W	F	202
Borrach	N Ayr	NS0326	55°29·5'	5°6·7'W	X	69
Borraichill Mór	Arg & Bt	NR3746	55°38·4'	6°10·3'W	X	60
Borraichill Mór (Fort)	Arg & Bt	NR3746	55°38·4'	6°10·3'W	A	60
Borrans	Cumbr	SD5690	54°18·5'	2°40·2'W	X	97
Borrans Hill	Cumbr	NY3644	54°47·5'	2°59·3'W	X	85
Borrans Resr	Cumbr	NY4201	54°24·3'	2°53·2'W	W	90
Borrans,The	Cumbr	SD5697	54°22·2'	2°40·2'W	X	97
Borras	Wrex	SJ3452	53°3·9'	2°58·7'W	T	117
Borras Hall	Wrex	SJ3752	53°3·9'	2°56·0'W	A	117
Borras Head	Wrex	SJ3653	53°4·5'	2°56·9'W	A	117
Borreraig	Highld	NG1853	57°29·0'	6°41·9'W	T	23
Borrett	Cumbr	SD6491	54°19·0'	2°32·8'W	X	97
Borrins	N Yks	SD7874	54°9·9'	2°19·8'W	X	98
Borrins Moor	N Yks	SD7675	54°10·5'	2°21·6'W	X	98
Borrins Wood	N Yks	SD8166	54°5·6'	2°17·0'W	X	98
Borrobol Forest	Highld	NC7925	58°12·1'	4°3·1'W	X	17
Borrobol Hill	Highld	NC8725	58°12·2'	3°54·9'W	H	17
Borrobol Lodge	Highld	NC8626	58°12·7'	3°55·9'W	X	17
Borrodale	Highld	NG1648	57°26·3'	6°43·5'W	T	23
Borrodale Burn	Highld	NM7086	56°54·8'	5°46·2'W	W	40
Borrodale House	Highld	NM6985	56°54·2'	5°47·2'W	X	40
Borrohill	Aberd	NJ9254	57°34·8'	2°7·6'W	X	30
Borron Point	D & G	NX9958	54°54·6'	3°34·1'W	X	84
Borrowash	Derby	SK4234	52°54·3'	1°22·1'W	T	129
Borrow Beck	Cumbr	NY5205	54°26·5'	2°44·0'W	W	90
Borrow Beck	Cumbr	NY5901	54°24·4'	2°37·5'W	W	91
Borrowby	N Yks	NZ7715	54°31·7'	0°48·2'W	T	94
Borrowby	N Yks	SE4289	54°17·9'	1°20·9'W	T	99
Borrowby Dale	N Yks	NZ7816	54°32·2'	0°47·2'W	X	94
Borrowby Grange	N Yks	NZ7717	54°32·8'	0°48·2'W	X	94
Borrowby Grange	N Yks	SE4189	54°17·9'	1°21·8'W	X	99
Borrowby Moor	N Yks	NZ7614	54°31·2'	0°49·1'W	X	94
Borrowdale	Cumbr	NY2417	54°32·8'	3°10·1'W	X	89,90
Borrowdale	Cumbr	NY5603	54°25·5'	2°40·3'W	X	90
Borrowdale Fells	Cumbr	NY2513	54°30·7'	3°9·1'W	X	89,90
Borrowdale Gates	Cumbr	NY2517	54°32·8'	3°9·1'W	X	89,90
Borrowdale Head	Cumbr	NY5404	54°26·0'	2°42·1'W	X	90
Borrowdale Ho	Cumbr	NY8315	54°32·0'	2°15·3'W	X	91,92
Borrowdale Moss	Cumbr	NY5106	54°27·1'	2°44·9'W	X	90
Borrowdale Yews	Cumbr	NY2312	54°30·1'	3°10·9'W	X	89,90
Borrowfield	Aberd	NO8293	57°1·9'	2°17·3'W	X	38,45
Borrowfield	Angus	NO7059	56°43·6'	2°29·0'W	X	54
Borrow Moss	D & G	NX4357	54°53·2'	4°26·4'W	X	83
Borrowmoss	D & G	NX4357	54°53·2'	4°26·4'W	X	83
Borrowmoss Burn	D & G	NX4357	54°53·2'	4°26·4'W	W	83
Borrowscale	Cumbr	NY1938	54°44·1'	3°15·1'W	X	89,90
Borrowston	Highld	ND3243	58°22·2'	3°9·3'W	T	12
Borrowstone	Aberd	NJ5514	57°13·1'	2°44·3'W	X	37
Borrowstone	C of Aber	NJ8407	57°9·5'	2°15·4'W	X	38
Borrowstonehill	Orkney	HY4407	58°57·1'	2°57·9'W	X	6,7
Borrowstone Ho	Aberd	NO5999	57°5·1'	2°40·1'W	X	37,44
Borrowston Mains	Highld	ND0168	58°35·6'	3°41·7'W	X	11,12
Borrowston Rig	Scot Bord	NT5552	55°45·8'	2°42·6'W	X	66,73
Borrowstoun Mains	Falk	NS9980	56°0·4'	3°36·7'W	T	65
Borsdane Wood	Bolton	SD6206	53°33·2'	2°34·0'W	F	109
Borse Skerry	Shetld	HU1562	60°20·8'	1°43·2'W	X	3
Borsham	N Eil	NG0885	57°45·8'	6°54·1'W	T	18
Borstal	Medway	TQ7366	51°22·2'	0°29·5'E	T	178
Borth	Cered	SN6089	52°29·1'	4°3·3'W	T	135
Borthaugh	Scot Bord	NT4713	55°24·7'	2°49·8'W	X	79
Borthaugh Hill	Scot Bord	NT4614	55°25·3'	2°50·8'W	H	79
Borth Fawr	Gwyn	SH3227	52°49·1'	4°29·2'W	W	123
Borth Sands	Cered	SN6092	52°30·7'	4°3·4'W	X	135
Borth Wen	Gwyn	SH2741	52°56·6'	4°34·1'W	W	123
Borthwen	I of Angl	SH2774	53°14·3'	4°35·1'W	W	114
Borthwen	I of Angl	SH2987	53°21·4'	4°33·8'W	X	114
Borth-wen	I of Angl	SH5283	53°19·6'	4°12·9'W	W	114,115
Borthwen Fm	Gwyn	SH5809	52°39·9'	4°5·6'W	FM	124
Borthwick	Midlo	NT3659	55°49·5'	3°0·9'W	T	66,73
Borthwickbrae	Scot Bord	NT4113	55°24·7'	2°55·5'W	X	79
Borthwick Castle (Hotel)	Midlo	NT3659	55°49·5'	3°0·9'W	A	66,73
Borthwick Hall	Scot Bord	NT3852	55°45·7'	2°58·8'W	X	66,73
Borthwick Mains	Midlo	NT3760	55°50·0'	2°59·9'W	X	66
Borthwick Mains	Scot Bord	NT4314	55°25·2'	2°53·6'W	X	79
Borthwickshiels	Scot Bord	NT4315	55°25·8'	2°53·6'W	X	79
Borthwickshiels Horn	Scot Bord	NT4316	55°26·3'	2°53·6'W	X	79
Borthwick Water	Scot Bord	NT3508	55°22·0'	3°1·1'W	W	79
Borthwnog	Gwyn	SH6819	52°45·4'	3°57·0'W	X	124
Borthwood Fm	I of W	SZ5784	50°39·4'	1°11·2'W	FM	196
Borth-y-Gest	Gwyn	SH5637	52°54·9'	4°8·1'W	T	124
Borthyn	Carm	SN6637	52°1·2'	3°56·8'W	X	146
Bortree Stile	Cumbr	SD2779	54°12·3'	3°6·7'W	X	96,97
Borve	Highld	NG3452	57°29·1'	6°25·8'W	X	23
Borve	Highld	NG4448	57°27·3'	6°15·6'W	T	23
Borve	N Eil	NF6601	56°59·0'	7°29·5'W	T	31
Borve	N Eil	NF9181	57°43·0'	7°10·9'W	T	18
Borve	N Eil	NG0394	57°50·5'	6°59·8'W	T	18
Borvebeg Burn	N Eil	NG0494	57°50·5'	6°58·8'W	W	18
Borve Castle	Highld	NC7264	58°33·0'	4°11·5'W	A	10
Borve Corry	Highld	NG4548	57°27·3'	6°14·6'W	X	23
Borve Hill	N Eil	NF9181	57°43·0'	7°10·9'W	H	18
Borve Lodge	N Eil	NG0394	57°50·5'	6°59·8'W	X	18
Borve Point	N Eil	NF6401	56°58·9'	7°31·5'W	X	31
Borwens	Cumbr	SD6283	54°14·7'	2°34·6'W	X	97
Borwick	Lancs	SD5273	54°9·3'	2°43·7'W	T	97
Bor Wick	Orkney	HY2216	59°1·7'	3°21·0'W	W	6
Borwick	Orkney	HY2216	59°1·7'	3°21·0'W	X	6
Borwick Fold	Cumbr	SD4497	54°22·2'	2°51·3'W	X	97
Borwick Rails	Cumbr	SD1879	54°12·3'	3°15·0'W	T	96
Borwick Rails Harbour	Cumbr	SD1880	54°12·8'	3°15·0'W	W	96
Borwicks	Lancs	SD5455	53°59·6'	2°41·7'W	X	102
Borwick's Aynsome	Cumbr	SD3879	54°12·4'	2°56·6'W	X	96,97
Borwins	N Yks	SD9190	54°18·6'	2°7·9'W	X	98
Bosahan	Corn	SW7626	50°5·7'	5°7·6'W	X	204
Bosan	Orkney	HY4047	59°18·6'	3°2·7'W	X	5
Bosanath Mill	Corn	SW7628	50°6·8'	5°7·6'W	X	204
Bosanketh	Corn	SW3826	50°4·8'	5°39·4'W	X	203
Bosavern	Corn	SW3730	50°6·9'	5°40·4'W	X	203
Bosawsack	Corn	SW7530	50°7·9'	5°8·5'W	X	204
Bosbury	Heref	SO6943	52°5·3'	2°26·8'W	T	149
Bosbury Ho	Heref	SO7044	52°5·8'	2°25·9'W	X	149
Boscadjack	Corn	SW6631	50°8·2'	5°16·1'W	T	203
Boscar Flatts	N Yks	SE5073	54°9·3'	1°13·6'W	X	100
Boscar Grange	N Yks	SE5072	54°8·7'	1°13·7'W	X	100
Boscar Moor Fm	N Yks	SE5071	54°8·2'	1°13·7'W	FM	100
Boscarn	Corn	SW3927	50°5·4'	5°38·6'W	X	203
Boscarne	Corn	SX0367	50°28·4'	4°46·2'W	X	200
Boscarne Junction Station	Corn	SX0467	50°28·4'	4°45·4'W	X	200
Boscarnon	Corn	SW7819	50°2·0'	5°5·6'W	X	204
Boscastle	Corn	SX0990	50°40·9'	4°41·8'W	T	190
Boscathnoe Resr	Corn	SW4531	50°7·7'	5°33·7'W	W	203
Boscawen Fm	Corn	SW7345	50°15·9'	5°10·7'W	FM	204
Boscawen-noon	Corn	SW4127	50°5·4'	5°36·9'W	X	203
Boscawen Point	Corn	SW4322	50°2·8'	5°35·0'W	X	203
Boscawen Rose	Corn	SW4323	50°3·3'	5°35·1'W	X	203
Boscean	Corn	SW3632	50°8·0'	5°41·3'W	T	203
Boscobel House	Shrops	SJ8308	52°40·4'	2°14·7'W	A	127
Boscolla	Corn	SW8046	50°16·6'	5°4·9'W	X	204
Boscombe	Bourne	SZ1191	50°43·3'	1°50·3'W	T	195
Boscombe	Wilts	SU2038	51°8·7'	1°42·5'W	T	184
Boscombe Down Airfield	Wilts	SU1839	51°9·2'	1°44·2'W	X	184
Boscombe Down East	Wilts	SU2337	51°8·1'	1°39·9'W	X	184
Boscombe Down West	Wilts	SU1840	51°9·8'	1°44·2'W	X	184
Boscomoor	Staffs	SJ9213	52°43·1'	2°6·7'W	T	127
Boscoppa	Corn	SX0353	50°20·9'	4°45·8'W	T	200,204
Boscreege	Corn	SW5930	50°7·5'	5°21·9'W	T	203
Boscreege Fm	Corn	SW4634	50°9·3'	5°33·0'W	FM	203
Boseley Court	Glos	SO7015	51°50·2'	2°25·7'W	X	162
Bose Low	Derby	SK1652	53°4·1'	1°45·3'W	A	119
Bosence	Corn	SW4030	50°7·0'	5°37·9'W	X	203
Bosendale Wood	N Yks	SE7162	54°3·2'	0°54·5'W	F	100
Bosent	Corn	SX2163	50°26·6'	4°30·9'W	X	201
Bosfranken	Corn	SW3825	50°4·3'	5°39·3'W	X	203
Bosham	W Susx	SU8004	50°50·0'	0°51·5'W	T	197
Bosham Channel	W Susx	SU7903	50°49·5'	0°52·3'W	W	197
Bosham Hoe	W Susx	SU8101	50°48·4'	0°50·6'W	T	197
Bosham Sta	W Susx	SU8105	50°50·6'	0°50·6'W	X	197
Bosherston	Pemb	SR9694	51°36·7'	4°56·4'W	T	158
Boshill Cross	Devon	SY2692	50°43·6'	3°2·5'W	X	192,193
Boship Fm Hotel	E Susx	TQ5711	50°52·9'	0°14·3'E	X	199
Bosigran Castle	Corn	SW4136	50°10·3'	5°37·3'W	A	203
Bosigran Fm	Corn	SW4236	50°10·3'	5°36·4'W	FM	203
Bosiliack	Corn	SW4333	50°8·7'	5°35·5'W	X	203
Bosistow	Corn	SW3623	50°3·2'	5°40·9'W	X	203
Bosithow	Corn	SW9952	50°20·3'	4°49·1'W	X	200,204
Boskednan	Corn	SW4434	50°9·3'	5°34·7'W	T	203
Boskenna	Corn	SW4223	50°3·3'	5°35·9'W	T	203
Boskennal	Corn	SW4125	50°4·4'	5°36·8'W	X	203
Boskennal	Corn	SW5034	50°9·4'	5°29·6'W	X	203
Boskensoe Fm	Corn	SW7728	50°6·8'	5°6·8'W	FM	204
Boskenwyn Downs	Corn	SW6927	50°6·1'	5°13·5'W	X	203
Boskenwyn Manor	Corn	SW6827	50°6·1'	5°14·3'W	X	203
Boskeydyke Fm	N Lincs	SE8313	53°36·7'	0°44·3'W	FM	112
Bosleake	Corn	SW6740	50°13·1'	5°15·6'W	T	203
Bosley	Ches	SJ9165	53°11·2'	2°7·7'W	T	118
Bosley Fields	Derby	SK1370	53°13·9'	1°47·9'W	X	119
Bosley Locks	Ches	SJ9066	53°11·7'	2°8·6'W	X	118
Bosley Minn	Ches	SJ9366	53°11·7'	2°5·9'W	X	118
Bosley Reservoir	Ches	SJ9266	53°11·7'	2°6·8'W	W	118
Bosliven	Corn	SW4125	50°4·4'	5°36·8'W	X	203
Bosloggas	Corn	SW8434	50°10·2'	5°1·1'W	X	204
Boslow	Corn	SW3932	50°8·1'	5°38·8'W	X	203
Boslowick	Corn	SW7931	50°8·5'	5°5·2'W	T	204
Boslymon	Corn	SX0861	50°25·3'	4°41·8'W	T	200
Bosmaugon	Corn	SX1162	50°25·9'	4°39·3'W	X	200
Bosmere Hall	Suff	TM1054	52°8·9'	1°4·6'E	X	155
Bosmore Fm	Bucks	SU7487	51°34·8'	0°55·5'W	FM	175
Bosney Fm	E Susx	TQ9224	50°59·2'	0°44·5'E	FM	189
Bosoljack	Corn	SW4532	50°8·2'	5°33·8'W	X	203
Bosorne	Corn	SW3630	50°6·9'	5°41·2'W	X	203
Bosoughan	Corn	SW8760	50°24·3'	4°59·5'W	T	200
Bosparva	Corn	SW6135	50°10·2'	5°20·5'W	X	203
Bosporthennis	Corn	SW4336	50°10·3'	5°35·6'W	T	203
Bosprowal	Corn	SW6237	50°11·3'	5°19·7'W	X	203
Bossack	Orkney	HY5008	58°57·6'	2°51·7'W	X	6,7
Bossall	N Yks	SE7160	54°2·1'	0°54·5'W	T	100
Bossava	Corn	SW4424	50°3·9'	5°34·3'W	X	203
Bossenden Fm	Kent	TR0859	51°17·7'	0°59·4'E	FM	179
Bosses	Staffs	SK0802	52°37·2'	1°52·5'W	X	139
Bossholes	Aberd	NO8188	56°59·2'	2°18·3'W	X	45
Bossillian	Corn	SW9348	50°18·0'	4°54·0'W	X	204
Bossiney	Corn	SX0688	50°39·8'	4°44·3'W	T	200
Bossiney Haven	Corn	SX0689	50°40·3'	4°44·4'W	W	200
Bossingham	Kent	TR1548	51°11·7'	1°5·0'E	T	179,189
Bossington	Hants	SU3331	51°4·9'	1°31·3'W	T	185
Bossington	Kent	TR2355	51°15·3'	1°12·1'E	T	179
Bossington	Somer	SS8947	51°12·9'	3°35·0'W	T	181
Bossington Hill	Somer	SS9048	51°13·5'	3°34·1'W	X	181
Boss Lane Fm	Bucks	SU8696	51°39·6'	0°45·0'W	FM	165
Boss Moor	N Yks	SD9662	54°3·5'	2°3·3'W	X	98
Bosstree Hill	D & G	NY3190	55°12·2'	3°4·6'W	H	79
Bosta	N Eil	NB1440	58°15·6'	6°52·1'W	X	13
Bostal Hill	E Susx	TQ4904	50°49·2'	0°7·3'E	X	199
Bostal Hill (Tumuli)	E Susx	TQ4904	50°49·2'	0°7·3'E	A	199
Bostall Woods	Gren	TQ4677	51°28·6'	0°6·5'E	F	177
Bostern Grange Fm	Derby	SK1553	53°4·7'	1°46·2'W	FM	119
Bostle, The	Bri & Hov	TQ3705	50°49·9'	0°2·9'W	X	198
Bostock Barns Fm	Ches	SJ7978	53°18·2'	2°18·5'W	FM	118
Bostock Green	Ches	SJ6769	53°13·3'	2°29·2'W	T	118
Bostock Hall	Ches	SJ6768	53°12·7'	2°29·2'W	X	118
Bostock Hall	Shrops	SJ5134	52°54·3'	2°43·3'W	X	126
Bostock Ho	Ches	SJ7756	53°6·3'	2°20·2'W	X	118
Bostock House Fm	Ches	SJ6966	53°11·7'	2°27·4'W	FM	118
Boston	Lincs	TF3344	52°58·8'	0°0·7'W	T	131
Boston Aerodrome	Lincs	TF2943	52°58·4'	0°4·3'W	X	131
Boston Corporation Fm	Lincs	TF3859	53°6·9'	0°4·1'E	FM	122
Boston Deeps	Lincs	TF5148	53°0·7'	0°15·5'E	W	131
Boston Deeps	Lincs	TF5652	53°2·8'	0°20·0'E	W	122
Boston Fm	N Yks	SE1195	54°21·3'	1°49·4'W	FM	99
Boston Fm	Worcs	SP0143	52°5·4'	1°58·7'W	FM	150
Boston Lodge	Gwyn	SH5837	52°54·9'	4°6·3'W	X	124
Boston Lodge	Leic	SP5586	52°28·4'	1°11·0'W	X	140
Boston Long Hedges	Lincs	TF3547	53°0·4'	0°1·1'E	T	131
Boston Park	Donc	SE6704	53°31·9'	0°58·9'W	X	111
Boston Spa	Leeds	SE4245	53°54·2'	1°21·2'W	T	105
Boston West	Lincs	TF2945	52°59·4'	0°4·3'W	T	131
Bostraze	Corn	SW3831	50°7·5'	5°39·6'W	X	203
Bosue	Corn	SW9847	50°17·5'	4°49·8'W	X	204
Bosullow Common	Corn	SW4134	50°9·2'	5°37·2'W	X	203
Bosulval	Corn	SW4634	50°9·3'	5°33·0'W	X	203
Bosvargus	Corn	SW3731	50°7·5'	5°40·4'W	X	203
Bosvarren	Corn	SW7530	50°7·9'	5°8·5'W	X	204
Bosvathick	Corn	SW7530	50°7·9'	5°8·5'W	X	204
Bosveal	Corn	SW7727	50°6·3'	5°6·8'W	X	204
Bosvenning	Corn	SW4231	50°7·6'	5°36·2'W	X	203
Boswallow	Corn	SW8856	50°22·2'	4°58·5'W	X	200
Boswarthen	Corn	SW4128	50°6·0'	5°36·9'W	X	203
Boswarthen	Corn	SW4433	50°8·7'	5°34·6'W	X	203
Boswarva	Corn	SW4332	50°8·2'	5°35·4'W	X	203
Boswarva Carn	Corn	SW4233	50°8·7'	5°36·3'W	X	203
Boswednack	Corn	SW4437	50°10·9'	5°34·8'W	T	203
Boswednan	Corn	SW4431	50°7·7'	5°34·5'W	X	203
Boswell	Devon	SY1490	50°42·4'	3°12·7'W	X	192,193
Boswell Ho	Lincs	TF2790	53°23·7'	0°5·0'W	X	113
Boswellick	Corn	SW8150	50°18·8'	5°4·2'W	X	200,204
Boswells Fm	Bucks	SP8806	51°45·0'	0°43·1'W	FM	165
Boswells Fm	Surrey	TQ1337	51°7·5'	0°22·7'W	FM	187
Boswell's Monument	Aberd	NO8897	57°4·1'	2°11·4'W	X	38,45
Boswens	Corn	SW4033	50°8·6'	5°38·0'W	X	203
Boswens Common	Corn	SW4132	50°8·1'	5°37·1'W	X	203
Boswiddle	Corn	SW8651	50°19·4'	5°0·0'W	X	200,204
Boswidjack	Corn	SW7129	50°7·3'	5°11·8'W	X	203
Boswin	Corn	SW6934	50°9·9'	5°13·7'W	T	203
Boswinger	Corn	SW9941	50°14·3'	4°48·8'W	T	204
Boswold Hall	Suff	TM1275	52°20·1'	1°7·1'E	A	144
Bosworgey	Corn	SW9063	50°26·0'	4°57·1'W	X	200
Bosworlas	Corn	SW3730	50°6·9'	5°40·4'W	X	203
Bosworth Field	Leic	SK3900	52°36·0'	1°25·0'W	A	140
Bosworth Fm	Notts	SK6641	52°58·0'	1°0·6'W	FM	129
Bosworth Gorse	Leic	SP6486	52°28·3'	1°3·1'W	F	140
Bosworth Grange	Leic	SP6386	52°28·3'	1°3·9'W	X	140
Bosworth Lodge	Leic	SP6386	52°28·3'	1°3·9'W	X	140
Bosworth Mill Fm	Leic	SP6382	52°26·2'	1°4·0'W	FM	140
Bosworth Park	Leic	SK4102	52°37·1'	1°23·3'W	X	140
Boswyn	Corn	SW6636	50°10·9'	5°16·3'W	T	203
Botallack	Corn	SW3632	50°8·0'	5°41·3'W	T	203
Botallack Head	Corn	SW3633	50°8·5'	5°41·3'W	X	203
Botallick	Corn	SX1658	50°23·8'	4°35·0'W	X	201
Botany	Durham	NY9521	54°35·3'	2°4·2'W	X	91,92
Botany	Northum	NU0924	55°30·8'	1°51·0'W	X	75
Botany Bay	Cambs	TL3795	52°32·4'	0°1·6'E	X	142,143
Botany Bay	Derby	SK2615	52°44·2'	1°36·5'W	X	128
Botany Bay	Donc	SE6309	53°34·7'	1°2·5'W	X	111
Botany Bay	Enf	TQ2999	51°40·7'	0°7·7'W	T	166,176
Botany Bay	Kent	TR3971	51°23·5'	1°26·5'E	W	179
Botany Bay	Leic	SK4015	52°44·1'	1°24·1'W	X	129
Botany Bay	Monm	SO5102	51°43·1'	2°42·2'W	T	162
Botany Bay	N Yks	SE6095	54°21·1'	1°4·2'W	X	94,100
Botany Bay	N Yks	SE6229	53°45·5'	1°3·2'W	X	105
Botany Bay	Suff	TL6785	52°26·5'	0°27·8'E	X	143
Botany Bay Barn	Dorset	SY8896	50°46·0'	2°9·8'W	X	194
Botany Bay Fm	Herts	TL2527	51°55·9'	0°10·5'W	FM	166
Botany Bay Fm	Norf	TG1623	52°45·9'	1°12·5'E	FM	133
Botany Bay Fm	Notts	SK6882	53°20·1'	0°58·3'W	FM	111,120
Botany Bay Fox Covert	Leic	SK7004	52°38·0'	0°57·5'W	F	141
Botany Bay Wood	Salf	SJ7298	53°28·9'	2°24·9'W	F	109
Botany Fm	Dorset	SY8682	50°38·5'	2°11·5'W	FM	194
Botany Fm	Northnts	SP6571	52°20·2'	1°2·4'W	FM	141
Botany Fm	Suff	TM0370	52°17·7'	0°59·0'E	FM	144,155
Botany Fm	Wilts	ST8643	51°11·4'	2°11·6'W	FM	183
Botany Spinney	Leic	SK3702	52°37·1'	1°26·8'W	F	140
Botarua	N Eil	NF7873	57°38·2'	7°23·3'W	X	18
Botary Mains	Aberd	NJ4745	57°29·8'	2°52·6'W	X	28,29

Botathan	Corn	SX2981	50°36·5′	4°24·6′W	X	201
Botcherby	Cumbr	NY4155	54°53·4′	2°54·8′W	T	85
Botcheston	Leic	SK4804	52°38·1′	1°17·0′W	T	140
Botelet Fm	Corn	SX1860	50°24·9′	4°33·3′W	FM	201
Botesdale	Suff	TM0475	52°20·3′	1°0·1′E	T	144
Botesdale Lodge	Suff	TM0675	52°20·3′	1°1·8′E	X	144
Bothal	Northum	NZ2386	55°10·3′	1°37·9′W	T	81
Bothal Barns	Northum	NZ2486	55°10·3′	1°37·0′W	X	81
Bothal Castle	Northum	NZ2486	55°10·3′	1°37·0′W	A	81
Bothalhaugh	Northum	NZ2486	55°10·3′	1°37·0′W	X	81
Bothal Park	Northum	NZ2387	55°10·9′	1°37·9′W	X	81
Bothampstead	W Berks	SU5076	51°29·1′	1°16·4′W	T	174
Bothampstead Fm	W Berks	SU5076	51°29·1′	1°16·4′W	FM	174
Bothams	N Yks	SE1555	53°59·7′	1°45·9′W	X	104
Bothamsall	Notts	SK6773	53°15·2′	0°59·3′W	T	120
Botham's Hall	Tames	SJ9892	53°25·7′	2°1·4′W	X	109
Bothel	Cumbr	NY1838	54°44·1′	3°16·0′W	T	89,90
Bothel Craggs	Cumbr	NY1837	54°43·5′	3°16·0′W	X	89,90
Bothen	Shetld	HP6312	60°47·4′	0°50·1′W	T	1
Bothenhampton	Dorset	SY4691	50°43·2′	2°45·5′W	T	193
Bothenwood Fm	Dorset	SU0202	50°49·3′	1°57·9′W	FM	195
Botherickfield	Renf	NS3867	55°52·4′	4°34·9′W	X	63
Both Hellia	Orkney	HY6121	59°4·7′	2°40·3′W	X	5
Both Hill	Aberd	NJ4440	57°27·1′	2°55·5′W	H	28
Bothiewells	Highld	NH9752	57°33·0′	3°42·8′W	X	27
Bothlin Burn	N Lanak	NS7069	55°54·1′	4°4·3′W	W	64
Bothrigg Burn	Cumbr	NY5576	55°4·8′	2°41·9′W	W	86
Bothwell	Scot Bord	NT6864	55°52·3′	2°30·2′W	X	67
Bothwell	S Lanak	NS7058	55°48·1′	4°4·0′W	T	64
Bothwell Br	S Lanak	NS7157	55°47·6′	4°3·0′W	X	64
Bothwell Hill	Scot Bord	NT6764	55°52·3′	2°31·2′W	X	67
Bothwell Park Fm	S Lanak	NS7159	55°48·7′	4°3·1′W	FM	64
Bothwellseat	Aberd	NJ5536	57°25·0′	2°44·5′W	X	29
Bothwell Service Area	S Lanak	NS7059	55°48·7′	4°4·0′W	X	64
Bothwellshields	N Lanak	NS8062	55°50·4′	3°54·5′W	X	65
Bothwell Water	Scot Bord	NT6766	55°53·4′	2°31·2′W	W	67
Bothy	Aberd	NJ2202	57°6·4′	3°16·8′W	X	36
Bothy Geo	Orkney	ND4898	58°52·2′	2°53·6′W	X	6,7
Bothyhill	Highld	NH7149	57°31·0′	4°8·8′W	X	27
Botich	Pth & Kin	NN9231	56°27·8′	3°44·7′W	H	52
Botley	Bucks	SP9802	51°42·7′	0°34·5′W	T	165
Botley	Hants	SU5113	50°55·1′	1°16·1′W	T	196
Botley	Oxon	SP4805	51°44·7′	1°17·9′W	T	164
Botley Copse	Oxon	SU2880	51°31·3′	1°35·4′W	F	174
Botley Down	Wilts	SU2960	51°20·5′	1°34·6′W	X	174
Botley Hill	Surrey	TQ3955	51°16·9′	0°0·0′W	X	187
Botley Hill	Warw	SP1467	52°18·1′	1°47·3′W	X	151
Botley Hill Fm	Warw	SP1468	52°18·8′	1°47·3′W	FM	139,151
Botley Mill Stables	Warw	SP1468	52°18·8′	1°47·3′W	X	139,151
Botley's Fm	Wilts	SU1421	50°59·5′	1°47·6′W	FM	184
Botley Wood	Hants	SU5410	50°53·4′	1°13·5′W	F	196
Botloe's Green	Glos	SO7228	51°57·2′	2°24·1′W	T	149
Botney Hill Fm	Essex	TQ6591	51°35·8′	0°23·3′E	FM	177,178
Botney Lodge	Leic	SP5882	52°26·2′	1°8·4′W	X	140
Botney Meadows	Oxon	SU3993	51°38·3′	1°25·8′W	X	164,174
Botolph Claydon	Bucks	SP7324	51°54·8′	0°55·9′W	T	165
Botolphs	W Susx	TQ1909	50°52·3′	0°18·1′W	T	198
Botolph's Bridge	Kent	TR1233	51°3·6′	1°1·9′E	X	179,189
Bottacks	Highld	NH4860	57°36·5′	4°32·2′W	T	20
Bottengoms	Essex	TL9432	51°57·4′	0°49·8′E	X	168
Botterleyhill	Ches	SJ5951	53°3·5′	2°36·3′W	X	117
Botternell	Corn	SX2774	50°32·6′	4°26·1′W	T	201
Botter's Fm	Essex	TL7809	51°45·3′	0°35·1′E	FM	167
Bottesford	Leic	SK8038	52°56·2′	0°48·2′W	T	130
Bottesford	N Lincs	SE8907	53°33·2′	0°39·0′W	T	112
Bottesford Beck	N Lincs	SE8806	53°32·8′	0°39·9′W	W	112
Bottesford Moor	N Lincs	SE8507	53°33·4′	0°42·6′W	X	112
Bottin Fms	Lancs	SD8733	53°47·8′	2°11·4′W	FM	103
Bottings Fm	W Susx	TQ2018	50°57·2′	0°17·1′W	FM	198
Bottisam Hall	Cambs	TL5561	52°13·7′	0°16·6′E	A	154
Bottisham	Cambs	TL5460	52°13·2′	0°15·7′E	T	154
Bottisham Fen	Cambs	TL5264	52°15·4′	0°14·0′E	X	154
Bottisham Lode	Cambs	TL5264	52°15·4′	0°14·0′E	W	154
Bottlebrook Houses	Derby	SK3846	53°0·8′	1°25·6′W	X	119,128
Bottlebush Down	Dorset	SU0215	50°56·3′	1°57·9′W	X	184
Bottle & Glass Wood	Suff	TM3986	52°25·4′	1°31·3′E	F	156
Bottle Hill	Devon	SX5658	50°24·5′	4°1·2′W	X	202
Bottle Hill	Stock on T	NZ4224	54°36·8′	1°20·6′W	X	93
Bottlehouse Fm	Bucks	SP8133	51°59·6′	0°48·8′W	FM	152,165
Bottle Island	Highld	NB9502	57°57·9′	5°27·5′W	X	15
Bottlesford	Wilts	SU1159	51°20·0′	1°50·1′W	T	173
Bottles Hall	Essex	TM0724	51°52·8′	1°0·9′E	X	168,169
Bottleswell Point	Somer	ST2164	51°22·4′	3°7·7′W	X	182
Bottom	Angus	NO2853	56°40·1′	3°10·0′W	X	53
Bottom	N Yks	NZ6904	54°25·8′	0°55·8′W	X	94
Bottom Barn	W Berks	SU3868	51°24·8′	1°26·8′W	X	174
Bottom Boat	Wakf	SE3524	53°42·9′	1°27·8′W	T	104
Bottom Burn	E Ayr	NS6607	55°20·6′	4°6·3′W	W	71,77
Bottom Burn	Fife	NT2089	56°5·5′	3°16·7′W	W	66
Bottom Copse	Hants	SU5820	50°58·8′	1°10·0′W	F	185
Bottom Copse	W Berks	SU3372	51°27·0′	1°31·1′W	F	174
Bottomcraig	Fife	NO3624	56°24·5′	3°1·8′W	T	54,59
Bottom Fen Fm	Lincs	TF1628	52°50·5′	0°16·3′W	FM	130
Bottom Flash	Ches	SJ6565	53°11·1′	2°31·0′W	W	118
Bottom Fm	Brad	SE1838	53°50·5′	1°43·2′W	FM	104
Bottom Fm	Cambs	TL1382	52°25·7′	0°19·9′W	FM	142
Bottom Fm	Cambs	TL4584	52°26·3′	0°8·4′E	FM	143
Bottom Fm	Hants	SU5124	51°1·0′	1°16·0′W	FM	185
Bottom Fm	Herts	TL0006	51°44·9′	0°32·7′W	FM	166
Bottom Fm	Monm	SO3912	51°48·4′	2°52·7′W	FM	161
Bottom Fm	Notts	SK5854	53°5·0′	1°7·6′W	FM	120
Bottom Fm	N Yks	SE7197	54°22·1′	0°54·0′W	FM	94,100
Bottom Fm	Oxon	SU6483	51°32·8′	1°4·2′W	FM	175
Bottom Fm	Oxon	SU6777	51°29·5′	1°1·7′W	FM	175
Bottomhead	Falk	NS7780	56°0·1′	3°57·9′W	X	64
Bottom Head Fell	Lancs	SD6559	54°1·8′	2°30·7′W	X	103
Bottom Ho	Cumbr	NY4447	54°49·1′	2°51·9′W	X	85
Bottom Ho	Darl	NZ2617	54°33·1′	1°35·5′W	X	93
Bottom Ho	N Yks	NZ9407	54°27·2′	0°32·6′W	X	94
Bottom House	Staffs	SK0452	53°4·2′	1°56·0′W	T	119

Bottom House Fm	Ches	SJ6358	53°7·3′	2°32·8′W	FM	118
Bottomhouse Fm	Notts	SK5748	53°1·8′	1°8·6′W	FM	129
Bottomhouse Fm	W Berks	SU5974	51°27·9′	1°8·6′W	FM	174
Bottom Laddus Fm	Cambs	TF4601	52°35·5′	0°9·7′E	FM	143
Bottomlane Fm	Staffs	SK0251	53°3·6′	1°57·8′W	FM	119
Bottomley	Cald	SD9421	53°41·4′	2°5·0′W	X	103
Bottomley	Cald	SE0619	53°40·3′	1°54·1′W	T	110
Bottom Lodge	Northnts	TL0277	52°23·1′	0°29·7′W	X	141
Bottom Lodge Fm	Cambs	TL1981	52°25·1′	0°14·6′W	FM	142
Bottom Lodge Fm	Northnts	SP8478	52°23·8′	0°45·5′W	FM	141
Bottom of Hutton	Lancs	SD4827	53°44·5′	2°46·9′W	T	102
Bottom-of-the-Oven	Ches	SJ9872	53°14·9′	2°1·4′W	X	118
Bottom o' th' Moor	Bolton	SD6610	53°35·4′	2°30·4′W	T	109
Bottom Plantation	Leic	SK8724	52°48·6′	0°42·2′W	F	130
Bottom Pond	Kent	TQ8958	51°17·6′	0°43·0′E	T	178
Bottoms	Brad	SE0036	53°49·5′	1°59·6′W	X	104
Bottoms	Corn	SW3824	50°3·7′	5°39·3′W	T	203
Bottoms	E Ayr	NS3844	55°40·0′	4°34·1′W	X	63,70
Bottoms	Shetld	HU3264	60°21·8′	1°24·7′W	X	3
Bottoms Beck	Lancs	SD7456	54°0·2′	2°23·4′W	W	103
Bottoms Fm	Ches	SJ7158	53°7·3′	2°25·6′W	FM	118
Bottoms Fm	Lancs	SD4675	54°10·3′	2°49·2′W	FM	97
Bottoms Fm	S Glos	ST7174	51°28·1′	2°24·7′W	FM	172
Bottom's Hall	Stock	SJ9688	53°23·6′	2°3·2′W	X	109
Bottoms Resr	Derby	SK0296	53°27·9′	1°57·8′W	W	110
Bottoms Rigg	N Yks	SD7573	54°9·4′	2°22·6′W	X	98
Bottom Wood	Bucks	TQ0293	51°37·8′	0°31·2′W	F	176
Bottom Wood	Dorset	SY4792	50°43·7′	2°44·7′W	F	193
Bottom Wood	Oxon	SU6678	51°30·1′	1°2·6′W	F	175
Bottom Woodbeck Fm	Notts	SK7678	53°17·8′	0°51·2′W	FM	120
Bottom Yard Fm	Lincs	TF2416	52°43·9′	0°9·4′W	FM	131
Bottomyre	Angus	NO4545	56°35·9′	2°53·3′W	X	54
Botton Cross	N Yks	NZ6901	54°24·2′	0°55·8′W	A	94
Botton Fm	Brad	SE1838	53°50·5′	1°43·2′W	FM	104
Botton Head	Lancs	SD6661	54°2·9′	2°30·7′W	X	98
Botton Head	N Yks	NZ5901	54°24·3′	1°5·0′W	X	93
Botton Head Fell	Lancs	SD6559	54°1·8′	2°31·6′W	X	102,103
Botton Mill	Lancs	SD6463	54°3·9′	2°32·6′W	X	97
Bottonnet	Corn	SX3178	50°34·9′	4°22·9′W	X	201
Bottor Rock	Devon	SX8280	50°36·7′	3°39·7′W	X	191
Bottreaux Mill	Devon	SS8226	51°1·5′	3°40·6′W	T	181
Bottrells Close	Bucks	SU9893	51°37·9′	0°34·6′W	T	175,176
Botts Green	Warw	SP2492	52°31·8′	1°38·4′W	T	139
Boturich Castle	W Dunb	NS3884	56°1·6′	4°35·5′W	X	56
Botusfleming	Corn	SX4061	50°25·9′	4°14·8′W	T	201
Botvyle	Shrops	SO4796	52°33·8′	2°46·5′W	X	137,138
Botwnnog	Gwyn	SH2631	52°51·1′	4°34·6′W	T	123
Botwright's Fm	Suff	TM2881	52°23·0′	1°21·4′E	FM	156
Boucherett Fm	Lincs	TF1888	53°22·8′	0°13·2′W	FM	113,122
Bouchers Hill	Devon	SS6602	50°48·4′	3°53·7′W	H	191
Bouch Ho	Cumbr	NY1429	54°39·2′	3°19·6′W	X	89
Bouchier's Grange	Essex	TL8524	51°53·3′	0°41·7′E	X	168
Bouchland Fm	Devon	SS6418	50°57·0′	3°55·8′W	FM	180
Boudiestone	Aberd	NJ8327	57°20·2′	2°16·5′W	X	38
Bougang Fm	S Ayr	NX1185	55°7·7′	4°57·4′W	FM	76
Bouges Fm	W Susx	TQ1225	51°1·0′	0°23·8′W	FM	187,198
Bough Beech	Kent	TQ4946	51°11·9′	0°8·3′E	T	188
Bough Beech Resr	Kent	TQ4948	51°12·9′	0°8·4′E	W	188
Boughrood	Powys	SO1339	52°2·8′	3°15·7′W	T	161
Boughrood Brest	Powys	SO1438	52°2·3′	3°14·8′W	T	161
Boughrood Castle	Powys	SO1339	52°2·8′	3°15·7′W	X	161
Boughspring	Glos	ST5597	51°40·4′	2°38·7′W	T	162
Boughthill	Northum	NY7986	55°10·3′	2°19·4′W	X	80
Boughton	Ches	SJ4166	53°11·5′	2°52·6′W	T	117
Boughton	Lincs	TF1245	52°59·7′	0°19·5′W	T	130
Boughton	Norf	TF7001	52°35·0′	0°31·0′E	T	143
Boughton	Northnts	SP7565	52°16·9′	0°53·6′W	T	152
Boughton	Notts	SK6768	53°12·5′	0°59·4′W	T	120
Boughton Aluph	Kent	TR0348	51°11·9′	0°54·7′E	T	179,189
Boughton Bottom	Kent	TQ7748	51°12·4′	0°32·4′E	X	188
Boughton Brake	Notts	SK6669	53°13·1′	1°0·3′W	F	120
Boughton Church Fm	Kent	TR0458	51°17·3′	0°55·9′E	FM	178,179
Boughton Corner	Kent	TR0448	51°11·9′	0°55·6′E	T	179,189
Boughton Grange	Northnts	SP7465	52°16·9′	0°54·5′W	X	152
Boughton Green	Kent	TQ7651	51°14·1′	0°31·7′E	T	188
Boughton Green	Northnts	SP7665	52°16·9′	0°52·8′W	X	152
Boughton Hall	Surrey	TQ0355	51°17·3′	0°31·0′W	X	186
Boughton Heath	Ches	SJ4265	53°11·0′	2°51·7′W	T	117
Boughton Hill	Kent	TR0759	51°17·8′	0°58·5′E	X	179
Boughton House	Northnts	SP9081	52°25·4′	0°40·2′W	A	141
Boughton Lees	Kent	TR0247	51°11·4′	0°53·8′E	T	189
Boughton Lodge Fm	Cambs	TL1964	52°15·9′	0°15·0′W	FM	153
Boughton Malherbe	Kent	TQ8849	51°12·8′	0°41·9′E	T	189
Boughton Mill Fm	Northnts	SP7365	52°16·9′	0°55·4′W	FM	152
Boughton Monchelsea	Kent	TQ7651	51°14·1′	0°31·7′E	T	188
Boughton Monchelsea Place	Kent	TQ7749	51°13·0′	0°32·5′E	A	188
Boughton Mount	Kent	TQ7752	51°14·6′	0°32·5′E	X	188
Boughton Park	Northnts	SP8981	52°25·4′	0°41·1′W	X	141
Boughton Street	Kent	TR0659	51°17·8′	0°57·7′E	T	179
Boughton Village	Cambs	TL1964	52°15·9′	0°15·0′W	A	153
Boughton Wood	Norf	TF7001	52°35·0′	0°31·0′E	F	143
Bought, The	Orkney	HY5708	58°57·7′	2°44·4′W	X	6
Boughurst Street Fm	Kent	TQ6663	51°20·7′	0°23·4′E	FM	177,178,188
Bougton End	Beds	SP9837	52°1·6′	0°33·9′W	T	153
Bouilag Hill	Highld	ND0932	58°16·3′	3°32·6′W	H	11,17
Bouilane	I of M	SC2873	54°7·7′	4°37·5′W	X	95
Boulby	Red & Cl	NZ7619	54°33·9′	0°49·1′W	T	94
Boulby Mine	Red & Cl	NZ7518	54°33·4′	0°50·0′W	X	94
Bould	Oxon	SP2421	51°53·5′	1°38·7′W	T	163
Boulder Clough	Cald	SE0323	53°42·4′	1°56·9′W	T	104
Bouldershaw Ho	N Yks	NY9901	54°24·5′	2°0·5′W	X	92
Bouldershaw Well	Cumbr	SD6885	54°15·8′	2°29·1′W	W	98
Boulderwall Fm	Kent	TR0619	50°56·2′	0°56·3′E	FM	189
Bouldnor	I of W	SZ3789	50°42·2′	1°28·2′W	T	196
Bouldnor Cliff	I of W	SZ3890	50°42·7′	1°27·3′W	X	196
Bouldon	Shrops	SO5485	52°27·9′	2°40·2′W	T	137,138
Boulge	Suff	TM2552	52°7·5′	1°17·6′E	X	156
Boulmer	Northum	NU2614	55°25·4′	1°34·9′W	T	81
Boulmer Haven	Northum	NU2613	55°24·9′	1°34·9′W	W	81

Boulmer Steel	Northum	NU2614	55°25·4′	1°34·9′W	X	81
Boulsbury Fm	Hants	SU0716	50°56·8′	1°53·6′W	FM	184
Boulsbury Wood	Hants	SU0715	50°56·3′	1°53·6′W	F	184
Boulsdon	Glos	SO7024	51°55·1′	2°25·8′W	T	162
Boulston	Pemb	SM9712	51°46·4′	4°56·2′W	T	157,158
Boulsworth Dyke	Lancs	SD9236	53°49·5′	2°6·9′W	X	103
Boulsworth Hill	Lancs	SD9335	53°48·9′	2°6·0′W	H	103
Boultbee's Fm	Warw	SP2696	52°33·9′	1°36·6′W	FM	140
Boultenstone	Aberd	NJ4110	57°10·9′	2°58·1′W	X	37
Boulter's Barn	Oxon	SP2925	51°55·6′	1°34·3′W	X	164
Boulter's Lock	Win & Maid	SU9082	51°32·0′	0°41·8′W	X	175
Boulters Tor	Devon	SX5278	50°35·2′	4°5·1′W	X	191,201
Boultham	Lincs	SK9669	53°12·8′	0°33·3′W	T	121
Boultham Moor	Lincs	SK9568	53°12·3′	0°34·3′W	T	121
Boulthurst Fm	Surrey	TQ4151	51°14·7′	0°1·6′E	FM	187
Boultibrooke	Powys	SO3165	52°17·0′	3°0·3′W	X	137,148
Boulton	C of Derb	SK3832	52°53·3′	1°25·7′W	T	128
Boulton Moor	C of Derb	SK3832	52°53·3′	1°25·7′W	T	128
Boults Green Fm	Ches	SJ7659	53°7·9′	2°21·1′W	FM	118
Boultwood's Fm	Essex	TL7827	51°55·0′	0°35·7′E	FM	167
Bouncers Bank	Kent	TQ6343	51°10·0′	0°20·3′E	X	188
Bounce's Fm	Essex	TL7630	51°56·7′	0°34·0′E	FM	167
Bouncing Hill	Lincs	TF0545	52°59·8′	0°25·7′W	X	130
Boundary	Derby	SK3318	52°45·8′	1°30·3′W	T	128
Boundary	Staffs	SJ9842	52°58·8′	2°1·4′W	T	118
Boundary Belt	Suff	TL8580	52°23·5′	0°44·3′E	F	144
Boundary Dyke	Suff	TM4991	52°27·8′	1°40·3′E	W	134
Boundary Fm	Bucks	SP7041	52°4·0′	0°58·3′W	FM	152
Boundary Fm	Ches	SJ6970	53°13·8′	2°27·5′W	FM	118
Boundary Fm	E Yorks	SE7342	53°52·4′	0°53·0′W	FM	105,106
Boundary Fm	Lancs	SD4019	53°40·1′	2°54·1′W	FM	108
Boundary Fm	Lincs	SK8648	53°1·6′	0°42·7′W	FM	130
Boundary Fm	Lincs	TF0871	53°13·7′	0°22·5′W	FM	121
Boundary Fm	Lincs	TF3045	52°59·4′	0°3·4′W	FM	131
Boundary Fm	Norf	TG3600	52°33·0′	1°29·3′E	FM	134
Boundary Fm	Norf	TM4293	52°29·1′	1°34·3′E	FM	134
Boundary Fm	Notts	SK6056	53°6·1′	1°5·8′W	FM	120
Boundary Fm	N Yks	SE5062	54°3·3′	1°13·8′W	FM	100
Boundary Fm	Staffs	SO8699	52°35·6′	2°12·0′W	FM	139
Boundary Fm	Suff	TM0866	52°15·4′	1°3·3′E	FM	155
Boundary Fm	Suff	TM1262	52°13·1′	1°6·6′E	FM	155
Boundary Fm	Suff	TM1860	52°11·9′	1°11·8′E	FM	156
Boundary Fm	Suff	TM3164	52°13·8′	1°23·4′E	FM	156
Boundary Fm	Suff	TM3583	52°23·9′	1°27·7′E	FM	156
Boundary Fm	Warw	SP3551	52°9·6′	1°28·9′W	FM	151
Boundary Fm	Warw	SP5264	52°16·5′	1°13·9′W	FM	151
Boundary Fms	Ches	SJ8268	53°12·8′	2°15·8′W	FM	118
Boundary Ho	Norf	TG4015	52°41·0′	1°33·5′E	X	134
Bounder Ho	Durham	NZ1139	54°45·0′	1°49·3′W	X	92
Bounderlands	Northum	NY8162	54°57·4′	2°17·4′W	X	86,87
Boundless Copse	Surrey	SU9036	51°7·2′	0°42·5′W	F	186
Bounds Cliff	Corn	SX0281	50°35·9′	4°47·5′W	X	200
Bounds Cross	Devon	SS2801	50°47·2′	4°26·0′W	X	190
Bounds End Fm	Kent	TQ7740	51°8·1′	0°32·2′E	FM	188
Bound's Fm	Essex	TL9008	51°44·5′	0°45·5′E	FM	168
Bounds Fm	Essex	TM0729	51°55·5′	1°1·0′E	FM	168,169
Bound Skerry	Shetld	HU7071	60°25·3′	0°43·2′W	X	2
Bounds, The	Heref	SO6433	51°59·9′	2°31·1′W	X	149
Boundstone	Surrey	SU8344	51°11·6′	0°48·3′W	T	186
Bountisthorne	Devon	SS3715	50°54·9′	4°18·8′W	X	190
Bouprie Banks	Fife	NT1785	56°3·3′	3°19·5′W	X	65,66
Bourblach	Highld	NM6793	56°58·4′	5°49·6′W	X	40
Bourblach Hill	Highld	NM6794	56°58·9′	5°49·6′W	H	40
Bourblaige	Highld	NM5462	56°41·4′	6°0·6′W	X	47
Bourbon Tower	Bucks	SP6837	52°1·9′	1°0·1′W	X	152
Bourchiers	Essex	TL6621	51°52·0′	0°25·1′E	X	167
Bourchier's Hall	Essex	TL9126	51°54·2′	0°47·0′E	X	168
Bourchier's Hall	Essex	TL9411	51°46·1′	0°49·1′E	X	168
Bourden Fm	Leic	SK6312	52°42·4′	1°3·7′W	FM	129
Bourley Hill	Hants	SU8350	51°14·8′	0°48·3′W	X	186
Bourn	Cambs	TL3256	52°11·4′	0°3·7′W	T	153
Bourna	Devon	SS5410	50°52·5′	4°4·1′W	X	191
Bourn Br	Cambs	TL5249	52°7·3′	0°13·6′E	X	154
Bourn Brook	Birm	SP0183	52°26·9′	1°58·7′W	W	139
Bournbrook	Birm	SP0482	52°26·4′	1°56·1′W	T	139
Bourn Brook	Cambs	TL3555	52°10·8′	0°1·1′W	W	154
Bourn Brook	Staffs	SK0225	52°49·6′	1°57·8′W	W	128
Bourne	Devon	SS6514	50°54·8′	3°54·8′W	X	180
Bourne	Lincs	TF0920	52°46·2′	0°22·7′W	T	130
Bourne	N Som	ST4859	51°19·9′	2°44·4′W	T	172,182
Bourne Bank	Worcs	SO8942	52°4·8′	2°9·2′W	X	150
Bourne Barn Fm	Essex	TL9626	51°54·1′	0°51·3′E	FM	168
Bourne Bottom	Wilts	SU1948	51°14·1′	1°43·3′W	X	184
Bourne Brook	Essex	TL8028	51°55·5′	0°37·5′E	W	168
Bourne Brook	Herts	TL4823	51°53·4′	0°9·4′E	W	167
Bourne Brook	Staffs	SK1014	52°43·7′	1°50·7′W	W	128
Bourne Brook	Staffs	SK1702	52°37·2′	1°44·5′W	W	139
Bourne Brook	Warw	SP2890	52°30·7′	1°34·8′W	W	140
Bourne Court	Hants	SU4250	51°15·1′	1°23·5′W	X	185
Bourne Eau	Lincs	TF1319	52°45·6′	0°19·1′W	W	130
Bourne End	Beds	SP9644	52°5·4′	0°35·5′W	T	153
Bourne End	Beds	TL0160	52°14·0′	0°30·9′W	T	153
Bourne End	Bucks	SU8987	51°34·7′	0°42·5′W	T	175
Bourne End	Herts	TL0206	51°44·8′	0°31·0′W	T	166
Bourne End Fm	Beds	SP9745	52°5·9′	0°34·6′W	FM	153
Bourne Fm	Dorset	SY7397	50°46·5′	2°22·6′W	FM	194
Bourne Fm	Essex	TL6040	52°2·3′	0°20·4′E	FM	154
Bourne Fm	E Susx	TQ7525	51°0·1′	0°30·0′E	FM	188,199
Bourne Fm	Hill	TQ0689	51°35·6′	0°27·8′W	FM	176
Bourne Fm	Kent	TQ6054	51°16·0′	0°18·0′E	FM	188
Bourne Fm	Kent	TQ7827	51°1·1′	0°32·7′E	FM	188,199
Bourne Fm	Norf	TL6492	52°30·3′	0°25·4′E	FM	143
Bourne Fm	Wals	SK0700	52°36·1′	1°53·4′W	FM	139
Bourne Fm	Wilts	SU0991	51°37·3′	1°51·8′W	FM	163,173
Bourne Fm	Worcs	SO9041	52°4·3′	2°8·4′W	FM	150
Bourne Grange Fm	Kent	TQ6249	51°13·3′	0°19·6′E	FM	188
Bourne Hill	Suff	TM1541	52°1·8′	1°8·5′E	X	169
Bournehill Ho	W Susx	TQ1728	51°2·6′	0°19·5′W	X	187,198
Bourne Ho	Hants	SU4363	51°22·1′	1°22·5′W	X	174
Bournelake Fm	Wilts	SU0793	51°38·4′	1°53·5′W	FM	163,173

Bournemill Fm	Kent	TQ5944	51°10·6'	0°16·9'E	FM	188
Bournemouth	Bourne	SZ0891	50°43·3'	1°52·8'W	T	195
Bournemouth International Airport	Dorset	SZ1198	50°47·1'	1°50·3'W	X	195
Bourne North Fen	Lincs	TF1421	52°46·7'	0°18·2'W	X	130
Bourne Park	Devon	SS7518	50°57·1'	3°46·4'W	X	180
Bourne Park	Hants	SU3751	51°15·6'	1°27·8'W	X	185
Bourne Park	Kent	TR1853	51°14·3'	1°7·8'E	X	179,189
Bourne Park	Suff	TM1542	52°2·3'	1°8·5'E	X	169
Bourne Park House	Kent	TR1853	51°14·3'	1°7·8'E	A	179,189
Bourne Place	Kent	TQ5549	51°13·4'	0°13·6'E	X	188
Bourne Rivulet	Hants	SU3952	51°16·2'	1°26·1'W	W	185
Bournes	Lancs	SD3941	53°51·9'	2°55·2'W	X	102
Bournes Green	Glos	SO9004	51°44·3'	2°8·3'W	T	163
Bournes Green	Sou-on-Sea	TQ9186	51°32·7'	0°45·7'E	T	178
Bournes Green	Worcs	SO9174	52°22·1'	2°7·5'W	T	139
Bourneside Fm	Kent	TQ6348	51°12·7'	0°20·4'E	FM	188
Bourne South Fen	Lincs	TF1218	52°45·1'	0°20·0'W	X	130
Bourne, The	Monm	SO4609	51°46·9'	2°46·6'W	X	161
Bourne, The	Surrey	TQ0268	51°24·3'	0°31·6'W	W	176
Bourne, The	Surrey	TQ0462	51°21·1'	0°30·0'W	W	176,186
Bourne Vale	Wals	SP0699	52°35·6'	1°54·3'W	T	139
Bourne Valley	Poole	SZ0693	50°44·4'	1°54·5'W	T	195
Bourne Wood	Brom	TQ4968	51°23·7'	0°8·9'E	F	177
Bourne Wood	Lincs	TF0721	52°46·8'	0°24·4'W	F	130
Bournfield Fm	W Berks	SU6171	51°26·3'	1°7·0'W	FM	175
Bournheath	Worcs	SO9474	52°22·1'	2°4·9'W	T	139
Bourn Lodge	Cambs	TL3257	52°12·0'	0°3·7'W	X	153
Bournmoor	Durham	NZ3151	54°51·4'	1°30·6'W	T	88
Bournside	Glos	SO9321	51°53·5'	2°5·7'W	T	163
Bournstream	Glos	ST7494	51°38·9'	2°22·2'W	T	162,172
Bournville	Birm	SP0481	52°25·9'	1°56·1'W	T	139
Bourn Windmill	Cambs	TL3158	52°12·5'	0°4·6'W	A	153
Bourock	D & G	NX8871	55°1·5'	3°44·7'W	X	84
Bourock	E Ayr	NS4051	55°43·8'	4°32·4'W	X	64
Boursa Island	Highld	NC8067	58°34·7'	4°3·3'W	X	10
Bourtie Ho	Aberd	NJ7824	57°18·6'	2°21·5'W	X	38
Bourton	Bucks	SP7033	51°59·7'	0°58·4'W	T	152,165
Bourton	Devon	SX8160	50°25·9'	3°40·2'W	X	202
Bourton	Dorset	ST7630	51°4·4'	2°20·2'W	T	183
Bourton	N Som	ST3764	51°22·5'	2°53·9'W	T	182
Bourton	Oxon	SU2387	51°35·1'	1°39·7'W	T	174
Bourton	Shrops	SO5996	52°33·9'	2°35·9'W	T	137,138
Bourton	Wilts	SU0464	51°22·7'	1°56·2'W	T	173
Bourton Combe	N Som	ST5068	51°24·8'	2°42·7'W	F	172,182
Bourton Downs	Glos	SP1432	51°59·4'	1°47·4'W	X	151
Bourton Far Hill Fm	Glos	SP1332	51°59·4'	1°48·2'W	FM	151
Bourtonfields Fm	Oxon	SP4445	52°6·3'	1°21·1'W	FM	151
Bourton Fm	Somer	ST4155	51°17·7'	2°50·4'W	FM	172,182
Bourton Grange	Shrops	SO6096	52°33·9'	2°35·0'W	X	138
Bourton Grounds	Bucks	SP7232	51°59·1'	0°56·7'W	X	152,165
Bourton Heath	Warw	SP4371	52°20·4'	1°21·7'W	X	140
Bourton Heights	Oxon	SP4446	52°6·9'	1°21·0'W	X	151
Bourton Hill Fm	Glos	SP1518	51°51·9'	1°46·5'W	FM	163
Bourton Hill Ho	Glos	SP1432	51°59·4'	1°47·4'W	X	151
Bourton Ho	Oxon	SP4645	52°6·3'	1°19·3'W	X	151
Bourton on Dunsmore	Warw	SP4370	52°19·8'	1°21·7'W	T	140
Bourton-on-the-Hill	Glos	SP1732	51°59·4'	1°44·8'W	T	151
Bourton-on-the-Water	Glos	SP1620	51°52·9'	1°45·7'W	T	163
Bourton Woods	Glos	SP1633	51°59·9'	1°45·6'W	F	151
Bourtreebush	Angus	NO4756	56°41·8'	2°51·5'W	X	54
Bourtreebush	S Ayr	NS4028	55°31·4'	4°31·6'W	X	70
Bourtreehill	N Ayr	NS3439	55°37·2'	4°37·7'W	T	70
Bourtrees	N Ayr	NS2155	55°45·6'	4°50·7'W	X	63
Bousd	Arg & Bt	NM2563	56°40·9'	6°29·0'W	T	46,47
Bousdale Fm	Red & Cl	NZ5814	54°31·3'	1°5·8'W	FM	93
Bousdale Woods	Red & Cl	NZ5814	54°31·3'	1°5·8'W	F	93
Bousfield	Cumbr	NY6008	54°28·2'	2°36·6'W	X	91
Bousta	Shetld	HU2257	60°18·1'	1°35·6'W	T	3
Boustead Hill	Cumbr	NY2959	54°55·5'	3°6·0'W	T	85
Boust Hill	Highld	NG3537	57°21·0'	6°23·9'W	H	23,32
Boustie Ley	Angus	NO3276	56°52·5'	3°6·5'W	H	44
Bouth	Cumbr	SD3285	54°15·6'	3°2·2'W	T	96,97
Bouth Fall Stile	Cumbr	SD3385	54°15·6'	3°1·3'W	X	96,97
Bouthwaite	Cumbr	SD5498	54°22·8'	2°42·1'W	X	97
Bouthwaite	N Yks	SE1271	54°8·3'	1°48·6'W	T	99
Bouts	Worcs	SP0358	52°13·4'	1°57·0'W	T	150
Bovacott	Devon	SS4204	50°49·1'	4°14·2'W	X	190
Bovaglie	Aberd	NO3091	57°0·5'	3°8·7'W	X	44
Bovain	Stir	NN5430	56°26·6'	4°21·7'W	X	51
Bovehill Fm	Swan	SS4693	51°37·1'	4°13·1'W	FM	159
Boveney	Bucks	SU9377	51°29·3'	0°39·2'W	T	175
Boveney Court	Bucks	SU9377	51°29·3'	0°39·2'W	X	175
Boveney Lock	Bucks	SU9477	51°29·3'	0°38·4'W	X	175
Boveridge	Dorset	SU0614	50°55·8'	1°54·5'W	T	195
Boveridge Heath	Dorset	SU0909	50°53·1'	1°51·9'W	F	195
Boveridge Ho	Dorset	SU0614	50°55·8'	1°54·5'W	X	195
Boverton	V of Glam	SS9868	51°24·3'	3°27·6'W	T	170
Boverton Mill Fm	V of Glam	SS9967	51°23·8'	3°26·7'W	FM	170
Bove Wood	Cumbr	NY5549	54°50·3'	2°41·6'W	F	86
Bovey	Devon	SX4494	50°43·7'	4°12·2'W	X	190
Bovey Down	Devon	SY2091	50°43·0'	3°7·6'W	X	192,193
Bovey Heath	Devon	SX8276	50°34·5'	3°39·6'W	X	191
Bovey Ho (Hotel)	Devon	SY2090	50°42·5'	3°7·6'W	X	192,193
Bovey Tracey	Devon	SX8178	50°35·6'	3°40·5'W	T	191
Boville Park	N Yks	SE4496	54°21·7'	1°19·0'W	X	99
Bovill's Hall	Essex	TM1517	51°48·8'	1°7·6'E	X	168,169
Bovill Uplands	Essex	TL9200	51°40·2'	0°47·0'E	X	168
Bovingdon	Herts	TL0103	51°43·2'	0°31·9'W	T	166
Bovingdon Green	Bucks	SU8386	51°34·2'	0°47·8'W	T	175
Bovingdon Green	Herts	TL0102	51°42·7'	0°31·9'W	T	166
Bovingdon Hall	Essex	TL7427	51°55·1'	0°32·2'E	X	167
Bovingdon Wood	Essex	TL7528	51°55·6'	0°33·1'E	F	167
Bovinger	Essex	TL5205	51°43·6'	0°12·4'E	T	167
Bovinger Lodge	Essex	TL5206	51°44·2'	0°12·5'E	X	167
Bovington Camp	Dorset	SY8389	50°42·3'	2°14·1'W	T	194
Bovington Fm	Dorset	SY8288	50°41·7'	2°14·9'W	FM	194
Bovington Heath	Dorset	SY8289	50°42·3'	2°14·9'W	X	194
Bovingtons	Essex	TL8011	51°46·3'	0°36·9'E	X	168
Bovisand Bay	Devon	SX4950	50°20·1'	4°6·9'W	W	201
Bovisand Lodge	Devon	SX4950	50°20·1'	4°6·9'W	X	201
Bovone	Glos	SO7622	51°54·0'	2°20·5'W	X	162
Bovuy	Arg & Bt	NN1022	56°21·4'	5°4·1'W	X	50
Bow	Cumbr	NY3356	54°53·9'	3°2·3'W	X	85
Bow	Devon	SS7201	50°47·9'	3°48·6'W	T	191
Bow	Devon	SX8049	50°20·0'	3°40·8'W	X	202
Bow	Devon	SX8156	50°23·7'	3°40·1'W	T	202
Bow	D & G	NX5092	55°12·2'	4°21·0'W	H	77
Bow	Orkney	ND4587	58°46·3'	2°56·6'W	X	7
Bow	Orkney	ND4897	58°51·7'	2°53·6'W	X	6,7
Bow	Oxon	SU3494	51°38·9'	1°30·1'W	T	164,174
Bow	T Ham	TQ3682	51°31·5'	0°2·0'W	T	177
Bowacre	Devon	SX7396	50°45·2'	3°47·6'W	X	191
Bowanhill	Scot Bord	NT4005	55°20·4'	2°56·3'W	X	79
Bowaters Fm	Thurr	TQ6777	51°28·3'	0°24·7'E	FM	177,178
Bowbank	Cumbr	NY5659	54°55·7'	2°40·8'W	X	86
Bowbank	Cumbr	SD5296	54°21·7'	2°43·9'W	X	97
Bowbank	Durham	NY9423	54°36·4'	2°5·2'W	T	91,92
Bow Barn Fm	Somer	ST4513	50°55·1'	2°46·6'W	FM	193
Bowbeat Hill	Scot Bord	NT2946	55°42·4'	3°7·4'W	H	73
Bow Beck	N Yks	SE1249	53°56·5'	1°48·6'W	W	104
Bowbeck	Suff	TL9475	52°20·5'	0°51·3'E	T	144
Bowbeer	Devon	SX7191	50°42·5'	3°49·2'W	X	191
Bowbeer	Devon	SX7198	50°46·3'	3°49·4'W	X	191
Bowber Head	Cumbr	NY7403	54°25·6'	2°23·6'W	X	91
Bowber Hill	Cumbr	NY8110	54°29·3'	2°17·2'W	X	91,92
Bowbierhill	Devon	SS9521	50°59·0'	3°29·4'W	X	181
Bow Br	Heref	SO4373	52°21·4'	2°49·8'W	X	137,148
Bow Br	N Yks	SD9963	54°4·0'	2°0·5'W	X	98
Bow Brickhill	Mil Key	SP9034	52°0·1'	0°40·9'W	T	152,165
Bow Brickhill Sta	Mil Key	SP8934	52°0·1'	0°41·8'W	X	152,165
Bow Bridge	Cumbr	SD2271	54°8·0'	3°11·2'W	A	96
Bow Bridge	Fife	NT2094	56°8·2'	3°16·8'W	X	58
Bowbridge	Glos	SO8504	51°44·3'	2°12·6'W	T	162
Bowbridge	Pth & Kin	NO1930	56°27·6'	3°18·4'W	X	53
Bowbridge Fields Fm	Derby	SK3038	52°56·6'	1°32·8'W	FM	128
Bowbridge Fm	N Yks	SE5144	53°53·6'	1°13·0'W	FM	105
Bowbridge Ho	Cumbr	NY6814	54°31·5'	2°29·2'W	X	91
Bowbridge House Fm	Derby	SK3038	52°56·6'	1°32·8'W	FM	128
Bow Brook	Hants	SU6558	51°19·3'	1°3·6'W	W	175,186
Bowbrook	Shrops	SJ4512	52°42·4'	2°48·4'W	T	126
Bow Brook	Somer	ST7124	51°1·1'	2°24·4'W	W	183
Bow Brook	Somer	ST7321	50°59·5'	2°22·7'W	W	183
Bow Brook	Worcs	SO9351	52°9·7'	2°5·7'W	W	150
Bow Broom	Roth	SK4599	53°29·4'	1°18·9'W	T	111
Bowbrow	Cumbr	NY6208	54°28·2'	2°34·8'W	X	91
Bow Burn	D & G	NX5799	55°16·1'	4°14·6'W	W	77
Bow Burn	D & G	NX6099	55°16·2'	4°11·8'W	W	77
Bowburn	Durham	NZ3038	54°44·4'	1°31·6'W	T	93
Bow Burn	E Ayr	NS4413	55°23·4'	4°27·3'W	W	70
Bowburnet	Heref	SO4571	52°20·3'	2°48·0'W	X	137,138,148
Bow Castle	Scot Bord	NT4641	55°39·8'	2°51·1'W	X	73
Bow Castle (Broch)	Scot Bord	NT4641	55°39·8'	2°51·1'W	A	73
Bowcheek	Orkney	HY3529	59°8·8'	3°7·7'W	X	6
Bowcliffe Hall	Leeds	SE4242	53°52·6'	1°21·3'W	X	105
Bowcombe	Devon	SX6655	50°23·0'	3°52·7'W	X	202
Bowcombe	Devon	SX7544	50°17·2'	3°44·9'W	X	202
Bowcombe	I of W	SZ4686	50°40·5'	1°20·6'W	T	196
Bowcombe Down	I of W	SZ4687	50°41·1'	1°20·5'W	X	196
Bow Common	T Ham	TQ3781	51°30·9'	0°1·1'W	T	177
Bowcott Fm	Glos	ST7896	51°40·0'	2°18·7'W	FM	162
Bow Creek	Devon	SX8256	50°23·8'	3°39·2'W	W	202
Bow Cross	Devon	SX8065	50°28·6'	3°41·1'W	X	202
Bowd	Devon	SY1089	50°41·9'	3°16·1'W	X	192
Bowd	Devon	SY1090	50°42·4'	3°16·1'W	T	192,193
Bowdah	Corn	SS2400	50°46·6'	4°29·4'W	X	190
Bowdell	Kent	TQ9927	51°0·7'	0°50·6'E	X	189
Bowden	Corn	SX2068	50°29·3'	4°31·9'W	X	201
Bowden	Corn	SS4121	50°58·2'	4°15·5'W	X	180,190
Bowden	Devon	SS4717	50°56·2'	4°10·3'W	X	180
Bowden	Devon	SS8322	50°59·4'	3°39·6'W	X	181
Bowden	Devon	SX7067	50°29·5'	3°49·6'W	X	202
Bowden	Devon	SX7492	50°43·1'	3°46·7'W	X	191
Bowden	Devon	SX7544	50°17·2'	3°44·9'W	X	202
Bowden	Devon	SX7951	50°21·0'	3°41·7'W	X	202
Bowden	Devon	SX8448	50°19·5'	3°37·4'W	T	202
Bowden	Dorset	ST7723	51°0·6'	2°19·3'W	T	183
Bowden	Scot Bord	NT5530	55°33·9'	2°42·4'W	T	73
Bowden	Somer	SS9940	51°9·3'	3°26·3'W	X	181
Bowden Bank Fm	Ches	SJ7975	53°16·5'	2°18·5'W	FM	118
Bowden Burn	Scot Bord	NT5630	55°34·0'	2°41·4'W	W	73
Bowden Corner	Devon	SS5740	51°8·7'	4°2·3'W	X	180
Bowden Derra Hotel	Corn	SX2581	50°36·4'	4°28·0'W	X	201
Bowden Doors	Northum	NU0732	55°35·1'	1°52·9'W	X	75
Bowden Fm	Devon	SS5645	51°11·4'	4°3·3'W	FM	180
Bowden Fm	Devon	SS5740	51°8·7'	4°2·3'W	FM	180
Bowden Fm	Devon	SX7190	50°42·0'	3°49·2'W	FM	191
Bowden Fm	Devon	SX7283	50°38·2'	3°48·2'W	FM	191
Bowden Fm	Devon	SX7488	50°40·9'	3°46·6'W	FM	191
Bowden Fm	Somer	ST0631	51°4·5'	3°20·1'W	FM	181
Bowden Fm	Wilts	SU2262	51°21·6'	1°40·7'W	FM	174
Bowden Hall	Derby	SK0681	53°19·8'	1°54·2'W	X	110
Bowden Hall (Hotel)	Glos	SO8715	51°50·2'	2°10·9'W	X	162
Bowden Hill	Devon	SX4682	50°37·3'	4°10·2'W	X	201
Bowden Hill	Wilts	ST9367	51°24·4'	2°5·6'W	T	173
Bowden Hill Ho	Wilts	ST9367	51°24·4'	2°5·6'W	X	173
Bowden Ho	Devon	SX8058	50°24·8'	3°41·0'W	X	202
Bowden House Fm	Ches	SJ8781	53°19·8'	2°11·3'W	FM	109
Bowden Moor	Scot Bord	NT5231	55°34·5'	2°45·2'W	X	73
Bowdenmoor	Scot Bord	NT5331	55°34·5'	2°44·3'W	X	73
Bowden Park	Wilts	ST9368	51°24·9'	2°5·7'W	X	173
Bowdens	Devon	SS8921	50°58·9'	3°34·5'W	X	181
Bowdens	Dorset	ST7302	50°49·2'	2°22·6'W	X	194
Bowdens	Essex	TL9433	51°57·9'	0°49·8'E	X	168
Bowdens	Somer	ST4128	51°3·1'	2°50·1'W	T	193
Bowden's Fm	Newp	ST4189	51°35·9'	2°50·7'W	FM	171,172
Bowden's Fm	Somer	ST3922	50°59·9'	2°51·8'W	FM	193
Bowden View Fm	Ches	SJ7183	53°20·8'	2°25·7'W	FM	109
Bowderdale	Cumbr	NY1607	54°27·3'	3°17·3'W	X	89
Bowderdale	Cumbr	NY6704	54°26·1'	2°30·1'W	T	91
Bowderdale Beck	Cumbr	NY6701	54°24·4'	2°30·1'W	W	91
Bowder Stone	Cumbr	NY2516	54°32·3'	3°9·1'W	X	89,90
Bowd Fm	S Glos	ST7274	51°28·1'	2°23·8'W	FM	172
Bowditch Fm	Devon	ST2505	50°50·6'	3°3·5'W	FM	192,193
Bowd Lane Wood	Northnts	SP8086	52°28·2'	0°48·9'W	F	141
Bowdley	Devon	SX7472	50°32·3'	3°46·3'W	X	191
Bowd Lodge	Northnts	SP8085	52°27·7'	0°49·0'W	X	141
Bowdon	Traf	SJ7586	53°22·5'	2°22·1'W	T	109
Bowdon View Fm	Ches	SJ7484	53°21·4'	2°23·0'W	FM	109
Bowdown Ho	W Berks	SU5065	51°23·1'	1°16·5'W	X	174
Bowd's Fm	Wilts	SU0180	51°31·4'	1°58·7'W	FM	173
Bowdun Head	Aberd	NO8884	56°57·1'	2°11·4'W	X	45
Bowduns	Aberd	NO8884	56°57·1'	2°11·4'W	X	45
Bowens Fm	Kent	TQ5342	51°9·6'	0°11·7'E	FM	188
Bowen's Hall	Wrex	SJ4442	52°58·6'	2°49·6'W	X	117
Bower	Devon	SS3915	50°55·0'	4°17·0'W	X	190
Bower	Highld	ND2363	58°33·2'	3°18·9'W	T	11,12
Bower	Northum	NY7583	55°8·7'	2°23·1'W	H	80
Bower	Northum	NY7583	55°8·7'	2°23·1'W	X	80
Bower	Renf	NS3762	55°49·7'	4°35·7'W	X	63
Bower	Scot Bord	NT4250	55°44·6'	2°55·0'W	X	66,73
Bower Ashton	C of Bris	ST5671	51°26·4'	2°37·6'W	T	172
Bowerbank	Cumbr	NY4724	54°36·8'	2°48·8'W	X	90
Bower Brook	Oxon	SU2589	51°36·2'	1°37·9'W	W	174
Bower Brook	Oxon	SU2590	51°36·7'	1°37·9'W	W	163,174
Bowerchalke	Wilts	SU0223	51°0·6'	1°57·9'W	T	184
Bowerclough Head	Tames	SE0201	53°30·6'	1°57·8'W	X	110
Bowercourt Fm	Worcs	SO7370	52°19·9'	2°23·4'W	FM	138
Bowerdale Beck	Cumbr	SD6799	54°23·4'	2°30·1'W	W	98
Bowerdon	Devon	SX7066	50°29·0'	3°49·6'W	X	202
Bower End	Staffs	SJ7644	52°59·8'	2°21·1'W	X	118
Bower Fm	Essex	TQ5496	51°38·7'	0°13·9'E	FM	167,177
Bower Fm	E Susx	TQ3719	50°57·5'	0°2·6'W	FM	198
Bower Fm	Hants	SU6926	51°2·0'	1°0·6'W	FM	186,197
Bower Fm	Hav	TQ5093	51°37·2'	0°10·4'E	FM	177
Bower Fm	Monm	SO3723	51°54·4'	2°54·6'W	FM	161
Bower Fm	Shrops	SO5572	52°20·9'	2°39·2'W	FM	137,138
Bower Fm	Staffs	SK0319	52°46·4'	1°56·9'W	FM	128
Bower Fm	Suff	TM1449	52°6·1'	1°7·9'E	FM	169
Bower Fm	W Berks	SU5580	51°31·2'	1°12·0'W	FM	174
Bower Hall	Essex	TL6740	52°2·2'	0°26·5'E	X	154
Bower Hall	Essex	TL8045	52°4·7'	0°38·0'E	X	155
Bower Hall	Essex	TM0214	51°47·5'	0°56·1'E	X	168
Bowerhayes Fm	Devon	ST1408	50°52·1'	3°12·9'W	FM	192,193
Bower Heath	Herts	TL1416	51°50·1'	0°20·3'W	T	166
Bower Hill	S Ayr	NS2918	55°25·8'	4°41·7'W	H	70
Bower Hill	Somer	ST2439	51°8·9'	3°4·8'W	H	182
Bowerhill	Wilts	ST9162	51°21·7'	2°7·4'W	T	173
Bowerhill Lodge Fm	Wilts	ST9163	51°22·2'	2°7·4'W	FM	173
Bower Hinton	Somer	ST4518	50°57·8'	2°46·6'W	T	193
Bower Ho	Hav	TQ5192	51°36·6'	0°11·2'E	X	177
Bowerhope	Scot Bord	NT2522	55°29·4'	3°10·8'W	T	73
Bowerhope Burn	Scot Bord	NT2521	55°28·9'	3°10·8'W	W	73
Bowerhope Law	Scot Bord	NT2521	55°28·9'	3°10·8'W	H	73
Bowerhouse	E Loth	NT6676	55°58·8'	2°32·3'W	X	67
Bowerhouse	Scot Bord	NT4950	55°44·7'	2°48·3'W	X	66,73
Bower House Fm	Suff	TL9840	52°1·6'	0°53·6'E	FM	155
Bower House Tye	Suff	TL9840	52°1·6'	0°53·6'E	T	155
Bowerland	Devon	SX5493	50°43·3'	4°3·7'W	X	191
Bowerland Fm	Kent	TR0854	51°15·1'	0°59·2'E	FM	179,189
Bowerland Fm	Surrey	TQ3945	51°11·5'	0°0·3'W	FM	187
Bowermadden	Highld	ND2464	58°33·7'	3°17·9'W	X	11,12
Bowerman's Nose	Devon	SX7480	50°36·6'	3°46·5'W	X	191
Bower of Wandel	S Lanak	NS9528	55°32·3'	3°39·4'W	A	72
Bower Park Fm	Kent	TQ5563	51°20·9'	0°13·9'E	FM	177,188
Bowers	Cumbr	SD6295	54°21·2'	2°34·7'W	X	97
Bowers	Staffs	SJ8135	52°55·0'	2°16·6'W	T	127
Bowers Fm	Bucks	SU9594	51°38·4'	0°37·2'W	FM	175,176
Bower's Fm	Somer	ST5627	51°2·7'	2°37·3'W	FM	183
Bowers Gifford	Essex	TQ7588	51°34·0'	0°31·9'E	T	178
Bowers Hall	Derby	SK2364	53°10·6'	1°38·9'W	X	119
Bowers Hall	Essex	TQ7587	51°33·5'	0°31·9'E	X	178
Bowershall	Fife	NT0991	56°6·4'	3°27·4'W	T	58
Bowershield	Northum	NY9494	55°14·7'	2°5·2'W	X	80
Bowers Hill	Worcs	SP0842	52°4·8'	1°52·6'W	X	150
Bower's House Fm	N Yks	SE5228	53°45·0'	1°12·3'W	FM	105
Bowers Marshes	Essex	TQ7586	51°33·0'	0°31·8'E	X	178
Bowers, The	Lancs	SD4645	53°54·1'	2°48·9'W	X	102
Bowerswain Fm	Dorset	SU0009	50°53·1'	1°59·6'W	FM	195
Bower, The	Heref	SO2958	52°13·2'	3°2·0'W	X	148
Bowerthy	Devon	SS7209	50°52·2'	3°48·8'W	X	191
Bowerthy Wood	Devon	SS7209	50°52·2'	3°48·8'W	F	191
Bowertower	Highld	ND2262	58°32·6'	3°19·9'W	X	11,12
Bowertrapping	N Ayr	NS3249	55°42·6'	4°40·0'W	X	63
Bower Wood	Bucks	SU9588	51°35·2'	0°37·3'W	F	175,176
Bower Wood	Kent	TR0856	51°16·1'	0°59·3'E	F	179
Bowery, The	Aberd	NO7899	57°5·1'	2°21·3'W	X	38,45
Bowes	Durham	NY9913	54°31·0'	2°0·5'W	T	92
Bowes	E Ayr	NS5618	55°26·3'	4°16·1'W	X	71
Bowes	Scot Bord	NT6643	55°41·0'	2°32·0'W	X	74
Bowes Close	Durham	NY8332	54°41·2'	2°15·4'W	X	91,92
Bowes Close	Durham	NZ1426	54°38·0'	1°46·6'W	X	92
Bowes Edge	Lancs	SD9442	53°52·7'	2°5·1'W	X	103
Bowesfield Fm	Cumbr	SD2271	54°8·0'	3°11·2'W	FM	96
Bowesfield Industrial Estate	Stock on T	NZ4316	54°32·5'	1°19·7'W	X	93
Bowe's Gate	Ches	SJ5758	53°7·3'	2°38·1'W	X	117
Bowes Green Fm	N Yks	SE2563	54°4·0'	1°36·7'W	FM	99
Boweshill	Northum	NY8085	55°9·8'	2°18·4'W	X	80
Bowes Hill	N Yks	SE3396	54°21·7'	1°29·1'W	X	99
Bowes Ho	Durham	NZ3052	54°52·0'	1°31·5'W	X	88
Bowes Lodge	Cumbr	SD4283	54°14·6'	2°53·0'W	X	96,97
Bowes Moor	Durham	NY9211	54°29·9'	2°7·0'W	X	91,92
Bowes Moor Hotel	Durham	NY9212	54°30·4'	2°7·0'W	X	91,92
Bowes Museum, The	Durham	NZ0516	54°32·6'	1°54·9'W	X	92
Bowes Park	Enf	TQ3091	51°36·4'	0°7·0'W	T	176,177
Bowes Rly	Sund	NZ2858	54°55·2'	1°33·4'W	X	88
Bowett	Pemb	SM9600	51°39·9'	4°56·6'W	X	157,158
Bow Farm	Inverc	NS2576	55°57·0'	4°47·7'W	FM	63
Bow Fell	Cumbr	NY2406	54°26·9'	3°9·9'W	H	89,90

Bowfell Links	Cumbr	NY2406	54°26·9′	3°9·9′W	X	89,90
Bowfield	Durham	NZ0312	54°30·4′	1°56·8′W	X	92
Bowfield	E Renf	NS4055	55°46·0′	4°32·6′W	X	64
Bowfield	Renf	NS3958	55°47·6′	4°33·6′W	X	63
Bow Field	Shetld	HU4657	60°17·9′	1°9·6′W	H	2,3
Bow Fm	Scot Bord	NT4541	55°39·8′	2°52·0′W	FM	73
Bow Fm	Worcs	SO8736	52°1·6′	2°11·0′W	FM	150
Bowford Fm	W Susx	TQ1218	50°57·3′	0°23·9′W	FM	198
Bowforth	N Yks	SE6883	54°14·5′	0°57·0′W	X	100
Bow Grange	Devon	SX8364	50°28·1′	3°38·5′W	X	202
Bowgreave	Lancs	SD4943	53°53·1′	2°46·1′W	T	102
Bow Green	Somer	ST2517	50°57·1′	3°3·7′W	X	193
Bowgreen	Traf	SJ7586	53°22·5′	2°22·1′W	T	109
Bow Hall	Cumbr	NY7025	54°37·4′	2°27·5′W	X	91
Bowhayes Fm	Devon	ST1012	50°54·3′	3°16·4′W	FM	181,193
Bowhay Fm	Devon	SX8988	50°41·1′	3°33·9′W	FM	192
Bow Head	Orkney	HY4552	59°21·3′	2°57·6′W	X	5
Bow Hill	D & G	NY0184	55°8·7′	3°32·8′W	X	78
Bow Hill	D & G	NY1786	55°9·9′	3°17·7′W	H	79
Bow Hill	E Ayr	NS4412	55°22·9′	4°27·3′W	X	70
Bowhill	Fife	NT2195	56°8·7′	3°15·8′W	T	58
Bow Hill	Norf	TG1307	52°37·4′	1°9·2′E	X	144
Bowhill	Scot Bord	NT4227	55°32·2′	2°54·7′W	T	73
Bowhill	W Susx	SU8109	50°52·7′	0°50·5′W	X	197
Bow Hill	W Susx	SU8211	50°53·8′	0°49·7′W	X	197
Bowhill Fm	Devon	ST0004	50°49·8′	3°24·8′W	FM	192
Bowhill Fm	Staffs	SJ7648	53°2·0′	2°21·1′W	FM	118
Bow Hill Ho	Kent	TQ6951	51°14·2′	0°25·6′E	X	188
Bowhill House	Fife	NO4608	56°15·9′	2°51·9′W	X	59
Bow Hills	N Yks	NY9609	54°28·8′	2°3·3′W	X	91,92
Bowhills	Shrops	SO7784	52°27·4′	2°19·9′W	X	138
Bowhills Dingle	Shrops	SO7884	52°27·4′	2°19·0′W	X	138
Bow Hills Head	Durham	NY9609	54°28·8′	2°3·3′W	X	91,92
Bow Ho	Shrops	SO3689	52°29·9′	2°56·2′W	X	137
Bowhouse	Clackm	NS8992	56°6·7′	3°46·7′W	X	58
Bowhouse	D & G	NY0265	54°58·5′	3°31·4′W	X	84
Bowhouse	Falk	NS9475	55°57·6′	3°41·4′W	X	65
Bowhouse	Fife	NO5101	56°12·2′	2°46·9′W	X	59
Bowhouse	Fife	NT3195	56°8·8′	3°6·2′W	X	59
Bowhouse	N Lanak	NS7863	55°50·9′	3°56·5′W	X	64
Bowhouse	Pth & Kin	NO2001	56°11·9′	3°16·9′W	X	58
Bowhouse	S Lanak	NS9438	55°37·7′	3°40·6′W	X	71,72
Bowhousebog or Liquo	N Lanak	NS8558	55°48·4′	3°49·7′W	T	65,72
Bowhouse Fm	E Ayr	NS3847	55°41·6′	4°34·2′W	FM	63
Bowhouse Fm	Fife	NO2610	56°16·9′	3°11·3′W	FM	59
Bowhouse Fm	Fife	NT2397	56°9·8′	3°14·0′W	FM	58
Bowiebank	Aberd	NJ6959	57°37·5′	2°30·7′W	X	29
Bowie's Plantn	Scot Bord	NT8959	55°49·7′	2°10·1′W	F	67,74
Bowing Park	Know	SJ4289	53°23·9′	2°51·9′W	T	108
Bowismiln	Scot Bord	NT5023	55°30·1′	2°47·1′W	T	73
Bowithick	Corn	SX1882	50°36·8′	4°34·0′W	T	201
Bowker's Green	Lancs	SD4004	53°32·0′	2°53·9′W	T	108
Bowkerstead Fm	Cumbr	SD3391	54°18·9′	3°1·4′W	FM	96,97
Bowlacre Fm	Stock	SJ9492	53°25·7′	2°5·0′W	FM	109
Bow Laithe	Lancs	SD7747	53°55·4′	2°20·6′W	X	103
Bowlams Fox Covert	E Yorks	TA1244	53°53·0′	0°17·3′W	F	107
Bowland	Scot Bord	NT4439	55°38·7′	2°53·0′W	X	73
Bowland	Scot Bord	NT4540	55°39·3′	2°52·0′W	X	73
Bowland Bridge	Cumbr	SD4189	54°17·8′	2°54·0′W	T	96,97
Bowland Ho	N Yks	SE6733	53°47·6′	0°58·6′W	X	105,106
Bowland Knotts	N Yks	SD7261	54°2·9′	2°25·2′W	X	98
Bowlas Wood	Glos	ST8299	51°41·6′	2°15·2′W	F	162
Bowldish Pond	Dorset	SU0315	50°56·3′	1°57·1′W	W	184
Bowldown	Wilts	ST9277	51°29·7′	2°6·5′W	T	173
Bowldown Fm	Glos	ST8392	51°37·8′	2°14·3′W	FM	162,173
Bowldown Wood	Glos	ST8491	51°37·3′	2°13·5′W	F	162,173
Bowleaze Common	Newp	ST3785	51°33·9′	2°54·1′W	X	171
Bowleaze Cove	Dorset	SY7081	50°37·9′	2°25·1′W	W	194
Bowlee	Roch	SD8406	53°33·3′	2°14·1′W	T	109
Bowlees	Durham	NY9028	54°39·1′	2°8·9′W	T	91,92
Bowlees	Durham	NZ0937	54°43·9′	1°51·2′W	X	92
Bowler's Town	E Susx	TQ9122	50°58·2′	0°43·6′E	T	189
Bowle's Fm	Essex	TL7341	52°2·6′	0°31·8′E	FM	155
Bowles Fm	Hants	SU2820	50°59·0′	1°35·7′W	FM	184
Bowles Fm	Oxon	SP4111	51°48·0′	1°23·9′W	FM	164
Bowles Fm	Surrey	TQ0838	51°8·1′	0°27·0′W	FM	187
Bowley	Devon	SS9004	50°49·7′	3°33·3′W	X	192
Bowley	Heref	SO5452	52°10·1′	2°40·0′W	T	149
Bowley Fm	Kent	TQ8949	51°12·8′	0°42·8′E	FM	189
Bowley Fm	W Susx	SU8525	51°1·3′	0°46·9′W	FM	186,197
Bowley Fm	W Susx	SZ8899	50°47·3′	0°44·7′W	FM	197
Bowley Hill	Lancs	SD7233	53°48·0′	2°25·1′W	X	103
Bowley Lane	Heref	SO6843	52°5·3′	2°27·6′W	T	149
Bowleys	Fife	NT0992	56°7·0′	3°27·4′W	X	58
Bowley Scout Camp	Lancs	SD7333	53°47·8′	2°24·2′W	X	103
Bowley's Fm	Notts	SK5222	52°47·8′	1°13·3′W	FM	129
Bowley's Wood	Bucks	SU7494	51°38·6′	0°55·4′W	F	175
Bowley Town	Heref	SO5353	52°10·6′	2°40·8′W	T	149
Bowl Fm	Essex	TM1729	51°55·3′	1°9·7′E	FM	168,169
Bowl Fm	Glos	SP1726	51°56·2′	1°44·8′W	FM	163
Bowlhead Green	Surrey	SU9138	51°8·3′	0°41·6′W	T	186
Bowlhole Wood	Stock on T	NZ3709	54°28·7′	1°25·3′W	F	93
Bowling	Brad	SE1731	53°46·7′	1°44·1′W	T	104
Bowling	W Dunb	NS4479	55°55·7′	4°29·4′W	T	64
Bowling Alley	Hants	SU7949	51°14·3′	0°51·7′W	T	186
Bowling Bank	Wrex	SJ3948	53°1·8′	2°54·2′W	T	117
Bowling Fm	Pemb	SM9620	51°50·7′	4°57·3′W	FM	157,158
Bowling Green	Corn	SX0258	50°23·5′	4°46·8′W	T	200
Bowling Green	Corn	SX3670	50°30·6′	4°18·4′W	T	201
Bowling Green	Dudley	SO9486	52°28·6′	2°4·9′W	T	139
Bowling Green	Glos	SP0202	51°43·2′	1°57·9′W	T	163
Bowling Green	Hants	SZ2996	50°46·0′	1°34·9′W	T	196
Bowling Green	Shrops	SJ6225	52°49·5′	2°33·4′W	T	127
Bowling Green	Worcs	SO8151	52°9·7′	2°16·3′W	T	150
Bowling Green Fm	Derby	SK2366	53°11·7′	1°38·9′W	FM	119
Bowling Green Fm	Oxon	SU3095	51°39·4′	1°33·6′W	FM	164
Bowling Green Fm	Suff	TM3268	52°15·9′	1°24·4′E	FM	156
Bowling Green Ho	Shrops	SJ7904	52°38·2′	2°18·2′W	X	127
Bowling Park	Brad	SE1731	53°46·7′	1°44·1′W	X	104
Bowlins	Moray	NJ3851	57°33·0′	3°1·7′W	X	28
Bowlish	Devon	SX8595	50°44·8′	3°37·4′W	X	191
Bowlish	Somer	ST6143	51°11·3′	2°33·1′W	T	183
Bowl Rock, The	Corn	SW5236	50°10·6′	5°28·0′W	X	203
Bowls	Cered	SN2747	52°5·9′	4°31·2′W	X	145
Bowls Barrow	Wilts	ST9446	51°13·0′	2°4·8′W	X	184
Bowls Barrow (Long Barrow)	Wilts	ST9446	51°13·0′	2°4·8′W	A	184
Bowlturner Ho	N Yks	NZ3004	54°26·1′	1°31·8′W	X	93
Bowl Wood Fm	Norf	TF6808	52°38·8′	0°29·4′E	FM	143
Bowman Hill	Notts	SK6781	53°19·5′	0°59·2′W	X	111,120
Bowman-hillock	Aberd	NJ4839	57°26·6′	2°51·5′W	X	28,29
Bowmans	Kent	TQ5273	51°26·4′	0°11·6′E	T	177
Bowmans	Moray	NJ3526	57°19·5′	3°4·3′W	X	37
Bowman's Fm	E Susx	TQ6822	50°58·6′	0°24·0′E	FM	199
Bowmansgreen Fm	Herts	TL1804	51°43·6′	0°17·1′W	FM	166
Bowmanstead	Cumbr	SD2996	54°21·5′	3°5·1′W	T	96,97
Bowmanston	S Ayr	NS3918	55°26·0′	4°32·2′W	X	70
Bowmillholm	D & G	NY1274	55°3·4′	3°22·2′W	X	85
Bowmont Forest	Scot Bord	NT7328	55°32·9′	2°25·2′W	F	74
Bowmont Hill	Northum	NT8331	55°34·6′	2°15·7′W	X	74
Bowmont Water	Scot Bord	NT8329	55°33·5′	2°15·7′W	W	74
Bowmont Water	Scot Bord	NT8419	55°28·1′	2°14·8′W	W	80
Bowmore	Arg & Bt	NR3159	55°45·2′	6°16·8′W	T	60
Bowmuir	S Lanak	NS9942	55°39·9′	3°35·9′W	X	72
Bowness	Cumbr	NY1015	54°31·6′	3°23·0′W	X	89
Bowness Common	Cumbr	NY1959	54°55·4′	3°15·4′W	X	85
Bowness Fm	Cumbr	NY2229	54°39·3′	3°12·1′W	FM	89,90
Bowness Hall	Cumbr	NY2261	54°56·5′	3°12·6′W	X	85
Bowness Knott	Cumbr	NY1115	54°31·6′	3°22·1′W	H	89
Bowness-on-Solway	Cumbr	NY2262	54°57·0′	3°12·6′W	T	85
Bowness-On-Windermere	Cumbr	SD4096	54°21·6′	2°55·0′W	T	96,97
Bowness Wath	Cumbr	NY2163	54°57·6′	3°13·6′W	W	85
Bown Hill	Glos	SO8202	51°43·2′	2°15·2′W	H	162
Bown Scar Wood	N Yks	SD9172	54°8·9′	2°7·9′W	F	98
Bown's Fm	Glos	SP0503	51°43·8′	1°55·3′W	FM	163
Bow of Cavequoy	Orkney	HY4533	59°11·1′	2°57·3′W	X	5,6
Bow of Fife	Fife	NO3212	56°18·0′	3°5·5′W	T	59
Bow of Hascosay, The	Shetld	HU5492	60°36·7′	1°0·3′W	X	1,2
Bowood	Devon	SS4225	51°0·4′	4°14·7′W	X	180,190
Bowood Fm	Devon	ST2004	50°50·0′	3°7·8′W	FM	192,193
Bowood Ho	Wilts	ST9769	51°25·4′	2°2·2′W	A	173
Bowood Lake	Wilts	ST9769	51°25·4′	2°2·2′W	W	173
Bow or Vault Beach	Corn	SX0040	50°13·8′	4°47·9′W	X	204
Bowrake Fm	N Yks	SE3548	53°55·9′	1°27·6′W	FM	104
Bowridge	Falk	NS7880	56°0·1′	3°56·9′W	X	64
Bowridge	S Lanak	NS8552	55°45·1′	3°49·5′W	X	65,72
Bowridge Hill	Dorset	ST8127	51°2·8′	2°15·9′W	T	183
Bowriefauld	Angus	NO5148	56°37·5′	2°47·5′W	T	54
Bowringsleigh	Devon	SX7144	50°17·1′	3°48·3′W	A	202
Bows	Aberd	NO6778	56°53·8′	2°32·1′W	X	45
Bowsber	N Yks	SD7468	54°6·7′	2°23·4′W	X	98
Bowscale	Cumbr	NY0942	54°46·1′	3°24·4′W	X	85
Bowscale	Cumbr	NY3531	54°40·4′	3°0·1′W	X	90
Bowscale Fell	Cumbr	NY3330	54°39·9′	3°1·9′W	H	90
Bowscale Tarn	Cumbr	NY3331	54°40·4′	3°1·9′W	W	90
Bowscar	Cumbr	NY5134	54°42·2′	2°45·2′W	X	90
Bowsden	Northum	NT9941	55°40·0′	2°0·5′W	T	75
Bowsden Moor	Northum	NT9642	55°40·5′	2°3·4′W	X	74,75
Bowsden West Farm	Northum	NT9841	55°40·0′	2°1·5′W	FM	75
Bowsers	Essex	TL5643	52°4·0′	0°17·0′E	X	154
Bowsers Fm	Lincs	TF3257	53°5·9′	0°1·3′W	FM	122
Bowser's Hole	Ghead	NZ1059	54°55·8′	1°50·2′W	X	88
Bowse's Hill Fm	Lancs	SD3744	53°53·5′	2°57·1′W	FM	102
Bowsey Hill	Wok	SU8080	51°31·0′	0°50·4′W	T	175
Bowseywood Fm	Staffs	SJ7646	53°0·9′	2°21·1′W	FM	118
Bowshank	Scot Bord	NT4541	55°39·8′	2°52·0′W	T	73
Bowshank Hill	Scot Bord	NT4340	55°39·3′	2°53·9′W	H	73
Bowshaw	Derby	SK3479	53°18·6′	1°29·0′W	X	119
Bow Shaw	N Yks	SE1251	53°57·5′	1°48·6′W	X	104
Bowshaws, The	Leeds	SE2843	53°53·2′	1°34·0′W	X	104
Bowshiel	Scot Bord	NT7867	55°54·0′	2°20·7′W	X	67
Bowshiel Wood	Scot Bord	NT7867	55°54·0′	2°20·7′W	F	67
Bow's Hill	Dorset	SY6798	50°47·1′	2°27·7′W	X	194
Bowshot Wood	Warw	SP3053	52°10·7′	1°33·3′W	F	151
Bowside Lodge	Highld	NC8261	58°31·5′	4°1·1′W	X	10
Bow Skerries	Orkney	HY2328	59°8·2′	3°20·3′W	X	6
Bowstead Gates	Cumbr	SD2981	54°13·4′	3°4·9′W	X	96,97
Bows, The	Stir	NN7306	56°14·0′	4°2·5′W	X	57
Bowston	Cumbr	SD4996	54°21·7′	2°46·7′W	T	97
Bowstonegate	Ches	SJ9781	53°19·8′	2°2·3′W	X	109
Bow Stones	Ches	SJ9781	53°19·8′	2°2·3′W	A	109
Bow Street	Cered	SN6284	52°26·4′	4°1·4′W	T	135
Bow Street	Norf	TM0197	52°32·2′	0°58·2′E	T	144
Bowstridge	Bucks	SU9992	51°37·3′	0°33·8′W	X	175,176
Bow, The	Aberd	NK1036	57°25·1′	1°49·6′W	X	30
Bow, The	I Scilly	SV8908	49°53·7′	6°19·5′W	X	203
Bowthorn Fm	Cumbr	NY0116	54°32·0′	3°31·4′W	FM	89
Bowthorpe	Norf	TG1709	52°38·3′	1°12·8′E	T	134
Bowthorpe Hall	N Yks	SE6933	53°47·6′	0°56·7′W	X	105,106
Bowthorpe Park Fm	Lincs	TF0615	52°43·6′	0°25·4′W	FM	130
Bowton	E Ayr	NS5117	55°25·7′	4°20·8′W	X	70
Bowtrees	Falk	NS9086	56°3·5′	3°45·5′W	X	65
Bow Wood	Derby	SK3156	53°6·3′	1°31·8′W	F	119
Bow Wood	Worcs	SO9455	52°11·8′	2°4·9′W	F	150
Bowyer's Common	Hants	SU7626	51°1·9′	0°54·6′W	T	186,197
Bowzell Fm	Kent	TQ5150	51°14·0′	0°10·2′E	FM	188
Box	Glos	SO8600	51°42·1′	2°11·8′W	T	162
Box	Wilts	ST8268	51°24·9′	2°15·1′W	T	173
Boxalland Fm	W Susx	SU9331	51°4·5′	0°40·0′W	FM	186
Boxalland Fm	W Susx	TQ0227	51°2·2′	0°32·3′W	FM	186,197
Box Br	Wilts	ST8067	51°24·3′	2°16·9′W	X	173
Boxbury Fm	Herts	TL2726	51°55·3′	0°8·8′W	FM	166
Boxbush	Glos	SO6720	51°52·9′	2°28·4′W	T	162
Boxbush	Glos	SO7412	51°48·6′	2°22·2′W	X	162
Boxbush	Powys	SO1537	52°1·7′	3°13·9′W	X	161
Boxbush	Powys	SO2431	51°58·6′	3°6·0′W	X	161
Box Bush Fm	N Som	ST4062	51°21·5′	2°51·3′W	FM	172,182
Boxbush Fm	Suff	TM1867	52°15·7′	1°12·1′E	FM	156
Boxedge Fm	Traf	SJ7288	53°23·5′	2°24·9′W	FM	109
Box End	Beds	TL0048	52°7·5′	0°32·0′W	T	153
Boxend Ho	Beds	TL0148	52°7·5′	0°31·1′W	X	153
Box Fm	Glos	SO6808	51°46·4′	2°27·4′W	FM	162
Box Fm	Hants	SU3357	51°18·9′	1°31·2′W	FM	174
Box Fm	Powys	SO1253	52°10·3′	3°16·8′W	FM	148
Boxford	Suff	TL9640	52°1·6′	0°51·8′E	T	155
Boxford	W Berks	SU4271	51°26·4′	1°23·4′W	T	174
Boxford Common	W Berks	SU4471	51°26·4′	1°21·6′W	X	174
Boxgrove	W Susx	SU9007	50°51·6′	0°42·9′W	T	197
Boxgrove Common	W Susx	SU9108	50°52·1′	0°42·0′W	X	197
Box Hall	Herts	TL2924	51°54·2′	0°7·1′W	X	166
Box Hall	Suff	TM3444	52°2·9′	1°25·2′E	X	169
Boxhedge Fm	Beds	SP9645	52°5·9′	0°35·5′W	FM	153
Box Hedge Fm	Swin	SU1794	51°38·9′	1°44·9′W	FM	163,173
Box Hill	Surrey	TQ1951	51°15·0′	0°17·3′W	T	187
Box Hill	Wilts	ST8369	51°25·4′	2°14·3′W	T	173
Box Hill Country Park	Surrey	TQ1751	51°15·0′	0°19·0′W	X	187
Box Ho	Glos	ST8699	51°41·6′	2°11·8′W	X	162
Boxhurst	Kent	TQ8027	51°1·1′	0°34·4′E	X	188,199
Boxhurst	Surrey	TQ1850	51°14·4′	0°18·2′W	X	187
Box Knowe	E Dunb	NS6679	55°59·4′	4°8·4′W	X	64
Box Law	N Ayr	NS2561	55°48·9′	4°47·1′W	H	63
Boxley	Kent	TQ7758	51°17·8′	0°32·7′E	T	178,188
Boxley Abbey	Kent	TQ7658	51°17·9′	0°31·9′E	A	178,188
Boxley Ho	Kent	TQ7759	51°18·4′	0°32·8′E	X	178,188
Boxmoor	Herts	TL0406	51°44·8′	0°29·2′W	T	166
Box Rock	Glos	SO6909	51°47·0′	2°26·6′W	X	162
Box's Shop	Corn	SS2101	50°47·1′	4°32·0′W	T	190
Boxted	Essex	TL9933	51°57·8′	0°54·2′E	T	168
Boxted	Essex	TM0031	51°56·7′	0°55·0′E	T	168
Boxted	Kent	TQ8566	51°22·0′	0°39·9′E	X	178
Boxted	Suff	TL8251	52°7·9′	0°39·9′E	T	155
Boxted Cross	Essex	TM0032	51°57·3′	0°55·0′E	T	168
Boxted Fm	Herts	TL0308	51°45·9′	0°30·0′W	FM	166
Boxted Lodge	Essex	TL9932	51°57·3′	0°54·2′E	X	168
Boxted Wood	Essex	TL6923	51°53·0′	0°27·7′E	F	167
Boxtree	Cumbr	SD4495	54°21·1′	2°51·3′W	X	97
Box Tree	Lancs	SD6270	54°7·7′	2°34·5′W	X	97
Boxtree Fm	Suff	TL9750	52°7·0′	0°53·0′E	FM	155
Box Trees	Sol	SP1474	52°22·1′	1°47·3′W	T	139
Box Tunnel	Wilts	ST8369	51°25·4′	2°14·3′W	X	173
Boxwell	Glos	ST8192	51°37·8′	2°16·1′W	T	162,173
Box Wood	Herts	TL2626	51°55·3′	0°9·7′W	F	166
Box Wood	Herts	TL3509	51°46·0′	0°2·2′W	F	166
Boxworth	Cambs	TL3464	52°15·7′	0°1·8′W	T	154
Boxworth End	Cambs	TL3667	52°17·3′	0°0·0′E	T	154
Boyach	D & G	NX4736	54°42·0′	4°22·0′W	X	83
Boyah Grange	Derby	SK4437	52°56·0′	1°20·3′W	X	129
Boyatt Wood	Hants	SU4420	50°58·9′	1°22·0′W	T	185
Boyce Ct	Glos	SO7029	51°57·8′	2°25·8′W	X	149
Boyce Fen Fm	Norf	TF5205	52°37·5′	0°15·1′E	FM	143
Boyce Fm, The	Heref	SO6952	52°10·2′	2°26·8′W	FM	149
Boyce's Dyke	Norf	TG4100	52°32·9′	1°33·7′E	W	134
Boycombe Fm	Devon	SY1696	50°45·7′	3°11·1′W	A	192,193
Boycott	Shrops	SJ3807	52°39·7′	2°54·6′W	X	126
Boycott Fm	Bucks	SP6636	52°1·3′	1°1·9′W	FM	152
Boycott Manor	Bucks	SP6637	52°1·9′	1°1·9′W	X	152
Boycott Manor Fm	Bucks	SP6537	52°1·9′	1°2·8′W	FM	152
Boy Court	Kent	TQ8446	51°11·2′	0°38·4′E	X	188
Boydell's Fm	Essex	TL7230	51°56·7′	0°30·6′E	FM	167
Boyden End	Suff	TL7355	52°10·2′	0°32·2′E	T	155
Boyden Gate	Kent	TR2265	51°20·7′	1°11·7′E	T	179
Boyd Fm	S Glos	ST6870	51°25·9′	2°27·2′W	FM	172
Boyds Fm	Wilts	ST8867	51°24·3′	2°10·0′W	FM	173
Boydston	S Ayr	NS4532	55°33·7′	4°27·0′W	X	70
Boydstone	Renf	NS3655	55°45·9′	4°36·4′W	X	63
Boydston Fm	N Ayr	NS2245	55°40·2′	4°49·4′W	FM	63
Boyington Court	Kent	TR2242	51°8·3′	1°10·8′E	X	179,189
Boyken Burn	D & G	NY2988	55°11·1′	3°6·5′W	W	79
Boykenhopehead	D & G	NY2788	55°11·1′	3°8·4′W	X	79
Boyland	Devon	SX7989	50°41·5′	3°42·4′W	X	191
Boyland Common	Norf	TM0884	52°25·1′	1°3·9′E	T	144
Boyland New Fm	Norf	TM0885	52°25·6′	1°4·0′E	FM	144
Boyles Court	Essex	TQ5791	51°36·0′	0°16·4′E	X	177
Boyles Fm	W Susx	TQ3936	51°6·6′	0°0·5′W	FM	187
Boylestone	Derby	SK1835	52°55·0′	1°43·5′W	T	128
Boylestonfield	Derby	SK1836	52°55·5′	1°43·5′W	T	128
Boylston	E Ayr	NS5920	55°27·5′	4°13·4′W	X	71
Boynal Copse	Oxon	SP3117	51°51·3′	1°32·6′W	F	164
Boyndie	Aberd	NJ6463	57°39·6′	2°35·7′W	T	29
Boyndie Bay	Aberd	NJ6765	57°40·7′	2°32·7′W	W	29
Boyndlie Ho	Aberd	NJ9162	57°39·1′	2°8·6′W	X	30
Boynds	Aberd	NJ7822	57°17·5′	2°21·4′W	X	38
Boyne Bay	Aberd	NJ6266	57°41·2′	2°37·8′W	W	29
Boyne Castle	Aberd	NJ6165	57°40·7′	2°38·8′W	A	29
Boyne Fm	Pth & Kin	NO2628	56°26·6′	3°11·6′W	FM	53,59
Boynes, The	Worcs	SO8340	52°3·7′	2°14·5′W	X	150
Boyne Water	Shrops	SO5984	52°27·4′	2°35·8′W	W	137,138
Boyn Hill	Win & Maid	SU8780	51°31·0′	0°44·4′W	T	175
Boynton	E Yorks	TA1368	54°6·0′	0°15·9′W	T	101
Boynton Hall	Suff	TM0937	51°59·7′	1°3·1′E	A	155,169
Boysack	Angus	NO6249	56°38·1′	2°36·7′W	T	54
Boysackhill	Angus	NO5943	56°34·9′	2°39·6′W	X	54
Boysack Mills	Angus	NO6249	56°38·1′	2°36·7′W	X	54
Boy's Grove	Glos	SP0113	51°49·2′	1°58·7′W	F	163
Boy's Hall	Suff	TM0464	52°14·4′	0°59·7′E	X	155
Boy's Hill	Aberd	NO7182	56°56·0′	2°28·1′W	X	45
Boys Hill	Dorset	ST6710	50°53·5′	2°27·8′W	T	194
Boys Village	V of Glam	ST0267	51°23·9′	3°24·1′W	T	170
Boys Wood	Dorset	SU0509	50°53·1′	1°55·4′W	F	195
Boys Wood	Oxon	SP3606	51°45·3′	1°28·3′W	F	164
Boythorpe	Derby	SK3770	53°13·8′	1°26·3′W	T	119
Boythorpe	N Yks	SE9972	54°8·3′	0°28·7′W	X	101
Boythorpe Cott	N Yks	TA0072	54°8·3′	0°27·7′W	X	101
Boyton	Corn	SX3191	50°41·9′	4°23·2′W	T	190
Boyton	Suff	TM3747	52°4·5′	1°27·9′E	T	169
Boyton	Wilts	ST9539	51°9·2′	2°3·9′W	T	184
Boyton Court	Kent	TQ8248	51°12·4′	0°36·7′E	X	188
Boyton Cross	Essex	TL6509	51°45·5′	0°23·8′E	T	167
Boyton Down	Wilts	ST9438	51°8·7′	2°4·8′W	X	184
Boyton End	Essex	TL6232	51°58·0′	0°21·9′E	T	167

Boyton End	Suff	TL7144	52°4·3'	0°30·1'E	T	154
Boyton Hall	Essex	TL6509	51°45·5'	0°23·8'E	X	167
Boyton Hall	Essex	TL7034	51°58·9'	0°28·9'E	X	154
Boyton Hall	Suff	TL6746	52°5·5'	0°26·7'E	X	154
Boyton Hall	Suff	TL9746	52°4·9'	0°52·9'E	X	155
Boyton Hall	Suff	TM0257	52°10·7'	0°57·7'E	X	155
Boyton Hall Fm	Suff	TM3846	52°3·9'	1°28·7'E	FM	169
Boyton Marshes	Suff	TM3946	52°3·9'	1°29·6'E	X	169
Boyton Mill	Devon	SX3392	50°42·5'	4°21·5'W	X	190
Boywood Fm	Dorset	ST7307	50°51·9'	2°22·6'W	FM	194
Bozard's Fm	Glos	SO9330	51°58·3'	2°5·7'W	FM	150
Bozeat	Northnts	SP9058	52°13·0'	0°40·6'W	T	152
Bozeat Grange	Northnts	SP9056	52°11·9'	0°40·6'W	X	152
Bozedown Fm	Oxon	SU6477	51°29·5'	1°4·3'W	FM	175
Bozedown Ho	Oxon	SU6378	51°30·1'	1°5·1'W	X	175
Bozen Green	Herts	TL4027	51°55·7'	0°2·6'E	T	167
Bozenham Mill	Northnts	SP7648	52°7·7'	0°53·0'W	X	152
Bozion Fm	Corn	SX0170	50°30·0'	4°48·0'W	FM	200
Bozomzeal	Devon	SX8653	50°22·2'	3°35·8'W	X	202
Bozomzeal Cross	Devon	SX8554	50°22·7'	3°36·7'W	X	202
Braaid	I of M	SC3276	54°9·4'	4°34·0'W	T	95
Braaid	I of M	SC3380	54°11·6'	4°33·2'W	X	95
Braal Castle	Highld	ND1360	58°31·4'	3°29·2'W	T	11,12
Braava Skerries	Shetld	HP5707	60°44·8'	0°56·8'W	X	1
Brabands	E Susx	TQ9022	50°58·2'	0°42·8'E	X	189
Braban Ho	Cumbr	SD5097	54°22·2'	2°45·8'W	X	97
Brabbin Wood	Lancs	SD7150	53°57·0'	2°26·1'W	F	103
Brabling Green	Suff	TM2964	52°13·8'	1°21·6'E	X	156
Brabourne	Kent	TR1041	51°8·0'	1°0·5'E	T	179,189
Brabourne Coomb	Kent	TR0942	51°8·6'	0°59·7'E	X	179,189
Brabourne Lees	Kent	TR0840	51°7·5'	0°58·7'E	T	179,189
Brabster	Highld	ND3269	58°36·5'	3°9·7'W	X	12
Brabsterdorran	Highld	ND2360	58°31·5'	3°18·9'W	T	11,12
Brabsterdorran Mains	Highld	ND2260	58°31·5'	3°19·9'W	X	11,12
Brabstermire Ho	Highld	ND3169	58°36·5'	3°10·8'W	X	12
Brabster Moss	Highld	ND2359	58°31·0'	3°18·8'W	X	11,12
Brabyns Park	Stock	SJ9689	53°24·1'	2°3·2'W	X	109
Bracadale	Highld	NG3538	57°21·6'	6°23·9'W	T	23,32
Bracadale Point	Highld	NG3337	57°21·0'	6°25·9'W	X	23,32
Braceborough	Lincs	TF0813	52°42·5'	0°23·7'W	T	130,142
Braceborough Great Wood	Lincs	TF0613	52°42·5'	0°25·5'W	F	130,142
Bracebridge	Lincs	SK9668	53°12·3'	0°33·4'W	T	121
Bracebridge Heath	Lincs	SK9867	53°11·7'	0°31·6'W	T	121
Bracebridge Pool	Birm	SP0998	52°35·0'	1°51·6'W	W	139
Braceby	Lincs	TF0135	52°54·4'	0°29·5'W	T	130
Brace Field	Shetld	HU2552	60°15·4'	1°32·4'W	H	3
Brace Garth	Orkney	HY7546	59°18·2'	2°25·9'W	X	5
Braceland	Glos	SO5513	51°49·1'	2°38·8'W	X	162
Bracelet Bay	Swan	SS6387	51°34·2'	3°58·2'W	W	159
Bracelet Hall	Cumbr	SD2391	54°18·8'	3°10·6'W	X	96
Brace's Leigh	Worcs	SO7950	52°9·1'	2°18·0'W	X	150
Bracewell	Lancs	SD8648	53°55·9'	2°12·4'W	T	103
Bracey Bridge	E Yorks	TA0762	54°2·8'	0°21·5'W	X	101
Brachlach Hill	Highld	NC8163	58°32·6'	4°2·2'W	H	10
Brachyriach	Highld	NH5131	57°21·0'	4°28·1'W	X	26
Brack-a-broom	I of M	SC2782	54°12·5'	4°38·8'W	X	95
Brack Barrow	Cumbr	SD2294	54°20·4'	3°11·6'W	X	96
Bracken	E Yorks	SE9850	53°56·4'	0°30·0'W	X	106
Bracken Bank	Brad	SE0439	53°51·1'	1°55·9'W	T	104
Brackenbank	Cumbr	NY4852	54°51·9'	2°48·2'W	X	86
Brackenbank	Cumbr	NY5339	54°44·9'	2°43·4'W	X	90
Brackenbarrow Fm	Cumbr	SD2994	54°20·4'	3°5·1'W	FM	96,97
Bracken Bay	S Ayr	NS2718	55°25·8'	4°43·6'W	W	70
Brackenber	Cumbr	NY6906	54°27·2'	2°28·3'W	X	91
Brackenber	Cumbr	NY7219	54°34·2'	2°25·6'W	T	91
Brackenber Lo	Cumbr	NY5614	54°31·4'	2°40·4'W	X	90
Brackenber Moor	Cumbr	NY7119	54°34·2'	2°26·5'W	X	91
Brackenberry Wyke	N Yks	NZ7918	54°33·3'	0°46·3'W	W	94
Brackenborough Hall	Lincs	TF3390	53°23·6'	0°0·4'E	X	113
Brackenborough Lawn	Lincs	TF3289	53°23·1'	0°0·5'W	X	113,122
Brackenborough Village	Lincs	TF3390	53°23·6'	0°0·4'E	A	113
Brackenbottom	N Yks	SD8172	54°8·9'	2°17·0'W	T	98
Brackenbraes	Aberd	NJ5943	57°28·8'	2°40·6'W	X	29
Brackenburgh	Cumbr	NY4738	54°44·3'	2°49·0'W	X	90
Brackenburgh Cottages	Cumbr	NY4739	54°44·8'	2°49·0'W	X	90
Brackenbury Ditches	Glos	ST7494	51°38·9'	2°22·2'W	X	162,172
Brackenbury Ditches (Fort)	Glos	ST7494	51°38·9'	2°22·2'W	A	162,172
Brackenbury Leazes Fm	Durham	NZ1923	54°36·4'	1°41·9'W	FM	92
Brackenclose	Cumbr	NY1807	54°27·4'	3°15·5'W	X	89,90
Bracken Cott	Northum	NU1310	55°23·3'	1°47·3'W	X	81
Brackendale Fm	E Yorks	TA1463	54°3·3'	0°15·1'W	FM	101
Bracken End Fm	Leeds	SE1843	53°53·2'	1°43·2'W	FM	104
Brackenfield	Derby	SK3759	53°7·8'	1°26·4'W	T	119
Brackenfield Green	Derby	SK3758	53°7·3'	1°26·4'W	X	119
Bracken Fold	Cumbr	SD5697	54°22·2'	2°40·2'W	X	97
Bracken Garth	N Yks	SD7263	54°4·0'	2°25·3'W	X	98
Bracken Gill	N Yks	SD9273	54°9·4'	2°6·9'W	X	98
Bracken Hall	Brad	SE1339	53°51·1'	1°47·7'W	X	104
Bracken Hall	Cumbr	SD5586	54°16·3'	2°41·0'W	X	97
Bracken Hall	Cumbr	SD5796	54°21·7'	2°39·3'W	X	97
Brackenhall	Kirk	SE1519	53°40·3'	1°46·0'W	T	110
Brackenhill	Cumbr	NY5906	54°27·1'	2°37·5'W	X	91
Bracken Hill	Durham	NZ0925	54°37·4'	1°51·2'W	X	92
Brackenhill	E Ayr	NS5224	55°29·5'	4°20·1'W	X	70
Bracken Hill	E Yorks	SE8219	53°39·9'	0°45·1'W	X	112
Bracken Hill	E Yorks	TA2834	53°47·4'	0°3·0'W	X	107
Bracken Hill	Kirk	SE1821	53°41·3'	1°43·2'W	T	104
Bracken Hill	Lincs	TF3585	53°20·9'	0°2·1'E	X	122
Bracken Hill	N Lincs	SE9606	53°32·7'	0°32·7'W	X	112
Bracken Hill	Notts	SK6575	53°16·3'	1°1·1'W	X	120
Brackenhill	Notts	SK6845	53°0·1'	0°58·8'W	X	129
Bracken Hill	Notts	SK6896	53°27·6'	0°58·1'W	X	111
Bracken Hill	N Som	ST4664	51°22·6'	2°46·2'W	X	172,182
Bracken Hill	N Yks	SD6570	54°7·7'	2°31·7'W	X	97
Bracken Hill	N Yks	SE5895	54°21·1'	1°6·0'W	X	100
Bracken Hill	N Yks	SE6365	54°4·9'	1°1·8'W	X	100
Brackenhill	Pth & Kin	NN9114	56°18·6'	3°45·3'W	X	58
Brackenhill	S Ayr	NX2399	55°15·5'	4°46·7'W	X	76
Brackenhill	S Lanak	NS7052	55°44·9'	4°3·8'W	X	64
Brackenhill	S Lanak	NS8252	55°45·1'	3°52·4'W	X	65,72
Bracken Hill Fm	Lincs	TF0368	53°12·2'	0°27·1'W	FM	121
Brackenhill Rigg	Cumbr	NY4469	55°1·0'	2°52·1'W	X	85
Brackenhills	Aberd	NJ5859	57°37·4'	2°41·7'W	X	29
Brackenhirst	N Lanak	NS7468	55°53·6'	4°0·5'W	X	64
Brackenholme	N Yks	SE7030	53°45·9'	0°55·9'W	X	105,106
Brackenholmes	N Lincs	SE9215	53°37·6'	0°36·1'W	F	112
Brackenhowes	Moray	NJ2143	57°28·5'	3°18·6'W	X	28
Brackenhow Fm	Cumbr	NY3748	54°49·6'	2°58·4'W	FM	85
Brackenhurst	Notts	SK6952	53°3·9'	0°57·8'W	X	120
Brackenlands	Cumbr	NY2547	54°49·0'	3°9·6'W	T	85
Bracken Lea	Lancs	SD5251	53°57·4'	2°43·5'W	X	102
Brackenlees	Falk	NS9185	56°3·0'	3°44·6'W	X	65
Bracken Noits	Moray	NJ2350	57°32·3'	3°16·7'W	H	28
Bracken Park	Leeds	SE3541	53°52·1'	1°27·6'W	T	104
Bracken Ridge	N Yks	SE1076	54°11·0'	1°50·4'W	X	99
Brackenridge	S Lanak	NS6643	55°40·0'	4°7·4'W	X	71
Brackenrigg	Aberd	NO7367	56°47·9'	2°26·1'W	X	45
Brackenrigg	Cumbr	NY2361	54°56·5'	3°11·7'W	X	85
Brackenrigg	Cumbr	NY2921	54°35·0'	3°5·5'W	X	89,90
Brackenrigg	N Yks	SE0480	54°13·2'	1°55·9'W	X	98
Bracken Riggs	Cumbr	NY2920	54°34·5'	3°5·5'W	X	89,90
Brackenrow Sike	Cumbr	NY5779	55°6·5'	2°40·0'W	W	86
Brackens	Aberd	NJ7553	57°34·2'	2°24·6'W	X	29
Brackenscales Fm	Lancs	SD3937	53°49·8'	2°55·2'W	FM	102
Brackens Fm	Lincs	TF2984	53°20·5'	0°3·3'W	FM	122
Brackensgill	Cumbr	SD6689	54°18·0'	2°30·9'W	X	98
Brackenside	Cumbr	NY5660	54°56·2'	2°40·8'W	X	86
Brackenside	Northum	NT9740	55°39·5'	2°2·4'W	X	75
Brackenside	S Lanak	NS8033	55°34·8'	3°53·8'W	X	71,72
Brackenslack	Cumbr	NY6316	54°32·5'	2°33·9'W	X	91
Brackenslack	Moray	NJ2952	57°33·4'	3°10·7'W	X	28
Brackenstake	Aberd	NO5292	57°1·3'	2°47·0'W	H	44
Brackenthwaite	Cumbr	NY0410	54°28·8'	3°28·5'W	X	89
Brackenthwaite	Cumbr	NY1522	54°35·4'	3°18·5'W	T	89
Brackenthwaite	Cumbr	NY2946	54°48·5'	3°5·9'W	T	85
Brackenthwaite	Cumbr	NY5453	54°52·4'	2°42·6'W	X	86
Brackenthwaite	Cumbr	NY7122	54°35·8'	2°26·5'W	X	91
Brackenthwaite	Lancs	SD4977	54°11·4'	2°46·5'W	X	97
Brackenthwaite	N Yks	SE2751	53°57·5'	1°34·9'W	T	104
Brackenthwaite Fell	Cumbr	NY1721	54°34·9'	3°16·6'W	X	89,90
Brackenwood	D & G	NY2866	54°59·3'	3°7·1'W	X	85
Bracken Wood	Lincs	TF2064	53°9·8'	0°11·9'W	F	122
Brack Hill	E Ayr	NS7427	55°31·5'	3°59·3'W	X	71
Brackies Burn	Northum	NY7666	54°59·5'	2°22·1'W	W	86,87
Brackla	Aberd	NJ6122	57°17·5'	2°38·4'W	X	37
Brackla (Bragle)	Brig	SS9279	51°30·2'	3°33·0'W	T	170
Bracklach	Moray	NJ3824	57°18·4'	3°1·3'W	X	37
Brackla Hill	Brig	SS9280	51°30·8'	3°33·0'W	X	170
Brackla Ho	Highld	NH8651	57°32·3'	3°53·8'W	X	27
Bracklamore	Aberd	NJ8458	57°37·0'	2°15·6'W	X	29,30
Bracklamore Hill	Aberd	NJ8359	57°37·5'	2°16·6'W	H	29,30
Bracklesham	W Susx	SZ8096	50°45·7'	0°51·6'W	T	197
Bracklesham Bay	W Susx	SZ8195	50°45·2'	0°50·7'W	W	197
Brackletter	Highld	NN1882	56°53·9'	4°58·8'W	X	34,41
Brackley	Arg & Bt	NN1826	56°23·7'	4°56·5'W	X	50
Brackley	Arg & Bt	NR7941	55°37·0'	5°30·1'W	X	62,69
Brackley	Arg & Bt	NR8587	56°1·9'	5°26·6'W	X	55
Brackley	Arg & Bt	NS0973	55°55·0'	5°2·9'W	X	63
Brackley	Highld	NH8052	57°32·8'	3°59·8'W	X	27
Brackley	Northnts	SP5837	52°1·9'	1°8·9'W	T	152
Brackley Fields Fm	Northnts	SP5838	52°2·5'	1°8·9'W	FM	152
Brackley Gate Fm	Derby	SK3842	52°58·7'	1°25·6'W	FM	119,128
Brackley Grange	Northnts	SP5738	52°2·5'	1°9·7'W	X	152
Brackley Hatch	Northnts	SP6441	52°4·1'	1°3·6'W	X	152
Brackley Point	Arg & Bt	NS0973	55°55·0'	5°2·9'W	X	63
Bracklinn Falls	Stir	NN6408	56°15·0'	4°11·3'W	W	57
Brackloch	Highld	NC1123	58°9·6'	5°12·3'W	X	15
Brackloch Craig	Aberd	NO5295	57°2·9'	2°47·0'W	H	37,44
Brackmills	Northnts	SP7758	52°13·1'	0°52·0'W	X	152
Brackmont	Fife	NO4222	56°23·5'	2°55·9'W	X	54,59
Brackmont Mill	Fife	NO4322	56°23·5'	2°55·0'W	X	54,59
Brackmuirhill	Aberd	NO8683	56°56·5'	2°13·4'W	X	45
Bracknell	Brackn	SU8668	51°24·5'	0°45·4'W	T	175
Bracknell-Croft	Wilts	SU1833	51°6·0'	1°44·2'W	X	184
Bracknell Fm	Leic	SP4798	52°34·9'	1°18·0'W	FM	140
Brackness Hole	S Ayr	NX0576	55°2·7'	5°2·7'W	X	76
Brackrevach	Highld	ND0663	58°33·0'	3°36·4'W	X	11,12
Bracks	Fife	NO2206	56°14·7'	3°15·1'W	X	58
Brackside Burn	Highld	NC9462	58°32·3'	3°48·8'W	W	11
Brack, The	Arg & Bt	NN2403	56°11·5'	4°49·7'W	H	56
Brackwell Fm	Bucks	SP7112	51°48·4'	0°57·8'W	FM	165
Braco	Aberd	NJ7222	57°17·5'	2°27·4'W	X	38
Braco	Aberd	NJ9357	57°36·4'	2°6·6'W	X	30
Braco	Aberd	NK0638	57°26·2'	1°53·5'W	X	30
Braco	Angus	NO5070	56°49·4'	2°48·7'W	X	44
Braco	D & G	NX8687	55°10·1'	3°47·0'W	X	78
Braco	D & G	NX8775	55°3·7'	3°45·7'W	X	84
Braco	E Renf	NS4155	55°46·0'	4°31·6'W	X	64
Braco	Moray	NJ4951	57°33·0'	2°50·7'W	X	28,29
Braco	Pth & Kin	NN8309	56°15·8'	3°52·9'W	T	57
Braco	Pth & Kin	NN9932	56°28·4'	3°37·9'W	X	52,53
Bracobrae	Moray	NJ5052	57°33·6'	2°49·7'W	X	29
Braco Castle	Pth & Kin	NN8211	56°16·9'	3°53·9'W	A	57
Braco Cott	Aberd	NK0637	57°25·7'	1°53·5'W	X	30
Bracon	N Lincs	SE7807	53°33·5'	0°48·9'W	T	112
Bracon Ash	Norf	TM1899	52°32·9'	1°13·2'E	T	134
Bracon Hall	Norf	TG1800	52°33·5'	1°13·4'E	X	134
Braco Park	Aberd	NJ9266	57°41·3'	2°7·6'W	X	30
Bracora	Highld	NM7192	56°58·0'	5°45·6'W	T	33,40
Bracorina	Highld	NM7292	56°58·0'	5°44·6'W	T	33,40
Bracs, The	S Lanak	NT0331	55°34·0'	3°31·9'W	X	72
Bractullo	Angus	NO4740	56°33·2'	2°51·3'W	X	54
Bractullo	Angus	NO5247	56°37·0'	2°46·5'W	X	54
Bractullo Mill	Angus	NO5246	56°36·5'	2°46·5'W	X	54
Bractullo Muir	Angus	NO4741	56°33·7'	2°51·3'W	X	54
Brada	Northum	NU2538	55°38·3'	1°35·7'W	W	75
Bradaford	Devon	SX3994	50°43·6'	4°16·5'W	T	190
Bradastac	N Eil	NA0900	57°49·4'	8°34·8'W	X	18
Bradavin	Devon	SS4727	51°1·6'	4°10·5'W	X	180
Bradbourne	Derby	SK2152	53°4·1'	1°40·8'W	T	119
Bradbourne Brook	Derby	SK1950	53°3·1'	1°42·6'W	W	119
Bradbourne Ho	Kent	TQ7057	51°17·4'	0°26·7'E	A	178,188
Brad Brook	Flint	SJ3360	53°8·2'	2°59·7'W	W	117
Bradbrook Fm	Flint	SJ3260	53°8·2'	3°0·6'W	FM	117
Bradbury	Durham	NZ3128	54°39·0'	1°30·9'W	T	93
Bradbury Barton	Devon	SS6626	51°1·3'	3°54·3'W	X	180
Bradbury Carrs	Durham	NZ3125	54°37·4'	1°30·8'W	X	93
Bradbury Fm	Herts	TL3930	51°57·3'	0°1·8'E	FM	166
Bradbury Grange	Leeds	SE3833	53°47·8'	1°25·0'W	X	104
Bradburys	W Susx	TQ2228	51°2·5'	0°15·2'W	X	187,198
Bradbury's Fm	Staffs	SO8087	52°29·1'	2°17·3'W	FM	138
Bradda East	I of M	SC1970	54°5·9'	4°45·7'W	T	95
Bradda Head	I of M	SC1869	54°5·3'	4°46·6'W	H	95
Bradda Hill	I of M	SC1971	54°6·4'	4°45·7'W	H	95
Braddan Bridge	I of M	SC3676	54°9·5'	4°30·3'W	X	95
Bradda West	I of M	SC1970	54°5·9'	4°45·7'W	T	95
Bradden	Northnts	SP6448	52°7·8'	1°3·5'W	T	152
Braddicksknap Hill	Devon	ST1807	50°51·6'	3°9·5'W	X	192,193
Braddock	Corn	SX1662	50°26·0'	4°35·1'W	T	201
Braddocks Barn	Staffs	SK1020	52°46·9'	1°50·7'W	X	128
Braddocks Hay	Staffs	SJ8857	53°6·8'	2°10·4'W	T	118
Braddon	Devon	SX3998	50°45·8'	4°16·6'W	X	190
Braddup Fm	Lancs	SD7044	53°53·7'	2°27·0'W	FM	103
Braddup Ho	Lancs	SD7144	53°53·7'	2°26·1'W	X	103
Bradeley	C of Stoke	SJ8851	53°3·6'	2°10·3'W	T	118
Bradeley Fm	Shrops	SO5994	52°32·8'	2°35·9'W	FM	137,138
Bradeley Green	Ches	SJ5344	52°59·7'	2°41·6'W	T	117
Bradeley Hall	Ches	SJ7256	53°6·3'	2°24·7'W	X	118
Bradenbury	Kent	TQ7246	51°11·5'	0°28·1'E	X	188
Bradenham	Bucks	SU8297	51°40·2'	0°48·5'W	T	165
Bradenham	Norf	TF9208	52°38·4'	0°50·7'E	T	144
Bradenham Hall	Norf	TF9209	52°38·9'	0°50·7'E	X	144
Bradenham Hill	Norf	TF9210	52°39·4'	0°50·7'E	X	132
Bradenstoke	Wilts	SU0079	51°30·8'	1°59·6'W	T	173
Bradenstoke Abbey	Wilts	ST9979	51°30·8'	2°0·5'W	X	173
Brades Fm, The	Shrops	SJ5432	52°53·2'	2°40·6'W	FM	126
Bradeshade	Aberd	NO7379	56°54·3'	2°26·1'W	X	45
Bradeston Marsh	Norf	TG3307	52°36·9'	1°26·9'E	W	134
Brades Village	Sand	SO9790	52°30·7'	2°2·3'W	T	139
Bradfield	Devon	ST0509	50°52·6'	3°20·6'W	T	192
Bradfield	Essex	TM1430	51°55·9'	1°7·2'E	T	168,169
Bradfield	Norf	TG2733	52°51·0'	1°22·7'E	T	133
Bradfield	W Berks	SU6072	51°26·9'	1°7·8'W	T	175
Bradfield Barn	Oxon	SU4191	51°37·2'	1°24·1'W	X	164,174
Bradfield Br	Norf	TG2732	52°50·5'	1°22·6'E	X	133
Bradfield Combust	Suff	TL8957	52°11·0'	0°46·3'E	T	155
Bradfield Dale	Sheff	SK2491	53°25·2'	1°37·9'W	X	110
Bradfield Green	Ches	SJ6859	53°7·9'	2°28·3'W	T	118
Bradfield Grove Fm	Oxon	SU4091	51°37·2'	1°24·9'W	FM	164,174
Bradfield Hall	Essex	TM1329	51°55·3'	1°6·3'E	X	168,169
Bradfield Hall	Norf	TG2733	52°51·0'	1°22·7'E	X	133
Bradfield Hall	W Berks	SU5871	51°26·3'	1°9·5'W	X	174
Bradfield Heath	Essex	TM1329	51°55·3'	1°6·3'E	T	168,169
Bradfield Ho	W Berks	SU5872	51°26·9'	1°9·5'W	X	174
Bradfield House	Devon	ST0509	50°52·6'	3°20·6'W	A	192
Bradfield Lodge	Essex	TM1228	51°54·8'	1°5·4'E	X	168,169
Bradfield Manor Fm	Wilts	ST8982	51°32·4'	2°9·1'W	A	173
Bradfield Moors	Sheff	SK2392	53°25·7'	1°38·8'W	X	110
Bradfield Moors	Sheff	SK2489	53°24·1'	1°37·9'W	X	110
Bradfield Park	Suff	TL8957	52°11·0'	0°46·3'E	X	155
Bradfield's	Essex	TL7236	52°0·0'	0°30·7'E	X	154
Bradfield's Fm	Essex	TL8143	52°3·6'	0°38·8'E	FM	155
Bradfield's Fm	Essex	TQ7590	51°35·1'	0°32·0'E	FM	178
Bradfield St Clare	Suff	TL9057	52°10·9'	0°47·2'E	T	155
Bradfield St George	Suff	TL9160	52°12·5'	0°48·1'E	T	155
Bradfield Wood	Wilts	ST9084	51°33·5'	2°8·3'W	F	173
Bradfield Woods (Nature Reserve)	Suff	TL9357	52°10·9'	0°49·8'E	X	155
Bradford	Brad	SE1632	53°47·3'	1°45·0'W	T	104
Bradford	Corn	SX1175	50°32·9'	4°39·7'W	T	200
Bradford	Derby	SK2164	53°10·6'	1°40·7'W	T	119
Bradford	Devon	SS4207	50°50·7'	4°14·3'W	T	190
Bradford	Man	SJ8698	53°29·0'	2°12·2'W	T	109
Bradford	Northum	NU1532	55°35·1'	1°45·3'W	X	75
Bradford	Northum	NZ0679	55°6·6'	1°53·9'W	X	87
Bradford Abbas	Dorset	ST5814	50°55·7'	2°35·5'W	T	194
Bradford Barton	Devon	SS8216	50°56·1'	3°40·4'W	X	181
Bradford Down	Dorset	SY6490	50°42·7'	2°30·2'W	X	194
Bradford Fell	Lancs	SD7247	53°55·3'	2°25·2'W	X	103
Bradford Fm	Devon	SS9914	50°55·2'	3°25·8'W	FM	181
Bradford Fm	Dorset	ST9705	50°50·9'	2°2·2'W	FM	195
Bradford Ho	Ches	SJ8576	53°17·1'	2°13·1'W	X	118
Bradford Ho	Devon	SS4104	50°49·1'	4°15·1'W	X	190
Bradford Ho	Worcs	SO8671	52°20·5'	2°11·9'W	X	139
Bradford Ho	Worcs	SO9276	52°23·2'	2°6·7'W	X	139
Bradford Kaims	Northum	NU1631	55°34·6'	1°44·3'W	X	75
Bradford Leigh	Wilts	ST8362	51°21·6'	2°14·3'W	T	173
Bradford Manor	Devon	SS2801	50°47·2'	4°26·0'W	X	190
Bradford Mill	Ches	SJ6468	53°12·7'	2°31·9'W	X	118
Bradford Mill	Devon	SS8216	50°56·1'	3°40·4'W	X	181
Bradford-On-Avon	Wilts	ST8261	51°21·1'	2°15·1'W	T	173
Bradford-on-Tone	Somer	ST1722	50°59·7'	3°10·6'W	T	181,193
Bradford Peverell	Dorset	SY6592	50°43·8'	2°29·4'W	T	194
Bradford's Brook	Oxon	SU5988	51°35·5'	1°8·5'W	W	174
Bradford's Fm	E Susx	TQ4817	50°56·2'	0°6·8'E	FM	198
Bradford's Fm	W Berks	SU4168	51°24·8'	1°24·2'W	FM	174
Bradford Tracy	Devon	SS8116	50°56·1'	3°41·2'W	X	181
Bradford Wood Fm	Ches	SJ6468	53°12·7'	2°31·9'W	FM	118
Bradford Wood Ho	Ches	SJ6367	53°12·2'	2°32·8'W	X	118
Bradgate	Leic	SK5310	52°41·3'	1°12·5'W	A	129
Bradgate	Roth	SK4193	53°26·2'	1°22·6'W	T	111
Bradgate Ho	Leic	SK5009	52°40·8'	1°15·2'W	X	140
Bradgate Home Fm	Leic	SK5108	52°40·3'	1°14·3'W	FM	140
Bradgate Park Country Park	Leic	SK5210	52°41·3'	1°13·4'W	X	129
Bradholme	Donc	SE6911	53°35·7'	0°57·0'W	X	111
Bradiford	Devon	SS5534	51°5·5'	4°3·9'W	T	180
Bradiford Fm	Devon	SS7306	50°50·6'	3°47·9'W	FM	191
Bradiford Ho	Devon	SS5434	51°5·4'	4°4·7'W	X	180
Bradiford Water	Devon	SS5636	51°6·6'	4°3·0'W	W	180

Brading	I of W	SZ6086	50°40·5′	1°8·7′W	T	196
Brading Down	I of W	SZ5986	50°40·5′	1°9·5′W	X	196
Bradkirk Hall	Lancs	SD4033	53°47·6′	2°54·2′W	X	102
Bradle Fm	Dorset	SY9380	50°37·4′	2°5·6′W	FM	195
Bradleigh	Devon	SX7595	50°44·7′	3°45·9′W	X	191
Bradleigh Down	Devon	SS9013	50°54·6′	3°33·5′W	X	181
Bradleigh Old Hall	Warr	SJ5793	53°26·2′	2°38·4′W	X	108
Bradlem Pond	Northnts	SP7344	52°5·6′	0°55·7′W	W	152
Bradley	Ches	SJ5377	53°17·5′	2°41·9′W	X	117
Bradley	Cumbr	NY5723	54°36·3′	2°39·5′W	X	91
Bradley	Derby	SK2246	53°0·9′	1°39·9′W	T	119,128
Bradley	Devon	SS8912	50°54·0′	3°34·3′W	X	181
Bradley	Devon	SX8277	50°35·1′	3°39·6′W	X	191
Bradley	Durham	NZ1036	54°43·4′	1°50·3′W	X	92
Bradley	Glos	ST7593	51°38·3′	2°21·3′W	T	162,172
Bradley	Hants	SU6341	51°10·1′	1°5·5′W	T	185
Bradley	Kirk	SE1620	53°40·8′	1°45·1′W	T	104
Bradley	NE Lincs	TA2406	53°32·4′	0°7·3′W	T	113
Bradley	NE Lincs	TA2407	53°32·9′	0°7·3′W	T	113
Bradley	Staffs	SJ8817	52°45·3′	2°10·3′W	T	127
Bradley	Wolv	SO9595	52°33·4′	2°4·0′W	T	139
Bradley	Wrex	SJ3253	53°4·4′	3°0·5′W	T	117
Bradley Barton	Devon	SS5007	50°50·8′	4°7·5′W	X	191
Bradley Brook	Ches	SJ5046	53°0·8′	2°44·3′W	X	117
Bradley Brook	Ches	SJ6785	53°21·9′	2°29·3′W	W	109
Bradley Brook	Derby	SK2244	52°59·8′	1°39·9′W	W	119,128
Bradley Brook	S Glos	ST6381	51°31·8′	2°31·6′W	W	172
Bradley Cott	Durham	NZ1035	54°42·8′	1°50·3′W	X	92
Bradley Cottage	Essex	TL7931	51°57·1′	0°36·7′E	X	167
Bradley Court	Glos	SO6620	51°52·9′	2°29·2′W	X	162
Bradley Court	W Berks	SU4974	51°28·0′	1°17·3′W	X	174
Bradley Cross	Somer	ST4753	51°16·7′	2°45·2′W	T	182
Bradley Elms	Staffs	SK0442	52°58·8′	1°56·0′W	X	119,128
Bradleyfield	Cumbr	SD4991	54°19·0′	2°46·6′W	X	97
Bradleyfield Ho	Cumbr	SD4992	54°19·5′	2°46·6′W	X	97
Bradley Fields Fm	Bucks	SP7140	52°3·5′	0°57·5′W	FM	152
Bradley Fm	Devon	SS8502	50°48·6′	3°37·6′W	FM	191
Bradley Fm	Hants	SU5442	51°10·7′	1°13·3′W	FM	185
Bradley Fm	Oxon	SP4603	51°43·7′	1°19·6′W	FM	164
Bradley Fm	Shrops	SJ6301	52°36·6′	2°32·4′W	FM	127
Bradley Fm	Shrops	SO7179	52°24·7′	2°25·2′W	FM	138
Bradley Fold	Bury	SD7508	53°34·3′	2°22·2′W	T	109
Bradley Gairs	NE Lincs	TA2404	53°31·3′	0°7·4′W	X	113
Bradley Green	Ches	SJ5145	53°0·2′	2°43·4′W	T	117
Bradley Green	Glos	ST7493	51°38·3′	2°22·2′W	T	162,172
Bradley Green	Somer	ST2538	51°8·4′	3°3·9′W	T	182
Bradley Green	Warw	SK2800	52°36·1′	1°34·8′W	T	140
Bradley Green	Worcs	SO9861	52°15·1′	2°1·4′W	T	150
Bradley Hall	Durham	NZ1253	54°52·5′	1°48·4′W	X	88
Bradley Hall	Essex	TM1623	51°52·0′	1°8·6′E	X	168,169
Bradley Hall	Ghead	NZ1263	54°57·9′	1°48·3′W	X	88
Bradley Hall	Lancs	SD5217	53°39·1′	2°43·2′W	X	108
Bradley Hall	Lancs	SD6541	53°52·1′	2°31·5′W	X	102,103
Bradley Hall	Northum	NY7767	55°0·1′	2°21·1′W	X	86,87
Bradley Hall	Staffs	SJ8816	52°44·7′	2°10·3′W	X	127
Bradley Hall	Warr	SJ6584	53°21·3′	2°31·1′W	X	109
Bradley Hall Fm	Ghead	NZ1163	54°57·9′	1°49·3′W	FM	88
Bradley Hill	Glos	SO6609	51°47·0′	2°29·2′W	X	162
Bradley Hill	Hants	SU4453	51°16·7′	1°21·8′W	X	185
Bradley Hill	Hants	SU6442	51°10·6′	1°4·7′W	X	185
Bradley Hill	Lancs	SD5041	53°52·0′	2°45·2′W	X	102
Bradley Hill	Somer	ST4729	51°3·7′	2°45·0′W	X	193
Bradley Hill	Somer	ST4730	51°4·2′	2°45·0′W	H	182
Bradleyhill Fm	Essex	TL7643	52°3·7′	0°34·4′E	FM	155
Bradley Ho	Wilts	ST8038	51°8·7′	2°16·8′W	X	183
Bradley House Fm	Warw	SP4187	52°29·0′	1°23·4′W	FM	140
Bradley Ings	N Yks	SD9948	53°55·9′	2°0·5′W	X	103
Bradley in the Moors	Staffs	SK0641	52°58·2′	1°54·2′W	T	119,128
Bradleylane Fm	Derby	SK3275	53°16·5′	1°30·8′W	FM	119
Bradley Lodge	Derby	SK2246	53°0·9′	1°39·9′W	X	119,128
Bradley Manor	Devon	SX8470	50°31·3′	3°37·8′W	A	202
Bradley Mills	Kirk	SE1517	53°39·2′	1°46·0′W	T	110
Bradley Moor	Derby	SK2045	53°0·4′	1°41·7′W	X	119,128
Bradley Mount	Ches	SJ9177	53°17·6′	2°7·7′W	T	118
Bradley Nook Fm	Derby	SK2347	53°1·4′	1°39·0′W	FM	119,128
Bradley Oldpark	Derby	SK2344	52°59·8′	1°39·0′W	X	119,128
Bradley Orchard	Ches	SJ5477	53°17·5′	2°41·0′W	X	117
Bradley Park Wood	Suff	TL6754	52°9·8′	0°26·9′E	F	154
Bradley Pastures	Derby	SK2246	53°0·9′	1°39·9′W	X	119,128
Bradley's Coppice	Shrops	SO6999	52°35·5′	2°27·1′W	F	138
Bradley's Corner	Heref	SO5960	52°14·4′	2°35·6′W	X	137,138,149
Bradleys Fm	Lancs	SD6239	53°51·0′	2°34·2′W	FM	102,103
Bradley's Fm	Shrops	SO6181	52°25·8′	2°34·0′W	FM	138
Bradley's Fm	Wilts	ST8762	51°21·6′	2°10·8′W	FM	173
Bradley Stoke	S Glos	ST6281	51°31·8′	2°32·5′W	T	172
Bradley Wood	Derby	SK1946	53°0·9′	1°42·6′W	F	119,128
Bradley Wood	Hants	SU4552	51°16·2′	1°20·9′W	F	185
Bradley Wood	Kirk	SE1521	53°41·4′	1°46·0′W	F	104
Bradley Wood	NE Lincs	TA2405	53°31·9′	0°7·3′W	F	113
Bradley Wood Fm	Hants	SU4552	51°16·2′	1°20·9′W	FM	185
Bradleywood Fm	W Berks	SU4373	51°27·5′	1°22·5′W	FM	174
Bradlow	Heref	SO7138	52°2·6′	2°25·0′W	T	149
Bradmer Hill	Notts	SK5866	53°11·5′	1°7·5′W	X	120
Bradmoor Fm	Norf	TG2630	52°49·4′	1°21·7′E	FM	133
Bradmoor Plantn	Norf	TF7514	52°41·9′	0°35·8′E	F	132
Bradmore	Notts	SK5831	52°52·6′	1°7·9′W	T	129
Bradmore	Wolv	SO8997	52°34·5′	2°9·3′W	T	139
Bradmore Moor	Notts	SK5730	52°52·1′	1°8·8′W	X	129
Bradney	Shrops	SO7695	52°33·4′	2°20·8′W	T	138
Bradney	Somer	ST3338	51°8·5′	2°57·1′W	T	182
Bradney Fm	Cambs	TL3794	52°31·8′	0°1·6′E	FM	142,143
Bradninch	Devon	SS6133	51°5·0′	3°58·7′W	X	180
Bradninch	Devon	SS9903	50°49·3′	3°25·7′W	T	192
Bradnock's Marsh	Sol	SP2279	52°24·7′	1°40·2′W	T	139
Bradnop	Staffs	SK0155	53°5·8′	1°58·7′W	T	119
Bradnor Green	Heref	SO2957	52°12·6′	3°2·0′W	T	148
Bradnor Hill	Heref	SO2858	52°13·2′	3°2·8′W	H	148
Bradock	D & G	NX0173	55°1·0′	5°6·3′W	X	76,82
Bradpole	Dorset	SY4794	50°44·8′	2°44·7′W	T	193
Bradridge	Corn	SX3193	50°43·0′	4°23·3′W	X	190
Bradridge Ho	Devon	SX7357	50°24·2′	3°46·9′W	X	202
Bradridge Wood	Corn	SX3293	50°43·0′	4°22·4′W	F	190
Bradshaw	Bolton	SD7312	53°36·5′	2°24·1′W	T	109
Bradshaw	Cald	SE0730	53°46·2′	1°53·2′W	T	104
Bradshaw	Kirk	SE0514	53°37·6′	1°55·1′W	T	110
Bradshaw	Kirk	SE0907	53°33·8′	1°51·4′W	X	110
Bradshaw	N Ayr	NS2453	55°44·6′	4°47·8′W	X	63
Bradshaw	Staffs	SJ9455	53°5·8′	2°5·0′W	T	118
Bradshaw Brook	Bolton	SD7311	53°35·9′	2°24·1′W	W	109
Bradshaw Hall	Wigan	SD6106	53°33·2′	2°34·9′W	X	109
Bradshaw Hall Fm	Derby	SK0380	53°19·3′	1°56·9′W	FM	110
Bradshaw Hill	Sheff	SK1898	53°28·9′	1°43·3′W	X	110
Bradshaw Ho	Ches	SJ7472	53°14·9′	2°23·0′W	X	118
Bradshaw Lane Head	Lancs	SD4145	53°54·1′	2°53·5′W	X	102
Bradshaws, The	Staffs	SJ8401	52°36·6′	2°13·8′W	X	127
Bradshott Hall	Hants	SU7632	51°5·2′	0°54·5′W	X	186
Bradstone	Devon	SX3880	50°36·1′	4°17·0′W	T	201
Bradstone Brook	Surrey	TQ0146	51°12·5′	0°32·9′W	X	186
Bradup	Brad	SE0944	53°53·8′	1°51·4′W	X	104
Bradup Beck	Brad	SE0943	53°53·2′	1°51·4′W	W	104
Bradville	Mil Key	SP8341	52°3·9′	0°47·0′W	T	152
Bradwall Green	Ches	SJ7563	53°10·1′	2°22·0′W	T	118
Bradwall Ho	Ches	SJ7562	53°9·5′	2°22·0′W	X	118
Bradwall Manor	Ches	SJ7563	53°10·1′	2°22·0′W	X	118
Bradway	Sheff	SK3280	53°19·2′	1°30·8′W	T	110,111
Bradwell	Derby	SK1781	53°19·8′	1°44·3′W	T	110
Bradwell	Devon	SS4942	51°9·7′	4°9·2′W	T	180
Bradwell	Essex	TL8023	51°52·8′	0°37·3′E	T	168
Bradwell	Mil Key	SP8339	52°2·8′	0°47·0′W	T	152
Bradwell	Norf	TG5004	52°34·8′	1°41·8′E	T	134
Bradwell	Staffs	SJ8449	53°2·5′	2°13·9′W	T	118
Bradwell Brook	Essex	TL9905	51°42·7′	0°53·2′E	W	168
Bradwell Common	Mil Key	SP8439	52°2·8′	0°46·1′W	T	152
Bradwell Creek	Essex	TL9807	51°43·8′	0°52·4′E	W	168
Bradwell Dale	Derby	SK1780	53°19·2′	1°44·3′W	X	110
Bradwell Edge	Derby	SK1880	53°19·2′	1°43·4′W	X	110
Bradwell Grove	Oxon	SP2308	51°46·4′	1°39·6′W	X	163
Bradwell Grove Wood	Oxon	SP2407	51°45·9′	1°38·7′W	F	163
Bradwell Hall	Essex	TL8122	51°52·3′	0°38·2′E	X	168
Bradwell Hall	Essex	TL9805	51°42·7′	0°52·4′E	X	168
Bradwell Hall	Norf	TG5005	52°35·3′	1°41·9′E	X	134
Bradwell Hills	Derby	SK1780	53°19·2′	1°44·3′W	T	110
Bradwell Lodge	Essex	TM0006	51°43·2′	0°54·1′E	X	168
Bradwell Marshes	Essex	TM0105	51°42·7′	0°55·0′E	X	168
Bradwell Moor	Derby	SK1480	53°19·2′	1°47·0′W	X	110
Bradwell on Sea	Essex	TM0006	51°43·2′	0°54·1′E	T	168
Bradwell Waterside	Essex	TL9907	51°43·8′	0°53·3′E	T	168
Bradwell Wick	Essex	TL9705	51°42·8′	0°51·5′E	X	168
Bradworthy	Devon	SS3213	50°53·8′	4°23·0′W	T	190
Bradworthy Common	Devon	SS3214	50°54·3′	4°23·0′W	X	190
Bradworthy Cross	Devon	SS3112	50°53·2′	4°23·8′W	X	190
Bradwys	Powys	SO1735	52°0·7′	3°12·2′W	X	161
Bradyston	Pth & Kin	NO0938	56°31·8′	3°28·3′W	X	52,53
Brae	D & G	NX8674	55°3·1′	3°46·6′W	X	84
Brae	D & G	NY0689	55°11·4′	3°28·2′W	X	78
Brae	E Ayr	NS3747	55°41·6′	4°35·2′W	X	63
Brae	Highld	NC4301	57°58·5′	4°38·8′W	X	16
Brae	Highld	NG5541	57°23·9′	6°4·2′W	X	24
Brae	Highld	NG8185	57°48·3′	5°40·7′W	X	19
Brae	N Yks	SE1258	54°1·3′	1°48·6′W	X	104
Brae	S Ayr	NX2098	55°14·9′	4°49·5′W	X	76
Brae	Shetld	HU3668	60°23·9′	1°20·3′W	T	2,3
Brae	S Lanak	NS8538	55°37·6′	3°49·1′W	X	71,72
Braeantra	Highld	NH5677	57°45·8′	4°24·8′W	X	21
Braebuster	Orkney	HY5405	58°56·1′	2°47·5′W	X	6,7
Braebuster Ness	Orkney	HY5404	58°55·5′	2°47·5′W	X	6,7
Brae-callasay	N Eil	NF9272	57°38·2′	7°9·2′W	X	18
Braecock	Pth & Kin	NO0939	56°32·3′	3°28·3′W	X	52,53
Brae Cott	Aberd	NJ5110	57°11·0′	2°48·2′W	X	37
Braecroft	D & G	NX9277	55°4·8′	3°41·1′W	X	84
Braedmarloch Hill	Highld	ND2439	58°20·2′	3°17·4′W	X	11,12
Braedown	Highld	NH6455	57°34·1′	4°16·0′W	X	26
Braedownie	Angus	NO2875	56°51·9′	3°10·4′W	X	44
Brae Dunstan	Scot Bord	NT7740	55°39·4′	2°21·5′W	X	74
Braeface	Falk	NS7880	56°0·1′	3°56·9′W	T	64
Braeface Fm	E Renf	NS4555	55°46·1′	4°27·8′W	FM	64
Brae Fell	Cumbr	NY2835	54°42·5′	3°6·6′W	X	89,90
Braefield	D & G	NT1400	55°17·4′	3°20·8′W	X	78
Braefield	Highld	NH4230	57°20·3′	4°37·0′W	X	26
Braefield	Shetld	HU4018	59°57·0′	1°16·5′W	X	4
Braefindon	Highld	NH6259	57°36·3′	4°18·1′W	T	26
Brae Fm	Aberd	NJ8015	57°13·8′	2°19·4′W	FM	38
Braefolds	Aberd	NJ5329	57°21·2′	2°46·4′W	X	37
Braefoot	Aberd	NJ4307	57°9·3′	2°56·1′W	X	37
Braefoot	Aberd	NJ7046	57°30·5′	2°29·6′W	X	29
Braefoot	D & G	NX7263	54°57·0′	3°59·5′W	X	83,84
Braefoot	D & G	NY0778	55°5·5′	3°27·0′W	X	85
Braefoot	Orkney	HY5117	59°2·5′	2°50·8′W	X	6
Braefoot Bay	Fife	NT1883	56°2·2′	3°18·5′W	W	65,66
Braefoot Point	Fife	NT1783	56°2·2′	3°19·5′W	X	65,66
Braefoot Wood	D & G	NT0711	55°23·3′	3°27·7′W	F	78
Braefordie	Pth & Kin	NN7925	56°24·4′	3°57·2′W	X	51,52
Braegarie	Aberd	NO1089	56°59·3′	3°28·4′W	T	43
Brae Geo	Orkney	HY6430	59°9·6′	2°37·3′W	X	5
Braegrudie	Highld	NC7109	58°3·3′	4°10·7′W	X	16
Braegrum	Pth & Kin	NO0025	56°24·7′	3°36·8′W	T	52,53,58
Braehead	Aberd	NJ4504	57°7·7′	2°54·1′W	X	37
Braehead	Aberd	NJ4746	57°30·3′	2°52·6′W	X	28,29
Braehead	Aberd	NJ5206	57°8·8′	2°47·1′W	X	37
Braehead	Aberd	NJ5925	57°19·1′	2°40·4′W	X	37
Braehead	Aberd	NJ6035	57°24·5′	2°39·5′W	X	29
Braehead	Aberd	NJ6817	57°14·8′	2°31·4′W	X	38
Braehead	Aberd	NJ8658	57°37·0′	2°13·6′W	X	30
Braehead	Aberd	NJ9135	57°24·6′	2°8·5′W	X	30
Braehead	Aberd	NJ9216	57°14·3′	2°7·5′W	X	38
Braehead	Aberd	NJ9830	57°21·9′	2°1·5′W	X	30
Braehead	Aberd	NK0248	57°31·6′	1°57·5′W	X	30
Braehead	Angus	NO8785	56°57·6′	2°12·4′W	X	45
Braehead	Beds	SP9755	52°11·3′	0°34·5′W	X	153
Braehead	D & G	NX4252	54°50·5′	4°27·2′W	T	83
Braehead	D & G	NX9584	55°8·6′	3°38·4′W	X	78
Braehead	D & G	NY0376	55°4·4′	3°30·7′W	X	84
Braehead	D & G	NY2873	55°3·0′	3°7·2′W	X	85
Braehead	E Ayr	NS4534	55°34·8′	4°27·1′W	X	70
Braehead	E Ayr	NS4924	55°29·4′	4°23·0′W	X	70
Braehead	E Ayr	NS5713	55°23·7′	4°15·0′W	X	71
Braehead	E Ayr	NS5921	55°28·0′	4°13·4′W	X	71
Braehead	Moray	NJ2557	57°36·1′	3°14·8′W	X	28
Braehead	Moray	NJ2645	57°29·6′	3°13·6′W	X	28
Braehead	Moray	NJ3843	57°28·6′	3°1·6′W	X	28
Braehead	Moray	NJ4249	57°31·9′	2°57·7′W	X	28
Braehead	N Ayr	NS3541	55°38·3′	4°36·9′W	X	70
Braehead	N Lanak	NS7063	55°50·8′	4°4·1′W	X	64
Braehead	N Lanak	NS7078	55°58·9′	4°4·6′W	X	64
Braehead	Orkney	HY4447	59°18·6′	2°58·5′W	T	5
Braehead	Orkney	HY5101	58°53·9′	2°50·5′W	X	6,7
Braehead	Pth & Kin	NO0626	56°25·3′	3°31·0′W	X	52,53,58
Braehead	S Ayr	NS2303	55°17·6′	4°46·8′W	X	76
Braehead	S Ayr	NS3422	55°28·1′	4°37·1′W	T	70
Brae Head	Scot Bord	NT3706	55°20·9′	2°59·2′W	H	79
Braehead	Scot Bord	NT4000	55°17·7′	2°56·3′W	X	79
Braehead	Shetld	HP6515	60°49·0′	0°47·8′W	X	1
Braehead	S Lanak	NS5955	55°46·3′	4°14·4′W	T	64
Braehead	S Lanak	NS8134	55°35·4′	3°52·9′W	X	71,72
Braehead	S Lanak	NS9550	55°44·2′	3°39·9′W	T	65,72
Braehead	Stir	NS8092	56°6·6′	3°55·3′W	T	57
Braehead Moss	S Lanak	NS9651	55°44·7′	3°39·0′W	X	65,72
Braehead of Lunan	Angus	NO6852	56°39·8′	2°30·9′W	T	54
Braehill	D & G	NY1271	55°1·8′	3°22·2′W	X	85
Braehiller	Highld	ND1432	58°16·4′	3°27·5′W	X	11,17
Braehoulland	Shetld	HU2479	60°29·9′	1°33·3′W	T	3
Braehour	Highld	ND0953	58°27·6′	3°33·1′W	X	11,12
Braehouse	Highld	NM5267	56°44·0′	6°2·8′W	X	47
Braehouse	Scot Bord	NT8228	55°33·0′	2°16·7′W	X	74
Braehouse	Stir	NS7491	56°6·0′	4°1·1′W	X	57
Braehungie	Highld	ND1837	58°19·1′	3°23·5′W	X	11
Braeintra	Highld	NG8632	57°20·0′	5°32·9′W	X	24
Brae Kirkiboll	Highld	NC5956	58°28·4′	4°24·6′W	X	10
Braelangwell	Highld	NH6964	57°39·1′	4°11·2′W	X	21
Braelangwell Lodge	Highld	NH5192	57°53·8′	4°30·4′W	X	20
Braeleny	Stir	NN6311	56°16·6′	4°12·3′W	X	57
Braeloine	Aberd	NO4896	57°3·4′	2°51·0′W	X	37,44
Braemar	Aberd	NO1292	57°0·9′	3°26·5′W	X	43
Braemar	Aberd	NO1491	57°0·4′	3°24·5′W	T	43
Braemar	Aberd	NO2692	57°1·1′	3°12·7′W	X	44
Braemar	Cumbr	NY5924	54°36·8′	2°37·7′W	X	91
Braemar	Shetld	HU3817	59°56·4′	1°18·7′W	X	4
Braemar Castle	Aberd	NO1592	57°0·9′	3°23·5′W	A	43
Brae Meadale	Highld	NG4035	57°20·1′	6°18·8′W	X	32
Braeminzion	Angus	NO3666	56°47·1′	3°2·4′W	X	44
Braemoor Knowe	Scot Bord	NT7921	55°29·2′	2°19·5′W	H	74
Braemoray Lodge	Moray	NH9942	57°27·7′	3°40·6′W	X	27
Braemore	Highld	NC5503	57°59·8′	4°26·7′W	X	16
Braemore	Highld	ND0730	58°15·2′	3°34·6′W	T	11,17
Braemore	Highld	NH1979	57°46·1′	5°2·1′W	X	20
Braemore	Orkney	HY3210	58°58·6′	3°10·5′W	X	6
Braemore Forest	Highld	NH2276	57°44·6′	4°59·0′W	X	20
Braemore Lodge	Highld	ND0630	58°15·2′	3°35·6′W	X	11,17
Braemore Square	Highld	NH1979	57°46·1′	5°2·1′W	X	20
Braemore Wood	Highld	NC5401	57°58·7′	4°27·7′W	F	16
Braemount	Renf	NS4760	55°48·8′	4°26·1′W	X	64
Braenaloin	Aberd	NO2799	57°4·8′	3°11·8′W	X	37,44
Braendam Ho	Stir	NN6401	56°11·2′	4°11·0′W	X	57
Braeneil	Aberd	NJ7212	57°12·1′	2°27·4′W	X	38
Braens	Shetld	HU3348	60°13·2′	1°23·8′W	X	3
Braentrian	Stir	NN6634	56°29·0′	4°10·1′W	X	51
Brae of Achnahaird	Highld	NC0013	58°3·9′	5°23·0′W	T	15
Brae of Airlie	Angus	NO3052	56°39·5′	3°8·1′W	X	53
Brae of Auchendrane	S Ayr	NS3315	55°24·3′	4°37·8′W	X	70
Brae of Balnabeen	Highld	NH5955	57°34·0′	4°21·0′W	X	26
Brae of Biffie	Aberd	NJ9646	57°30·5′	2°3·5′W	X	30
Brae of Boquhapple	Stir	NN6501	56°11·2′	4°10·1′W	X	57
Brae of Cessintully	Stir	NN6701	56°11·2′	4°8·1′W	X	57
Brae of Cluny	Pth & Kin	NN8752	56°39·0′	3°50·1′W	X	52
Brae of Conon	Angus	NO5742	56°34·3′	2°41·5′W	X	54
Brae of Coynach	Aberd	NJ9844	57°29·4′	2°1·5′W	X	30
Brae of Crombie	Aberd	NJ5852	57°33·6′	2°41·7′W	X	29
Brae of Cultullich	Pth & Kin	NN8849	56°37·4′	3°49·1′W	X	52
Brae of Downie	Angus	NO5137	56°31·6′	2°47·3′W	X	54
Brae of Easter Kinkell	Highld	NH5754	57°33·5′	4°22·9′W	X	26
Brae of Fordyce	Aberd	NJ5563	57°39·5′	2°44·8′W	X	29
Brae of Glenbervie	Aberd	NO7685	56°57·6′	2°23·2′W	X	45
Brae of Largue	Aberd	NJ6341	57°27·7′	2°36·5′W	X	29
Brae of Moan	Orkney	HY3733	59°11·0′	3°5·7′W	H	6
Brae of Montgrew	Moray	NJ4452	57°33·5′	2°55·7′W	X	28
Brae of Monzie	Pth & Kin	NN8725	56°24·5′	3°49·4′W	X	52,58
Brae of Monzievaird	Pth & Kin	NN8424	56°23·9′	3°52·3′W	X	52,58
Brae of Pert	Angus	NO6465	56°46·8′	2°34·9′W	T	45
Brae of Pitcastle	Pth & Kin	NN9054	56°40·1′	3°47·2′W	X	52
Brae of Restensgeo	Shetld	HZ2172	59°32·3′	1°37·2′W	X	4
Brae of Scurdargue	Aberd	NJ4728	57°20·6′	2°52·4′W	X	37
Braepark	C of Edin	NT1875	55°57·9′	3°18·4′W	T	65,66
Brae Park	Highld	NH6056	57°34·6′	4°20·0′W	X	26
Braeriach or Braigh Riabhach	Aberd	NN9599	57°4·5′	3°43·5′W	H	36,43
Braeroddach	Aberd	NO4899	57°5·0′	2°51·0′W	X	37,44
Braeroddach Loch	Aberd	NJ4800	57°5·5′	2°51·0′W	W	37
Braeroy Forest	Highld	NN3791	56°59·1′	4°40·5′W	X	34
Braes	Falk	NS7984	56°2·3′	3°56·1′W	X	57,64
Braes Cairn	Moray	NJ3958	57°36·7′	3°0·8′W	X	28
Braes Fm	Suff	TL9339	52°1·2′	0°49·2′E	FM	155
Braeshellach	Angus	NO3166	56°47·1′	3°7·3′W	X	44
Braeside	Aberd	NJ4420	57°16·3′	2°55·3′W	X	37
Braeside	Aberd	NJ5310	57°11·0′	2°46·2′W	X	37
Braeside	Aberd	NJ5460	57°37·9′	2°45·8′W	X	29
Braeside	Aberd	NJ6011	57°11·5′	2°39·3′W	X	37
Braeside	Aberd	NJ6337	57°25·6′	2°36·5′W	X	29
Braeside	Aberd	NJ6342	57°28·3′	2°36·6′W	X	29
Braeside	Aberd	NJ6502	57°6·7′	2°34·2′W	X	38
Braeside	Aberd	NJ6922	57°17·5′	2°30·4′W	X	38

Braeside	Aberd	NJ7140	57°27·2′	2°28·5′W	X	29
Braeside	Aberd	NJ7420	57°16·5′	2°25·4′W	X	38
Braeside	Aberd	NJ8354	57°34·8′	2°16·6′W	X	29,30
Braeside	Aberd	NJ8629	57°21·3′	2°13·5′W	X	38
Braeside	Aberd	NJ9038	57°26·2′	2°9·5′W	T	30
Braeside	Aberd	NO5898	57°4·5′	2°41·1′W	X	37,44
Braeside	Angus	NO4537	56°31·6′	2°53·2′W	X	54
Braeside	C of Aber	NJ9104	57°7·9′	2°8·5′W	T	38
Braeside	D & G	NX8883	55°8·0′	3°45·0′W	X	78
Braeside	E Ayr	NS4133	55°34·1′	4°30·9′W	X	70
Braeside	Fife	NO2714	56°19·0′	3°10·4′W	X	59
Braeside	Fife	NT0683	56°2·1′	3°30·1′W	X	65
Braeside	Highld	NG8719	57°13·0′	5°31·2′W	X	33
Braeside	Highld	NH9251	57°32·4′	3°47·8′W	X	27
Braeside	Inverc	NS2375	55°56·4′	4°49·6′W	T	63
Braeside	Moray	NJ2737	57°25·3′	3°12·5′W	X	28
Braeside	Orkney	HY2824	59°6·1′	3°14·9′W	X	6
Braeside	Shetld	HP5303	60°42·7′	1°1·2′W	X	1
Braeside	Shetld	HU3579	60°29·9′	1°21·3′W	X	2,3
Braeside Auchmachar	Aberd	NJ9450	57°32·7′	2°5·6′W	X	30
Braeside Fm	Kent	TR0037	51°6·1′	0°51·8′E	FM	189
Braeside of Balnakettle	Aberd	NJ9020	57°16·5′	2°9·5′W	X	38
Braeside of Fetterangus	Aberd	NJ9751	57°33·2′	2°2·5′W	X	30
Braeside of Lindores	Fife	NO2517	56°20·6′	3°12·4′W	X	59
Braeside of Rothmaise	Aberd	NJ6832	57°22·9′	2°31·5′W	X	29
Braeside Wood	Aberd	NJ3212	57°11·9′	3°7·1′W	F	37
Braeside Woods	Aberd	NJ4420	57°16·3′	2°55·3′W	F	37
Braes of Abernethy	Highld	NJ0715	57°13·2′	3°31·9′W	X	36
Braes of Aglath	Orkney	HY3518	59°2·9′	3°7·5′W	X	6
Braes of Balquhidder	Stir	NN4821	56°21·7′	4°27·2′W	X	51,57
Braes of Coul	Angus	NO2757	56°42·2′	3°11·1′W	T	53
Braes of Doune	Stir	NN6905	56°13·4′	4°6·3′W	X	57
Braes of Enzie	Moray	NJ3959	57°37·3′	3°0·8′W	X	28
Braes of Fintock	Aberd	NJ3605	57°8·1′	3°3·0′W	X	37
Braes of Foss	Pth & Kin	NN7556	56°41·0′	4°2·0′W	X	42,51,52
Braes of Fowlis	Pth & Kin	NN9324	56°24·0′	3°43·6′W	X	52,58
Braes of Gight	Aberd	NJ8238	57°26·2′	2°17·5′W	X	29,30
Braes of Glenlivet	Moray	NJ2421	57°16·7′	3°15·2′W	X	36
Braes of Glenlivet	Moray	NJ2521	57°16·7′	3°14·2′W	X	37
Braes of Greenock	Stir	NN6305	56°13·3′	4°12·1′W	X	57
Braes of Lorn	Arg & Bt	NM8716	56°17·6′	5°26·1′W	X	55
Braes of Minnonie	Aberd	NJ7937	57°25·6′	2°20·5′W	X	29,30
Braes of Mullachgeny	D & G	NX4084	55°7·7′	4°30·1′W	X	77
Braes of Ogilvie	Pth & Kin	NN8907	56°14·8′	3°47·0′W	X	58
Braes of the Carse	Pth & Kin	NO2126	56°25·4′	3°16·4′W	H	53,58
Braes of Ullapool	Highld	NH1493	57°53·5′	5°7·8′W	T	20
Braes o'Lochaber	Highld	NN3180	56°53·1′	4°46·0′W	X	34,41
Braestairie	Aberd	NJ6637	57°25·6′	2°33·5′W	X	29
Braesteads	Cumbr	NY3715	54°31·8′	2°58·0′W	X	90
Brae Stein	Highld	NG2656	57°30·9′	6°34·1′W	X	23
Braes, The	D & G	NY2373	55°3·0′	3°11·9′W	X	85
Braes, The	Highld	NG5234	57°20·0′	6°6·8′W	X	24,32
Braes, The	Pth & Kin	NO1552	56°39·4′	3°22·7′W	X	53
Braes, The	Renf	NS3964	55°50·8′	4°33·9′W	X	63
Braes Wick	Orkney	HY6137	59°13·3′	2°40·5′W	W	5
Braeswick	Orkney	HY6137	59°13·3′	2°40·5′W	T	5
Brae, The	Aberd	NJ6906	57°8·9′	2°30·3′W	X	38
Braetollie	Highld	NH6175	57°44·9′	4°19·7′W	X	21
Braetongue	Highld	NC5957	58°29·0′	4°24·6′W	X	10
Braetown	Moray	NJ3938	57°26·0′	3°0·5′W	X	28
Braevail	Highld	NH9550	57°31·9′	3°44·8′W	X	27
Braeval	Highld	ND0630	58°15·2′	3°35·6′W	X	11,17
Braeval	Moray	NJ2220	57°16·1′	3°17·1′W	X	36
Braeval	Stir	NN5300	56°10·5′	4°21·6′W	X	57
Braevallich	Arg & Bt	NM9507	56°12·9′	5°17·9′W	T	55
Brae Wick	Shetld	HU2477	60°28·8′	1°33·3′W	W	3
Braewick	Shetld	HU2478	60°29·4′	1°33·3′W	T	3
Braewick	Shetld	HU3357	60°18·0′	1°23·7′W	T	2,3
Brafferton	Darl	NZ2921	54°35·2′	1°32·7′W	T	93
Brafferton	N Yks	SE4370	54°7·7′	1°20·1′W	T	99
Brafferton Spring Wood	N Yks	SE4571	54°8·2′	1°18·3′W	F	99
Braffords Fm	E Yorks	SE9830	53°45·7′	0°30·4′W	FM	106
Braffords Hall	E Yorks	SE9830	53°45·7′	0°30·4′W	X	106
Brafield-on-the-Green	Northnts	SP8258	52°13·1′	0°47·6′W	T	152
Brafle Fm	Carm	SN3937	52°0·7′	4°20·4′W	FM	145
Braga	Orkney	HY2109	58°57·9′	3°21·9′W	X	6,7
Braga	Shetld	HU3140	60°8·9′	1°26·0′W	X	4
Braga	Shetld	HU5362	60°20·6′	1°1·9′W	X	2,3
Braga	Shetld	HU5995	60°38·3′	0°54·8′W	X	1,2
Braga Ness	Shetld	HU1948	60°13·2′	1°38·9′W	X	3
Braga Ness	Shetld	HU3160	60°19·6′	1°25·8′W	X	3
Bragar	N Eil	NB2947	58°19·9′	6°37·3′W	T	8
Bragasetter	Shetld	HU1759	60°19·2′	1°41·0′W	X	3
Bragborough Hall	Northnts	SP5666	52°17·6′	1°10·3′W	X	152
Bragbury End	Herts	TL2621	51°52·6′	0°9·8′W	T	166
Bragdale	Leeds	SE4435	53°48·8′	1°19·5′W	X	105
Bragenham	Bucks	SP9028	51°56·8′	0°41·0′W	T	165
Braggamarsh	Devon	SS6419	50°57·5′	3°55·8′W	X	180
Braggan Point	I of M	SC4481	54°12·3′	4°23·1′W	X	95
Braggers Hill	Shrops	SJ6405	52°38·7′	2°31·5′W	X	127
Bragg Fm	N Yks	SE6797	54°22·1′	0°57·7′W	FM	94,100
Bragg Ho	Durham	NZ0709	54°28·8′	1°53·1′W	X	92
Braggington Hall Fm	Shrops	SJ3313	52°42·9′	2°59·1′W	FM	126
Braggington House	Warw	SP1350	52°9·1′	1°48·2′W	X	151
Braggon's Fm	Suff	TL8249	52°6·8′	0°39·9′E	FM	155
Braggs Fm	Devon	SX4861	50°26·0′	4°8·0′W	FM	201
Bragleenbeg Ho	Arg & Bt	NM9120	56°19·8′	5°22·4′W	X	49
Bragleenmore	Arg & Bt	NM9020	56°19·8′	5°23·4′W	X	49
Bragmere Pits	Norf	TL9391	52°29·2′	0°51·0′E	F	144
Bragty	Carm	SN3418	51°50·4′	4°24·2′W	X	159
Braham Fm	Cambs	TL5377	52°22·4′	0°15·3′E	FM	143
Braham Hall	Essex	TM1028	51°54·9′	1°3·6′E	X	168,169
Braham Hall	N Yks	SE3552	53°58·0′	1°27·6′W	X	104
Braham Hall	Suff	TM0933	51°57·6′	1°2·9′E	X	168,169
Brahan Ho	Highld	NH5154	57°33·4′	4°29·0′W	X	26
Brahan Wood	Highld	NH5055	57°33·9′	4°30·0′W	F	26
Brahunisary	Arg & Bt	NR3746	55°38·4′	6°10·3′W	X	60
Braibruich	Arg & Bt	NR2559	55°45·0′	6°22·5′W	X	60
Braich	Denb	SJ0551	53°3·1′	3°24·6′W	X	116
Braich	Gwyn	SH6421	52°46·4′	4°0·6′W	X	124

Braich Anelog	Gwyn	SH1427	52°48·8′	4°45·2′W	X	123
Braich Ddu	Gwyn	SH6411	52°41·0′	4°0·3′W	H	124
Braich Ddu	Gwyn	SH6701	52°35·7′	3°57·4′W	H	135
Braich Ddu	Gwyn	SJ0141	52°57·7′	3°28·0′W	X	125
Braich-llwyd	Gwyn	SH9012	52°41·9′	3°37·3′W	X	125
Braich-lwyd	I of Angl	SH3367	53°10·7′	4°29·5′W	X	114
Braichmelyn	Gwyn	SH6265	53°10·1′	4°3·5′W	T	115
Braich-Odnant	Powys	SH9001	52°36·0′	3°37·1′W	X	136
Braich-y-big	Gwyn	SH5443	52°58·1′	4°10·0′W	X	124
Braich-y-ceunant	Gwyn	SH7618	52°45·0′	3°49·8′W	X	124
Braich y Cymmer	Brig	SS9090	51°36·1′	3°34·9′W	X	170
Braich-y-Dinas	Gwyn	SH5348	53°0·8′	4°11·1′W	X	115
Braichyfedw	Powys	SN8991	52°30·6′	3°37·7′W	T	135,136
Braich y Golwydd	Gwyn	SH7001	52°35·7′	3°54·8′W	H	135
Braich y Noddfa	Gwyn	SH1326	52°48·2′	4°46·0′W	X	123
Braich-y-parc	Gwyn	SH6444	52°58·8′	4°1·1′W	X	124
Braich y Pwll	Gwyn	SH1325	52°47·7′	4°46·0′W	X	123
Braich-yr-hwch	Gwyn	SH8723	52°47·8′	3°40·2′W	H	124,125
Braich yr Hydd	Brig	SS9294	51°38·3′	3°33·3′W	X	170
Braich-yr Owen	Powys	SH9625	52°49·0′	3°32·2′W	X	125
Braich-y-saint	Gwyn	SH5140	52°56·4′	4°12·6′W	X	124
Braich y Tarw	Conwy	SH8656	53°5·6′	3°41·7′W	H	116
Braich-y-waen	Powys	SJ0817	52°44·8′	3°21·4′W	X	125
Braid	C of Edin	NT2569	55°54·8′	3°11·6′W	X	66
Braida Garth	N Yks	SD7077	54°11·5′	2°27·2′W	X	98
Braida Garth Scar	N Yks	SD7077	54°11·5′	2°27·2′W	X	98
Braidbog	Moray	NJ4963	57°39·5′	2°50·8′W	X	28,29
Braid Burn	C of Edin	NT2871	55°55·9′	3°8·7′W	W	66
Braid Cairn	Aberd	NO4287	56°58·5′	2°56·8′W	H	44
Braidenhill Fm	N Lanak	NS7467	55°53·0′	4°0·4′W	FM	64
Braidenoch	D & G	NX5690	55°11·3′	4°15·3′W	X	77
Braidenoch Lane	D & G	NX5690	55°11·3′	4°15·3′W	W	77
Braides	Lancs	SD4451	53°57·5′	2°50·8′W	X	102
Braideston	Angus	NO3147	56°36·8′	3°7·0′W	X	53
Braidfauld	C of Glas	NS6363	55°50·7′	4°10·8′W	T	64
Braid Fell	D & G	NX1166	54°57·4′	4°56·7′W	H	82
Braidfield	W Dunb	NS4972	55°55·3′	4°24·5′W	X	64
Braidhaugh	Scot Bord	NT5910	55°23·2′	2°38·4′W	X	80
Braid Hill	Arg & Bt	NR7334	55°33·1′	5°35·5′W	H	68
Braid Hill	S Lanak	NS8921	55°28·5′	3°44·9′W	H	71,72
Braid Hills	C of Edin	NT2569	55°54·8′	3°11·6′W	X	66
Braid Knowe	S Lanak	NS8525	55°30·6′	3°48·8′W	X	71,72
Braidknowe Burn	S Lanak	NS8625	55°30·6′	3°47·9′W	W	71,72
Braidland	E Ayr	NS4447	55°41·7′	4°28·5′W	X	64
Braidlane Burn	D & G	NX9591	55°12·4′	3°38·6′W	W	78
Braid Law	Midlo	NT1859	55°49·3′	3°18·1′W	H	65,66,72
Braidlea	S Lanak	NS8231	55°33·8′	3°51·8′W	X	71,72
Braidley	N Yks	SE0380	54°13·2′	1°56·8′W	T	98
Braidley Burn	Scot Bord	NY4798	55°16·6′	2°49·6′W	W	79
Braidley Moor	N Yks	SE0280	54°13·2′	1°57·7′W	X	98
Braidley Moss	E Ayr	NS5941	55°38·8′	4°14·0′W	X	71
Braidlie	Scot Bord	NY4796	55°15·6′	2°49·6′W	X	79
Braidliehope	Scot Bord	NY4798	55°16·6′	2°49·6′W	X	79
Braidnie Burn	S Lanak	NS8325	55°30·5′	3°50·7′W	W	71,72
Braidon Bay	Aberd	NO8677	56°53·2′	2°13·3′W	W	45
Braids	Arg & Bt	NR7144	55°38·4′	5°37·9′W	X	62
Braidshaw Rig	D & G	NX9397	55°15·6′	3°40·6′W	X	78
Braidshawrig	Scot Bord	NT5852	55°45·8′	2°39·7′W	X	67,73,74
Braidway	Shrops	SJ5118	52°45·7′	2°43·2′W	X	126
Braidwood	E Loth	NT7273	55°57·2′	2°26·5′W	X	67
Braidwood	Midlo	NT1959	55°49·3′	3°17·1′W	X	65,66,72
Braidwood	Midlo	NT3158	55°48·9′	3°5·6′W	X	66,73
Braidwood	S Lanak	NS8447	55°42·4′	3°50·3′W	T	72
Braidwood Br	Midlo	NT3158	55°48·9′	3°5·6′W	X	66,73
Braidwood Ho	S Lanak	NS8448	55°42·9′	3°50·4′W	X	72
Braigh a' Chaoil	Arg & Bt	NM5833	56°25·9′	5°55·1′W	X	47,48
Braigh a' Choire Bhig	Highld	NH1533	57°21·3′	5°4·1′W	X	25
Braigh à Choire Bhuidhe	Highld	NM9797	57°1·4′	5°20·9′W	X	33,40
Braigh a' Choire Mhóir	Arg & Bt	NM5643	56°31·2′	5°57·6′W	H	47,48
Braigh a' Gharraidh	Arg & Bt	NM6020	56°19·0′	5°52·4′W	X	49
Bràigh Aluinn	Highld	NG4132	57°18·6′	6°17·6′W	X	32
Bràigh an Dùin	Highld	NG2649	57°27·2′	6°33·6′W	X	23
Bràigh an Fhàis	N Eil	NB1006	57°57·2′	6°53·7′W	H	13,14
Bràigh an Fhirich	Arg & Bt	NM6530	56°24·5′	5°48·1′W	X	49
Bràigh an Fhraoich	Highld	NN0472	56°48·2′	5°12·2′W	X	41
Bràigh an Ruisg	N Eil	NB1804	57°56·4′	6°45·4′W	X	13,14
Bràigh Bac	Highld	NN3088	56°57·4′	4°47·3′W	X	34,41
Bràigh Bheagarais	N Eil	NB0412	58°0·2′	7°0·2′W	X	13
Bràigh Bhlàich	Highld	NN0273	56°48·6′	5°14·2′W	H	41
Bràigh Buidhe	N Eil	NB0012	58°0·0′	7°4·2′W	X	13
Bràigh Buidhe	N Eil	NF7671	57°37·0′	7°25·2′W	X	18
Bràigh Buidhe	N Eil	NG0292	57°49·4′	7°0·7′W	X	18
Bràigh Clais Daimh	Pth & Kin	NN8974	56°50·9′	3°48·7′W	H	43
Bràigh Coille na Droighniche	Highld	NG3832	57°18·5′	6°20·6′W	X	32
Bràigh Coire Caochan nan Laogh	Pth & Kin	NN9581	56°54·8′	3°43·0′W	H	43
Bràigh Coire Chruinn-bhalgain	Pth & Kin	NN9472	56°49·9′	3°43·8′W	H	43
Bràigh Coire na Conlaich	Pth & Kin	NN9377	56°52·6′	3°44·9′W	H	43
Bràigh Dubh Dhoire	Highld	NM7148	56°34·3′	5°43·2′W	X	49
Bràighe Beag	N Eil	NB5265	58°30·4′	6°15·0′W	X	8
Bràighe Mòr	N Eil	NB5365	58°30·5′	6°14·0′W	X	8
Bràigh Fèith Ghiubhsachain	Pth & Kin	NO0073	56°50·5′	3°37·9′W	H	43
Bràigh Fèith Hemigal	Highld	ND0253	58°27·5′	3°40·3′W	X	11,12
Bràigh Lochan	Highld	NH3359	57°35·7′	4°47·2′W	W	26
Bràigh Mór	N Eil	NA9916	58°2·1′	7°5·5′W	W	13
Bràigh Mór	N Eil	NG1994	57°51·1′	6°43·7′W	W	14
Bràigh na Cloiche	Highld	NG1745	57°24·7′	6°42·3′W	X	23
Bràigh na Frithe	Arg & Bt	NM8420	56°19·6′	5°29·2′W	H	49
Bràigh na Glaice Móire	Highld	NM7248	56°34·4′	5°42·3′W	X	49
Bràigh na h-Aoidhe	N Eil	NB4632	58°12·5′	6°19·0′W	T	8
Bràigh na h-Eaglaise	Highld	ND0622	58°10·9′	3°35·4′W	H	17
Bràigh na Leitire	Highld	NH1852	57°31·6′	5°1·9′W	X	25
Bràigh-nam-bagh	N Eil	NG0789	57°47·9′	6°55·4′W	X	14,18
Bràigh nan Creagan Breac	Pth & Kin	NN8975	56°51·5′	3°48·8′W	H	43
Bràigh nan Stacannan	N Eil	NB1341	58°16·1′	6°53·2′W	X	13
Bràigh nan Uamhachan	Highld	NM9786	56°55·5′	5°19·7′W	H	40

Braigh Riabhach or Braeriach	Aberd	NN9599	57°4·5′	3°43·5′W	H	36,43
Bràigh Rubha an t-Sasunnaich	Highld	NM7142	56°31·1′	5°42·9′W	X	49
Bràigh Skulamus	Highld	NG6521	57°13·4′	5°53·1′W	X	32
Bràigh Sròn Ghorm	Pth & Kin	NN9078	56°53·1′	3°47·9′W	H	43
Braigh Uaine	Highld	NN1899	57°3·0′	4°59·6′W	X	34
Bràigh Uladail	Highld	NM7252	56°36·5′	5°42·5′W	X	49
Braigh Varr	Arg & Bt	NR9695	56°6·5′	5°16·4′W	X	55
Braigiewell	Aberd	NJ7604	57°7·8′	2°23·3′W	X	38
Braigo	Arg & Bt	NR2369	55°50·3′	6°25·0′W	X	60
Braikie Castle	Angus	NO6250	56°38·7′	2°36·7′W	A	54
Braiklay	Aberd	NJ8336	57°25·1′	2°16·5′W	X	29,30
Braiklay	Aberd	NJ8530	57°21·9′	2°14·5′W	X	30
Brailes Hill	Warw	SP2939	52°3·2′	1°34·2′W	H	151
Brail Fm	Wilts	SU2763	51°22·2′	1°36·3′W	FM	174
Brailsford	Derby	SK2541	52°58·2′	1°37·3′W	T	119,128
Brailsford Brook	Derby	SK2441	52°58·2′	1°38·2′W	W	119,128
Brailsford Common	Derby	SK2642	52°58·7′	1°36·4′W	X	119,128
Brailsford Green	Derby	SK2541	52°58·2′	1°37·3′W	X	119,128
Brainge	Heref	SO6438	52°2·6′	2°31·1′W	A	149
Braingortan	Arg & Bt	NS0775	55°56·0′	5°4·9′W	X	63
Brainley	Aberd	NJ5714	57°13·1′	2°42·3′W	X	37
Brainport Bay	Arg & Bt	NR9795	56°6·5′	5°15·4′W	W	55
Brains Fm	Somer	ST7127	51°2·7′	2°24·4′W	FM	183
Brain's Green	Glos	SO6608	51°46·4′	2°29·2′W	T	162
Brainshaugh	Northum	NU2003	55°19·5′	1°40·7′W	X	81
Braintree	Essex	TL7623	51°52·9′	0°33·8′E	T	167
Braintris	Essex	TL5517	51°50·0′	0°15·4′E	X	167
Brainwood Fm	Essex	TL6305	51°43·4′	0°22·0′E	FM	167
Braiseworth	Suff	TM1371	52°18·0′	1°7·8′E	T	144,156
Braiseworth Hall	Suff	TM2467	52°15·6′	1°17·3′E	X	156
Braishfield	Hants	SU3725	51°1·6′	1°28·0′W	T	185
Braisthwaite Br	N Yks	SE7262	54°3·2′	0°53·6′W	X	100
Braisthwaites Wood	N Yks	SE7262	54°3·2′	0°53·6′W	F	100
Braisty Woods	N Yks	SE2063	54°4·0′	1°41·2′W	F	99
Braiswick	Essex	TL9826	51°54·1′	0°53·1′E	T	168
Braithwaite	Brad	SE0441	53°52·2′	1°55·9′W	T	104
Braithwaite	Cumbr	NY2323	54°36·0′	3°11·1′W	T	89,90
Braithwaite	Donc	SE6112	53°36·3′	1°4·3′W	T	111
Braithwaite	N Yks	NZ8203	54°25·2′	0°43·8′W	X	94
Braithwaite Hall	Cumbr	NY4141	54°45·9′	2°54·6′W	X	85
Braithwaite Hall	N Yks	SE1185	54°15·9′	1°49·4′W	A	99
Braithwaite Hall	N Yks	SE2473	54°9·4′	1°37·5′W	X	99
Braithwaite Moor	N Yks	SE1184	54°15·3′	1°49·5′W	X	99
Braithwaite Moor	N Yks	SE1461	54°2·9′	1°46·8′W	X	99
Braithwaite Shields	Cumbr	NY4241	54°45·9′	2°53·7′W	X	85
Braithwaite Sike	N Yks	SE1965	54°5·1′	1°42·2′W	W	99
Braithwaite Wife Hole	N Yks	SD7476	54°11·0′	2°23·5′W	X	98
Braithwell	Donc	SK5394	53°26·6′	1°11·7′W	T	111
Braiton of Leys	Highld	NH6740	57°26·1′	4°12·5′W	X	26
Brake	Shetld	HU3714	59°54·8′	1°19·8′W	T	4
Brake	Shetld	HU3735	60°6·1′	1°19·6′W	X	4
Brakefield Fm	Suff	TM0751	52°7·3′	1°1·8′E	FM	155
Brakefield Green	Norf	TG0209	52°38·7′	0°59·6′E	T	144
Brake Hill	Norf	TF8106	52°37·5′	0°40·9′E	X	144
Brake Hill Fm	Northnts	SP9382	52°25·9′	0°37·5′W	FM	141
Brakehill Lodge Fm	Norf	TF9403	52°35·6′	0°52·3′E	FM	144
Brakehope Rig	Scot Bord	NT2728	55°32·7′	3°9·0′W	H	73
Brakelands Fm	Oxon	SP3738	52°2·6′	1°27·2′W	FM	151
Brake Mill Fm	Worcs	SO8979	52°24·8′	2°9·3′W	FM	139
Brakenhill	Wakf	SE4216	53°38·6′	1°21·5′W	T	111
Brakenhurst Fm	Staffs	SK1423	52°48·5′	1°47·1′W	FM	128
Brake Plantns	Devon	SS5031	51°3·8′	4°8·1′W	F	180
Brakes Coppice Fm	E Susx	TQ7613	50°53·6′	0°30·5′E	FM	199
Brakes Fm	Bucks	SP7733	51°59·6′	0°52·3′W	FM	152,165
Brakes Fm	Durham	NZ3328	54°39·0′	1°28·9′W	FM	93
Brake's Fm	Essex	TL9319	51°50·4′	0°48·5′E	FM	168
Brakes Fm	Heref	SO4475	52°22·5′	2°49·0′W	FM	137,148
Brakeshill	Aberd	NK0049	57°32·1′	1°59·5′W	X	30
Brakes of Barras	Aberd	NO8378	56°53·8′	2°16·3′W	X	45
Brake, The	Fife	NO5210	56°17·1′	2°46·1′W	X	59
Brakey Hills Fm	Suff	TL7284	52°25·8′	0°32·2′E	FM	143
Brakey Pin Hall Fm	Suff	TL8068	52°17·1′	0°38·7′E	FM	155
Brakey Wood	Essex	TL7709	51°45·3′	0°34·3′E	F	167
Braleckan	Arg & Bt	NN0202	56°10·4′	5°10·9′W	X	55
Bramah Edge	Derby	SK0597	53°28·4′	1°55·1′W	X	110
Bramaskew	Cumbr	SD6393	54°20·1′	2°33·7′W	X	97
Bramber	W Susx	TQ1810	50°52·9′	0°19·0′W	T	198
Bramber Fm	W Susx	SZ8799	50°47·3′	0°45·6′W	FM	197
Bramble	Pemb	SM8722	51°51·6′	5°5·2′W	X	157
Bramble Bottom	Dorset	SY6799	50°47·6′	2°27·7′W	X	194
Brambleburn	Moray	NJ5156	57°35·7′	2°48·7′W	X	29
Bramblecombe	Dorset	ST7700	50°48·2′	2°19·2′W	T	194
Brambledown	Kent	TQ9671	51°24·5′	0°49·5′E	X	178
Bramble Fm	Hav	TQ5683	51°31·7′	0°15·3′E	FM	177
Bramble Garr	N Yks	NZ7007	54°27·5′	0°54·8′W	X	94
Bramble Hall	Essex	TQ8288	51°33·9′	0°38·0′E	X	178
Bramble Hall Fm	Essex	TL8704	51°42·4′	0°42·8′E	FM	168
Brambleham	Devon	SX5084	50°38·4′	4°6·9′W	X	191,201
Bramble Hill	Norf	TG4722	52°44·6′	1°40·0′E	X	134
Bramblehill Fm	W Susx	TQ3434	51°5·6′	0°4·8′W	FM	187
Bramble Hill Hotel	Hants	SU2615	50°56·3′	1°37·4′W	X	184
Bramble Hills	Lincs	TF5659	53°6·6′	0°20·2′E	X	122
Brambles Chine	I of W	SZ3288	50°41·7′	1°32·4′W	X	196
Brambles Farm	Midd	NZ5219	54°34·1′	1°11·3′W	FM	93
Brambles Fm	Kent	TR1562	51°19·2′	1°5·5′E	FM	179
Brambles Fm	Somer	ST7843	51°11·4′	2°18·5′W	FM	183
Brambles, The	E Yorks	SE8850	53°56·6′	0°39·1′W	F	106
Brambles Wildlife Park	Kent	TR1663	51°19·7′	1°6·4′E	X	179
Brambletye	Surrey	TQ4136	51°6·6′	0°1·2′E	X	187
Brambletye House	E Susx	TQ4135	51°6·0′	0°1·2′E	A	187
Bramble Wood	Corn	SX3565	50°27·9′	4°19·1′W	X	201
Bramble Wood	Devon	SS4105	50°49·6′	4°15·1′W	F	190
Brambling Fields	N Yks	SE8272	54°8·5′	0°44·3′W	X	100
Brambridge	Hants	SU4721	50°59·4′	1°19·4′W	T	185
Brambridge Ho	Hants	SU4622	51°0·0′	1°20·3′W	X	185
Bramcote	Notts	SK5137	52°55·9′	1°14·1′W	T	129
Bramcote	Warw	SP4088	52°29·5′	1°24·3′W	T	140
Bramcote Covert	Warw	SK2705	52°38·8′	1°35·7′W	F	140

Bramcote Fields Fm	Warw	SP4088	52°29·5'	1°24·3'W	FM	140
Bramcote Hall	Warw	SK2704	52°38·2'	1°35·7'W	X	140
Bramcote Hills	Notts	SK5138	52°56·5'	1°14·1'W	T	129
Bramcote Mains	Warw	SP4087	52°29·0'	1°24·3'W	T	140
Bram Crag	Cumbr	NY3121	54°35·0'	3°3·6'W	X	90
Bramdean	Hants	SU6128	51°3·1'	1°7·4'W	T	185
Bramdean Common	Hants	SU6329	51°3·6'	1°5·7'W	F	185
Bramdown Copse	Hants	SU5247	51°13·4'	1°14·9'W	F	185
Bramelane	N Yks	SE2053	53°58·6'	1°41·3'W	X	104
Bramerton	Norf	TG2905	52°35·9'	1°23·3'E	T	134
Bramery	Cumbr	NY5445	54°48·1'	2°42·5'W	X	86
Brames Hall	Suff	TM1367	52°15·8'	1°7·7'E	X	156
Bramfield	Herts	TL2915	51°49·4'	0°7·3'W	T	166
Bramfield	Suff	TM4073	52°18·4'	1°31·6'E	T	156
Bramfieldbury	Herts	TL2815	51°49·4'	0°8·2'W	A	166
Bramfieldhall Wood	Suff	TM4073	52°18·4'	1°31·6'E	F	156
Bramfield Ho	Herts	TL2915	51°49·4'	0°7·3'W	X	166
Bramfield Ho	Suff	TM3873	52°18·4'	1°29·9'E	X	156
Bramfield Place Fm	Herts	TL2915	51°49·4'	0°7·3'W	FM	166
Bramfield Woods	Herts	TL2816	51°49·9'	0°8·1'W	F	166
Bramford	Dudley	SO9393	52°32·3'	2°5·8'W	T	139
Bramford	Suff	TM1246	52°4·5'	1°6·0'E	T	155,169
Bramhall	Stock	SJ8984	53°21·4'	2°9·5'W	T	109
Bramhall Moor	Stock	SJ9186	53°22·5'	2°7·7'W	T	109
Bramhall Park	Stock	SJ8886	53°22·5'	2°10·4'W	T	109
Bramham	Leeds	SE4243	53°53·1'	1°21·2'W	T	105
Bramham Biggin	Leeds	SE4242	53°52·6'	1°21·3'W	X	105
Bramham Lodge	Leeds	SE4242	53°52·6'	1°21·3'W	X	105
Bramham Moor	Leeds	SE4442	53°52·6'	1°19·4'W	X	105
Bramham Park	Leeds	SE4141	53°52·1'	1°22·2'W	A	105
Bramhope	Leeds	SE2543	53°53·2'	1°36·8'W	T	104
Bramhope Grove Fm	Leeds	SE2542	53°52·7'	1°36·8'W	FM	104
Bramhope Moor	Leeds	SE2442	53°52·7'	1°37·7'W	X	104
Bramlands	W Susx	TQ2314	50°55·0'	0°14·6'W	X	198
Bramley	Cumbr	NY1023	54°35·9'	3°23·2'W	X	89
Bramley	Derby	SK4079	53°18·6'	1°23·6'W	T	120
Bramley	Hants	SU6559	51°19·8'	1°3·6'W	T	175,186
Bramley	Leeds	SE2434	53°48·3'	1°37·7'W	T	104
Bramley	Roth	SK4892	53°25·6'	1°16·2'W	T	111
Bramley	Surrey	TQ0044	51°11·4'	0°33·7'W	T	186
Bramley Corner	Hants	SU6359	51°19·8'	1°5·4'W	T	175
Bramley Dale	Derby	SK2372	53°14·9'	1°38·9'W	X	119
Bramley Fall	Leeds	SE2436	53°49·4'	1°37·7'W	F	104
Bramley Fm	Derby	SK2473	53°15·4'	1°38·0'W	FM	119
Bramley Fm	Lincs	TF2955	53°4·8'	0°4·0'W	FM	122
Bramley Grange	Leeds	SE3638	53°50·5'	1°26·8'W	X	104
Bramley Grange	N Yks	SE2076	54°11·0'	1°41·2'W	X	99
Bramley Grange Fm	Roth	SK4992	53°25·6'	1°15·3'W	FM	111
Bramley Green	Hants	SU6658	51°19·3'	1°2·8'W	T	175,186
Bramley Head	N Yks	SE1258	54°1·3'	1°48·6'W	T	104
Bramleyhill Fm	Derby	SK4079	53°18·6'	1°23·6'W	FM	120
Bramley Moor	Derby	SK3979	53°18·6'	1°24·5'W	X	119
Bramley Vale	Derby	SK4666	53°11·6'	1°18·3'W	T	120
Bramling	Kent	TR2256	51°15·8'	1°11·3'E	T	179
Bramling Downs	Kent	TR2255	51°15·3'	1°11·3'E	X	179
Bramper Fm	N Yks	SE3193	54°20·1'	1°31·0'W	FM	99
Brampford Speke	Devon	SX9298	50°46·5'	3°31·5'W	T	192
Brampton	Cambs	TL2070	52°19·1'	0°14·0'W	T	153
Brampton	Cumbr	NY5261	54°56·7'	2°44·5'W	T	86
Brampton	Cumbr	NY6723	54°36·3'	2°30·2'W	T	91
Brampton	Derby	SK3670	53°13·8'	1°27·2'W	T	119
Brampton	Heref	SO4036	52°1·4'	2°52·1'W	X	149,161
Brampton	Lincs	SK8479	53°18·3'	0°44·0'W	T	121
Brampton	Norf	TG2224	52°46·3'	1°17·9'E	T	133,134
Brampton	Roth	SE4101	53°30·5'	1°22·5'W	T	111
Brampton	Suff	TM4381	52°22·6'	1°34·6'E	T	156
Brampton Abbotts	Heref	SO6026	51°56·1'	2°34·5'W	T	162
Brampton Ash	Northnts	SP7987	52°28·7'	0°49·8'W	T	141
Brampton Bryan	Heref	SO3772	52°20·8'	2°55·1'W	T	137,148
Brampton Bryan Park	Heref	SO3571	52°20·2'	2°56·8'W	X	137,148
Brampton Common	Roth	SK4887	53°22·9'	1°16·3'W	X	111,120
Brampton East Moor	Derby	SK2970	53°13·8'	1°33·5'W	X	119
Brampton en le Morthen	Roth	SK4888	53°23·4'	1°16·3'W	T	111,120
Bramptonfell	Cumbr	NY5459	54°55·7'	2°42·6'W	X	86
Brampton Grange	Lincs	SK8480	53°18·9'	0°43·9'W	X	121
Brampton Grange	Northnts	SP7365	52°16·9'	0°55·4'W	X	152
Brampton Hall	N Yks	SE3666	54°5·6'	1°26·6'W	X	99
Brampton Hill	Heref	SO4035	52°0·8'	2°52·1'W	H	149,161
Brampton Hill	Northnts	SP7166	52°17·5'	0°57·1'W	X	152
Brampton Lodge	Cambs	TL1970	52°19·1'	0°14·8'W	X	153
Brampton Lodge	C of Edin	NT1570	55°55·2'	3°21·2'W	X	65
Brampton Old Hall	Suff	TM4183	52°23·7'	1°32·9'E	X	156
Brampton Park	Cambs	TL2070	52°19·1'	0°14·0'W	T	153
Brampton Sta	Cumbr	NY5459	54°55·7'	2°42·6'W	X	86
Brampton Sta	Suff	TM4183	52°23·7'	1°32·9'E	X	156
Brampton Street	Suff	TM4281	52°22·6'	1°33·7'E	T	156
Brampton, The	Staffs	SJ8446	53°0·9'	2°13·9'W	T	118
Brampton Tower	Cumbr	NY6822	54°35·8'	2°29·3'W	X	91
Brampton Valley Way	Northnts	SP7368	52°18·5'	0°55·4'W	X	152
Brampton Wood	Cambs	TL1770	52°19·2'	0°16·6'W	F	153
Brampton Wood	Northnts	SP7985	52°27·7'	0°49·8'W	F	141
Bram Rigg	Cumbr	SD6596	54°21·7'	2°31·9'W	X	97
Bram Rigg Beck	Cumbr	SD6595	54°21·2'	2°31·9'W	W	97
Bram Rigg Top	Cumbr	SD6696	54°21·7'	2°31·0'W	X	98
Bramshall	Staffs	SK0633	52°53·9'	1°54·2'W	T	128
Bramshaw	Hants	SU2715	50°56·3'	1°36·6'W	T	184
Bramshaw Telegraph	Hants	SU2216	50°56·8'	1°40·8'W	X	184
Bramshaw Wood	Hants	SU2516	50°56·8'	1°38·3'W	F	184
Bramshill	Hants	SU7461	51°20·8'	0°55·9'W	T	175,186
Bramshill Ho	Hants	SU7559	51°19·7'	0°55·0'W	A	175,186
Bramshill Park	Hants	SU7559	51°19·7'	0°55·0'W	X	175,186
Bramshill Plantation	Hants	SU7562	51°21·4'	0°55·0'W	F	175,186
Bramshott	Hants	SU8432	51°5·1'	0°47·7'W	T	186
Bramshott Chase	Hants	SU8633	51°5·6'	0°45·9'W	X	186
Bramshott Common	Hants	SU8633	51°5·6'	0°45·9'W	F	186
Bramshott Court	Hants	SU8333	51°5·6'	0°48·5'W	X	186
Bramshott Vale	Hants	SU8332	51°5·1'	0°48·5'W	X	186
Bramwell	Somer	ST4329	51°3·7'	2°48·4'W	T	193
Branas Isaf	Denb	SJ0238	52°56·1'	3°27·1'W	X	125
Branas Uchaf	Denb	SJ0137	52°55·5'	3°28·0'W	X	125
Branault	Highld	NM5269	56°45·1'	6°3·0'W	T	47
Branbridges	Kent	TQ6748	51°12·6'	0°23·8'E	T	188
Bran Burn	D & G	NX9796	55°15·1'	3°36·8'W	W	78
Brancaster	Norf	TF7743	52°57·5'	0°38·5'E	T	132
Brancaster Bay	Norf	TF7546	52°59·2'	0°36·8'E	W	132
Brancaster Hall	Norf	TF7843	52°57·5'	0°39·4'E	X	132
Brancaster Harbour	Norf	TF7845	52°58·6'	0°39·5'E	W	132
Brancaster Marsh	Norf	TF7944	52°58·0'	0°40·3'E	W	132
Brancaster Staithe	Norf	TF7944	52°58·0'	0°40·3'E	T	132
Brance	Orkney	ND4893	58°49·5'	2°53·6'W	X	7
Brancepeth	Durham	NZ2237	54°43·9'	1°39·1'W	T	93
Brancepeth Park	Durham	NZ2337	54°43·9'	1°38·1'W	X	93
Branch Cleuch	Scot Bord	NY4689	55°11·8'	2°50·5'W	X	79
Branchend	Northum	NY8561	54°56·9'	2°13·6'W	X	87
Branch End	Northum	NZ0661	54°56·9'	1°54·0'W	T	87
Branches Park	Suff	TL7055	52°10·2'	0°29·6'E	X	154
Branch Fm	Somer	ST7250	51°15·1'	2°23·7'W	FM	183
Branchill	Moray	NJ0852	57°33·2'	3°31·8'W	X	27
Branchton	Inverc	NS2475	55°56·4'	4°48·6'W	T	63
Brancliffe Grange	Roth	SK5481	53°19·6'	1°10·9'W	X	111,120
Brancote Fm	Staffs	SJ9622	52°48·0'	2°3·2'W	FM	127
Brancroft	Donc	SK6697	53°28·2'	0°59·9'W	X	111
Brandarsaig Bay	Highld	NG2539	57°21·8'	6°33·9'W	W	23
Brandedleys	D & G	NX8372	55°2·0'	3°49·4'W	X	84
Brandelhow Park	Cumbr	NY2520	54°34·4'	3°9·2'W	X	89,90
Branden	Kent	TQ8037	51°6·5'	0°34·7'E	X	188
Brand End	Derby	SK0568	53°12·8'	1°55·1'W	X	119
Brand End	Lincs	TF3745	52°59·3'	0°2·9'E	T	131
Brand End Fm	Lincs	TF2141	52°57·4'	0°11·5'W	FM	131
Brander	Scot Bord	NT8770	55°55·6'	2°12·0'W	X	67
Branderburgh	Moray	NJ2371	57°43·6'	3°17·1'W	T	28
Brandesburton	E Yorks	TA1147	53°54·7'	0°18·2'W	T	107
Brandeston	Suff	TM2460	52°11·8'	1°17·1'E	T	156
Brandeston Hall	Suff	TL9146	52°5·0'	0°47·7'E	X	155
Brandfold	Kent	TQ7239	51°7·7'	0°27·9'E	X	188
Brand Green	Glos	SO7428	51°57·2'	2°22·3'W	T	150
Brand Green	Heref	SO7641	52°4·2'	2°20·6'W	T	150
Brand Hall	Shrops	SJ6938	52°56·6'	2°27·3'W	A	127
Brand Hall Fm	Shrops	SJ6938	52°56·6'	2°27·3'W	FM	127
Brand Heald	Lancs	SD4020	53°40·6'	2°54·1'W	X	102
Brandhill	Shrops	SO4278	52°24·1'	2°50·8'W	T	137,148
Brandhouse Fm	Glos	ST8698	51°41·1'	2°11·8'W	FM	162
Brandicar	N Lincs	TA0503	53°31·0'	0°24·6'W	X	112
Brandier	Wilts	SU0191	51°37·3'	1°58·7'W	X	163,173
Brandiquoy	Orkney	ND4592	58°49·0'	2°56·7'W	X	7
Brandirons Corner	Devon	SS7802	50°48·5'	3°43·5'W	X	191
Brandis Corner	Devon	SS4103	50°48·5'	4°15·0'W	T	190
Brandis Cross	Devon	SX6893	50°43·5'	3°51·8'W	X	191
Brandish	I of M	SC3880	54°11·7'	4°28·6'W	X	95
Brandish Street	Somer	SS9046	51°12·4'	3°34·1'W	T	181
Brandiston	Norf	TG1321	52°44·9'	1°9·8'E	T	133
Brandleside	E Ayr	NS4050	55°43·3'	4°32·4'W	X	64
Brandleys	D & G	NS8110	55°22·4'	3°52·2'W	X	71,78
Brandleys Cott	D & G	NS8111	55°23·0'	3°52·3'W	X	71,78
Brandlingill	Cumbr	NY1226	54°37·5'	3°21·4'W	T	89
Brandlodge Coppice	Worcs	SO7375	52°22·6'	2°23·4'W	F	138
Brandmyres	Aberd	NJ9201	57°6·2'	2°7·5'W	X	38
Brandon	Durham	NZ2339	54°45·0'	1°38·1'W	T	93
Brandon	Lincs	SK9048	53°1·5'	0°39·1'W	T	130
Brandon	Northum	NU0417	55°27·1'	1°55·8'W	X	81
Brandon	Suff	TL7886	52°26·8'	0°37·6'E	T	144
Brandon	Warw	SP4076	52°23·1'	1°24·3'W	T	140
Brandon Bank	Cambs	TL6288	52°28·2'	0°23·5'E	T	143
Brandon Brook	Worcs	SP0160	52°14·5'	1°58·7'W	W	150
Brandon Camp	Heref	SO4072	52°20·8'	2°52·5'W	A	137,148
Brandon Country Park	Suff	TL7885	52°26·3'	0°37·5'E	F	144
Brandon Creek	Norf	TL6091	52°29·8'	0°21·8'E	T	143
Brandon Drain	Leeds	SE3340	53°51·6'	1°29·5'W	W	104
Brandon Fen	Suff	TL7185	52°26·4'	0°31·4'E	X	143
Brandon Grange Fm	Warw	SP4276	52°23·1'	1°22·6'W	FM	140
Brandon Hall	Leeds	SE3340	53°51·6'	1°29·5'W	X	104
Brandon Hall	Suff	TL7786	52°26·8'	0°36·7'E	X	144
Brandon Hillhead	Northum	NU0517	55°27·1'	1°54·8'W	X	81
Brandon Ho	Durham	NZ3034	54°42·3'	1°31·6'W	X	93
Brandon Lodge	Leeds	SE3440	53°51·5'	1°28·6'W	X	104
Brandon Park	Suff	TL7784	52°25·7'	0°36·6'E	X	144
Brandon Parva	Norf	TG0707	52°37·5'	1°3·9'E	T	144
Brandon Villa	Heref	SO3971	52°20·3'	2°53·3'W	X	137,148
Brandon-Walk Bishop Auckland	Durham	NZ2440	54°45·5'	1°37·2'W	X	88
Brandon Walls	Durham	NY9441	54°46·1'	2°5·2'W	X	87
Brandon White Ho	Northum	NU0517	55°27·1'	1°54·8'W	X	81
Brandon Wood	Warw	SP3976	52°23·1'	1°25·2'W	F	140
Brandon Wood Fm	Warw	SP3976	52°23·1'	1°25·2'W	FM	140
Brandreth	Cumbr	NY2111	54°29·5'	3°12·8'W	H	89,90
Brandrick's Green	Glos	SO6409	51°46·9'	2°30·9'W	F	162
Brandrith Crags	N Yks	SE1456	54°0·2'	1°46·8'W	X	104
Brandrith Fm	N Yks	SE6969	54°7·0'	0°56·2'W	FM	100
Brandrith Wood	N Yks	SE7068	54°6·4'	0°55·3'W	F	100
Brand's Bay	Dorset	SZ0185	50°40·1'	1°58·8'W	W	195
Brandsby	N Yks	SE5872	54°8·7'	1°6·3'W	T	100
Brandsby Hall	N Yks	SE5971	54°8·1'	1°5·4'W	X	100
Brandsby Lodge	N Yks	SE6072	54°8·7'	1°4·5'W	X	100
Brands Fm	Essex	TL6019	51°51·0'	0°19·8'E	FM	167
Brand's Fm	Herts	TL4119	51°51·3'	0°3·2'E	FM	167
Brand's Fm	Roth	SK5484	53°21·2'	1°10·9'W	FM	111,120
Brands Hatch Circuit	Kent	TQ5764	51°21·4'	0°15·7'E	X	177,188
Brand's Hill	Essex	TL5237	52°0·9'	0°13·3'E	X	154
Brands Hill	Northum	NT9723	55°30·3'	2°2·4'W	H	75
Brands Hill	Notts	SK5333	52°53·7'	1°12·3'W	H	129
Brands Hill	Slough	TQ0177	51°29·2'	0°32·3'W	T	176
Brandshill Wood	Aberd	NO7267	56°47·9'	2°27·1'W	F	45
Brands Ho	Bucks	SU8795	51°39·1'	0°44·2'W	X	165
Brand Side	Derby	SK0468	53°12·8'	1°56·0'W	X	119
Brand Spinney	Suff	TL8772	52°19·1'	0°45·0'E	F	144,155
Brandston	Moray	NJ2865	57°40·4'	3°12·0'W	X	28
Brandstone Beck	N Yks	SE1265	54°5·1'	1°48·6'W	W	99
Brand Top	Derby	SK0468	53°12·8'	1°56·0'W	X	119
Brandvnvm (Roman Fort)	Norf	TF7843	52°57·5'	0°39·4'E	R	132
Brandwith Howe	N Yks	SE1877	54°11·5'	1°43·0'W	X	99
Brandwood	Shrops	SJ4726	52°50·0'	2°46·8'W	T	126
Brand Wood	Shrops	SO7276	52°23·1'	2°24·3'W	F	138
Brandwood End	Birm	SP0779	52°24·8'	1°53·4'W	T	139
Brandwood Ho	Shrops	SJ4725	52°49·4'	2°46·8'W	X	126
Brandwood Moor	Lancs	SD8520	53°40·8'	2°13·2'W	X	103
Brandy Bay	Dorset	SY8879	50°36·9'	2°9·8'W	W	194
Brandy Bottle Spring	Cumbr	NY6736	54°43·3'	2°30·3'W	W	91
Brandy Brook	Pemb	SM8825	51°53·2'	5°4·5'W	W	157
Brandyburn	D & G	NX9285	55°9·1'	3°41·3'W	X	78
Brandy Carr	Wakf	SE3023	53°42·4'	1°32·3'W	T	104
Brandy Cove	Swan	SS5887	51°34·1'	4°2·5'W	W	159
Brandy Cove Point	Devon	SS5047	51°12·4'	4°8·5'W	X	180
Brandy Crag	Cumbr	SD2298	54°22·5'	3°11·6'W	X	96
Brandy Head	Devon	SY0883	50°38·6'	3°17·7'W	X	192
Brandy Hill	Carm	SN2113	51°47·5'	4°35·3'W	H	158
Brandy Hole	Essex	TQ8295	51°37·7'	0°38·2'E	T	168
Brandy House Fm	Powys	SO1780	52°24·9'	3°12·8'W	FM	136
Brandy-Lee	Staffs	SJ9463	53°10·1'	2°5·0'W	X	118
Brandys	Corn	SW4136	50°10·3'	5°37·3'W	X	203
Brandywell	E Yorks	TA1833	53°47·0'	0°12·1'W	X	107
Brandywell	I of M	SC3985	54°14·4'	4°27·8'W	X	95
Brandy Well	S Ayr	NX3492	55°11·9'	4°36·1'W	W	76
Brandy Well Hall	Northum	NZ0478	55°6·0'	1°55·8'W	X	87
Brandy Wharf	Lincs	TF0196	53°27·3'	0°28·3'W	T	112
Brane	Corn	SW4028	50°5·9'	5°37·8'W	T	203
Bran End	Essex	TL6525	51°54·2'	0°24·3'E	T	167
Branetrigg	D & G	NX8668	54°59·9'	3°46·5'W	X	84
Branetrigg	D & G	NY0379	55°6·0'	3°30·8'W	X	84
Brangan	Aberd	NJ6164	57°40·1'	2°38·8'W	X	29
Bran Hills	Leic	SK7016	52°44·5'	0°57·4'W	X	129
Brankam Hill	Angus	NO2955	56°41·1'	3°9·1'W	H	53
Brankanentham	Aberd	NJ5466	57°41·2'	2°45·8'W	X	29
Brankanentum	Aberd	NJ6530	57°21·8'	2°34·5'W	X	29
Branken Wall	Cumbr	SD0996	54°21·3'	3°23·6'W	X	96
Brankfleet	Essex	TQ9894	51°36·8'	0°52·0'E	W	168,178
Brankinentum	Aberd	NJ6615	57°13·7'	2°33·3'W	X	38
Brankley Fm	Staffs	SK1520	52°46·9'	1°46·3'W	FM	128
Branklyn Gardens	Pth & Kin	NO1222	56°23·2'	3°25·1'W	X	53,58
Branksea Castle	Dorset	SZ0287	50°41·2'	1°57·9'W	X	195
Branksome	Darl	NZ2616	54°32·6'	1°35·5'W	T	93
Branksome	Poole	SZ0592	50°43·9'	1°55·4'W	T	195
Branksome Chine	Poole	SZ0689	50°42·3'	1°54·5'W	X	195
Branksome Park	Poole	SZ0590	50°42·8'	1°55·4'W	T	195
Brankston	Aberd	NJ5931	57°22·3'	2°40·4'W	X	29,37
Brankston	S Lanak	NS7544	55°40·7'	3°58·8'W	X	71
Brankstone Grange	Fife	NS9790	56°5·8'	3°38·9'W	X	58
Brankumhall	S Lanak	NS6555	55°46·4'	4°8·7'W	X	64
Brankumleys	Moray	NJ4364	57°40·0'	2°56·9'W	X	28
Bran Law	D & G	NT1815	55°25·6'	3°17·3'W	X	79
Brannel	Corn	SW9551	50°19·6'	4°52·4'W	X	200,204
Brann Fm	Staffs	SJ7828	52°51·2'	2°19·2'W	FM	127
Brannie Burn	Arg & Bt	NN1716	56°18·3'	4°57·0'W	W	50,56
Brannie, The	Arg & Bt	NN1714	56°17·2'	4°57·0'W	X	50,56
Branogenium (Leintwardine)	Heref	SO4074	52°21·9'	2°52·5'W	R	137,148
Branrigg	D & G	NX9995	55°14·6'	3°34·9'W	X	78
Bran Sands	Red & Cl	NZ5526	54°37·8'	1°8·5'W	X	93
Bransbog	Aberd	NJ9455	57°35·4'	2°5·6'W	X	30
Bransbury	Hants	SU4242	51°10·8'	1°23·6'W	T	185
Bransbury Common	Hants	SU4141	51°10·2'	1°24·4'W	X	185
Bransby	Lincs	SK8979	53°18·3'	0°39·5'W	T	121
Branscombe	Devon	SY1988	50°41·4'	3°8·4'W	T	192
Branscombe Cross	Devon	SY1790	50°42·5'	3°10·1'W	X	192,193
Branscombe Ebb	Devon	SY1987	50°40·9'	3°8·4'W	X	192
Branscombe Mouth	Devon	SY2088	50°41·4'	3°7·6'W	X	192
Branscombe's Loaf	Devon	SX5589	50°41·2'	4°2·8'W	H	191
Bransdale	N Yks	SE6296	54°21·6'	1°2·3'W	X	94,100
Bransdale Lodge	N Yks	SE6198	54°22·7'	1°3·2'W	X	94,100
Bransdale Moor	N Yks	SE6199	54°23·2'	1°3·2'W	X	94,100
Bransdown Hill	Wilts	ST8787	51°35·1'	2°10·9'W	X	173
Bransfarm	Aberd	NJ9556	57°35·9'	2°4·6'W	X	30
Bransfield Fm	E Ayr	NS5837	55°36·6'	4°14·8'W	FM	71
Bransford	Worcs	SO7952	52°10·2'	2°18·0'W	T	150
Bransford Br	Warw	SP5182	52°26·2'	1°14·6'W	X	140
Bransford Br	Worcs	SO8053	52°10·7'	2°17·2'W	X	150
Bransford Court	Worcs	SO8152	52°10·2'	2°16·3'W	X	150
Bransgore	Hants	SZ1897	50°46·6'	1°44·3'W	T	195
Bransgore Ho	Hants	SZ1998	50°47·1'	1°43·4'W	X	195
Bransgrove	Devon	SS6510	50°52·7'	3°54·8'W	X	191
Branshaw	Northum	NY8899	55°17·3'	2°10·9'W	X	80
Branshaw Moor	Brad	SE0339	53°51·1'	1°56·8'W	X	104
Branshill	Clackm	NS8894	56°7·8'	3°47·7'W	T	58
Branshill Fm	E Susx	TQ7615	50°54·7'	0°30·6'E	FM	199
Bransholme	K upon H	TA1033	53°47·1'	0°19·4'W	X	107
Bransley	Shrops	SO6575	52°22·6'	2°30·5'W	X	138
Bransley Fm	Worcs	SO7372	52°21·0'	2°23·4'W	FM	138
Bransly Hill	E Loth	NT6770	55°55·6'	2°31·2'W	H	67
Branson's Cross	Worcs	SP0870	52°19·9'	1°52·6'W	T	139
Branston	Leic	SK8129	52°51·4'	0°47·4'W	T	130
Branston	Lincs	TF0267	53°11·7'	0°28·0'W	T	121
Branston	Staffs	SK2221	52°47·4'	1°40·0'W	T	128
Branston Booths	Lincs	TF0669	53°12·7'	0°24·4'W	T	121
Branston Delph	Lincs	TF0770	53°13·2'	0°23·4'W	W	121
Branstone	I of W	SZ5583	50°38·9'	1°12·9'W	T	196
Branstone Beck	N Yks	SD6768	54°6·7'	2°29·9'W	X	98
Branstone Fen	Lincs	TF0869	53°12·7'	0°22·6'W	X	121
Branston Island	Lincs	TF0970	53°13·2'	0°21·6'W	X	121
Branston Lodge	Lincs	TF0668	53°12·1'	0°24·4'W	X	121
Branston Moor	Lincs	TF0467	53°11·6'	0°26·2'W	X	121
Branstree	Cumbr	NY4709	54°28·7'	2°48·7'W	H	90
Bransty	Cumbr	NX9719	54°33·6'	3°35·1'W	T	89
Bran's Walls	Northum	NY6697	55°16·2'	2°31·7'W	X	80
Bran's Walls (Settlements)	Northum	NY6697	55°16·2'	2°31·7'W	A	80
Brantbeck Fm	Lancs	SD4757	54°0·6'	2°48·1'W	FM	102
Brant Broughton	Lincs	SK9154	53°4·8'	0°38·1'W	T	121
Brantcas	N Yks	NZ1511	54°29·9'	1°45·7'W	X	92
Branteth	D & G	NY2875	55°4·1'	3°7·2'W	X	85
Brant Fell	Cumbr	SD4096	54°21·6'	2°55·0'W	H	96,97
Brant Fell	Cumbr	SD6695	54°21·2'	2°31·0'W	X	98
Brantham	Suff	TM1034	51°58·1'	1°3·8'E	T	155,169

Brantham Court	Suff	TM1234	51°58·1′	1°5·6′E	X	155,169
Brantham Glebe	Suff	TM1134	51°58·1′	1°4·7′E	X	155,169
Brantham Hall	Suff	TM1233	51°57·5′	1°5·5′E	X	168,169
Branthill Cottages	Norf	TF9040	52°55·7′	0°50·0′E	X	132
Brant Hill Fm	Leic	SP6392	52°31·6′	1°3·9′W	FM	140
Branthill Fm	Norf	TF9040	52°55·7′	0°50·0′E	FM	132
Branthwaite	Cumbr	NY0524	54°36·4′	3°27·8′W	T	89
Branthwaite	Cumbr	NY2937	54°43·6′	3°5·7′W	T	89,90
Branthwaite	Cumbr	SD6393	54°20·1′	2°33·7′W	X	97
Branthwaite Edge	Cumbr	NY0524	54°36·4′	3°27·8′W	T	89
Branthwaite Outgang	Cumbr	NY0525	54°36·9′	3°27·8′W	X	89
Branthwaite Rigg	Cumbr	NY0523	54°35·8′	3°27·8′W	X	89
Branthwaite Row Fm	Cumbr	NY0424	54°36·4′	3°28·8′W	FM	89
Branthwaites	Cumbr	SD6891	54°19·1′	2°29·1′W	X	98
Brantingham	E Yorks	SE9429	53°45·2′	0°34·0′W	T	106
Brantingham Grange	E Yorks	SE9328	53°44·6′	0°35·0′W	X	106
Brantinghamthorpe	E Yorks	SE9429	53°45·2′	0°34·0′W	X	106
Brantingham Wold	E Yorks	SE9530	53°45·7′	0°33·1′W	X	106
Branton	Donc	SE6401	53°30·3′	1°1·7′W	T	111
Branton	Northum	NU0416	55°26·5′	1°55·8′W	T	81
Branton Bldgs	Northum	NU0415	55°26·0′	1°55·8′W	X	81
Branton Court	N Yks	SE3460	54°2·3′	1°28·4′W	X	99
Branton Grange	Donc	SE6403	53°31·4′	1°1·7′W	X	111
Branton Green	N Yks	SE4462	54°3·4′	1°19·3′W	T	99
Branton Middlesteads	Northum	NU0414	55°25·4′	1°55·8′W	X	81
Branton's Fm	E Yorks	TA0164	54°4·0′	0°27·0′W	FM	101
Brantrake	Cumbr	SD1498	54°22·5′	3°19·0′W	X	96
Brantridge Forest	W Susx	TQ2832	51°4·6′	0°10·0′W	F	187
Brantridge Forest Fm	W Susx	TQ2831	51°4·1′	0°10·0′W	FM	187
Brantridge Park	W Susx	TQ2830	51°3·5′	0°10·0′W	X	187
Brants Gill Head	N Yks	SD8172	54°8·9′	2°17·0′W	X	98
Brant Side	Cumbr	SD7786	54°16·4′	2°20·8′W	X	98
Brantwood	Cumbr	SD3195	54°21·0′	3°3·3′W	X	96,97
Branxholm	Scot Bord	NT4712	55°24·2′	2°49·8′W	X	79
Branxholm Braes	Scot Bord	NT4511	55°23·6′	2°51·7′W	X	79
Branxholme	Scot Bord	NT4611	55°23·7′	2°50·7′W	T	79
Branxholme Castle	Scot Bord	NT4611	55°23·7′	2°50·7′W	A	79
Branxholme Easter Loch	Scot Bord	NT4311	55°23·6′	2°53·6′W	W	79
Branxholme Wester Loch	Scot Bord	NT4211	55°23·6′	2°54·5′W	W	79
Branxholm Park	Scot Bord	NT4612	55°24·2′	2°50·7′W	X	79
Branxholmpark Hill	Scot Bord	NT4612	55°24·2′	2°50·7′W	H	79
Branxholmtown	Scot Bord	NT4511	55°23·6′	2°51·7′W	X	79
Branxton	E Loth	NT7472	55°56·7′	2°24·5′W	X	67
Branxton	Fife	NO4006	56°14·8′	2°57·7′W	X	59
Branxton	Fife	NT3094	56°8·3′	3°7·1′W	X	59
Branxton	Northum	NT8937	55°37·8′	2°10·0′W	T	74
Branxton Bldgs	Northum	NT8837	55°37·8′	2°11·0′W	X	74
Branxton Hill	Northum	NT8936	55°37·3′	2°10·0′W	X	74
Branxton Moor	Northum	NT8936	55°37·3′	2°10·0′W	X	74
Branxton Stead	Northum	NT8836	55°37·3′	2°11·0′W	X	74
Braodmoor Bottom	Brackn	SU8562	51°21·3′	0°46·4′W	X	175,186
Braomisaig	Highld	NM7895	56°59·8′	5°38·9′W	X	33,40
Braon a' Mheallan	Highld	NG3840	57°22·8′	6°21·1′W	H	23
Brascote	Leic	SK4402	52°37·1′	1°20·6′W	T	140
Brascote Ho	Leic	SK4402	52°37·1′	1°20·6′W	X	140
Brasenose Fm	Oxon	SP4626	51°56·1′	1°19·5′W	FM	164
Brasenose Wood	Oxon	SP5605	51°44·7′	1°10·9′W	F	164
Brashfield Ho	Oxon	SP5925	51°55·5′	1°8·1′W	X	164
Brass Castle	Brad	SE0844	53°53·8′	1°52·3′W	X	104
Brass Castle	N Yks	SE0257	54°0·8′	1°57·8′W	X	104
Brass Castle	N Yks	SE2051	53°57·5′	1°41·3′W	X	104
Brassey Green	Ches	SJ5260	53°8·3′	2°42·6′W	T	117
Brassington	Derby	SK2354	53°5·2′	1°39·0′W	T	119
Brass Knoll	Heref	SO3030	51°58·1′	3°0·7′W	X	161
Brass Mill	Glos	SO7425	51°55·6′	2°22·3′W	X	162
Brasted	Kent	TQ4755	51°16·7′	0°6·9′E	T	188
Brasted Chart	Kent	TQ4653	51°15·7′	0°5·9′E	T	188
Brasted Hill Fm	Kent	TQ4657	51°17·8′	0°6·0′E	FM	188
Brasted Lands	Kent	TQ4746	51°11·9′	0°6·6′E	X	188
Braston	S Ayr	NS3619	55°26·5′	4°35·1′W	X	70
Bratanais Mòr	N Eil	NB2032	58°11·5′	6°45·4′W	X	8,13
Brat Bheinn	Arg & Bt	NR4966	55°49·6′	6°0·0′W	H	60,61
Bratch Copse	Dorset	SU0813	50°55·2′	1°52·8′W	F	195
Bratch Copse	Glos	SP1407	51°45·9′	1°47·4′W	F	163
Brathay Hall (Training Centre)	Cumbr	NY3603	54°25·4′	2°58·9′W	X	90
Brathens	Aberd	NO6798	57°4·6′	2°32·2′W	T	38,45
Brathens Moss	Aberd	NO6697	57°4·0′	2°33·2′W	X	38,45
Brathens, The	Aberd	NO6798	57°4·6′	2°32·2′W	X	38,45
Brat Hill	N Lincs	SE9108	53°33·9′	0°37·1′W	X	112
Brathinch	Angus	NO5864	56°46·2′	2°40·8′W	X	44
Bratlands	Lincs	TA1607	53°33·0′	0°14·5′W	X	113
Bratley Arch	Hants	SU2309	50°53·0′	1°40·0′W	X	195
Bratley Inclosure	Hants	SU2208	50°52·5′	1°40·9′W	F	195
Bratley Plain	Hants	SU2108	50°52·5′	1°41·7′W	X	195
Bratley Water	Hants	SU2307	50°52·0′	1°40·0′W	W	195
Bratley Wood	Hants	SU2208	50°52·5′	1°40·9′W	F	195
Bratoft	Lincs	TF4764	53°9·4′	0°12·3′E	T	122
Bratoft Corner	Lincs	TF4964	53°9·4′	0°14·1′E	X	122
Bratta Field	Shetld	HU3859	60°19·1′	1°18·2′W	X	2,3
Bratta Stack	Shetld	HU5989	60°35·1′	0°54·9′W	X	1,2
Brattibreck	Shetld	HU2844	60°11·0′	1°29·2′W	X	4
Brattle	Kent	TQ9433	51°4·0′	0°46·5′E	T	189
Brattleburn	D & G	NT0106	55°20·5′	3°33·2′W	X	78
Brattleby	Lincs	SK9480	53°18·7′	0°34·9′W	T	121
Brattleby Thorns	Lincs	SK9281	53°19·3′	0°36·7′W	F	121
Brattle Ho	Kent	TQ9826	51°0·2′	0°49·7′E	X	189
Brattles Grange	Kent	TQ6740	51°8·3′	0°23·6′E	X	188
Bratton	Somer	SS9446	51°12·4′	3°30·7′W	T	181
Bratton	Wilts	ST9152	51°16·3′	2°7·4′W	T	184
Bratton	Wrekin	SJ6314	52°43·6′	2°32·5′W	T	127
Bratton Ball	Somer	SS9447	51°13·0′	3°30·7′W	H	181
Bratton Camp	Wilts	ST9051	51°15·7′	2°8·2′W	A	184
Bratton Clovelly	Devon	SX4691	50°42·1′	4°10·5′W	T	190
Bratton Court	Somer	SS9446	51°12·4′	3°30·7′W	A	181
Bratton Cross	Devon	SS6236	51°6·6′	3°57·9′W	X	180
Bratton Down	Devon	SS6638	51°7·8′	3°54·5′W	H	180
Bratton Fleming	Devon	SS6437	51°7·2′	3°56·2′W	T	180
Bratton Hill	Somer	ST6729	51°3·8′	2°27·9′W	H	183
Bratton House Fm	NE Lincs	TA2701	53°29·7′	0°4·7′W	FM	113

Bratton Seymour	Somer	ST6729	51°3·8′	2°27·9′W	T	183
Brat Tor	Devon	SX5385	50°39·0′	4°4·4′W	X	191,201
Bratt Wood	E Yorks	SE8448	53°55·5′	0°42·8′W	F	106
Brauchhill	Moray	NJ2548	57°31·2′	3°14·7′W	X	28
Braughing	Herts	TL3924	51°54·1′	0°1·6′E	T	166
Braughing Friars	Herts	TL4124	51°54·0′	0°3·4′E	T	167
Braughty Fm	Pth & Kin	NO0403	56°12·9′	3°32·4′W	FM	58
Braughty Hill	Pth & Kin	NO0303	56°12·8′	3°33·4′W	H	58
Braulen Lodge	Highld	NH2338	57°24·1′	4°56·3′W	X	25
Brauncewell	Lincs	TF0152	53°3·6′	0°29·2′W	X	121
Brauncewell Village	Lincs	TF0452	53°3·5′	0°26·5′W	A	121
Braunder	Devon	SX4366	50°28·6′	4°12·4′W	X	201
Braundsworthy	Devon	SS4305	50°49·6′	4°13·4′W	X	190
Braunston	Northnts	SP5466	52°17·6′	1°12·1′W	T	152
Braunston Cleves	Northnts	SP5468	52°18·7′	1°12·1′W	F	152
Braunston Covert	Northnts	SP5464	52°16·5′	1°12·1′W	F	152
Braunstone	Leic	SK5502	52°37·0′	1°10·9′W	T	140
Braunstone Park	C of Leic	SK5503	52°37·6′	1°10·8′W	X	140
Braunston Fields	Northnts	SP5368	52°18·7′	1°13·0′W	X	152
Braunston-in-Rutland	Rut	SK8306	52°39·0′	0°46·0′W	T	141
Braunston Lodge Fm	Northnts	SP5567	52°18·1′	1°11·2′W	FM	152
Braunston Tunnel	Northnts	SP5665	52°17·1′	1°10·3′W	X	152
Braunton	Devon	SS4836	51°6·4′	4°9·9′W	T	180
Braunton Burrows	Devon	SS4535	51°5·8′	4°12·4′W	X	180
Braunton Down	Devon	SS4936	51°6·4′	4°9·0′W	H	180
Braunton Great Field	Devon	SS4735	51°5·9′	4°10·7′W	A	180
Braunton Marsh	Devon	SS4734	51°5·3′	4°10·7′W	X	180
Braushie Cree	Moray	NJ2532	57°22·6′	3°14·4′W	H	37
Braust	I of M	NX4200	54°22·5′	4°25·5′W	X	95
Bravoniacvm (Roman Fort)	Cumbr	NY6325	54°37·4′	2°34·0′W	R	91
Brawby	N Yks	SE7378	54°11·8′	0°52·4′W	T	100
Brawby Grange	N Yks	SE7379	54°12·3′	0°52·4′W	X	100
Brawdy Airfield	Pemb	SM8524	51°52·6′	5°7·0′W	X	157
Brawdy Fm	Pemb	SM8523	51°52·1′	5°7·0′W	FM	157
Brawith	N Yks	NZ5007	54°27·6′	1°13·3′W	T	93
Brawith Hall	N Yks	SE4187	54°16·9′	1°21·8′W	X	99
Brawl	Highld	NC8066	58°34·2′	4°3·3′W	X	10
Brawland	Aberd	NJ4726	57°19·5′	2°52·4′W	X	37
Brawlandknowes	Aberd	NJ5036	57°25·0′	2°49·5′W	X	29
Brawlands	Moray	NJ3343	57°28·6′	3°6·6′W	X	28
Brawlbin	Highld	ND0757	58°29·7′	3°35·3′W	X	11,12
Brawlbin Fm	Highld	ND0757	58°29·7′	3°35·3′W	FM	11,12
Brawleymuir	Aberd	NO7770	56°49·5′	2°22·2′W	X	45
Brawliemuir	Aberd	NO7484	56°57·0′	2°25·2′W	X	45
Brawlings Fm	Bucks	TQ0192	51°37·3′	0°32·1′W	FM	176
Brawn Fm	Glos	SO8224	51°55·1′	2°15·3′W	FM	162
Brawn's Den	Durham	NZ2038	54°44·4′	1°40·9′W	X	93
Brawns Dod	Scot Bord	NT1019	55°27·6′	3°25·0′W	H	78
Brawns Ho	Oxon	SU7384	51°33·2′	0°56·4′W	X	175
Brawn, The	Corn	SX3353	50°21·4′	4°20·5′W	X	201
Brax	Angus	NO5843	56°34·9′	2°40·6′W	X	54
Braxfield Ho	Glos	SP2039	52°3·2′	1°42·1′W	X	151
Braxted Park Ho	Essex	TL8515	51°48·4′	0°41·4′E	X	168
Bray	Win & Maid	SU9079	51°30·4′	0°41·8′W	T	175
Bray Bridge	Devon	SS6725	51°0·8′	3°53·4′W	X	180
Braybrooke	Northnts	SP7684	52°27·2′	0°52·5′W	T	141
Braybrooke Lower Lodge	Northnts	SP7585	52°27·7′	0°53·4′W	X	141
Braybrook Fm	Lincs	TA3402	53°30·1′	0°1·6′E	FM	113
Bray Clough	Derby	SK0591	53°25·2′	1°55·1′W	X	110
Bray Common	Devon	SS7138	51°7·8′	3°50·2′W	X	180
Brayden Marshes	Norf	TG4422	52°44·7′	1°37·3′E	W	134
Braydeston Hall	Norf	TG3408	52°37·4′	1°27·8′E	X	134
Braydon Brook Fm	Wilts	ST9891	51°37·3′	2°1·3′W	FM	163,173
Braydon Burn	Northum	NT8821	55°29·2′	2°11·0′W	W	74
Braydon Crag	Northum	NT8921	55°29·2′	2°10·0′W	X	74
Braydon Green Fm	Wilts	SU0587	51°35·1′	1°55·3′W	FM	173
Braydon Hall	Wilts	SU0290	51°36·8′	1°57·9′W	X	163,173
Braydon Hook	Wilts	SU2167	51°24·3′	1°41·5′W	X	174
Braydon Manor	Wilts	SU0487	51°35·1′	1°56·1′W	X	173
Braydon Pond	Wilts	ST9987	51°35·1′	2°0·5′W	W	173
Braydon Side	Wilts	SU0185	51°34·1′	1°58·7′W	T	173
Braydon Wood	Wilts	ST9987	51°35·1′	2°0·5′W	F	173
Bray Down	Corn	SX1882	50°36·8′	4°34·0′W	H	201
Brayfield Ho	Mil Key	SP9252	52°9·7′	0°38·9′W	X	152
Bray Fm	Norf	TG3923	52°45·3′	1°32·9′E	FM	133,134
Brayford	Devon	SS6834	51°5·6′	3°52·7′W	T	180
Brayfordhill	Devon	SS6834	51°5·6′	3°52·7′W	T	180
Brayley Barton	Devon	SS6830	51°3·5′	3°52·6′W	X	180
Brayley Hill	Devon	SS6830	51°3·5′	3°52·6′W	X	180
Brayne Hall	Ches	SJ6657	53°6·8′	2°30·1′W	X	118
Bray Roy Lodge	Highld	NN3391	56°59·1′	4°44·4′W	X	34
Brays	Essex	TQ8792	51°36·0′	0°42·4′E	X	178
Brays Fm	Devon	ST2601	50°48·5′	3°2·6′W	FM	192,193
Brays Grove	Essex	TL4608	51°45·3′	0°7·3′E	T	167
Brayshaw	Cumbr	NY0409	54°28·3′	3°28·5′W	X	89
Brayshaw	N Yks	SD7758	54°1·3′	2°20·6′W	X	103
Brayshill	Corn	SS2404	50°48·8′	4°29·5′W	X	190
Bray's Hill	E Susx	TQ6714	50°54·3′	0°22·9′E	X	199
Bray Shop	Corn	SX3374	50°32·8′	4°21·1′W	T	201
Bray's Point	Corn	SX1396	50°44·2′	4°38·6′W	X	190
Braystones	Cumbr	NY0005	54°26·1′	3°32·1′W	T	89
Brayswick	Worcs	SO8249	52°8·6′	2°15·4′W	T	150
Bray's Wood	Bucks	SP9104	51°43·9′	0°40·5′W	F	165
Braythorn	N Yks	SE2449	53°56·4′	1°37·6′W	T	104
Brayton	N Yks	SE6030	53°46·0′	1°5·0′W	T	105
Brayton Barff	N Yks	SE5830	53°46·0′	1°6·8′W	F	105
Brayton Park	Cumbr	NY1642	54°46·2′	3°17·9′W	X	85
Braytown	Dorset	SY8386	50°40·6′	2°14·1′W	T	194
Bray Wick	Win & Maid	SU8979	51°30·4′	0°42·7′W	T	175
Braywood Fm	Corn	SX2490	50°41·2′	4°29·1′W	FM	190
Braywood Ho	Win & Maid	SU9175	51°28·2′	0°41·0′W	X	175
Braywoodside	Win & Maid	SU8775	51°28·3′	0°44·5′W	T	175
Brazacott	Corn	SX2691	50°41·8′	4°27·5′W	T	190
Brazen Church Hill	Glos	SU1897	51°40·5′	1°44·0′W	X	163
Brazenhead Fm	Essex	TL6528	51°55·8′	0°24·4′E	FM	167
Brazenhill	Staffs	SJ8621	52°47·4′	2°12·1′W	T	127
Brazen Ward	Devon	SS1346	51°11·2′	4°40·2′W	X	180
Brazen Ward (Battery)	Devon	SS1346	51°11·2′	4°40·2′W	A	180
Braziers Common	Oxon	SU6583	51°32·8′	1°3·4′W	X	175
Braziers End Ho	Bucks	SP9306	51°44·9′	0°38·8′W	X	165

Brazier's Fm	Essex	TM1215	51°47·8′	1°4·9′E	FM	168,169
Brazier's Hall	Suff	TM0758	52°11·1′	1°2·1′E	X	155
Braziers Park	Oxon	SU6384	51°33·3′	1°5·1′W	X	175
Brazils	Essex	TL8000	51°40·4′	0°36·6′E	X	168
Brea	Corn	SW6640	50°13·1′	5°16·4′W	T	203
Breabag	Highld	NC2917	58°6·8′	4°53·7′W	H	15
Breabag Tasuinn	Highld	NC2919	58°7·9′	4°53·8′W	X	15
Breabost	Highld	NG3653	57°29·7′	6°23·9′W	X	23
Breabost Burn	Highld	NG3652	57°29·1′	6°23·8′W	W	23
Breac-achadh	Arg & Bt	NM3318	56°17·0′	6°18·4′W	X	48
Breac Achadh	Arg & Bt	NM5428	56°23·1′	5°58·7′W	X	48
Breac-achadh	Highld	NC8411	58°4·6′	3°57·5′W	X	17
Breac-Bheinn	Highld	NH4995	57°55·4′	4°32·5′W	H	20
Breach	Aberd	NJ5463	57°39·5′	2°45·8′W	X	29
Breach	Bath & NE Somer	ST6260	51°20·5′	2°32·3′W	T	172
Breach	Essex	TL6226	51°54·8′	0°21·7′E	X	167
Breach	Kent	TQ8465	51°21·5′	0°39·0′E	T	178
Breach	Kent	TR1947	51°11·0′	1°8·4′E	X	179,189
Breach	W Susx	SU7706	50°51·1′	0°54·0′W	T	197
Breachacha Castle	Arg & Bt	NM1553	56°35·2′	6°38·1′W	A	46
Breach Barns	Essex	TL4002	51°42·2′	0°2·0′E	X	167
Breach Brook	Warw	SP3285	52°28·0′	1°31·3′W	W	140
Breach Copse	W Berks	SU3672	51°27·0′	1°28·5′W	F	174
Breach Downs	Kent	TR2048	51°11·5′	1°9·3′E	X	179,189
Breaches Fm	Essex	TL3902	51°42·2′	0°1·1′E	FM	166
Breache's Wood	Lincs	TF0424	52°48·4′	0°27·0′W	F	130
Breach Farm Cott	Oxon	SP3705	51°44·8′	1°27·5′W	X	164
Breach Fm	Derby	SK2453	53°4·7′	1°38·1′W	FM	119
Breach Fm	Derby	SK2618	52°45·8′	1°36·5′W	FM	128
Breach Fm	Dorset	ST8117	50°57·4′	2°15·8′W	FM	183
Breach Fm	Hants	SU5843	51°11·2′	1°9·8′W	FM	185
Breach Fm	Hants	SU5849	51°14·5′	1°9·8′W	FM	185
Breach Fm	Hants	SU6235	51°6·9′	1°6·5′W	FM	185
Breach Fm	Leic	SK3715	52°44·1′	1°26·7′W	FM	128
Breach Fm	Leic	SP6086	52°28·4′	1°6·6′W	FM	140
Breach Fm	Oxon	SP3312	51°48·6′	1°30·9′W	FM	164
Breach Fm	Rut	SP8798	52°34·6′	0°42·6′W	FM	141
Breach Fm	Swin	SU2184	51°33·5′	1°41·4′W	FM	174
Breach Fm	Wilts	SU0273	51°27·6′	1°57·9′W	FM	173
Breach Fm	Worcs	SO9177	52°23·7′	2°7·5′W	FM	139
Breach Fm	Worcs	SO9250	52°9·1′	2°6·6′W	FM	150
Breach Hill	Bath & NE Somer	ST5459	51°19·9′	2°39·2′W	X	172,182
Breach Hill	Hants	SU5214	50°55·6′	1°15·2′W	X	196
Breach Hill	Wilts	SU0046	51°13·0′	1°59·6′W	X	184
Breach Ho	N Yks	SE2983	54°14·8′	1°32·9′W	X	99
Breach Ho	Oxon	SU5784	51°33·4′	1°10·3′W	X	174
Breach House Fm	Ches	SJ7882	53°20·3′	2°19·4′W	FM	109
Breach Law	Scot Bord	NT1833	55°35·3′	3°17·6′W	H	72
Breachloch	Highld	NH6358	57°35·7′	4°17·1′W	X	26
Breach Oak Fm	Warw	SP3087	52°29·0′	1°33·1′W	FM	140
Breach Wood	Dorset	ST7503	50°49·8′	2°20·9′W	F	194
Breach Wood	Herts	TL0213	51°48·6′	0°30·8′W	F	166
Breach wood	Somer	ST4030	51°4·2′	2°51·0′W	F	182
Breach Wood	Somer	ST7041	51°10·3′	2°25·4′W	F	183
Breachwood Green	Herts	TL1522	51°53·3′	0°19·3′W	T	166
Breackerie Water	Arg & Bt	NR6511	55°20·5′	5°41·9′W	W	68
Breackue	Highld	NC7205	58°1·2′	4°9·5′W	X	16
Breac Leac	Stir	NN4493	56°6·5′	4°30·1′W	X	57
Breac Leathad	Arg & Bt	NM6725	56°21·9′	5°45·9′W	X	49
Breac Leathad	Moray	NJ2119	57°15·6′	3°18·1′W	X	36
Breaclete	N Eil	NB1536	58°13·5′	6°50·8′W	T	13
Breaclete	N Eil	NB1636	58°13·5′	6°49·8′W	W	13
Breac-reidh	Pth & Kin	NO0573	56°50·6′	3°33·0′W	H	43
Breacrie	Highld	NC8951	58°26·3′	3°53·6′W	X	10
Breaday Gill	N Yks	SE9692	54°19·1′	0°31·0′W	W	94,101
Bread & Beer Cott	D & G	NX6979	55°5·5′	4°2·7′W	X	77,84
Breaden Heath	Shrops	SJ4436	52°55·4′	2°49·6′W	T	126
Breadsall	Derby	SK3739	52°57·1′	1°26·6′W	T	128
Breadsall Hilltop	C of Derb	SK3638	52°56·5′	1°27·5′W	T	128
Breadsall Lodge	Derby	SK3740	52°57·6′	1°26·5′W	X	119,128
Breadsall Moor	Derby	SK3742	52°58·7′	1°26·5′W	X	119,128
Breadsall Priory (Hotel)	Derby	SK3841	52°58·1′	1°25·6′W	X	119,128
Breadsell Fm	E Susx	TQ7713	50°53·6′	0°31·4′E	FM	199
Breadstone	Glos	SO7100	51°42·1′	2°24·8′W	T	162
Bread Street	Glos	SO8306	51°45·4′	2°14·4′W	T	162
Brea Fm	Corn	SW3728	50°5·9′	5°40·3′W	FM	203
Breagach Hill	Aberd	NJ3313	57°12·4′	3°6·1′W	H	37
Breage	Corn	SW6128	50°6·5′	5°20·2′W	T	203
Brea Hill	Corn	SW9277	50°33·6′	4°55·8′W	H	200
Breakachy	Arg & Bt	NR6726	55°28·6′	5°40·8′W	X	68
Breakachy	Highld	NH4644	57°27·9′	4°33·6′W	X	26
Breakachy	Highld	NN6392	57°0·2′	4°14·9′W	X	35
Breaker Hill	S Ayr	NX1788	55°9·4′	4°51·9′W	H	76
Breakheart Bottom	Wilts	ST9745	51°12·5′	2°2·2′W	X	184
Breakheart Hill	Beds	TL0137	52°1·6′	0°31·3′W	X	153
Break Heart Hill	Dorset	SY6198	50°47·0′	2°32·8′W	X	194
Breakheart Hill	Glos	SO6719	51°52·4′	2°28·4′W	H	162
Breakheart Hill	Glos	ST7596	51°40·0′	2°21·3′W	H	162
Breakheart Hill	Wilts	ST9744	51°11·9′	2°2·2′W	X	184
Break House Fm	N Yks	NZ3308	54°28·2′	1°29·0′W	FM	93
Breakneck Bank	Shrops	SO7176	52°23·1′	2°25·2′W	X	138
Breakneck Hole	Devon	SS7140	51°8·9′	3°50·3′W	X	180
Breakough	N Ayr	NS1655	55°45·5′	4°55·5′W	X	63
Breaksea Point	V of Glam	ST0265	51°22·8′	3°24·1′W	X	170
Breaks Fold Fm	N Yks	SE1457	54°0·8′	1°46·8′W	FM	104
Breaks Hall	Cumbr	NY7013	54°30·9′	2°27·4′W	X	91
Breakshaw Hill	Cumbr	NY6377	55°5·4′	2°34·4′W	X	86
Breaks Moss	Cumbr	NY4965	54°58·9′	2°47·4′W	X	86
Breakspear Ho	Hill	TQ0689	51°35·6′	0°27·8′W	X	176
Breaks, The	Cumbr	NY4964	54°58·3′	2°47·4′W	X	86
Breakwell	Highld	NH6391	57°53·5′	4°18·2′W	X	21
Breaky Bottom	E Susx	TQ4005	50°49·9′	0°0·3′W	X	198
Brealeys	Devon	SS5415	50°55·2′	4°4·3′W	T	180
Bream	Glos	SO6005	51°44·8′	2°34·4′W	T	162
Bream Cove	Corn	SW7928	50°6·9′	5°5·1′W	W	204
Bream Cross	Glos	SO5905	51°44·8′	2°35·2′W	X	162
Breamore	Hants	SU1518	50°57·9′	1°46·8′W	T	184
Breamore Down	Hants	SU1320	50°59·0′	1°48·5′W	X	184

Breamore Ho	Hants	SU1519	50°58·4'	1°46·8'W	A	184
Breamore Wood	Hants	SU1419	50°58·4'	1°47·6'W	F	184
Breams Fm	Essex	TL7217	51°49·7'	0°30·2'E	FM	167
Bream's Meend	Glos	SO5905	51°44·8'	2°35·2'W	T	162
Bream Wood	E Susx	TQ5233	51°4·8'	0°10·6'E	F	188
Brean	Somer	ST2956	51°18·2'	3°0·7'W	T	182
Brean Down	Somer	ST2958	51°19·2'	3°0·7'W	X	182
Brean Down Fm	Somer	ST3058	51°19·2'	2°59·9'W	FM	182
Brean Fm	Somer	ST2957	51°18·7'	3°0·7'W	FM	182
Breapadail	Arg & Bt	NM5832	56°25·4'	5°55·0'W	X	48
Brearlands	N Yks	SD9173	54°9·4'	2°7·9'W	X	98
Brearley	Cald	SE0226	53°44·1'	1°57·8'W	T	104
Brearton	N Yks	SE3260	54°2·3'	1°30·3'W	T	99
Brearton Moor	N Yks	SE3260	54°2·3'	1°30·3'W	X	99
Breary Banks	N Yks	SE1680	54°13·2'	1°44·9'W	X	99
Breary Grange	Leeds	SE2642	53°52·7'	1°35·9'W	X	104
Breary Marsh	Leeds	SE2541	53°52·1'	1°36·8'W	X	104
Breascleit	N Eil	NB2135	58°13·2'	6°44·6'W	T	8,13
Breaskay Moss	Cumbr	SD7092	54°19·6'	2°27·3'W	W	98
Breasthigh Road	Cumbr	NY5604	54°26·0'	2°40·3'W	X	90
Breast Mill	C of Edin	NT1274	55°57·3'	3°24·1'W	X	65
Breast Mill Beck	Cumbr	SD2172	54°8·5'	3°12·1'W	X	96
Breaston	Derby	SK4633	52°53·8'	1°18·6'W	T	129
Breaston Fields Fm	Derby	SK4633	52°53·8'	1°18·6'W	FM	129
Breast Sand	Norf	TF5427	52°49·3'	0°17·5'E	X	131
Breasty Haw	Cumbr	SD3492	54°19·4'	3°0·5'W	X	96,97
Breazle Fms	Devon	SX4492	50°42·6'	4°12·2'W	FM	190
Breazle Water	Devon	SX4590	50°41·6'	4°11·3'W	W	190
Brebast	Cered	SN4250	52°7·8'	4°18·1'W	X	146
Bre Brough	Orkney	HY1803	58°54·7'	3°24·9'W	X	7
Brechfa	Carm	SN5230	51°57·2'	4°8·8'W	T	146
Brechfa	Pemb	SN0922	51°52·1'	4°46·1'W	X	145,158
Brechfa	Powys	SO1136	52°1·2'	3°17·4'W	X	161
Brechfa Common	Powys	SO1138	52°2·2'	3°17·5'W	X	161
Brechfafach	Cered	SN6059	52°12·9'	4°2·6'W	X	146
Brechfa Fawr	Cered	SN6060	52°13·5'	4°2·6'W	X	146
Brechfa Forest	Carm	SN5334	51°59·3'	4°8·1'W	F	146
Brechfa Pool	Powys	SO1137	52°1·7'	3°17·4'W	W	161
Brechin	Angus	NO5960	56°44·0'	2°39·8'W	T	44
Brechin	Angus	NO6059	56°43·5'	2°38·8'W	T	54
Brechin Castle	Angus	NO5959	56°43·5'	2°39·8'W	X	54
Breck	Orkney	HY3412	58°59·7'	3°8·4'W	X	6
Breck	Orkney	HY3607	58°57·0'	3°6·3'W	X	6,7
Breck	Orkney	HY4431	59°10·0'	2°58·3'W	X	5,6
Breck	Orkney	HY4552	59°21·3'	2°57·6'W	X	5
Breck	Orkney	HY5106	58°56·6'	2°50·6'W	X	6,7
Breck	Orkney	HY5805	58°56·1'	2°43·3'W	X	6
Breck	Shetld	HU2148	60°13·2'	1°36·8'W	X	3
Breckagh Burn	D & G	NS8408	55°21·4'	3°49·4'W	W	71,78
Breckamore	N Yks	SE2872	54°8·8'	1°33·9'W	X	99
Breckan	Orkney	HY2506	58°56·3'	3°17·7'W	X	6,7
Breckan	Orkney	HY3216	59°1·8'	3°10·6'W	X	6
Breckan	Orkney	HY3833	59°11·0'	3°4·6'W	X	6
Breckan	Orkney	HY5807	58°57·2'	2°43·3'W	X	6
Breckan	Orkney	HY6745	59°17·7'	2°34·3'W	X	5
Breckaskaill	Orkney	HY4550	59°20·2'	2°57·5'W	X	5
Breck Cott	Orkney	HY2425	59°6·6'	3°19·1'W	X	6
Breck Edge	Derby	SK0882	53°20·3'	1°52·4'W	X	110
Breckenborough Hall	N Yks	SE3883	54°14·7'	1°24·6'W	X	99
Breckenbrough	N Yks	SE2096	54°21·8'	1°41·1'W	X	99
Breckenbrough	N Yks	SE3783	54°14·7'	1°25·5'W	X	99
Breckenbrough Grange	N Yks	SE3982	54°14·2'	1°23·7'W	X	99
Brecken Hill	N Yks	NZ4301	54°24·4'	1°19·8'W	X	93
Breckenhurst	N Yks	SE9594	54°20·2'	0°31·9'W	X	94,101
Brecken Shank	D & G	NY4093	55°13·9'	2°56·2'W	X	79
Breckeny Knowe	D & G	NY3882	55°8·0'	2°57·9'W	X	79
Breck Fm	Derby	SK2049	53°2·5'	1°41·7'W	FM	119
Breck Fm	Norf	TG0438	52°54·3'	1°2·4'E	FM	133
Breck Fm	Norf	TG0733	52°51·5'	1°4·9'E	FM	133
Breck Fm	Norf	TG1615	52°41·6'	1°12·2'E	FM	133
Breck Fm	Norf	TG1621	52°44·8'	1°12·4'E	FM	133
Breckhead	Derby	SK0582	53°20·3'	1°55·1'W	X	110
Breck Ho	N Yks	SE6197	54°22·1'	1°3·2'W	X	94,100
Brecklach Hill	D & G	NX3384	55°7·6'	4°36·7'W	H	76
Breckland Fm	Norf	TL7392	52°30·1'	0°33·3'E	FM	143
Brecklands	N Yks	SE7182	54°14·0'	0°54·2'W	X	100
Brecklate	Arg & Bt	NR6912	55°21·1'	5°38·2'W	X	68
Breckles	Norf	TL9594	52°30·8'	0°52·8'E	T	144
Breckle's Grange	Norf	TL9494	52°30·8'	0°51·9'E	X	144
Breckles Hall	Norf	TL9694	52°30·7'	0°53·7'E	A	144
Breckles Heath	Norf	TL9394	52°30·8'	0°51·1'E	X	144
Breck Ness	Orkney	HY2209	58°57·9'	3°20·9'W	X	6,7
Breckness Ho	Orkney	HY2209	58°57·9'	3°20·9'W	A	6,7
Breckney Bed	Cumbr	NY6167	55°0·0'	2°36·2'W	X	86
Breckney Fm	N Yks	SE8375	54°10·1'	0°43·3'W	FM	100
Breckney Hill	Northum	NZ1368	55°0·6'	1°47·4'W	X	88
Brecknish	Highld	NH7148	57°30·5'	4°8·7'W	X	27
Breck of Cruan	Orkney	HY3718	59°2·9'	3°5·4'W	T	6
Breck of Linkquoy	Orkney	HY2315	59°1·2'	3°20·0'W	X	6
Breck of Mailand	Shetld	HP6002	60°42·1'	0°53·6'W	X	1
Breck of Newgord	Shetld	HP5706	60°44·2'	0°56·8'W	X	1
Breck of Ramnageo	Shetld	HP6200	60°41·0'	0°51·4'W	X	1
Breck of Rendall	Orkney	HY4120	59°4·0'	3°1·3'W	X	5,6
Breck of Voesgrind	Shetld	HP6201	60°41·5'	0°51·4'W	X	1
Breckon	Shetld	HP5204	60°43·2'	1°2·3'W	X	1
Breckon	Shetld	HU4269	60°24·4'	1°13·8'W	X	2,3
Breckonbrough	N Yks	SE8090	54°18·2'	0°45·8'W	X	94,100
Breckonhill	D & G	NY1576	55°4·5'	3°19·5'W	X	85
Breckon Hill	Durham	NZ1026	54°38·0'	1°50·3'W	X	92
Breckon Hill	Durham	NZ3050	54°50·9'	1°31·5'W	X	88
Breckon Hill	Durham	NZ3526	54°37·9'	1°27·0'W	X	93
Breckon Hill	Northum	NY9063	54°57·9'	2°8·9'W	X	87
Breckonholme	Northum	NY8547	54°49·3'	2°13·6'W	X	87
Breckon Howe	N Yks	NZ8503	54°25·2'	0°41·0'W	A	94
Breckoniehill	D & G	NX8259	54°55·0'	3°50·0'W	X	84
Breckowall	Orkney	HY4348	59°19·1'	2°59·6'W	X	5
Breck Plantation	Notts	SK6978	53°17·9'	0°57·5'W	F	120
Breckquoy	Orkney	HY5100	58°53·3'	2°50·5'W	X	6,7
Breckquoy	Orkney	HY5302	58°54·4'	2°48·5'W	X	6,7
Breckrey	Highld	NG5062	57°35·0'	6°10·5'W	T	23,24
Brecks	Orkney	HY4917	59°2·5'	2°52·8'W	X	6
Brecks	Orkney	HY5507	58°57·1'	2°46·4'W	X	6
Brecks	Orkney	ND4793	58°49·5'	2°54·6'W	X	7
Brecks	Roth	SK4692	53°25·6'	1°18·1'W	T	111
Brecks	Shetld	HU3253	60°15·9'	1°24·8'W	X	3
Breck's Bridge	Lancs	SD4551	53°57·4'	2°49·9'W	X	102
Brecks Fm	Leeds	SE3931	53°46·7'	1°24·1'W	FM	104
Brecks Fm	Notts	SK7061	53°8·7'	0°56·8'W	FM	120
Breck's Fm	Notts	SK7467	53°11·9'	0°53·1'W	FM	120
Brecks Fm	N Yks	SE5229	53°45·5'	1°12·3'W	FM	105
Brecks Fm	N Yks	SE6384	54°15·1'	1°1·6'W	FM	100
Brecks Fm	York	SE5956	54°0·0'	1°5·6'W	FM	105
Brecks Fms	Notts	SK7573	53°15·2'	0°52·1'W	FM	120
Brecks o' Banks	Orkney	HY4430	59°9·5'	2°58·3'W	X	5,6
Brecks of Bigton	Shetld	HU3721	59°58·6'	1°19·7'W	X	4
Breckstreet Fm	E Yorks	SE7641	53°51·8'	0°50·2'W	FM	105,106
Brecks Wood	Notts	SK6387	53°22·8'	1°2·8'W	F	111,120
Brecks Wood	N Yks	SE6485	54°15·6'	1°0·6'W	F	94,100
Breck, The	Derby	SK4276	53°17·0'	1°21·8'W	X	120
Breck,The	Orkney	HY3403	58°54·8'	3°8·3'W	X	6,7
Breck, The	Shetld	HU3292	60°36·9'	1°24·4'W	X	1
Brecktor	Derby	SK1279	53°18·7'	1°48·8'W	X	119
Brecon (Aberhonddu)	Powys	SO0428	51°56·8'	3°23·4'W	T	160
Brecon Beacons (Bannau Brycheiniog)	Pemb	SN0021	51°51·3'	4°53·9'W	H	160
Brecon Beacons (Bannau Brycheiniog)	Powys	SO0021	51°53·0'	3°26·8'W	H	160
Breconbeds	D & G	NY2271	55°1·9'	3°12·8'W	X	85
Brecon Court	Monm	SO4501	51°42·5'	2°47·4'W	X	171
Brecongill	N Yks	SE0886	54°16·4'	1°52·2'W	X	99
Breconhill	Cumbr	NY3744	54°47·5'	2°58·4'W	X	85
Breconhill	Cumbr	NY5262	54°57·3'	2°44·5'W	X	86
Brecon Ho	N Yks	NZ1809	54°28·8'	1°42·9'W	X	92
Brecon Mountain Rly	Merth Tyd	SO0610	51°47·1'	3°21·4'W	X	160
Breconrae	D & G	NY0574	55°3·3'	3°28·8'W	X	85
Breconridge	D & G	NY1073	55°2·9'	3°24·1'W	X	85
Breconside	D & G	NS8302	55°18·1'	3°50·1'W	X	78
Breconside	D & G	NT1002	55°18·5'	3°24·6'W	X	78
Breconside	D & G	NX8488	55°10·6'	3°48·9'W	X	78
Breconside	D & G	NX8866	54°58·8'	3°44·6'W	X	84
Breconside Burn	D & G	NS8202	55°18·1'	3°51·1'W	W	78
Breconside Burn	D & G	NT1102	55°18·5'	3°23·7'W	W	78
Breconside Hill	D & G	NS8102	55°18·1'	3°52·0'W	H	78
Breconside Hill	D & G	NX8966	54°58·8'	3°43·6'W	H	84
Breda Hill	Aberd	NJ5216	57°14·2'	2°47·3'W	H	37
Breda Ho	Aberd	NJ5416	57°14·2'	2°45·3'W	X	37
Bredaig	Highld	NH4842	57°26·8'	4°31·5'W	X	26
Bredbury	Stock	SJ9291	53°25·2'	2°6·8'W	T	109
Bredbury Green	Stock	SJ9390	53°24·6'	2°5·9'W	T	109
Breddock Bay	D & G	NX0937	54°41·8'	4°57·4'W	W	82
Brede	E Susx	TQ8218	50°56·2'	0°35·8'E	T	199
Brede Barn Fm	E Susx	TQ7918	50°56·2'	0°33·3'E	FM	199
Brede High Green	E Susx	TQ8020	50°57·3'	0°34·2'E	X	199
Brede High Wood	E Susx	TQ7920	50°57·3'	0°33·3'E	F	199
Brede Level	E Susx	TQ8417	50°55·6'	0°37·5'E	X	199
Brede Level	E Susx	TQ8617	50°55·6'	0°39·2'E	X	189,199
Bredenbury	Heref	SO6056	52°12·3'	2°34·7'W	T	149
Brede Place	E Susx	TQ8318	50°56·2'	0°36·7'E	A	199
Bredfield	Suff	TM2652	52°7·4'	1°18·5'E	T	156
Bredgar	Kent	TQ8860	51°18·7'	0°42·2'E	T	178
Bredhurst	Kent	TQ7962	51°20·0'	0°34·6'E	T	178,188
Bredhurst Hurst	Kent	TQ8061	51°19·4'	0°35·4'E	F	178,188
Bredicot	Worcs	SO9054	52°11·3'	2°8·4'W	X	150
Bredlands Fm	Kent	TR1961	51°18·6'	1°8·9'E	FM	179
Bredon	Worcs	SO9236	52°1·6'	2°6·6'W	T	150
Bredon Field Fm	Worcs	SO9038	52°2·7'	2°8·4'W	FM	150
Bredon Hill	Worcs	SO9639	52°3·2'	2°3·1'W	H	150
Bredon School	Worcs	SO8636	52°1·6'	2°11·8'W	X	150
Bredon's Hardwick	Worcs	SO9135	52°1·0'	2°7·5'W	T	150
Bredon's Norton	Worcs	SO9339	52°3·2'	2°5·7'W	T	150
Bredwardine	Heref	SO2855	52°11·6'	3°2·8'W	X	148
Bredwardine	Heref	SO3344	52°5·7'	2°58·3'W	T	148,149,161
Bredwardine Hill	Heref	SO3144	52°5·6'	3°0·0'W	X	148,161
Bredy Fm	Dorset	SY5089	50°42·1'	2°42·1'W	FM	194
Bredy North Hill	Dorset	SY5090	50°42·7'	2°42·1'W	X	194
Breeches Fm	Somer	ST3204	50°50·1'	2°57·6'W	FM	193
Breeches Rock	Scot Bord	NT9562	55°51·3'	2°4·3'W	X	67
Breeder Hills Fm	Lincs	SK8436	52°55·1'	0°44·6'W	FM	130
Breedless Fm	Aberd	NJ7036	57°25·8'	2°29·7'W	FM	29
Breedon Brand Fm	Leic	SK4220	52°46·8'	1°22·2'W	FM	129
Breedon Hill	Leic	SK4023	52°48·4'	1°24·0'W	X	129
Breedon Lodge Fm	Leic	SK4222	52°47·9'	1°22·2'W	FM	129
Breedon on the Hill	Leic	SK4022	52°47·9'	1°24·0'W	T	129
Breeds	Essex	TL6812	51°47·1'	0°26·5'E	T	167
Breedy Butts	Lancs	SD3440	53°51·4'	2°59·8'W	T	102
Breens Cottages	E Susx	TQ3719	50°57·5'	0°2·6'W	X	198
Breeran	Orkney	HY3424	59°6·1'	3°8·6'W	X	6
Breever's Br	E Yorks	SE6618	53°39·5'	0°59·7'W	X	111
Breewood Hall	Essex	TL9730	51°56·2'	0°52·4'E	X	168
Breeze Fm	E Yorks	TA1354	53°58·4'	0°16·2'W	FM	107
Breeze Hill	Dorset	ST8920	50°59·0'	2°9·0'W	H	184
Bregach	Moray	NJ2632	57°22·6'	3°13·4'W	X	37
Bregsell's Fm	Surrey	TQ1743	51°10·7'	0°19·2'W	FM	187
Breibhig	N Eil	NB4158	58°26·3'	6°25·8'W	X	8
Breibhig	N Eil	NB4839	58°16·3'	6°17·4'W	T	8
Breibister	Shetld	HU2149	60°13·8'	1°36·8'W	X	3
Breich	W Loth	NS9660	55°49·6'	3°39·2'W	T	65
Breich Water	W Loth	NS9460	55°49·6'	3°41·1'W	W	65
Breich Water	W Loth	NT0063	55°51·2'	3°35·4'W	W	65
Breidden Forest	Powys	SJ2914	52°43·4'	3°2·7'W	F	126
Breidden Hill	Powys	SJ2914	52°43·4'	3°2·7'W	H	126
Brei Geo	Shetld	HP5602	60°42·1'	0°57·9'W	X	1
Brei Geo	Shetld	HU3193	60°37·4'	1°25·5'W	X	1
Brei Geo	Shetld	HU3546	60°12·1'	1°21·6'W	X	4
Brei Geo	Shetld	HU3942	60°9·9'	1°17·3'W	X	4
Brei Geo	Shetld	HU4079	60°29·8'	1°15·8'W	X	2,3
Brei Geo	Shetld	HU4117	59°56·4'	1°15·5'W	X	4
Brei Geo	Shetld	HU5066	60°22·8'	1°5·1'W	X	2,3
Brei Geo	Shetld	HU6772	60°25·8'	0°46·5'W	X	2
Breigeo Head	Shetld	HU1560	60°19·7'	1°43·2'W	X	3
Breightmet	Bolton	SD7409	53°34·9'	2°23·2'W	T	109
Breighton	E Yorks	SE7134	53°48·1'	0°54·9'W	T	105,106
Breihascro	N Eil	NB4955	58°24·9'	6°17·4'W	X	8
Brei-hevda	Shetld	HU5381	60°30·8'	1°1·6'W	X	1,2,3
Brei Holm	Shetld	HU1860	60°19·7'	1°39·9'W	X	3
Breil Nook	E Yorks	TA2471	54°7·4'	0°5·7'W	X	101
Brei Mires	Shetld	HU4889	60°35·2'	1°6·9'W	X	1,2
Brei Ness	Shetld	HU3167	60°23·4'	1°25·8'W	X	3
Breinish	N Eil	NF8563	57°33·1'	7°15·5'W	X	18
Brein Phort	Arg & Bt	NR4677	55°55·4'	6°3·5'W	W	60,61
Brein Phort	Arg & Bt	NR5083	55°58·8'	6°0·0'W	W	61
Breinton Common	Heref	SO4539	52°3·0'	2°47·7'W	T	149,161
Breiti Stack	Shetld	HZ2072	59°32·3'	1°38·3'W	X	4
Brei Water	Shetld	HU3171	60°25·6'	1°25·7'W	W	3
Brei Water	Shetld	HU5064	60°21·7'	1°5·1'W	W	2,3
Brei Water of Nibon	Shetld	HU3171	60°25·6'	1°25·7'W	W	3
Brei Wick	Shetld	HP5305	60°43·7'	1°1·2'W	W	1
Brei Wick	Shetld	HP6317	60°50·1'	0°50·0'W	W	1
Breiwick	Shetld	HU2648	60°13·2'	1°31·3'W	X	3
Brei Wick	Shetld	HU3876	60°28·2'	1°18·0'W	W	2,3
Brei Wick	Shetld	HU4546	60°12·0'	1°10·8'W	W	4
Breiwick	Shetld	HU4547	60°12·6'	1°10·8'W	T	3
Brei Wick	Shetld	HU4740	60°8·8'	1°8·7'W	W	4
Brei Wick	Shetld	HU5560	60°19·5'	0°59·8'W	W	2
Brei Wick	Shetld	HU6198	60°39·9'	0°52·5'W	W	1
Breiwick Stack	Shetld	HP6301	60°41·5'	0°50·3'W	X	1
Breja Fm	Corn	SW4838	50°11·5'	5°31·5'W	FM	203
Brelston Green	Heref	SO5620	51°52·8'	2°38·0'W	T	162
Bremenda	Carm	SN5120	51°51·8'	4°9·4'W	X	159
Bremenivm (Roman Fort)	Northum	NY8398	55°16·8'	2°15·6'W	R	80
Bremere Rife	W Susx	SU8600	50°47·8'	0°46·4'W	W	197
Bremeridge Fm	Wilts	ST8450	51°15·2'	2°13·4'W	FM	183
Bremetennacvm (Roman Fort)	Lancs	SD6434	53°48·3'	2°32·4'W	R	102,103
Bremhill	Wilts	ST9773	51°27·6'	2°2·2'W	T	173
Bremhill Grove	Wilts	ST9774	51°28·1'	2°2·2'W	F	173
Bremhill Ho	Wilts	ST9974	51°28·1'	2°0·5'W	X	173
Bremhill Wick	Wilts	ST9674	51°28·1'	2°3·1'W	T	173
Bremia (Roman Fort)	Cered	SN6456	52°11·4'	3°59·0'W	R	146
Bremirehoull	Shetld	HU4229	60°2·9'	1°14·3'W	T	4
Bremley	Devon	SS8128	51°2·6'	3°41·5'W	X	181
Bremridge	Devon	SS6929	51°3·0'	3°51·8'W	A	180
Bremridge	Devon	ST0025	51°1·2'	3°25·2'W	X	181
Bremridge	Devon	SX7870	50°31·3'	3°42·9'W	X	202
Bremridge Fm	Devon	SS5824	51°0·1'	4°1·0'W	FM	180
Bremridge Fm	Devon	SS8404	50°49·7'	3°38·4'W	FM	191
Bremridge Wood	Devon	SS6828	51°2·4'	3°52·6'W	F	180
Brenachie	Highld	NH7676	57°45·7'	4°4·6'W	T	21
Brenachoile Lodge	Stir	NN4709	56°15·2'	4°27·7'W	X	57
Brenan	Cered	SN6476	52°22·2'	3°59·5'W	X	135
Brenchley	Kent	TQ6741	51°8·9'	0°23·7'E	T	188
Brenchoillie	Arg & Bt	NN0102	56°10·4'	5°11·9'W	X	55
Brendale	Orkney	HY4331	59°10·0'	2°59·3'W	X	5,6
Brendon	Corn	SX3968	50°29·6'	4°15·8'W	X	201
Brendon	Devon	SS2806	50°49·9'	4°26·2'W	X	190
Brendon	Devon	SS3513	50°53·8'	4°20·4'W	T	190
Brendon	Devon	SS3607	50°50·6'	4°19·4'W	T	190
Brendon	Devon	SS3919	50°57·1'	4°17·2'W	X	190
Brendon	Devon	SS7647	51°12·8'	3°46·1'W	T	180
Brendon	Devon	SX4299	50°46·4'	4°14·1'W	X	190
Brendon Barton	Corn	SX2594	50°43·4'	4°28·4'W	X	190
Brendon Barton	Devon	SS7447	51°12·7'	3°47·9'W	X	180
Brendon Common	Devon	SS7644	51°11·1'	3°46·1'W	X	180
Brendon Hill	Somer	ST0234	51°6·1'	3°23·6'W	X	181
Brendon Hill Fm	Somer	SS9237	51°7·6'	3°32·2'W	FM	181
Brendon Hill Fm	Somer	ST0133	51°5·5'	3°24·4'W	FM	181
Brendon Hills	Somer	SS9935	51°6·6'	3°26·2'W	H	181
Brendon Two Gates	Somer	SS7643	51°10·6'	3°46·1'W	X	180
Breney Fm	Corn	SX0660	50°24·7'	4°43·5'W	FM	200
Brenfield	Arg & Bt	NR8482	55°59·2'	5°27·3'W	X	55
Brenfield Bay	Arg & Bt	NR8582	55°59·2'	5°26·4'W	W	55
Brenfield Point	Arg & Bt	NR8582	55°59·2'	5°26·4'W	X	55
Brenham Fm	Essex	TQ8595	51°37·6'	0°40·8'E	FM	168
Brenish	N Eil	NA9926	58°7·5'	7°6·3'W	T	13
Brenish Point	N Eil	NF9089	57°47·3'	7°12·5'W	X	18
Brenish River	N Eil	NA9925	58°7·0'	7°6·2'W	W	13
Brenk Ho	N Yks	SE5478	54°11·9'	1°9·9'W	X	100
Brenk House Fm	N Yks	SE4591	54°19·0'	1°18·1'W	FM	99
Brenkley	N upon Ty	NZ2175	55°4·4'	1°39·8'W	T	88
Brenley Corner	Kent	TR0359	51°17·9'	0°55·1'E	X	178,179
Brenley Ho	Kent	TR0359	51°17·9'	0°55·1'E	X	178,179
Brennand Fell	Lancs	SD6355	53°59·6'	2°33·4'W	X	102,103
Brennand Fm	Lancs	SD6454	53°59·1'	2°32·5'W	FM	102,103
Brennand Great Hill	Lancs	SD6256	54°0·2'	2°34·4'W	X	102,103
Brennand River	Lancs	SD6354	53°59·1'	2°33·4'W	W	102,103
Brennand Round Hill	Lancs	SD6356	54°0·2'	2°33·5'W	X	102,103
Brennand Tarn	Lancs	SD6254	53°59·1'	2°34·4'W	W	102,103
Brenscombe Fm	Dorset	SY9782	50°38·5'	2°2·2'W	FM	195
Brenscombe Hill	Dorset	SY9882	50°38·5'	2°1·3'W	X	195
Brent	Corn	SX2151	50°20·1'	4°30·5'W	T	201
Brent Ditch	Cambs	TL5147	52°6·3'	0°12·7'E	A	154
Brent Eleigh	Suff	TL9447	52°5·5'	0°50·3'E	T	155
Brent Fm	Somer	ST3246	51°12·8'	2°58·0'W	FM	182
Brentford	Houns	TQ1877	51°29·0'	0°17·6'W	T	176
Brentford End	Houns	TQ1677	51°29·0'	0°19·4'W	T	176
Brentford Grange	Bucks	SU9694	51°38·4'	0°36·4'W	X	175,176
Brent Fore Hill	Devon	SX6661	50°26·2'	3°52·8'W	X	202
Brent Hall	Essex	TL6733	51°58·4'	0°26·3'E	X	167
Brent Hall	Essex	TL7512	51°47·0'	0°32·6'E	X	167
Brent Hill	Devon	SX7061	50°26·3'	3°49·5'W	H	202
Brentingby	Leic	SK7818	52°45·5'	0°50·2'W	T	129
Brentingby Lodge	Leic	SK7719	52°46·0'	0°51·1'W	X	129
Brent Knoll	Somer	ST3350	51°14·9'	2°57·2'W	T	182
Brent Knoll	Somer	ST3450	51°15·0'	2°56·4'W	H	182
Brentlands	Glos	SO8412	51°48·6'	2°13·5'W	X	162
Brent Mill	Devon	SX6959	50°25·2'	3°50·3'W	T	202
Brent Moor	Devon	SX6663	50°27·3'	3°52·9'W	X	202
Brenton	Devon	SX9086	50°40·0'	3°33·0'W	X	192
Brent Pelham	Herts	TL4330	51°57·2'	0°5·3'E	T	167
Brent Reservoir	Brent	TQ2187	51°34·4'	0°14·8'W	W	176

Brentry	C of Bris	ST5779	51°30·7'	2°36·8'W	T	172
Brent Sta	Barnet	TQ2387	51°34·3'	0°13·1'W	X	176
Brent Tor	Devon	SX4780	50°36·2'	4°9·4'W	H	191,201
Brentwood	Essex	TQ6093	51°37·0'	0°19·1'E	T	177
Brenzett	Kent	TR0027	51°0·7'	0°51·5'E	T	189
Brenzett Green	Kent	TR0128	51°1·2'	0°52·3'E	T	189
Brenzett Place	Kent	TR0127	51°0·7'	0°52·3'E	X	189
Brenzieshill	Aberd	NO7979	56°54·4'	2°20·2'W	X	45
Breoch	D & G	NX7859	54°54·9'	3°53·8'W	X	84
Breoch Cott	D & G	NX7759	54°54·9'	3°54·7'W	X	84
Brerachan Water	Pth & Kin	NN9963	56°45·1'	3°38·7'W	W	43
Brereton	Staffs	SK0516	52°44·7'	1°55·2'W	T	128
Brereton Cross	Staffs	SK0615	52°44·2'	1°54·3'W	T	128
Brereton Fm	Ches	SJ9069	53°13·3'	2°8·6'W	FM	118
Brereton Green	Ches	SJ7764	53°10·6'	2°20·2'W	T	118
Brereton Hall	Ches	SJ7865	53°11·1'	2°19·3'W	A	118
Brereton Hayes Wood	Staffs	SK0414	52°43·7'	1°56·0'W	F	128
Brereton Heath	Ches	SJ8064	53°10·6'	2°17·5'W	T	118
Brereton Heath Park	Ches	SJ7965	53°11·1'	2°18·4'W	X	118
Breretonhill	Staffs	SK0515	52°44·2'	1°55·2'W	T	128
Brereton Park Fm	Ches	SJ4962	53°9·4'	2°45·4'W	FM	117
Bresby Ho	Lincs	TF2433	52°53·0'	0°9·0'W	X	131
Bresdale	Shetld	HU5988	60°34·5'	0°54·9'W	X	1,2
Brè-Sgorr	Highld	NG2104	57°2·8'	6°35·6'W	X	39
Bressay	Shetld	HU5040	60°8·8'	1°5·5'W	X	4
Bressay Sound	Shetld	HU4841	60°9·3'	1°7·6'W	W	4
Bressigarth	Orkney	HY6940	59°15·0'	2°32·1'W	X	5
Bressingham	Norf	TM0780	52°23·0'	1°2·9'E	T	144
Bressingham Common	Norf	TM0982	52°24·0'	1°4·7'E	T	144
Bressingham Fen	Norf	TM0680	52°23·0'	1°2·0'E	X	144
Brestbaily	Powys	SN9838	52°2·1'	3°28·8'W	X	160
Brest Cwm-Llwyd	Carm	SN7019	51°51·5'	3°52·9'W	X	160
Brest Rhiw-ddu	Carm	SN7319	51°51·5'	3°50·3'W	X	160
Brest Rocks	S Ayr	NS1905	55°18·6'	4°50·7'W	X	70,76
Brest Twrch	Carm	SN8020	51°52·2'	3°44·2'W	X	160
Brest y Rhôs	Carm	SN7621	51°52·7'	3°47·7'W	X	160
Bretasker	N Eil	NF9593	57°49·6'	7°7·8'W	X	18
Bretby	Derby	SK2923	52°48·5'	1°33·8'W	T	128
Bretby Hall (Hospital)	Derby	SK3022	52°47·9'	1°32·9'W	X	128
Bretchel	Shrops	SJ3311	52°41·8'	2°59·1'W	X	126
Bretch, The	Oxon	SP4339	52°3·1'	1°22·0'W	X	151
Bretford	Warw	SP4277	52°23·6'	1°22·6'W	T	140
Bretforton	Worcs	SP0943	52°5·4'	1°51·7'W	T	150
Bretherdale Bank	Cumbr	NY5605	54°26·6'	2°40·3'W	X	90
Bretherdale Beck	Cumbr	NY5804	54°26·0'	2°38·4'W	W	91
Bretherdale Common	Cumbr	NY5803	54°25·5'	2°38·4'W	X	91
Bretherdale Hall	Cumbr	NY5904	54°26·0'	2°37·5'W	X	91
Bretherdale Head	Cumbr	NY5705	54°26·6'	2°39·4'W	X	91
Bretherton	Lancs	SD4720	53°40·7'	2°47·7'W	T	102
Brethren	Shetld	HU4847	60°12·5'	1°7·5'W	X	3
Bretney	I of M	SC3699	54°21·9'	4°30·0'W	X	95
Bretons	Hav	TQ5184	51°32·3'	0°11·0'E	X	177
Brettabister	Shetld	HU4857	60°17·9'	1°7·4'W	T	2,3
Brettanby Fm	N Yks	NZ2210	54°29·3'	1°39·2'W	FM	93
Brettanby Manor	N Yks	NZ2209	54°28·8'	1°39·2'W	X	93
Brettanby Plantn	N Yks	NZ2210	54°29·3'	1°39·2'W	F	93
Brettavale	Orkney	HY3020	59°3·9'	3°12·8'W	X	6
Brettenham	Norf	TL9383	52°24·9'	0°50·7'E	T	144
Brettenham	Suff	TL9653	52°8·7'	0°52·3'E	T	155
Brettenham Heath	Norf	TL9286	52°26·5'	0°49·9'E	X	144
Bretto	Shetld	HU4252	60°15·3'	1°14·0'W	X	3
Brettobreck	Orkney	HY2414	59°0·6'	3°18·9'W	X	6
Brettobreck	Orkney	HY4021	59°4·6'	3°2·3'W	X	5,6
Bretton	Derby	SK2077	53°17·6'	1°41·6'W	T	119
Bretton	Flint	SJ3563	53°9·9'	2°57·9'W	T	117
Bretton	Peterb	TF1600	52°35·4'	0°16·9'W	T	142
Bretton Brook	Derby	SK1978	53°18·2'	1°42·5'W	W	119
Bretton Clough	Derby	SK2078	53°18·2'	1°41·6'W	X	119
Bretton Country Park	Wakf	SE2812	53°36·5'	1°34·2'W	X	110
Bretton Hall	Flint	SJ3663	53°9·9'	2°57·0'W	X	117
Bretton Hall (College)	Wakf	SE2812	53°36·5'	1°34·2'W	X	110
Bretton Wood	Ches	SJ3662	53°9·3'	2°57·0'W	F	117
Brett's Fm	Essex	TL9128	51°55·3'	0°47·1'E	FM	168
Bretts Fm	Thurr	TQ5681	51°30·6'	0°15·3'E	FM	177
Brett's Hall	Essex	TM1323	51°52·1'	1°6·0'E	X	168,169
Brevig	N Eil	NL6998	56°57·5'	7°26·3'W	T	31
Brevig Bay	N Eil	NL6998	56°57·5'	7°26·3'W	W	31
Brew	Corn	SW3725	50°4·3'	5°40·2'W	X	203
Brewers	Devon	SX4288	50°40·5'	4°13·8'W	X	190
Brewers Castle	Somer	SS8829	51°3·2'	3°35·5'W	A	181
Brewer's End	Essex	TL5521	51°52·2'	0°15·5'E	T	167
Brewers Fm	Somer	ST1028	51°2·9'	3°16·7'W	FM	181,193
Brewer's Grave	Lincs	SK8433	52°53·5'	0°44·7'W	X	130
Brewers Green	Norf	TM1080	52°22·9'	1°5·5'E	T	144
Brewer's Hall Fm	Beds	TL1152	52°9·5'	0°22·2'W	FM	153
Brewer's Oak	Shrops	SJ7510	52°41·5'	2°21·8'W	X	127
Brewer Street	Surrey	TQ3251	51°14·8'	0°6·1'W	T	187
Brewers Wood	Kent	TQ7839	51°7·6'	0°33·0'E	F	188
Brewery Fm	Leeds	SE2342	53°52·7'	1°38·6'W	FM	104
Brewery Fm	Suff	TM1554	52°8·8'	1°8·9'E	FM	156
Brewham Brake Fm	Somer	ST7334	51°6·5'	2°22·8'W	FM	183
Brewhamfield Fm	Somer	ST7138	51°8·7'	2°24·5'W	FM	183
Brewham Ho	Somer	ST7237	51°8·1'	2°23·6'W	X	183
Brewham Lodge Fm	Somer	ST7436	51°7·6'	2°21·9'W	FM	183
Brew Ho	Suff	TM3345	52°3·5'	1°24·3'E	X	169
Brewhurst Mill	W Susx	TQ0431	51°4·4'	0°30·5'W	X	186
Brewing Scar	D & G	NY1263	54°57·5'	3°22·0'W	X	85
Brewlands	Angus	NO1960	56°43·7'	3°19·0'W	X	43
Brewlands Bridge	Angus	NO1961	56°44·3'	3°19·0'W	X	43
Brewood	Staffs	SJ8808	52°40·4'	2°10·2'W	T	127
Brewood Park Fm	Staffs	SJ8906	52°39·3'	2°9·4'W	FM	127,139
Brewsdale	N Yks	NZ4610	54°29·2'	1°17·0'W	X	93
Brewshott	S Lanak	NS9350	55°44·2'	3°41·8'W	X	65,72
Brewster Hill	N Yks	SE5292	54°19·5'	1°11·6'W	X	100
Brewsterwells	Fife	NO4809	56°16·5'	2°49·9'W	X	59
Brewston	Angus	NO5867	56°47·8'	2°40·8'W	X	44
Brewthin	Aberd	NJ7805	57°8·4'	2°21·4'W	X	38
Brexworthy	Devon	SS2813	50°53·7'	4°26·4'W	X	190
Breydon Water	Norf	TG4806	52°35·9'	1°40·1'E	W	134
Briach	Moray	NJ0954	57°34·3'	3°30·8'W	X	27
Briach Ty Du	Gwyn	SH6562	53°8·5'	4°0·7'W	X	115
Briaghlann	Highld	NM4166	56°43·1'	6°13·5'W	W	47
Brian Choille	Highld	NM8570	56°46·6'	5°30·7'W	X	40
Brian Choille	Highld	NN0684	56°54·7'	5°10·7'W	X	41
Briantspuddle	Dorset	SY8193	50°44·4'	2°15·8'W	T	194
Briarcroft Fm	Devon	SS4511	50°52·9'	4°11·8'W	FM	190
Briar Dene	Ghead	NZ2357	54°54·7'	1°38·0'W	X	88
Briar Dykes	Durham	NY9519	54°34·2'	2°4·2'W	X	91,92
Briar Edge	Shrops	SO4286	52°28·4'	2°50·8'W	X	137
Briar Fm	Norf	TM2583	52°24·1'	1°18·9'E	FM	156
Briarhill	Bucks	SP6826	51°55·9'	1°0·3'W	X	164,165
Briar Hill	Northnts	SP7359	52°13·7'	0°55·5'W	T	152
Briar Hill Fm	Glos	SP1637	52°2·1'	1°45·6'W	FM	151
Briar Hill Fm	N Yks	SE4773	54°9·3'	1°16·4'W	FM	100
Briarlands	Stir	NS7498	56°9·7'	4°1·3'W	X	57
Briarlea	Orkney	HY6822	59°5·3'	2°33·0'W	X	5
Briarpool Fm	Ches	SJ7265	53°11·1'	2°24·7'W	FM	118
Briarsbank Fm	Bucks	SP7932	51°59·1'	0°50·6'W	FM	152,165
Briars, The	Derby	SK3453	53°4·6'	1°29·1'W	X	119
Briar Stockings	Beds	SP9934	52°0·0'	0°33·1'W	F	153,165
Briarwood	Northum	NY7962	54°57·4'	2°19·2'W	X	86,87
Briarwood Fm	Somer	ST4035	51°6·9'	2°51·0'W	FM	182
Briary Wood	Northnts	SP7242	52°4·5'	0°56·6'W	F	152
Briary Wood	W Berks	SU3372	51°27·0'	1°31·1'W	F	174
Briary Wood Fm	Bucks	SP7241	52°4·0'	0°56·6'W	FM	152
Bribwll	Pemb	SN2029	51°56·1'	4°36·7'W	X	145,158
Brickbarns Fm	Essex	TL6808	51°45·0'	0°26·4'E	FM	167
Brickbarns Fm	Worcs	SO7842	52°4·8'	2°18·9'W	FM	150
Brickbarns Fm	Worcs	SO9052	52°10·2'	2°8·4'W	FM	150
Brick End	Essex	TL5725	51°54·3'	0°17·3'E	T	167
Brickendon	Herts	TL3207	51°45·0'	0°4·9'W	T	166
Brickendonbury	Herts	TL3310	51°46·6'	0°3·9'W	A	166
Brickendon Grange	Herts	TL3107	51°45·0'	0°5·7'W	X	166
Bricket Wood	Herts	TL1302	51°42·5'	0°21·5'W	T	166
Bricket Wood Common	Herts	TL1200	51°41·5'	0°22·4'W	F	166
Brickfield Fm	Leic	SK7915	52°43·8'	0°49·4'W	FM	129
Brickfield Fm	Oxon	SP4034	52°0·4'	1°24·6'W	FM	151
Brickfield Ho	N Yks	SE4165	54°5·0'	1°22·0'W	X	99
Brickfields	Worcs	SO8656	52°12·4'	2°11·9'W	T	150
Brick Garth Plantn	N Yks	SE0990	54°18·6'	1°51·3'W	F	99
Brickhall	Pth & Kin	NO1316	56°20·0'	3°24·0'W	X	58
Brickhill	Beds	TL0552	52°9·6'	0°27·5'W	T	153
Brick Hill	Dorset	SY7485	50°40·1'	2°21·7'W	X	194
Brick Hill	Surrey	SU9564	51°22·3'	0°37·7'W	T	175,176,186
Brick Hill	Wilts	ST8646	51°13·0'	2°11·6'W	X	183
Brickhill Fm	N Yks	SE6824	53°42·7'	0°57·8'W	FM	105,106
Brickhill Pastures	Beds	TL0539	52°2·6'	0°27·7'W	X	153
Brickhills Fm	N Lincs	SE9708	53°33·8'	0°31·7'W	FM	112
Brick Ho	Ches	SJ8256	53°6·3'	2°15·7'W	X	118
Brick Ho	Essex	TL5311	51°46·8'	0°13·5'E	X	167
Brick Ho	Essex	TL6011	51°46·7'	0°19·6'E	X	167
Brick Ho	Essex	TL6520	51°51·5'	0°24·2'E	X	167
Brick Ho	Essex	TQ8991	51°35·4'	0°44·1'E	X	178
Brick Ho	Lancs	SD3643	53°53·0'	2°58·0'W	X	102
Brick Ho	Lancs	SD6834	53°48·3'	2°28·7'W	X	103
Brick Ho	Newp	ST4084	51°33·3'	2°51·5'W	X	171,172
Brick Ho	N Yks	SE3596	54°21·7'	1°27·3'W	X	99
Brick Ho	Shrops	SO4674	52°21·9'	2°47·2'W	X	137,138,148
Brick Ho	Shrops	SO6174	52°22·0'	2°34·0'W	X	138
Brickhouse	D & G	NX9760	54°55·7'	3°36·0'W	X	84
Brick House	Essex	TL4933	51°58·8'	0°10·6'E	A	167
Brick House End	Essex	TL4628	51°56·1'	0°7·8'E	T	167
Brick House Fm	Essex	TL5434	51°59·2'	0°15·0'E	FM	154
Brickhouse Fm	Essex	TL8516	51°48·9'	0°41·4'E	FM	168
Brick House Fm	Essex	TL8531	51°57·0'	0°41·9'E	FM	168
Brick House Fm	Essex	TL8903	51°41·9'	0°44·5'E	FM	168
Brick House Fm	Essex	TL9603	51°41·7'	0°50·6'E	FM	168
Brickhouse Fm	Essex	TM0127	51°54·5'	0°55·7'E	FM	168
Brickhouse Fm	Essex	TQ5996	51°38·6'	0°18·3'E	FM	167,177
Brickhouse Fm	Essex	TQ8595	51°37·6'	0°40·8'E	FM	168
Brickhouse Fm	E Susx	TQ5936	51°6·3'	0°16·7'E	FM	188
Brick House Fm	Hants	SU7860	51°20·3'	0°52·4'W	FM	175,186
Brickhouse Fm	Heref	SO6457	52°12·8'	2°31·2'W	FM	149
Brick House Fm	Herts	TL4131	51°57·8'	0°3·5'E	FM	167
Brick House Fm	Herts	TL4211	51°47·0'	0°3·9'E	FM	167
Brick House Fm	Medway	TQ8277	51°28·0'	0°37·6'E	FM	178
Brick House Fm	N Yks	SE1749	53°56·5'	1°44·0'W	FM	104
Brickhouse Fm	Somer	ST6941	51°10·3'	2°26·2'W	FM	183
Brickhouse Fm	Somer	ST7431	51°4·9'	2°21·9'W	FM	183
Brickhouse Fm	Suff	TL7954	52°9·5'	0°37·4'E	FM	155
Brickhouse Fm	Suff	TL8351	52°7·8'	0°40·8'E	FM	155
Brickhouse Fm	Suff	TL9851	52°7·5'	0°54·0'E	FM	155
Brickhouse Fm	Worcs	SO8663	52°16·1'	2°11·9'W	FM	150
Brickhouse Fm	Worcs	SO9467	52°18·3'	2°4·9'W	FM	150
Brickhouses	Ches	SJ7762	53°9·5'	2°20·2'W	T	118
Brick Houses	Sheff	SK3081	53°19·7'	1°32·6'W	T	110,111
Brickhurst Fm	E Susx	TQ5013	50°54·0'	0°8·4'E	FM	199
Brickhurst Wood	E Susx	TQ7527	51°1·2'	0°30·1'E	F	188,199
Brickhurst Wood	E Susx	TQ8526	51°0·4'	0°38·6'E	F	189,199
Brickkiln Copse	Wilts	SU3169	51°25·4'	1°32·9'W	F	174
Brickkiln Cott	Herts	SP9910	51°47·0'	0°33·5'W	X	165
Brickkiln Covert	Norf	TL9291	52°29·2'	0°50·1'E	F	144
Brick-kiln End	Notts	SK5856	53°6·1'	1°7·6'W	T	120
Brickkiln Fm	Essex	TM1829	51°55·2'	1°10·6'E	FM	168,169
Brick Kiln Fm	E Susx	TQ6730	51°2·9'	0°23·3'E	FM	188
Brick Kiln Fm	Hants	SU6629	51°3·6'	1°3·1'W	FM	185,186
Brick Kiln Fm	Norf	TF9102	52°35·2'	0°49·6'E	FM	144
Brick Kiln Fm	Norf	TF9509	52°38·8'	0°53·4'E	FM	144
Brick Kiln Fm	Norf	TF9815	52°42·0'	0°56·2'E	FM	132
Brick Kiln Fm	Norf	TG0723	52°46·1'	1°4·5'E	FM	133
Brick Kiln Fm	Norf	TG1301	52°34·1'	1°9·0'E	FM	144
Brickkiln Fm	Norf	TL7489	52°28·5'	0°34·5'E	FM	143
Brickkiln Fm	Norf	TL7889	52°28·4'	0°37·7'E	FM	144
Brick Kiln Fm	Northnts	SP7547	52°7·2'	0°53·9'W	FM	152
Brick Kiln Fm	Shrops	SJ5543	52°59·2'	2°40·0'W	FM	117
Brickkiln Fm	Suff	TL7585	52°26·3'	0°34·9'E	FM	143
Brick Kiln Fm	Suff	TM3168	52°15·9'	1°23·5'E	FM	156
Brick Kiln Fm	Suff	TM3472	52°18·0'	1°26·3'E	FM	156
Brick Kiln Fm	Suff	TM4180	52°22·1'	1°32·8'E	FM	156
Brick Kiln Fm	Suff	TM4186	52°25·4'	1°33·1'E	FM	156
Brick Kiln Fm	Suff	TM4980	52°21·9'	1°39·9'E	FM	156
Brick Kiln Fm	Warw	SP2848	52°8·0'	1°35·1'W	FM	151
Brickkiln Fm	W Susx	SU8312	50°54·3'	0°48·8'W	FM	197
Brick Kiln Fm	W Susx	TQ1524	51°0·5'	0°21·3'W	FM	198
Brick Kiln Gorse	Warw	SP2848	52°8·0'	1°35·1'W	F	151
Brickkiln Green	Essex	TL7331	51°57·3'	0°31·5'E	T	167
Brick Kiln Hill	Leic	SP4495	52°33·3'	1°20·7'W	X	140
Brick Kiln Inclosure	Hants	SU2906	50°51·4'	1°34·9'W	F	196
Brick Kiln Plantation	Donc	SE5510	53°35·3'	1°9·7'W	F	111
Brick Kiln Plantn	Northum	NT9142	55°40·5'	2°8·2'W	F	74,75
Brick Kiln Plantn	Suff	TL8567	52°16·4'	0°43·1'E	F	155
Brick Kilns Fm	Cambs	TL2987	52°28·2'	0°5·7'W	FM	142
Brick Kiln Walks	Suff	TM4471	52°17·2'	1°35·1'E	X	156
Brickkiln Wood	Hants	SU4845	51°12·4'	1°18·4'W	F	185
Brick Kiln Wood	Heref	SO5434	52°0·4'	2°39·8'W	F	149
Brickkiln Wood	Herts	TL1323	51°53·9'	0°21·1'W	F	166
Brickkiln Wood	W Berks	SU4769	51°25·3'	1°19·1'W	F	174
Bricklands Fm	Northnts	SP5233	51°59·8'	1°14·2'W	FM	151
Brickledon's Fm	Hants	SU6561	51°20·9'	1°3·6'W	FM	175,186
Bricklehampton	Worcs	SO9842	52°4·8'	2°1·4'W	T	150
Bricklehurst Manor	E Susx	TQ6529	51°2·4'	0°21·6'E	X	188,199
Brickles Wood	Dorset	ST7312	50°54·6'	2°22·7'W	F	194
Brickles Wood	Essex	TL5510	51°46·3'	0°15·2'E	F	167
Bricksbury Hill	Surrey	SU8349	51°14·3'	0°48·3'W	X	186
Brickshed Cott	N Yks	SE4688	54°17·4'	1°17·2'W	X	100
Brickwall Fm	Beds	TL0838	52°2·0'	0°25·1'W	FM	153
Brickwall Fm	Ches	SJ6443	52°59·2'	2°31·8'W	FM	118
Brickwall Fm	Essex	TL9622	51°52·0'	0°51·2'E	FM	168
Brickwall Fm	Kent	TR0418	50°55·7'	0°54·6'E	FM	189
Brickwalls	Shrops	SJ5137	52°55·9'	2°43·3'W	X	126
Brickworth Ho	Wilts	SU2224	51°1·1'	1°40·8'W	X	184
Brickyard Fm	Cambs	TL1677	52°23·0'	0°17·3'W	FM	142
Brickyard Fm	Cambs	TL1881	52°25·1'	0°15·5'W	FM	142
Brickyard Fm	E Yorks	SE7542	53°52·4'	0°51·1'W	FM	105,106
Brickyard Fm	Lincs	TF1975	53°15·8'	0°12·5'W	FM	122
Brickyard Fm	Monm	ST4398	51°40·9'	2°49·1'W	FM	171
Brickyard Fm	Notts	SK7150	53°2·8'	0°56·0'W	FM	120
Brickyard Fm	N Yks	SE2983	54°14·8'	1°32·9'W	FM	99
Brickyard Fm	N Yks	SE6976	54°10·7'	0°56·1'W	FM	100
Brickyard Fm	N Yks	SE7474	54°9·6'	0°51·6'W	FM	100
Brick Yard Fm	N Yks	SE7884	54°15·0'	0°47·8'W	FM	100
Briddellarw	Gwyn	SH7106	52°38·4'	3°54·0'W	X	124
Briddicott Fm	Somer	ST0041	51°9·8'	3°25·4'W	FM	181
Briddlesford Lodge	I of W	SZ5390	50°42·7'	1°14·6'W	X	196
Briddon Weir Fm	Ches	SJ7584	53°21·4'	2°22·1'W	FM	109
Bride	I of M	NX4401	54°23·1'	4°23·7'W	T	95
Bride Cross Ho	N Yks	SE1949	53°56·4'	1°42·2'W	X	104
Bride Hall	Herts	TL1915	51°49·5'	0°16·0'W	X	166
Bridehead	Dorset	SY5888	50°41·6'	2°35·3'W	X	194
Bridekirk	Cumbr	NY1133	54°41·3'	3°22·4'W	T	89
Bridell	Pemb	SN1742	52°3·0'	4°39·7'W	X	145
Briden's Camp	Herts	TL0411	51°47·5'	0°29·1'W	X	166
Brides Fm	Herts	TL3510	51°46·6'	0°2·2'W	FM	166
Bride's Hole	Northum	NU1442	55°40·5'	1°46·2'W	X	75
Bride's Ness	Orkney	HY7752	59°21·5'	2°23·8'W	X	5
Bride Stones	N Yks	SE5797	54°22·2'	1°6·9'W	A	100
Bridestones	N Yks	SE8791	54°18·7'	0°39·3'W	X	94,101
Bridestones	Staffs	SJ9062	53°9·5'	2°8·6'W	X	118
Bride Stones Moor	Cald	SD9326	53°44·1'	2°6·0'W	H	103
Bridestowe	Devon	SX5189	50°41·1'	4°6·2'W	T	191
Bridestowe and Sourton Common	Devon	SX5588	50°40·7'	4°2·8'W	X	191
Brideswell	Aberd	NJ5739	57°26·6'	2°42·5'W	T	29
Bridewell	Devon	SY3699	50°47·5'	2°54·1'W	X	193
Bridewell Fm	Oxon	SP3714	51°49·6'	1°27·4'W	FM	164
Bridford	Devon	SX8186	50°39·9'	3°40·7'W	T	191
Bridfordmills	Devon	SX8387	50°40·5'	3°39·0'W	T	191
Bridford Wood	Devon	SX8088	50°41·0'	3°41·5'W	F	191
Bridge	Corn	SW6744	50°15·2'	5°15·8'W	T	203
Bridge	Corn	SW7229	50°7·3'	5°11·0'W	T	204
Bridge	Kent	TR1854	51°14·8'	1°7·8'E	T	179,189
Bridge	Powys	SJ2312	52°42·3'	3°8·0'W	X	126
Bridge	Somer	ST3605	50°50·7'	2°54·2'W	T	193
Bridge Ball	Devon	SS7446	51°12·2'	3°47·8'W	T	180
Bridgebank	D & G	NX0756	54°51·9'	5°0·0'W	X	82
Bridge Barn	Warw	SP3668	52°18·8'	1°27·9'W	X	151
Bridge Castle	W Loth	NS9470	55°54·9'	3°41·3'W	X	65
Bridgechapel	Cambs	TL3167	52°17·4'	0°4·4'W	A	153
Bridge Close Fm	Somer	ST5011	50°54·0'	2°42·3'W	FM	194
Bridge Cottages	Cumbr	SD7198	54°22·8'	2°26·4'W	X	98
Bridge Court	Heref	SO2448	52°7·7'	3°6·2'W	X	148
Bridge Court	Heref	SO4236	52°1·4'	2°50·3'W	X	149,161
Bridgecourt	I of W	SZ5281	50°37·8'	1°15·5'W	X	196
Bridgedale Brow	Cumbr	NY6416	54°32·5'	2°33·0'W	X	91
Bridge End	Beds	TL0050	52°8·6'	0°31·9'W	T	153
Bridge End	Cumbr	NY3748	54°49·6'	2°58·4'W	T	85
Bridge End	Cumbr	NY5100	54°23·8'	2°44·9'W	X	90
Bridge End	Cumbr	NY5905	54°26·6'	2°37·5'W	X	91
Bridge End	Cumbr	NY6325	54°37·4'	2°34·0'W	X	91
Bridge End	Cumbr	SD2490	54°18·2'	3°9·7'W	X	96
Bridge End	Cumbr	SD6392	54°19·6'	2°33·7'W	X	97
Bridge End	Derby	SK2472	53°14·9'	1°38·0'W	X	119
Bridge End	Devon	SX6946	50°18·2'	3°50·0'W	T	202
Bridge End	Devon	SY0989	50°41·8'	3°16·9'W	T	192
Bridge End	Durham	NY9650	54°50·9'	2°3·3'W	X	87
Bridge End	Durham	NZ0136	54°43·4'	1°58·6'W	T	92
Bridge End	Essex	TL6731	51°57·4'	0°26·2'E	T	167
Bridge-end	Falk	NS8786	56°3·5'	3°48·4'W	X	65
Bridge End	Flint	SJ3157	53°6·6'	3°1·4'W	T	117
Bridge End	Heref	SO6246	52°6·9'	2°32·9'W	T	149
Bridge End	Lancs	SD8240	53°51·6'	2°16·0'W	X	103
Bridge End	Lincs	TF1436	52°54·8'	0°17·9'W	T	130
Bridge End	Northum	NT9631	55°34·6'	2°3·4'W	X	74,75
Bridge End	Northum	NU1013	55°24·9'	1°50·1'W	X	81
Bridge End	Northum	NY6761	54°56·8'	2°30·5'W	X	86,87
Bridge End	Northum	NY9166	54°59·6'	2°8·0'W	T	87
Bridge End	Northum	NY9464	54°58·5'	2°5·2'W	T	87
Bridge End	Northum	NZ0871	55°2·3'	1°52·1'W	X	88
Bridge End	Oxon	SU5793	51°38·2'	1°10·2'W	T	164,174
Bridge End	Powys	SO2666	52°17·5'	3°4·7'W	X	137,148

Bridge End	Shetld	HU3733	60°5·1′	1°19·6′W	T	4
Bridge End	Staffs	SK0862	53°9·5′	1°52·4′W	X	119
Bridge-end	Staffs	SK1260	53°8·5′	1°48·8′W	X	119
Bridge End	Surrey	TQ0757	51°18·3′	0°27·5′W	T	187
Bridge End	Warw	SP2864	52°16·6′	1°35·0′W	T	151
Bridge End	W Loth	NT0768	55°54·0′	3°28·8′W	X	65
Bridge End	Worcs	SO8031	51°58·9′	2°17·1′W	T	150
Bridge End Causeway	Lincs	TF1536	52°54·8′	0°17·0′W	X	130
Bridge-end Cleuch	D & G	NS7711	55°22·9′	3°56·1′W	X	71,78
Bridge End Cott	Cumbr	SD7784	54°15·3′	2°20·8′W	X	98
Bridge End East	Cumbr	SD7290	54°18·5′	2°25·4′W	X	98
Bridge End Fm	Cumbr	NY3119	54°33·9′	3°3·6′W	FM	90
Bridge End Fm	N Yks	SD9944	53°53·8′	2°0·5′W	FM	103
Bridge End Fm	N Yks	SE0082	54°14·3′	1°59·6′W	FM	98
Bridge End Fm	N Yks	SE2659	54°1·8′	1°35·8′W	FM	104
Bridge End Fm	N Yks	SE3679	54°12·6′	1°26·5′W	FM	99
Bridge End Hill	Scot Bord	NT2322	55°29·4′	3°12·7′W	H	73
Bridge End Ho	Cumbr	NY7145	54°48·2′	2°26·6′W	X	86,87
Bridge-end Pasture	Derby	SK1788	53°23·6′	1°44·3′W	X	110
Bridgefield	C of Aber	NJ9012	57°12·2′	2°9·5′W	T	38
Bridgefield	Cumbr	SD2986	54°16·1′	3°5·0′W	X	96,97
Bridgefield	Derby	SK0479	53°18·7′	1°56·0′W	X	119
Bridge Fm	Bucks	SP7527	51°56·4′	0°54·1′W	FM	165
Bridge Fm	Caer	ST2385	51°33·8′	3°6·3′W	FM	171
Bridge Fm	Cambs	TL2846	52°6·1′	0°7·5′W	FM	153
Bridge Fm	Cambs	TL4073	52°20·5′	0°3·7′E	FM	154
Bridge Fm	Cambs	TL5887	52°27·7′	0°19·9′E	FM	143
Bridge Fm	Ches	SJ3462	53°9·3′	2°58·8′W	FM	117
Bridge Fm	Ches	SJ6149	53°2·5′	2°34·5′W	FM	118
Bridge Fm	Ches	SJ6450	53°3·0′	2°31·8′W	FM	118
Bridge Fm	Ches	SJ6870	53°13·8′	2°28·4′W	FM	118
Bridge Fm	Ches	SJ7263	53°10·0′	2°24·7′W	FM	118
Bridge Fm	Corn	SX3975	50°33·4′	4°16·0′W	FM	201
Bridge Fm	Devon	SS6502	50°48·3′	3°54·6′W	FM	191
Bridge Fm	Devon	SX9397	50°46·0′	3°30·7′W	FM	192
Bridge Fm	Dorset	SU0708	50°52·5′	1°53·6′W	FM	195
Bridge Fm	Essex	TL5400	51°40·9′	0°14·1′E	FM	167
Bridge Fm	Essex	TL6106	51°44·0′	0°20·3′E	FM	167
Bridge Fm	Essex	TL9412	51°46·6′	0°49·1′E	FM	168
Bridge Fm	E Yorks	TA2331	53°45·9′	0°7·6′W	FM	107
Bridge Fm	Heref	SO4430	51°58·2′	2°48·5′W	FM	149,161
Bridge Fm	Herts	TL3024	51°54·2′	0°6·2′W	FM	166
Bridge Fm	I of W	SZ5181	50°37·8′	1°16·4′W	FM	196
Bridge Fm	Kent	TQ9239	51°7·3′	0°45·0′E	FM	189
Bridge Fm	Kent	TQ9629	51°1·8′	0°48·1′E	FM	189
Bridge Fm	Kent	TQ9931	51°2·9′	0°50·7′E	FM	189
Bridge Fm	Kent	TR0227	51°0·6′	0°53·2′E	FM	189
Bridge Fm	Kent	TR0433	51°3·8′	0°55·1′E	FM	179,189
Bridge Fm	Leic	SK7026	52°49·9′	0°57·3′W	FM	129
Bridge Fm	Leic	SP4595	52°33·3′	1°19·8′W	FM	140
Bridge Fm	Lincs	SK8346	53°0·5′	0°45·4′W	FM	130
Bridge Fm	Lincs	TA0308	53°33·7′	0°26·3′W	FM	112
Bridge Fm	Lincs	TA0407	53°33·2′	0°25·4′W	FM	112
Bridge Fm	Lincs	TF2556	53°5·4′	0°7·6′W	FM	122
Bridge Fm	Lincs	TF4823	52°47·3′	0°12·1′E	FM	131
Bridge Fm	Lincs	TF5369	53°12·0′	0°17·8′E	FM	122
Bridge Fm	N Ayr	NR9231	55°32·0′	5°17·3′W	FM	68,69
Bridge Fm	N Lincs	SE9810	53°34·9′	0°30·8′W	FM	112
Bridge Fm	N Lincs	SK7797	53°28·1′	0°50·0′W	FM	112
Bridge Fm	Norf	TF5903	52°36·3′	0°21·3′E	FM	143
Bridge Fm	Norf	TG2437	52°53·3′	1°20·2′E	FM	133
Bridge Fm	Norf	TG2732	52°50·5′	1°22·6′E	FM	133
Bridge Fm	Norf	TM1482	52°23·9′	1°9·1′E	FM	144,156
Bridge Fm	N Yks	SE4777	54°11·4′	1°16·4′W	FM	100
Bridge Fm	N Yks	SE6364	54°4·3′	1°1·8′W	FM	100
Bridge Fm	N Yks	SE7381	54°13·4′	0°52·4′W	FM	100
Bridge Fm	Oxon	SP6218	51°51·7′	1°5·6′W	FM	164,165
Bridge Fm	Oxon	SU5293	51°38·2′	1°14·5′W	FM	164,174
Bridge Fm	Pemb	SN0238	52°0·6′	4°52·7′W	FM	145,157
Bridge Fm	Pth & Kin	NO1638	56°31·8′	3°21·5′W	FM	53
Bridge Fm	Shrops	SJ5232	52°53·2′	2°42·4′W	FM	126
Bridge Fm	Somer	ST3252	51°16·0′	2°58·1′W	FM	182
Bridge Fm	Somer	ST5536	51°7·5′	2°38·2′W	FM	182,183
Bridge Fm	St Hel	SJ5289	53°24·0′	2°42·9′W	FM	108
Bridge Fm	Suff	TL8761	52°13·2′	0°44·7′E	FM	155
Bridge Fm	Suff	TL9147	52°5·5′	0°47·7′E	FM	155
Bridge Fm	Suff	TL9270	52°17·9′	0°49·4′E	FM	144,155
Bridge Fm	Suff	TL9348	52°6·0′	0°49·5′E	FM	155
Bridge Fm	Suff	TL9468	52°16·8′	0°51·0′E	FM	155
Bridge Fm	Suff	TM0156	52°10·2′	0°56·8′E	FM	155
Bridge Fm	Suff	TM0460	52°12·3′	0°59·5′E	FM	155
Bridge Fm	Suff	TM3577	52°20·7′	1°27·4′E	FM	156
Bridge Fm	Suff	TM3973	52°18·4′	1°30·8′E	FM	156
Bridge Fm	Suff	TM4770	52°16·6′	1°37·7′E	FM	156
Bridge Fm	Warw	SP1547	52°7·5′	1°46·5′W	FM	151
Bridge Fm	Wilts	SU1528	51°3·3′	1°46·8′W	FM	184
Bridge Fm	Wok	SU7467	51°24·1′	0°55·8′W	FM	175
Bridge Fm	Worcs	SO7966	52°17·7′	2°18·1′W	FM	138,150
Bridge Fm	Wrekin	SJ7118	52°45·8′	2°25·4′W	FM	127
Bridge Fm	W Susx	SU8501	50°48·4′	0°47·2′W	FM	197
Bridgefoot	Aberd	NJ4103	57°7·1′	2°58·0′W	X	37
Bridgefoot	Aberd	NJ7114	57°13·2′	2°28·4′W	X	38
Bridgefoot	Aberd	NJ9017	57°14·9′	2°9·5′W	X	38
Bridgefoot	Aberd	NJ9232	57°23·0′	2°7·5′W	X	30
Bridgefoot	Aberd	NK0034	57°24·0′	1°59·5′W	X	30
Bridgefoot	Angus	NO3735	56°30·4′	3°1·0′W	T	54
Bridgefoot	Cambs	TL4042	52°3·7′	0°2·9′E	X	154
Bridgefoot	Cumbr	NY0529	54°39·1′	3°27·9′W	T	89
Bridgefoot	Herts	TL2300	51°41·3′	0°12·8′W	X	166
Bridgefoot	Herts	TL4321	51°52·4′	0°5·0′E	X	167
Bridgefoot Fm	Essex	TL5418	51°50·6′	0°14·5′E	FM	167
Bridgeford	Northum	NY8582	55°8·2′	2°13·7′W	X	80
Bridge Grange Fm	N Yks	SE2887	54°16·9′	1°33·8′W	FM	99
Bridge Green	Essex	TL4636	52°0·4′	0°8·0′E	T	154
Bridge Green	Norf	TM1483	52°24·4′	1°9·2′E	T	144,156
Bridgeham Grange	Surrey	TQ3142	51°10·0′	0°7·2′W	X	187
Bridgehampton	Somer	ST5624	51°1·1′	2°37·3′W	T	183
Bridgehaugh	Moray	NJ3435	57°24·3′	3°5·4′W	X	28
Bridge Hewick	N Yks	SE3370	54°7·7′	1°29·3′W	T	99
Bridgehill	Durham	NZ0951	54°51·5′	1°51·2′W	T	88
Bridgehill	N Lanak	NS8765	55°52·2′	3°47·9′W	X	65
Bridge Hill	N Lincs	TA0921	53°40·7′	0°20·6′W	X	107,112
Bridge Hill	Surrey	SU9154	51°16·9′	0°41·3′W	X	186
Bridgehill Fm	W Susx	TQ1122	50°59·4′	0°24·7′W	FM	198
Bridge Ho	Arg & Bt	NR3156	55°43·6′	6°16·6′W	X	60
Bridge Ho	Brad	SE0247	53°55·4′	1°57·8′W	X	104
Bridge Ho	Cumbr	NY2749	54°50·1′	3°7·8′W	X	85
Bridge Ho	Cumbr	NY3022	54°35·5′	3°4·6′W	X	90
Bridge Ho	Cumbr	SD4288	54°17·3′	2°53·0′W	X	96,97
Bridge Ho	Durham	NZ1824	54°36·9′	1°42·9′W	X	92
Bridge Ho	Durham	NZ3731	54°40·6′	1°25·1′W	X	93
Bridge Ho	Lincs	TF2760	53°7·6′	0°5·7′W	X	122
Bridge Ho	Mil Key	SP8845	52°6·0′	0°42·5′W	X	152
Bridge Ho	Northum	NY8279	55°6·6′	2°16·5′W	X	86,87
Bridge Ho	Notts	SK6688	53°23·3′	1°0·0′W	X	111,120
Bridge Ho	Shrops	SO5271	52°20·3′	2°41·9′W	X	137,138
Bridgeholm Fm	S Lanak	NS7345	55°41·2′	4°0·8′W	FM	64
Bridgeholm Green	Derby	SK0481	53°19·8′	1°56·0′W	T	110
Bridge House	Cumbr	NY3704	54°25·9′	2°57·9′W	X	90
Bridgehouse	D & G	NX4344	54°46·2′	4°26·0′W	X	83
Bridgehouse Fm	Cambs	TL3397	52°33·5′	0°1·9′W	FM	142
Bridgehouse Fm	Ches	SJ7553	53°4·7′	2°22·0′W	FM	118
Bridgehouse Fm	Ches	SJ7656	53°6·3′	2°21·1′W	FM	118
Bridgehouse Fm	E Ayr	NS4334	55°34·7′	4°29·0′W	FM	70
Bridge House Fm	E Yorks	TA0349	53°55·8′	0°25·5′W	FM	107
Bridge House Fm	Lincs	TF2915	52°43·3′	0°5·0′W	FM	131
Bridgehouse Gate	N Yks	SE1565	54°5·1′	1°45·8′W	T	99
Bridgelands	Scot Bord	NT4830	55°33·9′	2°49·0′W	T	73
Bridgelands Fm	Suff	TL7156	52°10·8′	0°30·5′E	FM	154
Bridgelands Fm	W Susx	SU8421	50°59·2′	0°47·8′W	FM	197
Bridge Lane	Dorset	SY6082	50°38·4′	2°33·6′W	X	194
Bridgemacote	Glos	SO7615	51°50·2′	2°20·5′W	X	162
Bridgemans Fm	Essex	TM0003	51°41·6′	0°54·0′E	FM	168
Bridgemark	D & G	NX6290	55°11·4′	4°9·6′W	X	77
Bridgemarsh Creek	Essex	TQ8897	51°38·6′	0°43·4′E	W	168
Bridgemarsh Island	Essex	TQ8996	51°38·1′	0°44·3′E	X	168
Bridgemary	Hants	SU5803	50°49·6′	1°10·2′W	T	196
Bridgemere	Ches	SJ7145	53°0·3′	2°25·5′W	T	118
Bridgemere Fm	Ches	SJ7244	52°59·8′	2°24·6′W	FM	118
Bridgemere Fm	Leic	SP6187	52°28·9′	1°5·7′W	FM	140
Bridgemere Garden World	Ches	SJ7243	52°59·3′	2°24·6′W	X	118
Bridgemere Hall	Ches	SJ7145	53°0·3′	2°25·5′W	X	118
Bridge Mill	Northum	NU0244	55°41·6′	1°57·7′W	X	75
Bridgemont	Derby	SK0182	53°20·3′	1°58·7′W	T	110
Bridgemuir	D & G	NY0984	55°8·8′	3°25·2′W	X	78
Bridgend	Aberd	NJ4203	57°7·1′	2°57·0′W	X	37
Bridgend	Aberd	NJ4719	57°15·8′	2°52·3′W	X	37
Bridgend	Aberd	NJ5002	57°6·6′	2°49·1′W	X	37
Bridgend	Aberd	NJ5135	57°24·4′	2°48·5′W	T	29
Bridgend	Aberd	NJ5711	57°11·5′	2°42·2′W	X	37
Bridgend	Aberd	NJ7141	57°27·8′	2°28·5′W	X	29
Bridgend	Aberd	NJ7226	57°19·7′	2°27·4′W	X	38
Bridgend	Aberd	NJ7249	57°32·1′	2°27·6′W	X	29
Bridgend	Aberd	NJ7256	57°35·8′	2°27·6′W	X	29
Bridgend	Aberd	NJ7816	57°14·3′	2°21·4′W	X	38
Bridgend	Aberd	NJ8825	57°19·2′	2°11·5′W	X	38
Bridgend	Aberd	NJ9263	57°39·7′	2°7·6′W	X	30
Bridgend	Aberd	NJ9626	57°19·7′	2°3·5′W	X	38
Bridgend	Aberd	NJ9648	57°31·6′	2°3·5′W	X	30
Bridgend	Aberd	NK0348	57°31·6′	1°56·5′W	X	30
Bridgend	Aberd	NK0636	57°25·1′	1°53·5′W	X	30
Bridgend	Aberd	NO5895	57°2·9′	2°41·1′W	X	37,44
Bridgend	Aberd	NO6498	57°4·6′	2°35·2′W	X	37,45
Bridgend	Aberd	NO8078	56°53·8′	2°19·2′W	X	45
Bridgend	Aberd	NO8481	56°55·5′	2°15·3′W	X	45
Bridgend	Angus	NO3747	56°36·9′	3°1·1′W	T	54
Bridgend	Angus	NO5368	56°48·3′	2°45·7′W	T	44
Bridgend	Arg & Bt	NR3362	55°46·9′	6°15·1′W	T	60,61
Bridgend	Arg & Bt	NR7937	55°34·8′	5°29·9′W	T	68,69
Bridgend	Arg & Bt	NR8592	56°4·6′	5°26·9′W	T	55
Bridgend	Cered	SN1745	52°4·6′	4°39·8′W	T	145
Bridgend	Corn	SX1059	50°24·2′	4°40·1′W	T	200
Bridgend	Cumbr	NY3914	54°31·3′	2°56·1′W	T	90
Bridgend	Devon	SX5548	50°19·1′	4°1·8′W	T	202
Bridgend	E Loth	NT4878	55°59·8′	2°49·6′W	X	66
Bridgend	Fife	NO3912	56°18·0′	2°58·7′W	T	59
Bridgend	Glos	SO8004	51°44·3′	2°17·0′W	T	162
Bridgend	Highld	NH3255	57°33·5′	4°48·0′W	X	26
Bridgend	Highld	NH5459	57°36·1′	4°26·1′W	X	26
Bridgend	Highld	NH7794	57°55·4′	4°4·1′W	X	21
Bridgend	Inverc	NS2172	55°54·7′	4°51·8′W	X	63
Bridgend	Inverc	NS2975	55°56·5′	4°43·8′W	X	63
Bridgend	Moray	NJ1466	57°40·8′	3°26·1′W	X	28
Bridgend	Moray	NJ3731	57°22·2′	3°2·4′W	X	37
Bridgend	N Lanak	NS6870	55°54·6′	4°6·3′W	T	64
Bridgend	Orkney	HY3911	58°59·2′	3°3·2′W	X	6
Bridgend	Pth & Kin	NO0464	56°45·7′	3°33·8′W	X	43
Bridgend	Renf	NS3459	55°48·0′	4°38·5′W	X	63
Bridgend	S Ayr	NS4220	55°27·2′	4°29·5′W	X	70
Bridgend	Scot Bord	NT4712	55°24·2′	2°49·8′W	X	79
Bridgend	W Loth	NT0475	55°57·8′	3°31·8′W	T	65
Bridgend Fm	W Loth	NT0476	55°58·3′	3°31·9′W	FM	65
Bridgend Mains	S Ayr	NS3921	55°27·6′	4°32·4′W	X	70
Bridgend of Kildarroch	D & G	NX6050	54°49·8′	4°10·3′W	X	83
Bridgend of Lintrathen	Angus	NO2854	56°40·6′	3°10·1′W	T	53
Bridgend (Pen-y-bont Ar Ogwr)	Brig	SS9080	51°30·7′	3°34·7′W	T	170
Bridgeness	Falk	NT0181	56°1·0′	3°34·8′W	T	65
Bridge O'Ess	Aberd	NO5097	57°3·9′	2°49·0′W	X	37,44
Bridge of Aird	D & G	NX0760	54°54·1′	5°0·2′W	X	82
Bridge of Alford	Aberd	NJ5617	57°14·8′	2°43·3′W	T	37
Bridge of Allan	Stir	NS7997	56°9·3′	3°56·4′W	T	57
Bridge of Alvah	Aberd	NJ6861	57°38·5′	2°31·7′W	X	29
Bridge of Avon	Moray	NJ1420	57°16·0′	3°25·1′W	X	36
Bridge of Avon	Moray	NJ1835	57°24·1′	3°21·4′W	X	28
Bridge of Awe	Arg & Bt	NN0329	56°25·0′	5°11·2′W	T	50
Bridge of Balgie	Pth & Kin	NN5746	56°35·3′	4°19·3′W	T	51
Bridge of Bogendreip	Aberd	NO6690	57°0·3′	2°33·1′W	X	38,45
Bridge of Brown	Highld	NJ1220	57°16·0′	3°27·1′W	T	36
Bridge of Buthlaw	Aberd	NK0647	57°31·0′	1°53·5′W	X	30
Bridge of Cally	Pth & Kin	NO1451	56°38·8′	3°23·7′W	T	53
Bridge of Canny	Aberd	NO6597	57°4·0′	2°34·2′W	T	38,45
Bridge of Coe	Highld	NN1058	56°40·8′	5°5·6′W	X	41
Bridge of Craigisla	Angus	NO2553	56°40·0′	3°13·0′W	T	53
Bridge of Crathies	Pth & Kin	NO2745	56°35·7′	3°10·9′W	X	53
Bridge of Dee	Aberd	NO1890	56°59·9′	3°20·5′W	X	43
Bridge of Dee	Aberd	NO6995	57°3·0′	2°30·2′W	X	38,45
Bridge of Dee	C of Aber	NJ9203	57°7·3′	2°7·5′W	A	38
Bridge of Dee	D & G	NX7360	54°55·4′	3°58·5′W	T	83,84
Bridge of DERRYBEG	Moray	NJ2440	57°26·9′	3°15·5′W	X	28
Bridge of Don	C of Aber	NJ9409	57°10·6′	2°5·5′W	T	38
Bridge of Dun	Angus	NO6658	56°43·0′	2°32·9′W	T	54
Bridge of Dye	Aberd	NO6586	56°58·1′	2°34·1′W	X	45
Bridge of Earn	Pth & Kin	NO1318	56°21·0′	3°24·0′W	T	58
Bridge of Ericht	Pth & Kin	NN5258	56°41·7′	4°24·6′W	X	42,51
Bridge of Feugh	Aberd	NO7094	57°2·4′	2°29·2′W	X	38,45
Bridge of Fitch	Shetld	HU4341	60°9·3′	1°13·0′W	X	4
Bridge of Forss	Highld	ND0368	58°35·6′	3°39·7′W	X	11,12
Bridge of Gairn	Aberd	NO3597	57°3·8′	3°3·9′W	T	37,44
Bridge of Gaur	Pth & Kin	NN5056	56°40·6′	4°26·4′W	T	42,51
Bridge of Grudie	Highld	NG9667	57°39·1′	5°24·7′W	X	19
Bridge of Horn	Highld	NC7904	58°0·8′	4°2·4′W	X	17
Bridge of Isla	Pth & Kin	NO1638	56°31·8′	3°21·5′W	X	53
Bridge of Kair	Aberd	NO7675	56°52·2′	2°23·2′W	X	45
Bridge of Leachd	Moray	NJ2314	57°12·9′	3°16·0′W	X	36
Bridge of Lossie	Moray	NJ1251	57°32·7′	3°27·8′W	X	28
Bridge of Lyon	Pth & Kin	NN7246	56°35·6′	4°4·6′W	X	51,52
Bridge of Muchalls	Aberd	NO8991	57°0·9′	2°10·4′W	T	38,45
Bridge of Mucomir	Highld	NN1883	56°54·4′	4°58·9′W	X	34,41
Bridge of Muick	Aberd	NO3694	57°2·2′	3°2·8′W	X	37,44
Bridge of Oich	Highld	NH3303	57°5·5′	4°44·9′W	X	34
Bridge of Orchy	Arg & Bt	NN2939	56°31·0′	4°46·3′W	T	50
Bridge of Ruthven	Angus	NO2848	56°37·4′	3°10·0′W	X	53
Bridge of Slateford	Moray	NJ2221	57°16·6′	3°17·2′W	X	36
Bridge of Tilt	Pth & Kin	NN8765	56°46·0′	3°50·5′W	X	43
Bridge of Twatt	Shetld	HU3252	60°15·3′	1°24·8′W	X	3
Bridge of Tynet	Moray	NJ3861	57°38·3′	3°1·8′W	T	28
Bridge of Waithe	Orkney	HY2811	58°59·1′	3°14·7′W	X	6
Bridge of Walls	Shetld	HU2651	60°14·8′	1°31·3′W	T	3
Bridge of Weir	Renf	NS3965	55°51·3′	4°33·9′W	T	63
Bridgepark	Highld	NH4751	57°31·7′	4°32·8′W	X	26
Bridge Petton	Cumbr	NY0703	54°25·1′	3°25·6′W	X	89
Bridge Reach	Medway	TQ7368	51°23·3′	0°29·6′E	W	178
Bridge Reeve	Devon	SS6613	50°54·3′	3°54·0′W	T	180
Bridger's Fm	W Susx	TQ2718	50°57·1′	0°11·1′W	FM	198
Bridgerule	Devon	SS2702	50°47·7′	4°26·9′W	T	190
Bridges	Aberd	NJ5642	57°28·2′	2°43·6′W	X	29
Bridges	Corn	SX0457	50°23·1′	4°45·1′W	T	200
Bridges	Shrops	SO3996	52°33·7′	2°53·6′W	T	137
Bridges Fm	Glos	SO6732	51°59·4′	2°28·4′W	FM	149
Bridges Fm	Northum	NZ0457	54°54·7′	1°55·8′W	FM	87
Bridges Fm	Suff	TL9843	52°3·2′	0°53·7′E	FM	155
Bridge Sollers	Heref	SO4142	52°4·6′	2°51·3′W	T	148,149,161
Bridges, The	Corn	SX2050	50°19·6′	4°31·4′W	X	201
Bridgestone	Aberd	NK0045	57°30·0′	1°59·5′W	X	30
Bridgestone	D & G	NX7266	54°58·6′	3°59·6′W	X	83,84
Bridge Street	Suff	TL8749	52°6·7′	0°44·3′E	T	155
Bridge Street Fm	Suff	TL8748	52°6·1′	0°44·2′E	FM	155
Bridge, The	Corn	SX4652	50°21·1′	4°9·5′W	X	201
Bridgeton	Aberd	NJ5512	57°12·1′	2°44·2′W	X	37
Bridgeton	C of Glas	NS6164	55°51·2′	4°12·8′W	T	64
Bridgeton	Moray	NJ3151	57°32·9′	3°8·7′W	X	28
Bridgeton Castle	Aberd	NO7766	56°47·4′	2°22·1′W	X	45
Bridgetown	Corn	SX3489	50°40·9′	4°20·6′W	T	190
Bridge Town	Devon	SS5507	50°50·9′	4°3·2′W	X	191
Bridgetown	Devon	SS5726	51°1·2′	4°2·0′W	X	180
Bridgetown	Devon	SX8160	50°25·9′	3°40·2′W	T	202
Bridgetown	Somer	SS9233	51°5·4′	3°32·1′W	T	181
Bridgetown	Staffs	SJ9808	52°40·4′	2°1·4′W	T	127
Bridge Town	Warw	SP2054	52°11·3′	1°42·0′W	T	151
Bridge Trafford	Ches	SJ4571	53°14·2′	2°49·0′W	X	117
Bridgets Fm	Hants	SU5134	51°6·4′	1°15·9′W	FM	185
Bridgewarth Beck	N Yks	NZ2401	54°24·5′	1°37·4′W	W	93
Bridgewater and Taunton Canal	Somer	ST2825	51°1·4′	3°1·2′W	W	193
Bridgewater and Taunton Canal	Somer	ST3134	51°6·3′	2°58·7′W	W	182
Bridgewater Canal	Halton	SJ5682	53°20·2′	2°39·2′W	W	108
Bridgewater Canal	Warr	SJ7187	53°23·0′	2°25·8′W	W	109
Bridgewater Ho	Lincs	SK9240	52°57·2′	0°37·4′W	X	130
Bridgewick Arts Centre	Essex	TR0199	51°39·5′	0°54·8′E	X	168
Bridge Wood	Suff	TM1840	52°1·2′	1°11·0′E	F	169
Bridge Woods	Kent	TQ7363	51°20·6′	0°29·4′E	F	178,188
Bridge Yate	S Glos	ST6873	51°27·5′	2°27·2′W	T	172
Bridgham	Norf	TL9585	52°25·9′	0°52·5′E	T	144
Bridgham Heath	Norf	TL9286	52°26·5′	0°49·9′E	X	144
Bridgnorth	Shrops	SO7193	52°32·3′	2°25·3′W	T	138
Bridgwalton	Shrops	SO6892	52°31·7′	2°27·9′W	X	138
Bridgwater	Somer	ST3037	51°7·9′	2°59·6′W	T	182
Bridgwater Bar	Somer	ST2249	51°14·3′	3°6·7′W	X	182
Bridgwater Bay		ST1450	51°14·8′	3°13·5′W	W	181
Bridgwater Bay		ST2051	51°15·4′	3°8·4′W	W	182
Bridin	I of Angl	SH5072	53°13·7′	4°14·4′W	X	114,115
Bridlefolds	Aberd	NJ9318	57°15·4′	2°6·5′W	X	38
Bridle Green	Northum	NY7161	54°56·8′	2°26·7′W	X	86,87
Bridleway Gate	Shrops	SJ5426	52°50·0′	2°40·6′W	X	126
Bridley Manor	Surrey	SU9655	51°17·4′	0°37·0′W	X	175,186
Bridlington	E Yorks	TA1867	54°5·4′	0°11·3′W	T	101
Bridlington Bay	E Yorks	TA2165	54°4·2′	0°8·6′W	W	101
Bridport	Dorset	SY4692	50°43·7′	2°45·5′W	T	193
Bridstow	Heref	SO5824	51°55·0′	2°36·2′W	T	162
Bridwell	Devon	ST0512	50°54·2′	3°20·7′W	X	181
Bridwick Fm	Devon	SS6442	51°9·9′	3°56·3′W	FM	180
Bridzor Fm	Wilts	ST9327	51°2·8′	2°5·6′W	FM	184
Briercliffe	Lancs	SD8441	53°52·1′	2°14·2′W	X	103
Brierdene Burn	N Tyne	NZ3272	55°2·7′	1°29·5′W	W	88
Brier Dene Fm	N Tyne	NZ3374	55°3·8′	1°28·6′W	FM	88
Briereridge	Northum	NY8083	55°8·7′	2°18·4′W	X	80
Brierfield	Lancs	SD8436	53°49·4′	2°14·2′W	T	103
Briergrove Fm	Derby	SK0088	53°23·6′	1°59·6′W	FM	110

Brier Hill	Northum	NY7879	55°6·5′	2°20·3′W	X	86,87
Brier Hills Fm	Donc	SE7008	53°34·1′	0°56·2′W	FM	112
Brierholme Carr	Donc	SE6810	53°35·2′	0°58·0′W	T	111
Brierley	Barns	SE4110	53°35·3′	1°22·4′W	T	111
Brierley	Glos	SO6215	51°50·2′	2°32·7′W	T	162
Brierley	Heref	SO4955	52°11·7′	2°44·4′W	T	148,149
Brierley Beck	Stock on T	NZ4026	54°37·9′	1°22·4′W	W	93
Brierley Common	Barns	SE4210	53°35·3′	1°21·5′W	X	111
Brierley Gap	Barns	SE4210	53°35·3′	1°21·5′W	X	111
Brierley Grange	Glos	SO7728	51°57·2′	2°19·7′W	X	150
Brierley Hill	Dudley	SO9286	52°28·5′	2°6·7′W	T	139
Brierley Hill	Heref	SO3468	52°18·6′	2°57·7′W	X	137,148
Brierley Hulme Fm	Ches	SJ7365	53°11·1′	2°23·8′W	FM	118
Brierley Manor	Barns	SE4210	53°35·3′	1°21·5′W	X	111
Brierley Wood	Heref	SO4955	52°11·7′	2°44·4′W	F	148,149
Brierley Wood	Stock on T	NZ3927	54°38·4′	1°23·3′W	F	93
Brier Low	Derby	SK0868	53°12·8′	1°52·4′W	X	119
Brierlow Bar	Derby	SK0869	53°13·3′	1°52·4′W	X	119
Brierlow Bar Fm	Derby	SK0869	53°13·3′	1°52·4′W	FM	119
Brierlow Grange	Derby	SK0969	53°13·3′	1°51·5′W	X	119
Brierton	Hartpl	NZ4730	54°40·0′	1°15·9′W	T	93
Brier Wood	Suff	TM4886	52°25·2′	1°39·2′E	F	156
Briery	Cumbr	NY2824	54°36·6′	3°6·5′W	T	89,90
Briery Bank	D & G	NY3791	55°12·8′	2°59·0′W	X	79
Briery Cave	Devon	SS5548	51°13·0′	4°4·2′W	X	180
Briery Close	Cumbr	NY3901	54°24·3′	2°56·0′W	X	90
Briery Cott	D & G	NY2482	55°7·8′	3°11·1′W	X	79
Briery Hall Fm	Wakf	SE3515	53°38·1′	1°27·8′W	FM	110,111
Briery Hill	Blae Gw	SO1608	51°46·1′	3°12·6′W	T	161
Brieryhill	D & G	NY1185	55°9·3′	3°23·4′W	X	78
Briery Hill	Glos	SO6924	51°55·1′	2°26·7′W	X	162
Briery Hill	Northum	NZ2279	55°6·5′	1°38·9′W	X	88
Brieryhill	Scot Bord	NT4814	55°25·3′	2°48·9′W	X	79
Brieryhill	Scot Bord	NT8153	55°46·4′	2°17·7′W	X	67,74
Brieryhurst	Staffs	SJ8456	53°6·3′	2°13·9′W	X	118
Briery Leys Spinney	Leic	SK7400	52°35·8′	0°54·0′W	F	141
Brieryshaw	D & G	NY3790	55°12·3′	2°59·0′W	X	79
Brieryshaw Hill	D & G	NY3691	55°12·8′	2°59·9′W	X	79
Briery Wood	Leic	SK8233	52°53·5′	0°46·5′W	F	130
Briery Wood Fm	Brad	SE0947	53°55·4′	1°51·4′W	FM	104
Briery Yards	Scot Bord	NT5317	55°26·9′	2°44·2′W	X	79
Briestfield	Kirk	SE2317	53°39·2′	1°38·7′W	T	110
Briestonhill Ho	W Loth	NT0164	55°51·8′	3°34·5′W	X	65
Briga Head	Highld	ND1875	58°39·6′	3°24·3′W	X	7,12
Brigalee	Shetld	HU2745	60°11·6′	1°30·3′W	X	4
Brigam Fm	V of Glam	SS9979	51°30·3′	3°26·9′W	FM	170
Brigden Hill Fm	E Susx	TQ6615	50°54·9′	0°22·1′E	FM	199
Brigflatts	Cumbr	SD6491	54°19·0′	2°32·8′W	T	97
Brigg	N Lincs	TA0007	53°33·2′	0°29·0′W	T	112
Briggate	Norf	TG3127	52°47·7′	1°26·0′E	T	133,134
Briggate Fm	N Lincs	SE9004	53°31·7′	0°38·1′W	FM	112
Brigg Burn	Northum	NY8889	55°12·0′	2°10·9′W	W	80
Brigg End	N Yks	TA1381	54°13·0′	0°15·6′W	X	101
Briggen (Hotel)	Herts	TL4111	51°47·0′	0°3·0′E	X	167
Briggle	Cumbr	NY5834	54°42·2′	2°38·7′W	X	91
Briggle Beck	Cumbr	NY5745	54°48·1′	2°39·7′W	W	86
Briggle Beck	Cumbr	NY5833	54°41·7′	2°38·7′W	W	91
Briggs	Aberd	NJ8044	57°29·4′	2°19·6′W	X	29,30
Briggs House Fm	Cumbr	SD4989	54°17·9′	2°46·6′W	FM	97
Briggs of Criggie	Aberd	NO8482	56°56·0′	2°15·3′W	X	45
Briggs of Fidra	E Loth	NT5186	56°4·1′	2°46·8′W	W	66
Briggswath	N Yks	NZ8608	54°27·8′	0°40·0′W	T	94
Brigg, The	Northum	NY8989	55°12·0′	2°9·9′W	X	80
Brigham	Cumbr	NY0830	54°39·7′	3°25·2′W	T	89
Brigham	Cumbr	NY2723	54°36·1′	3°7·4′W	T	89,90
Brigham	E Yorks	TA0753	53°58·0′	0°21·7′W	T	107
Brigham Bank	Cumbr	NY6024	54°36·8′	2°36·7′W	X	91
Brig Head	Northum	NZ3093	55°14·1′	1°31·3′W	X	81
Brighead Bush	Aberd	NO8371	56°50·1′	2°16·3′W	X	45
Brighouse	Cald	SE1423	53°42·4′	1°46·9′W	T	104
Brighouse	Cumbr	SD0895	54°20·8′	3°24·5′W	X	96
Brighouse	Cumbr	SD1994	54°20·4′	3°14·3′W	X	96
Brighouse	D & G	NX6445	54°47·1′	4°6·5′W	X	83
Brighouse	D & G	NX6978	55°5·0′	4°2·7′W	X	77,84
Brighouse	Fife	NO4021	56°22·9′	2°57·9′W	X	54,59
Brighouse Bay	D & G	NX6345	54°47·1′	4°7·4′W	W	83
Brighstone	I of W	SZ4282	50°38·4′	1°24·0′W	T	196
Brighstone Bay	I of W	SZ4280	50°37·3′	1°24·0′W	W	196
Brighstone Down	I of W	SZ4384	50°39·5′	1°23·1′W	X	196
Brighstone Forest	I of W	SZ4284	50°39·5′	1°24·0′W	F	196
Brightall Common	Heref	SO4769	52°19·2′	2°46·3′W	X	137,138,148
Brightenflat	Cumbr	NY4563	54°57·8′	2°51·1′W	X	86
Brightgate	Derby	SK2659	53°7·9′	1°36·3′W	T	119
Brighthampton	Oxon	SP3803	51°43·7′	1°26·6′W	T	164
Bright Hill Plantn	Warw	SP3048	52°8·0′	1°33·3′W	F	151
Brightholmlee	Sheff	SK2995	53°27·3′	1°33·4′W	T	110
Brighthouse Fm	Suff	TL8553	52°8·9′	0°42·6′E	FM	155
Brightley	Devon	SS5411	50°53·0′	4°4·2′W	X	191
Brightley	Devon	SX5997	50°45·6′	3°59·6′W	T	191
Brightley Barton	Devon	SS6122	50°59·1′	3°58·4′W	X	180
Brightling	E Susx	TQ6821	50°58·1′	0°24·0′E	T	199
Brightling Down	E Susx	TQ6620	50°57·6′	0°22·2′E	X	199
Brightling Hall	E Susx	TQ7022	50°58·6′	0°25·7′E	X	199
Brightling Park	E Susx	TQ6820	50°57·5′	0°23·9′E	X	199
Brightlingsea	Essex	TM0817	51°48·5′	1°1·5′E	T	168,169
Brightlingsea Creek	Essex	TM0916	51°48·4′	1°2·3′E	W	168,169
Brightlingsea Reach	Essex	TM0814	51°47·4′	1°1·4′E	W	168,169
Brightlycott Fm	Devon	SS5735	51°6·0′	4°2·2′W	FM	180
Brightmans Hayes	Devon	SS4810	50°52·4′	4°9·2′W	X	191
Brightmony	Highld	NH9253	57°33·5′	3°47·8′W	X	27
Brightmoor	Bucks	SP7331	51°58·6′	0°55·8′W	X	152,165
Brighton	Bri & Hov	TQ3106	50°50·5′	0°8·0′W	T	198
Brighton	Corn	SW9054	50°21·1′	4°56·8′W	T	200
Brighton	Derby	SK1359	53°7·9′	1°47·9′W	X	119
Brighton Hill	Hants	SU6249	51°14·4′	1°6·3′W	T	185
Brighton le Sands	Sefton	SJ3099	53°29·2′	3°2·9′W	T	108
Brightons	Falk	NS9377	55°58·7′	3°42·4′W	T	65
Brighton Wood	Brad	SE0243	53°53·2′	1°57·8′W	F	104
Brightor	Corn	SX3561	50°25·8′	4°19·0′W	X	201
Bright Pitts Fm	Northnts	TL0683	52°26·3′	0°26·0′W	FM	142
Bright's Corner	Shrops	SO6185	52°27·9′	2°34·0′W	X	138
Bright's Fm	Suff	TL8949	52°6·6′	0°46·0′E	FM	155
Bright's Fm	Wilts	ST9879	51°30·8′	2°1·3′W	FM	173
Brights Hill	Glos	SO7020	51°52·9′	2°25·8′W	H	162
Brightside	Sheff	SK3789	53°24·0′	1°26·2′W	T	110,111
Brightwalton	W Berks	SU4279	51°30·7′	1°23·3′W	T	174
Brightwalton Common	W Berks	SU4280	51°31·3′	1°23·3′W	X	174
Brightwalton Green	W Berks	SU4278	51°30·2′	1°23·3′W	T	174
Brightwalton Holt	W Berks	SU4377	51°29·6′	1°22·4′W	T	174
Brightwell	Suff	TM2443	52°2·6′	1°16·4′E	T	169
Brightwell Baldwin	Oxon	SU6595	51°39·2′	1°3·2′W	T	164,165
Brightwell Barrow	Oxon	SU5791	51°37·1′	1°10·2′W	H	164,174
Brightwell-cum-Sotwell	Oxon	SU5890	51°36·6′	1°9·4′W	T	164,174
Brightwell Fm	W Susx	TQ2828	51°2·4′	0°10·1′W	FM	187,198
Brightwell Grove	Oxon	SU6593	51°38·2′	1°3·3′W	X	164,175
Brightwell Park	Oxon	SU6595	51°39·2′	1°3·2′W	X	164,165
Brightworthy	Somer	SS8335	51°6·4′	3°39·9′W	X	181
Brightworthy Barrows	Somer	SS8135	51°6·4′	3°41·6′W	A	181
Brigland	E Ayr	NS5128	55°31·6′	4°21·2′W	X	70
Briglands	Pth & Kin	NT0299	56°10·7′	3°34·3′W	X	58
Brigmerston	Wilts	SU1645	51°12·5′	1°45·9′W	T	184
Brigmerston Down	Wilts	SU2047	51°13·5′	1°42·4′W	X	184
Brigmerston Field	Wilts	SU1846	51°13·0′	1°44·1′W	X	184
Brignall	Durham	NZ0712	54°30·4′	1°53·1′W	T	92
Brignall Banks	Durham	NZ0511	54°29·9′	1°54·9′W	X	92
Brignam Park	N Yks	SE8081	54°13·3′	0°46·0′W	X	100
Brig o' Turk	Stir	NN5306	56°13·7′	4°21·8′W	T	57
Brigshillock	Aberd	NJ6756	57°35·8′	2°32·7′W	X	29
Brigsley	NE Lincs	TA2501	53°29·7′	0°6·5′W	T	113
Brigsley Top	NE Lincs	TA2602	53°30·2′	0°5·6′W	X	113
Brigstanes	Aberd	NO8578	56°53·8′	2°14·3′W	X	45
Brigsteer	Cumbr	SD4889	54°17·9′	2°47·5′W	T	97
Brigsteer Park	Cumbr	SD4888	54°17·3′	2°47·5′W	F	97
Brigs, The	Shetld	HU3058	60°18·6′	1°26·9′W	W	3
Brigstock	Northnts	SP9485	52°27·5′	0°36·6′W	T	141
Brigtham's Fm	W Susx	TQ1917	50°56·6′	0°18·0′W	FM	198
Brig, The	Shetld	HU3584	60°32·5′	1°21·2′W	X	1,2,3
Brigton	Aberd	NO6770	56°49·5′	2°32·0′W	X	45
Brigton	Angus	NO2948	56°37·4′	3°9·0′W	X	53
Brigton	D & G	NX3674	55°2·3′	4°33·6′W	X	77
Brigton	Fife	NO5111	56°17·6′	2°47·1′W	X	59
Brigton	Pth & Kin	NO1922	56°23·3′	3°18·3′W	X	53,58
Brigton Fm	Aberd	NO7595	57°3·0′	2°24·3′W	FM	38,45
Brigton Ho	Angus	NO4146	56°36·4′	2°57·2′W	X	54
Brigurd Point	N Ayr	NS1752	55°43·9′	4°54·4′W	X	63
Brigwellt-y-coed	Carm	SN4617	51°50·1′	4°13·7′W	X	159
Brill	Bucks	SP6513	51°48·9′	1°3·0′W	T	164,165
Brill	Carm	SN2808	51°44·9′	4°29·1′W	X	158
Brill	Corn	SW7229	50°7·3′	5°11·0′W	T	204
Brillbury Hall Fm	Bucks	SP6514	51°49·5′	1°3·0′W	FM	164,165
Brilley	Heref	SO2649	52°8·3′	3°4·5′W	T	148
Brilley Court Fm	Heref	SO2548	52°7·8′	3°5·3′W	FM	148
Brilley Green	Heref	SO2648	52°7·8′	3°4·5′W	X	148
Brilley Mountain	Powys	SO2651	52°9·4′	3°4·5′W	T	148
Brill Hill	Corn	SW7129	50°7·3′	5°11·8′W	X	203
Brill Ho	Bucks	SP6513	51°48·9′	1°3·0′W	X	164,165
Brills Fm	Lincs	SK8559	53°7·5′	0°43·4′W	FM	121
Brills Fm	Surrey	TQ4149	51°13·6′	0°1·6′E	FM	187
Brimaston	Pemb	SM9325	51°53·4′	5°0·1′W	T	157,158
Brimblecombe	Devon	SS5609	50°52·0′	4°2·4′W	X	191
Brimblecombe Brake	Devon	SS5508	50°51·4′	4°3·2′W	F	191
Brim Brook	Devon	SX5887	50°40·2′	4°0·2′W	W	191
Brimfast Fm	W Susx	SZ8599	50°47·3′	0°47·3′W	FM	197
Brim Fell	Cumbr	SD2798	54°22·6′	3°7·0′W	H	96,97
Brimfield	Heref	SO5267	52°18·2′	2°41·8′W	T	137,138,149
Brimfield Common	Heref	SO5166	52°17·6′	2°42·7′W	X	137,138,149
Brimfieldcross	Heref	SO5368	52°18·7′	2°41·0′W	X	137,138
Brimfield Hill	Heref	SO5366	52°17·6′	2°41·0′W	X	137,138,149
Brimford Bridge	Devon	SS2817	50°55·8′	4°26·5′W	X	190
Brimford Ho	Powys	SJ3014	52°43·4′	3°1·8′W	X	126
Brimham	N Yks	SE2164	54°4·5′	1°40·3′W	X	99
Brimham Hall Fm	N Yks	SE2262	54°3·5′	1°39·4′W	FM	99
Brimham Lodge	N Yks	SE2263	54°4·0′	1°39·4′W	A	99
Brimham Moor	N Yks	SE2164	54°4·5′	1°40·3′W	X	99
Brimham Rocks	N Yks	SE2164	54°4·5′	1°40·3′W	X	99
Brim Hill	Devon	SX8855	50°23·3′	3°34·2′W	H	202
Brim House Fm	N Yks	SE2168	54°6·7′	1°40·3′W	FM	99
Brimington	Derby	SK4073	53°15·4′	1°23·6′W	T	120
Brimington Common	Derby	SK4072	53°14·8′	1°23·6′W	T	120
Brimley	Devon	ST3300	50°48·0′	2°56·7′W	T	193
Brimley	Devon	SX7977	50°35·0′	3°42·2′W	T	191
Brimley Coombe	Dorset	ST4300	50°48·0′	2°48·1′W	X	193
Brimley Corner	Devon	SX8779	50°36·2′	3°35·4′W	X	192
Brimley Hill	Devon	ST1714	50°55·4′	3°10·5′W	X	181,193
Brimlin Wood	Suff	TM0740	52°1·4′	1°1·4′E	F	155,169
Brimmer Beck	Lincs	TF1089	53°23·4′	0°20·3′W	W	113
Brimmer Head Fm	Cumbr	NY3208	54°28·0′	3°2·5′W	A	90
Brimmers Fm	Bucks	SP8102	51°42·9′	0°49·3′W	FM	165
Brimmicroft	Lancs	SD6224	53°42·9′	2°34·1′W	X	102,103
Brimmond Hill	C of Aber	NJ8509	57°10·6′	2°14·4′W	H	38
Brim Ness	Shetld	HP6117	60°50·1′	0°52·2′W	X	1
Brim Ness	Shetld	HU4648	60°13·1′	1°9·7′W	X	3
Brimpit Fm	Devon	ST2205	50°50·6′	3°6·1′W	FM	192,193
Brimpool Rocks	Devon	SX7835	50°12·4′	3°42·2′W	X	202
Brimpsfield	Glos	SO9312	51°48·6′	2°5·7′W	T	163
Brimpsfield Park	Glos	SO9412	51°48·6′	2°4·8′W	X	163
Brimps Hill	Glos	SO6718	51°51·8′	2°28·4′W	T	162
Brimpton	W Berks	SU5564	51°22·6′	1°12·2′W	T	174
Brimpton Common	W Berks	SU5663	51°22·0′	1°11·3′W	T	174
Brimpton Mill	W Berks	SU5565	51°23·1′	1°12·2′W	X	174
Brimpts Fm	Devon	SX6673	50°32·7′	3°53·1′W	FM	191
Brims	Orkney	ND2888	58°46·7′	3°14·2′W	X	7
Brims Castle	Highld	ND0471	58°37·2′	3°38·7′W	A	12
Brimscombe	Glos	SO8702	51°43·2′	2°10·9′W	T	162
Brimsdown	Enf	TQ3697	51°39·5′	0°1·6′W	T	166,177
Brims Down	Wilts	ST8539	51°9·2′	2°12·5′W	X	183
Brimsdown Hill	Wilts	ST8239	51°9·2′	2°15·1′W	H	183
Brims Hill	Highld	ND0770	58°36·7′	3°35·6′W	H	12
Brimslade Fm	Wilts	SU2063	51°22·2′	1°42·4′W	FM	174
Brims Ness	Highld	ND0471	58°37·2′	3°38·7′W	X	12
Brims Ness	Orkney	ND2988	58°46·7′	3°13·2′W	X	7
Brimstage	Wirral	SJ3082	53°20·1′	3°2·7′W	T	108
Brimstone Fm	Oxon	SU2595	51°39·4′	1°37·9′W	FM	163
Brimstone Inclosure	Hants	SU8032	51°5·1′	0°51·1′W	F	186
Brimstone Wood	Kent	TQ6565	51°21·8′	0°22·6′E	F	177,178
Brimstree Hill	Shrops	SJ7505	52°38·8′	2°21·8′W	X	127
Brinacory	Highld	NM7591	56°57·6′	5°41·6′W	X	33,40
Brinacory Island	Highld	NM7590	56°57·1′	5°41·5′W	X	33,40
Brince	Pemb	SN0606	51°43·4′	4°48·1′W	X	158
Brincliffe	Sheff	SK3385	53°21·9′	1°29·8′W	T	110,111
Brind	E Yorks	SE7431	53°46·4′	0°52·2′W	T	105,106
Brindacks	Shetld	HP5711	60°46·9′	0°56·7′W	X	1
Brindham	Somer	ST5140	51°9·7′	2°41·7′W	T	182,183
Brindifield	Devon	SS8210	50°52·9′	3°40·3′W	X	191
Brindister	Shetld	HU2857	60°18·0′	1°29·1′W	T	3
Brindister	Shetld	HU4337	60°7·2′	1°13·1′W	T	4
Brindister Voe	Shetld	HU2857	60°18·0′	1°29·1′W	W	3
Brindiwell	Devon	SS8907	50°51·3′	3°34·2′W	X	192
Brindle	Lancs	SD5924	53°42·9′	2°36·9′W	T	102
Brindle Heath	Salf	SD8000	53°30·0′	2°17·7′W	T	109
Brindle Lodge	Lancs	SD6026	53°44·0′	2°36·0′W	X	102,103
Brindley	Ches	SJ5953	53°4·6′	2°36·3′W	T	117
Brindley Croft	Staffs	SK0459	53°7·9′	1°56·0′W	X	119
Brindley Ford	C of Stoke	SJ8854	53°5·2′	2°10·3′W	X	118
Brindley Green	Ches	SJ7762	53°9·5′	2°20·2′W	X	118
Brindley Hall Fm	Ches	SJ5854	53°5·1′	2°37·2′W	FM	117
Brindley Heath	Staffs	SJ9914	52°43·7′	2°0·5′W	X	127
Brindley Lea Hall	Ches	SJ5853	53°4·6′	2°37·2′W	X	117
Brind Leys Fm	E Yorks	SE7332	53°47·0′	0°53·1′W	FM	105,106
Brindleys Plantn	E Yorks	SE7431	53°46·4′	0°52·2′W	F	105,106
Brindley Valley	Staffs	SK0014	52°43·7′	1°59·6′W	X	128
Brindwoodgate	Derby	SK3376	53°17·0′	1°29·9′W	T	119
Brindy	Aberd	NJ6120	57°16·4′	2°38·3′W	X	37
Brindy Hill	Aberd	NJ6021	57°16·9′	2°39·4′W	H	37
Brindymuir	Aberd	NJ6120	57°16·4′	2°38·3′W	X	37
Brinepits Fm	Ches	SJ6646	53°0·9′	2°30·0′W	FM	118
Brine Pits Fm	Worcs	SO9065	52°17·2′	2°8·4′W	FM	150
Brines	Ches	SJ9883	53°20·9′	2°1·4′W	X	109
Brine's Brow	Ches	SJ5270	53°13·7′	2°42·7′W	X	117
Brineton	Staffs	SJ8013	52°43·1′	2°17·4′W	T	127
Bringan	E Ayr	NS4540	55°38·0′	4°27·3′W	X	70
Bring Deeps	Orkney	HY2902	58°54·2′	3°13·5′W	W	6,7
Bringers	Shetld	HU5563	60°21·1′	0°59·7′W	X	2
Bringewood	Shrops	SO4673	52°21·4′	2°47·2′W	F	137,138,148
Bringewood Forge	Heref	SO4574	52°21·9′	2°48·1′W	T	137,138,148
Bring Head	Orkney	HY2702	58°54·2′	3°15·5′W	X	6,7
Bring Head	Orkney	HY3733	59°11·0′	3°5·7′W	X	6
Bringhurst	Leic	SP8492	52°31·4′	0°45·3′W	T	141
Brings	Orkney	HY3834	59°11·6′	3°4·6′W	X	6
Bringsty Common	Heref	SO7055	52°11·8′	2°25·9′W	T	149
Bring, The	Orkney	HY2601	58°53·7′	3°16·6′W	X	6,7
Brington	Cambs	TL0875	52°22·0′	0°24·4′W	T	142
Brin Ho	Highld	NH6629	57°20·2′	4°13·1′W	X	26,35
Brinian	Orkney	HY4327	59°7·8′	2°59·3′W	T	5,6
Brinian Ho	Orkney	HY4427	59°7·8′	2°58·2′W	X	5,6
Brinningham	Norf	TG0334	52°52·1′	1°1·4′E	T	133
Brink Brow	Ches	SJ9679	53°18·7′	2°3·2′W	X	118
Brinkburn Lodge	Northum	NZ1199	55°17·3′	1°49·2′W	X	81
Brinkburn Priory	Northum	NZ1198	55°16·8′	1°49·2′W	A	81
Brink Ends	Lancs	SD9437	53°50·0′	2°5·1′W	X	103
Brinken Wood	Hants	SU2705	50°50·9′	1°36·6′W	F	195
Brink Fm	Ches	SJ9574	53°16·0′	2°4·1′W	FM	118
Brink Fm	Ches	SJ9679	53°18·7′	2°3·2′W	FM	118
Brink Hall Fm	Lincs	SK9980	53°18·7′	0°30·4′W	FM	121
Brinkheugh	Northum	NZ1298	55°16·8′	1°48·2′W	X	81
Brinkhill	Lincs	TF3773	53°14·4′	0°3·6′E	T	122
Brink Hill	Norf	TF7520	52°45·2′	0°36·0′E	X	132
Brink Hill	N Yks	SE5478	54°11·9′	1°9·9′W	H	100
Brink Hill Farm	N Yks	SE5478	54°11·9′	1°9·9′W	FM	100
Brinkies Brae	Orkney	HY2509	58°58·0′	3°17·8′W	H	6,7
Brinkley	Cambs	TL6254	52°9·9′	0°22·5′E	T	154
Brinkley	Notts	SK7152	53°3·9′	0°56·0′W	T	120
Brinkley Fm	Notts	SK7152	53°3·9′	0°56·0′W	FM	120
Brinkley Hill	Heref	SO5831	51°58·8′	2°36·3′W	T	149
Brinkley Wood	Cambs	TL6155	52°10·4′	0°21·7′E	F	154
Brinklow	Mil Key	SP9037	52°1·7′	0°40·9′W	T	152
Brinklow	Warw	SP4379	52°24·7′	1°21·7′W	T	140
Brinklow Heath	Warw	SP4177	52°23·6′	1°23·4′W	X	140
Brinksole	W Susx	SU9922	50°59·6′	0°35·0′W	X	197
Brinkwall	Orkney	HY4955	59°23·0′	2°53·4′W	X	5
Brinkwells	W Susx	TQ0221	50°59·0′	0°32·4′W	X	197
Brinkworth	Wilts	SU0184	51°33·5′	1°58·7′W	T	173
Brinkworth Brook	Wilts	ST9983	51°33·0′	2°0·5′W	W	173
Brinkworth Hall	York	SE6848	53°55·7′	0°57·4′W	X	105,106
Brin Mains	Highld	NH6630	57°20·7′	4°13·1′W	X	26
Brinmore	Highld	NH6628	57°19·6′	4°13·1′W	X	26,35
Brinnaval	N Eil	NB0228	58°8·7′	7°3·4′W	H	13
Brinnigar	Orkney	HY2308	58°57·4′	3°19·8′W	X	6,7
Brinning	Devon	SX7585	50°39·3′	3°45·7′W	X	191
Brinnington	Stock	SJ9192	53°25·7′	2°7·7′W	T	109
Brinns Fm	Cumbr	NY5517	54°33·0′	2°41·3′W	FM	90
Brin Rock	Highld	NH6629	57°20·2′	4°13·1′W	X	26,35
Brinsabach Fm	Devon	SX4879	50°35·7′	4°8·5′W	FM	191,201
Brinsbury Estate (Coll of Agriculture)	W Susx	TQ0622	50°59·5′	0°29·0′W	X	197
Brinscall	Lancs	SD6221	53°41·3′	2°34·1′W	T	102,103
Brinscall Hall	Lancs	SD6221	53°41·3′	2°34·1′W	X	102,103
Brinscombe	Devon	SS6340	51°8·8′	3°57·1′W	X	180
Brinscombe	Somer	ST4252	51°16·1′	2°49·5′W	X	182
Brinscombe Fm	Devon	ST2804	50°50·1′	3°1·0′W	FM	193
Brinscombe Hill	Somer	ST4251	51°15·5′	2°49·5′W	H	182
Brinscott	Devon	SS5843	51°10·4′	4°1·5′W	X	180
Brinsea	N Som	ST4462	51°21·5′	2°47·9′W	T	172,182
Brinsford	Staffs	SJ9105	52°38·8′	2°7·6′W	T	127,139
Brinshope	Heref	SO4267	52°18·1′	2°50·6′W	X	137,148,149
Brinsley	Notts	SK4649	53°2·4′	1°18·4′W	T	129
Brinsley Hall	Notts	SK4549	53°2·4′	1°19·3′W	X	129
Brinsop	Heref	SO4444	52°5·7′	2°48·7′W	T	148,149,161
Brinsop Common	Heref	SO4344	52°5·7′	2°49·5′W	T	148,149,161
Brinsop Court	Heref	SO4445	52°6·3′	2°48·7′W	A	148,149

Brinstone	Heref	SO4823	51°54·4′	2°45·0′W	X	161
Brinsworth	Roth	SK4190	53°24·6′	1°22·6′W	T	111
Brinsworthy	Devon	SS7530	51°3·6′	3°46·6′W	T	180
Brinton	Norf	TG0335	52°52·7′	1°1·4′E	T	133
Brionn Pholl	Arg & Bt	NM3839	56°28·5′	6°14·8′W	X	47,48
Brisbane Mains	N Ayr	NS2062	55°49·3′	4°52·0′W	X	63
Brisco	Cumbr	NY4251	54°51·3′	2°53·8′W	T	85
Briscoe	Cumbr	NY0211	54°29·3′	3°30·4′W	T	89
Briscoe Bank	Cumbr	NX9720	54°34·1′	3°35·2′W	X	89
Briscoe Fm	N Yks	NZ8109	54°28·4′	0°44·6′W	FM	94
Briscoerigg	N Yks	SE2550	53°57·0′	1°36·7′W	T	104
Briscoerigg Fm	N Yks	SE2551	53°57·5′	1°36·7′W	FM	104
Brisco Hill	Cumbr	NY3967	54°59·9′	2°56·8′W	X	85
Brisco Hill	Cumbr	NY4251	54°51·3′	2°53·8′W	X	85
Briscwm	Cered	SN1745	52°4·6′	4°39·8′W	X	145
Brisdeadh a Mhill Dhuibh	Highld	NH1275	57°43·8′	5°9·0′W	H	19
Brisderg	N Ayr	NR9832	55°32·7′	5°11·7′W	X	69
Brisgen	Carm	SN5828	51°56·2′	4°3·5′W	X	146
Brishie Burn	D & G	NX4783	55°7·3′	4°23·5′W	W	77
Brishing Court	Kent	TQ7751	51°14·1′	0°32·5′E	X	188
Brisley	Norf	TF9521	52°45·3′	0°53·8′E	T	132
Brisley Fm	Kent	TQ9940	51°7·7′	0°51·0′E	FM	189
Brisley Green	Norf	TF9521	52°45·3′	0°53·8′E	X	132
Brislington	C of Bris	ST6270	51°25·9′	2°32·4′W	T	172
Brislington Ho	C of Bris	ST6370	51°25·9′	2°31·5′W	X	172
Brisons, The	Corn	SW3431	50°7·4′	5°42·9′W	X	203
Brissenden	Kent	TQ9439	51°7·3′	0°46·7′E	X	189
Brissenden Fm	Kent	TQ8139	51°7·5′	0°35·6′E	FM	188
Brissenden Fm	Kent	TQ9034	51°4·7′	0°43·1′E	FM	189
Brissenden Green	Kent	TQ9339	51°7·3′	0°45·9′E	T	189
Bristnall Fields	Sand	SO9986	52°28·6′	2°0·5′W	T	139
Bristol	C of Bris	ST6075	51°28·6′	2°34·2′W	T	172
Bristoland Bath Railway Path	Bath & NE Somer	ST6868	51°24·8′	2°27·2′W	X	172
Bristol Belt	Suff	TL7369	52°17·7′	0°32·6′E	F	155
Bristol Channel		SS9951	51°15·2′	3°26·5′W	W	181
Bristol Channel		ST1465	51°22·9′	3°13·8′W	W	171
Bristol Channel		ST2062	51°21·3′	3°8·5′W	W	182
Bristol Channel		ST2461	51°20·8′	3°5·1′W	W	182
Bristol Channel or Mòr Hafren		SS4784	51°32·3′	4°12·0′W	W	159
Bristol International Airport	N Som	ST5065	51°23·1′	2°42·7′W	X	172,182
Bristol Parkway Sta	S Glos	ST6279	51°30·8′	2°32·5′W	X	172
Bristol Plain Fm	Somer	ST5052	51°16·1′	2°42·6′W	FM	182,183
Briston	Corn	SX3964	50°27·5′	4°15·7′W	X	201
Briston	Norf	TG0632	52°51·0′	1°4·0′E	T	133
Briston Common	Norf	TG0631	52°50·5′	1°3·9′E	X	133
Bristow Br	Wilts	SU1561	51°21·1′	1°46·7′W	X	173
Brisworthy	Devon	SX5565	50°28·2′	4°2·2′W	X	202
Britain Bottom	S Glos	ST7886	51°34·6′	2°18·7′W	T	172
Britannia	Lancs	SD8821	53°41·4′	2°10·5′W	T	103
Britannia Fm	Norf	TG4708	52°37·0′	1°39·3′E	FM	134
Britannia Inn (PH)	Denb	SJ1945	53°0·0′	3°12·0′W	X	116
Britannia Quarries	Lancs	SD8720	53°40·8′	2°11·4′W	X	103
Britannia RN College	Devon	SX8752	50°21·7′	3°34·9′W	X	202
Britchcombe Fm	Oxon	SU3087	51°35·1′	1°33·6′W	FM	174
Britcher Fm	Kent	TQ8629	51°2·0′	0°39·6′E	FM	189,199
Britcher Fm	Kent	TQ9046	51°11·1′	0°43·5′E	FM	189
Britford	Wilts	SU1628	51°3·3′	1°45·9′W	T	184
Brithayes	Devon	SS9607	50°51·4′	3°28·3′W	X	192
Brithdir	Brig	SS8988	51°35·0′	3°35·7′W	X	170
Brithdir	Caer	SO1501	51°42·3′	3°13·4′W	T	171
Brithdir	Carm	SN5335	51°59·9′	4°8·1′W	X	146
Brithdir	Cered	SN3447	52°6·0′	4°25·0′W	T	145
Brithdir	Conwy	SJ0245	52°59·8′	3°27·2′W	X	116
Brithdir	Flint	SJ1863	53°9·7′	3°13·2′W	X	116
Brithdir	Gwyn	SH4751	53°2·3′	4°16·5′W	X	115,123
Brithdir	Gwyn	SH5346	52°59·7′	4°11·0′W	X	115
Brithdir	Gwyn	SH5569	53°12·1′	4°9·9′W	X	114,115
Brithdir	Gwyn	SH5758	53°6·2′	4°7·8′W	X	115
Brithdir	Gwyn	SH7618	52°45·0′	3°49·8′W	T	124
Brithdir	Powys	SJ1224	52°48·6′	3°17·9′W	X	125
Brithdir	Powys	SN8985	52°27·3′	3°37·6′W	X	135,136
Brithdir	Powys	SN9075	52°22·0′	3°36·5′W	X	136,147
Brithdir	Powys	SO1097	52°34·0′	3°19·3′W	X	136
Brithdir	Powys	SO3095	52°33·1′	3°1·5′W	X	137
Brithdir Coch	Gwyn	SH8313	52°42·4′	3°43·5′W	X	124,125
Brithdir Hall	Powys	SJ1902	52°36·8′	3°11·4′W	X	136
Brithdir Mawr	Pemb	SN0737	52°0·1′	4°48·3′W	X	145
Brithem Bottom	Devon	ST0110	50°53·1′	3°24·1′W	T	192
Brither Rocks	N Ayr	NS1946	55°40·7′	4°52·3′W	X	63
Brithers, The	Angus	NO5935	56°30·6′	2°39·5′W	X	54
British	Torf	SO2503	51°43·5′	3°4·8′W	T	171
British Geological Survey	Carm	SN6231	51°57·9′	4°0·1′W	X	146
British Horse Racing School	Suff	TL6465	52°15·7′	0°24·6′E	X	154
British Museum	Camden	TQ3081	51°31·0′	0°7·2′W	X	176,177
Britland Edge Hill	Derby	SE1002	53°31·1′	1°50·5′W	H	110
Briton Ferry	Nth Pt Talb	SS7394	51°38·1′	3°49·7′W	T	170
Britta Geo	Shetld	HP6406	60°44·2′	0°49·1′W	X	1
Brittain	Orkney	HY2423	59°5·5′	3°19·1′W	X	6
Britten's	Bath & NE Somer	ST6556	51°18·4′	2°29·7′W	T	172
Brittle Down	Devon	SX7595	50°44·7′	3°45·9′W	H	191
Brittle's Fm	Worcs	SO7982	52°26·4′	2°18·1′W	FM	138
Brittleware Fm	Surrey	TQ2443	51°10·6′	0°13·2′W	FM	187
Britton Fm	Kent	TR2358	51°16·9′	1°12·3′E	FM	179
Britton House Stud	Somer	ST4910	50°53·5′	2°43·1′W	X	193
Britton's Fm	Norf	TG1104	52°35·8′	1°7·3′E	FM	144
Britton's Fm	Suff	TL8154	52°9·5′	0°39·2′E	FM	155
Brittons Hall Fm	Essex	TL6709	51°45·5′	0°25·6′E	FM	167
Britty Common	Somer	ST2515	50°56·0′	3°3·7′W	X	193
Britwell	Slough	SU9582	51°32·0′	0°37·4′W	T	175,176
Britwell Hill	Oxon	SU6891	51°37·1′	1°0·7′W	X	164,175
Britwell Priory	Oxon	SU6793	51°38·1′	1°1·5′W	X	164,175
Britwell Salome	Oxon	SU6793	51°38·1′	1°1·5′W	T	164,175
Britwell Salome Ho	Oxon	SU6692	51°37·6′	1°2·4′W	X	164,175
Briwnant	Powys	SH8402	52°36·4′	3°42·4′W	X	135,136
Briwnant	Powys	SN8982	52°25·7′	3°37·6′W	X	135,136
Briwnant	Powys	SO1942	52°4·5′	3°10·5′W	X	148,161
Brixedone Fm	Hants	SU4910	50°53·5′	1°17·8′W	FM	196
Brixey's Fm	Hants	SU1602	50°49·3′	1°46·0′W	FM	195
Brixfield Fm	Warw	SP3447	52°7·4′	1°29·8′W	FM	151
Brixham	Torbay	SX9255	50°23·3′	3°30·8′W	T	202
Brixtarw	Carm	SN3012	51°47·1′	4°27·5′W	X	159
Brixter Hill	Northum	NZ0872	55°2·8′	1°52·1′W	X	88
Brixton	Carm	SN2812	51°47·1′	4°29·2′W	X	158
Brixton	Devon	SX5552	50°21·2′	4°1·9′W	T	202
Brixton	Lam	TQ3175	51°27·8′	0°6·5′W	T	176,177
Brixton Barton	Devon	SS6005	50°49·9′	3°58·9′W	X	191
Brixton Barton	Devon	SX5460	50°25·5′	4°3·0′W	X	201
Brixton Deverill	Wilts	ST8638	51°8·7′	2°11·6′W	T	183
Brixton Fm	Oxon	SU3098	51°41·0′	1°33·6′W	FM	164
Brixton Hill	Oxon	SU6587	51°34·9′	1°3·3′W	X	175
Brixworth	Northnts	SP7470	52°19·6′	0°54·4′W	T	141
Brixworth Fox Covert	Northnts	SP7770	52°19·6′	0°51·8′W	F	141
Brizen Fm	Glos	SO9319	51°52·4′	2°5·7′W	FM	163
Brize Norton	Oxon	SP3007	51°45·9′	1°33·5′W	T	164
Brize Norton Airfield	Oxon	SP2805	51°44·8′	1°35·3′W	X	163
Brize Norton Airfield	Oxon	SP2905	51°44·8′	1°34·4′W	X	164
Brize's Lodge	Oxon	SP3315	51°50·2′	1°30·9′W	X	164
Brizlee Hill	Northum	NU1514	55°25·4′	1°45·3′W	H	81
Brizlee Wood	Northum	NU1414	55°25·4′	1°46·3′W	F	81
Broach Dale	E Yorks	TA0467	54°5·5′	0°24·2′W	X	101
Broachrigg Fm	Midlo	NT2861	55°50·5′	3°8·5′W	FM	66
Broadacre	Somer	ST4431	51°4·8′	2°47·6′W	X	182
Broad Acres	E Yorks	TA0459	54°1·2′	0°24·3′W	X	107
Broadacres Fm	Devon	SY1698	50°46·8′	3°11·1′W	FM	192,193
Broadaford	Devon	SX6976	50°34·4′	3°50·6′W	X	191
Broad Alley	Worcs	SO8867	52°18·3′	2°10·2′W	T	150
Broadall Gulf	Devon	SX6064	50°27·8′	3°58·0′W	X	202
Broadall Lake	Devon	SX6162	50°26·7′	3°57·1′W	W	202
Broadall's District	Cambs	TL3189	52°29·2′	0°3·8′W	X	142
Broadall's Fm	Cambs	TL3188	52°28·7′	0°3·9′W	FM	142
Broad Barrow	Devon	SX7079	50°36·0′	3°49·8′W	A	191
Broad Bay or Loch a Tuath	N Eil	NB4936	58°14·7′	6°16·2′W	W	8
Broad Beach	Devon	SS2225	51°0·1′	4°31·8′W	X	190
Broad Beck	N Yks	SE4288	54°17·4′	1°20·9′W	W	99
Broadbeck Ho	N Yks	SE4188	54°17·4′	1°21·8′W	X	99
Broadbeck Mill	Cumbr	NY5248	54°49·7′	2°44·4′W	X	86
Broad Bench	Dorset	SY8978	50°36·3′	2°8·9′W	X	195
Broad Blunsdon	Swin	SU1590	51°36·8′	1°46·6′W	T	163,173
Broadbog	Aberd	NJ5109	57°10·4′	2°48·2′W	X	37
Broad Bog	Scot Bord	NT8168	55°54·5′	2°17·8′W	X	67
Broad Border	Suff	TM0161	52°12·9′	0°56·9′E	F	155
Broadbottom	Tames	SJ9894	53°26·8′	2°1·4′W	T	109
Broadbrae	Highld	NH5350	57°31·2′	4°26·8′W	X	26
Broadbridge	Surrey	TQ3142	51°10·0′	0°7·2′W	X	187
Broadbridge	W Susx	SU8105	50°50·6′	0°50·6′W	T	197
Broadbridge Fm	W Susx	SU8005	50°50·6′	0°51·4′W	FM	197
Broadbridge Fm	W Susx	TQ1430	51°3·7′	0°22·0′W	FM	187
Broadbridge Heath	W Susx	TQ1431	51°4·2′	0°22·0′W	T	187
Broad Bridges	Oxon	SP4002	51°43·1′	1°24·9′W	X	164
Broad Burn	Moray	NJ2650	57°32·3′	3°13·7′W	W	28
Broadbury	Devon	SX4796	50°44·8′	4°9·7′W	T	191
Broadbury Banks	Wilts	SU0955	51°17·9′	1°51·9′W	A	173
Broadbury Castle	Devon	SX4895	50°44·3′	4°8·9′W	A	191
Broadbush	Swin	SU1590	51°36·8′	1°46·6′W	T	163,173
Broad Cairn	Angus	NO2481	56°55·1′	3°14·5′W	H	44
Broad Campden	Glos	SP1537	52°2·1′	1°46·5′W	T	151
Broad Carr	Cald	SE0919	53°40·3′	1°51·4′W	T	110
Broad Carr	N Yks	NZ4505	54°26·5′	1°17·9′W	X	93
Broadcarse	Clackm	NS9189	56°5·1′	3°44·7′W	X	65
Broad Chalke	Wilts	SU0325	51°1·7′	1°57·0′W	T	184
Broadclose	Derby	SK1652	53°4·1′	1°45·3′W	X	119
Broad Close	Derby	SK2536	52°55·5′	1°37·3′W	X	128
Broad Close	N Yks	SE2695	54°21·2′	1°35·6′W	X	99
Broadclose	V of Glam	ST0670	51°25·5′	3°20·7′W	X	170
Broad Clough	Derby	SK0687	53°23·0′	1°54·2′W	X	110
Broad Clough	Lancs	SD8623	53°42·4′	2°12·3′W	T	103
Broadclough Hall	Lancs	SD8623	53°42·4′	2°12·3′W	X	103
Broadclyst	Devon	SX9897	50°46·1′	3°26·4′W	T	192
Broadclyst Moor	Devon	SX9797	50°46·0′	3°27·3′W	X	192
Broad Colney	Herts	TL1703	51°43·0′	0°18·0′W	T	166
Broad Common	Worcs	SO8767	52°18·3′	2°11·0′W	T	150
Broad Crag	Cumbr	NY2207	54°27·4′	3°11·8′W	X	89,90
Broad Craig	S Ayr	NS2415	55°24·1′	4°46·3′W	X	70
Broad Croft	Devon	ST2805	50°50·6′	3°1·0′W	X	193
Broadcroft	Devon	SX4893	50°43·2′	4°8·8′W	X	191
Broad Down	Devon	SX6280	50°36·4′	3°56·6′W	H	191
Broad Down	Devon	SY1793	50°44·1′	3°10·2′W	X	192,193
Broad Down	Worcs	SO7639	52°3·2′	2°20·6′W	X	150
Broad Downs	Kent	TR0745	51°10·2′	0°58·1′E	X	179,189
Broad Ebb	Orkney	HY5539	59°14·4′	2°46·8′W	X	5
Broad Edge	D & G	NY4383	55°8·5′	2°53·2′W	X	79
Broad End	Cumbr	NY2528	54°38·7′	3°9·3′W	X	89,90
Broad End	Cumbr	NY2530	54°39·8′	3°9·3′W	X	89,90
Broad End	Cumbr	NY4007	54°27·5′	2°55·1′W	X	90
Broad End Fm	Suff	TM2674	52°19·3′	1°19·4′E	FM	156
Broadenham Fm	Dorset	SY4596	50°45·9′	2°46·4′W	FM	193
Broadenham Fm	Somer	ST3806	50°51·2′	2°52·5′W	FM	193
Broad Fall	Lancs	SD5047	53°55·2′	2°45·3′W	X	102
Broadfans Fm	Essex	TL6028	51°55·9′	0°20·0′E	FM	167
Broadfaulds	Angus	NO5451	56°39·2′	2°44·6′W	X	54
Broadfell	Cumbr	NY6209	54°28·7′	2°34·8′W	X	91
Broad Fen	Norf	TG3425	52°46·5′	1°28·6′E	W	133,134
Broad Fen Fm	Norf	TL6996	52°32·4′	0°29·9′E	FM	143
Broad Field	Cumbr	NY4244	54°47·5′	2°53·7′W	X	85
Broadfield	D & G	NX4256	54°52·7′	4°27·3′W	X	83
Broadfield	Dorset	ST7903	50°49·8′	2°17·5′W	X	194
Broadfield	Inverc	NS3473	55°55·5′	4°39·0′W	T	63
Broadfield	Kent	TQ5643	51°10·1′	0°14·3′E	X	188
Broadfield	Kent	TQ6153	51°15·4′	0°18·8′E	X	188
Broadfield	Lancs	SD5322	53°41·8′	2°42·3′W	T	102
Broadfield	Lancs	SD7427	53°44·6′	2°23·2′W	T	103
Broadfield	Moray	NJ4048	57°31·4′	2°59·6′W	X	28
Broadfield	Pemb	SN1303	51°41·9′	4°42·0′W	T	158
Broadfield	Roch	SD8410	53°35·4′	2°14·1′W	T	109
Broadfield	S Lanak	NS9833	55°35·1′	3°36·7′W	X	72
Broadfield	W Susx	TQ2534	51°5·7′	0°12·5′W	T	187
Broadfield Court	Heref	SO5453	52°10·6′	2°40·0′W	A	149
Broadfield Covert	Glos	SP1211	51°48·1′	1°49·2′W	F	163
Broadfield Fm	Bath & NE Somer	ST7658	51°19·5′	2°20·3′W	FM	172
Broadfield Fm	Glos	SP1211	51°48·1′	1°49·2′W	FM	163
Broadfield Fm	Herts	TL3301	51°41·7′	0°4·1′W	FM	166
Broadfield Fm	Northnts	SP8994	52°32·4′	0°40·9′W	FM	141
Broadfield Fm	N Som	ST4964	51°22·6′	2°43·6′W	FM	172,182
Broadfield Fm	N Yks	NZ5602	54°24·9′	1°7·8′W	FM	93
Broadfield Fm	Wilts	SU1935	51°7·1′	1°43·3′W	FM	184
Broadfield Hall	Herts	TL3231	51°57·9′	0°4·3′W	X	166
Broadfield Height	D & G	NY1399	55°16·9′	3°21·8′W	H	78
Broadfield Ho	Cumbr	NY4344	54°47·5′	2°52·8′W	X	85
Broadfield Lodge Fm	Herts	TL3231	51°57·9′	0°4·3′W	FM	166
Broadfields	Heref	SO5768	52°18·7′	2°37·4′W	X	137,138
Broadfields	Staffs	SK1813	52°43·1′	1°43·6′W	X	128
Broadfields Fm	Essex	TL7122	51°52·4′	0°29·4′E	FM	167
Broadfields Fm	Hav	TQ5886	51°33·3′	0°17·1′E	FM	177
Broadfields Fm	N Yks	SE3168	54°6·7′	1°31·1′W	FM	99
Broadfields Fm	Staffs	SK2112	52°42·6′	1°40·9′W	FM	128
Broadfield Wood	N Yks	SE4259	54°1·8′	1°21·1′W	F	105
Broadflash Fm	Norf	TL9198	52°33·0′	0°49·4′E	FM	144
Broad Fleet	Essex	TM0415	51°48·0′	0°57·9′E	W	168
Broad Flow	Northum	NT7912	55°24·3′	2°19·5′W	X	80
Broad Fm	E Susx	TQ5712	50°53·4′	0°14·3′E	FM	199
Broadfold	Cald	SE0327	53°44·6′	1°56·9′W	X	104
Broadfold	Cumbr	SD4797	54°22·2′	2°48·5′W	X	97
Broadfold	Pth & Kin	NN9613	56°18·1′	3°40·4′W	X	58
Broadfoot	Shetld	HT9637	60°7·3′	2°3·8′W	X	4
Broadford	Aberd	NJ4305	57°8·2′	2°56·1′W	X	37
Broadford	D & G	NX9184	55°8·6′	3°42·2′W	X	78
Broadford	Highld	NG6423	57°14·5′	5°54·2′W	T	32
Broad Ford	Kent	TQ7139	51°7·7′	0°27·0′E	T	188
Broadford	Surrey	SU9761	51°20·6′	0°36·0′W	X	175,176,186
Broadford	Surrey	SU9946	51°12·5′	0°34·6′W	T	186
Broadford Airstrip	Highld	NG6924	57°15·2′	5°49·3′W	X	32
Broadford Bay	Highld	NG6523	57°14·5′	5°53·2′W	W	32
Broadford Bridge	W Susx	TQ0921	50°58·9′	0°26·4′W	T	198
Broadford River	Highld	NG6222	57°13·9′	5°56·2′W	W	32
Broad Forstal Fm	Kent	TQ7446	51°11·4′	0°29·8′E	FM	188
Broadgairhill	Scot Bord	NT2010	55°22·9′	3°15·3′W	X	79
Broadgairhill Burn	Scot Bord	NT1911	55°23·4′	3°16·3′W	W	79
Broadgair Knowe	Scot Bord	NT3917	55°26·8′	2°57·4′W	H	79
Broadgate	Aberd	NJ5528	57°20·7′	2°44·4′W	X	37
Broadgate	Corn	SX3873	50°32·3′	4°16·8′W	X	201
Broadgate	Cumbr	SD1886	54°16·0′	3°15·1′W	X	96
Broadgate	D & G	NY0671	55°1·7′	3°27·8′W	X	85
Broadgate	Hants	SU4122	51°0·0′	1°24·6′W	T	185
Broadgate	Lancs	SD5545	53°54·2′	2°40·7′W	X	102
Broad Gate	Northum	NY8351	54°51·5′	2°15·5′W	X	86,87
Broadgate Fm	Cumbr	SD4399	54°23·2′	2°52·2′W	FM	97
Broadgate Fm	E Yorks	TA0137	53°49·4′	0°27·5′W	FM	106,107
Broad Gate Fm	N Yks	NZ6704	54°25·9′	0°57·6′W	FM	94
Broadgate Fm	Suff	TL8158	52°11·7′	0°39·3′E	FM	155
Broadgate Hill	Staffs	SK0438	52°56·6′	1°56·0′W	X	128
Broadgate Ho	Lincs	TF2823	52°47·6′	0°5·7′W	X	131
Broadgate Ho	Lincs	TF3916	52°43·7′	0°3·9′E	X	131
Broadgate Ho	Lincs	TF4023	52°47·4′	0°5·0′E	X	131
Broadgates	Derby	SK3052	53°4·1′	1°32·7′W	X	119
Broadgates	Devon	SX8355	50°23·2′	3°38·4′W	X	202
Broadgates	Essex	TL6117	51°49·9′	0°20·6′E	X	167
Broad Geo	Highld	ND3544	58°23·0′	3°6·2′W	X	12
Broad Geo	Orkney	HY4731	59°10·0′	2°55·1′W	X	5,6
Broad Geo	Orkney	HY5215	59°1·4′	2°49·7′W	X	6
Broad Geo	Orkney	ND2888	58°46·7′	3°14·2′W	X	7
Broadgrass Green	Suff	TL9663	52°14·0′	0°52·6′E	T	155
Broad Green	Beds	SP9543	52°4·9′	0°36·4′W	T	153
Broad Green	Cambs	TL6859	52°12·4′	0°27·9′E	T	154
Broad Green	Croy	TQ3266	51°22·9′	0°5·8′W	T	176,177
Broad Green	Essex	TL4439	52°2·1′	0°6·4′E	T	154
Broad Green	Essex	TL8723	51°52·7′	0°43·4′E	T	168
Broad Green	Heref	SO4767	52°18·2′	2°46·2′W	X	137,138,148
Broad Green	Liv	SJ4090	53°24·4′	2°53·7′W	T	108
Broadgreen	Pth & Kin	NO1435	56°30·2′	3°23·4′W	X	53
Broad Green	Suff	TL7859	52°12·3′	0°36·7′E	T	155
Broad Green	Suff	TM0959	52°11·6′	1°3·9′E	T	155
Broad Green	Suff	TM1464	52°14·2′	1°8·5′E	X	156
Broad Green	Worcs	SO7655	52°11·8′	2°20·7′W	T	150
Broad Green	Worcs	SO9970	52°19·9′	2°0·5′W	T	139
Broad Green Fm	E Susx	TQ6909	50°51·6′	0°24·5′E	FM	199
Broadgreens	Aberd	NJ7645	57°29·9′	2°23·6′W	X	29
Broadgreens	Aberd	NJ9101	57°6·2′	2°8·5′W	X	38
Broadgreen Wood	Herts	TL3109	51°46·1′	0°5·7′W	T	166
Broadgroves	Essex	TL6420	51°51·5′	0°23·3′E	X	167
Broadhag Burn	E Ayr	NS5112	55°23·0′	4°20·7′W	W	70
Broad Halfpenny	W Susx	SU9817	50°56·9′	0°35·9′W	X	197
Broadhalfpenny Down	Hants	SU6715	50°56·1′	1°2·4′W	X	196
Broadhalgh	Roch	SD8713	53°37·0′	2°11·4′W	T	109
Broadham Green	Surrey	TQ3851	51°14·7′	0°1·0′W	T	187
Broadham Ho	W Susx	SU8814	50°55·4′	0°44·5′W	X	197
Broadhanger	Hants	SU7125	51°1·4′	0°58·9′W	X	186,197
Broadhaugh	Scot Bord	NT4509	55°22·6′	2°51·6′W	T	79
Broadhaugh	Scot Bord	NT8654	55°47·0′	2°13·0′W	X	67,74
Broadhaugh Hill	Scot Bord	NT4508	55°22·0′	2°51·6′W	H	79
Broad Haven	Aberd	NK0530	57°21·9′	1°54·6′W	W	30
Broadhaven	Highld	ND3751	58°26·8′	3°4·3′W	T	12
Broad Haven	Highld	ND3851	58°26·8′	3°3·3′W	W	12
Broad Haven	Pemb	SM8613	51°46·7′	5°5·8′W	T	157
Broad Haven	Pemb	SR9794	51°36·7′	4°55·5′W	W	158
Broadhay	Shrops	SJ5731	52°52·7′	2°37·9′W	X	126
Broad Haye	Staffs	SK0144	52°59·8′	1°58·7′W	X	119,128
Broadhayes Ho	Devon	ST2302	50°49·0′	3°5·2′W	X	192,193
Broadhay Fm	Derby	SK2280	53°19·2′	1°39·8′W	FM	110
Broadhead	Black w Dar	SD7320	53°40·8′	2°24·1′W	X	103
Broad Head	Cumbr	SD5896	54°21·7′	2°38·4′W	X	97
Broad Head	D & G	NY3494	55°14·4′	3°1·8′W	H	79

Broad Head	D & G	NY3988	55°11·2'	2°57·1'W	X	79
Broadhead	S Ayr	NS3821	55°27·6'	4°33·3'W	X	70
Broadhead Brook	Black w					
	Dar	SD7318	53°39·7'	2°24·1'W	W	109
Broadhead Cottage	Midlo	NT3157	55°48·3'	3°5·6'W	X	66,73
Broad Head Drain	Roch	SD9616	53°38·7'	2°3·2'W	W	109
Broad Head Fm	Brad	SE0139	53°51·1'	1°58·7'W	FM	104
Broadhead Fm	Lancs	SD7251	53°57·5'	2°25·2'W	FM	103
Broad Head Fm	N Yks	SE9088	54°17·0'	0°36·6'W	FM	94,101
Broadheadfold	Pth & Kin	NO0410	56°16·6'	3°32·6'W	X	58
Broad Head Moor	Lancs	SD9436	53°49·5'	2°5·1'W	X	103
Broadhead Noddle	Oldham	SD9910	53°35·4'	2°0·5'W	X	109
Broad Heath	Powys	SO3363	52°15·9'	2°58·5'W	T	137,148,149
Broad Heath	Staffs	SJ8525	52°49·6'	2°13·0'W	T	127
Broadheath	Traf	SJ7689	53°24·1'	2°21·2'W	T	109
Broad Heath	Worcs	SO6665	52°17·2'	2°29·5'W	X	138,149
Broadhembury	Devon	ST1004	50°49·9'	3°16·3'W	T	192,193
Broadhempston	Devon	SX8066	50°29·1'	3°41·1'W	T	202
Broadhey Hill	Derby	SJ9983	53°20·9'	2°0·5'W	X	109
Broad Hill	Cambs	TL5976	52°21·8'	0°20·5'E	T	143
Broad Hill	Ches	SJ8168	53°12·8'	2°16·7'W	X	118
Broadhill	Devon	SS7824	51°0·4'	3°44·0'W	X	180
Broad Hill	Leic	SK4725	52°49·5'	1°17·7'W	X	129
Broad Hill	Leic	SK5714	52°43·5'	1°9·0'W	X	129
Broad Hill	S Glos	ST7686	51°34·6'	2°20·4'W	X	172
Broad Hill	S Lanak	NT0029	55°32·9'	3°34·7'W	H	72
Broad Hill	S Lanak	NT0219	55°27·6'	3°32·6'W	H	78
Broadhill	Staffs	SJ8019	52°46·3'	2°17·4'W	X	127
Broadhill	W Susx	TQ3116	50°55·9'	0°7·8'W	X	198
Broad Hill Fm	Somer	ST4911	50°54·0'	2°43·1'W	FM	193,194
Broad Hill Fm	Worcs	SO9144	52°5·9'	2°7·5'W	FM	150
Broadhills	Arg & Bt	NM1755	56°36·3'	6°36·3'W	X	46
Broad Hinton	Wilts	SU1076	51°29·2'	1°51·0'W	T	173
Broad Ho	Norf	TG3016	52°41·8'	1°24·6'E	X	133,134
Broadhoath Wood	Kent	TQ5753	51°15·5'	0°15·4'E	F	188
Broadholm	Derby	SK3449	53°2·5'	1°29·2'W	T	119
Broadholm	D & G	NY1083	55°8·5'	3°24·3'W	X	78
Broadholme	Lincs	SK8974	53°15·6'	0°39·5'W	T	121
Broadholme	Northnts	SP9369	52°18·9'	0°37·7'W	X	153
Broadholme Fm	N Yks	SE8358	54°0·9'	0°43·6'W	FM	106
Broadhope Hill	Northum	NT9323	55°30·3'	2°6·2'W	H	74,75
Broadhouselea	S Lanak	NS9150	55°44·1'	3°43·7'W	X	65,72
Broadhurst	E Susx	TQ6224	50°59·8'	0°18·9'E	X	199
Broadhurst Fm	Lincs	TF1741	52°57·4'	0°15·1'W	FM	130
Broadhurst Green	Staffs	SJ9815	52°44·2'	2°1·4'W	X	127
Broadhurst Manor	W Susx	TQ3830	51°3·4'	0°1·5'W	X	187
Broadi Face	Orkney	HY2000	58°53·1'	3°22·8'W	X	7
Broad Ing	Cumbr	NY4926	54°37·8'	2°47·0'W	X	90
Broad Ing	Lancs	SD7751	53°57·5'	2°20·6'W	X	103
Broad Ings	E Yorks	SE8051	53°57·2'	0°46·4'W	T	106
Broad Ings	N Yks	NZ5800	54°23·8'	1°6·0'W	X	93
Broad Ings Fm	Lincs	TF2339	52°56·3'	0°9·8'W	FM	131
Broad Islands	N Ayr	NS1551	55°43·3'	4°56·3'W	X	63,69
Broadith Lane	Lancs	SD5638	53°50·4'	2°39·7'W	X	102
Broad Lake	Hants	SU7004	50°50·1'	1°0·0'W	W	197
Broadlake	Kent	TQ8042	51°9·2'	0°34·8'E	X	188
Broadland	Aberd	NJ4841	57°27·6'	2°51·5'W	X	28,29
Broadland	Brig	SS8879	51°30·2'	3°36·4'W	X	170
Broadland	Pemb	SM9012	51°46·3'	5°2·2'W	X	157,158
Broadland Fm	Norf	TF7007	52°38·3'	0°31·1'E	FM	143
Broadland Row	E Susx	TQ8319	50°56·7'	0°36·7'E	T	199
Broadlands	Devon	SX8571	50°31·9'	3°37·0'W	T	202
Broadlands	Hants	SU3520	50°58·9'	1°29·7'W	X	185
Broadlands	Hants	SU6335	51°6·9'	1°5·6'W	X	185
Broadlands	W Susx	SU9432	51°5·0'	0°39·1'W	X	186
Broadlands Fm	Wakf	SE3217	53°39·2'	1°30·5'W	FM	110,111
Broadlands Lake	Hants	SU3416	50°56·8'	1°30·6'W	W	185
Broadlands, The	Shrops	SJ4021	52°47·2'	2°53·0'W	X	126
Broadlane	Corn	SW6130	50°7·6'	5°20·3'W	T	203
Broad Lane	Corn	SW6742	50°14·2'	5°15·7'W	T	203
Broadlane Fm	Ches	SJ7365	53°11·1'	2°23·8'W	FM	118
Broad Lane Fm	Somer	ST3225	51°1·5'	2°57·8'W	FM	193
Broad Lane Fm	Wakf	SE4509	53°34·8'	1°18·8'W	FM	111
Broad Lane Fm	Wilts	ST9462	51°21·7'	2°4·8'W	FM	173
Broad Lanes	Shrops	SO7788	52°29·6'	2°19·9'W	T	138
Broad Law	Durham	NY9539	54°45·0'	2°4·2'W	X	91,92
Broadlaw	Northum	NZ1679	55°6·6'	1°44·5'W	X	88
Broad Law	Scot Bord	NT1423	55°29·8'	3°21·2'W	H	72
Broad Law	Scot Bord	NT3453	55°46·2'	3°2·7'W	H	66,73
Broad Law	Scot Bord	NT7913	55°24·9'	2°19·5'W	X	80
Broad Law	S Lanak	NS8915	55°25·2'	3°44·8'W	H	71,78
Broadlay	Carm	SN3709	51°45·6'	4°21·3'W	T	159
Broad Layings	Hants	SU4362	51°21·6'	1°22·6'W	T	174
Broad Lea	Cumbr	NY6623	54°36·3'	2°31·2'W	X	91
Broad Lea	Darl	NZ3521	54°35·2'	1°27·1'W	X	93
Broadlea	D & G	NX8366	54°58·7'	3°49·3'W	X	84
Broadlea	D & G	NY2274	55°3·5'	3°12·8'W	X	85
Broadlea	Scot Bord	NT3911	55°23·6'	2°57·4'W	X	79
Broadleaze Fm	Dorset	ST4904	50°50·2'	2°43·1'W	FM	193,194
Broadleaze Fm	Oxon	SU2296	51°40·0'	1°40·5'W	FM	163
Broadleaze Fm	Oxon	SU2689	51°36·2'	1°37·1'W	FM	174
Broadleaze Fm	Oxon	SU3489	51°36·2'	1°30·2'W	FM	174
Broadleaze Fm	Somer	ST4920	50°58·9'	2°43·2'W	FM	183,193
Broadleaze Fm	Somer	ST5214	50°55·6'	2°40·6'W	FM	194
Broadleaze Fm	Wilts	SU0992	51°37·8'	1°51·8'W	FM	163,173
Broad Ledge	Dorset	SY3492	50°43·7'	2°55·7'W	X	193
Broad Ledge	I Scilly	SV9115	49°57·5'	6°18·2'W	X	203
Broadlee	Northum	NY7850	54°50·9'	2°20·1'W	X	86,87
Broadlee-bank Tor	Derby	SK1185	53°21·9'	1°49·7'W	X	110
Broadlee Fm	Derby	SK0376	53°17·1'	1°56·9'W	FM	119
Broadlee Hill	Scot Bord	NT4521	55°29·0'	2°51·8'W	X	73
Broadlee Loch	Scot Bord	NT4010	55°23·1'	2°56·4'W	W	79
Broadlees	E Renf	NS5353	55°45·1'	4°20·1'W	X	64
Broadlees	S Lanak	NS9835	55°36·1'	3°36·7'W	X	72
Broadleigh	Somer	ST0918	50°57·5'	3°17·4'W	X	181
Broadley	Aberd	NJ4518	57°15·2'	2°54·2'W	X	37
Broadley	Devon	SS9206	50°50·8'	3°31·7'W	X	192
Broadley	Devon	SX4963	50°27·1'	4°7·2'W	X	201
Broadley	Devon	SX7254	50°22·6'	3°47·6'W	X	202
Broadley	Highld	NH8754	57°34·0'	3°52·9'W	X	27
Broadley	Lancs	SD8816	53°38·7'	2°10·5'W	T	109
Broadley	Monm	SO2828	51°57·0'	3°2·5'W	X	161
Broadley	Moray	NJ3961	57°38·3'	3°0·8'W	T	28
Broadley	Pemb	SN0109	51°44·9'	4°52·6'W	X	157,158
Broadley Bridge	Aberd	NJ6063	57°39·6'	2°39·8'W	X	29
Broadley Common	Essex	TL4206	51°44·3'	0°3·8'E	T	167
Broadley Fm	Swan	SS5990	51°35·7'	4°1·8'W	FM	159
Broadley Grange	York	SE5349	53°56·3'	1°11·1'W	X	105
Broadleyhill	Aberd	NK0532	57°23·0'	1°54·6'W	X	30
Broadley Hill	Devon	ST2307	50°51·7'	3°5·3'W	X	192,193
Broadley Ho	Hants	SZ2697	50°46·5'	1°37·5'W	X	195
Broadley Inclosure	Hants	SZ2599	50°47·6'	1°38·3'W	F	195
Broadleys	Aberd	NJ8660	57°38·0'	2°13·6'W	X	30
Broad Leys	Cumbr	NY0407	54°27·2'	3°28·4'W	X	89
Broadleys	Fife	NT2689	56°5·5'	3°10·9'W	X	66
Broadleys	Pth & Kin	NN9914	56°18·7'	3°37·5'W	X	58
Broadleys Fm	Denb	SJ0365	53°10·6'	3°26·7'W	FM	116
Broadley's Gate	Durham	NY9029	54°39·6'	2°8·9'W	X	91,92
Broadley Wood	Dorset	ST8406	50°51·4'	2°13·3'W	F	194
Broadlie	E Ayr	NS4251	55°43·9'	4°30·5'W	X	64
Broadlie Ho	N Ayr	NS2849	55°42·5'	4°43·8'W	X	63
Broad Low	Derby	SK1778	53°18·2'	1°44·3'W	X	119
Broadlowash	Derby	SK1550	53°3·1'	1°46·2'W	X	119
Broad Marston	Worcs	SP1446	52°7·0'	1°47·3'W	T	151
Broadmayne	Dorset	SY7286	50°40·6'	2°23·6'W	T	194
Broad Mea	Northum	NY6448	54°49·8'	2°33·2'W	X	86
Broadmea Crag	N Yks	SD8396	54°21·8'	2°15·3'W	X	98
Broadmead	Devon	SS5310	50°52·5'	4°5·0'W	X	191
Broad Mead	Newp	ST3983	51°32·8'	2°52·4'W	X	171
Broad Mead	Newp	ST4083	51°32·8'	2°51·5'W	X	171,172
Broad Mead	Somer	SS7141	51°9·5'	3°50·3'W	X	180
Broadmead Brook	Wilts	ST7976	51°29·2'	2°17·8'W	W	172
Broadmead Brook	Wilts	ST8076	51°29·2'	2°16·9'W	W	173
Broadmead Fm	Devon	SS8818	50°57·3'	3°35·3'W	FM	181
Broadmead Fm	Herts	SP8917	51°50·9'	0°42·1'W	FM	165
Broadmead Fm	Wilts	ST8531	51°4·9'	2°12·5'W	FM	183
Broad Meadow	Staffs	SJ8348	53°2·0'	2°14·8'W	T	118
Broad Meadow	Staffs	SK1904	52°38·2'	1°42·8'W	X	139
Broadmeadow	W Loth	NT0361	55°50·2'	3°32·5'W	X	65
Broadmeadow Common	Norf	TF8215	52°42·3'	0°42·0'E	X	132
Broadmeadow Fm	Black w					
	Dar	SD7419	53°40·3'	2°23·2'W	FM	109
Broadmeadow Hall	Staffs	SK1163	53°10·1'	1°49·7'W	A	119
Broadmeadows	Cumbr	NY5937	54°43·8'	2°37·8'W	X	91
Broadmeadows	D & G	NY3876	55°4·7'	2°57·8'W	X	85
Broadmeadows	Durham	NZ1045	54°48·2'	1°50·2'W	X	88
Broad Meadows	Northum	NY7648	54°49·8'	2°22·0'W	X	86,87
Broadmeadows	Scot Bord	NT4130	55°33·9'	2°55·7'W	T	73
Broadmeadows	Scot Bord	NT9151	55°45·4'	2°8·2'W	X	67,74,75
Broadmeadows	Staffs	SJ9258	53°7·4'	2°6·8'W	X	118
Broadmeadows Ho	Scot Bord	NT9154	55°47·0'	2°8·2'W	X	67,74,75
Broadmeads Plantn	Devon	SX4496	50°44·8'	4°12·3'W	F	190
Broad Mea Head	Cumbr	SD7789	54°18·0'	2°20·8'W	X	98
Broad Mea Top	N Yks	SD9193	54°20·2'	2°7·9'W	X	98
Broad Meend	Monm	SO5004	51°44·2'	2°43·1'W	F	162
Broadmere	Hants	SU6147	51°13·4'	1°7·3'W	T	185
Broad Mere	Northum	NY8753	54°52·5'	2°11·7'W	X	87
Broad Meres	Durham	NY8242	54°46·6'	2°16·4'W	X	86,87
Broadmire	Cumbr	SD7486	54°16·4'	2°23·5'W	X	98
Broadmoor	Cumbr	NY0815	54°31·6'	3°24·9'W	X	89
Broadmoor	Cumbr	NY3144	54°47·4'	3°4·0'W	X	85
Broad Moor	Cumbr	NY3242	54°46·3'	3°3·0'W	X	85
Broadmoor	Devon	SS6323	50°59·6'	3°56·8'W	X	180
Broadmoor	Devon	SS7517	50°56·6'	3°46·4'W	X	180
Broad Moor	D & G	NX0158	54°52·9'	5°5·7'W	X	82
Broad Moor	Norf	TF9601	52°34·5'	0°54·0'E	X	144
Broadmoor	Pemb	SM8212	51°46·1'	5°9·2'W	X	157
Broadmoor	Pemb	SM9428	51°55·0'	4°59·3'W	X	157,158
Broad Moor	Pemb	SM9609	51°44·8'	4°56·9'W	X	157,158
Broadmoor	Pemb	SN0905	51°42·9'	4°45·5'W	T	158
Broadmoor	Surrey	TQ1345	51°11·8'	0°22·6'W	T	187
Broadmoor Common	Heref	SO6036	52°1·5'	2°34·6'W	T	149
Broadmoor Fm	Brackn	SU8563	51°21·8'	0°46·4'W	FM	175,186
Broadmoor Fm	Corn	SX3960	50°25·3'	4°15·6'W	FM	201
Broadmoor Fm	Devon	SX5278	50°35·2'	4°5·1'W	FM	191,201
Broadmoor Fm	Glos	SP1717	51°51·3'	1°44·8'W	FM	163
Broadmoor Fm	Northnts	SP6780	52°25·1'	1°0·5'W	FM	141
Broadmoor Hospital	Brackn	SU8564	51°22·3'	0°46·3'W	X	175,186
Broadmore Green	Worcs	SO8153	52°10·7'	2°16·3'W	T	150
Broadmore, The	Staffs	SK0126	52°50·1'	1°58·7'W	X	128
Broad Moss	Pth & Kin	NO1947	56°36·7'	3°18·7'W	X	53
Broadmuir	Aberd	NK0533	57°23·5'	1°54·6'W	X	30
Broadmuir	Angus	NO3255	56°41·2'	3°6·2'W	X	53
Broadmuir Fm	Aberd	NJ8158	57°37·0'	2°18·6'W	FM	29,30
Broadmyre	Aberd	NJ5324	57°18·5'	2°46·4'W	X	37
Broadmyre	Aberd	NJ6225	57°19·1'	2°37·4'W	X	37
Broadness	Kent	TQ6076	51°27·8'	0°18·6'E	X	177
Broadness Fm	Cumbr	NY2229	54°39·3'	3°12·1'W	FM	89,90
Broadnymett	Devon	SS7000	50°47·3'	3°50·3'W	X	191
Broadnymett Moor	Devon	SS7000	50°47·3'	3°50·3'W	X	191
Broad Oak	Barns	SE2406	53°33·2'	1°37·9'W	A	110
Broad Oak	Bucks	SP9027	51°56·3'	0°41·1'W	X	165
Broad Oak	Carm	SN5722	51°52·9'	4°4·3'W	T	159
Broad Oak	Cumbr	SD1194	54°20·3'	3°21·7'W	T	96
Broad Oak	Cumbr	SD4389	54°17·9'	2°52·1'W	X	97
Broadoak	Cumbr	SD4691	54°19·0'	2°49·4'W	X	97
Broad Oak	Devon	SY0693	50°44·0'	3°19·5'W	T	192
Broad Oak	Dorset	ST7812	50°54·7'	2°18·4'W	T	194
Broadoak	Dorset	SY4396	50°45·9'	2°48·1'W	T	193
Broad Oak	E Susx	TQ6022	50°58·7'	0°17·1'E	T	199
Broad Oak	E Susx	TQ8220	50°57·3'	0°35·9'E	T	199
Broadoak	Glos	SO7012	51°48·6'	2°25·7'W	T	162
Broadoak	Hants	SU5013	50°55·1'	1°16·9'W	T	196
Broad Oak	Hants	SU7551	51°15·4'	0°55·1'W	T	186
Broad Oak	Heref	SO4821	51°53·3'	2°44·9'W	T	161
Broadoak	Kent	TQ9060	51°18·7'	0°44·0'E	X	178
Broad Oak	Kent	TR0438	51°6·5'	0°55·3'E	T	179,189
Broad Oak	Kent	TR1661	51°18·6'	1°6·4'E	T	179
Broadoak	Shrops	SJ4917	52°45·1'	2°44·9'W	T	126
Broad Oak	Shrops	SO7888	52°29·6'	2°19·0'W	T	138
Broad Oak	Somer	ST2907	50°51·7'	3°0·1'W	X	193
Broadoak	Staffs	SJ9747	53°1·5'	2°2·3'W	X	118
Broad Oak	St Hel	SJ5395	53°27·2'	2°42·1'W	T	108
Broadoak	Wrex	SJ3658	53°7·2'	2°57·0'W	T	117
Broad Oak	York	SE5960	54°2·2'	1°5·5'W	X	100
Broadoak Brake	Notts	SK6365	53°10·9'	1°3·0'W	X	120
Broadoak End	Herts	TL3013	51°48·3'	0°6·5'W	T	166
Broad Oak Fm	Ches	SJ7084	53°21·4'	2°26·6'W	FM	109
Broad Oak Fm	Ches	SJ7780	53°19·2'	2°20·3'W	FM	109
Broadoak Fm	Dorset	SY4395	50°45·3'	2°48·1'W	FM	193
Broad Oak Fm	Northum	NZ1056	54°54·2'	1°50·2'W	FM	88
Broadoak Fm	Staffs	SK0535	52°55·0'	1°55·1'W	FM	128
Broadoak Fm	Stock	SJ9487	53°23·0'	2°5·0'W	FM	109
Broadoak Fm	Suff	TM1365	52°14·7'	1°7·6'E	FM	156
Broad Oak Fm	Suff	TM3368	52°15·9'	1°25·3'E	FM	156
Broad Oak Fm	Suff	TM3874	52°19·0'	1°29·9'E	FM	156
Broad Oak Fm	Traf	SJ7290	53°24·6'	2°24·9'W	FM	109
Broad Oak Fm	Wilts	ST9026	51°2·2'	2°8·2'W	FM	184
Broad Oak Fm	Wrex	SJ4940	52°57·5'	2°45·1'W	FM	117
Broad Oak Fm	York	SE6948	53°55·7'	0°56·5'W	FM	105,106
Broadoak Hill	Derby	SK4564	53°10·5'	1°19·2'W	X	120
Broadoak Park	Salf	SD7600	53°30·0'	2°21·3'W	T	109
Broad Oaks	Cumbr	NY4001	54°24·3'	2°55·0'W	X	90
Broad Oaks Fm	Derby	SK3953	53°4·6'	1°24·7'W	FM	119
Broad Oaks Fm	N Yks	SE5861	54°2·7'	1°6·4'W	FM	100
Broadoaks Manor	Essex	TL5933	51°58·6'	0°19·3'E	A	167
Broad Orchard Fm	Dorset	SY4298	50°47·0'	2°49·0'W	FM	193
Broad Parkham	Devon	SS3722	50°58·7'	4°18·9'W	T	190
Broad Park Ho	N Yks	SE0356	54°0·2'	1°56·8'W	X	104
Broadpiece Fm	Cambs	TL4280	52°24·2'	0°5·6'E	FM	142,143
Broadplace	Aberd	NJ7427	57°20·2'	2°25·5'W	X	38
Broadplat	Oxon	SU7383	51°32·7'	0°56·4'W	T	175
Broadpool	Cambs	TL3382	52°25·4'	0°2·2'W	X	142
Broad Pool	Swan	SS5091	51°36·1'	4°9·6'W	W	159
Broadpool Common	Northum	NY8175	55°4·4'	2°17·4'W	X	86,87
Broadpool Fm	Cambs	TL3483	52°25·9'	0°1·3'W	FM	142
Broad Raine	Cumbr	SD6290	54°18·5'	2°34·6'W	X	97
Broadrake	N Yks	SD7479	54°12·6'	2°23·5'W	X	98
Broadrashes	Moray	NJ3747	57°30·8'	3°2·6'W	X	28
Broadrashes	Moray	NJ4354	57°34·6'	2°56·7'W	X	28
Broadreed Fm	E Susx	TQ5425	51°0·4'	0°12·1'E	FM	188,199
Broadreed Fm	W Susx	SU7711	50°53·8'	0°53·9'W	FM	197
Broad Ride	Glos	SO9502	51°43·2'	2°4·0'W	X	163
Broadridge	Devon	SX8254	50°22·7'	3°39·2'W	X	202
Broadridge Fm	Devon	SS7509	50°52·3'	3°46·2'W	FM	191
Broadridge Fm	Devon	SS7916	50°56·1'	3°42·9'W	FM	180
Broadridge Fm	Devon	SS8508	50°51·8'	3°37·7'W	FM	191
Broadridge Wood	Devon	SX8371	50°31·9'	3°38·7'W	F	202
Broad Rife	W Susx	SZ8395	50°45·1'	0°49·0'W	W	197
Broad River	Somer	ST4811	50°54·0'	2°44·0'W	W	193
Broad Rock		NS2142	55°38·6'	4°50·2'W	X	63,70
Broad Rock	Devon	SX6167	50°29·4'	3°57·2'W	X	202
Broadrock	Glos	ST5496	51°39·9'	2°39·5'W	T	162
Broad Rushes	Devon	SX6664	50°27·9'	3°52·9'W	X	202
Broad Salts	Kent	TR3459	51°17·1'	1°21·7'E	X	179
Broad Sands	Devon	SS4632	51°4·2'	4°11·5'W	X	180
Broad Sands	E Loth	NT5285	56°3·6'	2°45·8'W	X	66
Broadsands	Torbay	SX8957	50°24·4'	3°33·3'W	T	202
Broadsea	Aberd	NJ7020	57°16·4'	2°29·4'W	X	38
Broadsea	Aberd	NJ9867	57°41·8'	2°1·6'W	T	30
Broadsea Bay	D & G	NW9659	54°53·3'	5°10·4'W	W	82
Broads Fm	Corn	SX0870	50°30·1'	4°42·1'W	FM	200
Broad's Green	Essex	TL6912	51°47·1'	0°27·4'E	T	167
Broad's Green	Wilts	ST9867	51°24·4'	2°1·3'W	T	173
Broadshade	Aberd	NJ8107	57°9·5'	2°18·4'W	X	38
Broadshard	Somer	ST4410	50°53·4'	2°47·4'W	T	193
Broad Shaw	Durham	NY9018	54°33·7'	2°8·9'W	X	91,92
Broadshaw	Highld	NH9750	57°32·0'	3°42·8'W	X	27
Broad Shaw	N Yks	SD7161	54°2·9'	2°26·2'W	X	98
Broadshaw	N Yks	SE0857	54°0·8'	1°52·3'W	X	104
Broadshaw	W Loth	NT0462	55°50·8'	3°31·6'W	X	65
Broadshaw Bottom	N Yks	NY9407	54°27·7'	2°5·1'W	X	91,92
Broadshaw Rig	D & G	NY0498	55°16·3'	3°30·2'W	X	78
Broadshaw Water	D & G	NY0497	55°15·7'	3°30·2'W	W	78
Broadshean	S Ayr	NS2406	55°19·3'	4°46·0'W	X	70,76
Broadshed	Aberd	NJ8518	57°15·4'	2°14·5'W	X	38
Broadshell Cross	Devon	SS3102	50°47·8'	4°23·5'W	X	190
Broads Ho	N Yks	SE4188	54°17·4'	1°21·8'W	X	99
Broad Shoal	Orkney	HY4939	59°14·3'	2°53·1'W	X	5
Broad Shore	Orkney	HY2209	58°57·9'	3°20·9'W	X	6,7
Broadside	Falk	NS7783	56°1·7'	3°58·0'W	X	57,64
Broadside Park Fm	Suff	TM5077	52°20·3'	1°40·6'E	FM	156
Broadslap	Pth & Kin	NN9915	56°19·3'	3°37·5'W	X	58
Broad Sound	I Scilly	SV8308	49°53·5'	6°24·5'W	W	203
Broad Sound	Pemb	SM7206	51°42·6'	5°17·6'W	W	157
Broadsruther	Northum	NT9424	55°30·8'	2°5·3'W	X	74,75
Broad Stack	Shetld	HU3411	59°53·2'	1°23·1'W	X	4
Broadstairs	Kent	TR3967	51°21·3'	1°26·4'E	T	179
Broad Stand	Cumbr	NY2106	54°26·8'	3°12·7'W	X	89,90
Broads, The	Cambs	TL5969	52°18·0'	0°20·3'E	X	154
Broad Stone	Glos	ST5797	51°40·4'	2°36·9'W	A	162
Broadstone	Kent	TQ8647	51°11·7'	0°40·1'E	T	189
Broadstone	Monm	SO5003	51°43·6'	2°43·0'W	T	162
Broadstone	N Ayr	NS3653	55°44·8'	4°36·3'W	X	63
Broadstone	Poole	SZ0095	50°45·5'	1°59·6'W	T	195
Broadstone	Shrops	SO4996	52°33·8'	2°44·7'W	X	137,138
Broadstone	Shrops	SO5489	52°30·1'	2°40·3'W	T	137,138
Broadstone Fm	E Susx	TQ3720	50°58·0'	0°2·5'W	FM	198
Broadstone Fm	E Susx	TQ4332	51°4·4'	0°2·9'E	FM	187
Broadstone Fm	Shrops	SO5489	52°30·1'	2°40·3'W	FM	137,138
Broadstone Fm	Surrey	TQ1236	51°7·0'	0°23·6'W	FM	187
Broadstonehall	N Ayr	NS3552	55°44·3'	4°37·3'W	X	63
Broadstone Hill	Oldham	SE0207	53°33·8'	1°57·8'W	X	110
Broadstone Hill	Oxon	SP3526	51°56·1'	1°29·1'W	X	164
Broadstone Lodge	Kirk	SE2006	53°33·3'	1°41·5'W	X	110
Broadstone Resr	Barns	SE1906	53°33·3'	1°42·4'W	W	110
Broad Stone Rigg	Durham	NY8619	54°34·2'	2°12·6'W	X	91,92
Broad Stones	Northum	NU1442	55°40·5'	1°46·2'W	X	75
Broad Stone, The	Dorset	SY5990	50°42·7'	2°34·5'W	A	194
Broadstone Village	Oxon	SP3525	51°55·6'	1°29·1'W	A	164

Broadstone Warren	E Susx	TQ4232	51°4·4'	0°2·0'E	F	187
Broad Street	E Susx	TQ8616	50°55·0'	0°39·2'E	T	189,199
Broad Street	Kent	TQ8356	51°16·6'	0°37·8'E	T	178,188
Broad Street	Kent	TR1140	51°7·4'	1°1·3'E	T	179,189
Broad Street	Kent	TR1640	51°7·3'	1°5·6'E	T	179,189
Broad Street	Medway	TQ7671	51°24·9'	0°32·3'E	T	178
Broad Street	Suff	TL9643	52°3·3'	0°51·9'E	T	155
Broad Street	Wilts	SU1059	51°20·0'	1°51·0'W	T	173
Broadstreet Common	Newp	ST3584	51°33·3'	2°55·9'W	T	171
Broadstreet Common	Surrey	SU9650	51°14·7'	0°37·1'W	X	186
Broad Street Fm	Oxon	SU6382	51°32·2'	1°5·1'W	FM	175
Broad Street Green	Essex	TL8609	51°45·2'	0°42·1'E	T	168
Broad Taing	Orkney	HY4217	59°2·4'	3°0·2'W	X	6
Broad Tenterden	Kent	TQ8832	51°3·6'	0°41·4'E	T	189
Broad, The	Heref	SO4960	52°14·4'	2°44·4'W	T	137,138,148
Broadthorn	Cumbr	SD5496	54°21·7'	2°42·1'W	X	97
Broad Tongue	Cumbr	NY1905	54°26·3'	3°14·5'W	X	89,90
Broad Town	Wilts	SU0977	51°29·7'	1°51·8'W	T	173
Broadtown Hill	Wilts	SU0977	51°29·7'	1°51·8'W	X	173
Broadun Ring	Devon	SX6380	50°36·5'	3°55·8'W	A	191
Broadview Fm	Bucks	SP9503	51°43·3'	0°37·1'W	FM	165
Broadward	Aberd	NJ7426	57°19·7'	2°25·5'W	X	38
Broadward	Aberd	NJ8936	57°25·1'	2°10·5'W	X	30
Broadward Br	Heref	SO4957	52°12·8'	2°44·4'W	X	148,149
Broadward Hall	Shrops	SO3876	52°23·0'	2°54·3'W	X	137,148
Broadwas	Worcs	SO7655	52°11·8'	2°20·7'W	T	150
Broadwas Court	Worcs	SO7555	52°11·8'	2°21·5'W	X	150
Broadwash Fm	Norf	TM2785	52°25·2'	1°20·7'E	FM	156
Broadwater	Aberd	NJ8004	57°7·8'	2°19·4'W	X	38
Broadwater	Cumbr	SD0889	54°17·5'	3°24·4'W	X	96
Broad Water	Glos	SP1501	51°42·7'	1°46·6'W	W	163
Broad Water	Gwyn	SH5702	52°36·1'	4°6·3'W	W	135
Broadwater	Herts	TL2522	51°53·2'	0°10·6'W	T	166
Broad Water	Norf	TF7144	52°58·2'	0°33·2'E	W	132
Broadwater	Suff	TM2961	52°12·2'	1°21·5'E	X	156
Broad Water	Surrey	TQ0865	51°22·7'	0°26·5'W	W	176
Broadwater	Warw	SP2285	52°28·0'	1°40·2'W	W	139
Broadwater	W Susx	TQ1404	50°49·7'	0°22·5'W	T	198
Broadwater Bottom	Glos	SP1317	51°51·3'	1°48·3'W	X	163
Broadwater Br	Bucks	SP9700	51°41·7'	0°35·4'W	X	165
Broadwater Down	Kent	TQ5737	51°6·9'	0°15·0'E	T	188
Broadwater Fm	Kent	TQ6856	51°16·9'	0°24·9'E	FM	178,188
Broadwater Fm	Suff	TM2861	52°12·2'	1°20·6'E	FM	156
Broadwater Forest	E Susx	TQ5537	51°6·9'	0°13·3'E	F	188
Broadwater House Fm	Lincs	TF3021	52°46·5'	0°4·0'W	FM	131
Broadwaters	Worcs	SO8478	52°24·2'	2°13·7'W	T	138
Broadwaters Fm	Notts	SK7563	53°9·8'	0°52·3'W	FM	120
Broadwaters Wood	Notts	SK7563	53°9·8'	0°52·3'W	F	120
Broadwath	Cumbr	NY4855	54°53·5'	2°48·2'W	T	86
Broadway	Carm	SN2910	51°46·0'	4°28·3'W	T	159
Broadway	Carm	SN3808	51°45·1'	4°20·4'W	T	159
Broad Way	Northum	NY8851	54°51·5'	2°10·8'W	X	87
Broadway	Pemb	SM8713	51°46·8'	5°4·9'W	T	157
Broadway	Pemb	SM9124	51°52·8'	5°1·8'W	X	157,158
Broadway	Pemb	SN0618	51°49·9'	4°48·5'W	X	158
Broadway	Powys	SO2993	52°32·1'	3°2·4'W	X	137
Broadway	Shrops	SJ4011	52°41·8'	2°52·9'W	X	126
Broadway	Somer	ST3215	50°56·1'	2°57·7'W	T	193
Broadway	Suff	TM3978	52°21·1'	1°31·0'E	T	156
Broadway	Worcs	SP0937	52°2·1'	1°51·7'W	T	150
Broadway Fm	Cambs	TL3358	52°12·5'	0°2·8'W	FM	154
Broadway Fm	Ches	SJ7969	53°13·3'	2°18·5'W	FM	118
Broadway Fm	Hants	SU6713	50°55·0'	1°2·4'W	FM	196
Broadway Fm	Herts	TL0106	51°44·8'	0°31·8'W	FM	166
Broadway Fm	Norf	TF9711	52°39·9'	0°55·2'E	FM	132
Broadway Fm	Suff	TM3979	52°21·6'	1°31·0'E	FM	156
Broadway Foot	N Yks	SE5688	54°17·3'	1°8·0'W	X	100
Broadway Green Fm	Kent	TR1251	51°13·3'	1°2·6'E	FM	179,189
Broadway Hall	Suff	TM2674	52°19·3'	1°19·4'E	X	156
Broadway Head Fm	Somer	ST0632	51°5·0'	3°20·1'W	FM	181
Broadway Hill	Worcs	SP1136	52°1·6'	1°50·0'W	H	150
Broadway Lands	Heref	SO5530	51°58·2'	2°38·9'W	T	149
Broadways	Devon	ST0818	50°57·5'	3°18·2'W	X	181
Broadway Tower Country Park	Worcs	SP1035	52°1·0'	1°50·9'W	X	150
Broadway Wood	Bucks	SP8132	51°59·1'	0°48·8'W	F	152,165
Broadway Wood	Worcs	SP1034	52°0·5'	1°50·9'W	F	150
Broadwell	Devon	SX4670	50°30·8'	4°10·0'W	X	201
Broadwell	Glos	SO5811	51°48·0'	2°36·2'W	T	162
Broadwell	Glos	SP2027	51°56·7'	1°42·1'W	T	163
Broadwell	Monm	ST4991	51°37·2'	2°43·8'W	X	162,172
Broadwell	Oxon	SP2503	51°43·7'	1°37·9'W	T	163
Broadwell	Warw	SP4565	52°17·1'	1°20·0'W	T	151
Broadwell Brook	Oxon	SP2403	51°43·7'	1°38·8'W	W	163
Broadwell Hill	Glos	SP2026	51°56·2'	1°42·2'W	X	163
Broadwell Ho	Northum	NY9153	54°52·5'	2°8·0'W	X	87
Broadwell Mill	Oxon	SP2502	51°43·2'	1°37·9'W	X	163
Broadwey	Dorset	SY6683	50°39·0'	2°28·5'W	T	194
Broadwigg	D & G	NX4343	54°45·7'	4°26·0'W	X	83
Broadwindsor	Dorset	ST4302	50°49·1'	2°48·2'W	T	193
Broadwood	Devon	SS6121	50°58·5'	3°58·4'W	X	180
Broadwood	Durham	NZ1245	54°48·2'	1°48·4'W	X	88
Broad Wood	E Loth	NT4984	56°3·0'	2°48·7'W	F	66
Broad Wood	Northum	NU1726	55°31·9'	1°43·4'W	F	75
Broadwood	S Ayr	NS4122	55°28·2'	4°30·5'W	X	70
Broadwood Fm	Somer	SS9841	51°9·8'	3°27·1'W	FM	181
Broadwood Halls	Northum	NY8255	54°53·6'	2°16·4'W	X	86,87
Broadwoodkelly	Devon	SS6105	50°49·9'	3°58·1'W	T	191
Broadwoodside	E Loth	NT5268	55°54·4'	2°45·6'W	X	66
Broadwoodwidger	Devon	SX4189	50°41·0'	4°14·7'W	T	190
Broadyards Fm	S Ayr	NS4331	55°33·1'	4°28·9'W	FM	70
Broallan	Highld	NH4945	57°28·5'	4°30·6'W	X	26
Broathill	D & G	NY2669	55°0·9'	3°9·0'W	X	85
Broats	Cumbr	NY6231	54°40·6'	2°34·9'W	X	91
Broats	D & G	NY2569	55°0·8'	3°9·9'W	X	85
Broats	Durham	NZ0113	54°31·0'	1°58·7'W	X	92
Broats	N Yks	SE1191	54°19·1'	1°49·4'W	X	99
Broats Fm	N Yks	SE6985	54°15·6'	0°56·0'W	FM	94,100
Broats Fm	N Yks	SE7279	54°12·3'	0°53·3'W	FM	100
Broats Fm	N Yks	SE7987	54°16·6'	0°46·8'W	FM	94,100
Broats Ho	N Yks	SD6871	54°8·3'	2°29·0'W	X	98
Brobury	Heref	SO3444	52°5·7'	2°57·4'W	T	148,149,161
Brocair	N Eil	NB5536	58°14·9'	6°10·1'W	T	8
Brocas Fm	Kent	TQ4645	51°11·4'	0°5·7'E	FM	188
Brocas Lands Fm	Hants	SU6563	51°22·0'	1°3·6'W	FM	175,186
Brocastle	V of Glam	SS9377	51°29·1'	3°32·1'W	X	170
Brocastle Barn	V of Glam	SS9476	51°28·6'	3°31·2'W	X	170
Brocavvm (Roman Fort)	Cumbr	NY5328	54°38·9'	2°43·3'W	R	90
Broc-bheinn	Highld	NG4433	57°19·2'	6°14·7'W	H	32
Brochdhu	Aberd	NO3493	57°1·7'	3°4·8'W	X	37,44
Brochel	Highld	NG5846	57°26·7'	6°1·5'W	T	24
Brochel Castle	Highld	NG5846	57°26·7'	6°1·5'W	A	24
Brochen	Powys	SN9958	52°12·9'	3°28·3'W	X	147
Broc Hill	Staffs	SJ9720	52°46·9'	2°2·3'W	H	127
Brochloch	D & G	NX5396	55°14·4'	4°18·3'W	X	77
Brochneil	S Ayr	NX1895	55°13·2'	4°51·2'W	X	76
Broch of Burland	Shetld	HU4436	60°6·6'	1°12·0'W	A	4
Broch of Culswick	Shetld	HU2544	60°11·0'	1°32·5'W	A	4
Broch of Mousa	Shetld	HU4523	59°59·6'	1°11·1'W	A	4
Broch (rems of)	S Lanak	NS9848	55°43·1'	3°37·0'W	X	72
Brochroy	Arg & Bt	NN0031	56°26·0'	5°14·2'W	T	50
Brock	Arg & Bt	NM0647	56°31·6'	6°46·4'W	X	46
Brock	Lancs	SD5140	53°51·5'	2°44·3'W	T	102
Brocka	Cumbr	SD4180	54°13·0'	2°53·9'W	X	96,97
Brockabank	N Yks	SD9356	54°0·2'	2°6·0'W	X	103
Brockabarrow Common	Corn	SX1575	50°33·0'	4°36·3'W	X	201
Brocka Beck	N Yks	NZ8500	54°23·5'	0°41·0'W	W	94
Brocka Laithe	N Yks	SD8958	54°1·3'	2°9·7'W	X	103
Brockamin	Worcs	SO7653	52°10·7'	2°20·7'W	T	150
Brockan	Orkney	HY2309	58°57·9'	3°19·9'W	X	6,7
Brockan	Orkney	HY2324	59°6·0'	3°20·2'W	X	6
Brockbridge	Hants	SU6118	50°57·7'	1°7·5'W	T	185
Brockbridge Fm	Hants	SU7732	51°5·2'	0°53·6'W	FM	186
Brock Burn	C of Glas	NS5360	55°48·9'	4°20·3'W	W	64
Brock Burn	E Renf	NS5055	55°46·2'	4°23·0'W	W	64
Brock Burn	S Lanak	NS6344	55°40·5'	4°10·3'W	W	71
Brockbury Hall	Heref	SO7441	52°4·2'	2°22·4'W	X	150
Brock Close	Lancs	SD5544	53°53·7'	2°40·7'W	X	102
Brock Cott Fm	Lancs	SD5443	53°53·1'	2°41·6'W	FM	102
Brock Crag	Cumbr	NY2102	54°24·7'	3°12·6'W	X	89,90
Brock Crag	Cumbr	NY4519	54°34·0'	2°50·6'W	X	90
Brock Crags	Cumbr	NY4113	54°30·8'	2°54·3'W	H	90
Brockdam Fm	Northum	NU1624	55°30·8'	1°44·4'W	FM	75
Brockdam Moor	Northum	NU1524	55°30·8'	1°45·3'W	X	75
Brockdish	Norf	TM2079	52°22·1'	1°14·3'E	T	156
Brockdish Hall	Norf	TM2180	52°22·6'	1°15·2'E	A	156
Brockenbarrow Fm	Devon	SS6641	51°9·4'	3°54·6'W	FM	180
Brocken Burn	Shetld	HU4893	60°37·3'	1°6·9'W	W	1,2
Brockencote	Worcs	SO8873	52°21·5'	2°10·2'W	T	139
Brockenhurst	Hants	SU2902	50°49·2'	1°34·9'W	T	196
Brockenhurst Park	Hants	SU3101	50°48·7'	1°33·2'W	X	196
Brocker Fm	Leic	SK7912	52°42·2'	0°49·4'W	FM	129
Brocker Fm	Notts	SK7239	52°56·8'	0°55·3'W	FM	129
Brockeridge Common	Glos	SO8838	52°2·7'	2°10·1'W	X	150
Brockers Gill Fm	Durham	NY9227	54°38·5'	2°7·0'W	FM	91,92
Brocket	S Ayr	NS3629	55°31·9'	4°35·5'W	X	70
Brocket Hall	Herts	TL2113	51°48·4'	0°14·3'W	A	166
Brocket Holes Pasture	N Yks	SD7480	54°13·1'	2°23·5'W	X	98
Brocketsbrae	S Lanak	NS8239	55°38·1'	3°52·0'W	T	71,72
Brocketts Hall	Essex	TM1426	51°53·7'	1°7·0'E	X	168,169
Brocket Wood	N Yks	SE5644	53°53·6'	1°8·5'W	F	105
Brockey Fm	Leic	SP4499	52°35·5'	1°20·6'W	FM	140
Brockey Fm	Leic	SP4598	52°34·9'	1°19·7'W	FM	140
Brockey River	Somer	SS9025	51°1·1'	3°33·7'W	W	181
Brockey, The	Leic	SP4498	52°34·9'	1°20·6'W	X	140
Brockfield	Devon	ST3005	50°50·7'	2°59·3'W	T	193
Brockfield	N Yks	SE6655	53°59·4'	0°59·2'W	X	105,106
Brock Fm	Glos	SO8823	51°54·6'	2°10·1'W	FM	162
Brockford Green	Suff	TM1265	52°14·8'	1°6·7'E	T	155
Brockford Ho	Suff	TM1263	52°13·7'	1°6·7'E	X	155
Brockford Street	Suff	TM1166	52°15·3'	1°5·9'E	T	155
Brock Hall	Heref	SO5358	52°13·3'	2°40·9'W	X	149
Brockhall	Northnts	SP6362	52°15·4'	1°4·2'W	T	152
Brock Hall	Shrops	SO7285	52°28·0'	2°24·3'W	X	138
Brockhall Fm	Lancs	SD7037	53°49·9'	2°26·9'W	FM	103
Brock Hall Fm	N Yks	NZ9202	54°24·5'	0°34·5'W	FM	94
Brockhall Village	Lancs	SD7036	53°49·4'	2°26·9'W	T	103
Brockham	Cumbr	NY6522	54°35·8'	2°32·1'W	X	91
Brockham	Surrey	TQ1949	51°13·9'	0°17·3'W	T	187
Brockham End	Bath & NE Somer	ST7169	51°25·4'	2°24·6'W	T	172
Brockham Fm	Kent	TR0740	51°7·5'	0°57·9'E	FM	179,189
Brockham Hill Barn	Hants	SU7242	51°10·6'	0°57·8'W	X	186
Brockham Park	Surrey	TQ2047	51°12·8'	0°16·5'W	T	187
Brockhampton	Glos	SO9426	51°56·2'	2°4·8'W	T	163
Brockhampton	Glos	SP0322	51°54·0'	1°57·0'W	T	163
Brockhampton	Hants	SU7106	50°51·2'	0°59·1'W	T	197
Brockhampton	Heref	SO5931	51°58·8'	2°35·4'W	T	149
Brockhampton	Heref	SO6855	52°11·8'	2°27·7'W	X	149
Brockhampton Green	Dorset	ST7106	50°51·4'	2°24·3'W	T	194
Brockhampton Park	Glos	SP0322	51°54·0'	1°57·0'W	X	163
Brockham Warren	Surrey	TQ1951	51°15·0'	0°17·3'W	X	187
Brockhill	Devon	SX9895	50°45·0'	3°26·4'W	X	192
Brock Hill	D & G	NT1100	55°17·4'	3°23·7'W	H	78
Brockhill	Dorset	SY8392	50°43·9'	2°14·1'W	X	194
Brock Hill	Dorset	SY9397	50°46·6'	2°5·6'W	X	195
Brock Hill	Essex	TQ7396	51°38·4'	0°30·4'E	T	167
Brock Hill	Glos	ST8193	51°38·4'	2°16·1'W	X	162,173
Brock Hill	Leic	SK7426	52°49·8'	0°53·7'W	X	129
Brockhill	Scot Bord	NT3924	55°30·6'	2°57·5'W	T	73
Brock Hill	Surrey	SU9259	51°19·6'	0°40·4'W	X	175,186
Brockhill	Worcs	SP0069	52°19·4'	1°59·6'W	X	139
Brockhill Barm	Glos	SP1223	51°54·6'	1°49·1'W	X	163
Brockhill Cote	N Yks	SD9291	54°19·1'	2°7·0'W	X	98
Brockhill Country Park	Kent	TR1436	51°5·2'	1°3·7'E	X	179,189
Brockhill Court	Worcs	SO7263	52°16·2'	2°24·2'W	X	138,149
Brock Hill Fm	Leic	SK7527	52°50·4'	0°52·8'W	FM	129
Brockhill Fm	Worcs	SP0169	52°19·4'	1°58·7'W	FM	139
Brockhill Fm	Worcs	SP0771	52°20·5'	1°53·4'W	FM	139
Brockhill Hagg	N Yks	SE6687	54°16·7'	0°58·8'W	X	94,100
Brockhill Hall Fm	Leic	SK7426	52°49·8'	0°53·7'W	FM	129
Brockhill Ho	Brackn	SU8971	51°26·1'	0°42·8'W	X	175
Brockhills	Devon	SX7857	50°24·2'	3°42·6'W	X	202
Brockhill Stone	D & G	NX8685	55°9·0'	3°46·9'W	X	78
Brockhill Wood	Worcs	SP0268	52°18·8'	1°57·8'W	F	139
Brockholds	Essex	TL6135	51°59·6'	0°21·1'E	X	154
Brockhold's Fm	Herts	TL3622	51°53·0'	0°1·0'W	FM	166
Brockhole	Devon	SS9626	51°1·7'	3°28·6'W	X	181
Brockhole	Donc	SE6301	53°30·4'	1°2·6'W	X	111
Brockhole Burn	Northum	NZ0264	54°58·5'	1°57·7'W	W	87
Brockhole (National Park Centre)	Cumbr	NY3800	54°23·7'	2°56·9'W	X	90
Brockholes	Aberd	NJ6307	57°9·4'	2°36·2'W	X	37
Brock Holes	Barns	SE2201	53°30·6'	1°39·7'W	X	110
Brockholes	Cumbr	NY6101	54°24·4'	2°35·6'W	X	91
Brockholes	Kirk	SE1411	53°36·0'	1°46·9'W	T	110
Brock Holes	N Yks	SE6725	53°43·3'	0°58·7'W	X	105,106
Brockholes	Scot Bord	NT8263	55°51·8'	2°16·8'W	X	67
Brockholes Gill	N Yks	NY8100	54°24·0'	2°17·1'W	W	91,92
Brockholes Hill	Scot Bord	NT8165	55°52·9'	2°17·8'W	X	67
Brockholes Wood	Scot Bord	NT8165	55°52·9'	2°17·8'W	F	67
Brockhollands	Glos	SO6105	51°44·8'	2°33·5'W	T	162
Brockholme	E Yorks	TA1847	53°54·6'	0°11·8'W	X	107
Brockholme Fm	N Yks	SE3197	54°22·3'	1°30·9'W	FM	99
Brockholme Fm	N Yks	SE3889	54°18·0'	1°24·5'W	FM	99
Brockhope Burn	Scot Bord	NT2113	55°24·5'	3°14·4'W	W	79
Brockhoperig	Scot Bord	NT2312	55°24·0'	3°12·5'W	X	79
Brockhouse	Scot Bord	NT4250	55°44·6'	2°55·0'W	X	73
Brockhouse Burn	Scot Bord	NT4051	55°45·2'	2°56·9'W	W	66,73
Brockhurst	Derby	SK3364	53°10·6'	1°30·0'W	T	119
Brockhurst	Hants	SU5901	50°48·6'	1°9·4'W	T	196
Brockhurst	Staffs	SJ8211	52°42·0'	2°15·6'W	X	127
Brockhurst	Warw	SP4683	52°26·8'	1°19·0'W	T	140
Brockhurst	W Susx	TQ4037	51°7·1'	0°0·4'E	X	187
Brockhurst Castle	Shrops	SO4492	52°31·6'	2°49·1'W	A	137
Brockhurst Fm	Bucks	SP9702	51°42·7'	0°35·4'W	FM	165
Brockhurst Fm	Shrops	SJ5428	52°51·1'	2°40·6'W	FM	126
Brockhurst Fm	Staffs	SK1501	52°36·6'	1°46·3'W	FM	139
Brockhurst School	W Berks	SU5271	51°26·4'	1°14·7'W	X	174
Brockhurst Wood	Bucks	SU9684	51°33·0'	0°36·5'W	F	175,176
Brockhurst Wood	Wilts	SU0686	51°34·6'	1°54·4'W	F	173
Brockie Law	Scot Bord	NT5905	55°20·5'	2°38·4'W	H	80
Brockieside	N Lanak	NS7279	55°59·5'	4°2·7'W	X	64
Brockilow Fm	Notts	SK7165	53°10·9'	0°55·8'W	FM	120
Brockington Down	Dorset	SU0111	50°54·1'	1°58·9'W	X	195
Brockington Fm	Dorset	SU0110	50°53·6'	1°58·8'W	FM	195
Brockis Hill	Hants	SU2911	50°54·1'	1°34·9'W	X	196
Brockishill Inclosure	Hants	SU3011	50°54·1'	1°34·0'W	F	196
Brocklar	E Ayr	NS5627	55°31·2'	4°16·4'W	X	71
Brocklas	Angus	NO3863	56°45·5'	3°0·4'W	X	44
Brocklaw Burn	D & G	NS8019	55°27·3'	3°53·4'W	W	71,78
Brocklaw Rig	D & G	NS8019	55°27·3'	3°53·4'W	X	71,78
Brockle	Corn	SX3180	50°36·0'	4°22·9'W	X	201
Brocklebank	Cumbr	NY3043	54°46·9'	3°4·9'W	X	85
Brocklebank Ground	Cumbr	SD2793	54°19·9'	3°6·9'W	X	96,97
Brockle Beck	Cumbr	NY2822	54°35·5'	3°6·4'W	W	89,90
Brocklecrag	Cumbr	NY2532	54°40·9'	3°9·4'W	X	89,90
Brocklees	E Ayr	NS5541	55°38·7'	4°17·8'W	X	71
Brocklees Loch	E Ayr	NS5441	55°38·7'	4°18·8'W	W	70
Brocklehill	S Ayr	NS4023	55°28·7'	4°31·5'W	X	70
Brocklehirst	D & G	NY0574	55°3·3'	3°28·8'W	T	85
Brocklehurst	Lancs	SD7445	53°54·3'	2°23·3'W	X	103
Brocklerigg	D & G	NY1473	55°2·9'	3°20·3'W	X	85
Brocklesby	Lincs	TA1411	53°35·2'	0°16·3'W	T	113
Brocklesby Park	Lincs	TA1311	53°35·2'	0°17·2'W	X	113
Brocklesby Sta	N Lincs	TA1113	53°36·3'	0°18·9'W	X	113
Brocklewath	Cumbr	NY4851	54°51·3'	2°48·2'W	X	86
Brockley	Lew	TQ3674	51°27·1'	0°2·2'W	T	177
Brockley	N Som	ST4666	51°23·7'	2°46·2'W	T	171,172,182
Brockley	Suff	TL8371	52°18·6'	0°41·5'E	T	144,155
Brockley Combe	N Som	ST4766	51°23·7'	2°45·3'W	X	171,172,182
Brockley Court	N Som	ST4667	51°24·2'	2°46·2'W	X	171,172,182
Brockley Elm Fm	N Som	ST4667	51°24·2'	2°46·2'W	FM	171,172,182
Brockley Fm	Notts	SK6654	53°5·0'	1°0·5'W	FM	120
Brockley Green	Suff	TL7247	52°5·9'	0°31·1'E	T	154
Brockley Green	Suff	TL8254	52°9·5'	0°40·0'E	T	155
Brockleyhall	Northum	NU1620	55°28·7'	1°44·4'W	X	75
Brockley Hall	Suff	TL8255	52°10·0'	0°40·1'E	X	155
Brockleyhall Moor	Northum	NU1520	55°28·7'	1°45·3'W	X	75
Brockley Hill Fm	Harrow	TQ1794	51°38·2'	0°18·2'W	FM	166,176
Brockleymoor	Cumbr	NY4936	54°43·2'	2°47·1'W	T	90
Brockleys Fm	Leic	SK7215	52°43·9'	0°55·6'W	FM	129
Brockley Warren	Hants	SU4236	51°7·5'	1°23·6'W	X	185
Brockley Wood	N Som	ST4766	51°23·7'	2°45·3'W	F	171,172,182
Brockley Wood	Suff	TM0075	52°20·4'	0°56·6'E	F	144
Brockley Wood	Suff	TM1139	52°0·8'	1°4·9'E	F	155,169
Brocklie	S Ayr	NS4531	55°33·1'	4°27·0'W	X	70
Brocklinns Bank	D & G	NY3282	55°7·9'	3°3·6'W	X	79
Brockloch	D & G	NX7972	55°1·9'	3°53·2'W	X	84
Brockloch	E Ayr	NS5910	55°22·1'	4°13·1'W	X	71
Brockloch	Moray	NJ0654	57°34·2'	3°33·8'W	X	27
Brockloch	S Ayr	NS2911	55°22·0'	4°41·5'W	X	70
Brockloch	S Ayr	NX2495	55°13·3'	4°45·6'W	X	76
Brockloch Craig	D & G	NX5397	55°14·9'	4°18·3'W	X	77
Brockloch Fell	D & G	NX0970	54°59·5'	4°58·7'W	X	76
Brockloch Hill	D & G	NX5173	55°2·0'	4°19·5'W	H	77
Brockloch Hill	D & G	NX8179	55°5·7'	3°51·5'W	H	84
Brockloch Rig	D & G	NS5801	55°17·2'	4°13·7'W	H	77
Brockly Hall	Northum	NZ0898	55°16·8'	1°52·0'W	X	81
Brockmanton	Heref	SO5459	52°13·9'	2°40·0'W	T	149
Brockmill	Lancs	SD5443	53°53·1'	2°41·6'W	X	102
Brockmill Fm	Northum	NU0543	55°41·1'	1°54·8'W	FM	75
Brockmoor	Dudley	SO9187	52°29·1'	2°7·6'W	T	139
Brock of Borwick	Orkney	HY2216	59°1·7'	3°21·0'W	A	6
Brock of Gurness	Orkney	HY3826	59°7·2'	3°4·5'W	A	6
Brockrigg	N Yks	NZ8214	54°31·1'	0°43·6'W	X	94
Brocks Burn	Northum	NZ2390	55°12·5'	1°37·9'W	W	81
Brocks Bushes	Northum	NZ0264	54°58·5'	1°57·7'W	X	87
Brock Scar	Durham	NY9322	54°35·8'	2°6·1'W	X	91,92

Brockscombe	Devon	SX4694	50°43·7′	4°10·5′W	T	190
Brock's Common	Devon	SX4694	50°43·7′	4°10·5′W	X	190
Brocks Cross	Devon	SX7699	50°46·9′	3°45·2′W	X	191
Brock's Fm	Essex	TL7905	51°43·1′	0°35·9′E	FM	167
Brocks Fm	Essex	TQ6798	51°39·6′	0°25·3′E	FM	167,177
Brock's Fm	N Yks	SE6632	53°47·0′	0°59·5′W	FM	105,106
Brocksford Hall	Derby	SK1333	52°53·9′	1°48·0′W	X	128
Brock's Green	Hants	SU5061	51°21·0′	1°16·5′W	T	174
Brock's Holes	D & G	NX8047	54°48·5′	3°51·6′W	X	84
Brock's Holes	Northum	NT8510	55°23·3′	2°13·8′W	H	80
Brock Side	Lancs	SD5241	53°52·0′	2°43·4′W	X	102
Brocks, The	Northum	NZ2099	55°17·3′	1°40·7′W	X	81
Brocks, The	Northum	NZ2388	55°11·4′	1°37·9′W	X	81
Brockstones	Cumbr	NY4605	54°26·5′	2°49·5′W	X	90
Brock's Watering	Norf	TM1492	52°29·3′	1°9·5′E	T	144
Brocks Wood	E Susx	TQ3414	50°54·8′	0°5·2′W	F	198
Brock Thorn	Lancs	SD7555	53°59·7′	2°22·5′W	X	103
Brockton	Aberd	NO6899	57°5·1′	2°31·2′W	X	38,45
Brockton	Shrops	SJ3104	52°38·0′	3°0·8′W	T	126
Brockton	Shrops	SJ7203	52°37·7′	2°24·4′W	T	127
Brockton	Shrops	SO3285	52°27·8′	2°59·7′W	T	137
Brockton	Shrops	SO5793	52°32·2′	2°37·6′W	T	137,138
Brockton	Staffs	SJ8131	52°52·8′	2°16·5′W	T	127
Brockton	Wrekin	SJ7216	52°44·7′	2°24·5′W	T	127
Brockton Brook	Staffs	SJ8132	52°53·3′	2°16·5′W	W	127
Brockton Fm	Kent	TQ9248	51°12·2′	0°45·3′E	FM	189
Brockton Grange	Staffs	SJ8013	52°43·1′	2°17·4′W	X	127
Brockton Leasows	Wrekin	SJ7216	52°44·7′	2°24·5′W	X	127
Brockweir	Glos	SO5401	51°42·6′	2°39·6′W	T	162
Brockwell	Somer	SS9243	51°10·8′	3°32·3′W	T	181
Brockwell Fm	Bucks	SP8304	51°43·9′	0°47·5′W	FM	165
Brockwellmuir	E Ayr	NS4151	55°43·8′	4°31·5′W	X	64
Brockwell Park	Lam	TQ3174	51°27·2′	0°6·5′W	X	176,177
Brockwells Fm	E Susx	TQ4716	50°55·7′	0°5·9′E	FM	198
Brockwells Fm	Monm	ST4789	51°36·1′	2°45·5′W	FM	171,172
Brockwood Fm	Notts	SK6649	53°2·3′	1°0·5′W	FM	129
Brockwood Hall	Cumbr	SD1684	54°14·9′	3°16·9′W	X	96
Brockwood Hill Fm	Staffs	SJ7852	53°4·1′	2°19·3′W	FM	118
Brockwoodlees	D & G	NY3878	55°5·8′	2°57·9′W	X	85
Brockwood Park	Hants	SU6226	51°2·0′	1°6·6′W	X	185
Brockworth	Glos	SO8916	51°50·8′	2°9·2′W	T	163
Brockworth Wood	Glos	SO8914	51°49·7′	2°9·2′W	F	163
Brocky Burn	Aberd	NO6183	56°56·5′	2°38·0′W	W	45
Broclach Hill	Aberd	NJ6222	57°17·5′	2°38·4′W	H	37
Brocolitia (Roman Fort)	Northum	NY8571	55°2·2′	2°13·7′W	R	87
Brocstedes Fm	Wigan	SD5500	53°29·9′	2°40·3′W	FM	108
Brocton	Corn	SX0168	50°28·9′	4°47·9′W	T	200
Brocton	Staffs	SJ9619	52°46·4′	2°3·2′W	T	127
Brocton Coppice	Staffs	SJ9819	52°46·4′	2°1·4′W	F	127
Brocton Field	Staffs	SJ9817	52°45·3′	2°1·4′W	X	127
Brocton Lodge	Staffs	SJ9720	52°46·9′	2°2·3′W	X	127
Brocton's Fm	Essex	TL5532	51°58·1′	0°15·8′E	FM	167
Bro-dawel	Cered	SN6781	52°24·9′	3°56·9′W	X	135
Broddebb	Orkney	ND4992	58°49·0′	2°52·5′W	X	7
Brode Hall	Ches	SJ8169	53°13·3′	2°16·7′W	X	118
Broden Hill	Devon	SS6623	50°59·8′	3°54·6′W	X	180
Brodgar	Orkney	HY3012	58°59·6′	3°12·6′W	X	6
Brodiach	Aberd	NJ8407	57°9·5′	2°15·4′W	X	38
Brodick	N Ayr	NS0136	55°34·9′	5°9·0′W	T	69
Brodick Bay	N Ayr	NS0236	55°34·9′	5°8·1′W	W	69
Brodick Castle	N Ayr	NS0137	55°35·4′	5°9·0′W	A	69
Brodie Castle	Moray	NH9757	57°35·7′	3°42·9′W	X	27
Brodieshill	Moray	NJ1059	57°37·0′	3°29·9′W	X	28
Brodieshill Cotts	Moray	NJ0960	57°37·5′	3°31·0′W	X	27
Brodiesord	Aberd	NJ5760	57°37·9′	2°42·7′W	T	29
Brodiesord Fm	Aberd	NJ5660	57°37·9′	2°43·7′W	FM	29
Brodnyx	Kent	TR0727	51°0·5′	0°57·4′E	X	189
Brodoclea	N Ayr	NS2753	55°44·6′	4°44·9′W	X	63
Brodsworth	Donc	SE5007	53°33·7′	1°14·3′W	T	111
Brodynex Fm	Kent	TR0626	51°0·0′	0°56·6′E	FM	189
Brofair	Denb	SJ1160	53°8·0′	3°19·4′W	X	116
Brofiscin Fm	Rho Cyn Taf	ST0681	51°31·4′	3°20·9′W	FM	170
Broford Fm	Somer	SS9131	51°4·3′	3°33·0′W	FM	181
Brogaig	Highld	NG4768	57°38·1′	6°13·9′W	T	23
Brog an Eich	N Eil	NB1844	58°17·9′	6°48·3′W	X	8
Brogan, The	Powys	SJ1919	52°46·0′	3°11·6′W	W	125
Brogborough	Beds	SP9638	52°2·2′	0°35·6′W	T	153
Brogborough Manor Fm	Beds	SP9639	52°2·7′	0°35·6′W	FM	153
Brogden	Kent	TQ8253	51°15·0′	0°36·9′E	X	188
Brogden Fm	N Yks	SE3397	54°22·3′	1°29·1′W	FM	99
Brogden Hall	Lancs	SD8547	53°55·4′	2°13·3′W	X	103
Brogging Moss	Sheff	SK2191	53°25·2′	1°40·6′W	X	110
Broginin	Cered	SN6684	52°26·5′	3°57·9′W	X	135
Brograve Fm	Norf	TG4425	52°46·3′	1°37·4′E	FM	134
Brograve Level	Norf	TG4424	52°45·7′	1°37·4′E	X	134
Brogues, The	Kent	TQ8435	51°5·3′	0°38·0′E	F	188
Brogyntyn	Shrops	SJ2731	52°52·5′	3°4·7′W	X	126
Broich	Pth & Kin	NN8620	56°21·8′	3°50·3′W	X	52,58
Broich Burn	Clackm	NN9103	56°12·7′	3°45·0′W	W	58
Broich Fm	Stir	NN6901	56°11·3′	4°6·2′W	FM	57
Broisgill Beg	Highld	NG3440	57°22·6′	6°25·1′W	X	23
Broisgill More	Highld	NG3441	57°23·2′	6°25·1′W	X	23
Broke Hall	Suff	TM1943	52°2·7′	1°12·0′E	T	169
Broke Hall	Suff	TM2239	52°0·5′	1°14·5′E	X	169
Broken Back	D & G	NT1300	55°17·4′	3°21·8′W	H	78
Brokenback	Lincs	TF0688	53°22·9′	0°24·0′W	X	112,121
Brokenborough	Wilts	ST9189	51°36·2′	2°7·4′W	T	173
Broken Brae	N Yks	NZ2000	54°23·9′	1°41·1′W	X	93
Broken Brough	Shetld	HU4013	59°54·3′	1°16·6′W	X	4
Broken Burns	Highld	NC5152	58°26·1′	4°32·7′W	X	9
Broken Cross	Ches	SJ6873	53°15·4′	2°28·4′W	T	118
Broken Cross	Ches	SJ8973	53°15·5′	2°9·5′W	T	118
Broken Cross	Norf	TF5216	52°43·4′	0°15·5′E	X	131
Broken Cross Fm	Glos	SO7316	51°50·8′	2°23·1′W	FM	162
Broken Cross Muir	S Lanak	NS8437	55°37·0′	3°50·1′W	H	71,72
Broken Flatts	Derby	SK3024	52°49·0′	1°32·9′W	X	128
Brokenfolds	Aberd	NJ6550	57°32·6′	2°34·6′W	X	29
Broken Green	Herts	TL4122	51°52·9′	0°3·3′E	T	167
Broken Ground	Tames	SE0002	53°31·1′	1°59·6′W	X	110
Broken Hatch Fm	Oxon	SP3412	51°48·6′	1°30·0′W	FM	164

Brokenheugh	Northum	NY8566	54°59·5′	2°13·6′W	X	87
Brokenstones	Shrops	SO4287	52°28·9′	2°50·8′W	X	137
Brokentore	Moray	NJ1854	57°34·4′	3°21·8′W	X	28
Brokenwind	Aberd	NJ8918	57°15·4′	2°10·5′W	X	38
Brokerswood	Wilts	ST8351	51°15·7′	2°14·2′W	T	183
Brokes	N Yks	SE1599	54°23·4′	1°45·7′W	T	99
Broke Wood	Dorset	ST6612	50°54·6′	2°28·6′W	F	194
Broland	Orkney	HY4331	59°10·0′	2°59·3′W	X	5,6
Brolass	Arg & Bt	NM4923	56°20·2′	6°3·2′W	X	48
Broll	Orkney	ND4587	58°46·3′	2°56·6′W	X	7
Bromaking Grange	N Yks	SE2887	54°16·9′	1°33·8′W	X	99
Broman's Fm	Essex	TM0614	51°47·4′	0°59·6′E	FM	168
Brombil	Nth Pt Talb	SS7987	51°34·4′	3°44·4′W	T	170
Bromborough	Wirral	SJ3482	53°20·1′	2°59·1′W	T	108
Bromborough Pool	Wirral	SJ3484	53°21·2′	2°59·1′W	T	108
Bromborough Rake Sta	Wirral	SJ3481	53°19·6′	2°59·0′W	X	108
Bromborough Sta	Wirral	SJ3481	53°19·6′	2°59·0′W	X	108
Bromdon	Shrops	SO6080	52°25·2′	2°34·9′W	T	138
Brome	Suff	TM1376	52°20·7′	1°8·0′E	T	144,156
Brome Hall	Suff	TM1576	52°20·6′	1°9·8′E	X	144,156
Brome Hall	Warw	SP1870	52°19·9′	1°43·8′W	X	139
Bromehill Cott	Norf	TL8089	52°28·4′	0°39·4′E	X	144
Brome Park Fm	Suff	TM1575	52°20·1′	1°9·7′E	FM	144,156
Bromesberrow Place	Glos	SO7534	52°0·5′	2°21·5′W	X	150
Brome Street	Suff	TM1576	52°20·6′	1°9·8′E	T	144,156
Bromeswell	Suff	TM3050	52°6·2′	1°21·9′E	T	156
Bromeswell Heath	Suff	TM3049	52°5·7′	1°21·9′E	X	169
Bromfield	Cumbr	NY1746	54°48·4′	3°17·1′W	T	85
Bromfield	Shrops	SO4876	52°23·0′	2°45·4′W	T	137,138,148
Bromford	Birm	SP1290	52°30·7′	1°49·0′W	T	139
Bromham	Beds	TL0051	52°9·1′	0°31·9′W	T	153
Bromham	Wilts	ST9665	51°23·3′	2°3·2′W	T	173
Bromham Fm	Somer	SS8645	51°11·8′	3°37·5′W	FM	181
Bromham Grange	Beds	TL0050	52°8·6′	0°31·9′W	X	153
Bromham House Fm	Wilts	ST9765	51°23·3′	2°2·2′W	FM	173
Bromhey Fm	Medway	TQ7657	51°27·6′	0°32·4′E	FM	178
Bromiley	Black w Dar	SD6616	53°38·6′	2°30·4′W	X	109
Bromley	Barns	SK3298	53°28·9′	1°30·7′W	T	110,111
Bromley	Brom	TQ4069	51°24·4′	0°1·2′E	T	177
Bromley	Dudley	SO9088	52°29·6′	2°8·4′W	T	139
Bromley	Herts	TL4121	51°52·4′	0°3·3′E	T	167
Bromley	Shrops	SJ4026	52°49·9′	2°53·0′W	T	126
Bromley	Shrops	SO7395	52°33·4′	2°23·5′W	T	138
Bromley	T Ham	TQ3782	51°31·4′	0°1·1′W	T	177
Bromley Barn	Kent	TQ7841	51°8·7′	0°33·1′E	X	188
Bromley Common	Brom	TQ4167	51°23·3′	0°2·0′E	T	177
Bromley Common	Herts	TL3120	51°52·0′	0°5·4′W	X	166
Bromley Court	Heref	SO5329	51°57·7′	2°40·6′W	X	149
Bromley Cross	Bolton	SD7313	53°37·0′	2°24·1′W	T	109
Bromley Cross	Essex	TM0627	51°54·4′	1°0·1′E	T	168
Bromley Fm	Bath & NE Somer	ST6061	51°21·0′	2°34·1′W	FM	172
Bromley Fm	Worcs	SO7581	52°25·8′	2°21·7′W	FM	138
Bromley Forge	Shrops	SJ4316	52°44·6′	2°50·3′W	X	126
Bromley Green	Kent	TQ9936	51°5·5′	0°50·9′E	T	189
Bromley Green	Staffs	SJ8043	52°59·3′	2°17·5′W	X	118
Bromley Hall	Herts	TL4121	51°52·4′	0°3·3′E	X	167
Bromley Hall	Shrops	SJ4025	52°49·4′	2°53·0′W	X	126
Bromley Hall	Staffs	SJ7734	52°54·4′	2°20·1′W	T	127
Bromley Heath	S Glos	ST6578	51°30·2′	2°29·9′W	T	172
Bromley Hurst	Staffs	SK0822	52°48·0′	1°52·5′W	X	128
Bromley Lodge	Essex	TQ7598	51°39·4′	0°32·2′E	X	167
Bromley Mill Fm	Staffs	SJ7835	52°55·0′	2°19·2′W	FM	127
Bromley Muir	W Dunb	NS3680	55°59·4′	4°37·3′W	H	63
Bromley Park	Brom	TQ3969	51°24·4′	0°0·3′E	T	177
Bromley Park	Staffs	SK1125	52°49·6′	1°49·8′W	X	128
Bromleysmill	Shrops	SO3391	52°31·0′	2°58·8′W	X	137
Bromley Wood	Staffs	SJ9735	52°55·0′	2°2·3′W	F	127
Bromley Wood	Staffs	SK1024	52°49·0′	1°50·7′W	T	128
Bromlow	Shrops	SJ3201	52°36·4′	2°59·8′W	T	126
Bromlow Callow	Shrops	SJ3201	52°36·4′	2°59·8′W	H	126
Brompton	C of West	TQ2779	51°30·0′	0°9·8′W	T	176
Brompton	Medway	TQ7668	51°23·2′	0°32·2′E	T	178
Brompton	N Yks	SE3796	54°21·7′	1°25·4′W	T	99
Brompton	Shrops	SJ5407	52°39·8′	2°40·4′W	T	126
Brompton Beck	N Yks	SE2192	54°19·6′	1°40·2′W	W	99
Brompton Beck	N Yks	SE3897	54°22·3′	1°24·5′W	W	99
Brompton Beck	N Yks	SE9380	54°12·7′	0°34·0′W	W	101
Brompton Br	N Yks	SE2199	54°23·4′	1°40·2′W	X	99
Brompton-by-Sawdon	N Yks	SE9482	54°13·7′	0°33·1′W	T	101
Brompton Dale	Lincs	TA1205	53°32·0′	0°18·2′W	F	113
Brompton Dale	N Yks	SE9383	54°14·3′	0°33·9′W	X	101
Brompton Fm	N Yks	NZ3700	54°23·9′	1°25·4′W	FM	93
Brompton Hall	Shrops	SO2593	52°32·0′	3°5·9′W	X	137
Brompton Ings	N Yks	SE9479	54°12·1′	0°33·1′W	X	101
Brompton Moor Ho	N Yks	SE9388	54°17·0′	0°33·9′W	X	94,101
Brompton-on-Swale	N Yks	SE2199	54°23·4′	1°40·2′W	T	99
Brompton Ralph	Somer	ST0832	51°5·0′	3°19·4′W	T	181
Brompton Regis	Somer	SS9531	51°4·4′	3°29·5′W	T	181
Bromsash	Heref	SO6424	51°55·0′	2°31·0′W	T	162
Bromsberrow	Glos	SO7434	52°0·5′	2°22·3′W	T	150
Bromsberrow Heath	Glos	SO7332	51°59·4′	2°23·1′W	T	150
Bromsden Fm	Oxon	SU7184	51°33·3′	0°58·2′W	FM	175
Bromsgrove	Worcs	SO9570	52°19·9′	2°4·0′W	T	139
Bromsgrove Sta	Worcs	SO9669	52°19·4′	2°3·1′W	X	139
Bromson Hall	Warw	SP3257	52°12·9′	1°31·5′W	X	151
Bromson Hill	Warw	SP3258	52°13·4′	1°31·5′W	X	151
Bromstead Common	Staffs	SJ8018	52°45·8′	2°17·4′W	T	127
Bromstead Heath	Staffs	SJ8017	52°45·3′	2°17·4′W	T	127
Bromstone	Kent	TR3867	51°21·3′	1°25·5′E	T	179
Bromtrees Fm	Northnts	SP5156	52°12·2′	1°14·8′W	FM	151
Bromtree's Hall	Heref	SO6447	52°7·4′	2°31·2′W	X	149
Bromwich Park	Shrops	SJ3225	52°49·3′	3°0·1′W	X	126
Bromwich Wood	Birm	SO9981	52°25·9′	2°0·5′W	F	139
Bromyard	Heref	SO6554	52°11·2′	2°30·3′W	T	149
Bromyard Downs	Heref	SO6655	52°11·8′	2°29·5′W	T	149
Bromyard & Linton Light Railway	Heref	SO6654	52°11·2′	2°29·4′W	X	149
Brom-y-Court	Heref	SO5028	51°57·1′	2°43·3′W	X	149

Bronaber	Gwyn	SH7131	52°51·9′	3°54·6′W	T	124
Bronaeron	Cered	SN6059	52°12·9′	4°2·6′W	X	146
Bronafon	Powys	SJ2219	52°46·0′	3°9·0′W	X	126
Bron Alarch	Conwy	SH8554	53°4·5′	3°42·6′W	X	116
Bronant	Cered	SN3844	52°4·5′	4°21·4′W	X	145
Bronasgellog	Gwyn	SH7335	52°54·1′	3°52·9′W	X	124
Bronbanadl	Cered	SN6469	52°18·4′	3°59·4′W	X	135
Bron-Bannog	Denb	SJ0352	53°3·6′	3°26·4′W	X	116
Bronbyrfe	Cered	SN7152	52°9·3′	3°52·7′W	X	146,147
Bronclydwr	Gwyn	SH5704	52°37·1′	4°6·3′W	X	135
Broncoed-isaf	Flint	SJ2362	53°9·2′	3°8·7′W	X	117
Broncroft	Shrops	SO5486	52°28·4′	2°40·2′W	T	137,138
Broncroft Lodge	Shrops	SO5386	52°28·4′	2°41·1′W	X	137,138
Broncroft Parks	Shrops	SO5386	52°28·4′	2°41·1′W	X	137,138
Bron-ddel	I of Angl	SH2676	53°15·4′	4°36·1′W	X	114
Brondesbury	Brent	TQ2484	51°32·7′	0°12·3′W	T	176
Brondesbury Park	Brent	TQ2383	51°32·2′	0°13·2′W	T	176
Brondini	Carm	SN4906	51°44·2′	4°10·8′W	X	159
Brondre Fach	Powys	SO0376	52°22·6′	3°25·1′W	X	136,147
Brondre Fawr	Powys	SO0377	52°23·2′	3°25·1′W	X	136,147
Brondre-fawr Hill	Powys	SO0477	52°23·2′	3°24·2′W	H	136,147
Brondyffryn (Sch)	Denb	SJ0665	53°10·7′	3°24·0′W	X	116
Broneifion	Gwyn	SH4838	52°55·3′	4°15·3′W	X	123
Broneirion	Powys	SO0288	52°29·1′	3°26·2′W	T	136
Bronfelin Hall	Powys	SO0491	52°30·7′	3°24·5′W	X	136
Bronferiaeth	Conwy	SH8273	53°14·7′	3°45·7′W	X	116
Bronffynnon	Powys	SN9047	52°6·9′	3°36·0′W	X	147
Bronfre	Cered	SN4858	52°12·2′	4°13·1′W	X	146
Brongain	Powys	SJ1920	52°46·5′	3°11·6′W	X	125
Brongarth	Powys	SN9455	52°11·2′	3°32·6′W	X	147
Brongest	Cered	SN3245	52°4·9′	4°26·7′W	T	145
Brongoll Fm	Shrops	SJ2529	52°51·4′	3°6·4′W	FM	126
Bronguddio	Denb	SJ0340	52°57·2′	3°26·2′W	X	125
Brongwyn	Cered	SN2048	52°6·3′	4°37·3′W	X	145
Brongwyn	Cered	SN2843	52°3·8′	4°30·2′W	T	145
Bronhafod	Powys	SO0798	52°34·6′	3°21·9′W	X	136
Bron Haul	Carm	SN3118	51°50·3′	4°26·8′W	X	159
Bron Haul	Conwy	SH8454	53°4·5′	3°43·5′W	X	116
Bron-haul	Conwy	SH9572	53°14·3′	3°34·0′W	X	116
Bron Haul	Conwy	SH9669	53°12·7′	3°33·0′W	X	116
Bron Heulog	Conwy	SH7258	53°6·5′	3°54·3′W	X	115
Bron Heulog	Conwy	SH9371	53°13·8′	3°35·8′W	X	116
Bronheulog	Gwyn	SH2837	52°54·4′	4°33·1′W	X	123
Bron-heulog	I of Angl	SH3487	53°21·5′	4°29·3′W	X	114
Bronheulwen	Powys	SN9285	52°27·4′	3°35·0′W	X	136
Bronheulwen	Powys	SN9478	52°23·6′	3°33·1′W	X	136,147
Bronhyddon	Powys	SJ2220	52°46·6′	3°9·0′W	X	126
Bronial	Cered	SN2847	52°5·9′	4°30·3′W	X	145
Broniarth	Powys	SJ2113	52°42·8′	3°9·8′W	X	125
Broniarth Hill	Powys	SJ1612	52°42·2′	3°14·2′W	H	125
Bronie Burn	Aberd	NJ9228	57°20·8′	2°7·5′W	W	38
Bronington	Wrex	SJ4839	52°57·0′	2°46·0′W	T	126
Bronkham Hill	Dorset	SY6287	50°41·1′	2°31·9′W	H	194
Bron-llan	Conwy	SH9266	53°11·1′	3°36·6′W	X	116
Bron Llan	Conwy	SH9644	52°59·2′	3°32·6′W	X	125
Bronllan	Powys	SO0789	52°29·7′	3°21·8′W	X	136
Bron-llety-Ifan	Gwyn	SH6312	52°41·5′	4°1·2′W	X	124
Bronllwyd	Gwyn	SH2430	52°50·6′	4°36·4′W	X	123
Bronllys	Powys	SO1435	52°0·6′	3°14·8′W	T	161
Bronllys Castle	Powys	SO1434	52°0·1′	3°14·8′W	A	161
Bron Menai	I of Angl	SH4564	53°9·3′	4°18·7′W	X	114,115
Bronmiod Fm	Gwyn	SH4144	52°58·4′	4°21·7′W	FM	123
Bronmwyn	Cered	SN7164	52°15·8′	3°53·0′W	X	146,147
Bronnant	Cered	SN6467	52°17·3′	3°59·2′W	T	135
Bronphilip Fm	Gwyn	SH2631	52°51·1′	4°34·6′W	FM	123
Bron Pistyll	Conwy	SH8873	53°14·8′	3°40·3′W	X	116
Bron-prŷs	Gwyn	SH5900	52°35·0′	4°4·5′W	X	135
Bronsil	Heref	SO7437	52°2·1′	2°22·3′W	X	150
Bronte Waterfall	Brad	SD9935	53°48·9′	2°0·5′W	W	103
Bronte Way	Brad	SE0236	53°49·5′	1°57·8′W	X	104
Bronte Way	Cald	SE1524	53°43·0′	1°45·9′W	X	104
Bronte Way	Lancs	SD9637	53°50·0′	2°3·2′W	X	103
Bronwenllwyd	Cered	SN6666	52°16·8′	3°57·5′W	X	135
Bronwion	Cered	SN2845	52°4·8′	4°30·2′W	X	145
Bronwion	Cered	SN7192	52°30·9′	3°53·7′W	X	135
Bronwydd	Cered	SN3543	52°3·9′	4°24·0′W	T	145
Bronwydd	Powys	SN8910	51°46·9′	3°36·2′W	X	160
Bronwydd Arms	Carm	SN4124	51°53·8′	4°18·3′W	T	159
Bron Wylfa	Gwyn	SH4557	53°5·5′	4°18·5′W	X	115,123
Bronwylfa	Wrex	SJ2848	53°1·7′	3°4·0′W	X	117
Bron-y-aur	Gwyn	SH7302	52°36·3′	3°52·1′W	X	135
Bron y Berllan	Carm	SN5017	51°50·1′	4°10·2′W	X	159
Bronydd	Cered	SN2145	52°4·7′	4°36·3′W	X	145
Bronydd	Pemb	SN1342	52°2·9′	4°43·2′W	X	145
Bronydd	Powys	SO2245	52°6·1′	3°7·9′W	T	148
Bronydd Isaf	Gwyn	SH6270	53°12·8′	4°3·6′W	X	115
Bronydd-mawr	Powys	SN8830	51°57·7′	3°37·4′W	X	160
Bron-y-fedw	Gwyn	SH5754	53°4·1′	4°7·7′W	X	115
Bron-y-felin	Denb	SJ1461	53°8·6′	3°16·7′W	X	116
Bron-y-foel	Gwyn	SH5438	52°55·4′	4°9·9′W	X	124
Bron-y-foel	Gwyn	SH6024	52°48·0′	4°4·2′W	X	124
Bron-y-gaer	Carm	SN3019	51°50·9′	4°27·7′W	X	159
Bronygarth	Shrops	SJ2637	52°55·8′	3°5·6′W	T	126
Bron-y-glyn	Carm	SN5427	51°55·6′	4°7·0′W	X	146
Bron-y-gof	Denb	SJ0856	53°5·8′	3°22·0′W	X	116
Bron-y-main	Powys	SJ1614	52°43·3′	3°14·2′W	X	125
Bronyn	Carm	SN3712	51°47·2′	4°21·4′W	X	159
Bron-yr-haul	Conwy	SH8565	53°10·4′	3°42·8′W	X	116
Bron-yr-Helm	Cered	SN7954	52°10·5′	3°45·8′W	X	146,147
Bronyscawen	Carm	SN2125	51°53·9′	4°35·7′W	X	145,158
Bronyvastre	Powys	SO1190	52°30·3′	3°18·3′W	X	136
Brooches, The	Shrops	SO4182	52°26·2′	2°51·7′W	X	137
Brood Low	Derby	SK1279	53°18·7′	1°48·8′W	A	119
Broodview	N Yks	SE7985	54°15·5′	0°46·8′W	X	94,100
Broogh, The	I of M	SC3174	54°8·3′	4°34·8′W	A	95
Broo Gill	Shetld	HU2678	60°29·4′	1°31·1′W	X	3
Brook	Carm	SN2609	51°45·4′	4°30·9′W	T	158
Brook	Devon	SX4772	50°31·9′	4°9·2′W	T	191,201
Brook	Devon	SX6054	50°22·4′	3°57·8′W	X	202
Brook	Devon	SX8091	50°42·6′	3°41·6′W	T	191

Brook	Devon	SX8190	50°42·1′	3°40·7′W	X	191
Brook	Hants	SU2714	50°55·7′	1°36·6′W	T	195
Brook	Hants	SZ3428	51°3·2′	1°30·5′W	T	185
Brook	I of W	SZ3983	50°39·0′	1°26·5′W	T	196
Brook	Kent	TR0644	51°9·7′	0°57·2′E	T	179,189
Brook	Powys	SJ8902	52°36·5′	3°38·0′W	X	135,136
Brook	Surrey	SU9337	51°7·7′	0°39·9′W	T	186
Brook	Surrey	TQ0646	51°12·4′	0°28·6′W	T	187
Brook	Wilts	ST8551	51°15·7′	2°12·5′W	X	183
Brookbank	W Loth	NT0759	55°49·2′	3°28·6′W	X	65,72
Brook Barn Fm	W Susx	TQ0103	50°49·3′	0°33·6′W	FM	197
Brook Bay	I of W	SZ3883	50°39·0′	1°27·4′W	W	196
Brook Bottom	Derby	SJ9886	53°22·5′	2°1·4′W	T	109
Brook Bottom	Derby	SK1476	53°17·1′	1°47·0′W	X	119
Brook Bottom	Lancs	SD5442	53°52·6′	2°41·6′W	T	102
Brook Bottom	Lancs	SD6740	53°51·6′	2°29·7′W	X	103
Brook Bottom	Tames	SD9602	53°31·1′	2°3·2′W	T	109
Brook Bridge	Heref	SO4361	52°14·9′	2°49·7′W	X	137,148,149
Brook Common	Hants	SU2613	50°55·2′	1°37·4′W	X	195
Brook Coppice	Shrops	SJ3901	52°36·4′	2°53·6′W	F	126
Brook Cottage	Lancs	SD5638	53°50·4′	2°39·7′W	X	102
Brook Covert	Staffs	SJ7821	52°47·4′	2°19·2′W	F	127
Brookdale Fm	Ches	SJ4664	53°10·5′	2°48·1′W	FM	117
Brookdale Plantation	I of M	SC4392	54°18·2′	4°24·4′W	X	95
Brook Down	I of W	SZ3885	50°40·0′	1°27·4′W	X	196
Brooke	Norf	TM2899	52°32·7′	1°22·2′E	T	134
Brooke	Rut	SK8405	52°38·4′	0°45·1′W	T	141
Brooke Hall	Suff	TL9456	52°10·3′	0°50·6′E	X	155
Brooke Ho	Norf	TM2898	52°32·1′	1°22·1′E	X	134
Brooke Lodge	Norf	TM2899	52°32·7′	1°22·2′E	X	134
Brookenby	Lincs	TF2095	53°26·5′	0°11·2′W	T	113
Brook End	Beds	TL0763	52°15·5′	0°25·5′W	T	153
Brook End	Beds	TL1647	52°6·8′	0°18·0′W	T	153
Brook End	Cambs	TL0873	52°20·9′	0°24·5′W	T	153
Brookend	Essex	TL5824	51°53·8′	0°18·2′E	X	167
Brookend	Essex	TL6522	51°52·6′	0°24·2′E	X	167
Brookend	Glos	SO6802	51°43·2′	2°27·4′W	T	162
Brookend	Glos	SO7333	51°59·9′	2°23·2′W	X	150
Brookend	Glos	ST5999	51°41·5′	2°35·2′W	T	162
Brook End	Herts	TL3228	51°56·3′	0°4·4′W	T	166
Brook End	Mil Key	SP9144	52°5·4′	0°39·9′W	T	152
Brookend	Oxon	SP3221	51°53·4′	1°31·7′W	T	164
Brookend	Staffs	SK0937	52°56·1′	1°51·6′W	X	128
Brook End	Warw	SP2594	52°32·8′	1°37·5′W	X	140
Brook End	Wilts	ST8384	51°33·5′	2°14·3′W	T	173
Brook End	Worcs	SO8649	52°8·6′	2°11·9′W	T	150
Brook End Fm	Bucks	SU9385	51°33·6′	0°39·1′W	FM	175
Brook End Fm	Staffs	SP1999	52°35·5′	1°42·8′W	FM	139
Brook End Fm	Warw	SP2494	52°32·8′	1°38·4′W	FM	139
Brook End Green Fm	Beds	TL0731	51°58·3′	0°26·1′W	FM	166
Brookend Ho	Oxon	SP2331	51°58·9′	1°39·5′W	X	151
Brooke Priory	Rut	SK8406	52°38·9′	0°45·1′W	X	141
Brooker Fm	Kent	TR0431	51°2·7′	0°55·0′E	FM	189
Brookes Croft	Kent	TR0457	51°16·8′	0°55·9′E	X	178,179
Brooke's Hill	Hants	SU3315	50°56·2′	1°31·4′W	X	196
Brookes's Fm	Essex	TL8126	51°54·4′	0°38·3′E	FM	168
Brookestreet Fm	Kent	TR3059	51°17·2′	1°18·3′E	FM	179
Brooke Wood	Norf	TM2798	52°32·2′	1°21·2′E	F	134
Brook Field	Cambs	TL4167	52°17·2′	0°4·4′E	X	154
Brookfield	Derby	SK0195	53°27·3′	1°58·7′W	T	110
Brookfield	Heref	SO4334	52°0·3′	2°49·4′W	X	149,161
Brookfield	I of M	SC2778	54°10·4′	4°38·6′W	X	95
Brookfield	Lancs	SD5631	53°46·7′	2°39·6′W	T	102
Brookfield	Midd	NZ4815	54°31·9′	1°15·1′W	T	93
Brookfield	Renf	NS4164	55°50·8′	4°31·9′W	T	64
Brookfield	Worcs	SO9177	52°23·7′	2°7·5′W	X	139
Brookfield	W Susx	TQ0205	50°50·4′	0°32·7′W	X	197
Brookfield Common	Herts	TL3220	51°52·0′	0°4·6′W	X	166
Brookfield Fm	Cambs	TL2172	52°20·2′	0°13·0′W	FM	153
Brookfield Fm	Cambs	TL4067	52°17·2′	0°3·6′E	FM	154
Brookfield Fm	Glos	SP0803	51°43·8′	1°52·7′W	FM	163
Brookfield Fm	Shrops	SJ3230	52°52·0′	3°0·2′W	FM	126
Brookfield Fm	Warw	SP3883	52°26·9′	1°26·1′W	FM	140
Brookfield Ho	Ches	SJ7474	53°16·0′	2°23·0′W	X	118
Brookfield Ho	Lancs	SD3904	53°32·0′	2°54·8′W	X	108
Brookfield Ho	Pth & Kin	NN9009	56°15·9′	3°46·1′W	X	58
Brookfield Manor	Derby	SK2382	53°20·3′	1°38·9′W	X	110
Brookfield Plantation	Northnts	SP8991	52°30·8′	0°40·9′W	F	141
Brookfields Fm	Ches	SJ6845	53°0·3′	2°28·2′W	FM	118
Brookfields Fm	N Yks	NZ3607	54°27·7′	1°26·3′W	FM	93
Brook Fm	Beds	SP9544	52°5·4′	0°36·4′W	FM	153
Brook Fm	Beds	SP9958	52°12·9′	0°32·7′W	FM	153
Brook Fm	Beds	TL0857	52°12·3′	0°24·8′W	FM	153
Brook Fm	Beds	TL1357	52°12·2′	0°20·4′W	FM	153
Brook Fm	Bucks	SP7622	51°53·7′	0°53·3′W	FM	165
Brook Fm	Bucks	SP8207	51°45·6′	0°48·3′W	FM	165
Brook Fm	Cambs	TL4053	52°9·7′	0°3·2′E	FM	154
Brook Fm	Ches	SJ5954	53°5·1′	2°36·3′W	FM	117
Brook Fm	Ches	SJ5979	53°18·6′	2°36·5′W	FM	117
Brook Fm	Ches	SJ6359	53°7·9′	2°32·8′W	FM	118
Brook Fm	Ches	SJ6653	53°4·6′	2°30·0′W	FM	118
Brook Fm	Ches	SJ6870	53°13·8′	2°28·4′W	FM	118
Brook Fm	Ches	SJ7259	53°7·9′	2°24·7′W	FM	118
Brook Fm	Ches	SJ7859	53°7·9′	2°19·3′W	FM	118
Brook Fm	Ches	SJ7977	53°17·6′	2°18·5′W	FM	118
Brook Fm	Ches	SJ8579	53°18·7′	2°13·1′W	FM	118
Brook Fm	Derby	SK1636	52°55·5′	1°45·3′W	FM	128
Brook Fm	Devon	SY1290	50°42·4′	3°14·4′W	FM	192,193
Brook Fm	Essex	TL6721	51°52·0′	0°25·9′E	FM	167
Brook Fm	Essex	TL7202	51°41·6′	0°29·7′E	FM	167
Brook Fm	Essex	TL8306	51°43·6′	0°39·4′E	FM	168
Brook Fm	Essex	TL8430	51°56·5′	0°41·0′E	FM	168
Brook Fm	Essex	TL9932	51°57·3′	0°54·2′E	FM	168
Brook Fm	Essex	TM0000	51°40·0′	0°53·9′E	FM	168
Brook Fm	Essex	TM0721	51°51·2′	1°0·7′E	FM	168,169
Brook Fm	Essex	TM1022	51°51·6′	1°3·4′E	FM	168,169
Brook Fm	Essex	TQ5296	51°38·8′	0°12·2′E	FM	167,177
Brook Fm	Essex	TQ9597	51°38·5′	0°49·5′E	FM	168
Brook Fm	E Susx	TQ8617	50°55·6′	0°39·2′E	FM	189,199
Brook Fm	E Yorks	SE8731	53°46·3′	0°40·4′W	FM	106

Brook Fm	Flint	SJ2963	53°9·8′	3°3·3′W	FM	117
Brook Fm	Glos	SO7114	51°49·7′	2°24·9′W	FM	162
Brook Fm	Halton	SJ4582	53°20·2′	2°49·2′W	FM	108
Brook Fm	Hants	SU3524	51°1·1′	1°29·7′W	FM	185
Brook Fm	Heref	SO3328	51°57·0′	2°58·1′W	FM	149,161
Brook Fm	Heref	SO3457	52°12·7′	2°57·6′W	FM	148,149
Brook Fm	Heref	SO5460	52°14·4′	2°40·0′W	FM	137,138,149
Brook Fm	Heref	SO6736	52°1·5′	2°28·5′W	FM	149
Brook Fm	Kent	TQ7245	51°10·9′	0°28·1′E	FM	188
Brook Fm	Kent	TQ8735	51°5·2′	0°40·6′E	FM	189
Brook Fm	Kent	TR1137	51°5·8′	1°1·2′E	FM	179,189
Brook Fm	Kent	TR2268	51°22·3′	1°11·8′E	FM	179
Brook Fm	Lancs	SD4045	53°54·1′	2°54·4′W	FM	102
Brook Fm	Lancs	SD4544	53°53·6′	2°49·8′W	FM	102
Brook Fm	Lancs	SD5638	53°50·4′	2°39·7′W	FM	102
Brook Fm	Leic	SK4612	52°42·5′	1°18·7′W	FM	129
Brook Fm	Leic	SK7128	52°50·9′	0°56·3′W	FM	129
Brook Fm	Leic	SK7850	52°38·5′	0°50·4′W	FM	141
Brook Fm	Lincs	TF2773	53°14·6′	0°5·4′W	FM	122
Brook Fm	Lincs	TF3679	53°17·7′	0°2·8′E	FM	122
Brook Fm	Newp	ST3392	51°37·6′	2°57·7′W	FM	171
Brook Fm	Norf	TF6708	52°38·9′	0°28·5′E	FM	143
Brook Fm	Norf	TG2810	52°38·8′	1°22·6′E	FM	133,134
Brook Fm	Northnts	SP5372	52°20·8′	1°12·9′W	FM	140
Brook Fm	Northnts	SP7257	52°12·6′	0°56·4′W	FM	152
Brook Fm	N Som	ST4970	51°25·8′	2°43·6′W	FM	172
Brook Fm	Rut	SK9111	52°41·6′	0°38·8′W	FM	130
Brook Fm	S Glos	ST5682	51°32·3′	2°37·7′W	FM	172
Brook Fm	S Glos	ST6993	51°38·3′	2°26·5′W	FM	162,172
Brook Fm	Shrops	SJ7501	52°36·6′	2°21·8′W	FM	127
Brook Fm	Somer	ST2319	50°58·2′	3°5·4′W	FM	193
Brook Fm	Somer	ST4744	51°11·8′	2°45·1′W	FM	182
Brook Fm	Staffs	SJ7851	53°3·6′	2°19·3′W	FM	118
Brook Fm	Staffs	SK0155	53°5·8′	1°58·7′W	FM	119
Brook Fm	Staffs	SK0511	52°42·0′	1°55·2′W	FM	128
Brook Fm	Staffs	SP1899	52°35·5′	1°43·7′W	FM	139
Brook Fm	Suff	TL9362	52°13·6′	0°50·0′E	FM	155
Brook Fm	Suff	TL9757	52°10·8′	0°53·3′E	FM	155
Brook Fm	Suff	TL9869	52°17·2′	0°54·6′E	FM	155
Brook Fm	Suff	TM0058	52°11·3′	0°56·0′E	FM	155
Brook Fm	Suff	TM1461	52°12·6′	1°8·3′E	FM	156
Brook Fm	Suff	TM1636	51°59·0′	1°9·1′E	FM	169
Brook Fm	Suff	TM2455	52°9·1′	1°16·9′E	FM	156
Brook Fm	Suff	TM2560	52°11·8′	1°17·9′E	FM	156
Brook Fm	Suff	TM3282	52°23·4′	1°25·0′E	FM	156
Brook Fm	Suff	TM3772	52°17·9′	1°29·0′E	FM	156
Brook Fm	Suff	TM3861	52°12·0′	1°29·4′E	FM	156
Brook Fm	Suff	TM3983	52°23·8′	1°31·2′E	FM	156
Brook Fm	Suff	TM4279	52°21·6′	1°33·7′E	FM	156
Brook Fm	Surrey	TQ2145	51°11·7′	0°15·7′W	FM	187
Brook Fm	Surrey	TQ3749	51°13·6′	0°1·9′W	FM	187
Brook Fm	Thurr	TQ6580	51°29·9′	0°23·0′E	FM	177,178
Brook Fm	W Berks	SU6965	51°23·0′	1°0·1′W	FM	175
Brook Fm	Wok	SU7866	51°23·5′	0°52·3′W	FM	175
Brook Fm	Worcs	SO6167	52°18·2′	2°33·9′W	FM	138,149
Brook Fm	Worcs	SO7850	52°9·1′	2°18·9′W	FM	150
Brook Fm	Worcs	SO8264	52°16·7′	2°15·4′W	FM	138,150
Brook Fm	Worcs	SP0670	52°19·9′	1°54·3′W	FM	139
Brook Fm	Wrex	SJ4146	53°0·7′	2°52·4′W	FM	117
Brook Fm	W Susx	TQ1824	51°0·4′	0°18·7′W	FM	198
Brookfoot	Cald	SE1323	53°42·4′	1°47·8′W	T	104
Brook Furlong Fm	Notts	SK5626	52°50·0′	1°9·7′W	FM	129
Brookfurlong Fm	Oxon	SP5315	51°50·1′	1°13·5′W	FM	164
Brookgate Fm	E Susx	TQ7229	51°2·3′	0°27·6′E	FM	188,199
Brook Green	Ham & Ful	TQ2379	51°29·9′	0°13·3′W	T	176
Brookgreen	I of W	SZ3883	50°39·0′	1°27·4′W	T	196
Brook Green	Somer	ST3618	50°57·7′	2°54·3′W	X	193
Brook Green	Suff	TL8658	52°11·6′	0°43·7′E	T	155
Brook Hall	Ches	SJ4859	53°7·8′	2°46·2′W	X	117
Brook Hall	Essex	TL8443	52°3·5′	0°41·4′E	X	155
Brook Hall	Essex	TL8900	51°40·2′	0°44·4′E	X	168
Brook Hall	Norf	TM1591	52°28·7′	1°10·4′E	X	144
Brook Hall	N Yks	SE4746	53°54·7′	1°16·7′W	X	105
Brook Hall	Suff	TM0167	52°16·1′	0°57·2′E	X	155
Brook Hall	Suff	TM3974	52°18·9′	1°30·8′E	X	156
Brook Hall Fm	Suff	TM1458	52°10·9′	1°8·2′E	FM	156
Brookhall Fm	Suff	TM3781	52°22·8′	1°29·3′E	FM	156
Brookham	Devon	SS5129	51°2·7′	4°7·2′W	X	180
Brookhampton	Oxon	SU6098	51°40·9′	1°7·5′W	T	164,165
Brookhampton	Shrops	SO5690	52°30·6′	2°38·5′W	T	137,138
Brookhampton	Somer	ST6327	51°2·7′	2°31·3′W	T	183
Brookhampton	Warw	SP3150	52°9·1′	1°32·4′W	X	151
Brookhay	Staffs	SK1611	52°42·0′	1°45·4′W	X	128
Brookhead Fm	Essex	TL8305	51°43·1′	0°39·4′E	FM	168
Brook Head Fm	Warr	SJ5792	53°25·6′	2°38·4′W	FM	108
Brookheath	Hants	SU1316	50°56·8′	1°48·5′W	X	184
Brookheyes Fm	Traf	SJ7490	53°24·6′	2°23·1′W	FM	109
Brook Hill	Hants	SU2714	50°55·7′	1°36·6′W	T	195
Brook Hill	I of W	SZ3984	50°39·5′	1°26·5′W	X	196
Brook Hill	N Lincs	TA1122	53°41·2′	0°18·7′W	X	107,113
Brook Hill	Notts	SK5633	52°53·7′	1°9·6′W	T	129
Brook Hill	Suff	TM2043	52°2·7′	1°12·9′E	X	169
Brook Hill Fm	Leic	SP4397	52°34·4′	1°21·5′W	FM	140
Brookhill Fm	Worcs	SO8661	52°15·1′	2°11·9′W	FM	150
Brookhill Hall	Derby	SK4656	53°6·2′	1°18·4′W	X	120
Brookhill Ho	W Susx	TQ2122	50°59·3′	0°16·2′W	X	198
Brookhill Wood	Suff	TM2143	52°2·7′	1°13·8′E	F	169
Brook Ho	Ches	SJ5850	53°3·0′	2°37·2′W	X	117
Brook Ho	Ches	SJ5973	53°15·4′	2°36·5′W	X	117
Brook Ho	Ches	SJ6367	53°12·2′	2°32·8′W	X	118
Brook Ho	Ches	SJ6969	53°13·3′	2°27·5′W	X	118
Brook Ho	Ches	SJ8660	53°8·5′	2°12·2′W	X	118
Brook Ho	Ches	SJ9079	53°18·7′	2°8·6′W	X	118
Brook Ho	Devon	SX5270	50°30·9′	4°9·9′W	X	201
Brook Ho	Devon	SX7861	50°26·4′	3°42·7′W	X	202
Brook Ho	Essex	TL7026	51°54·6′	0°28·7′E	X	167
Brook Ho	Essex	TL9033	51°58·0′	0°46·3′E	X	168
Brook Ho	Essex	TQ4798	51°39·9′	0°7·9′E	X	167,177
Brook Ho	E Susx	TQ4919	50°57·3′	0°7·7′E	X	199
Brook Ho	E Susx	TQ5127	51°1·6′	0°9·6′E	X	188,199

Brook Ho	Hants	SU8156	51°18·1′	0°49·9′W	X	175,186
Brook Ho	I of W	SZ3984	50°39·5′	1°26·5′W	X	196
Brook Ho	Kent	TQ8148	51°12·4′	0°35·9′E	X	188
Brook Ho	Lancs	SD5455	53°59·6′	2°41·7′W	X	102
Brook Ho	Lancs	SD6440	53°51·5′	2°32·4′W	X	102,103
Brook Ho	Norf	TM2084	52°24·8′	1°14·5′E	X	156
Brook Ho	N Yks	SE6469	54°7·0′	1°0·8′W	X	100
Brook Ho	Roth	SK5189	53°24·0′	1°13·6′W	X	111,120
Brook Ho	Shrops	SJ2726	52°49·8′	3°4·6′W	X	126
Brook Ho	Shrops	SJ3509	52°40·7′	2°57·3′W	X	126
Brook Ho	Shrops	SJ4237	52°55·9′	2°51·4′W	X	126
Brook Ho	Shrops	SJ5229	52°51·6′	2°42·4′W	X	126
Brook Ho	Shrops	SJ5234	52°54·3′	2°42·4′W	X	126
Brook Ho	Shrops	SO2285	52°27·7′	3°8·5′W	X	137
Brook Ho	Shrops	SO4797	52°34·3′	2°46·5′W	X	137,138
Brook Ho	Shrops	SO5287	52°29·0′	2°42·0′W	X	137,138
Brook Ho	Shrops	SO5477	52°23·6′	2°40·2′W	X	137,138
Brook Ho	Staffs	SJ9651	53°3·6′	2°3·2′W	X	118
Brook Ho	Staffs	SK0231	52°52·8′	1°57·8′W	X	128
Brook Ho	Suff	TL9243	52°3·3′	0°48·4′E	X	155
Brook Ho	Suff	TM3584	52°24·4′	1°27·7′E	X	156
Brook Ho	Wilts	ST8476	51°29·2′	2°13·4′W	X	173
Brook Ho	W Susx	TQ2412	50°53·9′	0°13·8′W	X	198
Brook Ho	W Susx	TQ3529	51°2·9′	0°4·1′W	X	187,198
Brook Ho	W Susx	TQ3837	51°7·2′	0°1·3′W	X	187
Brook Ho Fm	Shrops	SO3396	52°33·7′	2°58·9′W	FM	137
Brookhouse	Black w Dar	SD6828	53°45·1′	2°28·7′W	T	103
Brookhouse	Cald	SE0629	53°45·7′	1°54·1′W	T	104
Brookhouse	Ches	SJ9475	53°16·6′	2°5·0′W	T	118
Brookhouse	Ches	SJ9872	53°14·9′	2°1·4′W	X	118
Brookhouse	Denb	SJ0765	53°10·7′	3°23·1′W	T	116
Brookhouse	E Susx	TQ3715	50°55·3′	0°2·7′W	X	198
Brookhouse	Lancs	SD5464	54°4·4′	2°41·8′W	T	97
Brookhouse	Roth	SK5188	53°23·4′	1°13·6′W	T	111,120
Brookhouse	Staffs	SJ9349	53°2·5′	2°5·9′W	X	118
Brookhouse Fm	Ches	SJ4964	53°10·5′	2°45·4′W	FM	117
Brookhouse Fm	Ches	SJ5264	53°10·5′	2°42·7′W	FM	117
Brookhouse Fm	Ches	SJ6078	53°18·1′	2°35·6′W	FM	118
Brookhouse Fm	Ches	SJ6165	53°11·1′	2°34·6′W	FM	118
Brook House Fm	Ches	SJ6377	53°17·6′	2°32·9′W	FM	118
Brook House Fm	Ches	SJ6684	53°21·3′	2°30·2′W	FM	109
Brook House Fm	Ches	SJ6761	53°8·9′	2°29·2′W	FM	118
Brook House Fm	Ches	SJ7166	53°11·7′	2°25·6′W	FM	118
Brook House Fm	Ches	SJ7257	53°6·8′	2°24·7′W	FM	118
Brook House Fm	Ches	SJ7471	53°14·4′	2°23·0′W	FM	118
Brook House Fm	Ches	SJ7876	53°17·1′	2°19·4′W	FM	118
Brook House Fm	Ches	SJ8779	53°18·7′	2°11·3′W	FM	118
Brook House Fm	Ches	SJ8862	53°9·5′	2°10·4′W	FM	118
Brookhouse Fm	Derby	SK2049	53°2·5′	1°41·7′W	FM	119
Brook House Fm	Essex	TL9210	51°45·6′	0°47·3′E	FM	168
Brook House Fm	Heref	SO6652	52°10·2′	2°29·4′W	FM	149
Brook House Fm	Know	SJ4685	53°21·8′	2°48·3′W	FM	108
Brookhouse Fm	Lancs	SD7237	53°50·0′	2°25·1′W	FM	103
Brook House Fm	Lincs	TF4227	52°49·5′	0°6·9′E	FM	131
Brookhouse Fm	N Yks	NZ2406	54°27·2′	1°37·4′W	FM	93
Brook House Fm	N Yks	SD6668	54°6·7′	2°30·8′W	FM	98
Brookhouse Fm	Staffs	SK1030	52°52·3′	1°50·7′W	FM	128
Brook House Fm	Suff	TM1653	52°8·2′	1°9·8′E	FM	156
Brook House Fm	Warw	SP1171	52°20·5′	1°49·9′W	FM	139
Brook House Fm	Warw	SP2892	52°31·7′	1°34·8′W	FM	140
Brook House Fm	Wilts	ST8553	51°16·8′	2°12·5′W	FM	183
Brookhouse Fm	W Susx	TQ1320	50°58·3′	0°23·0′W	FM	198
Brookhouse Green	Ches	SJ8161	53°9·0′	2°16·6′W	T	118
Brook House Green	Lancs	SD7354	53°59·1′	2°24·3′W	X	103
Brookhouse Moss	Ches	SJ8061	53°9·0′	2°17·5′W	F	118
Brookhouses	Derby	SK0289	53°24·1′	1°57·8′W	T	110
Brookhouses	Derby	SK0478	53°18·2′	1°56·0′W	X	119
Brookhouses	Staffs	SJ9943	52°59·3′	2°0·5′W	T	118
Brookhurst	Surrey	TQ1041	51°9·7′	0°25·2′W	X	187
Brookhurst	Wirral	SJ3480	53°19·0′	2°59·0′W	T	108
Brookhurst Fm	W Susx	TQ1332	51°4·8′	0°22·8′W	FM	187
Brooking	Devon	SX7560	50°25·8′	3°45·2′W	X	202
Brookland	Devon	SS7015	50°55·4′	3°50·6′W	X	180
Brookland	Glos	SO6730	51°58·3′	2°28·4′W	X	149
Brookland	Kent	TQ9825	50°59·6′	0°49·7′E	T	189
Brookland Hall	Powys	SJ2110	52°41·2′	3°9·7′W	X	126
Brooklands	Cambs	TL1874	52°21·3′	0°15·6′W	X	142
Brooklands	Carm	SN3625	51°54·2′	4°22·6′W	X	145
Brooklands	D & G	NX8173	55°2·5′	3°51·3′W	X	84
Brooklands	Essex	TM1726	51°53·6′	1°9·6′E	X	168,169
Brooklands	E Susx	TQ4338	51°7·6′	0°3·0′E	X	187
Brooklands	E Susx	TQ6519	50°57·0′	0°21·3′E	X	199
Brooklands	Hants	SU4908	50°52·4′	1°17·8′W	X	196
Brooklands	Hants	SU7961	51°20·8′	0°51·5′W	X	175
Brooklands	Leeds	SE3435	53°48·9′	1°28·6′W	T	104
Brooklands	N Yks	SE9579	54°12·1′	0°32·2′W	X	101
Brooklands	Shrops	SJ5242	52°58·6′	2°42·5′W	T	117
Brooklands	Shrops	SJ7507	52°39·8′	2°21·8′W	X	127
Brooklands	Suff	TM2474	52°19·3′	1°17·6′E	X	156
Brooklands	Surrey	TQ0662	51°21·1′	0°28·3′W	T	176,187
Brooklands	Traf	SJ7990	53°24·6′	2°18·5′W	T	109
Brooklands	V of Glam	ST0873	51°27·1′	3°19·1′W	X	170
Brooklands Burn	D & G	NX8071	55°1·4′	3°52·2′W	W	84
Brooklands Fm	Cambs	TL2277	52°22·9′	0°12·1′W	FM	142
Brooklands Fm	Cambs	TL3157	52°12·0′	0°4·6′W	FM	153
Brooklands Fm	Dorset	SY6695	50°45·4′	2°28·5′W	FM	194
Brooklands Fm	Hants	SU5416	50°56·7′	1°13·5′W	FM	185
Brooklands Fm	Surrey	TQ0340	51°9·2′	0°31·2′W	FM	186
Brooklands Fm	Worcs	SP0342	52°4·8′	1°57·0′W	FM	150
Brooklands Fm	W Susx	TQ2521	50°58·7′	0°12·8′W	FM	198
Brooklands Fm	W Susx	TQ3221	50°58·6′	0°6·8′W	FM	198
Brooklands Hill	D & G	NX8173	55°2·5′	3°51·3′W	H	84
Brooklands, The	Derby	SK2268	53°12·8′	1°39·8′W	X	119
Brookleigh	Devon	SX9598	50°46·6′	3°29·0′W	T	192
Brook Lodge	Cambs	TL1477	52°23·0′	0°19·1′W	X	142
Brook Lodge	Ches	SJ5162	53°9·4′	2°43·6′W	X	117
Brook Lodge Fm	E Susx	TQ8018	50°56·2′	0°34·1′E	FM	199
Brook Lodge Fm	Surrey	TQ1845	51°11·7′	0°18·3′W	FM	187
Brooklyns	Devon	SS5902	50°48·3′	3°59·7′W	X	191

Brook Manor	Devon	SX7167	50°29·6′	3°48·7′W	X	202
Brookmans Park	Herts	TL2404	51°43·5′	0°11·9′W	T	166
Brookman's Valley	Dorset	ST8714	50°55·7′	2°10·7′W	X	194
Brookmead Fm	Essex	TL8803	51°41·9′	0°43·6′E	FM	168
Brookmill	Shrops	SJ4138	52°56·4′	2°52·3′W	X	126
Brookover Fm	Somer	ST7649	51°14·6′	2°20·2′W	FM	183
Brookpits	W Susx	TQ0001	50°48·2′	0°34·5′W	T	197
Brook Place	Kent	TQ4952	51°15·1′	0°8·5′E	X	188
Brook Place	Surrey	SU9561	51°20·6′	0°37·8′W	T	175,176,186
Brookrow	Shrops	SO6074	52°22·0′	2°34·9′W	T	138
Brooks	Corn	SX1560	50°24·9′	4°35·9′W	T	201
Brooks	Lancs	SD5645	53°54·2′	2°39·8′W	X	102
Brooks	Powys	SO1499	52°35·2′	3°15·8′W	T	136
Brooksbottoms	Bury	SD7915	53°38·1′	2°18·6′W	T	109
Brooksby	Leic	SK6716	52°44·5′	1°0·0′W	T	129
Brooksby Grange Fm	Leic	SK6615	52°44·0′	1°1·0′W	FM	129
Brooks End	Kent	TR2967	51°21·6′	1°17·8′E	T	179
Brooks Fm	Ches	SJ9267	53°12·2′	2°6·8′W	FM	118
Brooks Fm	Monm	SO4708	51°46·3′	2°45·7′W	FM	161
Brooks Green	W Susx	TQ1225	51°1·0′	0°23·8′W	T	187,198
Brooksgrove	Pemb	SM9314	51°47·4′	4°59·7′W	X	157,158
Brook's Hill	Shrops	SJ6303	52°37·6′	2°32·4′W	X	127
Brooks Hill	Shrops	SO3496	52°33·7′	2°58·0′W	X	137
Brookshill Marsh	Shrops	SO3596	52°33·7′	2°57·1′W	X	137
Brooks Ho	Arg & Bt	NS3378	55°58·2′	4°40·1′W	X	63
Brooks House	Devon	SS3101	50°47·3′	4°23·5′W	X	190
Brookside	Brackn	SU9170	51°25·5′	0°41·1′W	T	175
Brookside	Derby	SK3570	53°13·8′	1°28·1′W	T	119
Brookside	E Susx	TQ5917	50°56·1′	0°16·2′E	X	199
Brookside	N Yks	SE1391	54°19·1′	1°47·6′W	X	99
Brook Side	Shrops	SJ3319	52°46·1′	2°59·2′W	X	126
Brookside	Wrekin	SJ6905	52°38·8′	2°27·1′W	T	127
Brookside Burn	E Loth	NT5663	55°51·7′	2°41·7′W	W	67
Brookside Fm	Ches	SJ3858	53°7·2′	2°55·2′W	FM	117
Brookside Fm	Ches	SJ8369	53°13·3′	2°14·9′W	FM	118
Brookside Fm	Ches	SJ9584	53°21·4′	2°4·1′W	FM	109
Brookside Fm	Derby	SK1830	52°52·3′	1°43·6′W	FM	128
Brookside Fm	E Susx	TQ5422	50°58·9′	0°12·0′E	FM	199
Brookside Fm	Surrey	TQ2747	51°12·7′	0°10·5′W	FM	187
Brookside Fm	Warr	SJ6689	53°24·0′	2°30·3′W	FM	109
Brookside Fm	W Susx	TQ2014	50°55·0′	0°17·2′W	FM	198
Brooksmarle	E Susx	TQ6725	51°0·2′	0°23·2′E	X	188,199
Brooks Mill	Ches	SJ6343	52°59·2′	2°32·7′W	X	118
Brooks, The	E Susx	TQ4208	50°51·5′	0°1·4′E	X	198
Brook Street	Essex	TQ5793	51°37·1′	0°16·5′E	T	177
Brook Street	Kent	TQ5745	51°11·2′	0°15·2′E	T	188
Brook Street	Kent	TQ9333	51°4·1′	0°45·7′E	T	189
Brook Street	Suff	TL8248	52°6·2′	0°39·9′E	T	155
Brook Street	W Susx	TQ3026	51°1·3′	0°8·4′W	T	187,198
Brook Street Fm	Essex	TL7931	51°57·1′	0°36·7′E	FM	167
Brook Street Fm	Kent	TQ4543	51°10·3′	0°4·8′E	FM	188
Brook, The	Orkney	ND3884	58°44·6′	3°3·8′W	X	7
Brook, The	Wrex	SJ4543	52°59·1′	2°48·8′W	X	117
Brook, The	Wrex	SJ4741	52°58·1′	2°46·9′W	X	117
Brookthorpe	Glos	SO8312	51°48·6′	2°14·4′W	T	162
Brookvale	Halton	SJ5480	53°19·1′	2°41·0′W	T	108
Brook Vale	Suff	TL9859	52°11·8′	0°54·2′E	X	155
Brook Vale Fm	Lancs	SD4739	53°50·9′	2°47·9′W	FM	102
Brookville	Norf	TL7396	52°32·2′	0°33·0′E	T	143
Brook Waters	Wilts	ST9123	51°0·6′	2°7·3′W	T	184
Brookway Fm	Dorset	ST6001	50°48·7′	2°33·7′W	FM	194
Brookwell	Surrey	TQ0142	51°10·3′	0°32·9′W	X	186
Brook Wood	Devon	SX7167	50°29·6′	3°48·7′W	F	202
Brook Wood	Kent	TQ9237	51°6·2′	0°44·9′E	F	189
Brookwood	Surrey	SU9557	51°18·5′	0°37·8′W	T	175,186
Brookwood Br	Surrey	SU9557	51°18·5′	0°37·8′W	X	175,186
Brookwood Cemetery	Surrey	SU9556	51°17·9′	0°37·8′W	X	175,186
Brookwood Fm	Derby	SK1750	53°3·1′	1°44·4′W	FM	119
Brookwood Fm	W Susx	TQ1617	50°56·7′	0°20·5′W	FM	198
Broo Loch	Shetld	HU4044	60°11·0′	1°16·2′W	W	4
Broom	Aberd	NJ5466	57°41·2′	2°45·8′W	X	29
Broom	Angus	NO4758	56°42·9′	2°51·5′W	X	54
Broom	Beds	TL1743	52°4·6′	0°17·2′W	T	153
Broom	Cumbr	NY0501	54°24·0′	3°27·4′W	X	89
Broom	Cumbr	NY6623	54°36·3′	2°31·2′W	T	91
Broom	D & G	NY1474	55°3·4′	3°20·4′W	X	85
Broom	Dorset	ST3202	50°49·0′	2°57·5′W	T	193
Broom	E Renf	NS5456	55°46·8′	4°19·2′W	T	64
Broom	Falk	NS8974	55°57·0′	3°46·2′W	X	65
Broom	Fife	NO3701	56°12·1′	3°0·5′W	T	59
Broom	Heref	SO4059	52°13·8′	2°52·3′W	X	148,149
Broom	Pemb	SN1108	51°44·6′	4°43·9′W	T	158
Broom	Pth & Kin	NS9896	56°9·0′	3°38·1′W	X	58
Broom	Roth	SK4491	53°25·1′	1°19·9′W	T	111
Broom	Scot Bord	NT6123	55°30·2′	2°36·6′W	X	74
Broom	Stir	NS8194	56°7·7′	3°54·4′W	X	57
Broom	Warw	SP0953	52°10·7′	1°51·7′W	T	150
Broombank	Aberd	NJ5006	57°8·8′	2°49·1′W	X	37
Broombank	Aberd	NO7880	56°54·9′	2°21·2′W	X	45
Broom Bank	Ches	SJ4966	53°11·6′	2°45·4′W	X	117
Broombank	C of Aber	NJ8311	57°11·6′	2°16·4′W	X	38
Broombank	Highld	NH9255	57°34·6′	3°47·9′W	X	27
Broombank	Worcs	SO6770	52°19·9′	2°28·7′W	T	138
Broombarns	Pth & Kin	NO0718	56°21·0′	3°29·8′W	X	58
Broomber Rigg	N Yks	SE0793	54°20·2′	1°53·1′W	X	99
Broomberry	S Ayr	NS3516	55°24·9′	4°36·0′W	X	70
Broomborough House Fm	Devon	SX7960	50°25·9′	3°41·8′W	FM	202
Broombrae	Aberd	NJ4504	57°7·7′	2°54·1′W	X	37
Broombrae	Aberd	NJ5617	57°14·8′	2°43·3′W	X	37
Broombrae	Aberd	NJ5901	57°6·1′	2°40·2′W	X	37
Broombrae	Aberd	NJ6727	57°20·2′	2°32·4′W	X	38
Broombrae	Aberd	NJ7431	57°22·4′	2°25·5′W	X	29
Broombrae	Aberd	NJ8718	57°15·4′	2°12·5′W	X	38
Broombrae	Fife	NO2412	56°17·9′	3°13·2′W	X	59
Broombriggs Hill	Leic	SK5114	52°43·5′	1°14·5′W	X	129
Broom Channel	C of Port	SU6703	50°49·6′	1°2·5′W	W	196
Broom Close	N Yks	SE3767	54°6·1′	1°25·6′W	X	99
Broom Close Fm	N Yks	SE3492	54°19·6′	1°28·2′W	FM	99
Broom Close Fm	N Yks	SE4070	54°7·7′	1°22·9′W	FM	99
Broomclose Fm	Wilts	ST8540	51°9·8′	2°12·5′W	FM	183

Broom Cott	Suff	TL8670	52°18·0′	0°44·1′E	X	144,155
Broom Court	Warw	SP0852	52°10·2′	1°52·6′W	X	150
Broom Covert	Norf	TF7300	52°34·4′	0°33·6′E	F	143
Broom Covert	Norf	TM0286	52°26·3′	0°58·7′E	F	144
Broom Covert	Notts	SK6083	53°20·7′	1°5·5′W	F	111,120
Broom Covert	Scot Bord	NT6023	55°30·2′	2°37·6′W	F	74
Broom Covert	Suff	TM4576	52°19·9′	1°36·2′E	F	156
Broom Craig	Angus	NO4673	56°51·0′	2°52·7′W	H	44
Broomcroft	Shrops	SJ5601	52°36·5′	2°38·6′W	X	126
Broomden	E Susx	TQ6730	51°2·9′	0°23·3′E	X	188
Broomdykes	D & G	NX9883	55°8·1′	3°35·6′W	X	78
Broomdykes	Scot Bord	NT8753	55°46·5′	2°12·0′W	X	67,74
Broom Dykes North	Darl	NZ2321	54°35·3′	1°38·2′W	X	93
Broome	Norf	TM3491	52°28·2′	1°27·1′E	T	134
Broome	Shrops	SO4080	52°25·1′	2°52·5′W	T	137
Broome	Shrops	SO5298	52°34·9′	2°42·1′W	T	137,138
Broome	Worcs	SO9078	52°24·2′	2°8·4′W	T	139
Broome Beck	Norf	TM3492	52°28·8′	1°27·2′E	W	134
Broome Common	Norf	TM3591	52°28·2′	1°28·0′E	X	134
Broomedge	Warr	SJ7085	53°21·9′	2°26·6′W	T	109
Broome Fm	Shrops	SJ3731	52°52·6′	2°55·8′W	FM	126
Broome Hall	Surrey	TQ1542	51°10·2′	0°20·9′W	X	187
Broome Heath	Norf	TM3491	52°28·2′	1°27·1′E	X	134
Broome Hill	Northum	NU1312	55°24·4′	1°47·3′W	X	81
Broome House Fm	Norf	TM3394	52°29·9′	1°26·4′E	FM	134
Broomell's Fm	Surrey	TQ1841	51°9·6′	0°18·4′W	FM	187
Broomelton	S Lanak	NS7450	55°43·9′	4°0·0′W	X	64
Broome Manor	Swin	SU1682	51°32·4′	1°45·8′W	X	173
Broome Marshes	Norf	TM3490	52°27·7′	1°27·1′E	X	134
Broomend	Aberd	NJ6325	57°19·1′	2°36·4′W	X	37
Broomend	Aberd	NJ7719	57°15·9′	2°22·4′W	X	38
Broomend	Pth & Kin	NO2843	56°34·7′	3°9·9′W	X	53
Broome Park	Kent	TR2148	51°11·5′	1°10·2′E	F	179,189
Broome Park	Northum	NU1012	55°24·4′	1°50·1′W	X	81
Broome Park	Shrops	SO6676	52°23·1′	2°29·4′W	X	138
Broome Park	Surrey	TQ2150	51°14·4′	0°15·6′W	X	187
Broome Park Hotel	Kent	TR2148	51°11·5′	1°10·2′E	X	179,189
Broome Place	Norf	TM3492	52°28·8′	1°27·2′E	X	134
Broomer's Corner	W Susx	TQ1221	50°58·9′	0°23·9′W	T	198
Broomershill	W Susx	TQ0619	50°57·9′	0°29·0′W	T	197
Broomerside Hill	S Lanak	NS7930	55°33·2′	3°54·7′W	H	71
Broome Wood	Northum	NU1311	55°23·8′	1°47·3′W	X	81
Broomey Croft Fm	Warw	SP2097	52°34·5′	1°41·9′W	FM	139
Broom Farm	Cumbr	NY0602	54°24·5′	3°26·5′W	FM	89
Broomfauld	Angus	NO4060	56°43·9′	2°58·4′W	X	44
Broom Fell	Cumbr	NY1927	54°38·1′	3°14·9′W	H	89,90
Broomfield	Aberd	NJ7700	57°5·7′	2°22·3′W	X	38
Broomfield	Aberd	NJ9532	57°23·0′	2°4·5′W	T	30
Broomfield	Aberd	NJ9633	57°23·5′	2°3·5′W	X	30
Broomfield	Angus	NO5760	56°44·0′	2°41·7′W	X	44
Broomfield	Ches	SJ8873	53°15·5′	2°10·4′W	X	118
Broomfield	Cumbr	NY3448	54°49·6′	3°1·2′W	T	85
Broom Field	Cumbr	SD5078	54°12·0′	2°45·6′W	X	97
Broomfield	Derby	SK3758	53°7·3′	1°26·4′W	X	119
Broomfield	Essex	TL7010	51°46·0′	0°28·2′E	T	167
Broomfield	Fife	NO3003	56°13·1′	3°7·3′W	X	59
Broomfield	Kent	TQ8352	51°14·5′	0°37·7′E	T	188
Broomfield	Kent	TR1966	51°21·3′	1°9·1′E	T	179
Broomfield	S Lanak	NS7847	55°42·3′	3°56·1′W	X	64
Broomfield	S Lanak	NS8834	55°35·5′	3°46·2′W	X	71,72
Broomfield	Somer	ST2232	51°5·2′	3°6·4′W	T	182
Broomfield	Wilts	ST8778	51°30·3′	2°10·8′W	T	173
Broomfield Fell	Northum	NZ0690	55°12·5′	1°53·9′W	X	81
Broomfield Fm	Ches	SJ8267	53°12·2′	2°15·8′W	FM	118
Broomfield Fm	Ghead	NZ1259	54°55·8′	1°48·3′W	FM	88
Broomfield Fm	Kent	TR0052	51°14·1′	0°52·3′E	FM	189
Broomfield Fm	N Yks	SE4169	54°7·2′	1°21·9′W	FM	99
Broomfield Fm	Warw	SP2794	52°32·8′	1°35·7′W	FM	140
Broomfield Hall	Somer	ST2334	51°6·2′	3°5·6′W	X	182
Broomfield Hall (College)	Derby	SK3840	52°57·6′	1°25·7′W	X	119,128
Broomfield Hill	Somer	ST2132	51°5·1′	3°7·3′W	H	182
Broomfield Ho	Hants	SU6507	50°51·8′	1°4·2′W	X	196
Broomfield Ho	N Yks	SE3393	54°20·1′	1°29·1′W	X	99
Broomfield Park	Enf	TQ3092	51°36·9′	0°6·9′W	X	176,177
Broomfields	N Yks	NZ9008	54°27·8′	0°36·3′W	X	94
Broomfields	Shrops	SJ4217	52°45·1′	2°51·2′W	T	126
Broomfields	Surrey	SU8342	51°10·5′	0°48·4′W	X	186
Broomfield's Fm	Essex	TL8414	51°47·9′	0°40·5′E	FM	168
Broomfields Fm	Staffs	SK0728	52°51·2′	1°53·4′W	FM	128
Broomflat	N Yks	NZ5302	54°24·9′	1°10·6′W	X	93
Broomfleet	E Yorks	SE8827	53°44·2′	0°39·5′W	T	106
Broomfleet Ho	E Yorks	SE8728	53°44·7′	0°40·4′W	X	106
Broomfleet Hope	E Yorks	SE8826	53°43·6′	0°39·6′W	X	106
Broomfleet Island	E Yorks	SE8926	53°43·6′	0°38·6′W	X	106
Broom Fm	Hants	SU6215	50°56·1′	1°6·7′W	FM	196
Broom Fm	Heref	SO5017	51°51·2′	2°43·2′W	FM	162
Broom Fm	Heref	SO7049	52°8·5′	2°25·9′W	FM	149
Broom Fm	Norf	TG1210	52°39·0′	1°8·5′E	FM	133
Broom Fm	Norf	TM3499	52°32·5′	1°27·5′E	FM	134
Broom Fm	Notts	SK5882	53°20·1′	1°7·3′W	FM	111,120
Broom Fm	N Yks	SE9270	54°7·3′	0°35·1′W	FM	101
Broomfold	Aberd	NJ5743	57°28·8′	2°42·6′W	X	29
Broomfold	Aberd	NJ6207	57°9·4′	2°37·2′W	X	37
Broomfold	Aberd	NJ6212	57°12·1′	2°37·3′W	X	37
Broomfold	C of Aber	NJ8404	57°7·9′	2°15·4′W	X	38
Broomford Manor	Devon	SS5701	50°47·7′	4°1·4′W	X	191
Broom Green	Norf	TF9824	52°46·9′	0°56·6′E	T	132
Broomgreen Covert	Suff	TM3474	52°19·1′	1°26·4′E	F	156
Broomhall	Ches	SJ6247	53°1·4′	2°33·6′W	T	118
Broom Hall	Durham	NZ2342	54°46·6′	1°38·1′W	X	88
Broomhall	Fife	NO4302	56°12·7′	2°54·7′W	X	59
Broomhall	Fife	NT0783	56°2·1′	3°29·1′W	X	65
Broom Hall	Gwyn	SH4137	52°54·7′	4°21·5′W	X	123
Broomhall	Pth & Kin	NO2927	56°26·0′	3°8·6′W	X	53,59
Broomhall	Scot Bord	NT6131	55°34·5′	2°36·7′W	X	74
Broom Hall	Staffs	SJ8710	52°41·5′	2°11·1′W	X	127
Broom Hall	Suff	TL9159	52°12·0′	0°48·1′E	X	155
Broomhall	Win & Maid	SU9566	51°23·3′	0°37·7′W	T	175,176
Broomhall	W Susx	TQ1532	51°4·8′	0°21·1′W	X	187
Broom Hall Fm	Herts	TL2819	51°51·5′	0°8·1′W	FM	166

Broomhall Fm	N upon Ty	NZ1669	55°1·2′	1°44·6′W	FM	88
Broomhall Fms	Worcs	SO8651	52°9·7′	2°11·9′W	FM	150
Broomhall Grange	Staffs	SJ6834	52°54·4′	2°28·1′W	X	127
Broomhall Green	Ches	SJ6247	53°1·4′	2°33·6′W	T	118
Broomham	Devon	SS7021	50°58·7′	3°50·7′W	X	180
Broomham	E Susx	TQ5212	50°53·5′	0°10·1′E	T	199
Broomham	E Susx	TQ6024	50°59·8′	0°17·2′E	X	199
Broomham	E Susx	TQ7213	50°53·7′	0°27·1′E	X	199
Broomham Fm	E Susx	TQ5212	50°53·5′	0°10·1′E	FM	199
Broomham Moor	Devon	SS7020	50°58·1′	3°50·7′W	X	180
Broomham Sch	E Susx	TQ8515	50°54·5′	0°38·3′E	X	189,199
Broomhaugh	Northum	NZ0161	54°56·9′	1°58·6′W	T	87
Broomhaugh Island	Northum	NY9464	54°58·5′	2°5·2′W	X	87
Broomhead	Aberd	NJ9863	57°39·7′	2°1·6′W	X	30
Broomhead Hall	Sheff	SK2496	53°27·9′	1°37·9′W	X	110
Broomhead Moor	Sheff	SK2295	53°27·3′	1°39·7′W	X	110
Broomhead Reservoir	Sheff	SK2695	53°27·3′	1°36·1′W	W	110
Broomhhaugh	Northum	NZ2290	55°12·5′	1°38·8′W	X	81
Broomhill	Aberd	NJ4012	57°12·0′	2°59·1′W	X	37
Broom Hill	Aberd	NJ4318	57°15·2′	2°56·2′W	H	37
Broom Hill	Aberd	NJ4609	57°10·4′	2°53·1′W	H	37
Broom Hill	Aberd	NJ5704	57°7·8′	2°42·2′W	H	37
Broomhill	Aberd	NJ5713	57°12·6′	2°42·3′W	X	37
Broomhill	Aberd	NJ5834	57°23·9′	2°41·5′W	X	29
Broom Hill	Aberd	NJ6237	57°25·6′	2°37·5′W	H	29
Broomhill	Aberd	NJ7209	57°10·5′	2°27·3′W	X	38
Broomhill	Aberd	NJ7458	57°36·9′	2°25·7′W	X	29
Broomhill	Aberd	NJ7611	57°11·6′	2°23·4′W	X	38
Broomhill	Aberd	NJ8540	57°27·3′	2°14·5′W	X	30
Broomhill	Aberd	NJ8753	57°34·3′	2°12·6′W	X	30
Broomhill	Aberd	NO8490	57°0·3′	2°15·4′W	X	38,45
Broom Hill	Angus	NO2257	56°42·2′	3°16·0′W	H	53
Broom Hill	Angus	NO2371	56°49·7′	3°15·3′W	X	44
Broom Hill	Angus	NO2779	56°54·1′	3°11·5′W	X	44
Broom Hill	Angus	NO3263	56°45·5′	3°6·3′W	X	44
Broom Hill	Angus	NO6040	56°33·3′	2°38·6′W	X	54
Broomhill	Barns	SE4102	53°31·0′	1°22·5′W	T	111
Broomhill	Brom	TQ4566	51°22·7′	0°5·4′E	T	177
Broom Hill	Ches	SJ4769	53°13·2′	2°47·2′W	T	117
Broom Hill	Ches	SJ9565	53°11·2′	2°4·1′W	X	118
Broom Hill	C of Bris	ST6271	51°26·4′	2°32·4′W	T	172
Broom Hill	C of Bris	ST6276	51°29·1′	2°32·4′W	T	172
Broomhill	Corn	SS2206	50°49·8′	4°31·3′W	X	190
Broomhill	Cumbr	NY0800	54°23·5′	3°24·6′W	X	89
Broomhill	Cumbr	NY4866	54°59·4′	2°48·3′W	X	86
Broomhill	Cumbr	SD1187	54°16·5′	3°21·6′W	X	96
Broomhill	Devon	SS2908	50°51·0′	4°25·4′W	X	190
Broomhill	Devon	SS5636	51°6·6′	4°3·0′W	X	180
Broomhill	Devon	SS7601	50°48·0′	3°45·2′W	X	191
Broomhill	Devon	SS9901	50°48·2′	3°25·6′W	X	192
Broomhill	Devon	SX6358	50°24·6′	3°55·3′W	X	202
Broomhill	Devon	SX8550	50°20·6′	3°36·6′W	X	202
Broomhill	D & G	NY0983	55°8·2′	3°25·2′W	X	78
Broomhill	D & G	NY3789	55°11·7′	2°59·0′W	X	79
Broomhill	Dorset	SU0302	50°49·3′	1°57·1′W	T	195
Broomhill	Durham	NZ1054	54°53·1′	1°50·2′W	T	88
Broom Hill	Durham	NZ1539	54°45·0′	1°45·6′W	H	92
Broomhill	E Ayr	NS5938	55°37·2′	4°13·9′W	X	71
Broomhill	E Yorks	TA2043	53°52·4′	0°10·1′W	X	107
Broomhill	Fife	NO2013	56°18·4′	3°17·1′W	X	58
Broom Hill	Hants	SU2614	50°55·7′	1°37·4′W	X	195
Broom Hill	Hants	SU4521	50°59·4′	1°21·1′W	X	185
Broomhill	Highld	NH5150	57°31·2′	4°28·8′W	X	26
Broomhill	Highld	NH6151	57°31·9′	4°18·8′W	X	26
Broomhill	Highld	NH7171	57°42·9′	4°9·5′W	T	21
Broomhill	Highld	NH7256	57°34·8′	4°8·0′W	X	27
Broomhill	Highld	NH8751	57°32·4′	3°52·8′W	X	27
Broom Hill	Kent	TQ8131	51°3·2′	0°35·3′E	X	188
Broomhill	Kent	TR2458	51°16·8′	1°13·1′E	T	179
Broom Hill	Lancs	SD7547	53°55·4′	2°22·4′W	X	103
Broom Hill	Medway	TQ7369	51°23·8′	0°29·6′E	X	178
Broomhill	Moray	NJ1667	57°41·4′	3°24·1′W	X	28
Broomhill	Moray	NJ2965	57°40·4′	3°11·0′W	X	28
Broomhill	Moray	NJ4254	57°34·6′	2°57·7′W	X	28
Broomhill	N Ayr	NS2846	55°40·9′	4°43·7′W	X	63
Broom Hill	Norf	TF6104	52°36·8′	0°23·1′E	T	143
Broom Hill	Norf	TF9519	52°44·2′	0°53·7′E	X	132
Broom Hill	Norf	TG3800	52°33·0′	1°31·0′E	X	134
Broomhill	Northum	NU2401	55°18·4′	1°36·9′W	T	81
Broomhill	Northum	NY9085	55°9·8′	2°9·0′W	X	80
Broom Hill	Northum	NZ1282	55°8·2′	1°48·3′W	X	81
Broomhill	Notts	SK5448	53°1·8′	1°11·3′W	T	129
Broomhill	Notts	SK6390	53°24·4′	1°2·7′W	X	111
Broomhill	Notts	SK6874	53°15·8′	0°58·4′W	X	120
Broom Hill	N Yks	SE6597	54°22·1′	0°59·6′W	X	94,100
Broomhill	Pth & Kin	NO0417	56°20·4′	3°32·7′W	X	58
Broomhill	Pth & Kin	NO1337	56°31·3′	3°24·4′W	X	53
Broomhill	S Ayr	NS3733	55°34·1′	4°34·7′W	X	70
Broomhill	Scot Bord	NT2432	55°34·8′	3°11·9′W	H	73
Broomhill	Scot Bord	NT4829	55°33·4′	2°49·0′W	T	73
Broomhill	Scot Bord	NT7046	55°42·6′	2°28·2′W	X	74
Broomhill	Scot Bord	NT8055	55°47·5′	2°18·7′W	X	67,74
Broomhill	Shrops	SJ3208	52°40·2′	2°59·9′W	X	126
Broom Hill	Shrops	SJ4103	52°37·5′	2°51·9′W	H	126
Broom Hill	Staffs	SO8385	52°28·0′	2°14·6′W	X	138
Broom Hill	Suff	TL9076	52°21·2′	0°47·8′E	X	144
Broom Hill	Suff	TM0440	52°1·5′	0°58·8′E	X	155
Broom Hill	Suff	TM1348	52°5·6′	1°7·0′E	X	169
Broom Hill	Suff	TM2647	52°4·7′	1°18·3′E	T	169
Broom Hill	Suff	TM4670	52°16·6′	1°36·8′E	X	156
Broom Hill	Warw	SP3441	52°4·2′	1°29·8′W	X	151
Broomhill	W Loth	NT0361	55°50·2′	3°32·5′W	X	65
Broom Hill	Worcs	SO9175	52°22·6′	2°7·5′W	T	139
Broom Hill	Wrekin	SJ7519	52°46·3′	2°21·8′W	X	127
Broomhillbank	D & G	NY1290	55°12·0′	3°22·5′W	X	78
Broomhillbank	Kent	TQ5640	51°8·5′	0°14·2′E	T	188
Broomhillbank Hill	D & G	NY1391	55°12·6′	3°21·6′W	H	78
Broomhill Br	Dorset	SY8188	50°41·7′	2°15·8′W	X	194
Broomhill Burrows	Pemb	SM8800	51°39·8′	5°3·5′W	X	157,158
Broomhill Farm	S Lanak	NT0046	55°42·1′	3°35·0′W	FM	72

Broomhill Fm	Derby	SK1832	52°53·3'	1°43·5'W	FM	128
Broomhill Fm	Dorset	ST5602	50°49·2'	2°37·1'W	FM	194
Broom Hill Fm	Durham	NZ2935	54°42·8'	1°32·6'W	FM	93
Broom Hill Fm	E Susx	TQ9718	50°55·9'	0°48·6'E	FM	189
Broomhill Fm	Lincs	SK9368	53°12·3'	0°36·0'W	FM	121
Broom Hill Fm	Norf	TL9299	52°33·5'	0°50·4'E	FM	144
Broomhill Fm	Oxon	SP3441	52°4·2'	1°29·8'W	FM	151
Broomhill Fm	Pemb	SM8005	51°42·3'	5°10·7'W	FM	157
Broomhill Fm	Pemb	SN0312	51°46·6'	4°51·0'W	FM	157,158
Broom Hill Fm	Roch	SD8308	53°34·3'	2°15·0'W	FM	109
Broomhill Fm	Warw	SP4372	52°20·9'	1°21·7'W	FM	140
Broomhill Grange	Notts	SK6066	53°11·5'	1°5·7'W	X	120
Broomhill Ho	Highld	NH9922	57°16·9'	3°40·1'W	X	36
Broomhill Ho	Midlo	NT3166	55°53·2'	3°5·7'W	X	66
Broomhill Level	E Susx	TQ9818	50°55·9'	0°49·5'E	X	189
Broomhill Moss	Cumbr	NY4966	54°59·4'	2°47·4'W	X	86
Broomhillock	Aberd	NJ5826	57°19·6'	2°41·4'W	X	37
Broomhillock	Aberd	NJ9220	57°16·5'	2°7·5'W	X	38
Broomhill Plantn	E Yorks	SE7044	53°53·5'	0°55·7'W	F	105,106
Broomhills	Aberd	NJ5764	57°40·1'	2°42·8'W	X	29
Broomhills	Aberd	NJ9567	57°41·8'	2°4·6'W	X	30
Broomhills	C of Edin	NT2667	55°53·7'	3°10·6'W	X	66
Broomhills	Cumbr	NY3654	54°52·8'	2°59·4'W	X	85
Broomhills	Cumbr	NY4268	55°0·4'	2°54·0'W	X	85
Broomhills	D & G	NY1185	55°9·3'	3°23·4'W	X	78
Broomhills	D & G	NY1196	55°15·3'	3°23·6'W	X	78
Broomhills	D & G	NY2664	54°58·2'	3°8·9'W	X	85
Broomhills	Essex	TQ6791	51°35·8'	0°25·1'E	X	177,178
Broomhills	Essex	TQ8890	51°34·9'	0°43·2'E	X	178
Broom Hills	Lincs	SK8376	53°16·7'	0°44·9'W	X	121
Broomhills	Scot Bord	NT6310	55°23·2'	2°34·6'W	X	80
Broom Hills	Suff	TM0476	52°20·9'	1°0·1'E	X	144
Broomhill Sands	E Susx	TQ9817	50°55·3'	0°49·4'E	X	189
Broomhills Fm	Beds	SP9226	51°55·7'	0°39·3'W	FM	165
Broomhills Fm	Leic	SK4701	52°36·5'	1°18·0'W	FM	140
Broom Hill Wood	Notts	SK6283	53°20·7'	1°3·7'W	F	111,120
Broom Ho	Derby	SK3856	53°6·2'	1°25·5'W	X	119
Broom Ho	Durham	NZ2147	54°49·3'	1°40·0'W	X	88
Broom Ho	Durham	NZ3047	54°49·3'	1°31·6'W	X	88
Broom Ho	Essex	TL9027	51°54·8'	0°46·2'E	X	168
Broom Ho	Monm	SO4006	51°45·2'	2°51·8'W	X	161
Broom Ho	Northum	NU1914	55°25·4'	1°41·6'W	X	81
Broom Ho	Northum	NZ0184	55°9·3'	1°58·6'W	X	81
Broom Ho	Northum	NZ1084	55°9·3'	1°50·2'W	X	81
Broom Ho	Notts	SK6150	53°2·9'	1°5·0'W	X	120
Broom Ho	N Yks	NZ8011	54°29·5'	0°45·5'W	X	94
Broom Ho	Scot Bord	NT8056	55°48·1'	2°18·7'W	X	67,74
Broomholm	D & G	NY3781	55°7·4'	2°58·8'W	X	79
Broomholm	Norf	TG3433	52°50·8'	1°28·9'E	T	133
Broomholmshiels	D & G	NY3882	55°8·0'	2°57·9'W	X	79
Broomhope	Northum	NY8883	55°8·7'	2°10·9'W	X	80
Broomhope Burn	Northum	NY8982	55°8·2'	2°9·9'W	W	80
Broomhope Mill	Northum	NY8883	55°8·7'	2°10·9'W	X	80
Broomhouse	C of Glas	NS6662	55°50·2'	4°7·9'W	T	64
Broom House	Devon	SX9378	50°35·7'	3°30·3'W	X	192
Broomhouse	Essex	TM0334	51°58·3'	0°57·7'E	X	155
Broomhouse	Northum	NU0427	55°32·5'	1°55·8'W	X	75
Broomhouse	Northum	NU1019	55°28·1'	1°50·1'W	X	81
Broomhouse	Northum	NY6962	54°57·3'	2°28·6'W	X	86,87
Broomhouse Common	Northum	NY7061	54°56·8'	2°27·7'W	X	86,87
Broomhouse Fm	Devon	SS7023	50°59·7'	3°50·8'W	FM	180
Broom House Fm	Lancs	SD9245	53°54·3'	2°6·9'W	FM	103
Broom House Fm	Northum	NU0344	55°41·6'	1°56·7'W	FM	75
Broomhouse Fm	Suff	TL7682	52°24·7'	0°35·7'E	FM	143
Broomhouse Mains	Scot Bord	NT8056	55°48·1'	2°18·7'W	X	67,74
Broomhurst Fm	Hants	SU8056	51°18·1'	0°50·8'W	FM	175,186
Broomhurst Fm	W Susx	TQ0205	50°50·4'	0°32·7'W	FM	197
Broomiebank	Scot Bord	NT6348	55°43·7'	2°34·9'W	X	74
Broomieknowe	D & G	NY3980	55°6·9'	2°57·0'W	X	79
Broomielaw	Durham	NZ0818	54°33·7'	1°52·2'W	X	92
Broomieside	Fife	NT1586	56°3·8'	3°21·5'W	X	65
Brooming Crook	Northum	NT8113	55°24·9'	2°17·6'W	X	80
Broomisle	D & G	NX4165	54°57·5'	4°28·6'W	X	83
Broomisle	D & G	NX8259	54°55·0'	3°50·0'W	X	84
Broomknowe	Angus	NO5658	56°43·0'	2°42·7'W	X	54
Broomknowe	Fife	NS9289	56°5·2'	3°43·7'W	X	65
Broom Knowe	Moray	NJ3525	57°18·9'	3°4·3'W	X	37
Broomknowe of Garbet	Moray	NJ3621	57°16·8'	3°3·2'W	X	37
Broomknowes	Moray	NJ3532	57°22·7'	3°4·4'W	X	37
Broomknowes	N Lanak	NS6670	55°54·5'	4°8·2'W	X	64
Broomknowes	S Ayr	NS2809	55°21·0'	4°42·3'W	X	70,76
Broomlands	Ches	SJ6846	53°0·9'	2°28·2'W	X	118
Broomlands	D & G	NT0801	55°17·9'	3°26·5'W	X	78
Broomlands	Kent	TQ5438	51°7·5'	0°12·4'E	X	188
Broomlands	N Ayr	NS3438	55°36·7'	4°37·7'W	T	70
Broomlands	Scot Bord	NT7334	55°36·2'	2°25·3'W	X	74
Broomlands Fm	Surrey	TQ4253	51°15·7'	0°2·5'E	FM	187
Broomlee Centre	Scot Bord	NT1550	55°44·4'	3°20·8'W	X	65,72
Broomlee Lough	Northum	NY7969	55°1·2'	2°19·3'W	W	86,87
Broomlee Mains	Scot Bord	NT1551	55°44·9'	3°20·8'W	X	65,72
Broomlees	Fife	NO4801	56°12·2'	2°49·8'W	X	59
Broomley	Angus	NO6759	56°43·5'	2°31·9'W	X	54
Broomley	Angus	NO6864	56°46·2'	2°31·0'W	X	45
Broomley	Northum	NZ0360	54°56·3'	1°56·8'W	T	87
Broomley-Fell Fm	Northum	NZ0259	54°55·8'	1°57·7'W	FM	87
Broomleyfell Plantation	Northum	NZ0159	54°55·8'	1°58·6'W	F	87
Broomley Pit Ho	Northum	NZ0159	54°55·8'	1°58·6'W	X	87
Broomlye	E Susx	TQ4319	50°57·4'	0°2·6'E	X	198
Broom of Dalreoch	Pth & Kin	NO0017	56°20·3'	3°36·6'W	X	58
Broom of Moy	Moray	NJ0159	57°36·9'	3°39·0'W	X	27
Broompark	Cumbr	NY1952	54°51·6'	3°15·3'W	X	85
Broompark	D & G	NX2352	54°50·1'	4°44·9'W	X	82
Broompark	D & G	NX4340	54°44·1'	4°25·9'W	X	83
Broompark	Durham	NZ2441	54°46·0'	1°37·2'W	T	88
Broom Park	Northum	NY9266	54°59·6'	2°7·1'W	X	87
Broompark	Pth & Kin	NO0939	56°32·3'	3°28·3'W	X	52,53
Broompark	W Loth	NS9671	55°55·5'	3°39·4'W	X	65
Broompatch	Shrops	SJ4206	52°39·2'	2°51·0'W	X	126
Broom Plantation	Suff	TL8763	52°14·2'	0°44·7'E	F	155
Broom Point	D & G	NX4734	54°40·9'	4°22·0'W	X	83
Broomridding Wood	Derby	SK4264	53°10·5'	1°21·9'W	F	120
Broomridge	Stir	NS8091	56°6·1'	3°55·3'W	T	57
Broomrigg	Cumbr	NY5445	54°48·1'	2°42·5'W	X	86
Broomrigg	D & G	NX9779	55°5·9'	3°36·4'W	X	84
Broomrigg	E Loth	NT4368	55°54·4'	2°54·3'W	X	66
Broomrigg End	Cumbr	NY7715	54°32·0'	2°20·9'W	X	91
Broomrigg Plantn	Cumbr	NY5446	54°48·7'	2°42·5'W	F	86
Broomriggs	Cumbr	NY5058	54°55·1'	2°46·4'W	X	86
Broom Royd Wood	Barns	SE3202	53°31·1'	1°30·6'W	F	110,111
Brooms	Aberd	NJ5956	57°35·8'	2°40·7'W	X	29
Brooms	Aberd	NJ7625	57°19·2'	2°23·5'W	X	38
Brooms	Ches	SJ9467	53°12·2'	2°5·0'W	X	118
Broom's Barn	Suff	TL7565	52°15·5'	0°34·3'E	T	155
Brooms Coppice	Shrops	SJ5821	52°47·3'	2°37·0'W	F	126
Broomscot Common	Norf	TM0080	52°23·1'	0°56·7'E	X	144
Broomscott	Devon	SS6231	51°3·9'	3°57·8'W	X	180
Broom's Fm	Wilts	ST8677	51°29·7'	2°11·7'W	FM	173
Brooms Fm	W Susx	SU8315	50°55·9'	0°48·7'W	FM	197
Broom's Green	Glos	SO7133	51°59·9'	2°25·0'W	T	149
Broomsgrove	E Susx	TQ8210	50°51·9'	0°35·6'E	T	199
Broomsgrove Fm	Wilts	SU1762	51°21·6'	1°45·0'W	FM	173
Broomsgrove Wood	Wilts	SU1763	51°22·2'	1°45·0'W	F	173
Broomshawbury	Essex	TL5716	51°49·5'	0°17·1'E	X	167
Broomsheils Hall	Durham	NZ1142	54°46·6'	1°49·3'W	X	88
Brooms Ho	N Yks	SE3962	54°3·4'	1°23·8'W	X	99
Broomside Ho	Durham	NZ3143	54°47·1'	1°30·7'W	X	88
Broomsleigh	Kent	TQ5756	51°17·1'	0°15·5'E	X	188
Broomsmead	Devon	SS7510	50°52·8'	3°46·2'W	X	191
Brooms, The	N Yks	SE3676	54°11·0'	1°26·5'W	X	99
Broomsthorpe	Norf	TF8428	52°49·3'	0°44·3'E	T	132
Broomston	N Lincs	SK7397	53°28·1'	0°53·6'W	X	112
Broom Street	Kent	TR0462	51°19·5'	0°56·1'E	T	178,179
Broomstreet Fm	Somer	SS8148	51°13·4'	3°41·9'W	FM	181
Broom,The	Cumbr	SD4592	54°19·5'	2°50·3'W	X	97
Broom, The	D & G	NY0779	55°6·1'	3°27·0'W	X	85
Broom, The	Suff	TM4049	52°5·5'	1°30·6'E	X	169
Broomton	Highld	NH8575	57°45·3'	3°55·5'W	X	21
Broomton	Highld	NH9654	57°34·1'	3°43·9'W	X	27
Broomtown Ho	Highld	NH6161	57°37·3'	4°19·2'W	X	21
Broomvale Fm	Suff	TM1249	52°6·1'	1°6·1'E	FM	155,169
Broom Walks	Suff	TM5079	52°21·3'	1°40·7'E	X	156
Broomway, The	Essex	TR0089	51°34·1'	0°53·5'E	X	178
Broomwell	Heref	SO4751	52°9·5'	2°46·1'W	X	148,149
Broom Wood	Essex	TL5129	51°56·6'	0°12·2'E	F	167
Broom Wood	Notts	SK6379	53°18·5'	1°2·9'W	F	120
Broomy Fields Fm	Worcs	SO6865	52°17·2'	2°27·8'W	FM	138,149
Broomy Furlong	Derby	SK3120	52°46·8'	1°32·0'W	X	128
Broomy Hall	Northum	NZ0971	55°2·3'	1°51·1'W	X	88
Broomy Hill	Heref	SO4939	52°3·1'	2°44·2'W	T	149
Broomy Hill	Northum	NY6385	55°9·7'	2°34·4'W	H	80
Broomy Holm	Durham	NZ2350	54°50·9'	1°38·1'W	X	88
Broomy Inclosure	Hants	SU2011	50°54·1'	1°42·5'W	F	195
Broomyknowes	W Loth	NT0174	55°57·2'	3°34·7'W	X	65
Broomy Law	Scot Bord	NT0727	55°31·9'	3°28·0'W	H	72
Broomy Law	Scot Bord	NT2223	55°29·9'	3°13·7'W	H	73
Broomy Law	Scot Bord	NT4131	55°34·4'	2°55·7'W	H	73
Broomy Law	S Lanak	NT0842	55°40·0'	3°27·3'W	H	72
Broomy Lea	Aberd	NJ6023	57°18·0'	2°39·4'W	H	37
Broomylees Rig	Scot Bord	NT3942	55°40·3'	2°57·8'W	H	73
Broomylinn	Northum	NY6384	55°9·2'	2°34·4'W	X	80
Broomy Lodge	Hants	SU2111	50°54·1'	1°41·7'W	X	195
Broomy Plain	Hants	SU2110	50°53·6'	1°41·7'W	X	195
Broomyshaw	Staffs	SK0649	53°2·5'	1°54·2'W	T	119
Broomy Side	Scot Bord	NT1239	55°38·4'	3°23·5'W	H	72
Brootes Barn	N Yks	SD9271	54°8·3'	2°6·9'W	X	98
Brora	Highld	NC9004	58°1·0'	3°51·2'W	T	17
Brosdale	Arg & Bt	NR4963	55°48·0'	5°59·9'W	X	60,61
Brosdale Island	Arg & Bt	NR4962	55°47·4'	5°59·8'W	X	60,61
Broseley	Shrops	SJ6701	52°36·6'	2°28·8'W	T	127
Brosterfield Fm	Derby	SK1876	53°17·1'	1°43·4'W	FM	119
Brotherfield	C of Aber	NJ8304	57°7·9'	2°16·4'W	X	38
Brotherhill	Pemb	SN0002	51°41·1'	4°53·2'W	X	157,158
Brotherhouse Bar	Lincs	TF2614	52°42·8'	0°7·7'W	T	131
Brotheridge Green	Worcs	SO8241	52°4·3'	2°15·4'W	T	150
Brotherilkeld	Cumbr	NY2101	54°24·1'	3°12·6'W	X	89,90
Brother Isle	Shetld	HU4281	60°30·9'	1°13·6'W	X	1,2,3
Brotherlee	Durham	NY9237	54°43·9'	2°7·0'W	T	91,92
Brother Loch	E Renf	NS5052	55°44·5'	4°22·9'W	W	64
Brothers	I Scilly	SV8607	49°53·1'	6°21·9'W	X	203
Brothershiels	Scot Bord	NT4255	55°47·3'	2°55·1'W	X	66,73
Brothershiels Burn	Midlo	NT4256	55°47·9'	2°55·1'W	W	66,73
Brotherstone	Scot Bord	NT6135	55°36·7'	2°36·7'W	X	74
Brotherstone Moor	Scot Bord	NT6137	55°37·8'	2°36·7'W	X	74
Brotherston Hill	Scot Bord	NT6136	55°37·2'	2°36·7'W	H	74
Brotherston's Hole	Northum	NU0054	55°47·0'	1°59·6'W	X	75
Brothers Water	Cumbr	NY4012	54°30·2'	2°55·2'W	W	90
Brothertoft	Lincs	TF2746	53°0·0'	0°6·0'W	T	131
Brotherton	N Yks	SE4825	53°43·4'	1°15·9'W	T	105
Brotherton	W Loth	NT0364	55°51·8'	3°32·6'W	X	65
Brotherwick	Northum	NU2205	55°20·6'	1°38·8'W	X	81
Brothybeck	Cumbr	NY3443	54°46·9'	3°1·1'W	T	85
Broti Ber	Orkney	ND4678	58°41·4'	2°55·4'W	X	7
Brotton	Red & Cl	NZ6819	54°33·9'	0°56·5'W	T	94
Brottos	Gwyn	SH8743	52°58·6'	3°40·6'W	X	124,125
Br o' Turk	Stir	NN5206	56°13·7'	4°22·8'W	X	57
Brotus	Fife	NO3408	56°15·9'	3°3·5'W	X	59
Broubster	Highld	ND0360	58°31·3'	3°39·4'W	T	11,12
Broubster Cottage	Highld	ND0262	58°32·4'	3°40·5'W	X	11,12
Broubster Hill	Highld	ND0260	58°31·3'	3°40·5'W	X	11,12
Broubster Village (ruins)	Highld	ND0359	58°30·8'	3°39·4'W	X	11,12
Brough	Cumbr	NY7914	54°31·5'	2°19·0'W	T	91
Brough	Derby	SK1882	53°20·3'	1°43·4'W	T	110
Brough	E Yorks	SE9326	53°43·6'	0°35·0'W	T	106
Brough	Highld	ND2273	58°38·5'	3°20·1'W	T	7,12
Brough	Notts	SK8358	53°7·0'	0°45·2'W	T	121
Brough	Orkney	HY3118	59°2·9'	3°11·7'W	T	6
Brough	Orkney	HY4447	59°18·6'	2°58·5'W	X	5
Brough	Orkney	HY4709	58°58·2'	2°54·8'W	X	6,7
Brough	Orkney	ND4483	58°44·1'	2°57·6'W	X	7
Brough	Shetld	HP5304	60°43·2'	1°1·2'W	T	1
Brough	Shetld	HU2051	60°14·8'	1°37·8'W	X	3
Brough	Shetld	HU3735	60°6·1'	1°19·6'W	X	4
Brough	Shetld	HU4377	60°28·7'	1°12·6'W	T	2,3
Brough	Shetld	HU4754	60°16·3'	1°8·5'W	T	3
Brough	Shetld	HU5141	60°9·3'	1°4·4'W	X	4
Brough	Shetld	HU5179	60°29·8'	1°3·8'W	T	2,3
Brough	Shetld	HU5564	60°21·6'	0°59·7'W	T	2
Broughall	Shrops	SJ5641	52°58·1'	2°38·9'W	T	117
Broughall Fields	Shrops	SJ5540	52°57·6'	2°39·8'W	X	117
Broughall Fm	Shrops	SJ5841	52°58·1'	2°37·1'W	FM	117
Broughall Ho	Shrops	SJ5541	52°58·1'	2°39·8'W	X	117
Brougham	Cumbr	NY5327	54°38·4'	2°43·3'W	X	90
Brougham Castle	Cumbr	NY5328	54°38·9'	2°43·3'W	A	90
Broughanreid	Pth & Kin	NO1462	56°44·8'	3°23·9'W	X	43
Brough Beck	N Yks	SE2297	54°22·3'	1°39·3'W	W	99
Broughdearg	Pth & Kin	NO1367	56°47·4'	3°25·0'W	X	43
Brough Fm	N Yks	SE1488	54°17·5'	1°46·7'W	FM	99
Brough Hall	N Yks	SE2197	54°22·3'	1°40·2'W	A	99
Brough Hall	Staffs	SJ8322	52°48·0'	2°14·7'W	X	127
Brough Head	Highld	ND3763	58°33·3'	3°4·5'W	X	12
Brough Head	Orkney	HY2328	59°8·2'	3°20·3'W	X	6
Brough Head	Shetld	HU4011	59°53·2'	1°16·6'W	X	4
Brough Head	Shetld	HU5464	60°21·6'	1°0·8'W	X	2
Brough Hill	Cumbr	NY7615	54°32·0'	2°21·8'W	H	91
Brough Hill Fm	Cumbr	NY2344	54°47·3'	3°11·4'W	FM	85
Brough Hill Plantn	N Yks	SE8269	54°6·9'	0°44·3'W	F	100
Brough Holm	Shetld	HP5605	60°43·7'	0°57·9'W	X	1
Brough House Fm	Red & Cl	NZ6821	54°35·0'	0°56·4'W	FM	94
Brough Intake	Cumbr	NY8115	54°32·0'	2°17·2'W	X	91,92
Broughjairg Beg	I of M	SC3393	54°18·6'	4°33·6'W	X	95
Brough Law	Northum	NT9916	55°26·5'	2°0·5'W	X	81
Brough Lodge	Shetld	HU5892	60°36·7'	0°55·9'W	X	1,2
Brough Moor	N Yks	NZ2102	54°25·0'	1°40·2'W	X	93
Broughmore	Stir	NS5888	56°4·1'	4°16·4'W	X	57
Brough Ness	Orkney	ND4482	58°43·6'	2°57·5'W	X	7
Brough of Bigging	Orkney	HY2115	59°1·2'	3°22·1'W	X	6
Brough of Birsay	Orkney	HY2328	59°8·2'	3°20·3'W	X	6
Brough of Deerness	Orkney	HY5908	58°57·7'	2°42·3'W	X	6
Brough of Deerness (Settlement)	Orkney	HY5908	58°57·7'	2°42·3'W	A	6
Brough Pasture	N Yks	SD9489	54°18·0'	2°5·1'W	X	98
Brough Plantn	N Yks	SE7161	54°2·6'	0°54·5'W	F	100
Brough Roads	E Yorks	SE9424	53°42·5'	0°34·1'W	W	106,112
Brough Skerries	Shetld	HU2158	60°18·6'	1°36·7'W	X	3
Brough Sowerby	Cumbr	NY7912	54°30·4'	2°19·0'W	T	91
Broughsplace	Ches	SJ9871	53°14·4'	2°1·4'W	X	118
Brough Taing	Shetld	HP6304	60°43·1'	0°50·2'W	X	1
Brough, The	Highld	ND3648	58°25·2'	3°5·3'W	W	12
Brough, The	Orkney	HY5410	58°58·7'	2°47·5'W	X	6
Brough, The	Orkney	HY6922	59°5·3'	2°32·0'W	X	5
Brough, The	Orkney	ND4587	58°46·3'	2°56·6'W	X	7
Brough, The	Orkney	ND4687	58°46·3'	2°55·5'W	X	7
Brough, The	Shetld	HU2982	60°31·5'	1°27·8'W	X	1,3
Brough,The	Shetld	HU4488	60°34·7'	1°11·3'W	X	1,2
Brough, The (Broch)	Shetld	HU4488	60°34·7'	1°11·3'W	A	1,2
Brough, The (Fort)	Orkney	ND4587	58°46·3'	2°56·6'W	A	7
Broughton	Bucks	SP8413	51°48·8'	0°46·5'W	T	165
Broughton	Cambs	TL2877	52°22·8'	0°6·8'W	T	142
Broughton	C of Edin	NT2575	55°58·0'	3°11·7'W	T	66
Broughton	Flint	SJ3463	53°9·8'	2°58·8'W	T	117
Broughton	Hants	SU3032	51°5·4'	1°33·9'W	T	185
Broughton	Kent	TQ5758	51°18·2'	0°15·5'E	X	188
Broughton	Lancs	SD5235	53°48·8'	2°43·3'W	T	102
Broughton	Mil Key	SP8940	52°3·3'	0°41·7'W	X	152
Broughton	N Lincs	SE9608	53°33·8'	0°32·6'W	T	112
Broughton	Northnts	SP8375	52°22·2'	0°46·5'W	T	141
Broughton	N Yks	SD9451	53°57·5'	2°5·1'W	T	103
Broughton	N Yks	SE7673	54°9·1'	0°49·8'W	T	100
Broughton	Orkney	HY4448	59°19·1'	2°58·5'W	T	5
Broughton	Oxon	SP4238	52°2·6'	1°22·9'W	T	151
Broughton	Scot Bord	NT1136	55°36·8'	3°24·3'W	T	72
Broughton	Shrops	SO8091	52°31·2'	2°17·3'W	T	138
Broughton	Staffs	SJ7634	52°54·4'	2°21·0'W	T	127
Broughton	V of Glam	SS9271	51°25·9'	3°32·8'W	T	170
Broughton Astley	Leic	SP5292	52°31·6'	1°13·6'W	T	140
Broughton Bank	Cumbr	SD3780	54°13·0'	2°57·5'W	X	96,97
Broughton Banks Fm	N Yks	NZ5404	54°26·0'	1°9·6'W	FM	93
Broughton Bay	Swan	SS4293	51°37·1'	4°16·5'W	W	159
Broughton Beck	Cumbr	SD2882	54°14·0'	3°5·9'W	T	96,97
Broughton Beck	N Yks	NZ5406	54°27·0'	1°9·6'W	W	93
Broughton Br	N Lincs	SE9810	53°34·9'	0°30·8'W	X	112
Broughton Br	N Yks	NZ5408	54°28·1'	1°9·6'W	X	93
Broughton Bridge Beck	N Yks	NZ5408	54°28·1'	1°9·6'W	W	93
Broughton Brook	Somer	ST2420	50°58·7'	3°4·6'W	W	193
Broughton Burn	Scot Bord	NT1038	55°37·9'	3°25·3'W	W	72
Broughton Burrows	Swan	SS4192	51°36·5'	4°17·4'W	X	159
Broughton Carrs	N Lincs	SE9910	53°34·9'	0°29·9'W	X	112
Broughton Clays	Lincs	SK8855	53°5·3'	0°40·8'W	X	121
Broughton Common	N Lincs	SE9710	53°34·9'	0°31·7'W	T	112
Broughton Cross	Cumbr	NY0730	54°39·6'	3°26·1'W	T	89
Broughton Decoy Fm	N Lincs	SE9710	53°34·9'	0°31·7'W	FM	112
Broughton Down	Hants	SU2833	51°6·0'	1°35·6'W	X	184
Broughton Down Fm	Hants	SU2933	51°6·0'	1°34·8'W	FM	185
Broughtondowns Plantation	Oxon	SP2107	51°45·9'	1°41·3'W	F	163
Broughton Fields Fm	N Yks	SD9250	53°57·0'	2°6·9'W	FM	103
Broughton Fm	Ches	SJ6952	53°4·1'	2°27·4'W	FM	118
Broughton Fm	Shrops	SJ4924	52°48·9'	2°45·0'W	FM	126
Broughton Fm	Somer	ST2522	50°59·8'	3°3·7'W	FM	193
Broughton Fm	Worcs	SO9347	52°7·5'	2°5·7'W	FM	150
Broughton Folly	Staffs	SJ7534	52°54·4'	2°21·9'W	X	127
Broughton Gifford	Wilts	ST8763	51°22·2'	2°10·8'W	T	173
Broughton Grange	N Lincs	SE9710	53°34·9'	0°31·7'W	X	112
Broughton Grange	Northnts	SP8576	52°22·8'	0°44·7'W	X	141
Broughton Grange	N Yks	NZ5505	54°26·5'	1°8·7'W	X	93
Broughton Grange	Oxon	SP4237	52°2·0'	1°22·9'W	X	151
Broughton Grange Fm	Notts	SK6527	52°50·4'	1°1·7'W	FM	129
Broughton Green	Worcs	SO9561	52°15·1'	2°4·0'W	T	150
Broughton Grounds	Mil Key	SP9240	52°3·3'	0°39·1'W	X	152
Broughton Grounds Fm	Oxon	SP4039	52°3·1'	1°24·6'W	FM	151

Broughton Hackett	Worcs	SO9254	52°11·3′	2°6·6′W	T	150
Broughton Hall	Lancs	SD5434	53°48·3′	2°41·5′W	X	102
Broughton Heights	Scot Bord	NT1240	55°39·0′	3°23·5′W	H	72
Broughton Hill	Hants	SU3031	51°4·9′	1°33·9′W	X	185
Broughton Hill	Leic	SK7124	52°48·8′	0°56·4′W	X	129
Broughton Ho	Cumbr	SD3981	54°13·5′	2°55·7′W	X	96,97
Broughton Ho	Kent	TQ5158	51°18·3′	0°10·4′E	X	188
Broughton Ho	Lancs	SD5234	53°48·2′	2°43·3′W	X	102
Broughton in Furness	Cumbr	SD2187	54°16·6′	3°12·4′W	T	96
Broughtonknowe	Scot Bord	NT0939	55°38·4′	3°26·3′W	X	72
Broughton Lane Plantation	N Lincs	SE9706	53°32·7′	0°31·8′W	F	112
Broughton Lodge	Cumbr	NY0633	54°41·2′	3°27·1′W	X	89
Broughton Lodge	Cumbr	SD3980	54°13·0′	2°55·7′W	X	96,97
Broughton Lodge	Notts	SK6425	52°49·4′	1°2·6′W	X	129
Broughton Lodge Fm	Wrex	SJ4346	53°0·7′	2°50·6′W	FM	117
Broughton Lodges	Leic	SK7024	52°48·8′	0°57·3′W	T	129
Broughton Mains	D & G	NX4544	54°46·3′	4°24·2′W	X	83
Broughton Manor	Mil Key	SP8939	52°2·8′	0°41·7′W	X	152
Broughton Manor Fm	Norf	TM2388	52°26·9′	1°17·3′E	FM	156
Broughton Mills	Cumbr	SD2290	54°18·2′	3°11·5′W	T	96
Broughton Moor	Cumbr	NY0533	54°41·2′	3°28·0′W	T	89
Broughton Moor	Cumbr	SD2593	54°19·9′	3°8·8′W	X	96
Broughton Moor	N Yks	SE7674	54°9·6′	0°49·7′W	X	100
Broughton Park	Oxon	SP4138	52°2·6′	1°23·7′W	X	151
Broughton Park	Salf	SD8301	53°30·6′	2°15·0′W	T	109
Broughton Place	Scot Bord	NT1137	55°37·4′	3°24·4′W	X	72
Broughton Plantn	N Yks	NZ5503	54°25·4′	1°8·7′W	F	93
Broughton Poggs	Oxon	SP2303	51°43·7′	1°39·6′W	T	163
Broughtons	Glos	SO7014	51°49·7′	2°25·7′W	X	162
Broughton Skeog	D & G	NX4544	54°46·3′	4°24·2′W	X	83
Broughton Vale	N Lincs	SE9607	53°33·3′	0°32·6′W	X	112
Broughton Wood	Worcs	SO9661	52°15·1′	2°3·1′W	F	150
Broughtown	Orkney	HY6541	59°15·5′	2°36·3′W	T	5
Broughty Castle	C of Dun	NO4630	56°27·8′	2°52·1′W	A	54
Broughty Ferry	C of Dun	NO4630	56°27·8′	2°52·1′W	T	54
Brouncey	E Yorks	SE8342	53°52·3′	0°43·8′W	X	106
Brouncker's Down	Wilts	ST9550	51°15·2′	2°3·9′W	X	184
Brouncker's Well	Wilts	ST9550	51°15·2′	2°3·9′W	W	184
Brounshill	E Loth	NT5369	55°55·0′	2°44·7′W	X	66
Brousentor Fm	Devon	SX5480	50°36·3′	4°3·4′W	FM	191,201
Brouster	Shetld	HU2551	60°14·8′	1°32·4′W	X	3
Brow	Cumbr	NY3103	54°25·3′	3°4·3′W	X	90
Brow	Cumbr	NY4825	54°37·3′	2°47·9′W	X	90
Brow	Lancs	SD7652	53°58·1′	2°21·5′W	X	103
Brow	N Lanak	NS8755	55°46·8′	3°47·7′W	X	65,72
Brow Burn	S Lanak	NS9741	55°39·4′	3°37·8′W	W	72
Browda	Corn	SX3071	50°31·1′	4°23·5′W	X	201
Brow Edge	Cumbr	SD3584	54°15·1′	2°59·4′W	T	96,97
Brow Fm	N Yks	SE8471	54°7·9′	0°42·4′W	FM	100
Brow Fm	Shrops	SO3692	52°31·6′	2°56·2′W	FM	137
Browfoot	Cumbr	NY4500	54°23·8′	2°50·4′W	X	90
Brow Foot	Cumbr	NY6914	54°31·5′	2°28·3′W	X	91
Brow Foot	Cumbr	SD4995	54°21·1′	2°46·7′W	X	97
Browfoot	Cumbr	SD5497	54°22·2′	2°42·1′W	X	97
Brow Foot Fm	Lancs	SD4975	54°10·3′	2°46·5′W	FM	97
Brow Gill	Cumbr	SD6386	54°16·3′	2°33·7′W	W	97
Browgill Cave	N Yks	SD8077	54°11·5′	2°18·0′W	X	98
Brow Head Fm	Cumbr	NY3604	54°25·9′	2°58·8′W	FM	90
Brow Hill	E Ayr	NS5834	55°35·0′	4°14·7′W	X	71
Browhill Fm	Lincs	TA0301	53°30·0′	0°26·4′W	FM	112
Brow House Fm	N Yks	NZ8300	54°23·6′	0°42·9′W	FM	94
Browhouses	D & G	NY2864	54°58·2′	3°7·1′W	T	85
Browick Hall	Norf	TG1201	52°34·2′	1°8·1′E	X	144
Browland	Shetld	HU2750	60°14·3′	1°30·2′W	T	3
Brow Moor	Brad	SE0436	53°49·5′	1°55·9′W	X	104
Brow Moor	N Yks	NZ9601	54°24·0′	0°30·9′W	X	94
Browna Paddocks	N Yks	SD8990	54°18·6′	2°9·7′W	X	98
Brown Band	Cumbr	NY1310	54°28·9′	3°20·1′W	X	89
Brownbank	Cumbr	NY0502	54°24·5′	3°27·4′W	X	89
Brown Bank	N Yks	SD7461	54°2·9′	2°23·4′W	X	98
Brown Bank	N Yks	SE0057	54°0·8′	1°59·6′W	X	104
Brown Bank	N Yks	SE0957	54°0·8′	1°51·3′W	X	104
Brown Bank	N Yks	SE2153	53°58·6′	1°40·4′W	T	104
Brown Bank Bow	N Yks	SE0057	54°0·8′	1°59·6′W	X	104
Brown Bank Brow	N Yks	SD9957	54°0·8′	2°0·5′W	X	103
Brown Bank Fm	Staffs	SK0442	52°58·8′	1°56·0′W	FM	119,128
Brown Bank Head	N Yks	SE1058	54°1·3′	1°50·4′W	X	104
Brown Barn Fm	Bolton	SD7413	53°37·0′	2°23·2′W	FM	109
Brown Beck	Cumbr	NY4820	54°34·6′	2°47·8′W	W	90
Brown Beck Crags	N Yks	SE1282	54°14·3′	1°48·5′W	X	99
Brownber	Cumbr	NY7005	54°26·6′	2°27·3′W	T	91
Brownber	Cumbr	NY8507	54°27·7′	2°13·5′W	X	91,92
Brownber Edge	Cumbr	NY8406	54°27·2′	2°14·4′W	H	91,92
Brownber Hill	Cumbr	NY7027	54°38·5′	2°27·5′W	H	91
Brownberries, The	Leeds	SE2339	53°51·0′	1°38·6′W	X	104
Brownberry	Durham	NY9321	54°35·3′	2°6·1′W	X	91,92
Brown Berry Plain	Lancs	SD6047	53°55·3′	2°36·1′W	X	102,103
Brownber Tarn	Cumbr	NY8506	54°27·2′	2°13·5′W	W	91,92
Brown Birch Fm	Know	SJ4599	53°29·3′	2°49·3′W	FM	108
Brownbread Street	E Susx	TQ6815	50°54·8′	0°23·8′E	T	199
Brown Brook Fm	Lancs	SD5842	53°52·6′	2°37·9′W	FM	102
Brown Candover	Hants	SU5739	51°9·1′	1°10·7′W	T	185
Brown Carrick Hill	S Ayr	NS2916	55°24·7′	4°41·6′W	H	70
Browncastle Burn	S Lanak	NS6145	55°41·0′	4°12·2′W	W	64
Browncastle Burn	S Lanak	NS6244	55°40·4′	4°11·2′W	W	71
Brown Caterthun	Angus	NO5566	56°47·3′	2°43·7′W	X	44
Brown Caterthun (Fort)	Angus	NO5566	56°47·3′	2°43·7′W	A	44
Brownchesters	Northum	NY8892	55°13·6′	2°10·9′W	X	80
Brown Clee Hill	Shrops	SO5985	52°27·9′	2°35·8′W	H	137,138
Brown Cove	Cumbr	NY3415	54°31·8′	3°0·8′W	X	90
Browncove Crags	Cumbr	NY3315	54°31·8′	3°1·7′W	X	90
Brown Cow Hill	Aberd	NJ2204	57°7·5′	3°16·8′W	H	36
Brown Crag	Cumbr	NY2710	54°29·1′	3°7·2′W	X	89,90
Brown Crag	Cumbr	NY3217	54°32·9′	3°2·7′W	X	90
Browndale Beck	Cumbr	NY3419	54°34·0′	3°0·8′W	W	90
Brown Dod	Scot Bord	NT1341	55°39·5′	3°22·5′W	H	72
Brown Dod	S Lanak	NS8818	55°26·8′	3°45·8′W	H	71,78
Brown Dodd	Cumbr	NY2617	54°32·8′	3°8·2′W	H	89,90
Brown Dodd	Durham	NY9928	54°39·1′	2°0·5′W	X	92
Brown Dod Wood	E Loth	NT4962	55°51·2′	2°48·4′W	F	66
Browndown	Hants	SZ5799	50°47·5′	1°11·1′W	X	196
Brown Down	Somer	ST2214	50°55·4′	3°6·2′W	X	193
Brown Down Lodge	Devon	ST2312	50°54·4′	3°5·3′W	X	193
Browndown Point	Hants	SZ5798	50°47·0′	1°11·1′W	X	196
Brown Dyke	Cumbr	NY4665	54°58·9′	2°50·2′W	X	86
Brownedge	Ches	SJ7763	53°10·1′	2°20·2′W	T	118
Brown Edge	Derby	SK0675	53°16·6′	1°54·2′W	H	119
Brown Edge	Derby	SK2879	53°18·7′	1°34·4′W	X	119
Brown Edge	Lancs	SD3614	53°37·4′	2°57·6′W	T	108
Brown Edge	Lancs	SD5673	54°9·3′	2°40·0′W	X	97
Brown Edge	Lancs	SD8832	53°47·3′	2°10·5′W	X	103
Brown Edge	Sheff	SK2586	53°22·5′	1°37·0′W	X	110
Brown Edge	Staffs	SJ9053	53°4·7′	2°8·6′W	T	118
Brown Edge	Staffs	SK1246	53°0·9′	1°48·9′W	X	119,128
Brown Edge	St Hel	SJ5093	53°26·1′	2°44·7′W	T	108
Brown Edge Fm	Sheff	SK2784	53°21·4′	1°35·3′W	FM	110
Brown Edge Fm	Staffs	SK0252	53°4·2′	1°57·8′W	FM	119
Brownelson	Cumbr	NY3852	54°51·8′	2°57·5′W	X	85
Browne's Lodge	Rut	SK8014	52°43·3′	0°48·5′W	X	130
Browney Gill	Cumbr	NY2604	54°25·8′	3°8·0′W	W	89,90
Brown Fell	Cumbr	NY5856	54°54·1′	2°38·9′W	X	86
Brownfield	D & G	NX9880	55°6·5′	3°35·5′W	X	78
Brown Fms	Somer	ST0231	51°4·4′	3°23·5′W	FM	181
Brown Gelly	Corn	SX1972	50°31·4′	4°32·8′W	H	201
Browngelly Downs	Corn	SX1972	50°31·4′	4°32·8′W	H	201
Browngill	Cumbr	NY7646	54°48·7′	2°22·0′W	X	86,87
Brownhart Law	Scot Bord	NT7809	55°22·7′	2°20·4′W	H	80
Brown Haw	Cumbr	SD2293	54°19·8′	3°11·6′W	X	96
Brown Haw	N Yks	SD9979	54°12·6′	2°0·5′W	X	98
Brownhayes Fm	Ches	SJ7069	53°13·3′	2°26·6′W	FM	118
Brown Head	N Ayr	NR8925	55°28·7′	5°19·9′W	X	68,69
Brown Head	N Yks	SE8095	54°20·9′	0°45·7′W	X	94,100
Brown Heath	Ches	SJ4564	53°10·5′	2°49·0′W	T	117
Brownheath	Devon	ST1415	50°55·9′	3°13·0′W	T	181,193
Brown Heath	Devon	SX6465	50°28·4′	3°54·6′W	X	202
Brown Heath	Hants	SU5216	50°56·7′	1°15·2′W	T	185
Brownheath	Shrops	SJ4629	52°51·6′	2°47·7′W	T	126
Brownheath Common	Worcs	SO8960	52°14·5′	2°9·3′W	T	150
Brownheath Moss	Shrops	SJ4530	52°52·1′	2°48·6′W	F	126
Brown Hill	Aberd	NJ4436	57°24·9′	2°55·5′W	H	28
Brownhill	Aberd	NJ4542	57°28·2′	2°54·6′W	X	28,29
Brown Hill	Aberd	NJ4638	57°26·0′	2°53·5′W	H	28,29
Brownhill	Aberd	NJ6700	57°5·6′	2°32·2′W	X	38
Brownhill	Aberd	NJ6944	57°29·4′	2°30·6′W	X	29
Brown Hill	Aberd	NJ7001	57°6·2′	2°29·3′W	H	38
Brown Hill	Aberd	NJ7337	57°25·6′	2°26·5′W	X	29
Brown Hill	Aberd	NJ7338	57°26·2′	2°26·5′W	H	29
Brownhill	Aberd	NJ7418	57°15·4′	2°25·4′W	X	38
Brownhill	Aberd	NJ7844	57°29·4′	2°21·6′W	X	29,30
Brownhill	Aberd	NJ8640	57°27·3′	2°13·5′W	X	30
Brownhill	Aberd	NJ8953	57°34·3′	2°10·6′W	X	30
Brownhill	Aberd	NJ9343	57°28·9′	2°6·5′W	T	30
Brownhill	Aberd	NJ9349	57°32·1′	2°6·6′W	X	30
Brownhill	Aberd	NJ9951	57°33·2′	2°0·5′W	X	30
Brown Hill	Aberd	NO5595	57°2·9′	2°44·1′W	H	37,44
Brownhill	Black w Dar	SD6830	53°46·2′	2°28·7′W	T	103
Brownhill	Ches	SJ5764	53°10·5′	2°38·2′W	X	117
Brownhill	Cumbr	NY5276	55°4·8′	2°44·7′W	X	86
Brownhill	Cumbr	NY5465	54°58·9′	2°42·7′W	X	86
Brown Hill	Cumbr	NY6635	54°42·8′	2°31·2′W	X	91
Brownhill	D & G	NS5502	55°17·7′	4°16·6′W	X	77
Brown Hill	D & G	NS6501	55°17·3′	4°7·1′W	X	77
Brown Hill	D & G	NS6913	55°23·9′	4°3·7′W	X	71
Brown Hill	D & G	NS7706	55°20·2′	3°55·9′W	H	71,78
Brown Hill	D & G	NS8311	55°23·0′	3°50·4′W	H	71,78
Brownhill	D & G	NX4643	54°45·8′	4°23·2′W	X	83
Brown Hill	D & G	NX7346	54°47·8′	3°58·1′W	H	83,84
Brown Hill	D & G	NX7488	55°10·5′	3°58·3′W	H	77
Brown Hill	D & G	NX7999	55°16·5′	3°53·9′W	X	78
Brownhill	D & G	NX9091	55°12·3′	3°43·3′W	X	78
Brown Hill	E Ayr	NS5104	55°18·7′	4°20·4′W	X	77
Brownhill	E Ayr	NS5439	55°37·6′	4°18·7′W	X	70
Brown Hill	E Dunb	NS6678	55°58·8′	4°8·4′W	H	64
Brown Hill	E Renf	NS5348	55°42·4′	4°19·9′W	H	64
Brown Hill	Highld	NH7460	57°37·0′	4°6·1′W	X	21,27
Brown Hill	Inverc	NS2370	55°53·7′	4°49·4′W	H	63
Brown Hill	Lancs	SD8341	53°52·1′	2°15·1′W	X	103
Brown Hill	Moray	NJ3834	57°23·8′	3°1·4′W	X	28
Brown Hill	Moray	NJ5948	57°31·5′	2°40·6′W	H	29
Brown Hill	N Ayr	NS2456	55°46·2′	4°47·9′W	H	63
Brown Hill	N Ayr	NS2460	55°48·3′	4°48·1′W	X	63
Brownhill	N Lanak	NS8060	55°49·4′	3°54·5′W	X	65
Brown Hill	N Yks	NZ6711	54°29·6′	0°57·5′W	H	94
Brown Hill	N Yks	SD9362	54°3·5′	2°6·0′W	X	98
Brown Hill	N Yks	SE0870	54°7·8′	1°52·2′W	X	99
Brown Hill	N Yks	SE9297	54°21·9′	0°34·6′W	X	94,101
Brown Hill	Orkney	HY3008	58°57·5′	3°12·5′W	X	6,7
Brown Hill	Orkney	HY4030	59°9·4′	3°2·5′W	X	5,6
Brownhill	S Ayr	NS4127	55°30·9′	4°30·7′W	X	70
Brownhill	Shrops	SJ4022	52°47·8′	2°53·0′W	T	126
Brown Hill	S Lanak	NS6733	55°34·6′	4°6·1′W	X	71
Brown Hill	S Lanak	NS8530	55°33·3′	3°49·0′W	X	71,72
Brown Hill	S Lanak	NS9513	55°24·2′	3°39·1′W	H	78
Brown Hill	W Dunb	NS4476	55°57·4′	4°29·5′W	X	64
Brown Hill	W Susx	TQ1415	50°55·6′	0°22·3′W	X	198
Brownhill Burn	D & G	NS5302	55°17·7′	4°18·5′W	W	77
Brown Hill Fm	Brad	SE0536	53°49·5′	1°55·0′W	FM	104
Brownhill Fm	Carm	SN6930	51°57·4′	3°54·0′W	FM	146,160
Brownhill Fm	N Ayr	NS3151	55°43·6′	4°41·0′W	FM	63
Brownhill Fm	N Lanak	NS8862	55°50·5′	3°46·9′W	FM	65
Brown Hill Fm	N Yks	SE0954	53°59·2′	1°51·3′W	FM	104
Brownhill Fm	S Lanak	NS9944	55°41·0′	3°35·9′W	FM	72
Brownhill Ho	N Ayr	NS3151	55°43·6′	4°41·0′W	X	63
Brownhill Inclosure	Hants	SZ2399	50°47·6′	1°40·0′W	F	195
Brown Hill Plain	N Yks	SE0967	54°6·2′	1°51·3′W	X	99
Brownhill Plantation	Aberd	NJ5045	57°29·8′	2°49·6′W	F	29
Brown Hill Plantn	N Yks	SD8957	54°0·8′	2°9·7′W	F	103
Brownhill Resr	Kirk	SE1106	53°33·3′	1°49·6′W	W	110
Brownhill Rig	D & G	NS5401	55°17·1′	4°17·5′W	X	77
Brownhills	Aberd	NJ6527	57°20·2′	2°34·4′W	X	38
Brownhills	Aberd	NJ8316	57°14·3′	2°16·4′W	X	38
Brownhills	Aberd	NJ8818	57°15·4′	2°11·5′W	X	38
Brown Hills	Cumbr	NY3719	54°34·0′	2°58·0′W	X	90
Brown Hills	Cumbr	NY4233	54°41·6′	2°53·6′W	X	90
Brown Hills	Cumbr	NY6716	54°32·5′	2°30·2′W	X	91
Brownhills	Fife	NO5215	56°19·8′	2°46·1′W	T	59
Brown Hills	Lancs	SD6950	53°57·0′	2°27·9′W	X	103
Brownhills	N Ayr	NS3851	55°43·8′	4°34·4′W	X	63
Brownhills	Shrops	SJ6735	52°54·9′	2°29·0′W	T	127
Brownhills	Wals	SK0405	52°38·8′	1°56·1′W	T	139
Brownhills Fm	Ches	SJ8971	53°14·4′	2°9·5′W	FM	118
Brownhills Fm	York	SE6554	53°58·9′	1°0·1′W	FM	105,106
Brown Hill Wood	N Yks	SE3553	53°58·6′	1°27·6′W	F	104
Brownhill Wood	Shrops	SJ6632	52°53·3′	2°29·9′W	F	127
Brown Ho	N Yks	SD9148	53°55·9′	2°7·8′W	X	103
Brown Holm	Angus	NO3473	56°50·9′	3°4·5′W	X	44
Brownhouse Fm	Derby	SK2950	53°3·0′	1°33·6′W	FM	119
Brown How	Cumbr	NY1115	54°31·6′	3°22·1′W	X	89
Brown Howe	Cumbr	NY2604	54°25·8′	3°8·0′W	X	89,90
Brown Howe	Cumbr	NY4608	54°28·1′	2°49·6′W	H	90
Brown Howe	Cumbr	NY4812	54°30·3′	2°47·8′W	H	90
Brown Howe	Cumbr	NY5108	54°28·1′	2°44·9′W	X	90
Brown Howe	Cumbr	NY5525	54°37·3′	2°41·4′W	X	90
Brown Howe	Cumbr	NY5718	54°33·6′	2°39·5′W	X	91
Brown Howe	Cumbr	SD2890	54°18·3′	3°6·0′W	X	96,97
Brown Howe	N Yks	SE8194	54°20·3′	0°44·8′W	X	94,100
Brownieleys	Aberd	NO7772	56°50·6′	2°22·2′W	X	45
Brownie's Chair	Arg & Bt	NR6343	55°37·6′	5°45·5′W	X	62
Brownies Chair	Fife	NO2012	56°17·9′	3°17·1′W	X	58
Brownieshill	Aberd	NJ6613	57°12·6′	2°33·3′W	X	38
Brownieside	Northum	NU1623	55°30·3′	1°44·4′W	X	75
Browning Hill	Hants	SU5860	51°20·4′	1°9·6′W	X	174
Browninghill Green	Hants	SU5859	51°19·9′	1°9·7′W	T	174
Brownings	W Susx	TQ0124	51°0·6′	0°33·2′W	X	197
Browning's	W Susx	TQ2022	50°59·3′	0°17·0′W	X	198
Browning's Fm	Cambs	TL6141	52°2·9′	0°21·3′E	FM	154
Brownings Fm	Devon	ST1213	50°54·8′	3°14·7′W	FM	181,193
Brownings Fm	Essex	TQ4694	51°37·8′	0°7·0′E	FM	167,177
Brownings Fm	E Susx	TQ6613	50°53·8′	0°22·0′E	FM	199
Brownings Fm	Kent	TQ5147	51°12·4′	0°10·1′E	FM	188
Browning's Manor	E Susx	TQ5220	50°57·8′	0°10·3′E	X	199
Brown Jewel	Aberd	NO9092	57°1·4′	2°9·4′W	X	38,45
Brown Knoll	Derby	SK0885	53°21·9′	1°52·4′W	H	110
Brown Knott	Cumbr	SD6588	54°17·4′	2°31·8′W	X	97
Brown Knotts	Cumbr	NY2719	54°33·9′	3°7·3′W	X	89,90
Brown Knowe	D & G	NX5477	55°4·2′	4°16·8′W	X	77
Brown Knowe	D & G	NX7895	55°14·3′	3°54·7′W	X	78
Brownknowe	Northum	NY7986	55°10·3′	2°19·4′W	X	80
Brown Knowe	Scot Bord	NT3013	55°24·6′	3°5·9′W	X	79
Brown Knowe	Scot Bord	NT3303	55°19·2′	3°2·9′W	X	79
Brown Knowe	Scot Bord	NT3832	55°34·9′	2°58·6′W	H	73
Brown Knowl	Ches	SJ4953	53°4·5′	2°45·3′W	T	117
Brown Law	Northum	NT8306	55°21·1′	2°15·7′W	X	80
Brownlee	S Ayr	NS3733	55°34·1′	4°34·7′W	X	70
Brownlee Ho	S Lanak	NS8051	55°44·5′	3°54·3′W	X	65,72
Brown Lees	Staffs	SJ8756	53°6·3′	2°11·2′W	T	118
Brownley Hill	Lancs	SD5659	54°1·8′	2°39·9′W	X	102
Brownley Hill	Northum	NY7950	54°50·9′	2°19·2′W	H	86,87
Brownley Park	Lancs	SD8541	53°52·1′	2°13·3′W	X	103
Brownlow	Ches	SJ8261	53°9·0′	2°15·7′W	T	118
Brownlow	Ches	SJ9570	53°13·9′	2°4·1′W	X	118
Brownlow	Staffs	SK0757	53°6·8′	1°53·3′W	X	119
Brownlow	St Hel	SD5201	53°30·5′	2°43·0′W	T	108
Brown Low	Stock	SJ9890	53°24·6′	2°1·4′W	A	109
Brownlow Fold	Bolton	SD7010	53°35·4′	2°26·8′W	T	109
Brownlow Heath	Ches	SJ8260	53°8·5′	2°15·7′W	T	118
Brown Moor	Cumbr	SD6496	54°21·7′	2°32·8′W	X	97
Brownmoor	D & G	NY2072	55°2·4′	3°14·7′W	X	85
Brown Moor	Leeds	SE3733	53°47·8′	1°25·9′W	T	104
Brown Moor	Northum	NY8370	55°1·7′	2°15·5′W	X	86,87
Brown Moor	N Yks	SD8790	54°18·6′	2°11·6′W	X	98
Brown Moor	N Yks	SE6165	54°4·9′	1°3·6′W	X	100
Brownmoor	Scot Bord	NT4626	55°31·7′	2°50·9′W	X	73
Brownmoor Fm	N Yks	SE6165	54°4·9′	1°3·6′W	FM	100
Brown Moor Fm	N Yks	SE8062	54°3·1′	0°46·3′W	FM	100
Brown Moor Heights	Scot Bord	NT4624	55°30·7′	2°50·9′W	H	73
Brown Moor Hill	D & G	NX9991	55°12·4′	3°34·8′W	H	78
Brown Moss	Ches	SJ6945	53°0·3′	2°27·3′W	X	118
Brown Moss	Shrops	SJ5639	52°57·0′	2°38·9′W	X	126
Brownmoss Fm	Ches	SJ5572	53°14·8′	2°40·1′W	FM	117
Brownmuir	Aberd	NO7377	56°53·3′	2°26·1′W	X	45
Brown Muir	Moray	NJ2555	57°35·0′	3°14·8′W	H	28
Brownmuir	N Ayr	NS3756	55°46·4′	4°35·5′W	X	63
Brownmuir Plantn	N Ayr	NS3756	55°46·4′	4°35·5′W	F	63
Brown Nab	Lancs	SD6350	53°56·9′	2°33·4′W	X	102,103
Brown Pike	Cumbr	SD2696	54°21·5′	3°7·9′W	X	96,97
Brown Queen	Corn	SX1062	50°25·9′	4°40·1′W	X	200
Brownridge	Northum	NU0137	55°37·8′	1°58·6′W	X	75
Brownridge	Northum	NU1028	55°33·0′	1°50·1′W	X	75
Brown Ridge	N Yks	SE1077	54°11·6′	1°50·4′W	X	99
Brownridge Burn	Northum	NU1028	55°33·0′	1°50·1′W	W	75
Brown Rig	E Ayr	NS4811	55°22·4′	4°23·5′W	X	70
Brown Rig	Scot Bord	NT2717	55°26·7′	3°8·8′W	H	79
Brown Rig	Scot Bord	NT4946	55°42·5′	2°48·3′W	H	73
Brown Rig	Scot Bord	NT8669	55°55·1′	2°13·0′W	X	67
Brown Rig	S Lanak	NS8022	55°28·9′	3°53·5′W	X	71,72
Brownrigg	Cumbr	NY0420	54°34·2′	3°28·7′W	X	89
Brownrigg	Cumbr	NY0539	54°44·5′	3°28·1′W	X	89
Brownrigg	Cumbr	NY1652	54°51·6′	3°18·1′W	X	85
Brown Rigg	Cumbr	NY3014	54°31·2′	3°4·5′W	H	90
Brownrigg	Cumbr	NY3040	54°45·3′	3°4·8′W	X	85
Brown Rigg	Cumbr	NY4464	54°58·3′	2°52·1′W	X	85
Brown Rigg	Cumbr	NY4720	54°34·6′	2°48·8′W	X	90
Brown Rigg	Cumbr	SD1896	54°21·4′	3°15·3′W	X	96
Brownrigg	D & G	NX9977	55°4·9′	3°34·5′W	X	84
Brownrigg	E Loth	NT5580	56°0·9′	2°42·9′W	X	66
Brown Rigg	Northum	NT8435	55°36·8′	2°14·8′W	X	74
Brown Rigg	Northum	NY7356	54°54·1′	2°24·8′W	X	86,87
Brown Rigg	Northum	NY7565	54°59·0′	2°23·0′W	X	86,87

Brown Rigg	N Yks	SE1283	54°14·8′	1°48·5′W	X	99
Brownrigg	Scot Bord	NT4207	55°21·5′	2°54·5′W	X	79
Brownrigg	Scot Bord	NT7024	55°30·8′	2°28·1′W	X	74
Brownrigg	S Lanak	NS9348	55°43·1′	3°41·8′W	X	72
Brown Rigg Beck	N Yks	NZ9200	54°23·5′	0°34·6′W	W	94
Brown Rigg End	N Yks	NZ7409	54°28·5′	0°51·1′W	X	94
Brownrigg Fm	Cumbr	NY4024	54°36·7′	2°55·3′W	FM	90
Brownrigg Hall Fm	Cumbr	NY0943	54°46·7′	3°24·5′W	FM	85
Brownrigg Hall Fm	Cumbr	NY3140	54°45·3′	3°3·9′W	A	85
Brownrigg Head	Northum	NY8194	55°14·6′	2°17·5′W	H	80
Brown Rigg Howe	N Yks	NZ7409	54°28·5′	0°51·1′W	A	94
Brown Rigg Moss	Durham	NY9416	54°32·6′	2°5·1′W	X	91,92
Brownrigg Well	Cumbr	NY3315	54°31·8′	3°1·7′W	W	90
Brown's Bank	Ches	SJ6443	52°59·2′	2°31·8′W	T	118
Brownsbank	S Lanak	NT0742	55°40·0′	3°28·3′W	X	72
Browns Brook Fm	Shrops	SJ5034	52°54·3′	2°44·2′W	FM	126
Brownscombe	Devon	SS5024	51°0·0′	4°7·9′W	X	180
Brownscombe Hill	Devon	SX8565	50°28·6′	3°36·9′W	X	202
Brown's Covert	Norf	TG0030	52°50·0′	0°58·6′E	F	133
Brown's Covert	Notts	SK6161	53°8·8′	1°4·9′W	F	120
Brownsea Island	Dorset	SZ0288	50°41·7′	1°57·9′W	X	195
Brown's End	Glos	SO7434	52°0·5′	2°22·3′W	T	150
Brownsett	Staffs	SJ9963	53°10·1′	2°0·5′W	X	118
Brownsey Ho	N Yks	SD9698	54°22·9′	2°3·3′W	X	98
Brownsey Moor	N Yks	SD9699	54°23·4′	2°3·3′W	X	98
Brownsfield	Renf	NS4667	55°52·6′	4°27·3′W	X	64
Brownsfields Fm	Staffs	SK1211	52°42·0′	1°48·9′W	FM	128
Brown's Fm	Devon	SX9085	50°39·5′	3°33·0′W	FM	192
Brown's Fm	Essex	TL7942	52°3·1′	0°37·0′E	FM	155
Browns Fm	Essex	TQ6993	51°36·9′	0°26·9′E	FM	177,178
Brown's Fm	E Susx	TQ7322	50°58·5′	0°28·2′E	FM	199
Brown's Fm	Hants	SU5759	51°19·9′	1°10·5′W	FM	174
Browns Fm	Lincs	TF4531	52°51·6′	0°9·6′E	FM	131
Brown's Fm	Wilts	SU1967	51°24·3′	1°43·2′W	FM	173
Brown's Folly	Bath & NE Somer	ST7966	51°23·8′	2°17·7′W	X	172
Brown's Green	Birm	SP0491	52°31·2′	1°56·1′W	T	139
Brown's Green	Warw	SP1271	52°20·5′	1°49·0′W	X	139
Brownshall	Scot Bord	NT6146	55°42·6′	2°36·8′W	X	74
Brownsham	Devon	SS2825	51°0·2′	4°26·7′W	A	190
Brownshill	Aberd	NJ9161	57°38·6′	2°8·6′W	X	30
Brown's Hill	Cambs	TL4390	52°29·6′	0°6·8′E	X	142,143
Brownshill	Glos	SO8802	51°43·2′	2°10·0′W	T	162
Brown's Hill	Leic	SK7423	52°48·2′	0°53·7′W	X	129
Browns Hill	Norf	TG3518	52°42·7′	1°29·2′E	X	133,134
Brown's Hill	Scot Bord	NT5305	55°20·5′	2°44·0′W	H	79
Brownshill Green	Cov	SP3082	52°26·3′	1°33·1′W	T	140
Brown's Hill Head	Devon	SS5723	50°59·6′	4°1·9′W	H	180
Brownshill Staunch	Cambs	TL3672	52°20·0′	0°0·2′E	X	154
Brown's Hole	D & G	NX4946	54°47·4′	4°20·5′W	X	83
Brown's Ho (ruin)	Devon	SX6179	50°35·9′	3°57·5′W	X	191
Brownside	Aberd	NJ6754	57°34·8′	2°32·6′W	X	29
Brownside	Aberd	NJ9153	57°34·3′	2°8·6′W	X	30
Brownside	Cumbr	NY7044	54°47·6′	2°27·6′W	X	86,87
Brownside	E Renf	NS5151	55°44·0′	4°21·9′W	X	64
Brownside	Lancs	SD8632	53°47·3′	2°12·3′W	T	103
Brownside	Renf	NS4358	55°47·6′	4°29·8′W	X	64
Brownside	Renf	NS4860	55°48·8′	4°25·1′W	X	64
Brownside Braes	Renf	NS4860	55°48·8′	4°25·1′W	X	64
Brownside Moss	Cumbr	NY6944	54°47·6′	2°28·5′W	X	86,87
Brownside Wood	Aberd	NJ6754	57°34·8′	2°32·6′W	F	29
Brownsills	Lancs	SD7532	53°47·3′	2°22·4′W	X	103
Brownslade	Pemb	SR9097	51°38·2′	5°1·7′W	X	158
Brownslade	Surrey	TQ2946	51°12·1′	0°8·8′W	X	187
Brownslade Burrows	Pemb	SR8998	51°38·7′	5°2·6′W	X	158
Brownsland	Devon	SX7199	50°46·8′	3°49·4′W	X	191
Brownsland	Heref	SO5053	52°10·6′	2°43·5′W	X	149
Brownsland	Scot Bord	NT1641	55°39·6′	3°19·7′W	X	72
Brownslate	Pemb	SM9501	51°40·5′	4°57·5′W	X	157,158
Brown's Law	Northum	NT9727	55°32·5′	2°2·4′W	X	75
Brownsleazes	Northum	NY8379	55°6·6′	2°15·6′W	X	86,87
Brownslow Ho	Ches	SJ6577	53°17·6′	2°31·1′W	X	118
Brownsman	Northum	NU2337	55°37·8′	1°37·6′W	X	75
Brownsmill Fm	Glos	ST6898	51°41·0′	2°27·4′W	FM	162
Brown's Muir	E Ayr	NS5432	55°33·8′	4°18·5′W	X	70
Brown's Oak Fm	E Susx	TQ6822	50°58·6′	0°24·0′E	FM	199
Brownsover	Warw	SP5177	52°23·6′	1°14·6′W	T	140
Brownspit	Corn	SS2315	50°54·7′	4°30·7′W	X	190
Brownspit	Staffs	SK0863	53°10·1′	1°52·4′W	X	119
Brownspring Coppice	Cumbr	SD4597	54°22·2′	2°50·4′W	F	97
Brownstay Ridge	N Yks	SE1766	54°5·6′	1°44·0′W	X	99
Brownston	Devon	SX6952	50°21·4′	3°50·1′W	T	202
Brownstone	Devon	SX5949	50°19·7′	3°58·5′W	X	202
Brownston Fm	Devon	SX7562	50°26·9′	3°45·3′W	FM	202
Brown Street	Suff	TM0663	52°13·8′	1°1·4′E	T	155
Brownswell	Devon	SX7671	50°31·8′	3°44·6′W	X	202
Brown's Wood	Bucks	SU9492	51°37·4′	0°38·1′W	F	175
Brown's Wood	E Susx	TQ6137	51°6·8′	0°18·4′E	F	188
Browns Wood	Mil Key	SP9035	52°0·6′	0°40·9′W	T	152
Brown Syke	Lancs	SD6158	54°1·2′	2°35·3′W	W	102,103
Brown Syke	Lancs	SD6356	54°0·2′	2°33·5′W	W	102,103
Brown Syke Hill	Lancs	SD6457	54°0·7′	2°32·5′W	X	102,103
Brownthwaite	Cumbr	SD6480	54°13·1′	2°32·7′W	H	97
Brownthwaites	Lancs	SD7847	53°55·4′	2°19·7′W	X	103
Browntod	S Lanak	NS7150	55°43·8′	4°2·8′W	X	64
Brown Wardle Hill	Lancs	SD8918	53°39·7′	2°9·6′W	H	109
Brownwich Fm	Hants	SU5103	50°49·7′	1°16·2′W	FM	196
Brown Willy	Corn	SX1579	50°35·1′	4°36·4′W	H	201
Brownwilly Downs	Corn	SX1579	50°35·1′	4°36·4′W	X	201
Brow of The Hill	Northum	NT9654	55°47·0′	2°3·4′W	X	74,75
Brow Plantation	N Yks	SE9876	54°10·5′	0°29·5′W	F	101
Brow Plantn	N Yks	SE9075	54°10·0′	0°36·9′W	F	101
Brows	Lancs	SD4157	54°0·6′	2°53·6′W	X	102
Brows	Lancs	SD7645	53°54·3′	2°21·5′W	X	103
Browsburn	N Lanak	NS7664	55°51·5′	3°58·4′W	T	64
Browsholme Hall	Lancs	SD6845	53°54·3′	2°28·8′W	A	103
Browsholme Moor	Lancs	SD7047	53°55·3′	2°27·0′W	X	103
Browshott	S Lanak	NS9351	55°44·7′	3°41·8′W	X	65,72
Brow Side Fell	Cumbr	NY2500	54°23·6′	3°8·9′W	X	89,90
Brow Side Syke	N Yks	SD7363	54°4·0′	2°24·3′W	W	98

Browson Bank	N Yks	NZ1210	54°29·4′	1°48·5′W	X	92
Brows, The	Cumbr	SD3789	54°17·8′	2°57·7′W	X	96,97
Browston Green	Norf	TG4901	52°33·2′	1°40·8′E	T	134
Brow, The	Cumbr	NY2500	54°23·6′	3°8·9′W	X	89,90
Brow, The	N Yks	SE6689	54°17·8′	0°58·7′W	X	94,100
Browtop	Cumbr	NY0624	54°36·4′	3°26·9′W	T	89
Brow Top	Lancs	SD5241	53°52·0′	2°43·4′W	X	102
Brow Top Fm	Lancs	SD5258	54°1·2′	2°43·5′W	FM	102
Brow Well	D & G	NY0867	54°59·6′	3°25·9′W	X	85
Brow Wood	N Yks	NZ8104	54°25·7′	0°44·7′W	F	94
Brow Wood	N Yks	SE6271	54°8·1′	1°2·6′W	F	100
Brox	Scot Bord	NY4989	55°11·8′	2°47·6′W	X	79
Broxa	N Yks	SE9491	54°18·6′	0°32·9′W	X	94,101
Broxbourne	Herts	TL3607	51°44·9′	0°1·4′W	T	166
Broxbournebury Sch	Herts	TL3507	51°45·0′	0°2·3′W	X	166
Broxbourne Wood	Herts	TL3207	51°45·0′	0°4·9′W	F	166
Broxburn	E Loth	NT6977	55°59·4′	2°29·4′W	T	67
Brox Burn	W Loth	NT0671	55°55·6′	3°29·8′W	W	65
Broxburn	W Loth	NT0872	55°56·2′	3°27·9′W	T	65
Broxden	Pth & Kin	NO0822	56°23·1′	3°29·0′W	X	52,53,58
Broxendale Fm	Derby	SK2754	53°5·2′	1°35·4′W	FM	119
Broxfield	Northum	NU2016	55°26·5′	1°40·6′W	T	81
Broxhall Fm	Kent	TR1551	51°13·3′	1°5·1′E	FM	179,189
Broxham Ho	Kent	TQ4547	51°12·5′	0°4·9′E	X	188
Broxham Manor	Kent	TQ4548	51°13·0′	0°5·0′E	X	188
Broxhead Common	Hants	SU8037	51°7·8′	0°51·0′W	X	186
Broxholme	Lincs	SK9177	53°17·2′	0°37·7′W	T	121
Broxholme	N Yks	SE2761	54°2·9′	1°34·8′W	X	99
Broxmead	W Susx	TQ2724	51°0·3′	0°11·0′W	X	198
Broxmouth	E Loth	NT6977	55°59·4′	2°29·4′W	X	67
Broxtead Ho	Suff	TM3146	52°4·1′	1°22·6′E	X	169
Broxted	Essex	TL5726	51°54·8′	0°17·4′E	T	167
Broxted Hall	Essex	TL5726	51°54·8′	0°17·4′E	X	167
Broxted Hill	Essex	TL5728	51°55·9′	0°17·4′E	X	167
Broxted Hill	Essex	TL5824	51°53·8′	0°18·2′E	X	167
Broxton	Ches	SJ4754	53°5·1′	2°47·1′W	T	117
Broxton Old Hall	Ches	SJ4853	53°4·5′	2°46·2′W	X	117
Broxtowe	C of Nott	SK5242	52°58·6′	1°13·1′W	T	129
Broxty Ho	Cumbr	NY8211	54°29·9′	2°16·3′W	X	91,92
Broxwater	Corn	SS2713	50°53·7′	4°27·2′W	X	190
Broxwood	Heref	SO3654	52°11·1′	2°55·8′W	T	148,149
Broxy Burn	Moray	NJ5064	57°40·0′	2°49·8′W	W	29
Broyle Mill Fm	E Susx	TQ4713	50°54·1′	0°5·8′E	FM	198
Broyle Place	E Susx	TQ4712	50°53·5′	0°5·8′E	X	198
Broyle Side	E Susx	TQ4613	50°54·1′	0°5·0′E	T	198
Broynach	Highld	ND1567	58°35·2′	3°27·2′W	X	11,12
Brù	N Eil	NB3449	58°21·2′	6°32·3′W	T	8
Bruach an Fhraoich	Highld	NC3940	58°19·4′	4°44·5′W	X	9
Bruach an Sgriodain	Highld	NH1938	57°24·0′	5°0·3′W	X	25
Bruach Bad na h-Iorguil	Highld	NC3355	58°27·3′	4°51·3′W	X	9
Bruach Bhuidhe	Highld	NG7438	57°22·8′	5°45·1′W	X	24
Bruach Bhuidhe	Highld	NM6888	56°55·8′	5°48·3′W	X	40
Bruach Caorainn	Stir	NN4000	56°10·2′	4°34·2′W	W	56
Bruach Dhubh	Highld	NN7688	56°58·3′	4°1·9′W	H	42
Bruach Màiri	N Eil	NB4033	58°12·8′	6°25·1′W	T	8
Bruachmary	Highld	NH8846	57°29·7′	3°51·7′W	X	27
Bruach Mholach	Moray	NJ1406	57°8·5′	3°24·8′W	X	36
Bruach Mhór	Aberd	NO0996	57°3·0′	3°29·6′W	X	36,43
Bruach Mhór	Arg & Bt	NM4541	56°29·8′	6°8·1′W	X	47,48
Bruach na Frithe	Highld	NG4625	57°15·0′	6°12·2′W	H	32
Bruach na' Maorach	Highld	NM6467	56°44·4′	5°51·1′W	X	40
Bruach nam Biodag	Highld	NN5899	57°3·9′	4°20·1′W	X	35
Bruach nam Bò	Highld	NG5226	57°15·7′	6°6·3′W	X	32
Bruach nan-Imrichean	Highld	NH7007	57°8·4′	4°8·4′W	H	35
Bruach nan Iomairean	Pth & Kin	NN6075	56°51·0′	4°17·3′W	X	42
Bruach na Sean-pheighinne	Arg & Bt	NM3652	56°35·4′	6°17·6′W	X	47
Bruach Shobhach	Highld	NC4442	58°20·6′	4°39·4′W	X	9
Bruach, The	Moray	NJ1105	57°7·9′	3°27·8′W	H	36
Bruaichean Losgaintir	N Eil	NG0699	57°53·3′	6°57·2′W	X	14,18
Bruan	Highld	ND3139	58°20·3′	3°10·2′W	T	11,12
Bruar	Pth & Kin	NN8265	56°46·0′	3°55·4′W	T	43
Bruar Lodge	Pth & Kin	NN8376	56°51·9′	3°54·7′W	X	43
Bruar Water	Pth & Kin	NN8274	56°50·8′	3°55·6′W	W	43
Bruce Castle	Hargy	TQ3390	51°35·8′	0°4·4′W	A	176,177
Bruce Down	Wilts	SU1656	51°18·4′	1°45·8′W	X	173
Brucefield	Clackm	NS9591	56°6·3′	3°40·9′W	X	58
Brucefield	Fife	NT1086	56°3·8′	3°26·3′W	T	65
Brucefield	Highld	NH9386	57°51·3′	3°47·7′W	X	21
Brucefield	W Loth	NT0364	55°51·8′	3°32·6′W	X	65
Bruce Field Barn	Wilts	SU1556	51°18·4′	1°46·7′W	X	173
Bruce Haven	Fife	NT0882	56°1·6′	3°28·1′W	W	65
Brucehaven	Fife	NT0983	56°2·1′	3°27·2′W	X	65
Brucehill	Aberd	NJ8547	57°31·0′	2°14·6′W	X	30
Brucehill	Stir	NS5997	56°8·9′	4°15·7′W	X	57
Brucehill	W Dunb	NS3875	55°56·7′	4°35·2′W	T	63
Bruce Ho	N Yks	SE4577	54°11·4′	1°18·2′W	X	99
Bruceland	Moray	NJ1962	57°38·7′	3°21·0′W	X	28
Bruce's Camp (Fort)	Aberd	NJ7618	57°15·4′	2°23·4′W	A	38
Bruce's Castle Fm	Cambs	TL1884	52°26·7′	0°15·4′W	FM	142
Bruce's Cave	D & G	NY2670	55°1·4′	3°9·0′W	X	85
Bruce's Haven	Aberd	NK0631	57°22·4′	1°53·6′W	W	30
Bruce's Stone	D & G	NX5576	55°3·7′	4°15·8′W	A	77
Bruce's Well	D & G	NX9491	55°12·4′	3°39·5′W	W	78
Bruceton	Pth & Kin	NO2850	56°38·4′	3°10·0′W	X	53
Brucewells	Aberd	NO8393	57°1·9′	2°16·4′W	X	38,45
Bruchag	Arg & Bt	NS1157	55°46·4′	5°0·4′W	X	63
Bruchag Point	Arg & Bt	NS1157	55°46·4′	5°0·4′W	X	63
Bruche	Warr	SJ6289	53°24·0′	2°33·9′W	T	109
Bruckhills	Aberd	NJ6937	57°25·6′	2°30·5′W	X	29
Bruckley Castle	Aberd	NJ9150	57°32·7′	2°8·6′W	X	30
Brucklay Ho	Aberd	NJ9048	57°31·6′	2°9·6′W	X	30
Brucklaywaird	Aberd	NO8284	56°57·1′	2°17·3′W	X	45
Brucklebog	Aberd	NO7498	57°4·6′	2°25·3′W	T	38,45
Bruckles	Moray	NJ5350	57°32·4′	2°46·6′W	X	29
Bruckleseat	Aberd	NJ8341	57°27·8′	2°16·5′W	X	29,30
Bruckleseat	Aberd	NK0443	57°28·9′	1°55·5′W	X	30
Bruckley	Fife	NO4318	56°21·3′	2°54·9′W	X	59
Bruckton	Devon	SX8452	50°21·6′	3°37·5′W	X	202
Bructor	Aberd	NJ7824	57°18·6′	2°21·5′W	X	38

Bruddans, The	Shetld	HU2077	60°28·8′	1°37·7′W	X	3
Brudhach Buaile an Tùir	Highld	NG4021	57°12·6′	6°17·9′W	X	32
Brue	Orkney	HY6527	59°8·0′	2°36·2′W	X	5
Brue Fm	Somer	ST5931	51°4·8′	2°34·7′W	FM	182,183
Bruera	Ches	SJ4360	53°8·3′	2°50·7′W	T	117
Bruern Abbey	Oxon	SP2620	51°52·9′	1°36·9′W	T	163
Bruernish	N Eil	NF7102	56°59·8′	7°24·7′W	T	31
Bruernish	N Eil	NF7201	56°59·3′	7°23·6′W	H	31
Bruernish Point	N Eil	NF7300	56°58·8′	7°22·5′W	X	31
Bruern Wood	Oxon	SP2619	51°52·4′	1°36·9′W	F	163
Bruff Fm	Lincs	TA0300	53°29·4′	0°26·4′W	FM	112
Brugarth	Shetld	HU3946	60°12·1′	1°17·3′W	X	4
Brughs	Aberd	NJ3512	57°11·9′	3°4·1′W	X	37
Bruiach	Highld	NH5041	57°26·3′	4°29·5′W	X	26
Bruiach Burn	Highld	NH4938	57°24·7′	4°30·4′W	W	26
Bruichladdich	Arg & Bt	NR2661	55°46·1′	6°21·7′W	T	60
Bruichnain	Highld	NH6345	57°28·7′	4°16·6′W	X	26
Bruiland	Arg & Bt	NR8658	55°46·3′	5°24·3′W	X	62
Bruist	N Eil	NF9282	57°43·6′	7°10·0′W	X	18
Bruisyard	Suff	TM3266	52°14·8′	1°24·3′E	T	156
Bruisyard Vinery	Suff	TM3266	52°14·8′	1°24·3′E	X	156
Bruisyard Wood	Suff	TM3367	52°15·3′	1°25·2′E	F	156
Bruiths Skerry	Shetld	HU3787	60°34·2′	1°19·0′W	X	1,2
Brumber Hill	N Yks	SE5343	53°53·1′	1°11·2′W	X	105
Brumby	N Lincs	SE8909	53°34·4′	0°38·9′W	T	112
Brumby Common West	N Lincs	SE8509	53°34·5′	0°42·6′W	X	112
Brumby Grange	N Lincs	SE8410	53°35·0′	0°43·5′W	X	112
Brumby Grove	N Lincs	SE8709	53°34·5′	0°40·8′W	X	112
Brumby Hall	N Lincs	SE8810	53°35·0′	0°39·8′W	A	112
Brumstead Common	Norf	TG3626	52°47·0′	1°30·4′E	X	133,134
Brùnabhal	N Eil	NB1206	57°57·3′	6°51·6′W	H	13,14
Brunachan	Highld	NN3189	56°57·9′	4°46·3′W	X	34,41
Bruna Fea	Orkney	HY2610	58°58·5′	3°16·7′W	X	6
Brunan an Uillt	Highld	NG6822	57°14·1′	5°50·2′W	W	32
Bruna Ness	Shetld	HU3837	60°7·2′	1°18·5′W	X	4
Brunant	Carm	SN2114	51°48·0′	4°35·4′W	X	158
Brunant	Carm	SN6741	52°3·3′	3°56·0′W	X	146
Brunant	Powys	SJ2809	52°40·7′	3°3·5′W	T	126
Brunatwatt	Shetld	HU2450	60°14·3′	1°33·5′W	T	3
Brund	Staffs	SK1061	53°9·0′	1°50·6′W	T	119
Brundall	Norf	TG3208	52°37·4′	1°26·1′E	T	134
Brundall Gdns	Norf	TG3108	52°37·5′	1°25·2′E	X	134
Brundcliffe	Derby	SK1661	53°9·0′	1°45·2′W	X	119
Brundeanlaws	Scot Bord	NT7211	55°23·8′	2°26·1′W	X	80
Brund Fell	Cumbr	NY2616	54°32·3′	3°8·2′W	H	89,90
Brund Hays	Staffs	SK0557	53°6·8′	1°55·1′W	X	119
Brund Hill	Staffs	SK0264	53°10·6′	1°57·8′W	X	119
Brundholme	Cumbr	NY2924	54°36·6′	3°5·5′W	X	89,90
Brundholme Wood	Cumbr	NY2824	54°36·6′	3°6·5′W	F	89,90
Brundish	Norf	TM3995	52°30·3′	1°31·7′E	T	134
Brundish	Suff	TM2769	52°16·6′	1°20·1′E	T	156
Brundish Lodge	Suff	TM2770	52°17·1′	1°20·1′E	X	156
Brundish Street	Suff	TM2670	52°17·1′	1°19·2′E	T	156
Brundon	Suff	TL8642	52°2·9′	0°43·2′E	T	155
Brundrigg	Cumbr	SD4895	54°21·1′	2°47·6′W	X	97
Brunerican	Arg & Bt	NR6908	55°19·0′	5°38·0′W	X	68
Brunerican Bay	Arg & Bt	NR6907	55°18·4′	5°38·0′W	W	68
Brunery	Highld	NM7271	56°46·7′	5°43·5′W	T	40
Brunery Burn	Highld	NM6887	56°55·2′	5°48·3′W	W	40
Brunery Hill	Highld	NM7373	56°47·9′	5°42·6′W	X	40
Brune's Purlieu	Hants	SU1815	50°56·3′	1°44·2′W	X	184
Brunett	Wrex	SJ4742	52°58·6′	2°47·0′W	A	117
Brungerley Br	Lancs	SD7342	53°52·7′	2°24·2′W	X	103
Brunghill Moor	Lancs	SD6852	53°58·0′	2°28·9′W	X	103
Brun-goleu	Conwy	SH9867	53°11·7′	3°31·2′W	X	116
Brun Grange	Bucks	SP9006	51°45·0′	0°41·4′W	X	165
Brunk Wood	Notts	SK7461	53°8·7′	0°53·2′W	F	120
Brunning's Fm	Suff	TL9635	51°59·0′	0°51·7′E	FM	155
Brunnion	Corn	SW5036	50°10·5′	5°29·7′W	T	203
Brunsell Knap Fm	Dorset	ST7214	50°55·7′	2°23·5′W	FM	194
Brunshaw	Lancs	SD8532	53°47·3′	2°13·2′W	T	103
Brunslow	Shrops	SO3684	52°27·3′	2°56·1′W	X	137
Brunsow Beck	Cumbr	NY0839	54°44·5′	3°25·3′W	W	89
Brunstane	C of Edin	NT3172	55°56·4′	3°5·8′W	T	66
Brunstane	Midlo	NT2058	55°48·8′	3°16·2′W	X	66,73
Brunstead Grange	Norf	TG3727	52°47·5′	1°31·3′E	X	133,134
Brunstead Hall	Norf	TG3626	52°47·0′	1°30·4′E	X	133,134
Brunstock	Cumbr	NY4159	54°55·6′	2°54·8′W	T	85
Brunstock Beck	Cumbr	NY4261	54°56·7′	2°53·9′W	W	85
Brunston Castle	S Ayr	NS2601	55°16·6′	4°43·9′W	A	76
Brunswick	Man	SJ8497	53°28·4′	2°14·1′W	T	109
Brunswick Fm	Suff	TM2662	52°12·8′	1°18·9′E	FM	156
Brunswick Park	Barnet	TQ2893	51°37·5′	0°8·7′W	T	176
Brunswick Village	N upon Ty	NZ2372	55°2·8′	1°38·0′W	T	88
Brunswood Fm	Derby	SK4037	52°56·0′	1°23·9′W	FM	129
Brunta Burn	Scot Bord	NT5948	55°43·7′	2°38·7′W	W	73,74
Bruntaburn Mill	Scot Bord	NT5949	55°44·2′	2°38·7′W	X	73,74
Bruntbrae	Aberd	NJ6458	57°36·9′	2°35·7′W	X	29
Bruntcliffe	Leeds	SE2527	53°44·6′	1°36·8′W	T	104
Bruntcliffe Fm	N Yks	SE4398	54°22·8′	1°19·9′W	FM	99
Brunt Fm	Pemb	SM8004	51°41·7′	5°10·6′W	FM	157
Brunthall	Aberd	NJ7146	57°30·5′	2°28·6′W	X	29
Brunthall	Moray	NJ4353	57°34·1′	2°56·7′W	X	28
Brunt Hamarsland	Shetld	HU4452	60°15·3′	1°11·8′W	X	3
Brunthass Burn	D & G	NY0496	55°15·2′	3°30·2′W	W	78
Brunt Hill	Aberd	NJ4712	57°12·0′	2°52·2′W	H	37
Brunthill	Aberd	NJ8422	57°17·6′	2°15·5′W	X	38
Brunthill	Aberd	NK0338	57°26·2′	1°56·5′W	X	30
Brunt Hill	Aberd	NO6376	56°52·7′	2°36·0′W	X	45
Brunt Hill	Cumbr	NY7402	54°25·0′	2°23·6′W	X	91
Brunt Hill	D & G	NX7496	55°14·8′	3°58·5′W	H	77
Brunt Hill	D & G	NY1693	55°13·7′	3°18·8′W	H	79
Brunthill	E Ayr	NS4740	55°38·0′	4°25·4′W	X	70
Brunt Hill	E Loth	NT6874	55°57·7′	2°30·3′W	H	67
Brunt Hill	Orkney	HY2311	58°59·0′	3°19·9′W	X	6
Brunthill	Pth & Kin	NO1100	56°11·3′	3°25·6′W	X	58
Brunt Hill	Shetld	HU3693	60°37·4′	1°20·0′W	X	1,2
Brunt Hill	Shetld	HU5279	60°29·7′	1°2·7′W	X	2,3
Brunthill Fm	Aberd	NJ8552	57°33·7′	2°14·6′W	FM	30
Brunthwaite	Brad	SE0546	53°54·8′	1°55·0′W	T	104

Brunthwaite	Cumbr	SD5788	54°17·4'	2°39·2'W	X	97
Brunthwaite Br	Brad	SE0545	53°54·3'	1°55·0'W	X	104
Brunthwaite Crag	Brad	SE0546	53°54·8'	1°55·0'W	X	104
Bruntingthorpe	Leic	SP6089	52°30·0'	1°6·6'W	T	140
Bruntis Loch	D & G	NX4465	54°57·6'	4°25·8'W	W	83
Brunt Knott	Cumbr	NY4800	54°23·8'	2°47·6'W	H	90
Brunt Knott Fm	Cumbr	NY4700	54°23·8'	2°48·6'W	FM	90
Bruntland	Aberd	NJ4528	57°20·6'	2°54·4'W	X	37
Bruntland	E Ayr	NS4743	55°39·6'	4°25·5'W	X	70
Bruntland	Moray	NJ1264	57°39·7'	3°28·0'W	X	28
Bruntland	Shetld	HU5142	60°9·8'	1°4·4'W	X	4
Bruntlandpark	Aberd	NJ9218	57°15·4'	2°7·5'W	X	38
Brunton	Angus	NO6646	56°36·5'	2°32·8'W	X	54
Brunton	Fife	NO3220	56°22·3'	3°5·6'W	T	53,59
Brunton	Northum	NU2024	55°30·8'	1°40·6'W	X	75
Brunton	Wilts	SU2456	51°18·4'	1°39·0'W	T	174
Brunton Bank	Northum	NY9269	55°1·2'	2°7·1'W	X	87
Brunton Barns	Fife	NO3002	56°12·6'	3°7·3'W	X	59
Brunton Bridge Fm	N upon Ty	NZ2169	55°1·2'	1°39·9'W	FM	88
Brunton Burn	Northum	NU2226	55°31·9'	1°38·7'W	W	75
Brunton Burn	W Loth	NS9572	55°56·0'	3°40·4'W	W	65
Brunton Fm	W Loth	NS9573	55°56·6'	3°40·4'W	FM	65
Brunton Ho	Northum	NY9269	55°1·2'	2°7·1'W	X	87
Brunton Ho	N Yks	SD7866	54°5·6'	2°19·8'W	X	98
Brunton Laithe	Lancs	SD7157	54°0·7'	2°26·1'W	X	103
Bruntons Hill	Cumbr	NY4173	55°3·1'	2°55·0'W	X	85
Bruntown	Moray	NJ4966	57°41·1'	2°50·9'W	X	28,29
Brunt Rig	D & G	NS7208	55°21·2'	4°0·7'W	X	71,77
Brunt Rig	D & G	NT3102	55°18·7'	3°4·8'W	X	79
Brunt Riggs	Cumbr	SD2583	54°14·5'	3°8·6'W	X	96
Brunt Riggs Moss	N Yks	SD7573	54°9·4'	2°22·6'W	X	98
Bruntscar	N Yks	SD7378	54°12·1'	2°24·4'W	X	98
Bruntsfield Links	C of Edin	NT2572	55°56·4'	3°11·6'W	X	66
Bruntshielbog	D & G	NY4082	55°8·0'	2°56·0'W	X	79
Bruntshields	Angus	NO2668	56°48·1'	3°12·3'W	H	44
Bruntshields	D & G	NY0283	55°8·2'	3°31·8'W	X	78
Bruntshiel Hill	D & G	NY4182	55°8·0'	2°55·1'W	H	79
Bruntshiels	Fife	NO4310	56°17·0'	2°55·8'W	X	59
Brunt Sike	Cumbr	SD6297	54°22·3'	2°34·7'W	X	97
Bruntskerry	Shetld	HU2250	60°14·3'	1°35·7'W	X	3
Bruntstane	Aberd	NJ5539	57°26·6'	2°44·5'W	X	29
Brunt, The	E Loth	NT6873	55°57·2'	2°30·3'W	X	67
Brunt Tongue	Cumbr	NY5009	54°28·7'	2°45·9'W	X	90
Bruntwood	E Ayr	NS5032	55°33·8'	4°22·3'W	X	70
Bruntwood Hall	Stock	SJ8587	53°23·0'	2°13·1'W	X	109
Bruntwoodhill	E Ayr	NS5032	55°33·8'	4°22·3'W	X	70
Bruntwood Mains	E Ayr	NS5032	55°33·8'	4°22·3'W	X	70
Bruntwood Tap	Aberd	NJ6621	57°17·0'	2°33·4'W	X	38
Brunty	Pth & Kin	NO1938	56°31·9'	3°18·6'W	X	53
Bruntyairds Wood	Aberd	NO8193	57°1·9'	2°18·3'W	F	38,45
Bruntyards	Aberd	NJ7359	57°37·5'	2°26·7'W	X	29
Bruray	Shetld	HU6972	60°25·8'	0°44·3'W	T	2
Bruray Taing	Shetld	HU6972	60°25·8'	0°44·3'W	X	2
Bruse Holm	Shetld	HU5263	60°21·1'	1°3·0'W	X	2,3
Brush	N Yks	SD9843	53°53·2'	2°1·4'W	X	103
Brushes	Tames	SJ9799	53°29·5'	2°2·3'W	T	109
Brushes	Tames	SJ9999	53°29·5'	2°0·5'W	X	109
Brushes Clough Resr	Oldham	SD9509	53°34·9'	2°4·1'W	W	109
Brushfield	Derby	SK1571	53°14·4'	1°46·1'W	T	119
Brushfield Hough	Derby	SK1671	53°14·4'	1°45·2'W	X	119
Brushford	Devon	SS6707	50°51·1'	3°53·0'W	T	191
Brushford	Somer	SS9225	51°1·1'	3°32·0'W	T	181
Brush Hills	Suff	TL8773	52°19·6'	0°45·1'E	F	144,155
Brushy Burn	D & G	NX4361	54°55·4'	4°26·6'W	W	83
Brusselton Wood	Durham	NZ2025	54°37·4'	1°41·0'W	F	93
Bruthach an Sgùilein	Highld	NN7684	56°56·1'	4°1·8'W	H	42
Bruthach Chiulam	Pth & Kin	NN6980	56°53·8'	4°8·6'W	X	42
Bruthach Dhomhnuillean	N Eil	NF9566	57°35·1'	7°5·8'W	W	18
Bruthach Mór	Arg & Bt	NR2741	55°35·4'	6°19·5'W	X	60
Bruthach na Garbh Choille	Highld	NH1285	57°49·2'	5°9·5'W	H	19
Bruthach nan Uamh	Highld	NH1912	57°10·1'	4°59·2'W	X	34
Bruthwaite Forest	Cumbr	NY6057	54°54·6'	2°37·0'W	X	86
Bruton	Somer	ST6834	51°6·5'	2°27·0'W	T	183
Bruts Moss	Cumbr	NY3521	54°35·1'	2°59·9'W	X	90
Brux	Aberd	NJ4918	57°15·2'	2°50·3'W	X	37
Brux Hill	Aberd	NJ5021	57°16·9'	2°49·3'W	H	37
Bruxie Hill	Aberd	NO8280	56°54·9'	2°17·3'W	H	45
Bruxie Lodge	Aberd	NJ9548	57°31·6'	2°4·6'W	X	30
Brwynen	Powys	SJ0321	52°46·9'	3°25·9'W	X	125
Brwyno	Cered	SN7096	52°33·0'	3°54·6'W	X	135
Brwynog	Conwy	SH7564	53°9·8'	3°51·8'W	X	115
Brwynog	I of Angl	SH3586	53°21·0'	4°28·3'W	X	114
Bryameadow	Orkney	HY2522	59°5·0'	3°18·0'W	X	6
Bryan Beck	Cumbr	SD4090	54°18·4'	2°54·9'W	X	96,97
Bryan Mills Beck	E Yorks	TA0146	53°54·3'	0°27·3'W	W	106,107
Bryan Mills Fm	E Yorks	TA0146	53°54·3'	0°27·3'W	FM	106,107
Bryans	Midlo	NT3464	55°52·1'	3°2·8'W	T	66
Bryan's Green	Worcs	SO8868	52°18·8'	2°10·2'W	T	139
Bryan's Heights	E Ayr	NS4902	55°17·6'	4°22·3'W	H	77
Bryanston	Dorset	ST8706	50°51·4'	2°10·7'W	T	194
Bryanston Park	Dorset	ST8706	50°51·4'	2°10·7'W	X	194
Bryanston School	Dorset	ST8707	50°52·0'	2°10·7'W	X	194
Bryanton	Angus	NO6548	56°37·6'	2°33·8'W	X	54
Bryant's Bottom	Bucks	SU8599	51°41·2'	0°45·8'W	T	165
Bryant's Br	Norf	TM0088	52°27·4'	0°57·0'E	X	144
Bryant's Fm	E Susx	TQ6632	51°4·0'	0°22·5'E	FM	188
Bryant's Fm	Oxon	SU7277	51°29·5'	0°57·4'W	FM	175
Bryant's Fm	Somer	ST1218	50°57·5'	3°14·8'W	FM	181,193
Bryant's Heath	Norf	TG2529	52°48·9'	1°20·7'E	F	133,134
Bryants Puddle Heath	Dorset	SY8091	50°43·3'	2°16·6'W	X	194
Bryars Fm	Lancs	SD4831	53°46·6'	2°46·9'W	FM	102
Bryaton	Corn	SS2115	50°54·6'	4°32·4'W	X	190
Bryce's Fm	Hants	SU2823	51°0·6'	1°35·7'W	FM	184
Brychgoed Fm	Powys	SN9224	51°54·5'	3°33·8'W	FM	160
Brychyni	Gwyn	SH4444	52°58·5'	4°19·0'W	X	123
Bryckden Place	E Susx	TQ5420	50°57·8'	0°12·0'E	X	199
Brydekirk	D & G	NY1870	55°1·3'	3°16·5'W	T	85
Brydekirk Mains	D & G	NY1871	55°1·9'	3°16·5'W	X	85
Bryers	Suff	TL8558	52°11·6'	0°42·8'E	X	155
Bryers Fold	Cumbr	SD3895	54°21·1'	2°56·8'W	X	96,97
Bryffin	Cered	SN6066	52°16·7'	4°2·7'W	X	135
Bryher	I Scilly	SV8715	49°57·4'	6°21·5'W	X	203
Bryiau	Powys	SH9614	52°43·1'	3°32·0'W	X	125
Brylach Hill	Moray	NJ2352	57°33·4'	3°16·7'W	H	28
Bryland	Scot Bord	NT1143	55°40·6'	3°24·5'W	X	72
Brymbo	Conwy	SH8071	53°13·6'	3°47·5'W	T	116
Brymbo	Wrex	SJ2953	53°4·4'	3°3·2'W	T	117
Brymire	Orkney	HY4906	58°56·6'	2°52·7'W	X	6,7
Brymore School	Somer	ST2439	51°8·9'	3°4·8'W	X	182
Brympton D'Evercy	Somer	ST5115	50°56·2'	2°41·5'W	T	183
Brympton Hill	Somer	ST4714	50°55·6'	2°44·9'W	H	193
Brympton House	Somer	ST5215	50°56·2'	2°40·6'W	X	183
Bryn	Caer	ST1695	51°39·1'	3°12·5'W	T	171
Bryn	Carm	SN4024	51°53·7'	4°19·1'W	X	159
Bryn	Carm	SN5041	52°3·1'	4°10·9'W	X	146
Bryn	Carm	SN5400	51°41·0'	4°6·3'W	T	159
Bryn	Carm	SN5510	51°46·4'	4°5·7'W	X	159
Bryn	Carm	SN6730	51°57·4'	3°55·7'W	X	146
Bryn	Carm	SN7114	51°48·8'	3°51·9'W	X	160
Bryn	Cered	SN6659	52°13·0'	3°57·3'W	X	146
Bryn	Cered	SN7672	52°20·2'	3°48·8'W	X	135,147
Bryn	Cered	SN7774	52°21·3'	3°48·0'W	X	135,147
Bryn	Ches	SJ6072	53°14·9'	2°35·6'W	T	118
Bryn	Conwy	SH8060	53°7·7'	3°47·2'W	X	116
Bryn	Conwy	SH8355	53°5·0'	3°44·4'W	X	116
Bryn	Conwy	SH8949	53°1·9'	3°38·9'W	X	116
Bryn	Conwy	SH9362	53°8·9'	3°35·6'W	X	116
Bryn	Flint	SJ1767	53°11·9'	3°14·1'W	X	116
Bryn	Gwyn	SH3540	52°56·2'	4°26·9'W	X	123
Bryn	Gwyn	SH5165	53°9·9'	4°13·3'W	X	114,115
Bryn	Gwyn	SH5803	52°36·6'	4°5·4'W	X	135
Bryn	Gwyn	SH5970	53°12·7'	4°6·3'W	T	114,115
Bryn	Gwyn	SH6344	52°58·8'	4°2·0'W	X	124
Bryn	Gwyn	SH9019	52°45·7'	3°37·4'W	X	125
Bryn	Heref	SO3329	51°57·6'	2°58·1'W	X	149,161
Bryn	Monm	SO3301	51°42·5'	2°57·8'W	X	171
Bryn	Nth Pt Talb	SS8192	51°37·1'	3°42·7'W	T	170
Bryn	Powys	SJ1602	52°36·8'	3°14·0'W	T	136
Bryn	Powys	SJ2506	52°39·0'	3°6·1'W	X	126
Bryn	Powys	SN8852	52°9·5'	3°37·8'W	X	147
Bryn	Powys	SN9055	52°11·2'	3°36·1'W	H	147
Bryn	Powys	SO0170	52°19·4'	3°26·8'W	X	136,147
Bryn	Powys	SO0357	52°12·4'	3°24·8'W	X	147
Bryn	Powys	SO0565	52°16·7'	3°23·2'W	X	136,147
Bryn	Powys	SO0722	51°53·6'	3°20·7'W	H	160
Bryn	Powys	SO1092	52°31·3'	3°19·2'W	X	136
Bryn	Powys	SO1155	52°11·4'	3°17·7'W	X	148
Bryn	Powys	SO1584	52°27·1'	3°14·6'W	H	136
Bryn	Powys	SO1694	52°32·5'	3°13·9'W	X	136
Bryn	Powys	SO1696	52°33·6'	3°13·9'W	X	136
Bryn	Powys	SO2257	52°12·6'	3°8·1'W	X	148
Bryn	Powys	SO2260	52°14·2'	3°8·1'W	X	137,148
Bryn	Rho Cyn Taf	SN9205	51°44·2'	3°33·5'W	T	160
Bryn	Shrops	SJ2224	52°48·7'	3°9·0'W	X	126
Bryn	Shrops	SO2985	52°27·7'	3°2·3'W	T	137
Bryn	Swan	SS5293	51°37·2'	4°7·9'W	T	159
Bryn	Wigan	SD5600	53°29·9'	2°39·4'W	T	108
Bryn-aber	Powys	SJ1024	52°48·6'	3°19·7'W	X	125
Brynadda	Gwyn	SH5268	53°11·6'	4°12·5'W	X	114,115
Bryn- Adda	Wrex	SJ2544	52°59·5'	3°6·6'W	X	117
Bryn-Adda Flat	Wrex	SJ2445	53°0·1'	3°7·5'W	X	117
Brynaerau	Gwyn	SH3738	52°55·1'	4°25·1'W	X	123
Brynaere	Powys	SH8903	52°37·0'	3°38·0'W	X	135,136
Brynaeron	Pemb	SN1221	51°51·6'	4°43·4'W	X	145,158
Brynafan	Cered	SN7173	52°20·6'	3°53·2'W	T	135,147
Bryn-afel	Swan	SS5590	51°35·7'	4°5·2'W	X	159
Bryn Afon	Wrex	SJ3646	53°0·7'	2°56·8'W	X	117
Bryn Ala	I of Angl	SH3977	53°16·2'	4°24·5'W	X	114
Bryn Aled	Conwy	SH9570	53°13·2'	3°34·0'W	X	116
Brynallt	Shrops	SJ3732	52°53·1'	2°55·8'W	X	126
Bryn Alyn	Flint	SJ2066	53°11·3'	3°11·4'W	X	117
Bryn-Alyn	Wrex	SJ3354	53°5·0'	2°59·6'W	X	117
Bryn-ambor	Cered	SN7450	52°8·3'	3°50·1'W	X	146,147
Brynamlwg	Carm	SN2214	51°48·0'	4°34·5'W	X	158
Bryn-amlwg	Cered	SN5164	52°15·5'	4°10·6'W	X	146
Brynamlwg	Cered	SN6063	52°15·1'	4°2·7'W	X	146
Bryn Amlwg	Powys	SN9297	52°33·8'	3°35·2'W	H	136
Brynamman	Carm	SN7114	51°48·8'	3°51·9'W	T	160
Bryn Arau Duon	Carm	SN7248	52°7·2'	3°51·8'W	H	146,147
Brynarddyn	Wrex	SJ2238	52°56·3'	3°9·2'W	X	126
Brynard's Hill	Wilts	SU0781	51°31·9'	1°53·6'W	X	173
Brynarth	Cered	SN6669	52°18·4'	3°57·5'W	X	135
Brynarth	Powys	SN9050	52°8·5'	3°36·1'W	X	147
Bryn Arw	Monm	SO3019	51°52·1'	3°0·6'W	X	161
Bryn Asaph	Denb	SJ0473	53°15·0'	3°25·9'W	X	116
Brynau	Rho Cyn Taf	ST1384	51°33·1'	3°14·9'W	X	171
Brynawel	Caer	ST1991	51°37·0'	3°9·8'W	T	171
Bryn-awel	Nth Pt Talb	SN8404	51°43·6'	3°40·4'W	X	170
Brynawel	V of Glam	SS8975	51°28·0'	3°35·5'W	X	170
Brynawelon	Cered	SN4451	52°8·4'	4°16·4'W	X	146
Bryn-Awelon	Pemb	SM9937	51°59·9'	4°55·3'W	X	157
Brynbach	Denb	SJ0258	53°6·9'	3°27·4'W	X	116
Bryn Bach	Flint	SJ2470	53°13·5'	3°7·9'W	X	117
Bryn Bach	Gwyn	SH3034	52°52·8'	4°31·2'W	X	123
Bryn Bach	Nth Pt Talb	SN9000	51°41·5'	3°35·1'W	X	170
Brynbach	Powys	SN9099	52°34·9'	3°37·0'W	X	136
Bryn-bach-Common	Swan	SN6103	51°42·8'	4°0·3'W	X	159
Bryn Bach Park	Blae Gw	SO1209	51°46·6'	3°16·1'W	X	161
Brynbala	Cered	SN5986	52°27·5'	4°4·1'W	X	135
Bryn-banal	Carm	SN5109	51°45·8'	4°9·2'W	X	159
Bryn-banc	Carm	SN1918	51°50·1'	4°37·2'W	X	158
Brynbanedd	Powys	SO0149	52°7·9'	3°26·4'W	X	147
Brynbank Fm	Suff	TL7848	52°6·3'	0°36·3'E	FM	155
Bryn-Banon	Gwyn	SH9536	52°54·9'	3°33·3'W	X	125
Bryn Barcut	Conwy	SH8866	53°11·0'	3°40·2'W	X	116
Bryn Beddau	Conwy	SH8258	53°6·6'	3°45·4'W	X	116
Bryn-Bedw	Cered	SN3550	52°7·7'	4°24·2'W	X	145
Bryn-bedw	Denb	SJ1363	53°9·7'	3°17·7'W	X	116
Bryn-bedwog	Gwyn	SH9332	52°52·7'	3°35·0'W	X	125
Bryn-beili	Powys	SN8944	52°5·2'	3°36·8'W	X	147,160
Brynbella	Denb	SJ0872	53°14·5'	3°22·3'W	A	116
Brynberian	Pemb	SN1035	51°59·1'	4°45·6'W	T	145
Bryn Betws	Conwy	SH8264	53°9·8'	3°45·5'W	X	116
Bryn-biettyn	Carm	SN4329	51°56·5'	4°16·7'W	X	146
Bryn Bigad	Conwy	SH9664	53°10·0'	3°32·9'W	X	116
Bryn Blaen-y-glyn	Powys	SN9181	52°25·2'	3°35·8'W	X	136
Brynblodau	Cered	SN6056	52°11·3'	4°2·5'W	X	146
Bryn-bod	Conwy	SH9965	53°10·6'	3°30·3'W	X	116
Brynbolgoed	Powys	SN9725	51°55·1'	3°29·5'W	X	160
Bryn-Bowlio	Denb	SJ1861	53°8·6'	3°13·2'W	X	116
Bryn-Brân	Carm	SN6644	52°4·9'	3°56·9'W	X	146
Bryn Bras	Cered	SN7479	52°23·9'	3°50·7'W	H	135,147
Bryn-bras	Gwyn	SH8543	52°58·6'	3°42·4'W	X	124,125
Bryn Bras Castle	Gwyn	SH5462	53°8·4'	4°10·6'W	X	114,115
Bryn Brawd	Cered	SN6951	52°8·7'	3°54·5'W	H	146
Bryn Brith	Gwyn	SH6615	52°43·2'	3°58·6'W	H	124
Bryn-brŷch	Gwyn	SH4445	52°59·0'	4°19·0'W	X	115,123
Brynbryddan	Nth Pt Talb	SS7792	51°37·0'	3°46·2'W	T	170
Brynbuga or Usk	Monm	SO3700	51°41·9'	2°54·3'W	T	171
Bryn Bugeiliaid	Gwyn	SH4749	53°1·2'	4°16·5'W	X	115,123
Bryn Bugeiliaid	Powys	SN8513	51°48·5'	3°39·7'W	X	160
Brynbwa	Pemb	SN1538	52°0·8'	4°41·4'W	X	145
Bryn Bwbach	Gwyn	SH6236	52°54·5'	4°2·7'W	T	124
Bryn-bŵl	Cered	SN6086	52°27·5'	4°3·2'W	X	135
Brynbychan	Gwyn	SH4143	52°57·9'	4°21·6'W	X	123
Bryn Cader Faner	Gwyn	SH6435	52°54·0'	4°0·9'W	H	124
Bryn Cadwgan	Carm	SN7248	52°7·2'	3°51·8'W	H	146,147
Bryncae	Rho Cyn Taf	SS9982	51°31·9'	3°27·0'W	T	170
Bryncaemaeshir	Powys	SJ1100	52°35·7'	3°18·4'W	X	136
Bryncaled	Gwyn	SH8631	52°52·1'	3°41·2'W	X	124,125
Bryncalled	Shrops	SO3376	52°22·9'	2°58·7'W	X	137,148
Bryn-Camlo	Powys	SO0668	52°18·4'	3°22·3'W	X	136,147
Bryncar	Conwy	SH8973	53°14·8'	3°39·4'W	X	116
Bryn-Carnarfon	Carm	SS5498	51°39·9'	4°6·3'W	X	159
Bryncarnedd	Cered	SN6082	52°25·3'	4°3·1'W	X	135
Bryncarne Fm	Nth Pt Talb	SN7505	51°44·0'	3°48·2'W	FM	160
Bryn Carregog	Cered	SN7153	52°9·9'	3°52·8'W	X	146,147
Bryn-Carrog Fm	Denb	SJ0176	53°16·5'	3°28·7'W	FM	116
Bryn Cau	Gwyn	SH8133	52°53·1'	3°45·7'W	X	124,125
Bryn-caws Fm	Nth Pt Talb	SN7701	51°41·9'	3°46·4'W	FM	170
Bryn Ceffyl	Gwyn	SH7837	52°55·2'	3°48·5'W	X	124
Bryn Ceiliogau	Cered	SN6949	52°7·7'	3°54·4'W	X	146
Bryn Ceinon	Powys	SN9558	52°12·9'	3°31·8'W	X	147
Brynceir	Carm	SN4526	51°54·9'	4°14·8'W	X	146
Bryn-ceirch	Carm	SN4739	52°1·9'	4°13·4'W	X	146
Bryncelli Ddu	I of Angl	SH5070	53°12·6'	4°14·4'W	X	114,115
Bryn Celyn	Denb	SJ1260	53°8·0'	3°18·5'W	X	116
Bryn Celyn	Flint	SJ1876	53°16·7'	3°13·4'W	T	116
Bryn-celyn	Gwyn	SH3025	52°48·0'	4°30·9'W	X	123
Bryn Celyn	I of Angl	SH6079	53°17·6'	4°5·6'W	T	114,115
Bryn Celyn Hall	Gwyn	SH3134	52°52·9'	4°30·3'W	X	123
Bryncenarth	Powys	SN9775	52°22·0'	3°30·4'W	X	136,147
Bryncene	Carm	SN4226	51°54·8'	4°17·4'W	X	146
Bryn Cerbyd	Conwy	SH8545	52°59·6'	3°42·4'W	H	116
Bryn-Cerdin	Cered	SN3848	52°6·6'	4°21·6'W	X	145
Brynceri	Cered	SN3351	52°8·2'	4°26·0'W	X	145
Bryn-cesig	Cered	SN4953	52°9·5'	4°12·1'W	X	146
Bryncethin	Brig	SS9184	51°32·9'	3°33·9'W	T	170
Bryn-cethin	Cered	SN6262	52°14·6'	4°0·9'W	X	146
Bryn Cethin	Gwyn	SH3028	52°49·6'	4°31·0'W	X	123
Bryn-chwareu	Denb	SJ1553	53°4·3'	3°15·7'W	X	116
Bryn-chwith	Brig	SS9584	51°32·9'	3°30·5'W	X	170
Bryn-chwith	Brig	SS9788	51°35·1'	3°28·8'W	X	170
Brynchwyth	Cered	SN6171	52°19·4'	4°2·0'W	X	135
Bryncian	I of Angl	SH3472	53°13·4'	4°28·8'W	X	114
Bryncir	Gwyn	SH4844	52°58·6'	4°15·4'W	T	123
Bryncleddau	Pemb	SM9129	51°55·5'	5°2·0'W	X	157,158
Brynclettwr	Cered	SN4444	52°4·6'	4°16·2'W	X	146
Bryn Clun	Powys	SN8653	52°10·1'	3°39·6'W	H	147
Bryn-clŷd	I of Angl	SH3982	53°18·9'	4°24·6'W	X	114
Bryn-clygo	Powys	SH7801	52°35·8'	3°47·7'W	X	135
Bryn-cnap	Conwy	SH9465	53°10·5'	3°34·8'W	X	116
Bryn Cnewyllyn	Denb	SJ0678	53°17·7'	3°24·2'W	X	116
Bryncoch	Brig	SS9183	51°32·4'	3°33·9'W	T	170
Bryncoch	Carm	SN3810	51°46·2'	4°20·5'W	X	159
Bryncoch	Carm	SN4114	51°48·4'	4°18·0'W	X	159
Bryncoch	Carm	SN4509	51°45·7'	4°14·4'W	X	159
Bryn Coch	Cered	SN6751	52°8·7'	3°56·2'W	X	146
Bryn-coch	Flint	SJ1378	53°17·8'	3°17·9'W	X	116
Bryn-coch	Gwyn	SH4037	52°54·6'	4°22·4'W	X	123
Bryn-coch	Gwyn	SH8732	52°52·7'	3°40·3'W	X	124,125
Bryn-coch	I of Angl	SH5072	53°13·7'	4°14·4'W	X	114,115
Bryn côch	Nth Pt Talb	SS7499	51°40·8'	3°49·0'W	T	170
Bryn-coch	Powys	SH7602	52°36·3'	3°49·5'W	H	135
Bryn-coch	Powys	SH8902	52°36·5'	3°38·0'W	X	135,136
Bryn-coch	Powys	SJ0322	52°47·5'	3°25·9'W	H	125
Bryncoch	Powys	SJ1321	52°47·0'	3°17·0'W	X	125
Bryn Coch	Powys	SJ1327	52°50·3'	3°17·1'W	X	125
Bryn Côch	Powys	SJ2019	52°46·0'	3°10·7'W	X	126
Bryncoch	Powys	SJ2330	52°52·0'	3°8·2'W	X	126
Bryn-côch	Powys	SN9396	52°33·3'	3°34·3'W	X	136
Bryncoch	Powys	SN9859	52°13·4'	3°29·2'W	X	147
Bryn-coch	Powys	SO0183	52°26·4'	3°27·0'W	X	136
Bryn-coch	Powys	SO0598	52°34·5'	3°23·7'W	X	136
Bryn-coch	Powys	SO1196	52°33·5'	3°18·4'W	X	136
Bryn Coch	Powys	SO1284	52°27·1'	3°17·3'W	X	136
Bryn-côch Fm	Nth Pt Talb	SN7400	51°41·3'	3°49·0'W	FM	170
Bryn-cocyn	Conwy	SH9968	53°12·2'	3°30·4'W	X	116
Bryn Cogail	I of Angl	SH5878	53°17·0'	4°7·4'W	X	114,115
Bryn Common	Flint	SJ2656	53°6·0'	3°5·9'W	T	117
Bryn Copa	Cered	SN8175	52°21·9'	3°44·5'W	H	135,136,147
Bryncothi	Carm	SN5632	51°58·3'	4°5·4'W	X	146
Bryn-Cothi Lodge	Carm	SN5632	51°58·3'	4°5·4'W	X	146
Bryn Cownwy	Powys	SJ0117	52°44·7'	3°27·6'W	X	125
Bryn-cras	Cered	SN8189	52°29·4'	3°44·8'W	X	135,136
Bryn-Crâs	Conwy	SJ0146	53°0·4'	3°28·1'W	X	116
Bryn Crîn	Gwyn	SH3735	52°53·5'	4°25·0'W	X	123
Bryncroes	Gwyn	SH2231	52°51·1'	4°38·2'W	T	123
Bryncroiau	Cered	SN6164	52°15·6'	4°1·8'W	X	146
Bryncrug	Gwyn	SH6003	52°36·6'	4°3·7'W	T	135

Bryn Crugog	Powys	SN9492	52°31·2'	3°33·3'W	H	136
Bryn Crwn	Powys	SN8258	52°12·7'	3°43·2'W	X	147
Bryn-cûl	Powys	SN9310	51°46·9'	3°32·7'W	X	160
Bryncut	Gwyn	SH9434	52°53·8'	3°34·1'W	X	125
Bryn-cŵm	Conwy	SH7872	53°14·1'	3°49·3'W	H	115
Bryn Cwmrhiwdre	Powys	SO0783	52°26·5'	3°21·7'W	H	136
Bryn Cwnin Fm	Denb	SJ0279	53°18·2'	3°27·8'W	FM	116
Bryncws	Cered	SN1545	52°4·6'	4°41·6'W	X	145
Bryn-Cynan	Brig	SS8687	51°34·5'	3°38·3'W	X	170
Bryn Cyncoed	Powys	SN9358	52°12·8'	3°33·6'W	X	147
Bryncyn-felen	Powys	SJ2019	52°46·0'	3°10·7'W	X	126
Bryn-Cynon	Powys	SO1849	52°8·2'	3°11·5'W	X	148
Bryncyrch	Powys	SJ0010	52°41·0'	3°28·4'W	X	125
Bryn Cysegrfa	Cered	SN6452	52°9·2'	3°58·9'W	H	146
Brynda	Cered	SN6366	52°16·7'	4°0·1'W	X	135
Bryn Dadlau	Powys	SO0583	52°26·4'	3°23·5'W	X	136
Bryndafydd	Carm	SN6039	52°2·1'	4°2·1'W	X	146
Bryn Dafydd	Cered	SN7871	52°19·7'	3°47·0'W	H	135,147
Bryn-Dafydd	Swan	SS6197	51°39·5'	4°0·2'W	X	159
Bryn Daith	Powys	SN8285	52°27·3'	3°43·8'W	X	135,136
Bryn Dansi	Conwy	SH8674	53°15·3'	3°42·1'W	X	116
Brynddenwen	Powys	SN9791	52°30·7'	3°30·7'W	X	136
Bryn Ddol	I of Angl	SH5980	53°18·1'	4°6·6'W	X	114,115
Brynddu	I of Angl	SH3791	53°23·7'	4°26·7'W	X	114
Bryn-ddwy-nant	Powys	SO2035	52°0·7'	3°9·5'W	X	161
Bryndedwydd	Conwy	SJ0144	52°59·3'	3°28·1'W	X	125
Bryndefaid	Brig	SS8891	51°36·6'	3°36·7'W	X	170
Bryn Deildre	Powys	SN8986	52°27·9'	3°37·6'W	X	135,136
Brynderi	Monm	SO3917	51°51·1'	2°52·7'W	X	161
Brynderlwyn	Powys	SN9599	52°35·0'	3°32·6'W	X	136
Bryn-derw	Gwyn	SH9838	52°56·0'	3°30·7'W	X	125
Bryn Derw	Gwyn	SJ0041	52°57·7'	3°28·9'W	X	125
Brynderw	Powys	SH8502	52°36·5'	3°41·5'W	X	135,136
Bryn Derwen	Conwy	SH8159	53°7·1'	3°46·3'W	H	116
Bryn-derwen	Monm	SO3507	51°45·7'	2°56·1'W	X	161
Bryn-derwen	Powys	SJ0009	52°40·4'	3°28·3'W	X	125
Brynderwen	Powys	SJ1618	52°45·4'	3°14·3'W	X	125
Brynderwen	Powys	SO1027	51°56·3'	3°18·2'W	X	161
Brynderwen	Powys	SO1695	52°33·0'	3°13·9'W	T	136
Bryn Derwent	Gwyn	SH6166	53°10·6'	4°4·4'W	X	115
Bryn Derwydd	Conwy	SH7374	53°15·1'	3°53·8'W	X	115
Bryn-deunydd	Conwy	SH9969	53°12·8'	3°30·3'W	X	116
Bryn-dial	Powys	SJ1712	52°42·2'	3°13·3'W	X	125
Bryndias Fm	Carm	SN4303	51°42·5'	4°16·0'W	FM	159
Bryn Diliw	Cered	SN8377	52°23·0'	3°42·7'W	H	135,136,147
Bryn Dinas	Gwyn	SH6250	53°2·0'	4°3·1'W	X	115
Bryn Dinas	Gwyn	SN6499	52°34·6'	4°0·0'W	H	135
Bryndioddef	Cered	SN3141	52°2·7'	4°27·5'W	X	145
Bryndraenog	Powys	SO2078	52°23·9'	3°10·2'W	X	137,148
Bryn-Dreiniog	Denb	SJ0550	53°2·6'	3°24·6'W	X	116
Bryndreiniog	Powys	SJ0825	52°49·1'	3°21·5'W	X	125
Bryndrinog	Shrops	SO2582	52°26·1'	3°5·8'W	X	137
Bryndu	Carm	SN5309	51°45·9'	4°7·4'W	T	159
Bryndu	Carm	SN5716	51°49·7'	4°4·1'W	X	159
Bryn-dû	Cered	SN6077	52°22·6'	4°3·0'W	X	135
Bryn Du	Cered	SN6751	52°8·7'	3°56·2'W	X	146
Bryn Du	Cered	SN6957	52°12·0'	3°54·6'W	X	146
Bryn Du	Cered	SN7655	52°11·0'	3°48·4'W	X	146,147
Bryn-du	Conwy	SH9251	53°3·0'	3°36·3'W	X	116
Bryn-du	Denb	SJ0847	53°1·0'	3°21·9'W	X	116
Bryn Du	Gwyn	SH8341	52°57·5'	3°44·1'W	X	124,125
Bryn Du	I of Angl	SH3472	53°13·4'	4°28·8'W	T	114
Bryn-du	Powys	SH9809	52°40·4'	3°30·1'W	X	125
Bryn Du	Powys	SN8356	52°11·6'	3°42·3'W	H	147
Bryn Du	Powys	SN8380	52°24·6'	3°42·8'W	X	135,136
Bryn Du	Powys	SN9097	52°33·8'	3°37·0'W	H	136
Bryn Du	Powys	SN9259	52°13·4'	3°34·5'W	X	147
Bryn Du	Powys	SN9342	52°4·2'	3°33·3'W	H	147,160
Bryndu	Powys	SN9683	52°26·3'	3°31·4'W	X	136
Bryn Du	Powys	SN9719	51°51·8'	3°29·4'W	X	160
Bryn Du	Powys	SO0297	52°34·0'	3°26·4'W	X	136
Bryndu	Powys	SO0877	52°23·2'	3°20·7'W	X	136,147
Bryndu	Powys	SO1206	51°44·9'	3°16·6'W	X	161
Bryn-du	Rho Cyn Taf	SS9099	51°41·0'	3°35·1'W	X	170
Bryn Du	Rho Cyn Taf	SS9799	51°41·1'	3°29·0'W	X	170
Bryn Du	Wrex	SJ1535	52°54·6'	3°15·4'W	X	125
Bryndu Fach	Nth Pt Talb	SS8383	51°32·3'	3°40·8'W	X	170
Bryndulais	Nth Pt Talb	SN8108	51°45·7'	3°43·1'W	X	160
Bryn Dulas	Conwy	SH9077	53°17·0'	3°38·6'W	T	116
Bryn-Dwyryd	Gwyn	SH6239	52°56·1'	4°2·8'W	H	124
Bryndy	Denb	SJ1249	53°2·1'	3°18·3'W	X	116
Bryndyffryn	Conwy	SH8161	53°8·2'	3°46·3'W	X	116
Bryn Dyfrydog	I of Angl	SH4385	53°20·6'	4°21·1'W	X	114
Bryn Eden	Gwyn	SH7129	52°50·8'	3°54·5'W	X	124
Bryn Edwin	Flint	SJ2369	53°13·0'	3°8·8'W	X	117
Bryn Eglur	Denb	SJ0861	53°8·5'	3°22·1'W	X	116
Bryneglwys	Denb	SJ1447	53°1·0'	3°16·5'W	T	116
Bryn Eglwys	Gwyn	SH6066	53°10·6'	4°5·3'W	T	115
Bryneglwys	I of Angl	SH3084	53°19·8'	4°32·8'W	X	114
Bryn-Eglwys Quarry	Gwyn	SH6905	52°37·9'	3°55·7'W	X	124
Bryneifed	Cered	SN2344	52°4·2'	4°34·6'W	X	145
Bryneira	Powys	SO1190	52°30·3'	3°18·3'W	X	136
Bryn Eisteddfod	Conwy	SH8076	53°16·3'	3°47·6'W	X	116
Bryn Eithen	Denb	SJ1861	53°8·6'	3°13·2'W	X	116
Bryneithin	Carm	SN6325	51°54·6'	3°59·1'W	X	146
Bryn Eithin	Conwy	SH8151	53°2·8'	3°46·1'W	X	116
Bryneithin	Gwyn	SH1829	52°49·9'	4°41·7'W	X	123
Bryn-eithin	Pemb	SN1930	51°56·6'	4°37·6'W	X	145
Bryn Eithin Fm	Flint	SJ2269	53°13·0'	3°9·7'W	FM	117
Bryneithinog	Cered	SN7363	52°15·3'	3°51·2'W	X	146,147
Bryn Eithinog	Cered	SN7866	52°17·0'	3°46·9'W	H	135,147
Bryn Eithinog	Powys	SN8468	52°18·1'	3°41·7'W	X	135,136,147
Bryn-Eithyn Hall	Cered	SN5878	52°23·1'	4°4·8'W	X	135
Bryneiyhyn Outward Bound	Gwyn	SN6296	52°32·9'	4°1·7'W	X	135
Brynele	Cered	SN5660	52°13·4'	4°6·1'W	X	146
Brynelen	Powys	SJ1307	52°39·5'	3°16·8'W	X	125
Brynelltyn	Powys	SJ1519	52°46·0'	3°15·2'W	X	125
Bryn-ellyll	Powys	SJ2129	52°51·4'	3°10·0'W	X	126
Bryn-engan	Gwyn	SH4543	52°58·0'	4°18·1'W	X	123

Bryn Eryr	Denb	SJ0049	53°2·0'	3°29·1'W	X	116
Bryn-eryr	I of Angl	SH5375	53°15·3'	4°11·8'W	X	114,115
Bryn Esgob	Conwy	SH8355	53°5·0'	3°44·4'W	X	116
Bryneurin	Cered	SN2743	52°3·7'	4°31·0'W	X	145
Bryn Euryn	Conwy	SH8379	53°17·9'	3°44·9'W	X	116
Bryn Euryn	Conwy	SH8860	53°7·8'	3°40·0'W	H	116
Bryn Fagas Fm	Flint	SJ2762	53°9·3'	3°5·1'W	FM	117
Bryn-ffanigl-ganol	Conwy	SH9175	53°15·9'	3°37·6'W	X	116
Brynffanigl Isaf	Conwy	SH9074	53°15·3'	3°38·5'W	X	116
Brynffo Fm	Carm	SN8540	52°3·0'	3°40·2'W	FM	147,160
Brynffordd	Conwy	SH9272	53°14·3'	3°36·7'W	X	116
Bryn-Ffyn	Powys	SO0360	52°14·0'	3°24·8'W	X	147
Bryn-ffynnon	Conwy	SH9445	52°59·8'	3°34·4'W	X	116
Bryn-ffynnon	Flint	SJ1467	53°11·8'	3°16·8'W	X	116
Brynffynnon	Gwyn	SH4642	52°57·4'	4°17·2'W	X	123
Bryn-ffynnon	Gwyn	SH4749	53°1·2'	4°16·5'W	X	115,123
Bryn Fm	Carm	SN2740	52°2·1'	4°30·9'W	FM	145
Bryn Fm	Gwyn	SH1926	52°48·3'	4°40·7'W	FM	123
Bryn Fm	Pemb	SN1518	51°50·0'	4°40·7'W	FM	158
Bryn Fm	Powys	SJ0700	52°35·6'	3°22·0'W	FM	136
Bryn Fm	V of Glam	ST0677	51°29·3'	3°20·8'W	FM	170
Brynford	Flint	SJ1774	53°15·6'	3°14·3'W	T	116
Bryn Fuches	I of Angl	SH4890	53°23·3'	4°16·7'W	X	114
Bryn Gareg	Carm	SN6144	52°4·9'	4°1·3'W	F	146
Bryngarn	Brig	SS9683	51°32·4'	3°29·6'W	X	170
Bryn Garreg-lwyd	Cered	SN7053	52°9·8'	3°53·6'W	H	146,147
Bryn Garw	Cered	SN8077	52°22·9'	3°45·4'W	X	135,136,147
Bryn Garw	Powys	SN8361	52°14·3'	3°42·4'W	X	147
Bryn Garw	Powys	SN8471	52°19·7'	3°41·7'W	H	135,136,147
Bryngarw Country Park	Brig	SS9084	51°32·9'	3°34·8'W	X	170
Bryn Gates	Wigan	SD5901	53°30·5'	2°36·7'W	T	108
Bryn Gefeilia	Conwy	SH7456	53°5·4'	3°52·5'W	X	115
Bryn Geinach	Gwyn	SH2034	52°52·6'	4°40·1'W	X	123
Bryn Gelli	Carm	SN5610	51°46·4'	4°4·8'W	X	159
Brynglas	Carm	SN6027	51°55·7'	4°1·8'W	X	146
Bryn Glas	Carm	SN7149	52°7·7'	3°52·7'W	X	146,147
Bryn-glâs	Carm	SN7426	51°55·3'	3°49·5'W	X	146,160
Bryn Glas	Cered	SN6752	52°9·3'	3°56·3'W	X	146
Bryn-glas	Cered	SN7351	52°8·8'	3°51·0'W	X	146,147
Bryn-glas	Cered	SN7681	52°25·0'	3°49·0'W	X	135
Bryn Glas	Cered	SN7682	52°25·6'	3°49·0'W	H	135
Bryn Glas	Conwy	SH8065	53°10·4'	3°47·3'W	X	116
Bryn-glâs	Conwy	SJ0145	52°59·8'	3°28·1'W	X	116
Bryn Glas	Denb	SJ0877	53°17·2'	3°22·4'W	X	116
Bryn-glas	Gwyn	SH5770	53°12·7'	4°8·1'W	X	114,115
Bryn Glâs	Gwyn	SH6137	52°55·0'	4°3·6'W	X	124
Bryn Glas	I of Angl	SH5877	53°16·5'	4°7·4'W	X	114,115
Bryn Glâs	Merth Tyd	SO0411	51°47·6'	3°23·1'W	X	160
Brynglas	Newp	ST3089	51°36·0'	3°0·3'W	T	171
Bryn-glas	Powys	SH8810	52°40·8'	3°39·0'W	X	124,125
Bryn-glas	Powys	SJ0617	52°44·8'	3°23·2'W	H	125
Bryn-glas	Powys	SJ0905	52°38·3'	3°20·3'W	X	125
Bryn-glâs	Powys	SN7499	52°34·7'	3°51·2'W	X	135
Bryn Glas	Powys	SN8657	52°12·2'	3°39·7'W	X	147
Bryn Glâs	Powys	SO2568	52°18·5'	3°5·6'W	H	137,148
Bryn-glas Hall	Powys	SJ0809	52°40·5'	3°21·2'W	X	125
Brynglas Sta	Gwyn	SH6203	52°36·7'	4°1·9'W	T	135
Brynglessy	Powys	SO2138	52°2·3'	3°8·7'W	X	161
Bryn Gloch Farm	Gwyn	SH5357	53°5·6'	4°11·3'W	FM	115
Bryn Gôf	I of Angl	SH5171	53°13·2'	4°13·5'W	X	114,115
Bryn-gogledd	Powys	SJ0416	52°44·2'	3°24·9'W	X	125
Bryngolau	Carm	SN2837	52°0·5'	4°30·0'W	X	145
Bryngolau	Cered	SN4443	52°4·0'	4°16·2'W	X	146
Bryn Golau	Denb	SJ0260	53°7·9'	3°27·5'W	X	116
Bryn Golau	Flint	SJ1469	53°12·9'	3°16·9'W	H	116
Bryngolau	Pemb	SN1440	52°1·9'	4°42·3'W	X	145
Bryn Golau	Rho Cyn Taf	ST0088	51°35·2'	3°26·2'W	T	170
Bryn-goleu	Cered	SN5453	52°9·6'	4°7·7'W	X	146
Bryn-goleu	Cered	SN6984	52°26·5'	3°55·2'W	X	135
Bryn-goleu	Conwy	SH8762	53°8·8'	3°41·0'W	X	116
Bryn-goleu	Conwy	SH9165	53°10·5'	3°37·4'W	X	116
Bryngoleu	Gwyn	SH3837	52°54·6'	4°24·1'W	X	123
Bryn Goleu	Gwyn	SH7134	52°53·5'	3°54·6'W	X	124
Bryngoleu	I of Angl	SH4290	53°23·2'	4°22·1'W	X	114
Bryn-goleu	I of Angl	SH4581	53°18·4'	4°19·2'W	X	114,115
Bryngoleu	Rho Cyn Taf	ST0591	51°36·8'	3°21·9'W	X	170
Bryn Goleu	Shrops	SJ3337	52°55·8'	2°59·4'W	X	126
Bryn Goleu	Wrex	SJ2747	53°1·2'	3°4·9'W	X	117
Bryn Gollen	I of Angl	SH4083	53°19·4'	4°23·7'W	X	114,115
Bryn Gors	I of Angl	SH4473	53°14·1'	4°19·8'W	X	114,115
Bryngranod	Cered	SN4748	52°6·8'	4°13·7'W	X	146
Bryngrunin	Powys	SN7712	51°47·8'	3°46·6'W	X	160
Bryngwallan	I of Angl	SH4875	53°15·3'	4°16·3'W	X	114,115
Bryn-gwas	Swan	SS5493	51°37·3'	4°6·2'W	X	159
Bryngwdyn	Gwyn	SH4139	52°55·7'	4°21·5'W	X	123
Bryngwelltyn	Carm	SN1919	51°50·7'	4°37·3'W	X	158
Bryn Gwenallt	Denb	SJ0647	53°1·0'	3°23·7'W	X	116
Bryngwenith	Brig	SS9682	51°31·9'	3°29·6'W	X	170
Bryn-gwenyn	Carm	SN5210	51°46·4'	4°8·3'W	X	159
Bryn-Gwerfil	Powys	SJ1628	52°50·8'	3°14·4'W	X	125
Bryn-gwian	Conwy	SH8267	53°11·5'	3°45·6'W	X	116
Bryn Gwnog	Conwy	SH8255	53°5·0'	3°45·3'W	X	116
Bryngwran	I of Angl	SH3577	53°16·1'	4°28·0'W	T	114
Bryngwrog	Cered	SN2844	52°4·3'	4°30·2'W	X	145
Bryn Gwydd	Gwyn	SH2639	52°55·5'	4°34·9'W	X	123
Bryngwyddil	Pemb	SN2229	51°56·1'	4°35·0'W	X	145,158
Bryn-gwyddon	I of Angl	SH4281	53°18·4'	4°21·9'W	H	114,115
Bryn-gwyddon	I of Angl	SH4281	53°18·4'	4°21·9'W	X	114
Bryngwydion	Gwyn	SH4453	53°3·3'	4°19·3'W	X	115,123
Bryn-Gwylan	Conwy	SH8869	53°12·6'	3°40·2'W	X	116
Bryngwyn	Carm	SN4725	51°54·4'	4°13·1'W	X	146
Bryn-gwyn	Carm	SN5814	51°48·6'	4°3·2'W	X	159
Bryngwyn	Carm	SN6434	51°59·5'	3°58·5'W	X	146
Bryn-gwyn	Carm	SN6548	52°7·1'	3°57·9'W	X	146
Bryngwyn	Cered	SN2945	52°4·9'	4°29·3'W	T	145
Bryngwyn	Cered	SN3743	52°3·9'	4°22·3'W	X	145
Bryn-gwyn	Cered	SN4661	52°13·8'	4°14·9'W	X	146
Bryngwyn	Cered	SN5365	52°16·1'	4°8·9'W	X	135
Bryn-gwyn	Cered	SN5754	52°10·2'	4°5·1'W	X	146
Bryngwyn	Cered	SN5771	52°19·4'	4°5·5'W	X	135

Bryngwyn	Cered	SN6074	52°21·0'	4°2·9'W	X	135
Bryngwyn	Cered	SN6264	52°15·7'	4°0·9'W	X	146
Bryngwyn	Cered	SN6478	52°23·2'	3°59·5'W	X	135
Bryngwyn	Cered	SN6486	52°27·5'	3°59·7'W	X	135
Bryn Gwyn	Cered	SN7389	52°29·3'	3°51·8'W	H	135
Bryn Gwyn	Cered	SN7486	52°27·7'	3°50·9'W	H	135
Bryn-gwyn	Conwy	SH8749	53°1·8'	3°40·7'W	X	116
Bryngwyn	Denb	SJ0853	53°4·2'	3°22·0'W	X	116
Bryn-gwyn	Flint	SJ2768	53°12·5'	3°5·2'W	X	117
Bryn Gwyn	Gwyn	SH3133	52°52·3'	4°30·3'W	X	123
Bryngwyn	Gwyn	SH4956	53°5·0'	4°14·9'W	X	115,123
Bryngwyn	Gwyn	SH5362	53°8·3'	4°11·5'W	X	114,115
Bryn-gwyn	Gwyn	SH6106	52°38·3'	4°2·9'W	X	124
Bryn Gwyn	Gwyn	SH8630	52°51·6'	3°41·2'W	X	124,125
Bryngwyn	Heref	SO4830	51°58·2'	2°45·0'W	X	149,161
Bryngwyn	I of Angl	SH3371	53°12·8'	4°29·7'W	X	114
Bryngwyn	I of Angl	SH4566	53°10·4'	4°18·7'W	X	114,115
Bryngwyn	Monm	SO3909	51°46·8'	2°52·7'W	T	161
Bryngwyn	Pemb	SM8424	51°52·6'	5°7·9'W	X	157
Bryngwyn	Pemb	SN1730	51°56·5'	4°39·4'W	X	145
Bryn Gwyn	Powys	SH9302	52°36·6'	3°34·4'W	X	136
Bryngwyn	Powys	SH9902	52°36·6'	3°29·1'W	X	136
Bryn-gwyn	Powys	SJ1029	52°51·3'	3°19·8'W	X	125
Bryngwyn	Powys	SJ1817	52°44·9'	3°12·5'W	X	125
Bryn Gwyn	Powys	SO0487	52°28·6'	3°24·4'W	X	136
Bryn-gwyn	Powys	SO1075	52°22·2'	3°18·9'W	X	136,148
Bryngwyn	Powys	SO1849	52°8·2'	3°11·5'W	T	148
Bryn Gwynant	Gwyn	SH6451	53°2·6'	4°1·3'W	X	115
Bryngwyn Bach	Cered	SN7262	52°14·7'	3°52·1'W	X	146,147
Bryngwyn Bach	Denb	SJ0975	53°16·1'	3°21·5'W	X	116
Bryngwyn Fm	Carm	SN6926	51°55·3'	3°53·9'W	FM	146,160
Bryngwyn Fm	Denb	SJ2061	53°8·7'	3°11·4'W	FM	117
Bryngwyn Hall	Flint	SJ1073	53°15·0'	3°20·5'W	X	116
Bryngwyn Hall	Powys	SJ1718	52°45·4'	3°13·4'W	X	125
Bryngwyn Hill	Powys	SO1750	52°8·8'	3°12·4'W	H	148
Bryngwyn Manor	Monm	SO3908	51°46·3'	2°52·7'W	X	161
Bryngwynne	Carm	SN6721	51°52·5'	3°55·5'W	X	159
Bryngwynne Uchaf	Carm	SN5817	51°50·3'	4°3·3'W	X	159
Bryngydfa	Powys	SO1280	52°24·9'	3°17·2'W	H	136
Bryngyrnos	Nth Pt Talb	SS8191	51°36·6'	3°42·7'W	X	170
Bryn-hael	Powys	SO0929	51°57·4'	3°19·1'W	X	161
Bryn Hafod	Conwy	SH8067	53°11·4'	3°47·4'W	X	116
Bryn Hafod	Conwy	SH8962	53°8·9'	3°39·2'W	X	116
Bryn Hafod	Gwyn	SH4349	53°1·2'	4°20·0'W	X	115,123
Bryn Hafod	Powys	SN8519	52°45·6'	3°41·9'W	H	124,125
Bryn Hafod	Powys	SO0079	52°24·2'	3°27·8'W	X	136,147
Brynhafod	Conwy	SH7448	53°1·1'	3°52·3'W	X	115
Bryn Hafod-fraith	Denb	SJ1958	53°7·0'	3°12·2'W	H	116
Bryn-haidd	Denb	SJ0448	53°1·5'	3°25·5'W	X	116
Brynhalen	Gwyn	SH6369	53°12·3'	4°2·7'W	X	115
Bryn Hall	Wigan	SD5801	53°30·5'	2°37·6'W	A	108
Bryn Hall	Cered	SN4741	52°3·0'	4°13·5'W	X	146
Brynhawc	Carm	SN5118	51°50·7'	4°9·4'W	X	159
Brynhawddgar	Cered	SN3344	52°4·4'	4°25·8'W	X	145
Brynhawen	Carm	SN5131	51°57·7'	4°9·7'W	X	146
Brynhebog	Flint	SJ1076	53°16·6'	3°20·6'W	X	116
Bryn Hedydd	Newp	ST2586	51°34·3'	3°4·5'W	X	171
Brynhedydd	Powys	SO0589	52°29·7'	3°23·6'W	X	136
Bryn-helyg	V of Glam	ST0578	51°29·8'	3°21·7'W	X	170
Brynhelygen	Denb	SH9973	53°14·9'	3°30·4'W	X	116
Bryn-hên	Pemb	SN0039	52°1·0'	4°54·5'W	T	145,157
Bryn-henllan	Brig	SS8594	51°38·2'	3°39·3'W	T	170
Brynheulog	Carm	SN2915	51°48·7'	4°28·4'W	X	159
Bryn-heulog	Powys	SO0797	52°34·0'	3°21·9'W	X	136
Brynheulog	Pemb	SN1013	51°47·2'	4°44·9'W	X	158
Bryn Hill	Shrops	SO2986	52°28·3'	3°2·3'W	H	137
Bryn Hill	Cered	SN3449	52°7·1'	4°25·1'W	X	145
Brynhinlle	Cered	SN5873	52°20·4'	4°4·7'W	X	135
Brynhir	Cered	SN6186	52°27·5'	4°2·4'W	H	135
Bryn-hir	Cered	SN6257	52°11·9'	4°0·8'W	X	146
Bryn-Hir						
Bryn Hir	Powys	SN8368	52°18·1'	3°42·6'W	X	135,136,147
Brynhir	Powys	SO0658	52°13·0'	3°22·2'W	X	147
Bryn-hir	Swan	SS5594	51°37·8'	4°5·3'W	X	159
Bryn-hirfaen	Cered	SN6246	52°5·9'	4°0·5'W	X	146
Brynhoffnant	Cered	SN3351	52°8·2'	4°26·0'W	T	145
Bryn Hogfaen	Cered	SN4947	52°6·3'	4°11·9'W	X	146
Brynhonddu	Monm	SO3222	51°53·8'	2°58·9'W	X	161
Brynhope	Cered	SN7165	52°16·3'	3°53·0'W	X	135,147
Brynhovah	Wrex	SJ3843	52°59·1'	2°55·0'W	X	117
Brynhovah Bank	Wrex	SJ3843	52°59·1'	2°55·0'W	X	117
Brynhoveth	Powys	SO1066	52°17·3'	3°18·8'W	X	136,148
Bryn-hownant	Cered	SN6959	52°13·1'	3°54·7'W	X	146
Brynhunog Fawr	Gwyn	SH2030	52°50·5'	4°40·0'W	X	123
Brynhwdog	Powys	SJ1304	52°37·8'	3°16·7'W	X	136
Bryn-hyfryd	Carm	SN6324	51°54·1'	3°59·1'W	X	159
Bryn Hyfryd	Denb	SJ0162	53°9·0'	3°28·4'W	X	116
Brynhyfryd	Denb	SJ0351	53°3·1'	3°26·4'W	X	116
Brynhyfryd	Denb	SJ2143	52°59·0'	3°10·2'W	X	117
Bryn Hyfryd	I of Angl	SH3475	53°15·0'	4°28·9'W	X	114
Brynhyfryd	I of Angl	SH4670	53°12·5'	4°18·0'W	X	114,115
Brynhyfryd	Pemb	SM9627	51°54·5'	4°57·6'W	X	157,158
Brynhyfryd	Pemb	SN0137	52°0·0'	4°53·6'W	X	145,157
Bryn-hyfryd	Powys	SO0891	52°30·8'	3°20·9'W	X	136
Brynhynae	Powys	SO0147	52°7·0'	3°26·4'W	X	147
Bryn-hynod	Gwyn	SH9132	52°52·7'	3°36·8'W	X	125
Brynhynog	Gwyn	SH3636	52°54·0'	4°25·9'W	X	123
Bryn-hynog	Powys	SN8643	52°4·7'	3°39·4'W	X	147,160
Bryn Hywel	Gwyn	SH5141	52°57·0'	4°12·7'W	H	124
Bryniau	Carm	SN5839	52°2·1'	4°3·8'W	X	146
Bryniau	Conwy	SH7880	53°18·4'	3°49·5'W	X	115
Bryniau	Conwy	SH7974	53°15·2'	3°48·4'W	X	115
Bryniau	Denb	SJ0680	53°18·8'	3°24·2'W	T	116
Bryniau	Denb	SJ1752	53°3·8'	3°13·9'W	X	116
Bryniau	Gwyn	SH2639	52°55·5'	4°34·9'W	X	123
Bryniau	I of Angl	SH4267	53°10·8'	4°21·5'W	X	114,115
Bryniau	Merth Tyd	SO0508	51°46·0'	3°22·2'W	X	160
Bryniau-bâch	Cered	SN4854	52°10·0'	4°13·0'W	X	146
Bryniau Brithion	Conwy	SH8652	53°3·4'	3°41·7'W	X	116
Bryniau Bugeiliaid	Conwy	SH8654	53°4·5'	3°41·7'W	X	116
Bryniau Defaid	Conwy	SH8550	53°2·3'	3°42·5'W	X	116

Bryniau Duon	Conwy	SH7846	53°0·1'	3°48·7'W	X	115
Bryniau Duon	Conwy	SH8854	53°4·5'	3°39·9'W	X	116
Bryniau-ednyfed	I of Angl	SH3975	53°15·1'	4°24·4'W	X	114
Bryniau Fm	Wrex	SJ2235	52°54·6'	3°9·2'W	FM	126
Bryniau Gleision	Conwy	SH8468	53°12·0'	3°43·8'W	X	116
Bryniau Gleision	Denb	SJ0032	52°52·8'	3°28·8'W	X	125
Bryniau Gleision	Powys	SO0715	51°49·8'	3°20·6'W	X	160
Bryniau Golau	Gwyn	SH9133	52°53·2'	3°36·8'W	X	125
Bryniau Pair	Conwy	SH8562	53°8·8'	3°42·8'W	X	116
Bryniau Pica	Cered	SN8066	52°17·0'	3°45·2'W	X	135,136,147
Bryniau Poethion	Gwyn	SH7939	52°56·3'	3°47·6'W	X	124
Bryniau Rhyddion	Cered	SN7489	52°29·3'	3°50·9'W	X	135
Bryniau'r-plas	Denb	SJ1749	53°2·2'	3°13·9'W	H	116
Bryniau Ystumcegid	Gwyn	SH5041	52°57·0'	4°13·6'W	H	124
Brynich	Powys	SO0727	51°56·3'	3°20·8'W	X	160
Brynieuau	Powys	SN9756	52°11·8'	3°30·0'W	X	147
Bryn Ifan	Conwy	SH8255	53°5·0'	3°45·3'W	X	116
Bryn Ifan	Gwyn	SH4449	53°1·2'	4°19·1'W	X	115,123
Bryn-Ifan	Gwyn	SH8539	52°56·4'	3°42·3'W	X	124,125
Bryning	Lancs	SD4029	53°45·5'	2°54·2'W	T	102
Bryning Hall Fm	Lancs	SD3929	53°45·5'	2°55·1'W	FM	102
Bryniog	Powys	SO1922	51°53·7'	3°10·2'W	X	161
Bryniog Isaf	Conwy	SH8260	53°7·7'	3°45·4'W	X	116
Bryniog Uchaf	Conwy	SH8360	53°7·7'	3°44·5'W	X	116
Bryn-Isaf Fm	Denb	SJ1556	53°5·9'	3°15·8'W	FM	116
Brynithel	Blae Gw	SO2101	51°42·4'	3°8·2'W	T	171
Bryn Iwan	Carm	SN3131	51°57·4'	4°27·2'W	T	145
Bryn-Kenrick	Conwy	SH9469	53°12·7'	3°34·8'W	X	116
Brynkinalt	Wrex	SJ3037	52°55·8'	3°2·1'W	X	126
Brynkir	Gwyn	SH5243	52°58·1'	4°11·8'W	X	124
Brynleaze Fm	S Glos	ST5783	51°32·9'	2°36·8'W	FM	172
Brynllaeth	Gwyn	SH3737	52°54·6'	4°25·0'W	X	123
Bryn Llech	Conwy	SH8149	53°1·7'	3°46·1'W	H	116
Brynllech	Gwyn	SH8531	52°52·1'	3°42·1'W	X	124,125
Bryn Llefrith	Cered	SN4847	52°6·3'	4°12·8'W	X	146
Brynllefrith	Gwyn	SH4340	52°56·3'	4°19·8'W	X	123
Bryn-llefrith	Nth Pt Talb	SN7312	51°47·8'	3°50·1'W	X	160
Brynllefrith	Powys	SO1066	52°17·3'	3°18·8'W	X	136,148
Bryn Llewelyn	Gwyn	SH2730	52°50·6'	4°33·7'W	X	123
Bryn Llewelyn	I of Angl	SH3994	53°25·3'	4°25·0'W	X	114
Bryn-lliarth	Denb	SJ0561	53°8·5'	3°24·8'W	X	116
Bryn-llici	Powys	SO1126	51°55·8'	3°17·3'W	X	161
Bryn-llin-fawr	Gwyn	SH7729	52°50·9'	3°49·2'W	X	124
Brynllithrig Hall	Denb	SJ0775	53°16·1'	3°23·3'W	X	116
Bryn-llo	Carm	SN5343	52°4·2'	4°8·3'W	X	146
Bryn-llus	Denb	SJ0841	52°57·8'	3°21·8'W	X	125
Brynllwyd	Cered	SN4547	52°6·2'	4°15·4'W	X	146
Bryn-llwyd	Cered	SN7684	52°26·6'	3°49·1'W	H	135
Bryn-llwyd	Cered	SN7776	52°22·3'	3°48·0'W	H	135,147
Bryn-llwyd	Denb	SJ9861	53°8·4'	3°31·1'W	X	116
Bryn-llwyd	Gwyn	SH7407	52°39·0'	3°51·4'W	X	124
Bryn-llwyd	I of Angl	SH3964	53°9·2'	4°24·1'W	X	114
Bryn Llwyd	I of Angl	SH4192	53°24·3'	4°23·1'W	X	114
Bryn Llwyd	I of Angl	SH4967	53°11·0'	4°15·2'W	X	114,115
Bryn-llwyd	Powys	SN9554	52°10·7'	3°31·7'W	X	147
Bryn-llwyd	Powys	SO1253	52°10·3'	3°16·8'W	X	148
Brynllwydwyn	Powys	SN7898	52°34·2'	3°47·6'W	X	135
Bryn-Llwyn	Denb	SJ0641	52°57·7'	3°23·6'W	X	125
Bryn-llwyn	Flint	SJ0781	53°19·3'	3°23·4'W	X	116
Bryn Llychese	Cered	SN8280	52°24·6'	3°43·7'W	X	135,136
Bryn Llydan	Nth Pt Talb	SN8700	51°41·5'	3°37·7'W	X	170
Brynllygoed	Powys	SO0867	52°17·8'	3°20·6'W	X	136,147
Bryn Llyndwr	Powys	SO0683	52°26·5'	3°22·6'W	X	136
Bryn Llyn Egnant	Cered	SN7966	52°17·0'	3°46·0'W	H	135,147
Bryn Llynwyn-ddwr	Nth Pt Talb	SS9099	51°41·0'	3°35·1'W	X	170
Brynllys	Gwyn	SH8515	52°43·5'	3°41·8'W	X	124,125
Brynllys Fm	Cered	SN6288	52°28·6'	4°1·5'W	FM	135
Brynllystyn	Flint	SJ1182	53°19·9'	3°19·8'W	X	116
Brynllywarch	Brig	SS8787	51°34·5'	3°37·5'W	X	170
Brynllywarch	Powys	SO1589	52°29·8'	3°14·7'W	T	136
Bryn-Llywelyn	Carm	SN5136	52°0·4'	4°9·9'W	X	146
Brynlow	Ches	SJ8577	53°17·6'	2°13·1'W	X	118
Bryn Madog	Cered	SN5852	52°9·1'	4°4·1'W	X	146
Bryn-Madog	Conwy	SH8264	53°9·8'	3°45·5'W	X	116
Bryn Madyn Hall	Flint	SJ2174	53°15·7'	3°10·7'W	X	117
Bryn Maelgwyn	Conwy	SH7980	53°18·4'	3°48·6'W	H	115
Brynmaen	Carm	SN5506	51°44·3'	4°5·6'W	X	159
Bryn Maen	Powys	SN9459	52°13·4'	3°32·7'W	X	147
Bryn Maethlu	I of Angl	SH3187	53°21·4'	4°32·0'W	X	114
Brynmarlais	Carm	SN6214	51°48·7'	3°59·7'W	X	159
Bryn-mawndy	Denb	SJ0348	53°1·5'	3°26·4'W	X	116
Bryn-Mawr	Blae Gw	SO1811	51°47·7'	3°11·0'W	T	161
Bryn-mawr	Brig	SS8491	51°36·6'	3°40·1'W	X	170
Bryn-mawr	Carm	SN6046	52°5·9'	4°2·2'W	X	146
Bryn-mawr	Carm	SN6646	52°6·0'	3°57·0'W	X	146
Bryn Mawr	Carm	SN6649	52°7·6'	3°57·1'W	H	146
Bryn Mawr	Carm	SN8024	51°54·3'	3°44·3'W	H	160
Bryn Mawr	Carm	SN8025	51°54·9'	3°44·3'W	H	160
Bryn Mawr	Cered	SN7290	52°29·8'	3°52·7'W	H	135
Bryn Mawr	Cered	SN7452	52°9·4'	3°50·1'W	X	146,147
Bryn Mawr	Cered	SN7772	52°20·2'	3°47·9'W	X	135,147
Bryn Mawr	Cered	SN7953	52°10·0'	3°45·8'W	X	146,147
Bryn Mawr	Cered	SN7956	52°11·6'	3°45·8'W	X	146,147
Bryn-mawr	Conwy	SH7676	53°16·2'	3°51·2'W	X	115
Bryn-mawr	Conwy	SH8044	52°59·0'	3°46·8'W	H	124,125
Bryn-mawr	Conwy	SH9864	53°10·0'	3°31·1'W	X	116
Bryn Mawr	Flint	SJ1873	53°15·1'	3°13·3'W	X	116
Bryn Mawr	Flint	SJ2470	53°13·5'	3°7·9'W	X	117
Bryn-mawr	Gwyn	SH1528	52°49·3'	4°44·3'W	X	123
Bryn-mawr	Gwyn	SH2433	52°52·2'	4°36·5'W	T	123
Bryn Mawr	Gwyn	SH4243	52°57·9'	4°20·8'W	X	123
Bryn Mawr	Gwyn	SH6440	52°56·7'	4°1·0'W	X	124
Bryn Mawr	Gwyn	SH8220	52°46·1'	3°44·5'W	H	124,125
Bryn Mawr	Gwyn	SH8325	52°48·8'	3°43·8'W	X	124,125
Bryn Mawr	Gwyn	SH9018	52°45·1'	3°37·4'W	H	125
Bryn-mawr	I of Angl	SH4078	53°16·7'	4°23·6'W	X	114,115
Bryn Mawr	Nth Pt Talb	SN6908	51°45·6'	3°53·5'W	H	160
Bryn Mawr	Powys	SH9421	52°46·8'	3°33·9'W	H	125
Bryn Mawr	Powys	SH9919	52°45·8'	3°29·4'W	X	125
Bryn Mawr	Powys	SJ0528	52°50·7'	3°24·2'W	H	125
Brynmawr	Powys	SJ0714	52°43·2'	3°22·2'W	X	125
Bryn-mawr	Powys	SJ1104	52°37·8'	3°18·5'W	X	136
Bryn-mawr	Powys	SJ2014	52°43·3'	3°10·7'W	X	126
Bryn-mawr	Powys	SJ2518	52°45·5'	3°6·3'W	T	126
Bryn Mawr	Powys	SN8656	52°11·7'	3°39·7'W	X	147
Bryn Mawr	Powys	SN8853	52°10·1'	3°37·9'W	H	147
Bryn Mawr	Powys	SN8886	52°27·9'	3°38·5'W	H	135,136
Bryn Mawr	Powys	SN9193	52°31·7'	3°36·0'W	X	136
Bryn Mawr	Powys	SN9480	52°24·7'	3°33·1'W	H	136
Bryn Mawr	Powys	SO1382	52°26·0'	3°16·4'W	X	136
Bryn-mawr	Shrops	SO2184	52°27·1'	3°9·4'W	X	137
Bryn-Meherin	Cered	SN6767	52°17·3'	3°56·6'W	X	135
Brynmeini	Carm	SN3326	51°54·7'	4°25·3'W	X	145
Brynmelin	Heref	SO2441	52°4·0'	3°6·1'W	X	148,161
Brynmelyn	Carm	SN4926	51°55·0'	4°11·3'W	X	146
Bryn-melyn	Gwyn	SH8928	52°50·5'	3°38·5'W	X	124,125
Bryn-melyn	Gwyn	SH9936	52°55·0'	3°29·7'W	X	125
Bryn-melyn	Nth Pt Talb	SN7310	51°46·7'	3°50·1'W	X	160
Brynmelyn	Powys	SH8005	52°38·0'	3°46·0'W	X	124,125
Bryn-melyn	Powys	SN7498	52°34·2'	3°51·1'W	X	135
Bryn Melyn	Powys	SN9319	51°51·8'	3°32·8'W	X	160
Brynmelyn	Powys	SO1018	51°51·4'	3°18·0'W	X	161
Brynmelyn	Powys	SO1473	52°21·1'	3°15·4'W	X	136,148
Brynmelys	Powys	SO1357	52°12·5'	3°16·0'W	X	148
Brynmenyn	Brig	SS9084	51°32·9'	3°34·8'W	T	170
Bryn Meurig	I of Angl	SH5774	53°14·9'	4°8·2'W	X	114,115
Brynmeurig	Powys	SH8505	52°38·1'	3°41·6'W	X	124,125
Bryn Mill	Corn	SW9863	50°26·2'	4°50·3'W	X	200
Brynmill	Swan	SS6392	51°36·8'	3°58·3'W	T	159
Bryn Moel	Cered	SN6952	52°9·3'	3°54·5'W	X	146
Bryn-moel	Conwy	SH7453	53°3·8'	3°52·4'W	X	115
Bryn-moel	Powys	SH8504	52°37·5'	3°41·6'W	X	135,136
Bryn Moel	Powys	SN7791	52°30·4'	3°48·3'W	H	135
Bryn Moel	Powys	SN8594	52°32·1'	3°41·3'W	H	135,136
Bryn Moel	Powys	SN9359	52°13·4'	3°33·6'W	X	147
Brynmoelddu	Powys	SN9352	52°9·6'	3°33·5'W	X	147
Bryn-moelyn Ho	Gwyn	SH3336	52°54·0'	4°28·6'W	X	123
Bryn Môr	I of Angl	SH4791	53°23·9'	4°17·7'W	X	114
Brynmorfudd	Conwy	SH8064	53°9·8'	3°47·3'W	T	116
Bryn-Morfydd	Conwy	SH8876	53°16·4'	3°40·4'W	X	116
Bryn Morfydd Hotel	Denb	SJ0762	53°9·1'	3°23·0'W	X	116
Brynmorlo	Gwyn	SN6698	52°34·0'	3°58·2'W	X	135
Bryn Mulan	Denb	SJ0563	53°9·6'	3°24·8'W	H	116
Bryn Mwysau	Cered	SN7050	52°8·2'	3°53·6'W	X	146,147
Brynmyllt	Conwy	SH8453	53°3·9'	3°43·5'W	X	116
Bryn Myrddin	Carm	SN4421	51°52·2'	4°15·6'W	T	159
Brynna	Rho Cyn Taf	SS9883	51°32·4'	3°27·9'W	T	170
Bryn-nantllech	Conwy	SH9468	53°12·2'	3°34·8'W	X	116
Brynnau Gwynion	Rho Cyn Taf	SS9782	51°31·9'	3°28·7'W	T	170
Bryn-Neuadd	Gwyn	SH5241	52°57·0'	4°11·8'W	X	124
Bryn-newydd	Denb	SJ1841	52°57·8'	3°12·8'W	T	125
Bryn Newydd	Wrex	SJ4241	52°58·0'	2°51·4'W	X	117
Bryn Hill	Corn	SW9762	50°25·6'	4°51·1'W	X	200
Bryn Nicol	Carm	SN8244	52°5·1'	3°42·9'W	H	147,160
Bryn-Oawe	Carm	SN5226	51°55·0'	4°8·7'W	X	146
Bryn Ocyn	Denb	SJ0258	53°6·9'	3°27·4'W	H	116
Bryn-ocyn Fm	Denb	SJ0358	53°6·9'	3°26·6'W	FM	116
Brynodol	Gwyn	SH2536	52°53·8'	4°35·7'W	X	123
Bryn-oer Patch	Caer	SO1209	51°46·6'	3°16·1'W	X	161
Bryn Offa	Wrex	SJ3249	53°2·3'	3°0·4'W	T	117
Brynog	Cered	SN5257	52°11·7'	4°9·5'W	X	146
Brynonnen	Cered	SN3757	52°11·5'	4°22·7'W	X	145
Brynore	Shrops	SJ3635	52°54·8'	2°56·7'W	T	126
Brynowen	Cered	SN6088	52°28·6'	4°3·3'W	X	135
Brynoyre	Powys	SO1022	51°53·6'	3°18·1'W	X	161
Bryn Pabo	I of Angl	SH3888	53°22·1'	4°25·7'W	X	114
Brynpedol	Carm	SN6914	51°48·8'	3°53·6'W	X	160
Bryn-penarth	Powys	SJ1004	52°37·8'	3°19·4'W	T	136
Bryn Pen-y-lan	Wrex	SJ3342	52°58·5'	2°59·5'W	T	117
Bryn Person	Conwy	SH8676	53°16·4'	3°42·2'W	X	116
Bryn-Perthy	Powys	SJ2515	52°43·9'	3°6·2'W	X	126
Bryn-picca	Powys	SO0684	52°27·0'	3°22·6'W	X	136
Bryn-pig	Gwyn	SH7630	52°51·4'	3°50·1'W	H	124
Bryn Poeth	Conwy	SH9060	53°7·8'	3°38·2'W	X	116
Bryn-Polyn	Denb	SJ0473	53°15·0'	3°25·9'W	X	116
Brynposteg Hill	Powys	SN9682	52°25·8'	3°31·4'W	H	136
Bryn-prydydd	Gwyn	SH7422	52°47·1'	3°51·7'W	X	124
Bryn Pydew	Conwy	SH8079	53°17·9'	3°47·6'W	T	116
Bryn-re	Gwyn	SH7033	52°53·0'	3°55·5'W	X	124
Brynrefail	Gwyn	SH5562	53°8·4'	4°9·7'W	T	114,115
Brynrefail	I of Angl	SH4886	53°21·2'	4°16·6'W	T	114
Brynreidon	Carm	SN5030	51°57·1'	4°10·6'W	X	146
Bryn Rhedyn	Conwy	SH7677	53°16·8'	3°51·2'W	X	115
Brynrhedyn	Conwy	SH9764	53°10·0'	3°32·0'W	X	116
Bryn-rhôs	Swan	SS6297	51°39·5'	3°59·3'W	X	159
Bryn Rhudd	Cered	SN6955	52°10·9'	3°54·6'W	H	146
Bryn Rhudd	Cered	SN8278	52°23·5'	3°43·6'W	X	135,136,147
Bryn-rhudd	Conwy	SH7964	53°9·8'	3°48·2'W	X	115
Bryn Rhudd	Powys	SN8858	52°12·8'	3°38·0'W	X	147
Bryn Rhug	Conwy	SH8256	53°5·5'	3°45·3'W	X	116
Brynrhug	Gwyn	SH7116	52°43·8'	3°54·2'W	X	124
Brynrhug	Powys	SJ1104	52°37·8'	3°18·5'W	X	136
Bryn-Rhug Fm	Brig	SS8691	51°36·6'	3°38·4'W	FM	170
Bryn Rhydd	Gwyn	SH2638	52°54·9'	4°34·9'W	X	123
Brynrhydd	Gwyn	SH4239	52°55·8'	4°20·6'W	X	123
Brynrhydderch	Monm	SO3310	51°47·3'	2°57·9'W	X	161
Bryn Rhyd-yr-Arian	Conwy	SH9567	53°11·6'	3°33·9'W	T	116
Bryn-rhys	Conwy	SH8076	53°16·3'	3°47·6'W	T	116
Bryn Robin	Conwy	SJ0063	53°9·5'	3°29·3'W	X	116
Brynrodyn	Cered	SN6088	52°28·6'	4°3·3'W	X	135
Bryn Rodyn	Conwy	SH8776	53°16·4'	3°41·3'W	X	116
Bryn Rodyn	Gwyn	SH3538	52°55·1'	4°26·9'W	X	123
Bryn Rodyn	I of Angl	SH4570	53°12·5'	4°18·9'W	X	114,115
Brynrorin	Powys	SO1495	52°33·0'	3°15·7'W	X	136
Bryn Rosa	Denb	SJ0563	53°9·6'	3°24·8'W	X	116
Bryn Rossett	Wrex	SJ4640	52°57·5'	2°47·8'W	X	117
Bryn Rug	Flint	SJ1670	53°13·5'	3°15·1'W	X	116
Brynsadler	Rho Cyn Taf	ST0280	51°30·9'	3°24·4'W	T	170
Brynsadwrn	Powys	SO0456	52°11·9'	3°23·9'W	X	147
Bryn Saer	Flint	SJ2769	53°13·0'	3°5·2'W	X	117
Bryn Saint	Denb	SJ0642	52°58·3'	3°23·6'W	X	125
Bryn Saith Marchog	Denb	SJ0750	53°2·6'	3°22·8'W	T	116
Brynscolfa	Powys	SO0070	52°19·4'	3°27·6'W	X	136,147
Brynsegur	Cered	SN4742	52°3·6'	4°13·5'W	X	146
Bryn-seir	Cered	SN6570	52°18·9'	3°58·4'W	X	135
Bryn-sela	Powys	SO1054	52°10·9'	3°18·6'W	X	148
Bryn-selwrn	Gwyn	SH9735	52°54·4'	3°31·5'W	X	125
Bryn Serth	Blae Gw	SO1410	51°47·2'	3°14·4'W	H	161
Bryn Sgurboriau	Denb	SJ1047	53°1·0'	3°20·1'W	X	116
Bryn Shop	Shrops	SO1783	52°26·6'	3°12·9'W	X	136
Brynsiencyn	I of Angl	SH4867	53°10·9'	4°16·1'W	T	114,115
Brynsifiog	Powys	SO1441	52°3·9'	3°14·9'W	X	148,161
Bryn Sion	Flint	SJ1371	53°14·0'	3°17·8'W	A	116
Bryn-Sion	Gwyn	SH8616	52°44·0'	3°40·9'W	X	124,125
Bryn Siriol	Flint	SJ1970	53°13·5'	3°12·4'W	X	116
Brynsiriol	Pemb	SN2042	52°3·1'	4°37·1'W	X	145
Bryn Siwrnai	Brig	SS8793	51°37·7'	3°37·6'W	X	170
Brynspard Fm	Heref	SO2841	52°4·0'	3°2·6'W	FM	148,161
Brynsworthy	Devon	SS5331	51°3·8'	4°5·5'W	T	180
Bryn-sych	Powys	SO1585	52°27·6'	3°14·7'W	X	136
Bryn-sych	V of Glam	SS9570	51°25·4'	3°30·2'W	X	170
Bryn Syldy	Conwy	SH8261	53°8·2'	3°45·4'W	X	116
Bryntail	Powys	SN9187	52°28·4'	3°35·9'W	X	136
Bryn Tail	Rho Cyn Taf	ST0989	51°35·8'	3°18·4'W	X	171
Bryntaldwyn	Caer	ST1193	51°38·0'	3°16·8'W	X	171
Bryn-tân	Conwy	SH8861	53°8·3'	3°40·1'W	X	116
Bryn Tanat	Powys	SJ2421	52°47·1'	3°7·2'W	T	126
Bryn Tangor	Denb	SJ1146	53°0·5'	3°19·2'W	X	116
Bryn-teg	Carm	SN4903	51°42·6'	4°10·7'W	X	159
Brynteg	Carm	SN6522	51°53·1'	3°57·3'W	X	159
Brynteg	Carm	SN6843	52°4·4'	3°55·2'W	X	146
Bryn-teg	Cered	SN3551	52°8·2'	4°24·3'W	X	145
Brynteg	Cered	SN4843	52°4·1'	4°12·7'W	X	146
Brynteg	Gwyn	SH7032	52°52·4'	3°55·5'W	X	124
Brynteg	I of Angl	SH4982	53°19·1'	4°15·6'W	T	114,115
Brynteg	Pemb	SN0426	51°54·1'	4°50·6'W	X	145,157,158
Bryn-teg	Powys	SJ1022	52°47·5'	3°19·7'W	X	125
Bryn Teg	Powys	SO0222	51°53·5'	3°25·1'W	X	160
Brynteg	Rho Cyn Taf	ST0584	51°33·1'	3°21·8'W	X	170
Brynteg	Wrex	SJ3052	53°3·9'	3°2·3'W	T	117
Bryntegid	Gwyn	SH9134	52°53·8'	3°36·8'W	X	125
Bryn-Teifi	Cered	SN3839	52°1·8'	4°21·3'W	X	145
Brynteilo	Carm	SN6024	51°54·1'	4°1·7'W	X	159
Brynteilog	Cered	SN3553	52°9·3'	4°24·3'W	X	145
Brynterfyn	Flint	SJ0979	53°18·3'	3°21·5'W	X	116
Bryn, The	Caer	ST1390	51°36·4'	3°15·0'W	X	171
Bryn, The	Wrex	SJ4241	52°58·0'	2°51·4'W	A	117
Brynthomas	Powys	SO1062	52°15·2'	3°18·7'W	X	148
Bryntirion	Brig	SS8880	51°30·7'	3°36·5'W	T	170
Bryntirion	Gwyn	SH5368	53°11·6'	4°11·6'W	A	114,115
Bryntirion	Gwyn	SH9133	52°53·2'	3°36·8'W	X	125
Bryntirion	I of Angl	SH4565	53°9·8'	4°18·7'W	X	114,115
Bryn Tirion	I of Angl	SH4981	53°18·5'	4°15·6'W	X	114,115
Bryn-tirion	I of Angl	SH5086	53°21·2'	4°14·8'W	X	114
Bryntirion	Powys	SJ1005	52°38·4'	3°19·4'W	X	125
Bryntirion Hall	Flint	SJ2958	53°7·1'	3°3·2'W	X	117
Bryn Titi	Powys	SN9375	52°22·0'	3°33·9'W	H	136,147
Bryntowyn	Carm	SN2918	51°50·3'	4°28·5'W	X	159
Bryn Trapau	Cered	SN8265	52°16·5'	3°43·4'W	H	135,136,147
Bryn Trillyn	Conwy	SH9459	53°7·3'	3°34·6'W	H	116
Bryn-Tudur	Powys	SH7701	52°35·8'	3°48·6'W	X	135
Bryn Twr	I of Angl	SH4174	53°14·6'	4°22·6'W	X	114,115
Bryntwrog	I of Angl	SH4179	53°17·3'	4°22·7'W	X	114,115
Bryn Tygg Fm	Flint	SJ3063	53°9·8'	3°2·4'W	FM	117
Bryn Tyn-llwyn	Cered	SN7577	52°22·8'	3°49·8'W	H	135,147
Bryn-tywarch	Powys	SN8426	51°55·5'	3°40·8'W	X	160
Bryn-tywydd	Conwy	SH9473	53°14·9'	3°34·9'W	X	116
Bryn-uchel-isaf	Powys	SH8508	52°39·7'	3°41·6'W	X	124,125
Bryn Villa	Wrex	SJ4049	53°2·3'	2°53·3'W	X	117
Bryn Vyrnwy Fm	Powys	SJ2320	52°46·6'	3°8·1'W	FM	126
Brynwell	V of Glam	ST1474	51°27·7'	3°13·9'W	X	171
Brynwern Br	Powys	SO0156	52°11·8'	3°26·5'W	X	147
Bryn-wern Hall	Powys	SO0055	52°11·3'	3°27·4'W	X	147
Bryn Wg	Powys	SH7901	52°35·8'	3°46·8'W	H	135
Brynwgan	Carm	SN6425	51°54·7'	3°58·2'W	X	146
Bryn-wg-isaf	Powys	SH7901	52°35·8'	3°46·8'W	X	135
Bryn-whilach	Swan	SN6400	51°41·2'	3°57·7'W	X	159
Brynwicket Fm	Carm	SN5209	51°45·8'	4°8·3'W	FM	159
Bryn-Withan	Carm	SN5507	51°44·8'	4°5·6'W	X	159
Brynwl	Carm	SN2922	51°52·5'	4°28·7'W	X	145,159
Bryn-y-baal	Flint	SJ2664	53°10·3'	3°6·0'W	X	117
Bryn-y-bar	I of Angl	SH2875	53°14·9'	4°34·3'W	X	114
Bryn y Beddau	Cered	SN7787	52°28·3'	3°48·3'W	X	135
Bryn-y-Brain	Powys	SN8199	52°34·8'	3°45·0'W	H	135,136
Bryn y Brath	Powys	SH9501	52°36·0'	3°32·6'W	X	136
Bryn y Cae	Brig	SS9490	51°36·2'	3°31·4'W	X	170
Bryn-y-castell	Gwyn	SH6101	52°35·6'	4°2·7'W	X	135
Bryn y Castell	Powys	SH9704	52°37·7'	3°30·9'W	H	136
Bryn y Castell	Powys	SH9705	52°38·2'	3°30·9'W	X	125
Bryn y Castell	Powys	SO2972	52°20·7'	3°2·1'W	A	137,148
Bryn-ychain	Gwyn	SH4649	53°1·2'	4°17·4'W	X	115,123
Brynycil	Powys	SO1397	52°34·1'	3°16·6'W	X	136
Bryn-y-clochydd	Conwy	SH8760	53°7·8'	3°40·9'W	X	116
Bryn-y-cochin	Shrops	SJ3635	52°54·8'	2°56·7'W	T	126
Bryn-y-crofftau	Cered	SN7463	52°15·3'	3°50·4'W	H	146,147
Bryn y Fan	Powys	SN9388	52°29·0'	3°34·1'W	H	136
Bryn-y-fawnog	Conwy	SH7759	53°7·1'	3°49·9'W	X	115
Bryn-y-fawnog	Conwy	SH8256	53°5·5'	3°45·3'W	X	116
Bryn y Fawnog	Powys	SO0397	52°34·0'	3°25·5'W	X	136
Bryn-y-fedwen	I of Angl	SH4670	53°12·5'	4°18·0'W	X	114,115
Bryn-y-fedwen	Powys	SJ0318	52°45·3'	3°25·8'W	X	125
Bryn y Fedwen	Powys	SN8495	52°32·7'	3°42·2'W	H	135,136
Bryn-y-fedwen	Shrops	SJ2322	52°47·6'	3°8·1'W	X	126
Bryn-y-ffynnon	Denb	SJ0853	53°4·2'	3°22·0'W	X	116
Bryn-y-ffynnon	Wrex	SJ2439	52°56·8'	3°7·5'W	X	126
Brynyffynnon Fm	Flint	SJ2460	53°8·1'	3°7·8'W	FM	117
Bryn y Gadair	Powys	SN9594	52°32·3'	3°32·5'W	H	136
Bryn-y-Garn	Powys	SN8836	52°0·9'	3°37·5'W	H	160
Bryn-y-garreg	Flint	SJ2370	53°13·5'	3°8·8'W	X	117
Bryn-y-garth	Powys	SO1844	52°5·5'	3°11·4'W	X	148,161

Bryn y Gorlan	Cered	SN7454	52°10·4′	3°50·2′W	X	146,147
Bryn y Gors-goch	Conwy	SH9555	53°5·2′	3°33·7′W	X	116
Bryn-y-groes	Carm	SN4904	51°43·1′	4°10·8′W	X	159
Bryn-y-groes	Powys	SO0557	52°12·4′	3°23·0′W	X	147
Bryn-y-groes	Powys	SO0694	52°32·4′	3°22·8′W	X	136
Bryn-y-grog	Wrex	SJ3448	53°1·8′	2°58·6′W	X	117
Bryn-y-gwalia	Powys	SJ1924	52°48·7′	3°11·7′W	X	125
Brynygwenin	Monm	SO3316	51°50·6′	2°58·0′W	T	161
Bryn-y-gwin	Gwyn	SH7117	52°44·4′	3°54·2′W	X	124
Bryn-y-gwrgi	Conwy	SH9950	53°2·5′	3°30·0′W	X	116
Bryn-y-gwynt Isaf	Denb	SJ0563	53°9·6′	3°24·8′W	X	116
Bryn-y-gwynt Uchaf	Denb	SJ0463	53°9·6′	3°25·7′W	X	116
Bryn y Lloi	Powys	SH9604	52°37·7′	3°31·8′W	X	136
Bryn-y-maen	Conwy	SH8376	53°16·3′	3°44·9′W	T	116
Bryn-y-maen	Powys	SO1657	52°12·5′	3°13·4′W	X	148
Bryn-y-maen Fm	Conwy	SH8375	53°15·8′	3°44·8′W	FM	116
Bryn-y-mor	Carm	SN3807	51°44·5′	4°20·4′W	X	159
Bryn-y-mor	Gwyn	SH5700	52°35·0′	4°6·2′W	T	135
Bryn-y-mor	Gwyn	SH5706	52°38·2′	4°6·4′W	X	124
Brynynyd	Carm	SN4716	51°49·5′	4°12·8′W	X	159
Bryn-Ynyr	Conwy	SH8967	53°11·6′	3°39·3′W	X	116
Bryn-ynys	Gwyn	SH3835	52°53·5′	4°24·1′W	X	123
Bryn-y-pentre Wood	Powys	SO0793	52°31·9′	3°21·9′W	F	136
Bryn-y-pin	Denb	SH9873	53°14·9′	3°31·3′W	X	116
Bryn-y-plentyn	Shrops	SJ3229	52°51·5′	3°0·2′W	X	126
Bryn yr Aran	Powys	SN9395	52°32·8′	3°34·3′W	X	136
Bryn-yr-aur	Conwy	SH8869	53°12·6′	3°40·2′W	X	116
Bryn-yr-efail uchaf	Gwyn	SH4843	52°58·0′	4°15·4′W	X	123
Bryn-yr-eglwys	Carm	SN5528	51°56·1′	4°6·2′W	X	146
Bryn-yr-Eglwys	Cered	SN4848	52°6·8′	4°12·8′W	X	146
Bryn yr Eithin	Flint	SJ1370	53°13·4′	3°17·8′W	H	116
Bryn-yr-eithin	Wrex	SJ3155	53°5·5′	3°1·4′W	X	117
Bryn-yr-Eos	Wrex	SJ2840	52°57·4′	3°3·9′W	T	117
Bryn-yr-Eryr	Gwyn	SH3947	53°0·0′	4°23·6′W	X	123
Bryn yr Hen Bobl	I of Angl	SH5169	53°12·1′	4°13·4′W	X	114,115
Bryn yr Hen Bobl (Chambered Cairn)	I of Angl	SH5169	53°12·1′	4°13·4′W	A	114,115
Bryn-y-rhyd	Carm	SN5908	51°45·4′	4°2·2′W	X	159
Bryn-y-rhyd	Cered	SN6852	52°9·3′	3°55·4′W	X	146
Bryn yr Hydd	Cered	SN7787	52°28·3′	3°48·3′W	X	135
Bryn-yr-hydd	Powys	SO1841	52°3·9′	3°11·4′W	X	148,161
Bryn yr Hydd Common	Powys	SO1841	52°3·9′	3°11·4′W	X	148,161
Bryn yr Hyrddod	Cered	SN8169	52°18·6′	3°44·3′W	X	135,136,147
Bryn yr Ieir	Powys	SN8372	52°20·3′	3°42·6′W	H	135,136,147
Brynyrodyn	Denb	SJ1759	53°7·5′	3°14·0′W	X	116
Bryn-yr-odyn	Denb	SJ2048	53°1·6′	3°11·2′W	X	117
Bryn yr Oerfa	Powys	SN9094	52°32·2′	3°36·9′W	H	136
Bryn-yr-ogof	Denb	SJ1956	53°5·9′	3°12·2′W	T	116
Bryn-yr-orsedd	Denb	SJ1548	53°1·6′	3°15·6′W	X	116
Bryn yr wyn	Powys	SN8392	52°31·0′	3°43·1′W	X	135,136
Brynyrychain	Cered	SN5777	52°22·6′	4°5·7′W	X	135
Bryn Ysbio	Powys	SJ0029	52°51·2′	3°28·7′W	X	125
Bryn Ysguthan	Powys	SH9311	52°41·4′	3°34·6′W	X	125
Bryn-y-tail	Powys	SN9187	52°28·4′	3°35·9′W	H	136
Bryn-y-Wrach	Brig	SS9286	51°34·0′	3°33·1′W	X	170
Bryn y Wyntyll	Powys	SO0275	52°22·1′	3°26·0′W	X	136,147
Bryn-y-wystyn	Shrops	SJ3223	52°48·3′	3°0·1′W	X	126
Bryony Hill	Devon	SS5908	50°51·5′	3°59·8′W	X	191
Brysgyni-uchaf	Gwyn	SH4249	53°1·1′	4°20·9′W	X	115,123
Bry yr wyn	Powys	SN8392	52°31·0′	3°43·1′W	X	135,136
Bu	Orkney	HY2304	58°55·2′	3°19·8′W	X	6,7
Bu	Orkney	HY4119	59°3·5′	3°1·2′W	X	6
Bu	Orkney	HY5041	59°15·4′	2°52·1′W	X	5
Bu	Orkney	HY6224	59°6·3′	2°39·3′W	X	5
Buachailean	Arg & Bt	NS1270	55°53·4′	4°59·9′W	H	63
Buachaill Breige	Stir	NN5418	56°20·2′	4°21·3′W	H	57
Buachaille Bréige	Aberd	NO0285	56°57·0′	3°36·2′W	H	43
Buachaille Brèige	Arg & Bt	NN2443	56°33·0′	4°51·3′W	X	50
Buachaille Breige	Arg & Bt	NN3143	56°33·2′	4°44·5′W	X	50
Buachaille Etive Beag	Highld	NN1854	56°38·8′	4°57·7′W	H	41
Buachaille Etive Mór	Highld	NN2053	56°38·3′	4°55·7′W	H	41
Buail' a' Ghioll	N Eil	NF8130	57°15·2′	7°17·0′W	X	22
Buail a Muigh	N Eil	NB5363	58°29·4′	6°13·8′W	X	8
Buaile an Fharaidh	Highld	NG3330	57°17·2′	6°25·4′W	X	32
Buailebhal Mòr	N Eil	NB1940	58°15·8′	6°47·0′W	H	8,13
Buaile Caragarry	N Eil	NF9263	57°33·4′	7°8·5′W	X	18
Buaile Dubh	N Eil	NF7846	57°23·7′	7°21·2′W	T	22
Buaile Dubh Ard	Highld	NG3041	57°23·0′	6°29·1′W	X	23
Buaile Mhór	N Eil	NB4025	58°8·5′	6°24·6′W	X	14
Buaile-mhòr	N Eil	NF8856	57°29·5′	7°12·0′W	X	22
Buaile na Cloiche	N Eil	NB4431	58°11·9′	6°20·9′W	X	8
Buaile na h-Ochd	N Eil	NB4839	58°16·3′	6°17·4′W	X	8
Buaile nan Caorach	N Eil	NB5166	58°30·9′	6°16·1′W	X	8
Buaile Rairnis	N Eil	NF8649	57°25·6′	7°13·5′W	X	22
Buailteach	Aberd	NO2793	57°1·6′	3°11·7′W	X	37,44
Bualintur	Highld	NG4020	57°12·1′	6°17·8′W	T	32
Bualnaluib	Highld	NG8690	57°51·2′	5°35·9′W	X	19
Buan	Orkney	HY3209	58°58·0′	3°10·5′W	X	6,7
Buarthau	Denb	SJ1060	53°8·0′	3°20·3′W	X	116
Buarthau	Flint	SJ2460	53°8·1′	3°7·8′W	X	117
Buarthau	Gwyn	SH6247	53°0·4′	4°3·0′W	X	115
Buarth Berran	Gwyn	SH5764	53°9·5′	4°7·9′W	X	114,115
Buarth Maen	Torf	ST2599	51°41·3′	3°4·7′W	X	171
Buarthmeini	Gwyn	SH8232	52°52·6′	3°44·8′W	X	124,125
Buarthre	Gwyn	SH7426	52°49·3′	3°51·8′W	X	124
Buarth y Caerau	Powys	SO0713	51°48·7′	3°20·6′W	X	160
Buarth y Gaer	Nth Pt Talb	SS7693	51°37·6′	3°47·1′W	A	170
Buarth-yr-ê	Powys	SJ0931	52°52·4′	3°20·7′W	X	125
Bubb Down Hill	Dorset	ST5906	50°51·4′	2°34·6′W	X	194
Bubbenhall	Warw	SP3672	52°20·9′	1°27·9′W	T	140
Bubbenhall Br	Warw	SP3572	52°20·9′	1°28·8′W	X	140
Bubbenhall Ho	Warw	SP3771	52°20·4′	1°27·0′W	X	140
Bubbenhall Wood	Warw	SP3671	52°20·4′	1°27·9′W	F	140
Bubble Hill	N Yks	SD8095	54°21·3′	2°18·0′W	X	98
Bubbleton	Pemb	SS0998	51°39·1′	4°45·3′W	X	158
Bubblewell	Glos	SO8700	51°42·2′	2°10·9′W	T	162
Bubbly Buss	E Loth	NT5285	56°3·6′	2°45·8′W	X	66
Bubb's Hill	Glos	SO9613	51°49·2′	2°3·1′W	X	163
Bubhurst	Kent	TQ8241	51°8·6′	0°36·5′E	X	188
Bubnell	Derby	SK2472	53°14·9′	1°38·0′W	T	119
Bubnell Cliff	Derby	SK2471	53°14·4′	1°38·0′W	X	119
Bubney	Shrops	SJ5142	52°58·6′	2°43·4′W	X	117
Bubney Moor	Shrops	SJ5141	52°58·1′	2°43·4′W	X	117
Bubwith	E Yorks	SE7136	53°49·2′	0°54·9′W	T	105,106
Bubwith Rail Trail	E Yorks	SE7437	53°49·7′	0°52·1′W	X	105,106
Buccleuch	Scot Bord	NT3214	55°25·2′	3°4·0′W	T	79
Buccleuch Fm	Northnts	SP9073	52°21·1′	0°40·3′W	FM	141
Bucehayes Fm	Devon	ST2105	50°50·6′	3°6·9′W	FM	192,193
Buces	Suff	TM1165	52°14·8′	1°5·9′E	X	155
Buchaam	Aberd	NJ3913	57°12·5′	3°0·1′W	X	37
Buchal	Pth & Kin	NO2751	56°39·0′	3°11·0′W	X	53
Buchan	D & G	NS7104	55°19·0′	4°1·5′W	X	77
Buchan	D & G	NX4180	55°5·6′	4°29·1′W	X	77
Buchan	D & G	NX7661	54°55·9′	3°55·7′W	X	84
Buchanan Castle	Stir	NS4688	56°3·9′	4°28·0′W	X	57
Buchanan Home Fm	Stir	NS4688	56°3·9′	4°28·0′W	FM	57
Buchanan Old Ho	Stir	NS4588	56°3·8′	4°28·9′W	X	57
Buchanan Smithy	Stir	NS4689	56°4·4′	4°28·0′W	T	57
Buchan Burn	D & G	NX4282	55°6·7′	4°28·2′W	W	77
Buchan Country Park	W Susx	TQ2434	51°5·7′	0°13·4′W	F	187
Buchanhaven	Aberd	NK1247	57°31·0′	1°47·5′W	T	30
Buchan Hill	D & G	NX4281	55°6·1′	4°28·2′W	H	77
Buchan Hill	W Susx	TQ2533	51°5·2′	0°12·5′W	T	187
Buchan Line Walkway	Aberd	NJ9243	57°28·9′	2°7·5′W	X	30
Buchan Ness	Aberd	NK1342	57°28·3′	1°46·5′W	X	30
Buchans, The	C of Edin	NT1779	56°0·1′	3°19·4′W	X	65,66
Buchanstone	Aberd	NJ6526	57°19·7′	2°34·4′W	X	38
Buchanty	Pth & Kin	NN9328	56°26·2′	3°43·7′W	T	52,58
Buchanty Burn	Pth & Kin	NN9326	56°25·1′	3°43·6′W	W	52,58
Buchany	Stir	NN7102	56°11·8′	4°4·3′W	T	57
Bucharn	Aberd	NJ5236	57°25·0′	2°47·5′W	X	29
Bucharn	Aberd	NO6593	57°1·9′	2°34·1′W	X	38,45
Buchesydd	Gwyn	SH7721	52°46·6′	3°49·0′W	X	124
Buches y Foelortho	Powys	SJ0421	52°46·9′	3°25·0′W	X	125
Buchley	E Dunb	NS5972	55°55·5′	4°15·0′W	T	64
Buchlyvie	Stir	NS5793	56°6·8′	4°17·5′W	T	57
Buchlyvie Muir	Stir	NS5891	56°5·7′	4°16·5′W	X	57
Buchromb	Moray	NJ3144	57°29·1′	3°8·6′W	X	28
Buchtrig	Scot Bord	NT7714	55°25·4′	2°21·4′W	X	80
Buchts	Aberd	NJ9958	57°37·0′	2°0·5′W	X	30
Bucinch	Stir	NS3891	56°5·3′	4°35·8′W	X	56
Buck	Moray	NJ3924	57°18·4′	3°0·3′W	X	37
Buckabank	Cumbr	NY3749	54°50·2′	2°58·4′W	T	85
Buckabarrow Downs	Corn	SX1760	50°24·9′	4°34·2′W	X	201
Bucka Hill	Derby	SK2877	53°17·6′	1°34·4′W	X	119
Buckanay Fm	Suff	TM3542	52°1·8′	1°26·0′E	FM	169
Buckator	Corn	SX1193	50°42·6′	4°40·2′W	X	190
Buckbarrow	Cumbr	NY1305	54°26·2′	3°20·1′W	X	89
Buckbarrow	Cumbr	NY1306	54°26·8′	3°20·1′W	X	89
Buck Barrow	Cumbr	SD1591	54°18·7′	3°18·0′W	H	96
Buckbarrow Beck	Cumbr	SD1391	54°18·7′	3°19·8′W	W	96
Buckbarrow Crag	Cumbr	NY4807	54°27·6′	2°47·7′W	X	90
Buck Beck	NE Lincs	TA2705	53°31·8′	0°4·6′W	W	113
Buck Beck	N Yks	SD7280	54°13·1′	2°25·3′W	W	98
Buck Br	Norf	TG2232	52°50·6′	1°18·2′E	X	133
Buck Burn	Northum	NY5890	55°12·4′	2°39·2′W	W	80
Buckbury	Worcs	SO8434	52°0·5′	2°13·6′W	T	150
Buckby Folly	Northnts	SP6568	52°18·6′	1°2·4′W	X	152
Buckby Lodge	Northnts	SP6369	52°19·2′	1°4·1′W	X	152
Buckcastle Hill	Heref	SO5625	51°55·5′	2°38·0′W	X	162
Buck Cleuch	D & G	NS7401	55°17·5′	3°58·6′W	X	77
Buck Cleugh	Scot Bord	NT3314	55°25·2′	3°3·1′W	X	79
Buck Crag	Cumbr	NY4214	54°31·3′	2°53·3′W	X	90
Buck Crag	Cumbr	NY4304	54°25·9′	2°52·3′W	X	90
Buck Crag	Cumbr	SD4081	54°13·5′	2°54·8′W	X	96,97
Buck Crags	Cumbr	NY5007	54°27·6′	2°45·9′W	X	90
Buck Craig	Stir	NN3522	56°22·0′	4°39·8′W	X	50
Buckdas of Cairnbaber	D & G	NX4876	55°3·6′	4°22·4′W	X	77
Buckden	Cambs	TL1967	52°17·5′	0°14·9′W	T	153
Buckden	N Yks	SD9477	54°11·6′	2°5·1′W	T	98
Buckden	N Yks	SD9579	54°12·6′	2°4·2′W	X	98
Buckden Beck	N Yks	SD9477	54°11·6′	2°5·1′W	W	98
Buckden Pike	N Yks	SD9678	54°12·1′	2°3·3′W	H	98
Buckden Wood	Cambs	TL1767	52°17·5′	0°16·7′W	X	153
Buckenham	Norf	TG3505	52°35·7′	1°28·6′E	T	134
Buckenham Carrs	Norf	TG3505	52°35·7′	1°28·6′E	X	134
Buckenham Ho	Norf	TM0790	52°28·3′	1°3·3′E	X	144
Buckenham Tofts Park	Norf	TL8495	52°31·5′	0°43·1′E	X	144
Buckenhill Manor	Heref	SO6556	52°12·3′	2°30·3′W	X	149
Buckerell	Devon	ST1200	50°47·8′	3°14·5′W	T	192,193
Buckerell Knap	Devon	ST1201	50°48·3′	3°14·6′W	H	192,193
Bucket Corner	Hants	SU4021	50°59·4′	1°25·4′W	T	185
Bucket Fm	N Yks	SD9945	53°54·3′	2°0·5′W	FM	103
Buckethole Fm	Somer	SS8745	51°11·8′	3°36·7′W	FM	181
Bucket Rocks	Northum	NU0053	55°46·5′	1°59·6′W	X	75
Buckets Down Fm	Hants	SU4453	51°16·7′	1°21·8′W	FM	185
Buckette	Pemb	SM9531	51°56·6′	4°58·6′W	X	157
Buck Farm Ho	Win & Maid	SU8574	51°27·7′	0°46·2′W	X	175
Buckfast	Devon	SX7367	50°29·6′	3°47·1′W	T	202
Buckfastleigh	Devon	SX7366	50°29·0′	3°47·0′W	T	202
Buckfastleigh Moor	Devon	SX6767	50°29·5′	3°52·1′W	X	202
Buck Fell	Northum	NY5990	55°12·4′	2°38·2′W	H	80
Buck Fm	Wrex	SJ4342	52°58·6′	2°50·5′W	FM	117
Buck Gates, The	Notts	SK6369	53°13·1′	1°3·0′W	X	120
Buckhall	Kent	TQ9139	51°7·3′	0°44·2′E	X	189
Buckham	Dorset	ST4703	50°49·7′	2°44·8′W	T	193
Buckham Down	Dorset	ST4703	50°49·7′	2°44·8′W	X	193
Buckham Hill	E Susx	TQ4520	50°57·9′	0°4·3′E	X	198
Buckham Hill Fm	E Susx	TQ4420	50°57·9′	0°3·4′E	FM	198
Buckham Hill Ho	E Susx	TQ4420	50°57·9′	0°3·4′E	X	198
Buckham Mills	Dorset	ST4704	50°50·2′	2°44·8′W	X	193
Buckham's Walls	Northum	NT7911	55°23·8′	2°19·5′W	X	80
Buckham's Walls Burn	Northum	NT8111	55°23·8′	2°17·6′W	W	80
Buckhatch Fm	Essex	TQ7799	51°39·9′	0°34·0′E	FM	167
Buckhaven	Fife	NT3598	56°10·5′	3°2·4′W	T	59
Buck Haw Brow	N Yks	SD7965	54°5·1′	2°18·8′W	X	98
Buckhayes	Devon	SS9718	50°57·4′	3°27·6′W	X	181
Buck Hazels	Derby	SK2840	52°57·6′	1°34·6′W	X	119,128
Buck Head	Durham	NZ1424	54°36·9′	1°46·6′W	X	92
Buckherd Bottom	Hants	SU2008	50°52·5′	1°42·6′W	X	195
Buck Hill	Dorset	SY6899	50°47·6′	2°26·9′W	H	194
Buck Hill	Leic	SK5016	52°44·6′	1°15·2′W	X	129
Buck Hill	Wilts	ST9770	51°26·0′	2°2·2′W	T	173
Buckhole Fm	Medway	TQ7775	51°27·0′	0°33·2′E	FM	178
Buckholm	Scot Bord	NT4838	55°38·2′	2°49·1′W	T	73
Buckholme Island	Cumbr	NY1933	54°41·4′	3°15·0′W	X	89,90
Buckholme Wood	Cumbr	NY5225	54°37·3′	2°44·2′W	F	90
Buckholm Hill	Scot Bord	NT4937	55°37·7′	2°48·2′W	H	73
Buckholt	Monm	SO5016	51°50·7′	2°43·2′W	T	162
Buckholt Fm	E Susx	TQ6520	50°57·6′	0°21·4′E	FM	199
Buckholt Fm	E Susx	TQ7411	50°52·6′	0°28·8′E	FM	199
Buckholt Fm	Hants	SU2732	51°5·4′	1°36·5′W	FM	184
Buckholt Fm	Kent	TR1050	51°12·9′	1°0·8′E	FM	179,189
Buckholt, The	Glos	SO8913	51°49·2′	2°9·2′W	X	163
Buckholt Wood	Glos	SO8913	51°49·2′	2°9·2′W	F	163
Buckholt Wood	Monm	SO5016	51°50·7′	2°43·2′W	F	162
Buckhood	Angus	NO3563	56°45·5′	3°3·3′W	X	44
Buckhorn	Devon	SX3799	50°46·3′	4°18·3′W	T	190
Buckhorn Weston	Dorset	ST7524	51°1·1′	2°21·0′W	T	183
Buckhurst	Kent	TQ8340	51°8·0′	0°37·3′E	T	188
Buckhurst Fm	E Susx	TQ4833	51°4·9′	0°7·2′E	FM	188
Buckhurst Fm	Kent	TQ7837	51°6·5′	0°33·0′E	FM	188
Buckhurst Fm	Lancs	SD8115	53°38·1′	2°16·8′W	A	109
Buckhurst Hill	Essex	TQ4193	51°37·3′	0°2·6′E	T	177
Buckhurst Park	E Susx	TQ5035	51°5·9′	0°8·9′E	X	188
Buckhurst Place	E Susx	TQ6032	51°4·1′	0°17·4′E	X	188
Buckie	Aberd	NJ8916	57°14·3′	2°10·5′W	X	38
Buckie	Moray	NJ4165	57°40·5′	2°58·9′W	T	28
Buckie Braes	Pth & Kin	NO1022	56°23·2′	3°27·0′W	X	53,58
Buckie Cottage	D & G	NY1673	55°2·9′	3°18·5′W	X	85
Buckiemill	Angus	NO6953	56°40·3′	2°29·9′W	X	54
Buckies	Angus	NO4164	56°46·1′	2°57·5′W	X	44
Buckies	Highld	ND1063	58°33·0′	3°32·3′W	X	11,12
Buckies Hill	Highld	ND1062	58°32·5′	3°32·3′W	H	11,12
Buckies Leys	Aberd	NO7082	56°56·0′	2°29·1′W	X	45
Buckie's Mill	Aberd	NO7883	56°56·5′	2°21·2′W	X	45
Buckingham	Bucks	SP6933	51°59·7′	0°59·3′W	T	152,165
Buckingham Barn	W Susx	TQ2106	50°50·7′	0°16·5′W	X	198
Buckingham Palace	C of West	TQ2979	51°29·9′	0°8·1′W	X	176
Buckingham's Fm	Essex	TL6029	51°56·4′	0°20·1′E	FM	167
Buckinghams Leary	Devon	SS6529	51°2·9′	3°55·2′W	X	180
Buckingham Thick Copse	Northnts	SP7043	52°5·1′	0°58·3′W	F	152
Buckinghill Fm	Surrey	TQ1541	51°9·6′	0°20·9′W	FM	187
Buckland	Bucks	SP8812	51°48·2′	0°43·0′W	T	165
Buckland	Devon	SX6743	50°16·6′	3°51·6′W	T	202
Buckland	Devon	SX8147	50°18·9′	3°39·9′W	X	202
Buckland	Devon	SX8771	50°31·9′	3°35·3′W	T	202
Buckland	Glos	SP0836	52°1·6′	1°52·6′W	T	150
Buckland	Hants	SZ3196	50°46·0′	1°33·2′W	T	196
Buckland	Heref	SO5556	52°12·3′	2°39·1′W	X	149
Buckland	Herts	TL3533	51°59·0′	0°1·7′W	T	166
Buckland	Kent	TR3042	51°8·1′	1°17·7′E	T	179
Buckland	Oxon	SU3498	51°41·0′	1°30·1′W	T	164
Buckland	Surrey	TQ2250	51°14·4′	0°14·7′W	T	187
Buckland	Thurr	TQ6777	51°28·3′	0°24·7′E	X	177,178
Buckland Abbey	Devon	SX4866	50°28·7′	4°8·2′W	A	201
Buckland Bank	E Susx	TQ3611	50°53·2′	0°3·6′W	X	198
Buckland Barton	Devon	SX8871	50°31·9′	3°34·4′W	X	202
Buckland Beacon	Devon	SX7373	50°32·8′	3°47·2′W	X	191
Buckland Brewer	Devon	SS4120	50°57·7′	4°15·5′W	T	180,190
Buckland Burn	D & G	NX6948	54°48·8′	4°1·9′W	W	83,84
Buckland Common	Bucks	SP9206	51°44·9′	0°39·6′W	T	165
Buckland Common	Devon	SX7374	50°33·4′	3°47·2′W	X	191
Buckland Dinham	Somer	ST7551	51°15·7′	2°21·1′W	T	183
Buckland Down	Devon	SS4840	51°8·6′	4°10·0′W	X	180
Buckland Down	Somer	ST7251	51°15·7′	2°23·7′W	T	183
Buckland End	Birm	SP1488	52°29·6′	1°47·2′W	T	139
Buckland Fields	Glos	SP0537	52°2·1′	1°55·2′W	X	150
Buckland Filleigh	Devon	SS4609	50°51·8′	4°10·9′W	T	190
Buckland Fleet	Medway	TQ7777	51°28·1′	0°33·3′E	W	178
Buckland Fm	Devon	SS5613	50°54·1′	4°2·5′W	FM	180
Buckland Fm	Kent	TR3156	51°15·6′	1°19·1′E	FM	179
Buckland Fm	Medway	TQ7374	51°26·5′	0°29·8′E	FM	178
Buckland Fm	Powys	SO1322	51°53·6′	3°15·5′W	FM	161
Buckland Fm	Somer	ST1819	50°58·1′	3°9·7′W	FM	181,193
Buckland Fm	Somer	ST2415	50°56·0′	3°4·5′W	FM	193
Buckland Fm	Somer	ST3028	51°3·1′	2°59·5′W	FM	193
Buckland Fm	Wok	SU8073	51°27·2′	0°50·5′W	FM	175
Buckland Hill	Powys	SO1321	51°53·1′	3°15·5′W	H	161
Buckland Hill	Somer	ST1617	50°57·0′	3°11·4′W	H	181,193
Buckland Hill	Somer	ST2713	50°54·9′	3°1·9′W	X	193
Buckland Hill Fm	E Susx	TQ6434	51°5·1′	0°20·9′E	FM	188
Buckland Hills	Surrey	TQ2352	51°15·5′	0°13·8′W	X	187
Buckland Ho	Powys	SO1321	51°53·1′	3°15·5′W	X	161
Buckland Ho (Coll)	Oxon	SU3498	51°41·0′	1°30·1′W	X	164
Buckland Hollow	Derby	SK3651	53°3·5′	1°27·4′W	X	119
Buckland in the Moor	Devon	SX7273	50°32·8′	3°48·0′W	T	191
Buckland Manor	Devon	SS4837	51°7·0′	4°9·9′W	A	180
Buckland Marsh	Oxon	SU3399	51°41·6′	1°31·0′W	T	164
Buckland Marsh Fm	Oxon	SU3299	51°41·6′	1°31·8′W	FM	164
Buckland Mill	Devon	SS4708	50°51·3′	4°10·0′W	X	191
Buckland Monachorum	Devon	SX4868	50°29·8′	4°8·2′W	T	201
Buckland Newton	Dorset	ST6905	50°50·9′	2°26·0′W	T	194
Buckland Park	Devon	SX6844	50°17·1′	3°50·8′W	X	202
Buckland Rings	Hants	SZ3196	50°46·0′	1°33·2′W	A	196
Buckland Ripers	Dorset	SY6482	50°38·4′	2°30·2′W	T	194
Bucklands	Scot Bord	NT5116	55°26·4′	2°46·0′W	T	79
Buckland St Mary	Somer	ST2713	50°54·9′	3°1·9′W	T	193
Buckland-Tout-Saints	Devon	SX7545	50°17·7′	3°44·9′W	X	202
Buckland Valley	Kent	TR3043	51°8·6′	1°17·7′E	T	179
Buckland Warren	Oxon	SU3396	51°39·9′	1°31·0′W	F	164
Bucklandwharf	Bucks	SP8911	51°47·7′	0°42·2′W	T	165
Buckland Wood	Bucks	SP9107	51°45·5′	0°40·5′W	F	165
Buckland Wood	Glos	SP0935	52°1·0′	1°51·7′W	F	150
Buckland Wood	Somer	ST1817	50°57·0′	3°9·7′W	F	181,193
Bucklandwood Fm	Bucks	SP9107	51°45·5′	0°40·5′W	FM	165
Bucklawren	Corn	SX2755	50°22·4′	4°25·6′W	X	201
Bucklebury	W Berks	SU5570	51°25·8′	1°12·1′W	T	174
Bucklebury Alley	W Berks	SU5170	51°25·8′	1°15·6′W	T	174
Bucklebury Common	W Berks	SU5568	51°24·7′	1°12·2′W	X	174

Bucklebury Farm Park	W Berks	SU5570	51°25·8′	1°12·1′W	X	174
Bucklebury Place	W Berks	SU5668	51°24·7′	1°11·3′W	X	174
Bucklegate	Lincs	TF3335	52°54·0′	0°1·0′W	T	131
Buckle Grove	Beds	TL0834	51°59·9′	0°25·2′W	F	153
Buckleigh	Devon	SS4328	51°2·0′	4°14·0′W	T	180
Bucklerheads	Angus	NO4636	56°31·0′	2°52·2′W	T	54
Buckler's Fm	Essex	TL8724	51°53·2′	0°43·4′E	FM	168
Bucklers Hall Fm	Herts	TL4417	51°50·2′	0°5·8′E	FM	167
Bucklers Hard	Hants	SU4000	50°48·1′	1°25·6′W	T	196
Buckler's Wood	Wilts	ST8543	51°11·4′	2°12·5′W	F	183
Buckle's Gap	Surrey	TQ2259	51°19·2′	0°14·6′W	X	187
Bucklesham	Suff	TM2441	52°1·6′	1°16·3′E	T	169
Bucklesham Hall	Suff	TM2542	52°2·1′	1°17·2′E	X	169
Buckle Street	Worcs	SP1048	52°8·0′	1°50·8′W	X	150
Buckle's Wood	Suff	TM4363	52°12·9′	1°33·8′E	F	156
Buckle Wood	Glos	SO9113	51°49·2′	2°7·4′W	F	163
Buckle Wood	Monm	SO5100	51°42·0′	2°42·2′W	F	162
Buckley	Brad	SD9936	53°49·5′	2°0·5′W	X	103
Buckley	Roch	SD9015	53°38·1′	2°8·7′W	T	109
Buckley	Shrops	SJ3027	52°50·4′	3°2·0′W	X	126
Buckley Fm	Devon	SY1490	50°42·4′	3°12·7′W	FM	192,193
Buckley Fm	Shrops	SJ3617	52°45·1′	2°56·5′W	FM	126
Buckley Green	Warw	SP1567	52°18·3′	1°46·4′W	T	151
Buckley Hall	Lancs	SD6336	53°49·4′	2°33·3′W	X	102,103
Buckley Hill	Sefton	SJ3499	53°29·3′	2°59·3′W	T	108
Buckley Hill Fm	Tames	SJ9199	53°29·5′	2°7·7′W	FM	109
Buckley Mountain	Flint	SJ2764	53°10·3′	3°5·1′W	X	117
Buckley or Bwcle	Flint	SJ2764	53°10·3′	3°5·1′W	T	117
Buckley Wood	Bath & NE Somer	ST5754	51°17·2′	2°36·6′W	F	182,183
Bucklow Fm	Ches	SJ7375	53°16·5′	2°23·9′W	FM	118
Bucklow Hill	Ches	SJ7383	53°20·8′	2°23·9′W	T	109
Buckman Corner	W Susx	TQ1028	51°2·7′	0°25·5′W	X	187,198
Buckman Green Fm	Kent	TQ8841	51°8·5′	0°41·6′E	FM	189
Buckman's Fms	Worcs	SO7849	52°8·6′	2°18·9′W	FM	150
Buckminster	Leic	SK8722	52°47·5′	0°42·2′W	T	130
Buckminster Lodge	Leic	SK8720	52°46·5′	0°42·2′W	X	130
Buckminster Park	Leic	SK8723	52°48·1′	0°42·2′W	X	130
Buckmoorend	Bucks	SP8404	51°43·9′	0°46·6′W	T	165
Buckmore Park	Kent	TQ7463	51°20·6′	0°30·3′E	X	178,188
Bucknall	C of Stoke	SJ9047	53°1·5′	2°8·5′W	T	118
Bucknall	Lincs	TF1768	53°12·0′	0°14·5′W	T	121
Bucknell	Oxon	SP5625	51°55·5′	1°10·7′W	T	164
Bucknell	Shrops	SO3573	52°21·3′	2°56·9′W	T	137,148
Bucknell Ct	Heref	SO4454	52°11·1′	2°48·8′W	X	148,149
Bucknell Hill	Shrops	SO3475	52°22·4′	2°57·8′W	H	137,148
Bucknell Lodge	Oxon	SP5423	51°54·4′	1°12·5′W	X	164
Bucknell Wood	Northnts	SP6544	52°5·7′	1°2·7′W	F	152
Bucknell Wood	Shrops	SO3374	52°21·8′	2°58·6′W	F	137,148
Bucknole Fm	Devon	SY1896	50°45·7′	3°9·4′W	FM	192,193
Bucknowle Ho	Dorset	SY9481	50°38·0′	2°4·7′W	X	195
Buckny Burn	Pth & Kin	NO0548	56°37·1′	3°32·4′W	W	52,53
Buckoak	Ches	SJ5172	53°14·8′	2°43·7′W	T	117
Buckover	S Glos	ST6690	51°36·7′	2°29·1′W	T	162,172
Buckover Fms	S Glos	ST6690	51°36·7′	2°29·1′W	FM	162,172
Buck Park	Brad	SE0635	53°48·9′	1°54·1′W	X	104
Buck Plantn	Norf	TM3087	52°26·2′	1°23·4′E	F	156
Buckpool	Dudley	SO8986	52°28·5′	2°9·3′W	T	139
Buckpool	Moray	NJ4165	57°40·5′	2°58·9′W	T	28
Buckquoy	Orkney	HY3115	59°1·3′	3°11·6′W	X	6
Buckquoy	Orkney	HY3627	59°7·8′	3°6·6′W	X	6
Buckridge	Worcs	SO7274	52°22·0′	2°24·3′W	T	138
Buckrig	D & G	NY0899	55°16·8′	3°26·5′W	X	78
Buck Riggs	Durham	NY9124	54°36·9′	2°7·9′W	X	91,92
Buck Rush Fm	Red & Cl	NZ6916	54°32·3′	0°55·6′W	FM	94
Bucks	Lancs	SD7346	53°54·8′	2°24·2′W	X	103
Bucksburn	C of Aber	NJ8909	57°10·6′	2°10·5′W	T	38
Bucksburn Fm	C of Aber	NJ8908	57°10·0′	2°10·5′W	FM	38
Bucksburn Ho	C of Aber	NJ8908	57°10·0′	2°10·5′W	X	38
Buck's Cross	Devon	SS3423	50°59·2′	4°21·5′W	T	190
Bucks Fm	Herts	TL2907	51°45·0′	0°7·5′W	FM	166
Bucks Fm	I of W	SZ4781	50°37·8′	1°19·7′W	FM	196
Bucksford Manor	Kent	TQ9842	51°8·8′	0°50·2′E	X	189
Buck's Green	Suff	TM1767	52°15·7′	1°11·2′E	X	156
Bucks Green	W Susx	TQ0732	51°4·9′	0°28·0′W	T	187
Buck's Hall	Suff	TM1667	52°15·7′	1°10·3′E	X	156
Buckshaw	Northum	NZ1287	55°10·9′	1°48·3′W	X	81
Buckshaw Fm	Dorset	ST6811	50°54·1′	2°26·9′W	FM	194
Buckshaw Fm	Notts	SK7163	53°9·8′	0°55·9′W	FM	120
Buckshaw Ho	Dorset	ST6811	50°54·1′	2°26·9′W	X	194
Buckshead	Corn	SW8346	50°16·7′	5°2·4′W	X	204
Buck's Head	Dorset	ST4400	50°48·0′	2°47·3′W	X	193
Bucks Head	W Susx	TQ2129	51°3·1′	0°16·0′W	X	187,198
Buck's Head Fm	Staffs	SK1403	52°37·7′	1°47·2′W	FM	139
Buck's Hill	Ches	SJ8570	53°13·9′	2°13·1′W	X	118
Bucks Hill	Herts	TL0500	51°41·6′	0°28·5′W	T	166
Buck's Hill Bottom	Herts	TQ0699	51°41·0′	0°27·6′W	X	166,176
Bucks Horn Oak	Hants	SU8041	51°10·0′	0°51·0′W	T	186
Buckshott	Durham	NY9749	54°50·4′	2°2·4′W	X	87
Buckshott Fell	Durham	NY9748	54°49·9′	2°2·4′W	X	87
Buckside Knowe	Scot Bord	NY5992	55°13·5′	2°38·2′W	X	80
Buckskin	Hants	SU6051	51°15·5′	1°8·0′W	T	185
Bucks Linn	D & G	NX6079	55°5·4′	4°11·2′W	W	77
Buck's Mill	Devon	SS5624	51°0·1′	4°2·8′W	X	180
Buck's Mills	Devon	SS3523	50°59·2′	4°20·7′W	T	190
Buck's Nook	Ghead	NZ1161	54°56·9′	1°49·3′W	X	88
Buckspool	Pemb	SR9694	51°36·7′	4°56·4′W	X	158
Buckstall	Lancs	SD7145	53°54·3′	2°26·1′W	X	103
Bucksteep Manor	E Susx	TQ6516	50°55·4′	0°21·3′E	X	199
Buck Stone	Derby	SK2384	53°21·4′	1°38·9′W	X	110
Buck Stone	Glos	SO5412	51°48·5′	2°39·6′W	X	162
Buck Stone	N Yks	SD9942	53°52·7′	2°0·5′W	X	103
Buck Stone	Scot Bord	NY5096	55°15·6′	2°46·8′W	A	79
Buckstone Ho	Lancs	SD5274	54°9·8′	2°43·7′W	X	97
Buck Stones	Brad	SE0945	53°54·3′	1°51·4′W	X	104
Buckstones Ho	Kirk	SE0113	53°37·1′	1°58·7′W	X	110
Buckstones Moss	Kirk	SE0013	53°37·1′	1°59·6′W	X	110
Buck, The	Moray	NJ4123	57°17·9′	2°58·3′W	H	37
Buckton	E Yorks	TA1872	54°8·1′	0°11·2′W	T	101
Buckton	Heref	SO3873	52°21·3′	2°54·2′W	T	137,148
Buckton	Northum	NU0838	55°38·4′	1°51·9′W	X	75
Buckton Castle	Tames	SD9801	53°30·6′	2°1·4′W	A	109
Buckton Cliffs	E Yorks	TA1774	54°9·1′	0°12·1′W	X	101
Buckton Fm	Devon	SY1490	50°42·4′	3°12·7′W	FM	192,193
Buckton Hall	E Yorks	TA1773	54°8·6′	0°12·1′W	X	101
Buckton Hill	Devon	SY1490	50°42·4′	3°12·7′W	X	192,193
Buckton Moor	Northum	NU0637	55°37·8′	1°53·8′W	X	75
Buckton Moor	Tames	SD9901	53°30·6′	2°0·5′W	X	109
Buckton Park	Heref	SO3973	52°21·3′	2°53·3′W	X	137,148
Buckton Vale	Tames	SD9800	53°30·0′	2°1·4′W	T	109
Bucktor	Devon	SX4869	50°30·3′	4°8·2′W	X	201
Buckwell	Kent	TR1963	51°19·7′	1°9·0′E	X	179
Buckwell	Monm	ST4296	51°39·8′	2°49·9′W	X	171
Buckwell Fm	E Susx	TQ6717	50°55·9′	0°23·0′E	FM	199
Buckwell Fm	Kent	TR0448	51°11·9′	0°55·6′E	FM	179,189
Buckwell Lodge	Leic	SP5983	52°26·7′	1°7·5′W	X	140
Buckwell Place	E Susx	TQ6211	50°52·8′	0°18·6′E	X	199
Buck Wood	Brad	SE1739	53°51·1′	1°44·1′W	F	104
Buck Wood	E Yorks	SE8057	54°0·4′	0°46·3′W	F	106
Buckwood Stubs	Herts	TL0416	51°50·2′	0°29·0′W	X	166
Buckworth	Cambs	TL1476	52°22·4′	0°19·1′W	T	142
Buckworth Wood	Cambs	TL1376	52°22·5′	0°20·0′W	F	142
Buckworthy	Somer	SS8437	51°7·5′	3°39·1′W	X	181
Buckwyns Fm	Essex	TQ6696	51°38·5′	0°24·3′E	FM	167,177
Buckyette	Devon	SX8163	50°27·5′	3°40·2′W	X	202
Buctor	Devon	SX4572	50°31·9′	4°10·8′W	X	201
Buda	Devon	SS4018	50°56·6′	4°16·3′W	X	180,190
Buda	Devon	SS4515	50°55·1′	4°11·9′W	X	180,190
Budbrooke	Warw	SP2565	52°17·2′	1°37·6′W	T	151
Budbrooke Fm	Warw	SP2465	52°17·2′	1°38·5′W	FM	151
Budbrooke Village	Warw	SP2565	52°17·2′	1°37·6′W	A	151
Budby	Notts	SK6170	53°13·6′	1°4·8′W	T	120
Budby Carr	Notts	SK6170	53°13·6′	1°4·8′W	F	120
Budby Castle	Notts	SK6269	53°13·1′	1°3·9′W	X	120
Budby Corner Plantations	Notts	SK6272	53°14·7′	1°3·8′W	X	120
Budby North Forest	Notts	SK6171	53°14·2′	1°4·8′W	X	120
Budby South Forest	Notts	SK6169	53°13·1′	1°4·8′W	X	120
Buddabrake	Shetld	HP6114	60°48·5′	0°52·2′W	X	1
Buddacombe	Devon	SS5126	51°1·1′	4°7·1′W	X	180
Budden's Fm	Dorset	ST8519	50°58·4′	2°12·4′W	FM	183
Budden's Fm	Dorset	SY8789	50°42·3′	2°10·7′W	FM	194
Buddileigh	Staffs	SJ7549	53°2·5′	2°22·0′W	T	118
Buddington Fm	W Susx	SU8823	51°0·2′	0°44·4′W	FM	197
Buddle	Devon	SX4090	50°41·5′	4°15·5′W	X	190
Buddlehayes	Devon	SY1791	50°43·0′	3°10·2′W	X	192,193
Buddle Ho	N Yks	NZ1304	54°26·1′	1°47·6′W	X	92
Buddles Fm	Kent	TR3768	51°21·9′	1°24·7′E	FM	179
Buddleswick	Devon	SS8414	50°55·1′	3°38·6′W	X	181
Buddlewall	Devon	ST3302	50°49·1′	2°56·7′W	X	193
Buddon Burn	Angus	NO5034	56°30·0′	2°48·3′W	W	54
Buddo Ness	Fife	NO5515	56°19·8′	2°43·2′W	X	59
Buddon Ness	Angus	NO5430	56°27·8′	2°44·3′W	X	54
Buddon Wood	Leic	SK5615	52°44·0′	1°9·8′W	F	129
Buddo Rock	Fife	NO5615	56°19·8′	2°42·3′W	X	59
Budds	Kent	TQ5752	51°15·0′	0°15·4′E	X	188
Budd's Fm	Essex	TL6303	51°42·3′	0°21·9′E	FM	167
Budd's Fm	Hants	SU4660	51°20·5′	1°20·0′W	FM	174
Budd's Fm	Kent	TQ9026	51°0·3′	0°42·9′E	FM	189
Bude	Corn	SS2106	50°49·8′	4°32·1′W	T	190
Bude	Devon	SS6103	50°48·8′	3°58·0′W	X	191
Bude	Devon	SX6394	50°44·0′	3°56·1′W	X	191
Bude Aqueduct	Devon	SS3009	50°51·6′	4°24·6′W	W	190
Bude Bay		SS1607	50°50·2′	4°36·4′W	W	190
Bude Fm	Devon	SS5906	50°50·4′	3°59·8′W	FM	191
Bude Fm	Devon	SX5559	50°25·0′	4°2·1′W	FM	202
Bude Haven	Corn	SS2006	50°49·8′	4°33·0′W	W	190
Budgate	Highld	NH8349	57°31·2′	3°56·7′W	X	27
Budgehill Wood	Glos	SP1712	51°48·6′	1°44·8′W	F	163
Budgells Fm	Devon	ST1906	50°51·1′	3°8·7′W	FM	192,193
Budgenor Lodge	W Susx	SU8923	51°0·2′	0°43·5′W	X	197
Budge's Shop	Corn	SX3259	50°24·6′	4°21·5′W	T	201
Budgett Fm	Hants	SU4246	51°12·9′	1°23·5′W	FM	185
Budgett's Cross	Somer	ST1719	50°58·1′	3°10·5′W	X	181,193
Budigarth	Shetld	HP6212	60°47·4′	0°51·2′W	X	1
Budlake	Devon	SS9800	50°47·7′	3°26·5′W	T	192
Budle	Northum	NU1535	55°36·8′	1°45·3′W	X	75
Budle Bay	Northum	NU1535	55°36·8′	1°45·3′W	W	75
Budleigh	Somer	ST1819	50°58·1′	3°9·7′W	T	181,193
Budleigh Fm	Devon	SX7685	50°39·3′	3°44·9′W	FM	191
Budleigh Salterton	Devon	SY0682	50°38·0′	3°19·4′W	T	192
Budle Point	Northum	NU1636	55°37·3′	1°44·3′W	X	75
Budlett's Common	E Susx	TQ4723	50°59·5′	0°6·1′E	T	198
Budloy	Pemb	SN0628	51°55·2′	4°48·9′W	X	145,158
Budna	Beds	TL1447	52°6·8′	0°19·7′W	X	153
Budnall Fm	Bucks	SP7410	51°47·3′	0°55·2′W	FM	165
Budock Water	Corn	SW7832	50°9·0′	5°6·1′W	T	204
Budshaw	N Lanak	NS7962	55°50·4′	3°55·5′W	X	64
Budworth Heath	Ches	SJ6678	53°18·1′	2°30·2′W	T	118
Budworth Mere	Ches	SJ6576	53°17·0′	2°31·1′W	W	118
Budworth Pool	Ches	SJ5965	53°11·1′	2°36·4′W	W	117
Buel Houll	Shetld	HP6214	60°48·5′	0°51·1′W	X	1
Buersil Head	Roch	SD9110	53°35·4′	2°7·7′W	T	109
Buerton	Ches	SJ6843	52°59·2′	2°28·2′W	T	118
Buerton Approach	Ches	SJ4260	53°8·3′	2°51·6′W	X	117
Buerton Hall	Ches	SJ6843	52°59·2′	2°28·2′W	X	118
Buerton Moss	Ches	SJ6844	52°59·8′	2°28·2′W	X	118
Buffet Hill	N Yks	SD6967	54°6·1′	2°28·0′W	X	98
Buffitt	N Yks	SE8383	54°14·4′	0°43·2′W	X	100
Buffler's Holt	Bucks	SP6635	52°0·8′	1°1·9′W	T	152
Bufton	Corn	SW7028	50°6·7′	5°12·7′W	X	203
Bufton	Leic	SK4005	52°38·7′	1°24·1′W	T	140
Bugarth	Shetld	HU5190	60°35·7′	1°3·6′W	X	1,2
Bugbrooke	Northnts	SP6757	52°12·7′	1°0·8′W	T	152
Bugbrooke Mill	Northnts	SP6758	52°13·2′	1°0·8′W	X	152
Bugby's Fm	Herts	TL3423	51°53·6′	0°2·8′W	FM	166
Bugeilyn	Powys	SN8292	52°31·0′	3°43·9′W	W	135,136
Bugeilyn	Powys	SN8292	52°31·0′	3°43·9′W	X	135,136
Bugeulus Fawr	Gwyn	SH1829	52°49·9′	4°41·7′W	X	123
Bugford	Devon	SS6043	51°10·4′	3°59·8′W	T	180
Bugford Fm	Devon	SX8351	50°21·1′	3°38·3′W	FM	202
Buggie	Shetld	HU4226	60°1·3′	1°14·3′W	X	4
Bugglesden	Kent	TQ8636	51°5·8′	0°39·8′E	X	189
Bughead Cross	Devon	SX7385	50°39·3′	3°47·4′W	X	191
Bught Burn	D & G	NX5179	55°5·2′	4°19·6′W	W	77
Bught Fell	D & G	NX2062	54°55·5′	4°48·1′W	H	82
Bught Geo	Orkney	HY6520	59°4·2′	2°36·1′W	X	5
Bught Hill	D & G	NS7819	55°27·2′	3°55·3′W	H	71,78
Bught Hill	Scot Bord	NT1810	55°22·9′	3°17·2′W	H	79
Bught Knowe	D & G	NS7903	55°18·6′	3°54·0′W	X	78
Bught Knowe	D & G	NT0307	55°21·1′	3°31·4′W	H	78
Bught Knowe	D & G	NY3997	55°16·1′	2°57·2′W	H	79
Bughtknowe	E Loth	NT4864	55°52·2′	2°49·4′W	X	66
Bught Knowe	Scot Bord	NT6707	55°21·6′	2°30·8′W	X	80
Bught Knowe	Scot Bord	NT7010	55°23·2′	2°28·0′W	X	80
Bught Knowe	Scot Bord	NY4796	55°15·6′	2°49·6′W	X	79
Bught Knowe	Scot Bord	NY5395	55°15·1′	2°43·9′W	X	79
Bught Knowes	D & G	NT2100	55°17·5′	3°14·2′W	H	79
Bughtknowes	S Lanak	NS9755	55°46·9′	3°38·1′W	X	65,72
Bughtlin	C of Edin	NT1874	55°57·4′	3°18·4′W	T	65,66
Bught Park	Highld	NH6643	57°27·7′	4°13·6′W	X	26
Bught Rig	D & G	NY4189	55°11·8′	2°55·2′W	X	79
Bught Rig	Scot Bord	NT2628	55°32·7′	3°9·9′W	H	73
Bughtrig	Scot Bord	NT7944	55°41·6′	2°19·6′W	X	74
Bught Shank	Scot Bord	NT0617	55°26·5′	3°28·7′W	X	78
Bught Shank	Scot Bord	NY4597	55°16·1′	2°51·5′W	X	79
Bught Sike	Scot Bord	NY5593	55°14·0′	2°42·0′W	W	80
Bught, The	Orkney	HY5729	59°9·0′	2°44·6′W	X	5,6
Buglawton	Ches	SJ8763	53°10·1′	2°11·3′W	T	118
Buglawton Hall Sch	Ches	SJ8864	53°10·6′	2°10·4′W	X	118
Bugle	Corn	SX0158	50°23·5′	4°47·6′W	T	200
Bugle Gate	Worcs	SO8267	52°18·3′	2°15·4′W	T	138,150
Buglehole	Aberd	NJ5843	57°28·8′	2°41·6′W	X	29
Bugle Hole	Devon	SX6046	50°18·1′	3°57·6′W	X	202
Bugley	Dorset	ST7824	51°1·1′	2°18·4′W	T	183
Bugley	Wilts	ST8544	51°11·9′	2°12·5′W	T	183
Bugmore Hill	Hants	SU5937	51°8·0′	1°9·0′W	X	185
Bugsby's Hole	Kent	TQ9773	51°25·5′	0°50·4′E	X	178
Bugsby's Reach	Newham	TQ3980	51°30·3′	0°0·6′E	W	177
Bugsell Mill Fm	E Susx	TQ7225	51°0·1′	0°27·5′E	FM	188,199
Bug Spit	Wirral	SJ2379	53°18·4′	3°8·9′W	X	117
Bugthorpe	E Yorks	SE7757	54°0·4′	0°49·1′W	T	105,106
Bugthorpe Beck	E Yorks	SE7657	54°0·4′	0°50·0′W	W	105,106
Bugthorpe Grange	E Yorks	SE7658	54°1·0′	0°50·0′W	X	105,106
Bu Hill	Orkney	HY2304	58°55·2′	3°19·8′W	X	6,7
Bu'house	Orkney	HY4818	59°3·0′	2°53·9′W	X	6
Buidheanach of Cairntoul	Aberd	NN9695	57°2·3′	3°42·4′W	X	36,43
Buidhe Bheinn	Highld	NG9508	57°7·3′	5°22·7′W	H	33
Building End	Essex	TL4337	52°1·0′	0°5·4′E	T	154
Building Fm	Ghead	NZ1364	54°58·5′	1°47·4′W	FM	88
Building Fm	Shrops	SJ3733	52°53·7′	2°55·8′W	FM	126
Buildings Fm	Donc	SE7011	53°35·7′	0°56·1′W	FM	112
Buildings Fm	Norf	TF8333	52°52·0′	0°43·5′E	FM	132
Buildings Fm	Oxon	SU4698	51°41·0′	1°19·7′W	FM	164
Buildings Fm	Suff	TL7453	52°9·1′	0°33·0′E	FM	155
Buildings Fm, The	Derby	SK3322	52°47·9′	1°30·2′W	FM	128
Buildings, The	Monm	ST3495	51°39·2′	2°56·9′W	X	171
Buildings, The	Shrops	SJ3628	52°51·0′	2°56·6′W	X	126
Buildwas	Shrops	SJ6304	52°38·2′	2°32·4′W	T	127
Buildwas Park	Shrops	SJ6203	52°37·6′	2°33·3′W	X	127
Builg Burn	Aberd	NO6786	56°58·1′	2°32·1′W	W	45
Builg Burn	Moray	NJ1805	57°8·0′	3°20·8′W	W	36
Builg, The	Aberd	NO6985	56°57·6′	2°30·1′W	X	45
Built Fm	Bucks	SU7787	51°34·8′	0°52·9′W	FM	175
Builth Castle	Powys	SO0451	52°9·2′	3°23·8′W	A	147
Builth Road	Powys	SO0253	52°10·2′	3°25·6′W	T	147
Builth Wells or (Llanfair-Ym-Muallt)	Powys	SO0350	52°8·6′	3°24·7′W	T	147
Buinach Hill	Moray	NJ1856	57°35·5′	3°21·8′W	H	28
Buinnach	Moray	NJ4160	57°37·8′	2°58·8′W	X	28
Buistean	N Eil	NB2548	58°20·3′	6°41·5′W	X	8
Buiston	N Ayr	NS4143	55°39·5′	4°31·2′W	X	70
Buistonhead	N Ayr	NS4243	55°39·5′	4°30·3′W	X	70
Buittle Br	D & G	NX8260	54°55·5′	3°50·1′W	X	84
Buittle Burn	D & G	NX8063	54°57·1′	3°52·0′W	W	84
Buittle Hill	D & G	NX8161	54°56·0′	3°51·0′W	H	84
Buittle Mains	D & G	NX8160	54°55·5′	3°51·0′W	X	84
Buittle Place	D & G	NX8161	54°56·0′	3°51·0′W	A	84
Buke Horn Fm	Peterb	TF2605	52°37·9′	0°7·9′W	FM	142
Bukthorn	N Yks	SE7981	54°13·4′	0°46·9′W	X	100
Bulabhall	N Eil	NG0593	57°50·0′	6°57·8′W	H	14,18
Bula-charpach	N Eil	NA9516	58°2·0′	7°9·6′W	X	13
Bul Barrow	Dorset	ST7705	50°50·9′	2°19·2′W	A	194
Bulbarrow Fm	Dorset	ST7805	50°50·9′	2°18·4′W	FM	194
Bulbarrow Hill	Dorset	ST7605	50°50·9′	2°20·1′W	H	194
Bulbeck Common	Northum	NY9352	54°52·0′	2°6·1′W	X	87
Bulbeck Cottage	Northum	NZ0751	54°51·5′	1°53·0′W	X	88
Bulbourne	Herts	SP9313	51°48·7′	0°38·7′W	T	165
Bulbridge	Wilts	SU0830	51°4·4′	1°52·8′W	T	184
Bulbury	Dorset	SY9294	50°45·0′	2°6·4′W	A	195
Bulby	Lincs	TF0526	52°49·5′	0°26·1′W	T	130
Bulby Hall	Lincs	TF0525	52°49·0′	0°26·1′W	X	130
Bulby Hall Wood	Lincs	TF0426	52°49·5′	0°27·0′W	F	130
Bulcamp	Suff	TM4376	52°19·9′	1°34·4′E	X	156
Bulcamp Ho	Suff	TM4675	52°19·3′	1°37·0′E	X	156
Bulcote	Notts	SK6544	52°59·6′	1°1·5′W	T	129
Bulcote Lodge Fm	Notts	SK6444	52°59·6′	1°2·4′W	FM	129
Bulcote Wood	Notts	SK6445	53°0·1′	1°2·4′W	F	129
Buldoo	Highld	NC9967	58°35·0′	3°43·8′W	T	11
Buleney	Highld	ND1255	58°28·7′	3°30·1′W	X	11,12
Bulford	Pemb	SM9110	51°45·2′	5°1·3′W	X	157,158
Bulford	Somer	ST2617	50°57·1′	3°2·8′W	X	193
Bulford	Wilts	SU1743	51°11·4′	1°45·0′W	T	184
Bulford Camp	Wilts	SU1943	51°11·4′	1°43·3′W	T	184
Bulford Field	Wilts	SU1745	51°12·5′	1°45·0′W	X	184
Bulford Mill	Essex	TL7720	51°51·3′	0°34·6′E	X	167
Bulg	Angus	NO5476	56°52·6′	2°44·8′W	H	44
Bulgham Bay	I of M	SC4585	54°14·5′	4°22·3′W	W	95
Bulkamore	Devon	SX7462	50°26·9′	3°46·1′W	X	202
Bulkeley	Ches	SJ5354	53°5·1′	2°41·7′W	T	117
Bulkeley Hall	Ches	SJ5253	53°4·6′	2°42·6′W	X	117

Bulkeley Hall	Shrops	SJ7342	52°58·7'	2°23·7'W	T	118
Bulkeleyhay	Ches	SJ5353	53°4·6'	2°41·7'W	X	117
Bulkeley Hill	Ches	SJ5255	53°5·6'	2°42·6'W	H	117
Bulkeley Memorial	I of Angl	SH5977	53°16·5'	4°6·5'W	X	114,115
Bulkington	Warw	SP3986	52°28·5'	1°25·1'W	T	140
Bulkington	Wilts	ST9458	51°19·5'	2°4·8'W	T	173
Bulkington Fields Fm	Warw	SP4086	52°28·5'	1°24·3'W	FM	140
Bulkworthy	Devon	SS3914	50°54·4'	4°17·0'W	T	190
Bullacebush Fm	Norf	TG3410	52°38·5'	1°27·9'E	FM	133,134
Bullace Trees Fm	Kirk	SE1923	53°42·4'	1°42·3'W	FM	104
Bullaford	Devon	SS8125	51°1·0'	3°41·4'W	X	181
Bullamoor	N Yks	SE3994	54°20·6'	1°23·6'W	T	99
Bulla na h-Acairseid Fhalaich	N Eil	NG2396	57°52·3'	6°39·8'W	X	14
Bulland	Devon	SS4222	50°58·8'	4°14·7'W	X	180,190
Bull and Butcher Fm	Warw	SP3971	52°20·4'	1°25·3'W	FM	140
Bulland Lodge	Somer	ST0527	51°2·3'	3°20·9'W	X	181
Bullapit	Corn	SX3289	50°40·8'	4°22·3'W	X	190
Bullaton Fm	Devon	SX8082	50°37·8'	3°41·4'W	FM	191
Bullatree Hill Fm	Roth	SK5390	53°24·5'	1°11·8'W	FM	111
Bullaval	N Eil	NF9999	57°53·0'	7°4·2'W	H	18
Bull Bank	Lancs	SD6171	54°8·2'	2°35·4'W	X	97
Bull Banks	Glos	SO9408	51°46·5'	2°4·8'W	X	163
Bullbanks Fm	Essex	TL9326	51°54·2'	0°48·7'E	FM	168
Bull Barrow	Dorset	SU0505	50°50·9'	1°55·4'W	A	195
Bull Bay or Porth Llechog	I of Angl	SH4393	53°24·9'	4°21·3'W	W	114
Bull Br	Suff	TL9467	52°16·2'	0°51·0'E	X	155
Bullbridge	Derby	SK3552	53°4·1'	1°28·3'W	T	119
Bullbrook	Brackn	SU8869	51°25·0'	0°43·7'W	T	175
Bullby Hill	Cambs	TL2355	52°11·0'	0°11·7'W	X	153
Bull Cleugh	Cumbr	NY5976	55°4·9'	2°38·1'W	X	86
Bullcleugh Gate	Cumbr	NY5976	55°4·9'	2°38·1'W	X	86
Bull Cliff	V of Glam	ST0966	51°23·4'	3°18·1'W	X	171
Bull Cliff Fm	Wakf	SE2815	53°38·1'	1°34·2'W	FM	110
Bull Close	Cumbr	NY3402	54°24·8'	3°0·6'W	X	90
Bull Close Fm	Derby	SK3576	53°17·0'	1°28·1'W	FM	119
Bull Clough	Sheff	SK1895	53°27·3'	1°43·3'W	X	110
Bull Clough	Sheff	SK1897	53°28·4'	1°43·3'W	X	110
Bullclough	Staffs	SK0554	53°5·2'	1°55·1'W	X	119
Bull Crag	Cumbr	NY2710	54°29·1'	3°7·2'W	X	89,90
Bull Crag	Cumbr	NY2712	54°30·1'	3°7·2'W	X	89,90
Bullcrag Edge	Northum	NY6786	55°10·3'	2°30·7'W	H	80
Bull Dog Channel		TF5933	52°52·5'	0°22·2'E	W	131
Bull Dog Sand	Norf	TF5927	52°49·3'	0°22·0'E	X	131
Bull Dog Sand	Norf	TF6027	52°49·2'	0°22·9'E	X	132
Bullechach	Highld	ND1254	58°28·2'	3°30·0'W	X	11,12
Bulleigh Barton	Devon	SX8565	50°28·6'	3°36·9'W	X	202
Bulleign	Kent	TQ8830	51°2·5'	0°41·3'E	T	189
Bullen Fm	Kent	TQ6649	51°13·2'	0°23·0'E	FM	188
Bullen Green	Suff	TM0946	52°4·6'	1°3·4'E	X	155,169
Bullenhall Fm	Suff	TM1046	52°4·6'	1°4·3'E	FM	155,169
Bullenhill	Wilts	ST8957	51°19·0'	2°9·1'W	T	173
Bullen Ho	I of W	SZ6190	50°42·6'	1°7·8'W	X	196
Bullen's Bank	Heref	SO2741	52°4·0'	3°3·5'W	X	148,161
Bullens Fm	Cambs	TL2165	52°16·4'	0°13·2'W	FM	153
Bullens Fm	Lancs	SD4202	53°30·9'	2°52·1'W	FM	108
Bullen's Fm	Norf	TF9501	52°34·5'	0°53·1'E	FM	144
Bullen's Green	Herts	TL2105	51°44·1'	0°14·5'W	T	166
Bullen's Hill Fm	E Yorks	SE9337	53°49·5'	0°34·8'W	FM	106
Bullen Wood	N Yks	SE4538	53°50·4'	1°18·6'W	F	105
Buller Downs	Corn	SW7039	50°12·6'	5°13·0'W	X	203
Buller's Hill	Devon	SX8884	50°38·9'	3°34·7'W	H	192
Bullersike	Cumbr	NY4662	54°57·2'	2°50·2'W	X	86
Bullers of Buchan	Aberd	NK1038	57°26·2'	1°49·5'W	X	30
Bulley	Glos	SO7619	51°52·4'	2°20·5'W	T	162
Bull Farm	Notts	SK5162	53°9·4'	1°13·8'W	FM	120
Bull Farm Ho	Hants	SU4934	51°6·4'	1°17·6'W	X	185
Bullfer Grove	Norf	TG0135	52°52·7'	0°59·6'E	F	133
Bullfinches	E Susx	TQ5234	51°5·3'	0°10·6'E	X	188
Bull Flag	Orkney	HY5050	59°20·3'	2°52·2'W	X	5
Bullflatt	Cumbr	NY6209	54°28·7'	2°34·8'W	X	91
Bull Fm	Beds	SP9726	51°55·7'	0°35·0'W	FM	165
Bull Fm	Devon	ST2003	50°49·5'	3°7·8'W	FM	192,193
Bull Fm	Kent	TQ6653	51°15·3'	0°23·1'E	FM	188
Bull Fm	Shrops	SJ5501	52°36·5'	2°39·5'W	FM	126
Bull Gate	Ches	SJ9066	53°11·7'	2°8·6'W	X	118
Bullgill	Cumbr	NY0938	54°44·0'	3°24·4'W	T	89
Bullgill	Cumbr	NY7605	54°26·6'	2°21·8'W	X	91
Bull Green	Suff	TL8459	52°12·1'	0°42·0'E	X	155
Bullhall Wood	Devon	SY1793	50°44·1'	3°10·2'W	F	192,193
Bull Hassocks Fm	N Lincs	SE7200	53°29·7'	0°54·5'W	FM	112
Bull Haw Moss	Cumbr	SD2794	54°20·4'	3°7·0'W	X	96,97
Bullhead Fm	Devon	SS5807	50°50·9'	4°0·7'W	FM	191
Bull Hill	Black w Dar	SD7019	53°40·2'	2°26·8'W	X	109
Bull Hill	Derby	SK2046	53°0·9'	1°41·7'W	X	119,128
Bull Hill	Hants	SZ3398	50°47·1'	1°31·5'W	T	196
Bull Hill	Lancs	SD7618	53°39·7'	2°21·4'W	H	109
Bull Hill	Roth	SK5081	53°19·7'	1°14·5'W	X	111,120
Bull Hill Fm	Dorset	SU1013	50°55·2'	1°51·1'W	FM	195
Bull Hole	Arg & Bt	NM3024	56°20·1'	6°21·7'W	W	48
Bull Hole	Lancs	SD8138	53°50·5'	2°16·9'W	X	103
Bull Hole	Pemb	SM7109	51°44·2'	5°18·6'W	W	157
Bullhook	Pemb	SN0520	51°50·9'	4°49·5'W	X	145,158
Bullhope Law	E Loth	NT5460	55°50·1'	2°43·6'W	X	66
Bull House Fm	Lincs	TA0705	53°32·1'	0°22·7'W	FM	112
Bull Hurst	N Yks	SD7760	54°2·4'	2°20·7'W	X	98
Bullhurst Hill	Derby	SK2943	52°59·3'	1°33·7'W	T	119,128
Bullia Skerry	Shetld	HU3536	60°6·7'	1°21·7'W	X	4
Bulliber Down	Pemb	SR9095	51°37·1'	5°1·6'W	X	158
Bullie Burn	Pth & Kin	NN7909	56°15·7'	3°56·8'W	W	57
Bulliemore	Highld	ND1364	58°33·6'	3°29·2'W	X	11,12
Bullimore Fm	Somer	ST6342	51°10·8'	2°31·4'W	FM	183
Bullinghope	Heref	SO5137	52°2·0'	2°42·5'W	T	149
Bullingstone	Kent	TQ5341	51°9·1'	0°11·7'E	X	188
Bullington	Lincs	TF0977	53°17·0'	0°21·5'W	T	121
Bullington Cross Inn	Hants	SU4642	51°10·8'	1°20·1'W	X	185
Bullington End	Mil Key	SP8145	52°6·1'	0°48·6'W	X	152
Bull in the Oak	Leic	SK4203	52°37·6'	1°22·4'W	X	140
Bulliondale Fm	Falk	NS9072	55°56·0'	3°45·2'W	FM	65
Bullions	Fife	NT0384	56°2·6'	3°33·0'W	X	65
Bullions	Northum	NZ0353	54°52·6'	1°56·8'W	X	87
Bullions	Stir	NS8687	56°4·0'	3°49·4'W	X	65
Bull Lane Br	N Yks	SE5761	54°2·7'	1°7·4'W	X	100
Bull Loch	Arg & Bt	NS0173	55°54·8'	5°10·6'W	W	63
Bullman Hills	Cumbr	NY7037	54°43·9'	2°27·5'W	X	91
Bullmire Fm	N Yks	NZ2508	54°28·2'	1°36·4'W	FM	93
Bull Nose Coppice	Northnts	TL0681	52°25·2'	0°26·1'W	F	142
Bullo	Glos	SO6809	51°47·0'	2°27·4'W	T	162
Bulloak Fm	Warw	SP2569	52°19·3'	1°37·6'W	FM	151
Bulloch	Highld	NN2588	56°57·3'	4°52·2'W	X	34,41
Bullock Br	Heref	SO5847	52°7·4'	2°36·4'W	X	149
Bullock Down	E Susx	TQ4103	50°48·8'	0°0·5'E	X	198
Bullock Down	E Susx	TV5896	50°44·7'	0°14·8'E	X	199
Bullock Hill	Bri & Hov	TQ3606	50°50·5'	0°3·7'W	X	198
Bullockhurst Fm	Worcs	SO7371	52°20·4'	2°23·4'W	FM	138
Bullock Lodge Fm	Suff	TL7967	52°16·5'	0°37·8'E	FM	155
Bullocks	Essex	TL5720	51°51·6'	0°17·2'E	X	167
Bullocks Fm	Bucks	SU8193	51°38·0'	0°49·4'W	FM	175
Bullock's Fm	Hants	SU7650	51°14·9'	0°54·3'W	FM	186
Bullocks Fm	N Som	ST4067	51°24·2'	2°51·4'W	FM	171,172,182
Bullock's Hall	Northum	NZ2497	55°16·2'	1°36·9'W	X	81
Bullock's Hill	Somer	ST6848	51°14·1'	2°27·1'W	X	183
Bullock's Horn	Wilts	ST9890	51°36·8'	2°1·3'W	T	163,173
Bullock Steads	N upon Ty	NZ2069	55°1·2'	1°40·8'W	X	88
Bullockstone	Kent	TR1665	51°20·8'	1°6·5'E	T	179
Bullo Pill	Glos	SO6909	51°47·0'	2°26·6'W	W	162
Bulloway's Fm	Wok	SU7563	51°21·9'	0°55·0'W	FM	175,186
Bullow Brook	Devon	SS6507	50°51·0'	3°54·7'W	W	191
Bullpark Wood	Wilts	ST8186	51°34·6'	2°16·1'W	F	173
Bull Piece Plantn	N Yks	TA0084	54°14·8'	0°27·5'W	F	101
Bull Pit	Derby	SK1081	53°19·8'	1°50·6'W	X	110
Bull Point	Devon	SS4646	51°11·8'	4°11·9'W	X	180
Bull Point	Devon	SX4357	50°23·8'	4°12·2'W	X	201
Bull Pot	N Yks	SD7078	54°12·1'	2°27·2'W	X	98
Bullpot Fm	Cumbr	SD6681	54°13·7'	2°30·9'W	FM	98
Bullrenney	I of M	SC3692	54°18·1'	4°30·8'W	X	95
Bull Ring	Derby	SK0778	53°18·2'	1°53·3'W	X	119
Bull Ring Fm	Warw	SP3760	52°14·5'	1°27·1'W	FM	151
Bull Ring (Henge)	Derby	SK0778	53°18·2'	1°53·3'W	A	119
Bull Rock	Arg & Bt	NS1674	55°55·7'	4°56·3'W	X	63
Bull Rock	Glos	ST6599	51°41·6'	2°30·0'W	X	162
Bull Sand Fort		TA3709	53°33·8'	0°4·5'E	X	113
Bull's Ash Corner	Suff	TM0550	52°6·8'	1°0·0'E	X	155
Bull's Br	Somer	ST7744	51°11·9'	2°19·4'W	X	183
Bull's Bridge	Hill	TQ1079	51°30·2'	0°24·5'W	X	176
Bulls Bridge Fm	Essex	TL6639	52°1·7'	0°25·6'E	FM	154
Bull's Bushes Copse	Hants	SU5748	51°13·9'	1°10·6'W	F	185
Bull's Bushes Fm	Hants	SU5748	51°13·9'	1°10·6'W	FM	185
Bull Scar	N Yks	SE0193	54°20·2'	1°58·7'W	X	98
Bullscross	Enf	TL3400	51°41·2'	0°3·3'W	X	166
Bulls Cross	Enf	TQ3499	51°40·7'	0°3·3'W	T	166,176,177
Bulls Cross	Glos	SO8708	51°46·5'	2°10·9'W	X	162
Bull's Cross Wood	Suff	TL9544	52°3·8'	0°51·1'E	F	155
Bulls Fm	Cambs	TL5263	52°14·9'	0°14·0'E	FM	154
Bull's Fm	W Susx	TQ1828	51°2·6'	0°18·6'W	FM	187,198
Bull's Green	Herts	TL2717	51°50·5'	0°9·0'W	T	166
Bull's Green	Norf	TM4194	52°29·7'	1°33·4'E	T	134
Bulls Green	Somer	ST7146	51°13·0'	2°24·5'W	T	183
Bullsgreen Fm	Ches	SJ6156	53°6·2'	2°34·5'W	FM	118
Bull's Hall	Suff	TM1173	52°19·1'	1°6·2'E	X	144,155
Bull's Hall	Suff	TM2167	52°15·6'	1°14·7'E	X	156
Bull's Hall	Suff	TM4260	52°11·3'	1°32·8'E	X	156
Bullshead Fm	Mil Key	SP8151	52°9·3'	0°48·6'W	FM	152
Bull's Hill	Dorset	SY4997	50°46·5'	2°43·0'W	H	193,194
Bull's Hill	Heref	SO5920	51°52·9'	2°35·3'W	T	162
Bulls Hill	Northum	NY8456	54°54·2'	2°14·5'W	X	86,87
Bullsland Fm	Herts	TQ0194	51°38·4'	0°32·0'W	FM	166,176
Bullslaughter Bay	Pemb	SR9494	51°36·7'	4°58·1'W	X	158
Bulls Lodge	Essex	TL7310	51°45·9'	0°30·8'E	X	167
Bullsmill	Herts	TL3115	51°49·3'	0°5·6'W	X	166
Bullsnape Hall	Lancs	SD5740	53°51·5'	2°38·8'W	X	102
Bullspark Wood	Staffs	SK1428	52°51·2'	1°47·1'W	F	128
Bull Spinney	Leic	SP6791	52°31·0'	1°0·4'W	F	141
Bulls' Run	Norf	TL8693	52°30·4'	0°44·8'E	F	144
Bullstone Bed	Cumbr	SD1577	54°11·2'	3°17·7'W	X	96
Bull Stones	Sheff	SK1796	53°27·9'	1°44·2'W	X	110
Bullswater Common	Surrey	SU9554	51°16·9'	0°37·9'W	F	186
Bulls Wood	I of W	SZ4488	50°41·6'	1°22·2'W	F	196
Bull's Wood	Suff	TL9254	52°9·3'	0°48·8'E	F	155
Bullswood Fm	Suff	TL9254	52°9·3'	0°48·8'E	FM	155
Bull, The	Corn	SW8476	50°32·9'	5°2·6'W	X	200
Bull, The	Devon	SX7437	50°13·4'	3°45·6'W	X	202
Bull, The	S Glos	ST5285	51°33·9'	2°41·2'W	X	172
Bull Tor	Derby	SK1472	53°14·9'	1°47·0'W	X	119
Bulltown Fm	Kent	TR0843	51°9·1'	0°58·8'E	FM	179,189
Bullwell Bay	Pemb	SM9003	51°41·4'	5°1·9'W	W	157,158
Bullwood	Arg & Bt	NS1674	55°55·7'	4°56·3'W	T	63
Bull Wood	Beds	TL0918	51°51·2'	0°24·6'W	F	166
Bull Wood	Renf	NS5162	55°50·0'	4°22·3'W	F	64
Bullwood Hall	Essex	TQ8291	51°35·5'	0°38·0'E	X	178
Bully Hill	Lincs	TF1792	53°24·9'	0°14·0'W	X	113
Bully Hill	Lincs	TF3382	53°19·3'	0°0·2'E	X	122
Bully Hill Fm	Lincs	TF1692	53°25·0'	0°14·9'W	FM	113
Bully Hill (Tumuli)	Lincs	TF3382	53°19·3'	0°0·2'E	A	122
Bully Ho	Cumbr	NY1831	54°40·3'	3°15·9'W	X	89,90
Bullyhole Bottom	Monm	ST4696	51°39·8'	2°46·5'W	T	171
Bullymore's Lodge	Northnts	SP9383	52°26·5'	0°37·5'W	X	141
Bully Trees Fm	Brad	SE0036	53°49·5'	1°59·6'W	FM	104
Bulman Hill	Cumbr	NY3543	54°46·9'	3°0·2'W	X	85
Bulman's Rigg	Northum	NY8558	54°55·2'	2°13·6'W	X	87
Bulman Strands	Cumbr	SD4393	54°20·0'	2°52·2'W	X	97
Bulmer	Essex	TL8440	52°1·9'	0°41·3'E	T	155
Bulmer	N Yks	SE6967	54°5·9'	0°56·3'W	T	100
Bulmer Beck	N Yks	SE6967	54°5·9'	0°56·3'W	W	100
Bulmer Hag	N Yks	SE7167	54°5·9'	0°54·4'W	F	100
Bulmer Moss	S Lanak	NS9017	55°26·3'	3°43·9'W	X	71,78
Bulmer Tye	Essex	TL8438	52°0·8'	0°41·3'E	T	155
Bulmoor	Devon	SY2994	50°44·7'	3°0·0'W	X	193
Bulmoor Cross	Devon	SY2994	50°44·7'	3°0·0'W	X	193
Bulmore	Newp	ST3591	51°37·1'	2°55·9'W	X	171
Bulphan	Thurr	TQ6486	51°33·2'	0°22·3'E	T	177
Bulreanrob	Highld	ND2138	58°19·7'	3°20·5'W	X	11
Bulstone	Devon	SY1789	50°41·9'	3°10·1'W	X	192
Bulstrode	Herts	TL0302	51°42·7'	0°30·2'W	T	166
Bulstrode Park	Bucks	SU9888	51°35·2'	0°34·7'W	X	175,176
Bulsworthy Fm	Corn	SX3584	50°38·2'	4°19·6'W	FM	201
Bulta Sound	Shetld	HU3437	60°7·2'	1°22·8'W	W	4
Bulthy	Shrops	SJ3113	52°42·9'	3°0·9'W	T	126
Bulthy Fm	Shrops	SJ3113	52°42·9'	3°0·9'W	FM	126
Bulthy Hill	Shrops	SJ3013	52°42·8'	3°1·8'W	X	126
Bulverhythe	E Susx	TQ7708	50°50·9'	0°31·3'E	T	199
Bulverton	Devon	SY1188	50°41·3'	3°15·2'W	T	192
Bulverton Hill	Devon	SY1088	50°41·3'	3°16·1'W	H	192
Bulwardine	Shrops	SO7991	52°31·2'	2°18·2'W	X	138
Bulwark	Monm	ST5392	51°37·7'	2°40·4'W	T	162,172
Bulwark Croft	Aberd	NJ9345	57°30·0'	2°6·5'W	X	30
Bulwarks, The	Glos	SO8208	51°46·5'	2°15·3'W	X	162
Bulwarks, The	Glos	SO8601	51°42·7'	2°11·8'W	A	162
Bulwarks, The	Leic	SK4023	52°48·4'	1°24·0'W	X	129
Bulwarks, The	V of Glam	ST0866	51°23·4'	3°18·9'W	A	170
Bulwarks, The (Fort)	Leic	SK4023	52°48·4'	1°24·0'W	A	129
Bulwark, The	Cambs	TL3975	52°21·6'	0°2·9'E	A	142,143
Bulwark, The	Swan	SS4492	51°36·6'	4°14·8'W	A	159
Bulwell	C of Nott	SK5345	53°0·2'	1°12·2'W	T	129
Bulwell Forest	C of Nott	SK5445	53°0·2'	1°11·3'W	T	129
Bulwick	Leic	SP6694	52°32·6'	1°1·2'W	T	141
Bulwick Lodge	Northnts	SP9693	52°31·8'	0°34·7'W	X	141
Bulwith Rail Trail	E Yorks	SE7336	53°49·1'	0°53·1'W	X	105,106
Bulworks, The (Fort)	Glos	SO8208	51°46·5'	2°15·3'W	A	162
Bulworthy	Devon	SS5026	51°1·1'	4°7·9'W	X	180
Bulworthy Fms	Devon	SS8517	50°56·7'	3°37·8'W	FM	181
Bulworthy Knap	Devon	SS8618	50°57·2'	3°37·0'W	X	181
Bumblebee Fm	Essex	TL9417	51°49·3'	0°49·3'E	FM	168
Bumble Rock	Corn	SW7011	49°57·5'	5°12·0'W	X	203
Bumble's Green	Essex	TL4005	51°43·8'	0°2·0'E	T	167
Bummers Hill	Herts	TL3928	51°56·2'	0°1·7'E	X	166
Bummers Hill (Tumulus)	Herts	TL3928	51°56·2'	0°1·7'E	A	166
Bumper Castle	Derby	SK2865	53°11·1'	1°34·5'W	X	119
Bumper Castle	N Yks	SE5592	54°19·5'	1°8·8'W	X	100
Bumper Castle	N Yks	SE5871	54°8·1'	1°6·3'W	X	100
Bumper Fm	Carm	SN2324	51°53·4'	4°33·9'W	FM	145,158
Bumper Hall	Darl	NZ3416	54°32·5'	1°28·0'W	X	93
Bumpers	Bucks	SP7605	51°44·5'	0°53·6'W	X	165
Bumpstead Hall	Essex	TL6641	52°2·8'	0°25·6'E	X	154
Bumpstead's Fm	Essex	TL6704	51°42·8'	0°25·4'E	FM	167
Bumpston Cross	Devon	SX7765	50°28·5'	3°43·6'W	X	202
Bumwell Hill	Norf	TM1291	52°28·8'	1°7·7'E	T	144
Bun Abhainn Eadarra	N Eil	NB1304	57°56·2'	6°50·5'W	T	13,14
Bun Abhainn na Cloich	N Eil	NB5350	58°22·4'	6°13·0'W	W	8
Bunacaimb	Highld	NM6588	56°55·7'	5°51·3'W	T	40
Bun a' Ghlinne	N Eil	NB5244	58°19·1'	6°13·6'W	X	8
Bunahoun	Highld	NC8952	58°26·8'	3°53·6'W	X	10
Bun Allt na Criche	Highld	NM9256	56°39·3'	5°23·1'W	W	49
Bunalteachan	Highld	NM7362	56°41·9'	5°42·0'W	X	40
Bun an Amair	N Eil	NF8224	57°12·0'	7°15·5'W	W	22
Bun an Leoib	Arg & Bt	NM4023	56°19·9'	6°11·9'W	W	48
Bun an Lòin	Highld	NM6993	56°58·5'	5°47·6'W	W	40
Bun an t-Sruith	N Eil	NF7100	56°58·7'	7°24·5'W	W	31
Bun-an-uillt	Arg & Bt	NR2969	55°50·5'	6°19·3'W	X	60
Bun an Uillt	N Eil	NF8219	57°9·4'	7°15·1'W	W	31
Bunarkaig	Highld	NN1887	56°56·6'	4°59·1'W	T	34,41
Bunbury	Ches	SJ5658	53°7·3'	2°39·0'W	T	117
Bunbury Heath	Ches	SJ5557	53°6·7'	2°39·9'W	T	117
Bunbury Locks	Ches	SJ5759	53°7·8'	2°38·2'W	X	117
Bun Casgro	N Eil	NB5559	58°27·3'	6°11·5'W	W	8
Bunce Common	Surrey	TQ2046	51°12·3'	0°16·5'W	T	187
Bunce Court	Kent	TQ9353	51°14·8'	0°46·3'E	X	189
Bun Challagrich	N Eil	NG1596	57°52·0'	6°47·9'W	W	14
Bunchrew	Highld	NH6145	57°28·7'	4°18·6'W	T	26
Bunchrew Burn	Highld	NH6143	57°27·6'	4°18·6'W	W	26
Bunchrew Ho	Highld	NH6245	57°28·7'	4°17·6'W	X	26
Buncombe Wood	Somer	ST2032	51°5·1'	3°8·1'W	F	182
Buncton Manor Fm	W Susx	TQ1413	50°54·5'	0°22·3'W	FM	198
Bundalloch	Highld	NG8927	57°17·4'	5°29·6'W	T	33
Bundell's Hill	St Hel	SJ4890	53°24·5'	2°46·5'W	H	108
Bundish Hall	Essex	TL5505	51°43·6'	0°15·1'E	X	167
Bundle Head	Devon	SX9371	50°32·0'	3°30·2'W	X	202
Buness	Shetld	HP6209	60°45·8'	0°51·2'W	X	1
Bu Ness	Shetld	HZ2272	59°32·3'	1°36·2'W	X	4
Bunessan	Arg & Bt	NM3821	56°18·8'	6°13·8'W	T	48
Bungalow	I of M	SC3986	54°14·9'	4°27·9'W	X	95
Bungalow Br	I of M	SC4087	54°15·5'	4°27·0'W	X	95
Bungalow Fm	Cambs	TL5858	52°12·1'	0°19·1'E	FM	154
Bungalow Fm	Leic	SP4899	52°35·4'	1°17·1'W	FM	140
Bungalow Fm	Northnts	SP5742	52°4·6'	1°9·7'W	FM	152
Bungalow Fm	Somer	ST7338	51°8·7'	2°22·8'W	FM	183
Bungalow Fm	Suff	TM1775	52°20·0'	1°11·5'E	FM	156
Bungalow Hill	Cambs	TL5858	52°12·1'	0°19·1'E	X	154
Bungalow Sta	I of M	SC3986	54°14·9'	4°27·9'W	X	95
Bungalow, The	Cumbr	NY4316	54°32·4'	2°52·4'W	X	90
Bungalow, The	Denb	SJ1551	53°3·2'	3°15·7'W	X	116
Bungalow, The	Oxon	SP3743	52°5·3'	1°27·2'W	X	151
Bungate Wood	Essex	TL8324	51°53·3'	0°40·0'E	F	168
Bungay	Suff	TM3389	52°27·2'	1°26·2'E	T	156
Bungay Lake Fm	Worcs	SO9270	52°19·9'	2°6·6'W	FM	139
Bungays Fm	Dorset	ST7417	50°57·3'	2°21·8'W	FM	183
Bungdale Head Fm	N Yks	SE5583	54°14·6'	1°8·9'W	FM	100
Bungehurst Fm	E Susx	TQ5924	50°59·8'	0°16·3'E	FM	199
Bungla Burn	Shetld	HU5293	60°37·3'	1°2·5'W	W	1,2
Bunglan	Shetld	HU4676	60°28·2'	1°9·3'W	X	2,3
Bungsie Burn	D & G	NX1372	55°0·7'	4°55·0'W	W	76
Bûn-idein	Highld	NG4276	57°42·3'	6°19·4'W	X	23
Bunjups Wood	Glos	SO5311	51°48·0'	2°40·5'W	F	162
Bunkegivie	Highld	NH5017	57°13·4'	4°28·6'W	T	35
Bunker Hill	Durham	NZ1152	54°52·0'	1°49·3'W	X	88
Bunker Hill Fm	Leic	SK6319	52°46·1'	1°3·6'W	FM	129
Bunker's Barn	Suff	TL7770	52°18·2'	0°36·2'E	X	144,155
Bunkers Fm	Herts	TL0805	51°44·2'	0°25·8'W	FM	166
Bunkers Fm	Lincs	TF2886	53°21·6'	0°4·2'W	FM	113,122

Bunker's Hill	Beds	TL1948	52°7·3'	0°15·3'W	X	153
Bunkers Hill	Bexley	TQ4972	51°25·9'	0°9·0'E	X	177
Bunker's Hill	Black w Dar	SD6625	53°43·5'	2°30·5'W	X	103
Bunker's Hill	Brad	SE0339	53°51·1'	1°56·8'W	X	104
Bunkers Hill	Brad	SE1336	53°49·4'	1°47·7'W	X	104
Bunker's Hill	Cambs	TF4007	52°38·8'	0°4·6'E	T	142,143
Bunkers Hill	Cambs	TL1071	52°19·8'	0°22·7'W	X	153
Bunkershill	Cumbr	NY3654	54°52·8'	2°59·4'W	X	85
Bunkers Hill	Cumbr	NY4530	54°40·0'	2°50·7'W	X	90
Bunker's Hill	Derby	SK3441	52°58·2'	1°29·2'W	X	119,128
Bunker's Hill	E Yorks	TA2827	53°43·7'	0°3·2'W	X	107
Bunker's Hill	Hants	SU3015	50°56·2'	1°34·0'W	X	196
Bunkers Hill	Hants	SU3801	50°48·7'	1°27·3'W	X	196
Bunkers Hill	Hants	SU6511	50°53·9'	1°4·2'W	X	196
Bunker's Hill	Heref	SO6138	52°2·6'	2°33·7'W	X	149
Bunker's Hill	Kent	TQ9253	51°14·9'	0°45·5'E	X	189
Bunkers Hill	Lancs	SD8739	53°51·1'	2°11·4'W	X	103
Bunkers Hill	Lincs	TF2653	53°3·8'	0°6·8'W	T	122
Bunker's Hill	Norf	TF7525	52°47·9'	0°36·2'E	X	132
Bunker's Hill	Norf	TF7628	52°49·5'	0°37·1'E	X	132
Bunker's Hill	Norf	TF9038	52°54·6'	0°49·9'E	X	132
Bunker's Hill	Norf	TG0231	52°50·5'	1°0·4'E	X	133
Bunker's Hill	Norf	TG0835	52°52·6'	1°5·9'E	X	133
Bunker's Hill	Norf	TG1629	52°49·1'	1°12·7'E	X	133
Bunker's Hill	Norf	TG1809	52°38·3'	1°13·7'E	T	134
Bunkers Hill	Norf	TG1810	52°38·9'	1°13·8'E	X	133,134
Bunkers Hill	Notts	SK5672	53°14·8'	1°9·2'W	X	120
Bunker's Hill	Notts	SK6975	53°16·3'	0°57·5'W	X	120
Bunkers Hill	N Yks	SE3051	53°57·5'	1°32·2'W	X	104
Bunkers Hill	Oxon	SP4717	51°51·2'	1°18·7'W	T	164
Bunker's Hill	Rut	SK9507	52°39·4'	0°35·3'W	X	141
Bunkers Hill	Stock	SJ9389	53°24·1'	2°5·9'W	T	109
Bunker's Hill	Suff	TG5000	52°32·6'	1°41·6'E	T	134
Bunkers Hill	Warw	SP1350	52°9·1'	1°48·2'W	X	151
Bunker's Hill	Warw	SP3658	52°13·4'	1°28·0'W	X	151
Bunkers Hill	Warw	SP4869	52°19·3'	1°17·3'W	X	151
Bunker's Hill Fm	Corn	SW4026	50°4·9'	5°37·7'W	FM	203
Bunker's Hill Fm	Hants	SU7256	51°18·1'	0°57·6'W	FM	175,186
Bunkershill Fm	Kent	TR1946	51°10·5'	1°8·4'E	FM	179,189
Bunker's Hill Fm	Lincs	SK8297	53°28·0'	0°45·5'W	FM	112
Bunkers Hill Fm	Northnts	SP7666	52°17·4'	0°52·7'W	FM	152
Bunkers Hill Fm	Northnts	SP8381	52°25·5'	0°46·4'W	FM	141
Bunkers Hill Fm	Suff	TM3972	52°17·9'	1°30·7'E	FM	156
Bunkers Hill Fm	Warw	SP3764	52°16·6'	1°27·1'W	FM	151
Bunkershill Plantn	E Susx	TQ3709	50°52·1'	0°2·8'W	F	198
Bunkershill Plantn	Norf	TL8396	52°32·1'	0°42·3'E	F	144
Bunkers Hill Wood	Derby	SK2770	53°13·8'	1°35·3'W	F	119
Bunker's Hill Wood	Staffs	SO8782	52°26·4'	2°11·1'W	F	139
Bunkersland	Devon	SS9113	50°54·6'	3°32·6'W	X	181
Bunkers Wood	Leic	SK8131	52°52·5'	0°47·4'W	F	130
Bunkingie	Highld	NH0900	57°3·4'	5°8·5'W	X	33
Bunkle Castle	Scot Bord	NT8059	55°49·7'	2°18·7'W	A	67,74
Bunkle Wood	Scot Bord	NT8158	55°49·1'	2°17·8'W	F	67,74
Bunksland Fm	Devon	SS8526	51°1·5'	3°38·0'W	FM	181
Bunlarie	Arg & Bt	NR7830	55°31·1'	5°30·6'W	X	68,69
Bunloinn Forest	Highld	NH1707	57°7·3'	5°0·9'W	X	34
Bunloit	Highld	NH5025	57°17·7'	4°28·9'W	T	26,35
Bun Loyne	Highld	NH2109	57°8·5'	4°57·0'W	X	34
Bunmhullin	N Eil	NF7911	57°4·9'	7°17·5'W	T	31
Bun na Feathlach	N Eil	NF7536	57°18·2'	7°23·4'W	W	22
Bunnahabhain	Arg & Bt	NR4273	55°53·1'	6°7·1'W	T	60,61
Bun na Leige	N Eil	NG1894	57°51·1'	6°44·7'W	W	14
Bun nan Tri-allt	Highld	NC6121	58°9·6'	4°21·3'W	W	16
Bunneford Cross	Devon	SS9806	50°50·9'	3°26·6'W	X	192
Bunnett's Moat	Norf	TM1586	52°26·0'	1°10·2'E	A	144,156
Bunning's Park	Corn	SX1872	50°31·4'	4°33·7'W	X	201
Bunn's Bank	Norf	TM0693	52°30·0'	1°2·5'E	A	144
Bunn's Bank	Norf	TM0794	52°30·5'	1°3·4'E	A	144
Bunn's Hill	Norf	TM2194	52°30·2'	1°15·8'E	X	134
Bunn's Lane	Heref	SO3847	52°7·3'	2°53·9'W	X	148,149
Bunny	Notts	SK5829	52°51·6'	1°7·9'W	T	129
Bunny Hill	E Yorks	SE8535	53°48·5'	0°42·1'W	X	106
Bunny Hill	Notts	SK5728	52°51·0'	1°8·8'W	X	129
Bunny Moor	Notts	SK5730	52°52·1'	1°8·8'W	X	129
Bunoich	Highld	NH3709	57°8·8'	4°41·2'W	X	34
Bunrannoch Ho	Pth & Kin	NN6558	56°41·9'	4°11·8'W	X	42,51
Bunree	Highld	NN0262	56°42·7'	5°13·7'W	T	41
Bunroy	Highld	NN2780	56°53·0'	4°49·9'W	X	34,41
Bunsal Cob	Derby	SK0175	53°16·6'	1°58·7'W	X	119
Bunshill	Heref	SO4342	52°4·6'	2°49·5'W	X	148,149,161
Bunsley Bank	Ches	SJ6744	52°59·8'	2°29·1'W	T	118
Bunson	Devon	SS6917	50°56·5'	3°51·5'W	X	180
Bunsons Wood	Cov	SP3184	52°27·4'	1°32·2'W	F	140
Bun Sruth	N Eil	NF8414	57°6·8'	7°12·8'W	W	31
Bunstead	Hants	SU4324	51°1·1'	1°22·8'W	T	185
Bunster Hill	Staffs	SK1451	53°3·6'	1°47·1'W	X	119
Bunsty Fm	Mil Key	SP8347	52°7·1'	0°46·9'W	FM	152
Buntait	Highld	NH3931	57°20·7'	4°40·1'W	X	26
Bunting Field	Derby	SK3265	53°11·1'	1°30·9'W	X	119
Buntingford	Herts	TL3629	51°56·8'	0°0·9'W	T	166
Buntingsdale Hall	Shrops	SJ6532	52°53·2'	2°30·8'W	A	127
Bunting's Fm	Cambs	TL2395	52°32·6'	0°10·8'W	FM	142
Bunting's Fm	Essex	TL8244	52°4·1'	0°39·7'E	FM	155
Bunting's Green	Essex	TL8330	51°56·5'	0°40·1'E	T	168
Buntonhill	E Ayr	NS4241	55°38·5'	4°30·2'W	X	70
Bun Uisleitir	N Eil	NB0901	57°54·5'	6°54·3'W	W	14
Bunwell	Norf	TM1293	52°29·8'	1°7·8'E	T	144
Bunwell	Shetld	HU6691	60°36·1'	0°47·2'W	X	1,2
Bunwell Bottom	Norf	TM1095	52°31·0'	1°6·1'E	T	144
Bu' of Aith	Orkney	ND2989	58°47·2'	3°13·2'W	X	7
Bu of Burray, The	Orkney	ND4897	58°51·7'	2°53·6'W	X	6,7
Bu of Cairston	Orkney	HY2709	58°58·0'	3°15·7'W	X	6,7
Buoldhu	Highld	ND1434	58°17·4'	3°27·5'W	X	11,17
Buolfruich	Highld	ND1535	58°18·0'	3°26·5'W	X	11,17
Buolloch	Highld	ND0661	58°31·9'	3°36·4'W	X	11,12
Buoltach	Highld	ND1735	58°18·0'	3°24·5'W	X	11
Bu Point	Orkney	HY2709	58°58·0'	3°15·7'W	X	6,7
Bupton Fm	Derby	SK2237	52°56·0'	1°40·0'W	FM	128
Bupton Hill Fm	Wilts	SU0675	51°28·7'	1°54·4'W	FM	173
Bupton Village	Wilts	SU0576	51°29·2'	1°55·3'W	A	173
Burabhal	N Eil	NF9062	57°32·8'	7°10·5'W	H	22
Burach	Highld	NH3814	57°11·6'	4°40·4'W	H	34
Burandie	Orkney	HY2501	58°53·7'	3°17·6'W	X	6,7
Burbage	Derby	SK0472	53°14·9'	1°56·0'W	T	119
Burbage	Leic	SP4492	52°31·7'	1°20·7'W	T	140
Burbage	Wilts	SU2361	51°21·1'	1°39·8'W	T	174
Burbage Brook	Derby	SK2680	53°19·2'	1°36·2'W	W	110
Burbage Common	Leic	SP4495	52°33·3'	1°20·7'W	X	140
Burbage Edge	Derby	SK0273	53°15·5'	1°57·8'W	H	119
Burbage Ho	Leic	SP4491	52°31·1'	1°20·7'W	X	140
Burbage Moor	Sheff	SK2782	53°20·3'	1°35·3'W	X	110
Burbage Rocks	Sheff	SK2682	53°20·3'	1°36·2'W	X	110
Burbage Wharf	Wilts	SU2263	51°22·2'	1°40·6'W	X	174
Burbage Wood	Leic	SP4594	52°32·8'	1°19·8'W	F	140
Burble Fm	Cumbr	NY4344	54°47·5'	2°52·8'W	FM	85
Burbles Hill	Lancs	SD7045	53°54·3'	2°27·0'W	X	103
Burblethwaite Hall	Cumbr	SD4189	54°17·8'	2°54·0'W	X	96,97
Burch	Devon	SS7729	51°3·1'	3°44·9'W	X	180
Burcher	Heref	SO3360	52°14·3'	2°58·5'W	T	137,148,149
Burchetts	W Susx	TQ3123	50°59·7'	0°7·6'W	X	198
Burchett's Fm	W Susx	TQ0428	51°2·7'	0°30·6'W	FM	186,197
Burchett's Green	Win & Maid	SU8381	51°31·5'	0°47·8'W	T	175
Burch's Rough	Kent	TR0836	51°5·4'	0°58·6'E	F	179,189
Burcombe	Corn	SX4166	50°28·6'	4°14·1'W	X	201
Burcombe	Devon	SS7228	51°2·5'	3°49·2'W	X	180
Burcombe	Devon	SS7819	50°57·7'	3°43·9'W	X	180
Burcombe	Devon	SX4782	50°37·3'	4°9·4'W	X	191,201
Burcombe	Dorset	SY5198	50°47·0'	2°41·3'W	X	194
Burcombe	Somer	SS7537	51°7·4'	3°46·8'W	X	180
Burcombe	Wilts	SU0730	51°4·4'	1°53·6'W	T	184
Burcombe Ivers	Wilts	SU0529	51°3·9'	1°55·3'W	X	184
Burcot	Oxon	SU5695	51°39·3'	1°11·0'W	T	164
Burcot	Worcs	SO9871	52°20·5'	2°1·4'W	T	139
Burcot	Wrekin	SJ6210	52°41·4'	2°33·3'W	X	127
Burcote	Shrops	SO7495	52°33·4'	2°22·6'W	T	138
Burcote Ho	Shrops	SO7494	52°32·8'	2°22·6'W	X	138
Burcote Villa	Shrops	SO7394	52°32·8'	2°23·5'W	X	138
Burcotewood Fm	Northnts	SP6846	52°6·7'	1°0·0'W	FM	152
Burcot Fm	Hants	SU5438	51°8·6'	1°13·3'W	FM	185
Burcot Fm	Oxon	SU5696	51°39·8'	1°11·0'W	FM	164
Burcott	Bucks	SP8415	51°49·9'	0°46·5'W	T	165
Burcott	Bucks	SP8723	51°54·2'	0°43·7'W	T	165
Burcott	Somer	ST5245	51°12·4'	2°40·8'W	T	182,183
Burcott Hall Fm	Bucks	SP8823	51°54·1'	0°42·9'W	FM	165
Burcott Lodge Fm	Bucks	SP8624	51°54·7'	0°44·6'W	FM	165
Burcott, The	Heref	SO5242	52°4·7'	2°41·6'W	X	149
Burcroft Fm	Wakf	SE3719	53°40·2'	1°26·0'W	FM	110,111
Burdale House Fm	N Yks	SE8762	54°3·0'	0°39·9'W	FM	101
Burdale North Wold	N Yks	SE8863	54°3·6'	0°38·9'W	X	101
Burdale Tunnel	N Yks	SE8663	54°3·6'	0°40·7'W	X	101
Burdale Warren	N Yks	SE8762	54°3·0'	0°39·9'W	X	101
Burden Fm	Devon	SX4996	50°44·9'	4°8·0'W	FM	191
Burdenham Fm	Somer	ST3734	51°6·3'	2°53·6'W	FM	182
Burden Head Fm	Leeds	SE2843	53°53·2'	1°34·0'W	FM	104
Burderop Down	Swin	SU1676	51°29·1'	1°45·8'W	X	173
Burderop Hackpen	Swin	SU1678	51°30·3'	1°45·8'W	X	173
Burderop Park	Swin	SU1680	51°31·4'	1°45·8'W	X	173
Burderop Wood	Swin	SU1681	51°31·9'	1°45·8'W	F	173
Burdey's Gill	N Yks	NZ1008	54°28·3'	1°50·3'W	W	92
Burdiehouse	C of Edin	NT2767	55°53·7'	3°9·6'W	T	66
Burdiehouse	N Ayr	NS3856	55°46·5'	4°34·5'W	X	63
Burdiehouse Burn	C of Edin	NT2867	55°53·7'	3°8·6'W	W	66
Bur Dike	York	SE5954	53°59·0'	1°5·6'W	W	105
Burdocks	W Susx	TQ0323	50°59·8'	0°31·5'W	X	197
Burdon	Sund	NZ3851	54°51·4'	1°24·1'W	T	88
Burdon Court Fm	Glos	ST7991	51°37·3'	2°17·8'W	FM	162,172
Burdon Grange	Devon	SS4703	50°48·6'	4°9·9'W	X	191
Burdon Hall	Darl	NZ3217	54°33·1'	1°29·9'W	X	93
Burdonshill	V of Glam	ST1171	51°26·1'	3°16·4'W	T	171
Burdon Side	Northum	NY8090	55°12·5'	2°18·4'W	X	80
Burdrop	Oxon	SP3537	52°2·1'	1°29·0'W	T	151
Burell Ho	Corn	SX3958	50°24·2'	4°15·6'W	A	201
Bure Marshes	Norf	TG3516	52°41·7'	1°29·1'E	W	133,134
Bures	Essex	TL9034	51°58·5'	0°46·4'E	T	155
Bures Green	Suff	TL9135	51°59·1'	0°47·3'E	T	155
Bures Manor	Surrey	TQ2446	51°12·2'	0°13·1'W	X	187
Bure Valley Railway and Walk	Norf	TG2223	52°45·8'	1°17·8'E	X	133,134
Burfa	Powys	SO2761	52°14·8'	3°3·8'W	X	137,148
Burfa Camp	Powys	SO2860	52°14·2'	3°2·9'W	A	137,148
Burf Castle	Shrops	SO7690	52°30·7'	2°20·8'W	A	138
Burfield	Shrops	SO2680	52°25·0'	3°4·9'W	X	137
Burfield Hall	Norf	TM0999	52°33·1'	1°5·4'E	A	144
Burfields	Suff	TM0573	52°19·2'	1°0·9'E	X	144,155
Burfoot	Derby	SK1672	53°14·9'	1°45·2'W	X	119
Burfoot Leazes	Durham	NZ0724	54°36·9'	1°53·1'W	X	92
Burford	Ches	SJ6253	53°4·6'	2°33·6'W	T	118
Burford	Devon	SS3022	50°58·6'	4°24·9'W	T	190
Burford	Oxon	SP2512	51°48·6'	1°37·8'W	T	163
Burford	Shrops	SO5868	52°18·7'	2°36·6'W	T	137,138
Burford	Somer	ST5941	51°10·2'	2°34·8'W	T	182,183
Burford Cross	Somer	ST5941	51°10·2'	2°34·8'W	X	182,183
Burford Down	Devon	SX6360	50°25·7'	3°55·4'W	X	202
Burford Fm	Kent	TQ7349	51°13·1'	0°29·0'E	FM	188
Burford Ho Gardens	Shrops	SO5867	52°18·2'	2°36·6'W	X	137,138,149
Burfordlane Fm	Warr	SJ7086	53°22·4'	2°26·6'W	FM	109
Burford Lodge	Surrey	SU9143	51°11·0'	0°41·5'W	X	186
Burg	Arg & Bt	NM3845	56°31·7'	6°15·2'W	X	47,48
Burg	Arg & Bt	NM4226	56°21·6'	6°10·2'W	X	48
Burgadies	Shetld	HU4019	59°57·5'	1°16·5'W	X	4
Burgan	Shetld	HU3477	60°28·8'	1°22·4'W	X	2,3
Burgany Hall	E Yorks	TA3025	53°42·5'	0°1·4'W	X	107,113
Burgar	Orkney	HY3427	59°7·8'	3°8·7'W	X	6
Burgar	Shetld	HP6614	60°48·5'	0°46·7'W	X	1
Burgar Hill	Orkney	HY3426	59°7·2'	3°8·7'W	H	6
Burga Stacks	Shetld	HU2544	60°11·0'	1°32·5'W	X	4
Burgastoo	Shetld	HU3465	60°22·3'	1°22·5'W	X	2,3
Burgate	Suff	TM0875	52°20·2'	1°3·6'E	T	144
Burgate Fm	N Yks	SE9795	54°20·7'	0°30·0'W	FM	94,101
Burgate Ho	Surrey	SU9838	51°8·2'	0°35·6'W	X	186
Burgates	Hants	SU7728	51°3·0'	0°53·7'W	T	186,197
Burgate Wood	Suff	TM0775	52°20·3'	1°2·7'E	F	144
Burga Water	Shetld	HU2354	60°16·4'	1°34·6'W	W	3
Burga Water	Shetld	HU4864	60°21·7'	1°7·3'W	W	2,3
Burga Wick	Shetld	HP6203	60°42·6'	0°51·3'W	W	1
Burgedin	Powys	SJ2414	52°43·3'	3°7·1'W	T	126
Burgedin Fm	Powys	SJ2315	52°43·9'	3°8·0'W	FM	126
Burgedin Hall	Powys	SJ2413	52°42·8'	3°7·1'W	X	126
Burgedin Locks	Powys	SJ2514	52°43·3'	3°6·2'W	X	126
Burge End	Herts	TL1432	51°58·7'	0°20·0'W	T	166
Burge Fm	Somer	ST1627	51°2·4'	3°11·5'W	FM	181,193
Burgess Fm	Cambs	TL5093	52°31·1'	0°13·0'E	FM	143
Burgess Fm	Heref	SO6552	52°10·1'	2°30·3'W	FM	149
Burgess Fm	Kent	TR1163	51°19·8'	1°2·1'E	FM	179
Burgess Hall	N Lincs	SE8410	53°35·0'	0°43·5'W	X	112
Burgess Hill	W Susx	TQ3119	50°57·6'	0°7·7'W	T	198
Burgess Outon	D & G	NX4541	54°44·7'	4°24·1'W	X	83
Burgess's Fm	W Berks	SU3375	51°28·6'	1°31·1'W	FM	174
Burgh	Suff	TM2351	52°7·0'	1°15·8'E	T	156
Burgham	E Susx	TQ7027	51°1·3'	0°25·8'E	X	188,199
Burgham	Northum	NZ1796	55°15·7'	1°43·5'W	X	81
Burgh by Sands	Cumbr	NY3259	54°55·5'	3°3·2'W	T	85
Burgh Castle	Norf	TG4804	52°34·9'	1°40·0'E	T	134
Burgh Castle Marshes	Norf	TG4805	52°35·4'	1°40·1'E	X	134
Burgh Castle Reach	Norf	TG4704	52°34·9'	1°39·2'E	W	134
Burghclere	Hants	SU4761	51°21·0'	1°19·1'W	T	174
Burghclere Common	Hants	SU4762	51°21·5'	1°19·1'W	T	174
Burgh Common	Norf	TG4412	52°39·3'	1°36·9'E	W	134
Burgh Common	Norf	TM0694	52°30·5'	1°2·5'E	T	144
Burghead	Moray	NJ1169	57°42·4'	3°29·1'W	T	28
Burghead Bay	Moray	NJ0867	57°41·3'	3°32·1'W	W	27
Burghfield	W Berks	SU6668	51°24·7'	1°2·7'W	T	175
Burghfield Common	W Berks	SU6566	51°23·6'	1°3·6'W	T	175
Burghfield Hill	W Berks	SU6567	51°24·1'	1°3·5'W	T	175
Burghfield Mill	W Berks	SU6670	51°25·7'	1°2·6'W	X	175
Burghfield Place	W Berks	SU6768	51°24·7'	1°1·8'W	X	175
Burgh Hall	Lancs	SD5715	53°38·0'	2°38·6'W	X	108
Burgh Hall	Norf	TG0433	52°51·6'	1°2·2'E	A	133
Burgh Hall	Norf	TG2127	52°47·9'	1°17·1'E	X	133,134
Burgh Hall	Norf	TG4904	52°34·8'	1°40·9'E	X	134
Burgh Head	Orkney	HY6923	59°5·8'	2°32·0'W	X	5
Burgh Heath	Surrey	TQ2457	51°18·1'	0°12·9'W	T	187
Burgh Hill	E Susx	TQ5412	50°53·4'	0°11·8'E	T	199
Burgh Hill	E Susx	TQ7226	51°0·7'	0°27·5'E	T	188,199
Burgh Hill	Orkney	HY6823	59°5·8'	2°33·0'W	H	5
Burghill	Angus	NO5959	56°43·5'	2°39·8'W	X	54
Burghill	Heref	SO4744	52°5·7'	2°46·0'W	T	148,149,161
Burghill Wood	Angus	NO5958	56°43·0'	2°39·7'W	F	54
Burgh Island	Devon	SX6443	50°16·5'	3°54·1'W	X	202
Burghlee	Midlo	NT2765	55°52·6'	3°9·6'W	X	66
Burgh le Marsh	Lincs	TF5064	53°9·4'	0°15·0'E	T	122
Burghley Ho	Peterb	TF0406	52°38·7'	0°27·4'W	A	141
Burghley Park	Peterb	TF0405	52°38·2'	0°27·4'W	X	141
Burgh Marsh	Cumbr	NY3060	54°56·0'	3°5·1'W	W	85
Burgh Marsh	Lincs	TF5264	53°9·3'	0°16·8'E	X	122
Burgh Marshes	Norf	TM4894	52°29·5'	1°39·6'E	X	134
Burghmarsh Point	Cumbr	NY3161	54°56·6'	3°4·2'W	X	85
Burgh Moor Ho	Cumbr	NY3157	54°54·4'	3°4·1'W	X	85
Burgh Muir	Aberd	NJ7716	57°14·3'	2°22·4'W	T	38
Burghmuir	W Loth	NT0278	55°59·4'	3°33·8'W	X	65
Burghmuir Fm	S Lanak	NT0438	55°37·8'	3°31·1'W	FM	72
Burghnamary	Moray	NJ3352	57°33·4'	3°6·7'W	X	28
Burgh next Aylsham	Norf	TG2225	52°46·8'	1°17·9'E	T	133,134
Burgh on Bain	Lincs	TF2186	53°21·6'	0°9·6'W	T	113,122
Burghope	Heref	SO5050	52°9·0'	2°43·5'W	X	149
Burghope Wood	Heref	SO4950	52°9·0'	2°44·3'W	F	148,149
Burgh St Margaret (Fleggburgh)	Norf	TG4414	52°40·3'	1°37·0'E	T	134
Burgh St Peter	Norf	TM4693	52°29·0'	1°37·8'E	T	134
Burgh Stubbs	Norf	TG0434	52°52·1'	1°2·3'E	T	133
Burgh, The	W Susx	TQ0411	50°53·6'	0°30·9'W	X	197
Burgh Top	Lincs	TF2185	53°21·1'	0°10·5'W	X	122
Burghwallis	Donc	SE5311	53°35·8'	1°11·5'W	T	111
Burghwallis Grange	Donc	SE5211	53°35·8'	1°12·4'W	X	111
Burgh Wood	E Susx	TQ7227	51°1·2'	0°27·5'E	F	188,199
Burgi Ayre	Shetld	HU4523	59°59·6'	1°11·1'W	X	4
Burgiehill	Moray	NJ0956	57°35·4'	3°30·9'W	X	27
Burgie Ho	Moray	NJ0959	57°37·0'	3°30·9'W	X	27
Burgie Lodge	Moray	NJ0859	57°37·0'	3°31·9'W	X	27
Burgie Wood	Moray	NJ0958	57°36·4'	3°30·9'W	F	27
Burgi Geos	Shetld	HP4703	60°42·7'	1°7·8'W	X	1
Burgins	Shetld	HU3556	60°17·5'	1°21·5'W	H	2,3
Burgir	Orkney	HY3507	58°57·0'	3°7·3'W	X	6,7
Burgi Stacks	Shetld	HU3623	59°59·7'	1°20·8'W	X	4
Burgois	Corn	SW9272	50°30·9'	4°55·7'W	T	200
Burgo Taing	Shetld	HU3789	60°35·2'	1°19·0'W	X	1,2
Burgs, The	Shrops	SJ4808	52°40·3'	2°45·7'W	X	126
Burgs, The (Fort)	Shrops	SJ4808	52°40·3'	2°45·7'W	A	126
Burgundy Chapel	Somer	SS9448	51°13·5'	3°30·7'W	A	181
Burham	Kent	TQ7262	51°20·1'	0°28·5'E	T	178,188
Burham Court	Kent	TQ7162	51°20·1'	0°27·7'E	T	178,188
Burham Hill Fm	Kent	TQ7363	51°20·6'	0°29·4'E	FM	178,188
Burhill	Glos	SP0836	52°1·6'	1°52·6'W	H	150
Burhill	Surrey	TQ1062	51°21·0'	0°24·8'W	X	176,187
Burhill (Fort)	Glos	SP0836	52°1·6'	1°52·6'W	A	150
Burholme	Lancs	SD6648	53°55·9'	2°30·7'W	X	103
Burholme Br	Lancs	SD6547	53°55·3'	2°31·6'W	X	102,103
Burhunt Fm	Hants	SU7532	51°5·2'	0°55·4'W	FM	186
Burian Hill	D & G	NY3681	55°7·4'	2°59·8'W	X	79
Burican Hill	N Ayr	NR9526	55°29·3'	5°14·3'W	X	68,69
Burifa' Hill	Highld	ND2075	58°39·6'	3°22·3'W	H	7,12
Buriton	Hants	SU7320	50°58·7'	0°57·2'W	T	197
Buriton Fm	W Susx	SU8117	50°57·0'	0°50·4'W	FM	197
Burkham Ho	Hants	SU6542	51°10·6'	1°3·8'W	X	185,186
Burkinshaw's Covert	N Lincs	TA1618	53°39·0'	0°14·3'W	F	113
Burki Skerries	Shetld	HU3162	60°20·7'	1°25·8'W	X	3
Burki Taing	Shetld	HU3162	60°20·7'	1°25·8'W	X	3
Burki Waters	Shetld	HU3164	60°21·8'	1°25·8'W	W	3
Burland	Ches	SJ6153	53°4·6'	2°34·5'W	T	118

Burland	E Yorks	SE7730	53°45·9′	0°49·5′W	X	105,106
Burland	Shetld	HU3937	60°7·2′	1°17·4′W	T	4
Burland Fm	Ches	SJ6053	53°4·6′	2°35·4′W	FM	118
Burland Fm	Devon	SS5341	51°9·2′	4°5·7′W	FM	180
Burland Hall	E Yorks	SE7730	53°45·9′	0°49·5′W	X	105,106
Burland Hall Fm	Ches	SJ6053	53°4·6′	2°35·4′W	FM	118
Burland Ho	Warw	SP3245	52°6·4′	1°31·6′W	X	151
Burlands	Somer	ST2027	51°2·4′	3°8·1′W	X	193
Burlands Beck	Lincs	TF4771	53°13·2′	0°12·5′E	W	122
Burlands Fm	York	SE5453	53°58·5′	1°10·2′W	FM	105
Burland Skerry	Shetld	HU3836	60°6·7′	1°18·5′W	X	4
Burlawn	Corn	SW9970	50°30·0′	4°49·7′W	T	200
Burleaze Fm	Somer	ST3516	50°56·6′	2°55·1′W	FM	193
Burledge Hill	Bath & NE Somer	ST5858	51°19·4′	2°35·8′W	H	172,182
Burleigh	Glos	SO8601	51°42·7′	2°11·8′W	T	162
Burleigh	Pth & Kin	NO1204	56°13·5′	3°24·7′W	X	58
Burleigh	Wrekin	SJ6621	52°47·4′	2°29·8′W	X	127
Burleigh Common	Herts	TL3817	51°50·3′	0°0·6′E	X	166
Burleigh Fm	Devon	SX7040	50°15·0′	3°49·0′W	FM	202
Burleigh Fm	Herts	TL2221	51°52·7′	0°13·3′W	FM	166
Burleigh Fm	Herts	TL3104	51°43·4′	0°5·8′W	FM	166
Burleigh Fm	Kent	TQ9249	51°12·7′	0°45·3′E	FM	189
Burleigh Fm	Oxon	SP4412	51°48·5′	1°21·3′W	FM	164
Burleigh Fm	Wrekin	SJ6621	52°47·4′	2°29·8′W	FM	127
Burleigh Hill Fm	Cambs	TL3174	52°21·1′	0°4·2′W	FM	142
Burleigh House Fm	W Susx	TQ3537	51°7·2′	0°3·9′W	FM	187
Burleigh Wood	Oxon	SP4413	51°49·1′	1°21·3′W	F	164
Burlescombe	Devon	ST0716	50°56·4′	3°19·0′W	T	181
Burleston	Dorset	SY7794	50°44·9′	2°19·2′W	T	194
Burlestone	Devon	SX8248	50°19·4′	3°39·1′W	T	202
Burley	Hants	SU2103	50°49·8′	1°41·7′W	T	195
Burley	Heref	SO6653	52°10·7′	2°29·4′W	X	149
Burley	Leeds	SE2734	53°48·3′	1°35·0′W	T	104
Burley	Rut	SK8810	52°41·1′	0°41·5′W	T	130
Burley	Shrops	SO4781	52°25·7′	2°46·4′W	T	137,138
Burley Bank Fm	N Yks	SE2656	54°0·2′	1°35·8′W	FM	104
Burley Beacon	Hants	SU2002	50°49·3′	1°42·6′W	T	195
Burley Bushes	Rut	SK9010	52°41·0′	0°39·7′W	F	130
Burleydam	Ches	SJ6042	52°58·7′	2°35·3′W	T	118
Burley Down	Devon	SX4986	50°39·5′	4°7·8′W	X	191,201
Burleyfields	Staffs	SJ9023	52°48·5′	2°8·5′W	X	127
Burley Fields Fm	Derby	SK2764	53°10·6′	1°35·4′W	FM	119
Burley Gate	Heref	SO5947	52°7·4′	2°35·5′W	T	149
Burley Grange	Derby	SK3441	52°58·2′	1°29·2′W	X	119,128
Burleyheyes Fm	Warr	SJ6482	53°20·3′	2°32·0′W	FM	109
Burley Hill	Derby	SK3541	52°58·1′	1°28·3′W	X	119,128
Burley Hill	Hants	SU1903	50°49·8′	1°43·4′W	X	195
Burleyhurst Fm	Ches	SJ8181	53°19·8′	2°16·7′W	FM	109
Burley in Wharfedale	Brad	SE1646	53°54·8′	1°45·0′W	T	104
Burley Lawn	Hants	SU2203	50°49·8′	1°40·9′W	T	195
Burley Lodge	Hants	SU2305	50°50·9′	1°40·0′W	X	195
Burley Meadows	Derby	SK3441	52°58·2′	1°29·2′W	X	119,128
Burley Moor	Brad	SE1344	53°53·8′	1°47·7′W	X	104
Burley Moor	Hants	SU2104	50°50·3′	1°41·7′W	X	195
Burley New Inclosure	Hants	SU2304	50°50·3′	1°40·0′W	F	195
Burley Old Inclosure	Hants	SU2404	50°50·3′	1°39·2′W	F	195
Burley on the Hill	Rut	SK8810	52°41·1′	0°41·5′W	A	130
Burley Outer Rails Inclosure	Hants	SU2305	50°50·9′	1°40·0′W	F	195
Burley Park	Leeds	SE2735	53°48·9′	1°35·0′W	X	104
Burley Street	Hants	SU2004	50°50·3′	1°42·6′W	T	195
Burleys Wood	W Susx	TQ3037	51°7·3′	0°8·2′W	F	187
Burleywhag	D & G	NS9700	55°17·3′	3°36·9′W	X	78
Burley Wood	Devon	SX4987	50°40·0′	4°7·8′W	F	191
Burley Wood	Hants	SU5348	51°14·0′	1°14·1′W	F	185
Burley Wood	Rut	SK8909	52°40·5′	0°40·6′W	F	141
Burley Woodhead	Brad	SE1544	53°53·8′	1°45·9′W	T	104
Burl Fm	Dorset	ST5803	50°49·7′	2°35·4′W	FM	194
Burl Hill	Powys	SO2057	52°12·6′	3°9·9′W	H	148
Burlinch	Somer	ST2629	51°3·6′	3°3·0′W	T	193
Burlingham Green	Norf	TG3610	52°38·4′	1°29·7′E	T	133,134
Burlingham Ho	Norf	TG3510	52°38·4′	1°28·8′E	X	133,134
Burlingham Lodge Fm	Norf	TG3710	52°38·4′	1°30·6′E	FM	133,134
Burlingham Lodge Fm	Norf	TM2589	52°27·4′	1°19·1′E	FM	156
Burlingham's Fm	Somer	ST5021	50°59·4′	2°42·4′W	FM	183
Burlingjobb	Powys	SO2558	52°13·1′	3°5·5′W	T	148
Burlings	Brom	TQ4558	51°18·4′	0°5·2′E	X	188
Burlington	Shrops	SJ7711	52°42·0′	2°20·0′W	X	127
Burlington Fm	Shrops	SJ7710	52°41·5′	2°20·0′W	FM	127
Burlish Fm	Worcs	SO7972	52°21·0′	2°18·1′W	FM	138
Burlish Park	Worcs	SO8072	52°21·0′	2°17·2′W	T	138
Burloes Fm	Herts	TL3740	52°2·7′	0°0·3′E	FM	154
Burloes Hall	Herts	TL3740	52°2·7′	0°0·3′E	X	154
Burlorne Pillow	Corn	SX0168	50°28·9′	4°47·9′W	X	200
Burlorne Tregoose	Corn	SX0169	50°29·5′	4°48·0′W	T	200
Burlow	E Susx	TQ5716	50°55·5′	0°14·4′E	T	199
Burlton	Shrops	SJ4526	52°50·0′	2°48·6′W	T	126
Burlton Court	Heref	SO4844	52°5·8′	2°45·2′W	X	148,149,161
Burlton Grange	Shrops	SJ4527	52°50·5′	2°48·6′W	X	126
Burltonlane Fm	Shrops	SJ4624	52°48·9′	2°47·7′W	FM	126
Burlyns	Hants	SU4162	51°21·6′	1°24·3′W	X	174
Burmantofts	Leeds	SE3234	53°48·3′	1°30·4′W	T	104
Burmarsh	Heref	SO5346	52°6·9′	2°40·8′W	T	149
Burmarsh	Kent	TR1031	51°2·6′	1°0·1′E	T	189
Burmead	Somer	ST4049	51°14·5′	2°51·2′W	X	182
Burmieston	Pth & Kin	NO0032	56°28·4′	3°37·0′W	X	52,53
Burmington	Warw	SP2637	52°2·1′	1°36·9′W	T	151
Burmington Grange	Warw	SP2837	52°2·1′	1°35·1′W	X	151
Burmoor	Northum	NY8277	55°5·5′	2°16·5′W	X	86,87
Burmsdon	Corn	SS2706	50°49·9′	4°27·0′W	X	190
Burn	Corn	SS2106	50°49·8′	4°32·1′W	X	190
Burn	Corn	SS2603	50°48·3′	4°27·8′W	X	190
Burn	Devon	SS9405	50°50·3′	3°29·9′W	X	192
Burn	D & G	NX9098	55°16·1′	3°43·4′W	X	78
Burn	E Ayr	NS5133	55°34·3′	4°21·4′W	X	70
Burn	N Ayr	NS2952	55°44·1′	4°43·0′W	X	63
Burn	N Yks	SE5928	53°44·9′	1°5·9′W	T	105
Burn	Orkney	ND4583	58°44·1′	2°56·5′W	X	7
Burn	Shetld	HU3366	60°22·9′	1°23·6′W	X	2,3
Burnage	Man	SJ8692	53°25·7′	2°12·2′W	T	109
Burn Anne	E Ayr	NS5334	55°34·9′	4°19·5′W	W	70
Burnard's Ho	Devon	SS3104	50°48·9′	4°23·6′W	T	190
Burnaston	Derby	SK2832	52°53·3′	1°34·6′W	T	128
Burnbank	D & G	NY0581	55°7·1′	3°28·9′W	X	78
Burnbank	Inverc	NS3567	55°52·3′	4°37·8′W	X	63
Burnbank	Moray	NJ2256	57°35·5′	3°17·8′W	X	28
Burnbank	N Ayr	NR9936	55°34·8′	5°10·9′W	X	69
Burnbank	N Lanak	NS8660	55°49·4′	3°48·7′W	X	65
Burnbank	Northum	NY7987	55°10·9′	2°19·4′W	X	80
Burnbank	S Ayr	NS3512	55°22·7′	4°35·8′W	X	70
Burnbank	S Ayr	NS3931	55°33·0′	4°32·7′W	X	70
Burnbank	Scot Bord	NT9256	55°48·1′	2°7·2′W	X	67,74,75
Burnbank	S Lanak	NS6949	55°43·3′	4°4·7′W	X	64
Burnbank	S Lanak	NS7056	55°47·0′	4°3·9′W	T	64
Burnbank Fell	Cumbr	NY1121	54°34·8′	3°22·2′W	H	89
Burnbank Fm	Cumbr	SD4180	54°13·0′	2°53·9′W	FM	96,97
Burnbank Fm	Inverc	NS3169	55°53·3′	4°41·7′W	FM	63
Burnbanks	Cumbr	NY5016	54°32·5′	2°45·9′W	H	90
Burnbanks Haven	C of Aber	NJ9602	57°6·8′	2°3·5′W	W	38
Burnbank Water	Inverc	NS2968	55°52·7′	4°43·6′W	W	63
Burn Barrow Wood	Cumbr	SD3582	54°14·0′	2°59·4′W	F	96,97
Burn betwixt Laws	Scot Bord	NT5959	55°49·6′	2°38·8′W	W	67,73,74
Burnbrae	D & G	NX7565	54°58·1′	3°56·7′W	X	84
Burnbrae	D & G	NX8470	55°0·9′	3°48·4′W	X	84
Burnbrae	Fife	NO5509	56°16·5′	2°43·2′W	X	59
Burnbrae	N Lanak	NS8759	55°48·9′	3°47·8′W	X	65,72
Burnbrae	Pth & Kin	NN9623	56°23·5′	3°40·6′W	X	52,53,58
Burnbrae	Pth & Kin	NO0803	56°12·9′	3°28·6′W	X	58
Burnbrae	Pth & Kin	NO2036	56°30·8′	3°17·6′W	X	53
Burnbrae	S Ayr	NS3732	55°33·5′	4°34·6′W	X	70
Burnbrae	Scot Bord	NT6837	55°37·8′	2°30·1′W	X	74
Burnbrae	S Lanak	NS7141	55°39·0′	4°2·6′W	X	71
Burnbrae	S Lanak	NS7250	55°43·8′	4°1·9′W	X	64
Burnbrae	S Lanak	NS8241	55°39·1′	3°52·1′W	X	71,72
Burnbrae	W Dunb	NS4285	56°2·2′	4°31·7′W	X	56
Burnbrae	W Loth	NS9764	55°51·7′	3°38·3′W	X	65
Burnbrae	W Loth	NT0163	55°51·3′	3°34·5′W	X	65
Burnbrae	W Loth	NT1065	55°52·4′	3°25·9′W	X	65
Burnbrae Burn	Inverc	NS3365	55°51·2′	4°39·6′W	W	63
Burnbrae Fm	N Lanak	NS6771	55°55·1′	4°7·3′W	FM	64
Burnbrae Ho	Midlo	NT3163	55°51·6′	3°5·7′W	X	66
Burnbrae Lodge	E Ayr	NS4724	55°29·4′	4°24·9′W	X	70
Burn Bridge	N Yks	SE3051	53°57·5′	1°32·2′W	T	104
Burn Butts	E Yorks	SE9951	53°57·0′	0°29·1′W	X	106
Burnby	E Yorks	SE8346	53°54·4′	0°43·8′W	T	106
Burnby Gate Ho	E Yorks	SE8247	53°55·0′	0°44·7′W	X	106
Burn Carrs	Northum	NU2328	55°33·0′	1°37·7′W	X	75
Burncastle	Scot Bord	NT5351	55°45·3′	2°44·5′W	X	66,73
Burncleuch	D & G	NT2301	55°18·1′	3°12·3′W	X	79
Burncoose	Corn	SW6923	50°4·0′	5°13·3′W	X	203
Burncoose	Corn	SW7439	50°12·7′	5°9·7′W	X	204
Burn Coppice	Northnts	SP9791	52°30·7′	0°33·8′W	F	141
Burn Cott	D & G	NY3387	55°10·6′	3°2·7′W	X	79
Burn Cottage	Devon	SX4982	50°37·3′	4°7·7′W	X	191,201
Burncrooks	S Lanak	NS7545	55°41·2′	3°58·9′W	X	64
Burn Crooks	W Dunb	NS4780	55°59·6′	4°26·7′W	W	64
Burncrooks Reservoir	W Dunb	NS4879	55°59·1′	4°25·7′W	W	64
Burncross	Sheff	SK3496	53°27·8′	1°28·9′W	T	110,111
Burncruinach	Aberd	NJ5035	57°24·4′	2°49·5′W	X	29
Burndale	Midlo	NT3067	55°53·7′	3°6·7′W	X	66
Burndell	W Susx	SU9802	50°48·8′	0°36·1′W	T	197
Burnden	Bolton	SD7307	53°33·8′	2°24·0′W	T	109
Burn Divot	Northum	NY6970	55°1·7′	2°28·7′W	X	86,87
Burn Edge	N Yks	SE1067	54°6·2′	1°50·4′W	X	99
Burnedge	Roch	SD9210	53°35·4′	2°6·8′W	T	109
Burnedge Bent Fm	Oldham	SD9805	53°32·7′	2°1·4′W	FM	109
Burned I	D & G	NX6572	55°1·7′	4°6·3′W	X	77,84
Burne Fm	Devon	SX7970	50°31·3′	3°42·0′W	FM	202
Burne Fm	Roth	SK5085	53°21·8′	1°14·5′W	FM	111,120
Burnells	Somer	SS9643	51°10·8′	3°28·9′W	X	181
Burnend	Aberd	NJ5138	57°26·0′	2°48·5′W	X	29
Burnend	Aberd	NJ6849	57°32·1′	2°31·6′W	X	29
Burnend	Aberd	NJ8341	57°27·8′	2°16·5′W	X	29,30
Burnend	Aberd	NJ9733	57°23·5′	2°2·5′W	X	30
Burnend	Aberd	NJ9742	57°28·4′	2°2·5′W	X	30
Burnend	Moray	NJ4955	57°35·2′	2°50·7′W	X	28,29
Burnervie	Aberd	NJ5851	57°33·1′	2°41·6′W	X	29
Burneside	Cumbr	SD5095	54°21·1′	2°45·7′W	T	97
Burness	Orkney	HY3815	59°1·3′	3°4·3′W	X	6
Burness	Orkney	HY4248	59°19·1′	3°0·7′W	X	5
Burness	Orkney	HY6644	59°17·1′	2°35·3′W	T	5
Burneston	N Yks	SE3085	54°15·8′	1°31·9′W	T	99
Burneston Grange	N Yks	SE3185	54°15·8′	1°31·0′W	X	99
Burnetland Fm	Scot Bord	NT1036	55°36·8′	3°25·3′W	FM	72
Burnet Plantns	N Yks	SE1694	54°20·7′	1°44·8′W	F	99
Burnett	Bath & NE Somer	ST6665	51°23·2′	2°28·9′W	T	172
Burnett's Hill	Pemb	SN0109	51°44·9′	4°52·6′W	X	157,158
Burneven Hill	Inverc	NS2175	55°56·3′	4°51·5′W	H	63
Burnewhall	Corn	SW4023	50°3·3′	5°37·6′W	X	203
Burney	Cumbr	SD2585	54°15·6′	3°8·7′W	X	96
Burney Fm	Wilts	SU2372	51°27·0′	1°39·8′W	FM	174
Burney Hill	Cumbr	NY6830	54°40·1′	2°29·3′W	H	91
Burnfarm	Highld	NH6757	57°35·3′	4°13·0′W	X	26
Burn Fell	Lancs	SD6753	53°58·6′	2°29·8′W	X	103
Burnfield	Aberd	NJ5447	57°30·9′	2°45·6′W	X	29
Burnfield	Cumbr	SD1781	54°13·3′	3°16·0′W	X	96
Burn Fm	Aberd	NO6072	56°50·5′	2°38·9′W	FM	45
Burn Fm	S Ayr	NS4224	55°29·3′	4°29·6′W	FM	70
Burn Fm	S Lanak	NS6949	55°43·3′	4°4·7′W	FM	64
Burnfold	Aberd	NJ7828	57°20·8′	2°21·5′W	X	38
Burnfold	Aberd	NO5490	57°0·2′	2°45·0′W	X	44
Burnfoot	Angus	NO4880	56°54·8′	2°50·8′W	X	44
Burnfoot	Angus	NO5367	56°47·8′	2°45·7′W	X	44
Burnfoot	Cumbr	NY3666	54°59·3′	2°59·6′W	X	85
Burnfoot	D & G	NS7610	55°22·4′	3°57·0′W	X	71,78
Burnfoot	D & G	NX5864	54°57·3′	4°12·6′W	X	83
Burnfoot	D & G	NX5992	55°12·4′	4°12·5′W	X	77
Burnfoot	D & G	NX9791	55°12·4′	3°36·7′W	X	78
Burnfoot	D & G	NX9863	54°57·3′	3°35·1′W	X	84
Burnfoot	D & G	NY2574	55°3·5′	3°10·0′W	T	85
Burnfoot	D & G	NY3388	55°11·2′	3°2·7′W	X	79
Burnfoot	D & G	NY3996	55°15·5′	2°57·2′W	X	79
Burnfoot	E Ayr	NS4209	55°21·2′	4°29·1′W	T	70,77
Burnfoot	E Ayr	NS4444	55°40·1′	4°28·4′W	X	70
Burnfoot	E Ayr	NS6728	55°31·9′	4°6·0′W	X	71
Burnfoot	E Dunb	NS6776	55°57·8′	4°7·4′W	X	64
Burnfoot	E Loth	NT5069	55°54·9′	2°47·6′W	X	66
Burnfoot	Highld	NC8630	58°14·9′	3°56·1′W	X	17
Burnfoot	N Lanak	NS7566	55°52·5′	3°59·4′W	T	64
Burnfoot	Northum	NY6660	54°56·3′	2°31·4′W	X	86
Burnfoot	Northum	NY9065	54°59·0′	2°8·9′W	X	87
Burnfoot	Pth & Kin	NN9804	56°13·3′	3°38·3′W	X	58
Burnfoot	Renf	NS3458	55°47·5′	4°38·4′W	X	63
Burn Foot	S Ayr	NX0576	55°2·7′	5°2·7′W	X	76
Burnfoot	S Ayr	NX1686	55°8·3′	4°52·8′W	X	76
Burnfoot	Scot Bord	NT4113	55°24·7′	2°55·5′W	X	79
Burnfoot	Scot Bord	NT4520	55°28·5′	2°51·8′W	X	73
Burnfoot	Scot Bord	NT4952	55°45·8′	2°48·3′W	X	66,73
Burnfoot	Scot Bord	NT5116	55°26·4′	2°46·0′W	T	79
Burnfoot	S Lanak	NS8043	55°40·2′	3°54·0′W	X	71,72
Burnfoot	S Lanak	NS9730	55°33·4′	3°37·5′W	X	72
Burnfoot	S Lanak	NS9855	55°46·9′	3°37·1′W	X	65,72
Burnfoot	S Lanak	NS9940	55°38·8′	3°35·9′W	X	72
Burnfoot	Stir	NS6788	56°4·2′	4°7·8′W	X	57
Burnfoot Belt	D & G	NS7509	55°21·8′	3°57·9′W	X	71,78
Burnfoot Br	E Ayr	NS4725	55°29·9′	4°24·9′W	X	70
Burnfoot Burn	D & G	NX5965	54°57·8′	4°11·7′W	W	83
Burnfoot Burn	Stir	NS6889	56°4·8′	4°6·8′W	W	57
Burnfoot Cottage	D & G	NY2088	55°11·0′	3°15·0′W	X	79
Burnfoot Fm	Durham	NY9823	54°36·4′	2°1·4′W	FM	92
Burnfoot Fm	E Ayr	NS5540	55°38·2′	4°17·8′W	FM	71
Burnfoot Fm	Scot Bord	NT0636	55°36·8′	3°29·1′W	FM	72
Burnfoot Hall	D & G	NY2074	55°3·5′	3°14·7′W	X	85
Burnfoot Hill	Clackm	NN9003	56°12·7′	3°46·0′W	X	58
Burnfoothill	D & G	NY2673	55°3·0′	3°9·1′W	X	85
Burnfoot Moor	E Ayr	NS6727	55°31·4′	4°6·0′W	X	71
Burnfoot Plantation	D & G	NY3490	55°12·2′	3°1·8′W	F	79
Burnfoot Resr	E Ayr	NS4544	55°40·1′	4°27·4′W	W	70
Burnford	Devon	SX4978	50°35·2′	4°7·6′W	X	191,201
Burngate Fm	Dorset	SY8381	50°37·9′	2°14·0′W	FM	194
Burn Gill	N Ayr	NS1951	55°43·4′	4°52·5′W	W	63
Burn Gill	N Yks	SE1068	54°6·7′	1°50·4′W	W	99
Burn Gill Head Moss	N Yks	SE0868	54°6·7′	1°52·2′W	X	99
Burngrains	Aberd	NJ8218	57°15·4′	2°17·4′W	X	38
Burngrains	Aberd	NJ9339	57°26·7′	2°6·5′W	X	30
Burngrains	D & G	NY3693	55°13·9′	2°59·9′W	X	79
Burngrains Fm	Aberd	NJ8336	57°25·1′	2°16·5′W	FM	29,30
Burn Grange	Northum	NY7294	55°14·6′	2°26·0′W	X	80
Burngrange	Pth & Kin	NO2035	56°30·3′	3°17·5′W	X	53
Burngrange	S Lanak	NT0248	55°43·2′	3°33·2′W	X	72
Burngrange Moor	Northum	NY7294	55°14·6′	2°26·0′W	X	80
Burngreave	Sheff	SK3588	53°23·5′	1°28·0′W	T	110,111
Burn Ground	N Yks	SE1168	54°6·7′	1°49·5′W	X	99
Burngullow	Corn	SW9852	50°20·2′	4°50·2′W	X	200,204
Burn Hall	Durham	NZ2638	54°44·4′	1°35·3′W	X	93
Burn Hall	N Yks	SE5365	54°4·9′	1°11·0′W	X	100
Burn Hall Fm	Sund	NZ3951	54°51·4′	1°23·1′W	FM	88
Burnham	Bucks	SU9282	51°32·0′	0°40·0′W	T	175
Burnham	N Lincs	TA0517	53°38·6′	0°24·3′W	T	112
Burnham Abbey	Bucks	SU9280	51°30·9′	0°40·1′W	X	175
Burnham Beeches	Bucks	SU9485	51°33·6′	0°38·2′W	F	175
Burnham Beeches	Bucks	SU9585	51°33·6′	0°37·4′W	F	175,176
Burnham Beeches Fm	N Lincs	TA0416	53°38·0′	0°25·2′W	FM	112
Burnham Deepdale	Norf	TF8044	52°58·0′	0°41·2′E	T	132
Burnham Green	Herts	TL2616	51°49·9′	0°9·9′W	T	166
Burnham Grove	Bucks	SU9383	51°32·5′	0°39·1′W	X	175
Burnham Harbour	Norf	TF8546	52°59·0′	0°45·8′E	W	132
Burnham Level	Somer	ST3148	51°13·9′	2°58·9′W	X	182
Burnham Lodge	N Lincs	TA0617	53°38·6′	0°23·4′W	X	112
Burnham Market	Norf	TF8342	52°56·9′	0°43·8′E	T	132
Burnham Norton	Norf	TF8243	52°57·4′	0°43·0′E	T	132
Burnham-On-Crouch	Essex	TQ9596	51°38·0′	0°49·5′E	T	168
Burnham-on-Sea	Somer	ST3049	51°14·4′	2°59·8′W	T	182
Burnham Overy Staithe	Norf	TF8444	52°57·9′	0°44·8′E	T	132
Burnham Overy Town	Norf	TF8442	52°56·9′	0°44·7′E	T	132
Burnham Sta	Slough	SU9381	51°31·4′	0°39·2′W	X	175
Burnham Thorpe	Norf	TF8541	52°56·3′	0°45·6′E	T	132
Burnham Wick	Essex	TQ9695	51°37·4′	0°50·3′E	X	168
Burnhayes	Devon	SS9406	50°50·9′	3°30·0′W	X	192
Burnhead	Aberd	NJ6800	57°5·6′	2°31·2′W	X	38
Burnhead	Aberd	NJ8123	57°18·1′	2°18·5′W	X	38
Burnhead	Aberd	NJ8422	57°17·6′	2°15·5′W	X	38
Burnhead	Aberd	NK0439	57°26·7′	1°55·5′W	X	30
Burnhead	Aberd	NK0652	57°33·7′	1°53·5′W	X	30
Burnhead	Aberd	NK0941	57°27·8′	1°50·5′W	X	30
Burnhead	Aberd	NO7270	56°49·5′	2°27·1′W	X	45
Burnhead	Aberd	NO7681	56°55·4′	2°23·2′W	X	45
Burnhead	Aberd	NO8693	57°1·9′	2°13·4′W	T	38,45
Burnhead	Aberd	NO8798	57°4·6′	2°12·4′W	X	38,45
Burnhead	Angus	NO4963	56°45·6′	2°49·6′W	X	44
Burnhead	Angus	NO5544	56°35·4′	2°43·5′W	X	54
Burnhead	D & G	NX5485	55°8·5′	4°17·0′W	X	77
Burnhead	D & G	NX8695	55°14·4′	3°47·1′W	T	78
Burnhead	D & G	NX9184	55°8·6′	3°42·2′W	T	78
Burnhead	D & G	NY1981	55°7·3′	3°15·8′W	X	79
Burnhead	D & G	NY2473	55°3·0′	3°10·9′W	X	85
Burnhead	E Ayr	NS4509	55°21·3′	4°26·3′W	X	70,77
Burnhead	E Ayr	NS6036	55°36·1′	4°12·9′W	X	71
Burnhead	Falk	NS8969	55°54·3′	3°46·1′W	X	65
Burnhead	Inverc	NS2872	55°54·9′	4°44·7′W	X	63
Burnhead	Moray	NJ3141	57°27·5′	3°8·5′W	X	28
Burnhead	N Lanak	NS6878	55°58·9′	4°6·5′W	X	64
Burnhead	Pth & Kin	NO2345	56°35·7′	3°14·8′W	X	53
Burnhead	S Ayr	NS2200	55°16·0′	4°47·7′W	T	76
Burnhead	Scot Bord	NT5116	55°26·4′	2°46·0′W	T	79
Burnhead	Scot Bord	NT8425	55°31·4′	2°14·8′W	X	74
Burnhead	S Lanak	NS6951	55°44·3′	4°4·8′W	X	64
Burnhead	S Lanak	NS7141	55°39·0′	4°2·6′W	X	71

Burnhead	S Lanak	NS7651	55°44·4'	3°58·1'W	X	64
Burnhead	S Lanak	NS7946	55°41·8'	3°55·1'W	X	64
Burnhead	S Lanak	NS8440	55°38·6'	3°50·2'W	X	71,72
Burnhead	Stir	NS8490	56°5·6'	3°51·4'W	X	58
Burnhead	W Loth	NS9561	55°50·1'	3°40·2'W	X	65
Burnhead Burn	E Ayr	NS4510	55°21·8'	4°26·3'W	W	70
Burnhead Cottages	Scot Bord	NT5117	55°26·9'	2°46·0'W	X	79
Burnhead Dam	Durham	NY9445	54°48·2'	2°5·2'W	W	87
Burnhead Fm	Scot Bord	NT2646	55°42·4'	3°10·2'W	FM	73
Burnhead Fm	S Lanak	NS8649	55°43·5'	3°48·5'W	FM	72
Burnhead Moor	Inverc	NS2873	55°55·4'	4°44·7'W	X	63
Burnhead of Cloquhat	Pth & Kin	NO1552	56°39·4'	3°22·7'W	X	53
Burnhead of Perkhill	Aberd	NJ5606	57°8·8'	2°43·2'W	X	37
Burnheads	Moray	NJ4960	57°37·9'	2°50·8'W	X	28,29
Burnhervie	Aberd	NJ7319	57°15·9'	2°26·4'W	X	38
Burn Hill	Bucks	SP7713	51°48·8'	0°52·6'W	X	165
Burnhill	D & G	NY0573	55°2·8'	3°28·8'W	X	85
Burn Hill	Durham	NZ0644	54°47·7'	1°54·0'W	X	87
Burn Hill	Somer	ST1124	51°0·7'	3°15·7'W	X	181,193
Burnhill Fm	Devon	ST0719	50°58·0'	3°19·1'W	FM	181
Burnhill Green	Staffs	SJ7800	52°36·1'	2°19·1'W	T	127
Burnhill Ho	Wakf	SE4617	53°39·1'	1°17·8'W	X	111
Burn Ho	Durham	NZ1717	54°33·1'	1°43·8'W	X	92
Burn Ho	Lancs	SD6852	53°58·0'	2°28·9'W	X	103
Burn Ho	Northum	NY7058	54°55·2'	2°27·7'W	X	86,87
Burn Ho	Northum	NY7963	54°57·9'	2°19·3'W	X	86,87
Burn Ho	Northum	NY8673	55°3·3'	2°12·7'W	X	87
Burn Hope	Durham	NY8139	54°45·0'	2°17·3'W	X	91,92
Burnhope	Durham	NZ1848	54°49·8'	1°42·8'W	T	88
Burn Hope	E Loth	NT6969	55°55·0'	2°29·3'W	X	67
Burnhope Burn	Durham	NY8238	54°44·4'	2°16·4'W	W	91,92
Burnhope Burn	Durham	NY9747	54°49·3'	2°2·4'W	W	87
Burnhope Burn	Durham	NZ0149	54°50·4'	1°58·6'W	W	87
Burnhope Dam	Durham	NY9646	54°48·8'	2°3·3'W	W	87
Burnhope Fm	Stock on T	NZ4117	54°33·0'	1°21·5'W	FM	93
Burnhope Moor	Durham	NY8138	54°44·4'	2°17·3'W	X	91,92
Burnhope Reservoir	Durham	NY8438	54°44·4'	2°14·5'W	W	91,92
Burnhope Seat	Cumbr	NY7837	54°43·9'	2°20·1'W	H	91
Burnhopeside Hall	Durham	NZ1846	54°48·8'	1°42·8'W	X	88
Burnhouse	E Ayr	NS5035	55°35·4'	4°22·4'W	X	70
Burnhouse	E Renf	NS5554	55°45·7'	4°18·2'W	X	64
Burnhouse	Falk	NS7984	56°2·3'	3°56·1'W	X	57,64
Burnhouse	N Ayr	NS3850	55°43·2'	4°34·3'W	T	63
Burnhouse	Northum	NU2130	55°34·0'	1°39·6'W	X	75
Burnhouse	Orkney	ND3090	58°47·8'	3°12·2'W	X	7
Burnhouse	Orkney	ND3095	58°50·5'	3°12·3'W	X	7
Burnhouse	S Ayr	NS3114	55°23·7'	4°39·7'W	X	70
Burnhouse	Scot Bord	NT4349	55°44·1'	2°54·0'W	X	73
Burnhouse	S Lanak	NS6150	55°43·7'	4°12·4'W	X	64
Burnhouse	S Lanak	NS6248	55°42·6'	4°11·4'W	X	64
Burnhouse	S Lanak	NS8937	55°37·1'	3°45·3'W	X	71,72
Burnhouse	S Lanak	NS9332	55°34·4'	3°41·4'W	X	71,72
Burnhouse	S Lanak	NS9745	55°41·5'	3°37·9'W	X	72
Burnhouse	W Loth	NS9364	55°51·7'	3°42·1'W	X	65
Burnhouse	W Loth	NT0371	55°55·6'	3°32·7'W	X	65
Burnhouse Fm	W Loth	NT0967	55°53·5'	3°26·9'W	FM	65
Burnhouse Mains	Scot Bord	NT4449	55°44·1'	2°53·1'W	T	73
Burnhouses	Scot Bord	NT7558	55°49·1'	2°23·5'W	X	67,74
Burn Howe	N Yks	SE9199	54°22·9'	0°35·5'W	A	94,101
Burn Howe Moor	N Yks	SE9498	54°22·4'	0°32·8'W	X	94,101
Burn Howe Rigg	N Yks	SE9198	54°22·4'	0°35·5'W	X	94,101
Burnicombe	Devon	SX8087	50°40·5'	3°41·5'W	X	191
Burniere	Corn	SW9873	50°31·6'	4°50·6'W	T	200
Burniestrype	Moray	NJ3163	57°39·4'	3°8·9'W	T	28
Burnigill	Durham	NZ2537	54°43·9'	1°36·3'W	X	93
Burning Cliff	Dorset	SY7681	50°37·9'	2°20·0'W	X	194
Burningfold Manor Stud	Surrey	TQ0034	51°6·0'	0°33·9'W	A	186
Burniston	N Yks	TA0193	54°19·6'	0°26·4'W	T	101
Burniston Beck	N Yks	TA0192	54°19·1'	0°26·4'W	W	101
Burn Knott	Cumbr	SD3286	54°16·2'	3°2·2'W	X	96,97
Burn Lane Fm	N Yks	SE5927	53°44·4'	1°5·9'W	FM	105
Burnlaw	Northum	NY7957	54°54·7'	2°19·2'W	X	86,87
Burnlee	Kirk	SE1207	53°33·8'	1°48·7'W	T	110
Burnley	Lancs	SD8332	53°47·3'	2°15·1'W	T	103
Burnley Hall	Norf	TG4719	52°43·0'	1°39·8'E	A	134
Burnley Lane	Lancs	SD8434	53°48·4'	2°14·2'W	T	103
Burnley Wood	Lancs	SD8431	53°46·7'	2°14·2'W	T	103
Burn Lodge Fm	N Yks	SE5827	53°44·4'	1°6·8'W	FM	105
Burnmakiman Burn	Arg & Bt	NS1472	55°54·6'	4°58·1'W	W	63
Burnmill	Aberd	NK0751	57°33·2'	1°52·5'W	X	30
Burn Mill	Scot Bord	NT5247	55°43·1'	2°45·4'W	X	73
Burn Moor	Cumbr	SD1492	54°19·2'	3°18·9'W	H	96
Burn Moor	Lancs	SD6964	54°4·5'	2°28·0'W	X	98
Burn Moor	Lancs	SD8443	53°53·2'	2°14·2'W	X	103
Burn Moor End	Lancs	SD8442	53°52·7'	2°14·2'W	X	103
Burn Moor Fell	N Yks	SD7064	54°4·5'	2°27·1'W	X	98
Burnmoor Lodge	Cumbr	NY1804	54°25·7'	3°15·4'W	X	89,90
Burnmoor Tarn	Cumbr	NY1804	54°25·7'	3°15·4'W	W	89,90
Burnmouth	Angus	NO3042	56°34·1'	3°7·9'W	X	53
Burnmouth	D & G	NS8305	55°19·8'	3°50·2'W	X	71,78
Burnmouth	Moray	NJ4850	57°32·5'	2°51·7'W	X	28,29
Burnmouth	Northum	NY7958	54°55·2'	2°19·2'W	X	86,87
Burnmouth	Northum	NY7988	55°11·4'	2°19·4'W	X	80
Burnmouth	Orkney	ND2098	58°52·0'	3°22·7'W	X	7
Burnmouth	S Ayr	NS3312	55°22·7'	4°37·7'W	X	70
Burnmouth	Scot Bord	NT9561	55°50·8'	2°4·4'W	T	67
Burnmouth Cottages	Northum	NY8974	55°3·9'	2°9·9'W	X	87
Burnmouth Ferry	Pth & Kin	NO1133	56°29·1'	3°26·3'W	X	53
Burnmouth Fm	Scot Bord	NY5595	55°15·1'	2°42·0'W	FM	80
Burnmouth Hill	Scot Bord	NT9561	55°50·8'	2°4·4'W	X	67
Burn Naze	Lancs	SD3343	53°53·0'	3°0·7'W	T	102
Burnockhead	E Ayr	NS5114	55°24·1'	4°20·8'W	X	70
Burnock Mill	E Ayr	NS5017	55°25·7'	4°21·8'W	X	70
Burnock Water	E Ayr	NS5018	55°26·2'	4°21·8'W	W	70
Burn of Aberlour	Moray	NJ2739	57°26·4'	3°12·5'W	W	28
Burn of Acharole	Highld	ND2251	58°26·7'	3°19·7'W	W	11,12
Burn of Achlais	Stir	NS4591	56°5·5'	4°29·0'W	W	57
Burn of Adedazzle	Angus	NO4785	56°57·5'	2°51·8'W	W	44
Burn of Adekimore	Angus	NO4585	56°57·4'	2°53·8'W	W	44
Burn of Adikinear	Angus	NO4272	56°50·4'	2°56·6'W	W	44

Burn of Agie	Highld	NN3790	56°58·6'	4°40·5'W	W	34
Burn of Aith	Shetld	HU6490	60°35·6'	0°49·4'W	W	1,2
Burn of Allanstank	Aberd	NO5189	56°59·6'	2°47·9'W	W	44
Burn of Altavallie	Moray	NJ2831	57°22·1'	3°11·4'W	W	37
Burn of Altibrair	D & G	NX1470	54°59·6'	4°54·0'W	W	76
Burn of Ample	Stir	NN5918	56°20·3'	4°16·4'W	W	57
Burn of Arisdale	Shetld	HU4783	60°31·9'	1°8·1'W	W	1,2,3
Burn of Asleid	Aberd	NJ8342	57°28·3'	2°16·5'W	W	29,30
Burn of Atlascord	Shetld	HU3753	60°15·8'	1°19·4'W	W	3
Burn of Auchentumb	Aberd	NJ9357	57°36·4'	2°6·6'W	W	30
Burn of Auchintoul	Aberd	NJ6052	57°33·6'	2°39·7'W	W	29
Burn of Auchrannie	Pth & Kin	NO2752	56°39·5'	3°11·0'W	W	53
Burn of Auldmad	Aberd	NO4989	56°59·6'	2°49·9'W	W	44
Burn of Aultmore	Moray	NJ4554	57°34·6'	2°54·7'W	W	28,29
Burn of Aultmore	Moray	NJ4556	57°35·7'	2°54·7'W	X	28,29
Burn of Badanseaneach	Aberd	NJ3907	57°9·2'	3°0·0'W	W	37
Burn of Badymicks	Aberd	NO5883	56°56·4'	2°41·0'W	W	44
Burn of Bailiefea	Orkney	ND2796	58°51·0'	3°15·4'W	W	6,7
Burn of Balmakelly	Aberd	NO6967	56°47·9'	2°30·0'W	W	45
Burn of Balmakelly	Aberd	NO7068	56°48·4'	2°29·0'W	X	45
Burn of Balquholly	Aberd	NJ7846	57°30·5'	2°21·6'W	W	29,30
Burn of Bank	Moray	NJ3923	57°17·9'	3°0·3'W	W	37
Burn of Basta	Shetld	HU5194	60°37·8'	1°3·6'W	W	1,2
Burn of Bathie	Angus	NO4677	56°53·1'	2°52·7'W	W	44
Burn of Beag	Angus	NO5276	56°52·6'	2°46·8'W	W	44
Burn of Berryhill	Angus	NO4976	56°52·6'	2°49·8'W	W	44
Burn of Birse	Aberd	NO5496	57°3·4'	2°45·1'W	W	37,44
Burn of Black Butten	Shetld	HU3084	60°32·6'	1°26·7'W	W	1,3
Burn of Blackpots	Angus	NO5680	56°54·8'	2°42·9'W	W	44
Burn of Blaranduall	Highld	NH8848	57°30·8'	3°51·7'W	W	27
Burn of Boyndie	Aberd	NJ6463	57°39·6'	2°35·7'W	W	29
Burn of Boyne	Aberd	NJ5658	57°36·9'	2°43·7'W	W	29
Burn of Boyne	Aberd	NJ5960	57°37·9'	2°40·7'W	W	29
Burn of Braco	Moray	NJ5053	57°34·1'	2°49·7'W	W	29
Burn of Branny	Angus	NO4484	56°56·9'	2°54·8'W	W	44
Burn of Breitoe	Shetld	HU4025	60°0·7'	1°16·5'W	W	4
Burn of Brown	Highld	NJ1117	57°14·4'	3°28·0'W	W	36
Burn of Brydock	Aberd	NJ6558	57°36·9'	2°34·7'W	W	29
Burn of Buckie	Moray	NJ4363	57°39·5'	2°56·9'W	W	28
Burn of Cairnie	Aberd	NJ4945	57°29·8'	2°50·6'W	W	28,29
Burn of Calanach	Angus	NO4681	56°55·3'	2°52·8'W	W	44
Burn of Caldback	Shetld	HP5906	60°44·2'	0°54·6'W	W	1
Burn of Calletar	Angus	NO4969	56°48·8'	2°49·7'W	W	44
Burn of Cambus	Stir	NN7003	56°12·4'	4°5·3'W	T	57
Burn of Cammie	Aberd	NO5187	56°58·6'	2°47·9'W	W	44
Burn of Canny	Aberd	NO6598	57°4·6'	2°34·2'W	W	38,45
Burn of Carron	Moray	NJ2340	57°26·9'	3°16·5'W	W	28
Burn of Cat	Angus	NO4884	56°56·9'	2°50·8'W	W	44
Burn of Cattie	Aberd	NO5693	57°1·8'	2°43·0'W	W	37,44
Burn of Cattiksimires	Shetld	HU2253	60°15·9'	1°35·6'W	W	3
Burn of Cauldcots	Aberd	NO6374	56°51·6'	2°36·0'W	W	45
Burn of Clashgour	Moray	NJ1146	57°30·0'	3°28·6'W	W	28
Burn of Clashmad	Aberd	NO6189	56°59·7'	2°38·1'W	W	45
Burn of Claver	Shetld	HU3923	59°59·7'	1°17·6'W	W	4
Burn of Clearach	Angus	NO4983	56°56·4'	2°49·8'W	W	44
Burn of Cobairdy	Aberd	NJ5742	57°28·2'	2°42·6'W	W	29
Burn of Cochlie	Angus	NO4576	56°52·6'	2°53·7'W	W	44
Burn of Coirebreac	Moray	NJ2622	57°17·2'	3°13·2'W	W	37
Burn of Coire Seileach	Highld	NJ1332	57°22·5'	3°26·3'W	W	36
Burn of Collieston	Aberd	NK0130	57°21·9'	1°58·5'W	W	30
Burn of Colp	Aberd	NJ7448	57°31·5'	2°25·6'W	W	29
Burn of Cook	Aberd	NJ7956	57°35·9'	2°20·6'W	X	29,30
Burn of Corchinnan	Aberd	NJ4322	57°17·4'	2°56·3'W	W	37
Burn of Corfinnoch	Aberd	NO6076	56°52·7'	2°38·9'W	W	45
Burn of Corn	Aberd	NO5090	57°0·2'	2°48·9'W	W	44
Burn of Coroglie	Angus	NO3459	56°43·3'	3°4·3'W	W	54
Burn of Coroglie	Angus	NO3560	56°43·9'	3°3·3'W	W	44
Burn of Corrhatnich	Moray	NJ1749	57°31·7'	3°22·7'W	W	28
Burn of Corrichie	Aberd	NJ7101	57°6·2'	2°28·3'W	W	38
Burn of Corriedoune	Angus	NO4376	56°52·6'	2°55·7'W	W	44
Burn of Corriehausherun	Angus	NO4379	56°54·2'	2°55·7'W	W	44
Burn of Corries	Moray	NJ1849	57°31·7'	3°21·7'W	W	28
Burn of Corrigall	Orkney	HY3319	59°3·4'	3°9·6'W	W	6
Burn of Corscarie	Angus	NO4470	56°49·3'	2°54·6'W	W	44
Burn of Couster	Shetld	HU4236	60°6·7'	1°14·2'W	W	4
Burn of Craig	Aberd	NJ4625	57°19·0'	2°53·3'W	W	37
Burn of Crookadale	Shetld	HU4254	60°16·3'	1°13·9'W	W	3
Burn of Crooksetter	Shetld	HU4075	60°27·7'	1°15·9'W	W	2,3
Burn of Curran	Aberd	NO6990	57°0·3'	2°30·2'W	W	38,45
Burn of Dairy	Angus	NO3060	56°43·8'	3°8·2'W	W	44
Burn of Dalamut	Shetld	HU4687	60°34·1'	1°9·1'W	W	1,2
Burn of Dalbrack	Angus	NO4677	56°53·1'	2°52·7'W	W	44
Burn of Dale	Shetld	HU2053	60°15·9'	1°37·8'W	W	3
Burn of Dale	Shetld	HU4342	60°9·9'	1°13·0'W	W	4
Burn of Dalforth	Angus	NO5777	56°53·2'	2°41·9'W	W	44
Burn of Darnich	Angus	NO5172	56°50·5'	2°47·7'W	W	44
Burn of Davidston	Aberd	NJ4144	57°29·2'	2°58·6'W	W	28
Burn of Day	Aberd	NO8087	56°58·7'	2°19·3'W	X	45
Burn of Deepdale	Shetld	HU3825	60°0·7'	1°18·6'W	W	4
Burn of Deskford	Moray	NJ5162	57°39·0'	2°48·8'W	W	29
Burn of Deuchary	Angus	NO5175	56°52·1'	2°47·8'W	W	44
Burn of Doune	Angus	NO3984	56°56·9'	2°59·7'W	W	44
Burn of Drimmie	Pth & Kin	NO1752	56°39·4'	3°20·8'W	W	53
Burn of Drumblade	Aberd	NJ5942	57°28·2'	2°40·6'W	W	29
Burn of Drumcairn	Angus	NO5370	56°49·4'	2°45·8'W	W	44
Burn of Drumhendry	Moray	NJ3544	57°29·2'	3°4·6'W	W	28
Burn of Duchrey	Angus	NO4278	56°53·6'	2°56·7'W	W	44
Burn of Duglenny	Aberd	NO6885	56°57·6'	2°31·1'W	W	45
Burn of Durn	Aberd	NJ5661	57°38·5'	2°43·8'W	W	29
Burn of Duskintry	Angus	NO4272	56°50·4'	2°56·6'W	W	44
Burn of Easterbutton	Shetld	HU3969	60°24·4'	1°17·0'W	W	2,3
Burn of East Mires	Shetld	HU4995	60°38·4'	1°5·7'W	W	1,2
Burn of Edendocher	Aberd	NO5983	56°56·4'	2°40·0'W	W	44
Burn of Edendocher	Aberd	NO6084	56°57·0'	2°39·0'W	W	45
Burn of Edinglassie	Moray	NJ4138	57°26·0'	2°58·5'W	W	28
Burn of Edramucky	Pth & Kin	NN6137	56°30·5'	4°15·1'W	W	51
Burn of Eelawater	Shetld	HU3177	60°28·8'	1°25·7'W	W	3
Burn of Elsick	Aberd	NO8994	57°2·5'	2°10·4'W	W	38,45
Burn of Etheriegeo	Orkney	HY3225	59°6·7'	3°10·8'W	W	6
Burn of Farchal	Angus	NO2869	56°48·7'	3°10·3'W	W	44

Burn of Fasheilach	Angus	NO3585	56°57·4'	3°3·7'W	W	44
Burn of Favat	Moray	NJ2632	57°22·6'	3°13·4'W	W	37
Burn of Favat	Moray	NJ2733	57°23·2'	3°12·4'W	W	28
Burn of Fialzioch	Angus	NO2276	56°52·4'	3°16·3'W	W	44
Burn of Fishrie	Aberd	NJ7758	57°36·9'	2°22·6'W	W	29,30
Burn of Fitch	Shetld	HU4240	60°8·8'	1°14·1'W	W	4
Burn of Fochabers	Moray	NJ3656	57°35·6'	3°3·8'W	W	28
Burn of Forbie	Angus	NO5675	56°52·1'	2°42·9'W	W	44
Burn of Fordyce	Aberd	NJ5563	57°39·5'	2°44·8'W	W	29
Burn of Forgue	Aberd	NJ5944	57°29·3'	2°40·6'W	W	29
Burn of Forse	Orkney	ND2294	58°49·9'	3°20·6'W	W	7
Burn of Forse	Shetld	HU4457	60°18·0'	1°11·7'W	W	2,3
Burn of Forvie	Aberd	NK0132	57°23·0'	1°58·5'W	W	30
Burn of Frakkafield	Shetld	HU4342	60°9·9'	1°13·0'W	W	4
Burn of Freoch	Angus	NO5171	56°49·9'	2°47·7'W	W	44
Burn of Funzie	Shetld	HU6589	60°35·0'	0°48·3'W	W	1,2
Burn of Garrat	Angus	NO5275	56°52·1'	2°46·8'W	W	44
Burn of Garrol	Aberd	NO6576	56°52·7'	2°34·0'W	W	45
Burn of Garth	Shetld	HP5401	60°41·6'	1°0·2'W	W	1
Burn of Gask	Aberd	NJ7247	57°31·0'	2°27·6'W	W	29
Burn of Geosetter	Shetld	HU3820	59°58·1'	1°18·7'W	W	4
Burn of Gerdie	Shetld	HP6207	60°44·7'	0°51·3'W	W	1
Burn of Glansie	Angus	NO4469	56°48·8'	2°54·6'W	W	44
Burn of Glascorrie	Angus	NO4382	56°55·8'	2°55·7'W	W	44
Burn of Glendui	Aberd	NO4293	57°1·7'	2°56·9'W	W	37,44
Burn of Glenmoye	Angus	NO4064	56°46·1'	2°58·4'W	W	44
Burn of Glenny	Aberd	NJ4423	57°17·9'	2°55·3'W	W	37
Burn of Gossawater	Shetld	HU5099	60°40·5'	1°4·6'W	W	1
Burn of Goster	Shetld	HU1851	60°14·8'	1°40·0'W	W	3
Burn of Gowal	Angus	NO2380	56°54·6'	3°15·4'W	W	44
Burn of Greendams	Aberd	NO6389	56°59·7'	2°36·1'W	W	45
Burn of Greenheads	Orkney	ND2392	58°48·8'	3°19·5'W	W	7
Burn of Griesta	Shetld	HU4144	60°11·0'	1°15·2'W	W	4
Burn of Grunnafirth	Shetld	HU4559	60°19·0'	1°10·6'W	W	2,3
Burn of Guinea	Aberd	NO7481	56°55·4'	2°25·2'W	X	45
Burn of Hamarifield	Shetld	HU4026	60°1·3'	1°16·5'W	W	4
Burn of Hamnavoe	Shetld	HU4981	60°30·8'	1°6·0'W	W	1,2,3
Burn of Heldale	Orkney	ND2791	58°48·3'	3°15·3'W	W	7
Burn of Heughs	Angus	NO3771	56°49·8'	3°1·5'W	W	44
Burn of Hillside	Orkney	HY3123	59°5·6'	3°11·8'W	W	6
Burn of Hillwell	Shetld	HU3614	59°54·8'	1°20·9'W	W	4
Burn of Hogston	Aberd	NJ5144	57°29·3'	2°48·6'W	W	29
Burn of Holmhead	Angus	NO5577	56°53·2'	2°43·9'W	W	44
Burn of Holsas	Shetld	HU4132	60°4·5'	1°15·3'W	W	4
Burn of Houlland	Shetld	HU3687	60°34·2'	1°20·1'W	W	1,2
Burn of Houstry	Highld	ND1534	58°17·4'	3°26·5'W	W	11,17
Burn of Hummelton	Shetld	HU5282	60°31·4'	1°2·7'W	W	1,2,3
Burn of Inchmill	Angus	NO3368	56°48·2'	3°5·4'W	W	44
Burn of Kaywick	Shetld	HU5292	60°36·7'	1°2·5'W	W	1,2
Burn of Keddloch	Angus	NO4985	56°57·5'	2°49·9'W	W	44
Burn of Keenie	Angus	NO5176	56°52·6'	2°47·8'W	W	44
Burn of Kergord	Shetld	HU4059	60°19·1'	1°16·1'W	W	2,3
Burn of Kilbo	Angus	NO2674	56°51·4'	3°12·4'W	W	44
Burn of Kilry	Angus	NO2354	56°40·5'	3°15·0'W	W	53
Burn of Kirkhouse	Shetld	HU3961	60°20·1'	1°17·1'W	W	2,3
Burn of Kirny	Angus	NO4582	56°55·8'	2°53·8'W	W	44
Burn of Knock	Aberd	NO7091	57°0·8'	2°29·2'W	W	38,45
Burn of Lambawater	Shetld	HU3756	60°17·5'	1°19·3'W	W	2,3
Burn of Latheronwheel	Highld	ND1835	58°18·0'	3°23·5'W	W	11
Burn of Laurie	Angus	NO5279	56°54·2'	2°46·8'W	W	44
Burn of Laxdale	Shetld	HU4131	60°4·0'	1°15·3'W	W	4
Burn of Laxobigging	Shetld	HU4172	60°26·1'	1°14·8'W	W	2,3
Burn of Leuchary	Aberd	NO5580	56°54·8'	2°43·9'W	W	44
Burn of Little Fergie	Moray	NJ1711	57°11·2'	3°21·9'W	W	36
Burn of Lochans	Moray	NJ1648	57°31·1'	3°23·7'W	W	28
Burn of Lochy	Moray	NJ1323	57°17·6'	3°26·2'W	W	36
Burn of Loin	Moray	NJ1409	57°10·1'	3°24·9'W	W	36
Burn of Loinherry	Aberd	NJ2410	57°10·7'	3°15·0'W	W	36
Burn of Longley	Aberd	NJ4227	57°20·1'	2°57·3'W	W	37
Burn of Longshank	Angus	NO3577	56°53·0'	3°3·6'W	W	44
Burn of Louie	Angus	NO2671	56°49·7'	3°12·3'W	W	44
Burn of Luchray	Aberd	NO6983	56°56·5'	2°30·1'W	W	45
Burn of Ludquharn	Aberd	NK0143	57°28·9'	1°58·5'W	W	30
Burn of Lungatou	Shetld	HU2054	60°16·4'	1°37·8'W	W	3
Burn of Lunklet	Shetld	HU3757	60°18·0'	1°19·3'W	W	2,3
Burn of Lushan	Orkney	HY3323	59°5·6'	3°9·7'W	W	6
Burn of Lyneriach	Moray	NJ2135	57°24·2'	3°18·4'W	W	28
Burn of Lyth	Highld	ND2961	58°32·1'	3°12·7'W	W	11,12
Burn of Mail	Shetld	HU4128	60°2·3'	1°15·4'W	W	4
Burn of Mailand	Shetld	HP6008	60°45·3'	0°53·4'W	W	1
Burn of Mangaster	Shetld	HU3372	60°26·1'	1°23·5'W	W	2,3
Burn of Mar	Stir	NS4392	56°6·0'	4°31·0'W	W	56
Burn of Mar	Stir	NS4492	56°6·0'	4°30·0'W	W	57
Burn of Marno	Aberd	NJ9460	57°38·1'	2°5·6'W	W	30
Burn of Marrofield-water	Shetld	HU3758	60°18·5'	1°19·3'W	W	2,3
Burn of Meallie	Angus	NO5679	56°54·3'	2°42·9'W	W	44
Burn of Melmannoch	Aberd	NO6989	56°59·7'	2°30·2'W	W	45
Burn of Melrose	Aberd	NJ7564	57°40·2'	2°24·7'W	W	29
Burn of Monboys	Aberd	NO8590	57°0·3'	2°14·4'W	W	38,45
Burn of Monquhitter	Aberd	NJ8151	57°33·2'	2°18·6'W	W	29,30
Burn of Mooran	Angus	NO5574	56°51·6'	2°43·8'W	W	44
Burn of Muchalls	Aberd	NO8891	57°0·9'	2°11·4'W	W	38,45
Burn of Mulben	Moray	NJ3351	57°32·9'	3°6·7'W	W	28
Burn of Myrehouse	Aberd	NJ7163	57°39·6'	2°28·7'W	W	29
Burn of Nevie	Moray	NJ2228	57°20·4'	3°17·3'W	W	36
Burn of Ola's Loch	Shetld	HU3485	60°33·1'	1°22·3'W	W	1,2,3
Burn of Olas Voe	Shetld	HU2946	60°12·1'	1°28·1'W	W	4
Burn of Oldtown	Angus	NO5470	56°49·4'	2°44·8'W	W	44
Burn of Ore	Orkney	ND2893	58°49·4'	3°14·3'W	W	7
Burn of Orrwick	Shetld	HU3381	60°30·9'	1°23·4'W	W	1,2,3
Burn of Paithnick	Moray	NJ4752	57°33·6'	2°52·7'W	W	28,29
Burn of Pettawater	Shetld	HU4156	60°17·4'	1°15·0'W	W	2,3
Burn of Quaichly	Angus	NO2960	56°43·8'	3°9·2'W	W	44
Burn of Quoys	Shetld	HU4455	60°16·9'	1°11·8'W	W	3
Burn of Ranoch	Angus	NO5576	56°52·6'	2°43·8'W	W	44
Burn of Reafirth	Shetld	HU5189	60°35·1'	1°3·6'W	W	1,2
Burn of Redglen	Orkney	HY2101	58°53·6'	3°21·8'W	W	6,7
Burn of Redshank	Angus	NO4589	56°59·6'	2°53·9'W	W	44
Burn of Roerwater	Shetld	HU3585	60°33·1'	1°21·2'W	W	1,2,3
Burn of Rothes	Moray	NJ2348	57°31·2'	3°16·7'W	W	28

Burn of Rothes	Moray	NJ2547	57°30·7′	3°14·7′W	X	28
Burn of Rusht	Orkney	HY3421	59°4·5′	3°8·6′W	W	6
Burn of Russdale	Shetld	HU4128	60°2·3′	1°15·4′W	W	4
Burn of Ruthven	Highld	NN7697	57°3·1′	4°2·2′W	W	35
Burn of Sandgarth	Shetld	HU4067	60°23·4′	1°16·0′W	W	2,3
Burn of Sandvoe	Shetld	HU3590	60°35·8′	1°21·2′W	W	1,2
Burn of Sandwater	Shetld	HU4152	60°15·3′	1°15·1′W	W	3
Burn of Sandwick	Shetld	HU5497	60°39·4′	1°0·2′W	W	1
Burn of Saughs	Aberd	NO5683	56°56·4′	2°42·9′W	W	44
Burn of Scatsta	Shetld	HU3871	60°25·5′	1°18·1′W	W	2,3
Burn of Scrooie	Shetld	HU3146	60°12·1′	1°26·0′W	W	4
Burn of Scutta Voe	Shetld	HU2849	60°13·7′	1°29·2′W	W	3
Burn of Segal	Orkney	HY2002	58°54·1′	3°22·8′W	W	7
Burn of Selivoe	Shetld	HU3049	60°13·7′	1°27·0′W	W	3
Burn of Selta	Orkney	HY2212	58°59·5′	3°21·0′W	W	6
Burn of Setter	Shetld	HU2150	60°14·3′	1°36·7′W	W	3
Burn of Setter	Shetld	HU4889	60°35·2′	1°6·9′W	W	1,2
Burn of Sevdale	Shetld	HU3921	59°58·6′	1°17·6′W	W	4
Burn of Sheeoch	Aberd	NO7490	57°0·3′	2°25·2′W	W	38,45
Burn of Skaw	Shetld	HP6416	60°49·6′	0°48·9′W	W	1
Burn of Skinna	Aberd	NO4793	57°1·8′	2°51·9′W	W	37,44
Burn of Slidderies	Angus	NO3677	56°53·1′	3°2·6′W	W	44
Burn of Sligatu	Shetld	HU4781	60°30·9′	1°8·1′W	W	1,2,3
Burn of Sorrow	Clackm	NS9599	56°10·6′	3°41·0′W	W	58
Burn of Strand	Shetld	HU4245	60°11·5′	1°14·1′W	W	4
Burn of Sundibanks	Shetld	HU4037	60°7·2′	1°16·3′W	W	4
Burn of Swartabeck	Orkney	HY3808	58°57·5′	3°4·2′W	W	6,7
Burn of Sweenalay	Orkney	HY3819	59°3·5′	3°4·4′W	W	6
Burn of Tactigill	Shetld	HU3751	60°14·8′	1°19·4′W	W	3
Burn of Teckmires	Shetld	HU1954	60°16·5′	1°38·9′W	W	3
Burn of Tennet	Angus	NO5183	56°56·4′	2°47·9′W	W	44
Burn of Tervie	Moray	NJ2230	57°21·5′	3°17·3′W	W	36
Burn of the Boitan	Shetld	HU4030	60°3·4′	1°16·4′W	W	4
Burn of the Cowlatt	Moray	NJ1644	57°29·0′	3°23·6′W	W	28
Burn of the Dupin	S Ayr	NX0874	55°1·7′	4°59·8′W	W	76
Burn of the Greystane	Shetld	HU4026	60°1·3′	1°16·5′W	W	4
Burn of the Run	Shetld	HU4028	60°2·4′	1°16·4′W	W	4
Burn of the Twa-roes	Shetld	HU3484	60°32·6′	1°22·3′W	W	1,2,3
Burn of the White Horse	Orkney	ND2797	58°51·5′	3°15·4′W	W	6,7
Burn of Tingon	Shetld	HU2482	60°31·5′	1°33·3′W	W	3
Burn of Tippochs	Moray	NJ1648	57°31·1′	3°23·7′W	W	28
Burn of Tonburn	Aberd	NJ4726	57°19·5′	2°52·4′W	W	37
Burn of Tornahaish	Aberd	NJ2906	57°8·6′	3°9·9′W	W	37
Burn of Towie	Moray	NJ3846	57°30·3′	3°1·6′W	W	28
Burn of Tronamoor	Shetld	HU4884	60°32·5′	1°7·0′W	W	1,2,3
Burn of Tronister	Shetld	HU4665	60°22·2′	1°9·5′W	W	2,3
Burn of Tulchan	Highld	NJ1136	57°24·6′	3°28·4′W	W	28
Burn of Turret	Angus	NO5481	56°55·3′	2°44·9′W	W	44
Burn of Turriff	Aberd	NJ7348	57°31·5′	2°26·6′W	W	29
Burn of Twatt	Shetld	HU3253	60°15·9′	1°24·8′W	W	3
Burn of Tynet	Moray	NJ3861	57°38·3′	3°1·8′W	W	28
Burn of Urie	Shetld	HU5993	60°37·2′	0°54·8′W	W	1,2
Burn of Valayre	Shetld	HU3769	60°24·5′	1°19·2′W	W	2,3
Burn of Veng	Shetld	HU5036	60°6·6′	1°5·5′W	W	4
Burn of Voesgarth	Shetld	HP6107	60°44·7′	0°52·4′W	W	1
Burn of Voxter	Shetld	HU3760	60°19·6′	1°19·3′W	W	2,3
Burn of Waterhead	Aberd	NO6284	56°57·0′	2°37·0′W	W	45
Burn of Weisdale	Shetld	HU4054	60°16·4′	1°16·1′W	W	3
Burn of Weisdale	Shetld	HU4057	60°18·0′	1°16·1′W	W	2,3
Burn of Westerbutton	Shetld	HU3969	60°24·4′	1°17·0′W	W	2,3
Burn of Windhouse	Shetld	HU4993	60°37·3′	1°5·8′W	W	1,2
Burn of Winnaswarta Dale	Shetld	HP6015	60°49·1′	0°53·3′W	W	1
Burn of Withigill	Orkney	ND2696	58°51·0′	3°16·5′W	W	6,7
Burn of Woodwick	Orkney	HY3722	59°5·1′	3°5·5′W	W	6
Burn o' Need	E Ayr	NS5630	55°32·8′	4°16·5′W	W	71
Burn o' Need Rig	E Ayr	NS5630	55°32·8′	4°16·5′W	X	71
Burnoon	Corn	SW7022	50°3·5′	5°12·4′W	X	203
Burnopfield	Durham	NZ1656	54°54·2′	1°44·6′W	T	88
Burnorrachie	Aberd	NO8791	57°0·9′	2°12·4′W	X	38,45
Burn o' Vat	Aberd	NO4299	57°5·0′	2°57·0′W	X	37,44
Burnow	Corn	SW6623	50°3·9′	5°15·8′W	X	203
Burn Park	E Yorks	TA0334	53°47·8′	0°25·8′W	X	107
Burn Rew Fm	Devon	ST0210	50°53·1′	3°23·2′W	FM	192
Burnrigg	Cumbr	NY4755	54°53·5′	2°49·2′W	T	86
Burn River	Devon	SS9607	50°51·4′	3°28·3′W	W	192
Burnroot	Aberd	NO4897	57°3·9′	2°51·0′W	X	37,44
Burnroot	Aberd	NO6970	56°49·5′	2°30·0′W	X	45
Burns	Aberd	NJ4213	57°12·5′	2°57·2′W	X	37
Burns	Aberd	NJ5558	57°36·8′	2°44·7′W	X	29
Burns	D & G	NX4859	54°54·4′	4°21·8′W	X	83
Burns	Scot Bord	NT6406	55°21·1′	2°33·6′W	X	80
Burns	Shetld	HT9639	60°8·4′	2°3·8′W	X	4
Burnsall	N Yks	SE0361	54°2·9′	1°56·8′W	T	98
Burnsall and Thorpe Fell	N Yks	SE0159	54°1·9′	1°58·7′W	X	104
Burnsands	D & G	NS8403	55°18·7′	3°49·2′W	X	78
Burnsands Burn	D & G	NS8304	55°19·2′	3°50·2′W	W	78
Burns Cott	S Ayr	NS3318	55°25·9′	4°37·9′W	X	70
Burnseat	Aberd	NJ7309	57°10·5′	2°26·3′W	X	38
Burns Fm	Cumbr	NY3024	54°36·6′	3°4·6′W	FM	90
Burns Fm	Cumbr	SD3679	54°12·4′	2°58·5′W	FM	96,97
Burns Fm	Lancs	SD5147	53°55·3′	2°44·4′W	FM	102
Burn's Fm	Leeds	SE3444	53°53·7′	1°28·5′W	FM	104
Burns Fm	Notts	SK5768	53°12·6′	1°8·4′W	FM	120
Burnsford	Moray	NJ5063	57°39·5′	2°49·8′W	X	29
Burn's Green	Herts	TL3022	51°53·1′	0°6·3′W	T	166
Burns Hall	Devon	SX4482	50°37·2′	4°11·9′W	X	201
Burnshangie	Aberd	NJ9555	57°35·4′	2°4·6′W	X	30
Burnshot	Falk	NT0479	55°59·9′	3°31·9′W	X	65
Burnshot Wood	C of Edin	NT1677	55°59·0′	3°20·3′W	F	65,66
Burnside	Aberd	NJ2808	57°9·7′	3°11·0′W	X	37
Burnside	Aberd	NJ4601	57°6·1′	2°53·0′W	X	37
Burnside	Aberd	NJ4723	57°17·9′	2°52·3′W	X	37
Burnside	Aberd	NJ5008	57°9·9′	2°49·1′W	X	37
Burnside	Aberd	NJ5560	57°37·9′	2°44·8′W	X	29
Burnside	Aberd	NJ5722	57°17·5′	2°42·3′W	X	37
Burnside	Aberd	NJ6018	57°15·3′	2°39·3′W	X	37
Burnside	Aberd	NJ6027	57°20·2′	2°39·4′W	X	37
Burnside	Aberd	NJ6439	57°26·7′	2°35·5′W	X	29
Burnside	Aberd	NJ6444	57°29·3′	2°35·6′W	X	29
Burnside	Aberd	NJ6561	57°38·5′	2°34·7′W	X	29
Burnside	Aberd	NJ6911	57°11·6′	2°30·3′W	X	38
Burnside	Aberd	NJ7363	57°39·6′	2°26·7′W	X	29
Burnside	Aberd	NJ7552	57°33·7′	2°24·6′W	X	29
Burnside	Aberd	NJ7606	57°8·9′	2°23·3′W	X	38
Burnside	Aberd	NJ7633	57°23·5′	2°23·5′W	X	29
Burnside	Aberd	NJ7712	57°12·1′	2°22·4′W	X	38
Burnside	Aberd	NJ8049	57°32·1′	2°19·6′W	X	29,30
Burnside	Aberd	NJ8244	57°29·4′	2°17·6′W	X	29,30
Burnside	Aberd	NJ8245	57°29·9′	2°17·6′W	X	29,30
Burnside	Aberd	NJ8518	57°15·4′	2°14·5′W	X	38
Burnside	Aberd	NJ8723	57°18·1′	2°12·5′W	X	38
Burnside	Aberd	NJ9017	57°14·9′	2°9·5′W	X	38
Burnside	Aberd	NJ9853	57°34·3′	2°1·5′W	X	30
Burnside	Aberd	NK0259	57°37·5′	1°57·5′W	X	30
Burnside	Aberd	NK0651	57°33·2′	1°53·5′W	X	30
Burnside	Aberd	NO4797	57°3·9′	2°52·0′W	X	37,44
Burnside	Aberd	NO5496	57°3·4′	2°45·1′W	X	37,44
Burnside	Aberd	NO7271	56°50·0′	2°27·1′W	X	45
Burnside	Aberd	NO8393	57°1·9′	2°16·4′W	X	38,45
Burnside	Aberd	NO8597	57°4·1′	2°14·4′W	X	38,45
Burnside	Aberd	NO8791	57°0·9′	2°12·4′W	X	38,45
Burnside	Angus	NO2254	56°40·5′	3°15·9′W	X	53
Burnside	Angus	NO3850	56°38·5′	3°0·2′W	X	54
Burnside	Angus	NO4259	56°43·4′	2°56·4′W	X	54
Burnside	Angus	NO4782	56°55·8′	2°51·8′W	X	44
Burnside	Angus	NO5050	56°38·6′	2°48·5′W	X	54
Burnside	Angus	NO5946	56°36·5′	2°39·6′W	X	54
Burnside	Angus	NO6053	56°40·3′	2°38·7′W	X	54
Burnside	Clackm	NS8997	56°9·4′	3°46·8′W	X	58
Burnside	D & G	NX8587	55°10·1′	3°47·9′W	X	78
Burnside	D & G	NX8675	55°3·6′	3°46·7′W	X	84
Burnside	D & G	NX8857	54°54·0′	3°44·4′W	X	84
Burnside	D & G	NX9283	55°8·0′	3°41·2′W	X	78
Burnside	D & G	NX9571	55°1·6′	3°38·1′W	X	84
Burnside	D & G	NX9988	55°10·8′	3°34·7′W	X	78
Burnside	D & G	NY0487	55°10·3′	3°30·0′W	X	78
Burnside	D & G	NY0682	55°7·7′	3°28·0′W	X	78
Burnside	D & G	NY1668	55°0·2′	3°18·4′W	X	85
Burnside	D & G	NY4177	55°5·3′	2°55·0′W	X	85
Burnside	E Ayr	NS4314	55°23·9′	4°28·3′W	X	70
Burnside	E Ayr	NS4516	55°25·1′	4°26·5′W	X	70
Burnside	E Ayr	NS5811	55°22·6′	4°14·0′W	T	71
Burnside	E Renf	NS4955	55°46·1′	4°24·0′W	X	64
Burnside	Fife	NO1608	56°15·7′	3°20·9′W	T	58
Burnside	Fife	NO3203	56°13·1′	3°5·3′W	X	59
Burnside	Fife	NO3704	56°13·7′	3°0·5′W	X	59
Burnside	Fife	NO4422	56°23·5′	2°54·0′W	X	54,59
Burnside	Fife	NO4527	56°26·2′	2°53·1′W	X	54,59
Burnside	Fife	NO4615	56°19·7′	2°52·0′W	X	59
Burnside	Fife	NT0193	56°7·4′	3°35·1′W	X	58
Burnside	Herts	TL2610	51°46·7′	0°10·0′W	X	166
Burnside	Highld	ND2661	58°32·1′	3°15·8′W	X	11,12
Burnside	Highld	NH6292	57°54·0′	4°19·2′W	X	21
Burnside	Highld	NH6859	57°36·4′	4°12·1′W	X	26
Burnside	Highld	NH7158	57°35·9′	4°9·0′W	X	27
Burnside	Highld	NH9440	57°26·5′	3°45·5′W	X	27
Burnside	Highld	NH9452	57°33·0′	3°45·8′W	X	27
Burnside	Highld	NJ0826	57°19·2′	3°31·2′W	X	36
Burnside	Inverc	NS3673	55°55·6′	4°37·1′W	X	63
Burn Side	Lancs	SD6853	53°58·6′	2°28·9′W	X	103
Burnside	Midlo	NT3962	55°51·1′	2°58·0′W	X	66
Burnside	Moray	NJ0856	57°35·3′	3°31·9′W	X	27
Burnside	Moray	NJ1250	57°32·2′	3°27·7′W	X	28
Burnside	Moray	NJ1669	57°42·4′	3°24·1′W	X	28
Burnside	Moray	NJ1759	57°37·1′	3°22·9′W	X	28
Burnside	Moray	NJ1938	57°25·8′	3°20·5′W	X	28
Burnside	Moray	NJ2755	57°35·0′	3°12·8′W	X	28
Burnside	Moray	NJ3444	57°29·1′	3°5·6′W	X	28
Burnside	Moray	NJ4151	57°33·0′	2°58·7′W	X	28
Burnside	Northum	NZ0471	55°2·3′	1°55·8′W	X	87
Burnside	Northum	NZ0778	55°6·0′	1°53·0′W	X	88
Burnside	Orkney	HY2610	58°58·5′	3°16·7′W	X	6
Burnside	Orkney	HY3608	58°57·5′	3°6·3′W	X	6,7
Burnside	Orkney	HY5004	58°55·5′	2°51·6′W	X	6,7
Burnside	Orkney	HY5009	58°58·2′	2°51·7′W	X	6,7
Burnside	Pth & Kin	NN8807	56°14·8′	3°48·0′W	X	58
Burnside	Pth & Kin	NO0125	56°24·7′	3°35·8′W	T	52,53,58
Burnside	Pth & Kin	NO0125	56°24·7′	3°35·8′W	X	52,53,58
Burnside	Pth & Kin	NO0945	56°35·5′	3°28·5′W	X	52,53
Burnside	Pth & Kin	NO1033	56°29·1′	3°27·2′W	X	53
Burnside	Pth & Kin	NO1435	56°30·2′	3°23·4′W	X	53
Burnside	Pth & Kin	NO1543	56°34·5′	3°22·6′W	X	53
Burnside	Pth & Kin	NO3228	56°26·6′	3°5·7′W	X	53,59
Burnside	Renf	NS3958	55°47·6′	4°33·6′W	X	63
Burnside	S Ayr	NX2778	55°4·2′	4°42·1′W	X	76
Burnside	Shetld	HP6209	60°45·8′	0°51·2′W	X	1
Burnside	Shetld	HU2778	60°29·4′	1°30·0′W	T	3
Burnside	Shetld	HU2952	60°15·3′	1°28·1′W	X	3
Burnside	S Lanak	NS6260	55°49·1′	4°11·7′W	X	64
Burnside	S Lanak	NS6638	55°37·3′	4°7·2′W	X	71
Burnside	S Lanak	NS8541	55°39·2′	3°49·2′W	X	71,72
Burnside	S Lanak	NS8824	55°30·1′	3°46·0′W	X	71,72
Burnside	Stir	NN8105	56°13·6′	3°54·7′W	X	57
Burnside	Sund	NZ3350	54°50·9′	1°28·7′W	T	88
Burnside	W Loth	NT0575	55°57·8′	3°30·9′W	X	65
Burnside	W Loth	NT0971	55°55·7′	3°26·9′W	T	65
Burnside Cottage	Aberd	NJ6022	57°17·5′	2°39·4′W	X	37
Burnside Cottage	Highld	NN3580	56°53·2′	4°42·0′W	X	34,41
Burnside Croft	Aberd	NJ7120	57°16·6′	2°28·4′W	X	38
Burnside Fm	Fife	NO5714	56°19·2′	2°41·3′W	FM	59
Burnside Fm	Moray	NJ1662	57°38·7′	3°24·0′W	FM	28
Burnside Fm	S Ayr	NS1901	55°16·5′	4°50·5′W	FM	76
Burnside of Allachie	Moray	NJ2841	57°27·5′	3°11·5′W	X	28
Burnside of Ballintomb	Moray	NJ2143	57°28·5′	3°18·6′W	X	28
Burnside of Baltersan	D & G	NX9180	55°6·4′	3°42·1′W	X	78
Burnside of Birnie	Moray	NJ2259	57°37·1′	3°17·9′W	X	28
Burnside of Blackhills	Aberd	NJ5007	57°9·3′	2°49·1′W	X	37
Burnside of Carnousie	Aberd	NJ6553	57°34·2′	2°34·6′W	X	29
Burnside of Cassindilly	Fife	NO4009	56°16·4′	2°57·7′W	X	59
Burnside of Culshan	D & G	NX8069	55°0·3′	3°52·1′W	X	84
Burnside of Deskie	Moray	NJ2130	57°21·5′	3°18·3′W	X	36
Burnside of Dipple	Moray	NJ3256	57°35·6′	3°7·8′W	X	28
Burnside of Drimmie	Pth & Kin	NO1751	56°38·9′	3°20·8′W	X	53
Burnside of Duntrune	Angus	NO4434	56°29·9′	2°54·1′W	T	54
Burnside of Ennets	Aberd	NJ6106	57°8·9′	2°38·2′W	X	37
Burnside of Enzie	Moray	NJ3960	57°37·8′	3°0·8′W	X	28
Burnside of Folla	Aberd	NJ7134	57°24·0′	2°28·5′W	X	29
Burnside of Geddes	Highld	NH8851	57°32·4′	3°51·8′W	X	27
Burnside of Gight	Aberd	NJ8341	57°27·8′	2°16·5′W	X	29,30
Burnside of Idoch	Aberd	NJ7748	57°31·6′	2°22·6′W	X	29,30
Burnside of Kirkbuddo	Angus	NO4942	56°34·3′	2°49·4′W	X	54
Burnside of Lethenty	Aberd	NJ8141	57°27·8′	2°18·5′W	X	29,30
Burnside of Newhall	Aberd	NO8794	57°2·5′	2°12·4′W	X	38,45
Burnside of Pitcaple	Aberd	NJ7227	57°20·2′	2°27·5′W	X	38
Burnside of Thain	Moray	NJ2422	57°17·2′	3°15·2′W	X	36
Burnside of Tulloes	Angus	NO5044	56°35·4′	2°48·4′W	X	54
Burnside of Tynet	Moray	NJ3960	57°37·8′	3°0·8′W	X	28
Burnside of Urr	D & G	NX8469	55°0·4′	3°48·4′W	X	84
Burnside of Whitefield	Aberd	NJ6553	57°34·2′	2°34·6′W	X	29
Burn Sike	N Yks	NZ2807	54°27·7′	1°33·7′W	W	93
Burnslack	Lancs	SD6146	53°54·8′	2°35·2′W	X	102,103
Burnslack Fell	Lancs	SD6246	53°54·8′	2°34·3′W	X	102,103
Burns Mon	E Ayr	NS4338	55°36·9′	4°29·1′W	X	70
Burns of Gutcher	Shetld	HP5300	60°41·0′	1°1·3′W	W	1
Burns of Kinminitie	Moray	NJ4253	57°34·1′	2°57·7′W	X	28
Burn's Plain	Hants	SU8350	51°14·8′	0°48·3′W	X	186
Burnsquare	Fife	NO4312	56°18·1′	2°54·8′W	X	59
Burns, The	Shetld	HU2055	60°17·0′	1°37·8′W	X	3
Burnston	E Ayr	NS5412	55°23·1′	4°17·8′W	X	70
Burnston Burn	E Ayr	NS5412	55°23·1′	4°17·8′W	W	70
Burnstone	Devon	SS3223	50°59·2′	4°23·2′W	T	190
Burnstones	Northum	NY6754	54°53·0′	2°30·4′W	X	86,87
Burnswark	D & G	NY1979	55°6·2′	3°15·7′W	X	85
Burntack	Moray	NJ0450	57°32·1′	3°35·7′W	X	27
Burnt Allotment	Norf	TG1718	52°43·2′	1°13·2′E	F	133,134
Burnt Ash	Glos	SO8801	51°42·7′	2°10·0′W	T	162
Burnt Axon	Hants	SU1902	50°49·3′	1°43·4′W	X	195
Burnt Barns Fm	E Susx	TQ7013	50°53·7′	0°25·4′E	FM	199
Burnt Bottom	Dorset	ST5200	50°48·1′	2°40·5′W	X	194
Burntbrae	Aberd	NJ9444	57°29·4′	2°5·5′W	X	30
Burnt Bridge Fm	Lincs	SK8093	53°25·9′	0°47·3′W	FM	112
Burnt Burn	Scot Bord	NY4791	55°12·9′	2°49·5′W	W	79
Burnt Chimney Fm	E Susx	TQ7715	50°54·7′	0°31·5′E	FM	199
Burntcliff Top	Ches	SJ9966	53°11·7′	2°0·5′W	X	118
Burntcommon	Surrey	TQ0354	51°16·8′	0°31·0′W	T	186
Burnt Craig	Scot Bord	NT5005	55°20·4′	2°46·9′W	H	79
Burnter's Covert	Suff	TM3658	52°10·4′	1°27·5′E	F	156
Burnt Fen	Cambs	TL6087	52°27·7′	0°21·7′E	X	143
Burntfen Broad	Norf	TG3318	52°42·8′	1°27·4′E	W	133,134
Burnt Fm	Herts	TL3101	51°41·8′	0°5·9′W	FM	166
Burntfold Copse	Northnts	SP6053	52°10·6′	1°7·0′W	F	152
Burnt Gill	Durham	NY9310	54°29·4′	2°6·1′W	W	91,92
Burnt Grove	Hants	SU3320	50°58·9′	1°31·4′W	F	185
Burnt, The	Devon	SS9207	50°51·4′	3°31·7′W	W	192
Burn, The	Moray	NJ4039	57°26·5′	2°59·5′W	X	28
Burnt Heath	Derby	SK2075	53°16·5′	1°41·6′W	X	119
Burntheath	Derby	SK2431	52°52·8′	1°38·2′W	T	128
Burnt Heath	Essex	TM0628	51°55·0′	1°0·1′E	T	168
Burnt Heath Fm	Warw	SP3765	52°17·1′	1°27·1′W	FM	151
Burnt Heath Fm	Wilts	ST9185	51°34·1′	2°7·4′W	FM	173
Burnt Hengoed	Heref	SO2652	52°9·9′	3°4·5′W	X	148
Burnthill	Aberd	NJ9465	57°40·7′	2°5·6′W	X	30
Burnt Hill	Angus	NO4177	56°53·1′	2°57·6′W	H	44
Burnt Hill	Cambs	TL4780	52°24·1′	0°10·1′E	X	143
Burnt Hill	Derby	SK0490	53°24·6′	1°56·0′W	X	110
Burnt Hill	D & G	NY2584	55°8·9′	3°10·2′W	H	79
Burnt Hill	E Ayr	NS6131	55°33·4′	4°11·8′W	H	71
Burnt Hill	E Ayr	NS6311	55°22·7′	4°9·3′W	X	71
Burnt Hill	N Ayr	NS2563	55°50·0′	4°47·2′W	H	63
Burnt Hill	N Ayr	NS3058	55°47·4′	4°42·2′W	X	63
Burnt Hill	Pth & Kin	NO0006	56°14·4′	3°36·4′W	H	58
Burnt Hill	Suff	TM5091	52°27·8′	1°41·2′E	X	134
Burnt Hill	W Berks	SU5674	51°28·0′	1°11·2′W	T	174
Burnthill Fm	Sheff	SK2992	53°25·7′	1°33·4′W	FM	110
Burnthillock	Aberd	NK0650	57°32·7′	1°53·5′W	X	30
Burnthills	Renf	NS3756	55°46·4′	4°35·5′W	X	63
Burnt Ho	Cumbr	NY1103	54°25·1′	3°21·9′W	X	89
Burnt Ho	I of W	SZ5187	50°41·1′	1°16·3′W	X	196
Burnt Ho	Kent	TQ8744	51°10·1′	0°40·9′E	X	189
Burnt Ho	Lincs	TF2630	52°51·4′	0°7·3′W	X	131
Burnt Ho	Newp	ST3484	51°33·3′	2°56·7′W	X	171
Burnt Ho	Northum	NZ0058	54°59·6′	1°59·6′W	X	87
Burnt Ho	Northum	NZ2383	55°8·7′	1°37·9′W	X	81
Burnt Ho	N Yks	NZ4405	54°26·6′	1°18·9′W	X	93
Burnt Ho	N Yks	SE1456	54°0·2′	1°46·8′W	X	104
Burnt Ho	Powys	SJ2214	52°43·3′	3°8·9′W	X	126
Burnt Ho	Powys	SO2354	52°11·0′	3°7·2′W	X	148
Burnt Ho	Shrops	SO5070	52°19·8′	2°43·6′W	X	137,138
Burnt Ho	Suff	TM0172	52°18·8′	0°57·3′E	X	144,155
Burnt Ho	Suff	TM2871	52°17·6′	1°21·0′E	X	156
Burnt Horse	Cumbr	NY2928	54°38·8′	3°5·6′W	X	89,90
Burnthouse	Corn	SW7636	50°11·1′	5°7·9′W	T	204
Burnthouse	Shrops	SO5471	52°20·3′	2°40·1′W	X	137,138
Burnthouse Br	W Berks	SU6868	51°24·6′	1°0·9′W	X	175
Burnt House Fm	Cambs	TL3394	52°31·9′	0°2·0′W	FM	142
Burnthouse Fm	Ches	SJ7278	53°18·1′	2°24·8′W	FM	118
Burnt House Fm	Ches	SJ9666	53°11·7′	2°3·2′W	FM	118
Burnthouse Fm	Devon	SY0987	50°40·8′	3°16·9′W	FM	192
Burnt House Fm	Essex	TL7534	51°58·8′	0°33·3′E	FM	155
Burnthouse Fm	Essex	TM2229	51°55·1′	1°14·1′E	FM	169
Burnt House Fm	E Susx	TQ6523	50°59·2′	0°21·4′E	FM	199
Burnt House Fm	Kent	TQ9649	51°12·6′	0°48·8′E	FM	189
Burnt House Fm	Lancs	SD8641	53°52·1′	2°12·4′W	FM	103
Burnthouse Fm	Norf	TG0629	52°49·4′	1°3·9′E	FM	133
Burnt House Fm	Somer	ST6145	51°12·4′	2°33·1′W	FM	183
Burnt House Fm	Somer	ST6921	50°59·5′	2°26·1′W	FM	183
Burnt House Fm	Suff	TL9755	52°9·7′	0°53·2′E	FM	155
Burnt House Fm	Suff	TM1674	52°19·5′	1°10·6′E	FM	144,156
Burnt House Fm	Suff	TM3758	52°10·4′	1°28·4′E	FM	156
Burnt House Fm	Suff	TM3763	52°13·1′	1°28·6′E	FM	156

Burnthouse Plantn	N Yks	NZ1914	54°31·5′	1°42·0′W	F	92
Burnt Houses	Durham	NZ1223	54°36·4′	1°48·4′W	X	92
Burnthouse Wood	E Susx	TQ7318	50°56·3′	0°28·1′E	F	199
Burnthurst Fm	Warw	SP3871	52°20·4′	1°26·1′W	FM	140
Burnthwaite	Cumbr	NY1909	54°28·4′	3°14·6′W	X	89,90
Burntisland	Fife	NT2386	56°3·9′	3°13·8′W	T	66
Burnt Island	I Scilly	SV8708	49°53·7′	6°21·1′W	X	203
Burnt Islands	Arg & Bt	NS0175	55°55·9′	5°10·7′W	X	63
Burnt Leys Fm	Derby	SK5477	53°17·5′	1°11·0′W	FM	120
Burnt Mill	Halton	SJ4783	53°20·7′	2°47·4′W	X	108
Burnt Mills	Essex	TQ7390	51°35·2′	0°30·2′E	T	178
Burnt Moor	Cumbr	NY0500	54°23·4′	3°27·4′W	X	89
Burnt Moor	N Yks	NY8300	54°24·0′	2°15·3′W	X	91,92
Burnt Mound	Orkney	ND4684	58°44·7′	2°55·5′W	A	7
Burnt Norton	Glos	SP1441	52°4·3′	1°47·3′W	X	151
Burnt Oak	Barnet	TQ2091	51°36·5′	0°15·6′W	T	176
Burnt Oak	E Susx	TQ5127	51°1·6′	0°9·6′E	T	188,199
Burntoak	Kent	TQ9539	51°7·2′	0°47·6′E	X	189
Burnt Oak	Kent	TQ9934	51°4·5′	0°50·8′E	X	189
Burntoak Gate	W Susx	SU8814	50°55·4′	0°44·5′W	X	197
Burntoak Hollins	Staffs	SJ9760	53°8·5′	2°2·3′W	X	118
Burn Tod	Cumbr	NY2832	54°40·9′	3°6·6′W	X	89,90
Burnton	Aberd	NO7270	56°49·5′	2°27·1′W	X	45
Burnton	E Ayr	NS3715	55°24·4′	4°34·0′W	X	70
Burnton	E Ayr	NS4706	55°19·7′	4°24·3′W	T	70,77
Burnton	E Ayr	NS4917	55°25·7′	4°22·7′W	X	70
Burnton	E Ayr	NS6313	55°23·8′	4°9·4′W	X	71
Burnton	Highld	NH8128	57°19·9′	3°58·1′W	X	35
Burnton	S Ayr	NS3104	55°18·3′	4°39·3′W	X	76
Burnton	S Ayr	NS3620	55°27·0′	4°35·2′W	X	70
Burntongues	N Ayr	NS2750	55°43·0′	4°44·8′W	X	63
Burn Tongues	Northum	NY8056	54°54·1′	2°18·3′W	X	86,87
Burntonhill	E Ayr	NS6412	55°23·2′	4°8·4′W	X	71
Burntown	Moray	NJ2342	57°28·0′	3°16·6′W	X	28
Burnt Plantation	Scot Bord	NT5613	55°24·8′	2°41·3′W	F	80
Burnt Platt	Oxon	SU6983	51°32·7′	0°59·9′W	F	175
Burn Treble	Moray	NJ3632	57°22·7′	3°3·4′W	W	37
Burntreble	Moray	NJ3731	57°22·2′	3°2·4′W	X	37
Burnt Ridge	Northum	NY8956	54°54·2′	2°9·9′W	X	87
Burntridge Moor	Northum	NY8755	54°53·6′	2°11·7′W	X	87
Burnt Rig	S Lanak	NS8031	55°33·7′	3°53·7′W	X	71,72
Burntroots Plantn	N Yks	SE2774	54°9·9′	1°34·8′W	F	99
Burntshield	E Ayr	NS5926	55°30·7′	4°13·5′W	X	71
Burntshield Haugh	Northum	NY9253	54°52·5′	2°7·1′W	X	87
Burntshieldhaugh Fell	Northum	NY9352	54°52·0′	2°6·1′W	X	87
Burnt Shields	Cumbr	NY5083	55°8·6′	2°46·6′W	X	79
Burntshields	Renf	NS3862	55°49·7′	4°34·7′W	X	63
Burntstalk	Norf	TF7437	52°54·4′	0°35·6′E	X	132
Burntstalk Plantation	Norf	TF7811	52°40·3′	0°38·4′E	F	132
Burntstump Country Park	Notts	SK5750	53°2·9′	1°8·6′W	X	120
Burnt Tom	Northum	NY6286	55°10·3′	2°35·4′W	X	80
Burnt Tom	Northum	NY7278	55°6·0′	2°25·9′W	X	86,87
Burnt Tom Crags	Northum	NY5982	55°8·1′	2°38·2′W	H	80
Burnt Tree	Sand	SO9590	52°30·7′	2°4·0′W	T	139
Burnturk	Fife	NO3208	56°15·8′	3°5·4′W	X	59
Burnt Walls	Durham	NY9540	54°45·5′	2°4·2′W	X	87
Burnt Walls	Northnts	SP5861	52°14·9′	1°8·6′W	A	152
Burnt Walls	Northnts	SP5861	52°14·9′	1°8·6′W	X	152
Burnt Walls	Northum	NY6566	54°59·5′	2°32·4′W	X	86
Burntwick Island	Kent	TQ8672	51°25·2′	0°40·9′E	X	178
Burnt Wood	Derby	SK2766	53°11·7′	1°35·3′W	F	119
Burnt Wood	Hants	SU5035	51°7·0′	1°16·8′W	F	185
Burnt Wood	I of W	SZ4492	50°43·8′	1°22·2′W	F	196
Burntwood	Oxon	SU6180	51°31·2′	1°6·9′W	X	175
Burnt Wood	Roth	SK4487	53°22·9′	1°19·9′W	F	111,120
Burnt Wood	S Glos	ST7486	51°34·6′	2°22·1′W	F	172
Burnt Wood	Staffs	SJ7434	52°54·4′	2°22·8′W	F	127
Burntwood	Staffs	SK0509	52°41·0′	1°55·2′W	T	128
Burnt Wood	Wilts	SU2669	51°25·4′	1°37·2′W	F	174
Burnt Wood	Worcs	SO7673	52°21·5′	2°20·7′W	F	138
Burntwood Fm	Hants	SU5034	51°6·4′	1°16·8′W	FM	185
Burntwood Grange	Donc	SE5303	53°31·5′	1°11·6′W	X	111
Burntwood Green	Staffs	SK0708	52°40·4′	1°53·4′W	T	128
Burntwood Hall	Barns	SE4209	53°34·8′	1°21·5′W	X	111
Burntwood Pentre	Flint	SJ2964	53°10·3′	3°3·3′W	T	117
Burnt Yates	N Yks	SE2561	54°2·9′	1°36·7′W	T	99
Burnuick Fm	Corn	SW6624	50°4·4′	5°15·9′W	FM	203
Burnums Fm	Northnts	SP5869	52°19·2′	1°8·5′W	FM	152
Burnville	Devon	SX4882	50°37·3′	4°8·6′W	X	191,201
Burnwell	Devon	SX8287	50°40·5′	3°39·8′W	X	191
Burnwood	Derby	SK4238	52°56·5′	1°22·1′W	X	129
Burn Wood	Stock on T	NZ3815	54°32·0′	1°24·3′W	F	93
Burnworthy	Somer	ST1815	50°56·0′	3°9·6′W	T	181,193
Burnwynd	C of Edin	NT1368	55°54·1′	3°23·0′W	T	65
Burons Laithe	Lancs	SD8650	53°57·0′	2°12·4′W	X	103
Burpham	Surrey	TQ0152	51°15·7′	0°32·8′W	T	186
Burpham	W Susx	TQ0408	50°52·0′	0°30·9′W	T	197
Burpham Court Fm	Surrey	TQ0053	51°16·3′	0°33·6′W	FM	186
Burpham High Barn	W Susx	TQ0509	50°52·5′	0°30·1′W	X	197
Burrach Mór	Highld	NH5808	57°8·7′	4°20·4′W	H	35
Burracott	Corn	SS2200	50°46·6′	4°31·1′W	X	190
Burra Dale	Shetld	HU4242	60°9·9′	1°14·1′W	H	4
Burradon	Northum	NT9806	55°21·1′	2°1·5′W	T	81
Burradon	N Tyne	NZ2772	55°2·8′	1°34·2′W	T	88
Burradon Ho	N Tyne	NZ2773	55°3·3′	1°34·2′W	X	88
Burradon Mains	Northum	NT9606	55°21·1′	2°3·4′W	X	81
Burradon Windyside Fm	Northum	NT9805	55°20·6′	2°1·5′W	FM	81
Burrafirth	Shetld	HP6113	60°48·0′	0°52·2′W	T	1
Burra Firth	Shetld	HP6116	60°49·6′	0°52·2′W	W	1
Burragarth	Shetld	HP5703	60°42·6′	0°56·8′W	X	1
Burra Ho	Orkney	HY2304	58°55·2′	3°19·8′W	X	6,7
Burrain Skelton	D & G	NY1387	55°10·4′	3°21·5′W	X	78
Burraland	Shetld	HU2249	60°13·7′	1°35·7′W	X	3
Burraland	Shetld	HU3475	60°27·7′	1°22·4′W	X	2,3
Burralie	Orkney	HY3207	58°57·0′	3°10·4′W	X	6,7
Burral Knowe	Shetld	HP6104	60°43·1′	0°52·4′W	X	1
Burrance	D & G	NY0490	55°11·9′	3°30·1′W	X	78
Burrance	D & G	NY0985	55°9·3′	3°25·3′W	X	78
Burrance Br	D & G	NY0490	55°11·9′	3°30·1′W	X	78
Burra Ness	Shetld	HU4475	60°27·6′	1°11·5′W	X	2,3

Burra Ness	Shetld	HU5179	60°29·8′	1°3·8′W	X	2,3
Burra Ness	Shetld	HU5595	60°38·3′	0°59·2′W	X	1,2
Burras	Corn	SW6734	50°9·9′	5°15·4′W	T	203
Burrashield	Shetld	HZ2072	59°32·3′	1°38·3′W	X	4
Burra Sound	Orkney	HY2404	58°55·3′	3°18·7′W	W	6,7
Burrastow	Shetld	HU2247	60°12·7′	1°35·7′W	T	3
Burraton	Corn	SX3474	50°32·8′	4°20·2′W	X	201
Burraton	Corn	SX4067	50°29·1′	4°14·9′W	X	201
Burraton	Corn	SX4159	50°24·8′	4°13·9′W	T	201
Burraton	Devon	SX6152	50°21·3′	3°56·9′W	X	202
Burraton Coombe	Corn	SX4158	50°24·3′	4°13·9′W	T	201
Burrator	Devon	SX5567	50°29·3′	4°2·3′W	X	202
Burrator Reservoir	Devon	SX5568	50°29·9′	4°2·3′W	W	202
Burravoe	Shetld	HU3567	60°23·4′	1°21·4′W	T	2,3
Burra Voe	Shetld	HU3688	60°34·7′	1°20·1′W	W	1,2
Burravoe	Shetld	HU3789	60°35·2′	1°19·0′W	X	1,2
Burra Voe	Shetld	HU5279	60°29·7′	1°2·7′W	W	2,3
Burravoe	Shetld	HU5279	60°29·7′	1°2·7′W	T	2,3
Burray	Orkney	ND4496	58°51·1′	2°57·8′W	X	6,7
Burray Haas	Orkney	ND4998	58°52·2′	2°52·6′W	X	6,7
Burray Ness	Orkney	ND5096	58°51·2′	2°51·5′W	X	6,7
Burray Village	Orkney	ND4795	58°50·6′	2°54·6′W	T	7
Burreldale Moss	Aberd	NJ8223	57°18·1′	2°17·5′W	X	38
Burreldales	Aberd	NJ6755	57°35·3′	2°32·7′W	X	29
Burreldales	Aberd	NJ7439	57°26·7′	2°25·5′W	X	29
Burrell Collection	C of Glas	NS5562	55°50·0′	4°18·5′W	X	64
Burrell Green	Cumbr	NY5435	54°42·7′	2°42·4′W	X	90
Burrellhill	Cumbr	NY6333	54°41·7′	2°34·0′W	X	91
Burrells	Cumbr	NY6818	54°33·6′	2°29·3′W	T	91
Burrells Fm	Essex	TQ7793	51°36·7′	0°33·8′E	FM	178
Burrelton	Pth & Kin	NO2037	56°31·4′	3°17·6′W	T	53
Burrelton Burn	Pth & Kin	NO1733	56°29·2′	3°20·4′W	W	53
Burrenrig	D & G	NY0590	55°12·0′	3°29·1′W	X	78
Burreth Village	Lincs	TF1569	53°12·6′	0°16·3′W	A	121
Burretts Grove	Hants	SU2634	51°6·5′	1°37·3′W	F	184
Burrey Brae	Orkney	HY3910	58°58·6′	3°3·2′W	X	6
Burr Fm	Kent	TQ9933	51°3·9′	0°50·8′E	FM	189
Burr Green	Lancs	SD6333	53°47·8′	2°33·3′W	X	102,103
Burr Hill	Donc	SK5797	53°28·2′	1°8·1′W	X	111
Burrian	Orkney	HY2918	59°2·9′	3°13·8′W	X	6
Burrian	Shetld	HU3536	60°6·7′	1°21·7′W	X	4
Burrian (Broch)	Orkney	HY2918	59°2·9′	3°13·8′W	A	6
Burrian, The	Shetld	HZ2069	59°30·7′	1°38·3′W	X	4
Burridge	Devon	SS5635	51°6·0′	4°3·0′W	T	180
Burridge	Devon	SS7412	50°53·9′	3°47·1′W	X	180
Burridge	Devon	SS9211	50°53·5′	3°31·8′W	X	192
Burridge	Devon	ST3106	50°51·2′	2°58·4′W	T	193
Burridge	Hants	SU5110	50°53·5′	1°16·1′W	T	196
Burridge Fm	Corn	SS2311	50°52·5′	4°30·6′W	FM	190
Burridge Fm	Devon	SS8105	50°50·2′	3°41·0′W	FM	191
Burridge Fm	Hants	SU5110	50°53·5′	1°16·1′W	FM	196
Burridge Heath	Wilts	SU2964	51°22·7′	1°34·6′W	X	174
Burrien Hill	Orkney	HY3516	59°1·8′	3°7·5′W	H	6
Burrier Head	Shetld	HU1651	60°14·8′	1°42·2′W	X	3
Burrier Wick	Shetld	HU3192	60°36·9′	1°25·5′W	W	1
Burries Ness	Shetld	HU2783	60°32·0′	1°30·0′W	X	3
Burrigill	Highld	ND2234	58°17·5′	3°19·4′W	T	11
Burri Hill	Shetld	HU4491	60°36·3′	1°11·3′W	X	1,2
Burrill	N Yks	SE2387	54°16·9′	1°38·4′W	T	99
Burrill Beck	N Yks	SE2486	54°16·4′	1°37·5′W	W	99
Burringham	N Lincs	SE8309	53°34·5′	0°44·4′W	T	112
Burringham South Grange	N Lincs	SE8307	53°33·4′	0°44·4′W	X	112
Burrington	Devon	SS6316	50°55·9′	3°56·6′W	T	180
Burrington	Heref	SO4472	52°20·8′	2°48·9′W	T	137,148
Burrington	N Som	ST4859	51°19·9′	2°44·4′W	T	172,182
Burrington Combe	N Som	ST4858	51°19·4′	2°44·4′W	X	172,182
Burrington Common	Heref	SO4472	52°20·8′	2°48·9′W	X	137,148
Burrington Ham	N Som	ST4858	51°19·4′	2°44·4′W	X	172,182
Burrington Moor Cross	Devon	SS6016	50°55·8′	3°59·2′W	X	180
Burriott Barton	Devon	SS5821	50°58·5′	4°1·0′W	X	180
Burrista	Shetld	HZ2072	59°32·3′	1°38·3′W	X	4
Burrody's Hill	Orkney	HY4804	58°55·5′	2°53·7′W	X	6,7
Burroo	I of M	SC1564	54°2·6′	4°49·1′W	X	95
Burroo Ned	I of M	SC1766	54°3·7′	4°47·4′W	X	95
Burrough	Devon	SS4221	50°58·2′	4°14·6′W	X	180,190
Burrough Court	Leic	SK7510	52°41·2′	0°53·0′W	X	129
Burrough Court Fm	Leic	SK7509	52°40·6′	0°53·0′W	FM	141
Burrough End	Cambs	TL6255	52°10·4′	0°22·5′E	T	154
Burrough Green	Cambs	TL6355	52°10·4′	0°23·4′E	T	154
Burrough Hall	Leic	SK7611	52°41·7′	0°52·1′W	X	129
Burrough Hill Country Park	Leic	SK7612	52°42·3′	0°52·1′W	X	129
Burrough Hill Fm	Glos	ST7393	51°38·3′	2°23·0′W	FM	162,172
Burrough on the Hill	Leic	SK7510	52°41·2′	0°53·0′W	T	129
Burroughs Grove	Bucks	SU8589	51°35·8′	0°46·0′W	T	175
Burroughs Grove Hill	Bucks	SU8589	51°35·8′	0°46·0′W	X	175
Burroughs Hill	Wilts	SU1630	51°4·4′	1°45·9′W	X	184
Burroughston	Orkney	HY5320	59°4·1′	2°48·7′W	T	5,6
Burrow	Devon	SS3408	50°51·1′	4°21·1′W	X	190
Burrow	Devon	SS7002	50°48·4′	3°50·3′W	X	191
Burrow	Devon	SS7717	50°56·6′	3°44·7′W	X	180
Burrow	Devon	SX3899	50°46·3′	4°17·5′W	X	190
Burrow	Devon	SX9997	50°46·1′	3°25·6′W	T	192
Burrow	Devon	SY0789	50°41·8′	3°18·6′W	T	192
Burrow	Shrops	SO3782	52°26·2′	2°55·2′W	F	137
Burrow	Somer	SS9342	51°10·3′	3°31·4′W	T	181
Burrow	Somer	ST4120	50°58·8′	2°50·3′W	T	193
Burroway Brook	Oxon	SP3000	51°42·1′	1°33·6′W	W	164
Burrowbridge	Somer	ST3529	51°3·6′	2°55·3′W	T	193
Burrowbridge	Somer	ST3530	51°4·2′	2°55·3′W	T	182
Burrow Corner	Devon	SS9609	50°52·5′	3°28·3′W	X	192
Burrow Cross	Devon	SS7617	50°56·6′	3°45·5′W	X	180
Burrow Farm	Bucks	SU7985	51°33·7′	0°51·2′W	FM	175
Burrow Fields	Notts	SK6942	52°58·5′	0°57·9′W	X	129
Burrow Fm	Devon	ST0619	50°58·0′	3°19·9′W	FM	181
Burrow Fm	Devon	SX7491	50°42·5′	3°46·7′W	FM	191
Burrow Fm	Devon	SX9399	50°47·1′	3°30·7′W	FM	192
Burrow Fm	Devon	SX9998	50°46·6′	3°25·6′W	FM	192
Burrow Fm	Devon	SY2499	50°47·3′	3°4·3′W	FM	192,193
Burrow Fm	Somer	ST0034	51°6·0′	3°25·3′W	FM	181
Burrow Fm	Somer	ST0321	50°59·0′	3°22·5′W	FM	181

Burrow Fm	Somer	ST0523	51°0·1′	3°20·9′W	FM	181
Burrow Gap	Norf	TF8745	52°58·4′	0°47·5′E	X	132
Burrow Head	D & G	NX4534	54°40·9′	4°23·8′W	X	83
Burrow Heights	Lancs	SD4758	54°1·2′	2°48·1′W	X	102
Burrow Hill	Devon	ST1412	50°54·3′	3°13·0′W	X	181,193
Burrow Hill	Lancs	SD5558	54°1·2′	2°40·8′W	X	102
Burrow Hill	Norf	TF8417	52°43·4′	0°43·9′E	X	132
Burrow Hill	Norf	TF9628	52°49·1′	0°54·9′E	X	132
Burrow Hill	Suff	TM3848	52°5·0′	1°28·8′E	X	169
Burrowhill	Surrey	SU9763	51°21·7′	0°36·0′W	T	175,176,186
Burrow Hill	Warw	SP3085	52°28·0′	1°33·1′W	X	140
Burrow Hill Fm	Devon	SY1193	50°44·0′	3°15·3′W	FM	192,193
Burrow Hill Fm	Somer	ST1029	51°3·4′	3°16·7′W	FM	181,193
Burrow Hill Fort	Warw	SP3085	52°28·0′	1°33·1′W	A	140
Burrow Ho	Cumbr	SD3891	54°18·9′	2°56·8′W	X	96,97
Burrow House Fm	E Yorks	SE9866	54°5·1′	0°29·7′W	FM	101
Burrowine	Fife	NS9789	56°5·2′	3°38·9′W	X	65
Burrow Island	C of Port	SU6200	50°48·0′	1°6·8′W	X	196
Burrowland	N Ayr	NS3344	55°39·9′	4°38·9′W	X	63,70
Burrowley	Aberd	NJ9834	57°24·0′	2°1·5′W	X	30
Burrow Moor	Cambs	TL3995	52°32·3′	0°3·4′E	X	142,143
Burrow Mump	Somer	ST3530	51°4·2′	2°55·3′W	A	182
Burrow Nose	Devon	SS5548	51°13·0′	4°4·2′W	X	180
Burrow Park	Corn	SW9778	50°34·2′	4°51·6′W	X	200
Burrows Cross	Surrey	TQ0846	51°12·4′	0°26·8′W	T	187
Burrows Fm	C of Nott	SK5333	52°53·7′	1°12·3′W	FM	129
Burrow's Fm	Devon	ST1610	50°53·2′	3°11·3′W	FM	192,193
Burrows Fm	Dorset	SU0810	50°53·6′	1°52·8′W	FM	195
Burrow's Fm	Lancs	SD3544	53°53·5′	2°58·9′W	FM	102
Burrows Hill	Somer	ST3712	50°54·5′	2°53·4′W	X	193
Burrowshill Fm	Suff	TM3563	52°13·1′	1°26·8′E	FM	156
Burrows Hole	Northum	NU1340	55°39·4′	1°47·2′W	W	75
Burrows Lea	Surrey	TQ0746	51°12·4′	0°27·7′W	X	187
Burrowsmoor Holt	Notts	SK7041	52°57·9′	0°57·1′W	T	129
Burrows Pasture	N Yks	SE0167	54°6·2′	1°58·7′W	X	98
Burrows, The	Pemb	SS1299	51°39·7′	4°42·7′W	X	158
Burrows, The or Tywyn	Pemb	SM7326	51°53·4′	5°17·5′W	X	157
Burrowstown Moss	D & G	NY4286	55°10·1′	2°54·2′W	X	79
Burrow Walls (Roman Fort)	Cumbr	NY0030	54°39·6′	3°32·6′W	R	89
Burrow Wood	Somer	SS8934	51°5·9′	3°34·7′W	F	181
Burrs Country Park	Bury	SD7912	53°36·5′	2°18·6′W	X	109
Burrs Fm	Derby	SK1071	53°14·4′	1°50·6′W	FM	119
Burrs Fm	Roth	SK5585	53°21·8′	1°10·0′W	FM	111,120
Burrs Green Fm	Herts	TL3217	51°50·4′	0°4·6′W	FM	166
Burrs Hill	Kent	TQ6840	51°8·3′	0°24·5′E	X	188
Burrs Mount	Derby	SK1778	53°18·2′	1°44·3′W	X	119
Burrsville Park	Essex	TM1817	51°48·8′	1°10·2′E	T	168,169
Burrs Wood	Derby	SK3075	53°16·5′	1°32·6′W	F	119
Burrswood	Kent	TQ5237	51°7·0′	0°10·7′E	T	188
Burr, The	Shetld	HU2180	60°30·5′	1°36·6′W	X	3
Burry	Swan	SS4590	51°35·5′	4°13·9′W	T	159
Burry Green	Swan	SS4691	51°36·0′	4°13·0′W	T	159
Burryhillock	Aberd	NJ6426	57°19·6′	2°35·4′W	X	37
Burry Holms	Swan	SS3992	51°36·5′	4°19·1′W	X	159
Burry Pill	Swan	SS4692	51°36·6′	4°13·1′W	W	159
Burry Port (Porth Tywyn)	Carm	SN4401	51°41·4′	4°15·0′W	T	159
Burscombe Fm	Devon	SY1291	50°43·0′	3°14·4′W	FM	192,193
Burscombe Fm	Kent	TQ9048	51°12·2′	0°43·6′E	FM	189
Burscott	Devon	SS3124	50°59·7′	4°24·1′W	T	190
Burscott	Devon	SS3407	50°50·6′	4°21·1′W	X	190
Burscough	Lancs	SD4310	53°35·3′	2°51·3′W	T	108
Burscough Bridge	Lancs	SD4411	53°35·8′	2°50·4′W	T	108
Burscough Moss	Lancs	SD4413	53°36·9′	2°50·4′W	X	108
Bursdon	Devon	SS2620	50°56·9′	4°28·2′W	T	190
Bursdon Moor	Devon	SS2620	50°57·4′	4°28·3′W	X	190
Bursea	E Yorks	SE8033	53°47·5′	0°46·7′W	T	106
Bursea Grange	E Yorks	SE8134	53°48·0′	0°45·8′W	X	106
Bursea Ho	E Yorks	SE8133	53°47·5′	0°45·8′W	X	106
Bursea Lane Ends	E Yorks	SE7935	53°48·6′	0°47·6′W	X	105,106
Bursea Lodge	E Yorks	SE8134	53°48·0′	0°45·8′W	X	106
Burshill	E Yorks	TA0948	53°55·2′	0°20·0′W	T	107
Burshill and Barff Drain	E Yorks	TA0946	53°54·2′	0°20·0′W	W	107
Bursledon	Hants	SU4809	50°52·9′	1°18·7′W	T	196
Burslem	C of Stoke	SJ8749	53°2·5′	2°11·2′W	T	118
Burstall	Suff	TM0944	52°3·5′	1°3·3′E	T	155,169
Burstall Br	Suff	TM1043	52°3·0′	1°4·2′E	X	155,169
Burstall Hall	Suff	TM1045	52°4·0′	1°4·2′E	X	155,169
Burstallhill	Suff	TM0845	52°4·1′	1°2·5′E	T	155,169
Bursteads	Herts	TL4717	51°50·2′	0°8·4′E	X	167
Bursted Manor	Kent	TR1651	51°13·3′	1°6·0′E	X	179,189
Bursted Wood	Kent	TR1650	51°12·7′	1°6·0′E	F	179,189
Burstheart Hill	Notts	SK6467	53°12·0′	1°2·1′W	X	120
Burstock	Dorset	ST4203	50°49·7′	2°49·0′W	T	193
Burstock Down	Dorset	ST4301	50°48·6′	2°48·2′W	X	193
Burstock Grange	Dorset	ST4202	50°49·1′	2°49·0′W	X	193
Burston	Devon	SS7102	50°48·4′	3°49·5′W	T	191
Burston	Devon	SS9425	51°1·1′	3°30·3′W	X	181
Burston	Norf	TM1383	52°24·4′	1°8·3′E	T	144,156
Burston	Staffs	SJ9430	52°52·3′	2°4·9′W	T	127
Burstone	Devon	SS4514	50°54·5′	4°11·9′W	X	180,190
Burston Hill	Bucks	SP8318	51°51·5′	0°47·3′W	X	165
Burston Hill Fm	Bucks	SP8318	51°51·5′	0°47·3′W	FM	165
Burston Village	Bucks	SP8418	51°51·5′	0°46·4′W	A	165
Burstow	Surrey	TQ3041	51°9·4′	0°8·1′W	T	187
Burstow Hall	W Susx	TQ3040	51°8·9′	0°8·1′W	X	187
Burstow Lodge	Surrey	TQ3144	51°11·0′	0°7·1′W	X	187
Burstow Park Fm	Surrey	TQ3147	51°12·7′	0°7·1′W	FM	187
Burstwick	E Yorks	TA2227	53°43·7′	0°8·6′W	T	107
Burstwick Drain	E Yorks	TA2128	53°44·3′	0°9·5′W	W	107
Burstwick Grange	E Yorks	TA2428	53°44·3′	0°6·8′W	X	107
Burtenshaw Fm	E Susx	TQ4217	50°56·3′	0°1·7′E	FM	198
Burtersett	N Yks	SD8989	54°18·0′	2°9·7′W	T	98
Burtersett Bottoms	N Yks	SD8989	54°18·0′	2°9·7′W	X	98
Burtersett High Pasture	N Yks	SD8888	54°17·5′	2°10·6′W	X	98
Burthinghurst	Cumbr	NY5466	54°59·4′	2°42·7′W	X	86
Burtholme	Cumbr	NY5463	54°57·8′	2°42·7′W	T	86
Burthorpe	Suff	TL7764	52°15·0′	0°36·0′E	T	155
Burthwaite	Cumbr	NY1828	54°38·7′	3°15·8′W	X	89,90
Burthwaite	Cumbr	NY4149	54°50·2′	2°54·7′W	T	85

Burthwaite	Cumbr	NY6923	54°36·3'	2°28·4'W	X	91
Burthwaite Hill	Cumbr	NY4150	54°50·7'	2°54·7'W	X	85
Burthy Fm	Corn	SW9155	50°21·7'	4°55·9'W	FM	200
Burthy Row Fm	Corn	SW9156	50°22·2'	4°56·0'W	FM	200
Burtis Wood	N Yks	SE5679	54°12·5'	1°8·1'W	F	100
Burtle	Somer	ST3942	51°10·7'	2°52·0'W	T	182
Burtle Hill	Somer	ST3943	51°11·2'	2°52·0'W	T	182
Burtley Wood	Bucks	SU9588	51°35·2'	0°37·3'W	F	175,176
Burtness Combe	Cumbr	NY1714	54°31·1'	3°16·5'W	X	89,90
Burtness Wood	Cumbr	NY1715	54°31·7'	3°16·5'W	F	89,90
Burtoft	Lincs	TF2635	52°54·1'	0°7·2'W	T	131
Burton	Ches	SJ3174	53°15·8'	3°1·7'W	T	117
Burton	Ches	SJ5063	53°9·9'	2°44·5'W	T	117
Burton	Devon	SX6940	50°15·0'	3°49·9'W	X	202
Burton	Dorset	SY6891	50°43·3'	2°26·8'W	T	194
Burton	Dorset	SZ1694	50°45·0'	1°46·0'W	T	195
Burton	Lincs	SK9674	53°15·5'	0°33·2'W	T	121
Burton	Northum	NU1733	55°35·7'	1°43·4'W	X	75
Burton	Pemb	SM9805	51°42·7'	4°55·1'W	T	157,158
Burton	S Ayr	NS3117	55°25·3'	4°39·8'W	X	70
Burton	Somer	ST1944	51°11·6'	3°9·2'W	T	181
Burton	Somer	ST5313	50°55·1'	2°39·7'W	T	194
Burton	V of Glam	ST0367	51°23·9'	3°23·3'W	T	170
Burton	Wilts	ST8179	51°30·8'	2°16·0'W	T	173
Burton	Wilts	ST8232	51°5·5'	2°15·0'W	T	183
Burton	Wrex	SJ3557	53°6·8'	2°57·8'W	T	117
Burton Agnes	E Yorks	TA1063	54°3·3'	0°18·8'W	T	101
Burton Agnes Field	E Yorks	TA0964	54°3·9'	0°19·7'W	X	101
Burton Agnes Stud Fm	E Yorks	TA1162	54°2·8'	0°17·9'W	FM	101
Burton Bandalls	Leic	SK5620	52°46·7'	1°9·8'W	X	129
Burton Beach	Dorset	SY4888	50°41·6'	2°43·8'W	X	193
Burton Beck	N Yks	SE1790	54°18·6'	1°43·9'W	W	99
Burton Beck Fm	Durham	NZ2434	54°42·3'	1°37·2'W	FM	93
Burton Bower	Essex	TL5224	51°53·9'	0°12·9'E	X	167
Burton Br	Lincs	TF1241	52°57·5'	0°19·6'W	X	130
Burton Bradstock	Dorset	SY4889	50°42·1'	2°43·8'W	T	193
Burton Brook	Leic	SK7716	52°44·4'	0°51·2'W	W	129
Burton Brook Fm	Leic	SP6796	52°33·7'	1°0·3'W	FM	141
Burton Bushes	E Yorks	TA0139	53°50·5'	0°27·5'W	F	106,107
Burtoncarr Ho	E Yorks	TA1261	54°2·2'	0°17·0'W	X	101
Burton Cliff	Dorset	SY4889	50°42·1'	2°43·8'W	X	193
Burton Cliff	Lincs	TF1141	52°57·5'	0°20·4'W	X	130
Burton Closes	Derby	SK2167	53°12·2'	1°40·7'W	X	119
Burton Common	Hants	SZ1995	50°45·5'	1°43·5'W	X	195
Burton Common Fm	N Yks	SE5127	53°44·5'	1°13·2'W	FM	105
Burton Constable	E Yorks	TA1836	53°48·6'	0°12·1'W	X	107
Burton Corner	Lincs	TF3345	52°59·4'	0°0·7'W	T	131
Burton Cottages	N Yks	SE4169	54°7·2'	1°21·9'W	X	99
Burton Court	Heref	SO4257	52°12·7'	2°50·5'W	X	148,149
Burton Court	Heref	SO6623	51°54·5'	2°29·3'W	X	162
Burton Court	Worcs	SO6962	52°15·6'	2°26·9'W	X	138,149
Burton Cross	Dorset	SY8386	50°40·6'	2°14·1'W	X	194
Burton Dairy Fm	Somer	ST3725	51°1·5'	2°53·5'W	FM	193
Burton Dassett	Warw	SP3951	52°9·6'	1°25·4'W	T	151
Burton Down	W Susx	SU9613	50°54·7'	0°37·7'W	X	197
Burton End	Cambs	TL6249	52°7·2'	0°22·4'E	T	154
Burton End	Essex	TL5323	51°53·3'	0°13·8'E	T	167
Burton Fell	Cumbr	NY7821	54°35·3'	2°20·0'W	X	91
Burton Ferry	Pemb	SM9805	51°42·7'	4°55·1'W	T	157,158
Burtonfield Hall	E Yorks	SE7255	53°59·4'	0°53·7'W	X	105,106
Burton Fields	Warw	SP4289	52°30·1'	1°22·5'W	X	140
Burton Fields	Warw	SP4290	52°30·6'	1°22·5'W	X	140
Burton Fleming	E Yorks	TA0872	54°8·2'	0°20·4'W	T	101
Burton Fleming Grange	E Yorks	TA0773	54°8·7'	0°21·3'W	X	101
Burton Fm	Lincs	TF1242	52°58·1'	0°19·5'W	FM	130
Burton Fm	Somer	ST3724	51°1·0'	2°53·5'W	FM	193
Burton Fm	Warw	SP1856	52°12·4'	1°43·8'W	FM	151
Burton Freshwater	Dorset	SY4789	50°42·1'	2°44·6'W	X	193
Burton Grange	Leic	SP6697	52°34·2'	1°1·2'W	X	141
Burton Grange	N Yks	SE4269	54°7·1'	1°21·0'W	X	99
Burton Green	Essex	TL8226	51°54·4'	0°39·1'E	T	168
Burton Green	Warw	SP2675	52°22·6'	1°36·7'W	T	140
Burton Green	Wrex	SJ3458	53°7·1'	2°58·8'W	T	117
Burton Grove Fm	Swin	SU1988	51°35·7'	1°43·2'W	FM	173
Burton Hall	N Yks	SE5829	53°45·5'	1°6·8'W	X	105
Burton Hastings	Warw	SP4189	52°30·1'	1°23·4'W	T	140
Burton Hill	Cumbr	SD6789	54°18·0'	2°30·0'W	X	98
Burton Hill	Heref	SO3948	52°7·9'	2°53·1'W	H	148,149
Burton Hill	Wilts	ST9386	51°34·6'	2°5·7'W	X	173
Burton Hill	W Susx	SU9718	50°57·4'	0°36·7'W	X	197
Burton Hill Fm	Warw	SP3849	52°8·5'	1°26·3'W	FM	151
Burton Hills	Warw	SP3951	52°9·6'	1°25·4'W	X	151
Burton Hill Wood	Dorset	ST6510	50°53·5'	2°29·5'W	F	194
Burton Ho	Durham	NZ1421	54°35·3'	1°46·6'W	X	92
Burton Ho	Lincs	TF3336	52°54·5'	0°0·9'W	X	131
Burton Ho	N Yks	SE2281	54°13·7'	1°39·3'W	X	99
Burton Ho	N Yks	SE5673	54°9·2'	1°8·1'W	X	100
Burton Ho	Wrex	SJ3557	53°6·6'	2°57·9'W	X	117
Burtonhole Fm	Barnet	TQ2392	51°37·0'	0°13·0'W	FM	176
Burton Howe	N Yks	NZ6003	54°25·4'	1°4·1'W	A	94
Burton-in-Kendal	Cumbr	SD5376	54°10·9'	2°42·8'W	T	97
Burton in Lonsdale	N Yks	SD6572	54°8·8'	2°31·7'W	T	97
Burton Joyce	Notts	SK6443	52°59·1'	1°2·4'W	T	129
Burton Latimer	Northnts	SP8974	52°21·6'	0°41·2'W	T	141
Burton Lazars	Leic	SK7616	52°44·4'	0°52·1'W	T	129
Burton-le-Coggles	Lincs	SK9725	52°49·1'	0°33·2'W	T	130
Burton Leonard	N Yks	SE3263	54°4·0'	1°30·2'W	T	99
Burton Lodge	Wrex	SJ3359	53°7·7'	2°59·7'W	X	117
Burton Lodge Fm	Leic	SP6696	52°33·7'	1°1·2'W	FM	141
Burton Manor	Derby	SK2067	53°12·2'	1°41·6'W	X	119
Burton Manor	Staffs	SJ9120	52°46·9'	2°7·6'W	T	127
Burton Meadows	Notts	SK6643	52°59·1'	1°0·6'W	X	129
Burton Meadows	Wrex	SJ3559	53°7·7'	2°57·9'W	X	117
Burton Mere	Dorset	SY5087	50°41·1'	2°42·1'W	W	194
Burton Mill Pond	W Susx	SU9717	50°56·9'	0°36·8'W	W	197
Burton Moor	Derby	SK2067	53°12·2'	1°41·6'W	X	119
Burton Moor	N Yks	SE0385	54°15·9'	1°56·8'W	X	98
Burton Mountain	Pemb	SM9905	51°42·7'	4°54·2'W	X	157,158
Burton on the Wolds	Leic	SK5921	52°47·2'	1°7·1'W	T	129
Burton Overy	Leic	SP6798	52°34·8'	1°0·3'W	T	141
Burton Park	N Yks	SE1591	54°19·1'	1°45·7'W	X	99
Burton Park	W Susx	SU9617	50°56·9'	0°37·6'W	X	197
Burton Pasture	N Yks	SE0184	54°15·3'	1°58·7'W	X	98
Burton Pedwardine	Lincs	TF1142	52°58·1'	0°20·4'W	T	130
Burton Pidsea	E Yorks	TA2531	53°45·9'	0°5·8'W	T	107
Burton Point	Ches	SJ3073	53°15·2'	3°2·5'W	X	117
Burton Point Fm	Ches	SJ3074	53°15·7'	3°2·6'W	FM	117
Burton Pynsent	Somer	ST3724	51°1·0'	2°53·5'W	X	193
Burton Rakes	E Yorks	SE9539	53°50·5'	0°33·0'W	X	106
Burton Round	Notts	SK8085	53°21·6'	0°47·5'W	W	112,121
Burton Row Fm	Somer	ST3352	51°16·0'	2°57·2'W	FM	182
Burton Salmon	N Yks	SE4927	53°44·5'	1°15·0'W	T	105
Burton Service Area	Cumbr	SD5276	54°10·9'	2°43·7'W	X	97
Burton's Fm	Bucks	TQ0096	51°39·5'	0°32·9'W	FM	166,176
Burtons Fm	Heref	SO7040	52°3·7'	2°25·9'W	FM	149
Burton's Fm	Norf	TG0249	53°0·2'	1°1·0'E	FM	134
Burton's Fm	Suff	TL8446	52°5·1'	0°41·5'E	FM	155
Burton Shutts Fm	Derby	SK2544	52°59·8'	1°37·2'W	FM	119,128
Burton Stather	N Lincs	SE8618	53°39·3'	0°41·5'W	T	112
Burton's Wood	Wrex	SJ4343	52°59·1'	2°50·5'W	F	117
Burton Tower	Wrex	SJ3457	53°6·6'	2°58·8'W	X	117
Burton upon Stather	N Lincs	SE8717	53°38·8'	0°40·6'W	T	112
Burton upon Trent	Staffs	SK2422	52°47·9'	1°38·2'W	T	128
Burton Westwood	Shrops	SO6097	52°34·4'	2°35·0'W	T	138
Burton Wold	Northnts	SP9274	52°21·6'	0°38·5'W	X	141
Burton Wolds	Leic	SK6221	52°47·2'	1°4·4'W	X	129
Burton Wood	Lancs	SD5466	54°5·5'	2°41·8'W	F	97
Burton Wood	Lincs	SK8483	53°20·5'	0°43·9'W	F	121
Burton Wood	N Lincs	SE8616	53°38·2'	0°41·5'W	F	112
Burton Wood	N Yks	SE3464	54°4·5'	1°28·4'W	F	99
Burtonwood	Warr	SJ5692	53°25·6'	2°39·3'W	T	108
Burtonwood Fm	Essex	TL5343	52°4·1'	0°14·3'E	FM	154
Burtonwood Service Area	Warr	SJ5791	53°25·1'	2°38·4'W	X	108
Burtree	Cumbr	NY6910	54°29·3'	2°28·3'W	X	91
Burtree Fell	Durham	NY8542	54°46·6'	2°13·6'W	X	87
Burtree Ford	Durham	NY8540	54°45·5'	2°13·6'W	X	87
Burtree Gate	Darl	NZ2518	54°33·6'	1°36·4'W	X	93
Burtree Ho	Darl	NZ2618	54°33·6'	1°35·5'W	X	93
Burtree Ho	N Yks	SE2490	54°18·5'	1°37·4'W	X	99
Burtree Ho	N Yks	SE4876	54°10·9'	1°15·5'W	X	100
Burts Fm	Somer	ST1419	50°58·1'	3°13·1'W	FM	181,193
Burts Fm	Suff	TL9660	52°12·4'	0°52·5'E	FM	155
Burvale Fm	Surrey	TQ1063	51°21·6'	0°24·8'W	FM	176,187
Burwain Hall	Cumbr	NY6420	54°34·7'	2°33·0'W	X	91
Burwains Fm	Lancs	SD8835	53°48·9'	2°10·5'W	FM	103
Burwardsley	Ches	SJ5156	53°6·2'	2°43·5'W	T	117
Burwardsley Hill	Ches	SJ5055	53°5·6'	2°44·4'W	X	117
Burwarton	Shrops	SO6185	52°27·9'	2°34·0'W	T	138
Burwarton Park	Shrops	SO6185	52°27·9'	2°34·0'W	X	138
Burwash	E Susx	TQ6724	50°59·7'	0°23·2'E	T	199
Burwash Common	E Susx	TQ6423	50°59·2'	0°20·6'E	T	199
Burwash Weald	E Susx	TQ6523	50°59·2'	0°21·4'E	T	199
Burway Fm	Shrops	SO5075	52°22·5'	2°43·7'W	FM	137,138
Burway Hill	Shrops	SO4494	52°32·7'	2°49·1'W	X	137
Burwell	Cambs	TL5866	52°16·4'	0°19·3'E	T	154
Burwell	Devon	SS7527	51°2·0'	3°46·6'W	X	180
Burwell	Lincs	TF3579	53°17·7'	0°1·9'E	T	122
Burwell Fen	Cambs	TL5666	52°16·4'	0°17·6'E	X	154
Burwell Fen	Cambs	TL5767	52°16·9'	0°18·5'E	X	154
Burwell Lode	Cambs	TL5668	52°17·5'	0°17·6'E	W	154
Burwell Wood	Lincs	TF3680	53°18·2'	0°2·9'E	F	122
Burwen	I of Angl	SH4193	53°24·8'	4°23·1'W	T	114
Burwen Cas	N Yks	SD9249	53°56·5'	2°6·9'W	X	103
Burwen Cas (Roman Fort)	N Yks	SD9249	53°56·5'	2°6·9'W	R	103
Bur Wick	Orkney	ND4383	58°44·1'	2°58·6'W	W	7
Burwick	Orkney	ND4384	58°44·7'	2°58·6'W	X	7
Bur Wick	Shetld	HU3840	60°8·8'	1°18·4'W	W	4
Burwick	Shetld	HU3940	60°8·8'	1°17·4'W	T	4
Burwick Holm	Shetld	HU3840	60°8·8'	1°18·4'W	X	4
Burwood	Devon	SS5018	50°56·8'	4°7·7'W	X	180
Burwood	Dorset	SU0614	50°55·8'	1°54·5'W	F	195
Burwood	Shrops	SO4887	52°28·9'	2°45·5'W	X	137,138
Burwood Hall	Norf	TF9119	52°44·3'	0°50·2'E	X	132
Burwood Park	Surrey	TQ1064	51°22·1'	0°24·8'W	X	176,187
Bury	Bury	SD8010	53°35·4'	2°17·7'W	T	109
Bury	Cambs	TL2883	52°26·0'	0°6·6'W	T	142
Bury	Heref	SO4756	52°12·2'	2°46·1'W	X	148,149
Bury	Heref	SO4968	52°18·7'	2°44·5'W	X	137,138,148
Bury	Somer	SS9427	51°2·2'	3°30·3'W	T	181
Bury	W Susx	TQ0113	50°54·7'	0°33·4'W	T	197
Buryas Br	Corn	SW4429	50°6·6'	5°34·5'W	T	203
Bury Bank	Staffs	SJ8835	52°55·0'	2°10·3'W	A	127
Burybank	Staffs	SJ8835	52°55·0'	2°10·3'W	T	127
Bury Barns	Herts	TL3035	52°0·1'	0°6·0'W	X	153
Bury Barton	Devon	SS7307	50°51·2'	3°47·9'W	X	191
Bury Camp	Leic	SK4905	52°38·7'	1°16·1'W	A	140
Bury Camp	Wilts	ST8173	51°27·6'	2°16·0'W	A	173
Bury Castle	Corn	SX1369	50°29·7'	4°37·8'W	A	200
Bury Castle	Somer	SS9147	51°12·9'	3°33·3'W	A	181
Bury Castle	Somer	SS9326	51°1·6'	3°31·2'W	X	181
Bury Castle (Motte & Bailey)	Somer	SS9326	51°1·6'	3°31·2'W	A	181
Bury Court	Glos	SO7632	51°59·4'	2°20·6'W	A	150
Bury Court	Hants	SU7845	51°12·2'	0°52·6'W	X	186
Bury Court	Heref	SO4168	52°18·7'	2°51·5'W	X	137,148
Burycroft Fm	Oxon	SP3411	51°48·0'	1°30·0'W	FM	164
Bury Ditches	Shrops	SO3283	52°26·7'	2°59·6'W	X	137
Bury Ditches (Fort)	Shrops	SO3283	52°26·7'	2°59·6'W	A	137
Bury Down	Corn	SX1859	50°24·4'	4°33·3'W	X	201
Bury Down	W Berks	SU4784	51°33·4'	1°18·9'W	X	174
Bury End	Beds	SP9850	52°8·6'	0°33·7'W	T	153
Bury End	Beds	TL1234	51°59·8'	0°21·7'W	T	153
Bury End	Worcs	SP0936	52°1·6'	1°51·7'W	T	150
Buryend Fm	Worcs	SO8539	52°3·2'	2°12·7'W	FM	150
Bury Fen	Cambs	TL2984	52°26·6'	0°5·7'W	X	142
Bury Field	Mil Key	SP8644	52°5·5'	0°44·3'W	X	152
Buryfields Fm	Beds	TL0561	52°14·5'	0°27·3'W	FM	153
Bury Fm	Barnet	TQ1994	51°38·2'	0°16·4'W	FM	166,176
Bury Fm	Beds	SP9824	51°54·6'	0°34·1'W	FM	165
Bury Fm	Beds	TL0215	51°49·7'	0°30·8'W	FM	166
Bury Fm	Beds	TL0519	51°51·8'	0°28·1'W	FM	166
Bury Fm	Beds	TL0540	52°3·1'	0°27·7'W	FM	153
Bury Fm	Beds	TL1130	51°57·7'	0°22·7'W	FM	166
Bury Fm	Bucks	SP9002	51°42·8'	0°41·4'W	FM	165
Bury Fm	Bucks	SP9321	51°53·0'	0°38·5'W	FM	165
Bury Fm	Cambs	TL3143	52°4·4'	0°4·9'W	FM	153
Bury Fm	Cambs	TL3443	52°4·4'	0°2·3'W	FM	154
Bury Fm	Cambs	TL4751	52°8·5'	0°9·3'E	FM	154
Bury Fm	Essex	TL4403	51°42·7'	0°5·5'E	FM	167
Bury Fm	Essex	TL5918	51°50·5'	0°18·9'E	FM	167
Bury Fm	Essex	TL6720	51°51·4'	0°25·9'E	FM	167
Bury Fm	Essex	TL8404	51°42·5'	0°40·2'E	FM	168
Bury Fm	Hants	SU3711	50°54·1'	1°28·0'W	FM	196
Bury Fm	Hants	SU5211	50°54·0'	1°15·2'W	FM	196
Bury Fm	Hav	TQ6086	51°33·2'	0°18·9'E	FM	177
Bury Fm	Heref	SO4862	52°15·5'	2°45·3'W	FM	137,138,148
Bury Fm	Herts	TL2619	51°51·5'	0°9·8'W	FM	166
Bury Fm	Lancs	SD5823	53°42·3'	2°37·8'W	A	102
Bury Fm	Shrops	SJ5828	52°51·1'	2°37·0'W	FM	126
Bury Fm, The	Heref	SO5052	52°10·1'	2°43·5'W	FM	149
Bury Grange	Herts	TL3027	51°55·8'	0°6·2'W	X	166
Bury Green	Herts	TL3401	51°41·7'	0°3·3'W	T	166
Bury Green	Herts	TL4521	51°52·3'	0°6·8'E	T	167
Bury Green Fm	Cambs	TL2685	52°27·1'	0°8·3'W	FM	142
Bury Hall	Norf	TM0297	52°32·2'	0°59·1'E	X	144
Bury Hill	Hants	SU3443	51°11·3'	1°30·4'W	X	185
Bury Hill	Heref	SO6423	51°54·5'	2°31·0'W	X	162
Bury Hill	Oxon	SP3224	51°55·0'	1°31·7'W	X	164
Bury Hill	Oxon	SU2396	51°40·0'	1°39·7'W	X	163
Bury Hill	S Glos	ST6579	51°30·8'	2°29·9'W	X	172
Bury Hill	S Glos	ST7285	51°34·0'	2°23·8'W	X	172
Bury Hill	Somer	SS9328	51°2·7'	3°31·2'W	X	181
Bury Hill	Suff	TL6664	52°15·2'	0°26·3'E	X	154
Bury Hill	Surrey	TQ1548	51°13·4'	0°20·8'W	X	187
Bury Hill	Wilts	SU0590	51°36·8'	1°55·3'W	X	163,173
Bury Hill	W Susx	TQ0012	50°54·2'	0°34·3'W	X	197
Buryhill Fm	Wilts	SU0589	51°36·2'	1°55·3'W	FM	173
Bury Hill (Fort)	Hants	SU3443	51°11·3'	1°30·4'W	A	185
Bury Hill (Fort)	S Glos	ST6579	51°30·8'	2°29·9'W	A	172
Bury Hill Ho	Surrey	TQ1447	51°12·9'	0°21·7'W	X	187
Bury Hill (Settlement)	Wilts	SU0590	51°36·8'	1°55·3'W	A	163,173
Bury Holme Fm	Beds	TL2645	52°5·6'	0°9·2'W	FM	153
Bury Lodge	Essex	TL5222	51°52·8'	0°12·9'E	X	167
Bury Lodge	Hants	SU6414	50°55·5'	1°5·0'W	X	196
Bury Lug Fen	Cambs	TL2983	52°26·0'	0°5·7'W	X	142
Bury Mill Fm	W Susx	TQ0015	50°55·8'	0°34·2'W	FM	197
Bury Park	Luton	TL0821	51°52·9'	0°25·5'W	T	166
Bury's Bank	W Berks	SU4965	51°23·1'	1°17·4'W	T	174
Bury's Court School	Surrey	TQ2347	51°12·8'	0°13·9'W	X	187
Bury's Fm	Lancs	SD6135	53°48·8'	2°35·1'W	FM	102,103
Bury's Hall	Norf	TF8806	52°37·4'	0°47·1'E	X	144
Bury's Hall	Norf	TM0993	52°29·9'	1°5·2'E	X	144
Bury St Austen's	W Susx	TQ1034	51°5·9'	0°25·4'W	X	187
Burystead Fm	Cambs	TL4378	52°23·1'	0°6·5'E	FM	142,143
Bury St Edmunds	Suff	TL8564	52°14·8'	0°43·0'E	T	155
Bury, The	Beds	TL0147	52°7·0'	0°31·1'W	X	153
Bury, The	Bucks	SP9501	51°42·2'	0°37·1'W	X	165
Bury, The	Cambs	TL5260	52°13·3'	0°13·9'E	X	154
Bury, The	Herts	TL1821	51°52·7'	0°16·7'W	X	166
Bury, The	Herts	TL2426	51°55·4'	0°11·4'W	X	166
Burythorpe	N Yks	SE7964	54°4·2'	0°47·1'W	T	100
Burythorpe Ho	N Yks	SE7965	54°4·7'	0°47·1'W	X	100
Burytown Fms	Swin	SU1591	51°37·3'	1°46·6'W	FM	163,173
Bury Walls	Shrops	SJ5727	52°50·6'	2°37·9'W	X	126
Bury Walls (Fort)	Shrops	SJ5727	52°50·6'	2°37·9'W	A	126
Busbiehead	E Ayr	NS3940	55°37·9'	4°33·0'W	X	70
Busbiehill	E Ayr	NS3839	55°37·3'	4°33·9'W	T	70
Busbie Mains	E Ayr	NS3940	55°37·9'	4°33·0'W	X	70
Busbie Muir	N Ayr	NS2346	55°40·8'	4°48·5'W	X	63
Busbridge	Surrey	SU9742	51°10·4'	0°36·4'W	T	186
Busbridge Hall	Surrey	SU9742	51°10·4'	0°36·4'W	X	186
Busbridge Lakes	Surrey	SU9741	51°9·8'	0°36·4'W	W	186
Busby	E Renf	NS5756	55°46·8'	4°16·4'W	T	64
Busby	Pth & Kin	NO0326	56°25·2'	3°33·9'W	X	52,53,58
Busby Hall	N Yks	NZ5104	54°26·0'	1°12·4'W	X	93
Busby Ho	N Yks	NZ5006	54°27·1'	1°13·3'W	X	93
Busby Moor	N Yks	NZ5203	54°25·4'	1°11·5'W	X	93
Busby Stoop	N Yks	SE3880	54°13·1'	1°24·6'W	X	99
Busby Wood	N Yks	NZ5103	54°25·4'	1°12·4'W	F	93
Buscaverran	Corn	SW6434	50°9·8'	5°17·9'W	X	203
Buscoe Beck Fm	N Yks	NZ7506	54°26·9'	0°50·2'W	FM	94
Buscoe Sike	Cumbr	NY2505	54°26·3'	3°9·0'W	W	89,90
Buscombe	Devon	SS6839	51°8·3'	3°52·8'W	X	180
Buscot	Oxon	SU2397	51°40·5'	1°39·7'W	T	163
Buscot Ho	Oxon	SU2496	51°40·0'	1°38·8'W	X	163
Buscott	Somer	ST4438	51°8·5'	2°47·6'W	T	182
Buscott's Lodge	Northnts	SP9867	52°17·8'	0°33·4'W	X	153
Buscot Wick	Oxon	SU2197	51°40·5'	1°41·4'W	X	163
Bush	Aberd	NJ6537	57°25·6'	2°34·5'W	X	29
Bush	Aberd	NO7298	57°4·6'	2°27·3'W	X	38,45
Bush	Aberd	NO7665	56°46·8'	2°23·1'W	T	45
Bush	Aberd	NO8090	57°0·3'	2°19·3'W	X	38,45
Bush	Corn	SS2307	50°50·4'	4°30·5'W	T	190
Bush	Cumbr	NY5774	55°3·8'	2°40·0'W	X	86
Bush	D & G	NY0978	55°5·5'	3°25·1'W	X	85
Bush	D & G	NY1773	55°2·9'	3°17·5'W	X	85
Bush	D & G	NY3792	55°13·3'	2°59·0'W	X	79
Bush	Moray	NJ2640	57°26·9'	3°13·5'W	X	28
Bush	Pemb	SN0309	51°44·9'	4°50·8'W	X	157,158
Bush	Pth & Kin	NO1728	56°26·5'	3°20·3'W	X	53,58
Bush	Somer	ST2136	51°7·3'	3°7·3'W	X	182
Bushayes Fm	Devon	SX9988	50°41·2'	3°25·4'W	FM	192
Bush Bank	Heref	SO4551	52°9·5'	2°47·8'W	T	148,149
Bush Barn	E Susx	TQ7325	51°0·1'	0°28·3'E	X	188,199
Bushbarns	Essex	TL6216	51°49·3'	0°21·4'E	X	167
Bush Barrow	Dorset	SY7981	50°37·9'	2°17·4'W	A	194
Bush Blades	Durham	NZ1653	54°52·5'	1°44·6'W	X	88
Bushbury	E Susx	TQ5219	50°57·2'	0°10·2'E	X	199
Bushbury	Surrey	TQ1947	51°12·8'	0°17·4'W	T	187
Bushbury	Wolv	SJ9203	52°37·7'	2°6·7'W	T	127,139

Bushby	Leic	SK6504	52°38·0′	1°2·0′W	T	141
Bushbyside Fm	S Lanak	NS5855	55°46·3′	4°15·4′W	FM	64
Bushby Spinney	Leic	SK6503	52°37·5′	1°2·0′W	F	141
Bushcliff Ho	Wakf	SE3313	53°37·0′	1°29·7′W	X	110,111
Bushcombe Bottom	Wilts	ST8338	51°8·7′	2°14·2′W	X	183
Bush Crathie	Aberd	NO2596	57°3·2′	3°13·7′W	X	37,44
Bush Down	Devon	SX6882	50°37·6′	3°51·6′W	X	191
Bush Down	Hants	SU7234	51°6·3′	0°57·9′W	H	186
Bushelhill	Scot Bord	NT7263	55°51·8′	2°26·4′W	X	67
Bush End	Essex	TL5519	51°51·1′	0°15·4′E	T	167
Bushes	Essex	TL5207	51°44·7′	0°12·5′E	A	167
Bushes Barn	Dorset	SY6497	50°46·5′	2°30·3′W	X	194
Bushes Fm	Dorset	SY8998	50°47·1′	2°9·0′W	FM	195
Bushes Fm	Kent	TQ5149	51°13·4′	0°10·1′E	FM	188
Bush Estate	Norf	TG4029	52°48·5′	1°34·1′E	T	134
Bushes, The	Leic	SK8134	52°54·1′	0°47·3′W	F	130
Bushes, The	Monm	SO2906	51°45·1′	3°1·3′W	F	161
Bushes, The	Oxon	SP5120	51°52·8′	1°15·1′W	F	164
Bushes, The	Somer	ST7641	51°10·3′	2°20·2′W	F	183
Bushett Fm	Essex	TL6728	51°55·8′	0°26·1′E	FM	167
Bushey	Dorset	SY9883	50°39·0′	2°1·3′W	T	195
Bushey	Herts	TQ1395	51°38·8′	0°21·6′W	T	166,176
Bushey Close	Kent	TR0559	51°17·8′	0°56·8′E	X	179
Bushey Ground	Oxon	SP3109	51°47·0′	1°32·6′W	T	164
Bushey Heath	Herts	TQ1594	51°38·2′	0°19·9′W	T	166,176
Bushey Leys	Bucks	SP8307	51°45·6′	0°47·4′W	X	165
Bushey Mead	Merton	TQ2368	51°24·1′	0°13·5′W	T	176
Bushey Wood	Peterb	TF0902	52°36·5′	0°23·0′W	F	142
Bushfield	Cumbr	NY4780	55°6·9′	2°49·4′W	T	79
Bush Fm	Essex	TM0726	51°53·9′	1°0·9′E	FM	168,169
Bush Fm	Hants	SU2844	51°11·9′	1°35·6′W	FM	184
Bush Fm	Herts	TL2907	51°45·0′	0°7·5′W	FM	166
Bush Fm	Kent	TR0125	50°59·6′	0°52·2′E	FM	189
Bush Fm	Kent	TR3465	51°20·4′	1°22·0′E	FM	179
Bush Fm	Lincs	TF1279	53°18·0′	0°18·8′W	FM	121
Bush Fm	Moray	NJ3850	57°32·4′	3°1·7′W	FM	28
Bush Fm	Norf	TF9302	52°35·1′	0°51·3′E	FM	144
Bush Fm	Norf	TM2393	52°29·6′	1°17·5′E	FM	134
Bush Fm	Norf	TM3596	52°30·9′	1°28·2′E	FM	134
Bush Fm	Northum	NY8665	54°59·0′	2°12·7′W	FM	87
Bush Fm	N Yks	SE2476	54°11·0′	1°37·5′W	FM	99
Bush Fm	Pemb	SN1222	51°52·1′	4°43·5′W	FM	145,158
Bush Fm	Shrops	SO5691	52°31·1′	2°38·5′W	FM	137,138
Bush Fm	Somer	ST5528	51°3·2′	2°38·1′W	FM	183
Bush Fm	Suff	TM0150	52°6·9′	0°56·5′E	FM	155
Bush Fm	Suff	TM1773	52°19·0′	1°11·4′E	FM	156
Bush Fm	Wilts	ST8431	51°4·9′	2°13·3′W	FM	183
Bushford	Pemb	SM8310	51°45·0′	5°8·2′W	X	157
Bushfurlong Fm	Somer	ST3721	50°59·3′	2°53·5′W	FM	193
Bushgillhead	Cumbr	NY2647	54°49·0′	3°8·7′W	X	85
Bushglen	N Ayr	NS2049	55°42·3′	4°51·4′W	X	63
Bush Green	Norf	TM0298	52°32·8′	0°59·2′E	T	144
Bush Green	Norf	TM2187	52°26·4′	1°15·5′E	T	156
Bush Green	Suff	TL9157	52°10·9′	0°48·0′E	T	155
Bush Hill	Enf	TQ3295	51°38·5′	0°5·1′W	X	166,176,177
Bush Hill	Oxon	SP3946	52°6·9′	1°25·4′W	X	151
Bush Hill	Warw	SP5163	52°16·0′	1°14·8′W	X	151
Bush Hill Fm	Suff	TM3476	52°20·1′	1°26·5′E	FM	156
Bush Hill Park	Enf	TQ3395	51°38·5′	0°4·3′W	T	166,176,177
Bush Ho	Midlo	NT2463	55°51·5′	3°12·4′W	X	66
Bush Ho	Swin	SU1979	51°30·8′	1°43·2′W	X	173
Bush Howe	Cumbr	SD6598	54°22·8′	2°31·9′W	X	97
Bushie Law	Scot Bord	NT1809	55°22·3′	3°17·2′W	H	79
Bush Knowe	Northum	NT9314	55°25·4′	2°6·2′W	H	80
Bushley	Worcs	SO8734	52°0·5′	2°11·0′W	T	150
Bushley Bank	Cumbr	NY5773	55°3·2′	2°40·0′W	X	86
Bushley Green	Worcs	SO8634	52°0·5′	2°11·8′W	T	150
Bushley Park	Worcs	SO8733	52°0·0′	2°11·0′W	X	150
Bush Loch	D & G	NX6155	54°52·5′	4°9·6′W	W	83
Bushman's Crag	Northum	NT8403	55°19·5′	2°14·7′W	X	80
Bushmead	Beds	TL1160	52°13·8′	0°22·1′W	T	153
Bushmead Cross	Beds	TL1160	52°13·8′	0°22·1′W	X	153
Bushmead Priory	Beds	TL1160	52°13·8′	0°22·1′W	A	153
Bushmoor	Shrops	SO4387	52°28·9′	2°50·0′W	T	137
Bushnells Green	W Berks	SU5670	51°25·8′	1°11·3′W	X	174
Bush Nook	Cumbr	NY6265	54°58·9′	2°35·2′W	X	86
Bush o' Bield	D & G	NX7968	54°59·8′	3°53·1′W	X	84
Bush of Craigs	D & G	NY0171	55°1·7′	3°32·5′W	X	84
Bush of Killylour	D & G	NX8676	55°4·2′	3°46·7′W	X	84
Bush-on-Lyne Fm	Cumbr	NY4066	54°59·3′	2°55·8′W	FM	85
Bushovel Fm	W Susx	TQ1413	50°54·5′	0°22·3′W	FM	198
Bush Pasture	Beds	TL1119	51°51·7′	0°22·9′W	F	166
Bush Street Fm	Glos	ST7295	51°39·4′	2°23·9′W	FM	162
Bush, The	Heref	SO2249	52°8·3′	3°8·0′W	X	148
Bush, The	Northum	NU2336	55°37·1′	1°37·7′W	X	75
Bush, The	Orkney	HY2810	58°58·5′	3°14·7′W	W	6
Bushton	Devon	SS6430	51°3·4′	3°56·1′W	X	180
Bushton	Staffs	SK2026	52°50·1′	1°41·8′W	X	128
Bushton	Wilts	SU0677	51°29·7′	1°54·4′W	T	173
Bush Walk	Northnts	SP8371	52°20·1′	0°46·5′W	F	141
Bushwood	Essex	TQ6495	51°38·0′	0°22·6′E	X	167,177
Bush Wood	Oxon	SU6884	51°33·3′	1°0·8′W	F	175
Bush Wood	Shrops	SO7082	52°26·3′	2°26·1′W	F	138
Bush Wood	Suff	TM2877	52°20·8′	1°21·3′E	F	156
Bush Wood	Warw	SP1768	52°18·8′	1°44·6′W	F	139,151
Bushwood Grange	Warw	SP1869	52°19·4′	1°43·8′W	X	139,151
Bushwood Hall	Warw	SP1769	52°19·4′	1°44·6′W	X	139,151
Bushwood Ho	Warw	SP1867	52°18·3′	1°43·8′W	X	151
Bushy Barn	Oxon	SU3695	51°39·4′	1°28·4′W	X	164
Bushy Bog	N Ayr	NS2460	55°48·3′	4°48·1′W	X	63
Bushy Bottom	W Susx	TQ2209	50°52·3′	0°15·6′W	X	198
Bushy Bratley	Hants	SU2308	50°52·5′	1°40·0′W	X	195
Bushy Common	Norf	TF9513	52°41·0′	0°53·5′E	T	132
Bushycommon Wood	Beds	SP9330	51°57·9′	0°38·4′W	F	165
Bushy Copse	Hants	SU3934	51°6·5′	1°26·2′W	F	185
Bushy Down Fm	Hants	SU6218	50°57·7′	1°6·6′W	FM	185
Bushy Flat	Durham	NY9938	54°44·5′	2°0·5′W	X	92
Bushygap	Northum	NZ0998	55°16·8′	1°51·1′W	X	81
Bushy Grove	Glos	SO6900	51°42·1′	2°26·5′W	F	162
Bushy Heath	Oxon	SU2396	51°40·0′	1°39·7′W	F	163
Bushy Heath Fm	Derby	SK1478	53°18·2′	1°47·0′W	FM	119
Bushy Hill	Essex	TQ8198	51°39·3′	0°37·4′E	X	168
Bushy Hill	Hants	SU7426	51°1·9′	0°56·3′W	X	186,197
Bushy Hill	Surrey	SU9450	51°14·7′	0°38·8′W	X	186
Bushy Hill	Surrey	TQ0251	51°15·2′	0°31·9′W	T	186
Bushy Hill	Worcs	SP1344	52°5·9′	1°48·2′W	X	151
Bushy Hill Fm	E Yorks	SE9437	53°49·5′	0°33·9′W	FM	106
Bushy Knap	Devon	ST1301	50°48·4′	3°13·7′W	F	192,193
Bushy Knowe	D & G	NY3199	55°17·1′	3°4·8′W	H	79
Bushy Leaze Wood	Hants	SU6837	51°7·9′	1°1·3′W	F	185,186
Bushy Lodge Fm	E Susx	TQ4808	50°51·4′	0°6·6′E	FM	198
Bushy Park	N Yks	SE1099	54°23·4′	1°50·3′W	X	99
Bushy Park	Rich	TQ1569	51°24·7′	0°20·4′W	X	176
Bushypark Fm	Derby	SK4162	53°9·5′	1°22·8′W	FM	120
Bushy Ruff Ho	Kent	TR2843	51°8·7′	1°16·0′E	X	179
Bushy Wood	Essex	TL7318	51°50·3′	0°31·1′E	F	167
Bushy Wood	Essex	TL7501	51°41·1′	0°32·3′E	F	167
Busk	Cumbr	NY6042	54°46·5′	2°36·9′W	T	86
Busk	Cumbr	NY7610	54°29·3′	2°21·8′W	X	91
Busk	N Yks	SD8687	54°17·0′	2°12·5′W	X	98
Busk	Oldham	SD9105	53°32·7′	2°7·7′W	T	109
Busketts Lawn Inclosure	Hants	SU3110	50°53·5′	1°33·2′W	F	196
Busketts Wood	Hants	SU3110	50°53·5′	1°33·2′W	F	196
Buskey Ho	N Yks	NZ8807	54°27·3′	0°38·1′W	X	94
Buskhead	Angus	NO4978	56°53·7′	2°49·8′W	X	44
Busk Hill	N Yks	SE7763	54°3·7′	0°49·0′W	X	100
Buskhill Plantn	N Yks	SE7760	54°2·1′	0°49·0′W	F	100
Busk Ho	Cumbr	NY3003	54°25·3′	3°4·3′W	X	90
Buskin	Scot Bord	NT8867	55°54·0′	2°11·1′W	X	67
Buskin Burn	Scot Bord	NT8866	55°53·5′	2°11·1′W	W	67
Buskinburn Ho	Scot Bord	NT8867	55°54·0′	2°11·1′W	X	67
Buskin Fm	Devon	SS5901	50°47·7′	3°59·7′W	FM	191
Busk Moss	N Yks	SD9384	54°15·3′	2°6·0′W	X	98
Busk Pike	Cumbr	NY3003	54°25·3′	3°4·3′W	X	90
Busky Dale	Red & Cl	NZ6615	54°31·8′	0°58·4′W	X	94
Busky Fm	Leic	SK4706	52°39·2′	1°17·9′W	FM	140
Busland Wood	Heref	SO6235	52°1·0′	2°32·8′W	F	149
Buslingthorpe	Lincs	TF0885	53°21·3′	0°22·2′W	T	112,121
Buslingthorpe Wood	Lincs	TF0784	53°20·8′	0°23·2′W	F	121
Busnant	Powys	SO0564	52°16·2′	3°23·1′W	X	147
Busnant	Powys	SO1351	52°9·3′	3°15·9′W	X	148
Bussage	Glos	SO8803	51°43·8′	2°10·0′W	T	162
Bussavean	Corn	SW8047	50°17·2′	5°4·9′W	X	204
Buss Craig	Scot Bord	NT9465	55°52·9′	2°5·3′W	X	67
Buss Creek	Suff	TM4976	52°19·8′	1°39·7′E	W	156
Bussells	Devon	SX9598	50°46·6′	3°29·0′W	X	192
Busses Fm	Fife	NT0294	56°8·0′	3°34·2′W	FM	58
Busses Fm	Suff	TL7557	52°11·2′	0°34·0′E	FM	155
Busses Fm	W Susx	TQ3935	51°6·1′	0°0·5′W	FM	187
Bussex	Somer	ST3535	51°6·9′	2°55·3′W	T	182
Busseys Stool Fm	Dorset	ST9214	50°55·8′	2°6·4′W	FM	195
Buss Fm	Kent	TQ9141	51°8·4′	0°44·2′E	FM	189
Bussock Hill Ho	W Berks	SU4671	51°26·4′	1°19·9′W	X	174
Bussock Mayne	W Berks	SU4672	51°26·9′	1°19·9′W	X	174
Bussock Wood	W Berks	SU4672	51°26·9′	1°19·9′W	F	174
Bussock Woods	Suff	TM3345	52°3·5′	1°24·3′E	F	169
Bussow Resr	Corn	SW5039	50°12·1′	5°29·8′W	W	203
Buss's Green	E Susx	TQ6435	51°5·7′	0°20·9′E	X	188
Buss, The	Shetld	HP6615	60°49·0′	0°46·7′W	X	1
Busta	Shetld	HU3466	60°22·9′	1°22·5′W	T	2,3
Busta	Shetld	HZ2070	59°31·2′	1°38·3′W	X	4
Bustabeck	Cumbr	NY3741	54°45·8′	2°58·3′W	X	85
Busta Fm	Hants	SU7860	51°20·3′	0°52·4′W	FM	175
Busta Hill	Shetld	HU6394	60°37·7′	0°50·4′W	X	1,2
Bustard Green	Essex	TL6428	51°55·8′	0°23·5′E	T	167
Bustard Hill	Cambs	TL0869	52°18·7′	0°24·5′W	X	153
Bustard Inn	Wilts	SU0946	51°13·0′	1°51·9′W	X	184
Bustard Nest Fm	E Yorks	SE9952	53°57·5′	0°29·1′W	FM	106
Bustards Fm	Norf	TF5117	52°44·0′	0°14·6′E	FM	131
Bustard's Green	Norf	TM1792	52°29·2′	1°12·2′E	T	134
Bustatoun	Orkney	HY7652	59°21·5′	2°24·8′W	T	5
Busta Voe	Shetld	HU3566	60°22·9′	1°21·4′W	W	2,3
Buster	Shetld	HU4691	60°36·3′	1°9·1′W	X	1,2
Buston Barns	Northum	NU2307	55°21·6′	1°37·8′W	X	81
Buston Fm	Northnts	SP5038	52°2·5′	1°15·9′W	FM	151
Buston Manor	Kent	TQ7150	51°13·6′	0°27·3′E	X	188
Busveal	Corn	SW7141	50°13·7′	5°12·3′W	T	203
Bu Taing	Shetld	HU4014	59°54·8′	1°16·6′W	X	4
Butchercote	Scot Bord	NT6234	55°36·1′	2°35·8′W	X	74
Butcher Fold	Lancs	SD6235	53°48·8′	2°34·2′W	X	102,103
Butcher Hill	Northum	NZ0570	55°1·7′	1°54·9′W	X	87
Butcher Ho	N Yks	SE4188	54°17·4′	1°21·8′W	X	99
Butcherland Fm	W Susx	SU9827	51°2·3′	0°35·7′W	FM	186,197
Butcherlawn Pond	Derby	SK4878	53°18·0′	1°16·4′W	W	120
Butchers Bank Fm	Ches	SJ7758	53°7·4′	2°20·2′W	FM	118
Butcher's Common	Norf	TG3420	52°43·8′	1°28·4′E	T	133,134
Butcher's Cove	Devon	SX5946	50°18·1′	3°58·4′W	W	202
Butcher's Cross	E Susx	TQ5525	51°0·4′	0°13·0′E	T	188,199
Butcher's Hill Fm	Cambs	TL5391	52°30·0′	0°15·6′E	FM	143
Butchersick Fm	Derby	SK3977	53°17·5′	1°24·5′W	FM	119
Butcher's Row	W Susx	TQ1720	50°58·3′	0°19·6′W	X	198
Butcher's Wood	W Susx	TQ3014	50°54·9′	0°8·7′W	F	198
Butcombe	N Som	ST5161	51°21·0′	2°41·8′W	T	172,182
Butcombe Court	N Som	ST5163	51°22·1′	2°41·8′W	X	172,182
Butcombe Fm	N Som	ST5060	51°20·4′	2°42·7′W	FM	172,182
Buteland	Northum	NY8781	55°7·6′	2°11·8′W	X	80
Buteland Fell	Northum	NY8882	55°8·2′	2°10·9′W	H	80
Buteland Fm	C of Edin	NT1364	55°51·9′	3°23·0′W	FM	65
Buteland Hill	C of Edin	NT1163	55°51·4′	3°24·9′W	H	65
Buteland Ho	W Loth	NT1264	55°51·9′	3°23·9′W	X	65
Bute Town	Caer	SO1009	51°46·6′	3°17·9′W	T	161
Butetown	Card	ST1874	51°27·8′	3°10·4′W	T	171
Butford Fm	Heref	SO5453	52°10·6′	2°40·0′W	FM	149
Bu, The	Orkney	HY4426	59°7·3′	2°58·2′W	X	5,6
Bu, The	Orkney	ND4093	58°49·5′	3°1·9′W	X	7
Buthill	Moray	NJ1365	57°40·3′	3°27·0′W	X	28
Butland	Devon	SX6450	50°20·3′	3°54·3′W	X	202
Butland Wood	Devon	SX6051	50°20·8′	3°57·7′W	F	202
Butlane Head	Shrops	SJ4113	52°42·9′	2°52·0′W	T	126
Butlas	Devon	SX5554	50°22·3′	4°2·0′W	X	202
Butleigh	Somer	ST5233	51°5·9′	2°40·7′W	T	182,183
Butleigh Court	Somer	ST5133	51°5·9′	2°41·6′W	X	182,183
Butleigh Cross	Somer	ST5232	51°5·4′	2°40·7′W	X	182,183
Butleigh Moor	Somer	ST4434	51°6·4′	2°47·6′W	X	182
Butleigh Wood	Somer	ST5033	51°5·9′	2°42·5′W	F	182,183
Butleigh Wootton	Somer	ST5035	51°7·0′	2°42·5′W	T	182,183
Butler Hill	N Yks	SD9849	53°56·5′	2°1·4′W	X	103
Butlers	Essex	TL8010	51°45·8′	0°36·9′E	X	168
Butlersbank	Shrops	SJ5822	52°47·9′	2°37·0′W	X	126
Butlers Court	Bucks	SU9390	51°36·3′	0°39·0′W	X	175
Butler's Court	Glos	SO9024	51°55·1′	2°8·3′W	X	163
Butler's Court	Glos	SP2000	51°42·1′	1°42·2′W	X	163
Butler's Cross	Bucks	SP8407	51°45·6′	0°46·6′W	T	165
Butlers Cross	Bucks	SU9792	51°37·3′	0°35·5′W	T	175,176
Butler's Cross	Norf	TF6726	52°48·6′	0°29·1′E	A	132
Butler's Ct	Kent	TR1261	51°18·7′	1°2·9′E	X	179
Butler's End	Warw	SP2484	52°27·4′	1°38·4′W	X	139
Butler's Fm	Essex	TL5640	52°2·4′	0°16·9′E	FM	154
Butlers Fm	Essex	TL7011	51°46·5′	0°28·2′E	FM	167
Butler's Fm	Essex	TL7742	52°3·1′	0°35·3′E	FM	155
Butler's Fm	Essex	TL8932	51°57·5′	0°45·4′E	FM	168
Butler's Fm	Essex	TM1730	51°55·8′	1°9·8′E	FM	168,169
Butler's Fm	Essex	TQ8989	51°34·3′	0°44·0′E	FM	178
Butlers Fm	Herts	TL1108	51°45·8′	0°23·1′W	FM	166
Butler's Fm	W Berks	SU5969	51°25·2′	1°8·7′W	FM	174
Butlersgreen Ho	W Susx	TQ3123	50°59·7′	0°7·6′W	X	198
Butler's Hall	Herts	TL4619	51°51·3′	0°7·6′E	X	167
Butler's Hall	Suff	TL8557	52°11·0′	0°42·8′E	X	155
Butler's Hall Fm	Essex	TL8337	52°0·3′	0°40·4′E	FM	155
Butler's Hill	Notts	SK5448	53°1·8′	1°11·3′W	T	129
Butler's Hill	Worcs	SP0269	52°19·4′	1°57·8′W	X	139
Butlers Hill Fm	Warw	SP3031	51°58·8′	1°33·4′W	FM	151
Butler's Hill Wood	Worcs	SP0269	52°19·4′	1°57·8′W	F	139
Butlers Lands	W Berks	SU6662	51°21·4′	1°2·7′W	X	175,186
Butlers Lane Sta	Birm	SP1199	52°35·6′	1°49·9′W	X	139
Butler's Manor	Bucks	SP9519	51°51·9′	0°36·8′W	X	165
Butlers Marston	Warw	SP3150	52°9·1′	1°32·4′W	T	151
Butlers Road Fm	Warw	SP3031	51°58·8′	1°33·4′W	FM	151
Butley	Suff	TM3651	52°6·6′	1°27·2′E	T	156
Butley Abbey	Suff	TM3749	52°5·5′	1°28·0′E	X	169
Butleyferry Fm	Suff	TM3848	52°5·0′	1°28·8′E	FM	169
Butley High Corner	Suff	TM3849	52°5·5′	1°28·9′E	T	169
Butley Low Corner	Suff	TM3849	52°5·5′	1°28·9′E	T	169
Butley Mills	Suff	TM3851	52°6·6′	1°29·0′E	X	156
Butley River	Suff	TM3850	52°6·0′	1°28·9′E	W	156
Butley River	Suff	TM3949	52°5·5′	1°29·7′E	W	169
Butley Town	Ches	SJ9177	53°17·6′	2°7·7′W	T	118
Butlocks Heath	Hants	SU4608	50°52·4′	1°20·4′W	T	196
Butsa	Shetld	HU6688	60°34·5′	0°47·2′W	X	1,2
Butser Hill	Hants	SU7120	50°58·7′	0°58·9′W	H	197
Butsfield Abbey	Durham	NZ1043	54°47·2′	1°50·2′W	X	88
Butsfield Burn	Durham	NZ1044	54°47·7′	1°50·2′W	X	88
Butsford Barton	Devon	SS7600	50°47·4′	3°45·2′W	X	191
Butstone	Devon	SS5010	50°52·4′	4°7·5′W	X	191
Butter Bank	Staffs	SJ8723	52°48·5′	2°11·2′W	T	127
Butterbent	Cumbr	SD5591	54°19·0′	2°41·1′W	X	97
Butter Bog	Scot Bord	NT6606	55°21·1′	2°31·7′W	X	80
Butterbridge	Arg & Bt	NN2309	56°14·7′	4°50·9′W	X	56
Butter Burn	Cumbr	NY6774	55°3·8′	2°30·6′W	W	86,87
Butterburn	Cumbr	NY6774	55°3·8′	2°30·6′W	X	86,87
Butter Burn	D & G	NX3583	55°7·1′	4°34·8′W	W	77
Butterburn Flow	Cumbr	NY6776	55°4·9′	2°30·6′W	X	86,87
Butterburn Hill	Cumbr	NY6173	55°3·2′	2°36·2′W	X	86
Buttercombe Barton	Devon	SS4942	51°9·7′	4°9·2′W	X	180
Buttercombe Fm	Oxon	SP3830	51°58·3′	1°26·4′W	FM	151
Butter Cove	Devon	SX6643	50°16·5′	3°52·5′W	W	202
Buttercrambe	N Yks	SE7358	54°1·0′	0°52·7′W	T	105,106
Buttercrambe Moor	N Yks	SE7157	54°0·5′	0°54·6′W	X	105,106
Buttercrambe Moor Wood	N Yks	SE7057	54°0·5′	0°55·5′W	F	105,106
Butter Cross	Shrops	SO7485	52°28·0′	2°22·6′W	A	138
Butterdales	D & G	NY2465	54°58·7′	3°10·8′W	X	85
Butterdean	E Loth	NT4572	55°56·5′	2°52·4′W	X	66
Butterdean	Scot Bord	NT7964	55°52·4′	2°19·7′W	X	67
Butterdon Ball Wood	Devon	SX7589	50°41·5′	3°45·8′W	F	191
Butterdon Hill	Devon	SX6558	50°24·6′	3°53·6′W	X	202
Butterdon Hill	Devon	SX7588	50°40·9′	3°45·8′W	H	191
Butterfield Cott	N Yks	SD7263	54°4·0′	2°25·3′W	X	98
Butterfield Gap	N Yks	SD7663	54°4·0′	2°21·6′W	X	98
Butterfield Green	Luton	TL1024	51°54·4′	0°23·7′W	X	166
Butterfields	Essex	TL8801	51°40·8′	0°43·6′E	X	168
Butterfly Farm	Hants	SU3509	50°53·0′	1°29·8′W	FM	196
Butterfly World	I of W	SZ5290	50°42·7′	1°15·4′W	X	196
Butterford	Devon	SX7056	50°23·6′	3°49·4′W	X	202
Buttergask	Pth & Kin	NN8708	56°15·3′	3°49·0′W	X	58
Butterglen	Pth & Kin	NO0645	56°35·5′	3°31·4′W	X	52,53
Butterhall	Scot Bord	NT5721	55°29·1′	2°40·4′W	X	73,74
Butter Haw	N Yks	SD9352	53°58·1′	2°6·0′W	X	103
Butter Hill	Ches	SJ4070	53°13·7′	2°53·5′W	X	117
Butter Hill	Devon	SS7043	51°10·5′	3°51·2′W	H	180
Butter Hill	D & G	NY4196	55°15·5′	2°55·3′W	H	79
Butter Hill	Oxon	SP3733	51°59·9′	1°27·3′W	X	151
Butter Hill	Staffs	SJ8919	52°46·3′	2°9·4′W	H	127
Butterhill	Staffs	SJ8919	52°46·3′	2°9·4′W	X	127
Butterhill Bank	Staffs	SJ9330	52°52·3′	2°5·8′W	X	127
Butterhill Fm	Pemb	SM8208	51°43·9′	5°9·0′W	FM	157
Butter Hole	Corn	SW9077	50°33·5′	4°57·5′W	X	200
Butterhole	D & G	NX8160	54°55·5′	3°51·0′W	X	84
Butterhole	D & G	NX9570	55°1·1′	3°38·1′W	X	84
Butterhole Bridge	D & G	NX6488	55°10·3′	4°7·7′W	X	77
Butter Howe	N Yks	NZ8215	54°31·7′	0°43·6′W	A	94
Butteriss Downs	Corn	SW7232	50°8·9′	5°11·1′W	X	204
Butteriss Gate	Corn	SW7133	50°9·4′	5°12·0′W	T	203
Butter Knowe	Orkney	HY7040	59°15·0′	2°31·1′W	X	5
Butter Knowe (Burnt Mound)	Orkney	HY7040	59°15·0′	2°31·1′W	A	5
Butterknowes	Northum	NZ0999	55°17·3′	1°51·1′W	X	81
Butterknowle	Durham	NZ1025	54°37·4′	1°50·3′W	T	92
Butterlands	Ches	SJ9467	53°12·2′	2°5·0′W	X	118
Butterlands	Staffs	SJ9159	53°7·9′	2°7·7′W	X	118
Butterlands Park	Devon	SS7000	50°47·3′	3°50·3′W	X	191

Butterlaw	N upon Ty	NZ1868	55°0·6'	1°42·7'W	X	88
Butterlaw	Scot Bord	NT8344	55°41·6'	2°15·8'W	X	74
Butterlees Fm	W Susx	SU9001	50°48·3'	0°43·0'W	FM	197
Butterleigh	Devon	SS9708	50°52·0'	3°27·4'W	T	192
Butterley	Derby	SK3460	53°8·4'	1°29·1'W	T	119
Butterley	Derby	SK4051	53°3·5'	1°23·8'W	T	120
Butterley Court	Heref	SO6157	52°12·8'	2°33·9'W	X	149
Butterley Heys	Ches	SJ6441	52°58·1'	2°31·8'W	A	118
Butterley Moss	Derby	SE0901	53°30·6'	1°51·4'W	X	110
Butterley Resr	Kirk	SE0410	53°35·4'	1°56·0'W	W	110
Butter Lump	N Ayr	NS1855	55°45·5'	4°53·6'W	X	63
Butterly	Kirk	SE0409	53°34·9'	1°56·0'W	X	110
Butterman's Bay	Suff	TM2238	52°0·0'	1°14·4'E	W	169
Buttermere	Cumbr	NY1717	54°32·7'	3°16·6'W	T	89,90
Buttermere	Cumbr	NY1815	54°31·7'	3°15·6'W	W	89,90
Buttermere	Wilts	SU3461	51°21·1'	1°30·3'W	T	174
Buttermere Fell	Cumbr	NY1915	54°31·7'	3°14·7'W	X	89,90
Buttermere Moss	Cumbr	NY1916	54°32·2'	3°14·7'W	X	89,90
Buttermere Wood	Wilts	SU3460	51°20·5'	1°30·3'W	F	174
Buttermilk Fm	Herts	TL3429	51°56·8'	0°2·6'W	FM	166
Buttermilk Hall	Bucks	SP6612	51°48·4'	1°2·2'W	X	164,165
Buttermilkhall Fm	Bucks	SP7923	51°54·2'	0°50·7'W	FM	165
Buttermilk Hall Fm	Northnts	SP7351	52°9·4'	0°55·6'W	FM	152
Buttermilk Hill	Staffs	SK1028	52°51·2'	1°50·7'W	X	128
Buttermilk Stud	Oxon	SP4132	51°59·3'	1°23·8'W	X	151
Buttermilk Wood	Mil Key	SP9231	51°58·4'	0°39·2'W	F	152,165
Buttermoor	Devon	SS4010	50°52·3'	4°16·1'W	X	190
Buttern Hill	Corn	SX1781	50°36·2'	4°34·8'W	H	201
Buttern Hill	Devon	SX6588	50°40·8'	3°54·3'W	H	191
Butter Park	N Yks	NZ7804	54°25·8'	0°47·4'W	X	94
Butterrow	Glos	SO8503	51°43·8'	2°12·6'W	T	162
Buttersend	Glos	SO7725	51°55·6'	2°19·7'W	X	162
Butters Green	Staffs	SJ8150	53°3·1'	2°16·6'W	T	118
Buttershaw	Brad	SE1329	53°45·7'	1°47·8'W	T	104
Butterstocks Fm	W Susx	TQ1322	50°59·4'	0°23·0'W	FM	198
Butter Stone	Durham	NY9918	54°33·7'	2°0·5'W	A	92
Butterstone	Pth & Kin	NO0645	56°35·5'	3°31·4'W	X	52,53
Butter Stone	Shetld	HU3856	60°17·4'	1°18·3'W	X	2,3
Butterstone House School	Pth & Kin	NO0645	56°35·5'	3°31·4'W	X	52,53
Butter's Tor	Corn	SX1578	50°34·6'	4°36·4'W	H	201
Butterstor Downs	Corn	SX1577	50°34·0'	4°36·4'W	X	201
Butterton	Staffs	SJ8342	52°58·7'	2°14·8'W	T	118
Butterton	Staffs	SK0756	53°6·3'	1°53·3'W	T	119
Butterton Grange Fm	Staffs	SJ8442	52°58·7'	2°13·9'W	FM	118
Butterton-lane Fm	Ches	SJ7554	53°5·2'	2°22·0'W	FM	118
Butterton Moor	Staffs	SK0556	53°6·3'	1°55·1'W	X	119
Butterton Moor End	Staffs	SK0555	53°5·8'	1°55·1'W	X	119
Butter Tubs	N Yks	SD8796	54°21·8'	2°11·6'W	X	98
Butterwell	Pth & Kin	NO1506	56°14·6'	3°21·8'W	X	58
Butterwell Fm	N Yks	SE2090	54°18·6'	1°41·1'W	FM	99
Butterwick	Cumbr	NY5119	54°34·1'	2°45·1'W	T	90
Butterwick	Dorset	ST6710	50°53·5'	2°27·8'W	X	194
Butterwick	Durham	NZ3829	54°39·5'	1°24·2'W	T	93
Butterwick	Lincs	TF3845	52°59·3'	0°3·8'E	T	131
Butterwick	N Yks	SE7377	54°11·3'	0°52·5'W	T	100
Butterwick	N Yks	SE9971	54°7·8'	0°28·7'W	T	101
Butterwick Common	N Lincs	SE8506	53°32·9'	0°42·6'W	X	112
Butterwick Ings Fm	Lincs	TF3747	53°0·4'	0°2·9'E	FM	131
Butterwick Low	Lincs	TF4243	52°58·2'	0°7·3'E	X	131
Butterwick Moor	Durham	NZ3931	54°40·6'	1°23·3'W	X	93
Butterwicks	N Yks	NZ7206	54°26·9'	0°53·0'W	X	94
Butterwicks Fm	E Yorks	TA2071	54°7·5'	0°9·4'W	FM	101
Butterwick Whins	N Yks	SE9772	54°8·3'	0°30·5'W	X	101
Butter Wood	Hants	SU7152	51°16·0'	0°58·5'W	F	186
Buttery	Devon	SS7535	51°6·7'	3°46·7'W	X	180
Buttery Fm	Wrekin	SJ6817	52°45·2'	2°28·0'W	FM	127
Butteryhaugh	Northum	NY6393	55°14·0'	2°34·5'W	T	80
Butterytack	Aberd	NJ5661	57°38·5'	2°43·8'W	X	29
Butt Fm	E Yorks	TA0137	53°49·4'	0°27·5'W	FM	106,107
Butt Green	Ches	SJ6651	53°3·6'	2°30·0'W	T	118
Butt Hatch Fm	Essex	TL5708	51°45·1'	0°16·9'E	FM	167
Butt Hatch Fm	Essex	TL6207	51°44·5'	0°21·2'E	FM	167
Butt Hill	Cumbr	NY6250	54°50·9'	2°35·1'W	X	86
Butt Hill	Lancs	SD5344	53°53·6'	2°42·5'W	X	102
Butt Hill	Warw	SP4661	52°14·9'	1°19·2'W	X	151
Butthill Sike	Northum	NY7377	55°5·5'	2°25·0'W	W	86,87
Butt Ho	Derby	SK2437	52°56·0'	1°38·2'W	X	128
Butthouse	Heref	SO4448	52°7·9'	2°48·7'W	FM	148,149
Butthouse Knapp	Heref	SO4349	52°8·4'	2°49·6'W	X	148,149
Buttington	Powys	SJ2408	52°40·1'	3°7·0'W	T	126
Buttington Hall	Powys	SJ2509	52°40·7'	3°6·2'W	X	126
Butt Lane	Staffs	SJ8254	53°5·2'	2°15·7'W	T	118
Buttlane Fm	Staffs	SJ8522	52°48·0'	2°12·9'W	FM	127
Buttle's Fm	Somer	ST1911	50°53·8'	3°8·7'W	FM	192,193
Butt Moor	Somer	ST5235	51°7·0'	2°40·8'W	X	182,183
Butt Moor Br	Somer	ST5235	51°7·0'	2°40·8'W	X	182,183
Butt Mound	Lincs	TF0543	52°58·7'	0°25·8'W	A	130
Buttock	Lancs	SD8040	53°51·6'	2°17·8'W	X	103
Buttock Point	Arg & Bt	NS0174	55°55·6'	5°10·7'W	X	63
Buttockspire Wood	Northnts	SP6541	52°4·0'	1°2·7'W	F	152
Butt of Blackburn	Northum	NY6356	54°54·1'	2°34·2'W	X	86
Butt of Lewis (Rubha Robhanais)	N Eil	NB5166	58°30·9'	6°16·1'W	X	8
Button	Devon	SS6438	51°7·7'	3°56·2'W	X	180
Button	Devon	SX7167	50°29·6'	3°48·7'W	X	202
Button	Orkney	HY2908	58°57·5'	3°13·6'W	X	6,7
Buttonbridge	Shrops	SO7379	52°24·7'	2°23·4'W	T	138
Buttoner Ho	N Yks	SE2250	53°57·0'	1°39·5'W	X	104
Button Fen	Norf	TF6910	52°39·9'	0°30·4'E	X	132,143
Button Haugh Green	Suff	TL9966	52°15·6'	0°55·4'E	T	155
Button Hill Fm	N Yks	SE5638	53°50·4'	1°8·5'W	FM	105
Button Hills	Shetld	HU3968	60°23·9'	1°17·0'W	H	2,3
Buttonhook, The	N Lincs	SE9115	53°37·7'	0°37·0'W	F	112
Buttonoak	Shrops	SO7477	52°23·7'	2°22·5'W	T	138
Buttons	E Susx	TQ6329	51°2·5'	0°19·9'E	X	188,199
Button's Fm	E Susx	TQ5623	50°59·3'	0°13·8'E	FM	199
Button's Green	Suff	TL9153	52°8·8'	0°48·3'E	T	155
Button's Hill	Essex	TQ9199	51°39·7'	0°46·1'E	X	168
Buttridge	Hants	SU7649	51°14·3'	0°54·3'W	X	186
Butt Roads	Scot Bord	NT8716	55°26·5'	2°11·9'W	X	80
Butts	Derby	SK3463	53°10·0'	1°29·1'W	X	119
Butts	Devon	SX8089	50°41·5'	3°41·6'W	T	191
Buttsash	Hants	SU4205	50°50·8'	1°23·8'W	T	196
Buttsbear Cross	Corn	SS2604	50°48·8'	4°27·8'W	T	190
Buttsbury	Essex	TQ6698	51°39·6'	0°24·4'E	T	167,177
Butt's Close	Herts	TL1829	51°57·0'	0°16·6'W	X	166
Butts Fm	Ches	SJ5966	53°11·6'	2°36·4'W	FM	117
Butts Fm	Leic	SP5585	52°27·8'	1°11·0'W	FM	140
Butts Fm	Wilts	SU1257	51°19·0'	1°49·3'W	FM	173
Butt's Green	Essex	TL7603	51°42·1'	0°33·2'E	T	167
Butt's Green	Hants	SU3026	51°2·2'	1°33·9'W	T	185
Butts Hill	Herts	TL1029	51°57·1'	0°23·6'W	X	166
Butts Hill	Surrey	SU9863	51°21·7'	0°35·2'W	X	175,176,186
Butts Lawn	Hants	SU2902	50°49·2'	1°34·9'W	X	196
Butts Lawn	Hants	SU2905	50°50·9'	1°34·9'W	X	196
Buttsole	Kent	TR3054	51°14·5'	1°18·1'E	T	179
Butts Park	Devon	SX5548	50°19·1'	4°1·8'W	X	202
Buttspill	Devon	SX4368	50°29·7'	4°12·4'W	X	201
Butts, The	Ches	SJ8476	53°17·1'	2°14·0'W	X	118
Butts, The	Hants	SU2115	50°56·3'	1°41·7'W	X	184
Butts, The	Shrops	SO4877	52°23·6'	2°45·5'W	X	137,138,148
Butts, The (Tumuli)	Hants	SU2115	50°56·3'	1°41·7'W	A	184
Butt, The	Hants	SU2413	50°55·2'	1°39·1'W	X	195
Butt Yeats	Lancs	SD5867	54°6·1'	2°38·1'W	T	97
Butty Moss	Ches	SJ8768	53°12·8'	2°11·3'W	X	118
Bu Water	Shetld	HU5461	60°20·0'	1°0·8'W	W	2
Buxa	Orkney	HY2905	58°55·9'	3°13·5'W	X	6,7
Buxbury Fm	Wilts	ST9827	51°2·8'	2°1·3'W	FM	184
Buxey Sand		TM1002	51°40·9'	1°2·7'E	X	168
Buxhall	Suff	TL9957	52°10·7'	0°55·0'E	T	155
Buxhall Fen Street	Suff	TM0059	52°11·8'	0°56·0'E	T	155
Buxley	E Loth	NT4171	55°56·0'	2°56·2'W	X	66
Buxley	Scot Bord	NT8054	55°47·0'	2°18·7'W	T	67,74
Buxlow Fm	Bucks	SP7925	51°55·3'	0°50·7'W	FM	165
Buxshalls	W Susx	TQ3527	51°1·8'	0°4·1'W	X	187,198
Buxted	E Susx	TQ4923	50°59·4'	0°7·8'E	T	199
Buxted Park	E Susx	TQ4822	50°58·9'	0°6·9'E	X	198
Buxton	Derby	SK0673	53°15·5'	1°54·2'W	T	119
Buxton	Norf	TG2322	52°45·2'	1°18·7'E	T	133,134
Buxton Brow	Staffs	SJ9864	53°10·6'	2°1·4'W	X	118
Buxton Country Park	Derby	SK0472	53°14·9'	1°56·0'W	X	119
Buxton Heath	Norf	TG1721	52°44·8'	1°13·3'E	X	133,134
Buxton Lodge	Norf	TG2323	52°45·7'	1°18·7'E	X	133,134
Buxton Wood	Northnts	TL0098	52°34·5'	0°31·1'W	F	141
Buxworth	Derby	SK0282	53°20·3'	1°57·8'W	T	110
Buzbury Rings	Dorset	ST9105	50°50·9'	2°7·3'W	A	195
Buzzacott Manor Ho	Devon	SS6046	51°12·0'	3°59·8'W	X	180
Buzzard Hill	Durham	NY8913	54°31·0'	2°9·8'W	X	91,92
Buzzards Nest	E Yorks	TA2631	53°45·8'	0°4·9'W	X	107
Buzzard's, The	Heref	SO4263	52°16·0'	2°50·6'W	X	137,148,149
Buzzart Dikes	Pth & Kin	NO1248	56°37·2'	3°25·6'W	A	53
Bvrrivm (Usk or Brynbuga)	Monm	SO3700	51°41·9'	2°54·3'W	R	171
Bwa-drain	Cered	SN7179	52°23·9'	3°53·4'W	X	135,147
Bwa Du	I of Angl	SH2576	53°15·4'	4°37·0'W	X	114
Bwcle or Buckley	Flint	SJ2764	53°10·3'	3°5·1'W	T	117
Bwich Isaf	Monm	SO2627	51°56·4'	3°4·2'W	X	161
Bwich y Garn	Blae Gw	SO1809	51°46·7'	3°10·9'W	X	161
Bwlan	I of Angl	SH3669	53°11·8'	4°26·9'W	X	114
Bwlch	Carm	SN3136	52°0·0'	4°27·3'W	X	145
Bwlch	Cered	SN5960	52°13·5'	4°3·5'W	X	146
Bwlch	Cered	SN6079	52°23·7'	4°3·1'W	X	135
Bwlch	Denb	SJ0361	53°8·5'	3°26·6'W	X	116
Bwlch	Denb	SJ0777	53°17·2'	3°23·3'W	X	116
Bwlch	Denb	SJ1168	53°12·3'	3°19·5'W	X	116
Bwlch	Denb	SJ1941	52°57·9'	3°12·0'W	X	125
Bwlch	Flint	SJ1765	53°10·8'	3°14·1'W	X	116
Bwlch	Flint	SJ1771	53°14·0'	3°14·2'W	T	116
Bwlch	Gwyn	SH2927	52°49·1'	4°31·9'W	X	123
Bwlch	Gwyn	SH3443	52°57·8'	4°27·9'W	X	123
Bwlch	Gwyn	SH5705	52°37·7'	4°6·4'W	T	124
Bwlch	I of Angl	SH3591	53°23·7'	4°28·5'W	X	114
Bwlch	Nth Pt Talb	SS7693	51°37·6'	3°47·1'W	X	170
Bwlch	Powys	SJ2130	52°51·9'	3°10·0'W	X	126
Bwlch	Powys	SN7597	52°33·6'	3°50·2'W	X	135
Bwlch	Powys	SN9214	51°49·1'	3°33·6'W	X	160
Bwlch	Powys	SO0068	52°18·3'	3°27·6'W	X	136,147
Bwlch	Powys	SO1421	51°53·1'	3°14·6'W	T	161
Bwlch	Powys	SO1679	52°24·4'	3°13·7'W	X	136,148
Bwlch	Powys	SO1953	52°10·4'	3°10·7'W	X	148
Bwlch	Shrops	SJ2525	52°49·3'	3°6·4'W	X	126
Bwlch	Shrops	SJ2529	52°51·4'	3°6·4'W	X	126
Bwlch	Shrops	SO2377	52°23·4'	3°7·5'W	X	137,148
Bwlchau	Powys	SO1158	52°13·0'	3°17·8'W	X	148
Bwlch Bach	Monm	SO2628	51°57·0'	3°4·2'W	X	161
Bwlchbryndinam	Powys	SO0667	52°17·8'	3°22·3'W	X	136,147
Bwlch Bryn-rhudd	Powys	SN8619	51°51·7'	3°38·9'W	X	160
Bwlchbychan	Cered	SN4743	52°4·1'	4°13·5'W	X	146
Bwlch-cae-haidd	Powys	SO0496	52°33·4'	3°24·6'W	X	136
Bwlch Cam	Powys	SH9727	52°50·1'	3°31·3'W	X	125
Bwlch-castell	Cered	SN5259	52°12·8'	4°9·6'W	X	146
Bwlchcefnsarth	Carm	SN6837	52°1·2'	3°55·0'W	X	146
Bwlch Cerrig Duon	Powys	SN8522	51°53·3'	3°39·9'W	X	160
Bwlch-chwyrn	Powys	SN9554	52°10·7'	3°31·7'W	X	147
Bwlchciliau	Powys	SN9555	52°11·2'	3°31·8'W	X	147
Bwlch-clawdd	Carm	SN3835	51°59·6'	4°21·2'W	X	145
Bwlch-clawdd	Carm	SN4837	52°0·9'	4°12·5'W	X	146
Bwlch-clawdd	Cered	SN3353	52°9·2'	4°26·1'W	X	145
Bwlch Côch	Denb	SJ1144	52°59·4'	3°19·2'W	X	125
Bwlch Coch	Powys	SN8496	52°33·2'	3°42·3'W	X	135,136
Bwlch Coch	Powys	SN9564	52°16·1'	3°31·9'W	X	147
Bwlch-coediog	Gwyn	SH8815	52°43·5'	3°39·1'W	X	124,125
Bwlch Corog	Cered	SN7394	52°32·0'	3°51·9'W	H	135
Bwlchcrwys	Cered	SN7177	52°22·9'	3°53·3'W	X	135,147
Bwlch Cwmdulyn	Gwyn	SH5048	53°0·7'	4°13·8'W	X	115
Bwlch-derwin	Gwyn	SH4646	52°59·6'	4°17·3'W	T	115,123
Bwlch Drws Ardudwy	Gwyn	SH6628	52°50·2'	3°59·0'W	X	124
Bwlch-du	Denb	SH9858	53°6·8'	3°31·0'W	X	116
Bwlch Duwynt	Powys	SO0021	51°53·0'	3°26·8'W	X	160
Bwlch Einion	Cered	SN6994	52°31·9'	3°55·5'W	X	135
Bwlch Esgair Gelli	Cered	SN7857	52°12·1'	3°46·7'W	X	146,147
Bwlch Fm	Carm	SN3121	51°52·0'	4°26·9'W	FM	145,159
Bwlch Fm	Carm	SN3822	51°52·6'	4°20·8'W	FM	145,159
Bwlch Fm	Heref	SO2641	52°4·0'	3°4·4'W	FM	148,161
Bwlch Fm	Shrops	SO2776	52°22·9'	3°4·0'W	FM	137,148
Bwlch-garneddog	Gwyn	SH9839	52°56·6'	3°30·7'W	X	125
Bwlchgarreg-lwyd	Pemb	SN1539	52°1·4'	4°41·4'W	X	145
Bwlchgarth	Powys	SN9855	52°11·3'	3°29·1'W	X	147
Bwlchgarw	Brig	SS8994	51°38·3'	3°35·9'W	X	170
Bwlch Giedd	Powys	SN8221	51°52·7'	3°42·5'W	X	160
Bwlch-glas	Cered	SN7087	52°28·2'	3°54·4'W	X	135
Bwlch Glynmynydd	Powys	SN8699	52°34·9'	3°40·6'W	X	135,136
Bwlch golau	Powys	SJ0812	52°42·1'	3°21·3'W	X	125
Bwlch Goriwared	Gwyn	SH7624	52°48·2'	3°50·0'W	X	124
Bwlch Graianog	Gwyn	SH8942	52°58·1'	3°38·8'W	X	124,125
Bwlch Greolen	Powys	SJ0823	52°48·0'	3°21·5'W	X	125
Bwlchgwallter	Cered	SN7672	52°20·2'	3°48·8'W	X	135,147
Bwlchgwernog	Gwyn	SH6145	52°59·3'	4°3·8'W	X	115
Bwlch-gwyn	Carm	SN4028	51°55·9'	4°19·2'W	X	146
Bwlch Gwyn	Cered	SN7478	52°23·4'	3°50·7'W	X	135,147
Bwlch Gwyn	Conwy	SH9054	53°4·6'	3°38·1'W	X	116
Bwlchgwyn	Gwyn	SH6213	52°42·1'	4°2·1'W	X	124
Bwlchgwyn	Gwyn	SN6197	52°33·4'	4°2·6'W	X	135
Bwlch-gwyn	I of Angl	SH4872	53°13·6'	4°16·2'W	X	114,115
Bwlchgwyn	Powys	SN9472	52°20·4'	3°33·0'W	X	136,147
Bwlch Gwyn	Powys	SO0315	51°49·8'	3°24·1'W	X	160
Bwlch-gwyn	Rho Cyn Taf	ST0388	51°35·2'	3°23·6'W	X	170
Bwlchgwyn	Wrex	SJ2653	53°4·4'	3°5·9'W	T	117
Bwlchgwyn Cottages	Powys	SN9472	52°20·4'	3°33·0'W	X	136,147
Bwlch Gwyn Fm	V of Glam	ST0277	51°29·2'	3°24·3'W	FM	170
Bwlch-gwyn-isaf	Powys	SN9472	52°20·4'	3°33·0'W	X	136,147
Bwlchgwynt	Carm	SN2722	51°52·4'	4°30·4'W	X	145,158
Bwlchgwynt	Carm	SN6745	52°5·5'	3°56·1'W	X	146
Bwlch Gwynt	Gwyn	SH3241	52°56·7'	4°29·6'W	X	123
Bwlchgylfin	Gwyn	SH5553	53°3·5'	4°9·4'W	X	115
Bwlch-henllan	Powys	SO0337	52°1·6'	3°24·4'W	X	160
Bwlch-Llan	Cered	SN5758	52°12·3'	4°5·2'W	T	146
Bwlch-llwyn Bank	Powys	SO1159	52°13·6'	3°17·8'W	X	148
Bwlch Llyn Bach	Gwyn	SH7412	52°41·7'	3°51·5'W	X	124
Bwlch Maen Gwynedd	Denb	SJ0734	52°54·0'	3°22·6'W	X	125
Bwlch Main	Gwyn	SH6053	53°3·6'	4°4·9'W	X	115
Bwlch-mawr	Denb	SJ1946	53°0·6'	3°12·0'W	X	116
Bwlch Mawr	Gwyn	SH4247	53°0·1'	4°20·9'W	H	115,123
Bwlchmawr	Pemb	SM8225	51°53·1'	5°9·7'W	X	157
Bwlchmawr	Pemb	SN0038	52°0·5'	4°54·5'W	X	145,157
Bwlchmawr	Powys	SN8950	52°8·5'	3°36·9'W	X	147
Bwlch-mawr	Powys	SO0467	52°17·8'	3°24·1'W	X	136,147
Bwlchmelyn	Carm	SN2640	52°2·1'	4°31·8'W	X	145
Bwlch Nant-gwyn	Rho Cyn Taf	SS9197	51°39·9'	3°34·2'W	X	170
Bwlch-newydd	Carm	SN3624	51°53·7'	4°22·6'W	T	145,159
Bwlch Oerddrws	Gwyn	SH7917	52°44·5'	3°47·1'W	X	124
Bwlchog-isaf	Carm	SN4438	52°1·4'	4°16·0'W	X	146
Bwlch Penbarras	Denb	SJ1660	53°8·1'	3°14·9'W	X	116
Bwlchserth Fm	Powys	SN9937	52°1·6'	3°27·9'W	FM	160
Bwlch Siglen	Gwyn	SH8313	52°42·4'	3°43·5'W	X	124,125
Bwlch Sirddyn	Gwyn	SH8823	52°47·8'	3°39·3'W	X	124,125
Bwlch Sych	Powys	SJ0223	52°48·0'	3°26·8'W	X	125
Bwlchteulu	Cered	SN6867	52°17·4'	3°55·7'W	X	135
Bwlchtocyn	Gwyn	SH3026	52°48·5'	4°30·9'W	T	123
Bwlch-tre-banau	Carm	SN7237	52°1·2'	3°51·5'W	X	146,160
Bwlch Tyddiad	Gwyn	SH6530	52°51·3'	3°59·9'W	X	124
Bwlch Ungwr	Pemb	SN1332	51°57·5'	4°42·9'W	X	145
Bwlchwernen Fawr	Cered	SN6055	52°10·8'	4°2·5'W	X	146
Bwlchwern Hir	Conwy	SH8174	53°15·2'	3°46·6'W	X	116
Bwlch y Bedol	Gwyn	SH5044	52°58·6'	4°13·6'W	X	124
Bwlch-y-beudy	Conwy	SH9648	53°1·4'	3°32·6'W	X	116
Bwlch y Brecan	Gwyn	SH6261	53°7·9'	4°3·4'W	X	115
Bwlchybryngolan	Powys	SO1865	52°16·9'	3°11·7'W	X	136,148
Bwlch-y-cefn Bank	Powys	SO1260	52°14·1'	3°16·9'W	H	148
Bwlch-y-cibau	Powys	SJ1717	52°44·9'	3°13·4'W	T	125
Bwlch y Clawdd	Rho Cyn Taf	SS9494	51°38·3'	3°31·5'W	X	170
Bwlch y Cribwr	Gwyn	SH9230	52°51·6'	3°35·8'W	X	125
Bwlch y Crogfa	Powys	SJ1315	52°43·8'	3°16·9'W	X	125
Bwlch-y-cwm	Card	ST1483	51°32·6'	3°14·0'W	T	171
Bwlchyddar	Powys	SJ1622	52°47·6'	3°14·3'W	T	125
Bwlch y Ddau Faen	Powys	SN8958	52°12·8'	3°37·1'W	X	147
Bwlch y Ddeufaen	Conwy	SH7171	53°13·5'	3°55·5'W	X	115
Bwlch y Ddeuwynt	Powys	SN7917	51°50·5'	3°45·0'W	H	160
Bwlch-y-ddwyallt	Cered	SN6688	52°28·7'	3°58·0'W	X	135
Bwlchyddwyallt	Cered	SN7163	52°15·2'	3°53·0'W	X	146,147
Bwlch-y-ddwy-elor	Gwyn	SH5550	53°1·9'	4°9·3'W	X	115
Bwlch y Ddwy-Glyder	Gwyn	SH6558	53°6·4'	4°0·6'W	X	115
Bwlch-y-diarth	Powys	SO0161	52°14·5'	3°26·6'W	X	147
Bwlch y Dolydd	Wrex	SJ1337	52°55·6'	3°17·3'W	X	125
Bwlchydomen	Carm	SN2516	51°49·2'	4°31·9'W	X	158
Bwlchydomen	Carm	SN3237	52°0·6'	4°26·5'W	X	145
Bwlchydonge	Powys	SJ2231	52°52·5'	3°9·1'W	X	126
Bwlch y Duwynt	Powys	SN9019	51°51·8'	3°35·5'W	X	160
Bwlch y Dŵr	Gwyn	SH9829	52°51·2'	3°30·5'W	X	125
Bwlch-y-fadfa	Cered	SN4349	52°7·3'	4°17·2'W	X	146
Bwlchyfan	Powys	SN9489	52°29·6'	3°33·3'W	X	136
Bwlchyfedwen Fm	Carm	SN4902	51°42·0'	4°10·7'W	FM	159
Bwlch-y-fen-bentir	I of Angl	SH4177	53°16·2'	4°22·7'W	X	114,115
Bwlch y Fenni	Gwyn	SH9733	52°53·3'	3°31·5'W	X	125
Bwlch-y-ffordd	Gwyn	SH7228	52°50·3'	3°53·6'W	X	124
Bwlch-y-ffridd	Powys	SO0695	52°32·9'	3°22·8'W	T	136
Bwlch y Fign	Gwyn	SH8218	52°45·0'	3°44·5'W	H	124,125
Bwlch-y-fwlet	Gwyn	SH9030	52°51·6'	3°37·6'W	X	125
Bwlch y Gadair	Powys	SN8866	52°17·1'	3°38·1'W	X	135,136,147
Bwlch-y-gaer	Conwy	SH7469	53°12·4'	3°52·8'W	X	115
Bwlch-y-garnedd	Denb	SJ1645	53°0·0'	3°14·7'W	X	116
Bwlch y Garreg	Powys	SO0196	52°33·4'	3°27·2'W	X	136
Bwlch y Gaseg	Denb	SJ0940	52°57·2'	3°20·9'W	X	125
Bwlch y Gesail	Gwyn	SH8318	52°45·1'	3°43·6'W	H	124,125
Bwlch-y-gilwen	Carm	SN6643	52°4·4'	3°56·9'W	X	146
Bwlch-y-gle Dam	Powys	SN9288	52°29·0'	3°35·0'W	X	136
Bwlch y Gorddinan or Crimea Pass	Conwy	SH7049	53°1·6'	3°55·9'W	X	115
Bwlch-y-graig	Cered	SN5759	52°12·9'	4°5·2'W	X	146
Bwlch-y-graig	Powys	SJ1222	52°47·5'	3°17·9'W	X	125
Bwlch y Greigwen	Gwyn	SH9342	52°58·1'	3°35·2'W	X	125

Bwlch y Groes	Conwy	SH7551	53°2·7′	3°51·5′W	X	115
Bwlch y Groes	Denb	SJ1445	53°0·0′	3°16·5′W	X	116
Bwlch-y-groes	Gwyn	SH5559	53°6·8′	4°9·6′W	X	115
Bwlch y Groes	Gwyn	SH9123	52°47·9′	3°36·6′W	X	125
Bwlchygroes	Pemb	SN2336	51°59·9′	4°34·3′W	X	145
Bwlch y Gwyddel	Gwyn	SH6555	53°4·8′	4°0·5′W	X	115
Bwlchygwynt	Carm	SN5141	52°3·1′	4°10·0′W	X	146
Bwlch-y-gwynt	Conwy	SH8260	53°7·7′	3°45·4′W	X	116
Bwlch y Llan	Gwyn	SH6217	52°44·2′	4°2·2′W	H	124
Bwlch-y-llan	Powys	SJ1420	52°46·5′	3°16·1′W	X	125
Bwlchyllyn	Gwyn	SH5055	53°4·5′	4°13·9′W	T	115
Bwlchyllyn	Powys	SN9788	52°29·1′	3°30·6′W	X	136
Bwlch-y-maen	Conwy	SH7853	53°3·9′	3°48·8′W	X	115
Bwlch-y-maen	Gwyn	SH6506	52°38·3′	3°59·3′W	X	124
Bwlch-y-maen-melyn	Conwy	SH8947	53°0·8′	3°38·9′W	X	116
Bwlch y Main	Powys	SJ0524	52°48·6′	3°24·2′W	X	125
Bwlch-y-mawn	Conwy	SH9247	53°0·8′	3°36·2′W	X	116
Bwlchymynydd	Carm	SN4417	51°50·0′	4°15·5′W	X	159
Bwlchymynydd	Swan	SS5798	51°40·0′	4°3·7′W	X	159
Bwlch-yn-horeb	Gwyn	SH9634	52°53·8′	3°32·4′W	X	125
Bwlch-y-pant	Pemb	SN1029	51°55·9′	4°45·4′W	X	145,158
Bwlch-y-parc	Denb	SJ1658	53°7·0′	3°14·9′W	X	116
Bwlch y Pawl	Gwyn	SH9126	52°49·5′	3°36·7′W	X	125
Bwlch y Pentre	Conwy	SH8746	53°0·2′	3°40·6′W	X	116
Bwlch-y-Plain	Powys	SO2475	52°22·3′	3°6·6′W	T	137,148
Bwlch yr Eifl	Gwyn	SH3645	52°58·9′	4°26·2′W	X	123
Bwlch-yr-haiarn	Conwy	SH7759	53°7·1′	3°49·9′W	X	115
Bwlchyrhandir	Cered	SN5973	52°20·5′	4°3·8′W	X	135
Bwlch y Rhediad	Gwyn	SH6652	53°3·2′	3°59·6′W	X	115
Bwlch-y-rhiw	Carm	SN7246	52°6·1′	3°51·7′W	X	146,147
Bwlch-y-rhiw	Powys	SJ2229	52°51·4′	3°9·1′W	X	126
Bwlch y Rhiwgyr	Gwyn	SH6220	52°45·8′	4°2·3′W	H	124
Bwlch-y-rhôs	Pemb	SM9338	52°0·4′	5°0·6′W	X	157
Bwlchysaethau	Gwyn	SH6154	53°4·2′	4°4·1′W	X	115
Bwlch-y-sarnau	Powys	SO0274	52°21·6′	3°25·9′W	T	136,147
Bwlchystyllen	Cered	SN7386	52°27·7′	3°51·8′W	X	135
Bwlch y Tri Marchog	Conwy	SH7062	53°8·6′	3°56·2′W	X	115
Bwlch-y-waun	Powys	SO1118	51°51·4′	3°17·1′W	X	161
Bwllfa Fm	Rho Cyn Taf	SS9794	51°38·4′	3°28·9′W	FM	170
Bwn Bach	Pemb	SN0944	52°3·9′	4°46·8′W	X	145
Bwrdd Arthur	Conwy	SH9667	53°11·6′	3°33·0′W	X	116
Bwrdd Arthur	Denb	SJ0734	52°54·0′	3°22·6′W	X	125
Bwrdd Arthur	I of Angl	SH5881	53°18·7′	4°7·5′W	A	114,115
Bwrdd Arthur (Cairn)	Denb	SJ0734	52°54·0′	3°22·6′W	A	125
Bwrdd Arthur (Fort)	I of Angl	SH5881	53°18·7′	4°7·5′W	A	114,115
Bwrdd y Rhyfel	Flint	SJ1475	53°16·1′	3°17·0′W	A	116
Bwysfa	Powys	SN8828	51°56·6′	3°37·4′W	X	160
Byall Fen	Cambs	TL4586	52°27·4′	0°8·4′E	X	143
Byall Fen	Cambs	TL4682	52°25·2′	0°9·2′E	X	143
Byall Fen	Cambs	TL4984	52°26·2′	0°11·9′E	X	143
Byall Fen Fm	Cambs	TL4487	52°27·9′	0°7·6′E	FM	142,143
Byanna	Staffs	SJ8329	52°51·7′	2°14·7′W	X	127
Byard's Leap Fm	Lincs	SK9949	53°2·0′	0°31·0′W	FM	130
Byatts, The	Ches	SJ4567	53°12·1′	2°49·0′W	X	117
Bybeck	Cumbr	NY6105	54°26·6′	2°35·7′W	X	91
Bybrook	Kent	TR0144	51°9·8′	0°52·9′E	T	189
By Brook	Wilts	ST8370	51°26·0′	2°14·3′W	W	173
Bybrook Lodge Fm	Leic	SK5511	52°41·9′	1°10·8′W	FM	129
Bycell Fm	Bucks	SP6936	52°1·3′	0°59·3′W	FM	152
Bycliffe	N Yks	SE0169	54°7·3′	1°58·7′W	X	98
Bycliff Hill	N Yks	SE0268	54°6·7′	1°57·7′W	X	98
Bycott	Devon	SS7117	50°56·5′	3°49·8′W	X	180
Bycross	Heref	SO3742	52°4·6′	2°54·8′W	T	148,149,161
Byddegai	Powys	SN9823	51°54·0′	3°28·6′W	W	160
Byddwn	Powys	SO0827	51°56·3′	3°19·9′W	X	160
Bydean Fm	Hants	SU7026	51°2·0′	0°59·7′W	FM	186,197
Byde Fm	Wilts	SU0259	51°20·0′	1°57·9′W	FM	173
Bydemill Brook	Swin	SU1893	51°38·4′	1°44·0′W	W	163,173
Bydemill Fm	Swin	SU1892	51°37·8′	1°44·0′W	FM	163,173
Byden Copse	Hants	SU7018	50°57·7′	0°59·8′W	F	197
Bydown Ho	Devon	SS6229	51°2·9′	3°57·7′W	X	180
Byeastwood	Brig	SS9281	51°31·3′	3°33·0′W	T	170
Byeballs Fm	Essex	TL6335	51°59·6′	0°22·8′E	FM	154
Byebush	Aberd	NJ7733	57°23·5′	2°22·5′W	X	29,30
Bye Common	Somer	SS8835	51°6·4′	3°35·6′W	H	181
Bye Fm	Dorset	ST7623	51°0·6′	2°20·1′W	FM	183
Bye Fm	Somer	ST0542	51°10·4′	3°21·2′W	FM	181
Byegill Fm	Cumbr	NY4958	54°55·1′	2°47·3′W	FM	86
Bye Green	Bucks	SP8611	51°47·7′	0°44·8′W	T	165
Byehass Fell	Scot Bord	NT3403	55°19·3′	3°2·0′W	H	79
Bye Hill	Scot Bord	NY4199	55°17·1′	2°55·3′W	H	79
Bye Law Hill	W Loth	NS9557	55°47·9′	3°40·1′W	X	65,72
Byelet Coppice	Shrops	SO6597	52°34·4′	2°30·6′W	F	138
Byeloch	D & G	NY0773	55°2·8′	3°26·9′W	X	85
Byerhope	Northum	NY8646	54°48·8′	2°12·6′W	T	87
Byerhope Bank	Northum	NY8647	54°49·3′	2°12·6′W	X	87
Byerhope Fm	Northum	NY8646	54°48·8′	2°12·6′W	FM	87
Byerhope Moss	Northum	NY8747	54°49·3′	2°11·7′W	X	87
Byerhope Resr	Northum	NY8546	54°48·8′	2°13·6′W	W	87
Byerley Stud, The	Northum	NZ0575	55°4·4′	1°54·9′W	X	87
Byermoor	Ghead	NZ1857	54°54·7′	1°42·7′W	T	88
Byermoor	Ghead	NZ1858	54°55·2′	1°42·7′W	X	88
Byers Fell	Northum	NY6557	54°54·6′	2°32·3′W	X	86
Byers Fm	D & G	NY0269	55°0·6′	3°31·5′W	FM	84
Byers Garth	Durham	NZ3141	54°46·0′	1°30·7′W	X	88
Byers' Gill Wood	Darl	NZ3320	54°34·7′	1°28·9′W	F	93
Byers Green	Durham	NZ2234	54°42·3′	1°39·1′W	T	93
Byers Hall	Northum	NY6560	54°56·2′	2°32·4′W	X	86
Byers Hill	N Yks	NZ0707	54°27·7′	1°53·1′W	X	92
Byers Pike	Cumbr	NY6357	54°54·6′	2°34·2′W	X	86
Byerstead	Cumbr	NX9613	54°30·3′	3°35·9′W	X	89
Byerstead	Cumbr	NY1428	54°38·6′	3°19·5′W	X	89
Byerworth Fm	Lancs	SD4944	53°53·6′	2°46·1′W	FM	102
Byes Fm	Devon	ST1414	50°55·4′	3°13·0′W	FM	181,193
Byes Fm	Essex	TM1126	51°53·8′	1°4·4′E	FM	168,169
Byesteads	Cumbr	NY6021	54°35·2′	2°36·7′W	X	91
Byfield	Northnts	SP5153	52°10·6′	1°14·9′W	T	151
Byfleet	Surrey	TQ0661	51°20·5′	0°28·3′W	T	176,187
Byford	Heref	SO3942	52°4·6′	2°53·0′W	T	148,149,161
Byford Common	Heref	SO3843	52°5·2′	2°53·9′W	T	148,149,161
Byfords Fm	Glos	SO7221	51°53·4′	2°24·0′W	FM	162
Bygate	Northum	NZ0776	55°5·0′	1°53·0′W	X	88
Bygate Hall Cottages	Northum	NT8608	55°22·2′	2°12·8′W	X	80
Bygone Village	Norf	TG4513	52°39·8′	1°37·8′E	X	134
Bygot House Fm	E Yorks	SE9943	53°52·7′	0°29·2′W	FM	106
Bygot Wood	E Yorks	TA0043	53°52·6′	0°28·3′W	F	106,107
Bygrave	Herts	TL2635	52°0·2′	0°9·5′W	T	153
Bygrave Lodge Fm	Herts	TL2835	52°0·1′	0°7·7′W	FM	153
Byham Hall	Essex	TL8135	51°59·3′	0°38·6′E	X	155
Byhams	Essex	TL9904	51°42·2′	0°53·2′E	X	168
Byholme Fm	E Yorks	SE7645	53°54·0′	0°50·2′W	FM	105,106
Bykenhillock	Angus	NO3660	56°43·9′	3°2·3′W	X	44
Byker	N upon Ty	NZ2764	54°58·4′	1°34·3′W	T	88
Byke Yards	Highld	ND3866	58°34·9′	3°3·5′W	X	12
Bylam Fm	Suff	TM1936	51°59·0′	1°11·8′E	FM	169
Bylan	Gwyn	SH7615	52°43·4′	3°49·8′W	X	124
Byland Abbey	N Yks	SE5478	54°11·9′	1°9·9′W	T	100
Byland Moor	N Yks	SE5481	54°13·6′	1°9·9′W	X	100
Bylands	Aberd	NK0754	57°34·8′	1°52·5′W	X	30
Bylands Fm	Hants	SU7059	51°19·8′	0°59·3′W	FM	175,186
Bylane End	Corn	SX2759	50°24·6′	4°25·7′W	X	201
Bylaugh Park	Norf	TG0319	52°44·1′	1°0·8′E	X	133
Bylaugh Wood	Norf	TG0319	52°44·1′	1°0·8′E	F	133
Bylbster	Highld	ND2553	58°27·8′	3°16·7′W	X	11,12
Bylbster Moss	Highld	ND2652	58°27·3′	3°15·6′W	X	11,12
Bylchau	Conwy	SH9762	53°9·0′	3°32·0′W	T	116
Bylchau	Powys	SN8443	52°4·6′	3°41·2′W	X	147,160
Bylchau Blaenclydach	Carm	SN8026	51°55·4′	3°44·3′W	H	160
Bylchau Rhos-fain	Carm	SN7517	51°50·5′	3°48·5′W	X	160
Byletts	Heref	SO3858	52°13·2′	2°54·1′W	X	148,149
Byley	Ches	SJ7169	53°13·3′	2°25·7′W	T	118
Byley Hall	Ches	SJ7167	53°12·2′	2°25·6′W	X	118
Byley Hill Fm	Ches	SJ7167	53°12·2′	2°25·6′W	FM	118
Bylsborough Fm	W Susx	TQ2216	50°56·1′	0°15·4′W	FM	198
Bynack Beg	Highld	NJ0306	57°8·3′	3°35·7′W	X	36
Bynack Burn	Aberd	NN9785	56°56·9′	3°41·1′W	W	43
Bynack Lodge	Aberd	NO0085	56°57·0′	3°38·2′W	X	43
Bynack More	Highld	NJ0406	57°8·4′	3°34·7′W	H	36
Bynack Stable	Highld	NJ0210	57°10·5′	3°36·8′W	X	36
Byndes	Essex	TL8433	51°58·1′	0°41·1′E	X	168
Bynea	Carm	SS5499	51°40·5′	4°6·3′W	T	159
Byne Brook	Shrops	SO4687	52°28·9′	2°47·3′W	W	137,138
Byne Hill	S Ayr	NX1894	55°12·7′	4°51·2′W	H	76
Bynehill Burn	S Ayr	NX1894	55°12·7′	4°51·2′W	W	76
Byne's Fm	E Susx	TQ7511	50°52·5′	0°29·6′E	FM	199
Byng Hall	Suff	TM2853	52°7·9′	1°20·3′E	X	156
Bynorth Cliff	Corn	SX1799	50°45·9′	4°35·3′W	X	190
Byra Hill	E Ayr	NS4144	55°40·1′	4°31·2′W	X	70
Byram	N Yks	SE4825	53°43·4′	1°15·9′W	T	105
Byram Fm	N Yks	SE5026	53°43·9′	1°14·1′W	FM	105
Byram Hall	N Yks	SE4926	53°43·9′	1°15·0′W	X	105
Byrds Fm	Essex	TL5440	52°2·4′	0°15·1′E	FM	154
Byre Bank Wood	N Yks	SD9372	54°8·9′	2°6·0′W	F	98
Byreburn	D & G	NY3979	55°6·4′	2°56·9′W	X	85
Byre Burn	D & G	NY3980	55°6·9′	2°57·0′W	W	79
Byreburnfoot	D & G	NY3877	55°5·3′	2°57·9′W	X	85
Byreburnside	D & G	NY3978	55°5·8′	2°56·9′W	X	85
Byre Cleuch	D & G	NY2682	55°7·9′	3°9·2′W	X	79
Byrecleuch Burn	D & G	NY4192	55°13·4′	2°55·2′W	W	79
Byrecleugh	Scot Bord	NT6258	55°49·1′	2°35·9′W	X	67,74
Byrecleugh Ridge	Scot Bord	NT6159	55°49·6′	2°36·9′W	X	67,74
Byrecroft	D & G	NX8668	54°59·9′	3°46·5′W	X	84
Byrehill	Cumbr	NY4753	54°52·4′	2°49·1′W	X	86
Byreholm	D & G	NX8594	55°13·9′	3°48·1′W	X	78
Byreholm	Scot Bord	NY5089	55°11·8′	2°46·7′W	X	79
Byrehope Mount	Scot Bord	NT1054	55°46·5′	3°25·7′W	H	65,72
Byreleask	Aberd	NK0333	57°23·5′	1°56·5′W	X	30
Byrelee Burn	Scot Bord	NT3613	55°24·7′	3°0·2′W	W	79
Byrelee Hill	Scot Bord	NT3713	55°24·7′	2°59·3′W	H	79
Byre of Scord	Shetld	HP5807	60°44·8′	0°55·7′W	X	1
Byres	E Ayr	NS5738	55°37·1′	4°15·8′W	X	71
Byres	E Loth	NT4976	55°58·7′	2°48·6′W	X	66
Byres	Fife	NO3524	56°24·5′	3°2·8′W	X	54,59
Byres	Moray	NJ3562	57°38·9′	3°4·9′W	X	28
Byres	Pth & Kin	NO1332	56°28·6′	3°24·3′W	X	53
Byres	W Loth	NT0070	55°55·0′	3°35·6′W	X	65
Byreshaw Hill	Northum	NY7572	55°2·8′	2°23·0′W	X	86,87
Byreshield Hill	Northum	NY6783	55°8·7′	2°30·6′W	H	80
Byresloan	Fife	NT3199	56°11·0′	3°6·3′W	X	59
Byres Loan	Midlo	NT3865	55°52·7′	2°59·0′W	X	66
Byres of Murthly	Pth & Kin	NO0538	56°31·7′	3°32·2′W	X	52,53
Byretown	S Lanak	NS8742	55°39·8′	3°47·3′W	X	71,72
Byrewalls	Scot Bord	NT6642	55°40·5′	2°32·0′W	X	74
Byrgoed	Gwyn	SH9837	52°55·5′	3°30·6′W	X	125
Byrgwm	Torf	SO2303	51°43·5′	3°6·5′W	X	171
Byrgwm Bach	Carm	SN5431	51°57·7′	4°7·1′W	X	146
Byrhedyn-fawr	Gwyn	SH5906	52°38·2′	4°4·6′W	X	124
Byrkley Park	Staffs	SK1623	52°48·5′	1°45·4′W	X	128
Byrkley Park Centre	Staffs	SK1723	52°48·5′	1°44·5′W	X	128
Byrlip	Cered	SN3658	52°12·0′	4°23·6′W	X	145
Byrlymau Elan	Cered	SN8274	52°21·3′	3°43·6′W	X	135,136,147
Byrness	Northum	NT7602	55°18·9′	2°22·3′W	T	80
Byrness Hill	Northum	NT7703	55°19·5′	2°21·3′W	H	80
Byrom Hall	Wigan	SJ6298	53°28·9′	2°33·9′W	X	109
Byron's Pool	Cambs	TL4354	52°10·2′	0°5·9′E	W	154
Byrwydd	Powys	SJ1504	52°37·9′	3°15·0′W	X	136
Byslips	Beds	TL0316	51°50·2′	0°29·9′W	X	166
Bysshe Court	Surrey	TQ3342	51°9·9′	0°5·5′W	X	187
Bystock	Devon	SY0283	50°38·5′	3°22·8′W	X	192
Bytham Fm	Wilts	SU2072	51°27·0′	1°42·3′W	FM	174
By the Crossways	Suff	TM4064	52°13·5′	1°31·3′E	X	156
By The Down	Devon	SX5272	50°32·0′	4°4·9′W	X	191,201
Byth Ho	Aberd	NJ8156	57°35·9′	2°18·6′W	X	29,30
Bything	Devon	SS8115	50°55·6′	3°41·2′W	X	181
Bythorn	Cambs	TL0575	52°22·0′	0°27·1′W	T	142
Bythstone	Aberd	NJ6659	57°37·4′	2°33·7′W	X	29
Byton	Heref	SO3663	52°15·9′	2°55·9′W	T	137,148,149
Byton Hand	Heref	SO3663	52°15·9′	2°55·9′W	T	137,148,149
Bywater Fm	Leeds	SE2838	53°50·5′	1°34·1′W	FM	104
Bywell	Northum	NZ0461	54°56·9′	1°55·8′W	T	87
Bywell	Northum	NZ1697	55°16·3′	1°44·5′W	X	81
Bywell Home Fm	Northum	NZ0463	54°57·9′	1°55·8′W	FM	87
Bywell Letch	Northum	NZ1797	55°16·3′	1°43·5′W	W	81
Bywood Copse	Devon	ST1509	50°52·7′	3°12·1′W	F	192,193
Bywood Fm	Devon	ST1608	50°52·2′	3°11·2′W	FM	192,193
Byworth	W Susx	SU9820	50°58·5′	0°35·9′W	T	197

C

C2C Cycle Route	Durham	NZ2053	54°52·5′	1°40·9′W	X	88
Caa Field	Shetld	HU2482	60°31·5′	1°33·3′W	X	3
Caaf Resr	N Ayr	NS2550	55°43·0′	4°46·7′W	W	63
Caaf Wafer	N Ayr	NS2748	55°41·9′	4°44·7′W	W	63
Caaf Water	N Ayr	NS2353	55°44·5′	4°48·7′W	W	63
Caagil Bay	N Eil	NA9900	57°53·5′	7°4·3′W	W	18
Cabaan Forest	Highld	NH3550	57°30·9′	4°44·8′W	X	26
Cabal	Heref	SO3458	52°13·2′	2°57·6′W	X	148,149
Cabalva Fm	Powys	SO2345	52°6·1′	3°7·1′W	FM	148
Cabalva Ho	Powys	SO2446	52°6·7′	3°6·2′W	X	148
Caban-coch Reservoir	Powys	SN9163	52°15·5′	3°35·4′W	W	147
Cabbachs	Moray	NJ3648	57°31·3′	3°3·7′W	X	28
Cabbacott	Devon	SS4021	50°58·2′	4°16·4′W	T	180,190
Cabbage Creek	Norf	TF9645	52°58·2′	0°55·5′E	W	132
Cabbagehall	Fife	NO5408	56°16·0′	2°44·1′W	X	59
Cabbage Hill	Brackn	SU8671	51°26·1′	0°45·4′W	T	175
Cabbage Hill	Lincs	SK9820	52°46·4′	0°32·4′W	X	130
Cabbage Hill Fm	Lincs	SK9920	52°46·3′	0°31·5′W	FM	130
Cabbylatch or Muir of Drumshade	Angus	NO3850	56°38·5′	3°0·2′W	X	54
Caber Fm	Cumbr	NY5646	54°48·7′	2°40·7′W	FM	86
Caberslack	Cumbr	NY5646	54°48·7′	2°40·7′W	X	86
Caberstongrains	Scot Bord	NT3740	55°39·2′	2°59·6′W	X	73
Cabharstadh	N Eil	NB3619	58°5·1′	6°28·3′W	T	14
Cabilla Moorland	Corn	SX1469	50°29·7′	4°37·0′W	X	200
Cabilla Wood	Corn	SX1365	50°27·5′	4°37·7′W	F	200
Cabin	Shrops	SO3189	52°29·9′	3°0·6′W	T	137
Cabinet Wood	Worcs	SO8146	52°7·0′	2°16·3′W	F	150
Cabin Hill	Durham	NZ0732	54°41·2′	1°53·1′W	X	92
Cabin Hill	Redbr	TQ4793	51°37·2′	0°7·8′E	H	177
Cabin Ho	Darl	NZ2116	54°32·6′	1°40·1′W	X	93
Cabin, The	Cumbr	SD3093	54°19·9′	3°4·2′W	W	96,97
Cabin, The	D & G	NX7551	54°50·5′	3°56·4′W	X	84
Cabin, The	Durham	NZ1121	54°35·3′	1°49·4′W	X	92
Cabin Wood	Gwyn	SH4638	52°55·3′	4°17·0′W	F	123
Cablea	Pth & Kin	NN9138	56°31·5′	3°45·9′W	X	52
Cable Rake	Cumbr	SD7381	54°13·7′	2°24·4′W	X	98
Cab Liogan	Arg & Bt	NN1402	56°10·7′	4°59·4′W	W	56
Cablyd	Gwyn	SH9740	52°57·1′	3°31·6′W	X	125
Cabot Twr	C of Bris	ST5772	51°27·0′	2°36·7′W	X	172
Cabourne	Lincs	TA1301	53°29·8′	0°17·4′W	T	113
Cabourne High Woods	Lincs	TA1304	53°31·5′	0°17·3′W	F	113
Cabourne Mount	Lincs	TA1202	53°30·4′	0°18·3′W	X	113
Cabourne Parva	Lincs	TA1503	53°30·9′	0°15·5′W	X	113
Cabourne Vale	Lincs	TA1300	53°29·3′	0°17·4′W	X	113
Cabourne Wold	Lincs	TA1403	53°30·9′	0°16·4′W	X	113
Cabrach	Arg & Bt	NR4964	55°48·5′	5°59·9′W	X	60,61
Cabrach	Moray	NJ3827	57°20·0′	3°1·3′W	T	37
Cabrach Ho	Moray	NJ3926	57°19·5′	3°0·3′W	X	37
Cabrich	Highld	NH5343	57°27·5′	4°26·6′W	T	26
Cabrook	Bucks	SU9285	51°33·6′	0°40·0′W	X	175
Caburn Wood	N Yks	SE8166	54°5·3′	0°45·3′W	F	100
Cabus	Lancs	SD4947	53°55·2′	2°46·2′W	T	102
Cabus Cross Roads	Lancs	SD4848	53°55·8′	2°47·1′W	X	102
Cabus Nook	Lancs	SD4848	53°55·8′	2°47·1′W	X	102
Cac Carn Beag	Aberd	NO2486	56°57·8′	3°14·5′W	H	44
Cac Carn Mór	Aberd	NO2485	56°57·3′	3°14·5′W	H	44
Cachenhead Fm	Moray	NJ3745	57°29·7′	3°2·6′W	FM	28
Cachlaidh Mhór	Arg & Bt	NR3961	55°46·6′	6°9·3′W	X	60
Cacket's Fm	Brom	TQ4559	51°18·9′	0°5·2′E	FM	188
Cackle Hill	Derby	SK1442	52°58·7′	1°47·1′W	X	119,128
Cackle Hill	Lincs	TF3526	52°49·1′	0°0·6′E	T	131
Cackleshaw	Brad	SE0438	53°50·5′	1°55·9′W	T	104
Cackle Street	E Susx	TQ4526	51°1·1′	0°4·4′E	T	188,198
Cackle Street	E Susx	TQ6919	50°57·0′	0°24·7′E	T	199
Cackle Street	E Susx	TQ8218	50°56·2′	0°35·8′E	T	199
Cacrabank	Scot Bord	NT3017	55°26·8′	3°6·0′W	X	79
Cacrabank Hill	D & G	NY1491	55°12·6′	3°20·7′W	H	78
Cacra Hill	Scot Bord	NT3117	55°26·8′	3°5·0′W	H	79
Cacraside	Scot Bord	NT3017	55°26·8′	3°6·0′W	X	79
Cada an Tuill	Highld	NG5066	57°37·1′	6°10·7′W	X	23,24
Cada Burn	Shetld	HU4780	60°30·3′	1°8·2′W	W	1,2,3
Cadach Geodha Nighean Aigh	N Eil	NB5345	58°19·7′	6°12·7′W	X	8
Cadair Benllyn	Gwyn	SH9045	52°59·7′	3°37·9′W	H	116
Cadair Berwyn	Powys	SJ0732	52°52·9′	3°22·5′W	H	125
Cadair Bronwen	Denb	SJ0734	52°54·0′	3°22·6′W	H	125
Cadairfarch	Brig	SS9784	51°33·0′	3°28·7′W	X	170
Cadair Fawr	Rho Cyn Taf	SN9712	51°48·1′	3°29·2′W	H	160
Cadair Idris	Gwyn	SH7113	52°42·2′	3°54·2′W	H	124
Cadair Ifan Goch	Conwy	SH7866	53°10·9′	3°49·1′W	X	115
Cadam Law	Scot Bord	NT5256	55°47·9′	2°45·5′W	X	66,73
Cadboll	Highld	NH8777	57°46·4′	3°53·5′W	X	21
Cadboll Mount	Highld	NH8879	57°47·5′	3°52·6′W	X	21
Cadborough Fm	E Susx	TQ9119	50°56·5′	0°43·5′E	FM	189
Cadborough Fm	Warw	SP1166	52°17·8′	1°49·9′W	FM	150
Cadborough Hill	Derby	SK2914	52°43·6′	1°33·8′W	X	128
Cadbury	Devon	SS9104	50°49·8′	3°32·5′W	T	192
Cadbury	Shrops	SO6173	52°21·5′	2°34·0′W	X	138
Cadbury Barton	Devon	SS6917	50°56·5′	3°51·5′W	X	180

Cadbury Camp	N Som	ST4572	51°26·9′	2°47·1′W	A	171,172
Cadbury Castle	Devon	SS9105	50°50·3′	3°32·5′W	X	192
Cadbury Castle	Somer	ST6225	51°1·6′	2°32·1′W	A	183
Cadbury Castle (Fort)	Devon	SS9105	50°50·3′	3°32·5′W	A	192
Cadbury Court Fm	N Som	ST4371	51°26·3′	2°48·8′W	FM	171,172
Cadbury Fm	Hants	SU3127	51°2·7′	1°33·1′W	FM	185
Cadbury Heath	S Glos	ST6672	51°27·0′	2°29·0′W	T	172
Cadbury Hill	N Som	ST4464	51°22·6′	2°47·9′W	X	172,182
Cadbury Hill (Fort)	N Som	ST4464	51°22·6′	2°47·9′W	A	172,182
Cadbury Park Fm	Somer	ST6127	51°2·7′	2°33·0′W	FM	183
Caddaford	Devon	SX7565	50°28·5′	3°45·3′W	X	202
Caddam	Angus	NO3372	56°50·3′	3°5·4′W	X	44
Caddam	Angus	NO3756	56°41·7′	3°1·3′W	X	54
Caddam	Pth & Kin	NO2039	56°32·4′	3°17·6′W	X	53
Caddam Wood	Angus	NO3855	56°41·2′	3°0·3′W	F	54
Caddell	N Ayr	NS2647	55°41·4′	4°45·7′W	X	63
Caddell Burn	N Ayr	NS2647	55°41·4′	4°45·7′W	W	63
Cadder	E Dunb	NS6172	55°55·5′	4°13·0′W	T	64
Cadderlie	Arg & Bt	NN0436	56°28·8′	5°10·5′W	X	50
Cadderlie Burn	Arg & Bt	NN0337	56°29·3′	5°11·5′W	W	50
Cadder's Hill	Norf	TG0617	52°42·9′	1°3·4′E	X	133
Caddicroft Fm	Worcs	SO9247	52°7·5′	2°6·6′W	FM	150
Caddiford Fm	Devon	SX7795	50°44·7′	3°44·2′W	FM	191
Caddington	Beds	TL0619	51°51·8′	0°27·2′W	T	166
Caddington Hall	Herts	TL0617	51°50·7′	0°27·3′W	X	166
Caddiston	Devon	SS6404	50°49·4′	3°55·5′W	X	191
Caddleton	Arg & Bt	NM7816	56°17·3′	5°34·8′W	X	55
Caddonfoot	Scot Bord	NT4434	55°36·0′	2°52·9′W	X	73
Caddon Head	Scot Bord	NT3743	55°40·8′	2°59·7′W	X	73
Caddonhead	Scot Bord	NT4041	55°39·8′	2°56·8′W	X	73
Caddonlee	Scot Bord	NT4435	55°36·6′	2°52·9′W	T	73
Caddon Mill	Scot Bord	NT4436	55°37·1′	2°52·9′W	X	73
Caddon Water	Scot Bord	NT4140	55°39·2′	2°55·8′W	W	73
Caddow Fm	Notts	SK7581	53°19·5′	0°52·0′W	FM	120
Caddow Wood	Notts	SK7581	53°19·5′	0°52·0′W	F	120
Caddroun Burn	Scot Bord	NY5899	55°17·3′	2°39·2′W	W	80
Caddroun Rig	Scot Bord	NY5899	55°17·3′	2°39·2′W	H	80
Caddsdown	Devon	SS4325	51°0·4′	4°13·9′W	X	180,190
Caddy Well	Cumbr	NY1402	54°24·6′	3°19·1′W	W	89
Cadeby	Donc	SE5100	53°29·9′	1°13·5′W	T	111
Cadeby	Leic	SK4202	52°37·1′	1°22·4′W	T	140
Cadeby Hall	Lincs	TF2695	53°26·4′	0°5·8′W	X	113
Cadeby Village	Lincs	TF2795	53°26·4′	0°4·9′W	A	113
Cadeleigh	Devon	SS9107	50°51·4′	3°32·5′W	T	192
Cadeleigh Court	Devon	SS9107	50°51·4′	3°32·5′W	X	192
Cademan Wood	Leic	SK4316	52°44·6′	1°21·4′W	F	129
Cademuir	Scot Bord	NT2236	55°36·9′	3°13·9′W	T	73
Cademuir Hill	Scot Bord	NT2337	55°37·5′	3°12·9′W	H	73
Cademuir Plantation	Scot Bord	NT2437	55°37·5′	3°12·0′W	F	73
Cadenham Fm	Cambs	TL5762	52°14·3′	0°18·4′E	FM	154
Cadenham Manor	Wilts	ST9877	51°29·7′	2°1·3′W	X	173
Cadenham Park Fm	Wilts	ST9877	51°29·7′	2°1·3′W	FM	173
Cader	Denb	SJ0061	53°8·5′	3°29·3′W	T	116
Caderg	Angus	NO1976	56°52·4′	3°19·3′W	X	43
Cade's Fm	Somer	ST1421	50°59·2′	3°13·1′W	FM	181,193
Cade Street	E Susx	TQ6020	50°57·7′	0°17·1′E	T	199
Cadfor	Monm	SO2714	51°49·4′	3°3·2′W	X	161
Cadger Beck	N Yks	SE0764	54°4·6′	1°53·2′W	W	99
Cadger Bog	Northum	NT7301	55°18·4′	2°25·1′W	X	80
Cadgerford	Fife	NS9892	56°6·8′	3°38·0′W	X	58
Cadger Ford	Northum	NY7683	55°8·7′	2°22·2′W	X	80
Cadgerford Fm	C of Aber	NJ8305	57°8·4′	2°16·4′W	FM	38
Cadgerhill	Aberd	NK0647	57°31·0′	1°53·5′W	X	30
Cadger Path	Angus	NO4957	56°42·4′	2°49·5′W	T	54
Cadgers Burn	Northum	NZ1276	55°4·9′	1°48·3′W	W	88
Cadger's Road	Aberd	NJ6634	57°24·0′	2°33·5′W	X	29
Cadge's Wood	Cambs	TL6349	52°7·1′	0°23·2′E	F	154
Cadge Wood	Northnts	SP9794	52°32·3′	0°33·8′W	F	141
Cadgill	D & G	NY3173	55°3·1′	3°4·4′W	X	85
Cadgill Burn	D & G	NY3075	55°4·1′	3°5·3′W	W	85
Cadgillfoot	D & G	NY3273	55°3·1′	3°3·4′W	X	85
Cadgillhead	D & G	NY3175	55°4·1′	3°4·4′W	X	85
Cadgillside	D & G	NY3075	55°4·1′	3°5·3′W	X	85
Cadgill Wood	D & G	NY3174	55°3·6′	3°4·4′W	F	85
Cad Green	Somer	ST3417	50°57·2′	2°56·0′W	T	193
Cadgwith	Corn	SW7214	49°59·2′	5°10·5′W	T	204
Cadha	N Eil	NB5561	58°28·4′	6°11·6′W	X	8
Cadha	N Eil	NG1599	57°53·6′	6°48·1′W	X	14
Cadha an da Luain	Arg & Bt	NM4819	56°18·0′	6°4·0′W	X	48
Cadha an t-Sagairt	Highld	ND0726	58°13·0′	3°34·5′W	X	17
Cadha Bàn	Highld	NH0330	57°19·3′	5°15·9′W	X	25
Cadha Buidhe	Highld	NH1184	57°48·6′	5°10·4′W	X	19
Cadha Buidhe	Highld	NH3096	57°55·5′	4°51·8′W	X	20
Cadhachan Riabhach	Highld	NH0079	57°45·6′	5°21·2′W	X	19
Cadha Cleit	N Eil	NB2615	58°2·6′	6°38·1′W	H	13,14
Cadha Dearg	Highld	NH2886	57°50·1′	4°53·4′W	X	20
Cadha Dubh	Moray	NJ2337	57°25·3′	3°16·5′W	X	28
Cadha Dubh	Moray	NJ2627	57°19·9′	3°13·3′W	X	37
Cadha Fhionn	Highld	ND0923	58°11·5′	3°32·4′W	X	17
Cadha Gobhlach	Highld	NH0782	57°47·4′	5°14·3′W	X	19
Cadha Leum-dharaich	Highld	NG8648	57°28·6′	5°33·7′W	X	24
Cadham	Devon	SS5802	50°48·2′	4°0·5′W	X	191
Cadham	Fife	NO2702	56°12·6′	3°10·2′W	T	59
Cadha Mór	Highld	NH6585	57°50·3′	4°16·0′W	X	21
Cadha Mór	Highld	NH9005	57°7·6′	3°48·6′W	X	36
Cadha Mòr	N Eil	NF6600	56°58·5′	7°29·4′W	H	31
Cadha na Beucaich	Highld	NC3248	58°23·6′	4°52·0′W	X	9
Cadha na Gaoidhsich	N Eil	NG4399	57°54·6′	6°19·9′W	X	14
Cadha nan Ingrean	Highld	NG5516	57°10·4′	6°2·7′W	X	32
Cadhan dubha	N Eil	NB2003	57°56·0′	6°43·4′W	X	13,14
Cadha Raineach	Highld	NH2241	57°25·7′	4°57·4′W	X	25
Cadha Riabhach	Highld	NM9697	57°1·4′	5°21·2′W	X	33,40
Cadha Ruadh	Highld	NH0133	57°20·9′	5°18·0′W	H	25
Cadha Ruadh	Highld	NM6948	56°34·3′	5°45·2′W	X	49
Cadhay Ho	Devon	SY0896	50°45·6′	3°17·9′W	A	192
Cadhay Wood	Devon	SY0795	50°45·1′	3°18·7′W	F	192
Cadifor Hall	Pemb	SN2832	51°57·8′	4°29·8′W	X	145
Cadira Beeches	Monm	ST4294	51°38·7′	2°49·9′W	F	171,172
Cadishead	Salf	SJ7092	53°25·7′	2°26·7′W	T	109
Cadlan	Gwyn	SH1926	52°48·3′	4°40·7′W	X	123
Cadland Creek	Hants	SU4505	50°50·8′	1°21·3′W	W	196
Cadland Ho	Hants	SZ4699	50°47·6′	1°20·5′W	X	196
Cadle	Swan	SS6297	51°39·5′	3°59·3′W	T	159
Cadleigh Lodge	Devon	SX6156	50°23·5′	3°57·0′W	X	202
Cadleighpark	Devon	SX6155	50°22·9′	3°56·9′W	X	202
Cadley	Lancs	SD5231	53°46·6′	2°43·3′W	T	102
Cadley	Wilts	SU2066	51°23·8′	1°42·4′W	T	174
Cadley	Wilts	SU2454	51°17·3′	1°39·0′W	T	184
Cadley Fm	Wilts	ST9956	51°18·4′	2°0·5′W	FM	173
Cadley Hill	Derby	SK2718	52°45·8′	1°35·6′W	X	128
Cadley Hill	Glos	SP1834	52°0·5′	1°43·9′W	X	151
Cadlington Ho	Hants	SU7113	50°55·0′	0°59·0′W	X	197
Cadman's Fm	Kent	TQ9953	51°14·7′	0°51·5′E	FM	189
Cadman's Pool	Hants	SU2212	50°54·7′	1°40·8′W	W	195
Cadman's Wood	Kent	TR0843	51°9·1′	0°58·8′E	X	179,189
Cadmoor Copse	Glos	SP0906	51°45·4′	1°51·8′W	F	163
Cadmore End	Bucks	SU7892	51°37·5′	0°52·0′W	T	175
Cadnam	Hants	SU2913	50°55·2′	1°34·9′W	T	196
Cadnam Common	Hants	SU2815	50°56·3′	1°35·7′W	X	184
Cadnam Common	Hants	SU2915	50°56·3′	1°34·9′W	X	196
Cadnam Green	Hants	SU2914	50°55·7′	1°34·9′W	X	196
Cadnam River	Hants	SU2915	50°56·3′	1°34·9′W	W	196
Cadnam River	Hants	SU3016	50°56·8′	1°34·0′W	W	185
Cadnant	Powys	SJ0925	52°49·1′	3°20·6′W	X	125
Cadnant	Powys	SJ1418	52°45·4′	3°16·1′W	W	125
Cadney	N Lincs	TA0103	53°31·1′	0°28·2′W	T	112
Cadney Bank	Wrex	SJ4634	52°54·3′	2°47·8′W	T	126
Cadney Bridge	N Lincs	TA0002	53°30·5′	0°29·1′W	X	112
Cadney Carrs	N Lincs	TA0104	53°31·6′	0°28·2′W	X	112
Cadney Moss	Wrex	SJ4734	52°54·3′	2°46·9′W	F	126
Cadole	Flint	SJ2062	53°9·2′	3°11·4′W	T	117
Cadon Bank	Scot Bord	NT3435	55°36·5′	3°2·4′W	H	73
Cadover Br	Devon	SX5564	50°27·7′	4°2·2′W	X	202
Cadoxton	V of Glam	ST1269	51°25·0′	3°15·5′W	T	171
Cadoxton-Juxta-Neath	Nth Pt Talb	SS7598	51°40·3′	3°48·1′W	T	170
Cadoxton River	V of Glam	ST1569	51°25·1′	3°13·0′W	W	171
Cadshaw	Black w Dar	SD7018	53°39·7′	2°26·8′W	T	109
Cadson	Corn	SX3467	50°29·0′	4°20·0′W	X	201
Cadson Bury	Corn	SX3467	50°29·0′	4°20·0′W	A	201
Cadster	Derby	SK0279	53°18·7′	1°57·8′W	X	119
Cadubh	Highld	NH2194	57°54·2′	5°0·8′W	X	20
Ca-du Ford	Highld	NJ1313	57°12·2′	3°25·9′W	X	36
Cadwell	Heref	SO3565	52°17·0′	2°56·8′W	X	137,148,149
Cadwell	Herts	TL1832	51°58·7′	0°16·5′W	T	166
Cadwell Covert	Oxon	SU6395	51°39·2′	1°5·0′W	F	164,165
Cadwell Fm	Oxon	SU6495	51°39·2′	1°4·1′W	FM	164,165
Cadwell Highfield	Lincs	TF2881	53°18·9′	0°4·3′W	X	122
Cadwell Hill	S Glos	ST7675	51°28·6′	2°20·3′W	X	172
Cadwell Park	Lincs	TF2981	53°18·8′	0°3·4′W	X	122
Cadwell Slates	Lincs	TF2880	53°18·3′	0°4·3′W	X	122
Cadwgan	Monm	SO2725	51°55·4′	3°3·3′W	X	161
Cadwgan	Powys	SN9190	52°30·1′	3°35·9′W	X	136
Cadwgan Fawr	Carm	SN4615	51°49·0′	4°13·7′W	X	159
Cadwgan Fm	Powys	SO2339	52°2·9′	3°7·0′W	FM	161
Cadwgan Hall	Wrex	SJ2948	53°1·7′	3°3·1′W	X	117
Cadwin	Corn	SX0264	50°26·8′	4°47·0′W	X	200
Cadwst	Denb	SJ0335	52°54·5′	3°26·1′W	X	125
Cadythew Rock	Corn	SX0140	50°13·8′	4°47·0′W	X	204
Cadzow	S Lanak	NS7153	55°45·4′	4°2·9′W	T	64
Cadzow Castle	S Lanak	NS7353	55°45·5′	4°1·0′W	A	64
Cae	Gwyn	SH7622	52°47·1′	3°49·9′W	X	124
Cae-ab-Edward	Denb	SJ1856	53°5·9′	3°13·1′W	X	116
Cae Adar Fm	Wrex	SJ2652	53°3·9′	3°5·9′W	FM	117
Caeadda	Powys	SH7906	52°38·5′	3°46·9′W	X	124
Cae Afon	Gwyn	SH8114	52°42·9′	3°45·3′W	X	124,125
Cae-ap-Edward	Flint	SJ2755	53°5·5′	3°5·0′W	X	117
Caeathro	Gwyn	SH5061	53°7·8′	4°14·1′W	T	114,115
Caeau	Conwy	SH8375	53°15·8′	3°44·8′W	X	116
Caeau	Flint	SJ1972	53°14·6′	3°12·4′W	X	116
Caeau	Powys	SO2149	52°8·3′	3°8·9′W	X	148
Caeau	V of Glam	ST0176	51°28·7′	3°25·1′W	X	170
Caeau-brychion	I of Angl	SH4366	53°10·3′	4°20·5′W	X	114,115
Caeaubychain Bach	Carm	SN7226	51°55·3′	3°51·3′W	X	146,160
Caeaubychain Mawr	Carm	SN7225	51°54·8′	3°51·3′W	X	146,160
Caeauduon	Powys	SN9499	52°35·0′	3°33·5′W	X	136
Caeau Fm	Flint	SJ3158	53°7·1′	3°1·5′W	FM	117
Caeau Gleision	Flint	SJ2170	53°13·5′	3°10·6′W	X	117
Caeaugwynedd	Powys	SJ1219	52°45·9′	3°17·9′W	X	125
Caeaugwynion	Gwyn	SH5555	53°4·6′	4°9·5′W	X	115
Caeaugwynion	Wrex	SJ2739	52°56·8′	3°4·8′W	X	126
Caeaugwynion Mawr	Denb	SJ0564	53°10·1′	3°24·9′W	X	116
Cae-awr	Conwy	SH7456	53°5·4′	3°52·5′W	X	115
Caebalciog	Powys	SN9972	52°20·4′	3°28·6′W	X	136,147
Caebalcog	Cered	SN6666	52°16·8′	3°57·5′W	X	135
Caebanaol	Powys	SO1758	52°13·1′	3°12·5′W	X	148
Caebardd	Powys	SJ1912	52°42·2′	3°11·5′W	X	125
Caebetran	Powys	SO0835	52°0·6′	3°20·0′W	X	160
Caebislan Isaf	Cered	SN4862	52°14·4′	4°13·2′W	X	146
Caebitra	Powys	SO2392	52°31·5′	3°7·7′W	W	137
Cae Burdydd	Merth Tyd	SO0410	51°47·1′	3°23·1′W	A	160
Caebwd	Cered	SN7058	52°12·5′	3°53·8′W	X	146,147
Cae Camp	Monm	ST3593	51°38·2′	2°56·0′W	A	171
Caecanol mawr	Gwyn	SH7243	52°58·4′	3°54·0′W	X	124
Cae Caradog	Carm	SN6546	52°6·0′	3°57·9′W	X	146
Cae Caradog Fm	V of Glam	SS9173	51°27·0′	3°33·7′W	FM	170
Cae Castell	Card	ST2280	51°31·0′	3°7·1′W	A	171
Caeceinach	Gwyn	SN6799	52°34·6′	3°57·4′W	X	135
Cae-ceirch	Gwyn	SH7719	52°45·5′	3°49·0′W	X	124
Caecethin	Powys	SN9678	52°23·7′	3°31·3′W	X	136,147
Cae Clyd	Gwyn	SH7144	52°58·9′	3°54·9′W	T	124
Cae Cnap	Monm	ST3697	51°40·3′	2°55·1′W	F	171
Cae Coch	Conwy	SH7371	53°13·5′	3°53·7′W	X	115
Cae-côch	Gwyn	SH8324	52°48·3′	3°43·7′W	X	124,125
Cae-coed	Conwy	SH8864	53°9·9′	3°40·1′W	X	116
Cae-coed	Conwy	SH9463	53°9·5′	3°34·7′W	X	116
Cae-coryn	Gwyn	SH9838	52°56·0′	3°30·7′W	X	125
Cae Cottrel	Powys	SO1527	51°56·3′	3°13·8′W	X	161
Cae Crwn	Conwy	SH7562	53°8·7′	3°51·7′W	X	115
Caecynddelw	Gwyn	SH9835	52°54·4′	3°30·6′W	X	125
Caecyno	Powys	SH8107	52°39·1′	3°45·1′W	X	124,125
Cae Dafydd	Gwyn	SH6145	52°59·3′	4°3·8′W	X	115
Caedelyn	Carm	SN5806	51°44·3′	4°3·0′W	X	159
Caederwen	Monm	SO3014	51°49·5′	3°0·5′W	X	161
Caedicws Fm	Wrex	SJ2035	52°54·6′	3°11·0′W	FM	126
Caedildre	Powys	SO1263	52°15·7′	3°17·0′W	X	148
Cae-Drain	Denb	SJ0368	53°12·3′	3°26·7′W	X	116
Cae-du	Conwy	SH9363	53°9·4′	3°35·6′W	X	116
Cae-du	Denb	SJ1046	53°0·5′	3°20·1′W	X	116
Cae-du	Flint	SJ2560	53°8·2′	3°6·9′W	X	117
Cae-du	Gwyn	SH5605	52°37·7′	4°7·3′W	X	124
Cae-dû	Powys	SN8945	52°5·8′	3°36·8′W	X	147
Cae-Dyah	Wrex	SJ3842	52°58·5′	2°55·0′W	X	117
Cae Elen	I of Angl	SH3277	53°16·1′	4°30·7′W	X	114
Cae Forys	Conwy	SH8172	53°14·1′	3°46·6′W	X	116
Cae Gaer	Powys	SN8281	52°25·1′	3°43·7′W	X	135,136
Cae Gaer (Roman Fort)	Cered	SN8281	52°25·1′	3°43·7′W	R	135,136
Caegarw	Nth Pt Talb	SS8283	51°32·3′	3°41·7′W	X	170
Cae Garw	Powys	SN9138	52°2·0′	3°34·9′W	X	160
Caegarw	Powys	SN9762	52°15·0′	3°30·1′W	X	147
Cae-glâs	Carm	SN7237	52°1·2′	3°51·5′W	X	146,160
Cae Glas	Gwyn	SH6939	52°56·2′	3°56·6′W	X	124
Cae-glâs	Gwyn	SH9333	52°53·3′	3°35·0′W	X	125
Cae-glâs	I of Angl	SH2680	53°17·6′	4°36·2′W	X	114
Cae Glas	Wrex	SJ2652	53°3·9′	3°5·9′W	X	117
Cae Glas	Wrex	SJ2848	53°1·7′	3°4·0′W	X	117
Cae-Goronwy	Conwy	SH9563	53°9·5′	3°33·8′W	X	116
Cae Gors	Gwyn	SH4545	52°59·0′	4°18·1′W	X	115,123
Caegroes	Carm	SN6124	51°54·1′	4°0·8′W	X	159
Cae Grugog	Flint	SJ2555	53°5·5′	3°6·8′W	X	117
Caegwernog	Gwyn	SH7121	52°46·5′	3°54·3′W	X	124
Caegwian	Gwyn	SH6419	52°45·3′	4°0·5′W	X	124
Cae Gwydd	Flint	SJ2357	53°6·5′	3°8·6′W	X	117
Cae-gwydd	Wrex	SJ3343	52°59·1′	2°59·5′W	X	117
Cae-gwyn	Carm	SN7431	51°58·0′	3°49·7′W	X	146,160
Cae-gwyn	Conwy	SH8951	53°2·9′	3°39·0′W	X	116
Cae-gwyn	Denb	SJ0456	53°5·8′	3°25·6′W	X	116
Cae-gwyn	Denb	SJ0872	53°14·5′	3°22·3′W	X	116
Cae-gwyn	Denb	SJ2155	53°5·4′	3°10·4′W	X	117
Cae-gwyn	Gwyn	SH4963	53°8·8′	4°15·1′W	X	114,115
Cae Gwyn	Gwyn	SH7129	52°50·8′	3°54·5′W	X	124
Cae-haidd	Cered	SN4660	52°13·2′	4°14·9′W	X	146
Cae Haidd	Conwy	SH8454	53°4·5′	3°43·5′W	X	116
Cae Haidd	Gwyn	SH4956	53°5·0′	4°14·9′W	X	115,123
Cae-hedydd Fm	Monm	ST4595	51°39·3′	2°47·3′W	FM	171
Cae Hên	Gwyn	SH4958	53°6·1′	4°14·9′W	X	115,123
Cae-Heulen	Powys	SN7899	52°34·8′	3°47·6′W	X	135
Cae-Heylin	Powys	SO1089	52°29·7′	3°19·1′W	X	136
Cae Hic	Flint	SJ2456	53°6·0′	3°7·7′W	X	117
Cae-hir	Powys	SJ1530	52°51·9′	3°15·4′W	X	125
Cae-hogyn	Powys	SN9955	52°11·3′	3°28·3′W	X	147
Caehopkin	Powys	SN8212	51°47·9′	3°42·3′W	T	160
Caehowel	Gwyn	SH9734	52°53·9′	3°31·5′W	X	125
Cae Howel	Shrops	SJ3417	52°45·0′	2°58·3′W	X	126
Cae Hywel	I of Angl	SH3377	53°16·1′	4°29·8′W	X	114
Caeiago	Powys	SN9587	52°28·5′	3°32·4′W	X	136
Caeiocyn	Wrex	SJ2538	52°56·3′	3°6·6′W	X	126
Caeiron	Heref	SO2738	52°2·4′	3°3·5′W	X	161
Caeliber Isaf	Powys	SO2192	52°31·5′	3°9·5′W	X	137
Cae-lica	Wrex	SJ4344	52°59·7′	2°50·6′W	X	117
Cae-llea	Powys	SJ2415	52°43·9′	3°7·1′W	X	126
Cae-llwyd	Wrex	SJ1532	52°53·0′	3°15·4′W	X	125
Cae Llwyd Resr	Wrex	SJ2647	53°1·2′	3°5·8′W	W	117
Cae-mab-seifion	Gwyn	SH6820	52°45·9′	3°57·0′W	X	124
Caemabynyr	Gwyn	SH5159	53°6·7′	4°13·2′W	X	115
Cae Madoc Uchaf	Denb	SJ1849	53°2·2′	3°13·0′W	X	116
Caemadog	Cered	SN7566	52°16·9′	3°49·6′W	X	135,147
Cae Madog	Denb	SJ1862	53°9·2′	3°13·2′W	X	116
Cae Madog	Powys	SN8899	52°34·9′	3°38·8′W	X	135,136
Cae Maen	Rho Cyn Taf	ST0494	51°38·4′	3°22·9′W	X	170
Caemaen Fm	V of Glam	ST0572	51°26·6′	3°21·6′W	FM	170
Cae-march	Conwy	SH9572	53°14·3′	3°34·0′W	X	116
Cae-mawr	Carm	SN5002	51°42·0′	4°9·9′W	X	159
Cae-MAWR	Carm	SN6041	52°3·2′	4°2·1′W	X	146
Cae-mawr	Carm	SN6625	51°54·7′	3°56·5′W	X	146
Cae-mawr	Denb	SJ1850	53°2·7′	3°13·0′W	X	116
Cae Mawr	Flint	SJ2457	53°6·5′	3°7·7′W	X	117
Cae Mawr	Gwyn	SH4959	53°6·7′	4°15·0′W	X	115,123
Cae-mawr	Gwyn	SH5865	53°10·0′	4°7·1′W	X	114,115
Cae Mawr	Heref	SO2938	52°2·4′	3°1·7′W	X	161
Cae-mawr	I of Angl	SH2383	53°19·1′	4°39·0′W	X	114
Cae-mawr	I of Angl	SH3570	53°12·3′	4°27·8′W	X	114
Cae Mawr	I of Angl	SH4080	53°17·8′	4°23·6′W	X	114,115
Cae Mawr	I of Angl	SH4286	53°21·1′	4°22·0′W	X	114
Cae Mawr	I of Angl	SH4664	53°9·3′	4°17·8′W	X	114,115
Caemawr	Powys	SJ1325	52°49·2′	3°17·1′W	X	125
Cae-mawr Fm	Denb	SJ1559	53°7·5′	3°15·8′W	FM	116
Cae-Melwr	Conwy	SH8060	53°7·7′	3°47·2′W	X	116
Cae Morfa Fm	Gwyn	SH4251	53°2·2′	4°21·0′W	FM	115,123
Caemorgan	Cered	SN1947	52°5·7′	4°38·2′W	T	145
Cae-Morgan	Swan	SS5091	51°36·1′	4°9·6′W	X	159
Caemor Wood	Wrex	SJ2235	52°54·6′	3°9·2′W	F	126
Caen	Highld	ND0117	58°8·1′	3°40·4′W	X	17
Caenant	Powys	SJ1125	52°49·2′	3°18·8′W	X	125
Caenant	Powys	SO1528	51°56·9′	3°13·8′W	X	161
Caenantmelyn	Powys	SO2240	52°3·4′	3°7·9′W	X	148,161
Caen Burn	Highld	ND0119	58°9·2′	3°40·5′W	W	17
Caenby	Lincs	TF0089	53°23·6′	0°29·4′W	T	112,121
Caenby Cliff Fm	Lincs	SK9789	53°23·6′	0°32·1′W	FM	112,121
Caenby Corner	Lincs	SK9689	53°23·6′	0°33·0′W	X	112,121
Cae Newydd	Flint	SJ1664	53°10·2′	3°15·0′W	X	116
Caenewydd	Gwyn	SN6397	52°33·5′	4°0·9′W	X	135
Caenfedw	Powys	SN9284	52°26·8′	3°34·9′W	X	136
Caen-hen	Powys	SN8101	52°35·9′	3°45·6′W	X	135,136
Caen Hill	Highld	ND0118	58°8·7′	3°40·4′W	X	17
Caen Hill	Lincs	TA1305	53°32·0′	0°17·3′W	X	113
Caen Hill Locks	Wilts	ST9861	51°21·1′	2°1·3′W	X	173
Caenlochan Forest	Angus	NO1775	56°51·8′	3°21·2′W	X	43
Caenlochan Glen	Angus	NO1876	56°52·3′	3°20·3′W	X	43

Caenlochan National Nature Reserve	Angus	NO1977	56°52·9′	3°19·3′W	X	43
Caenlochan National Nature Reserve	Angus	NO2177	56°52·9′	3°17·3′W	X	44
Caenog	Denb	SJ0945	52°59·9′	3°21·0′W	X	116
Caen Wood	Surrey	TQ1759	51°19·3′	0°18·9′W	X	187
Cae'n-y-bwlch	Gwyn	SH6235	52°53·9′	4°2·7′W	X	124
Cae'n-y-cefn	Gwyn	SH7029	52°50·8′	3°55·4′W	X	124
Cae'n-y-coed	Conwy	SH7657	53°6·0′	3°50·7′W	X	115
Caen-y-mynydd	Powys	SJ0610	52°41·0′	3°23·0′W	X	125
Caen-y-waun	Powys	SN9946	52°6·4′	3°28·1′W	X	147
Caeo Forest	Carm	SN7140	52°2·8′	3°52·5′W	F	146,147,160
Cae-pant	Gwyn	SH9937	52°55·5′	3°29·7′W	X	125
Cae-penfras	Powys	SJ0214	52°43·1′	3°26·7′W	X	125
Cae-poeth	Gwyn	SH7525	52°48·7′	3°50·9′W	X	124
Cae-poeth	Gwyn	SH8827	52°50·0′	3°39·4′W	X	124,125
Caeprior	Shrops	SO2695	52°33·1′	3°5·1′W	X	137
Cae Pwtto	Monm	ST4699	51°41·5′	2°46·5′W	F	171
Caer Allt-gôch	Cered	SN6388	52°28·6′	4°0·6′W	A	135
Caer-arglwyddes	Cered	SN6991	52°30·3′	3°55·4′W	X	135
Caer Argoed	Cered	SN6170	52°18·9′	4°2·0′W	A	135
Caer Arianrhod	Gwyn	SH4254	53°3·8′	4°21·1′W	X	115,123
Caerau	Brig	SS8594	51°38·2′	3°39·3′W	T	170
Caerau	Card	ST1375	51°28·3′	3°14·8′W	T	171
Caerau	Cered	SN3649	52°7·1′	4°23·3′W	A	145
Caerau	Cered	SN4744	52°4·6′	4°13·6′W	X	146
Caerau	Gwyn	SH2636	52°53·8′	4°34·8′W	X	123
Caerau	Gwyn	SH2935	52°53·4′	4°32·1′W	X	123
Caerau	Gwyn	SH4748	53°0·7′	4°16·4′W	X	115,123
Caerau	I of Angl	SH3291	53°23·6′	4°31·2′W	X	114
Caerau	Powys	SN8840	52°3·1′	3°37·6′W	X	147,160
Caerau	Powys	SN9250	52°8·5′	3°34·3′W	X	147
Caerau	Powys	SO0084	52°26·9′	3°27·9′W	X	136
Caerau	Rho Cyn Taf	ST0683	51°32·5′	3°20·9′W	A	170
Caerau Gaer	Pemb	SN1316	51°48·9′	4°42·4′W	A	158
Caerau Isaf	Gwyn	SH9739	52°56·6′	3°31·6′W	X	125
Caerau Park	Newp	ST2987	51°34·9′	3°1·1′W	T	171
Caer bach	Conwy	SH7472	53°14·1′	3°52·9′W	X	115
Caer bach (Fort)	Conwy	SH7472	53°14·1′	3°52·9′W	A	115
Caer Beris	Powys	SO0250	52°8·6′	3°25·5′W	A	147
Caerberllan	Gwyn	SH6607	52°38·9′	3°58·4′W	X	124
Caerbigyn Fm	Carm	SN4806	51°44·2′	4°11·7′W	FM	159
Cae'r-blaidd	Carm	SN5133	51°58·8′	4°9·8′W	X	146
Cae'r-bont	Powys	SN8011	51°47·3′	3°44·0′W	T	160
Caer Brân	Corn	SW4029	50°6·5′	5°37·8′W	A	203
Caerbre	Shrops	SO2796	52°33·7′	3°4·2′W	A	137
Cae'r-Brenin	I of Angl	SH4669	53°12·0′	4°17·9′W	X	114,115
Cae'r-bryn	Carm	SN5913	51°48·1′	4°2·3′W	T	159
Caer Bwdy Bay	Pemb	SM7624	51°52·4′	5°14·9′W	W	157
Caerbwla	Powys	SJ0008	52°39·9′	3°28·3′W	X	125
Caercappin	Powys	SO0996	52°33·5′	3°20·1′W	X	136
Caer Caradoc	Shrops	SO3075	52°22·4′	3°1·3′W	A	137,148
Caer Caradoc	Shrops	SO4795	52°33·3′	2°46·5′W	A	137,138
Caer Caradoc Hill	Shrops	SO4795	52°33·3′	2°46·5′W	H	137,138
Caer Caradog	Conwy	SH9647	53°0·9′	3°32·6′W	A	116
Caer Carreg-y-fran	Gwyn	SH5462	53°8·4′	4°10·6′W	A	114,115
Cae'r-ceiliog	Conwy	SH8162	53°8·8′	3°46·4′W	X	116
Caer-Cynog	Gwyn	SH6227	52°49·6′	4°2·5′W	X	124
Caer Dane	Corn	SW7752	50°19·8′	5°7·6′W	A	200,204
Caer Ddunod	Conwy	SH9851	53°3·0′	3°30·9′W	A	116
Cae'r Defaid	Gwyn	SH7923	52°47·7′	3°47·3′W	X	124
Caerdegog Isaf	I of Angl	SH3492	53°24·2′	4°29·4′W	X	114
Caerdegog Uchaf	I of Angl	SH3491	53°23·6′	4°29·4′W	X	114
Caerdeon	Gwyn	SH6518	52°44·8′	3°59·6′W	T	124
Caer Din	Shrops	SO2789	52°29·9′	3°4·1′W	A	137
Caer-din Ring	Shrops	SO2385	52°27·7′	3°7·6′W	A	137
Caer Drewyn	Denb	SJ0844	52°59·4′	3°21·8′W	A	125
Caer Du	Powys	SO0559	52°13·5′	3°23·1′W	A	147
Caerdydd or Cardiff	Card	ST1876	51°28·9′	3°10·5′W	T	171
Cae'r-dynyn	Gwyn	SH8224	52°48·3′	3°44·6′W	X	124,125
Caer Eini	Gwyn	SH9941	52°57·7′	3°29·8′W	A	125
Caer Einon	Powys	SO0653	52°10·3′	3°22·1′W	A	147
Caeremi	Brig	SS8489	51°35·5′	3°40·1′W	X	170
Caeremlyn	Carm	SN1720	51°51·2′	4°39·0′W	X	145,158
Caer Engan	Gwyn	SH4752	53°2·8′	4°16·5′W	A	115,123
Caer Estyn	Flint	SJ3157	53°6·6′	3°1·4′W	A	117
Caer-Estyn	Wrex	SJ3257	53°6·6′	3°0·5′W	T	117
Caer Faban	Conwy	SH8164	53°9·8′	3°46·4′W	X	116
Caerfai	Pemb	SM7524	51°52·4′	5°15·7′W	X	157
Caerfai Bay	Pemb	SM7524	51°52·4′	5°15·7′W	W	157
Caerfallen	Denb	SJ1259	53°7·5′	3°18·5′W	A	116
Caerfanell	Powys	SO0618	51°51·4′	3°21·5′W	W	160
Caer-Farchell	Pemb	SM7926	51°53·6′	5°12·3′W	T	157
Caer Fawr	Powys	SO0553	52°10·3′	3°23·0′W	A	147
Cae'r-fedwen	Denb	SJ1067	53°11·8′	3°20·4′W	X	116
Cae'r-ferch	Gwyn	SH4243	52°57·9′	4°20·8′W	X	123
Caerffili or Caerphilly	Caer	ST1586	51°34·2′	3°13·2′W	T	171
Caerffynnon	Gwyn	SH6024	52°48·0′	4°4·2′W	X	124
Cae'r-ffynnon	Gwyn	SH6135	52°53·9′	4°3·6′W	X	124
Caerforiog	Pemb	SM8126	51°53·6′	5°10·6′W	X	157
Caerfyrddin-fâch	Cered	SN5161	52°13·9′	4°10·5′W	X	146
Caer Gai	Gwyn	SH8731	52°52·1′	3°40·3′W	X	124,125
Caer Gai (Roman Fort)	Gwyn	SH8731	52°52·1′	3°40·3′W	A	124,125
Cae'r-geifr	Gwyn	SH1628	52°49·3′	4°43·4′W	X	123
Caergeiliog	I of Angl	SH3078	53°16·6′	4°32·6′W	T	114
Cae'r-gerreg	Gwyn	SH9043	52°58·6′	3°37·9′W	X	125
Caer-glaw	I of Angl	SH3776	53°15·6′	4°26·2′W	X	114
Caergribin	Gwyn	SH3643	52°57·8′	4°26·1′W	X	123
Cae'r-groes	Conwy	SH8061	53°8·2′	3°47·2′W	X	116
Cae'r groes	Conwy	SH9668	53°12·2′	3°33·0′W	X	116
Cae'r-groes	Denb	SJ1358	53°7·0′	3°17·6′W	X	116
Caergwanaf-isaf	Rho Cyn Taf	ST0480	51°30·9′	3°22·6′W	X	170
Cae'r-gweision	Powys	SH9813	52°42·5′	3°30·2′W	X	125
Caergwrle	Flint	SJ3057	53°6·6′	3°2·3′W	T	117
Caergwrli	I of Angl	SH3784	53°19·9′	4°26·5′W	X	114
Cae'r-hedd	Denb	SJ0656	53°5·8′	3°23·8′W	X	116
Caerhafod	Pemb	SM8231	51°56·3′	5°9·9′W	X	157
Caerhays Castle	Corn	SW9741	50°14·3′	4°50·4′W	X	204
Caerhedyn	Cered	SN7097	52°33·6′	3°54·7′W	X	135
Cae Rheinallt	Flint	SJ2555	53°5·5′	3°6·8′W	X	117
Cae'r-Helygen	Gwyn	SH4859	53°6·6′	4°15·8′W	X	115,123
Caerhendy	Nth Pt Talb	SS7791	51°36·5′	3°46·2′W	T	170
Cae-rhos	Gwyn	SH4760	53°7·2′	4°16·8′W	X	114,115
Caerhoslligwy	I of Angl	SH4884	53°20·1′	4°16·6′W	X	114,115
Caerhowel Hall	Powys	SO2098	52°34·7′	3°10·4′W	X	137
Caerhowell	Rho Cyn Taf	SN9409	51°46·4′	3°31·8′W	X	160
Caerhûn	Conwy	SH7770	53°13·0′	3°50·1′W	X	115
Caerhun	Gwyn	SH5769	53°12·2′	4°8·1′W	T	114,115
Caerhyn	Carm	SN7127	51°55·8′	3°52·2′W	X	146,160
Cae Rhys	Gwyn	SH6834	52°53·5′	3°57·3′W	X	124
Caerhys	Pemb	SM7930	51°55·7′	5°12·5′W	X	157
Cae-Rhys-ddu	V of Glam	SS9878	51°29·7′	3°27·8′W	X	170
Cae Rhys Fm	Denb	SJ1075	53°16·1′	3°20·6′W	FM	116
Caer Idris	I of Angl	SH4967	53°11·0′	4°15·2′W	A	114,115
Caerketton Hill	Midlo	NT2366	55°53·1′	3°13·4′W	H	66
Caer Kief	Corn	SW7852	50°19·8′	5°6·8′W	A	200,204
Cae'r-Lan	Powys	SN8012	51°47·9′	3°44·0′W	T	160
Cae'r-lan	Rho Cyn Taf	SS9988	51°35·1′	3°27·1′W	X	170
Caerlan Tibot	Gwyn	SH5064	53°9·4′	4°14·2′W	A	114,115
Caerlaverock	Pth & Kin	NN8916	56°19·7′	3°47·3′W	X	58
Caerlaverock Castle	D & G	NY0265	54°58·5′	3°31·4′W	A	84
Caerlaverock Nature Reserve	D & G	NY0365	54°58·5′	3°30·5′W	X	84
Caer Leb	I of Angl	SH4767	53°10·9′	4°17·0′W	A	114,115
Caerlem	Pemb	SM9039	52°0·8′	5°3·2′W	X	157
Cae'r-leon	Gwyn	SH8839	52°56·4′	3°39·6′W	X	124,125
Caerleon or Caerllion	Newp	ST3390	51°36·5′	2°57·7′W	T	171
Caer Licyn	Newp	ST3892	51°37·6′	2°53·4′W	X	171
Caer Licyn (Motte & Bailey)	Newp	ST3892	51°37·6′	2°53·4′W	A	171
Caer Llan	Monm	SO4908	51°46·3′	2°44·0′W	X	162
Caerlleon	Carm	SN2522	51°52·4′	4°32·1′W	X	145,158
Caer Lletty-llwyd	Cered	SN6588	52°28·6′	3°58·9′W	A	135
Caerllion or Caerleon	Newp	ST3390	51°36·5′	2°57·7′W	T	171
Cae'r-llo	Conwy	SH8666	53°11·0′	3°42·0′W	X	116
Cae'r-lloi	Conwy	SJ0146	53°0·4′	3°28·1′W	X	116
Caerllugest	Cered	SN6161	52°14·0′	4°1·7′W	X	146
Caer Llugwy	Conwy	SH7457	53°6·0′	3°52·5′W	X	115
Caer Llugwy (Roman Fort)	Conwy	SH7457	53°6·0′	3°52·5′W	R	115
Caerloch Dhu	S Ayr	NX3992	55°12·0′	4°31·4′W	X	77
Caerloda	Gwyn	SH4354	53°3·9′	4°20·2′W	X	115,123
Caermaenau Fawr	Pemb	SN1217	51°49·4′	4°43·3′W	X	158
Caermalwas	Carm	SN5640	52°2·6′	4°5·6′W	X	146
Caermead	V of Glam	SS9569	51°24·9′	3°30·2′W	T	170
Caermeini	Pemb	SN1431	51°57·0′	4°42·0′W	T	145
Caermeirch	Cered	SN7573	52°20·7′	3°49·7′W	X	135,147
Caer-moel	Caer	ST1091	51°36·9′	3°17·6′W	X	171
Caer Mote	Cumbr	NY1937	54°43·5′	3°15·0′W	X	89,90
Cae'rmynach	Gwyn	SH6007	52°38·8′	4°3·8′W	X	124
Cae'r-mynach	Powys	SN9847	52°7·0′	3°29·0′W	X	147
Cae'r Mynyd	Nth Pt Talb	SS8292	51°37·1′	3°41·9′W	X	170
Caernarfon	Gwyn	SH4862	53°8·3′	4°15·9′W	T	114,115
Caernarfon Bay		SH3254	53°3·7′	4°30·0′W	W	123
Caernarfon Bay	I of Angl	SH3064	53°9·0′	4°32·1′W	W	114
Cae'rneuadd	Powys	SN9674	52°21·5′	3°31·2′W	X	136,147
Cae'rneuadd Hill	Powys	SO2147	52°7·2′	3°8·8′W	H	148
Caer Noddfa	Powys	SN9696	52°33·4′	3°31·6′W	A	136
Cae-Robin	Monm	SO4121	51°53·3′	2°51·0′W	X	161
Caeronwy	Gwyn	SH5154	53°4·0′	4°13·0′W	X	115
Cae Rosser	Brig	SS9587	51°34·6′	3°30·5′W	X	170
Caer Penrhos	Cered	SN5569	52°18·2′	4°7·2′W	A	135
Caerphilly Common	Caer	ST1585	51°33·7′	3°13·2′W	H	171
Caerphilly or Caerffil	Caer	ST1586	51°34·2′	3°13·2′W	T	171
Caer Pwll-glâs	Cered	SN6386	52°27·5′	4°0·6′W	A	135
Cae'r-Sais	Gwyn	SH5057	53°5·6′	4°14·0′W	X	115
Cae'r Sais	I of Angl	SH2677	53°15·9′	4°36·1′W	X	114
Caersegan	Pemb	SM9036	51°59·2′	5°3·1′W	X	157
Caersiac	Powys	SO1297	52°34·1′	3°17·5′W	A	136
Caerswall Fm	Heref	SO6433	51°59·9′	2°31·1′W	FM	149
Caersws	Powys	SO0392	52°31·3′	3°25·4′W	T	136
Cae'r-tyddyn	Gwyn	SH7817	52°44·5′	3°48·0′W	X	124
Caer-uchedydd	Carm	SN2527	51°55·1′	4°32·3′W	X	145,158
Caer Vallack	Corn	SW7224	50°4·6′	5°10·8′W	A	204
Caervallack	Corn	SW7224	50°4·6′	5°10·8′W	X	204
Caervega	Pemb	SM8125	51°53·1′	5°10·5′W	X	157
Caerwedros	Cered	SN3755	52°10·4′	4°22·6′W	T	145
Caerwen	Card	ST1083	51°32·6′	3°17·5′W	X	171
Caerwen	Pemb	SM8226	51°53·6′	5°9·7′W	X	157
Caerwenlli	Cered	SN3953	52°9·4′	4°20·8′W	X	145
Caerwent	Monm	ST4690	51°36·6′	2°46·4′W	T	171,172
Caerwent Brook	Monm	ST4789	51°36·1′	2°45·5′W	T	171,172
Caerwents	Glos	SO7324	51°55·1′	2°23·2′W	X	162
Caerwigau	V of Glam	ST0675	51°28·2′	3°20·8′W	X	170
Caerwnon Ho	Powys	SO0154	52°10·8′	3°26·5′W	X	147
Cae'r-wrach	Gwyn	SH4044	52°58·4′	4°22·6′W	X	123
Caerwych	Gwyn	SH6336	52°54·5′	4°1·8′W	X	124
Caerwys	Flint	SJ1272	53°14·5′	3°18·7′W	T	116
Caerwys Hall	Flint	SJ1374	53°15·6′	3°17·8′W	X	116
Caer y Cwr	I of Angl	SH2182	53°18·5′	4°40·8′W	A	114
Caerynwch	Gwyn	SH7617	52°44·4′	3°49·8′W	X	124
Caesamson	Powys	SN9993	52°31·8′	3°28·9′W	X	136
Caesaromagvs (Chelmsford)	Essex	TL7006	51°43·8′	0°28·1′E	R	167
Caesar's Belt	Hants	SU4853	51°16·7′	1°18·3′W	F	185
Caesar's Camp	Brackn	SU8665	51°22·9′	0°45·5′W	A	175
Caesar's Camp	Brom	TQ4263	51°21·1′	0°2·7′E	A	177,187
Caesar's Camp	Dorset	ST9315	50°56·3′	2°5·6′W	A	184
Caesar's Camp	Merton	TQ2271	51°25·7′	0°14·3′W	A	176
Caesar's Camp (Fort)	Dorset	ST9315	50°56·3′	2°5·6′W	A	184
Caesar's Camp (Fort)	Merton	TQ2271	51°25·7′	0°14·3′W	A	176
Caesiencyn	Powys	SJ1124	52°48·6′	3°18·8′W	X	125
Caestwbwrn	Powys	SJ0006	52°38·8′	3°28·3′W	X	125
Caethle	Gwyn	SN6099	52°34·5′	4°3·6′W	X	135
Caethle	I of Angl	SH3268	53°11·2′	4°30·5′W	W	114
Caethro	Powys	SJ2209	52°40·6′	3°8·8′W	X	126
Caety Traylow	Powys	SO1956	52°12·0′	3°10·7′W	H	148
Cae Uchaf	Gwyn	SH4854	53°3·9′	4°15·7′W	X	115,123
Cae Weirglodd	Denb	SJ0555	53°5·2′	3°24·7′W	X	116
Cafan Fm	Cered	SN3142	52°3·3′	4°27·5′W	FM	145
Caffell Side	Cumbr	NY2617	54°32·8′	3°8·2′W	X	89,90
Caffyns Fm	Devon	SS6948	51°13·2′	3°52·2′W	FM	180
Caffyns Heanton Down	Devon	SS6947	51°12·7′	3°52·1′W	H	180
Cafnan	I of Angl	SH3493	53°24·7′	4°29·4′W	X	114
Cafnau	Pemb	SM9940	52°1·6′	4°55·4′W	X	145,157
Cafnau	Pemb	SN0040	52°1·6′	4°54·5′W	X	145,157
Cafn Enlli	Gwyn	SH1120	52°44·9′	4°47·6′W	W	123
Cafuam	N Eil	NF9174	57°39·3′	7°10·4′W	X	18
Cagar Feosaig	Highld	NC8404	58°0·9′	3°57·3′W	H	17
Cag Burn	Northum	NZ1075	55°4·4′	1°50·2′W	W	88
Cage Brook	Heref	SO4337	52°1·9′	2°49·5′W	W	149,161
Cage Fm	Cumbr	SD7186	54°16·4′	2°26·3′W	FM	98
Cage Green	Kent	TQ5947	51°12·2′	0°17·0′E	T	188
Cage Grove	Suff	TL8869	52°17·4′	0°45·8′E	F	155
Cage Hill	Ches	SJ9683	53°20·9′	2°3·2′W	X	109
Cage Hill	Staffs	SK0028	52°51·2′	1°59·6′W	X	128
Cages, The	Northum	NU0841	55°40·0′	1°51·9′W	X	75
Caggan	Highld	NH8216	57°13·4′	3°56·8′W	X	35
Caggle Street	Monm	SO3617	51°51·1′	2°55·4′W	T	161
Caggypole Fm	Dorset	ST7523	51°0·6′	2°21·0′W	FM	183
Caia Fm	Shrops	SJ3337	52°55·8′	2°59·4′W	FM	126
Caia Fm	Wrex	SJ3454	53°5·0′	2°58·7′W	FM	117
Caia, The	V of Glam	ST0974	51°27·7′	3°18·2′W	X	171
Caidge Fm	Essex	TQ9499	51°39·6′	0°48·7′E	FM	168
Caiesmill	C of Aber	NJ8314	57°13·2′	2°16·4′W	X	38
Caigeann Doire nan Cuilean	Arg & Bt	NM5729	56°23·7′	5°55·8′W	X	48
Caigher Point	I of M	SC1564	54°2·6′	4°49·1′W	X	95
Caigionn	N Eil	NF8357	57°29·8′	7°17·1′W	X	22
Caigton Hill	D & G	NX7959	54°54·9′	3°52·8′W	H	84
Cailiness Point	D & G	NX1535	54°40·8′	4°51·8′W	X	82
Cailleach a' Bheathrach	Arg & Bt	NS0090	56°3·9′	5°12·3′W	X	55
Cailleach Head	Highld	NG9898	57°55·8′	5°24·2′W	X	19
Cailleach Uragaig	Arg & Bt	NR3898	56°6·4′	6°12·4′W	X	61
Cailleveanach	Arg & Bt	NR0248	56°35·2′	5°13·0′W	X	50
Càil Mhór	Highld	NH3484	57°49·2′	4°47·2′W	X	20
Cailness	Stir	NN3406	56°13·3′	4°40·2′W	X	56
Cailness Burn	Stir	NN3505	56°12·8′	4°39·2′W	W	56
Cailternis	N Eil	NF8658	57°30·5′	7°14·1′W	X	22
Caim	I of Angl	SH6280	53°18·2′	4°3·9′W	T	114,115
Caimhlin Mor	Highld	NH6814	57°12·1′	4°10·6′W	H	35
Cain an Fhuarain Mhóir	Highld	NJ0637	57°25·1′	3°33·4′W	H	27
Cain Br	Warw	SP0760	52°14·5′	1°53·5′W	X	150
Cain Hill	Beds	TL0935	52°0·4′	0°24·3′W	X	153
Cainhoe Manor Fm	Beds	TL1036	52°0·9′	0°23·4′W	FM	153
Cainscross	Glos	SO8305	51°44·8′	2°14·4′W	T	162
Cain's Folly	Dorset	SY3792	50°43·7′	2°53·2′W	X	193
Cain's Hill	Suff	TL7244	52°4·3′	0°31·0′E	X	154
Caio	Carm	SN6739	52°2·2′	3°56·0′W	T	146
Caiplach	Highld	NG4731	57°18·2′	6°11·6′W	X	32
Caiplich	Highld	NH5437	57°24·3′	4°25·3′W	X	26
Caiplie	Fife	NO5805	56°14·4′	2°40·2′W	X	59
Cair	Corn	SX3155	50°22·5′	4°22·2′W	X	201
Cairdhillock	C of Aber	NJ8406	57°8·9′	2°15·4′W	X	38
Caird Park	C of Dun	NO4032	56°28·8′	2°58·0′W	X	54
Cairdseat	Aberd	NJ8727	57°20·3′	2°12·5′W	X	38
Cairds Hill	Moray	NJ4247	57°30·8′	2°57·6′W	H	28
Cairds Wood	Moray	NJ4247	57°30·8′	2°57·6′W	F	28
Càiream	N Eil	NG1690	57°48·8′	6°46·5′W	X	14
Cairidh Ghlumaig	Highld	NG4073	57°40·6′	6°21·2′W	X	23
Cairidh Mhór	Arg & Bt	NR5580	55°57·3′	5°55·1′W	X	61
Cairidh nan Òb	Highld	NG3570	57°38·8′	6°26·0′W	X	23
Cairinis	N Eil	NF8160	57°31·3′	7°19·3′W	T	22
Cairn	E Ayr	NS5618	55°26·3′	4°16·1′W	X	71
Cairn	Pth & Kin	NN8814	56°18·6′	3°48·2′W	X	58
Cairnacay	Moray	NJ2032	57°22·5′	3°19·4′W	H	36
Cairnadailly	Aberd	NJ9436	57°25·1′	2°5·5′W	X	30
Cairnadloch	S Ayr	NX3994	55°13·1′	4°31·4′W	X	77
Cairnagour Hill	Aberd	NJ3205	57°8·1′	3°7·0′W	H	37
Cairnandrew	Aberd	NJ7460	57°38·0′	2°25·7′W	X	29
Cairn Ardachy	Highld	NH5825	57°17·9′	4°20·9′W	H	26,35
Cairnargat	Aberd	NJ4539	57°26·5′	2°54·5′W	X	28,29
Cairn Avel	D & G	NX5592	55°12·3′	4°16·3′W	A	77
Cairnbaan	Arg & Bt	NR8390	56°3·5′	5°28·7′W	T	55
Cairnbaber	D & G	NX4876	55°3·6′	4°22·4′W	X	77
Cairn Baddoch	Angus	NO2770	56°49·2′	3°11·3′W	X	44
Cairn Ballantruan	Moray	NJ1524	57°18·2′	3°24·2′W	H	36
Cairnballoch	Aberd	NJ5613	57°12·6′	2°43·2′W	X	37
Cairnbank	Aberd	NO8189	56°59·8′	2°18·3′W	X	45
Cairnbank	Scot Bord	NT7953	55°46·4′	2°19·6′W	X	67,74
Cairn Bannoch	Angus	NO2282	56°55·6′	3°16·4′W	H	44
Cairnbanno Ho	Aberd	NJ8444	57°29·4′	2°15·6′W	X	29,30
Cairnbeathie	Aberd	NJ5703	57°7·2′	2°42·2′W	X	37
Cairn Beck	Cumbr	NY5153	54°52·4′	2°45·4′W	W	86
Cairnbeddie	Pth & Kin	NO1431	56°28·1′	3°23·3′W	X	53
Cairn Bleamnach	Pth & Kin	NO1555	56°41·0′	3°22·8′W	A	53
Cairnbo	Aberd	NJ7661	57°38·6′	2°23·7′W	X	29
Cairnbog	N Lanak	NS6878	55°58·9′	4°6·5′W	X	64
Cairnborrow Lodge	Aberd	NJ4541	57°27·6′	2°54·5′W	X	28,29
Cairnbo Stewart	Pth & Kin	NO0404	56°13·4′	3°32·5′W	X	58
Cairnbowie	D & G	NW9969	54°58·8′	5°8·0′W	X	82
Cairnbowie Hill	D & G	NW9870	54°59·3′	5°9·0′W	H	76,82
Cairnbrallan	Moray	NJ3224	57°18·4′	3°7·3′W	X	37
Cairnbrallan	Moray	NJ3324	57°18·4′	3°6·3′W	H	37
Cairnbridge	Cumbr	NY5054	54°52·9′	2°46·3′W	X	86
Cairn Broadlands	Angus	NO2777	56°53·0′	3°11·4′W	X	44
Cairnbrogie	Aberd	NJ8527	57°20·3′	2°14·5′W	X	38
Cairnbulg	Aberd	NK0365	57°40·7′	1°56·5′W	T	30
Cairnbulg Castle	Aberd	NK0163	57°39·7′	1°58·5′W	A	30
Cairnbulg Mains	Aberd	NK0263	57°39·7′	1°57·5′W	X	30
Cairnbulg Point	Aberd	NK0366	57°41·3′	1°56·5′W	X	30
Cairn Burn	D & G	NS7902	55°18·1′	3°53·9′W	W	78
Cairn Burn	Scot Bord	NT1752	55°45·5′	3°18·9′W	W	65,66,72
Cairn Buy	D & G	NX2650	54°49·1′	4°42·1′W	A	82
Cairn Caidloch	Angus	NO4378	56°53·6′	2°55·7′W	H	44
Cairncatto	Aberd	NK0742	57°28·3′	1°52·5′W	X	30
Cairn Cattoch	Moray	NJ2346	57°30·1′	3°16·6′W	X	28
Cairn Catto Long Cairn	Aberd	NK0742	57°28·3′	1°52·5′W	A	30
Cairnchina	Aberd	NK0055	57°35·4′	1°59·5′W	X	30
Cairn Cleugh	Northum	NT7300	55°17·9′	2°25·1′W	X	80
Cairnconon Hill	Angus	NO5645	56°35·9′	2°42·5′W	H	54

Cairn Corse	Angus	NO2864	56°46·0′	3°10·2′W	H	44
Cairncortie	Angus	NO5440	56°33·2′	2°44·5′W	X	54
Cairncosh	Aberd	NJ5719	57°15·8′	2°42·3′W	X	37
Cairncoullie	E Ayr	NS4813	55°23·5′	4°23·6′W	X	70
Cairncross	Angus	NO4979	56°54·2′	2°49·8′W	T	44
Cairncross	Scot Bord	NT8963	55°51·9′	2°10·1′W	X	67
Cairn Culchavie	Aberd	NJ2007	57°9·1′	3°18·9′W	H	36
Cairncurran	Inverc	NS3169	55°53·3′	4°41·7′W	X	63
Cairncurran Hill	Inverc	NS2970	55°53·8′	4°43·7′W	H	63
Cairndaie	Aberd	NJ6909	57°10·5′	2°30·3′W	X	38
Cairndale	Aberd	NJ9348	57°31·6′	2°6·6′W	X	30
Cairn Damff	Angus	NO2477	56°52·9′	3°14·4′W	H	44
Cairn Daunie	Angus	NO2468	56°48·1′	3°14·2′W	X	44
Cairn Derg	Angus	NO3076	56°52·5′	3°8·5′W	X	44
Cairn Derig	Pth & Kin	NO1566	56°46·9′	3°23·0′W	X	43
Cairnderry	D & G	NX3279	55°4·9′	4°37·5′W	X	76
Cairndhu Point	Arg & Bt	NS2782	56°0·2′	4°46·0′W	X	56
Cairndinnis	E Loth	NT5774	55°57·7′	2°40·9′W	X	67
Cairndoon	D & G	NX3838	54°42·9′	4°30·5′W	X	83
Cairndoon Bank	D & G	NX3939	54°43·5′	4°29·6′W	X	83
Cairndoor Hill	Aberd	NJ3002	57°6·5′	3°8·9′W	H	37
Cairndow	Arg & Bt	NN1810	56°15·1′	4°55·8′W	T	50,56
Cairn Dregnie	Moray	NJ2526	57°19·4′	3°14·3′W	H	37
Cairndrum	Angus	NO5866	56°47·3′	2°40·8′W	X	44
Cairn Duhie	Highld	NH9842	57°27·7′	3°41·6′W	H	27
Cairn Dulnan	Highld	NH7510	57°10·1′	4°3·6′W	H	35
Cairn Dye	Angus	NO2472	56°50·3′	3°14·3′W	X	44
Cairn Edward	D & G	NX6273	55°2·2′	4°9·1′W	A	77
Cairn Edward	D & G	NX6375	55°3·3′	4°8·3′W	X	77
Cairn Edward Hill	D & G	NX6273	55°2·2′	4°9·1′W	H	77
Cairn Edward Well	D & G	NX6373	55°2·2′	4°8·2′W	W	77
Cairn Ellick	Moray	NJ1823	57°17·7′	3°21·2′W	H	36
Cairnend	Moray	NJ3158	57°36·7′	3°8·8′W	X	28
Cairn End	Northum	NY7160	54°56·3′	2°26·7′W	X	86,87
Cairn Eney	Moray	NJ0244	57°28·8′	3°37·6′W	X	27
Cairnerzean	D & G	NX1467	54°58·0′	4°53·9′W	X	82
Cairnerzean Fell	D & G	NX1366	54°57·5′	4°54·8′W	H	82
Cairness	Aberd	NK0360	57°38·1′	1°56·5′W	X	30
Cairneve	Aberd	NJ9237	57°25·7′	2°7·5′W	X	30
Cairn Ewen	Highld	NH5802	57°5·5′	4°20·2′W	H	35
Cairneyhall	Fife	NO2715	56°19·6′	3°10·4′W	X	59
Cairneyhead	N Lanak	NS8960	55°49·5′	3°45·9′W	X	65
Cairney Hill	D & G	NX7159	54°54·8′	4°0·3′W	X	83,84
Cairneyhill	Fife	NT0486	56°3·7′	3°32·1′W	T	65
Cairneyhillock	Moray	NJ2658	57°36·6′	3°13·8′W	X	28
Cairney Knowe	D & G	NX7697	55°15·3′	3°56·6′W	X	78
Cairney Lodge	Fife	NO3716	56°20·2′	3°0·7′W	X	59
Cairneymount	Scot Bord	NT5439	55°38·8′	2°43·4′W	X	73
Cairneywhin	Aberd	NO7199	57°5·1′	2°28·3′W	X	38,45
Cairnfauld	Aberd	NO7593	57°1·9′	2°24·3′W	X	38,45
Cairnfechel	Aberd	NJ8626	57°19·7′	2°13·5′W	X	38
Cairn Fell	D & G	NX1036	54°41·2′	4°56·4′W	H	82
Cairn Fichlie	Aberd	NJ4514	57°13·1′	2°54·2′W	A	37
Cairnfield	Aberd	NJ8318	57°15·4′	2°16·5′W	X	38
Cairnfield	D & G	NX3948	54°48·3′	4°29·9′W	X	83
Cairnfield	Fife	NO3010	56°16·9′	3°7·4′W	X	59
Cairnfield	Highld	ND1464	58°33·6′	3°28·2′W	X	11,12
Cairnfield Ho	Moray	NJ4162	57°38·9′	2°58·8′W	X	28
Cairn Fm	Angus	NO4456	56°41·8′	2°54·4′W	FM	54
Cairn Fm	D & G	NX9187	55°10·2′	3°42·2′W	FM	78
Cairnfold	Aberd	NJ7011	57°11·6′	2°29·3′W	X	38
Cairnfold	Pth & Kin	NT0095	56°8·5′	3°36·1′W	X	58
Cairnford	Aberd	NJ4940	57°27·1′	2°50·5′W	X	28,29
Cairnford	E Ayr	NS4819	55°26·7′	4°23·8′W	X	70
Cairnfore	S Ayr	NX3587	55°9·2′	4°34·9′W	A	77
Cairnfore Burn	S Ayr	NX3487	55°9·2′	4°35·9′W	W	76
Cairnfore Hill	S Ayr	NX3587	55°9·2′	4°34·9′W	X	77
Cairnfore Loch	S Ayr	NX3486	55°8·7′	4°35·9′W	W	76
Cairngaan	D & G	NX1232	54°39·1′	4°54·4′W	X	82
Cairngall	Aberd	NK0447	57°31·0′	1°55·5′W	X	30
Cairn Galtar	N Eil	NL6491	56°53·6′	7°30·7′W	H	31
Cairngarroch	D & G	NX0549	54°48·1′	5°1·6′W	X	82
Cairngarroch	D & G	NX1335	54°40·8′	4°53·6′W	X	82
Cairngarroch	D & G	NX4977	55°4·1′	4°21·5′W	H	77
Cairngarroch Bay	D & G	NX0449	54°48·1′	5°2·5′W	W	82
Cairn Geddes	Pth & Kin	NO1113	56°18·3′	3°25·9′W	A	58
Cairn Geldie	Aberd	NN9988	56°58·6′	3°39·2′W	H	43
Cairn Gibbs	Angus	NO1859	56°43·2′	3°19·9′W	H	53
Cairnglass	Aberd	NK0462	57°39·1′	1°55·5′W	X	30
Cairnglass	Highld	NH8151	57°32·3′	3°58·8′W	X	27
Cairnglass	Highld	NH9646	57°29·8′	3°43·7′W	X	27
Cairn Glass	Moray	NJ1748	57°31·1′	3°22·7′W	X	28
Cairnglastenhope	Northum	NY7580	55°7·1′	2°23·1′W	H	80
Cairnglastenhope	Northum	NY7580	55°7·1′	2°23·1′W	X	80
Cairn Gleamnach	Pth & Kin	NO1555	56°41·0′	3°22·8′W	A	53
Cairn Gorm	Highld	NJ0004	57°7·2′	3°38·6′W	H	36
Cairngorm Club Footbridge	Highld	NH9207	57°8·7′	3°46·6′W	X	36
Cairngorm Mountains	Moray	NH9901	57°5·6′	3°39·6′W	X	36
Cairngorm National Nature Reserve	Aberd	NN9496	57°2·8′	3°44·4′W	X	36,43
Cairngreen Wood	Fife	NO4013	56°18·6′	2°57·7′W	F	59
Cairn Greg	C of Dun	NO4633	56°29·4′	2°52·2′W	A	54
Cairngryffe Hill	S Lanak	NS9441	55°39·3′	3°40·6′W	H	71,72
Cairn Guish	Moray	NJ2237	57°25·3′	3°17·5′W	X	28
Cairnhall	Aberd	NJ7817	57°14·8′	2°21·4′W	X	38
Cairnhall	Angus	NO2753	56°40·0′	3°11·0′W	X	53
Cairnhall	D & G	NX9085	55°9·1′	3°43·1′W	X	78
Cairnhall	Stir	NS5589	56°4·6′	4°19·3′W	X	57
Cairnhandy	D & G	NX0945	54°46·1′	4°57·7′W	X	82
Cairnharrow	D & G	NX5356	54°52·9′	4°17·1′W	H	83
Cairnhead	Aberd	NJ4620	57°16·3′	2°53·3′W	X	37
Cairn Head	D & G	NX4838	54°43·1′	4°21·2′W	X	83
Cairnhead	D & G	NX4838	54°43·1′	4°21·2′W	X	83
Cairnhead	D & G	NX7097	55°15·3′	4°2·3′W	X	77
Cairn Head	Orkney	HY5051	59°20·8′	2°52·3′W	X	5
Cairnhead Fm	Cumbr	NY5548	54°49·7′	2°41·6′W	FM	86
Cairn Head, The	Orkney	ND4396	58°51·1′	2°58·8′W	X	6,7
Cairnhigh	Aberd	NJ8954	57°34·8′	2°10·6′W	X	30
Cairn Hill	Aberd	NJ4630	57°21·7′	2°53·4′W	H	29,37
Cairnhill	Aberd	NJ5438	57°26·1′	2°45·5′W	X	29
Cairnhill	Aberd	NJ5809	57°10·5′	2°41·2′W	X	37
Cairnhill	Aberd	NJ6459	57°37·4′	2°35·7′W	X	29
Cairnhill	Aberd	NJ6632	57°22·9′	2°33·5′W	T	29
Cairnhill	Aberd	NJ6751	57°33·1′	2°32·6′W	X	29
Cairn Hill	Aberd	NJ7536	57°25·1′	2°24·5′W	H	29
Cairnhill	Aberd	NJ7851	57°33·2′	2°21·6′W	X	29,30
Cairnhill	Aberd	NJ8119	57°15·9′	2°18·4′W	X	38
Cairnhill	Aberd	NJ8933	57°23·5′	2°10·5′W	X	30
Cairnhill	Aberd	NJ9427	57°20·3′	2°5·5′W	X	38
Cairnhill	Aberd	NJ9838	57°26·2′	2°1·5′W	X	30
Cairnhill	Aberd	NK0949	57°32·1′	1°50·5′W	X	30
Cairnhill	Aberd	NO7393	57°1·9′	2°26·2′W	X	38,45
Cairnhill	Aberd	NO8893	57°1·9′	2°11·4′W	X	38,45
Cairn Hill	Angus	NO2261	56°44·3′	3°16·1′W	H	44
Cairn Hill	D & G	NS7606	55°20·2′	3°56·9′W	H	71,78
Cairn Hill	D & G	NS8507	55°20·9′	3°48·4′W	H	71,78
Cairn Hill	D & G	NT0303	55°18·9′	3°31·3′W	X	78
Cairnhill	D & G	NX0450	54°48·6′	5°2·6′W	X	82
Cairn Hill	D & G	NX0769	54°58·9′	5°0·5′W	H	82
Cairn Hill	D & G	NX4747	54°47·9′	4°22·4′W	X	83
Cairn Hill	D & G	NX5949	54°49·2′	4°11·2′W	H	83
Cairn Hill	D & G	NX6898	55°15·8′	4°4·2′W	X	77
Cairn Hill	D & G	NX7949	54°49·5′	3°52·6′W	X	84
Cairn Hill	D & G	NY0396	55°15·2′	3°31·1′W	X	78
Cairnhill	E Ayr	NS5234	55°34·9′	4°20·4′W	H	70
Cairn Hill	E Ayr	NS6623	55°29·2′	4°6·8′W	X	71
Cairnhill	Fife	NO4610	56°17·0′	2°51·9′W	X	59
Cairn Hill	Highld	ND3576	58°40·3′	3°6·8′W	H	7,12
Cairnhill	Moray	NJ5051	57°33·0′	2°49·7′W	X	29
Cairnhill	Moray	NJ5348	57°31·4′	2°46·6′W	X	29
Cairnhill	N Lanak	NS7564	55°51·4′	3°59·4′W	T	64
Cairn Hill	Northum	NT9019	55°28·1′	2°9·1′W	H	80
Cairn Hill	Orkney	ND2691	58°48·3′	3°16·4′W	H	7
Cairn Hill	Orkney	ND4385	58°45·2′	2°58·6′W	X	7
Cairnhill	S Ayr	NS2300	55°16·0′	4°46·7′W	X	76
Cairn Hill	S Ayr	NS3201	55°16·7′	4°38·3′W	X	76
Cairnhill	S Ayr	NS3609	55°21·1′	4°34·8′W	X	70,77
Cairn Hill	S Ayr	NS4104	55°18·5′	4°29·9′W	X	77
Cairn Hill	S Ayr	NX1383	55°6·6′	4°55·5′W	H	76
Cairn Hill	S Ayr	NX1793	55°12·1′	4°52·1′W	H	76
Cairn Hill	S Ayr	NX3090	55°10·8′	4°39·8′W	H	76
Cairn Hill	Scot Bord	NT3638	55°38·1′	3°0·6′W	H	73
Cairnhill	Scot Bord	NT8052	55°45·9′	2°18·7′W	X	67,74
Cairn Hill	S Lanak	NS8520	55°27·9′	3°48·7′W	H	71,72
Cairn Hillock	Aberd	NO3688	56°59·0′	3°2·7′W	H	44
Cairn Ho	Northum	NZ1172	55°2·8′	1°49·2′W	X	88
Cairnholy	D & G	NX5154	54°51·8′	4°18·9′W	X	83
Cairnholy Hill	D & G	NX5155	54°52·3′	4°18·9′W	H	83
Cairnhouse	D & G	NX4158	54°53·7′	4°28·3′W	X	83
Cairnhouses	S Lanak	NS8435	55°35·9′	3°50·0′W	X	71,72
Cairnie	Aberd	NJ4844	57°29·3′	2°51·6′W	T	28,29
Cairnie	Aberd	NJ8517	57°14·9′	2°14·5′W	X	38
Cairnie	Angus	NO6342	56°34·4′	2°35·7′W	X	54
Cairnie	Pth & Kin	NO1920	56°22·2′	3°18·2′W	X	53,58
Cairnie Burn	Aberd	NO8295	57°3·0′	2°17·3′W	W	38,45
Cairnieburn	Aberd	NO8495	57°3·0′	2°15·4′W	X	38,45
Cairniedrouth	Arg & Bt	NS3579	55°58·8′	4°38·2′W	X	63
Cairnie Finnart	D & G	NX0841	54°43·9′	4°58·5′W	X	82
Cairniehill	D & G	NX6246	54°47·6′	4°8·4′W	H	83
Cairniehill	D & G	NX6346	54°47·7′	4°7·4′W	X	83
Cairnie Ho	Fife	NO4803	56°13·3′	2°49·9′W	X	59
Cairnie Mill	Pth & Kin	NO1920	56°22·2′	3°18·2′W	X	53,58
Cairnie Pier	Pth & Kin	NO1919	56°21·6′	3°18·2′W	X	58
Cairnies Fm	Pth & Kin	NN9628	56°26·2′	3°40·8′W	FM	52,53,58
Cairnies, The	Pth & Kin	NN9628	56°26·2′	3°40·8′W	X	52,53,58
Cairnies, The	Pth & Kin	NN9728	56°26·2′	3°39·8′W	X	52,53,58
Cairnie Wood	Pth & Kin	NO0219	56°21·4′	3°34·7′W	F	58
Cairn Inks	Angus	NO3072	56°50·3′	3°8·4′W	H	44
Cairn Kenny	D & G	NX1775	55°2·4′	4°51·4′W	X	76
Cairn Kenny (Chambered Cairn)	D & G	NX1775	55°2·4′	4°51·4′W	A	76
Cairn Kincraig	Highld	NH8236	57°24·2′	3°57·4′W	X	27
Cairnkinna Hill	D & G	NS7901	55°17·5′	3°53·9′W	H	78
Cairn Kinny	S Lanak	NS7821	55°28·3′	3°55·4′W	H	71
Cairn Knowe	D & G	NY1997	55°15·9′	3°16·1′W	H	79
Cairnknowe	D & G	NY2686	55°10·0′	3°9·4′W	X	79
Cairnknowe	S Lanak	NT0851	55°44·9′	3°27·5′W	X	65,72
Cairn Law	Scot Bord	NT1421	55°28·8′	3°21·2′W	H	72
Cairnlea	S Ayr	NX2281	55°5·7′	4°46·9′W	X	76
Cairnlea	Stir	NS5088	56°3·9′	4°24·1′W	X	57
Cairnlea Hill	Aberd	NJ3007	57°9·2′	3°9·0′W	H	37
Cairn Lee	Aberd	NJ7562	57°39·1′	2°24·7′W	A	29
Cairnleith	Aberd	NJ9136	57°25·1′	2°8·5′W	X	30
Cairnleith	Angus	NO3453	56°40·1′	3°4·2′W	X	54
Cairn Leith	Angus	NO3464	56°46·0′	3°4·3′W	X	44
Cairn Leith	Angus	NO3468	56°48·2′	3°4·4′W	H	44
Cairnleith	Pth & Kin	NN8720	56°21·8′	3°49·3′W	X	52,58
Cairnleith Crofts	Aberd	NJ9035	57°24·6′	2°9·5′W	T	30
Cairnleith Moss	Pth & Kin	NO0736	56°30·7′	3°30·2′W	X	52,53
Cairn Leuchan	Aberd	NO3891	57°0·6′	3°0·8′W	X	44
Cairn Ley	Aberd	NJ4614	57°13·1′	2°53·2′W	A	37
Cairnley	Aberd	NJ7017	57°14·8′	2°29·4′W	X	38
Cairnleys	D & G	NX7563	54°57·0′	3°56·7′W	X	84
Cairn Lick	Angus	NO3978	56°53·6′	2°59·6′W	H	44
Cairnlob	Aberd	NK0255	57°35·4′	1°57·5′W	X	30
Cairn Lochan	Highld	NH9802	57°6·1′	3°40·6′W	H	36
Cairn Lunkard	Angus	NO2378	56°53·5′	3°15·4′W	H	44
Cairn Macneilie	D & G	NX0961	54°54·7′	4°58·4′W	X	82
Cairn MacNeilie	D & G	NX1762	54°55·4′	4°50·9′W	A	82
Cairnmill	D & G	NX8494	55°13·8′	3°49·0′W	X	78
Cairn Molly	D & G	NX6982	55°7·2′	4°2·8′W	H	77
Cairn-mon-earn	Aberd	NO7891	57°0·8′	2°21·3′W	H	38,45
Cairnmon Fell	D & G	NX0448	54°47·6′	5°2·5′W	H	82
Cairnmore	Aberd	NJ4206	57°8·7′	2°57·1′W	X	37
Cairnmore	Aberd	NJ4304	57°7·7′	2°56·0′W	X	37
Cairn More	Aberd	NJ5024	57°18·5′	2°49·3′W	X	37
Cairn More	Aberd	NO4797	57°3·9′	2°52·0′W	A	37,44
Cairn More	D & G	NX1036	54°41·2′	4°56·4′W	A	82
Cairn More (Fort)	Aberd	NJ5024	57°18·5′	2°49·3′W	A	37
Cairnmore Hillock	Highld	ND0567	58°35·1′	3°37·6′W	H	11,12
Cairnmorris Hill	Pth & Kin	NN9301	56°11·6′	3°43·0′W	H	58
Cairn Motherie	Angus	NO2759	56°43·3′	3°11·1′W	A	53
Cairn Mude	Aberd	NJ5802	57°6·7′	2°41·2′W	A	37
Cairnmude	Aberd	NJ5802	57°6·7′	2°41·2′W	X	37
Cairnmuir	Aberd	NJ9862	57°39·1′	2°1·5′W	X	30
Cairnmuir	Clackm	NS9695	56°8·4′	3°40·0′W	X	58
Cairn Muir	Scot Bord	NT1157	55°48·1′	3°24·8′W	X	65,72
Cairn Muldonich	Moray	NJ2326	57°19·3′	3°16·3′W	X	36
Cairn Mulgainich	Moray	NJ2334	57°23·7′	3°16·4′W	X	28
Cairnmurnan	Aberd	NJ9161	57°38·6′	2°8·6′W	X	30
Cairnmyre	Aberd	NJ7929	57°21·3′	2°20·5′W	X	38
Cairn na Burgh Beg	Arg & Bt	NM3044	56°30·9′	6°22·9′W	X	46,47,48
Cairn na Burgh More	Arg & Bt	NM3044	56°30·9′	6°22·9′W	X	46,47,48
Cairn na Gath	D & G	NX2167	54°58·2′	4°47·4′W	A	82
Cairn Nairvie	Aberd	NO4293	57°1·7′	2°56·9′W	H	37,44
Cairnoch	Stir	NS6984	56°2·1′	4°5·7′W	X	57,64
Cairnoch Hill	Stir	NS6985	56°2·7′	4°5·7′W	H	57
Cairn of Achoy	Highld	ND2253	58°27·8′	3°19·7′W	A	11,12
Cairn of Ballindean	Moray	NJ1546	57°30·0′	3°24·6′W	H	28
Cairn of Barns	Angus	NO3171	56°49·8′	3°7·4′W	H	44
Cairn of Claise	Aberd	NO1878	56°53·4′	3°20·3′W	H	43
Cairn of Clune	Moray	NJ1445	57°29·5′	3°25·6′W	X	28
Cairn of Craigs	D & G	NY0073	55°2·7′	3°33·5′W	X	84
Cairn of Finglenny	Aberd	NO6184	56°57·0′	2°38·0′W	X	45
Cairn of Gowal	Angus	NO2281	56°55·1′	3°16·4′W	H	44
Cairn of Knockglass	D & G	NX4761	54°55·5′	4°22·8′W	A	83
Cairn of Meadows	Angus	NO4374	56°51·5′	2°55·6′W	H	44
Cairn of Mey	Highld	ND2873	58°38·6′	3°13·9′W	A	7,12
Cairn of Milduan	Aberd	NJ4730	57°21·7′	2°52·4′W	X	29,37
Cairn o' Mount	Aberd	NO6480	56°54·9′	2°35·0′W	X	45
Cairnorrie	Aberd	NJ8640	57°27·3′	2°13·5′W	T	30
Cairnorrie Mains	Aberd	NJ8641	57°27·8′	2°13·5′W	X	30
Cairnpapple Hill	W Loth	NS9871	55°55·5′	3°37·5′W	X	65
Cairnpark	Aberd	NJ8318	57°15·4′	2°16·5′W	X	38
Cairnpark	D & G	NX8698	55°16·0′	3°47·2′W	T	78
Cairn Pat	D & G	NX0456	54°51·9′	5°2·8′W	H	82
Cairnpat	D & G	NX0556	54°51·9′	5°1·9′W	X	82
Cairn Plew	Angus	NO2658	56°42·7′	3°12·1′W	A	53
Cairn Point	D & G	NX0668	54°58·4′	5°1·4′W	X	82
Cairn Pool	Highld	NM6571	56°46·5′	5°50·3′W	W	40
Cairn Poullachie	Highld	NH6324	57°17·4′	4°15·9′W	H	26,35
Cairnraws	D & G	NX6274	55°2·7′	4°9·2′W	X	77
Cairn Robie	Angus	NO4680	56°54·7′	2°52·8′W	H	44
Cairnryan	D & G	NX0668	54°58·4′	5°1·4′W	T	82
Cairn Rynettin	Highld	NJ0014	57°12·6′	3°38·9′W	H	36
Cairns	Aberd	NJ8136	57°25·1′	2°18·5′W	X	29,30
Cairns	Aberd	NJ8544	57°29·4′	2°14·6′W	X	30
Cairns	Pth & Kin	NO1146	56°36·1′	3°26·5′W	X	53
Cairnsaigh	E Ayr	NS6136	55°36·1′	4°11·9′W	H	71
Cairn Sawvie	Aberd	NJ2104	57°7·5′	3°17·8′W	H	36
Cairnscadden Hill	E Ayr	NS6116	55°25·3′	4°11·3′W	H	71
Cairnscarrow	D & G	NX1364	54°56·4′	4°54·7′W	H	82
Cairnscluse	Fife	NO5309	56°16·5′	2°45·1′W	X	59
Cairnsgarroch	D & G	NX5191	55°11·7′	4°20·0′W	H	77
Cairn Sgùmain	Highld	NH8740	57°26·4′	3°52·5′W	H	27
Cairnshee	Aberd	NO7494	57°2·4′	2°25·3′W	X	38,45
Cairnshee Wood	Aberd	NO7393	57°1·9′	2°26·2′W	F	38,45
Cairn Shiel	Angus	NO3069	56°48·7′	3°8·3′W	X	44
Cairns Hill	D & G	NX9198	55°16·1′	3°42·5′W	X	78
Cairns Ho	W Loth	NT0960	55°49·7′	3°26·7′W	X	65
Cairnside	D & G	NW9870	54°59·3′	5°9·0′W	X	76,82
Cairnsmill	Fife	NO4914	56°19·2′	2°49·0′W	X	59
Cairn's Mill	Scot Bord	NT7849	55°44·3′	2°20·6′W	X	74
Cairnsmore	D & G	NX4763	54°56·5′	4°22·9′W	X	83
Cairnsmore Burn	D & G	NX4764	54°57·1′	4°22·9′W	W	83
Cairnsmore of Carsphairn	D & G	NX5998	55°15·6′	4°12·7′W	H	77
Cairnsmore of Fleet	D & G	NX5065	54°57·7′	4°20·1′W	X	83
Cairnsmore or Black Craig of Dee	D & G	NX5875	55°3·2′	4°13·0′W	H	77
Cairns of Aberbothrie	Pth & Kin	NO2346	56°36·2′	3°14·8′W	X	53
Cairns of Coll	Arg & Bt	NM2866	56°42·6′	6°26·2′W	X	46,47
Cairns of Cùl nan Gad, The	Aberd	NO3287	56°58·4′	3°6·7′W	H	44
Cairns of Drimmie	Pth & Kin	NO1751	56°38·9′	3°20·8′W	X	53
Cairns of Melrose	Aberd	NJ7462	57°39·1′	2°25·7′W	X	29
Cairns of Memsie	Aberd	NJ9762	57°39·1′	2°2·6′W	X	30
Cairns of Ord	Aberd	NJ6158	57°36·9′	2°38·7′W	X	29
Cairns of Stirkoke	Highld	ND3348	58°25·2′	3°8·3′W	X	12
Cairnston	S Ayr	NS4318	55°26·1′	4°28·5′W	X	70
Cairnston	Stir	NN7903	56°12·5′	3°56·6′W	X	57
Cairn Table	E Ayr	NS7224	55°29·8′	4°1·1′W	H	71
Cairntack	Aberd	NJ9517	57°14·9′	2°4·5′W	X	38
Cairn, The	S Ayr	NX0199	55°15·0′	5°7·4′W	X	76
Cairnton	Aberd	NJ5463	57°39·5′	2°45·8′W	X	29
Cairnton	Aberd	NJ5504	57°7·7′	2°44·1′W	X	37
Cairnton	Aberd	NJ5844	57°29·3′	2°41·6′W	X	29
Cairnton	Aberd	NJ6163	57°39·6′	2°38·8′W	X	29
Cairnton	Aberd	NJ8519	57°15·9′	2°14·5′W	X	38
Cairnton	Aberd	NO7276	56°52·7′	2°27·1′W	X	45
Cairnton	Angus	NO6646	56°36·5′	2°32·8′W	X	54
Cairnton	C of Aber	NO8198	57°4·6′	2°18·4′W	X	38,45
Cairnton	Orkney	HY3405	58°55·9′	3°8·3′W	X	6,7
Cairnton	Pth & Kin	NO0727	56°25·8′	3°30·0′W	X	52,53,58
Cairnton Fm	Aberd	NJ7518	57°15·4′	2°24·4′W	FM	38
Cairnton Ho	Aberd	NO6595	57°2·9′	2°34·2′W	X	38,45
Cairnton of Balbegno	Aberd	NO6372	56°50·5′	2°35·9′W	X	45
Cairntosh Hill	D & G	NX6358	54°54·1′	4°7·8′W	H	83
Cairn Toul or Carn an t-Sabhail	Aberd	NN9697	57°3·4′	3°42·4′W	H	36,43
Cairntradlin	Aberd	NJ8213	57°12·7′	2°17·4′W	X	38
Cairn Trench	Angus	NO3974	56°51·5′	2°59·6′W	X	44
Cairnty Croft	Moray	NJ3352	57°33·4′	3°6·7′W	X	28
Cairn Uish	Moray	NJ1750	57°32·2′	3°22·7′W	H	28
Cairnurenan	Highld	NH5652	57°32·4′	4°23·9′W	X	26
Cairn Vachich	Aberd	NJ2611	57°11·3′	3°13·0′W	H	37
Cairn Vaich	Aberd	NJ2310	57°10·7′	3°16·0′W	X	36
Cairnvickuie	Arg & Bt	NR6551	55°42·0′	5°44·0′W	X	62
Cairnview Mains	W Loth	NT0061	55°50·2′	3°35·4′W	X	65
Cairn Vungie	Highld	NH4507	57°7·9′	4°33·2′W	H	34
Cairn Water	D & G	NX8189	55°11·1′	3°51·7′W	W	78

Cairn Water	D & G	NX8582	55°7·4′	3°47·8′W	W	78
Cairnweil	D & G	NX0948	54°47·7′	4°57·8′W	X	82
Cairnweil Burn	D & G	NX0849	54°48·2′	4°58·8′W	W	82
Cairnwell	Aberd	NO9096	57°3·6′	2°9·4′W	X	38,45
Cairnwell Burn	Aberd	NO1478	56°53·4′	3°24·2′W	W	43
Cairnwell, The	Pth & Kin	NO1377	56°52·8′	3°25·2′W	H	43
Cairnwhelp	Aberd	NJ4845	57°29·8′	2°51·6′W	X	28,29
Cairnwhin	S Ayr	NX2491	55°11·2′	4°45·4′W	X	76
Cairn William	Aberd	NJ6516	57°14·3′	2°34·3′W	H	38
Cairnyard	D & G	NX9070	55°1·0′	3°42·8′W	X	84
Cairny Croft	Northum	NY6667	55°0·0′	2°31·5′W	X	86
Cairnyfarrach	Aberd	NJ4624	57°18·5′	2°53·3′W	X	37
Cairny Hill	Angus	NO5570	56°49·4′	2°43·8′W	X	44
Cairnywellan Head	D & G	NX0939	54°42·8′	4°57·5′W	X	82
Cairnywhing	Aberd	NJ8656	57°35·9′	2°13·6′W	X	30
Cairston	Orkney	HY2611	58°59·1′	3°16·8′W	T	6
Cairston Roads	Orkney	HY2608	58°57·4′	3°16·7′W	W	6,7
Cais-bhaigh	Highld	NC0618	58°6·8′	5°17·1′W	W	15
Caiseachan	Highld	NH2360	57°36·0′	4°57·3′W	X	20
Caisteal Abhail	N Ayr	NR9644	55°39·1′	5°14·1′W	X	62,69
Caisteal a' Mhorair	N Eil	NB5349	58°21·9′	6°12·9′W	A	8
Caisteal an Fhithich	Highld	NG2664	57°35·2′	6°34·6′W	X	23
Caisteal Ard	N Eil	NB1809	57°59·1′	6°45·8′W	H	13,14
Caisteal Beag	Arg & Bt	NM4138	56°28·0′	6°11·9′W	X	47,48
Caisteal Bharraich	Highld	NC5856	58°28·4′	4°25·6′W	A	10
Caisteal Bheagram	N Eil	NF7637	57°18·8′	7°22·5′W	A	22
Caisteal Bhuirgh	N Eil	NF7750	57°25·8′	7°22·5′W	A	22
Caisteal Corrach	Stir	NN4207	56°14·0′	4°32·5′W	H	56
Caisteal Corrach	Stir	NN4625	56°23·8′	4°29·3′W	H	51
Caisteal Dubh	Arg & Bt	NS1598	56°8·6′	4°58·2′W	X	56
Caisteal Dubh	Pth & Kin	NN9458	56°42·4′	3°43·4′W	A	52,53
Caisteal Dùin	Arg & Bt	NR9097	56°7·4′	5°22·3′W	X	55
Caisteal Grugaig	Highld	NG8625	57°16·2′	5°32·5′W	X	33
Caisteal Liath	Highld	NC1518	58°7·0′	5°8·0′W	H	15
Caisteal Maol	Highld	NG7526	57°16·4′	5°43·5′W	A	33
Caisteal Mór	Arg & Bt	NM4037	56°27·5′	6°12·8′W	X	47,48
Caisteal Mór	Highld	NG9869	57°40·2′	5°22·8′W	X	19
Caisteal na Caillich	Aberd	NO2887	56°58·4′	3°10·6′W	H	44
Caisteal nan Con	Arg & Bt	NM7613	56°15·7′	5°36·6′W	A	55
Caisteal nan Con	Highld	NM5848	56°34·0′	5°55·9′W	A	47,48
Caisteal nan Corr	Highld	NC4601	57°58·6′	4°35·8′W	A	16
Caisteal Odair	N Eil	NF7376	57°39·6′	7°28·6′W	X	18
Caisteal Ormacleit	N Eil	NF7331	57°15·4′	7°25·0′W	X	22
Caisteal Samhraidh	Stir	NN5138	56°30·9′	4°24·8′W	X	51
Caisteal Sloc nam Ban	Arg & Bt	NM4231	56°24·3′	6°10·5′W	X	48
Caisteal Uamh an t-Sagait	Arg & Bt	NM4231	56°24·3′	6°10·5′W	X	48
Caisteal Uisdein	Highld	NG3858	57°32·4′	6°22·2′W	A	23
Caister Hall	Norf	TG5012	52°39·1′	1°42·2′E	X	134
Caister-on-Sea	Norf	TG5212	52°39·0′	1°43·9′E	T	134
Caister Point	Norf	TG5211	52°38·5′	1°43·9′E	X	134
Caiston Beck	Cumbr	NY3910	54°29·1′	2°56·1′W	W	90
Caistor	Lincs	TA1101	53°29·9′	0°19·2′W	T	113
Caistor Moor	Lincs	TA0902	53°30·4′	0°21·0′W	X	112
Caistor Moor Fm	Lincs	TA1002	53°30·4′	0°20·1′W	FM	113
Caistor St Edmund	Norf	TG2303	52°35·0′	1°17·9′E	T	134
Caistron	Northum	NT9901	55°18·4′	2°0·5′W	X	81
Caiteseal	N Eil	NB2404	57°56·7′	6°39·4′W	H	13,14
Caitha Hill	Scot Bord	NT4640	55°39·3′	2°51·1′W	H	73
Caithlim	Arg & Bt	NM7617	56°17·8′	5°36·8′W	X	55
Caitiosbhal	N Eil	NB4017	58°4·2′	6°24·1′W	H	14
Caitloch	D & G	NX7691	55°12·1′	3°56·5′W	X	78
Caius Fm	Cambs	TL4754	52°10·1′	0°9·4′E	FM	154
Cakebole	Worcs	SO8772	52°21·0′	2°11·1′W	T	139
Cakebole House Fm	Worcs	SO8772	52°21·0′	2°11·1′W	FM	139
Cakeham Manor Ho	W Susx	SZ7897	50°46·3′	0°53·2′W	A	197
Cakelaw Burn	S Lanak	NS9718	55°27·0′	3°37·3′W	W	78
Cakelaw Rig	S Lanak	NS9818	55°27·0′	3°36·3′W	X	78
Cakemuir Burn	Midlo	NT4159	55°49·5′	2°56·1′W	W	66,73
Cakemuir Castle	Midlo	NT4159	55°49·5′	2°56·1′W	A	66,73
Cake Pill Gout	S Glos	ST5688	51°35·6′	2°37·7′W	X	162,172
Cakes of Bread	Derby	SK1990	53°24·6′	1°42·4′W	X	110
Cake Wood	W Berks	SU3068	51°24·8′	1°33·7′W	F	174
Calabhagh	N Eil	NF8654	57°28·3′	7°13·8′W	X	22
Cala Burn	Scot Bord	NT4716	55°26·4′	2°49·8′W	W	79
Calaburn Fm	Scot Bord	NT4716	55°26·4′	2°49·8′W	FM	79
Calacvm (Roman Fort)	Lancs	SD6175	54°10·4′	2°35·4′W	R	97
Caladh	Highld	NH5754	57°33·5′	4°22·9′W	X	26
Cala Ghlumaig	N Eil	NB4230	58°11·3′	6°22·9′W	W	8
Calair Burn	Stir	NN5318	56°20·2′	4°22·2′W	W	57
Calais	Fife	NT1286	56°3·8′	3°24·4′W	X	65
Calais Muir Wood	Fife	NT1386	56°3·8′	3°23·4′W	F	65
Calais Street	Suff	TL9739	52°1·1′	0°52·7′E	T	155
Calaman	Highld	NG5815	57°10·0′	5°59·7′W	X	32
Calaman Cave	Highld	NG5815	57°10·0′	5°59·7′W	X	32
Calamansack	Corn	SW7427	50°6·2′	5°9·3′W	X	204
Calanais	N Eil	NB2133	58°12·1′	6°44·5′W	T	8,13
Cala Steòrnabhaigh	N Eil	NB4331	58°11·8′	6°22·0′W	W	8
Calback Ness	Shetld	HU3977	60°28·8′	1°16·9′W	X	2,3
Calbha Beag	Highld	NC1536	58°16·7′	5°8·8′W	X	15
Calbhach Coire	Highld	NC3456	58°27·9′	4°50·3′W	X	9
Calbhaigh	N Eil	NF7728	57°14·0′	7°20·8′W	X	22
Calbha Mór	Highld	NC1636	58°16·7′	5°7·8′W	X	15
Calbost	N Eil	NB4117	58°4·3′	6°23·1′W	T	14
Calbourne	I of W	SZ4286	50°40·6′	1°24·0′W	T	196
Calcaria (Tadcaster)	N Yks	SE4843	53°53·1′	1°15·8′W	R	105
Calceby	Lincs	TF3975	53°15·5′	0°5·4′E	T	122
Calcethorpe Ho	Lincs	TF2388	53°22·7′	0°8·6′W	X	113,122
Calcethorpe Manor Fm	Lincs	TF2488	53°22·7′	0°7·7′W	FM	113,122
Calcethorpe Village	Lincs	TF2488	53°22·7′	0°7·7′W	A	113,122
Calceto Fm	W Susx	TQ0305	50°50·3′	0°31·8′W	FM	197
Calcoed	Flint	SJ1774	53°15·6′	3°14·3′W	T	116
Calcot	Glos	SP0810	51°47·5′	1°52·6′W	T	163
Calcot	W Berks	SU6671	51°26·3′	1°2·6′W	T	175
Calcote Fm	Wilts	SU0362	51°21·7′	1°57·0′W	FM	173
Calcot Fm	Glos	ST8494	51°38·9′	2°13·5′W	FM	162,173
Calcot Fm	Shrops	SO2795	52°33·1′	3°4·2′W	FM	137
Calcot Fm	W Susx	TQ1714	50°55·0′	0°19·7′W	FM	198
Calcot Hall	Flint	SJ1674	53°15·6′	3°15·2′W	X	116
Calcot Hill	Worcs	SO9478	52°24·2′	2°4·9′W	X	139
Calcot Ho	Hants	SU5315	50°56·1′	1°14·4′W	X	196
Calcot Peak Fm	Glos	SP1010	51°47·5′	1°50·9′W	FM	163
Calcot Row	W Berks	SU6671	51°26·3′	1°2·6′W	T	175
Calcott	Kent	TR1762	51°19·2′	1°7·3′E	T	179
Calcott	Shrops	SJ4413	52°42·9′	2°49·3′W	T	126
Calcott Hall	Powys	SJ2819	52°46·1′	3°3·6′W	X	126
Calcott's Green	Glos	SO7817	51°51·3′	2°18·8′W	T	162
Calcot Wood	W Susx	TQ1714	50°55·0′	0°19·7′W	F	198
Calcrafts Barn	Leic	SK7833	52°53·6′	0°50·0′W	X	129
Calcutt	N Yks	SE3455	53°59·6′	1°28·5′W	T	104
Calcutt	Wilts	SU1193	51°38·4′	1°50·1′W	T	163,173
Calcutt Elms Fm	Warw	SP4764	52°16·6′	1°18·3′W	FM	151
Calcutt Fm	Warw	SP4664	52°16·6′	1°19·1′W	FM	151
Calcutt House Fm	Warw	SP4763	52°16·0′	1°18·3′W	FM	151
Calcutt Locks	Warw	SP4663	52°16·0′	1°19·2′W	X	151
Calcutt Spinney	Warw	SP4763	52°16·0′	1°18·3′W	F	151
Calcutt Village	Warw	SP4664	52°16·6′	1°19·1′W	A	151
Calda House	Highld	NC2423	58°9·9′	4°59·0′W	A	15
Caldale	Orkney	HY4110	58°58·7′	3°1·1′W	X	6
Caldarvan	W Dunb	NS4384	56°1·6′	4°30·7′W	X	56,64
Caldarvan Loch	W Dunb	NS4283	56°1·1′	4°31·6′W	W	56,64
Caldback	Shetld	HP6006	60°44·2′	0°53·5′W	X	1
Caldbec Hill	E Susx	TQ7516	50°55·2′	0°29·8′E	X	199
Caldbeck	Cumbr	NY3239	54°44·7′	3°3·0′W	T	90
Caldbeck Fells	Cumbr	NY3135	54°42·6′	3°3·8′W	H	90
Caldbergh	N Yks	SE0985	54°15·9′	1°51·3′W	T	99
Cald Burn	Angus	NO2977	56°53·0′	3°9·5′W	W	44
Caldcoats	E Renf	NS5155	55°46·2′	4°22·1′W	X	64
Caldcot Plantn	Scot Bord	NT4148	55°43·6′	2°55·9′W	F	73
Caldcots	Angus	NO6360	56°44·1′	2°35·8′W	X	45
Caldecote	Cambs	TL1488	52°28·9′	0°18·9′W	T	142
Caldecote	Cambs	TL3457	52°11·9′	0°2·0′W	T	154
Caldecote	Herts	TL2338	52°1·8′	0°12·0′W	T	153
Caldecote	Mil Key	SP8842	52°4·4′	0°42·6′W	X	152
Caldecote	Northnts	SP6851	52°9·4′	1°0·0′W	T	152
Caldecote	Warw	SP3594	52°32·8′	1°28·6′W	T	140
Caldecote Dyke Fm	Cambs	TL1788	52°28·9′	0°16·2′W	FM	142
Caldecote Fen	Cambs	TL1889	52°29·4′	0°15·3′W	X	142
Caldecote Fm	Norf	TF7403	52°36·0′	0°34·6′E	FM	143
Caldecote Hill	Herts	TQ1594	51°38·2′	0°19·9′W	T	166,176
Caldecote Manor Fm	Cambs	TL2258	52°12·6′	0°12·5′W	FM	153
Caldecott	Northnts	SP9868	52°18·3′	0°33·4′W	T	153
Caldecott	Oxon	SU4996	51°39·9′	1°17·1′W	T	164
Caldecott	Rut	SP8693	52°31·9′	0°43·5′W	T	141
Caldecotte	Mil Key	SP8935	52°0·6′	0°41·8′W	T	152
Caldecotte Village	Mil Key	SP8935	52°0·6′	0°41·8′W	A	152
Caldecott Fm	Kent	TR0524	50°59·0′	0°55·6′E	FM	189
Caldecott Green	Ches	SJ4251	53°3·4′	2°51·5′W	X	117
Caldecott Hall	Ches	SJ4351	53°3·4′	2°50·6′W	X	117
Caldecott Hall	Norf	TG4701	52°33·3′	1°39·0′E	X	134
Calder	Cumbr	NY0303	54°25·0′	3°29·3′W	T	89
Calder	Northum	NU0119	55°28·1′	1°58·6′W	X	81
Calder Abbey	Cumbr	NY0406	54°26·7′	3°28·4′W	A	89
Calder and Hebble Navigation	Wakf	SE2817	53°39·2′	1°34·2′W	W	110
Calderbank	N Lanak	NS7662	55°50·4′	3°58·4′W	T	64
Calderbergh Moor	N Yks	SE1083	54°14·8′	1°50·4′W	X	99
Calder Bridge	Cumbr	NY0405	54°26·1′	3°28·4′W	T	89
Calderbrook	Cered	SN3345	52°4·9′	4°25·8′W	X	145
Calderbrook	Roch	SD9418	53°39·7′	2°5·0′W	T	109
Calder Burn	E Ayr	NS5941	55°38·8′	4°14·0′W	W	71
Calder Burn	Highld	NH3401	57°4·5′	4°43·9′W	W	34
Caldercleugh	Scot Bord	NT6666	55°53·4′	2°32·2′W	X	67
Caldercruix	N Lanak	NS8268	55°53·7′	3°52·8′W	T	65
Calderdale Way	Cald	SD9425	53°43·5′	2°5·0′W	X	103
Calderdale Way	Cald	SE0829	53°45·7′	1°52·3′W	X	104
Calder Dyke	Lancs	SD5448	53°55·8′	2°41·6′W	W	102
Calder Fell	Lancs	SD5548	53°55·8′	2°40·7′W	X	102
Calderglen	S Lanak	NS6759	55°48·6′	4°6·9′W	X	64
Calderglen Country Park	S Lanak	NS6552	55°44·8′	4°8·6′W	X	64
Caldergreen	S Lanak	NS6444	55°40·5′	4°9·3′W	X	71
Caldergrove	S Lanak	NS6758	55°48·1′	4°6·9′W	X	64
Calder Grove	Wakf	SE3016	53°38·6′	1°32·4′W	T	110,111
Calder Hall	Cumbr	NY0303	54°25·0′	3°29·3′W	X	89
Calderhead	Orkney	HY4107	58°57·0′	3°1·0′W	X	6,7
Calder & Hebble Navigation	Cald	SE1322	53°41·9′	1°47·8′W	W	104
Calder Ho	W Loth	NT0767	55°53·5′	3°28·8′W	A	65
Calder Mains	Highld	ND0959	58°30·8′	3°33·2′W	T	11,12
Caldermill	S Lanak	NS6641	55°38·9′	4°7·3′W	T	71
Calder Moor	Lancs	SD6452	53°58·0′	2°32·5′W	X	102,103
Caldermoor	Roch	SD9316	53°38·7′	2°5·9′W	T	109
Calder Moss	E Ayr	NS5940	55°38·2′	4°14·0′W	X	71
Calders	Cumbr	SD6796	54°21·8′	2°30·1′W	X	98
Calder's Geo	Shetld	HU2078	60°29·4′	1°37·7′W	X	3
Calder's Head	Shetld	HU3491	60°36·3′	1°22·2′W	X	1,2
Calder Side	Lancs	SD5348	53°55·8′	2°42·5′W	X	102
Calderside	S Lanak	NS6654	55°45·9′	4°7·7′W	X	64
Calderstones	Liv	SJ4087	53°22·8′	2°53·7′W	T	108
Calderstones Hospital	Lancs	SD7237	53°50·0′	2°25·1′W	X	103
Calder Vale	Lancs	SD5345	53°54·2′	2°42·5′W	T	102
Calder Water	N Ayr	NS2765	55°51·1′	4°45·4′W	W	63
Calder Water	S Lanak	NS6242	55°39·4′	4°11·2′W	W	71
Calder Water	S Lanak	NS6451	55°44·3′	4°9·5′W	W	64
Calderwood	S Lanak	NS6455	55°46·4′	4°9·7′W	T	64
Calder Wood	W Loth	NT0766	55°52·9′	3°28·8′W	F	65
Caldewbeck	Cumbr	NY3644	54°47·5′	2°59·3′W	X	85
Caldewell House	Worcs	SO9148	52°8·0′	2°7·5′W	X	150
Caldew Wood	Cumbr	NY4431	54°40·5′	2°51·7′W	F	90
Caldey Island (Ynys Bŷr)	Pemb	SS1396	51°38·1′	4°41·8′W	X	158
Caldey Point	Pemb	SS1496	51°38·2′	4°40·9′W	X	158
Caldey Roads	Pemb	SS1298	51°39·2′	4°42·7′W	W	158
Caldey Sound	Pemb	SS1297	51°38·7′	4°42·6′W	W	158
Caldhambank	Angus	NO4748	56°37·5′	2°51·4′W	X	54
Caldhame	Angus	NO4748	56°37·5′	2°51·4′W	T	54
Caldicot	Monm	ST4788	51°35·5′	2°45·5′W	T	171,172
Caldicot Level	Monm	ST5290	51°36·6′	2°41·2′W	X	162,172
Caldicot Level	Newp	ST3984	51°33·3′	2°52·4′W	X	171
Caldicot Level	Newp	ST4285	51°33·9′	2°49·8′W	X	171,172
Caldicot Moor	Monm	ST4586	51°34·4′	2°47·2′W	X	171,172
Caldicot Pill	Monm	ST4987	51°35·0′	2°43·8′W	W	172
Caldicott	Heref	SO5232	51°59·3′	2°41·5′W	X	149
Caldicott Fm	Heref	SO4820	51°52·8′	2°44·9′W	FM	161
Caldmore	Wals	SP0197	52°34·5′	1°58·7′W	T	139
Caldon Canal	Staffs	SJ9353	53°4·7′	2°5·9′W	W	118
Caldon Canal	Staffs	SK0048	53°2·0′	1°59·6′W	W	119
Caldon Grange	Staffs	SK0848	53°2·0′	1°52·4′W	X	119
Caldon Low	Staffs	SK0848	53°2·0′	1°52·4′W	X	119
Caldons	D & G	NX4078	55°4·5′	4°29·9′W	X	77
Caldons Burn	D & G	NX4177	55°4·0′	4°29·0′W	W	77
Caldonshill	D & G	NX0753	54°50·3′	4°59·9′W	X	82
Caldons Park	D & G	NX0754	54°50·9′	4°59·9′W	X	82
Caldons Wood	D & G	NX4078	55°4·5′	4°29·9′W	F	77
Caldow Lodge	D & G	NX7278	55°5·0′	3°59·9′W	X	77,84
Caldow Moor	D & G	NX7378	55°5·1′	3°59·0′W	X	77,84
Caldra	Scot Bord	NT7057	55°48·6′	2°28·3′W	X	67,74
Caldra Fm	Scot Bord	NT7749	55°44·3′	2°21·5′W	FM	74
Caldra House	Scot Bord	NT7749	55°44·3′	2°21·5′W	X	74
Caldronbrae	Scot Bord	NT7238	55°38·3′	2°26·3′W	X	74
Caldron Burn	D & G	NX4386	55°8·9′	4°27·4′W	W	77
Caldron Burn	N Ayr	NS2351	55°43·5′	4°48·7′W	W	63
Caldrongill	S Ayr	NS4130	55°32·5′	4°30·8′W	X	70
Caldron Hill	N Ayr	NS2251	55°43·4′	4°49·6′W	H	63
Caldronlea	D & G	NY2676	55°4·6′	3°9·1′W	X	85
Caldron Sike	D & G	NY3796	55°15·5′	2°59·0′W	W	79
Caldside	Scot Bord	NT7042	55°40·5′	2°28·2′W	X	74
Caldslope	Cumbr	NY5678	55°5·9′	2°40·9′W	X	86
Caldwell	Derby	SK2517	52°45·2′	1°37·4′W	T	128
Caldwell	N Yks	NZ1613	54°31·0′	1°44·7′W	T	92
Caldwell Beck	N Yks	NZ1512	54°30·4′	1°45·7′W	W	92
Caldwell Burn	D & G	NY1693	55°13·7′	3°18·8′W	W	79
Caldwell Hall (School)	Derby	SK2517	52°45·2′	1°37·4′W	X	128
Caldwell Ho	E Renf	NS4154	55°45·5′	4°31·6′W	X	64
Caldwell Law	E Renf	NS4255	55°46·0′	4°30·7′W	X	64
Caldwells	Fife	NO2613	56°18·5′	3°11·3′W	X	59
Caldwellside	S Lanak	NS8944	55°40·9′	3°45·5′W	X	71,72
Caldwell Sike	Cumbr	NY5383	55°8·6′	2°43·8′W	W	79
Caldy	Wirral	SJ2285	53°21·6′	3°9·9′W	T	108
Caldy Bank	Shrops	SO2383	52°26·6′	3°7·6′W	X	137
Caldy Blacks	Wirral	SJ2284	53°21·1′	3°9·9′W	X	108
Caldy Brook	Ches	SJ4364	53°10·4′	2°50·8′W	W	117
Calebrack	Cumbr	NY3435	54°42·6′	3°1·0′W	X	90
Caledffrwd	Gwyn	SH5663	53°8·9′	4°8·8′W	W	114,115
Caledonian Canal	Highld	NH6441	57°26·6′	4°15·5′W	W	26
Caledonian Canal	Highld	NN1481	56°53·2′	5°2·7′W	W	34,41
Caledonian Canal	Highld	NN2896	57°1·6′	4°49·6′W	W	34
Caledonian Rly	Angus	NO6359	56°43·5′	2°35·8′W	X	54
Caledrhydiau	Cered	SN4753	52°9·5′	4°13·8′W	X	146
Calees	Cumbr	NY5664	54°58·4′	2°40·8′W	X	86
Cale Green	Stock	SJ8988	53°23·6′	2°9·5′W	T	109
Calehill Ho	Kent	TQ9447	51°11·6′	0°47·0′E	X	189
Calendra	Corn	SW9240	50°13·6′	4°54·6′W	X	204
Calenick	Corn	SW8243	50°15·0′	5°3·1′W	T	204
Calerick	Corn	SW8347	50°17·2′	5°2·4′W	X	204
Cales Dale	Derby	SK1764	53°10·6′	1°44·3′W	X	119
Cales Fm	Derby	SK1664	53°10·6′	1°45·2′W	FM	119
Caley Crags	Leeds	SE2344	53°53·7′	1°38·6′W	X	104
Caley Hall Fm	Leeds	SE2344	53°53·7′	1°38·6′W	FM	104
Caleys Fields	Warw	SP2144	52°5·9′	1°41·2′W	X	151
Calf	Cumbr	SD6585	54°15·8′	2°31·8′W	X	97
Calf Allen Rocks	N Yks	TA0884	54°14·7′	0°20·1′W	X	101
Calf Beck	Cumbr	SD6596	54°21·7′	2°31·9′W	W	97
Calf Br	Lincs	TF1832	52°52·6′	0°14·4′W	X	130
Calf Close	Northum	NY8884	55°9·3′	2°10·9′W	X	80
Calf Clough	Lancs	SD6755	53°59·6′	2°29·8′W	X	103
Calf Cop	N Yks	SD6470	54°7·7′	2°32·6′W	X	97
Calf Cove	Cumbr	NY3510	54°29·1′	2°59·8′W	X	90
Calf Crag	Cumbr	NY3010	54°29·1′	3°4·4′W	H	90
Calfcraig Bog	D & G	NX9389	55°11·3′	3°40·4′W	X	78
Calf Edge Fm	N Yks	SD9446	53°54·8′	2°5·1′W	FM	103
Calf Hall	Durham	NZ0449	54°50·4′	1°55·8′W	X	87
Calf Haugh	N Yks	SE2465	54°5·1′	1°37·6′W	X	99
Calfhay Fm	Dorset	ST6106	50°51·4′	2°32·9′W	FM	194
Calf Heath	Staffs	SJ9308	52°40·4′	2°5·8′W	T	127
Calf Hey Resr	Lancs	SD7522	53°41·9′	2°22·3′W	W	103
Calfhill	Scot Bord	NT5138	55°38·2′	2°46·3′W	X	73
Calf Holes	N Yks	SD8077	54°11·5′	2°18·0′W	X	98
Calfhope Burn	Scot Bord	NT4045	55°41·9′	2°56·8′W	W	73
Calfhope Hill	Scot Bord	NT4045	55°41·9′	2°56·8′W	H	73
Calfhow Pike	Cumbr	NY3321	54°35·0′	3°1·8′W	H	90
Calfield	D & G	NY3384	55°9·0′	3°2·7′W	X	79
Calfield Rig	D & G	NY3284	55°9·0′	3°3·6′W	H	79
Calf Lee	Northum	NT9005	55°20·6′	2°9·0′W	H	80
Calf of Cava	Orkney	HY3200	58°53·2′	3°10·3′W	X	6,7
Calf of Daaey	Shetld	HU6095	60°38·3′	0°53·7′W	X	1,2
Calf of Eday	Orkney	HY5839	59°14·4′	2°43·7′W	X	5
Calf of Flotta	Orkney	ND3896	58°51·1′	3°4·0′W	X	6,7
Calf of Linga	Shetld	HU5363	60°21·1′	1°1·9′W	X	2,3
Calf of Linga	Shetld	HU6162	60°20·5′	0°53·2′W	X	2
Calf of Man	I of M	SC1565	54°3·1′	4°49·2′W	X	95
Calford Green	Suff	TL6945	52°4·9′	0°28·4′E	T	154
Calf Park	D & G	NX0755	54°51·4′	5°0·0′W	X	82
Calfpark	D & G	NY0673	55°2·8′	3°27·8′W	X	85
Calf Rock	N Som	ST2360	51°20·3′	3°5·9′W	X	182
Calfshaw	Scot Bord	NT4633	55°35·5′	2°51·0′W	X	73
Calfshaw Head	Scot Bord	NT3807	55°21·4′	2°58·2′W	H	79
Calf Sike	Cumbr	NY6275	55°4·3′	2°35·3′W	W	86
Calf Sound	I of M	SC1766	54°3·7′	4°47·4′W	W	95
Calfsound	Orkney	HY5737	59°13·3′	2°44·7′W	T	5
Calf Sound	Orkney	HY5738	59°13·9′	2°44·7′W	W	5
Calf Sound	Orkney	ND3896	58°51·1′	3°4·0′W	W	6,7
Calf, The	Cumbr	SD6697	54°22·3′	2°31·0′W	H	98
Calf Top	Cumbr	SD6685	54°15·8′	2°30·9′W	H	98
Calfward	Aberd	NJ5011	57°11·5′	2°49·2′W	X	37
Calfward	Pth & Kin	NN9315	56°19·2′	3°43·4′W	X	58
Calfward Wood	Angus	NO3942	56°34·2′	2°59·1′W	F	54
Calf Way	Glos	SO9110	51°47·5′	2°7·4′W	X	163
Calfway Fm	Glos	SO9107	51°45·9′	2°7·4′W	FM	163
Calgarry Beg	Highld	NC8959	58°30·6′	3°53·8′W	X	10
Calgarth Hall	Cumbr	SD3999	54°23·2′	2°55·9′W	A	96,97
Calgary	Arg & Bt	NM3751	56°34·9′	6°16·5′W	T	47

Calgary Bay	Arg & Bt	NM3650	56°34·3′	6°17·4′W	W	47
Calgary Point	Arg & Bt	NM1052	56°34·5′	6°42·9′W	X	46
Calgow	D & G	NX4365	54°57·5′	4°26·7′W	X	83
Calhayes Fm	Devon	ST1606	50°51·1′	3°11·2′W	FM	192,193
Caliach	Arg & Bt	NM3553	56°35·9′	6°18·6′W	X	47
Caliach Point	Arg & Bt	NM3454	56°36·4′	6°19·6′W	X	47
Calier	Moray	NJ2220	57°16·1′	3°17·1′W	X	36
Califer	Moray	NJ0857	57°35·9′	3°31·9′W	T	27
Califermoss	Moray	NJ0856	57°35·3′	3°31·9′W	X	27
California	Birm	SP0183	52°26·9′	1°58·7′W	T	139
California	Cambs	TL5384	52°26·2′	0°15·4′E	T	143
California	D & G	NX4241	54°44·6′	4°26·8′W	X	83
California	Falk	NS9076	55°58·1′	3°45·3′W	T	65
California	Norf	TG5115	52°40·7′	1°43·2′E	T	134
California	Shrops	SO5280	52°25·2′	2°42·0′W	X	137,138
California	Suff	TM1844	52°3·3′	1°11·2′E	T	169
California	Suff	TM2855	52°9·0′	1°20·4′E	X	156
California Country Park	Wok	SU7865	51°22·9′	0°52·4′W	X	175
California Cross	Devon	SX7053	50°22·0′	3°49·3′W	X	202
California Fm	Dorset	SZ0177	50°35·8′	1°58·8′W	FM	195
California Fm	Notts	SK5225	52°49·4′	1°13·3′W	FM	129
California Fm	Notts	SK8472	53°14·5′	0°44·1′W	FM	121
California Fm	N Yks	SE8181	54°13·3′	0°45·0′W	FM	100
California Fm	Suff	TL7445	52°4·8′	0°32·8′E	FM	155
California Fm	W Berks	SU4380	51°31·3′	1°22·4′W	FM	174
Caliness	D & G	NX1435	54°40·8′	4°52·7′W	X	82
Calke	Derby	SK3722	52°47·9′	1°26·7′W	T	128
Calke Abbey	Derby	SK3622	52°47·9′	1°27·6′W	A	128
Calke Park	Derby	SK3622	52°47·9′	1°27·6′W	X	128
Calke Wood	Suff	TM0274	52°19·8′	0°58·3′E	F	144
Calkin	D & G	NY3088	55°11·1′	3°5·5′W	X	79
Calkin Rig	D & G	NY2987	55°10·6′	3°6·5′W	H	79
Calla	S Lanak	NS9949	55°43·7′	3°36·1′W	X	72
Callabarrett Wood	Corn	SX1067	50°28·6′	4°40·3′W	F	200
Callachally	Arg & Bt	NM5942	56°30·8′	5°54·6′W	X	47,48
Callachy Hill	Highld	NH7460	57°37·0′	4°6·1′W	H	21,27
Callacott Barton	Devon	SS6507	50°51·0′	3°54·7′W	X	191
Calladrum	Aberd	NO7794	57°2·4′	2°22·3′W	T	38,45
Calla Geodha	N Eil	NF7655	57°28·4′	7°23·9′W	X	22
Callakille	Highld	NG6954	57°31·3′	5°51·0′W	T	24
Callaly	Northum	NU0509	55°22·7′	1°54·8′W	T	81
Callaly Burn	Northum	NU0510	55°23·3′	1°54·8′W	W	81
Callaly Crag	Northum	NU0609	55°22·7′	1°53·9′W	X	81
Callaly Mill	Northum	NU0511	55°23·8′	1°54·8′W	X	81
Callander	Stir	NN6307	56°14·4′	4°12·2′W	T	57
Callander Craig	Stir	NN6308	56°14·9′	4°12·2′W	X	57
Callandrade	Stir	NN6207	56°14·4′	4°13·2′W	X	57
Callands	Warr	SJ5890	53°24·6′	2°37·5′W	T	108
Callands Ho	Scot Bord	NT1545	55°41·7′	3°20·7′W	X	72
Callan's Close	Devon	ST0302	50°48·8′	3°22·2′W	X	192
Callan's Lane Wood	Lincs	TF0626	52°49·5′	0°25·2′W	F	130
Callard	Devon	SS6215	50°55·3′	3°57·4′W	X	180
Callas Hill	Swin	SU2183	51°33·0′	1°41·4′W	X	174
Callater Burn	Aberd	NO1686	56°57·7′	3°22·4′W	W	43
Callaughton	Shrops	SO6197	52°34·4′	2°34·1′W	T	138
Callaughton Ho	Shrops	SO6297	52°34·4′	2°33·2′W	X	138
Callaw Cairn	Scot Bord	NT8014	55°25·4′	2°18·5′W	H	80
Callelochan	Pth & Kin	NN7142	56°33·4′	4°5·5′W	X	51,52
Callendar Fm	Northnts	SP6974	52°21·8′	0°58·8′W	FM	141
Callendar Fm	Warw	SP3893	52°32·2′	1°26·0′W	FM	140
Callendar House	Falk	NS8979	55°59·7′	3°46·3′W	A	65
Callendar Park	Falk	NS8979	55°59·7′	3°46·3′W	T	65
Callender	Highld	NJ1436	57°24·6′	3°25·4′W	X	28
Callendoun	Arg & Bt	NS3384	56°1·4′	4°40·3′W	X	56
Callercove Pt	Scot Bord	NT9365	55°52·9′	2°6·3′W	X	67
Caller Crag	Northum	NU1106	55°21·1′	1°49·2′W	X	81
Callerhues Crag	Northum	NY8586	55°10·3′	2°13·7′W	H	80
Callernish	N Eil	NF7476	57°39·6′	7°27·6′W	X	18
Callers	Northum	NU2437	55°37·8′	1°36·7′W	X	75
Caller's Corner	E Susx	TQ6119	50°57·1′	0°17·9′E	X	199
Callert Cottage	Highld	NN1060	56°41·8′	5°5·7′W	X	41
Callert Ho	Highld	NN0960	56°41·8′	5°6·7′W	X	41
Callerton	N upon Ty	NZ1768	55°0·6′	1°43·6′W	T	88
Callerton Grange	Northum	NZ1569	55°1·2′	1°45·5′W	X	88
Callerton Hall	Northum	NZ1670	55°1·7′	1°44·6′W	X	88
Callerton Lane End	N upon Ty	NZ1669	55°1·2′	1°44·6′W	T	88
Callestick	Corn	SW7750	50°18·7′	5°7·6′W	T	200,204
Callestick Vean	Corn	SW7749	50°18·2′	5°7·5′W	X	204
Calleva (Roman Town)	Hants	SU6362	51°21·4′	1°5·3′W	R	175
Calleynough	Corn	SX0870	50°30·1′	4°42·1′W	X	200
Call Hill	Stock on T	NZ3814	54°31·4′	1°24·4′W	X	93
Calliburn	Arg & Bt	NR7225	55°28·2′	5°36·0′W	X	68
Callies	Aberd	NJ8042	57°28·3′	2°19·5′W	X	29,30
Calligarry	Highld	NG6203	57°3·7′	5°55·1′W	T	32
Calligeo	N Eil	NF8681	57°42·8′	7°15·9′W	W	18
Callimore Fm	Worcs	SO8770	52°19·9′	2°11·0′W	FM	139
Calling Low	Derby	SK1765	53°11·1′	1°44·3′W	X	119
Callington	Corn	SX3669	50°30·1′	4°18·4′W	T	201
Callingwood	Staffs	SK1923	52°48·5′	1°42·7′W	T	128
Callipers Hall	Herts	TL0500	51°41·6′	0°28·5′W	X	166
Callisham Down	Devon	SX5366	50°28·8′	4°3·9′W	X	201
Callisterhall	D & G	NY2881	55°7·3′	3°7·3′W	X	79
Callochant	Renf	NS3961	55°49·2′	4°33·8′W	X	63
Calloose	Corn	SW5935	50°10·2′	5°22·1′W	T	203
Callop	Highld	NM9278	56°51·1′	5°24·2′W	X	40
Callow	Derby	SK2481	53°19·8′	1°38·0′W	X	110
Callow	Derby	SK2652	53°4·1′	1°36·3′W	T	119
Callow	Heref	SO4934	52°0·4′	2°44·2′W	T	149
Callow	Shrops	SO4391	52°31·1′	2°50·0′W	H	137
Calloways	W Susx	SU9217	50°56·9′	0°41·0′W	X	197
Callow Bank	Derby	SK2582	53°20·3′	1°37·1′W	X	110
Callow Brook	Cambs	TL3760	52°13·5′	0°0·7′E	W	154
Callow Down Fm	Bucks	SU7899	51°41·3′	0°51·9′W	FM	165
Callowell	Glos	SO8406	51°45·4′	2°13·5′W	X	162
Callow End	Worcs	SO8349	52°8·6′	2°14·5′W	T	150
Callow Fm	Derby	SK2180	53°19·2′	1°40·7′W	FM	110
Callow Fm	Glos	SO7231	51°58·8′	2°24·1′W	FM	149
Callow Fm	Oxon	SP3918	51°51·8′	1°25·6′W	FM	164
Callowgate	Shrops	SO5979	52°24·7′	2°35·8′W	X	137,138
Callow Green	Norf	TG3521	52°44·4′	1°29·3′E	X	133,134

Callow Hall (Hotel)	Derby	SK1647	53°1·4′	1°45·3′W	X	119,128
Callow Hill	Heref	SO5116	51°50·7′	2°42·3′W	T	162
Callow Hill	Shrops	SJ3804	52°38·1′	2°54·6′W	X	126
Callow Hill	Shrops	SO4685	52°27·9′	2°47·3′W	H	137,138
Callow Hill	Somer	ST4455	51°17·7′	2°47·8′W	H	172,182
Callow Hill	Somer	ST5044	51°11·8′	2°42·5′W	T	182,183
Callowhill	Staffs	SK0526	52°50·1′	1°55·1′W	X	128
Callow Hill	Surrey	SU9969	51°24·9′	0°34·2′W	H	175,176
Callow Hill	Wilts	SU0384	51°33·5′	1°57·0′W	T	173
Callow Hill	Worcs	SO7473	52°21·5′	2°22·5′W	T	138
Callow Hill	Worcs	SP0264	52°16·7′	1°57·8′W	X	150
Callow Hill Fm	Heref	SO6739	52°3·1′	2°28·7′W	FM	149
Callow Hill Fm	Staffs	SJ9742	52°58·8′	2°2·3′W	FM	118
Callow Hollow	Shrops	SO4292	52°31·6′	2°50·9′W	X	137
Callow Marsh	Heref	SO6546	52°6·9′	2°30·3′W	T	149
Callow Moor	Derby	SK2651	53°3·6′	1°36·3′W	X	119
Callows Grave	Worcs	SO5966	52°17·7′	2°35·7′W	X	137,138,149
Callows Hill	Bucks	SU8199	51°41·3′	0°49·3′W	X	165
Callow, The	Heref	SO5721	51°53·4′	2°37·1′W	X	162
Call, The	Angus	NO2072	56°50·2′	3°18·2′W	X	44
Callum Hill	Kent	TQ8766	51°22·0′	0°41·6′E	H	178
Callumkill	Arg & Bt	NR4046	55°38·5′	6°7·5′W	X	60
Callum Park	Kent	TQ8667	51°22·5′	0°40·7′E	X	178
Callybarrett	Corn	SX0868	50°29·1′	4°42·0′W	X	200
Cally Ho	Pth & Kin	NO1252	56°39·3′	3°25·7′W	X	53
Cally House	D & G	NX5955	54°52·4′	4°11·4′W	A	83
Cally Lake	D & G	NX6055	54°52·5′	4°10·5′W	W	83
Cally Loch	Pth & Kin	NO0243	56°34·4′	3°35·3′W	W	52,53
Cally Mains	D & G	NX5954	54°51·9′	4°11·4′W	X	83
Cally Palace Hotel	D & G	NX5954	54°51·9′	4°11·4′W	X	83
Cally Park	D & G	NX6054	54°51·9′	4°10·5′W	F	83
Callywith	Corn	SX0867	50°28·5′	4°42·0′W	X	200
Callywith Wood	Corn	SX0967	50°28·5′	4°41·1′W	F	200
Calmanach Wood	Pth & Kin	NO0765	56°46·3′	3°30·8′W	F	43
Calmore	Hants	SU3414	50°55·7′	1°30·6′W	T	196
Calmsden	Glos	SP0408	51°46·5′	1°56·1′W	T	163
Calmsden Gorse	Glos	SP0307	51°45·9′	1°57·0′W	F	163
Calm Slate	N Yks	SE0354	53°59·2′	1°56·8′W	X	104
Calna Taing	Shetld	HU3672	60°26·1′	1°20·3′W	X	2,3
Calne	Wilts	ST9971	51°26·5′	2°0·5′W	T	173
Calne Marsh	Wilts	SU0071	51°26·5′	1°59·6′W	T	173
Calow	Derby	SK4171	53°14·3′	1°22·7′W	T	120
Calow Brook	Derby	SK4169	53°13·2′	1°22·7′W	W	120
Calow Green	Derby	SK4169	53°13·2′	1°22·7′W	T	120
Calpa Mòr	Highld	NH6610	57°9·9′	4°12·5′W	H	35
Calrofold	Ches	SJ9474	53°16·0′	2°5·0′W	T	118
Calrossie	Highld	NH8077	57°46·3′	4°0·6′W	X	21
Calrossie Woods	Highld	NH7978	57°46·8′	4°1·6′W	F	21
Calroust	Scot Bord	NT8219	55°28·1′	2°16·7′W	X	80
Calroust Burn	Scot Bord	NT8317	55°27·0′	2°15·7′W	W	80
Calroust Hopehead	Scot Bord	NT8316	55°26·5′	2°15·7′W	X	80
Calshot	Hants	SU4701	50°48·6′	1°19·6′W	T	196
Calshot Buoy	Hants	SU5001	50°48·6′	1°17·0′W	X	196
Calshot Castle	Hants	SU4802	50°49·2′	1°18·7′W	A	196
Calside	D & G	NX7490	55°11·5′	3°58·3′W	X	77
Calside	D & G	NX9875	55°3·8′	3°35·4′W	X	84
Calstock	Devon	SX4368	50°29·7′	4°12·4′W	T	201
Calstone Down	Wilts	SU0468	51°24·9′	1°56·2′W	X	173
Calstone Wellington	Wilts	SU0268	51°24·9′	1°57·9′W	T	173
Caltanais	N Eil	NF8341	57°21·2′	7°15·8′W	X	22
Calternach	Moray	NJ3244	57°29·1′	3°7·6′W	X	28
Calternach	Moray	NJ3650	57°32·4′	3°3·7′W	X	28
Calthorpe	Norf	TG1831	52°50·2′	1°14·6′E	T	133
Calthorpe	Oxon	SP4639	52°3·1′	1°19·4′W	T	151
Calthorpe Broad	Norf	TG4125	52°46·3′	1°34·8′E	W	134
Calthorpes Fm	Essex	TL6536	52°0·1′	0°24·6′E	FM	154
Calthorpe Street	Norf	TG4025	52°46·4′	1°33·9′E	X	134
Calthwaite	Cumbr	NY4640	54°45·4′	2°49·9′W	T	86
Calton	Arg & Bt	NR7121	55°26·0′	5°36·8′W	T	68
Calton	C of Glas	NS6064	55°51·2′	4°13·8′W	T	64
Calton	N Yks	SD9059	54°1·9′	2°8·7′W	T	103
Calton	Staffs	SK1050	53°3·1′	1°50·6′W	T	119
Calton Fm	Derby	SK1171	53°14·4′	1°49·7′W	FM	119
Calton Fm	E Ayr	NS5916	55°25·3′	4°13·2′W	FM	71
Calton Gill Syke	N Yks	SD9259	54°1·9′	2°6·9′W	W	103
Calton Green	Staffs	SK1049	53°2·5′	1°50·6′W	X	119
Calton Hill	C of Edin	NT2674	55°57·5′	3°10·7′W	X	66
Calton Hill	Derby	SK1171	53°14·4′	1°49·7′W	X	119
Calton Houses	Derby	SK2468	53°12·7′	1°38·0′W	X	119
Calton Lees	Derby	SK2568	53°12·7′	1°37·1′W	X	119
Calton Moor	N Yks	SD9261	54°2·9′	2°6·9′W	X	98
Caltonmoor Ho	Staffs	SK1148	53°2·0′	1°49·8′W	X	119
Calton Pastures	Derby	SK2368	53°12·8′	1°38·9′W	X	119
Calurg Wood	Aberd	NO6092	57°1·2′	2°39·1′W	F	45
Calvadnack	Corn	SW6935	50°10·4′	5°13·7′W	T	203
Calva Hall	Cumbr	NY0526	54°37·5′	3°27·9′W	X	89
Calvay	N Eil	NF8012	57°5·5′	7°16·6′W	X	31
Calvay	N Eil	NF8118	57°8·8′	7°16·0′W	X	31
Calve Island	Arg & Bt	NM5254	56°37·0′	6°2·1′W	X	47
Calveley	Ches	SJ5958	53°7·3′	2°36·4′W	T	117
Calveley Fm	Ches	SJ5959	53°7·8′	2°36·4′W	FM	117
Calveley Green Fm	Ches	SJ6160	53°8·4′	2°34·6′W	FM	118
Calveley Hall	Ches	SJ4558	53°7·2′	2°48·9′W	X	117
Calveley Hall	Norf	TG0105	52°36·6′	0°58·5′E	X	144
Calveley Hall Fm	Ches	SJ6059	53°7·8′	2°35·5′W	FM	118
Calver	Derby	SK2474	53°16·0′	1°38·0′W	T	119
Calverhall	Shrops	SJ6037	52°56·0′	2°35·3′W	T	127
Calver Hill	Heref	SO3748	52°7·8′	2°54·8′W	T	148,149
Calver Hill	N Yks	NZ0100	54°24·0′	1°58·7′W	H	92
Calverleigh	Devon	SS9214	50°55·2′	3°31·8′W	T	181
Calverley	Leeds	SE2036	53°49·4′	1°41·4′W	T	104
Calverley House Fm	Leeds	SE2137	53°50·0′	1°40·4′W	FM	104
Calverley Wood	Leeds	SE2037	53°50·0′	1°41·4′W	F	104
Calver Peak	Derby	SK2374	53°16·0′	1°38·9′W	H	119
Calver Sough	Derby	SK2475	53°16·5′	1°38·0′W	T	119
Calvert	Bucks	SP6824	51°54·9′	1°0·3′W	T	164,165
Calvert End	Cumbr	NY7335	54°42·8′	2°24·7′W	X	91
Calvert Hos	N Yks	SD9297	54°22·4′	2°7·0′W	X	98
Calverton	Mil Key	SP7939	52°2·9′	0°50·5′W	T	152
Calverton	Notts	SK6149	53°2·3′	1°5·0′W	T	129

Calvert's Fm	Lancs	SD6023	53°42·4′	2°35·9′W	FM	102,103
Calvertsholm	D & G	NY2868	55°0·3′	3°7·1′W	X	85
Calves Bridge	Devon	SS7408	50°51·7′	3°47·0′W	X	191
Calves Croft Fm	Derby	SK2417	52°45·2′	1°38·3′W	FM	128
Calveslake Tor	Devon	SX6067	50°29·4′	3°58·0′W	X	202
Calvesland	Pemb	SS0498	51°39·0′	4°49·6′W	X	158
Calvesleys Fm	W Berks	SU5675	51°28·5′	1°11·2′W	FM	174
Calves Wood	Suff	TM0348	52°5·8′	0°58·2′E	F	155
Calvine	Pth & Kin	NN8065	56°45·9′	3°57·3′W	T	43
Calvington	Wrekin	SJ7022	52°47·9′	2°26·3′W	X	127
Calvis Hall	N Yks	SE4184	54°15·2′	1°21·8′W	X	99
Calvo	Cumbr	NY1453	54°52·1′	3°20·0′W	T	85
Calvo Marsh	Cumbr	NY1554	54°52·7′	3°19·1′W	X	85
Calway's Fm	Somer	ST1418	50°57·5′	3°13·1′W	FM	181,193
Calwich Abbey	Staffs	SK1243	52°59·3′	1°48·9′W	X	119,128
Calxton Manor	Norf	TG3303	52°34·7′	1°26·7′E	X	134
Calziebohalzie	Stir	NN7207	56°14·6′	4°3·5′W	X	57
Calziemuck	Stir	NN6200	56°10·6′	4°12·9′W	X	57
Calzieveg	Pth & Kin	NN8109	56°15·8′	3°54·8′W	X	57
Cam	Glos	ST7499	51°41·6′	2°22·2′W	T	162
Cam a' Bhealaich	Highld	NH5188	57°51·7′	4°30·2′W	H	20
Cama' Choire	Pth & Kin	NN6978	56°52·8′	4°8·5′W	X	42
Camaes	Conwy	SH8667	53°11·5′	3°42·0′W	X	116
Camaghael	Highld	NN1276	56°50·5′	5°4·5′W	T	41
Camalaig Bay	Highld	NG2350	57°27·6′	6°36·7′W	W	23
Cam Allt	Arg & Bt	NN2614	56°17·5′	4°48·2′W	W	50,56
Cam Allt	Arg & Bt	NR6939	55°35·6′	5°39·5′W	W	68
Cam-allt	Highld	NG9240	57°24·4′	5°27·3′W	X	25
Cam Allt	Stir	NN3613	56°17·1′	4°38·5′W	W	50,56
Cam Allt	Stir	NS4195	56°7·5′	4°33·0′W	W	57
Cam Alltan	Highld	NC2420	58°8·3′	4°58·9′W	W	15
Cam Alltan	Highld	NM8155	56°38·4′	5°33·8′W	W	49
Cama-loch	N Eil	NF9472	57°38·3′	7°7·2′W	W	18
Cama-lochan	N Eil	NF9074	57°39·2′	7°11·4′W	W	18
Camalynes	Aberd	NJ7543	57°28·9′	2°24·6′W	X	29
Cam-ard-Mór	N Eil	NF9167	57°35·5′	7°9·8′W	X	18
Camas a' Bhata	Highld	NG7371	57°40·6′	5°48·0′W	W	19
Camas a' Bhuailidh	Highld	NH0998	57°56·1′	5°13·1′W	W	19
Camas a'Bhuailte	Arg & Bt	NR6690	56°3·0′	5°45·0′W	W	55,61
Camas a' Bhualt	N Eil	NG1992	57°50·0′	6°43·6′W	W	14
Camas a' Bhuic	N Eil	NA9910	57°58·9′	7°5·1′W	W	13
Camas a'Chaiginn	Highld	NM8551	56°36·4′	5°29·7′W	W	49
Camas a' Challtuinn	Highld	NM8373	56°48·1′	5°32·8′W	W	40
Camas a' Charraig	Highld	NG8995	57°53·9′	5°33·2′W	W	19
Camas a' Chàrsair	Highld	NG8354	57°31·7′	5°37·0′W	W	24
Camas a' Chòis	Highld	NN0460	56°41·7′	5°11·6′W	W	41
Camas A' Chonnaidh	Highld	NH1391	57°52·4′	5°8·7′W	W	19
Camas a' Chruthaich	Highld	NG9591	57°52·0′	5°26·9′W	W	19
Camas a' ghlais' lean	Highld	NB9615	58°4·9′	5°27·1′W	X	15
Camas Aird nam Fiasgan	Highld	NM6793	56°58·4′	5°49·6′W	W	40
Camas Airigh Shamhraidh	Highld	NM8449	56°35·3′	5°30·6′W	W	49
Camas Allt a' Choire	Highld	NM6850	56°35·3′	5°46·3′W	W	49
Camas Allt Eoin Thòmais	Highld	NG8189	57°50·5′	5°40·9′W	W	19
Camas Allt nam Bearnach	N Eil	NB3608	57°59·2′	6°27·5′W	W	14
Camas a' Mhoil	N Eil	NA9825	58°6·9′	7°7·2′W	W	13
Camas a' Mhór-bheòil	Highld	NG5235	57°20·5′	6°6·8′W	W	24,32
Camas a'Mhor-Fhir	Arg & Bt	NM7007	56°12·3′	5°42·1′W	W	55
Camas a' Mhùrain	Highld	NG3916	57°9·9′	6°18·6′W	W	32
Camasan Dearga	Highld	NG7390	57°50·9′	5°49·0′W	W	19
Camas an Diamh	Highld	NH1491	57°52·5′	5°7·7′W	W	20
Camas an Dùin	Highld	NC4458	58°29·2′	4°40·1′W	W	9
Camas an Eilean	Highld	NG7558	57°33·6′	5°45·2′W	W	24
Camas an Eireannaich	Highld	NM8575	56°49·3′	5°30·9′W	W	40
Camas an Fhéidh	Arg & Bt	NM4027	56°22·1′	6°12·2′W	W	48
Camas an Lagain	Arg & Bt	NM4441	56°29·7′	6°9·1′W	W	47,48
Camas an Léim	Highld	NG8155	57°32·2′	5°39·1′W	W	24
Camas-an-Léim	Highld	NG8155	57°32·2′	5°39·1′W	X	24
Camas an Lighe	Highld	NM6168	56°44·8′	5°54·1′W	W	40
Camas an Lochain	Highld	NG8797	57°55·0′	5°35·3′W	W	19
Camas an Lochain	N Eil	NF8313	57°6·2′	7°13·7′W	W	31
Camas an Losgainn	Stir	NS3795	56°7·5′	4°36·9′W	W	56
Camas an Staca	Arg & Bt	NR4664	55°48·4′	6°2·8′W	X	60,61
Camas an t-Salainn	Highld	NM6585	56°54·1′	5°51·1′W	W	40
Camas an t-Seilisdeir	Arg & Bt	NM6828	56°23·5′	5°45·1′W	W	49
Camas Bàn	Arg & Bt	NM8532	56°26·1′	5°28·8′W	W	49
Camas Bàn	Highld	NG2841	57°23·0′	6°31·1′W	W	23
Camas Bàn	Highld	NG4942	57°24·2′	6°10·3′W	W	23
Camas Bàn	Highld	NG8410	57°8·1′	5°33·7′W	W	33
Camas Bàn	Highld	NM5661	56°40·9′	5°58·6′W	W	47
Camas Bàn	N Eil	NF6663	57°32·3′	7°34·5′W	W	22
Camas Barabhaig	Highld	NG6909	57°7·1′	5°48·5′W	W	32
Camas Beag	Highld	NG3761	57°34·0′	6°23·4′W	W	23
Camas Bhlathain	Highld	NM7668	56°45·3′	5°39·4′W	W	40
Camas Bosta	N Eil	NB1340	58°15·6′	6°53·1′W	W	13
Camas Bruaich Ruaidhe	Arg & Bt	NM8934	56°27·3′	5°25·0′W	W	49
Camas Chalaboist	N Eil	NB4117	58°4·3′	6°23·1′W	W	14
Camas Chala Moil	N Eil	NA9923	58°5·9′	7°6·1′W	W	13
Camas Chil Mhalieu	Highld	NM9055	56°38·6′	5°25·1′W	W	49
Camas Chlèidir	N Eil	NA9928	58°8·6′	7°6·5′W	W	13
Camas Choimhleachain	Highld	NM8489	56°56·8′	5°32·6′W	W	40
Camas Chonalain Beag	Highld	NG8507	57°6·5′	5°32·6′W	W	33
Camas Chrònaig	Highld	NM8145	56°33·0′	5°33·3′W	W	49
Camas Clachach	Highld	NM6368	56°44·9′	5°52·1′W	W	40
Camas Coille	Highld	NC0016	58°5·5′	5°23·1′W	W	15
Camas Cròm	Highld	NM8274	56°48·6′	5°33·8′W	W	40
Camas Crubaig	N Eil	NF9470	57°37·2′	7°7·1′W	W	18
Camas Cuil an t-Saimh	Arg & Bt	NM2623	56°19·5′	6°25·5′W	W	48
Camas Daoine Loch	Arg & Bt	NN0206	56°12·6′	5°11·1′W	W	55
Camas Daraich	Highld	NG5709	57°6·7′	6°0·4′W	W	32,39
Camas Daraich	Highld	NM5699	57°1·3′	6°0·8′W	W	32,39
Camas Deannd	Highld	NG7933	57°20·3′	5°39·9′W	W	24
Camas Domhain	Highld	NG8307	57°6·4′	5°34·5′W	W	33
Camas Driseach	Highld	NG8310	57°8·0′	5°34·7′W	W	33
Camas Driseach	Highld	NM7582	56°52·8′	5°41·1′W	W	40
Camas Drollaman	Highld	NM6382	56°52·4′	5°52·9′W	W	40
Camas Dubh	Highld	NN5372	56°49·2′	4°24·1′W	X	42
Camas Dubh	N Eil	NF9276	57°40·4′	7°9·5′W	W	18
Camas Dubh-aird	Highld	NG7833	57°20·3′	5°40·9′W	W	24
Camas Eigneig	Highld	NM7943	56°31·9′	5°35·2′W	W	49
Camas Eilean Ghlais	Highld	NB9615	58°4·9′	5°27·1′W	W	15

Camas Eunay	N Eil	NB1340	58°15·6'	6°53·1'W	W	13
Camas Fearna	Highld	NM5761	56°40·9'	5°57·6'W	W	47
Camas Fhionnairigh	Highld	NG5118	57°11·4'	6°6·8'W	W	32
Camas Garbh	Highld	NG7408	57°6·7'	5°43·5'W	W	33
Camas Geodhachan an Duilisg	N Eil	NB0438	58°14·1'	7°2·1'W	W	13
Camas Ghaoideil	Highld	NM6683	56°53·0'	5°50·0'W	W	40
Camas Glas	Highld	NG8582	57°46·8'	5°36·5'W	W	19
Camas Glas	Highld	NM6458	56°39·5'	5°50·6'W	W	49
Camas Gorm	Highld	NM7742	56°31·3'	5°37·1'W	W	49
Camas Grianach	Highld	NM7972	56°47·5'	5°36·7'W	W	40
Camas h-Atha	Highld	NM3099	57°0·5'	6°26·4'W	W	39
Camashie	Highld	NH1858	57°34·8'	5°2·2'W	X	25
Camasinas	Highld	NM6561	56°41·2'	5°49·8'W	X	40
Camas Islivig	N Eil	NA9828	58°8·5'	7°7·5'W	W	13
Camas Leathann	Highld	NM6483	56°53·0'	5°52·0'W	W	40
Camas Lèim an Taghain	Highld	NM8245	56°33·0'	5°32·4'W	W	49
Camas Leirageo	N Eil	NA9721	58°4·7'	7°7·9'W	W	13
Camas Luinge	Highld	NM7889	56°56·6'	5°38·5'W	W	40
Camas Luinge	Highld	NM8777	56°50·4'	5°29·1'W	W	40
Camas-luinie	Highld	NG9428	57°18·0'	5°24·7'W	T	25,33
Camas Malag	Highld	NG5819	57°12·1'	5°59·9'W	W	32
Camas Mhic a' Phi	Highld	NM9962	56°42·6'	5°16·6'W	W	40
Camas Mhic Chullaich	Highld	NH1362	57°36·8'	5°7·4'W	X	19
Camas Mó	N Eil	NF7676	57°39·7'	7°25·6'W	W	18
Camas Mol Griom	N Eil	NA9726	58°7·4'	7°8·3'W	W	13
Camas Mór	Arg & Bt	NM7316	56°17·2'	5°39·6'W	W	55
Camas Mór	Arg & Bt	NM7335	56°27·4'	5°40·6'W	W	49
Camas Mór	Highld	NC1000	57°57·2'	5°12·2'W	W	15
Camas Mór	Highld	NG3655	57°30·8'	6°24·0'W	W	23
Camas Mòr	Highld	NG3670	57°38·8'	6°25·0'W	W	23
Camas Mòr	Highld	NG7591	57°51·4'	5°47·1'W	W	19
Camas Mòr	Highld	NM4078	56°49·5'	6°15·2'W	W	39
Camas na Ban-tighearna	Arg & Bt	NR8965	55°50·2'	5°21·7'W	W	62
Camas na Cairidh	Highld	NM4180	56°50·6'	6°14·4'W	W	39
Camas na Ceardaich	Arg & Bt	NR9162	55°48·6'	5°19·7'W	W	62
Camas na Cille	Highld	NG2836	57°20·3'	6°30·8'W	W	23
Camas na Clibhe	N Eil	NB0837	58°13·8'	6°58·0'W	W	13
Camas na Cloiche Ruadhe	Highld	NN1596	56°58·3'	6°40·9'W	W	39
Camas na Criche	N Eil	NF7676	57°39·7'	7°25·6'W	W	18
Camasnacroise	Highld	NM8552	56°36·9'	5°29·8'W	T	49
Camas na Croise	Highld	NM8652	56°36·9'	5°28·8'W	W	49
Camas na Cùirte	Arg & Bt	NN0436	56°28·8'	5°10·5'W	W	50
Camas na Fisteodh	Highld	NG6328	57°17·1'	5°55·5'W	W	32
Camas na Geadaig	Highld	NG5832	57°19·1'	6°0·7'W	W	24,32
Camas na h-Airbhe	Highld	NM7360	56°40·9'	5°41·9'W	W	40
Camas na h-Airde	N Eil	NB0538	58°14·2'	7°1·1'W	W	13
Camas na h-Airigh	Highld	NG7973	57°41·8'	5°42·1'W	W	19
Camas na h-Annait	Highld	NG6934	57°20·5'	5°49·9'W	W	24,32
Camas na h-Eilde	Highld	NM7084	56°53·7'	5°46·1'W	W	40
Camas na h-Uamha	Highld	NG2537	57°20·7'	6°33·8'W	W	23
Camas na Leideig	Arg & Bt	NM7431	56°25·3'	5°39·4'W	W	49
Camas nam Bad	Highld	NC1534	58°15·6'	5°8·7'W	W	15
Camas nam Meanbh-chuileag	Arg & Bt	NR6689	56°2·5'	5°45·0'W	W	55,61
Camas nam Mult	Highld	NG7013	57°9·3'	5°47·7'W	W	32,33
Camas nan Alltan	Highld	NG7615	57°10·5'	5°41·9'W	W	33
Camas nan Clacha' Mora	Highld	NM5262	56°41·3'	6°2·5'W	W	47
Camas nan Gall	Arg & Bt	NM7307	56°12·3'	5°39·2'W	W	55
Camas nan Gall	Highld	NG4514	57°9·0'	6°12·5'W	W	32
Camas nan Gall	Highld	NG8123	57°15·0'	5°37·4'W	W	33
Camas nan Geall	Highld	NM5561	56°40·9'	5°59·6'W	W	47
Camas nan Gobher	Highld	NG8491	57°51·6'	5°38·0'W	W	19
Camas nan Sidhean	Highld	NG1347	57°25·6'	6°46·4'W	W	23
Camas na Roide	N Eil	NG1893	57°50·5'	6°44·7'W	W	14
Camas na Ruthaig	Highld	NN0098	57°55·9'	5°22·2'W	W	19
Camas na Sgianadin	Highld	NG6225	57°15·5'	5°56·3'W	W	32
Camas Nathais	Arg & Bt	NM8737	56°28·9'	5°27·1'W	W	49
Camas na Togalach	Highld	NM7491	56°57·6'	5°42·6'W	W	33,40
Camas Phail	Highld	NG8583	57°47·4'	5°36·6'W	W	19
Camas Pliasgaig	Highld	NG4002	57°2·4'	6°16·7'W	W	32,39
Camas-ruadh	Highld	NG8155	57°32·2'	5°39·1'W	X	24
Camas Ruadh	Highld	NM6891	56°57·4'	5°48·5'W	W	40
Camas Rubha' a' Mhurain	Highld	NM6590	56°56·8'	5°51·4'W	W	40
Camas Rubha na Liathaig	Arg & Bt	NM8734	56°27·3'	5°27·0'W	W	49
Camas Salach	Highld	NM6861	56°41·3'	5°46·9'W	X	40
Camas Sandig	N Eil	NB1337	58°14·0'	6°52·9'W	W	13
Camas Sgiotaig	Highld	NM4789	56°55·7'	6°9·0'W	W	39
Camas Shalachain	Highld	NM6146	56°33·0'	5°52·9'W	W	49
Camas Shallachain	Highld	NM9862	56°42·6'	5°17·6'W	W	40
Camas Shamhairidh	Highld	NM6345	56°32·5'	5°50·9'W	W	49
Camas Shannageadh	N Eil	NB0837	58°13·8'	6°58·0'W	W	13
Camas Sliginish	N Eil	NF8222	57°11·0'	7°15·4'W	W	31
Camas Thairbearnais	Highld	NG2306	57°4·0'	6°33·7'W	W	39
Camas Thomascro	N Eil	NB3303	57°56·4'	6°30·2'W	W	13,14
Camastianavaig	Highld	NG5039	57°22·6'	6°9·1'W	T	23,24,32
Camas Torr na Dùile	Highld	NM8246	56°33·6'	5°32·4'W	W	49
Camas Tuath	Arg & Bt	NM3524	56°20·3'	6°16·8'W	W	48
Camas Uig	N Eil	NB0233	58°11·4'	7°3·8'W	W	13
Camasunary	Highld	NG5118	57°11·4'	6°6·8'W	X	32
Camault Muir	Highld	NH5040	57°25·8'	4°29·4'W	T	26
Camb	Shetld	HU5092	60°36·8'	1°4·7'W	T	1,2
Camb	Shetld	HU5192	60°36·8'	1°3·6'W	T	1,2
Camba	N Eil	NF8440	57°20·7'	7°14·8'W	X	22
Camban	Highld	NH0518	57°12·9'	5°13·3'W	X	33
Cambeak	Corn	SX1296	50°44·2'	4°39·5'W	X	190
Cam Beck	Cumbr	NY5369	55°1·0'	2°43·7'W	W	86
Cam Beck	N Yks	SD8079	54°12·6'	2°18·0'W	W	98
Cambeckhill	Cumbr	NY5063	54°57·8'	2°46·4'W	X	86
Camber	E Susx	TQ9618	50°55·9'	0°47·8'E	T	189
Camber Castle	E Susx	TQ9218	50°56·0'	0°44·3'E	A	189
Camberley	Surrey	SU8860	51°20·2'	0°43·8'W	T	175,186
Camberlot Hall	E Susx	TQ5511	50°52·9'	0°12·6'E	X	199
Camber Sands	E Susx	TQ9518	50°55·9'	0°46·9'E	X	189
Camberwell	Sthwk	TQ3377	51°28·8'	0°4·7'W	T	176,177
Càm Bhealach	Highld	NN2493	56°59·9'	4°53·4'W	X	34
Cambir, The	N Eil	NA0701	57°49·8'	8°36·9'W	X	18
Camblee	Shetld	HU3552	60°15·3'	1°21·6'W	X	3
Camblesforth	N Yks	SE6426	53°43·8'	1°1·4'W	T	105,106
Camblesforth Common	N Yks	SE6227	53°44·4'	1°3·2'W	X	105

Cambo	Fife	NO6011	56°17·6'	2°38·3'W	X	59
Cambo	Northum	NZ0285	55°9·8'	1°57·7'W	T	81
Cambo Brigs	Fife	NO6012	56°18·2'	2°38·3'W	X	59
Cambo Fm	Fife	NO5911	56°17·6'	2°39·3'W	FM	59
Camboglanna	Cumbr	NY5163	54°57·8'	2°45·5'W	R	86
Cambois	Northum	NZ3083	55°8·7'	1°31·3'W	T	81
Cambo Ness	Fife	NO6011	56°17·6'	2°38·3'W	X	59
Camborne	Corn	SW6440	50°13·0'	5°18·1'W	T	203
Cambo Sands	Fife	NO6012	56°18·2'	2°38·3'W	X	59
Cambray Fm	Kent	TQ8866	51°21·9'	0°42·4'E	FM	178
Cambret	D & G	NX5156	54°52·8'	4°18·9'W	X	83
Cambret Hill	D & G	NX5257	54°53·4'	4°18·0'W	H	83
Cambret Moor	D & G	NX5257	54°53·4'	4°18·0'W	X	83
Cambrian Cott	Wrex	SJ4736	52°55·4'	2°46·9'W	X	126
Cambrick Hill	D & G	NX4277	55°4·0'	4°28·0'W	X	77
Cambridge	Cambs	TL4658	52°12·3'	0°8·6'E	T	154
Cambridge	Glos	SO7403	51°43·7'	2°22·2'W	T	162
Cambridge	Leeds	SE2045	53°54·3'	1°41·3'W	T	104
Cambridge	Scot Bord	NT5848	55°43·7'	2°39·7'W	T	73,74
Cambridge Airport	Cambs	TL4858	52°12·2'	0°10·4'E	X	154
Cambridge Batch	N Som	ST5269	51°25·3'	2°41·0'W	T	172,182
Cambridge Brook	Essex	TL8931	51°56·9'	0°45·4'E	W	168
Cambridge Hill	Cambs	TL6057	52°11·5'	0°20·8'E	X	154
Cambridge Hill	Suff	TL6262	52°14·2'	0°22·7'E	X	154
Cambridge Town	Sou-on-Sea	TQ9284	51°31·6'	0°46·5'E	T	178
Cam Brook	Bath & NE Somer	ST7058	51°19·5'	2°25·4'W	W	172
Cambrook Ho	Bath & NE Somer	ST6257	51°18·9'	2°32·3'W	X	172
Cambrose	Corn	SW6845	50°15·8'	5°14·9'W	T	203
Camb, The	Shetld	HU4993	60°37·3'	1°5·8'W	X	1,2
Cambus	Clackm	NS8594	56°7·8'	3°50·6'W	T	58
Cambusavie Fm	Highld	NH7796	57°56·5'	4°4·2'W	FM	21
Cambusbarron	Stir	NS7792	56°6·6'	3°58·2'W	T	57
Cambusbeg	Stir	NN6605	56°13·4'	4°9·2'W	X	57
Cambuscurrie Bay	Highld	NH7285	57°50·4'	4°8·9'W	W	21
Cambusdrenny	Stir	NS7594	56°7·6'	4°0·2'W	T	57
Cambushinnie	Pth & Kin	NN7807	56°14·7'	3°57·7'W	X	57
Cambushinnie Hill	Pth & Kin	NN7808	56°15·2'	3°57·7'W	H	57
Cambuskenneth	Stir	NS8094	56°7·7'	3°55·4'W	T	57
Cambuslang	S Lanak	NS6459	55°48·6'	4°9·8'W	T	64
Cambusmichael	Pth & Kin	NO1132	56°28·6'	3°26·2'W	X	53
Cambusmoon	W Dunb	NS4285	56°2·2'	4°31·7'W	X	56
Cambusmore	Stir	NN6506	56°13·9'	4°10·2'W	X	57
Cambusmore Lodge	Highld	NH7697	57°57·0'	4°5·2'W	X	21
Cambusnethan	N Lanak	NS8155	55°46·7'	3°53·4'W	T	65,72
Cambusnethan Ho	N Lanak	NS7853	55°45·6'	3°56·2'W	X	64
Cambus O'May	Aberd	NO4198	57°4·4'	2°57·9'W	X	37,44
Cambussorray	Highld	NH2938	57°24·3'	4°50·3'W	X	25
Cambuswallace	S Lanak	NT0438	55°37·8'	3°31·1'W	X	72
Cambwell	Scot Bord	NT0740	55°38·9'	3°28·2'W	X	72
Camcase	Fife	NO2820	56°22·3'	3°9·5'W	X	53,59
Càm Chreag	Arg & Bt	NN3033	56°27·8'	4°45·1'W	X	50
Càm Chreag	Pth & Kin	NN5349	56°36·8'	4°23·3'W	H	51
Càm Chreag	Pth & Kin	NN5838	56°31·0'	4°18·0'W	X	51
Càm Chreag	Stir	NN3734	56°28·5'	4°38·3'W	H	50
Càm Chreag	Stir	NN5424	56°23·4'	4°21·5'W	X	51
Cam Chriochan	Pth & Kin	NN4766	56°45·9'	4°29·7'W	W	42
Cam Crag	Cumbr	NY2511	54°29·6'	3°9·1'W	X	89,90
Camddwr	Cered	SN6566	52°16·8'	3°58·3'W	W	135
Camddwr	Cered	SN7754	52°10·5'	3°47·5'W	W	146,147
Camddwr	Gwyn	SH8520	52°46·2'	3°41·9'W	W	124,125
Camddwr	Powys	SO1373	52°21·1'	3°16·2'W	W	136,148
Camddwr Bleiddiad	Powys	SN8455	52°11·1'	3°41·4'W	X	147
Camddwr Fâch	Cered	SN6866	52°16·8'	3°55·7'W	W	135
Camden Fm	Oxon	SU2798	51°41·0'	1°36·2'W	FM	163
Camden Hill	Kent	TQ7938	51°7·0'	0°33·8'E	T	188
Camden Park	Brom	TQ4370	51°24·9'	0°3·8'E	X	177
Camden Park	Kent	TQ5938	51°7·4'	0°16·7'E	T	188
Camden Town	Camden	TQ2984	51°32·6'	0°8·0'W	T	176
Camden Wood	E Susx	TQ6134	51°5·2'	0°18·3'E	F	188
Cam Dhoire	Highld	NN0486	56°55·7'	5°12·8'W	X	41
Camdore Fm	Heref	SO4526	51°56·0'	2°47·6'W	FM	161
Cam & Dursley Station	Glos	SO7502	51°43·2'	2°21·3'W	X	162
Came Down	Dorset	SY6886	50°40·6'	2°26·8'W	X	194
Came Ho	Dorset	SY7088	50°41·7'	2°25·1'W	A	194
Camela Ho	E Yorks	SE6420	53°40·6'	1°1·5'W	X	105,106
Camela Ho	N Yks	SE6426	53°43·8'	1°1·4'W	X	105,106
Cameleon Lodge	Notts	SK6270	53°13·6'	1°3·9'W	X	120
Cameley	Bath & NE Somer	ST6157	51°18·9'	2°33·2'W	T	172
Cameley Ho	Bath & NE Somer	ST6057	51°18·9'	2°34·0'W	X	172
Camel Fm	Somer	ST5924	51°1·1'	2°34·7'W	FM	183
Camelford	Corn	SX1083	50°37·2'	4°40·8'W	T	200
Camel Green	Dorset	SU1212	50°54·7'	1°49·4'W	T	195
Camel Hill	Somer	ST5825	51°1·6'	2°35·5'W	H	183
Camelon	Falk	NS8680	56°0·2'	3°49·2'W	T	65
Camelon Lane	D & G	NX6864	54°57·4'	4°3·3'W	W	83,84
Camels	Corn	SW9239	50°13·1'	4°54·6'W	X	204
Camelsdale	W Susx	SU8832	51°5·1'	0°44·2'W	T	186
Camel's Path	Northum	NT7907	55°21·6'	2°19·4'W	A	80
Camel Trail	Corn	SX0070	50°30·0'	4°48·8'W	X	200
Cam End	N Yks	SD8080	54°13·2'	2°18·0'W	X	98
Camer	Kent	TQ6567	51°22·9'	0°22·7'E	T	177,178
Camer-fawr	Cered	SN6861	52°14·1'	3°55·6'W	X	146
Cameron	Fife	NO4711	56°17·6'	2°50·9'W	X	59
Cameron	Fife	NT3499	56°11·0'	3°3·4'W	T	59
Cameron	N Lanak	NS7770	55°54·7'	3°57·6'W	X	64
Cameron	W Dunb	NS3783	56°1·0'	4°36·5'W	X	56
Cameron Bridge	Fife	NT3499	56°11·0'	3°3·4'W	T	59
Cameron Burn	Fife	NO5012	56°18·1'	2°48·0'W	W	59
Cameron Fm	W Dunb	NS3782	56°0·5'	4°36·4'W	FM	56
Cameron Muir	Stir	NS4683	56°1·2'	4°27·8'W	X	57,64
Cameron Reservoir	Fife	NO4711	56°17·6'	2°50·9'W	W	59
Cameron's Moss	E Ayr	NS5242	55°39·2'	4°20·7'W	X	70
Cameron Toll	C of Edin	NT2771	55°55·9'	3°9·7'W	X	66
Cameron Wood	W Dunb	NS3682	56°0·4'	4°37·4'W	F	56
Camerory	Highld	NJ0231	57°21·8'	3°37·3'W	X	27,36

Camer Park (Country Park)	Kent	TQ6566	51°22·4'	0°22·6'E	X	177,178
Camer's Green	Worcs	SO7734	52°0·5'	2°19·7'W	T	150
Camerton	Bath & NE Somer	ST6857	51°18·9'	2°27·2'W	T	172
Camerton	Cumbr	NY0330	54°39·6'	3°29·8'W	T	89
Camerton	E Yorks	TA2226	53°43·2'	0°8·7'W	T	107
Camerton Court	Bath & NE Somer	ST6857	51°18·9'	2°27·2'W	X	172
Camerton Fm	Bath & NE Somer	ST6856	51°18·4'	2°27·2'W	FM	172
Camerton Grange	Cumbr	NY0332	54°40·7'	3°29·8'W	X	89
Camerton Hall	Cumbr	NY0330	54°39·6'	3°29·8'W	X	89
Cames Meads	Somer	ST3327	51°2·5'	2°57·0'W	X	193
Camesworth	Dorset	SY4797	50°46·4'	2°44·7'W	T	193
Came Wood	Dorset	SY6985	50°40·1'	2°25·9'W	F	194
Cam Fell	N Yks	SD8180	54°13·2'	2°17·1'W	X	98
Camffrwd	Swan	SN6004	51°43·3'	4°1·2'W	W	159
Camfield Pl	Herts	TL2606	51°44·5'	0°10·1'W	X	166
Cam Fm	N Yks	SE5481	54°13·6'	1°9·9'W	FM	100
Camford	D & G	NX3846	54°47·2'	4°30·7'W	X	83
Camforth Hall Fm	Lancs	SD5637	53°49·9'	2°39·7'W	FM	102
Càm Ghleann	Highld	NN2452	56°37·9'	4°51·7'W	X	41
Camghouran	Pth & Kin	NN5456	56°40·6'	4°22·5'W	X	42,51
Cam Gill Beck	N Yks	SD9575	54°10·5'	2°4·2'W	W	98
Cam Head	N Yks	SD9775	54°10·5'	2°2·3'W	X	98
Cam-helyg	Wrex	SJ1835	52°54·6'	3°12·8'W	X	125
Cam Ho	N Yks	SE5697	54°22·2'	1°7·9'W	X	100
Cam Houses	N Yks	SD8282	54°14·2'	2°16·2'W	X	98
Camies Stone	Aberd	NJ7617	57°14·8'	2°23·4'W	A	38
Camieston	Scot Bord	NT5729	55°33·4'	2°40·5'W	X	73,74
Camiestone	Aberd	NJ7618	57°15·4'	2°23·4'W	X	38
Camilla	Fife	NT2190	56°6·0'	3°15·8'W	X	58
Camilla Loch	Fife	NT2291	56°6·6'	3°14·8'W	W	58
Camilty Hill	W Loth	NT0459	55°49·1'	3°31·5'W	X	65,72
Camilty Plantation	W Loth	NT0559	55°49·2'	3°30·5'W	F	65,72
Camilty Water	W Loth	NT0661	55°50·2'	3°29·6'W	W	65
Camis Eskan Fm	Arg & Bt	NS3281	55°59·8'	4°41·2'W	FM	63
Camis Eskan Ho	Arg & Bt	NS3281	55°59·8'	4°41·2'W	X	63
Camisky	Highld	NN1480	56°52·7'	5°2·7'W	X	34,41
Camlad	Powys	SJ2100	52°35·8'	3°9·6'W	W	126
Camlad	Powys	SO2992	52°31·5'	3°2·4'W	W	137
Camlad	Shrops	SJ2600	52°35·8'	3°5·2'W	W	126
Camlan	Gwyn	SH8116	52°44·0'	3°45·3'W	H	124,125
Camlan	Gwyn	SH8511	52°41·3'	3°41·7'W	X	124,125
Camlet	Aberd	NO3093	57°1·6'	3°8·7'W	X	37,44
Camlet	Angus	NO4081	56°55·2'	2°58·7'W	X	44
Camling	D & G	NX8394	55°13·8'	3°50·0'W	X	78
Camlo Brook	Powys	SO0566	52°17·3'	3°23·2'W	W	136,147
Càm Loch	Arg & Bt	NM9009	56°13·9'	5°22·8'W	W	55
Càm Loch	Arg & Bt	NM9301	56°9·7'	5°19·6'W	W	55
Cam Loch	Arg & Bt	NR8287	56°1·8'	5°29·5'W	W	55
Cam Loch	Highld	NC2113	58°4·5'	5°1·6'W	W	15
Camlo Hill	Powys	SO0369	52°18·9'	3°25·0'W	H	136,147
Cam Long Down	Glos	ST7799	51°41·6'	2°19·6'W	H	162
Camlork	I of M	SC3578	54°10·5'	4°31·3'W	X	95
Cammachmore	Aberd	NO9094	57°2·5'	2°9·4'W	T	38,45
Cammachmore Bay	Aberd	NO9295	57°3·0'	2°7·5'W	W	38,45
Cammal Burn	Stir	NS6487	56°3·6'	4°10·6'W	W	57
Cammall	I of M	SC3288	54°15·9'	4°34·4'W	X	95
Cammarnaint	Conwy	SH6973	53°14·5'	3°57·4'W	X	115
Cammas Hall	Essex	TL5615	51°48·9'	0°16·2'E	A	167
Cammen Mawr	Powys	SJ0719	52°45·9'	3°22·3'W	X	125
Cammen Ucha	Powys	SJ0619	52°45·9'	3°23·2'W	X	125
Cammeringham	Lincs	SK9482	53°19·8'	0°34·9'W	T	121
Cammeringham Grange	Lincs	SK9581	53°19·3'	0°34·0'W	X	121
Cammerlaws	Scot Bord	NT6550	55°44·8'	2°33·0'W	X	67,74
Camm Ho	Lancs	SD5552	53°58·0'	2°40·7'W	X	102
Cammo	C of Edin	NT1774	55°57·4'	3°19·3'W	X	65,66
Cammock Hill	Pth & Kin	NN8959	56°42·8'	3°48·4'W	H	52
Cammock Burn	S Ayr	NX2683	55°6·9'	4°43·3'W	W	76
Cammock Fm	Angus	NO2358	56°42·7'	3°15·0'W	FM	53
Cammock Lodge	Angus	NO2259	56°43·2'	3°16·0'W	X	53
Cammock Rigg	Cumbr	NY6177	55°5·4'	2°36·2'W	X	86
Cammon Stone	N Yks	SE6299	54°23·2'	1°2·3'W	A	94,100
Camnant	Carm	SN6343	52°4·3'	3°59·5'W	W	146
Camnant	Cered	SN4445	52°5·1'	4°16·2'W	X	146
Camnant	Powys	SN9532	51°58·8'	3°31·3'W	X	160
Camnant	Powys	SO0783	52°26·5'	3°21·7'W	W	136
Camnant	Powys	SO0883	52°26·5'	3°20·8'W	X	136
Camnant	Powys	SO0956	52°11·9'	3°19·5'W	T	147
Camnant Brook	Powys	SO0955	52°11·4'	3°19·5'W	W	147
Camock Hill	Aberd	NJ2604	57°7·5'	3°12·9'W	H	37
Camois Hall	Cambs	TL6558	52°12·0'	0°25·3'E	X	154
Camomile Fm	N Yks	SE7290	54°18·3'	0°53·2'W	FM	94,100
Camoquhill	Stir	NS5389	56°4·5'	4°21·3'W	T	57
Camoquhill Douglas	Stir	NS5389	56°4·5'	4°21·3'W	X	57
Camore	Highld	NH7790	57°53·2'	4°4·0'W	T	21
Camore Burn	Aberd	NJ2411	57°11·3'	3°15·0'W	W	36
Camore Wood	Highld	NH7789	57°52·7'	4°4·0'W	F	21
Camoys Court	E Susx	TQ4215	50°55·2'	0°1·6'E	X	198
Camoys Court	Oxon	SU5998	51°40·9'	1°8·4'W	X	164
Camp	Devon	SX3888	50°40·4'	4°17·2'W	X	190
Camp	Lincs	SK8854	53°4·8'	0°40·8'W	T	121
Camp	Shetld	HP6413	60°48·0'	0°48·9'W	X	1
Campa	Arg & Bt	NR1965	55°48·1'	6°28·6'W	X	60
Campaign Fm	Lincs	TF3575	53°15·5'	0°1·8'E	FM	122
Cam Pasture	N Yks	SD8282	54°14·2'	2°16·2'W	X	98
Cam Pasture	N Yks	SD9673	54°9·4'	2°3·3'W	X	98
Campay	N Eil	NB1442	58°16·7'	6°52·3'W	X	13
Camp Barn	Glos	SP1812	51°48·6'	1°43·9'W	X	163
Campbarn	Shrops	SO4581	52°25·7'	2°48·1'W	X	137,138
Campbell Cleuch	D & G	NX9699	55°16·7'	3°37·8'W	X	78
Campbell Park	Mil Key	SP8639	52°2·8'	0°44·4'W	X	152
Campbell's Burn	D & G	NX4670	55°0·3'	4°24·1'W	W	77
Campbells Fm	Warw	SP3670	52°19·8'	1°27·9'W	FM	140
Campbells Hill	E Ayr	NS5202	55°17·6'	4°19·4'W	H	77
Campbell's Platform	Gwyn	SH6741	52°57·2'	3°58·4'W	X	124
Campbelton	D & G	NX6552	54°50·9'	4°5·7'W	X	83,84
Campbelton	N Ayr	NS1950	55°42·8'	4°52·4'W	X	63
Campbeltown	Arg & Bt	NR7120	55°25·5'	5°36·7'W	T	68

Campbeltown Loch	Arg & Bt	NR7420	55°25·6'	5°33·9'W	W	68
Campbeltown Loch	Arg & Bt	NR7520	55°25·6'	5°32·9'W	W	68,69
Camp Burn	Scot Bord	NT3910	55°23·1'	2°57·3'W	W	79
Camp Burn Fm	Leic	SP5986	52°28·4'	1°7·5'W	FM	140
Camp Close	Suff	TL7673	52°19·8'	0°35·4'E	F	155
Camp Corner	Oxon	SP6403	51°43·6'	1°4·0'W	T	164,165
Camp Cottage	Arg & Bt	NR9965	55°50·4'	5°12·2'W	X	62
Camp Cottages	Wilts	SU0937	51°8·2'	1°51·9'W	X	184
Camp Dale	N Yks	TA0577	54°10·9'	0°23·0'W	X	101
Campdalmore	Moray	NJ1519	57°15·5'	3°24·1'W	X	36
Campden Ashes	Glos	SP1334	52°0·5'	1°48·2'W	X	151
Campden Hill Fm	Glos	SP1436	52°1·6'	1°47·4'W	FM	151
Campden Ho	Glos	SP1337	52°2·1'	1°48·2'W	X	151
Campden Tunnel	Glos	SP1640	52°3·7'	1°45·6'W	X	151
Campdouglas	D & G	NX7265	54°58·0'	3°59·5'W	X	83,84
Camp down	Dorset	ST8808	50°52·5'	2°9·8'W	X	194
Camp Down	Wilts	SU1133	51°6·0'	1°50·2'W	X	184
Campend	Midlo	NT3168	55°54·3'	3°5·8'W	X	66
Camperdown	Northum	NZ0653	54°52·5'	1°54·0'W	X	87
Camperdown	N Tyne	NZ2772	55°2·8'	1°34·2'W	T	88
Camperdown Country Park	C of Dun	NO3632	56°28·8'	3°1·9'W	X	54
Camperdown Fm	Corn	SX1279	50°35·1'	4°39·0'W	FM	200
Camperdown Hill	Shetld	HU4569	60°24·4'	1°10·5'W	H	2,3
Campers' Corner	Cumbr	NY3672	55°2·6'	2°59·7'W	X	85
Campfield	Northum	NT8538	55°38·4'	2°13·9'W	X	74
Campfield Fm	Cumbr	NY1960	54°55·9'	3°15·4'W	FM	85
Campfield Ho	Aberd	NJ6600	57°5·6'	2°33·2'W	X	38
Campfield Place	Surrey	TQ1342	51°10·2'	0°22·6'W	X	187
Camp Fm	Bucks	SP6812	51°48·4'	1°0·4'W	FM	164,165
Camp Fm	Essex	TL5115	51°49·0'	0°11·8'E	FM	167
Camp Fm	Glos	SP1415	51°50·2'	1°47·4'W	FM	163
Camp Fm	Glos	SP1420	51°52·9'	1°47·4'W	FM	163
Camp Fm	Lincs	SK9926	52°49·6'	0°31·4'W	FM	130
Camp Fm	Northnts	SP5335	52°0·9'	1°13·3'W	FM	152
Camp Fm	Staffs	SJ7324	52°49·0'	2°23·6'W	FM	127
Camp Fm	Staffs	SK1101	52°36·6'	1°49·9'W	FM	139
Camp Fm	Staffs	SO8489	52°30·2'	2°13·7'W	FM	138
Camp Fm	Warw	SP2395	52°33·4'	1°39·2'W	FM	139
Camp Fm	Warw	SP2873	52°21·5'	1°34·9'W	FM	140
Camp Fm	Worcs	SO7465	52°17·2'	2°22·5'W	FM	138,150
Camp Green	Derby	SK2381	53°19·8'	1°38·9'W	A	110
Camp Green Fm	Suff	TM1863	52°13·5'	1°11·9'E	FM	156
Camphill	Aberd	NJ5607	57°9·4'	2°43·2'W	X	37
Camphill	C of Aber	NJ8500	57°5·7'	2°14·4'W	X	38
Camphill	Derby	SK1878	53°18·2'	1°43·4'W	T	119
Camphill	D & G	NX8668	54°59·9'	3°46·5'W	X	84
Camp Hill	E Susx	TQ4628	51°2·2'	0°5·3'E	H	188,198
Camp Hill	Kent	TQ5146	51°11·8'	0°10·1'E	X	188
Camp Hill	Kirk	SE0516	53°38·7'	1°55·1'W	T	110
Camp Hill	Liv	SJ4285	53°21·8'	2°51·9'W	X	108
Camp Hill	Northum	NT8232	55°35·1'	2°16·7'W	X	74
Camphill	Northum	NT9754	55°47·0'	2°2·4'W	X	75
Camp Hill	Northum	NU1322	55°29·7'	1°47·2'W	X	75
Camphill	Northum	NY9176	55°4·9'	2°8·0'W	X	87
Camp Hill	Notts	SK6658	53°7·1'	1°0·4'W	X	120
Camp Hill	N Yks	SE3182	54°14·2'	1°31·0'W	T	99
Camp Hill	Pemb	SN1113	51°47·3'	4°44·0'W	T	158
Camp Hill	Somer	ST5214	50°55·6'	2°40·6'W	X	194
Camp Hill	Staffs	SJ7740	52°57·7'	2°20·1'W	H	118
Camp Hill	Warw	SP3392	52°31·7'	1°30·4'W	T	140
Camp Hill	W Susx	TQ0311	50°53·6'	0°31·7'W	X	197
Camphill Fm	Norf	TM3088	52°26·7'	1°23·5'E	FM	156
Camp Hill Plantn	N Yks	SE3082	54°14·2'	1°32·0'W	F	99
Camp Hill Prison	I of W	SZ4890	50°42·7'	1°18·8'W	X	196
Camphill Resr	N Ayr	NS2655	55°45·7'	4°46·0'W	W	63
Camp Ho	Durham	NZ3432	54°41·2'	1°27·9'W	X	93
Camp Ho	Lancs	SD5767	54°6·1'	2°39·0'W	X	97
Camp Ho	Northum	NZ1382	55°8·2'	1°47·3'W	X	81
Camp Ho	N Yks	SE2879	54°12·6'	1°33·8'W	X	99
Camp House	Glos	SO7623	51°54·5'	2°20·5'W	A	162
Camphouse	Scot Bord	NT6713	55°24·8'	2°30·8'W	X	80
Camp House Fm	Leeds	SE2442	53°52·7'	1°37·7'W	FM	104
Camphouses	Northum	NT9746	55°42·7'	2°2·4'W	X	75
Campi Geo	Orkney	HY4813	59°0·3'	2°53·8'W	X	6
Camping Hill	Norf	TF9743	52°57·1'	0°56·4'E	X	132
Campingholm	D & G	NY3371	55°2·0'	3°2·5'W	X	85
Campion Hills	Warw	SP3266	52°17·7'	1°31·4'W	T	151
Campions	Essex	TL4812	51°47·4'	0°9·2'E	T	167
Camp Knowe	Scot Bord	NT5335	55°36·6'	2°44·3'W	X	73
Campland Hill	D & G	NT0210	55°22·7'	3°32·4'W	H	78
Cample	D & G	NX8993	55°13·4'	3°44·3'W	X	78
Cample Burn	Renf	NS3062	55°49·5'	4°42·4'W	W	63
Cample Cleuch	D & G	NX9199	55°16·6'	3°42·5'W	X	78
Cample Water	D & G	NX9094	55°13·9'	3°43·4'W	W	78
Camp Moor	Scot Bord	NT7251	55°45·3'	2°26·3'W	X	67,74
Campmuir	Pth & Kin	NO2137	56°31·4'	3°16·6'W	X	53
Campney Grange Fm	Lincs	TF1567	53°11·5'	0°16·3'W	FM	121
Camp Plantns	Scot Bord	NT5637	55°37·7'	2°41·5'W	F	73
Camp Ring	Shrops	SO4982	52°26·3'	2°44·6'W	X	137,138
Camp Ring (Motte & Bailey)	Shrops	SO4982	52°26·3'	2°44·6'W	A	137,138
Camps	W Loth	NT1068	55°54·1'	3°25·9'W	X	65
Campsall	Donc	SE5413	53°36·9'	1°10·6'W	T	111
Campscott Fms	Devon	SS4945	51°11·3'	4°9·3'W	FM	180
Camps End	Cambs	TL6142	52°3·4'	0°21·3'E	T	154
Campsey Ash	Suff	TM3356	52°9·4'	1°24·8'E	X	156
Campsfield	Oxon	SP4615	51°50·1'	1°19·5'W	T	164
Camps Hall	Cambs	TL6143	52°3·9'	0°21·3'E	X	154
Campshead	S Lanak	NT0121	55°28·6'	3°33·5'W	X	72
Camps Heath	Suff	TM5194	52°29·4'	1°42·2'E	T	134
Camp Shiel	Scot Bord	NT3432	55°34·9'	3°2·4'W	X	73
Campshill Fm	Pemb	SN0509	51°45·0'	4°49·1'W	FM	158
Campsie	Pth & Kin	NN9828	56°26·2'	3°38·8'W	X	52,53,58
Campsie	Pth & Kin	NO1233	56°29·1'	3°25·3'W	X	53
Campsie Dene	Stir	NS5580	55°59·7'	4°19·1'W	X	64
Campsie Fells	Stir	NS6083	56°1·4'	4°14·3'W	X	57,64
Campsie Glen	E Dunb	NS6180	55°59·8'	4°13·3'W	X	64
Campsie Hill	Pth & Kin	NO1333	56°29·1'	3°24·3'W	X	53
Campsie Linn	Pth & Kin	NO1234	56°29·6'	3°25·3'W	W	53

Campsie Muir	Stir	NS6383	56°1·5'	4°11·5'W	X	57,64
Camps Knowe Wood	S Lanak	NT0122	55°29·2'	3°33·6'W	F	72
Campsmount Home Fm	Donc	SE5314	53°37·4'	1°11·5'W	FM	111
Camps Reservoir	S Lanak	NT0022	55°29·1'	3°34·5'W	W	72
Campston	Orkney	HY5303	58°55·0'	2°48·5'W	X	6,7
Camp Stone, The	Stir	NN6906	56°14·0'	4°6·4'W	A	57
Campston Hill	Monm	SO3622	51°53·8'	2°55·4'W	X	161
Camps Water	S Lanak	NS9822	55°29·1'	3°36·4'W	W	72
Camps Wood	Suff	TL9346	52°4·9'	0°49·4'E	F	155
Camp, The	Heref	SO3866	52°17·6'	2°54·1'W	H	137,148,149
Camp, The	N Yks	TA0676	54°10·4'	0°22·1'W	X	101
Camp, The (Earthworks)	N Yks	TA0676	54°10·4'	0°22·1'W	A	101
Campton	Beds	TL1338	52°2·0'	0°20·8'W	T	153
Camptonbury Fm	Beds	TL1237	52°1·4'	0°21·7'W	FM	153
Camptoun	E Loth	NT5077	55°59·3'	2°47·6'W	T	66
Camp Town	Leeds	SE3039	53°51·0'	1°32·2'W	T	104
Camptown	Scot Bord	NT6713	55°24·8'	2°30·8'W	T	80
Campville	Northum	NT9402	55°19·0'	2°5·2'W	X	80
Campville Ho	Staffs	SK2609	52°40·9'	1°36·5'W	X	128,140
Camquhart	Arg & Bt	NR9985	56°1·2'	5°13·1'W	X	55
Cam Rakes	N Yks	SD8281	54°13·7'	2°16·1'W	X	98
Camregan	S Ayr	NX2199	55°15·4'	4°48·6'W	X	76
Camregan Hill	S Ayr	NX2197	55°14·3'	4°48·5'W	X	76
Camriach	Highld	NJ1134	57°23·5'	3°28·4'W	X	28
Camrie	D & G	NX2060	54°54·4'	4°48·0'W	X	82
Camrie Burn	D & G	NX1959	54°53·8'	4°48·9'W	W	82
Camrie Fell	D & G	NX1960	54°54·4'	4°49·0'W	H	82
Camrose	Pemb	SM9220	51°50·6'	5°0·8'W	T	157,158
Camrose Brook	Pemb	SM9120	51°50·6'	5°1·7'W	W	157,158
Cams	Hants	SU6314	50°55·5'	1°5·8'W	X	196
Camserney	Pth & Kin	NN8149	56°37·3'	3°55·9'W	T	52
Camserney Burn	Pth & Kin	NN7951	56°38·4'	3°57·9'W	W	42,51,52
Camserney Burn	Pth & Kin	NN8050	56°37·8'	3°56·9'W	W	52
Cam Sgeir	Arg & Bt	NR3842	55°36·3'	6°9·2'W	X	60
Cam Sgeir	Arg & Bt	NR4244	55°37·5'	6°5·5'W	X	60
Camsgill	Cumbr	SD5483	54°14·7'	2°41·9'W	X	97
Cams Hall	Hants	SU5805	50°50·7'	1°10·2'W	X	196
Camshaw's Plantation	Lincs	TF1274	53°15·3'	0°18·9'W	F	121
Cams Head	N Yks	SE5379	54°12·5'	1°10·8'W	X	100
Cam's Hill	Wilts	ST9385	51°34·1'	2°5·7'W	H	173
Cams Ho	N Yks	SD9190	54°18·6'	2°7·9'W	X	98
Camsiscan	S Ayr	NS4531	55°33·1'	4°27·0'W	X	70
Camsix Fm	Essex	TL6817	51°49·8'	0°26·7'E	FM	167
Cam Spout Crag	Cumbr	NY2105	54°26·3'	3°12·7'W	X	89,90
Cams Rock	Arg & Bt	NM8337	56°28·8'	5°31·0'W	X	49
Camster	Highld	ND2060	58°31·5'	3°21·9'W	X	11,12
Camster Burn	Highld	ND2446	58°24·0'	3°17·5'W	W	11,12
Camster Lodge	Highld	ND2641	58°21·3'	3°15·4'W	X	11,12
Camstone Rigg	Northum	NY7978	55°6·0'	2°19·3'W	X	86,87
Camstraddan Ho	Arg & Bt	NS3592	56°5·8'	4°38·7'W	X	56
Cam, The	Bath & NE Somer	ST6157	51°18·9'	2°33·2'W	W	172
Cam, The	Dorset	ST6611	50°54·1'	2°28·6'W	W	194
Camus a' Chuilinn	Highld	NN0469	56°46·5'	5°12·0'W	W	41
Camusaneighin	Highld	NM8393	56°58·9'	5°33·8'W	X	33,40
Camuschoirk	Highld	NM7660	56°40·9'	5°39·0'W	X	40
Camus Croise	Highld	NG7011	57°8·2'	5°47·6'W	W	32,33
Camuscross	Highld	NG6911	57°8·2'	5°48·6'W	T	32
Camusdarach	Highld	NM6691	56°57·3'	5°50·5'W	X	40
Camusericht Fm	Pth & Kin	NN5057	56°41·1'	4°26·5'W	FM	42,51
Camusericht Lodge	Pth & Kin	NN5158	56°41·7'	4°25·5'W	X	42,51
Camuslongart	Highld	NG8827	57°17·3'	5°30·6'W	X	33
Camuslusta	Highld	NG2655	57°30·4'	6°34·0'W	X	23
Camusnagaul	Highld	NH0689	57°51·2'	5°15·7'W	T	19
Camusnagaul	Highld	NN0974	56°49·4'	5°7·3'W	T	41
Camus nan Gall	Highld	NH0689	57°51·2'	5°15·7'W	W	19
Camusrory	Highld	NM8595	57°0·0'	5°32·0'W	X	33,40
Camus's Cross	Angus	NO5237	56°31·6'	2°46·4'W	A	54
Camus's Stone	Moray	NJ1568	57°41·9'	3°25·1'W	A	28
Camusteel	Highld	NG7042	57°24·9'	5°49·3'W	T	24
Camusterrach	Highld	NG7141	57°24·4'	5°48·3'W	T	24
Camusurich	Stir	NN6334	56°29·0'	4°13·0'W	X	51
Camusvrachan	Pth & Kin	NN6247	56°35·9'	4°14·4'W	T	51
Camvlodvnvm (Colchester)	Essex	TL9925	51°53·5'	0°53·9'E	R	168
Camwell Hall	Herts	TL4117	51°50·3'	0°3·2'E	X	167
Cam Woodlands	N Yks	SD8280	54°13·2'	2°16·1'W	X	98
Camy	Orkney	HY5301	58°53·9'	2°48·5'W	X	6,7
Cam-yr-Alyn	Wrex	SJ3657	53°6·6'	2°57·0'W	X	117
Canaan Fm	Leic	SP5287	52°28·9'	1°13·7'W	FM	140
Canaan Fm	Notts	SK5725	52°49·4'	1°8·8'W	FM	129
Canabony	D & G	NX9857	54°54·1'	3°35·0'W	X	84
Canada	E Yorks	SE8964	54°4·1'	0°38·0'W	X	101
Canada	Hants	SU2817	50°57·3'	1°35·7'W	T	184
Canada	Lincs	TA1201	53°29·9'	0°18·3'W	T	113
Canada	Northnts	SP5849	52°8·4'	1°8·8'W	X	152
Canada	Northum	NU1204	55°20·0'	1°48·2'W	X	81
Canada Bottom	W Susx	TQ1408	50°51·8'	0°22·4'W	X	198
Canada Common	Hants	SU2817	50°57·3'	1°35·7'W	X	184
Canada Cotts	Suff	TL9846	52°4·8'	0°53·8'E	X	155
Canada Cotts	W Susx	SU8613	50°54·8'	0°46·2'W	X	197
Canada Fm	Dorset	ST9914	50°55·8'	2°0·5'W	FM	195
Canada Fm	Lincs	TF2253	53°3·9'	0°10·4'W	FM	122
Canada Fm	Somer	ST4140	51°9·6'	2°50·2'W	FM	182
Canada Fm	Suff	TL7775	52°20·9'	0°36·3'E	FM	144
Canada Hill	Scot Bord	NT2235	55°36·4'	3°13·9'W	H	73
Canada West	Orkney	HY2825	59°6·6'	3°15·0'W	X	6
Canadia	E Susx	TQ7417	50°55·8'	0°29·0'E	T	199
Canaglaze	Corn	SX1981	50°36·3'	4°33·1'W	X	201
Canakey Wood	Corn	SX2060	50°25·0'	4°31·6'W	F	201
Canal Burn	Highld	NN3590	56°58·6'	4°42·4'W	W	34
Canal Fm	Leic	SK8516	52°44·3'	0°44·1'W	FM	130
Canal Fm	Notts	SK7029	52°51·5'	0°57·2'W	FM	129
Canal Foot	Cumbr	SD3177	54°11·3'	3°3·0'W	T	96,97
Canal Head	E Yorks	SE7947	53°55·0'	0°47·4'W	X	105,106
Canal Side	Donc	SE6812	53°36·2'	0°57·9'W	T	111
Canal, The	D & G	NX3950	54°49·4'	4°29·9'W	W	83
Canary Ledges	Dorset	SY3592	50°43·7'	2°54·9'W	X	193
Canary Wharf	T Ham	TQ3780	51°30·4'	0°1·2'W	X	177
Canaston	Pemb	SN0714	51°47·7'	4°47·5'W	X	158
Canaston Bridge	Pemb	SN0615	51°48·2'	4°48·4'W	X	158

Canaston Wood	Pemb	SN0813	51°47·2'	4°46·6'W	F	158
Canbus	Clackm	NS8593	56°7·2'	3°50·5'W	T	58
Cancleave Strand	Corn	SX1799	50°45·9'	4°35·3'W	X	190
Can Court Fm	Wilts	SU1081	51°31·9'	1°51·0'W	FM	173
Candacraig	Aberd	NO3399	57°4·9'	3°5·9'W	X	37,44
Candacraig Ho	Aberd	NJ3311	57°11·4'	3°6·1'W	X	37
Cander Moss	S Lanak	NS7846	55°41·8'	3°56·0'W	X	64
Canderside	S Lanak	NS7647	55°42·3'	3°58·0'W	X	64
Canderside Toll	S Lanak	NS7648	55°42·8'	3°58·0'W	X	64
Cander Water	S Lanak	NS7645	55°41·2'	3°57·9'W	W	64
Canderwater	S Lanak	NS7744	55°40·7'	3°56·9'W	X	71
Candie	Falk	NS9374	55°57·1'	3°42·4'W	X	65
Candie-end	Falk	NS9273	55°56·5'	3°43·3'W	X	65
Candiehead	Falk	NS9373	55°56·5'	3°42·4'W	X	65
Candie Ho	Falk	NS9374	55°57·1'	3°42·4'W	X	65
Candieshill	Aberd	NO7496	57°3·5'	2°25·3'W	X	38,45
Candle Hill	Aberd	NJ5929	57°21·2'	2°40·4'W	H	37
Candle of the Sale	Orkney	HY2701	58°53·7'	3°15·5'W	X	6,7
Candle of the Sneuk	Orkney	ND2195	58°50·4'	3°21·6'W	X	7
Candlesby	Lincs	TF4567	53°11·1'	0°10·6'E	T	122
Candlesby Hill	Lincs	TF4568	53°11·6'	0°10·6'E	X	122
Candleston Castle	Brig	SS8777	51°29·1'	3°37·3'W	A	170
Candle Stone	Aberd	NJ9234	57°24·0'	2°7·5'W	A	30
Candleston Fm	Brig	SS8777	51°29·1'	3°37·3'W	FM	170
Candle Street	Suff	TM0374	52°19·8'	0°59·2'E	T	144
Candlet	Suff	TM2936	51°58·7'	1°20·5'E	X	169
Candle, The	Orkney	ND3289	58°46·7'	3°10·1'W	X	7
Candover Copse	Hants	SU5540	51°9·6'	1°12·4'W	F	185
Candover Ho	Hants	SU5839	51°9·1'	1°9·9'W	X	185
Candovers	Hants	SU7535	51°6·8'	0°55·3'W	X	186
Can Down	Wilts	SU0550	51°15·2'	1°55·3'W	X	184
Candra	Corn	SX1177	50°34·0'	4°39·8'W	X	200
Candra Hill	Corn	SX1379	50°35·1'	4°38·1'W	X	200
Candrens	Renf	NS4565	55°51·5'	4°28·1'W	X	64
Candwr Brook	Torf	ST3295	51°39·2'	2°58·6'W	W	171
Candy	Aberd	NJ5330	57°21·7'	2°46·4'W	X	29,37
Candy	Aberd	NO7980	56°54·9'	2°20·2'W	X	45
Candy	Shrops	SJ2528	52°50·9'	3°6·4'W	X	126
Candybank	S Lanak	NT0741	55°39·5'	3°28·3'W	X	72
Candy Burn	S Lanak	NT0741	55°39·5'	3°28·3'W	W	72
Candycraig	Aberd	NO4797	57°3·9'	2°52·0'W	X	37,44
Candy Fm	Donc	SE6903	53°31·4'	0°57·1'W	FM	111
Candyglirach	Aberd	NJ7501	57°6·2'	2°24·3'W	X	38
Candy Mill	Denb	SJ1071	53°13·9'	3°20·5'W	X	116
Candy Mill	S Lanak	NT0741	55°39·5'	3°28·3'W	X	72
Candymill Burn	S Lanak	NS9050	55°44·1'	3°44·7'W	W	65,72
Cane End	Oxon	SU6779	51°30·6'	1°1·7'W	T	175
Cane End Fm	Oxon	SU6879	51°30·6'	1°0·8'W	FM	175
Canefield	Hants	SU3025	51°1·6'	1°33·9'W	X	185
Canegore Corner	Somer	ST5725	51°1·6'	2°36·4'W	X	183
Caneheath	E Susx	TQ5507	50°50·7'	0°12·5'E	T	199
Caner	Brig	SS9486	51°34·0'	3°31·4'W	X	170
Canerw	Carm	SN1924	51°53·4'	4°37·4'W	X	145,158
Canes Fm	Essex	TL4806	51°44·2'	0°9·0'E	FM	167
Canewdon	Essex	TQ8994	51°37·0'	0°44·2'E	T	168,178
Canfield End	Essex	TL5821	51°52·1'	0°18·1'E	T	167
Canfield Hart	Essex	TL5619	51°51·1'	0°16·3'E	F	167
Canford Cliffs	Poole	SZ0589	50°42·3'	1°55·4'W	T	195
Canford Cliffs Chine	Poole	SZ0589	50°42·3'	1°55·4'W	X	195
Canford Heath	Poole	SZ0294	50°45·0'	1°57·9'W	T	195
Canford Heath	Poole	SZ0395	50°45·5'	1°57·1'W	X	195
Canford Magna	Poole	SZ0398	50°47·1'	1°57·1'W	T	195
Canford School	Poole	SZ0398	50°47·1'	1°57·1'W	X	195
Cangate	Norf	TG3219	52°43·4'	1°26·5'E	T	133,134
Cangle, The	Essex	TL8331	51°57·1'	0°40·2'E	X	168
Canham's Fm	Suff	TL7445	52°4·8'	0°32·8'E	FM	155
Canham's Fm	Suff	TM2674	52°19·3'	1°19·4'E	FM	156
Canham's Green	Suff	TM0565	52°14·9'	1°0·6'E	T	155
Canholes	Derby	SK0471	53°14·4'	1°56·0'W	T	119
Canisbay	Highld	ND3472	58°38·1'	3°7·7'W	T	7,12
Canis Dale	Shetld	HU5082	60°31·4'	1°4·8'W	X	1,2,3
Canisp	Highld	NC2018	58°7·1'	5°2·9'W	H	15
Canister Fm	Leic	SK4412	52°42·5'	1°20·5'W	FM	129
Canister Fm	Norf	TF8514	52°41·7'	0°44·7'E	FM	132
Canister Fm	Norf	TF9114	52°41·6'	0°50·0'E	FM	132
Canister Hall	Lincs	TF2949	53°1·6'	0°4·2'W	X	131
Canister Hall	Norf	TF8927	52°48·7'	0°48·7'E	X	132
Canister Hall Fm	Norf	TF9335	52°52·9'	0°52·5'E	FM	132
Cank	Worcs	SP0456	52°12·4'	1°56·1'W	X	150
Canker	Orkney	HY6941	59°15·5'	2°32·1'W	X	5
Cank Fm	Northnts	SP7068	52°18·6'	0°58·0'W	FM	152
Canklow	Roth	SK4290	53°24·5'	1°21·7'W	T	111
Canley	Cov	SP3077	52°23·6'	1°33·1'W	T	140
Canllefaes	Cered	SN2148	52°6·3'	4°36·4'W	X	145
Cannamore	Angus	NO4547	56°37·0'	2°53·3'W	X	54
Cann	Dorset	ST8721	50°59·5'	2°10·7'W	T	183
Canna	Highld	NG2405	57°3·5'	6°32·7'W	X	39
Cannaframe Fm	Corn	SX2078	50°34·7'	4°32·2'W	FM	201
Canna Harbour	Highld	NG2804	57°3·1'	6°28·7'W	W	39
Cannalidgey	Corn	SW9369	50°29·3'	4°54·7'W	T	200
Cannamore Fm	Devon	SX6957	50°24·1'	3°50·2'W	FM	202
Canna Park	Devon	SX7183	50°38·2'	3°49·1'W	X	191
Cannard's Grave	Somer	ST6241	51°10·3'	2°32·2'W	T	183
Cannaway's Fm	N Som	ST3861	51°20·9'	2°53·0'W	FM	182
Cann Common	Dorset	ST8821	50°59·5'	2°9·9'W	T	183
Cannee	D & G	NX6850	54°49·9'	4°2·9'W	X	83,84
Cannerheugh	Cumbr	NY6141	54°46·0'	2°35·9'W	X	86
Cannes Fm	Monm	SO5114	51°49·6'	2°42·3'W	FM	162
Canness Burn	Angus	NO2077	56°52·9'	3°18·3'W	W	44
Canness Glen	Angus	NO2076	56°52·4'	3°18·3'W	X	44
Cannfield Fm	Dorset	ST8821	50°59·5'	2°9·9'W	FM	183
Cannich	Highld	NH3331	57°20·6'	4°46·0'W	T	26
Canniehole	W Loth	NT0463	55°51·3'	3°31·6'W	X	65
Canniemyre	Orkney	HY5003	58°54·9'	2°51·6'W	X	6,7
Canniesile	Orkney	HY5000	58°53·3'	2°51·6'W	X	6,7
Cannigal	Orkney	HY4407	58°57·1'	2°57·9'W	X	6,7
Cannimore	Wilts	ST8443	51°11·4'	2°13·4'W	X	183
Canning Knowe	Shetld	HU4592	60°36·8'	1°10·2'W	X	1,2
Cannings Court	Dorset	ST7107	50°51·9'	2°24·3'W	X	194
Cannings Cross Fm	Wilts	SU0763	51°22·2'	1°53·6'W	FM	173

Cannington	Somer	ST2539	51°9·0′	3°4·0′W	T	182
Cannington Brook	Somer	ST2739	51°9·0′	3°2·2′W	W	182
Cannington Fm	Devon	SY3192	50°43·6′	2°58·3′W	FM	193
Cannington Park	Somer	ST2440	51°9·5′	3°4·8′W	H	182
Canning Town	Newham	TQ4081	51°30·9′	0°1·5′E	T	177
Cannis	Corn	SX1049	50°18·9′	4°39·8′W	X	200,204
Cannlane Fm	Ches	SJ6879	53°18·7′	2°28·4′W	FM	118
Cannock	Staffs	SJ9810	52°41·5′	2°1·4′W	T	127
Cannock Chase	Staffs	SJ9917	52°45·3′	2°0·5′W	X	127
Cannock Chase Country Park	Staffs	SJ9718	52°45·8′	2°2·3′W	X	127
Cannock Chase Country Park	Staffs	SK0017	52°45·3′	1°59·6′W	X	128
Cannock Chase Forest	Staffs	SJ9915	52°44·2′	2°0·5′W	F	127
Cannock Hill	E Ayr	NS6404	55°18·9′	4°8·2′W	H	77
Cannock Wood	Staffs	SK0412	52°42·6′	1°56·0′W	T	128
Cann Office	Powys	SJ0110	52°41·0′	3°27·5′W	X	125
Canno Mill	Northum	NT9031	55°34·6′	2°9·1′W	X	74,75
Cannon	Powys	SH9507	52°39·3′	3°32·7′W	X	125
Cannon Barn	Devon	SX4487	50°39·9′	4°12·1′W	X	190
Cannon Court Fm	Win & Maid	SU8783	51°32·6′	0°44·3′W	FM	175
Cannon Fm	Kent	TQ7543	51°9·8′	0°30·6′E	FM	188
Cannon Hall Country Park	Barns	SE2708	53°34·3′	1°35·1′W	X	110
Cannon Heath Down	Hants	SU5056	51°18·3′	1°16·6′W	X	174
Cannon Heath Fm	Hants	SU5055	51°17·7′	1°16·6′W	FM	174,185
Cannon Hill	Devon	SS7044	51°11·1′	3°51·2′W	H	180
Cannon Hill	Merton	TQ2368	51°24·1′	0°13·5′W	X	176
Cannon Hill Park	Birm	SP0683	52°26·9′	1°54·3′W	X	139
Cannon Hill Plantation	Dorset	SU0401	50°48·7′	1°56·2′W	F	195
Cannonhills	Aberd	NJ9565	57°40·7′	2°4·6′W	X	30
Cannonholm	S Lanak	NS8145	55°41·3′	3°53·1′W	X	72
Cannon House Fm	York	SE6747	53°55·1′	0°58·4′W	FM	105,106
Cannon Ponds	Glos	SO6010	51°47·5′	2°34·4′W	W	162
Cannons	Essex	TL5517	51°50·0′	0°15·4′E	X	167
Cannon's Green	Essex	TL5706	51°44·1′	0°16·8′E	T	167
Cannon St Sta	C of Lon	TQ3280	51°30·4′	0°5·5′W	X	176,177
Cannon, The	Shetld	HU2077	60°28·8′	1°37·7′W	X	3
Cannonwalls Fm	Devon	SY0288	50°41·2′	3°22·9′W	FM	192
Cannop	Glos	SO6011	51°48·0′	2°34·4′W	T	162
Cannop Brook	Glos	SO6112	51°48·6′	2°33·5′W	W	162
Cann Orchard	Corn	SS2304	50°48·7′	4°30·4′W	X	190
Canns Hill	Heref	SO3931	51°58·7′	2°52·9′W	X	149,161
Cann's Mill Bridge	Devon	SS7810	50°52·8′	3°43·7′W	X	191
Cann Wood	Devon	SX5359	50°25·0′	4°3·8′W	F	201
Cann Wood	Powys	SO3063	52°15·9′	3°1·1′W	F	137,148
Canny Hill	Cumbr	SD3785	54°15·7′	2°57·6′W	H	96,97
Canolfan Blaencwm	Gwyn	SH6445	52°59·3′	4°1·2′W	X	115
Canon Barns	Essex	TQ7599	51°40·0′	0°32·2′E	X	167
Canonbie	D & G	NY3976	55°4·7′	2°56·9′W	T	85
Canon Bridge	Heref	SO4341	52°4·1′	2°49·5′W	T	148,149,161
Canonbury	Isling	TQ3284	51°32·6′	0°5·4′W	T	176,177
Canon Frome	Heref	SO6543	52°5·3′	2°30·3′W	T	149
Canonium (Kelvedon)	Essex	TL8618	51°50·0′	0°42·4′E	R	168
Canon Pyon	Heref	SO4648	52°7·9′	2°46·9′W	T	148,149
Canon Pyon Ho	Heref	SO4450	52°9·0′	2°48·7′W	X	148,149
Canons Ashby	Northnts	SP5750	52°9·0′	1°9·6′W	A	152
Canons Ashby	Northnts	SP5750	52°9·0′	1°9·6′W	T	152
Canon's Barn	Glos	SP0819	51°52·4′	1°52·6′W	X	163
Canonscourt Fm	Glos	ST7493	51°38·3′	2°22·2′W	FM	162,172
Canons Fm	Surrey	TQ2457	51°18·1′	0°12·9′W	FM	187
Canonsgrove	Somer	ST2121	50°59·2′	3°7·1′W	T	193
Canonsleigh Fm	Devon	ST0617	50°56·9′	3°19·9′W	FM	181
Canons Park	Harrow	TQ1891	51°36·6′	0°17·4′W	T	176
Canonstown	Corn	SW5335	50°10·1′	5°27·2′W	T	203
Canonteign Barton	Devon	SX8383	50°38·3′	3°38·9′W	A	191
Canonteign Ho	Devon	SX8382	50°37·8′	3°38·9′W	X	191
Canon Winder	Cumbr	SD3574	54°9·7′	2°59·3′W	X	96,97
Canopus	Corn	SW4226	50°4·9′	5°36·0′W	X	203
Canovium (Roman Fort)	Conwy	SH7770	53°13·0′	3°50·1′W	R	115
Canridden Wood	Shrops	SJ7142	52°58·7′	2°25·5′W	F	118
Cans Dale	N Yks	TA0674	54°9·3′	0°22·2′W	X	101
Cansdale FM	N Yks	TA0774	54°9·3′	0°21·3′W	FM	
Cansford Fm	Corn	SX1693	50°42·7′	4°36·0′W	FM	190
Cant	Pemb	SN0128	51°55·1′	4°53·2′W	X	145,157,158
Cantaba Fm	Denb	SJ1357	53°6·4′	3°17·6′W	FM	116
Cant Beck	Lancs	SD6374	54°9·9′	2°33·6′W	W	97
Cant Burn	D & G	NX7799	55°16·4′	3°55·7′W	W	78
Cant Clough Resr	Lancs	SD8930	53°46·2′	2°9·6′W	W	103
Cant Cove	Corn	SW9574	50°32·0′	4°53·2′W	W	200
Cantel Hall Fm	Powys	SO1473	52°21·1′	3°15·4′W	FM	136,148
Cantelupe Fm	Cambs	TL4254	52°10·2′	0°5·0′E	FM	154
Canterbury	Aberd	NJ5659	57°37·4′	2°43·7′W	X	29
Canterbury	Kent	TR1457	51°16·5′	1°4·5′E	T	179
Canterburys	Essex	TL6600	51°40·7′	0°24·5′E	X	167
Canterbury Tye Hall	Essex	TQ5996	51°38·6′	0°18·3′E	X	167,177
Canterland	Aberd	NO7064	56°46·3′	2°29·0′W	X	45
Cantern Brook	Shrops	SO6995	52°33·4′	2°27·0′W	W	138
Canter's Doles	Cambs	TL2595	52°32·5′	0°9·0′W	X	142
Canterton Manor	Hants	SU2713	50°55·2′	1°36·6′W	X	195
Cantfield's Fm	Essex	TL9120	51°51·0′	0°46·8′E	FM	168
Cant Fm	Corn	SW9574	50°32·0′	4°53·2′W	FM	200
Cant Hill	Corn	SW9474	50°32·0′	4°54·0′W	H	200
Cant Hills	N Lanak	NS8562	55°50·5′	3°49·8′W	X	65
Cantick	Orkney	ND3489	58°47·3′	3°8·0′W	X	7
Cantick Head	Orkney	ND3489	58°47·3′	3°8·0′W	X	7
Cantick Sound	Orkney	ND3590	58°47·8′	3°7·0′W	W	7
Cantlayhills	Aberd	NO8890	57°0·3′	2°11·4′W	X	38,45
Cantley	Donc	SE6202	53°30·9′	1°3·5′W	T	111
Cantley	Norf	TG3803	52°34·6′	1°31·2′E	T	134
Cantley Common	Donc	SE6302	53°30·9′	1°2·6′W	X	111
Cantley Fm	Norf	TG1804	52°35·6′	1°13·5′E	FM	134
Cantley Fm	Suff	TM3174	52°19·1′	1°23·8′E	FM	156
Cantley Grange	Norf	TG3803	52°34·6′	1°31·2′E	X	134
Cantlin Stone	Shrops	SO2086	52°28·2′	3°10·3′W	X	137
Cantlop	Shrops	SJ5205	52°38·7′	2°42·2′W	T	126
Cantlop Br	Shrops	SJ5106	52°39·2′	2°43·1′W	X	126
Cantlop Wood	Shrops	SJ5104	52°38·1′	2°43·0′W	F	126
Canton	Card	ST1676	51°28·8′	3°12·2′W	T	171
Cantraybruich	Highld	NH7746	57°29·5′	4°2·7′W	X	27

Cantraydoune	Highld	NH7946	57°29·5′	4°0·7′W	X	27
Cantray Ho	Highld	NH7948	57°30·6′	4°0·7′W	X	27
Cantraywood	Highld	NH7847	57°30·1′	4°1·7′W	T	27
Cantref Resr	Powys	SN9915	51°49·7′	3°27·5′W	W	160
Cantreyn	Shrops	SO7194	52°32·8′	2°25·3′W	X	138
Cantsdam	Fife	NT1493	56°7·6′	3°22·6′W	X	58
Cantsfield	Lancs	SD6272	54°8·8′	2°34·5′W	T	97
Cantsford	Moray	NJ0754	57°34·3′	3°32·8′W	X	27
Cant's Hill	Bucks	SU9383	51°32·5′	0°39·1′W	X	175
Cantsmill	Angus	NO3252	56°39·5′	3°6·1′W	X	53
Cants, The	Scot Bord	NT4327	55°32·3′	2°53·8′W	X	73
Canty Bay	E Loth	NT5885	56°3·6′	2°40·0′W	W	67
Canty Burn	E Loth	NT4374	55°57·6′	2°54·3′W	W	66
Cantyhall	E Loth	NT4375	55°58·1′	2°54·4′W	X	66
Cantyhall	Fife	NO3015	56°19·6′	3°7·5′W	X	59
Cantyhall	Fife	NO5204	56°13·8′	2°46·0′W	X	59
Cantyhaugh	S Lanak	NT0344	55°41·0′	3°32·1′W	X	72
Cantywheery	Stir	NS5481	56°0·2′	4°20·0′W	X	64
Canvers Fm	N Yks	SE4589	54°17·9′	1°18·1′W	FM	99
Canvey Island	Essex	TQ7883	51°31·3′	0°34·3′E	T	178
Canvey Point	Essex	TQ8383	51°31·2′	0°38·7′E	X	178
Canwell Hall	Staffs	SK1400	52°36·1′	1°47·2′W	X	139
Canwick	Lincs	SK9869	53°12·8′	0°31·5′W	T	121
Canwick Manor Fm	Lincs	SK9967	53°11·7′	0°30·7′W	FM	121
Canwood Fm	Heref	SO6037	52°2·0′	2°34·6′W	FM	149
Canwood Knoll	Heref	SO6137	52°2·0′	2°33·7′W	H	149
Canworthy	Corn	SX2292	50°42·3′	4°30·9′W	X	190
Canworthy Water	Corn	SX2291	50°41·7′	4°30·8′W	T	190
Canyards	Sheff	SK2595	53°27·3′	1°37·0′W	X	110
Caochan a' Chùil	Highld	NH6821	57°15·9′	4°10·9′W	W	26,35
Caochan an Eich Bhuidhe	Pth & Kin	NN4248	56°36·1′	4°34·0′W	W	51
Caochan an Leathaid Bhàin	Pth & Kin	NN6162	56°44·0′	4°15·9′W	W	42
Caochan an t-Sneachda	Highld	NH5617	57°13·5′	4°22·7′W	W	35
Caochan Bheithe	Highld	NJ0710	57°10·5′	3°31·8′W	W	36
Caochan Breac	Highld	NH7127	57°19·2′	4°8·1′W	W	35
Caochan Cam	Highld	NH1611	57°9·4′	5°2·1′W	W	34
Caochan Crom	Aberd	NJ2514	57°12·9′	3°14·1′W	W	37
Caochan Cròm	Highld	NH7517	57°13·9′	4°3·8′W	W	35
Caochan Cròm nan Eag	Highld	NH7714	57°12·3′	4°1·7′W	W	35
Caochan Dir na Lair	Highld	NH8943	57°28·1′	3°50·6′W	W	27
Caochan Donn Beag	Highld	NN4073	56°49·5′	4°36·9′W	W	42
Caochan Dubh	Highld	NN8786	56°57·3′	3°51·0′W	W	43
Caochan Dubh	Highld	NH8994	57°1·7′	3°49·3′W	W	35,36,43
Caochan Dubh	Moray	NJ2045	57°29·6′	3°19·6′W	W	28
Caochan Dubh	Pth & Kin	NN4652	56°38·3′	4°30·2′W	W	42,51
Caochan Duine	Highld	NH7911	57°10·7′	3°59·6′W	W	35
Caochandye Hill	Aberd	NJ3220	57°16·2′	3°7·2′W	H	37
Caochan Easg' àn Lochain	Highld	NH8012	57°11·2′	3°58·7′W	W	35
Caochan Glac na Criche	Highld	NN6389	56°58·6′	4°14·8′W	W	42
Caochan Glac na Criche	Highld	NN6390	56°59·1′	4°14·8′W	W	35
Caochan Greusaiche	Pth & Kin	NN4248	56°36·1′	4°34·0′W	W	51
Caochan Lùb	Pth & Kin	NN8182	56°55·1′	3°56·8′W	W	43
Caochan Meadhonach	Highld	NH6721	57°15·9′	4°11·9′W	W	26,35
Caochan Mór	Highld	NH7710	57°10·1′	4°1·6′W	W	35
Caochan na Feòraige	Highld	NH7814	57°12·3′	4°0·7′W	W	35
Caochan na Gaibhre	Highld	NH7409	57°9·5′	4°4·5′W	W	35
Caochan na Gaibhre	Highld	NH8018	57°14·5′	3°58·8′W	W	35
Caochan na Lùibe	Highld	NC6423	58°10·8′	4°18·1′W	W	16
Caochan nam Meann	Pth & Kin	NN4759	56°42·1′	4°29·5′W	W	42,51
Caochan nan Sac	Highld	NH7308	57°9·0′	4°5·5′W	W	35
Caochan Riabhach	Highld	NH2005	57°6·3′	4°57·9′W	W	34
Caochan Uchdach	Highld	NH5702	57°5·5′	4°21·1′W	W	35
Caochan Uilleim	Highld	NH4702	57°5·3′	4°31·0′W	W	34
Caoikain	Arg & Bt	NR7582	55°59·0′	5°36·0′W	H	55
Caol	Highld	NN1076	56°50·5′	5°6·4′W	T	41
Caol Abhainn	Arg & Bt	NR3652	55°41·6′	6°11·6′W	W	60
Caolas	Arg & Bt	NM0848	56°32·3′	6°44·6′W	T	46
Caolas a Deas	N Eil	NB3609	57°59·8′	6°27·6′W	W	14
Caolas a' Mhill Ghairbh	Highld	NB9708	58°1·2′	5°25·7′W	W	15
Caolas a' Mhòrain	N Eil	NF8480	57°42·2′	7°17·9′W	W	18
Caolas an Eilein	Arg & Bt	NM2255	56°36·5′	6°31·4′W	W	46,47
Caolas an Eilein	Arg & Bt	NR3844	55°37·4′	6°9·3′W	W	60
Caolas an Eilein	Highld	NA9821	58°4·8′	7°6·9′W	W	13
Caolas an Fhuraidh	Highld	NG7992	57°52·0′	5°43·1′W	X	19
Caolas an Iaruinn	N Eil	NF7907	57°2·8′	7°17·2′W	W	31
Caolas an Iasgaich	Arg & Bt	NR3686	55°59·9′	6°13·6′W	W	61
Caolas an Lamhachaidh	Highld	NG7920	57°13·3′	5°39·2′W	W	33
Caolas Annraidh	Arg & Bt	NM2926	56°21·2′	6°22·8′W	W	48
Caolas an Scarp	N Eil	NA9812	57°59·9′	7°6·2′W	W	13
Caolas a' Phlòtha	Arg & Bt	NR4763	55°47·9′	6°1·8′W	W	60,61
Caolas a Tuath	N Eil	NB3810	58°0·4′	6°25·6′W	W	14
Caolas Bàn	Arg & Bt	NM1151	56°34·0′	6°41·8′W	W	46
Caolas Beag	Highld	NG7478	57°44·4′	5°47·4′W	W	19
Caolas Beag	N Eil	NG1490	57°48·8′	6°48·5′W	W	14
Caolas Chèabhagh	N Eil	NB1935	58°13·1′	6°46·7′W	W	8,13
Caolas Craro	Arg & Bt	NR6248	55°40·3′	5°46·7′W	W	62
Caolas Eilean nan Caorach	Arg & Bt	NR3644	55°37·3′	6°11·2′W	W	60
Caolas Eilean Ràrsaidh	Highld	NG8111	57°8·5′	5°38·7′W	W	33
Caolas Eilean Ristol	Highld	NB9710	58°2·2′	5°25·9′W	W	15
Caolas Fhlodaigh	N Eil	NF8255	57°28·7′	7°17·9′W	X	22
Caolas Fhlodaigh	N Eil	NF8454	57°28·2′	7°15·8′W	W	22
Caolas Gigalum	Arg & Bt	NR6446	55°39·3′	5°44·7′W	W	62
Caolas Harsgir	N Eil	NB1141	58°16·0′	6°55·2′W	W	13
Caolas Isgeir	N Eil	NB5562	58°28·9′	6°11·7′W	W	8
Caolas Liubharsaigh	N Eil	NF8339	57°20·1′	7°15·7′W	X	22
Caolas Liursaigh	N Eil	NF8640	57°20·8′	7°12·8′W	W	22
Caolas Loch Portain	N Eil	NF9469	57°36·7′	7°6·7′W	W	18
Caolas Mhic an Athar	Arg & Bt	NR3686	55°59·9′	6°13·6′W	W	61
Caolas Mór	Arg & Bt	NR3686	55°59·9′	6°13·6′W	W	61
Caolas Mór	Highld	NG7035	57°21·1′	5°48·9′W	W	24
Caolas Mór	Highld	NG8806	57°6·0′	5°29·6′W	W	33
Caolasmór	Highld	NG8806	57°6·0′	5°29·6′W	H	33
Caolas Mòr	N Eil	NF8438	57°19·6′	7°14·6′W	W	22
Caolasnacon	Highld	NN1460	56°41·9′	5°1·8′W	X	41
Caolas na h-Airde	Highld	NM6844	56°32·1′	5°45·9′W	W	49
Caolas nan Gall	Arg & Bt	NR1651	55°40·4′	6°30·6′W	W	60
Caolas na Sgeir	N Eil	NB1301	57°54·6′	6°50·3′W	X	14
Caolas na Sgeire Leithe	N Eil	NB1137	58°13·9′	6°54·9′W	W	13
Caolas Orasaigh	N Eil	NF8650	57°26·2′	7°13·5′W	W	22

Caolas Port na Lice	Arg & Bt	NR4649	55°40·3′	6°1·9′W	W	60
Caolas Rahuaidh	Highld	NM6356	56°38·4′	5°51·5′W	W	49
Caolas Scalpaigh	N Eil	NG2198	57°53·8′	6°42·0′W	T	14
Caolas Scalpaigh	N Eil	NG2297	57°52·8′	6°40·9′W	W	14
Caolas Scalpay	Highld	NG6027	57°16·5′	5°58·4′W	W	32
Caolas-sgeire-buidhe	N Eil	NG1795	57°51·6′	6°45·8′W	X	14
Caolas Shaoidh	N Eil	NB0605	57°56·5′	6°57·6′W	W	13,14
Caolas Shiolaigh	N Eil	NF5962	57°31·4′	7°41·4′W	W	22
Caolas Soa	Arg & Bt	NM1551	56°34·1′	6°37·9′W	W	46
Caolas Stocinis	N Eil	NG1391	57°49·3′	6°49·6′W	T	14
Caolas Stulaigh	N Eil	NF8223	57°11·5′	7°15·4′W	W	22
Caolas Stulaigh	N Eil	NF8223	57°11·5′	7°15·4′W	X	22
Caol Beag	Highld	NC6664	58°32·9′	4°17·7′W	W	10
Caol Bheinn	Highld	NM7749	56°35·1′	5°37·4′W	H	49
Caol Chàrna	Highld	NM6258	56°39·5′	5°52·6′W	W	49
Caol Creran	Arg & Bt	NN0950	56°36·4′	5°6·3′W	X	41
Caoldairidh	Arg & Bt	NM4552	56°35·7′	6°8·8′W	X	47
Caoles	Arg & Bt	NM1252	56°34·6′	6°40·9′W	X	46
Caol Fladda	Highld	NG5950	57°28·8′	6°0·8′W	W	24
Caol-ghleann	Arg & Bt	NS0693	56°5·7′	5°6·7′W	X	56
Caol Ghleann	Moray	NJ1404	57°7·4′	3°24·8′W	W	36
Caol Ghleann	Stir	NS3798	56°9·1′	4°37·0′W	X	56
Caol Ila	Arg & Bt	NR4269	55°51·0′	6°6·9′W	T	60,61
Caolis	N Eil	NL6297	56°56·7′	7°33·1′W	X	31
Caol Lairig	Highld	NN2885	56°55·7′	4°49·1′W	X	34,41
Caol-loch	Highld	NC7659	58°30·4′	4°7·2′W	W	10
Caol-loch	Highld	NC8458	58°30·0′	3°58·9′W	W	10
Caol-loch	Highld	NC8555	58°28·4′	3°57·8′W	W	10
Caol-loch	Highld	NC9261	58°31·7′	3°50·8′W	W	11
Caol Loch	Highld	ND0248	58°24·8′	3°40·2′W	W	11,12
Caol Loch	N Eil	NB1023	58°6·3′	6°54·9′W	W	13,14
Caol Loch	N Eil	NB1531	58°10·8′	6°50·4′W	W	13
Caol Loch a' Mhind	Highld	NC2645	58°21·8′	4°58·0′W	W	9
Caol-Lochan	Arg & Bt	NM4444	56°31·4′	6°9·3′W	W	47,48
Caol-Lochan	Arg & Bt	NM5150	56°34·8′	6°2·8′W	W	47
Caol Lochan	Highld	NC2844	58°21·3′	4°55·9′W	W	9
Caol Lochan	Highld	NM7848	56°34·5′	5°36·4′W	W	49
Caol-loch Beag	Highld	NC7743	58°21·8′	4°5·7′W	W	10
Caol-loch Creag nan Laogh	Highld	NC7657	58°29·3′	4°7·1′W	W	10
Caol-loch Mór	Highld	NC7844	58°22·3′	4°4·7′W	W	10
Caol Mór	Highld	NG5733	57°19·6′	6°1·8′W	W	24,32
Caol Raineach	Highld	NC6364	58°32·8′	4°20·8′W	W	10
Caol Rona	Highld	NG6154	57°31·1′	5°59·0′W	W	24
Caol Ruadh	Arg & Bt	NS0175	55°55·9′	5°10·7′W	X	63
Caol Scotnish	Arg & Bt	NR7688	56°2·2′	5°35·3′W	W	55
Caonich	Highld	NN0692	56°59·0′	5°11·1′W	X	33
Caorainn Achaidh Burn	Stir	NN3704	56°12·3′	4°37·2′W	W	56
Capan Nathraichean	Aberd	NO2288	56°58·9′	3°16·5′W	H	44
Cape Cornwall	Corn	SW3431	50°7·4′	5°42·9′W	X	203
Cape Fm	S Glos	ST8082	51°32·4′	2°16·9′W	FM	173
Capehall Fm	Glos	SO7604	51°44·3′	2°20·5′W	FM	162
Capehope Burn	Scot Bord	NT7815	55°26·0′	2°20·4′W	W	80
Capel	Carm	SN5101	51°41·5′	4°9·0′W	T	159
Capel	Cered	SN1847	52°5·7′	4°39·0′W	X	145
Capel	Kent	TQ6344	51°10·5′	0°20·3′E	T	188
Capel	Powys	SO1528	51°56·9′	3°13·8′W	X	161
Capel	Shetld	HU4878	60°29·2′	1°7·1′W	X	2,3
Capel	Surrey	TQ1740	51°9·1′	0°19·2′W	T	187
Capel	V of Glam	SS9369	51°24·8′	3°31·9′W	X	170
Cape Law	Scot Bord	NT1315	55°25·5′	3°22·0′W	H	78
Capelaw Hill	C of Edin	NT2165	55°52·6′	3°15·3′W	H	66
Capel Bangor	Cered	SN6580	52°24·3′	3°58·7′W	T	135
Capel Bettws	Carm	SN2728	51°55·7′	4°30·6′W	A	145,158
Capel Betws Lleucu	Cered	SN6058	52°12·4′	4°2·5′W	T	146
Capel Burn	Angus	NO2978	56°53·5′	3°9·5′W	W	44
Capel Burn	D & G	NX9799	55°16·7′	3°36·9′W	W	78
Capel Burn	D & G	NY2585	55°9·5′	3°10·2′W	W	79
Capel Carmel	Gwyn	SH1628	52°49·3′	4°43·4′W	X	123
Capel Church Fm	Kent	TR2540	51°7·1′	1°13·3′E	FM	179
Capel Coch	I of Angl	SH4582	53°19·0′	4°19·2′W	T	114,115
Capel Cross	Kent	TQ7140	51°8·2′	0°27·1′E	T	188
Capel Ct	Kent	TR2538	51°6·0′	1°13·2′E	X	179
Capel Curig	Conwy	SH7258	53°6·5′	3°54·3′W	T	115
Capel Cynon	Cered	SN3849	52°7·2′	4°21·6′W	X	145
Capel Dewi	Carm	SN4720	51°51·7′	4°12·9′W	T	159
Capel Dewi	Carm	SN6517	51°50·4′	3°57·2′W	A	159
Capel Dewi	Cered	SN4542	52°3·5′	4°15·3′W	T	146
Capel Dewi	Cered	SN6282	52°25·4′	4°1·4′W	T	135
Capel-Dewi-uchaf	Carm	SN4820	51°51·7′	4°12·1′W	X	159
Capel Fell	D & G	NT1607	55°21·2′	3°19·1′W	H	79
Capel Fleet	Kent	TR0169	51°23·3′	0°53·7′E	W	178
Capel Fm	Kent	TR1151	51°13·4′	1°1·7′E	FM	179,189
Capel Fm	Suff	TL9256	52°10·4′	0°48·9′E	FM	155
Capelfoot	D & G	NY2386	55°10·0′	3°12·1′W	X	79
Capel Galltcoed	Gwyn	SH4740	52°56·4′	4°16·2′W	A	123
Capel Garmon	Conwy	SH8154	53°4·4′	3°46·2′W	X	116
Capel Garmon	Conwy	SH8155	53°5·0′	3°46·2′W	T	116
Capel Garmon (Chambered Long Cairn)	Conwy	SH8154	53°4·4′	3°46·2′W	A	116
Capel Grange	Kent	TQ6545	51°11·0′	0°22·0′E	X	188
Capel Green	Suff	TM3649	52°5·6′	1°27·1′E	T	169
Capelgrove	Suff	TM0937	51°59·7′	1°3·1′E	X	155,169
Capel Gwnda	Cered	SN3247	52°6·0′	4°26·8′W	X	145
Capel Gwyn	I of Angl	SH3475	53°15·0′	4°28·9′W	T	114
Capel Gwynfe	Carm	SN7222	51°53·2′	3°51·2′W	T	160
Capel Hall	Suff	TM2837	51°59·3′	1°19·6′E	X	169
Capel Hendre	Carm	SN5911	51°47·0′	4°2·3′W	T	159
Capel Hermon	Gwyn	SH7425	52°48·7′	3°51·8′W	X	124
Capel Hill	D & G	NS9006	55°20·4′	3°43·6′W	H	71,78
Capel Hill	Pth & Kin	NO0352	56°39·2′	3°34·5′W	H	52,53
Capel Hill Fm	Kent	TR0069	51°23·3′	0°52·9′E	FM	178
Capel Ho	Kent	TQ9935	51°5·0′	0°50·9′E	X	189
Capel Horeb	Powys	SJ0303	52°37·2′	3°25·6′W	X	136
Capel How	Cumbr	NY0427	54°38·0′	3°28·8′W	X	89
Capeli	Cered	SN5451	52°8·5′	4°7·6′W	X	146
Capel Ifan	Carm	SN4915	51°49·0′	4°11·1′W	X	159
Capel-isaf	Carm	SN6625	51°54·7′	3°56·5′W	X	146
Capel Issac	Carm	SN5827	51°55·6′	4°3·5′W	T	146
Capel Iwan	Carm	SN2936	52°0·0′	4°29·1′W	T	145

Capel-lago	Carm	SN5442	52°3·7′	4°7·4′W	X	146
Capell Crag	Cumbr	NY2411	54°29·6′	3°10·0′W	X	89,90
Capel-le-Ferne	Kent	TR2438	51°6·1′	1°12·4′E	T	179,189
Capel Leyse	Surrey	TQ1644	51°11·2′	0°20·0′W	X	187
Capellie Fm	E Renf	NS4658	55°47·7′	4°27·0′W	FM	64
Capel Llanilterne	Card	ST0979	51°30·4′	3°18·3′W	T	171
Capel Mawr	I of Angl	SH4171	53°13·0′	4°22·5′W	T	114,115
Capel Mounth	Aberd	NO2980	56°54·6′	3°9·5′W	X	44
Capel Mounth	Angus	NO2978	56°53·5′	3°9·5′W	X	44
Capel Newydd	Gwyn	SH2830	52°50·6′	4°32·8′W	X	123
Capel Parc	I of Angl	SH4486	53°21·1′	4°20·2′W	T	114
Capel Seion	Carm	SN5113	51°48·0′	4°9·3′W	T	159
Capel Seion	Cered	SN6379	52°23·8′	4°0·4′W	T	135
Capel Siloam	Conwy	SH8353	53°3·9′	3°44·4′W	T	116
Capel St Andrew	Suff	TM3748	52°5·0′	1°28·0′E	T	169
Capel St Mary	Suff	TM0938	52°0·3′	1°3·1′E	T	155,169
Capelstones	Aberd	NJ9145	57°30·0′	2°8·6′W	X	30
Capel-Tydist	Carm	SN6624	51°54·1′	3°56·5′W	X	159
Capel Tygwydd	Cered	SN2743	52°3·7′	4°31·0′W	T	145
Capel Uchaf	Gwyn	SH4349	53°1·2′	4°20·0′W	T	115,123
Capelulo	Conwy	SH7476	53°16·2′	3°53·0′W	T	115
Capel Vicar	Cered	SN4556	52°11·1′	4°15·6′W	X	146
Capel Water	D & G	NX9794	55°14·0′	3°36·7′W	W	78
Capel-y-ffin	Powys	SO2531	51°58·6′	3°5·1′W	T	161
Capel-y-graig	Gwyn	SH5469	53°12·1′	4°10·7′W	T	114,115
Capel-y-Groes	Cered	SN5247	52°6·3′	4°9·3′W	X	146
Capenhurst	Ches	SJ3673	53°15·3′	2°57·2′W	T	117
Capenoch	D & G	NX3850	54°49·4′	4°30·9′W	X	83
Capenoch	D & G	NX8493	55°13·3′	3°49·0′W	X	78
Capenoch Croft	D & G	NX3851	54°49·9′	4°30·9′W	X	83
Capenoch Loch	D & G	NX8392	55°12·8′	3°49·9′W	W	78
Capenoch Moor	D & G	NX8392	55°12·8′	3°49·9′W	X	78
Cape of Good Hope Fm	Ches	SJ7173	53°15·4′	2°25·7′W	FM	118
Cape of Good Hope Fm	N Yks	SE6568	54°6·5′	0°59·9′W	FM	100
Capernwray	Lancs	SD5371	54°8·2′	2°42·7′W	T	97
Capernwray Hall	Lancs	SD5472	54°8·8′	2°41·8′W	X	97
Caper's Fm	Surrey	TQ4148	51°13·1′	0°1·5′E	FM	187
Capesthorne Hall	Ches	SJ8472	53°14·9′	2°14·0′W	X	118
Capeston	Pemb	SM8609	51°44·6′	5°5·6′W	X	157
Cape, The	Ches	SJ4550	53°2·9′	2°48·8′W	X	117
Cape, The	Cumbr	NY3613	54°30·7′	2°58·9′W	H	90
Capet Law	Renf	NS2960	55°48·4′	4°43·3′W	H	63
Cape Wrath	Highld	NC2574	58°37·4′	5°0·3′W	X	9
Capheaton	Northum	NZ0380	55°7·1′	1°56·7′W	T	81
Caphill Moss	Cumbr	SD7193	54°20·2′	2°26·3′W	X	98
Capielaw	Midlo	NT3061	55°50·5′	3°6·6′W	X	66
Capilus Hill	Scot Bord	NT1118	55°27·1′	3°24·0′W	H	78
Capin	Shetld	HU2279	60°29·9′	1°35·5′W	X	3
Capite, The	W Susx	TQ1617	50°56·7′	0°20·5′W	X	198
Caplaich Burn	Highld	ND0938	58°19·5′	3°32·7′W	W	11,17
Caplaich Hill	Highld	ND1037	58°19·0′	3°31·7′W	H	11,17
Capland	Somer	ST3018	50°57·7′	2°59·4′W	T	193
Caplaw	E Renf	NS4458	55°47·7′	4°28·9′W	X	64
Cap Law	Midlo	NT1759	55°49·3′	3°19·0′W	X	65,66,72
Caplaw Burn	S Lanak	NT0225	55°30·8′	3°32·7′W	W	72
Caplaw Dam	Renf	NS4358	55°47·6′	4°29·8′W	W	64
Caplaw Rig	D & G	NS9107	55°21·0′	3°42·7′W	X	71,78
Caplecombe	Devon	SS6822	50°59·2′	3°52·5′W	X	180
Capledrae	Fife	NT1897	56°9·8′	3°18·8′W	X	58
Capler Camp	Heref	SO5932	51°59·3′	2°35·4′W	A	149
Caple Rig	D & G	NY3497	55°16·0′	3°1·9′W	X	79
Caple Rigg	Durham	NY8818	54°33·7′	2°10·7′W	X	91,92
Capler Wood	Heref	SO5832	51°59·3′	2°36·3′W	F	149
Caplestone Fell	Northum	NY5988	55°11·3′	2°38·2′W	H	80
Caple, The	D & G	NY1696	55°15·3′	3°18·9′W	W	79
Caple Tump	Heref	SO5528	51°57·2′	2°38·9′W	A	149
Capley Mea	N Yks	SD8296	54°21·8′	2°16·2′W	X	98
Caplich Wood	Highld	NC3701	57°58·4′	4°44·9′W	F	16
Capo	Aberd	NO6266	56°47·3′	2°36·9′W	X	45
Capon Hall	N Yks	SD8666	54°5·6′	2°12·4′W	X	98
Capon Hall Fm	Red & Cl	NZ6319	54°34·0′	1°1·1′W	FM	94
Capon's Fm	W Susx	TQ2022	50°59·3′	0°17·0′W	FM	198
Capon's Green	Suff	TM2867	52°15·5′	1°20·9′E	X	156
Capon's Hill Fm	W Susx	TQ2022	50°59·3′	0°17·0′W	FM	198
Capons Wood	Herts	TL3632	51°58·4′	0°0·8′W	F	166
Capon Wood	Red & Cl	NZ6318	54°33·4′	1°1·1′W	F	94
Cappelbank Plantation	N Yks	SE0787	54°17·0′	1°53·1′W	F	99
Cappele	Conwy	SH9047	53°0·8′	3°38·0′W	X	116
Cappenham Br	Northnts	SP7148	52°7·8′	0°57·4′W	X	152
Cappercleuch	Scot Bord	NT2423	55°29·9′	3°11·8′W	T	73
Capper Law	Scot Bord	NT2423	55°29·9′	3°11·8′W	H	73
Capperneuk	Aberd	NJ7022	57°17·5′	2°29·4′W	X	38
Capplebarrow	Cumbr	NY5003	54°25·4′	2°45·8′W	H	90
Capple Barrow	Cumbr	SD4295	54°21·1′	2°53·1′W	H	96,97
Capplefall	Cumbr	NY5203	54°25·5′	2°44·0′W	X	90
Capplegill	D & G	NT1409	55°22·3′	3°21·0′W	T	78
Capplerigg	Cumbr	SD4794	54°20·6′	2°48·5′W	X	97
Capplerigg	Cumbr	SD5492	54°19·5′	2°42·0′W	X	97
Cappleside	N Yks	SD7959	54°1·8′	2°18·8′W	X	103
Capple Stones	N Yks	SD9174	54°9·9′	2°7·9′W	X	98
Capplethwaite Hall	Cumbr	SD6291	54°19·0′	2°34·6′W	X	97
Capps Lodge Fm	Oxon	SP2714	51°49·7′	1°36·1′W	FM	163
Cappuck	Scot Bord	NT6920	55°28·6′	2°29·0′W	X	74
Cappuck Br	Scot Bord	NT6920	55°28·6′	2°29·0′W	X	74
Caprickhill	E Ayr	NS4637	55°36·4′	4°26·2′W	X	70
Caprington Castle	E Ayr	NS4036	55°35·7′	4°31·9′W	A	70
Capsall	Shrops	SJ3501	52°36·4′	2°57·2′W	X	126
Capstone	Medway	TQ7865	51°21·6′	0°33·8′E	T	178
Capstone	Stock	SJ9887	53°23·0′	2°1·4′W	X	109
Capstone Farm Country Park	Medway	TQ7864	51°21·1′	0°33·8′E	X	178,188
Capstone Point	Devon	SS5148	51°12·9′	4°7·6′W	X	180
Captain Blake's Point	Corn	SX4149	50°19·4′	4°13·6′W	X	201
Captain Cook's Monument	N Yks	NZ5810	54°29·2′	1°5·9′W	X	93
Captain Fold	Roch	SD8510	53°35·4′	2°13·2′W	T	109
Captain Moor	N Yks	SD9261	54°2·9′	2°6·9′W	X	98
Captain Robertson's Cairn	Highld	NM7270	56°46·2′	5°43·4′W	X	40
Captain's Barn	Staffs	SJ9445	53°0·4′	2°5·0′W	X	118
Captains Fm	Bury	SD8208	53°34·3′	2°15·9′W	FM	109
Captain's Fm	Devon	SS9008	50°51·9′	3°33·4′W	FM	192
Captains Fm	E Susx	TQ3517	50°56·4′	0°4·3′W	FM	198
Captain's Fm	Kent	TQ8558	51°17·7′	0°39·6′E	FM	178
Captain's Road	Scot Bord	NT2617	55°26·7′	3°9·8′W	X	79
Captain Style	Pemb	SN0913	51°47·2′	4°45·8′W	X	158
Captain's Wood	Essex	TL8510	51°45·7′	0°41·2′E	F	168
Captain's Wood	Suff	TM4254	52°8·1′	1°32·6′E	F	156
Captainton	D & G	NX8680	55°6·3′	3°46·8′W	X	78
Capthorne	Carm	SN2610	51°45·9′	4°30·9′W	X	158
Capton	Devon	SX7551	50°21·0′	3°45·0′W	X	202
Capton	Devon	SX8353	50°22·2′	3°38·3′W	T	202
Capton	Somer	ST0839	51°8·8′	3°18·5′W	T	181
Capull Cloiche	Arg & Bt	NS0387	56°2·4′	5°9·3′W	X	55
Capull Cloiche	Arg & Bt	NS1188	56°3·1′	5°1·7′W	X	56
Capull Corrach	Arg & Bt	NM4223	56°20·0′	6°10·0′W	X	48
Caputh	Pth & Kin	NO0840	56°32·8′	3°29·3′W	T	52,53
Cara	Orkney	ND4794	58°50·1′	2°54·6′W	X	7
Carabad	Pth & Kin	NN4851	56°37·8′	4°28·2′W	X	42,51
Carachan	Arg & Bt	NL9646	56°30·7′	6°56·1′W	X	46
Caradal	Highld	NG5604	57°4·0′	6°1·1′W	X	32,39
Caradoc	Heref	SO5527	51°56·6′	2°38·9′W	A	162
Caradon Hill	Corn	SX2770	50°30·5′	4°26·0′W	H	201
Caradon Town	Corn	SX2971	50°31·1′	4°24·4′W	T	201
Caragloose Fm	Corn	SW9238	50°12·6′	4°54·5′W	FM	204
Caragloose Point	Corn	SW9439	50°13·1′	4°52·9′W	X	204
Caragrich Island	N Eil	NL6596	56°56·3′	7°30·1′W	X	31
Cara Island	Arg & Bt	NR6343	55°37·6′	5°45·5′W	X	62
Car an Daimh	Highld	NM6583	56°53·0′	5°51·0′W	X	40
Caratacus Stone	Somer	SS8833	51°5·4′	3°35·6′W	A	181
Carbaglet	Corn	SX1274	50°32·4′	4°38·8′W	X	200
Carbellow	E Ayr	NS6122	55°28·6′	4°11·5′W	X	71
Carberry	Fife	NT2894	56°8·3′	3°9·1′W	X	59
Carberry Hall Fm	E Yorks	SE7452	53°57·8′	0°51·9′W	FM	105,106
Carberry Mains	E Loth	NT3570	55°55·4′	3°2·0′W	X	66
Carberry Tower	E Loth	NT3669	55°54·8′	3°1·0′W	A	66
Carbeth Ho	Stir	NS5279	55°59·1′	4°21·9′W	X	64
Carbeth Ho	Stir	NS5287	56°3·4′	4°22·2′W	X	57
Carbeth Loch	Stir	NS5379	55°59·1′	4°20·9′W	W	64
Carbieston Byres	S Ayr	NS3920	55°27·1′	4°32·3′W	X	70
Carbilly Tor	Corn	SX1275	50°32·9′	4°38·8′W	H	200
Carbins Wood	W Berks	SU5668	51°24·7′	1°11·3′W	F	174
Carbis	Corn	SX0059	50°24·0′	4°48·5′W	T	200
Carbis Bay	Corn	SW5238	50°11·6′	5°28·1′W	T	203
Carbis Common	Corn	SX0058	50°23·5′	4°48·5′W	X	200
Carbisdale Castle	Highld	NH5795	57°55·6′	4°24·4′W	X	21
Carbis Moor	Corn	SX0255	50°21·9′	4°46·7′W	X	200
Carbonells	Essex	TM1629	51°55·3′	1°8·9′E	X	168,169
Carbost	Highld	NG3831	57°17·9′	6°20·5′W	T	32
Carbost	Highld	NG4248	57°27·2′	6°17·6′W	T	23
Carbostbeg	Highld	NG3732	57°18·4′	6°21·6′W	X	32
Carbost Burn	Highld	NG3730	57°17·4′	6°21·4′W	W	32
Carbows Fm	Corn	SW5533	50°9·0′	5°25·4′W	FM	203
Carbrain	N Lanak	NS7674	55°56·8′	3°58·7′W	T	64
Carbreck	Highld	NC3359	58°29·5′	4°51·4′W	X	9
Carbrook	Sheff	SK3889	53°24·0′	1°25·3′W	T	110,111
Carbrooke	Norf	TF9402	52°35·1′	0°52·2′E	T	144
Carbrooke Hall	Norf	TF9600	52°34·0′	0°53·9′E	X	144
Carbrook Mains	Stir	NS8486	56°3·4′	3°51·3′W	X	65
Carbrotach	Aberd	NJ4243	57°28·7′	2°57·6′W	X	28
Carburrow Tor	Corn	SX1570	50°30·3′	4°36·2′W	H	201
Carburton	Notts	SK6173	53°15·3′	1°4·7′W	T	120
Carburton Corner	Notts	SK6272	53°14·7′	1°3·8′W	X	120
Carby Hill	Scot Bord	NY4988	55°11·3′	2°47·6′W	X	79
Carby Hill (Settlement)	Scot Bord	NY4984	55°9·1′	2°47·6′W	A	79
Carcade	Corn	SX1284	50°37·8′	4°39·1′W	X	200
Carcant	Scot Bord	NT3652	55°45·7′	3°0·8′W	X	66,73
Carcar Fm	N Lincs	SE8803	53°31·2′	0°39·9′W	FM	112
Carcarse	D & G	NS6908	55°21·2′	4°3·5′W	X	71,77
Carcary	Angus	NO6455	56°41·4′	2°34·8′W	X	54
Carcary Hill Cotts	Angus	NO6454	56°40·8′	2°34·8′W	X	54
Carci	Conwy	SH8772	53°14·2′	3°41·2′W	X	116
Carclaze	Corn	SX0254	50°21·4′	4°46·6′W	T	200
Carclaze Fm	Corn	SX0075	50°32·7′	4°49·0′W	FM	200
Carclew	Corn	SW7838	50°12·3′	5°6·3′W	T	204
Carcluie	S Ayr	NS3415	55°24·3′	4°36·9′W	X	70
Carcluie Loch	S Ayr	NS3416	55°24·8′	4°36·9′W	W	70
Carco	D & G	NS7813	55°24·0′	3°55·2′W	X	71,78
Carcoe	Corn	SX3155	50°22·5′	4°22·2′W	X	201
Car Colston	Notts	SK7242	52°58·5′	0°55·3′W	T	129
Carco Mains	D & G	NS7712	55°23·4′	3°56·1′W	X	71,78
Carcoside	D & G	NS7712	55°23·4′	3°56·1′W	X	71,78
Carcow Burn	E Ayr	NS6008	55°21·0′	4°12·1′W	W	71,77
Car Craig	Fife	NT1983	56°2·2′	3°17·6′W	X	65,66
Carcroft	Donc	SE5410	53°35·3′	1°10·6′W	T	111
Carcut Beck	Darl	NZ3317	54°33·1′	1°29·0′W	W	93
Carcwm	Powys	SN8850	52°8·5′	3°37·8′W	X	147
Cardale Woodland	N Yks	SE2754	53°59·1′	1°34·9′W	F	104
Cardean	Pth & Kin	NO2945	56°35·7′	3°8·9′W	X	53
Cardeast	Corn	SX1169	50°29·7′	4°39·5′W	X	200
Cardeeth	Pemb	SN0504	51°42·3′	4°48·9′W	X	158
Carden	Moray	NJ1462	57°38·6′	3°26·0′W	X	28
Carden	Pth & Kin	NT0498	56°10·2′	3°32·3′W	X	58
Cardenbarns	Fife	NT2294	56°8·2′	3°14·9′W	X	58
Carden Brook	Ches	SJ4553	53°4·5′	2°48·9′W	W	117
Cardenden	Fife	NT2295	56°8·7′	3°14·9′W	T	58
Carden Hill	Moray	NJ1462	57°38·6′	3°26·0′W	H	28
Cardensbrae	Aberd	NJ6020	57°16·4′	2°39·3′W	X	37
Cardenstone	Aberd	NJ5312	57°12·0′	2°46·2′W	X	37
Cardenwell	Aberd	NJ7740	57°27·2′	2°22·5′W	X	29,30
Carder Low	Derby	SK1362	53°9·5′	1°47·9′W	H	119
Cardeston	Shrops	SJ3912	52°42·4′	2°53·8′W	T	126
Cardeston Park Fm	Shrops	SJ3811	52°41·8′	2°54·6′W	FM	126
Cardew	Corn	SX0988	50°39·9′	4°41·8′W	X	190,200
Cardew	Corn	SX1891	50°41·6′	4°34·2′W	X	190
Cardew	Cumbr	NY3449	54°50·1′	3°1·2′W	T	85
Cardew Hall	Cumbr	NY3449	54°50·1′	3°1·2′W	X	85
Cardewlees	Cumbr	NY3451	54°51·2′	3°1·3′W	T	85
Cardew Lodge	Cumbr	NY3349	54°50·1′	3°2·2′W	X	85
Cardew Mires	Cumbr	NY3450	54°50·7′	3°1·2′W	X	85
Cardfield's Fm	Essex	TL7909	51°45·3′	0°36·0′E	FM	167
Cardie Hill	Scot Bord	NT2740	55°39·1′	3°9·2′W	X	73
Cardiff Flats	Card	ST2174	51°27·8′	3°7·8′W	X	171
Cardiff or Caerdydd	Card	ST1876	51°28·9′	3°10·5′W	T	171
Cardiff Wales Airport	V of Glam	ST0667	51°23·9′	3°20·7′W	X	170
Cardiff West Service Area	Card	ST0979	51°30·4′	3°18·3′W	X	171
Cardigan (Aberteifi)	Cered	SN1746	52°5·2′	4°39·9′W	T	145
Cardigan Island (Nature Reserve)	Cered	SN1651	52°7·8′	4°40·9′W	X	145
Cardigan Plantation	Norf	TL8796	52°32·0′	0°45·8′E	F	144
Cardinal's Green	Cambs	TL6146	52°5·6′	0°21·4′E	T	154
Cardinal Steps	Fife	NO5704	56°13·9′	2°41·2′W	X	59
Cardington	Beds	TL0847	52°6·9′	0°25·0′W	T	153
Cardington	Shrops	SO5095	52°33·3′	2°43·8′W	T	137,138
Cardington Cross	Beds	TL0848	52°7·4′	0°24·9′W	X	153
Cardington Hill	Shrops	SO4993	52°32·2′	2°44·7′W	X	137,138
Cardington Moor	Shrops	SO4994	52°32·7′	2°44·7′W	X	137,138
Cardinham	Corn	SX1268	50°29·1′	4°38·6′W	T	200
Cardinham Castle	Corn	SX1268	50°29·1′	4°38·6′W	A	200
Cardinham Downs	Corn	SX1069	50°29·6′	4°40·4′W	X	200
Cardinham Moor	Corn	SX1371	50°30·8′	4°37·9′W	X	200
Cardle	I of M	SC4590	54°17·2′	4°22·5′W	X	95
Cardnach Fm	Moray	NJ1942	57°27·9′	3°20·6′W	FM	28
Cardney Ho	Pth & Kin	NO0545	56°35·5′	3°32·4′W	X	52,53
Cardon	Scot Bord	NT0933	55°35·2′	3°26·2′W	X	72
Cardona	Stir	NN6800	56°10·7′	4°7·1′W	X	57
Cardonald	C of Glas	NS5364	55°51·1′	4°20·5′W	T	64
Cardon Burn	Scot Bord	NT0731	55°34·1′	3°28·1′W	W	72
Cardoness	D & G	NX5653	54°51·3′	4°14·2′W	X	83
Cardoness Cas	D & G	NX5855	54°52·4′	4°12·4′W	A	83
Cardoness Wood	D & G	NX5654	54°51·9′	4°14·2′W	F	83
Cardon Hill	Scot Bord	NT0631	55°34·1′	3°29·0′W	H	72
Cardon Law	Scot Bord	NT2745	55°41·8′	3°9·3′W	H	73
Cardoon Burn	D & G	NX5365	54°57·7′	4°17·3′W	W	83
Cardow	Moray	NJ1943	57°28·5′	3°20·6′W	T	28
Cardrain	D & G	NX1231	54°38·6′	4°54·4′W	X	82
Cardrona	Scot Bord	NT3039	55°38·6′	3°6·3′W	T	73
Cardrona Forest	Scot Bord	NT3036	55°37·0′	3°6·3′W	F	73
Cardrona Ho	Scot Bord	NT3037	55°37·5′	3°6·3′W	X	73
Cardross	Arg & Bt	NS3477	55°57·7′	4°39·1′W	T	63
Cardross	Stir	NS6097	56°9·0′	4°14·8′W	A	57
Cardross Moss	Stir	NS5799	56°10·0′	4°17·7′W	X	57
Cardrum	Aberd	NJ8231	57°22·4′	2°17·5′W	X	29,30
Cardryne	D & G	NX1132	54°39·1′	4°55·4′W	X	82
Cards Fm	Essex	TL7420	51°51·3′	0°32·0′E	FM	167
Cards Fm	Somer	ST7234	51°6·5′	2°23·6′W	FM	183
Cardsknolls	Fife	NO3005	56°14·2′	3°7·3′W	X	59
Cards Mill Fm	Dorset	SY3996	50°45·9′	2°51·5′W	FM	193
Cardunneth Pike	Cumbr	NY5552	54°51·9′	2°41·6′W	H	86
Cardurnock	Cumbr	NY1758	54°54·8′	3°17·3′W	T	85
Cardurnock Flatts	Cumbr	NY1660	54°55·9′	3°18·2′W	X	85
Cardwell	Devon	SX4379	50°35·6′	4°12·7′W	X	201
Cardwell Fm	Oxon	SP3331	51°58·8′	1°30·8′W	FM	151
Cardwell Ho	Lancs	SD6340	53°51·5′	2°33·3′W	X	102,103
Cardwell Ho	Lincs	TF4229	52°50·6′	0°6·9′E	X	131
Cardwell's Fm	Lancs	SD6029	53°45·6′	2°36·0′W	FM	102,103
Car Dyke	Cambs	TL4767	52°17·1′	0°9·7′E	A	154
Car Dyke	Lincs	TF1062	53°8·9′	0°20·9′W	W	121
Car Dyke	Lincs	TF1228	52°50·5′	0°19·8′W	X	130
Car Dyke	Notts	SK6845	53°0·1′	0°58·8′W	W	129
Car Dyke	Notts	SK7255	53°5·5′	0°55·1′W	W	120
Car Dyke	Notts	SK7443	52°59·0′	0°53·5′W	W	129
Car Dyke Br	Notts	SK7342	52°58·5′	0°54·4′W	X	129
Car Dyke Fm	Lincs	TF1227	52°50·0′	0°19·8′W	FM	130
Cardyke Fm	Lincs	TF1437	52°55·3′	0°17·9′W	FM	130
Cardyke Fm	N Lanak	NS6469	55°54·0′	4°10·1′W	FM	64
Car Dyke (Roman Canal)	Lincs	TF1062	53°8·9′	0°20·9′W	R	121
Car Dyke (Roman Canal)	Lincs	TF1228	52°50·5′	0°19·8′W	R	130
Car Dyke (Roman Canal)	Lincs	TF1540	52°56·9′	0°16·9′W	R	130
Car Dyke (Roman Canal)	Peterb	TF1803	52°36·9′	0°15·0′W	R	142
Careby	Lincs	TF0216	52°44·2′	0°29·0′W	T	130
Careby Wood	Lincs	TF0315	52°43·6′	0°28·1′W	F	130
Carefoot	Lancs	SD5039	53°50·9′	2°45·2′W	X	102
Careg Aderyn	Pemb	SN1349	52°6·7′	4°43·5′W	X	145
Careg Fawr	Carm	SN6929	51°56·9′	3°54·0′W	A	146,160
Careg y Bwci	Carm	SN6447	52°6·5′	3°58·8′W	A	146
Careg y Chwislen	Gwyn	SH2842	52°57·1′	4°33·2′W	X	123
Careg-y-fuddan	Powys	SH7902	52°36·4′	3°46·8′W	X	135
Careg-ywen	Powys	SO0052	52°9·7′	3°27·3′W	X	147
Carehouse Cross	Devon	SX8042	50°16·2′	3°40·7′W	X	202
Caresman Hill	Scot Bord	NT2842	55°40·2′	3°8·2′W	X	73
Careston	Angus	NO5360	56°44·0′	2°45·6′W	T	44
Careston Castle	Angus	NO5359	56°43·5′	2°45·6′W	A	54
Carestown	Moray	NJ5162	57°39·0′	2°48·8′W	X	29
Carevick	Corn	SW7958	50°23·1′	5°6·2′W	X	200
Care Village	Leic	SP7296	52°33·7′	0°55·9′W	T	141
Carew	Pemb	SN0403	51°41·7′	4°49·8′W	T	157,158
Carew Cheriton	Pemb	SN0402	51°41·2′	4°49·7′W	T	157,158
Carewell Fm	Surrey	TQ4043	51°10·4′	0°0·6′E	FM	187
Carew Fm	Pemb	SR9595	51°37·2′	4°57·3′W	FM	158
Carew Mountain	Pemb	SN0505	51°42·8′	4°49·0′W	X	158
Carew Newton	Pemb	SN0404	51°42·3′	4°49·8′W	T	157,158
Carewoodrig	D & G	NY4297	55°16·1′	2°54·3′W	X	79
Carewood Rig	D & G	NY4397	55°16·1′	2°53·4′W	X	79
Carewoodrig Burn	D & G	NY4196	55°15·5′	2°55·3′W	W	79
Carewoodrighope Burn	D & G	NY4298	55°16·6′	2°54·3′W	W	79
Carew River	Pemb	SN0205	51°42·8′	4°51·6′W	W	157,158
Carey	Dorset	SY9088	50°41·7′	2°8·1′W	X	195
Carey	Heref	SO5631	51°58·8′	2°38·0′W	T	149
Carey	Pth & Kin	NO1716	56°20·0′	3°20·1′W	X	58
Carey Barton	Devon	SX3691	50°42·0′	4°19·0′W	X	190
Carey Burn	Northum	NT9625	55°31·4′	2°3·4′W	W	74,75
Carey Heath	Dorset	SY9088	50°41·7′	2°8·1′W	X	195
Carey Park	Corn	SX2151	50°20·1′	4°30·5′W	T	201
Carey Tor	Corn	SX2377	50°34·2′	4°29·6′W	X	201
Carey Wood	Devon	SX3691	50°42·0′	4°19·0′W	F	190
Carfan	Gwyn	SH5666	53°10·5′	4°8·9′W	X	114,115
Carfax Conduit	Oxon	SU5397	51°40·4′	1°13·6′W	A	164
Carfield Fm	Norf	TL9397	52°32·4′	0°51·2′E	FM	144
Carfin	N Lanak	NS7758	55°48·2′	3°57·3′W	T	64
Carfin	S Lanak	NS8346	55°41·9′	3°51·3′W	X	72

Carfrae	E Loth	NT5769	55°55·0′	2°40·8′W	T	67
Carfrae	Scot Bord	NT5055	55°47·4′	2°47·4′W	X	66,73
Carfrae Common	Scot Bord	NT4858	55°49·0′	2°49·4′W	X	66,73
Carfraemill Hotel	Scot Bord	NT5053	55°46·3′	2°47·4′W	X	66,73
Carfury	Corn	SW4434	50°9·3′	5°34·7′W	T	203
Cargaie, The	S Ayr	NX4191	55°11·5′	4°29·4′W	X	77
Cargate	Suff	TL9358	52°11·4′	0°49·8′E	X	155
Cargate Common	Norf	TM1390	52°28·2′	1°8·6′E	T	144
Cargate Green	Norf	TG3912	52°39·4′	1°32·4′E	X	133,134
Cargates	Pth & Kin	NN9620	56°21·9′	3°40·6′W	X	52,53,58
Cargen	D & G	NX9672	55°2·2′	3°37·2′W	X	84
Cargenbank	D & G	NX9074	55°3·2′	3°42·9′W	X	84
Cargenbridge	D & G	NX9574	55°3·2′	3°38·2′W	T	84
Cargenholm	D & G	NX9673	55°2·7′	3°37·2′W	X	84
Cargen Pow	D & G	NX9673	55°2·7′	3°37·2′W	W	84
Cargentle	Corn	SX2987	50°39·7′	4°24·8′W	X	190
Cargen Water	D & G	NX9376	55°4·3′	3°40·1′W	W	84
Cargenwen Fm	Corn	SW6535	50°10·3′	5°17·1′W	FM	203
Cargenwen Resrs	Corn	SW6535	50°10·3′	5°17·1′W	W	203
Carghidown	D & G	NX4335	54°41·4′	4°25·7′W	X	83
Cargie's Plantation	Northum	NU0249	55°44·3′	1°57·7′W	X	75
Cargill	Pth & Kin	NO1536	56°30·8′	3°22·4′W	T	53
Cargilston	S Ayr	NS2911	55°22·0′	4°41·5′W	X	70
Carglonnon	Corn	SX2159	50°24·5′	4°30·8′W	X	201
Cargloth Fm	Corn	SX3354	50°22·0′	4°20·5′W	FM	201
Cargo	Cumbr	NY3659	54°55·5′	2°59·5′W	T	85
Cargo Fleet	Midd	NZ5120	54°34·6′	1°12·2′W	T	93
Cargohill	Cumbr	NY3660	54°56·1′	2°59·5′W	X	85
Cargoll	Corn	SW8156	50°22·0′	5°4·4′W	X	200
Cargreen	Corn	SX4362	50°26·4′	4°12·3′W	T	201
Cargurra Fm	Corn	SX1391	50°41·6′	4°38·5′W	FM	190
Carham	Northum	NT7938	55°38·4′	2°19·6′W	X	74
Carham Hall	Northum	NT8038	55°38·4′	2°18·6′W	X	74
Carhampton	Somer	ST0042	51°10·3′	3°25·4′W	T	181
Carharrack	Corn	SW7341	50°13·8′	5°10·6′W	T	204
Carhart	Corn	SW9573	50°31·5′	4°53·2′W	X	200
Carharthen	Corn	SW8745	50°16·2′	4°59·0′W	X	204
Car Head	Derby	SK2382	53°20·3′	1°38·9′W	X	110
Carhead Rocks	Derby	SK2482	53°20·3′	1°38·0′W	H	110
Car Hill	Notts	SK7342	52°58·5′	0°54·4′W	X	129
Carholme	Lancs	SD8252	53°58·1′	2°16·0′W	X	103
Carhullan	Cumbr	NY4818	54°33·5′	2°47·8′W	X	90
Carhurly	Fife	NO5609	56°16·5′	2°42·2′W	X	59
Carie	Pth & Kin	NN6157	56°41·3′	4°15·7′W	X	42,51
Carie	Pth & Kin	NN6437	56°30·6′	4°12·2′W	X	51
Carie Burn	Pth & Kin	NN6155	56°40·2′	4°15·7′W	W	42,51
Carim Lodge	Pth & Kin	NN8505	56°13·7′	3°50·9′W	X	58
Carines	Corn	SW7959	50°23·6′	5°6·2′W	X	200
Caring	Kent	TQ8053	51°15·1′	0°35·2′E	X	188
Caring	Kent	TQ8054	51°15·6′	0°35·2′E	X	188
Carisbrooke	I of W	SZ4888	50°41·6′	1°18·8′W	T	196
Carisbrooke Castle	I of W	SZ4887	50°41·1′	1°18·8′W	A	196
Carisbrooke Manor	N Lincs	SE8608	53°33·9′	0°41·7′W	X	112
Carishader	N Eil	NB0933	58°11·7′	6°56·7′W	T	13
Cark	Cumbr	SD3676	54°10·8′	2°58·4′W	T	96,97
Cark Airfield	Cumbr	SD3774	54°9·7′	2°57·5′W	X	96,97
Cark & Cartmel Sta	Cumbr	SD3676	54°10·8′	2°58·4′W	X	96,97
Carkeel	Corn	SX4160	50°25·3′	4°13·9′W	T	201
Carkeen	Corn	SX0680	50°35·5′	4°44·1′W	X	200
Carkees Tor	Corn	SX1376	50°33·5′	4°38·0′W	X	200
Carkeet	Corn	SX2173	50°32·0′	4°31·2′W	X	201
Cark Hall Allotment	Cumbr	SD3782	54°14·0′	2°57·6′W	X	96,97
Carkin Fields	N Yks	NZ1710	54°29·3′	1°43·8′W	X	92
Carkin Grange	N Yks	NZ1709	54°28·8′	1°43·8′W	X	92
Carkin Moor	N Yks	NZ1608	54°28·3′	1°44·8′W	X	92
Càrlabhagh	N Eil	NB2042	58°16·9′	6°46·1′W	T	8,13
Carlam Hill Fm	E Yorks	TA1036	53°48·8′	0°19·3′W	FM	107
Carland Cross	Corn	SW8454	50°21·0′	5°1·8′W	X	200
Carlannick	Corn	SW8539	50°13·0′	5°0·5′W	X	204
Carlatton Demesne	Cumbr	NY5252	54°51·9′	2°44·4′W	X	86
Carlatton Middle	Cumbr	NY5253	54°52·4′	2°44·5′W	X	86
Carlatton Mill	Cumbr	NY5251	54°51·3′	2°44·4′W	X	86
Carlaverock Fm	E Loth	NT4071	55°56·0′	2°57·2′W	FM	66
Carlavin Hill	Scot Bord	NT1418	55°27·2′	3°21·2′W	H	78
Carlbury	Darl	NZ2115	54°32·0′	1°40·1′W	T	93
Carlby	Lincs	TF0513	52°42·5′	0°26·3′W	T	130,142
Carlby Hawes	Lincs	TF0514	52°43·0′	0°26·3′W	F	130
Carl Crag	Cumbr	SD0499	54°22·9′	3°28·3′W	X	96
Carlcroft	Northum	NT8311	55°23·8′	2°15·7′W	X	80
Carlcroft Burn	Northum	NT8313	55°24·9′	2°15·7′W	W	80
Carlcroft Hill	Northum	NT8212	55°24·3′	2°16·6′W	H	80
Carl Cross	Cumbr	SD2281	54°13·4′	3°11·4′W	X	96
Carlean	Corn	SW6042	50°14·0′	5°21·6′W	X	203
Carleatheran	Stir	NS6891	56°5·9′	4°6·9′W	H	57
Carlecotes	Barns	SE1703	53°31·6′	1°44·2′W	T	110
Carle Edge	N Yks	SE1668	54°6·7′	1°44·9′W	X	99
Carleen	Corn	SW6130	50°7·6′	5°20·3′W	T	203
Carleen	Corn	SW7124	50°4·6′	5°11·7′W	X	203
Carle Fell	N Yks	SE0578	54°12·1′	1°55·0′W	X	98
Carle Fell	N Yks	SE0678	54°12·1′	1°54·1′W	X	99
Carle Ho	N Yks	SE4867	54°6·0′	1°15·5′W	X	100
Carleith Hill	Pth & Kin	NO0908	56°15·6′	3°27·7′W	X	58
Carlekemp	E Loth	NT5385	56°3·6′	2°44·8′W	X	66
Carle Moor	N Yks	SE1674	54°9·9′	1°44·9′W	X	99
Carlenrig	Scot Bord	NT3904	55°19·8′	2°57·3′W	T	79
Carleon Cove	Corn	SW7215	49°59·7′	5°10·5′W	W	204
Carlesgill	D & G	NY3388	55°11·2′	3°2·7′W	X	79
Carlesgill Hill	D & G	NY3186	55°10·1′	3°4·6′W	H	79
Carle Side	N Yks	SE0677	54°11·6′	1°54·1′W	X	99
Carlesmoor	N Yks	SE1873	54°9·4′	1°43·0′W	T	99
Carlesmoor Beck	N Yks	SE1873	54°9·4′	1°43·0′W	W	99
Carleton	Cumbr	NY0109	54°28·3′	3°31·2′W	T	89
Carleton	Cumbr	NY4252	54°51·8′	2°53·8′W	T	85
Carleton	Cumbr	NY5329	54°39·5′	2°43·3′W	T	90
Carleton	D & G	NX3937	54°42·4′	4°29·5′W	X	83
Carleton	D & G	NX6248	54°48·7′	4°8·4′W	X	83
Carleton	Lancs	SD3339	53°50·8′	3°0·7′W	T	102
Carleton	Wakf	SE4620	53°40·7′	1°17·8′W	T	105
Carleton Bay	S Ayr	NX1289	55°9·8′	4°56·7′W	W	76
Carleton Biggin	N Yks	SD9748	53°55·9′	2°2·3′W	X	103
Carleton Br	N Yks	SD9850	53°57·0′	2°1·4′W	X	103
Carleton Croft	D & G	NX6249	54°49·3′	4°8·5′W	X	83
Carleton Fen	Norf	TM1190	52°28·3′	1°6·8′E	F	144
Carleton Fishery	S Ayr	NX1289	55°9·8′	4°56·7′W	X	76
Carleton Forehoe	Norf	TG0905	52°36·4′	1°5·6′E	T	144
Carleton Hall	Cumbr	SD0898	54°22·4′	3°24·6′W	T	96
Carleton Head	Cumbr	SD0898	54°22·4′	3°24·6′W	X	96
Carleton Hill	Cumbr	NY4550	54°50·8′	2°51·0′W	X	86
Carletonhill	Cumbr	NY5330	54°40·0′	2°43·3′W	X	90
Carleton in Craven	N Yks	SD9749	53°56·5′	2°2·3′W	T	103
Carleton Lane Head	N Yks	SD9549	53°56·5′	2°4·2′W	X	103
Carleton Mains	S Ayr	NX1389	55°9·9′	4°55·7′W	X	76
Carleton Moor	N Yks	SD9547	53°55·4′	2°4·2′W	X	103
Carleton Park	N Yks	SD9748	53°55·9′	2°2·3′W	X	103
Carleton Port	D & G	NX3837	54°42·4′	4°30·4′W	W	83
Carleton Rode	Norf	TM1192	52°29·3′	1°6·9′E	T	144
Carleton St Peter	Norf	TG3402	52°34·1′	1°27·6′E	T	134
Carley	Devon	SX3786	50°39·3′	4°18·0′W	X	201
Carley Hill	Sund	NZ3859	54°55·7′	1°24·0′W	T	88
Carleys Fm	N Yks	SE4591	54°19·0′	1°18·1′W	FM	99
Carlhurey	Fife	NO3905	56°14·3′	2°58·6′W	X	59
Carlhurlie Resr	Fife	NO3904	56°13·7′	2°58·6′W	W	59
Carlidnack	Corn	SW7729	50°7·4′	5°6·8′W	T	204
Carlies	Bolton	SD6407	53°33·7′	2°32·2′W	X	109
Carlincraig	Aberd	NJ6744	57°29·4′	2°32·6′W	X	29
Carlindean	S Lanak	NS9946	55°42·1′	3°36·0′W	X	72
Carlin Foot	Orkney	HY6033	59°11·2′	2°41·5′W	X	5,6
Carling Burn	W Dunb	NS4680	55°59·6′	4°27·7′W	W	64
Carlingcott	Bath & NE Somer	ST6958	51°19·4′	2°26·3′W	T	172
Carlin Geo	Orkney	HY5227	59°7·9′	2°49·8′W	X	5,6
Carlin Geo	Orkney	HY6922	59°5·3′	2°32·0′W	X	5
Carlingheugh Bay	Angus	NO6742	56°34·4′	2°31·8′W	W	54
Carlingholme	N Yks	NZ3207	54°27·7′	1°30·0′W	X	93
Carlinghow	Kirk	SE2324	53°43·0′	1°38·7′W	T	104
Carlin Gill	Cumbr	SD6399	54°23·4′	2°33·8′W	X	97
Carling Knot	Cumbr	NY1120	54°34·3′	3°22·2′W	H	89
Carlingwark	Devon	ST1613	50°54·9′	3°11·3′W	T	181,193
Carlingwark Ho	D & G	NX7661	54°55·9′	3°55·7′W	X	84
Carlingwark Lane	D & G	NX7462	54°56·5′	3°57·6′W	W	83,84
Carlingwark Loch	D & G	NX7661	54°55·9′	3°55·7′W	W	84
Carlingwha	Cumbr	SD5781	54°13·6′	2°39·2′W	X	97
Carlin How	Red & Cl	NZ7019	54°33·9′	0°54·6′W	T	94
Carlin Howe Fm	Red & Cl	NZ6017	54°32·9′	1°3·9′W	FM	94
Carlin's Cairn	D & G	NX4988	55°10·1′	4°21·8′W	H	77
Carlin's Cairn	D & G	NX4988	55°10·1′	4°21·8′W	X	77
Carlinside	S Lanak	NS8445	55°41·3′	3°50·3′W	X	72
Carlinstane Burn	D & G	NS7801	55°17·5′	3°54·8′W	W	78
Carlin Stone	Aberd	NJ6746	57°30·4′	2°32·6′W	A	29
Carlin Stone	D & G	NX3249	54°48·7′	4°36·4′W	A	82
Carlin Tooth	D & G	NY4198	55°16·6′	2°55·3′W	H	79
Carlin Tooth	Scot Bord	NT6302	55°18·9′	2°34·5′W	X	80
Carlintooth Rig	Scot Bord	NY4495	55°15·0′	2°52·4′W	H	79
Carlisle	Cumbr	NY3955	54°53·4′	2°56·6′W	T	85
Carlisle Airport	Cumbr	NY4860	54°56·2′	2°48·3′W	X	86
Carlo	N Ayr	NS0240	55°37·1′	5°8·2′W	X	69
Carlochy	Angus	NO3978	56°53·6′	2°59·6′W	W	44
Carlochy	Angus	NO4183	56°56·3′	2°57·7′W	W	44
Carlock Hill	S Ayr	NX0877	55°3·3′	4°59·9′W	H	76
Carlock Ho	S Ayr	NX0977	55°3·3′	4°59·0′W	X	76
Carloggas	Corn	SW8765	50°27·0′	4°59·7′W	T	200
Carloggas	Corn	SW9063	50°26·0′	4°57·1′W	X	200
Carloggas	Corn	SW9554	50°21·3′	4°52·5′W	T	200
Carloggas	Corn	SX0256	50°22·5′	4°46·7′W	X	200
Carlogie Fm	Aberd	NO5899	57°5·1′	2°41·1′W	FM	37,44
Carloonan	Arg & Bt	NN0810	56°14·9′	5°5·5′W	X	50,56
Carlops	Scot Bord	NT1655	55°47·1′	3°19·9′W	T	65,66,72
Carlopshill	Scot Bord	NT1555	55°47·1′	3°20·9′W	X	65,72
Carlops Hill	Scot Bord	NT1556	55°47·6′	3°20·9′W	X	65,72
Carlownie Hill	Pth & Kin	NN9508	56°15·4′	3°41·3′W	H	58
Carlowrie	C of Edin	NT1474	55°57·3′	3°22·2′W	X	65
Carlowrie Fm	C of Edin	NT1475	55°57·9′	3°22·2′W	FM	65
Carlshead Ho	N Yks	SE3546	53°54·8′	1°27·6′W	X	104
Carl Side	Cumbr	NY2528	54°38·7′	3°9·3′W	H	89,90
Carlston	E Dunb	NS6374	55°56·6′	4°11·2′W	X	64
Carlstonhill Fm	N Yks	SE3546	53°54·8′	1°27·6′W	FM	104
Carl, The	Orkney	HY1801	58°53·6′	3°24·9′W	X	7
Carlton	Barns	SE3610	53°35·4′	1°27·0′W	T	110,111
Carlton	Beds	SP9555	52°11·3′	0°36·2′W	T	153
Carlton	Cambs	TL6453	52°9·3′	0°24·2′E	T	154
Carlton	Leeds	SE3327	53°44·5′	1°29·6′W	T	104
Carlton	Leic	SK3905	52°38·7′	1°25·0′W	T	140
Carlton	Notts	SK6041	52°58·0′	1°6·0′W	T	129
Carlton	N Yks	NZ1912	54°30·4′	1°42·0′W	X	92
Carlton	N Yks	SE0684	54°15·3′	1°54·1′W	T	99
Carlton	N Yks	SE6086	54°16·2′	1°4·3′W	T	94,100
Carlton	N Yks	SE6424	53°42·7′	1°1·4′W	T	105,106
Carlton	Stock on T	NZ3921	54°35·2′	1°23·4′W	T	93
Carlton	Suff	TM3864	52°13·6′	1°29·5′E	T	156
Carlton Ashes	Lincs	SK9244	52°59·4′	0°37·4′W	X	130
Carlton Bank	N Yks	NZ5102	54°24·9′	1°12·4′W	X	93
Carlton Br	Leic	SK3804	52°38·2′	1°25·9′W	X	140
Carlton Colville	Suff	TM5189	52°26·7′	1°42·0′E	T	156
Carlton Colville	Suff	TM5190	52°27·2′	1°42·1′E	T	134
Carlton Curlieu	Leic	SP6997	52°34·2′	0°58·5′W	T	141
Carlton Curlieu Manor Ho	Leic	SP7098	52°34·8′	0°57·6′W	X	141
Carlton Fm	Cambs	TF4110	52°40·4′	0°5·5′E	FM	130,142
Carlton Fm	Cambs	TF4110	52°40·4′	0°5·5′E	FM	143
Carlton Fm	N Yks	SE4858	54°1·2′	1°15·6′W	FM	105
Carlton Forest Fm	Notts	SK6082	53°20·1′	1°5·5′W	FM	111,120
Carlton Grange	Leic	SP7097	52°34·2′	0°57·6′W	X	141
Carlton Grange	Lincs	TF4488	53°22·4′	0°10·3′E	X	113,122
Carlton Grange	N Yks	NZ1913	54°31·0′	1°42·0′W	X	92
Carlton Grange	N Yks	SE6087	54°16·7′	1°4·3′W	X	94,100
Carlton Grange	Stock on T	NZ3922	54°35·7′	1°23·4′W	X	93
Carlton Green	Cambs	TL6451	52°8·2′	0°24·2′E	T	154
Carlton Grove	Norf	TM1681	52°23·3′	1°10·9′E	X	144,156
Carlton Grove	N Yks	NZ4905	54°26·5′	1°14·2′W	X	93
Carlton Ho	Hants	SU3213	50°55·2′	1°32·3′W	X	196
Carlton Ho	N Yks	SE4081	54°13·6′	1°22·8′W	X	99
Carlton Husthwaite	N Yks	SE4976	54°10·9′	1°14·5′W	T	100
Carlton in Cleveland	N Yks	NZ5004	54°26·0′	1°13·3′W	T	93
Carlton in Lindrick	Notts	SK5984	53°21·2′	1°6·4′W	T	111,120
Carlton Lake	Notts	SK5883	53°20·7′	1°7·3′W	W	111,120
Carlton-le-Moorland	Lincs	SK9057	53°6·4′	0°38·9′W	T	121
Carlton Lodge	N Yks	SE3981	54°13·6′	1°23·7′W	X	99
Carlton Lodge Fm	Leic	SK6814	52°43·4′	0°59·2′W	FM	129
Carlton Lowfield Fm	Lincs	SK9256	53°5·8′	0°37·2′W	FM	121
Carlton Manor	Leeds	SE2142	53°52·7′	1°40·4′W	X	104
Carlton Marsh	N Yks	SE6522	53°41·7′	1°0·5′W	X	105,106
Carlton Miniott	N Yks	SE3981	54°13·6′	1°23·7′W	T	99
Carlton Moor	N Yks	SE0384	54°15·3′	1°56·8′W	X	98
Carlton-on-Trent	Notts	SK7963	53°9·7′	0°48·7′W	T	120,121
Carlton Park Fm	N Yks	SE6188	54°17·3′	1°3·4′W	FM	94,100
Carlton Purlieus	Northnts	SP8387	52°28·7′	0°46·3′W	T	141
Carlton Rack	Notts	SK8164	53°10·3′	0°46·9′W	W	121
Carlton School	Beds	SP9554	52°10·8′	0°36·2′W	X	153
Carlton Scroop	Lincs	SK9545	52°59·9′	0°34·7′W	T	130
Carlton Towers	N Yks	SE6423	53°42·2′	1°1·4′W	X	105,106
Carlton Wood	Cambs	TL6552	52°8·7′	0°25·1′E	F	154
Carlton Wood	N Yks	SE4958	54°1·2′	1°14·7′W	F	105
Carluddon	Corn	SX0255	50°21·9′	4°46·7′W	T	200
Carluke	S Lanak	NS8450	55°44·0′	3°50·4′W	T	65,72
Carlung Fm	N Ayr	NS1949	55°42·3′	4°52·4′W	FM	63
Carlung Ho	N Ayr	NS1949	55°42·3′	4°52·4′W	X	63
Carlungie	Angus	NO5135	56°30·5′	2°47·3′W	X	54
Carlunie Hill	Angus	NO3643	56°34·7′	3°2·1′W	H	54
Carl Wark	Sheff	SK2581	53°19·8′	1°37·1′W	H	110
Carl Wark (Fort)	Sheff	SK2581	53°19·8′	1°37·1′W	A	110
Carlyon	Corn	SW9575	50°32·6′	4°53·2′W	X	200
Carlyon Bay	Corn	SX0552	50°20·4′	4°44·1′W	T	200,204
Carlyon Fm	Corn	SW8242	50°14·5′	5°3·1′W	FM	204
Carmacoup	S Lanak	NS7927	55°31·6′	3°54·6′W	X	71
Carmacoup Burn	S Lanak	NS7827	55°31·5′	3°55·5′W	W	71
Carmaddie Brae	S Ayr	NX4188	55°9·9′	4°29·3′W	X	77
Carman Muir	W Dunb	NS3678	55°58·3′	4°37·2′W	X	63
Carman Resr	W Dunb	NS3778	55°58·3′	4°36·3′W	W	63
Carmarthen Bay	Carm	SS2398	51°39·4′	4°33·1′W	W	158
Carmarthen (Caerfyrddin)	Carm	SN4120	51°51·6′	4°18·2′W	T	159
Carmel	Carm	SN5816	51°49·7′	4°3·3′W	T	159
Carmel	Flint	SJ1776	53°16·7′	3°14·3′W	T	116
Carmel	Gwyn	SH4954	53°4·0′	4°14·8′W	T	115,123
Carmel	I of Angl	SH3882	53°18·9′	4°25·5′W	T	114
Carmel	Powys	SO0566	52°17·3′	3°23·2′W	T	136,147
Carmel Bank	E Ayr	NS3837	55°36·2′	4°33·9′W	X	70
Carmel College	Oxon	SU6087	51°35·0′	1°7·6′W	X	175
Carmel Head or Trwyn y Gader	I of Angl	SH2993	53°24·6′	4°34·0′W	X	114
Carmelhill	C of Edin	NT1075	55°57·8′	3°26·1′W	X	65
Carmel Water	E Ayr	NS3837	55°36·2′	4°33·9′W	W	70
Carmen's Wood	Suff	TM3850	52°6·0′	1°28·9′E	F	156
Carmether Village	Corn	SX1079	50°35·0′	4°40·7′W	A	200
Carmichael	S Lanak	NS9238	55°37·7′	3°42·5′W	T	71,72
Carmichael Burn	S Lanak	NS9236	55°36·6′	3°42·4′W	W	71,72
Carmichael Hill	S Lanak	NS9239	55°38·2′	3°42·5′W	H	71,72
Carmichael Ho	S Lanak	NS9339	55°38·2′	3°41·6′W	X	71,72
Carmichaels Fm	Pth & Kin	NO3031	56°28·2′	3°7·7′W	FM	53
Carmichael's Rocks	Arg & Bt	NR4244	55°37·5′	6°5·5′W	X	60
Carminish	N Eil	NG0284	57°45·1′	7°0·1′W	T	18
Carminish Islands	N Eil	NG0185	57°45·6′	7°1·2′W	X	18
Carminnows	D & G	NX6090	55°11·3′	4°11·5′W	X	77
Carminow Cross	Corn	SX0865	50°27·4′	4°41·9′W	T	200
Carminowe	Corn	SW6623	50°3·9′	5°15·8′W	X	203
Carminowe Creek	Corn	SW6424	50°4·4′	5°17·5′W	W	203
Carmire Gate	N Yks	SE7168	54°6·4′	0°54·4′W	X	100
Carmodle	Pth & Kin	NO0305	56°13·9′	3°33·4′W	H	58
Carmont	Aberd	NO8184	56°57·1′	2°18·3′W	X	45
Carmont Hill	Aberd	NO8083	56°56·5′	2°19·3′W	H	45
Car Mór	Arg & Bt	NR7964	55°49·4′	5°31·3′W	X	62
Càr Mór	Pth & Kin	NN5063	56°44·3′	4°26·7′W	X	42
Carmore	Fife	NO1409	56°16·2′	3°22·9′W	X	58
Carmore Burn	Pth & Kin	NO1409	56°16·2′	3°22·9′W	W	58
Carmounthead	Staffs	SJ9249	53°2·5′	2°6·8′W	X	118
Carmunnock	C of Glas	NS5957	55°47·4′	4°14·5′W	T	64
Carmyle	C of Glas	NS6461	55°49·6′	4°9·8′W	T	64
Carmyllie	Angus	NO5442	56°34·3′	2°44·5′W	T	54
Carmyllie Hill	Angus	NO5443	56°34·9′	2°44·5′W	X	54
Carmyllie Moor	Angus	NO5444	56°35·4′	2°44·5′W	X	54
Carn	Arg & Bt	NR1958	55°44·3′	6°28·2′W	X	60
Carn	Arg & Bt	NR2457	55°43·9′	6°23·4′W	X	60
Carn	Monm	SO2712	51°48·4′	3°3·1′W	X	161
Carna	Highld	NM6259	56°40·0′	5°52·6′W	X	49
Carn a' Bhacain	Aberd	NJ2904	57°7·5′	3°9·9′W	H	37
Carn a' Bhadain	Highld	NN6092	57°0·1′	4°17·8′W	X	35
Carn a' Bhadhain	Highld	NH7728	57°19·8′	4°2·1′W	X	35
Carn a Bhaid-Rabhain	Highld	NG9791	57°52·0′	5°24·9′W	H	19
Carn a' Bhainne	Highld	NH4326	57°18·1′	4°35·9′W	H	26
Carn a' Bhalbhain	Highld	NM6867	56°44·5′	5°47·2′W	X	40
Carn a' Bhealaich	Pth & Kin	NN4468	56°46·9′	4°32·8′W	X	42
Carn a' Bhealaich	Pth & Kin	NN4568	56°46·9′	4°31·8′W	X	42
Carn a' Bhealaich Mhóir	Highld	NG8232	57°19·9′	5°36·8′W	H	24
Carn a' Bhealaidh	Aberd	NO3393	57°1·7′	3°5·8′W	H	37,44
Carn a' Bhiorain	Highld	NH1483	57°48·1′	5°7·3′W	H	20
Carn a' Bhodaich	Highld	NH5637	57°24·3′	4°23·3′W	H	26
Carn a' Bhodaich	Moray	NJ2628	57°20·5′	3°13·3′W	H	37
Carn a' Bhothain Duibh	Highld	NH7629	57°20·3′	4°3·2′W	X	35
Carn a' Bhothain Mholaich	Highld	NH7006	57°7·9′	4°8·4′W	H	35
Carn a' Bhreabadair	Highld	NH1183	57°48·1′	5°10·4′W	H	19
Carn a' Bhreabadiar	Highld	NH1767	57°39·6′	5°3·6′W	X	20
Carn a'Bhuilg	Arg & Bt	NR9372	55°54·1′	5°18·2′W	H	62
Carn a' Bhutha	Pth & Kin	NO0382	56°55·4′	3°35·2′W	H	43
Carnaby	E Yorks	TA1465	54°4·3′	0°15·0′W	T	101
Carnaby Ho	N Yks	SE2191	54°19·1′	1°40·2′W	X	99
Carnaby Moor	E Yorks	TA1563	54°3·2′	0°14·2′W	X	101
Carnaby Temple	E Yorks	TA1466	54°4·9′	0°15·0′W	X	101
Carnacailliche	Highld	NM5850	56°35·0′	5°56·0′W	X	47
Carnach	Highld	NH0196	57°54·8′	5°21·1′W	T	19
Carnach	Highld	NH0228	57°18·2′	5°16·8′W	X	25,33
Carnach	Highld	NH8046	57°29·6′	3°59·7′W	X	27
Carnach	Highld	NM6885	56°54·2′	5°48·2′W	X	40

Carnach	Moray	NJ0048	57°30·9′	3°39·7′W	T	27
Carnach	N Eil	NF8063	57°32·9′	7°20·5′W	X	18
Carnach	N Eil	NG2297	57°52·8′	6°40·9′W	T	14
Carn Achadh Gaibhre	Highld	NH9245	57°29·2′	3°47·6′W	X	27
Carnachadh Loch	Highld	NC7053	58°27·0′	4°13·2′W	W	10
Carnacha Fionna	Arg & Bt	NM5031	56°24·6′	6°2·7′W	X	48
Carn-achaidh	Highld	NC4744	58°21·7′	4°36·4′W	H	9
Càrn a' Chait	Highld	NH7180	57°47·7′	4°9·7′W	A	21
Carn a' Chaochain	Highld	NH2318	57°13·4′	4°55·4′W	H	34
Carn á Chaochain Chruaidh	Highld	NH2415	57°11·8′	4°54·3′W	H	34
Carn a' Chaorainn	Highld	NH1954	57°32·7′	5°1·0′W	X	25
Carn a' Cheatraimh Mhóir	Highld	NH9638	57°25·5′	3°43·5′W	H	27
Carnachen-lŵyd	Pemb	SM8733	51°57·5′	5°5·6′W	X	157
Carnachenwen	Pemb	SM8732	51°57·0′	5°5·6′W	X	157
Carn a' Chiaraidh	Pth & Kin	NN8777	56°52·5′	3°50·8′W	H	43
Carnachie	Moray	NJ1047	57°30·5′	3°29·7′W	H	28
Carn a' Chlaiginn	Highld	NH5387	57°51·2′	4°28·2′W	H	20
Carn a' Chlamain	Pth & Kin	NN9175	56°51·5′	3°46·8′W	H	43
Carn a' Chlarsaich	Pth & Kin	NO0677	56°52·8′	3°32·1′W	H	43
Carnach Mór	Arg & Bt	NS1499	56°9·1′	4°59·2′W	H	56
Càrnach Mór	Highld	NG2359	57°32·4′	6°37·3′W	X	23
Carnach Mór	Highld	NH0921	57°14·7′	5°9·5′W	X	25,33
Carn a' Chnuic	Highld	NJ0314	57°12·7′	3°35·9′W	H	36
Carn a' Choin Deirg	Highld	NH3992	57°53·6′	4°42·5′W	H	20
Carn a' Choire Bhuidhe	Highld	NH1816	57°12·2′	5°0·3′W	H	34
Carn a' Choire Ghairbh	Highld	NH1318	57°13·1′	5°5·4′W	H	34
Carn á Choire Ghlais	Highld	NH2519	57°14·0′	4°53·5′W	H	34
Carn a' Choire Ghlaise	Highld	NH5408	57°8·6′	4°24·3′W	X	35
Carn a' Choire Ghuirm	Highld	NH1317	57°12·6′	5°5·3′W	H	34
Carn a' Choire Léith	Highld	NH2618	57°13·4′	4°52·5′W	H	34
Carn a' Choire Mhóir	Highld	NH8429	57°20·5′	3°55·2′W	H	35
CARN a' Choire Odhair	Highld	NH7941	57°26·9′	4°0·5′W	H	27
Carn a' Choire Sheilich	Highld	NH5812	57°10·9′	4°20·5′W	H	35
Carn a' Chrasgie	Highld	NH8643	57°28·0′	3°53·6′W	H	27
Carn a Chuaille	Highld	NH8626	57°18·9′	3°53·1′W	H	35
Carn a Chùil	Highld	NH6721	57°15·9′	4°11·9′W	X	26,35
Carnachuin	Highld	NN8493	57°1·1′	3°54·2′W	T	35,43
Carnachy	Highld	NC7251	58°26·0′	4°11·1′W	T	10
Carnachy Burn	Highld	NC7050	58°25·4′	4°13·1′W	W	10
Carn Afr	Pemb	SN0930	51°56·4′	4°46·3′W	X	145
Carn a' Garbh-choire	Highld	NH8225	57°18·3′	3°57·1′W	H	35
Carn a' Ghaill	Highld	NG2606	57°4·1′	6°30·8′W	H	39
Carn a' Gharbh-ghlaic	Highld	NH8935	57°23·8′	3°50·4′W	H	27
Carn a' Gheòidh	Pth & Kin	NO1076	56°52·3′	3°28·1′W	H	43
Carn a Ghille Chearr	Highld	NJ1430	57°21·4′	3°25·3′W	H	36
Carn a' Ghlinne	Highld	NH0660	57°35·6′	5°14·3′W	H	19
Carn a Ghobhair	Highld	NM7196	57°0·2′	5°45·8′W	H	33,40
Carn a' Ghorm Loch	Highld	NH4093	57°54·1′	4°41·5′W	H	20
Carnagrie	I of M	SC2679	54°10·9′	4°39·6′W	X	95
Carnaich	Highld	NC4423	58°10·4′	4°38·7′W	X	16
Carn Aig Mhala	Pth & Kin	NO1372	56°50·1′	3°25·1′W	H	43
Carnain	Arg & Bt	NR3162	55°46·8′	6°17·0′W	X	60,61
Carn Aire	Corn	SW3628	50°5·8′	5°41·1′W	X	203
Carn Airigh an Easain	Highld	NH0083	57°47·8′	5°21·4′W	H	19
Carn Airighe nan Eag	Highld	NH7614	57°12·3′	4°2·7′W	H	35
Carn Airigh Shomhairle	Arg & Bt	NR3792	56°3·2′	6°13·0′W	X	61
Carn Ait	Pth & Kin	NO1473	56°50·7′	3°24·1′W	H	43
Carn Alladale	Highld	NH4089	57°52·0′	4°41·4′W	H	20
Carn Allt a' Chlaiginn	Moray	NJ3230	57°21·6′	3°7·4′W	H	37
Carn Allt an Aitinn	Aberd	NO1399	57°4·7′	3°25·7′W	H	43
Carn Allt Laoigh	Highld	NH9231	57°21·7′	3°47·3′W	H	27,36
Carn Allt nà Beinne	Aberd	NO0796	57°3·0′	3°31·5′W	H	43
Carn Allt na Bràdh	Highld	NG9535	57°21·8′	5°24·1′W	H	25
Carnalw	Pemb	SN1333	51°58·1′	4°42·9′W	X	145
Carn a Mhadaidh	Highld	NC5249	58°24·5′	4°31·5′W	H	10
Carn á Mhadaidh-ruaidh	Highld	NH1414	57°11·0′	5°4·2′W	H	34
Carn a' Mhadaidh-ruaidh	Highld	NH2449	57°30·1′	4°55·8′W	H	25
Carn a' Mhadaidh-ruaidh	Highld	NH2748	57°29·6′	4°52·7′W	H	25
Carn a' Mhadaidh-ruaidh	Highld	NM7088	56°55·8′	5°46·4′W	H	40
Carn a' Mhaim	Aberd	NN9995	57°2·4′	3°39·4′W	H	36,43
Carn a' Mhais Leathain	Highld	NH8441	57°26·9′	3°55·5′W	H	27
Carn a' Mharc	N Eil	NB4743	58°18·4′	6°18·7′W	A	8
Carn a' Mheallain Odhair	Highld	NH3720	57°14·8′	4°41·6′W	H	26
Carn a' Mhuilt	Highld	NH3436	57°23·3′	4°45·3′W	H	26
Carn a' Mhurraich	Pth & Kin	NN7375	56°51·2′	4°4·5′W	H	42
Carnan	Arg & Bt	NM0849	56°32·8′	6°44·6′W	X	46
Càrnan	N Eil	NF7946	57°23·7′	7°20·2′W	T	22
Carnan	N Eil	NL5582	56°48·3′	7°38·8′W	H	31
Carn an Ailean	Highld	NH8321	57°16·1′	3°56·0′W	H	35
Càrnan-aird-Fuidhaigh	N Eil	NF8447	57°24·5′	7°15·3′W	X	22
Carn an Alltain Riabhaich	Highld	NH2245	57°27·9′	4°57·6′W	H	25
Carnan Bàn	Highld	NH0076	57°44·0′	5°21·1′W	H	19
Càrnan Bàn	Highld	NH1289	57°51·3′	5°9·6′W	H	19
Carnan Cruithneachd	Highld	NG9925	57°16·6′	5°19·6′W	H	25,33
Carn an Dáimh	Aberd	NO2987	56°58·4′	3°9·6′W	X	44
Carn an Daimh	Pth & Kin	NO1371	56°49·6′	3°25·1′W	H	43
Carn an Daimh Bhàin	Highld	NH2240	57°25·2′	4°57·4′W	H	25
Carn an Doire Mhóir	Highld	NH3912	57°10·5′	4°39·3′W	H	34
Carn an Druim Ruaidh	Highld	NH9734	57°23·3′	3°42·4′W	H	27
Carnan Dubha	Arg & Bt	NM2057	56°37·5′	6°33·5′W	X	46,47
Carn an Dubh-ghlaic	Highld	NH5626	57°18·4′	4°23·0′W	X	26,35
Carnane	I of M	SC3774	54°8·4′	4°29·3′W	X	95
Carn an Eich Dheirg	Highld	NG8782	57°46·9′	5°34·5′W	H	19
Carnan Eoin	Arg & Bt	NR4098	56°6·5′	6°10·5′W	H	61
Carnan Eoin Mhaoil	Arg & Bt	NR9878	55°57·4′	5°13·7′W	X	62
Carnanes	I of M	SC2071	54°6·5′	4°44·8′W	X	95
Carn an Fheadain	Highld	NH5527	57°18·9′	4°24·0′W	X	26,35
Carn an Fheidh	Highld	NC5727	58°12·8′	4°25·6′W	H	16
Carn an Fheidh	Highld	NC6262	58°31·7′	4°21·7′W	H	10
Carn an Fhidhleir	Angus	NO1765	56°46·4′	3°21·0′W	H	43
Carn an Fhidhleir Lorgaidh	Highld	NN8587	56°57·9′	3°53·0′W	H	43
Carn an Fhidhleir or Carn Ealar	Pth & Kin	NN9084	56°56·3′	3°48·0′W	H	43
Carn an Fhiodha	Highld	NH2444	57°27·4′	4°55·6′W	X	25
Carn an Fhradhairc	Highld	NJ0735	57°24·0′	3°32·4′W	H	27
Carn an Fhreacadain	Highld	NH6531	57°21·2′	4°14·2′W	X	26
Carn an Fhreiceadain	Highld	NH7207	57°8·4′	4°6·5′W	H	35
Carn an Fhuarain Duibh	Highld	NH8111	57°10·7′	3°57·7′W	H	35
Carnan Fuar	Highld	NH2555	57°33·3′	4°55·0′W	H	25
Carn an Inbhire	Highld	NH1655	57°33·1′	5°4·0′W	H	25
Carn an 'Ic Duibhe	Aberd	NO0590	56°59·7′	3°33·4′W	H	43
Carn an Leanaidh	Highld	NH2153	57°32·2′	4°59·0′W	H	25
Carn an Leth-allt	Aberd	NO0588	56°58·7′	3°33·3′W	X	43
Carn an Leth-choin	Highld	NN6299	57°3·9′	4°16·1′W	H	35
Carn an Leth-uillt	Highld	NG7338	57°22·8′	5°46·1′W	H	24
Carn an Liath-bhiad	Highld	NH5487	57°51·2′	4°27·1′W	X	21
Carn an Lochain Duibh	Highld	NG9689	57°50·9′	5°25·8′W	H	19
Carn an Lochan	Highld	NH5083	57°49·0′	4°31·0′W	H	20
Carnan Maire	Highld	NG9374	57°42·8′	5°28·0′W	H	19
Carnan Mór	Arg & Bt	NL9640	56°27·5′	6°55·7′W	H	46
Carnan Mór	N Eil	NB3911	58°1·0′	6°24·7′W	H	14
Carnan Mòr	N Eil	NG1391	57°49·3′	6°49·6′W	X	14
Carnan Móra	Arg & Bt	NM2158	56°38·1′	6°32·6′W	X	46,47
Carnan Móra	Arg & Bt	NM2560	56°39·3′	6°28·8′W	X	46,47
Carn an Rathaid Dhuibh	Highld	NH6924	57°17·5′	4°10·0′W	H	26,35
Carn an Reidh-bhric	Highld	NG8231	57°19·3′	5°36·8′W	H	24
Carn an Righ	Highld	NC2063	58°31·3′	5°5·0′W	H	9
Carn an Righ	Highld	NC3757	58°28·5′	4°47·2′W	X	9
Carn an Righ	Pth & Kin	NO0277	56°52·7′	3°36·0′W	H	43
Carn an Ruidh Mhaoil	Highld	NG9385	57°48·7′	5°28·6′W	H	19
Carn an Sgianair	Highld	NH6822	57°16·4′	4°10·9′W	X	26,35
Carn Anthony	Highld	NG9757	57°33·7′	5°23·2′W	X	25
Carn an Tilgidh	Arg & Bt	NR9587	56°2·2′	5°17·0′W	H	55
Carn an Tionail	Highld	NC3939	58°18·9′	4°44·4′W	H	16
Carn an Tionail	Highld	NC5747	58°23·6′	4°26·3′W	H	10
Carnanton	Corn	SW8764	50°26·5′	4°59·6′W	X	200
Carn an t-Sabhail or Cairn Toul	Aberd	NN9697	57°3·4′	3°42·4′W	H	36,43
Carn an t-Sagairt Beag	Aberd	NO2184	56°56·7′	3°17·5′W	H	44
Carn an t-Saigairt Mór	Aberd	NO2084	56°56·7′	3°18·4′W	H	44
Carn an t-Saighdeir	Highld	NG8331	57°19·3′	5°35·8′W	H	24
Carn an t-Saluinn	Highld	NG7831	57°19·2′	5°40·8′W	X	24
Carn an t-Seachrain	Highld	NG7824	57°15·4′	5°40·4′W	H	33
Carn an t-Sean-liathanaich	Highld	NH8632	57°22·1′	3°53·3′W	H	27,36
Carn an t-Seididh	Highld	NG7201	57°2·9′	5°45·1′W	H	33
Carn an t-Seilich	Highld	NM7967	56°44·8′	5°36·4′W	X	40
Carn an t-Seillich	Highld	NH6813	57°11·6′	4°10·6′W	X	35
Carn an t-Sionnaich	Pth & Kin	NO0175	56°51·6′	3°37·0′W	H	43
Carn an t-Sleibhe	Moray	NJ1411	57°11·2′	3°24·9′W	H	36
Carn an t-Sluic Dhuibh	Highld	NH4125	57°17·5′	4°37·8′W	H	26
Carn an t-Snàth	Highld	NH3040	57°25·4′	4°49·4′W	X	26
Carn an t-Suidhe	Highld	NH4410	57°9·5′	4°34·3′W	H	34
Carn an t-Suidhe	Moray	NJ2626	57°19·4′	3°13·3′W	H	37
Carn an Tuairneir	Highld	NH3919	57°14·3′	4°39·6′W	H	34
Carn an Tuirc	Aberd	NO1780	56°54·5′	3°21·3′W	H	43
Carn an Uillt Bhric	Highld	NH8339	57°25·8′	3°56·5′W	H	27
Carn an Uillt Tharsuinn	Highld	NH7024	57°17·5′	4°9·0′W	H	35
Carn Aosda	Aberd	NO1379	56°53·9′	3°25·2′W	H	43
Carn a' Phris-ghiubhais	Highld	NH9303	57°6·6′	3°45·5′W	H	36
Carnaquheen	Aberd	NO2494	57°2·1′	3°14·7′W	X	36,44
Carnaquidden Downs	Corn	SW4635	50°9·9′	5°33·0′W	X	203
Carnaquidden Fm	Corn	SW4635	50°9·9′	5°33·0′W	FM	203
Carn Arthen	Corn	SW6739	50°12·5′	5°15·6′W	T	203
Carn Arthur	Pemb	SN1332	51°57·5′	4°42·9′W	A	145
Carn ar Wig	Pemb	SM7123	51°51·8′	5°19·2′W	X	157
Carnary Fm	Pemb	SN1714	51°47·9′	4°38·9′W	FM	158
Carnassarie	Arg & Bt	NM8301	56°9·4′	5°29·2′W	T	55
Carnassarie Castle	Arg & Bt	NM8300	56°8·9′	5°29·2′W	A	55
Carnau	Cered	SN6955	52°10·9′	3°54·6′W	X	146
Carnau	I of Angl	SH3076	53°15·5′	4°32·5′W	X	114
Carnau	Powys	SN8857	52°12·2′	3°37·9′W	X	147
Carnau	Powys	SN9334	51°59·9′	3°33·1′W	X	160
Carnau Cefn-y-ffordd	Powys	SN9560	52°13·9′	3°31·9′W	A	147
Carnau Gwynion	Powys	SN9214	51°49·1′	3°33·6′W	X	160
Carnau Gŵys	Powys	SN8120	51°52·2′	3°43·3′W	X	160
Carnau Lladron	Pemb	SN0932	51°57·5′	4°46·4′W	X	145
Carnau Nant-Menyn	Carm	SN7920	51°52·2′	3°45·1′W	X	160
Carnau'r Gareg-las	Carm	SN7720	51°52·1′	3°46·8′W	A	160
Carnavel	D & G	NX5692	55°12·3′	4°15·3′W	X	77
Carn Avie	Highld	NH8816	57°13·5′	3°50·8′W	X	35,36
Carn Bad a' Chreamha	Highld	NG9226	57°16·9′	5°26·6′W	H	25,33
Carn Bad a' Churaich	Highld	NH9637	57°25·0′	3°43·4′W	X	27
Carn Bad a' Ghad	Highld	NJ0336	57°24·5′	3°36·4′W	H	27
Carn Bad a' Ghuail	Moray	NJ1709	57°10·1′	3°21·9′W	H	36
Carn Bad an Daimh	Highld	NH7621	57°16·0′	4°2·9′W	H	35
Carn Bad an Fhraoich	Pth & Kin	NN8037	56°30·8′	3°56·6′W	X	52
Carn Bad Leabhraidh	Highld	NH3666	57°39·5′	4°44·5′W	H	20
Carn Bad na Caorach	Highld	NJ0335	57°24·0′	3°36·4′W	H	27
Carn Bad na Circe	Highld	NH3801	57°4·6′	4°39·9′W	H	34
Carn Bad na h-Achlaise	Highld	NG9085	57°48·6′	5°31·6′W	H	19
Carn Bad nan Clachan	Highld	NH9035	57°23·8′	3°49·4′W	H	27
Carn Bad nan Luibhean	Highld	NH8523	57°17·3′	3°54·0′W	H	35
Carnbahn	Pth & Kin	NN6748	56°36·6′	4°9·6′W	X	51
Carn Ballach	Highld	NH6404	57°6·7′	4°14·3′W	H	35
Carn Bàn	Arg & Bt	NM7228	56°23·6′	5°41·2′W	H	49
Càrn Bàn	Arg & Bt	NM8401	56°9·4′	5°28·3′W	A	55
Carn Ban	Arg & Bt	NR8490	56°3·5′	5°27·7′W	A	55
Càrn Bàn	Arg & Bt	NR9583	56°0·0′	5°16·8′W	A	55
Carn Bàn	Arg & Bt	NS0788	56°3·0′	5°5·5′W	H	56
Carn Bàn	Highld	NC1935	58°16·3′	5°4·7′W	X	15
Carn Bàn	Highld	NG4868	57°38·2′	6°12·9′W	A	23
Carn Bàn	Highld	NH2205	57°6·4′	4°55·9′W	H	34
Carn Bàn	Highld	NH3341	57°26·0′	4°46·5′W	H	26
Carn Bàn	Highld	NH3387	57°50·7′	4°48·4′W	H	20
Carn Bàn	Highld	NH4525	57°17·6′	4°33·9′W	H	26
Carn Bàn	Highld	NH6303	57°6·1′	4°15·2′W	H	35
Càrn Bàn	Highld	NH6325	57°18·0′	4°16·0′W	X	26,35
Càrn Bàn	N Ayr	NR9926	55°29·4′	5°10·5′W	X	69
Càrn Bàn	N Eil	NB2508	57°58·8′	6°38·7′W	H	13,14
Carn Bàn Beag	Highld	NN8698	57°3·8′	3°52·3′W	H	35,36,43
Càrn Bàn (Chambered Cairn)	N Ayr	NR9926	55°29·4′	5°10·5′W	A	69
Carnbane Castle	Pth & Kin	NN6747	56°36·0′	4°9·5′W	A	51
Carn Bàn Mór	Highld	NN8997	57°3·3′	3°49·3′W	H	35,36,43
Carnban Point	Arg & Bt	NS2487	56°2·9′	4°49·1′W	X	56
Carn Barges	Corn	SW3626	50°4·8′	5°41·0′W	X	203
Carn Barges	Corn	SW4423	50°3·4′	5°34·2′W	X	203
Càrn Bàrn	Pth & Kin	NN7039	56°31·8′	4°6·4′W	X	51,52
Carn Barra	Corn	SW3522	50°2·6′	5°41·7′W	X	203
Carn Barrow	Corn	SW7113	49°58·6′	5°11·3′W	X	203
Carn Beag	Arg & Bt	NM3850	56°34·4′	6°15·5′W	X	47
Carn Beag	Highld	NC4103	57°59·5′	4°40·9′W	H	16
Carn Beag	Highld	NH1055	57°33·0′	5°10·1′W	H	25
Carn Beag	Highld	NH5477	57°45·8′	4°26·8′W	H	21
Carn Beag Dearg	Highld	NN1773	56°49·0′	4°59·4′W	H	41
Càrn Beannachd	Arg & Bt	NR2567	55°49·3′	6°23·0′W	A	60
Carnbee	Fife	NO5306	56°14·9′	2°45·1′W	T	59
Carn Bentyrch	Gwyn	SH4241	52°56·8′	4°20·7′W	A	123
Carn Besi	Carm	SN1527	51°54·9′	4°41·0′W	X	145,158
Carn Bhac	Pth & Kin	NO0482	56°55·4′	3°34·2′W	H	43
Carn Bheadhair	Highld	NJ0511	57°11·1′	3°33·8′W	H	36
Carn Bhinnein	Pth & Kin	NO0976	56°52·2′	3°29·1′W	H	43
Carn Bhithir	Aberd	NO0786	56°57·6′	3°31·3′W	H	43
Carn Bhrain	Highld	NH5287	57°51·1′	4°29·2′W	H	20
Carn Bhrunachain	Highld	NN3389	56°58·0′	4°44·4′W	H	34,41
Carn Bica	Pemb	SN1232	51°57·5′	4°43·8′W	H	145
Carn Biga	Powys	SN8389	52°29·4′	3°43·0′W	A	135,136
Carn Bingally	Highld	NH3329	57°19·5′	4°46·0′W	H	26
Carn Biorach	Highld	NJ0139	57°26·1′	3°38·5′W	H	27
Carnbo	Pth & Kin	NO0503	56°12·9′	3°31·5′W	T	58
Carn Boel	Corn	SW3423	50°3·1′	5°42·6′W	X	203
Carnbooth Ho	C of Glas	NS5857	55°47·4′	4°15·4′W	X	64
Carn Braenrerich	Highld	NH8327	57°19·4′	3°56·1′W	H	35
Carn Bran	Highld	NC9412	58°5·3′	3°47·4′W	X	17
Carn Bran (Broch)	Highld	NC9412	58°5·3′	3°47·4′W	A	17
Carn Brâs	Corn	SW3125	50°4·1′	5°45·2′W	X	203
Carn Brea	Corn	SW3828	50°5·9′	5°39·5′W	H	203
Carn Brea	Corn	SW6840	50°13·1′	5°14·8′W	H	203
Carn Breac	Highld	NG7544	57°26·1′	5°44·5′W	X	24
Carn Breac	Highld	NH0453	57°31·7′	5°16·0′W	H	25
Carn Breac	Highld	NH4380	57°47·2′	4°38·0′W	X	20
Carn Breac	Moray	NJ2013	57°12·3′	3°19·0′W	H	36
Carn Breac	Pth & Kin	NN9568	56°47·8′	3°42·7′W	H	43
Carn Breac Beag	Highld	NH1779	57°46·1′	5°4·1′W	H	20
Carn Breac Meadhonach	Highld	NH1680	57°46·6′	5°5·2′W	H	20
Carn Breac Mór	Highld	NH1680	57°46·6′	5°5·2′W	H	20
Carn Brea (Fort)	Corn	SW6840	50°13·1′	5°14·8′W	A	203
Carn Breagach	Arg & Bt	NM8524	56°21·8′	5°28·4′W	H	49
Carn Brea Village	Corn	SW6841	50°13·6′	5°14·8′W	T	203
Carn Breseb	Pemb	SN1333	51°58·1′	4°42·9′W	X	145
Carn Breugach	Arg & Bt	NM8127	56°23·3′	5°32·4′W	H	49
Carn Briw	Pemb	SN0537	52°0·1′	4°50·1′W	A	145
Carnbroe	N Lanak	NS7463	55°50·9′	4°0·3′W	T	64
Carnbroe Mains Fm	N Lanak	NS7362	55°50·3′	4°1·2′W	FM	64
Carn Bryn-llwd	Powys	SO1082	52°26·0′	3°19·0′W	X	136
Carn Brynllydan	Nth Pt Talb	SN8701	51°42·0′	3°37·7′W	A	170
Carn Buachaille Bréig	Arg & Bt	NN3134	56°28·3′	4°44·2′W	X	50
Carnbwlchcloddiau	Powys	SN8578	52°23·5′	3°41·0′W	A	135,136,147
Carn Caca	Nth Pt Talb	SN8200	51°41·4′	3°42·0′W	X	170
Carn Cadh an Eididh	Highld	NG9146	57°27·6′	5°28·6′W	X	25
Carn Caglau	Nth Pt Talb	SN8600	51°41·5′	3°38·6′W	A	170
Carn Caol	Highld	NH7616	57°13·3′	4°2·8′W	X	35
Carn Cas nan Gabhar	Highld	NH5280	57°47·4′	4°28·9′W	H	20
Carn Cennen	Carm	SN7018	51°51·0′	3°52·9′W	X	160
Carn Chailein	Arg & Bt	NM9217	56°18·2′	5°21·3′W	X	55
Carn Chailein	Highld	NG7639	57°23·4′	5°43·2′W	X	24
Carn Chàiseachain	Highld	NH2560	57°36·0′	4°55·3′W	H	20
Carn Chaluim	Arg & Bt	NR8962	55°48·6′	5°21·6′W	X	62
Carn Chaointe	Arg & Bt	NR3692	56°3·1′	6°14·0′W	X	61
Carn Chaorainn	Highld	NH1853	57°32·1′	5°2·0′W	X	25
Carn Choire Odhair	Highld	NH7114	57°12·2′	4°7·7′W	H	35
Carn Choire Odhair	Highld	NH7528	57°19·8′	4°4·1′W	H	35
Carn Choire Riabhaich	Highld	NH5417	57°13·5′	4°24·6′W	H	35
Carn Choire Shaùilegaich	Highld	NH6315	57°12·6′	4°15·6′W	H	35
Carn Chòis	Pth & Kin	NN7927	56°25·4′	3°57·3′W	H	51,52
Carn Chomas-àirigh	Arg & Bt	NR3749	55°40·1′	6°10·5′W	H	60
Carn Chomh-Stri	Pth & Kin	NO1371	56°49·6′	3°25·1′W	H	43
Carn Chrionaidh	Aberd	NO1380	56°54·4′	3°25·3′W	H	43
Carn Chrom	Moray	NJ3433	57°23·2′	3°5·4′W	H	28
Carn Chuilinn	Highld	NH4103	57°5·7′	4°37·0′W	H	34
Carn Chuinneag	Highld	NH4883	57°48·9′	4°33·1′W	H	20
Carn Clach na Fearna	Highld	NH4308	57°8·4′	4°35·2′W	H	34
Carn Clew	Corn	SW7655	50°21·4′	5°8·6′W	X	200
Carncliff Top	N Yks	SE0758	54°1·3′	1°53·2′W	H	104
Carn Cloich-mhuilinn	Aberd	NN9690	56°59·6′	3°42·3′W	H	43
Carn Cloinn Mhic Cruimein	Highld	NG8222	57°14·5′	5°36·3′W	X	33
Carn Clough	Corn	SW3935	50°9·7′	5°38·9′W	H	203
Carn Clough (Cairn)	Corn	SW3935	50°9·7′	5°38·9′W	A	203
Carn Cobba	Corn	SW4538	50°11·5′	5°34·0′W	X	203
Carn Coed	Pemb	SM9439	52°0·9′	4°59·7′W	X	157
Carn Coire Dhealanaich	Highld	NH7119	57°14·9′	4°7·8′W	H	35
Carn Coire Dhugain	Highld	NH8009	57°9·6′	3°58·6′W	H	35
Carn Coire Easgrabath	Highld	NH7115	57°12·7′	4°7·7′W	H	35
Carn Coire na Caorach	Highld	NH8019	57°15·0′	3°58·9′W	H	35
Carn Coire na Creiche	Highld	NH6208	57°8·8′	4°16·4′W	H	35
Carn Coire na h-Easgainn	Highld	NH7313	57°11·7′	4°5·6′W	H	35
Carn Coire na h-Eirghe	Highld	NH7518	57°14·4′	4°3·8′W	H	35
Carn Coire na h-Inghinn	Highld	NH7104	57°6·8′	4°7·4′W	H	35
Carn Cornel	Nth Pt Talb	SN8106	51°44·6′	3°43·0′W	A	160
Carn Creagach	Aberd	NO0683	56°56·0′	3°32·2′W	H	43
Carn Crom	Aberd	NO0295	57°2·4′	3°36·4′W	H	36,43
Carn Crom	Moray	NJ2145	57°29·6′	3°18·6′W	X	28
Carn Cròm-gleann	Highld	NH6017	57°13·6′	4°18·7′W	H	35
Carn Crom-loch	Highld	NH3882	57°48·2′	4°43·1′W	H	20
Carn Cruinn	Aberd	NO0981	56°54·9′	3°29·2′W	H	43
Carn Cruinn	Highld	NH2959	57°35·6′	4°51·2′W	H	25
Carn Cùl-sgòr	Highld	NH3435	57°22·8′	4°45·2′W	H	26
Carn-cwcw	Pemb	SM9930	51°56·2′	4°55·1′W	X	157
Carn Daimh	Arg & Bt	NN4146	56°35·0′	4°34·9′W	X	51
Carn Daimh	Moray	NJ1824	57°18·2′	3°21·2′W	H	36
Carn Daimh	Moray	NJ3027	57°20·0′	3°9·3′W	X	37
Carn Damhaireach or Top of the Battery	Aberd	NO0585	56°57·1′	3°33·3′W	H	43
Carn Daraich	Highld	NH2363	57°37·6′	4°57·4′W	H	20
Carn Dar-riach	Highld	NH7131	57°21·3′	4°8·2′W	H	27
Carn-ddu	Merth Tyd	SO0312	51°48·1′	3°24·0′W	A	160
Carn Dearg	Aberd	NO0986	56°57·6′	3°29·3′W	X	43
Carn Dearg	Aberd	NO1293	57°1·4′	3°26·5′W	X	36,43

Carn Dearg	Aberd	NO3198	57°4·3′	3°7·8′W	H	37,44
Carn Dearg	Arg & Bt	NM8210	56°14·2′	5°30·6′W	H	55
Carn Dearg	Arg & Bt	NM8918	56°18·7′	5°24·2′W	H	55
Carn Dearg	Arg & Bt	NM9620	56°20·0′	5°17·6′W	X	49
Carn Dearg	Arg & Bt	NM9922	56°21·1′	5°14·7′W	H	49
Carn Dearg	Highld	NC3738	58°18·3′	4°46·4′W	H	16
Carn Dearg	Highld	NG5915	57°10·0′	5°58·7′W	H	32
Carn Dearg	Highld	NG7677	57°43·9′	5°45·3′W	X	19
Carn Dearg	Highld	NG7845	57°26·7′	5°41·5′W	X	24
Carn Dearg	Highld	NH0098	57°55·9′	5°22·2′W	H	19
Carn Dearg	Highld	NH2106	57°6·9′	4°56·9′W	X	34
Carn Dearg	Highld	NH4818	57°13·9′	4°30·6′W	H	34
Carn Dearg	Highld	NH6302	57°5·6′	4°15·2′W	H	35
Carn Dearg	Highld	NH7130	57°20·8′	4°8·2′W	H	27
Carn Dearg	Highld	NH8717	57°14·0′	3°51·9′W	H	35,36
Carn Dearg	Highld	NJ0722	57°17·0′	3°32·1′W	X	36
Carn Dearg	Highld	NJ0941	57°27·3′	3°30·5′W	H	27
Carn Dearg	Highld	NM8369	56°46·0′	5°32·6′W	X	40
Carn Dearg	Highld	NN1570	56°47·4′	5°1·3′W	X	41
Carn Dearg	Highld	NN1572	56°48·4′	5°1·4′W	H	41
Càrn Dearg	Highld	NN2666	56°45·5′	4°50·3′W	X	41
Carn Dearg	Highld	NN3488	56°57·5′	4°43·3′W	H	34,41
Carn Dearg	Highld	NN3496	57°1·8′	4°43·7′W	H	34
Carn Dearg	Highld	NN3594	57°0·7′	4°42·6′W	H	34
Carn Dearg	Highld	NN4165	56°45·2′	4°35·6′W	H	42
Carn Dearg	Highld	NN4189	56°58·2′	4°36·5′W	H	34,42
Carn Dearg	Highld	NN4898	57°3·1′	4°29·9′W	H	34
Carn Dearg	Highld	NN5076	56°51·3′	4°27·1′W	H	42
Carn Dearg	Highld	NN8190	56°59·4′	3°57·1′W	H	35,43
Carn Dearg	Moray	NJ1702	57°6·3′	3°21·8′W	H	36
Carn Dearg	Pth & Kin	NN5367	56°46·5′	4°23·9′W	H	42
Carn Dearg	Pth & Kin	NN6567	56°46·8′	4°12·1′W	H	42
Carn Dearg	Pth & Kin	NO0279	56°53·8′	3°36·1′W	H	43
Carn Dearg	Pth & Kin	NO0471	56°49·5′	3°33·9′W	H	43
Carn Dearg	Pth & Kin	NO1570	56°49·1′	3°23·1′W	H	43
Carn Dearg Ailein	Highld	NG9795	57°54·2′	5°25·1′W	H	19
Carn Dearg an Droma	Highld	NG9794	57°53·6′	5°25·0′W	H	19
Carn Dearg Beag	Highld	NN3694	57°0·7′	4°41·6′W	H	34
Carn Dearg Beag	Highld	NN8393	57°1·1′	3°55·2′W	H	35,43
Carn Dearg Beag	Pth & Kin	NN8470	56°48·7′	3°53·6′W	X	43
Carn Dearg Meadhonach	Highld	NN1772	56°48·5′	4°59·4′W	H	41
Carn Dearg Mór	Highld	NH8613	57°11·9′	3°52·7′W	H	35,36
Carn Dearg Mór	Highld	NN8291	57°0·0′	3°56·1′W	H	35,43
Carn Dearg Mór	Pth & Kin	NN8573	56°50·3′	3°52·7′W	H	43
Carn Deas	Highld	NB9602	57°57·9′	5°26·5′W	X	15
Carn Dhomhnaill Duibh	Pth & Kin	NN4250	56°37·2′	4°34·1′W	X	42,51
Carn Dhomhnaill Mhic a' Ghobha	Highld	NH0256	57°33·3′	5°18·1′W	H	25
Carn Dhonnachadh	Highld	NG9153	57°31·4′	5°29·0′W	X	25
Carn Doire Chaorach	Highld	NH4004	57°6·2′	4°38·0′W	H	34
Carn Doire Mhurchaidh	Highld	NH4249	57°30·5′	4°37·8′W	H	26
Carn Doire na h-Achlais	Highld	NH6423	57°16·9′	4°14·9′W	H	26,35
Carn Doire nan Aighean	Highld	NH5213	57°11·3′	4°26·5′W	X	35
Carn Dolgau	Cered	SN7082	52°25·5′	3°54·3′W	A	135
Carn Donnachaidh	Highld	NG7038	57°22·7′	5°49·1′W	H	24
Carn Donnachaidh Beag	Highld	NH5803	57°6·0′	4°20·2′W	H	35
Carn Downs	Corn	SW4134	50°9·2′	5°37·2′W	X	203
Carn Drochaid	Aberd	NJ1601	57°5·8′	3°22·7′W	H	36
Carn Du	Corn	SW3634	50°9·1′	5°41·4′W	X	203
Carn-du	Corn	SW4523	50°3·4′	5°33·4′W	X	203
Carndu	Highld	NG8927	57°17·4′	5°29·6′W	X	33
Carn Dubh	Aberd	NO1681	56°55·0′	3°22·3′W	H	43
Càrn Dubh	Arg & Bt	NN0017	56°18·5′	5°13·5′W	X	50,55
Carn Dubh	Highld	NG8006	57°5·8′	5°37·5′W	X	33
Carn Dubh	Highld	NH2659	57°35·5′	4°54·2′W	H	25
Carn Dubh	Highld	NH2699	57°57·0′	4°55·9′W	H	20
Carn Dubh	Highld	NH3017	57°13·0′	4°48·5′W	H	34
Carn Dubh	Highld	NH3512	57°10·4′	4°43·3′W	H	34
Carn Dubh	Highld	NH4886	57°50·5′	4°33·2′W	H	20
Carn Dubh	Highld	NH5109	57°9·1′	4°27·3′W	H	35
Carn Dubh	Highld	NH7428	57°19·8′	4°5·1′W	H	35
Carn Dubh	Highld	NH7513	57°11·7′	4°3·7′W	H	35
Carn Dubh	Highld	NH8220	57°15·6′	3°56·9′W	X	35
Carn Dubh	Highld	NH9026	57°18·9′	3°49·1′W	H	36
Carn Dubh	Highld	NJ0507	57°8·9′	3°33·8′W	H	36
Carn Dubh	Highld	NM8493	56°58·9′	5°32·8′W	X	33,40
Carn Dubh	Highld	NN1494	57°0·2′	5°3·3′W	H	34
Carn Dubh	Highld	NN5192	57°0·0′	4°26·7′W	X	35
Carn Dubh	Moray	NJ1512	57°11·7′	3°23·9′W	H	36
Carn Dubh	Moray	NJ1626	57°19·3′	3°23·2′W	H	36
Carn Dubh	Pth & Kin	NN9862	56°44·6′	3°39·6′W	H	43
Carn Dubh	Pth & Kin	NO0069	56°48·4′	3°37·8′W	H	43
Carn Dubh	Pth & Kin	NO1072	56°50·1′	3°28·1′W	H	43
Carn Dubh Beag	Highld	NH7740	57°26·3′	4°2·5′W	H	27
Carndubh Burn	Arg & Bt	NR8289	56°2·9′	5°29·6′W	W	55
Carn Dubh-chromagach	Highld	NH7529	57°20·3′	4°4·1′W	H	35
Carn Dubh-ghlaic	Highld	NH3333	57°21·7′	4°46·1′W	X	26
Carn Dubh 'Ic an Deòir	Highld	NH7719	57°15·0′	4°1·9′W	H	35
Carn Dubh Mór	Highld	NH7939	57°25·8′	4°0·5′W	H	27
Carn Dubh na Burrich	Highld	NH3221	57°15·2′	4°46·6′W	X	26
Carn Dubh nan Earban	Highld	NH8136	57°24·2′	3°58·4′W	H	27
Carn Duchara	Arg & Bt	NM8910	56°14·4′	5°23·9′W	H	55
Carnduff	S Lanak	NS6646	55°41·6′	4°7·5′W	X	64
Carn Dulack	Moray	NJ2316	57°14·0′	3°16·1′W	H	36
Carn Dulack Beag	Moray	NJ2115	57°13·4′	3°18·0′W	X	36
Carnduncan	Arg & Bt	NR2467	55°49·3′	6°24·0′W	X	60
Carn-du Rocks	Corn	SW8120	50°2·6′	5°3·2′W	X	204
Carne	Corn	SW7724	50°4·7′	5°6·6′W	T	204
Carne	Corn	SW9138	50°12·5′	4°55·4′W	T	204
Carne	Corn	SW9558	50°23·4′	4°52·7′W	T	200
Carne	Pemb	SM9237	51°59·8′	5°1·4′W	X	157
Carne	Pemb	SN0809	51°45·0′	4°46·5′W	X	158
Carn Eachie	Highld	NJ1328	57°20·3′	3°26·3′W	H	36
Carn Eag Dhubh	Aberd	NO1297	57°3·6′	3°26·6′W	X	36,43
Carn Ealar or Carn an Fhidhleir	Pth & Kin	NN9084	56°56·3′	3°48·0′W	H	43
Carn Ealasaid	Aberd	NJ2211	57°11·3′	3°17·0′W	H	36
Carn Eas	Aberd	NO1298	57°4·1′	3°26·6′W	X	36,43
Carn Easgainn Mór	Highld	NH7215	57°12·7′	4°6·7′W	H	35
Carn Easgann Bàna	Highld	NH4806	57°7·5′	4°30·2′W	H	34

Carne Beach	Corn	SW9038	50°12·5′	4°56·2′W	X	204
Carnebo Fm	Corn	SW7954	50°20·9′	5°6·0′W	FM	200
Carnebone	Corn	SW7031	50°8·3′	5°12·8′W	T	203
Carnedd	Powys	SO0291	52°30·7′	3°26·2′W	T	136
Carneddans Wood	E Dunb	NS5276	55°57·5′	4°21·8′W	F	64
Carneddau	Conwy	SH6762	53°8·6′	3°58·9′W	H	115
Carneddau	Powys	SO0654	52°10·8′	3°22·1′W	H	147
Carneddau	Powys	SO0755	52°11·4′	3°21·2′W	X	147
Carneddau Fm	Powys	SO0453	52°10·3′	3°23·8′W	FM	147
Carneddau Hengwm	Gwyn	SH6120	52°45·8′	4°3·2′W	A	124
Carneddau (ruin)	Powys	SN9999	52°35·0′	3°29·0′W	X	136
Carnedd Dafydd	Conwy	SH6662	53°8·5′	3°59·8′W	H	115
Carnedd Das Eithin	Powys	SJ0523	52°48·0′	3°24·1′W	A	125
Carnedd Fach	Gwyn	SH6562	53°8·5′	4°0·7′W	X	115
Carnedd Fychan	Pemb	SN0537	52°0·1′	4°50·1′W	X	145
Carnedd Iago	Gwyn	SH7840	52°56·9′	3°48·5′W	H	124
Carnedd Llwydion	Caer	ST1092	51°37·4′	3°17·6′W	A	171
Carnedd-Lleithr	Pemb	SM7428	51°54·5′	5°16·8′W	H	157
Carnedd Llewelyn	Conwy	SH6864	53°9·7′	3°58·1′W	H	115
Carnedd Meibion-Owen	Pemb	SN0936	51°59·6′	4°46·5′W	H	145
Carnedd Moel-siabod	Conwy	SH7054	53°4·3′	3°56·0′W	H	115
Carneddol	Gwyn	SH3033	52°52·3′	4°31·2′W	H	123
Carnedd Penyborth-goch	Gwyn	SH7069	53°12·4′	3°56·4′W	A	115
Carnedd Wen	Gwyn	SJ0035	52°54·4′	3°28·8′W	A	125
Carnedd Wen	Powys	SH9209	52°40·3′	3°35·4′W	X	125
Carnedd y Ci	Denb	SJ0534	52°53·9′	3°24·3′W	X	125
Carnedd y Cribau	Gwyn	SH6753	53°3·7′	3°58·7′W	H	115
Carnedd y Cylch	Powys	SH9309	52°40·3′	3°34·5′W	X	125
Carnedd y Ddelw	Gwyn	SH7070	53°12·9′	3°56·4′W	A	115
Carnedd y Filiast	Gwyn	SH6162	53°8·5′	4°4·3′W	H	115
Carnedd y Filiast	Gwyn	SH8744	52°59·1′	3°40·6′W	H	124,125
Carne Down	Corn	SX2081	50°36·3′	4°32·3′W	X	201
Carn Edward	Pemb	SN0536	51°59·5′	4°50·0′W	X	145
Carneggan Fm	Corn	SX1652	50°20·6′	4°34·8′W	FM	201
Carnegie	Angus	NO5341	56°33·8′	2°45·4′W	T	54
Carn Eididh	Highld	NG9747	57°28·3′	5°22·7′W	X	25
Carn Eige	Highld	NH1226	57°17·4′	5°6·7′W	H	25
Carneil Hill	Fife	NT0388	56°4·8′	3°33·1′W	H	65
Carn Eilrig	Highld	NH9305	57°7·7′	3°45·6′W	H	36
Carn Eite	Highld	NG9949	57°29·5′	5°20·8′W	H	25
Carn Eiteige	Highld	NH2043	57°26·8′	4°59·5′W	H	25
Carn Eitidh	Highld	NH7325	57°18·1′	4°6·0′W	H	35
Carneles Green	Herts	TL3406	51°44·4′	0°3·2′W	X	166
Carnell	S Ayr	NS4632	55°33·7′	4°26·1′W	A	70
Carnelloe	Corn	SW4438	50°11·4′	5°34·8′W	X	203
Carn Elrig Beag	Aberd	NO0993	57°1·4′	3°29·5′W	H	36,43
Carn Elrig Mór	Aberd	NO0994	57°1·9′	3°29·5′W	H	36,43
Carnemough Fm	Corn	SW9151	50°19·5′	4°55·8′W	FM	200,204
Carn Enoch	Pemb	SN0136	51°59·5′	4°53·5′W	X	145,157
Carness	Highld	NN0659	56°41·2′	5°9·6′W	X	41
Carness	Orkney	HY4613	59°0·3′	2°55·9′W	X	6
Car Ness	Orkney	HY4614	59°0·8′	2°55·9′W	X	6
Carn Etchachan	Aberd	NJ0000	57°5·1′	3°38·5′W	H	36
Carnethy Hill	Midlo	NT2061	55°50·4′	3°16·2′W	H	66
Carnetley	Cumbr	NY5861	54°56·8′	2°38·9′W	X	86
Carnetown	Rho Cyn Taf	ST0794	51°38·5′	3°20·3′W	T	170
Carn Euny	Corn	SW4028	50°5·9′	5°37·8′W	X	203
Carnevas	Corn	SW8672	50°30·8′	5°0·7′W	X	200
Carn Everis	Corn	SW5141	50°13·2′	5°29·1′W	X	203
Carnewas	Corn	SW8569	50°29·1′	5°1·5′W	X	200
Carnewas Island	Corn	SW8469	50°29·1′	5°2·3′W	X	200
Carne Wood	Corn	SX1568	50°29·2′	4°36·1′W	F	201
Carnfachbugeilyn	Cered	SN8290	52°30·0′	3°43·9′W	A	135,136
Carn Fada	Highld	NC5652	58°26·2′	4°27·5′W	X	10
Carn Fada	Highld	NG8530	57°18·9′	5°33·8′W	X	24
Carnfadog	Carm	SN7617	51°50·5′	3°47·6′W	A	160
Carn Fadrun	Gwyn	SH2735	52°53·3′	4°33·9′W	X	123
Carn Fadrun (Fort)	Gwyn	SH2735	52°53·3′	4°33·9′W	A	123
Carn Fadryn	Gwyn	SH2735	52°53·3′	4°33·9′W	H	123
Carn Faire nan Con	Highld	NH3959	57°35·8′	4°41·2′W	H	26
Carnfathach	Pemb	SM9340	52°1·4′	5°0·6′W	X	157
Carn Fawr	Carm	SN6650	52°8·2′	3°57·1′W	A	146
Carn Fawr	Cered	SN7057	52°12·0′	3°53·7′W	A	146,147
Carn Fawr	Cered	SN8190	52°29·9′	3°44·8′W	A	135,136
Carn Fawr	Powys	SO1215	51°49·8′	3°16·2′W	A	161
Carn Fearna	Highld	NH4261	57°36·9′	4°38·2′W	H	20
Carn Ferched	Pemb	SN1532	51°57·6′	4°41·2′W	A	145
Carnferg	Aberd	NO5293	57°1·8′	2°47·0′W	H	37,44
Carn Feur-lochain	Highld	NH4084	57°49·3′	4°41·2′W	H	20
Carn Feur-lochain	Highld	NH4578	57°46·2′	4°35·9′W	X	20
Carn-ffald	Pemb	SM7528	51°54·5′	5°15·9′W	H	157
Carn Fflur	Cered	SN7462	52°14·7′	3°50·3′W	H	146,147
Carn Fiaclach	Aberd	NO1096	57°3·0′	3°28·6′W	X	36,43
Carn Fiaclach	Highld	NH2727	57°18·3′	4°51·9′W	H	25
Carn Fiaclach	Moray	NJ1706	57°8·5′	3°21·8′W	X	36
Carn Fiaclach	Pth & Kin	NN6662	56°44·1′	4°11·0′W	H	42
Carnfield Hall	Derby	SK4256	53°6·2′	1°22·0′W	A	120
Carn Fliuch-bhaid	Highld	NH5512	57°10·8′	4°23·5′W	H	35
Carn Foesen	Nth Pt Talb	SN9002	51°42·6′	3°35·1′W	A	170
Carnforth	Lancs	SD4970	54°7·6′	2°46·4′W	T	97
Carn Fran	Pemb	SM9737	51°59·9′	4°57·0′W	X	157
Carn Fraoich	Highld	NH5501	57°4·9′	4°23·1′W	H	35
Carn Gafallt	Powys	SN9464	52°16·1′	3°32·8′W	H	147
Carn Gaibhre	Arg & Bt	NM9725	56°22·7′	5°16·8′W	H	49
Carn Gaineamhach	Highld	NH3968	57°40·6′	4°41·5′W	H	20
Carn Gairbhthinn	Highld	NH5215	57°12·4′	4°26·6′W	H	35
Carn Galver	Corn	SW4236	50°10·3′	5°36·4′W	X	203
Càrn Garbh	Highld	NC9013	58°5·8′	3°51·5′W	H	17
Carn Garbh	Highld	NH2858	57°35·0′	4°52·2′W	H	25
Càrn Garth	Highld	NC9013	58°5·8′	3°51·5′W	X	17
Carn Geal	Pth & Kin	NN9663	56°45·1′	3°41·6′W	H	43
Carn Gearresith	Highld	NH6211	57°10·4′	4°16·5′W	H	35
Carn Gelli	Pemb	SM9237	51°59·8′	5°1·4′W	H	157
Carn Geuradainn	Highld	NG9839	57°24·1′	5°21·3′W	H	25
Carn Gharbh-baid	Highld	NJ0639	57°26·2′	3°33·6′W	X	27
Carn Ghiubhais	Moray	NJ0845	57°29·4′	3°31·6′W	H	27
Carn Ghluasaid	Highld	NH1412	57°9·9′	5°4·1′W	H	34
Carn Ghrantaich	Moray	NJ1727	57°19·8′	3°22·3′W	H	36
Carn Ghriogair	Aberd	NO1183	56°56·0′	3°27·3′W	H	43
Carn Ghriogair	Highld	NH6519	57°14·8′	4°13·8′W	H	35

Carngillan	S Ayr	NS4225	55°29·9′	4°29·6′W	X	70
Carn Glac an Eich	Highld	NH6926	57°18·6′	4°10·0′W	H	26,35
Carn Glac nam Fiadh	Highld	NH3164	57°38·3′	4°49·4′W	H	20
Carn Glas	Arg & Bt	NR3592	56°3·1′	6°14·9′W	X	61
Càrn Glas	Arg & Bt	NS2199	56°9·3′	4°52·5′W	X	56
Carn Glas	Highld	NC7934	58°16·9′	4°3·3′W	A	17
Carn Glas	Highld	NG7016	57°10·9′	5°47·9′W	A	33
Carn Glas	Highld	NH5752	57°32·4′	4°22·9′W	X	26
Carn Glas	Highld	NH6438	57°25·0′	4°15·4′W	X	26
Carnglas	Swan	SS6193	51°37·4′	4°0·1′W	T	159
Carn Glas (Chambered Cairn)	Highld	NH5752	57°32·4′	4°22·9′W	A	26
Carn Glas (Chambered Cairns)	Highld	NH6438	57°25·0′	4°15·4′W	A	26
Carn Glas-choire	Highld	NH8929	57°20·5′	3°50·2′W	H	35,36
Carn Glas Iochdarach	Highld	NH1620	57°14·3′	5°2·5′W	H	25
Carn Glaze	Corn	SW3929	50°6·5′	5°38·7′W	X	203
Carnglaze Caverns	Corn	SX1866	50°28·2′	4°33·5′W	X	201
Carn Gleann an Tairbhidh	Highld	NH8532	57°22·1′	3°54·3′W	H	27,36
Carn Gloose	Corn	SW3531	50°7·4′	5°42·1′W	X	203
Carn Goch	Carm	SN6924	51°54·2′	3°53·9′W	H	160
Carn-Goch	Swan	SS6098	51°40·0′	4°1·1′W	A	159
Carn Goedog	Pemb	SN1233	51°58·1′	4°43·8′W	H	145
Carn Goraig	Highld	NG9986	57°49·4′	5°22·6′W	H	19
Carn-gorm	Highld	NG9520	57°13·8′	5°23·3′W	T	25,33
Carn Gorm	Highld	NH1350	57°30·4′	5°6·8′W	H	25
Carn Gorm	Highld	NH3235	57°22·7′	4°47·2′W	H	26
Carn Gorm	Highld	NH4362	57°37·5′	4°37·3′W	H	20
Carn Gorm	Highld	NH4570	57°41·9′	4°35·6′W	H	20
Carn Gorm	Pth & Kin	NN6350	56°37·6′	4°13·5′W	H	42,51
Carn Gorm-loch	Highld	NH3180	57°46·9′	4°50·1′W	H	20
Carngour	Fife	NO5212	56°18·1′	2°46·1′W	X	59
Carngowil	Pemb	SM9238	52°0·3′	5°1·4′W	X	157
Carn Gowla	Corn	SW6951	50°19·1′	5°14·3′W	X	203
Carn Grean	Corn	SW3828	50°5·9′	5°39·5′W	X	203
Carn Greannach	Highld	NG8230	57°18·8′	5°36·7′W	X	24
Carn Greannach	Pth & Kin	NN9582	56°55·3′	3°43·0′W	H	43
Carn Greeb	Corn	SW3424	50°3·6′	5°42·6′W	X	203
Carn Gruama Beag	Highld	NC6238	58°18·8′	4°20·9′W	H	16
Carn Gruamach	Highld	NH8830	57°21·1′	3°51·2′W	X	27,36
Càrn Gruama Mór	Highld	NC6037	58°18·2′	4°22·9′W	H	16
Carnguwch Bach	Gwyn	SH3642	52°57·3′	4°26·1′W	X	123
Carnguwch Fawr	Gwyn	SH3742	52°57·3′	4°25·2′W	X	123
Carn Gwilym	Powys	SN7990	52°29·9′	3°46·6′W	A	135
Carn Gyfrwy	Pemb	SN1432	51°57·6′	4°42·0′W	X	145
Carn Haut	Corn	SW7655	50°21·4′	5°8·6′W	X	200
Carnhedryn	Pemb	SM7927	51°54·1′	5°12·4′W	T	157
Carnhedryn Uchaf	Pemb	SM7927	51°54·1′	5°12·4′W	T	157
Carnhell Green	Corn	SW6137	50°11·3′	5°20·5′W	T	203
Carn Hen	Pemb	SM7327	51°54·0′	5°17·6′W	X	157
Carnhendy	Pemb	SM9439	52°0·9′	4°59·7′W	X	157
Carnhot	Corn	SW7445	50°15·9′	5°9·9′W	T	204
Carnhuan	Pemb	SN1337	52°0·2′	4°43·1′W	X	145
Carn Hyddgen	Powys	SN7990	52°29·9′	3°46·6′W	H	135
Carn Iar	Highld	NB9602	57°57·9′	5°26·5′W	X	15
Carn Icean Duibhe	Highld	NH7111	57°10·6′	4°7·6′W	H	35
Carnichal	Aberd	NJ9351	57°33·2′	2°6·6′W	X	30
Carn' Ic Loumhaidh	Pth & Kin	NN5772	56°49·3′	4°20·1′W	X	42
Carnie	Aberd	NJ8005	57°8·4′	2°19·4′W	X	38
Carnieston	Aberd	NJ6132	57°22·9′	2°38·5′W	X	29,37
Carnigill	Durham	NY9118	54°33·7′	2°7·9′W	X	91,92
Carnine	D & G	NS6803	55°18·5′	4°4·3′W	H	77
Carningli Common	Pemb	SN0536	51°59·5′	4°50·0′W	X	145
Carnirock Stone	D & G	NX3987	55°9·3′	4°31·2′W	X	77
Carnish	N Eil	NB0232	58°10·8′	7°3·7′W	X	13
Carnis Mhór	Highld	NH3116	57°12·5′	4°47·4′W	H	34
Carnivan Hill	E Ayr	NS5515	55°24·7′	4°17·0′W	X	71
Carn Kenidjack	Corn	SW3832	50°8·1′	5°39·6′W	X	203
Carn Kez	Corn	SW3424	50°3·6′	5°42·6′W	X	203
Carnkie	Corn	SW6839	50°12·6′	5°14·7′W	T	203
Carnkie	Corn	SW7134	50°9·9′	5°12·0′W	T	203
Carnkief	Corn	SW7852	50°19·8′	5°6·8′W	T	200,204
Carn Kitty	Moray	NJ0942	57°27·8′	3°30·6′W	H	27
Carn Labhruinn	Pth & Kin	NN6715	56°18·8′	4°8·6′W	H	57
Carnlaggie	Highld	ND0216	58°7·6′	3°39·4′W	X	17
Carn Iain Ruaidh	Highld	NH8728	57°20·0′	3°52·2′W	H	35
Carn Lairig Meachdainn	Pth & Kin	NN5248	56°36·3′	4°24·2′W	X	51
Carn Leac	Highld	NN4097	57°2·4′	4°37·8′W	H	34
Càrn Leacach	Highld	NC3054	58°26·7′	4°54·3′W	X	9
Carn Leacan Sleamhuinn	Highld	NH8011	57°10·7′	3°58·6′W	H	35
Carn Leachtar Dhubh	Highld	NH6816	57°13·2′	4°10·7′W	H	35
Carn Leachter	Highld	NH6424	57°17·4′	4°14·9′W	H	26,35
Carn Leachter Mór	Highld	NH7620	57°15·5′	4°2·9′W	X	35
Carn Leac Saighaeir	Aberd	NJ2706	57°8·6′	3°11·9′W	H	37
Carn Leathan	Highld	NH8530	57°21·0′	3°54·2′W	H	27
Carn Leitir Coire Chalich	Highld	NH6914	57°12·1′	4°9·6′W	X	35
Carn Leitir na Cloiche	Aberd	NJ2007	57°9·1′	3°18·9′W	X	36
Carn Lês Boel	Corn	SW3523	50°3·1′	5°41·8′W	X	203
Carn Leskys	Corn	SW3530	50°6·9′	5°42·0′W	X	203
Carn Lethendry	Highld	NH8920	57°15·7′	3°50·0′W	H	35,36
Carn Leum Niall	Highld	NG9890	57°51·5′	5°23·8′W	H	19
Carn Liath	Aberd	NO0386	56°57·6′	3°35·3′W	H	43
Carn Liath	Aberd	NO1697	57°3·6′	3°22·6′W	H	36,43
Càrn Liath	Highld	NG3768	57°37·8′	6°23·9′W	X	23
Carn Liath	Highld	NG4251	57°28·8′	6°17·8′W	X	23
Carn Liath	Highld	NG4956	57°31·7′	6°11·1′W	H	23
Carn Liath	Highld	NH1350	57°30·4′	5°6·8′W	H	25
Carn Liath	Highld	NH5518	57°14·0′	4°23·7′W	H	35
Carn Liath	Highld	NH5866	57°40·0′	4°22·4′W	X	21
Carn Liath	Highld	NH6669	57°41·7′	4°14·4′W	A	21
Carn Liath	Highld	NH6918	57°14·3′	4°9·8′W	X	35
Carnliath	Highld	NM6455	56°37·9′	5°50·4′W	X	49
Carn Liath	Highld	NN4790	56°58·8′	4°30·6′W	H	34
Carn Liath	Moray	NJ1826	57°19·3′	3°21·2′W	H	36
Carn Liath	Moray	NJ2515	57°13·4′	3°14·1′W	H	37
Carn Liath	Pth & Kin	NN9369	56°48·3′	3°44·7′W	H	43
Carn Liath	Pth & Kin	NN9966	56°46·7′	3°38·7′W	H	43
Carn Liath	Stir	NN3818	56°19·9′	4°36·8′W	X	50,56
Carn Liath-bhaid	Highld	NH5411	57°10·3′	4°24·4′W	H	35

Càrn Liath (Chambered Cairn)	Highld	NG3768	57°37·8'	6°23·9'W	A	23
Càrn Liath (Chambered Cairn)	Highld	NG4251	57°28·8'	6°17·8'W	A	23
Carn Liath (Chambered Cairn)	Highld	NH5866	57°40·0'	4°22·4'W	A	21
Carn Liathdoire	Highld	NH5718	57°14·1'	4°21·7'W	H	35
Carn Llechart	Swan	SN6906	51°44·5'	3°53·5'W	A	160
Carn Llidi	Pemb	SM7327	51°54·0'	5°17·6'W	X	157
Carnllundain	Pemb	SM6923	51°51·7'	5°20·9'W	H	157
Carn Loch a' Bhothain	Highld	NH3720	57°14·8'	4°41·6'W	H	26
Carn Loch a' Mhuilinn	Highld	NH3824	57°16·9'	4°40·8'W	H	26
Carn Loch an t-Sionnaich	Highld	NH4221	57°15·4'	4°36·7'W	H	26
Carn Loch an Tuirc	Highld	NH4262	57°37·5'	4°38·3'W	H	20
Carn Loch na Gobhlaig	Highld	NH2530	57°19·9'	4°54·0'W	H	25
Carn Loch na Leitir	Highld	NH6929	57°20·2'	4°10·1'W	H	26,35
Carn Loch nan Amhaichean	Highld	NH4175	57°44·5'	4°39·8'W	H	20
Carn Loch nan Eun	Highld	NG9527	57°17·5'	5°23·7'W	H	25,33
Carn Loch Srùban Móra	Highld	NH3184	57°49·1'	4°50·2'W	H	20
Carn Loisgte	Highld	NH0357	57°33·9'	5°17·2'W	H	25
Carn Loisgte	Highld	NH8728	57°20·0'	3°52·2'W	H	35,36
Carn Lub an Ath Ruaidh	Highld	NG9735	57°21·9'	5°22·1'W	X	25
Carn Luig	Highld	NJ0232	57°22·3'	3°37·3'W	H	27,36
Carn Lwyd	Cered	SN7583	52°26·1'	3°49·9'W	A	135
Carn Lwyd	Nth Pt Talb	SN7207	51°45·1'	3°50·9'W	A	160
Carn Macoul	Highld	NH6300	57°4·5'	4°15·1'W	H	35
Carn Macsna	Highld	NH4427	57°18·7'	4°34·9'W	H	26
Carn Maire	Highld	NH4883	57°48·9'	4°33·1'W	H	20
Carn Mairg	Pth & Kin	NN6851	56°38·2'	4°8·7'W	H	42,51
Carn Màiri	Highld	NG8805	57°5·5'	5°29·5'W	H	33
Carn Maol	Highld	NH8645	57°29·1'	3°53·6'W	H	27
Carn Marth	Corn	SW7140	50°13·2'	5°12·2'W	H	203
Carn Meadhonach	Aberd	NJ2411	57°11·3'	3°15·0'W	X	36
Carn Meadhonach	Aberd	NJ2505	57°8·0'	3°13·9'W	X	37
Carn Meadhonach	Highld	NH7525	57°18·2'	4°4·0'W	H	35
Carn Meadhonach	Moray	NJ1317	57°14·4'	3°26·0'W	H	36
Carnmeal Downs	Corn	SW6229	50°7·0'	5°19·4'W	X	203
Carn Meilich	Moray	NJ1623	57°17·7'	3°23·2'W	H	36
Carnmenellis	Corn	SW6936	50°11·0'	5°13·8'W	H	203
Carnmenyn	Pemb	SN1432	51°57·6'	4°42·0'W	X	145
Carn Mhartuin	Highld	NH1754	57°32·6'	5°3·0'W	H	25
Carn Mheadhoin	Highld	NH9130	57°21·1'	3°48·2'W	X	27,36
Carn Mhic a' Ghille-chaim	Highld	NM7195	56°59·6'	5°45·8'W	H	33,40
Carn Mhic an Toisich	Aberd	NJ2412	57°11·8'	3°15·0'W	X	36
Carn Mhic an Toisich	Highld	NH3118	57°13·6'	4°47·5'W	H	34
Carn Mhic Eoghainn	Arg & Bt	NR5883	55°59·0'	5°52·3'W	X	61
Carn Mhic Iamhair	Highld	NH6114	57°12·0'	4°17·6'W	H	35
Carn Mhic Labhraich	Highld	NM8779	56°51·5'	5°29·2'W	X	40
Carn Mhic Raonuill	Highld	NH2908	57°8·1'	4°49·1'W	H	34
Carn Mòine an Tighearn	Aberd	NO2296	57°3·2'	3°16·7'W	H	36,44
Carn Monadh nan da Allt	Highld	NH8138	57°25·3'	3°58·4'W	H	27
Carn Mòr	Aberd	NJ2607	57°9·1'	3°12·9'W	H	37
Carn Mòr	Aberd	NJ3111	57°11·3'	3°8·0'W	H	37
Carn Mòr	Aberd	NO0290	56°59·7'	3°36·3'W	H	43
Carn Mòr	Aberd	NO1087	56°58·2'	3°28·4'W	H	43
Carn Mòr	Arg & Bt	NM3948	56°33·2'	6°14·4'W	H	47,48
Càrn Mòr	Arg & Bt	NM8543	56°32·1'	5°29·3'W	A	49
Carn Mòr	Arg & Bt	NR1964	55°47·5'	6°28·5'W	X	60
Carn Mòr	Arg & Bt	NR2160	55°45·4'	6°26·4'W	X	60
Carn Mòr	Arg & Bt	NR2771	55°51·6'	6°21·3'W	X	60
Carn Mòr	Arg & Bt	NR3794	56°4·3'	6°13·1'W	H	61
Carn Mòr	Arg & Bt	NR4047	55°39·1'	6°7·5'W	X	60
Carn Mòr	Arg & Bt	NR4095	56°4·9'	6°10·3'W	H	61
Càrn Mòr	Arg & Bt	NR7182	55°58·8'	5°39·8'W	A	55
Carn Mòr	Highld	NC4004	58°0·1'	4°42·0'W	H	16
Carn Mòr	Highld	ND0228	58°14·1'	3°39·7'W	H	17
Carn Mòr	Highld	NG3917	57°10·4'	6°18·6'W	X	32
Carn Mòr	Highld	NG5215	57°9·8'	6°5·6'W	X	32
Carn Mor	Highld	NG9448	57°28·8'	5°25·7'W	X	25
Carn Mòr	Highld	NG9743	57°26·2'	5°22·5'W	X	25
Carn Mòr	Highld	NG9877	57°44·5'	5°23·2'W	X	19
Carn Mòr	Highld	NH0246	57°27·9'	5°17·6'W	H	25
Carn Mòr	Highld	NH2036	57°23·0'	4°59·2'W	H	25
Carn Mòr	Highld	NH2487	57°50·5'	4°57·4'W	H	20
Carn Mòr	Highld	NH4119	57°14·3'	4°37·6'W	H	34
Carn Mòr	Highld	NH4271	57°42·3'	4°38·6'W	H	20
Carn Mòr	Highld	NH4334	57°22·4'	4°36·2'W	H	26
Carn Mòr	Highld	NH4890	57°52·7'	4°33·3'W	A	20
Carn Mòr	Highld	NH4999	57°57·5'	4°32·7'W	A	20
Carn Mòr	Highld	NH5090	57°52·7'	4°31·3'W	H	20
Carn Mòr	Highld	NH5098	57°57·0'	4°31·6'W	X	20
Càrn Mòr	Highld	NH6191	57°53·5'	4°20·2'W	A	21
Carn Mòr	Highld	NH6527	57°19·1'	4°14·0'W	H	26,35
Carn Mòr	Highld	NH7216	57°13·3'	4°6·7'W	H	35
Carn Mòr	Highld	NH8546	57°29·6'	3°54·7'W	H	27
Carn Mòr	Highld	NH8636	57°24·3'	3°53·4'W	X	27
Carn Mòr	Highld	NH8715	57°13·0'	3°51·8'W	H	35,36
Carn Mòr	Highld	NH9238	57°25·4'	3°47·4'W	X	27
Carn Mòr	Highld	NM6271	56°46·4'	5°53·3'W	H	40
Carn Mòr	Highld	NM6786	56°54·7'	5°49·2'W	X	40
Carn Mòr	Highld	NM6877	56°49·9'	5°47·7'W	X	40
Carn Mòr	Highld	NM9090	56°57·5'	5°26·8'W	H	33,40
Carn Mòr	Moray	NJ2119	57°15·6'	3°18·1'W	X	36
Carn Mòr	Moray	NJ2618	57°15·1'	3°13·1'W	H	37
Carn Mòr	N Ayr	NR9645	55°39·6'	5°14·2'W	X	62,69
Carn Mòr	Pth & Kin	NO0365	56°46·2'	3°34·8'W	H	43
Carn Mòr	Pth & Kin	NO1175	56°51·7'	3°27·1'W	H	43
Carn Mòraig	Highld	NH3537	57°23·9'	4°44·3'W	H	26
Carn Mòraig	Highld	NH7630	57°20·9'	4°3·2'W	H	27
Càrn Mòr (Broch)	Highld	NH4999	57°57·5'	4°32·7'W	A	20
Carn Mòr (Broch)	Highld	NH5098	57°57·0'	4°31·6'W	A	20
Carn Mòr Dearg	Highld	NN1772	56°48·5'	4°59·4'W	H	41
Carnmore	Highld	NG9776	57°43·9'	5°24·1'W	X	19
Carn Mòr na Comhdhal	Highld	NM7666	56°44·2'	5°39·3'W	X	40
Carn Morval Point	I Scilly	SV9011	49°55·4'	6°18·8'W	X	203
Carn na Bèiste	Highld	NG9989	57°51·0'	5°22·8'W	H	19
Carn na Bèiste	Highld	NH2864	57°38·3'	4°52·4'W	H	20
Carn na Bo Maoile	Highld	NH4196	57°55·8'	4°40·6'W	H	20
Carn na Breabaig	Highld	NH0629	57°18·9'	5°12·8'W	X	25,33
Carn na Breabaig	Highld	NH0630	57°19·4'	5°12·9'W	H	25
Carn na Bruar	Moray	NJ2925	57°18·9'	3°10·3'W	H	37
Carn na Buaile	Highld	NH4156	57°34·2'	4°39·1'W	X	26
Carn na Caillich	Highld	NG9690	57°51·4'	5°25·8'W	H	19
Carn na Caillich	Highld	NG9690	57°51·4'	5°25·8'W	H	19
Carn na Caillich	Highld	NH7112	57°11·1'	4°7·6'W	H	35
Carn na Caillich	Highld	NH9042	57°27·6'	3°49·6'W	H	27
Carn na Cailliche	Highld	NM5750	56°35·0'	5°57·0'W	A	47
Carn na Cailliche	Moray	NJ1847	57°30·6'	3°21·7'W	H	28
Carn na Caim	Highld	NN6782	56°54·9'	4°10·6'W	H	42
Carn na Cainnle	Arg & Bt	NR3794	56°4·3'	6°13·1'W	X	61
Carn na Canaich	Highld	NH0982	57°47·5'	5°12·3'W	H	19
Carn na Caorach	Highld	NH3218	57°13·6'	4°46·5'W	H	34
Carn na Caorach	Highld	NH4220	57°14·9'	4°36·7'W	H	26
Carn na Ceardaich	Highld	NC3809	58°2·7'	4°44·2'W	H	16
Carn na Ceàrdaich	Highld	NN6187	56°57·5'	4°16·7'W	H	42
Carn na Cloiche	Highld	NH4702	57°5·3'	4°31·0'W	X	34
Carn na Cloiche	Highld	NJ0922	57°17·0'	3°30·1'W	H	36
Carn na Cloiche Mòire	Highld	NH3753	57°32·5'	4°42·9'W	H	26
Carn na Còinnich	Highld	NH3251	57°31·3'	4°47·9'W	H	26
Carn na Coinnse	Highld	NJ0423	57°17·5'	3°35·1'W	H	36
Carn na Coireig	Highld	NH1856	57°33·7'	5°2·1'W	X	25
Carn na Con Dhu	Highld	NH0724	57°16·2'	5°11·6'W	H	25,33
Carn na Còsaig	Highld	NH1540	57°25·0'	5°4·4'W	X	25
Carn na Craoibhe-caoruinn	Highld	NG9182	57°47·0'	5°30·5'W	X	19
Carn na Craoibhe Seileich	Aberd	NO1396	57°3·1'	3°25·6'W	H	36,43
Carn na Crè	Highld	NH2847	57°29·1'	4°51·7'W	H	25
Carn na Cre	Highld	NH3059	57°35·6'	4°50·2'W	H	26
Carn na Creige	Highld	NG8832	57°20·0'	5°30·9'W	H	24
Carn na Criche	Aberd	NO1194	57°2·0'	3°27·5'W	H	36,43
Carn na Criche	Highld	NH1972	57°42·3'	5°1·8'W	H	20
Carn na Criche	Highld	NH5802	57°5·5'	4°20·2'W	H	35
Carn na Croiche	Highld	NH6125	57°17·9'	4°18·0'W	X	26,35
Carn na Croiche	Highld	NH6572	57°43·3'	4°15·5'W	X	21
Carn na Croiche (Chambered Cairn)	Highld	NH6572	57°43·3'	4°15·5'W	A	21
Carn na Croite	Highld	NH8431	57°21·5'	3°55·2'W	H	27
Carn na Cuimbne	Aberd	NO2494	57°2·1'	3°14·7'W	A	36,44
Carn na Dalach	Moray	NJ1627	57°19·8'	3°23·3'W	H	36
Carn na Doire	Highld	NJ0933	57°23·0'	3°30·4'W	X	27
Carn na Dreamaig	Highld	NH4109	57°8·9'	4°37·2'W	X	34
Carn na Drochaide	Aberd	NO1286	56°57·7'	3°26·4'W	H	43
Carn na Drochaide	Aberd	NO1293	57°1·4'	3°26·5'W	H	36,43
Carn na Dubh-chlais	Moray	NJ1241	57°27·3'	3°27·5'W	X	28
Carn na Dubh Choille	Highld	NH3867	57°40·1'	4°42·5'W	H	20
Carn na Farraidh	Highld	NJ1114	57°12·7'	3°28·0'W	H	36
Carn na Farr Bheinne	Highld	NH7026	57°18·6'	4°9·0'W	H	35
Carn na Feannaige	Moray	NJ1008	57°9·5'	3°28·8'W	H	36
Carn na Fèith-rabhain	Highld	NH2257	57°34·3'	4°58·1'W	H	25
Carn na Feòla	Highld	NG9161	57°35·7'	5°29·4'W	H	19
Carn na Fiacail	Highld	NH4122	57°15·9'	4°37·7'W	H	26
Carn na Garbh Lice	Highld	NH0860	57°35·6'	5°12·3'W	H	19
Carn na Gèarraig	Highld	NH4137	57°24·0'	4°38·3'W	H	26
Carn na Gearrsaich	Highld	NH4045	57°28·3'	4°39·6'W	H	26
Carn na Geuraidean	Highld	NH0145	57°27·4'	5°18·6'W	X	25
Carn na Glaic Buidhe	Highld	NG9892	57°52·6'	5°23·9'W	H	19
Carn na Glaice Mòire	Highld	NH5217	57°13·5'	4°26·6'W	H	35
Carn na Glaic Fhluich	Highld	NH8124	57°17·7'	3°58·0'W	H	35
Carn na Glaisneach	Highld	NJ0236	57°24·5'	3°37·4'W	H	27
Carn na Glascoill	Moray	NJ2822	57°17·2'	3°11·2'W	H	37
Carn na Gobhlaig-beithe	Highld	NH4985	57°50·0'	4°32·1'W	H	20
Carn na Goibhre	Pth & Kin	NN7838	56°31·4'	3°58·5'W	X	51,52
Carn na Gourach	Highld	NH5102	57°5·4'	4°27·1'W	X	35
Carn na Grèine	Aberd	NO1581	56°55·0'	3°23·3'W	H	43
Carn na Guaille	Highld	NH7615	57°12·8'	4°2·7'W	X	35
Carn na Guaille	Highld	NH7817	57°13·9'	4°0·8'W	H	35
Carn na Guaille	Highld	NH8618	57°14·6'	3°52·9'W	H	35,36
Carn na h-Achlaise	Highld	NH0761	57°36·1'	5°13·3'W	H	19
Carn na h-Àilig	Highld	NJ0713	57°12·2'	3°31·9'W	H	36
Carn na h-Aire	Highld	NG9691	57°52·0'	5°25·9'W	H	19
Carn na h-Annaite Mór	Highld	NH3554	57°33·0'	4°45·0'W	H	26
Carn na h-Aon-chraoibhe	Highld	NH8441	57°26·9'	3°55·5'W	H	27
Carn na h-Ath-aoil	Highld	NH9835	57°23·9'	3°41·4'W	H	27
Carn na h-Earbaige Bige	Highld	NH3123	57°16·2'	4°47·7'W	H	26
Carn na h-Easgainn	Highld	NH7432	57°21·9'	4°5·2'W	H	27
Carn na h-Eige	Highld	NJ0938	57°25·7'	3°30·5'W	X	27
Carn na h-Elrig	Pth & Kin	NN9959	56°43·0'	3°38·6'W	H	52,53
Carn na h-Imrich	Highld	NH4127	57°18·6'	4°37·9'W	H	26
Carn na h-Iolaire	Highld	NJ1229	57°20·8'	3°27·3'W	H	36
Carn na h-Iolaire	Moray	NJ2223	57°17·7'	3°17·2'W	H	36
Carn na h-Onaich	Highld	NG9232	57°20·1'	5°26·9'W	H	25
Carn na h-Uamhaig	Highld	NC6462	58°31·8'	4°19·7'W	H	10
Carn na h-Uigeig	Highld	NH5684	57°49·6'	4°25·0'W	X	21
Carn na h-Ulach	Highld	NH1808	57°7·9'	5°0·0'W	X	34
Carn na Làir	Highld	NH8223	57°17·2'	3°57·0'W	H	35
Carn na Larach	Highld	NN3396	57°1·8'	4°44·6'W	H	34
Carn na Làraiche Maoile	Highld	NH5811	57°10·3'	4°20·5'W	H	35
Carn na Leacainn	Moray	NJ1542	57°27·9'	3°24·6'W	H	28
Carn na Leitire	Highld	NH5434	57°22·6'	4°25·2'W	H	26
Carn na Leitire	Highld	NH9330	57°21·1'	3°46·2'W	H	27
Carn na Lòine	Highld	NJ0736	57°24·6'	3°32·4'W	H	27
Carn na Loinne	Highld	NH7632	57°22·0'	4°3·2'W	H	27
Carn na Lòinne	Highld	NH8024	57°17·7'	3°59·0'W	H	35
Carn na Loinne	Highld	NJ0322	57°17·0'	3°36·1'W	H	36
Carn na Loinne	Highld	NJ0615	57°13·2'	3°32·9'W	H	36
Carn nam Bad	Highld	NH4033	57°21·8'	4°39·2'W	H	26
Carn nam Bain-tighearna	Highld	NH8425	57°18·3'	3°55·1'W	H	35
Carn nam Bò-airigh	Highld	NH7530	57°20·9'	4°4·2'W	H	27
Carn nam Bo Maola	Highld	NC4509	58°2·8'	4°37·1'W	H	16
Carn nam Builtean	Highld	NH0087	57°49·9'	5°21·6'W	H	19
Càrn nam Buth	Highld	NC9024	58°11·7'	3°51·8'W	X	17
Càrn nam Fèithean	Highld	NH1178	57°45·4'	5°10·1'W	H	19
Carn nam Feuaich	Highld	NH1712	57°10·0'	5°1·1'W	H	34
Carn nam Fiacail	Highld	NH2446	57°28·5'	4°55·6'W	X	25
Carn nam Fiacal	Highld	NH2036	57°23·0'	4°59·2'W	H	25
Carn nam Fiaclan	Highld	NH1245	57°27·6'	5°7·6'W	H	25
Carn nam Fiadh	Highld	NG8341	57°24·7'	5°36·3'W	H	24
Carn nam Fiadh	Pth & Kin	NN5150	56°37·4'	4°25·3'W	X	42,51
Carn nam Meirleach	Highld	NH6914	57°12·1'	4°9·6'W	X	35
Carn nam Moine	Aberd	NO0687	56°58·1'	3°32·3'W	H	43
Carn na Moine	Highld	NH8209	57°9·7'	3°56·6'W	X	35
Carn nan Abrach	Highld	NH0395	57°54·3'	5°19·0'W	X	19
Carn nan Aighean	Highld	NH3878	57°46·0'	4°42·9'W	H	20
Carn nan Nathrach	Highld	NM8869	56°46·1'	5°27·7'W	H	40
Carn nan Caorach	Highld	NG9108	57°7·2'	5°26·7'W	H	33
Carn nan Caorach	Highld	NH4602	57°5·3'	4°32·0'W	X	34
Càrn nan Ceannaichean	Highld	NC7325	58°12·0'	4°9·2'W	H	16
Carn nan Clach Garbha	Highld	NH9434	57°23·3'	3°45·3'W	H	27
Carn nan Coireachan Cruaidh	Highld	NH1818	57°13·3'	5°0·4'W	H	34
Carn nan Conbhairean	Highld	NC3217	58°6·9'	4°50·6'W	X	15
Carn nan Con-easan	Highld	NG9887	57°49·9'	5°23·7'W	H	19
Carn nan Con Ruadha	Highld	NH4174	57°43·9'	4°39·8'W	H	20
Carn nan Cuilleag	Highld	NG9486	57°49·2'	5°27·6'W	H	19
Carn nan Dubh Lochan	Highld	NH3713	57°11·0'	4°41·4'W	H	34
Carn nan Eag	Highld	NH8034	57°23·1'	3°59·3'W	H	27
Carn nan Eagan	Highld	NH8927	57°19·5'	3°50·1'W	H	35,36
Carn nan Earb	Highld	NH3019	57°14·1'	4°48·5'W	H	34
Carn nan Eun	Highld	NG5537	57°21·7'	6°4·0'W	X	24,32
Carn nan Gabhar	Highld	NH9733	57°22·8'	3°42·3'W	X	27
Carn nan Gabhar	Pth & Kin	NN9773	56°50·5'	3°40·9'W	H	43
Càrn nan Gillean	Arg & Bt	NR3567	55°49·7'	6°13·5'W	H	60,61
Càrn nan Gillean	Arg & Bt	NR6593	56°4·6'	5°46·1'W	H	55,61
Carn nan Gobhar	Highld	NH1834	57°21·9'	5°1·1'W	H	25
Carn nan Gobhar	Highld	NH2743	57°26·9'	4°52·5'W	H	25
Carn nan Iomairean	Highld	NG9135	57°21·7'	5°28·0'W	H	25
Carn nan Lùibean Glas	Highld	NH7618	57°14·4'	4°2·8'W	H	35
Carn nan Sac	Pth & Kin	NO1176	56°52·3'	3°27·2'W	H	43
Carn nan Seabhag	Pth & Kin	NN7472	56°49·6'	4°3·4'W	H	42
Carn nan Searrach	Highld	NH0132	57°20·4'	5°17·9'W	H	25
Càrn nan Sgeir	Highld	NC0101	57°57·5'	5°21·3'W	X	15
Carn nan Sgliat	Aberd	NO1690	56°59·9'	3°22·5'W	H	43
Carn nan Tri-tighearnan	Highld	NH8239	57°25·8'	3°57·5'W	H	27
Carn Nant-y-ffald	Powys	SN9073	52°20·9'	3°36·5'W	A	136,147
Carn Nant-yr-ast	Carm	SN7249	52°7·7'	3°51·8'W	H	146,147
Carn nan Uaighean	Highld	NG7339	57°23·4'	5°46·2'W	X	24
Carn na Ruabraich	Moray	NJ1210	57°10·6'	3°26·9'W	H	36
Carn na Ruighe Duibhe	Highld	NH3724	57°16·9'	4°41·8'W	H	26
Carn na Sàile Lèithe	Highld	NH1836	57°22·9'	5°1·2'W	X	25
Carn na Saobhaidh	Highld	NH6009	57°9·3'	4°18·4'W	H	35
Carn na Saobhaidh	Highld	NH6724	57°17·5'	4°12·0'W	H	26,35
Carn na Saobhaidhe	Highld	NH0333	57°21·0'	5°16·0'W	X	25
Carn na Saobhaidhe	Highld	NH4006	57°7·3'	4°38·1'W	H	34
Carn na Saobhaidhe	Highld	NH5304	57°6·5'	4°25·2'W	H	35
Carn na Saobhaidhe	Highld	NH5514	57°11·9'	4°23·5'W	H	35
Carn na Saohaidhe	Highld	NH6014	57°12·0'	4°18·6'W	H	35
Carn na Seanalaich	Highld	NH7726	57°18·7'	4°2·1'W	H	35
Carn na Sean-lùibe	Highld	NH0235	57°22·0'	5°17·1'W	H	25
Carn na Sguabaich	Highld	NH8736	57°24·3'	3°52·4'W	H	27
Carn na Sguabaig	Highld	NH7229	57°20·3'	4°7·1'W	X	35
Carn na Snaobhaig	Highld	NG7727	57°17·0'	5°41·5'W	X	33
Carn na Speireig	Highld	NH4388	57°51·5'	4°38·3'W	H	20
Carn na Squabaich	Highld	NH8222	57°16·7'	3°57·0'W	H	35
Carn na Sròine	Highld	NJ1020	57°16·0'	3°29·1'W	H	36
Carn na Toiteill	Highld	NH3035	57°22·7'	4°49·2'W	X	26
Carn Naun Point	Corn	SW4741	50°13·1'	5°32·4'W	X	203
Carn Near	I Scilly	SV8913	49°56·4'	6°19·7'W	X	203
Carn-Nwchwn	Pemb	SM7624	51°52·4'	5°14·9'W	X	157
Carno	Powys	SN9596	52°33·3'	3°32·5'W	T	136
Carno	Powys	SN9823	51°54·0'	3°28·6'W	X	160
Carnoch	Highld	NH2551	57°31·2'	4°54·9'W	X	25
Carnoch	Highld	NH3836	57°23·4'	4°41·3'W	X	26
Carnoch	Highld	NH5623	57°16·8'	4°22·9'W	X	26,35
Carnoch	Highld	NH8740	57°26·4'	3°52·5'W	X	27
Carnoch	Highld	NM8460	56°41·2'	5°31·2'W	X	40
Carnoch	Highld	NM8696	57°0·6'	5°31·0'W	X	33,40
Carnoch	Moray	NJ4565	57°40·6'	2°54·9'W	X	28,29
Carnochan	E Ayr	NS4112	55°22·8'	4°30·1'W	X	70
Carnoch Burn	Highld	NH8741	57°27·0'	3°52·5'W	W	27
Carnoch River	Highld	NM8660	56°41·2'	5°29·2'W	W	40
Carnoch Wood	Highld	NH3735	57°22·8'	4°42·2'W	F	26
Carnoch Wood	Moray	NJ4666	57°41·1'	2°53·9'W	F	28,29
Carnock	Fife	NT0488	56°4·8'	3°32·1'W	T	65
Carnock Burn	Stir	NS4783	56°1·2'	4°26·8'W	W	57,64
Carnock Ho	Fife	NT0489	56°5·3'	3°32·1'W	X	65
Carnock Ho	Stir	NS8688	56°4·5'	3°49·5'W	X	65
Carnock Moor	Fife	NT0490	56°5·8'	3°32·2'W	F	58
Carn Odhar	Arg & Bt	NN0813	56°16·5'	5°5·6'W	H	50,56
Carn Odhar	Highld	NH0049	57°29·5'	5°19·8'W	H	25
Carn Odhar	Highld	NH6317	57°13·7'	4°15·7'W	H	35
Carn Odhar	Highld	NH6925	57°18·1'	4°10·0'W	H	26,35
Carn Odhar	Highld	NH7228	57°19·7'	4°7·1'W	H	35
Carn Odhar	Highld	NH8241	57°26·9'	3°57·5'W	X	27
Carn Odhar	Highld	NH9404	57°7·1'	3°44·6'W	H	36
Carn Odhar na Criche	Highld	NH6003	57°6·1'	4°18·2'W	H	35
Carn Odhar Uaine Osein	Highld	NH4706	57°7·4'	4°31·2'W	X	34
Carn Oighreag	Aberd	NJ2407	57°9·1'	3°14·9'W	H	36
Carn Oighreagan	Highld	NH7224	57°17·6'	4°7·0'W	X	35
Carnon Downs	Corn	SW7940	50°13·4'	5°5·5'W	T	204
Carnon River	Corn	SW7741	50°13·9'	5°7·2'W	W	204
Carno Resr	Blae Gw	SO1613	51°48·8'	3°12·7'W	W	161
Carnousie Ho	Aberd	NJ6749	57°32·1'	2°32·6'W	X	29
Carnoustie	Angus	NO5634	56°30·0'	2°42·4'W	T	54
Carn Owen	Cered	SN7388	52°28·8'	3°51·8'W	A	135
Carn Pantmaenllwyd	Powys	SN9558	52°12·9'	3°31·8'W	A	147
Carn Pen-rhiw-ddu	Carm	SN7218	51°51·0'	3°51·1'W	A	160
Carn Penrhiwllwydog	Cered	SN7352	52°9·3'	3°51·0'W	A	146,147
Carn Pen-y-clogau	Carm	SN7118	51°51·0'	3°52·0'W	A	160
Carnpessack	Corn	SW7417	50°0·9'	5°8·9'W	X	204
Carn Pheigith	Highld	NN7593	57°0·9'	4°3·1'W	X	35
Carn Phris Mhóir	Highld	NH8021	57°16·1'	3°58·9'W	H	35
Carn Poll-eisg	Highld	NH0137	57°23·1'	5°18·2'W	H	25
Carn Ricet	Powys	SN8770	52°19·2'	3°39·1'W	X	135,136,147
Carn Richard	Highld	NC8332	58°15·9'	3°59·2'W	X	17
Càrn Richard (Chambered Cairn)	Highld	NC8332	58°15·9'	3°59·2'W	A	17
Carn Righean	Highld	NH5923	57°16·8'	4°19·9'W	H	26,35
Carn Rock	Pemb	SN0902	51°41·3'	4°45·4'W	X	158
Carn Ruabraich	Moray	NJ1312	57°11·7'	3°25·9'W	H	36
Carn Ruadh-bhreac	Highld	NJ1213	57°12·2'	3°26·9'W	H	36

Carn Ruairidh	Highld	NG9438	57°23·4'	5°25·2'W	H	25
Carn Ruigh an t-Seilich	Highld	NH4810	57°9·6'	4°30·3'W	H	34
Carn Ruigh Chorrach	Highld	NH9834	57°23·4'	3°41·4'W	H	27
Carn Ruighe an Uain	Highld	NJ0637	57°25·1'	3°33·4'W	H	27
Carn Ruighe na Gaoithe	Highld	NH5615	57°12·5'	4°22·6'W	X	35
Carn Ruighe Shamhraich	Highld	NH7822	57°16·6'	4°1·0'W	H	35
Carn Ruigh na Creadha	Highld	NH5313	57°11·3'	4°25·5'W	H	35
Carn Ruigh Thuim	Moray	NJ0239	57°26·1'	3°37·5'W	H	27
Carn Saethon	Gwyn	SH2933	52°52·3'	4°32·0'W	A	123
Carn Salachaidh	Highld	NH5187	57°51·1'	4°30·2'W	H	20
Carn Scathe	Corn	SW3721	50°2·1'	5°40·0'W	X	203
Carnsdale Fm	Wirral	SJ2882	53°20·0'	3°4·5'W	FM	108
Carnsefyll	Pemb	SN0137	52°0·0'	4°53·6'W	X	145,157
Carnsew Fm	Corn	SW7634	50°10·1'	5°7·8'W	FM	204
Carn Sgolbaidh	Highld	NH3953	57°32·6'	4°40·9'W	H	26
Carn Sgùlain	Highld	NH6805	57°7·3'	4°10·4'W	H	35
Carn Sgùlain	Highld	NH6909	57°9·5'	4°9·5'W	H	35
Carn Shalag	Moray	NJ1142	57°27·8'	3°28·6'W	H	28
Carnshalloch	D & G	NX9780	55°6·5'	3°36·4'W	X	78
Carn Sian	Pemb	SN1232	51°57·5'	4°43·8'W	H	145
Carn Slani	Pemb	SM9837	51°59·9'	4°56·2'W	X	157
Carn Sleamhuinn	Highld	NH8516	57°13·5'	3°53·8'W	H	35,36
Carn Slèibhe	Moray	NJ1821	57°16·6'	3°21·1'W	H	36
Carnsmerry	Corn	SX0158	50°23·5'	4°47·6'W	T	200
Carn Sònraichte	Highld	NH5179	57°46·8'	4°29·9'W	H	20
Carn Suidhe Ghoiri	Highld	NH5313	57°11·3'	4°25·5'W	H	35
Carn Tarmachain	Pth & Kin	NO0571	56°49·5'	3°32·9'W	X	43
Carn Tarsuinn	Highld	NH0028	57°18·2'	5°18·7'W	H	25,33
Carn Tarsuinn	Highld	NH2407	57°7·5'	4°54·0'W	H	34
Carn Tarsuinn	Highld	NH3411	57°9·9'	4°44·2'W	H	34
Carn Tarsuinn	Highld	NH3822	57°15·9'	4°40·7'W	H	26
Carn Tarsuinn	Highld	NJ0611	57°11·1'	3°32·9'W	H	36
Carn, The	Corn	SW4134	50°9·2'	5°37·2'W	X	203
Carn, The	I of M	SC1971	54°6·4'	4°45·7'W	X	95
Carn Thearlaich	Highld	NH7918	57°14·5'	3°59·8'W	X	35
Carn Thollaidh	Highld	NG8029	57°18·2'	5°38·7'W	H	33
Carn Thòmais	Highld	NH4408	57°8·4'	4°34·2'W	H	34
Carn Thòmais	Highld	NN7288	56°58·2'	4°5·9'W	X	42
Carn Tighearn	Moray	NJ2329	57°21·0'	3°16·3'W	H	36
Carn Torcaidh	Pth & Kin	NN9473	56°50·4'	3°43·8'W	H	43
Carn Torr Mheadhoin	Highld	NH8434	57°23·2'	3°55·3'W	H	27
Carn Towan	Corn	SW3626	50°4·8'	5°41·0'W	T	203
Carn Treglemaes	Pemb	SM8128	51°54·7'	5°10·7'W	H	157
Carn Treliwyd	Pemb	SM7528	51°54·5'	5°15·9'W	X	157
Carn Tuadhan	Highld	NJ1215	57°13·3'	3°27·0'W	X	36
Carn Tuairneir	Highld	NJ0923	57°17·6'	3°30·1'W	H	36
Carn Tullich	Moray	NJ2324	57°18·3'	3°16·2'W	H	36
Carn Twrch	Carm	SN8046	52°6·2'	3°44·7'W	A	147
Carntyne	C of Glas	NS6365	55°51·8'	4°10·9'W	T	64
Carn Ulie	Moray	NJ1904	57°7·4'	3°19·8'W	X	36
Carn Vellan	Corn	SW3634	50°9·1'	5°41·4'W	X	203
Carnwadric	C of Glas	NS5459	55°48·4'	4°19·3'W	T	64
Carnwath	S Lanak	NS9846	55°42·1'	3°36·9'W	T	72
Carnwath Burn	S Lanak	NS9747	55°42·6'	3°37·9'W	W	72
Carnwath Mill	S Lanak	NS9945	55°41·5'	3°36·0'W	X	72
Carnwath Moss	S Lanak	NS9748	55°43·1'	3°37·9'W	X	72
Carnweather Point	Corn	SW9580	50°35·3'	4°53·4'W	X	200
Carn Wen	Carm	SN1628	51°55·4'	4°40·2'W	H	145,158
Carn-wen	Carm	SN3534	51°59·1'	4°23·8'W	A	145
Carn-wen	Carm	SN3933	51°58·6'	4°20·3'W	A	145
Carn Wen	Powys	SN9073	52°20·9'	3°36·5'W	A	136,147
Carn-wen	Powys	SN9860	52°14·0'	3°29·2'W	A	147
Carn Wen	Powys	SN9866	52°17·2'	3°29·3'W	A	136,147
Carnwinnick	Corn	SW9251	50°19·6'	4°55·0'W	X	200,204
Carn y Bugail	Merth Tyd	SO1003	51°43·3'	3°17·8'W	A	171
Carn y Castell	Powys	SO1529	51°57·4'	3°13·8'W	A	161
Carn-y-celyn	Rho Cyn Taf	SS9890	51°36·2'	3°28·0'W	X	170
Carn-y-chain	Flint	SJ0880	53°18·8'	3°20·5'W	X	116
Carn-y-crochan	Powys	SN9109	51°46·4'	3°34·4'W	X	160
Carn y Defaid	Torf	SO2709	51°46·7'	3°3·1'W	X	161
Carn-y-geifr	Powys	SN9760	52°14·0'	3°30·1'W	A	147
Carn y Gigfran	Carm	SN7721	51°52·7'	3°46·8'W	A	160
Carn-y-gorfydd	Monm	SO2711	51°47·8'	3°3·1'W	X	161
Carnyorth	Corn	SW3733	50°8·6'	5°40·5'W	T	203
Carn-y-Parc	Conwy	SH8150	53°2·3'	3°46·1'W	X	116
Carn-y-pigwn	Rho Cyn Taf	ST0197	51°40·0'	3°25·5'W	A	170
Carn yr arian	Powys	SN9312	51°48·0'	3°32·7'W	A	160
Carn yr arian	Powys	SN9412	51°48·0'	3°31·8'W	A	160
Carn yr Helyg	Powys	SO0911	51°47·7'	3°18·8'W	X	161
Carn-yr-hyrddod	Brig	SS9193	51°37·8'	3°34·1'W	A	170
Carnyrhyrddod	Cered	SN7970	52°19·1'	3°46·1'W	A	135,147
Carn yr Onnen	Powys	SN8816	51°50·1'	3°37·1'W	X	160
Carnysgubor	Pemb	SM6924	51°52·2'	5°21·0'W	H	157
Carn-y-wiwer	Rho Cyn Taf	SS9099	51°41·0'	3°35·1'W	X	170
Carn-y-wiwer	Rho Cyn Taf	ST0294	51°38·4'	3°24·6'W	X	170
Caroe	Corn	SX1691	50°41·6'	4°35·9'W	T	190
Carol Green	Sol	SP2577	52°23·7'	1°37·6'W	T	140
Carol Ho	Norf	TF8307	52°38·0'	0°42·7'E	X	144
Carolina	Derby	SK3261	53°8·9'	1°30·9'W	X	119
Carolina Hill	Highld	NG4147	57°26·6'	6°18·5'W	H	23
Caroline Park	C of Edin	NT2277	55°59·0'	3°14·6'W	A	66
Carolside	Scot Bord	NT5639	55°38·8'	2°41·5'W	X	73
Caroy	Highld	NG3043	57°24·1'	6°29·2'W	T	23
Caroy River	Highld	NG3045	57°25·2'	6°29·4'W	W	23
Carpalla	Corn	SW9654	50°21·3'	4°51·7'W	T	200
Carpel Burn	Renf	NS3359	55°48·0'	4°39·4'W	W	63
Carpenders Park	Herts	TQ1293	51°37·7'	0°22·5'W	T	176
Carpenters Dock	Hants	SU3901	50°48·7'	1°26·4'W	X	196
Carpenters Down Wood	Hants	SU6455	51°17·7'	1°4·5'W	F	175,185
Carpenters Fm	I of W	SZ6188	50°41·5'	1°7·8'W	FM	196
Carpenter's Grove	Suff	TM0676	52°20·8'	1°1·9'E	F	144
Carpenter's Hill	Devon	ST1503	50°49·5'	3°12·0'W	X	192,193
Carpenter's Hill	Worcs	SP0770	52°20·1'	1°53·4'W	T	139
Carperby	N Yks	SD9991	54°19·1'	2°0·5'W	X	98
Carperby	N Yks	SE0089	54°18·1'	1°59·6'W	T	98
Carperby Moor	N Yks	SD9891	54°19·1'	2°1·4'W	X	98
Carperstane	E Loth	NT5582	56°2·0'	2°42·9'W	X	66
Carpet	Scot Bord	NT1655	55°47·1'	3°19·9'W	X	65,66,72
Carphin	Fife	NO3119	56°21·8'	3°6·6'W	X	59
Carpley Green	N Yks	SD9487	54°17·0'	2°5·1'W	X	98

Car Ponds	Derby	SK4764	53°10·5'	1°17·4'W	W	120
Carpow Bank	Pth & Kin	NO2018	56°21·1'	3°17·2'W	X	58
Carpow Ho	Pth & Kin	NO2017	56°20·6'	3°17·2'W	X	58
Carp Shield	Durham	NZ0447	54°49·3'	1°55·8'W	X	87
Carpuan	Corn	SX2069	50°29·8'	4°31·9'W	X	201
Carr	Bury	SD7817	53°39·2'	2°19·6'W	T	109
Carr	Roth	SK5190	53°24·5'	1°13·6'W	T	111
Carra Beag	Pth & Kin	NN9256	56°41·3'	3°45·3'W	H	52
Carraburn	Moray	NJ2954	57°34·5'	3°10·8'W	X	28
Carrabus	Arg & Bt	NR3163	55°47·4'	6°17·0'W	X	60,61
Carrabus Burn	Arg & Bt	NR3263	55°47·4'	6°16·1'W	W	60,61
Carracawn Fm	Corn	SX3257	50°23·6'	4°21·4'W	FM	201
Carrachan	Highld	NC4222	58°9·8'	4°40·7'W	X	16
Carrachan	Highld	NG6833	57°20·0'	5°50·8'W	X	24,32
Carrachan Dubh	Highld	NC4117	58°7·1'	4°41·5'W	H	16
Carrachan Mór	Arg & Bt	NM4027	56°22·1'	6°12·2'W	X	48
Carrach, The	Angus	NO3056	56°41·7'	3°8·1'W	H	53
Carrack Gladden	Corn	SW5338	50°11·7'	5°27·3'W	X	203
Carracks, The	Corn	SW4640	50°12·6'	5°33·2'W	X	203
Carra-crom	N Eil	NF7373	57°38·0'	7°28·3'W	H	18
Carradale	Arg & Bt	NR8138	55°35·4'	5°28·1'W	T	68,69
Carradale Bay	Arg & Bt	NR8036	55°34·3'	5°29·0'W	W	68,69
Carradale Ho	Arg & Bt	NR8037	55°34·9'	5°29·0'W	X	68,69
Carradale Point	Arg & Bt	NR8136	55°34·4'	5°28·0'W	X	68,69
Carradale Water	Arg & Bt	NR7839	55°35·9'	5°31·0'W	W	68,69
Carradale Water	Arg & Bt	NR7840	55°36·4'	5°31·0'W	W	62,69
Carraghan	I of M	SC3684	54°13·8'	4°30·5'W	H	95
Carragh an t-Sruith	Arg & Bt	NR4371	55°52·1'	6°6·0'W	X	60,61
Carragraich	N Eil	NG1998	57°53·2'	6°44·0'W	T	14
Carraig	Highld	NM5557	56°38·7'	5°59·3'W	X	47
Carraig a' Choire	Arg & Bt	NR7063	55°48·6'	5°39·8'W	X	61,62
Carraig an Daimh	Arg & Bt	NM2725	56°20·6'	6°24·6'W	X	48
Carraig an Daimh	Arg & Bt	NR6678	55°56·5'	5°44·4'W	X	61,62
Carraig an Ràtha	Arg & Bt	NR4658	55°45·2'	6°2·4'W	X	60
Carraig Bhàn	Arg & Bt	NR2572	55°52·0'	6°23·3'W	X	60
Carraig Bun Aibhne	Arg & Bt	NR3140	55°35·0'	6°15·7'W	X	60
Carraig Chorrach	Arg & Bt	NM4137	56°27·5'	6°11·8'W	X	47,48
Carraig Dhubh	Arg & Bt	NR3062	55°46·8'	6°17·9'W	X	60
Carraigean	Arg & Bt	NR3289	56°1·4'	6°17·6'W	X	61
Carraig Fhada	Arg & Bt	NR3444	55°37·3'	6°13·1'W	X	60
Carraig Gheal	Arg & Bt	NM9621	56°20·5'	5°17·6'W	X	49
Carraig Ghillìondrais	Arg & Bt	NM3524	56°20·3'	6°16·8'W	X	48
Carraigh Chorrach	Arg & Bt	NM3724	56°20·4'	6°14·9'W	X	48
Carraig Mhaol	Arg & Bt	NS2087	56°2·8'	4°53·0'W	X	56
Carraig Mhicheil	Arg & Bt	NM8531	56°25·6'	5°28·7'W	X	49
Carraig Mhic Thòmais	Arg & Bt	NM4026	56°21·6'	6°12·1'W	X	48
Carraig Mhór	Arg & Bt	NM3617	56°16·6'	6°15·4'W	X	48
Carraig Mhór	Arg & Bt	NM5521	56°19·3'	5°57·3'W	X	48
Carraig Mhór	Arg & Bt	NM6901	56°9·0'	5°42·7'W	X	55,61
Carraig Mhór	Arg & Bt	NR4655	55°43·6'	6°2·3'W	X	60
Carraig Mhór	Arg & Bt	NR4751	55°41·4'	6°1·1'W	X	60
Carraig Mhór	Arg & Bt	NR6248	55°40·3'	5°46·7'W	X	62
Carraig na h-Acairseid	Arg & Bt	NR6973	55°53·9'	5°41·3'W	X	61,62
Carraig na Maraig	Arg & Bt	NS2093	56°6·0'	4°53·2'W	X	56
Carraig nam Ban	Arg & Bt	NR9073	55°54·5'	5°21·2'W	X	62
Carraig nam Bodach	Arg & Bt	NR7067	55°50·7'	5°40·0'W	X	61,62
Carraig nam Fear	Arg & Bt	NR2170	55°50·8'	6°27·0'W	X	60
Carraig nam Marbh	Arg & Bt	NM8322	56°20·7'	5°30·2'W	X	49
Carraig nan Ròn	Arg & Bt	NS2193	56°6·0'	4°52·2'W	X	56
Carrallack	Corn	SW3630	50°6·9'	5°41·2'W	X	203
Carr Allt a'Chaise	Pth & Kin	NN8074	56°50·8'	3°57·6'W	H	43
Carra-mhòine	Arg & Bt	NR2667	55°49·4'	6°22·1'W	X	60
Carran	N Eil	NG0796	57°51·7'	6°56·0'W	H	14,18
Carran Hill	Moray	NJ3741	57°27·6'	3°2·5'W	H	28
Carrant Brook	Glos	SO9134	52°0·5'	2°7·5'W	W	150
Carrant Brook Fm	Worcs	SP0038	52°2·7'	1°59·6'W	FM	150
Carrastaoin	Arg & Bt	NL9447	56°31·2'	6°58·1'W	X	46
Carrat	Stir	NS7497	56°9·2'	4°1·3'W	X	57
Carraw	Northum	NY8471	55°2·2'	2°14·6'W	X	86,87
Carrawbrough	Northum	NY8671	55°2·2'	2°12·7'W	X	87
Carr Bàn	Highld	NH6736	57°24·0'	4°12·3'W	X	26
Carr Bank	Cumbr	SD4778	54°11·9'	2°48·3'W	T	97
Carr Banks Fm	Notts	SK6356	53°6·1'	1°3·1'W	FM	120
Carr Beck	Brad	SE1444	53°53·8'	1°46·8'W	W	104
Carr Beck	Leeds	SE3835	53°48·8'	1°25·0'W	W	104
Carr Beck	N Yks	SD7963	54°4·0'	2°18·8'W	W	98
Carr Beck	N Yks	SE4499	54°23·3'	1°18·9'W	W	99
Carr Bog Farm	Brad	SE0349	53°56·5'	1°56·8'W	FM	104
Carr Bottom	Derby	SK2083	53°20·8'	1°41·6'W	X	110
Carr Br	Leic	SK7008	52°40·1'	0°57·5'W	X	141
Carr Brae	Highld	NG8924	57°15·7'	5°29·5'W	X	33
Carr Brecks Fm	Notts	SK6466	53°11·5'	1°2·1'W	FM	120
Carrbridge	Highld	NH9022	57°16·8'	3°49·0'W	T	36
Carrbridge Fm	N Yks	NZ4104	54°26·0'	1°21·7'W	FM	93
Carr Brigs	Fife	NO6411	56°17·7'	2°34·5'W	X	59
Carr Brook	Lancs	SD4921	53°41·3'	2°45·9'W	W	102
Carrbrook	Tames	SD9801	53°30·6'	2°1·4'W	T	109
Carrbrook Fm	Derby	SK3049	53°2·5'	1°32·7'W	FM	119
Carr Brow Moor	Durham	NY8839	54°45·0'	2°10·8'W	H	91,92
Carr Cote	N Yks	SE5791	54°18·9'	1°7·0'W	X	100
Carr & Craggs Moor	Cald	SD8925	53°43·5'	2°9·6'W	X	103
Carr Cross	Lancs	SD3714	53°37·4'	2°56·7'W	T	108
Carr Delph	Brad	SE0643	53°53·2'	1°54·1'W	X	104
Carr Dike	N Yks	SE5136	53°49·3'	1°13·1'W	W	105
Càrr Dubh	Highld	NH6285	57°50·3'	4°19·0'W	X	21
Carr-Dyke Fm	Lincs	TF0768	53°12·1'	0°23·5'W	FM	121
Carrdyke Fm	Lincs	TF1124	52°48·4'	0°20·8'W	FM	130
Carr Dyke Fm	Lincs	TF1161	53°8·3'	0°20·0'W	FM	121
Carr Edge	Northum	NY8869	55°1·2'	2°10·8'W	X	87
Carreg	Gwyn	SH1628	52°49·3'	4°43·4'W	X	123
Carreg	Powys	SO0987	52°28·6'	3°20·0'W	X	136
Carreg Alltrem	Conwy	SH7450	53°2·2'	3°52·3'W	X	115
Carregberfedd	Conwy	SH9949	53°2·0'	3°30·0'W	X	116
Carreg Bica	Nth Pt Talb	SS7299	51°40·8'	3°50·7'W	A	170
Carreg Bica	Pemb	SN0944	52°3·9'	4°46·8'W	X	145
Carreg Blaen-Llym	Gwyn	SH6643	52°58·3'	3°59·3'W	X	124
Carreg Cadno	Powys	SN8715	51°49·6'	3°38·0'W	X	160
Carregcadwgan	Cered	SN6990	52°29·8'	3°55·4'W	X	135
Carreg Cennen	Carm	SN6519	51°51·4'	3°57·2'W	X	159
Carreg-Cennen Castle	Carm	SN6619	51°51·5'	3°56·4'W	A	159

Carreg Chwislen	Gwyn	SH1925	52°47·8'	4°40·7'W	X	123
Carreg Coetan	Pemb	SN0639	52°1·2'	4°49·3'W	A	145
Carreg-cyn-ffrydd	Carm	SN6622	51°53·1'	3°56·4'W	X	159
Carreg-ddu	Carm	SS5297	51°39·4'	4°8·0'W	X	159
Carreg Ddu	Gwyn	SH1423	52°46·6'	4°45·1'W	X	123
Carreg Ddu	Gwyn	SH2742	52°57·1'	4°34·1'W	X	123
Carreg-ddu	Powys	SJ1128	52°50·8'	3°18·9'W	X	125
Carreg Dwfn	Carm	SN6517	51°50·4'	3°57·2'W	X	159
Carregedrywy	Pemb	SN0441	52°2·2'	4°51·1'W	X	145
Carreg-fach	Carm	SS5197	51°39·4'	4°8·9'W	X	159
Carreg Fawr	Gwyn	SH1121	52°45·5'	4°47·7'W	X	123
Carreg Fawr	Gwyn	SH6229	52°50·7'	4°2·5'W	X	124
Carreg Fran	Pemb	SM7322	51°51·3'	5°17·4'W	X	157
Carreg-gafeiliog	Pemb	SM7126	51°53·4'	5°19·3'W	X	157
Carreg Goch	Powys	SN8116	51°50·0'	3°43·2'W	H	160
Carreg Golchfa	Pemb	SM8835	51°58·6'	5°4·8'W	X	157
Carreg-gwylan	Pemb	SM6923	51°51·7'	5°20·9'W	X	157
Carreg-gwylan-fach	Pemb	SM7730	51°55·7'	5°14·2'W	X	157
Carreg Gwyn	Powys	SO2054	52°10·9'	3°9·8'W	X	148
Carreg Gybi	Gwyn	SH1925	52°47·8'	4°40·7'W	X	123
Carreg Gybi	Pemb	SM9041	52°1·9'	5°3·3'W	X	157
Carreg Herefio	Pemb	SM8836	51°59·2'	5°4·9'W	X	157
Carreg Hirfaen	Carm	SN6246	52°5·9'	4°0·5'W	A	146
Carreghofa Hall	Powys	SJ2521	52°47·1'	3°6·3'W	X	126
Carreg Ifan	Cered	SN3154	52°9·7'	4°27·9'W	X	145
Carreglefn	I of Angl	SH3889	53°22·6'	4°25·7'W	T	114
Carreg Lem	Powys	SN8017	51°50·6'	3°44·1'W	X	160
Carreg Lleon	Conwy	SH8155	53°5·0'	3°46·2'W	X	116
Carregllys	Carm	SN4823	51°53·3'	4°12·1'W	X	159
Carreg Lusog	Gwyn	SH8126	52°49·3'	3°45·6'W	X	124,125
Carreglwyd	I of Angl	SH3087	53°21·4'	4°32·9'W	A	114
Carreg Lwyd	Powys	SN8615	51°49·6'	3°38·9'W	X	160
Carreg Lydan	Cered	SN1651	52°7·8'	4°40·9'W	X	145
Carreglydan	I of Angl	SH3271	53°12·8'	4°30·6'W	X	114
Carreg Maen Taro	Torf	SO2311	51°47·8'	3°6·6'W	A	161
Carreg Mianog	Conwy	SH6861	53°8·0'	3°58·0'W	X	115
Carreg Onnen	Pemb	SM8841	52°1·9'	5°5·0'W	X	157
Carreg Onnen Bay	Pemb	SM8940	52°1·3'	5°4·1'W	W	157
Carreg Rhoson	Pemb	SM6625	51°52·7'	5°23·6'W	X	157
Carreg Sampson	Pemb	SM8433	51°57·5'	5°8·2'W	A	157
Carreg Samson	Cered	SN6753	52°9·8'	3°56·3'W	A	146
Carreg-Sawdde Common	Carm	SN7027	51°55·8'	3°53·1'W	X	146,160
Carreg Ti-pw	Cered	SN5370	52°18·7'	4°9·0'W	X	135
Carreg-trai	Pemb	SM6927	51°53·9'	5°21·1'W	X	157
Carregwastad Point	Pemb	SM9240	52°1·4'	5°1·5'W	X	157
Carregwastad Point (French Landed AD 1797)	Pemb	SM9240	52°1·4'	5°1·5'W	X	157
Carreg Waun Llech	Powys	SO1617	51°51·0'	3°12·8'W	A	161
Carregwen	Carm	SN2831	51°57·3'	4°29·8'W	X	145
Carreg-wen	Pemb	SN2241	52°2·6'	4°35·3'W	T	145
Carreg Wen	Powys	SN8288	52°28·9'	3°43·9'W	A	135,136
Carreg Wen Fawr	Powys	SN8262	52°14·9'	3°43·3'W	H	147
Carregwiber	Powys	SO0859	52°13·5'	3°20·4'W	X	147
Carreg Wylan	Pemb	SN1045	52°4·5'	4°46·0'W	X	145
Carreg Wynt	Cered	SN2352	52°8·5'	4°34·8'W	X	145
Carreg y Barcud	Pemb	SM7724	51°52·4'	5°14·0'W	X	157
Carreg-y-big	Powys	SH9903	52°37·2'	3°29·1'W	X	136
Carreg-y-big	Shrops	SJ2532	52°53·1'	3°6·5'W	X	126
Carreg-y-blaidd	Conwy	SH8649	53°1·8'	3°41·6'W	X	116
Carreg y Ddafad	Cered	SN2751	52°8·1'	4°31·3'W	X	145
Carreg-y-Ddafad	Gwyn	SH9146	53°0·3'	3°37·1'W	X	116
Carreg y Defaid	Gwyn	SH3432	52°51·8'	4°27·6'W	X	123
Carregyderlwyn	Cered	SN8070	52°19·1'	3°45·2'W	X	135,136,147
Carreg y Diocyn	Gwyn	SH8336	52°54·8'	3°44·0'W	X	124,125
Carreg-y-ffordd	Conwy	SH7568	53°11·9'	3°51·9'W	X	115
Carreg y Foel-gron	Gwyn	SH7442	52°57·9'	3°52·2'W	X	124
Carreg y Frân	Gwyn	SH7344	52°58·9'	3°53·1'W	X	124
Carreg y Frân	I of Angl	SH2887	53°21·4'	4°34·7'W	X	114
Carreg y Frân	Powys	SH9514	52°43·1'	3°32·9'W	X	125
Carreg y Frân	Powys	SN8058	52°12·7'	3°45·0'W	X	147
Carreg-y-frân	Powys	SO1878	52°23·9'	3°11·9'W	X	136,148
Carreg-y-franc	Wrex	SJ3742	52°58·5'	2°55·9'W	X	117
Carreg y Garth	Gwyn	SH5865	53°10·0'	4°7·1'W	T	114,115
Carreg-y-gâth	Denb	SJ0559	53°7·4'	3°24·8'W	X	116
Carreg y Nodwydd	Cered	SN2953	52°9·2'	4°29·6'W	X	145
Carreg-y-pennill	Denb	SJ0862	53°9·1'	3°22·1'W	X	116
Carreg yr Adar	Powys	SN8357	52°12·2'	3°42·3'W	X	147
Carreg yr Aderyn	Gwyn	SH8324	52°48·3'	3°43·7'W	H	124,125
Carreg yr Afr	Pemb	SM7529	51°55·1'	5°15·9'W	X	157
Carreg yr Ast	Powys	SN8759	52°13·3'	3°38·9'W	X	147
Carreg yr Esgob	Pemb	SM7223	51°51·8'	5°18·3'W	X	157
Carreg yr Honwy	Gwyn	SH1021	52°45·4'	4°48·5'W	X	123
Carreg yr Imbill	Gwyn	SH3834	52°53·0'	4°24·1'W	X	123
Carreg Yr Ogof	Carm	SN7721	51°52·7'	3°46·8'W	H	160
Carreg-y-saeth	Gwyn	SH6430	52°51·3'	4°0·8'W	H	124
Carreg Yspar	Pemb	SN0945	52°4·5'	4°46·8'W	X	145
Carreg y Trai	Gwyn	SH3425	52°48·1'	4°27·3'W	X	123
Carreg-y-trai	I of Angl	SH3367	53°10·7'	4°29·5'W	X	114
Carreg-y-tŷ	Cered	SN3053	52°9·2'	4°28·7'W	X	145
Carr End	Lancs	SD3744	53°53·5'	2°57·1'W	X	102
Carr End	Northum	NU2232	55°35·1'	1°38·6'W	X	75
Carr End	N Yks	SD9186	54°16·4'	2°7·9'W	X	98
Carr Fm	Derby	SK0493	53°26·3'	1°56·0'W	FM	110
Carr Fm	Derby	SK3945	53°0·3'	1°24·7'W	FM	119,128
Carr Fm	E Yorks	SE7349	53°56·2'	0°52·9'W	FM	105,106
Carr Fm	E Yorks	SE8534	53°48·0'	0°42·2'W	FM	106
Carr Fm	E Yorks	SE8537	53°49·6'	0°42·1'W	FM	106
Carr Fm	E Yorks	TA0248	53°55·3'	0°26·4'W	FM	106,107
Carr Fm	E Yorks	TA2630	53°45·3'	0°4·9'W	FM	107
Carr Fm	E Yorks	TA3029	53°44·7'	0°1·3'W	FM	107
Carr Fm	Leeds	SE3639	53°51·0'	1°26·8'W	FM	104
Carr Fm	Lincs	SK8972	53°14·5'	0°39·6'W	FM	121
Carr Fm	N Lincs	TA0004	53°31·6'	0°29·1'W	FM	112
Carr Fm	Norf	TG4915	52°40·7'	1°41·4'E	FM	134
Carr Fm	Norf	TM0692	52°29·4'	1°2·5'E	FM	144
Carr Fm	Norf	TM4099	52°32·4'	1°32·8'E	FM	134
Carr Fm	Norf	TM4894	52°29·5'	1°39·6'E	FM	134
Carr Fm	Notts	SK7294	53°26·5'	0°54·6'W	FM	112
Carr Fm	N Yks	SE1851	53°57·5'	1°43·1'W	FM	104
Carr Fm	Roth	SK4979	53°18·6'	1°15·5'W	FM	120

Carr Fm	Wirral	SJ2489	53°23·8′	3°8·2′W	FM	108
Carr Gate	Wakf	SE3124	53°42·9′	1°31·4′W	T	104
Carr Grange Fm	N upon Ty	NZ2074	55°3·9′	1°40·8′W	FM	88
Carr Green	Traf	SJ7188	53°23·5′	2°25·8′W	T	109
Carr Hall	Lancs	SD7033	53°47·8′	2°26·9′W	X	103
Carr Hall	Lancs	SD8438	53°50·5′	2°14·2′W	X	103
Carr Hall	N Yks	NZ8708	54°27·8′	0°39·0′W	X	94
Carrhall Fm	Derby	SK2745	53°0·3′	1°35·5′W	FM	119,128
Carr Head Hall	N Yks	SD9744	53°53·8′	2°2·3′W	X	103
Carr Hill	Ghead	NZ2661	54°56·8′	1°35·2′W	T	88
Carr Hill	Northum	NY9467	55°0·1′	2°5·2′W	X	87
Carr Hill	Northum	NZ0168	55°0·6′	1°58·6′W	X	87
Carr Hill	Notts	SK6892	53°25·5′	0°58·2′W	X	111
Carr Hill	N Yks	SE4685	54°15·8′	1°17·2′W	X	100
Carr Hill Fm	Derby	SK4235	52°54·9′	1°22·1′W	FM	129
Carrhill Fm	E Yorks	SE8431	53°46·4′	0°43·1′W	FM	106
Carr Hill Wood	N Yks	NZ3402	54°25·0′	1°28·1′W	F	93
Carr Ho	Ches	SJ8980	53°19·2′	2°9·5′W	X	109
Carr Ho	Darl	NZ3320	54°34·7′	1°28·9′W	X	93
Carr Ho	Derby	SK1586	53°22·5′	1°46·1′W	X	110
Carr Ho	Durham	NZ1420	54°34·7′	1°46·6′W	X	92
Carr Ho	E Yorks	TA0758	54°0·7′	0°21·6′W	X	107
Carr Ho	E Yorks	TA0838	53°49·9′	0°21·1′W	X	107
Carr Ho	E Yorks	TA1050	53°56·3′	0°19·0′W	X	107
Carr Ho	Ghead	NZ1257	54°54·7′	1°48·3′W	X	88
Carr Ho	K upon H	TA1233	53°47·1′	0°17·6′W	X	107
Carr Ho	Lancs	SD4621	53°41·2′	2°48·6′W	X	102
Carr Ho	N Lincs	SE8114	53°37·2′	0°46·1′W	X	112
Carr Ho	N Yks	NZ3303	54°25·5′	1°29·1′W	X	93
Carr Ho	N Yks	NZ4909	54°28·7′	1°14·2′W	X	93
Carr Ho	N Yks	SE2173	54°9·4′	1°40·3′W	X	99
Carr Ho	N Yks	SE5678	54°11·9′	1°8·1′W	X	100
Carr Ho	N Yks	SE7980	54°12·8′	0°46·9′W	X	100
Carr Ho	N Yks	SE9281	54°13·2′	0°34·9′W	X	101
Carr Ho	N Yks	TA0980	54°12·5′	0°19·3′W	X	101
Carr Ho	Roth	SK5692	53°25·5′	1°9·0′W	X	111
Carr Ho	Staffs	SJ9231	52°52·8′	2°6·7′W	X	127
Carr Ho	Tames	SK0095	53°27·3′	1°59·6′W	X	110
Carrholme	Cumbr	NY5147	54°49·2′	2°45·3′W	X	86
Carrholme Bridge	N Yks	SE5064	54°4·4′	1°13·7′W	X	100
Carrhouse	Devon	SS7706	50°50·7′	3°44·4′W	T	191
Carr House	Lancs	SD4637	53°49·8′	2°48·8′W	X	102
Carr House Fm	E Yorks	TA0855	53°59·0′	0°20·8′W	FM	107
Carr House Fm	E Yorks	TA1042	53°52·0′	0°19·2′W	FM	107
Carr House Fm	E Yorks	TA2626	53°43·1′	0°5·0′W	FM	107
Carr House Fm	Lancs	SD3849	53°56·3′	2°56·3′W	FM	102
Carr House Fm	N Yks	SE1548	53°55·9′	1°45·9′W	FM	104
Carr House Fm	N Yks	SE2676	54°11·0′	1°35·7′W	FM	99
Carr House Fm	N Yks	SE8780	54°12·7′	0°39·5′W	FM	101
Carr House Fm	N Yks	SE9077	54°11·1′	0°36·8′W	FM	101
Carr House Fm	N Yks	TA0280	54°12·6′	0°25·7′W	FM	101
Carr House Fm	N Yks	TA0482	54°13·6′	0°23·9′W	FM	101
Carr House Fm	Sund	NZ3747	54°49·2′	1°25·0′W	FM	88
Carr Houses	Northum	NZ0168	55°0·6′	1°58·6′W	X	87
Carr Houses	Sefton	SD3203	53°31·4′	3°1·1′W	T	108
Carribber Mill	W Loth	NS9574	55°57·1′	3°40·5′W	X	65
Carrick	Arg & Bt	NR9087	56°2·1′	5°21·8′W	X	55
Carrick	D & G	NX5750	54°49·7′	4°13·1′W	X	83
Carrick	D & G	NY0491	55°12·5′	3°30·1′W	X	78
Carrick	Fife	NO4422	56°23·5′	2°54·0′W	T	54,59
Carrick	I of M	SC3893	54°18·7′	4°29·0′W	H	95
Carrick	S Ayr	NX3594	55°13·0′	4°35·2′W	X	77
Carrickaboys	D & G	NX4837	54°42·6′	4°21·1′W	X	83
Carrick Burn	Arg & Bt	NS1894	56°6·5′	4°55·2′W	W	56
Carrick Burn	D & G	NX3076	55°3·2′	4°39·3′W	W	76
Carrick Burnfoot	D & G	NX3176	55°3·2′	4°38·3′W	X	76
Carrick Castle	Arg & Bt	NS1994	56°6·5′	4°54·2′W	T	56
Carrick Fm	Orkney	HY5638	59°13·8′	2°45·8′W	FM	5
Carrick Forest	S Ayr	NX4296	55°14·2′	4°28·7′W	F	77
Carrick Heights	Northum	NY9096	55°15·7′	2°9·0′W	X	80
Carrick Ho	Orkney	HY5638	59°13·8′	2°45·8′W	X	5
Carrick Lane	E Ayr	NX4794	55°13·2′	4°23·9′W	W	77
Carrick Lûz	Corn	SW7516	50°0·3′	5°8·0′W	X	204
Carricknath Point	Corn	SW8432	50°9·2′	5°1·1′W	X	204
Carrickowel Point	Corn	SX0350	50°19·3′	4°45·7′W	X	200,204
Carrick Point	Arg & Bt	NR7726	55°28·9′	5°31·3′W	X	68,69
Carrick Point	Arg & Bt	NS0359	55°47·3′	5°8·1′W	X	63
Carrick Pt	D & G	NX5750	54°49·7′	4°13·1′W	X	83
Carrick Roads	Corn	SW8334	50°10·2′	5°2·0′W	W	204
Carrick's Hill	E Susx	TQ6519	50°57·0′	0°21·3′E	X	199
Carrickstone	N Lanak	NS7576	55°57·9′	3°59·7′W	X	64
Carrick, The	I of M	SC2267	54°4·3′	4°42·8′W	X	95
Carrick Villa	Fife	NO4302	56°12·7′	2°54·7′W	X	59
Carriden	Falk	NT0181	56°1·0′	3°34·8′W	T	65
Carriden House	Falk	NT0280	56°0·4′	3°33·9′W	A	65
Carrier's Hill	Aberd	NJ6227	57°20·2′	2°37·4′W	H	37
Carriers' Way	Northum	NY9351	54°51·5′	2°6·1′W	X	87
Carrifran	D & G	NT1611	55°23·4′	3°19·1′W	X	79
Carrifran Burn	D & G	NT1512	55°23·9′	3°20·1′W	W	79
Carrifran Gans	D & G	NT1513	55°24·5′	3°20·1′W	H	79
Carrimers Fm	Oxon	SU5584	51°33·4′	1°12·0′W	FM	174
Carrine Common	Corn	SW7943	50°15·0′	5°5·6′W	X	204
Carrington	C of Nott	SK5642	52°58·6′	1°9·6′W	T	129
Carrington	Lincs	TF3154	53°4·3′	0°2·3′W	T	122
Carrington	Midlo	NT3160	55°50·0′	3°5·7′W	T	66
Carrington	Traf	SJ7492	53°25·7′	2°23·1′W	T	109
Carrington Barns	Midlo	NT3261	55°50·5′	3°4·7′W	X	66
Carrington Fm	Essex	TL9510	51°45·5′	0°49·9′E	FM	168
Carrington Fm	Notts	SK6249	53°2·3′	1°4·1′W	FM	129
Carrington Grange	Lincs	TF3154	53°4·3′	0°2·3′W	X	122
Carrington Ho	Lincs	TF3155	53°4·8′	0°2·2′W	X	122
Carrington Mill	Midlo	NT3159	55°49·4′	3°5·6′W	X	66,73
Carrington Moss	Traf	SJ7491	53°25·2′	2°23·1′W	X	109
Carringtons Fm	Essex	TM0827	51°54·4′	1°1·8′E	FM	168,169
Carrisaval	N Eil	NF7618	57°8·6′	7°21·0′W	H	31
Carrish	N Eil	NF7603	57°0·5′	7°19·8′W	X	31
Carriston	Fife	NO3204	56°13·7′	3°5·4′W	X	59
Carriston Cotton	Fife	NO3204	56°13·7′	3°5·4′W	X	59
Carriston Resr	Fife	NO3203	56°13·1′	3°5·3′W	W	59
Carriteth Moor	Northum	NY7983	55°8·7′	2°19·3′W	X	80
Carr Laithe	Brad	SE0240	53°51·6′	1°57·8′W	X	104
Carr Lodge	N Yks	SE5778	54°11·9′	1°7·2′W	X	100
Carr Lodge Fm	N Yks	SE1759	54°1·8′	1°44·0′W	FM	104
Carrlow Ridge Plantn	N Yks	SE1757	54°0·8′	1°44·0′W	F	104
Carr Manor	Leeds	SE2937	53°49·9′	1°33·1′W	X	104
Carr Mill Dam	St Hel	SJ5298	53°28·8′	2°43·0′W	W	108
Carr Mór	Highld	NH9831	57°21·7′	3°41·3′W	X	27,36
Carr na Moine	Pth & Kin	NN7680	56°53·9′	4°1·7′W	X	42
Carroch	Angus	NO3658	56°42·8′	3°2·3′W	X	54
Carroch Hill	D & G	NX6792	55°12·5′	4°5·0′W	H	77
Carrock	D & G	NX6791	55°12·0′	4°5·0′W	X	77
Carrock Beck	Cumbr	NY3435	54°42·6′	3°1·0′W	W	90
Carrock Fell	Cumbr	NY3433	54°41·5′	3°1·0′W	H	90
Carrock Lane	D & G	NX6691	55°12·0′	4°5·9′W	W	77
Car Rocks	E Loth	NT6184	56°3·1′	2°37·1′W	X	67
Carrodell Ho	N Yks	SE4290	54°18·5′	1°20·8′W	X	99
Carrog	Cered	SN5672	52°19·9′	4°6·4′W	X	135
Carrog	Conwy	SH7647	53°0·6′	3°50·5′W	T	115
Carrog	Denb	SJ1043	52°58·9′	3°20·0′W	T	125
Carrog	Denb	SJ1242	52°58·3′	3°18·2′W	X	125
Carrog	Gwyn	SH2133	52°52·1′	4°39·2′W	X	123
Carrog	Gwyn	SH4657	53°5·5′	4°17·6′W	X	115,123
Carrog	I of Angl	SH3791	53°23·7′	4°26·7′W	X	114
Carrog	I of Angl	SH4372	53°13·6′	4°20·7′W	X	114,115
Carrog Fm	Cered	SN5672	52°19·9′	4°6·4′W	FM	135
Carroglen	Pth & Kin	NN7626	56°24·9′	4°0·1′W	X	51,52
Carrog Uchaf	I of Angl	SH4678	53°16·8′	4°18·2′W	X	114,115
Carrol	Highld	NC8406	58°1·9′	3°57·4′W	X	17
Carroll's Fm	Cambs	TL4990	52°29·5′	0°12·1′E	FM	143
Carrol Rock	Highld	NC8407	58°2·5′	3°57·4′W	H	17
Carron	Arg & Bt	NR9499	56°8·6′	5°18·5′W	X	55
Carron	Falk	NS8882	56°1·3′	3°47·4′W	T	65
Carron	Moray	NJ2241	57°27·4′	3°17·5′W	T	28
Carronbridge	D & G	NX8697	55°15·5′	3°47·2′W	T	78
Carron Bridge	Falk	NS7483	56°1·7′	4°0·9′W	X	64
Carronglen	D & G	NS8803	55°18·8′	3°45·5′W	X	78
Carron Glen	Falk	NS7883	56°1·7′	3°57·0′W	X	57,64
Carronhill	D & G	NX8798	55°16·0′	3°46·3′W	X	78
Carron Ho	Falk	NS8983	56°1·9′	3°46·4′W	X	65
Carron Ho	Moray	NJ2341	57°27·4′	3°16·5′W	X	28
Carron Lodge	Fife	NO4816	56°20·3′	2°50·0′W	X	59
Carronshore	Falk	NS8883	56°1·9′	3°47·4′W	T	65
Carronvale Ho	Falk	NS8682	56°1·3′	3°49·3′W	X	65
Carron Valley Forest	N Lanak	NS6982	56°1·0′	4°5·7′W	F	57,64
Carron Valley Reservoir	Stir	NS6983	56°1·6′	4°5·7′W	W	57,64
Carron Water	Aberd	NO8385	56°57·6′	2°16·3′W	W	45
Carron Water	D & G	NS8801	55°17·7′	3°45·4′W	W	78
Carrot	Angus	NO4641	56°33·7′	2°52·3′W	X	54
Carrot	E Renf	NS5748	55°42·5′	4°16·1′W	X	64
Carrot Burn	E Renf	NS5748	55°42·5′	4°16·1′W	W	64
Carrot Hill	Angus	NO4540	56°33·2′	2°53·2′W	H	54
Carrouch Burn	D & G	NX5366	54°58·3′	4°17·4′W	W	83
Carroway Head	Staffs	SP1599	52°35·6′	1°46·3′W	T	139
Carrow Bank	N Yks	SE1449	53°56·5′	1°46·8′W	X	104
Carrow Hill	Monm	ST4390	51°36·6′	2°49·0′W	T	171,172
Carrow Rigg	Northum	NY9595	55°15·2′	2°4·3′W	X	81
Carr Plantn	E Yorks	TA0738	53°49·9′	0°22·0′W	F	107
Carr Plantn	E Yorks	TA1167	54°5·5′	0°17·8′W	F	101
Carr Plantn	N Yks	NZ1814	54°31·5′	1°42·9′W	F	92
Carr Plantn	N Yks	SE3982	54°14·2′	1°23·7′W	F	99
Carrs	N Yks	SD7978	54°12·1′	2°18·9′W	X	98
Carr's Burn	Northum	NY7554	54°53·1′	2°23·0′W	W	86,87
Carr Seasg	Arg & Bt	NR7671	55°53·1′	5°34·5′W	X	62
Carr's Fm	Durham	NZ0635	54°42·8′	1°54·0′W	FM	92
Carrsgate	Northum	NY7464	54°58·4′	2°23·9′W	X	86,87
Carr Sheild	Northum	NY8047	54°49·3′	2°18·3′W	T	86,87
Carrshield Moor	Northum	NY8146	54°48·8′	2°17·3′W	X	86,87
Carrs Hill	Durham	NY9530	54°40·1′	2°4·2′W	H	91,92
Carr's Ho	N Yks	SE4856	54°0·1′	1°15·6′W	X	105
Carr Side	Donc	SE6507	53°33·6′	1°0·7′W	X	111
Carrside	N Lincs	SE7703	53°31·3′	0°49·9′W	X	112
Carr Side	N Yks	SE2048	53°55·9′	1°41·3′W	X	104
Carr Side Fm	Lancs	SD6442	53°52·6′	2°32·4′W	FM	102,103
Carrside Fm	N Lincs	SE9613	53°36·5′	0°32·5′W	FM	112
Carr Side Fm	Sefton	SD3303	53°31·4′	3°0·2′W	FM	108
Carrsides	Durham	NZ2927	54°38·5′	1°32·6′W	X	93
Carrs Rock	Pemb	SM9504	51°42·1′	4°57·6′W	X	157,158
Carrs, The	Ches	SJ8481	53°19·8′	2°14·0′W	X	109
Carrs, The	E Yorks	SE7753	53°58·3′	0°49·2′W	X	105,106
Carrs, The	Lincs	TF1555	53°5·0′	0°16·6′W	X	121
Carrs, The	N Yks	SE3874	54°9·9′	1°24·7′W	X	99
Carrs, The	N Yks	SE4467	54°6·1′	1°19·2′W	X	99
Carrs, The	N Yks	SE9779	54°12·1′	0°30·4′W	X	101
Carrs, The	Suff	TL9636	51°59·5′	0°51·7′E	X	155
Carrstone Pit	Norf	TF6834	52°52·9′	0°30·2′E	X	132
Carr, The	Derby	SK2645	53°0·3′	1°36·3′W	X	119,128
Carr, The	E Yorks	SE6320	53°40·6′	1°2·4′W	X	105,106
Carr, The	Norf	TF7729	52°50·0′	0°38·1′E	F	132
Carr, The	Norf	TF8623	52°46·6′	0°45·9′E	X	132
Carr, The	Norf	TG3124	52°46·1′	1°25·9′E	F	133,134
Carr, The	N Yks	SE4062	54°3·4′	1°22·9′W	W	99
Carr, The	N Yks	SE7966	54°5·3′	0°47·1′W	X	100
Carr, The	Suff	TL7483	52°25·3′	0°33·9′E	F	143
Carr Top Fm	N Yks	SE3663	54°3·9′	1°26·6′W	FM	99
Carruan	Corn	SW9578	50°34·2′	4°53·3′W	X	200
Carruchan	D & G	NX9473	55°2·7′	3°39·1′W	X	84
Carruchan Fm	D & G	NX9573	55°2·7′	3°38·2′W	FM	84
Carruggatt Wood	Corn	SX0856	50°22·6′	4°41·6′W	F	200
Carrum	Pth & Kin	NN9620	56°21·9′	3°40·6′W	X	52,53,58
Carruthers	D & G	NY2580	55°6·8′	3°10·1′W	X	79
Carrutherstown	D & G	NY1071	55°1·8′	3°24·1′W	T	85
Carruth Ho	Inverc	NS3566	55°51·9′	4°37·8′W	X	63
Carruthmuir	Inverc	NS3564	55°50·7′	4°37·7′W	X	63
Carr Vale	Derby	SK4669	53°13·2′	1°18·3′W	T	120
Carrville	Durham	NZ3043	54°47·1′	1°31·6′W	T	88
Carr Wood	Cumbr	NY1643	54°46·7′	3°17·9′W	F	85
Carr Wood	Derby	SK2038	52°56·6′	1°41·6′W	F	128
Carr Wood	Kirk	SE1813	53°37·0′	1°43·3′W	F	110
Carr Wood	N Yks	NZ8201	54°24·1′	0°43·8′W	F	94
Carr Wood	N Yks	SE4937	53°49·9′	1°14·9′W	F	105
Carry	Arg & Bt	NR9867	55°51·5′	5°13·2′W	X	62
Carry Br	Lancs	SD9039	53°51·1′	2°8·7′W	X	103
Carry Burn	Northum	NT6502	55°18·9′	2°32·7′W	W	80
Carry Burn	Northum	NY9279	55°6·6′	2°7·1′W	W	87
Carry Burn	Northum	NY9280	55°7·1′	2°7·1′W	W	80
Carrycoats Hall	Northum	NY9279	55°6·6′	2°7·1′W	X	87
Carry Moor	N Yks	NZ3505	54°26·6′	1°27·2′W	X	93
Carry Point	Arg & Bt	NR9967	55°51·5′	5°12·3′W	X	62
Carsaig	Arg & Bt	NM5421	56°19·3′	5°58·3′W	T	48
Carsaig	Arg & Bt	NR7387	56°1·6′	5°38·1′W	T	55
Carsaig Arches	Arg & Bt	NM4918	56°17·5′	6°2·9′W	X	48
Carsaig Bay	Arg & Bt	NM5321	56°19·3′	5°59·2′W	W	48
Carsaig Bay	Arg & Bt	NR7387	56°1·6′	5°38·1′W	W	55
Carsaig Ho	Arg & Bt	NM5421	56°19·3′	5°58·3′W	X	48
Carsaig Island	Arg & Bt	NR7389	56°2·7′	5°38·2′W	X	55
Carsamull	Arg & Bt	NM0646	56°31·1′	6°46·4′W	X	46
Carscallan	S Lanak	NS7252	55°44·9′	4°1·9′W	X	64
Carscliff Fm	Somer	ST4752	51°16·1′	2°45·2′W	FM	182
Carscombe	Devon	SS9219	50°57·9′	3°31·9′W	X	181
Carscreugh	D & G	NX2259	54°53·9′	4°46·1′W	X	82
Carscreugh Croft	D & G	NX2362	54°55·5′	4°45·3′W	X	82
Carscreugh Fell	D & G	NX2361	54°55·0′	4°45·3′W	H	82
Carse	D & G	NX6556	54°53·1′	4°5·8′W	X	83,84
Carse	D & G	NX9765	54°58·4′	3°36·1′W	X	84
Carse	Pth & Kin	NN8048	56°36·8′	3°56·9′W	X	52
Carse Bay	D & G	NX9860	54°55·7′	3°35·1′W	W	84
Carsebreck	Pth & Kin	NN8609	56°15·8′	3°50·0′W	X	58
Carsebreck Loch	Pth & Kin	NN8609	56°15·8′	3°50·0′W	W	58
Carsebuie	D & G	NX3365	54°57·4′	4°36·1′W	X	82
Carseburn	Angus	NO4652	56°39·7′	2°52·4′W	X	54
Carseglass Hill	D & G	NX6585	55°8·7′	4°6·7′W	H	77
Carsegour	Pth & Kin	NT1098	56°10·2′	3°26·5′W	X	58
Carsegowan	D & G	NX4258	54°53·8′	4°27·4′W	X	83
Carsegowan	D & G	NX9466	54°58·9′	3°39·0′W	X	84
Carsegowan Moss	D & G	NX4258	54°53·8′	4°27·4′W	X	83
Carsegownie	Angus	NO5054	56°40·8′	2°48·5′W	T	54
Carse Gray	Angus	NO4653	56°40·2′	2°52·4′W	X	54
Carsegreen	Pth & Kin	NO0333	56°29·0′	3°34·1′W	X	52,53
Carsehall	Pth & Kin	NO0400	56°11·2′	3°32·4′W	X	58
Carsehead	Pth & Kin	NN9523	56°23·5′	3°41·6′W	X	52,53,58
Carse Hill	Angus	NO4553	56°40·2′	2°53·4′W	H	54
Carsehope Burn	S Lanak	NS9404	55°19·4′	3°39·8′W	W	78
Carsehope Middens	S Lanak	NS9303	55°18·8′	3°40·7′W	X	78
Carse House	Arg & Bt	NR7461	55°47·6′	5°35·9′W	X	62
Carsella Fm	Corn	SW9457	50°22·8′	4°53·5′W	FM	200
Carsemeg	Pth & Kin	NN8109	56°15·8′	3°54·8′W	X	57
Carseminnoch	D & G	NX4463	54°56·5′	4°25·7′W	X	83
Carsenaw	D & G	NX4264	54°57·0′	4°27·6′W	X	83
Carsenestock	D & G	NX4461	54°55·4′	4°25·6′W	X	83
Carse of Ardersier	Highld	NH8057	57°35·5′	4°0·0′W	X	27
Carse of Barr	D & G	NX4363	54°56·5′	4°26·6′W	X	83
Carse of Clary	D & G	NX4260	54°54·8′	4°27·5′W	X	83
Carse of Delnies	Highld	NH8356	57°35·0′	3°56·9′W	X	27
Carse of Gowrie	Pth & Kin	NO2322	56°23·3′	3°14·4′W	X	53,58
Carse of Kinglands	Pth & Kin	NO0233	56°29·0′	3°35·0′W	X	52,53
Carse of Lecropt	Stir	NS7697	56°9·2′	3°59·3′W	X	57
Carse of Lennoch	Pth & Kin	NN7922	56°22·7′	3°57·1′W	X	51,52
Carse of Melbost	N Eil	NB4533	58°13·0′	6°20·0′W	X	8
Carse of Raddery	Highld	NH7158	57°35·9′	4°9·0′W	X	27
Carse of Shannochill	Stir	NS5398	56°9·4′	4°21·6′W	X	57
Carse of Trowan	Pth & Kin	NN8122	56°22·8′	3°55·2′W	X	52
Carseriggan	D & G	NX3167	54°58·4′	4°38·0′W	X	82
Carseriggan Moor	D & G	NX3169	54°59·5′	4°38·1′W	X	82
Carse Sands	D & G	NY0060	54°55·7′	3°33·2′W	X	84
Carsethorn	D & G	NX9959	54°55·2′	3°34·1′W	X	84
Carsewalloch	D & G	NX4561	54°55·4′	4°24·7′W	X	83
Carsewell	Midlo	NT2159	55°49·3′	3°15·2′W	X	66,73
Carse Wood	Highld	NH8156	57°35·0′	3°59·0′W	F	27
Carsfad Loch	D & G	NX6086	55°9·2′	4°11·4′W	W	77
Carsgailoch Hill	E Ayr	NS5514	55°24·2′	4°17·0′W	X	71
Carsgailoch Runner	E Ayr	NS5516	55°25·2′	4°17·0′W	W	71
Carsgoe	Highld	ND1363	58°33·0′	3°29·2′W	X	11,12
Carshalton	Sutton	TQ2764	51°21·9′	0°10·1′W	T	176,187
Carshalton Beeches	Sutton	TQ2763	51°21·3′	0°10·2′W	T	176,187
Carshalton on the Hill	Sutton	TQ2863	51°21·3′	0°9·3′W	T	176,187
Carshope	Northum	NT8411	55°23·8′	2°14·7′W	X	80
Carshope Plantation	Northum	NT8410	55°23·3′	2°14·7′W	F	80
Carsie	Pth & Kin	NO1742	56°34·0′	3°20·6′W	X	53
Carsie Mains	Pth & Kin	NO1741	56°33·5′	3°20·6′W	X	53
Carsington	Derby	SK2553	53°4·7′	1°37·2′W	T	119
Carsington Pasture	Derby	SK2554	53°5·2′	1°37·2′W	X	119
Carsington Water	Derby	SK2451	53°3·6′	1°38·1′W	W	119
Carsinker Law	Scot Bord	NT4548	55°43·6′	2°52·1′W	H	73
Carskeoch	E Ayr	NS4109	55°21·2′	4°30·0′W	X	70,77
Carskeoch Hill	E Ayr	NS4008	55°20·7′	4°31·0′W	X	70,77
Carskerdo	Fife	NO3908	56°15·9′	2°58·6′W	X	59
Carskey Bay	Arg & Bt	NR6607	55°18·3′	5°40·8′W	W	68
Carskiey	Arg & Bt	NR6507	55°18·3′	5°41·7′W	X	68
Carslae	D & G	NX4358	54°53·8′	4°26·5′W	X	83
Carsleddam	Cumbr	NY2527	54°38·2′	3°9·3′W	X	89,90
Carsloe	S Ayr	NS3105	55°18·9′	4°39·4′W	X	70,76
Carslogie	Fife	NO3514	56°19·1′	3°2·6′W	X	59
Carslogie House	Fife	NO3514	56°19·1′	3°2·6′W	A	59
Carsluith	D & G	NX4854	54°51·7′	4°21·7′W	T	83
Carsluith Burn	D & G	NX5055	54°52·3′	4°19·8′W	W	83
Carsluith Castle	D & G	NX4954	54°51·7′	4°20·7′W	A	83
Carsons Hill	D & G	NX6553	54°51·5′	4°5·8′W	X	83,84
Carsons Stone	D & G	NX4982	55°6·8′	4°21·6′W	X	77
Carsphairn	D & G	NX5693	55°12·9′	4°15·4′W	T	77
Carsphairn Forest	D & G	NS5702	55°17·7′	4°14·7′W	F	77
Carsphairn Lane	D & G	NX5495	55°13·9′	4°17·3′W	W	77
Carstairs	S Lanak	NS9346	55°42·0′	3°41·7′W	T	72
Carstairs Junction	S Lanak	NS9545	55°41·5′	3°39·8′W	T	72
Carstairs Mains	S Lanak	NS9444	55°40·9′	3°40·7′W	X	71,72
Carston	E Ayr	NS4518	55°26·1′	4°26·6′W	X	70
Carston	E Ayr	NS4921	55°27·8′	4°22·9′W	X	70
Carston	Stir	NS5084	56°1·8′	4°24·0′W	X	57,64
Carstramon	D & G	NX5860	54°55·1′	4°12·5′W	X	83
Carstran	Stir	NS5922	56°22·4′	4°16·5′W	X	51
Carswadda	D & G	NX8970	55°1·0′	3°43·7′W	X	84

Carswalls Manor	Glos	SO7427	51°56·7′	2°22·3′W	X	162
Carswell	E Renf	NS4653	55°45·0′	4°26·8′W	X	64
Carswell Fm	Devon	SX5847	50°18·6′	3°59·3′W	FM	202
Carswell Fm	Devon	SY3294	50°44·7′	2°57·4′W	FM	193
Carswell Marsh	Oxon	SU3298	51°41·0′	1°31·8′W	T	164
Carswells Moor	Devon	SY2295	50°45·2′	3°6·0′W	X	192,193
Cartbridge	Surrey	TQ0156	51°17·9′	0°32·7′W	T	186
Carter Bar	Northum	NT6906	55°21·1′	2°28·9′W	X	80
Carter Burn	Scot Bord	NT6507	55°21·6′	2°32·7′W	W	80
Carter Fell	Scot Bord	NT6603	55°19·4′	2°31·7′W	X	80
Carter Ground	Cumbr	SD2292	54°19·3′	3°11·5′W	X	96
Carterhall Fm	Derby	SK3981	53°19·7′	1°24·5′W	FM	110,111
Carterhaugh	Scot Bord	NT4326	55°31·7′	2°53·7′W	T	73
Carter Ho	Cumbr	SD5384	54°15·2′	2°42·9′W	X	97
Carter Ho	Lancs	SD5141	53°52·0′	2°44·3′W	X	102
Carter Ho	N Yks	NZ0708	54°28·3′	1°53·1′W	X	92
Carterhope Burn	Scot Bord	NT0916	55°26·0′	3°25·9′W	W	78
Carterhope Rig	Scot Bord	NT0918	55°27·1′	3°25·9′W	X	78
Carterhouse	Scot Bord	NT6707	55°21·6′	2°30·8′W	X	80
Carter Knowle	Sheff	SK3384	53°21·3′	1°29·8′W	T	110,111
Carter Lodge	Derby	SK3982	53°20·2′	1°24·4′W	X	110,111
Carter Moor	Northum	NZ1677	55°5·5′	1°44·5′W	X	88
Carter Moor	Stock on T	NZ4115	54°32·0′	1°21·6′W	X	93
Carters	Herts	TL4515	51°49·1′	0°6·6′E	X	167
Carters	Lancs	SD8151	53°57·5′	2°17·0′W	X	103
Carter's Clay	Hants	SU3024	51°1·1′	1°34·0′W	T	185
Carter's Corner Place	E Susx	TQ6012	50°53·3′	0°16·9′E	X	199
Carter's Fm	Essex	TL7634	51°58·8′	0°34·2′E	FM	155
Carter's Fm	E Susx	TQ8814	50°53·9′	0°40·8′E	FM	199
Carter's Fm	Lancs	SD3845	53°54·1′	2°56·2′W	FM	102
Carter's Fm	Powys	SO3069	52°19·1′	3°1·2′W	FM	137,148
Cartersford Br	Swan	SS5591	51°36·2′	4°5·2′W	X	159
Carter's Green	Essex	TL5110	51°46·3′	0°11·7′E	T	167
Carters Green	Pemb	SM8701	51°40·3′	5°4·4′W	X	157
Carters Green Fm	Ches	SJ7352	53°4·1′	2°23·8′W	FM	118
Carter's Hill	Kent	TQ5553	51°15·5′	0°13·7′E	X	188
Carter's Hill	Wok	SU7669	51°25·1′	0°54·0′W	T	175
Carter's Hill	Worcs	SO9663	52°16·1′	2°3·1′W	X	150
Carter's Hill Fm	Wok	SU7668	51°24·6′	0°54·0′W	FM	175
Carter's Ho	N Yks	SE8496	54°21·4′	0°42·0′W	X	94,100
Carterside	Northum	NU0400	55°17·9′	1°55·8′W	X	81
Carter's Lane	Lancs	SD8150	53°57·0′	2°17·0′W	X	103
Carter's Lodge	W Susx	TQ2329	51°3·1′	0°14·3′W	X	187,198
Carter's or Gull Rocks	Corn	SW7559	50°23·5′	5°9·6′W	X	200
Carterspiece	Glos	SO5914	51°49·6′	2°35·3′W	T	162
Carter's Rough	Leic	SK5008	52°40·3′	1°15·2′W	X	140
Carter Syke Fm	N Yks	SE2272	54°8·8′	1°39·4′W	FM	99
Carterton	D & G	NY2089	55°11·6′	3°15·0′W	X	79
Carterton	Oxon	SP2806	51°45·4′	1°35·3′W	T	163
Carterton Knowes	D & G	NY2192	55°13·2′	3°14·1′W	H	79
Carterway Heads	Northum	NZ0451	54°51·5′	1°55·8′W	T	87
Cartford Br	Lancs	SD4240	53°51·4′	2°52·5′W	X	102
Cart Gap	Norf	TG3929	52°48·6′	1°33·2′E	X	133,134
Cart Gap	Oxon	SU6387	51°34·9′	1°5·1′W	X	175
Carthagena	N Yks	NZ3706	54°27·1′	1°25·3′W	X	93
Carthagena Bank	Pth & Kin	NO2722	56°23·3′	3°10·5′W	X	53,59
Carthagena Fm	W Susx	SZ8198	50°46·8′	0°50·7′W	FM	197
Carthamartha	Corn	SX3677	50°34·4′	4°18·6′W	T	201
Carthat Hill	D & G	NY0677	55°5·0′	3°27·9′W	H	85
Carthew	Corn	SW6836	50°11·0′	5°14·6′W	T	203
Carthew	Corn	SX0055	50°21·9′	4°48·4′W	T	200
Carthew Fm	Corn	SW9571	50°30·4′	4°53·1′W	FM	200
Carthick Wood	Leeds	SE3446	53°54·8′	1°28·5′W	F	104
Cart Ho	Cumbr	SD2281	54°13·4′	3°11·4′W	X	96
Carthorpe	N Yks	SE3083	54°14·8′	1°32·0′W	T	99
Cartington	Northum	NU0304	55°20·1′	1°56·7′W	X	81
Cartington Castle	Northum	NU0304	55°20·1′	1°56·7′W	A	81
Cartington Hill	Northum	NU0405	55°20·6′	1°55·8′W	H	81
Cartland	S Lanak	NS8646	55°41·9′	3°48·4′W	T	72
Cartland Mains	S Lanak	NS8645	55°41·4′	3°48·4′W	X	72
Cartland Muir Plantation	S Lanak	NS8647	55°42·4′	3°48·4′W	F	72
Cartledge	Derby	SK3277	53°17·6′	1°30·8′W	T	119
Cartlett Brook	Pemb	SM9818	51°49·7′	4°55·5′W	W	157,158
Cart Low	Staffs	SK1051	53°3·6′	1°50·6′W	X	119
Cartmel	Cumbr	SD3878	54°11·9′	2°56·6′W	T	96,97
Cartmel Fell	Cumbr	SD4188	54°17·3′	2°54·0′W	T	96,97
Cartmell Fold	Cumbr	SD4491	54°18·9′	2°51·2′W	X	97
Cartmel Sands	Cumbr	SD3376	54°10·8′	3°1·2′W	X	96,97
Cartmel Wharf	Cumbr	SD3668	54°6·5′	2°58·3′W	X	96,97
Cartmire Gill	Cumbr	SD7593	54°20·2′	2°22·7′W	W	98
Cartmore	Fife	NT1794	56°8·1′	3°19·7′W	X	58
Cartoft	N Yks	SE7185	54°15·6′	0°54·2′W	X	94,100
Cartoft Lodge	N Yks	SE7185	54°15·6′	0°54·2′W	X	94,100
Cartole	Corn	SX1954	50°21·7′	4°32·3′W	X	201
Carton Fm	Worcs	SO7173	52°21·5′	2°25·2′W	FM	138
Car Top	Derby	SK2876	53°17·1′	1°34·4′W	X	119
Cartreglas Fm	V of Glam	ST0377	51°29·3′	3°23·4′W	FM	170
Cartridge Hill	Black w Dar	SD6719	53°40·2′	2°29·6′W	X	109
Cartsaddle Hill	Cumbr	SD6487	54°16·9′	2°32·8′W	X	97
Cartsdyke	Inverc	NS2875	55°56·5′	4°44·8′W	T	63
Cartsdyke	Inverc	NS2975	55°56·5′	4°43·8′W	T	63
Cartside	Renf	NS4061	55°49·2′	4°32·8′W	X	64
Cartside	S Lanak	NS5754	55°45·8′	4°16·3′W	X	64
Carts, The	Northum	NY8373	55°3·3′	2°15·5′W	X	86,87
Cartuther Barton	Corn	SX2663	50°26·7′	4°26·7′W	X	201
Cartworth	Kirk	SE1407	53°33·8′	1°46·9′W	T	110
Cartwright's Drumble	Staffs	SJ9644	52°59·8′	2°3·2′W	X	118
Carty Port	D & G	NX4362	54°55·9′	4°26·6′W	X	83
Carus Fm	Lancs	SD4864	54°4·4′	2°47·3′W	FM	97
Carus Lodge	Lancs	SD4864	54°4·4′	2°47·3′W	X	97
Carvannel	Corn	SW7138	50°12·1′	5°12·2′W	X	203
Carvannel Downs	Corn	SW6444	50°15·2′	5°18·3′W	X	203
Carvean	Corn	SW8847	50°17·3′	4°58·2′W	X	204
Carvear Moor	Corn	SX0554	50°21·5′	4°44·1′W	X	200
Carvedras	Corn	SW7231	50°8·4′	5°11·1′W	X	204
Carvenom	Fife	NO5405	56°14·4′	2°44·1′W	X	59
Carver Barracks	Essex	TL5634	51°59·2′	0°16·7′E	X	154
Carverel Copse	Wilts	SU1931	51°4·9′	1°43·3′W	F	184
Carvers Fm	Essex	TQ6690	51°35·3′	0°24·2′E	FM	177,178

Carver's Rocks	Derby	SK3322	52°47·9′	1°30·2′W	X	128
Carveth	Corn	SW7534	50°10·0′	5°8·7′W	X	204
Carveth	Corn	SW9345	50°16·4′	4°53·9′W	X	204
Carveth Wood	Corn	SW9346	50°16·9′	4°54·0′W	F	204
Carvichen	Aberd	NJ5438	57°26·1′	2°45·5′W	X	29
Carvinack	Corn	SW7747	50°17·1′	5°7·5′W	X	204
Carvinack	Corn	SW7935	50°10·7′	5°5·4′W	X	204
Carvinack	Corn	SW8147	50°17·2′	5°4·1′W	X	204
Carvoda	Corn	SX3478	50°34·9′	4°20·3′W	X	201
Carvoran	Northum	NY6665	54°59·0′	2°31·5′W	X	86
Carvossa	Corn	SW9148	50°17·9′	4°55·7′W	A	204
Carvynick	Corn	SW8756	50°22·2′	4°59·3′W	X	200
Carwad	I of Angl	SH5879	53°17·6′	4°7·4′W	X	114,115
Carwags	Lancs	SD5842	53°52·6′	2°37·9′W	X	102
Carwardine Fm	Heref	SO4040	52°3·5′	2°52·1′W	FM	148,149,161
Carwarthen	Corn	SW8437	50°11·9′	5°1·2′W	X	204
Carwath	Cumbr	NY3147	54°49·0′	3°4·0′W	X	85
Carway	Carm	SN4606	51°44·1′	4°13·4′W	T	159
Carwen	Corn	SX1173	50°31·8′	4°39·6′W	X	200
Carwen	Corn	SX1655	50°22·2′	4°34·9′W	X	201
Carwendy	Heref	SO4625	51°55·5′	2°46·7′W	X	161
Carwin	Corn	SW5838	50°11·8′	5°23·1′W	X	203
Carwinion	Corn	SW7728	50°6·8′	5°6·8′W	X	204
Carwinley	Cumbr	NY4072	55°2·6′	2°55·9′W	T	85
Carwinnick	Corn	SW9548	50°18·0′	4°52·3′W	X	204
Carwinshoch	S Ayr	NS2916	55°24·7′	4°41·6′W	X	70
Carwitham Barton	Corn	SX1592	50°42·1′	4°36·8′W	X	190
Carwood	S Lanak	NT0340	55°38·9′	3°32·0′W	X	72
Carworgie	Corn	SW9060	50°24·4′	4°57·0′W	X	200
Carwynnen	Corn	SW6537	50°11·4′	5°17·2′W	T	203
Carwythenack Fm	Corn	SW7128	50°6·7′	5°11·8′W	FM	203
Cary Br	Somer	ST4928	51°3·2′	2°43·3′W	X	183,193
Cary Fitzpaine	Somer	ST5427	51°2·7′	2°39·0′W	T	183
Carylls	W Susx	TQ2135	51°6·3′	0°15·9′W	X	187
Carylls Lea	W Susx	TQ2135	51°6·3′	0°15·9′W	X	187
Cary Moor	Somer	ST6030	51°4·3′	2°33·9′W	X	183
Carzield	D & G	NX9681	55°7·0′	3°37·4′W	T	78
Carzise	Corn	SW5934	50°9·7′	5°22·1′W	T	203
Casbrook Common	Hants	SU3525	51°1·6′	1°29·7′W	X	185
Cascade	Scot Bord	NT4832	55°35·0′	2°49·1′W	X	73
Cascade Ho	Caer	ST1497	51°40·1′	3°14·2′W	X	171
Cascade Plantn	N Yks	SE8066	54°5·3′	0°46·2′W	F	100
Cascob	Powys	SO2366	52°17·4′	3°7·3′W	T	137,148
Cas Dubh	Highld	NN4093	57°0·3′	4°35·9′W	X	34
Caseberry	Devon	SS9703	50°49·3′	3°27·4′W	X	192
Caseg Malltraeth	I of Angl	SH3764	53°9·1′	4°25·9′W	X	114
Casehill Downs	Corn	SX1278	50°34·5′	4°38·9′W	X	200
Caseley Court	Devon	SX7882	50°37·7′	3°43·1′W	X	191
Casemore Fm	Bucks	SP6528	51°57·0′	1°2·9′W	FM	164,165
Casewick Hall	Lincs	TF0709	52°40·3′	0°24·6′W	A	142
Casey Bridge	Ches	SJ7251	53°3·6′	2°24·7′W	X	118
Caseytown	Devon	SX5073	50°32·5′	4°6·6′W	X	191,201
Cas fo Dheas	N Eil	NF8231	57°15·8′	7°16·0′W	X	22
Cas fo Tuath	N Eil	NF8331	57°15·8′	7°15·1′W	X	22
Casfuar	Moray	NJ2016	57°13·9′	3°19·1′W	X	36
Cas-funch	Pemb	SN0229	51°55·7′	4°52·4′W	A	145,157,158
Casgan Dittw	Denb	SJ2352	53°3·8′	3°8·5′W	X	117
Cash Burn	Cumbr	NY7138	54°44·4′	2°26·6′W	W	91
Cashel Dhu	Highld	NC4549	58°24·4′	4°38·7′W	X	9
Cashel Fm	Stir	NS3994	56°7·0′	4°34·9′W	FM	56
Cashell Burn	Stir	NS4094	56°7·0′	4°34·0′W	W	56
Cashes Fm	Worcs	SO8969	52°19·4′	2°9·3′W	FM	139
Cashes Green	Glos	SO8205	51°44·8′	2°15·3′W	T	162
Cashfield	Pemb	SM9516	51°48·5′	4°58·0′W	X	157,158
Cashigarsh	Shetld	HU5190	60°35·7′	1°3·6′W	X	1,2
Cashley	Stir	NS5693	56°6·7′	4°18·5′W	X	57
Cashlie	Pth & Kin	NN4841	56°32·4′	4°27·9′W	T	51
Cash Loch	Fife	NO2409	56°16·3′	3°13·2′W	W	59
Cash Mill	Fife	NO2410	56°16·8′	3°13·2′W	X	59
Cashmoor	Dorset	ST9713	50°55·2′	2°2·2′W	T	195
Cashtal Lajer	I of M	SC3593	54°18·6′	4°31·8′W	X	95
Cashtal Lajer (Round House)	I of M	SC3593	54°18·6′	4°31·8′W	A	95
Cashtal yn Ard	I of M	SC4689	54°16·7′	4°21·5′W	X	95
Cashtal yn Ard (Chambered Long Cairn)	I of M	SC4689	54°16·7′	4°21·5′W	A	95
Cashtel Mooar	I of M	SC2383	54°13·0′	4°42·5′W	X	95
Cashtel Ree Corree	I of M	NX3902	54°23·5′	4°28·4′W	A	95
Caskald	Orkney	HY5220	59°4·1′	2°49·7′W	X	5,6
Caskieben	C of Aber	NJ8312	57°12·2′	2°16·4′W	X	38
Caskieberran	Fife	NO2500	56°11·5′	3°12·1′W	T	59
Caslub	N Eil	NF8241	57°21·2′	7°16·8′W	W	22
Cas na Smorrach	Moray	NJ1245	57°29·5′	3°27·6′W	H	28
Casnewydd or Newport	Newp	ST3188	51°35·4′	2°59·4′W	T	171
Caspin	D & G	NX0073	55°0·9′	5°7·3′W	X	76,82
Cassafuir	Stir	NN6102	56°11·6′	4°14·0′W	X	57
Cassencarie	D & G	NX4757	54°53·3′	4°22·7′W	X	83
Cassenvey	D & G	NX6877	55°4·4′	4°3·6′W	X	77,84
Cassenvey Burn	D & G	NX6977	55°4·4′	4°2·7′W	W	77,84
Cassey Compton	Glos	SP0415	51°50·2′	1°56·1′W	T	163
Cass Hagg	N Yks	SE7686	54°16·1′	0°49·6′W	X	94,100
Cass Hagg Wood	N Yks	SE7687	54°16·6′	0°49·5′W	F	94,100
Cassia Lodge	Ches	SJ6168	53°12·7′	2°34·6′W	X	118
Cassieford	Moray	NJ0559	57°36·9′	3°35·0′W	X	27
Cassiegills	Aberd	NJ9632	57°23·0′	2°3·5′W	X	30
Cassillis House	S Ayr	NS3412	55°22·7′	4°36·8′W	A	70
Cassillis View	S Ayr	NS3011	55°22·1′	4°40·5′W	X	70
Cassindilly	Fife	NO3909	56°16·4′	2°58·7′W	X	59
Cassindonald	Fife	NO4612	56°18·1′	2°51·9′W	X	59
Cassington	Oxon	SP4510	51°47·4′	1°20·5′W	T	164
Cassington	S Ayr	NS3511	55°22·2′	4°35·8′W	X	70
Cassiobury Park	Herts	TQ0996	51°39·4′	0°25·1′W	X	166,176
Cass-ny-Hawin Head	I of M	SC3069	54°5·6′	4°35·6′W	X	95
Cassochie	Pth & Kin	NN9926	56°25·2′	3°37·8′W	X	52,53,58
Cassock Hill	D & G	NT2204	55°19·7′	3°13·3′W	X	79
Casson Dyke Fm	Cumbr	NY3461	54°56·6′	3°1·4′W	FM	85
Cassop	Durham	NZ3438	54°44·4′	1°27·9′W	T	93
Cassop Grange	Durham	NZ3138	54°44·4′	1°30·7′W	X	93
Cassop Moor	Durham	NZ3239	54°44·9′	1°29·7′W	X	93
Cass Plantn	N Yks	SE5667	54°6·0′	1°8·2′W	F	100

Casswell's Br	Lincs	TF1627	52°49·9′	0°16·3′W	X	130
Cast	Fife	NO4622	56°23·5′	2°52·0′W	X	54,59
Castallack	Corn	SW4525	50°4·5′	5°33·5′W	T	203
Castaway Fm	Norf	TM1695	52°30·8′	1°11·4′E	FM	144
Castcliffe Hill	Lincs	TF3073	53°14·5′	0°2·7′W	X	122
Castell	Carm	SN6036	52°0·5′	4°2·0′W	X	146
Castell	Cered	SN3647	52°6·1′	4°23·3′W	X	145
Castell	Cered	SN5858	52°12·4′	4°4·3′W	X	146
Castell	Cered	SN5948	52°7·0′	4°3·2′W	X	146
Castell	Cered	SN6157	52°11·9′	4°1·6′W	X	146
Castell	Cered	SN7390	52°29·8′	3°51·9′W	X	135
Castell	Conwy	SH7669	53°12·5′	3°51·0′W	T	115
Castell	Conwy	SH9845	52°59·8′	3°30·8′W	X	116
Castell	Denb	SJ0672	53°14·4′	3°24·1′W	X	116
Castell	Denb	SJ1168	53°12·3′	3°19·5′W	T	116
Castell	Denb	SJ2057	53°6·5′	3°11·3′W	X	117
Castell	Flint	SJ2268	53°12·4′	3°9·7′W	X	117
Castell	Gwyn	SH5665	53°10·0′	4°8·8′W	X	114,115
Castell	Gwyn	SH5804	52°37·2′	4°5·5′W	X	135
Castell	Gwyn	SH6347	53°0·4′	4°2·1′W	X	115
Castell	Gwyn	SH8632	52°52·6′	3°41·2′W	X	124,125
Castell	I of Angl	SH4094	53°25·4′	4°24·1′W	X	114
Castell	I of Angl	SH5080	53°18·0′	4°14·6′W	X	114,115
Castell	I of Angl	SH5173	53°14·2′	4°13·6′W	X	114,115
Castell	Pemb	SN1732	51°57·6′	4°39·4′W	X	145
Castell	Powys	SN9596	52°33·3′	3°32·5′W	X	136
Castell Aberlleiniog	I of Angl	SH6179	53°17·6′	4°4·7′W	A	114,115
Castell Allt-goch	Cered	SN5950	52°8·1′	4°3·2′W	A	146
Castellau	Rho Cyn Taf	ST0586	51°34·1′	3°21·9′W	X	170
Castellau-ganol	Rho Cyn Taf	ST0487	51°34·7′	3°22·7′W	X	170
Castell-bach	Carm	SN2427	51°55·1′	4°33·2′W	A	145,158
Castell Bach	Cered	SN3658	52°12·0′	4°23·6′W	A	145
Castell Bach	Gwyn	SH3339	52°55·6′	4°28·7′W	X	123
Castell Blaenllynfi	Powys	SO1422	51°53·6′	3°14·6′W	A	161
Castell Brogyntyn	Shrops	SJ2731	52°52·5′	3°4·7′W	A	126
Castell Bron-niwl	Carm	SN2922	51°52·5′	4°28·7′W	A	145,159
Castell Bryn Amlwg	Shrops	SO1684	52°27·1′	3°13·8′W	A	136
Castell Bryn-gwyn	I of Angl	SH4667	53°10·9′	4°17·9′W	A	114,115
Castell Bwa-drain	Cered	SN7179	52°23·9′	3°53·4′W	A	135,147
Castell Caemardy	Powys	SO0353	52°10·2′	3°24·7′W	X	147
Castell Caerau	Gwyn	SH5043	52°58·0′	4°13·6′W	A	124
Castell Caeron	Gwyn	SH2230	52°50·5′	4°38·2′W	A	123
Castell-Caeronwy	Gwyn	SH5254	53°4·0′	4°12·1′W	X	115
Castell Caer Seion	Conwy	SH7577	53°16·8′	3°52·1′W	X	115
Castell Caer Seion (Fort)	Conwy	SH7577	53°16·8′	3°52·1′W	A	115
Castell Carndochan	Gwyn	SH8430	52°51·5′	3°43·0′W	A	124,125
Castell Cawr	Conwy	SH9376	53°16·5′	3°35·9′W	A	116
Castell Cenddu	Cered	SN4758	52°12·2′	4°13·9′W	X	146
Castell Coch	Card	ST1382	51°32·0′	3°14·9′W	A	171
Castell Coch	Monm	ST4288	51°35·5′	2°49·8′W	X	171,172
Castell Coch	Pemb	SM7730	51°55·7′	5°14·2′W	A	157
Castell Coch	Pemb	SM8433	51°57·5′	5°8·2′W	A	157
Castell Coch	Pemb	SM8734	51°58·1′	5°5·7′W	A	157
Castell Coch	Pemb	SN0713	51°47·2′	4°47·5′W	A	158
Castell Côch	Powys	SN9314	51°49·1′	3°32·8′W	A	160
Castell Coch	V of Glam	ST0274	51°27·6′	3°24·3′W	A	170
Castell Cogan	Carm	SN3214	51°48·2′	4°25·8′W	A	159
Castell Collen (Roman Fort)	Powys	SO0562	52°15·1′	3°23·1′W	R	147
Castell Crugerydd	Powys	SO1559	52°13·6′	3°14·3′W	A	148
Castellcrugiau	Cered	SN3652	52°8·8′	4°23·4′W	X	145
Castell Crwn	I of Angl	SH3390	53°23·1′	4°30·3′W	A	114
Castell Crychydd	Pemb	SN2634	51°58·9′	4°31·6′W	A	145
Castell Cwm-Aran (Motte & Baileys)	Powys	SO1570	52°19·5′	3°14·4′W	A	136,148
Castelldeudraeth	Gwyn	SH5937	52°55·0′	4°5·4′W	X	124
Castell Dinas	Powys	SO1730	51°58·0′	3°12·1′W	A	161
Castell Dinas Bran	Denb	SJ2243	52°59·0′	3°9·3′W	A	117
Castell Dol-wlff	Carm	SN5244	52°4·7′	4°9·2′W	A	146
Castell Draenog	Carm	SN2021	51°51·8′	4°36·5′W	X	145,158
Castell Du	Carm	SN4334	51°59·2′	4°16·8′W	A	146
Castell-du	Cered	SN5346	52°5·8′	4°8·4′W	X	146
Castell-du	Powys	SN9128	51°56·6′	3°34·8′W	A	160
Castell Dwyran	Carm	SN3323	51°53·1′	4°25·2′W	X	145,159
Castellfelorganol	Pemb	SN1642	52°3·0′	4°40·6′W	A	145
Castell Fferwynt	Monm	SO2808	51°46·2′	3°2·2′W	X	161
Castell Flemish	Cered	SN6563	52°15·2′	3°58·3′W	A	146
Castell Fm	Pemb	SM9737	51°59·9′	4°57·0′W	FM	157
Castell foel-allt	Powys	SO2567	52°18·0′	3°5·6′W	A	137,148
Castell Forlan	Pemb	SN0926	51°54·2′	4°46·2′W	A	145,158
Castell Garw	Carm	SN1426	51°54·3′	4°41·8′W	A	145,158
Castell Garw	Carm	SN1526	51°54·4′	4°41·0′W	X	145,158
Castell Goetre	Cered	SN6050	52°8·1′	4°2·3′W	A	146
Castell Gorfod	Carm	SN2620	51°51·3′	4°31·2′W	X	145,158
Castell Gorwyn	Carm	SN3025	51°54·1′	4°27·9′W	X	145
Castell-greidd	Powys	SN8883	52°26·3′	3°38·5′W	X	135,136
Castell Grogwynion	Cered	SN7272	52°20·1′	3°52·3′W	A	135,147
Castell Gwallter	Cered	SN6286	52°27·5′	4°1·5′W	A	135
Castell Gwgan	Gwyn	SH3940	52°56·2′	4°23·3′W	X	123
Castell Gwyn	Pemb	SN1021	51°51·6′	4°45·2′W	A	145,158
Castell-gwyn	Pemb	SN1021	51°51·6′	4°45·2′W	X	145,158
Castell Gwynionydd	Cered	SN4242	52°3·5′	4°17·9′W	A	146
Castell Gwythian	Cered	SN2649	52°7·0′	4°32·1′W	A	145
Castell Heinif	Pemb	SM7224	51°52·3′	5°18·3′W	A	157
Castell hendre-wen	Pemb	SM9233	51°57·6′	5°1·3′W	A	157
Castell Henllys	Pemb	SN1139	52°1·3′	4°44·9′W	A	145
Castell-Howel	Carm	SN6026	51°55·1′	4°1·8′W	X	146
Castell Howell	Cered	SN4448	52°6·7′	4°16·3′W	X	146
Castell Hywel	Cered	SN4447	52°6·2′	4°16·3′W	X	146
Castellior	I of Angl	SH5474	53°14·8′	4°10·9′W	X	114,115
Castell-isaf	Powys	SO0599	52°35·1′	3°23·7′W	X	136
Castell Llainfawr	Pemb	SN1537	52°0·3′	4°41·3′W	A	145
Castell Llwyd	Pemb	SN1137	52°0·2′	4°44·8′W	A	145
Castell Mael	Pemb	SN0029	51°55·7′	4°54·1′W	A	145,157,158
Castellmai	Gwyn	SH4960	53°7·2′	4°15·0′W	X	114,115
Castellmarch	Gwyn	SH3129	52°50·2′	4°30·1′W	A	123
Castell-mawr	Carm	SN2427	51°55·1′	4°33·2′W	A	145,158
Castell-mawr	Carm	SN2427	51°55·1′	4°33·2′W	A	145,158
Castell-mawr	Carm	SN2727	51°55·1′	4°30·5′W	A	145,158
Castell-mawr	Gwyn	SH3340	52°56·1′	4°28·7′W	X	123

Castell-mawr	I of Angl	SH5381	53°18·6′	4°12·0′W	X	114,115
Castell-Mawr	Pemb	SN1137	52°0·2′	4°44·8′W	A	145
Castell Mawry	Carm	SN2727	51°55·1′	4°30·5′W	X	145,158
Castell Meredydd	Newp	ST2288	51°35·4′	3°7·2′W	A	171
Castell Meurig	Carm	SN7027	51°55·8′	3°53·1′W	A	146,160
Castell Moeddyn	Cered	SN4851	52°8·4′	4°12·9′W	A	146
Castell Moel	V of Glam	ST0573	51°27·1′	3°21·6′W	A	170
Castell-moel (rems of)	Carm	SN3916	51°49·4′	4°19·8′W	A	159
Castell Morgraig	Caer	ST1684	51°33·2′	3°12·3′W	A	171
Castellnadolig	Cered	SN2950	52°7·6′	4°29·5′W	A	145
Castell Nanhyfer	Pemb	SN0840	52°1·8′	4°47·5′W	A	145
Castell Nant-y-garau	Cered	SN3642	52°3·4′	4°23·1′W	A	145
Castell Nonni	Carm	SN4939	52°2·0′	4°11·7′W	A	146
Castell Nos	Rho Cyn Taf	SN9600	51°41·6′	3°29·9′W	A	170
Castell Odo	Gwyn	SH1828	52°49·4′	4°41·7′W	A	123
Castell Olwen	Cered	SN5849	52°7·5′	4°4·1′W	A	146
Castell Pen yr allt	Pemb	SN1542	52°3·0′	4°41·5′W	A	145
Castell Pistog	Cered	SN3840	52°2·3′	4°21·3′W	X	145
Castell-poeth	Pemb	SM8937	51°59·7′	5°4·0′W	A	157
Castell-pridd	Cered	SN2949	52°7·0′	4°29·5′W	X	145
Castell Prysor	Gwyn	SH7536	52°54·7′	3°51·1′W	A	124
Castell Rhyfel	Cered	SN7359	52°13·1′	3°51·2′W	A	146,147
Castell Tal-y-van	V of Glam	ST0277	51°29·2′	3°24·3′W	A	170
Castelltinboeth	Powys	SO0975	52°22·2′	3°19·8′W	A	136,147
Castell Toch	Carm	SN2511	51°46·5′	4°31·8′W	X	158
Castell Tomen-y-mur	Gwyn	SH7038	52°55·7′	3°55·6′W	A	124
Castell Tomen-y-mur (Roman Fort)	Gwyn	SH7038	52°55·7′	3°55·6′W	R	124
Castell Trefilan	Cered	SN5457	52°11·8′	4°7·8′W	A	146
Castelltreruffydd	Pemb	SN1044	52°4·0′	4°45·9′W	A	145
Castell y Bere	Gwyn	SH6608	52°39·4′	3°58·5′W	A	124
Castell-y-blaidd	Powys	SO1279	52°24·4′	3°17·2′W	X	136,148
Castell-y-blaidd (Settlement)	Powys	SO1279	52°24·4′	3°17·2′W	A	136,148
Castell-y-bwch	Torf	ST2792	51°37·6′	3°2·9′W	T	171
Castell-y-dail	Powys	SO0989	52°29·7′	3°20·0′W	X	136
Castell-y-Dryw	V of Glam	SS9168	51°24·3′	3°33·6′W	X	170
Castell-y-gaer	Carm	SN3419	51°50·9′	4°24·2′W	A	159
Castell y Gaer	Gwyn	SH5909	52°39·9′	4°4·7′W	A	124
Castell-y-garn	Pemb	SN0742	52°2·8′	4°48·5′W	X	145
Castell-y-garn (Cairn)	Powys	SO0173	52°21·0′	3°26·8′W	A	136,147
Castell-y-geifr	Cered	SN4258	52°12·1′	4°18·3′W	X	146
Castell y Geifr	Powys	SN8216	51°50·0′	3°42·4′W	X	160
Castell-y-graig	Carm	SN6015	51°49·2′	4°1·5′W	X	159
Castell y Gwynt	Conwy	SH7760	53°7·6′	3°49·9′W	X	115
Castell-y-rhingyll	Carm	SN5714	51°48·6′	4°4·1′W	T	159
Castell y Rhodwydd	Denb	SJ1751	53°3·2′	3°13·9′W	A	116
Castell y Van	Caer	ST1686	51°34·2′	3°12·3′W	A	171
Castellywaun	Carm	SN3117	51°49·8′	4°26·8′W	X	159
Castercliff	Lancs	SD8838	53°50·5′	2°10·5′W	X	103
Castercliff (Fort)	Lancs	SD8838	53°50·5′	2°10·5′W	A	103
Casterley Camp	Wilts	SU1153	51°16·8′	1°50·1′W	A	184
Castern	Staffs	SK1252	53°4·1′	1°48·8′W	X	119
Casterton	Cumbr	SD6279	54°12·6′	2°34·5′W	T	97
Casterton Fell	Cumbr	SD6580	54°13·1′	2°31·8′W	X	97
Casterton Ho	Lincs	TF2536	52°54·6′	0°8·1′W	X	131
Cast Hills	N Yks	SE2071	54°8·3′	1°41·2′W	X	99
Cast Hills (Settlement)	N Yks	SE2071	54°8·3′	1°41·2′W	A	99
Casthorpe Fm	Lincs	SK8536	52°55·1′	0°43·7′W	FM	130
Casthorpe Hills	Lincs	SK8736	52°55·1′	0°42·0′W	X	130
Casthorpe House Fm	Lincs	SK8635	52°54·6′	0°42·9′W	FM	130
Casthorpe Lodge	Lincs	SK8635	52°54·6′	0°42·9′W	X	130
Castick Fm	Corn	SX2676	50°33·7′	4°27·0′W	FM	201
Castinicks	I Scilly	SV8511	49°55·2′	6°23·0′W	X	203
Castlake Fm	Somer	ST1136	51°7·2′	3°15·9′W	FM	181
Castlandhill	Fife	NT1182	56°1·6′	3°25·2′W	H	65
Castle	Corn	SX0958	50°23·7′	4°40·9′W	X	200
Castle	Cumbr	NY4330	54°40·0′	2°52·6′W	X	90
Castle	Devon	ST3301	50°48·5′	2°56·7′W	T	193
Castle	Glos	SO5707	51°45·8′	2°37·0′W	X	162
Castle	Monm	SO2913	51°48·9′	3°1·4′W	A	161
Castle	Monm	SO4108	51°46·3′	2°50·9′W	A	161
Castle	Somer	ST0928	51°2·9′	3°17·5′W	T	181
Castle	Somer	ST5044	51°11·8′	2°42·5′W	T	182,183
Castle Acre	Norf	TF8115	52°42·4′	0°41·2′E	T	132
Castle-an-Dinas	Corn	SW4835	50°9·9′	5°31·4′W	A	203
Castle-an-Dinas	Corn	SW9462	50°25·5′	4°53·6′W	X	200
Castle-an-Dinas (Fort)	Corn	SW9462	50°25·5′	4°53·6′W	A	200
Castle Ashby	Northnts	SP8659	52°13·6′	0°44·1′W	T	152
Castle Ashby Lodge	Northnts	SP8558	52°13·1′	0°44·9′W	X	152
Castle Ban	D & G	NW9667	54°57·6′	5°10·8′W	X	82
Castle Bank	Kent	TQ7840	51°8·1′	0°33·0′E	X	188
Castle Bank	N Yks	SE0391	54°19·1′	1°56·8′W	X	98
Castle Bank	Oxon	SP4040	52°3·6′	1°24·6′W	X	151
Castle Bank	Powys	SO0777	52°23·2′	3°21·6′W	H	136,147
Castle Bank	Powys	SO0855	52°11·4′	3°20·4′W	X	147
Castle Bank	Shrops	SO4598	52°34·9′	2°48·3′W	X	137,138
Castlebank	S Lanak	NS8743	55°40·3′	3°47·4′W	X	71,72
Castle Bank (Earthworks)	Kent	TQ7840	51°8·1′	0°33·0′E	A	188
Castle Bank (Enclosure)	Oxon	SP4040	51°3·6′	1°24·6′W	A	151
Castle Bank (Motte & Bailey)	Shrops	SO4598	52°34·9′	2°48·3′W	A	137,138
Castle Ban (Motte)	D & G	NW9667	54°57·6′	5°10·8′W	A	82
Castle Barn	S Glos	ST7982	51°32·4′	2°17·8′W	X	172
Castle Barn Fm	Glos	SP1016	51°50·8′	1°50·9′W	FM	163
Castle Barrow	Wilts	ST9644	51°11·9′	2°3·0′W	A	184
Castle Batch	N Som	ST3663	51°22·0′	2°54·8′W	A	182
Castle Bay	Highld	NG8635	57°21·6′	5°33·0′W	W	24
Castle Bay	N Ayr	NS2058	55°47·2′	4°51·8′W	W	63
Castle Bay	N Eil	NL6697	56°56·9′	7°29·2′W	W	31
Castlebay	N Eil	NL6698	56°57·4′	7°29·3′W	T	31
Castlebeach Bay	Pemb	SM8104	51°41·8′	5°9·8′W	W	157
Castlebeck Fm	N Yks	SE9597	54°21·8′	0°31·9′W	FM	94,101
Castlebeck Wood	N Yks	SE9497	54°21·8′	0°32·8′W	F	94,101
Castlebeck Wood	N Yks	SE9597	54°21·8′	0°31·9′W	F	94,101
Castle Bolton	N Yks	SE0391	54°19·1′	1°56·8′W	T	98
Castle Bourne	Worcs	SO9476	52°23·2′	2°4·9′W	X	139
Castle Br	Heref	SO4474	52°21·9′	2°48·9′W	X	137,148
Castlebrae	Aberd	NJ6354	57°34·7′	2°36·7′W	X	29
Castlebrae	D & G	NS7809	55°21·8′	3°55·1′W	X	71,78
Castlebrocket	S Lanak	NS7342	55°39·6′	4°0·7′W	X	71
Castle Bromwich	Sol	SP1589	52°30·2′	1°46·3′W	T	139
Castle Bryher	I Scilly	SV8614	49°56·9′	6°22·3′W	X	203
Castle Burn	Northum	NY8473	55°3·3′	2°14·6′W	W	86,87
Castle Burn	Stir	NN7608	56°15·2′	3°59·6′W	W	57
Castle Burn	Stir	NS4799	56°9·8′	4°27·4′W	W	57
Castlebury Fm	Herts	TL3917	51°50·3′	0°1·5′E	FM	166
Castle Butt	D & G	NW9667	54°57·6′	5°10·8′W	X	82
Castle Bytham	Lincs	SK9818	52°45·3′	0°32·5′W	T	130
Castlebythe	Pemb	SN0228	51°55·2′	4°52·4′W	T	145,157,158
Castlebythe Common	Pemb	SN0128	51°55·1′	4°53·2′W	X	145,157,158
Castle Caereinion	Powys	SJ1605	52°38·4′	3°14·1′W	T	125
Castle Campbell	Clackm	NS9699	56°10·6′	3°40·1′W	A	58
Castle Camps	Cambs	TL6343	52°3·9′	0°23·1′E	T	154
Castle Canyke	Corn	SX0865	50°27·4′	4°41·9′W	A	200
Castle Carlton	Lincs	TF3983	53°19·8′	0°5·6′E	T	122
Castle Carrock	Cumbr	NY5455	54°53·5′	2°42·6′W	T	86
Castle Carrock Fell	Cumbr	NY5654	54°53·0′	2°40·7′W	X	86
Castle Cary	Falk	NS7877	55°58·5′	3°56·9′W	A	64
Castlecary	N Lanak	NS7878	55°59·0′	3°56·9′W	T	64
Castle Cary	Somer	ST6332	51°5·4′	2°31·3′W	T	183
Castlecary Cottage	Falk	NS7877	55°58·5′	3°56·9′W	X	64
Castlecary High Wood	Falk	NS8077	55°58·5′	3°54·9′W	F	65
Castlecary Low Wood	Falk	NS7977	55°58·5′	3°55·9′W	F	64
Castle Cary Sta	Somer	ST6333	51°5·9′	2°31·3′W	X	183
Castle Cenlas	Pemb	SM8630	51°55·9′	5°6·4′W	X	157
Castle Chamber	N Yks	NZ9606	54°26·7′	0°30·8′W	X	94
Castle Clanyard	D & G	NX1037	54°41·8′	4°56·5′W	X	82
Castle Cliff	N Yks	TA0589	54°17·4′	0°22·8′W	X	101
Castle Close	Devon	SS9318	50°57·3′	3°31·0′W	X	181
Castle Close (Settlement)	Devon	SS9318	50°57·3′	3°31·0′W	A	181
Castle Cob	Ches	SJ5373	53°15·4′	2°41·9′W	X	117
Castle Coeffin	Arg & Bt	NM8543	56°32·1′	5°29·3′W	A	49
Castle Combe	Wilts	ST8477	51°29·7′	2°13·4′W	T	173
Castle Copse	Wilts	SU2863	51°22·2′	1°35·5′W	F	174
Castle Crab	Powys	SO0455	52°11·3′	3°23·9′W	X	147
Castle Crag	Cumbr	NY2415	54°31·7′	3°10·0′W	X	89,90
Castle Crag	Cumbr	NY2918	54°33·4′	3°5·4′W	X	89,90
Castle Crag	Cumbr	NY3011	54°29·6′	3°4·4′W	X	90
Castle Crag (Fort)	Cumbr	NY2918	54°33·4′	3°5·4′W	A	89,90
Castle Craig	Arg & Bt	NS1690	56°4·3′	4°56·9′W	X	56
Castle Craig	D & G	NX6892	55°12·5′	4°4·0′W	X	77
Castlecraig	Highld	NH6363	57°38·4′	4°17·2′W	A	21
Castlecraig	Highld	NH8269	57°42·0′	3°58·3′W	X	21,27
Castlecraig	Scot Bord	NT1344	55°41·2′	3°22·6′W	T	72
Castle Craigs	D & G	NY3884	55°9·0′	2°57·9′W	X	79
Castle Craigs	N Ayr	NS2241	55°38·1′	4°49·2′W	X	70
Castle Crawford Fm	S Lanak	NS9521	55°28·5′	3°39·2′W	FM	72
Castlecreavie	D & G	NX7248	54°48·9′	3°59·1′W	X	83,84
Castlecroft	Wolv	SO8797	52°34·5′	2°11·1′W	T	139
Castle Dewey	Corn	SX1670	50°30·3′	4°35·3′W	X	201
Castle Dike	Lincs	TF2651	53°2·7′	0°6·8′W	W	122
Castle Dike	Rut	TF0014	52°43·1′	0°30·8′W	A	130
Castle Dike	Sheff	SE2000	53°30·0′	1°41·5′W	A	110
Castle Dike Fm	Lincs	TF2750	53°2·2′	0°5·9′W	FM	122
Castle Dikes	N Yks	SE2975	54°10·4′	1°32·9′W	R	99
Castle Ditches	Hants	SU1219	50°58·4′	1°49·4′W	X	184
Castle Ditches	Shrops	SO3575	52°22·4′	2°56·9′W	X	137,148
Castle Ditches	Suff	TL9769	52°17·3′	0°53·7′E	X	155
Castle Ditches	Wilts	ST9628	51°3·3′	2°3·0′W	X	184
Castle Ditches (Earthwork)	Shrops	SO3575	52°22·4′	2°56·9′W	A	137,148
Castle Ditches (Fort)	Hants	SU1219	50°58·4′	1°49·4′W	A	184
Castle Ditches (Fort)	Wilts	ST9628	51°3·3′	2°3·0′W	A	184
Castledon Fm	Essex	TQ7393	51°36·8′	0°30·3′E	FM	178
Castle Donington	Leic	SK4427	52°50·6′	1°20·4′W	T	129
Castle Dore	Corn	SX1054	50°21·6′	4°39·9′W	A	200
Castle Douglas	D & G	NX7662	54°56·5′	3°55·7′W	T	84
Castle Dow	Pth & Kin	NN9251	56°38·6′	3°45·2′W	X	52
Castle Dow(fort)	Pth & Kin	NN9251	56°38·6′	3°45·2′W	A	52
Castle Down	I Scilly	SV8815	49°57·5′	6°20·7′W	X	203
Castle Downs	Corn	SW9462	50°25·5′	4°53·6′W	H	200
Castle Drogo	Devon	SX7290	50°42·0′	3°48·4′W	X	191
Castle Dyke	Devon	SX8778	50°35·7′	3°35·4′W	X	192
Castle Dyke	Devon	SX9277	50°35·2′	3°31·2′W	A	192
Castle Dyke	Sheff	SK3083	53°20·8′	1°32·6′W	X	110,111
Castle Dyke Fm	Lincs	TF2848	53°1·1′	0°5·1′W	FM	131
Castle Dyke (Fort)	Devon	SX8778	50°35·7′	3°35·4′W	A	192
Castledykes	D & G	NX6750	54°49·9′	4°3·8′W	A	83,84
Castle Dykes	Northnts	SP6156	52°12·2′	1°6·0′W	A	152
Castle Dykes	N Yks	SD9887	54°17·0′	2°1·4′W	X	98
Castledykes	S Lanak	NS9244	55°40·9′	3°42·6′W	X	71,72
Castledykes	S Lanak	NS9631	55°33·9′	3°38·5′W	X	72
Castle Dykes (Henge)	N Yks	SD9887	54°17·0′	2°1·4′W	A	98
Castledykes (Roman Fort)	S Lanak	NS9244	55°40·9′	3°42·6′W	R	71,72
Castle Earthworks	Denb	SJ0679	53°18·2′	3°24·2′W	A	116
Castle Eaton	Swin	SU1495	51°39·4′	1°47·5′W	T	163
Castle Eden	Durham	NZ4237	54°43·8′	1°20·4′W	T	93
Castle Eden Burn	Durham	NZ4138	54°44·4′	1°21·4′W	W	93
Castle Eden Walkway	Stock on T	NZ4025	54°37·4′	1°22·4′W	X	93
Castle Edge Fm	Derby	SJ9987	53°23·0′	2°0·5′W	FM	109
Castle End	Peterb	TF1208	52°39·7′	0°20·2′W	T	142
Castle End Fm	Glos	SO7613	51°49·1′	2°20·5′W	FM	162
Castle End Fm	Wok	SU8027	51°29·4′	0°50·5′W	FM	175
Castle Ewen	Highld	NG4162	57°34·7′	6°19·5′W	X	23
Castlefairn	D & G	NX7387	55°9·9′	3°59·2′W	X	77
Castlefairn Water	D & G	NX7688	55°10·5′	3°56·4′W	W	78
Castle Farm	Durham	NZ0514	54°31·5′	1°54·9′W	FM	92
Castle Feather	D & G	NX4434	54°40·9′	4°24·8′W	X	83
Castle Feather (Fort)	D & G	NX4434	54°40·9′	4°24·8′W	A	83
Castle Field	E Yorks	SE8154	53°58·8′	0°45·5′W	X	106
Castlefield Fm	Heref	SO4223	51°54·4′	2°50·2′W	FM	161
Castle Fields	Bucks	SP6934	52°0·2′	0°59·3′W	X	152,165
Castlefields	Halton	SJ5382	53°20·2′	2°41·9′W	T	108
Castle Fields	Shrops	SJ5013	52°43·0′	2°44·0′W	T	126
Castle Finlay	Highld	NH8851	57°32·4′	3°51·8′W	X	27
Castle Finlay (Fort)	Highld	NH8851	57°32·4′	3°51·8′W	A	27
Castle Fm	Angus	NO3035	56°30·4′	3°7·8′W	FM	53
Castle Fm	Bath & NE Somer	ST6760	51°20·5′	2°28·0′W	FM	172
Castle Fm	Cambs	TL2551	52°8·8′	0°10·0′W	FM	153
Castle Fm	Cambs	TL6242	52°3·4′	0°22·2′E	FM	154
Castle Fm	Ches	SJ3570	53°13·6′	2°58·0′W	FM	117
Castle Fm	Ches	SJ5351	53°3·5′	2°41·7′W	FM	117
Castle Fm	Ches	SJ8760	53°8·5′	2°11·3′W	FM	118
Castle Fm	Corn	SW9562	50°25·6′	4°52·8′W	FM	200
Castle Fm	Derby	SK4349	53°2·4′	1°21·1′W	FM	129
Castle Fm	Devon	SX6546	50°18·1′	3°53·4′W	FM	202
Castle Fm	D & G	NX9158	54°54·5′	3°41·6′W	FM	84
Castle Fm	E Renf	NS5555	55°46·3′	4°18·3′W	FM	64
Castle Fm	E Susx	TQ7220	50°57·4′	0°27·3′E	FM	199
Castle Fm	E Susx	TQ9117	50°55·5′	0°43·5′E	FM	189
Castle Fm	E Yorks	SE7031	53°46·5′	0°55·9′W	FM	105,106
Castle Fm	E Yorks	SE8138	53°50·2′	0°45·7′W	FM	106
Castle Fm	E Yorks	SE8838	53°50·1′	0°39·4′W	FM	106
Castle Fm	E Yorks	SE9033	53°47·4′	0°37·6′W	FM	106
Castle Fm	Hants	SU2639	51°9·2′	1°37·3′W	FM	184
Castle Fm	Hants	SU5710	50°53·4′	1°11·0′W	FM	196
Castle Fm	Heref	SO3233	51°59·7′	2°59·0′W	FM	161
Castle Fm	Heref	SO4038	52°2·5′	2°52·1′W	FM	149,161
Castle Fm	Heref	SO5942	52°4·7′	2°35·5′W	FM	149
Castle Fm	Heref	SO6428	51°57·2′	2°31·0′W	FM	149
Castle Fm	Herts	TL1725	51°54·9′	0°17·5′W	FM	166
Castle Fm	Kent	TQ5263	51°21·0′	0°11·4′E	FM	177,188
Castle Fm	Kent	TQ9945	51°10·4′	0°51·2′E	FM	189
Castle Fm	Leic	SK3606	52°39·3′	1°27·7′W	FM	140
Castle Fm	Lincs	SK8332	52°53·0′	0°45·6′W	FM	130
Castle Fm	Lincs	TF1491	53°24·4′	0°16·7′W	FM	113
Castle Fm	Lincs	TF3983	53°19·8′	0°5·6′E	FM	122
Castle Fm	Mil Key	SP9154	52°10·8′	0°39·7′W	FM	152
Castle Fm	Monm	SO3701	51°42·5′	2°54·3′W	FM	171
Castle Fm	Norf	TG0217	52°43·0′	0°59·9′E	FM	133
Castle Fm	Norf	TG4128	52°48·0′	1°34·9′E	FM	134
Castle Fm	Northnts	SP4942	52°4·7′	1°16·7′W	FM	151
Castle Fm	Northum	NT9910	55°23·3′	2°0·5′W	FM	81
Castle Fm	Northum	NY8362	54°57·4′	2°15·5′W	FM	86,87
Castle Fm	Notts	SK5777	53°17·5′	1°8·3′W	FM	120
Castle Fm	Notts	SK8772	53°14·5′	0°41·4′W	FM	121
Castle Fm	N Som	ST5466	51°23·7′	2°39·3′W	FM	172,182
Castle Fm	N Yks	SE3784	54°15·3′	1°25·5′W	FM	99
Castle Fm	N Yks	SE3858	54°1·2′	1°24·8′W	FM	104
Castle Fm	N Yks	SE4586	54°16·3′	1°18·1′W	FM	99
Castle Fm	N Yks	SE5118	53°39·6′	1°13·3′W	FM	111
Castle Fm	S Glos	ST7774	51°28·1′	2°19·5′W	FM	172
Castle Fm	Somer	ST2715	50°56·0′	3°1·9′W	FM	193
Castle Fm	Staffs	SJ9733	52°53·9′	2°2·3′W	FM	127
Castle Fm	Suff	TL8355	52°10·0′	0°41·0′E	FM	155
Castle Fm	Suff	TL9555	52°9·8′	0°51·5′E	FM	155
Castle Fm	Suff	TL9855	52°9·7′	0°54·1′E	FM	155
Castle Fm	Suff	TM0649	52°6·3′	1°0·9′E	FM	155
Castle Fm	Suff	TM3068	52°15·9′	1°22·6′E	FM	156
Castle Fm	Warw	SP0964	52°16·7′	1°51·7′W	FM	150
Castle Fm	Warw	SP2188	52°29·6′	1°41·0′W	FM	139
Castle Fm	Warw	SP2460	52°14·5′	1°38·5′W	FM	151
Castle Fm	Warw	SP3655	52°11·8′	1°28·0′W	FM	151
Castle Fm	Warw	SP4967	52°18·2′	1°16·5′W	FM	151
Castle Fm	Wilts	SU2651	51°15·7′	1°37·3′W	FM	184
Castle Fm	Worcs	SO7570	52°19·9′	2°21·6′W	FM	138
Castle Folds	Cumbr	NY6509	54°28·8′	2°32·0′W	A	91
Castle Forbes	Aberd	NJ6219	57°15·9′	2°37·3′W	X	37
Castleford	Wakf	SE4225	53°43·4′	1°21·4′W	T	105
Castleford Ings	Wakf	SE4326	53°44·0′	1°20·5′W	X	105
Castle Fraser	Aberd	NJ7212	57°12·1′	2°27·4′W	A	38
Castlefraser Moss	Aberd	NJ7510	57°11·1′	2°24·4′W	F	38
Castle Frome	Heref	SO6645	52°6·4′	2°29·4′W	T	149
Castle Gate	Corn	SW4934	50°9·4′	5°30·5′W	T	203
Castlegate Fm	Ches	SJ5459	53°7·8′	2°40·8′W	FM	117
Castlegate Stud Fm	Derby	SK1975	53°16·5′	1°42·5′W	FM	119
Castle Geo	Highld	ND3865	58°34·4′	3°3·5′W	X	12
Castle Girnigoe or Castle Sinclair	Highld	ND3754	58°28·4′	3°4·3′W	A	12
Castle Godwyn	Glos	SO8711	51°48·1′	2°10·9′W	X	162
Castle Goff	Corn	SX0882	50°36·4′	4°42·4′W	A	200
Castle Gogar	C of Edin	NT1672	55°56·3′	3°20·2′W	A	65,66
Castle Goring	W Susx	TQ1005	50°50·3′	0°25·9′W	A	198
Castle Gotha Fm	Corn	SX0249	50°18·7′	4°46·5′W	FM	204
Castlegower	D & G	NX7859	54°54·9′	3°53·8′W	X	84
Castle Grant	Highld	NJ0430	57°21·3′	3°35·3′W	X	27,36
Castle Green	Bark & Dag	TQ4783	51°31·8′	0°7·6′E	T	177
Castle Green	Barns	SE2502	53°31·1′	1°37·0′W	T	110
Castle Green	Cumbr	SD5392	54°19·5′	2°42·9′W	X	97
Castlegreen	Orkney	HY4613	59°0·3′	2°55·9′W	X	6
Castlegreen	Shrops	SO3289	52°29·9′	2°59·7′W	T	137
Castle Green	Surrey	SU9660	51°20·1′	0°36·9′W	T	175,176,186
Castle Green	Worcs	SO7851	52°9·6′	2°18·9′W	X	150
Castle Greg	W Loth	NT0559	55°49·2′	3°30·5′W	X	65,72
Castle Greg (Roman Fortlet)	W Loth	NT0559	55°49·2′	3°30·5′W	R	65,72
Castle Gresley	Derby	SK2718	52°45·8′	1°35·6′W	T	128
Castle Ground Fm	Wilts	ST7931	51°4·9′	2°17·6′W	FM	183
Castle Grounds	Heref	SO5165	52°17·1′	2°42·7′W	X	137,138,149
Castle Hall	Pemb	SM9105	51°42·5′	5°1·1′W	X	157,158
Castle Haugh	Lancs	SD8250	53°57·0′	2°16·0′W	A	103
Castle Haven	Aberd	NO8884	56°57·1′	2°11·4′W	W	45
Castle Haven Bay	D & G	NX5948	54°48·7′	4°11·2′W	W	83
Castlehaw	Cumbr	SD6692	54°19·6′	2°30·9′W	X	98
Castle Hayes Park Fm	Staffs	SK1927	52°50·6′	1°42·7′W	FM	128
Castlehead	Renf	NS4763	55°50·4′	4°26·2′W	T	64
Castle Head (Field Centre)	Cumbr	SD4279	54°12·5′	2°52·9′W	X	96,97
Castlehead Rocks	Northum	NU1344	55°41·6′	1°47·2′W	X	75
Castle Heather	Highld	NH6742	57°27·2′	4°12·5′W	X	26
Castle Heaton	Northum	NT9041	55°40·0′	2°9·1′W	X	74,75
Castle Hedingham	Essex	TL7835	51°59·3′	0°35·9′E	T	155
Castleheggie	Fife	NO3302	56°12·6′	3°4·4′W	X	59
Castle High	Pemb	SM8815	51°47·9′	5°4·1′W	X	157
Castlehill	Aberd	NJ5128	57°20·7′	2°48·4′W	X	37
Castlehill	Aberd	NJ6451	57°33·1′	2°35·6′W	X	29
Castlehill	Aberd	NJ7949	57°32·1′	2°20·6′W	X	29,30
Castle Hill	Aberd	NJ7964	57°40·2′	2°20·7′W	H	29,30
Castlehill	Aberd	NJ8739	57°26·7′	2°12·5′W	X	30
Castle Hill	Aberd	NO6592	57°1·3′	2°34·1′W	X	38,45

Castle Hill	Aberd	NO7796	57°3·5'	2°22·3'W	X	38,45
Castle Hill	Aberd	NO8474	56°51·7'	2°15·3'W	X	45
Castle Hill	Angus	NO3656	56°41·7'	3°2·3'W	H	54
Castle Hill	Angus	NO4457	56°42·3'	2°54·4'W	A	54
Castlehill	Arg & Bt	NR3650	55°40·6'	6°11·5'W	X	60
Castle Hill	Bucks	SP8822	51°53·6'	0°42·9'W	A	165
Castle Hill	Cambs	TL0967	52°17·6'	0°23·7'W	A	153
Castlehill	Cered	SN4955	52°10·6'	4°12·1'W	X	146
Castle Hill	Cered	SN6274	52°21·0'	4°1·2'W	H	135
Castle Hill	Ches	SJ4644	52°59·7'	2°47·9'W	A	117
Castle Hill	Ches	SJ5367	53°12·1'	2°41·8'W	X	117
Castle Hill	C of Leic	SK5609	52°40·8'	1°9·9'W	X	140
Castle Hill	Corn	SX0043	50°15·4'	4°48·0'W	X	204
Castle Hill	Cumbr	SD2577	54°11·2'	3°8·5'W	A	96,97
Castle Hill	Darl	NZ3620	54°34·7'	1°26·2'W	X	93
Castle Hill	Derby	SK3177	53°17·6'	1°31·7'W	A	119
Castle Hill	Derby	SK3972	53°14·9'	1°24·5'W	A	119
Castle Hill	Devon	SS4918	50°56·7'	4°8·6'W	H	180
Castle Hill	Devon	SS5216	50°55·7'	4°6·0'W	H	180
Castle Hill	Devon	SS6728	51°2·4'	3°53·4'W	A	180
Castle Hill	Devon	SS9904	50°49·8'	3°25·7'W	H	192
Castle Hill	Devon	ST1311	50°53·8'	3°13·8'W	H	192,193
Castle Hill	Devon	SY2199	50°47·3'	3°6·9'W	A	192,193
Castle Hill	D & G	NS7916	55°25·6'	3°54·3'W	H	71,78
Castlehill	D & G	NS8804	55°19·3'	3°45·5'W	X	78
Castle Hill	D & G	NX7294	55°13·7'	4°0·3'W	X	77
Castlehill	D & G	NX7555	54°52·7'	3°56·5'W	X	84
Castlehill	D & G	NX8188	55°10·6'	3°51·7'W	X	78
Castle Hill	D & G	NX8254	54°52·3'	3°49·9'W	H	84
Castle Hill	D & G	NX9275	55°3·7'	3°41·0'W	X	84
Castlehill	D & G	NX9784	55°8·6'	3°36·5'W	X	78
Castlehill	D & G	NY0881	55°7·1'	3°26·1'W	X	78
Castlehill	D & G	NY1278	55°5·6'	3°22·3'W	X	85
Castlehill	D & G	NY1881	55°7·2'	3°16·7'W	X	79
Castlehill	D & G	NY2494	55°14·3'	3°11·3'W	X	79
Castle Hill	D & G	NY2495	55°14·9'	3°11·3'W	H	79
Castle Hill	D & G	NY3686	55°10·1'	2°59·9'W	H	79
Castle Hill	Dorset	ST5505	50°50·8'	2°38·0'W	A	194
Castle Hill	Dorset	ST5900	50°48·1'	2°34·5'W	H	194
Castle Hill	Dorset	SY7492	50°43·9'	2°21·7'W	X	194
Castlehill	E Ayr	NS4838	55°37·0'	4°24·4'W	X	70
Castlehill	E Renf	NS5653	55°45·2'	4°17·2'W	X	64
Castle Hill	E Susx	TQ3707	50°51·0'	0°2·8'W	X	198
Castle Hill	E Susx	TQ5528	51°2·0'	0°13·0'E	T	188,199
Castle Hill	E Yorks	TA1234	53°47·7'	0°17·6'W	H	107
Castlehill	Falk	NS9575	55°57·6'	3°40·5'W	X	65
Castle Hill	Glos	SO8915	51°50·2'	2°9·2'W	X	163
Castle Hill	Hants	SU1616	50°56·8'	1°45·9'W	A	184
Castle Hill	Hants	SU1616	50°56·8'	1°45·9'W	X	184
Castle Hill	Hants	SU1903	50°49·8'	1°43·4'W	X	195
Castle Hill	Hants	SU4016	50°56·8'	1°25·5'W	A	185
Castle Hill	Highld	ND1528	58°14·2'	3°26·4'W	X	17
Castlehill	Highld	NH6944	57°28·3'	4°10·6'W	X	26
Castle Hill	Highld	NH9505	57°7·7'	3°43·6'W	H	36
Castlehill	Inverc	NS3572	55°55·0'	4°38·0'W	X	63
Castle Hill	Kent	TQ6043	51°10·1'	0°17·7'E	X	188
Castle Hill	Kent	TQ6942	51°9·4'	0°25·4'E	T	188
Castle Hill	Kent	TR2137	51°5·6'	1°9·8'E	X	179,189
Castle Hill	Kirk	SE1514	53°37·6'	1°46·0'W	H	110
Castle Hill	Leeds	SE3643	53°53·2'	1°26·7'W	A	104
Castle Hill	Leic	SK7805	52°38·5'	0°50·4'W	H	141
Castle Hill	Lincs	TF4282	53°19·2'	0°8·3'E	X	122
Castle Hill	Man	SJ8083	53°20·9'	2°17·6'W	X	109
Castlehill	Moray	NJ2157	57°36·0'	3°18·8'W	X	28
Castle Hill	Moray	NJ2763	57°39·3'	3°12·9'W	X	28
Castle Hill	Moray	NJ3060	57°37·7'	3°9·9'W	X	28
Castle Hill	N Ayr	NS2158	55°47·2'	4°50·8'W	X	63
Castlehill	N Ayr	NS2843	55°39·3'	4°43·6'W	X	63,70
Castle Hill	N Lincs	SE8000	53°29·7'	0°47·2'W	A	112
Castle Hill	Norf	TG0735	52°52·6'	1°5·0'E	A	133
Castle Hill	Norf	TG2015	52°41·5'	1°15·7'E	X	133,134
Castle Hill	Norf	TM2689	52°27·4'	1°20·0'E	X	156
Castlehill	Northum	NT9810	55°23·3'	2°1·5'W	X	81
Castle Hill	Northum	NU0609	55°22·7'	1°53·9'W	H	81
Castle Hill	Northum	NU0922	55°29·8'	1°51·0'W	H	75
Castle Hill	Northum	NY6393	55°14·0'	2°34·5'W	H	80
Castle Hill	Notts	SK4955	53°5·6'	1°15·7'W	X	120
Castle Hill	Notts	SK6941	52°58·0'	0°58·0'W	X	129
Castlehill	Notts	SK7864	53°10·3'	0°49·6'W	X	120,121
Castle Hill	N Som	ST4173	51°27·4'	2°50·6'W	F	171,172
Castle Hill	N Yks	NZ3609	54°28·7'	1°26·2'W	X	93
Castle Hill	N Yks	SE5333	53°47·7'	1°11·3'W	A	105
Castlehill	Orkney	HY2625	59°6·6'	3°17·0'W	X	6
Castlehill	Orkney	HY6640	59°15·0'	2°35·3'W	X	5
Castle Hill	Oxon	SP6004	51°44·1'	1°7·5'W	X	164,165
Castle Hill	Oxon	SU3884	51°33·4'	1°26·7'W	X	174
Castle Hill	Oxon	SU5792	51°37·6'	1°10·2'W	X	164,174
Castle Hill	Pemb	SN0538	52°0·6'	4°50·1'W	X	145
Castle Hill	Powys	SJ2113	52°42·8'	3°9·8'W	X	126
Castle Hill	Powys	SO0068	52°18·3'	3°27·6'W	H	136,147
Castle Hill	Powys	SO2058	52°13·1'	3°9·9'W	H	148
Castlehill	Pth & Kin	NO2730	56°27·6'	3°10·6'W	T	53
Castle Hill	Roth	SK5188	53°23·4'	1°13·6'W	A	111,120
Castle Hill	Rut	SK8500	52°35·7'	0°44·3'W	X	141
Castlehill	S Ayr	NS3520	55°27·0'	4°36·1'W	T	70
Castlehill	Scot Bord	NT2135	55°36·4'	3°14·8'W	T	73
Castle Hill	Sheff	SK2792	53°25·7'	1°35·2'W	A	110
Castlehill	Shrops	SJ5901	52°36·6'	2°35·9'W	X	126
Castle Hill	Shrops	SJ6536	52°55·5'	2°30·8'W	X	127
Castle Hill	Shrops	SJ7908	52°40·4'	2°18·2'W	A	127
Castle Hill	Shrops	SO4695	52°33·2'	2°47·4'W	A	137,138
Castlehill	S Lanak	NS7950	55°44·0'	3°55·2'W	X	64
Castle Hill	S Lanak	NS9422	55°29·1'	3°40·2'W	H	71,72
Castlehill	S Lanak	NS9934	55°35·6'	3°35·7'W	X	72
Castle Hill	Somer	ST0928	51°2·9'	3°17·5'W	H	181
Castle Hill	Somer	ST0940	51°9·4'	3°17·7'W	X	181
Castle Hill	Somer	ST4210	50°53·4'	2°49·1'W	H	193
Castle Hill	Staffs	SJ7637	52°56·0'	2°21·0'W	X	127
Castle Hill	Stock	SJ9293	53°26·3'	2°6·8'W	T	109
Castle Hill	Stock on T	NZ4610	54°29·2'	1°17·0'W	A	93

Castle Hill	Suff	TL9967	52°16·1'	0°55·4'E	A	155
Castle Hill	Suff	TM1547	52°5·0'	1°8·7'E	T	169
Castle Hill	Surrey	TQ1963	51°21·4'	0°17·1'W	A	176,187
Castle Hill	Surrey	TQ3250	51°14·3'	0°6·2'W	X	187
Castle Hill	Swin	SU1591	51°37·3'	1°46·6'W	X	163,173
Castle Hill	Traf	SJ7485	53°21·9'	2°23·0'W	H	109
Castle Hill	Warw	SP2560	52°14·5'	1°37·6'W	X	151
Castle Hill	Warw	SP3040	52°3·7'	1°33·3'W	A	151
Castlehill	W Dunb	NS3876	55°57·2'	4°35·2'W	T	63
Castle Hill	Wilts	SU1432	51°5·5'	1°47·6'W	H	184
Castle Hill	Worcs	SO7759	52°14·0'	2°19·8'W	T	150
Castle Hill	Worcs	SO8181	52°25·8'	2°16·4'W	X	138
Castle Hill Barton	Devon	SS6627	51°1·8'	3°54·3'W	X	180
Castle Hill Country Park	C of Leic	SK5609	52°40·8'	1°9·9'W	X	140
Castlehill Fm	Ches	SJ5374	53°15·9'	2°41·9'W	FM	117
Castle Hill Fm	Derby	SK5078	53°18·0'	1°14·6'W	FM	120
Castle Hill Fm	E Susx	TQ5528	51°2·0'	0°13·0'E	FM	188,199
Castle Hill Fm	Flint	SJ2967	53°12·0'	3°3·4'W	FM	117
Castle Hill Fm	Ghead	NZ1264	54°58·5'	1°48·3'W	FM	88
Castle Hill Fm	Glos	SU1197	51°40·5'	1°50·1'W	FM	163
Castle Hill Fm	Kent	TQ6143	51°10·0'	0°18·6'E	FM	188
Castle Hill Fm	N Yks	SE6726	53°43·8'	0°58·7'W	FM	105,106
Castlehill Fm	S Ayr	NS2511	55°22·0'	4°45·2'W	FM	70
Castle Hill Fm	Shrops	SO4699	52°35·4'	2°47·4'W	FM	137,138
Castlehill Fm	S Lanak	NS8746	55°41·9'	3°47·4'W	FM	72
Castle Hill (Fort)	D & G	NX7294	55°13·7'	4°0·3'W	A	77
Castle Hill (Fort)	Dorset	ST5900	50°48·1'	2°34·5'W	A	194
Castle Hill (Fort)	Kent	TQ6043	51°10·1'	0°17·7'E	A	188
Castle Hill (Fort)	Kirk	SE1514	53°37·6'	1°46·0'W	A	110
Castle Hill (Fort)	N Ayr	NS2158	55°47·2'	4°50·8'W	A	63
Castle Hill (Fort)	Somer	ST0928	51°2·9'	3°17·5'W	A	181
Castle Hill (Fort)	Swin	SU1591	51°37·3'	1°46·6'W	A	163,173
Castlehill Ho	Ches	SJ5374	53°15·9'	2°41·9'W	X	117
Castle Hill Ho	Devon	SY1391	50°43·0'	3°13·6'W	X	192,193
Castle Hill Hospital	Ghead	NZ1264	54°58·5'	1°48·3'W	X	88
Castle Hill (Motte & Bailey)	Darl	NZ3620	54°34·7'	1°26·2'W	A	93
Castle Hill (Motte & Bailey)	Leic	SK8500	52°35·7'	0°44·3'W	A	141
Castle Hill (Motte & Bailey)	Norf	TG2015	52°41·5'	1°15·7'E	A	133,134
Castle Hill (Motte & Bailey)	Norf	TM2689	52°27·4'	1°20·0'E	A	156
Castle Hill (Motte & Bailey)	Surrey	TQ3250	51°14·3'	0°6·2'W	A	187
Castlehill Point	D & G	NX8552	54°51·2'	3°47·1'W	X	84
Castlehill Resr	Pth & Kin	NN9903	56°12·8'	3°37·3'W	W	58
Castle Hill (Ring & Baileys)	Kent	TR2137	51°5·6'	1°9·8'E	A	179,189
Castlehill (ruin)	Highld	ND1968	58°35·8'	3°23·1'W	X	11,12
Castle Hills	Aberd	NJ9062	57°39·1'	2°9·6'W	H	30
Castle Hills	Cambs	TL1758	52°12·7'	0°16·9'W	A	153
Castle Hills	Cambs	TL2471	52°19·6'	0°10·4'W	A	153
Castle Hills	Durham	NZ0939	54°45·0'	1°51·2'W	X	92
Castle Hills	Lincs	SK8191	53°24·8'	0°46·5'W	A	112
Castle Hills	Lincs	TF0039	52°56·6'	0°30·3'W	X	130
Castle Hills	N Yks	SE2597	54°22·3'	1°36·5'W	X	99
Castle Hills	N Yks	SE4532	53°47·2'	1°18·6'W	X	105
Castle Hills	Sol	SP1782	52°26·4'	1°44·6'W	X	139
Castle Hills	Warw	SP2887	52°29·0'	1°34·9'W	X	140
Castle Hills Fm	N Yks	SE3594	54°20·7'	1°27·3'W	FM	99
Castle Hills (Motte & Bailey)	N Yks	SE2597	54°22·3'	1°36·5'W	A	99
Castle Hills (Ring & Bailey)	Warw	SP2887	52°29·0'	1°34·9'W	A	140
Castle Hill Wood	Glos	SO7120	51°52·9'	2°24·9'W	F	162
Castle Hill Wood	Notts	SK7380	53°18·9'	0°53·8'W	F	120
Castle Hill Wood	N Yks	SE4638	53°50·4'	1°17·6'W	F	105
Castlehill Wood	S Ayr	NS2512	55°22·5'	4°45·3'W	F	70
Castle Ho	Essex	TM0532	51°57·1'	0°59·4'E	X	168
Castle Ho	Surrey	TQ2354	51°16·5'	0°13·8'W	X	187
Castle Horneck	Corn	SW4530	50°7·2'	5°33·7'W	X	203
Castle Hotel	Blackp	SD3040	53°51·3'	3°3·4'W	X	102
Castle Hotel	Kent	TR3970	51°22·9'	1°26·5'E	X	179
Castle House Fm	N Yks	NZ5607	54°27·6'	1°7·7'W	FM	93
Castle Houses	N Yks	NZ7107	54°27·4'	0°53·9'W	X	94
Castle How	Cumbr	NY2300	54°23·6'	3°10·7'W	H	89,90
Castle How	Cumbr	NY2534	54°42·0'	3°9·4'W	X	89,90
Castle How	Cumbr	NY3007	54°27·5'	3°4·4'W	X	90
Castle How	Cumbr	NY3538	54°44·2'	3°0·1'W	A	90
Castle Howard	N Yks	SE7170	54°7·5'	0°54·4'W	A	100
Castle Howe	Cumbr	NY6105	54°26·6'	2°35·7'W	A	91
Castle Howe	Cumbr	SD5192	54°19·5'	2°44·8'W	A	97
Castle Howe	Orkney	HY5100	58°53·3'	2°50·5'W	A	6,7
Castlehowe Scar	Cumbr	NY5815	54°32·0'	2°38·5'W	X	91
Castle How (Fort)	Cumbr	NY2030	54°39·8'	3°14·0'W	A	89,90
Castlehows Point	Cumbr	NY4522	54°35·7'	2°50·7'W	X	90
Castlehungry	Aberd	NJ8317	57°14·9'	2°16·4'W	X	38
Castle Huntley	Pth & Kin	NO3029	56°27·1'	3°7·7'W	A	53,59
Castle Idris	Shrops	SO2382	52°26·1'	3°7·6'W	H	137
Castle Inn	Cumbr	NY2132	54°40·9'	3°13·1'W	X	89,90
Castle Island	N Ayr	NS1551	55°43·3'	4°56·3'W	X	63,69
Castle Island	Pth & Kin	NO1301	56°11·9'	3°23·7'W	X	58
Castle Kayle	Corn	SW5835	50°10·2'	5°23·0'W	A	203
Castle Kennedy	D & G	NX1059	54°53·6'	4°57·3'W	T	82
Castle Kennedy	D & G	NX1160	54°54·2'	4°56·4'W	A	82
Castle Killibury	Corn	SX0173	50°31·6'	4°48·1'W	A	200
Castle Knott	Cumbr	SD6584	54°15·3'	2°31·8'W	H	97
Castle Knowe	Fife	NO4521	56°22·9'	2°53·0'W	X	54,59
Castle Knowe	Scot Bord	NT7223	55°30·2'	2°26·2'W	X	74
Castle Lachlan	Arg & Bt	NS0195	56°6·6'	5°11·6'W	X	55
Castle Lake Camp	Pemb	SN0212	51°46·5'	4°51·8'W	A	157,158
Castlelaw	Midlo	NT2263	55°51·5'	3°14·3'W	X	66
Castle Law	Pth & Kin	NO1715	56°19·5'	3°20·1'W	X	58
Castlelaw	Scot Bord	NT1450	55°44·4'	3°21·8'W	X	65,72
Castlelaw	Scot Bord	NT8141	55°40·2'	2°17·7'W	X	74
Castle Law	Scot Bord	NT8230	55°34·1'	2°16·7'W	H	74
Castlelaw Hill	Midlo	NT2264	55°52·0'	3°14·3'W	H	66
Castle Leisure Park	Lincs	TF2056	53°5·5'	0°12·1'W	X	122
Castle Leod	Highld	NH4859	57°36·0'	4°32·1'W	A	26
Castle Lloyd Fm	Carm	SN2409	51°45·4'	4°32·6'W	FM	158

Castle Loch	D & G	NX2853	54°50·8'	4°40·3'W	W	82
Castle Loch (Nature Reserve)	D & G	NY0881	55°7·1'	3°26·1'W	W	78
Castlemaddy	D & G	NX5589	55°10·7'	4°16·2'W	X	77
Castlemaddy Gairy	D & G	NX4988	55°10·1'	4°21·8'W	X	77
Castle Madoc	Powys	SO0236	52°1·1'	3°25·3'W	A	160
Castle Mains	D & G	NY0880	55°6·6'	3°26·1'W	X	78
Castle Mains	E Loth	NT5183	56°2·5'	2°46·8'W	X	66
Castle Mains	E Loth	NT5566	55°53·4'	2°42·7'W	X	66
Castle Mains	Pth & Kin	NN9413	56°18·1'	3°42·3'W	X	58
Castle Mains	Scot Bord	NT7656	55°48·1'	2°22·5'W	X	67,74
Castle Mains	S Lanak	NS8632	55°34·4'	3°48·0'W	X	71,72
Castle Malgwyn Fm	Pemb	SN2243	52°3·6'	4°35·4'W	FM	145
Castle Manor Fm	Northnts	TL0278	52°23·7'	0°29·7'W	FM	141
Castleman's Hill Fm	Somer	ST1822	50°59·7'	3°9·7'W	FM	181,193
Castle Marsh	Suff	TM4791	52°27·9'	1°38·6'E	X	134
Castlemartin	Pemb	SR9198	51°38·8'	5°0·9'W	T	158
Castlemartin Corse	Pemb	SR9099	51°39·3'	5°1·8'W	X	158
Castle Maud	Aberd	NO6299	57°5·1'	2°37·2'W	A	37,45
Castlemawgan	Corn	SX1656	50°22·7'	4°34·9'W	X	201
Castle Menzies	Pth & Kin	NN8349	56°37·4'	3°54·0'W	A	52
Castle Mestag	Highld	ND3376	58°40·3'	3°8·8'W	A	7,12
Castlemilk	C of Glas	NS6058	55°48·0'	4°13·6'W	T	64
Castlemilk	D & G	NY1577	55°5·1'	3°19·5'W	T	85
Castlemilktown	D & G	NY1378	55°5·6'	3°21·4'W	X	85
Castle Mill	Scot Bord	NT7246	55°42·6'	2°26·3'W	X	74
Castle Mill	Suff	TM4792	52°28·4'	1°38·6'E	X	134
Castle Mill	Wrex	SJ2637	52°55·8'	3°5·6'W	X	126
Castle Mill Fm	Man	SJ8083	53°20·9'	2°17·6'W	FM	109
Castlemoch Fach	Powys	SJ1123	52°48·1'	3°18·8'W	X	125
Castle Moffat	E Loth	NT6069	55°55·0'	2°38·0'W	X	67
Castlemoor	Shrops	SO5588	52°29·5'	2°39·4'W	X	137,138
Castlemorris	Pemb	SM9031	51°56·5'	5°2·9'W	T	157
Castlemorton	Worcs	SO7937	52°2·1'	2°18·0'W	T	150
Castlemorton Common	Worcs	SO7839	52°3·2'	2°18·9'W	X	150
Castle Muir Point	D & G	NX7947	54°48·4'	3°52·5'W	X	84
Castle Naze	Derby	SK0578	53°18·2'	1°55·1'W	X	119
Castle Neroche	Somer	ST2715	50°56·0'	3°1·9'W	A	193
Castle Nimble	Powys	SO2459	52°13·7'	3°6·4'W	A	148
Castle Nook	Cumbr	NY2317	54°32·8'	3°11·0'W	X	89,90
Castle Nook	Northum	NY6949	54°50·3'	2°28·5'W	X	86,87
Castle o' Burrian	Orkney	HY5042	59°16·0'	2°52·1'W	X	5
Castle O'er	D & G	NY2492	55°13·2'	3°11·3'W	T	79
Castle O'er Forest	D & G	NY2393	55°13·8'	3°12·2'W	F	79
Castle O'er (Fort & Settlement)	D & G	NY2492	55°13·2'	3°11·3'W	A	79
Castle of Allardice	Aberd	NO8173	56°51·1'	2°18·2'W	A	45
Castle of Auchry	Aberd	NJ7850	57°32·6'	2°21·6'W	X	29,30
Castle of Ballzordie	Angus	NO5665	56°46·7'	2°42·8'W	X	44
Castle of Claisdie	Orkney	HY5301	58°53·9'	2°48·5'W	X	6,7
Castle of Comfort	Somer	ST1739	51°8·9'	3°10·8'W	X	181
Castle of Comfort (PH)	Somer	ST5453	51°16·7'	2°39·2'W	X	182,183
Castle of Esslemont	Aberd	NJ9329	57°21·3'	2°6·5'W	A	38
Castle of Fiddes	Aberd	NO8281	56°55·5'	2°17·3'W	A	45
Castle of King Edward	Aberd	NJ7256	57°35·8'	2°27·6'W	A	29
Castle of Mey	Highld	ND2873	58°38·6'	3°13·9'W	A	7,12
Castle of Old Wick	Highld	ND3748	58°25·2'	3°4·2'W	A	12
Castle of Old Wick	Highld	ND3748	58°25·2'	3°4·2'W	X	12
Castle of Park	D & G	NX1857	54°52·7'	4°49·8'W	A	82
Castle of Rednock	Stir	NN6002	56°11·7'	4°14·9'W	X	57
Castle on Oyne	S Ayr	NX4288	55°9·9'	4°28·4'W	X	77
Castle o' Trim	Lancs	SD5356	54°0·1'	2°42·6'W	X	102
Castle Park	Ches	SJ5177	53°17·5'	2°43·7'W	X	117
Castle Park	Warw	SP2863	52°16·1'	1°35·0'W	X	151
Castlepark Hill	Corn	SX3679	50°35·5'	4°18·6'W	H	201
Castle Pencaire	Corn	SW5930	50°7·5'	5°21·9'W	A	203
Castle Piece	Hants	SU1908	50°52·5'	1°43·4'W	A	195
Castle Place	Shrops	SJ4403	52°37·6'	2°49·2'W	X	126
Castle Plain	Somer	ST2615	50°56·0'	3°2·8'W	X	193
Castle Point	Arg & Bt	NS2782	56°0·2'	4°46·0'W	X	56
Castle Point	Corn	SW8432	50°9·2'	5°1·1'W	X	204
Castle Point	D & G	NX0053	54°50·2'	5°6·4'W	X	82
Castle Point	Northum	NU1441	55°40·0'	1°46·2'W	X	75
Castle Point	Northum	NU2522	55°29·7'	1°35·8'W	X	75
Castle Point	Pemb	SM9637	51°59·9'	4°57·9'W	X	157
Castle Port	S Ayr	NS1907	55°19·7'	4°50·8'W	W	70,76
Castle Qua	S Lanak	NS8744	55°40·8'	3°47·4'W	A	71,72
Castlerankine	Falk	NS7881	56°0·6'	3°57·0'W	X	64
Castlerankine Burn	Falk	NS7681	56°0·6'	3°58·9'W	W	64
Castle Reach	Pemb	SN0007	51°43·8'	4°53·4'W	W	157,158
Castlerigg	Cumbr	NY2822	54°35·5'	3°6·4'W	T	89,90
Castlerigg	N Lanak	NS8458	55°48·3'	3°50·6'W	X	65,72
Castlerigg Fell	Cumbr	NY2819	54°33·9'	3°6·4'W	H	89,90
Castlerigg Fm	Cumbr	NY5041	54°45·9'	2°46·2'W	FM	86
Castle Ring	Derby	SK2262	53°9·5'	1°39·9'W	A	119
Castle Ring	Powys	SO2663	52°15·9'	3°4·7'W	A	137,148
Castle Ring	Shrops	SJ3100	52°35·8'	3°0·7'W	X	126
Castle Ring	Shrops	SJ3701	52°36·4'	2°55·4'W	X	126
Castle Ring	Shrops	SO4097	52°34·3'	2°52·7'W	A	137
Castle Ring	Staffs	SK0412	52°42·6'	1°56·0'W	X	128
Castle Ring (Fort)	Shrops	SJ3100	52°35·8'	3°0·7'W	A	126
Castle Ring (Fort)	Shrops	SJ3701	52°36·4'	2°55·4'W	A	126
Castle Ring (Fort)	Staffs	SK0412	52°42·6'	1°56·0'W	A	128
Castle Rings	Wilts	ST8825	51°1·7'	2°9·9'W	A	183
Castle Rising	Norf	TF6624	52°47·5'	0°28·1'E	T	132
Castle Roborough	Devon	SS6137	51°7·2'	3°58·8'W	A	180
Castle Rock	Angus	NO6844	56°35·5'	2°30·8'W	X	54
Castle Rock	Cumbr	NY3219	54°33·9'	3°2·7'W	X	90
Castle Rock	Devon	SS7049	51°13·8'	3°51·3'W	X	180
Castle Rock of Muchalls	Aberd	NO8990	57°0·3'	2°10·4'W	X	38,45
Castle Rocks	N Yks	TA0983	54°14·1'	0°19·2'W	X	101
Castle Rough	Kent	TQ9166	51°21·9'	0°45·0'E	A	178
Castle Roy	Highld	NJ0022	57°16·9'	3°39·1'W	A	36
Castle Rushen	I of M	SC2667	54°4·4'	4°39·2'W	A	95
Castles Bay	Pemb	SM8401	51°40·2'	5°7·0'W	W	157
Castlesea Bay	Angus	NO6843	56°34·9'	2°30·8'W	W	54
Castle Semple Loch	Renf	NS3659	55°48·0'	4°36·5'W	W	63
Castles Fm	Arg & Bt	NN1329	56°25·2'	5°1·5'W	FM	50
Castles Fm	Cambs	TL6077	52°22·3'	0°21·4'E	FM	143
Castle Shaw	Oldham	SE0009	53°34·9'	1°59·6'W	X	110

Castleshaw Moor	Oldham	SD9911	53°36·0′	2°0·5′W	X	109
Castleshaw Resrs	Oldham	SD9909	53°34·9′	2°0·5′W	W	109
Castleshaw Tower	Cumbr	SD6692	54°19·6′	2°30·9′W	A	98
Castle Shuna	Arg & Bt	NM9148	56°34·9′	5°23·7′W	A	49
Castleside	Durham	NZ0848	54°49·9′	1°52·1′W	T	88
Castleside	Scot Bord	NT4620	55°28·5′	2°50·8′W	X	73
Castleside Fm	Ches	SJ5359	53°7·8′	2°41·7′W	FM	117
Castle Sinclair or Castle Girnigoe	Highld	ND3754	58°28·4′	3°4·3′W	A	12
Castle Sinniness	D & G	NX2153	54°50·6′	4°46·8′W	X	82
Castle Skerry	Orkney	ND4384	58°44·7′	2°58·6′W	X	7
Castle Spynie	Highld	NH5442	57°27·0′	4°25·5′W	A	26
Castle Stalker	Arg & Bt	NM9247	56°34·4′	5°22·7′W	A	49
Castlesteads	Cumbr	NY4938	54°44·3′	2°47·1′W	X	90
Castlesteads	Cumbr	NY5125	54°37·3′	2°45·1′W	A	90
Castlesteads	Cumbr	NY5163	54°57·8′	2°45·5′W	X	86
Castlesteads	Cumbr	SD5388	54°17·4′	2°42·9′W	X	97
Castle Steads	E Loth	NT3369	55°54·8′	3°3·9′W	X	66
Castle Steads	N Yks	NZ1107	54°27·7′	1°49·4′W	A	92
Castle Steads	N Yks	SE1085	54°15·9′	1°50·4′W	X	99
Castlesteads (Fort)	Cumbr	SD5388	54°17·4′	2°42·9′W	A	97
Castle Steads (Fort)	N Yks	SE1085	54°15·9′	1°50·4′W	A	99
Castle Stede	Lancs	SD5869	54°7·2′	2°38·1′W	X	97
Castle Stewart	D & G	NX3769	54°59·6′	4°32·5′W	A	83
Castle Stewart Burn	D & G	NX3671	55°0·6′	4°33·5′W	W	77
Castles, The	Arg & Bt	NR7410	55°20·2′	5°33·4′W	X	68
Castles, The	Durham	NZ1033	54°41·8′	1°50·3′W	A	92
Castles, The	E Loth	NT5364	55°52·3′	2°44·6′W	X	66
Castles, The	N Lincs	TA0622	53°41·3′	0°23·3′W	X	107,112
Castles, The	Northum	NT8710	55°23·3′	2°11·9′W	X	80
Castles, The	Orkney	HY5837	59°13·3′	2°43·7′W	X	5
Castles, The	Scot Bord	NT8219	55°28·1′	2°16·7′W	X	80
Castles, The (Fort)	E Loth	NT5364	55°52·3′	2°44·6′W	A	66
Castles, The (Motte & Baileys)	N Lincs	TA0622	53°41·3′	0°23·3′W	A	107,112
Castle Street	Cald	SD9524	53°43·0′	2°4·1′W	T	103
Castle Street Fm	Devon	SS4740	51°8·6′	4°10·9′W	FM	180
Castle Stuart	Highld	NH7449	57°31·1′	4°5·8′W	A	27
Castle Sween	Arg & Bt	NR7178	55°56·7′	5°39·6′W	A	62
Castlesween	Arg & Bt	NR7178	55°56·7′	5°39·6′W	X	62
Castle Tank	Pemb	SR9693	51°36·2′	4°56·4′W	X	158
Castle Tarbet	E Loth	NT5186	56°4·1′	2°46·8′W	X	66
Castle, The	Beds	SP9931	51°58·3′	0°33·1′W	X	165
Castle, The	Bucks	SP9000	51°41·7′	0°41·5′W	A	165
Castle, The	Ches	SJ4065	53°11·0′	2°53·5′W	A	117
Castle, The	Cumbr	NY4720	54°34·6′	2°48·8′W	X	90
Castle, The	Devon	SS4838	51°7·5′	4°9·9′W	A	180
Castle, The	Devon	SS5747	51°12·5′	4°2·4′W	A	180
Castle, The	Devon	SX8044	50°17·3′	3°40·7′W	X	202
Castle, The	Dorset	ST6307	50°51·9′	2°31·2′W	A	194
Castle, The	Durham	NZ4238	54°44·4′	1°20·4′W	X	93
Castle, The	Lancs	SD6213	53°37·0′	2°34·1′W	X	109
Castle, The	Moray	NJ1110	57°10·6′	3°27·9′W	X	36
Castle, The	Northnts	SP8659	52°13·6′	0°44·1′W	A	152
Castle, The	Orkney	HY6221	59°4·7′	2°39·3′W	X	5
Castle, The	Pemb	SM8919	51°50·0′	5°3·4′W	A	157,158
Castle, The	Pemb	SR9593	51°36·2′	4°57·2′W	X	158
Castle, The	S Glos	ST6688	51°35·6′	2°29·1′W	X	162,172
Castle, The	Shetld	HU3682	60°31·5′	1°20·1′W	X	1,2,3
Castle, The	Shetld	HU3787	60°34·2′	1°19·0′W	X	1,2
Castle, The	Suff	TM0051	52°7·5′	0°55·7′E	X	155
Castle, The	W Susx	TQ1934	51°5·8′	0°17·6′W	X	187
Castle, The (Earthwork)	W Susx	TQ1934	51°5·8′	0°17·6′W	A	187
Castle,The (Fort)	Pemb	SR9593	51°36·2′	4°57·2′W	A	158
Castlethorpe	Mil Key	SP7944	52°5·6′	0°50·4′W	T	152
Castlethorpe	N Lincs	SE9807	53°33·3′	0°30·8′W	T	112
Castlethorpe Bridge	N Lincs	SE9808	53°33·8′	0°30·8′W	X	112
Castlethwaite	Cumbr	NY7802	54°25·0′	2°19·9′W	X	91
Castle Tioram	Highld	NM6672	56°47·1′	5°49·4′W	A	40
Castle Toll	Kent	TQ8528	51°1·5′	0°38·7′E	A	189,199
Castleton	Aberd	NO1591	57°0·4′	3°23·5′W	T	43
Castleton	Aberd	NO7578	56°53·8′	2°24·2′W	X	45
Castleton	Angus	NO3346	56°36·3′	3°5·0′W	T	53
Castleton	Angus	NO6544	56°35·5′	2°33·7′W	X	54
Castleton	Arg & Bt	NR8884	56°0·4′	5°23·6′W	X	55
Castleton	Clackm	NN9800	56°11·2′	3°38·2′W	X	58
Castleton	Derby	SK1582	53°20·3′	1°46·1′W	T	110
Castleton	E Loth	NT5985	56°3·6′	2°39·1′W	X	67
Castleton	Heref	SO5945	52°6·3′	2°35·5′W	X	149
Castleton	Highld	NH6953	57°33·2′	4°10·9′W	X	26
Castleton	Midlo	NT3358	55°48·9′	3°3·7′W	X	66,73
Castleton	Moray	NJ1928	57°20·4′	3°20·3′W	X	36
Castleton	Newp	ST2583	51°32·7′	3°4·5′W	T	171
Castleton	N Yks	NZ6808	54°28·0′	0°56·6′W	T	94
Castleton	Pemb	SM9300	51°39·9′	4°59·2′W	X	157,158
Castleton	Pth & Kin	NN9313	56°18·1′	3°43·3′W	T	58
Castleton	Roch	SD8810	53°35·4′	2°10·5′W	T	109
Castleton	Shetld	HP6201	60°41·5′	0°51·4′W	X	1
Castleton	Stir	NS8588	56°4·5′	3°50·4′W	X	65
Castleton	V of Glam	ST0268	51°24·4′	3°24·2′W	A	170
Castleton Barn	Heref	SO2645	52°6·1′	3°4·4′W	X	148
Castleton Fm	Aberd	NJ7256	57°35·8′	2°27·6′W	FM	29
Castleton Hill	Clackm	NN9700	56°11·1′	3°39·1′W	X	58
Castleton Ho	Arg & Bt	NR8884	56°0·4′	5°23·6′W	X	55
Castleton Muir	Scot Bord	NY5189	55°11·8′	2°45·8′W	X	79
Castleton of Asloun	Aberd	NJ5414	57°13·1′	2°45·2′W	X	37
Castleton Rigg	N Yks	NZ6805	54°26·4′	0°56·7′W	H	94
Castle Toot	Shrops	SO2856	52°12·1′	3°2·7′W	A	138
Castletop Fm	Derby	SK3056	53°6·3′	1°32·7′W	FM	119
Castle Toward Sch	Arg & Bt	NS1168	55°52·3′	5°0·8′W	X	63
Castletown	Ches	SJ4351	53°3·4′	2°50·6′W	T	117
Castletown	Cumbr	NY5030	54°40·0′	2°46·1′W	T	90
Castletown	Dorset	SY6874	50°34·1′	2°26·7′W	T	194
Castletown	Highld	ND1967	58°35·3′	3°23·1′W	T	11,12
Castletown	Highld	NH7442	57°27·3′	4°5·5′W	X	27
Castletown	I of M	SC2667	54°4·4′	4°39·2′W	T	95
Castletown	Moray	NJ1835	57°24·1′	3°21·4′W	X	28
Castletown	Staffs	SJ9123	52°48·5′	2°7·6′W	T	127
Castletown	Sund	NZ3558	54°55·2′	1°26·8′W	T	88
Castle Town	W Susx	TQ2010	50°52·8′	0°17·3′W	T	198
Castletown Bay	I of M	SC2766	54°3·9′	4°38·2′W	W	95
Castletown Ho	Cumbr	NY3462	54°57·1′	3°1·4′W	X	85
Castlett Fm	Glos	SP0925	51°55·6′	1°51·8′W	FM	163
Castletump	Glos	SO7129	51°57·8′	2°24·9′W	T	149
Castle Twts	Heref	SO2755	52°11·5′	3°3·7′W	A	148
Castle-upon-Alun	V of Glam	SS9174	51°27·5′	3°33·7′W	T	170
Castle Vale	Birm	SP1491	52°31·2′	1°47·2′W	T	139
Castle View	Dorset	SY9978	50°36·3′	2°0·5′W	X	195
Castle View	Gwyn	SH5159	53°6·7′	4°13·2′W	X	115
Castle View	Leic	SK7028	52°50·9′	0°57·2′W	X	129
Castle Villa	Pemb	SM8827	51°54·3′	5°4·5′W	X	157
Castleward	Angus	NO3443	56°34·7′	3°4·0′W	H	54
Castleward	I of M	SC3678	54°10·5′	4°30·3′W	X	95
Castleweary	Scot Bord	NT4003	55°19·3′	2°56·3′W	T	79
Castlewell	Orkney	ND3693	58°49·5′	3°6·0′W	X	7
Castlewich	Corn	SX3668	50°29·6′	4°18·4′W	X	201
Castlewigg	D & G	NX4243	54°45·7′	4°26·9′W	X	83
Castle William	E Ayr	NS6205	55°19·4′	4°10·1′W	X	71,77
Castlewink	D & G	NY4097	55°16·1′	2°56·2′W	H	79
Castle Wood	E Loth	NT5567	55°53·9′	2°42·7′W	F	66
Castle Wood	E Yorks	SE9464	54°4·0′	0°33·4′W	F	101
Castle Wood	Scot Bord	NT7755	55°47·5′	2°21·6′W	F	67,74
Castle Wood	Wilts	ST7533	51°6·0′	2°21·0′W	F	183
Castlewood Fm	Devon	SY2793	50°44·2′	3°1·7′W	FM	193
Castlewood Ho	Durham	NZ1236	54°43·4′	1°48·4′W	X	92
Castley	Cumbr	SD6395	54°21·2′	2°33·7′W	X	97
Castley	N Yks	SE2645	53°54·3′	1°35·8′W	T	104
Castle Yard	Northnts	SP6983	52°26·7′	0°58·7′W	X	141
Castle Yard	Suff	TM4073	52°18·4′	1°31·6′E	A	156
Castle Yard (Motte & Bailey)	Northnts	SP6983	52°26·7′	0°58·7′W	A	141
Castleyards	D & G	NX7545	54°47·3′	3°56·2′W	X	84
Castleyards	D & G	NY0377	55°4·9′	3°30·7′W	X	84
Castleyards (Fort)	D & G	NX7545	54°47·3′	3°56·2′W	A	84
Castley Fm	N Yks	SE2646	53°54·8′	1°35·8′W	FM	104
Castley Hill	Somer	ST4930	51°4·3′	2°43·3′W	H	182,183
Castley Knotts	Cumbr	SD6496	54°21·7′	2°32·8′W	X	97
Castlezens Fm	Corn	SW9242	50°14·7′	4°54·7′W	FM	204
Castling's Hall	Suff	TL9743	52°3·2′	0°52·8′E	X	155
Castling's Heath	Suff	TL9743	52°3·2′	0°52·8′E	T	155
Caston	Norf	TL9597	52°32·4′	0°52·9′E	T	144
Castor	Peterb	TL1298	52°34·3′	0°20·4′W	T	142
Castor Hanglands	Peterb	TF1201	52°35·9′	0°20·4′W	F	142
Castramon Burn	D & G	NX7983	55°7·8′	3°53·4′W	W	78
Castramon Hill	D & G	NX7883	55°7·8′	3°54·4′W	H	78
Castramon Moor	D & G	NX7884	55°8·4′	3°54·4′W	X	78
Castramont Burn	D & G	NX5962	54°56·2′	4°11·6′W	W	83
Castramont Hill	D & G	NX6061	54°55·7′	4°10·7′W	H	83
Castramont Wood	D & G	NX5960	54°55·1′	4°11·6′W	F	83
Castrigg	Cumbr	NY6722	54°35·8′	2°30·2′W	X	91
Cas Troggy	Monm	ST4195	51°39·3′	2°50·8′W	A	171
Castrogi Brook	Monm	ST4593	51°38·2′	2°47·3′W	W	171,172
Castweazel Oast	Kent	TQ8337	51°6·4′	0°37·2′E	X	188
Casty Rock	N Yks	TA0983	54°14·1′	0°19·2′W	X	101
Caswell	Northnts	SP6550	52°8·9′	1°2·6′W	X	152
Caswell	Swan	SS5987	51°34·1′	4°1·7′W	T	159
Caswell Bay	Swan	SS5987	51°34·1′	4°1·7′W	W	159
Caswell Cross	N Som	ST4874	51°28·0′	2°44·5′W	X	171,172
Caswell Fm	Dorset	ST5809	50°53·0′	2°35·4′W	FM	194
Caswell Fm	Oxon	SP3208	51°46·4′	1°31·8′W	FM	164
Caswell Wood	Glos	SO5400	51°42·0′	2°39·5′W	F	162
Cataclews Point	Corn	SW8776	50°32·9′	5°0·0′W	X	200
Catacol	N Ayr	NR9149	55°41·6′	5°19·1′W	T	62,69
Catacol Bay	N Ayr	NR9049	55°41·6′	5°20·0′W	W	62,69
Cataractonivm (Roman Town)	N Yks	SE2299	54°23·4′	1°39·3′W	R	99
Cataraidh	N Eil	NF7623	57°11·3′	7°21·4′W	X	22
Cata Sand	Orkney	HY7040	59°15·0′	2°31·1′W	X	5
Cat Babbleton	N Yks	SE6228	53°44·9′	1°3·2′W	X	105
Cat Babbleton	N Yks	TA0074	54°9·4′	0°27·7′W	X	101
Cat Bank	Cumbr	SD3097	54°22·1′	3°4·2′W	T	96,97
Cat Bells	Cumbr	NY2419	54°33·9′	3°10·1′W	H	89,90
Cat Bields	Cumbr	NY1307	54°27·3′	3°20·1′W	X	89
Catbrain	S Glos	ST5780	51°31·3′	2°36·8′W	T	172
Catbrook	Monm	SO5002	51°43·1′	2°43·0′W	T	162
Catbrook Ho	Wilts	ST9574	51°28·1′	2°3·9′W	X	173
Catburn	N Ayr	NS2656	55°46·2′	4°46·0′W	X	63
Cat Cairn	C of Aber	NJ9503	57°7·3′	2°4·5′W	A	38
Cat Cairn	Northum	NY6192	55°13·5′	2°36·4′W	X	80
Catcairn Bushes	Scot Bord	NT9659	55°49·7′	2°3·4′W	X	74,75
Cat Castle	Durham	NZ0016	54°32·6′	1°59·6′W	X	92
Catch	Flint	SJ2070	53°13·5′	3°11·5′W	T	117
Catchall	Corn	SW4327	50°5·5′	5°35·2′W	T	203
Catch Burn	Northum	NZ2283	55°8·7′	1°38·9′W	W	81
Catchburn Fm	Northum	NZ2083	55°8·7′	1°40·7′W	FM	81
Catchdale Moss	St Hel	SJ4696	53°27·7′	2°48·4′W	X	108
Catchdale Moss	St Hel	SJ4696	53°27·7′	2°48·4′W	X	108
Catchean	Arg & Bt	NM3023	56°19·6′	6°21·6′W	X	48
Catchems Corner	Sol	SP2576	52°23·1′	1°37·6′W	T	140
Catchems End	Worcs	SO7975	52°22·6′	2°18·1′W	T	138
Catcherside	Northum	NY9987	55°10·9′	2°0·5′W	X	81
Catchet's Fm	Norf	TF9927	52°48·5′	0°57·6′E	FM	132
Catchfrench Manor	Corn	SX3059	50°24·6′	4°23·2′W	X	201
Catchgate	Durham	NZ1652	54°52·0′	1°44·6′W	T	88
Catch Hall	Cambs	TL4062	52°14·5′	0°3·4′E	X	154
Catch Hill	Scot Bord	NT7261	55°50·7′	2°26·4′W	X	67
Catchory	Highld	ND2557	58°29·9′	3°16·7′W	T	11,12
Catchpenny	Pth & Kin	NO0643	56°34·4′	3°31·4′W	X	52,53
Catchpenny Pool	Ches	SJ8171	53°14·4′	2°16·7′W	W	118
Catchwater Drain	Cald	SE0231	53°46·8′	1°57·8′W	W	104
Catchwater Drain	E Yorks	TA0344	53°53·2′	0°25·6′W	W	107
Catchwater Drain	Lincs	TF1668	53°12·0′	0°15·4′W	W	121
Catchwater Drain	Lincs	TF2556	53°5·4′	0°7·6′W	W	122
Catchwater Drain	Lincs	TF5163	53°8·8′	0°15·9′E	W	122
Catchwater Drain	Notts	SK7981	53°19·4′	0°48·4′W	W	120,121
Catcleuch	Northum	NT7406	55°21·1′	2°24·2′W	X	80
Catcleuch Shin	Scot Bord	NT6806	55°21·1′	2°29·8′W	X	80
Catcleugh	Northum	NT7403	55°19·5′	2°24·2′W	T	80
Catcleugh Ho	Northum	NT7403	55°19·5′	2°24·2′W	X	80
Catcleugh Reservoir	Northum	NT7303	55°19·5′	2°25·1′W	W	80
Catcliffe	Roth	SK4288	53°23·5′	1°21·7′W	T	111,120
Cat Clough	Derby	SE1101	53°30·6′	1°49·6′W	X	110
Catcomb	Wilts	SU0076	51°29·2′	1°59·6′W	T	173
Catcomb Wood	Wilts	SU0077	51°29·7′	1°59·6′W	F	173
Catcott	Somer	ST3939	51°9·1′	2°51·9′W	T	182
Cat Cottage	S Glos	ST7586	51°34·6′	2°21·3′W	X	172
Catcott Br	Somer	ST4042	51°10·7′	2°51·1′W	X	182
Catcott Grounds	Somer	ST4043	51°11·2′	2°51·1′W	X	182
Catcott Heath	Somer	ST4041	51°10·1′	2°51·1′W	X	182
Catcraig	Aberd	NJ9241	57°27·8′	2°7·5′W	X	30
Cat Craig	D & G	NX7570	55°0·8′	3°56·9′W	X	84
Catcraig	E Loth	NT7177	55°59·4′	2°27·5′W	X	67
Catcraig	S Ayr	NS4231	55°33·1′	4°29·8′W	X	70
Cat Craig	Scot Bord	NT3629	55°33·3′	3°0·4′W	H	73
Cat Craigs	Aberd	NJ4930	57°21·7′	2°50·4′W	H	29,37
Catcune	Midlo	NT3559	55°49·4′	3°1·8′W	X	66,73
Cat Ditch	Herts	TL2637	52°1·3′	0°9·4′W	W	153
Catebraid	D & G	NW9855	54°51·2′	5°8·4′W	X	82
Cateran Hill	Northum	NU1023	55°30·3′	1°50·1′W	H	75
Caterham	Surrey	TQ3355	51°16·9′	0°5·2′W	T	187
Cater's Beam	Devon	SX6369	50°30·5′	3°55·6′W	X	202
Catershook	Pemb	SN1109	51°45·1′	4°43·9′W	X	158
Catesby Ho	Northnts	SP5259	52°13·8′	1°13·9′W	X	151
Cate's Cove Corner	Lincs	TF3013	52°42·2′	0°4·2′W	X	131,142
Cat & Fiddle	Derby	SK4340	52°57·6′	1°21·2′W	X	129
Cat & Fiddle	Hants	SZ2095	50°45·5′	1°42·6′W	X	195
Cat & Fiddle (PH)	Ches	SK0071	53°14·4′	1°59·6′W	X	119
Catfield	Norf	TG3821	52°44·3′	1°31·9′E	T	133,134
Catfield Common	Norf	TG4021	52°44·2′	1°33·7′E	T	134
Catfield Hall	Norf	TG3721	52°44·3′	1°31·1′E	X	133,134
Catfirth	Shetld	HU4354	60°16·3′	1°12·9′W	T	3
Cat Firth	Shetld	HU4552	60°15·3′	1°10·7′W	W	3
Catford	Lew	TQ3873	51°26·6′	0°0·5′W	T	177
Catford	Somer	ST0229	51°3·4′	3°23·5′W	X	181
Catford Cott	Somer	ST0837	51°7·7′	3°18·5′W	X	181
Catfords Fm	Devon	ST0212	50°54·2′	3°23·2′W	FM	181
Catforth	Lancs	SD4735	53°48·8′	2°47·9′W	T	102
Catfoss Grange	E Yorks	TA1448	53°55·2′	0°15·4′W	X	107
Catfoss Hall Fm	E Yorks	TA1446	53°54·1′	0°15·5′W	FM	107
Catgair Edge	Scot Bord	NT3208	55°21·9′	3°3·9′W	X	79
Catgill	N Yks	SE0654	53°59·2′	1°54·1′W	X	104
Cat Gill	N Yks	SE0685	54°15·9′	1°54·1′W	W	99
Cat Gill	N Yks	SE1777	54°11·6′	1°43·9′W	W	99
Catgill Hall	Cumbr	NY0009	54°28·2′	3°32·2′W	X	89
Cathadail an Ear	N Eil	NB0910	57°59·3′	6°55·0′W	X	13,14
Cathadail Grànnda	N Eil	NB0909	57°58·8′	6°54·9′W	X	13,14
Cathair Mhic Dhiarmaid	Highld	NM5169	56°45·0′	6°3·9′W	X	47
Cathal	Cered	SN4647	52°6·2′	4°14·5′W	X	146
Catham	Devon	SS6416	50°55·9′	3°55·7′W	X	180
Catham Copse	Hants	SU7842	51°10·5′	0°52·7′W	F	186
Cathan	Swan	SS4390	51°35·5′	4°15·6′W	X	159
Cathanger	Somer	ST3422	50°59·9′	2°56·0′W	A	193
Cathanger Fm	W Susx	SU9519	50°58·0′	0°38·4′W	FM	197
Cathanger Wood	Wilts	SU3253	51°16·7′	1°32·1′W	F	185
Cathangings Letch	Northum	NU1138	55°38·4′	1°49·1′W	X	75
Càthar a'Mhuilichinn	Arg & Bt	NR7364	55°49·2′	5°37·0′W	X	62
Càthar an Leargain Bhric	Arg & Bt	NR5272	55°52·9′	5°57·5′W	X	61
Cathargoed uchaf	Carm	SN5918	51°50·8′	4°2·4′W	X	159
Catharine Bourne	Herts	TL2000	51°41·4′	0°15·4′W	W	166
Càthar Mór	Highld	NN6488	56°58·1′	4°13·8′W	X	42
Cathar nan Ean, Loch	Arg & Bt	NR6386	56°0·8′	5°47·7′W	W	61
Cathay	Moray	NJ0558	57°36·4′	3°34·9′W	X	27
Cathays	Card	ST1877	51°29·4′	3°10·5′W	T	171
Cathays Park	Card	ST1776	51°28·8′	3°11·3′W	T	171
Cathburn	N Lanak	NS8356	55°47·2′	3°51·5′W	X	65,72
Cathcart	C of Glas	NS5860	55°49·0′	4°15·5′W	T	64
Cath Dubh	Highld	NJ1214	57°12·8′	3°27·0′W	X	36
Cà, The	Aberd	NJ2805	57°8·1′	3°10·9′W	H	37
Cathebedron Cross	Corn	SW6236	50°10·8′	5°19·7′W	X	203
Cathedine	Powys	SO1425	51°55·3′	3°14·6′W	T	161
Cathedine fawr	Powys	SO1426	51°55·8′	3°14·7′W	X	161
Cathelyd-uchaf	Swan	SN6803	51°42·9′	3°54·3′W	X	159
Catherinebraes	Moray	NJ2544	57°29·1′	3°14·6′W	X	28
Catherine-de-Barnes	Sol	SP1780	52°25·3′	1°44·6′W	T	139
Catherinefield	D & G	NX9979	55°6·0′	3°34·5′W	X	84
Catherine Fm	Bucks	SP7125	51°55·4′	0°57·7′W	FM	165
Catherine Hill	S Glos	ST5986	51°34·5′	2°35·1′W	X	172
Catherine Ho	N Yks	SE6195	54°21·1′	1°3·3′W	X	94,100
Catherinehole Scar	Cumbr	NY0851	54°51·0′	3°25·5′W	X	85
Catherine or Katty White's Allotments	N Yks	SE1162	54°3·5′	1°49·5′W	X	99
Catherinepark Wood	Corn	SX2254	50°21·8′	4°29·8′W	F	201
Catherine Slack	Brad	SE0928	53°45·1′	1°51·4′W	T	104
Catherine's Loch	Highld	ND0438	58°19·5′	3°37·9′W	W	11,17
Catherine Wheel	Kent	TQ8140	51°8·1′	0°35·6′E	X	188
Catherington	Hants	SU6914	50°55·5′	1°0·7′W	T	197
Catherington Down	Hants	SU6813	50°55·0′	1°1·6′W	X	196
Catherington Down	Hants	SU6915	50°56·0′	1°0·7′W	T	197
Catherston Leweston	Dorset	SY3794	50°44·8′	2°53·2′W	T	193
Catherton	Shrops	SO6578	52°24·2′	2°30·5′W	X	138
Catherton Common	Shrops	SO6278	52°24·2′	2°33·1′W	X	138
Catherton Marshes	Shrops	SO6478	52°24·2′	2°31·4′W	X	138
Cat Heugh	Northum	NU1415	55°26·0′	1°46·3′W	X	81
Catheugh	Northum	NZ1599	55°17·3′	1°45·4′W	X	81
Cathilas	Carm	SN6414	51°48·7′	3°58·0′W	X	159
Cat Hill	Barns	SE2405	53°32·7′	1°37·9′W	T	110
Cat Hills Plantn	Notts	SK5872	53°14·7′	1°7·4′W	F	120
Cathiron	Warw	SP4678	52°24·1′	1°19·0′W	T	140
Cathkin Braes	S Lanak	NS6258	55°48·0′	4°11·7′W	X	64
Cathlawhill	W Loth	NS9872	55°56·1′	3°37·5′W	X	65
Cathlaw Ho	W Loth	NS9872	55°56·1′	3°37·5′W	X	65
Cat Ho	Suff	TM1938	52°0·1′	1°11·8′E	X	169
Cat Hole	Derby	SK3267	53°12·2′	1°30·8′W	X	119
Cat Hole	N Yks	SE0973	54°9·5′	1°51·3′W	X	99
Cathole	Warw	SP2041	52°4·3′	1°42·1′W	X	151
Cathole Cliff	Devon	SX6937	50°13·3′	3°49·8′W	X	202
Cathole Rock	Swan	SS5390	51°35·6′	4°6·9′W	X	159
Catholes	Cumbr	SD6590	54°18·5′	2°31·9′W	T	97
Catholme	Staffs	SK1916	52°44·7′	1°42·7′W	X	128

Cat Holme	Staffs	SK2015	52°44·2'	1°41·8'W	X	128
Catholme Br	Staffs	SK1916	52°44·7'	1°42·7'W	X	128
Cathouse Point	Suff	TM1939	52°0·6'	1°11·9'E	X	169
Cathow	Cumbr	NY0414	54°31·0'	3°28·6'W	X	89
Cathpair	Scot Bord	NT4646	55°42·5'	2°51·1'W	T	73
Cathrie	Fife	NO4505	56°14·3'	2°52·8'W	X	59
Càth Sgeir	Arg & Bt	NR6147	55°39·7'	5°47·6'W	X	62
Cati Geo	Orkney	HY4342	59°15·9'	2°59·5'W	X	5
Catisfield	Hants	SU5406	50°51·3'	1°13·6'W	T	196
Catkill	Devon	SS7920	50°58·2'	3°43·0'W	X	180
Cat Knot	Lancs	SD7159	54°1·8'	2°26·1'W	X	103
Catlake	Devon	SS8908	50°51·9'	3°34·3'W	X	192
Catlands Hill	Cumbr	NY2441	54°45·7'	3°10·4'W	H	85
Cat Law	Angus	NO3161	56°44·4'	3°7·2'W	H	44
Catless	Northum	NY8375	55°4·4'	2°15·5'W	X	86,87
Catley Cross	Essex	TL8435	51°59·2'	0°41·2'E	X	155
Catley Fms	Heref	SO6844	52°5·8'	2°27·6'W	FM	149
Catley Hill Ho	Durham	NZ3533	54°41·7'	1°27·0'W	X	93
Catley Lane Head	Roch	SD8715	53°38·1'	2°11·4'W	T	109
Catley's Fms	Essex	TL8731	51°57·0'	0°43·7'E	FM	168
Catley Southfield	Heref	SO6844	52°5·8'	2°27·6'W	T	149
Catlins	D & G	NY1683	55°8·3'	3°18·6'W	X	79
Catlips Fm	Herts	TQ0395	51°38·9'	0°30·3'W	FM	166,176
Catlock Burn	E Ayr	NS5608	55°21·0'	4°15·8'W	W	71,77
Catlodge	Highld	NN6392	57°0·2'	4°14·9'W	T	35
Catlow	Lancs	SD7158	54°1·3'	2°26·1'W	X	103
Catlow	Lancs	SD8836	53°49·5'	2°10·5'W	X	103
Catlow Brook	Lancs	SD8936	53°49·5'	2°9·6'W	W	103
Catlow Dod	S Lanak	NS9505	55°19·9'	3°38·9'W	X	78
Catlowdy	Cumbr	NY4576	55°4·8'	2°51·3'W	T	86
Catlow Fell	Lancs	SD7060	54°2·4'	2°27·1'W	X	98
Catlow Hall	Durham	NZ4134	54°42·2'	1°21·4'W	X	93
Catmere End	Essex	TL4939	52°2·0'	0°10·7'E	T	154
Catmore	W Berks	SU4580	51°31·3'	1°20·7'W	T	174
Catmoss	Scot Bord	NT7145	55°42·1'	2°27·3'W	X	74
Cat Nab	E Yorks	TA2173	54°8·6'	0°8·4'W	X	101
Catnish	Arg & Bt	NN2330	56°26·0'	4°51·8'W	X	50
Catochil Fm	Pth & Kin	NO1713	56°18·4'	3°20·0'W	FM	58
Caton	Devon	SX6454	50°22·4'	3°54·4'W	X	202
Caton	Devon	SX7871	50°31·8'	3°42·9'W	T	202
Caton	Lancs	SD5364	54°4·4'	2°42·7'W	T	97
Caton Green	Lancs	SD5465	54°5·0'	2°41·8'W	T	97
Caton Moor	Lancs	SD5763	54°3·9'	2°39·0'W	X	97
Cator Common	Devon	SX6777	50°34·9'	3°52·3'W	X	191
Cator Court	Devon	SX6876	50°34·4'	3°51·5'W	X	191
Catrail	Scot Bord	NT4010	55°23·1'	2°56·4'W	A	79
Catrail	Scot Bord	NT5102	55°18·8'	2°45·9'W	A	79
Catrake Force	N Yks	NY8901	54°24·5'	2°9·7'W	W	91,92
Catraw	Northum	NZ2079	55°6·5'	1°40·8'W	X	88
Catraw Burn	Northum	NZ1980	55°7·1'	1°41·7'W	W	81
Catreen	Northum	NY8878	55°6·0'	2°10·9'W	X	87
Catridge Fm	Wilts	ST8967	51°24·3'	2°9·1'W	FM	173
Cat Rig	D & G	NT3300	55°17·6'	3°2·9'W	X	79
Catrigg	N Yks	SD8467	54°6·2'	2°14·3'W	X	98
Catrigg Beck	N Yks	SD8367	54°6·2'	2°15·2'W	W	98
Catrigg Force	N Yks	SD8367	54°6·2'	2°15·2'W	W	98
Catriggs Fm	N Yks	SD8989	54°18·0'	2°9·7'W	FM	98
Catrine	E Ayr	NS5225	55°30·0'	4°20·2'W	T	70
Catrine Mains	E Ayr	NS5226	55°30·6'	4°20·2'W	X	70
Catrineshaw	E Ayr	NS5325	55°30·1'	4°19·2'W	X	70
Cat Rock	Pemb	SN0439	52°1·1'	4°51·0'W	X	145,157
Cats Abbey Fm	Glos	SP1113	51°49·2'	1°50·0'W	FM	163
Cat's Ash	Newp	ST3790	51°36·6'	2°54·2'W	T	171
Cat's Barn	Suff	TM3654	52°8·3'	1°27·3'E	X	156
Cat's Bottom	Norf	TF6727	52°49·1'	0°29·1'E	X	132
Catsbrain Fm	Bucks	SP6409	51°46·8'	1°3·9'W	FM	164,165
Catsbrain Hill	Oxon	SU6283	51°32·8'	1°6·0'W	X	175
Catsclough	Ches	SJ6467	53°12·2'	2°31·9'W	X	118
Cat's Common	Norf	TG3423	52°45·5'	1°28·5'E	T	133,134
Cat's Cove	Corn	SW8576	50°32·9'	5°1·7'W	W	200
Cat's Craig	Aberd	NJ4833	57°23·3'	2°51·4'W	X	28,29
Cats Craig	D & G	NX8783	55°8·0'	3°45·9'W	H	78
Cats Edge	Staffs	SJ9552	53°4·2'	2°4·1'W	T	118
Catsfield	E Susx	TQ7213	50°53·7'	0°27·1'E	T	199
Catsfield Manor	E Susx	TQ7213	50°53·7'	0°27·1'E	X	199
Catsfield Place	E Susx	TQ7312	50°53·1'	0°28·0'E	X	199
Catsfield Stream	E Susx	TQ7113	50°53·7'	0°26·3'E	T	199
Catsfold Fm	W Susx	TQ1915	50°55·6'	0°18·0'W	FM	198
Catsford Common	Somer	ST2345	51°12·2'	3°5·7'W	X	182
Catsgore	Somer	ST5025	51°1·6'	2°42·4'W	T	183
Catsham	Somer	ST5533	51°5·9'	2°38·2'W	T	182,183
Catshaw	Barns	SE2003	53°31·6'	1°41·5'W	T	110
Catshaw	Lancs	SD5453	53°58·5'	2°41·7'W	X	102
Catshaw Cross	Barns	SE2003	53°31·6'	1°41·5'W	A	110
Catshaw Fell	Lancs	SD5551	53°57·4'	2°40·7'W	X	102
Catshaw Greave	Lancs	SD5651	53°57·4'	2°39·8'W	X	102
Catshawhill	Scot Bord	NT5422	55°29·6'	2°43·3'W	X	73
Catshayes Fm	Devon	SY1397	50°46·2'	3°13·6'W	FM	192,193
Catshead Fm	Northnts	SP9583	52°26·4'	0°35·7'W	FM	141
Cat's Hill	Herts	TL3911	51°47·0'	0°1·3'E	X	166
Catshill	Wals	SK0505	52°38·8'	1°55·2'W	T	139
Cat's Hill	Wilts	ST8365	51°23·3'	2°14·3'W	X	173
Catshill	Worcs	SO9573	52°21·5'	2°4·0'W	T	139
Cat's Hill Cross	Staffs	SJ8230	52°52·3'	2°15·6'W	T	127
Catshole Tor	Corn	SX1678	50°34·6'	4°35·6'W	H	201
Catsholme Fm	Norf	TL6896	52°32·4'	0°29·0'E	FM	143
Cat Shoulder	S Lanak	NT0322	55°29·2'	3°31·7'W	H	72
Catsick Hill	Leic	SK5718	52°45·6'	1°8·9'W	X	129
Catslack Burn	Scot Bord	NT3226	55°31·6'	3°4·2'W	W	73
Catslackburn	Scot Bord	NT3425	55°31·1'	3°2·3'W	T	73
Catsland Fm	W Susx	TQ2313	50°54·4'	0°14·6'W	FM	198
Catsley Fm	Dorset	ST5203	50°49·7'	2°40·5'W	FM	194
Catsley Fm	Shrops	SO7279	52°24·7'	2°24·3'W	FM	138
Catslip	Oxon	SU7086	51°34·3'	0°59·0'W	T	175
Catson Hill	Devon	SY0784	50°39·1'	3°18·6'W	X	192
Cat Stane	C of Edin	NT1474	55°57·3'	3°22·2'W	A	65
Cat Stone	N Yks	SD9640	53°51·6'	2°3·2'W	X	103
Catstone	Scot Bord	NT0952	55°45·4'	3°26·6'W	H	65,72
Catstone Hill	Aberd	NJ5750	57°32·5'	2°42·6'W	H	29
Catstone Hill	Notts	SK5041	52°58·1'	1°14·9'W	X	129

Cat Stones	Cald	SD9917	53°39·2'	2°0·5'W	X	109
Cats Tor	Ches	SJ9975	53°16·6'	2°0·5'W	H	118
Catstor Down	Devon	SX5465	50°28·2'	4°3·1'W	X	201
Catstree	Shrops	SO7496	52°33·9'	2°22·6'W	T	138
Catstye Cam	Cumbr	NY3415	54°31·8'	3°0·8'W	X	90
Cat's Water	Peterb	TF2505	52°37·9'	0°8·8'W	W	142
Cats Wood	Kent	TQ6933	51°4·5'	0°25·1'E	F	188
Catswood Fm	Glos	SO8807	51°45·9'	2°10·0'W	FM	162
Cattadale	Arg & Bt	NR3860	55°46·0'	6°10·2'W	X	60
Cattal	N Yks	SE4454	53°59·1'	1°19·3'W	T	105
Cattal Grange	N Yks	SE4355	53°59·6'	1°20·2'W	X	105
Cattal Lodge	N Yks	SE4553	53°58·5'	1°18·4'W	X	105
Cattal Sta	N Yks	SE4455	53°59·6'	1°19·3'W	X	105
Catta Ness	Shetld	HU4967	60°23·3'	1°6·2'W	X	2,3
Cattawade	Suff	TM1033	51°57·6'	1°3·8'E	T	168,169
Cattedown	C of Plym	SX4953	50°21·7'	4°7·0'W	T	201
Cattens	Aberd	NJ5116	57°14·2'	2°48·3'W	X	37
Catteral Hall	N Yks	SD8064	54°4·5'	2°17·9'W	X	98
Catterall	Lancs	SD4942	53°52·5'	2°46·1'W	T	102
Catterall Lodge	Lancs	SD4942	53°52·5'	2°46·1'W	X	102
Catteralslane	Shrops	SJ5640	52°57·6'	2°38·9'W	X	117
Catter Burn	Stir	NS4685	56°2·2'	4°27·9'W	W	57
Catter Ho	Stir	NS4787	56°3·3'	4°27·0'W	X	57
Catterick	N Yks	SE2497	54°22·3'	1°37·4'W	T	99
Catterick Bridge	N Yks	SE2299	54°23·4'	1°39·3'W	A	99
Catterick Bridge	N Yks	SE2299	54°23·4'	1°39·3'W	T	99
Catterick Garrison	N Yks	SE1797	54°22·3'	1°43·9'W	X	99
Catterick Moss	Durham	NY9936	54°43·4'	2°0·5'W	H	92
Cattering Wood	Kent	TQ6854	51°15·8'	0°24·9'E	F	188
Catterlen	Cumbr	NY4833	54°41·6'	2°48·0'W	T	90
Catterlen Hall	Cumbr	NY4732	54°41·1'	2°48·9'W	A	90
Catterline	Aberd	NO8678	56°53·8'	2°13·3'W	T	45
Catterline Burn	Aberd	NO8579	56°54·4'	2°14·3'W	W	45
Catterloch	Aberd	NO7098	57°4·6'	2°29·2'W	X	38,45
Cattermuir Lodge	Stir	NS4686	56°2·8'	4°27·9'W	X	57
Cattersty Sands	Red & Cl	NZ7020	54°34·5'	0°54·6'W	X	94
Catterton	N Yks	SE5145	53°54·1'	1°13·0'W	T	105
Catterton Beck	N Yks	SE5046	53°54·7'	1°13·9'W	W	105
Catteshall	Surrey	SU9844	51°11·4'	0°35·5'W	T	186
Catteshall Manor	Surrey	SU9843	51°10·9'	0°35·5'W	X	186
Cattespool	Worcs	SP0071	52°20·5'	1°59·6'W	X	139
Cattewater	C of Plym	SX4953	50°21·7'	4°7·0'W	W	201
Catt Fm	Kent	TQ9327	51°0·8'	0°45·5'E	FM	189
Catthorpe	Leic	SP5578	52°24·1'	1°11·1'W	T	140
Catthorpe Manor	Leic	SP5578	52°24·1'	1°11·1'W	X	140
Cattie	Aberd	NJ6216	57°14·2'	2°37·3'W	X	37
Cattiehill	Aberd	NJ6216	57°14·2'	2°37·3'W	X	37
Catti Geo	Shetld	HU4325	60°0·7'	1°13·2'W	X	4
Catti Geo	Shetld	HU4484	60°32·5'	1°11·4'W	X	1,2,3
Catti Geos	Shetld	HU3830	60°3·4'	1°18·6'W	X	4
Cattishall	Suff	TL8865	52°15·3'	0°45·7'E	X	155
Cattistock	Dorset	SY5999	50°47·6'	2°34·5'W	T	194
Cattistock Lo	Dorset	SY5999	50°47·6'	2°34·5'W	X	194
Cattle Brook	Warw	SP2969	52°19·3'	1°34·1'W	W	151
Cattle End	Northnts	SP6643	52°5·1'	1°1·8'W	T	152
Cattle Fm	Notts	SK7494	53°26·5'	0°52·7'W	FM	112
Cattleford Br	Bucks	SP7436	52°1·3'	0°54·9'W	X	152
Cattlegate Fm	Herts	TL3001	51°41·8'	0°6·7'W	FM	166
Cattle Hill	Somer	ST6630	51°4·3'	2°28·7'W	X	183
Cattleholmes	E Yorks	TA0856	53°59·6'	0°20·7'W	X	107
Cattle Moss	Fife	NS9991	56°6·3'	3°37·0'W	X	58
Catto Hall	N Yks	SE4292	54°19·6'	1°20·8'W	X	99
Catton	Northum	NY8257	54°54·7'	2°16·4'W	T	86,87
Catton	N Yks	SE3778	54°12·0'	1°25·6'W	T	99
Catton Beacon	Northum	NY8259	54°55·8'	2°16·4'W	H	86,87
Catton Hall	Ches	SJ5576	53°17·0'	2°40·1'W	X	117
Catton Hall	Derby	SK2015	52°44·2'	1°41·8'W	X	128
Catton Hall	N Yks	SE3778	54°12·0'	1°25·6'W	X	99
Catton Moor	N Yks	SE3878	54°12·0'	1°24·6'W	X	99
Catton Park	E Yorks	SE7251	53°57·2'	0°53·8'W	X	105,106
Catton Park Fm	E Yorks	SE7352	53°57·8'	0°52·8'W	FM	105,106
Catton Wood	Derby	SK2014	52°43·6'	1°41·8'W	F	128
Cattows Fm	Leic	SK3811	52°42·0'	1°25·9'W	FM	128
Catt's Fms	Kent	TR1451	51°13·3'	1°4·3'E	FM	179,189
Cattsford	Kent	TQ8130	51°2·7'	0°35·3'E	X	188
Catts Green Fm	E Susx	TQ7820	50°57·3'	0°32·5'E	FM	199
Catt's Place	Kent	TQ6843	51°9·9'	0°24·6'E	X	188
Catts Place	Hants	SU5261	51°21·0'	1°14·8'W	X	174
Cattybrook Fm	S Glos	ST5883	51°32·9'	2°36·0'W	FM	172
Catwalls	Shetld	HU4145	60°11·5'	1°15·1'W	X	4
Catwater Fm	Peterb	TF2404	52°37·4'	0°9·7'W	FM	142
Catwhins	Notts	SK6472	53°14·7'	1°2·0'W	F	120
Catwick	E Yorks	TA1345	53°53·6'	0°16·4'W	T	107
Catwick	N Yks	NZ9005	54°26·2'	0°36·3'W	X	94
Catwick Grange	E Yorks	TA1246	53°54·1'	0°17·3'W	X	107
Catwick Ho	E Yorks	TA1345	53°53·6'	0°16·4'W	X	107
Catworth	Cambs	TL0873	52°20·9'	0°24·5'W	T	153
Catworth Hill	Cambs	TL0973	52°20·9'	0°23·6'W	X	153
Catworth Lodge	Cambs	TL0771	52°19·8'	0°25·4'W	X	153
Catyans	D & G	NX4340	54°44·1'	4°25·9'W	X	83
Catythisty Well	Stir	NS5181	56°0·2'	4°22·9'W	W	64
Caucabush Rigg	Durham	NY9315	54°32·1'	2°6·1'W	X	91,92
Caudale Beck	Cumbr	NY4011	54°29·7'	2°55·2'W	W	90
Caudalebeck Fm	Cumbr	NY4011	54°29·7'	2°55·2'W	FM	90
Caudale Head	Cumbr	NY4110	54°29·2'	2°54·2'W	X	90
Caudale Moor	Cumbr	NY4110	54°29·2'	2°54·2'W	X	90
Caud Beck	Cumbr	NY6172	55°2·7'	2°36·2'W	W	86
Caudbeck Flow	Cumbr	NY5872	55°2·7'	2°39·0'W	X	86
Caudle Common	Norf	TF8502	52°35·3'	0°44·3'E	X	144
Caudle Fm	Suff	TL7281	52°24·2'	0°32·1'E	FM	143
Caudle Green	Glos	SO9410	51°47·6'	2°4·8'W	T	163
Caudlesprings	Norf	TF9401	52°34·6'	0°52·2'E	T	144
Caudwell Fm	Glos	SO5507	51°45·8'	2°38·7'W	FM	162
Caudworthy Bridge	Corn	SX2492	50°42·3'	4°29·2'W	X	190
Caudworthy Water	Corn	SX2491	50°41·8'	4°29·1'W	W	190
Caughall Manor	Ches	SJ4170	53°13·7'	2°52·6'W	X	117
Caukleys Bank	N Yks	SE6778	54°11·8'	0°58·0'W	F	100
Caukleys Wood	N Yks	SE6678	54°11·9'	0°58·9'W	F	100
Caul Bourne	I of W	SZ4188	50°41·6'	1°24·8'W	W	196
Caulcott	Beds	SP9942	52°4·3'	0°32·9'W	T	153

Caulcott	Oxon	SP5024	51°55·0'	1°16·0'W	T	164
Cauld	Scot Bord	NT4427	55°32·3'	2°52·8'W	X	73
Cauld	Scot Bord	NT4914	55°25·3'	2°47·9'W	T	79
Cauld	Scot Bord	NT6524	55°30·8'	2°32·8'W	X	74
Cauld	Scot Bord	NT7133	55°35·6'	2°27·2'W	X	74
Cauldale Field Fm	Leic	SK7207	52°39·6'	0°55·7'W	FM	141
Cauldbarns	Stir	NS7988	56°4·4'	3°56·2'W	X	57
Cauld Burn	E Loth	NT6472	55°56·6'	2°34·1'W	W	67
Cauldcleuch Head	Scot Bord	NT4500	55°17·7'	2°51·5'W	H	79
Cauldcoats	Midlo	NT3070	55°55·3'	3°6·8'W	X	66
Cauldcoats Holdings	Falk	NT0379	55°59·6'	3°32·9'W	T	65
Cauldcots	Angus	NO6547	56°37·1'	2°33·8'W	X	54
Cauldcots	Fife	NO5504	56°13·8'	2°43·1'W	X	59
Cauldcots Fm	Aberd	NO6373	56°51·1'	2°35·9'W	FM	45
Cauld Face	Scot Bord	NT2411	55°23·5'	3°11·6'W	H	79
Cauld Face	Scot Bord	NT4137	55°37·6'	2°55·8'W	H	73
Cauldhall	Midlo	NT2858	55°48·8'	3°8·5'W	X	66,73
Cauldhall Moor	Midlo	NT2758	55°48·8'	3°9·5'W	X	66,73
Cauldham	Kent	TR2438	51°6·1'	1°12·4'E	X	179,189
Cauldhame	Aberd	NJ5206	57°8·8'	2°47·1'W	X	37
Cauldhame	Aberd	NJ8527	57°20·3'	2°14·5'W	X	38
Cauldhame	E Ayr	NS4346	55°41·2'	4°29·4'W	X	64
Cauldhame	N Ayr	NS3737	55°36·2'	4°34·8'W	X	70
Cauldhame	Orkney	HY2412	58°59·6'	3°18·9'W	X	6
Cauldhame	Orkney	HY2628	59°8·2'	3°17·1'W	X	6
Cauldhame	Orkney	HY5633	59°11·2'	2°45·7'W	X	5,6
Cauldhame	Shetld	HU3938	60°7·7'	1°17·4'W	X	4
Cauldhame	Stir	NN8201	56°11·5'	3°53·6'W	X	57
Cauldhame	Stir	NS6494	56°7·4'	4°10·8'W	T	57
Cauldhame	W Loth	NT0175	55°57·7'	3°34·7'W	X	65
Cauldhame Fm	E Ayr	NS3847	55°41·6'	4°34·2'W	FM	63
Cauldholm	D & G	NY0699	55°16·8'	3°28·4'W	X	78
Cauld Law	D & G	NT1804	55°19·6'	3°17·1'W	H	79
Cauld Law Grain	D & G	NT1903	55°19·1'	3°16·2'W	W	79
Cauldmill	Scot Bord	NT5315	55°25·8'	2°44·1'W	T	79
Cauldon	Staffs	SK0749	53°2·5'	1°53·3'W	T	119
Cauldon Lowe	Staffs	SK0847	53°1·5'	1°52·4'W	T	119,128
Cauld Rocks	N Ayr	NS2260	55°48·3'	4°50·0'W	X	63
Cauldron Snout	Durham	NY8128	54°39·1'	2°17·2'W	W	91,92
Cauldrus	Orkney	HY2216	59°1·7'	3°21·0'W	X	6
Cauldshiel	E Loth	NT4866	55°53·3'	2°49·4'W	X	66
Cauldshiels Hill	Scot Bord	NT5131	55°34·5'	2°46·2'W	H	73
Cauldshiels Loch	Scot Bord	NT5132	55°35·0'	2°46·2'W	W	73
Cauldside	D & G	NX5457	54°53·4'	4°16·2'W	X	83
Cauldside	E Loth	NT5979	56°0·4'	2°39·0'W	X	67
Cauldside	Fife	NO4716	56°20·3'	2°51·0'W	X	59
Cauldside	Inverc	NS3270	55°53·9'	4°40·8'W	X	63
Cauldside Burn	D & G	NX5357	54°53·4'	4°17·1'W	W	83
Cauldside Hill	D & G	NX8971	55°1·5'	3°43·8'W	H	84
Cauldstanes	E Ayr	NS4946	55°41·3'	4°23·7'W	X	64
Cauldstane Slap	Scot Bord	NT1158	55°48·7'	3°24·8'W	X	65,72
Cauldwell Brook	Notts	SK5359	53°7·8'	1°12·1'W	W	120
Cauldwell Fm	Leic	SP5487	52°28·9'	1°11·9'W	FM	140
Cauldwellknowe	D & G	NY2373	55°3·0'	3°11·9'W	X	85
Cauldwells	Aberd	NJ7855	57°35·3'	2°21·6'W	X	29,30
Cauldwells	Aberd	NJ7956	57°35·9'	2°20·6'W	T	29,30
Cauldwell Wood	Notts	SK5358	53°7·2'	1°12·1'W	F	120
Caulkerbush	D & G	NX9257	54°54·0'	3°40·6'W	T	84
Caulkerbush Burn	D & G	NX9158	54°54·5'	3°41·6'W	W	84
Caulker grain	Scot Bord	NY4495	55°15·0'	2°52·4'W	W	79
Caulkleys Grange	N Yks	SE6777	54°11·3'	0°58·0'W	X	100
Caulside	D & G	NX4438	54°43·0'	4°24·9'W	X	83
Caulside	D & G	NY4480	55°6·9'	2°52·2'W	T	79
Caulston	Devon	SX5647	50°18·6'	4°1·0'W	X	202
Caultons Fm	Lincs	TF2711	52°41·1'	0°6·9'W	FM	131,142
Caunce Grange	Lancs	SD4548	53°55·8'	2°49·8'W	X	102
Caundle Brook	Dorset	ST7113	50°55·2'	2°24·4'W	W	194
Caundle Marsh	Dorset	ST6713	50°55·2'	2°27·8'W	T	194
Caundle Wake	Dorset	ST7012	50°54·6'	2°25·2'W	X	194
Caunsall	Worcs	SO8581	52°25·8'	2°12·8'W	T	139
Caunton	Notts	SK7460	53°8·2'	0°53·2'W	T	120
Caunton Common Fm	Notts	SK7261	53°8·7'	0°55·0'W	FM	120
Causa Grange	Cumbr	NY3045	54°47·9'	3°4·9'W	X	85
Causamul	N Eil	NF6670	57°36·0'	7°35·1'W	X	18
Causar	Highld	NJ0120	57°15·9'	3°38·0'W	X	36
Caus Castle	Shrops	SJ3307	52°39·6'	2°59·0'W	A	126
Cause	Orkney	ND3985	58°45·2'	3°2·8'W	X	7
Causebeach	Shrops	SJ3408	52°40·2'	2°58·2'W	X	126
Causeland Sta	Corn	SX2459	50°24·5'	4°28·2'W	X	201
Causemountain	Shrops	SJ3308	52°40·2'	2°59·0'W	X	126
Causeway	Hants	SU6912	50°54·4'	1°0·7'W	T	197
Causeway	Hants	SU7422	50°59·8'	0°56·3'W	T	197
Causeway	Monm	ST4386	51°34·4'	2°49·0'W	T	171,172
Causeway Bank	Scot Bord	NT8759	55°49·7'	2°12·0'W	X	67,74
Causeway Br	Thurr	TQ5779	51°29·5'	0°16·1'E	X	177
Causeway Dyke	Notts	SK7047	53°1·2'	0°57·0'W	W	129
Causewayend	Aberd	NJ8419	57°15·9'	2°15·5'W	X	38
Causewayend	Aberd	NO6570	56°49·5'	2°34·0'W	X	45
Causewayend	C of Aber	NJ9212	57°12·2'	2°7·5'W	X	38
Causeway End	Cumbr	SD3079	54°12·4'	3°4·0'W	X	96,97
Causeway End	Cumbr	SD3484	54°15·1'	3°0·4'W	T	96,97
Causeway End	Cumbr	SD4885	54°15·7'	2°47·5'W	T	97
Causeway End	Devon	ST0904	50°49·9'	3°17·2'W	X	192
Causeway End	D & G	NX4260	54°54·8'	4°27·5'W	X	83
Causeway End	Essex	TL6819	51°50·9'	0°26·7'E	T	167
Causewayend	S Lanak	NT0336	55°36·7'	3°32·0'W	T	72
Causeway End	Wilts	SU0084	51°33·5'	1°59·6'W	T	173
Causeway End Fm	Essex	TL6033	51°58·6'	0°20·2'E	FM	167
Causeway Fm	Cambs	TL4275	52°21·5'	0°5·5'E	FM	142,143
Causeway Fm	Cambs	TL5479	52°23·5'	0°16·2'E	FM	143
Causeway Fm	Carm	SN2809	51°45·4'	4°29·1'W	FM	158
Causeway Fm	Donc	SE7013	53°36·8'	0°56·1'W	FM	112
Causeway Fm	Essex	TL7241	52°2·7'	0°30·9'E	FM	154
Causeway Fm	Lancs	SD4514	53°37·4'	2°49·5'W	FM	108
Causewayfold	Aberd	NJ7231	57°22·4'	2°27·5'W	X	29
Causeway Foot	Cald	SE0731	53°46·8'	1°53·2'W	T	104
Causeway Foot	Cumbr	NY2921	54°35·0'	3°5·5'W	X	89,90
Causeway Foot	Kirk	SE1912	53°36·5'	1°42·4'W	T	110
Causeway Grain Head	D & G	NY3598	55°16·6'	3°1·0'W	H	79
Causeway Green	Sand	SO9987	52°29·1'	2°0·5'W	T	139

Causeway Hag Plantn	E Yorks	SE9147	53°54·9′	0°36·5′W	F	106
Causewayhead	Cumbr	NY1252	54°51·6′	3°21·8′W	X	85
Causeway Head	D & G	NX7367	54°59·1′	3°58·7′W	X	83,84
Causewayhead	Fife	NO4327	56°26·2′	2°55·0′W	X	54,59
Causewayhead	Stir	NS5995	56°7·9′	4°15·7′W	X	57
Causewayhead	Stir	NS8095	56°8·2′	3°55·4′W	T	57
Causeway Hill	Durham	NY8335	54°42·8′	2°15·4′W	X	91,92
Causeway Ho	Cumbr	NY4548	54°49·7′	2°50·9′W	X	86
Causeway Ho	Northum	NY7666	54°59·5′	2°22·1′W	X	86,87
Causeway House Fm	Suff	TL9852	52°8·1′	0°54·0′E	FM	155
Causeway Sike	Durham	NY9029	54°39·6′	2°8·9′W	W	91,92
Causeway, The	Arg & Bt	NM3235	56°26·1′	6°20·4′W	X	46,47,48
Causeway Toll Fm	Peterb	TF2403	52°36·9′	0°9·7′W	FM	142
Causewaywood	Shrops	SO5298	52°34·9′	2°42·1′W	T	137,138
Causewell	Corn	SX2199	50°46·0′	4°31·9′W	X	190
Causewood	W Loth	NT0861	55°50·3′	3°27·7′W	X	65
Causey	Durham	NZ2056	54°54·1′	1°40·9′W	T	88
Causey Arch	Durham	NZ2055	54°53·6′	1°40·9′W	A	88
Causeyend	Aberd	NJ9519	57°16·0′	2°4·5′W	X	38
Causey Hall Fm	Durham	NZ2055	54°53·6′	1°40·9′W	FM	88
Causeyhead	E Ayr	NS4246	55°41·2′	4°30·4′W	X	64
Causeyhill	N Lanak	NS9057	55°47·9′	3°44·8′W	X	65,72
Causey Hill	Northum	NY9263	54°57·9′	2°7·1′W	X	87
Causey Moss	Cumbr	NY8710	54°29·4′	2°11·6′W	X	91,92
Causey Park	Northum	NZ1795	55°15·2′	1°43·5′W	X	81
Causey Park Bridge	Northum	NZ1894	55°14·6′	1°42·6′W	T	81
Causey Pike	Cumbr	NY2120	54°34·4′	3°12·9′W	H	89,90
Causeyport	Aberd	NO9098	57°4·6′	2°9·4′W	X	38,45
Causeyton	Aberd	NJ6511	57°11·6′	2°34·3′W	X	38
Causilgey	Corn	SW7747	50°17·1′	5°7·5′W	X	204
Causton Wood	Kent	TQ8236	51°5·9′	0°36·4′E	F	188
Caute	Devon	SS4310	50°52·3′	4°13·5′W	T	190
Cautley	Cumbr	SD6995	54°21·2′	2°28·2′W	T	98
Cautley Beck	Cumbr	SD6996	54°21·8′	2°28·2′W	X	98
Cautley Crag	Cumbr	SD6896	54°21·8′	2°29·1′W	X	98
Cautley Fm	E Yorks	SE7854	53°58·8′	0°48·2′W	FM	105,106
Cautley Spout	Cumbr	SD6897	54°22·3′	2°29·1′W	W	98
Cautley Thwaite	Cumbr	SD6996	54°21·8′	2°28·2′W	X	98
Cava	Orkney	ND3299	58°52·6′	3°10·3′W	X	6,7
Cavaliers, The	Lancs	SD7836	53°49·4′	2°19·6′W	X	103
Cavan's Wood	Staffs	SJ9712	52°42·6′	2°2·3′W	F	127
Cave Arthur	Aberd	NK0732	57°23·0′	1°52·6′W	X	30
Cave Common Fm	E Yorks	SE8930	53°45·8′	0°38·6′W	FM	106
Cave Cott	Derby	SK1633	52°53·9′	1°45·3′W	X	128
Cave Fm, The	Shrops	SO6688	52°29·6′	2°29·6′W	FM	138
Cave Gate	Herts	TL3832	51°58·4′	0°0·9′E	X	166
Cave Hill	N Yks	SD8078	54°12·1′	2°18·0′W	X	98
Cave Hole	Dorset	SY6869	50°31·4′	2°26·7′W	X	194
Cave Hole	N Yks	SD7866	54°5·6′	2°19·8′W	X	98
Cave Hole Wood	N Yks	SD7866	54°5·6′	2°19·8′W	F	98
Cavelstone	Pth & Kin	NO1200	56°11·3′	3°24·6′W	X	58
Cavendish	Suff	TL8046	52°5·2′	0°38·0′E	T	155
Cavendish Bridge	Leic	SK4429	52°51·6′	1°20·4′W	T	129
Cavendish Hall	Suff	TL7945	52°4·7′	0°37·1′E	X	155
Cavendish Lodge	Notts	SK5964	53°10·4′	1°6·6′W	X	120
Cavendish Wood	Notts	SK5864	53°10·4′	1°7·5′W	F	120
Cavenham	Suff	TL7669	52°17·7′	0°35·3′E	T	155
Cavenham Heath	Suff	TL7672	52°19·3′	0°35·4′E	X	155
Cavenham Ho	Norf	TF6802	52°35·6′	0°29·2′E	X	143
Cavenham Park	Suff	TL7669	52°17·7′	0°35·3′E	X	155
Caven Mill	E Ayr	NS3444	55°39·9′	4°37·9′W	X	63,70
Cavens	D & G	NX9758	54°54·6′	3°36·0′W	X	84
Cave of Banks	Orkney	ND3692	58°48·9′	3°6·0′W	X	7
Cave of the Bard	Shetld	HU5135	60°6·0′	1°4·5′W	X	4
Cave o' Meackie	Aberd	NK1240	57°27·3′	1°47·5′W	X	30
Caverhill	Scot Bord	NT2138	55°38·0′	3°14·9′W	X	73
Cavers	Scot Bord	NT5315	55°25·8′	2°44·1′W	X	79
Cavers Carre	Scot Bord	NT5526	55°31·8′	2°42·3′W	T	73
Caversfield	Oxon	SP5825	51°55·5′	1°9·0′W	T	164
Caversfield Ho	Oxon	SP5825	51°55·5′	1°9·0′W	X	164
Cavershall Common	Staffs	SJ9444	52°59·8′	2°5·0′W	X	118
Caversham	Read	SU7175	51°28·4′	0°58·3′W	T	175
Caversham Bridge	Read	SU7174	51°27·9′	0°58·3′W	X	175
Caversham Heights	Read	SU7075	51°28·4′	0°59·1′W	T	175
Caversham Park	Read	SU7276	51°28·9′	0°57·4′W	X	175
Caver's Hill	Scot Bord	NT3921	55°29·0′	2°57·5′W	H	73
Cavers Knowes	Scot Bord	NT5414	55°25·3′	2°43·2′W	X	79
Caverslee	Scot Bord	NT3921	55°29·0′	2°57·5′W	X	73
Cavers Mains	Scot Bord	NT5416	55°26·4′	2°43·2′W	X	79
Caverswall	Staffs	SJ9542	52°58·8′	2°4·1′W	T	118
Caverswall	Staffs	SK0431	52°52·8′	1°56·0′W	X	128
Caverswall Park	Staffs	SJ9442	52°58·8′	2°5·0′W	X	118
Caverton Hillhead	Scot Bord	NT7327	55°32·4′	2°25·2′W	X	74
Caverton Mains	Scot Bord	NT7527	55°32·4′	2°23·3′W	X	74
Caverton Mill	Scot Bord	NT7525	55°31·3′	2°23·3′W	X	74
Caves Fm	Cambs	TL5691	52°29·9′	0°18·3′E	FM	143
Caves Fm	Worcs	SO8561	52°15·1′	2°12·8′W	FM	150
Caves of Kilhern	D & G	NX1964	54°56·5′	4°49·1′W	X	82
Caves of Kilhern (Chambered Cairn)	D & G	NX1964	54°56·5′	4°49·1′W	A	82
Caves, The	N Som	ST3858	51°19·3′	2°53·0′W	X	182
Cave Wold	E Yorks	SE9432	53°46·8′	0°34·0′W	X	106
Cave Wood Grange	E Yorks	SE8830	53°45·8′	0°39·5′W	X	106
Cavick Ho	Norf	TG1001	52°34·2′	1°6·3′E	X	144
Cavil Head	Northum	NU2202	55°18·9′	1°38·8′W	X	81
Caville	E Yorks	SE7730	53°45·9′	0°49·5′W	X	105,106
Cavit	Orkney	HY4425	59°6·8′	2°58·2′W	X	5,6
Caw	Cumbr	SD2394	54°20·4′	3°10·6′W	H	96
Cawarden Springs Fm	Staffs	SK0618	52°45·8′	1°54·3′W	FM	128
Caw Burn	Northum	NY7468	55°0·6′	2°24·0′W	W	86,87
Cawburn Shield	Northum	NY7268	55°0·6′	2°25·8′W	X	86,87
Cawdale	Cumbr	NY4817	54°33·0′	2°47·8′W	X	90
Cawdale Beck	Cumbr	NY4817	54°33·0′	2°47·8′W	W	90
Cawdale Edge	Cumbr	NY4718	54°33·5′	2°48·8′W	X	90
Cawdearg	Highld	NH5691	57°53·4′	4°25·3′W	X	21
Cawder Cuilt	C of Glas	NS5670	55°54·4′	4°17·8′W	X	64
Cawder Gill	N Yks	SE0050	53°57·0′	1°59·6′W	W	104
Cawder Hall Fm	N Yks	SD9950	53°57·0′	2°0·5′W	FM	103
Cawderstanes	Scot Bord	NT9453	55°46·5′	2°5·3′W	X	67,74,75
Cawdey Field	N Yks	SE3792	54°19·6′	1°25·4′W	X	99

Cawdle Fen	Cambs	TL5378	52°22·9′	0°15·3′E	X	143
Cawdor	Highld	NH8449	57°31·2′	3°55·7′W	T	27
Cawdor Castle	Highld	NH8449	57°31·2′	3°55·7′W	A	27
Cawdor Wood	Highld	NH8448	57°30·7′	3°55·7′W	F	27
Caw Fell	Cumbr	NY1210	54°28·9′	3°21·1′W	H	89
Cawfell Beck	Cumbr	NY1009	54°28·4′	3°22·9′W	W	89
Cawfields	Northum	NY7167	55°0·1′	2°26·8′W	X	86,87
Cawg	Powys	SN8798	52°34·3′	3°39·6′W	X	135,136
Caw Gill	Cumbr	NY0909	54°28·3′	3°23·8′W	W	89
Cawhillan	E Ayr	NS4921	55°27·8′	4°22·9′W	X	70
Ca Whims	Angus	NO2078	56°53·4′	3°18·3′W	X	44
Cawin Burn	S Ayr	NS3704	55°18·4′	4°33·7′W	W	77
Cawin Hill	S Ayr	NS3703	55°17·9′	4°33·6′W	H	77
Cawkeld	E Yorks	SE9950	53°56·4′	0°29·1′W	T	106
Cawkeld Field	E Yorks	TA0051	53°57·0′	0°28·2′W	X	106,107
Cawkett Fm	Somer	SS8827	51°2·1′	3°35·5′W	FM	181
Cawkwell	Lincs	TF2879	53°17·8′	0°4·4′W	T	122
Cawledge Burn	Northum	NU1910	55°23·3′	1°41·6′W	W	81
Cawleys Coppice	Shrops	SO6094	52°32·8′	2°35·0′W	F	138
Caw Moss	Cumbr	SD2494	54°20·4′	3°9·7′W	X	96
Cawood	N Yks	SE5737	53°49·8′	1°7·6′W	T	105
Cawood Hagg Fm	N Yks	SE5634	53°48·2′	1°8·6′W	FM	105
Cawood Hall	Lincs	TF2230	52°51·5′	0°10·9′W	X	131
Cawood Hill	Cumbr	NY6941	54°46·0′	2°28·5′W	X	86,87
Cawood Ings	N Yks	SE5937	53°49·8′	1°5·8′W	X	105
Cawood Marshes	N Yks	SE5937	53°49·8′	1°5·8′W	X	105
Cawood Park	N Yks	SE5638	53°50·4′	1°8·5′W	X	105
Cawrence	Cered	SN2245	52°4·7′	4°35·5′W	X	145
Cawsand	Corn	SX4350	50°20·0′	4°12·0′W	T	201
Cawsand Bay	Corn	SX4450	50°20·0′	4°11·1′W	W	201
Cawston	Norf	TG1323	52°46·0′	1°9·8′E	T	133
Cawston	Warw	SP4773	52°21·4′	1°18·2′W	T	140
Cawston College	Norf	TG1624	52°46·4′	1°12·5′E	X	133
Cawston Grange Fm	Warw	SP4773	52°21·4′	1°18·2′W	FM	140
Cawston Heath	Norf	TG1623	52°45·9′	1°12·5′E	X	133
Cawston Ho	Warw	SP4772	52°20·9′	1°18·2′W	X	140
Cawthorne	Barns	SE2807	53°33·8′	1°34·2′W	T	110
Cawthorne	N Yks	SE7789	54°17·7′	0°48·6′W	T	94,100
Cawthorne Park	Barns	SE2807	53°33·8′	1°34·2′W	X	110
Cawthorn Moor	N Yks	SE7892	54°19·3′	0°47·6′W	X	94,100
Cawthorpe	Lincs	TF0922	52°47·3′	0°22·6′W	T	130
Cawton	N Yks	SE6476	54°10·8′	1°0·7′W	T	100
Caxton	Cambs	TL3058	52°12·5′	0°5·4′W	T	153
Caxton Common Fm	Cambs	TL3160	52°13·6′	0°4·5′W	FM	153
Caxton Gibbet	Cambs	TL2960	52°13·6′	0°6·3′W	X	153
Cay Brook	Shrops	SO5474	52°22·0′	2°40·1′W	W	137,138
Caydale Mill	N Yks	SE5486	54°16·2′	1°9·8′W	X	100
Cay Hill	Suff	TM0963	52°13·8′	1°4·0′E	X	155
Caynham	Shrops	SO5473	52°21·4′	2°40·1′W	A	137,138
Caynham	Shrops	SO5473	52°21·4′	2°40·1′W	T	137,138
Caynham Ho	Shrops	SO5372	52°20·9′	2°41·0′W	X	137,138
Caynton Hall	Shrops	SJ7702	52°37·2′	2°20·0′W	X	127
Caynton Ho	Wrekin	SJ7021	52°47·4′	2°26·3′W	X	127
Caynton Manor	Shrops	SJ6921	52°47·4′	2°27·2′W	X	127
Cayo	Heref	SO3128	51°57·0′	2°59·8′W	X	161
Cayo Fm	Heref	SO4130	51°58·2′	2°51·1′W	FM	149,161
Cayo, The	Monm	SO4004	51°44·1′	2°51·7′W	X	171
Cayo, The	Newp	ST4391	51°37·1′	2°49·0′W	X	171,172
Caysbriggs	Moray	NJ2466	57°40·9′	3°16·0′W	X	28
Caythorpe	Lincs	SK9348	53°1·5′	0°36·4′W	T	130
Caythorpe	Notts	SK6845	53°0·1′	0°58·8′W	T	129
Caythorpe Fm	Lincs	TF2236	52°54·7′	0°10·7′W	FM	131
Caythorpe Heath	Lincs	SK9748	53°1·5′	0°32·8′W	X	130
Cayton	N Yks	SE2963	54°4·0′	1°33·0′W	X	99
Cayton	N Yks	TA0583	54°14·2′	0°22·9′W	T	101
Cayton Bay	N Yks	TA0784	54°14·7′	0°21·1′W	W	101
Cayton Cliff	N Yks	TA0685	54°15·2′	0°22·0′W	X	101
Cayton Gill Fm	N Yks	SE2862	54°3·4′	1°33·9′W	FM	99
Cayton Gorse	Wrekin	SJ7021	52°47·4′	2°26·3′W	F	127
Cayton Grange	N Yks	SE2962	54°3·4′	1°33·0′W	X	99
Cayton Hall	N Yks	SE2962	54°3·4′	1°33·0′W	X	99
Cayton Hall	Shrops	SJ7702	52°37·2′	2°20·0′W	X	127
Cayton Park	Win & Maid	SU8080	51°31·0′	0°50·4′W	X	175
Cayton Village	N Yks	SE2863	54°4·0′	1°33·9′W	A	99
Ceabhagh	N Eil	NB1934	58°12·6′	6°46·6′W	X	8,13
Cealach na h-Atha	N Eil	NB0400	57°53·7′	6°59·3′W	W	18
Ceallan	N Eil	NF8755	57°28·9′	7°12·9′W	X	22
Cean Caol Beinn a'Chàisgein	Highld	NG9684	57°48·2′	5°25·5′W	X	19
Ceanghline	Pth & Kin	NO0263	56°45·2′	3°35·7′W	X	43
Ceannabeinne	Highld	NC4365	58°33·0′	4°41·4′W	X	9
Ceannabhaid	Highld	NC8225	58°12·1′	4°0·0′W	H	17
Ceann a' Bhàig	N Eil	NF7567	57°34·8′	7°25·8′W	W	18
Ceann-a-bhàigh	Arg & Bt	NM2463	56°40·9′	6°30·0′W	X	46,47
Ceann a' Bhàigh	N Eil	NF7873	57°38·2′	7°23·3′W	W	18
Ceann a Bhàigh	N Eil	NG1193	57°50·3′	6°51·7′W	T	14
Ceann a Bhàigh	N Eil	NG2395	57°51·8′	6°39·8′W	T	14
Ceann a' Chìnich	N Eil	NB4332	58°12·4′	6°22·0′W	T	8
Ceann a' Chlachain	Arg & Bt	NR2858	55°44·6′	6°19·6′W	X	60
Ceann a' Chreagain	Highld	NM8565	56°43·9′	5°30·4′W	X	40
Ceannacroc Bridge	Highld	NH2210	57°9·0′	4°56·1′W	X	34
Ceannacroc Forest	Highld	NH1713	57°10·5′	5°1·2′W	X	34
Ceannacroc Lodge	Highld	NH2211	57°9·6′	4°56·1′W	X	34
Ceanna Garbh	Highld	NM7769	56°45·8′	5°38·5′W	X	40
Ceann a' Gharaidh	N Eil	NF7315	57°6·8′	7°23·7′W	X	31
Ceann a' Ghàraidh	N Eil	NG2098	57°53·3′	6°43·0′W	T	14
Ceann Airigh an Obain	N Eil	NF8759	57°31·0′	7°13·2′W	X	22
Ceann a' Mhàim	Highld	NH2708	57°8·1′	4°51·1′W	H	34
Ceann a' Mhara	Arg & Bt	NL9340	56°27·4′	6°58·6′W	H	46
Ceannamhoir	N Eil	NB4014	58°2·6′	6°23·9′W	X	14
Ceannamhór	Highld	NC1339	58°18·3′	5°11·0′W	X	15
Ceanna Mór	Highld	NM8551	56°36·4′	5°29·7′W	X	49
Ceanna Mór	Highld	NM8552	56°36·9′	5°29·8′W	X	49
Ceann a-Muigh Chuil	N Eil	NB4640	58°16·8′	6°19·5′W	T	8
Ceann-an-òba	Highld	NG9230	57°19·1′	5°26·8′W	X	25
Ceann an Ora	N Eil	NB1303	57°55·7′	6°50·4′W	X	13,14
Ceann an t-Saideil	Highld	NM7092	56°58·0′	5°46·6′W	X	33,40
Ceann an t-Sailein	Arg & Bt	NR7079	55°57·2′	5°40·6′W	W	61,62
Ceann an t-Sailein	Arg & Bt	NR7080	55°57·7′	5°40·7′W	W	55,61
Ceann an Tùir	Arg & Bt	NM6041	56°30·3′	5°53·6′W	X	49

Ceannaraigh	N Eil	NF8655	57°28·9′	7°13·9′W	X	22
Ceann a-staigh Chuil	N Eil	NB4739	58°16·3′	6°18·4′W	T	8
Ceann Badaidh na Muic	Highld	ND1526	58°13·1′	3°26·3′W	X	17
Ceann Beag	Highld	NG8864	57°37·2′	5°32·5′W	H	19
Ceann Buidhe	Arg & Bt	NR5774	55°54·1′	5°52·8′W	X	61
Ceann Caol	Arg & Bt	NR3843	55°36·9′	6°9·2′W	X	60
Ceann Caol	Highld	NN0474	56°49·2′	5°12·2′W	X	41
Ceann Caol	N Ayr	NR8742	55°37·8′	5°22·6′W	X	62,69
Ceann Caol Beinn na Lap	Highld	NN3668	56°46·7′	4°40·6′W	X	41
Ceann Caol na Creige	Pth & Kin	NN6659	56°42·5′	4°10·9′W	X	42,51
Ceann Caol na Glas-bheinne	Highld	NN2766	56°45·5′	4°49·3′W	X	41
Ceann Chnocain	Arg & Bt	NM6433	56°26·1′	5°49·2′W	X	49
Ceann Chreagan	Arg & Bt	NN0914	56°17·1′	5°4·7′W	X	50,56
Ceanncoille	Pth & Kin	NN4456	56°40·4′	4°32·3′W	X	42,51
Ceann Creagach	Stir	NN6331	56°27·3′	4°12·9′W	H	51
Ceann Creag-airighe	Highld	NG2205	57°3·4′	6°34·7′W	X	39
Ceann Creige	Arg & Bt	NN0134	56°27·6′	5°13·3′W	H	50
Ceann Dibig	N Eil	NG1498	57°53·1′	6°49·0′W	X	14
Ceann Druiom na Garth-lertr	Highld	NH1708	57°7·9′	5°1·0′W	X	34
Ceann Dubh	Pth & Kin	NN6169	56°47·8′	4°16·1′W	X	42
Ceann Ear	N Eil	NF6361	57°31·1′	7°37·3′W	X	22
Ceànn Fàsachd	Arg & Bt	NM1653	56°35·2′	6°37·1′W	H	46
Ceann Garbh	Arg & Bt	NN2220	56°20·6′	4°52·4′W	H	50,56
Ceann Garbh	Arg & Bt	NR3943	55°36·9′	6°8·3′W	X	60
Ceann Garbh	Arg & Bt	NR4961	55°46·9′	5°59·7′W	X	60,61
Ceann Garbh	Highld	NC3151	58°25·2′	4°53·1′W	H	9
Ceann Garbh	Highld	NC7245	58°22·8′	4°10·9′W	H	10
Ceann Garbh	Highld	NM5758	56°39·3′	5°57·4′W	X	47
Ceann Garbh	Pth & Kin	NN4953	56°38·9′	4°27·3′W	X	42,51
Ceann Garbh à Chaillich	Highld	NH1370	57°41·1′	5°7·7′W	X	19
Ceann Garbh Meallan Chuaich	Highld	NH1169	57°40·5′	5°9·7′W	X	19
Ceann Garbh na Beinne Dirich	Highld	NC4037	58°17·8′	4°43·3′W	X	16
Ceann Gorm	Pth & Kin	NN6171	56°48·8′	4°16·2′W	H	42
Ceann Hilligeo	Highld	ND2535	58°18·1′	3°16·3′W	X	11
Ceann Iar	N Eil	NF6162	57°31·5′	7°39·4′W	X	22
Ceann Leathad nam Bò	Highld	ND1323	58°11·5′	3°28·3′W	X	17
Ceann Loch	Highld	NN2895	57°1·1′	4°49·5′W	W	34
Ceann-locha	Highld	NG8152	57°30·6′	5°38·9′W	X	24
Ceann Loch Caolisport	Arg & Bt	NR7677	55°56·3′	5°34·8′W	X	62
Ceann-loch-damh	Highld	NG8647	57°28·0′	5°33·6′W	X	24
Ceann Loch Reasort	N Eil	NB1017	58°3·1′	6°54·5′W	X	13,14
Ceann Loch Shealg	N Eil	NB3010	58°0·1′	6°33·7′W	W	13,14
Ceann Loch Uachdrach	Highld	NM7471	56°46·8′	5°41·5′W	X	40
Ceann Mara	Arg & Bt	NN0722	56°21·3′	5°7·0′W	X	50
Ceann Min na Beinne Brice	Arg & Bt	NR6092	56°3·9′	5°50·9′W	X	61
Ceann Mór	Arg & Bt	NM0549	56°32·7′	6°47·5′W	X	46
Ceann Mór	Arg & Bt	NM8313	56°15·9′	5°29·8′W	H	55
Ceann Mòr	Arg & Bt	NN3212	56°16·5′	4°42·4′W	X	50,56
Ceann Mór	Highld	NM1596	56°58·3′	6°40·9′W	X	39
Ceann Mòr	N Eil	NB2206	57°57·7′	6°41·5′W	X	13,14
Ceann na Baintighearna	Stir	NN4717	56°19·5′	4°28·0′W	H	57
Ceann na Beinne	Highld	NG4217	57°10·5′	6°15·7′W	H	32
Ceann-na-Cleithe	N Eil	NG1794	57°51·0′	6°45·7′W	X	14
Ceann na Coille	Highld	NC5413	58°5·2′	4°28·1′W	X	16
Ceann-na-coille	Highld	NC6740	58°20·0′	4°15·8′W	X	10
Ceann na Coille	Highld	NM8255	56°38·4′	5°32·9′W	X	49
Ceann nam Buailtean	N Eil	NB4531	58°11·9′	6°19·9′W	T	8
Ceann na Mòine, Lochain	Highld	NH0967	57°39·4′	5°11·6′W	W	19
Ceann nan Clachan	N Eil	NF7774	57°38·7′	7°24·4′W	X	18
Ceann nan Leac	N Eil	NF6400	56°58·4′	7°31·4′W	X	31
Ceann nan Sgeirean	Arg & Bt	NR4547	55°39·2′	6°2·8′W	X	60
Ceann Ousdale	Highld	ND0718	58°8·7′	3°34·3′W	X	17
Ceann Reamhar	N Ayr	NR8741	55°37·2′	5°22·5′W	H	62,69
Ceann Reamhar	N Eil	NG1199	57°53·5′	6°52·1′W	H	14
Ceann Reamhar na Sròine	N Eil	NG0993	57°50·2′	6°53·7′W	H	14
Ceann Riobha	Arg & Bt	NR3585	55°59·3′	6°14·5′W	X	61
Ceann Shiphoirt	N Eil	NB2916	58°3·3′	6°35·2′W	X	13,14
Ceann Tarabhaigh	N Eil	NB2317	58°3·6′	6°41·3′W	X	13,14
Ceann Tràghad	N Eil	NF7554	57°27·9′	7°24·8′W	X	22
Ceann Tràigh na Croise	N Eil	NF7414	57°6·3′	7°22·6′W	X	31
Cean Uachdarach	N Eil	NF7876	57°39·8′	7°23·5′W	X	18
Ceaplaich	Highld	NG3629	57°16·8′	6°22·4′W	X	32
Ceap Liath	Arg & Bt	NM6625	56°21·8′	5°46·9′W	X	49
Ceapmaol	Highld	NH5724	57°17·3′	4°21·9′W	X	26,35
Cearascleit Bheag	N Eil	NB1015	58°2·0′	6°54·3′W	H	13,14
Cearascleit Mòr	N Eil	NB1113	58°1·0′	6°53·2′W	H	13,14
Cearcall Dubh	Highld	NG8541	57°24·8′	5°34·3′W	H	24
Ceardach	Stir	NS3991	56°5·3′	4°34·8′W	X	56
Ceardach Ruadh	N Eil	NF7761	57°31·7′	7°23·4′W	X	22
Cearnabhal	N Eil	NB1815	58°2·3′	6°46·2′W	H	13,14
Cearsiadair	N Eil	NB3420	58°5·6′	6°30·4′W	T	13,14
Ceartaval	N Eil	NB0412	58°0·2′	7°0·2′W	H	13
Ceasar's Camp	Hants	SU8350	51°14·8′	0°48·3′W	A	186
Ceaseat Beck	Cumbr	SD7691	54°19·1′	2°21·7′W	W	98
Ceathramh Garbh	Highld	NC2251	58°24·9′	5°2·4′W	X	9
Cedar Fm	Derby	SK4462	53°9·4′	1°20·1′W	FM	120
Cedar Fm	Lancs	SD4913	53°36·9′	2°45·8′W	FM	108
Cedar Fm	Lincs	TF0788	53°22·9′	0°23·1′W	FM	112,121
Cedar Fm	Suff	TM3442	52°1·8′	1°25·1′E	FM	169
Cedar Hill	Leic	SK8230	52°51·9′	0°46·5′W	X	130
Cedar Lodge	Lincs	TF2812	52°41·7′	0°6·0′W	X	131,142
Cedars Fm	Northnts	SP4751	52°9·5′	1°18·4′W	FM	151
Cedars Fm, The	Essex	TM0922	51°51·7′	1°2·5′E	FM	168,169
Cedars, The	Beds	TL1737	52°1·4′	0°17·3′W	X	153
Cedars, The	Ches	SJ4959	53°7·8′	2°45·3′W	X	117
Cedars, The	Norf	TM2094	52°30·2′	1°14·9′E	X	134
Cedars, The	Notts	SK5224	52°48·9′	1°13·3′W	X	129
Cedars, The	Suff	TL9165	52°15·2′	0°48·3′E	X	155
Cedars, The	Suff	TM1266	52°15·3′	1°6·8′E	X	155
Cedars, The	W Berks	SU4463	51°22·1′	1°21·7′W	X	174
Cedar Tree	Cambs	TL5657	52°11·6′	0°17·3′E	X	154
Cedig	Powys	SH9922	52°47·4′	3°29·5′W	X	125
Cedni	Powys	SN8957	52°12·2′	3°37·1′W	W	147

Cedris Fm	Gwyn	SH6908	52°39·5′	3°55·8′W	FM	124
Cedryn	Conwy	SH7163	53°9·2′	3°55·3′W	X	115
Cefn	Cered	SN3249	52°7·1′	4°26·8′W	X	145
Cefn	Conwy	SH7670	53°13·0′	3°51·0′W	X	115
Cefn	Denb	SJ0261	53°8·5′	3°27·5′W	X	116
Cefn	Heref	SO2549	52°8·3′	3°5·4′W	X	148
Cefn	I of Angl	SH5876	53°16·0′	4°7·3′W	X	114,115
Cefn	I of Angl	SH5980	53°18·1′	4°6·6′W	X	114,115
Cefn	Monm	SO3420	51°52·7′	2°57·1′W	X	161
Cefn	Newp	ST2788	51°35·4′	3°2·8′W	T	171
Cefn	Powys	SH9202	52°36·5′	3°35·3′W	X	136
Cefn	Powys	SJ0522	52°47·5′	3°24·1′W	X	125
Cefn	Powys	SJ0902	52°36·7′	3°20·2′W	X	136
Cefn	Powys	SJ2610	52°41·2′	3°5·3′W	T	126
Cefn	Powys	SN8477	52°23·0′	3°41·9′W	H	135,136,147
Cefn	Powys	SN9144	52°5·3′	3°35·1′W	X	147,160
Cefn	Powys	SN9283	52°26·3′	3°34·9′W	X	136
Cefn	Powys	SN9664	52°16·1′	3°31·0′W	X	147
Cefn	Powys	SN9679	52°24·2′	3°31·3′W	X	136,147
Cefn	Powys	SO0086	52°28·0′	3°27·9′W	X	136
Cefn	Powys	SO2036	52°1·2′	3°9·6′W	X	161
Cefn	Rho Cyn Taf	ST0692	51°37·4′	3°21·1′W	X	170
Cefn-Aber-Tanat	Shrops	SJ2322	52°47·6′	3°8·1′W	X	126
Cefn Alltwinau	Powys	SN8649	52°7·9′	3°39·5′W	H	147
Cefnamwlch	Gwyn	SH2335	52°53·2′	4°37·5′W	X	123
Cefn Arthen	Carm	SN8333	51°59·2′	3°41·8′W	H	160
Cefnau	Powys	SJ0011	52°41·5′	3°28·4′W	X	125
Cefn Bach	Caer	SO1301	51°42·3′	3°15·2′W	X	171
Cefn Bach	Carm	SN7041	52°3·4′	3°53·4′W	H	146,147,160
Cefn-bach	Conwy	SH9562	53°8·9′	3°33·8′W	X	116
Cefn-bach	I of Angl	SH5069	53°12·1′	4°14·3′W	X	114,115
Cefn Bach	Powys	SN9073	52°20·9′	3°36·5′W	X	136,147
Cefn-bach	Powys	SN9786	52°28·0′	3°30·6′W	X	136
Cefn Bach	Powys	SO0038	52°2·1′	3°27·1′W	H	160
Cefn Bach	Powys	SO0621	51°53·0′	3°21·6′W	X	160
Cefn Bâch	Rho Cyn Taf	SO2004	51°44·0′	3°9·1′W	H	171
Cefn-banadl	Cered	SN6462	52°14·6′	3°59·1′W	X	146
Cefn-bangor	Cered	SN6879	52°23·8′	3°56·0′W	X	135
Cefnbannog	Denb	SJ0251	53°3·1′	3°27·3′W	X	116
Cefn Barhedyn	Powys	SN8298	52°34·3′	3°44·1′W	X	135,136
Cefn Berain	Conwy	SH9969	53°12·8′	3°30·3′W	T	116
Cefn-betingau	Swan	SN6601	51°41·7′	3°55·9′W	X	159
Cefnblaenau	Carm	SN5741	52°3·2′	4°4·7′W	X	146
Cefn Blaen-coel	Powys	SN8864	52°16·0′	3°38·1′W	X	147
Cefn Blaencwmhenog	Powys	SN8348	52°7·3′	3°42·1′W	X	147
Cefn Blaeneinon	Powys	SN8851	52°9·0′	3°37·8′W	X	147
Cefn Blewog	Cered	SN7072	52°20·1′	3°54·1′W	X	135,147
Cefnblewog	Powys	SO1599	52°35·2′	3°14·9′W	X	136
Cefn Bod-Gadfan	Gwyn	SH5706	52°38·2′	4°6·4′W	X	124
Cefn-bodig	Gwyn	SH8934	52°53·8′	3°38·6′W	X	124,125
Cefn Bola-maen	Powys	SN9734	51°59·9′	3°29·6′W	X	160
Cefn Bran	Powys	SJ0919	52°45·9′	3°20·5′W	X	125
Cefn'bran	Powys	SN9354	52°10·7′	3°33·5′W	X	147
Cefn Branddu	Carm	SN7146	52°6·1′	3°52·6′W	H	146,147
Cefn Brenig	Denb	SH9757	53°6·3′	3°31·9′W	X	116
Cefnbrisgen	Carm	SN5829	51°56·7′	4°3·6′W	X	146
Cefn-brith	Conwy	SH9350	53°2·4′	3°35·4′W	T	116
Cefn Brith	Powys	SH9800	52°35·5′	3°29·9′W	X	136
Cefn brith	Powys	SN9145	52°5·8′	3°35·1′W	A	147
Cefn Brith	Powys	SO1478	52°23·8′	3°15·4′W	X	136,148
Cefn Briw	Powys	SJ1124	52°48·6′	3°18·8′W	X	125
Cefn Briw	Powys	SJ2518	52°45·5′	3°6·3′W	X	126
Cefnbronllys	Powys	SO1070	52°19·5′	3°18·8′W	X	136,148
Cefn Brwynog	Cered	SN8265	52°16·5′	3°43·4′W	X	135,136,147
Cefnbryn	Carm	SN4804	51°43·1′	4°11·6′W	X	159
Cefn-bryn	Carm	SN5646	52°5·9′	4°5·7′W	X	146
Cefn-bryn-brain	Carm	SN7413	51°48·3′	3°49·3′W	T	160
Cefnbryntalch	Powys	SO1796	52°33·6′	3°13·1′W	X	136
Cefn Bugeilyn	Powys	SJ1317	52°44·9′	3°16·9′W	X	125
Cefn-bychan	Flint	SJ1964	53°10·3′	3°12·3′W	X	116
Cefnbychan	Powys	SN9670	52°19·3′	3°31·2′W	X	136,147
Cefnbychan	Powys	SO0855	52°11·4′	3°20·4′W	X	147
Cefn-bychan	Swan	SS5495	51°38·3′	4°6·2′W	T	159
Cefn-bychan	Wrex	SJ2741	52°57·9′	3°4·8′W	T	117
Cefn Bychan or Newbridge	Caer	ST2197	51°40·2′	3°8·2′W	T	171
Cefnbyrallt	Shrops	SJ2331	52°52·5′	3°8·2′W	X	126
Cefnbys	Cered	SN5653	52°9·6′	4°5·9′W	X	146
Cefn Cadlan	Rho Cyn Taf	SN9611	51°47·5′	3°30·1′W	X	160
Cefn Cadle Fm	Swan	SS6497	51°39·6′	3°57·6′W	FM	159
Cefncaeau	Carm	SS5399	51°40·5′	4°7·2′W	T	159
Cefn-caer	Gwyn	SH7000	52°35·2′	3°54·7′W	X	135
Cefn Caer-Euni	Gwyn	SH9940	52°57·1′	3°29·8′W	X	125
Cefn-caer-ferch	Gwyn	SH4242	52°57·4′	4°20·7′W	X	123
Cefn Caer For	I of Angl	SH3974	53°14·6′	4°24·4′W	X	114
Cefncaled	Powys	SO1491	52°30·8′	3°15·6′W	X	136
Cefn Cam	Gwyn	SH6825	52°48·6′	3°57·1′W	X	124
Cefncamberth	Gwyn	SH5603	52°36·6′	4°7·2′W	X	135
Cefn-Campstone	Monm	SO3421	51°53·3′	2°57·1′W	X	161
Cefn Canol	Powys	SJ2331	52°52·5′	3°8·2′W	T	126
Cefn Canol	Wrex	SJ1938	52°56·2′	3°11·9′W	X	125
Cefn Cantref	Powys	SO0426	51°55·7′	3°23·4′W	H	160
Cefn Car	Merth Tyd	SO0213	51°48·7′	3°24·9′W	X	160
Cefn Carfan	Brig	SS9285	51°33·5′	3°33·1′W	X	170
Cefn-carn	Gwyn	SH6925	52°48·6′	3°56·2′W	X	124
Cefncarnau	Caer	ST1684	51°33·2′	3°12·3′W	X	171
Cefn Carnedd (Fort)	Powys	SO0189	52°29·6′	3°27·1′W	A	136
Cefn Carn Fadog	Carm	SN7616	51°50·0′	3°47·6′W	H	160
Cefn Castell	Conwy	SH9075	53°15·9′	3°38·5′W	X	116
Cefn-ceirch	Denb	SJ0146	53°0·4′	3°28·1′W	X	116
Cefn-Ceist Fm	Heref	SO3135	52°0·8′	2°59·9′W	FM	161
Cefn Cenarth	Powys	SN9776	52°22·6′	3°30·4′W	X	136,147
Cefn-cenfi	Carm	SN6414	51°48·7′	3°58·0′W	X	159
Cefn-cerrig	Carm	SN7732	51°58·6′	3°47·1′W	X	146,160
Cefncerrig	Cered	SN7658	52°12·6′	3°48·5′W	X	146,147
Cefn Cerrigellgwm	Conwy	SH8547	53°0·7′	3°42·4′W	H	116
Cefn-Cestyll	Conwy	SH8353	53°3·9′	3°44·4′W	X	116
Cefncethin	Carm	SN6318	51°50·9′	3°58·9′W	X	159
Cefn Cil-Sanws	Merth Tyd	SO0209	51°46·5′	3°24·8′W	X	160
Cefn-cilwg	Carm	SN6327	51°55·7′	3°59·2′W	X	146

Cefn Clawdd	Gwyn	SH6733	52°52·9′	3°58·2′W	X	124
Cefn Clawdd	Powys	SO0440	52°3·2′	3°23·6′W	H	147,160
Cefncleisiog	Powys	SJ0816	52°44·3′	3°21·4′W	X	125
Cefn Clytha	Monm	SO3720	51°52·7′	2°54·5′W	X	161
Cefn Cnwc	Cered	SN7759	52°13·2′	3°47·6′W	H	146,147
Cefn Cnwcheithinog	Cered	SN7549	52°7·8′	3°49·2′W	X	146,147
Cefn Coch	Blae Gw	SO2109	51°46·7′	3°8·3′W	H	161
Cefn Coch	Carm	SN8539	52°2·5′	3°40·2′W	X	160
Cefncoch	Cered	SN6373	52°20·5′	4°0·3′W	X	135
Cefn Coch	Cered	SN7496	52°33·1′	3°51·1′W	H	135
Cefn Coch	Cered	SN7872	52°20·2′	3°47·0′W	H	135,147
Cefn Côch	Conwy	SH7274	53°15·1′	3°54·7′W	X	115
Cefn Côch	Conwy	SH8142	52°58·0′	3°45·9′W	X	124,125
Cefn-coch	Conwy	SH8668	53°12·1′	3°42·0′W	T	116
Cefn Coch	Denb	SJ1250	53°2·6′	3°18·4′W	X	116
Cefn coch	Denb	SJ1457	53°6·4′	3°16·7′W	X	116
Cefn-coch	Gwyn	SH5442	52°57·6′	4°10·0′W	X	124
Cefn-coch	Gwyn	SH9226	52°49·5′	3°35·8′W	H	125
Cefn Coch	Gwyn	SJ0035	52°54·4′	3°28·8′W	X	125
Cefn-coch	I of Angl	SH3490	53°23·1′	4°29·4′W	X	114
Cefn Coch	I of Angl	SH5676	53°15·9′	4°9·1′W	X	114,115
Cefn Côch	Powys	SH8202	52°36·4′	3°44·2′W	X	135,136
Cefn Côch	Powys	SH8203	52°37·0′	3°44·2′W	X	135,136
Cefn Côch	Powys	SH9718	52°45·2′	3°31·2′W	X	125
Cefn Coch	Powys	SJ0402	52°36·7′	3°24·7′W	T	136
Cefn côch	Powys	SJ1026	52°49·7′	3°19·7′W	X	125
Cefn Coch	Powys	SN8253	52°10·0′	3°43·1′W	X	147
Cefncoch	Powys	SN9992	52°31·2′	3°28·9′W	X	136
Cefncoch	Powys	SO2373	52°21·2′	3°7·4′W	X	137,148
Cefn Coch	Shrops	SJ2333	52°53·6′	3°8·3′W	F	126
Cefn Coch Fm	Cered	SN7496	52°33·1′	3°51·1′W	FM	135
Cefn Coch Fm	Monm	SO3712	51°48·4′	2°54·4′W	FM	161
Cefn Coch Fm	Monm	SO3907	51°45·7′	2°52·6′W	FM	161
Cefncoch-gwyllt	Powys	SH8203	52°37·0′	3°44·2′W	X	135,136
Cefncoed	Carm	SN8136	52°0·8′	3°43·6′W	X	160
Cefn-coed	Cered	SN4058	52°12·1′	4°20·1′W	X	146
Cefncoed	Cered	SN6258	52°12·4′	4°0·8′W	X	146
Cefncoed	Powys	SO0060	52°14·0′	3°27·5′W	X	147
Cefn-coed	Powys	SO0762	52°15·1′	3°21·3′W	X	147
Cefncoed Bach	Powys	SO0133	51°59·4′	3°26·1′W	X	160
Cefncoed Isaf	Carm	SN5140	52°2·5′	4°10·0′W	X	146
Cefncoed Uchaf	Carm	SN5140	52°2·5′	4°10·0′W	X	146
Cefn-coed-y-cymmer	Merth Tyd	SO0308	51°46·0′	3°24·0′W	T	160
Cefn Coleshill	Flint	SJ2173	53°15·1′	3°10·6′W	X	117
Cefn Colstyn	Card	ST1181	51°31·5′	3°16·6′W	X	171
Cefn Craig	Powys	SO2176	52°22·8′	3°9·2′W	X	137,148
Cefn Craig Amos	Rho Cyn Taf	SS9898	51°40·5′	3°28·1′W	X	170
Cefn Crew	Powys	SO0019	51°51·9′	3°26·7′W	X	160
Cefn Crib	Gwyn	SN6898	52°34·1′	3°56·5′W	X	135
Cefn Crib	Torf	SO2300	51°41·8′	3°6·5′W	X	171
Cefn-crib	Torf	ST2399	51°41·3′	3°6·4′W	T	171
Cefn Cribwr	Brig	SS8582	51°31·8′	3°39·1′W	T	170
Cefn-Crîn	Powys	SJ1404	52°37·9′	3°15·8′W	X	136
Cefn-crin	Powys	SO0272	52°20·5′	3°25·9′W	X	136,147
Cefn Croes	Cered	SN8180	52°24·5′	3°44·6′W	X	135,136
Cefn Cross	Brig	SS8682	51°31·8′	3°38·2′W	T	170
Cefn Crug	Carm	SN7835	52°0·2′	3°46·2′W	H	146,160
Cefn Crug	Powys	SN8651	52°9·0′	3°39·6′W	H	147
Cefn-crûg	Powys	SO0915	51°49·8′	3°18·8′W	X	161
Cefn-crwth	Carm	SN3120	51°51·4′	4°26·9′W	X	145,159
Cefn Cul	Powys	SN8618	51°51·2′	3°38·9′W	X	160
Cefn Cûl	Powys	SO0119	51°51·9′	3°25·9′W	X	160
Cefn Cwm-coel	Powys	SN8965	52°16·6′	3°37·2′W	X	135,136,147
Cefn Cwmirfon	Powys	SN8449	52°7·9′	3°41·3′W	X	147
Cefn Cwm Llwch	Powys	SO0122	51°53·5′	3°25·9′W	X	160
Cefn Cwm-y-geifr	Wrex	SJ1133	52°53·5′	3°19·0′W	X	125
Cefn-cwrt	Cered	SN3254	52°9·8′	4°27·0′W	X	145
Cefn Cyfarwydd	Conwy	SH7563	53°9·2′	3°51·8′W	X	115
Cefn Cyff	Powys	SO0422	51°53·5′	3°23·3′W	X	160
Cefncyfrifol	Powys	SN8095	52°32·6′	3°45·8′W	X	135,136
Cefncynfal	Powys	SO1268	52°18·4′	3°17·0′W	X	136,148
Cefn Cynllaith	Powys	SN8951	52°9·0′	3°36·9′W	X	147
Cefn Dderwen	I of Angl	SH4766	53°10·4′	4°16·9′W	X	114,115
Cefn Ddwy Ffrwd	I of Angl	SH4686	53°21·2′	4°18·4′W	X	114
Cefn-ddwygraig	Gwyn	SH9233	52°53·3′	3°35·9′W	X	125
Cefn-ddwysarn	Gwyn	SH9638	52°56·0′	3°32·4′W	T	125
Cefnderwen	Powys	SJ1026	52°49·7′	3°19·7′W	X	125
Cefndeuddwr	Gwyn	SH7326	52°49·2′	3°52·7′W	X	124
Cefn Dolgelynen	Gwyn	SH7200	52°35·2′	3°53·0′W	H	135
Cefndre	Powys	SJ0609	52°40·5′	3°23·0′W	X	125
Cefndreboeth	Powys	SO1799	52°35·2′	3°13·1′W	X	136
Cefn-dre-wern	Powys	SO1456	52°12·0′	3°15·1′W	H	148
Cefn Drum	Swan	SN6104	51°43·3′	4°0·4′W	X	159
Cefn-drydwy	Conwy	SH8770	53°13·1′	3°41·1′W	X	116
Cefn Du	Conwy	SH8373	53°14·7′	3°44·8′W	H	116
Cefn Du	Conwy	SH9258	53°6·7′	3°36·4′W	H	116
Cefn Du	Conwy	SH9866	53°11·1′	3°31·2′W	X	116
Cefn Du	Denb	SJ0454	53°4·7′	3°25·6′W	H	116
Cefn-du	Denb	SJ0454	53°4·7′	3°25·6′W	X	116
Cefn Du	Denb	SJ0972	53°14·5′	3°21·4′W	H	116
Cefn-du	Gwyn	SH5460	53°7·3′	4°10·5′W	H	114,115
Cefn-Du	I of Angl	SH3874	53°14·5′	4°25·3′W	X	114
Cefn Du	I of Angl	SH4872	53°13·6′	4°16·2′W	X	114,115
Cefn-du	Powys	SJ1509	52°40·6′	3°15·0′W	X	125
Cefn Du	Powys	SO0475	52°22·1′	3°24·2′W	H	136,147
Cefn Du Isaf	I of Angl	SH4973	53°14·2′	4°15·3′W	X	114,115
Cefn-du Mawr	I of Angl	SH4682	53°19·0′	4°18·3′W	X	114,115
Cefn du uchaf	Powys	SJ1508	52°40·0′	3°15·0′W	X	125
Cefn-dyrys	Powys	SO0352	52°9·7′	3°24·7′W	X	147
Cefndyrys	Powys	SO0473	52°21·0′	3°24·2′W	H	136,147
Cefn Edern	Gwyn	SH2838	52°55·0′	4°33·1′W	X	123
Cefn Edmwnt	Powys	SO0720	51°52·5′	3°20·7′W	X	160
Cefn Eglwysilan	Rho Cyn Taf	ST0990	51°36·3′	3°18·5′W	H	171
Cefn Einion	Shrops	SO2886	52°28·3′	3°3·2′W	T	137
Cefneithin	Carm	SN5513	51°48·1′	4°5·8′W	T	159
Cefn-Eithin	Gwyn	SH4656	53°5·0′	4°17·6′W	X	115,123
Cefn-Eithin	Gwyn	SJ0243	52°58·8′	3°27·2′W	X	125
Cefnen	Conwy	SH8758	53°6·7′	3°40·9′W	H	116
Cefnen	Conwy	SH8776	53°16·4′	3°41·3′W	X	116
Cefnen Wen	Conwy	SH8854	53°4·5′	3°39·9′W	H	116

Cefn-esgair	Powys	SN8744	52°5·2′	3°38·6′W	X	147,160
Cefn Esgair-carnau	Powys	SN9713	51°48·6′	3°29·3′W	X	160
Cefn Esgeronen	Cered	SN4157	52°11·5′	4°19·2′W	X	146
Cefn-eurgain	Flint	SJ2267	53°11·9′	3°9·7′W	T	117
Cefnfaes	Powys	SN9669	52°18·8′	3°31·1′W	X	136,147
Cefn Fannog	Powys	SN8151	52°8·9′	3°44·0′W	X	147
Cefnfarchen	Carm	SN1619	51°50·6′	4°39·9′W	X	158
Cefn Farm	I of Angl	SH4373	53°14·1′	4°20·7′W	FM	114,115
Cefn-fedw	Carm	SN6820	51°52·0′	3°54·6′W	X	159
Cefnfedw	Powys	SN9225	51°55·0′	3°33·8′W	X	160
Cefnfedwfawr	Powys	SN9324	51°54·5′	3°32·9′W	X	160
Cefnfeusydd Fm	Gwyn	SH6010	52°40·4′	4°3·8′W	FM	124
Cefnffordd	Nth Pt Talb	SN9003	51°43·1′	3°35·2′W	X	170
Cefn Ffordd	Nth Pt Talb	SS8599	51°40·9′	3°39·4′W	X	170
Cefn Fforest	Caer	ST1697	51°40·2′	3°12·5′W	T	171
Cefn-Fforest	Conwy	SH9561	53°8·4′	3°33·8′W	X	116
Cefn-fforest	Merth Tyd	ST0998	51°40·6′	3°18·6′W	X	171
Cefnfforest-fawr	Swan	SN6300	51°41·2′	3°58·5′W	X	159
Cefnfilltir	Gwyn	SH5830	52°51·2′	4°6·1′W	X	124
Cefn Fm	Carm	SN6932	51°58·5′	3°54·0′W	FM	146,160
Cefn Fm	Carm	SN8138	52°1·9′	3°43·7′W	FM	160
Cefn Fm	Cered	SN6261	52°14·0′	4°0·9′W	FM	146
Cefn Fm	Flint	SJ2074	53°15·7′	3°11·6′W	FM	117
Cefn Fm	Wrex	SJ2753	53°4·4′	3°5·0′W	FM	117
Cefn Fms	Heref	SO2837	52°1·8′	3°2·6′W	FM	161
Cefnfoelallt	Cered	SN6151	52°8·6′	4°1·5′W	X	146
Cefn-Gader	Powys	SH8206	52°38·6′	3°44·2′W	X	124,125
Cefngaer	Cered	SN7266	52°16·9′	3°52·2′W	X	135,147
Cefn Gafros Common	Powys	SO1040	52°3·3′	3°18·4′W	X	148,161
Cefn-gallt-y-cwm	Gwyn	SH7134	52°53·5′	3°54·6′W	X	124
Cefn Garlleg	Conwy	SH8276	53°16·3′	3°45·8′W	X	116
Cefngarw	Conwy	SH7942	52°57·9′	3°47·7′W	X	124
Cefngarw	Conwy	SH8851	53°2·9′	3°39·8′W	X	116
Cefn Garw	Powys	SN8855	52°11·2′	3°37·9′W	X	147
Cefn Garw Fm	Monm	SO4312	51°48·5′	2°49·2′W	FM	161
Cefngarw Wood	Monm	ST4797	51°40·4′	2°45·6′W	F	171
Cefngast	Powys	SN9147	52°6·9′	3°35·1′W	X	147
Cefn Gelligaer	Caer	SO1101	51°42·3′	3°16·9′W	H	171
Cefngeudrum	Carm	SN7727	51°55·9′	3°47·0′W	X	146,160
Cefn Glancamddwr	Powys	SN9147	52°6·9′	3°35·1′W	X	147
Cefn Glas	Brig	SS8980	51°30·7′	3°35·6′W	T	170
Cefn-glas	Conwy	SH7354	53°4·3′	3°53·3′W	X	115
Cefn-glas	Gwyn	SH8037	52°55·3′	3°46·7′W	X	124,125
Cefn-glas	Gwyn	SH8422	52°47·2′	3°42·8′W	H	124,125
Cefn-glâs	Merth Tyd	ST0797	51°40·1′	3°20·3′W	X	170
Cefn Glas	Powys	SH9420	52°46·3′	3°33·9′W	X	125
Cefn Glas	Rho Cyn Taf	SN9202	51°42·6′	3°33·4′W	X	170
Cefn-glasfryn	Carm	SN6728	51°56·3′	3°55·7′W	X	146
Cefn Gledwen	Powys	SO0342	52°4·3′	3°24·5′W	X	147,160
Cefn Gof	Powys	SN9131	51°58·2′	3°34·8′W	X	160
Cefn Gola	Newp	ST4193	51°38·2′	2°50·8′W	X	171,172
Cefn Golau	Blae Gw	SO1308	51°46·1′	3°15·3′W	T	161
Cefn Goleu	Powys	SJ1516	52°44·3′	3°15·1′W	X	125
Cefngoleu Fm	Swan	SS5795	51°38·4′	4°3·6′W	FM	159
Cefngoleugoed	Powys	SN9486	52°27·9′	3°33·2′W	X	136
Cefn Goleu Parc	Swan	SS5795	51°38·4′	4°3·6′W	X	159
Cefn Golog	Powys	SO1887	52°28·7′	3°12·0′W	X	136
Cefngornoeth	Carm	SN7128	51°56·4′	3°52·2′W	X	146,160
Cefn-gorwydd	Powys	SN9045	52°5·8′	3°36·0′W	T	147
Cefn-gorwydd	Swan	SS5995	51°38·4′	4°1·9′W	X	159
Cefngraigwen	Cered	SN5773	52°20·4′	4°5·5′W	X	135
Cefngranod	Cered	SN3051	52°8·1′	4°28·6′W	X	145
Cefn Gribin	Powys	SJ1118	52°45·4′	3°18·7′W	X	125
Cefn-Griolen	Denb	SJ1048	53°1·5′	3°20·1′W	X	116
Cefn Grug	Nth Pt Talb	SN8802	51°42·6′	3°36·9′W	X	170
Cefn Grugos	Powys	SJ0821	52°47·0′	3°21·4′W	X	125
Cefn Gunthly	Shrops	SO3394	52°32·6′	2°58·9′W	H	137
Cefngwaunhynog	Powys	SN8711	51°47·4′	3°37·9′W	X	160
Cefngweiriog	Cered	SN6793	52°31·4′	3°57·2′W	X	135
Cefn Gwenffrwd	Carm	SN7448	52°7·2′	3°50·0′W	X	146,147
Cefngwernfa	Powys	SJ1100	52°35·7′	3°18·4′W	X	136
Cefn-Gwili	Carm	SN5809	51°45·9′	4°3·1′W	X	159
Cefn Gwrhyd	Nth Pt Talb	SN7208	51°45·6′	3°50·9′W	H	160
Cefngwrthafarn Uchaf	Cered	SN5263	52°15·0′	4°9·7′W	X	146
Cefn-gwrych	Carm	SN7728	51°56·5′	3°47·0′W	X	146,160
Cefn-gwyddfod	Powys	SO0897	52°34·0′	3°21·0′W	X	136
Cefn-gwyn	Cered	SN5364	52°15·5′	4°8·8′W	X	146
Cefn-gwyn	Conwy	SH8170	53°13·1′	3°46·5′W	X	116
Cefngwyn	Conwy	SH8345	52°59·6′	3°44·2′W	X	116
Cefn-gwyn	Gwyn	SH2032	52°51·6′	4°40·0′W	X	123
Cefn Gwyn	Gwyn	SH5366	53°10·5′	4°11·6′W	X	114,115
Cefn-gwyn	Gwyn	SH8310	52°40·7′	3°43·4′W	X	124,125
Cefn Gwyn	Gwyn	SH9030	52°51·6′	3°37·6′W	H	125
Cefn Gwyn	Monm	SO3513	51°48·9′	2°56·2′W	X	161
Cefngwyn	Powys	SJ1123	52°48·1′	3°18·8′W	X	125
Cefn Gwyn	Powys	SJ1329	52°51·3′	3°17·1′W	X	125
Cefn Gwyn	Powys	SN9992	52°31·2′	3°28·9′W	X	136
Cefn-gwyn	Powys	SO1587	52°28·7′	3°14·7′W	X	136
Cefn Gwyngul	Rho Cyn Taf	ST0295	51°39·0′	3°24·6′W	X	170
Cefn Gwyntog	Powys	SH9726	52°49·5′	3°31·3′W	X	125
Cefn Gwynus	Gwyn	SH3441	52°56·7′	4°27·8′W	X	123
Cefn-hafdref	Powys	SN9253	52°10·1′	3°34·4′W	X	147
Cefn Hafod wen	Powys	SN8884	52°26·8′	3°38·5′W	X	135,136
Cefn Hedog	Gwyn	SH2030	52°50·5′	4°40·0′W	X	123
Cefn-hendre	Carm	SN6429	51°56·8′	3°58·3′W	X	146
Cefn Hendre	Powys	SN8580	52°24·6′	3°41·0′W	X	135,136
Cefn Hengoed	Caer	ST1495	51°39·1′	3°14·2′W	T	171
Cefn-hengoed	Swan	SS6895	51°38·5′	3°54·1′W	T	159
Cefn-henllan	Carm	SN4524	51°53·8′	4°14·8′W	X	159
Cefn-henllan	Monm	ST3693	51°38·2′	2°55·1′W	X	171
Cefn Hepreas	Shrops	SO2678	52°23·9′	3°4·9′W	H	137,148
Cefn-hilin	Powys	SJ1903	52°37·4′	3°11·4′W	X	136
Cefn Hill	Heref	SO2738	52°2·4′	3°3·5′W	H	161
Cefn Hill	Monm	ST3995	51°39·3′	2°52·5′W	H	171
Cefnhinog Fm	Powys	SO0848	52°7·6′	3°20·2′W	FM	147
Cefn-hir	Gwyn	SH6239	52°56·1′	4°2·8′W	X	124
Cefn-hir	Powys	SO0689	52°29·7′	3°22·7′W	X	136
Cefn-hir	Powys	SO2055	52°11·5′	3°9·8′W	H	148
Cefnhir	Powys	SO2055	52°11·5′	3°9·8′W	X	148
Cefn Hirbrysg	Powys	SN8981	52°25·2′	3°37·5′W	X	135,136

Cefnhirfach	Powys	SJ1526	52°49·7′	3°15·3′W	X	125
Cefnhirfawr	Powys	SJ1326	52°49·7′	3°17·1′W	X	125
Cefnhirfryn	Carm	SN7941	52°3·5′	3°45·5′W	X	146,147,160
Cefn Hir-fynydd	Wrex	SJ1531	52°52·4′	3°15·4′W	X	125
Cefnhirfynydd Isaf	Conwy	SH9149	53°1·9′	3°37·1′W	X	116
Cefnhirfynydd Uchaf	Conwy	SH9049	53°1·9′	3°38·0′W	X	116
Cefn Hirgoed	Brig	SS9383	51°32·4′	3°32·2′W	X	170
Cefn-hirwaun	Powys	SO0644	52°5·4′	3°21·9′W	X	147,160
Cefn Ila Fm	Monm	SO3600	51°41·9′	2°55·2′W	FM	171
Cefni Reservoir	I of Angl	SH4477	53°16·3′	4°20·0′W	W	114,115
Cefn-isa	Gwyn	SH4840	52°56·4′	4°15·3′W	X	123
Cefn-Isa	Wrex	SJ1937	52°55·7′	3°11·9′W	X	125
Cefn-isaf	Carm	SN3638	52°1·2′	4°23·0′W	X	145
Cefn Isaf	Cered	SN7754	52°10·5′	3°47·5′W	X	146,147
Cefn Isaf	Cered	SN7956	52°11·6′	3°45·8′W	X	146,147
Cefn Isaf	Conwy	SH8975	53°15·9′	3°39·4′W	X	116
Cefn Isaf	Gwyn	SH3541	52°56·7′	4°26·9′W	X	123
Cefn Isaf	Powys	SJ1525	52°49·2′	3°15·3′W	X	125
Cefn Isaf	Powys	SN9253	52°10·1′	3°34·4′W	X	147
Cefn-Isaf Fm	Nth Pt Talb	SN8807	51°45·3′	3°37·0′W	FM	160
Cefn Leisiog	Gwyn	SH2737	52°54·4′	4°34·0′W	X	123
Cefnllan	Carm	SN7938	52°1·9′	3°45·4′W	X	146,160
Cefn-llan	Powys	SN9347	52°6·9′	3°33·4′W	X	147
Cefnllan	Powys	SO2095	52°33·1′	3°10·4′W	X	137
Cefn Llandybo	Powys	SH8309	52°40·2′	3°43·4′W	H	124,125
Cefn Llanfair	Gwyn	SH3233	52°52·3′	4°29·4′W	X	123
Cefnllanio Fm	Cered	SN6557	52°11·9′	3°58·1′W	FM	146
Cefn-llêch	Cered	SN6277	52°22·7′	4°1·2′W	X	135
Cefn Llech	Conwy	SH8066	53°10·9′	3°47·3′W	X	116
Cefn Llech	Powys	SN9577	52°23·1′	3°32·2′W	X	136,147
Cefn Llechid	Powys	SN9427	51°56·1′	3°32·1′W	H	160
Cefn Lle-oer	Powys	SJ1023	52°48·1′	3°19·7′W	X	125
Cefn Lletyhywel	Powys	SN9673	52°21·0′	3°31·2′W	X	136,147
Cefnllidiart	Cered	SN6681	52°24·9′	3°57·8′W	X	135
Cefn Llogell	Newp	ST2684	51°33·2′	3°3·7′W	X	171
Cefn-llwyd	Caer	ST1290	51°36·4′	3°15·9′W	X	171
Cefn-llwyd	Caer	ST2284	51°33·2′	3°7·1′W	X	171
Cefn Llwyd	Cered	SN6483	52°25·9′	3°59·6′W	T	135
Cefn Llwyd	Conwy	SH9866	53°11·1′	3°31·2′W	X	116
Cefn Llwyd	Powys	SH8207	52°39·1′	3°44·3′W	H	124,125
Cefnllwyd	Powys	SJ1209	52°40·5′	3°17·7′W	X	125
Cefn Llwyd	Powys	SN8492	52°31·1′	3°42·2′W	X	135,136
Cefn Llwydallt	Powys	SO0740	52°3·3′	3°21·0′W	H	147,160
Cefn Llwydlo	Powys	SN8542	52°4·1′	3°40·3′W	X	147,160
Cefnllwyn	Cered	SN6766	52°16·8′	3°56·6′W	X	135
Cefnllwyni	Powys	SJ1017	52°44·8′	3°19·6′W	X	125
Cefn Llwyni	Powys	SJ1118	52°45·4′	3°18·7′W	X	125
Cefnllwynpiod	Cered	SN6075	52°21·6′	4°3·0′W	X	135
Cefn-llydan	Powys	SO0696	52°33·5′	3°22·8′W	X	136
Cefn-llyfnog	Powys	SJ1917	52°44·9′	3°11·6′W	X	125
Cefn Llys	V of Glam	ST0379	51°30·3′	3°23·5′W	X	170
Cefnllys Castle	Powys	SO0861	52°14·6′	3°20·5′W	A	147
Cefn Llys-gwr	Conwy	SH9358	53°6·8′	3°35·5′W	X	116
Cefnllysgwynne	Powys	SN9950	52°8·6′	3°28·2′W	X	147
Cefn-llys Isaf	Powys	SJ0006	52°38·8′	3°28·3′W	X	125
Cefn Llystyn	Denb	SJ0133	52°53·4′	3°27·9′W	X	125
Cefn llys Uchaf	Powys	SH9707	52°39·3′	3°31·0′W	X	125
Cefn Mably Woods	Caer	ST2184	51°33·2′	3°8·0′W	F	171
Cefnmabws	Cered	SN5768	52°17·7′	4°5·4′W	X	135
Cefnmachen-isaf	Brig	SS9186	51°34·0′	3°34·0′W	X	170
Cefnmachen-uchaf	Brig	SS9186	51°34·0′	3°34·0′W	X	170
Cefnmachllys	Powys	SO0735	52°0·6′	3°20·9′W	X	160
Cefn-madryn	Gwyn	SH2736	52°53·9′	4°33·9′W	X	123
Cefn Maen Amor	Conwy	SH7373	53°14·6′	3°53·8′W	X	115
Cefn-maen-llwyd	Denb	SJ0947	53°1·0′	3°21·0′W	X	116
Cefn-maen-uchaf	Denb	SJ0261	53°8·5′	3°27·5′W	X	116
Cefn Maes	Carm	SN6729	51°56·9′	3°55·7′W	X	146
Cefnmaes	Cered	SN3246	52°5·5′	4°26·7′W	X	145
Cefnmaes	Cered	SN4555	52°10·5′	4°15·6′W	X	146
Cefnmaesmawr	Powys	SN7298	52°34·1′	3°52·9′W	X	135
Cefn Manmoel	Caer	SO1606	51°45·0′	3°12·6′W	H	161
Cefn Mawr	Conwy	SH9057	53°6·2′	3°38·2′W	H	116
Cefn-mawr	Denb	SJ0357	53°6·3′	3°26·5′W	X	116
Cefn-mawr	Denb	SJ0550	53°2·6′	3°24·6′W	H	116
Cefn Mawr	Flint	SJ1963	53°9·7′	3°12·3′W	X	116
Cefn Mawr	Flint	SJ2063	53°9·7′	3°11·4′W	H	117
Cefn Mawr	I of Angl	SH4367	53°10·9′	4°20·6′W	X	114,115
Cefn Mawr	Monm	SO3303	51°43·5′	2°57·8′W	H	171
Cefnmawr	Nth Pt Talb	SS8599	51°40·9′	3°39·4′W	X	170
Cefn Mawr	Powys	SN7915	51°49·5′	3°45·0′W	X	160
Cefnmawr	Powys	SO0556	52°11·9′	3°23·0′W	X	147
Cefn Mawr	Powys	SO1194	52°32·4′	3°18·3′W	H	136
Cefn-mawr	Wrex	SJ2842	52°58·5′	3°3·9′W	T	117
Cefn Mawr Fm	Monm	SO3403	51°43·5′	2°56·9′W	FM	171
Cefn Meiriadog	Denb	SJ0172	53°14·4′	3°28·6′W	H	116
Cefnmelgoed	Cered	SN5774	52°21·0′	4°5·6′W	X	135
Cefn-melyn	Flint	SJ1866	53°11·3′	3°13·2′W	X	116
Cefn Merthyr	Merth Tyd	ST0899	51°41·2′	3°19·5′W	X	170
Cefn Merthyr Cynog	Powys	SN9738	52°2·1′	3°29·7′W	H	160
Cefnmeurig	Carm	SN2318	51°50·2′	4°33·8′W	X	158
Cefn Mine	Gwyn	SH3336	52°54·0′	4°28·6′W	X	123
Cefn Modfedd	Powys	SN7897	52°33·7′	3°47·6′W	H	135
Cefn Moel	Powys	SO1624	51°54·7′	3°12·9′W	H	161
Cefn Morfudd	Nth Pt Talb	SS7897	51°39·8′	3°45·4′W	X	170
Cefnmystrych	Carm	SN3721	51°52·1′	4°21·7′W	X	145,159
Cefn-nannau	Conwy	SH9645	52°59·8′	3°32·6′W	X	116
Cefn Nannerth	Powys	SN9272	52°20·4′	3°34·7′W	X	136,147
Cefnnantmel	Powys	SO0367	52°17·8′	3°24·9′W	X	136,147
Cefn Nantygeugarn	Rho Cyn Taf	SN9914	51°49·2′	3°27·5′W	X	160
Cefn Nant-y-gwair	Nth Pt Talb	SS9098	51°40·4′	3°35·1′W	X	170
Cefn Nant-yr-iau	Powys	SN8562	52°14·9′	3°40·7′W	X	147
Cefn-nen	Gwyn	SH2433	52°52·2′	4°36·5′W	X	123
Cefn-nith	Powys	SO0590	52°30·2′	3°23·6′W	X	136
Cefn Onn	Caer	ST1785	51°33·7′	3°11·5′W	X	171
Cefn Onnau	Powys	SO1616	51°50·4′	3°12·8′W	X	161
Cefn Padrig	Carm	SN4800	51°40·9′	4°11·5′W	X	159
Cefn Parc	Brig	SS8684	51°32·8′	3°38·3′W	X	170
Cefn Parc	Carm	SN6729	51°56·9′	3°55·7′W	X	146
Cefn-parc Fm	Rho Cyn Taf	ST0581	51°31·4′	3°21·8′W	FM	170
Cefn Park	Wrex	SJ3549	53°2·3′	2°57·8′W	X	117

Cefn-pawl	Powys	SO0670	52°19·4′	3°22·4′W	X	136,147
Cefn Pawl	Powys	SO1679	52°24·4′	3°13·7′W	X	136,148
Cefn Penagored	Denb	SJ0334	52°53·9′	3°26·1′W	X	125
Cefnpenarth	Powys	SN9285	52°27·4′	3°35·0′W	X	136
Cefn-Penarth	Powys	SO0966	52°17·3′	3°19·7′W	X	136,147
Cefn Pencoed	Gwyn	SH4542	52°57·4′	4°18·0′W	X	123
Cefn Pen-lan	Powys	SN9575	52°22·0′	3°32·1′W	X	136,147
Cefn-Pen-llety	Denb	SJ0336	52°55·0′	3°26·2′W	X	125
Cefn Pennar	Merth Tyd	SO0402	51°42·7′	3°23·0′W	X	170
Cefnpennar	Rho Cyn Taf	SO0300	51°41·7′	3°23·8′W	T	170
Cefn-pennar-uchaf	Rho Cyn Taf	SO0302	51°42·7′	3°23·9′W	X	170
Cefn Pentre	Gwyn	SH3740	52°56·2′	4°25·1′W	X	123
Cefn-pentre	Powys	SJ1611	52°41·7′	3°14·2′W	X	125
Cefn Pen-y-bont	Powys	SN8651	52°9·0′	3°39·6′W	H	147
Cefn Peraidd	Gwyn	SH5241	52°57·0′	4°11·8′W	X	124
Cefnperfa	Powys	SO1289	52°29·7′	3°17·4′W	X	136
Cefn Perfedd	Powys	SN9316	51°50·2′	3°32·8′W	X	160
Cefn Perfedd	Powys	SN9420	51°52·3′	3°32·0′W	X	160
Cefn-perfedd	Powys	SO0146	52°6·4′	3°26·3′W	X	147
Cefn-poeth	I of Angl	SH4974	53°14·7′	4°15·4′W	X	114,115
Cefn-poeth	Powys	SN9851	52°9·1′	3°29·1′W	X	147
Cefn Pool	Powys	SO0880	52°24·9′	3°20·8′W	W	136
Cefn Post	Conwy	SH9948	53°1·4′	3°29·9′W	X	116
Cefn Pwll-coch	Powys	SO1614	51°49·3′	3°12·7′W	X	161
Cefnpwllhen	Carm	SN8234	51°59·8′	3°42·7′W	X	160
Cefn Pyllau-duon	Blae Gw	SO1011	51°47·7′	3°17·9′W	X	161
Cefn Rhigos	Rho Cyn Taf	SN9106	51°44·8′	3°34·3′W	T	160
Cefnrhos-gwawr	Rho Cyn Taf	SN9701	51°42·1′	3°29·0′W	X	170
Cefn Rhouniarth	Powys	SJ2114	52°43·3′	3°9·8′W	X	126
Cefn-rhudd	Conwy	SH8558	53°6·7′	3°42·7′W	H	116
Cefn Rhudd	Powys	SN8220	51°52·2′	3°42·4′W	X	160
Cefnrhuddlan Uchaf	Cered	SN5044	52°4·7′	4°10·9′W	X	146
Cefn Rhydoldog	Powys	SN9368	52°18·2′	3°33·8′W	X	136,147
Cefn Rhyswg	Caer	ST2394	51°38·6′	3°6·4′W	X	171
Cefnrickett	Carm	SN7636	52°0·8′	3°48·0′W	X	146,160
Cefn Rofft	Denb	SJ0049	53°2·0′	3°29·1′W	X	116
Cefn-Roger	I of Angl	SH4282	53°18·9′	4°21·9′W	X	114,115
Cefns	Shrops	SO2783	52°26·6′	3°4·0′W	X	137
Cefn-Saeson	Nth Pt Talb	SS7796	51°39·2′	3°46·3′W	X	170
Cefn Sarnau	Powys	SO0133	51°59·4′	3°26·1′W	X	160
Cefn Sidan Sands	Carm	SN3405	51°43·4′	4°23·8′W	X	159
Cefn-suran	Powys	SO2271	52°20·1′	3°8·3′W	X	137,148
Cefn Sychbant	Rho Cyn Taf	SN9810	51°47·0′	3°28·3′W	X	160
Cefn Tan-y-graig	Conwy	SH9557	53°6·2′	3°33·7′W	H	116
Cefn Tarenni Cochion	Powys	SO0615	51°49·8′	3°21·5′W	H	160
Cefntelych	Carm	SN7932	51°58·6′	3°45·3′W	X	146,160
Cefn Tilla	Monm	ST3295	51°39·2′	2°58·6′W	X	171
Cefntilla Court	Monm	SO4002	51°43·0′	2°51·7′W	X	171
Cefn-treflech	Conwy	SH9469	53°12·7′	3°34·8′W	X	116
Cefn Trefor	Denb	SJ0256	53°5·8′	3°27·4′W	H	116
Cefn-trefor-fawr	Gwyn	SH6236	52°54·5′	4°2·7′W	X	124
Cefntrefor-isaf	Gwyn	SH4845	52°59·1′	4°15·5′W	X	115,123
Cefn-trenfa	Carm	SN7438	52°1·8′	3°49·8′W	X	146,160
Cefntreuddyn	Gwyn	SH2235	52°53·2′	4°38·3′W	X	123
Cefn Tre-ysbyty or Mynydd St John	Powys	SH9720	52°46·3′	3°31·2′W	H	125
Cefn Trum yr Hwch	Powys	SN9940	52°3·2′	3°28·0′W	H	147,160
Cefn Trybeddgwilym	Powys	SN8447	52°6·8′	3°41·2′W	X	147
Cefn-twlch	Powys	SJ1000	52°35·7′	3°19·3′W	X	136
Cefntwrch	Powys	SN9029	51°57·2′	3°35·6′W	X	160
Cefn Twrch	Powys	SN9031	51°58·2′	3°35·7′W	H	160
Cefntyle-brych	Nth Pt Talb	SN9001	51°42·1′	3°35·1′W	X	170
Cefntyncoed	Cered	SN4662	52°14·3′	4°14·9′W	X	146
Cefn Ty'n-y-graig	Powys	SN8052	52°9·4′	3°44·9′W	X	147
Cefn Ucha	Shrops	SJ2222	52°47·6′	3°9·0′W	X	126
Cefn-uchaf	Nth Pt Talb	SN8907	51°45·3′	3°36·1′W	X	160
Cefn Uchaf	Powys	SJ1525	52°49·2′	3°15·3′W	X	125
Cefn Uchaf	Powys	SN8349	52°7·9′	3°42·2′W	X	147
Cefn Uchaf	Wrex	SJ1938	52°56·2′	3°11·9′W	X	125
Cefnucheldre	Carm	SN7232	51°58·5′	3°51·4′W	X	146,160
Cefnvaes Fm	Nth Pt Talb	SS7599	51°40·8′	3°48·1′W	FM	170
Cefn Vaynor	Powys	SO1499	52°35·2′	3°15·8′W	X	136
Cefn Vron Hill	Shrops	SO1683	52°26·6′	3°13·8′W	H	136
Cefn Waun-lwyd	Powys	SN8652	52°9·5′	3°39·6′W	H	147
Cefn-wig	Cered	SN4761	52°13·8′	4°14·0′W	X	146
Cefn Wylfre	Powys	SO1451	52°9·3′	3°15·0′W	H	148
Cefnwyrygrug	Powys	SN8196	52°33·2′	3°44·9′W	X	135,136
Cefn-y-bedd	Flint	SJ3156	53°6·0′	3°1·4′W	T	117
Cefnybidwal	Denb	SJ1247	53°1·0′	3°18·3′W	X	116
Cefn-y-blaen	Powys	SO2047	52°7·2′	3°9·7′W	H	148
Cefn y blodwel	Shrops	SJ2424	52°48·7′	3°7·3′W	X	126
Cefn-y-braich	Powys	SJ1927	52°50·3′	3°11·7′W	X	125
Cefn-y-braich	Wrex	SJ1933	52°53·5′	3°11·8′W	X	125
Cefn y Brithdir	Caer	SO1203	51°43·4′	3°16·1′W	H	171
Cefn y Bryn	Carm	SN7043	52°4·4′	3°53·4′W	H	146,147,160
Cefn-y-bryn	Powys	SO0992	52°31·3′	3°20·1′W	X	136
Cefn-y-bwlch	Powys	SN9382	52°25·8′	3°34·0′W	X	136
Cefn y Capel	Conwy	SH7058	53°6·4′	3°56·1′W	X	115
Cefn-y-castell	Conwy	SH8763	53°9·4′	3°41·0′W	X	116
Cefnycerrig	Conwy	SH6754	53°4·2′	3°58·7′W	X	115
Cefn y Clawdd	Gwyn	SH7614	52°42·8′	3°49·7′W	X	124
Cefn-y-coed	Denb	SJ1643	52°58·9′	3°14·7′W	X	125
Cefn-y-coed	Gwyn	SH4660	53°7·1′	4°17·7′W	X	114,115
Cefn y Coed	Powys	SJ2024	52°48·7′	3°10·8′W	H	126
Cefn-y-coed	Powys	SO1993	52°32·0′	3°11·2′W	X	136
Cefn-y-coed Common	Carm	SN7026	51°55·3′	3°53·0′W	X	146,160
Cefn-y-Coed Isaf	Conwy	SH7868	53°12·0′	3°49·2′W	X	115
Cefn y Cylchau	Carm	SN7519	51°51·6′	3°48·5′W	H	160
Cefnydd	Gwyn	SH3342	52°57·2′	4°28·8′W	X	123
Cefn Ydfa	Brig	SS8786	51°33·9′	3°37·4′W	X	170
Cefn-y-don	Nth Pt Talb	SS7698	51°40·3′	3°47·2′W	X	170
Cefn-y-don	Rho Cyn Taf	SN9605	51°44·3′	3°30·0′W	X	160
Cefnydre	Pemb	SM9635	51°58·8′	4°57·8′W	X	157
Cefn y Fan	Merth Tyd	ST0698	51°40·6′	3°21·2′W	X	170
Cefn-y-fedw	Wrex	SJ2443	52°59·0′	3°7·5′W	X	117
Cefn-y-ffynnon	Conwy	SH8677	53°16·9′	3°42·2′W	X	116
Cefn-y-gader	Denb	SJ1050	53°2·6′	3°20·1′W	X	116
Cefn-y-gadfa	Conwy	SH8653	53°4·0′	3°41·7′W	X	116
Cefn-y-gaer	Cered	SN5361	52°13·9′	4°8·8′W	X	146
Cefn y Galchan	Monm	SO2610	51°47·3′	3°4·0′W	X	161

Cefn-y-garth	Powys	SO0543	52°4·9′	3°22·8′W	X	147,160
Cefn-y-Garth	Swan	SN7000	51°41·3′	3°52·5′W	T	170
Cefn-y-gefail	Carm	SN7838	52°1·9′	3°46·3′W	X	146,160
Cefn-y-groes-fawr	Conwy	SH9166	53°11·0′	3°37·5′W	X	116
Cefn-y-grug	Powys	SO1664	52°16·3′	3°13·5′W	H	148
Cefn-y-maes	Gwyn	SH8536	52°54·8′	3°42·2′W	X	124,125
Cefn-y-maes	Powys	SO0059	52°13·4′	3°27·4′W	X	147
Cefn-y-maes	Shrops	SJ2332	52°53·0′	3°8·3′W	X	126
Cefn-y-Meirch	Gwyn	SH9732	52°52·8′	3°31·4′W	X	125
Cefn Ynys-fawr	Merth Tyd	SO0114	51°49·2′	3°25·8′W	X	160
Cefn-y-pant	Carm	SN1925	51°53·9′	4°37·5′W	T	145,158
Cefn-y-parc	Powys	SO0028	51°56·7′	3°26·9′W	X	160
Cefn yr Arail	Blae Gw	SO1905	51°44·5′	3°10·0′W	X	161
Cefn yr Argoed	Nth Pt Talb	SS8294	51°38·2′	3°41·9′W	X	170
Cefn-yr-eryri	Powys	SO1772	52°20·6′	3°12·7′W	X	136,148
Cefn yr Esgair	Cered	SN7488	52°28·8′	3°50·9′W	H	135
Cefn yr Henriw	Powys	SN9718	51°51·3′	3°29·3′W	X	160
Cefn-y-rhodfa	Powys	SJ1230	52°51·9′	3°18·0′W	X	125
Cefn y Rhondda	Rho Cyn Taf	SS9797	51°40·0′	3°29·0′W	X	170
Cefn-yr-iwrch	Denb	SJ0757	53°6·4′	3°22·9′W	X	116
Cefn yr Ogof	Conwy	SH9177	53°17·0′	3°37·7′W	H	116
Cefn-yr-Owen	Gwyn	SH6815	52°43·2′	3°56·9′W	X	124
Cefnyrysgub	Carm	SN5723	51°53·5′	4°4·3′W	X	159
Cefn yr Ystrad	Powys	SO0813	51°48·7′	3°19·7′W	H	160
Cefnysgwydd Bach	I of Angl	SH3375	53°15·0′	4°29·8′W	X	114
Cefn Ystrad-ffin	Carm	SN8147	52°6·8′	3°43·9′W	H	147
Cefn y Truman	Carm	SN7419	51°51·6′	3°49·4′W	X	160
Cefn-y-wern-isaf	Powys	SO1428	51°56·9′	3°14·7′W	X	161
Cegidfa or Guilsfield	Powys	SJ2211	52°41·7′	3°8·8′W	T	126
Ceginan	Cered	SN3946	52°5·6′	4°20·6′W	X	145
Cei-bach	Cered	SN4059	52°12·6′	4°20·1′W	X	146
Cei Ballast	Gwyn	SH5737	52°54·9′	4°7·2′W	X	124
Ceibwr Bay	Pemb	SN1045	52°4·5′	4°46·0′W	W	145
Ceidio	I of Angl	SH4085	53°20·5′	4°23·8′W	X	114
Ceidio Bach	Gwyn	SH2837	52°54·4′	4°33·1′W	X	123
Cei Llydan Sta	Gwyn	SH5761	53°7·9′	4°7·8′W	X	114,115
Ceint	I of Angl	SH4874	53°14·7′	4°16·3′W	X	114,115
Ceinws	Powys	SH7605	52°38·0′	3°49·5′W	T	124
Ceiriog Ddu	Wrex	SJ1238	52°56·2′	3°18·2′W	W	125
Ceiriog Forest	Wrex	SJ1538	52°56·2′	3°15·5′W	F	125
Ceiro	Cered	SN7582	52°25·5′	3°49·9′W	X	135
Ceiswyn	Gwyn	SH7410	52°40·6′	3°51·4′W	X	124
Ceithinis	N Eil	NF8964	57°33·8′	7°11·6′W	X	18
Celfyddifan	Brig	SS8887	51°34·5′	3°36·6′W	X	170
Cellan	Cered	SN6149	52°7·6′	4°1·4′W	T	146
Cellardyke	Fife	NO5703	56°13·3′	2°41·2′W	T	59
Cellar Fm	Gwyn	SH2532	52°51·7′	4°35·6′W	FM	123
Cellarhead	Staffs	SJ9547	53°1·5′	2°4·1′W	T	118
Cellarhill	Kent	TQ9562	51°19·6′	0°48·3′E	T	178
Cellar, The	Shetld	HU4623	59°59·6′	1°10·0′W	X	4
Celleron	Cumbr	NY4925	54°37·3′	2°47·0′W	X	90
Cell Howel	Pemb	SN0843	52°3·4′	4°47·6′W	X	145
Cellifor	Carm	SN5617	51°50·2′	4°5·0′W	X	159
Cellws	Powys	SO0763	52°15·7′	3°21·4′W	X	147
Celmi	Gwyn	SH5904	52°37·2′	4°4·6′W	X	135
Celsau	Powys	SN9152	52°9·6′	3°35·2′W	X	147
Celyn	Gwyn	SH5663	53°8·9′	4°8·8′W	X	114,115
Celyn Fm	Flint	SJ2368	53°12·5′	3°8·8′W	FM	117
Celyn Fm	Flint	SJ2560	53°8·2′	3°6·9′W	FM	117
Celyn Fm	Monm	SO4121	51°53·3′	2°51·0′W	FM	161
Celyn-Mali	Flint	SJ1766	53°11·3′	3°14·1′W	T	116
Celynog	Powys	SJ1225	52°49·2′	3°17·9′W	X	125
Celynog Hill	Powys	SO0597	52°34·0′	3°23·7′W	H	136
Cemaes	Gwyn	SH6106	52°38·3′	4°2·9′W	X	124
Cemaes	I of Angl	SH3693	53°24·7′	4°27·6′W	T	114
Cemaes	I of Angl	SH3874	53°14·5′	4°25·3′W	X	114
Cemaes Bay	I of Angl	SH3694	53°25·3′	4°27·7′W	W	114
Cemaes Head	Pemb	SN1350	52°7·2′	4°43·5′W	X	145
Cemig	Conwy	SH9644	52°59·2′	3°32·6′W	W	125
Cemlyn Bay	I of Angl	SH3393	53°24·7′	4°30·3′W	W	114
Cemmaes	Powys	SH8306	52°38·6′	3°43·4′W	T	124,125
Cemmaes Road	Powys	SH8204	52°37·5′	3°44·2′W	T	135,136
Cenarth	Cered	SN2641	52°2·6′	4°31·8′W	T	145
Cencoed-uchaf	Carm	SN4803	51°42·5′	4°11·6′W	X	159
Ceniarth Fm	Powys	SN7797	52°33·7′	3°48·5′W	FM	135
Cennant	Cered	SN6977	52°22·8′	3°55·1′W	X	135
Cennin	Gwyn	SH4644	52°58·5′	4°17·2′W	X	123
Cenrhos	Carm	SN4402	51°41·9′	4°15·1′W	X	159
Centenary Circle	Essex	TL6808	51°45·0′	0°26·4′E	X	167
Centenary Walk	Essex	TQ4097	51°39·5′	0°1·8′E	X	167,177
Centenary Walk	Kent	TQ7358	51°17·9′	0°29·3′E	X	178,188
Centenary Walk	Redbr	TQ3993	51°37·3′	0°0·9′E	X	177
Centenary Walk Maidstone	Kent	TQ7660	51°18·9′	0°31·9′E	X	178,188
Centenary Walk Rochester	Medway	TQ7367	51°22·8′	0°29·6′E	X	178
Centenary Way	Warw	SP3763	52°16·1′	1°27·1′W	X	151
Centery Fm	Devon	SS5442	51°9·8′	4°4·9′W	FM	180
Central	Inverc	NS2775	55°56·5′	4°45·8′W	T	63
Central Fm	Northnts	SP5751	52°9·5′	1°9·6′W	FM	152
Central Forest Park	C of Stoke	SJ8848	53°2·0′	2°10·3′W	X	118
Central Milton Keynes	Mil Key	SP8438	52°2·3′	0°46·1′W	T	152
Central Milton Keynes	Mil Key	SP8538	52°2·3′	0°45·2′W	T	152
Central Park	C of Plym	SX4756	50°23·3′	4°8·8′W	X	201
Central Pier	Blackp	SD3035	53°48·6′	3°3·4′W	X	102
Central Sta	C of Glas	NS5865	55°51·7′	4°15·7′W	X	64
Central Sta	Sou-on-Sea	TQ8885	51°32·2′	0°43·0′E	X	178
Centre Fm	Lancs	SD4752	53°57·9′	2°48·1′W	FM	102
Centre for Alternative Technology	Powys	SH7504	52°37·4′	3°50·4′W	X	135
Centre of Rural Economy	Midlo	NT2463	55°51·5′	3°12·4′W	X	66
Centre Tree	Notts	SK6067	53°12·0′	1°5·7′W	X	120
Centry	Devon	SX7445	50°17·7′	3°45·8′W	X	202
Ceol na mara	Highld	NM7561	56°41·3′	5°40·0′W	X	40
Ceòs	N Eil	NB3521	58°6·2′	6°29·4′W	T	14
Ceosabh	Arg & Bt	NL9742	56°28·6′	6°54·8′W	X	46
Cerbid	Pemb	SM8227	51°54·2′	5°9·8′W	X	157
Cerbynau	Carm	SN4930	51°57·1′	4°11·4′W	X	146
Ceres	Fife	NO4011	56°17·5′	2°57·7′W	T	59
Ceres Burn	Fife	NO4113	56°18·6′	2°56·8′W	W	59
Ceres Lodge	Notts	SK6269	53°13·1′	1°3·9′W	X	120

Ceres Moor	Fife	NO3913	56°18·6′	2°58·7′W	X	59
Ceres Rock	Corn	SW5741	50°13·4′	5°24·0′W	X	203
Cerig Brith	I of Angl	SH3493	53°24·7′	4°29·4′W	X	114
Cerist	Gwyn	SH8416	52°44·0′	3°42·7′W	H	124,125
Cerist	Powys	SN9688	52°29·0′	3°31·5′W	X	136
Cerne Abbas	Dorset	ST6601	50°48·7′	2°28·6′W	T	194
Cerne Abbey	Dorset	ST6601	50°48·7′	2°28·6′W	A	194
Cerne Park	Dorset	ST6401	50°48·7′	2°30·3′W	F	194
Cernes Fm	Surrey	TQ4244	51°10·9′	0°2·3′E	FM	187
Cerney Ho	Glos	SP0107	51°45·9′	1°58·7′W	X	163
Cerney Wick	Glos	SU0796	51°40·0′	1°53·5′W	T	163
Cerniach	Conwy	SH8162	53°8·8′	3°46·4′W	X	116
Cerniau	Gwyn	SH7524	52°48·2′	3°50·9′W	H	124
Cerniau	Powys	SH9516	52°44·1′	3°32·9′W	X	125
Cerniau	Powys	SJ0013	52°42·6′	3°28·4′W	X	125
Cernioge	Conwy	SH9150	53°2·4′	3°37·1′W	X	116
Cerniog Ganol	Gwyn	SH3240	52°56·1′	4°29·6′W	X	123
Cernyfed	Denb	SJ0358	53°6·9′	3°26·6′W	X	116
Cerrig	Pemb	SN0337	52°0·0′	4°51·8′W	X	145,157
Cerrig Arthur	Gwyn	SH6318	52°44·8′	4°1·4′W	A	124
Cerrig Cafael	I of Angl	SH3774	53°14·5′	4°26·2′W	X	114
Cerrig-calch	Denb	SJ1751	53°3·2′	3°13·9′W	X	116
Cerrig Camog	I of Angl	SH3387	53°21·5′	4°30·2′W	X	114
Cerrig Caws	Denb	SH9556	53°5·7′	3°33·7′W	H	116
Cerrig Cedny	Carm	SN8046	52°6·2′	3°44·7′W	A	147
Cerrigceinwen	I of Angl	SH4273	53°14·1′	4°21·6′W	T	114,115
Cerrig Chwibanog	Gwyn	SH8230	52°51·5′	3°44·8′W	X	124,125
Cerrig Cochion	Gwyn	SH6651	53°2·6′	3°59·5′W	X	115
Cerrig Coediog	Wrex	SJ1138	52°56·2′	3°19·1′W	H	125
Cerrigcroes	Powys	SO0361	52°14·6′	3°24·8′W	X	147
Cerrig Cŵn	Powys	SH9214	52°43·0′	3°35·5′W	X	125
Cerrigcwplau	Powys	SN8663	52°15·4′	3°39·8′W	X	147
Cerrig Cyffion	Carm	SN6847	52°6·6′	3°55·3′W	H	146
Cerrig-duon	I of Angl	SH3964	53°9·2′	4°24·1′W	X	114
Cerrig Duon	Pemb	SM9939	52°1·0′	4°55·4′W	X	157
Cerrig Duon	Powys	SJ0530	52°51·8′	3°24·3′W	X	125
Cerrig-Duon	Wrex	SJ1238	52°56·2′	3°18·2′W	X	125
Cerrig Edmwnt	Powys	SO0519	51°51·9′	3°22·4′W	X	160
Cerrigellgwm Isaf	Conwy	SH8548	53°1·3′	3°42·5′W	X	116
Cerrigellgwm Uchaf	Conwy	SH8547	53°0·7′	3°42·4′W	X	116
Cerrig Engan	I of Angl	SH4073	53°14·0′	4°23·4′W	X	114,115
Cerrig Gwalch	Powys	SN9370	52°19·3′	3°33·6′W	X	136,147
Cerrig Gwaun-y-llan	Powys	SN8678	52°23·5′	3°40·1′W	H	135,136,147
Cerrig Gwinau	Powys	SN8564	52°16·0′	3°40·7′W	X	147
Cerrig Gwylan	Pemb	SM7932	51°56·8′	5°12·6′W	X	157
Cerrig Gwynion	Conwy	SH7274	53°15·1′	3°54·7′W	X	115
Cerrig Gwynion	Powys	SN9765	52°16·7′	3°30·2′W	X	136,147
Cerrig Lladron	Pemb	SN0632	51°57·4′	4°49·0′W	H	145
Cerrig Llwydion	Carm	SN3732	51°58·0′	4°22·0′W	X	145
Cerrig-llwydion	Gwyn	SH9033	52°53·2′	3°37·7′W	X	125
Cerrig Llwydion	Nth Pt Talb	SS7894	51°38·1′	3°45·4′W	T	170
Cerrig Llwydion	Powys	SN9173	52°20·9′	3°35·6′W	X	136,147
Cerrig Llwydion (Burial Chamber)	Carm	SN3732	51°58·0′	4°22·0′W	A	145
Cerrigllwydion Hall	Denb	SJ1063	53°9·6′	3°20·4′W	X	116
Cerrig Llwyd y Rhestr	Powys	SN8460	52°13·8′	3°41·5′W	X	147
Cerrig Maesycawnau	Cered	SN7658	52°12·6′	3°48·5′W	X	146,147
Cerrig-mân	I of Angl	SH4591	53°23·8′	4°19·5′W	T	114
Cerrig Mân	Swan	SS5494	51°37·8′	4°6·2′W	X	159
Cerrig-mawr	I of Angl	SH3964	53°9·2′	4°24·1′W	X	114
Cerrig-myna	I of Angl	SH3773	53°14·0′	4°26·1′W	X	114
Cerrig-oerion	Denb	SJ0555	53°5·3′	3°24·7′W	X	116
Cerrig-tranau	Cered	SN6390	52°29·7′	4°0·7′W	X	135
Cerrig y Barcdy	Gwyn	SH4335	52°53·6′	4°19·6′W	X	123
Cerrig-y-brain	I of Angl	SH3172	53°13·3′	4°31·5′W	X	114
Cerrig y Cledd	Gwyn	SH6419	52°45·4′	4°0·5′W	X	124
Cerrigydrudion	Conwy	SH9548	53°1·4′	3°33·5′W	T	116
Cerrig y Gof	Pemb	SN0338	52°0·6′	4°51·8′W	A	145,157
Cerrig y Gordref	Gwyn	SH9343	52°58·7′	3°35·2′W	X	125
Cerrig-y-gorllwyn	Gwyn	SH6214	52°42·6′	4°2·2′W	X	124
Cerrig y Gwŷr	I of Angl	SH2782	53°18·6′	4°35·4′W	X	114
Cerrig-y-Gwŷr	I of Angl	SH3073	53°13·9′	4°32·4′W	X	114
Cerrig y Ieirch	Gwyn	SH7542	52°57·9′	3°51·3′W	X	124
Cerrigypenrhyn	Cered	SN6095	52°32·3′	4°3·5′W	X	135
Cerrig yr Hafan	Cered	SN7388	52°28·8′	3°51·8′W	H	135
Cerrig-y-rhwydwr	Gwyn	SH5943	52°58·2′	4°5·6′W	X	124
Cerrig yr Iwrch	Gwyn	SH8229	52°51·0′	3°44·7′W	X	124,125
Cerrig yr Wyn	Powys	SN8186	52°27·8′	3°44·7′W	X	135,136
Cerrig y Tân	Powys	SH9104	52°37·6′	3°36·2′W	X	136
Cesail-gwm	Denb	SJ1444	52°59·4′	3°16·5′W	X	125
Cesailgwm	Gwyn	SH6921	52°46·5′	3°56·1′W	X	124
Cesailgwm	Conwy	SH9543	52°58·7′	3°33·4′W	X	125
Ceseiliau Moelwyn	Gwyn	SH6644	52°58·8′	3°59·4′W	X	124
Cesig duon	Pemb	SN0540	52°1·7′	4°50·2′W	X	145
Cess	Norf	TG4417	52°42·0′	1°37·1′E	T	134
Cessbank Common	Ches	SJ9568	53°12·8′	2°4·1′W	X	118
Cessford	Scot Bord	NT7323	55°30·3′	2°25·2′W	X	74
Cessford Burn	Scot Bord	NT7322	55°29·7′	2°25·2′W	W	74
Cessford Moor	Scot Bord	NT7223	55°30·2′	2°26·2′W	X	74
Cesslands	Essex	TL5100	51°40·9′	0°11·4′E	X	167
Cessnock Castle	E Ayr	NS5135	55°35·4′	4°21·4′W	A	70
Cessnock Water	E Ayr	NS4732	55°33·7′	4°25·1′W	W	70
Cessnock Water	E Ayr	NS5329	55°32·2′	4°19·3′W	W	70
Cestersover Fm	Warw	SP5081	52°25·7′	1°15·5′W	FM	140
Cestyll	I of Angl	SH3493	53°24·7′	4°29·4′W	X	114
Cesyg Aled	Conwy	SH9258	53°6·7′	3°36·4′W	X	116
Cethin Fm	Carm	SN2620	51°51·3′	4°31·2′W	FM	145,158
Ceulanau	Powys	SO1286	52°28·1′	3°17·3′W	X	136
Ceum Garbh	Highld	NG8109	57°7·4′	5°36·6′W	X	33
Ceum na Caillich	N Ayr	NR9744	55°39·1′	5°13·2′W	X	62,69
Ceunant	Gwyn	SH5361	53°7·8′	4°11·4′W	T	114,115
Ceunant	Powys	SH9909	52°40·4′	3°29·2′W	X	125
Ceunant	Powys	SJ0507	52°39·4′	3°23·9′W	X	125
Ceunant	Powys	SJ0618	52°45·3′	3°23·2′W	X	125
Ceunant	Powys	SJ2314	52°43·3′	3°8·0′W	X	126
Ceunant Bach	Gwyn	SH5758	53°6·2′	4°7·8′W	X	115
Ceunant Coch	Denb	SJ0331	52°52·3′	3°26·1′W	W	125
Ceunant-du	Powys	SJ1728	52°50·8′	3°13·5′W	X	125
Ceunant Geifr	Gwyn	SH6637	52°55·1′	3°59·2′W	X	124
Ceunant Llennyrch	Gwyn	SH6638	52°55·6′	3°59·2′W	X	124

Ceunant Mawr	Conwy	SH7645	52°59·5′	3°50·4′W	X	115
Ceunant Mawr	Gwyn	SH6653	53°3·7′	3°59·6′W	X	115
Ceunant Ty'n-y-ddol	Conwy	SH6852	53°3·2′	3°57·8′W	W	115
Ceunant y Briddell	Gwyn	SH8922	52°47·3′	3°38·4′W	X	124,125
Ceunant y Ddôl	Gwyn	SH5345	52°59·2′	4°11·0′W	W	115
Ceunant-y-Garnedd	Conwy	SH7052	53°3·2′	3°56·0′W	W	115
Ceunant y Gaseg	Gwyn	SH7737	52°55·2′	3°49·4′W	W	124
Cgreagan Glasa	N Eil	NB2008	57°58·7′	6°43·7′W	X	13,14
Chaa-ans, The	Shetld	HU3475	60°27·7′	1°22·4′W	X	2,3
Chabet Water	Moray	NJ1624	57°18·2′	3°23·2′W	W	36
Chaceley	Glos	SO8530	51°58·3′	2°12·7′W	T	150
Chaceley Hole	Glos	SO8430	51°58·3′	2°13·6′W	T	150
Chaceley Stock	Glos	SO8629	51°57·8′	2°11·8′W	T	150
Chace Stud Fm	Surrey	TQ1856	51°17·7′	0°18·1′W	FM	187
Chacewater	Corn	SW7544	50°15·4′	5°9·0′W	T	204
Chackmore	Bucks	SP6835	52°0·8′	1°0·2′W	T	152
Chacombe	Northnts	SP4943	52°5·2′	1°16·7′W	T	151
Chacombe Hill Fm	Northnts	SP5043	52°5·2′	1°15·8′W	FM	151
Chacombe Ho	Northnts	SP4943	52°5·2′	1°16·7′W	X	151
Chacombe Lodge Fm	Northnts	SP5144	52°5·8′	1°14·9′W	FM	151
Chadacre Park	Suff	TL8552	52°8·3′	0°42·6′E	X	155
Chad Brook	Suff	TL8650	52°7·2′	0°43·4′E	W	155
Chadbury	Worcs	SP0146	52°7·0′	1°58·7′W	T	150
Chadderton	Oldham	SD9005	53°32·7′	2°8·6′W	T	109
Chadderton Fold	Oldham	SD8906	53°33·3′	2°9·6′W	T	109
Chadderton Heights	Oldham	SD8907	53°33·8′	2°9·6′W	X	109
Chaddesden	C of Derb	SK3737	52°56·0′	1°26·6′W	T	128
Chaddesley Corbett	Worcs	SO8973	52°21·5′	2°9·3′W	T	139
Chaddesley Wood	Worcs	SO9073	52°21·5′	2°8·4′W	F	139
Chaddesley Wood Fm	Worcs	SO9073	52°21·5′	2°8·4′W	FM	139
Chaddlehanger	Devon	SX4677	50°34·6′	4°10·1′W	T	201
Chaddlewood	C of Plym	SX5556	50°23·4′	4°2·0′W	T	202
Chaddleworth	W Berks	SU4177	51°29·7′	1°24·2′W	T	174
Chaddleworth Ho	W Berks	SU4177	51°29·7′	1°24·2′W	X	174
Chadhurst Fm	Surrey	TQ1546	51°12·3′	0°20·8′W	FM	187
Chadkirk	Stock	SJ9489	53°24·1′	2°5·0′W	T	109
Chadley Ho	Warw	SP2653	52°10·7′	1°36·8′W	X	151
Chadlington	Oxon	SP3221	51°53·4′	1°31·7′W	T	164
Chadnor Court	Heref	SO4352	52°10·0′	2°49·6′W	X	148,149
Chadshunt	Warw	SP3452	52°10·1′	1°29·8′W	T	151
Chadsmoor	Staffs	SJ9811	52°42·0′	2°1·4′W	T	127
Chadstone	Northnts	SP8558	52°13·1′	0°44·9′W	T	152
Chadswell	Lancs	SD6742	53°52·6′	2°29·7′W	X	103
Chad Valley	Birm	SP0485	52°28·0′	1°56·1′W	T	139
Chadwell	Leic	SK7824	52°48·7′	0°50·2′W	T	129
Chadwell	Shrops	SJ7814	52°43·6′	2°19·1′W	T	127
Chadwell End	Beds	TL0865	52°16·6′	0°24·6′W	T	153
Chadwell Fm	Bucks	SP8730	51°57·9′	0°43·6′W	FM	152,165
Chadwell Heath	Bark & Dag	TQ4888	51°34·5′	0°8·5′E	T	177
Chadwell Hill	Bucks	SP7905	51°44·5′	0°51·0′W	X	165
Chadwell Mill	Shrops	SJ7814	52°43·6′	2°19·1′W	X	127
Chadwell Place	Thurr	TQ6378	51°28·9′	0°21·2′E	X	177
Chadwell St Mary	Thurr	TQ6478	51°28·9′	0°22·1′E	T	177
Chadwich Grange Fm	Worcs	SO9777	52°23·7′	2°2·2′W	FM	139
Chadwich Manor	Worcs	SO9776	52°23·2′	2°2·2′W	A	139
Chadwick	Worcs	SO8369	52°19·4′	2°14·6′W	T	138
Chadwick End	Sol	SP2073	52°21·5′	1°42·0′W	T	139
Chadwick Green	St Hel	SJ5399	53°29·4′	2°42·1′W	T	108
Chadwick Manor	Sol	SP2074	52°22·1′	1°42·0′W	X	139
Chadwick's Fm	Wigan	SD6100	53°30·0′	2°34·9′W	FM	109
Chaenish	N Eil	NF9883	57°44·4′	7°4·0′W	X	18
Chafer Wood	N Yks	SE8983	54°14·3′	0°37·6′W	F	101
Chaffcombe	Somer	ST3510	50°53·4′	2°55·1′W	T	193
Chaffcombe Gate Fm	Somer	ST3510	50°53·4′	2°55·1′W	FM	193
Chaffcombe Manor Fm	Devon	SS7503	50°49·0′	3°46·1′W	FM	191
Chaffeigh Fm	Dorset	ST3804	50°50·2′	2°52·4′W	FM	193
Chaffeymoor	Dorset	ST7630	51°4·4′	2°20·2′W	X	183
Chaff Hall	Ches	SJ9165	53°11·2′	2°7·7′W	X	118
Chaffhay Fm	Devon	ST2506	50°51·2′	3°3·5′W	FM	192,193
Chaffix	Essex	TL6820	51°51·4′	0°26·8′E	X	167
Chaffold's Fm	Surrey	TQ2038	51°7·9′	0°16·7′W	FM	187
Chafford Fm	Kent	TQ5240	51°8·6′	0°10·8′E	FM	188
Chafford Hundred	Thurr	TQ5979	51°29·5′	0°17·8′E	T	177
Chafford Park	Kent	TQ5139	51°8·0′	0°9·9′E	X	188
Chagford	Devon	SX7087	50°40·3′	3°50·0′W	T	191
Chagford Common	Devon	SX6782	50°37·6′	3°52·4′W	X	191
Chagford Ho	Devon	SX7087	50°40·3′	3°50·0′W	X	191
Chaigley Farm	Lancs	SD6941	53°52·1′	2°27·9′W	FM	103
Chaigley Manor	Lancs	SD6941	53°52·1′	2°27·9′W	X	103
Chailey	E Susx	TQ3919	50°57·4′	0°0·9′W	T	198
Chain Br	Devon	SS9320	50°58·4′	3°31·1′W	X	181
Chain Br	Monm	SO3405	51°44·6′	2°57·0′W	X	161
Chainbridge	Cambs	TF4200	52°35·0′	0°6·2′E	T	142,143
Chain Bridge	Lincs	TF3043	52°58·3′	0°3·4′W	X	131
Chainbridge Fm	Essex	TQ6296	51°38·6′	0°20·9′E	FM	167,177
Chain Bridge Lane	Notts	SK7085	53°21·7′	0°56·5′W	X	120
Chain Dene Fm	Kent	TQ7447	51°12·0′	0°29·8′E	FM	188
Chain Fm	Norf	TL6091	52°29·8′	0°21·8′E	FM	143
Chain Heads	Northum	NU0505	55°20·6′	1°54·8′W	X	81
Chain Hill	Oxon	SU4087	51°35·1′	1°25·0′W	X	174
Chain Hill	Wilts	SU0837	51°8·2′	1°52·8′W	X	184
Chain Hill Fm	Oxon	SU4086	51°34·5′	1°25·0′W	FM	174
Chainhurst	Kent	TQ7347	51°12·0′	0°29·0′E	T	188
Chains Barrow	Somer	SS7341	51°9·5′	3°48·6′W	A	180
Chains Fm	Kent	TQ4850	51°14·0′	0°7·6′E	FM	188
Chains, The	Somer	SS7342	51°10·0′	3°48·6′W	X	180
Chain Walk	Herts	TL3335	52°0·1′	0°3·4′W	X	154
Chain Wood	D & G	NX4960	54°55·0′	4°20·9′W	F	83
Chaipaval	N Eil	NF9692	57°49·1′	7°6·7′W	H	18
Chair Carn	Corn	SW4036	50°10·3′	5°38·1′W	X	203
Chairford Bridge	Northum	NY9086	55°10·3′	2°9·0′W	X	80
Chair Hill	E Ayr	NS5105	55°19·2′	4°20·5′W	X	70,77
Chair of Lyde	Orkney	HY3518	59°2·9′	3°7·5′W	X	6
Chair, The	Corn	SW6617	50°0·7′	5°15·6′W	X	203
Chair, The	Corn	SW7113	49°58·6′	5°11·3′W	X	203
Chaites Fm	W Susx	TQ2621	50°58·7′	0°11·9′W	FM	198
Chalbury	Dorset	SU0106	50°51·4′	1°58·9′W	T	195
Chalbury	Dorset	SY6983	50°39·0′	2°25·9′W	A	194
Chalbury Common	Dorset	SU0206	50°51·4′	1°57·9′W	T	195
Chalbury Fm	Dorset	SU0107	50°52·0′	1°58·8′W	FM	195

Chalcot Ho	Wilts	ST8448	51°14·1′	2°13·4′W	X	183
Chalcott Fm	Somer	ST2344	51°11·6′	3°5·7′W	FM	182
Chalcroft Fm	Hants	SU4816	50°56·7′	1°18·6′W	FM	185
Chalcroft Hill	Somer	ST4947	51°13·4′	2°43·4′W	H	182,183
Chaldean Fm	Herts	TL4220	51°51·9′	0°4·1′E	FM	167
Chalder Fm	W Susx	SZ8699	50°47·3′	0°46·4′W	FM	197
Chalder Ness	Shetld	HU4350	60°14·2′	1°12·9′W	X	3
Chaldon	Surrey	TQ3155	51°17·0′	0°6·9′W	T	187
Chaldon Down	Dorset	SY7882	50°38·5′	2°18·3′W	X	194
Chaldon Fm	Devon	ST0304	50°49·9′	3°22·3′W	FM	192
Chaldon Herring or East Chaldon	Dorset	SY7983	50°39·0′	2°17·4′W	T	194
Chaldra Rock	Orkney	HY7037	59°13·4′	2°31·0′W	X	5
Chale	I of W	SZ4877	50°35·7′	1°18·9′W	T	196
Chale Bay	I of W	SZ4677	50°35·7′	1°20·6′W	W	196
Chale Green	I of W	SZ4879	50°36·8′	1°18·9′W	T	196
Chaleshurst	Surrey	SU9432	51°5·0′	0°39·1′W	X	186
Chalêt Fm	E Yorks	SE9867	54°5·6′	0°29·7′W	FM	101
Chalet, The	S Glos	ST6388	51°35·6′	2°31·7′W	X	162,172
Chalfont Centre	Bucks	TQ0092	51°37·3′	0°32·9′W	X	176
Chalfont Common	Bucks	TQ0092	51°37·3′	0°32·9′W	T	176
Chalfont Grove	Bucks	SU9891	51°36·8′	0°34·7′W	T	175,176
Chalfont & Latimer Sta	Bucks	SU9997	51°40·0′	0°33·7′W	X	165,176
Chalfont Lodge	Bucks	TQ0189	51°35·7′	0°32·1′W	X	176
Chalfont Park	Bucks	TQ0189	51°35·7′	0°32·1′W	X	176
Chalfont St Giles	Bucks	SU9893	51°37·9′	0°34·6′W	T	175,176
Chalfont St Peter	Bucks	TQ0090	51°36·2′	0°33·0′W	T	176
Chalford	Glos	SO8902	51°43·2′	2°9·2′W	T	163
Chalford	Oxon	SP7100	51°41·9′	0°58·0′W	T	165
Chalford	Wilts	ST8650	51°15·2′	2°11·6′W	T	183
Chalford Green	Oxon	SP3424	51°55·0′	1°29·9′W	X	164
Chalford Hill	Glos	SO8903	51°43·8′	2°9·2′W	T	163
Chalford Oaks Fm	Oxon	SP3426	51°56·1′	1°29·9′W	FM	164
Chalgrave	Beds	TL0127	51°56·2′	0°31·5′W	T	166
Chalgrave Manor	Beds	TL0127	51°56·2′	0°31·5′W	X	166
Chalgrove	Oxon	SU6396	51°39·8′	1°5·0′W	T	164,165
Chalgrove Airfield	Oxon	SU6398	51°40·9′	1°4·9′W	X	164,165
Chalgrove Common	Oxon	SU6399	51°41·4′	1°4·9′W	X	164,165
Chalgrove Field	Oxon	SU6497	51°40·3′	1°4·1′W	X	164,165
Chalgrove Fm	Oxon	SU6396	51°39·8′	1°5·0′W	FM	164,165
Chalk	Kent	TQ6773	51°26·1′	0°24·6′E	T	177,178
Chalk Beck	Cumbr	NY3345	54°48·0′	3°2·1′W	W	85
Chalkbridge	Cumbr	NY3344	54°47·4′	3°2·1′W	X	85
Chalk Croft Fm	Hants	SU3348	51°14·0′	1°31·3′W	FM	185
Chalkdell Fm	Herts	TL1913	51°48·4′	0°16·0′W	FM	166
Chalk End	Essex	TL6310	51°46·1′	0°22·1′E	T	167
Chalket Fm	Kent	TQ6240	51°8·4′	0°19·3′E	FM	188
Chalk Fm	Cambs	TL5660	52°13·2′	0°17·4′E	FM	154
Chalk Fm	Cambs	TL6373	52°20·1′	0°23·9′E	FM	154
Chalk Fm	E Susx	TQ5802	50°48·0′	0°14·9′E	FM	199
Chalk Fm	Norf	TF7710	52°39·8′	0°37·4′E	FM	132
Chalk Fm	Suff	TL6881	52°24·3′	0°28·6′E	FM	143
Chalkfoot	Cumbr	NY3348	54°49·6′	3°2·1′W	T	85
Chalk Ford	Devon	SX6868	50°30·1′	3°51·3′W	X	202
Chalkhall Fm	Norf	TL7389	52°28·5′	0°33·2′E	FM	143
Chalk-Hall Fm	Norf	TL8297	52°32·7′	0°41·4′E	FM	144
Chalk Hall Fm	Suff	TL8078	52°22·5′	0°39·1′E	FM	144
Chalkham Fm	E Susx	TQ4212	50°53·6′	0°1·5′E	FM	198
Chalk Hill	Beds	TL0023	51°54·0′	0°32·4′W	X	166
Chalk Hill	Glos	SP1226	51°56·2′	1°49·1′W	X	163
Chalk Hill	Herts	TL1224	51°54·4′	0°21·9′W	X	166
Chalk Hill	Herts	TL1526	51°55·5′	0°19·3′W	X	166
Chalk Hill	Norf	TF8241	52°56·4′	0°42·9′E	X	132
Chalkhill	Norf	TF8501	52°34·7′	0°44·2′E	T	144
Chalk Hill	Suff	TL7072	52°19·4′	0°30·1′E	H	154
Chalkhill Barn	Oxon	SU4285	51°34·0′	1°23·3′W	X	174
Chalk Hill Fm	Kent	TQ8845	51°10·6′	0°41·8′E	FM	189
Chalk Hill Fm	Norf	TF9541	52°56·1′	0°54·5′E	FM	132
Chalkhole Fm	Kent	TR3468	51°22·0′	1°22·1′E	FM	179
Chalkhouse Green	Oxon	SU7178	51°30·0′	0°58·2′W	T	175
Chalkhurst	Kent	TQ5364	51°21·5′	0°12·2′E	X	177,188
Chalkielaw	Scot Bord	NT8054	55°47·0′	2°18·7′W	X	67,74
Chalkieside	E Loth	NT3668	55°54·3′	3°1·0′W	X	66
Chalk Lane	Suff	TL8474	52°20·2′	0°42·5′E	X	144
Chalk Lodge	Cumbr	NY3447	54°49·1′	3°1·2′W	X	85
Chalkney Wood	Essex	TL8727	51°54·8′	0°43·5′E	F	168
Chalkpit Fm	W Berks	SU6273	51°27·4′	1°6·1′W	FM	175
Chalkpit Hill	Wilts	SU2249	51°14·6′	1°40·7′W	X	184
Chalk Pit Hollow	Northnts	TF0203	52°37·1′	0°29·2′W	X	141
Chalkplains Wood	Cumbr	NY3242	54°46·3′	3°3·0′W	F	85
Chalk Pool Hill	Leic	SK7017	52°45·0′	0°57·4′W	X	129
Chalk Rig Edge	D & G	NT0713	55°24·4′	3°27·7′W	H	78
Chalkshire	Bucks	SP8407	51°45·6′	0°46·6′W	T	165
Chalkside	Cumbr	NY3245	54°48·0′	3°3·0′W	X	85
Chalksole	Kent	TR2543	51°8·7′	1°13·4′E	T	179
Chalkvale	Hants	SU3831	51°4·9′	1°27·1′W	X	185
Chalk Water	Somer	SS8145	51°11·7′	3°41·8′W	W	181
Chalkway	Somer	ST3707	50°51·8′	2°53·3′W	T	193
Chalkwell	Kent	TQ8964	51°20·8′	0°43·2′E	T	178
Chalkwell	Sou-on-Sea	TQ8585	51°32·2′	0°40·5′E	T	178
Chalkwell Oaze	Sou-on-Sea	TQ8585	51°32·2′	0°40·5′E	X	178
Chalk Wood	Bexley	TQ4970	51°24·8′	0°9·0′E	F	177
Challaborough	Devon	SX6544	50°17·1′	3°53·3′W	T	202
Challabrook Fm	Devon	SX8077	50°35·1′	3°41·3′W	FM	191
Challacombe	Devon	SS5847	51°12·5′	4°1·6′W	X	180
Challacombe	Devon	SS6940	51°8·9′	3°52·0′W	X	180
Challacombe	Devon	SS7115	50°55·4′	3°49·7′W	X	180
Challacombe Common	Devon	SS6842	51°10·0′	3°52·9′W	X	180
Challacombe Down	Devon	SX6879	50°36·0′	3°51·5′W	H	191
Challacombe Mill	Devon	SS6840	51°8·9′	3°52·9′W	X	180
Challacombe Resr	Devon	SS6942	51°10·0′	3°52·0′W	W	180
Challands Fm	Notts	SK6552	53°3·9′	1°1·4′W	FM	120
Challan Hall	Lancs	SD4776	54°10·9′	2°48·3′W	X	97
Challenger Fm	Devon	ST2804	50°50·1′	3°1·0′W	FM	193
Challick Fm	Somer	ST0627	51°2·3′	3°20·1′W	FM	181
Challister	Shetld	HU5665	60°22·2′	0°58·6′W	T	2
Challister Ness	Shetld	HU5767	60°23·2′	0°57·5′W	X	2
Challoch	D & G	NX0263	54°55·6′	5°5·0′W	X	82
Challoch	D & G	NX0748	54°47·6′	4°59·7′W	X	82
Challoch	D & G	NX3866	54°58·0′	4°31·4′W	X	83

Challoch	D & G	NX3867	54°58·5′	4°31·4′W	T	83
Challoch Burn	D & G	NX3865	54°57·5′	4°31·4′W	W	83
Challochglass	D & G	NX2954	54°51·3′	4°39·4′W	X	82
Challochglass Moor	D & G	NX2955	54°51·9′	4°39·4′W	X	82
Challochglass Moss	D & G	NX2955	54°51·9′	4°39·4′W	X	82
Challoch-hill	D & G	NX0356	54°51·9′	5°3·8′W	X	82
Challoch Hill	D & G	NX1657	54°52·7′	4°51·7′W	H	82
Challochmunn	D & G	NX2253	54°50·7′	4°45·9′W	X	82
Challock	Kent	TR0050	51°13·1′	0°52·2′E	T	189
Challock Fm	Northnts	SP6645	52°6·2′	1°1·8′W	FM	152
Challon's Combe	Devon	SX6748	50°19·3′	3°51·7′W	X	202
Challonsleigh	Devon	SX5955	50°22·9′	3°58·6′W	X	202
Challow Fm	Dorset	SY9682	50°38·5′	2°3·0′W	FM	195
Challow Marsh Fm	Oxon	SU3790	51°36·7′	1°27·5′W	FM	164,174
Chalmers Hope	Orkney	HY2800	58°53·1′	3°14·5′W	W	6,7
Chalmers Slack	Moray	NJ4965	57°40·6′	2°50·8′W	X	28,29
Chalmerston	E Ayr	NS4623	55°28·9′	4°25·8′W	X	70
Chalmerston	Stir	NS7395	56°8·1′	4°2·2′W	X	57
Chalmington	Dorset	ST5900	50°48·1′	2°34·5′W	T	194
Chalton	Beds	TL0326	51°55·6′	0°29·7′W	T	166
Chalton	Beds	TL1450	52°8·4′	0°19·6′W	T	153
Chalton	Hants	SU7316	50°56·6′	0°57·3′W	T	197
Chalton Cross Fm	Beds	TL0325	51°55·1′	0°29·7′W	FM	166
Chalton Down	Hants	SU7217	50°57·1′	0°58·1′W	X	197
Chalton Down	Hants	SU7315	50°56·0′	0°57·3′W	H	197
Chalvedon	Essex	TQ7388	51°34·1′	0°30·2′E	T	178
Chalvey	Slough	SU9679	51°30·3′	0°36·6′W	T	175,176
Chalvington	E Susx	TQ5209	50°51·9′	0°10·0′E	T	199
Chalybeate Spring	Leic	SK8426	52°49·7′	0°44·8′W	W	130
Chalybeate Spring	N Lincs	SE9421	53°40·9′	0°34·2′W	W	106,112
Chalybeate Spring	N Yks	SD6471	54°8·3′	2°32·6′W	W	97
Chalybeate Spring	N Yks	SD6471	54°8·3′	2°32·6′W	W	97
Chambercombe	Devon	SS5247	51°12·4′	4°6·7′W	T	180
Chambercombe Manor	Devon	SS5346	51°11·9′	4°5·9′W	A	180
Chamber Fm	Derby	SK1079	53°18·7′	1°50·6′W	FM	119
Chamberhouse Fm	W Berks	SU5265	51°23·1′	1°14·8′W	FM	174
Chamberlain Knowe	Angus	NO5142	56°34·3′	2°47·4′W	X	54
Chamberlain's Buildings Fm	Suff	TL7477	52°22·0′	0°33·7′E	FM	143
Chamberlain's Covert	Staffs	SJ8218	52°45·8′	2°15·6′W	F	127
Chamberlayne's Fm	Dorset	SY8492	50°43·9′	2°13·2′W	FM	194
Chamberlaynes Fm	Essex	TL4531	51°57·7′	0°7·0′E	FM	167
Chamberlayne's Heath	Dorset	SY8391	50°43·3′	2°14·1′W	X	194
Chamberline Wood	Shrops	SO7676	52°23·1′	2°20·8′W	F	138
Chamber's Common	Cumbr	NY5434	54°42·2′	2°42·4′W	X	90
Chambers Court	Worcs	SO8435	52°1·0′	2°13·6′W	X	150
Chambers Fm	Cambs	TL4976	52°21·9′	0°11·7′E	FM	143
Chambers' Fm	Glos	SO8211	51°48·1′	2°15·3′W	FM	162
Chamber's Green	Kent	TQ9243	51°9·5′	0°45·1′E	T	189
Chambers Green Fm	Bucks	SP9006	51°45·0′	0°41·4′W	FM	165
Chambers Manor Fm	Essex	TL4304	51°43·2′	0°4·6′E	FM	167
Chambers Wall	Kent	TR2567	51°21·7′	1°14·3′E	X	179
Chamber's Wood	Lincs	TF1573	53°14·7′	0°16·2′W	F	121
Chamberwells	Angus	NO3642	56°34·2′	3°2·0′W	X	54
Chammen's Hill	Dorset	SY5996	50°46·0′	2°34·5′W	X	194
Chamot Hill	Cumbr	NY4877	55°5·3′	2°48·5′W	H	86
Champany	Falk	NT0278	55°59·4′	3°33·8′W	X	65
Champerhaies	Devon	ST0104	50°49·9′	3°24·0′W	X	192
Champernhayes Fm	Dorset	SY3596	50°45·8′	2°54·9′W	FM	193
Champernhayes Marsh	Dorset	SY3597	50°46·4′	2°54·9′W	T	193
Champfleurie Ho	W Loth	NT0376	55°58·3′	3°32·8′W	X	65
Champion Court	Kent	TQ9558	51°17·5′	0°48·2′E	X	178
Champion Fm	Derby	SK3242	52°58·7′	1°31·0′W	FM	119,128
Champion Fm	I of W	SZ5084	50°39·4′	1°17·2′W	FM	196
Champion Fm	Lancs	SD7551	53°57·5′	2°22·4′W	FM	103
Champion Fm	Lincs	TF2551	53°2·7′	0°7·7′W	FM	122
Champions Fm	W Susx	TQ0916	50°56·2′	0°26·5′W	FM	198
Chample's Fm	Devon	SS9120	50°58·4′	3°32·8′W	FM	181
Champneys	Herts	SP9408	51°46·0′	0°37·9′W	X	165
Champneys Fm	E Susx	TQ6610	50°52·2′	0°21·9′E	FM	199
Champson	Devon	SS8028	51°2·6′	3°42·3′W	T	181
Chancefield	Fife	NO2308	56°15·8′	3°14·1′W	X	58
Chance Hall	Ches	SJ8259	53°7·9′	2°15·7′W	X	118
Chance Inn	Fife	NO3710	56°17·0′	3°0·6′W	T	59
Chance Inn	Pth & Kin	NO1100	56°11·3′	3°25·6′W	X	58
Chancel Covert	Suff	TM5282	52°22·9′	1°42·6′E	F	156
Chancellor's Dike	Norf	TF5508	52°39·1′	0°17·9′E	W	143
Chancellor's Fm	Somer	ST5252	51°16·1′	2°40·9′W	FM	182,183
Chancellor, The	Highld	NN1658	56°40·9′	4°59·8′W	X	41
Chancery	Cered	SN5876	52°22·1′	4°4·7′W	T	135
Chancery Fm	Essex	TM0628	51°55·0′	1°0·1′E	FM	168
Chancery Fm	Lancs	SD7244	53°53·7′	2°25·2′W	FM	103
Chance's Pitch	Heref	SO7440	52°3·7′	2°22·4′W	T	150
Chanctonbury Ring	W Susx	TQ1312	50°54·0′	0°23·2′W	A	198
Chanderhill	Derby	SK3270	53°13·8′	1°30·8′W	X	119
Chandler's Cross	Herts	TQ0698	51°40·5′	0°27·6′W	T	166,176
Chandler's Cross	Worcs	SO7738	52°2·6′	2°19·7′W	T	150
Chandler's Ford	Hants	SU4320	50°58·9′	1°22·9′W	T	185
Chandlers Green	Hants	SU7058	51°19·2′	0°59·3′W	T	175,186
Chandos	Heref	SO6434	52°0·4′	2°31·1′W	X	149
Chandos Fm	Suff	TM1072	52°18·6′	1°5·2′E	FM	144,155
Chandos Fm	Suff	TM2267	52°15·6′	1°15·6′E	FM	156
Chang Burn	D & G	NX3048	54°48·1′	4°38·3′W	W	82
Changehill	Aberd	NJ8722	57°17·6′	2°12·5′W	X	38
Chang Hill	E Ayr	NS5608	55°21·0′	4°15·8′W	X	71,77
Changue	D & G	NX2947	54°47·6′	4°39·2′W	X	82
Changue	E Ayr	NS5518	55°26·3′	4°17·1′W	X	71
Changue	E Ayr	NS5735	55°35·5′	4°15·7′W	X	71
Changue	S Ayr	NX2893	55°12·3′	4°41·7′W	X	76
Changue	S Ayr	NX3291	55°11·3′	4°37·9′W	X	76
Changue Burn	S Ayr	NX3093	55°12·4′	4°39·9′W	W	76
Changue Fell	D & G	NX3049	54°48·7′	4°38·3′W	H	82
Changue Glen	E Ayr	NS5835	55°35·5′	4°14·8′W	X	71
Changue Hill	E Ayr	NS5635	55°35·5′	4°16·7′W	X	71
Changue Plantation	S Ayr	NX3093	55°12·4′	4°39·9′W	F	76
Changue Port	D & G	NX2947	54°47·6′	4°39·2′W	W	82
Chanlock Burn	D & G	NS7400	55°16·9′	3°58·6′W	W	77
Chanlock Burn	D & G	NS7500	55°17·0′	3°57·7′W	W	78
Chanlock Craig	D & G	NX7999	55°16·5′	3°53·9′W	X	78
Chanlockfoot	D & G	NS7900	55°17·0′	3°53·9′W	X	78
Chanlockfoot Cott	D & G	NS7800	55°17·0′	3°54·8′W	X	78
Chanlockhead	D & G	NS7500	55°17·0′	3°57·7′W	X	78
Chanlock Rig	D & G	NS7700	55°17·0′	3°55·8′W	X	78
Channain Hill	Highld	NC9341	58°20·9′	3°49·2′W	H	11
Channel Fm	Devon	SS5246	51°11·9′	4°6·7′W	FM	180
Channel Fm	E Yorks	TA2919	53°39·3′	0°2·5′W	FM	113
Channel Fm	Pth & Kin	NO1504	56°13·5′	3°21·8′W	FM	58
Channel Head	Lancs	SD5067	54°6·0′	2°45·5′W	X	97
Channel Ho	Cumbr	SD2677	54°11·3′	3°7·6′W	X	96,97
Channel of Lochar Water	D & G	NY0863	54°57·4′	3°25·8′W	W	85
Channel of River Eden	D & G	NY1763	54°57·5′	3°17·3′W	W	85
Channel of River Esk	D & G	NY2763	54°57·6′	3°8·0′W	W	85
Channel of River Wampool	Cumbr	NY1756	54°53·8′	3°17·2′W	W	85
Channel of River Waver	Cumbr	NY1655	54°53·2′	3°18·1′W	W	85
Channel's End	Beds	TL1156	52°11·7′	0°22·2′W	T	153
Channels, The	Norf	TF7203	52°36·1′	0°32·8′E	F	143
Channel Tunnel Terminal	Kent	TR1937	51°5·6′	1°8·1′E	X	179,189
Channel View	N Som	ST3867	51°24·2′	2°53·1′W	X	171,182
Channel View Fm	V of Glam	SS9370	51°25·4′	3°32·0′W	FM	170
Channel Well	Northum	NY9160	54°56·3′	2°8·0′W	X	87
Channer Wick	Shetld	HU4022	59°59·1′	1°16·5′W	W	4
Channerwick	Shetld	HU4023	59°59·7′	1°16·5′W	T	4
Channocks Fm	Herts	TL4413	51°48·1′	0°5·7′E	FM	167
Channons Hall	Norf	TM1488	52°27·1′	1°9·4′E	A	144,156
Chanonry Ness	Highld	NH7456	57°34·9′	4°6·0′W	X	27
Chanonry Point	Highld	NH7455	57°34·3′	4°5·9′W	X	27
Chanryhill	Aberd	NK0357	57°36·4′	1°56·5′W	X	30
Chanstone Court Fm	Heref	SO3635	52°0·8′	2°55·6′W	FM	149,161
Chanstone Wood	Heref	SO3535	52°0·8′	2°56·4′W	F	149,161
Chantersluer Fm	Surrey	TQ2343	51°10·6′	0°14·0′W	FM	187
Chantlers	Kent	TQ5044	51°10·8′	0°9·2′E	X	188
Chantlers Fm	E Susx	TQ4638	51°7·6′	0°5·6′E	FM	188
Chantmarle (Police Training Centre)	Dorset	ST5802	50°49·2′	2°35·4′W	A	194
Chantries	Surrey	TQ0148	51°13·6′	0°32·8′W	F	186
Chantry	Devon	SS5823	50°59·6′	4°1·0′W	T	180
Chantry	Devon	ST1502	50°48·9′	3°12·0′W	A	192,193
Chantry	Devon	SX7049	50°19·8′	3°49·2′W	X	202
Chantry	N Yks	SE0588	54°17·5′	1°55·0′W	X	98
Chantry	Somer	ST1444	51°11·6′	3°13·5′W	A	181
Chantry	Somer	ST7247	51°13·5′	2°23·7′W	T	183
Chantry	Suff	TM1443	52°2·9′	1°7·7′E	T	169
Chantry	Wilts	SU2854	51°17·3′	1°35·5′W	X	184
Chantry Fm	Dorset	ST4702	50°49·1′	2°44·8′W	FM	193
Chantry Fm	Essex	TL7611	51°46·4′	0°33·5′E	FM	167
Chantry Fm	Heref	SO6228	51°57·2′	2°32·8′W	FM	149
Chantry Fm	Mil Key	SP7847	52°7·2′	0°51·2′W	FM	152
Chantry Fm	Northnts	SP7740	52°3·4′	0°52·2′W	FM	152
Chantry Fm	Northum	NY9866	54°59·6′	2°1·4′W	FM	87
Chantry Fm	N Yks	NZ2406	54°27·2′	1°37·4′W	FM	93
Chantry Fm	Suff	TM3255	52°8·9′	1°23·9′E	FM	156
Chantry Hill	W Susx	TQ0812	50°54·1′	0°27·5′W	X	197
Chantry Hills	Norf	TF8738	52°54·6′	0°47·3′E	X	132
Chantry Marshes	Suff	TM4249	52°5·4′	1°32·4′E	X	169
Chantry Park	Suff	TM1344	52°3·4′	1°6·8′E	X	169
Chantry Point	Suff	TM4248	52°4·9′	1°32·3′E	X	169
Chantry, The	Essex	TL9732	51°57·3′	0°52·4′E	X	168
Chantry, The	W Susx	TQ0912	50°54·1′	0°26·6′W	X	198
Chantry Wood	Essex	TL8412	51°46·8′	0°40·4′E	F	168
Chapel	Corn	SW8460	50°24·2′	5°2·0′W	T	200
Chapel	Cumbr	NY2231	54°40·3′	3°12·1′W	T	89,90
Chapel	D & G	NS8805	55°19·8′	3°45·5′W	X	71,78
Chapel	D & G	NT0705	55°20·1′	3°27·5′W	A	78
Chapel	D & G	NX6855	54°52·6′	4°3·0′W	X	83,84
Chapel	D & G	NX8384	55°8·4′	3°49·7′W	X	78
Chapel	Fife	NT2593	56°7·7′	3°12·0′W	T	59
Chapel	N Lanak	NS8354	55°46·2′	3°51·5′W	X	65,72
Chapel	Scot Bord	NT7657	55°48·6′	2°22·5′W	X	67,74
Chapel Allerton	Leeds	SE3037	53°49·9′	1°32·2′W	T	104
Chapel Allerton	Somer	ST4050	51°15·0′	2°51·2′W	T	182
Chapel Amble	Corn	SW9975	50°32·7′	4°49·8′W	T	200
Chapelarroch	Stir	NS5195	56°7·7′	4°23·4′W	X	57
Chapel Ascote	Warw	SP4157	52°12·8′	1°23·6′W	X	151
Chapel Bank	Kent	TQ9229	51°1·9′	0°44·7′E	X	189
Chapelbank	Pth & Kin	NO0017	56°20·3′	3°36·6′W	X	58
Chapel Bay	Pemb	SM8603	51°41·3′	5°5·4′W	W	157
Chapel Beck	Cumbr	NY2331	54°40·3′	3°11·2′W	W	89,90
Chapel Beck	Cumbr	NY6207	54°27·7′	2°34·8′W	W	91
Chapel Beck	Cumbr	SD6395	54°21·2′	2°33·7′W	W	97
Chapel Brampton	Northnts	SP7266	52°17·5′	0°56·3′W	T	152
Chapelbridge	Cambs	TL2894	52°32·0′	0°6·4′W	X	142
Chapel Brook	Ches	SJ8467	53°12·2′	2°14·0′W	W	118
Chapelburn	Cumbr	NY5964	54°58·4′	2°38·0′W	X	86
Chapel Burn	Pth & Kin	NO0709	56°16·1′	3°29·7′W	W	58
Chapel Burn	S Ayr	NS4102	55°17·4′	4°29·8′W	W	77
Chapel Chorlton	Staffs	SJ8137	52°56·0′	2°16·6′W	T	127
Chapel Cleeve	Somer	ST0342	51°10·4′	3°22·9′W	T	181
Chapel Cliff	Corn	SX2050	50°19·6′	4°31·4′W	X	201
Chapel Close	Wakf	SE2616	53°38·6′	1°36·0′W	X	110
Chapel Common	W Susx	SU8128	51°3·0′	0°50·3′W	X	186,197
Chapel Copse	Northnts	SP6842	52°4·6′	1°0·1′W	F	152
Chapel Cottage Fm	Kent	TR0830	51°2·1′	0°58·4′E	FM	189
Chapel Cottages	Wrex	SJ3356	53°6·1′	2°59·6′W	X	117
Chapel Court Fm	Dorset	ST4506	50°51·3′	2°46·5′W	FM	193
Chapel Crags	Cumbr	NY1615	54°31·6′	3°17·5′W	X	89
Chapelcroft	D & G	NX8054	54°52·2′	3°51·8′W	X	84
Chapelcroft	D & G	NY0684	55°8·7′	3°28·1′W	X	78
Chapel Croft	Lancs	SD7049	53°56·4′	2°27·0′W	X	103
Chapel Croft Plantn	D & G	NX8154	54°52·2′	3°50·8′W	F	84
Chapel Cross	E Susx	TQ6120	50°57·6′	0°17·9′E	T	199
Chapel Cross	Somer	ST6326	51°2·2′	2°31·3′W	X	183
Chapelden	Aberd	NJ8363	57°39·7′	2°16·6′W	X	29,30
Chapeldonan	S Ayr	NS1900	55°15·9′	4°50·5′W	X	76
Chapel Down	I Scilly	SV9415	49°57·6′	6°15·7′W	X	203
Chapel Down Fm	Dorset	ST9815	50°56·3′	2°1·3′W	FM	184
Chapel Downs	Devon	SS8100	50°47·5′	3°40·9′W	X	191
Chapel End	Beds	TL0542	52°4·2′	0°27·7′W	T	153
Chapel End	Beds	TL0948	52°7·4′	0°24·1′W	T	153
Chapel End	Beds	TL1058	52°12·8′	0°23·0′W	T	153
Chapel End	Cambs	TL1282	52°25·7′	0°20·8′W	T	142
Chapel End	Ches	SJ6743	52°59·2′	2°29·1′W	T	118
Chapel End	Essex	TL5624	51°53·8′	0°16·4′E	T	167
Chapel End	Northnts	TL1187	52°28·4′	0°21·5′W	T	142
Chapel End	Warw	SP3293	52°32·3′	1°31·3′W	T	140
Chapel-en-le-Frith	Derby	SK0580	53°19·3′	1°55·1′W	T	110
Chapel-En-Le-Frith-Sta	Derby	SK0579	53°18·7′	1°55·1′W	X	119
Chapelerne	D & G	NX7767	54°59·2′	3°54·9′W	X	84
Chapel Fell	Durham	NY8735	54°42·8′	2°11·7′W	X	91,92
Chapel Fell	N Yks	SD8867	54°6·2′	2°10·6′W	X	98
Chapelfell Top	Durham	NY8734	54°42·3′	2°11·7′W	H	91,92
Chapelfield	Aberd	NO7667	56°47·9′	2°23·1′W	X	45
Chapel Field	Bury	SD7906	53°33·3′	2°18·6′W	T	109
Chapel Field	Norf	TG3624	52°45·9′	1°30·3′E	T	133,134
Chapel Field Barn	Wilts	ST8733	51°6·0′	2°10·8′W	X	183
Chapel Fields	Cov	SP3179	52°24·7′	1°32·3′W	T	140
Chapel Fields	York	SE5651	53°57·4′	1°8·4′W	T	105
Chapel Finian	D & G	NX2748	54°48·1′	4°41·1′W	A	82
Chapel Fm	Cambs	TL3298	52°34·1′	0°2·7′W	FM	142
Chapel Fm	Ches	SJ7372	53°14·9′	2°23·9′W	FM	118
Chapel Fm	Corn	SX4165	50°28·0′	4°14·1′W	FM	201
Chapel Fm	Devon	SS9102	50°48·7′	3°32·4′W	FM	192
Chapel Fm	D & G	NT0705	55°20·1′	3°27·5′W	FM	78
Chapel Fm	Fife	NT2594	56°8·2′	3°12·0′W	FM	59
Chapel Fm	Glos	SO7529	51°57·8′	2°21·4′W	FM	150
Chapel Fm	Hants	SU2924	51°1·1′	1°34·8′W	FM	185
Chapel Fm	Hants	SU7635	51°6·8′	0°54·5′W	FM	186
Chapel Fm	Heref	SO3968	52°18·6′	2°53·9′W	FM	137,148
Chapel Fm	Heref	SO6230	51°58·3′	2°32·8′W	FM	149
Chapel Fm	Herts	TL3121	51°52·6′	0°5·4′W	FM	166
Chapel Fm	Kent	TQ9050	51°13·3′	0°43·6′E	FM	189
Chapel Fm	Lincs	SK9365	53°10·7′	0°36·1′W	FM	121
Chapel Fm	Lincs	TF1715	52°43·4′	0°15·6′W	FM	130
Chapel Fm	Lincs	TF2065	53°10·3′	0°11·9′W	FM	122
Chapel Fm	Lincs	TF2917	52°44·3′	0°4·9′W	FM	131
Chapel Fm	Lincs	TF2956	53°5·4′	0°4·0′W	FM	122
Chapel Fm	Monm	SO3609	51°46·8′	2°55·3′W	FM	161
Chapel Fm	Monm	SO4908	51°46·3′	2°44·0′W	FM	162
Chapel Fm	Monm	ST4485	51°33·9′	2°48·1′W	FM	171,172
Chapel Fm	Newp	ST4090	51°36·6′	2°51·6′W	FM	171,172
Chapel Fm	N Lincs	TA0118	53°39·2′	0°27·9′W	FM	112
Chapel Fm	N Lincs	TA1222	53°41·2′	0°17·8′W	FM	107,113
Chapel Fm	Norf	TG1308	52°37·9′	1°9·3′E	FM	144
Chapel Fm	Norf	TL8787	52°27·2′	0°45·5′E	FM	144
Chapel Fm	Northnts	SP5469	52°19·2′	1°12·1′W	FM	152
Chapel Fm	Northnts	SP7848	52°7·7′	0°51·2′W	FM	152
Chapel Fm	Northum	NZ0872	55°2·8′	1°52·1′W	FM	88
Chapel Fm	N Yks	SE9596	54°21·3′	0°31·9′W	FM	94,101
Chapel Fm	Pemb	SM9525	51°53·4′	4°58·4′W	FM	157,158
Chapel Fm	Pemb	SR9098	51°38·7′	5°1·7′W	FM	158
Chapel Fm	Powys	SO2247	52°7·2′	3°8·0′W	FM	148
Chapel Fm	Renf	NS4168	55°53·0′	4°32·1′W	FM	64
Chapel Fm	Rut	SK8912	52°42·1′	0°40·6′W	FM	130
Chapel Fm	Scot Bord	NT5425	55°31·2′	2°43·3′W	FM	73
Chapel Fm	S Lanak	NS7443	55°40·1′	3°59·8′W	FM	71
Chapel Fm	Somer	ST3551	51°15·5′	2°55·5′W	FM	182
Chapel Fm	Suff	TL9749	52°6·5′	0°53·0′E	FM	155
Chapel Fm	Suff	TM0451	52°7·4′	0°59·2′E	FM	155
Chapel Fm	Suff	TM0763	52°13·8′	1°2·3′E	FM	155
Chapel Fm	Suff	TM0973	52°19·1′	1°4·4′E	FM	144,155
Chapel Fm	Suff	TM1058	52°11·0′	1°4·7′E	FM	155
Chapel Fm	Suff	TM3377	52°20·7′	1°25·7′E	FM	156
Chapel Fm	Surrey	TQ1552	51°15·6′	0°20·7′W	FM	187
Chapel Fm	Swin	SU1291	51°37·3′	1°49·2′W	FM	163,173
Chapel Fm	W Berks	SU4475	51°28·6′	1°21·6′W	FM	174
Chapel Fm	Wilts	ST8732	51°5·5′	2°10·8′W	FM	183
Chapel Fm	Wilts	ST9421	50°59·5′	2°4·7′W	FM	184
Chapel Fm	Worcs	SO7671	52°20·4′	2°20·7′W	FM	138
Chapel Fm	Worcs	SO9480	52°25·3′	2°4·9′W	FM	139
Chapel Fm	Worcs	SO9941	52°4·3′	2°0·5′W	FM	150
Chapelfoot	Herts	TL1925	51°54·9′	0°15·8′W	X	166
Chapelford	Moray	NJ3860	57°37·8′	3°1·8′W	X	28
Chapelgarth	N Yks	NZ5606	54°27·0′	1°7·8′W	X	93
Chapel Garths	N Yks	SE3068	54°6·7′	1°32·0′W	X	99
Chapel Gate	Derby	SK1083	53°20·9′	1°50·6′W	X	110
Chapelgate	Lincs	TF4124	52°47·9′	0°5·9′E	T	131
Chapel Geo	Highld	ND1872	58°38·0′	3°24·3′W	X	7,12
Chapel Geo	Orkney	HY6715	59°1·5′	2°34·0′W	X	5
Chapelgill Hill	Scot Bord	NT0630	55°33·5′	3°29·0′W	H	72
Chapel Grain	Scot Bord	NY4495	55°15·0′	2°52·4′W	W	79
Chapel Green	Herts	TL3435	52°0·1′	0°2·5′W	T	154
Chapel Green	Warw	SP2685	52°28·0′	1°36·6′W	T	140
Chapel Green	Warw	SP4660	52°14·4′	1°19·2′W	T	151
Chapel Green	Wok	SU8167	51°24·0′	0°49·7′W	X	175
Chapel Haddlesey	N Yks	SE5826	53°43·9′	1°6·8′W	T	105
Chapelhaies	Devon	SS9705	50°50·4′	3°27·4′W	X	192
Chapelhall	Aberd	NJ9128	57°20·8′	2°8·5′W	X	38
Chapelhall	N Lanak	NS7862	55°50·4′	3°56·5′W	T	64
Chapelhaugh	Aberd	NJ8439	57°26·7′	2°15·5′W	X	29,30
Chapelhayes	Devon	ST1909	50°52·7′	3°8·7′W	X	192,193
Chapel Head	Cambs	TL3481	52°24·9′	0°1·4′W	T	142
Chapelhead	Moray	NJ4654	57°34·6′	2°53·7′W	X	28,29
Chapelheron	D & G	NX4541	54°44·7′	4°24·1′W	X	83
Chapel Hill	Aberd	NJ4036	57°24·9′	2°59·5′W	H	28
Chapel Hill	Aberd	NJ4217	57°14·7′	2°57·2′W	H	37
Chapelhill	Aberd	NJ6144	57°29·3′	2°38·6′W	X	29
Chapel Hill	Aberd	NK0635	57°24·6′	1°53·6′W	T	30
Chapel Hill	Brig	SS8878	51°29·6′	3°36·4′W	X	170
Chapel Hill	Cambs	TL4051	52°8·6′	0°3·2′E	X	154
Chapel Hill	Cambs	TL5375	52°21·3′	0°15·0′E	X	143
Chapel Hill	Cumbr	NY4676	55°4·8′	2°50·3′W	H	86
Chapel Hill	Cumbr	SD1097	54°21·9′	3°22·7′W	X	96
Chapel Hill	Derby	SK4466	53°11·6′	1°20·1′W	X	120
Chapel Hill	D & G	NX7246	54°47·8′	3°59·0′W	X	83,84
Chapelhill	D & G	NY0168	55°0·1′	3°32·4′W	X	84
Chapelhill	D & G	NY0891	55°12·5′	3°26·3′W	X	78
Chapelhill	D & G	NY2778	55°5·7′	3°8·2′W	X	85
Chapel Hill	Dorset	SY5784	50°39·5′	2°36·1′W	H	194
Chapel Hill	Glos	SO6102	51°43·2′	2°33·5′W	T	162
Chapelhill	Highld	NH8273	57°44·1′	3°58·4′W	X	21
Chapel Hill	Lancs	SD4355	53°59·5′	2°51·7′W	X	102

Chapel Hill	Lincs	SK9521	52°46·9′	0°35·1′W	X	130
Chapel Hill	Lincs	TF1389	53°23·4′	0°17·6′W	X	113,121
Chapel Hill	Lincs	TF2054	53°4·4′	0°12·1′W	T	122
Chapel Hill	Monm	SO5200	51°42·0′	2°41·3′W	T	162
Chapel Hill	Norf	TF7108	52°38·8′	0°32·1′E	X	143
Chapel Hill	Norf	TG2204	52°35·5′	1°17·1′E	X	134
Chapel Hill	N Yks	SE2979	54°12·6′	1°32·9′W	X	99
Chapel Hill	N Yks	SE3446	53°54·8′	1°28·5′W	X	104
Chapel Hill	N Yks	SE5818	53°39·6′	1°6·9′W	X	111
Chapel Hill	Pemb	SM9421	51°51·2′	4°59·1′W	X	157,158
Chapel Hill	Pemb	SN1211	51°46·2′	4°43·1′W	X	158
Chapelhill	Pemb	SR9598	51°38·8′	4°57·4′W	X	158
Chapelhill	Pth & Kin	NN9619	56°21·4′	3°40·5′W	X	58
Chapel Hill	Pth & Kin	NO0009	56°16·0′	3°36·4′W	X	58
Chapelhill	Pth & Kin	NO0030	56°27·4′	3°36·9′W	X	52,53
Chapelhill	Pth & Kin	NO2021	56°22·7′	3°17·3′W	T	53,58
Chapelhill	Pth & Kin	NO2445	56°35·7′	3°13·8′W	X	53
Chapel Hill	Rut	SK9508	52°39·9′	0°35·3′W	X	141
Chapel Hill	Scot Bord	NT4211	55°23·6′	2°54·5′W	H	79
Chapelhill	Scot Bord	NT4412	55°24·2′	2°52·6′W	X	79
Chapel Hill	S Lanak	NS7826	55°31·0′	3°55·5′W	X	71
Chapel Hill	S Lanak	NS9136	55°36·6′	3°43·4′W	H	71,72
Chapel Hill	Suff	TM0158	52°11·2′	0°56·8′E	X	155
Chapel Hill	Suff	TM0461	52°12·8′	0°59·6′E	X	155
Chapel Hill	Suff	TM2258	52°10·8′	1°15·2′E	X	156
Chapelhill Fm	Scot Bord	NT2442	55°40·2′	3°12·1′W	FM	73
Chapelhill Fm	Scot Bord	NT7770	55°55·6′	2°21·6′W	FM	67
Chapel Hill (Moat)	Lincs	TF1389	53°23·4′	0°17·6′W	A	113,121
Chapelhill Rough	Worcs	SO8347	52°7·5′	2°14·5′W	F	150
Chapelhills	D & G	NY3577	55°5·2′	3°0·7′W	X	85
Chapel Ho	Ches	SJ7471	53°14·4′	2°23·0′W	X	118
Chapel Ho	Cumbr	NY5457	54°54·6′	2°42·6′W	X	86
Chapel Ho	Cumbr	NY6207	54°27·7′	2°34·8′W	X	91
Chapel Ho	Cumbr	SD3785	54°15·7′	2°57·6′W	X	96,97
Chapel Ho	Cumbr	SD4692	54°19·5′	2°49·4′W	X	97
Chapel Ho	Cumbr	SD6278	54°12·0′	2°34·5′W	X	97
Chapel Ho	Durham	NZ1815	54°32·0′	1°42·9′W	X	92
Chapel Ho	Northum	NY6466	54°59·5′	2°33·3′W	X	86
Chapel Ho	Northum	NY8157	54°54·7′	2°17·4′W	X	86,87
Chapel Ho	N Yks	SD9766	54°5·6′	2°2·3′W	X	98
Chapel Ho	Oxon	SP3228	51°57·2′	1°31·7′W	X	164
Chapel Ho	S Glos	ST6196	51°39·9′	2°33·4′W	X	162
Chapel Ho	Shrops	SO5879	52°24·7′	2°36·7′W	X	137,138
Chapelhope	Scot Bord	NT2219	55°27·8′	3°13·6′W	X	79
Chapelhope Burn	Scot Bord	NT2218	55°27·2′	3°13·6′W	W	79
Chapel House	Lancs	SD4706	53°33·1′	2°47·6′W	T	108
Chapelhouse Fm	Ches	SJ3958	53°7·2′	2°54·3′W	FM	117
Chapelhouse Fm	Ches	SJ4360	53°8·3′	2°50·7′W	FM	117
Chapel House Fm	Cumbr	NY2536	54°43·1′	3°9·4′W	FM	89,90
Chapel House Fm	Derby	SK3247	53°1·4′	1°31·0′W	FM	119,128
Chapel House Fm	Lancs	SD5554	53°59·1′	2°40·8′W	FM	102
Chapel House Fm	Staffs	SK2027	52°50·6′	1°41·8′W	FM	128
Chapel House Fm	Traf	SJ8086	53°22·5′	2°17·6′W	FM	109
Chapelhouse Resr	Cumbr	NY2535	54°42·5′	3°9·4′W	W	89,90
Chapelhouses	Aberd	NJ8030	57°21·9′	2°19·5′W	X	29,30
Chapel Island	Cumbr	SD3275	54°10·2′	3°2·1′W	X	96,97
Chapel Knapp	Wilts	ST8868	51°24·9′	2°10·0′W	T	173
Chapelknowe	D & G	NY3173	55°3·1′	3°4·4′W	T	85
Chapelknowe	N Lanak	NS7858	55°48·2′	3°56·3′W	X	64
Chapel Lane	Cumbr	NY3744	54°47·5′	2°58·4′W	X	85
Chapel Lane Fm	N Yks	SE1890	54°18·6′	1°43·0′W	FM	99
Chapel Lawn	Shrops	SO3176	52°22·9′	3°0·4′W	T	137,148
Chapel-le-Dale	N Yks	SD7377	54°11·5′	2°24·4′W	T	98
Chapel Leigh	Somer	ST1229	51°3·5′	3°15·0′W	T	181,193
Chapel Mains	Scot Bord	NT5542	55°40·4′	2°42·5′W	T	73
Chapel Marsh	Dorset	ST4804	50°50·2′	2°43·9′W	X	193
Chapel Mere	Ches	SJ5351	53°3·5′	2°41·7′W	W	117
Chapel Milton	Derby	SK0581	53°19·8′	1°55·1′W	T	110
Chapel Moor	N Yks	SD9180	54°13·2′	2°7·9′W	X	98
Chapel Ness	Fife	NT4899	56°11·1′	2°49·8′W	X	59
Chapel Oak	Warw	SP0551	52°9·7′	1°55·2′W	X	150
Chapel of Barras	Aberd	NO8378	56°53·8′	2°16·3′W	X	45
Chapel of Ease	Caer	ST2295	51°39·1′	3°7·3′W	T	171
Chapel of Ease Fm	Cambs	TL4796	52°32·7′	0°10·5′E	FM	143
Chapel of Elrick	Aberd	NJ8718	57°15·4′	2°12·5′W	X	38
Chapel of Garioch	Aberd	NJ7123	57°18·1′	2°28·4′W	T	38
Chapel of Lethendy	Pth & Kin	NO1441	56°33·4′	3°23·5′W	X	53
Chapel of Seggat	Aberd	NJ7242	57°28·3′	2°27·6′W	X	29
Chapel of Stoneywood	C of Aber	NJ8610	57°11·1′	2°13·4′W	T	38
Chapel of Towie	Aberd	NJ4713	57°12·5′	2°52·2′W	X	37
Chapel on Leader	Scot Bord	NT5541	55°39·9′	2°42·5′W	T	73
Chapel o'Sink	Aberd	NJ7019	57°15·9′	2°29·4′W	H	38
Chapel Outon	D & G	NX4442	54°45·2′	4°25·0′W	X	83
Chapelpark	Aberd	NJ5945	57°29·9′	2°40·6′W	X	29
Chapelpark	Aberd	NJ8534	57°24·0′	2°14·5′W	X	30
Chapelpark	Highld	NH7801	57°5·3′	4°0·3′W	X	35
Chapel Pill Fm	N Som	ST5376	51°29·1′	2°40·2′W	FM	172
Chapel Plaister	Wilts	ST8467	51°24·3′	2°13·4′W	T	173
Chapel Point	Corn	SX0243	50°15·5′	4°46·3′W	X	204
Chapel Point	E Loth	NT7375	55°58·3′	2°25·5′W	X	67
Chapel Point	Lincs	TF5673	53°14·1′	0°20·7′E	X	122
Chapel Point	Pemb	SS1495	51°37·6′	4°40·9′W	X	158
Chapel & Popes Tower	Oxon	SP4105	51°44·8′	1°24·0′W	A	164
Chapel Porth	Corn	SW6949	50°18·0′	5°14·3′W	W	203
Chapel Rock	Corn	SW5130	50°7·3′	5°28·6′W	X	203
Chapel Rossan	D & G	NX1045	54°46·1′	4°56·8′W	X	82
Chapel Rossan Bay	D & G	NX1145	54°46·1′	4°55·9′W	W	82
Chapel Row	Essex	TL7900	51°40·4′	0°35·7′E	T	167
Chapel Row	E Susx	TQ6312	50°53·3′	0°19·4′E	T	199
Chapel Row	W Berks	SU5769	51°25·3′	1°10·4′W	T	174
Chapels	Black w Dar	SD6923	53°42·4′	2°27·8′W	T	103
Chapels	Cumbr	SD2383	54°14·5′	3°10·5′W	T	96
Chapel Six Marshes	Lincs	TF5574	53°14·7′	0°19·8′E	X	122
Chapel Stile	Cumbr	NY3205	54°26·4′	3°2·5′W	T	90
Chapel St Leonards	Lincs	TF5572	53°13·6′	0°19·7′E	T	122
Chapel Street Fm	Suff	TL7343	52°3·7′	0°31·8′E	FM	155
Chapel Taing	Orkney	HY5205	58°56·0′	2°49·6′W	X	6,7
Chapel, The	Orkney	HY5428	59°8·4′	2°47·8′W	X	5,6
Chapelthorpe	Wakf	SE3115	53°38·1′	1°31·5′W	T	110,111

Chapelton	Aberd	NJ3808	57°9·8′	3°1·1′W	X	37
Chapelton	Aberd	NJ4216	57°14·1′	2°57·2′W	X	37
Chapelton	Aberd	NJ5837	57°25·5′	2°41·5′W	X	29
Chapelton	Aberd	NJ5923	57°18·0′	2°40·4′W	X	37
Chapelton	Aberd	NJ8836	57°25·1′	2°11·5′W	X	30
Chapelton	Aberd	NJ9228	57°20·8′	2°7·5′W	X	38
Chapelton	Aberd	NJ9764	57°40·2′	2°2·6′W	X	30
Chapelton	Aberd	NO6168	56°48·4′	2°37·9′W	X	45
Chapelton	Aberd	NO7382	56°56·0′	2°26·2′W	X	45
Chapelton	Aberd	NO8582	56°56·0′	2°14·3′W	X	45
Chapelton	Aberd	NO8994	57°2·5′	2°10·4′W	T	38,45
Chapelton	Angus	NO3758	56°42·8′	3°1·3′W	X	54
Chapelton	Angus	NO5350	56°38·6′	2°45·5′W	X	54
Chapelton	Angus	NO5866	56°47·3′	2°40·8′W	X	44
Chapelton	Angus	NO6247	56°37·1′	2°36·7′W	T	54
Chapelton	Devon	SS5726	51°1·2′	4°2·0′W	T	180
Chapelton	D & G	NX4959	54°54·4′	4°20·9′W	X	83
Chapelton	D & G	NX7247	54°48·3′	3°59·1′W	X	83,84
Chapelton	D & G	NX7966	54°58·7′	3°53·0′W	X	84
Chapelton	Highld	NH5251	57°31·8′	4°27·8′W	X	26
Chapelton	Highld	NH7346	57°29·5′	4°6·7′W	X	27
Chapelton	Highld	NH9119	57°15·2′	3°47·9′W	X	36
Chapelton	Moray	NJ0457	57°35·8′	3°35·9′W	X	27
Chapelton	Moray	NJ1730	57°21·4′	3°22·3′W	X	36
Chapelton	N Ayr	NS2046	55°40·7′	4°51·3′W	X	63
Chapelton	Pth & Kin	NN8661	56°43·9′	3°51·3′W	X	43
Chapelton	Pth & Kin	NO1145	56°35·6′	3°26·5′W	X	53
Chapelton	S Ayr	NS2304	55°18·2′	4°46·9′W	X	76
Chapelton	S Ayr	NS3209	55°21·0′	4°38·6′W	X	70,76
Chapelton	S Lanak	NS6848	55°42·7′	4°5·6′W	T	64
Chapelton Burn	S Ayr	NS2204	55°18·1′	4°47·8′W	W	76
Chapelton Fm	Pth & Kin	NO2146	56°36·2′	3°16·8′W	FM	53
Chapeltonmoss	Moray	NJ0557	57°35·8′	3°34·9′W	X	27
Chapelton Row	D & G	NX6248	54°48·7′	4°8·4′W	X	83
Chapelton Wood	S Ayr	NS3103	55°17·8′	4°39·3′W	F	76
Chapeltoun Ho	E Ayr	NS3944	55°40·0′	4°33·2′W	X	63,70
Chapeltown	Aberd	NJ6247	57°31·0′	2°37·6′W	X	29
Chapeltown	Black w Dar	SD7315	53°38·1′	2°24·1′W	T	109
Chapel Town	Corn	SW8855	50°21·6′	4°58·5′W	T	200
Chapeltown	Cumbr	NY4371	55°2·1′	2°53·1′W	X	85
Chapeltown	Highld	NH9715	57°13·1′	3°41·9′W	X	36
Chapeltown	Leeds	SE3037	53°49·9′	1°32·2′W	T	104
Chapeltown	Sheff	SK3596	53°27·8′	1°28·0′W	T	110,111
Chapel Tump	Heref	SO5324	51°55·0′	2°40·6′W	X	162
Chapel Well	Cumbr	NY5250	54°50·8′	2°44·4′W	X	86
Chapelwell	Fife	NO4015	56°19·7′	2°57·8′W	X	59
Chapelwell Hill	Aberd	NJ6203	57°7·2′	2°37·2′W	H	37
Chapelwick Fm	Oxon	SU2587	51°35·1′	1°38·0′W	FM	174
Chapel Wood	Ches	SJ8273	53°15·5′	2°15·8′W	F	118
Chapel Wood	D & G	NY0890	55°12·0′	3°26·3′W	F	78
Chapel Wood	W Berks	SU4575	51°28·6′	1°20·7′W	F	174
Chapel Wood Fm	N Yks	SE4598	54°22·8′	1°18·0′W	FM	99
Chapelwood Manor	E Susx	TQ4328	51°2·2′	0°2·8′E	X	187,198
Chapel Yard	Beds	TL0966	52°17·1′	0°23·7′W	X	153
Chapelyard	Fife	NO2506	56°14·7′	3°12·2′W	X	59
Chapel Yard	Lincs	SK8993	53°25·8′	0°39·2′W	X	112
Chaplain's Fm	Suff	TM0836	51°59·2′	1°2·2′E	FM	155,169
Chapleton	Moray	NJ2421	57°16·7′	3°15·2′W	T	36
Chaplin's Yd	Lincs	TF3282	53°19·3′	0°0·7′W	X	122
Chapman Banks Wood	N Yks	SE9590	54°18·0′	0°32·0′W	F	94,101
Chapman Barrows	Devon	SS6943	51°10·5′	3°52·1′W	A	180
Chapman Hill	Durham	NZ1432	54°41·2′	1°46·5′W	X	92
Chapman Rock	Devon	SS2627	51°1·2′	4°28·5′W	X	190
Chapman Sands	Essex	TQ8383	51°31·2′	0°38·7′E	X	178
Chapman's Cross	Glos	SO9301	51°42·7′	2°5·7′W	X	163
Chapmans Fm	Hav	TQ5688	51°34·4′	0°15·5′E	FM	177
Chapman's Fm	Kent	TQ7741	51°8·7′	0°32·2′E	FM	188
Chapman's Fm	Lincs	TF5473	53°14·1′	0°18·9′E	FM	122
Chapman's Fm	Somer	ST0036	51°7·1′	3°25·3′W	FM	181
Chapmansford Fm	Hants	SU4248	51°14·0′	1°23·5′W	FM	185
Chapman's Hill	Worcs	SO9677	52°23·7′	2°3·1′W	T	139
Chapmanslade	Wilts	ST8247	51°13·5′	2°15·1′W	T	183
Chapman's Pool	Dorset	SY9576	50°35·3′	2°3·9′W	W	195
Chapman's Rocks	Devon	SY1487	50°40·8′	3°12·7′W	X	192
Chapman's Town	E Susx	TQ6118	50°56·6′	0°17·9′E	T	199
Chapmans Well	Devon	SX3593	50°43·0′	4°19·9′W	T	190
Chapmans Well	Durham	NZ1749	54°50·4′	1°43·7′W	X	88
Chapmanton	D & G	NX7664	54°57·6′	3°55·8′W	X	84
Chapmore End	Herts	TL3216	51°49·8′	0°4·7′W	T	166
Chapner Fm	Devon	SS8113	50°54·5′	3°41·2′W	FM	181
Chappel	Essex	TL8928	51°55·3′	0°45·3′E	T	168
Chappel and Wakes Colne Station	Essex	TL8928	51°55·3′	0°45·3′E	X	168
Chappel Fm	Essex	TL8809	51°45·1′	0°43·8′E	FM	168
Chappel House Fm	Shrops	SJ8004	52°38·2′	2°17·3′W	FM	127
Chappels Fm	Cumbr	SD1684	54°14·9′	3°16·9′W	FM	96
Chapperton Down	Wilts	ST9947	51°13·6′	2°0·5′W	X	184
Chapple	Devon	SS8411	50°53·4′	3°38·6′W	X	191
Chapple	Devon	SX6789	50°41·4′	3°52·6′W	X	191
Chapplecroft Fm	Devon	ST2802	50°49·0′	3°0·9′W	FM	193
Chapple Fm	Devon	SS5510	50°52·5′	4°3·3′W	FM	191
Chapple Fm	Devon	SS5621	50°58·5′	4°2·7′W	FM	180
Chapple Fm	Somer	SS9627	51°2·2′	3°28·6′W	FM	181
Chapple Moor	Devon	SS6200	50°47·2′	3°57·1′W	X	191
Chapter Fm	Kent	TQ7169	51°23·9′	0°27·9′E	FM	178
Chapyn Blaendrawsffos	Powys	SN8369	52°18·6′	3°42·6′W	X	135,136,147
Charaton	Corn	SX3069	50°30·0′	4°23·5′W	T	201
Charborough Ho	Dorset	SY9297	50°46·6′	2°6·4′W	A	195
Charborough Park	Dorset	SY9298	50°47·1′	2°6·4′W	X	195
Charcoal Plantn	Notts	SK6271	53°14·2′	1°3·9′W	F	120
Charcoals Wood	Cambs	TL6557	52°11·4′	0°25·2′E	F	154
Charcott	Kent	TQ5247	51°12·3′	0°10·9′E	T	188
Chard	Somer	ST3208	50°52·3′	2°57·6′W	T	193
Chard Junction	Somer	ST3404	50°50·1′	2°55·9′W	T	193
Chardleigh Green	Somer	ST3110	50°53·4′	2°58·5′W	T	193
Chardown Hill	Dorset	SY3993	50°44·2′	2°51·5′W	H	193
Chard Resr	Somer	ST3309	50°52·8′	2°56·8′W	W	193
Chardstock	Devon	ST3004	50°50·1′	2°59·3′W	T	193
Chardstock Court	Devon	ST3004	50°50·1′	2°59·3′W	A	193

Chardstock Ho	Somer	ST3106	50°51·2′	2°58·4′W	X	193
Chardwell Fm	Essex	TL4734	51°59·3′	0°8·8′E	FM	154
Chare Ends	Northum	NU1242	55°40·5′	1°48·1′W	X	75
Chareheads	Northum	NY7852	54°52·0′	2°20·1′W	X	86,87
Charfield	S Glos	ST7292	51°37·8′	2°23·9′W	T	162,172
Charfield Green	S Glos	ST7292	51°37·8′	2°23·9′W	T	162,172
Charfield Hall Fm	S Glos	ST7291	51°37·3′	2°23·9′W	FM	162,172
Charfield Hill	S Glos	ST7192	51°37·8′	2°24·7′W	T	162,172
Charford	Worcs	SO9569	52°19·4′	2°4·0′W	T	139
Charford Manor	Devon	SX7258	50°24·7′	3°47·7′W	X	202
Chargot Ho	Somer	SS9737	51°7·6′	3°27·9′W	X	181
Chargot Wood	Somer	SS9736	51°7·1′	3°27·9′W	F	181
Chargrove	Glos	SO9219	51°52·4′	2°6·6′W	T	163
Chargy Hill	Glos	SO8023	51°54·5′	2°17·1′W	X	162
Charing	Kent	TQ9549	51°12·6′	0°47·9′E	T	189
Charing Cross	Dorset	SU1112	50°54·7′	1°50·2′W	X	195
Charing Cross Sta	C of West	TQ3080	51°30·5′	0°7·2′W	X	176,177
Charing Heath	Kent	TQ9249	51°12·7′	0°45·3′E	T	189
Charing Hill	Kent	TQ9650	51°13·2′	0°48·8′E	T	189
Charingworth	Glos	SP2039	52°3·2′	1°42·1′W	T	151
Charingworth Grange	Glos	SP2139	52°3·2′	1°41·2′W	X	151
Charinton Fm	Lincs	TF2220	52°46·1′	0°11·1′W	FM	131
Charisworth	Dorset	ST8601	50°48·7′	2°11·5′W	X	194
Charity	Highld	ND3549	58°25·7′	3°6·3′W	X	12
Charity Bottom	Dorset	ST6000	50°48·1′	2°33·7′W	X	194
Charity Down Fm	Hants	SU3438	51°8·6′	1°30·4′W	FM	185
Charity Fm	Beds	SP9425	51°55·2′	0°37·6′W	FM	165
Charity Fm	Cambs	TL4151	52°8·6′	0°4·0′E	FM	154
Charity Fm	Essex	TL6629	51°56·3′	0°25·3′E	FM	167
Charity Fm	Essex	TL8100	51°40·4′	0°37·5′E	FM	168
Charity Fm	Hants	SU5708	50°52·3′	1°11·0′W	FM	196
Charity Fm	Hants	SU7331	51°4·6′	0°57·1′W	FM	186
Charity Fm	Heref	SO2831	51°58·6′	3°2·5′W	FM	161
Charity Fm	N Lincs	SE7201	53°30·3′	0°54·5′W	FM	112
Charity Fm	Norf	TG4512	52°39·2′	1°37·8′E	FM	134
Charity Fm	N Yks	SE6439	53°50·8′	1°1·2′W	FM	105,106
Charity Fm	N Yks	SE8480	54°12·8′	0°42·3′W	FM	100
Charity Fm	Somer	ST4132	51°5·3′	2°50·2′W	FM	182
Charity Fm	Suff	TL7369	52°17·7′	0°32·6′E	FM	155
Charity Fm	Suff	TL9451	52°7·6′	0°50·5′E	FM	155
Charity Fm	Suff	TM2336	51°58·9′	1°15·2′E	FM	169
Charity Fm	Suff	TM3485	52°25·0′	1°26·9′E	FM	156
Charity Fm	Warw	SP2893	52°32·3′	1°34·8′W	FM	140
Charity Hall	Northum	NT9604	55°20·1′	2°3·4′W	X	81
Charity Wood	Dorset	ST8203	50°49·8′	2°15·0′W	F	194
Chark	Corn	SX0860	50°24·7′	4°41·8′W	X	200
Chark Common	Hants	SU5702	50°49·1′	1°11·1′W	X	196
Charlacott	Devon	SS5327	51°1·7′	4°5·4′W	X	180
Charlaw Fell	Durham	NZ2248	54°49·8′	1°39·0′W	H	88
Charlaw Plantn	Durham	NZ2148	54°49·8′	1°40·0′W	F	88
Charlbury	Oxon	SP3519	51°52·3′	1°29·1′W	T	164
Charlbury Hill	Swin	SU2382	51°32·4′	1°39·7′W	H	174
Charlcombe	Bath & NE Somer	ST7467	51°24·3′	2°22·0′W	T	172
Charlcombe Bay	N Som	ST4375	51°28·5′	2°48·9′W	W	171,172
Charlcot	N Yks	SE2085	54°15·9′	1°41·2′W	X	99
Charlcotte	Shrops	SO6386	52°28·5′	2°32·3′W	X	138
Charlcutt	Wilts	ST9875	51°28·7′	2°1·3′W	T	173
Charlcutt Hill	Wilts	ST9875	51°28·7′	2°1·3′W	X	173
Charlecombe	Devon	SX9070	50°31·4′	3°32·7′W	X	202
Charlecote	Warw	SP2656	52°12·3′	1°36·8′W	T	151
Charlecote Park	Warw	SP2556	52°12·3′	1°37·7′W	A	151
Charlemont	Sand	SP0193	52°32·3′	1°58·7′W	T	139
Charles	Devon	SS6832	51°4·6′	3°52·7′W	T	180
Charles Bottom	Devon	SS6831	51°4·0′	3°52·7′W	T	180
Charlesbye	Lancs	SD4208	53°34·2′	2°52·1′W	X	108
Charlesfield	Aberd	NJ6942	57°28·3′	2°30·6′W	X	29
Charlesfield	D & G	NY1568	55°0·2′	3°19·3′W	X	85
Charlesfield	Pth & Kin	NO0019	56°21·4′	3°36·7′W	X	58
Charlesfield	Scot Bord	NT5829	55°33·4′	2°39·5′W	T	73,74
Charlesground	Cumbr	SD1192	54°19·2′	3°21·7′W	X	96
Charles Hall	Suff	TM0353	52°8·5′	0°58·4′E	X	155
Charles Head	Ches	SJ9779	53°18·7′	2°2·3′W	X	118
Charles Head Fm	Ches	SJ9778	53°18·2′	2°2·3′W	FM	118
Charleshill	Surrey	SU8944	51°11·5′	0°43·2′W	T	186
Charleshurst Fm	W Susx	TQ0130	51°3·9′	0°33·1′W	FM	186
Charles Pit Cottages	Durham	NZ2948	54°49·8′	1°32·5′W	X	88
Charleston	Angus	NO3845	56°35·8′	3°0·1′W	T	54
Charleston	Highld	ND2671	58°37·5′	3°16·0′W	X	7,12
Charleston	Highld	NH5723	57°16·8′	4°21·9′W	X	26,35
Charleston	Highld	NH6443	57°27·7′	4°15·6′W	X	26
Charleston	Pth & Kin	NO1135	56°30·2′	3°26·3′W	X	53
Charleston	Renf	NS4862	55°49·9′	4°25·2′W	T	64
Charleston	S Lanak	NS9241	55°39·3′	3°42·6′W	X	71,72
Charlestone Fm	E Yorks	TA1370	54°7·0′	0°15·9′W	FM	101
Charleston Farmhouse	E Susx	TQ4906	50°50·3′	0°7·4′E	X	199
Charleston Manor	E Susx	TQ5200	50°47·0′	0°9·8′E	A	199
Charlestown	Aberd	NK0563	57°39·7′	1°54·5′W	T	30
Charlestown	Brad	SE1538	53°50·5′	1°45·9′W	T	104
Charlestown	Cald	SD9726	53°44·1′	2°2·3′W	T	103
Charlestown	C of Aber	NJ9300	57°5·7′	2°6·5′W	T	38
Charlestown	Corn	SX0451	50°19·8′	4°44·9′W	T	200,204
Charlestown	Derby	SK0392	53°25·7′	1°56·9′W	T	110
Charlestown	Dorset	SY6479	50°36·8′	2°30·1′W	T	194
Charlestown	Fife	NT0683	56°2·1′	3°30·1′W	T	65
Charlestown	Highld	NG8075	57°42·9′	5°41·2′W	T	19
Charlestown	Highld	NH6448	57°30·4′	4°15·7′W	T	26
Charlestown	Man	SD8603	53°31·7′	2°12·3′W	T	109
Charlestown	Moray	NJ1367	57°41·3′	3°27·1′W	T	28
Charlestown	Pth & Kin	NO2427	56°26·0′	3°13·5′W	X	53,59
Charlestown	Salf	SJ8199	53°29·5′	2°16·8′W	T	109
Charlestown of Aberlour	Moray	NJ2642	57°28·0′	3°13·6′W	T	28
Charles Tye	Suff	TM0252	52°8·0′	0°57·5′E	T	155
Charlesworth	Derby	SK0093	53°26·3′	1°59·6′W	T	110
Charleton	Angus	NO7160	56°44·1′	2°28·0′W	X	45
Charleton and Kinnaber Links	Angus	NO7361	56°44·6′	2°26·0′W	X	45
Charleton Ho	Fife	NO4503	56°13·2′	2°52·8′W	X	59
Charle Wood	Beds	SP9232	51°59·0′	0°39·2′W	F	152,165
Charley Hall	Leic	SK4714	52°43·5′	1°17·8′W	X	129

Charley Houses	Cumbr	SD4193	54°20·0′	2°54·0′W	X	96,97
Charley Knoll	Leic	SK4815	52°44·1′	1°16·9′W	X	129
Charley Mill Fm	Leic	SK4714	52°43·5′	1°17·8′W	FM	129
Charlie's Knowe	Scot Bord	NT6407	55°21·6′	2°33·6′W	X	80
Charlie's Moss	D & G	NY3885	55°9·6′	2°58·0′W	X	79
Charlie's Taing	Orkney	HY6728	59°8·5′	2°34·1′W	X	5
Charlinch	Somer	ST2337	51°7·9′	3°5·6′W	T	182
Charlock Hill	Dorset	ST6118	50°57·8′	2°32·9′W	H	183
Charlottetown	Fife	NO2910	56°16·9′	3°8·4′W	X	59
Charlston Bottom	E Susx	TQ5300	50°47·0′	0°10·6′E	X	199
Charlton	Gren	TQ4178	51°29·2′	0°2·2′E	T	177
Charlton	Hants	SU3547	51°13·5′	1°29·5′W	T	185
Charlton	Herts	TL1728	51°56·5′	0°17·5′W	T	166
Charlton	Northnts	SP5236	52°1·4′	1°14·1′W	T	151
Charlton	Northum	NY8085	55°9·8′	2°18·4′W	T	80
Charlton	Oxon	SU4088	51°35·6′	1°25·0′W	T	174
Charlton	Red & Cl	NZ6415	54°31·8′	1°0·2′W	T	94
Charlton	Somer	ST2926	51°2·0′	3°0·4′W	T	193
Charlton	Somer	ST6343	51°11·3′	2°31·4′W	T	183
Charlton	Somer	ST6852	51°16·2′	2°27·1′W	T	183
Charlton	Surrey	TQ0869	51°24·8′	0°26·4′W	T	176
Charlton	Wilts	ST9022	51°0·1′	2°8·2′W	T	184
Charlton	Wilts	ST9688	51°35·7′	2°3·1′W	T	173
Charlton	Wilts	SU1156	51°18·4′	1°50·1′W	T	173
Charlton	Worcs	SO8371	52°20·4′	2°14·6′W	T	138
Charlton	Worcs	SP0145	52°6·4′	1°58·7′W	T	150
Charlton	Wrekin	SJ5911	52°41·9′	2°36·0′W	T	126
Charlton	W Susx	SU8812	50°54·3′	0°44·5′W	T	197
Charlton Abbots	Glos	SP0324	51°55·1′	1°57·0′W	T	163
Charlton Adam	Somer	ST5328	51°3·2′	2°39·8′W	T	183
Charlton-All-Saints	Wilts	SU1723	51°0·6′	1°45·1′W	T	184
Charlton Barrow	Dorset	ST8903	50°49·8′	2°9·0′W	X	195
Charltonbrook	Sheff	SK3496	53°27·8′	1°28·9′W	T	110,111
Charlton Clump	Wilts	SU0954	51°17·3′	1°51·9′W	F	184
Charlton Court	Kent	TQ8349	51°12·9′	0°37·6′E	X	188
Charlton Court	W Susx	TQ1611	50°53·4′	0°20·7′W	X	198
Charlton Down	Dorset	ST8700	50°48·2′	2°10·7′W	X	194
Charlton Down	Glos	ST8691	51°37·3′	2°11·7′W	X	162,173
Charlton Down	Wilts	ST9020	50°59·0′	2°8·2′W	X	184
Charlton Down	Wilts	SU0852	51°16·3′	1°52·7′W	X	184
Charlton Down	W Susx	SU8811	50°53·7′	0°44·5′W	X	197
Charltondown Covert	Glos	ST8591	51°37·3′	2°12·6′W	F	162,173
Charlton Down Fm	Hants	SU3549	51°14·6′	1°29·5′W	FM	185
Charlton Field	Bath & NE Somer	ST6366	51°23·7′	2°31·5′W	X	172
Charlton Fm	Kent	TQ7748	51°12·4′	0°32·4′E	FM	188
Charlton Fm	N Som	ST4973	51°27·5′	2°43·7′W	FM	172
Charlton Fm	Somer	ST7653	51°16·8′	2°20·3′W	FM	183
Charlton Fm	Wilts	ST9788	51°35·7′	2°2·2′W	FM	173
Charlton Forest	W Susx	SU8915	50°55·9′	0°43·6′W	F	197
Charlton Gorse Fm	Leic	SK6419	52°46·1′	1°2·7′W	FM	129
Charlton Hall	Northum	NU1722	55°29·7′	1°43·4′W	X	75
Charlton Higher Down	Dorset	SY6895	50°45·5′	2°26·8′W	X	194
Charlton Hill	Shrops	SJ5807	52°39·8′	2°36·9′W	H	126
Charlton Hill	Somer	ST6724	51°1·1′	2°27·8′W	X	183
Charlton Hill Fm	Somer	ST6524	51°1·1′	2°29·6′W	FM	183
Charlton Ho	Glos	ST8893	51°38·4′	2°10·0′W	X	162,173
Charlton Ho	Gren	TQ4177	51°28·7′	0°2·2′E	A	177
Charlton Ho	Shrops	SJ6010	52°41·4′	2°35·1′W	X	127
Charlton Horethorne	Somer	ST6623	51°0·6′	2°28·7′W	T	183
Charlton House Fm	Northnts	SP5336	52°1·4′	1°13·3′W	FM	152
Charlton Kings	Glos	SO9620	51°52·9′	2°3·1′W	T	163
Charlton Kings Common	Glos	SO9518	51°51·9′	2°4·0′W	X	163
Charlton Mackrell	Somer	ST5228	51°3·2′	2°40·7′W	T	183
Charlton Manor Fm	Wilts	SU1624	51°1·1′	1°45·9′W	FM	184
Charlton Marshall	Dorset	ST9003	50°49·8′	2°8·1′W	T	195
Charlton Mires	Northum	NU1720	55°28·7′	1°43·4′W	X	75
Charlton Musgrove	Somer	ST7231	51°4·9′	2°23·6′W	T	183
Charlton-on-Otmoor	Oxon	SP5615	51°50·1′	1°10·8′W	T	164
Charlton on the Hill	Dorset	ST8903	50°49·8′	2°9·0′W	T	195
Charlton Park	Glos	SO9520	51°52·9′	2°4·0′W	T	163
Charlton Park	Kent	TR1951	51°13·2′	1°8·6′E	X	179,189
Charlton Park	Wilts	ST9589	51°36·2′	2°3·9′W	A	173
Charlton Park	W Susx	SU8911	50°53·7′	0°43·7′W	F	197
Charlton Wood	Kent	TR1851	51°13·2′	1°7·7′E	F	179,189
Charlwood	E Susx	TQ3934	51°5·5′	0°0·5′W	T	187
Charlwood	Hants	SU6731	51°4·7′	1°2·2′W	T	185,186
Charlwood	Surrey	TQ2441	51°9·5′	0°13·2′W	T	187
Charlwood House	W Susx	TQ2639	51°8·4′	0°11·5′W	A	187
Charlwood Place	Surrey	TQ2441	51°9·5′	0°13·2′W	X	187
Charmandean School	Bucks	SP6839	52°2·9′	1°0·1′W	X	152
Charmans Fm	W Susx	TQ1335	51°6·4′	0°22·8′W	FM	187
Charmborough Fm	Somer	ST6751	51°15·7′	2°28·0′W	FM	183
Charminster	Bourne	SZ1094	50°45·0′	1°51·1′W	T	195
Charminster	Dorset	SY6892	50°43·8′	2°26·8′W	T	194
Charminster Down	Dorset	SY6694	50°44·9′	2°28·5′W	X	194
Charmouth	Dorset	SY3693	50°44·2′	2°54·0′W	T	193
Charm Park	N Yks	SE9883	54°14·2′	0°29·4′W	X	101
Charmwood Fm	Brom	TQ4662	51°20·5′	0°6·2′E	FM	177,188
Charmy Down	Bath & NE Somer	ST7669	51°25·4′	2°20·3′W	X	172
Charmydown Fm	Bath & NE Somer	ST7668	51°24·9′	2°20·3′W	FM	172
Charnaford Fm	Devon	SS8214	50°55·0′	3°40·3′W	FM	181
Charnage	Wilts	ST8331	51°4·9′	2°14·2′W	T	183
Charnage Down	Wilts	ST8433	51°6·0′	2°13·3′W	X	183
Charndon	Bucks	SP6724	51°54·9′	1°1·2′W	T	164,165
Charndon Grounds	Bucks	SP6524	51°54·9′	1°2·9′W	X	164,165
Charnes	Staffs	SJ7733	52°53·9′	2°20·1′W	T	127
Charnes Old Hall	Staffs	SJ7833	52°53·9′	2°19·2′W	R	127
Charney Bassett	Oxon	SU3894	51°38·8′	1°26·7′W	T	164,174
Charnock Green	Lancs	SD5516	53°38·6′	2°40·4′W	T	108
Charnock Hall	Sheff	SK3882	53°20·3′	1°25·3′W	T	110,111
Charnock Hill	Leic	SK4425	52°49·5′	1°20·4′W	X	129
Charnock Ho	Lancs	SD5516	53°38·6′	2°40·4′W	X	108
Charnock Richard	Lancs	SD5515	53°38·0′	2°40·4′W	T	108
Charnwood Forest	Leic	SK4814	52°43·5′	1°17·0′W	X	129
Charnwood Hall	Leic	SK5116	52°44·6′	1°14·3′W	X	129
Charnwood Lodge	Leic	SK4615	52°44·1′	1°18·7′W	X	129

Charr	Aberd	NO6183	56°56·5′	2°38·0′W	X	45
Charsfield	Suff	TM2556	52°9·6′	1°17·8′E	T	156
Char's Stone	Highld	NH3931	57°20·7′	4°40·1′W	A	26
Charston Rock	Monm	ST5288	51°35·6′	2°41·2′W	X	162,172
Charston Sands	Monm	ST5288	51°35·6′	2°41·2′W	X	162,172
Chart Bottom Fm	Kent	TQ7948	51°12·4′	0°34·1′E	FM	188
Chart Corner	Kent	TQ7950	51°13·5′	0°34·2′E	T	188
Chart Court	Kent	TQ9346	51°11·1′	0°46·1′E	X	189
Charter Alley	Hants	SU5957	51°18·8′	1°8·8′W	T	174
Charterhall	Scot Bord	NT7647	55°43·2′	2°22·5′W	X	74
Charterhall Wood	Scot Bord	NT7547	55°43·2′	2°23·4′W	F	74
Charterhouse	Scot Bord	NT6734	55°36·2′	2°31·0′W	X	74
Charterhouse	Somer	ST5055	51°17·8′	2°42·6′W	T	172,182
Charterhouse	Surrey	SU9645	51°12·0′	0°37·2′W	X	186
Charterhouse Fm	Cambs	TL2287	52°28·3′	0°11·8′W	FM	142
Chartershall	Stir	NS7990	56°5·5′	3°56·2′W	T	57
Chartershall	Stir	NS8090	56°5·5′	3°55·3′W	T	57
Charter's Moss Plantation	Black w Dar	SD6916	53°38·6′	2°27·7′W	F	109
Charterstone	Aberd	NJ6345	57°29·9′	2°36·6′W	X	29
Charterville Allotments	Oxon	SP3110	51°47·5′	1°32·6′W	T	164
Chartham	Kent	TR1054	51°15·0′	1°0·9′E	T	179,189
Chartham Downs	Kent	TR1253	51°14·4′	1°2·6′E	X	179,189
Chartham Hatch	Kent	TR1056	51°16·1′	1°1·0′E	T	179
Chartham Park	Surrey	TQ3840	51°8·8′	0°1·2′W	X	187
Chart Hill	Kent	TQ7949	51°12·9′	0°34·2′E	T	188
Chart Ho	Somer	ST7227	51°2·7′	2°23·6′W	X	183
Chartist Cave	Powys	SO1215	51°49·8′	3°16·2′W	X	161
Chart Knolle	Dorset	ST4501	50°48·6′	2°46·5′W	X	193
Chartley Barn Fm	Staffs	SK0029	52°51·7′	1°59·6′W	FM	128
Chartley Castle	Staffs	SK0128	52°51·2′	1°58·7′W	A	128
Chartley Hall	Staffs	SK0028	52°51·2′	1°59·6′W	X	128
Chartley Moss	Staffs	SK0228	52°51·2′	1°57·8′W	F	128
Chartner Burn	Northum	NZ0096	55°15·7′	1°59·6′W	W	81
Chartners	Northum	NZ0095	55°15·2′	1°59·6′W	X	81
Chartners Fm	E Susx	TQ4736	51°6·5′	0°6·4′E	FM	188
Charton	Devon	SY3090	50°42·6′	2°59·1′W	X	193
Charton	Kent	TQ5566	51°22·5′	0°14·0′E	X	177
Charton Cross	Devon	SY3091	50°43·1′	2°59·1′W	X	193
Chart Park	Surrey	TQ1748	51°13·4′	0°19·1′W	X	187
Chartridge	Bucks	SP9303	51°43·3′	0°38·8′W	T	165
Chartridge End Fm	Bucks	SP9204	51°43·9′	0°39·7′W	FM	165
Chart Sutton	Kent	TQ7950	51°13·5′	0°34·2′E	T	188
Chartwell	Kent	TQ4551	51°14·6′	0°5·0′E	X	188
Charvil	Wok	SU7776	51°28·9′	0°53·1′W	T	175
Charvil Fm	Wok	SU7776	51°28·9′	0°53·1′W	FM	175
Charwell Field	Somer	ST6324	51°1·1′	2°31·3′W	X	183
Charwelton	Northnts	SP5355	52°11·7′	1°13·1′W	T	152
Charwelton Hill	Northnts	SP5255	52°11·7′	1°14·0′W	X	151
Charwelton Lodge	Northnts	SP5354	52°11·1′	1°13·1′W	X	152
Chase	N Yks	SE2574	54°9·9′	1°36·6′W	X	99
Chase	Staffs	SJ8637	52°56·1′	2°12·1′W	X	127
Chase Barn	Wilts	ST9821	50°59·5′	2°1·3′W	X	184
Chase Cliffe	Derby	SK3453	53°4·6′	1°29·1′W	X	119
Chase Cross	Hav	TQ5092	51°36·6′	0°10·4′E	T	177
Chase End Hill	Worcs	SO7635	52°1·0′	2°20·6′W	H	150
Chase End Street	Worcs	SO7635	52°1·0′	2°20·6′W	T	150
Chase Fm	Beds	TL1937	52°1·3′	0°15·5′W	FM	153
Chase Fm	Bucks	SP8131	51°58·5′	0°48·8′W	FM	152,165
Chase Fm	Essex	TQ6591	51°35·8′	0°23·3′E	FM	177,178
Chase Fm	Glos	ST5598	51°41·0′	2°38·7′W	FM	162
Chase Fm	Herts	TQ2699	51°40·8′	0°10·3′W	FM	166,176
Chase Fm	Lincs	TF2173	53°14·6′	0°10·8′W	FM	122
Chase Fm	Lincs	TF2224	52°48·2′	0°11·0′W	FM	131
Chase Fm	Norf	TL9597	52°32·4′	0°52·9′E	FM	144
Chase Fm	Northnts	SP9285	52°27·5′	0°38·4′W	FM	141
Chase Fm	Notts	SK6044	52°59·6′	1°6·0′W	FM	129
Chase Fm	Warw	SP2673	52°21·5′	1°36·7′W	FM	140
Chase Fm	W Susx	TQ1426	51°1·5′	0°22·1′W	FM	187,198
Chasehayes	Devon	ST2404	50°50·1′	3°4·4′W	X	192,193
Chase Hill	Glos	ST7388	51°35·6′	2°23·0′W	T	162,172
Chase Hill Fm	N Lincs	TA1519	53°39·5′	0°15·2′W	FM	113
Chase Hill Wood	N Lincs	TA1519	53°39·5′	0°15·2′W	F	113
Chase Ho	Glos	ST5599	51°41·5′	2°38·7′W	X	162
Chase Park	Northnts	SP8455	52°11·4′	0°45·9′W	X	152
Chase Park Fm	Northnts	SP8554	52°10·9′	0°45·0′W	FM	152
Chasepool Fm	Staffs	SO8589	52°30·2′	2°12·9′W	FM	139
Chase Terrace	Staffs	SK0409	52°41·0′	1°56·0′W	T	128
Chase, The	Essex	TM0925	51°53·3′	1°2·6′E	X	168,169
Chase, The	Hants	SU4462	51°21·6′	1°21·7′W	F	174
Chase, The	Leic	SP5687	52°28·9′	1°10·1′W	X	140
Chase, The	Lincs	TF0691	53°24·5′	0°23·9′W	F	112
Chase, The	S Glos	ST7385	51°34·0′	2°23·0′W	X	172
Chase, The	Sol	SP1677	52°23·7′	1°45·5′W	X	139
Chasetown	Staffs	SK0508	52°40·4′	1°55·2′W	T	128
Chase View	Staffs	SJ9215	52°44·2′	2°6·7′W	X	127
Chasewater	Staffs	SK0307	52°39·9′	1°56·9′W	W	139
Chase Wood	E Susx	TQ5836	51°6·3′	0°15·8′E	F	188
Chase Wood	Heref	SO6022	51°53·9′	2°34·5′W	F	162
Chase Wood	N Lincs	TA1212	53°35·8′	0°18·0′W	F	113
Chase Wood	Warw	SP2572	52°21·0′	1°37·6′W	F	140
Chasewood Fm	Oxon	SP3314	51°49·7′	1°30·9′W	FM	164
Chase Woods	Wilts	ST9719	50°58·5′	2°2·2′W	F	184
Chase Woods Fm	Wilts	SU2174	51°28·1′	1°41·5′W	FM	174
Chasleton Glebe	Oxon	SP2330	51°58·3′	1°39·5′W	X	151
Chasms, The	I of M	SC1966	54°3·7′	4°45·5′W	X	95
Chastleton	Oxon	SP2429	51°57·8′	1°38·6′W	T	163
Chastleton Barrow	Oxon	SP2528	51°57·2′	1°37·8′W	X	163
Chastleton Barrow (Fort)	Glos	SP2528	51°57·2′	1°37·8′W	A	163
Chastleton Hill	Oxon	SP2528	51°57·2′	1°37·8′W	X	163
Chastleton House	Oxon	SP2429	51°57·8′	1°38·6′W	A	163
Chaston Fm	Dorset	ST7105	50°50·9′	2°24·3′W	FM	194
Chasty	Devon	SS3402	50°47·9′	4°21·0′W	T	190
Chatburn	Lancs	SD7644	53°53·7′	2°21·5′W	T	103
Chatburn Fm	Suff	TM4269	52°16·2′	1°33·2′E	FM	156
Chatburn Ho	Lancs	SD4954	53°59·0′	2°46·2′W	X	102
Chatcombe Wood	Glos	SO9717	51°51·3′	2°2·2′W	F	163
Chatcull	Staffs	SJ7934	52°54·4′	2°18·3′W	T	127
Chatcull Brook	Staffs	SJ8034	52°54·4′	2°17·4′W	W	127
Chatcull Wood	Staffs	SJ8034	52°54·4′	2°17·4′W	F	127

Chateau Impney	Worcs	SO9164	52°16·7′	2°7·5′W	X	150
Chatelherault Country Park	S Lanak	NS7353	55°45·5′	4°1·0′W	F	64
Chates	W Susx	TQ1916	50°56·1′	0°18·0′W	X	198
Chates	W Susx	TQ2021	50°58·8′	0°17·0′W	X	198
Chatfield's Fm	W Susx	TQ2124	51°0·4′	0°16·1′W	FM	198
Chatfolds	W Susx	TQ1435	51°6·4′	0°21·9′W	X	187
Chatford	Shrops	SJ4705	52°38·6′	2°46·6′W	T	126
Chatham	Caer	ST2189	51°35·9′	3°8·0′W	T	171
Chatham	Medway	TQ7665	51°21·6′	0°32·1′E	T	178
Chatham Green	Essex	TL7115	51°48·7′	0°29·2′E	T	167
Chatham Hall	Essex	TL7013	51°47·6′	0°28·3′E	X	167
Chatham Reach	Medway	TQ7569	51°23·8′	0°31·3′E	W	178
Chat Hill	Brad	SE1132	53°47·3′	1°49·6′W	T	104
Chathill	Northum	NU1826	55°31·9′	1°42·5′W	T	75
Chathill	Surrey	TQ3748	51°13·1′	0°1·9′W	X	187
Chathill Fm	Lancs	SD4144	53°53·6′	2°53·5′W	FM	102
Chatleigh Ho	Wilts	ST7861	51°21·1′	2°18·6′W	X	172
Chatley	Worcs	SO8561	52°15·1′	2°12·8′W	T	150
Chatley Fm	Surrey	TQ0859	51°19·4′	0°26·6′W	FM	187
Chatley Ho	Somer	ST7855	51°17·9′	2°18·5′W	X	172
Chatmore	Shrops	SO6285	52°27·9′	2°33·2′W	X	138
Chat Moss	Salf	SJ7096	53°27·8′	2°26·7′W	X	109
Chatsworth House	Derby	SK2670	53°13·8′	1°36·2′W	A	119
Chatsworth Park	Derby	SK2570	53°13·8′	1°37·1′W	X	119
Chattafin	Devon	SS6102	50°48·3′	3°58·0′W	X	191
Chattan	Devon	SY3097	50°46·3′	2°59·2′W	X	193
Chattenden	Medway	TQ7571	51°24·9′	0°31·4′E	T	178
Chattenden Fm	Medway	TQ7573	51°26·0′	0°31·5′E	FM	178
Chatter End	Essex	TL4725	51°54·5′	0°8·6′E	T	167
Chatteris	Cambs	TL3985	52°26·9′	0°3·1′E	T	142,143
Chatteris Fen	Cambs	TL3979	52°23·7′	0°3·0′E	X	142,143
Chatterley	Durham	NZ0735	54°42·8′	1°53·1′W	X	92
Chatterley	Staffs	SJ8451	53°3·6′	2°13·9′W	T	118
Chattern Hill	Surrey	TQ0871	51°25·9′	0°26·4′W	T	176
Chatterton	Lancs	SD7918	53°39·7′	2°18·7′W	T	109
Chatterton Fm	Donc	SE6618	53°39·5′	0°59·7′W	FM	111
Chatt Ho	E Yorks	TA2531	53°45·9′	0°5·8′W	X	107
Chattisham	Suff	TM0942	52°2·4′	1°3·3′E	T	155,169
Chattis Hill	Hants	SU3236	51°7·6′	1°32·2′W	H	185
Chattis Hill Ho	Hants	SU3235	51°7·0′	1°32·2′W	X	185
Chattle Hill	Warw	SP1990	52°30·7′	1°42·8′W	T	139
Chattlehope	Northum	NT7302	55°18·9′	2°25·1′W	X	80
Chattlehope Burn	Northum	NT7102	55°18·9′	2°27·0′W	W	80
Chatto	Scot Bord	NT7717	55°27·0′	2°21·4′W	T	80
Chatto Craig	Scot Bord	NT7616	55°26·5′	2°22·3′W	H	80
Chatto Craigs	Scot Bord	NT5238	55°38·2′	2°45·3′W	X	73
Chatton	Northum	NU0528	55°33·0′	1°54·8′W	T	75
Chatton Moor	Northum	NU0928	55°33·0′	1°51·0′W	X	75
Chatton Park	Northum	NU0628	55°33·0′	1°53·9′W	X	75
Chattonpark Hill	Northum	NU0729	55°33·5′	1°52·9′W	H	75
Chatton Sandyfords	Northum	NU1026	55°31·9′	1°50·1′W	X	75
Chat Tor	Devon	SX5585	50°39·0′	4°2·7′W	H	191
Chattlehope Crag	Northum	NT7302	55°18·9′	2°25·1′W	X	80
Chatwall Lawn	Shrops	SO5197	52°34·4′	2°43·0′W	X	137,138
Chatwell Hall	Shrops	SO5197	52°34·4′	2°43·0′W	X	137,138
Chatwell Park Fm	Staffs	SJ7913	52°43·1′	2°18·3′W	FM	127
Chaucers	Kent	TQ6159	51°18·7′	0°19·0′E	X	188
Chaulden	Herts	TL0306	51°44·8′	0°30·1′W	T	166
Chaul End	Beds	TL0521	51°52·9′	0°28·1′W	T	166
Chaureth Hall Fm	Essex	TL5828	51°55·9′	0°18·3′E	FM	167
Chavel	Shrops	SJ4213	52°42·9′	2°51·1′W	T	126
Chavenage Green	Glos	ST8695	51°39·5′	2°11·8′W	T	162
Chavenage Ho	Glos	ST8795	51°39·5′	2°10·9′W	A	162
Chavey Down	Brackn	SU8969	51°25·0′	0°42·8′W	T	175
Chawleigh	Devon	SS7112	50°53·8′	3°49·7′W	T	180
Chawleigh Week	Devon	SS6813	50°54·3′	3°52·3′W	X	180
Chawley	Oxon	SP4704	51°44·2′	1°18·8′W	T	164
Chawley Manor Fm	Bucks	SP8195	51°44·9′	0°49·4′W	FM	165
Chawners Yard	Staffs	SJ9660	53°8·5′	2°3·2′W	X	118
Chawridge Manor Fm	Brackn	SU9073	51°27·2′	0°41·9′W	FM	175
Chawson	Worcs	SO8862	52°15·6′	2°10·2′W	T	150
Chawston	Beds	TL1556	52°11·6′	0°18·7′W	T	153
Chawton	Hants	SU7037	51°7·9′	0°59·6′W	T	186
Chawton House	Hants	SU7037	51°7·9′	0°59·6′W	A	186
Chawton Park Fm	Hants	SU6937	51°7·9′	1°0·4′W	FM	186
Chawton Park Wood	Hants	SU6736	51°7·4′	1°2·2′W	F	185,186
Chaxhill	Glos	SO7414	51°49·7′	2°22·2′W	T	162
Chazey Court	Read	SU6975	51°28·4′	1°0·0′W	X	175
Chazey Heath	Oxon	SU6977	51°29·5′	1°0·0′W	T	175
Chazey Wood	Oxon	SU6876	51°29·0′	1°0·9′W	F	175
Cheadle	Staffs	SK0143	52°59·3′	1°58·7′W	T	119,128
Cheadle	Stock	SJ8688	53°23·6′	2°12·2′W	T	109
Cheadle Fm	Ches	SJ7273	53°15·4′	2°24·8′W	FM	118
Cheadle Heath	Stock	SJ8789	53°24·1′	2°11·3′W	T	109
Cheadle Hulme	Stock	SJ8786	53°22·5′	2°11·3′W	T	109
Cheadle Orchard	Shrops	SJ6336	52°55·4′	2°32·6′W	X	127
Cheadle Park	Staffs	SK0043	52°59·3′	1°59·6′W	T	119,128
Chealamy	Highld	NC7250	58°25·4′	4°11·0′W	X	10
Cheal Br	Lincs	TF2229	52°50·9′	0°10·9′W	X	131
Cheal House Fm	Lincs	TF2328	52°50·4′	0°10·0′W	FM	131
Cheam	Croy	TQ2462	51°20·8′	0°12·8′W	T	176,187
Cheam Hawtreys School	Hants	SU5161	51°21·0′	1°15·7′W	X	174
Cheapside	Herts	TL4033	51°58·9′	0°2·7′E	T	167
Cheapside	Win & Maid	SU9469	51°25·0′	0°38·5′W	T	175
Cheapside Fm	Herts	TL1510	51°46·8′	0°19·6′W	FM	166
Chear Fen	Cambs	TL4971	52°19·2′	0°11·6′E	X	154
Chear Fen Fms	Cambs	TL5071	52°19·2′	0°12·5′E	FM	154
Chearsley	Bucks	SP7110	51°47·3′	0°57·8′W	T	165
Chearsley Furze	Bucks	SP7112	51°48·4′	0°57·8′W	F	165
Chearsley Hill Ho	Bucks	SP7110	51°47·3′	0°57·8′W	X	165
Cheat Hill	Heref	SO5648	52°8·0′	2°38·2′W	X	149
Cheaton Brook	Heref	SO5159	52°13·9′	2°42·7′W	W	149
Cheaveleyhall Fm	Ches	SJ4161	53°8·8′	2°52·5′W	FM	117
Chebbard Fm	Dorset	SY7698	50°47·1′	2°20·0′W	FM	194
Chebsey	Staffs	SJ8628	52°51·2′	2°12·1′W	T	127
Checkendon	Oxon	SU6683	51°32·8′	1°2·5′W	T	175
Checkendon Court	Oxon	SU6683	51°32·8′	1°2·5′W	X	175
Checker Leazes	Durham	NZ1625	54°37·3′	1°44·7′W	X	92
Checkers Fm	Notts	SK6849	53°2·3′	0°58·7′W	FM	129
Checkhill Fm	Staffs	SO8587	52°29·1′	2°12·9′W	FM	139

Checkhole	Orkney	HY5101	58°53·9'	2°50·5'W	X	6,7
Checkley	Ches	SJ7346	53°0·9'	2°23·7'W	T	118
Checkley	Heref	SO5938	52°2·6'	2°35·5'W	T	149
Checkley	Staffs	SK0237	52°56·1'	1°57·8'W	T	128
Checkleybank	Staffs	SK0237	52°56·1'	1°57·8'W	X	128
Checkley Brook	Ches	SJ7246	53°0·9'	2°24·6'W	W	118
Checkleyfields	Staffs	SK0238	52°56·6'	1°57·8'W	X	128
Checkley Green	Ches	SJ7245	53°0·3'	2°24·6'W	T	118
Checkley Hall	Ches	SJ7346	53°0·9'	2°23·7'W	A	118
Checkley's Fm	Essex	TL8926	51°54·3'	0°45·2'E	FM	168
Checkley Wood	Ches	SJ7345	53°0·3'	2°23·7'W	F	118
Checkley Wood Fm	Ches	SJ7444	52°59·8'	2°22·8'W	FM	118
Chedburgh	Suff	TL7957	52°11·2'	0°37·5'E	T	155
Cheddar	Somer	ST4553	51°16·6'	2°46·9'W	T	182
Cheddar Cliffs	Somer	ST4754	51°17·2'	2°45·2'W	H	182
Cheddar Gorge	Somer	ST4754	51°17·2'	2°45·2'W	X	182
Cheddar Head Fm	Somer	ST5052	51°16·1'	2°42·6'W	FM	182,183
Cheddar Moor	Somer	ST4551	51°15·6'	2°46·9'W	X	182
Cheddar Reservoir	Somer	ST4453	51°16·6'	2°47·8'W	W	182
Cheddar Wood	Somer	ST4455	51°17·7'	2°47·8'W	F	172,182
Cheddar Yeo	Somer	ST4253	51°16·6'	2°49·5'W	W	182
Cheddington	Bucks	SP9217	51°50·9'	0°39·5'W	T	165
Cheddington Sta	Bucks	SP9218	51°51·4'	0°39·5'W	X	165
Cheddleton	Staffs	SJ9752	53°4·2'	2°2·3'W	T	118
Cheddleton Heath	Staffs	SJ9853	53°4·7'	2°1·4'W	T	118
Cheddon Down	Somer	ST2230	51°4·1'	3°6·4'W	X	182
Cheddon Fitzpaine	Somer	ST2427	51°2·5'	3°4·7'W	T	193
Chedglow	Wilts	ST9493	51°38·4'	2°4·8'W	T	163,173
Chedgrave	Norf	TM3699	52°32·5'	1°29·2'E	T	134
Chedgrave Marshes	Norf	TG4502	52°33·9'	1°37·3'E	X	134
Chedington	Dorset	ST4805	50°50·8'	2°43·9'W	T	193
Chedington Court	Dorset	ST4805	50°50·8'	2°43·9'W	X	193
Chedington Woods	Dorset	ST4907	50°51·8'	2°43·1'W	F	193,194
Chediston	Suff	TM3577	52°20·7'	1°27·4'E	T	156
Chediston Grange	Suff	TM3576	52°20·1'	1°27·4'E	X	156
Chediston Green	Suff	TM3578	52°21·2'	1°27·5'E	T	156
Chediston Hall	Suff	TM3777	52°20·6'	1°29·2'E	X	156
Chedworth	Glos	SP0511	51°48·1'	1°55·3'W	T	163
Chedworth Beacon	Glos	SP0412	51°48·6'	1°56·1'W	X	163
Chedworth Laines	Glos	SP0311	51°48·1'	1°57·0'W	T	163
Chedworth Woods	Glos	SP0513	51°49·2'	1°55·3'W	F	163
Chedzoy	Somer	ST3437	51°7·9'	2°56·2'W	T	182
Chee Dale	Derby	SK1273	53°15·5'	1°48·8'W	X	119
Cheeklaw	Scot Bord	NT7852	55°45·9'	2°20·6'W	X	67,74
Cheeks Fm	Hants	SU8045	51°12·1'	0°50·9'W	FM	186
Cheeks Hill	Derby	SK0269	53°13·3'	1°57·8'W	X	119
Cheerbrook Fm	Ches	SJ6752	53°4·1'	2°29·1'W	FM	118
Cheesden	Roch	SD8216	53°38·7'	2°15·9'W	X	109
Cheesden Brook	Roch	SD8313	53°37·0'	2°15·0'W	W	109
Cheese Bay	N Eil	NF9673	57°38·9'	7°5·3'W	T	18
Cheese Burn	Cumbr	NY6273	55°3·3'	2°35·3'W	W	86
Cheese Burn	D & G	NY2686	55°10·0'	3°9·3'W	W	79
Cheeseburn Grange	Northum	NZ0971	55°2·3'	1°51·1'W	X	88
Cheeseburn Hill	Cumbr	NY6273	55°3·3'	2°35·3'W	X	86
Cheesecake Fm	York	SE6945	53°54·0'	0°56·6'W	FM	105,106
Cheesecake Ho	E Yorks	SE7957	54°0·4'	0°47·3'W	X	105,106
Cheese Cake Wold	E Yorks	SE8057	54°0·4'	0°46·3'W	X	106
Cheese Copse	Northnts	SP6842	52°4·6'	1°0·1'W	F	152
Cheesedown Fm	Hants	SU5449	51°14·5'	1°13·2'W	FM	185
Cheese Fm	Corn	SX2972	50°31·6'	4°24·4'W	FM	201
Cheesefoot Head	Hants	SU5327	51°2·6'	1°14·3'W	H	185
Cheese Hill	Somer	ST7545	51°12·5'	2°21·1'W	X	183
Cheeseman's Fm	Kent	TR3266	51°21·0'	1°20·3'E	FM	179
Cheeseman's Green	Kent	TR0238	51°6·6'	0°53·5'E	X	189
Cheese Press Stone	N Yks	SD6876	54°11·0'	2°29·0'W	X	98
Cheese Vat Fm	N Yks	SE6468	54°6·5'	1°0·8'W	FM	100
Cheese Well	Scot Bord	NT3533	55°35·4'	3°1·4'W	W	73
Cheesewring	Corn	SX2572	50°31·5'	4°27·8'W	X	201
Cheetall Fm	Lancs	SD7141	53°52·1'	2°26·0'W	FM	103
Cheetam Hill	Man	SD8400	53°30·0'	2°14·1'W	T	109
Cheetham Ho	Lancs	SD6132	53°47·2'	2°35·1'W	X	102,103
Chee Tor	Derby	SK1273	53°15·5'	1°48·8'W	X	119
Cheeveley	Northum	NZ2199	55°17·3'	1°39·7'W	X	81
Cheglinch	Devon	SS5143	51°10·2'	4°7·5'W	T	180
Chegworth	Kent	TQ8452	51°14·5'	0°38·6'E	T	188
Cheke's Ct	Kent	TQ9464	51°20·7'	0°47·5'E	X	178
Chelborough Hill	Dorset	ST5404	50°50·3'	2°38·8'W	H	194
Chelburn Moor	Roch	SD9518	53°39·7'	2°4·1'W	X	109
Chelburn Resrs	Roch	SD9518	53°39·7'	2°4·1'W	W	109
Cheldon	Devon	SS7313	50°54·4'	3°48·0'W	T	180
Cheldon Ho	Devon	SS7213	50°54·4'	3°48·9'W	X	180
Cheley Well	Northnts	SP7743	52°5·0'	0°52·2'W	W	152
Chelfham	Devon	SS6135	51°6·1'	3°58·7'W	T	180
Chelfham Barton	Devon	SS6136	51°6·6'	3°58·8'W	X	180
Chelford	Ches	SJ8174	53°16·0'	2°16·7'W	T	118
Chelker House Fm	N Yks	SE0551	53°57·5'	1°55·0'W	FM	104
Chelker Resr	N Yks	SE0551	53°57·5'	1°55·0'W	W	104
Chellaston	C of Derb	SK3730	52°52·2'	1°26·6'W	T	128
Chell Heath	C of Stoke	SJ8752	53°4·1'	2°11·2'W	T	118
Chellington	Beds	SP9555	52°11·3'	0°36·2'W	T	153
Chellow Dean	Brad	SE1134	53°48·4'	1°49·6'W	X	104
Chellow Heights	Brad	SE1135	53°48·9'	1°49·6'W	X	104
Chellows Fm	Surrey	TQ3946	51°12·0'	0°0·2'W	FM	187
Chellows Park	Surrey	TQ4046	51°12·0'	0°0·6'E	X	187
Chells	Herts	TL2625	51°54·8'	0°9·7'W	T	166
Chellshill	Ches	SJ7958	53°7·4'	2°18·4'W	X	118
Chells Manor	Herts	TL2625	51°54·8'	0°9·7'W	A	166
Chelmarsh	Shrops	SO7287	52°29·1'	2°24·3'W	T	138
Chelmarsh Common	Shrops	SO7286	52°28·5'	2°24·3'W	X	138
Chelmarsh Coppice	Shrops	SO7187	52°29·0'	2°25·2'W	F	138
Chelmarsh Reservoir	Shrops	SO7387	52°29·1'	2°23·5'W	W	138
Chelmer & Blackwater Navigation	Essex	TL7909	51°45·3'	0°36·0'E	W	167
Chelmer Village	Essex	TL7307	51°44·3'	0°30·7'E	T	167
Chelmick	Shrops	SO4691	52°31·1'	2°47·4'W	T	137,138
Chelmondiston	Suff	TM2037	51°59·5'	1°12·7'E	T	169
Chelmorton	Derby	SK1169	53°13·3'	1°49·7'W	T	119
Chelmorton Flat	Derby	SK1171	53°14·4'	1°49·7'W	X	119
Chelmscote Manor	Bucks	SP8927	51°56·3'	0°41·9'W	X	165
Chelmsford	Essex	TL7006	51°43·8'	0°28·1'E	T	167
Chelmshoe House Fm	Essex	TL8035	51°59·3'	0°37·7'E	FM	155
Chelmsine	Somer	ST1918	50°57·6'	3°8·8'W	T	181,193
Chelmsley Wood	Sol	SP1886	52°28·5'	1°43·7'W	T	139
Chelsdon	Devon	SS4710	50°52·4'	4°10·1'W	X	191
Chelsea	King	TQ2777	51°28·9'	0°9·9'W	T	176
Chelsea Br	Wan	TQ2877	51°28·9'	0°9·0'W	X	176
Chelsfield	Brom	TQ4664	51°21·6'	0°6·2'E	T	177,188
Chelsham	Surrey	TQ3759	51°19·0'	0°1·7'W	T	187
Chelsham Court Fm	Surrey	TQ3858	51°18·5'	0°0·8'W	FM	187
Chelsham Place Fm	Surrey	TQ3658	51°18·5'	0°2·5'W	FM	187
Chelsing Fm	Herts	TL3417	51°50·4'	0°2·9'W	FM	166
Chelson	Devon	SY1691	50°43·0'	3°11·0'W	X	192,193
Chelston	Somer	ST1521	50°59·2'	3°12·3'W	T	181,193
Chelston	Torbay	SX8964	50°28·2'	3°33·5'W	T	202
Chelston Heathfield	Somer	ST1621	50°59·2'	3°11·4'W	T	181,193
Chelsworth	Suff	TL9847	52°5·4'	0°53·8'E	T	155
Chelsworth Common	Suff	TL9847	52°5·4'	0°53·8'E	T	155
Chelsworth Hall	Suff	TL9847	52°5·4'	0°53·8'E	X	155
Cheltenham	Glos	SO9422	51°54·0'	2°4·8'W	T	163
Chelveston	Northnts	SP9969	52°18·8'	0°32·5'W	T	153
Chelveston Lodge	Northnts	SP9769	52°18·9'	0°34·2'W	X	153
Chelvey	N Som	ST4668	51°24·7'	2°46·2'W	T	171,172,182
Chelvey Batch	N Som	ST4767	51°24·2'	2°45·3'W	T	171,172,182
Chelwood	Bath & NE Somer	ST6361	51°21·0'	2°31·5'W	T	172
Chelwood Beacon	E Susx	TQ4229	51°2·8'	0°1·9'E	X	187,198
Chelwood Common	E Susx	TQ4128	51°2·3'	0°1·1'E	T	187,198
Chelwood Gate	E Susx	TQ4129	51°2·8'	0°1·1'E	T	187,198
Chelwood Ho	Bath & NE Somer	ST6261	51°21·0'	2°32·4'W	X	172
Chelwood Vachery	E Susx	TQ4330	51°3·3'	0°2·8'E	X	187
Chelworth	Wilts	ST9794	51°38·9'	2°2·2'W	T	163,173
Chelworth Lawns	Wilts	ST9694	51°38·9'	2°3·1'W	X	163,173
Chelworth Lower Green	Wilts	SU0892	51°37·8'	1°52·7'W	T	163,173
Chelworth Upper Green	Wilts	SU0892	51°37·8'	1°52·7'W	T	163,173
Chelynch	Somer	ST6543	51°11·3'	2°29·7'W	T	183
Chemistry	Shrops	SJ5341	52°58·1'	2°41·6'W	T	117
Chenery's Fm	Suff	TM4388	52°26·4'	1°34·9'E	FM	156
Cheney Court	Wilts	ST8169	51°25·4'	2°16·0'W	X	173
Cheney Longville	Shrops	SO4284	52°27·3'	2°50·8'W	T	137
Cheney Water	Cambs	TL2943	52°4·4'	0°6·7'W	W	153
Chenhalls	Corn	SW5535	50°10·1'	5°25·5'W	T	203
Chenies	Bucks	TQ0198	51°40·5'	0°32·0'W	T	166,176
Chenies Place	Bucks	TQ0198	51°40·5'	0°32·0'W	X	166,176
Chensil Grove	Suff	TL9158	52°11·5'	0°48·1'E	F	155
Chenson	Devon	SS7009	50°52·2'	3°50·5'W	X	191
Chenson Fm	Devon	SS7009	50°52·2'	3°50·5'W	FM	191
Chepstow (Cas-Gwent)	Monm	ST5393	51°38·3'	2°40·4'W	T	162,172
Chepstow Hill	Newp	ST3590	51°36·5'	2°55·9'W	H	171
Chepstow Park Wood	Monm	ST4897	51°40·4'	2°44·7'W	F	171
Chepstow Park Wood	Monm	ST4997	51°40·4'	2°43·9'W	F	162
Chequerbent	Bolton	SD6706	53°33·2'	2°29·5'W	T	109
Chequer Br	Notts	SK6481	53°19·6'	1°1·5'W	X	111,120
Chequer Court	Kent	TR2859	51°17·3'	1°16·6'E	A	179
Chequerfield	Wakf	SE4620	53°40·7'	1°17·8'W	T	105
Chequer Hall	N Yks	SE6443	53°53·0'	1°1·2'W	X	105,106
Chequer Hill Coppice	Northnts	TL0578	52°23·6'	0°27·0'W	W	142
Chequers	Bucks	SP8405	51°44·5'	0°46·6'W	A	165
Chequers	Hants	SU6963	51°21·9'	1°0·1'W	X	175,186
Chequers	N Yks	SE4797	54°22·2'	1°16·2'W	X	100
Chequers Corner	Norf	TF4908	52°39·2'	0°12·6'E	T	143
Chequers Fm	Lincs	TF3294	53°25·8'	0°0·4'W	FM	113
Chequers Fm	Norf	TM0480	52°23·0'	1°0·3'E	FM	144
Chequers Fm	Norf	TM0789	52°27·8'	1°3·2'E	FM	144
Chequers Manor Fm	Bucks	SU7793	51°38·1'	0°52·9'W	FM	175
Chequers (PH)	Kent	TR3655	51°14·9'	1°23·3'E	X	179
Chequertree	Kent	TR0337	51°6·0'	0°54·4'E	T	179,189
Chequertree Fm	Kent	TQ7834	51°4·9'	0°32·9'E	FM	188
Chequertree Fm	Kent	TQ9238	51°6·8'	0°45·0'E	FM	189
Cherbury	Oxon	SU3796	51°39·9'	1°27·5'W	A	164
Cherbury Ho	Oxon	SU3896	51°39·9'	1°26·6'W	X	164
Chercombe Br	Devon	SX8371	50°31·9'	3°38·7'W	X	202
Cherfold	Surrey	SU9534	51°6·1'	0°38·2'W	X	186
Cherhill	Wilts	SU0370	51°26·0'	1°57·0'W	T	173
Cherhill Down	Wilts	SU0569	51°25·4'	1°55·3'W	H	173
Cherhill Field	Wilts	SU0370	51°26·0'	1°57·0'W	X	173
Cherington	Glos	ST9098	51°41·1'	2°8·3'W	T	163
Cherington	Warw	SP2936	52°1·5'	1°34·2'W	T	151
Cherington Butts	Warw	SP2837	52°2·1'	1°35·1'W	X	151
Cheristow	Devon	SS2525	51°0·1'	4°29·3'W	T	190
Cheriton	Devon	SS7346	51°12·2'	3°48·7'W	T	180
Cheriton	Hants	SU5828	51°3·1'	1°10·0'W	T	185
Cheriton	Kent	TR1936	51°5·1'	1°8·0'E	T	179,189
Cheriton	Swan	SS4593	51°37·1'	4°13·9'W	T	159
Cheriton Barton	Devon	SS8606	50°50·8'	3°36·8'W	X	191
Cheriton Bishop	Devon	SX7793	50°43·7'	3°44·2'W	T	191
Cheriton Cross	Devon	SS8504	50°49·7'	3°37·6'W	X	191
Cheriton Cross	Devon	SX7792	50°43·1'	3°44·2'W	T	191
Cheriton Fitzpaine	Devon	SS8606	50°50·8'	3°36·8'W	T	191
Cheriton Mill	Hants	SU5729	51°3·7'	1°10·8'W	X	185
Cheriton Mill Cross	Devon	SS8507	50°51·3'	3°37·6'W	X	191
Cheriton or Stackpole Elidor	Pemb	SR9897	51°38·4'	4°54·8'W	T	158
Cheriton Ridge	Devon	SS7444	51°11·1'	3°47·8'W	H	180
Cheriton Wood	Hants	SU6029	51°3·7'	1°8·2'W	F	185
Cherkley Court	Surrey	TQ1754	51°16·6'	0°19·0'W	X	187
Cherridge	Devon	SS7620	50°58·2'	3°45·6'W	X	180
Cherrington	Wrekin	SJ6619	52°46·3'	2°29·8'W	T	127
Cherrington Manor	Wrekin	SJ6620	52°46·8'	2°29·8'W	X	127
Cherrington Moor	Wrekin	SJ6718	52°45·8'	2°28·9'W	X	127
Cherrybank	Pth & Kin	NO1022	56°23·2'	3°27·0'W	T	53,58
Cherrybank Gardens	Pth & Kin	NO0922	56°23·1'	3°28·0'W	X	52,53
Cherrybank Gardens	Pth & Kin	NO0922	56°23·1'	3°28·0'W	X	53,58
Cherrybridge	Devon	SS7147	51°12·7'	3°50·4'W	X	180
Cherry Brook	Devon	SX6376	50°34·3'	3°55·7'W	W	191
Cherrybrook House	Devon	SX4878	50°35·2'	4°8·5'W	X	191,201
Cherryburn	Northum	NZ0762	54°57·4'	1°53·0'W	X	88
Cherry Burton	E Yorks	SE9942	53°52·1'	0°29·2'W	T	106
Cherry Burton Wold	E Yorks	SE9541	53°51·6'	0°32·9'W	X	106
Cherry Cobb Sands	E Yorks	TA2121	53°40·5'	0°9·7'W	X	107,113
Cherry Croft Fm	E Susx	TQ6310	50°52·2'	0°19·4'E	FM	199
Cherryfield	Angus	NO4848	56°37·5'	2°50·4'W	X	54
Cherryfield Plantn	Suff	TM0672	52°18·7'	1°1·7'E	F	144,155
Cherry Fm	Bucks	SP8813	51°48·8'	0°43·0'W	FM	165
Cherry Fm	Ches	SJ3079	53°18·4'	3°2·6'W	FM	117
Cherry Fm	Lincs	TF5173	53°14·2'	0°16·2'E	FM	122
Cherry Fm	N Lincs	SE9802	53°30·6'	0°30·9'W	FM	112
Cherry Fm	Norf	TF5118	52°44·5'	0°14·6'E	FM	131
Cherry Fm	N Yks	SE7770	54°7·4'	0°48·9'W	FM	100
Cherry Garden Fm	E Susx	TQ8612	50°52·9'	0°39·0'E	FM	199
Cherry Gardens	Kent	TQ9134	51°4·6'	0°44·0'E	X	189
Cherry Gardens Fm	E Susx	TQ5135	51°5·9'	0°9·8'E	FM	188
Cherry Garth Fm	Lincs	TA1500	53°29·3'	0°15·6'W	FM	113
Cherry Green	Essex	TL5729	51°56·5'	0°17·4'E	T	167
Cherry Green	Herts	TL3525	51°54·7'	0°1·8'W	T	166
Cherry Grove	Somer	ST2522	50°59·8'	3°3·7'W	X	193
Cherry Hall Fm	Warr	SJ6785	53°21·9'	2°29·3'W	FM	109
Cherryhill	Ches	SJ4547	53°1·3'	2°48·8'W	X	117
Cherry Hill	Heref	SO5735	52°0·9'	2°37·2'W	H	149
Cherry Hill	N Yks	SE5872	54°8·7'	1°6·3'W	X	100
Cherry Hill	Suff	TM0045	52°4·3'	0°55·5'E	X	155
Cherry Hinton	Cambs	TL4856	52°11·2'	0°10·3'E	T	154
Cherry Island	Highld	NH3810	57°9·4'	4°40·2'W	X	34
Cherry Lair	D & G	NT3005	55°20·3'	3°5·8'W	H	79
Cherrylane Fm	Warr	SJ6786	53°22·4'	2°29·4'W	FM	109
Cherry Lodge	Wilts	SU0642	51°10·9'	1°54·5'W	X	184
Cherry Orchard	Monm	ST4495	51°39·3'	2°48·2'W	X	171
Cherry Orchard	Shrops	SJ4912	52°42·4'	2°44·9'W	T	126
Cherry Orchard	Wilts	ST8184	51°33·5'	2°16·1'W	F	173
Cherry Orchard	Worcs	SO8553	52°10·7'	2°12·8'W	T	150
Cherry Orchard	Wrex	SJ3040	52°57·4'	3°2·1'W	X	117
Cherry Orchard Fm	Beds	TL0958	52°12·8'	0°23·9'W	FM	153
Cherry Orchard Fm	Dorset	ST8422	51°0·1'	2°13·3'W	FM	183
Cherry Orchard Fm	N Yks	SE6332	53°47·1'	1°2·2'W	FM	105,106
Cherry Orchard Ho	Flint	SJ3163	53°9·8'	3°1·5'W	X	117
Cherryrock Fm	Glos	ST7389	51°36·2'	2°23·0'W	FM	162,172
Cherryslack	Derby	SK1275	53°16·6'	1°48·8'W	X	119
Cherrystone Cott	Lincs	TF0465	53°10·5'	0°26·2'W	X	121
Cherry Tree	Black w Dar	SD6525	53°43·5'	2°31·4'W	T	102,103
Cherry Tree	Bucks	SP9306	51°44·9'	0°38·8'W	X	165
Cherry Tree	Heref	SO4534	52°0·3'	2°47·7'W	X	149,161
Cherry Tree	Northnts	SP5551	52°9·5'	1°11·4'W	X	152
Cherry Tree	Stock	SJ9590	53°24·6'	2°4·1'W	T	109
Cherry Tree Fm	Bucks	SU8798	51°40·7'	0°44·1'W	FM	165
Cherrytree Fm	Ches	SJ7484	53°21·4'	2°23·0'W	FM	109
Cherry Tree Fm	Kent	TQ8041	51°8·6'	0°34·8'E	FM	188
Cherry Tree Fm	Norf	TL9595	52°31·3'	0°52·9'E	FM	144
Cherry Tree Fm	Norf	TM0195	52°31·2'	0°58·2'E	FM	144
Cherry Tree Fm	N Yks	SE5917	53°39·0'	1°6·0'W	FM	111
Cherry Tree Fm	N Yks	SE6590	54°18·3'	0°59·6'W	FM	94,100
Cherry Tree Fm	Suff	TM3169	52°16·5'	1°23·6'E	FM	156
Cherrytree Hill	C of Derb	SK3836	52°55·4'	1°25·7'W	T	128
Cherrytree Ho	Kent	TQ9727	51°0·7'	0°48·9'E	X	189
Cherrytree Lodge	Northnts	SP7442	52°4·5'	0°54·8'W	X	152
Cherrytrees	Scot Bord	NT8129	55°33·5'	2°17·6'W	X	74
Cherrytree Slade	Staffs	SJ9819	52°46·4'	2°1·4'W	X	127
Cherry Valley Fm	Lincs	TF1699	53°28·7'	0°14·7'W	FM	113
Cherry Willingham	Lincs	TF0372	53°14·3'	0°27·0'W	T	121
Cherry Wood	E Yorks	SE9465	54°4·6'	0°33·4'W	F	101
Cherry Yate	Lancs	SD6536	53°49·4'	2°31·5'W	X	102,103
Chertsey	Surrey	TQ0466	51°23·2'	0°29·9'W	T	176
Chertsey Common	Surrey	SU9965	51°22·8'	0°34·3'W	X	175,176
Chertsey Meads	Surrey	TQ0566	51°23·2'	0°29·1'W	T	176
Cherubeer	Devon	SS5912	50°53·7'	3°59·9'W	X	180
Cherwell Barn	Oxon	SP3629	51°57·7'	1°28·2'W	X	164
Cherwell Fm	Northnts	SP5157	52°12·8'	1°14·8'W	FM	151
Cherwell Fm	Oxon	SP5209	51°46·9'	1°14·4'W	FM	164
Chescombe Bottom	Glos	SO9814	51°49·7'	2°1·3'W	F	163
Chescombe Fm	Dorset	ST8200	50°48·2'	2°14·9'W	FM	194
Cheselbourne	Dorset	SY7699	50°47·6'	2°20·0'W	T	194
Cheselbourne West Down	Dorset	SY7498	50°47·1'	2°21·7'W	X	194
Cheseldyne Spinney	Leic	SK8006	52°39·0'	0°48·6'W	F	141
Cheseridge Fm	W Berks	SU5078	51°30·2'	1°16·4'W	FM	174
Cheseridge Wood	W Berks	SU5078	51°30·2'	1°16·4'W	F	174
Chesfield Park	Herts	TL2427	51°55·9'	0°11·4'W	X	166
Chesford Br	Warw	SP3069	52°19·3'	1°33·2'W	X	151
Chesham	Bucks	SP9601	51°42·2'	0°36·3'W	T	165
Chesham	Bury	SD8112	53°36·5'	2°16·8'W	T	109
Chesham Bois	Bucks	SU9699	51°41·1'	0°36·3'W	T	165,176
Chesham Vale	Bucks	SP9603	51°43·3'	0°36·2'W	X	165
Cheshire College of Agriculture	Ches	SJ6454	53°5·2'	2°31·8'W	X	118
Cheshire Coppice	Wrekin	SJ6214	52°43·6'	2°33·4'W	F	127
Cheshire Cycle Way	Ches	SJ5355	53°5·7'	2°41·7'W	X	117
Cheshire Fields	Ches	SJ6140	52°57·6'	2°34·4'W	X	118
Cheshire Fm	Ches	SJ4959	53°7·8'	2°45·3'W	FM	117
Cheshire Fm	Flint	SJ2670	53°13·6'	3°6·1'W	FM	117
Cheshire Kennels	Ches	SJ5969	53°13·2'	2°36·4'W	X	117
Cheshire Ring Canal Walk	Ches	SJ7359	53°7·9'	2°23·8'W	X	118
Cheshire Ring Canal Walk	Traf	SJ7995	53°27·3'	2°18·6'W	X	109
Cheshire Ring Canal Work	Ches	SJ5778	53°18·1'	2°38·3'W	X	117
Cheshire's Close	Staffs	SJ8658	53°7·4'	2°12·1'W	X	118
Cheshire Wood	Staffs	SK1153	53°4·7'	1°49·7'W	F	119
Cheshunt	Herts	TL3502	51°42·3'	0°2·4'W	T	166
Cheshunt Common	Herts	TL3103	51°42·9'	0°5·8'W	X	166
Cheshunt field	Essex	TL9622	51°52·0'	0°51·2'E	X	168
Cheshunt Marsh	Herts	TL3600	51°41·2'	0°1·6'W	X	166
Cheshunt Park	Herts	TL3404	51°43·3'	0°3·2'W	X	166
Cheshunts	Essex	TM0033	51°57·8'	0°55·1'E	X	168
Chesil	Dorset	SY6873	50°33·6'	2°26·7'W	T	194
Chesil Beach	Dorset	SY6081	50°37·9'	2°33·6'W	X	194
Chesley	Kent	TQ8563	51°20·4'	0°39·8'E	T	178
Cheslyn Hay	Staffs	SJ9707	52°39·9'	2°2·3'W	T	127,139
Chesney Farm	E Yorks	TA0357	54°0·2'	0°25·3'W	FM	107
Chespool Ho	Lincs	TF2130	52°51·5'	0°11·8'W	X	131
Chessell Fm	I of W	SZ3985	50°40·0'	1°26·5'W	FM	196
Chessetts Wood	Warw	SP1873	52°21·5'	1°43·7'W	T	139
Chessgrove	Glos	SO6819	51°52·4'	2°27·5'W	X	162
Chessington	King	TQ1863	51°21·5'	0°17·9'W	T	176,187

Chessington World of Adventures	King	TQ1762	51°20·9′	0°18·8′W	X	176,187
Chessley Hill Fm	Wilts	SU0381	51°31·9′	1°57·0′W	FM	173
Chessmount	Bucks	SP9601	51°42·2′	0°36·3′W	T	165
Chesson's Fm	E Susx	TQ6631	51°3·5′	0°22·5′E	FM	188
Chestal	Glos	ST7698	51°41·0′	2°20·4′W	X	162
Chestall	Staffs	SK0512	52°42·6′	1°55·2′W	T	128
Chested	Kent	TQ5046	51°11·8′	0°9·2′E	X	188
Chester	Ches	SJ4066	53°11·5′	2°53·5′W	T	117
Chesterbank	Scot Bord	NT9460	55°50·2′	2°5·3′W	X	67
Chesterblade	Somer	ST6641	51°10·3′	2°28·8′W	T	183
Chester Business Park	Ches	SJ4063	53°9·9′	2°53·4′W	X	117
Chestercourt Hall Fm	N Yks	SE6227	53°44·4′	1°3·2′W	FM	105
Chestercourt House Fm	N Yks	SE6226	53°43·8′	1°3·2′W	FM	105
Chesterfield	Derby	SK3871	53°14·3′	1°25·4′W	T	119
Chesterfield	Scot Bord	NT9453	55°46·5′	2°5·3′W	X	67,74,75
Chesterfield	Staffs	SK1005	52°38·8′	1°50·7′W	T	139
Chesterfield Canal	Notts	SK7492	53°25·4′	0°52·8′W	W	112
Chesterfield Canal	Roth	SK5182	53°20·2′	1°13·6′W	W	111,120
Chesterford Park	Essex	TL5342	52°3·5′	0°14·3′E	X	154
Chestergarth Ho	Durham	NY9442	54°46·6′	2°5·2′W	X	87
Chesterhall	E Loth	NT4374	55°57·6′	2°54·3′W	X	66
Chesterhall	Scot Bord	NT5531	55°34·5′	2°42·4′W	X	73
Chesterhall	S Lanak	NS9632	55°34·5′	3°38·5′W	X	72
Chesterhill	Fife	NO4327	56°26·2′	2°55·0′W	X	54,59
Chesterhill	Fife	NO5714	56°19·2′	2°41·3′W	X	59
Chester Hill	Midlo	NT3456	55°47·8′	3°2·7′W	X	66,73
Chesterhill	Midlo	NT3765	55°52·7′	3°0·0′W	T	66
Chesterhill	Northum	NU1334	55°36·2′	1°47·2′W	X	75
Chesterhill	Northum	NU1604	55°20·0′	1°44·4′W	X	81
Chester Hill	Scot Bord	NT5246	55°42·6′	2°45·4′W	X	73
Chester Hill	Scot Bord	NT9560	55°50·2′	2°4·4′W	X	67
Chester Hill	S Lanak	NS9539	55°38·2′	3°39·6′W	H	72
Chesterhill Ho	E Loth	NT4561	55°50·6′	2°52·3′W	X	66
Chesterhill Slakes	Northum	NU1435	55°36·8′	1°46·2′W	X	75
Chester Ho	Durham	NY9138	54°44·5′	2°8·0′W	X	91,92
Chester Ho	Northnts	SP9166	52°17·3′	0°39·5′W	X	152
Chester Ho	N Yks	SE4193	54°20·1′	1°21·7′W	X	99
Chesterholm	Northum	NY7766	54°59·5′	2°21·1′W	X	86,87
Chesterhope	Northum	NY8985	55°9·8′	2°9·9′W	T	80
Chester Hope	Northum	NZ0299	55°17·4′	1°57·7′W	X	81
Chesterhope Common	Northum	NY9184	55°9·3′	2°8·0′W	X	80
Chesterhouse	Scot Bord	NT7720	55°28·6′	2°21·4′W	X	74
Chesterhouse Hill	Scot Bord	NT7620	55°28·6′	2°22·3′W	H	74
Chesterknowes	Scot Bord	NT5226	55°31·8′	2°45·2′W	T	73
Chesterlane Brook	Ches	SJ6165	53°11·1′	2°34·6′W	W	118
Chesterlane Fm	Ches	SJ6165	53°11·6′	2°34·6′W	FM	118
Chester-Le-Street	Durham	NZ2751	54°51·4′	1°34·3′W	T	88
Chester Moor	Durham	NZ2649	54°50·4′	1°35·3′W	T	88
Chester New Bridge	Durham	NZ2852	54°52·0′	1°33·4′W	A	88
Chester Road Sta	Birm	SP1193	52°32·3′	1°49·9′W	X	139
Chesters	Fife	NO5209	56°16·5′	2°46·1′W	X	59
Chesters	Northum	NT9814	55°25·4′	2°1·5′W	X	81
Chesters	Northum	NU1035	55°36·8′	1°50·0′W	X	75
Chesters	Northum	NY9170	55°1·7′	2°8·0′W	X	87
Chesters	Northum	NZ0087	55°10·9′	1°59·6′W	X	81
Chesters	N Yks	SD7068	54°6·7′	2°27·1′W	X	98
Chesters	Scot Bord	NT6022	55°29·7′	2°37·6′W	X	74
Chesters	Scot Bord	NT6210	55°23·2′	2°35·6′W	T	80
Chesters	Scot Bord	NT7447	55°43·2′	2°24·4′W	X	74
Chesters Burn	Northum	NT9914	55°25·4′	2°0·5′W	W	81
Chesters Fm	E Loth	NT5670	55°55·5′	2°41·8′W	FM	67
Chesters Grange	Scot Bord	NT6022	55°29·7′	2°37·6′W	X	74
Chesters Hill	Dorset	SY5883	50°38·9′	2°35·3′W	H	194
Chesters Pike	Northum	NY7067	55°0·0′	2°27·7′W	X	86,87
Chesters, The	E Loth	NT5078	55°59·8′	2°47·7′W	X	66
Chesters, The	E Loth	NT6673	55°57·2′	2°32·2′W	X	67
Chesters, The (Fort)	E Loth	NT5078	55°59·8′	2°47·7′W	A	66
Chesters, The (Fort)	E Loth	NT6673	55°57·2′	2°32·2′W	A	67
Chesterstone	Fife	NO4204	56°13·8′	2°55·7′W	X	59
Chesterton	Cambs	TL1295	52°32·7′	0°20·5′W	T	142
Chesterton	Cambs	TL4660	52°13·4′	0°8·6′E	T	154
Chesterton	Glos	SP0100	51°42·2′	1°58·7′W	T	163
Chesterton	Oxon	SP5621	51°53·3′	1°10·8′W	T	164
Chesterton	Shrops	SO7897	52°34·5′	2°19·1′W	T	138
Chesterton	Staffs	SJ8349	53°2·5′	2°14·8′W	T	118
Chesterton	Warw	SP3558	52°13·4′	1°28·9′W	T	151
Chesterton Fields Fm	Oxon	SP5422	51°53·9′	1°12·5′W	FM	164
Chesterton Fields Fm	Warw	SP3359	52°13·9′	1°30·6′W	FM	151
Chesterton Fm	Glos	SP0100	51°42·2′	1°58·7′W	FM	163
Chesterton Green	Warw	SP3458	52°13·4′	1°29·7′W	T	151
Chesterton Hill	Warw	SP3456	52°12·3′	1°29·7′W	X	151
Chesterton Lodge	Cambs	TL1195	52°32·7′	0°21·4′W	X	142
Chesterton Lodge	Oxon	SP5621	51°53·3′	1°10·8′W	X	164
Chesterton Mill Fm	Shrops	SO7997	52°34·5′	2°18·2′W	FM	138
Chesterton Plantn	Glos	SU0099	51°41·6′	1°59·6′W	F	163
Chesterton Wood	Warw	SP3457	52°12·8′	1°29·7′W	F	151
Chester Villa	N Yks	SE8381	54°13·3′	0°43·2′W	X	100
Chesterwood	Northum	NY8265	54°59·0′	2°16·4′W	T	86,87
Chestfield	Kent	TR1365	51°20·9′	1°3·9′E	T	179
Chestham Park	W Susx	TQ2117	50°56·6′	0°16·3′W	X	198
Chesthill	Pth & Kin	NN6947	56°36·1′	4°7·6′W	X	51
Chestnut	S Glos	ST7093	51°38·3′	2°25·6′W	A	162,172
Chestnut Avenue	Lincs	TF0320	52°46·3′	0°28·0′W	X	130
Chestnut Centre	Derby	SK0782	53°20·3′	1°53·3′W	X	110
Chestnut Copse	Hants	SU8251	51°15·4′	0°49·1′W	F	186
Chestnutfield Wood	E Susx	TQ6928	51°1·8′	0°25·0′E	F	188,199
Chestnut Fm	Cambs	TF4204	52°37·1′	0°6·3′E	FM	142,143
Chestnut Fm	Cambs	TL4869	52°18·2′	0°10·6′E	FM	154
Chestnut Fm	Glos	SO9125	51°55·6′	2°7·5′W	FM	163
Chestnut Fm	Leic	SK6112	52°42·4′	1°5·4′W	FM	129
Chestnut Fm	Lincs	TF1420	52°46·2′	0°18·2′W	FM	130
Chestnut Fm	Norf	TM1787	52°26·5′	1°12·0′E	FM	156
Chestnut Fm	Notts	SK6132	52°53·2′	1°5·2′W	FM	129
Chestnut Fm	Suff	TL6578	52°22·7′	0°25·9′E	FM	143
Chestnut Hill	Cumbr	NY2723	54°36·1′	3°7·4′W	T	89,90
Chestnut Hill	Herts	TL3134	51°59·6′	0°5·1′W	X	153
Chestnut Hill	Notts	SK6580	53°19·0′	1°1·0′W	F	111,120
Chestnut Ho	Cambs	TF3913	52°42·0′	0°3·8′E	X	131,142,143
Chestnut Ho	Lincs	TF1813	52°42·3′	0°14·8′W	X	130,142

Chestnut Ho	Lincs	TF2323	52°47·7′	0°10·1′W	X	131
Chestnut House Fm	Ches	SJ7270	53°13·8′	2°24·8′W	FM	118
Chestnut House Fm	Lincs	TF2048	53°1·2′	0°12·3′W	FM	131
Chestnut Lodge	Suff	TM2470	52°17·2′	1°17·5′E	X	156
Chestnuts Fm	Essex	TL9715	51°48·2′	0°51·8′E	FM	168
Chestnuts Fm	Leic	SP7899	52°35·2′	0°50·5′W	FM	141
Chestnuts Fm	Lincs	SK8955	53°5·3′	0°39·9′W	FM	121
Chestnuts Fm	Lincs	TF2194	53°26·0′	0°10·3′W	FM	113
Chestnuts Fm	Peterb	TF3108	52°39·5′	0°3·4′W	FM	142
Chestnuts Fm	Suff	TM0252	52°8·0′	0°57·5′E	FM	155
Chestnuts Fm	Suff	TM0472	52°18·7′	1°0·0′E	FM	144,155
Chestnuts Fm	Suff	TM5087	52°25·6′	1°41·0′E	FM	156
Chestnuts Hill	Glos	SO6714	51°49·7′	2°28·3′W	H	162
Chestnuts, The	Cambs	TL3287	52°28·1′	0°3·0′W	X	142
Chestnuts, The	Leic	SP6592	52°31·6′	1°2·1′W	X	141
Chestnuts, The	Lincs	TF0930	52°51·6′	0°22·5′W	X	130
Chestnuts, The	Norf	TM4496	52°30·7′	1°36·2′E	X	134
Chestnuts, The	Suff	TL9659	52°11·9′	0°52·5′E	X	155
Chestnuts, The	Suff	TM2157	52°10·2′	1°14·3′E	X	156
Chestnuts, The	Suff	TM2458	52°10·7′	1°17·0′E	X	156
Chestnuts, The	Suff	TM2468	52°16·1′	1°17·4′E	X	156
Chestnuts, The	Suff	TM2566	52°15·0′	1°18·2′E	X	156
Chestnut Street	Kent	TQ8763	51°20·3′	0°41·5′E	T	178
Chestnut Tree Fm	Norf	TM1282	52°23·9′	1°7·4′E	FM	144
Chestnut Tree Fm	Suff	TM2872	52°18·1′	1°21·1′E	FM	156
Chestnut Wood	Somer	ST7540	51°9·8′	2°21·1′W	F	183
Chest of Dee	Aberd	NO0188	56°58·6′	3°37·3′W	W	43
Cheston	Devon	SX6858	50°24·7′	3°51·1′W	T	202
Chestwood	Devon	SS5631	51°3·9′	4°2·9′W	X	180
Chest Wood	Essex	TL9620	51°50·9′	0°51·1′E	F	168
Cheswardine	Shrops	SJ7129	52°51·7′	2°25·4′W	T	127
Cheswardine Hall	Shrops	SJ7230	52°52·2′	2°24·6′W	X	127
Cheswardine Park Fm	Shrops	SJ7031	52°52·8′	2°26·3′W	FM	127
Cheswell	Wrekin	SJ7117	52°45·2′	2°25·4′W	T	127
Cheswell Grange	Wrekin	SJ7116	52°44·7′	2°25·4′W	X	127
Cheswick	Northum	NU0346	55°42·7′	1°56·7′W	T	75
Cheswick Black Rocks	Northum	NU0347	55°43·2′	1°56·7′W	X	75
Cheswick Buildings	Northum	NU0245	55°42·2′	1°57·7′W	T	75
Cheswick Green	Sol	SP1275	52°22·6′	1°49·0′W	T	139
Cheswick Ho	Northum	NU0246	55°42·7′	1°57·7′W	X	75
Cheswick Sands	Northum	NU0546	55°42·7′	1°54·8′W	X	75
Cheswick Shiel	Northum	NU0546	55°42·7′	1°54·8′W	X	75
Cheswood Grange	Warw	SP1872	52°21·0′	1°43·7′W	X	139
Chesworth Fm	W Susx	TQ1729	51°3·1′	0°19·5′W	FM	187,198
Chetney Cotts	Kent	TQ8969	51°23·5′	0°43·4′E	X	178
Chetney Hill	Kent	TQ8869	51°23·6′	0°42·5′E	X	178
Chetney Marshes	Kent	TQ8871	51°24·6′	0°42·6′E	X	178
Chetnole	Dorset	ST6008	50°52·4′	2°33·7′W	T	194
Chetsford Water	Somer	SS8542	51°10·2′	3°38·3′W	W	181
Chetterwood	Dorset	ST9708	50°52·5′	2°2·2′W	F	195
Chettiscombe	Devon	SS9614	50°55·2′	3°28·4′W	T	181
Chettisham	Cambs	TL5483	52°25·6′	0°16·3′E	T	143
Chettle	Dorset	ST9513	50°55·2′	2°3·9′W	T	195
Chettle Down	Dorset	ST9414	50°55·8′	2°4·7′W	X	195
Chettle Ho	Dorset	ST9513	50°55·2′	2°3·9′W	X	195
Chettle Long Barrow	Dorset	ST9313	50°55·2′	2°5·6′W	A	195
Chetton	Shrops	SO6690	52°30·6′	2°29·7′W	T	138
Chetwode	Bucks	SP6429	51°57·6′	1°3·7′W	T	164,165
Chetwode Grange	Bucks	SP6328	51°57·0′	1°4·6′W	X	164,165
Chetwynd Aston	Wrekin	SJ7517	52°45·2′	2°21·8′W	T	127
Chetwynd Grange	Wrekin	SJ7121	52°47·4′	2°25·4′W	X	127
Chetwynd Heath	Wrekin	SJ7122	52°47·9′	2°25·4′W	F	127
Chetwynd or Salter's Br	Staffs	SK1813	52°43·1′	1°43·6′W	X	128
Chetwynd Park	Wrekin	SJ7321	52°47·4′	2°23·6′W	X	127
Chetwynd's Coppice	Staffs	SK0415	52°44·2′	1°56·0′W	F	128
Chevaux de frise Point	Essex	TM2217	51°48·7′	1°13·6′E	X	169
Cheveley	Cambs	TL6860	52°13·0′	0°28·0′E	T	154
Cheveley Park	Cambs	TL6760	52°13·0′	0°27·1′E	X	154
Cheveley Park Stud	Cambs	TL6761	52°13·5′	0°27·1′E	X	154
Cheveney	Kent	TQ7049	51°13·1′	0°26·5′E	X	188
Cheveney Fm	Kent	TQ7050	51°13·7′	0°26·5′E	FM	188
Chevening	Kent	TQ4857	51°17·8′	0°7·8′E	T	188
Chevening Cross	Kent	TQ4957	51°17·8′	0°8·6′E	X	188
Chevening Park	Kent	TQ4857	51°17·8′	0°7·8′E	X	188
Cheveralton	Pemb	SM9101	51°40·4′	5°1·0′W	X	157,158
Cheveral Wood	Notts	SK7356	53°6·0′	0°54·2′W	F	120
Cheverell Down	Wilts	ST9650	51°15·2′	2°3·1′W	X	184
Cheverells	Herts	TL0515	51°49·7′	0°28·2′W	X	166
Cheverells Fm	Surrey	TQ3956	51°17·4′	0°0·0′W	FM	187
Cheverell's Green	Herts	TL0515	51°49·7′	0°28·2′W	T	166
Cheverell Wood	Wilts	ST9755	51°17·9′	2°2·2′W	F	173
Cheveridge Fm	Worcs	SO6464	52°16·6′	2°31·3′W	FM	138,149
Chevers Hall	Essex	TL5803	51°42·4′	0°17·6′E	X	167
Cheverton Down	I of W	SZ4484	50°39·5′	1°22·3′W	X	196
Cheverton Fm	I of W	SZ4584	50°39·5′	1°21·4′W	FM	196
Cheverton Fm	I of W	SZ5783	50°38·9′	1°11·2′W	FM	196
Chevet Grange	Wakf	SE3414	53°37·5′	1°28·7′W	X	110,111
Chevet Park	Wakf	SE3415	53°38·1′	1°28·7′W	X	110,111
Chevin End	Brad	SE1844	53°53·8′	1°43·2′W	T	104
Chevin Forest Park	Leeds	SE2144	53°53·7′	1°40·4′W	F	104
Chevington	Suff	TL7859	52°12·3′	0°36·7′E	T	155
Chevington Burn	Northum	NZ2598	55°16·8′	1°36·0′W	W	81
Chevington Hall Fm	Suff	TL7860	52°12·8′	0°36·7′E	FM	155
Chevington Lodge	Northum	NZ2298	55°16·8′	1°38·8′W	X	81
Chevington Lodge Fm	Suff	TL7860	52°12·8′	0°36·7′E	FM	155
Chevington Moor	Northum	NZ2196	55°15·7′	1°39·7′W	X	81
Chevington Wood	Northum	NZ2299	55°17·3′	1°38·8′W	F	81
Chevin House Fm	Derby	SK3346	53°0·9′	1°30·1′W	FM	119,128
Chevinside	Derby	SK3446	53°0·9′	1°29·2′W	X	119,128
Chevin's Wood	Suff	TL9262	52°13·6′	0°49·1′E	F	155
Chevin, The	Leeds	SE2044	53°53·7′	1°41·3′W	X	104
Cheviot Burn	Scot Bord	NT8619	55°28·1′	2°12·9′W	W	80
Cheviot Fm	Northum	NY9776	55°5·0′	2°2·4′W	FM	87
Cheviot Hills, The	Northum	NT9022	55°29·8′	2°9·1′W	H	74,75
Cheviot Hills, The	Scot Bord	NT7811	55°23·8′	2°20·4′W	H	80
Cheviot, The	Northum	NT9020	55°28·7′	2°9·1′W	H	74,75
Cheviot View	Scot Bord	NT4736	55°37·1′	2°50·1′W	X	73
Chevithorne	Devon	SS9715	50°55·8′	3°27·6′W	T	181
Chevithorne Barton	Devon	SS9815	50°55·8′	3°26·7′W	X	181
Chew	Derby	SJ9992	53°25·7′	2°0·5′W	X	109

Chew Brook	Oldham	SE0202	53°31·1′	1°57·8′W	W	110
Chew Green	Scot Bord	NT7808	55°22·2′	2°20·4′W	X	80
Chew Hill	Bath & NE Somer	ST5764	51°22·6′	2°36·7′W	X	172,182
Chew Magna	Bath & NE Somer	ST5763	51°22·1′	2°36·7′W	T	172,182
Chew Mill	Lancs	SD7136	53°49·4′	2°26·0′W	X	103
Chew Moor	Bolton	SD6607	53°33·8′	2°30·4′W	T	109
Chew Resr	Oldham	SE0301	53°30·6′	1°56·9′W	W	110
Chew Stoke	Bath & NE Somer	ST5561	51°21·0′	2°38·4′W	T	172,182
Chewton Bunny	Dorset	SZ2193	50°44·4′	1°41·8′W	X	195
Chewton Field Fm	Somer	ST6153	51°16·7′	2°33·2′W	FM	183
Chewton Keynsham	Bath & NE Somer	ST6566	51°23·8′	2°29·8′W	T	172
Chewton Mendip	Somer	ST5953	51°16·7′	2°34·9′W	T	182,183
Chewton Place	Bath & NE Somer	ST6566	51°23·8′	2°29·8′W	X	172
Chewton Wood	Somer	ST6155	51°17·8′	2°33·2′W	F	172
Chew Valley Lake	Bath & NE Somer	ST5760	51°20·5′	2°36·7′W	W	172,182
Cheylesmore	Cov	SP3377	52°23·6′	1°30·5′W	T	140
Cheyne	Aberd	NO8486	56°58·2′	2°15·3′W	X	45
Cheyne Hill	Aberd	NO8387	56°58·7′	2°16·3′W	X	45
Cheyney Br	Cambs	TF4109	52°39·9′	0°5·5′E	X	142,143
Cheyney Fm	Northnts	SP8351	52°9·3′	0°46·8′W	FM	152
Cheyney Rock	Kent	TQ9375	51°26·7′	0°47·0′E	X	178
Cheyneys Lodge	Cambs	TL2939	52°2·3′	0°6·8′W	X	153
Cheynies	Shetld	HU3438	60°7·8′	1°22·8′W	X	4
Chibbanagh Plantation	I of M	SC3275	54°8·9′	4°33·9′W	F	95
Chibbet	Somer	SS8337	51°7·5′	3°39·9′W	X	181
Chibbet Post	Somer	SS8437	51°7·5′	3°39·1′W	X	181
Chibburn Fm	Northum	NZ2597	55°16·2′	1°36·0′W	FM	81
Chibley Fm	Somer	ST3811	50°53·9′	2°52·5′W	FM	193
Chicell's Hurst	Peterb	TF2602	52°36·3′	0°8·0′W	X	142
Chichacott	Devon	SX6096	50°45·0′	3°58·7′W	T	191
Chicheley	Mil Key	SP9045	52°6·0′	0°40·8′W	T	152
Chicheley Brook	Mil Key	SP9044	52°5·5′	0°40·8′W	W	152
Chicheley Brook	Mil Key	SP9346	52°6·5′	0°38·1′W	W	153
Chicheley Hill	Mil Key	SP8945	52°6·0′	0°41·6′W	X	152
Chichester	W Susx	SU8604	50°50·0′	0°46·3′W	T	197
Chichester and the Downs Cycle Route	W Susx	SU7914	50°55·4′	0°52·2′W	X	197
Chichester Canal	W Susx	SU8401	50°48·4′	0°48·1′W	W	197
Chichester Channel	W Susx	SU7801	50°48·4′	0°53·2′W	W	197
Chichester Hall (Hotel)	Kent	TQ7729	51°2·2′	0°31·9′E	X	188,199
Chichester Harbour	W Susx	SU7500	50°47·9′	0°55·8′W	W	197
Chickenden Fm	Kent	TQ8143	51°9·7′	0°35·7′E	FM	188
Chickengrove Bottom	Wilts	SU0321	50°59·5′	1°57·0′W	X	184
Chickenley	Kirk	SE2621	53°41·3′	1°36·0′W	T	104
Chicken Rock	I of M	SC1463	54°2·0′	4°50·0′W	X	95
Chickerell	Dorset	SY6480	50°37·3′	2°30·2′W	T	194
Chickering	Suff	TM2176	52°20·5′	1°15·1′E	X	156
Chicklade	Wilts	ST9134	51°6·5′	2°7·3′W	T	184
Chicklade Bottom Fm	Wilts	ST9334	51°6·5′	2°5·6′W	FM	184
Chickney	Essex	TL5728	51°55·9′	0°17·4′E	T	167
Chicksands	Beds	TL1239	52°2·5′	0°21·6′W	T	153
Chicksands Priory	Beds	TL1239	52°2·5′	0°21·6′W	X	153
Chicksands Wood	Beds	TL1040	52°3·1′	0°23·4′W	F	153
Chicksgrove	Wilts	ST9729	51°3·9′	2°2·2′W	T	184
Chick, The	Corn	SW7661	50°24·6′	5°8·8′W	X	200
Chickward	Heref	SO2853	52°10·5′	3°2·8′W	T	148
Chickwell Fm	Somer	ST7554	51°17·3′	2°21·1′W	FM	183
Chickwell New Fm	Somer	ST7554	51°17·3′	2°21·1′W	FM	183
Chidden	Hants	SU6517	50°57·2′	1°4·1′W	T	185
Chidden Down	Hants	SU6619	50°58·2′	1°3·2′W	X	185
Chidden Holt	Hants	SU6516	50°56·6′	1°4·1′W	F	185
Chiddingfold	Surrey	SU9535	51°6·6′	0°38·2′W	T	186
Chiddingly	E Susx	TQ5414	50°54·5′	0°11·8′E	T	199
Chiddinglye	W Susx	TQ3532	51°4·5′	0°4·0′W	X	187
Chiddingly Place	E Susx	TQ5414	50°54·5′	0°11·8′E	X	199
Chiddingstone	Kent	TQ4945	51°11·3′	0°8·3′E	T	188
Chiddingstone Causeway	Kent	TQ5246	51°11·8′	0°10·9′E	T	188
Chiddingstone Hoath	Kent	TQ4942	51°9·7′	0°8·2′E	T	188
Chiddlecombe	Devon	SS3924	50°59·8′	4°17·3′W	X	190
Chideock	Dorset	SY4292	50°43·7′	2°48·9′W	T	193
Chideock Fm	Dorset	SY7981	50°37·9′	2°17·4′W	FM	194
Chideock Manor	Dorset	SY4293	50°44·3′	2°48·9′W	X	193
Chidgley	Somer	ST0436	51°7·2′	3°21·9′W	T	181
Chidham	W Susx	SU7903	50°49·5′	0°52·3′W	T	197
Chidham Point	W Susx	SU7704	50°50·1′	0°54·0′W	X	197
Chidswell	Kirk	SE2623	53°42·4′	1°36·0′W	T	104
Chiefswood	Scot Bord	NT5333	55°35·6′	2°44·3′W	X	73
Chieveley	W Berks	SU4773	51°27·5′	1°19·0′W	T	174
Chieveley Service Area	W Berks	SU4872	51°26·9′	1°18·2′W	X	174
Chiflik Fm	Ches	SJ5154	53°5·1′	2°43·5′W	FM	117
Chigborough Fm	Essex	TL8708	51°44·6′	0°42·9′E	FM	168
Chignall Hall	Essex	TL6610	51°46·1′	0°24·7′E	X	167
Chignall Smealy	Essex	TL6611	51°46·6′	0°24·8′E	T	167
Chignall St James	Essex	TL6709	51°45·5′	0°25·6′E	T	167
Chigwell	Essex	TQ4393	51°37·3′	0°4·3′E	T	177
Chigwell Row	Essex	TQ4693	51°37·2′	0°6·9′E	T	177
Chilaway Fm	Oxon	SP3539	52°3·1′	1°29·0′W	FM	151
Chilbolton	Hants	SU3939	51°9·2′	1°26·2′W	T	185
Chilbolton Down	Hants	SU4136	51°7·5′	1°24·5′W	T	185
Chilboro Hill Fm	Bucks	SP7810	51°47·2′	0°51·8′W	FM	165
Chilbridge	Dorset	ST9901	50°48·7′	2°0·5′W	T	195
Chilbridge Fm	Devon	SS5937	51°7·1′	4°0·5′W	FM	180
Chilbridge Fm	Dorset	ST9802	50°49·3′	2°1·3′W	FM	195
Chil Brook	Oxon	SP4009	51°46·9′	1°24·8′W	W	164
Chilbury Hill	Wilts	ST8186	51°34·6′	2°16·1′W	X	173
Chilcarroch	D & G	NX3549	54°48·8′	4°33·6′W	X	83
Chilcomb	Hants	SU5028	51°3·2′	1°16·8′W	T	185
Chilcomb Down	Hants	SU5229	51°3·7′	1°15·1′W	X	185
Chilcombe	Devon	SY1895	50°45·2′	3°9·4′W	X	192,193
Chilcombe	Dorset	SY5291	50°43·2′	2°40·4′W	T	194
Chilcombe	Somer	ST1138	51°8·3′	3°15·9′W	T	181
Chilcombe Bottom	Bath & NE Somer	ST7668	51°24·9′	2°20·3′W	X	172

Chilcombe Hill	Dorset	SY5391	50°43·2'	2°39·6'W	H	194
Chilcombe Hill (Fort)	Dorset	SY5391	50°43·2'	2°39·6'W	A	194
Chilcompton	Somer	ST6451	51°15·7'	2°30·6'W	T	183
Chilcote	Leic	SK2811	52°42·0'	1°34·7'W	T	128
Chilcote Manor	Somer	ST5846	51°12·9'	2°35·7'W	X	182,183
Chilcott	Somer	SS8827	51°2·1'	3°35·5'W	X	181
Childerditch	Essex	TQ6089	51°34·9'	0°19·0'E	T	177
Childer Hill Fm	Hants	SU6739	51°9·0'	1°2·1'W	FM	185,186
Childerley Gate	Cambs	TL3559	52°13·0'	0°1·0'W	T	154
Childerley Hall	Cambs	TL3561	52°14·1'	0°1·0'W	A	154
Childer Thornton	Ches	SJ3677	53°17·4'	2°57·2'W	T	117
Childer Wood	Heref	SO6643	52°5·3'	2°29·4'W	F	149
Childe's Tomb	Devon	SX6270	50°31·0'	3°56·4'W	X	202
Childhay	Dorset	ST4103	50°49·6'	2°49·9'W	X	193
Child Okeford	Dorset	ST8312	50°54·7'	2°14·1'W	T	194
Child Pit Fm	Shrops	SJ7515	52°44·2'	2°21·8'W	FM	127
Children's Village, The	E Loth	NT4662	55°51·1'	2°51·3'W	X	66
Childrey	Oxon	SU3687	51°35·1'	1°28·4'W	T	174
Childrey Brook	Oxon	SU4294	51°38·8'	1°23·2'W	W	164,174
Childrey Field	Oxon	SU3586	51°34·5'	1°29·3'W	X	174
Childrey Warren	Oxon	SU3584	51°33·5'	1°29·3'W	X	174
Childsbridge	Kent	TQ5557	51°17·7'	0°13·8'E	T	188
Child's Court Fm	W Berks	SU5775	51°28·5'	1°10·4'W	FM	174
Childscourt School	Somer	ST6927	51°2·7'	2°26·1'W	X	183
Childs Ercall	Shrops	SJ6625	52°49·5'	2°29·9'W	T	127
Child's Fm	Cambs	TL2964	52°15·8'	0°6·2'W	FM	153
Child's Hill	Barnet	TQ2486	51°33·8'	0°12·3'W	T	176
Child's Seat, The or Suidh' an Fhir-bhig	Highld	NC9625	58°12·4'	3°45·7'W	H	17
Childswickham	Worcs	SP0738	52°2·7'	1°53·5'W	T	150
Childwall	Liv	SJ4189	53°23·9'	2°52·8'W	T	108
Childwick Bury	Herts	TL1310	51°46·9'	0°21·3'W	T	166
Childwick Green	Herts	TL1410	51°46·9'	0°20·4'W	T	166
Childwick Hall	Herts	TL1311	51°47·4'	0°21·3'W	X	166
Chilfinch Hill	Wilts	ST9235	51°7·1'	2°6·5'W	X	184
Chilford Hall Vineyard	Cambs	TL5648	52°6·7'	0°17·1'E	X	154
Chilfrome	Dorset	SY5898	50°47·0'	2°35·4'W	T	194
Chilgrove	W Susx	SU8214	50°55·4'	0°49·6'W	T	197
Chilgrove Hill	W Susx	SU8214	50°55·4'	0°49·6'W	X	197
Chilham	Kent	TR0653	51°14·6'	0°57·5'E	T	179,189
Chilhampton	Wilts	SU0933	51°6·0'	1°51·9'W	X	184
Chilla	Devon	SS4402	50°48·0'	4°12·4'W	X	190
Chilla Carr	Derby	SK2943	52°59·3'	1°33·7'W	X	119,128
Chillacombe Fm	Devon	SX9998	50°46·6'	3°25·6'W	FM	192
Chilla Moor	Devon	SS4602	50°48·1'	4°10·7'W	X	190
Chilland	Hants	SU5232	51°5·3'	1°15·1'W	X	185
Chillaton	Devon	SX4381	50°36·7'	4°12·8'W	T	201
Chillaton	Devon	SX6950	50°20·4'	3°50·1'W	X	202
Chillaton Ho	Devon	SX4281	50°36·7'	4°13·6'W	X	201
Chilleirivagh	N Eil	NF7620	57°9·6'	7°21·1'W	X	31
Chillenden	Kent	TR2653	51°14·1'	1°14·6'E	T	179
Chillerton	I of W	SZ4884	50°39·4'	1°18·9'W	T	196
Chillerton Down	I of W	SZ4783	50°38·9'	1°19·7'W	X	196
Chillerton Fm	I of W	SZ4883	50°38·9'	1°18·9'W	FM	196
Chillesford	Suff	TM3852	52°7·1'	1°29·0'E	T	156
Chillesford Lodge	Suff	TM3950	52°6·0'	1°29·8'E	X	156
Chilley	Devon	SX7650	50°20·4'	3°44·2'W	X	202
Chilley Fm	E Susx	TQ6306	50°50·1'	0°19·3'E	FM	199
Chillies	E Susx	TQ4927	51°1·6'	0°7·9'E	X	188,199
Chilling	Hants	SU5004	50°50·2'	1°17·0'W	X	196
Chillingford	Devon	SS7508	50°51·7'	3°46·2'W	X	191
Chillingham	Northum	NU0626	55°31·9'	1°53·9'W	T	75
Chillingham Barns	Northum	NU0526	55°31·9'	1°54·8'W	X	75
Chillingham Castle	Northum	NU0625	55°31·4'	1°53·9'W	A	75
Chillingham Park	Northum	NU0625	55°31·4'	1°53·9'W	X	75
Chilling Place Stud	Oxon	SP6416	51°50·6'	1°3·9'W	X	164,165
Chillington	Devon	SX7942	50°16·2'	3°41·5'W	T	202
Chillington	Somer	ST3811	50°53·9'	2°52·5'W	T	193
Chillington Fm	Staffs	SJ8607	52°39·9'	2°12·0'W	FM	127,139
Chillington Hall	Staffs	SJ8606	52°39·3'	2°12·0'W	A	127,139
Chillingwood Fm	I of W	SZ5588	50°41·6'	1°12·9'W	FM	196
Chilliswood Fm	Somer	ST1922	50°59·7'	3°8·9'W	FM	181,193
Chillmill	Kent	TQ6540	51°8·3'	0°23·6'E	T	188
Chilly Bridge	Somer	SS9230	51°3·8'	3°32·1'W	X	181
Chilly Hill	Cambs	TL5854	52°9·9'	0°19·0'E	X	154
Chilmark	Wilts	ST9632	51°5·5'	2°3·0'W	T	184
Chilmark Common	Wilts	ST9731	51°4·9'	2°2·2'W	X	184
Chilmark Down	Wilts	ST9635	51°7·1'	2°3·0'W	X	184
Chilmead Fm	Surrey	TQ2951	51°14·8'	0°8·7'W	FM	187
Chilmington Green	Kent	TQ9840	51°7·7'	0°50·2'E	T	189
Chilmore	Dorset	ST7603	50°49·8'	2°20·1'W	X	194
Chilpark	Corn	SX1796	50°44·3'	4°35·2'W	X	190
Chilsey	Highld	NC8955	58°28·4'	3°53·7'W	X	10
Chilsey Green	Lancs	SD6740	53°51·6'	2°29·7'W	X	102
Chilsham	E Susx	TQ6313	50°53·8'	0°19·5'E	T	199
Chilson	Oxon	SP3119	51°52·4'	1°32·6'W	T	164
Chilson	Somer	ST3203	50°49·6'	2°57·5'W	T	193
Chilson Common	Somer	ST3304	50°50·1'	2°56·7'W	T	193
Chilstone	Heref	SO3939	52°3·0'	2°53·0'W	X	149,161
Chilston Park	Kent	TQ8950	51°13·3'	0°42·8'E	X	189
Chilswell Fm	Oxon	SP4903	51°43·6'	1°17·0'W	FM	164
Chilswell Ho (Priory)	Oxon	SP4803	51°43·7'	1°17·9'W	X	164
Chilsworthy	Corn	SX4172	50°31·8'	4°14·2'W	T	201
Chilsworthy	Devon	SS3206	50°50·0'	4°22·8'W	T	190
Chiltern	Devon	SS9523	51°0·0'	3°29·4'W	X	181
Chiltern Fm	Bucks	SP9817	51°50·8'	0°34·2'W	FM	165
Chiltern Green	Beds	TL1319	51°51·7'	0°21·1'W	T	166
Chiltern Hall	Beds	TL1220	51°52·3'	0°22·0'W	X	166
Chiltern Hills	Bucks	SP8305	51°44·5'	0°47·5'W	H	165
Chiltern Hills	Oxon	SU7192	51°37·6'	0°58·1'W	H	175
Chiltern Hundreds	Bucks	SU9489	51°35·7'	0°38·2'W	X	175
Chiltern Hundreds	Bucks	SU9588	51°35·2'	0°37·3'W	X	175,176
Chilterns, The	Bucks	SP8509	51°46·6'	0°45·7'W	X	165
Chilthorne Domer	Somer	ST5219	50°58·3'	2°40·6'W	T	183
Chiltington	E Susx	TQ3815	50°55·3'	0°1·8'W	T	198
Chilton	Bucks	SP6811	51°47·8'	1°0·4'W	T	164,165
Chilton	Devon	SS8604	50°49·7'	3°36·7'W	X	191
Chilton	Devon	SS9205	50°50·3'	3°31·6'W	X	192
Chilton	Durham	NZ2829	54°39·6'	1°33·5'W	T	93
Chilton	Kent	TR3664	51°19·8'	1°23·7'E	T	179

Chilton	Oxon	SU4885	51°33·9'	1°18·1'W	T	174
Chilton	Shrops	SJ5309	52°40·8'	2°41·3'W	X	126
Chilton	Shrops	SO6778	52°24·2'	2°28·7'W	X	138
Chilton	Suff	TL8942	52°2·9'	0°45·8'E	T	155
Chilton	W Berks	SU3370	51°25·9'	1°31·1'W	X	174
Chilton Candover	Hants	SU5940	51°9·6'	1°9·0'W	T	185
Chilton Cantelo	Somer	ST5722	51°0·0'	2°36·4'W	T	183
Chilton Chine	I of W	SZ4082	50°38·4'	1°25·7'W	X	196
Chilton Downs	Oxon	SU4784	51°33·4'	1°18·9'W	X	174
Chilton East Ho	Durham	NZ3030	54°40·1'	1°31·7'W	X	93
Chilton Fm	I of W	SZ4182	50°38·4'	1°24·8'W	FM	196
Chilton Fm	Kent	TR2743	51°8·7'	1°15·1'E	FM	179
Chilton Fm	Swin	SU1280	51°31·4'	1°49·2'W	FM	173
Chilton Foliat	Wilts	SU3170	51°25·9'	1°32·9'W	T	174
Chilton Grange	Durham	NZ3029	54°39·6'	1°31·7'W	X	93
Chilton Grounds	Bucks	SP6911	51°47·8'	0°59·6'W	X	165
Chilton Grove	Bucks	SP6712	51°48·4'	1°1·3'W	X	164,165
Chilton Grove	Shrops	SJ5209	52°40·8'	2°42·2'W	X	126
Chilton Grove	Suff	TL8943	52°3·4'	0°45·8'E	X	155
Chilton Lane	Durham	NZ3030	54°40·1'	1°31·7'W	T	93
Chilton Leys	Suff	TM0259	52°11·8'	0°57·7'E	X	155
Chilton Leys	Suff	TM0259	52°11·8'	0°57·7'E	X	155
Chilton Manor	Hants	SU5840	51°9·6'	1°9·8'W	X	185
Chilton Moor	Somer	ST3742	51°10·7'	2°53·7'W	X	182
Chilton Moor	Sund	NZ3249	54°50·3'	1°29·7'W	T	88
Chiltonpark Fm	Bucks	SP6612	51°48·4'	1°2·2'W	FM	164,165
Chilton Park Fm	Wilts	SU3270	51°25·9'	1°32·0'W	FM	174
Chilton Polden	Somer	ST3739	51°9·0'	2°53·7'W	T	182
Chilton Priory	Somer	ST3738	51°8·5'	2°53·6'W	X	182
Chilton Street	Suff	TL7546	52°5·3'	0°33·7'E	T	155
Chilton Trinity	Somer	ST2939	51°9·0'	3°0·5'W	T	182
Chilton Trivett	Somer	ST2538	51°8·4'	3°3·9'W	X	182
Chilton Wood	Hants	SU5841	51°10·1'	1°9·8'W	F	185
Chilturst	E Susx	TQ6512	50°53·3'	0°21·1'E	X	199
Chilver House Fm	Norf	TF6820	52°45·3'	0°29·8'E	FM	132
Chilvers Coton	Warw	SP3590	52°30·6'	1°28·7'W	T	140
Chilverton	Devon	SS6906	50°50·6'	3°51·3'W	X	191
Chilverton Elms	Kent	TR2840	51°7·1'	1°15·9'E	X	179
Chilwell	Notts	SK5135	52°54·8'	1°14·1'W	T	129
Chilwell Dam Fm	C of Nott	SK5142	52°58·6'	1°14·0'W	FM	129
Chilworth	Hants	SU4118	50°57·8'	1°24·6'W	T	185
Chilworth	Surrey	TQ0247	51°13·0'	0°32·0'W	T	186
Chilworth Common	Hants	SU4117	50°57·3'	1°24·6'W	F	185
Chilworth Fm	Oxon	SP6303	51°43·6'	1°4·9'W	FM	164,165
Chilworth Manor	Hants	SU4018	50°57·8'	1°25·4'W	X	185
Chilworth Manor	Surrey	TQ0247	51°13·0'	0°32·0'W	X	186
Chilworth Old Village	Hants	SU4018	50°57·8'	1°25·4'W	X	185
Chilworth Ring	Hants	SU4117	50°57·3'	1°24·6'W	A	185
Chilworth Tower	Hants	SU4017	50°57·3'	1°25·4'W	X	185
Chilworthy Ho	Somer	ST3112	50°54·4'	2°58·5'W	X	193
Chimballs	Essex	TL6216	51°49·4'	0°21·4'E	X	167
Chimney	Oxon	SP3500	51°42·1'	1°29·2'W	T	164
Chimney Barn	N Yks	SE2862	54°3·4'	1°33·9'W	X	99
Chimney Down	Devon	ST0219	50°58·0'	3°23·4'W	X	181
Chimney-end	Oxon	SP3115	51°50·2'	1°32·6'W	T	164
Chimney Fm	Lincs	TF1717	52°44·5'	0°15·6'W	FM	130
Chimney Hill	Northum	NU0230	55°34·1'	1°57·7'W	H	75
Chimney Mill	Suff	TL8269	52°17·6'	0°40·5'E	X	155
Chimney Rocks	I Scilly	SV9415	49°57·6'	6°15·7'W	X	203
Chimneys, The	Norf	TG3631	52°49·7'	1°30·6'E	X	133
Chimney Street	Suff	TL7248	52°6·4'	0°31·1'E	T	154
Chimsworthy Fm	Devon	SX4693	50°43·2'	4°10·5'W	A	190
China Hall Fm	Durham	NZ0946	54°48·8'	1°51·2'W	FM	88
Chineham	Hants	SU6555	51°17·7'	1°3·7'W	T	175,185,186
Chine Way Fm	Devon	SY1395	50°45·1'	3°13·6'W	FM	192,193
Chineway Hill	Devon	SY1295	50°45·1'	3°14·5'W	X	192,193
Chingford	Wal F	TQ3994	51°37·9'	0°0·9'E	T	166,177
Chingford Green	Wal F	TQ3894	51°37·9'	0°0·0'E	T	166,177
Chingford Hatch	Wal F	TQ3892	51°36·8'	0°0·0'W	T	177
Chinglebraes	Orkney	HY4208	58°57·6'	3°0·0'W	X	6,7
Chingle Hall	Lancs	SD5535	53°48·8'	2°40·6'W	X	102
Chingley Manor	Kent	TQ6933	51°4·5'	0°25·1'E	X	188
Chingley Wood	Kent	TQ6833	51°4·5'	0°24·3'E	F	188
Chinham Fm	Oxon	SU3194	51°38·9'	1°32·7'W	FM	164,174
Chink Fm	Wilts	ST9685	51°34·1'	2°3·1'W	FM	173
Chinkwell Spinney	Northnts	SP6764	52°16·4'	1°0·7'W	F	152
Chinkwell Tor	Devon	SX7278	50°35·5'	3°48·1'W	H	191
Chinkwell Wood	Bucks	SP6614	51°49·5'	1°2·1'W	F	164,165
Chinley	Derby	SK0482	53°20·3'	1°56·0'W	T	110
Chinley Churn	Derby	SK0383	53°20·9'	1°56·9'W	H	110
Chinley Head	Derby	SK0484	53°21·4'	1°56·0'W	T	110
Chinley Ho	Derby	SK0282	53°20·3'	1°57·8'W	X	110
Chinnel Fm	Shrops	SJ5543	52°59·2'	2°39·8'W	FM	117
Chinnock Brook	Somer	ST4813	50°55·1'	2°44·0'W	W	193
Chinnor	Oxon	SP7500	51°41·9'	0°54·5'W	T	165
Chinnor Hill	Bucks	SU7699	51°41·3'	0°53·6'W	X	165
Chinn's Wood	Warw	SP2369	52°19·4'	1°39·4'W	F	139,151
Chinslade Fm	Warw	SP3236	52°1·5'	1°31·6'W	FM	151
Chinthurst Hill	Surrey	TQ0145	51°11·9'	0°32·9'W	H	186
Chipchase Castle	Northum	NY8875	55°4·4'	2°10·8'W	A	87
Chipchase Mill	Northum	NY8874	55°3·9'	2°10·8'W	X	87
Chipchase Strothers	Northum	NY8874	55°3·9'	2°10·8'W	X	87
Chipknowe	D & G	NY1286	55°9·9'	3°22·5'W	X	78
Chipley	Devon	SX8072	50°32·4'	3°41·2'W	X	191
Chipley	Somer	ST1123	51°0·2'	3°15·7'W	T	181,193
Chipley Abbey	Suff	TL7649	52°6·9'	0°34·6'E	X	155
Chipmans Platt	Glos	SO7806	51°45·4'	2°18·7'W	T	162
Chipman Strand	Corn	SX1598	50°45·4'	4°37·0'W	X	190
Chipnall	Shrops	SJ7231	52°52·8'	2°24·6'W	T	127
Chipnall Lees	Shrops	SJ7332	52°53·3'	2°23·7'W	X	127
Chipnall Wood	Shrops	SJ7131	52°52·8'	2°25·5'W	F	127
Chippenhall Green	Suff	TM2875	52°19·8'	1°21·2'E	T	156
Chippenham	Cambs	TL6669	52°17·9'	0°26·5'E	T	154
Chippenham	Wilts	ST9173	51°27·6'	2°7·4'W	T	173
Chippenham Fen	Cambs	TL6469	52°17·9'	0°24·7'E	F	154
Chippenham Hill	Suff	TL6965	52°15·7'	0°29·0'E	X	154
Chippenham Lodge	Cambs	TL6669	52°17·9'	0°26·5'E	X	154
Chippenham Park	Cambs	TL6668	52°17·3'	0°26·4'E	X	154
Chipperfield	Herts	TL0401	51°42·1'	0°29·3'W	T	166
Chipperfield Common	Herts	TL0401	51°42·1'	0°29·3'W	F	166

Chipperfield Ho	Herts	TL0302	51°42·7'	0°30·2'W	X	166
Chipperkyle	D & G	NX7868	54°59·8'	3°54·0'W	X	84
Chipperkyle Hill	D & G	NX7769	55°0·3'	3°55·0'W	H	84
Chipperlagan	E Ayr	NS4520	55°27·2'	4°26·6'W	X	70
Chippermore	D & G	NX2948	54°48·1'	4°39·2'W	X	82
Chippermore Point	D & G	NX2947	54°47·6'	4°39·2'W	X	82
Chippermore Port	D & G	NX2848	54°48·1'	4°40·1'W	W	82
Chippetts Fm	Essex	TL9225	51°53·7'	0°47·8'E	FM	168
Chipping	Herts	TL3532	51°58·4'	0°1·7'W	T	166
Chipping	Lancs	SD6243	53°53·2'	2°34·3'W	T	102,103
Chipping Barnet	Barnet	TQ2496	51°39·2'	0°12·1'W	T	166,176
Chipping Campden	Glos	SP1539	52°3·2'	1°46·5'W	T	151
Chipping Court	Warw	SP2253	52°10·7'	1°40·3'W	X	151
Chipping Fm	Oxon	SP5215	51°50·1'	1°14·3'W	FM	164
Chipping Hill	Essex	TL8115	51°48·5'	0°37·9'E	T	168
Chipping Hill	Herts	TL3532	51°58·4'	0°1·7'W	X	166
Chipping Ho	Lancs	SD5053	53°58·5'	2°45·3'W	X	102
Chippinghurst Manor	Oxon	SP6001	51°42·5'	1°7·5'W	X	164,165
Chipping Lawn	Lancs	SD6244	53°53·7'	2°34·3'W	X	102,103
Chipping Norton	Oxon	SP3126	51°56·1'	1°32·6'W	T	164
Chipping Ongar	Essex	TL5503	51°42·5'	0°15·0'E	T	167
Chipping Sodbury	S Glos	ST7282	51°32·4'	2°23·8'W	T	172
Chipping Warden	Northnts	SP4948	52°7·9'	1°16·7'W	T	151
Chipp's Manor	Bucks	SU8093	51°38·0'	0°50·3'W	X	175
Chipshop	Devon	SX4375	50°33·5'	4°12·6'W	X	201
Chipstable	Somer	ST0427	51°2·3'	3°21·8'W	T	181
Chipstead	Kent	TQ4956	51°17·2'	0°8·6'E	T	188
Chipstead	Surrey	TQ2757	51°18·1'	0°10·3'W	T	187
Chipstead Bottom	Surrey	TQ2657	51°18·1'	0°11·2'W	X	187
Chipton	Devon	SX8552	50°21·6'	3°36·6'W	X	202
Chirbury	Shrops	SO2698	52°34·7'	3°5·1'W	T	137
Chirdon	Northum	NY7683	55°8·7'	2°22·2'W	X	80
Chirdon Burn	Northum	NY7381	55°7·6'	2°25·0'W	W	80
Chirdonhead	Northum	NY7181	55°7·6'	2°26·9'W	X	80
Chirdon Moor	Northum	NY7682	55°8·2'	2°22·2'W	X	80
Chirk	Wrex	SJ2937	52°55·8'	3°3·0'W	T	126
Chirk Bank	Shrops	SJ2936	52°55·2'	3°3·0'W	T	126
Chirk Castle	Wrex	SJ2638	52°56·3'	3°5·7'W	A	126
Chirk Green	Wrex	SJ2938	52°56·3'	3°3·0'W	T	126
Chirmorie Cairn	S Ayr	NX2076	55°3·0'	4°48·6'W	X	76
Chirmorrie	S Ayr	NX2076	55°3·0'	4°48·6'W	X	76
Chirm, The	Northum	NZ0895	55°15·2'	1°52·0'W	X	81
Chirnside	Scot Bord	NT8756	55°48·1'	2°12·0'W	T	67,74
Chirnsidebridge	Scot Bord	NT8556	55°48·1'	2°13·9'W	T	67,74
Chirnside Hall (Hotel)	Scot Bord	NT8856	55°48·1'	2°11·0'W	X	67,74
Chirton	N Tyne	NZ3468	55°0·6'	1°27·7'W	T	88
Chirton	Wilts	SU0757	51°19·0'	1°53·6'W	T	173
Chirton Bottom	Wilts	SU0655	51°17·9'	1°54·4'W	X	173
Chirton Down	Wilts	SU0754	51°17·3'	1°53·6'W	X	184
Chirton Gorse	Wilts	SU0653	51°16·8'	1°54·5'W	X	184
Chirton Maggot	Wilts	SU0655	51°17·9'	1°54·4'W	X	173
Chisbridge	Bucks	SU8088	51°35·3'	0°50·3'W	X	175
Chisbridge Cross	Bucks	SU8189	51°35·9'	0°49·4'W	T	175
Chisbury	Wilts	SU2765	51°23·2'	1°36·3'W	A	174
Chisbury	Wilts	SU2766	51°23·8'	1°36·3'W	T	174
Chisbury Lane Fm	Wilts	SU2666	51°23·8'	1°37·2'W	FM	174
Chisbury Wood	Wilts	SU2765	51°23·2'	1°36·3'W	F	174
Chiscan	Arg & Bt	NR6718	55°24·3'	5°40·4'W	X	68
Chiscan Water	Arg & Bt	NR6916	55°23·3'	5°38·4'W	W	68
Chiselborough	Somer	ST4614	50°55·6'	2°45·7'W	T	193
Chiselborough Hill	Somer	ST4814	50°55·6'	2°44·0'W	X	193
Chiselborough Ho	Somer	ST4614	50°55·6'	2°45·7'W	X	193
Chiselbury	Wilts	SU0128	51°3·3'	1°58·8'W	A	184
Chiselbury Bay	Devon	SY0984	50°39·1'	3°16·9'W	W	192
Chiseldon	Swin	SU1879	51°30·8'	1°44·0'W	T	173
Chiseldown	W Susx	SU9111	50°53·7'	0°42·0'W	H	197
Chiselhampton Ho	Oxon	SU5999	51°41·4'	1°8·4'W	X	164
Chisel Hill	Norf	TG2417	52°42·5'	1°19·4'E	X	133,134
Chisel Rocks	Somer	ST2649	51°14·4'	3°3·2'W	X	182
Chiserley	Cald	SE0028	53°45·1'	1°59·6'W	T	104
Chishill Windmill	Cambs	TL4138	52°1·6'	0°3·7'E	X	154
Chisholme	Scot Bord	NT4112	55°24·2'	2°55·5'W	X	79
Chislehampton	Oxon	SU5998	51°40·9'	1°8·4'W	T	164
Chislehurst	Brom	TQ4470	51°24·9'	0°4·6'E	T	177
Chislehurst Common	Brom	TQ4470	51°24·9'	0°4·6'E	F	177
Chislehurst West	Brom	TQ4371	51°25·4'	0°3·8'E	T	177
Chislet	Kent	TR2264	51°20·1'	1°11·6'E	T	179
Chislet Forstal	Kent	TR2164	51°20·1'	1°10·8'E	T	179
Chislet Marshes	Kent	TR2366	51°21·2'	1°12·6'E	X	179
Chislet Park	Kent	TR2062	51°19·1'	1°9·8'E	X	179
Chisley Vale	Norf	TL8585	52°26·1'	0°43·7'E	F	144
Chisman's Cleeve	Wilts	SU1455	51°17·9'	1°47·6'W	X	173
Chisnall Hall	Lancs	SD5312	53°36·4'	2°42·2'W	X	108
Chiswell Green	Herts	TL1304	51°43·6'	0°21·4'W	T	166
Chiswell Hall	Kent	TQ4444	51°10·8'	0°4·0'E	X	187
Chiswick	Houns	TQ2078	51°29·5'	0°15·9'W	T	176
Chiswick Br	Rich	TQ2076	51°28·4'	0°15·9'W	X	176
Chiswick End	Cambs	TL3745	52°5·4'	0°0·4'E	T	154
Chiswick Hall	Essex	TL4437	52°1·0'	0°6·3'E	X	154
Chiswick Ho	Houns	TQ2177	51°29·0'	0°15·1'W	A	176
Chiswick's Fm	Norf	TF6407	52°38·4'	0°25·8'E	FM	143
Chisworth	Derby	SJ9992	53°25·7'	2°0·5'W	T	109
Chitcombe	E Susx	TQ8120	50°57·5'	0°35·0'E	T	199
Chitcombe Fm	Somer	ST0230	51°3·9'	3°23·5'W	FM	181
Chithis Mhòr	N Eil	NB2312	58°0·9'	6°41·0'W	H	13,14
Chithurst	W Susx	SU8423	51°0·2'	0°47·8'W	T	197
Chithurst Fm	Surrey	TQ3342	51°9·9'	0°5·5'W	FM	187
Chit Rocks	Devon	SY1286	50°40·3'	3°14·3'W	X	192
Chittenden	Kent	TQ4849	51°13·5'	0°7·6'E	X	188
Chittenden Fm	Kent	TQ8034	51°4·8'	0°34·6'E	FM	188
Chittenden Wood	Kent	TQ8135	51°5·4'	0°35·5'E	F	188
Chitten Hill	Dorset	SY9193	50°44·4'	2°7·3'W	X	195
Chittening Warth	C of Bris	ST5382	51°32·3'	2°40·3'W	X	172
Chittering	Cambs	TL4970	52°18·7'	0°11·5'E	T	154
Chittering Fm	Cambs	TL5171	52°19·2'	0°13·3'E	FM	154
Chitterley	Devon	SS9404	50°49·8'	3°29·9'W	T	192
Chitterman Hill Fm	Leic	SK4911	52°41·9'	1°16·1'W	FM	129
Chitterne	Wilts	ST9944	51°11·9'	2°0·5'W	T	184
Chitterne Down	Wilts	SU0243	51°11·4'	1°57·9'W	X	184
Chitterwell	Somer	ST1019	50°58·0'	3°16·5'W	X	181,193

Chittinghurst	E Susx	TQ6129	51°2·5'	0°18·2'E	X	188,199
Chittlegrove	Glos	SP0310	51°47·6'	1°57·0'W	X	163
Chittlehamholt	Devon	SS6420	50°58·0'	3°55·8'W	T	180
Chittlehampton	Devon	SS6325	51°0·7'	3°56·8'W	T	180
Chittlehampton	Devon	SS6512	50°53·7'	3°54·8'W	X	180
Chittoe	Wilts	ST9566	51°23·8'	2°3·9'W	T	173
Chitts Hills	Essex	TL9525	51°53·6'	0°50·4'E	T	168
Chitty	Kent	TR2264	51°20·1'	1°11·6'E	T	179
Chivel Fm	Oxon	SP3628	51°57·2'	1°28·2'W	FM	164
Chivelstone	Devon	SX7838	50°14·0'	3°42·3'W	T	202
Chivenor	Devon	SS5034	51°5·4'	4°8·1'W	T	180
Chivenor Airfield	Devon	SS4934	51°5·4'	4°9·0'W	X	180
Chivenor Ridge	Devon	SS5033	51°4·8'	4°8·1'W	X	180
Chiverlins Ho	Wilts	ST8973	51°27·6'	2°9·1'W	X	173
Chiverstone Fm	Devon	SX9484	50°39·0'	3°29·6'W	FM	192
Chivery	Bucks	SP9007	51°45·5'	0°41·4'W	T	165
Chivery Hall Fm	Bucks	SP9008	51°46·0'	0°41·3'W	FM	165
Chivrick's Brook	Dorset	ST7917	50°57·4'	2°17·6'W	W	183
Chlenry	D & G	NX1261	54°54·7'	4°55·6'W	X	82
Chlenry Burn	D & G	NX1260	54°54·2'	4°55·5'W	W	82
Chlinaig	Highld	NN2880	56°53·0'	4°48·9'W	X	34,41
Chno Dearg	Highld	NN3774	56°50·0'	4°39·8'W	H	41
Choakford	Devon	SX5854	50°22·4'	3°59·4'W	X	202
Chobbing's Fm	Essex	TL6809	51°45·5'	0°26·5'E	FM	167
Chobham	Surrey	SU9761	51°20·6'	0°36·0'W	T	175,176,186
Chobham Common	Surrey	SU9665	51°22·8'	0°36·8'W	X	175,176
Chobham Park Fm	Surrey	SU9862	51°21·1'	0°35·2'W	FM	175,176,186
Chobham Place	Surrey	SU9663	51°21·7'	0°36·9'W	X	175,176,186
Chobham Ridges	Surrey	SU9059	51°19·6'	0°42·1'W	X	175,186
Choc Feadaige	Arg & Bt	NM9007	56°12·8'	5°22·7'W	H	55
Choc na h-Iolaire	Highld	NC9310	58°4·2'	3°48·4'W	X	17
Chocolate Fm	Carm	SN2125	51°53·9'	4°35·7'W	FM	145,158
Choicehill Fm	Oxon	SP3029	51°57·8'	1°33·4'W	FM	164
Choicelee	Scot Bord	NT7451	55°45·4'	2°24·4'W	X	67,74
Choin	Orkney	HY2224	59°6·0'	3°21·2'W	W	6
Choin	Orkney	HY2427	59°7·7'	3°19·2'W	W	6
Choinneachain Hill	Pth & Kin	NN8128	56°26·0'	3°55·3'W	H	52
Choire Leacaich	Highld	NC3250	58°24·6'	4°52·1'W	X	9
Cholash Fm	Devon	SS4316	50°55·6'	4°13·7'W	FM	180,190
Cholderton	Wilts	SU2242	51°10·8'	1°40·7'W	T	184
Cholderton Hill	Hants	SU2543	51°11·4'	1°38·1'W	H	184
Cholderton Ho	Wilts	SU2242	51°10·8'	1°40·7'W	X	184
Cholderton Lodge	Hants	SU2342	51°10·8'	1°39·9'W	X	184
Choldertoo	Orkney	HY2224	59°6·0'	3°21·2'W	X	6
Cholditch	Devon	SX3597	50°45·2'	4°20·0'W	X	190
Cholesbury	Bucks	SP9307	51°45·5'	0°38·8'W	T	165
Cholhouse	Devon	SS6604	50°49·4'	3°53·8'W	X	191
Chollaton	Devon	SS3713	50°53·8'	4°18·7'W	X	190
Chollerford	Northum	NY9170	55°1·7'	2°8·0'W	T	87
Chollerton	Northum	NY9372	55°2·8'	2°6·1'W	T	87
Cholley's Fm	Thurr	TQ6682	51°31·0'	0°23·9'E	FM	177,178
Cholmondeley Castle	Ches	SJ5351	53°3·5'	2°41·7'W	X	117
Cholmondeston	Ches	SJ6259	53°7·8'	2°33·7'W	T	118
Cholmondeston Hall	Ches	SJ6458	53°7·3'	2°31·9'W	X	118
Cholsey	Oxon	SU5886	51°34·4'	1°9·4'W	T	174
Cholsey Downs	Oxon	SU5683	51°32·8'	1°11·2'W	X	174
Cholsey Grange	Bucks	SU7593	51°38·1'	0°54·6'W	X	175
Cholsey Hill	Oxon	SU5787	51°35·0'	1°10·2'W	H	174
Cholstrey	Heref	SO4659	52°13·8'	2°47·0'W	T	148,149
Cholwell	Bath & NE Somer	ST6158	51°19·4'	2°33·2'W	T	172
Cholwell	Devon	SX4375	50°33·5'	4°12·6'W	X	201
Cholwell	Devon	SX5181	50°36·8'	4°6·0'W	X	191,201
Cholwell	Devon	SX7859	50°25·3'	3°42·7'W	X	202
Cholwell Fm	Devon	SX4285	50°38·8'	4°13·7'W	FM	201
Cholwells	Devon	SX7141	50°15·5'	3°48·2'W	X	202
Cholwichtown Fm	Devon	SX5861	50°26·2'	3°59·6'W	FM	202
Chonar Fm	Ches	SJ8579	53°18·7'	2°13·1'W	FM	118
Choon	Corn	SW7524	50°4·6'	5°8·3'W	X	204
Choon	Corn	SW7848	50°17·6'	5°6·6'W	X	204
Choone	Corn	SW4224	50°3·8'	5°35·9'W	X	203
Chop Gate	N Yks	SE5599	54°23·3'	1°8·8'W	T	100
Chop Hardy	Durham	NY9748	54°49·9'	2°2·4'W	X	87
Choppington	Northum	NZ2583	55°8·7'	1°36·0'W	T	81
Choppins Hill	Suff	TM1455	52°9·3'	1°8·1'E	X	156
Chopwell	Ghead	NZ1158	54°55·2'	1°49·3'W	T	88
Chopwell Wood	Ghead	NZ1358	54°55·2'	1°47·4'W	F	88
Chorland Fm	Devon	SS9909	50°52·5'	3°25·8'W	FM	192
Chorley	Ches	SJ5751	53°3·5'	2°38·1'W	T	117
Chorley	Lancs	SD5817	53°39·1'	2°37·7'W	T	108
Chorley	Shrops	SO6983	52°26·9'	2°27·0'W	T	138
Chorley	Staffs	SK0710	52°41·5'	1°53·4'W	T	128
Chorley Bank	Ches	SJ5650	53°3·0'	2°39·0'W	X	117
Chorley Common	W Susx	SU8326	51°1·9'	0°48·6'W	T	186,197
Chorley Cop	Northnts	SP6570	52°19·7'	1°2·4'W	X	141
Chorley Covert	Shrops	SO7083	52°26·9'	2°26·1'W	F	138
Chorley Fm	Bucks	SU8195	51°39·1'	0°49·4'W	FM	165
Chorley Green	Ches	SJ5751	53°3·5'	2°38·1'W	X	117
Chorley Hall	Ches	SJ5849	53°2·4'	2°37·2'W	X	117
Chorley Hall	Ches	SJ8378	53°18·2'	2°14·9'W	X	118
Chorley Hill	Somer	ST6735	51°7·0'	2°27·9'W	H	183
Chorley Ho	Lancs	SD7342	53°52·7'	2°24·2'W	X	103
Chorley Place Fm	Staffs	SK0710	52°41·5'	1°53·4'W	FM	128
Chorley's	Somer	ST0729	51°3·4'	3°19·2'W	X	181
Chorley Stock	Ches	SJ5650	53°3·0'	2°39·0'W	X	117
Chorleywood	Herts	TQ0296	51°39·4'	0°31·1'W	T	166,176
Chorleywood Bottom	Herts	TQ0295	51°38·9'	0°31·1'W	T	166,176
Chorleywood Common	Herts	TQ0396	51°39·4'	0°30·3'W	X	166,176
Chorleywood Ho	Herts	TQ0396	51°39·4'	0°30·3'W	X	166,176
Chorleywood West	Herts	TQ0196	51°39·5'	0°32·0'W	T	166,176
Chorlton	Ches	SJ7250	53°3·0'	2°24·7'W	T	118
Chorlton Brook	Man	SJ8193	53°26·2'	2°16·8'W	W	109
Chorlton-cum-Hardy	Man	SJ8193	53°26·2'	2°16·8'W	T	109
Chorlton Fold	Ches	SJ4071	53°14·2'	2°53·5'W	X	117
Chorlton Hall	Ches	SJ4648	53°1·8'	2°47·9'W	X	117
Chorlton Lane	Ches	SJ4547	53°1·3'	2°48·8'W	T	117
Chorlton Lodge	Ches	SJ4647	53°1·3'	2°47·9'W	X	117
Chorlton Moss	Staffs	SJ7939	52°57·1'	2°18·4'W	X	127
Chorlton Water Park	Man	SJ8291	53°25·2'	2°15·8'W	X	109
Chorravein	N Eil	NF7615	57°7·0'	7°20·7'W	H	31
Choseley Fm	Norf	TF7540	52°56·0'	0°36·6'E	FM	132
Chosen Hill Ho	Glos	SO8818	51°51·9'	2°10·1'W	X	162
Chosley Fm	Hants	SU7250	51°14·9'	0°57·7'W	FM	186
Choulton	Shrops	SO3788	52°29·4'	2°55·3'W	T	137
Chourdon Point	Durham	NZ4446	54°48·7'	1°18·5'W	X	88
Chowdene	Ghead	NZ2559	54°55·7'	1°36·2'W	T	88
Chowder Ness	N Lincs	TA0023	53°41·9'	0°28·7'W	X	106,107,112
Chowles	W Susx	TQ2137	51°7·4'	0°15·9'W	X	187
Chowley	Ches	SJ4756	53°6·2'	2°47·1'W	X	117
Chownes Mead	W Susx	TQ3123	50°59·7'	0°7·6'W	T	198
Chraad	Aberd	NJ5306	57°8·8'	2°46·2'W	X	37
Chreag Cham-allt	Arg & Bt	NN2714	56°17·5'	4°47·3'W	X	50,56
Chrishall	Essex	TL4439	52°2·1'	0°6·4'E	T	154
Chrishall Common	Essex	TL4336	52°0·5'	0°5·4'E	X	154
Chrishall Grange	Cambs	TL4442	52°3·7'	0°6·4'E	X	154
Chrismo	Orkney	HY3128	59°8·3'	3°11·9'W	X	6
Chriswell	Inverc	NS2274	55°55·8'	4°50·5'W	X	63
Christchurch	Cambs	TL4996	52°32·7'	0°12·2'E	T	143
Christchurch	Dorset	SZ1592	50°43·9'	1°46·9'W	T	195
Christchurch	Glos	SO5712	51°48·5'	2°37·0'W	T	162
Christchurch	Newp	ST3489	51°36·0'	2°56·8'W	T	171
Christchurch Bay	Hants	SZ2391	50°43·3'	1°40·1'W	W	195
Christchurch Fm	Cambs	TL4799	52°34·4'	0°10·6'E	FM	143
Christchurch Harbour	Dorset	SZ1791	50°43·3'	1°45·2'W	W	195
Christchurch Park	Suff	TM1645	52°3·9'	1°9·5'E	X	169
Christianbury Crag	Cumbr	NY5782	55°8·1'	2°40·0'W	X	80
Christian Malford	Wilts	ST9678	51°30·3'	2°3·1'W	T	173
Christian's Cross	Somer	ST5230	51°4·3'	2°40·7'W	X	182,183
Christian's River	E Susx	TQ6516	50°55·4'	0°21·3'E	W	199
Christie Ho	Lincs	TF3931	52°51·7'	0°4·3'E	X	131
Christielands	D & G	NY2468	55°0·3'	3°10·9'W	X	85
Christies Bog	Northum	NT8300	55°17·9'	2°15·6'W	X	80
Christie's Hole	Shetld	HU1560	60°19·7'	1°43·2'W	W	3
Christie Wood	N Yks	SE1999	54°23·4'	1°42·0'W	F	99
Christlach	Arg & Bt	NR7011	55°20·6'	5°37·2'W	X	68
Christleton	Ches	SJ4465	53°11·0'	2°49·9'W	T	117
Christmas Common	Oxon	SU7193	51°38·1'	0°58·1'W	T	175
Christmas Cross	Shrops	SO5084	52°27·3'	2°43·8'W	X	137,138
Christmas Fm	E Susx	TQ6719	50°57·0'	0°23·0'E	FM	199
Christmas Gorse	Bucks	SP7825	51°55·3'	0°51·6'W	F	165
Christmas Hill	Warw	SP3756	52°12·3'	1°27·1'W	X	151
Christmas Hill Fm	Suff	TL7185	52°26·4'	0°31·4'E	FM	143
Christmas Mill	Kent	TQ4443	51°10·3'	0°4·0'E	X	187
Christmaspie	Surrey	SU9249	51°14·2'	0°40·5'W	X	186
Christon	N Som	ST3757	51°18·8'	2°53·8'W	T	182
Christon Bank	Northum	NU2022	55°29·7'	1°40·6'W	X	75
Christon Bank Fm	Northum	NU2122	55°29·7'	1°39·6'W	FM	75
Christon Plantn	N Som	ST3758	51°19·3'	2°53·9'W	F	182
Christow	Devon	SX8384	50°38·9'	3°38·9'W	T	191
Christow Common	Devon	SX8285	50°39·4'	3°39·8'W	X	191
Christ's Hospital	N Yks	SE2686	54°16·4'	1°35·6'W	A	99
Christ's Hospital (Sch)	W Susx	TQ1428	51°2·6'	0°22·0'W	X	187,198
Christ's Kirk	Aberd	NJ6026	57°19·6'	2°39·4'W	A	37
Christskirk	Aberd	NJ6026	57°19·6'	2°39·4'W	X	37
Christy Bank	Cumbr	NY7720	54°34·7'	2°20·9'W	X	91
Christy's Crags	Northum	NY6882	55°8·1'	2°29·7'W	X	80
Chrome Hill	Derby	SK0667	53°12·2'	1°54·2'W	X	119
Chryston	N Lanak	NS6870	55°54·6'	4°6·3'W	T	64
Chubag	N Eil	NB4531	58°11·9'	6°19·9'W	W	8
Chubb's Fm	Devon	SY3198	50°46·9'	2°58·3'W	FM	193
Chubden	Northum	NU0213	55°24·9'	1°57·7'W	H	81
Chub Tor	Devon	SX5166	50°28·7'	4°5·6'W	T	201
Chubworthy Fm	Somer	ST0326	51°1·7'	3°22·6'W	FM	181
Chuccaby	Orkney	ND3190	58°47·8'	3°11·2'W	X	7
Chuck Hatch	E Susx	TQ4733	51°4·9'	0°6·3'E	T	188
Chuck's Fm	W Susx	TQ1920	50°58·3'	0°17·9'W	FM	198
Chudleigh	Devon	SX8679	50°36·2'	3°36·3'W	T	191
Chudleigh Knighton	Devon	SX8477	50°35·1'	3°37·9'W	T	191
Chudleigh Rocks	Devon	SX8678	50°35·7'	3°36·3'W	X	191
Chuley Cross	Devon	SX7568	50°30·1'	3°45·4'W	X	202
Chullin	Highld	NH3061	57°36·7'	4°50·3'W	X	20
Chumleigh	Devon	SS6814	50°54·9'	3°52·3'W	T	180
Chumhill	Devon	SS6236	51°6·6'	3°57·9'W	X	180
Chûn	Corn	SW4034	50°9·2'	5°38·0'W	X	203
Chunal	Derby	SK0391	53°25·2'	1°56·9'W	T	110
Chunal Moor	Derby	SK0491	53°25·2'	1°56·0'W	X	110
Chûn Castle	Corn	SW4033	50°8·6'	5°38·0'W	A	203
Chûn Quoit	Corn	SW4034	50°9·2'	5°38·0'W	A	203
Church	Lancs	SD7429	53°45·6'	2°23·3'W	T	103
Churcham	Glos	SO7618	51°51·8'	2°20·5'W	T	162
Churcham Ho	Glos	SO7519	51°52·4'	2°21·4'W	X	162
Church Aston	Wrekin	SJ7417	52°45·2'	2°22·7'W	T	127
Churchbalk	Derby	SK2436	52°55·5'	1°38·2'W	X	128
Churchbank	Shrops	SO2979	52°24·5'	3°2·2'W	T	137,148
Church Bay or Porth Swtan	I of Angl	SH2989	53°22·5'	4°33·8'W	W	114
Church Beck	Cumbr	SD2998	54°22·6'	3°5·2'W	W	96,97
Church Bottom	Wilts	SU0424	51°1·2'	1°56·2'W	X	184
Church Bowers	Durham	NY8632	54°41·2'	2°12·6'W	X	91,92
Church Brampton	Northnts	SP7165	52°16·9'	0°57·2'W	T	152
Churchbridge	Corn	SX2158	50°23·9'	4°30·7'W	T	201
Churchbridge	Shrops	SO6172	52°20·9'	2°34·0'W	X	138
Churchbridge	Staffs	SJ9808	52°40·4'	2°1·4'W	T	127
Church Brook Fm	Hants	SU5960	51°20·4'	1°8·8'W	FM	174
Church Brough	Cumbr	NY7913	54°31·0'	2°19·0'W	T	91
Church Broughton	Derby	SK2033	52°53·9'	1°41·8'W	T	128
Church Burn	Northum	NY7658	54°55·2'	2°22·0'W	W	86,87
Church Charwelton	Northnts	SP5455	52°11·7'	1°12·2'W	T	152
Church Clough	Lancs	SD8839	53°51·1'	2°10·5'W	T	103
Churchcombe Fm	Devon	SS5321	50°58·4'	4°5·2'W	FM	180
Church Common	Hants	SU7325	51°1·4'	0°57·2'W	T	186,197
Church Common	Suff	TM3959	52°10·9'	1°30·2'E	X	156
Church Coombe	Corn	SW6940	50°13·1'	5°13·9'W	T	203
Church Coppice	Heref	SO5152	52°10·1'	2°42·6'W	F	149
Church Cove	Corn	SW6620	50°2·3'	5°15·7'W	W	203
Church Cove	Corn	SW7112	49°58·1'	5°11·2'W	T	203
Church Covert	Suff	TM5184	52°24·0'	1°41·8'E	F	156
Church Croft	Surrey	SU9246	51°12·6'	0°40·6'W	F	186
Church Crookham	Hants	SU8152	51°15·9'	0°50·0'W	T	186
Church Dale Fm	N Yks	NZ7806	54°26·8'	0°47·4'W	FM	94
Churchdale Hall	Derby	SK2070	53°13·8'	1°41·6'W	X	119
Churchdown	Glos	SO8720	51°52·9'	2°10·9'W	T	162
Churchdown Hill	Glos	SO8818	51°51·9'	2°10·1'W	H	162
Church Eaton	Staffs	SJ8417	52°45·3'	2°13·8'W	T	127
Church Eaton Brook	Staffs	SJ8615	52°44·2'	2°12·0'W	W	127
Church Eaton Common	Staffs	SJ8517	52°45·3'	2°12·9'W	X	127
Church End	Barnet	TQ2490	51°35·9'	0°12·2'W	T	176
Church End	Beds	SP9536	52°1·1'	0°36·5'W	T	153
Church End	Beds	SP9626	51°55·7'	0°35·8'W	X	165
Church End	Beds	SP9832	51°58·9'	0°34·0'W	T	165
Church End	Beds	SP9921	51°53·0'	0°33·3'W	T	165
Church End	Beds	TL0318	51°51·3'	0°29·9'W	T	166
Church End	Beds	TL0558	52°12·8'	0°27·4'W	T	153
Church End	Beds	TL0754	52°10·7'	0°25·7'W	T	153
Church End	Beds	TL1058	52°12·8'	0°23·0'W	T	153
Church End	Beds	TL1653	52°10·0'	0°17·8'W	T	153
Church End	Beds	TL1937	52°1·3'	0°15·5'W	T	153
Church End	Brent	TQ2184	51°32·7'	0°14·9'W	T	176
Church End	Bucks	SP7407	51°45·6'	0°55·3'W	T	165
Church End	Bucks	SP9415	51°49·8'	0°37·8'W	T	165
Church End	Cambs	TF3808	52°39·4'	0°2·8'E	T	142,143
Church End	Cambs	TL0973	52°20·9'	0°23·6'W	T	153
Church End	Cambs	TL2082	52°25·6'	0°13·7'W	T	142
Church End	Cambs	TL3669	52°18·4'	0°0·1'E	T	154
Church End	Cambs	TL3770	52°18·9'	0°1·0'E	T	154
Church End	Cov	SP3579	52°24·7'	1°28·7'W	T	140
Church End	Essex	TL5727	51°55·4'	0°17·4'E	T	167
Church End	Essex	TL5841	52°2·9'	0°18·6'E	T	154
Churchend	Essex	TL6322	51°52·6'	0°22·5'E	T	167
Church End	Essex	TL7227	51°55·1'	0°30·5'E	T	167
Church End	Essex	TL7316	51°49·2'	0°31·0'E	T	167
Churchend	Essex	TR0092	51°35·7'	0°53·7'E	T	178
Church End	E Yorks	TA0953	53°57·9'	0°19·9'W	T	107
Church End	Glos	SO7406	51°45·4'	2°22·2'W	T	162
Churchend	Glos	SO7805	51°44·8'	2°18·7'W	T	162
Church End	Glos	SO8936	52°1·6'	2°9·2'W	T	150
Church End	Hants	SU6756	51°18·2'	1°1·9'W	T	175,186
Church End	Herts	TL1011	51°47·4'	0°23·9'W	T	166
Church End	Herts	TL2630	51°57·5'	0°9·6'W	T	166
Church End	Herts	TL4422	51°52·9'	0°5·9'E	T	167
Church End	Herts	TQ0398	51°40·5'	0°30·2'W	T	166,176
Church End	Lincs	TF2234	52°53·6'	0°10·8'W	T	131
Church End	Lincs	TF4295	53°26·2'	0°8·7'E	T	113
Church End	Norf	TF5115	52°42·9'	0°14·5'E	T	131
Church End	Oxon	SP3231	51°58·8'	1°31·6'W	T	151
Church End	Oxon	SP3908	51°46·4'	1°25·7'W	T	164
Churchend	Read	SU6772	51°26·8'	1°1·8'W	T	175
Churchend	S Glos	ST7191	51°37·3'	2°24·7'W	T	162,172
Church End	Suff	TM2336	51°58·9'	1°15·2'E	T	169
Church End	Surrey	TQ0656	51°17·8'	0°28·4'W	T	187
Church End	Warw	SP2490	52°30·7'	1°38·4'W	T	139
Church End	Warw	SP2992	52°31·7'	1°34·0'W	T	140
Church End	Wilts	SU0278	51°30·3'	1°57·9'W	T	173
Church End	Worcs	SO8341	52°4·3'	2°14·5'W	T	150
Churchend Common	Herts	TL2727	51°55·8'	0°8·8'W	X	166
Church end Ring	Wilts	SU0135	51°7·1'	1°58·8'W	A	184
Church Enstone	Oxon	SP3725	51°55·6'	1°27·3'W	T	164
Churches Fm	Glos	SO7634	52°0·5'	2°20·6'W	FM	150
Churches Green	E Susx	TQ6417	50°56·0'	0°20·4'E	T	199
Churche's Mansion	Ches	SJ6552	53°4·1'	2°30·9'W	X	118
Churchfarm Marshes	Norf	TG4705	52°35·4'	1°39·2'E	X	134
Churchfarm Marshes	Suff	TM5185	52°24·5'	1°41·8'E	X	156
Church Fenton	N Yks	SE5136	53°49·3'	1°13·1'W	T	105
Churchfield	Heref	SO7346	52°6·9'	2°23·3'W	T	150
Churchfield	Sand	SP0192	52°31·8'	1°58·7'W	T	139
Churchfield Fm	Northnts	TL0087	52°28·5'	0°31·3'W	FM	141
Churchfield Ho	Lancs	SD6174	54°9·9'	2°35·4'W	X	97
Churchfields	Wilts	SU1329	51°3·8'	1°48·5'W	T	184
Churchfields Fm	Derby	SK2440	52°57·6'	1°38·2'W	FM	119,128
Churchfields Fm	Worcs	SO8761	52°15·1'	2°11·0'W	FM	150
Church Flatts Fm	Derby	SK2514	52°43·6'	1°37·4'W	FM	128
Church Fm	Beds	SP9940	52°3·2'	0°33·0'W	FM	153
Church Fm	Beds	TL2549	52°7·7'	0°10·0'W	FM	153
Church Fm	Bucks	SP6407	51°45·7'	1°4·0'W	FM	164,165
Church Fm	Bucks	SP9115	51°49·8'	0°40·4'W	FM	165
Church Fm	Bucks	SU8695	51°39·1'	0°45·0'W	FM	165
Church Fm	Caer	ST1994	51°38·6'	3°9·8'W	FM	171
Church Fm	Cambs	TL1571	52°19·7'	0°18·3'W	FM	153
Church Fm	Cambs	TL2789	52°29·3'	0°7·4'W	FM	142
Church Fm	Cambs	TL3855	52°10·8'	0°1·5'E	FM	154
Church Fm	Cambs	TL5483	52°25·6'	0°16·3'E	FM	143
Church Fm	Cambs	TL6288	52°28·2'	0°23·5'E	FM	143
Church Fm	Card	ST1983	51°32·7'	3°9·7'W	FM	171
Church Fm	Ches	SJ8468	53°12·8'	2°14·0'W	FM	118
Church Fm	Dorset	ST5710	50°53·5'	2°36·3'W	FM	194
Church Fm	Dorset	ST5818	50°57·8'	2°35·5'W	A	183
Church Fm	Dorset	ST8415	50°56·3'	2°13·3'W	FM	183
Church Fm	Essex	TL7926	51°54·4'	0°36·5'E	FM	167
Church Fm	Essex	TM1424	51°52·6'	1°6·9'E	FM	168,169
Church Fm	E Susx	TQ5202	50°48·1'	0°9·8'E	FM	199
Church Fm	E Susx	TQ6410	50°52·2'	0°20·2'E	FM	199
Church Fm	E Susx	TQ8514	50°54·0'	0°38·2'E	FM	199
Church Fm	E Yorks	TA0455	53°59·1'	0°24·4'W	FM	107
Church Fm	E Yorks	TA0942	53°52·0'	0°20·1'W	FM	107
Church Fm	E Yorks	TA1450	53°56·2'	0°15·4'W	FM	107
Church Fm	E Yorks	TA2619	53°39·4'	0°5·2'W	FM	113
Church Fm	Flint	SJ3568	53°12·5'	2°58·0'W	FM	117
Church Fm	Glos	ST9192	51°37·8'	2°7·4'W	FM	163,173
Church Fm	Hants	SU3032	51°5·4'	1°33·9'W	FM	185
Church Fm	Hants	SU3908	50°52·4'	1°26·4'W	FM	196
Church Fm	Hants	SU4156	51°18·3'	1°24·3'W	FM	174
Church Fm	Hants	SU7229	51°3·6'	0°58·0'W	FM	186,197
Church Fm	Hants	SU7761	51°20·8'	0°53·3'W	FM	175,186
Church Fm	Herts	SP9612	51°48·1'	0°36·1'W	FM	165
Church Fm	Herts	SP9913	51°48·6'	0°33·4'W	FM	165
Church Fm	Kent	TQ7445	51°10·9'	0°27·7'E	FM	188
Church Fm	Kent	TQ8250	51°13·4'	0°36·8'E	FM	188
Church Fm	Leic	SK7123	52°48·2'	0°56·4'W	FM	129
Church Fm	Lincs	SK8960	53°8·0'	0°39·8'W	FM	121

Church Fm	Lincs	TF2116	52°43·9'	0°12·1'W	FM	131
Church Fm	Lincs	TF5061	53°7·7'	0°14·9'E	FM	122
Church Fm	Mil Key	SP9348	52°7·6'	0°38·1'W	FM	153
Church Fm	Monm	SO4905	51°44·7'	2°43·9'W	FM	162
Church Fm	Norf	TF5520	52°45·6'	0°18·2'E	FM	131
Church Fm	Norf	TF6620	52°45·4'	0°28·0'E	FM	132
Church Fm	Norf	TF6938	52°55·0'	0°31·2'E	FM	132
Church Fm	Norf	TF7334	52°52·8'	0°34·7'E	FM	132
Church Fm	Norf	TF8915	52°42·2'	0°48·3'E	FM	132
Church Fm	Norf	TF9512	52°40·5'	0°53·5'E	FM	132
Church Fm	Norf	TG1120	52°44·4'	1°8·0'E	FM	133
Church Fm	Norf	TG1617	52°42·7'	1°12·3'E	FM	133
Church Fm	Norf	TG2128	52°48·5'	1°17·1'E	FM	133,134
Church Fm	Norf	TG3122	52°45·0'	1°25·8'E	FM	133,134
Church Fm	Norf	TG3323	52°45·5'	1°27·6'E	FM	133,134
Church Fm	Norf	TG3708	52°37·3'	1°30·5'E	FM	134
Church Fm	Norf	TG4205	52°35·6'	1°34·8'E	FM	134
Church Fm	Norf	TL9892	52°29·6'	0°55·4'E	FM	144
Church Fm	Norf	TM1196	52°31·5'	1°7·0'E	FM	144
Church Fm	Norf	TM2186	52°25·9'	1°15·5'E	FM	156
Church Fm	Norf	TM3288	52°26·7'	1°25·2'E	FM	156
Church Fm	Norf	TM3498	52°32·0'	1°27·4'E	FM	134
Church Fm	Norf	TM3792	52°28·7'	1°29·8'E	FM	134
Church Fm	Norf	TM3895	52°30·3'	1°30·8'E	FM	134
Church Fm	Norf	TM4494	52°29·6'	1°36·1'E	FM	134
Church Fm	Northnts	SP8053	52°10·4'	0°49·4'W	FM	152
Church Fm	Oxon	SU3190	51°36·7'	1°32·7'W	FM	164,174
Church Fm	Oxon	SU3591	51°37·2'	1°29·3'W	FM	164,174
Church Fm	Oxon	SU6482	51°32·2'	1°4·2'W	FM	175
Church Fm	Peterb	TF0501	52°36·0'	0°26·6'W	FM	142
Church Fm	Shrops	SJ5740	52°57·6'	2°38·0'W	FM	117
Church Fm	Somer	ST7957	51°18·9'	2°17·7'W	FM	172
Church Fm	Suff	TL8559	52°12·1'	0°42·8'E	FM	155
Church Fm	Suff	TL9849	52°6·5'	0°53·9'E	FM	155
Church Fm	Suff	TL9977	52°21·5'	0°55·8'E	FM	144
Church Fm	Suff	TM0948	52°5·7'	1°3·5'E	FM	155,169
Church Fm	Suff	TM1556	52°9·8'	1°9·0'E	FM	156
Church Fm	Suff	TM2159	52°11·3'	1°14·4'E	FM	156
Church Fm	Suff	TM2880	52°22·5'	1°21·4'E	FM	156
Church Fm	Suff	TM3068	52°15·9'	1°22·6'E	FM	156
Church Fm	Suff	TM3074	52°19·2'	1°22·9'E	FM	156
Church Fm	Suff	TM3176	52°20·2'	1°23·9'E	FM	156
Church Fm	Suff	TM3282	52°23·4'	1°25·0'E	FM	156
Church Fm	Suff	TM3356	52°9·4'	1°24·8'E	FM	156
Church Fm	Suff	TM3686	52°25·5'	1°28·7'E	FM	156
Church Fm	Suff	TM3889	52°27·0'	1°30·6'E	FM	156
Church Fm	Suff	TM4251	52°6·5'	1°32·5'E	FM	156
Church Fm	Suff	TM4276	52°19·9'	1°33·5'E	FM	156
Church Fm	Suff	TM4383	52°23·7'	1°34·7'E	FM	156
Church Fm	Suff	TM4387	52°25·8'	1°34·9'E	FM	156
Church Fm	Suff	TM4479	52°21·5'	1°35·4'E	FM	156
Church Fm	Suff	TM4481	52°22·6'	1°35·5'E	FM	156
Church Fm	Suff	TM4560	52°11·2'	1°35·5'E	FM	156
Church Fm	Suff	TM4580	52°22·0'	1°36·3'E	FM	156
Church Fm	Suff	TM4878	52°20·9'	1°38·9'E	FM	156
Church Fm	Suff	TM4981	52°22·4'	1°39·9'E	FM	156
Church Fm	Suff	TM5084	52°24·0'	1°40·9'E	FM	156
Church Fm	Suff	TM5281	52°22·4'	1°42·5'E	FM	156
Church Fm	Surrey	TQ0264	51°22·2'	0°31·7'W	FM	176,186
Church Fm	V of Glam	SS9977	51°29·2'	3°26·9'W	FM	170
Church Fm	Warw	SP2045	52°6·4'	1°42·1'W	FM	151
Church Fm	Warw	SP2565	52°17·2'	1°37·6'W	FM	151
Church Fm	Warw	SP2937	52°2·1'	1°34·2'W	FM	151
Church Fm	Warw	SP3090	52°30·7'	1°33·1'W	FM	140
Church Fm	W Berks	SU6179	51°30·6'	1°6·9'W	FM	175
Church Fm	Wilts	ST7938	51°8·7'	2°17·6'W	FM	183
Church Fm	Wilts	ST8352	51°16·2'	2°14·2'W	FM	183
Church Fm	Wilts	ST8887	51°35·1'	2°10·0'W	FM	173
Church Fm	Wilts	SU3158	51°19·4'	1°32·9'W	FM	174
Church Fm	Worcs	SO9144	52°5·9'	2°7·5'W	FM	150
Church Fm	Worcs	SO9159	52°14·0'	2°7·5'W	FM	150
Church Fm	Worcs	SO9655	52°11·8'	2°3·1'W	FM	150
Church Fm	Wrex	SJ4536	52°55·4'	2°48·7'W	FM	126
Church Fm	W Susx	SU8202	50°48·9'	0°49·8'W	FM	197
Church Fm	W Susx	SU8601	50°48·4'	0°46·4'W	FM	197
Church Fm	W Susx	SU9806	50°50·9'	0°36·1'W	FM	197
Churchford Hall	Suff	TM0838	52°0·3'	1°2·2'E	X	155,169
Churchgate	Herts	TL3402	51°42·3'	0°3·2'W	T	166
Churchgate Street	Essex	TL4811	51°46·9'	0°9·1'E	T	167
Church Gorse	Staffs	SO8287	52°29·1'	2°15·5'W	X	138
Church Green	Devon	SY1796	50°45·7'	3°10·2'W	T	192,193
Church Green	Norf	TM0691	52°28·9'	1°2·4'E	T	144
Church Gresley	Derby	SK2918	52°45·8'	1°33·8'W	T	128
Church Grounds	Dorset	SY4596	50°45·9'	2°46·4'W	X	193
Church Hall	Essex	TL5827	51°55·4'	0°18·3'E	A	167
Church Hall	Essex	TL8518	51°50·0'	0°41·5'E	X	168
Church Hanborough	Oxon	SP4212	51°48·5'	1°23·1'W	T	164
Church Hill	Bucks	SP8033	51°59·6'	0°49·7'W	X	152,165
Church Hill	Bucks	SP8128	51°56·9'	0°48·9'W	X	165
Church Hill	Ches	SJ6464	53°10·6'	2°31·9'W	X	118
Church Hill	Cumbr	NY2744	54°47·4'	3°7·7'W	X	85
Church Hill	Dorset	ST7103	50°49·8'	2°24·3'W	H	194
Church Hill	E Yorks	SE8238	53°50·1'	0°44·8'W	H	106
Church Hill	Glos	SO6208	51°46·4'	2°32·7'W	X	162
Church Hill	Heref	SO4173	52°21·4'	2°51·6'W	X	137,148
Church Hill	Highld	NH5988	57°51·8'	4°22·1'W	H	21
Church Hill	Leic	SP7695	52°33·1'	0°52·3'W	X	141
Church Hill	Notts	SK6762	53°9·3'	0°59·5'W	X	120
Church Hill	N Som	ST3970	51°25·8'	2°52·3'W	H	171,172
Church Hill	N Yks	NZ3302	54°25·0'	1°29·1'W	X	93
Church Hill	Pemb	SM8621	51°51·0'	5°6·0'W	H	157
Church Hill	Pemb	SM9714	51°47·5'	4°56·2'W	T	157,158
Church Hill	Sand	SO9895	52°33·4'	2°1·4'W	T	139
Church Hill	Somer	ST5843	51°11·3'	2°35·7'W	X	182,183
Church Hill	Staffs	SK0012	52°42·6'	1°59·6'W	T	128
Church Hill	Warw	SP4051	52°9·6'	1°24·5'W	H	151
Church Hill	Wilts	SU0352	51°16·3'	1°57·0'W	X	184
Church Hill	Worcs	SO7073	52°21·5'	2°26·0'W	X	138
Church Hill	Worcs	SP0668	52°18·8'	1°54·3'W	T	139
Church Hill	W Susx	TQ1108	50°51·9'	0°25·0'W	X	198
Church Hill Cross	Devon	SX6296	50°45·1'	3°57·0'W	X	191
Church-hill Fm	Bucks	SP6828	51°57·0'	1°0·2'W	FM	164,165
Church Hill Fm	Kent	TR2659	51°17·3'	1°14·9'E	FM	179
Church Hill Fm	Wilts	SU0883	51°33·0'	1°52·7'W	FM	173
Church-hill Wood	S Glos	ST6594	51°38·9'	2°30·0'W	F	162,172
Church Hill Wood	Shrops	SJ4104	52°38·1'	2°51·9'W	F	126
Church Ho	Cumbr	SD1993	54°19·8'	3°14·3'W	X	96
Church Ho	Heref	SO5663	52°16·0'	2°38·3'W	X	137,138,149
Church Ho	N Yks	NZ6906	54°26·9'	0°55·7'W	X	94
Church Ho	Pemb	SN0012	51°46·5'	4°53·6'W	X	157,158
Church Ho	Powys	SJ2604	52°38·0'	3°5·2'W	X	126
Church Hole	Derby	SK5374	53°15·9'	1°11·9'W	A	120
Church Hope Hill	Scot Bord	NT8115	55°26·0'	2°17·6'W	H	80
Church Hougham	Kent	TR2740	51°7·1'	1°15·0'E	T	179
Church House	Somer	ST1336	51°7·2'	3°14·2'W	A	181
Church House Fm	Ches	SJ5756	53°6·2'	2°38·1'W	FM	117
Church House Fm	Ches	SJ6550	53°3·0'	2°30·9'W	FM	118
Church House Fm	Cumbr	NY0405	54°26·1'	3°28·4'W	FM	89
Church House Fm	Essex	TL9025	51°53·7'	0°46·1'E	FM	168
Church House Fm	Heref	SO5753	52°10·7'	2°37·3'W	FM	149
Church House Fm	Powys	SO2450	52°8·8'	3°6·2'W	FM	148
Church House Fm	Worcs	SO7161	52°15·0'	2°25·1'W	FM	138,149
Church Houses	N Yks	SE6697	54°22·1'	0°58·6'W	T	94,100
Churchill	Devon	SS5940	51°8·8'	4°0·6'W	T	180
Churchill	Devon	SS9016	50°56·2'	3°33·6'W	X	181
Churchill	Devon	ST2901	50°48·5'	3°0·1'W	T	193
Churchill	N Som	ST4560	51°20·4'	2°47·0'W	T	172,182
Churchill	Oxon	SP2824	51°55·1'	1°35·2'W	T	163
Churchill	Pemb	SN0218	51°49·8'	4°52·0'W	X	157,158
Churchill	Worcs	SO8879	52°24·8'	2°10·2'W	T	139
Churchill	Worcs	SO9253	52°10·7'	2°6·6'W	T	150
Churchill Barrier No 1	Orkney	HY4800	58°53·3'	2°53·7'W	X	6,7
Churchill Barrier No 2	Orkney	ND4899	58°53·6'	2°53·6'W	X	6,7
Churchill Barrier No 3	Orkney	ND4798	58°52·2'	2°54·7'W	X	6,7
Churchill Barrier No 4	Orkney	ND4795	58°51·2'	2°54·6'W	X	7
Churchill Copse	Oxon	SP3316	51°50·7'	1°30·9'W	F	164
Churchill Cottage	Warw	SP1757	52°12·9'	1°44·7'W	X	151
Churchill Down	Devon	SS5940	51°8·8'	4°0·6'W	H	180
Churchill Fm	Somer	ST2931	51°4·7'	3°0·4'W	FM	182
Churchill Fm	Warw	SP2249	52°8·6'	1°40·3'W	FM	151
Churchill Fms	Devon	SY0297	50°46·1'	3°23·0'W	FM	192
Churchill Green	N Som	ST4360	51°20·4'	2°48·7'W	T	172,182
Churchill Grounds Fm	Oxon	SP2825	51°55·6'	1°35·2'W	FM	163
Churchill Heath Fm	Oxon	SP2622	51°54·0'	1°36·9'W	FM	163
Churchills Fm	I of W	SZ3986	50°40·6'	1°26·5'W	FM	196
Churchill Wood	Worcs	SO9154	52°11·3'	2°7·5'W	F	150
Churchinford	Somer	ST2112	50°54·4'	3°7·0'W	T	193
Church Knowle	Dorset	SY9381	50°37·9'	2°5·6'W	T	195
Churchland	Devon	SS6516	50°55·9'	3°54·9'W	X	180
Churchland	Pemb	SM9824	51°52·9'	4°55·7'W	X	157,158
Churchland Green	Devon	SX7052	50°21·4'	3°49·3'W	X	202
Church Lands	Northum	NY8458	54°55·2'	2°14·6'W	X	86,87
Churchlands Fm	E Yorks	TA2926	53°43·1'	0°2·3'W	FM	107
Church Lane Fm	York	SE6650	53°56·8'	0°59·2'W	FM	105,106
Church Laneham	Notts	SK8176	53°16·7'	0°46·7'W	T	121
Church Langley	Essex	TL4809	51°45·8'	0°9·1'E	X	167
Church Langton	Leic	SP7293	52°32·0'	0°55·9'W	T	141
Church Lawford	Warw	SP4476	52°23·0'	1°20·8'W	T	140
Church Lawton	Ches	SJ8155	53°5·8'	2°16·6'W	T	118
Church Leigh	Staffs	SK0235	52°55·0'	1°57·8'W	T	128
Church Lench	Worcs	SP0251	52°9·7'	1°57·8'W	T	150
Churchman's Fm	Kent	TQ9958	51°17·4'	0°51·6'E	FM	178
Church Mayfield	Staffs	SK1544	52°59·8'	1°46·2'W	T	119,128
Churchmead Fm	S Glos	ST6291	51°37·2'	2°32·5'W	FM	162,172
Church Mill	Oxon	SP3903	51°43·7'	1°25·7'W	X	164
Church Minshull	Ches	SJ6660	53°8·4'	2°30·1'W	T	118
Church Moor	Hants	SU2406	50°51·4'	1°39·2'W	X	195
Churchmoor Hall	Shrops	SO4188	52°29·4'	2°51·7'W	X	137
Churchmoor Hill	Shrops	SO4089	52°30·0'	2°52·6'W	X	137
Churchmoor Rough	Shrops	SO4088	52°29·4'	2°52·6'W	T	137
Church Norton	W Susx	SZ8695	50°45·1'	0°46·5'W	T	197
Church Oakley	Hants	SU5650	51°15·3'	1°11·5'W	T	185
Church Ope Cove	Dorset	SY6970	50°32·0'	2°25·9'W	W	194
Churchover	Warw	SP5180	52°25·2'	1°14·6'W	T	140
Church Path Oak	Northnts	SP8052	52°9·9'	0°49·4'W	X	152
Church Place	Hants	SU3306	50°51·4'	1°31·5'W	A	196
Church Place	Hants	SU3409	50°53·0'	1°30·6'W	A	196
Churchplace Inclosure	Hants	SU3409	50°53·0'	1°30·6'W	F	196
Church Point	I Scilly	SV9209	49°54·4'	6°17·0'W	X	203
Church Preen	Shrops	SO5498	52°34·9'	2°40·3'W	T	137,138
Church Pulverbatch	Shrops	SJ4302	52°37·0'	2°50·1'W	T	126
Church Rock	Pemb	SR9893	51°36·2'	4°54·6'W	X	158
Church Scar	Lancs	SD3526	53°43·8'	2°58·7'W	X	102
Churchsettle Fm	E Susx	TQ6429	51°2·4'	0°20·8'E	FM	188,199
Church Site Fm	Notts	SK6025	52°49·4'	1°6·2'W	FM	129
Church Slade	Northnts	SP8553	52°10·4'	0°45·0'W	F	152
Churchstanton	Somer	ST1914	50°55·4'	3°8·8'W	T	181,193
Churchstanton Hill	Somer	ST2114	50°55·4'	3°7·1'W	X	193
Churchstile	Cumbr	NY3735	54°42·6'	2°58·2'W	X	90
Church Stile	Cumbr	SD0799	54°22·9'	3°25·5'W	X	96
Churchstile Fm	Shrops	SO6173	52°21·5'	2°34·0'W	FM	138
Church Stoke	Powys	SO2794	52°32·6'	3°4·2'W	T	137
Churchstow	Devon	SX7145	50°17·7'	3°48·3'W	T	202
Church Stowe	Northnts	SP6357	52°12·7'	1°4·3'W	T	152
Church Street	Essex	TL7943	52°3·6'	0°37·1'E	T	155
Church Street	Kent	TQ7174	51°26·6'	0°28·0'E	T	178
Church Stretton	Shrops	SO4593	52°32·2'	2°48·3'W	T	137,138
Church Thorns	Leic	SK8033	52°53·5'	0°48·2'W	F	130
Churchton	Pemb	SN1305	51°43·0'	4°42·0'W	T	158
Churchton	Shetld	HU3947	60°12·6'	1°17·3'W	X	3
Churchton Bay	Highld	NG5436	57°21·1'	6°4·9'W	W	24,32
Church Top Fm	Lincs	TF2989	53°23·2'	0°3·2'W	FM	113,122
Church Town	Corn	SW6941	50°13·7'	5°14·0'W	T	203
Churchtown	Corn	SX0977	50°33·9'	4°41·4'W	T	200
Churchtown	Cumbr	NY3641	54°45·8'	2°59·3'W	T	85
Churchtown	Derby	SK2662	53°9·5'	1°36·3'W	T	119
Churchtown	Devon	SS2803	50°48·3'	4°26·1'W	T	190
Churchtown	Devon	SS6744	51°11·0'	3°53·8'W	T	180
Churchtown	I of M	SC4294	54°19·3'	4°25·3'W	T	95
Churchtown	Lancs	SD4843	53°53·1'	2°47·1'W	T	102
Church Town	Leic	SK3916	52°44·6'	1°24·9'W	T	128
Church Town	N Lincs	SE7806	53°32·9'	0°49·0'W	T	112
Churchtown	Sefton	SD3518	53°39·5'	2°58·6'W	T	108
Churchtown	Shrops	SO2687	52°28·8'	3°5·0'W	T	137
Churchtown	Somer	SS9738	51°8·2'	3°27·9'W	T	181
Church Town	Surrey	TQ3551	51°14·8'	0°3·6'W	T	187
Churchtown Fm	Corn	SX1451	50°20·0'	4°36·4'W	FM	200
Churchtown Hill	Shrops	SO2587	52°28·8'	3°5·9'W	X	137
Church Village	Rho Cyn Taf	ST0886	51°34·2'	3°19·3'W	T	170
Church Walks	Suff	TM4151	52°6·5'	1°31·6'E	X	156
Churchwalls	Devon	ST0417	50°56·9'	3°21·6'W	X	181
Church Warsop	Notts	SK5668	53°12·6'	1°9·3'W	T	120
Churchwater	Devon	SS6113	50°54·2'	3°58·2'W	X	180
Church Westcote	Glos	SP2220	51°52·9'	1°40·4'W	T	163
Church Whitfield	Kent	TR3145	51°9·7'	1°18·6'E	T	179
Church Wilne	Derby	SK4431	52°52·7'	1°20·4'W	T	129
Church Wood	E Yorks	TA0860	54°1·7'	0°20·7'W	F	101
Church Wood	Kent	TQ8659	51°18·2'	0°40·5'E	F	178
Church Wood	Kent	TR1059	51°17·7'	1°1·1'E	F	179
Church Wood	Norf	TF9021	52°45·4'	0°49·3'E	F	132
Church Wood	Northnts	SP5754	52°11·1'	1°9·6'W	F	152
Church Wood	Northum	NU0626	55°31·9'	1°53·9'W	F	75
Churchwood	W Susx	TQ0119	50°57·9'	0°33·3'W	T	197
Churn Clough Resr	Lancs	SD7838	53°50·5'	2°19·6'W	W	103
Churncote	Shrops	SJ4413	52°42·9'	2°49·3'W	X	126
Churndon	Devon	SX4889	50°41·1'	4°8·7'W	X	191
Churnet Grange	Staffs	SJ9852	53°4·2'	2°1·4'W	T	118
Churnet Valley	Staffs	SK0742	52°58·8'	1°53·3'W	X	119,128
Churn Fm	Oxon	SU5183	51°32·8'	1°15·5'W	FM	174
Churngill Beck	Cumbr	NY6401	54°24·4'	2°32·9'W	W	91
Churn Hill	Oxon	SU5284	51°33·4'	1°14·6'W	X	174
Churn Hole	Derby	SK1071	53°14·4'	1°50·6'W	X	119
Churn Knob	Oxon	SU5284	51°33·4'	1°14·6'W	A	174
Churn Milk Hole	N Yks	SD8371	54°8·3'	2°15·2'W	X	98
Churn Sike	Northum	NY6777	55°5·4'	2°30·6'W	W	86,87
Churnsike Lodge	Northum	NY6677	55°5·4'	2°31·5'W	X	86
Churn Wood	Essex	TM0325	51°53·4'	0°57·4'E	F	168
Churscombe	Torbay	SX8762	50°27·1'	3°35·1'W	T	202
Churston Cove	Torbay	SX9156	50°23·9'	3°31·6'W	W	202
Churston Ferrers	Torbay	SX9055	50°23·3'	3°32·5'W	T	202
Churston Sta	Torbay	SX8956	50°23·8'	3°33·3'W	X	202
Churt	Surrey	SU8538	51°8·3'	0°46·7'W	T	186
Churt Common	Surrey	SU8539	51°8·9'	0°46·7'W	F	186
Churt Ho	Hants	SU8439	51°8·9'	0°47·6'W	X	186
Churton	Ches	SJ4156	53°6·1'	2°52·5'W	T	117
Churt Place	Surrey	SU8739	51°8·8'	0°45·0'W	X	186
Churwell	Leeds	SE2729	53°45·6'	1°35·0'W	T	104
Chute Cadley	Wilts	SU3153	51°16·7'	1°32·9'W	T	185
Chute Causeway	Wilts	SU2955	51°17·8'	1°34·7'W	X	174,185
Chute Down	Wilts	SU2853	51°16·8'	1°35·5'W	X	184
Chute Fm	Beds	TL0018	51°51·3'	0°32·5'W	FM	166
Chute Lodge	Wilts	SU3051	51°15·7'	1°33·8'W	X	185
Chute Standen	Wilts	SU3053	51°16·8'	1°33·8'W	T	185
Chwaen Bach	I of Angl	SH3983	53°19·4'	4°24·6'W	X	114
Chwaen-gôch	I of Angl	SH3884	53°19·9'	4°25·6'W	X	114
Chwaen Hên	I of Angl	SH3683	53°19·4'	4°27·3'W	X	114
Chwaen-wen	I of Angl	SH3682	53°18·8'	4°27·3'W	X	114
Chwarelau	I of Angl	SH4665	53°9·8'	4°17·8'W	X	114,115
Chwarel y Fan	Monm	SO2529	51°57·5'	3°5·1'W	X	161
Chwefford	Conwy	SH8372	53°14·2'	3°44·8'W	T	116
Chwerfri	Powys	SN9953	52°10·2'	3°28·2'W	W	147
Chwibren	Conwy	SH9362	53°8·9'	3°35·6'W	X	116
Chwilog	Gwyn	SH4338	52°55·2'	4°19·7'W	T	123
Chwilog Fawr	Gwyn	SH4438	52°55·3'	4°18·8'W	X	123
Chwipin	I of Angl	SH4569	53°12·0'	4°18·8'W	X	114,115
Chwythlyn	Conwy	SH8364	53°9·9'	3°44·6'W	W	116
Chyandour	Corn	SW4730	50°7·2'	5°32·0'W	T	203
Chyanvounder	Corn	SW6522	50°3·3'	5°16·6'W	T	203
Chybilly	Corn	SW7123	50°4·0'	5°11·6'W	X	203
Chybucca	Corn	SW7848	50°17·6'	5°6·6'W	X	204
Chycoose	Corn	SW8038	50°12·3'	5°4·6'W	T	204
Chyenhâl	Corn	SW4528	50°6·1'	5°33·6'W	X	203
Chygarkye	Corn	SW7023	50°4·0'	5°12·5'W	X	203
Chygwyne	Corn	SW8041	50°13·9'	5°4·7'W	X	204
Chyknell	Shrops	SO7793	52°32·3'	2°19·9'W	X	138
Chymder	Corn	SW6721	50°2·8'	5°14·9'W	X	203
Chyngton Fm	E Susx	TV5098	50°46·0'	0°8·0'E	FM	199
Chynhale	Corn	SW6430	50°7·6'	5°17·8'W	T	203
Chynhale	Corn	SW7749	50°18·2'	5°7·5'W	X	204
Chynhalls Point	Corn	SW7817	50°0·9'	5°5·6'W	X	204
Chynoweth	Corn	SW5431	50°7·9'	5°26·2'W	T	203
Chypons	Corn	SW6820	50°2·3'	5°14·0'W	X	203
Chypraze	Corn	SW3935	50°9·7'	5°38·9'W	X	203
Chysauster	Corn	SW4734	50°9·4'	5°32·2'W	X	203
Chysauster	Corn	SW4735	50°9·9'	5°32·2'W	X	203
Chysauster (Settlement)	Corn	SW4735	50°9·9'	5°32·2'W	A	203
Chytane Fm	Corn	SW9155	50°21·7'	4°55·9'W	FM	200
Chyvarloe	Corn	SW6523	50°3·9'	5°16·7'W	T	203
Chyverton Ho	Corn	SW7951	50°19·3'	5°5·9'W	X	200,204
Chywoon	Corn	SW7435	50°10·6'	5°9·5'W	X	204
Chywoone	Corn	SW7820	50°2·6'	5°5·7'W	X	204
Chywoone Grove	Corn	SW4527	50°5·5'	5°33·6'W	X	203
Ciapagro	N Eil	NB4658	58°26·5'	6°20·7'W	W	8
Ciaran Water	Highld	NN2862	56°43·3'	4°48·2'W	W	41
Cicelyford	Monm	SO5003	51°43·6'	2°43·0'W	T	162
Cicely Houghton School	Staffs	SJ9550	53°3·1'	2°4·1'W	X	118
Cicely Mill	Ches	SJ7383	53°20·8'	2°23·9'W	X	109
Ciche na Beinne Deirge	Highld	NG5126	57°15·7'	6°7·3'W	H	32
Cichle	I of Angl	SH6078	53°17·1'	4°5·6'W	X	114,115
Cicvcivm (Roman Fort)	Powys	SO0029	51°57·3'	3°26·9'W	R	160
Ciddy Hall	Hants	SU7828	51°3·0'	0°52·8'W	X	186,197
Cider Ho	Powys	SO1084	52°27·0'	3°19·1'W	X	136
Cidermill Fm	Surrey	TQ2140	51°9·0'	0°15·8'W	FM	187
Cider Mill Fm	W Susx	TQ1534	51°5·9'	0°21·1'W	FM	187
Cidigill	Pemb	SN1835	51°59·3'	4°38·6'W	X	145
Cil	Powys	SJ1701	52°36·3'	3°13·1'W	X	136
Cilan	Denb	SJ0237	52°55·5'	3°27·1'W	X	125
Cilan Uchaf	Gwyn	SH2923	52°46·9'	4°31·7'W	X	123
Cilanw	Carm	SN2122	51°52·3'	4°35·6'W	X	145,158
Cilarddu	Powys	SO0147	52°7·0'	3°26·4'W	X	147

Cilast-isaf	Pemb	SN2140	52°2·0′	4°36·2′W	X	145
Cilast-uchaf	Pemb	SN2139	52°1·5′	4°36·2′W	X	145
Cilau	Carm	SN1224	51°53·2′	4°43·5′W	X	145,158
Cilau	Pemb	SM9439	52°0·9′	4°59·7′W	T	157
Cilaufach	Carm	SN1224	51°53·2′	4°43·5′W	X	145,158
Cilau-fawr	Carm	SN1225	51°53·8′	4°43·6′W	X	145,158
Cilau Fm	Powys	SO2017	51°51·0′	3°9·3′W	FM	161
Cilaugwyn	Carm	SN4902	51°42·0′	4°10·7′W	X	159
Cilberllan	Carm	SN5422	51°52·9′	4°6·9′W	X	159
Cilberllan	Powys	SO0854	52°10·8′	3°20·3′W	X	147
Cilbronnau	Cered	SN2045	52°4·7′	4°37·2′W	X	145
Cilbwn	Cered	SN5456	52°11·2′	4°7·8′W	X	146
Cilcain	Flint	SJ1765	53°10·8′	3°14·1′W	T	116
Cilcain Hall	Flint	SJ1868	53°12·4′	3°13·3′W	X	116
Cilcarn	Nth Pt Talb	SS7992	51°37·1′	3°44·5′W	X	170
Cilcarw	Carm	SN4810	51°46·3′	4°11·8′W	X	159
Cilcarw	Carm	SN4912	51°47·4′	4°11·0′W	X	159
Cil-cemmaes	Gwyn	SH6204	52°37·2′	4°1·9′W	X	135
Cilcenni Dingle	Powys	SO1741	52°3·9′	3°12·3′W	X	148,161
Cilcennin	Cered	SN5260	52°13·3′	4°9·6′W	T	146
Cilcert	Cered	SN4461	52°13·7′	4°16·7′W	X	146
Cilcert	Cered	SN6061	52°14·0′	4°2·6′W	X	146
Cilcewydd	Powys	SJ2204	52°37·9′	3°8·8′W	T	126
Cilcoed	Carm	SN3121	51°52·0′	4°26·9′W	X	145,159
Cilcoed	Gwyn	SH4250	53°1·7′	4°21·0′W	X	115,123
Cilcoll Fm	Carm	SN6215	51°49·2′	3°59·7′W	FM	159
Cilcrug	Carm	SN3624	51°53·7′	4°22·6′W	X	145,159
Cil Cwm	Gwyn	SH9017	52°44·6′	3°37·4′W	X	125
Cilcwn	Powys	SN8796	52°33·2′	3°39·6′W	X	135,136
Cil-cychwyn	Gwyn	SH6325	52°48·6′	4°1·6′W	X	124
Cil-Ddewi-fawr	Carm	SN5405	51°43·7′	4°6·5′W	X	159
Cil-Ddewi uchaf	Carm	SN5406	51°44·3′	4°6·5′W	X	159
Cil-dyfnog	Powys	SH7700	52°35·3′	3°48·5′W	X	135
Cildywyll	Carm	SN2212	51°46·9′	4°34·4′W	X	158
Cilely Fm	Rho Cyn Taf	ST0189	51°35·7′	3°25·4′W	FM	170
Cileos	Powys	SJ0825	52°49·1′	3°21·5′W	X	125
Cilerwysg	Cered	SN5654	52°10·2′	4°5·9′W	X	146
Cilevan	Carm	SN2628	51°55·6′	4°31·5′W	X	145,158
Cilfach-allt	Powys	SN9683	52°26·3′	3°31·4′W	X	136
Cilfaenor	Powys	SO1624	51°54·7′	3°12·9′W	X	161
Cilfaesty Hill	Powys	SO1284	52°27·1′	3°17·3′W	H	136
Cilfallen	Cered	SN2943	52°3·8′	4°29·3′W	X	145
Cilfeigan	Monm	SO3500	51°41·9′	2°56·0′W	X	171
Cilfeigan Park	Monm	SO3400	51°41·9′	2°56·9′W	F	171
Cilfeithy Fm	Carm	SN3910	51°46·2′	4°19·6′W	FM	159
Cilfery Isaf	Carm	SN4705	51°43·6′	4°12·5′W	X	159
Cilffara	Carm	SN7233	51°59·1′	3°51·4′W	X	146,160
Cilfforch	Cered	SN4461	52°13·7′	4°16·7′W	X	146
Cilfodeg	Powys	SN9955	52°11·3′	3°28·3′W	X	147
Cilfodig Fm	Powys	SO1036	52°1·1′	3°18·3′W	FM	161
Cilfowyr	Pemb	SN2142	52°3·1′	4°36·2′W	X	145
Cilfrew	Nth Pt Talb	SN7700	51°41·4′	3°46·4′W	T	170
Cil-fwnwr	Swan	SS6398	51°40·1′	3°58·5′W	X	159
Cilfynydd	Rho Cyn Taf	ST0892	51°37·4′	3°19·4′W	T	170
Cilgadan	Carm	SN4011	51°46·7′	4°18·8′W	X	159
Cilgee	Powys	SO0162	52°15·1′	3°26·6′W	X	147
Cilgell	Carm	SN5645	52°5·3′	4°5·7′W	X	146
Cilgelynen	Pemb	SM9834	51°58·3′	4°56·1′W	X	157
Cilgerran	Pemb	SN1942	52°3·1′	4°38·0′W	T	145
Cilgerran Castle	Pemb	SN1943	52°3·6′	4°38·0′W	A	145
Cilglassyn	Conwy	SH8176	53°16·3′	3°46·7′W	X	116
Cilgoed	Denb	SJ0550	53°2·6′	3°24·6′W	X	116
Cilgryman	Carm	SN2325	51°54·0′	4°34·0′W	X	145,158
Cilgwnfydd Fm	Powys	SO0354	52°10·8′	3°24·7′W	FM	147
Cil-Gwrgan	Powys	SN9178	52°23·6′	3°35·7′W	X	136,147
Cil-Gwrgan	Powys	SO1493	52°31·9′	3°15·7′W	X	136
Cilgwyn	Carm	SN3522	51°52·6′	4°23·4′W	X	145,159
Cilgwyn	Carm	SN7429	51°57·0′	3°49·6′W	T	146,160
Cilgwyn	Cered	SN3141	52°2·7′	4°27·5′W	T	145
Cilgwyn	Cered	SN6054	52°10·2′	4°2·4′W	X	146
Cilgwyn	Gwyn	SH4954	53°4·0′	4°14·8′W	T	115,123
Cilgwyn	I of Angl	SH4183	53°19·5′	4°22·8′W	X	114,115
Cilgwyn	Pemb	SN0736	51°59·6′	4°48·3′W	X	145
Cilgwyn	Pemb	SN2338	52°1·0′	4°34·4′W	X	145
Cilgwyn	Powys	SH7704	52°37·4′	3°48·6′W	X	135
Cilgwyn	Powys	SN9733	51°59·4′	3°29·6′W	X	160
Cilgwyn	Powys	SO1439	52°2·8′	3°14·8′W	X	161
Cilgwyn-mawr	Conwy	SH8476	53°16·3′	3°44·0′W	X	116
Cilgwyn-uchaf	Powys	SN9479	52°24·2′	3°33·1′W	X	136,147
Cilgwyn Wood	Carm	SN7529	51°57·0′	3°48·7′W	F	146,160
Cilgynlle	Cered	SN3958	52°12·0′	4°21·0′W	X	145
Cilgynydd	Carm	SN1823	51°52·8′	4°38·3′W	X	145,158
CIL Haul	Gwyn	SH5158	53°6·1′	4°13·1′W	X	115
Cil-haul	Powys	SJ1305	52°38·4′	3°16·7′W	X	125
Cilhaul	Powys	SN9590	52°30·1′	3°32·4′W	X	136
Cil-helyg	Powys	SO1823	51°54·2′	3°11·1′W	X	161
Cilhendre	Nth Pt Talb	SN7202	51°42·4′	3°50·8′W	X	170
Cilhengroes	Carm	SN1921	51°51·7′	4°37·3′W	X	145,158
Cilhernin	Carm	SN1725	51°53·9′	4°39·2′W	X	145,158
Cilhir Isaf	Carm	SN3123	51°53·0′	4°26·9′W	X	145,159
Cilhir-Uchaf	Carm	SN3224	51°53·6′	4°26·1′W	X	145,159
Cilian-uchaf	Powys	SO0642	52°4·3′	3°21·9′W	X	147,160
Ciliau	Powys	SN9554	52°10·7′	3°31·7′W	X	147
Ciliau	Powys	SO1042	52°4·4′	3°18·4′W	X	148,161
Ciliau Aeron	Cered	SN5058	52°12·2′	4°11·3′W	T	146
Ciliau-hwnt	Cered	SN3455	52°10·3′	4°25·3′W	X	145
Ciliau-uchaf	Cered	SN5057	52°11·7′	4°11·3′W	X	146
Ciliauwen	Pemb	SM9432	51°57·1′	4°59·5′W	X	157
Cilie	Cered	SN3556	52°10·9′	4°24·4′W	X	145
Cilieni	Powys	SN9134	51°59·9′	3°34·9′W	W	160
Cilifor Top	Swan	SS5092	51°36·7′	4°9·6′W	H	159
Cill Amhlaidh	N Eil	NF7545	57°23·0′	7°24·1′W	T	22
Cillchriosd	Arg & Bt	NM3753	56°36·0′	6°16·6′W	X	47
Cill Chriosd	Highld	NG6120	57°12·8′	5°57·0′W	A	32
Cill Donnain	N Eil	NF7427	57°13·3′	7°23·7′W	T	22
Cille-a-mhoraire	Arg & Bt	NM4547	56°33·0′	6°8·5′W	X	47,48
Cille-bharra	N Eil	NF7007	57°2·4′	7°26·0′W	A	31
Cill Eireabhagh	N Eil	NF8248	57°24·9′	7°17·4′W	T	22
Cille Mhaodain	Highld	NN0165	56°44·3′	5°14·8′W	A	41
Cille Mhic Foghainn	Arg & Bt	NM3938	56°28·0′	6°13·8′W	A	47,48
Cille Mhuire	Highld	NH5277	57°45·8′	4°28·8′W	A	20
Cillibion	Swan	SS5191	51°36·1′	4°8·7′W	X	159
Cillibion Plantn	Swan	SS5292	51°36·7′	4°7·9′W	F	159
Cil-llidiart	Conwy	SH8972	53°14·3′	3°39·4′W	X	116
Cil-Llwch	Cered	SN4756	52°11·1′	4°13·9′W	X	146
Cillmairi	Highld	NM7359	56°40·3′	5°41·9′W	X	49
Cill mo Chormaig	Stir	NN6735	56°29·6′	4°9·2′W	A	51
Cill Naoimh	Arg & Bt	NR2871	55°51·6′	6°20·4′W	A	60
Cil-lonydd	Caer	ST2297	51°40·2′	3°7·3′W	X	171
Cilmachau	Carm	SN3829	51°56·4′	4°21·0′W	X	145
Cilmaen	Carm	SN7625	51°54·8′	3°47·8′W	X	146,160
Cilmaengwyn	Nth Pt Talb	SN7406	51°44·6′	3°49·1′W	T	160
Cilmaenllwyd	Carm	SN6619	51°51·5′	3°56·4′W	X	159
Cilmanharen	Powys	SO0334	52°0·0′	3°24·4′W	X	160
Cilmarch	Carm	SN4013	51°47·8′	4°18·8′W	X	159
Cilmaren	Carm	SN6938	52°1·7′	3°54·2′W	X	146,160
Cilmawr	Powys	SJ1725	52°49·2′	3°13·5′W	X	125
Cilmawr	Powys	SJ1814	52°43·3′	3°12·4′W	X	125
Cilmeityn	Conwy	SH8079	53°17·9′	3°47·6′W	X	116
Cilmery	Powys	SO0051	52°9·1′	3°27·3′W	T	147
Cilmery Fm	Powys	SN9951	52°9·1′	3°28·2′W	FM	147
Cil-moor	Pemb	SN0826	51°54·2′	4°47·1′W	X	145,158
Cilnant	Wrex	SJ2336	52°55·2′	3°8·3′W	X	126
Ciloerwynt	Powys	SN8862	52°14·9′	3°38·0′W	X	147
Cilolwg	Cered	SN6187	52°28·0′	4°2·4′W	X	135
Cil-onen	Swan	SS5493	51°37·3′	4°6·2′W	X	159
Cilonw	Powys	SO2338	52°2·3′	3°7·0′W	X	161
Cilonw Brook	Powys	SO2239	52°2·9′	3°7·9′W	W	161
Cilowen	Carm	SN1722	51°52·2′	4°39·1′W	X	145,158
Cilowen	Conwy	SH9368	53°12·1′	3°35·7′W	X	116
Cil-Owen Brook	Powys	SO1480	52°24·9′	3°15·5′W	W	136
Cilpebyll	Powys	SN9836	52°1·0′	3°28·8′W	X	160
Cilpost Fm	Carm	SN1918	51°50·1′	4°37·2′W	FM	158
Cilrath	Pemb	SN1117	51°49·4′	4°44·2′W	X	158
Cilrhedyn	Pemb	SN0034	51°58·4′	4°54·3′W	X	145,157
Cilrhedyn Br	Pemb	SN0034	51°58·4′	4°54·3′W	X	145,157
Cilrhiw Ho	Pemb	SN1413	51°47·3′	4°41·4′W	X	158
Cilrhue	Pemb	SN1939	52°1·4′	4°37·9′W	X	145
Cilrhue Fach	Pemb	SN2240	52°2·0′	4°35·3′W	X	145
Cilrhye	Powys	SN9675	52°22·0′	3°31·3′W	X	136,147
Cilrhyg	Cered	SN6059	52°12·9′	4°2·6′W	X	146
Cilsan	Carm	SN5922	51°53·0′	4°2·5′W	T	159
Cilsan Br	Carm	SN5821	51°52·4′	4°3·4′W	X	159
Cilsant	Carm	SN2623	51°52·9′	4°31·3′W	X	145,158
Cilshafe	Pemb	SM9736	51°59·4′	4°57·0′W	X	157
Ciltalgarth	Gwyn	SH8840	52°57·0′	3°39·6′W	X	124,125
Ciltrew	Powys	SJ2119	52°46·0′	3°9·9′W	X	126
Ciltriew	Powys	SO1588	52°29·2′	3°14·7′W	X	136
Ciltwrch	Powys	SO1540	52°3·4′	3°14·0′W	T	148,161
Cil-voynog	Monm	ST4494	51°38·8′	2°48·2′W	X	171,172
Cilvrnvm (Roman Fort)	Northum	NY9170	55°1·7′	2°8·0′W	R	87
Cilwaunydd	Carm	SN4218	51°50·5′	4°17·2′W	X	159
Cilwaunydd	Carm	SN6219	51°51·4′	3°59·8′W	X	159
Cil-waunydd Fawr	Carm	SN2935	51°59·5′	4°29·0′W	X	145
Cilwen	Carm	SN3424	51°53·6′	4°24·4′W	X	145,159
Cilwendeg	Pemb	SN2238	52°1·0′	4°35·2′W	T	145
Cilwern	Carm	SN5823	51°53·5′	4°3·4′W	X	159
Cilwern	Carm	SN6325	51°54·6′	3°59·1′W	X	146
Cilwhybert	Powys	SO0126	51°55·7′	3°26·0′W	X	160
Cil-wnwg	Carm	SN5104	51°43·1′	4°9·0′W	X	159
Cil-wnwg	Carm	SN5105	51°43·7′	4°9·1′W	X	159
Cilwr Fm	Carm	SN6032	51°58·4′	4°1·9′W	FM	146
Cilybebyll	Nth Pt Talb	SN7404	51°43·5′	3°49·1′W	T	170
Cilyblaidd	Carm	SN5445	52°5·3′	4°7·5′W	X	146
Cilycwm	Carm	SN7540	52°2·9′	3°49·0′W	T	146,147,160
Cil-y-Gofid	Nth Pt Talb	SS7991	51°36·5′	3°44·5′W	X	170
Cilyllynfawr	Carm	SN6233	51°58·9′	4°0·2′W	X	146
Cim	Gwyn	SH3125	52°48·0′	4°30·0′W	X	123
Cimla	Nth Pt Talb	SS7696	51°39·2′	3°47·2′W	T	170
Cimwch	Flint	SJ1269	53°12·9′	3°18·7′W	X	116
Cinderbarrow	Lancs	SD5175	54°10·4′	2°44·6′W	X	97
Cinderdale Beck	Cumbr	NY1619	54°33·8′	3°17·5′W	W	89
Cinder Fm	E Susx	TQ4019	50°57·4′	0°0·0′W	FM	198
Cinderford	Glos	SO6513	51°49·1′	2°30·1′W	T	162
Cinder Hill	Barns	SE2808	53°34·3′	1°34·2′W	X	110
Cinder Hill	Bolton	SD7605	53°32·7′	2°21·3′W	T	109
Cinderhill	C of Nott	SK5343	52°59·1′	1°12·2′W	T	129
Cinderhill	Derby	SK3646	53°0·8′	1°27·4′W	T	119,128
Cinder Hill	Kent	TQ5346	51°11·8′	0°11·8′E	T	188
Cinder Hill	Lancs	SD5572	54°8·8′	2°40·9′W	X	97
Cinder Hill	Lincs	TF3669	53°12·3′	0°2·6′E	X	122
Cinder Hill	Somer	ST2611	50°53·9′	3°2·8′W	X	192,193
Cinder Hill	Wolv	SO9294	52°32·9′	2°6·7′W	T	139
Cinder Hill	W Susx	TQ3729	51°2·9′	0°2·3′W	X	187,198
Cinderhill Fm	E Susx	TQ6128	51°2·0′	0°18·2′E	FM	188,199
Cinder Hill Fm	Oldham	SD9007	53°33·8′	2°8·6′W	FM	109
Cinder Hills	N Yks	SE2158	54°1·3′	1°40·4′W	X	104
Cinder Lane Fm	Ches	SJ7973	53°15·5′	2°18·5′W	FM	118
Cinder Plot	Lincs	SK9168	53°12·3′	0°37·8′W	F	121
Cinders	Heref	SO5864	52°16·6′	2°36·5′W	X	137,138,149
Cinders	Wrex	SJ3243	52°59·0′	3°0·4′W	X	117
Cinders Fm	Derby	SK5077	53°17·5′	1°14·6′W	FM	120
Cinders Wood	Heref	SO5865	52°17·1′	2°36·5′W	X	137,138,149
Cindery Island	Essex	TM0915	51°47·9′	1°2·3′E	X	168,169
Cindra How	N Yks	SE1976	54°11·0′	1°42·1′W	X	99
Cinnamire Fm	N Yks	SE3597	54°22·3′	1°27·3′W	FM	99
Cinnamon Brow	Warr	SJ6291	53°25·1′	2°33·9′W	T	109
Cinque Cliff Grange	N Yks	SE4884	54°15·2′	1°15·4′W	X	100
Cinque Cliff Ho	N Yks	SE4884	54°15·2′	1°15·4′W	X	100
Cinque Fm	Suff	TL9878	52°22·1′	0°54·9′E	FM	144
Cinquefoil Lodge	Northnts	SP9179	52°24·3′	0°39·3′W	X	141
Ciochan Beinn Laoigh	Arg & Bt	NN2627	56°24·5′	4°48·8′W	X	50
Cioch Beinn an Eion	Highld	NC1206	58°0·5′	5°10·4′W	H	15
Cioch Beinn nan Eun	Highld	NH4375	57°44·5′	4°37·8′W	H	20
Cioch Mhór	Arg & Bt	NN1806	56°13·0′	4°55·7′W	X	56
Cioch Mhor	Highld	NC3557	58°28·5′	4°49·3′W	H	9
Cioch Mhór	Highld	NH5063	57°38·2′	4°30·3′W	H	20
Cioch na h-Oighe	N Ayr	NR9943	55°38·6′	5°11·2′W	X	62,69
Ciolle Uisge	Highld	NH4654	57°33·3′	4°34·0′W	X	26
Ciopeagail Mòr	N Eil	NB2406	57°57·7′	6°39·5′W	H	13,14
Ciopeagal Bheag	N Eil	NB2406	57°57·7′	6°39·5′W	H	13,14
Ciorabhal	N Eil	NB0623	58°6·2′	6°59·0′W	H	13,14
Ciorabhal	N Eil	NB2124	58°7·3′	6°43·8′W	H	13,14
Cippenham	Slough	SU9480	51°30·9′	0°38·3′W	T	175
Cippyn	Pemb	SN1347	52°5·6′	4°43·4′W	T	145
Cipyllygwynt	Pemb	SN1340	52°1·9′	4°43·2′W	X	145
Cirbhig	N Eil	NB2041	58°16·4′	6°46·1′W	T	8,13
Circebost	N Eil	NB1834	58°12·5′	6°47·6′W	T	8,13
Cirean Geardail	Highld	NC0034	58°15·2′	5°24·0′W	X	15
Cirein Mór	Highld	NG2859	57°32·6′	6°32·3′W	X	23
Cirein Seileageo	N Eil	NB5655	58°25·2′	6°10·2′W	X	8
Cirencester	Glos	SP0201	51°42·7′	1°57·9′W	T	163
Cirencester Park	Glos	SO9901	51°42·7′	2°0·5′W	X	163
Cir Mhòr	N Ayr	NR9743	55°38·5′	5°13·1′W	H	62,69
Cissbury	W Susx	TQ1208	50°51·9′	0°24·1′W	X	198
Cissbury Ring	W Susx	TQ1308	50°51·9′	0°23·3′W	A	198
Ciss Green	Ches	SJ8460	53°8·5′	2°13·9′W	X	118
Cist Cerrig	Gwyn	SH5438	52°55·4′	4°9·9′W	A	124
Ciste Dhubh	Highld	NH0616	57°11·9′	5°12·2′W	H	33
Ciste Dhubh	Highld	NH1124	57°16·3′	5°7·6′W	X	25
Cistercian Way	Cumbr	SD2775	54°10·2′	3°6·7′W	X	96
Cistfaen	Gwyn	SH9938	52°56·0′	3°29·8′W	X	125
Cistfaen	Powys	SN8677	52°23·0′	3°40·1′W	H	135
Cistfaen	Powys	SN8677	52°23·0′	3°40·1′W	H	135,136,147
Citadel	Orkney	HY2408	58°57·4′	3°18·8′W	X	6,7
Citadel, The	C of Plym	SX4853	50°21·7′	4°7·8′W	A	201
Citadel, The	Shrops	SJ5728	52°51·1′	2°37·9′W	X	126
Cithis Bheag	N Eil	NB2314	58°2·0′	6°41·1′W	H	13,14
Citron Seat	Durham	NY9710	54°29·4′	2°2·4′W	H	92
City	Powys	SO2189	52°29·8′	3°9·4′W	T	137
City	V of Glam	SS9878	51°29·7′	3°27·8′W	T	170
City Dulas	I of Angl	SH4687	53°21·7′	4°18·4′W	T	114
City Fm	Beds	TL1159	52°13·3′	0°22·1′W	FM	153
City Fm	Oxon	SP4211	51°48·0′	1°23·1′W	FM	164
City Fm	Oxon	SP5803	51°43·6′	1°9·2′W	FM	164
City Fm	W Loth	NT0164	55°51·8′	3°34·5′W	FM	65
City of London Cemetery	Newham	TQ4286	51°33·5′	0°3·3′E	X	177
City of Whiteborough Fm	Notts	SK4660	53°8·3′	1°18·3′W	FM	120
City, The	Suff	TM3988	52°26·5′	1°31·4′E	X	156
Civit Hills Fm	Ches	SJ9368	53°12·8′	2°5·9′W	FM	118
Clabhach	Arg & Bt	NM1858	56°38·0′	6°35·5′W	T	46
Clach a' Bhadain	Arg & Bt	NM5132	56°25·1′	6°1·8′W	X	48
Clach a' Bhealaich	Arg & Bt	NR7637	55°34·8′	5°32·8′W	X	68,69
Clach a' Bhein	Arg & Bt	NN2938	56°30·4′	4°46·3′W	X	50
Clach a Bhein	Arg & Bt	NN3038	56°30·5′	4°45·3′W	X	50
Clach a' Bhoineid	Highld	NC2753	58°26·1′	4°57·3′W	X	9
Clach-a-Charra	Highld	NN0261	56°42·2′	5°13·6′W	A	41
Clach a' Charridh	Highld	NH8574	57°44·7′	3°55·5′W	A	21
Clach a' Chomharraidh	Highld	NH1844	57°27·3′	5°1·6′W	X	25
Clach a' Cléirich	Aberd	NO1199	57°4·7′	3°27·6′W	X	36,43
Clachadubh	Arg & Bt	NM9427	56°23·7′	5°19·8′W	X	49
Clachaig	Arg & Bt	NM5636	56°27·4′	5°57·2′W	X	47,48
Clachaig	Arg & Bt	NR7762	55°48·2′	5°33·1′W	X	62
Clachaig	Arg & Bt	NS1181	55°59·3′	5°1·4′W	T	63
Clachaig	Highld	NJ0218	57°14·8′	3°37·0′W	T	36
Clachaig	N Ayr	NR9421	55°26·6′	5°15·0′W	X	68,69
Clachaig	N Ayr	NR9522	55°27·2′	5°14·1′W	X	68,69
Clachaig	N Ayr	NR9623	55°27·8′	5°13·2′W	X	68,69
Clachaig Hill	Arg & Bt	NS1082	55°59·9′	5°2·4′W	H	56
Clachaig Inn (PH)	Highld	NN1256	56°39·7′	5°3·6′W	X	41
Clachaig Mhór	Arg & Bt	NR6596	56°6·2′	5°46·3′W	H	55,61
Clachaig Water	Arg & Bt	NR6941	55°36·7′	5°39·6′W	W	62
Clach-airigh	Arg & Bt	NR4072	55°52·5′	6°9·0′W	X	60,61
Clach Alasdair	Highld	NM4588	56°55·1′	6°10·9′W	X	39
Clachamish	Highld	NG3853	57°29·8′	6°21·9′W	X	23
Clachan	Arg & Bt	NM7819	56°18·9′	5°34·9′W	X	55
Clachan	Arg & Bt	NM8643	56°32·1′	5°28·4′W	T	49
Clachan	Arg & Bt	NN0901	56°10·1′	5°4·1′W	T	56
Clachan	Arg & Bt	NR7656	55°45·0′	5°33·7′W	T	62
Clachan	D & G	NX0270	54°59·4′	5°5·3′W	X	76,82
Clachan	D & G	NX8880	55°6·4′	3°44·9′W	X	78
Clachan	Highld	NC7062	58°31·9′	4°13·5′W	T	10
Clachan	Highld	NG3971	57°39·5′	6°22·1′W	X	23
Clachan	Highld	NG4966	57°37·1′	6°11·7′W	T	23
Clachan	Highld	NG5436	57°21·1′	6°4·9′W	T	24,32
Clachan	Highld	NH1784	57°48·8′	5°4·4′W	T	20
Clachan	Highld	NH6532	57°21·8′	4°14·2′W	X	26
Clachan	N Ayr	NR9648	55°41·2′	5°13·4′W	H	62,69
Clachan	N Eil	NF7746	57°23·6′	7°22·2′W	T	22
Clachanach	Arg & Bt	NM2824	56°20·1′	6°23·6′W	X	48
Clachan a' Ghobha	N Eil	NB5141	58°17·5′	6°14·5′W	X	8
Clachan-a-Luib	N Eil	NF8163	57°32·9′	7°19·5′W	T	18
Clachan Beag	Arg & Bt	NN1812	56°16·2′	4°55·9′W	X	50,56
Clachanbirnie Burn	D & G	NY0092	55°13·0′	3°33·9′W	W	78
Clachan Bridge	Arg & Bt	NM7819	56°18·9′	5°34·9′W	X	55
Clachan Burn	Highld	NC7360	58°30·8′	4°10·3′W	W	10
Clachan Burrival	N Eil	NF8963	57°33·3′	7°11·5′W	H	18
Clachan Comair	Highld	NH3330	57°20·1′	4°46·0′W	X	26
Clachan Craonaval	N Eil	NF8463	57°33·1′	7°16·5′W	X	18
Clach an Daimh	Highld	NH1336	57°22·8′	5°6·2′W	X	25
Clachandhu	Arg & Bt	NM4535	56°26·6′	6°7·8′W	X	47,48
Clachandow Rig	D & G	NX6688	55°10·3′	4°5·8′W	X	77
Clachandubh Burn	Arg & Bt	NM8700	56°9·0′	5°25·3′W	W	55
Clachandubh Hill	Arg & Bt	NM8601	56°9·5′	5°26·3′W	H	55
Clach an Easbuig	Arg & Bt	NR8676	55°56·0′	5°25·1′W	X	62
Clachaneasy	D & G	NX3574	55°2·2′	4°34·5′W	T	77
Clachan Fhalbhain	Arg & Bt	NM4523	56°20·1′	6°7·1′W	X	48
Clach an Fhuarain	Highld	NN4162	56°43·6′	4°35·5′W	X	42
Clachan Fm	Arg & Bt	NN1812	56°16·2′	4°55·9′W	FM	50,56
Clachan Fm	Arg & Bt	NS2582	56°0·2′	4°48·0′W	FM	56
Clachan Gorma	Highld	NG3627	57°15·7′	6°22·2′W	X	32
Clachan Heughs	D & G	NX0370	54°59·4′	5°4·3′W	X	76,82
Clachan Hill	Arg & Bt	NN1815	56°17·8′	4°56·1′W	H	50,56
Clachan Hill Fm	D & G	NX0270	54°59·4′	5°5·3′W	FM	76,82
Clach an Lochain	Highld	NM5366	56°43·5′	6°1·8′W	W	47
Clachan Mór	Arg & Bt	NL9847	56°31·3′	6°54·2′W	X	46
Clachanmore	D & G	NX0846	54°46·6′	4°58·7′W	X	82
Clachan More	Pth & Kin	NN9948	56°37·0′	3°38·3′W	A	52,53
Clachan of Campsie	E Dunb	NS6179	55°59·3′	4°13·3′W	T	64
Clachan of Glendaruel	Arg & Bt	NR9984	56°0·7′	5°13·0′W	T	55

Clachan of Myrton	D & G	NX3643	54°45·6'	4°32·5'W	X	83
Clachanpluck	D & G	NX0961	54°54·7'	4°58·4'W	X	82
Clach an Righ	Highld	NC6739	58°19·4'	4°15·8'W	A	16
Clachanry	Stir	NS5188	56°4·0'	4°23·2'W	X	57
Clachan Sands	N Eil	NF8775	57°39·6'	7°14·5'W	X	18
Clachan-Seil	Arg & Bt	NM7819	56°18·9'	5°34·9'W	T	55
Clachanshiels	Aberd	NO7987	56°58·7'	2°20·3'W	X	45
Clachan Sound	Arg & Bt	NM7819	56°18·9'	5°34·9'W	W	55
Clachan Sound	Arg & Bt	NM7820	56°19·5'	5°35·0'W	W	49
Clachantachree	Arg & Bt	NR3057	55°44·1'	6°17·6'W	X	60
Clach an Teampuill	N Eil	NB0100	57°53·6'	7°2·3'W	A	18
Clach an Tigh Bhuairidh	Pth & Kin	NN4857	56°41·1'	4°28·4'W	X	42,51
Clach an Tiompain	Arg & Bt	NR3469	55°50·7'	6°14·5'W	A	60,61
Clachanton	S Ayr	NX1586	55°8·3'	4°53·7'W	X	76
Clach an Truiseil	N Eil	NB3753	58°23·5'	6°29·6'W	A	8
Clach an t-Sagairt	N Eil	NF8776	57°40·2'	7°14·5'W	A	18
Clach-an-Tuirc	Pth & Kin	NN7244	56°34·5'	4°4·6'W	X	51,52
Clachanturn	Aberd	NO2794	57°2·1'	3°11·7'W	X	37,44
Clach an Tursa	N Eil	NB2042	58°16·9'	6°46·1'W	A	8,13
Clachan Uaine	Highld	NG4715	57°9·6'	6°10·6'W	X	32
Clachan Yell	Aberd	NO4491	57°0·7'	2°54·9'W	H	44
Clach Ard	Highld	NG4249	57°27·7'	6°17·7'W	X	23
Clachbain	Highld	NH9728	57°20·1'	3°42·2'W	X	36
Clach Bhadan	Arg & Bt	NM9523	56°21·6'	5°18·7'W	X	49
Clach Bhàn	Moray	NJ1511	57°11·2'	3°23·9'W	X	36
Clach Bhàn	Moray	NJ1605	57°8·0'	3°22·8'W	X	36
Clach Bhàrr	Arg & Bt	NM7804	56°10·9'	5°34·2'W	H	55
Clach Bheag na Faraid	Highld	NC3971	58°36·1'	4°45·8'W	X	9
Clach Bheinn	Arg & Bt	NS1288	56°3·1'	5°0·7'W	H	56
Clach Bheinn	Arg & Bt	NS2195	56°7·1'	4°52·3'W	H	56
Clach-bheinn	Highld	NH2720	57°14·5'	4°51·6'W	H	25
Clachbrake	Moray	NJ2646	57°30·2'	3°13·6'W	X	28
Clachbreck	Arg & Bt	NR7675	55°55·2'	5°34·7'W	T	62
Clach Bun Rudhtair	Moray	NJ1303	57°6·8'	3°25·7'W	X	36
Clach Choutsaich	Aberd	NJ1401	57°5·8'	3°24·7'W	X	36
Clach Choutsaich	Aberd	NJ2205	57°8·0'	3°16·9'W	X	36
Clach Choutsaich	Highld	NH9003	57°6·5'	3°48·5'W	X	36
Clach Criche	Highld	NH2206	57°6·9'	4°55·9'W	H	34
Clachcurr	Aberd	NJ4013	57°12·5'	2°59·1'W	H	37
Clach-dhruim Beag	Arg & Bt	NR7277	55°56·2'	5°38·6'W	X	62
Clach-dhruim Mór	Arg & Bt	NR7278	55°56·7'	5°38·6'W	H	62
Clach Dubh	Highld	NG5241	57°23·8'	6°7·2'W	X	23,24
Clacherdean Wood	E Loth	NT5270	55°55·5'	2°45·7'W	F	66
Clachertyfarlie Knowes	Stir	NS5583	56°1·3'	4°19·1'W	X	57,64
Clach Fiaraidh	Moray	NJ1505	57°7·9'	3°23·8'W	X	36
Clachfin Glen	Arg & Bt	NR7229	55°30·4'	5°36·2'W	X	68
Clachgeal Hill	Highld	NC9657	58°29·6'	3°46·6'W	X	11
Clach Gharbh	Arg & Bt	NR9287	56°2·1'	5°19·9'W	X	55
Clachghlas	Pth & Kin	NN9172	56°49·9'	3°46·7'W	X	43
Clach Goil	Highld	NH5781	57°48·0'	4°23·9'W	X	21
Clachie Burn	Aberd	NJ6921	57°17·0'	2°30·4'W	W	38
Clachie Burn	Stir	NS6383	56°1·5'	4°11·5'W	X	57,64
Clachindruim	Highld	NH6534	57°22·8'	4°14·3'W	X	26
Clach Leathad	Highld	NN2349	56°36·2'	4°52·6'W	H	50
Clach Loundrain	Highld	NH2751	57°31·2'	4°52·9'W	H	25
Clach MacKenny	Arg & Bt	NS2383	56°0·7'	4°49·9'W	X	56
Clach Mhallaichte	Highld	NH8067	57°40·9'	4°0·3'W	X	21,27
Clach-mheall	Highld	NN7793	57°1·0'	4°1·1'W	H	35
Clach-mheall Beag	Highld	NN7391	56°59·8'	4°5·0'W	H	35
Clach-mheall Dubh	Highld	NN7290	56°59·3'	4°5·9'W	H	35
Clach Mhic Cailein or The Argyll Stone	Highld	NH9004	57°7·1'	3°48·5'W	X	36
Clach Mhic Leòid	N Eil	NG0497	57°52·1'	6°59·1'W	A	18
Clach Mhic Mhios	Highld	NC9415	58°6·9'	3°47·5'W	A	17
Clach Mhór a Che	N Eil	NF7666	57°34·3'	7°24·8'W	A	18
Clach Mhór na Faraid	Highld	NC3971	58°36·1'	4°45·8'W	X	9
Clach Mhór Sheamsgeir	N Eil	NF9377	57°40·9'	7°8·6'W	X	18
Clach Mór	Highld	NC0711	58°3·0'	5°15·8'W	X	15
Clachnaben	Aberd	NO6186	56°58·1'	2°38·0'W	H	45
Clach na Boile	Pth & Kin	NN6658	56°41·9'	4°10·9'W	A	42,51
Clachnabrain	Angus	NO3766	56°47·1'	3°1·4'W	X	44
Clach na Briton	Stir	NN3321	56°21·4'	4°41·7'W	X	50,56
Clach-na-Coileach	Pth & Kin	NO1464	56°45·8'	3°24·0'W	X	43
Clach na Frithealaidh	Highld	NH0277	57°44·6'	5°19·1'W	X	19
Clach na Gile	Arg & Bt	NR4678	55°55·9'	6°3·6'W	X	60,61
Clach na h-Annait	Highld	NG5920	57°12·7'	5°59·0'W	A	32
Clach na h-Armaichd	Highld	NC5551	58°25·7'	4°28·5'W	X	10
Clachnaharry	Highld	NH6546	57°29·3'	4°14·7'W	T	26
Clach na h' Jobairte	Pth & Kin	NN6159	56°42·4'	4°15·8'W	A	42,51
Clach nam Ban	Highld	NH5281	57°47·9'	4°28·9'W	X	20
Clach nam Piòbair	Highld	NJ1026	57°19·2'	3°29·2'W	X	36
Clach nan Con-fionn	Highld	NG9448	57°28·8'	5°25·7'W	X	25
Clach nan Ràmh	Highld	NG4673	57°40·8'	6°15·2'W	X	23
Clach nan Taillear (Stone)	Aberd	NN9896	57°2·9'	3°40·4'W	X	36,43
Clach na Tiompan	Pth & Kin	NN8333	56°28·7'	3°53·5'W	X	52
Clach na Tiompan (Chambered Cairn)	Pth & Kin	NN8333	56°28·7'	3°53·5'W	A	52
Clach Oscar	Highld	NG5622	57°13·7'	6°2·1'W	X	32
Clach Ossian	Pth & Kin	NN8930	56°27·2'	3°47·6'W	A	52
Clachrum Rig	D & G	NX6371	55°1·1'	4°8·1'W	X	77
Clach Sgoilte	Highld	NH3181	57°47·5'	4°50·1'W	X	20
Clach Sgoilte	Highld	NH4176	57°45·0'	4°39·8'W	H	20
Clach Sgorach	Pth & Kin	NO1361	56°44·2'	3°24·9'W	X	43
Clach Stei Lin	N Eil	NB3954	58°24·1'	6°27·6'W	A	8
Clach Stein	N Eil	NB5131	58°12·1'	6°13·8'W	A	8
Clach Stein	N Eil	NB5364	58°29·9'	6°13·9'W	A	8
Clachtoll	Highld	NC0427	58°11·6'	5°19·6'W	T	15
Clach Uaine	N Eil	NG4399	57°54·6'	6°19·9'W	X	14
Clach Uilleim	N Eil	NB4014	58°2·6'	6°23·9'W	X	14
Clachville	Highld	NH4653	57°32·7'	4°33·9'W	X	26
Clack Hill	D & G	NX6267	54°59·0'	4°9·0'W	H	83
Clack Hill	Leic	SP7586	52°28·2'	0°53·4'W	X	141
Clack Ho	N Yks	SE4497	54°22·2'	1°18·9'W	X	99
Clackleith	D & G	NS8217	55°26·2'	3°51·5'W	X	71,78
Clackleith Hill	D & G	NS8217	55°26·2'	3°51·5'W	H	71,78
Clackmae	Scot Bord	NT5639	55°38·8'	2°41·5'W	X	73
Clackmannan	Clackm	NS9191	56°6·2'	3°44·7'W	T	58
Clackmarras	Moray	NJ2458	57°36·6'	3°15·9'W	T	28
Clack Mount	Wilts	ST9979	51°30·8'	2°0·5'W	A	173
Clacknockater	Angus	NO1962	56°44·8'	3°19·0'W	X	43

Clack's Fm	Oxon	SU6389	51°36·0'	1°5·0'W	FM	175
Clack's Fm	Worcs	SO8265	52°17·2'	2°15·4'W	FM	138,150
Clacton Grove Fm	Essex	TM1719	51°49·9'	1°9·4'E	FM	168,169
Clacton-On-Sea	Essex	TM1715	51°47·7'	1°9·2'E	T	168,169
Cladach	N Ayr	NS0137	55°35·4'	5°9·0'W	T	69
Cladach a' Bhaile Shear	N Eil	NF8162	57°32·4'	7°19·4'W	T	22
Cladach a' Ghlinne	Highld	NG5216	57°10·3'	6°5·7'W	X	32
Cladach an Eilein	N Eil	NB5365	58°30·5'	6°14·0'W	X	8
Cladach Chaidhsaidair	N Eil	NB5561	58°28·4'	6°11·6'W	X	8
Cladach Chairinis	N Eil	NF8558	57°30·4'	7°15·1'W	X	22
Cladach Chuidhsiadair	N Eil	NB5558	58°26·8'	6°11·4'W	X	8
Cladach Dhiobadail	N Eil	NB5554	58°24·6'	6°11·2'W	X	8
Cladach Fionn	Arg & Bt	NR2571	55°51·5'	6°23·2'W	X	60
Cladach Lag na Greine	N Eil	NB3855	58°24·6'	6°28·7'W	X	8
Cladach Mór	N Eil	NF7174	57°38·4'	7°30·4'W	X	18
Cladach na Luinge	N Eil	NB4661	58°28·1'	6°20·9'W	X	8
Cladance	S Lanak	NS6548	55°42·7'	4°8·5'W	X	64
Cladance Moss	S Lanak	NS6649	55°43·2'	4°7·6'W	X	64
Claddach	Arg & Bt	NR1653	55°41·5'	6°30·7'W	T	60
Claddach Cumhang	N Eil	NF8064	57°33·4'	7°20·6'W	X	18
Claddach Illeray	N Eil	NF7964	57°33·4'	7°21·6'W	T	18
Claddach Kirkibost	N Eil	NF7865	57°33·9'	7°22·7'W	T	18
Claddach-knockline	N Eil	NF7567	57°34·8'	7°25·8'W	T	18
Claddach-kyles	N Eil	NF7666	57°34·3'	7°24·8'W	X	18
Claddach-vallay	N Eil	NF7773	57°38·1'	7°24·3'W	X	18
Claddagh, The	I of M	SC3893	54°18·4'	4°30·7'W	X	95
Claddy House Burn	D & G	NX0768	54°58·4'	5°0·5'W	W	82
Cladh a'Bhile	Arg & Bt	NR7375	55°55·1'	5°37·5'W	A	62
Cladh a' Mhanaich	Highld	NG3581	57°44·7'	6°26·7'W	X	23
Cladh an Diseart	Arg & Bt	NM2824	56°20·1'	6°23·6'W	A	48
Cladh Chiarain	Highld	NM5661	56°40·9'	5°58·6'W	A	47
Cladh Churadain	Highld	NH5867	57°40·5'	4°22·4'W	A	21
Cladh Mhuire	N Eil	NB3551	58°22·3'	6°31·5'W	A	8
Cladh na-h-Annait	Arg & Bt	NN0029	56°24·9'	5°14·1'W	A	50
Cladich	Arg & Bt	NN0921	56°20·8'	5°5·0'W	T	50,56
Cladich River	Arg & Bt	NN1021	56°20·9'	5°4·0'W	W	50,56
Cladich Steading	Arg & Bt	NN0922	56°21·4'	5°5·0'W	X	50
Cladswell	Worcs	SP0458	52°13·4'	1°56·1'W	T	150
Cladville	Arg & Bt	NR1754	55°42·1'	6°29·8'W	X	60
Claerddu	Cered	SN7968	52°18·0'	3°46·1'W	X	135,147
Claerwen	Powys	SN8267	52°17·5'	3°43·4'W	X	135,136,147
Claerwen	Powys	SO2391	52°30·9'	3°7·7'W	X	137
Claerwen Reservoir	Powys	SN8465	52°16·5'	3°41·6'W	W	135,136,147
Clafdy	I of Angl	SH3569	53°11·8'	4°27·8'W	X	114
Claggain Bay	Arg & Bt	NR4653	55°42·5'	6°2·2'W	W	60
Claggain River	Arg & Bt	NR4453	55°42·4'	6°4·1'W	W	60
Claggan	Arg & Bt	NR3461	55°46·5'	6°14·1'W	X	60
Claggan	Highld	NC8532	58°16·0'	3°57·1'W	X	17
Claggan	Highld	NM6949	56°34·8'	5°45·2'W	X	49
Claggan	Highld	NN1174	56°49·4'	5°5·4'W	T	41
Claggan	Moray	NJ2643	57°28·5'	3°13·6'W	X	28
Claggan	Pth & Kin	NN7138	56°31·2'	4°5·4'W	X	51,52
Claggan Burn	Highld	NC8533	58°16·5'	3°57·2'W	W	17
Clagganghoul	Aberd	NO2191	57°0·5'	3°17·6'W	X	44
Claggersnich	Highld	NJ0928	57°20·3'	3°30·2'W	X	36
Claggersnich Wood	Highld	NJ0926	57°19·2'	3°30·2'W	F	36
Claggy Cott	Herts	TL1618	51°51·1'	0°18·5'W	X	166
Claghbane	I of M	SC2577	54°9·8'	4°40·4'W	X	95
Clagh Ouyr	I of M	SC4188	54°16·0'	4°26·1'W	H	95
Clahar Barton Fm	Corn	SW6819	50°1·8'	5°14·0'W	FM	203
Claife Heights	Cumbr	SD3797	54°22·1'	2°57·8'W	H	96,97
Claigan	Highld	NG2353	57°29·2'	6°36·9'W	T	23
Claigan	Highld	NG2354	57°29·8'	6°36·9'W	X	23
Claig Castle	Arg & Bt	NR4762	55°47·4'	6°1·7'W	X	60,61
Claim Fm	Ches	SJ5173	53°15·3'	2°43·7'W	FM	117
Claines	Worcs	SO8558	52°13·4'	2°12·8'W	T	150
Clairinsh	Stir	NS4189	56°4·3'	4°32·8'W	X	56
Clair View Fm	Norf	TL5398	52°33·7'	0°15·8'E	FM	143
Clais	Highld	NC1313	58°4·3'	5°9·8'W	X	15
Clais a' Bhaid Choille	Highld	NH5889	57°52·3'	4°23·2'W	X	21
Clais Bhàn	Highld	NC1546	58°22·1'	5°9·3'W	X	9
Clais Bheag	Pth & Kin	NO0674	56°51·1'	3°32·0'W	H	43
Clais Bhreac	Highld	NM7247	56°33·8'	5°42·2'W	X	49
Clais-Cairn Hill	Highld	ND1327	58°13·7'	3°28·4'W	X	17
Clais Chàrnach	Highld	NC2673	58°36·9'	4°59·3'W	X	9
Clais Dhearg	Arg & Bt	NM9331	56°25·8'	5°21·0'W	X	49
Claiseanglas	Highld	NH6891	57°53·6'	4°13·1'W	X	21
Claisfearn	Highld	NC1946	58°22·2'	5°5·2'W	X	9
Clais Fhearnaig	Aberd	NO0693	57°1·4'	3°32·4'W	X	36,43
Clais Ghàrbh	Highld	NJ0732	57°22·4'	3°32·3'W	H	27
Claish Moss	Highld	NM7167	56°44·6'	5°44·2'W	X	40
Clais mór	Highld	NC3903	57°59·5'	4°42·9'W	X	16
Clais na Cuinneig	Highld	NH6895	57°55·8'	4°13·3'W	X	21
Clais na Gaibhre	Moray	NJ1042	57°27·9'	3°29·6'W	X	28
Clamandswells	Aberd	NJ9836	57°25·1'	2°1·5'W	X	30
Clamerkin	I of W	SZ4390	50°42·7'	1°23·1'W	X	196
Clamerkin Lake	I of W	SZ4390	50°42·7'	1°23·1'W	W	196
Clammel Knowes	Shetld	HP5806	60°44·2'	0°55·7'W	X	1
Clammer	Somer	SS9428	51°2·7'	3°30·3'W	X	181
Clammer Hill	Surrey	SU9234	51°6·1'	0°40·8'W	H	186
Clamoak	Devon	SX4364	50°27·5'	4°12·3'W	X	201
Clamp Fm	Suff	TM0757	52°10·6'	1°2·1'E	FM	155
Clamp Ho	Suff	TM2137	51°59·5'	1°13·5'E	X	169
Clampit	Corn	SX3075	50°33·2'	4°23·6'W	X	201
Clampitt	Devon	SS8203	50°49·1'	3°40·1'W	X	191
Clampitt	Devon	SX8184	50°38·8'	3°40·6'W	X	191
Clampitts, The	Devon	SS5232	51°4·3'	4°6·4'W	X	180
Clamps Heath	Suff	TL7870	52°18·2'	0°37·0'E	X	144,155
Clamps, The	Suff	TM0748	52°5·7'	1°1·7'E	X	155,169
Clamps, The	Suff	TM4477	52°20·4'	1°35·3'E	F	156
Clamshell Cave	Arg & Bt	NM3235	56°26·1'	6°20·4'W	X	46,47,48
Clanacombe	Devon	SX6844	50°17·1'	3°50·8'W	X	202
Clanden Hill	Dorset	ST4402	50°49·3'	2°47·3'W	X	193
Clandon	Dorset	SY6689	50°42·2'	2°28·5'W	X	194
Clan Donald Visitor Centre	Highld	NG6304	57°4·2'	5°54·1'W	X	32
Clandon Barrow	Dorset	SY6589	50°42·2'	2°29·4'W	A	194
Clandon Downs	Surrey	TQ0550	51°14·6'	0°29·4'W	X	187
Clandon Park	Surrey	TQ0451	51°15·1'	0°30·2'W	X	186
Clan Down	Bath & NE Somer	ST6756	51°18·4'	2°28·0'W	X	172

Clandown	Bath & NE Somer	ST6855	51°17·8'	2°27·2'W	T	172,183
Clandown Bottom	Bath & NE Somer	ST6756	51°18·4'	2°28·0'W	X	172
Clanery	D & G	NX4862	54°56·0'	4°21·9'W	X	83
Clanery Hill	D & G	NX4963	54°56·6'	4°21·0'W	X	83
Clanfield	Hants	SU7016	50°56·6'	0°59·8'W	T	197
Clanfield	Oxon	SP2801	51°42·7'	1°35·3'W	T	163
Clanfin	E Ayr	NS4944	55°40·2'	4°23·6'W	X	70
Clanford Brook	Staffs	SJ8624	52°49·0'	2°12·1'W	W	127
Clanford Hall Fm	Staffs	SJ8724	52°49·0'	2°11·2'W	FM	127
Clanger Wood	Wilts	ST8754	51°17·3'	2°10·8'W	F	183
Clanking	Bucks	SP8207	51°45·6'	0°48·3'W	T	165
Clanna	Glos	SO5902	51°43·1'	2°35·2'W	X	162
Clannaborough Barton	Devon	SS7402	50°48·5'	3°46·9'W	X	191
Clannaborough Cross	Devon	SS7402	50°48·5'	3°46·9'W	X	191
Clannaborough Fm	Devon	SX6691	50°42·4'	3°53·5'W	FM	191
Clanna Lodge	Glos	SO5802	51°43·1'	2°36·1'W	X	162
Clannochdyke	S Lanak	NS8040	55°38·6'	3°54·0'W	X	71,72
Clannon Ball	Devon	SS7543	51°10·6'	3°46·9'W	X	180
Clantibuies	D & G	NX3351	54°49·8'	4°35·6'W	X	82
Clanverend Fm	Essex	TL4936	52°0·4'	0°10·6'E	FM	154
Clanville	Hants	SU3149	51°14·6'	1°33·0'W	T	185
Clanville	Somer	ST6232	51°5·4'	2°32·2'W	T	183
Clanville	Wilts	ST9279	51°30·8'	2°6·5'W	T	173
Clanville Lodge	Hants	SU3248	51°14·0'	1°32·1'W	X	185
Clanville Manor	Somer	ST6133	51°5·9'	2°33·0'W	X	183
Clanyard Bay	D & G	NX0937	54°41·8'	4°57·4'W	W	82
Clanyard Mill	D & G	NX1037	54°41·8'	4°56·5'W	X	82
Claonaig	Arg & Bt	NR8756	55°45·3'	5°23·2'W	T	62
Claonaig Bay	Arg & Bt	NR8755	55°44·8'	5°23·2'W	W	62
Claonaig Water	Arg & Bt	NR8657	55°45·8'	5°24·2'W	W	62
Claonairigh	Arg & Bt	NN0504	56°11·6'	5°8·1'W	X	56
Claonel	Highld	NC5604	58°0·4'	4°25·7'W	X	16
Claon Leiter	Highld	NH1100	57°3·4'	5°6·5'W	X	34
Clapcote Cotts	Wilts	ST8780	51°31·4'	2°10·9'W	X	173
Clapdale	N Yks	SD7570	54°7·8'	2°22·5'W	X	98
Clapdale Scars	N Yks	SD7470	54°7·8'	2°23·5'W	X	98
Clapgate	Dorset	SU0102	50°49·3'	1°58·8'W	T	195
Clap Gate	Hants	SU4652	51°16·1'	1°20·0'W	X	185
Clapgate	Herts	TL4425	51°54·5'	0°6·0'E	T	167
Clap Gate	N Yks	SE3447	53°55·3'	1°28·5'W	X	104
Clapgate Fm	Herts	TL0701	51°42·1'	0°26·7'W	FM	166
Clapgate Fm	Lincs	TF3271	53°13·4'	0°1·0'W	FM	122
Clapgate Gill	N Yks	NZ1102	54°25·0'	1°49·4'W	W	92
Clapgate Spring Plantn	N Yks	NZ1102	54°25·0'	1°49·4'W	F	92
Clapham	Beds	TL0253	52°10·2'	0°30·1'W	T	153
Clapham	Devon	SX8987	50°40·6'	3°33·9'W	T	192
Clapham	Lam	TQ2975	51°27·8'	0°8·2'W	T	176
Clapham	N Yks	SD7469	54°7·2'	2°23·5'W	T	98
Clapham	W Susx	TQ0906	50°50·8'	0°26·7'W	T	198
Clapham Beck	N Yks	SD7570	54°7·8'	2°22·5'W	W	98
Clapham Bents	N Yks	SD7473	54°9·4'	2°23·5'W	X	98
Clapham Bottoms	N Yks	SD7572	54°8·8'	2°22·5'W	X	98
Clapham Common	N Yks	SD7261	54°2·9'	2°25·2'W	X	98
Clapham Common	Wan	TQ2874	51°27·3'	0°9·1'W	X	176
Clapham Dams	Norf	TG2638	52°53·7'	1°22·0'E	T	133
Clapham Green	Beds	TL0352	52°9·6'	0°29·3'W	T	153
Clapham Green	N Yks	SE2458	54°1·3'	1°37·6'W	T	104
Clapham Hill	Kent	TR1064	51°20·4'	1°1·3'E	T	179
Clapham Ho	E Susx	TQ5201	50°47·5'	0°9·8'E	X	199
Clapham Junc Sta	Wan	TQ2775	51°27·8'	0°9·9'W	X	176
Clapham Lodge	N Yks	SE2988	54°17·5'	1°32·8'W	X	99
Clapham Moor	N Yks	SD7267	54°6·1'	2°25·3'W	X	98
Clapham Park	Beds	TL0452	52°9·6'	0°28·4'W	X	153
Clapham Park	Lam	TQ2974	51°27·2'	0°8·2'W	T	176
Clapham Sta	N Yks	SD7367	54°6·1'	2°24·4'W	X	98
Clapham Wood	W Susx	TQ1007	50°51·3'	0°25·8'W	F	198
Clapham Wood Hall	N Yks	SD7166	54°5·6'	2°26·2'W	X	98
Clapham Woods	N Yks	SD7167	54°6·1'	2°26·2'W	F	98
Clap Hill	Kent	TR0536	51°5·4'	0°56·0'E	T	179,189
Clapnall Hill	Notts	SK6360	53°8·2'	1°3·1'W	X	120
Clapper	Corn	SX0071	50°30·5'	4°48·9'W	T	200
Clapper	Shetld	HU4796	60°38·9'	1°7·9'W	X	1
Clapper	Shrops	SO3594	52°32·6'	2°57·1'W	X	137
Clapper Br	Corn	SX3565	50°27·9'	4°19·1'W	A	201
Clapper Br	Devon	SX7582	50°37·7'	3°45·7'W	X	191
Clapper Bridge	Devon	SX6277	50°34·8'	3°56·6'W	A	191
Clapper Bridge	Devon	SX6478	50°35·4'	3°54·9'W	A	191
Clapper Bridge	Devon	SX6566	50°28·9'	3°53·8'W	A	202
Clapper Cross	Devon	SS7102	50°48·4'	3°49·5'W	X	191
Clapperdown	Devon	SS6604	50°49·4'	3°53·8'W	X	191
Clapper Fm	Kent	TQ7845	51°10·8'	0°33·2'E	FM	188
Clapper Fm	Suff	TM0734	51°58·2'	1°1·2'E	FM	155,169
Clapper Hill	Kent	TQ8436	51°5·8'	0°38·1'E	T	188
Clappers	Cumbr	NY1446	54°48·3'	3°19·9'W	X	85
Clappers	Scot Bord	NT9455	55°47·5'	2°5·3'W	X	67,74,75
Clappers Fm	W Berks	SU6965	51°23·0'	1°0·1'W	FM	175
Clappersgate	Cumbr	NY3603	54°25·4'	2°58·8'W	T	90
Clappers Wood	E Susx	TQ5916	50°55·5'	0°16·1'E	F	199
Clapper, The	Shetld	HP4806	60°44·3'	1°6·7'W	X	1
Clapperton Hall	W Loth	NT0869	55°54·6'	3°27·9'W	X	65
Clapphoull	Shetld	HU4228	60°2·3'	1°14·3'W	X	4
Clapp Mill Fm	Devon	SY0199	50°47·2'	3°23·9'W	FM	192
Clapstile Fm	Suff	TL8950	52°7·2'	0°46·0'E	FM	155
Clapton	Somer	ST4106	50°51·3'	2°49·9'W	T	193
Clapton	Somer	ST6453	51°16·7'	2°30·6'W	T	183
Clapton	W Berks	SU3870	51°25·9'	1°26·8'W	T	174
Clapton Court	N Som	ST4673	51°27·4'	2°46·2'W	X	171,172
Clapton Fm	Somer	ST7529	51°3·8'	2°21·0'W	FM	183
Clapton Hall	Essex	TL6220	51°51·5'	0°21·5'E	X	167
Clapton in Gordano	N Som	ST4774	51°28·0'	2°45·4'W	T	171,172
Clapton Moor	N Som	ST4573	51°27·4'	2°47·1'W	X	171,172
Clapton-on-the-Hill	Glos	SP1617	51°51·3'	1°45·7'W	T	163
Clapton Park	Hack	TQ3585	51°33·1'	0°2·8'W	T	177
Clapton Wick	N Som	ST4472	51°26·9'	2°48·0'W	X	171,172
Clapwater Ho	E Susx	TQ4325	51°0·6'	0°2·7'E	X	187,198
Clapworthy	Devon	SS6724	51°0·2'	3°53·4'W	T	180
Clapworthy Cross	Devon	SS6525	51°0·7'	3°55·1'W	X	180
Clarabad	Scot Bord	NT9254	55°47·0'	2°7·2'W	X	67,74,75

Clarabad Mill	Scot Bord	NT9354	55°47·0'	2°6·3'W	X	67,74,75
Clarach	Cered	SN6083	52°25·9'	4°3·2'W	T	135
Clarach Bay	Cered	SN5883	52°25·8'	4°4·9'W	W	135
Clarack	Aberd	NO4598	57°4·4'	2°54·0'W	X	37,44
Clara Vale	Ghead	NZ1364	54°58·5'	1°47·4'W	T	88
Clàr Beag	N Eil	NB1115	58°2·1'	6°53·3'W	X	13,14
Clarbeston	Pemb	SN0421	51°51·4'	4°50·4'W	T	145,157,158
Clarbeston Grange	Pemb	SN0620	51°50·9'	4°48·6'W	X	145,158
Clarbeston Road	Pemb	SN0120	51°50·8'	4°53·0'W	T	145,157,158
Clarborough	Notts	SK7383	53°20·6'	0°53·8'W	T	120
Clarborough Grange	Notts	SK7483	53°20·6'	0°52·9'W	X	120
Clarborough Hall	Notts	SK7382	53°20·0'	0°53·8'W	X	120
Clarborough Hill Fm	Notts	SK7483	53°20·6'	0°52·9'W	FM	120
Clardon	Highld	ND1469	58°36·3'	3°28·3'W	X	12
Clardon Haven	Highld	ND1570	58°36·8'	3°27·3'W	W	7,12
Clardon Head	Highld	ND1570	58°36·8'	3°27·3'W	X	7,12
Clardon Hill	Highld	ND1469	58°36·3'	3°28·3'W	H	12
Clare	Oxon	SU6798	51°40·8'	1°1·5'W	X	164,165
Clare	Suff	TL7645	52°4·7'	0°34·5'E	T	155
Clarebrand	D & G	NX7666	54°58·6'	3°55·8'W	X	84
Clare Camp	Suff	TL7645	52°4·7'	0°34·5'E	A	155
Clare Castle Country Park	Suff	TL7745	52°4·7'	0°35·4'E	X	155
Clare College Fm	Cambs	TL3664	52°15·7'	0°0·0'W	FM	154
Claredon Palace	Wilts	SU1830	51°4·7'	1°44·2'W	A	184
Claredown Fm	Essex	TL7744	52°4·2'	0°35·3'E	FM	155
Clare Fm	Cambs	TL4680	52°24·1'	0°9·2'E	FM	143
Claregate	Wolv	SJ8901	52°36·6'	2°9·3'W	T	127,139
Clare Hill	Oxon	SU6797	51°40·3'	1°1·5'W	X	164,165
Clare Ho	Kent	TQ6957	51°17·4'	0°25·8'E	X	178,188
Clareland	Worcs	SO8269	52°19·4'	2°15·4'W	X	138
Claremont	Fife	NO4514	56°19·2'	2°52·9'W	X	59
Claremont Park	Surrey	TQ1363	51°21·5'	0°22·2'W	T	176,187
Claremont Pier	Suff	TM5491	52°27·7'	1°44·8'E	X	134
Claremont School	E Susx	TQ7914	50°54·1'	0°33·1'E	X	199
Claremount	Cald	SE0925	53°43·5'	1°51·4'W	T	104
Clarencefield	D & G	NY0968	55°0·1'	3°24·9'W	T	85
Clarence Hills	Norf	TF8307	52°38·0'	0°42·7'E	X	144
Clarence Park	N Som	ST3160	51°20·3'	2°59·0'W	T	182
Clarence Pier	C of Port	SZ6398	50°46·9'	1°6·0'W	X	196
Clarendon Hill	Wilts	SU2248	51°14·1'	1°40·7'W	H	184
Clarendon Ho	Wilts	SU1928	51°3·3'	1°43·3'W	X	184
Clarendon Ho	W Loth	NT0076	55°58·3'	3°35·7'W	X	65
Clarendon Park	C of Leic	SK5902	52°37·0'	1°7·3'W	T	140
Clarendon School	Beds	TL0741	52°3·7'	0°26·0'W	X	153
Clarendon Way	Hants	SU4029	51°3·8'	1°25·4'W	X	185
Clarendon Way	Hants	SU4229	51°3·8'	1°23·7'W	X	185
Clarendon Way	Wilts	SU2232	51°5·4'	1°40·8'W	X	184
Clare Park	Hants	SU8047	51°13·2'	0°50·9'W	X	186
Clare Plantation	Highld	NH5464	57°38·8'	4°26·3'W	F	21
Clarepool Moss	Shrops	SJ4334	52°54·3'	2°50·4'W	F	126
Clare's Barn Fm	Leic	SK3304	52°38·2'	1°30·3'W	FM	140
Clares Fm	Warr	SJ6493	53°26·2'	2°32·1'W	FM	109
Clareston	Pemb	SM9510	51°45·3'	4°57·8'W	T	157,158
Claret Hall	Essex	TL7643	52°3·7'	0°34·4'E	X	155
Clareton	N Yks	SE3959	54°1·8'	1°23·9'W	X	104
Clarewood	Northum	NZ0170	55°1·7'	1°58·6'W	X	87
Clarghyll Hall	Cumbr	NY7249	54°50·4'	2°25·7'W	X	86,87
Clargillhead	Cumbr	NY7349	54°50·4'	2°24·8'W	X	86,87
Claridges Barn	Oxon	SP3324	51°55·0'	1°30·8'W	X	164
Claridge Spinney	Northnts	SP7875	52°22·3'	0°50·9'W	F	141
Clarilaw	Scot Bord	NT5218	55°27·5'	2°45·1'W	X	79
Clarilaw	Scot Bord	NT5527	55°32·3'	2°42·4'W	T	73
Clarilawmuir	Scot Bord	NT5128	55°32·8'	2°46·2'W	X	73
Clarion Ho	Lancs	SD8937	53°50·3'	2°9·6'W	X	103
Clarke Ho	Ches	SJ9576	53°17·1'	2°4·1'W	X	118
Clarken Green	Hants	SU5650	51°15·0'	1°11·5'W	T	185
Clarke's Bottom	Oxon	SP3620	51°52·9'	1°28·2'W	X	164
Clarke's Bush	Leic	SK6502	52°36·9'	1°2·0'W	F	141
Clarkes Common Fm	E Yorks	SE8243	53°52·8'	0°44·7'W	FM	106
Clarke's Fm	Glos	SO7713	51°49·1'	2°19·6'W	FM	162
Clarke's Fm	Norf	TF7724	52°47·3'	0°37·9'E	FM	132
Clarke's Green	Warw	SP0965	52°17·2'	1°51·7'W	X	150
Clarke's Hill	Cambs	TL4753	52°9·8'	0°9·3'E	X	154
Clarke's Thorne	Devon	ST0505	50°50·4'	3°20·6'W	X	192
Clarkestown	Devon	SS6205	50°49·9'	3°57·2'W	X	191
Clark Fell	D & G	NY3486	55°10·1'	3°1·7'W	H	79
Clark Green	Ches	SJ9379	53°18·7'	2°5·9'W	T	118
Clark Hall	Wakf	SE3422	53°41·8'	1°28·7'W	A	104
Clarkham Cross	Dorset	ST5507	50°51·9'	2°38·0'W	X	194
Clarkly Hill	Moray	NJ1368	57°41·9'	3°27·1'W	X	28
Clark's Carr	N Yks	SE1862	54°3·5'	1°43·1'W	X	99
Clarksfield	Oldham	SD9404	53°32·2'	2°5·0'W	T	109
Clark's Fm	Essex	TL5301	51°41·4'	0°13·2'E	FM	167
Clark's Fm	Essex	TL8241	52°2·5'	0°39·6'E	FM	155
Clarks Fm	Essex	TL8418	51°50·0'	0°40·6'E	FM	168
Clarks Fm	Essex	TL8810	51°45·6'	0°43·9'E	FM	168
Clarks Fm	Lincs	TF5023	52°47·3'	0°13·9'E	FM	131
Clark's Green	Surrey	TQ1739	51°8·5'	0°19·3'W	T	187
Clark's Hard	Essex	TR0094	51°36·8'	0°53·7'E	X	168,178
Clarks Hill	Cumbr	NY5867	55°0·0'	2°39·0'W	X	86
Clark's Hill	Lincs	TF3820	52°45·8'	0°3·1'E	T	131
Clark's Hill	Wilts	ST9769	51°25·4'	2°2·2'W	X	173
Clark's Hill	Worcs	SP0243	52°5·4'	1°57·9'W	X	150
Clarks Lane Fm	Surrey	TQ4156	51°17·4'	0°1·7'E	FM	187
Clarkson's Carr Fm	N Lincs	SE9913	53°36·5'	0°29·8'W	FM	112
Clarkson's Fm	Lancs	SD3324	53°59·0'	2°51·7'W	FM	102
Clarkson's Fold	Lancs	SD5733	53°47·7'	2°38·8'W	X	102
Clark's Sike	Scot Bord	NY5689	55°11·8'	2°41·0'W	W	80
Clarkston	E Renf	NS5656	55°46·8'	4°17·3'W	T	64
Clarkston	N Lanak	NS7766	55°52·5'	3°57·5'W	T	64
Clarkston Fm	S Lanak	NS8342	55°39·7'	3°51·2'W	FM	71,72
Clarkton	Stir	NN7102	56°11·8'	4°4·3'W	X	57
Clarkwood	N Yks	SE4474	54°9·8'	1°19·1'W	X	99
Clàr Loch	Highld	NC1847	58°22·7'	5°6·3'W	W	9
Clàr Loch	Highld	NC9544	58°22·6'	3°47·2'W	W	11
Clàr Loch	N Eil	NB2813	58°1·6'	6°36·0'W	W	13,14
Clàr Lochan	Highld	NC2400	57°57·5'	4°58·0'W	W	15
Clar Lochan	Highld	NH2595	57°54·9'	4°56·8'W	W	20
Clàr Loch Beag	Highld	NB9915	58°5·0'	5°24·1'W	W	15
Clar Loch Beag	Highld	NC1808	58°1·7'	5°4·5'W	W	15
Clàr-loch Beag	Highld	NC6558	58°29·6'	4°18·5'W	W	10
Clàr Loch Cnoc Thormaid	Highld	NC2041	58°19·5'	5°3·9'W	W	9
Clàr Loch Mór	Highld	NB9914	58°4·4'	5°24·0'W	W	15
Clàr Loch Mór	Highld	NC1707	58°1·1'	5°5·4'W	W	15
Clàr Loch Mór	Highld	NC2042	58°20·0'	5°4·0'W	W	9
Clàr-loch Mór	Highld	NC6458	58°29·6'	4°19·5'W	W	10
Claro Ho	N Yks	SE4060	54°2·3'	1°22·9'W	X	99
Clarrick House Fm	N Yks	SD6872	54°8·8'	2°29·0'W	FM	98
Clarum, The	I of M	SC4485	54°14·5'	4°23·2'W	X	95
Clas Brook	Powys	SO1351	52°9·3'	3°15·9'W	W	148
Clase	Swan	SS6597	51°39·6'	3°56·7'W	T	159
Clash	Angus	NO3459	56°43·3'	3°4·3'W	X	54
Clash	Angus	NO3860	56°43·9'	3°0·4'W	X	44
Clash	Stir	NN6306	56°13·9'	4°12·2'W	X	57
Clashach Cove	Moray	NJ1570	57°43·0'	3°25·1'W	W	28
Clashandorran	Highld	NH5148	57°30·1'	4°28·7'W	T	26
Clashanruich	Aberd	NJ3101	57°5·9'	3°7·9'W	X	37
Clashbenny	Pth & Kin	NO2121	56°22·7'	3°16·3'W	X	53,58
Clashbhan	Highld	NH6496	57°56·2'	4°17·4'W	X	21
Clashbuie	Highld	NC6563	58°32·3'	4°18·7'W	X	10
Clashcoig	Highld	NH6393	57°54·6'	4°18·3'W	X	21
Clashconnachie	Moray	NJ1654	57°34·4'	3°23·8'W	X	28
Clashcraggan	Highld	ND2139	58°20·2'	3°20·5'W	X	11,12
Clash Damph	Moray	NJ2033	57°23·1'	3°19·4'W	X	28
Clashdhu	Moray	NJ0352	57°33·1'	3°36·8'W	X	27
Clash Don	Moray	NJ1451	57°32·7'	3°25·7'W	X	28
Clashdon	Moray	NJ1551	57°32·7'	3°24·7'W	X	28
Clasheddy	Highld	NC6663	58°32·3'	4°17·6'W	X	10
Clashendamer	Aberd	NJ5461	57°38·5'	2°45·8'W	X	29
Clashendrum	Aberd	NO8375	56°52·2'	2°16·3'W	X	45
Clashenteple Hill	Aberd	NJ3516	57°14·1'	3°4·2'W	H	37
Clashfarland Point	N Ayr	NS1856	55°46·0'	4°53·6'W	X	63
Clashfarquhar Bay	Aberd	NO9294	57°2·5'	2°7·5'W	W	38,45
Clashgal	Highld	ND1558	58°30·4'	3°27·0'W	X	11,12
Clashgour	Arg & Bt	NN2342	56°32·5'	4°52·3'W	X	50
Clashholm	Aberd	NJ5907	57°9·4'	2°40·2'W	X	37
Clashindarroch	Aberd	NJ4831	57°22·2'	2°51·4'W	X	29,37
Clashindarroch	Moray	NJ1442	57°27·9'	3°25·6'W	X	28
Clashmach Hill	Aberd	NJ4938	57°26·0'	2°50·5'W	H	28,29
Clashman Hillock	Moray	NJ5348	57°31·4'	2°46·6'W	X	29
Clashmerlich	Moray	NJ2633	57°23·1'	3°13·4'W	X	28
Clashmore	Highld	NC0331	58°13·7'	5°20·8'W	T	15
Clashmore	Highld	ND2239	58°20·2'	3°19·5'W	X	11,12
Clashmore	Highld	NH7489	57°52·6'	4°7·0'W	T	21
Clash More	Moray	NJ1451	57°32·7'	3°25·7'W	X	28
Clashmore	Stir	NS4997	56°8·8'	4°25·4'W	X	57
Clashmore Wood	Highld	NH7490	57°53·2'	4°7·0'W	F	21
Clashmugach	Highld	NH7490	57°53·2'	4°7·0'W	X	21
Clashnabuiac	Highld	NH6368	57°41·1'	4°17·4'W	X	21
Clashnagrave	Highld	NH7594	57°55·3'	4°6·2'W	X	21
Clashnamuiach	Highld	NH8677	57°46·4'	3°54·5'W	X	21
Clash na Mush	Moray	NJ1552	57°33·3'	3°24·8'W	X	28
Clashnarae Burn	Aberd	NJ4119	57°15·7'	2°58·2'W	W	37
Clashnessie	Highld	NC0530	58°13·2'	5°18·7'W	T	15
Clashnessie Bay	Highld	NC0631	58°13·8'	5°17·8'W	W	15
Clashnoir	Moray	NJ2222	57°17·2'	3°17·2'W	T	36
Clash of Scalan	Moray	NJ2418	57°15·0'	3°15·1'W	X	36
Clash of Wirren	Angus	NO4975	56°52·1'	2°49·7'W	X	44
Clashrodney	Aberd	NO9499	57°5·2'	2°5·5'W	W	38,45
Clashverains	S Ayr	NX3799	55°15·7'	4°33·5'W	X	77
Clash Wan	Moray	NJ2533	57°23·1'	3°14·4'W	X	28
Clashwinne	S Ayr	NS4200	55°16·4'	4°28·8'W	X	77
Clash Wood	D & G	NX5154	54°51·8'	4°18·9'W	F	83
Clash Wood	Highld	NH5051	57°31·7'	4°29·8'W	F	26
Classlochie	Pth & Kin	NT1399	56°10·8'	3°23·6'W	X	58
Claston Fm	Heref	SO5840	52°3·6'	2°36·4'W	FM	149
Clate	Shetld	HU5461	60°20·0'	1°0·8'W	T	2
Clate Point	Arg & Bt	NS0068	55°52·1'	5°11·4'W	X	63
Clatequoy	Highld	ND1064	58°33·6'	3°32·3'W	X	11,12
Clater Park	Heref	SO6854	52°11·2'	2°27·7'W	X	149
Clatfields	Kent	TQ4443	51°10·3'	0°4·0'E	X	187
Clatford	Wilts	SU1568	51°24·9'	1°46·7'W	T	173
Clatford Bottom	Wilts	SU1569	51°25·4'	1°46·7'W	X	173
Clatford Down	Wilts	SU1470	51°26·0'	1°47·5'W	X	173
Clatford Oakcuts	Hants	SU3339	51°9·2'	1°31·3'W	T	185
Clatford Park Fm	Wilts	SU1666	51°23·8'	1°45·8'W	FM	173
Clathick	Pth & Kin	NN8022	56°22·8'	3°56·2'W	X	52
Clathy	Pth & Kin	NN9919	56°21·4'	3°37·6'W	T	58
Clathybeg	Pth & Kin	NN9920	56°22·0'	3°37·7'W	X	52,53,58
Clathymore	Pth & Kin	NO0121	56°22·5'	3°35·7'W	X	52,53,58
Clatt	Aberd	NJ5325	57°19·0'	2°46·4'W	T	37
Clatter	Powys	SN9994	52°32·3'	3°29·0'W	T	136
Clatterbridge Hospital	Wirral	SJ3182	53°20·1'	3°1·8'W	X	108
Clattercote	Oxon	SP4549	52°8·5'	1°20·1'W	X	151
Clattercote Resr	Oxon	SP4548	52°7·9'	1°20·2'W	W	151
Clatterdishes Fm	Ches	SJ6056	53°6·2'	2°35·4'W	FM	118
Clatterford	I of W	SZ4887	50°41·1'	1°18·8'W	T	196
Clatterford End	Essex	TL5202	51°42·0'	0°12·4'E	T	167
Clatterford End	Essex	TL5606	51°44·1'	0°15·9'E	T	167
Clatterford End	Essex	TL6113	51°47·8'	0°20·5'E	T	167
Clatterha	Angus	NO4855	56°41·3'	2°50·5'W	X	54
Clatterin Brig	Aberd	NO6678	56°53·8'	2°33·0'W	X	45
Clatteringbrigs	Pth & Kin	NO3228	56°26·6'	3°5·7'W	X	53,59
Clattering Burn	N Lanak	NS7963	55°51·0'	3°55·5'W	W	64
Clatteringford	Pth & Kin	NN8410	56°16·4'	3°52·0'W	X	58
Clatteringhouses	Northum	NU1326	55°31·9'	1°47·2'W	X	75
Clatteringshaws	D & G	NX5576	55°3·7'	4°15·8'W	X	77
Clatteringshaws Fell	D & G	NX5575	55°3·2'	4°15·8'W	X	77
Clatteringshaws Loch	D & G	NX5477	55°4·2'	4°16·8'W	W	77
Clatterin Kist	Aberd	NJ5422	57°17·4'	2°45·3'W	X	37
Clatternbriggs	Moray	NJ2958	57°36·6'	3°10·8'W	X	28
Clatterstanes Burn	D & G	NY0288	55°10·8'	3°31·9'W	W	78
Clattinger Fm	Wilts	SU0193	51°38·4'	1°58·7'W	FM	163,173
Clatto	Fife	NO3507	56°15·3'	3°2·5'W	X	59
Clatto	Fife	NO4315	56°19·7'	2°54·9'W	T	59
Clatto Barns	Fife	NO3606	56°14·8'	3°1·5'W	X	59
Clatto Country Park	C of Dun	NO3734	56°29·9'	3°1·0'W	X	54
Clatto Hill	Fife	NO3506	56°14·8'	3°2·5'W	H	59
Clatto Hill	Fife	NO4315	56°19·7'	2°54·9'W	H	59
Clatto Resr	Fife	NO3607	56°15·3'	3°1·5'W	W	59
Clattsmore Fm	Worcs	SO9340	52°3·7'	2°5·7'W	FM	150
Clatworthy	Devon	SS6828	51°2·4'	3°52·6'W	X	180
Clatworthy	Somer	ST0530	51°3·9'	3°21·0'W	T	181
Clatworthy Reservoir	Somer	ST0431	51°4·5'	3°21·8'W	W	181
Clauchan Glen	N Ayr	NR9430	55°31·5'	5°15·4'W	X	68,69
Clauchanton Hill	S Ayr	NX1486	55°7·6'	4°54·7'W	H	76
Clauchan Water	N Ayr	NR9330	55°31·4'	5°16·3'W	W	68,69
Clauchendolly	D & G	NX6447	54°48·2'	4°6·5'W	X	83
Clauchland Hills	N Ayr	NS0333	55°33·3'	5°7·0'W	H	69
Clauchlands	N Ayr	NS0432	55°32·8'	5°6·0'W	T	69
Clauchlands Fm	N Ayr	NS0433	55°33·3'	5°6·0'W	FM	69
Clauchlands Point	N Ayr	NS0532	55°32·8'	5°5·0'W	X	69
Clauchrie	D & G	NX4053	54°51·0'	4°29·1'W	X	83
Clauchrie	D & G	NX4056	54°52·6'	4°29·2'W	X	83
Clauchrie	D & G	NX9188	55°10·7'	3°42·3'W	X	78
Clauchrie Burn	D & G	NX9189	55°11·2'	3°42·3'W	W	78
Clauchrie Burn	S Ayr	NX2884	55°7·5'	4°41·4'W	W	76
Clauchrie Burn	S Ayr	NX3087	55°9·1'	4°39·7'W	W	76
Clauchrie Hill	D & G	NX9289	55°11·3'	3°41·4'W	H	78
Clauchrie Hill	S Ayr	NS3401	55°16·8'	4°36·4'W	H	76
Clauchrie Moor	D & G	NX4057	54°53·2'	4°29·2'W	X	83
Clauchrie Plantation	D & G	NX9289	55°11·3'	3°41·4'W	F	78
Claughreid	D & G	NX5255	54°52·3'	4°18·0'W	X	83
Claughton	Lancs	SD5242	53°52·6'	2°44·2'W	T	102
Claughton	Lancs	SD5666	54°5·5'	2°39·9'W	T	97
Claughton	Wirral	SJ3088	53°23·3'	3°2·7'W	T	108
Claughton Moor	Lancs	SD5864	54°4·5'	2°38·1'W	X	97
Claunch	D & G	NX4248	54°48·4'	4°27·1'W	X	83
Clautschip	Angus	NO2364	56°45·9'	3°15·1'W	H	44
Clava Lodge Hotel	Highld	NH7644	57°28·4'	4°3·6'W	X	27
Clave	Shetld	HU2776	60°28·3'	1°30·0'W	X	3
Clavel	Shetld	HU3719	59°57·5'	1°19·8'W	X	4
Clavell's Hard	Dorset	SY9277	50°35·8'	2°6·4'W	X	195
Clavelshay	Somer	ST2531	51°4·6'	3°3·9'W	T	182
Clavengers Fm	Somer	ST1522	50°59·7'	3°12·3'W	FM	181,193
Claver	Shetld	HU3725	60°0·8'	1°19·7'W	X	4
Claverdon	Warw	SP1964	52°16·7'	1°42·9'W	T	151
Claverdon Leys	Warw	SP2065	52°17·2'	1°42·0'W	X	151
Claverdon Lodge	Warw	SP2164	52°16·7'	1°41·1'W	X	151
Claverham	N Som	ST4466	51°23·7'	2°47·9'W	T	171,172,182
Claverhambury	Essex	TL4003	51°42·7'	0°2·0'E	T	167
Claver Hill	Northum	NY7479	55°6·5'	2°24·0'W	X	86,87
Claverhouse	C of Dun	NO4034	56°29·9'	2°58·0'W	X	54
Claverhouse's Stone	Pth & Kin	NN9063	56°45·0'	3°47·5'W	A	43
Clavering	Essex	TL4731	51°57·7'	0°8·8'E	T	167
Clavering	Northum	NU0229	55°33·5'	1°57·7'W	X	75
Clavering Fm	Essex	TL4634	51°59·3'	0°8·0'E	FM	154
Clavering Hall	Essex	TL4730	51°57·2'	0°8·7'E	X	167
Clavering Place Fm	Essex	TL4633	51°58·8'	0°8·0'E	FM	167
Clavering's Cross	Northum	NZ1391	55°13·0'	1°47·3'W	A	81
Clavering's Fm	Essex	TL8226	51°54·4'	0°39·1'E	FM	168
Claverley	Shrops	SO7993	52°32·3'	2°18·2'W	T	138
Claverton	Bath & NE Somer	ST7864	51°22·7'	2°18·6'W	T	172
Claverton Down	Bath & NE Somer	ST7763	51°22·2'	2°19·4'W	T	172
Clave, The	Shetld	HU1853	60°15·9'	1°40·0'W	W	3
Clavey's Fm	Somer	ST7148	51°14·1'	2°24·5'W	FM	183
Claw	Devon	SS8709	50°52·4'	3°36·0'W	X	192
Clawbelly Hill	D & G	NX8760	54°55·6'	3°45·4'W	H	84
Claw Bridge	Devon	SS3700	50°46·8'	4°18·4'W	X	190
Claw Cross	Devon	SS3318	50°56·5'	4°22·2'W	X	190
Clawdd Brythonig	Powys	SN8636	52°0·9'	3°39·3'W	A	160
Clawddcam	Pemb	SM8728	51°54·8'	5°5·4'W	X	157
Clawddcam	Pemb	SN1446	52°5·1'	4°42·5'W	X	145
Clawdd Coch	Powys	SJ2520	52°46·6'	3°6·3'W	X	126
Clawdd Côch	Powys	SO0723	51°54·1'	3°20·7'W	X	160
Clawdd-côch	V of Glam	ST0577	51°29·3'	3°21·7'W	T	170
Clawdd-du	Carm	SN5909	51°46·0'	4°2·2'W	X	159
Clawdd-du-bach	Powys	SN8670	52°19·2'	3°40·0'W	X	135,136,147
Clawdd Du Mawr	Powys	SN8569	52°18·7'	3°40·8'W	H	135,136,147
Clawdd-llesg	Powys	SJ1511	52°41·6'	3°15·1'W	X	125
Clawdd-mawr	Carm	SN3733	51°58·5'	4°22·0'W	A	145
Clawdd Mawr	Powys	SJ0621	52°46·9'	3°23·2'W	A	125
Clawdd-melyn	Cered	SN3748	52°6·6'	4°22·4'W	X	145
Clawdd-newydd	Denb	SJ0852	53°3·7'	3°22·0'W	T	116
Clawdd-Offa	Flint	SJ2467	53°11·9'	3°7·9'W	X	117
Clawddowen	Carm	SN5730	51°57·2'	4°4·5'W	X	146
Clawdd Poncen	Denb	SJ0744	52°59·4'	3°22·7'W	T	125
Clawfin	E Ayr	NS5007	55°20·3'	4°21·5'W	X	70,77
Clawfin Hill	E Ayr	NS5206	55°19·8'	4°19·6'W	H	70,77
Clawford	Devon	SS3700	50°46·8'	4°18·4'W	X	190
Clawmoor Fm	Devon	SS4001	50°47·4'	4°15·8'W	FM	190
Claw Moor Plantation	Devon	SS3902	50°47·9'	4°16·7'W	F	190
Clawson Hill	Leic	SK7225	52°49·3'	0°55·5'W	X	129
Clawson Lodge	Leic	SK7125	52°49·3'	0°56·4'W	X	129
Clawthorpe	Cumbr	SD5377	54°11·4'	2°42·8'W	T	97
Clawthorpe Fell	Cumbr	SD5478	54°12·0'	2°41·9'W	X	97
Clawton	Devon	SX3599	50°46·3'	4°20·0'W	T	190
Claxby	Lincs	TF1194	53°26·1'	0°19·3'W	T	113
Claxby	Lincs	TF4571	53°13·2'	0°10·7'E	T	122
Claxby Grange	Lincs	TF4472	53°13·8'	0°9·8'E	X	122
Claxby Grange Fm	Lincs	TF0996	53°27·2'	0°21·1'W	FM	112
Claxby House Fm	Lincs	TF1193	53°25·6'	0°19·4'W	FM	113
Claxby Moor	Lincs	TF0996	53°27·2'	0°21·1'W	X	112
Claxby Platts	Lincs	TF1094	53°26·1'	0°20·2'W	F	113
Claxby Pluckacre	Lincs	TF3064	53°9·7'	0°2·9'W	X	122
Claxby Wood	Lincs	TF1194	53°26·1'	0°19·3'W	F	113
Claxton	Norf	TG3303	52°34·7'	1°26·7'E	T	134
Claxton	N Yks	SE6959	54°1·6'	0°56·4'W	X	105,106
Claxton	N Yks	SE6960	54°2·1'	0°56·4'W	T	100
Claxton Grange	Hartpl	NZ4728	54°38·9'	1°15·9'W	X	93
Claxton Hall	N Yks	SE6860	54°2·1'	0°57·3'W	X	100
Claxton House Fm	Hartpl	NZ4727	54°38·4'	1°15·9'W	FM	93
Claxy Ho	Lincs	TF4454	53°4·1'	0°9·4'E	X	122
Clay Bank	Ches	SJ7571	53°14·4'	2°22·1'W	X	118
Clay Bank	N Yks	NZ5704	54°25·9'	1°6·9'W	X	93
Claybank Fm	Notts	SK6992	53°25·5'	0°57·3'W	FM	111
Clay Bank Fm	Warw	SP1273	52°21·5'	1°49·0'W	FM	139
Claybokie	Aberd	NO0889	56°59·2'	3°30·4'W	X	43

Clay Br	Lincs	TF0878	53°17·5′	0°22·4′W	X	121
Claybrook	Shrops	SO4991	52°31·1′	2°44·7′W	X	137,138
Claybrooke Grange	Leic	SP5089	52°30·0′	1°15·4′W	X	140
Claybrooke Lodge Fm	Leic	SP4890	52°30·6′	1°17·2′W	FM	140
Claybrooke Magna	Leic	SP4988	52°29·5′	1°16·3′W	T	140
Claybrooke Parva	Leic	SP4987	52°29·0′	1°16·3′W	T	140
Clay Burn	Northum	NT8915	55°26·0′	2°10·0′W	W	80
Claybush Hill	Herts	TL2638	52°1·8′	0°9·4′W	H	153
Claycart Bottom	Hants	SU8451	51°15·3′	0°47·4′W	X	186
Clay Chimneys	Herts	TL4427	51°55·6′	0°6·1′E	X	167
Clay Common	Suff	TM4781	52°22·5′	1°38·1′E	T	156
Clay Coton	Northnts	SP5977	52°23·5′	1°7·6′W	T	140
Claycroft	D & G	NX8260	54°55·5′	3°50·1′W	X	84
Claycroft Fm	Ches	SJ6476	53°17·0′	2°32·0′W	FM	118
Claycrop	D & G	NX4150	54°49·4′	4°28·1′W	X	83
Clay Cross	Derby	SK3963	53°10·0′	1°24·6′W	T	119
Claydaubing Bridge	D & G	NY1487	55°10·4′	3°20·6′W	X	78
Claydene	Kent	TQ4641	51°9·2′	0°5·7′E	X	188
Clay Dike	Lincs	TF2345	52°59·5′	0°9·6′W	W	131
Claydon	Glos	SO9331	51°58·9′	2°5·7′W	T	150
Claydon	Oxon	SP4550	52°9·0′	1°20·1′W	T	151
Claydon	Suff	TM1349	52°6·1′	1°7·0′E	T	169
Claydon Brook	Bucks	SP7427	51°56·4′	0°55·0′W	W	165
Claydon Fields	Glos	SP1900	51°42·1′	1°43·1′W	X	163
Claydon Hay Fm	Oxon	SP4551	52°9·6′	1°20·1′W	FM	151
Claydon Hill	Oxon	SP4040	52°3·6′	1°24·6′W	X	151
Claydon Hill Fm	Bucks	SP7127	51°56·4′	0°57·6′W	FM	165
Claydon Ho	Bucks	SP7225	51°55·4′	0°56·8′W	A	165
Claydon Ho	Glos	SP1900	51°42·1′	1°43·1′W	X	163
Claydon Lawn	Bucks	SP7323	51°54·3′	0°55·9′W	X	165
Claydons Fm	Essex	TL7601	51°41·0′	0°33·2′E	FM	167
Claydons Fm	Warw	SP2352	52°10·2′	1°39·4′W	FM	151
Claydykes	Aberd	NJ6306	57°8·9′	2°36·2′W	X	37
Clay End	Herts	TL3025	51°54·7′	0°6·2′W	T	166
Clayesmore School	Dorset	ST8614	50°55·7′	2°11·6′W	X	194
Clayfelton	Shrops	SO5076	52°23·0′	2°43·7′W	X	137,138
Clayfield Fm	Cambs	TL2966	52°16·8′	0°6·1′W	FM	153
Clayfield Fm	E Yorks	SE8148	53°55·5′	0°45·6′W	FM	106
Clayfield Fm	E Yorks	TA1049	53°55·8′	0°19·1′W	FM	107
Clayfields Fm	Lincs	TF0951	53°2·9′	0°22·0′W	FM	121
Clayflat Plantn	E Yorks	SE8142	53°52·3′	0°45·7′W	F	106
Clay Fm	Cambs	TL4455	52°10·7′	0°6·8′E	FM	154
Clay Fm	E Yorks	SE8251	53°57·2′	0°44·6′W	FM	106
Clay Fm	Lincs	SK8583	53°20·5′	0°43·0′W	FM	121
Clay Fm	Mil Key	SP8949	52°8·2′	0°41·6′W	FM	152
Clay Fm	Notts	SK8565	53°10·8′	0°43·3′W	FM	121
Clayfolds	Aberd	NJ6860	57°38·0′	2°31·7′W	X	29
Clayfolds	Aberd	NO8792	57°1·4′	2°12·4′W	X	38,45
Clayford	Somer	SS9026	51°1·6′	3°33·7′W	X	181
Clayfords	Aberd	NJ9655	57°35·4′	2°3·6′W	X	30
Clayfurlong Fm	Glos	ST9997	51°40·5′	2°0·5′W	FM	163
Clay Gap	Cumbr	NY2938	54°44·2′	3°5·7′W	X	89,90
Clay Gap	Lancs	SD3843	53°53·0′	2°56·2′W	X	102
Claygate	D & G	NY3979	55°6·4′	2°56·9′W	T	85
Claygate	Kent	TQ6051	51°14·4′	0°17·9′E	T	188
Claygate	Kent	TQ7144	51°10·4′	0°27·2′E	T	188
Claygate	Surrey	TQ1663	51°21·5′	0°19·6′W	T	176,187
Claygate Cross	Kent	TQ6155	51°16·5′	0°18·9′E	T	188
Claygate Fm	E Susx	TQ4726	51°1·1′	0°6·1′E	FM	188,198
Clay Gates	Staffs	SJ9009	52°41·0′	2°8·5′W	X	127
Clay Geo	Orkney	HY3428	59°8·3′	3°8·7′W	X	6
Clayhall	Essex	TM1628	51°54·7′	1°8·8′E	X	168,169
Clay Hall	E Yorks	TA0535	53°48·3′	0°23·9′W	X	107
Clayhall	Hants	SZ6198	50°46·9′	1°7·7′W	T	196
Clayhall	Redbr	TQ4290	51°35·7′	0°3·4′E	T	177
Clay Hall	Suff	TM0939	52°0·8′	1°3·1′E	X	155,169
Clayhall Fm	Norf	TG0919	52°43·9′	1°6·1′E	FM	133
Clayhall Fm	Surrey	TQ2448	51°13·3′	0°13·1′W	FM	187
Clay Hall Fm	Warw	SP1049	52°8·6′	1°50·8′W	FM	150
Clayhanger	Devon	ST0222	50°59·6′	3°23·4′W	T	181
Clayhanger	Dorset	ST6916	50°56·8′	2°26·1′W	X	183
Clayhanger	Dorset	SY5289	50°42·2′	2°40·4′W	X	194
Clayhanger	Somer	ST3111	50°53·9′	2°58·5′W	T	193
Clayhanger	Wals	SK0404	52°38·3′	1°56·1′W	T	139
Clayhanger Fm	Dorset	SY5884	50°39·5′	2°35·3′W	FM	194
Clayhanger Hall	Ches	SJ7257	53°6·8′	2°24·7′W	X	118
Clay Head	I of M	SC4480	54°11·8′	4°23·1′W	H	95
Clayhead Fm	I of M	SC4380	54°11·8′	4°24·0′W	FM	95
Clayhedges	S Lanak	NS6149	55°43·1′	4°12·3′W	X	64
Clayhidon	Devon	ST1615	50°55·9′	3°11·3′W	T	181,193
Clayhidon Hill	Devon	ST1614	50°55·4′	3°11·3′W	X	181,193
Clayhidon Turbary	Devon	ST1515	50°55·9′	3°12·2′W	X	181,193
Clay Hill	Cambs	TL4140	52°2·7′	0°3·8′E	X	154
Clay Hill	C of Bris	ST6274	51°28·1′	2°32·4′W	T	172
Clay Hill	Dorset	SU0105	50°50·9′	1°58·8′W	X	195
Clay Hill	Enf	TQ3298	51°40·1′	0°5·1′W	T	166,176,177
Clay Hill	Essex	TL4007	51°44·9′	0°2·1′E	X	167
Clay Hill	Essex	TL8637	52°0·2′	0°43·0′E	X	155
Clayhill	E Susx	TQ8423	50°58·8′	0°37·7′E	T	199
Clay Hill	Flint	SJ3167	53°12·0′	3°1·6′W	X	117
Clay Hill	Glos	SO7617	51°51·3′	2°20·5′W	X	162
Clay Hill	Hants	SU2302	50°49·3′	1°40·0′W	X	195
Clayhill	Hants	SU3007	50°51·9′	1°34·0′W	T	196
Clayhill	Kent	TQ7829	51°2·2′	0°32·7′E	X	188,199
Clay Hill	Kent	TR0961	51°18·8′	1°0·3′E	H	179
Clay Hill	Norf	TF9627	52°48·5′	0°54·9′E	X	132
Clay Hill	Rut	TF0212	52°42·0′	0°29·0′W	X	130
Clay Hill	S Glos	ST7788	51°35·7′	2°19·5′W	X	162,172
Clay Hill	Suff	TL9747	52°5·4′	0°52·9′E	X	155
Clay Hill	Suff	TM1259	52°11·5′	1°6·5′E	X	155
Clay Hill	W Berks	SU4868	51°24·8′	1°18·2′W	X	174
Clay Hill	W Berks	SU5770	51°25·8′	1°10·4′W	T	174
Clayhill Bottom	Hants	SU2301	50°48·7′	1°40·0′W	X	195
Clay Hill Burn	D & G	NX7079	55°5·6′	4°1·8′W	W	77,84
Clayhill Copse	Wilts	SU0494	51°38·9′	1°56·1′W	F	163,173
Clay Hill Cotts	Kent	TQ6537	51°6·7′	0°21·8′E	X	188
Clayhill Fm	Beds	TL0432	51°58·8′	0°28·7′W	FM	166
Clayhill Fm	Somer	ST2637	51°7·9′	3°3·1′W	FM	182
Clayhill Fm	Suff	TL9249	52°6·6′	0°48·6′E	FM	155
Clayhill Fm	Surrey	TQ2246	51°12·2′	0°14·8′W	FM	187

Clayhill Fm	Warw	SP4676	52°23·0′	1°19·0′W	FM	140
Clay Hill Ho	Dorset	ST8023	51°0·6′	2°16·7′W	X	183
Clayhill Ho	E Susx	TQ4414	50°54·7′	0°3·3′E	X	198
Clayhill Plantn	E Yorks	TA1138	53°49·8′	0°18·4′W	F	107
Clayhills	Aberd	NK0244	57°29·4′	1°57·5′W	X	30
Clay Hills	Suff	TM4164	52°13·5′	1°32·1′E	X	156
Clayhithe	Cambs	TL5064	52°15·4′	0°12·3′E	T	154
Clay Ho	Lancs	SD7943	53°53·2′	2°18·8′W	X	103
Clay Ho	Northum	NZ1284	55°9·3′	1°48·3′W	X	81
Clay Ho	Oxon	SU7680	51°31·1′	0°53·9′W	X	175
Clay Hole		TF4039	52°56·0′	0°5·4′E	W	131
Clayholes	Aberd	NO6596	57°3·5′	2°34·2′W	X	38,45
Clayholes	Angus	NO5535	56°30·6′	2°43·4′W	T	54
Clayhooter Hill	Aberd	NJ4323	57°17·9′	2°56·3′W	H	37
Clay House Fm	Ches	SJ7177	53°17·6′	2°25·7′W	FM	118
Clayhusbandry	Highld	ND1367	58°35·2′	3°29·3′W	X	11,12
Clay Lake	Lincs	TF2421	52°46·6′	0°9·3′W	T	131
Clayland	Stir	NS5587	56°3·5′	4°19·3′W	T	57
Clayland Cross	Torbay	SX8759	50°25·4′	3°35·1′W	X	202
Claylands	Stir	NS6394	56°7·4′	4°11·8′W	X	57
Claylands Fm	Cambs	TL1166	52°17·1′	0°22·0′W	FM	153
Claylands Fm	C of Edin	NT1271	55°55·7′	3°24·1′W	FM	65
Claylands Fm	Cumbr	NY7303	54°25·5′	2°24·5′W	FM	91
Claylands Fm	W Susx	TQ1717	50°56·7′	0°19·7′W	FM	198
Clay Lane Fm	Bucks	SU8390	51°36·4′	0°47·7′W	FM	175
Claylane Fm	Ches	SJ6067	53°12·2′	2°35·5′W	FM	118
Claylane Fm	Herts	TL4715	51°49·1′	0°8·4′E	FM	167
Clay Lane Head	Lancs	SD4947	53°55·2′	2°46·2′W	X	102
Claylanes Fm	Ches	SJ7358	53°7·4′	2°23·8′W	FM	118
Claylane Wood	Kent	TQ6670	51°24·5′	0°23·6′E	F	177,178
Clayley Hall	Ches	SJ4758	53°7·2′	2°47·1′W	X	117
Claymill	Aberd	NJ5811	57°11·5′	2°41·2′W	X	37
Clay Mills	Staffs	SK2627	52°50·6′	1°36·4′W	T	128
Claymires	Aberd	NJ5757	57°36·3′	2°42·7′W	X	29
Claymires	Aberd	NJ7251	57°33·2′	2°27·6′W	X	29
Claymires	Aberd	NJ9428	57°20·8′	2°5·5′W	X	38
Claymires	Moray	NJ5349	57°32·0′	2°46·6′W	X	29
Claymires	Stir	NS5994	56°7·3′	4°15·6′W	X	57
Claymoddie	D & G	NX4237	54°42·4′	4°26·7′W	X	83
Claymoor	N Yks	NZ8214	54°31·1′	0°43·6′W	X	94
Clayock	Highld	ND1759	58°30·9′	3°25·0′W	X	11,12
Clay of Allan	Highld	NH8276	57°45·8′	3°58·5′W	X	21
Clay Ope	Dorset	SY6872	50°33·0′	2°26·7′W	W	194
Claypenny Hospital	N Yks	SE5370	54°7·6′	1°10·9′W	X	100
Clay Pit	V of Glam	SS9376	51°28·6′	3°32·1′W	X	170
Claypit Fm	Hants	SU7028	51°3·1′	0°59·7′W	FM	186,197
Claypit Hall	Essex	TL6830	51°56·8′	0°27·1′E	X	167
Claypit Hall	Essex	TL8343	52°3·5′	0°40·6′E	X	155
Claypit Hill	Cambs	TL3554	52°10·3′	0°1·2′W	T	154
Claypit Hill	Derby	SK2132	52°53·3′	1°40·9′W	X	128
Clay Pit Hill	Wilts	ST9942	51°10·9′	2°0·5′W	H	184
Claypit Moor	Norf	TF8718	52°43·9′	0°46·6′E	X	132
Claypits	Essex	TL5436	52°0·3′	0°15·0′E	X	154
Claypits	Glos	SO7605	51°44·8′	2°20·5′W	T	162
Claypits	Heref	SO3947	52°7·3′	2°53·1′W	X	148,149
Claypits	Kent	TR2555	51°15·2′	1°13·9′E	T	179
Claypits	Suff	TL7181	52°24·2′	0°31·2′E	T	143
Claypits Fm	Essex	TL8627	51°54·9′	0°42·7′E	FM	168
Clay Pits Plantation	N Yks	SD8265	54°5·1′	2°16·1′W	F	98
Claypitts Fm	Devon	SY1092	50°43·5′	3°16·1′W	FM	192,193
Claypole	Lincs	SK8549	53°2·1′	0°43·5′W	T	130
Claypole Fen	Lincs	SK8650	53°2·7′	0°42·6′W	X	121
Claypond Cottage	Suff	TM3250	52°6·2′	1°23·7′E	X	156
Claypots	Aberd	NJ8319	57°15·9′	2°16·5′W	X	38
Claypots	Moray	NJ4553	57°34·1′	2°54·6′W	X	28,29
Claypots Croft	Aberd	NK0041	57°27·8′	1°59·5′W	X	30
Claypow	Shetld	HU3687	60°34·2′	1°20·1′W	X	1,2
Clays	Wrex	SJ3751	53°3·4′	2°56·0′W	X	117
Clays End	Bath & NE Somer	ST7064	51°22·7′	2°25·5′W	T	172
Clays Fm	Ches	SJ5858	53°7·3′	2°37·3′W	FM	117
Clay's Fm	Hants	SU7438	51°8·4′	0°56·1′W	FM	186
Clayshant	D & G	NX1152	54°49·9′	4°56·1′W	X	82
Clayshot Hill	Aberd	NJ4428	57°20·6′	2°55·4′W	H	37
Clays, The	Lincs	SK9055	53°5·3′	0°39·0′W	X	121
Claystiles	Aberd	NJ9759	57°37·5′	2°2·6′W	X	30
Clay Street	Suff	TM0171	52°18·2′	0°57·3′E	X	144,155
Clay Street Fm	Essex	TQ9187	51°33·2′	0°45·7′E	FM	178
Clay's Wood	E Susx	TQ6034	51°5·2′	0°17·5′E	F	188
Claysyke Fm	Pth & Kin	NO0301	56°11·8′	3°33·4′W	FM	58
Claythorpe	Lincs	TF4179	53°17·6′	0°7·3′E	T	122
Clayton	Brad	SE1231	53°46·8′	1°48·7′W	T	104
Clayton	Donc	SE4507	53°33·7′	1°18·8′W	T	111
Clayton	Fife	NO4318	56°21·3′	2°54·9′W	T	59
Clayton	Man	SJ8898	53°29·0′	2°10·4′W	T	109
Clayton	Staffs	SJ8543	52°59·3′	2°13·0′W	T	118
Clayton	W Susx	TQ3014	50°54·9′	0°8·7′W	T	198
Clayton Beck	Brad	SE1232	53°47·3′	1°48·7′W	W	104
Clayton Brook	Lancs	SD5724	53°42·9′	2°38·7′W	T	102
Clayton Court	W Susx	SU7826	51°1·9′	0°52·9′W	X	186,197
Clayton Fm	E Susx	TQ8921	50°57·7′	0°41·9′E	FM	189
Clayton Fm	W Susx	TQ1013	50°54·6′	0°25·7′W	FM	198
Clayton Fold Fm	Ches	SJ9979	53°18·7′	2°0·5′W	FM	118
Clayton Green	Lancs	SD5723	53°42·3′	2°38·7′W	T	102
Clayton Hall Fm	Kirk	SE2711	53°35·9′	1°35·1′W	FM	110
Clayton Heights	Brad	SE1130	53°46·2′	1°49·6′W	T	104
Clayton Hey Fold	Lancs	SD6732	53°47·2′	2°29·6′W	X	103
Clayton Hill	Essex	TL3805	51°43·8′	0°0·3′E	X	166
Clayton Ho	Staffs	SK0857	53°6·8′	1°52·4′W	X	119
Clayton Le Dale	Lancs	SD6733	53°47·8′	2°29·6′W	T	103
Clayton-Le-Moors	Lancs	SD7431	53°46·7′	2°23·3′W	T	103
Clayton-le-Woods	Lancs	SD5622	53°41·8′	2°39·6′W	T	102
Clayton Priory	W Susx	TQ3017	50°56·5′	0°8·6′W	X	198
Clayton's Fm	E Susx	TQ5825	51°0·4′	0°15·5′E	FM	188,199
Clayton Tunnel	W Susx	TQ2913	50°54·3′	0°9·5′W	X	198
Clayton Vale	Man	SJ8899	53°29·5′	2°10·4′W	X	109
Clayton West	Kirk	SE2510	53°35·4′	1°36·9′W	T	110
Claytown	Devon	SS6322	50°59·1′	3°56·7′W	X	180
Clay Tye Fm	Hav	TQ5986	51°33·3′	0°18·0′E	FM	177
Clay Walls	Northum	NY9879	55°6·6′	2°1·5′W	X	87

Clayway Fm	Cambs	TL5783	52°25·6′	0°18·9′E	FM	143
Claywell	Dorset	SY9984	50°39·6′	2°0·5′W	X	195
Claywell Fm	Oxon	SP3505	51°44·8′	1°29·2′W	FM	164
Claywell Hill	Oxon	SP3405	51°44·8′	1°30·1′W	X	164
Clayworth	Notts	SK7288	53°23·3′	0°54·6′W	T	112,120
Clayworth Woodhouse	Notts	SK7588	53°23·2′	0°51·9′W	X	112,120
Cleabarrow	Cumbr	SD4296	54°21·6′	2°53·1′W	X	96,97
Clea Burn	N Ayr	NS2356	55°46·2′	4°48·9′W	W	63
Cleaburn or Musgrove Pasture	N Yks	NZ0800	54°24·0′	1°52·2′W	X	92
Cleadale	Highld	NM4788	56°55·1′	6°9·0′W	T	39
Cleadon	S Tyne	NZ3862	54°57·3′	1°24·0′W	T	88
Cleadon Grange	S Tyne	NZ3862	54°57·3′	1°24·0′W	X	88
Cleadon Hills Fm	S Tyne	NZ3963	54°57·9′	1°23·0′W	FM	88
Cleadon Park	S Tyne	NZ3863	54°57·9′	1°24·0′W	T	88
Cleagreen	Cumbr	NY2643	54°46·8′	3°8·6′W	X	85
Clea Hall	Cumbr	NY2742	54°46·3′	3°7·7′W	X	85
Cleamire	Cumbr	NY2741	54°45·8′	3°7·6′W	X	85
Cleanbrae	Aberd	NJ5142	57°28·2′	2°48·6′W	X	29
Cleanhill	Aberd	NJ6251	57°33·1′	2°37·6′W	X	29
Cleanhill	Moray	NJ4364	57°40·0′	2°56·9′W	X	28
Cleanhill	Pth & Kin	NO0227	56°25·8′	3°34·9′W	X	52,53,58
Cleanhill Wood	Aberd	NO8699	57°5·2′	2°13·4′W	F	38,45
Cleap, The	Shetld	HU3612	59°53·8′	1°20·9′W	H	4
Clearbank	Angus	NO5344	56°35·4′	2°45·5′W	X	54
Clearbank Ho	Angus	NO6264	56°46·2′	2°36·9′W	X	45
Clearbrook	Carm	SN5317	51°50·2′	4°7·6′W	X	159
Clearbrook	Devon	SX5265	50°28·2′	4°4·8′W	T	201
Clear Burn	Scot Bord	NT3314	55°25·2′	3°3·1′W	W	79
Clearburn Cott	Scot Bord	NT3314	55°25·2′	3°3·1′W	X	79
Clearburn Loch	Scot Bord	NT3415	55°25·7′	3°2·1′W	W	79
Clearbury Down	Wilts	SU1524	51°1·1′	1°46·8′W	X	184
Clearbury Ring	Wilts	SU1524	51°1·1′	1°46·8′W	A	184
Clearfield	Aberd	NO4699	57°5·0′	2°53·0′W	X	37,44
Clearfields Fm	Bucks	SP6716	51°50·5′	1°1·3′W	FM	164,165
Clearie Woods	Angus	NO5339	56°32·7′	2°45·4′W	F	54
Clearmount	E Ayr	NS5237	55°36·5′	4°20·5′W	X	70
Clearmount	Surrey	SU9763	51°21·7′	0°36·0′W	X	175,176,186
Clearspring Fm	Derby	SK3152	53°4·1′	1°31·8′W	FM	119
Clearview Fm	E Susx	TQ3317	50°56·4′	0°6·0′W	FM	198
Clearwell	Newp	ST2585	51°33·8′	3°4·5′W	T	171
Clearwell Caves	Glos	SO5708	51°46·4′	2°37·0′W	X	162
Clearwood	Wilts	ST8349	51°14·6′	2°14·2′W	T	183
Clear Wood	Wilts	ST8446	51°13·0′	2°13·4′W	F	183
Clearymuir	Aberd	NO8081	56°55·4′	2°19·3′W	X	45
Cleasby	N Yks	NZ2513	54°30·9′	1°36·4′W	T	93
Cleasby Grange	N Yks	NZ2511	54°29·9′	1°36·4′W	X	93
Cleasby Hill	N Yks	NY9707	54°27·7′	2°2·4′W	H	92
Cleascro	N Eil	NB3328	58°9·9′	6°31·9′W	X	8,13
Cleat	Highld	NG4466	57°36·9′	6°16·7′W	H	23
Cleat	N Eil	NF6604	57°0·6′	7°29·7′W	T	31
Cleat	Orkney	HY4601	58°53·8′	2°55·7′W	X	6,7
Cleat	Orkney	HY4612	58°59·8′	2°55·9′W	X	6
Cleat	Orkney	HY4646	59°18·1′	2°56·4′W	X	5
Cleat	Orkney	HY6822	59°5·3′	2°33·0′W	X	5
Cleat	Orkney	HY7042	59°16·1′	2°31·1′W	X	5
Cleat	Orkney	ND4584	58°44·7′	2°56·5′W	T	7
Cleatham	N Lincs	SE9300	53°29·5′	0°35·5′W	X	112
Cleatham Hall	N Lincs	SE9301	53°30·1′	0°35·5′W	X	112
Cleatham Hall Fm	N Lincs	SE9201	53°30·1′	0°36·4′W	FM	112
Cleatham House Fm	N Lincs	SE9300	53°29·5′	0°35·5′W	FM	112
Cleat Hill	Beds	TL0653	52°10·1′	0°26·6′W	X	153
Cleat Hill Fm	Staffs	SK0912	52°42·6′	1°51·6′W	FM	128
Cleatlam	Durham	NZ1118	54°33·7′	1°49·4′W	T	92
Cleatonbrae	Orkney	HY4546	59°18·1′	2°57·5′W	X	5
Cleatop	N Yks	SD8161	54°2·9′	2°17·0′W	X	98
Cleator	Cumbr	NY0113	54°30·4′	3°31·3′W	T	89
Cleator Moor	Cumbr	NY0214	54°31·0′	3°30·4′W	T	89
Cleat Skerry	Highld	NG2742	57°23·5′	6°32·2′W	X	23
Cleats Shore	N Ayr	NR9420	55°26·1′	5°14·9′W	X	68,69
Cleats, The	Highld	NG3679	57°43·7′	6°25·6′W	X	23
Cleave	Corn	SX1597	50°44·8′	4°37·0′W	X	190
Cleave	Corn	SX4068	50°29·6′	4°15·0′W	X	201
Cleave	Devon	SS4014	50°54·4′	4°16·2′W	X	180,190
Cleave	Devon	SS4718	50°56·7′	4°10·3′W	X	180
Cleave	Devon	SS6415	50°55·3′	3°55·7′W	X	180
Cleave	Devon	SS7510	50°52·8′	3°46·2′W	X	191
Cleave	Devon	ST2000	50°47·9′	3°7·7′W	X	192,193
Cleave	Devon	SX4082	50°37·2′	4°15·3′W	X	201
Cleave	Devon	SX5290	50°41·7′	4°5·4′W	X	191
Cleaveanger	Devon	SS7107	50°51·1′	3°49·6′W	X	191
Cleave Dike	N Yks	SE5183	54°14·6′	1°12·6′W	A	100
Cleave Fm	Corn	SX3969	50°30·2′	4°15·8′W	FM	201
Cleave Fm	Devon	SS5302	50°48·2′	4°4·8′W	FM	191
Cleave Fm	Devon	SS5524	51°0·1′	4°3·6′W	FM	180
Cleave Fm	Devon	SS5943	51°10·4′	4°0·6′W	FM	180
Cleave Fm	Devon	SS6624	51°0·2′	3°54·2′W	FM	180
Cleave Fm	Devon	SS7221	50°58·7′	3°49·0′W	FM	180
Cleave Fm	Devon	SS8714	50°55·1′	3°36·1′W	FM	181
Cleave Fm	Devon	ST2008	50°52·2′	3°7·8′W	FM	192,193
Cleave Fm	Devon	SX8495	50°44·8′	3°38·3′W	FM	191
Cleave Hill	Hants	SU3538	51°8·6′	1°29·6′W	X	185
Cleave Hill	Somer	ST2709	50°52·8′	3°1·9′W	X	193
Cleave Ho	Devon	SX6194	50°44·0′	3°57·8′W	X	191
Cleavelands	Essex	TM0222	51°51·8′	0°56·4′E	X	168
Cleavel Point	Dorset	SZ0086	50°40·6′	1°59·6′W	X	195
Cleaven Dyke	Pth & Kin	NO1640	56°32·9′	3°21·5′W	R	53
Cleaver's Clump	Northnts	SP5654	52°11·1′	1°10·5′W	F	152
Cleaver's Fm	E Susx	TQ5011	50°53·0′	0°8·3′E	FM	199
Cleaver's Mining Ground	N Yks	SE0094	54°20·7′	1°59·6′W	X	98
Cleaver, The	Heref	SO5129	51°57·7′	2°42·4′W	T	149
Cleaves	Devon	SS8608	50°51·9′	3°36·8′W	X	191
Cleaves Fm	E Yorks	TA0554	53°58·5′	0°23·5′W	FM	107
Cleaves Fm	Renf	NS4068	55°53·0′	4°33·0′W	FM	64
Cleaves Strand	Corn	SX1598	50°45·4′	4°37·0′W	X	190
Cleaves Wood	Bath & NE Somer	ST7557	51°18·9′	2°21·1′W	F	172
Cleaving Coombe	E Yorks	SE8646	53°54·4′	0°41·0′W	H	106
Cleaving Grange	E Yorks	SE8545	53°53·9′	0°42·0′W	X	106
Cleber Wick	Shetld	HU3784	60°32·5′	1°19·0′W	W	1,2,3

Clebrig	Highld	NC5834	58°16·6'	4°24·8'W	X	16
Clechden	Aberd	NJ7463	57°39·6'	2°25·7'W	X	29
Cleckheaton	Kirk	SE1825	53°43·5'	1°43·2'W	T	104
Cledan	Powys	SJ0006	52°38·8'	3°28·3'W	W	125
Cledan	Powys	SN8444	52°5·2'	3°41·2'W	W	147,160
Cledan	Powys	SN8745	52°5·7'	3°38·6'W	W	147
Cleddans	N Lanak	NS7470	55°54·7'	4°0·5'W	X	64
Cleddau Lodge	Pemb	SM9419	51°50·1'	4°59·0'W	X	157,158
Cleddon	Monm	SO5003	51°43·6'	2°43·0'W	X	162
Cleddon	Monm	SO5103	51°43·7'	2°42·2'W	T	162
Cleddon Hall	Monm	SO5104	51°44·2'	2°42·2'W	X	162
Cledford Hall	Ches	SJ7165	53°11·1'	2°25·6'W	X	118
Clee Brook	Shrops	SO5584	52°27·4'	2°39·3'W	W	137,138
Cleedownton	Shrops	SO5880	52°25·2'	2°36·7'W	T	137,138
Cleehill	Shrops	SO5975	52°22·5'	2°35·7'W	T	137,138
Clee Hill	Shrops	SO5976	52°23·1'	2°35·7'W	X	137,138
Clee Hill	Shrops	SO6076	52°23·1'	2°34·9'W	X	138
Cleekhimin	N Lanak	NS7757	55°47·7'	3°57·3'W	T	64
Cleekhimin Br	Scot Bord	NT5252	55°45·8'	2°45·5'W	X	66,73
Cleekhimin Burn	Scot Bord	NT5252	55°45·8'	2°45·5'W	W	66,73
Clee Liberty	Shrops	SO5884	52°27·4'	2°36·7'W	X	137,138
Cleemarsh	Shrops	SO5684	52°27·4'	2°38·5'W	T	137,138
Cleers	Corn	SW9758	50°23·4'	4°51·0'W	X	200
Cleese Fm	Corn	SX2656	50°22·9'	4°26·5'W	FM	201
Clees Hall	Essex	TL8834	51°58·6'	0°44·6'E	X	155
Cleestanton	Shrops	SO5779	52°24·7'	2°37·5'W	T	137,138
Clee St Margaret	Shrops	SO5684	52°27·4'	2°38·5'W	T	137,138
Cleethorpes	NE Lincs	TA3008	53°33·4'	0°1·8'W	T	113
Cleeton Court	Shrops	SO6079	52°24·7'	2°34·9'W	X	138
Cleetongate	Shrops	SO6078	52°24·2'	2°34·9'W	X	138
Cleeton St Mary	Shrops	SO6178	52°24·2'	2°34·0'W	T	138
Cleeton Vallets	Shrops	SO6178	52°24·2'	2°34·0'W	X	138
Cleeve	Devon	SX6355	50°23·0'	3°55·2'W	X	202
Cleeve	Glos	SO7212	51°48·6'	2°24·0'W	T	162
Cleeve	N Som	ST4666	51°23·7'	2°46·2'W	T	171,172,182
Cleeve	Oxon	SU6081	51°31·7'	1°7·7'W	T	175
Cleeve Abbey	Somer	ST0440	51°9·3'	3°22·0'W	A	181
Cleeve Cloud	Glos	SO9825	51°55·6'	2°1·4'W	X	163
Cleeve Common	Glos	SO9925	51°55·6'	2°0·5'W	X	163
Cleeve Court	N Som	ST4665	51°23·1'	2°46·2'W	X	171,172,182
Cleeve Hill	Glos	SO9826	51°56·2'	2°1·4'W	T	163
Cleeve Hill	N Som	ST4666	51°23·7'	2°46·2'W	X	171,172,182
Cleeve Hill	W Berks	SU3376	51°29·2'	1°31·1'W	X	174
Cleeve Hill	Wilts	ST8632	51°5·5'	2°11·6'W	X	183
Cleeve Hill	Wilts	SU1055	51°17·9'	1°51·0'W	X	173
Cleeve Hill	Worcs	SP0748	52°8·1'	1°53·5'W	X	150
Cleeve Ho	Wilts	ST9360	51°20·6'	2°5·6'W	X	173
Cleeve Ho	Wilts	ST9382	51°32·4'	2°5·7'W	X	173
Cleeve Ho	Worcs	SO7932	51°59·4'	2°18·0'W	X	150
Cleevely Wood	Glos	SP0317	51°51·3'	1°57·0'W	F	163
Cleeve Mill	Glos	SO7326	51°56·1'	2°23·2'W	X	162
Cleeve Prior	Worcs	SP0849	52°8·6'	1°52·6'W	T	150
Cleeves	N Ayr	NS3148	55°42·0'	4°40·9'W	X	63
Cleeves Cove	N Ayr	NS3147	55°41·5'	4°40·9'W	A	63
Cleeves Fm	Wilts	ST9922	51°0·1'	2°0·5'W	FM	184
Cleeves, The	Oxon	SP4823	51°54·4'	1°17·7'W	X	164
Cleeve Toot	N Som	ST4665	51°23·1'	2°46·2'W	X	171,172,182
Cleggars	Pemb	SS0299	51°39·5'	4°51·4'W	X	158
Clegg Hall	Roch	SD9214	53°37·6'	2°6·8'W	A	109
Clegg Moor	Roch	SD9615	53°38·1'	2°3·2'W	X	109
Cleggswood Hill	Roch	SD9315	53°38·1'	2°5·9'W	H	109
Cleghorn	S Lanak	NS8946	55°41·9'	3°45·5'W	X	72
Cleghorn	S Lanak	NS9045	55°41·4'	3°44·6'W	T	72
Clegir Canol	Denb	SJ0447	53°0·9'	3°25·5'W	X	116
Clegir-Gwynion	I of Angl	SH3679	53°17·2'	4°27·2'W	X	114
Clegir Isaf	Denb	SJ0447	53°0·9'	3°25·5'W	X	116
Clegir Mawr	I of Angl	SH3090	53°23·0'	4°33·0'W	X	114
Clegir Mawr	I of Angl	SH3777	53°16·1'	4°26·2'W	X	114
Clegir Uchaf	Denb	SJ0447	53°0·9'	3°25·5'W	X	116
Clegyr	Pemb	SM7725	51°53·0'	5°14·0'W	X	157
Clegyr-Boia	Pemb	SM7325	51°52·9'	5°17·5'W	X	157
Clegyrdy-bâch	I of Angl	SH4777	53°16·3'	4°17·3'W	X	114,115
Clegyrdy-mawr	I of Angl	SH4776	53°15·8'	4°17·2'W	X	114,115
Clegyr-mawr	Denb	SJ0549	53°2·0'	3°24·6'W	X	116
Clegyrn	Pemb	SM9134	51°58·2'	5°2·2'W	X	157
Clegyrnant	Powys	SH9207	52°39·2'	3°35·4'W	X	125
Clegyrog Blas	I of Angl	SH3890	53°23·2'	4°25·7'W	X	114
Clegyrog Ganol	I of Angl	SH3889	53°22·6'	4°25·7'W	X	114
Clehonger	Heref	SO4537	52°2·0'	2°47·7'W	T	149,161
Clehonger Court	Heref	SO4737	52°2·0'	2°46·0'W	X	149,161
Cleibesgeir	N Eil	NB1841	58°16·3'	6°48·1'W	X	8,13
Cleifiog Fawr	I of Angl	SH2980	53°17·6'	4°33·5'W	X	114
Cleifiog Isaf	I of Angl	SH3079	53°17·1'	4°32·6'W	X	114
Cleigh	Arg & Bt	NM8725	56°22·4'	5°26·5'W	T	49
Cleikeminn	Midlo	NT2458	55°48·8'	3°12·3'W	X	66,73
Cleikiminn	Pth & Kin	NO0936	56°30·7'	3°28·3'W	X	52,53
Cleiriach	Conwy	SH9262	53°8·9'	3°36·5'W	X	116
Cleiriau	Powys	SN7996	52°33·1'	3°46·7'W	X	135
Cleiseabhal	N Eil	NB0708	57°58·2'	6°56·8'W	H	13,14
Cleish	Pth & Kin	NT0998	56°10·2'	3°27·5'W	T	58
Cleish Castle	Pth & Kin	NT0897	56°9·7'	3°28·4'W	X	58
Cleish Hills	Pth & Kin	NT0796	56°9·1'	3°29·4'W	H	58
Cleish Mains	Pth & Kin	NT0797	56°9·7'	3°29·4'W	X	58
Cleish Mill Fm	Pth & Kin	NT1097	56°9·7'	3°26·5'W	FM	58
Cleisteir	N Eil	NB0809	57°58·7'	6°55·9'W	X	13,14
Cleit a' Bhaile	N Eil	NB3309	57°59·7'	6°30·6'W	X	13,14
Cleit a' Bràigh	N Eil	NR1892	57°50·0'	6°44·6'W	H	14
Cleit a' Ghlaisrig	Arg & Bt	NR2741	55°35·4'	6°19·5'W	X	60
Cleit a' Ghlinn-mhóir	N Eil	NF8225	57°12·6'	7°15·6'W	X	22
Cleit a' Ghobha	N Eil	NG0091	57°48·7'	7°2·6'W	H	18
Cleit Aighearail	N Eil	NB3105	57°57·4'	6°32·4'W	X	13,14
Cleit an Ruisg	N Eil	NB1704	57°56·4'	6°46·5'W	H	13,14
Cléit an t-Seabhaig	Highld	NC5268	58°34·8'	4°32·2'W	X	10
Cleit Ard	N Eil	NB1808	57°58·6'	6°45·7'W	H	13,14
Cleit Chathadail	N Eil	NB0910	57°59·3'	6°55·0'W	H	13,14
Cleit Conachro	N Eil	NB0108	57°57·9'	7°2·9'W	X	13
Cleit Dhubh	Arg & Bt	NR6843	55°37·8'	5°40·7'W	X	62
Cleit Dhubh	Highld	NC3273	58°37·0'	4°53·1'W	X	9
Cleit Duastal	N Eil	NB0919	58°4·1'	6°55·6'W	H	13,14
Cleiteachan	N Eil	NG1999	57°53·8'	6°44·1'W	H	14

Cleite Adam	N Eil	NB0528	58°8·8'	7°0·4'W	H	13
Cleiteadh Buidhe	N Ayr	NR8834	55°33·5'	5°21·3'W	X	68,69
Cleiteadh Buidhe	N Ayr	NR9520	55°26·1'	5°14·0'W	X	68,69
Cleiteadh Dubh	N Ayr	NR9222	55°27·1'	5°16·9'W	X	68,69
Cleiteadh nan Sgarbh	N Ayr	NR8830	55°31·3'	5°21·1'W	X	68,69
Cleit Earscleit	N Eil	NB1613	58°1·2'	6°48·1'W	H	13,14
Cleite Beag	N Eil	NB5448	58°21·4'	6°11·8'W	X	8
Cleite Catriona	N Eil	NB3111	58°0·7'	6°32·8'W	H	13,14
Cleite Dubh	N Eil	NB5448	58°21·4'	6°11·8'W	X	8
Cleite Fhidigidh	N Eil	NB0622	58°5·6'	6°58·9'W	H	13,14
Cleite Ghiosla	N Eil	NB1026	58°7·9'	6°55·1'W	H	13
Cleite Gile	N Eil	NB5266	58°31·0'	6°15·0'W	X	8
Cleite Leathann	N Eil	NB0428	58°8·8'	7°1·4'W	H	13
Cleite Loisgte	N Eil	NF9876	57°40·6'	7°3·5'W	X	18
Cleite Mileavat	N Eil	NB0727	58°8·4'	6°58·3'W	H	13
Cleite na Beiste	N Eil	NB1829	58°9·9'	6°47·2'W	H	8,13
Cleite na Cloich Ard	N Eil	NB1730	58°10·4'	6°48·3'W	H	8,13
Cleite na Cos Cleit	N Eil	NB1516	58°2·8'	6°49·3'W	H	13,14
Cleite nan Caorach	N Eil	NB0826	58°7·9'	6°57·2'W	H	13
Cleite nan Luch	N Eil	NF9575	57°40·0'	7°6·4'W	X	18
Cleite nan Ràmh	N Eil	NB0719	58°4·1'	6°57·7'W	H	13,14
Cleite Tiorsdam	N Eil	NB2015	58°2·4'	6°44·2'W	H	13,14
Cleit Faobh	N Eil	NB1818	58°3·9'	6°46·4'W	H	13,14
Cleit-feòra	N Eil	NF8359	57°30·9'	7°17·2'W	X	22
Cleitichean Beag	N Eil	NB2736	58°14·0'	6°38·6'W	H	8,13
Cleit Lonndabhat	N Eil	NB1800	57°54·3'	6°45·2'W	H	14
Cleit Mhór	Highld	ND1730	58°15·3'	3°24·4'W	X	11
Cleit Mhòr	N Eil	NF8546	57°24·0'	7°14·2'W	X	22
Cleit na Ceardaich	N Eil	NB3115	58°2·8'	6°33·1'W	H	13,14
Cleit na Duaich	N Eil	NG0996	57°51·8'	6°53·9'W	H	14
Cleit nan Cnocan Fraoich	N Eil	NB2113	58°1·4'	6°43·0'W	H	13,14
Cleit nan Uan	N Eil	NB1304	57°56·2'	6°50·5'W	H	13,14
Cleit Ruadh	N Eil	NF8482	57°43·3'	7°18·0'W	X	18
Cleit Ruaig	Arg & Bt	NM0745	56°30·6'	6°45·3'W	X	46
Clèitseal a Deas	N Eil	NB2528	58°9·6'	6°40·1'W	H	8,13
Cleit Steiseigh	N Eil	NF8444	57°22·9'	7°15·1'W	X	22
Cleiver, The	Shetld	HU2785	60°33·1'	1°30·0'W	X	3
Cleland	N Lanak	NS7958	55°48·3'	3°55·4'W	T	64
Cleland Ho	N Lanak	NS7857	55°47·7'	3°56·3'W	X	64
Cleland Townhead	N Lanak	NS7859	55°48·8'	3°56·4'W	X	64
Clemenstone	V of Glam	SS9273	51°27·0'	3°32·9'W	X	170
Clement Fm	Brig	SS8578	51°29·6'	3°39·0'W	FM	170
Clementhorpe	E Yorks	SE8229	53°45·3'	0°45·0'W	X	106
Clement Leazes	Cumbr	NY5859	54°55·7'	2°38·9'W	X	86
Clement's End	Beds	TL0215	51°49·7'	0°30·8'W	T	166
Clements End	Glos	SO5807	51°45·8'	2°36·1'W	T	162
Clement's Fm	Devon	ST1114	50°55·4'	3°15·6'W	FM	181,193
Clements Fm	Herts	TL3209	51°46·1'	0°4·8'W	FM	166
Clement's Fm	Lincs	TF2363	53°9·2'	0°9·2'W	FM	122
Clementsgreen Creek	Essex	TQ8296	51°38·2'	0°38·2'E	W	168
Clements Hill	Devon	SS4617	50°56·2'	4°11·1'W	X	180,190
Clements Marsh	Essex	TQ9493	51°36·4'	0°48·5'E	X	178
Clement Street	Kent	TQ5370	51°24·7'	0°12·4'E	T	177
Clemy's Cairn	Northum	NT8800	55°17·9'	2°10·9'W	X	80
Clench	Wilts	SU1862	51°21·6'	1°44·1'W	T	173
Clench Common	Wilts	SU1765	51°23·3'	1°45·0'W	T	173
Clencher's Mill	Heref	SO7335	52°1·0'	2°23·2'W	T	150
Clenchwarton	Norf	TF5920	52°45·5'	0°21·8'E	T	131
Clendrie	D & G	NX0267	54°57·8'	5°5·1'W	X	82
Clenenney	Gwyn	SH5342	52°57·6'	4°10·9'W	X	124
Clennell	Northum	NT9207	55°21·7'	2°7·1'W	T	80
Clennell Hill	Northum	NT9308	55°22·2'	2°6·2'W	H	80
Clennell Street	Northum	NT8909	55°22·7'	2°10·0'W	A	80
Clennellstreet	Northum	NT9207	55°21·7'	2°7·1'W	X	80
Clennoch Burn	D & G	NS6000	55°16·7'	4°11·8'W	W	77
Clennon Hill	Torbay	SX8859	50°25·4'	3°34·2'W	H	202
Clenrie	D & G	NX5582	55°6·9'	4°16·0'W	X	77
Clenries	D & G	NS8012	55°23·3'	3°53·2'W	X	71,78
Clent	Worcs	SO9279	52°24·8'	2°6·7'W	T	139
Clenterty	Aberd	NJ7760	57°38·0'	2°22·6'W	X	29,30
Clent Grange	Worcs	SO9278	52°24·2'	2°6·7'W	X	139
Clent Grove	Worcs	SO9280	52°25·3'	2°6·7'W	X	139
Clent Hills	Worcs	SO9379	52°24·8'	2°5·8'W	H	139
Clentrie Fm	Fife	NT2291	56°6·6'	3°14·8'W	FM	58
Clentry	Fife	NT1294	56°8·1'	3°24·5'W	X	58
Cleobury Brook	Shrops	SO6485	52°27·9'	2°31·4'W	W	138
Cleobury Coppice	Shrops	SO7074	52°22·0'	2°26·0'W	F	138
Cleobury Fm	Sol	SP1175	52°22·6'	1°49·9'W	FM	139
Cleobury Lodge Fm	Shrops	SO6977	52°23·6'	2°26·9'W	FM	138
Cleobury Mortimer	Shrops	SO6775	52°22·6'	2°28·7'W	T	138
Cleobury North	Shrops	SO6286	52°28·5'	2°33·2'W	T	138
Cleongart	Arg & Bt	NR6634	55°32·9'	5°42·1'W	X	68
Clephanton	Fife	NO5504	56°13·8'	2°43·1'W	X	59
Clephanton	Highld	NH8150	57°31·7'	3°58·8'W	T	27
Cleppa Park	Newp	ST2784	51°33·2'	3°2·8'W	X	171
Cleras Geo	Shetld	HU3090	60°35·8'	1°26·6'W	X	1
Clere Wood	Hants	SU4460	51°20·5'	1°21·7'W	F	174
Clerkenhill	Pemb	SN0415	51°48·2'	4°50·2'W	X	157,158
Clerkenleap Fm	Worcs	SO8551	52°9·7'	2°12·8'W	FM	150
Clerkenville	Scot Bord	NT7446	55°42·7'	2°24·4'W	X	74
Clerkenwater	Corn	SX0668	50°29·0'	4°43·7'W	T	200
Clerkenwell	Isling	TQ3182	51°31·5'	0°6·3'W	T	176,177
Clerk Grain	D & G	NX9998	55°16·2'	3°34·9'W	X	78
Clerk Green	Kirk	SE2323	53°42·4'	1°38·7'W	T	104
Clerkhill	Aberd	NK1245	57°30·0'	1°47·5'W	T	30
Clerkhill	D & G	NY2597	55°15·9'	3°10·4'W	X	79
Clerk Hill	D & G	NY2598	55°16·5'	3°10·4'W	H	79
Clerkhill	Highld	NC7162	58°31·9'	4°12·5'W	X	10
Clerk Hill	Lancs	SD7436	53°49·4'	2°23·3'W	X	103
Clerkhill Burn	D & G	NY2698	55°16·5'	3°9·5'W	W	79
Clerkhillgrains	D & G	NY2698	55°16·5'	3°9·5'W	X	79
Clerkington	E Loth	NT5072	55°56·6'	2°47·6'W	X	66
Clerkington Mains	E Loth	NT5072	55°56·6'	2°47·6'W	X	66
Clerk Laithe	Lancs	SD6950	53°57·0'	2°27·9'W	X	103
Clerkland	E Ayr	NS4147	55°41·7'	4°31·3'W	X	64
Clerklands	Scot Bord	NT5024	55°30·7'	2°47·1'W	T	73
Clerklands Fm	S Lanak	NS7541	55°39·0'	3°58·8'W	FM	71
Clerkseat	Moray	NJ4752	57°33·6'	2°52·7'W	X	28,29
Clerkston	D & G	NY2765	54°58·7'	3°8·0'W	X	85
Clerk, The	Cumbr	NY2126	54°37·6'	3°13·0'W	X	89,90

Clermiston	C of Edin	NT1974	55°57·4'	3°17·4'W	T	65,66
Clermont	Norf	TL8799	52°33·6'	0°45·9'E	X	144
Clervaux Castle	N Yks	NZ2709	54°28·8'	1°34·6'W	X	93
Clerwood	C of Edin	NT2074	55°57·4'	3°16·4'W	X	66
Cleskett Beck	Cumbr	NY5858	54°55·1'	2°38·9'W	W	86
Clesketts	Cumbr	NY5858	54°55·1'	2°38·9'W	X	86
Clestrain	Orkney	HY3006	58°56·4'	3°12·5'W	X	6,7
Clestrain	Orkney	HY4953	59°21·9'	2°53·3'W	X	5
Clestrain	Orkney	HY6327	59°8·0'	2°38·3'W	X	5
Clestrain Sound	Orkney	HY2806	58°56·4'	3°14·6'W	W	6,7
Clethloch	N Eil	NB4637	58°15·2'	6°19·3'W	X	8
Clett	Highld	ND1071	58°37·3'	3°32·5'W	X	12
Clett	Highld	NG2258	57°31·9'	6°38·2'W	X	23
Clett	N Eil	NF8022	57°10·9'	7°17·3'W	H	31
Clett	N Eil	NF8574	57°39·0'	7°16·4'W	X	18
Clett	Orkney	HY2604	58°55·3'	3°16·6'W	X	6,7
Clett	Shetld	HU1652	60°15·4'	1°42·2'W	X	3
Clett	Shetld	HU2941	60°9·4'	1°28·2'W	X	4
Cletta	N Eil	NL6489	56°52·5'	7°30·5'W	X	31
Clettack Skerry	Orkney	ND4877	58°40·9'	2°53·3'W	X	7
Clett a' Ghrunnda Dhuibh	N Eil	NG1393	57°50·3'	6°49·7'W	H	14
Clett an Dùin	N Eil	NG0399	57°53·2'	7°0·2'W	X	18
Clette Dho' uill	N Eil	NG0191	57°48·8'	7°1·6'W	H	18
Cletter	N Eil	NB0112	58°0·1'	7°3·2'W	X	13
Cletter Bay	N Eil	NB0102	57°54·7'	7°2·5'W	W	18
Cletters, The	Shetld	HU5541	60°9·3'	1°0·1'W	X	4
Cletterwood	Powys	SJ2608	52°40·1'	3°5·3'W	X	126
Clett Head	Shetld	HU5560	60°19·5'	0°59·8'W	X	2
Clett More	N Eil	NB0201	57°54·2'	7°1·4'W	H	18
Clettnadal	Shetld	HU3530	60°3·5'	1°21·8'W	X	4
Clettna Taing	Shetld	HU3730	60°3·4'	1°19·6'W	X	4
Clett Nisabost	N Eil	NG0495	57°51·1'	6°58·9'W	H	18
Clett of Crura	Orkney	ND4687	58°46·3'	2°55·5'W	X	7
Cletts	Orkney	ND4691	58°48·5'	2°55·6'W	X	7
Clett Skerry	Orkney	ND3095	58°50·5'	3°12·3'W	X	7
Cletts of Ramnageo	Shetld	HU5053	60°15·8'	1°5·3'W	X	3
Cletts, The	Shetld	HU4012	59°53·7'	1°16·6'W	X	4
Clett, The	I of M	SC4479	54°11·2'	4°23·0'W	X	95
Clett, The	Orkney	HY4532	59°10·5'	2°57·2'W	X	5,6
Clett, The	Shetld	HU6494	60°37·7'	0°49·3'W	X	1,2
Clettwr Fach	Cered	SN4347	52°6·2'	4°17·1'W	W	146
Clettwr Fawr	Cered	SN4248	52°6·7'	4°18·1'W	W	146
Cletwr	Cered	SN4351	52°8·3'	4°17·3'W	X	146
Cleuch	D & G	NX8888	55°10·7'	3°45·1'W	X	78
Cleuch	Scot Bord	NT0736	55°36·8'	3°28·2'W	X	72
Cleuch	S Lanak	NS8821	55°28·5'	3°45·9'W	X	71,72
Cleuchbrae	D & G	NY0993	55°13·6'	3°25·4'W	X	78
Cleuchbrae Mill	D & G	NY2075	55°4·0'	3°14·7'W	X	85
Cleuch Burn	D & G	NT1508	55°21·8'	3°20·0'W	W	79
Cleuch Burn	E Ayr	NS5729	55°32·3'	4°15·5'W	W	71
Cleuch Burn	S Lanak	NS9208	55°21·5'	3°41·8'W	W	71,78
Cleuch Burn	S Lanak	NS9434	55°35·5'	3°40·5'W	W	71,72
Cleuch Burn	S Lanak	NS9436	55°36·6'	3°40·5'W	W	71,72
Cleuch Burn	S Lanak	NS9438	55°37·7'	3°40·6'W	W	71,72
Cleuchead	Aberd	NO7684	56°57·1'	2°23·2'W	X	45
Cleuchfoot	D & G	NY3182	55°7·9'	3°4·5'W	X	79
Cleuchhead	D & G	NS8200	55°17·1'	3°51·0'W	X	78
Cleuchhead	D & G	NY1970	55°1·3'	3°15·6'W	X	85
Cleuchhead	Scot Bord	NT5720	55°28·6'	2°40·4'W	X	73,74
Cleuch Head	Scot Bord	NT5910	55°23·2'	2°38·4'W	T	80
Cleuch-head	Scot Bord	NY5293	55°14·0'	2°44·9'W	X	79
Cleuchhead Hill Plantation	D & G	NS8201	55°17·6'	3°51·1'W	F	78
Cleuchheads	D & G	NY0995	55°14·7'	3°25·5'W	X	78
Cleuchheads	D & G	NY1387	55°10·4'	3°21·5'W	X	78
Cleuch Mill	S Lanak	NS9553	55°45·8'	3°40·0'W	X	65,72
Cleuch Reservoir	S Lanak	NS9335	55°36·1'	3°41·5'W	W	71,72
Cleuchside	D & G	NY1578	55°5·6'	3°19·5'W	X	85
Cleuchside	Scot Bord	NT7019	55°28·1'	2°28·0'W	X	80
Cleughbrae	D & G	NX6186	55°9·2'	4°10·5'W	X	77
Cleughbrae	D & G	NX9175	55°3·7'	3°42·0'W	X	84
Cleughbrae	D & G	NY0673	55°2·8'	3°27·8'W	X	85
Cleughbrae	Northum	NY8396	55°15·7'	2°15·6'W	X	80
Cleugh Burn	D & G	NX4982	55°6·8'	4°21·6'W	W	77
Cleugh Burn	D & G	NX5862	54°56·2'	4°12·6'W	W	83
Cleughearn Lodge	S Lanak	NS6248	55°42·6'	4°11·4'W	X	64
Cleughfoot	Northum	NY7167	55°0·1'	2°26·8'W	X	86,87
Cleughfoot Wood	Cumbr	NY3971	55°2·0'	2°56·8'W	F	85
Cleughhead	Cumbr	NY4470	55°1·5'	2°52·1'W	X	85
Cleugh Head	Cumbr	NY5961	54°56·8'	2°38·0'W	X	86
Cleugh Head	Northum	NY8087	55°10·9'	2°18·4'W	X	80
Cleughhead	Scot Bord	NT7546	55°42·7'	2°23·4'W	X	74
Cleughhead	S Lanak	NS7737	55°36·9'	3°56·7'W	X	71
Cleugh Ho	Durham	NY8243	54°47·1'	2°16·4'W	X	86,87
Cleugh Ho	S Lanak	NS9554	55°46·3'	3°40·0'W	X	65,72
Cleughie Burn	Fife	NO3821	56°22·9'	2°59·8'W	W	54,59
Cleugh of Eglon	D & G	NX5467	54°58·8'	4°16·5'W	X	83
Cleughs	S Lanak	NS7624	55°29·9'	3°57·3'W	X	71
Cleughside	Cumbr	NY5179	55°6·4'	2°45·7'W	X	86
Cleulow Cross	Ches	SJ9467	53°12·2'	2°5·0'W	X	118
Clevage	Pth & Kin	NO0414	56°18·8'	3°32·7'W	X	58
Clevage Hills	Pth & Kin	NO0513	56°18·3'	3°31·7'W	H	58
Clevage Loch	Pth & Kin	NO0513	56°18·3'	3°31·7'W	W	58
Clevance	S Ayr	NS3532	55°33·5'	4°36·5'W	X	70
Clevancy	Wilts	SU0575	51°28·7'	1°55·3'W	T	173
Clevancy Hill	Wilts	SU0575	51°28·7'	1°55·3'W	X	173
Clevans	Renf	NS3765	55°51·3'	4°35·8'W	T	63
Cleve Beck	Durham	NY8420	54°34·7'	2°14·4'W	W	91,92
Cleve Court	Kent	TR3166	51°21·0'	1°19·4'E	X	179
Clevedon	N Som	ST3971	51°26·3'	2°52·3'W	T	171,172
Clevedon Bay	N Som	ST3971	51°26·3'	2°52·3'W	W	171,172
Clevedon Court	N Som	ST4271	51°26·3'	2°49·7'W	A	171,172
Clevedon Moor	N Som	ST4270	51°25·8'	2°49·7'W	X	171,172
Cleve Hill Fm	Bath & NE Somer	ST5357	51°18·8'	2°40·1'W	FM	172,182
Cleveland	N Yks	NZ6112	54°30·2'	1°3·1'W	X	94
Cleveland	Red & Cl	NZ7315	54°31·7'	0°51·9'W	X	94
Cleveland Fm	Oxon	SU2790	51°36·7'	1°36·2'W	FM	163,174
Cleveland Fm	Wilts	SU0694	51°38·9'	1°54·4'W	FM	163,173
Cleveland Hills	N Yks	NZ5901	54°24·3'	1°5·0'W	H	93
Cleveland Hills	N Yks	NZ6005	54°26·5'	1°4·1'W	H	94

Cleveland Hills	N Yks	SE5097	54°22·2′	1°13·4′W	H	100
Clevelandhouse Fm	Notts	SK7077	53°17·4′	0°56·6′W	FM	120
Cleveland Lodge	N Yks	NZ5611	54°29·7′	1°7·7′W	X	93
Clevelands	Kent	TQ8334	51°4·8′	0°37·1′E	X	188
Cleveland Tontine Inn	N Yks	SE4499	54°23·3′	1°18·9′W	X	99
Cleveland View	N Yks	NZ4006	54°27·1′	1°22·6′W	X	93
Cleveland Way	N Yks	NZ5503	54°25·4′	1°8·7′W	X	93
Cleveland Way	N Yks	SE4599	54°23·3′	1°18·0′W	X	99
Cleveland Way	N Yks	SE5083	54°14·7′	1°13·5′W	X	100
Cleveland Way	N Yks	TA0586	54°15·8′	0°22·9′W	X	101
Cleveland Way	Red & Cl	NZ6721	54°35·0′	0°57·4′W	X	94
Cleveland Way	Red & Cl	NZ7319	54°33·9′	0°51·8′W	X	94
Cleveley	Oxon	SP3824	51°55·0′	1°26·5′W	T	164
Cleveley Bank Fm	Lancs	SD4950	53°56·9′	2°46·2′W	FM	102
Cleveleys	Lancs	SD3143	53°53·0′	3°2·6′W	T	102
Clevelode	Worcs	SO8346	52°7·0′	2°14·5′W	X	150
Cleve Marshes	Kent	TR0464	51°20·5′	0°56·1′E	X	178,179
Cleverdon	Devon	SS3313	50°53·8′	4°22·1′W	X	190
Cleverhayes Fm	Devon	ST1901	50°48·4′	3°8·6′W	FM	192,193
Cleverton	Wilts	ST9785	51°34·1′	2°2·2′W	T	173
Cleves Copse	Wilts	SU3155	51°17·8′	1°32·9′W	F	174,185
Cleves Hill	Northnts	SP5468	52°18·7′	1°12·1′W	X	152
Clevies, The	Orkney	ND2989	58°47·2′	3°13·2′W	X	7
Clevison Currick	Durham	NY8343	54°47·1′	2°15·4′W	X	86,87
Clewer	Somer	ST4451	51°15·6′	2°47·8′W	T	182
Clewer Green	Win & Maid	SU9475	51°28·2′	0°38·4′W	T	175
Clewer New Town	Win & Maid	SU9576	51°28·7′	0°37·5′W	T	175,176
Clewers Hill	Hants	SU5515	50°56·1′	1°12·6′W	X	196
Clewer Village	Win & Maid	SU9577	51°29·3′	0°37·5′W	T	175,176
Clew Head	Shetld	HU2485	60°33·1′	1°33·2′W	X	3
Clews Gill	Cumbr	NY1315	54°31·6′	3°20·2′W	W	89
Clews Hill	Scot Bord	NT1521	55°28·8′	3°20·3′W	H	72
Cley Channel	Norf	TG0345	52°58·1′	1°1·8′E	W	133
Cley Eye	Norf	TG0445	52°58·0′	1°2·7′E	X	133
Cleygate Common	Surrey	SU9153	51°16·4′	0°41·3′W	X	186
Cley Hill	Wilts	ST8344	51°11·9′	2°14·2′W	H	183
Cley Hill Fm	Wilts	ST8345	51°12·5′	2°14·2′W	FM	183
Cley next the Sea	Norf	TG0443	52°57·0′	1°2·6′E	T	133
Cley Park	Norf	TG0640	52°55·3′	1°4·3′E	F	133
Cliad	Arg & Bt	NM2059	56°38·6′	6°33·6′W	X	46,47
Cliad Bay	Arg & Bt	NM1960	56°39·1′	6°34·6′W	W	46
Cliasay Beg	N Eil	NF9270	57°37·1′	7°9·1′W	X	18
Cliasay More	N Eil	NF9370	57°37·2′	7°8·1′W	X	18
Cliasmaol	N Eil	NB0706	57°57·1′	6°56·7′W	X	13,14
Cliastul	N Eil	NB4044	58°18·7′	6°25·9′W	W	8
Cliatasay	N Eil	NB1333	58°11·8′	6°52·6′W	X	13
Clibberswick	Shetld	HP6412	60°47·4′	0°49·0′W	T	1
Cliburn	Cumbr	NY5824	54°36·8′	2°38·6′W	T	91
Cliburn Moss	Cumbr	NY5725	54°37·3′	2°39·5′W	F	91
Click' em in	Northum	NZ0072	55°2·8′	1°59·6′W	X	87
Clickemin	Northum	NZ1772	55°2·8′	1°43·6′W	X	88
Click-em-Inn Fm	Durham	NZ1644	54°47·7′	1°44·6′W	FM	88
Clicket Hill	Suff	TL9133	51°58·0′	0°47·2′E	X	168
Clickett Hill	Suff	TM2835	51°58·2′	1°19·6′E	X	169
Clickimin	Orkney	HY6644	59°17·1′	2°35·3′W	X	5
Clickland	Devon	SX6152	50°21·3′	3°56·9′W	X	202
Click Mill	Orkney	HY3222	59°5·0′	3°10·7′W	X	6
Clicknafea	Orkney	HY1900	58°53·1′	3°23·8′W	X	7
Cliddesden	Hants	SU6349	51°14·4′	1°5·5′W	T	185
Clies Fm	Corn	SW6523	50°3·9′	5°16·7′W	FM	203
Clieves Hills	Lancs	SD3807	53°33·6′	2°55·8′W	X	108
Cliff	Carm	SN3609	51°45·6′	4°22·2′W	X	159
Cliff	Ches	SJ9881	53°19·8′	2°1·4′W	X	109
Cliff	Corn	SX1255	50°22·1′	4°38·2′W	X	200
Cliff	Derby	SK0287	53°23·0′	1°57·8′W	T	110
Cliff	Highld	NM6769	56°45·5′	5°48·3′W	T	40
Cliff	N Eil	NB0835	58°12·7′	6°57·8′W	T	13
Cliff	Shetld	HP6011	60°46·9′	0°53·4′W	X	1
Cliff	Staffs	SJ9762	53°9·5′	2°2·3′W	X	118
Cliff	Warw	SP2098	52°35·0′	1°41·9′W	T	139
Cliffash	Derby	SK2848	53°2·0′	1°34·5′W	X	119
Cliff Bank	Ches	SJ4753	53°4·5′	2°47·1′W	X	117
Cliff Beck	Lincs	TF0943	52°58·6′	0°22·2′W	W	130
Cliff Beck	N Yks	SD8897	54°22·3′	2°10·7′W	W	98
Cliff Brook	Ches	SJ5875	53°16·5′	2°37·4′W	W	117
Cliffburn	Angus	NO6541	56°33·8′	2°33·7′W	T	54
Cliff Carr	Lincs	TF3170	53°12·9′	0°1·9′W	F	122
Cliff College	Derby	SK2473	53°15·4′	1°38·0′W	X	119
Cliffe	Lancs	SD7232	53°47·3′	2°25·1′W	T	103
Cliffe	Medway	TQ7376	51°27·6′	0°29·8′E	T	178
Cliffe	N Yks	NZ2115	54°32·0′	1°40·1′W	T	93
Cliffe	N Yks	SE6632	53°47·0′	0°59·5′W	T	105,106
Cliffe Bank	N Yks	NZ2114	54°31·5′	1°40·1′W	X	93
Cliffe Castle	Brad	SE0541	53°52·2′	1°55·0′W	X	104
Cliffe Creek	Medway	TQ7077	51°28·2′	0°27·3′E	W	178
Cliffe Dales	E Yorks	SE8835	53°48·5′	0°39·4′W	X	106
Cliffe Fleet	Medway	TQ7478	51°28·7′	0°30·9′E	W	178
Cliffe Fm	Barns	SE3101	53°30·5′	1°31·5′W	FM	110,111
Cliffe Fm	Lancs	SD4916	53°38·5′	2°45·9′W	FM	108
Cliffe Fort	Medway	TQ7076	51°27·7′	0°27·2′E	A	178
Cliffe Hall	N Yks	NZ2015	54°32·0′	1°41·0′W	X	93
Cliffe Hill	E Susx	TQ4310	50°52·5′	0°2·3′E	H	198
Cliffe Hill	Leic	SK4710	52°41·4′	1°17·9′W	X	129
Cliffe House Fm	N Yks	SE7265	54°4·8′	0°53·6′W	FM	100
Cliffe House Fm	Sheff	SK2791	53°25·1′	1°35·2′W	FM	110
Cliffe Marshes	Medway	TQ7278	51°28·7′	0°29·0′E	X	178
Cliff End	E Susx	TQ8813	50°53·4′	0°40·8′E	T	199
Cliff End	E Susx	TV5297	50°45·4′	0°9·7′E	X	199
Cliff End	I of W	SZ3289	50°42·2′	1°32·4′W	X	196
Cliff End	Kirk	SE1216	53°38·7′	1°48·7′W	T	110
Cliffe Park	Staffs	SJ9359	53°7·9′	2°5·9′W	X	118
Clifferdine Wood	Glos	SP0111	51°48·1′	1°58·7′W	F	163
Cliffe, The	Shrops	SJ3920	52°46·7′	2°53·9′W	X	126
Cliffe Woods	Medway	TQ7373	51°26·0′	0°29·7′E	T	178
Cliffey Wood	Worcs	SO8444	52°5·9′	2°13·6′W	F	150
Cliff Field Ho	N Yks	SE6371	54°8·1′	1°1·7′W	X	100
Cliff Fm	Ches	SJ5074	53°15·9′	2°44·6′W	FM	117
Cliff Fm	Derby	SK2162	53°9·5′	1°40·7′W	FM	119
Cliff Fm	E Yorks	TA3822	53°40·8′	0°5·8′E	FM	107,113
Cliff Fm	Glos	SO6502	51°43·2′	2°30·0′W	FM	162

Cliff Fm	I of W	SZ4695	50°45·4′	1°20·5′W	FM	196
Cliff Fm	Kent	TQ9326	51°0·3′	0°45·4′E	FM	189
Cliff Fm	Lincs	SK8941	52°57·8′	0°40·1′W	FM	130
Cliff Fm	Lincs	SK9676	53°16·6′	0°33·2′W	FM	121
Cliff Fm	Lincs	TF0168	53°12·2′	0°28·9′W	FM	121
Cliff Fm	Lincs	TF0244	52°59·3′	0°28·4′W	FM	130
Cliff Fm	N Lincs	SK9597	53°27·9′	0°33·7′W	FM	112
Cliff Fm	N Yks	NZ7818	54°33·3′	0°47·2′W	FM	94
Cliff Fm	N Yks	SE7584	54°15·0′	0°50·5′W	FM	100
Cliff Fm	S Glos	ST6978	51°30·2′	2°26·4′W	FM	172
Cliff Fm	S Glos	ST7180	51°31·3′	2°24·7′W	FM	172
Cliff Fm	Suff	TM2946	52°4·1′	1°20·9′E	FM	169
Cliff Fms	Ches	SJ9880	53°19·3′	2°1·4′W	FM	109
Cliff Grange	Shrops	SJ6432	52°53·3′	2°31·7′W	X	127
Cliff Grange Fm	N Yks	SE1866	54°5·6′	1°43·1′W	FM	99
Cliff Hill	Ches	SJ9374	53°16·0′	2°5·9′W	X	118
Cliff Hill	Donc	SE5315	53°38·0′	1°11·5′W	X	111
Cliff Hill	Lincs	TF0244	52°59·3′	0°28·4′W	X	130
Cliff Hill	N Lincs	SE7701	53°30·2′	0°49·9′W	X	112
Cliff Hill	Somer	ST6832	51°5·4′	2°27·0′W	H	183
Cliff Hill or Meáll a' Cluith	Highld	NG8480	57°45·7′	5°37·4′W	H	19
Cliff Ho	Barns	SE2401	53°30·5′	1°37·9′W	X	110
Cliff Ho	E Yorks	TA1756	53°59·4′	0°12·5′W	X	107
Cliff Ho	Leic	SK3403	52°37·7′	1°29·5′W	X	140
Cliff Ho	Lincs	SK9683	53°20·3′	0°33·1′W	X	121
Cliff Ho	Lincs	SK9695	53°26·8′	0°32·9′W	X	112
Cliff Ho	Lincs	SK9881	53°19·2′	0°31·3′W	X	121
Cliff Ho	Suff	TM4768	52°15·5′	1°37·6′E	X	156
Cliff Ho	V of Glam	ST0468	51°24·4′	3°22·4′W	X	170
Cliffhope Burn	Scot Bord	NT5600	55°17·8′	2°41·1′W	W	80
Cliff House Fm	Leic	SK6021	52°47·2′	1°6·2′W	FM	129
Cliff House Fm	Lincs	SK9493	53°25·8′	0°34·7′W	FM	112
Clifflane Fm	Warr	SJ6584	53°21·3′	2°31·1′W	FM	109
Cliff Lodge	N Yks	SE1189	54°18·0′	1°49·4′W	X	99
Cliff Marsh Fm	Kent	TQ9425	50°59·7′	0°46·3′E	FM	189
Clifforch	Carm	SN2724	51°53·5′	4°30·5′W	X	145,158
Clifford	Devon	SS3021	50°58·0′	4°24·9′W	T	190
Clifford	Heref	SO2445	52°6·1′	3°6·2′W	T	148
Clifford	Leeds	SE4244	53°53·7′	1°21·2′W	T	105
Clifford Barton	Devon	SX7890	50°42·0′	3°43·3′W	A	191
Clifford Bottom	Wilts	SU0438	51°8·7′	1°56·2′W	X	184
Clifford Br	Devon	SX7889	50°41·5′	3°43·3′W	A	191
Clifford Castle	Heref	SO2445	52°6·1′	3°6·2′W	A	148
Clifford Chambers	Warw	SP1952	52°10·2′	1°42·9′W	T	151
Clifford Hall	N Yks	SD6471	54°8·3′	2°32·6′W	X	97
Clifford Hill	Northnts	SP8060	52°14·2′	0°49·3′W	A	152
Clifford Hill Fm	Warw	SP1851	52°9·7′	1°43·8′W	FM	151
Clifford Manor	Glos	SO7021	51°53·4′	2°25·8′W	X	162
Clifford Moor Fm	Leeds	SE4144	53°53·7′	1°22·2′W	FM	105
Clifford's Fm	Durham	NZ1314	54°31·5′	1°47·5′W	FM	92
Cliffords Fort	N Tyne	NZ3668	55°0·6′	1°25·8′W	A	88
Clifford's Hill	Wilts	SU0863	51°22·2′	1°52·7′W	H	173
Clifford's Ho	Durham	NZ1743	54°47·1′	1°43·7′W	X	88
Clifford's Mesne	Glos	SO7023	51°54·5′	2°25·8′W	T	162
Cliffords, The	Shrops	SO5971	52°20·4′	2°35·7′W	X	137,138
Clifford's Wood	Staffs	SJ8337	52°56·0′	2°14·8′W	F	127
Clifford Water	Devon	SS3020	50°57·5′	4°24·9′W	W	190
Clifforest Fm	Carm	SN3238	52°1·1′	4°26·5′W	FM	145
Cliff Plantation	Suff	TM4357	52°9·7′	1°33·6′E	F	156
Cliff Quay	Suff	TM1642	52°2·3′	1°9·4′E	X	169
Cliff Reach	Essex	TQ9296	51°38·0′	0°46·9′E	W	168
Cliff Reach	Suff	TM4056	52°9·2′	1°30·9′E	W	156
Cliff Ridge Wood	N Yks	NZ5711	54°29·7′	1°6·8′W	F	93
Cliffs End	Kent	TR3464	51°19·8′	1°21·9′E	T	179
Cliffside	Derby	SK3455	53°5·7′	1°29·1′W	X	119
Cliffs, The	S Glos	ST7188	51°35·6′	2°24·7′W	X	162,172
Cliffs, The	Shetld	HP6515	60°49·0′	0°47·8′W	X	1
Cliffs, The	Staffs	SK1546	53°0·9′	1°46·2′W	X	119,128
Cliff Stud	N Yks	SE6185	54°15·7′	1°3·4′W	X	94,100
Cliff, The	Ches	SJ5875	53°16·5′	2°37·4′W	X	117
Cliff, The	Derby	SK2275	53°16·5′	1°39·8′W	X	119
Cliff, The	Dorset	ST8107	50°52·0′	2°15·8′W	X	194
Cliff, The	Dorset	ST8706	50°51·4′	2°10·7′W	X	194
Cliff, The	Dorset	ST9407	50°52·0′	2°4·7′W	X	195
Cliff, The	Leic	SK6021	52°47·2′	1°6·2′W	X	129
Cliff, The	N Lincs	SE8619	53°39·9′	0°41·5′W	X	112
Cliff, The	Notts	SK4655	53°5·7′	1°18·4′W	X	120
Cliff, The	Suff	TM3948	52°4·9′	1°29·7′E	X	169
Cliff Top	N Yks	SE1865	54°5·1′	1°43·1′W	X	99
Cliff Top	Staffs	SK1348	53°2·0′	1°48·0′W	H	119
Cliff Top Ho	N Yks	TA0293	54°19·6′	0°25·5′W	X	101
Clifftown	Sou-on-Sea	TQ8785	51°32·2′	0°42·2′E	T	178
Cliffwell Cotts	Glos	SO8309	51°47·0′	2°14·4′W	X	162
Cliff Wood	Lincs	SK8434	52°54·0′	0°44·7′W	F	130
Cliff Wood	N Yks	SE5488	54°17·3′	1°9·8′W	F	100
Clift	Dorset	SY5498	50°47·0′	2°38·8′W	X	194
Cliftbog	Aberd	NJ6945	57°29·9′	2°30·6′W	X	29
Clifthayne Fm	Devon	ST2511	50°53·9′	3°3·6′W	FM	192,193
Clift Hills	Shetld	HU3931	60°4·0′	1°17·5′W	H	4
Clift Ho	Cumbr	NY4166	54°59·4′	2°54·9′W	X	85
Clifton	Beds	TL1638	52°1·9′	0°18·1′W	T	153
Clifton	Cald	SE1522	53°41·9′	1°46·0′W	T	104
Clifton	Ches	SJ5279	53°18·6′	2°42·8′W	T	117
Clifton	C of Bris	ST5673	51°27·5′	2°37·6′W	T	172
Clifton	C of Nott	SK5434	52°54·3′	1°11·4′W	T	129
Clifton	Corn	SX4264	50°27·5′	4°13·2′W	X	201
Clifton	Cumbr	NY5326	54°37·9′	2°43·3′W	T	90
Clifton	Derby	SK1644	52°59·8′	1°45·3′W	T	119,128
Clifton	Devon	SS5941	51°9·3′	4°0·6′W	T	180
Clifton	Donc	SK5196	53°27·7′	1°13·5′W	T	111
Clifton	Lancs	SD4630	53°46·1′	2°48·7′W	T	102
Clifton	Northum	NZ2082	55°8·2′	1°40·7′W	T	81
Clifton	N Yks	SE1948	53°55·9′	1°42·2′W	T	104
Clifton	Orkney	HY5042	59°16·0′	2°52·1′W	X	5
Clifton	Oxon	SP4831	51°58·8′	1°17·7′W	T	151
Clifton	Roth	SK4392	53°25·6′	1°20·8′W	T	111
Clifton	Salf	SD7703	53°31·6′	2°20·4′W	T	109
Clifton	Scot Bord	NT8126	55°31·9′	2°17·6′W	X	74
Clifton	Stir	NN3230	56°26·2′	4°43·0′W	T	50
Clifton	Worcs	SO8446	52°7·0′	2°13·6′W	T	150

Clifton	York	SE5953	53°58·4′	1°5·6′W	T	105
Clifton Beck	Cald	SE1424	53°43·0′	1°46·9′W	W	104
Clifton Br	C of Nott	SK5636	52°55·3′	1°9·6′W	X	129
Clifton Bury Fm	Beds	TL1639	52°2·5′	0°18·1′W	FM	153
Clifton Campville	Staffs	SK2510	52°41·5′	1°37·4′W	T	128
Clifton Castle	N Yks	SE2184	54°15·3′	1°40·2′W	X	99
Cliftoncote	Scot Bord	NT8023	55°30·3′	2°18·6′W	X	74
Clifton Country Park	Salf	SD7704	53°32·2′	2°20·4′W	X	109
Clifton Court	Newp	ST3782	51°32·2′	2°54·1′W	X	171
Clifton Craig	D & G	NX9156	54°53·5′	3°41·5′W	X	84
Clifton Cut	Oxon	SU5494	51°38·8′	1°12·8′W	W	164,174
Clifton Down	C of Bris	ST5674	51°28·0′	2°37·6′W	X	172
Clifton Dykes	Cumbr	NY5427	54°38·4′	2°42·3′W	X	90
Clifton Fm	Dorset	ST5812	50°54·6′	2°35·5′W	FM	194
Clifton Fm	N Yks	SE7763	54°3·7′	0°49·0′W	FM	100
Clifton Green	Salf	SD7802	53°31·1′	2°19·5′W	T	109
Clifton Hall	C of Edin	NT1070	55°55·1′	3°26·0′W	X	65
Clifton Hall	Cumbr	NY0429	54°39·1′	3°28·9′W	X	89
Clifton Hall	Staffs	SK2611	52°42·0′	1°36·5′W	X	128
Clifton Hall	Warw	SP5375	52°22·5′	1°12·9′W	X	140
Clifton Hampden	Oxon	SU5495	51°39·3′	1°12·8′W	T	164
Clifton Heath	Oxon	SU5597	51°40·4′	1°11·9′W	F	164
Clifton Hill	Lancs	SD4851	53°57·4′	2°47·1′W	X	102
Clifton Hill	Notts	SK8269	53°12·9′	0°45·9′W	X	121
Cliftonhill	Scot Bord	NT7437	55°37·8′	2°24·3′W	X	74
Clifton Hill	Worcs	SO7261	52°15·0′	2°24·2′W	X	138,149
Clifton Ho	Shrops	SJ3921	52°47·2′	2°53·9′W	X	126
Clifton House Fm	N Yks	SE6269	54°7·0′	1°2·7′W	FM	100
Clifton Ings	York	SE5853	53°58·4′	1°6·5′W	X	105
Clifton Junction	Salf	SD7903	53°31·6′	2°18·6′W	T	109
Clifton Lock	Oxon	SU5494	51°38·8′	1°12·8′W	X	164,174
Clifton Lodge	Staffs	SK2710	52°41·5′	1°35·6′W	X	128
Clifton Mains	C of Edin	NT1170	55°55·1′	3°25·0′W	X	65
Clifton Marsh Fm	Lancs	SD4629	53°45·5′	2°48·7′W	FM	102
Clifton Maubank	Dorset	ST5713	50°55·1′	2°36·3′W	A	194
Clifton Maybank	Dorset	ST5713	50°55·1′	2°36·3′W	T	194
Clifton Pasture	Notts	SK5432	52°53·2′	1°11·4′W	X	129
Clifton Pastures	Mil Key	SP9050	52°8·7′	0°40·7′W	X	152
Clifton Reynes	Mil Key	SP9051	52°9·2′	0°40·7′W	T	152
Clifton Rigg	Northum	NT8606	55°21·1′	2°12·8′W	H	80
Cliftons	Lancs	SD5150	53°56·9′	2°44·4′W	X	102
Cliftons	Lancs	SD5439	53°51·0′	2°41·5′W	X	102
Clifton's Br	Lincs	TF3718	52°44·8′	0°2·2′E	X	131
Clifton Spinney	Mil Key	SP9250	52°8·7′	0°38·9′W	F	152
Cliftonthorpe	Leic	SK3518	52°45·7′	1°28·5′W	X	128
Clifton upon Dunsmore	Warw	SP5376	52°23·0′	1°12·9′W	T	140
Clifton Upton Teme	Worcs	SO7161	52°15·0′	2°25·1′W	T	138,149
Cliftonville	Kent	TR3671	51°23·6′	1°23·9′E	T	179
Cliftonville	N Lanak	NS7465	55°52·0′	4°0·4′W	T	64
Cliftonville	Norf	TG3037	52°53·1′	1°25·5′E	T	133
Clifton Wood	Cald	SE1622	53°41·9′	1°45·0′W	F	104
Clifton Wood	Dorset	ST5712	50°54·6′	2°36·3′W	F	194
Clift Sound	Shetld	HU3933	60°5·1′	1°17·4′W	W	4
Clifts, The	Shetld	HU3281	60°30·9′	1°24·5′W	X	1,3
Cligga Head	Corn	SW7353	50°20·2′	5°11·0′W	X	204
Climbing Tree Fm	Northum	NZ2186	55°10·3′	1°39·8′W	FM	81
Climb Stile	Cumbr	SD2590	54°18·3′	3°8·7′W	X	96
Climer's Hill	Worcs	SO9156	52°12·4′	2°7·5′W	X	150
Climnie	Shetld	HU5055	60°16·8′	1°5·3′W	X	3
Climperwell Fm	Glos	SO9112	51°48·6′	2°7·4′W	FM	163
Climping	W Susx	SU9902	50°48·8′	0°35·3′W	T	197
Climpy	S Lanak	NS9255	55°46·8′	3°42·9′W	X	65,72
Climsett's Fm	E Susx	TQ7526	51°0·6′	0°30·1′E	FM	188,199
Climson	Corn	SX3674	50°32·8′	4°18·5′W	X	201
Clinch	Northum	NU0314	55°25·4′	1°56·7′W	X	81
Clinches Fm	Kent	TQ6846	51°11·5′	0°24·6′E	FM	188
Clinchorn Fm	Hants	SU3655	51°17·8′	1°28·6′W	FM	174,185
Clinchstreet Fm	Medway	TQ7876	51°27·5′	0°34·1′E	FM	178
Clinchyard	E Ayr	NS4835	55°35·4′	4°24·3′W	X	70
Clingera	Shetld	HP6208	60°45·3′	0°51·2′W	X	1
Clinger Fm	Dorset	ST6605	50°50·8′	2°28·6′W	FM	194,194
Clinger Fm	Somer	ST7526	51°2·2′	2°21·0′W	FM	183
Clingra Stack	Shetld	HP5917	60°50·2′	0°54·4′W	X	1
Clingre Fm	Glos	ST7299	51°41·6′	2°23·9′W	FM	162
Clingre Ho	Glos	SO7200	51°42·1′	2°23·9′W	X	162
Clingri Geo	Shetld	HU1759	60°19·2′	1°41·0′W	X	3
Clingri Geo	Shetld	HU5441	60°9·3′	1°1·1′W	X	4
Clings Water	Shetld	HU3055	60°17·0′	1°27·0′W	W	3
Clinigin Rocks	Highld	NG3456	57°31·2′	6°26·1′W	X	23
Clinkham Wood	St Hel	SJ5198	53°28·8′	2°43·9′W	T	108
Clinking Cauldron	Angus	NO2962	56°44·9′	3°9·2′W	X	44
Clinkstone	Aberd	NJ5834	57°23·9′	2°41·5′W	X	29
Clink, The	Fife	NO2113	56°18·4′	3°16·2′W	X	58
Clink, The	Fife	NO2213	56°18·4′	3°15·2′W	X	58
Clint	Cumbr	SD7385	54°15·8′	2°24·5′W	X	98
Clint	N Yks	SE2559	54°1·8′	1°36·7′W	T	104
Clintburn	Northum	NY7179	55°6·5′	2°26·3′W	F	86,87
Clintburn	Northum	NY7279	55°6·5′	2°25·9′W	X	86,87
Clint Burn	Northum	NY7380	55°7·1′	2°25·0′W	W	80
Clintergate	Norf	TM2487	52°26·3′	1°18·1′E	X	156
Clinterty Fm	Aberd	NJ8764	57°40·2′	2°12·6′W	FM	30
Clinterty Home Fm	C of Aber	NJ8410	57°11·1′	2°15·4′W	FM	38
Clint Fm	Suff	TM1471	52°17·9′	1°8·7′E	FM	144,156
Clint Grange Fm	N Yks	SE2660	54°2·4′	1°35·8′W	FM	99
Clint Green	Norf	TG0211	52°39·8′	0°59·6′E	T	133
Clint Hall Fm	N Yks	SE2559	54°1·8′	1°36·7′W	FM	104
Clint Head Fm	Cumbr	NY4852	54°51·9′	2°48·2′W	FM	86
Clinthill	Fife	NT1585	56°3·3′	3°21·5′W	X	65
Clint Hill	Northnts	SP7473	52°21·2′	0°54·4′W	H	141
Clinthill	Scot Bord	NT6032	55°35·1′	2°37·6′W	X	74
Clint Ho	Durham	NY9814	54°31·5′	2°1·4′W	X	92
Clintlaw	Angus	NO2953	56°40·1′	3°9·1′W	X	53
Clintmains	Scot Bord	NT6132	55°35·1′	2°36·7′W	X	74
Clintons	Herts	TL4421	51°52·4′	0°5·9′E	X	167
Clints	N Yks	NZ1000	54°24·0′	1°50·3′W	T	92
Clints	Scot Bord	NT4453	55°46·3′	2°53·1′W	X	66,73
Clints Crags	Cumbr	NY1635	54°42·4′	3°17·8′W	H	89
Clints Crags	N Yks	SE1677	54°11·6′	1°44·9′W	X	99
Clints Dod	E Loth	NT6268	55°54·5′	2°36·0′W	X	67
Clintsfield	Lancs	SD6269	54°7·2′	2°34·5′W	X	97

Clints Hill	N Yks	SE1677	54°11·6′	1°44·9′W	X	99
Clints Hill	Scot Bord	NT4453	55°46·3′	2°53·1′W	H	66,73
Clints of Clenrie	D & G	NX5282	55°6·9′	4°18·8′W	X	77
Clints of Dromore	D & G	NX5464	54°57·2′	4°16·4′W	X	83
Clinty Ford	Cumbr	NY4368	55°0·4′	2°53·0′W	X	85
Clip	Gwyn	SH6532	52°52·4′	3°59·9′W	H	124
Clip'd Thorn	N Yks	SE2669	54°7·2′	1°35·7′W	X	99
Clip Hedge Fm	Essex	TM1025	51°53·3′	1°3·5′E	FM	168,169
Clipiau	Gwyn	SH4146	52°59·5′	4°21·7′W	X	115,123
Clipiau	Gwyn	SH8410	52°40·8′	3°42·6′W	T	124,125
Clippens	Renf	NS4364	55°50·9′	4°30·0′W	X	64
Clipper Down	Bucks	SP9614	51°49·2′	0°36·0′W	F	165
Clippesby	Norf	TG4214	52°40·4′	1°35·2′E	T	134
Clippesby Ho	Norf	TG4214	52°40·4′	1°35·2′E	X	134
Clippesby Mill	Norf	TG4012	52°39·4′	1°33·3′E	X	134
Clippings Green	Norf	TG0412	52°40·3′	1°1·4′E	T	133
Clipsham	Leic	SK9616	52°44·2′	0°34·3′W	T	130
Clipsham Park Wood	Leic	SK9716	52°44·2′	0°33·4′W	F	130
Clipshead Fm	Derby	SK2252	53°4·1′	1°39·9′W	FM	119
Clipson's Fm	Cambs	TL4399	52°34·4′	0°7·0′E	FM	142,143
Clipston	Northnts	SP7181	52°25·6′	0°56·9′W	T	141
Clipston	Notts	SK6334	52°54·2′	1°3·4′W	T	129
Clipstone	Beds	SP9426	51°55·7′	0°37·6′W	T	165
Clipstone	Notts	SK5863	53°9·9′	1°7·5′W	T	120
Clipstone Brook	Beds	SP9426	51°55·7′	0°37·6′W	W	165
Clipstone Forest	Notts	SK6062	53°9·3′	1°5·8′W	F	120
Clipstone Ho	Norf	TF9730	52°50·1′	0°55·9′E	X	132
Clipston Grange	Northnts	SP7179	52°24·5′	0°57·0′W	X	141
Clipston Wolds	Notts	SK6432	52°53·1′	1°2·5′W	X	129
Clipstreet Fm	Norf	TG0137	52°53·8′	0°59·7′E	FM	133
Clipt Bushes Fm	Suff	TL9053	52°8·8′	0°47·0′E	FM	155
Cliston	Devon	SS5717	50°56·3′	4°1·7′W	X	180
Cliston	Devon	SS6101	50°47·8′	3°58·0′W	X	191
Cliston	Devon	SX7851	50°21·0′	3°42·5′W	X	202
Clitchbury Manor	Wilts	ST9885	51°34·1′	2°0·5′W	X	173
Clitherbeck	N Yks	NZ7109	54°28·5′	0°53·8′W	X	94
Clitheroe	E Yorks	TA0161	54°2·3′	0°27·0′W	X	101
Clitheroe	Lancs	SD7441	53°52·1′	2°23·3′W	T	103
Cliton Manor	Beds	TL1639	52°2·5′	0°18·1′W	T	153
Clitsome Fm	Somer	ST0339	51°8·8′	3°22·8′W	FM	181
Clitters	Corn	SX3772	50°31·7′	4°17·6′W	X	201
Cliuthar	N Eil	NG1490	57°48·8′	6°48·5′W	T	14
Cliva	Orkney	HY6825	59°6·9′	2°33·0′W	X	5
Cliva Hill	Shetld	HU3468	60°23·9′	1°22·5′W	H	2,3
Cliva Lochs	Shetld	HU3281	60°30·9′	1°24·5′W	W	1,3
Cliva Skerries	Shetld	HU5999	60°40·5′	0°54·7′W	X	1
Clive	Ches	SJ6766	53°11·6′	2°29·2′W	T	118
Clive	Shrops	SJ5124	52°48·9′	2°43·2′W	T	126
Cliveden	Bucks	SU9185	51°33·6′	0°40·8′W	X	175
Clive Green	Ches	SJ6765	53°11·1′	2°29·2′W	T	118
Clivehayes Fm	Somer	ST1812	50°54·3′	3°9·6′W	FM	181,193
Clive Ho	Ches	SJ6765	53°11·1′	2°29·2′W	X	118
Cliver Wood	Corn	SX2162	50°26·1′	4°30·9′W	F	201
Clive, The	Staffs	SO8297	52°34·5′	2°15·5′W	X	138
Clive Vale	E Susx	TQ8310	50°51·9′	0°36·4′E	T	199
Clive Wood	Shrops	SJ5124	52°48·9′	2°43·2′W	X	126
Clivie Bay	Orkney	HY5402	58°54·4′	2°47·4′W	W	6,7
Cliviger Laithe	Lancs	SD8631	53°46·8′	2°12·3′W	X	103
Clivland Bay	Shetld	HU3629	60°2·9′	1°20·7′W	W	4
Clivocast	Shetld	HP6000	60°41·0′	0°53·6′W	T	1
Clixby	Lincs	TA1004	53°31·5′	0°20·0′W	T	113
Clixby Manor Fm	Lincs	TA0904	53°31·5′	0°20·9′W	FM	112
Clixby Top Fm	Lincs	TA1005	53°32·0′	0°20·0′W	FM	113
Cloag	Pth & Kin	NO0126	56°25·2′	3°35·8′W	X	52,53,58
Cloak	Aberd	NJ5804	57°7·8′	2°41·2′W	X	37
Cloak	Aberd	NO8679	56°54·4′	2°13·3′W	X	45
Cloak Cott	Angus	NO6155	56°41·4′	2°37·8′W	X	54
Cloakham	Devon	SY2999	50°47·4′	3°0·1′W	X	193
Cloak Hill	D & G	NX8558	54°54·5′	3°47·2′W	H	84
Cloak Knowe	D & G	NY4291	55°12·8′	2°54·3′W	X	79
Cloak Moss	D & G	NX8559	54°55·0′	3°47·2′W	X	84
Cloak Wood	Aberd	NJ5906	57°8·8′	2°40·2′W	F	37
Cloan	Pth & Kin	NN9611	56°17·1′	3°40·4′W	X	58
Cloan Burn	Pth & Kin	NN9609	56°16·0′	3°40·3′W	W	58
Cloatley	Wilts	ST9890	51°36·8′	2°1·3′W	T	163,173
Cloatley End	Wilts	ST9990	51°36·8′	2°0·5′W	T	163,173
Cloatley Manor	Wilts	ST9790	51°36·8′	2°2·2′W	A	173
Clobb	Hants	SZ4099	50°47·6′	1°25·6′W	X	196
Cloburn	S Lanak	NS9440	55°38·8′	3°40·6′W	X	71,72
Cloburnwood	S Lanak	NS9340	55°38·8′	3°41·6′W	X	71,72
Clo Cadno	Powys	SO1116	51°50·4′	3°17·1′W	X	161
Clocaenog	Denb	SJ0854	53°4·8′	3°22·0′W	T	116
Clocaenog Forest	Conwy	SJ0053	53°4·1′	3°29·1′W	F	116
Clochan	Moray	NJ4060	57°37·8′	2°59·8′W	T	28
Clochandighter	Aberd	NO8998	57°4·6′	2°10·4′W	X	38,45
Clochcan	Aberd	NJ9443	57°28·9′	2°5·5′W	X	30
Clochfaen	Powys	SN9078	52°23·6′	3°36·6′W	X	136,147
Clochfoldich	Pth & Kin	NN8953	56°39·6′	3°48·2′W	X	52
Cloch Hill	Aberd	NO7867	56°47·9′	2°21·2′W	H	45
Clochie Fm	Angus	NO5468	56°48·3′	2°44·7′W	FM	44
Clochkan	Pth & Kin	NN8861	56°43·9′	3°49·4′W	X	43
Clochkeil	Arg & Bt	NR6623	55°27·0′	5°41·6′W	X	68
Clochmacreich	Moray	NJ4958	57°36·8′	2°50·8′W	X	28,29
Cloch-na Hill	Aberd	NO8182	56°56·0′	2°18·3′W	X	45
Clochnahill	Aberd	NO8282	56°56·0′	2°17·3′W	X	45
Clochnant	Denb	SJ0534	52°53·9′	3°24·3′W	W	125
Clochnant	Powys	SJ0422	52°47·5′	3°25·0′W	X	125
Clochodrick	Renf	NS3761	55°49·1′	4°35·7′W	X	63
Cloch Point	Inverc	NS2076	55°56·8′	4°52·5′W	X	63
Clochridgestone	Pth & Kin	NO1413	56°18·4′	3°23·0′W	X	58
Clochtow	Aberd	NK0530	57°21·9′	1°54·6′W	X	30
Clochtow	Angus	NO4752	56°39·7′	2°51·4′W	X	54
Clochyrie Fm	Carm	SN5304	51°43·2′	4°7·3′W	FM	159
Clockburn	Stir	NS5988	56°4·1′	4°15·5′W	X	57
Clockclownie	E Ayr	NS5817	55°25·8′	4°14·2′W	X	71
Clockeasy	Moray	NJ2962	57°38·8′	3°10·9′W	X	28
Clocken Syke Fm	N Yks	SE1860	54°2·4′	1°43·1′W	FM	99
Clockerhall	Scot Bord	NT5521	55°29·1′	2°42·3′W	X	73
Clock Face	St Hel	SJ5291	53°25·1′	2°42·9′W	T	108
Clock Fm	York	SE6550	53°56·8′	1°0·2′W	FM	105,106
Clock Hall	Suff	TL7247	52°5·9′	0°31·1′E	X	154
Clock Hall	Suff	TL7347	52°5·9′	0°31·9′E	X	155
Clockhill	Aberd	NJ8945	57°30·0′	2°10·6′W	X	30
Clockhill Fm	N Yks	SE4257	54°0·7′	1°21·1′W	FM	105
Clock Ho	Essex	TL8502	51°41·4′	0°41·0′E	X	168
Clock Ho	Kent	TQ7450	51°13·6′	0°29·9′E	X	188
Clock Ho	Lancs	SD4305	53°32·6′	2°51·2′W	X	108
Clock Ho	Lancs	SD5623	53°42·3′	2°39·6′W	X	102
Clock Ho	Lincs	SK9995	53°26·8′	0°30·2′W	X	112
Clock Ho	Surrey	TQ1738	51°8·0′	0°19·3′W	X	187
Clock Ho	Worcs	SO9473	52°21·5′	2°4·9′W	X	139
Clock Ho	W Susx	TQ1922	50°59·3′	0°17·9′W	X	198
Clock House	Croy	TQ2860	51°19·7′	0°9·4′W	T	176,187
Clock House Fm	Ches	SJ8677	53°17·6′	2°12·2′W	FM	118
Clock House Fm	Lancs	SD5633	53°47·7′	2°39·7′W	FM	102
Clock House Fm	Suff	TM1161	52°12·6′	1°5·7′E	FM	155
Clocklowie	E Ayr	NS6916	55°25·5′	4°3·8′W	X	71
Clocklowie Burn	E Ayr	NS6916	55°25·5′	4°3·8′W	W	71
Clocklowie Hill	E Ayr	NS6917	55°26·0′	4°3·8′W	H	71
Clockmaden	Pth & Kin	NO1931	56°28·1′	3°18·4′W	X	53
Clockmadron	Fife	NO4208	56°15·9′	2°55·7′W	X	59
Clock Mill	Northum	NZ0281	55°7·6′	1°57·7′W	X	81
Clockmill	Scot Bord	NT7753	55°46·4′	2°21·6′W	X	67,74
Clock Mills	Heref	SO2945	52°6·2′	3°1·8′W	T	148
Clockmore	Scot Bord	NT1822	55°29·3′	3°17·4′W	H	72
Clock's Cleugh	Northum	NY6881	55°7·6′	2°29·7′W	X	80
Clocksters	Aberd	NK0162	57°39·1′	1°58·5′W	X	30
Clockston	S Ayr	NS4128	55°31·4′	4°30·7′W	X	70
Clock Tower	Worcs	SO7466	52°17·7′	2°22·5′W	X	138,150
Cloddach	Moray	NJ1958	57°36·5′	3°20·9′W	X	28
Clodderoch Burn	D & G	NX7893	55°13·2′	3°54·6′W	W	78
Cloddiau	Gwyn	SH8736	52°54·8′	3°40·4′W	X	124,125
Cloddiau	Powys	SJ2009	52°40·6′	3°10·6′W	T	126
Cloddiau	Powys	SO1394	52°32·5′	3°16·6′W	X	136
Cloddiau Duon	Flint	SJ2354	53°4·9′	3°8·6′W	X	117
Cloddisdale	Shetld	HU3919	59°57·5′	1°17·6′W	X	4
Cloddymoss	Moray	NH9860	57°37·4′	3°42·0′W	T	27
Clodgy Point	Corn	SW5041	50°13·2′	5°29·9′W	X	203
Clod Hall Fm	Derby	SK2972	53°14·9′	1°33·5′W	FM	119
Clodisdale	Shetld	HU5041	60°9·3′	1°5·5′W	X	4
Clodisdale (ruin)	Shetld	HU2350	60°14·3′	1°34·6′W	X	3
Clodis Field	Shetld	HP5301	60°41·6′	1°1·3′W	X	1
Clodis Lee	Shetld	HP6612	60°47·4′	0°46·8′W	X	1
Clodis Water	Shetld	HU5184	60°32·4′	1°3·7′W	W	1,2,3
Clodmore Hill	Essex	TL4635	51°59·9′	0°8·0′E	X	154
Clodock	Heref	SO3227	51°56·5′	2°59·0′W	T	161
Cloffin Burn	D & G	NT0206	55°20·5′	3°32·3′W	W	78
Cloffrickford	Aberd	NJ9139	57°26·7′	2°8·5′W	X	30
Cloford	Somer	ST7243	51°11·4′	2°23·7′W	T	183
Cloford Common	Somer	ST7243	51°11·4′	2°23·7′W	T	183
Cloford Manor	Somer	ST7244	51°11·9′	2°23·7′W	X	183
Clogau	Gwyn	SH6720	52°45·9′	3°57·9′W	H	124
Clogau	Powys	SO0196	52°33·4′	3°27·2′W	X	136
Clogau Mawr	Carm	SN7119	51°51·5′	3°52·0′W	X	160
Clôg Fm	Powys	SO0985	52°27·6′	3°20·0′W	FM	136
Clogfryn	Cered	SN4462	52°14·3′	4°16·7′W	X	146
Cloggau	Powys	SO1852	52°9·9′	3°11·5′W	X	148
Clogg's Down	Somer	SS8331	51°4·2′	3°39·8′W	X	181
Cloggs Fm	Somer	SS8331	51°4·2′	3°39·8′W	FM	181
Cloggshill Cross	Devon	SS5322	50°59·0′	4°5·3′W	X	180
Clogg, The	Orkney	HY7039	59°14·5′	2°31·1′W	W	5
Cloghill	C of Aber	NJ8507	57°9·5′	2°14·4′W	X	38
Clog Knowe	D & G	NX9496	55°15·1′	3°39·6′W	H	78
Clogwyn	Gwyn	SH3937	52°54·6′	4°23·3′W	X	123
Clogwyn	Gwyn	SH7217	52°44·4′	3°53·4′W	X	124
Clogwyn-brith	Conwy	SH7954	53°4·4′	3°48·0′W	H	115
Clogwyn Bwlch-y-maen	Conwy	SH6754	53°4·2′	3°58·7′W	X	115
Clogwyn Candryll	Gwyn	SH7244	52°58·9′	3°54·0′W	X	124
Clogwyn Cyrau	Conwy	SH7857	53°6·0′	3°48·9′W	X	115
Clogwyn Du'r Arddu	Gwyn	SH5955	53°4·7′	4°5·9′W	X	115
Clogwyn Graig-ddu	Conwy	SH8346	53°0·2′	3°44·2′W	X	116
Clogwyn-mawr	Conwy	SH7358	53°6·5′	3°53·4′W	X	115
Clogwyn Melyn	Gwyn	SH4853	53°3·4′	4°15·7′W	X	115,123
Clogwyn Sta	Gwyn	SH6056	53°5·2′	4°5·0′W	X	115
Clogwynygarreg	Gwyn	SH5553	53°3·5′	4°9·4′W	X	115
Clogwyn y Person	Gwyn	SH6155	53°4·7′	4°4·1′W	X	115
Clogwynyreryr	Conwy	SH7266	53°10·8′	3°54·5′W	H	115
Clog-y-fran	Carm	SN2416	51°49·1′	4°32·8′W	X	158
Cloich	Scot Bord	NT2149	55°43·9′	3°15·0′W	X	73
Cloiche Dubh	Aberd	NJ4230	57°21·7′	2°57·4′W	X	37
Cloichedubh Hill	Aberd	NJ4330	57°21·7′	2°56·4′W	H	37
Cloich Hills	Scot Bord	NT2048	55°43·4′	3°16·0′W	H	73
Cloich Rig	Scot Bord	NT2248	55°43·4′	3°14·1′W	H	73
Cloidach	Carm	SN5126	51°55·0′	4°9·6′W	W	146
Cloigyn	Carm	SN4314	51°48·4′	4°16·2′W	T	159
Cloined	N Ayr	NR9622	55°27·2′	5°13·1′W	X	68,69
Cloisterseat	Aberd	NJ9026	57°19·7′	2°9·5′W	X	38
Cloisters Fm	Northnts	SP5934	52°0·3′	1°8·0′W	FM	152
Cloka Burn	Shetld	HU2450	60°14·3′	1°33·5′W	W	3
Cloke	Orkney	HY2922	59°5·0′	3°13·8′W	X	6
Cloki Stack	Shetld	HU3518	59°57·0′	1°21·9′W	X	4
Clola	Aberd	NK0043	57°28·9′	1°59·5′W	T	30
Clolyn	Powys	SJ1713	52°42·7′	3°13·3′W	X	125
Clombe Beck	N Yks	SE8066	54°5·3′	0°46·2′W	W	100
Clomendy	Carm	SN3814	51°48·3′	4°20·6′W	X	159
Clô Môr	Highld	NC3073	58°37·0′	4°55·1′W	X	9
Clonbeith Castle	N Ayr	NS3345	55°40·4′	4°38·9′W	A	63
Cloncaird	E Ayr	NS3817	55°25·5′	4°33·2′W	X	70
Cloncaird Castle	S Ayr	NS3507	55°20·0′	4°35·6′W	X	70,77
Cloncaird Mains	S Ayr	NS3607	55°20·0′	4°34·7′W	X	70,77
Cloncaird Moor	S Ayr	NS3807	55°20·1′	4°32·8′W	X	70,77
Clone	D & G	NX3345	54°46·6′	4°35·4′W	X	82
Clone	D & G	NX8158	54°54·3′	3°50·9′W	X	84
Clone Burn	D & G	NX6374	55°2·8′	4°8·2′W	W	77
Clonehead	D & G	NX8291	55°12·2′	3°50·8′W	X	78
Clone Moor	D & G	NX8391	55°12·2′	3°49·9′W	X	78
Clone Point	D & G	NX3345	54°46·6′	4°35·4′W	X	82
Cloney	Stir	NS6294	56°7·4′	4°12·8′W	X	57
Clonfeckle	D & G	NX9585	55°9·1′	3°38·4′W	X	78
Clonherb	E Ayr	NS4546	55°41·2′	4°27·5′W	X	64
Clonhie	D & G	NX8396	55°14·9′	3°50·0′W	X	78
Clonrae	D & G	NX8293	55°13·3′	3°50·9′W	X	78
Clonterbrook Fm	Ches	SJ8267	53°12·2′	2°15·8′W	FM	118
Clonter Opera Fm	Ches	SJ8267	53°12·2′	2°15·8′W	FM	118
Clonyard	D & G	NX9157	54°54·0′	3°41·6′W	X	84
Clonyard Fm	D & G	NX8555	54°52·8′	3°47·1′W	FM	84
Clonyard Loch	D & G	NX8555	54°52·8′	3°47·1′W	W	84
Clonyards	D & G	NX8158	54°54·4′	3°50·9′W	X	84
Clook	Orkney	HY2308	58°57·4′	3°19·8′W	X	6,7
Clook	Orkney	HY3328	59°8·3′	3°9·8′W	X	6
Cloon	Pth & Kin	NO0304	56°13·4′	3°33·4′W	H	58
Cloot Ho	Lincs	TF2414	52°42·8′	0°9·5′W	X	131
Clophill	Beds	TL0837	52°1·5′	0°25·2′W	T	153
Clopton	Northnts	TL0680	52°24·7′	0°26·1′W	T	142
Clopton Corner	Suff	TM2254	52°8·6′	1°15·1′E	T	156
Clopton Green	Suff	TL7654	52°9·6′	0°34·8′E	T	155
Clopton Green	Suff	TL9760	52°12·4′	0°53·4′E	T	155
Clopton Green	Suff	TM2154	52°8·6′	1°14·2′E	X	156
Clopton Hall	Suff	TL7649	52°6·9′	0°34·6′E	X	155
Clopton Hall	Suff	TL7654	52°9·6′	0°34·8′E	X	155
Clopton Hall	Suff	TL9859	52°11·8′	0°54·2′E	X	155
Clopton Ho	Warw	SP2056	52°12·3′	1°42·0′W	X	151
Clopton Tower	Warw	SP2056	52°12·3′	1°42·0′W	X	151
Clopton Village	Cambs	TL3048	52°7·1′	0°5·7′W	A	153
Clopton Way	Cambs	TL3350	52°8·2′	0°3·0′W	X	154
Cloquhairnan	S Ayr	NS4317	55°25·6′	4°28·4′W	X	70
Cloquhat	Pth & Kin	NO1452	56°39·4′	3°23·7′W	X	53
Clorach	I of Angl	SH4484	53°20·0′	4°20·2′W	X	114,115
Clorridge Hill	Devon	SS5846	51°12·0′	4°1·6′W	H	180
Cloryn	Powys	SN9697	52°33·9′	3°31·7′W	X	136
Clos	Pemb	SN1840	52°2·0′	4°38·8′W	X	145
Clos-bâch	Gwyn	SH5804	52°37·2′	4°5·5′W	X	135
Closcedi	Powys	SN9927	51°56·2′	3°27·8′W	X	160
Close a burns	Northum	NY7267	55°0·1′	2°25·8′W	X	86,87
Closeburn	D & G	NX8992	55°12·8′	3°44·2′W	T	78
Closeburn Castle	D & G	NX9092	55°12·9′	3°43·3′W	A	78
Closeburn Mains	D & G	NX9092	55°12·9′	3°43·3′W	X	78
Closeburnmill	D & G	NX9094	55°13·9′	3°43·4′W	X	78
Close Chairn	I of M	SC3995	54°19·8′	4°28·1′W	X	95
Close Clark	I of M	SC2774	54°8·2′	4°38·5′W	X	95
Close-e-Kewin	I of M	SC3896	54°20·3′	4°29·1′W	X	95
Close End	Cumbr	NY0428	54°38·5′	3°28·8′W	X	89
Close e Volley	I of M	SC3794	54°19·2′	4°30·0′W	X	95
Close Fm	Ches	SJ8457	53°6·8′	2°13·9′W	FM	118
Close Fm	Glos	SO9615	51°50·3′	2°3·1′W	FM	163
Close Fm	Glos	ST8891	51°37·3′	2°10·0′W	FM	162,173
Close Fm	Hartpl	NZ4228	54°39·0′	1°20·5′W	FM	93
Close Fm	N Yks	SE3995	54°21·2′	1°23·6′W	FM	99
Close Fm	N Yks	SE7671	54°8·0′	0°49·8′W	FM	100
Closegill	Cumbr	NY6063	54°57·9′	2°37·1′W	X	86
Closehead	Cumbr	NY5155	54°53·5′	2°45·4′W	X	86
Closehead	Northum	NY9093	55°14·1′	2°9·0′W	X	80
Closehill	Northum	NY8185	55°9·8′	2°17·5′W	X	80
Close Hills	N Yks	NY8602	54°25·0′	2°12·5′W	X	91,92
Close Ho	Cumbr	NY6727	54°38·5′	2°30·3′W	X	91
Close Ho	Durham	NY8322	54°35·8′	2°15·4′W	X	91,92
Close Ho	Lancs	SD6323	53°42·4′	2°33·2′W	X	102,103
Close Ho	Northum	NZ1265	54°59·0′	1°48·3′W	X	88
Close Ho	N Yks	SD6568	54°6·6′	2°31·7′W	X	97
Close Ho	N Yks	SD8063	54°4·0′	2°17·9′W	X	98
Close Ho	N Yks	SE0151	53°57·5′	1°58·7′W	X	104
Close Ho	N Yks	SE5672	54°8·7′	1°8·1′W	X	100
Close Hos	Northum	NZ0285	55°9·8′	1°57·7′W	X	81
Close House	Durham	NZ2327	54°38·5′	1°38·2′W	T	93
Close House Crags	Durham	NY8422	54°35·8′	2°14·4′W	X	91,92
Close Ing	N Yks	SD8785	54°15·9′	2°11·6′W	X	98
Closelake	I of M	SC4195	54°19·8′	4°26·3′W	X	95
Close Lea	Northum	NZ1266	54°59·6′	1°48·3′W	X	88
Close Mooar Fm	I of M	SC4085	54°14·4′	4°26·9′W	FM	95
Close Moss	Kirk	SE0111	53°36·0′	1°58·7′W	X	110
Close ny Chollagh	I of M	SC2467	54°4·4′	4°41·0′W	X	95
Closes	D & G	NX3268	54°59·0′	4°37·1′W	X	82
Closes Barn	Lancs	SD6550	53°56·9′	2°31·6′W	X	102,103
Closes Fm	Derby	SK2050	53°3·1′	1°41·7′W	FM	119
Closes Hall	Lancs	SD8050	53°57·0′	2°17·9′W	X	103
Closes, The	Derby	SK2448	53°2·0′	1°38·1′W	X	119
Close Taggart	I of M	SC3695	54°19·7′	4°30·9′W	X	95
Close, The	Cumbr	NY1151	54°51·0′	3°22·7′W	X	85
Close, The	Cumbr	NY1830	54°39·8′	3°15·9′W	X	89,90
Close, The	Cumbr	NY2341	54°45·7′	3°11·4′W	X	85
Close Turf Fm	Glos	SO5804	51°44·2′	2°36·1′W	FM	162
Close Wood	Hants	SU5813	50°55·0′	1°10·1′W	F	196
Closewood	Hants	SU6610	50°53·4′	1°3·3′W	X	196
Close Wood	Warw	SP2584	52°27·4′	1°37·5′W	F	140
Close Wood	Wilts	ST9671	51°26·5′	2°3·1′W	F	173
Close yn Ellan	I of M	SC4095	54°19·8′	4°27·2′W	X	95
Closglas	Carm	SN5219	51°51·2′	4°8·5′W	X	159
Clos-glâs	Carm	SN5417	51°50·2′	4°6·8′W	X	159
Closglas	Carm	SN6424	51°54·1′	3°58·2′W	X	159
Clos-isaf	Carm	SN5212	51°47·5′	4°8·4′W	X	159
Closs	D & G	NY1793	55°13·7′	3°17·9′W	X	79
Closs Burn	E Ayr	NS5016	55°25·2′	4°21·8′W	W	70
Closs Hill	D & G	NX1967	54°58·1′	4°49·2′W	H	82
Closter	Orkney	HY5805	58°56·1′	2°43·3′W	X	6
Clôs, The	Carm	SN2621	51°51·9′	4°31·2′W	X	145,158
Closworth	Somer	ST5610	50°53·5′	2°37·2′W	T	194
Clos-y-graig	Cered	SN1951	52°7·9′	4°38·3′W	X	145
Closyrefail	Cered	SN6453	52°9·8′	3°58·9′W	X	146
Clothall	Herts	TL2731	51°58·0′	0°8·7′W	T	166
Clothall Bury	Herts	TL2732	51°58·5′	0°8·7′W	X	166
Clothall Common	Herts	TL2533	51°59·1′	0°10·4′W	T	166
Clothalls Fm	W Susx	TQ1719	50°57·7′	0°19·6′W	FM	198
Clotherholme Fm	N Yks	SE2872	54°8·8′	1°33·9′W	FM	99
Clothister	Shetld	HU3473	60°26·6′	1°22·4′W	X	2,3
Clothister Hill	Shetld	HU3473	60°26·6′	1°22·4′W	H	2,3
Clott House Fm	N Yks	SE4267	54°6·1′	1°21·0′W	FM	99
Clotton	Ches	SJ5263	53°10·0′	2°42·7′W	T	117
Clotton Common	Ches	SJ5264	53°10·5′	2°42·7′W	T	117
Clotworthy Fm	Devon	SS7008	50°51·7′	3°50·5′W	FM	191
Cloud Br	Warw	SP3472	52°20·9′	1°29·7′W	X	140

Cloudesley Bush	Warw	SP4686	52°28·4′	1°19·0′W	T	140
Cloudesley Fm	Warw	SP4585	52°27·9′	1°19·9′W	FM	140
Cloud Fm	Somer	SS7946	51°12·3′	3°43·5′W	FM	180
Cloud Hill	D & G	NS7305	55°19·6′	3°59·7′W	H	71,77
Cloud Hill	Glos	SP0923	51°54·6′	1°51·8′W	X	163
Cloud Ho	Derby	SK4737	52°55·9′	1°17·6′W	X	129
Cloud Ho	Staffs	SJ9163	53°10·1′	2°7·7′W	X	118
Cloudlam Beck	Durham	NZ0129	54°39·6′	1°58·6′W	W	92
Clouds	Heref	SO5838	52°2·6′	2°36·3′W	T	149
Clouds Gill	Cumbr	SD7499	54°23·4′	2°23·6′W	W	98
Clouds Hill	Dorset	SY8290	50°42·8′	2°14·9′W	X	194
Cloudshill	Herts	TL1327	51°56·0′	0°21·0′W	X	166
Clouds Ho	Wilts	ST8730	51°4·4′	2°10·7′W	X	183
Cloud Side	Staffs	SJ9162	53°9·5′	2°7·7′W	T	118
Clouds Lane Fm	N Lincs	SE8106	53°32·9′	0°46·2′W	FM	112
Cloudsmoor Rocks	S Glos	ST5894	51°38·8′	2°36·0′W	X	162,172
Clouds, The	Derby	SK3044	52°59·8′	1°32·8′W	X	119,128
Cloud, The	Ches	SJ9063	53°10·1′	2°8·6′W	H	118
Cloud Wood	Leic	SK4121	52°47·3′	1°23·1′W	F	129
Clough	Cumbr	SD7891	54°19·1′	2°19·9′W	X	98
Clough	Kirk	SE0913	53°37·0′	1°51·4′W	T	110
Clough	Lancs	SD7055	53°59·7′	2°27·0′W	X	103
Clough	Oldham	SD9408	53°34·4′	2°5·0′W	T	109
Clough	Roch	SD9317	53°39·2′	2°5·9′W	T	109
Clougha Pike	Lancs	SD5459	54°1·7′	2°41·7′W	H	102
Clougha Scar	Lancs	SD5459	54°1·7′	2°41·7′W	X	102
Clougha Scar	Lancs	SD5459	54°1·7′	2°41·7′W	X	102
Clough Bank	Brad	SE0240	53°51·6′	1°57·8′W	X	104
Cloughbank Fm	Man	SJ8184	53°21·4′	2°16·7′W	FM	109
Clough Bottom	Lancs	SD7043	53°53·2′	2°27·0′W	X	103
Clough Bottom Resr	Lancs	SD8426	53°44·1′	2°14·1′W	W	103
Clough Brook	Ches	SJ9767	53°12·2′	2°2·3′W	W	118
Clough Dene	Durham	NZ1755	54°53·6′	1°43·7′W	T	88
Clough Edge	Derby	SK0697	53°28·4′	1°54·2′W	X	110
Clough Fm	Derby	SK1486	53°22·5′	1°47·0′W	FM	110
Cloughfold	Lancs	SD8122	53°41·9′	2°16·9′W	T	103
Clough Foot	Cald	SD9023	53°42·4′	2°8·7′W	T	103
Clough Gill	N Yks	NZ6603	54°25·3′	0°58·5′W	W	94
Clough Hall	Staffs	SJ8353	53°4·7′	2°14·8′W	T	118
Clough Head	Cald	SE0622	53°41·9′	1°54·1′W	T	104
Clough Head	Cumbr	NY3322	54°35·6′	3°1·8′W	H	90
Cloughhead	Derby	SK0283	53°20·9′	1°57·8′W	X	110
Clough Head	Kirk	SE0815	53°38·1′	1°52·3′W	T	110
Clough Head	Lancs	SD8243	53°53·2′	2°16·0′W	X	103
Clough Head	N Yks	SE0042	53°52·7′	1°59·6′W	X	104
Clough Head	Staffs	SJ9864	53°10·6′	2°1·4′W	X	118
Cloughhead	Staffs	SK0248	53°2·0′	1°57·8′W	X	119
Clough Head	Staffs	SK0859	53°7·9′	1°52·4′W	X	119
Clough Heads Brook	Lancs	SD5647	53°55·3′	2°39·8′W	W	102
Clough Heads Cotts	Lancs	SD5646	53°54·7′	2°39·8′W	X	102
Clough Hey	Brad	SD9939	53°51·1′	2°0·5′W	X	103
Clough Hey Allotment	Brad	SD9939	53°51·1′	2°0·5′W	X	103
Clough Ho	Ches	SJ9869	53°13·3′	2°1·4′W	X	118
Clough Ho	Staffs	SJ9452	53°4·2′	2°5·0′W	X	118
Clough Ho	Staffs	SK0554	53°5·2′	1°55·1′W	X	119
Clough House Fm	Lincs	TF5459	53°6·6′	0°18·5′E	FM	122
Cloughmor	Highld	NH6736	57°24·0′	4°12·3′W	X	26
Clough River	Cumbr	SD7389	54°18·0′	2°24·5′W	W	98
Cloughs	Lancs	SD8151	53°57·5′	2°17·0′W	X	103
Cloughs Cross	Cambs	TF3609	52°39·9′	0°1·1′E	X	142
Cloughs, The	Derby	SK0886	53°22·5′	1°52·4′W	X	110
Cloughton	N Yks	TA0094	54°20·1′	0°27·3′W	T	101
Cloughton Fields Fm	N Yks	TA0294	54°20·1′	0°25·5′W	FM	101
Cloughton Moor	N Yks	SE9996	54°21·2′	0°28·2′W	X	94,101
Cloughton Newlands	N Yks	TA0195	54°20·7′	0°26·4′W	T	101
Cloughton Plantns	N Yks	SE9995	54°20·7′	0°28·2′W	F	94,101
Cloughton Wyke	N Yks	TA0295	54°20·7′	0°25·4′W	W	101
Clough Wood	Derby	SK2561	53°9·0′	1°37·2′W	F	119
Clough Wood	Lancs	SD7650	53°57·0′	2°21·5′W	F	103
Clough Wood	N Yks	SD8693	54°20·2′	2°12·5′W	F	98
Clounlaid	Highld	NM7452	56°36·6′	5°40·5′W	X	49
Clousta	Shetld	HU3057	60°18·0′	1°26·9′W	T	3
Clouston	Orkney	HY3011	58°59·1′	3°12·6′W	T	6
Clouting's Fm	Suff	TM4162	52°12·4′	1°32·0′E	FM	156
Cloutsham	Somer	SS8943	51°10·8′	3°34·9′W	X	181
Cloutsham Ball	Somer	SS8943	51°10·8′	3°34·9′W	X	181
Clouts Wood	Swin	SU1379	51°30·8′	1°48·4′W	F	173
Clova	Aberd	NJ4522	57°17·4′	2°54·3′W	X	37
Clova	Angus	NO3273	56°50·9′	3°6·4′W	T	44
Clova Castle	Angus	NO3273	56°50·9′	3°6·4′W	A	44
Clova Hill	Aberd	NJ4322	57°17·4′	2°56·3′W	H	37
Clova Hill	Aberd	NJ5023	57°18·0′	2°49·3′W	H	37
Clove Car	Northum	NU2438	55°38·3′	1°36·7′W	X	75
Clovelly	Devon	SS3124	50°59·7′	4°24·1′W	T	190
Clovelly Court	Devon	SS3025	51°0·2′	4°25·0′W	X	190
Clovelly Dykes	Devon	SS3123	50°59·1′	4°24·1′W	A	190
Clove Lodge	Durham	NY9317	54°33·1′	2°6·1′W	X	91,92
Cloven Crag	N Yks	SE0757	54°0·8′	1°53·2′W	X	104
Cloven Craig	Scot Bord	NT1057	55°48·1′	3°25·7′W	X	65,72
Clovenfords	Scot Bord	NT4436	55°37·1′	2°52·9′W	T	73
Cloven Hill	Lincs	TF3573	53°14·4′	0°1·8′E	X	122
Cloven Hill Plantation	Wilts	SU2318	50°57·9′	1°40·0′W	F	184
Cloven Rocks	Somer	SS7839	51°8·5′	3°44·3′W	X	180
Clovenrocks Bridge	Somer	SS7839	51°8·5′	3°44·3′W	X	180
Clovenstone	Aberd	NJ7717	57°14·8′	2°22·4′W	T	38
Cloven Stone	Cumbr	NY3028	54°38·8′	3°4·7′W	X	90
Cloven Stone	E Ayr	NS6204	55°18·9′	4°10·0′W	X	77
Clovenstone	Moray	NJ5451	57°33·1′	2°45·7′W	X	29
Clovenstone	Renf	NS3361	55°49·1′	4°39·5′W	X	63
Clover	Dorset	SY6185	50°40·0′	2°32·7′W	X	194
Clover	Moray	NJ1159	57°37·0′	3°28·9′W	X	28
Cloverdale	Shrops	SJ5238	52°56·5′	2°42·5′W	X	126
Clover Fm	E Susx	TQ5510	50°52·3′	0°12·6′E	FM	199
Clover Fm	Somer	ST6542	51°10·8′	2°29·7′W	FM	183
Cloverhill	C of Aber	NJ9412	57°12·2′	2°5·5′W	X	38
Clover Hill	Northum	NY6559	54°55·7′	2°32·3′W	X	86
Clover Hill	Pemb	SM9919	51°50·2′	4°54·7′W	X	157,158
Clover Hill	Pemb	SN0725	51°53·7′	4°47·9′W	X	145,158
Clover Hill	Pemb	SN1836	51°59·8′	4°38·7′W	X	145
Cloverhill	Scot Bord	NT1138	55°37·9′	3°24·4′W	X	72

Cloverhill	S Lanak	NS6946	55°41·6′	4°4·6′W	X	64
Cloverhill Fm	Pemb	SN0909	51°45·1′	4°45·6′W	FM	158
Clover Law	Scot Bord	NT1238	55°37·9′	3°23·4′W	H	72
Cloverleaf Fm	Somer	ST5014	50°55·6′	2°42·3′W	FM	194
Cloverley Dole	Shrops	SJ6238	52°56·5′	2°33·5′W	X	127
Cloverley Hall	Shrops	SJ6137	52°56·0′	2°34·4′W	X	127
Cloverley Pool	Shrops	SJ6136	52°55·4′	2°34·4′W	W	127
Cloverycrook	Aberd	NJ7635	57°24·5′	2°23·5′W	X	29
Cloves	Moray	NJ1361	57°38·1′	3°27·0′W	X	28
Clovigarth	Orkney	HY2414	59°0·6′	3°18·9′W	X	6
Clovile Hall	Essex	TL7100	51°40·6′	0°28·8′E	A	167
Clovullin	Highld	NN0063	56°43·2′	5°15·7′W	T	41
Clowally	Orkney	HY3104	58°55·3′	3°11·4′W	X	6,7
Clowance (Hotel)	Corn	SW6334	50°9·8′	5°18·7′W	X	203
Clowance Wood	Corn	SW6234	50°9·7′	5°19·6′W	T	203
Clow Beck	N Yks	NZ2410	54°29·3′	1°37·3′W	W	93
Clowbeck Fm	N Yks	NZ2310	54°29·3′	1°38·3′W	FM	93
Clow Bridge	Lancs	SD8228	53°45·1′	2°16·0′W	T	103
Clow Bridge	Pth & Kin	NO0510	56°16·6′	3°31·6′W	X	58
Clowbridge Resr	Lancs	SD8228	53°45·1′	2°16·0′W	W	103
Clowder	N Yks	SD9270	54°7·8′	2°6·9′W	X	98
Clowes Fm	Kent	TR1262	51°19·3′	1°3·0′E	FM	179
Clowes's Corner	Suff	TM2163	52°13·5′	1°14·6′E	X	156
Clowes Wood	Kent	TR1263	51°19·8′	1°3·0′E	F	179
Clowes Wood	Warw	SP0973	52°21·5′	1°51·7′W	F	139
Clow Hill	Pth & Kin	NO0511	56°17·2′	3°31·6′W	X	58
Clowne	Derby	SK4975	53°16·4′	1°15·5′W	T	120
Clowne Common	Derby	SK4775	53°16·4′	1°17·3′W	X	120
Clown Hill Plantn	Notts	SK5873	53°15·3′	1°7·4′W	F	120
Clowsgill Holme	Cumbr	NY5859	54°55·7′	2°38·9′W	X	86
Clows Top	Worcs	SO7171	52°20·4′	2°25·1′W	T	138
Clow, The	Highld	ND2352	58°27·2′	3°18·7′W	X	11,12
Cloy	Highld	NH6959	57°36·4′	4°11·1′W	X	26
Cloy	Wrex	SJ3943	52°59·1′	2°54·1′W	T	117
Cloybank	Falk	NS7779	55°59·5′	3°57·9′W	X	64
Cloy Fm	Wrex	SJ3944	52°59·6′	2°54·1′W	FM	117
Cloy Hall	Wrex	SJ4043	52°59·1′	2°53·2′W	X	117
Cloy Ho	Wrex	SJ3944	52°59·6′	2°54·1′W	X	117
Cloyntie	S Ayr	NS3305	55°18·9′	4°37·5′W	X	70,76
Cluaisnahadig	Highld	NH8847	57°30·2′	3°51·7′W	X	27
Cluan	Stir	NS3697	56°8·5′	4°37·9′W	X	56
Cluanach	Arg & Bt	NR3659	55°45·4′	6°12·0′W	X	60
Cluanie	Highld	NH4644	57°27·9′	4°33·6′W	X	26
Cluanie Forest	Highld	NH0409	57°8·1′	5°13·9′W	X	33
Cluanie Inn	Highld	NH0711	57°9·2′	5°11·0′W	X	33
Cluanie Lodge	Highld	NH0910	57°8·7′	5°9·0′W	X	33
Cluas Deas	Highld	NC0032	58°14·1′	5°23·9′W	X	15
Cluas Mhin	Arg & Bt	NM6936	56°27·8′	5°44·5′W	X	49
Clubba Water	Shetld	HU4468	60°23·9′	1°11·6′W	W	2,3
Clubbie Craig	Aberd	NJ9867	57°41·8′	2°1·6′W	X	30
Clubbiedean Resr	C of Edin	NT2066	55°53·1′	3°16·3′W	W	66
Clubbi Shuns	Shetld	HU3386	60°33·6′	1°23·4′W	W	1,2,3
Clubb of Mulla	Shetld	HU3964	60°21·8′	1°17·1′W	X	2,3
Clubb of Tronister	Shetld	HU4565	60°22·3′	1°10·5′W	H	2,3
Clubb,The	Shetld	HU0964	60°21·9′	1°49·7′W	X	3
Clubb, The	Shetld	HU3165	60°22·3′	1°25·8′W	H	3
Clu Ber	Orkney	HY5908	58°57·7′	2°42·3′W	X	6
Club Fm	Shrops	SO5690	52°30·6′	2°38·5′W	FM	137,138
Club Gill	Durham	NY9428	54°39·1′	2°5·2′W	X	91,92
Clubley's Plantn	E Yorks	TA1249	53°55·7′	0°17·2′W	F	107
Clubmoor	Liv	SJ3893	53°26·1′	2°55·6′W	T	108
Club Nook Fm	N Yks	SE0558	54°1·3′	1°55·0′W	FM	104
Club Point	N Yks	TA1182	54°13·5′	0°17·4′W	X	101
Clubscross	Aberd	NK0845	57°30·0′	1°51·5′W	X	30
Clubston	Fife	NO3619	56°21·8′	3°1·7′W	X	59
Club, The	Shetld	HU3896	60°39·0′	1°17·8′W	X	1
Clubworthy	Corn	SX2792	50°42·4′	4°26·6′W	T	190
Cluddley	Wrekin	SJ6310	52°41·4′	2°32·4′W	T	127
Cluden	D & G	NX9479	55°5·9′	3°39·2′W	X	84
Cluden Lodge	D & G	NX9379	55°5·9′	3°40·2′W	X	84
Cluden Water	D & G	NX9279	55°5·9′	3°41·1′W	W	84
Clue Hills Fm	Oxon	SP6216	51°50·6′	1°5·6′W	FM	164,165
Clugston	D & G	NX3557	54°53·1′	4°33·9′W	X	83
Clugston Loch	D & G	NX3457	54°53·1′	4°34·8′W	W	82
Clumber Br	Notts	SK6273	53°15·3′	1°3·8′W	X	120
Clumber Lake	Notts	SK6274	53°15·8′	1°3·8′W	W	120
Clumber Park (Country Park)	Notts	SK6275	53°16·3′	1°3·8′W	X	120
Clumber Park Hotel	Notts	SK6474	53°15·8′	1°2·0′W	X	120
Clumlie	Shetld	HU4018	59°57·0′	1°16·5′W	X	4
Clumly	Orkney	HY2416	59°1·7′	3°19·0′W	X	6
Clump	Shetld	HU4423	59°59·6′	1°12·2′W	X	4
Clumpcliffe	Leeds	SE3626	53°44·0′	1°26·8′W	X	104
Clumpers	Shetld	HU1757	60°18·1′	1°41·0′W	X	3
Clump Fm	Hants	SU5946	51°12·8′	1°8·9′W	FM	185
Clump Fm	Leic	SP4999	52°35·4′	1°16·2′W	FM	140
Clump Hill	Dorset	SU0606	50°51·4′	1°54·5′W	X	195
Clump Hill	Leic	SP5391	52°31·1′	1°12·7′W	X	140
Clump Hill	Warw	SP2360	52°14·5′	1°39·4′W	X	151
Clump Hill Fm	Lincs	TF1584	53°20·7′	0°15·9′W	FM	121
Clump of Backber	Orkney	HY5428	59°8·4′	2°47·8′W	X	5,6
Clump o' The Ness, The	Orkney	ND3885	58°45·2′	3°3·8′W	X	7
Clumps, The	Herts	TL3318	51°50·9′	0°3·7′W	F	166
Clumps, The	Orkney	HY4838	59°13·8′	2°54·2′W	X	5
Clump, The	Lincs	TF1689	53°23·3′	0°14·9′W	F	113,121
Clumpton	D & G	NX9977	55°4·9′	3°34·5′W	X	84
Clun	Shrops	SO3080	52°25·1′	3°1·4′W	T	137
Clunaisbhal	N Eil	NG0893	57°50·1′	6°54·7′W	X	14,18
Clunas Reservoir	Highld	NH8545	57°29·1′	3°54·6′W	W	27
Clunbele	Carm	SN3433	51°58·5′	4°24·6′W	X	145
Clunbury	Shrops	SO3780	52°25·1′	2°55·2′W	T	137
Clunbury Hill	Shrops	SO3779	52°24·6′	2°55·2′W	H	137,148
Clun Castle	Shrops	SO2980	52°25·0′	3°2·2′W	A	137
Clunch Pit Hill	Cambs	TL4450	52°8·0′	0°6·6′E	X	154
Cluncoch	Carm	SN3732	51°58·0′	4°22·0′W	X	145
Clunderwen	Carm	SN1219	51°50·5′	4°43·4′W	T	158
Clune	Highld	NH7925	57°18·2′	4°0·0′W	T	35
Clune	Moray	NJ1445	57°29·5′	3°25·6′W	X	28
Clune	Moray	NJ5163	57°39·5′	2°48·8′W	X	29
Clune	S Ayr	NS3725	55°29·8′	4°34·4′W	X	70

Clune	S Ayr	NS4424	55°29·4′	4°27·7′W	X	70
Clunebeg Ho	Highld	NH5028	57°19·3′	4°29·0′W	X	26,35
Clune Burn	Highld	NH8024	57°17·7′	3°59·0′W	W	35
Clunehill	Moray	NJ5163	57°39·5′	2°48·8′W	X	29
Clune Hill	Moray	NJ5164	57°40·1′	2°48·8′W	H	29
Clunehill Wood	Angus	NO3557	56°42·3′	3°3·2′W	F	54
Clunemore	Highld	NH4927	57°18·8′	4°30·0′W	X	26
Clune Plantn	Fife	NT1794	56°8·1′	3°19·7′W	F	58
Clunes	Highld	NN2088	56°57·2′	4°57·1′W	T	34,41
Clunes Forest	Highld	NN2189	56°57·7′	4°56·2′W	F	34,41
Clunes Forest	Highld	NN2290	56°58·3′	4°55·2′W	F	34
Clunes Lodge	Pth & Kin	NN7867	56°47·0′	3°59·4′W	X	42
Clunevackie	Highld	NH4837	57°24·1′	4°31·3′W	X	26
Clun Forest	Shrops	SO2286	52°28·2′	3°8·5′W	X	137
Clungarthen	Carm	SN3030	51°56·8′	4°28·0′W	X	145
Clung Point	D & G	NX6270	55°0·6′	4°9·1′W	X	77
Clungunford	Shrops	SO3978	52°24·0′	2°53·4′W	T	137,148
Clungwyn	Pemb	SN2732	51°57·8′	4°30·7′W	X	145
Clun Hill	Shrops	SO3079	52°24·5′	3°1·3′W	H	137,148
Clunie	D & G	NX9276	55°4·3′	3°41·1′W	X	84
Clunie	Pth & Kin	NO1043	56°34·5′	3°27·4′W	T	53
Clunie Castle	Pth & Kin	NO1144	56°35·0′	3°26·5′W	A	53
Clunie Cott	Aberd	NO1891	57°0·4′	3°20·6′W	X	43
Clunie Dam	Pth & Kin	NN8860	56°43·4′	3°49·4′W	X	43
Clunie Field	Pth & Kin	NO2217	56°20·6′	3°15·3′W	X	58
Clunie Hill	Aberd	NJ6450	57°32·6′	2°35·6′W	H	29
Cluniemore	Pth & Kin	NN9258	56°42·3′	3°45·4′W	X	52
Clunie Water	Aberd	NO1486	56°57·7′	3°24·4′W	W	43
Clunie Wood	Pth & Kin	NN9257	56°41·8′	3°45·4′W	F	52
Cluniter	Arg & Bt	NS1572	55°54·6′	4°57·2′W	X	63
Cluniter Ho	Arg & Bt	NS1572	55°54·6′	4°57·2′W	X	63
Clunpurfaith	Carm	SN3228	51°55·8′	4°26·2′W	X	145
Clunskea	Pth & Kin	NO0063	56°45·1′	3°37·7′W	X	43
Clunskea Burn	Pth & Kin	NN9965	56°46·2′	3°38·7′W	W	43
Clunton	Shrops	SO3381	52°25·6′	2°58·7′W	T	137
Clunton Hill	Shrops	SO3482	52°26·2′	2°57·9′W	H	137
Cluny	Fife	NT2495	56°8·8′	3°13·0′W	T	59
Cluny	Moray	NJ0753	57°33·7′	3°32·8′W	X	27
Clunybeg	Moray	NJ3640	57°27·0′	3°3·5′W	X	28
Cluny Castle	Aberd	NJ6812	57°12·1′	2°31·3′W	X	38
Cluny Castle	Highld	NN6494	57°1·3′	4°14·0′W	X	35
Cluny Crichton Castle	Aberd	NO6899	57°5·1′	2°31·2′W	A	38,45
Cluny Ho	Pth & Kin	NN8751	56°38·5′	3°50·1′W	X	52
Cluny Rock	Pth & Kin	NN8651	56°38·5′	3°51·1′W	X	52
Cluny's Cave or Uamh Chluanaidh	Highld	NN6796	57°2·4′	4°11·1′W	X	35
Cluny Villa	Arg & Bt	NM9033	56°26·8′	5°24·0′W	X	49
Clury	Highld	NH9623	57°17·4′	3°43·1′W	X	36
Cluseburn	Aberd	NO8176	56°52·8′	2°18·3′W	X	45
Clushmill	Angus	NO3037	56°31·4′	3°7·8′W	X	53
Clushmill Burn	Angus	NO3136	56°30·9′	3°6·8′W	W	53
Cluster	Shetld	HU5990	60°35·6′	0°54·9′W	X	1,2
Clust-y-blaidd	Conwy	SH9349	53°1·9′	3°35·3′W	X	116
Cluther Rocks	Derby	SK0787	53°23·0′	1°53·3′W	X	110
Clutter's Cave	Heref	SO7639	52°3·2′	2°20·6′W	X	150
Clutton	Bath & NE Somer	ST6259	51°20·0′	2°32·3′W	T	172
Clutton	Ches	SJ4654	53°5·1′	2°48·0′W	T	117
Clutton Hall Fm	Ches	SJ4654	53°5·1′	2°48·0′W	FM	117
Clutton Hill	Bath & NE Somer	ST6359	51°20·0′	2°31·5′W	T	172
Clwch	I of Angl	SH3681	53°18·3′	4°27·3′W	X	114
Clwch Dernog	I of Angl	SH3386	53°20·9′	4°30·1′W	X	114
Clwt	Conwy	SH9074	53°15·3′	3°38·5′W	X	116
Clwt	Wrex	SJ3245	53°0·1′	3°0·4′W	X	117
Clwt-grugoer	Conwy	SH9663	53°9·5′	3°32·9′W	X	116
Clwt-y-bont	Gwyn	SH5762	53°8·4′	4°7·9′W	T	114,115
Clwt-y-ddafad-ddu	Conwy	SH9265	53°10·5′	3°36·5′W	X	116
Clwyd Hall	Denb	SJ1161	53°8·6′	3°19·4′W	X	116
Clwyd Ho	Wrex	SJ3651	53°3·4′	2°56·9′W	X	117
Clwydyfagwyr	Merth Tyd	SO0206	51°44·9′	3°24·8′W	T	160
Clwydygraig	Powys	SO1624	51°54·7′	3°12·9′W	X	161
Clwytrawscae Fm	Merth Tyd	SO1100	51°41·7′	3°16·9′W	FM	171
Clyan's Dam	Aberd	NJ6715	57°13·7′	2°32·3′W	W	38
Clybane	I of M	SC3476	54°9·4′	4°32·1′W	X	95
Clydach	Monm	SO2213	51°48·8′	3°7·5′W	T	161
Clydach	Monm	ST4799	51°41·5′	2°45·6′W	X	171
Clydach	Powys	SO0821	51°53·0′	3°19·8′W	W	160
Clydach	Swan	SN6801	51°41·8′	3°54·2′W	T	159
Clydach Brook	Nth Pt Talb	SN8302	51°42·5′	3°41·2′W	W	170
Clydach Terrace	Blae Gw	SO1813	51°48·8′	3°11·0′W	T	161
Clydach Vale	Rho Cyn Taf	SS9793	51°37·8′	3°28·9′W	T	170
Clyddai	Cered	SN5252	52°9·0′	4°9·4′W	X	146
Clydebank	S Lanak	NS8345	55°41·3′	3°51·2′W	X	72
Clydebank	W Dunb	NS4970	55°54·2′	4°24·5′W	T	64
Clyde Fm	Cambs	TL2469	52°18·5′	0°10·5′W	FM	153
Clyde Law	S Lanak	NT0217	55°26·5′	3°32·5′W	H	78
Clydenoch	E Ayr	NS4719	55°26·7′	4°24·7′W	X	70
Clydes Burn	S Lanak	NS9716	55°25·9′	3°37·2′W	W	78
Clydes Burn	S Lanak	NT0115	55°25·4′	3°33·4′W	W	78
Clydesdale	S Lanak	NS7951	55°44·5′	3°55·2′W	X	64
Clydesdale	S Lanak	NS8645	55°41·4′	3°48·4′W	X	72
Clydesdale	S Lanak	NS8744	55°40·8′	3°47·4′W	X	71,72
Clydfannau	Powys	SN9884	52°26·9′	3°29·7′W	X	136
Clyeen	I of M	SC3289	54°16·4′	4°34·4′W	X	95
Clyffe Fm	Dorset	SY7791	50°43·3′	2°19·2′W	FM	194
Clyffe Hall	Wilts	SU0053	51°16·8′	1°59·6′W	X	184
Clyffe Hanging	Wilts	SU0776	51°29·2′	1°53·6′W	X	173
Clyffe Ho	Dorset	SY7892	50°43·9′	2°18·3′W	X	194
Clyffe Pypard	Wilts	SU0776	51°29·2′	1°53·6′W	T	173
Clyffe Pypard Wood	Wilts	SU0679	51°30·8′	1°54·4′W	F	173
Clynblewog Fm	Carm	SN2530	51°56·7′	4°32·4′W	FM	145
Clyncemmaes	Pemb	SN0725	51°53·7′	4°47·9′W	X	145,158
Clyncoch	Cered	SN4747	52°6·3′	4°13·6′W	X	146
Clyncoch	Cered	SN4950	52°7·9′	4°12·0′W	X	146
Clynder	Arg & Bt	NS2484	56°1·3′	4°49·0′W	T	56
Clynderwen	Carm	SN1319	51°50·5′	4°42·5′W	X	158
Clyn-du	Cered	SN4950	52°7·9′	4°12·0′W	X	146
Clyne	Aberd	NJ8521	57°17·0′	2°14·5′W	X	38

Clyne	Nth Pt Talb	SN8000	51°41·4'	3°43·8'W	T	170
Clyne Common	Swan	SS5990	51°35·7'	4°1·8'W	X	159
Clyne Fm	Swan	SS6090	51°35·7'	4°0·9'W	FM	159
Clynelish	Highld	NC8905	58°1·5'	3°52·3'W	X	17
Clynelish Moss	Highld	NC8804	58°0·9'	3°53·3'W	X	17
Clynemilton	Highld	NC9106	58°2·1'	3°50·3'W	X	17
Clyne River	Swan	SS5993	51°37·3'	4°1·8'W	W	159
Clyne Valley Country Park	Swan	SS6091	51°36·3'	4°0·9'W	X	159
Clyne Wood	Swan	SS6091	51°36·3'	4°0·9'W	F	159
Clyn felin-fach	Pemb	SN2733	51°58·4'	4°30·7'W	X	145
Clynfelin Fawr	Carm	SN2934	51°58·9'	4°29·0'W	X	145
Clynfyw	Pemb	SN2439	52°1·5'	4°33·5'W	X	145
Clyngarw	Cered	SN3653	52°9·3'	4°23·4'W	X	145
Clyngim	Pemb	SM9235	51°58·7'	5°1·3'W	X	157
Clyng Mill	Devon	SX6348	50°19·2'	3°55·1'W	X	202
Clyngwyn	Carm	SN1225	51°53·8'	4°43·6'W	X	145,158
Clyngwyn	Carm	SN1908	51°44·7'	4°36·9'W	X	158
Clyngwyn	Carm	SN4023	51°53·2'	4°19·1'W	X	159
Clyngwyn	Cered	SN3751	52°8·2'	4°22·5'W	X	145
Clyngwynne	Carm	SN2322	51°52·4'	4°33·9'W	X	145,158
Clyniau	Carm	SN4936	52°0·4'	4°11·6'W	X	146
Clyn-lâr	Carm	SN5040	52°2·5'	4°10·8'W	X	146
Clynmawr	Carm	SN7740	52°2·9'	3°47·2'W	X	146,147,160
Clyn Meinog	Pemb	SN0135	51°58·9'	4°53·5'W	X	145,157
Clynmelyn	Carm	SN4434	51°59·2'	4°15·9'W	X	146
Clyn-melyn	Carm	SN4938	52°1·4'	4°11·7'W	X	146
Clynnog	I of Angl	SH4365	53°9·8'	4°20·5'W	X	114,115
Clynnog-fawr	Gwyn	SH4149	53°1·1'	4°21·8'W	T	115,123
Clynpebyll	Carm	SN2321	51°51·8'	4°33·9'W	X	145,158
Clynsaer	Carm	SN8241	52°3·5'	3°42·9'W	X	147,160
Clyn, The	Powys	SN9363	52°15·5'	3°33·7'W	X	147
Clyn-yr-ynys	Cered	SN1650	52°7·3'	4°40·9'W	X	145
Clypse Moar	I of M	SC3980	54°11·7'	4°27·7'W	X	95
Clyro	Powys	SO2143	52°5·0'	3°8·8'W	T	148,161
Clyro Castle	Powys	SO2143	52°5·0'	3°8·8'W	A	148,161
Clyro Court	Powys	SO2042	52°4·5'	3°9·6'W	X	148,161
Clyro Hill	Powys	SO1946	52°6·6'	3°10·6'W	H	148
Clyrun	Powys	SJ2030	52°51·9'	3°10·9'W	X	126
Clyst Honiton	Devon	SX9893	50°43·9'	3°26·3'W	T	192
Clyst Hydon	Devon	ST0301	50°48·3'	3°22·2'W	T	192
Clyst St George	Devon	SX9888	50°41·2'	3°26·3'W	T	192
Clyst St Lawrence	Devon	ST0200	50°47·7'	3°23·1'W	T	192
Clyst St Mary	Devon	SX9791	50°42·8'	3°27·2'W	T	192
Clyst Valley	Devon	SX9892	50°43·4'	3°26·3'W	X	192
Clyst William	Devon	ST0602	50°48·8'	3°19·7'W	X	192
Clyth	Highld	ND2736	58°18·7'	3°14·3'W	X	11
Clytha Castle	Monm	SO3608	51°46·3'	2°55·3'W	X	161
Clytha Fm	Monm	SO3709	51°46·8'	2°54·4'W	FM	161
Clytha Hill	Monm	SO3607	51°45·7'	2°55·3'W	X	161
Clytha Park	Monm	SO3609	51°46·8'	2°55·3'W	X	161
Clyth Burn	Highld	ND2639	58°20·3'	3°15·4'W	W	11,12
Clyth Mains	Highld	ND2836	58°18·7'	3°13·3'W	X	11
Clytiau-gleision	Conwy	SH9460	53°7·8'	3°34·7'W	X	116
Clytiau-têg	Conwy	SH8458	53°6·6'	3°43·6'W	X	116
Clywedog Brook	Powys	SO0770	52°19·5'	3°21·5'W	W	136,147
Clywedog Plantation	Cered	SN6449	52°7·6'	3°58·8'W	F	146
Cnap a' Chailbhe	Arg & Bt	NM5253	56°36·5'	6°2·0'W	X	47
Cnap a' Chleirich	Aberd	NJ1000	57°5·2'	3°28·6'W	X	36
Cnap a' Choire Bhuidhe	Aberd	NO2290	56°59·5'	3°16·6'W	H	44
Cnap à Choire Leith Bhig	Highld	NM9371	56°47·3'	5°22·9'W	X	40
Cnap Allt an Laoigh	Moray	NJ1307	57°9·0'	3°25·8'W	X	36
Cnapan a' Choire Odhair Bhig	Highld	NH9131	57°21·6'	3°48·3'W	H	27
Cnapan a' Mheirlich	Moray	NJ0807	57°8·9'	3°30·8'W	H	36
Cnapan Beag	Highld	NN9389	56°59·0'	3°45·2'W	X	43
Cnapan Breaca	Highld	NM3997	56°59·6'	6°17·4'W	X	39
Cnap an Dòbhrain	Moray	NJ0806	57°8·4'	3°30·8'W	H	36
Cnapan Eas	Arg & Bt	NR8066	55°50·5'	5°30·4'W	X	62
Cnapan Garbh	Aberd	NN9886	56°57·5'	3°40·2'W	H	43
Cnapan Mór	Highld	NN9390	56°59·6'	3°45·2'W	H	43
Cnapan nan Laogh	Pth & Kin	NN9580	56°54·2'	3°43·0'W	X	43
Cnapau Hafodllywelyn	Powys	SN8347	52°6·8'	3°42·1'W	X	147
Cnap Breac	Pth & Kin	NN4767	56°46·4'	4°29·8'W	X	42
Cnap Chaochan Aitinn	Moray	NJ1409	57°10·1'	3°24·9'W	H	36
Cnap Coire Loch Tuath	Highld	NH2882	57°47·5'	4°53·2'W	H	20
Cnap Coire na Spreidhe	Highld	NJ0104	57°7·2'	3°37·6'W	H	36
Cnap Cruinn	Highld	NN3077	56°51·5'	4°46·8'W	H	41
Cnapiau'r Ferlen	Powys	SN9260	52°13·9'	3°34·5'W	X	147
Cnap Leum an Easaich	Moray	NJ0803	57°6·8'	3°30·7'W	X	36
Cnap Mór	Arg & Bt	NN3216	56°18·7'	4°42·5'W	H	50,56
Cnap na Criche	Arg & Bt	NN2715	56°18·0'	4°47·3'W	X	50,56
Cnap na Cùl-àth	Moray	NJ0708	57°9·5'	3°31·8'W	X	36
Cnap na Feola	Highld	NH2253	57°32·2'	4°58·0'W	H	25
Cnap nan Gobhar	Arg & Bt	NM6027	56°22·7'	5°52·8'W	H	49
Cnap nan Laogh	Highld	NN9093	57°1·2'	3°48·3'W	H	43
Cnap na Stri	Highld	NH1919	57°13·8'	4°59·5'W	H	34
Cnap Rheamhar	Arg & Bt	NS1787	56°2·7'	4°55·8'W	H	56
Cnap Ruigh Dubh	N Eil	NF9269	57°36·6'	7°9·0'W	X	18
Cneiddion	Powys	SO0149	52°8·1'	3°26·4'W	W	147
Cnewr	Powys	SN8922	51°53·4'	3°36·4'W	X	160
Cnicht	Gwyn	SH6446	52°59·9'	4°1·2'W	X	115
Cnoc	Arg & Bt	NN2613	56°16·9'	4°48·2'W	X	50,56
Cnoc a' Bhac Fhalaichte	Highld	NM8092	56°58·3'	5°36·7'W	H	33,40
Cnoc a' Bhaid Bhàin	Highld	NC4219	58°8·2'	4°40·5'W	H	16
Cnoc a' Bhaid-bheithe	Highld	NC5165	58°33·1'	4°33·2'W	H	9
Cnoc a' Bhaid-rallaich	Highld	NH0693	57°53·3'	5°15·9'W	H	19
Cnoc a' Bhaile-shios	Arg & Bt	NR8662	55°48·5'	5°24·5'W	H	62
Cnoc a' Bhainne	Highld	NC1527	58°11·8'	5°8·4'W	H	15
Cnoc a'Bharaille	Arg & Bt	NR8072	55°53·7'	5°30·7'W	H	62
Cnoc a' Bharra Leathainn	Arg & Bt	NR7762	55°48·2'	5°33·1'W	X	62
Cnoc a' Bhealaich Mhóir	Arg & Bt	NM6524	56°21·3'	5°47·8'W	X	49
Cnoc à Bhior	Arg & Bt	NR7362	55°48·1'	5°36·9'W	X	62
Cnoc a' Bhith	Highld	NC3300	57°57·7'	4°48·9'W	H	15
Cnoc a' Bholainn-airigh	Arg & Bt	NR8766	55°50·7'	5°23·7'W	X	62
Cnoc a' Bhothain	Highld	NC6954	58°27·7'	4°14·2'W	H	10
Cnoc a' Bhothain	Highld	ND0847	58°24·4'	3°34·0'W	X	11,12
Cnoc a' Bhràghad	Arg & Bt	NM5222	56°19·8'	6°0·3'W	H	48
Cnoc a'Bhraidein	Arg & Bt	NR7649	55°41·2'	5°33·4'W	H	62,69
Cnoc a' Bhraighe	N Eil	NF7716	57°7·5'	7°19·8'W	H	31
Cnoc a' Bhreacaich	Highld	NH5462	57°37·7'	4°26·2'W	H	21
Cnoc a' Bhreac-leathaid	Highld	NC5813	58°5·3'	4°24·0'W	H	16
Cnoc a' Bhreac Leathaid	Highld	NH5389	57°52·2'	4°28·2'W	H	20
Cnoc a' Bhreun-bhaid	Highld	NC8545	58°23·0'	3°57·5'W	X	10
Cnoc a' Bhuachaille	Highld	NH4828	57°19·3'	4°31·0'W	H	26
Cnoca Breac	N Eil	NF7333	57°16·5'	7°25·1'W	X	22
Cnoc Acaidh Raibhach	Arg & Bt	NR7572	55°53·6'	5°35·5'W	X	62
Cnoc Achadh na Teanga	Highld	NC6508	58°2·7'	4°16·8'W	X	16
Cnoc a Chaduldaidh	Arg & Bt	NR3646	55°38·4'	6°11·3'W	X	60
Cnoc Achaidh Bhuidhe	Arg & Bt	NR9798	56°8·2'	5°15·6'W	H	55
Cnoc a' Chàise	Highld	NC1743	58°20·5'	5°7·1'W	H	9
Cnoc a' Chàise Mór	Highld	NG6609	57°7·0'	5°51·5'W	H	32
Cnoc a' Chaisteil	Arg & Bt	NM3649	56°33·8'	6°17·4'W	X	47,48
Cnoc a' Chaisteil	Highld	NH1892	57°53·1'	5°3·7'W	X	20
Cnoc a' Chaisteil	N Eil	NB1410	57°59·5'	6°49·9'W	H	13,14
Cnoc a' Chaisteil	N Eil	NF8580	57°42·2'	7°16·9'W	X	18
Cnoc a' Chait	Arg & Bt	NM4657	56°38·4'	6°8·1'W	X	47
Cnoc a' Chaol-loch	Highld	ND0349	58°25·4'	3°39·2'W	X	11,12
Cnoc a' Chaorainn	Arg & Bt	NR2562	55°46·6'	6°22·7'W	X	60
Cnoc a' Chaorainn	Pth & Kin	NO1064	56°45·8'	3°27·9'W	H	43
Cnoc a' Chapuill	Highld	NG4033	57°19·1'	6°18·6'W	H	32
Cnoc a' Chapuill	N Ayr	NR9630	55°31·5'	5°13·5'W	H	68,69
Cnoc a' Charraich	Arg & Bt	NR4674	55°53·8'	6°3·3'W	H	60,61
Cnoc a' Chatha	Highld	NC5809	58°3·1'	4°23·9'W	H	16
Cnoc a' Chatha	Highld	NG2360	57°33·0'	6°37·4'W	X	23
Cnoc a' Cheàird	Arg & Bt	NR4075	55°54·1'	6°9·1'W	X	60,61
Cnoc a' Chinn	Highld	NH5945	57°28·7'	4°20·6'W	X	26
Cnoc a' Chlachain	Highld	NG4375	57°41·7'	6°18·3'W	X	23
Cnoc a' Chlaidheimh	Arg & Bt	NR3469	55°50·8'	6°14·5'W	X	60,61
Cnoc a' Chlaiginn	Highld	NH6386	57°50·8'	4°18·0'W	X	21
Cnoc a' Chlàrsàir	Highld	NG8129	57°18·2'	5°37·7'W	H	33
Cnoc Ach' na h-Uai'	Highld	NC8133	58°16·4'	4°1·3'W	H	17
Cnoc a' Choilich	Highld	NC3734	58°16·1'	4°46·3'W	H	16
Cnoc a' Choilich	Highld	NH1799	57°56·8'	5°5·1'W	H	20
Cnoc a' Choin Deirg	Highld	NC1324	58°10·2'	5°10·3'W	H	15
Cnoc a' Choire	Arg & Bt	NR6526	55°28·5'	5°42·7'W	X	68
Cnoc a' Choire	Highld	NC5004	58°0·3'	4°31·8'W	H	16
Cnoc a' Choire Beag	N Ayr	NR8939	55°36·2'	5°20·5'W	X	68,69
Cnoc a' Choire Bhig	Highld	NR8863	58°32·7'	3°55·0'W	H	10
Cnoc a' Choire Bhuidhe	Highld	NH6095	57°55·6'	4°21·4'W	H	21
Cnoc a' Choire Leacach	Highld	NC5110	58°3·5'	4°31·0'W	H	16
Cnoc a' Choire Mhoir	N Ayr	NR9036	55°34·6'	5°19·5'W	H	68,69
Cnoc a' Chomh-ruith	Highld	NG8021	57°13·9'	5°38·2'W	H	33
Cnoc a' Chomh-stri	Arg & Bt	NM9310	56°14·5'	5°20·0'W	X	55
Cnoc a' Chòrr-bhealach	Arg & Bt	NR4149	55°40·2'	6°6·7'W	X	60
Cnoc a' Chòta	Arg & Bt	NR5387	56°1·0'	5°57·4'W	X	61
Cnoc a' Chraois	Highld	NC4540	58°19·5'	4°38·3'W	H	9
Cnoc a' Chrochair	Arg & Bt	NR7261	55°47·6'	5°37·8'W	X	62
Cnoc a' Chrochaire	Highld	NG3144	57°24·7'	6°28·3'W	H	23
Cnoc a' Chrochaire	Highld	NG4944	57°25·3'	6°10·4'W	X	23
Cnoc a' Chromain	Arg & Bt	NR2058	55°44·3'	6°27·2'W	H	60
Cnoc a Chròm-uillt	Highld	NC7231	58°15·2'	4°10·4'W	H	16
Cnoc a' Chrom-uillt	Highld	NC7328	58°13·6'	4°9·3'W	H	16
Cnoc a' Chrònain	Arg & Bt	NM6223	56°20·6'	5°50·6'W	X	49
Cnoc a' Chrùbaich Bhig	Highld	NC8617	58°7·9'	3°55·7'W	X	17
Cnoc a' Chrùbaich Mhóir	Highld	NC8716	58°7·4'	3°54·6'W	H	17
Cnoc a' Chuail	Highld	NC4352	58°26·0'	4°40·9'W	X	9
Cnoc a' Chùil	Arg & Bt	NR2560	55°45·6'	6°22·6'W	X	60
Cnoc a' Chuirn	Arg & Bt	NR2356	55°43·4'	6°24·2'W	X	60
Cnoc a' Chùirn	Arg & Bt	NR4650	55°40·9'	6°2·0'W	X	60
Cnoc a'Chùirn Mhòir	Arg & Bt	NR6894	56°5·2'	5°43·3'W	H	55,61
Cnoc Adharcain	Arg & Bt	NM9700	56°9·2'	5°15·7'W	H	55
Cnoc a' Fhradhaire	Highld	NG3341	57°23·1'	6°26·1'W	H	23
Cnoc a'Garbh-bhaid Mhóir	Highld	NC2648	58°23·4'	4°58·1'W	H	9
Cnoc a' Garbh-leathaid	Highld	NC7510	58°4·0'	4°6·7'W	H	16
Cnoc a' Ghamhna Chaim	Arg & Bt	NR3368	55°50·1'	6°15·4'W	X	60,61
Cnoc a' Ghaorr'	Highld	NG7786	57°48·7'	5°44·8'W	H	19
Cnoc a' Gharbh-bhaid Beag	Highld	NC2651	58°25·0'	4°58·3'W	X	9
Cnoc a' Gharbh-loch	Highld	ND0346	58°23·8'	3°39·1'W	H	11,12
Cnoc a' Gharbh-uillt	Highld	NG5706	57°5·1'	6°0·2'W	H	32,39
Cnoc a' Gheodha Ruaidh	Highld	NC2467	58°33·6'	5°1·1'W	H	9
Cnoc a' Ghille	Arg & Bt	NM6020	56°19·0'	5°52·4'W	H	49
Cnoc a' Ghille Bhuidhe	Highld	NM7070	56°46·2'	5°45·4'W	X	40
Cnoc a' Ghiubhais	Highld	NC2670	58°35·3'	4°59·1'W	H	9
Cnoc a' Ghiubhais	Highld	NC5423	58°10·6'	4°28·5'W	H	16
Cnoc a' Ghlinnein	Highld	NC1623	58°9·7'	5°7·2'W	H	15
Cnoc a' Ghriama	Highld	NC4026	58°11·9'	4°42·9'W	H	16
Cnoc a' Ghrianain	Highld	NC8311	58°4·6'	3°58·6'W	H	17
Cnoc Airigh Giorsail	Highld	NB9615	58°4·9'	5°27·1'W	X	15
Cnoc Airigh Leathaid	Highld	NC9940	58°20·5'	3°43·0'W	X	11
Cnoc Airigh Luachraich	Arg & Bt	NR7248	55°40·6'	5°37·1'W	H	62
Cnoc Airigh na Meinne	Highld	NC6255	58°28·0'	4°21·5'W	X	10
Cnoc Allt a' Chait	Highld	ND0540	58°20·6'	3°36·9'W	H	11,12
Cnoc Alltan Iain Duinn	Highld	ND1045	58°23·3'	3°31·9'W	X	11,12
Cnoc Allt an Ulbhaidh	Highld	NC4726	58°12·0'	4°35·7'W	H	16
Cnoc Allt na Beithe	Highld	ND0422	58°10·8'	3°37·5'W	H	17
Cnoc Allt na Seilge	Highld	NM8797	57°1·2'	5°30·1'W	H	33,40
Cnoc Amanta	Arg & Bt	NR3558	55°44·8'	6°12·9'W	X	60
Cnoc a' Mhadaidh	Arg & Bt	NR7634	55°33·2'	5°32·7'W	X	68,69
Cnoc a'Mhadaidh	Arg & Bt	NS1683	56°0·5'	4°56·6'W	X	56
Cnoc a' Mhadaidh	Highld	NC3252	58°25·7'	4°52·2'W	H	9
Cnoc a' Mhadaidh	Highld	NH5878	57°46·4'	4°22·8'W	X	21
Cnoc a' Mhadaidh-ruaidh	Highld	NG7325	57°15·8'	5°45·4'W	X	33
Cnoc a' Mhadaih	Arg & Bt	NS1371	55°54·0'	4°59·0'W	X	63
Cnoc a' Mhaoil Ruaidh	Highld	NC4725	58°11·5'	4°35·7'W	H	16
Cnoc a' Mhargadaidh	Highld	NH5567	57°40·4'	4°25·4'W	H	21
Cnoc a' Mheadhoin	Highld	NC9224	58°11·8'	3°49·8'W	H	17
Cnoc a' Mhinisteir	Arg & Bt	NR7647	55°40·1'	5°33·3'W	X	62,69
Cnoc Amhlaigh	N Eil	NB5536	58°14·9'	6°10·1'W	T	8
Cnoc a' Mhóid	Highld	NC5740	58°19·8'	4°26·0'W	H	10
Cnoc a' Mhoil Bhàin	Highld	NC0934	58°15·5'	5°14·9'W	X	15
Cnoc a' Mhoraire	Highld	NH0736	57°22·7'	5°12·2'W	X	25
Cnoc a' Mhuilinn	Highld	NC8855	58°28·4'	3°54·7'W	X	10
Cnocan	Highld	NC6414	58°5·9'	4°18·0'W	X	16
Cnocan	Highld	NC7721	58°9·9'	4°5·0'W	X	17
Cnocan-a-Bealaidh	Highld	NJ0731	57°21·9'	3°32·3'W	X	27,36
Cnocan a' Bhuachaill	Arg & Bt	NR7932	55°32·2'	5°29·7'W	X	68,69
Cnoc an Achaidh Mhóir	Highld	NC5803	57°59·9'	4°23·7'W	H	16
Cnocan a'Chorra	Arg & Bt	NR9766	55°50·9'	5°14·1'W	X	62
Cnoc an Airbhe	Highld	NC5861	58°31·1'	4°25·8'W	X	10
Cnoc an Alaskie	Highld	NC4926	58°12·1'	4°33·7'W	H	16
Cnoc an Alltain Leacaich	Highld	NC5239	58°19·1'	4°31·1'W	H	16
Cnoc an Altan	Arg & Bt	NR7887	56°1·7'	5°33·3'W	H	55
Cnoc an Amais	Arg & Bt	NR8991	56°4·2'	5°23·0'W	H	55
Cnoc an Arbhair	Highld	NC6657	58°29·1'	4°17·4'W	H	10
Cnocan Bhrannabuis	Arg & Bt	NR3347	55°38·8'	6°14·2'W	X	60
Cnocan Biorach	Arg & Bt	NR6214	55°22·0'	5°44·9'W	X	68
Cnocan Biorach	N Ayr	NR9331	55°32·0'	5°16·4'W	X	68,69
Cnocan Buidhe	Arg & Bt	NM5019	56°18·1'	6°2·0'W	X	48
Cnocan Buidhe	Arg & Bt	NM5041	56°29·9'	6°3·3'W	X	47,48
Cnocan Buidhe	Highld	ND2547	58°24·6'	3°16·5'W	X	11,12
Cnocan Burn	N Ayr	NS0038	55°35·9'	5°10·0'W	W	69
Cnocan Chrannchuir	N Ayr	NR9127	55°29·8'	5°18·1'W	X	68,69
Cnocan Conachreag	Highld	ND1136	58°18·5'	3°30·7'W	H	11,17
Cnocan Cuallaich	N Ayr	NR8935	55°34·0'	5°20·4'W	H	68,69
Cnoc an dà Chinn	Arg & Bt	NM4445	56°31·9'	6°9·4'W	H	47,48
Cnoc an Dail Bhric	Highld	NC7216	58°7·1'	4°9·9'W	H	16
Cnoc an Daimh	Arg & Bt	NR7458	55°46·0'	5°35·7'W	H	62
Cnoc an Daimh	Highld	NC2252	58°25·5'	5°2·4'W	H	9
Cnoc an Daimh	Highld	NC2768	58°34·2'	4°58·0'W	H	9
Cnoc an Daimh	Pth & Kin	NO1062	56°44·7'	3°27·8'W	H	43
Cnoc an Daimh Beag	Highld	NC5240	58°19·7'	4°31·2'W	H	10
Cnoc an Daimh Mór	Highld	NC5342	58°20·8'	4°30·2'W	H	10
Cnoc an da Lunnain	Arg & Bt	NM4944	56°31·5'	6°4·4'W	X	47,48
Cnoc an Doire Dharaich	Arg & Bt	NR5877	55°55·8'	5°52·0'W	X	61
Cnocan Donn	N Ayr	NR9124	55°28·2'	5°18·0'W	H	68,69
Cnocan Donna	N Ayr	NR9946	55°40·2'	5°11·3'W	X	62,69
Cnoc an Droighinn	Highld	NC2623	58°10·0'	4°57·0'W	H	15
Cnoc an Droighinn	Highld	NH1488	57°50·8'	5°7·6'W	H	20
Cnoc an Droma Fhada	Highld	NG2848	57°26·7'	6°31·6'W	X	23
Cnocan Dubh	Highld	NH1703	57°5·2'	5°0·7'W	H	34
Cnocan Dubha	Arg & Bt	NM8203	56°10·4'	5°30·3'W	X	55
Cnoc an Dubharlainn	Highld	NC1128	58°12·3'	5°12·5'W	H	15
Cnoc an Dubh Chathair	Highld	NH7178	57°46·7'	4°9·7'W	X	21
Cnoc an Dubh-locha	Highld	NC5560	58°30·5'	4°28·8'W	H	10
Cnoc an Duin	Highld	NH6976	57°45·5'	4°11·6'W	X	21
Cnoc an Dùin	Pth & Kin	NO0362	56°44·6'	3°34·7'W	H	43
Cnoc an Duin (Fort)	Highld	NH6976	57°45·5'	4°11·6'W	A	21
Cnoc an Earrannaiche	Highld	ND2441	58°21·3'	3°17·4'W	H	11,12
Cnoc an Eich	Highld	ND0544	58°22·7'	3°37·0'W	X	11,12
Cnoc an Eireannaich	Highld	NC9527	58°13·4'	3°46·8'W	H	17
Cnoc an Eisg-brachaidh	Highld	NC0718	58°6·8'	5°16·1'W	H	15
Cnoc an Fheidh	N Ayr	NS0125	55°29·0'	5°8·5'W	H	69
Cnoc an Fheòir	Highld	NC4923	58°10·5'	4°33·6'W	H	16
Cnoc an Fheòir Mhaol	Highld	NC4924	58°11·0'	4°33·6'W	H	16
Cnoc an Fhionn	Arg & Bt	NR8562	55°48·5'	5°25·4'W	X	62
Cnoc an Fhir Bhreige	Highld	NC1441	58°19·4'	5°10·1'W	H	9
Cnoc an Fhir Bhreige	Highld	NC1750	58°24·3'	5°7·4'W	H	9
Cnoc an Fhir Mhóir	Arg & Bt	NR6189	56°2·3'	5°49·8'W	X	61
Cnoc an Fhithich	Arg & Bt	NL9445	56°30·1'	6°58·0'W	H	46
Cnoc an Fhithich	Arg & Bt	NR9874	55°55·3'	5°13·5'W	X	62
Cnoc an Fhithich	Highld	NM7170	56°46·2'	5°44·4'W	X	40
Cnoc an Fhithich	N Eil	NF6504	57°0·6'	7°30·7'W	H	31
Cnoc an Fhithich	Pth & Kin	NN7156	56°40·9'	4°5·9'W	H	42,51,52
Cnoc an Fhluichaidh	Highld	NG4252	57°29·4'	6°17·9'W	X	23
Cnoc an Fhraoich	Highld	NC9858	58°30·2'	3°44·5'W	X	11
Cnoc an Fhraoich Shùgain	Arg & Bt	NR2671	55°51·5'	6°22·3'W	X	60
Cnoc an Fhreacadain	Arg & Bt	NR7565	55°49·8'	5°35·1'W	X	62
Cnoc an Fhreacadain	Arg & Bt	NR8565	55°50·1'	5°25·6'W	X	62
Cnoc an Fhreiceadain	Highld	NC3259	58°29·5'	4°52·5'W	X	9
Cnoc an Fhreiceadain	Highld	NC6159	58°30·1'	4°22·6'W	H	10
Cnoc an Fhreiceadain	Highld	NC8853	58°27·3'	3°54·7'W	H	10
Cnoc an Fhuarain	Highld	NG7471	57°40·6'	5°47·0'W	H	19
Cnoc an Fhuarain Bhàin	Highld	NC3126	58°11·7'	4°52·0'W	H	15
Cnoc an Fhuarain Bhàin	Highld	NC9553	58°27·4'	3°47·5'W	H	11
Cnocan Gean	Arg & Bt	NR6828	55°29·7'	5°39·9'W	X	68
Cnoc an Ime	Arg & Bt	NR5880	55°57·4'	5°52·2'W	X	61
Cnocan Imheir	Arg & Bt	NR7264	55°49·2'	5°37·9'W	X	62
Cnoc an Laoigh	Arg & Bt	NM8415	56°17·0'	5°28·9'W	X	55
Cnoc an Laoigh	Arg & Bt	NM8515	56°17·0'	5°28·0'W	H	55
Cnoc an Laoigh	Highld	NC4720	58°8·8'	4°35·5'W	H	16
Cnoc an Leathaid Bhig	Highld	NC2214	58°5·0'	5°0·7'W	H	15
Cnoc an Leathaid Bhuidhe	Highld	NC2315	58°5·6'	4°59·7'W	H	15
Cnoc an Leòid	Highld	NH5971	57°42·7'	4°21·5'W	H	21
Cnoc an Leòthaid	Highld	NC1423	58°9·7'	5°9·2'W	H	15
Cnoc an Leòthaid Bhuidhe	Highld	NC1823	58°9·8'	5°5·2'W	H	15
Cnoc an Liath-bhaid	Highld	NC7310	58°3·9'	4°8·7'W	H	16
Cnoc an Liath-bhaid	Highld	NH6385	57°50·3'	4°18·0'W	X	21
Cnoc an Liath-bhaid Mhóir	Highld	NC7529	58°14·2'	4°7·3'W	H	16
Cnocan Lin	Arg & Bt	NR6710	55°20·0'	5°40·0'W	X	68
Cnoc an Lochain	Arg & Bt	NR8663	55°49·0'	5°24·5'W	X	62
Cnoc an Lochain-dèabhaidh	Highld	NB9816	58°5·5'	5°25·1'W	H	15
Cnoc an Lochain Duibh	Highld	NC2748	58°23·4'	4°57·1'W	X	9
Cnoc an Lùib Bhig	Highld	NC7419	58°8·8'	4°8·0'W	H	16
Cnoc an Luig Mhóir	N Eil	NB3203	57°56·4'	6°31·2'W	H	13,14
Cnocan Mealbhain	Highld	NH8183	57°49·5'	3°59·8'W	X	21
Cnocan na Caillich	N Ayr	NR9726	55°29·4'	5°12·4'W	X	69
Cnocan na Circe	Arg & Bt	NM6925	56°21·9'	5°44·0'W	X	49
Cnocan nan Sgitheag	Highld	NM5653	56°36·6'	5°58·1'W	X	47
Cnoc an Oir	Arg & Bt	NR5075	55°54·4'	5°59·6'W	X	61
Cnocan Ruar	Highld	ND1240	58°20·6'	3°29·7'W	H	11,12
Cnoc an Rubha	Highld	NC2054	58°26·5'	5°4·6'W	H	9
Cnoc an Ruffer	Highld	NC8563	58°32·7'	3°58·1'W	X	10
Cnocan Ruigh Ruaidh	Highld	NH5986	57°50·7'	4°22·1'W	X	21
Cnocan Sgeir'e	Arg & Bt	NS0285	56°1·3'	5°10·2'W	H	55
Cnoc an Sgolaidh	Arg & Bt	NR8066	55°50·5'	5°30·4'W	X	62
Cnoc an Sgùmain	Highld	NG6104	57°4·2'	5°56·1'W	H	32
Cnoc an Sgùmain	N Eil	NG0787	57°46·9'	6°55·3'W	X	14,18
Cnoc an Staca	Highld	NC1861	58°30·2'	5°6·9'W	H	9
Cnoc an Teampuill	Highld	NH5863	57°38·3'	4°22·3'W	A	21
Cnoc an Teine	Arg & Bt	NM5547	56°33·3'	5°58·8'W	X	47,48
Cnoc an Teine	Arg & Bt	NM6541	56°30·4'	5°48·7'W	H	49
Cnoc an Teine	Highld	NG3622	57°13·0'	6°21·9'W	X	32
Cnoc an Tighe	Arg & Bt	NR3767	55°49·7'	6°11·3'W	X	60,61
Cnoc an Tigh Odhair	Arg & Bt	NR8266	55°50·5'	5°28·5'W	H	62
Cnoc an Tigh-sgoile	Arg & Bt	NR2255	55°42·8'	6°25·1'W	X	60
Cnoc an Tiumpain	Highld	NH7808	57°9·1'	4°0·5'W	H	35
Cnoc an Tobair	Arg & Bt	NR8562	55°48·5'	5°25·4'W	X	62
Cnoc an Tobair	Highld	NG2756	57°31·0'	6°33·1'W	X	23

Cnoc an Torra Mhóir	Highld	NC7710	58°4·0′	4°4·6′W	H	17
Cnoc an Tosgaire	Highld	NC3504	57°59·9′	4°47·0′W	H	15
Cnoc an Tota	Arg & Bt	NM5144	56°31·6′	6°2·5′W	X	47,48
Cnoc an t-Sabhail	Arg & Bt	NR8557	55°45·8′	5°25·2′W	X	62
Cnoc an t-Sabhail	Highld	NC4644	58°21·7′	4°37·5′W	X	9
Cnoc an t-Sabhail	Highld	NC5233	58°15·9′	4°30·9′W	H	16
Cnoc an t-Sabhail	Highld	NH6978	57°46·6′	4°11·7′W	H	21
Cnoc an t-Sabhail	Highld	NH7281	57°48·3′	4°8·8′W	H	21
Cnoc an t-Saic	Highld	NH3398	57°56·7′	4°48·8′W	H	20
Cnoc an t-Samhlaidh	Arg & Bt	NR3369	55°50·7′	6°15·5′W	H	60,61
Cnoc an t-Samhlaidh	Arg & Bt	NR3973	55°53·0′	6°10·0′W	X	60,61
Cnoc an t-Samhlaidh	Arg & Bt	NR7287	56°1·6′	5°39·1′W	H	55
Cnoc an t-Samhlaidh	Arg & Bt	NR7949	55°41·3′	5°30·5′W	H	62,69
Cnoc an t- Sasunnaich	Highld	NC1908	58°1·7′	5°3·4′W	H	15
Cnoc an t-Seabhaig	N Ayr	NR9527	55°29·9′	5°14·3′W	X	68,69
Cnoc an t-Seallaidh Bhig	Arg & Bt	NR8254	55°44·1′	5°27·9′W	H	62
Cnoc an t-Searraich	Highld	ND1236	58°18·5′	3°29·6′W	X	11,17
Cnoc an t-Seilich	Arg & Bt	NR7339	55°35·8′	5°35·7′W	H	68
Cnoc an t-Sìdhean Beag	Highld	NH6076	57°45·4′	4°20·7′W	X	21
Cnoc an t-Sidhean Mór	Highld	NH5977	57°45·9′	4°21·7′W	H	21
Cnoc an t-Sìdhein	Highld	NH1553	57°32·0′	5°5·0′W	H	25
Cnoc an t-Sìthein	Highld	NC7526	58°12·6′	4°7·2′W	H	16
Cnoc an t-Sìthein	Highld	NG3621	57°12·5′	6°21·9′W	X	32
Cnoc an t-Sìthein	Highld	NG3932	57°18·5′	6°19·6′W	H	32
Cnoc an t-Sìthein	Highld	NG4931	57°18·3′	6°9·6′W	X	32
Cnoc an t-Sléibh	Arg & Bt	NR4169	55°50·9′	6°7·8′W	X	60,61
Cnoc an t-Socaich	Highld	NC7709	58°3·4′	4°4·6′W	H	17
Cnoc an t-Solais	N Eil	NB4740	58°16·8′	6°18·5′W	T	8
Cnoc an t-Srathaidh	Highld	NH6376	57°45·4′	4°17·7′W	H	21
Cnoc an t-Suidhe	Arg & Bt	NM3120	56°18·0′	6°20·5′W	X	48
Cnoc an t-Suidhe	Arg & Bt	NM3622	56°19·3′	6°15·7′W	H	48
Cnoc an t-Suidhe	Arg & Bt	NR8858	55°46·4′	5°22·4′W	X	62
Cnoc an Tubait	Highld	NH3293	57°54·0′	4°49·6′W	H	20
Cnoc an Tubhadair	Highld	ND0518	58°8·7′	3°36·4′W	X	17
Cnoc an Uillt Tharsuinn	Highld	NC5063	58°32·0′	4°34·1′W	H	9
Cnoc an Ulbhaidh	Highld	NC4822	58°9·9′	4°34·6′W	H	16
Cnoc a' Phollain Bheithe	Highld	NC0932	58°14·4′	5°14·8′W	H	15
Cnoc à Phrop	Arg & Bt	NR7573	55°54·1′	5°35·5′W	H	62
Cnoc Ard	Arg & Bt	NR3245	55°37·7′	6°15·0′W	X	60
Cnoc Ard	N Eil	NB5364	58°29·9′	6°13·9′W	T	8
Cnoc Ard an Tionail	Highld	NC7507	58°2·3′	4°6·6′W	H	16
Cnoc Ard an t-Siùil	Highld	NC4967	58°34·2′	4°35·3′W	H	9
Cnoc Ascaig	Highld	NC8623	58°11·1′	3°55·9′W	X	17
Cnoc a' Sga	Highld	NG3140	57°22·5′	6°28·0′W	H	23
Cnoc Bad-a-bhacaidh	Highld	NH6187	57°51·3′	4°20·1′W	X	21
Cnoc Bad a' Bhainne	Highld	NC1024	58°10·1′	5°13·3′W	H	15
Cnoc Bad a' Choille	Highld	NH3499	57°57·2′	4°47·8′W	H	20
Cnoc Bad a' Chrasgaidh	Highld	NC7502	57°59·6′	4°6·4′W	H	16
Cnoc Bad a' Ghille Dhuibh	Highld	NC7936	58°18·0′	4°3·4′W	H	17
Cnoc Badaireach na Gaoithe	Highld	NC8451	58°26·2′	3°58·7′W	H	10
Cnoc Bad an Amair	Highld	NC8543	58°21·9′	3°57·5′W	H	10
Cnoc Badan Eachainn	Highld	NC5535	58°17·1′	4°27·9′W	H	16
Cnoc Bad an Leathaid	Highld	NC7035	58°17·3′	4°12·6′W	H	16
Cnoc Bad an t-Slamain	Highld	NC7835	58°17·5′	4°4·4′W	H	17
Cnoc Bad Asgaraidh	Highld	ND0822	58°10·9′	3°33·4′W	H	17
Cnoc Bad Cholla	Highld	ND0635	58°17·9′	3°35·7′W	X	11,17
Cnoc Bad Mhairtein	Highld	NC9355	58°28·5′	3°49·6′W	H	11
Cnoc Bad na Caorach	Highld	ND1049	58°25·5′	3°32·0′W	H	11,12
Cnoc Bad na Coille	Highld	NC5336	58°17·5′	4°30·0′W	H	16
Cnoc Bad na Conaire	Highld	NC1125	58°10·7′	5°12·4′W	X	15
Cnoc Bad na Fainne	Highld	NC7135	58°17·3′	4°11·5′W	H	16
Cnoc Bad na Gallaig	Highld	NC6241	58°20·4′	4°21·0′W	H	10
Cnoc Bad na h-Achlaise	Highld	NC2411	58°3·5′	4°58·5′W	H	15
Cnoc Bad na h- Achlaise	Highld	NC2444	58°21·2′	5°0·0′W	H	9
Cnoc Bad na h-Eirig	Highld	NC8826	58°12·8′	3°53·9′W	H	17
Cnoc Bad na h-Eirig	Highld	NC8826	58°12·8′	3°53·9′W	X	17
Cnoc Bad nan Cuilleag	Highld	NG9488	57°50·3′	5°27·8′W	H	19
Cnoc Bad On T-Slamain	Highld	NC7835	58°17·5′	4°4·4′W	X	17
Cnoc Balavreed	Highld	ND1042	58°21·7′	3°31·8′W	H	11,12
Cnoc Ballygown	N Ayr	NR9229	55°30·9′	5°17·2′W	H	68,69
Cnoc Bàn	Highld	NG7507	57°6·2′	5°42·5′W	H	33
Cnoc Bàn	Highld	NM7166	56°44·0′	5°44·2′W	X	40
Cnoc Bann nan Sgàilein	Arg & Bt	NR4655	55°43·6′	6°2·3′W	X	60
Cnocbarbh	Highld	NC1859	58°29·1′	5°6·8′W	X	9
Cnoc Beag	Highld	NG2647	57°26·1′	6°33·5′W	H	23
Cnoc Beag	Highld	NH8115	57°12·9′	3°57·8′W	X	35
Cnoc Beag Milleho	N Eil	NB4237	58°15·0′	6°23·4′W	X	8
Cnoc Bealach nan Cas	Highld	NG6612	57°8·6′	5°51·6′W	H	32
Cnoc Bealach Sithe	Arg & Bt	NR7262	55°48·1′	5°37·8′W	X	62
Cnoc Beinn na Lice	Highld	NH4649	57°30·6′	4°33·8′W	X	26
Cnoc Beithe	Pth & Kin	NN8626	56°25·0′	3°50·4′W	H	52,58
Cnoc Beul na Faire	Highld	ND0147	58°24·3′	3°41·2′W	H	11,12
Cnoc Bharr	N Eil	NF6162	57°31·5′	7°39·4′W	X	22
Cnoc Bhi-bùirn	Arg & Bt	NR1653	55°41·5′	6°30·7′W	X	60
Cnoc Bhiosta	Arg & Bt	NL9746	56°30·8′	6°55·1′W	H	46
Cnoc Bhirceapol	Arg & Bt	NL9644	56°29·7′	6°55·9′W	H	46
Cnoc Biodaig	Highld	NH0417	57°12·4′	5°14·2′W	X	33
Cnoc Biorach	Arg & Bt	NM8026	56°22·8′	5°33·4′W	H	49
Cnoc Biorach	Arg & Bt	NR7589	56°2·7′	5°36·3′W	H	55
Cnoc Biorach	N Eil	NG1293	57°50·3′	6°50·7′W	H	14
Cnoc Blàrach	Highld	NC7820	58°9·4′	4°3·9′W	H	17
Cnoc Blàr an Dubhaidh	Highld	NC7211	58°4·4′	4°9·7′W	H	16
Cnoc Brannan	Pth & Kin	NN7215	56°18·9′	4°3·7′W	H	57
Cnoc Braonach	Highld	NC0823	58°9·5′	5°15·3′W	H	15
Cnoc Breac	Arg & Bt	NM3846	56°32·2′	6°15·3′W	X	47,48
Cnoc Breac	Arg & Bt	NR1857	55°43·7′	6°29·1′W	H	60
Cnoc Breac	Arg & Bt	NR2562	55°46·6′	6°22·7′W	X	60
Cnoc Breac	Arg & Bt	NR3268	55°50·1′	6°16·4′W	X	60,61
Cnocbreac	Arg & Bt	NR4473	55°53·2′	6°5·2′W	T	60,61
Cnoc Breac	Arg & Bt	NR7837	55°34·8′	5°30·9′W	X	68,69
Cnoc Breac	Arg & Bt	NR8663	55°49·0′	5°24·5′W	X	62
Cnoc Breac	Arg & Bt	NR8767	55°51·2′	5°23·7′W	X	62
Cnoc Breac	Highld	NC1115	58°5·3′	5°11·9′W	H	15
Cnoc Breac	Highld	NC2111	58°3·4′	5°1·5′W	H	15
Cnoc Breac	Highld	ND1633	58°16·9′	3°25·5′W	H	11
Cnoc Breac	Highld	NG2858	57°32·1′	6°32·2′W	H	23
Cnoc Breac	Highld	NG6912	57°8·7′	5°48·7′W	X	32
Cnoc Breac	Highld	NG7884	57°47·7′	5°43·7′W	H	19

Cnoc Breac	Highld	NH1297	57°55·6′	5°10·0′W	H	19
Cnoc Breac	Highld	NH5997	57°56·7′	4°22·5′W	X	21
Cnoc Breac	Highld	NM5661	56°40·9′	5°58·6′W	X	47
Cnoc Breac	N Ayr	NR9240	55°36·8′	5°17·7′W	X	62,69
Cnoc Breac	N Ayr	NR9739	55°36·4′	5°12·9′W	X	69
Cnoc Breac	N Ayr	NR9832	55°32·7′	5°11·7′W	X	69
Cnoc Breac Beag	N Eil	NB0314	58°1·2′	7°1·3′W	H	13
Cnoc Breac Gamhainn	N Ayr	NR9242	55°37·9′	5°17·8′W	X	62,69
Cnoc Breamanach	Arg & Bt	NS0377	55°57·0′	5°8·9′W	H	63
Cnoc Buidhe	Arg & Bt	NR6930	55°30·8′	5°39·1′W	H	68
Cnoc Buidhe	Arg & Bt	NR8866	55°50·7′	5°22·7′W	X	62
Cnoc Buidhe	Arg & Bt	NR9495	56°6·5′	5°18·3′W	H	55
Cnoc Buidhe	Arg & Bt	NR9687	56°2·2′	5°16·0′W	X	55
Cnoc Buidhe	Arg & Bt	NR9790	56°3·8′	5°15·2′W	H	55
Cnoc Camquhart	Arg & Bt	NR9884	56°0·6′	5°14·0′W	X	55
Cnoc Caol	Highld	NC7422	58°10·4′	4°8·1′W	X	16
Cnoc Caoruinn	Highld	NC7020	58°9·3′	4°12·1′W	H	16
Cnoc Cappullach	Arg & Bt	NM5153	56°36·4′	6°3·0′W	X	47
Cnoc Carach	Highld	NM6547	56°33·6′	5°49·0′W	H	49
Cnoc Carn a Bhodaich	Highld	NC2152	58°25·5′	5°3·4′W	X	9
Cnoc Càrnach	Highld	NG6519	57°12·4′	5°53·0′W	H	32
Cnoc Carnachadh	Highld	NC7152	58°26·5′	4°12·1′W	H	10
Cnoc Càrn an Léim	Highld	NC3272	58°36·5′	4°53·0′W	X	9
Cnoc Carrach	Arg & Bt	NM5427	56°22·5′	5°58·6′W	X	48
Cnoc Carrach	Arg & Bt	NM6038	56°28·6′	5°53·4′W	X	49
Cnoc Carrach	Arg & Bt	NM6828	56°23·5′	5°45·1′W	X	49
Cnoc Ceann nam Bad	Highld	NC5500	57°58·2′	4°26·6′W	H	16
Cnoc Ceann Tamhuis	Arg & Bt	NR9160	55°47·5′	5°19·6′W	X	62
Cnoc Céislein	Highld	NH5870	57°42·1′	4°22·5′W	H	21
Cnoc Chalbha	Highld	NC1838	58°17·8′	5°5·9′W	H	15
Cnoc Challtuinn	Arg & Bt	NM6831	56°25·1′	5°45·3′W	X	49
Cnoc Chalmac	Aberd	NJ2600	57°5·4′	3°12·8′W	H	37
Cnoc Cháluim Mhoir	Arg & Bt	NR1953	55°41·6′	6°27·9′W	H	60
Cnoc Chaornaidh	Highld	NC3008	58°2·0′	4°52·3′W	H	15
Cnoc Chaorunn Bheag	Highld	NC9629	58°14·5′	3°45·8′W	X	11,17
Cnoc Chlarsair	Highld	NG8030	57°18·7′	5°38·7′W	X	24
Cnoc Choisprig	Arg & Bt	NR1959	55°44·8′	6°28·2′W	H	60
Cnoc Cille Pheadair	Highld	NC7812	58°5·1′	4°3·7′W	H	17
Cnoc Clach-na-ciste	Arg & Bt	NM4640	56°29·3′	6°7·1′W	X	47,48
Cnoc Clauchog	N Ayr	NR9625	55°28·8′	5°13·3′W	X	68,69
Cnoc Coinnich	Arg & Bt	NN2300	56°9·8′	4°50·6′W	H	56
Cnoc Coir' an Eoin	Highld	NC8214	58°6·2′	3°59·7′W	X	17
Cnoc Coir' á Phuill	Highld	ND0420	58°9·8′	3°37·4′W	H	17
Cnoc Coire a' Bhaic	Highld	NC2429	58°13·1′	4°59·3′W	H	15
Cnoc Coire na Feàrna	Highld	NC9329	58°14·5′	3°48·9′W	H	11,17
Cnoc Corr	Arg & Bt	NR4299	56°7·1′	6°8·6′W	X	61
Cnoc Corr Guinie	Highld	NH6775	57°45·0′	4°13·6′W	H	21
Cnoc Cracail	Highld	NC6201	57°58·9′	4°19·6′W	H	16
Cnoc Cragaidh	Highld	NC8610	58°4·1′	3°55·5′W	H	17
Cnoc Craggie	Highld	NC6052	58°26·3′	4°23·4′W	H	10
Cnoc Craggie	Highld	NC8919	58°9·0′	3°52·7′W	H	17
Cnoc Craobhach	N Ayr	NS0023	55°27·9′	5°9·4′W	H	69
Cnoc Creach	Arg & Bt	NM8302	56°9·9′	5°29·3′W	H	55
Cnoc Creagach	Arg & Bt	NR8455	55°44·7′	5°26·0′W	X	62
Cnoc Creagach	Highld	NM4685	56°53·5′	6°9·8′W	X	39
Cnoc Creagain	Arg & Bt	NR8556	55°45·2′	5°25·1′W	X	62
Cnoc Crò a' Mhàil	Arg & Bt	NR3659	55°45·4′	6°12·0′W	H	60
Cnoc Croin-bhaid	Highld	NH5291	57°53·3′	4°29·3′W	X	20
Cnoc Croit na Macile	Highld	NH4949	57°30·6′	4°30·8′W	H	26
Cnoc Cròm-uillt	Highld	NC9439	58°19·9′	3°48·1′W	H	11,17
Cnoc Cruinn	Arg & Bt	NR9089	56°3·1′	5°21·9′W	H	55
Cnoc Cruinn	N Eil	NB0724	58°6·7′	6°58·0′W	H	13,14
Cnoc Crun na Maoil	Arg & Bt	NR4148	55°39·6′	6°6·6′W	H	60
Cnoc Cuidhein	N Eil	NF8459	57°30·9′	7°16·2′W	X	22
Cnoc Cùl nan Uamh	Arg & Bt	NM8317	56°18·0′	5°30·0′W	H	55
Cnoc Dail a' Bhàthaidh	Highld	NC8009	58°3·5′	4°1·5′W	X	17
Cnoc Dail a' Thuraich	Highld	NC6439	58°19·4′	4°18·8′W	X	16
Cnoc Dail-chairn	Highld	NC8528	58°13·8′	3°57·0′W	H	17
Cnoc Daimh	Highld	NC0928	58°12·2′	5°14·6′W	H	15
Cnoc Daimh	Highld	NH0053	57°31·6′	5°20·0′W	H	25
Cnoc Dalveghouse	Highld	NC7155	58°28·1′	4°12·2′W	H	10
Cnoc Damh	Arg & Bt	NM6541	56°30·4′	5°48·7′W	X	49
Cnoc Damh	Highld	NH2796	57°55·5′	4°54·8′W	H	20
Cnoc Deuchainn	Arg & Bt	NM4730	56°23·9′	6°5·6′W	X	48
Cnoc Deuchainneach	Arg & Bt	NM3423	56°19·7′	6°17·7′W	H	48
Cnoc Dhiarmaid	Arg & Bt	NR3768	55°50·3′	6°11·6′W	X	60,61
Cnoc Dhomhnuill	Arg & Bt	NM7413	56°15·6′	5°38·5′W	H	55
Cnoc Donn	Arg & Bt	NR3358	55°44·8′	6°14·8′W	H	60
Cnoc Donn	Arg & Bt	NR3761	55°46·5′	6°11·2′W	H	60
Cnoc Donn	Arg & Bt	NR7452	55°42·8′	5°35·4′W	H	62
Cnoc Donn	Arg & Bt	NR7537	55°34·7′	5°33·7′W	H	68,69
Cnoc Donn	Arg & Bt	NR8044	55°38·6′	5°29·3′W	X	62,69
Cnoc Donn	N Ayr	NR8739	55°36·1′	5°22·4′W	X	68,69
Cnoc Donn	N Ayr	NR9925	55°28·9′	5°10·4′W	X	69
Cnoc Donn Mór	Arg & Bt	NR3264	55°48·0′	6°16·1′W	X	60,61
Cnoc Dronnach	Arg & Bt	NR4247	55°39·1′	6°5·6′W	X	60
Cnoc Druidean	Arg & Bt	NM2723	56°19·5′	6°24·5′W	X	48
Cnoc Duaig	Highld	NH6274	57°44·3′	4°18·6′W	X	21
Cnoc Dùail	Highld	NC3351	58°25·2′	4°51·1′W	H	9
Cnoc Dubh	Aberd	NO4299	57°5·0′	2°57·0′W	H	37,44
Cnoc Dubh	Arg & Bt	NM3420	56°18·1′	6°17·6′W	X	48
Cnoc Dubh	Arg & Bt	NR1852	55°41·0′	6°28·8′W	X	60
Cnoc Dubh	Arg & Bt	NR2362	55°46·6′	6°24·6′W	H	60
Cnoc Dubh	Arg & Bt	NR4175	55°54·2′	6°8·2′W	X	60,61
Cnoc Dubh	Arg & Bt	NR4456	55°44·0′	6°4·2′W	X	60
Cnoc Dubh	Arg & Bt	NR7482	55°58·9′	5°36·9′W	X	55
Cnoc Dubh	Arg & Bt	NR7678	55°56·8′	5°34·8′W	X	62
Cnoc Dubh	Arg & Bt	NR8045	55°39·2′	5°29·4′W	X	62,69
Cnoc Dubh	Arg & Bt	NR8249	55°41·4′	5°27·7′W	X	62,69
Cnoc Dubh	Arg & Bt	NR8555	55°44·7′	5°25·1′W	X	62
Cnoc Dubh	Arg & Bt	NR9676	55°56·3′	5°15·5′W	X	62
Cnoc Dubh	Highld	NC5443	58°21·3′	4°29·2′W	X	10
Cnoc Dubh	Highld	NC5462	58°31·6′	4°30·0′W	H	10
Cnoc Dubh	Highld	NC5637	58°18·1′	4°27·0′W	X	16
Cnoc Dubh	Highld	NC7106	58°1·7′	4°10·6′W	H	16
Cnoc Dubh	Highld	NC8526	58°12·7′	3°57·0′W	X	17
Cnoc Dubh	Highld	ND1839	58°20·2′	3°23·6′W	H	11,12
Cnoc Dubh	Highld	NH4358	57°35·3′	4°37·1′W	H	26
Cnoc Dubh	Moray	NJ2117	57°14·5′	3°18·1′W	X	36
Cnoc Dubh	N Ayr	NR9735	55°34·2′	5°12·8′W	X	69

Cnoc Dubh	N Ayr	NR9928	55°30·5′	5°10·6′W	H	69
Cnoc Dubh	N Ayr	NS0032	55°32·7′	5°9·8′W	X	69
Cnoc Dubh	N Eil	NB4339	58°16·1′	6°22·5′W	X	8
Cnoc Dubhaidh	Highld	NC4252	58°25·9′	4°41·9′W	H	9
Cnoc Dubh an Locha	Arg & Bt	NR7867	55°51·0′	5°32·4′W	X	62
Cnoc Dubh Beag	Highld	NH6792	57°54·1′	4°14·2′W	H	21
Cnoc Dubh Heilla	Highld	NG3533	57°18·9′	6°23·6′W	H	32
Cnoc Duchaire	Highld	NH6171	57°42·7′	4°19·5′W	H	21
Cnoc Dùin	Highld	ND1128	58°14·2′	3°30·5′W	X	17
Cnoc Eachain	Highld	NC7919	58°8·9′	4°2·9′W	X	17
Cnoc Eadar Dà Beinn	N Eil	NB1402	57°55·2′	6°49·3′W	H	14
Cnoc Eadar-mi	Highld	NC5301	57°58·7′	4°28·7′W	X	16
Cnoc Eilig	Highld	NC5561	58°31·0′	4°28·9′W	H	10
Cnoc Eille Mór	Highld	NH4547	57°29·5′	4°34·7′W	H	26
Cnoc Eipteil	Highld	NC8662	58°32·1′	3°57·0′W	H	10
Cnoc Eirionnaich	Pth & Kin	NO1157	56°42·0′	3°26·8′W	H	53
Cnoc Eoghainn	Arg & Bt	NR7135	55°33·6′	5°37·4′W	H	68
Cnoc Eòghainn	Pth & Kin	NN5554	56°39·6′	4°21·5′W	H	42,51
Cnoc Fada	Arg & Bt	NR2565	55°48·3′	6°22·9′W	X	60
Cnoc Fada	Highld	NH1220	57°14·2′	5°6·4′W	X	25
Cnoc Fadail	Highld	NG3760	57°33·5′	6°23·4′W	H	23
Cnoc Fall	Highld	NG6205	57°4·7′	5°55·2′W	X	32
Cnoc Feannaig	Highld	NM6677	56°49·8′	5°49·7′W	X	40
Cnoc Féith na Fola	Highld	NC8229	58°14·3′	4°0·1′W	H	17
Cnoc Fergan	Moray	NJ1323	57°17·6′	3°26·2′W	H	36
Cnoc Fhionn	Highld	NG8719	57°13·0′	5°31·2′W	X	33
Cnoc Fhoirnigial	Arg & Bt	NL9845	56°30·3′	6°54·1′W	H	46
Cnoc Fodha	Highld	NC6609	58°3·3′	4°15·8′W	X	16
Cnoc Fraing	Highld	NH8014	57°12·3′	3°58·7′W	H	35
Cnoc Fraorach	Arg & Bt	NS1692	56°5·4′	4°57·0′W	X	56
Cnoc Fuar	Highld	NG1740	57°22·0′	6°42·0′W	H	23
Cnoc Fuarain	Highld	ND1134	58°17·4′	3°30·6′W	H	11,17
Cnoc Fyrish	Highld	NH6069	57°41·6′	4°20·5′W	H	21
Cnoc Gaineimh	Highld	NC9233	58°16·6′	3°50·0′W	X	11,17
Cnoc Garbh	Highld	NC1859	58°29·1′	5°6·8′W	H	9
Cnoc Garbh	Highld	NC2135	58°16·3′	5°2·6′W	X	15
Cnoc Garbh a' Mhill	Arg & Bt	NR2055	55°42·7′	6°27·0′W	H	60
Cnoc Garbh Beag	Highld	NC7321	58°9·8′	4°9·0′W	H	16
Cnoc Garbh-leathaid	Highld	NC9636	58°18·3′	3°46·0′W	X	11,17
Cnoc Geumasgairbhe	N Eil	NG1191	57°49·2′	6°51·6′W	H	14
Cnoc Ghual	Highld	NC8349	58°25·1′	3°59·7′W	H	10
Cnoc Gille Mo Bhrianaig	Highld	NH5671	57°42·6′	4°24·6′W	H	21
Cnoc Glac na Luachrach	Highld	NG6921	57°13·6′	5°49·2′W	H	32
Cnoc Gias	Arg & Bt	NR8379	55°57·6′	5°28·1′W	X	62
Cnoc Glas	Arg & Bt	NR8867	55°51·2′	5°22·8′W	X	62
Cnoc-glas	Highld	ND0452	58°27·0′	3°38·2′W	X	11,12
Cnoc Glas	Highld	NG8945	57°27·0′	5°30·5′W	X	24
Cnoc Glas	N Eil	NA0601	57°49·7′	8°38·0′W	H	18
Cnoc Glas Heilla	Highld	NG3434	57°19·4′	6°24·7′W	H	32
Cnoc Glas na Crionaiche	Highld	NC3919	58°8·1′	4°43·6′W	H	16
Cnocglas Water	Highld	ND0452	58°27·0′	3°38·2′W	W	11,12
Cnoc Gleannain	Highld	ND0333	58°16·8′	3°38·8′W	X	11,17
Cnoc Gorm	Highld	NG7708	57°6·8′	5°40·5′W	X	33
Cnoc Gorm	Highld	NG8844	57°26·5′	5°31·5′W	X	24
Cnoc Gorm	Highld	NM8788	56°56·3′	5°29·6′W	H	40
Cnoc Gorm Mór	Highld	NC2053	58°26·0′	5°4·5′W	H	9
Cnoc Grianail	Arg & Bt	NR3352	55°41·5′	6°14·5′W	X	60
Cnoc Heara	Highld	ND1731	58°15·9′	3°24·4′W	X	11
Cnoc Iaruinn	Arg & Bt	NR8047	55°40·3′	5°29·5′W	X	62,69
Cnoc Ibrig	Arg & Bt	NM0244	56°29·9′	6°50·1′W	H	46
Cnoc Iseabail	Highld	NG8791	57°51·7′	5°35·0′W	X	19
Cnoc Laoighscan	Arg & Bt	NR7850	55°41·8′	5°31·5′W	X	62,69
Cnoc Leacach	Highld	NC4211	58°3·9′	4°40·2′W	X	16
Cnoc Leac a' Ghille	Highld	NC6536	58°17·8′	4°17·7′W	X	16
Cnoc Leacainn Duibhe	N Ayr	NR9149	55°41·6′	5°19·1′W	X	62,69
Cnoc Leamhnachd	Highld	NC7511	58°4·5′	4°6·7′W	H	16
Cnoc Lean na Meine	N Ayr	NR9726	55°29·4′	5°12·4′W	X	69
Cnoc Leathad na Siorramachd	Highld	NH5981	57°48·1′	4°21·9′W	X	21
Cnoc Leathan	Arg & Bt	NM4254	56°36·7′	6°11·8′W	H	47
Cnoc Leathan	Highld	NC2550	58°24·5′	4°59·2′W	H	9
Cnoc Leathan	Highld	NG4417	57°10·6′	6°13·7′W	H	32
Cnoc Leathan	N Eil	NB1405	57°56·8′	6°49·6′W	X	13,14
Cnoc Leathann	Highld	NC3963	58°31·8′	4°45·4′W	X	9
Cnoc Leinish	Highld	NG2050	57°27·5′	6°39·7′W	X	23
Cnoc Liath	Arg & Bt	NR3067	55°49·5′	6°18·2′W	X	60
Cnoc Liath	Highld	NC2851	58°25·1′	4°56·2′W	H	9
Cnoc Liath	Highld	ND0136	58°18·4′	3°40·9′W	H	11,17
Cnoc Liath	Highld	NH3014	57°11·4′	4°48·3′W	X	34
Cnoc Liath	Pth & Kin	NO1366	56°46·9′	3°25·0′W	X	43
Cnoc Lochan Iain Bhuidhe	Highld	NC6801	57°59·0′	4°13·5′W	X	16
Cnoc Lochan nan Clach Geala	Highld	NC9350	58°25·8′	3°49·5′W	H	11
Cnoc Lochan na Seanaig	Highld	NC5660	58°30·5′	4°27·8′W	H	10
Cnoc Loch an Roìn	Highld	NC1953	58°25·9′	5°5·5′W	X	9
Cnoc Loch Eileanaich	Highld	ND0647	58°24·3′	3°36·0′W	X	11,12
Cnoc Loch Mhadadh	Highld	NC9932	58°16·2′	3°42·8′W	H	11,17
Cnoc Lochy	Moray	NJ1621	57°16·6′	3°23·1′W	H	36
Cnoc Lodge	Arg & Bt	NM9844	56°32·9′	5°16·7′W	X	49
Cnoc Loisgte	Arg & Bt	NR3360	55°45·8′	6°15·0′W	X	60
Cnoc Loisgte	Arg & Bt	NR6350	55°41·4′	5°45·8′W	X	62
Cnoc Loisgte	Highld	NG3726	57°15·2′	6°21·2′W	X	32
Cnocloisgte Water	Highld	ND0150	58°25·9′	3°41·2′W	W	11,12
Cnoc Lomain	Arg & Bt	NN0424	56°22·3′	5°10·0′W	H	50
Cnoc Lòn nan Eildean	Highld	NC5457	58°28·9′	4°29·8′W	H	10
Cnoc Luachair	Highld	ND0057	58°29·7′	3°42·5′W	H	11,12
Cnoc Madaidh	Arg & Bt	NS0681	55°59·2′	5°6·2′W	H	63
Cnoc Madaidh	Arg & Bt	NS1593	56°5·9′	4°58·0′W	H	56
Cnoc Màiri	N Eil	NB4034	58°13·3′	6°25·2′W	T	8
Cnoc Mairi Mùileir	Highld	NC9455	58°28·5′	3°48·6′W	H	11
Cnoc Malagan	Highld	NG6508	57°6·4′	5°52·4′W	H	32
Cnocmalavilach	Arg & Bt	NR7735	55°33·7′	5°31·8′W	H	68,69
Cnoc Mall-lairig	Highld	NH2750	57°30·7′	4°52·8′W	H	25
Cnoc Maol-dhùin	Highld	NC9534	58°17·2′	3°47·0′W	X	11,17
Cnoc Maol Donn	Highld	NC9745	58°23·1′	3°45·2′W	H	11
Cnoc Maol Donn	Highld	NC9855	58°28·5′	3°44·5′W	H	11
Cnoc Maol Malpelly	Highld	NC6949	58°24·9′	4°14·1′W	H	10
Cnoc Maol Mhucaig	Arg & Bt	NM5742	56°30·7′	5°56·5′W	X	47,48
Cnoc Maol na Cloiche Gile	Highld	NC4328	58°13·0′	4°39·9′W	H	16
Cnoc Maol nan Ròn	Arg & Bt	NR2669	55°50·4′	6°22·2′W	X	60

Cnoc Maovally	Highld	NC5060	58°30·4′	4°34·0′W	H	9
Cnoc Marlain	Highld	ND0730	58°15·2′	3°34·6′W	X	11,17
Cnoc Meadhon	Pth & Kin	NO1064	56°45·8′	3°27·9′W	H	43
Cnoc Meadhonach	Highld	NC8417	58°7·9′	3°57·7′W	H	17
Cnoc Meadhonach or Mid Hill	Highld	NC9820	58°9·7′	3°43·5′W	X	17
Cnoc Meala	Highld	NC7856	58°28·8′	4°5·1′W	H	10
Cnoc Mhàbairn	Highld	NH5563	57°38·3′	4°25·3′W	H	21
Cnoc Mhic Eoghainn	N Eil	NF8474	57°39·0′	7°17·4′W	X	18
Cnoc Mhichie	Highld	NC1746	58°22·1′	5°7·3′W	H	9
Cnoc Mòine Raibeirt	Arg & Bt	NR9059	55°47·0′	5°20·5′W	X	62
Cnoc Mór	Arg & Bt	NM2920	56°18·0′	6°22·4′W	H	48
Cnoc Mór	Arg & Bt	NM3424	56°20·3′	6°17·8′W	H	48
Cnoc Mór	Arg & Bt	NM3618	56°17·1′	6°15·5′W	X	48
Cnoc Mór	Arg & Bt	NM4019	56°17·8′	6°11·7′W	H	48
Cnoc Mór	Arg & Bt	NM4323	56°20·0′	6°9·0′W	X	48
Cnoc Mór	Arg & Bt	NM7309	56°13·4′	5°39·3′W	H	55
Cnoc Mór	Arg & Bt	NM8827	56°23·5′	5°25·6′W	H	49
Cnoc Mór	Arg & Bt	NR1752	55°41·0′	6°29·7′W	H	60
Cnoc Mór	Arg & Bt	NR2057	55°43·8′	6°27·2′W	H	60
Cnoc Mór	Arg & Bt	NR2064	55°47·5′	6°27·6′W	H	60
Cnoc Mór	Arg & Bt	NR3244	55°37·2′	6°15·0′W	X	60
Cnoc Mór	Arg & Bt	NR6808	55°18·9′	5°39·0′W	H	68
Cnoc Mór	Arg & Bt	NR7076	55°55·6′	5°40·5′W	X	61,62
Cnoc Mor	Arg & Bt	NR8667	55°51·2′	5°24·7′W	X	62
Cnoc Mór	Arg & Bt	NR9467	55°51·4′	5°17·0′W	H	62
Cnoc Mòr	Arg & Bt	NS0094	56°6·1′	5°12·5′W	H	55
Cnoc Mór	Highld	NC0014	58°4·5′	5°23·0′W	H	15
Cnoc Mór	Highld	NC0308	58°1·3′	5°19·7′W	H	15
Cnoc Mór	Highld	NC4108	58°2·2′	4°41·1′W	H	16
Cnoc Mór	Highld	NC7563	58°32·5′	4°8·4′W	H	10
Cnoc Mór	Highld	NG2505	57°3·5′	6°31·7′W	X	39
Cnoc Mór	Highld	NG2548	57°26·6′	6°34·5′W	H	23
Cnoc Mór	Highld	NG2549	57°27·1′	6°34·6′W	H	23
Cnoc Mór	Highld	NG8320	57°13·4′	5°35·2′W	H	33
Cnoc Mór	Highld	NH4956	57°34·4′	4°31·0′W	H	26
Cnoc Mòr	N Ayr	NS0225	55°29·0′	5°7·6′W	H	69
Cnoc Mór	N Eil	NA9811	57°59·4′	7°6·2′W	H	13
Cnoc Mór	N Eil	NB0010	57°58·9′	7°4·1′W	H	13
Cnoc Mòr	N Eil	NF6163	57°32·1′	7°39·5′W	X	22
Cnoc Mòr	N Eil	NF8761	57°32·1′	7°13·4′W	X	22
Cnoc Mór	N Eil	NG0785	57°45·8′	6°55·2′W	X	18
Cnoc Mór	N Eil	NG1595	57°51·5′	6°47·8′W	H	14
Cnoc Mòr	N Eil	NG1696	57°52·1′	6°46·9′W	H	14
Cnoc Mór	Stir	NN6410	56°16·0′	4°11·3′W	H	57
Cnoc Mór an Rubha Bhig	Highld	NC0214	58°4·5′	5°21·0′W	H	15
Cnoc Mór an t-Sagairt	N Eil	NF9472	57°38·3′	7°7·2′W	H	18
Cnoc Mór Ghrasdail	Arg & Bt	NR3047	55°38·7′	6°17·0′W	H	60
Cnocmor Lodge	Highld	NH4857	57°34·9′	4°32·1′W	X	26
Cnoc Mór na Claigin	Arg & Bt	NR4553	55°42·5′	6°3·1′W	H	60
Cnoc Mór nan Cnoc	Arg & Bt	NR5578	55°56·2′	5°54·9′W	H	61
Cnoc Mòr Shòbhail	N Eil	NB3324	58°7·7′	6°31·6′W	H	13,14
Cnoc Mór Thormaid	N Eil	NF9276	57°40·4′	7°9·5′W	X	18
Cnoc Moy	Arg & Bt	NR6115	55°22·5′	5°45·9′W	H	68
Cnoc Muigh-bhlàraidh	Highld	NH6382	57°48·7′	4°17·9′W	H	21
Cnoc na Bagh Choille	Highld	NC1733	58°15·1′	5°6·6′W	H	15
Cnoc na Bana-mhorair	Highld	NH4368	57°40·7′	4°37·5′W	H	20
Cnoc na Banaraich	Highld	NC1542	58°19·9′	5°9·1′W	H	9
Cnoc na Beinne	Highld	NG1748	57°26·3′	6°42·5′W	H	23
Cnoc na Béiste	Highld	NC9128	58°13·9′	3°50·9′W	H	17
Cnoc na Bò Ruaidhe	Arg & Bt	NM5925	56°21·6′	5°53·7′W	X	48
Cnoc na Braclaich	Arg & Bt	NM5825	56°21·6′	5°54·6′W	X	48
Cnoc na Brathain	N Eil	NF9173	57°38·7′	7°10·3′W	X	18
Cnoc na Brathan	N Eil	NG1089	57°48·1′	6°52·4′W	X	14
Cnoc na Breun-choille	Highld	NC7824	58°11·5′	4°4·0′W	H	17
Cnoc na Buaile	Arg & Bt	NR2258	55°44·4′	6°25·3′W	X	60
Cnoc na Buaile-fraoich	Highld	NC6907	58°2·2′	4°12·7′W	X	16
Cnoc na Buaile Salaich	Arg & Bt	NR8149	55°41·4′	5°28·6′W	H	62,69
Cnoc na Cachaille	Highld	NG6324	57°15·0′	5°55·3′W	H	32
Cnoc na Caillich	Arg & Bt	NR7734	55°33·2′	5°31·7′W	X	68,69
Cnoc na Caillich	Highld	NC2355	58°27·1′	5°1·5′W	H	9
Cnoc na Cairidh	Highld	NC2232	58°14·7′	5°1·5′W	H	15
Cnoc na Cairs	Arg & Bt	NR7563	55°48·7′	5°35·0′W	X	62
Cnoc na Caorach	Arg & Bt	NR8463	55°49·0′	5°26·4′W	X	62
Cnoc na Carraige	Arg & Bt	NR9768	55°52·0′	5°14·2′W	H	62
Cnoc na Ceàrdaich	Highld	NC8355	58°28·3′	3°59·9′W	H	10
Cnoc na Ceille	N Ayr	NR9135	55°34·1′	5°18·5′W	X	68,69
Cnoc na Circe	Highld	NC1219	58°7·5′	5°11·1′W	H	15
Cnoc-na-ciste	Arg & Bt	NM3124	56°20·2′	6°20·7′W	X	48
Cnoc na Claise Brice	Highld	ND0059	58°30·7′	3°42·5′W	H	11,12
Cnoc na Cloich-bhuaile	Highld	NC5204	58°0·3′	4°29·8′W	H	16
Cnoc na Cloiche	N Eil	NB1400	57°54·1′	6°49·2′W	H	14
Cnoc na Cloiche-muilinn	Arg & Bt	NR3647	55°38·9′	6°11·3′W	X	60
Cnoc na Coileach	Highld	NC4941	58°20·2′	4°34·3′W	H	9
Cnoc na Coille-beithe	Highld	NG3433	57°18·9′	6°24·6′W	X	32
Cnoc na Comhairle	N Ayr	NS0323	55°27·9′	5°6·5′W	H	69
Cnoc na Corpaich	Arg & Bt	NR5791	56°3·3′	5°53·7′W	X	61
Cnoc na Craoibhe	Arg & Bt	NR4171	55°52·0′	6°8·0′W	X	60,61
Cnoc na Craoibhe	Highld	ND0750	58°26·0′	3°35·1′W	X	11,12
Cnoc na Craoibh-fearna	Arg & Bt	NR9898	56°8·2′	5°14·6′W	H	55
Cnoc na Creige	Highld	NC2628	58°12·7′	4°57·2′W	H	15
Cnoc na Croiche	Highld	ND1021	58°10·4′	3°31·3′W	H	17
Cnoc na Crois	Highld	ND1039	58°20·1′	3°31·7′W	X	11,12,17
Cnoc na Croise	Arg & Bt	NR4272	55°52·6′	6°7·1′W	H	60,61
Cnoc na Croise	N Ayr	NR9731	55°32·1′	5°12·6′W	X	69
Cnoc na Cruime	Arg & Bt	NR9769	55°52·5′	5°14·3′W	X	62
Cnoc na Cuagaich	Highld	NG2643	57°24·0′	6°33·2′W	H	23
Cnoc na Cuairte	Arg & Bt	NR8059	55°46·7′	5°30·1′W	X	62
Cnoc na Cuairtich	Arg & Bt	NM4547	56°33·0′	6°8·5′W	X	47,48
Cnoc na Cubhaige	Highld	NG6421	57°13·4′	5°54·1′W	X	32
Cnoc na Cuthaige	Highld	NC1649	58°23·7′	5°8·4′W	H	9
Cnoc na Dail	N Ayr	NR9729	55°31·0′	5°12·5′W	H	69
Cnoc na Dalach Baite	Highld	NC8264	58°33·2′	4°1·2′W	X	10
Cnoc na Di-chuimhne	Arg & Bt	NM4840	56°29·3′	6°5·2′W	H	47,48
Cnoc na Doire	Highld	NC5521	58°9·5′	4°27·4′W	H	16
Cnoc na Dubh-chlaise	Highld	NC8059	58°30·4′	4°3·1′W	H	10
Cnoc na Faire	Arg & Bt	NM7927	56°23·3′	5°34·4′W	H	49
Cnoc na Faire	Arg & Bt	NM8223	56°21·2′	5°31·3′W	H	49
Cnoc na Faire	Arg & Bt	NR2974	55°53·2′	6°19·6′W	X	60
Cnoc na Faire	Arg & Bt	NR4278	55°55·8′	6°7·4′W	X	60,61
Cnoc na Faire	Arg & Bt	NR4298	56°6·6′	6°8·5′W	X	61
Cnoc na Faire	Arg & Bt	NR7489	56°2·7′	5°37·3′W	H	55
Cnoc na Faire	Arg & Bt	NR8756	55°45·3′	5°23·2′W	X	62
Cnoc na Faire	Arg & Bt	NR8865	55°50·2′	5°22·7′W	X	62
Cnoc na Faoilinn	Arg & Bt	NM6727	56°22·9′	5°46·0′W	H	49
Cnoc na Fardaich	Highld	NC7009	58°3·3′	4°11·7′W	H	16
Cnoc na Feadaige	Highld	ND0929	58°14·7′	3°32·5′W	H	11,17
Cnoc na Feadaige	Highld	NH7095	57°55·8′	4°11·2′W	X	21
Cnoc na Feannaig	Highld	NC7119	58°8·7′	4°11·0′W	H	16
Cnoc na Feudalach	Arg & Bt	NR6210	55°19·8′	5°44·7′W	X	68
Cnoc na Fliuch-airigh	Highld	NC8930	58°14·9′	3°53·0′W	H	17
Cnoc na Fuarachad	Highld	NG6213	57°9·0′	5°55·6′W	H	32
Cnoc na Fuaralachd	Highld	NC6115	58°6·4′	4°21·1′W	H	16
Cnoc na Gamhna	Highld	NC7703	58°0·2′	4°4·4′W	H	17
Cnoc na Gaoithe	Highld	NC7235	58°17·4′	4°10·5′W	H	16
Cnoc na Gaoithe	Highld	NH5839	57°25·4′	4°21·4′W	H	26
Cnoc na Garbad	N Ayr	NS0223	55°27·9′	5°7·5′W	H	69
Cnoc na Gearraisich	Highld	NH4762	57°37·6′	4°33·3′W	H	20
Cnoc na Glaice Móire	Highld	NC1844	58°21·1′	5°6·1′W	H	9
Cnoc na Glaic Móire	Arg & Bt	NR6589	56°2·4′	5°45·9′W	H	55,61
Cnoc na Glaic Tarsuinn	Highld	NC2964	58°32·1′	4°55·8′W	H	9
Cnoc na Glas Choile	Highld	NC2708	58°1·9′	4°55·3′W	H	15
Cnoc na Gréine	Arg & Bt	NR6313	55°21·5′	5°43·9′W	X	68
Cnoc na h-Acairseid	Highld	NG4414	57°9·0′	6°13·5′W	X	32
Cnoc na h-Airigh	Highld	NC9028	58°13·9′	3°51·9′W	H	17
Cnoc na h-Airigh	Highld	NG2643	57°24·0′	6°33·2′W	H	23
Cnoc na h-Airigh Duibhe	N Eil	NF8260	57°31·4′	7°18·3′W	X	22
Cnoc na h - Airighe	Arg & Bt	NS2290	56°4·4′	4°51·2′W	H	56
Cnoc na h-Airigh-seilich	Arg & Bt	NR6793	56°4·6′	5°44·2′W	H	55,61
Cnoc na h-Airigh-sléibh	Highld	NC7208	58°2·8′	4°9·6′W	H	16
Cnoc na h-Aodainn	Highld	NG7002	57°3·4′	5°47·1′W	X	33
Cnoc na h-Atha	Highld	NG9345	57°27·2′	5°26·6′W	H	25
Cnoc na h- Eannaiche	Highld	NC2156	58°27·6′	5°3·6′W	H	9
Cnoc na h-Earra	Highld	NG9885	57°48·8′	5°23·6′W	X	19
Cnoc na h-Eighich	Highld	NG3131	57°17·7′	6°27·5′W	H	32
Cnoc na h-Eilde	Arg & Bt	NR3459	55°45·3′	6°13·9′W	X	60
Cnoc na h-Eilde	Highld	NG7247	57°27·6′	5°47·6′W	X	24
Cnoc na h-Eireige	Arg & Bt	NR8757	55°45·8′	5°23·3′W	X	62
Cnoc na h-Imriche	Highld	ND1240	58°20·6′	3°29·7′W	H	11,12
Cnoc na h-Inghinn	Highld	NC6104	58°0·5′	4°20·7′W	H	16
Cnoc na h-Innse Móire	Highld	NC8219	58°8·9′	3°59·8′W	H	17
Cnoc na h-Iolaire	Arg & Bt	NR5371	55°52·4′	5°56·5′W	X	61
Cnoc na h-Iolaire	Highld	NC5406	58°1·4′	4°27·8′W	H	16
Cnoc na h-Iolaire	Highld	NG3330	57°17·2′	6°25·4′W	X	32
Cnoc na h-Iolaire	Highld	NH2978	57°45·8′	4°52·0′W	X	20
Cnoc na h-Iolaire	Highld	NH3664	57°38·4′	4°44·4′W	H	20
Cnoc na h-Iolaire	Highld	NH3860	57°36·3′	4°42·2′W	H	20
Cnoc na h-Iolaire	Arg & Bt	NR8277	55°56·5′	5°29·0′W	X	62
Cnoc na h-Iolaire	Highld	NC5551	58°25·7′	4°28·5′W	X	10
Cnoc na h-Iolaire	Pth & Kin	NN5342	56°33·1′	4°23·0′W	X	51
Cnoc na h-Osnaiche	Arg & Bt	NM1958	56°38·0′	6°34·5′W	H	46
Cnoc na h-Uamha	Arg & Bt	NR2362	55°46·6′	6°24·6′W	H	60
Cnoc na h-Uamha	Arg & Bt	NR5279	55°56·7′	5°57·9′W	X	61
Cnoc na h-Uidhe	Highld	NC7436	58°17·9′	4°8·5′W	H	16
Cnoc na Loch	Highld	NG7525	57°15·9′	5°43·4′W	X	33
Cnoc na Màine	Arg & Bt	NR7279	55°57·3′	5°38·7′W	X	62
Cnoc na Maoile	Highld	ND0021	58°10·3′	3°41·5′W	H	17
Cnoc na Maranaich	Highld	ND1333	58°16·9′	3°28·5′W	X	11,17
Cnoc nam Bad Bog	Highld	NH3597	57°56·2′	4°46·7′W	H	20
Cnoc nam Binneag	Arg & Bt	NR5775	55°54·7′	5°52·9′W	X	61
Cnoc nam Bo Riabhach	Highld	NC9039	58°19·8′	3°52·2′W	X	17
Cnoc nam Bothag	N Eil	NG1591	57°49·3′	6°47·5′W	X	14
Cnoc nam Brac	Highld	NC2241	58°19·6′	5°1·9′W	H	9
Cnoc nam Braonan	Highld	NG3339	57°22·1′	6°26·0′W	X	23,32
Cnoc nam Broc	Highld	NG8643	57°25·9′	5°33·4′W	X	24
Cnoc nam Broighleag	Arg & Bt	NR9493	56°5·4′	5°18·2′W	H	55
Cnoc nam Buth	Highld	NG8186	57°48·9′	5°40·8′W	H	19
Cnoc nam Càrnach	Arg & Bt	NM9006	56°12·3′	5°22·7′W	H	55
Cnoc na Mèine	Arg & Bt	NR9060	55°47·5′	5°20·6′W	H	62
Cnoc nam Faobh	Highld	NM6051	56°35·6′	5°54·1′W	X	49
Cnoc nam FEINN	Highld	NC9124	58°11·7′	3°50·8′W	X	17
Cnoc nam Fiadh	N Eil	NB3835	58°13·8′	6°27·3′W	X	8
Cnoc nam Fitheach	Highld	NG5921	57°13·2′	5°59·1′W	X	32
Cnoc nam Muc	Arg & Bt	NR8382	55°59·2′	5°28·3′W	H	55
Cnoc nam Mult	Highld	NG9036	57°22·2′	5°29·1′W	H	25
Cnoc na Moil Deirge	Highld	NG4314	57°9·0′	6°14·5′W	H	32
Cnoc na Moine	Arg & Bt	NM1656	56°36·8′	6°37·3′W	H	46
Cnoc na Mòine	Arg & Bt	NM7130	56°24·7′	5°42·3′W	X	49
Cnoc na Mòine	Arg & Bt	NM7915	56°16·8′	5°33·8′W	H	55
Cnoc na Mòine	Arg & Bt	NR4764	55°48·4′	6°1·8′W	X	60,61
Cnoc na Móine	Arg & Bt	NR7481	55°58·4′	5°36·9′W	X	55
Cnoc na Mòine	Arg & Bt	NR7684	56°0·1′	5°35·1′W	H	55
Cnoc na Moine	Arg & Bt	NR8391	56°4·0′	5°28·7′W	H	55
Cnoc na Moine	Highld	NC0623	58°9·5′	5°17·4′W	H	15
Cnoc na Mòine	Highld	NC3965	58°32·9′	4°45·5′W	X	9
Cnoc na Mòine	Highld	NC6252	58°26·3′	4°21·4′W	H	10
Cnoc na Moine	Highld	NH1096	57°55·0′	5°12·0′W	H	19
Cnoc na Mòine	Highld	NH1151	57°30·8′	5°8·9′W	H	25
Cnoc na Mòine	Highld	NH2934	57°22·1′	4°50·2′W	X	25
Cnoc na Moine	Highld	NH5942	57°27·0′	4°20·5′W	X	26
Cnoc na Moine	N Eil	NF7568	57°35·4′	7°25·9′W	X	18
Cnoc na Mòine Gile	Arg & Bt	NR7570	55°52·5′	5°35·4′W	X	62
Cnoc-na-Monadh	N Eil	NF7850	57°25·8′	7°21·5′W	X	22
Cnoc nam Partan	Arg & Bt	NM6440	56°29·8′	5°49·6′W	X	49
Cnoc nam Piob	Arg & Bt	NM4820	56°18·6′	6°4·0′W	X	48
Cnoc nam Sac	Highld	NH4988	57°51·6′	4°32·2′W	H	20
Cnoc nan Adag	N Eil	NG1693	57°50·4′	6°46·7′W	H	14
Cnoc nan Agh	Arg & Bt	NR7031	55°31·4′	5°38·2′W	X	68
Cnoc nan Aighean	Pth & Kin	NN7355	56°40·4′	4°3·9′W	H	42,51,52
Cnoc nan Airigh	Highld	NC9860	58°31·2′	3°44·6′W	H	11
Cnoc nan Cabar	Arg & Bt	NR8572	55°53·8′	5°25·9′W	X	62
Cnoc nan Caorach	Arg & Bt	NM6724	56°21·3′	5°45·8′W	X	49
Cnoc nan Caorach	Arg & Bt	NR3259	55°45·3′	6°15·9′W	H	60
Cnoc nan Caorach	Arg & Bt	NR8767	55°51·2′	5°23·7′W	X	62
Cnoc nan Caorach	Highld	NH4097	57°56·3′	4°41·7′W	H	20
Cnoc nan Caorach	Highld	NM7160	56°40·8′	5°43·9′W	X	40
Cnoc nan Caorach	Highld	NM8146	56°33·6′	5°33·4′W	H	49
Cnoc nan Caorach Beaga	Highld	NC0925	58°10·6′	5°14·4′W	X	15
Cnoc nan Capull	Highld	NG3729	57°16·8′	6°21·4′W	H	32
Cnoc nan Ceann Móra	Highld	NN2777	56°51·4′	4°49·8′W	X	41
Cnoc nan Cnamhag	Arg & Bt	NR8064	55°49·4′	5°30·3′W	X	62
Cnoc nan Colunnan	Highld	NG8889	57°50·7′	5°33·9′W	H	19
Cnoc nan Craobh	Arg & Bt	NR7345	55°39·0′	5°36·0′W	H	62
Cnoc nan Cro	Highld	NC2446	58°22·3′	5°0·1′W	H	9
Cnoc nan Cùb	Arg & Bt	NM5326	56°22·0′	5°59·5′W	X	48
Cnoc nan Cùbairean	Arg & Bt	NM7037	56°28·4′	5°43·6′W	X	49
Cnoc nan Cuigeal	N Eil	NF8969	57°36·5′	7°12·0′W	X	18
Cnoc nan Cùilean	Highld	NC5946	58°23·1′	4°24·2′W	H	10
Cnoc nan Darach	Arg & Bt	NR9981	55°59·1′	5°12·9′W	X	55
Cnoc nan Dubh Leitire	Arg & Bt	NM4947	56°33·1′	6°4·6′W	H	47,48
Cnocnaneach	Highld	NC1021	58°8·5′	5°13·2′W	X	15
Cnoc nan Each	Highld	NG9645	57°27·2′	5°23·6′W	H	25
Cnoc nan Each	Highld	NH5265	57°39·3′	4°28·4′W	H	20
Cnoc nan Each Mór	Highld	NH4564	57°38·6′	4°35·3′W	H	20
Cnoc nan Gabhar	Arg & Bt	NM4419	56°17·9′	6°7·8′W	X	48
Cnoc nan Gabhar	Arg & Bt	NR6614	55°22·1′	5°41·1′W	H	68
Cnoc nan Gabhar	Arg & Bt	NR8039	55°36·0′	5°29·1′W	H	68,69
Cnoc nan Gabhar	Arg & Bt	NR8959	55°47·0′	5°21·5′W	X	62
Cnoc nan Gaimhnean	Highld	NH6781	57°48·2′	4°13·8′W	H	21
Cnoc nan Gall	Highld	NC9442	58°21·5′	3°48·2′W	H	11
Cnoc nan Geoidh	Arg & Bt	NR2055	55°42·7′	6°27·0′W	X	60
Cnoc nan Gobhar	Arg & Bt	NM9117	56°18·2′	5°22·3′W	H	55
Cnoc nan Gobhar	Arg & Bt	NR6653	55°43·1′	5°43·1′W	H	62
Cnoc nan Gobhar	Highld	NC4251	58°25·4′	4°41·8′W	X	9
Cnoc nan Gobhar	Highld	NC4963	58°32·0′	4°35·1′W	H	9
Cnoc nan Gobhar	N Eil	NB4333	58°12·9′	6°22·1′W	T	8
Cnoc nan Imrichean	Highld	NC4910	58°3·5′	4°33·1′W	H	16
Cnoc nan Iteag	Arg & Bt	NR7149	55°41·1′	5°38·1′W	X	62
Cnoc nan Làrach cloiche	Arg & Bt	NM8416	56°17·5′	5°29·0′W	H	55
Cnoc nan Nathrach	Arg & Bt	NR2964	55°47·9′	6°19·0′W	X	60
Cnoc nan Oighreag	Pth & Kin	NN7415	56°18·9′	4°1·8′W	H	57
Cnoc nan Saobhaidhean	Highld	NM6151	56°35·7′	5°53·1′W	H	49
Cnoc nan Sgliat	Highld	NC3971	58°36·1′	4°45·8′W	X	9
Cnoc nan Sgolb	Arg & Bt	NM6332	56°25·5′	5°50·2′W	X	49
Cnoc nan Sgrath	N Ayr	NR9451	55°42·8′	5°16·3′W	X	62,69
Cnoc nan Sguab	Highld	NM6371	56°46·5′	5°52·3′W	X	40
Cnoc nan Sguabag	Highld	NC9551	58°26·3′	3°47·4′W	H	11
Cnoc nan Sithean	Highld	ND0342	58°21·6′	3°39·0′W	H	11,12
Cnoc nan Sltheag	Stir	NN5307	56°14·2′	4°21·9′W	X	57
Cnoc nan Speireag	Highld	NG3631	57°17·9′	6°22·5′W	H	32
Cnoc nan Stac	Highld	NG7491	57°51·3′	5°48·1′W	H	19
Cnoc nan Tobha	Highld	NC2157	58°28·1′	5°3·7′W	H	9
Cnoc nan Tobhaichean	Arg & Bt	NM6931	56°25·1′	5°44·3′W	X	49
Cnoc nan Tri-chlach	Highld	NC7943	58°21·8′	4°3·6′W	H	10
Cnoc nan Tri-mile	Highld	NC2771	58°35·8′	4°58·1′W	H	9
Cnoc nan Trì Tom	N Eil	NB3124	58°7·7′	6°33·7′W	H	13,14
Cnoc nan Uan	Arg & Bt	NM4745	56°32·0′	6°6·4′W	X	47,48
Cnoc nan Uan	Arg & Bt	NR3862	55°47·1′	6°10·3′W	X	60,61
Cnoc nan Uan	Highld	NG2955	57°30·5′	6°31·0′W	X	23
Cnoc nan Uan	Highld	NG3720	57°12·0′	6°20·8′W	X	32
Cnoc nan Uan	Highld	NG9741	57°25·1′	5°22·4′W	X	25
Cnoc na Pairce	Highld	NG2441	57°22·8′	6°35·1′W	H	23
Cnoc na Piobaireachd	Arg & Bt	NR4174	55°53·6′	6°8·1′W	X	60,61
Cnoc na Saile	Highld	NC2542	58°20·2′	4°58·9′W	H	9
Cnoc na Saobhaidhe	Highld	ND0235	58°17·8′	3°39·8′W	H	11,17
Cnoc na Saobhaidhe	Highld	ND0321	58°10·3′	3°38·5′W	X	17
Cnoc na Sealg	Moray	NJ2134	57°23·6′	3°18·4′W	X	28
Cnoc na Seamraig	Arg & Bt	NN1721	56°21·0′	4°57·2′W	H	50,56
Cnoc na Seamraig	Arg & Bt	NR8077	55°56·4′	5°30·9′W	H	62
Cnoc na Sean-leacainn	Arg & Bt	NR8469	55°52·2′	5°26·7′W	X	62
Cnoc na Seilg	Arg & Bt	NR7140	55°36·2′	5°37·7′W	H	62
Cnoc na Seilg	Highld	NJ1228	57°20·3′	3°27·3′W	X	36
Cnoc na Seilge	Arg & Bt	NR3971	55°51·9′	6°9·9′W	X	60,61
Cnoc na Sgratha	Arg & Bt	NR9159	55°47·0′	5°19·6′W	X	62
Cnoc na Sgrioba	Arg & Bt	NR4875	55°54·4′	6°1·5′W	H	60,61
Cnoc na Sguaibe	Highld	NC6910	58°3·9′	4°12·8′W	H	16
Cnoc na Sròine	Highld	NC2612	58°4·0′	4°56·5′W	H	15
Cnoc na Sròine	Highld	NC5440	58°19·7′	4°29·1′W	H	10
Cnoc na Sròine	Highld	NH5775	57°44·8′	4°23·7′W	H	21
Cnoc na Staing	Highld	NM5556	56°38·2′	5°59·3′W	H	47
Cnoc na Stri	Highld	ND0618	58°8·7′	3°35·3′W	X	17
Cnoc na Sùil Chruthaiche	Highld	NC2051	58°24·9′	5°4·4′W	H	9
Cnoc na Tobaireach	Highld	NC9361	58°31·7′	3°49·8′W	H	11
Cnoc na Tricriche	Arg & Bt	NS1696	56°7·5′	4°57·2′W	H	56
Cnoc na tri-dail	Arg & Bt	NR3755	55°43·3′	6°10·9′W	X	60
Cnoc na Tri-dail (fort)	Arg & Bt	NR3755	55°43·3′	6°10·9′W	A	60
Cnoc na Tuathrach	Highld	NC9033	58°16·6′	3°52·1′W	X	17
Cnoc na Tuirbhe	Highld	NH4786	57°50·5′	4°34·2′W	H	20
Cnoc na Tuppat	Highld	NH4787	57°51·0′	4°34·2′W	H	20
Cnoc Navie	Highld	NH6672	57°43·3′	4°14·5′W	H	21
Cnoc Neill	Highld	NC6010	58°3·7′	4°21·9′W	H	16
Cnocnicoll Wood	Arg & Bt	NS0960	55°48·0′	5°2·4′W	F	63
Cnoc Odhar	Arg & Bt	NM3952	56°35·5′	6°14·6′W	X	47
Cnoc Odhar	Arg & Bt	NR6612	55°21·0′	5°41·0′W	H	68
Cnoc Odhar	Arg & Bt	NR7042	55°37·3′	5°38·7′W	X	62
Cnoc Odhar	Arg & Bt	NR8485	56°0·8′	5°27·5′W	H	55
Cnoc Odhar	Arg & Bt	NR9088	56°2·6′	5°21·9′W	H	55
Cnoc Odhar	Highld	NC2238	58°17·9′	5°1·8′W	H	15
Cnoc Odhar	Highld	NC5664	58°32·7′	4°28·0′W	X	10
Cnoc Odhar	Highld	NH7596	57°56·4′	4°6·2′W	H	21
Cnoc Odhar	Stir	NN4813	56°17·4′	4°26·9′W	H	57
Cnoc Odhar Auchaluskin	Arg & Bt	NR7043	55°37·8′	5°38·8′W	X	62
Cnoc Olasdail	Highld	NC5418	58°7·9′	4°28·3′W	H	16
Cnoc Phadruig	Highld	NH1993	57°53·7′	5°2·8′W	X	20
Cnoc Poll a' Mhuilt	Highld	NC0329	58°12·6′	5°20·7′W	H	15
Cnoc Poll a' Mhurain	Highld	NC1961	58°30·2′	5°5·9′W	H	9
Cnoc Poll nam Muc	Highld	NC1525	58°10·8′	5°8·3′W	X	15
Cnoc Preas a' Mhadaidh	Highld	NC9848	58°24·8′	3°44·3′W	H	11
Cnoc Preas an Daimh	Highld	NC8519	58°9·0′	3°56·8′W	X	17
Cnoc Preas an Tairbh	Highld	NC7224	58°11·4′	4°10·2′W	H	16
Cnoc Ramascaig	Highld	NC5216	58°6·8′	4°30·3′W	X	16
Cnoc Reamhar	Arg & Bt	NM4422	56°19·5′	6°8·0′W	X	48
Cnoc Reamhar	Arg & Bt	NM4722	56°19·6′	6°5·1′W	X	48
Cnoc Reamhar	Arg & Bt	NM6125	56°21·7′	5°51·7′W	X	49
Cnoc Reamhar	Arg & Bt	NR4170	55°51·5′	6°7·9′W	X	60,61
Cnoc Reamhar	Arg & Bt	NR4665	55°48·9′	6°2·8′W	H	60,61
Cnoc Reamhar	Arg & Bt	NR6113	55°21·4′	5°45·8′W	X	68
Cnoc Reamhar	Arg & Bt	NR7035	55°33·5′	5°38·4′W	H	68
Cnoc Reamhar	Arg & Bt	NR7366	55°50·3′	5°37·1′W	X	62
Cnoc Reamhar	Arg & Bt	NR7690	56°3·3′	5°35·4′W	H	55

Cnoc Reamhar	Arg & Bt	NR7746	55°39·6′	5°32·3′W	H	62,69
Cnoc Reamhar	Arg & Bt	NR7942	55°37·5′	5°30·2′W	X	62,69
Cnoc Reamhar	N Ayr	NR9224	55°28·2′	5°17·0′W	H	68,69
Cnoc Réilereidhe	Arg & Bt	NR7945	55°39·2′	5°30·3′W	X	62,69
Cnoc Rhaonastil	Arg & Bt	NR4348	55°39·7′	6°4·7′W	H	60
Cnoc Riabhach	Highld	NC0232	58°14·2′	5°21·9′W	H	15
Cnoc Riabhach	Highld	NC5307	58°1·9′	4°28·9′W	H	16
Cnoc Riabhach	Highld	NC9237	58°18·8′	3°50·1′W	X	11,17
Cnoc Roll	Highld	NG4173	57°40·6′	6°20·2′W	H	23
Cnoc Rolum	N Eil	NF7855	57°28·5′	7°21·9′W	X	22
Cnoc Rubh' a'Choire	Arg & Bt	NR5580	55°57·3′	5°55·1′W	H	61
Cnoc Ruigh a' Chàirn	Highld	NC0431	58°13·7′	5°19·8′W	H	15
Cnoc Ruighean na Sgainn	Highld	NC8013	58°5·7′	4°1·7′W	X	17
Cnoc Ruigh nan Copag	Highld	NC6335	58°17·2′	4°19·7′W	H	16
Cnoc Salislade	Highld	NC9423	58°11·3′	3°47·7′W	H	17
Cnoc Salltraim	N Eil	NF7972	57°37·7′	7°22·2′W	X	18
Cnoc Sàstail	Arg & Bt	NM5024	56°20·8′	6°2·3′W	X	48
Cnoc Scarall	Highld	NG3828	57°16·3′	6°20·3′W	H	32
Cnoc Seasaimh	Highld	NC9942	58°21·6′	3°43·1′W	H	11
Cnoc Sgarabais	Arg & Bt	NR3973	55°53·0′	6°10·0′W	H	60,61
Cnoc Sgliatach	Arg & Bt	NM8706	56°12·2′	5°25·6′W	H	55
Cnoc Sgoraig	Highld	NH0097	57°55·3′	5°22·2′W	H	19
Cnoc Sgriodain	Highld	NC5527	58°12·7′	4°27·6′W	H	16
Cnoc Shalachry	Arg & Bt	NM6424	56°21·2′	5°48·8′W	H	49
Cnoc Sheangan	Highld	ND1633	58°16·9′	3°25·5′W	X	11
Cnoc Shieveina	N Ayr	NR9529	55°31·0′	5°14·4′W	H	68,69
Cnoc Shoirbidh	Arg & Bt	NM1953	56°35·3′	6°34·2′W	H	46
Cnoc Simid	Highld	NG3930	57°17·4′	6°19·5′W	X	32
Cnoc Slapin	Highld	NG5721	57°13·2′	6°1·1′W	H	32
Cnoc Snàtaig	Highld	NH5232	57°21·5′	4°27·2′W	H	26
Cnoc Soilleir	N Eil	NG1593	57°50·4′	6°47·7′W	H	14
Cnoc Spàrdain	Highld	ND0723	58°11·4′	3°34·4′W	H	17
Cnoc Squabach Cadha	Highld	NC9632	58°16·1′	3°45·9′W	X	11,17
Cnoc Sròn à Mhartuinn	Highld	NC5564	58°32·7′	4°29·0′W	H	10
Cnoc Staing	Highld	NC5841	58°20·3′	4°25·1′W	X	10
Cnoc Stanger	Highld	NC9665	58°33·9′	3°46·8′W	A	11
Cnoc Steud	Highld	NG3860	57°33·5′	6°22·4′W	H	23
Cnoc Stighseir	Arg & Bt	NR7176	55°55·6′	5°39·5′W	H	62
Cnoc Taillir	Arg & Bt	NR6691	56°3·5′	5°45·1′W	H	55,61
Cnoc Thorcaill	Highld	NH5984	57°49·7′	4°22·0′W	X	21
Cnoc Thormaid	Highld	NC1842	58°20·0′	5°6·0′W	X	9
Cnoc Thornasaig	Arg & Bt	NR2360	55°45·5′	6°24·5′W	X	60
Cnoc Thulagain	Highld	NH7422	57°16·5′	4°4·9′W	H	35
Cnoc Thull	Highld	NC2449	58°23·9′	5°0·2′W	H	9
Cnoc Tigh Mhic Fhionnlaidh	Arg & Bt	NR5269	55°51·3′	5°57·3′W	X	61
Cnoc Tigh-sealga	Arg & Bt	NR6089	56°2·3′	5°50·7′W	H	61
Cnoc Toiteach	Highld	NC5556	58°28·4′	4°28·7′W	H	10
Cnoc Torr an Leamhain	Highld	NC5900	57°58·3′	4°22·6′W	H	16
Cnoc Tuarie	Highld	NC8221	58°10·0′	3°59·9′W	H	17
Cnoc Uaine	Arg & Bt	NR9674	55°55·2′	5°15·4′W	X	62
Cnoc Uamh nam Fear	Arg & Bt	NR2170	55°50·8′	6°27·0′W	H	60
Cnoc Udais	Highld	NH4849	57°30·6′	4°31·8′W	H	26
Cnoc Udmail	Arg & Bt	NM3551	56°34·8′	6°18·5′W	X	47
Cnoc Uidh a' Chlàrain	Highld	NC7534	58°16·9′	4°7·4′W	H	16
Cnoc Undail	Arg & Bt	NR1851	55°40·5′	6°28·7′W	X	60
Cnoc Urray	Highld	NC9866	58°34·5′	3°44·8′W	A	11
Cnoc Vigas	Highld	ND2141	58°21·3′	3°20·5′W	X	11,12
Cnuic Charrach	Arg & Bt	NR5172	55°52·9′	5°58·4′W	X	61
Cnuic na Braclach	Highld	NC1211	58°3·2′	5°10·7′W	H	15
Cnuic nan Eildean	Highld	NG8401	57°3·2′	5°33·2′W	H	33
Cnù Lochanan	Arg & Bt	NM0247	56°31·5′	6°50·3′W	W	46
Cnuwch	Powys	SN8154	52°10·5′	3°44·0′W	X	147
Cnwc	Cered	SN5865	52°16·1′	4°4·5′W	X	135
Cnwc	Merth Tyd	SO0601	51°42·2′	3°21·2′W	X	170
Cnwc	Pemb	SN0830	51°56·4′	4°47·2′W	H	145
Cnwcdeilog	Carm	SN7435	52°0·2′	3°49·7′W	X	146,160
Cnwce	Carm	SN2213	51°47·5′	4°34·5′W	X	158
Cnŵch	Carm	SN7844	52°5·1′	3°46·4′W	H	146,147,160
Cnwch	Powys	SN9364	52°16·1′	3°33·7′W	X	147
Cnwch	Powys	SO1575	52°22·2′	3°14·5′W	X	136,148
Cnwch Bank	Powys	SO1774	52°21·7′	3°12·7′W	X	136,148
Cnwch Bank	Powys	SO1854	52°10·9′	3°11·6′W	X	148
Cnwch Coch	Cered	SN6775	52°21·7′	3°56·8′W	T	135
Cnwch Fm	Powys	SO1853	52°10·4′	3°11·6′W	FM	148
Cnwch Rhiwhalog	Cered	SN7952	52°9·4′	3°45·7′W	X	146,147
Cnwch yr Arian	Cered	SN6978	52°23·3′	3°55·1′W	H	135
Cñwclas Castle	Powys	SO2574	52°21·8′	3°5·7′W	A	137,148
Cnwc Rhudd	Pemb	SN1030	51°56·4′	4°45·5′W	X	145
Cnwc y Barcus	Cered	SN5870	52°18·8′	4°4·6′W	X	135
Cnwcymanal	Cered	SN2650	52°7·5′	4°32·1′W	X	145
Cnwcymorfol	Pemb	SM9633	51°57·7′	4°57·8′W	X	157
Cnych Mawr	Powys	SN9976	52°22·6′	3°28·6′W	X	136,147
Cnydfa	Powys	SO0081	52°25·3′	3°27·8′W	X	136
Coachan Donn Beag	Highld	NN3974	56°50·0′	4°37·9′W	W	41
Coachan Fearna	Highld	NN6088	56°58·0′	4°17·7′W	W	42
Coachan Riabhach	Highld	NN4593	57°0·4′	4°32·7′W	W	34
Coachan Roibidh	Aberd	NN9792	57°0·7′	3°41·3′W	W	43
Coacher Cleugh	Northum	NY6498	55°16·7′	2°33·6′W	X	80
Coachford	Aberd	NJ4645	57°29·8′	2°53·6′W	X	28,29
Coachford Burn	E Ayr	NS5118	55°26·2′	4°20·9′W	W	70
Coachlands	Pemb	SN0603	51°41·8′	4°48·0′W	X	158
Coachroad Coppice	Shrops	SO7076	52°23·1′	2°26·0′W	F	138
Coachroad Plantation	Notts	SK6381	53°19·6′	1°2·8′W	F	111,120
Coad's Green	Corn	SX2976	50°33·8′	4°24·5′W	T	201
Coag	Highld	NH7076	57°45·6′	4°10·6′W	X	21
Coakham Fm	Kent	TQ4449	51°13·5′	0°4·1′E	FM	187
Coal Ash	Cumbr	SD2484	54°15·0′	3°9·6′W	X	96
Coal Aston	Derby	SK3679	53°18·6′	1°27·2′W	T	119
Coal Bank	Darl	NZ3521	54°35·2′	1°27·1′W	T	93
Coal Bank	Sund	NZ3446	54°48·7′	1°27·8′W	X	88
Coalbog	Renf	NS3965	55°51·3′	4°33·9′W	X	63
Coal Brook	Nth Pt Talb	SS8184	51°32·8′	3°42·6′W	W	170
Coal Brook	Staffs	SJ7132	52°53·3′	2°25·5′W	W	127
Coalbrook	Swan	SN5900	51°41·1′	4°2·0′W	X	159
Coalbrookdale	Wrekin	SJ6604	52°38·2′	2°29·7′W	T	127
Coalbrookvale	Blae Gw	SO1909	51°46·7′	3°10·1′W	T	161
Coal Burn	E Ayr	NS6218	55°26·4′	4°10·5′W	W	71
Coalburn	N Ayr	NS3351	55°43·7′	4°39·1′W	X	63
Coal Burn	Northum	NT9845	55°42·2′	2°1·5′W	W	75
Coal Burn	Northum	NU0335	55°36·8′	1°56·7′W	W	75
Coal Burn	Northum	NY6977	55°5·4′	2°28·7′W	W	86,87
Coal Burn	Northum	NY9076	55°4·9′	2°9·0′W	W	87
Coal Burn	Northum	NY9474	55°3·9′	2°5·2′W	W	87
Coal Burn	Northum	NZ0477	55°5·5′	1°55·8′W	W	87
Coalburn	S Lanak	NS8134	55°35·4′	3°52·9′W	T	71,72
Coal Burn	S Lanak	NS8235	55°35·9′	3°51·9′W	W	71,72
Coalburn Fm	Ghead	NZ1260	54°56·3′	1°48·3′W	FM	88
Coalburn Fm	Northum	NZ2183	55°8·7′	1°39·8′W	FM	81
Coalburns	Ghead	NZ1261	54°56·9′	1°48·3′W	T	88
Coal Cleugh	Cumbr	NY6543	54°47·1′	2°32·2′W	X	86
Coal Cleugh	Northum	NY7873	55°3·3′	2°20·2′W	X	86,87
Coalcleugh	Northum	NY7974	55°3·9′	2°19·3′W	X	86,87
Coalcleugh	Northum	NY8045	54°48·2′	2°18·2′W	T	86,87
Coalcleugh Moor	Northum	NY8044	54°47·7′	2°18·2′W	X	86,87
Coal Clough Fm	Lancs	SD9027	53°44·6′	2°8·7′W	FM	103
Coal Clough Wind Fm	Lancs	SD8928	53°45·1′	2°9·6′W	FM	103
Coalcraigy Hill	Pth & Kin	NO0407	56°15·0′	3°32·5′W	H	58
Coalden	Fife	NT2495	56°8·8′	3°13·0′W	X	59
Coal Dike	E Yorks	TA0346	53°54·2′	0°25·5′W	W	107
Coal Dyke End	N Lincs	SE9807	53°33·3′	0°30·8′W	X	112
Coales Lodge	Northnts	TL0377	52°23·1′	0°28·8′W	X	141
Coaley	Glos	SO7701	51°42·7′	2°19·6′W	T	162
Coaley Peak	Glos	SO7901	51°42·7′	2°17·8′W	T	162
Coaley Wood	Glos	ST7899	51°41·6′	2°18·7′W	F	162
Coalfell	Cumbr	NY5959	54°55·7′	2°38·0′W	X	86
Coalfell Beck	Cumbr	NY6059	54°55·7′	2°37·0′W	W	86
Coalfin	Arg & Bt	NR8958	55°46·4′	5°21·4′W	X	62
Coal Fm	Fife	NO5302	56°12·8′	2°45·0′W	FM	59
Coalford	Aberd	NO8299	57°5·2′	2°17·4′W	T	38,45
Coalgarth Fm	Stock on T	NZ4020	54°34·7′	1°22·4′W	FM	93
Coal Gate	Cumbr	SD2186	54°16·1′	3°12·4′W	X	96
Coal Gate	Durham	NZ0448	54°49·9′	1°55·8′W	X	87
Coalgate Burn	Durham	NZ0348	54°49·9′	1°56·8′W	W	87
Coalgill	S Lanak	NS8632	55°34·4′	3°48·0′W	X	71,72
Coal Grain	Northum	NY5790	55°12·4′	2°40·1′W	W	80
Coalhall	E Ayr	NS4419	55°26·7′	4°27·5′W	T	70
Coal Harbour	Northum	NT9740	55°39·5′	2°2·4′W	X	75
Coalheughhead	W Loth	NT0361	55°50·2′	3°32·5′W	X	65
Coalhill	Essex	TQ7597	51°38·9′	0°32·2′E	T	167
Coalhill	N Ayr	NS2446	55°40·8′	4°47·5′W	X	63
Coal Hill	N Yks	SE1971	54°8·3′	1°42·1′W	X	99
Coal Hill	Orkney	HY4107	58°57·0′	3°1·0′W	X	6,7
Coal Hos	Northum	NZ0992	55°13·6′	1°51·1′W	X	81
Coalhouse Fort	Thurr	TQ6976	51°27·7′	0°26·4′E	A	177,178
Coalhouse Point	Thurr	TQ6876	51°27·7′	0°25·5′E	X	177,178
Coal Houses Fm	Northum	NU2401	55°18·4′	1°36·9′W	FM	81
Coall Head	Shetld	HU4433	60°5·0′	1°12·1′W	X	4
Coall, The	Shetld	HU4333	60°5·0′	1°13·1′W	X	4
Coalmeer Gutter	Hants	SU2613	50°55·2′	1°37·4′W	W	195
Coalmire	N Yks	NZ4800	54°23·8′	1°15·2′W	X	93
Coalmoor	Wrekin	SJ6607	52°39·8′	2°29·8′W	T	127
Coalmoss	Aberd	NJ9237	57°25·7′	2°7·5′W	X	30
Coalpark Gill	Durham	NZ2146	54°48·8′	1°40·0′W	F	88
Coalpit Field	Warw	SP3686	52°28·5′	1°27·8′W	T	140
Coalpit Heath	S Glos	ST6780	51°31·3′	2°28·1′W	T	172
Coalpit Hill	Cumbr	NY6011	54°29·8′	2°36·6′W	X	91
Coalpit Hill	Glos	SO5512	51°48·5′	2°38·8′W	X	162
Coalpit Hill	N Yks	SE1298	54°22·9′	1°48·5′W	X	99
Coalpit Hill	Staffs	SJ8253	53°4·7′	2°15·7′W	T	118
Coal Pit Lane	Lancs	SD8447	53°55·4′	2°14·2′W	X	103
Coal Pit Moor	N Yks	SE0495	54°21·3′	1°55·9′W	X	98
Coalpits	Monm	ST4992	51°37·7′	2°43·8′W	X	162,172
Coalpits Copse	Wilts	SU2429	51°3·8′	1°39·1′W	F	184
Coalpit Wood	N Yks	NZ4408	54°28·2′	1°18·8′W	F	93
Coal Pool	Wals	SK0100	52°36·1′	1°58·7′W	T	139
Coalport	Wrekin	SJ6902	52°37·1′	2°27·1′W	T	127
Coal Ridge	N Yks	SE5097	54°22·2′	1°13·4′W	X	100
Coal Sike	Cumbr	NY7724	54°36·9′	2°20·9′W	W	91
Coalsnaughton	Clackm	NS9295	56°8·4′	3°43·8′W	T	58
Coaltown of Balgonie	Fife	NT3099	56°11·0′	3°7·2′W	T	59
Coaltown of Burnturk	Fife	NO3207	56°15·3′	3°5·4′W	T	59
Coaltown of Callange	Fife	NO4111	56°17·5′	2°56·7′W	X	59
Coaltown of Wemyss	Fife	NT3295	56°8·8′	3°5·2′W	T	59
Coalville	Leic	SK4213	52°43·0′	1°22·3′W	T	129
Coalway	Glos	SO5810	51°47·5′	2°36·1′W	T	162
Coan Dubh	Highld	ND1425	58°12·6′	3°27·3′W	X	17
Coanwood	Northum	NY6859	54°55·7′	2°29·5′W	T	86,87
Coanwood Burn	Northum	NY7157	54°54·7′	2°26·7′W	W	86,87
Coanwood Common	Northum	NY7157	54°54·7′	2°26·7′W	X	86,87
Coar Holm	Shetld	HU3620	59°58·1′	1°20·8′W	X	4
Coars	Lancs	SD7954	53°59·1′	2°18·8′W	X	103
Coarsebarn Fm	E Susx	TQ7516	50°55·2′	0°29·8′E	FM	199
Coarsewell	Devon	SX7054	50°22·5′	3°49·3′W	T	202
Coast	Highld	NG8287	57°49·4′	5°39·8′W	X	19
Coastal Path	I of W	SZ4082	50°38·4′	1°25·7′W	X	196
Coastley	Northum	NY8965	54°59·0′	2°9·9′W	X	87
Coat	Somer	ST4520	50°58·8′	2°46·6′W	T	193
Coatbridge	N Lanak	NS7265	55°51·9′	4°2·3′W	T	64
Coatdyke	N Lanak	NS7564	55°51·4′	3°59·4′W	T	64
Coate	Swin	SU1882	51°32·4′	1°44·0′W	T	173
Coate	Wilts	SU0461	51°21·1′	1°56·2′W	T	173
Coate Fm	Somer	ST0727	51°2·3′	3°19·2′W	FM	181
Coate Moor	N Yks	NZ5910	54°29·2′	1°4·9′W	X	93
Coate Moor	N Yks	NZ6010	54°29·1′	1°4·0′W	X	94
Coatenhill	Northum	NY8448	54°49·8′	2°14·5′W	X	86,87
Coates	Cambs	TL3097	52°33·5′	0°4·5′W	T	142
Coates	E Loth	NT4775	55°58·2′	2°50·5′W	X	66
Coates	Fife	NO4403	56°13·2′	2°53·7′W	X	59
Coates	Glos	SO9800	51°42·2′	2°1·3′W	T	163
Coates	Lancs	SD8847	53°55·4′	2°10·5′W	T	103
Coates	Lincs	SK9183	53°20·4′	0°37·6′W	T	121
Coates	Midlo	NT2161	55°50·4′	3°15·3′W	T	66
Coates	Notts	SK8281	53°19·4′	0°45·7′W	T	121
Coates	Shrops	SO3995	52°33·2′	2°53·6′W	X	137
Coates	W Susx	SU9917	50°56·9′	0°35·1′W	T	197
Coates Barn	Warw	SP2733	51°59·9′	1°36·0′W	X	151
Coates Castle	W Susx	SU9917	50°56·9′	0°35·1′W	X	197
Coate's Cave	N Yks	SD8570	54°7·8′	2°13·4′W	X	98
Coates Common	W Susx	TQ0017	50°56·9′	0°34·2′W	X	197
Coates Copse	Oxon	SU6890	51°36·5′	1°0·7′W	F	164,175
Coates Fm	Oxon	SU6990	51°36·5′	0°59·8′W	FM	175
Coates Fm	Shrops	SO5890	52°30·6′	2°36·7′W	FM	137,138
Coates Fm	Shrops	SO6786	52°28·5′	2°28·8′W	FM	138
Coates Hall Fm	N Yks	SE6323	53°42·2′	1°2·3′W	FM	105,106
Coate's House Fm	E Yorks	TA2623	53°41·5′	0°5·1′W	FM	107,113
Coates of Fingask	Pth & Kin	NO1520	56°22·1′	3°22·1′W	X	53,58
Coatestown	Staffs	SK0666	53°11·7′	1°54·2′W	X	119
Coate Water Country Park	Swin	SU1782	51°32·4′	1°44·9′W	X	173
Coatfield	Staffs	SK0919	52°46·3′	1°51·6′W	X	128
Coatflat Hall	Cumbr	NY6205	54°26·6′	2°34·7′W	X	91
Coat Green	Cumbr	SD5375	54°10·4′	2°42·8′W	X	97
Coatham	Red & Cl	NZ5925	54°37·2′	1°4·8′W	T	93
Coatham Beck	Stock on T	NZ3916	54°32·5′	1°23·4′W	W	93
Coatham House Fm	Darl	NZ2819	54°34·2′	1°33·6′W	FM	93
Coatham Marsh	Red & Cl	NZ5824	54°36·7′	1°5·7′W	X	93
Coatham Mundeville	Darl	NZ2820	54°34·7′	1°33·6′W	T	93
Coatham Rocks	Red & Cl	NZ5925	54°37·2′	1°4·8′W	X	93
Coatham Rocks	Red & Cl	NZ6025	54°37·2′	1°3·8′W	X	94
Coatham Sands	Red & Cl	NZ5626	54°37·8′	1°7·5′W	X	93
Coatham Stob	Stock on T	NZ4016	54°32·5′	1°22·5′W	X	93
Coathill	N Lanak	NS7672	55°55·8′	3°58·6′W	X	64
Coat Hill	Northum	NZ1472	55°2·8′	1°46·4′W	X	88
Coatlith Hill	Cumbr	NY7147	54°49·3′	2°26·7′W	X	86,87
Coat Rakes Br	Lancs	SD7358	54°1·3′	2°24·3′W	X	103
Coatsay Moor	Darl	NZ2420	54°34·7′	1°37·3′W	X	93
Coatsgate	D & G	NT0605	55°20·1′	3°28·5′W	X	78
Coats Hill	D & G	NT0704	55°19·5′	3°27·5′W	X	78
Coatsike Fm	Cumbr	NY6825	54°37·4′	2°29·3′W	FM	91
Coats, The	Shrops	SO5292	52°31·7′	2°42·1′W	X	137,138
Coatston	D & G	NX8486	55°9·5′	3°48·8′W	X	78
Coat Walls Fm	Lancs	SD3546	53°54·6′	2°59·0′W	FM	102
Coat Weggs	Cumbr	SD7590	54°18·5′	2°22·6′W	X	144
Coat Yards Fm	Northum	NZ0893	55°14·1′	1°52·0′W	FM	81
Coaxdon Hall	Devon	ST3100	50°48·0′	2°58·4′W	A	193
Cobairdy	Aberd	NJ5743	57°28·8′	2°42·6′W	X	29
Cobairdy Wood	Aberd	NJ5744	57°29·3′	2°42·6′W	F	29
Cobalder Fm	Cambs	TL2085	52°27·2′	0°13·6′W	FM	142
Cobb	Dorset	SY3391	50°43·1′	2°56·6′W	T	193
Cobbaton	Devon	SS6126	51°1·2′	3°58·5′W	T	180
Cobb Court	E Susx	TQ5208	50°51·3′	0°10·0′E	X	199
Cobbe Place	E Susx	TQ4407	50°50·9′	0°3·1′E	X	198
Cobbershill	Bucks	SP8603	51°43·4′	0°44·9′W	X	165
Cobbett Hill	Surrey	SU9453	51°16·3′	0°38·8′W	X	186
Cobbetts Fm	Surrey	TQ1140	51°9·1′	0°24·4′W	FM	187
Cobb Flatts Fm	E Yorks	SE7350	53°56·7′	0°52·9′W	FM	105,106
Cobbie Row's Lade	Orkney	HY6021	59°4·7′	2°41·4′W	X	5,6
Cobbi Geo	Shetld	HU6671	60°25·3′	0°47·6′W	X	2
Cobbin's Bridge	Essex	TL4403	51°42·7′	0°5·5′E	X	167
Cobbin's Brook	Essex	TL4303	51°42·7′	0°4·6′E	W	167
Cobbinshaw Hill	W Loth	NT0357	55°48·0′	3°32·4′W	X	65,72
Cobbinshaw Reservoir	W Loth	NT0158	55°48·6′	3°34·3′W	W	65,72
Cobble Cott	C of Edin	NT1877	55°59·0′	3°18·4′W	X	65,66
Cobble Dump	N Yks	NZ8116	54°32·2′	0°44·5′W	X	94
Cobble Hall	Cumbr	NY3556	54°53·9′	3°0·4′W	X	85
Cobble Hall	E Yorks	TA1444	53°53·0′	0°15·5′W	X	107
Cobble Hall	Leeds	SE3438	53°50·5′	1°28·6′W	X	104
Cobble Hall	N Yks	NZ6709	54°28·6′	0°57·5′W	X	94
Cobble Hall Fm	Cumbr	NY1347	54°48·9′	3°20·8′W	FM	85
Cobblehaugh Fm	S Lanak	NS9242	55°39·8′	3°42·6′W	FM	71,72
Cobbleheugh	Aberd	NO4798	57°4·5′	2°52·0′W	X	37,44
Cobble Hey	Lancs	SD5344	53°53·6′	2°42·5′W	X	102
Cobblehouse	Aberd	NJ6347	57°31·0′	2°36·6′W	X	29
Cobbler's Coppice	Worcs	SO9269	52°19·4′	2°6·6′W	F	139
Cobbler's Corner	Suff	TM0742	52°2·5′	1°1·5′E	X	155,169
Cobbler's Corner	Worcs	SO7756	52°12·3′	2°19·8′W	T	150
Cobblers Gate	Powys	SO0387	52°28·6′	3°25·3′W	X	136
Cobbler's Green	Norf	TM2892	52°28·9′	1°21·9′E	T	134
Cobbler's Hall	Durham	NZ2626	54°38·0′	1°35·4′W	X	93
Cobbler's Hill	Notts	SK5548	53°1·8′	1°10·4′W	X	129
Cobbler's Lock	Lincs	TF1249	53°1·8′	0°19·4′W	X	130
Cobblers of Lorn	Arg & Bt	NM7209	56°13·4′	5°40·2′W	X	55
Cobbler's Pieces	Essex	TL5510	51°46·3′	0°15·2′E	X	167
Cobbler's Plain	Monm	SO4700	51°42·0′	2°45·6′W	T	171
Cobbler, The	Arg & Bt	NN2505	56°12·6′	4°48·9′W	X	56
Cobbles	Ches	SJ6180	53°19·2′	2°34·7′W	X	109
Cobbles Fm	Bucks	SU8891	51°36·9′	0°43·3′W	FM	175
Cobbolds Fm	Suff	TM0543	52°3·1′	0°59·8′E	FM	155
Cobbs	Warr	SJ6185	53°21·9′	2°34·8′W	T	109
Cobb's Cross	Glos	SO7633	51°59·9′	2°20·6′W	T	150
Cobb's Cross Stream	Somer	ST2634	51°6·3′	3°3·0′W	W	182
Cobbs Fenn	Essex	TL7733	51°58·3′	0°35·0′E	T	167
Cobb's Fm	Essex	TL8635	51°59·2′	0°42·9′E	FM	155
Cobb's Fm	Essex	TL8908	51°44·6′	0°44·7′E	FM	168
Cobb's Hall	Suff	TL7861	52°13·3′	0°36·8′E	X	155
Cobb's Hill	Kent	TR1241	51°8·0′	1°2·2′E	X	179,189
Cobb's Leaze Rhyne	Somer	ST2743	51°11·1′	3°2·3′W	W	182
Cobb's Mill	W Susx	TQ2719	50°57·6′	0°11·1′W	X	198
Cobb's Wood Fm	Cambs	TL3451	52°8·7′	0°2·1′W	FM	154
Cobby Syke	N Yks	SE1955	53°59·7′	1°42·2′W	T	104
Cob Castle	Lancs	SD7146	53°54·8′	2°26·1′W	X	103
Cobdale Fm	E Yorks	SE8553	53°58·2′	0°41·8′W	FM	106
Cobden	Devon	SX3889	50°40·9′	4°17·2′W	X	190
Cobden	Devon	SY0396	50°45·6′	3°22·1′W	X	192
Cobden Burn	Northum	NT9814	55°25·4′	2°1·5′W	W	81
Cobden Fm	Lancs	SD7736	53°49·4′	2°20·6′W	FM	103
Cobden Fm	W Susx	SU9225	51°1·2′	0°40·9′W	FM	186,197
Cobden Fm	W Susx	TQ1010	50°53·0′	0°25·8′W	FM	198
Cobditch Hill	Oxon	SU6893	51°38·1′	1°0·7′W	X	164,175
Coberley	Glos	SO9616	51°50·8′	2°3·1′W	T	163
Cobers Laithe	N Yks	SD8653	53°58·6′	2°12·4′W	X	103
Cobgate Fm	Lincs	TF2924	52°48·1′	0°4·8′W	FM	131
Cobhall Common	Heref	SO4535	52°0·9′	2°47·7′W	T	149,161
Cobhall Court	Heref	SO4535	52°0·9′	2°47·7′W	X	149,161
Cobham	Kent	TQ6768	51°23·4′	0°24·4′E	T	177,178
Cobham	Surrey	TQ1160	51°19·9′	0°24·0′W	T	176,187
Cobhambury Fm	Kent	TQ4543	51°10·3′	0°4·8′E	FM	188
Cobhambury Wood	Kent	TQ6767	51°22·9′	0°24·4′E	F	177,178
Cobham College	Kent	TQ6668	51°23·4′	0°23·5′E	A	177,178
Cobham Court	Surrey	TQ1059	51°19·4′	0°24·9′W	X	187

Cobham Fm	Kent	TQ9351	51°13·8′	0°46·3′E	FM	189
Cobham Fm	Wrex	SJ4149	53°2·3′	2°52·4′W	FM	117
Cobham Frith	Wilts	SU2567	51°24·3′	1°38·0′W	F	174
Cobham Hall (Sch)	Kent	TQ6868	51°23·4′	0°25·3′E	A	177,178
Cobham Lodge	Surrey	TQ1158	51°18·8′	0°24·0′W	X	187
Cobham Manor Fm	Kent	TQ8157	51°17·2′	0°36·1′E	FM	178,188
Cobham Park	Kent	TQ6868	51°23·4′	0°25·3′E	X	177,178
Cobham Park	Surrey	TQ1059	51°19·4′	0°24·9′W	X	187
Cobha Sgeir	N Eil	NB4762	58°28·6′	6°19·9′W	X	8
Cobhay Fm	Somer	ST0924	51°0·7′	3°17·4′W	FM	181
Cob Hill	Lincs	TF5378	53°16·8′	0°18·1′E	X	122
Cob Ho	Lancs	SD7446	53°54·8′	2°23·3′W	X	103
Cobholm Island	Norf	TG5107	52°36·4′	1°42·8′E	T	134
Cob House Fm	Lancs	SD8114	53°37·6′	2°16·8′W	FM	109
Cobhouse Fm	Worcs	SO7758	52°13·4′	2°19·8′W	FM	150
Cob Island	Suff	TM4456	52°9·1′	1°34·4′E	X	156
Cobland Hill	Corn	SX3454	50°22·0′	4°19·7′W	H	201
Coblands Fm	Devon	SS9504	50°49·8′	3°29·1′W	FM	192
Coblands Fm	Suff	TL7755	52°10·1′	0°35·7′E	FM	155
Coble Ho Point	Fife	NO4619	56°21·9′	2°52·0′W	X	59
Cobleland	Stir	NS5398	56°9·4′	4°21·6′W	X	57
Cobler's Green	Essex	TL6819	51°50·9′	0°26·7′E	T	167
Coblers Hill	Oxon	SU6286	51°34·4′	1°5·9′W	X	175
Cobles	Cumbr	SD6698	54°22·8′	2°31·0′W	X	98
Coble Shore	Fife	NO4619	56°21·9′	2°52·0′W	X	59
Cobley	Devon	SS7409	50°52·2′	3°47·1′W	X	191
Cobley	Dorset	SU0220	50°59·0′	1°57·9′W	T	184
Cobley Fm	Devon	SS7512	50°53·9′	3°46·3′W	FM	180
Cobley Hill	Worcs	SP0171	52°20·5′	1°58·7′W	T	139
Cobley Lodge Fm	Northnts	SP8985	52°27·6′	0°41·0′W	FM	141
Cobley Wood	Hants	SU5244	51°11·8′	1°15·0′W	F	185
Cobling Fm	Brad	SE0433	53°47·8′	1°55·9′W	FM	104
Cobmarsh Island	Essex	TM0012	51°46·5′	0°54·3′E	X	168
Cobnash	Heref	SO4560	52°14·4′	2°47·9′W	T	137,138,148
Cobnor	W Susx	TQ2137	51°7·4′	0°15·9′W	X	187
Cobnor Fm	W Susx	SU7902	50°49·0′	0°52·3′W	FM	197
Cobnor Ho	W Susx	SU7902	50°49·0′	0°52·3′W	X	197
Cobnor Point	W Susx	SU7901	50°48·4′	0°52·3′W	X	197
Cobra Castle	Cumbr	NY0211	54°29·3′	3°30·4′W	X	89
Cobrahamsole Fm	Kent	TR0056	51°16·3′	0°52·4′E	FM	178
Cobrance	Orkney	HY5009	58°58·2′	2°51·7′W	X	6,7
Cobrey Park	Heref	SO6021	51°53·4′	2°34·5′W	X	162
Cobridge	C of Stoke	SJ8748	53°2·0′	2°11·2′W	T	118
Cobs Ash	Herts	TL2103	51°43·0′	0°14·5′W	F	166
Cobscot	Shrops	SJ6838	52°56·5′	2°28·2′W	T	127
Cobshaw Fm	N Yks	SE2691	54°19·1′	1°35·6′W	FM	99
Coburg	Devon	SX8679	50°36·2′	3°36·3′W	X	191
Coburn's Fm	Devon	ST2411	50°53·8′	3°4·5′W	FM	192,193
Coburty	Aberd	NJ9264	57°40·2′	2°7·6′W	X	30
Cochill Burn	Pth & Kin	NN9042	56°33·7′	3°46·9′W	W	52
Cochno	W Dunb	NS4974	55°56·4′	4°24·6′W	X	64
Cochno Burn	W Dunb	NS5074	55°56·4′	4°23·7′W	W	64
Cochno Hill	W Dunb	NS4875	55°56·9′	4°25·6′W	H	64
Cochno Loch	W Dunb	NS4976	55°57·5′	4°24·7′W	W	64
Cochrage Muir	Pth & Kin	NO1249	56°37·7′	3°25·6′W	X	53
Cochrane Pike	Northum	NU0013	55°24·9′	1°59·6′W	H	81
Cochsidan	Powys	SO0698	52°34·5′	3°22·8′W	X	136
Cochwillan	Gwyn	SH6069	53°12·2′	4°5·4′W	A	115
Cochwillan	I of Angl	SH4788	53°22·3′	4°17·6′W	X	114
Coch-y-barlys	Carm	SN3813	51°47·8′	4°20·6′W	X	159
Coch Y Ceiliog	Pemb	SM9737	51°59·9′	4°57·0′W	X	157
Cochydwst	Powys	SO0563	52°15·7′	3°23·1′W	X	147
Côch-y-moel	Gwyn	SH2330	52°50·6′	4°37·3′W	X	123
Coch y Rhŵd	Gwyn	SH4654	53°3·9′	4°17·5′W	X	115,123
Cock	N Ayr	NR9651	55°42·8′	5°14·4′W	X	62,69
Cock Abingdon Fm	Leic	SP7796	52°33·6′	0°51·4′W	FM	141
Cockairney	Pth & Kin	NT0999	56°10·8′	3°27·5′W	X	58
Cockairney Feus	Pth & Kin	NT0998	56°10·2′	3°27·5′W	X	58
Cockairnie	Fife	NT1685	56°3·3′	3°20·5′W	X	65,66
Cockalane	Arg & Bt	NR7411	55°20·7′	5°33·4′W	X	68
Cock Alley	Derby	SK4170	53°13·8′	1°22·7′W	T	120
Cockan	Cumbr	NY0718	54°33·2′	3°25·9′W	X	89
Cockardie	Aberd	NO6199	57°5·1′	2°38·2′W	X	37,45
Cock Ash	Kent	TR1139	51°6·9′	1°1·3′E	X	179,189
Cockayne	N Yks	SE6298	54°22·7′	1°2·3′W	T	94,100
Cockayne Hatley	Beds	TL2649	52°7·7′	0°9·2′W	T	153
Cockayne Hatley Wood	Beds	TL2650	52°8·3′	0°9·1′W	F	153
Cockayne Ridge	N Yks	NZ6100	54°23·7′	1°3·2′W	H	94
Cockaynes	Essex	TM0621	51°51·2′	0°59·9′E	X	168
Cock Bank	Wrex	SJ3545	53°0·1′	2°57·7′W	T	117
Cock Beck	Leeds	SE4137	53°49·9′	1°22·2′W	W	105
Cock Beck	N Yks	SE4739	53°50·9′	1°16·7′W	W	105
Cock Bevington	Warw	SP0552	52°10·2′	1°55·2′W	T	150
Cock Br	Lancs	SD7434	53°48·3′	2°23·3′W	X	103
Cock Bridge	Aberd	NJ2508	57°9·7′	3°13·9′W	X	37
Cockbrook Fm	Cambs	TL0879	52°24·1′	0°24·3′W	FM	142
Cockbrook Lodge	Cambs	TL0878	52°23·6′	0°24·4′W	X	142
Cock Burn	Aberd	NJ2507	57°9·1′	3°13·9′W	W	37
Cock Burn	C of Edin	NT1363	55°51·4′	3°23·0′W	W	65
Cockburn	C of Edin	NT1465	55°52·5′	3°22·0′W	X	65
Cockburn	Scot Bord	NT7658	55°49·1′	2°22·5′W	H	67,74
Cockburn East	Scot Bord	NT7759	55°49·7′	2°21·6′W	X	67,74
Cockburnhill	C of Edin	NT1464	55°51·9′	3°22·0′W	X	65
Cockburn Law	Scot Bord	NT7659	55°49·7′	2°22·5′W	H	67,74
Cockburn Mill	Scot Bord	NT7758	55°49·1′	2°21·6′W	X	67,74
Cockburnspath	Scot Bord	NT7770	55°55·6′	2°21·6′W	T	67
Cockbury Court	Glos	SO9927	51°56·7′	2°0·5′W	X	163
Cock Bush Hall Fm	N Yks	NZ4400	54°23·9′	1°18·9′W	FM	93
Cock Bush Hall Fm	N Yks	SE4499	54°23·3′	1°18·9′W	FM	99
Cock Cairn	Angus	NO4688	56°59·1′	2°52·9′W	H	44
Cock Clarks	Essex	TL8102	51°41·5′	0°37·5′E	T	168
Cockclay	E Ayr	NS4941	55°38·6′	4°23·5′W	X	70
Cockclay	E Ayr	NS5006	55°19·8′	4°21·4′W	H	70,77
Cock Croft	Heref	SO4957	52°12·8′	2°44·4′W	X	148,149
Cockden	Lancs	SD8734	53°48·4′	2°11·4′W	T	103
Cockdurno	C of Edin	NT1564	55°52·0′	3°21·1′W	X	65
Cocked Hat	N Yks	SE1988	54°17·5′	1°42·1′W	X	99
Cocked Hat Fm	Lincs	SK9853	53°4·1′	0°31·8′W	FM	121
Cocked Hat Fm	N Yks	SE4280	54°13·1′	1°20·9′W	FM	99
Cocked Hat Plantn	Lincs	SK9953	53°4·1′	0°30·9′W	F	121

Cock & End	Suff	TL7253	52°9·1′	0°31·3′E	T	154
Cockenheugh	Northum	NU0634	55°36·2′	1°53·9′W	X	75
Cockenskell	Cumbr	SD2789	54°17·7′	3°6·9′W	X	96,97
Cocken White House Fm	Durham	NZ2947	54°49·3′	1°32·5′W	FM	88
Cockenzie	N Ayr	NS3046	55°40·9′	4°41·8′W	X	63
Cockenzie and Port Seton	E Loth	NT4075	55°58·1′	2°57·2′W	T	66
Cocker	N Yks	NY9307	54°27·7′	2°6·1′W	X	91,92
Cocker Bar	Lancs	SD5022	53°41·8′	2°45·0′W	T	102
Cocker Beck	Darl	NZ2416	54°32·6′	1°37·3′W	W	93
Cocker Beck	Notts	SK6546	53°0·7′	1°1·5′W	W	129
Cockercombe	Somer	ST1836	51°7·3′	3°9·9′W	X	181
Cockerdale Fm	N Yks	SE5381	54°13·6′	1°10·8′W	FM	100
Cockerells Hall	Suff	TL9857	52°10·8′	0°54·2′E	X	155
Cockerham	Lancs	SD4652	53°57·9′	2°49·0′W	T	102
Cockerham	N Yks	SD9961	54°2·9′	2°0·5′W	X	98
Cockerham Marsh	Lancs	SD4351	53°57·4′	2°51·7′W	W	102
Cockerham Moss	Lancs	SD4448	53°55·8′	2°50·8′W	X	102
Cockerham Sands	Lancs	SD4152	53°57·9′	2°53·5′W	X	102
Cocker Hill	D & G	NS7515	55°25·0′	3°58·1′W	H	71,78
Cocker Hill	Lancs	SD8842	53°52·7′	2°10·5′W	X	103
Cocker Hill	N Yks	NZ0406	54°27·2′	1°55·9′W	H	92
Cocker Hill Fm	Leeds	SE2641	53°52·1′	1°35·9′W	FM	104
Cocker Ho Bridge	Lancs	SD4751	53°57·4′	2°48·0′W	X	102
Cockering Fm	Kent	TR1356	51°16·0′	1°3·6′E	FM	179
Cockermount	Northum	NY8285	55°9·8′	2°16·5′W	X	80
Cockermouth	Cumbr	NY1230	54°39·7′	3°21·4′W	T	89
Cockernhoe	Herts	TL1223	51°53·9′	0°21·9′W	T	166
Cockersand Abbey Fm	Lancs	SD4253	53°58·4′	2°52·6′W	FM	102
Cockersdale	Leeds	SE2329	53°45·7′	1°38·7′W	T	104
Cockers Dale	Leeds	SE2330	53°46·2′	1°38·6′W	X	104
Cocker's Dyke Houses	Lancs	SD3749	53°56·2′	2°57·2′W	X	102
Cockersfauld	Pth & Kin	NO0210	56°16·6′	3°34·5′W	X	58
Cocker Shield	Northum	NY8954	54°53·1′	2°9·9′W	X	87
Cockerstone	Pth & Kin	NO0233	56°29·0′	3°35·0′W	X	52,53
Cockerton	Darl	NZ2715	54°32·0′	1°34·5′W	T	93
Cockethill	D & G	NY0778	55°5·5′	3°27·0′W	X	85
Cocket Moss	N Yks	SD7861	54°2·9′	2°19·7′W	X	98
Cockett	Swan	SS6294	51°37·9′	3°59·2′W	T	159
Cockett Fm	Notts	SK6457	53°6·6′	1°2·2′W	FM	120
Cockett Hill	Dorset	SY9295	50°45·5′	2°6·4′W	X	195
Cockett Wick Fm	Essex	TM1314	51°47·3′	1°5·7′E	FM	168,169
Cocketty	Aberd	NO7778	56°53·8′	2°22·2′W	X	45
Cockey Fm	Derby	SK1979	53°18·7′	1°42·5′W	FM	119
Cock Fen Fm	Norf	TL5396	52°32·6′	0°15·8′E	FM	143
Cockfield	Durham	NZ1224	54°36·9′	1°48·4′W	T	92
Cockfield	Suff	TL9054	52°9·3′	0°47·1′E	T	155
Cockfield Fell	Durham	NZ1224	54°36·9′	1°48·4′W	X	92
Cockfield Hall	Suff	TM1750	52°6·6′	1°10·5′E	X	156
Cockfield Hall	Suff	TM3969	52°16·3′	1°30·6′E	X	156
Cockfields Fm	Oldham	SD9402	53°31·1′	2°5·0′W	FM	109
Cock Flat	N Yks	NZ5500	54°23·8′	1°8·8′W	X	93
Cock Fm	Lancs	SD4607	53°33·7′	2°48·5′W	FM	108
Cock Fms	Somer	ST2243	51°11·1′	3°6·6′W	FM	182
Cockfosters	Barnet	TQ2796	51°39·1′	0°9·5′W	T	166,176
Cockgair Hill	D & G	NY2984	55°9·0′	3°6·4′W	H	79
Cock Gate	Heref	SO4665	52°17·1′	2°47·1′W	T	137,138,148
Cock Green	Essex	TL6919	51°50·9′	0°27·6′E	T	167
Cock Hag	Cumbr	SD4493	54°20·0′	2°51·3′W	X	97
Cockhaise Mill Fm	W Susx	TQ3725	51°0·7′	0°2·4′W	FM	187,198
Cockhall	Northum	NU1019	55°28·1′	1°50·1′W	X	81
Cock Hall Fm	Lancs	SD4753	53°58·5′	2°48·1′W	FM	102
Cockhampstead	Herts	TL4125	51°54·6′	0°3·4′E	X	167
Cockhayes	Devon	ST2010	50°53·3′	3°7·9′W	X	192,193
Cockhead	Ches	SJ9783	53°20·9′	2°2·3′W	X	109
Cock Heads	N Yks	NZ7100	54°23·7′	0°54·0′W	H	94
Cock Hill	Aberd	NO5387	56°58·6′	2°45·9′W	H	44
Cock Hill	Aberd	NO5586	56°58·0′	2°44·0′W	X	44
Cock Hill	Aberd	NO5783	56°56·4′	2°42·0′W	X	44
Cock Hill	Aberd	NO5979	56°54·3′	2°39·9′W	H	44
Cockhill	Angus	NO5244	56°35·4′	2°46·4′W	X	54
Cock Hill	Cald	SE0022	53°41·9′	1°59·6′W	X	104
Cock Hill	Cald	SE0132	53°47·3′	1°58·7′W	X	104
Cock Hill	Derby	SK0696	53°27·9′	1°54·2′W	X	110
Cockhill	Devon	SS5445	51°11·4′	4°5·0′W	X	180
Cock Hill	D & G	NS8508	55°21·4′	3°48·4′W	H	71,78
Cock Hill	E Ayr	NS5943	55°39·9′	4°14·1′W	X	71
Cock Hill	Lancs	SD9041	53°52·1′	2°8·7′W	X	103
Cock Hill	N Lanak	NS7182	56°1·1′	4°3·7′W	H	57,64
Cock Hill	Northum	NZ1681	55°7·6′	1°44·5′W	X	81
Cock Hill	N Yks	SE5155	53°59·6′	1°12·9′W	T	105
Cockhill	S Ayr	NS3617	55°25·4′	4°35·1′W	X	70
Cockhill	S Ayr	NS3736	55°35·7′	4°34·8′W	X	70
Cock Hill	Somer	ST3738	51°8·5′	2°53·6′W	H	182
Cockhill	Somer	ST6231	51°4·9′	2°32·2′W	T	183
Cock Hill	Stir	NN6105	56°13·3′	4°14·1′W	H	57
Cock Hill	Warw	SP1697	52°34·5′	1°45·4′W	X	139
Cockhill Cott	Stir	NN6205	56°13·3′	4°13·1′W	X	57
Cockhill Fm	Donc	SK5496	53°27·7′	1°10·8′W	FM	111
Cockhill Fm	Dorset	ST7016	50°56·8′	2°25·2′W	FM	183
Cockhill Fm	Kent	TQ8161	51°19·4′	0°36·3′E	FM	178,188
Cockhill Wood	Aberd	NJ7438	57°26·2′	2°25·5′W	F	29
Cockholme Burn	Scot Bord	NT4646	55°42·5′	2°51·1′W	W	73
Cock Howe	N Yks	SE5498	54°22·7′	1°9·7′W	A	100
Cockiland Hill	Scot Bord	NT1024	55°30·3′	3°25·1′W	H	72
Cockin	Cumbr	SD5799	54°23·3′	2°39·3′W	X	97
Cocking	W Susx	SU8717	50°57·0′	0°45·3′W	T	197
Cocking Causeway	W Susx	SU8819	50°58·0′	0°44·4′W	T	197
Cocking Down	W Susx	SU8616	50°56·4′	0°46·2′W	X	197
Cockingford	Devon	SX7275	50°33·9′	3°48·1′W	X	191
Cocking Moor	Notts	SK6966	53°11·4′	0°57·6′W	X	120
Cocking Park	W Susx	SU8719	50°58·1′	0°45·3′W	X	197
Cockington	Torbay	SX8963	50°27·6′	3°33·5′W	T	202
Cockington Fm	Devon	SS4025	51°0·4′	4°16·5′W	FM	180,190
Cocking Tor	Derby	SK3461	53°8·9′	1°29·1′W	X	119
Cockinhead Moss	N Ayr	NS3548	55°42·1′	4°37·1′W	X	63
Cock Inn	D & G	NX2351	54°49·6′	4°44·9′W	X	82
Cock Inn Fm	Cambs	TL6279	52°23·3′	0°23·2′E	FM	143
Cockintake	Staffs	SK0450	53°3·1′	1°56·0′W	X	119
Cockit Hill	Powys	SO1627	51°56·3′	3°12·9′W	X	161
Cock Knarr	Tames	SJ9998	53°29·0′	2°0·5′W	X	109

Cock-knoll	Ches	SJ9882	53°20·3′	2°1·4′W	X	109
Cock Knowe	Scot Bord	NT3406	55°20·9′	3°2·0′W	X	79
Cocklake	Cumbr	NY6204	54°26·0′	2°34·7′W	X	91
Cocklake	Cumbr	NY7537	54°43·9′	2°22·9′W	X	91
Cock Lake	Durham	NY8822	54°35·8′	2°10·7′W	X	91,92
Cocklake	Northum	NY9656	54°54·2′	2°3·3′W	X	87
Cocklake	Somer	ST4349	51°14·5′	2°48·6′W	T	182
Cocklakes	Cumbr	NY4551	54°51·3′	2°51·0′W	X	86
Cocklakes	Cumbr	SD2683	54°14·5′	3°7·7′W	X	96,97
Cocklake Side	Durham	NY8822	54°35·8′	2°10·7′W	X	91,92
Cock Lake Side	N Yks	SD8884	54°15·3′	2°10·6′W	X	98
Cock Lane Side	N Yks	NZ9000	54°23·5′	0°36·4′W	X	94
Cocklarachy	Aberd	NJ5337	57°25·5′	2°46·5′W	X	29
Cocklaw	C of Edin	NT1668	55°54·1′	3°20·2′W	X	65,66
Cock Law	D & G	NY2982	55°7·9′	3°6·4′W	H	79
Cocklaw	E Loth	NT7371	55°56·1′	2°25·5′W	X	67
Cocklaw	Fife	NO5809	56°16·6′	2°40·3′W	X	59
Cock Law	N Ayr	NS2453	55°44·6′	4°47·8′W	X	63
Cock Law	N Ayr	NS2555	55°45·7′	4°46·9′W	X	63
Cock Law	Northum	NU2122	55°29·7′	1°39·6′W	X	75
Cock Law	Pth & Kin	NO0310	56°16·6′	3°33·6′W	H	58
Cocklaw	Pth & Kin	NT0197	56°9·6′	3°35·2′W	X	58
Cock Law	Scot Bord	NT8517	55°27·0′	2°13·8′W	H	80
Cocklaw	Scot Bord	NT9360	55°50·2′	2°6·3′W	X	67
Cock Law	Scot Bord	NY5090	55°12·4′	2°46·7′W	H	79
Cocklaw	S Lanak	NT0441	55°39·4′	3°31·1′W	X	72
Cocklaw Dean	Northum	NU1128	55°33·0′	1°49·1′W	X	75
Cocklaw Fell	Cumbr	NY4803	54°25·4′	2°47·7′W	X	90
Cocklawfoot	Scot Bord	NT8518	55°27·6′	2°13·8′W	X	80
Cocklaw Hill	E Loth	NT7171	55°56·1′	2°27·4′W	H	67
Cocklaw Knowe	D & G	NT0812	55°23·9′	3°26·7′W	H	78
Cocklaw Mains	Aberd	NK1045	57°30·0′	1°49·5′W	X	30
Cocklaw Walls	Northum	NZ0078	55°6·0′	1°59·6′W	X	87
Cockleach	Lancs	SD6038	53°50·4′	2°36·1′W	X	102,103
Cock Leach	Lancs	SD8838	53°50·5′	2°10·5′W	X	103
Cockle Bank	Inverc	NS3175	55°56·6′	4°41·9′W	X	63
Cocklebarrow Fm	Glos	SP1410	51°47·5′	1°47·4′W	FM	163
Cockleberry Fm	N Yks	NZ2904	54°26·1′	1°32·8′W	FM	93
Cockleberry Fm	Oxon	SU3683	51°32·9′	1°28·5′W	FM	174
Cocklebury	Durham	NZ0412	54°30·4′	1°55·9′W	X	92
Cocklebury Fm	Wilts	SU1260	51°20·6′	1°49·3′W	FM	173
Cocklee	Scot Bord	NT5441	55°39·9′	2°43·4′W	X	73
Cocklee Fell	N Yks	SD8581	54°13·7′	2°13·4′W	X	98
Cockleford	Glos	SO9614	51°49·7′	2°3·1′W	T	163
Cockleford Fm	Glos	SO9713	51°49·2′	2°2·2′W	FM	163
Cockle Hill	Cambs	TL4449	52°7·5′	0°6·6′E	X	154
Cocklehill	Moray	NJ2267	57°41·4′	3°18·0′W	X	28
Cockle Hill	N Yks	SE1173	54°9·4′	1°49·5′W	X	99
Cockle Loch	N Ayr	NS2358	55°47·2′	4°48·9′W	W	63
Cocklemill Burn	Fife	NO4701	56°12·2′	2°50·8′W	W	59
Cocklemore Brook	Wilts	ST9370	51°26·0′	2°5·7′W	W	173
Cockle Park	Northum	NZ2091	55°13·0′	1°40·7′W	X	81
Cockleridge	Devon	SX6644	50°17·1′	3°52·5′W	X	202
Cockleroy	W Loth	NS9874	55°57·1′	3°37·6′W	X	65
Cockleroy (Fort)	W Loth	NS9874	55°57·1′	3°37·6′W	A	65
Cockles	E Loth	NT5371	55°56·1′	2°44·7′W	X	66
Cockle Sand	Devon	SX9982	50°38·0′	3°25·3′W	X	192
Cockleshell Beach	Medway	TQ8778	51°28·4′	0°42·0′E	X	178
Cockles, The	Northum	NZ2191	55°13·0′	1°39·8′W	X	81
Cocklet Hill	D & G	NX9688	55°10·8′	3°37·6′W	H	78
Cocklet Hill	Lancs	SD7455	53°59·7′	2°23·4′W	X	103
Cocklet Hill Fm	Cumbr	NY4967	54°59·9′	2°47·4′W	FM	86
Cocklett Rigg	Cumbr	NY5573	55°3·2′	2°41·8′W	X	86
Cockley	Aberd	NO8396	57°3·5′	2°16·4′W	X	38,45
Cockleybank	Cumbr	NY4953	54°52·4′	2°47·3′W	X	86
Cockley Beck	Cumbr	NY2401	54°24·2′	3°9·8′W	T	89,90
Cockley Beck	Cumbr	NY3840	54°45·3′	2°57·4′W	W	85
Cockley Beck Fell	Cumbr	NY2501	54°24·2′	3°8·9′W	X	89,90
Cockley Brook	Oxon	SP4426	51°56·1′	1°21·2′W	W	164
Cockley Cley	Norf	TF7904	52°36·5′	0°39·0′E	T	144
Cockleycley Heath	Norf	TF7905	52°37·0′	0°39·1′E	X	144
Cockleycley Warren	Norf	TF8204	52°36·4′	0°41·7′E	X	144
Cockleycley Wood	Norf	TF7705	52°37·1′	0°37·3′E	F	144
Cockleygill	Cumbr	NY0819	54°33·7′	3°24·9′W	X	89
Cockley Hill	Kirk	SE1817	53°39·2′	1°43·2′W	T	110
Cockleyhill Fm	Northnts	SP5441	52°4·1′	1°12·3′W	FM	152
Cockley Moor	Cumbr	NY3822	54°35·6′	2°57·2′W	X	90
Cocklethwaite	Cumbr	NY3841	54°45·9′	2°57·4′W	X	85
Cocklick End	Lancs	SD7358	54°1·3′	2°24·3′W	X	103
Cocklicks	D & G	NY1168	55°0·2′	3°23·1′W	X	85
Cocklie Rig Head	Scot Bord	NT0928	55°32·5′	3°26·1′W	H	72
Cockliffe House	Notts	SK5850	53°2·9′	1°7·7′W	X	120
Cocklit Hill	Cumbr	NY6360	54°56·2′	2°34·2′W	X	86
Cocklode Wood	Lincs	TF1076	53°16·4′	0°20·6′W	F	121
Cockly Knowes	Northum	NU1338	55°38·4′	1°47·2′W	X	75
Cock Marling	E Susx	TQ8818	50°56·1′	0°40·9′E	T	189,199
Cock Marsh	Win & Maid	SU8886	51°34·2′	0°43·4′W	X	175
Cockmartin's Fm	E Susx	TQ8014	50°54·1′	0°34·0′E	FM	199
Cockmill Croft Fm	Somer	ST6038	51°8·6′	2°33·9′W	FM	183
Cockmoor Cott	N Yks	SE9385	54°15·4′	0°33·9′W	X	94,101
Cockmoor Wood	Midlo	NT3254	55°46·7′	3°4·6′W	F	66,73
Cockmount Hill	Northum	NY6966	54°59·5′	2°28·6′W	X	86,87
Cockmuir	Aberd	NJ6931	57°22·4′	2°30·5′W	X	29
Cockmuir	Aberd	NJ9855	57°35·4′	2°1·5′W	X	30
Cockmuir	Midlo	NT2654	55°46·7′	3°10·3′W	X	66,73
Cockmuir Fm	Moray	NJ2357	57°36·3′	3°16·8′W	FM	28
Cockmurra	Orkney	HY4604	58°55·5′	2°55·8′W	X	6,7
Cockmylane	W Loth	NT0966	55°53·0′	3°26·8′W	X	65
Cocknage Fm	Staffs	SJ9140	52°57·7′	2°7·6′W	FM	118
Cocknowle	Dorset	SY9381	50°37·9′	2°5·6′W	T	195
Cock of Arran	N Ayr	NR9552	55°43·3′	5°15·4′W	X	62,69
Cockpen Fm	Midlo	NT3263	55°51·6′	3°4·7′W	FM	66
Cockpit	Gwyn	SH6307	52°38·9′	4°1·1′W	A	124
Cockpit Fm, The	Hants	SU5017	50°57·2′	1°16·9′W	FM	185
Cockpit Hall	N Yks	SE6888	54°17·2′	0°56·9′W	X	94,100
Cockpit Hill	Dorset	ST4101	50°48·6′	2°49·9′W	X	193
Cockpit, The	Cumbr	NY4822	54°35·7′	2°47·9′W	A	90
Cock Play	Cumbr	NY6077	55°5·4′	2°37·2′W	X	86
Cockplay	Northum	NY8872	55°2·8′	2°10·8′W	X	87
Cock Play	Northum	NY8982	55°8·2′	2°9·9′W	X	80

Cock Play	Northum	NZ0175	55°4·4′	1°58·6′W	X	87
Cockplay	Scot Bord	NT3913	55°24·7′	2°57·4′W	H	79
Cockplay Hill	D & G	NY3085	55°9·5′	3°5·5′W	X	79
Cockplay Hill	D & G	NY4094	55°14·4′	2°56·2′W	H	79
Cockplay Hill	Scot Bord	NY4495	55°15·0′	2°52·4′W	H	79
Cockpole Green	Wok	SU7981	51°31·6′	0°51·3′W	T	175
Cockpool	D & G	NY0667	54°59·6′	3°27·7′W	X	85
Cockpool Plantn	D & G	NY0667	54°59·6′	3°27·7′W	F	85
Cockrah Foot	N Yks	SE9689	54°17·5′	0°31·1′W	X	94,101
Cockrah Wood	N Yks	SE9688	54°17·0′	0°31·1′W	F	94,101
Cockrell's Fm	Essex	TL9431	51°56·8′	0°49·8′E	FM	168
Cock Ridge	Northum	NY8790	55°12·5′	2°11·8′W	X	80
Cock Rig	Midlo	NT1559	55°49·3′	3°21·0′W	H	65,72
Cockrig	S Lanak	NS9249	55°43·6′	3°42·7′W	X	72
Cockrigg	Cumbr	SD5487	54°16·8′	2°42·0′W	X	97
Cockrigg Crags	Cumbr	NY3017	54°32·9′	3°4·5′W	X	90
Cockroad Fm	Dorset	ST9808	50°52·5′	2°1·3′W	FM	195
Cock Road Fm	Somer	ST7652	51°16·2′	2°20·3′W	FM	183
Cockroad Wood	Somer	ST7432	51°5·4′	2°21·9′W	F	183
Cock Robin Cott	N Yks	SD9085	54°15·9′	2°8·8′W	X	98
Cock Robin Fm	Glos	SP0129	51°57·8′	1°58·7′W	FM	150,163
Cockrobin Hill	N Ayr	NS2552	55°44·0′	4°46·8′W	X	63
Cockroost Fm	Wilts	SU1077	51°29·7′	1°51·0′W	FM	173
Cockroost Hill	Bri & Hov	TQ2408	50°51·7′	0°13·9′W	X	198
Cocks	Corn	SW7652	50°19·8′	5°8·5′W	T	200,204
Cocksbrook Wood	Heref	SO4828	51°57·1′	2°45·0′W	F	149,161
Cocksburn Resr	Stir	NS8098	56°9·8′	3°55·5′W	W	57
Cocks Close	Cumbr	SD5299	54°23·3′	2°43·9′W	X	97
Cocksedge Fm	Cambs	TL6352	52°8·8′	0°23·3′E	FM	154
Cocksford	N Yks	SE4739	53°50·9′	1°16·7′W	X	105
Cocks Green	Suff	TL8858	52°11·5′	0°45·4′E	T	155
Cockshades	Ches	SJ7050	53°3·0′	2°26·4′W	X	118
Cockshades Hill	Lancs	SD4955	53°59·6′	2°46·3′W	X	102
Cockshall Cotts	Shrops	SO6384	52°27·4′	2°32·3′W	X	138
Cockshaw Plantn	E Yorks	SE7346	53°54·5′	0°52·9′W	F	105,106
Cockshead	Cered	SN6355	52°10·8′	3°59·8′W	T	146
Cock's Hill	Bucks	SP8906	51°45·0′	0°42·2′W	X	165
Cocks Hill	Devon	SX5679	50°35·8′	4°1·7′W	X	191
Cocks Hill	Oxon	SU6681	51°31·7′	1°2·5′W	X	175
Cock's Ho	Durham	NZ1327	54°38·5′	1°47·5′W	X	92
Cockshoot	Glos	SO8809	51°47·0′	2°10·0′W	X	162
Cockshoot	Heref	SO5838	52°2·6′	2°36·3′W	T	149
Cockshoot	Heref	SO6039	52°3·1′	2°34·6′W	X	149
Cockshoot Broad	Norf	TG3415	52°41·1′	1°28·1′E	W	133,134
Cockshoot Fm	Worcs	SO7761	52°15·0′	2°19·8′W	FM	138,150
Cockshoot Hill	Beds	TL1439	52°2·5′	0°19·9′W	X	153
Cockshoots Wood	Bucks	SP8703	51°43·4′	0°44·0′W	F	165
Cockshoots Woods	Bucks	SU8194	51°38·6′	0°49·4′W	F	175
Cockshoot Wood	Glos	SO6407	51°45·9′	2°30·9′W	F	162
Cockshot	Northum	NZ1199	55°17·3′	1°49·2′W	X	81
Cockshot Camp	Durham	NZ1214	54°31·5′	1°48·5′W	A	92
Cockshot Fm	Worcs	SO9856	52°12·4′	2°1·4′W	FM	150
Cockshot Hill	Heref	SO7446	52°6·9′	2°22·4′W	X	150
Cock Shots	Red & Cl	NZ7017	54°32·8′	0°54·6′W	X	94
Cockshott Point	Cumbr	SD3996	54°21·6′	2°55·9′W	X	96,97
Cockshotts Wood	Lancs	SD6070	54°7·7′	2°36·3′W	F	97
Cockshutford	Shrops	SO5885	52°27·9′	2°36·7′W	T	137,138
Cocks-hut-hill	Derby	SK3142	52°58·7′	1°31·9′W	X	119,128
Cockshut Rough	Shrops	SJ6103	52°37·6′	2°34·2′W	X	127
Cockshutt	Shrops	SJ4329	52°51·6′	2°50·4′W	T	126
Cockshutt	Shrops	SO7383	52°26·9′	2°23·4′W	T	138
Cocks Moss Fm	Ches	SJ8567	53°12·2′	2°13·1′W	FM	118
Cock's Park	Heref	SO4347	52°7·3′	2°49·6′W	F	148,149
Cocksport	Corn	SX1692	50°42·1′	4°36·0′W	X	190
Cockspur Hall	Worcs	SO5862	52°15·5′	2°36·5′W	X	137,138,149
Cockston	N Ayr	NS3158	55°47·4′	4°41·3′W	X	63
Cock Street	Kent	TQ7750	51°13·5′	0°32·5′E	T	188
Cock Street	Suff	TL9636	51°59·5′	0°51·7′E	T	155
Cockstreet	Swan	SS4292	51°36·5′	4°16·5′W	X	159
Cockthorne Fm	Lincs	TF0687	53°22·4′	0°24·0′W	FM	112,121
Cockthorn Fm	Lincs	SK8899	53°29·1′	0°40·0′W	FM	112
Cockthorpe	Norf	TF9842	52°56·6′	0°57·2′E	T	132
Cockthorpe Common	Norf	TF9843	52°57·1′	0°57·3′E	X	132
Cocktop	Derby	SK4361	53°8·9′	1°21·0′W	X	120
Cocktree Moor	Devon	SX6799	50°46·8′	3°52·8′W	X	191
Cocktree Throat	Devon	SX6697	50°45·7′	3°53·6′W	X	191
Cockup	Cumbr	NY2531	54°40·4′	3°9·4′W	X	89,90
Cockwells	Corn	SW5234	50°9·5′	5°28·0′W	T	203
Cockwood	Devon	SX9780	50°36·9′	3°27·0′W	T	192
Cock Wood	Northum	NY9563	54°57·9′	2°4·3′W	F	87
Cockwood	Somer	ST2242	51°10·6′	3°6·6′W	T	182
Cockwood Fm	Donc	SE6503	53°31·4′	1°0·8′W	FM	111
Cockyard	Derby	SK0479	53°18·7′	1°56·0′W	T	119
Cockyard	Heref	SO4133	51°59·8′	2°51·2′W	T	149,161
Cocum Fm	Hants	SU4439	51°9·1′	1°21·9′W	FM	185
Codale Tarn	Cumbr	NY2908	54°28·0′	3°5·3′W	W	89,90
Codau Mawr	Conwy	SH8670	53°13·1′	3°42·0′W	X	116
Cod Beck	N Yks	SE4189	54°17·9′	1°21·8′W	W	99
Cod Beck Reservoir	N Yks	SE4698	54°22·8′	1°17·1′W	W	100
Codborough Fm	E Susx	TQ9019	50°56·6′	0°42·7′E	FM	189
Codda	Corn	SX1878	50°34·6′	4°33·9′W	X	201
Codda Tor	Corn	SX1779	50°35·2′	4°34·7′W	X	201
Coddem Island	N Eil	NF9884	57°44·9′	7°4·1′W	X	18
Codden	Devon	SS5730	51°3·3′	4°2·0′W	X	180
Coddenham	Suff	TM1354	52°8·8′	1°7·2′E	T	156
Coddenham Green	Suff	TM1155	52°9·4′	1°5·5′E	T	155
Coddenham Hall	Suff	TL9539	52°1·1′	0°50·9′E	X	155
Codden Hill	Devon	SS5829	51°2·8′	4°1·2′W	H	180
Codd Hall	E Yorks	SE8929	53°45·2′	0°38·6′W	X	106
Coddiford	Devon	SS8607	50°51·3′	3°36·8′W	X	191
Coddington	Ches	SJ4555	53°5·6′	2°48·9′W	T	117
Coddington	Derby	SK3354	53°5·2′	1°30·0′W	X	119
Coddington	Heref	SO7142	52°4·8′	2°25·0′W	T	149
Coddington	Notts	SK8354	53°4·8′	0°45·2′W	T	121
Coddington Brook	Ches	SJ4456	53°6·1′	2°48·9′W	W	117
Coddington Cross	Heref	SO7243	52°5·3′	2°24·1′W	X	149
Coddington Moor	Notts	SK8454	53°4·8′	0°44·4′W	X	121
Coddingtons Yard	Lincs	TF5261	53°7·7′	0°16·7′E	X	122
Coddow Combe	Devon	SS7550	51°14·4′	3°47·1′W	X	180
Codeshayes Fm	Devon	SY1798	50°46·8′	3°10·3′W	FM	192,193
Codford Circle	Wilts	ST9840	51°9·8′	2°1·3′W	A	184
Codford Down	Wilts	ST9742	51°10·9′	2°2·2′W	X	184
Codford St Mary	Wilts	ST9739	51°9·2′	2°2·2′W	T	184
Codford St Peter	Wilts	ST9640	51°9·8′	2°3·0′W	T	184
Codger Fort	Northum	NZ0490	55°12·5′	1°55·8′W	X	81
Codhall	Kent	TR0028	51°1·2′	0°51·5′E	X	189
Codham Hall	Essex	TQ5888	51°34·3′	0°17·2′E	X	177
Codicote	Herts	TL2118	51°51·1′	0°14·2′W	T	166
Codicote Bottom	Herts	TL2017	51°50·5′	0°15·1′W	T	166
Codicote Heath	Herts	TL2018	51°51·1′	0°15·1′W	X	166
Codicote Lo	Herts	TL2118	51°51·1′	0°14·2′W	X	166
Codlafield	Shetld	HT9540	60°8·9′	2°4·9′W	X	4
Codlaw Dene	Northum	NY9468	55°0·6′	2°5·2′W	X	87
Codlaw Hill	Northum	NY9468	55°0·6′	2°5·2′W	X	87
Codmore	Bucks	SP9702	51°42·8′	0°35·4′W	T	165
Codmore Hill	W Susx	TQ0520	50°58·4′	0°29·9′W	T	197
Codmore Hill Fm	W Susx	TQ0420	50°58·4′	0°30·7′W	FM	197
Codnor	Derby	SK4149	53°2·4′	1°22·9′W	T	129
Codnor Breach	Derby	SK4047	53°1·4′	1°23·8′W	T	129
Codnor Gate	Derby	SK4150	53°3·0′	1°22·9′W	T	120
Codnor Park	Derby	SK4351	53°3·5′	1°21·1′W	T	120
Codnors Rocks	I Scilly	SV8207	49°53·0′	6°25·3′W	X	203
Codrington	S Glos	ST7278	51°30·2′	2°23·8′W	T	172
Cod Rock	Torbay	SX9455	50°23·4′	3°29·1′W	X	202
Cod Rocks	Devon	SX9252	50°21·7′	3°30·7′W	X	202
Codsall	Staffs	SJ8703	52°37·7′	2°11·1′W	T	127,139
Codsall Wood	Staffs	SJ8405	52°38·8′	2°13·8′W	T	127
Codsend	Somer	SS8839	51°8·6′	3°35·7′W	T	181
Codsend Moors	Somer	SS8740	51°9·1′	3°36·6′W	X	181
Codson Hill	Suff	TL7376	52°21·5′	0°32·8′E	X	143
Coduinn	N Eil	NB1223	58°6·4′	6°52·9′W	H	13,14
Cod Wood	Devon	SX7888	50°41·0′	3°43·2′W	F	191
Coe	Angus	NO5262	56°45·1′	2°46·6′W	X	44
Coe Burn	Angus	NO5162	56°45·1′	2°47·6′W	W	44
Coe Burn	Northum	NU0909	55°22·7′	1°51·0′W	W	81
Coe Crags	Northum	NU0707	55°21·7′	1°52·9′W	H	81
Coed	Cered	SN5060	52°13·2′	4°11·4′W	X	146
Coed	Denb	SJ1657	53°6·5′	3°14·9′W	X	116
Coed	Gwyn	SH6168	53°11·7′	4°4·4′W	X	115
Coed	Gwyn	SH7517	52°44·4′	3°50·7′W	X	124
Coed	Powys	SO0929	51°57·4′	3°19·1′W	X	161
Coed Aberartro	Gwyn	SH5926	52°49·0′	4°5·1′W	F	124
Coed-Acas	Denb	SJ0364	53°10·1′	3°26·7′W	X	116
Coed Adam	Carm	SN4616	51°49·5′	4°13·7′W	X	159
Coedanghred Hill	Monm	SO4619	51°52·3′	2°46·7′W	X	161
Coedarhydyglyn	V of Glam	ST1075	51°28·2′	3°17·4′W	X	171
Coed Arthur	V of Glam	ST0371	51°26·0′	3°23·3′W	F	170
Coed Bald	Newp	ST2790	51°36·5′	3°2·9′W	F	171
Coed Beddick	Monm	SO5302	51°43·1′	2°40·4′W	F	162
Coed Bodfel	Gwyn	SH3437	52°54·5′	4°27·7′W	F	123
Coed Bryn Banon	Gwyn	SH9637	52°55·5′	3°32·4′W	F	125
Coed Bryndansi	Conwy	SH8574	53°15·3′	3°43·0′W	F	116
Coed Bryn-mawr	Conwy	SH8871	53°13·7′	3°40·3′W	F	116
Coed Bwlchgwallter	Cered	SN7771	52°19·6′	3°47·9′W	F	135,147
Coedcae	Blae Gw	SO1909	51°46·7′	3°10·1′W	T	161
Coedcae	Carm	SN3318	51°50·4′	4°25·1′W	X	159
Coed-cae	Gwyn	SH8917	52°44·6′	3°38·3′W	X	124,125
Coed Cae	Merth Tyd	ST0999	51°41·2′	3°18·6′W	X	171
Coedcae	Torf	SO2608	51°46·2′	3°4·0′W	T	161
Coed Cae Aberaman	Rho Cyn Taf	ST0198	51°40·6′	3°25·5′W	F	170
Coed cae bach	Gwyn	SH4342	52°57·4′	4°19·8′W	X	123
Coed Cae Cendl	Blae Gw	SO1805	51°44·5′	3°10·9′W	X	161
Coed Caecorrwg	Rho Cyn Taf	ST1089	51°35·8′	3°17·6′W	X	171
Coed Caeddafydd	Gwyn	SH6146	52°59·8′	4°3·9′W	F	115
Coed Cae Ddu Fm	Rho Cyn Taf	SN9510	51°47·0′	3°30·9′W	FM	160
Coed Cae Du	Gwyn	SH4643	52°58·0′	4°17·2′W	X	123
Coedcae-du	Rho Cyn Taf	ST0686	51°34·1′	3°21·0′W	X	170
Coed Cae Fali	Gwyn	SH6340	52°56·6′	4°1·9′W	F	124
Coedcae Fm	Brig	SS9685	51°33·5′	3°29·6′W	FM	170
Coedcae Fm	Rho Cyn Taf	SO0104	51°43·8′	3°25·6′W	FM	170
Coed Cae Fm	Rho Cyn Taf	ST0183	51°32·5′	3°25·3′W	FM	170
Coedcaehaidd	Powys	SJ0709	52°40·5′	3°22·1′W	X	125
Coed Caeper-corn	Powys	SN9050	52°8·5′	3°36·1′W	F	147
Coed Cae Pica	Caer	ST1288	51°35·3′	3°15·8′W	F	171
Coed Caer Bedw	Carm	SN7227	51°55·8′	3°51·1′W	X	146,160
Coedcanlas Fm	Pemb	SN0008	51°44·3′	4°53·4′W	FM	157,158
Coedcanol	Monm	SO4016	51°50·6′	2°51·9′W	X	161
Coed Canol	Monm	ST3499	51°41·4′	2°56·9′W	F	171
Coed Cefn	I of Angl	SH5775	53°15·4′	4°8·2′W	F	114,115
Coedcefnlas	Pemb	SN1534	51°58·7′	4°41·2′W	X	145
Coed Cefn-pwll-du	Caer	ST2187	51°34·8′	3°8·0′W	F	171
Coed Cil-lonydd	Caer	ST2297	51°40·2′	3°7·3′W	F	171
Coed Clunmelyn	Powys	SN9349	52°8·0′	3°33·4′W	F	147
Coed Coch	Conwy	SH8874	53°15·3′	3°40·3′W	X	116
Coed Cochion	Conwy	SH9169	53°12·7′	3°37·5′W	X	116
Coed Cochion	Gwyn	SH9120	52°46·2′	3°36·5′W	X	125
Coed Cochion	Shrops	SJ2228	52°50·9′	3°9·1′W	F	126
Coed Coesau-whips	Caer	ST1985	51°33·7′	3°9·7′W	F	171
Coed-cowrhyd	Powys	SJ1212	52°42·2′	3°17·7′W	X	125
Coed Cowyn Fm	Powys	SN9849	52°8·0′	3°29·0′W	FM	147
Coed Cox	Monm	SO3402	51°43·0′	2°56·9′W	F	171
Coed Crafnant	Gwyn	SH6128	52°50·1′	4°3·4′W	F	124
Coed Craig Ruperra	Caer	ST2286	51°34·3′	3°7·1′W	F	171
Coed Craigyrogof	Cered	SN7071	52°19·5′	3°54·1′W	F	135,147
Coed Creigiau	Conwy	SH7763	53°9·2′	3°50·0′W	F	115
Coed Cwm	Denb	SJ0776	53°16·6′	3°23·3′W	F	116
Coed Cwmbrân	Carm	SN8031	51°58·1′	3°44·4′W	X	160
Coed Cwm Gloyne	Pemb	SN1039	52°1·3′	4°45·8′W	F	145
Coed Cwnwr	Monm	ST4199	51°41·4′	2°50·8′W	T	171
Coedcynheliar Fm	Conwy	SH7856	53°5·5′	3°48·9′W	FM	115
Coed-cyw-fawr	Carm	SN5207	51°44·8′	4°8·2′W	X	159
Coed-ddôl	Powys	SH7903	52°36·9′	3°46·8′W	X	135
Coed Deri-Newydd	Caer	SO1202	51°42·8′	3°16·0′W	F	171
Coed-detton	Shrops	SO2973	52°21·3′	3°2·2′W	F	137,148
Coed-dias	Monm	SO2724	51°54·8′	3°3·5′W	X	161
Coed Dolfudr	Gwyn	SH8332	52°52·6′	3°43·9′W	F	124,125
Coed Dolgarrog	Conwy	SH7666	53°10·8′	3°50·9′W	F	115
Coed Dôl-gëiliau	Gwyn	SH7127	52°49·7′	3°54·5′W	F	124
Coed-du	Nth Pt Talb	SN8005	51°44·1′	3°43·9′W	F	160
Coed Du Hospital	Flint	SJ1966	53°11·3′	3°12·3′W	X	116
Coed-duon	Monm	SO3600	51°41·9′	2°55·2′W	F	171
Coed Duon or Blackwood	Caer	ST1797	51°40·2′	3°11·6′W	T	171
Coedeiddig	Carm	SN5845	52°5·3′	4°4·0′W	X	146
Coedely	Rho Cyn Taf	ST0185	51°33·5′	3°25·3′W	T	170
Coeden	I of Angl	SH3789	53°22·6′	4°26·6′W	X	114
Coederyr	Gwyn	SH6350	53°2·0′	4°2·2′W	X	115
Coed Eva	Torf	ST2793	51°38·1′	3°2·9′W	T	171
Coed Felinrhyd	Gwyn	SH6438	52°55·6′	4°1·0′W	F	124
Coed Ffridd-fawr	Powys	SH8603	52°37·0′	3°40·6′W	F	135,136
Coed Fm	Carm	SN3813	51°47·8′	4°20·6′W	FM	159
Coed Fm	Powys	SO2823	51°54·3′	3°2·4′W	FM	161
Coed Foel	Cered	SN4242	52°3·5′	4°17·9′W	F	146
Coedfoel-Uchaf	Cered	SN4243	52°4·0′	4°17·9′W	X	146
Coedgain	Carm	SN4718	51°50·6′	4°12·9′W	X	159
Coed Garw	Newp	ST2889	51°36·0′	3°2·0′W	F	171
Coed Gawdir	Nth Pt Talb	SN7800	51°41·4′	3°45·5′W	F	170
Coed Gelli	Powys	SJ1414	52°43·3′	3°16·0′W	X	125
Coedgenau	Powys	SN9933	51°59·4′	3°27·9′W	X	160
Coedgenau	Powys	SO0033	51°59·4′	3°27·0′W	X	160
Coedglasson	Powys	SO0767	52°17·8′	3°21·4′W	X	136,147
Coed Golynos	Torf	ST2699	51°41·3′	3°3·8′W	F	171
Coed Gordderw	Gwyn	SH8333	52°53·1′	3°43·9′W	F	124,125
Coed Gruffydd	Cered	SN6784	52°26·5′	3°57·0′W	F	135
Coedgwgan Hall	Powys	SO0865	52°16·8′	3°20·5′W	X	136,147
Coedgwilym Park	Swan	SN7001	51°41·8′	3°52·5′W	X	170
Coed Gwydyr	Conwy	SH7765	53°10·3′	3°50·0′W	F	115
Coed Hafod	Cered	SN7573	52°20·7′	3°49·7′W	F	135,147
Coed Hafod	Conwy	SH8057	53°6·0′	3°47·1′W	F	116
Coed Hafod-las	Conwy	SH8347	53°0·7′	3°44·2′W	F	116
Coed-harbour	Powys	SO2271	52°20·1′	3°8·3′W	X	137,148
Coed Helen	Gwyn	SH4762	53°8·2′	4°16·8′W	X	114,115
Coed Hills	V of Glam	ST0272	51°26·5′	3°24·2′W	X	170
Coed-hir	Powys	SO0514	51°49·2′	3°22·3′W	X	160
Coedhirion	Carm	SN6632	51°58·5′	3°56·7′W	X	146
Coed Howell	Carm	SN2019	51°50·7′	4°36·4′W	X	158
Coed Howell	Monm	SO2904	51°44·1′	3°1·3′W	F	171
Coed Howell	Monm	SO2905	51°44·6′	3°1·3′W	F	161
Coed Hyrddyn	Denb	SJ2043	52°58·9′	3°11·1′W	X	117
Coed Hywel	Gwyn	SH4453	53°3·3′	4°19·3′W	X	115,123
Coed Hywel	Gwyn	SH5869	53°12·2′	4°7·2′W	X	114,115
Coed Iâl	Denb	SJ1543	52°58·9′	3°15·6′W	X	125
Coed-Ifan	Carm	SN8141	52°3·5′	3°43·8′W	X	147,160
Coed isa	Flint	SJ1579	53°18·3′	3°16·1′W	X	116
Coed Isaf	Conwy	SH8080	53°18·4′	3°47·7′W	F	116
Coed Ithel	Monm	SO2803	51°43·5′	3°2·2′W	X	171
Coed-Ithel Weir	Glos	SO5303	51°43·7′	2°40·4′W	X	162
Coedkernew	Newp	ST2783	51°32·7′	3°2·8′W	T	171
Coed-ladyr	Gwyn	SH8827	52°50·0′	3°39·4′W	X	124,125
Coedlannau	Cered	SN4648	52°6·8′	4°14·5′W	X	146
Coedlannau Fawr	Carm	SN4734	51°59·2′	4°13·3′W	X	146
Coed Leision	V of Glam	ST0476	51°28·7′	3°22·6′W	X	170
Coedleoddi Ucha	Wrex	SJ3140	52°57·4′	3°1·2′W	X	117
Coedleoedd-isaf	Wrex	SJ3139	52°56·9′	3°1·2′W	X	126
Coed-Llai or Leeswood	Flint	SJ2759	53°7·6′	3°5·1′W	T	117
Coed Lletywalter	Gwyn	SH5927	52°49·6′	4°5·2′W	F	124
Coed-llifos Fm	Monm	ST4696	51°39·8′	2°46·5′W	FM	171
Coed-llwyd	Pemb	SN2433	51°58·3′	4°33·3′W	X	145
Coed Llwynifan	Cered	SN6348	52°7·0′	3°59·7′W	F	146
Coed Llynlloedd	Powys	SN7599	52°34·7′	3°50·3′W	F	135
Coed Llyn y Garnedd	Gwyn	SH6441	52°57·2′	4°1·1′W	F	124
Coedllys	Cered	SN6273	52°20·5′	4°1·1′W	X	135
Coed Llys	Flint	SJ2369	53°13·0′	3°8·8′W	X	117
Coed Llywelyn	I of Angl	SH3868	53°11·3′	4°25·1′W	F	114
Coed Maenarthur	Cered	SN7272	52°20·1′	3°52·3′W	F	135,147
Coed Maen Bleddyn	Conwy	SH8152	53°3·4′	3°46·1′W	F	116
Coed Maes-y-pandy	Gwyn	SH7009	52°40·0′	3°54·9′W	F	124
Coed-major	Heref	SO2537	52°1·8′	3°5·2′W	X	161
Coed-mawr	Carm	SN7324	51°54·2′	3°50·4′W	X	160
Coedmawr	Cered	SN6257	52°11·9′	4°0·8′W	X	146
Coed Mawr	Conwy	SH6951	53°2·7′	3°56·8′W	X	115
Coed Mawr	Gwyn	SH4963	53°8·8′	4°15·1′W	X	114,115
Coed Mawr	Gwyn	SH5670	53°12·7′	4°9·0′W	T	114,115
Coed-mawr	Gwyn	SH5808	52°39·3′	4°5·6′W	X	124
Coed-mawr	Gwyn	SH8111	52°41·3′	3°45·2′W	F	124,125
Coed Mawr	Monm	ST3498	51°40·9′	2°56·9′W	F	171
Coed Mawr	Newp	ST2488	51°35·4′	3°5·4′W	F	171
Coed-Mawr	Powys	SH8104	52°37·5′	3°45·1′W	X	135,136
Coed-Mawr	Powys	SJ1213	52°42·7′	3°17·8′W	X	125
Coed-mawr	Powys	SJ2418	52°45·5′	3°7·2′W	X	126
Coedmawr	Powys	SN9151	52°9·0′	3°35·2′W	X	147
Coedmawr	Powys	SN9989	52°29·6′	3°28·9′W	X	136
Coed Mawr	Powys	SO0187	52°28·6′	3°27·1′W	X	136
Coedmawr	Powys	SO0234	52°0·0′	3°25·3′W	X	160
Coedmawr	Powys	SO0454	52°10·8′	3°23·8′W	X	147
Coed Mawr Hall	Conwy	SH7572	53°14·1′	3°52·0′W	X	115
Coed Medart	Caer	ST2392	51°37·5′	3°6·4′W	F	171
Coedmor	Cered	SN4146	52°5·6′	4°18·9′W	X	146
Coedmore	Cered	SN1943	52°3·6′	4°38·0′W	X	145
Coed More Fm	Heref	SO4634	52°0·3′	2°46·8′W	FM	149,161
Coedmor Fawr	Carm	SN5946	52°5·9′	4°3·1′W	X	146
Coed Morgan	Monm	SO3511	51°47·9′	2°56·2′W	T	161
Coed Morgannwg Way	Merth Tyd	SO0304	51°43·8′	3°23·9′W	X	
Coed Morgannwg Way	Nth Pt Talb	SN8702	51°42·6′	3°37·7′W	X	170
Coed Morgannwg Way	Nth Pt Talb	SS8393	51°37·7′	3°41·0′W	X	170
Coed-mynydd-isaf	Flint	SJ1370	53°13·4′	3°17·8′W	X	116
Coed Nant-yr-hwch	Powys	SN8254	52°10·5′	3°43·1′W	F	147
Coed-oer-le	Powys	SJ1617	52°44·9′	3°14·3′W	X	125
Coed-orros	Conwy	SH9666	53°11·1′	3°33·0′W	X	116
Coed Pant-glas	Conwy	SH8370	53°13·1′	3°44·7′W	F	116
Coed-parc gaer	Cered	SN5851	52°8·6′	4°4·1′W	A	146
Coed Pen-lan	Powys	SH7807	52°39·1′	3°47·8′W	F	124
Coed Penmaen	Gwyn	SH6033	52°52·8′	4°4·4′W	F	124
Coed Pennant	Denb	SJ0754	53°4·8′	3°22·9′W	F	116
Coedperthi	Cered	SN3147	52°6·0′	4°27·7′W	X	145
Coedpoeth	Wrex	SJ2851	53°3·3′	3°4·1′W	T	117
Coed-poeth Fm	Heref	SO3235	52°0·8′	2°59·1′W	FM	161
Coed-pryfydau	Nth Pt Talb	SN8900	51°41·5′	3°36·0′W	X	170
Coed Pwll-y-blawd	Denb	SJ1962	53°9·2′	3°12·3′W	F	116
Coed Rhos	Powys	SJ1014	52°43·2′	3°19·5′W	X	125
Coed Rhos-fawr	Gwyn	SH3739	52°55·7′	4°25·1′W	F	123

Coed Robin	Heref	SO2936	52°1·3′	3°1·7′W	X	161
Coed-saithpren	Carm	SN5223	51°53·4′	4°8·7′W	X	159
Coed Sara	Caer	ST2396	51°39·7′	3°6·4′W	F	171
Coed-Shôn	Carm	SN7125	51°54·8′	3°52·1′W	X	146,160
Coed Siencyn	Powys	SJ1018	52°45·4′	3°19·6′W	F	125
Coedstre	Carm	SN3739	52°1·8′	4°22·2′W	X	145
Coedstreisaf	Carm	SN3739	52°1·8′	4°22·2′W	X	145
Coed Swch y Pentre	Gwyn	SH8732	52°52·7′	3°40·3′W	F	124,125
Coed-swydd	Powys	SO1464	52°16·3′	3°15·2′W	H	148
Coed Taf Fawr	Rho Cyn Taf	SN9913	51°48·6′	3°27·5′W	F	160
Coed Tafol	Powys	SJ1400	52°35·7′	3°15·8′W	F	136
Coed Tai-isaf	Conwy	SH9454	53°4·6′	3°34·5′W	F	116
Coedtalog	Powys	SJ0511	52°41·5′	3°23·9′W	X	125
Coed-talon	Flint	SJ2658	53°7·1′	3°5·9′W	T	117
Coed-talon Banks	Flint	SJ2658	53°7·1′	3°5·9′W	X	117
Coed Tangaer	Cered	SN6247	52°6·5′	4°0·5′W	F	146
Coed Teg	Conwy	SH8476	53°16·3′	3°44·0′W	X	116
Coed Trecastell	Rho Cyn Taf	ST0281	51°31·4′	3°24·4′W	F	170
Coedtrefe	Powys	SO0896	52°33·5′	3°21·0′W	X	136
Coed Trinan	Caer	ST2199	51°41·3′	3°8·2′W	X	171
Coed Ty Canol	Monm	SO2824	51°54·8′	3°2·4′W	X	161
Coed Ty coch	Gwyn	SH6641	52°57·2′	3°59·3′W	F	124
Coed Tyfos Isaf	Denb	SJ0339	52°56·6′	3°26·2′W	F	125
Coed Tyglas	Gwyn	SH7207	52°39·0′	3°53·1′W	F	124
Coed Tŷ-mawr	Powys	SN9723	51°54·0′	3°29·4′W	F	160
Coedty Resr	Conwy	SH7566	53°10·8′	3°51·8′W	W	115
Coed Victoria	Gwyn	SH5859	53°6·8′	4°6·9′W	F	115
Coedwallter-fawr	Carm	SN4414	51°48·4′	4°15·4′W	X	159
Coedway	Powys	SJ3414	52°43·4′	2°58·2′W	T	126
Coed Wenallt	Gwyn	SH8431	52°52·1′	3°43·0′W	F	124,125
Coedwynog	Pemb	SN0940	52°1·8′	4°46·7′W	X	145
Coed-y-bedo	Gwyn	SH9640	52°57·1′	3°32·5′W	X	125
Coed-y-Bleiddiau	Gwyn	SH6641	52°57·2′	3°59·3′W	X	124
Coed-y-Bont	Caer	ST1791	51°36·9′	3°11·5′W	F	171
Coed-y-brain	Caer	SO1500	51°41·8′	3°13·4′W	X	171
Coed-y-brain	Carm	SN4010	51°46·2′	4°18·7′W	X	159
Coed-y-brain	Monm	SO3902	51°43·0′	2°52·6′W	X	171
Coed-y-Brenin	Cered	SN4959	52°12·8′	4°12·2′W	X	146
Coed-y-Brenin Forest	Gwyn	SH7326	52°49·2′	3°52·7′W	F	124
Coed-y-bryn	Cered	SN3545	52°5·0′	4°24·1′W	T	145
Coed y Bwnydd	Monm	SO3606	51°45·2′	2°55·2′W	X	161
Coed y Bwyndd (Fort)	Monm	SO3606	51°45·2′	2°55·2′W	A	161
Coed-y-caerau	Newp	ST3891	51°37·1′	2°53·3′W	T	171
Coed-y-celyn	Conwy	SH7955	53°5·0′	3°48·0′W	X	115
Coed-y-celyn	Conwy	SH8055	53°5·0′	3°47·1′W	F	116
Coed y Ciliau	Powys	SN9553	52°10·2′	3°31·7′W	F	147
Coed y Colwn	V of Glam	ST0370	51°25·5′	3°23·3′W	F	170
Coed-y-cra Uchaf	Flint	SJ2270	53°13·5′	3°9·7′W	A	117
Coed-y-cwm	Powys	SJ1705	52°38·4′	3°13·2′W	X	125
Coedydd Branas	Denb	SJ0138	52°56·1′	3°28·0′W	X	125
Coed-y-dinas	Powys	SJ2205	52°38·5′	3°8·8′W	X	126
Coed-y-Fawnog	Conwy	SH8452	53°3·4′	3°43·4′W	F	116
Coed-y-fedw	Monm	SO4408	51°46·3′	2°48·3′W	T	161
Coed y Fferm	Monm	ST3698	51°40·9′	2°55·2′W	F	171
Coed-y-foel Isaf	Gwyn	SH9138	52°55·9′	3°36·9′W	X	125
Coed-y-foel uchaf	Gwyn	SH9139	52°56·5′	3°36·9′W	X	125
Coed-y-fon	Monm	ST3694	51°38·7′	2°55·1′W	X	171
Coed y Fron	Denb	SJ0544	52°59·3′	3°24·5′W	F	125
Coed y Fron	Denb	SJ0654	53°4·7′	3°23·8′W	F	116
Coed y Fron	Denb	SJ0755	53°5·3′	3°22·9′W	F	116
Coed-y-fron	Gwyn	SH2930	52°50·7′	4°31·9′W	X	123
Coed y Fron-wyllt	Denb	SJ0856	53°5·8′	3°22·0′W	F	116
Coed y gaer	Powys	SO0084	52°26·9′	3°27·9′W	H	136
Coed y Gaer	Powys	SO1724	51°54·7′	3°12·0′W	A	161
Coed y Gaer	Shrops	SJ2328	52°50·9′	3°8·2′W	A	126
Coed y Garth	Cered	SN6894	52°31·9′	3°56·4′W	T	135
Coed-y-garth	Gwyn	SH6616	52°43·7′	3°58·7′W	F	124
Coed-y-gawen	Denb	SJ1256	53°5·9′	3°18·5′W	F	116
Coed y Gedrys	Rho Cyn Taf	ST1185	51°33·6′	3°16·6′W	F	171
Coed-y-gelli	Monm	SO3711	51°47·9′	2°54·4′W	X	161
Coed y Gesail	Gwyn	SH8210	52°40·7′	3°44·3′W	F	124,125
Coed y Glyn	Denb	SJ0538	52°56·1′	3°24·4′W	F	125
Coed-y-glyn	Nth Pt Talb	SN7804	51°43·5′	3°45·6′W	X	170
Coed y Glyn	Powys	SH8107	52°39·1′	3°45·1′W	F	124,125
Coed y go	Shrops	SJ2727	52°50·4′	3°4·6′W	T	126
Coed-y-gof	Carm	SN6339	52°2·2′	3°59·4′W	X	146
Coed-y-gôf	Cered	SN6354	52°10·3′	3°59·8′W	X	146
Coed-y-gôf	Gwyn	SH6405	52°37·8′	4°0·2′W	X	124
Coed y Grabla	V of Glam	SS9972	51°26·5′	3°26·8′W	F	170
Coed y Graig	Caer	ST1393	51°38·0′	3°15·0′W	F	171
Coed y Graig	Gwyn	SH6407	52°38·9′	4°0·2′W	F	124
Coed y Gribin	Gwyn	SH6716	52°43·8′	3°57·8′W	F	124
Coed y Gwernydd	Powys	SJ1115	52°43·8′	3°18·7′W	F	125
Coed y Gwmannog	Conwy	SH7762	53°8·7′	3°49·9′W	F	115
Coed y Llan	Powys	SJ1319	52°45·9′	3°17·0′W	X	125
Coed y Llanerch	Caer	SO1704	51°44·0′	3°11·7′W	F	171
Coed-y-llyn	Gwyn	SH5338	52°55·4′	4°10·8′W	F	124
Coed-y-maen	Powys	SJ1514	52°43·3′	3°15·1′W	X	125
Coed y Marchog	Powys	SO1541	52°3·9′	3°14·0′W	X	148,161
Coed y Mon	Monm	ST3999	51°41·4′	2°52·6′W	F	171
Coedymwstwr Ganol	Brig	SS9481	51°31·3′	3°31·3′W	X	170
Coed-y-mwstwr (Hotel)	Brig	SS9480	51°30·8′	3°31·3′W	X	170
Coed-y-mynydd Ucha	Flint	SJ1269	53°12·9′	3°18·7′W	X	116
Coed-y-paen	Monm	ST3398	51°40·8′	2°57·8′W	T	171
Coed-y-parc	Gwyn	SH6166	53°10·6′	4°4·4′W	T	115
Coed y Pentre	Denb	SJ0557	53°6·3′	3°24·7′W	X	116
Coed-y-person	Monm	SO2713	51°48·9′	3°3·1′W	X	161
Coed y Prior	Monm	SO2909	51°46·7′	3°1·4′W	X	161
Coed-y-Prior Field	Monm	SO2910	51°47·3′	3°1·4′W	X	161
Coed-y-pwll	Monm	SO4420	51°52·8′	2°48·4′W	F	161
Coed yr Allt	Conwy	SH7862	53°8·7′	3°49·0′W	F	115
Coed-yr-allt	Gwyn	SH6251	53°2·6′	4°3·1′W	X	115
Coed yr Allt	Shrops	SJ3239	52°56·9′	3°0·3′W	X	126
Coed y Rhaiadr	Powys	SN9011	51°47·4′	3°35·3′W	X	160
Coed-yr-hendy	Rho Cyn Taf	ST0481	51°31·4′	3°22·6′W	F	170
Coed y Rhiw-las	Powys	SN9631	51°58·3′	3°30·4′W	X	160
Coed y Rhygen	Gwyn	SH6836	52°54·6′	3°57·4′W	F	124
Coed-yr-ynys	Powys	SO1520	51°52·6′	3°13·7′W	T	161
Coed yr Ystrad	Powys	SJ0515	52°43·7′	3°24·0′W	F	125
Coed y Squire	Newp	ST2589	51°35·9′	3°4·6′W	F	171

Coed Ystumgwern	Gwyn	SH5823	52°47·4′	4°5·9′W	T	124
Coed-y-Trafelgwyn	Powys	SN8876	52°22·5′	3°38·3′W	F	135,136,147
Coed-y-tye	Shrops	SJ3332	52°53·1′	2°59·3′W	X	126
Coed-y-wenallt	Card	ST1583	51°32·6′	3°13·2′W	F	171
Coed y Wenallt	Gwyn	SH8223	52°47·7′	3°44·6′W	F	124,125
Coed-y-wlad	Powys	SJ2209	52°40·6′	3°8·8′W	T	126
Coe Fm	Lincs	SK8536	52°55·1′	0°43·7′W	FM	130
Coe Hill	Northum	NU0707	55°21·7′	1°52·9′W	H	81
Coelard	Arg & Bt	NM9243	56°32·2′	5°22·5′W	X	49
Coelbren	Powys	SN8511	51°47·4′	3°39·7′W	T	160
Coer Fm	Carm	SN4616	51°49·5′	4°13·7′W	FM	159
Coes-faen	Gwyn	SH6215	52°43·1′	4°2·2′W	X	124
Coetgae	Blae Gw	SO2103	51°43·4′	3°8·2′W	H	171
Coetgae	Monm	ST4796	51°39·9′	2°45·6′W	F	171
Coetgae Du	Powys	SO0316	51°50·3′	3°24·1′W	X	160
Coetgae-hen	Caer	ST2398	51°40·8′	3°6·4′W	X	171
Coetgae Isaf	Nth Pt Talb	SS8896	51°39·3′	3°36·8′W	H	170
Coetgae-llwyn	Powys	SO0516	51°50·3′	3°22·3′W	X	160
Coetgae'r Derlwyn	Nth Pt Talb	SN8801	51°42·0′	3°36·9′W	F	170
Coetty-mawr	Gwyn	SH6336	52°54·5′	4°1·8′W	X	124
Coety Bank	Powys	SO1580	52°24·9′	3°14·6′W	H	136
Coety Green	Swan	SS4291	51°36·0′	4°16·5′W	X	159
Coe Wood	Suff	TM3667	52°15·3′	1°27·9′E	F	156
Cofa Pike	Cumbr	NY3512	54°30·2′	2°59·8′W	X	90
Coffee Hall	Mil Key	SP8636	52°1·2′	0°44·4′W	T	152
Coffins	Devon	SX7096	50°45·2′	3°50·2′W	X	191
Coffin Stone	Devon	SX6773	50°32·7′	3°52·3′W	X	191
Coffinswell	Devon	SX8968	50°30·3′	3°33·5′W	T	202
Cofflete Creek	Devon	SX5450	50°20·1′	4°2·7′W	W	201
Cofford Fm	Devon	SX9680	50°36·9′	3°27·8′W	FM	192
Coft Hall	Essex	TL6628	51°55·8′	0°25·3′E	X	167
Cofton	Devon	SX9680	50°36·9′	3°27·8′W	T	192
Cofton Common	Birm	SP0177	52°23·7′	1°58·7′W	T	139
Cofton Hackett	Worcs	SP0075	52°22·6′	1°59·6′W	T	139
Cofton Hall	Worcs	SP0175	52°22·6′	1°58·7′W	X	139
Cofton Hill	Worcs	SO9975	52°22·6′	2°0·5′W	H	139
Cofton Richards Fm	Worcs	SP0175	52°22·6′	1°58·7′W	FM	139
Cog	V of Glam	ST1668	51°24·5′	3°12·1′W	T	171
Cogan	V of Glam	ST1772	51°26·7′	3°11·3′W	T	171
Cogarth	D & G	NX7268	54°59·7′	3°59·6′W	X	83,84
Cogbrae	Pth & Kin	NN9927	56°25·7′	3°37·8′W	X	52,53,58
Cog Burn	D & G	NS8313	55°24·1′	3°50·4′W	W	71,78
Cogden Beach	Dorset	SY5087	50°41·1′	2°42·1′W	X	194
Cogden Fm	Dorset	SY5088	50°41·6′	2°42·1′W	FM	194
Cogden Gill	N Yks	SE0496	54°21·8′	1°55·9′W	W	98
Cogden Hall	N Yks	SE0597	54°22·4′	1°55·0′W	X	98
Cogden Heugh	N Yks	SE0597	54°22·4′	1°55·0′W	X	98
Cogden Moor	N Yks	SE0596	54°21·8′	1°55·0′W	X	98
Cogenhoe	Northnts	SP8260	52°14·2′	0°47·6′W	T	152
Coggers Fm	E Susx	TQ5815	50°55·0′	0°15·3′E	FM	199
Cogges	Oxon	SP3609	51°46·9′	1°28·3′W	T	164
Coggeshall	Essex	TL8522	51°52·2′	0°41·6′E	T	168
Coggeshall Hall	Essex	TL8620	51°51·1′	0°42·4′E	X	168
Coggeshall Hamlet	Essex	TL8521	51°51·6′	0°41·6′E	T	168
Cogges Wood	Oxon	SP3811	51°48·0′	1°26·5′W	F	164
Coggins Mill	E Susx	TQ5927	51°1·4′	0°16·4′E	T	188,199
Coghill Hill	N Yks	NY8404	54°26·1′	2°14·4′W	X	91,92
Coghill Loch	Highld	ND0970	58°36·8′	3°33·5′W	W	12
Coghurst	E Susx	TQ8313	50°53·5′	0°36·5′E	X	199
Coghurst Hall	E Susx	TQ8313	50°53·5′	0°36·5′E	X	199
Cogie Hill Fm	Lancs	SD4446	53°54·7′	2°50·7′W	FM	102
Cogill Beck	N Yks	SD9094	54°20·7′	2°8·8′W	W	98
Cogill Closes	N Yks	SD9192	54°19·7′	2°7·9′W	X	98
Cogle	Highld	ND2657	58°30·0′	3°15·7′W	X	11,12
Cogley Wood	Somer	ST7035	51°7·0′	2°25·3′W	F	183
Cogload Fm	Somer	ST3027	51°2·5′	2°59·5′W	FM	193
Cog Mill Fm	S Glos	ST6682	51°32·4′	2°29·0′W	FM	172
Cog Moors	V of Glam	ST1569	51°25·1′	3°13·0′W	X	171
Cognor Wood	W Susx	SU8830	51°4·0′	0°44·3′W	F	186
Cogra Moss	Cumbr	NY0919	54°33·7′	3°24·0′W	W	89
Cogrie Moor	D & G	NY0997	55°15·8′	3°25·5′W	X	78
Cogries Fm	D & G	NY1097	55°15·8′	3°24·5′W	FM	78
Cogshall Brook	Ches	SJ6476	53°17·0′	2°32·0′W	W	118
Cogshall Hall	Ches	SJ6377	53°17·6′	2°32·9′W	X	118
Cogshead	D & G	NS8213	55°24·1′	3°51·4′W	X	71,78
Cogsmill	Scot Bord	NT5108	55°22·1′	2°46·0′W	X	79
Cogtail Burn	E Loth	NT5276	55°58·7′	2°45·7′W	W	66
Cogwell	Devon	SS9517	50°56·8′	3°29·3′W	X	181
Cogwell	Devon	SS9610	50°53·0′	3°28·3′W	X	192
Cogwell Brook	Heref	SO5160	52°14·4′	2°42·7′W	W	137,138,149
Cogworthy	Devon	SS5522	50°59·0′	4°3·6′W	X	180
Coham	Devon	SS4505	50°49·7′	4°11·7′W	X	190
Coigach	Highld	NC1104	57°59·4′	5°11·4′W	X	15
Coignafearn	Highld	NH7017	57°13·8′	4°8·8′W	X	35
Coignafearn Forest	Highld	NH6412	57°11·0′	4°14·5′W	X	35
Coignafearn Lodge	Highld	NH6815	57°12·7′	4°10·7′W	X	35
Coignafeuinternich	Highld	NH7217	57°13·8′	4°6·8′W	X	35
Coignascallan	Highld	NH7318	57°14·4′	4°5·8′W	X	35
Coig Peighinnean	N Eil	NB5264	58°29·9′	6°14·9′W	T	8
Coig Peighinnean Bhuirgh	N Eil	NB4056	58°25·2′	6°26·7′W	T	8
Coilachra	Stir	NN4111	56°16·2′	4°33·6′W	X	56
Coilacriech	Aberd	NO3296	57°3·3′	3°6·8′W	X	37,44
Coilantogle	Stir	NN5906	56°13·8′	4°16·0′W	X	57
Coilavoulin Fm	Pth & Kin	NN9557	56°41·8′	3°42·4′W	FM	52,53
Coileanais	N Eil	NF8126	57°13·1′	7°16·6′W	X	22
Coile na Dalach	Arg & Bt	NR3763	55°47·6′	6°11·3′W	F	60,61
Coilessan	Arg & Bt	NN2601	56°10·5′	4°47·7′W	X	56
Coilessan Glen	Arg & Bt	NN2401	56°10·4′	4°49·7′W	X	56
Coiletir	Highld	NN1446	56°34·4′	5°1·2′W	X	50
Coiliamy	Angus	NO3759	56°43·4′	3°1·3′W	X	54
Coilintuie	Highld	NH8103	57°6·4′	3°57·4′W	X	35
Coiliochbhar Hill	Aberd	NJ5015	57°13·6′	2°49·2′W	H	37
Coill a' Bhealaich Mhóir	Arg & Bt	NM6523	56°20·7′	5°47·7′W	X	49
Coill a' Bhun	Highld	NH1383	57°48·1′	5°8·3′W	X	19
Coillabus	Arg & Bt	NR3143	55°36·6′	6°15·9′W	X	60
Coill Ach' a' Chùil	Highld	NC6437	58°18·3′	4°18·8′W	F	16
Coill' a Chaiginn	Arg & Bt	NM5824	56°21·0′	5°54·6′W	X	48
Coill a' Choire	Highld	NN4689	56°58·3′	4°31·6′W	X	34,42
Coill' a' Chorra Ghoirtein	Arg & Bt	NR3069	55°50·6′	6°18·4′W	F	60
Coill a' Ghasgain	Highld	NG6412	57°8·6′	5°53·6′W	F	32

Coill' a' Ghuail	Arg & Bt	NR3760	55°46·0′	6°11·1′W	X	60
Coill'an Achaidh Mhóir	Highld	NH4159	57°35·8′	4°39·2′W	F	26
Coill'an Fhraoich Mhóir	Arg & Bt	NM7036	56°27·9′	5°43·6′W	X	49
Coill'an Righe	Highld	NH5258	57°35·5′	4°28·1′W	X	26
Coill' a' Phuill	Highld	NC6451	58°25·8′	4°19·3′W	X	10
Coill' Brian Léitir	Highld	NH2794	57°54·4′	4°54·7′W	X	20
Coille	Arg & Bt	NR2468	55°49·8′	6°24·0′W	X	60
Coille a' Bhad Leith	Highld	NC3724	58°10·8′	4°45·8′W	F	16
Coille a' Chorcaidh	Highld	NH3929	57°19·7′	4°40·0′W	X	26
Coille a' Chùirn Mhóir	Highld	NM8489	56°56·8′	5°32·6′W	F	40
Coilleag	N Eil	NF7810	57°4·4′	7°18·4′W	T	31
Coilleag a' Phrionnsa	N Eil	NF7810	57°4·4′	7°18·4′W	X	31
Coille a' Ghlinne Mhóir	Arg & Bt	NM3420	56°18·1′	6°17·6′W	X	48
Coille a' Ghonaidh	Arg & Bt	NM3421	56°18·7′	6°17·6′W	X	48
Coille Allmha	Highld	NM7589	56°56·5′	5°41·5′W	F	40
Coille a' Mheadhoin	Highld	NN5982	56°54·7′	4°18·5′W	X	42
Coille an Ath	Highld	NH3238	57°24·3′	4°47·3′W	X	26
Coille an Leth-uillt	Highld	NH2623	57°16·1′	4°52·7′W	F	25
Coille an Ruighe Mhóir	Highld	NN0588	56°56·8′	5°11·9′W	X	41
Coille an Torra Chruaidh	Highld	NN7799	57°4·2′	4°1·3′W	F	35
Coille an Tuathanaich	Highld	NH2823	57°16·2′	4°50·7′W	F	25
Coille Bhàn	Highld	NH0652	57°31·3′	5°13·9′W	X	25
Coille Bheag	Highld	NM8292	56°58·3′	5°34·8′W	X	33,40
Coille Bhienie	Pth & Kin	NN4857	56°41·1′	4°28·4′W	F	42,51
Coille Bhlàraidh	Highld	NH3616	57°12·6′	4°42·5′W	F	34
Coille-bhràghad	Arg & Bt	NN0808	56°13·8′	5°5·4′W	F	56
Coille Bhreac	Highld	NH0752	57°31·3′	5°12·9′W	X	25
Coille Bhreac-liath	Arg & Bt	NN3135	56°28·9′	4°44·2′W	F	50
Coille Bhrodainn	Highld	NM8778	56°50·9′	5°29·1′W	F	40
Coille Braigh Ichrachan	Arg & Bt	NN0128	56°24·4′	5°13·1′W	X	50
Coille Bràigh na Cille	Arg & Bt	NM9928	56°24·3′	5°15·0′W	X	49
Coille Brochain	Pth & Kin	NN9061	56°43·9′	3°47·4′W	F	43
Coille Chaolais	Highld	NM8294	56°59·4′	5°34·9′W	F	33,40
Coille Charnuis	Highld	NN0760	56°41·8′	5°8·7′W	X	41
Coillechat Burn	Stir	NN6705	56°13·4′	4°8·3′W	W	57
Coille Chill'a' Mhoraire	Arg & Bt	NM4447	56°33·0′	6°9·5′W	X	47,48
Coille Chriche	Pth & Kin	NN6222	56°22·5′	4°13·6′W	X	51
Coille Chuil	Arg & Bt	NM9813	56°16·3′	5°15·3′W	X	55
Coille Coire Chrannaig	Highld	NN4888	56°57·8′	4°29·5′W	F	34,42
Coille Coire Chuilc	Stir	NN3328	56°25·1′	4°42·0′W	X	50
Coille Coire Mhuilidh	Highld	NH3662	57°37·4′	4°44·3′W	X	20
Coille Coire nam Feuran	Highld	NC6634	58°16·7′	4°16·6′W	F	16
Coille Creag-loch	Highld	NG8252	57°30·6′	5°37·9′W	F	24
Coille Dalavil	Highld	NG5905	57°4·6′	5°58·1′W	F	32,39
Coille Dhubh	Highld	NG8745	57°27·0′	5°32·5′W	X	24
Coille Dhubh	Highld	NH1800	57°3·6′	4°59·6′W	X	34
Coille Dhubh	Highld	NM8564	56°43·4′	5°30·4′W	F	40
Coille Dhubh	Highld	NN0253	56°37·9′	5°13·2′W	X	41
Coille Dhubh	Pth & Kin	NN7148	56°36·6′	4°5·7′W	X	51,52
Coille Doir-àth	Highld	NN5286	56°56·8′	4°25·5′W	F	42
Coille Driseig	Arg & Bt	NN1127	56°24·1′	5°3·3′W	X	50
Coille Druim an Laoigh	Highld	NM7569	56°45·8′	5°40·4′W	F	40
Coille Druim na Saille	Highld	NM9579	56°51·7′	5°21·3′W	X	40
Coille-eughain Hill	Arg & Bt	NS3292	56°5·7′	4°41·6′W	H	56
Coille Gaireallach	Highld	NG6019	57°12·2′	5°58·0′W	F	32
Coille Garbh-leac	Highld	NH2438	57°24·2′	4°55·3′W	F	25
Coille Gharbh	Highld	NH3538	57°24·4′	4°44·3′W	H	26
Coille Ghormaig	Highld	NH2310	57°9·1′	4°55·1′W	F	34
Coille-ghuail	Highld	NG3334	57°19·4′	6°25·7′W	X	32
Coillegillie	Highld	NG7038	57°22·7′	5°49·1′W	X	24
Coilleigar	N Eil	NB0420	58°4·5′	7°0·8′W	X	13
Coille Innis na Sine	Highld	NH1849	57°29·9′	5°1·8′W	X	25
Coille Kynachan	Pth & Kin	NN7458	56°42·1′	4°3·0′W	F	42,51,52
Coille Lèanachain	Highld	NN2277	56°51·3′	4°54·7′W	F	41
Coille Leitire	Arg & Bt	NN0926	56°23·5′	5°5·2′W	X	50
Coille Leitir nan Lub	Highld	NM7689	56°56·5′	5°40·5′W	F	40
Coille Levishie	Highld	NH3817	57°13·2′	4°40·5′W	F	34
Coillelyal	Highld	NC7159	58°30·3′	4°12·4′W	X	10
Coille Meall Onfhaidh	Highld	NN0084	56°54·5′	5°16·6′W	F	41
Coille Mheadhonach	Arg & Bt	NN0249	56°35·7′	5°13·1′W	F	50
Coille Mheadhonach	Arg & Bt	NS1790	56°4·3′	4°56·0′W	F	56
Coille Mhialairigh	Highld	NG8112	57°9·1′	5°36·8′W	X	33
Coille Mhinnean	Arg & Bt	NR9998	56°8·2′	5°13·6′W	X	55
Coille Mhòr	Arg & Bt	NM7707	56°12·5′	5°35·3′W	X	55
Coille Mhór	Arg & Bt	NR3167	55°49·5′	6°17·3′W	X	60,61
Coille Mhór	Arg & Bt	NR6284	55°59·7′	5°48·6′W	X	61
Coille Mhór	Arg & Bt	NR8291	56°4·0′	5°29·7′W	F	55
Coille Mhór	Arg & Bt	NS0282	55°59·7′	5°10·0′W	X	55
Coille Mhór	Highld	NG8129	57°18·2′	5°37·7′W	X	33
Coille Mhór	Highld	NG8709	57°7·6′	5°30·7′W	X	33
Coille Mhór	Highld	NH2722	57°15·6′	4°51·6′W	F	25
Coille Mhór	Highld	NH4041	57°26·1′	4°39·5′W	X	26
Coille Mhór	Highld	NH4453	57°32·7′	4°35·9′W	X	26
Coille Mhór	Highld	NH6321	57°15·8′	4°15·8′W	H	26,35
Coille Mhór	Highld	NN0382	56°53·5′	5°13·6′W	X	41
Coille Mhór	Pth & Kin	NN5456	56°40·6′	4°22·5′W	F	42,51
Coillemhor	Pth & Kin	NN6523	56°23·1′	4°10·7′W	X	51
Coille Mhòr	Pth & Kin	NN8759	56°42·8′	3°50·3′W	X	52
Coille Mhór	Stir	NN4408	56°14·6′	4°30·6′W	X	57
Coille Mhór Hill	Stir	NS3798	56°9·1′	4°37·0′W	H	56
Coille Mhoruisge	Highld	NH1052	57°31·4′	5°9·9′W	X	25
Coillemore	Highld	NG8028	57°17·6′	5°38·6′W	X	33
Coillemore	Highld	NH7072	57°43·4′	4°10·5′W	X	21
Coillemore Point	N Ayr	NR9250	55°42·2′	5°18·2′W	X	62,69
Coille na Ceardaich	Highld	NH3629	57°19·6′	4°43·0′W	X	26
Coille na Creige Duibhe	Arg & Bt	NM5635	56°26·9′	5°57·1′W	X	47,48
Coille na Creige Duibhe	Highld	NN6998	57°3·5′	4°9·1′W	F	35
Coille na Cùile	Highld	NC5649	58°24·6′	4°27·4′W	X	10
Coille na Cùile	Highld	NM9863	56°43·2′	5°17·6′W	F	40
Coille na Dubh Chlaise	Highld	NH0165	57°38·1′	5°19·6′W	F	19
Coille na Dubh Leitire	Arg & Bt	NM4748	56°33·6′	6°6·6′W	X	47,48
Coille na Feinne	Highld	NH3815	57°12·1′	4°40·4′W	F	34
Coille na Glas-leitire	Highld	NG9964	57°37·5′	5°21·5′W	F	19
Coille na h-Uanaire	Arg & Bt	NR4471	55°52·1′	6°5·1′W	F	60,61
Coille na h-Ulaidh	Highld	NH2623	57°16·1′	4°52·7′W	F	25
Coille na Leitire Duibhe	Highld	NH2837	57°23·7′	4°51·3′W	F	25
Coille na Leitre Bige	Highld	NC6250	58°25·3′	4°21·3′W	X	10
Coille nam Bruach	Arg & Bt	NR4450	55°40·8′	6°3·9′W	F	60
Coillenangabhar	Arg & Bt	NM4323	56°20·0′	6°9·0′W	X	48
Coille nan Geur-oirean	Highld	NN0491	56°58·4′	5°13·0′W	X	33

Coille na Sidhe	Arg & Bt	NR9669	55°52·5′	5°15·2′W	X	62
Coille na Sròine	Arg & Bt	NM5637	56°28·0′	5°57·2′W	F	47,48
Coille na Totaig	Highld	NG8724	57°15·7′	5°31·5′W	X	33
Coille Phuiteachain	Highld	NN0984	56°54·7′	5°7·8′W	X	41
Coille Poll Losgannan	Highld	NM7789	56°56·6′	5°39·5′W	F	40
Coille Reidh nan Làir	Highld	NH3205	57°6·6′	4°46·0′W	F	34
Coille-righ	Highld	NG9627	57°17·5′	5°22·7′W	X	25,33
Coille Ropach	Highld	NM7185	56°54·2′	5°45·2′W	F	40
Coille Ruigh na Cuileige	Highld	NH2326	57°17·7′	4°55·8′W	F	25
Coille Sròn nam Boc	Arg & Bt	NM6424	56°21·2′	5°48·8′W	X	49
Coille Torr Dhùin	Highld	NH3306	57°7·1′	4°45·0′W	F	34
Coillore	Highld	NG3537	57°21·0′	6°23·9′W	T	23,32
Coilsfield Mains	S Ayr	NS4426	55°30·4′	4°27·8′W	X	70
Coilsholm	S Ayr	NS4525	55°29·9′	4°26·8′W	X	70
Coilsmore	Aberd	NJ9449	57°32·1′	2°5·6′W	X	30
Coiltry	Highld	NH3506	57°7·2′	4°43·1′W	X	34
Coinlach Burn	Aberd	NJ4003	57°7·1′	2°59·0′W	W	37
Coinneach Mhor	Highld	NG9460	57°35·2′	5°26·3′W	X	19
Coir' a' Bhaid Léith	Highld	NC4812	58°4·5′	4°34·2′W	X	16
Coir' a' Bharr' Reamhair	Arg & Bt	NM4528	56°22·8′	6°7·4′W	X	48
Coir' a' Bhathaich	Highld	NG9582	57°47·1′	5°26·4′W	X	19
Coir' a' Bhric Beag	Highld	NN3264	56°44·5′	4°44·4′W	X	41
Coir' a' Bhric Mor	Highld	NN3163	56°43·9′	4°45·3′W	X	41
Coir' Achadh nan Sac	Highld	NC6349	58°24·7′	4°20·2′W	X	10
Coir' a' Chaoruinn	Highld	NG4620	57°12·3′	6°11·9′W	X	32
Coir' a' Charrain	Arg & Bt	NM4832	56°25·0′	6°4·7′W	X	48
Coir' a' Chearcaill	Highld	NG8503	57°4·3′	5°32·4′W	X	33
Coir' a' Chinn-chlach	Arg & Bt	NR4056	55°43·9′	6°8·1′W	X	60
Coir' a' Chrom Uillt	Highld	NC2404	57°59·7′	4°58·2′W	X	15
Coir' a' Chruachain	Highld	NG4540	57°23·0′	6°14·1′W	X	23
Coir' a' Chruiteir	Highld	NC3247	58°23·0′	4°51·9′W	X	9
Coir' a'Ghallaich	Highld	NC4850	58°25·0′	4°35·7′W	X	9
Coir' a' Ghamhna	Highld	NH0583	57°47·9′	5°16·4′W	X	19
Coir' a' Ghlinne	Highld	NG4638	57°22·0′	6°13·0′W	X	23,32
Coir' a' Ghobhainn	Highld	NG4133	57°19·1′	6°17·7′W	X	32
Coir' a' Ghrianain	Highld	NH3575	57°44·3′	4°45·8′W	X	20
Coir' a' Ghrunnda	Highld	NG4419	57°11·7′	6°13·8′W	X	32
Coir' a' Ghuibhsachain	Highld	NH0983	57°48·0′	5°12·4′W	X	19
Coir' Allt a' Ghille	Highld	NG2850	57°27·8′	6°31·7′W	X	23
Coir' a' Mhadaidh	Highld	NG4424	57°14·4′	6°14·1′W	X	32
Coir' a' Mhàim	Arg & Bt	NM5831	56°24·8′	5°55·0′W	X	48
Coir' an Eas	Highld	NC6925	58°11·9′	4°13·3′W	X	16
Coir' an Eich	Highld	NG4322	57°13·3′	6°15·0′W	X	32
Coir' an Fhamair	Highld	NG8045	57°26·8′	5°39·5′W	X	24
Coir' an Laoigh	Highld	NC4005	58°0·6′	4°42·0′W	X	16
Coir' an Lochain	Highld	NG4521	57°12·8′	6°12·9′W	X	32
Coir' an Rathaid	Highld	NG3828	57°16·3′	6°20·3′W	X	32
Coir' an Stangain Mhòir	Highld	NN0296	57°1·0′	5°15·2′W	X	33
Coir' an Taoibh Riabhaich	Highld	NG9673	57°42·3′	5°25·0′W	X	19
Coir' an t-Sagairt	N Eil	NF8333	57°16·9′	7°15·2′W	X	22
Coir' an t-Saileín	Arg & Bt	NM5632	56°25·3′	5°56·9′W	X	48
Coir'an t-Seasgaich	Highld	NG4757	57°32·2′	6°13·2′W	X	23
Coir an t-Sneachda	Highld	NM6674	56°48·2′	5°49·5′W	X	40
Coir' an Uillt Mholaich	Arg & Bt	NM6231	56°24·9′	5°51·1′W	X	49
Coir'an Uisge Dheirg	Arg & Bt	NR5068	55°50·7′	5°59·2′W	X	61
Coir' a' Tairneilear	Highld	NG4524	57°14·4′	6°13·1′W	X	32
Coirc Bheinn	Arg & Bt	NM4832	56°25·0′	6°4·7′W	H	48
Coire a' Bhachaill	Arg & Bt	NN0629	56°25·1′	5°8·3′W	X	50
Coire a' Bhaile	Pth & Kin	NO1163	56°45·3′	3°26·9′W	X	43
Coire a' Bhainne	Highld	NH2706	57°7·0′	4°51·0′W	X	34
Coire a' Bhalachain	Highld	NN0895	57°0·6′	5°9·3′W	X	33
Coire a' Bhàsteir	Highld	NG4725	57°15·0′	6°11·2′W	X	32
Coire a Bhathaich	Stir	NN3702	56°11·2′	4°37·2′W	X	56
Coire a' Bhealaich	Highld	NN4469	56°47·4′	4°32·8′W	X	42
Coire a' Bhéin	Highld	NN5092	57°0·0′	4°27·7′W	H	35
Coire a' Bheithe	Highld	NM8989	56°56·9′	5°27·7′W	X	40
Coire a' Bheoil-airigh	Highld	NG8419	57°12·9′	5°34·2′W	X	33
Coire a Bhinnein	Arg & Bt	NN1740	56°31·2′	4°58·0′W	X	50
Coire a' Bhradain	N Ayr	NR9639	55°36·4′	5°13·9′W	X	68,69
Coire a'Bhradain	N Ayr	NR9640	55°36·9′	5°13·9′W	X	62,69
Coire a' Bhrait	Arg & Bt	NN0532	56°26·7′	5°9·4′W	X	50
Coire a' Bhuic	Highld	NH1851	57°31·0′	5°1·9′W	X	25
Coire a' Bhùiridh	Highld	NM7778	56°50·7′	5°38·9′W	X	40
Coir' Each	Highld	NH2769	57°40·9′	4°53·6′W	X	20
Coireach a' Bà	Highld	NN2347	56°35·2′	4°52·5′W	X	50
Coire a' Chadha Ruaidh Mór	Highld	NH0331	57°19·9′	5°15·9′W	X	25
Coire a' Chait	Highld	NH1013	57°10·4′	5°8·1′W	X	34
Coire Achaladair	Arg & Bt	NN3341	56°32·1′	4°42·5′W	X	50
Coireachan Buidhe	Arg & Bt	NM6423	56°20·7′	5°48·7′W	X	49
Coireachan Garbh	Highld	NN3685	56°55·9′	4°41·3′W	X	34,41
Coireachan Gorma	Arg & Bt	NM4230	56°23·8′	6°10·4′W	X	47
Coireachan Gorma	Highld	NH0808	57°7·6′	5°9·9′W	X	33
Coireachan Odhar	Highld	NH1827	57°18·1′	5°0·8′W	X	25
Coire a' Chaorachain	Highld	NG7942	57°25·1′	5°40·4′W	X	24
Coire a' Chaorainn	Highld	NM9895	57°0·4′	5°19·1′W	X	33,40
Coire a' Chaorainn	Highld	NN0086	56°55·6′	5°16·7′W	X	41
Coire a' Chaoruinn	Highld	NC2703	57°59·2′	4°55·1′W	X	15
Coire a Chapuill	Highld	NH8122	57°16·7′	3°58·0′W	X	35
Coire a' Charadh	Arg & Bt	NN1240	56°31·1′	5°2·9′W	X	50
Coire a' Charra	Highld	NH0840	57°24·9′	5°11·3′W	X	25
Coire a' Chàrra Bhig	Highld	NN4673	56°49·6′	4°31·0′W	X	42
Coire a' Chearcaill	Highld	NN0272	56°48·1′	5°14·1′W	X	41
Coire a' Cheud-chnoic	Highld	NG9555	57°32·6′	5°25·1′W	X	25
Coire a' Chiulinn	Highld	NM7659	56°40·4′	5°38·9′W	X	49
Coire a' Chlaiginn	Highld	NH1048	57°29·2′	5°9·7′W	X	25
Coire à Chochuill	Arg & Bt	NN1033	56°27·3′	5°4·6′W	X	50
Coire a' Choin Duinn	Highld	NM8479	56°51·4′	5°32·1′W	X	40
Coire a' Choire	Pth & Kin	NN6918	56°20·4′	4°6·7′W	X	57
Coire a' Chonachair	Highld	NC3302	57°58·8′	4°49·0′W	X	15
Coire a' Chonnaidh	Pth & Kin	NN6239	56°31·6′	4°14·2′W	X	51
Coire a' Chriochairein	Highld	NN4489	56°58·2′	4°33·5′W	X	34,42
Coireachrombie	Stir	NN5809	56°15·4′	4°17·1′W	X	57
Coire a' Chròtha	Highld	NH1946	57°28·4′	5°0·6′W	X	25
Coire-a' Chruidh	Highld	NG4718	57°11·2′	6°10·8′W	X	32
Coire a' chuil Droma Mór	Highld	NH0209	57°8·0′	5°15·9′W	X	33
Coire a' Chuilinn	Stir	NN3619	56°20·4′	4°38·7′W	X	50,56
Coire a' Chuilinn	Stir	NN3717	56°19·3′	4°37·7′W	X	50,56
Coire a' Chùil Mhàim	Highld	NM8557	56°39·6′	5°30·0′W	X	49
Coireag Bheag	Highld	NH1756	57°33·7′	5°3·1′W	X	25
Coireag Bhuidhe	Highld	NH1952	57°31·6′	5°0·9′W	X	25
Coireag Chaorainn	Highld	NG9678	57°45·0′	5°25·2′W	H	19
Coireag Dhearg	Highld	NG9058	57°34·1′	5°30·2′W	X	25
Coireag Dubh Mór	Highld	NG9358	57°34·1′	5°27·2′W	X	25
Coire a' Ghabhalach	Arg & Bt	NN3340	56°31·6′	4°42·5′W	X	50
Coire Aghaisgeig	Highld	NC8405	58°1·4′	3°57·4′W	X	17
Coire a' Ghearraig	Pth & Kin	NO0869	56°48·5′	3°30·0′W	X	43
Coire a' Ghiubhais	Pth & Kin	NN4662	56°43·7′	4°30·6′W	X	42
Coire a' Ghlas-thuill	Highld	NH0815	57°11·4′	5°10·2′W	X	33
Coire a' Ghraigh-fhear	Highld	NH0739	57°24·3′	5°12·3′W	X	25
Coire a' Ghreadaidh	Highld	NG4323	57°13·8′	6°15·0′W	X	32
Coireag Mhór	Highld	NG3840	57°22·8′	6°21·1′W	X	23
Coireag nan Each	Highld	NH0432	57°20·4′	5°15·0′W	X	25
Coireag Riabhach	Highld	NG9682	57°47·1′	5°25·4′W	X	19
Coireag Riabhach	Highld	NG9979	57°45·6′	5°22·3′W	X	19
Coire Aird	Highld	NH0826	57°17·3′	5°10·7′W	X	25,33
Coire Allt a' Chlair	Aberd	NO1288	56°58·7′	3°26·4′W	X	43
Coire Allt a Mharcaidh	Highld	NH8901	57°5·5′	3°49·5′W	X	35,36
Coire Allt an Tuirc	Highld	NH0522	57°15·1′	5°13·5′W	X	25,33
Coire Allt Donaich	Highld	NH1017	57°12·5′	5°8·3′W	X	34
Coire a' Mhadaidh	Highld	NC3021	58°9·0′	4°52·8′W	X	15
Coire a' Mhadaidh	Highld	NH3107	57°7·6′	4°47·1′W	X	34
Coire a' Mhaigh	Highld	NN4982	56°54·5′	4°28·3′W	X	34,42
Coire a' Mhuilt	Highld	NG7830	57°18·7′	5°40·7′W	X	24
Coire an Achaidh	Highld	NC3741	58°19·9′	4°46·6′W	X	9
Coire Anaic	Highld	NN5982	56°54·7′	4°18·5′W	X	42
Coirean an Eich Bhric	Highld	NH0808	57°7·6′	5°9·9′W	X	33
Coire an Athair	Highld	NH0617	57°12·4′	5°12·3′W	X	33
Coirean Bàn	Highld	NC2915	58°5·7′	4°53·6′W	X	15
Coire an Dòthaidh	Arg & Bt	NN3239	56°31·0′	4°43·4′W	X	50
Coire an Duich	Pth & Kin	NN5044	56°34·1′	4°26·0′W	X	51
Coire an Eas	Moray	NJ1707	57°9·0′	3°21·9′W	X	36
Coire an Eas Bhàin	Highld	NM7186	56°54·8′	5°45·3′W	X	40
Coire an Eich	Highld	NH5406	57°7·6′	4°24·3′W	X	35
Coire an Eich	Highld	NM9291	56°58·1′	5°24·9′W	X	33,40
Coire an Eich	Highld	NN2296	57°1·5′	4°55·5′W	X	34
Coire an Eich Bhàin	Highld	NG8405	57°5·4′	5°33·5′W	X	33
Coire an Eòin	Highld	NH2509	57°8·6′	4°53·1′W	X	34
Coire an Fhaicnich	Highld	NC7016	58°7·1′	4°11·9′W	X	16
Coire an Fheòir	Highld	NM7672	56°47·4′	5°39·6′W	X	40
Coire an Fhir Bhogha	Aberd	NO0497	57°3·5′	3°34·5′W	X	36,43
Coire an Fhir Leith	Highld	NN1343	56°32·8′	5°2·1′W	X	50
Coire an Fhraoich	Highld	NG7721	57°13·8′	5°41·2′W	X	33
Coire an Fhuarain	N Eil	NB2332	58°11·7′	6°42·4′W	T	8,13
Coire an Fhùdair	Arg & Bt	NM4554	56°36·8′	6°8·9′W	X	47
Coire an Fhuidhir	Highld	NN0682	56°53·6′	5°10·6′W	X	41
Coire an Iubhair	Highld	NM9261	56°41·9′	5°23·4′W	X	40
Coire an Lagain	Highld	NM5948	56°34·0′	5°54·9′W	X	47,48
Coire an Laoigh	Highld	NG9659	57°34·8′	5°24·3′W	X	25
Coire an Leth-uillt	Highld	NG9754	57°32·1′	5°23·0′W	X	25
Coire an Lightuinn	Highld	NN1082	56°53·7′	5°6·7′W	X	34,41
Coire an Liomhain	Highld	NM6354	56°37·3′	5°51·4′W	X	49
Coire an Loch	Pth & Kin	NN9883	56°55·9′	3°40·1′W	X	43
Coire an Lochain	Arg & Bt	NN3744	56°33·8′	4°38·7′W	X	50
Coire an Lochain	Highld	NH9803	57°6·7′	3°40·6′W	X	36
Coire an Lochain	Highld	NM7996	57°0·4′	5°37·9′W	X	33,40
Coire an Lochain	Highld	NN2265	56°44·8′	4°54·2′W	X	41
Coire an Lochain Sgeirich	Highld	NH2585	57°49·5′	4°56·3′W	X	20
Coire an Lochain Uaine	Aberd	NO0298	57°4·0′	3°36·5′W	X	36,43
Coire Annaich	Stir	NN2525	56°23·4′	4°49·6′W	X	50
Coirean Odhar	Arg & Bt	NM4843	56°31·0′	6°5·3′W	X	47,48
Coirean Riabhach	Highld	NN1845	56°34·0′	4°57·3′W	X	50
Coire an Stacain	Arg & Bt	NN1722	56°21·6′	4°57·3′W	X	50
Coire an Tàilleir	Highld	NH1839	57°24·6′	5°1·3′W	X	25
Coire AN Tobair	Aberd	NN9384	56°56·4′	3°45·1′W	X	43
Coire an t-Sabhail	Aberd	NN9697	57°3·4′	3°42·4′W	X	36,43
Coire ant-Sagairt	Highld	NG4433	57°19·2′	6°14·7′W	X	32
Coire an t-Sagairt	Highld	NM8296	57°0·5′	5°35·0′W	X	33,40
Coire an t-Saighdeir	Aberd	NN9696	57°2·9′	3°42·4′W	X	36,43
Coire an t-Searraich	Highld	NM8772	56°47·7′	5°28·8′W	X	40
Coire an t-Searraich Dhuibh	Highld	NM8675	56°49·3′	5°30·0′W	X	40
Coire àn-t-Seasaich	Highld	NG4228	57°16·5′	6°16·4′W	X	32
Coire an t-Seasgaich	Highld	NH0703	57°4·9′	5°10·6′W	X	33
Coire an t - Seilich	Highld	NH0749	57°29·7′	5°12·8′W	X	25
Coire an t-Seilich	Highld	NH4204	57°6·3′	4°36·1′W	X	34
Coire an t'Seilich	Highld	NN2685	56°55·7′	4°51·1′W	X	34,41
Coire an t-Seilich	Highld	NN2987	56°56·8′	4°48·2′W	X	34,41
Coire an t-Sidhein	Highld	NN3095	57°1·2′	4°47·6′W	X	34
Coire an t-Siosalaich	Highld	NH0319	57°13·4′	5°15·3′W	X	33
Coire an t-Sith	Arg & Bt	NS1289	56°3·7′	5°0·7′W	W	56
Coire an t-Sith	Highld	NH1933	57°21·4′	5°0·1′W	X	25
Coire an t-Slugain	Aberd	NJ2802	57°6·5′	3°10·9′W	X	37
Coire an t-Slugain	Highld	NH0609	57°8·1′	5°11·9′W	X	33
Coire an t-Sneachda	Highld	NH2027	57°18·2′	4°58·8′W	X	25
Coire an t-Sneachda	Highld	NH9903	57°6·7′	3°39·6′W	X	36
Coire an t-Sneachda	Highld	NM7260	56°40·8′	5°42·9′W	X	40
Coire an t-Suidhe	Highld	NM7966	56°44·3′	5°36·4′W	X	40
Coire an Tuill Bhàin	Highld	NH0948	57°29·2′	5°10·7′W	X	25
Coire an Tuim	Highld	NM6756	56°38·5′	5°47·6′W	X	49
Coire an Uaigneis	Highld	NG4523	57°13·9′	6°13·1′W	X	32
Coire an Uillt Dheirg	Highld	NH0450	57°30·1′	5°15·8′W	X	25
Coire an Uillt Mhóir	Highld	NJ0913	57°12·2′	3°29·9′W	X	36
Coire an Uinnseinn	Highld	NC3655	58°27·4′	4°48·2′W	X	9
Coire an Uruisge	Arg & Bt	NM5941	56°30·2′	5°54·5′W	X	47,48
Coire Aodainn	Arg & Bt	NS1398	56°8·5′	5°0·2′W	W	56
Coire a' Phiobaire	Highld	NH0855	57°32·9′	5°12·1′W	X	25
Coire a' Phuill	Highld	NG8402	57°3·8′	5°33·3′W	X	33
Coire Arcain	Highld	NN8698	57°3·8′	3°52·3′W	X	35,36,43
Coire Ardachaidh	Highld	NH2104	57°5·8′	4°56·8′W	X	34
Coire Ardair	Highld	NN4387	56°57·1′	4°34·4′W	X	34,42
Coire Arla	Arg & Bt	NM5248	56°33·8′	6°1·7′W	X	47,48
Coire as Airde	Highld	NH5295	57°55·5′	4°29·5′W	X	20
Coire Attadale	Highld	NG7845	57°26·7′	5°41·5′W	X	24
Coire Bàn	Arg & Bt	NM4646	56°32·5′	6°7·5′W	X	47,48
Coire Bàn	Arg & Bt	NM6132	56°25·4′	5°52·1′W	X	49
Coire Bàn	Highld	NM8052	56°36·8′	5°34·7′W	X	49
Coire Bàn	Pth & Kin	NN5045	56°34·6′	4°26·1′W	X	51
Coire Bàn	Pth & Kin	NN6144	56°34·3′	4°15·3′W	X	51
Coire Bàn Beag	Pth & Kin	NN4239	56°31·3′	4°33·7′W	X	51
Coire Bàn Mór	Pth & Kin	NN4238	56°30·7′	4°33·6′W	X	51
Coire Beag	Highld	NG4619	57°11·7′	6°11·8′W	X	32
Coire Beag	Highld	NG8667	57°38·8′	5°34·7′W	X	19
Coire Beag	Highld	NH2069	57°40·8′	5°0·7′W	X	20
Coire Beag	Highld	NM8150	56°35·7′	5°33·6′W	X	49
Coire Beag	N Ayr	NR9739	55°36·4′	5°12·9′W	X	69
Coire Beanaidh	Highld	NH9501	57°5·5′	3°43·5′W	X	36
Coire Bearnach	Arg & Bt	NM6733	56°26·2′	5°46·3′W	X	49
Coire Beinn Lunndaidh	Highld	NC7801	57°59·2′	4°3·3′W	X	17
Coire Beinn na h-Uamha	Highld	NM6754	56°37·5′	5°47·5′W	X	49
Coire Beithe	Arg & Bt	NN1940	56°31·3′	4°56·1′W	X	50
Coire Beithe	Highld	NG6022	57°13·8′	5°58·1′W	X	32
Coire Beithe	Highld	NG9703	57°4·7′	5°20·5′W	X	33
Coire Beithe	Highld	NH0443	57°26·4′	5°15·5′W	X	25
Coire Beithe	Highld	NH1148	57°29·2′	5°8·7′W	X	25
Coire Beithe	Highld	NH1408	57°7·8′	5°3·9′W	X	34
Coire Beithe	Highld	NM8284	56°54·0′	5°34·3′W	X	40
Coire Beithe	Pth & Kin	NN5147	56°35·7′	4°25·2′W	X	51
Coire Beitheach	Highld	NM7852	56°36·7′	5°36·6′W	X	49
Coire Beithe Beag	Highld	NH1349	57°29·8′	5°6·8′W	X	25
Coire Beul an Sporain	Highld	NN5979	56°53·1′	4°18·4′W	X	42
Coire Bhachdaidh	Pth & Kin	NN5571	56°48·7′	4°22·1′W	X	42
Coire Bhachdaidh Lodge	Pth & Kin	NN5472	56°49·3′	4°23·1′W	X	42
Coire Bhalach	Highld	NN2557	56°40·6′	4°50·9′W	X	41
Coire Bhàn	Highld	NN2090	56°58·2′	4°57·2′W	X	34
Coire Bhànain	Highld	NN4491	56°59·3′	4°33·6′W	X	34
Coire Bhealaich	Highld	NH7792	57°0·4′	4°1·1′W	X	35
Coire Bhearnaist	Aberd	NO0483	56°56·0′	3°34·2′W	X	43
Coire Bheithe	Highld	NH0341	57°25·3′	5°16·4′W	X	25
Coire Bhiocair	Arg & Bt	NN2237	56°29·7′	4°53·0′W	X	50
Coire Bhlàir	Highld	NN8992	57°0·6′	3°49·2′W	X	35,43
Coire Bhorradail	Highld	NM6250	56°35·2′	5°52·1′W	X	49
Coire Bhothain	Highld	NN7685	56°56·6′	4°1·8′W	X	42
Coire Bhotrais	Highld	NN1286	56°55·9′	5°4·9′W	X	34,41
Coire Bhran	Highld	NN8085	56°56·7′	3°57·9′W	X	43
Coire Bhrochain	Aberd	NN9599	57°4·5′	3°43·5′W	X	36,43
Coire Bhuidhe	Highld	NM6054	56°37·2′	5°54·3′W	X	49
Coire Bhùirich	Pth & Kin	NN5571	56°48·7′	4°22·1′W	X	42
Coire Bhuraich	Highld	NM8491	56°57·9′	5°32·7′W	X	33,40
Coire Bleaval	N Eil	NG0392	57°49·4′	6°59·7′W	X	18
Coire Bog	Highld	NC4705	58°0·7′	4°34·9′W	X	16
Coire Bog	Highld	NH1361	57°36·3′	5°7·3′W	X	19
Coire Bog	Highld	NH1532	57°20·7′	5°4·0′W	X	25
Coire Bog	Highld	NH5386	57°50·6′	4°28·1′W	X	20
Coire Bogha-cloiche	Highld	NN9399	57°4·4′	3°45·4′W	X	36,43
Coire Bohaskey	Highld	NN3087	56°56·8′	4°47·2′W	X	34,41
Coire Boidheach	Aberd	NO2384	56°56·7′	3°15·5′W	X	44
Coire Breac	Angus	NO4674	56°51·5′	2°52·7′W	X	44
Coire Breac	Highld	NH1671	57°41·7′	5°4·8′W	X	20
Coire Briste	Highld	NG9465	57°37·9′	5°26·6′W	X	19
Coire Buidhe	Aberd	NN9984	56°56·4′	3°39·1′W	X	43
Coire Buidhe	Arg & Bt	NM4228	56°22·7′	6°10·3′W	X	48
Coire Buidhe	Arg & Bt	NM4648	56°33·6′	6°7·6′W	X	47,48
Coire Buidhe	Arg & Bt	NM4655	56°37·3′	6°8·0′W	X	47
Coire Buidhe	Arg & Bt	NM4656	56°37·9′	6°8·1′W	X	47
Coire Buidhe	Arg & Bt	NM5322	56°19·8′	5°59·3′W	X	48
Coire Buidhe	Arg & Bt	NN0344	56°33·1′	5°11·9′W	X	50
Coire Buidhe	Arg & Bt	NN2019	56°20·0′	4°54·3′W	X	50,56
Coire Buidhe	Arg & Bt	NR4198	56°6·5′	6°9·5′W	X	61
Coire Buidhe	Highld	NC4510	58°3·4′	4°37·1′W	X	16
Coire Buidhe	Highld	NC6138	58°18·8′	4°21·9′W	X	16
Coire Buidhe	Highld	NC7042	58°21·1′	4°12·8′W	X	10
Coire Buidhe	Highld	NG6520	57°12·9′	5°53·1′W	X	32
Coire Buidhe	Highld	NG7722	57°14·3′	5°41·3′W	X	33
Coire Buidhe	Highld	NG8429	57°18·3′	5°34·7′W	X	33
Coire Buidhe	Highld	NG8912	57°9·3′	5°28·9′W	X	33
Coire Buidhe	Highld	NH1365	57°38·4′	5°7·5′W	X	19
Coire Buidhe	Highld	NH1529	57°19·1′	5°3·9′W	X	25
Coire Buidhe	Highld	NH4126	57°18·1′	4°37·9′W	X	26
Coire Buidhe	Highld	NH4297	57°56·3′	4°39·7′W	X	20
Coire Buidhe	Highld	NH9005	57°7·6′	3°48·6′W	X	36
Coire Buidhe	Highld	NM6358	56°39·5′	5°51·6′W	X	49
Coire Buidhe	Highld	NM7288	56°55·9′	5°44·4′W	X	40
Coire Buidhe	Highld	NM8478	56°50·9′	5°32·1′W	X	40
Coire Buidhe	Highld	NM9898	57°2·0′	5°19·3′W	X	33,40
Coire Buidhe	Highld	NN2597	57°2·1′	4°52·6′W	X	34
Coire Buidhe	Highld	NN3886	56°56·5′	4°39·3′W	X	34,41
Coire Buidhe	Pth & Kin	NN6220	56°21·4′	4°13·6′W	W	51,57
Coire Buidhe	Stir	NN2926	56°24·0′	4°45·8′W	X	50
Coire Buidhe Mór	Highld	NH1736	57°22·9′	5°2·2′W	X	25
Coire Cadderlie	Arg & Bt	NN0338	56°29·8′	5°11·6′W	X	50
Coire Camas Drollaman	Highld	NM6383	56°52·9′	5°53·0′W	X	40
Coire Caol	Highld	NC9427	58°13·4′	3°47·8′W	X	17
Coire Caol	Highld	NG9930	57°19·2′	5°19·8′W	X	25
Coire Caorach	Arg & Bt	NN0730	56°25·6′	5°7·3′W	X	50
Coire Carie	Pth & Kin	NN6253	56°39·2′	4°14·6′W	W	42,51
Coire Carlaig	Arg & Bt	NS3196	56°7·9′	4°42·7′W	X	56
Coire Càrnaig	Highld	NM9086	56°55·3′	5°26·6′W	X	40
Coire Carn na Saobhaidhe	Highld	NG9778	57°45·0′	5°24·2′W	H	19
Coire Cas	Highld	NH9904	57°7·2′	3°39·6′W	X	36
Coire Cas-eagallach	Pth & Kin	NN9773	56°50·5′	3°40·9′W	X	43
Coire Cath nam Fionn	Aberd	NN9593	57°1·2′	3°43·3′W	X	36,43
Coire Ceann Loch	Highld	NC3526	58°11·8′	4°48·0′W	X	15
Coire Ceirsle Hill	Highld	NN2485	56°55·6′	4°53·1′W	H	34,41
Coire Chailein	Arg & Bt	NN0048	56°35·1′	5°15·0′W	X	50
Coire Chailein	Arg & Bt	NN3133	56°27·8′	4°44·1′W	X	50
Coire Chaillich	Highld	NM8367	56°44·9′	5°32·5′W	X	40
Coire Chaiplin	Highld	NG4459	57°33·2′	6°16·3′W	X	23
Coire Challum	Stir	NN3831	56°26·9′	4°37·3′W	H	50
Coire Chaorach	Arg & Bt	NN1844	56°33·4′	4°57·2′W	X	50
Coire Chaorachaidh	Highld	NC6612	58°4·9′	4°15·9′W	X	16
Coire Chat	Arg & Bt	NN0630	56°25·6′	5°8·3′W	X	50
Coire-chat-achan	Highld	NG6222	57°13·9′	5°56·2′W	X	32
Coire Chatan	N Ayr	NR9940	55°37·0′	5°11·1′W	X	62,69
Coire Cheanna Mhuir	Highld	NN0994	57°0·1′	5°8·2′W	X	33
Coire-cheathaich	Stir	NN3935	56°29·0′	4°36·4′W	X	50
Coire Chicheanais	Highld	NM9594	56°59·8′	5°22·0′W	X	33,40
Coire Chirdle	Pth & Kin	NN3837	56°30·1′	4°37·5′W	X	50
Coire Chnàmh	Highld	NN1485	56°55·4′	5°2·9′W	X	34,41
Coire Choimhlidh	Highld	NN2475	56°50·3′	4°52·7′W	X	41

Coire Choinnich	Highld	NG5425	57°15·2′	6°4·3′W	X	32
Coire Choinnich	Highld	NH0845	57°27·5′	5°11·6′W	X	25
Coire Chòinnichean	Highld	NG7801	57°3·1′	5°39·2′W	X	33
Coire Chomhlain	Highld	NN4870	56°48·1′	4°28·9′W	X	42
Coire Chorsalain	Highld	NG8711	57°8·7′	5°30·8′W	X	33
Coire Chorse	Pth & Kin	NN4647	56°35·6′	4°30·0′W	X	51
Coire Chouplaig	Highld	NN3188	56°57·4′	4°46·3′W	X	34,41
Coire Chraoibhe	Highld	NN1584	56°54·9′	5°1·9′W	X	34,41
Coire Chrid	Aberd	NO1282	56°55·5′	3°26·3′W	X	43
Coire Chrìon-alltain	Highld	NN8495	57°2·2′	3°54·2′W	X	35,43
Coire Chroisg	Stir	NN6117	56°19·8′	4°14·4′W	X	57
Coire Chuaich	Highld	NN7186	56°57·1′	4°6·8′W	X	42
Coire Chùirn	Highld	NN6479	56°53·2′	4°13·5′W	X	42
Coire Chùr	Highld	NM9981	56°52·9′	5°17·5′W	X	40
Coire Circe	Arg & Bt	NM9943	56°32·4′	5°15·7′W	X	49
Coire Clachach	Arg & Bt	NM6130	56°24·4′	5°52·0′W	X	49
Coire Clachach	Arg & Bt	NM6637	56°28·3′	5°47·5′W	X	49
Coire Clachaig	Highld	NN3883	56°54·9′	4°39·2′W	X	34,41
Coire Cloiche Finne	Highld	NN2153	56°38·3′	4°54·7′W	X	41
Coire Cnoc na Gamhna	Highld	NC7803	58°0·2′	4°3·4′W	X	17
Coire Coinghil	Arg & Bt	NS2992	56°5·7′	4°44·5′W	X	56
Coire Coinnich	Arg & Bt	NN1439	56°30·6′	5°0·9′W	X	50
Coire Coulavie	Highld	NH1223	57°15·8′	5°6·6′W	X	25
Coire Craobh an Oir	Aberd	NO0294	57°1·9′	3°36·4′W	X	36,43
Coire Creagach	Arg & Bt	NN2745	56°34·2′	4°48·5′W	X	50
Coire Creagach	Arg & Bt	NN3013	56°17·0′	4°44·3′W	X	50,56
Coire Creagach	Highld	NN4166	56°45·8′	4°35·6′W	X	42
Coire Creagach	Highld	NN8783	56°55·7′	3°51·0′W	X	43
Coire Creagach	Pth & Kin	NN6073	56°49·9′	4°17·2′W	X	42
Coire Cròm	Highld	NH1520	57°14·3′	5°3·5′W	X	25
Coire Cruachan	Arg & Bt	NN0829	56°25·1′	5°6·3′W	X	50
Coire Cruinn	Highld	NC6717	58°7·6′	4°15·0′W	X	16
Coire Cruinn	Highld	NM6866	56°43·9′	5°47·1′W	X	40
Coire Cruinn	Pth & Kin	NN8630	56°27·2′	3°50·5′W	X	52
Coire Cùil	Highld	NN4096	57°1·9′	4°37·7′W	X	34
Coire Cuinne	Arg & Bt	NS3090	56°4·6′	4°43·5′W	X	56
Coire da Choimhid	Highld	NN1244	56°33·3′	5°3·1′W	X	50
Coire Dail Aiteil	Highld	NG9732	57°20·3′	5°21·9′W	X	25
Coire Daimh	Arg & Bt	NN2733	56°27·7′	4°48·0′W	X	50
Coire Daingean	Arg & Bt	NN3341	56°32·1′	4°42·5′W	X	50
Coire Daingean	Highld	NH2306	57°6·9′	4°54·9′W	X	34
Coire Daingean	N Ayr	NR9641	55°37·4′	5°14·0′W	X	62,69
Coire dà Leathaid	Highld	NN3650	56°37·1′	4°39·9′W	X	41
Coire Daraich	Highld	NG4529	57°17·1′	6°13·4′W	X	32
Coire Dearg	Arg & Bt	NN0729	56°25·1′	5°7·3′W	X	50
Coire Dearg	Highld	NH0594	57°53·8′	5°16·9′W	X	19
Coire Dho	Highld	NH1913	57°10·6′	4°59·2′W	X	34
Coire Dhomhain	Pth & Kin	NN6074	56°50·4′	4°17·3′W	X	42
Coire Dhomhnaill	Highld	NN2346	56°34·6′	4°52·4′W	X	50
Coire Dhondail	Highld	NN9298	57°3·9′	3°46·4′W	X	36,43
Coire Dhorrcail	Highld	NG8303	57°4·3′	5°34·3′W	X	33
Coire Dhruim nam Bò	Highld	NG8612	57°9·2′	5°31·8′W	X	33
Coire Dhubhchlair	Stir	NN4933	56°28·2′	4°26·6′W	X	51
Coire Dhuinnid	Highld	NG9225	57°16·4′	5°26·5′W	X	25,33
Coire Dhùnan	Arg & Bt	NR8299	56°8·3′	5°30·1′W	X	55
Coire Dibadale	N Eil	NB0424	58°6·6′	7°1·1′W	X	13
Coire Doe	Highld	NH4305	57°6·8′	4°35·1′W	X	34
Coire Doinn Mór	Highld	NH0941	57°25·4′	5°10·4′W	X	25
Coire Doir' Uillt	Highld	NM6874	56°48·2′	5°47·6′W	X	40
Coire-domhain	Highld	NG9734	57°21·3′	5°22·0′W	X	25
Coire Domhain	Highld	NG9815	57°11·1′	5°20·1′W	X	33
Coire Domhain	Highld	NG9860	57°35·4′	5°22·3′W	X	19
Coire Domhain	Highld	NH1528	57°18·6′	5°3·8′W	X	25
Coire Domhain	Highld	NN8792	57°0·6′	3°51·2′W	X	35,43
Coire Domhain	Moray	NH9902	57°6·1′	3°39·6′W	X	36
Coire Domhain	Pth & Kin	NO0570	56°49·0′	3°32·9′W	X	43
Coire Dorcha	Highld	NC6824	58°11·4′	4°14·2′W	X	16
Coire Dùail	Highld	NC3351	58°25·2′	4°51·1′W	X	9
Coire Dubh	Arg & Bt	NN2119	56°20·0′	4°53·3′W	X	50,56
Coire Dubh	Highld	NC3808	58°2·2′	4°44·2′W	X	16
Coire Dubh	Highld	NG5222	57°13·6′	6°6·1′W	X	32
Coire Dubh	Highld	NG7539	57°23·4′	5°44·2′W	X	24
Coire Dubh	Highld	NG8001	57°3·1′	5°37·2′W	X	33
Coire Dubh	Highld	NG8413	57°9·7′	5°33·9′W	X	33
Coire Dubh	Highld	NG8846	57°27·6′	5°31·6′W	X	24
Coire Dubh	Highld	NG9847	57°28·4′	5°21·7′W	X	25
Coire Dubh	Highld	NH0132	57°20·4′	5°17·9′W	X	25
Coire Dubh	Highld	NH0504	57°5·4′	5°12·6′W	X	33
Coire Dubh	Highld	NH0547	57°28·5′	5°14·7′W	X	25
Coire Dubh	Highld	NH2252	57°31·7′	4°57·9′W	X	25
Coire Dubh	Highld	NH2336	57°23·1′	4°56·2′W	X	25
Coire Dubh	Highld	NH2831	57°20·5′	4°51·0′W	X	25
Coire Dubh	Highld	NH2856	57°33·9′	4°52·1′W	X	25
Coire Dubh	Highld	NH4908	57°8·5′	4°29·3′W	X	34
Coire Dubh	Highld	NH5269	57°41·5′	4°28·5′W	X	20
Coire Dubh	Highld	NM3897	56°59·7′	6°18·4′W	X	39
Coire Dubh	Highld	NM7256	56°38·7′	5°42·7′W	X	49
Coire Dubh	Highld	NM7664	56°43·1′	5°39·2′W	X	40
Coire Dubh	Highld	NM7666	56°44·2′	5°39·3′W	X	40
Coire Dubh	Highld	NM8095	56°59·9′	5°36·9′W	X	33,40
Coire Dubh	Highld	NM8165	56°43·8′	5°34·4′W	X	40
Coire Dubh	Highld	NM8191	56°57·8′	5°35·7′W	X	33,40
Coire Dubh	Highld	NM8389	56°56·7′	5°33·6′W	X	40
Coire Dubh	Highld	NM8793	56°59·0′	5°29·9′W	X	33,40
Coire Dubh	Highld	NM9865	56°44·2′	5°17·7′W	X	40
Coire Dubh	Highld	NN0252	56°37·3′	5°13·2′W	X	41
Coire Dubh	Highld	NN0273	56°48·6′	5°14·2′W	X	41
Coire Dubh	Highld	NN0882	56°53·6′	5°8·7′W	X	41
Coire Dubh	Highld	NN1386	56°55·9′	5°3·9′W	X	34,41
Coire Dubh	Highld	NN2687	56°56·8′	4°51·2′W	X	34,41
Coire Dubh	Highld	NN3192	56°59·6′	4°46·5′W	X	34
Coire Dubh	Highld	NN3288	56°57·4′	4°45·3′W	X	34,41
Coire Dubh	Highld	NN3585	56°55·9′	4°42·2′W	X	34,41
Coire Dubh	Highld	NN4576	56°51·2′	4°32·1′W	X	42
Coire Dubh	Highld	NN4991	56°59·4′	4°28·7′W	H	34
Coire Dubh	N Eil	NB1406	57°57·4′	6°49·6′W	X	13,14
Coire Dubh	N Eil	NB2508	57°58·8′	6°38·7′W	X	13,14
Coire Dubh	N Eil	NF7616	57°7·5′	7°20·8′W	X	31
Coire Dubh	N Eil	NF7932	57°16·2′	7°19·1′W	X	22
Coire Dubh	N Eil	NF8121	57°10·4′	7°16·3′W	X	31
Coire Dubh	Pth & Kin	NN4648	56°36·2′	4°30·1′W	X	51
Coire Dubh Ealcha	Arg & Bt	NN1734	56°28·0′	4°57·8′W	X	50
Coire Dubh Garbh	Pth & Kin	NN4663	56°44·3′	4°30·6′W	X	42
Coire Dubh-ghlas	Arg & Bt	NN0207	56°13·1′	5°11·2′W	X	55
Coire Dubh Mòr	Arg & Bt	NN3845	56°34·4′	4°37·8′W	X	50
Coire Dubh Mór	Highld	NC2701	57°58·1′	4°55·0′W	X	15
Coire Dubh Mór	Highld	NG9459	57°34·7′	5°26·3′W	X	25
Coire Dubh-mór	Highld	NN1748	56°35·6′	4°58·4′W	X	50
Coire Dubh na Giubhsaich	Highld	NN0789	56°57·4′	5°10·0′W	X	41
Coire Dubh-riabhach	Highld	NH0551	57°30·7′	5°14·9′W	X	25
Coire Dubh Sguadaig	Highld	NN3686	56°56·4′	4°41·3′W	X	34,41
Coire Each	Highld	NG8105	57°5·3′	5°36·4′W	X	33
Coire Each	Highld	NG8243	57°25·8′	5°37·4′W	X	24
Coire Ealt	Arg & Bt	NS1496	56°7·5′	4°59·1′W	W	56
Coire Earb	Stir	NN3820	56°20·9′	4°36·8′W	X	50,56
Coire Earba	Highld	NG9948	57°28·9′	5°20·7′W	X	25
Coire Eich	Stir	NN3820	56°20·9′	4°36·8′W	X	50,56
Coire Eigheach	Pth & Kin	NN4365	56°45·3′	4°33·6′W	X	42
Coire Eindart	Highld	NN9091	57°0·1′	3°48·2′W	X	43
Coire Eòghainn	Highld	NH2233	57°21·4′	4°57·1′W	X	25
Coire Eoghannan	Pth & Kin	NN4144	56°33·9′	4°34·8′W	X	51
Coire Fada	Highld	NN0482	56°53·5′	5°12·6′W	X	41
Coire Faoin	Highld	NG4266	57°36·9′	6°18·7′W	X	23
Coire Faoin	Highld	NG4953	57°30·1′	6°10·9′W	H	23
Coire Fearchair	Highld	NG6023	57°14·4′	5°58·2′W	X	32
Coire Fearna	Arg & Bt	NN2040	56°31·3′	4°55·1′W	X	50
Coire Fearna	Highld	NM7473	56°47·9′	5°41·6′W	X	40
Coire Fhearnasdail	Highld	NN8296	57°2·7′	3°56·2′W	X	35,43
Coire Fhearneasg	Aberd	NO1181	56°55·0′	3°27·3′W	X	43
Coire Fhionn Lochan	N Ayr	NR9045	55°39·4′	5°19·9′W	W	62,69
Coire Fhiuran	Pth & Kin	NN4045	56°34·4′	4°35·8′W	X	51
Coire Fionnarach	Highld	NH1644	57°27·2′	5°3·6′W	X	25
Coire Fionnaraich	Highld	NG9450	57°29·9′	5°25·8′W	X	25
Coire Fionn Làirige	Stir	NN5637	56°30·4′	4°19·9′W	X	51
Coire Forsaidh	Highld	NG6021	57°13·3′	5°58·1′W	X	32
Coire Fraineach	Highld	NG9931	57°19·8′	5°19·9′W	X	25
Coire Fraoich	Arg & Bt	NM6438	56°28·8′	5°49·5′W	X	49
Coirefrois Burn	Highld	NC6916	58°7·1′	4°13·0′W	W	16
Coire Fuar	Highld	NG4557	57°32·1′	6°15·2′W	X	23
Coire Gabhar	Highld	NM8371	56°47·1′	5°32·7′W	X	40
Coire Gaothach	Stir	NN2726	56°23·9′	4°47·7′W	X	50
Coire Garbh	Highld	NG5823	57°14·3′	6°0·2′W	X	32
Coire Garbh	Highld	NG8004	57°4·7′	5°37·4′W	X	33
Coire Garbh	Highld	NG9349	57°29·3′	5°26·8′W	X	25
Coire Garbh	Pth & Kin	NN8231	56°27·6′	3°54·5′W	X	52
Coire Garbh	Stir	NN2925	56°23·4′	4°45·8′W	X	50
Coire Garbhlach	Highld	NN8794	57°1·7′	3°51·2′W	X	35,36,43
Coire Gasgain	Highld	NG7216	57°11·0′	5°45·9′W	X	33
Coire Ghabhar	Arg & Bt	NN2245	56°34·1′	4°53·4′W	X	50
Coire Ghaibhre	Arg & Bt	NM6334	56°26·6′	5°50·3′W	X	49
Coire Ghàidheil	Highld	NH0922	57°15·2′	5°9·5′W	X	25,33
Coire Ghaisgeach	Highld	NG4931	57°18·3′	6°9·6′W	X	32
Coire Ghamhnain	Arg & Bt	NN2933	56°27·7′	4°46·1′W	X	50
Coire Ghardail	Highld	NM8455	56°38·5′	5°30·9′W	X	49
Coire Ghiubhsachain	Highld	NM8976	56°49·9′	5°27·1′W	X	40
Coire Ghiusachan	Arg & Bt	NN1139	56°30·6′	5°3·8′W	X	50
Coire Glas	Arg & Bt	NN1028	56°24·6′	5°4·3′W	X	50
Coire Glas	Arg & Bt	NN1233	56°27·4′	5°2·6′W	X	50
Coire Glas	Highld	NC3608	58°2·1′	4°46·2′W	X	16
Coire Glas	Highld	NG7248	57°28·2′	5°47·7′W	X	24
Coire Glas	Highld	NG8701	57°3·3′	5°30·3′W	X	33
Coire Glas	Highld	NG9908	57°7·4′	5°18·8′W	X	33
Coire Glas	Highld	NH0603	57°4·9′	5°11·6′W	X	33
Coire Glás	Highld	NM9998	57°2·0′	5°18·3′W	X	33,40
Coire Glas	Highld	NN0689	56°57·4′	5°11·0′W	X	41
Coire Glas	Highld	NN1645	56°33·9′	4°59·2′W	X	50
Coire Glas	Highld	NN2295	57°1·0′	4°55·5′W	X	34
Coire Glas Mór	Highld	NH2642	57°26·4′	4°53·5′W	X	25
Coire Gleann na Muice	Highld	NC3711	58°3·8′	4°45·3′W	X	16
Coire Gnada	Highld	NH1436	57°22·9′	5°5·2′W	X	25
Coire Gorm	Aberd	NO3178	56°53·6′	3°7·5′W	X	44
Coire Gorm	Arg & Bt	NM5132	56°25·1′	6°1·8′W	X	48
Coire Gorm	Arg & Bt	NM6428	56°23·4′	5°49·0′W	X	49
Coire Gorm	Arg & Bt	NR6394	56°5·1′	5°48·1′W	X	61
Coire Gorm	Highld	NC1010	58°2·6′	5°12·7′W	X	15
Coire Gorm	Highld	NC1512	58°3·8′	5°7·7′W	X	15
Coire Gorm	Highld	NC3729	58°13·4′	4°46·1′W	X	16
Coire Gorm	Highld	NG6022	57°13·8′	5°58·1′W	X	32
Coire Gorm	Highld	NH9502	57°6·1′	3°43·5′W	X	36
Coire Gorm	Highld	NN3998	57°3·0′	4°38·8′W	X	34
Coire Gorm	Highld	NN5199	57°3·7′	4°27·0′W	X	35
Coire Gorm	Highld	NN8796	57°2·7′	3°51·3′W	X	35,36,43
Coire Gorm	Pth & Kin	NN4748	56°36·2′	4°29·1′W	X	51
Coire Gorm	Pth & Kin	NN6043	56°33·7′	4°16·2′W	X	51
Coire Gorm Beag	Highld	NG7948	57°28·4′	5°40·7′W	X	24
Coire Gorm Mór	Highld	NH1034	57°21·7′	5°9·1′W	X	25
Coire Grànda	Highld	NC3543	58°20·9′	4°48·7′W	X	9
Coire Granda	Highld	NC4139	58°18·9′	4°42·4′W	X	16
Coire Grannda	Highld	NG9552	57°31·0′	5°24·9′W	X	25
Coire Grealach	Moray	NJ1407	57°9·0′	3°24·8′W	X	36
Coiregrogain	Arg & Bt	NN3009	56°14·8′	4°44·2′W	X	56
Coire Heasgarnich	Pth & Kin	NN4138	56°30·7′	4°34·6′W	X	51
Coire Iain Oig	Highld	NN5198	57°3·2′	4°26·9′W	X	35
Coirein Lochain	N Ayr	NR9045	55°39·4′	5°19·9′W	X	62,69
Coirein nan Spainteach	Highld	NG9915	57°11·2′	5°19·1′W	X	33
Coire Iomhair	Highld	NG4458	57°32·6′	6°16·2′W	X	23
Coire Ionndrainn	Highld	NN2786	56°56·2′	4°50·2′W	W	34,41
Coire Ladhair Mhór	Highld	NM7577	56°50·1′	5°40·9′W	X	40
Coire Làgan	Highld	NG4320	57°12·2′	6°14·9′W	X	32
Coire Làir	Highld	NG9651	57°30·5′	5°23·9′W	X	25
Coire Làir	Highld	NH1212	57°9·9′	5°6·1′W	X	34
Coire Làire	Highld	NN3175	56°50·4′	4°45·8′W	X	41
Coire Lairige	Pth & Kin	NO1068	56°47·9′	3°28·0′W	X	43
Coire Lan	N Ayr	NR9942	55°38·1′	5°11·2′W	X	62,69
Coire Laogh	Highld	NG5823	57°14·3′	6°0·2′W	X	32
Coire Laoghan	Highld	NN2046	56°34·5′	4°55·4′W	X	50
Coire Laogh Mór	Highld	NJ0106	57°8·3′	3°37·7′W	X	36
Coire Laoigh	Stir	NN2725	56°23·4′	4°47·7′W	X	50
Coire Leacach	Highld	NM8658	56°40·2′	5°29·1′W	X	49
Coire Leacach	Highld	NN0187	56°56·2′	5°15·8′W	X	41
Coire Leacachain	Highld	NN2292	56°59·4′	4°55·3′W	X	34
Coire Leachavie	Highld	NH1324	57°16·4′	5°5·6′W	X	25
Coire Leaf	Arg & Bt	NM4931	56°24·5′	6°3·7′W	X	48
Coire Leathaid	N Ayr	NR9827	55°30·0′	5°11·5′W	X	69
Coire Leiridh	Highld	NH0146	57°27·9′	5°18·6′W	X	25
Coire Leis	Highld	NN1771	56°47·9′	4°59·4′W	X	41
Coire Leth Dhearc-ola	Arg & Bt	NM6538	56°28·8′	5°48·5′W	X	49
Coire Liath	Arg & Bt	NM6341	56°30·3′	5°50·6′W	X	49
Coire Liath	Highld	NH0100	57°3·1′	5°16·4′W	X	33
Coire Liath	Highld	NM7297	57°0·7′	5°44·9′W	X	33,40
Coire Liath	Highld	NN7686	56°57·2′	4°1·9′W	X	42
Coire Liath	Pth & Kin	NN6143	56°33·8′	4°15·3′W	X	51
Coire Liath Beag	Highld	NH2507	57°7·5′	4°53·0′W	X	34
Coire Lobhaidh	Stir	NN4832	56°27·6′	4°27·6′W	X	51
Coire Loch	Highld	NC3639	58°18·8′	4°47·5′W	W	16
Coire Loch	Highld	NH2928	57°18·9′	4°49·9′W	W	25
Coire Lochain	Arg & Bt	NN0931	56°26·2′	5°5·4′W	X	50
Coire Lochain	Highld	NH4870	57°41·9′	4°32·6′W	X	20
Coire Lochain	Highld	NN2291	56°58·8′	4°55·3′W	X	34
Coire Lochan	Highld	NH0423	57°15·6′	5°14·5′W	X	25,33
Coire Lochan	Highld	NH1227	57°18·0′	5°6·8′W	W	25
Coire Loch Blàir	Highld	NN0494	57°0·0′	5°13·2′W	X	33
Coire Loch Kander	Aberd	NO1881	56°55·0′	3°20·4′W	H	43
Coire Loch na Geala	Highld	NG8966	57°38·3′	5°31·6′W	X	19
Coire Loin Bheag	Moray	NJ1107	57°9·0′	3°27·8′W	X	36
Coire Lotha	Highld	NN1142	56°32·2′	5°4·0′W	X	50
Coire Luachrach	Highld	NG8810	57°8·2′	5°29·8′W	X	33
Coire Luaidh	Arg & Bt	NN3334	56°28·4′	4°42·2′W	X	50
Coire Lungard	Highld	NH0931	57°20·0′	5°9·9′W	X	25
Coire Lùnndie	Highld	NM6450	56°35·2′	5°50·2′W	X	49
Coire Mac Mhuirich	Highld	NH1811	57°9·5′	5°0·1′W	X	34
Coire Madagan Mór	Highld	NN7485	56°56·6′	4°3·8′W	X	42
Coire Màm a' Ghaill	Highld	NM5067	56°43·9′	6°4·8′W	X	47
Coire Mashie	Highld	NN5781	56°54·2′	4°20·4′W	X	42
Coire Meadhon	Highld	NN3572	56°48·9′	4°41·7′W	X	41
Coire Mhàim	Arg & Bt	NR7971	55°53·1′	5°31·6′W	X	62
Coire Mhàim	Highld	NH1131	57°20·1′	5°7·9′W	X	25
Coire Mharconaich	Highld	NN9193	57°1·2′	3°47·3′W	X	36,43
Coire Mhàrtuin	Arg & Bt	NN1135	56°28·4′	5°3·7′W	X	50
Coire Mheadoin	Highld	NH1515	57°11·6′	5°3·2′W	X	34
Coire Mheall Challuim	Highld	NM8958	56°40·2′	5°26·2′W	X	49
Coire Mhèil	Highld	NH0403	57°4·8′	5°13·6′W	X	33
Coire Mheobhith	Stir	NN6020	56°21·4′	4°15·5′W	X	51,57
Coire Mhic Eachainn	Highld	NG4471	57°39·6′	6°17·1′W	H	23
Coire Mhic Fhearchair	Highld	NH0572	57°42·0′	5°15·9′W	X	19
Coire Mhic Fhearchair	Highld	NH1054	57°32·4′	5°10·0′W	X	25
Coire Mhic Fhearchair	Highld	NH1526	57°17·5′	5°3·7′W	X	25
Coire Mhic Fhearghais	Highld	NG9145	57°27·1′	5°28·6′W	X	25
Coire Mhic Mhathain	Highld	NH2987	57°50·7′	4°52·4′W	X	20
Coire Mhic Mhìcheil	Highld	NG2141	57°22·7′	6°38·1′W	H	23
Coire Mhic Nòbuil	Highld	NG8758	57°34·0′	5°33·2′W	X	24
Coiremhonachan	Arg & Bt	NR9579	55°57·9′	5°16·6′W	X	62
Coire Mhóraigein	Highld	NH1949	57°30·0′	5°0·8′W	X	25
Coire Mhuic	Highld	NN1393	56°59·7′	5°4·3′W	X	34
Coire Mhuilinn	Highld	NN1285	56°55·4′	5°4·9′W	X	34,41
Coire Mhuillidh	Highld	NH2741	57°25·8′	4°52·4′W	X	25
Coire Min	Highld	NG8412	57°9·1′	5°33·8′W	X	33
Coire Moireach	Highld	NH1129	57°19·0′	5°7·9′W	X	25
Coire Molach	Highld	NM7988	56°56·1′	5°37·5′W	X	40
Coire Mór	Arg & Bt	NM5542	56°30·6′	5°58·5′W	X	47,48
Coire Mór	Arg & Bt	NM5832	56°25·4′	5°55·0′W	X	48
Coire Mór	Arg & Bt	NM6735	56°27·2′	5°46·4′W	X	49
Coire Mór	Highld	NC1218	58°6·9′	5°11·0′W	X	15
Coire Mór	Highld	NG2140	57°22·2′	6°38·0′W	H	23
Coire Mór	Highld	NG3823	57°13·6′	6°20·0′W	X	32
Coire Mor	Highld	NG8765	57°37·7′	5°33·6′W	X	19
Coire Mór	Highld	NG9731	57°19·7′	5°21·9′W	X	25
Coire Mór	Highld	NH1971	57°41·8′	5°1·8′W	X	20
Coire Mór	Highld	NH3187	57°50·7′	4°50·4′W	X	20
Coire Mór	Highld	NH4867	57°40·3′	4°32·4′W	X	20
Coire Mór	Highld	NM7273	56°47·8′	5°43·6′W	X	40
Coire Mór an Teallaich	Highld	NH0585	57°49·0′	5°16·5′W	X	19
Coire Mór Chlachair	Highld	NN4778	56°52·4′	4°30·2′W	X	42
Coire Muchdaroch	Highld	NG7349	57°28·7′	5°46·7′W	X	24
Coire Murean	Aberd	NJ4624	57°18·5′	2°53·3′W	X	37
Coire na Bà	Highld	NG7941	57°24·6′	5°40·3′W	X	24
Coire na Baintighearna	Arg & Bt	NN3011	56°15·9′	4°44·3′W	X	50,56
Coire na Banachdich	Highld	NG4321	57°12·7′	6°14·9′W	X	32
Coire na Beinne	Highld	ND1540	58°20·7′	3°26·6′W	H	11,12
Coire na Bèiste	Arg & Bt	NM5839	56°29·1′	5°55·4′W	X	47,48
Coire na Beithe	Arg & Bt	NM4347	56°32·9′	6°10·4′W	X	47,48
Coire na Bò Baine	Arg & Bt	NN1938	56°30·2′	4°56·0′W	X	50
Coire na Breabaig	Highld	NH0730	57°19·4′	5°11·9′W	X	25
Coire na Brogaichain	Highld	NH1132	57°20·6′	5°8·0′W	X	25
Coire na Bruaiche	Highld	NC6317	58°7·5′	4°19·1′W	X	16
Coire na Buaile Brucaiche	Highld	NM6453	56°36·8′	5°50·3′W	X	49
Coire na Buidheig	Highld	NH2033	57°21·4′	4°59·1′W	X	25
Coire na Cabaig	Highld	NN2974	56°49·8′	4°47·7′W	X	41
Coire na Caillich	Highld	NG7906	57°5·8′	5°38·4′W	X	33
Coire na Caillich	Highld	NN9098	57°3·9′	3°48·4′W	X	36,43
Coire na Caime	Arg & Bt	NN1641	56°31·8′	4°59·1′W	X	50
Coire na Caise	Arg & Bt	NM6925	56°21·9′	5°44·0′W	X	49
Coire na Caithris	Highld	NM8493	56°58·9′	5°32·8′W	X	33,40
Coire na Ceannain	Highld	NN2675	56°50·3′	4°50·7′W	X	41
Coire na Céire	Highld	NN4199	57°3·5′	4°36·9′W	X	34
Coire na Ciche	Aberd	NO0998	57°4·1′	3°29·6′W	X	36,43
Coire na Ciche	Aberd	NO2686	56°57·8′	3°12·6′W	X	44
Coire na Ciche	Highld	NG5126	57°15·7′	6°7·3′W	X	32
Coire na Ciche	Highld	NM8995	57°0·1′	5°28·0′W	X	33,40
Coire na Ciche	Highld	NN7986	56°57·2′	3°58·9′W	X	42
Coire na Ciche	N Ayr	NS0043	55°38·6′	5°10·3′W	X	63,69
Coire na Circe	Arg & Bt	NM6837	56°28·3′	5°45·6′W	X	49
Coire na Circe	Highld	NG4527	57°16·0′	6°13·3′W	X	32
Coire na Circe	Highld	NG7608	57°6·8′	5°41·5′W	X	33
Coire na Ciste	Highld	NJ0006	57°8·3′	3°38·7′W	X	36
Coire na Cloiche	Aberd	NO0296	57°2·9′	3°36·5′W	X	36,43
Coire na Cloiche	Highld	NG7800	57°2·5′	5°39·1′W	X	33
Coire na Cloiche	Highld	NH0822	57°15·2′	5°10·5′W	X	25,33
Coire na Cloiche	Highld	NH8700	57°4·9′	3°51·4′W	X	35,36
Coire na Cloiche	Highld	NM7475	56°49·0′	5°41·7′W	X	40

Coire na Cloiche	Highld	NM8398	57°1·6′	5°34·1′W	X	33,40
Coire na Cloiche	Highld	NN1647	56°35·0′	4°59·3′W	W	50
Coire na Cloiche	Pth & Kin	NN4669	56°47·5′	4°30·8′W	X	42
Coire na Cloiche	Pth & Kin	NN6619	56°20·9′	4°9·7′W	X	57
Coire na Cnamha	Highld	NM7578	56°50·6′	5°40·9′W	X	40
Coire na Coichille	Highld	NN4674	56°50·2′	4°31·0′W	X	42
Coire na Coille	Highld	NG9626	57°17·0′	5°22·6′W	X	25,33
Coire na Coinnich	Highld	NG7621	57°13·8′	5°42·2′W	X	33
Coire na Còir	Highld	NN7886	56°57·2′	3°59·9′W	X	42
Coire na Còsaig	Highld	NN1792	56°59·2′	5°0·3′W	X	34
Coire na Còsaig	Highld	NN4273	56°49·6′	4°34·9′W	X	42
Coire na Cradh-lice	Highld	NN2657	56°40·6′	4°50·0′W	X	41
Coire na Cràlaig	Highld	NH0916	57°12·0′	5°9·2′W	X	33
Coire na Craoibhe	Highld	NM8567	56°45·0′	5°30·5′W	X	40
Coire na Creag Rainich	Highld	NH0976	57°44·3′	5°12·0′W	X	19
Coire na Creiche	Highld	NG4325	57°14·9′	6°15·2′W	X	32
Coire na Creiche	Highld	NM7766	56°44·2′	5°38·3′W	X	40
Coire na Creige	Pth & Kin	NN9781	56°54·8′	3°41·0′W	H	43
Coire na Criche	Highld	NG9618	57°12·7′	5°22·2′W	X	33
Coire na Criche	Highld	NM6356	56°38·4′	5°51·5′W	X	49
Coire na Cuairtich	Highld	NM8996	57°0·7′	5°28·1′W	X	33,40
Coire na Cuilc	N Eil	NF8020	57°9·8′	7°17·2′W	X	31
Coire na Cuile	Highld	NC3653	58°26·3′	4°48·1′W	X	9
Coire na Cuiseig	N Ayr	NR9639	55°36·4′	5°13·9′W	X	68,69
Coire na Dheiragainn	Highld	NH0925	57°16·8′	5°9·7′W	X	25,33
Coire na Diollaide	Highld	NG8104	57°4·8′	5°36·4′W	X	33
Coire na Dubharaiche	Highld	NN8096	57°2·6′	3°58·2′W	X	35,43
Coire na Falain	Highld	NM4890	56°56·2′	6°8·1′W	X	39
Coire na Fearna	Highld	NM8398	57°1·6′	5°34·1′W	X	33,40
Coire na Féithe Riabhaich	Highld	NH4565	57°39·2′	4°35·4′W	X	20
Coire na Féithe Seilich	Highld	NH2635	57°22·6′	4°53·2′W	X	25
Coire na Feòla	Arg & Bt	NM6527	56°22·9′	5°47·9′W	X	49
Coire na Feòla	Highld	NG8144	57°26·3′	5°38·5′W	X	24
Coire na Feòla	Highld	NH2149	57°30·0′	4°58·8′W	X	25
Coire na Feòla	Highld	NH4667	57°40·3′	4°34·5′W	X	20
Coire na Fiar Bhealaich	Highld	NH0505	57°5·9′	5°12·7′W	X	33
Coire na Fionnarachd	Pth & Kin	NN6913	56°17·7′	4°6·6′W	X	57
Coire na Gadha	Highld	NH0513	57°10·2′	5°13·1′W	X	33
Coire na Gaoithe'n Ear	Highld	NM8799	57°2·2′	5°30·2′W	X	33,40
Coire na Garbhlaich	Arg & Bt	NN1432	56°26·9′	5°0·6′W	X	50
Coire na Garidha	Pth & Kin	NN6070	56°48·3′	4°17·1′W	X	42
Coire na Geurdain	Highld	NH1016	57°12·0′	5°8·3′W	X	34
Coire na Glas-lic	Highld	NH1050	57°30·3′	5°9·8′W	X	25
Coire na h-Airighe	Highld	NG5130	57°17·8′	6°7·5′W	X	24,32
Coire na h-Aisre	Highld	NG7708	57°6·8′	5°40·5′W	X	33
Coire na h-Eanachan	Arg & Bt	NS3296	56°7·9′	4°41·8′W	X	56
Coire na h-Eilde	Highld	NH0345	57°27·4′	5°16·6′W	X	25
Coire na h-Eiridh	Highld	NH0617	57°12·4′	5°12·3′W	X	33
Coire na h-Eitich	N Eil	NF8335	57°18·0′	7°15·4′W	X	22
Coire na h-Iolaire	Highld	NH6776	57°45·5′	4°13·6′W	X	21
Coire na h-Iolaire	Highld	NN0785	56°55·2′	5°9·8′W	X	41
Coire na h-Uamha	Highld	NM7743	56°31·8′	5°37·1′W	X	49
Coire na h-Uamha	Highld	NN3985	56°56·0′	4°38·3′W	X	34,41
Coire na h-Umha	Highld	NG9953	57°31·6′	5°21·0′W	X	25
Coire na Lairige	Aberd	NO1283	56°56·1′	3°26·3′W	X	43
Coire na Leirg	Highld	NH6431	57°21·2′	4°15·2′W	X	26
Coire na Lethchois	Highld	NN5073	56°49·7′	4°27·0′W	X	42
Coire na Lice Duibhe	Arg & Bt	NM5832	56°25·4′	5°55·0′W	X	48
Coire na Longairt	Highld	NN5680	56°53·6′	4°21·4′W	X	42
Coire na Lotha	Highld	NM8578	56°50·9′	5°31·1′W	X	40
Coire na Lurgainn	Highld	NC3349	58°24·1′	4°51·0′W	X	9
Coire nam Ban	Arg & Bt	NN1842	56°32·3′	4°57·2′W	X	50
Coire nam Bothan	Highld	NM4966	56°43·4′	6°5·7′W	X	47
Coire nam Brach	Highld	NH2105	57°6·3′	4°56·9′W	X	34
Coire nam Bruadaran	Highld	NG5225	57°15·2′	6°6·2′W	X	32
Coire nam Buabhall	N Ayr	NR8941	55°37·3′	5°20·6′W	X	62,69
Coire nam Buidheag	Pth & Kin	NN6645	56°34·9′	4°10·4′W	X	51
Coire nam Meanneasg	Aberd	NO1387	56°58·2′	3°25·4′W	X	43
Coire na Mèinne	Highld	NN3851	56°37·6′	4°38·0′W	X	41
Coire nam Fiadh	Arg & Bt	NM4555	56°37·3′	6°9·0′W	X	47
Coire nam Fiadh	Arg & Bt	NM5251	56°35·4′	6°1·9′W	X	47
Coire nam Fraochag	Pth & Kin	NN6248	56°36·5′	4°14·4′W	X	51
Coire nam Freumh	Aberd	NJ2803	57°7·0′	3°10·9′W	X	37
Coire nam Freumh	Aberd	NO1286	56°57·7′	3°26·4′W	X	43
Coire nam Fuaran	Arg & Bt	NM5133	56°25·7′	6°1·9′W	X	47,48
Coire nam Fuaran	Arg & Bt	NM6636	56°27·7′	5°47·5′W	X	49
Coire nam Fuaran	Highld	NM7867	56°44·8′	5°37·4′W	X	40
Coire nam Fuaran	Highld	NN0488	56°56·8′	5°12·9′W	X	41
Coire nam Fuaran	N Ayr	NR9843	55°38·6′	5°12·2′W	X	62,69
Coire nam Mang	Highld	NC2742	58°20·2′	4°56·8′W	X	9
Coire nam Mang	Highld	NC4133	58°15·7′	4°42·1′W	X	16
Coire nam Mart	Highld	NN8191	57°0·0′	3°57·1′W	X	35,43
Coire nam Meall	Highld	NM7863	56°42·6′	5°37·2′W	X	40
Coire nam Meann	N Ayr	NR9639	55°36·4′	5°13·9′W	X	68,69
Coire nam Meann	N Ayr	NR9940	55°37·0′	5°11·1′W	X	62,69
Coire nam Meann	Stir	NN4924	56°23·3′	4°26·3′W	X	51
Coire nam Mial-chu	Highld	NN7893	57°1·0′	4°0·1′W	X	35
Coire nam Miseach	Pth & Kin	NN5048	56°36·3′	4°26·2′W	X	51
Coire nam Muc	Arg & Bt	NM6141	56°30·3′	5°52·6′W	X	49
Coire Nam Muc	Highld	NM7350	56°35·5′	5°41·4′W	X	49
Coire na Muic	Arg & Bt	NN2444	56°33·6′	4°51·4′W	X	50
Coire na Murrach	Highld	NM8392	56°58·4′	5°33·8′W	X	33,40
Coire nan Allt Beithe	Highld	NM8572	56°47·7′	5°30·8′W	X	40
Coire nan Arr	Highld	NG7943	57°25·7′	5°40·4′W	X	24
Coire nan Caorach	Arg & Bt	NM4446	56°32·4′	6°9·4′W	X	47,48
Coire nan Caorach	Arg & Bt	NM4544	56°31·4′	6°8·3′W	X	47,48
Coire nan Capull	Arg & Bt	NR8561	55°47·9′	5°25·4′W	X	62
Coire nan Capull	Highld	NM7055	56°38·1′	5°44·6′W	X	49
Coire nan Ceum	N Ayr	NR9745	55°39·6′	5°13·2′W	X	62,69
Coire nan Cisteachan	Highld	NN8583	56°55·7′	3°52·9′W	X	43
Coire nan Clach	Aberd	NJ0900	57°5·2′	3°29·6′W	X	36
Coire nan Clach	Arg & Bt	NM6634	56°26·7′	5°47·4′W	X	49
Coire nan Clach	Highld	NH0480	57°46·3′	5°17·3′W	X	19
Coire nan Clach	Highld	NH1312	57°9·9′	5°5·1′W	X	34
Coire Nan Clach	Highld	NH9674	57°44·9′	3°44·4′W	X	19
Coire nan Clach	Highld	NM7989	56°56·6′	5°37·6′W	X	40
Coire nan Clach	Highld	NM8578	56°50·9′	5°31·1′W	X	40
Coire nan Clach	Highld	NN9399	57°4·4′	3°45·4′W	H	36,43
Coire nan Clach	Moray	NJ0502	57°6·2′	3°33·6′W	X	36
Coire nan-Clach	Pth & Kin	NN3442	56°32·7′	4°41·6′W	X	50
Coire nan Cnamh	Arg & Bt	NN1945	56°34·0′	4°56·3′W	X	50
Coire nan Cnaimhean	Highld	NH0595	57°54·4′	5°17·0′W	X	19
Coire nan Cnamhan	Highld	NG8949	57°29·2′	5°30·8′W	X	24
Coire nan Con	Highld	NM8370	56°46·5′	5°32·6′W	X	40
Coire nan Cuileag	Highld	NG7743	57°25·6′	5°42·4′W	X	24
Coire nan Cùileagan Dubha	Highld	NH2869	57°40·9′	4°52·6′W	X	20
Coire nan Cuilean	Highld	NG7319	57°12·6′	5°45·1′W	X	33
Coire nan Damh	Arg & Bt	NM4545	56°31·9′	6°8·4′W	X	47,48
Coire nan Darach	Highld	NM8554	56°38·0′	5°29·9′W	X	49
Coire nan Dearc	Arg & Bt	NM6935	56°27·3′	5°44·5′W	X	49
Coire nan Dearcag	Arg & Bt	NM4543	56°30·9′	6°8·3′W	X	47,48
Coire nan Dearcag	Arg & Bt	NM4629	56°23·4′	6°6·5′W	X	48
Coire nan Dearcag	Highld	NG9177	57°44·3′	5°30·2′W	X	19
Coire nan Dearcag	Highld	NN5598	57°3·3′	4°23·0′W	X	35
Coire nan Dearcag	Highld	NN7786	56°57·2′	4°0·9′W	X	42
Coire nan Each	Arg & Bt	NM4554	56°36·8′	6°8·9′W	X	47
Coire nan Each	Arg & Bt	NM4628	56°22·8′	6°6·4′W	X	48
Coire nan Each	Arg & Bt	NM5231	56°24·6′	6°0·8′W	X	48
Coire nan Each	Arg & Bt	NM6128	56°23·3′	5°51·9′W	X	49
Coire nan Each	Arg & Bt	NM6240	56°29·8′	5°51·6′W	X	49
Coire nan Each	Arg & Bt	NM6633	56°26·1′	5°47·3′W	X	49
Coire nan Each	Arg & Bt	NM6835	56°27·3′	5°45·5′W	X	49
Coire nan Each	Arg & Bt	NM7026	56°22·5′	5°43·0′W	X	49
Coire nan Each	Arg & Bt	NN3110	56°15·4′	4°43·2′W	X	50,56
Coire nan Each	Highld	NH0445	57°27·4′	5°15·6′W	X	25
Coire nan Each	Highld	NH0832	57°20·5′	5°11·0′W	X	25
Coire nan Each	Highld	NH1122	57°15·2′	5°7·5′W	X	25
Coire nan Each	Highld	NH1635	57°22·4′	5°3·1′W	H	25
Coire nan Each	Highld	NH2357	57°34·4′	4°57·1′W	X	25
Coire nan Each	Highld	NH2744	57°27·5′	4°52·6′W	X	25
Coire nan Each	Highld	NM8051	56°36·2′	5°34·6′W	X	49
Coire nan Each	Highld	NM8572	56°47·7′	5°30·8′W	X	40
Coire nan Eireacheanach	Highld	NH0409	57°8·1′	5°13·9′W	X	33
Coire nan Eiricheallach	Highld	NG9904	57°5·3′	5°18·6′W	X	33
Coire nan Eùn	Highld	NH0414	57°10·8′	5°14·1′W	X	33
Coire nan Eun	Highld	NH2047	57°28·9′	4°59·7′W	X	25
Coire nan Eun	Highld	NN2989	56°57·9′	4°48·3′W	X	34,41
Coire nan Gabhar	Arg & Bt	NM5336	56°27·3′	6°0·1′W	X	47,48
Coire nan Gael	Highld	NM6262	56°41·6′	5°52·8′W	X	40
Coire nan Gall	Highld	NG9725	57°16·5′	5°21·6′W	X	25,33
Coire nan Gall	Highld	NM8079	56°51·3′	5°36·1′W	X	40
Coire nan Gall	Highld	NM9297	57°1·3′	5°25·2′W	X	33,40
Coire nan Gall	Highld	NN4890	56°58·8′	4°29·6′W	X	34
Coire nan Gearran	Highld	NH2907	57°7·6′	4°49·0′W	X	34
Coire nan Geur-oirean	Highld	NN0589	56°57·3′	5°12·0′W	X	41
Coire nan Giomach	Pth & Kin	NN4563	56°44·2′	4°31·6′W	X	42
Coire nan Gobhar	Highld	NM7997	57°0·9′	5°38·0′W	X	33,40
Coire nan Greusaichean	Highld	NM7667	56°44·7′	5°39·3′W	X	40
Coire nan Griogag	Arg & Bt	NM4430	56°23·8′	6°8·5′W	X	48
Coire nan Grunnd	Highld	NM4095	56°58·6′	6°16·3′W	X	39
Coire nan Laogh	Highld	NG4619	57°11·7′	6°11·8′W	X	32
Coire nan Laogh	Highld	NG5125	57°15·1′	6°7·2′W	X	32
Coire nan Laogh	Highld	NG5228	57°16·8′	6°6·4′W	X	32
Coire nan Laogh	Highld	NG8203	57°4·3′	5°35·3′W	X	33
Coire nan Laogh	Highld	NH6200	57°4·5′	4°16·1′W	X	35
Coire nan Laogh	Highld	NN4086	56°56·5′	4°37·4′W	X	34,42
Coire nan Laogh	Highld	NN4086	56°56·5′	4°37·4′W	X	34,42
Coire nan Larach	N Ayr	NS0042	55°38·1′	5°10·2′W	X	63,69
Coire nan Leac	Highld	NH0707	57°7·1′	5°10·8′W	X	33
Coire nan Lochan	Highld	NN1555	56°39·3′	5°0·6′W	X	41
Coire nan Saighead	Stir	NN6015	56°18·7′	4°15·3′W	X	57
Coire nan Sgùlan	Highld	NH4778	57°46·2′	4°33·9′W	X	20
Coire nan Tiobairtean	Arg & Bt	NM6635	56°27·2′	5°47·4′W	X	49
Coire na Poite	Aberd	NO0094	57°1·8′	3°38·4′W	X	36,43
Coire na Poite	Highld	NG8145	57°26·8′	5°38·5′W	X	24
Coire na Rainich	Highld	NM4969	56°45·0′	6°5·9′W	X	47
Coire na Reinich	Highld	NN3489	56°58·0′	4°43·4′W	X	34,41
Coire na Saidhe Duibhe	Highld	NC6928	58°13·5′	4°13·4′W	X	16
Coire na Saobhaidh	Aberd	NO0295	57°2·4′	3°36·4′W	X	36,43
Coire na Saobhaidhe	Stir	NN2829	56°25·6′	4°46·9′W	X	50
Coire na Seilg	Highld	NG5324	57°14·7′	6°5·2′W	X	32
Coire na Seilge	Highld	NC6020	58°9·1′	4°22·3′W	X	16
Coire na Seilge	Highld	NC6426	58°12·4′	4°18·4′W	X	16
Coire na Sgairde	Highld	NG5029	57°17·3′	6°8·5′W	X	32
Coire na Sleaghaich	Highld	NH0168	57°39·7′	5°19·7′W	X	19
Coire na Sleaghaich	Highld	NH2843	57°26·9′	4°51·5′W	X	25
Coire na Sorna	Highld	NH0339	57°24·2′	5°16·3′W	X	25
Coire na Taothuirt	Highld	NM7671	56°46·9′	5°39·6′W	X	40
Coire na Tulaich	Highld	NN2154	56°38·9′	4°54·7′W	X	41
Coire-n-eassan	Pth & Kin	NN9151	56°38·5′	3°46·2′W	X	52
Coire Neurlain	Highld	NN2990	56°58·4′	4°48·3′W	X	34
Coire No	Arg & Bt	NN1506	56°12·9′	4°58·6′W	X	56
Coire Nochd Mór	Pth & Kin	NN7411	56°16·7′	4°1·7′W	H	57
Coire Nuis	N Ayr	NR9539	55°36·3′	5°14·8′W	X	68,69
Coire Odhar	Aberd	NN9795	57°2·3′	3°41·4′W	X	36,43
Coire Odhar	Arg & Bt	NN1333	56°27·4′	5°1·6′W	X	50
Coire Odhar	Arg & Bt	NR8173	55°54·3′	5°29·8′W	X	62
Coire Odhar	Highld	NG5922	57°13·8′	5°59·1′W	X	32
Coire Odhar	Highld	NG7623	57°14·8′	5°42·3′W	X	33
Coire Odhar	Highld	NG8305	57°5·4′	5°34·4′W	X	33
Coire Odhar	Highld	NG9840	57°24·6′	5°21·3′W	X	25
Coire Odhar	Highld	NH0436	57°22·6′	5°15·1′W	X	25
Coire Odhar	Highld	NH0816	57°11·9′	5°10·2′W	X	33
Coire Odhar	Highld	NH4506	57°7·4′	4°33·2′W	X	34
Coire Odhar	Highld	NH5006	57°7·5′	4°28·2′W	X	35
Coire Odhar	Highld	NH7306	57°7·9′	4°5·4′W	X	35
Coire Odhar	Highld	NJ0407	57°8·9′	3°34·7′W	X	36
Coire Odhar	Highld	NJ0722	57°17·0′	3°32·1′W	X	36
Coire Odhar	Highld	NM7058	56°39·7′	5°44·7′W	X	49
Coire Odhar	Highld	NM8370	56°46·5′	5°32·6′W	X	40
Coire Odhar	Highld	NM8579	56°51·4′	5°31·0′W	X	40
Coire Odhar	Highld	NN0882	56°53·6′	5°8·7′W	X	41
Coire Odhar	Highld	NN2249	56°36·2′	4°53·5′W	X	50
Coire Odhar	Highld	NN6086	56°56·9′	4°17·6′W	X	42
Coire Odhar	Highld	NN8194	57°1·6′	3°57·2′W	X	35,43
Coire Odhar	Highld	NN9197	57°3·3′	3°47·4′W	X	36,43
Coire Odhar	Pth & Kin	NN5248	56°36·3′	4°24·2′W	X	51
Coire Odhar	Pth & Kin	NN5548	56°36·3′	4°21·3′W	X	51
Coire Odhar	Pth & Kin	NN6140	56°32·1′	4°15·2′W	X	51
Coire Odhar	Pth & Kin	NN8213	56°17·9′	3°54·0′W	X	57
Coire Odhar Beag	Highld	NM8886	56°55·3′	5°28·5′W	X	40
Coire Odhar Beag	Highld	NN2192	56°59·3′	4°56·3′W	X	34
Coire Odhar Beag	Highld	NN3797	57°2·4′	4°40·7′W	X	34
Coire Odhar Beag	Pth & Kin	NN5464	56°44·9′	4°22·8′W	X	42
Coire Odhar Ghlas-bheinne	Highld	NM8356	56°39·0′	5°31·9′W	X	49
Coire Odhar Mór	Highld	NH9030	57°21·1′	3°49·2′W	X	27,36
Coire Odhar Mór	Highld	NM8987	56°55·8′	5°27·6′W	X	40
Coire Odhar Mór	Highld	NN2092	56°59·3′	4°57·3′W	X	34
Coire Odhar Mór	Pth & Kin	NN5466	56°46·0′	4°22·9′W	X	42
Coire of Corn Arn	Aberd	NO3994	57°2·2′	2°59·9′W	X	37,44
Coire Ordren	Stir	NN3021	56°21·3′	4°44·6′W	X	50,56
Coire Peitireach	Highld	NH0304	57°5·4′	5°14·6′W	X	33
Coire Pharlain	Pth & Kin	NN4948	56°36·2′	4°27·1′W	X	51
Coire Pollach	Highld	NN2551	56°37·4′	4°50·7′W	X	41
Coire Raibeirt	Moray	NJ0003	57°6·7′	3°38·6′W	X	36
Coire Raibhachain	Highld	NH1234	57°21·7′	5°7·1′W	X	25
Coire Raineach	Highld	ND0929	58°14·7′	3°32·5′W	X	11,17
Coire Rainich	Highld	NH2556	57°33·9′	4°55·1′W	X	25
Coire Rath	Highld	NN2672	56°48·7′	4°50·6′W	X	41
Coire Rèidh	Highld	NC3220	58°8·5′	4°50·8′W	X	15
Coire Rèidh	Highld	NG5923	57°14·3′	5°59·2′W	X	32
Coire Rèidh	Highld	NG9509	57°7·8′	5°22·8′W	X	33
Coire Rèidh	Highld	NM7978	56°50·7′	5°37·0′W	X	40
Coire Rèidh	Highld	NM8350	56°35·8′	5°31·6′W	X	49
Coire Rèidh	Highld	NM9496	57°0·8′	5°23·1′W	X	33,40
Coire Rèidh	Highld	NN3889	56°58·1′	4°39·4′W	X	34,41
Coire Rèidh nan Loch	Highld	NG4434	57°19·7′	6°14·7′W	X	32
Coire Riabhach	Aberd	NJ2512	57°11·8′	3°14·0′W	X	37
Coire Riabhach	Highld	NC2126	58°11·5′	5°2·2′W	X	15
Coire Riabhach	Highld	NG4726	57°15·5′	6°11·3′W	X	32
Coire Riabhach	Highld	NG4821	57°12·9′	6°10·0′W	X	32
Coire Riabhach	Highld	NH2268	57°40·3′	4°58·6′W	X	20
Coire Riabhach	Highld	NM6956	56°38·6′	5°45·6′W	X	49
Coire Riabhach	Highld	NM8250	56°35·7′	5°32·6′W	X	49
Coire Riabhach	Highld	NN1267	56°45·7′	5°4·1′W	X	41
Coire Riadhailt	Pth & Kin	NN5739	56°31·5′	4°19·0′W	X	51
Coire Roill	Highld	NG8951	57°30·3′	5°30·9′W	X	24
Coire Ròineabhail	N Eil	NG0486	57°46·2′	6°58·2′W	X	18
Coire Roinn	N Ayr	NR8943	55°38·3′	5°20·7′W	X	62,69
Coire Ruadail	N Eil	NF8135	57°17·9′	7°17·3′W	X	22
Coire Ruadh	Highld	NH9400	57°5·0′	3°44·5′W	X	36
Coire Ruadh	Highld	NN8897	57°3·3′	3°50·3′W	X	35,36,43
Coire Ruadh-bhruthaich	Arg & Bt	NM6225	56°21·7′	5°50·7′W	X	49
Coire Ruairidh	Moray	NJ0701	57°5·7′	3°31·6′W	X	36
Coiresa	Arg & Bt	NM7400	56°8·6′	5°37·8′W	X	55
Coire Salach	Highld	NM7899	57°2·0′	5°39·1′W	X	33,40
Coire Scamadal	Highld	NG4954	57°30·7′	6°11·0′W	H	23
Coire Screamhach	Highld	NN0188	56°56·7′	5°15·8′W	X	41
Coire Screin	N Eil	NB1704	57°56·4′	6°46·5′W	X	13,14
Coire Seamraig	Highld	NG5924	57°14·9′	5°59·2′W	X	32
Coire Seasgach	Highld	NH0441	57°25·3′	5°15·4′W	X	25
Coire Seileach	Highld	NG7403	57°4·0′	5°43·2′W	X	33
Coire Seilich	Arg & Bt	NN0432	56°26·6′	5°10·3′W	X	50
Coire Seilich	Arg & Bt	NN2339	56°30·8′	4°52·2′W	X	50
Coire Seilich	Highld	NG8522	57°14·6′	5°33·3′W	X	33
Coire Seilich	Highld	NH5912	57°10·9′	4°19·5′W	X	35
Coire Sgamadail	Arg & Bt	NM4653	56°36·3′	6°7·9′W	H	47
Coire Sgamadail	Highld	NG7907	57°6·3′	5°38·5′W	X	33
Coire Sgamhadail	Highld	NG7839	57°23·5′	5°41·2′W	X	24
Coire Sgeilm	Highld	NH0025	57°16·6′	5°18·6′W	X	25,33
Coire Sgeir	Highld	NM4369	56°44·8′	6°11·8′W	X	47
Coire Sgiathach	Arg & Bt	NR4262	55°47·2′	6°6·5′W	X	60,61
Coire Sgreamhach	Highld	NG5822	57°13·7′	6°0·1′W	X	32
Coire Sgreamhach	Highld	NM8957	56°39·7′	5°26·1′W	X	49
Coire Sgùrra-breac	N Eil	NB1210	57°59·4′	6°51·9′W	X	13,14
Coire Shaile	Highld	NH1043	57°26·5′	5°9·5′W	X	25
Coire Shalachain	Highld	NM8053	56°37·3′	5°34·7′W	X	49
Coire Sheilach	Arg & Bt	NN0249	56°35·7′	5°13·1′W	X	50
Coire Shesgnan	Highld	NN4197	57°2·5′	4°36·8′W	X	34
Coire Shith	Pth & Kin	NO1073	56°50·6′	3°28·1′W	X	43
Coire Shlat	Highld	NG9930	57°19·2′	5°19·8′W	X	25
Coire Shomhairle	Highld	NN3274	56°49·9′	4°44·8′W	X	41
Coire Shùbh	Highld	NG9404	57°5·1′	5°23·5′W	X	33
Coireshùbh	Highld	NG9505	57°5·7′	5°22·6′W	X	33
Coire Shùbh Beag	Highld	NG9403	57°4·6′	5°23·5′W	X	33
Coire Slabhaig	Highld	NM7244	56°32·2′	5°42·0′W	X	49
Coire Slatach	Arg & Bt	NN1638	56°30·1′	4°58·9′W	X	50
Coire Socrach	Highld	NH1433	57°21·2′	5°5·0′W	X	25
Coire Sputan Dearg	Aberd	NO0098	57°4·0′	3°38·5′W	X	36,43
Coire Sròn an Nid	Highld	NN5277	56°51·9′	4°25·2′W	X	42
Coire Stochdnaich	Highld	NN2787	56°56·8′	4°50·2′W	X	34,41
Coire Taodail	Highld	NG9943	57°26·2′	5°20·5′W	X	25
Coire Tathaidh	Highld	NG7802	57°3·6′	5°39·2′W	X	33
Coire Thòin	Stir	NN3332	56°27·3′	4°42·1′W	X	50
Coire Thollaidh	Highld	NM9187	56°55·9′	5°25·6′W	X	40
Coire Thollaidh	Highld	NN0399	57°2·7′	5°14·4′W	X	33
Coire Thomag	Arg & Bt	NR7974	55°54·8′	5°31·7′W	X	62
Coire Thormaid	Highld	NM8472	56°47·6′	5°31·8′W	X	40
Coire Thuill Easaich	Highld	NH0422	57°15·1′	5°14·5′W	X	25,33
Coire Thuill Sgeilceich	Highld	NH0220	57°13·9′	5°16·4′W	X	25,33
Coire Toaig	Arg & Bt	NN2445	56°34·1′	4°51·4′W	X	50
Coire Toll a' Chaorainn	Highld	NH0632	57°20·5′	5°13·0′W	X	25
Coire Toll a' Mhadaidh	Highld	NH0219	57°13·4′	5°16·3′W	X	33
Coire Toll a' Mhèine	Highld	NG8047	57°27·9′	5°39·6′W	X	24
Coire Toll nam Bian	Highld	NH0949	57°29·7′	5°10·8′W	X	25
Coire Torr an Asgaill	Highld	NG8302	57°3·7′	5°34·3′W	X	33
Coire Uaigneich	Highld	NG5321	57°13·1′	6°5·0′W	X	32
Coire Uaimh	Pth & Kin	NN4847	56°35·7′	4°28·1′W	X	51
Coire Uchdachan	Highld	NN4198	57°3·0′	4°36·8′W	X	34
Coireun Lochain	Highld	NN2345	56°34·1′	4°52·4′W	X	50
Coire Yaltie	Aberd	NO1385	56°57·1′	3°25·4′W	X	43
Coirmoir	Aberd	NJ6502	57°6·7′	2°34·2′W	X	38
Coir nan Laogh	Highld	NG8659	57°34·5′	5°34·3′W	X	24
Coir' Odhar	Arg & Bt	NM5332	56°25·2′	5°59·9′W	X	48
Coir' Odhar	Arg & Bt	NM5733	56°25·9′	5°56·0′W	X	47,48
Coir' Odhar	Arg & Bt	NM6329	56°23·9′	5°50·0′W	X	49
Coir' Odhar	Arg & Bt	NR4077	55°55·2′	6°9·3′W	X	60,61
Coir' Odhar Beag	Arg & Bt	NR6091	56°3·4′	5°50·8′W	X	61
Coir' Odhar Mór	Arg & Bt	NR6091	56°3·4′	5°50·8′W	X	61

Coir Orain	Arg & Bt	NN2638	56°30·4'	4°49·2'W	X	50
Coir Phollachie	Arg & Bt	NM5342	56°30·6'	6°0·4'W	X	47,48
Coirshellach	Highld	NH6096	57°56·1'	4°21·4'W	X	21
Coir'-uisg	Highld	NG4622	57°13·4'	6°12·0'W	X	32
Coishavachan	Pth & Kin	NN7427	56°25·4'	4°2·1'W	X	51,52
Coishletter	Highld	NG3450	57°28·0'	6°25·7'W	X	23
Coisley Hill	Sheff	SK4184	53°21·3'	1°22·6'W	T	111,120
Coity	Brig	SS9281	51°31·3'	3°33·0'W	T	170
Coity-Bach	Powys	SO1023	51°54·1'	3°18·1'W	X	161
Coity Mountain	Blae Gw	SO2307	51°45·6'	3°6·6'W	H	161
Coity Pond	Torf	SO2308	51°46·2'	3°6·6'W	W	161
Cokenach	Herts	TL3936	52°0·5'	0°1·9'E	T	154
Coker Court	Somer	ST5312	50°54·6'	2°39·7'W	A	194
Coker Hill	Somer	ST5113	50°55·1'	2°41·4'W	H	194
Cokerhurst Fm	Somer	ST2737	51°7·9'	3°2·2'W	FM	182
Coker's Frome	Dorset	SY6991	50°43·3'	2°26·0'W	X	194
Coker Wood	Somer	ST5310	50°53·5'	2°39·7'W	F	194
Coke's Fm	Bucks	SU9896	51°39·5'	0°34·6'W	FM	165,176
Cokesford Fm	Norf	TF8920	52°44·9'	0°48·4'E	FM	132
Coke's Yeld Dingle	Heref	SO3251	52°9·4'	2°59·2'W	X	148
Coke's Yeld Fm	Heref	SO3251	52°9·4'	2°59·2'W	FM	148
Cokethorpe Park	Oxon	SP3606	51°45·3'	1°28·3'W	X	164
Cokethorpe School	Oxon	SP3706	51°45·3'	1°27·4'W	X	164
Cokhay Green	Derby	SK2926	52°50·1'	1°33·8'W	T	128
Coking Fm	Dorset	ST7621	50°59·5'	2°20·1'W	FM	183
Col	Highld	NN3192	56°59·6'	4°46·5'W	X	34
Col	Highld	NN3383	56°54·8'	4°44·1'W	X	34,41
Col	Highld	NN4194	57°0·8'	4°36·7'W	X	34
Col	N Eil	NB4640	58°16·8'	6°19·5'W	T	8
Colaboll	Highld	NC5610	58°3·6'	4°26·0'W	X	16
Colachla	Arg & Bt	NR9568	55°52·0'	5°16·1'W	X	62
Coladoir River	Arg & Bt	NM5730	56°24·2'	5°55·9'W	W	48
Colaisd Caisteal Leodhais	N Eil	NB4133	58°12·8'	6°24·1'W	X	8
Colam Stream	Devon	SS5542	51°9·8'	4°4·0'W	W	180
Colan	Corn	SW8661	50°24·8'	5°0·4'W	T	200
Colana Beach	Corn	SX0243	50°15·5'	4°46·3'W	X	204
Colaouse Hill	Inverc	NS2570	55°53·7'	4°47·5'W	X	63
Colaton Raleigh	Devon	SY0787	50°40·7'	3°18·6'W	T	192
Colaton Raleigh Common	Devon	SY0487	50°40·7'	3°21·1'W	X	192
Colbeggie	Pth & Kin	NO2440	56°33·0'	3°13·7'W	X	53
Colber Fm	Dorset	ST7714	50°55·7'	2°19·3'W	FM	194
Col-bheinn	Highld	NC8811	58°4·7'	3°53·5'W	H	17
Colborne	Derby	SK0983	53°20·9'	1°51·5'W	X	110
Colborough Hill	Leic	SK7605	52°38·5'	0°52·2'W	H	141
Colbost	Highld	NG2149	57°27·0'	6°38·6'W	T	23
Colbost Point	Highld	NG3039	57°21·9'	6°29·0'W	X	23,32
Colbrans Fm	E Susx	TQ4812	50°53·5'	0°6·7'E	FM	198
Colburn	N Yks	SE2098	54°22·9'	1°41·1'W	T	99
Colburn Beck	N Yks	SE1998	54°22·9'	1°42·0'W	W	99
Colbury	Hants	SU3410	50°53·5'	1°30·6'W	X	196
Colbury Fm	Hants	SU3511	50°54·1'	1°29·8'W	FM	196
Colbury Ho	Hants	SU3416	50°56·8'	1°30·6'W	X	185
Colby	Cumbr	NY6620	54°34·7'	2°31·1'W	T	91
Colby	I of M	SC2370	54°6·0'	4°42·0'W	T	95
Colby	Norf	TG2231	52°50·1'	1°18·2'E	T	133
Colby Fm	Pemb	SN0316	51°48·7'	4°51·1'W	FM	157,158
Colby Glen	I of M	SC2370	54°6·0'	4°42·0'W	X	95
Colby Hall Fm	Norf	TG2130	52°49·6'	1°17·2'E	FM	133
Colby Laithes	Cumbr	NY6721	54°35·2'	2°30·2'W	X	91
Colby Lodge Garden	Pemb	SN1508	51°44·7'	4°40·4'W	X	158
Colby Mill	Pemb	SN0516	51°48·8'	4°49·3'W	X	158
Colby Moor	Pemb	SN0417	51°49·3'	4°50·3'W	X	157,158
Colby River	I of M	SC2371	54°6·5'	4°42·0'W	W	95
Colby's Fm	Norf	TM2385	52°25·3'	1°17·2'E	FM	156
Colcerrow	Corn	SX0657	50°23·1'	4°43·4'W	X	200
Colcharton	Devon	SX4573	50°32·4'	4°10·9'W	X	201
Colchester	Essex	TL9925	51°53·5'	0°53·9'E	T	168
Colchester Garrison	Essex	TL9924	51°53·0'	0°53·9'E	X	168
Colchester Green	Suff	TL9255	52°9·8'	0°48·8'E	T	155
Colcombe	Devon	SY2494	50°44·7'	3°4·3'W	X	192,193
Colcombe Fm	Devon	SS9717	50°56·8'	3°27·6'W	FM	181
Colcot	V of Glam	ST1169	51°25·0'	3°16·4'W	T	171
Coldale	E Loth	NT5573	55°57·1'	2°42·8'W	X	66
Cold Arbour	Cambs	TL1954	52°10·5'	0°15·2'W	X	153
Cold Arbour	Medway	TQ8074	51°26·4'	0°35·8'E	X	178
Coldarbour Fm	Essex	TL5827	51°55·4'	0°18·3'E	FM	167
Cold Ash	W Berks	SU5169	51°25·3'	1°15·6'W	T	174
Cold Ashby	Northnts	SP6576	52°22·9'	1°2·3'W	T	141
Cold Ashby Lodge	Northnts	SP6476	52°22·9'	1°3·2'W	X	140
Cold Ash Fm	W Berks	SU5070	51°25·8'	1°16·5'W	FM	174
Cold Ash Hill	Hants	SU8432	51°5·1'	0°47·7'W	T	186
Cold Ashton	S Glos	ST7472	51°27·0'	2°22·1'W	T	172
Cold Aston	Glos	SP1219	51°52·4'	1°49·1'W	T	163
Coldbackie	Highld	NC6159	58°30·1'	4°22·6'W	T	10
Coldbarrow Fell	Cumbr	NY2813	54°30·7'	3°6·3'W	X	89,90
Coldbeck	Cumbr	NY7204	54°26·1'	2°25·5'W	X	91
Coldbergh Edge	N Yks	NY8204	54°26·1'	2°16·2'W	X	91,92
Coldbergh Side	N Yks	NY8203	54°25·6'	2°16·2'W	X	91,92
Coldberry	Durham	NY9329	54°39·6'	2°6·1'W	X	91,92
Coldberry End	Durham	NY8235	54°42·8'	2°16·3'W	X	91,92
Coldberry Hill	Northum	NT9627	55°32·5'	2°3·4'W	H	74,75
Cold Berwick Hill	Wilts	ST9234	51°6·5'	2°6·5'W	X	184
Coldblow	Bexley	TQ5073	51°26·4'	0°9·9'E	T	177
Coldblow	Kent	TQ8258	51°17·7'	0°37·0'E	X	178,188
Coldblow	Kent	TQ9635	51°5·1'	0°48·3'E	X	189
Cold Blow	Kent	TR0844	51°9·7'	0°58·9'E	X	179,189
Cold Blow	Pemb	SM9222	51°51·7'	5°0·9'W	X	157,158
Coldblow	Pemb	SN0114	51°47·6'	4°52·8'W	X	157,158
Cold Blow	Pemb	SN1212	51°46·7'	4°43·1'W	T	158
Coldblow Fm	Kent	TR3549	51°11·7'	1°22·2'E	FM	179
Coldborough Hill	W Berks	SU3577	51°29·7'	1°29·4'W	X	174
Coldborough Park	Heref	SO6429	51°57·7'	2°31·0'W	X	149
Coldborough Park Fm	Heref	SO6328	51°57·2'	2°31·9'W	FM	149
Cold Brayfield	Mil Key	SP9252	52°9·7'	0°38·9'W	T	152
Coldbridge Fm	Kent	TQ8847	51°11·7'	0°41·8'E	FM	189
Coldbridge Wood	Kent	TQ8848	51°12·2'	0°41·9'E	F	189
Coldbrook	Heref	SO4925	51°55·5'	2°44·1'W	X	162
Coldbrook	Monm	SO4005	51°44·7'	2°51·8'W	X	161
Coldbrook	Powys	SO1536	52°1·2'	3°13·9'W	T	161
Coldbrook Fm	Heref	SO3127	51°56·5'	2°59·8'W	FM	161
Coldbrook Park	Monm	SO3112	51°48·4'	2°59·7'W	X	161
Coldburn	Moray	NJ1449	57°31·6'	3°25·7'W	X	28
Coldburn	Northum	NT8924	55°30·8'	2°10·0'W	X	74
Coldburn Hill	Northum	NT9024	55°30·8'	2°9·1'W	H	74,75
Cold Chapel	S Lanak	NS9324	55°30·1'	3°41·2'W	X	71,72
Coldchapel Burn	S Lanak	NS9424	55°30·2'	3°40·3'W	W	71,72
Cold Christmas	Herts	TL3816	51°49·8'	0°0·6'E	T	166
Cold Coats	Lancs	SD7538	53°50·5'	2°22·4'W	X	103
Coldcoats Burn	Northum	NZ1474	55°3·9'	1°46·4'W	W	88
Coldcoats Sike	Northum	NY8759	54°55·8'	2°11·7'W	W	87
Cold Comfort	Darl	NZ3211	54°29·8'	1°29·9'W	X	93
Cold Comfort	Pemb	SR9297	51°38·2'	5°0·0'W	X	158
Coldcomfort Fm	Warw	SP0757	52°12·9'	1°53·5'W	FM	150
Cold Comfort Fm	Warw	SP1951	52°9·7'	1°42·9'W	FM	151
Coldcomfort Wood	Warw	SP0658	52°13·4'	1°54·3'W	F	150
Coldcotes	Northum	NY7576	55°4·9'	2°23·1'W	X	86,87
Coldcotes	Northum	NY7675	55°4·4'	2°22·1'W	X	86,87
Cold Cotes	N Yks	SD7171	54°8·3'	2°26·2'W	T	98
Cold Cotes	N Yks	SE2156	54°0·2'	1°40·4'W	X	104
Coldcotes Hill	Northum	NY7675	55°4·4'	2°22·1'W	X	86,87
Coldcotes Moor	Northum	NZ1473	55°3·3'	1°46·4'W	X	88
Coldcot Fm	Wilts	ST7834	51°6·5'	2°18·5'W	FM	183
Coldcothill	S Ayr	NS4530	55°32·6'	4°27·0'W	X	70
Coldean	Bri & Hov	TQ3308	50°51·6'	0°6·2'W	T	198
Coldeast	Devon	SX8175	50°34·0'	3°40·4'W	T	191
Cold East Cross	Devon	SX7474	50°33·4'	3°46·3'W	X	191
Coldeaton	Derby	SK1456	53°6·3'	1°47·0'W	T	119
Cold Edge	Cald	SE0430	53°46·2'	1°55·9'W	X	104
Cold Edge Dams	Cald	SE0429	53°45·7'	1°55·9'W	W	104
Cold Elm	Worcs	SO8432	51°59·4'	2°13·6'W	T	150
Coldelm Fm	Glos	ST6998	51°41·0'	2°26·5'W	FM	162
Colden	Cald	SD9628	53°45·1'	2°3·2'W	T	103
Colden	I of M	SC3484	54°13·7'	4°32·4'W	H	95
Colden Common	Hants	SU4722	51°0·0'	1°19·4'W	T	185
Colden Plantation	I of M	SC3584	54°13·8'	4°31·5'W	F	95
Colden Water	Cald	SD9429	53°45·7'	2°5·0'W	W	103
Coldfair Green	Suff	TM4361	52°11·8'	1°33·8'E	T	156
Coldfall Wood	Hargy	TQ2790	51°35·9'	0°9·6'W	F	176
Cold Fell	Cumbr	NY0509	54°28·3'	3°27·5'W	H	89
Cold Fell	Cumbr	NY6055	54°53·5'	2°37·0'W	H	86
Cold Fm	Leic	SP5785	52°27·8'	1°9·3'W	FM	140
Coldgate Mill	Northum	NT9924	55°30·8'	2°0·5'W	X	75
Cold Grain	D & G	NT1213	55°24·4'	3°23·0'W	W	78
Cold Green	Heref	SO6842	52°4·8'	2°27·6'W	X	149
Coldgreen	N Ayr	NS2856	55°46·3'	4°44·1'W	X	63
Coldgreen	Shrops	SO5981	52°25·8'	2°35·8'W	X	137,138
Cold Hall	Essex	TM0825	51°53·2'	1°1·8'E	X	168,169
Cold Hall	Herts	TL3406	51°44·4'	0°3·2'W	X	166
Cold Hall Fm	Essex	TL4903	51°42·6'	0°9·8'E	FM	167
Cold Hall Fm	Essex	TL7225	51°54·0'	0°30·4'E	FM	167
Coldham	Cambs	TF4302	52°36·0'	0°7·1'E	T	142,143
Coldham	Staffs	SJ8508	52°40·4'	2°12·9'W	T	127
Coldham Field	Cambs	TF4402	52°36·0'	0°8·0'E	X	142,143
Coldham Grove	Suff	TM0871	52°18·1'	1°3·4'E	F	144,155
Coldham Hall	Cambs	TF4402	52°36·0'	0°8·0'E	X	142,143
Coldham Hall	Norf	TG2127	52°47·9'	1°17·1'E	X	133,134
Coldham Hall	Norf	TM2587	52°26·3'	1°19·0'E	X	156
Coldham Hall	Suff	TL8656	52°10·5'	0°43·6'E	A	155
Coldham Ho	Cambs	TF4504	52°37·1'	0°8·9'E	X	143
Coldham Lodge Fm	Beds	TL0563	52°15·5'	0°27·3'W	FM	153
Coldham's Common	Cambs	TL4758	52°12·3'	0°9·5'E	T	154
Coldhams Fm	Essex	TL4932	51°58·2'	0°10·5'E	FM	167
Coldham's Fm	Norf	TF6402	52°35·7'	0°25·7'E	FM	143
Coldham Wood	Suff	TM1973	52°18·9'	1°13·2'E	F	156
Cold Hanworth	Lincs	TF0383	53°20·3'	0°26·8'W	T	121
Cold Hanworth Village	Lincs	TF0383	53°20·3'	0°26·8'W	A	121
Coldharbour	Bucks	SU8388	51°35·3'	0°47·7'W	X	175
Cold Harbour	Cambs	TL2741	52°3·4'	0°8·5'W	X	153
Coldharbour	Corn	SW7548	50°17·6'	5°9·2'W	T	204
Cold Harbour	Cumbr	SD4793	54°20·0'	2°48·5'W	X	97
Coldharbour	Devon	SS6012	50°53·7'	3°59·1'W	X	180
Coldharbour	Devon	SS9423	51°0·0'	3°30·3'W	X	181
Coldharbour	Devon	ST0612	50°54·2'	3°19·8'W	T	181
Cold Harbour	Dorset	SY6581	50°37·9'	2°29·3'W	T	194
Cold Harbour	Dorset	SY9089	50°42·3'	2°8·1'W	T	195
Cold Harbour	E Susx	TQ7428	51°1·7'	0°29·3'E	X	188,199
Cold Harbour	E Yorks	SE9738	53°50·0'	0°31·1'W	X	106
Coldharbour	Glos	SO5503	51°43·7'	2°38·7'W	T	162
Cold Harbour	Hants	SU4251	51°15·6'	1°23·5'W	X	185
Coldharbour	Hav	TQ5278	51°29·1'	0°11·7'E	T	177
Coldharbour	Heref	SO4555	52°11·7'	2°47·9'W	X	148,149
Cold Harbour	Herts	TL1416	51°50·1'	0°20·3'W	T	166
Coldharbour	Kent	TQ5141	51°9·1'	0°9·9'E	X	188
Coldharbour	Kent	TQ5750	51°13·9'	0°15·3'E	T	188
Coldharbour	Kent	TQ6738	51°7·2'	0°23·6'E	X	188
Coldharbour	Kent	TQ8257	51°17·2'	0°37·0'E	X	178,188
Cold Harbour	Kent	TQ8342	51°9·1'	0°37·4'E	X	188
Cold Harbour	Kent	TQ8732	51°3·6'	0°40·5'E	X	189
Coldharbour	Kent	TQ8764	51°20·9'	0°41·5'E	T	178
Coldharbour	Kent	TR3251	51°12·9'	1°19·7'E	X	179
Cold Harbour	Lincs	SK9281	53°19·3'	0°36·7'W	X	121
Cold Harbour	Lincs	SK9534	52°53·9'	0°34·9'W	T	130
Cold Harbour	Lincs	TF2395	53°26·5'	0°8·5'W	X	113
Cold Harbour	Lincs	TF3096	53°26·9'	0°2·1'W	X	113
Cold Harbour	Lincs	TF3943	52°58·2'	0°4·6'E	X	131
Cold Harbour	Northum	NU2022	55°29·7'	1°40·6'W	X	75
Cold Harbour	Notts	SK7557	53°6·5'	0°52·4'W	X	120
Cold Harbour	N Yks	SE4475	54°10·4'	1°19·1'W	X	99
Cold Harbour	N Yks	SE6374	54°9·7'	1°1·7'W	X	100
Coldharbour	Oxon	SU6199	51°41·4'	1°6·7'W	X	164,165
Cold Harbour	Oxon	SU6379	51°30·6'	1°5·1'W	T	175
Coldharbour	Somer	ST0135	51°6·6'	3°24·5'W	X	181
Coldharbour	Somer	ST3414	50°55·5'	2°56·0'W	X	193
Coldharbour	Surrey	TQ1443	51°10·7'	0°21·8'W	T	187
Cold Harbour	W Berks	SU3466	51°23·8'	1°30·3'W	X	174
Cold Harbour	Wilts	ST8645	51°12·5'	2°11·6'W	T	183
Coldharbour	Wilts	ST8958	51°19·5'	2°9·1'W	T	173
Cold Harbour	Win & Maid	SU8378	51°29·9'	0°47·9'W	T	175
Cold Harbour Br	Somer	ST4840	51°9·6'	2°44·2'W	X	182
Coldharbour Common	Surrey	TQ1443	51°10·7'	0°21·8'W	X	187
Cold Harbour Corner	Cambs	TF4206	52°38·2'	0°6·3'E	X	142,143
Coldharbour Cross	Devon	SX7152	50°21·5'	3°48·4'W	X	202
Coldharbour Fm	Bucks	SP6614	51°49·5'	1°2·1'W	FM	164,165
Coldharbour Fm	Bucks	SP7913	51°48·8'	0°50·8'W	FM	165
Coldharbour Fm	Bucks	TQ0189	51°35·7'	0°32·1'W	FM	176
Cold Harbour Fm	Cambs	TL1482	52°25·7'	0°19·0'W	FM	142
Cold Harbour Fm	Cambs	TL3260	52°13·6'	0°3·6'W	FM	153
Cold Harbour Fm	Cambs	TL3969	52°18·3'	0°2·7'E	FM	154
Cold Harbour Fm	Derby	SK0185	53°22·0'	1°58·7'W	FM	110
Coldharbour Fm	Essex	TL5819	51°51·1'	0°18·0'E	FM	167
Cold Harbour Fm	Hants	SU5611	50°54·0'	1°11·8'W	FM	196
Coldharbour Fm	Herts	SP9811	51°47·6'	0°34·3'W	FM	165
Coldharbour Fm	Herts	TL2805	51°44·0'	0°8·4'W	FM	166
Coldharbour Fm	Kent	TQ8846	51°11·2'	0°41·8'E	FM	189
Coldharbour Fm	Kent	TR0024	50°59·1'	0°51·4'E	FM	189
Coldharbour Fm	Kent	TR0646	51°10·8'	0°57·2'E	FM	179,189
Cold Harbour Fm	Kent	TR2053	51°14·2'	1°9·5'E	FM	179,189
Cold Harbour Fm	Leeds	SE2140	53°51·6'	1°40·4'W	FM	104
Cold Harbour Fm	Lincs	SK8995	53°26·9'	0°39·2'W	FM	112
Cold Harbour Fm	Lincs	TF2681	53°18·9'	0°6·1'W	FM	122
Cold Harbour Fm	Norf	TG3917	52°42·1'	1°32·7'E	FM	133,134
Coldharbour Fm	Northnts	SP5940	52°3·5'	1°8·0'W	FM	152
Cold Harbour Fm	Notts	SK5224	52°48·9'	1°13·3'W	FM	129
Cold Harbour Fm	N Yks	SE4973	54°9·3'	1°14·6'W	FM	100
Coldharbour Fm	Oxon	SP3430	51°58·3'	1°29·9'W	FM	151
Coldharbour Fm	Oxon	SP4729	51°57·7'	1°18·6'W	FM	164
Coldharbour Fm	Oxon	SP6031	51°58·7'	1°7·2'W	FM	152,165
Coldharbour Fm	Oxon	SU3495	51°39·4'	1°30·1'W	FM	164
Coldharbour Fm	Oxon	SU6389	51°36·0'	1°5·0'W	FM	175
Coldharbour Fm	S Glos	ST7071	51°26·5'	2°25·5'W	FM	172
Coldharbour Fm	Somer	ST6842	51°10·8'	2°27·1'W	FM	183
Coldharbour Fm	Surrey	TQ3349	51°13·7'	0°5·3'W	FM	187
Coldharbour Fm	W Susx	SU9713	50°54·7'	0°36·8'W	FM	197
Cold Harbour Fm	W Susx	TQ0323	51°0·1'	0°31·5'W	FM	197
Coldharbour Fm	W Susx	TQ2914	50°54·9'	0°9·5'W	FM	198
Coldharbour Fm	W Susx	TQ3234	51°5·6'	0°6·5'W	FM	187
Cold Harbour Heath	Dorset	SY8989	50°42·3'	2°9·0'W	X	195
Coldharbour Hill	Beds	SP9356	52°11·9'	0°38·0'W	X	153
Coldharbour Manor	E Susx	TQ3932	51°4·5'	0°0·6'W	X	187
Coldharbour Marshes	Kent	TQ9167	51°22·4'	0°45·1'E	X	178
Coldharbour Moor	Derby	SK0793	53°26·3'	1°53·3'W	X	110
Coldharbour Pill	Newp	ST4384	51°33·4'	2°48·9'W	W	171,172
Coldharbour Wood	Norf	TL7898	52°33·3'	0°37·9'E	F	144
Cold Hatton	Wrekin	SJ6221	52°47·4'	2°33·4'W	T	127
Cold Hatton Heath	Wrekin	SJ6321	52°47·4'	2°32·5'W	T	127
Coldhayes	Hants	SU7526	51°1·9'	0°55·4'W	X	186,197
Coldheart	Worcs	SO5760	52°14·5'	2°37·4'W	X	137,138,149
Cold Hesledon	Durham	NZ4047	54°49·2'	1°22·2'W	T	88
Cold Hiendley	Wakf	SE3714	53°37·5'	1°26·0'W	T	110,111
Cold Hiendley Fm	Wakf	SE2514	53°37·6'	1°36·9'W	FM	110
Cold Hiendley Resr	Wakf	SE3614	53°37·5'	1°26·9'W	W	110,111
Cold Higham	Northnts	SP6653	52°10·5'	1°1·7'W	T	152
Coldhill Fm	N Yks	SE4635	53°48·8'	1°17·7'W	FM	105
Cold Hill Fm	Shrops	SO3696	52°33·7'	2°56·2'W	FM	137
Coldholm	Highld	NH6758	57°35·8'	4°13·1'W	X	26
Coldhome	Aberd	NJ4307	57°9·3'	2°56·1'W	X	37
Coldhome	Aberd	NJ5930	57°21·8'	2°40·4'W	X	29,37
Coldhome	Aberd	NJ6456	57°35·8'	2°35·7'W	X	29
Coldhome	Aberd	NJ9460	57°38·1'	2°5·6'W	X	30
Coldhome	Moray	NJ0951	57°32·7'	3°30·8'W	X	27
Coldhome	Moray	NJ3247	57°30·7'	3°7·6'W	X	28
Coldhome	Moray	NJ3639	57°26·5'	3°3·5'W	X	28
Coldhome	Moray	NJ4148	57°31·4'	2°58·6'W	X	28
Coldhome	Moray	NJ5250	57°32·5'	2°47·7'W	X	29
Cold Hurst	Durham	NZ1027	54°38·5'	1°50·3'W	X	92
Coldicote Fm	Glos	SP2131	51°58·9'	1°41·3'W	FM	151
Coldicott Fm	Kent	TR0422	50°57·9'	0°54·7'E	FM	189
Coldingham	Scot Bord	NT9066	55°53·5'	2°9·2'W	T	67
Coldingham Bay	Scot Bord	NT9166	55°53·5'	2°8·2'W	W	67
Coldingham Common	Scot Bord	NT8568	55°54·5'	2°14·0'W	X	67
Coldingham Loch	Scot Bord	NT8968	55°54·5'	2°10·1'W	W	67
Coldingham Moor	Scot Bord	NT8667	55°54·0'	2°13·0'W	X	67
Cold Inn	Pemb	SN1005	51°42·9'	4°44·6'W	T	158
Coldkeld	Cumbr	NY8210	54°29·3'	2°16·3'W	X	91,92
Cold Keld	Cumbr	SD7399	54°23·4'	2°24·5'W	X	98
Cold Kirby	N Yks	SE5384	54°15·2'	1°10·8'W	T	100
Cold Kitchen Hill	Wilts	ST8438	51°8·7'	2°13·3'W	H	183
Cold Knap Point	V of Glam	ST1066	51°23·4'	3°17·2'W	X	171
Cold Knoll	Brad	SE0036	53°49·5'	1°59·6'W	X	104
Cold Knuckles	N Yks	NZ2312	54°30·4'	1°38·3'W	X	93
Coldlands	Scot Bord	NT8461	55°50·8'	2°14·9'W	X	67
Cold Law	Northum	NT9203	55°19·5'	2°7·1'W	H	80
Cold Law	Northum	NT9509	55°22·7'	2°4·3'W	H	81
Cold Law	Northum	NT9523	55°30·3'	2°4·3'W	H	74,75
Coldlaw Burn	Northum	NT9317	55°27·1'	2°6·2'W	W	80
Coldlaw Cairn	Northum	NT9118	55°27·6'	2°8·1'W	X	80
Coldlaw Hope	Northum	NT9218	55°27·6'	2°7·2'W	X	80
Coldmartin	Northum	NU0027	55°32·5'	1°59·6'W	X	75
Coldmartin Loughs	Northum	NU0127	55°32·5'	1°58·6'W	W	75
Coldmeece	Staffs	SJ8532	52°53·4'	2°13·0'W	T	127
Cold Moor	N Yks	NZ5502	54°24·9'	1°8·7'W	X	93
Cold Moor Cote	N Yks	NZ5401	54°24·3'	1°9·7'W	X	93
Coldmoor Fm	Cambs	TL5180	52°24·1'	0°13·6'E	FM	143
Cold Moss	D & G	NS8909	55°22·0'	3°44·6'W	H	71,78
Cold Moss Heath	Ches	SJ7660	53°8·4'	2°21·1'W	T	118
Cold Nab Plantn	E Yorks	TA0562	54°2·8'	0°23·4'W	F	101
Cold Newton	Leic	SK7106	52°39·1'	0°56·6'W	T	141
Cold Newton Lodge	Leic	SK7105	52°38·5'	0°56·6'W	X	141
Cold Newton Village	Leic	SK7106	52°39·1'	0°56·6'W	A	141
Cold Northcott	Corn	SX2086	50°39·0'	4°32·4'W	T	201
Cold Norton	Essex	TL8400	51°40·3'	0°40·1'E	T	168
Cold Norton Fm	Staffs	SJ8732	52°53·4'	2°11·2'W	FM	127
Cold Norton Fm	Surrey	TQ0957	51°18·3'	0°25·8'W	FM	187
Cold Oak	Heref	SO4953	52°10·6'	2°44·4'W	X	148,149
Cold Oak	Powys	SO2963	52°15·9'	3°2·0'W	X	137,148
Cold Oak Copse	Northnts	SP8757	52°12·5'	0°43·2'W	F	152
Coldoch	Stir	NS6998	56°9·7'	4°6·1'W	T	57
Coldomo	Orkney	HY2909	58°58·0'	3°13·6'W	X	6,7
Coldon	Pth & Kin	NT1399	56°10·8'	3°23·6'W	X	58
Cold Overton	Leic	SK8110	52°41·1'	0°47·7'W	T	130

Cold Overton Grange	Leic	SK8011	52°41·7'	0°48·6'W	X	130
Cold Overton Park Wood	Leic	SK8208	52°40·0'	0°46·8'W	F	141
Cold Park Wood	Lancs	SD5966	54°5·5'	2°37·2'W	F	97
Cold Park Wood	Lancs	SD7948	53°55·9'	2°18·8'W	F	103
Cold Pike	Cumbr	NY2603	54°25·3'	3°8·0'W	H	89,90
Coldpool Beck	N Yks	NZ5011	54°29·8'	1°13·3'W	W	93
Coldra	Newp	ST3589	51°36·0'	2°55·9'W	T	171
Coldrach	Stir	NS4690	56°4·9'	4°28·0'W	X	57
Coldrain	Pth & Kin	NO0800	56°11·3'	3°28·5'W	X	58
Coldred	Kent	TR2746	51°10·3'	1°15·2'E	T	179
Coldred Court Fm	Kent	TR2747	51°10·8'	1°15·3'E	FM	179
Coldrenick	Corn	SX0971	50°30·7'	4°41·3'W	X	200
Coldrenick	Corn	SX2961	50°25·7'	4°24·1'W	X	201
Coldrey	Hants	SU7743	51°11·1'	0°53·5'W	A	186
Coldridge	Devon	SS6907	50°51·1'	3°51·3'W	T	191
Coldridge Barton	Devon	SS7007	50°51·1'	3°50·4'W	X	191
Coldridge Down	Wilts	SU2951	51°15·7'	1°34·7'W	X	185
Coldridge Wood	Wilts	SU2852	51°16·2'	1°35·5'W	F	184
Coldridge Wood	Worcs	SO8082	52°26·4'	2°17·3'W	F	138
Coldriding	C of Stoke	SJ9140	52°57·7'	2°7·6'W	X	118
Coldrife	Northum	NZ0694	55°14·7'	1°53·9'W	X	81
Coldrife Fm	Northum	NU1828	55°33·0'	1°42·4'W	FM	75
Coldrinnick Woods	Corn	SX0971	50°30·7'	4°41·3'W	F	200
Coldrochie	Pth & Kin	NO0729	56°26·9'	3°30·1'W	X	52,53,58
Coldron Brook	Oxon	SP3421	51°53·4'	1°30·0'W	W	164
Cold Row	Lancs	SD3744	53°53·6'	2°57·1'W	T	102
Coldshield	Northum	NY7158	54°55·2'	2°26·7'W	X	86,87
Coldside	Cumbr	NY5178	55°5·9'	2°45·6'W	X	86
Coldside	D & G	NX9083	55°8·0'	3°43·1'W	X	78
Coldside	Northum	NZ0669	55°1·2'	1°53·9'W	X	87
Coldside	Northum	NZ0695	55°15·2'	1°53·9'W	X	81
Cold Side	Sheff	SK1794	53°26·8'	1°44·2'W	X	110
Coldside Hill	Northum	NT9032	55°35·1'	2°9·1'W	H	74,75
Coldsides	Darl	NZ2518	54°33·6'	1°36·4'W	X	93
Cold Sike	Cumbr	NY5568	55°0·5'	2°41·8'W	W	86
Cold Slad	Glos	SO9216	51°50·8'	2°6·6'W	X	163
Coldsmouth Hill	Northum	NT8528	55°33·0'	2°13·8'W	H	74
Cold Springs Fm	Derby	SK0474	53°16·0'	1°56·0'W	FM	119
Coldstead Fm	Lincs	TF0875	53°15·9'	0°22·4'W	FM	121
Cold Stone	Lancs	SD7160	54°2·4'	2°26·2'W	X	98
Cold Stone	N Yks	SD7160	54°2·4'	2°26·2'W	X	98
Coldstone Beck	Brad	SE1445	53°54·3'	1°46·8'W	W	104
Coldstone Common	Heref	SO4336	52°1·4'	2°49·4'W	X	149,161
Coldstone Fm	Devon	SX5561	50°26·1'	4°2·1'W	FM	202
Coldstone Ho	N Yks	SE3379	54°12·6'	1°29·2'W	X	99
Cold Stone Plain	N Yks	SD7161	54°2·9'	2°26·2'W	X	98
Coldstorms	N Yks	SE1196	54°21·8'	1°49·4'W	X	99
Coldstream	Aberd	NO6672	56°50·5'	2°33·0'W	X	45
Coldstream	Angus	NO3939	56°32·6'	2°59·1'W	X	54
Coldstream	Fife	NO3802	56°12·6'	2°59·5'W	X	59
Coldstream	Scot Bord	NT8439	55°38·9'	2°14·8'W	T	74
Coldstream	S Lanak	NS6946	55°41·6'	4°4·6'W	X	64
Coldstream Burn	D & G	NX4070	55°0·2'	4°29·7'W	W	77
Coldstream Burn	D & G	NX7771	55°1·4'	3°55·0'W	W	84
Coldstream Fm	Durham	NZ2536	54°43·3'	1°36·3'W	FM	93
Coldstream Mains	Scot Bord	NT8440	55°39·4'	2°14·8'W	X	74
Coldswood Fm	Kent	TR3566	51°20·9'	1°22·9'E	FM	179
Coldthorn	Northnts	SP6942	52°4·6'	0°59·2'W	X	152
Coldtown	Northum	NY8988	55°11·4'	2°9·9'W	X	80
Coldvreath	Corn	SW9858	50°23·5'	4°50·1'W	T	200
Coldwakning	S Lanak	NS6440	55°38·3'	4°9·2'W	X	71
Coldwakning Burn	S Lanak	NS6340	55°38·3'	4°10·2'W	W	71
Coldwall	Staffs	SK1449	53°2·5'	1°47·1'W	X	119
Coldwall Br	Staffs	SK1449	53°2·5'	1°47·1'W	X	119
Coldwaltham	W Susx	TQ0216	50°56·3'	0°32·5'W	T	197
Coldwaltham Fm	W Susx	TQ0116	50°56·3'	0°33·4'W	FM	197
Cold Weather Ho	Lancs	SD8544	53°53·8'	2°13·3'W	X	103
Coldwell	Aberd	NJ5622	57°17·4'	2°43·3'W	X	37
Coldwell	Carm	SN1911	51°46·3'	4°37·0'W	X	158
Cold Well	Cumbr	NY6054	54°53·0'	2°37·0'W	W	86
Coldwell	Northum	NY9073	55°3·3'	2°9·0'W	X	87
Coldwell	Northum	NZ0086	55°10·3'	1°59·6'W	X	81
Cold Well	Staffs	SK0511	52°42·0'	1°55·2'W	T	128
Coldwell Bottom	Glos	SO9515	51°50·2'	2°4·0'W	X	163
Coldwell Burn	Durham	NZ3644	54°47·6'	1°26·0'W	W	88
Coldwell Clough	Derby	SK0585	53°22·0'	1°55·1'W	X	110
Coldwell Copse	Shrops	SO7479	52°24·7'	2°22·5'W	F	138
Coldwell Fm	Lancs	SD4777	54°11·4'	2°48·3'W	FM	97
Coldwell Hill	Northum	NZ2082	55°8·2'	1°40·7'W	X	81
Coldwell Plantn	N Yks	SE7566	54°5·3'	0°50·8'W	F	100
Coldwell Resrs	Lancs	SD9036	53°49·5'	2°8·7'W	W	103
Coldwell Rocks	Glos	SO5615	51°50·1'	2°37·9'W	X	162
Coldwells	Aberd	NJ7520	57°16·5'	2°24·4'W	X	38
Coldwells	Aberd	NK1140	57°27·3'	1°48·5'W	X	30
Coldwells	Highld	NH6449	57°30·9'	4°15·8'W	X	26
Coldwells	Midlo	NT3665	55°52·7'	3°0·9'W	X	66
Coldwells	Moray	NJ1050	57°32·1'	3°29·7'W	X	28
Coldwells	Moray	NJ1448	57°31·1'	3°25·7'W	X	28
Coldwells	Pth & Kin	NO0820	56°22·1'	3°28·9'W	X	52,53,58
Coldwells Croft	Aberd	NJ5622	57°17·4'	2°43·3'W	X	37
Cold Weston	Shrops	SO5483	52°26·8'	2°40·2'W	X	137,138
Cold Weston Court	Shrops	SO5483	52°26·8'	2°40·2'W	X	137,138
Coldwind	Corn	SX2065	50°27·7'	4°31·8'W	X	201
Coldwind Cross	Corn	SW7740	50°13·3'	5°7·2'W	X	204
Cold Wold	E Yorks	SE8552	53°57·7'	0°41·9'W	X	106
Coldwold Fm	E Yorks	SE8451	53°57·1'	0°42·8'W	FM	106
Cole	Shetld	HU3661	60°20·2'	1°20·4'W	X	2,3
Cole	Somer	ST6633	51°6·0'	2°28·7'W	T	183
Cò-leac	Arg & Bt	NM6032	56°25·4'	5°53·1'W	X	49
Colebarn Fm	Kent	TQ8333	51°4·2'	0°37·1'E	FM	188
Colebatch	Shrops	SO3187	52°28·8'	3°0·6'W	T	137
Colebatch Hill	Shrops	SO2987	52°28·8'	3°2·3'W	H	137
Colebrook	Devon	ST0006	50°50·9'	3°24·9'W	T	192
Colebrooke	Devon	SS7700	50°47·4'	3°44·3'W	T	191
Colebrooke	Kent	TQ6142	51°9·5'	0°18·5'E	X	188
Colebrook Fm	Corn	SS2307	50°50·4'	4°30·5'W	FM	190
Coleburn	Moray	NJ2455	57°35·0'	3°15·8'W	X	28
Coleby	Lincs	SK9760	53°7·9'	0°32·6'W	T	121
Coleby	N Lincs	SE8919	53°39·8'	0°38·8'W	T	112
Coleby Hall	N Yks	SD9391	54°19·1'	2°6·0'W	X	98
Coleby Heath	Lincs	SK9960	53°7·9'	0°30·8'W	X	121
Coleby Lodge Fm	Lincs	TF0061	53°8·4'	0°29·9'W	FM	121
Coleby Low Fields	Lincs	SK9560	53°8·0'	0°34·4'W	X	121
Coleby Wood	N Lincs	SE8719	53°39·9'	0°40·6'W	F	112
Cole Cross	Somer	ST5019	50°58·3'	2°42·3'W	X	183
Coledale Beck	Cumbr	NY2122	54°35·5'	3°12·9'W	W	89,90
Coledale Hause	Cumbr	NY1821	54°34·9'	3°15·7'W	X	89,90
Cole Deep	Shetld	HU3562	60°20·7'	1°21·5'W	W	2,3
Coledrain	Arg & Bt	NR7208	55°19·1'	5°35·2'W	X	68
Cole End	Essex	TL5636	52°0·3'	0°16·8'E	T	154
Cole End	Warw	SP1989	52°30·2'	1°42·8'W	T	139
Cole Fm	Kent	TR1939	51°6·7'	1°8·1'E	FM	179,189
Coleford	Devon	SS7701	50°48·0'	3°44·3'W	T	191
Coleford	Glos	SO5710	51°47·5'	2°37·0'W	T	162
Coleford	Somer	ST6849	51°14·6'	2°27·1'W	T	183
Coleford Bottom	Devon	SS9019	50°57·8'	3°33·6'W	X	181
Coleford Fm	Somer	ST1133	51°5·6'	3°15·9'W	FM	181
Coleford Water	Somer	ST1133	51°5·6'	3°15·9'W	T	181
Colegate End	Norf	TM1988	52°27·0'	1°13·8'E	T	156
Coleg Elidyr	Carm	SN7843	52°4·6'	3°46·4'W	X	146,147,160
Cole Green	Herts	TL2811	51°47·2'	0°8·3'W	T	166
Cole Green	Herts	TL4331	51°57·8'	0°5·3'E	T	167
Colehall	Birm	SP1488	52°29·6'	1°47·2'W	T	139
Coleham Green	Kent	TQ9537	51°6·2'	0°47·5'E	X	189
Colehanger	Devon	SX7846	50°18·3'	3°42·4'W	X	202
Colehayes Park	Devon	SX7977	50°35·0'	3°42·2'W	X	191
Cole Henley	Hants	SU4650	51°15·1'	1°20·1'W	T	185
Cole Henley Manor Fm	Hants	SU4651	51°15·6'	1°20·1'W	FM	185
Colehill	Aberd	NJ9732	57°23·0'	2°2·5'W	X	30
Colehill	Dorset	SU0200	50°48·2'	1°57·9'W	T	195
Cole Hill	Somer	ST7944	51°11·9'	2°17·6'W	X	183
Cole Hill Fm	Durham	NZ4231	54°40·6'	1°20·5'W	FM	93
Colehill Wood	Corn	SX3291	50°41·9'	4°22·4'W	F	190
Cole Hill Wood	Dorset	SY7087	50°41·1'	2°25·1'W	F	194
Cole Ho	Lincs	TF3916	52°43·5'	0°3·9'E	X	131
Colehouse	Devon	SS5905	50°49·9'	3°59·8'W	X	191
Colehouse Fm	Devon	SS5013	50°54·1'	4°7·6'W	FM	180
Colehurst	Heref	SO5525	51°55·5'	2°38·9'W	X	162
Colehurst Cottages	Shrops	SJ6630	52°52·2'	2°29·9'W	X	127
Colehurst Manor	Shrops	SJ6631	52°52·8'	2°29·9'W	X	127
Colehurst Wood	Shrops	SJ6631	52°52·8'	2°29·9'W	F	127
Colekitchen Fm	Surrey	TQ0848	51°13·5'	0°26·8'W	FM	187
Coleman Green	Herts	TL1912	51°47·9'	0°16·1'W	T	166
Colemans Cross	Devon	SX3586	50°39·3'	4°19·7'W	X	201
Coleman's Fm	Essex	TL5201	51°41·5'	0°12·3'E	FM	167
Coleman's Fm	Essex	TL8315	51°48·4'	0°39·7'E	FM	168
Coleman's Fm	Essex	TQ4999	51°40·4'	0°9·7'E	FM	167,177
Coleman's Fm	I of W	SZ4590	50°42·7'	1°21·4'W	FM	196
Coleman's Hatch	E Susx	TQ4533	51°4·9'	0°4·6'E	T	188
Coleman's Hill	Warw	SP1844	52°5·9'	1°43·8'W	X	151
Colemere	Shrops	SJ4332	52°53·2'	2°50·4'W	T	126
Cole Mere	Shrops	SJ4333	52°53·7'	2°50·4'W	W	126
Colemere Country Park	Shrops	SJ4233	52°53·7'	2°51·3'W	X	126
Colemere Woods	Shrops	SJ4231	52°52·6'	2°51·3'W	X	126
Colemore	Hants	SU7030	51°4·1'	0°59·7'W	T	186
Colemore Common	Hants	SU6929	51°3·6'	1°0·5'W	X	186,197
Colemore Fm	Shrops	SO7097	52°34·4'	2°26·2'W	FM	138
Colemore Green	Shrops	SO7097	52°34·4'	2°26·2'W	T	138
Colemouth Creek	Medway	TQ8574	51°26·3'	0°40·1'E	W	178
Colen	Pth & Kin	NO1030	56°27·5'	3°27·2'W	X	53
Colenden Cotts	Pth & Kin	NO1029	56°26·9'	3°27·2'W	X	53,58
Cole Ness	Shetld	HU3562	60°20·7'	1°21·5'W	X	2,3
Colenso	Corn	SW5630	50°7·4'	5°24·5'W	X	203
Colen Wood	Pth & Kin	NO1130	56°27·5'	3°26·2'W	F	53
Coleorton	Leic	SK4017	52°45·2'	1°24·0'W	T	129
Coleorton Hall	Leic	SK3917	52°45·2'	1°24·9'W	X	128
Coleorton Moor	Leic	SK4016	52°44·6'	1°24·0'W	T	129
Cole Park	Rich	TQ1673	51°26·9'	0°19·4'W	T	176
Cole Park	Wilts	ST9485	51°34·1'	2°4·8'W	A	173
Colepike Hall	Durham	NZ1446	54°48·8'	1°46·5'W	X	88
Cole Pool	Somer	ST1943	51°11·1'	3°9·2'W	X	181
Coleraine Fm	Heref	SO6121	51°53·4'	2°33·6'W	FM	162
Coleridge Cott	Somer	ST1939	51°8·9'	3°9·1'W	X	181
Coleridge Ho	Devon	SX7943	50°16·7'	3°41·5'W	X	202
Colerne	Wilts	ST8171	51°26·5'	2°16·0'W	T	173
Colerne Down	Wilts	ST8373	51°27·6'	2°14·3'W	X	173
Colerne Park	Wilts	ST8372	51°27·0'	2°14·3'W	X	173
Coles	Hants	SU6928	51°3·1'	1°0·5'W	X	186,197
Colesbourne	Glos	SO9913	51°49·2'	2°0·5'W	T	163
Colesbourne Park	Glos	SP0013	51°49·2'	1°59·6'W	X	163
Colesbridge Fm	Cambs	TF3509	52°39·9'	0°0·2'E	FM	142
Colesbrook	Dorset	ST8027	51°2·8'	2°16·7'W	T	183
Cole's Common	Norf	TM2088	52°27·0'	1°14·7'E	X	156
Cole's Cross	Devon	SX7746	50°18·3'	3°43·3'W	X	202
Cole's Cross	Dorset	ST3902	50°49·1'	2°51·6'W	T	193
Colesdale Fm	Herts	TL2901	51°41·8'	0°7·6'W	FM	166
Coles Dane	Kent	TQ8753	51°15·0'	0°41·2'E	X	189
Colesden	Beds	TL1255	52°11·1'	0°21·3'W	T	153
Colesden Grange Fm	Beds	TL1256	52°11·7'	0°21·3'W	FM	153
Colesden Lodge Fm	Beds	TL1455	52°11·1'	0°19·5'W	FM	153
Coleseed Ho	Cambs	TL4395	52°32·3'	0°6·9'E	X	142,143
Colesent	Corn	SX0774	50°32·3'	4°43·0'W	X	200
Coles Farm Ho	Somer	ST5852	51°16·2'	2°35·7'W	X	182,183
Coles Fm	Kent	TQ5047	51°12·4'	0°9·2'E	FM	188
Cole's Fm	W Berks	SU5371	51°26·4'	1°13·9'W	FM	174
Cole's Fm	Worcs	SO7931	51°58·9'	2°18·0'W	FM	150
Coles Fm	W Susx	SZ8694	50°44·6'	0°46·5'W	FM	197
Coles Green	Suff	TM0941	52°1·9'	1°3·2'E	T	155,169
Cole's Green	Suff	TM2862	52°12·8'	1°20·7'E	T	156
Coles Green	Worcs	SO7651	52°9·6'	2°20·7'W	T	150
Coles Green Fm	Herts	TL3229	51°56·9'	0°4·4'W	FM	166
Colesgrove Manor	Herts	TL3302	51°42·3'	0°4·1'W	X	166
Coles Hall	E Susx	TQ5523	50°59·4'	0°12·9'E	X	199
Coleshall	Kent	TQ8967	51°22·5'	0°43·3'E	X	178
Coleshill	Bucks	SU9495	51°39·0'	0°38·1'W	T	165
Coleshill	Flint	SJ2373	53°15·1'	3°8·8'W	X	117
Cole's Hill	Glos	SP0425	51°55·6'	1°56·1'W	X	163
Cole's Hill	Heref	SO3465	52°17·0'	2°57·7'W	H	137,148,149
Coles Hill	Herts	TL2901	51°41·8'	0°7·6'W	X	166
Coleshill	Oxon	SU2393	51°38·4'	1°39·7'W	T	163,174
Coleshill	Warw	SP1989	52°30·2'	1°42·8'W	T	139
Coleshill Fm	Surrey	TQ2047	51°12·8'	0°16·5'W	FM	187
Coleshill Fm	Wok	SU7764	51°22·4'	0°53·2'W	FM	175,186
Coleshill Hall Fm	Warw	SP1988	52°29·6'	1°42·8'W	FM	139
Coleshill Ho	Bucks	SU9595	51°39·0'	0°37·2'W	X	165,176
Coleshill Park	Oxon	SU2493	51°38·3'	1°38·8'W	X	163,174
Coleshill Pool	Sol	SP1986	52°28·5'	1°42·8'W	W	139
Coles Lane Fm	Dorset	ST8421	50°59·5'	2°13·3'W	FM	183
Coles Meads	Surrey	TQ2751	51°14·9'	0°10·4'W	T	187
Colesmoor Fm	Dorset	SY5596	50°45·9'	2°37·9'W	FM	194
Coles Oak Ho	Essex	TM0532	51°57·1'	0°59·4'E	X	168
Coles Park	Herts	TL3725	51°54·6'	0°0·1'W	X	166
Cole's Pits	Oxon	SU2993	51°38·3'	1°34·5'W	F	164,174
Coles's Fm	Devon	SY3297	50°46·3'	2°57·5'W	FM	193
Colestocks	Devon	ST0900	50°47·8'	3°17·1'W	T	192
Cole's Tump	Heref	SO4628	51°57·1'	2°46·8'W	X	149,161
Coles Wood	Hants	SU4258	51°19·4'	1°23·4'W	F	174
Coleswood	Heref	SO4174	52°21·9'	2°51·6'W	F	137,148
Colesworth	Devon	SY0899	50°47·2'	3°17·9'W	X	192
Colesworthy	Devon	SX8075	50°34·0'	3°41·3'W	X	191
Colethrop	Glos	SO8210	51°47·5'	2°15·3'W	T	162
Colethrop Fm	Glos	SO8011	51°48·1'	2°17·0'W	FM	162
Coleton Fishacre	Devon	SX9050	50°20·6'	3°32·4'W	X	202
Coleton Fm	Devon	SX9051	50°21·2'	3°32·4'W	FM	202
Cole Wood	Dorset	SY8585	50°40·1'	2°12·4'W	F	194
Cole Wood	E Susx	TQ7410	50°52·0'	0°28·8'E	F	199
Cole Wood	Kent	TQ9535	51°5·1'	0°47·4'E	F	189
Coley	Bath & NE Somer	ST5855	51°17·8'	2°35·8'W	T	172,182
Coley	Cald	SE1227	53°44·6'	1°48·7'W	T	104
Coley	Read	SU7172	51°26·8'	0°58·3'W	T	175
Coley	Staffs	SK0122	52°48·0'	1°58·7'W	X	128
Coley Lane Fm	Roth	SK4099	53°29·4'	1°23·4'W	FM	111
Coley Mill	Staffs	SJ7819	52°46·3'	2°19·2'W	X	127
Coley Pits Fm	Worcs	SO9167	52°18·3'	2°7·5'W	FM	150
Colfin	D & G	NX0555	54°51·4'	5°1·9'W	X	82
Colfryn Fm	Powys	SJ2117	52°44·9'	3°9·8'W	FM	126
Colgate	W Susx	TQ2332	51°4·7'	0°14·3'W	T	187
Colgate Fm	Glos	SO9820	51°52·9'	2°1·3'W	FM	163
Colgate Hill	W Susx	TQ2232	51°4·7'	0°15·1'W	X	187
Colgate Lodge	W Susx	TQ2332	51°4·7'	0°14·3'W	X	187
Colgates	Kent	TQ4961	51°19·9'	0°8·7'E	X	177,188
Colgrain	Arg & Bt	NS3280	55°59·3'	4°41·2'W	X	63
Colgrave Sound	Shetld	HU5790	60°35·6'	0°57·1'W	W	1,2
Colgrims	Hants	SZ3895	50°45·4'	1°27·3'W	X	196
Colham Green	Hill	TQ0781	51°31·3'	0°27·1'W	T	176
Colhayes	Devon	SY1299	50°47·3'	3°14·5'W	X	192,193
Colhayne Fm	Devon	SY2398	50°46·8'	3°5·2'W	FM	192,193
Colhender Fm	Corn	SX2357	50°23·4'	4°29·0'W	FM	201
Colhook Common	W Susx	SU9626	51°1·7'	0°37·5'W	F	186,197
Col-huw Point	V of Glam	SS9567	51°23·8'	3°30·2'W	X	170
Colifordhill	Scot Bord	NT5111	55°23·7'	2°46·0'W	X	79
Colin Craig	Scot Bord	NT0615	55°25·4'	3°28·7'W	X	78
Colindale	Brent	TQ2189	51°35·4'	0°14·8'W	T	176
Colinette Fm	Kent	TQ4754	51°16·2'	0°6·8'E	FM	188
Colingate	Cumbr	NY0323	54°35·8'	3°29·7'W	X	89
Colin Hill	Scot Bord	NT1020	55°28·2'	3°25·0'W	H	72
Colinsburgh	Fife	NO4703	56°13·3'	2°50·8'W	T	59
Colinshaugh	Angus	NO5558	56°42·9'	2°43·7'W	X	54
Colinshays Manor	Somer	ST7036	51°7·6'	2°25·3'W	X	183
Colinshiel	W Loth	NS9469	55°54·4'	3°41·3'W	X	65
Colin's Rig	Scot Bord	NT1355	55°47·1'	3°22·8'W	X	65,72
Colinton	C of Edin	NT2168	55°54·2'	3°15·4'W	T	66
Colintraive	Arg & Bt	NS0374	55°55·4'	5°8·7'W	T	63
Colislinn	Scot Bord	NT5111	55°23·7'	2°46·0'W	X	79
Colkins	Kent	TR0359	51°17·9'	0°55·1'E	X	178,179
Colkirk	Norf	TF9126	52°48·1'	0°50·4'E	T	132
Colk's Fm	Norf	TG2621	52°44·6'	1°21·3'E	FM	133,134
Coll	Arg & Bt	NM1956	56°37·0'	6°34·4'W	X	46
Colla	N Eil	NF7402	56°59·9'	7°21·7'W	X	31
Colla	N Eil	NF7604	57°1·1'	7°19·9'W	X	31
Collabear	Devon	SS5428	51°2·2'	4°4·6'W	X	180
Collabridge	Devon	SX8089	50°41·5'	3°41·6'W	X	191
Collace	Pth & Kin	NO2032	56°28·7'	3°17·5'W	X	53
Colla Cleit	N Eil	NB3106	57°58·0'	6°32·4'W	H	13,14
Collacombe Down	Devon	SX4377	50°34·5'	4°12·7'W	X	201
Collacombe Manor	Devon	SX4376	50°34·0'	4°12·6'W	A	201
Collacott	Corn	SX2792	50°42·4'	4°26·6'W	X	190
Collacott	Devon	SS4515	50°55·1'	4°11·9'W	X	180,190
Collacott	Devon	SS6428	51°2·4'	3°56·0'W	X	180
Collacott	Devon	SS6511	50°53·2'	3°54·8'W	X	191
Collacott Fm	Devon	SS5130	51°3·2'	4°7·2'W	FM	180
Collacott Fm	Devon	SS5641	51°9·2'	4°3·2'W	FM	180
Collacott Fm	Devon	SS6920	50°58·1'	3°51·6'W	FM	180
Collafield	Glos	SO6614	51°49·7'	2°29·2'W	T	162
Colla Field	Shetld	HU1953	60°15·9'	1°38·9'W	X	3
Colla Firth	Shetld	HU3683	60°32·0'	1°20·1'W	W	1,2,3
Collafirth	Shetld	HU4268	60°23·9'	1°13·8'W	T	2,3
Colla Firth	Shetld	HU4469	60°24·4'	1°11·6'W	W	2,3
Collafirth Hill	Shetld	HU3383	60°32·0'	1°23·4'W	H	1,2,3
Collafirth Hill	Shetld	HU4368	60°23·9'	1°12·7'W	H	2,3
Collafirth Ness	Shetld	HU4569	60°24·4'	1°10·5'W	X	2,3
Collairnie	Fife	NO3017	56°20·7'	3°7·5'W	X	59
Collairniehill	Fife	NO2916	56°20·1'	3°8·5'W	X	59
Collalis	W Dunb	NS4584	56°1·7'	4°28·8'W	X	64
Collam	N Eil	NF8450	57°26·1'	7°15·5'W	X	22
Collam	N Eil	NG1591	57°49·3'	6°47·5'W	T	14
Collamoor Head	Corn	SX1793	50°42·7'	4°35·1'W	T	190
Collan's Cross	Corn	SX1285	50°38·3'	4°39·2'W	X	200
Collapit Br	Devon	SX7242	50°16·1'	3°47·4'W	X	202
Collard	Devon	SX5561	50°26·1'	4°2·1'W	X	202
Collard Hill	Devon	ST1311	50°53·8'	3°13·8'W	X	192,193
Collard Hill	Somer	ST4834	51°6·4'	2°44·2'W	H	182
Collard Tor	Devon	SX5562	50°26·6'	4°2·2'W	X	202
Collar Law	E Loth	NT6062	55°51·2'	2°37·9'W	H	67
Collar Stoop	N Yks	SE2066	54°5·6'	1°41·2'W	X	99
Colla Sgairbh	N Eil	NB2606	57°57·8'	6°37·5'W	H	13,14
Collas Sgairbhe	N Eil	NB0609	57°58·6'	6°57·9'W	H	13,14
Collation Fm	Corn	SS2409	50°51·5'	4°29·7'W	FM	190
Collaton	Devon	SX5175	50°33·6'	4°5·8'W	X	191,201

Collaton	Devon	SX7139	50°14·4′	3°48·2′W	T	202
Collaton	Devon	SX7952	50°21·6′	3°41·7′W	X	202
Collaton Fm	Devon	SX5749	50°19·6′	4°0·2′W	FM	202
Collatons	Devon	SS7301	50°47·9′	3°47·8′W	X	191
Collaton St Mary	Torbay	SX8660	50°26·0′	3°35·9′W	T	202
Collaven Manor	Devon	SX5289	50°41·1′	4°5·3′W	X	191
College	Carm	SN3034	51°58·9′	4°28·1′W	X	145
College	Denb	SJ0570	53°13·4′	3°25·0′W	X	116
College Br	N Lincs	TA1119	53°39·6′	0°18·8′W	X	113
College Burn	Northum	NT8824	55°30·8′	2°11·0′W	W	74
College Coppice	Shrops	SJ3503	52°37·5′	2°57·2′W	F	126
College Cott	Peterb	TF1304	52°37·6′	0°19·4′W	X	142
College Down	Dorset	SY6898	50°47·1′	2°26·9′W	X	194
College Down Fm	Hants	SU5924	51°1·0′	1°9·1′W	FM	185
College Fields	Shrops	SJ7141	52°58·2′	2°25·5′W	X	118
College Fm	Beds	TL0152	52°9·7′	0°31·0′W	FM	153
College Fm	Beds	TL0761	52°14·4′	0°25·6′W	FM	153
College Fm	Bucks	SP6729	51°57·6′	1°1·1′W	FM	164,165
College Fm	Bucks	SP8713	51°48·8′	0°43·9′W	FM	165
College Fm	Cambs	TL2263	52°15·3′	0°12·4′W	FM	153
College Fm	Cambs	TL3578	52°23·2′	0°0·6′W	FM	142
College Fm	Cambs	TL4644	52°4·7′	0°8·2′E	FM	154
College Fm	Carm	SN1420	51°51·1′	4°41·7′W	FM	145,158
College Fm	Carm	SN3417	51°49·9′	4°24·2′W	FM	159
College Fm	Carm	SN5921	51°52·4′	4°2·5′W	FM	159
College Fm	Essex	TM1320	51°50·5′	1°5·9′E	FM	168,169
College Fm	E Yorks	SE7620	53°40·5′	0°50·6′W	FM	105,106,112
College Fm	Hants	SU6444	51°11·7′	1°4·7′W	FM	185
College Fm	Heref	SO2736	52°1·3′	3°3·4′W	FM	161
College Fm	Kent	TR0733	51°3·8′	0°57·6′E	FM	179,189
College Fm	Kent	TR2967	51°21·6′	1°17·8′E	FM	179
College Fm	Lincs	SK8840	52°57·2′	0°41·0′W	FM	130
College Fm	Lincs	TF0297	53°27·8′	0°27·4′W	FM	112
College Fm	Lincs	TF1626	52°49·4′	0°16·3′W	FM	130
College Fm	Lincs	TF3536	52°54·5′	0°0·9′E	FM	131
College Fm	Lincs	TF4677	53°16·4′	0°11·8′E	FM	122
College Fm	N Lincs	TA1019	53°39·6′	0°19·7′W	FM	113
College Fm	Norf	TF6308	52°38·9′	0°25·0′E	FM	143
College Fm	Norf	TF9303	52°35·7′	0°51·4′E	FM	144
College Fm	Norf	TG0002	52°35·0′	0°57·5′E	FM	144
College Fm	Norf	TL9396	52°31·9′	0°51·1′E	FM	144
College Fm	Norf	TM4194	52°29·7′	1°33·4′E	FM	134
College Fm	Norf	TM4692	52°28·4′	1°37·7′E	FM	134
College Fm	Notts	SK6585	53°21·7′	1°1·0′W	FM	111,120
College Fm	Oxon	SP2206	51°45·4′	1°40·5′W	FM	163
College Fm	Oxon	SP4007	51°45·8′	1°24·8′W	FM	164
College Fm	Oxon	SP4312	51°48·5′	1°22·2′W	FM	164
College Fm	Oxon	SP5217	51°51·2′	1°14·3′W	FM	164
College Fm	Oxon	SU3685	51°34·0′	1°28·4′W	FM	174
College Fm	Powys	SO1432	51°59·0′	3°14·7′W	FM	161
College Fm	Rut	SK8002	52°36·8′	0°48·7′W	FM	141
College Fm	Staffs	SO8089	52°30·2′	2°17·3′W	FM	138
College Fm	Suff	TL7859	52°12·3′	0°36·7′E	FM	155
College Fm	Suff	TL9450	52°7·1′	0°50·4′E	FM	155
College Fm	Suff	TM0743	52°3·0′	1°1·5′E	FM	155,169
College Fm	Suff	TM1056	52°10·0′	1°4·6′E	FM	155
College Fm	Suff	TM1059	52°11·6′	1°4·8′E	FM	155
College Fm	Suff	TM1161	52°12·6′	1°5·7′E	FM	155
College Fm	Suff	TM1974	52°19·4′	1°13·2′E	FM	156
College Fm	Suff	TM2984	52°24·6′	1°22·4′E	FM	156
College Fm	Swin	SU2095	51°39·4′	1°42·3′W	FM	163
College Fm	Warw	SP1760	52°14·5′	1°44·7′W	FM	151
College Fm	Warw	SP4248	52°8·0′	1°22·8′W	FM	151
College Fm	Warw	SP4482	52°26·3′	1°20·8′W	FM	140
College Fm	W Berks	SU3480	51°31·3′	1°30·2′W	FM	174
College Fm	W Susx	TQ1906	50°50·7′	0°18·2′W	FM	198
College Fm, The	Northum	NY6664	54°58·4′	2°31·4′W	FM	86
College Green	Cumbr	SD4884	54°15·2′	2°47·5′W	X	97
College Green	Somer	ST5736	51°7·5′	2°36·5′W	X	182,183
College Lake Wildlife Centre	Bucks	SP9314	51°49·2′	0°38·6′W	X	165
College Mawr	Cered	SN3248	52°6·5′	4°26·8′W	X	145
College Milton	S Lanak	NS6155	55°46·4′	4°12·5′W	T	64
College of Roseisle	Moray	NJ1366	57°40·8′	3°27·1′W	T	28
College of Scalan	Moray	NJ2419	57°15·1′	3°15·1′W	X	36
College or Abbot's Wood	Oxon	SU6580	51°31·1′	1°3·4′W	F	175
College Park	Ham & Ful	TQ2282	51°31·6′	0°14·1′W	T	176
College Resr	Corn	SW7633	50°9·5′	5°7·8′W	W	204
College, The	Glos	SO8109	51°47·0′	2°16·1′W	X	162
College Town	Brackn	SU8561	51°20·7′	0°46·4′W	T	175,186
College Wood	Beds	TL1446	52°6·3′	0°19·7′W	F	153
College Wood	Bucks	SP7933	51°59·6′	0°50·6′W	F	152,165
College Wood	Essex	TL6201	51°41·3′	0°21·0′E	F	167
College Wood	Hants	SU5642	51°10·7′	1°11·5′W	F	185
College Wood	Kent	TQ9658	51°17·5′	0°49·1′E	F	178
College Wood	Lincs	TF1275	53°15·8′	0°18·8′W	F	121
College Wood Fm	W Susx	TQ1614	50°55·1′	0°20·6′W	FM	198
Collegiate Church	S Ayr	NS3009	55°21·0′	4°40·4′W	A	70,76
Collegiate School	Harrow	TQ1892	51°37·1′	0°17·3′W	X	176
Collennan	S Ayr	NS3432	55°33·5′	4°37·5′W	T	70
Collery Fm	Corn	SS2310	50°52·0′	4°30·5′W	FM	190
Collessie	Fife	NO2813	56°18·5′	3°9·4′W	T	59
Collessie Den	Fife	NO2713	56°18·5′	3°10·4′W	X	59
Colleton Hall	Devon	SS8516	50°56·2′	3°37·8′W	X	181
Colleton Manor	Devon	SS6614	50°54·8′	3°54·0′W	A	180
Colleton Mills	Devon	SS6615	50°55·4′	3°54·0′W	T	180
Collets Brook	Birm	SP1498	52°35·0′	1°47·2′W	W	139
Collett's Br	Cambs	TF4806	52°38·1′	0°11·6′E	T	143
Collett's Green	Worcs	SO8251	52°9·7′	2°15·4′W	T	150
Colleybridge Fm	Essex	TL6205	51°43·4′	0°21·1′E	FM	167
Colley Fm	Somer	ST2514	50°55·5′	3°3·6′W	FM	193
Colley Hill	Lincs	TF2580	53°18·4′	0°7·0′W	X	122
Colley Hill	Norf	TF9117	52°43·2′	0°50·1′E	X	132
Colley Hill	Surrey	TQ2452	51°15·4′	0°13·0′W	X	187
Colley Lake	Devon	SS6820	50°58·1′	3°52·4′W	W	180
Colleymore Fm	Oxon	SU2594	51°38·9′	1°37·9′W	FM	163,174
Colleywell Bottom	Devon	SX9281	50°37·4′	3°31·2′W	X	192
Collfryn	Powys	SJ2116	52°44·4′	3°9·8′W	X	126
Collibeer	Devon	SX6697	50°45·7′	3°53·6′W	X	191

Collickmoor Fm	Surrey	TQ1545	51°11·8′	0°20·9′W	FM	187
Collie Fm	Moray	NJ3151	57°32·9′	3°8·7′W	FM	28
Collie Head	Aberd	NJ8167	57°41·8′	2°18·7′W	X	29,30
Collie Hill	Aberd	NJ5708	57°9·9′	2°42·2′W	H	37
Colliehill	Aberd	NK0940	57°27·3′	1°50·5′W	X	30
Collie Law	Scot Bord	NT2544	55°41·3′	3°11·1′W	H	73
Collie Law	Scot Bord	NT4850	55°44·7′	2°49·3′W	H	66,73
Collielaw	Scot Bord	NT4951	55°45·2′	2°48·3′W	X	66,73
Collielaw	S Lanak	NS9047	55°42·5′	3°44·6′W	X	72
Colliergate Beck	Cumbr	NY0619	54°33·7′	3°26·8′W	W	89
Collier Gill	N Yks	NZ7900	54°23·6′	0°46·6′W	W	94
Collier Hag Wood	N Yks	SE5986	54°16·2′	1°5·2′W	F	100
Collierhall	S Lanak	NS8735	55°36·0′	3°47·2′W	X	71,72
Collier Law	Durham	NZ0141	54°46·1′	1°58·6′W	H	87
Collierley	Durham	NZ1554	54°53·1′	1°45·5′W	X	88
Collie Rocks	Aberd	NJ7065	57°40·7′	2°29·7′W	X	29
Collier Row	Hav	TQ5090	51°35·6′	0°10·3′E	T	177
Collier's Elm	Glos	SO7520	51°52·9′	2°21·4′W	X	162
Colliers End	Herts	TL3720	51°51·9′	0°0·2′W	T	166
Colliers Far Wood	N Yks	SE2866	54°5·6′	1°33·9′W	F	99
Collier's Fm	Oxon	SU3290	51°36·7′	1°31·9′W	FM	164,174
Collier's Fm	Suff	TL9449	52°6·5′	0°50·4′E	FM	155
Collier's Fm	W Susx	SU8927	51°2·4′	0°43·4′W	FM	186,197
Collier's Green	E Susx	TQ7822	50°58·4′	0°32·5′E	T	199
Colliers Green	Kent	TQ7538	51°7·1′	0°30·4′E	X	188
Colliers Hatch	Essex	TL5002	51°42·0′	0°10·6′E	T	167
Collier's Hill	Kent	TR0337	51°6·0′	0°54·4′E	X	179,189
Colliers Hill	Oxon	SU6790	51°36·5′	1°1·6′W	X	164,175
Colliershill Fm	Worcs	SO7072	52°21·0′	2°26·0′W	FM	138
Collier's Reach	Essex	TL8807	51°44·0′	0°43·8′E	W	168
Collier Street	Kent	TQ7145	51°10·9′	0°27·2′E	T	188
Collier's Wood	Glos	SO8300	51°42·1′	2°14·4′W	F	162
Collier's Wood	Merton	TQ2770	51°25·1′	0°10·0′W	T	176
Collierswood Fm	Essex	TM0527	51°54·4′	0°59·2′E	FM	168
Colliery Fm	Northum	NU1809	55°22·7′	1°42·5′W	FM	81
Colliery Fm	Warw	SP2897	52°34·4′	1°34·8′W	FM	140
Colliery Row	Sund	NZ3249	54°50·3′	1°29·7′W	T	88
Collieston	Aberd	NK0328	57°20·8′	1°56·6′W	T	38
Collieston	Angus	NO8081	56°55·4′	2°19·3′W	X	45
Collieston Burn	D & G	NX8182	55°7·3′	3°51·5′W	W	78
Collieston Hill	D & G	NX8182	55°7·3′	3°51·5′W	H	78
Collieston Moor	D & G	NX8182	55°7·3′	3°51·5′W	X	78
Colliestown	Aberd	NJ6002	57°7·2′	2°39·2′W	X	37
Collifield Ness	Shetld	HU4960	60°19·5′	1°6·3′W	X	2,3
Colliford Downs	Corn	SX1871	50°30·9′	4°33·7′W	X	201
Colliford Lake Park	Corn	SX1773	50°31·9′	4°34·6′W	X	201
Colliford Lake (reservoir)	Corn	SX1772	50°31·4′	4°34·5′W	W	201
Colligarth	Orkney	HY6841	59°15·5′	2°33·2′W	X	5
Collihill	Devon	SX7995	50°44·8′	3°42·5′W	X	191
Collihole Fm	Devon	SX6885	50°39·2′	3°51·7′W	FM	191
Collimer Pt	Suff	TM2437	51°59·4′	1°16·2′E	X	169
Collin	D & G	NY0276	55°4·4′	3°31·7′W	T	84
Collin Bank	Cumbr	NY5772	55°2·7′	2°39·9′W	X	86
Collin Burn	D & G	NY3081	55°7·4′	3°5·4′W	W	79
Colli Ness	Orkney	HY6842	59°16·1′	2°33·2′W	X	5
Collin Fm	D & G	NX7951	54°50·6′	3°52·6′W	FM	84
Collingbourne Ducis	Wilts	SU2453	51°16·8′	1°39·0′W	T	184
Collingbourne Kingston	Wilts	SU2455	51°17·8′	1°39·0′W	T	174
Collingbourne Wood	Wilts	SU2753	51°16·8′	1°36·4′W	F	184
Collinge Fm	Ches	SJ4071	53°14·2′	2°53·5′W	FM	117
Collingham	Leeds	SE3845	53°54·2′	1°24·9′W	T	104
Collingham	Notts	SK8361	53°8·6′	0°45·1′W	T	121
Collingholme	Lancs	SD6374	54°9·9′	2°33·6′W	X	97
Collin Green Fm	Norf	TG0816	52°42·3′	1°5·1′E	FM	133
Collingsdown	Devon	SS3917	50°56·0′	4°17·1′W	X	190
Collingsford Br	Suff	TM1267	52°15·8′	1°6·8′E	X	155
Collings Hanger Fm	Bucks	SP8700	51°41·7′	0°44·1′W	FM	165
Collingthwaite Fm	Notts	SK5572	53°14·8′	1°10·1′W	FM	120
Collington	Heref	SO6460	52°14·5′	2°31·2′W	T	138,149
Collington Station	E Susx	TQ7307	50°50·4′	0°27·8′E	X	199
Collingtree	Northnts	SP7555	52°11·5′	0°53·8′W	T	152
Collingtree Park	Northnts	SP7554	52°11·0′	0°53·8′W	X	152
Collingwood	E Yorks	SE9566	54°5·1′	0°32·4′W	X	101
Collingwood	Northum	NZ2775	55°4·4′	1°34·2′W	T	88
Collingwood Fm	Thurr	TQ6680	51°29·9′	0°23·9′E	FM	177,178
Collingwood Ho	Kent	TQ7529	51°2·2′	0°30·2′E	X	188,199
Collin Hags	D & G	NY2980	55°6·8′	3°6·4′W	H	79
Collin Hill	D & G	NX7952	54°51·1′	3°52·7′W	H	84
Collin Ho	D & G	NX7952	54°51·1′	3°52·7′W	X	84
Collinpark Wood	Glos	SO7527	51°56·7′	2°21·4′W	F	162
Collins	Devon	SS6320	50°58·0′	3°56·7′W	X	180
Collins Burn	S Lanak	NS9418	55°26·9′	3°40·1′W	W	71,78
Collin's Coppice	Essex	TL5319	51°51·1′	0°13·7′E	F	167
Collin's Cross	Essex	TL5211	51°46·8′	0°12·6′E	X	167
Collins End	Oxon	SU6578	51°30·1′	1°3·4′W	T	175
Collin's Fm	Essex	TL8434	51°58·7′	0°41·1′E	FM	155
Collins Fm	Surrey	TQ0736	51°7·0′	0°27·9′W	FM	187
Collins Green	Warr	SJ5594	53°26·7′	2°40·2′W	T	108
Collins Green	Worcs	SO7357	52°12·9′	2°23·3′W	T	150
Collinson's Hill	Durham	NY9210	54°29·4′	2°7·0′W	X	91,92
Collipriest	Devon	SS9511	50°53·6′	3°29·2′W	T	192
Collis Ridge	N Yks	SE6091	54°18·9′	1°4·2′W	H	94,100
Collister Pill	Monm	ST4585	51°33·9′	2°47·2′W	W	171,172
Colliston	Angus	NO6045	56°36·0′	2°38·6′W	T	54
Colliston	Pth & Kin	NO1308	56°15·6′	3°23·8′W	X	58
Colliston	Pth & Kin	NO1407	56°15·1′	3°22·8′W	X	58
Colliston Castle	Angus	NO6146	56°36·5′	2°37·7′W	X	54
Colliston Hill	Fife	NO3605	56°14·2′	3°1·5′W	H	59
Colliston Mill	Angus	NO6045	56°36·0′	2°38·6′W	X	54
Colliter's Brook	N Som	ST5568	51°24·8′	2°38·4′W	W	172,182
Collith Hole	Northum	NU2329	55°33·5′	1°37·7′W	W	75
Colliton	Devon	ST0804	50°49·9′	3°18·0′W	T	192
Colliton Cross	Devon	ST0803	50°49·4′	3°18·0′W	X	192
Coll Melyn	Powys	SJ1321	52°47·0′	3°17·0′W	H	125
Collmuir	Aberd	NJ5306	57°8·8′	2°46·2′W	X	37
Collochan	D & G	NX9175	55°3·7′	3°42·0′W	X	84
Colloggett	Corn	SX4162	50°26·4′	4°14·0′W	X	201
Collon	Corn	SX1457	50°23·2′	4°36·6′W	X	200
Collonach	Aberd	NO7699	57°5·1′	2°23·3′W	X	38,45
Collonach Burn	Aberd	NJ4839	57°26·6′	2°51·5′W	W	28,29

Collordon	Aberd	NJ4404	57°7·7′	2°55·0′W	X	37
Collow	Lincs	TF1383	53°20·1′	0°17·8′W	X	121
Colloway Fm	Lancs	SD4459	54°1·7′	2°50·9′W	FM	102
Colloway Marsh	Lancs	SD4458	54°1·1′	2°50·9′W	W	102
Collow Grange	Lincs	TF1383	53°20·1′	0°17·8′W	X	121
Collow Holt	Lincs	TF1282	53°19·6′	0°18·7′W	F	121
Collum Fm	N Som	ST3565	51°23·1′	2°55·7′W	FM	171,182
Collusca	Arg & Bt	NR7132	55°31·9′	5°37·3′W	X	68
Collusca Water	Arg & Bt	NR7233	55°32·5′	5°36·4′W	W	68
Colluthie	Fife	NO3319	56°21·8′	3°4·6′W	X	59
Colluthie Hill	Fife	NO3418	56°21·2′	3°3·6′W	H	59
Colly	Merth Tyd	ST1099	51°41·2′	3°17·7′W	X	171
Colly Brook	Shrops	SO5873	52°21·4′	2°36·6′W	W	137,138
Collybrook Green	Shrops	SO5874	52°22·0′	2°36·6′W	X	137,138
Collycroft	Warw	SP3588	52°29·6′	1°28·7′W	T	140
Collycroft Fm	Derby	SK1643	52°59·3′	1°45·3′W	FM	119,128
Collydean	Fife	NO2602	56°12·5′	3°11·1′W	X	59
Collyers	Bucks	SP9816	51°50·3′	0°34·3′W	X	165
Collyers	Hants	SU7324	51°0·9′	0°57·2′W	X	197
Collyer's Fm	E Susx	TQ9522	50°58·1′	0°47·0′E	FM	189
Collyer's Wood	Suff	TM0772	52°18·6′	1°2·6′E	F	144,155
Colly Fm	Glos	ST8995	51°39·5′	2°9·1′W	FM	163
Collyhill	Aberd	NJ7231	57°22·4′	2°27·5′W	X	29
Collyhill	Aberd	NJ7724	57°18·6′	2°22·5′W	X	38
Colly Hill	Somer	SS9537	51°7·6′	3°29·6′W	X	181
Collyholme Wood	Lancs	SD7157	54°0·7′	2°26·1′W	F	103
Collyhurst	Man	SD8500	53°30·0′	2°13·2′W	T	109
Collyland	Clackm	NS8895	56°8·3′	3°47·7′W	X	58
Collymoon Moss	Stir	NS5896	56°8·4′	4°16·7′W	F	57
Collynie	Aberd	NJ8436	57°25·1′	2°15·5′W	X	29,30
Collytown	Devon	SX4665	50°28·1′	4°9·8′W	X	201
Collyweston	Northnts	SK9902	52°36·6′	0°31·9′W	T	141
Collyweston Br	Northnts	SK9903	52°37·2′	0°31·9′W	X	141
Collyweston Cross Roads	Northnts	TF0100	52°35·5′	0°30·1′W	X	141
Collyweston Great Wood	Northnts	TF0000	52°35·5′	0°31·0′W	F	141
Colman Hill	Notts	SK7639	52°56·8′	0°51·7′W	X	129
Colmans	Devon	SX4084	50°38·3′	4°15·4′W	X	201
Colman's Fm	Glos	SO9126	51°56·2′	2°7·5′W	FM	163
Colmeallie	Angus	NO5678	56°53·7′	2°42·9′W	X	44
Colmer	Devon	SX7053	50°22·0′	3°49·3′W	X	202
Colmer Fm	Devon	ST3700	50°48·0′	2°53·3′W	FM	193
Colmer Rocks	Corn	SX2753	50°21·3′	4°25·5′W	X	201
Colmer's Hill	Dorset	SY4493	50°44·3′	2°47·2′W	H	193
Colmire Sough	Cumbr	NY2250	54°50·6′	3°12·5′W	W	85
Colmonell	S Ayr	NX1485	55°7·7′	4°54·6′W	T	76
Colmslie	Scot Bord	NT5139	55°38·8′	2°46·3′W	T	73
Colmsliehill	Scot Bord	NT5141	55°39·9′	2°46·3′W	T	73
Colmworth	Beds	TL1058	52°12·8′	0°23·0′W	T	153
Colnabaichin	Aberd	NJ2908	57°9·7′	3°10·0′W	X	37
Colnbrook	Bucks	TQ0277	51°29·2′	0°31·5′W	T	176
Colne	Cambs	TL3775	52°21·6′	0°1·1′E	T	142,143
Colne	Lancs	SD8940	53°51·6′	2°9·6′W	T	103
Colne Bar	Essex	TM0912	51°46·3′	1°2·2′E	X	168,169
Colne Bridge	Kirk	SE1720	53°40·8′	1°44·1′W	T	104
Colne Brook	Bucks	TQ0482	51°31·9′	0°29·6′W	W	176
Colne Brook	Win & Maid	TQ0276	51°28·7′	0°31·5′W	W	176
Colne Edge	Lancs	SD8841	53°52·1′	2°10·5′W	T	103
Colne Engaine	Essex	TL8530	51°56·5′	0°41·9′E	T	168
Colne Fen	Cambs	TL3682	52°25·4′	0°0·4′E	X	142
Colne Fen	Cambs	TL3878	52°23·2′	0°2·1′E	X	142,143
Colne Fen Fm	Cambs	TL3878	52°23·2′	0°2·1′E	FM	142,143
Colnefields	Cambs	TL3777	52°22·7′	0°1·2′E	T	142,143
Colne Park	Essex	TL8730	51°56·4′	0°43·6′E	X	168
Colne Point	Essex	TM1012	51°46·3′	1°3·0′E	X	168,169
Colne Valley	Essex	TL8629	51°55·9′	0°42·7′E	X	168
Colne Valley Circular Walk	Kirk	SE0413	53°37·1′	1°56·0′W	X	110
Colne Valley Railway	Essex	TL7736	51°59·9′	0°35·1′E	X	155
Colne Water	Lancs	SD9140	53°51·6′	2°7·8′W	W	103
Colney	Norf	TG1807	52°37·2′	1°13·6′E	T	134
Colney Fm	Hill	TQ0490	51°36·2′	0°29·5′W	FM	176
Colney Hatch	Barnet	TQ2791	51°36·4′	0°9·6′W	T	176
Colney Heath	Herts	TL2005	51°44·1′	0°15·3′W	T	166
Colney Street	Herts	TL1502	51°42·5′	0°19·7′W	T	166
Colnpen Copse	Glos	SP0707	51°45·9′	1°53·5′W	F	163
Coln Rogers	Glos	SP0809	51°47·0′	1°52·6′W	T	163
Coln St Aldwyns	Glos	SP1405	51°44·8′	1°47·4′W	T	163
Coln St Dennis	Glos	SP0810	51°47·5′	1°52·6′W	T	163
Cologin	Arg & Bt	NM8526	56°22·9′	5°28·5′W	X	49
Colomendy	Denb	SJ0540	52°57·2′	3°24·4′W	X	125
Colomendy	Flint	SJ1369	53°12·9′	3°17·8′W	A	116
Colomendy	Wrex	SJ3045	53°0·1′	3°2·2′W	X	117
Colomendy Fm	Monm	ST3594	51°38·7′	2°56·0′W	FM	171
Colonel's Bed, The	Aberd	NO0887	56°58·2′	3°30·3′W	X	43
Colonsay	Arg & Bt	NR3794	56°4·3′	6°13·1′W	X	61
Colonsay Ho	Arg & Bt	NR3996	56°5·4′	6°11·3′W	X	61
Colony	Highld	NH7263	57°38·6′	4°8·2′W	X	21,27
Colony	Pth & Kin	NN8822	56°22·9′	3°48·4′W	X	52,58
Colony Bog	Surrey	SU9159	51°19·6′	0°41·2′W	X	175,186
Colony Fm	Cambs	TL5092	52°30·5′	0°13·0′E	FM	143
Colony Gate	Surrey	SU9158	51°19·1′	0°41·3′W	X	175,186
Colony, The	Powys	SO3167	52°18·0′	3°0·3′W	X	137,148
Colooneys	I of M	SC3375	54°8·9′	4°33·0′W	X	95
Colors Cove	Corn	SX1850	50°19·5′	4°33·0′W	W	201
Colpitts Grange	Northum	NY9855	54°53·6′	2°1·4′W	T	87
Colpman's Fm	Northnts	SP9779	52°24·3′	0°34·0′W	FM	141
Colpy	Aberd	NJ6432	57°22·9′	2°35·5′W	T	29,37
Colpy Fm	Aberd	NJ6332	57°22·9′	2°36·5′W	FM	29,37
Colquhalzie	Pth & Kin	NN9117	56°20·2′	3°45·3′W	X	58
Colquhar	Scot Bord	NT3341	55°39·7′	3°3·5′W	X	73
Colquhonnie Hotel	Aberd	NJ3612	57°11·9′	3°3·1′W	X	37
Colquite	Corn	SX0570	50°30·1′	4°44·6′W	X	200
Colquite	Corn	SX1673	50°31·9′	4°35·4′W	X	201
Colquite Woods	Corn	SX0570	50°30·1′	4°44·6′W	F	200
Colrig	Pth & Kin	NN6764	56°45·2′	4°10·1′W	X	42
Colrig	Pth & Kin	NN8068	56°47·5′	3°57·4′W	H	43
Colsay	Shetld	HU3618	59°57·0′	1°20·0′W	X	4
Colscott	Devon	SS3614	50°54·4′	4°19·6′W	T	190
Colsea Yawn	C of Aber	NJ9500	57°5·7′	2°4·5′W	W	38
Colsey Wood	Suff	TM1169	52°16·9′	1°6·0′E	X	155
Colshaw	Staffs	SK0467	53°12·2′	1°56·0′W	T	119

Colshaw Hall	Ches	SJ7874	53°16·0'	2°19·4'W	X	118
Colsnaur Hill	Clackm	NS8699	56°10·5'	3°49·7'W	H	58
Colsta	Shetld	HZ2072	59°32·3'	1°38·3'W	X	4
Colsterdale	N Yks	SE1381	54°13·7'	1°47·6'W	T	99
Colsterdale Moor	N Yks	SE1181	54°13·7'	1°49·5'W	X	99
Colsterworth	Lincs	SK9224	52°48·6'	0°37·7'W	T	130
Colstey	Shrops	SO3083	52°26·7'	3°1·4'W	X	137
Colston	Devon	SX7564	50°28·0'	3°45·3'W	X	202
Colston	E Dunb	NS6069	55°53·9'	4°13·9'W	T	64
Colston	Pemb	SM8812	51°46·2'	5°4·0'W	X	157
Colston	Pemb	SM9828	51°55·1'	4°55·9'W	T	157,158
Colston Barton	Devon	SS8614	50°55·1'	3°36·9'W	X	181
Colston Bassett	Notts	SK7033	52°53·6'	0°57·2'W	T	129
Colston Fm	Carm	SN2510	51°45·9'	4°31·8'W	FM	158
Colston Hall	Suff	TM3167	52°15·4'	1°23·5'E	X	156
Colstons Fm	Cumbr	NY6036	54°43·3'	2°36·8'W	FM	91
Colstoun Ho	E Loth	NT5171	55°56·0'	2°46·6'W	X	66
Colstoun Mains	E Loth	NT5271	55°56·0'	2°45·7'W	X	66
Colstoun Water	E Loth	NT5170	55°55·5'	2°46·6'W	W	66
Colstoun Wood	E Loth	NT5370	55°55·5'	2°44·7'W	F	66
Colstrope	Bucks	SU7888	51°35·4'	0°52·1'W	T	175
Colt Close	Cumbr	NY4342	54°46·4'	2°52·7'W	X	85
Colt Crag	Northum	NY9278	55°6·0'	2°7·1'W	X	87
Colt Crag Reservoir	Northum	NY9378	55°6·0'	2°6·2'W	W	87
Coltcrooks	Scot Bord	NT6540	55°39·4'	2°32·9'W	X	74
Colterscleuch	Scot Bord	NT4106	55°20·9'	2°55·4'W	X	79
Colterscleuch Shiel	Scot Bord	NT4204	55°19·8'	2°54·4'W	X	79
Coltfield	Moray	NJ1163	57°39·2'	3°29·0'W	T	28
Colt Hill	D & G	NX6999	55°16·3'	4°3·3'W	H	77
Colt Hill	Hants	SU7451	51°15·4'	0°56·0'W	T	186
Colt Ho	Notts	SK6950	53°2·8'	0°57·8'W	X	120
Colt Ho	N Yks	SE1269	54°7·2'	1°48·6'W	X	99
Colthouse	Cumbr	SD3598	54°22·6'	2°59·6'W	T	96,97
Colt House Fm	N Yks	SE6197	54°22·1'	1°3·2'W	FM	94,100
Colt House Gill	N Yks	SE1068	54°6·7'	1°50·4'W	W	99
Colthouse Heights	Cumbr	SD3697	54°22·1'	2°58·7'W	X	96,97
Colthrop	W Berks	SU5366	51°23·7'	1°13·9'W	T	174
Colthrop Manor	W Berks	SU5467	51°24·2'	1°13·0'W	X	174
Colthurst Hall	Lancs	SD7144	53°53·7'	2°26·1'W	X	103
Coltishall	Norf	TG2720	52°44·0'	1°22·1'E	T	133,134
Coltishall Airfield	Norf	TG2622	52°45·1'	1°21·3'E	X	133,134
Coltishall Hall	Norf	TG2819	52°43·5'	1°23·0'E	X	133,134
Coltleigh Fm	Dorset	SY5199	50°47·5'	2°41·3'W	FM	194
Coltness	N Lanak	NS8056	55°47·2'	3°54·6'W	X	65,72
Colton	Cumbr	SD3186	54°16·1'	3°3·2'W	T	96,97
Colton	Leeds	SE3632	53°47·2'	1°26·8'W	T	104
Colton	Norf	TG1009	52°38·5'	1°6·6'E	T	144
Colton	N Yks	SE5444	53°53·6'	1°10·3'W	T	105
Colton	Staffs	SK0520	52°46·9'	1°55·1'W	T	128
Colton	Suff	TL8766	52°15·8'	0°44·8'E	T	155
Colton Beck	Cumbr	SD3186	54°16·1'	3°3·2'W	W	96,97
Colton Br	N Yks	SE5443	53°53·1'	1°10·3'W	X	105
Colton Breck Fm	N Yks	SE5544	53°53·6'	1°9·4'W	FM	105
Colton Common	Leeds	SE3733	53°47·8'	1°25·9'W	X	104
Colton Fm	Fife	NT0989	56°5·4'	3°27·3'W	FM	65
Colton Fm	Somer	ST0535	51°6·6'	3°21·0'W	FM	181
Colton Haggs Fm	N Yks	SE5445	53°54·1'	1°10·3'W	FM	105
Colton Hall Fm	Staffs	SK0519	52°46·4'	1°55·2'W	FM	128
Colton Hills	Wolv	SO9095	52°33·4'	2°8·4'W	T	139
Colton Ho	Fife	NT0989	56°5·4'	3°27·3'W	X	65
Colton Lodge	N Yks	SE5344	53°53·6'	1°11·2'W	X	105
Colton Plantn	Durham	NZ0614	54°31·5'	1°54·0'W	F	92
Colton Wood	Norf	TG1108	52°37·9'	1°7·5'E	F	144
Colt Park	Cumbr	SD2770	54°7·5'	3°6·6'W	T	96,97
Coltpark	Northum	NZ0693	55°14·1'	1°53·9'W	X	81
Colt Park	N Yks	SD7777	54°11·5'	2°20·7'W	X	98
Colt Park Wood	N Yks	SE0698	54°22·9'	1°54·0'W	F	99
Colt Plain	N Yks	SE1168	54°6·7'	1°49·5'W	X	99
Coltraiseal Beag	N Eil	NB1424	58°7·0'	6°50·9'W	H	13,14
Coltraiseal Mòr	N Eil	NB1522	58°6·0'	6°49·8'W	H	13,14
Coltrannie	Pth & Kin	NO0635	56°30·1'	3°31·2'W	X	52,53
Coltscombe	Oxon	SP3530	51°58·3'	1°29·0'W	X	151
Coltsfoot	Herts	TL4132	51°58·3'	0°3·6'E	X	167
Coltsfoot Fm	Devon	SX7497	50°45·8'	3°46·8'W	FM	191
Coltsford Mill	Surrey	TQ3950	51°14·2'	0°0·1'W	X	187
Colt's Green	S Glos	ST7481	51°31·9'	2°22·1'W	T	172
Colt's Hall	Suff	TL7947	52°5·8'	0°37·2'E	X	155
Colt's Hill	Kent	TQ6443	51°10·0'	0°21·1'E	T	188
Colts Hill	Swan	SS6088	51°34·6'	4°0·8'W	X	159
Coltsmoor Fm	Glos	SP1607	51°45·9'	1°45·7'W	FM	163
Coltsmoor Fm	Staffs	SK0057	53°6·9'	1°59·6'W	FM	119
Coltstaple Fm	W Susx	TQ1727	51°2·1'	0°19·5'W	FM	187,198
Coltstone	Staffs	SK0150	53°3·1'	1°58·7'W	X	119
Col Uarach	N Eil	NB4539	58°16·2'	6°20·4'W	T	8
Columbia	Sund	NZ3155	54°53·6'	1°30·6'W	T	88
Columbie	S Lanak	NS9446	55°42·0'	3°40·8'W	X	72
Columbine Hall	Suff	TM0660	52°12·2'	1°1·3'E	A	155
Columbjohn	Devon	SX9599	50°47·1'	3°29·0'W	T	192
Column Field Quarry	Suff	TM1150	52°6·7'	1°5·3'E	X	155
Column of Victory	Oxon	SP4317	51°51·2'	1°22·1'W	X	164
Column Ride	Wilts	SU2364	51°22·7'	1°39·8'W	X	174
Column, The	Somer	ST7252	51°16·2'	2°23·7'W	X	183
Colva	Powys	SO2053	52°10·4'	3°9·8'W	T	148
Colvadale	Shetld	HP6204	60°43·1'	0°51·3'W	X	1
Colva Hill	Powys	SO1954	52°10·9'	3°10·7'W	H	148
Colvannick Tor	Corn	SX1271	50°30·8'	4°38·7'W	X	200
Colvase	Corn	SX2858	50°24·0'	4°24·8'W	X	201
Colvend	D & G	NX8654	54°52·3'	3°46·2'W	X	84
Colvennor	Corn	SW6821	50°2·9'	5°14·1'W	X	203
Colveston Manor Fm	Norf	TL7995	52°31·6'	0°38·7'E	FM	144
Colvigirts	Shetld	HU5863	60°21·1'	0°56·4'W	X	2
Colville Hall	Essex	TL5513	51°47·9'	0°15·3'E	A	167
Colville Park	N Lanak	NS7558	55°48·2'	3°59·2'W	X	64
Colville's Grove	Suff	TL9161	52°13·1'	0°48·2'E	F	155
Colvinston	S Ayr	NS4022	55°28·2'	4°31·4'W	X	70
Colvister	Shetld	HU5197	60°39·4'	1°3·5'W	T	1
Colvithick Wood	Corn	SX1253	50°21·1'	4°38·2'W	F	200
Colvorry	Corn	SW6027	50°5·9'	5°21·0'W	X	203
Colwall	Heref	SO7342	52°4·8'	2°23·2'W	T	150
Colwall Green	Heref	SO7541	52°4·2'	2°21·5'W	T	150

Colwall Mill Fm	Heref	SO7343	52°5·3'	2°23·2'W	FM	150
Colwall Stone	Heref	SO7542	52°4·8'	2°21·5'W	T	150
Colways Fm	Glos	SO8226	51°56·2'	2°15·3'W	FM	162
Colwell	Northum	NY9575	55°4·4'	2°4·3'W	T	87
Colwell Barton	Devon	SY1998	50°46·8'	3°8·6'W	X	192,193
Colwell Bay	I of W	SZ3288	50°41·7'	1°32·4'W	W	196
Colwell Fm	Somer	ST0833	51°5·6'	3°18·4'W	FM	181
Colwellhill	Northum	NY9194	55°14·7'	2°8·1'W	X	80
Colwich	Staffs	SK0121	52°47·4'	1°58·7'W	T	128
Colwick	Notts	SK6140	52°57·5'	1°5·1'W	T	129
Colwick Country Park	C of Nott	SK6039	52°56·9'	1°6·0'W	X	129
Colwinston	V of Glam	SS9475	51°28·1'	3°31·2'W	T	170
Colwith	Corn	SX0956	50°22·6'	4°40·8'W	X	200
Colwith	Cumbr	NY3303	54°25·3'	3°1·5'W	X	90
Colwood	Corn	SX1458	50°23·8'	4°36·7'W	X	200
Colwood Manor	W Susx	TQ2424	51°0·3'	0°13·6'W	X	198
Colwood Park Ho	W Susx	TQ2524	51°0·3'	0°12·7'W	X	198
Colworth	W Susx	SU9102	50°48·8'	0°42·1'W	T	197
Colworth Down	W Susx	SU8414	50°55·4'	0°47·9'W	X	197
Colworth Fm	W Susx	SU8514	50°55·4'	0°47·1'W	FM	197
Colworth Fm	W Susx	SU9003	50°49·4'	0°42·9'W	FM	197
Colworth Ho	Beds	SP9860	52°14·0'	0°33·5'W	T	153
Colwyn	Cered	SN1544	52°4·1'	4°41·6'W	X	145
Colwyn Bay or Bae Colwyn	Conwy	SH8678	53°17·4'	3°42·2'W	T	116
Colwyn Brook	Powys	SJ1616	52°44·3'	3°14·3'W	X	125
Colwyn Brook	Powys	SN9992	52°31·2'	3°28·9'W	W	136
Colwyn Castle	Powys	SO1053	52°10·3'	3°18·6'W	A	148
Colychurch	Brig	SS9479	51°30·2'	3°31·2'W	T	
Colyers Wents	Kent	TQ8557	51°17·1'	0°39·6'E	F	178
Colyford	Devon	SY2492	50°43·6'	3°4·2'W	T	192,193
Colyne	Aberd	NJ6141	57°27·7'	2°38·5'W	X	29
Colyton	Devon	SY2493	50°44·1'	3°4·2'W	T	192,193
Colyton Hill	Devon	SY2392	50°43·6'	3°5·1'W	X	192,193
Coly-uchaf	Merth Tyd	SO0902	51°42·8'	3°18·6'W	X	171
Colzie	Fife	NO2114	56°19·0'	3°16·2'W	X	58
Colzie Hill	Fife	NO2214	56°19·0'	3°15·2'W	H	58
Colzium	W Loth	NT0858	55°48·6'	3°27·6'W	X	65,72
Colzium Hill	W Loth	NT0956	55°47·6'	3°26·6'W	X	65,72
Colzium Ho	N Lanak	NS7278	55°58·9'	4°2·7'W	X	64
Comar	Highld	NH3331	57°20·6'	4°46·0'W	X	26
Comar Wood	Highld	NH3231	57°20·6'	4°47·0'W	F	26
Comb	Cumbr	SD6594	54°20·7'	2°31·9'W	X	97
Comb	Northum	NY7690	55°12·5'	2°22·2'W	X	80
Comb	Northum	NY7693	55°14·1'	2°22·2'W	X	80
Comb	Scot Bord	NT3205	55°20·3'	3°3·9'W	X	79
Comb Beck	Cumbr	NY2125	54°37·1'	3°13·0'W	W	89,90
Comb Crags	Cumbr	NY3313	54°30·7'	3°1·7'W	X	90
Combe	Devon	SS4227	51°1·5'	4°14·8'W	X	180
Combe	Devon	SS5801	50°47·7'	4°0·5'W	X	191
Combe	Devon	SS8228	51°2·6'	3°40·6'W	X	181
Combe	Devon	SX4174	50°32·9'	4°14·3'W	X	201
Combe	Devon	SX5452	50°21·2'	4°2·8'W	T	201
Combe	Devon	SX6997	50°45·7'	3°51·1'W	X	191
Combe	Devon	SX7068	50°30·1'	3°49·6'W	T	202
Combe	Devon	SX7138	50°13·9'	3°48·2'W	T	202
Combe	Devon	SX7250	50°20·4'	3°47·6'W	X	202
Combe	Devon	SX7640	50°15·1'	3°44·0'W	X	202
Combe	Devon	SX7864	50°28·0'	3°42·8'W	X	202
Combe	Devon	SX8448	50°19·5'	3°37·4'W	X	202
Combe	Devon	SX8775	50°34·1'	3°35·4'W	X	192
Combe	E Susx	TQ6228	51°1·9'	0°19·0'E	T	188,199
Combe	Heref	SO3463	52°15·9'	2°57·6'W	T	137,148,149
Combe	Oxon	SP4115	51°50·2'	1°23·9'W	T	164
Combe	Somer	SS9126	51°1·6'	3°32·9'W	X	181
Combe	Somer	ST0536	51°7·2'	3°21·1'W	X	181
Combe	Somer	ST4127	51°2·6'	2°50·1'W	T	193
Combe	W Berks	SU3760	51°20·5'	1°27·7'W	T	174
Combe Almer	Dorset	SY9597	50°46·6'	2°3·9'W	T	195
Combe Bank Fm	Kent	TQ4756	51°17·3'	0°6·9'E	FM	188
Combe Bank (Sch)	Kent	TQ4755	51°16·7'	0°6·9'E	X	188
Combe Beacon	Somer	ST2912	50°54·4'	3°0·2'W	H	193
Combe Beacon (Tumulus)	Somer	ST2912	50°54·4'	3°0·2'W	A	193
Combe Bottom	Dorset	ST8715	50°56·3'	2°10·7'W	X	183
Combe Bottom	Dorset	SY6098	50°47·0'	2°33·7'W	X	194
Combe Bottom	Dorset	SY6591	50°43·3'	2°29·4'W	X	194
Combe Bottom	Somer	ST0830	51°4·0'	3°18·4'W	F	181
Combe Bottom	Surrey	TQ0649	51°14·0'	0°28·5'W	X	187
Combebow	Devon	SX4887	50°40·0'	4°8·7'W	T	191
Combe Brook	Somer	ST6836	51°7·6'	2°27·1'W	W	183
Combe Common	Surrey	SU9535	51°6·6'	0°38·2'W	T	186
Combe Court	Surrey	SU9436	51°7·2'	0°39·0'W	X	186
Combe Cross	Devon	SX7870	50°31·3'	3°42·9'W	X	202
Combe Cross	Devon	SX8348	50°19·5'	3°38·2'W	X	202
Combe Davey	Somer	ST0732	51°5·0'	3°19·3'W	X	181
Combe Door	Cumbr	NY2510	54°29·0'	3°9·0'W	X	89,90
Combe Down	Bath & NE Somer	ST7662	51°21·6'	2°20·3'W	T	172
Combe Downs	Somer	ST0323	51°0·1'	3°22·6'W	H	181
Combe Fishacre	Devon	SX8464	50°28·1'	3°37·7'W	T	202
Combefishacre Ho	Devon	SX8465	50°28·6'	3°37·7'W	X	202
Combe Florey	Somer	ST1531	51°4·6'	3°12·4'W	T	181
Combe Fm	Devon	SX6748	50°19·3'	3°51·7'W	FM	202
Combe Fm	Devon	SX8248	50°19·4'	3°39·1'W	FM	202
Combe Fm	Devon	SX8289	50°41·6'	3°39·9'W	FM	191
Combe Fm	Somer	ST0040	51°9·3'	3°25·4'W	FM	181
Combe Gibbet	W Berks	SU3662	51°21·6'	1°28·6'W	X	174
Combe Gill	Cumbr	NY2513	54°30·7'	3°9·1'W	W	89,90
Combe Gill	Cumbr	SD7282	54°14·2'	2°25·4'W	W	98
Combe Hay	Bath & NE Somer	ST7359	51°20·0'	2°22·9'W	T	172
Combehayes	Devon	SY1699	50°47·3'	3°11·1'W	X	192,193
Combehayes Fm	Devon	ST1101	50°48·3'	3°15·4'W	FM	192,193
Combe Head	Cumbr	NY2410	54°29·0'	3°10·0'W	X	89,90
Combe Head	Devon	SS9322	50°59·5'	3°31·1'W	X	181
Combe Head	Somer	ST2911	50°53·9'	3°0·2'W	X	193
Combe Hill	Devon	ST1415	50°55·9'	3°13·0'W	X	181,193
Combe Hill	Devon	ST1503	50°49·5'	3°12·0'W	X	192,193
Combe Hill	Dorset	SY6298	50°47·1'	2°32·0'W	X	194

Combe Hill	E Susx	TQ5702	50°48·0'	0°14·1'E	H	199
Combe Hill	Lancs	SD9539	53°51·1'	2°4·1'W	X	103
Combe Hill	Northnts	SP8560	52°14·1'	0°44·9'W	X	152
Combe Hill	W Berks	SU3860	51°20·5'	1°26·9'W	H	174
Combe Hill	Wilts	ST9151	51°15·7'	2°7·4'W	X	184
Combe Hill	W Susx	SU7926	51°1·9'	0°52·0'W	H	186,197
Combe Hill Ho	Somer	ST5531	51°4·8'	2°38·2'W	X	182,183
Combe Hill (Tumuli)	E Susx	TQ5702	50°48·0'	0°14·1'E	A	199
Combe Ho	Cumbr	SD6887	54°16·9'	2°29·1'W	X	98
Combe Ho	Devon	SX8464	50°28·1'	3°37·7'W	X	202
Combe Ho	Devon	SY1497	50°46·2'	3°12·8'W	A	192,193
Combe Ho	Lancs	SD9538	53°50·5'	2°4·1'W	X	103
Combeinteignhead	Devon	SX9071	50°31·9'	3°32·7'W	T	202
Combe Lacey	Devon	SS8101	50°48·0'	3°40·9'W	X	191
Combeland	Devon	SS9426	51°1·7'	3°30·3'W	X	181
Combeleigh Fm	Somer	SS9039	51°8·6'	3°34·0'W	FM	181
Combe Martin	Devon	SS5846	51°12·0'	4°1·6'W	T	180
Combe Martin Bay	Devon	SS5748	51°13·0'	4°2·5'W	W	180
Combe Moor	Heref	SO3663	52°15·9'	2°55·9'W	T	137,148,149
Combend Manor	Glos	SO9811	51°48·1'	2°1·3'W	X	163
Combe Pafford	Torbay	SX9166	50°29·3'	3°31·8'W	T	202
Combepark	Corn	SS2304	50°48·7'	4°30·4'W	X	190
Combe Park	Devon	SS7347	51°12·7'	3°48·7'W	X	180
Combe Point	Devon	SX8848	50°19·5'	3°34·0'W	X	202
Combe Raleigh	Devon	ST1502	50°48·9'	3°12·0'W	T	192,193
Comberbach	Ches	SJ6477	53°17·6'	2°32·0'W	T	118
Comberford	Staffs	SK1907	52°39·9'	1°42·7'W	T	139
Comberford Hall	Staffs	SK1906	52°39·3'	1°42·7'W	X	139
Comber Mere	Ches	SJ5844	52°59·7'	2°37·1'W	W	117
Combermere Abbey	Ches	SJ5844	52°59·7'	2°37·1'W	A	117
Combermere Park	Ches	SJ5843	52°59·2'	2°37·1'W	X	117
Comberow	Somer	ST0235	51°6·6'	3°23·6'W	X	181
Combe Royal	Devon	SX7245	50°17·7'	3°47·5'W	X	202
Comberton	Cambs	TL3856	52°11·3'	0°1·5'E	T	154
Comberton	Heref	SO4967	52°18·2'	2°44·5'W	T	137,138,148
Comberton	Worcs	SO8476	52°23·1'	2°13·7'W	X	138
Comberton Fm	Shrops	SO5169	52°19·3'	2°42·7'W	FM	137,138
Comberwood Fm	Derby	SK4679	53°18·6'	1°18·2'W	FM	120
Combes Brook	Staffs	SK0052	53°4·2'	1°59·6'W	W	119
Combe Scar	Cumbr	SD6787	54°16·9'	2°30·0'W	X	98
Combe Scar	N Yks	SD7379	54°12·6'	2°24·4'W	X	98
Combeshead	Devon	ST1607	50°51·6'	3°11·2'W	X	192,193
Combes Head	Devon	SX8889	50°41·6'	3°34·8'W	X	192
Combeshead	Somer	SS9039	51°8·6'	3°34·0'W	X	181
Combeshead Cross	Devon	SX7455	50°23·1'	3°46·0'W	X	202
Combes Head Fm	Devon	ST2200	50°47·9'	3°6·0'W	FM	192,193
Combeshead Fm	Somer	SS9333	51°5·4'	3°31·3'W	FM	181
Combe Sta	Oxon	SP4115	51°50·2'	1°23·9'W	X	164
Combe St Nicholas	Somer	ST3011	50°53·9'	2°59·3'W	T	193
Combestone	Devon	SX6772	50°32·2'	3°52·2'W	X	191
Combestone Tor	Devon	SX6671	50°31·6'	3°53·1'W	X	202
Combe Sydenham	Somer	ST0736	51°7·2'	3°19·3'W	X	181
Combe, The	Somer	ST7345	51°12·4'	2°22·8'W	X	183
Combe Throop	Somer	ST7123	51°0·6'	2°24·4'W	T	183
Combe Tors	Devon	SX5277	50°34·7'	4°5·0'W	X	191,201
Combe Walker	Devon	SS4127	51°1·5'	4°15·7'W	X	180
Combe Water	Devon	SS8822	50°59·4'	3°35·4'W	W	181
Combe Wood	E Susx	TQ6128	51°2·0'	0°18·2'E	F	188,199
Combe Wood	Heref	SO3462	52°15·4'	2°57·6'W	F	137,148,149
Combe Wood	Herts	TL1801	51°41·9'	0°17·2'W	F	166
Combe Wood	Somer	ST1431	51°4·5'	3°13·3'W	F	181
Combe Wood	W Berks	SU3559	51°20·0'	1°29·5'W	F	174
Comb Fell	Northum	NT9118	55°27·6'	2°8·1'W	H	80
Combfield Ho	Durham	NZ0549	54°50·4'	1°54·9'W	X	87
Comb Head	D & G	NS9009	55°22·0'	3°43·7'W	X	71,78
Comb Hill	Northum	NY7692	55°13·5'	2°22·2'W	H	80
Combhill	Northum	NZ0692	55°13·6'	1°53·9'W	X	81
Comb Hill	Scot Bord	NT3900	55°17·7'	2°57·2'W	H	79
Combhills	Northum	NY9757	54°54·7'	2°2·4'W	X	87
Comb Law	S Lanak	NS9407	55°21·0'	3°39·9'W	H	71,78
Combley Fm	I of W	SZ5488	50°41·6'	1°13·7'W	FM	196
Combley Great Wood	I of W	SZ5488	50°41·6'	1°13·7'W	F	196
Combourne Fm	Kent	TQ7439	51°7·7'	0°29·6'E	FM	188
Combpyne	Devon	SY2992	50°43·6'	3°0·0'W	T	193
Combpyne Hill	Devon	SY2992	50°43·6'	3°0·0'W	X	193
Combrew	Devon	SS5232	51°4·3'	4°6·4'W	T	180
Combridge	Staffs	SK0937	52°56·1'	1°51·6'W	T	128
Comb Rigg	Northum	NY9687	55°10·9'	2°3·3'W	H	81
Combrook	Warw	SP3051	52°9·6'	1°33·3'W	T	151
Combs	Derby	SK0478	53°18·2'	1°56·0'W	T	119
Combs	Kirk	SE2419	53°40·3'	1°37·8'W	T	110
Combs	Suff	TM0456	52°10·1'	0°59·4'E	T	155
Combs Ditch	Dorset	ST8502	50°49·3'	2°12·4'W	A	194
Combs Ditch	Dorset	ST8700	50°48·2'	2°10·7'W	A	194
Combs Edge	Derby	SK0476	53°17·1'	1°56·0'W	H	119
Combs Fm	Notts	SK6355	53°5·5'	1°3·1'W	FM	120
Combs Ford	Suff	TM0557	52°10·6'	1°0·3'E	T	155
Combshead Tor	Devon	SX5868	50°29·9'	3°59·8'W	X	202
Combs Hollow	Cumbr	NY5602	54°24·9'	2°40·3'W	H	90
Combsland Cross	Devon	SS7725	51°0·9'	3°44·8'W	X	180
Combs Moss	Derby	SK0576	53°17·1'	1°55·1'W	X	119
Combs Plantation	Leic	SK7730	52°52·0'	0°51·0'W	F	129
Combs Resr	Derby	SK0379	53°18·7'	1°56·9'W	W	119
Combs, The	Cumbr	NY5948	54°49·8'	2°37·9'W	X	86
Combs, The	Durham	NZ0011	54°29·9'	1°59·6'W	X	92
Combs, The	Northum	NY8549	54°50·4'	2°13·6'W	X	87
Comb's Wood	Herts	TL3121	51°52·6'	0°5·4'W	F	166
Combs Wood	Notts	SK6354	53°5·0'	1°3·2'W	F	120
Combs Wood (Nature Reserve)	Suff	TM0556	52°10·1'	1°0·3'E	X	155
Combwell Priory Fm	Kent	TQ7033	51°4·5'	0°26·0'E	FM	188
Combwell Wood	Kent	TQ7133	51°4·5'	0°26·9'E	F	188
Combwich	Somer	ST2542	51°10·6'	3°4·0'W	T	182
Combwich Reach	Somer	ST2642	51°10·6'	3°3·1'W	W	182
Combyheugh	Northum	NY8874	55°3·9'	2°10·9'W	X	87
Comely	Orkney	HY5404	58°55·5'	2°47·5'W	X	6,7
Comelyburn	Pth & Kin	NN9009	56°15·9'	3°46·1'W	X	58
Comely Burn	Scot Bord	NT4149	55°44·1'	2°55·9'W	W	73
Comenden Manor	Kent	TQ7939	51°7·6'	0°33·9'E	X	188
Comer	Stir	NN3804	56°12·3'	4°36·3'W	X	56

Comers	Aberd	NJ6707	57°9·4′	2°32·3′W	T	38
Comer's Cross	Somer	SS8635	51°6·4′	3°37·3′W	X	181
Comer's Gate	Somer	SS8635	51°6·4′	3°37·3′W	X	181
Comers Hill	N Ayr	NS2665	55°51·1′	4°46·3′W	X	63
Comerslade	Somer	SS7337	51°7·3′	3°48·5′W	X	180
Comerton	Fife	NO4621	56°22·9′	2°52·0′W	X	54,59
Comerton Ho	Fife	NO4325	56°25·1′	2°55·0′W	X	54,59
Comer Wood	Shrops	SO7589	52°30·1′	2°21·7′W	F	138
Come-to-Good	Corn	SW8140	50°13·4′	5°3·8′W	T	204
Comet Stone	Orkney	HY2913	59°0·2′	3°13·7′W	A	6
Comeytrowe	Somer	ST2023	51°0·3′	3°8·0′W	T	193
Comford	Corn	SW7339	50°12·7′	5°10·5′W	T	204
Comfort	Corn	SW7329	50°7·3′	5°10·2′W	T	204
Comfort Law	Aberd	NJ7061	57°38·5′	2°29·7′W	X	29
Comfortlee	Scot Bord	NT6859	55°49·6′	2°30·2′W	X	67,74
Comforts Place	Surrey	TQ3746	51°12·0′	0°2·0′W	X	187
Comhampton	Worcs	SO8366	52°17·7′	2°14·6′W	T	138,150
Com Head	Corn	SW9480	50°35·2′	4°54·2′W	X	200
Còmhnard Coire nan Geur-oirean	Highld	NN0390	56°57·8′	5°14·0′W	X	33
Comielaw	Fife	NO5204	56°13·8′	2°46·0′W	X	59
Comin Cefn-poeth	Powys	SN9852	52°9·7′	3°29·1′W	X	147
Comin Coch	Powys	SN9552	52°9·6′	3°31·7′W	X	147
Comin-coch	Powys	SN9954	52°10·7′	3°28·2′W	X	147
Comin Coed-y-moeth	Caer	SO1501	51°42·3′	3°13·4′W	X	171
Comins Bach	Powys	SH8003	52°36·9′	3°45·9′W	X	135,136
Comins Capel Betws	Cered	SN6157	52°11·9′	4°1·6′W	X	146
Comins Coch	Cered	SN6182	52°25·3′	4°2·3′W	T	135
Comins Pen-y-banc	Cered	SN6668	52°17·9′	3°57·5′W	X	135
Comin-y-garth	Powys	SN9854	52°10·7′	3°29·1′W	X	147
Comin y Rhos	Powys	SN9109	51°46·4′	3°34·4′W	X	160
Comiston	C of Edin	NT2468	55°54·2′	3°12·5′W	T	66
Comisty	Aberd	NJ5941	57°27·7′	2°40·5′W	X	29
Comley	Orkney	HY6726	59°7·4′	2°34·1′W	X	5
Comley	Shrops	SO4896	52°33·8′	2°45·6′W	T	137,138
Comlongon Castle (Hotel)	D & G	NY0768	55°0·1′	3°26·8′W	X	85
Comlongon Mains	D & G	NY0769	55°0·7′	3°26·8′W	X	85
Comlongon Wood	D & G	NY0868	55°0·1′	3°25·9′W	F	85
Comlybank	Orkney	HY3416	59°1·8′	3°8·5′W	X	6
Commandery, The	Worcs	SO8554	52°11·3′	2°12·8′W	A	150
Commandry Fm	Worcs	SO9256	52°12·4′	2°6·6′W	FM	150
Commerce Common	Corn	SW9849	50°18·6′	4°49·9′W	X	204
Commercial End	Cambs	TL5563	52°14·8′	0°16·6′E	T	154
Commerrans Fm	Corn	SW8437	50°11·9′	5°1·2′W	FM	204
Commieston	Aberd	NO7263	56°45·7′	2°27·0′W	X	45
Commins	Denb	SJ1262	53°9·1′	3°18·6′W	T	116
Commins	Powys	SJ1027	52°50·2′	3°19·8′W	X	125
Commins Coch	Powys	SH8403	52°37·0′	3°42·4′W	T	135,136
Commins Gwalia	Powys	SH8504	52°37·5′	3°41·5′W	X	135,136
Commissarybog	Aberd	NJ6555	57°35·3′	2°34·7′W	X	29
Commissioners' Drain	Norf	TG4223	52°45·2′	1°35·6′E	W	134
Commissioners Fm	Cambs	TL5267	52°17·0′	0°14·1′E	FM	154
Commodore Wood	Norf	TF7028	52°49·6′	0°31·8′E	F	132
Common	E Ayr	NS5822	55°28·5′	4°14·4′W	X	71
Common Allotments	N Yks	SD8786	54°16·4′	2°11·6′W	X	98
Common Allotments	N Yks	SD8887	54°17·0′	2°10·6′W	X	98
Common Bach	Heref	SO3040	52°3·5′	3°0·9′W	X	148,161
Commonbank	Pth & Kin	NO1724	56°24·3′	3°20·3′W	X	53,58
Common Barn	Cambs	TL1765	52°16·5′	0°16·7′W	X	153
Common Barn	Ches	SJ9676	53°17·1′	2°3·2′W	X	118
Common Barn	Oxon	SU4394	51°38·8′	1°22·3′W	X	164,174
Common Barn	Staffs	SK1604	52°38·2′	1°45·4′W	X	139
Common Barn	Wok	SU7783	51°32·7′	0°53·0′W	X	175
Common Barn Cotts	W Berks	SU5174	51°28·0′	1°15·6′W	X	174
Common Barn Fm	Hants	SU6933	51°5·8′	1°0·5′W	FM	186
Common Barn Fm	Oxon	SP2102	51°43·2′	1°41·4′W	FM	163
Common Beck	E Yorks	SE7252	53°57·8′	0°53·7′W	W	105,106
Common Bottom Wood	N Yks	SE6742	53°52·4′	0°58·4′W	F	105,106
Commonbrae	Scot Bord	NT3701	55°18·2′	2°59·1′W	X	79
Common Burn	Northum	NT9226	55°31·9′	2°7·2′W	W	74,75
Commonburn Ho	Northum	NT9226	55°31·9′	2°7·2′W	X	74,75
Common Bychan	Powys	SO1835	52°0·7′	3°11·3′W	X	161
Common Carr Fm	Ches	SJ8378	53°18·2′	2°14·9′W	FM	118
Common Cefn-llwyn	Monm	ST3394	51°38·7′	2°57·7′W	T	171
Common Church Fm	Carm	SN2210	51°45·9′	4°34·4′W	FM	158
Common Cliff	Swan	SS4485	51°32·8′	4°14·6′W	X	159
Commondale	N Yks	NZ6610	54°29·1′	0°58·5′W	T	94
Commondale Moor	N Yks	NZ6411	54°29·7′	1°0·3′W	X	94
Commondale Moor	N Yks	NZ6608	54°28·0′	0°58·5′W	X	94
Commondyke Fm	E Ayr	NS5722	55°28·5′	4°15·3′W	FM	71
Common Edge	Lancs	SD3232	53°47·0′	3°1·5′W	T	102
Commonedge Hill	Clackm	NN9801	56°11·7′	3°38·2′W	H	58
Common End	Cumbr	NY0022	54°35·2′	3°32·4′W	T	89
Common End	Derby	SK4364	53°10·5′	1°21·0′W	T	120
Common End	Norf	TF9225	52°47·5′	0°51·3′E	X	132
Common End	Norf	TF9930	52°50·1′	0°57·7′E	X	132
Common End Fm	N Yks	SE6633	53°47·6′	0°59·5′W	FM	105,106
Common Fell	Cumbr	NY3820	54°34·5′	2°57·1′W	X	90
Common Fields	Glos	SO7125	51°55·6′	2°24·9′W	X	162
Commonflat	Northum	NU1425	55°31·4′	1°46·3′W	X	75
Common Fm	Beds	SP9739	52°2·7′	0°34·7′W	FM	153
Common Fm	Beds	TL2646	52°6·1′	0°9·2′W	FM	153
Common Fm	Cambs	TL2484	52°26·6′	0°10·1′W	FM	142
Common Fm	Cambs	TL2856	52°11·5′	0°7·2′W	FM	153
Common Fm	Cambs	TL3061	52°14·1′	0°5·4′W	FM	153
Common Fm	Cambs	TL3858	52°12·4′	0°1·6′E	FM	154
Common Fm	Cambs	TL4980	52°24·1′	0°11·8′E	FM	143
Common Fm	Ches	SJ5167	53°12·1′	2°43·6′W	FM	117
Common Fm	Ches	SJ5355	53°5·7′	2°41·7′W	FM	117
Common Fm	Ches	SJ6068	53°12·7′	2°35·5′W	FM	118
Common Fm	Ches	SJ7078	53°18·1′	2°26·6′W	FM	118
Common Fm	Essex	TQ7096	51°38·4′	0°27·8′E	FM	167
Common Fm	E Yorks	SE7252	53°57·8′	0°53·7′W	FM	105,106
Common Fm	E Yorks	SE7836	53°49·1′	0°48·5′W	FM	105,106
Common Fm	E Yorks	SE8243	53°52·8′	0°44·7′W	FM	106
Common Fm	E Yorks	SE8632	53°46·9′	0°41·3′W	FM	106
Common Fm	E Yorks	TA0351	53°56·9′	0°25·4′W	FM	107
Common Fm	Hants	SU6129	51°3·7′	1°7·4′W	FM	185
Common Fm	Heref	SO5960	52°14·4′	2°35·6′W	FM	137,138,149
Common Fm	Leic	SK6222	52°47·8′	1°4·4′W	FM	129
Common Fm	Lincs	TF4153	53°3·6′	0°6·6′E	FM	122
Common Fm	Lincs	TF4523	52°47·3′	0°9·4′E	FM	131
Common Fm	Mil Key	SP8038	52°2·3′	0°49·6′W	FM	152
Common Fm	Monm	SO4909	51°46·9′	2°44·0′W	FM	162
Common Fm	Monm	SO5108	51°46·3′	2°42·2′W	FM	162
Common Fm	N Lincs	SE7709	53°34·6′	0°49·8′W	FM	112
Common Fm	Norf	TG0029	52°49·5′	0°58·5′E	FM	133
Common Fm	Norf	TG4717	52°41·9′	1°39·7′E	FM	134
Common Fm	Norf	TM1294	52°30·4′	1°7·8′E	FM	144
Common Fm	Notts	SK7765	53°10·8′	0°50·5′W	FM	120
Common Fm	N Yks	SE6642	53°52·4′	0°59·4′W	FM	105,106
Common Fm	Oxon	SU3089	51°36·2′	1°33·6′W	FM	174
Common Fm	Roth	SK5086	53°22·3′	1°14·5′W	FM	111,120
Common Fm	Shrops	SJ7605	52°38·8′	2°20·9′W	FM	127
Common Fm	Shrops	SO4992	52°31·6′	2°44·7′W	FM	137,138
Common Fm	Shrops	SO7498	52°35·0′	2°22·6′W	FM	138
Common Fm	Suff	TM1667	52°15·7′	1°10·3′E	FM	156
Common Fm	Suff	TM3259	52°11·0′	1°24·0′E	FM	156
Common Fm	Swin	SU1381	51°31·9′	1°48·4′W	FM	173
Common Fm	Swin	SU2193	51°38·4′	1°41·4′W	FM	163,174
Common Fm	Warw	SP0866	52°17·8′	1°52·6′W	FM	150
Common Fm	W Berks	SU4776	51°29·1′	1°19·0′W	FM	174
Common Fm	Wilts	SU2522	51°0·0′	1°38·2′W	FM	184
Common Fm	Worcs	SO7942	52°4·8′	2°18·0′W	FM	150
Common Fm	Worcs	SO8880	52°25·3′	2°10·2′W	FM	139
Common Fm	Wrekin	SJ6722	52°47·9′	2°29·0′W	FM	127
Common Fms	E Yorks	SE8929	53°45·2′	0°38·6′W	FM	106
Common Grove	Glos	SO5816	51°50·7′	2°36·2′W	X	162
Common Hall	N Yks	SE4978	54°12·0′	1°14·5′W	X	100
Commonhead	S Ayr	NS3612	55°22·7′	4°34·9′W	X	70
Common Hill	Heref	SO5834	52°0·4′	2°36·3′W	T	149
Common Hill	Norf	TG0738	52°54·2′	1°5·1′E	X	133
Common Hill	Pth & Kin	NN9404	56°13·3′	3°42·1′W	X	58
Common Hill	S Lanak	NS7930	55°33·2′	3°54·7′W	H	71
Common Hill	S Lanak	NS8222	55°28·9′	3°51·6′W	H	71,72
Common Hill	Wilts	ST8474	51°28·1′	2°13·4′W	X	173
Common Hill	Wilts	SU0893	51°38·4′	1°52·7′W	H	163,173
Commonhill Wood	Bucks	SU7594	51°38·6′	0°54·6′W	F	175
Common Ho	Cumbr	NY5147	54°49·2′	2°45·3′W	X	86
Common Ho	Cumbr	NY6367	55°0·0′	2°34·3′W	X	86
Common Ho	Northum	NY7364	54°58·4′	2°24·9′W	X	86,87
Common Ho	N Yks	SE6427	53°44·4′	1°1·4′W	X	105,106
Common Ho	Surrey	TQ0135	51°6·5′	0°33·0′W	X	186
Common Lane Fm	Somer	ST7121	50°59·5′	2°24·4′W	FM	183
Common Lane Fm	Staffs	SK1315	52°44·2′	1°48·0′W	FM	128
Common Law	Scot Bord	NT0732	55°34·6′	3°28·1′W	H	72
Common Law	Scot Bord	NT1218	55°27·1′	3°23·1′W	X	78
Common Ley's FM	Bucks	SP7215	51°50·0′	0°56·9′W	X	165
Common Lode	Norf	TF5704	52°36·9′	0°19·5′E	W	143
Commonmire	Cumbr	SD5385	54°15·8′	2°42·9′W	X	97
Common Moor	Corn	SX2469	50°29·9′	4°28·5′W	T	201
Common Moor	Devon	SS3601	50°47·4′	4°19·2′W	X	190
Common Moor	Devon	SS3717	50°56·0′	4°18·8′W	X	190
Common Moor	Devon	SX6399	50°46·7′	3°56·2′W	X	191
Common Moor	N Yks	SE6859	54°1·6′	0°57·3′W	X	105,106
Common Moor	Somer	ST5040	51°9·7′	2°42·5′W	X	182,183
Common Moors	Devon	SS7026	51°1·4′	3°50·8′W	X	180
Common Moss	Cumbr	NY1447	54°48·9′	3°19·9′W	X	85
Common of Dunning	Pth & Kin	NO0109	56°16·0′	3°35·5′W	X	58
Common of Kirk	Orkney	ND4588	58°46·8′	2°56·6′W	X	7
Common Park	D & G	NX4540	54°44·1′	4°24·0′W	X	83
Common Plantation	E Loth	NT6170	55°55·5′	2°37·0′W	F	67
Common Plantation	Wilts	SU1927	51°2·8′	1°43·4′W	F	184
Common Plantn	N Lincs	SE9412	53°36·0′	0°34·4′W	F	112
Common Plantn	Norf	TG1838	52°53·9′	1°14·9′E	F	133
Common Plantn	Northum	NT8742	55°40·5′	2°12·0′W	F	74
Common Platt	Wilts	SU1086	51°34·6′	1°51·0′W	T	173
Common Rocks	Fife	NT2185	56°3·3′	3°15·7′W	X	66
Commons Fm	E Yorks	SE6920	53°40·6′	0°56·9′W	FM	105,106
Commons Fm	Northnts	SP7785	52°27·7′	0°51·6′W	FM	141
Commons Gate	Devon	SX3297	50°45·1′	4°22·5′W	X	190
Commonside	Ches	SJ5473	53°15·4′	2°41·0′W	T	117
Common Side	Ches	SJ5867	53°12·1′	2°37·3′W	T	117
Commonside	Derby	SK2442	52°58·7′	1°38·1′W	T	119,128
Common Side	Derby	SK3375	53°16·5′	1°29·9′W	T	119
Common Side	Derby	SK4346	53°0·8′	1°21·1′W	T	129
Commonside	Notts	SK4658	53°7·3′	1°18·4′W	T	120
Commonside	S Ayr	NS4124	55°29·3′	4°30·6′W	X	70
Commonside	Scot Bord	NT4207	55°21·5′	2°54·5′W	X	79
Commonside	Scot Bord	NT7357	55°48·6′	2°25·4′W	X	67,74
Commonside	Staffs	SJ9842	52°58·8′	2°1·4′W	X	118
Commonside Fm	Halton	SJ5982	53°20·2′	2°36·5′W	FM	108
Commonside Fm	N Yks	SE6329	53°45·5′	1°2·3′W	FM	105,106
Commonside Fm	N Yks	SE6535	53°48·7′	1°0·4′W	FM	105,106
Commonside Moor	Scot Bord	NT4108	55°22·0′	2°55·4′W	X	79
Common Stell	N Yks	SE3192	54°19·6′	1°31·0′W	W	99
Commons, The	Ches	SJ5267	53°12·1′	2°42·7′W	X	117
Commons Wood Fm	E Susx	TQ8222	50°58·3′	0°35·9′E	FM	199
Common, The	Cambs	TL6250	52°7·7′	0°22·4′E	X	154
Common,The	Cumbr	SD4299	54°23·2′	2°53·2′W	X	96,97
Common, The	Fife	NO2102	56°12·5′	3°16·0′W	F	58
Common, The	Fife	NO2102	56°12·5′	3°16·0′W	X	58
Common, The	Hants	SU4347	51°13·5′	1°22·7′W	X	185
Common, The	Herts	TL4524	51°54·0′	0°6·8′E	X	167
Common, The	Kent	TQ6350	51°13·8′	0°20·5′E	X	188
Common, The	Norf	TG0810	52°39·1′	1°4·9′E	X	133
Common, The	Norf	TM0990	52°28·3′	1°5·0′E	X	144
Common, The	N Yks	SE2985	54°15·8′	1°32·9′W	X	99
Common,The	N Yks	SE5964	54°4·4′	1°5·5′W	X	100
Common, The	Oxon	SP2927	51°56·7′	1°34·3′W	X	164
Common, The	Scot Bord	NT3339	55°38·6′	3°3·4′W	X	73
Common, The	Suff	TL8671	52°18·6′	0°44·1′E	X	144,155
Common, The	Suff	TM1248	52°5·6′	1°6·1′E	T	155
Common, The	Suff	TM1248	52°5·6′	1°6·1′E	T	155,169
Common, The	Swan	SS5092	51°36·7′	4°9·6′W	T	159
Common, The	Wilts	SU2432	51°5·4′	1°39·1′W	T	184
Commonty	Aberd	NJ8648	57°31·6′	2°13·6′W	X	30
Commonty	Aberd	NJ9632	57°23·0′	2°3·5′W	X	30
Commonwealth Pool	C of Edin	NT2672	55°56·4′	3°10·6′W	X	66
Common Wood	Bucks	SU8595	51°39·1′	0°45·9′W	F	165
Common Wood	Bucks	SU9194	51°38·5′	0°40·7′W	F	175
Common Wood	E Yorks	SE8131	53°46·4′	0°45·8′W	F	106
Commonwood	Herts	TL0400	51°41·6′	0°29·3′W	T	166
Common Wood	N Yks	SE6440	53°51·4′	1°1·2′W	F	105,106
Common Wood	Oxon	SU6580	51°31·1′	1°3·4′W	F	175
Commonwood	Shrops	SJ4828	52°51·1′	2°45·9′W	T	126
Commonwood	Wrex	SJ3853	53°4·5′	2°55·1′W	T	117
Commonwood Fm	Wilts	ST8584	51°33·5′	2°12·6′W	FM	173
Common-y-coed	Monm	ST4389	51°36·1′	2°49·0′W	T	171,172
Commore	E Renf	NS4654	55°45·5′	4°26·8′W	X	64
Commore Dam	E Renf	NS4654	55°45·5′	4°26·8′W	W	64
Communion Stones	D & G	NX8579	55°5·8′	3°47·7′W	A	84
Community Farm	Stock on T	NZ4922	54°35·7′	1°14·1′W	FM	93
Comogan Fm	Northum	NY8776	55°4·9′	2°11·8′W	FM	87
Comore	Devon	SS7200	50°47·4′	3°48·6′W	X	191
Comp	Kent	TQ6356	51°17·0′	0°20·6′E	T	188
Compact Fm	Dorset	SY9778	50°36·3′	2°2·2′W	FM	195
Compass	Highld	NH4916	57°12·9′	4°29·6′W	X	34
Compass	Somer	ST2933	51°5·7′	3°0·5′W	T	182
Compass Cove	Devon	SX8849	50°20·1′	3°34·0′W	W	202
Compasses	E Susx	TQ7720	50°57·4′	0°31·6′E	X	199
Compasses Corner	W Susx	TQ3236	51°6·7′	0°6·5′W	X	187
Compass Gardens & Saltcoats Park	Essex	TQ8197	51°38·8′	0°37·4′E	X	168
Compass Head	Shetld	HU4009	59°52·1′	1°16·7′W	X	4
Compass Hill	Angus	NO6249	56°38·1′	2°36·7′W	H	54
Compass Hill	Highld	NG2706	57°4·1′	6°29·8′W	H	39
Compass Point	Corn	SS1906	50°49·8′	4°33·8′W	X	190
Compass Slack	Scot Bord	NT4146	55°42·5′	2°55·9′W	X	73
Compass, The	Shetld	HU4009	59°52·1′	1°16·7′W	X	4
Compensation Resr	Inverc	NS2572	55°54·8′	4°47·6′W	W	63
Comp Fm	Kent	TQ6457	51°17·5′	0°21·5′E	FM	188
Comp Fm	Oxon	SU7378	51°30·0′	0°56·5′W	FM	175
Comphouse Fm	Hants	SU6408	50°52·3′	1°5·0′W	FM	196
Comphurst	E Susx	TQ6411	50°52·7′	0°20·3′E	X	199
Compstall	Stock	SJ9690	53°24·6′	2°3·2′W	T	109
Compstonend	D & G	NX6652	54°50·9′	4°4·8′W	X	83,84
Comp, The	E Susx	TQ4901	50°47·6′	0°7·2′E	X	199
Compton	C of Plym	SX4956	50°23·3′	4°7·1′W	T	201
Compton	Derby	SK1846	53°0·9′	1°43·5′W	T	119,128
Compton	Devon	SX8664	50°28·1′	3°36·0′W	T	202
Compton	Hants	SU3429	51°3·8′	1°30·5′W	T	185
Compton	Hants	SU4625	51°1·6′	1°20·3′W	T	185
Compton	Leeds	SE3944	53°53·7′	1°24·0′W	T	104
Compton	Staffs	SO8284	52°27·5′	2°15·5′W	T	138
Compton	Surrey	SU8546	51°12·6′	0°46·6′W	T	186
Compton	Surrey	SU9546	51°12·5′	0°38·0′W	T	186
Compton	W Berks	SU5280	51°31·2′	1°14·6′W	T	174
Compton	Wilts	SU1352	51°16·3′	1°48·4′W	T	184
Compton	Wolv	SO8898	52°35·0′	2°10·2′W	T	139
Compton	W Susx	SU7714	50°55·4′	0°53·9′W	T	197
Compton Abbas	Dorset	ST8718	50°57·9′	2°10·7′W	T	183
Compton Abdale	Glos	SP0616	51°50·8′	1°54·4′W	T	163
Compton Bassett	Wilts	SU0372	51°27·1′	1°57·0′W	T	173
Compton Bassett Ho	Wilts	SU0371	51°26·5′	1°57·0′W	X	173
Compton Bay	I of W	SZ3684	50°39·5′	1°29·1′W	W	196
Compton Beauchamp	Oxon	SU2887	51°35·1′	1°35·4′W	T	174
Compton Bishop	Somer	ST3955	51°17·7′	2°52·1′W	T	182
Compton Bottom	Oxon	SU2884	51°33·5′	1°35·4′W	X	174
Compton Castle	Somer	ST6425	51°1·6′	2°30·4′W	X	183
Compton Chamberlayne	Wilts	SU0229	51°3·9′	1°57·9′W	T	184
Compton Chine	I of W	SZ3685	50°40·0′	1°29·1′W	X	196
Compton Common	Bath & NE Somer	ST6463	51°22·1′	2°30·6′W	T	172
Compton Common	Surrey	SU9646	51°12·5′	0°37·2′W	X	186
Compton Dando	Bath & NE Somer	ST6464	51°22·7′	2°30·6′W	T	172
Compton Down	Dorset	ST8819	50°58·4′	2°9·9′W	H	183
Compton Down	Hants	SU4626	51°2·1′	1°20·2′W	X	185
Compton Down	I of W	SZ3785	50°40·0′	1°28·2′W	X	196
Compton Down	Wilts	SU0227	51°2·8′	1°57·9′W	X	184
Compton Down	Wilts	SU1051	51°15·7′	1°51·0′W	X	184
Compton Down	W Susx	SU7614	50°55·5′	0°54·7′W	H	197
Compton Downs	W Berks	SU5080	51°31·2′	1°16·4′W	X	174
Compton Downs	W Berks	SU5082	51°32·3′	1°16·4′W	X	174
Compton Dundon	Somer	ST4933	51°5·9′	2°43·3′W	T	182,183
Compton Durville	Somer	ST4117	50°57·2′	2°50·0′W	T	193
Compton End	Hants	SU4625	51°1·6′	1°20·3′W	T	185
Compton Fm	Glos	SP0716	51°50·8′	1°53·5′W	FM	163
Compton Fm	I of W	SZ3785	50°40·0′	1°28·2′W	FM	196
Compton Fm	Warw	SP3242	52°4·8′	1°31·6′W	FM	151
Compton Green	Glos	SO7328	51°57·2′	2°23·2′W	T	150
Compton Greenfield	S Glos	ST5681	51°31·8′	2°37·7′W	T	172
Compton Grove	Glos	SP0516	51°50·8′	1°55·3′W	F	163
Compton Grove	Leeds	SE3944	53°53·7′	1°24·0′W	X	104
Compton Hall	Norf	TF8635	52°53·0′	0°46·3′E	X	132
Compton Hill	Somer	ST3956	51°18·2′	2°52·1′W	H	182
Compton Hill	Wilts	SU0472	51°27·1′	1°56·2′W	X	173
Compton House	Oxon	SU2886	51°34·6′	1°35·4′W	A	174
Compton Manor	Hants	SU3429	51°3·8′	1°30·5′W	X	185
Compton Marsh Fm	Oxon	SU2787	51°35·1′	1°36·2′W	FM	174
Compton Martin	Bath & NE Somer	ST5457	51°18·8′	2°39·2′W	T	172,182
Compton Park	Wilts	SU0230	51°4·4′	1°57·9′W	A	184
Compton Park Fm	Staffs	SO8083	52°26·9′	2°17·3′W	FM	138
Compton Pauncefoot	Somer	ST6426	51°2·2′	2°30·4′W	T	183
Compton Pike	Warw	SP3241	52°4·2′	1°31·6′W	A	151
Compton Place	E Susx	TV6098	50°45·8′	0°16·5′E	X	199
Compton Pool	Devon	SX8665	50°28·7′	3°36·0′W	X	202
Comptons	E Susx	TQ5933	51°4·7′	0°16·6′E	X	188
Compton Scorpion Manor	Warw	SP2140	52°3·7′	1°41·2′W	X	151
Compton Valence	Dorset	SY5993	50°44·3′	2°34·5′W	T	194
Compton Verney	Warw	SP3152	52°10·2′	1°32·4′W	X	151
Compton Wood	Bath & NE Somer	ST5356	51°18·3′	2°40·1′W	F	172,182
Compton Wood	Glos	SP0514	51°49·7′	1°55·3′W	F	163
Compton Wood	Wilts	SU0130	51°4·4′	1°58·8′W	F	184
Compton Wynyates	Warw	SP3341	52°4·2′	1°30·7′W	A	151
Comrie	Fife	NT0289	56°5·3′	3°34·1′W	T	65
Comrie	Highld	NH4155	57°33·7′	4°39·0′W	X	26

Comrie	Pth & Kin	NN7722	56°22·7'	3°59·1'W	T	51,52
Comrie Burn	Fife	NT0089	56°5·3'	3°36·0'W	W	65
Comrie Castle	Pth & Kin	NN7848	56°36·7'	3°58·8'W	A	51,52
Comrie Fm	Pth & Kin	NN7748	56°36·7'	3°59·8'W	FM	51,52
Comrie Ho	Durham	NZ1536	54°43·4'	1°45·6'W	X	92
Comyns Fm	Warw	SP1958	52°13·4'	1°42·9'W	FM	151
Conachair	N Eil	NA0900	57°49·4'	8°34·8'W	H	18
Conachcraig	Aberd	NO2887	56°58·4'	3°10·6'W	H	44
Cona Chreag	Highld	NC0929	58°12·8'	5°14·6'W	H	15
Conachreag	Highld	ND0531	58°15·7'	3°36·7'W	H	11,17
Cona 'chreag nan Clach	Highld	NH5788	57°51·8'	4°24·2'W	X	21
Conaga Dingle	Pemb	SN0312	51°46·6'	4°51·0'W	X	157,158
Cona Ghleann	Arg & Bt	NS2898	56°8·9'	4°45·7'W	X	56
Conagleann	Highld	NH5820	57°15·2'	4°20·8'W	X	26,35
Cona Glen	Highld	NM9372	56°47·9'	5°22·9'W	X	40
Cona Glen	Highld	NN0069	56°46·4'	5°15·9'W	X	41
Conaglen Ho	Highld	NN0269	56°46·5'	5°14·0'W	X	41
Conamheall	Highld	NC3651	58°25·3'	4°48·0'W	H	9
Cona Mheall	Highld	NH2781	57°47·4'	4°54·1'W	H	20
Conanby	Roth	SK4998	53°28·8'	1°15·3'W	T	111
Conan Ho	Highld	NH5353	57°32·9'	4°26·9'W	X	26
Cona River	Highld	NM9372	56°47·9'	5°22·9'W	W	40
Conarst	Arg & Bt	NM3119	56°17·5'	6°20·4'W	X	48
Conbhar	Pth & Kin	NN8261	56°43·8'	3°55·3'W	H	43
Conce Moor	Corn	SX0461	50°25·2'	4°45·2'W	X	200
Conchieton	D & G	NX6353	54°51·4'	4°7·6'W	X	83
Conchra	Arg & Bt	NS0288	56°2·9'	5°10·3'W	T	55
Conchra	Highld	NG8827	57°17·3'	5°30·6'W	X	33
Conchra Fm	W Dunb	NS4584	56°1·7'	4°28·8'W	FM	64
Concle Bank	Cumbr	SD2265	54°4·7'	3°11·1'W	X	96
Concord	Sund	NZ3057	54°54·7'	1°31·5'W	T	88
Concord Ho	Bucks	SP8806	51°45·0'	0°43·1'W	X	165
Concord Park	Sheff	SK3792	53°25·6'	1°26·2'W	X	110,111
Concraig	Pth & Kin	NN8519	56°21·2'	3°51·2'W	X	58
Concraigs	Aberd	NK0161	57°38·6'	1°58·5'W	X	30
Condate (Northwich)	Ches	SJ6573	53°15·4'	2°31·1'W	R	118
Condercvm (Roman Fort)	N upon Ty	NZ2164	54°58·5'	1°39·9'W	R	88
Conder Green	Lancs	SD4655	53°59·5'	2°49·0'W	T	102
Conder Head	Lancs	SD5560	54°2·3'	2°40·8'W	X	97
Conderside Fm	Lancs	SD5058	54°1·2'	2°45·4'W	FM	102
Conderton	Worcs	SO9637	52°2·1'	2°3·1'W	T	150
Conderton Hill	Worcs	SO9638	52°2·7'	2°3·1'W	X	150
Condicote	Glos	SP1528	51°57·3'	1°46·5'W	T	163
Condie Wood	Pth & Kin	NO0713	56°18·3'	3°29·7'W	F	58
Condolden Barrow	Corn	SX0987	50°39·3'	4°41·8'W	A	190,200
Condolden Fm	Corn	SX0986	50°38·8'	4°41·7'W	FM	200
Condorrat	N Lanak	NS7373	55°56·3'	4°1·6'W	T	64
Condover	Shrops	SJ4906	52°39·2'	2°44·8'W	T	126
Condover Hall	Shrops	SJ4905	52°38·7'	2°44·8'W	A	126
Condover Park	Shrops	SJ4905	52°38·7'	2°44·8'W	X	126
Conduit Fm	Essex	TL9520	51°50·9'	0°50·3'E	FM	168
Conduit Fm	Surrey	SU9748	51°13·6'	0°36·3'W	FM	186
Conduit Hill	Bucks	SP7521	51°53·2'	0°54·2'W	X	165
Conduit House	Oxon	SP4905	51°44·7'	1°17·0'W	X	164
Conduit, The	Norf	TM0884	52°25·1'	1°3·9'E	A	144
Conduit Wood	Kent	TR0455	51°15·7'	0°55·8'E	F	178,179
Condurrow	Corn	SW7725	50°5·2'	5°6·7'W	X	204
Conegar Hill	Dorset	SY3795	50°45·3'	2°53·2'W	H	193
Conery	Shrops	SO3387	52°28·8'	2°58·8'W	X	137
Conery, The	Wrex	SJ4938	52°56·5'	2°45·1'W	X	126
Conesby Fm	N Lincs	SE8913	53°36·6'	0°38·9'W	FM	112
Coneyburrow Hill	Worcs	SO8337	52°2·1'	2°14·5'W	X	150
Coneybury	Worcs	SO6872	52°20·9'	2°27·8'W	X	138
Coneybury Hill	Northnts	SP6967	52°18·0'	0°58·9'W	X	152
Coney Byes Fm	Essex	TL9529	51°55·7'	0°50·6'E	FM	168
Coney Close	Kent	TR2867	51°21·6'	1°16·9'E	X	179
Coney Copse	W Berks	SU3372	51°27·0'	1°31·1'W	F	174
Coneygar	Dorset	SY4693	50°44·3'	2°45·5'W	T	193
Coneygar Fm	Glos	SP1305	51°44·8'	1°48·3'W	FM	163
Coney Garth	Cumbr	NY6825	54°37·4'	2°29·3'W	X	91
Coney Garth	N Lincs	SE7600	53°29·7'	0°50·9'W	X	112
Coney Garth	Northum	NZ2487	55°10·8'	1°37·0'W	X	81
Coney Garth	N Yks	SD7961	54°2·9'	2°18·8'W	X	98
Coney Garth	N Yks	SE3458	54°1·3'	1°28·4'W	X	104
Coneygarth Hill Fm	E Yorks	TA0951	53°56·9'	0°19·9'W	FM	107
Coney Garth Ho	Lincs	TF3727	52°49·6'	0°2·4'E	X	131
Coneygar Wood	Glos	SP1204	51°44·3'	1°49·2'W	F	163
Coney Greave	Staffs	SJ8040	52°57·7'	2°17·5'W	X	118
Coneygreave	Staffs	SJ9940	52°57·7'	2°0·5'W	X	118
Coneygreave Fm	Derby	SK3051	53°3·6'	1°32·7'W	FM	119
Coneygreaves Fm	Ches	SJ6066	53°11·6'	2°35·5'W	FM	118
Coney Green	Notts	SK8260	53°8·1'	0°46·0'W	X	121
Coney Green Fm	Derby	SK4063	53°10·0'	1°23·7'W	FM	120
Coneygree Wood	Heref	SO7237	52°2·1'	2°24·1'W	F	149
Coneygre Fm	Notts	SK7047	53°1·2'	0°57·0'W	FM	129
Coneygre Fm	Oxon	SP5829	51°57·6'	1°9·0'W	FM	164
Coneygrey Fm	Derby	SK3853	53°4·6'	1°25·6'W	FM	119
Coneygrey Fm	Notts	SK4748	53°1·9'	1°17·5'W	FM	129
Coney Hall	Brom	TQ3964	51°21·7'	0°0·2'E	T	177,187
Coney Hall	Essex	TR0096	51°37·9'	0°53·8'E	X	168
Coneyhatch	Aberd	NO8789	56°59·8'	2°12·4'W	X	45
Coney Hill	Glos	SO8517	51°51·3'	2°12·7'W	T	162
Coney Hill	Norf	TG0220	52°44·6'	1°0·0'E	X	133
Coney Hill	Suff	TM4767	52°15·0'	1°37·5'E	X	156
Coney Hill	Suff	TM5183	52°23·5'	1°41·7'E	X	156
Coney Hill Fm	Bucks	SP7615	51°49·9'	0°53·4'W	FM	165
Coneyhurst	W Susx	TQ1023	51°0·0'	0°25·6'W	T	198
Coney Lodge	Kent	TQ6661	51°19·7'	0°23·4'E	X	177,178,188
Coney Lodge Fm	Leeds	SE2241	53°52·1'	1°39·5'W	FM	104
Coney's Castle	Dorset	SY3797	50°46·4'	2°53·2'W	X	193
Coney's Castle (Fort)	Dorset	SY3797	50°46·4'	2°53·2'W	A	193
Coney Seat Hill	N Yks	NY9508	54°28·3'	2°4·2'W	H	91,92
Coneyside Ho	Cumbr	NX9809	54°28·2'	3°34·0'W	X	89
Coneysthorpe	N Yks	SE7171	54°8·0'	0°54·4'W	T	100
Coneysthorpe Banks Wood	N Yks	SE7172	54°8·6'	0°54·4'W	X	100
Coneythorpe	N Yks	SE3958	54°1·2'	1°23·9'W	T	104
Coney Weston	Suff	TL9578	52°22·1'	0°52·3'E	T	144
Coneywood Fen	Cambs	TL3992	52°30·7'	0°3·3'E	X	142,143
Conford	Hants	SU8232	51°5·1'	0°49·4'W	T	186

Confunderland	Aberd	NJ5109	57°10·4'	2°48·2'W	X	37
Congalton	Aberd	NJ7029	57°21·3'	2°29·5'W	X	38
Congalton Cotts	E Loth	NT5481	56°1·4'	2°43·8'W	X	66
Congalton Gardens	E Loth	NT5480	56°0·9'	2°43·8'W	X	66
Congalton Mains	E Loth	NT5480	56°0·9'	2°43·8'W	X	66
Congash	Highld	NJ0526	57°19·1'	3°34·2'W	X	36
Cong Burn	Durham	NZ2349	54°50·4'	1°38·1'W	W	88
Congburn Br	Durham	NZ2349	54°50·4'	1°38·1'W	X	88
Congdon's Shop	Corn	SX2778	50°34·8'	4°26·2'W	T	201
Congearaidh	Highld	NG2105	57°3·4'	6°35·6'W	X	39
Congeith	D & G	NX8765	54°58·3'	3°45·5'W	X	84
Congelow	Kent	TQ6949	51°13·1'	0°25·6'E	T	188
Conger Hill	Beds	TL0128	51°56·7'	0°31·4'W	A	166
Conger Rocks	Devon	SY0079	50°36·4'	3°24·4'W	X	192
Congerstone	Leic	SK3605	52°38·7'	1°27·7'W	T	140
Conger Stones	Cumbr	SD2563	54°3·7'	3°8·3'W	X	96
Congesquoy	Orkney	HY2710	58°58·5'	3°15·7'W	X	6
Congham	Norf	TF7123	52°46·9'	0°32·5'E	T	132
Congham Hall	Norf	TF7122	52°46·3'	0°32·5'E	X	132
Congham Heath	Norf	TF7322	52°46·3'	0°34·3'E	F	132
Congham Ho	Norf	TF7223	52°46·9'	0°33·4'E	X	132
Congham Lodge	Norf	TF7124	52°47·4'	0°32·6'E	X	132
Conghurst Fm	Kent	TQ7628	51°1·7'	0°31·0'E	FM	188,199
Conglas	Aberd	NJ7523	57°18·1'	2°24·4'W	X	38
Conglass Water	Moray	NJ1916	57°13·9'	3°20·0'W	W	36
Congleton	Ches	SJ8663	53°10·1'	2°12·2'W	T	118
Congleton Edge	Ches	SJ8760	53°8·5'	2°11·3'W	T	118
Congl-y-cae	Gwyn	SH2133	52°52·1'	4°39·2'W	X	123
Congl-y-wal	Gwyn	SH7044	52°58·9'	3°55·8'W	T	124
Congraigie	Pth & Kin	NO1044	56°35·0'	3°27·5'W	X	53
Congreave	Derby	SK2465	53°11·1'	1°38·0'W	X	119
Congresbury	N Som	ST4363	51°22·0'	2°48·7'W	T	172,182
Congresbury Moor	N Som	ST4364	51°22·6'	2°48·8'W	X	172,182
Congresbury Yeo	N Som	ST4861	51°21·0'	2°44·4'W	W	172,182
Congreve	Staffs	SJ9013	52°43·1'	2°8·5'W	T	127
Congrie Hill	Scot Bord	NT0729	55°33·0'	3°28·0'W	H	72
Conham	S Glos	ST6372	51°27·0'	2°31·6'W	T	172
Conheath	D & G	NX9969	55°0·6'	3°34·3'W	X	84
Conheath	Northum	NY8584	55°9·3'	2°13·7'W	X	80
Conheath Burn	Northum	NY8584	55°9·3'	2°13·7'W	W	80
Conhess	D & G	NY2778	55°5·7'	3°8·2'W	X	85
Conholt Hill	Wilts	SU3255	51°17·8'	1°32·1'W	X	174,185
Conholt Ho	Wilts	SU3255	51°17·8'	1°32·1'W	X	174,185
Conholt Park	Wilts	SU3254	51°17·3'	1°32·1'W	X	185
Conicavel	Moray	NH9953	57°33·6'	3°40·8'W	T	27
Conichan	Pth & Kin	NN8432	56°28·2'	3°52·5'W	X	52
Conic Hill	Stir	NS4392	56°6·0'	4°31·0'W	H	56
Coniecleugh	Aberd	NJ5443	57°28·8'	2°45·6'W	X	29
Conie Glen	Arg & Bt	NR6911	55°20·6'	5°38·2'W	X	68
Conieglen Water	Arg & Bt	NR6911	55°20·6'	5°38·2'W	W	68
Conies Dale	Derby	SK1280	53°19·2'	1°48·8'W	X	110
Conies Down Tor	Devon	SX5879	50°35·8'	4°0·0'W	X	191
Conies Fm	Derby	SK1180	53°19·2'	1°49·7'W	FM	110
Conies Fm	W Susx	TQ1923	50°59·9'	0°17·9'W	FM	198
Coniferhill	Norf	TM2484	52°24·7'	1°18·0'E	X	156
Conigar Point	Hants	SU7305	50°50·6'	0°57·4'W	X	197
Coniger, The	Wilts	SU0742	51°10·9'	1°53·6'W	X	184
Coniger, The (Tumuli)	Wilts	SU0742	51°10·9'	1°53·6'W	A	184
Conigree Court	Glos	SO7025	51°55·6'	2°25·8'W	X	162
Conigre Fm	Wilts	ST9871	51°26·5'	2°1·3'W	FM	173
Coning's Birks	N Yks	SE6189	54°17·8'	1°3·3'W	X	94,100
Coningsby	Lincs	TF2258	53°6·5'	0°10·2'W	T	122
Coningsby Airfield	Lincs	TF2256	53°5·5'	0°10·3'W	X	122
Coningsby Moor	Lincs	TF2457	53°6·0'	0°8·5'W	X	122
Conington	Cambs	TL1785	52°27·3'	0°16·3'W	T	142
Conington	Cambs	TL3266	52°16·8'	0°3·5'W	T	153
Conington Fen	Cambs	TL2085	52°27·2'	0°13·6'W	X	142
Conisbrough	Donc	SK5198	53°28·8'	1°13·5'W	T	111
Conisbrough Common	Donc	SK5298	53°28·8'	1°12·6'W	X	111
Conisbrough Lodge	Donc	SK5095	53°27·2'	1°14·4'W	X	111
Conisbrough Parks	Donc	SK5096	53°27·7'	1°14·4'W	X	111
Conisby	Arg & Bt	NR2661	55°46·1'	6°21·7'W	T	60
Coniscliffe Grange	Darl	NZ2515	54°32·0'	1°36·4'W	X	93
Coniser	N Yks	SE5695	54°21·1'	1°7·9'W	X	100
Conishead Priory	Cumbr	SD3075	54°10·2'	3°3·9'W	X	96,97
Conisholme	Lincs	TF4095	53°26·2'	0°6·9'E	T	113
Conisholme Fen	Lincs	TF3793	53°25·2'	0°4·1'E	X	113
Conister or St Mary's Rock	I of M	SC3875	54°9·0'	4°28·4'W	X	95
Coniston	Cumbr	SD3097	54°22·1'	3°4·2'W	T	96,97
Coniston	E Yorks	TA1535	53°48·1'	0°14·8'W	T	107
Coniston Cold	N Yks	SD9055	53°59·7'	2°8·7'W	T	103
Conistone	N Yks	SD9867	54°6·2'	2°1·4'W	T	98
Conistone Moor	N Yks	SE0170	54°7·8'	1°58·7'W	X	98
Coniston Fells	Cumbr	SD2999	54°23·1'	3°5·2'W	X	96,97
Coniston Hall	N Yks	SD8955	53°59·7'	2°9·7'W	X	103
Coniston Moor	Cumbr	SD3099	54°23·1'	3°4·3'W	X	96,97
Coniston Moor	N Yks	SD8855	53°59·7'	2°10·6'W	X	103
Coniston Water	Cumbr	SD3094	54°20·5'	3°4·2'W	W	96,97
Conival	Highld	NC3019	58°7·9'	4°52·8'W	H	15
Conjure Alders	Notts	SK6672	53°14·7'	1°0·2'W	F	120
Conkland Hill	Pemb	SN0217	51°49·2'	4°52·0'W	X	157,158
Conksbury	Derby	SK2065	53°11·1'	1°41·6'W	X	119
Conksbury Village	Derby	SK2165	53°11·1'	1°40·7'W	A	119
Conkwell	Wilts	ST7962	51°21·6'	2°17·7'W	T	172
Conkwell Grange	Wilts	ST7861	51°21·1'	2°18·6'W	X	172
Conkwell Wood	Wilts	ST7861	51°21·1'	2°18·6'W	F	172
Conlach Mhór	Pth & Kin	NN9376	56°52·0'	3°44·9'W	H	43
Conland	Aberd	NJ6043	57°28·8'	2°39·6'W	X	29
Conland	Pth & Kin	NO1411	56°17·3'	3°22·9'W	X	58
Conland Burn	Fife	NO2404	56°13·6'	3°13·1'W	W	59
Conlandmill	Aberd	NJ5943	57°28·8'	2°40·6'W	X	29
Conlan Hill	Pth & Kin	NO0547	56°36·6'	3°32·4'W	H	52,53
Conlawer Hill	Angus	NO4362	56°45·0'	2°55·5'W	H	44
Conmheall	Highld	NC0605	57°59·8'	5°16·5'W	H	15
Connachan	Pth & Kin	NN8827	56°25·6'	3°48·5'W	X	52,58
Connachan Lodge	Pth & Kin	NN8927	56°25·6'	3°47·5'W	X	52,58
Connachat Cottage	Aberd	NO2191	57°0·5'	3°17·6'W	X	44
Connage	Highld	NH7753	57°33·3'	4°2·9'W	X	27
Connage	Highld	NJ0523	57°17·5'	3°34·1'W	X	36
Connage	Moray	NJ4564	57°40·0'	2°54·9'W	X	28,29

Connagedale	Moray	NJ3363	57°39·4'	3°6·9'W	X	28
Connah's Quay	Flint	SJ2969	53°13·0'	3°3·4'W	T	117
Connaught Park	Kent	TR3142	51°8·1'	1°18·5'E	X	179
Connel	Arg & Bt	NM9134	56°27·4'	5°23·1'W	T	49
Connel Airfield	Arg & Bt	NM9035	56°27·9'	5°24·1'W	X	49
Connel Burn	E Ayr	NS5808	55°21·0'	4°13·9'W	W	71,77
Connel Burn	E Ayr	NS6011	55°22·6'	4°12·1'W	W	71
Connelburn Rig	E Ayr	NS5909	55°21·5'	4°13·0'W	X	71,77
Connelbush	D & G	NS7510	55°22·3'	3°57·9'W	X	71,78
Connel Park	E Ayr	NS6012	55°23·2'	4°12·2'W	T	71
Connelston	N Ayr	NS2954	55°45·2'	4°43·1'W	X	63
Connel's Well	D & G	NX7595	55°14·3'	3°57·5'W	X	78
Connetts	Kent	TQ9872	51°25·0'	0°51·2'E	X	178
Conniburrow	Mil Key	SP8539	52°2·8'	0°45·2'W	T	152
Conningbrook Manor	Kent	TR0343	51°9·2'	0°54·6'E	X	179,189
Conninghole	Orkney	HY6939	59°14·5'	2°32·1'W	X	5
Connista	Highld	NG4273	57°40·6'	6°19·2'W	T	23
Conniven	D & G	NX8566	54°58·8'	3°47·4'W	X	84
Connon	Corn	SX1962	50°26·0'	4°32·5'W	T	201
Connor Craigs	E Ayr	NS7019	55°27·1'	4°2·9'W	X	71
Connor Downs	Corn	SW5939	50°12·4'	5°22·3'W	T	203
Connor Hill	E Ayr	NS7120	55°27·7'	4°2·0'W	H	71
Conn's Fm	Beds	SP9340	52°3·3'	0°38·2'W	FM	153
Connypot Beck	Cumbr	NY8020	54°34·7'	2°18·1'W	W	91,92
Conny Tammy Currack	N Yks	SD9594	54°20·7'	2°4·2'W	X	98
Conock	Wilts	SU0657	51°19·0'	1°54·4'W	T	173
Conon	Angus	NO5643	56°34·9'	2°42·5'W	X	54
Cononbank Fm	Highld	NH5444	57°28·0'	4°25·6'W	FM	26
Conon Brae	Highld	NH5454	57°33·4'	4°26·0'W	X	26
Conon Bridge	Highld	NH5455	57°34·0'	4°26·0'W	T	26
Cononish	Stir	NN3028	56°25·1'	4°44·9'W	X	50
Cononley	N Yks	SD9847	53°55·4'	2°1·4'W	T	103
Cononley Moor	N Yks	SD9746	53°54·9'	2°2·3'W	X	103
Cononley Woodside	N Yks	SD9847	53°55·4'	2°1·4'W	T	103
Cononsyth	Angus	NO5646	56°36·5'	2°42·6'W	T	54
Conordan	Highld	NG5038	57°22·1'	6°9·0'W	T	23,24,32
Conostom	N Eil	NB1629	58°9·8'	6°49·3'W	H	13
Conquer Barrow	Dorset	SY7089	50°42·2'	2°25·1'W	A	194
Conquer Downs	Corn	SW4736	50°10·4'	5°32·2'W	X	203
Conquermoor Heath	Wrekin	SJ6719	52°46·3'	2°28·9'W	T	127
Conquest Fm	Cambs	TL2093	52°31·5'	0°13·5'W	FM	142
Conquest Fm	Somer	ST1828	51°3·0'	3°9·8'W	FM	181,193
Conquest Ho	Cambs	TL2193	52°31·5'	0°12·6'W	X	142
Conrhenny	I of M	SC4181	54°12·3'	4°25·9'W	X	95
Conrhenny Plantation	I of M	SC4182	54°12·8'	4°25·9'W	F	95
Conrick	D & G	NS7811	55°22·9'	3°55·1'W	X	71,78
Conrick Hill	D & G	NX7097	55°15·3'	4°2·3'W	X	77
Conrie Water	Aberd	NJ3309	57°10·3'	3°6·0'W	W	37
Conrig Hill	D & G	NS8112	55°23·5'	3°52·3'W	H	71,78
Conrock	Moray	NJ2747	57°30·7'	3°12·6'W	X	28
Consall	Staffs	SJ9848	53°2·0'	2°1·4'W	T	118
Consallforge	Staffs	SJ9949	53°2·5'	2°0·5'W	X	118
Consall Hall	Staffs	SJ9948	53°2·0'	2°0·5'W	X	118
Consall Wood	Staffs	SJ9849	53°2·5'	2°1·4'W	F	118
Consall Wood	Staffs	SJ9947	53°1·5'	2°0·5'W	F	118
Conscience Fm	Kent	TR0439	51°7·1'	0°55·3'E	FM	179,189
Conscience Hill	Lincs	TF3688	53°22·5'	0°3·1'E	X	113,122
Conscleuch Head	Scot Bord	NT2226	55°31·5'	3°13·7'W	H	73
Consett	Durham	NZ0951	54°51·5'	1°51·2'W	T	88
Consett & Sunderland Railway Path	Durham	NZ1953	54°52·5'	1°41·8'W	X	88
Conshield	Northum	NY8575	55°4·4'	2°13·7'W	X	87
Conslum	Arg & Bt	NL9347	56°31·1'	6°59·1'W	X	46
Constable Burton	N Yks	SE1690	54°18·6'	1°44·8'W	T	99
Constable Hill	Scot Bord	NT5754	55°46·9'	2°40·7'W	X	67,73,74
Constable Lee	Lancs	SD8123	53°42·4'	2°16·9'W	T	103
Constablewood	N Ayr	NS2163	55°49·9'	4°51·0'W	X	63
Constant	Cered	SN6564	52°15·7'	3°58·3'W	X	146
Constantia Manor	E Susx	TQ4519	50°57·4'	0°4·3'E	X	198
Constantine	Corn	SW7329	50°7·3'	5°10·2'W	T	204
Constantine Bay	Corn	SW8574	50°31·8'	5°1·6'W	W	200
Constantine Bay	Corn	SW8674	50°31·8'	5°0·8'W	T	200
Constantine Fm	Durham	NZ1733	54°41·7'	1°43·8'W	FM	92
Conster Manor	E Susx	TQ8220	50°57·3'	0°35·9'E	X	199
Constitutional Hill	Suff	TM0142	52°2·6'	0°56·3'E	X	155
Constitution Hill	Cered	SN5882	52°25·3'	4°4·9'W	H	135
Constitution Hill	Norf	TF6317	52°43·8'	0°25·2'E	X	132
Constitution Hill Fm	E Yorks	TA0141	53°51·6'	0°27·4'W	FM	106,107
Contin	Highld	NH4555	57°33·8'	4°35·0'W	T	26
Contin Mains	Highld	NH4655	57°33·8'	4°34·0'W	X	26
Contlach	Aberd	NJ4724	57°18·5'	2°52·3'W	X	37
Contlaw Mains	C of Aber	NJ8302	57°6·8'	2°16·4'W	X	38
Con Tom	Arg & Bt	NR7097	56°6·9'	5°41·5'W	H	55,61
Contrary Head	I of M	SC2282	54°12·4'	4°43·3'W	H	95
Contullich	Highld	NH6370	57°42·2'	4°17·5'W	X	21
Conundrum	Northum	NT9855	55°47·5'	2°1·5'W	X	75
Convalleys	Moray	NJ3037	57°25·3'	3°9·5'W	X	28
Convent of Notre Dame	Surrey	TQ0961	51°20·5'	0°25·7'W	X	176,187
Convent, The	Devon	SX8170	50°31·3'	3°40·3'W	X	202
Convent, The	Wilts	ST7534	51°6·5'	2°21·0'W	X	183
Conveth	Renf	NS3461	55°49·1'	4°38·5'W	X	63
Conveth Mains	Aberd	NO7272	56°50·6'	2°27·1'W	X	45
Convinth	Highld	NH5137	57°24·2'	4°28·3'W	X	26
Conwy	Conwy	SH7777	53°16·8'	3°50·3'W	T	115
Conwy Bay	Conwy	SH7079	53°17·8'	3°56·6'W	W	115
Conwy Castle	Conwy	SH7877	53°16·8'	3°49·4'W	A	115
Conwy Falls	Conwy	SH8053	53°3·9'	3°47·0'W	W	116
Conwy Morfa	Conwy	SH7678	53°17·3'	3°51·2'W	X	115
Conwy Mountain or Mynydd y Dref	Conwy	SH7677	53°16·8'	3°51·2'W	H	115
Conwy Sands	Conwy	SH7680	53°18·4'	3°51·3'W	X	115
Conyar	Orkney	HY3019	59°3·4'	3°12·7'W	X	6
Conyboro	E Susx	TQ4014	50°54·7'	0°1·0'W	X	198
Conyer	Kent	TQ9664	51°20·7'	0°49·3'E	T	178
Conyer Creek	Kent	TQ9565	51°21·3'	0°48·4'E	W	178
Conyer's Green	Suff	TL8867	52°16·4'	0°45·7'E	T	155
Conyers Spring	N Yks	SE1791	54°19·1'	1°43·9'W	X	99
Conygar	Dorset	SY7385	50°40·1'	2°22·5'W	X	194

Conygar Barn	Wilts	ST9737	51°8·2'	2°2·2'W	X	184
Conygar Coppice	Dorset	ST8111	50°54·1'	2°15·8'W	F	194
Conygar Hill	Dorset	SY6988	50°41·7'	2°26·0'W	H	194
Conygar Tower	Somer	SS9944	51°11·4'	3°26·3'W	X	181
Conygre Brook	Bath & NE Somer	ST6861	51°21·1'	2°27·2'W	W	172
Conygree Fm	Glos	SP1411	51°48·1'	1°47·4'W	FM	163
Conygree Fm	Oxon	SP3521	51°53·4'	1°29·1'W	FM	164
Conygre Fm	S Glos	ST6486	51°34·5'	2°30·8'W	FM	172
Conygre Fm	Wilts	SU2161	51°21·1'	1°41·5'W	FM	174
Conyngham Hall	N Yks	SE3457	54°0·7'	1°28·5'W	X	104
Cony Warren	N Yks	SE0657	54°0·8'	1°54·1'W	X	104
Coobe Grove Fm	Cambs	TL3252	52°9·3'	0°3·8'W	FM	153
Cooden	E Susx	TQ7107	50°50·5'	0°26·1'E	T	199
Coodham	S Ayr	NS3932	55°33·6'	4°32·7'W	X	70
Cooil	I of M	SC3476	54°9·4'	4°32·1'W	X	95
Cooilcam	I of M	SC3072	54°7·2'	4°35·7'W	X	95
Cooildarry	I of M	SC3189	54°16·4'	4°35·3'W	X	95
Cooildhoo	I of M	SC3899	54°21·9'	4°29·2'W	X	95
Cooilingel	I of M	SC3179	54°11·0'	4°35·0'W	X	95
Cooil Roi Mansion Ho	I of M	SC4181	54°12·3'	4°25·9'W	X	95
Cooilslieu	I of M	SC3082	54°12·6'	4°36·0'W	X	95
Cookbury	Devon	SS4006	50°50·1'	4°16·0'W	T	190
Cookbury Moor Plantation	Devon	SS3906	50°50·1'	4°16·8'W	F	190
Cookbury Wick	Devon	SS3805	50°49·6'	4°17·6'W	T	190
Cookeridge	Shrops	SO4577	52°23·5'	2°48·1'W	X	137,138,148
Cookham	Win & Maid	SU8985	51°33·6'	0°42·6'W	T	175
Cookham Dean	Win & Maid	SU8684	51°33·1'	0°45·2'W	T	175
Cookhamdean Common	Win & Maid	SU8684	51°33·1'	0°45·2'W	X	175
Cookham Rise	Win & Maid	SU8884	51°33·1'	0°43·5'W	T	175
Cookhill	Worcs	SP0558	52°13·4'	1°55·2'W	T	150
Cook Ho	N Yks	NZ9400	54°23·4'	0°32·7'W	X	94
Cook Ho	N Yks	SD9744	53°53·8'	2°2·3'W	X	103
Cooklaw	Northum	NY9371	55°2·3'	2°6·1'W	T	87
Cookley	Suff	TM3475	52°19·6'	1°26·5'E	X	156
Cookley	Worcs	SO8480	52°25·3'	2°13·7'W	T	138
Cookley Fm	Suff	TM1674	52°19·5'	1°10·6'E	FM	144,156
Cookley Grange	Suff	TM3676	52°20·1'	1°28·3'E	X	156
Cookley Green	Oxon	SU6990	51°36·5'	0°59·8'W	T	175
Cookley Green	Suff	TM3375	52°19·6'	1°25·6'E	X	156
Cookney	Aberd	NO8793	57°1·9'	2°12·4'W	T	38,45
Cookridge	Leeds	SE2540	53°51·6'	1°36·8'W	T	104
Cookridge Hall	Leeds	SE2540	53°51·6'	1°36·8'W	X	104
Cooksbridge	E Susx	TQ4013	50°54·2'	0°0·1'W	T	198
Cook's Bridge	Wrex	SJ3856	53°6·1'	2°55·2'W	X	117
Cook's Cairn	Moray	NJ3027	57°20·0'	3°9·3'W	H	37
Cooks Corner Fm	Oxon	SP4113	51°49·1'	1°23·9'W	FM	164
Cooksey Corner	Worcs	SO9168	52°18·8'	2°7·5'W	T	139
Cooksey Green	Worcs	SO9069	52°19·4'	2°8·4'W	T	139
Cooksey Lodge Fm	Worcs	SO9168	52°18·8'	2°7·5'W	FM	139
Cook's Fm	Dorset	ST7315	50°56·3'	2°22·7'W	FM	183
Cook's Fm	Kent	TR1552	51°13·8'	1°5·2'E	FM	179,189
Cooks Fm	Norf	TG2331	52°50·0'	1°19·0'E	FM	133
Cook's Fm	Somer	ST7336	51°7·6'	2°22·8'W	FM	183
Cooks Fm	Suff	TL8352	52°8·4'	0°40·9'E	FM	155
Cook's Fm	Suff	TL8658	52°11·6'	0°43·7'E	FM	155
Cooksgate	Staffs	SJ7748	53°2·0'	2°20·2'W	X	118
Cook's Grange	N Yks	SE7990	54°18·2'	0°46·7'W	X	94,100
Cook's Green	Essex	TM1818	51°49·3'	1°10·2'E	T	168,169
Cook's Green	Suff	TL9753	52°8·6'	0°53·1'E	T	155
Cook's Green Fm	Worcs	SO7375	52°22·6'	2°23·4'W	FM	138
Cook's Hall	Essex	TL9427	51°54·7'	0°49·6'E	X	168
Cookshall Fm	Bucks	SU8496	51°39·6'	0°46·7'W	FM	165
Cookshayes Fm	Devon	SY2197	50°46·3'	3°6·8'W	FM	192,193
Cookshill	Aberd	NJ4415	57°13·6'	2°55·2'W	X	37
Cook's Hill	Norf	TG2936	52°52·6'	1°24·6'E	X	133
Cookshill	Staffs	SJ9443	52°59·3'	2°5·0'W	T	118
Cook's Ho	Northum	NY9059	54°55·8'	2°8·9'W	X	87
Cook's Hold	Durham	NZ3342	54°46·6'	1°28·8'W	X	88
Cook's Hole	Peterb	TL0599	52°35·0'	0°26·6'W	X	142
Cooksland	Corn	SX0867	50°28·5'	4°42·0'W	T	200
Cooksland	Staffs	SJ8825	52°49·6'	2°10·3'W	X	127
Cook's Lodge	Leic	SP5299	52°35·4'	1°13·5'W	X	140
Cook's Mill	Essex	TL9427	51°54·7'	0°49·6'E	X	168
Cooksmill Green	Essex	TL6306	51°44·0'	0°22·0'E	T	167
Cooksoe Fm	Mil Key	SP9346	52°6·8'	0°38·1'W	FM	153
Cooksongreen	Ches	SJ5774	53°15·9'	2°38·3'W	T	117
Cookson Place	Cumbr	SD0899	54°22·9'	3°24·6'W	X	96
Cookson's Green	Durham	NZ2934	54°42·3'	1°32·6'W	X	93
Cooks Pit Fm	Ches	SJ5852	53°4·1'	2°37·2'W	FM	117
Cookstead	Northum	NT8838	55°38·4'	2°11·0'W	X	74
Cookston	Aberd	NJ9432	57°23·0'	2°5·5'W	X	30
Cookston	Aberd	NO9197	57°4·1'	2°8·5'W	X	38,45
Cookston	Angus	NO3348	56°37·4'	3°5·1'W	X	53
Cookston	Angus	NO5961	56°44·6'	2°39·8'W	X	44
Cookston	Fife	NO5810	56°17·1'	2°40·3'W	X	59
Cookston Fm	Angus	NO3448	56°37·4'	3°4·1'W	FM	54
Cook's Wood	Kent	TQ7637	51°6·5'	0°31·2'E	F	188
Cookwell Brook	Dorset	ST8111	50°54·1'	2°15·8'W	W	194
Cookworthy Buddle	Devon	SS4200	50°46·9'	4°14·1'W	X	190
Cookworthy Moor Plantation	Devon	SS4101	50°47·4'	4°15·0'W	F	190
Cool	N Yks	SD9667	54°6·2'	2°3·3'W	X	98
Coolam	N Yks	SD7856	54°0·2'	2°19·7'W	X	103
Coole Hall Fm	Ches	SJ6545	53°0·3'	2°30·9'W	FM	118
Cooles Fm	Wilts	SU0192	51°37·8'	1°58·7'W	FM	163,173
Coolham	Lancs	SD8143	53°53·2'	2°16·9'W	X	103
Coolham	W Susx	TQ1222	50°59·4'	0°23·9'W	T	198
Coolham Ho	W Susx	TQ1023	51°0·0'	0°25·6'W	X	198
Cool Hill Fm	Leic	SK3401	52°36·6'	1°29·5'W	FM	140
Coolhurst Wood	W Susx	TQ2029	51°3·1'	0°16·9'W	F	187,198
Coolhurst Wood	W Susx	TQ2029	51°3·1'	0°16·9'W	X	187,198
Cooling	Medway	TQ7576	51°27·6'	0°31·5'E	T	178
Cooling Court Fm	Medway	TQ7574	51°26·5'	0°31·5'E	FM	178
Coolinge	Kent	TR2036	51°5·1'	1°8·9'E	T	179,189
Cooling Marshes	Medway	TQ7677	51°28·1'	0°32·4'E	X	178
Cooling Street	Medway	TQ7474	51°26·5'	0°30·6'E	T	178
Coolington Fm	Northnts	SP5845	52°6·2'	1°8·8'W	FM	152
Coolmoor	Shrops	SJ6023	52°48·4'	2°35·2'W	X	127
Cool Oak Br	Brent	TQ2187	51°34·4'	0°14·8'W	X	176
Coo Lochans	D & G	NX5069	54°59·8'	4°20·3'W	W	83
Cools	Orkney	ND4489	58°47·4'	2°57·7'W	X	7
Coomb	Cumbr	NY3132	54°40·9'	3°3·8'W	X	90
Coomb	Pemb	SN0697	51°38·5'	4°47·8'W	X	158
Coomb Burn	D & G	NY1197	55°15·8'	3°23·6'W	W	78
Coomb Burn	Scot Bord	NT2009	55°22·4'	3°15·3'W	W	79
Coomb Cairn	D & G	NT1403	55°19·1'	3°20·9'W	X	78
Coomb (Cheshire Home)	Carm	SN3314	51°48·2'	4°24·9'W	X	159
Coomb Craig	D & G	NT1614	55°25·0'	3°19·2'W	X	79
Coomb Dale	Ches	SJ5054	53°5·1'	2°44·4'W	X	117
Coomb Dod	S Lanak	NT0423	55°29·7'	3°30·7'W	H	72
Coombe	Bucks	SP8406	51°45·0'	0°46·6'W	T	165
Coombe	Corn	SS2011	50°52·5'	4°33·1'W	T	190
Coombe	Corn	SW6242	50°14·0'	5°19·9'W	T	203
Coombe	Corn	SW7641	50°13·8'	5°8·1'W	T	204
Coombe	Corn	SW8340	50°13·4'	5°2·2'W	T	204
Coombe	Corn	SW9551	50°19·6'	4°52·4'W	T	200,204
Coombe	Corn	SX1151	50°20·0'	4°39·0'W	X	200,204
Coombe	Corn	SX2363	50°26·6'	4°29·2'W	T	201
Coombe	Corn	SX3163	50°26·8'	4°22·4'W	X	201
Coombe	Corn	SX3662	50°26·3'	4°18·2'W	X	201
Coombe	Devon	SS4713	50°54·0'	4°10·2'W	X	180
Coombe	Devon	SS4902	50°48·1'	4°8·2'W	X	191
Coombe	Devon	SS5020	50°58·0'	4°7·8'W	X	180
Coombe	Devon	SS6231	51°3·9'	3°57·8'W	X	180
Coombe	Devon	SS6237	51°7·2'	3°57·9'W	X	180
Coombe	Devon	SS6817	50°56·5'	3°52·3'W	X	180
Coombe	Devon	ST7028	51°2·4'	3°50·9'W	X	180
Coombe	Devon	SS8411	50°53·4'	3°38·6'W	X	191
Coombe	Devon	SS8908	50°51·9'	3°34·3'W	X	192
Coombe	Devon	SS9725	51°1·1'	3°27·7'W	X	181
Coombe	Devon	ST0017	50°56·9'	3°25·0'W	T	181
Coombe	Devon	SX3688	50°40·4'	4°18·9'W	X	190
Coombe	Devon	SX3885	50°38·8'	4°17·1'W	X	201
Coombe	Devon	SX4078	50°35·0'	4°15·2'W	X	201
Coombe	Devon	SX5096	50°44·9'	4°7·2'W	X	191
Coombe	Devon	SX5756	50°23·4'	4°0·3'W	X	202
Coombe	Devon	SX6853	50°22·0'	3°51·0'W	X	202
Coombe	Devon	SX6887	50°40·3'	3°51·7'W	X	191
Coombe	Devon	SX7177	50°34·9'	3°49·0'W	X	191
Coombe	Devon	SX7189	50°41·4'	3°49·2'W	X	191
Coombe	Devon	SX7848	50°19·4'	3°42·5'W	X	202
Coombe	Devon	SX8071	50°31·8'	3°41·2'W	X	202
Coombe	Devon	SX8156	50°23·7'	3°40·1'W	X	202
Coombe	Devon	SX8383	50°38·3'	3°38·9'W	X	191
Coombe	Devon	SX9374	50°33·6'	3°30·3'W	T	192
Coombe	Devon	SY1091	50°42·9'	3°16·1'W	T	192,193
Coombe	Dorset	ST5815	50°56·2'	2°35·5'W	X	183
Coombe	Dorset	SY3697	50°46·4'	2°54·1'W	T	193
Coombe	Dorset	SY9787	50°41·2'	2°2·2'W	X	195
Coombe	Glos	ST7694	51°38·9'	2°20·4'W	T	162,172
Coombe	Hants	SU6620	50°58·8'	1°3·2'W	T	185
Coombe	Kent	TR2957	51°16·2'	1°17·4'E	T	179
Coombe	King	TQ2070	51°25·2'	0°16·1'W	T	176
Coombe	Somer	ST2729	51°3·6'	3°2·1'W	T	193
Coombe	Somer	ST4009	50°52·9'	2°50·8'W	T	193
Coombe	Wilts	ST8922	51°0·1'	2°9·0'W	T	184
Coombe	Wilts	SU1450	51°15·2'	1°47·6'W	T	184
Coombe Abbey	Warw	SP4079	52°24·7'	1°24·3'W	A	140
Coombe Bank	Read	SU6974	51°27·9'	1°0·0'W	A	175
Coombe Bank Fm	Red & Cl	NZ6516	54°32·3'	0°59·3'W	FM	94
Coombe Barn Fm	Wilts	ST8036	51°7·6'	2°16·8'W	FM	183
Coombe Barton	Devon	SS5617	50°56·3'	4°2·6'W	A	180
Coombe Barton	Devon	SS8702	50°48·6'	3°35·9'W	X	192
Coombe Bissett	Wilts	SU1026	51°2·2'	1°51·1'W	T	184
Coombe Bissett Down	Wilts	SU1024	51°1·1'	1°51·1'W	X	184
Coombe Bottom	Bucks	SP9617	51°50·8'	0°36·0'W	X	165
Coombe Bottom	Dorset	ST7701	50°48·7'	2°19·2'W	X	194
Coombe Bottom	Dorset	ST8007	50°52·0'	2°16·7'W	X	194
Coombe Bottom	Dorset	ST8511	50°54·1'	2°12·4'W	X	194
Coombe Bottom	Dorset	SY7097	50°46·5'	2°25·1'W	X	194
Coombe Bottom	Dorset	SY9678	50°36·3'	2°3·0'W	X	195
Coombe Brook	Oxon	SP2314	51°49·7'	1°39·6'W	W	163
Coombe Cellars	Devon	SX9072	50°32·5'	3°32·8'W	X	192,202
Coombe Cott	Wilts	SU1056	51°18·4'	1°51·0'W	X	173
Coombe Countryside Park	Warw	SP3979	52°24·7'	1°25·2'W	X	140
Coombe Court	Devon	SX7587	50°40·4'	3°45·8'W	X	191
Coombe Cross	Hants	SU6620	50°58·8'	1°3·2'W	X	185
Coombe Cross	Somer	ST0837	51°7·7'	3°18·5'W	X	181
Coomb Edge	Scot Bord	NT5901	55°18·3'	2°38·3'W	H	80
Coombe Dingle	C of Bris	ST5577	51°29·6'	2°38·5'W	T	172
Coombe Down	Devon	SX7082	50°37·6'	3°49·9'W	H	191
Coombe Down	Wilts	SU1852	51°16·2'	1°44·1'W	X	184
Coombe Down	Wilts	SU1874	51°28·1'	1°44·1'W	H	173
Coombe Down Hill	Dorset	ST4800	50°48·1'	2°43·9'W	H	193
Coombe Eden	Cumbr	NY4945	54°48·1'	2°47·2'W	X	86
Coombe End	Somer	ST0229	51°3·4'	3°23·5'W	X	181
Coombe End Fm	Oxon	SU6279	51°30·6'	1°6·0'W	FM	175
Coombe Fields Fm	Warw	SP4381	52°25·8'	1°21·7'W	FM	140
Coombe Fm	Bri & Hov	TQ3903	50°48·8'	0°1·2'W	FM	198
Coombe Fm	Corn	SX0862	50°25·8'	4°41·8'W	FM	200
Coombe Fm	Corn	SX1359	50°24·3'	4°37·5'W	FM	200
Coombe Fm	Corn	SX2260	50°25·0'	4°30·0'W	FM	201
Coombe Fm	Corn	SX3568	50°29·6'	4°19·2'W	FM	201
Coombe Fm	Corn	SX4251	50°20·5'	4°12·9'W	FM	201
Coombe Fm	Devon	SS4212	50°53·4'	4°14·4'W	FM	180,190
Coombe Fm	Devon	SS4829	51°2·7'	4°9·7'W	FM	180
Coombe Fm	Devon	SS5709	50°52·0'	4°1·6'W	FM	191
Coombe Fm	Devon	SS5933	51°5·0'	4°0·4'W	FM	180
Coombe Fm	Devon	SS6526	51°1·3'	3°55·1'W	FM	180
Coombe Fm	Devon	SS7612	50°53·9'	3°45·4'W	FM	180
Coombe Fm	Devon	SS7648	51°13·3'	3°46·2'W	FM	180
Coombe Fm	Devon	SS8511	50°53·5'	3°37·7'W	FM	191
Coombe Fm	Devon	SS9608	50°52·0'	3°28·3'W	FM	192
Coombe Fm	Devon	SS9619	50°57·9'	3°28·5'W	FM	181
Coombe Fm	Devon	SS9906	50°50·9'	3°25·7'W	FM	192
Coombe Fm	Devon	SX5066	50°28·7'	4°6·5'W	FM	201
Coombe Fm	Devon	SX5251	50°20·7'	4°4·4'W	FM	201
Coombe Fm	Devon	SX6048	50°19·2'	3°57·6'W	FM	202
Coombe Fm	Devon	SX7345	50°17·7'	3°46·6'W	FM	202
Coombe Fm	Devon	SX7873	50°32·9'	3°42·9'W	FM	191
Coombe Fm	Devon	SX7893	50°43·7'	3°43·3'W	FM	191
Coombe Fm	Devon	SY0085	50°39·6'	3°24·5'W	FM	192
Coombe Fm	Dorset	ST6218	50°57·8'	2°32·1'W	FM	183
Coombe Fm	Glos	SP1336	52°1·6'	1°48·2'W	FM	151
Coombe Fm	Hants	SU5835	51°6·9'	1°9·9'W	FM	185
Coombe Fm	Herts	TL3137	52°1·2'	0°5·1'W	FM	153
Coombe Fm	I of W	SZ4283	50°38·9'	1°24·0'W	FM	196
Coombe Fm	Kent	TQ8734	51°4·7'	0°40·6'E	FM	189
Coombe Fm	Kent	TR1739	51°6·8'	1°6·4'E	FM	179,189
Coombe Fm	Kent	TR2239	51°6·7'	1°10·7'E	FM	179,189
Coombe Fm	N Som	ST3357	51°18·7'	2°57·3'W	FM	182
Coombe Fm	Oxon	SP3132	51°59·4'	1°32·5'W	FM	151
Coombe Fm	Shrops	SO6880	52°25·3'	2°27·8'W	FM	138
Coombe Fm	Somer	SS8539	51°8·6'	3°38·3'W	FM	181
Coombe Fm	Somer	ST6835	51°7·0'	2°27·0'W	FM	183
Coombe Fm	Warw	SP2351	52°9·6'	1°39·4'W	FM	151
Coombe Fm	Wilts	SU2369	51°25·4'	1°39·8'W	FM	174
Coombe Fm	W Susx	TQ2420	50°58·2'	0°13·6'W	FM	198
Coombe Fm	W Susx	TQ2617	50°56·5'	0°12·0'W	FM	198
Coombe Fms	Dorset	ST5603	50°49·7'	2°37·1'W	FM	194
Coombe Fms	Somer	ST0329	51°3·4'	3°22·7'W	FM	181
Coombe Grange	Win & Maid	SU9368	51°24·4'	0°39·4'W	X	175
Coombe Green	Wilts	ST9586	51°34·6'	2°3·9'W	X	173
Coombegreen Common	Worcs	SO7736	52°1·6'	2°19·7'W	X	150
Coombe Hall	Devon	SX7691	50°42·6'	3°45·0'W	X	191
Coombe Hall	W Susx	TQ3837	51°7·2'	0°1·3'W	X	187
Coombe Hawne	Corn	SX1150	50°19·4'	4°38·9'W	W	200,204
Coombehayes	Devon	SS9313	50°54·6'	3°30·9'W	X	181
Coombe Head	Devon	SX6294	50°44·0'	3°57·0'W	X	191
Coombe Head	Surrey	SU9034	51°6·1'	0°42·5'W	X	186
Coombe Head	W Susx	TQ1808	50°51·8'	0°19·0'W	X	198
Coombehead Fm	Devon	SS9212	50°54·1'	3°31·8'W	FM	181
Coombe Heath	Dorset	SY8684	50°39·6'	2°11·5'W	F	194
Coombe Hill	Bucks	SP8406	51°45·0'	0°46·6'W	H	165
Coombe Hill	Bucks	SP8909	51°46·6'	0°42·2'W	X	165
Coombe Hill	Dorset	ST7702	50°49·3'	2°19·2'W	X	194
Coombe Hill	Glos	SO8826	51°56·2'	2°10·1'W	X	162
Coombe Hill	Glos	ST7694	51°38·9'	2°20·4'W	X	162,172
Coombe Hill	Heref	SO7242	52°4·8'	2°24·1'W	X	149
Coombe Hill	Oxon	SP4533	51°59·8'	1°20·3'W	X	151
Coombe Hill	Wilts	SU1751	51°15·7'	1°45·0'W	X	184
Coombe Hill Fm	E Susx	TQ6913	50°53·7'	0°24·6'E	FM	199
Coombe Hill Ho	Somer	ST6835	51°7·0'	2°27·0'W	X	183
Coombe Ho	Devon	SS7801	50°48·0'	3°43·5'W	X	191
Coombe Ho	Devon	SS7913	50°54·5'	3°42·9'W	X	180
Coombe Ho	Devon	SX7055	50°23·1'	3°49·3'W	X	202
Coombe Ho	Oxon	SP5904	51°44·1'	1°8·3'W	X	164
Coombe Ho	W Susx	TQ2421	50°58·7'	0°13·6'W	X	198
Coombe Hole	Bucks	SP9617	51°50·8'	0°36·0'W	X	165
Coombekeale	Corn	SX2787	50°39·7'	4°26·5'W	X	190
Coombe Keynes	Dorset	SY8484	50°39·6'	2°13·2'W	T	194
Coombelake	Devon	SY0896	50°45·6'	3°17·9'W	T	192
Coombeland	Devon	SS9010	50°53·0'	3°33·4'W	X	192
Coombeland	Devon	SS9617	50°56·8'	3°28·4'W	X	181
Coombelands	W Susx	TQ0319	50°57·9'	0°31·6'W	X	197
Coombe Lodge	Essex	TQ5890	51°35·4'	0°17·2'E	X	177
Coombe Lodge	W Berks	SU4282	51°32·4'	1°23·3'W	X	174
Coombe Lodge (Coll)	N Som	ST4959	51°19·9'	2°43·5'W	X	172,182
Coombe Manor	Kent	TR0846	51°10·7'	0°59·0'E	X	179,189
Coombe Mill	Devon	SX3689	50°40·9'	4°18·9'W	X	190
Coombe Norris	Devon	SX7155	50°23·1'	3°48·5'W	X	202
Coombe Park	Devon	SX7843	50°16·7'	3°42·4'W	X	202
Coombe Park	Devon	SX8162	50°27·0'	3°40·2'W	X	202
Coombe Park	Oxon	SU6277	51°29·5'	1°6·0'W	X	175
Coombe Park Fm	Devon	SX8057	50°24·3'	3°40·9'W	FM	202
Coombe Place	E Susx	TQ3912	50°53·7'	0°1·0'W	X	198
Coombe Pool	Warw	SP3979	52°24·7'	1°25·2'W	W	140
Coombers Fm	W Susx	TQ2035	51°6·3'	0°16·8'W	FM	187
Coombes	W Susx	TQ1908	50°51·8'	0°18·2'W	T	198
Coombesdale	Staffs	SJ8038	52°56·6'	2°17·5'W	T	127
Coombes Edge	Derby	SK0192	53°25·7'	1°58·7'W	X	110
Coombe's Fm	Bucks	SU8596	51°39·6'	0°45·9'W	FM	165
Coombes Fm	Derby	SK0191	53°25·2'	1°58·7'W	FM	110
Coombeshead	Devon	SS6239	51°8·3'	3°58·0'W	X	180
Coombeshead	Devon	SS7230	51°3·5'	3°49·2'W	X	180
Coombes Head Fm	Devon	ST1115	50°55·9'	3°15·6'W	FM	181,193
Coombeshead Fm	Devon	SX8687	50°40·5'	3°36·4'W	FM	191
Coombeshead Park Fm	Devon	SX3891	50°42·0'	4°17·3'W	FM	190
Coombe Slade Fm	Warw	SP3338	52°2·6'	1°30·7'W	FM	151
Coombes, The	Northnts	SP6883	52°26·7'	0°59·6'W	F	141
Coombes,The	Wok	SU7767	51°24·0'	0°53·2'W	X	175
Coombeswood	Dudley	SO9785	52°28·0'	2°2·3'W	T	139
Coombe's Wood	Suff	TM3185	52°25·1'	1°24·2'E	F	156
Coombe, The	Dorset	SY6199	50°47·6'	2°32·8'W	X	194
Coombe Valley	Corn	SS2111	50°52·5'	4°32·3'W	X	190
Coombe Valley	Devon	SX8095	50°44·8'	3°41·7'W	X	191
Coombe View Fm	Warw	SP4181	52°25·8'	1°23·4'W	FM	140
Coombewick	W Susx	TQ1417	50°56·7'	0°22·2'W	X	198
Coombewillis	Devon	SS9209	50°52·5'	3°31·7'W	X	192
Coombe Wood	Dorset	SY8384	50°39·6'	2°14·0'W	F	194
Coombe Wood	Hants	SU6718	50°57·7'	1°2·4'W	F	185
Coombe Wood	Herts	TL2407	51°45·1'	0°11·8'W	F	166
Coombe Wood	Oxon	SP5904	51°44·1'	1°8·3'W	F	164
Coombe Wood	W Berks	SU5473	51°27·4'	1°13·0'W	F	174
Coombe Wood	W Susx	TQ0012	50°54·2'	0°34·3'W	F	197
Coombe Wood Fm	Devon	SY1488	50°41·4'	3°12·7'W	FM	192
Comb Height	Cumbr	NY3032	54°40·9'	3°4·7'W	H	90
Coomb Hill	Kent	TQ6664	51°21·3'	0°23·4'E	T	177,178,188
Coomb Hill	N Yks	SE5290	54°18·4'	1°11·6'W	H	100
Coomb Hill	Scot Bord	NT0626	55°31·4'	3°28·9'W	H	72
Coombland Wood	Devon	SX8796	50°45·4'	3°35·7'W	F	192
Coomboots	N Yks	SE9991	54°18·5'	0°28·3'W	X	94,101
Coomb or Neave Island	Highld	NC6664	58°32·9'	4°17·7'W	X	10
Coombs	Bucks	SP7332	51°59·1'	0°55·8'W	X	152,165
Coombs Dale	Derby	SK2274	53°16·0'	1°39·8'W	X	119
Coombs End	S Glos	ST7580	51°31·3'	2°21·2'W	T	172
Coombses	Somer	ST3305	50°50·7'	2°56·7'W	T	193
Coombs Fm	Derby	SK2367	53°12·2'	1°38·9'W	FM	119
Coombshead	Corn	SX2879	50°35·4'	4°25·4'W	X	201

Coombshead	Cumbr	NY5144	54°47·6'	2°45·3'W	X	86
Coombs Plantn	E Yorks	SE9033	53°47·4'	0°37·6'W	F	106
Coombs Wood	Cumbr	NY5144	54°47·6'	2°45·3'W	F	86
Coombs Wood	N Yks	NZ8102	54°24·7'	0°44·7'W	F	94
Coom Burn	D & G	NX6080	55°5·9'	4°11·2'W	W	77
Coombutler	Devon	SS9213	50°54·6'	3°31·8'W	X	181
Coomb Wood	Glos	SP2427	51°56·7'	1°38·7'W	F	163
Coom Dod	S Lanak	NS9018	55°26·9'	3°43·9'W	H	71,78
Coomery	Devon	SX8155	50°23·2'	3°40·1'W	X	202
Coom Law	Scot Bord	NT2818	55°27·3'	3°7·9'W	H	79
Coomlees	Scot Bord	NT1233	55°35·2'	3°23·3'W	X	72
Coom Rig	S Lanak	NS9409	55°22·1'	3°39·9'W	H	71,78
Cooms	D & G	NY4190	55°12·3'	2°55·2'W	X	79
Cooms Burn	D & G	NY4290	55°12·3'	2°54·3'W	W	79
Coomsdon Burn	Northum	NT7003	55°19·5'	2°27·9'W	W	80
Cooms Fell	D & G	NY4389	55°11·8'	2°53·3'W	H	79
Coomsfell End	D & G	NY4187	55°10·7'	2°55·2'W	X	79
Cooms Height	Scot Bord	NY4389	55°11·8'	2°53·3'W	X	79
Cooper	N Yks	NZ7717	54°32·8'	0°48·2'W	X	94
Co-operative Villas	Durham	NZ2153	54°52·5'	1°39·9'W	X	88
Cooper Cleuch	Scot Bord	NT5700	55°17·8'	2°40·2'W	X	80
Coopercleuch Knowe	Scot Bord	NT5700	55°17·8'	2°40·2'W	X	80
Cooper Fm	Kent	TQ9143	51°9·5'	0°44·3'E	FM	189
Cooperhall	Orkney	HY5629	59°9·0'	2°45·7'W	X	5,6
Cooperhill	Aberd	NJ6655	57°35·3'	2°33·7'W	X	29
Cooper Hill	Cumbr	SD7899	54°23·4'	2°19·9'W	X	98
Cooperhill	E Ayr	NS5119	55°26·8'	4°20·9'W	X	70
Cooper Ho	Cumbr	NY8214	54°31·5'	2°16·3'W	X	91,92
Cooper Ho	Cumbr	SD5399	54°23·3'	2°43·0'W	X	97
Cooper Ho	Durham	NZ0219	54°34·2'	1°57·7'W	X	92
Cooper Ho	Ghead	NZ2355	54°53·6'	1°38·1'W	X	88
Cooper Ho	N Yks	SE2052	53°58·1'	1°41·3'W	X	104
Coopers	Essex	TL6219	51°51·0'	0°21·5'E	X	167
Coopersale Common	Essex	TL4702	51°42·1'	0°8·0'E	T	167
Coopersale Hall	Essex	TL4600	51°41·0'	0°7·1'E	X	167
Coopersale Street	Essex	TL4701	51°41·5'	0°8·0'E	T	167
Cooper's Cleuch	Scot Bord	NT5504	55°19·9'	2°42·1'W	X	80
Cooper's Coppice	Shrops	SJ7312	52°42·5'	2°23·6'W	F	127
Cooper's Corner	E Susx	TQ7327	51°1·2'	0°28·4'E	X	188,199
Cooper's Corner	Kent	TQ4849	51°13·5'	0°7·6'E	T	188
Cooper's Covert	Suff	TL8573	52°19·7'	0°43·2'E	F	144,155
Cooper's Creek	Essex	TL9005	51°42·9'	0°45·4'E	W	168
Cooper's End	Essex	TL4635	51°59·9'	0°8·0'E	X	154
Cooper's Fm	Cambs	TL6241	52°2·8'	0°22·1'E	FM	154
Cooper's Fm	E Susx	TQ6509	50°51·6'	0°21·1'E	FM	199
Cooper's Fm	Kent	TQ8557	51°17·1'	0°39·6'E	FM	178
Coopers Fm	Lincs	TF3214	52°42·7'	0°2·4'W	FM	131
Coopers Fm	N Yks	NZ8207	54°27·3'	0°43·7'W	FM	94
Cooper's Fm	W Susx	TQ2223	50°59·8'	0°15·3'W	FM	198
Cooper's Green	E Susx	TQ4723	50°59·5'	0°6·1'E	T	198
Cooper's Green	Herts	TL1909	51°46·2'	0°16·1'W	T	166
Cooper's Hatch	E Susx	TQ4715	50°55·2'	0°5·9'E	X	198
Cooper's Hill	Beds	TL0237	52°1·6'	0°30·4'W	T	153
Cooper's Hill	Glos	SO8914	51°49·7'	2°9·2'W	H	163
Coopers Hill	Hants	SU2014	50°55·7'	1°42·5'W	X	195
Cooper's Hill	Surrey	SU9972	51°26·5'	0°34·1'W	T	175,176
Cooper's Knowe	Highld	NM7079	56°51·0'	5°45·9'W	H	40
Cooper Street	Kent	TR3059	51°17·2'	1°18·3'E	T	179
Coopers Wood	Hants	SZ3998	50°47·0'	1°26·4'W	F	196
Cooper's Wood	Kent	TQ5960	51°19·2'	0°17·3'E	F	177,188
Cooper Turning	Bolton	SD6308	53°34·3'	2°33·1'W	T	109
Coophurst Fm	Surrey	TQ1041	51°9·7'	0°25·2'W	FM	187
Coopwell Fm	Suff	TL8349	52°6·8'	0°40·8'E	FM	155
Cooran Lane	D & G	NX4782	55°6·8'	4°23·5'W	W	77
Coorsa, The	Orkney	HY6121	59°4·7'	2°40·3'W	X	5
Cooses, The	Shetld	HU3064	60°21·8'	1°26·9'W	H	3
Coosewartha Fm	Corn	SW7246	50°16·4'	5°11·6'W	FM	204
Coos Fm	Ches	SJ6344	52°59·8'	2°32·7'W	FM	118
Cootham	W Susx	TQ0714	50°55·2'	0°28·3'W	T	197
Cooting Downs	Kent	TR2252	51°13·7'	1°11·2'E	X	179,189
Cooting Fm	Kent	TR2253	51°14·2'	1°11·2'E	FM	179,189
Copa Ceiliog	Conwy	SH8748	53°1·3'	3°40·7'W	X	116
Copalder	Cambs	TL3589	52°29·2'	0°0·3'W	X	142
Copalder Corner	Cambs	TL3591	52°30·2'	0°0·3'W	X	142
Copalder Fm	Cambs	TL3592	52°30·2'	0°0·6'E	FM	142
Copa Shôn	Powys	SN7899	52°34·8'	3°47·6'W	H	135
Copcourt	Oxon	SP7001	51°42·4'	0°58·8'W	X	165
Cop Crag	N Yks	SE1456	54°0·2'	1°46·8'W	X	104
Copcut	Worcs	SO8861	52°15·1'	2°10·1'W	T	150
Copdock	Suff	TM1141	52°1·9'	1°5·0'E	T	155,169
Copdock Hill	Warw	SP2559	52°14·0'	1°37·6'W	X	151
Copdoe's Fm	Suff	TL8759	52°12·1'	0°44·6'E	FM	155
Coped Hall	Wilts	SU0783	51°33·0'	1°53·6'W	T	173
Copeland Forest	Cumbr	NY1407	54°27·3'	3°19·2'W	X	89
Copeland Ho	Durham	NZ1626	54°38·0'	1°44·7'W	X	92
Copelands	Lancs	SD3913	53°36·8'	2°54·9'W	X	108
Copelands's Fm	Norf	TF9505	52°36·7'	0°53·2'E	FM	144
Copelaw Gair	D & G	NY2795	55°14·9'	3°8·5'W	X	79
Copenagaeo	Orkney	HY5010	58°58·7'	2°51·7'W	X	6
Copenhagen	Denb	SJ0466	53°11·2'	3°25·8'W	T	116
Copenhagen	Devon	SS9405	50°50·3'	3°29·9'W	X	192
Copes	Kent	TQ8857	51°17·1'	0°42·2'E	X	178
Copes Fm	Bucks	SU8998	51°40·7'	0°42·4'W	FM	165
Copewood	D & G	NY1076	55°4·5'	3°24·1'W	X	85
Copford	Essex	TL9223	51°52·6'	0°47·8'E	T	168
Copford Green	Essex	TL9222	51°52·0'	0°47·7'E	T	168
Copford Hall	Essex	TL9322	51°52·0'	0°48·6'E	X	168
Copford Pl	Essex	TL9324	51°53·1'	0°48·7'E	X	168
Copgrove	N Yks	SE3463	54°4·0'	1°28·4'W	T	99
Cop Hall	N Yks	SE4774	54°9·8'	1°16·4'W	X	100
Cophall Fm	Cambs	TL5084	52°26·2'	0°12·8'E	FM	143
Cophall Fm	E Susx	TQ4626	51°1·1'	0°5·3'E	FM	188,198
Cophall Fm	Heref	SO4374	52°21·9'	2°49·8'W	FM	137,148
Copham's Hill Fm	Warw	SP1756	52°12·4'	1°44·7'W	FM	151
Cophill	Monm	ST5094	51°38·8'	2°43·0'W	X	162,172
Cophill Fm	Warw	SP2164	52°16·7'	1°41·1'W	FM	151
Cophole Fm	Somer	SS9832	51°4·9'	3°27·0'W	FM	181
Cop Holt Fm	Warr	SJ5993	53°26·2'	2°36·6'W	FM	108
Cop House Fm	Flint	SJ3566	53°11·5'	2°58·0'W	FM	117
Cophurst	Ches	SJ9469	53°13·3'	2°5·0'W	X	118

Copied Hall Fm	Hants	SU3214	50°55·7'	1°32·3'W	FM	196
Copince's Fen	Norf	TM0488	52°27·3'	1°0·6'E	X	144
Copinsay	Orkney	HY6101	58°53·9'	2°40·1'W	X	6
Copinsay Pass	Orkney	HY5903	58°55·0'	2°42·2'W	W	6
Copister	Shetld	HU4778	60°29·2'	1°8·2'W	T	2,3
Copkitchen's Fm	Essex	TL8603	51°41·9'	0°41·9'E	FM	168
Copland	Scot Bord	NT6324	55°30·8'	2°34·7'W	X	74
Coplandhill	Aberd	NK1146	57°30·5'	1°48·5'W	T	30
Cop Law	Scot Bord	NT3319	55°27·9'	3°3·1'W	H	79
Cople	Beds	TL1048	52°7·4'	0°23·2'W	T	153
Coplestone Ho	Devon	SS7701	50°48·0'	3°44·3'W	X	191
Copley	Cald	SE0822	53°41·9'	1°52·3'W	T	104
Copley	Durham	NZ0825	54°37·4'	1°52·1'W	T	92
Copley	Tames	SJ9798	53°29·0'	2°2·3'W	T	109
Copley Fm	Heref	SO7049	52°8·5'	2°25·9'W	FM	149
Copley Fm	Staffs	SO8198	52°35·0'	2°16·4'W	FM	138
Copley Hill	Cambs	TL5053	52°9·5'	0°12·0'E	X	154
Copley Hill	Kirk	SE2326	53°44·0'	1°38·7'W	T	104
Copley Hill Fm	Cambs	TL5052	52°9·0'	0°11·9'E	FM	154
Copley Hill (Tumulus)	Cambs	TL5053	52°9·5'	0°12·0'E	A	154
Copley House Fm	Kirk	SE1828	53°45·1'	1°43·2'W	FM	104
Copley Lodge	Durham	NZ1026	54°38·0'	1°50·3'W	X	92
Copley Wood	Somer	ST5031	51°4·8'	2°42·4'W	F	182,183
Coplie Hill	Inverc	NS3065	55°51·2'	4°42·5'W	X	63
Coploe Hill	Cambs	TL4942	52°3·6'	0°10·8'E	X	154
Coplow Dale	Derby	SK1679	53°18·7'	1°45·2'W	T	119
Coplowe Hall	Brad	SE0936	53°49·5'	1°51·4'W	X	104
Coplow Fm	Leic	SK7003	52°37·4'	0°57·6'W	FM	141
Coplow Hill	Warw	SP2561	52°15·0'	1°37·6'W	X	151
Copmanroyd Fm	N Yks	SE2047	53°55·4'	1°41·3'W	FM	104
Copmanthorpe	York	SE5647	53°55·2'	1°8·4'W	T	105
Copmanthorpe Grange	York	SE5644	53°53·6'	1°8·5'W	X	105
Copmanthorpe Lodge	York	SE5645	53°54·1'	1°8·4'W	X	105
Copmanthorpe Wood	York	SE5645	53°54·1'	1°8·4'W	F	105
Cop Mere	Staffs	SJ8029	52°51·7'	2°17·4'W	W	127
Copmere End	Staffs	SJ8029	52°51·7'	2°17·4'W	T	127
Copnor	C of Port	SU6602	50°49·1'	1°3·4'W	T	196
Copp	Lancs	SD4239	53°50·9'	2°52·5'W	T	102
Coppa Dolla Fm	Devon	SX8167	50°29·7'	3°40·3'W	FM	202
Coppagach	Pth & Kin	NN9365	56°46·1'	3°44·6'W	X	43
Coppa Ho	Flint	SJ2761	53°8·7'	3°5·1'W	X	117
Coppards	E Susx	TQ5807	50°50·7'	0°15·0'E	X	199
Coppath Burn	Northum	NT9812	55°24·4'	2°1·5'W	W	81
Coppa, The	Orkney	HY6225	59°6·9'	2°39·3'W	X	5
Coppathorne	Corn	SS2100	50°46·6'	4°32·0'W	T	190
Coppa View	Flint	SJ2763	53°9·8'	3°5·1'W	X	117
Coppa Wick	Shetld	HU1753	60°15·9'	1°41·1'W	W	3
Coppay	N Eil	NF9393	57°49·5'	7°9·8'W	X	18
Copped Hall	Essex	TL4301	51°41·6'	0°4·5'E	X	167
Copped Hall Fm	W Susx	TQ0827	51°2·2'	0°27·2'W	FM	187,197
Coppenhall	Ches	SJ7056	53°6·3'	2°26·5'W	T	118
Coppenhall	Staffs	SJ9019	52°46·3'	2°8·5'W	T	127
Coppenhall Moss	Ches	SJ7058	53°7·3'	2°26·5'W	T	118
Copperas Bay	Essex	TM1932	51°56·8'	1°11·6'E	W	168,169
Copperas Wood	Suff	TM3254	52°8·4'	1°23·8'E	F	156
Copper Fm	Corn	SX2093	50°42·8'	4°32·6'W	FM	190
Coppergill	N Yks	SE0363	54°4·0'	1°56·8'W	X	98
Copper Hall	E Yorks	TA0654	53°58·5'	0°22·6'W	X	107
Copper Hall Fm	N Yks	NZ5909	54°28·6'	1°4·9'W	FM	93
Copper Hill	Lincs	SK9741	52°57·7'	0°32·9'W	X	130
Copperhouse	Corn	SW5737	50°11·2'	5°23·9'W	T	203
Copperhouse Marshes	Medway	TQ7969	51°23·7'	0°34·8'E	W	178
Copperhurst	Kent	TR0735	51°4·8'	0°57·7'E	X	179,189
Copper's Hill	E Susx	TQ6623	50°59·2'	0°22·3'E	X	199
Copper Snout	Northum	NT8908	55°22·2'	2°10·0'W	H	80
Copperthwaite Allotment	N Yks	SE0599	54°23·4'	1°55·0'W	X	98
Copperthwaite Allotment	N Yks	SE0699	54°23·4'	1°54·0'W	X	99
Copper Top Fm	Derby	SK2336	52°55·5'	1°39·1'W	FM	128
Copperwalls Fm	Devon	SX8496	50°45·4'	3°38·3'W	FM	191
Coppet Hall Pt	Pemb	SN1405	51°43·0'	4°41·2'W	X	158
Coppet Hill	Dorset	SY4195	50°45·3'	2°49·8'W	H	193
Coppet Hill	Heref	SO5717	51°51·2'	2°37·1'W	X	162
Coppey Fm	Suff	TM1136	51°59·2'	1°4·8'E	FM	155,169
Copphall	Devon	SS8028	51°2·6'	3°42·3'W	X	181
Coppice	Oldham	SD9203	53°31·7'	2°6·8'W	T	109
Coppice Corner Fm	Warw	SP1767	52°18·3'	1°44·6'W	FM	151
Coppice Fm	Ches	SJ7685	53°21·9'	2°21·2'W	FM	109
Coppice Fm	Derby	SK1737	52°56·0'	1°44·4'W	FM	128
Coppice Fm	Derby	SK2343	52°59·3'	1°39·0'W	FM	119,128
Coppice Fm	Devon	SY0194	50°44·5'	3°23·8'W	FM	192
Coppice Fm	Essex	TM1320	51°50·5'	1°5·9'E	FM	168,169
Coppice Fm	Powys	SJ3016	52°44·5'	3°1·8'W	FM	126
Coppice Fm	Shrops	SJ4012	52°42·4'	2°52·9'W	FM	126
Coppice Fm	Shrops	SJ4401	52°36·5'	2°49·2'W	FM	126
Coppice Fm	Shrops	SJ4628	52°51·0'	2°47·7'W	FM	126
Coppice Fm	Shrops	SO4095	52°33·2'	2°52·7'W	FM	137
Coppice Fm	Shrops	SO4676	52°23·0'	2°47·2'W	FM	137,138
Coppice Fm	Shrops	SO4676	52°23·0'	2°47·2'W	FM	137,148
Coppice Fm	Shrops	SO5380	52°25·2'	2°41·1'W	FM	137,138
Coppice Fm	Staffs	SJ9615	52°44·2'	2°3·2'W	FM	127
Coppicegate	Shrops	SO7380	52°25·3'	2°23·4'W	T	138
Coppicegate Fm	Shrops	SO7479	52°24·7'	2°22·5'W	FM	138
Coppice Green	Shrops	SJ7508	52°40·4'	2°21·8'W	X	127
Coppice Hill	Staffs	SJ9819	52°46·4'	2°1·4'W	H	127
Coppice Ho	Bucks	SP8301	51°42·3'	0°47·5'W	X	165
Coppice Ho	Glos	SO7318	51°51·8'	2°23·1'W	X	162
Coppice Ho	Shrops	SJ4734	52°54·3'	2°46·9'W	X	126
Coppice Ho	Shrops	SO5198	52°34·9'	2°43·0'W	X	137,138
Coppice Hos	Wrekin	SJ5615	52°44·1'	2°38·7'W	X	126
Coppice House Fm	Derby	SK3321	52°47·4'	1°30·2'W	FM	128
Coppice House Wood	Heref	SO3053	52°10·5'	3°1·0'W	W	148
Coppice Howe Fm	Cumbr	SD5296	54°21·7'	2°43·9'W	FM	97
Coppice Leys	Rut	SK9501	52°36·1'	0°35·4'W	F	141
Coppice Lodge	Northnts	TL0085	52°27·5'	0°31·3'W	X	141
Coppice Mawr	Monm	ST4994	51°38·8'	2°43·8'W	F	162,172
Coppice of Linwood	Hants	SU2414	50°55·7'	1°39·1'W	F	195
Coppice, The	Derby	SK3823	52°48·4'	1°25·8'W	F	128
Coppice, The	Leic	SK6512	52°42·3'	1°1·9'W	X	129
Coppice, The	Oxon	SU5496	51°39·8'	1°12·8'W	F	164
Coppice, The	Powys	SJ2311	52°41·7'	3°8·0'W	X	126

Coppice, The	Staffs	SK1617	52°45·3'	1°45·4'W	F	128
Coppicetown	Devon	SX4868	50°29·8'	4°8·2'W	X	201
Coppice Wood	Beds	TL0364	52°16·1'	0°29·0'W	F	153
Coppice Wood	Notts	SK7258	53°7·1'	0°55·0'W	F	120
Coppid Hall	Oxon	SU7379	51°30·5'	0°56·5'W	X	175
Coppingford	Cambs	TL1680	52°24·6'	0°17·3'W	T	142
Coppingford Wood	Cambs	TL1780	52°24·6'	0°16·4'W	F	142
Copping Knoll	Oxon	SP4320	51°52·8'	1°22·1'W	X	164
Coppings Fm	Kent	TQ5348	51°12·9'	0°11·8'E	FM	188
Coppington Down	W Berks	SU3177	51°29·7'	1°32·8'W	X	174
Coppington Fm	Warw	SP2857	52°12·9'	1°35·0'W	FM	151
Coppington Hill	W Berks	SU3277	51°29·7'	1°32·0'W	X	174
Coppins	Bucks	TQ0381	51°31·3'	0°30·5'W	X	176
Coppins Corner	Kent	TQ9448	51°12·1'	0°47·0'E	T	189
Coppins Fm	Kent	TR0351	51°13·5'	0°54·8'E	FM	179,189
Coppleham	Somer	SS9234	51°5·9'	3°32·2'W	T	181
Copplesbury Fm	Somer	ST7037	51°8·1'	2°25·3'W	FM	183
Copplestone	Devon	SS7602	50°48·5'	3°45·2'W	T	191
Copplestone	Devon	SS9812	50°54·1'	3°26·7'W	X	181
Copplestone Fm	Corn	SX1189	50°40·4'	4°40·1'W	FM	190,200
Copplethwaite	Cumbr	SD7189	54°18·0'	2°26·3'W	X	98
Coppock House Fm	Ches	SJ8180	53°19·2'	2°16·7'W	FM	109
Coppull	Lancs	SD5614	53°37·5'	2°39·5'W	T	108
Coppull Moor	Lancs	SD5512	53°36·4'	2°40·4'W	T	108
Coppy	Cald	SD9630	53°46·2'	2°3·2'W	X	103
Coppy	Durham	NZ2155	54°53·6'	1°39·9'W	X	88
Coppybush	Pemb	SN0600	51°40·2'	4°47·9'W	X	158
Coppy Crooks	Durham	NZ2026	54°38·0'	1°41·0'W	X	93
Coppy Heads	Lancs	SD5856	54°0·1'	2°38·0'W	X	102
Coppy Hill	Derby	SK3525	52°49·5'	1°28·4'W	X	128
Coppy Ho	Lancs	SD8149	53°56·4'	2°17·0'W	X	103
Coppy Ho	Lancs	SD8546	53°54·8'	2°13·3'W	X	103
Coppy Ho	N Yks	SD7465	54°5·1'	2°23·4'W	X	98
Coppy Ho	Shrops	SO4278	52°24·1'	2°50·8'W	X	137,148
Copsale	W Susx	TQ1724	51°0·4'	0°19·5'W	T	198
Copsale Ct	W Susx	TQ1725	51°1·0'	0°19·5'W	X	187,198
Copse Barn	W Berks	SU4470	51°25·9'	1°21·6'W	X	174
Copse Fm	Hants	SU4161	51°21·0'	1°24·3'W	FM	174
Copse Fm	Somer	ST3133	51°5·8'	2°58·7'W	FM	182
Copse Fm	W Susx	SU8905	50°50·5'	0°43·8'W	FM	197
Copse Green Fm	Glos	SO8927	51°56·7'	2°9·2'W	FM	163
Copsegrove Fm	Glos	SO8905	51°44·9'	2°9·2'W	FM	163
Copse Hill	Cumbr	SD2679	54°12·3'	3°7·7'W	X	96,97
Copse Hill	Glos	SP1623	51°54·6'	1°45·6'W	X	163
Copse Hill	Merton	TQ2270	51°25·2'	0°14·3'W	T	176
Copse Ho	Dorset	ST3705	50°50·7'	2°53·3'W	X	193
Copse Ho	Dorset	ST7018	50°57·9'	2°25·2'W	X	183
Copse Lodge	Northnts	SP5541	52°4·1'	1°11·5'W	X	152
Copse, The	Norf	TF6206	52°37·9'	0°24·0'E	F	143
Copse Wood	Heref	SO4224	51°54·9'	2°50·2'W	F	161
Copse Wood	Hill	TQ0890	51°36·1'	0°26·0'W	F	176
Copshall	E Susx	TQ8415	50°54·5'	0°37·4'E	X	199
Copster	Barns	SE2802	53°31·1'	1°34·3'W	X	110
Copster Green	Lancs	SD6733	53°47·8'	2°29·6'W	T	103
Copster Hall	Lancs	SD6734	53°48·3'	2°29·7'W	X	103
Copster Hill	Oldham	SD9203	53°31·7'	2°6·8'W	T	109
Cop Stone	Cumbr	NY4921	54°35·1'	2°46·9'W	A	90
Copston Fields Fm	Warw	SP4587	52°29·0'	1°19·8'W	FM	140
Copston Fm	Warw	SP4488	52°29·5'	1°20·7'W	FM	140
Copston Magna	Warw	SP4588	52°29·5'	1°19·8'W	T	140
Cop Street	Kent	TR2959	51°17·3'	1°17·4'E	T	179
Coptcleugh	Durham	NY8641	54°46·1'	2°12·6'W	X	87
Coptfold Hall	Essex	TL6503	51°42·3'	0°23·7'E	X	167
Copt Green	Warw	SP1769	52°19·4'	1°44·6'W	T	139,151
Copt Hall	Beds	TL1219	51°51·7'	0°22·0'W	X	166
Copt Hall	Essex	TL5820	51°51·6'	0°18·1'E	X	167
Copt Hall	Essex	TL9814	51°47·6'	0°52·7'E	X	168
Copthall	Herts	TL4113	51°48·1'	0°3·1'E	X	167
Copthall Fm	Hill	TQ0686	51°34·0'	0°27·8'W	FM	176
Copthall Green	Essex	TL4201	51°41·6'	0°3·7'E	T	167
Copthall Grove	Essex	TL9815	51°48·1'	0°52·7'E	F	168
Copthall Saltings	Essex	TL9813	51°47·1'	0°52·6'E	W	168
Cop, The	Bucks	SP7700	51°41·8'	0°52·8'W	X	165
Cop, The	Derby	SK1279	53°18·7'	1°48·8'W	X	119
Copt Heath	Sol	SP1777	52°23·7'	1°44·6'W	T	139
Copt Hewick	N Yks	SE3371	54°8·3'	1°29·3'W	T	99
Copthill	Durham	NY8540	54°45·5'	2°13·6'W	T	87
Copt Hill	Hants	SU7340	51°9·5'	0°57·0'W	X	186
Copt Hill Fm	Kent	TR2641	51°7·6'	1°14·2'E	FM	179
Copthill Fm	Leic	SK7903	52°37·4'	0°49·6'W	FM	141
Copthill Fm	Lincs	TF0707	52°39·2'	0°24·7'W	FM	142
Copt Hill Fm	Notts	SK5656	53°6·1'	1°9·4'W	FM	120
Copthorne	Ches	SJ6543	52°59·2'	2°30·9'W	T	118
Copthorne	Corn	SX2692	50°42·3'	4°27·5'W	T	190
Copthorne	Lancs	SD4544	53°53·6'	2°49·8'W	X	102
Copthorne	Shrops	SJ4712	52°42·4'	2°46·7'W	T	126
Copthorne	W Susx	TQ3139	51°8·3'	0°7·3'W	T	187
Copthorne Common	W Susx	TQ3238	51°7·8'	0°6·4'W	X	187
Copthorne Fm	Notts	SK7466	53°11·4'	0°53·1'W	FM	120
Copthurst	Lancs	SD7936	53°49·4'	2°18·7'W	X	103
Coptiviney	Shrops	SJ4137	52°55·9'	2°52·3'W	T	126
Copt Oak	Leic	SK4812	52°42·4'	1°17·0'W	T	129
Copt Oak Fm	Leic	SP5397	52°34·3'	1°12·7'W	FM	140
Copton	Kent	TR0159	51°17·9'	0°53·4'E	T	178
Copton Ash Fm	Leic	SK3303	52°37·7'	1°30·3'W	FM	140
Copt Point	Kent	TR2436	51°5·0'	1°12·3'E	X	179,189
Copwood Fm	E Susx	TQ4621	50°58·4'	0°5·2'E	FM	198
Copy Fm	Bucks	SU8388	51°35·3'	0°47·7'W	FM	175
Copy Fm	Essex	TL6643	52°3·9'	0°25·7'E	FM	154
Copy Hill	N Yks	SD9452	53°58·1'	2°5·1'W	X	103
Copy Ho	Lancs	SD9143	53°53·2'	2°7·8'W	X	103
Copy Ho	Lancs	SD9338	53°50·5'	2°6·0'W	X	103
Copyhold	W Susx	TQ2326	51°1·4'	0°14·4'W	X	187,198
Copyhold Fm	Essex	TL5901	51°41·3'	0°18·4'E	FM	167
Copyhold Fm	E Susx	TQ5433	51°4·8'	0°12·3'E	FM	188
Copyhold Fm	W Berks	SU5768	51°24·7'	1°10·4'W	FM	174
Copyhold Fm	W Susx	SU8900	50°47·8'	0°43·8'W	FM	197
Copyhold Fm	W Susx	TQ3023	50°59·7'	0°8·5'W	FM	198
Copy Lake	Devon	SS6613	50°54·3'	3°54·0'W	X	180
Copy's Green	Norf	TF9439	52°55·0'	0°53·5'E	T	132

Copythorne	Hants	SU3014	50°55·7'	1°34·0'W	T	196
Copythorne Common	Hants	SU3015	50°56·2'	1°34·0'W	X	196
Copywood	Derby	SK2665	53°11·1'	1°36·2'W	X	119
Coquet Cairn	Northum	NZ0296	55°15·7'	1°57·7'W	X	81
Coquetdale	Northum	NU0001	55°18·4'	1°59·6'W	X	81
Coquet Head	Scot Bord	NT7708	55°22·2'	2°21·3'W	X	80
Coquet Island	Northum	NU2904	55°20·0'	1°32·1'W	X	81
Coquet Lodge	Northum	NU2306	55°21·1'	1°37·8'W	X	81
Coquet Moor Ho	Northum	NU2304	55°20·0'	1°37·8'W	X	81
Coquet Nook	N Yks	NZ7908	54°27·9'	0°46·4'W	X	94
Cora-bheinn	N Eil	NF6802	56°59·6'	7°27·6'W	X	31
Cora Campus	Renf	NS4172	55°55·1'	4°32·2'W	X	64
Corachan Burn	Arg & Bt	NR7109	55°19·6'	5°36·2'W	W	68
Coraddie	Arg & Bt	NS0477	55°57·0'	5°7·9'W	H	63
Coral Beaches	Highld	NG2254	57°29·7'	6°37·9'W	X	23
Coral Cottage	Moray	NJ2568	57°42·0'	3°15·0'W	X	28
Coralhill	Aberd	NK0561	57°38·6'	1°54·5'W	X	30
Coram Fm	Suff	TM0042	52°2·6'	0°55·4'E	FM	155
Coranbae Burn	D & G	NX6698	55°15·7'	4°6·1'W	W	77
Coranbae Hill	D & G	NX6799	55°16·3'	4°5·2'W	X	77
Coran of Portmark	D & G	NX5093	55°12·8'	4°21·0'W	H	77
Coranstilmore	Highld	NN8398	57°3·8'	3°55·3'W	X	35,43
Corarnstilbeg	Highld	NN8399	57°4·3'	3°55·3'W	T	35,43
Corarsik	Arg & Bt	NS1184	56°1·0'	5°1·5'W	X	56
Corarsik	Arg & Bt	NS1384	56°1·0'	4°59·6'W	X	56
Corarsik Burn	Arg & Bt	NS1284	56°1·0'	5°0·5'W	W	56
Corb	Pth & Kin	NO0008	56°15·5'	3°36·4'W	X	58
Corb	Pth & Kin	NO1656	56°41·5'	3°21·8'W	X	53
Corbanchory	Aberd	NJ4815	57°13·6'	2°51·2'W	X	37
Corbar Hill	Derby	SK0574	53°16·0'	1°55·1'W	H	119
Corb Br	Pth & Kin	NO0108	56°15·5'	3°35·4'W	X	58
Corbet Houses	Cumbr	NY2451	54°51·1'	3°10·6'W	X	85
Corbets	S Glos	ST6689	51°36·2'	2°29·1'W	X	162,172
Corbets Park	Shrops	SO7377	52°23·7'	2°23·4'W	F	138
Corbets Tey	Hav	TQ5585	51°32·8'	0°14·5'E	T	177
Corbett's Lodge	Norf	TF8811	52°40·1'	0°47·2'E	X	132
Corbet Wood	Shrops	SJ5223	52°48·4'	2°42·3'W	F	126
Corb Glen	Pth & Kin	NO0008	56°15·5'	3°36·4'W	X	58
Corbhainn	Highld	NN0851	56°37·0'	5°7·3'W	X	41
Corbie Geo	Shetld	HU2861	60°20·2'	1°29·1'W	X	3
Corbie Geo	Shetld	HU3517	59°56·5'	1°21·9'W	X	4
Corbie Geo	Shetld	HU3624	60°0·2'	1°20·8'W	X	4
Corbie Geo	Shetld	HU4422	59°59·1'	1°12·2'W	X	4
Corbie Geo	Shetld	HU6670	60°24·8'	0°47·6'W	X	2
Corbiegoe	Highld	ND3444	58°23·0'	3°7·2'W	X	12
Corbiehall	S Lanak	NS9244	55°40·9'	3°42·6'W	X	71,72
Corbie Head	Shetld	HU5891	60°36·2'	0°55·9'W	X	1,2
Corbiehilly	Fife	NO3322	56°23·4'	3°4·7'W	X	53,59
Corbie Knowe	Angus	NO6949	56°38·2'	2°29·9'W	A	54
Corbie Ness	Orkney	HY5539	59°14·4'	2°46·8'W	X	5
Corbie Nest	D & G	NX6949	54°49·4'	4°1·9'W	X	83,84
Corbie Shank	D & G	NY3598	55°16·6'	3°1·0'W	X	79
Corbies' Nest	Aberd	NJ3706	57°8·7'	3°2·0'W	X	37
Corbies Pot	Aberd	NO7878	56°53·8'	2°21·2'W	W	45
Corbieton Ho	D & G	NX7965	54°58·1'	3°53·0'W	X	84
Corbiewell	Moray	NJ3165	57°40·4'	3°8·9'W	X	28
Corbishley	Ches	SJ8275	53°16·5'	2°15·8'W	X	118
Corbitmere Dam	Durham	NY8744	54°47·7'	2°11·7'W	W	87
Corb Law	Pth & Kin	NO0009	56°16·0'	3°36·4'W	H	58
Corble Fm	Oxon	SP6315	51°50·0'	1°4·7'W	FM	164,165
Corblelack	Aberd	NJ4404	57°7·7'	2°55·0'W	X	37
Corbouies, The	Aberd	NJ4917	57°14·7'	2°50·3'W	X	37
Corbridge	Northum	NY9964	54°58·5'	2°0·5'W	T	87
Corbridge Common	Northum	NY9861	54°56·9'	2°1·4'W	X	87
Corbriggs	Derby	SK4168	53°12·7'	1°22·8'W	T	120
Corbrook Court	Ches	SJ6644	52°59·8'	2°30·0'W	X	118
Corbshill	Aberd	NJ8447	57°31·0'	2°15·6'W	X	29,30
Corby	Conwy	SH8575	53°15·8'	3°43·5'W	X	116
Corby	Northnts	SP8889	52°29·7'	0°41·8'W	T	141
Corby Castle	Cumbr	NY4754	54°52·9'	2°49·1'W	X	86
Corby Craig	D & G	NX4075	55°2·9'	4°29·8'W	X	77
Corby Gates Fm	Cumbr	NY7347	54°49·3'	2°24·8'W	FM	86,87
Corby Glen	Lincs	SK9925	52°49·0'	0°31·5'W	T	130
Corby Haugh	Aberd	NO2995	57°2·7'	3°9·8'W	X	37,44
Corby Hill	Cumbr	NY4857	54°54·5'	2°48·2'W	T	86
Corby Loch	C of Aber	NJ9214	57°13·3'	2°7·5'W	W	38
Corbyn's Head	Torbay	SX9063	50°27·6'	3°32·6'W	X	202
Corby Pasture Fm	Lincs	TF0026	52°49·6'	0°30·5'W	FM	130
Corby Pike	Northum	NT8401	55°18·4'	2°14·7'W	H	80
Corby's Crags	Northum	NU1210	55°23·3'	1°48·2'W	X	81
Corby Tunnel	Northnts	SP8991	52°30·8'	0°40·9'W	X	141
Corcasmol	N Eil	NB0618	58°3·5'	6°58·6'W	H	13,14
Cordach	Aberd	NO6097	57°4·0'	2°39·1'W	X	37,45
Cordale Beag	N Eil	NF7307	57°2·5'	7°23·1'W	X	31
Cordale Mór	N Eil	NF7308	57°3·1'	7°23·2'W	X	31
Cordale Mór	N Eil	NF7380	57°41·7'	7°28·9'W	X	18
Cordell Hall	Suff	TL7854	52°9·6'	0°36·5'E	X	155
Cordeman	I of M	SC2875	54°8·8'	4°37·6'W	X	95
Cordery's Fm	Hants	SU7462	51°21·4'	0°55·8'W	FM	175,186
Cord Hill	Leic	SK8417	52°44·9'	0°44·9'W	X	130
Cordilleras	N Yks	NZ0903	54°25·6'	1°51·3'W	X	92
Cording's Fm	Somer	ST0730	51°3·9'	3°19·3'W	FM	181
Cordon	N Ayr	NS0230	55°31·7'	5°7·8'W	T	69
Cordon	Pth & Kin	NO1817	56°20·6'	3°19·2'W	X	58
Cordons Fm	Kent	TQ4852	51°15·1'	0°7·6'E	FM	188
Cordorcan	D & G	NX3672	55°1·2'	4°33·5'W	X	77
Cordorcan Burn	D & G	NX4073	55°1·8'	4°29·8'W	W	77
Cordwell	Derby	SK3176	53°17·0'	1°31·7'W	X	119
Cordwell	Norf	TM1393	52°29·8'	1°8·7'E	T	144
Core	Moray	NJ3962	57°38·9'	3°0·9'W	X	28
Core Copse	Devon	SY1394	50°44·6'	3°13·6'W	F	192,193
Corehead	D & G	NT0712	55°23·8'	3°27·7'W	X	78
Coreheynan	Stir	NN3733	56°27·9'	4°38·3'W	X	50
Corehill	Aberd	NJ7533	57°23·5'	2°24·5'W	X	29
Core Hill	Aberd	NJ7633	57°23·5'	2°23·5'W	H	29
Core Hill	Devon	SY1290	50°42·4'	3°14·4'W	X	192,193
Core Hill	Pth & Kin	NN8804	56°13·2'	3°47·9'W	H	58
Corehouse	S Lanak	NS8841	55°39·2'	3°46·4'W	X	71,72
Coreley	Shrops	SO6173	52°21·5'	2°34·0'W	T	138
Coremachy	Angus	NO3370	56°49·3'	3°5·4'W	H	44

Core of Mayen	Moray	NJ5749	57°32·0'	2°42·6'W	X	29
Cores End	Bucks	SU9087	51°34·7'	0°41·7'W	T	175
Corfardine	D & G	NX7995	55°14·3'	3°53·7'W	H	78
Corfardine	D & G	NX8096	55°14·9'	3°52·8'W	X	78
Corfcott Green	Devon	SX3399	50°46·2'	4°21·7'W	X	190
Corfe	Somer	ST2319	50°58·2'	3°5·4'W	T	193
Corfe Barton	Somer	ST2320	50°58·7'	3°5·4'W	X	193
Corfe Castle	Dorset	SY9681	50°38·0'	2°3·0'W	T	195
Corfe Common	Dorset	SY9580	50°37·4'	2°3·9'W	X	195
Corfe Fm	Dorset	SY4995	50°45·4'	2°43·0'W	FM	193,194
Corfe Hill	Dorset	SY6681	50°37·9'	2°28·5'W	X	194
Corfe Hills	Dorset	SY9996	50°46·0'	2°0·5'W	X	195
Corfeidly	Aberd	NJ6700	57°5·6'	2°32·2'W	X	38
Corfe Mullen	Dorset	SY9897	50°46·6'	2°1·3'W	T	195
Corfe River	Dorset	SY9684	50°39·6'	2°3·0'W	W	195
Corffe	Devon	SS5429	51°2·7'	4°4·6'W	X	180
Corfham Castle	Shrops	SO5284	52°27·3'	2°42·0'W	A	137,138
Corfheath Firs	I of W	SZ4490	50°42·7'	1°22·2'W	F	196
Corfhouse	Arg & Bt	NN0132	56°26·6'	5°13·3'W	T	50
Corfield Fm	Shrops	SO5791	52°31·2'	2°37·6'W	FM	137,138
Corfton	Shrops	SO4984	52°27·3'	2°44·6'W	T	137,138
Corfton Bache	Shrops	SO4985	52°27·9'	2°44·6'W	X	137,138
Corgam	Cered	SN3352	52°8·7'	4°26·0'W	X	145
Corgarff	Aberd	NJ2708	57°9·7'	3°12·0'W	T	37
Corgarff Castle	Aberd	NJ2508	57°9·7'	3°13·9'W	A	37
Corgee	Corn	SX0460	50°24·7'	4°45·1'W	T	200
Corgelly Fm	Corn	SX1078	50°34·5'	4°40·6'W	FM	200
Corglass Fm	Moray	NJ1541	57°27·3'	3°24·5'W	FM	28
Corgrain Point	Highld	NH5948	57°30·3'	4°20·7'W	X	26
Corgyle	Moray	NJ2443	57°28·5'	3°15·6'W	X	28
Corhampton	Hants	SU6120	50°58·8'	1°7·5'W	T	185
Corhampton Down	Hants	SU5720	50°58·8'	1°10·9'W	X	185
Corhampton Forest	Hants	SU5821	50°59·4'	1°10·0'W	F	185
Corharncross	Angus	NO5178	56°53·7'	2°47·8'W	X	44
Corhill	Aberd	NK0851	57°33·2'	1°51·5'W	X	30
Corhulloch	D & G	NX3346	54°47·1'	4°35·4'W	X	82
Corhulloch Hill	D & G	NX3347	54°47·7'	4°35·4'W	H	82
Coriefeuran Hill	Highld	NC6633	58°16·2'	4°16·6'W	H	16
Coriestane	Aberd	NJ5338	57°26·1'	2°46·5'W	X	29
Corinivm (Cirencester)	Glos	SP0201	51°42·7'	1°57·9'W	R	163
Corinthian Arch	Bucks	SP6836	52°1·3'	1°0·1'W	X	152
Corkerhill	C of Glas	NS5462	55°50·0'	4°19·4'W	X	64
Corker's Fm	Oxon	SU6682	51°32·2'	1°2·5'W	FM	175
Corker Walls	Sheff	SK2689	53°24·1'	1°36·1'W	X	110
Cork Fm	Corn	SX0166	50°27·8'	4°47·9'W	FM	200
Cork Fm	Kent	TR0754	51°15·1'	0°58·4'E	FM	179,189
Corkham Beck	Cumbr	NY5803	54°25·5'	2°38·4'W	W	91
Cork Hill	Notts	SK6956	53°6·0'	0°57·8'W	X	120
Cork Hole	Norf	TF6033	52°52·5'	0°23·1'E	W	132
Corkickle	Cumbr	NX9717	54°32·5'	3°35·1'W	X	89
Corkindale Law	E Renf	NS4456	55°46·6'	4°28·8'W	X	64
Corkins Bank	Shrops	SO1882	52°26·0'	3°12·0'W	X	136
Corkley	Derby	SK2944	52°59·8'	1°33·7'W	X	119,128
Corkmere Bottom	Norf	TL8890	52°28·8'	0°46·5'E	F	144
Corkney Top	Inverc	NS2769	55°53·2'	4°45·5'W	X	63
Cork Sand	Essex	TM3326	51°53·2'	1°23·6'E	X	169
Corkscrew Hill	Devon	SX8255	50°23·2'	3°39·2'W	X	202
Cork's Fm	Oxon	SU7377	51°29·5'	0°56·5'W	FM	175
Corkwood Fm	E Susx	TQ9024	50°59·3'	0°42·8'E	FM	189
Corlabhadh	N Eil	NB3108	57°59·1'	6°32·6'W	H	13,14
Corlach	Arg & Bt	NM8305	56°11·6'	5°29·4'W	H	55
Corlach Hill	Aberd	NO5986	56°58·1'	2°40·0'W	X	44
Corlae	D & G	NX6597	55°15·2'	4°7·0'W	X	77
Corlae Burn	D & G	NX6794	55°13·6'	4°5·0'W	W	77
Corlae Hill	D & G	NX6995	55°14·2'	4°3·2'W	X	77
Corlan Fraith	Gwyn	SH6300	52°35·1'	4°0·9'W	H	135
Corlannau	Nth Pt Talb	SS7690	51°36·0'	3°47·0'W	T	170
Corlarach Hill	Arg & Bt	NS1374	55°55·6'	4°59·2'W	H	63
Corlaw	D & G	NY3197	55°16·0'	3°4·7'W	X	79
Corlaw Burn	D & G	NY3197	55°16·0'	3°4·7'W	W	79
Corlea Fm	I of M	SC2775	54°8·8'	4°38·5'W	FM	95
Corley	Warw	SP3085	52°28·0'	1°33·1'W	T	140
Corley Ash	Warw	SP2986	52°28·5'	1°34·0'W	T	140
Corley Fm	Derby	SK2147	53°1·4'	1°40·8'W	FM	119,128
Corley Hall	Warw	SP3085	52°28·0'	1°33·1'W	X	140
Corley Moor	Warw	SP2884	52°27·4'	1°34·9'W	T	140
Corley Service Area	Warw	SP3086	52°28·5'	1°33·1'W	X	140
Corlich Hill	Aberd	NJ3613	57°12·5'	3°3·1'W	H	37
Corlick Hill	Inverc	NS2973	55°55·4'	4°43·8'W	H	63
Corloch	N Ayr	NR9948	55°41·3'	5°11·4'W	X	62,69
Corly Craig	D & G	NX1874	55°1·9'	4°50·4'W	X	76
Cormaddie	D & G	NX9280	55°6·4'	3°41·1'W	X	78
Cormalet	Aberd	NJ5245	57°29·8'	2°47·6'W	X	29
Cormaud	Angus	NO3062	56°44·9'	3°8·2'W	H	44
Cormech	Aberd	NO6590	57°0·2'	2°34·1'W	W	38,45
Cormickhillock	Aberd	NJ6157	57°36·3'	2°38·7'W	X	29
Cormilligan	D & G	NX7495	55°14·2'	3°58·5'W	X	77
Cormilligan Bottom	D & G	NX7494	55°13·7'	3°58·4'W	X	77
Cormiston	S Lanak	NT0137	55°37·2'	3°33·9'W	X	72
Cormiston Mains	S Lanak	NT0037	55°37·2'	3°34·8'W	X	72
Cormiston Towers Fm	S Lanak	NT0037	55°37·2'	3°34·8'W	FM	72
Cormonachan	Arg & Bt	NS1996	56°7·6'	4°54·3'W	X	56
Cormonachan Glen	Arg & Bt	NS1897	56°8·1'	4°55·3'W	X	56
Cormuir	Angus	NO3066	56°47·1'	3°8·3'W	X	44
Cormunnoch Hill	D & G	NX7396	55°14·8'	3°59·4'W	H	77
Cornaa	I of M	SC4389	54°16·6'	4°24·3'W	T	95
Cornaa	I of M	SC4689	54°16·7'	4°21·5'W	X	95
Cornabo	Aberd	NJ6417	57°14·8'	2°35·3'W	X	37
Cornabus	Arg & Bt	NR3346	55°38·3'	6°14·1'W	X	60
Cornaig Bay	N Eil	NL6396	56°56·2'	7°32·0'W	W	31
Cornaigbeg	Arg & Bt	NL9846	56°30·8'	6°54·1'W	T	46
Cornaigbeg	Arg & Bt	NM2462	56°40·4'	6°29·9'W	X	46,47
Cornaigmore	Arg & Bt	NL9847	56°31·3'	6°54·2'W	T	46
Cornaigmore	Arg & Bt	NM2463	56°40·9'	6°30·0'W	X	46,47
Cornakey Cliff	Corn	SS2016	50°55·2'	4°33·3'W	X	190
Cornakey Fm	Corn	SS2116	50°55·2'	4°32·4'W	FM	190
Cornal Burn	D & G	NT1204	55°19·6'	3°22·8'W	W	78
Cornalees	Inverc	NS2571	55°54·3'	4°47·5'W	X	63
Cornalees Bridge Centre	Inverc	NS2472	55°54·8'	4°48·5'W	X	63
Cornan	Arg & Bt	NR7266	55°50·3'	5°38·0'W	X	62

Cornard Tye	Suff	TL9041	52°2·3'	0°46·6'E	T	155
Cornarroch Strand	D & G	NX4681	55°6·2'	4°24·4'W	W	77
Cornbank	Midlo	NT2260	55°49·9'	3°14·3'W	T	66
Cornborough	Devon	SS4128	51°2·0'	4°15·7'W	X	180
Cornborough Fm	N Yks	SE6266	54°5·4'	1°2·7'W	FM	100
Cornborough Hall	N Yks	SE6368	54°6·5'	1°1·8'W	X	100
Cornborough Range	Devon	SS4128	51°2·0'	4°15·7'W	X	180
Cornbrook	Shrops	SO6075	52°22·5'	2°34·9'W	T	138
Corn Brook	Shrops	SO6172	52°20·9'	2°34·0'W	W	138
Cornbrough Manor Fm	N Yks	SE6367	54°5·9'	1°1·8'W	FM	100
Cornbury Fm	Wilts	SU0049	51°14·6'	1°59·6'W	FM	184
Cornbury Ho	Oxon	SP3518	51°51·8'	1°29·1'W	A	164
Cornbury Park	Oxon	SP3517	51°51·3'	1°29·1'W	X	164
Corncatterach	Aberd	NJ5434	57°23·9'	2°45·5'W	X	29
Cornceres	Fife	NO5705	56°14·4'	2°41·2'W	X	59
Corn Close	Cumbr	SD6788	54°17·4'	2°30·0'W	X	98
Corn Close	Lancs	SD9441	53°52·2'	2°5·1'W	X	103
Corn Close	N Yks	SE1466	54°5·6'	1°46·7'W	X	99
Corn Close Fm	Leic	SK7707	52°39·5'	0°51·3'W	FM	141
Corncockle	D & G	NY0886	55°9·8'	3°26·2'W	X	78
Corndavon Lodge	Aberd	NJ2202	57°6·4'	3°16·8'W	X	36
Corndean Fm	Glos	SP0126	51°56·2'	1°58·7'W	FM	163
Corndean Hall	Glos	SP0126	51°56·2'	1°58·7'W	X	163
Corndon	Devon	SX6974	50°33·3'	3°50·6'W	X	191
Corndon	Devon	SX6985	50°39·2'	3°50·8'W	X	191
Corndon Fm	Powys	SO3095	52°33·1'	3°1·5'W	FM	137
Corndon Hill	Powys	SO3096	52°33·7'	3°1·6'W	H	137
Corndon Tor	Devon	SX6874	50°33·3'	3°51·4'W	H	191
Corn Dû	Powys	SO0021	51°53·0'	3°26·8'W	H	160
Corneal	Corn	SX3868	50°29·6'	4°16·7'W	X	201
Cornel	Conwy	SH7460	53°7·6'	3°52·6'W	X	115
Cornel	Denb	SJ0373	53°15·0'	3°26·8'W	X	116
Cornel	Powys	SN9863	52°15·6'	3°29·3'W	X	147
Cornelau	Gwyn	SH9233	52°53·3'	3°35·9'W	X	125
Cornelau	Powys	SO0140	52°3·2'	3°26·2'W	X	147,160
Cornelian Bay	N Yks	TA0686	54°15·8'	0°21·9'W	W	101
Cornell's Plantn	Norf	TL8891	52°29·3'	0°46·5'E	F	144
Cornelly Ho	I of M	SC2979	54°10·9'	4°36·8'W	X	95
Cornelyn	I of Angl	SH6179	53°17·6'	4°4·7'W	X	114,115
Corner Beck	Darl	NZ2223	54°36·3'	1°39·1'W	W	93
Corner Fm	Beds	TL0418	51°51·3'	0°29·0'W	FM	166
Corner Fm	Cambs	TL1776	52°22·4'	0°16·5'W	FM	142
Corner Fm	E Yorks	SE7751	53°57·2'	0°49·2'W	FM	105,106
Corner Fm	Glos	SO7602	51°43·2'	2°20·5'W	FM	162
Corner Fm	Hav	TQ6185	51°32·7'	0°19·7'E	FM	177
Corner Fm	Herts	TL0611	51°47·5'	0°27·4'W	FM	166
Corner Fm	Herts	TL0906	51°44·8'	0°24·9'W	FM	166
Corner Fm	Lincs	TF1976	53°16·3'	0°12·5'W	FM	122
Corner Fm	Lincs	TF5467	53°10·9'	0°18·7'E	FM	122
Corner Fm	Norf	TF4817	52°44·1'	0°11·9'E	FM	131
Corner Fm	Oxon	SP6011	51°47·9'	1°7·4'W	FM	164,165
Corner Fm	Pemb	SM9015	51°47·9'	5°2·3'W	FM	157,158
Corner Fm	Pemb	SN0317	51°49·3'	4°51·1'W	FM	157,158
Corner Fm	Peterb	TF3204	52°37·3'	0°2·6'W	FM	142
Corner Fm	Suff	TM3886	52°25·4'	1°30·4'E	FM	156
Corner Fm	Suff	TM4077	52°20·5'	1°31·8'E	FM	156
Corner Fm	Wilts	ST8728	51°3·3'	2°10·7'W	FM	183
Corner Fm	Wilts	SU0081	51°31·9'	1°59·6'W	FM	173
Corner Ho	D & G	NX0657	54°52·5'	5°1·0'W	X	82
Corner Ho	Kent	TQ9554	51°15·3'	0°48·1'E	X	189
Corner Lodge Fm	Leic	SP6091	52°31·0'	1°6·5'W	FM	140
Corner Pool	Highld	NM6950	56°35·4'	5°45·3'W	W	49
Cornerpool Fm	N Som	ST5064	51°22·6'	2°42·7'W	FM	172,182
Corner Quoit	Corn	SX1270	50°30·2'	4°38·7'W	X	200
Corner Row	Lancs	SD4134	53°48·2'	2°53·3'W	T	102
Corner, The	Dorset	ST8526	51°2·2'	2°12·5'W	X	183
Corner The	Dorset	SY4091	50°43·2'	2°50·6'W	X	193
Corner, The	Shrops	SO4387	52°28·9'	2°50·0'W	T	137
Cornerways Fm	Norf	TL6598	52°33·5'	0°26·4'E	FM	143
Cornescorn	Angus	NO5774	56°51·6'	2°41·9'W	X	44
Cornet Hill	Devon	ST0025	51°1·2'	3°25·2'W	X	181
Cornets End	Sol	SP2381	52°25·8'	1°39·3'W	X	139
Cornett	Heref	SO5749	52°8·5'	2°37·3'W	T	149
Corney	Cumbr	SD1191	54°18·7'	3°21·7'W	T	96
Corney Bury	Herts	TL3530	51°57·4'	0°1·7'W	A	166
Corney Fell	Cumbr	SD1391	54°18·7'	3°19·8'W	X	96
Corney Hall	Cumbr	SD1190	54°18·1'	3°21·6'W	X	96
Corney Hill	Lancs	SD5161	54°2·8'	2°44·5'W	X	97
Corneyside	Northum	NZ0273	55°3·3'	1°57·7'W	X	87
Cornfield Ho	Lancs	SD8134	53°48·4'	2°16·9'W	X	103
Cornfield Ho	N Yks	SE6197	54°22·1'	1°3·2'W	X	94,100
Corn Fm	Gwyn	SH3025	52°48·0'	4°30·9'W	FM	123
Corn Fm	Monm	SO4700	51°42·0'	2°45·6'W	FM	171
Cornford Bridge	Dorset	ST6912	50°54·6'	2°26·1'W	A	194
Cornforth	Durham	NZ3134	54°42·2'	1°30·7'W	T	93
Corngafr	Carm	SN2722	51°52·4'	4°30·4'W	X	145,158
Corngrave Fm	Red & Cl	NZ6420	54°34·5'	1°0·2'W	FM	94
Corn Hall	Suff	TL9135	51°59·1'	0°47·3'E	X	155
Corn Ham	Glos	SO7915	51°50·2'	2°17·9'W	X	162
Cornham Fm	Somer	SS7439	51°8·4'	3°47·7'W	FM	180
Cornharrow	D & G	NX6692	55°12·5'	4°5·9'W	X	77
Cornharrow Hill	D & G	NX6993	55°13·1'	4°3·1'W	H	77
Cornharrow Shoulder	D & G	NX6894	55°13·6'	4°4·1'W	X	77
Corn Hayes Fm	Staffs	SJ9452	53°4·2'	2°5·0'W	FM	118
Corn Head	Shetld	HU2257	60°18·1'	1°35·6'W	X	3
Cornheys Fm	Derby	SK0682	53°20·6'	1°54·2'W	FM	110
Corn Hill	Aberd	NJ5756	57°35·8'	2°42·7'W	H	29
Cornhill	Aberd	NJ5858	57°36·9'	2°41·7'W	T	29
Cornhill	Aberd	NJ7702	57°6·8'	2°22·3'W	X	38
Cornhill	C of Aber	NJ9107	57°9·5'	2°8·5'W	T	38
Cornhill	C of Stoke	SJ8952	53°4·1'	2°9·4'W	T	118
Cornhill	Cumbr	NY3656	54°53·9'	2°59·5'W	X	85
Cornhill	Fife	NO2713	56°18·5'	3°10·4'W	X	59
Cornhill	Highld	NH5891	57°53·4'	4°23·2'W	T	21
Cornhill	Kent	TQ8430	51°2·6'	0°37·9'E	X	188
Corn Hill	Monm	ST3996	51°39·8'	2°52·5'W	X	171
Corn Hill	Northnts	SP6655	52°11·6'	1°1·7'W	X	152
Corn Hill	N Yks	NZ3004	54°26·1'	1°31·8'W	X	93
Cornhill	Powys	SO1440	52°3·3'	3°14·9'W	T	148,161
Corn Hill	Powys	SO1460	52°14·1'	3°15·2'W	X	148

Cornhill	Pth & Kin	NN9410	56°16·5′	3°42·3′W	X	58
Corn Hill	Pth & Kin	NN9509	56°16·0′	3°41·3′W	X	58
Corn Hill	Shetld	HU5286	60°33·5′	1°2·6′W	X	1,2,3
Cornhill	Wrex	SJ4635	52°54·8′	2°47·8′W	X	126
Cornhill Fm	Aberd	NJ7264	57°40·2′	2°27·7′W	FM	29
Cornhill Fm	Ches	SJ4672	53°14·8′	2°48·1′W	FM	117
Cornhill Fm	Ches	SJ6066	53°11·6′	2°35·5′W	FM	118
Cornhill Fm	Corn	SW6140	50°12·9′	5°20·6′W	FM	203
Cornhill Fm	Corn	SX0654	50°21·5′	4°43·3′W	FM	200
Cornhill Fm	Kent	TQ9551	51°13·7′	0°48·0′E	FM	189
Cornhill Fm	N Lincs	TA0421	53°40·7′	0°25·1′W	FM	107,112
Cornhill Fm	Oxon	SU3787	51°35·1′	1°27·6′W	FM	174
Cornhill Fm	S Lanak	NT0235	55°36·2′	3°32·9′W	FM	72
Cornhill Ho	S Lanak	NT0135	55°36·2′	3°33·8′W	X	72
Cornhill Manor	Surrey	TQ0841	51°9·7′	0°26·9′W	X	187
Cornhill on-Tweed	Northum	NT8639	55°38·9′	2°12·9′W	T	74
Cornhills	Northum	NY9684	55°9·3′	2°3·3′W	X	81
Cornhills	S Lanak	NS7052	55°44·9′	4°3·8′W	X	64
Cornhills Fm	Lincs	SK9177	53°17·2′	0°37·7′W	FM	121
Corn Holm	Orkney	HY5901	58°53·9′	2°42·2′W	X	6
Cornholme	Cald	SD9026	53°44·1′	2°8·7′W	T	103
Cornhow	Cumbr	NY1422	54°35·4′	3°19·4′W	X	89
Cornhwrdd	Carm	SN5402	51°42·1′	4°6·4′W	X	159
Corniehaugh	Aberd	NJ5746	57°30·4′	2°42·6′W	X	29
Cornish Down	Pemb	SN1101	51°40·8′	4°43·6′W	X	158
Cornish Fm	E Susx	TV5696	50°44·8′	0°13·1′E	FM	199
Cornish Hall	Essex	TL6835	51°59·5′	0°27·2′E	X	154
Cornish Hall	Wrex	SJ3852	53°3·9′	2°55·1′W	X	117
Cornish Hall End	Essex	TL6836	52°0·0′	0°27·2′E	T	154
Cornish Hill	S Ayr	NX4094	55°13·1′	4°30·5′W	H	77
Cornish Loch	S Ayr	NX4094	55°13·1′	4°30·5′W	W	77
Cornist Ganol	Flint	SJ2272	53°14·6′	3°9·7′W	X	117
Cornlee	D & G	NX8478	55°5·2′	3°48·6′W	X	84
Cornlee Hill	D & G	NX8578	55°5·2′	3°47·7′W	H	84
Cornley	Notts	SK7495	53°27·0′	0°52·7′W	X	112
Corn Mill Fm	Brad	SE2330	53°46·2′	1°38·6′W	FM	104
Cornmill Stream	Essex	TL3801	51°41·7′	0°0·2′E	W	166
Cornmoor Fm	Somer	ST3444	51°11·7′	2°56·3′W	FM	182
Cornorion Fawr	Powys	SJ1121	52°47·0′	3°18·8′W	X	125
Corn Park	Durham	NY9919	54°34·2′	2°0·5′W	X	92
Cornpark	Staffs	SK1447	53°1·4′	1°47·1′W	X	119,128
Cornpit Fm	Hants	SU0915	50°56·3′	1°51·9′W	FM	184
Cornquoy	Orkney	ND5299	58°52·8′	2°49·5′W	X	6,7
Corn Ridge	Devon	SX5588	50°40·7′	4°2·8′W	H	191
Cornriggs	Durham	NY8441	54°46·1′	2°14·5′W	T	86,87
Cornsay	Durham	NZ1443	54°47·1′	1°46·5′W	T	88
Cornsay Colliery	Durham	NZ1643	54°47·1′	1°44·6′W	T	88
Cornsay House Fm	Durham	NZ1643	54°47·1′	1°44·6′W	FM	88
Cornsilloch	S Lanak	NS7851	55°44·5′	3°56·2′W	X	64
Cornton	Midlo	NT2158	55°48·8′	3°15·2′W	X	66,73
Cornton	Stir	NS7995	56°8·2′	3°56·4′W	T	57
Cornton Burn	Midlo	NT2059	55°49·3′	3°16·2′W	W	73
Corntown	Highld	NH5556	57°34·5′	4°25·0′W	T	26
Corntown	V of Glam	SS9177	51°29·1′	3°33·8′W	T	170
Corntown Fm	V of Glam	SS9276	51°28·6′	3°32·9′W	FM	170
Corntulloch	Aberd	NO4497	57°3·9′	2°55·0′W	X	37,44
Cornwal	Conwy	SH9063	53°9·4′	3°38·3′W	X	116
Cornwall Coast Path	Corn	SX3454	50°22·0′	4°19·7′W	X	201
Cornwall Fm	Powys	SO0924	51°54·7′	3°19·0′W	FM	161
Cornwall's Hill	Notts	SK6345	53°0·2′	1°3·3′W	X	129
Cornwell	Oxon	SP2727	51°56·7′	1°36·0′W	T	163
Cornwell Copse	Oxon	SP6600	51°41·9′	1°2·3′W	F	164,165
Cornwood	Devon	SX6059	50°25·1′	3°57·9′W	T	202
Cornworthy	Devon	SX8255	50°23·2′	3°39·2′W	T	202
Corn y Fan	Powys	SN9835	52°0·5′	3°28·8′W	X	160
Coronation Fm	Cambs	TL5980	52°23·9′	0°20·6′E	FM	143
Coronation Plantn	Durham	NZ0710	54°29·4′	1°53·1′W	F	92
Coronation Pot	N Yks	SD8570	54°7·8′	2°13·4′W	X	98
Coronation Whin	N Yks	SE3880	54°13·1′	1°24·6′W	F	99
Coronation Wood	Northum	NT9724	55°30·8′	2°2·4′W	F	75
Coronerage	Ches	SJ6246	53°0·8′	2°33·6′W	X	118
Cororion	Gwyn	SH5968	53°11·7′	4°4·9′W	X	114,115
Corpach	Highld	NN0976	56°50·4′	5°7·4′W	T	41
Corpach Bay	Arg & Bt	NR5691	56°3·2′	5°54·7′W	W	61
Corpach Hill	Highld	NN0978	56°51·5′	5°7·5′W	X	41
Corpach Moss	Highld	NN1176	56°50·5′	5°5·5′W	X	41
Corphin	S Ayr	NX2896	55°14·0′	4°41·9′W	X	76
Corporation Fm	Essex	TL8102	51°41·5′	0°37·5′E	FM	168
Corporation Fm	E Yorks	SE9647	53°54·9′	0°31·9′W	FM	106
Corporation Fm	E Yorks	TA0640	53°51·0′	0°22·9′W	FM	107
Corporation Fm	Norf	TM1599	52°33·0′	1°10·7′E	FM	144
Corporation Fm	Suff	TM2840	52°0·9′	1°19·8′E	FM	169
Corporation Marshes	Suff	TM4973	52°18·1′	1°39·5′E	W	156
Corps House Fm	N Yks	NZ4206	54°27·1′	1°20·7′W	FM	93
Corpslanding	E Yorks	TA0653	53°58·0′	0°22·6′W	X	107
Corpslanding Holme Fm	E Yorks	TA0452	53°57·5′	0°24·5′W	FM	107
Corpusty	Norf	TG1130	52°49·8′	1°8·3′E	T	133
Coruptechan	Arg & Bt	NR6633	55°32·3′	5°42·1′W	X	68
Corr	Highld	ND2035	58°18·0′	3°21·4′W	X	11
Corra	Arg & Bt	NR9765	55°50·4′	5°14·1′W	X	62
Corra	D & G	NX7861	54°56·0′	3°53·8′W	X	84
Corra	D & G	NX8666	54°58·8′	3°46·5′W	X	84
Corra	S Lanak	NS8639	55°38·1′	3°48·2′W	X	71,72
Corra-bheinn	Arg & Bt	NM5732	56°25·3′	5°56·0′W	H	48
Corra Bheinn	Arg & Bt	NR5275	55°54·5′	5°57·7′W	H	61
Corrach	Aberd	NO4087	56°58·5′	2°58·8′W	X	44
Corrachadh Mór	Highld	NM4166	56°43·1′	6°13·5′W	X	47
Corrachaive	Arg & Bt	NS1081	55°59·3′	5°2·3′W	X	63
Corrachaive Glen	Arg & Bt	NS0980	55°58·8′	5°3·2′W	X	63
Corrachan Buidhe	Highld	NH3049	57°30·2′	4°49·8′W	H	26
Corrach Bheinn	Arg & Bt	NM9321	56°20·4′	5°20·5′W	H	49
Corrachie	Highld	NH6754	57°33·7′	4°12·9′W	X	26
Corrachie Fm	Arg & Bt	NM9929	56°24·9′	5°15·1′W	FM	49
Corrachree	Aberd	NJ4604	57°7·7′	2°53·1′W	X	37
Corra Common	Shrops	SJ6138	52°56·5′	2°34·4′W	X	127
Corrafeckloch	D & G	NX3280	55°5·4′	4°37·5′W	X	76
Corrafeckloch Hill	D & G	NX3382	55°6·5′	4°36·7′W	X	76
Corraford Burn	D & G	NX6550	54°49·9′	4°5·7′W	W	83,84
Corrag Bhuidhe	Highld	NH0683	57°47·9′	5°15·4′W	X	19
Corra-ghoirtein	Arg & Bt	NR3169	55°50·6′	6°17·4′W	X	60,61

Corrahill	D & G	NX7145	54°47·3′	3°59·9′W	X	83,84
Corra Hill	D & G	NX7260	54°55·4′	3°59·4′W	H	83,84
Corraith	S Ayr	NS3631	55°33·0′	4°35·5′W	X	70
Corra Lane	D & G	NX7860	54°55·4′	3°53·8′W	W	84
Corra Linn	S Lanak	NS8841	55°39·2′	3°46·4′W	W	71,72
Corramore Fm	S Lanak	NS8640	55°38·7′	3°48·2′W	FM	71,72
Corran	Arg & Bt	NR7658	55°46·1′	5°33·8′W	X	62
Corran	Arg & Bt	NS2093	56°6·0′	4°53·2′W	X	56
Corran	Highld	NG8509	57°7·6′	5°32·7′W	T	33
Corran	Highld	NN0163	56°43·2′	5°14·7′W	T	41
Corran a' Chinn Uachdaraich	Highld	NG5829	57°17·5′	6°0·5′W	X	32
Corran Aird a' Mhòrain	N Eil	NF8376	57°40·0′	7°18·5′W	X	18
Corran Bàn	Arg & Bt	NR2973	55°52·7′	6°19·5′W	X	60
Corran Bàn	N Eil	NF7010	57°4·0′	7°26·3′W	X	31
Corran Buidhe	Arg & Bt	NR7179	55°57·2′	5°39·7′W	X	62
Corranbuie	Arg & Bt	NR8465	55°50·1′	5°26·5′W	X	62
Corran Dubh	Highld	NN0574	56°49·3′	5°11·3′W	X	41
Corran Fm	Corn	SW9946	50°17·0′	4°48·9′W	FM	204
Corran Goulaby	N Eil	NF8777	57°40·7′	7°14·6′W	X	18
Corran Lochan	Arg & Bt	NS2195	56°7·1′	4°52·3′W	W	56
Corran Mhànuis	N Eil	NF6461	57°31·1′	7°36·3′W	X	22
Corran Mór	N Eil	NB1033	58°11·7′	6°55·7′W	X	13
Corranmore	Arg & Bt	NM7903	56°10·4′	5°33·2′W	X	55
Corran na Beinne	N Eil	NB1733	58°12·0′	6°48·5′W	X	8,13
Corran Narrows	Highld	NN0163	56°43·2′	5°14·7′W	W	41
Corran Raah	N Eil	NB0400	57°53·7′	6°59·3′W	X	18
Corran River	Arg & Bt	NR5473	55°53·5′	5°55·6′W	W	61
Corran Rubha nan Lion	N Eil	NB3020	58°5·5′	6°34·4′W	X	13,14
Corran Sgoraig	Highld	NG9996	57°54·8′	5°23·1′W	X	19
Corran Sheileboist	N Eil	NG0698	57°52·7′	6°57·1′W	X	14,18
Corran Vallaquie	N Eil	NF8576	57°40·1′	7°16·5′W	X	18
Corran View	Arg & Bt	NM5341	56°30·0′	6°0·4′W	X	47,48
Corrany	I of M	SC4589	54°16·6′	4°22·4′W	T	95
Corrary	Arg & Bt	NR3157	55°44·2′	6°16·7′W	X	60
Corrary	Highld	NG8317	57°11·8′	5°35·1′W	X	33
Corrary Hill	Arg & Bt	NR3157	55°44·2′	6°16·7′W	X	60
Corravachie	Highld	NH4873	57°43·5′	4°32·7′W	X	20
Corr Bhàn	Arg & Bt	NR5910	55°19·8′	5°47·5′W	H	68
Corr Bheinn	Arg & Bt	NM9708	56°13·5′	5°16·0′W	H	55
Correchrevie	Arg & Bt	NR7353	55°43·3′	5°36·4′W	X	62
Correen Hills	Aberd	NJ5222	57°17·4′	2°47·3′W	H	37
Correen Wood	Aberd	NJ4922	57°17·4′	2°50·3′W	F	37
Còrr Eilean	Arg & Bt	NR6445	55°38·7′	5°44·6′W	X	62
Corr Eilean	Arg & Bt	NR6775	55°55·0′	5°43·3′W	X	61,62
Corr Eileanan	Highld	NG8606	57°6·0′	5°31·5′W	X	33
Corr-eileanan	N Eil	NF8640	57°20·8′	7°12·8′W	X	22
Correnie Forest	Aberd	NJ6410	57°11·0′	2°35·3′W	F	37
Correnie Moor	Aberd	NJ6109	57°10·5′	2°38·2′W	X	37
Corribeg	Highld	NM9978	56°51·3′	5°17·3′W	X	40
Corrichoich	Highld	ND0329	58°14·6′	3°38·7′W	X	11,17
Corrick	Highld	NH5139	57°25·3′	4°28·4′W	X	26
Corridge	Northum	NZ0683	55°8·7′	1°53·9′W	X	81
Corridge Fm	Devon	SX8190	50°42·1′	3°40·7′W	FM	191
Corridor Route	Cumbr	NY2108	54°27·9′	3°12·7′W	X	89,90
Corridow Hill	D & G	NS7605	55°19·7′	3°56·8′W	H	71,78
Corrie	Moray	NJ3942	57°28·1′	3°0·6′W	X	28
Corrie	N Ayr	NS0243	55°38·7′	5°8·4′W	T	63,69
Corrie	N Lanak	NS6979	55°59·4′	4°5·6′W	X	64
Corrie	Stir	NS4995	56°7·7′	4°25·3′W	X	57
Corrieachan	Stir	NN3708	56°14·5′	4°37·4′W	X	56
Corrie Amadal	Highld	NG4461	57°34·3′	6°16·4′W	X	23
Corriearklet	Stir	NN3709	56°15·0′	4°37·4′W	X	56
Corriearklet Burn	Stir	NN3611	56°16·0′	4°38·4′W	W	50,56
Corriebeagh Burn	Pth & Kin	NN7514	56°18·4′	4°0·8′W	W	57
Corriebreck	Aberd	NJ3314	57°13·0′	3°6·1′W	X	37
Corrie Burn	Angus	NO3274	56°51·4′	3°6·5′W	W	44
Corrie Burn	Arg & Bt	NS0578	55°57·6′	5°7·0′W	W	63
Corrie Burn	N Ayr	NS0041	55°37·5′	5°10·2′W	W	69
Corrie Burn	Stir	NS4795	56°7·7′	4°27·3′W	W	57
Corrie Chash	Aberd	NO2681	56°55·1′	3°12·5′W	X	44
Corriechoille	Highld	NN2580	56°53·0′	4°51·9′W	X	34,41
Corriechullie	Highld	NJ0621	57°16·5′	3°33·1′W	X	36
Corrie Common	D & G	NY2086	55°10·0′	3°14·9′W	T	79
Corriecravie	N Ayr	NR9223	55°27·7′	5°17·0′W	T	68,69
Corriecravie Moor	N Ayr	NR9224	55°28·2′	5°17·0′W	X	68,69
Corrie Cula	Aberd	NO1899	57°4·7′	3°20·7′W	X	36,43
Corriedoo	D & G	NX6882	55°7·1′	4°3·8′W	T	77
Corriedoo Forest	D & G	NX6882	55°7·1′	4°3·8′W	F	77
Corriedow	D & G	NX7293	55°13·1′	4°0·3′W	X	77
Corriedow	D & G	NX7693	55°13·2′	3°56·5′W	X	78
Corriedow Hill	D & G	NX7193	55°13·1′	4°1·2′W	H	77
Corriedow Hill	D & G	NX7693	55°13·2′	3°56·5′W	H	78
Corrie Duff	Angus	NO4683	56°56·4′	2°52·8′W	X	44
Corriefearn	Highld	NH6285	57°50·3′	4°19·0′W	X	21
Corriefeol	Highld	NH2050	57°30·5′	4°59·8′W	X	25
Corrie Feragie	Aberd	NO1691	57°0·4′	3°22·5′W	X	43
Corriefoulis	Highld	NH5764	57°38·9′	4°23·3′W	X	21
Corriegarth Lodge	Highld	NH5017	57°13·4′	4°28·6′W	X	35
Corriegills Point	N Ayr	NS0435	55°34·4′	5°6·1′W	X	69
Corriegour Lodge (Hotel)	Highld	NN2592	56°59·4′	4°52·4′W	X	34
Corriegrennan	Stir	NS4499	56°9·7′	4°30·3′W	X	57
Corriehall	Suff	TL8939	52°1·3′	0°45·7′E	X	155
Corrie Hallie	Highld	NH1185	57°49·1′	5°10·5′W	X	19
Corriehallie Forest	Highld	NH3848	57°29·9′	4°41·7′W	X	26
Corriehalls	D & G	NY2085	55°9·4′	3°14·9′W	X	79
Corriehead	Angus	NO3559	56°43·3′	3°3·3′W	X	54
Corriehiam Hill	N Ayr	NR9528	55°30·4′	5°14·3′W	X	68,69
Corrie Hill	Aberd	NJ6221	57°16·9′	2°37·4′W	H	37
Corriehills	D & G	NY1984	55°8·9′	3°15·8′W	X	79
Corrielaw	D & G	NY1784	55°8·9′	3°17·7′W	X	79
Corrielea	D & G	NY1985	55°9·4′	3°15·8′W	X	79
Corrielea	Pth & Kin	NO0134	56°29·5′	3°36·0′W	X	52,53
Corriemains	D & G	NY1982	55°7·8′	3°15·8′W	X	79
Corriemoillie	Highld	NH3563	57°37·9′	4°45·3′W	X	20
Corriemoillie Forest	Highld	NH3467	57°40·0′	4°46·5′W	X	20
Corriemoillie Lodge	Highld	NH3663	57°37·9′	4°44·3′W	X	20
Corriemulzie Burn	Aberd	NO1088	56°58·7′	3°28·4′W	W	43
Corriemulzie Lodge	Highld	NH3295	57°55·0′	4°49·7′W	X	20
Corriemulzie River	Highld	NH3193	57°53·9′	4°50·6′W	W	20

Corrie Murrin	Angus	NO4676	56°52·6′	2°52·7′W	X	44
Corrie na Berran	Angus	NO4472	56°50·4′	2°54·6′W	X	44
Corrie na Urisgean or Goblin's Cave	Stir	NN4807	56°14·1′	4°26·7′W	X	57
Corrienearn	Aberd	NO3994	57°2·2′	2°59·9′W	H	37,44
Corrie of Allt nan Aighean	Aberd	NJ2010	57°10·7′	3°18·9′W	X	36
Corrie of Balglass	Stir	NS5885	56°2·5′	4°16·3′W	X	57
Corrie of Bonhard	Angus	NO3175	56°51·9′	3°7·5′W	X	44
Corrie of Clova	Angus	NO3275	56°51·9′	3°6·5′W	X	44
Corrie of Creag Mheann	Aberd	NJ1910	57°10·7′	3°19·9′W	X	36
Corrie of Culchavie	Aberd	NJ2007	57°9·1′	3°18·9′W	X	36
Corrie of Morlich	Aberd	NJ4315	57°13·6′	2°56·2′W	X	37
Corries	Moray	NJ1635	57°24·1′	3°23·4′W	X	28
Corrieshalloch Gorge	Highld	NH2078	57°45·6′	5°1·1′W	X	20
Corrie Sike	Scot Bord	NT4002	55°18·8′	2°56·3′W	W	79
Corries Mill	D & G	NY3471	55°2·0′	3°1·5′W	X	85
Corriestand	D & G	NY2185	55°9·4′	3°14·0′W	X	79
Corrie Vanoch	Angus	NO1763	56°45·3′	3°21·0′W	X	43
Corrievorrie	Highld	NH7724	57°17·7′	4°2·0′W	X	35
Corrievuic	Highld	NH2051	57°31·1′	4°59·9′W	X	25
Corrie Water	D & G	NY1886	55°9·9′	3°16·8′W	W	79
Corrie Yairack	Highld	NN4398	57°3·0′	4°34·8′W	X	34
Corrieyairack Forest	Highld	NN4396	57°2·0′	4°34·8′W	X	34
Corrieyairack Hill	Highld	NN4299	57°3·6′	4°35·9′W	H	34
Corrieyairack Pass	Highld	NN4198	57°3·0′	4°36·8′W	X	34
Corrigall	Orkney	HY3219	59°3·4′	3°10·7′W	T	6
Corrimony	Highld	NH3730	57°20·1′	4°42·0′W	T	26
Corrimony Falls	Highld	NH3729	57°19·6′	4°42·0′W	X	26
Corringales	Essex	TL5216	51°49·5′	0°12·7′E	X	167
Corringdon Ball	Devon	SX6760	50°25·7′	3°52·0′W	H	202
Corringer Hill	N Yks	SD9251	53°57·5′	2°6·9′W	H	103
Corringham	Lincs	SK8791	53°24·8′	0°41·1′W	T	112
Corringham	Thurr	TQ7083	51°31·4′	0°27·4′E	T	178
Corringham Grange	Lincs	SK8891	53°24·7′	0°40·2′W	X	112
Corrins Hill	I of M	SC2383	54°13·0′	4°42·5′W	H	95
Corrinzion	Fife	NO1610	56°16·8′	3°21·0′W	X	58
Corris	Gwyn	SH7507	52°39·0′	3°50·5′W	T	124
Corrish Burn	Highld	NC6711	58°4·4′	4°14·8′W	W	16
Corrish Hill	Highld	NC8334	58°17·0′	3°59·2′W	X	17
Corris Uchaf	Gwyn	SH7408	52°39·5′	3°51·4′W	T	124
Corrlarach	Highld	NM9572	56°47·9′	5°21·0′W	X	40
Corr Leathad	Arg & Bt	NM8319	56°19·1′	5°30·1′W	X	55
Corr Mheall	Arg & Bt	NR9275	55°55·6′	5°19·3′W	X	62
CÒRR NA BEINNE	Highld	NN1051	56°37·0′	5°5·3′W	X	41
Corr nan Long	Arg & Bt	NR6410	55°19·9′	5°42·8′W	H	68
Corr Roy	S Ayr	NX3493	55°12·5′	4°36·1′W	W	76
Corrody Burn	Pth & Kin	NN9637	56°31·1′	3°41·0′W	W	52,53
Corrour	Moray	NJ2233	57°23·1′	3°17·4′W	X	28
Corrour Bothy	Aberd	NN9895	57°2·3′	3°40·4′W	X	36,43
Corrour Forest	Highld	NN4167	56°46·3′	4°35·7′W	X	42
Corrour Ho	Highld	NH8911	57°10·8′	3°49·7′W	X	35,36
Corrour Old Lodge	Highld	NN4064	56°44·7′	4°36·5′W	X	42
Corrour Shooting Lodge	Highld	NN4169	56°47·4′	4°35·7′W	X	42
Corrour Station	Highld	NN3566	56°45·6′	4°41·5′W	X	41
Corrow	Arg & Bt	NN1800	56°9·7′	4°55·4′W	X	56
Corr Sgeir	Arg & Bt	NR4345	55°38·1′	6°3·6′W	X	60
Corrunich	Moray	NJ2520	57°16·1′	3°14·2′W	X	37
Corry	Highld	NG6424	57°15·0′	5°54·3′W	T	32
Corry	Moray	NJ2520	57°16·1′	3°14·2′W	X	37
Corryachvrail	Highld	NC6802	57°59·5′	4°13·5′W	X	16
Corry Brook	Devon	SY2699	50°47·4′	3°2·6′W	W	192,193
Corrybrough	Highld	NH8129	57°20·4′	3°58·2′W	X	35
Corrycharcle	Highld	NH9734	57°23·3′	3°42·4′W	X	27
Corrycharmaig	Stir	NN5235	56°29·3′	4°23·8′W	X	51
Corrychurrachan	Highld	NN0466	56°44·9′	5°11·9′W	X	41
Corry Deanie	Highld	NH3041	57°25·9′	4°49·4′W	X	26
Corrydon	Pth & Kin	NO1366	56°46·9′	3°25·0′W	X	43
Corrydown	Aberd	NJ4333	57°23·3′	2°56·4′W	X	28
Corryfoyness	Highld	NH5533	57°22·1′	4°24·2′W	X	26
Corryghoil	Arg & Bt	NN1927	56°24·3′	4°55·6′W	X	50
Corryhabbie Burn	Moray	NJ2731	57°22·1′	3°12·4′W	W	37
Corryhabbie Hill	Moray	NJ2829	57°21·0′	3°11·3′W	H	37
Corryhill	Northum	NY7852	54°52·0′	2°20·1′W	X	86,87
Corry Ho	Cumbr	NY4956	54°54·0′	2°47·3′W	X	86
Corryhully	Highld	NM9184	56°54·3′	5°25·5′W	X	40
Corry Kinloch	Highld	NC3625	58°11·3′	4°46·9′W	X	16
Corrylach	Arg & Bt	NR7030	55°30·8′	5°38·2′W	X	68
Corrylair	Aberd	NJ4634	57°23·9′	2°53·5′W	X	28,29
Corry Lorn	Arg & Bt	NM8617	56°18·1′	5°27·1′W	X	55
Corrymoor Fm	Devon	ST2206	50°51·1′	3°6·1′W	FM	192,193
Corrymuckloch	Pth & Kin	NN8934	56°29·4′	3°47·7′W	X	52
Corryn	Powys	SN9648	52°7·5′	3°30·8′W	X	147
Corrynachenchy	Arg & Bt	NM6441	56°30·4′	5°49·7′W	X	49
Corrynahera	Arg & Bt	NR5979	55°56·9′	5°51·2′W	X	61
Corry of Ardnagrask	Highld	NH5048	57°30·1′	4°29·7′W	X	26
Corry Point	Highld	NH1492	57°53·0′	5°7·8′W	X	20
Corsairtly	Moray	NJ4249	57°31·9′	2°57·7′W	X	28
Corsankell	N Ayr	NS2643	55°39·2′	4°45·5′W	X	63,70
Corsback	Highld	ND2059	58°31·0′	3°21·9′W	X	11,12
Corsback	Highld	ND2372	58°38·0′	3°19·1′W	T	7,12
Corsback Hill	Highld	ND1960	58°31·5′	3°23·0′W	H	11,12
Corsbie	Scot Bord	NT6044	55°41·5′	2°37·7′W	X	74
Corsbie Moor	Scot Bord	NT5946	55°42·6′	2°38·7′W	X	73,74
Corsbie Moor	Scot Bord	NT6046	55°42·6′	2°37·8′W	X	74
Cors Bodwrog	I of Angl	SH4077	53°16·2′	4°23·6′W	W	114,115
Corscaplie	Stir	NN7602	56°11·9′	3°59·5′W	X	57
Cors Caron	Cered	SN6863	52°15·2′	3°55·6′W	W	146
Cors Caron	Cered	SN7065	52°16·3′	3°53·9′W	W	135,146
Corscombe	Devon	SX6296	50°45·1′	3°57·0′W	X	191
Corscombe	Dorset	ST5105	50°50·8′	2°41·4′W	T	194
Corscombe Court	Dorset	ST5205	50°50·8′	2°40·5′W	A	194
Corscombe Down	Devon	SX6195	50°44·5′	3°57·8′W	X	191
Cors Ddyga or Malltraeth Marsh	I of Angl	SH4571	53°13·1′	4°18·9′W	W	114,115
Corse	Aberd	NJ6040	57°27·2′	2°39·7′W	T	29
Corse	D & G	NX6776	55°3·9′	4°4·5′W	X	77,84
Corse	Glos	SO7826	51°56·2′	2°18·8′W	T	162
Corse	Glos	SO7828	51°57·2′	2°18·8′W	T	150
Corse	Orkney	HY3828	59°8·3′	3°4·5′W	X	6
Corse	Orkney	HY4310	58°58·7′	2°59·0′W	X	6

Corsebank	D & G	NS8016	55°25·6′	3°53·3′W	X	71,78
Corsebauld	Aberd	NO7282	56°56·0′	2°27·2′W	X	45
Corse Burn	Aberd	NJ5306	57°8·8′	2°46·2′W	W	37
Corse Burn	D & G	NS7911	55°22·9′	3°54·2′W	W	71,78
Corse Burn	D & G	NX4974	55°2·5′	4°21·4′W	W	77
Corse Castle	Aberd	NJ5507	57°9·4′	2°44·2′W	A	37
Corseclays Fm	S Ayr	NX0984	55°7·1′	4°59·3′W	FM	76
Corse Court Fm	Glos	SO7826	51°56·2′	2°18·8′W	FM	162
Corse Craig	D & G	NX4083	55°7·2′	4°30·1′W	X	77
Corsedardar Hill	Aberd	NO5994	57°2·4′	2°40·1′W	H	37,44
Corsefield	D & G	NX8883	55°8·0′	3°45·0′W	X	78
Corse Fm	Aberd	NK0153	57°34·3′	1°58·5′W	FM	30
Corsegate	D & G	NX7872	55°1·9′	3°54·1′W	X	84
Corsegight	Aberd	NJ8450	57°32·6′	2°15·6′W	X	29,30
Corsegreen	D & G	NY0779	55°6·1′	3°27·0′W	X	85
Corse Grove	Glos	SO8228	51°57·2′	2°15·3′W	F	150
Corsehead	D & G	NX2056	54°52·2′	4°47·9′W	X	82
Corse Hill	Aberd	NJ5406	57°8·8′	2°45·2′W	H	37
Corsehill	Aberd	NJ7945	57°29·9′	2°20·6′W	X	29,30
Corsehill	Aberd	NJ9015	57°13·8′	2°9·5′W	X	38
Corsehill	Aberd	NJ9159	57°37·5′	2°8·6′W	X	30
Corsehill	Aberd	NO8295	57°3·0′	2°17·3′W	X	38,45
Corsehill	C of Aber	NJ8511	57°11·6′	2°14·4′W	X	38
Corse Hill	D & G	NS6803	55°18·5′	4°4·3′W	H	77
Corse Hill	D & G	NX6684	55°8·2′	4°5·7′W	X	77
Corsehill	D & G	NY1789	55°11·6′	3°17·8′W	X	79
Corse Hill	E Renf	NS5946	55°41·5′	4°14·2′W	H	64
Corsehill	N Ayr	NS3638	55°36·7′	4°35·8′W	X	70
Corse Hill	Scot Bord	NT2215	55°25·6′	3°13·5′W	H	79
Corsehill Ho	D & G	NY2069	55°0·8′	3°14·6′W	X	85
Corsehope Burn	Scot Bord	NT3951	55°45·2′	2°57·9′W	W	66,73
Corsehope Fm	Scot Bord	NT3850	55°44·6′	2°58·8′W	FM	66,73
Corsehope Ho	Scot Bord	NT3952	55°45·7′	2°57·9′W	X	66,73
Corsehouse	E Ayr	NS4750	55°43·4′	4°25·7′W	X	64
Corse House Fm	Glos	SO7827	51°56·7′	2°18·8′W	FM	162
Corsehouse Resr	E Ayr	NS4749	55°42·9′	4°25·7′W	W	64
Corsekell Moss	Moray	NJ4157	57°36·2′	2°58·8′W	X	28
Corsekelly	Aberd	NK0561	57°38·6′	1°54·5′W	X	30
Corse Law	Scot Bord	NT7366	55°53·4′	2°25·5′W	X	67
Corse Law	S Lanak	NT0150	55°44·3′	3°34·2′W	X	65,72
Corse Lawn	Worcs	SO8330	51°58·3′	2°14·5′W	T	150
Corselet	E Ayr	NS4821	55°27·8′	4°23·8′W	X	70
Corsemaul	Aberd	NJ4040	57°27·0′	2°59·5′W	X	28
Corsemaul	Moray	NJ3840	57°27·0′	3°1·5′W	X	28
Corsencon	E Ayr	NS6613	55°23·8′	4°6·5′W	X	71
Corsencon Hill	E Ayr	NS6714	55°24·4′	4°5·6′W	H	71
Corsend	Aberd	NK0053	57°34·3′	1°59·5′W	X	30
Corsend Fm	Glos	SO7925	51°55·6′	2°17·9′W	FM	162
Corsenside	Northum	NY8889	55°12·0′	2°10·9′W	X	80
Corsenside Common	Northum	NY8788	55°11·4′	2°11·8′W	H	80
Corse of Balloch	Aberd	NK0441	57°27·8′	1°55·5′W	X	30
Corse of Garbet	Moray	NJ4127	57°20·0′	2°58·3′W	X	37
Corse of Slakes Road	D & G	NX5358	54°54·0′	4°17·1′W	X	83
Cors Erddreiniog	I of Angl	SH4780	53°17·9′	4°17·3′W	W	114,115
Corserig	D & G	NS7210	55°22·3′	4°0·8′W	X	71
Corserig Hill	D & G	NS7009	55°21·7′	4°2·6′W	H	71,77
Corserine	D & G	NX4987	55°9·5′	4°21·8′W	H	77
Corses	D & G	NY0288	55°10·8′	3°31·9′W	X	78
Corseside	Pemb	SM9000	51°39·8′	5°1·8′W	X	157,158
Corse Slack	Scot Bord	NT7609	55°22·7′	2°22·3′W	X	80
Corsewall	D & G	NX0369	54°58·9′	5°4·3′W	X	82
Corsewall Castle	D & G	NW9971	54°59·8′	5°8·1′W	A	76,82
Corsewall Point	D & G	NW9772	55°0·3′	5°10·0′W	X	76,82
Corse Wood Hill	Glos	SO8128	51°57·2′	2°16·2′W	H	150
Corseyard	D & G	NX5948	54°48·7′	4°11·2′W	X	83
Cors Farlais	Carm	SN6734	51°59·6′	3°55·8′W	X	146
Cors Fforchog	Powys	SH9205	52°38·2′	3°35·4′W	X	125
Cors Fochno	Cered	SN6391	52°30·2′	4°0·7′W	X	135
Cors Geirch	Gwyn	SH3136	52°53·9′	4°30·4′W	W	123
Cors Goch	I of Angl	SH4981	53°18·5′	4°15·6′W	W	114,115
Corshalloch	Aberd	NJ4141	57°27·6′	2°58·5′W	X	28
Corsham	Wilts	ST8670	51°26·0′	2°11·7′W	T	173
Corsham Court	Wilts	ST8770	51°26·0′	2°10·8′W	A	173
Corsham Park	Wilts	ST8771	51°26·5′	2°10·8′W	X	173
Corshelloch	Moray	NJ2232	57°22·6′	3°17·4′W	X	36
Corshellock	Moray	NJ2045	57°29·6′	3°19·6′W	X	28
Corshill	Stir	NS6899	56°10·2′	4°7·1′W	X	57
Corsiehill	Pth & Kin	NO1323	56°23·7′	3°24·1′W	T	53,58
Corsindae	Aberd	NJ6808	57°10·0′	2°31·3′W	X	38
Corskellie	Moray	NJ5547	57°30·9′	2°44·6′W	X	29
Corskie	Aberd	NJ7062	57°39·1′	2°29·7′W	X	29
Corskie	Moray	NJ3264	57°39·9′	3°7·9′W	X	28
Corsley	Wilts	ST8246	51°13·0′	2°15·1′W	T	183
Corsley Heath	Wilts	ST8245	51°12·5′	2°15·1′W	T	183
Corsley Hill Fm	Wilts	ST8147	51°13·5′	2°15·9′W	FM	183
Corsley Ho	Wilts	ST8245	51°12·5′	2°15·1′W	X	183
Corsley Mill	Wilts	ST8147	51°13·5′	2°15·9′W	X	183
Corsliehill	Renf	NS4069	55°53·5′	4°33·1′W	X	64
Corsock	D & G	NX7576	55°4·0′	3°57·0′W	T	84
Corsock	D & G	NX8656	54°53·4′	3°46·2′W	X	84
Corsock Ho	D & G	NX7575	55°3·5′	3°57·0′W	X	84
Corsock Loch	D & G	NX7575	55°3·5′	3°57·0′W	W	84
Cor Stack	I of M	SC4992	54°18·3′	4°18·8′W	X	95
Corstane	Scot Bord	NT1036	55°36·8′	3°25·3′W	X	72
Cors Tewgyll	Pemb	SN1331	51°57·0′	4°42·9′W	X	145
Corston	Bath & NE Somer	ST6965	51°23·2′	2°26·3′W	T	172
Corston	Orkney	HY3119	59°3·4′	3°11·7′W	X	6
Corston	Pemb	SR9299	51°39·3′	5°0·0′W	X	158
Corston	Wilts	ST9284	51°33·5′	2°6·5′W	T	173
Corston	W Loth	NT0763	55°51·3′	3°28·7′W	X	65
Corston Beacon	Pemb	SR9399	51°39·3′	4°59·2′W	X	158
Corston Beacon (Tumulus)	Pemb	SR9399	51°39·3′	4°59·2′W	A	158
Corstone	Devon	SS6104	50°49·4′	3°58·0′W	X	191
Corstone Moor	Devon	SS6104	50°49·4′	3°58·0′W	X	191
Corston Field	Bath & NE Somer	ST6864	51°22·7′	2°27·2′W	X	172
Corston Hill	W Loth	NT0963	55°51·4′	3°26·8′W	H	65
Corston Mill	Fife	NO2009	56°16·3′	3°17·1′W	X	58
Corstopitvm (Roman Fort)	Northum	NY9764	54°58·5′	2°2·4′W	R	87
Corstorphine	C of Edin	NT1972	55°56·3′	3°17·4′W	T	65,66
Corsua	D & G	NY0788	55°10·9′	3°27·2′W	X	78
Cors-y-bol	I of Angl	SH3784	53°19·9′	4°26·5′W	W	114
Cors-y-ceiliau	Gwyn	SH4144	52°58·4′	4°21·7′W	X	123
Corsyddalfa	Gwyn	SH4147	53°0·0′	4°21·8′W	W	115,123
Cors-y-garnedd	Gwyn	SH7623	52°47·7′	3°49·9′W	X	124
Cors y Gedol	Gwyn	SH6023	52°47·4′	4°4·2′W	A	124
Cors y Gwartheg-llwydion	Gwyn	SH8032	52°52·6′	3°46·6′W	X	124,125
Cors y Llyn	Gwyn	SH4850	53°1·8′	4°15·6′W	X	115,123
Cors y Llyn	Powys	SO0155	52°11·3′	3°26·5′W	W	147
Cors y Sarnau	Gwyn	SH9738	52°56·0′	3°31·5′W	W	125
Cors-y-wlad	Gwyn	SH4447	53°0·1′	4°19·1′W	X	115,123
Cortachy	Angus	NO3959	56°43·4′	2°59·4′W	T	54
Cortachy Castle	Angus	NO3959	56°43·4′	2°59·4′W	X	54
Cortes Ho	Aberd	NJ9959	57°37·5′	2°0·5′W	X	30
Corthant	Arg & Bt	NM7913	56°15·7′	5°33·7′W	X	55
Corthiemuir	Aberd	NJ8923	57°18·1′	2°10·5′W	X	38
Cortibrae	Aberd	NK0059	57°37·5′	1°59·5′W	X	30
Cortiecram	Aberd	NJ9641	57°27·8′	2°3·5′W	X	30
Cortiecram	Aberd	NK0251	57°33·2′	1°57·5′W	X	30
Cortleferry	Scot Bord	NT4350	55°44·7′	2°54·0′W	X	66,73
Cortleferry Hill	Scot Bord	NT4451	55°45·2′	2°53·1′W	X	66,73
Cort-ma Law	E Dunb	NS6579	55°59·4′	4°9·4′W	X	64
Corton	S Ayr	NS3517	55°25·4′	4°36·0′W	X	70
Corton	Suff	TM5497	52°30·9′	1°45·0′E	T	134
Corton	Wilts	ST9340	51°9·8′	2°5·6′W	T	184
Corton Cliffs	Suff	TM5398	52°31·5′	1°44·2′E	X	134
Corton Denham	Somer	ST6322	51°0·0′	2°31·3′W	T	183
Corton Down	Dorset	SY6386	50°40·6′	2°31·0′W	X	194
Corton Down	Wilts	ST9338	51°8·7′	2°5·6′W	X	184
Corton Farm	Dorset	SY6385	50°40·0′	2°31·0′W	A	194
Corton Hill	Somer	ST6323	51°0·5′	2°31·3′W	H	183
Corton Hill	Wilts	ST9339	51°9·2′	2°5·6′W	X	184
Corton Long Barrow	Wilts	ST9340	51°9·8′	2°5·6′W	A	184
Corton Manor Fm	Wilts	SU0575	51°28·7′	1°55·3′W	FM	173
Corton Ridge	Somer	ST6222	51°0·0′	2°32·1′W	H	183
Cor Tulloch	Highld	ND1535	58°18·0′	3°26·5′W	X	11,17
Cortworth	Roth	SK4098	53°28·9′	1°23·4′W	T	111
Coruanan	Highld	NN0668	56°46·1′	5°10·0′W	X	41
Coruanan Lodge	Highld	NN0668	56°46·1′	5°10·0′W	X	41
Coruisk Memorial Hut	Highld	NG4819	57°11·8′	6°9·8′W	X	32
Corunna	N Eil	NF8161	57°31·9′	7°19·4′W	X	22
Corunna Hill Plantn	Notts	SK5972	53°14·7′	1°6·5′W	F	120
Corun y Ffridd	Powys	SH8701	52°35·9′	3°39·7′W	H	135,136
Corvalley	I of M	SC3277	54°9·9′	4°34·0′W	X	95
Corvally	I of M	SC2986	54°14·7′	4°37·0′W	X	95
Corve Barn	Shrops	SO5993	52°32·2′	2°35·9′W	X	137,138
Corve Dale	Shrops	SO5388	52°29·5′	2°41·1′W	X	137,138
Corve Fm	I of W	SZ4780	50°37·3′	1°19·8′W	FM	196
Corvost	Highld	NH5392	57°53·9′	4°28·3′W	X	20
Corwall	D & G	NX2849	54°48·6′	4°40·2′W	X	82
Corwall Port	D & G	NX2748	54°48·1′	4°41·1′W	W	82
Corwar	D & G	NX4548	54°48·4′	4°24·3′W	X	83
Corwar	D & G	NX4769	54°59·8′	4°23·1′W	X	83
Corwar Burn	S Ayr	NX2878	55°4·3′	4°41·2′W	W	76
Corwar Fm	S Ayr	NX2878	55°4·3′	4°41·2′W	FM	76
Corwar Ho	S Ayr	NX2780	55°5·3′	4°42·2′W	X	76
Corwar Mains	S Ayr	NX2880	55°5·3′	4°41·3′W	X	76
Corwar Outon	D & G	NX4442	54°45·2′	4°25·0′W	X	83
Cor Water	Scot Bord	NT0616	55°26·0′	3°28·7′W	W	78
Corwen	Denb	SJ0743	52°58·8′	3°22·7′W	T	125
Corwharn	Angus	NO2865	56°46·5′	3°10·2′W	H	44
Corws	Carm	SN4231	51°57·5′	4°17·6′W	F	146
Cory	Corn	SS2116	50°55·2′	4°32·4′W	X	190
Cory	Devon	SS3516	50°55·4′	4°20·5′W	T	190
Coryates	Dorset	SY6285	50°40·0′	2°31·9′W	T	194
Coryhill	Devon	SX4683	50°37·8′	4°10·3′W	X	201
Coryton	Card	ST1481	51°31·5′	3°14·0′W	T	171
Coryton	Devon	SX4583	50°37·8′	4°11·1′W	T	201
Coryton	Devon	SY2798	50°46·9′	3°1·7′W	T	193
Coryton	Thurr	TQ7482	51°30·8′	0°30·9′E	X	178
Coryton Barton	Devon	SX4684	50°38·4′	4°10·3′W	X	201
Coryton's Cove	Devon	SX9675	50°34·2′	3°27·7′W	W	192
Coryton Wharves	Thurr	TQ7581	51°30·3′	0°31·7′E	X	178
Còsag	Highld	NG8219	57°12·9′	5°36·2′W	X	33
Cosby	Leic	SP5495	52°33·2′	1°11·8′W	T	140
Cosby Hill	Leic	SP5592	52°31·6′	1°11·0′W	X	140
Cosby Lodge	Leic	SP5592	52°31·6′	1°11·0′W	X	140
Cosby Spinneys	Leic	SP5395	52°33·2′	1°12·7′W	F	140
Coscote	Oxon	SU5188	51°35·5′	1°15·4′W	T	174
Cosdon Hill	Devon	SX6391	50°42·4′	3°56·0′W	H	191
Cose	Highld	NH8744	57°28·6′	3°52·6′W	X	27
Coseley	Dudley	SO9494	52°32·9′	2°4·9′W	T	139
Cosford	Warw	SP4979	52°24·6′	1°16·4′W	T	140
Cosford Airfield	Shrops	SJ7904	52°38·2′	2°18·2′W	X	127
Cosford Grange	Shrops	SJ7804	52°38·2′	2°19·1′W	X	127
Cosford Hall	Suff	TM0144	52°3·7′	0°56·3′E	X	155
Cosford Ho	Surrey	SU9138	51°8·3′	0°41·6′W	X	186
Cosgrove	Northnts	SP7942	52°4·5′	0°50·4′W	T	152
Cosgrove Leisure Park	Mil Key	SP8042	52°4·5′	0°49·6′W	X	152
Cosh	N Yks	SD8578	54°12·1′	2°13·4′W	X	98
Cosham	C of Port	SU6605	50°50·7′	1°3·4′W	T	196
Coshandrochaid	Arg & Bt	NR7082	55°58·8′	5°40·8′W	T	55,61
Cosh Beck	N Yks	SD8577	54°11·6′	2°13·4′W	W	98
Coshelly	Aberd	NJ7235	57°24·5′	2°27·5′W	X	29
Cosheston	Pemb	SN0003	51°41·6′	4°53·2′W	T	157,158
Cosheston Point	Pemb	SM9804	51°42·1′	4°55·0′W	X	157,158
Cosh Fm	Essex	TL4535	51°59·9′	0°7·1′E	FM	154
Coshieville	Pth & Kin	NN7749	56°37·3′	3°59·8′W	X	51,52
Coshieville	Pth & Kin	NN9052	56°39·1′	3°47·2′W	X	52
Cosh Inside	N Yks	SD8578	54°12·1′	2°13·4′W	X	98
Coshogle	D & G	NS8605	55°19·8′	3°47·4′W	X	71,78
Coshogle Rig	D & G	NS8606	55°20·3′	3°47·4′W	H	71,78
Cosh Outside	N Yks	SD8377	54°11·6′	2°15·2′W	X	98
Coskills	N Lincs	TA0410	53°34·8′	0°25·3′W	X	112
Cosmeston	V of Glam	ST1869	51°25·1′	3°10·4′W	T	171
Cosmeston Lakes Country Park	V of Glam	ST1769	51°25·1′	3°11·2′W	X	171
Cosmore	Dorset	ST6705	50°50·8′	2°27·7′W	T	194
Còs Raineach	Highld	NH1424	57°16·4′	5°4·6′W	X	25
Cossall	Notts	SK4842	52°58·6′	1°16·7′W	T	129
Cossall Marsh	Notts	SK4842	52°58·6′	1°16·7′W	T	129
Cossans	Angus	NO3949	56°38·0′	2°59·2′W	X	54
Cossars Hill	Scot Bord	NT2214	55°25·1′	3°13·5′W	H	79
Cossarshill	Scot Bord	NT2313	55°24·5′	3°12·5′W	X	79
Cossarshill Burn	Scot Bord	NT2314	55°25·1′	3°12·6′W	W	79
Cosses	S Ayr	NX1182	55°6·0′	4°57·3′W	X	76
Cossick Fm	Devon	SX7786	50°39·9′	3°44·0′W	FM	191
Cossington	Leic	SK6013	52°42·9′	1°6·3′W	T	129
Cossington	Somer	ST3540	51°9·6′	2°55·4′W	T	182
Cossington Fields	Kent	TQ7661	51°19·5′	0°32·0′E	X	178,188
Cosson	Arg & Bt	NS0958	55°46·9′	5°2·3′W	X	63
Costa	Orkney	HY3228	59°8·3′	3°10·8′W	T	6
Costa Beck	N Yks	SE7783	54°14·5′	0°48·7′W	W	100
Costa Beck	N Yks	SE7976	54°10·7′	0°47·0′W	W	100
Costa Fm	N Yks	SE7977	54°11·2′	0°46·9′W	FM	100
Costa Head	Orkney	HY3030	59°9·3′	3°13·0′W	X	6
Costa Hill	Lincs	SK8244	52°59·5′	0°46·3′W	X	130
Costa Hill	Orkney	HY3129	59°8·8′	3°11·9′W	H	6
Costains Fm	Brom	TQ4259	51°19·0′	0°2·7′E	FM	187
Costa Lodge	N Yks	SE7781	54°13·4′	0°48·7′W	X	100
Costa Manor Fm	N Yks	SE7876	54°10·7′	0°47·9′W	FM	100
Costens Hall	Suff	TL9038	52°0·7′	0°46·5′E	X	155
Costerton Mains	Midlo	NT4362	55°51·1′	2°54·2′W	X	66
Costessey	Norf	TG1712	52°40·0′	1°13·0′E	T	133,134
Costessey Park	Norf	TG1611	52°39·4′	1°12·0′E	T	133
Costhorpe	Notts	SK5886	53°22·3′	1°7·3′W	T	111,120
Costislost	Corn	SX0270	50°30·0′	4°47·1′W	T	200
Costislost Plantation	Corn	SX0270	50°30·0′	4°47·1′W	F	200
Costlyburn	Aberd	NJ5641	57°27·7′	2°43·5′W	X	29
Costock	Notts	SK5726	52°49·9′	1°8·8′W	T	129
Costock Hill	Notts	SK5727	52°50·5′	1°8·8′W	X	129
Coston	Leic	SK8422	52°47·6′	0°44·9′W	T	130
Coston	Norf	TG0606	52°37·0′	1°3·0′E	T	144
Coston Covert	Leic	SK8621	52°47·0′	0°43·1′W	F	130
Coston Lodge	Leic	SK8521	52°47·0′	0°44·0′W	X	130
Coston Lodge West	Leic	SK8523	52°48·1′	0°43·9′W	X	130
Coston Manor	Shrops	SO3980	52°25·1′	2°53·4′W	X	137
Costow Fm	Swin	SU1181	51°31·9′	1°50·1′W	FM	173
Costwell Fm	Northnts	SP6748	52°7·8′	1°0·9′W	FM	152
Costy Clough	Lancs	SD6654	53°59·1′	2°30·7′W	X	103
Coswarth	Corn	SW8659	50°23·8′	5°0·3′W	X	200
Coswinsawsin	Corn	SW6238	50°11·9′	5°19·7′W	T	203
Cotbank	Aberd	NJ8902	57°6·8′	2°10·4′W	X	38
Cotbank	Aberd	NO7682	56°56·0′	2°23·2′W	X	45
Cotbank of Barras	Aberd	NO8278	56°53·8′	2°17·3′W	X	45
Cotbank of Hilton	Aberd	NO8779	56°54·4′	2°12·4′W	X	45
Cotchet Fm	W Susx	SU9129	51°3·4′	0°41·7′W	FM	186,197
Cotcliffe Wood	N Yks	SE4291	54°19·0′	1°20·8′W	F	99
Cot Craigs	Aberd	NJ5321	57°16·9′	2°46·3′W	X	37
Cote	Brad	SE1638	53°50·5′	1°45·0′W	X	104
Cote	D & G	NY2595	55°14·9′	3°10·4′W	X	79
Cote	N Yks	SE0185	54°15·9′	1°58·7′W	X	98
Cote	Oxon	SP3502	51°43·2′	1°29·2′W	T	164
Cote	Somer	ST3444	51°11·7′	2°56·3′W	T	182
Cote	W Susx	TQ1105	50°50·3′	0°25·0′W	T	198
Cotebank	Derby	SK0282	53°20·3′	1°57·8′W	X	110
Cote Bank Fm	N Yks	NZ8207	54°27·3′	0°43·7′W	FM	94
Cote Bank Woods	N Yks	NZ8206	54°26·8′	0°43·7′W	F	94
Cote Beck	Lancs	SD5066	54°5·5′	2°45·5′W	W	97
Cote Bottom	N Yks	SD9885	54°15·9′	2°1·4′W	X	98
Cotebrook	Ches	SJ5765	53°11·1′	2°38·2′W	T	117
Cote Close	Cumbr	NY0211	54°29·3′	3°30·4′W	X	89
Cote Corner	Somer	ST3544	51°11·7′	2°55·4′W	X	182
Cotefield	Derby	SK1933	52°53·9′	1°42·6′W	X	128
Cotefield Ho	Oxon	SP4637	52°2·0′	1°19·4′W	X	151
Cote Fm	Cumbr	NY4418	54°33·5′	2°51·5′W	FM	90
Cote Fm	S Glos	ST5889	51°36·1′	2°36·0′W	FM	162,172
Cote Fm	Staffs	SK0744	52°59·8′	1°53·3′W	FM	119,128
Cote Garth	Cumbr	NY7909	54°28·8′	2°19·0′W	X	91
Cote Garth	N Yks	SE6683	54°14·5′	0°58·8′W	X	100
Cotegill	Cumbr	NY6504	54°26·1′	2°32·0′W	X	91
Cote Gill	N Yks	SD9469	54°7·3′	2°5·1′W	W	98
Cotehay	Glos	SP0322	51°54·0′	1°57·0′W	X	163
Cote Head	N Yks	SE9384	54°14·8′	0°33·9′W	X	101
Cotehele Ho	Corn	SX4268	50°29·7′	4°13·3′W	A	201
Cotehele Quay	Devon	SX4268	50°29·7′	4°13·3′W	X	201
Cotehill	Aberd	NK0229	57°21·3′	1°57·5′W	X	38
Cotehill	Cumbr	NY4650	54°50·8′	2°50·0′W	T	86
Cote Hill	Cumbr	NY5156	54°54·0′	2°45·4′W	X	86
Cotehill	Cumbr	NY5341	54°46·0′	2°43·4′W	X	86
Cote Hill	N Yks	NZ1614	54°31·5′	1°44·7′W	X	92
Cote Hill	N Yks	SE2157	54°0·8′	1°40·4′W	X	104
Cote Hill	N Yks	SE6796	54°21·5′	0°57·7′W	X	94,100
Cotehill Fm	Cumbr	NY5362	54°57·3′	2°43·6′W	FM	86
Cote Hill Fm	Leic	SP6382	52°26·2′	1°4·0′W	FM	140
Cote Hill Fm	Lincs	TF0792	53°25·1′	0°23·0′W	FM	112
Cotehill Loch	Aberd	NK0229	57°21·3′	1°57·5′W	W	38
Cote Ho	Cumbr	NY4752	54°51·8′	2°49·1′W	X	86
Cote Ho	Cumbr	NY7314	54°31·5′	2°24·6′W	X	91
Cote Ho	Durham	NY9523	54°36·4′	2°4·2′W	X	91,92
Cote Ho	N Yks	NZ5204	54°26·0′	1°11·5′W	X	93
Cote Ho	N Yks	SE1994	54°20·7′	1°42·0′W	X	99
Cote Ho	Oxon	SP3502	51°43·2′	1°29·2′W	A	164
Cote Ho Fm	Northum	NY9650	54°50·9′	2°3·3′W	FM	87
Cote How	Cumbr	NY3605	54°26·4′	2°58·8′W	X	90
Cotehow	Cumbr	NY4318	54°33·5′	2°52·5′W	X	90
Cote Lodge Fm	Oxon	SP3503	51°43·7′	1°29·2′W	FM	164
Cote Nook Fm	Durham	NZ3728	54°39·0′	1°25·2′W	FM	93
Cote Pasture	N Yks	SD9091	54°19·1′	2°8·8′W	X	98
Cote Pasture	N Yks	SE0891	54°19·1′	1°52·2′W	X	99
Cote Plantn	N Yks	SE1781	54°13·7′	1°43·9′W	F	99
Cotes	Cumbr	SD4886	54°16·3′	2°47·5′W	T	97
Cotes	Leic	SK5520	52°46·7′	1°10·7′W	T	129
Cotes	Staffs	SJ8434	52°54·4′	2°13·9′W	T	127
Cotesbach	Leic	SP5382	52°26·2′	1°12·8′W	T	140
Cotesbach Fields Fm	Leic	SP5381	52°25·7′	1°12·8′W	FM	140
Cotescue Park	N Yks	SE1086	54°16·4′	1°50·4′W	X	99
Cotes-de-val	Leic	SP5588	52°29·5′	1°11·0′W	X	140
Cotesfield	Derby	SK1364	53°10·6′	1°47·9′W	X	119

Cotes Fm	Black w Dar	SD7420	53°40·8'	2°23·2'W	FM	103
Cotes Grange	Lincs	TF2689	53°23·2'	0°5·9'W	X	113,122
Cotes Heath	Staffs	SJ8334	52°54·4'	2°14·8'W	T	127
Cotes Lodge	Staffs	SJ8335	52°55·0'	2°14·8'W	X	127
Cotes Park	Derby	SK4254	53°5·1'	1°22·0'W	T	120
Cote Stones	Lancs	SD4871	54°8·2'	2°47·3'W	X	97
Cote Syke	N Yks	SE2457	54°0·7'	1°37·6'W	X	104
Cote, The	Derby	SK0587	53°23·0'	1°55·1'W	X	110
Cotetown	Aberd	NJ5825	57°19·1'	2°41·4'W	X	37
Cote Walls	Northum	NT9707	55°21·7'	2°2·4'W	X	81
Cote Walls Plantn	E Yorks	TA1870	54°7·0'	0°11·3'W	F	101
Cotfield	Scot Bord	NT5322	55°29·6'	2°44·2'W	X	73
Cot Fm	Oxon	SP3111	51°48·0'	1°32·6'W	FM	164
Cotford	Devon	SY1492	50°43·5'	3°12·7'W	T	192,193
Cotgrave	Notts	SK6435	52°54·8'	1°2·5'W	T	129
Cotgrave Place	Notts	SK6337	52°55·8'	1°3·4'W	X	129
Cotgrave Wolds	Notts	SK6533	52°53·7'	1°1·6'W	X	129
Cothall	Aberd	NJ8715	57°13·8'	2°12·5'W	X	38
Cothall	Moray	NJ0154	57°34·2'	3°38·8'W	X	27
Cothall	Moray	NJ1160	57°37·5'	3°29·0'W	X	28
Cotham	C of Bris	ST5874	51°28·0'	2°35·9'W	T	172
Cotham	Notts	SK7947	53°1·1'	0°48·9'W	T	129
Cotham Grange	Notts	SK7846	53°0·6'	0°49·8'W	X	129
Cothayes Fm	Dorset	ST7503	50°49·8'	2°20·9'W	FM	194
Cothay Manor	Somer	ST0821	50°59·1'	3°18·3'W	A	181
Cothelhill	Angus	NO2854	56°40·6'	3°10·1'W	X	53
Cothelstone	Somer	ST1831	51°4·6'	3°9·8'W	T	181
Cothelstone Fm	Somer	ST1831	51°4·6'	3°9·8'W	FM	181
Cothelstone Hill	Somer	ST1832	51°5·1'	3°9·9'W	H	181
Cothelstone Hill (Tumuli)	Somer	ST1832	51°5·1'	3°9·9'W	A	181
Cothercott	Shrops	SJ4201	52°36·5'	2°51·0'W	X	126
Cothercott Hill	Shrops	SJ4100	52°35·9'	2°51·9'W	X	126
Cotheridge	Worcs	SO7854	52°11·3'	2°18·9'W	T	150
Cotheridge Court	Worcs	SO7854	52°11·3'	2°18·9'W	A	150
Cotherstone	Durham	NZ0119	54°34·2'	1°58·6'W	T	92
Cotherstone Moor	Durham	NY9317	54°33·1'	2°6·1'W	X	91,92
Cothill	Aberd	NJ6402	57°6·7'	2°35·2'W	X	37
Cothill	Aberd	NJ8417	57°14·9'	2°15·5'W	X	38
Cothill	Aberd	NJ9721	57°17·0'	2°2·5'W	X	38
Cothill	Angus	NO6651	56°39·2'	2°32·8'W	X	54
Cothill	C of Aber	NJ9011	57°11·6'	2°9·5'W	X	38
Cothill	Highld	NH5558	57°36·3'	3°45·0'W	X	27
Cot Hill	Northnts	SP6277	52°23·5'	1°4·9'W	X	140
Cothill	Oxon	SU4699	51°41·5'	1°19·7'W	T	164
Cothill	Scot Bord	NT7649	55°44·3'	2°22·5'W	X	74
Cothill Fm	Heref	SO3436	52°1·3'	2°57·3'W	FM	149,161
Cothon Leasows	Shrops	SJ4402	52°37·0'	2°49·2'W	X	126
Cotkerse	Stir	NS8396	56°8·8'	3°52·6'W	X	57
Cotlake Hill	Somer	ST2222	50°59·8'	3°6·3'W	H	193
Cotland	D & G	NX4254	54°51·6'	4°27·3'W	X	83
Cotland	D & G	NY0082	55°7·6'	3°33·7'W	X	78
Cotland	Monm	SO5004	51°44·2'	2°43·1'W	T	162
Cotland Fm	Pemb	SN0518	51°49·8'	4°49·4'W	FM	158
Cotland Mill	Pemb	SN0519	51°50·4'	4°49·4'W	X	158
Cotlands	W Susx	TQ2123	50°59·8'	0°16·2'W	X	198
Cotleigh	Devon	ST2002	50°49·0'	3°7·8'W	T	192,193
Cotleigh Br	Devon	ST2103	50°49·5'	3°6·9'W	X	192,193
Cotleigh Court	Devon	ST2001	50°48·4'	3°7·7'W	X	192,193
Cotley	Devon	SY0893	50°44·0'	3°17·8'W	X	192
Cotley	Somer	ST2906	50°51·2'	3°0·1'W	X	193
Cotley Castle	Devon	SX8689	50°41·6'	3°36·5'W	X	191
Cotley Hill	Wilts	ST9243	51°11·4'	2°6·5'W	H	184
Cotley Wood	Devon	SX8589	50°41·6'	3°37·3'W	F	191
Cotmanhay	Derby	SK4643	52°59·2'	1°18·5'W	T	129
Cotmarsh	Wilts	SU0979	51°30·8'	1°51·8'W	T	173
Cotmaton	Devon	SY1187	50°40·8'	3°15·2'W	T	192
Cotmoor Plantn	Notts	SK6752	53°3·9'	0°59·6'W	F	120
Cotmore	Devon	SX8041	50°15·6'	3°40·6'W	X	202
Cotmore Fm	Heref	SO3456	52°12·1'	2°57·5'W	FM	148,149
Cotmore Fm	Oxon	SP5826	51°56·0'	1°9·0'W	FM	164
Cotmore Ho	Oxon	SP5926	51°56·0'	1°8·1'W	X	164
Cotna	Corn	SW9942	50°14·9'	4°48·8'W	X	204
Cot Nab	E Yorks	SE8156	53°59·9'	0°45·4'W	X	106
Cotness	Dorset	SY9282	50°38·5'	2°6·4'W	X	195
Cotness Hall	E Yorks	SE7924	53°42·6'	0°47·8'W	X	105,106,112
Coton	Cambs	TL4058	52°12·4'	0°3·3'E	T	154
Coton	Northnts	SP6771	52°20·2'	1°0·6'W	T	141
Coton	Shrops	SJ5334	52°54·3'	2°41·5'W	T	126
Coton	Staffs	SJ8120	52°46·9'	2°16·5'W	T	127
Coton	Staffs	SJ9731	52°52·8'	2°2·0'W	T	127
Coton	Staffs	SK1805	52°38·8'	1°43·6'W	T	139
Coton Barn	Cambs	TL1373	52°20·8'	0°20·1'W	X	153
Coton Br	Leic	SK3802	52°37·1'	1°25·9'W	X	140
Coton Clanford	Staffs	SJ8723	52°48·5'	2°11·2'W	T	127
Coton End Fm	Staffs	SJ8119	52°46·3'	2°16·5'W	FM	127
Coton Fm	Oxon	SP4944	52°5·8'	1°16·7'W	FM	151
Coton Fm	Shrops	SJ3721	52°47·2'	2°55·6'W	FM	126
Coton Fm	Shrops	SO7786	52°28·5'	2°19·9'W	FM	138
Coton Fm	Warw	SP5279	52°24·6'	1°13·7'W	FM	140
Coton Hall	Shrops	SO7786	52°28·5'	2°19·9'W	X	138
Coton Hall	Warw	SP2194	52°32·8'	1°41·0'W	X	139
Coton Hall Fm	Staffs	SK1805	52°38·8'	1°43·6'W	FM	139
Coton Hayes	Staffs	SJ9932	52°53·4'	2°0·5'W	T	127
Cot-on-hill	Orkney	HY5216	59°2·0'	2°49·7'W	X	6
Coton Hill	Shrops	SJ4813	52°43·0'	2°45·8'W	T	126
Coton Hill	Staffs	SJ9832	52°53·4'	2°1·4'W	T	127
Coton Ho	Staffs	SJ8623	52°48·5'	2°12·1'W	X	127
Coton Ho (Coll)	Warw	SP5180	52°25·2'	1°14·6'W	X	140
Coton in the Clay	Staffs	SK1629	52°51·7'	1°45·3'W	T	128
Coton in the Elms	Derby	SK2415	52°44·2'	1°38·3'W	T	128
Coton Lawn	Warw	SP3490	52°30·6'	1°29·5'W	X	140
Coton Lodge	Northnts	SP6572	52°20·8'	1°2·3'W	X	141
Coton Park	Derby	SK2717	52°45·2'	1°35·6'W	T	128
Coton Park Fm	Shrops	SJ5233	52°53·8'	2°42·4'W	FM	126
Coton Priory	Leic	SK3902	52°37·1'	1°25·0'W	X	140
Cotons Fm	Shrops	SJ5506	52°39·2'	2°39·5'W	FM	126
Coton Side	Shrops	SJ3821	52°47·2'	2°54·8'W	X	126
Cotonwood	Shrops	SJ5336	52°55·4'	2°41·5'W	T	126
Cotonwood	Staffs	SJ8020	52°46·9'	2°17·4'W	T	127
Coton Wood Fm	Derby	SK1635	52°55·0'	1°45·3'W	FM	128
Cotril Fm	N Yks	SE6671	54°8·1'	0°59·0'W	FM	100
Cotsbrook Fm	Shrops	SJ7400	52°36·1'	2°22·6'W	FM	127
Cotsbrook Hall School	Shrops	SJ7500	52°36·1'	2°21·7'W	X	127
Cotside	Angus	NO5234	56°30·0'	2°46·3'W	X	54
Cots, The	Heref	SO4751	52°9·5'	2°46·1'W	X	148,149
Cots, The	Lincs	TF3736	52°54·5'	0°2·6'E	X	131
Cotswold Community	Wilts	SU0395	51°39·5'	1°57·0'W	T	163
Cotswold Crest Farm	Glos	SP2124	51°55·1'	1°41·3'W	FM	163
Cotswold Farm Park	Glos	SP1126	51°56·2'	1°50·0'W	X	163
Cotswold Fm	Glos	SO8705	51°44·8'	2°10·9'W	FM	162
Cotswold Fm	Glos	SO9809	51°47·0'	2°1·3'W	FM	163
Cotswold Fm	Lincs	SK9125	52°49·1'	0°38·6'W	FM	130
Cotswold Hills	Glos	SP0512	51°48·6'	1°55·3'W	H	163
Cotswold Hills	Glos	ST8897	51°40·5'	2°10·0'W	H	162
Cotswold Park	Glos	SO9809	51°47·0'	2°1·3'W	X	163
Cotswold Water Park	Glos	SU1899	51°41·6'	1°44·0'W	X	163
Cotswold Water Park	Wilts	SU0495	51°39·5'	1°56·1'W	X	163
Cotswold Way	Glos	SO9921	51°53·5'	2°0·5'W	X	163
Cotswold Way	Glos	SP0834	52°0·5'	1°52·6'W	X	150
Cotswold Way	Glos	SP1439	52°3·2'	1°47·4'W	X	151
Cotswold Way	Glos	ST7497	51°40·5'	2°22·2'W	X	162
Cotswold Way	Glos	ST7899	51°41·6'	2°18·7'W	X	162
Cott	Devon	ST0116	50°56·3'	3°24·2'W	X	181
Cott	Devon	SX7861	50°26·4'	3°42·7'W	T	202
Cott	Orkney	HY3005	58°55·9'	3°12·5'W	X	6,7
Cott	Orkney	HY3406	58°56·4'	3°8·3'W	X	6,7
Cott	Orkney	HY4121	59°4·6'	3°1·3'W	X	5,6
Cott	Orkney	HY4647	59°18·6'	2°56·4'W	X	5
Cott	Orkney	HY4952	59°21·3'	2°53·3'W	X	5
Cott	Orkney	HY5237	59°13·3'	2°50·0'W	X	5
Cott	Orkney	HY6723	59°5·8'	2°34·1'W	X	5
Cott	Shetld	HU3749	60°13·7'	1°19·4'W	X	3
Cottage Bridge	Conwy	SH9156	53°5·6'	3°37·3'W	X	116
Cottage Fen	Norf	TL7198	52°33·4'	0°31·8'E	X	143
Cottage Fm	Aberd	NJ7863	57°39·6'	2°21·7'W	FM	29,30
Cottage Fm	Cambs	TL1279	52°24·1'	0°20·8'W	FM	142
Cottage Fm	Cambs	TL2664	52°15·8'	0°8·8'W	FM	153
Cottage Fm	Cambs	TL3373	52°20·6'	0°2·5'W	FM	154
Cottage Fm	Derby	SK4534	52°54·3'	1°19·5'W	FM	129
Cottage Fm	E Yorks	SE7634	53°48·0'	0°50·3'W	FM	105,106
Cottage Fm	E Yorks	SE8348	53°55·5'	0°43·7'W	FM	106
Cottage Fm	Glos	SO5902	51°43·1'	2°35·2'W	FM	162
Cottage Fm	Leic	SK3207	52°39·8'	1°31·2'W	FM	140
Cottage Fm	Leic	SP4890	52°30·6'	1°17·2'W	FM	140
Cottage Fm	Lincs	TF0551	53°3·0'	0°25·6'W	FM	121
Cottage Fm	Lincs	TF3183	53°19·9'	0°1·6'W	FM	122
Cottage Fm	N Lincs	SE7714	53°37·2'	0°49·7'W	FM	112
Cottage Fm	Northnts	SP8266	52°17·4'	0°47·5'W	FM	152
Cottage Fm	Northum	NZ1384	55°9·3'	1°47·3'W	FM	81
Cottage Fm	Notts	SK5857	53°6·7'	1°7·6'W	FM	120
Cottage Fm	Notts	SK6145	53°0·2'	1°5·1'W	FM	129
Cottage Fm	Notts	SK6549	53°2·3'	1°1·4'W	FM	129
Cottage Fm	N Yks	SE3868	54°6·6'	1°24·7'W	FM	99
Cottage Fm	N Yks	SE5369	54°7·1'	1°10·9'W	FM	100
Cottage Fm	Scot Bord	NT1552	55°45·5'	3°20·8'W	FM	65,72
Cottage Fm	Suff	TM1149	52°6·2'	1°5·3'E	FM	155,169
Cottage Fm	Suff	TM4688	52°26·3'	1°37·6'E	FM	156
Cottage Fm	Warw	SP2138	52°2·6'	1°41·2'W	FM	151
Cottage Fm	Warw	SP2596	52°33·9'	1°37·5'W	FM	140
Cottage Fm	Warw	SP3088	52°29·6'	1°33·1'W	FM	140
Cottage Fm	Warw	SP4286	52°28·5'	1°22·5'W	FM	140
Cottage Fm	Wrekin	SJ6121	52°47·3'	2°34·3'W	FM	127
Cottage Gorse Fm	Wrex	SJ4045	53°0·2'	2°53·2'W	FM	117
Cottage Leas	N Yks	SE7887	54°16·6'	0°47·7'W	X	94,100
Cottage of Clunie	Pth & Kin	NO1344	56°35·0'	3°24·5'W	X	53
Cottage Pasture	E Yorks	TA0046	53°54·3'	0°28·3'W	X	106,107
Cottage Pasture Wood	E Yorks	TA1368	54°6·0'	0°15·9'W	F	101
Cottage Pool	Shrops	SJ4118	52°45·6'	2°52·1'W	W	126
Cottage Pool	Shrops	SO5794	52°32·8'	2°37·6'W	W	137,138
Cottagers Dale Wood	Lincs	TA1108	53°33·6'	0°19·0'W	F	113
Cottagers Hill	Notts	SK5230	52°52·1'	1°13·2'W	H	129
Cottagers Plot	NE Lincs	TA2307	53°32·9'	0°8·2'W	X	113
Cottage, The	Beds	TL0265	52°16·7'	0°29·9'W	X	153
Cottage, The	Ches	SJ6555	53°5·7'	2°31·0'W	X	118
Cottage, The	Cumbr	NY2461	54°56·5'	3°10·8'W	X	85
Cottage, The	Highld	NG2449	57°27·1'	6°35·6'W	X	23
Cottage, The	Lincs	SK9255	53°5·3'	0°37·2'W	X	121
Cottage, The	Shrops	SJ2702	52°36·9'	3°4·3'W	X	126
Cottage, The	Staffs	SK0864	53°10·6'	1°52·4'W	X	119
Cottage Wood	Norf	TG2340	52°54·9'	1°19·4'E	F	133
Cottam	E Yorks	SE9864	54°4·0'	0°29·7'W	X	101
Cottam	Lancs	SD5032	53°47·2'	2°45·1'W	T	102
Cottam	Notts	SK8179	53°18·3'	0°46·7'W	T	121
Cottam Grange	E Yorks	SE9865	54°4·5'	0°29·7'W	X	101
Cottam Ho	E Yorks	SE9964	54°4·0'	0°28·8'W	X	101
Cottam House Fm	Lancs	SD6238	53°50·5'	2°34·2'W	FM	102,103
Cottams	Lancs	SD7549	53°56·4'	2°22·4'W	X	103
Cottam Village	E Yorks	SE9964	54°4·0'	0°28·8'W	A	101
Cottam Warren	E Yorks	SE9862	54°2·9'	0°29·8'W	X	101
Cottam Warren Fm	E Yorks	SE9962	54°2·9'	0°28·9'W	FM	101
Cottarson Fm	Devon	ST1400	50°47·8'	3°12·8'W	FM	192,193
Cottarton	Pth & Kin	NO0632	56°28·5'	3°31·1'W	X	52,53
Cottartown	Highld	NH7442	57°27·3'	4°5·5'W	X	27
Cottartown	Highld	NJ0331	57°21·8'	3°36·3'W	X	27,36
Cottartown Moss	Moray	NJ5257	57°36·3'	2°47·7'W	X	29
Cottascarth	Orkney	HY3619	59°3·5'	3°6·5'W	X	6
Cottege Burn	Northum	NT9029	55°33·5'	2°9·1'W	W	74,75
Cottenden	E Susx	TQ6728	51°1·8'	0°23·3'E	X	188,199
Cottenham	Cambs	TL4567	52°17·1'	0°8·0'E	T	154
Cottenham Fm	Oxon	SP4030	51°58·3'	1°24·7'W	FM	151
Cottenham Lode	Cambs	TL4669	52°18·2'	0°8·9'E	W	154
Cottenham Park	Merton	TQ2269	51°24·6'	0°14·4'W	T	176
Cottenham Pastures	Cambs	TL4566	52°16·6'	0°7·9'E	X	154
Cotterbury	Devon	SX8150	50°20·5'	3°40·0'W	X	202
Cotterdale	N Yks	SD8393	54°20·2'	2°15·3'W	T	98
Cotterdale Common	N Yks	SD8296	54°21·8'	2°16·2'W	X	98
Cottered	Herts	TL3129	51°56·9'	0°5·2'W	T	166
Cottered Warren	Herts	TL3228	51°56·3'	0°4·4'W	X	166
Cotterell Ho	Surrey	TQ0746	51°12·4'	0°27·7'W	X	187
Cotter End	N Yks	SD8293	54°20·2'	2°16·2'W	X	98
Cotter End Tarn	N Yks	SD8193	54°20·2'	2°17·1'W	W	98
Cotter Force	N Yks	SD8492	54°19·6'	2°14·3'W	W	98
Cotterhill Woods	Roth	SK5582	53°20·2'	1°10·0'W	T	111,120
Cotteridge	Birm	SP0480	52°25·3'	1°56·1'W	T	139
Cotterill Fm	Derby	SK1459	53°7·9'	1°47·0'W	FM	119
Cotterill Fm	Leic	SK6701	52°36·4'	1°0·2'W	FM	141
Cotter Riggs	N Yks	SD8392	54°19·6'	2°15·3'W	X	98
Cotterstock	Northnts	TL0490	52°30·1'	0°27·7'W	T	141
Cotterstock Lodge	Northnts	TL0391	52°30·7'	0°28·5'W	X	141
Cotterton	Highld	NH6252	57°32·5'	4°17·9'W	X	26
Cotterton	Moray	NH9657	57°35·7'	3°43·9'W	X	27
Cotterton	Moray	NJ3644	57°29·2'	3°3·6'W	X	28
Cotterton	Pth & Kin	NO0363	56°45·2'	3°34·7'W	X	43
Cotterton	Pth & Kin	NO0627	56°25·8'	3°31·0'W	X	52,53,58
Cottertown	Angus	NO2254	56°40·5'	3°15·9'W	X	53
Cottesbrooke	Northnts	SP7073	52°21·3'	0°57·9'W	T	141
Cottesbrooke Park	Northnts	SP7074	52°21·8'	0°57·9'W	X	141
Cottesloe Fm	Bucks	SP8622	51°53·6'	0°44·6'W	FM	165
Cottesmore	Pemb	SM9418	51°49·6'	4°59·0'W	X	157,158
Cottesmore	Rut	SK9013	52°42·7'	0°39·7'W	T	130
Cottesmore	W Susx	TQ2433	51°5·2'	0°13·4'W	X	187
Cottesmore Airfield	Rut	SK9015	52°43·7'	0°39·6'W	X	130
Cottesmore Fm	Oxon	SU6392	51°37·6'	1°5·0'W	FM	164,175
Cottesmore Ho	Rut	SK9013	52°42·7'	0°39·7'W	X	130
Cottesmore Lodge Fm	Rut	SK9113	52°42·7'	0°38·8'W	FM	130
Cottesmore Wood	Rut	SK9112	52°42·1'	0°38·8'W	F	130
Cotteylands	Devon	SS9412	50°54·1'	3°30·1'W	T	181
Cott Fm	Devon	SX8554	50°22·7'	3°36·7'W	FM	202
Cott Fm	Pemb	SN0512	51°46·6'	4°49·2'W	FM	158
Cott Fm	Somer	ST4912	50°54·5'	2°43·1'W	FM	193,194
Cot, The	Heref	SO3761	52°14·9'	2°55·0'W	X	137,148,149
Cott Hill Spinney	Northnts	SP6974	52°21·8'	0°58·8'W	F	141
Cottingham	E Yorks	TA0633	53°47·2'	0°23·0'W	T	107
Cottingham	Northnts	SP8490	52°30·3'	0°45·3'W	T	141
Cottingham Fm	Herts	TL0202	51°42·7'	0°31·0'W	FM	166
Cottingley	Brad	SE1137	53°50·0'	1°49·6'W	T	104
Cottingley	Leeds	SE2730	53°46·2'	1°35·0'W	X	104
Cottingley Moor	Brad	SE1136	53°49·5'	1°49·6'W	X	104
Cottingley Wood Estate	Brad	SE1037	53°50·0'	1°50·5'W	F	104
Cottington Court Fm	Kent	TR3553	51°13·9'	1°22·4'E	FM	179
Cottington Hill	Kent	TR3363	51°19·3'	1°21·0'E	X	179
Cottington's Hill	Hants	SU5256	51°18·3'	1°14·9'W	H	174
Cottisford	Oxon	SP5831	51°58·7'	1°8·9'W	T	152
Cottisford Heath	Oxon	SP5732	51°59·2'	1°9·8'W	X	152
Cottleys	Pemb	SN0315	51°48·2'	4°51·1'W	X	157,158
Cott of Ness	Orkney	HY5409	58°58·2'	2°47·5'W	X	6,7
Cotton	Angus	NO5463	56°45·6'	2°44·7'W	X	44
Cotton	Devon	SX8550	50°20·6'	3°36·6'W	X	202
Cotton	Pth & Kin	NO0621	56°22·6'	3°30·9'W	X	52,53,58
Cotton	Staffs	SK0646	53°0·9'	1°54·2'W	T	119,128
Cotton	Suff	TM0667	52°16·0'	1°1·5'E	T	155
Cotton Abbotts	Ches	SJ4664	53°10·5'	2°48·1'W	X	117
Cotton Dale	N Yks	TA0276	54°10·4'	0°25·8'W	X	101
Cotton Edmunds Fm	Ches	SJ4665	53°11·0'	2°48·1'W	FM	117
Cotton End	Beds	TL0845	52°5·8'	0°25·0'W	T	153
Cotton End	Northnts	SP7559	52°13·7'	0°53·7'W	T	152
Cotton Fm	Cambs	TL2364	52°15·9'	0°11·5'W	FM	153
Cotton Fm	Ches	SJ4765	53°11·0'	2°47·2'W	FM	117
Cotton Fm	Devon	SS8807	50°51·3'	3°35·1'W	FM	192
Cotton Fm	Shrops	SJ6327	52°50·6'	2°32·6'W	FM	127
Cotton Fms	Devon	SS8909	50°52·4'	3°34·3'W	FM	192
Cotton Hall	Ches	SJ4666	53°11·5'	2°48·1'W	X	117
Cotton Hall	Ches	SJ7467	53°12·2'	2°22·9'W	A	118
Cotton Hall	Suff	TM0665	52°14·9'	1°1·5'E	X	155
Cotton Hill	Moray	NJ5262	57°39·0'	2°47·8'W	H	29
Cotton Mill	Northnts	SP6671	52°20·2'	1°1·5'W	X	141
Cotton Mill Fm	Notts	SK6555	53°5·5'	1°1·4'W	FM	120
Cotton of Brighty	Angus	NO4338	56°32·1'	2°55·2'W	T	54
Cotton of Carnegie	Angus	NO5241	56°33·8'	2°46·4'W	X	54
Cotton of Gardyne	Angus	NO5747	56°37·0'	2°41·6'W	T	54
Cotton of Guthrie	Angus	NO5650	56°38·6'	2°42·6'W	X	54
Cotton of Kirkbuddo	Angus	NO3943	56°34·8'	2°59·1'W	X	54
Cotton of Lownie	Angus	NO4848	56°37·5'	2°50·4'W	X	54
Cotton of Ovenstone	Angus	NO4742	56°34·3'	2°51·3'W	X	54
Cotton's Corner	Cambs	TL4999	52°34·3'	0°12·3'E	X	143
Cottons Field	Leic	SP7298	52°34·7'	0°55·8'W	X	141
Cotton's Fm	Essex	TL7032	51°57·9'	0°28·9'E	FM	167
Cotton's Fm	Glos	SP0335	52°1·0'	1°57·0'W	FM	150
Cottons Furze	Warw	SP4785	52°27·9'	1°18·1'W	F	140
Cottonshope	Northum	NT7904	55°20·0'	2°19·4'W	X	80
Cottonshope Burn	Northum	NT7803	55°19·5'	2°20·4'W	W	80
Cottonshopeburnfoot	Northum	NT7801	55°18·4'	2°20·4'W	X	80
Cottonshope Head	Northum	NT8006	55°21·1'	2°18·5'W	X	80
Cotton Spring Fm	Herts	TL0615	51°49·6'	0°27·3'W	FM	166
Cotton Stones	Cald	SE0221	53°41·4'	1°57·8'W	T	104
Cotton Tree	Lancs	SD9039	53°51·1'	2°8·7'W	T	103
Cottonworth	Hants	SU3739	51°9·2'	1°27·9'W	T	185
Cottorton	Highld	NH9620	57°15·8'	3°43·0'W	X	36
Cottown	Aberd	NJ5026	57°19·6'	2°49·4'W	X	37
Cottown	Aberd	NJ5721	57°16·9'	2°42·3'W	X	37
Cottown	Aberd	NJ8240	57°27·3'	2°17·5'W	T	29,30
Cottown	Aberd	NJ8323	57°18·1'	2°16·5'W	X	38
Cottown	Pth & Kin	NO2021	56°22·7'	3°17·3'W	T	53,58
Cottown Ardlogie	Aberd	NJ7837	57°25·6'	2°21·5'W	X	29,30
Cottown of Fetterletter	Aberd	NJ7939	57°26·7'	2°20·5'W	X	29,30
Cot-town Wood	Aberd	NJ7218	57°15·4'	2°27·4'W	F	38
Cottrell	V of Glam	ST0774	51°27·7'	3°19·9'W	X	170
Cotts	Devon	SX4365	50°28·1'	4°12·4'W	T	201
Cotts Fm	Heref	SO5441	52°4·2'	2°39·9'W	FM	149
Cotts of Innes	Moray	NJ2766	57°40·9'	3°13·0'W	X	28
Cotts Park	Pemb	SM9815	51°48·1'	4°55·4'W	X	157,158
Cotts, The	Pemb	SM8510	51°45·1'	5°6·5'W	X	157
Cott Street Fm	Hants	SU5915	50°56·1'	1°9·2'W	FM	196
Cotts Wood	Surrey	TQ0352	51°15·7'	0°31·0'W	F	186
Cott, The	E Yorks	SE8836	53°49·0'	0°39·4'W	X	106
Cottwood	Devon	SS6114	50°54·8'	3°58·3'W	T	180
Cotty Burn	Midlo	NT3766	55°53·2'	3°0·0'W	W	66
Cotty's Point	Corn	SW7555	50°21·4'	5°9·4'W	X	200
Cot Valley	Corn	SW3630	50°6·9'	5°41·2'W	X	203

Cotwall	Wrekin	SJ6017	52°45·2′	2°35·2′W	T	127
Cotwalton	Staffs	SJ9234	52°54·4′	2°6·7′W	T	127
Cotwells	Aberd	NJ7858	57°36·9′	2°21·6′W	X	29,30
Coubal	Shetld	HU3718	59°57·0′	1°19·8′W	X	4
Coubister	Orkney	HY3715	59°1·3′	3°5·4′W	T	6
Couch	W Loth	NS9164	55°51·7′	3°44·1′W	X	65
Couchercairn	Aberd	NJ7833	57°23·5′	2°21·5′W	X	29,30
Couch Green	Hants	SU5232	51°5·3′	1°15·1′W	T	185
Couchill Fm	Devon	SY2390	50°42·5′	3°5·1′W	FM	192,193
Couch's Mill	Corn	SX1459	50°24·3′	4°36·7′W	T	200
Couduit Spinney	Leic	SP7197	52°34·2′	0°56·7′W	F	141
Coughton	Heref	SO5921	51°53·4′	2°35·4′W	T	162
Coughton	Warw	SP0760	52°14·5′	1°53·5′W	T	150
Coughton Fields	Warw	SP0959	52°14·0′	1°51·7′W	T	150
Coughton Park	Warw	SP0660	52°14·5′	1°54·3′W	F	150
Cougie	Highld	NH2421	57°15·0′	4°54·6′W	X	25
Coukie Geo	Shetld	HU2345	60°11·6′	1°34·6′W	X	4
Coul	Fife	NO2703	56°13·1′	3°10·2′W	X	59
Coul	Highld	NH8194	57°55·4′	4°0·1′W	X	21
Coul	Pth & Kin	NN9612	56°17·6′	3°40·4′W	X	58
Coulachan Burn	Aberd	NO2598	57°4·3′	3°13·8′W	W	37,44
Coulaghailtro	Arg & Bt	NR7165	55°49·7′	5°38·9′W	X	62
Coulags	Highld	NG9645	57°27·2′	5°23·6′W	T	25
Coulalt Wood	Moray	NJ3438	57°25·9′	3°5·5′W	F	28
Coul Burn	Pth & Kin	NN9808	56°15·5′	3°38·3′W	W	58
Coulby Newham	Midd	NZ5014	54°31·4′	1°13·2′W	T	93
Coulderton	Cumbr	NX9809	54°28·2′	3°34·0′W	T	89
Couldoran	Highld	NG8444	57°26·4′	5°35·5′W	X	24
Coulererach	Arg & Bt	NR2065	55°48·1′	6°27·7′W	X	60
Coul Fm	Highld	NN5894	57°1·2′	4°19·9′W	FM	35
Coul Hill	Arg & Bt	NR7126	55°28·7′	5°37·0′W	X	68
Coul Hill	Highld	NH6470	57°42·2′	4°16·5′W	X	21
Coul Ho	Highld	NH4656	57°34·3′	4°34·0′W	X	26
Coulick Hill	Aberd	NJ3511	57°11·4′	3°4·1′W	H	37
Couligartan	Stir	NN4500	56°10·3′	4°29·4′W	X	57
Coulin	Highld	NH0154	57°32·2′	5°19·0′W	X	25
Coulin Forest	Highld	NH0054	57°32·2′	5°20·0′W	X	25
Coulin Lodge	Highld	NH0056	57°33·3′	5°20·1′W	T	25
Coulin Pass	Highld	NH0250	57°30·1′	5°17·8′W	X	25
Coulins Burn	Aberd	NJ3218	57°15·1′	3°7·2′W	W	37
Coull	Aberd	NJ5102	57°6·6′	2°48·1′W	T	37
Coull	Highld	NH8103	57°6·4′	3°57·4′W	X	35
Coullabus	Arg & Bt	NR2965	55°48·4′	6°19·1′W	X	60
Coull Fm	Arg & Bt	NR2064	55°47·5′	6°27·6′W	FM	60
Coull Ho	Aberd	NJ5201	57°6·1′	2°47·1′W	X	37
Coull Home Fm	Aberd	NJ5101	57°6·1′	2°48·1′W	FM	37
Coullie	Aberd	NJ8825	57°19·2′	2°11·5′W	X	38
Coulliehare	Aberd	NJ8928	57°20·8′	2°10·5′W	X	38
Coul Links	Highld	NH8194	57°55·4′	4°0·1′W	X	21
Coull of Newe	Aberd	NJ3712	57°11·9′	3°2·1′W	X	37
Coulmony Ho	Highld	NH9747	57°30·4′	3°42·7′W	X	27
Coulmore	Highld	NH6148	57°30·3′	4°18·7′W	X	26
Coulnacraggan	Highld	NG4345	57°25·6′	6°16·4′W	T	23
Coulnacraig	Aberd	NO6295	57°2·9′	2°37·1′W	X	37,45
Coulnagower	Highld	NH5858	57°35·6′	4°22·1′W	X	26
Coulnakyle	Highld	NH9921	57°16·4′	3°40·0′W	X	36
Coul of Fairburn	Highld	NH4753	57°32·7′	4°32·9′W	T	26
Coul Point	Arg & Bt	NR1864	55°47·5′	6°29·5′W	X	60
Coulport	Arg & Bt	NS2087	56°2·8′	4°53·0′W	T	56
Coul Resr	Fife	NO2603	56°13·1′	3°11·2′W	W	59
Coulscott	Devon	SS6046	51°12·0′	3°59·8′W	X	180
Coulsdon	Croy	TQ3058	51°18·6′	0°7·7′W	T	187
Coulsdon Common	Croy	TQ3257	51°18·0′	0°6·0′W	F	187
Coulshill	Pth & Kin	NN9709	56°16·0′	3°39·3′W	X	58
Coulsknowe	Pth & Kin	NO0105	56°13·9′	3°35·4′W	X	58
Coulson	Devon	SS6305	50°49·9′	3°56·3′W	X	191
Coulston	Wilts	ST9554	51°17·3′	2°3·9′W	T	184
Coulston Down	Wilts	ST9450	51°15·2′	2°4·8′W	X	184
Coulston Hill	Wilts	ST9452	51°16·3′	2°4·8′W	X	184
Coulston Old Mill	E Loth	NT5269	55°55·0′	2°45·6′W	X	66
Coulsworthy	Devon	SS6244	51°11·0′	3°58·1′W	X	180
Coultas Fm	Notts	SK6760	53°8·2′	0°59·5′W	FM	120
Coultas Fm	N Yks	SE7576	54°10·7′	0°50·6′W	FM	100
Coulter	S Lanak	NT0233	55°35·1′	3°32·9′W	T	72
Coulterfanny	Aberd	NJ9161	57°38·6′	2°8·6′W	X	30
Coulterhaugh	S Lanak	NT0034	55°35·6′	3°34·8′W	X	72
Coulter Mains	S Lanak	NT0134	55°35·6′	3°33·8′W	X	72
Coultermire Plantn	N Yks	SE1984	54°15·3′	1°42·1′W	F	99
Coulterna	Aberd	NJ8944	57°29·4′	2°10·6′W	X	30
Coulter Reservoir	S Lanak	NT0327	55°31·9′	3°31·8′W	W	72
Coulters Dean Fm	Hants	SU7419	50°58·2′	0°56·4′W	FM	197
Coulter Shaw	S Lanak	NT0333	55°35·1′	3°31·9′W	X	72
Coultershaw Bridge	W Susx	SU9719	50°58·0′	0°36·7′W	X	197
Coulters Hill	Staffs	SK1525	52°49·6′	1°46·2′W	X	128
Coultings	Somer	ST2241	51°10·0′	3°6·6′W	T	182
Coulton	N Yks	SE6374	54°9·7′	1°1·7′W	T	100
Coulton Moor	N Yks	SE6274	54°9·7′	1°2·6′W	F	100
Coulton Pale	N Yks	SE6375	54°10·3′	1°1·7′W	F	100
Coultoon	Arg & Bt	NR2057	55°43·8′	6°27·2′W	X	60
Coultorsay	Arg & Bt	NR2560	55°45·6′	6°22·6′W	X	60
Coultra	Fife	NO3523	56°23·9′	3°2·7′W	X	54,59
Coultra Fm	Fife	NO3422	56°23·4′	3°3·7′W	FM	54,59
Coulwood	Highld	NH4757	57°34·9′	4°33·1′W	X	26
Coumbs Wood	Derby	SK3157	53°6·8′	1°31·8′W	F	119
Coumes	Lancs	SD6659	54°1·8′	2°30·7′W	X	103
Coumes Fm	Sheff	SK2992	53°25·7′	1°33·4′W	FM	110
Council Hill	Oxon	SP3734	52°0·4′	1°27·3′W	X	151
Cound	Shrops	SJ5504	52°38·2′	2°39·5′W	T	126
Cound Brook	Shrops	SJ5006	52°39·2′	2°43·9′W	W	126
Coundlane	Shrops	SJ5705	52°38·7′	2°37·7′W	T	126
Coundmoor	Shrops	SJ5502	52°37·1′	2°39·5′W	T	126
Coundmoor Brook	Shrops	SJ5504	52°38·2′	2°39·5′W	W	126
Coundon	Cov	SP3181	52°25·8′	1°32·2′W	T	140
Coundon	Durham	NZ2429	54°39·6′	1°37·3′W	T	93
Coundon Burn	Durham	NZ2230	54°40·1′	1°39·1′W	W	93
Coundongate	Durham	NZ2229	54°39·6′	1°39·1′W	T	93
Coundon Grange	Durham	NZ2228	54°39·0′	1°39·1′W	T	93
Countam	D & G	NS7102	55°18·0′	4°1·5′W	H	77
Countam	D & G	NX7698	55°15·9′	3°56·7′W	H	78
Counter Drain	Lincs	TF1619	52°45·6′	0°16·5′W	W	130
Counter Fm	Kent	TQ9433	51°4·0′	0°46·5′E	FM	189
Counters End	Herts	TL0407	51°45·4′	0°29·2′W	T	166
Countersett	N Yks	SD9188	54°17·5′	2°7·9′W	T	98
Countersett Bardale	N Yks	SD8886	54°16·4′	2°10·6′W	X	98
Countess	Wilts	SU1542	51°10·9′	1°46·7′W	X	184
Countess Cliff	Derby	SK0570	53°13·9′	1°55·1′W	X	119
Countess Close	N Lincs	SE8721	53°40·9′	0°40·6′W	A	106,112
Countess Cross	Essex	TL8630	51°56·5′	0°42·8′E	T	168
Countesspark Wood	Northum	NY8681	55°7·6′	2°12·7′W	F	80
Countess' Pillar	Cumbr	NY5429	54°39·5′	2°42·4′W	A	90
Countess Wear	Devon	SX9490	50°42·2′	3°29·7′W	T	192
Countess Wells Fm	Suff	TM2864	52°13·8′	1°20·7′E	FM	156
Countesswells Ho	C of Aber	NJ8704	57°7·9′	2°12·4′W	X	38
Countesthorpe	Leic	SP5895	52°33·2′	1°8·3′W	T	140
Counthorpe Ho	Lincs	TF0020	52°46·3′	0°30·7′W	X	130
Counthorpe Lodge	Lincs	SK9821	52°46·9′	0°32·4′W	X	130
Countiesmeet	Somer	SS8724	51°0·5′	3°36·3′W	X	181
Counting Hill	Black w Dar	SD6714	53°37·5′	2°29·5′W	H	109
Countisbury	Devon	SS7449	51°13·8′	3°47·9′W	T	180
Countisbury Common	Devon	SS7549	51°13·8′	3°47·0′W	X	180
Countisbury Cove	Devon	SS7650	51°14·4′	3°46·2′W	W	180
Countlich	Pth & Kin	NN9949	56°37·6′	3°38·3′W	X	52,53
Count Rock	S Glos	ST5995	51°39·4′	2°35·2′W	X	162
Country Way	Leeds	SE4031	53°46·7′	1°23·2′W	X	105
County Cottage	Wilts	ST7943	51°11·4′	2°17·6′W	X	183
County Fm	Essex	TL6117	51°49·9′	0°20·6′E	FM	167
County Fm	Norf	TF9737	52°53·9′	0°56·1′E	FM	132
County Fm	Suff	TL6380	52°23·9′	0°24·1′E	FM	143
County Gate	Somer	SS7948	51°13·3′	3°43·6′W	X	180
County Hall	Kent	TQ7656	51°16·8′	0°31·8′E	X	178,188
County Hole	Norf	TL8880	52°23·4′	0°46·2′E	W	144
County School Station	Norf	TF9822	52°45·8′	0°56·5′E	X	132
Coupans	Pth & Kin	NN8107	56°14·7′	3°54·8′W	X	57
Coupar Angus	Pth & Kin	NO2240	56°33·0′	3°15·7′W	T	53
Coupar Grange	Pth & Kin	NO2342	56°34·1′	3°14·7′W	X	53
Coupar Grange Fm	Pth & Kin	NO2242	56°34·1′	3°15·7′W	FM	53
Couper Hill	Highld	ND2371	58°37·5′	3°19·1′W	X	7,12
Coup Green	Lancs	SD5927	53°44·5′	2°36·9′W	T	102
Coupland	Cumbr	NY7118	54°33·6′	2°26·5′W	T	91
Coupland	Northum	NT9331	55°34·6′	2°6·2′W	T	74,75
Coupland Gair	S Lanak	NS9414	55°24·8′	3°40·0′W	X	71,78
Coupland Hill	S Lanak	NS9720	55°28·0′	3°37·3′W	H	72
Couplaw	S Lanak	NS7543	55°40·1′	3°58·8′W	X	71
Couple Cross	Somer	SS9538	51°8·1′	3°29·7′W	X	181
Coupledyke Hall	Lincs	TF3842	52°57·7′	0°3·7′E	X	131
Coup Scar	Cumbr	SD2264	54°4·2′	3°11·1′W	X	96
Cour	Arg & Bt	NR8248	55°40·8′	5°27·6′W	X	62,69
Courage	Highld	NH9355	57°34·6′	3°46·9′W	X	27
Courance	D & G	NY0590	55°12·0′	3°29·1′W	T	78
Courancehill	D & G	NY0591	55°12·5′	3°29·1′W	X	78
Cour Bay	Arg & Bt	NR8248	55°40·8′	5°27·6′W	W	62,69
Cour Island	Arg & Bt	NR8247	55°40·3′	5°27·6′W	X	62,69
Courlands Cott	Corn	SX1358	50°23·8′	4°37·5′W	X	200
Courns Wood	Bucks	SU8498	51°40·7′	0°46·7′W	F	165
Coursan	Orkney	HY5233	59°11·1′	2°49·9′W	X	5,6
Coursebeer	Devon	SX6894	50°44·1′	3°51·9′W	X	191
Course Head	Scot Bord	NT3216	55°26·2′	3°4·1′W	X	79
Coursehill Fm	Oxon	SP3307	51°45·9′	1°30·9′W	FM	164
Coursehorn	Kent	TQ7935	51°5·4′	0°33·8′E	X	188
Coursers Fm	Herts	TL2004	51°43·5′	0°15·4′W	FM	166
Courses	Derby	SK0481	53°19·8′	1°56·0′W	X	110
Courshay	Devon	ST3400	50°48·0′	2°55·8′W	X	193
Cour-sheileach	Arg & Bt	NR7551	55°42·3′	5°34·4′W	X	62,69
Coursley	Somer	ST1433	51°5·6′	3°13·3′W	T	181
Courstein	D & G	NY1679	55°6·1′	3°18·6′W	X	85
Court	Brig	SS8579	51°30·1′	3°39·0′W	X	170
Court	Devon	SS9114	50°55·1′	3°32·7′W	X	181
Court	Devon	SS9725	51°1·1′	3°27·7′W	X	181
Court	Devon	SY0295	50°45·0′	3°23·0′W	X	192
Court	Glos	SO7433	51°59·9′	2°22·3′W	X	150
Court	Glos	SO7521	51°53·5′	2°21·4′W	X	162
Court	Glos	SO7618	51°51·8′	2°20·5′W	X	162
Court	Glos	SO7921	51°53·5′	2°17·9′W	X	162
Court	Glos	SO8917	51°51·3′	2°9·2′W	X	163
Court	Glos	SP0634	52°0·5′	1°54·4′W	X	150
Court	Heref	SO2553	52°10·4′	3°5·4′W	X	148
Court	Heref	SO3359	52°13·7′	2°58·5′W	X	148,149
Court	Heref	SO4062	52°15·4′	2°52·3′W	X	137,148,149
Court	Heref	SO4143	52°5·2′	2°51·3′W	X	148,149,161
Court	Heref	SO4443	52°5·2′	2°48·6′W	X	148,149,161
Court	Heref	SO4745	52°6·3′	2°46·0′W	X	148,149
Court	Heref	SO4863	52°16·0′	2°45·3′W	X	137,138,148
Court	Heref	SO5443	52°5·2′	2°39·9′W	X	149
Court	Heref	SO5727	51°56·6′	2°37·1′W	X	162
Court	Heref	SO7256	52°12·3′	2°24·2′W	X	149
Court	Monm	SO3010	51°47·3′	3°0·5′W	X	161
Court	Monm	SO4215	51°50·1′	2°50·1′W	X	161
Court	Monm	SO4810	51°47·4′	2°44·8′W	X	161
Court	Pemb	SM9835	51°58·8′	4°56·1′W	X	157
Court	Pemb	SN1339	52°1·3′	4°43·1′W	X	145
Court	Powys	SO1086	52°28·1′	3°19·1′W	X	136
Court	Powys	SO1239	52°2·8′	3°16·6′W	X	161
Court	Powys	SO1941	52°3·9′	3°10·5′W	X	148,161
Court	Powys	SO2416	51°50·5′	3°5·8′W	X	161
Court	S Glos	ST5882	51°32·4′	2°35·9′W	A	172
Court	Shrops	SO5473	52°21·4′	2°40·1′W	X	137,138
Court	Somer	ST1126	51°1·8′	3°15·8′W	X	181,193
Court	Warw	SP0753	52°10·7′	1°53·5′W	X	150
Court	Warw	SP1266	52°17·8′	1°49·0′W	A	150
Court	Worcs	SO7268	52°18·8′	2°24·2′W	X	138
Court	Worcs	SO7453	52°10·7′	2°22·4′W	X	150
Court	Worcs	SO8463	52°16·1′	2°13·7′W	X	138,150
Court	Worcs	SO9537	52°2·1′	2°4·0′W	X	150
Court-at-Street	Kent	TR0935	51°4·8′	0°59·4′E	T	179,189
Court-at-Wick	Kent	TR0129	51°1·7′	0°52·4′E	X	189
Court Barn	Somer	ST5437	51°8·1′	2°39·1′W	A	182,183
Court Barn Fm	Somer	ST5437	51°8·1′	2°39·1′W	FM	182,183
Court Barns Fm	Cambs	TL6459	52°12·5′	0°24·4′E	FM	154
Court Barton	Devon	SS5622	50°59·0′	4°2·7′W	X	180
Court Barton	Devon	SS9202	50°48·7′	3°31·6′W	X	192
Court Barton	Devon	SX6941	50°15·5′	3°49·9′W	X	202
Court Barton	Devon	SX8297	50°45·9′	3°40·0′W	X	191
Court Barton	Devon	SX8385	50°39·4′	3°38·9′W	T	191
Court Barton	Devon	SX8898	50°46·5′	3°34·9′W	X	192
Court Barton	Devon	SX8968	50°30·3′	3°33·5′W	X	202
Court Barton Fm	Corn	SX1856	50°22·8′	4°33·2′W	FM	201
Courtbrook Fm	Devon	SX9889	50°41·7′	3°26·3′W	FM	192
Courtcairn	Aberd	NJ7211	57°11·6′	2°27·3′W	X	38
Court Cairn	D & G	NX3051	54°49·8′	4°38·4′W	A	82
Court Calmore	Powys	SO1997	52°34·1′	3°11·3′W	X	136
Court Castle	Devon	SS6308	50°51·6′	3°56·4′W	A	191
Court & Castle	Powys	SO1821	51°53·1′	3°11·1′W	A	161
Court Colman	Brig	SS8881	51°31·2′	3°36·5′W	T	170
Court Copse	Hants	SU3016	50°56·8′	1°34·0′W	F	185
Court Corner	Hants	SU6059	51°19·8′	1°7·9′W	T	175
Court Down	Somer	SS9129	51°3·2′	3°32·9′W	X	181
Courteachan	Highld	NM6897	57°0·6′	5°48·8′W	T	40
Courteenhall	Northnts	SP7553	52°10·4′	0°53·8′W	T	152
Courteenhall Grange Fm	Northnts	SP7655	52°11·5′	0°52·9′W	FM	152
Courtenay	Devon	SS9216	50°56·2′	3°31·8′W	X	181
Courtenay Fm	Kent	TR0859	51°17·7′	0°59·4′E	FM	179
Court Evan Gwynne	Powys	SO2144	52°5·6′	3°8·8′W	X	148,161
Courtfall Loch	Highld	ND2174	58°39·1′	3°21·2′W	W	7,12
Court Farm Ho	Warw	SP2560	52°14·5′	1°37·6′W	X	151
Courtfield	Heref	SO5917	51°51·2′	2°35·3′W	X	162
Courtfield Fm	Bucks	SP6430	51°58·1′	1°3·7′W	FM	152,165
Court Field Ho	Bucks	SP8602	51°42·8′	0°44·9′W	X	165
Court Fm	Bucks	TQ0486	51°34·0′	0°29·6′W	FM	176
Court Fm	Carm	SN3938	52°1·3′	4°20·4′W	FM	145
Court Fm	Corn	SW9552	50°20·2′	4°52·5′W	FM	200,204
Court Fm	Dorset	ST6707	50°51·9′	2°27·8′W	FM	194
Court Fm	Dorset	ST6804	50°50·3′	2°26·9′W	FM	194
Court Fm	Dorset	SY8494	50°45·0′	2°13·2′W	FM	194
Court Fm	Essex	TL9503	51°41·7′	0°49·7′E	FM	168
Court Fm	Essex	TR0199	51°39·5′	0°54·8′E	FM	168
Court Fm	E Susx	TQ6925	51°0·2′	0°24·9′E	FM	188,199
Court Fm	Glos	SO6819	51°52·4′	2°27·5′W	FM	162
Court Fm	Glos	SO8313	51°49·2′	2°14·4′W	FM	162
Court Fm	Glos	SO8425	51°55·6′	2°13·6′W	FM	162
Court Fm	Glos	SO9328	51°57·3′	2°5·7′W	FM	150,163
Court Fm	Hants	SU1116	50°56·8′	1°50·2′W	FM	184
Court Fm	Hants	SU5150	51°15·0′	1°15·8′W	FM	185
Court Fm	Hants	SZ1597	50°46·6′	1°46·9′W	FM	195
Court Fm	Heref	SO2836	52°1·3′	3°2·6′W	FM	161
Court Fm	Heref	SO3636	52°1·4′	2°55·6′W	FM	149,161
Court Fm	Heref	SO5538	52°2·6′	2°39·0′W	FM	149
Court Fm	Heref	SO6133	51°59·9′	2°33·7′W	FM	149
Court Fm	Heref	SO6759	52°13·9′	2°28·6′W	FM	149
Court Fm	Kent	TQ8057	51°17·2′	0°35·3′E	FM	178,188
Court Fm	Kent	TR1435	51°4·7′	1°3·7′E	FM	179,189
Court Fm	Mil Key	SP8753	52°10·3′	0°43·3′W	FM	152
Court Fm	N Som	ST3860	51°20·4′	2°53·0′W	FM	182
Court Fm	Oxon	SP3332	51°59·4′	1°30·8′W	FM	151
Court Fm	Powys	SO0947	52°7·1′	3°19·4′W	FM	147
Court Fm	Powys	SO2143	52°5·0′	3°8·8′W	FM	148,161
Court Fm	Powys	SO2466	52°17·5′	3°6·5′W	FM	137,148
Court Fm	Rho Cyn Taf	SN9705	51°44·3′	3°29·1′W	FM	160
Court Fm	Shrops	SO5270	52°19·8′	2°41·9′W	FM	137,138
Court Fm	Somer	SS8537	51°7·5′	3°38·2′W	FM	181
Court Fm	Somer	ST1814	50°55·4′	3°9·6′W	FM	181,193
Court Fm	Somer	ST3232	51°5·2′	2°57·9′W	FM	182
Court Fm	Somer	ST4650	51°15·0′	2°46·0′W	FM	182
Court Fm	Suff	TM0548	52°5·8′	1°0·0′E	FM	155
Court Fm	Surrey	TQ3055	51°17·0′	0°7·8′W	FM	187
Court Fm	Warw	SP1547	52°7·5′	1°46·5′W	FM	151
Court Fm	W Berks	SU6064	51°22·5′	1°7·9′W	FM	175
Court Fm	Wilts	ST8553	51°16·8′	2°12·5′W	FM	183
Court Fm	Worcs	SO6568	52°18·8′	2°30·4′W	FM	138
Court Fm	Worcs	SO8065	52°17·2′	2°17·2′W	FM	138,150
Court Fm	Worcs	SO9849	52°8·6′	2°1·4′W	FM	150
Court Fm	W Susx	TQ1024	51°0·5′	0°25·5′W	FM	198
Court Fms	Somer	SS9936	51°7·1′	3°26·2′W	FM	181
Court Fm, The	Monm	SO4314	51°49·5′	2°49·2′W	FM	161
Court Garden	Bucks	SU8486	51°34·2′	0°46·9′W	X	175
Court Gardens Fm	E Susx	TQ3216	50°55·9′	0°6·9′W	FM	198
Court (Gdn)	Heref	SO3830	51°58·1′	2°53·8′W	X	149,161
Court Grange	Devon	SX8568	50°30·3′	3°36·9′W	X	202
Court Green Fm	N Yks	TA0194	54°20·1′	0°26·4′W	FM	101
Court Green Fm	Red & Cl	NZ5918	54°33·5′	1°4·8′W	FM	93
Court Green Howe	Red & Cl	NZ5818	54°33·5′	1°5·8′W	A	93
Court Green Woods	Red & Cl	NZ5818	54°33·5′	1°5·8′W	F	93
Court Hall Fm	Devon	ST0319	50°58·0′	3°22·5′W	FM	181
Court, The	Highld	NN2479	56°52·4′	4°52·8′W	W	41
Court Henry	Carm	SN5522	51°52·9′	4°6·0′W	T	159
Court Hey	Know	SJ4190	53°24·5′	2°52·8′W	T	108
Courthill	Angus	NO6751	56°39·2′	2°31·8′W	X	54
Court Hill	D & G	NX8154	54°52·2′	3°50·8′W	H	84
Courthill	D & G	NX8158	54°54·4′	3°50·9′W	X	84
Court Hill	D & G	NX8192	55°12·7′	3°51·8′W	H	78
Courthill	D & G	NX8571	55°1·5′	3°47·5′W	X	84
Courthill	Fife	NT0684	56°2·6′	3°30·1′W	X	65
Court Hill	Glos	SO8007	51°45·9′	2°17·0′W	X	162
Court Hill	N Ayr	NS3653	55°44·8′	4°35·4′W	A	63
Court Hill	Notts	SK5328	52°51·0′	1°12·4′W	X	129
Court Hill	N Som	ST4271	51°26·3′	2°49·7′W	X	171,172
Court Hill	Oxon	SU3886	51°34·5′	1°26·7′W	X	174
Court Hill	Pth & Kin	NO1437	56°31·3′	3°23·4′W	X	53
Courthill	Pth & Kin	NO1848	56°37·3′	3°19·7′W	X	53
Courthill	Scot Bord	NT5217	55°26·9′	2°45·1′W	X	79
Courthill	Scot Bord	NT6836	55°37·2′	2°30·1′W	X	74
Court Hill	Wilts	ST8336	51°7·6′	2°14·2′W	H	183
Court Hill	W Susx	SU8913	50°54·8′	0°43·7′W	H	197
Courthill Fm	W Susx	SU9508	50°52·0′	0°38·6′W	FM	197
Courthill Ho	Highld	NG8340	57°24·2′	5°36·3′W	X	24
Court Ho	Ches	SJ5668	53°12·7′	2°39·1′W	X	117
Court Ho	Ches	SJ6563	53°10·0′	2°31·0′W	X	118
Court Ho	Dorset	SY6299	50°47·6′	2°32·0′W	A	194
Court Ho	E Susx	TQ4428	51°2·2′	0°3·6′E	X	187,198
Court Ho	Hants	SU7653	51°16·5′	0°54·2′W	X	186

Court Ho	Powys	SJ2402	52°36·9'	3°7·0'W	X	126
Court Ho	Powys	SJ2418	52°45·5'	3°7·2'W	X	126
Court Ho	Powys	SO2692	52°31·5'	3°5·0'W	X	137
Court Ho	Wilts	ST9052	51°16·3'	2°8·2'W	A	184
Court Horeham	E Susx	TQ6015	50°55·0'	0°17·0'E	X	199
Courthouse	Cumbr	SD3598	54°22·6'	2°59·6'W	A	96,97
Court House	Dorset	SY9798	50°47·1'	2°2·2'W	A	195
Court House	Hants	SU6822	50°59·8'	1°1·5'W	A	185
Court House	Somer	ST1343	51°11·0'	3°14·3'W	A	181
Court House Dairy	Dorset	ST6214	50°55·7'	2°32·1'W	X	194
Courthouse Fm	Ches	SJ7565	53°11·1'	2°22·0'W	FM	118
Courthouse Fm	Derby	SK3445	53°0·3'	1°29·2'W	FM	119,128
Courthouse Fm	E Susx	TQ3812	50°53·7'	0°1·9'W	FM	198
Court House Fm	Lincs	TF0974	53°15·3'	0°21·6'W	FM	121
Court House Fm	N Yks	SE5260	54°2·2'	1°11·9'W	FM	100
Court House Fm	N Yks	SE5981	54°13·5'	1°5·3'W	FM	100
Court House Fm	Oxon	SU2694	51°38·9'	1°37·1'W	FM	163,174
Courthouse Fm	Swan	SS5690	51°35·7'	4°4·3'W	FM	159
Court House Fm	W Susx	TQ3024	51°0·3'	0°8·4'W	FM	198
Court House Green	Cov	SP3581	52°25·8'	1°28·7'W	T	140
Courtiestown	Aberd	NJ5624	57°18·5'	2°43·4'W	X	37
Court Knoll	Essex	TL9733	51°57·9'	0°52·5'E	A	168
Court Knoll	Suff	TL9734	51°58·4'	0°52·5'E	A	155
Courtland Fm	Somer	ST0931	51°4·5'	3°17·6'W	FM	181
Courtlands	Devon	ST0705	50°50·5'	3°18·9'W	X	192
Courtlands	Devon	SX9983	50°38·5'	3°25·3'W	X	192
Courtlands	Somer	ST1926	51°1·9'	3°8·9'W	X	181,193
Courtlands	Surrey	TQ3040	51°8·9'	0°8·1'W	X	187
Courtlands	Wilts	ST8869	51°25·4'	2°10·0'W	X	173
Courtlands	W Susx	TQ3832	51°4·5'	0°1·4'W	X	187
Court Lees	Kent	TR1163	51°19·8'	1°2·1'E	X	179
Court Leys	Lincs	SK9049	53°2·1'	0°39·1'W	X	130
Court-Llacca	Powys	SO0933	51°59·5'	3°19·1'W	X	161
Court Lodge	Brom	TQ4763	51°21·0'	0°7·1'E	X	177,188
Court Lodge	E Susx	TQ6808	50°51·0'	0°23·6'E	A	199
Court Lodge	E Susx	TQ6816	50°55·4'	0°23·8'E	X	199
Court Lodge	E Susx	TQ7825	51°0·0'	0°32·6'E	X	188,199
Court Lodge	E Susx	TQ8618	50°56·1'	0°39·2'E	X	189,199
Court Lodge	Kent	TQ4454	51°16·2'	0°4·2'E	X	187
Court Lodge	Kent	TQ5866	51°22·5'	0°16·6'E	X	177
Court Lodge	Kent	TQ6836	51°6·1'	0°24·4'E	X	188
Court Lodge	Kent	TQ7153	51°15·3'	0°27·4'E	X	188
Court Lodge	Kent	TQ7450	51°13·6'	0°29·9'E	X	188
Court Lodge	Kent	TQ8658	51°17·7'	0°40·5'E	A	178
Court Lodge	Kent	TR0063	51°20·1'	0°52·7'E	X	178
Court Lodge	Kent	TR0224	50°59·0'	0°53·1'E	X	189
Court Lodge	Kent	TR0340	51°7·6'	0°54·5'E	X	179,189
Court Lodge	Kent	TR1044	51°9·6'	1°0·6'E	X	179,189
Court Lodge	Medway	TQ7066	51°22·3'	0°26·9'E	X	178
Court Lodge Down	E Susx	TQ6037	51°6·8'	0°17·5'E	X	188
Court Lodge Fm	Kent	TQ4656	51°17·3'	0°6·0'E	FM	188
Court Lodge Fm	Kent	TR8653	51°15·0'	0°40·3'E	FM	189
Court Lodge Fm	Kent	TQ9047	51°11·7'	0°43·6'E	FM	189
Court Lodge Fm	Kent	TQ9652	51°14·2'	0°48·9'E	FM	189
Court Lodge Fm	Kent	TQ9939	51°7·2'	0°51·0'E	FM	189
Court Lodge Fm	Kent	TR0034	51°4·4'	0°51·7'E	FM	189
Court Lodge Fm	Kent	TR0736	51°5·4'	0°57·8'E	FM	179,189
Courtmoor Fm	Devon	ST2006	50°51·1'	3°7·8'W	FM	192,193
Court Oak Fm	W Berks	SU4374	51°28·0'	1°22·5'W	FM	174
Court of Gladestry	Powys	SO2256	52°12·0'	3°8·1'W	X	148
Court of Hill	Shrops	SO6072	52°20·9'	2°34·8'W	A	138
Court of Noke	Heref	SO3759	52°13·8'	2°54·9'W	X	148,149
Court Orchard	Dorset	SY4693	50°44·3'	2°45·5'W	T	193
Courtpark	Devon	SX6843	50°16·6'	3°50·8'W	X	202
Court Place	Devon	SS8808	50°51·9'	3°35·1'W	X	192
Court Place	Somer	SS8846	51°12·4'	3°35·8'W	X	181
Court Place	Somer	ST0521	50°59·1'	3°20·8'W	X	181
Court Place Fm	Devon	ST2101	50°48·4'	3°6·9'W	FM	192,193
Court Robert	Monm	SO4009	51°46·8'	2°51·8'W	X	161
Courtsend	Essex	TR0293	51°36·2'	0°55·4'E	T	178
Courts Fm	W Susx	SU9026	51°1·8'	0°42·6'W	FM	186,197
Court Stane	Aberd	NO7779	56°54·4'	2°22·2'W	A	45
Court St Lawrence	Monm	SO4505	51°44·7'	2°47·4'W	X	161
Courtstone	Aberd	NJ8433	57°23·5'	2°15·5'W	X	29,30
Court, The	Heref	SO6636	52°1·5'	2°29·3'W	X	149
Court, The	Monm	SO3517	51°51·1'	2°56·2'W	X	161
Court, The	Powys	SO0856	52°11·9'	3°20·4'W	X	147
Court, The	Powys	SO1594	52°32·5'	3°14·8'W	X	136
Court, The	W Berks	SU5767	51°24·2'	1°10·4'W	X	174
Court, The	Worcs	SO9343	52°5·4'	2°5·7'W	X	150
Court, The	Worcs	SP0153	52°10·8'	1°58·7'W	X	150
Courtway	Somer	ST2033	51°5·7'	3°8·2'W	T	182
Court Wick Park	W Susx	TQ0103	50°49·3'	0°33·6'W	X	197
Court Wood	Corn	SX1755	50°22·2'	4°34·0'W	F	201
Court Wood	Kent	TQ7071	51°25·0'	0°27·1'E	F	178
Court Wood	Kent	TR0757	51°16·7'	0°58·5'E	F	179
Courtyard Cotts	D & G	NX7758	54°54·3'	3°54·7'W	X	84
Courtyard Fm	Norf	TF7240	52°56·0'	0°34·0'E	FM	132
Court-y-Gaer	Powys	SO1130	51°57·9'	3°17·3'W	X	161
Court-y-park	Heref	SO6439	52°3·1'	2°31·1'W	X	149
Courtyplyfin	Powys	SO0931	51°58·4'	3°19·1'W	X	161
Cousens' Fm	Suff	TM1362	52°13·1'	1°7·5'E	FM	156
Couse Point	Orkney	HY4900	58°53·3'	2°52·6'W	X	6,7
Cousin's Cross	Devon	SX7839	50°14·5'	3°42·3'W	X	202
Cousland	Midlo	NT3768	55°54·3'	3°0·0'W	T	66
Cousland	W Loth	NT0166	55°52·9'	3°34·5'W	X	65
Cousland Park	Midlo	NT3968	55°54·3'	2°58·1'W	X	66
Cousley Wood	E Susx	TQ6533	51°4·6'	0°21·7'E	T	188
Couston	Angus	NO3239	56°32·5'	3°5·9'W	X	53
Couston Castle	Fife	NT1685	56°3·3'	3°20·5'W	A	65,66
Coustonn	Arg & Bt	NS0774	55°55·5'	5°4·9'W	X	63
Couston Water	W Loth	NS9671	55°55·5'	3°39·4'W	W	65
Coutens	Aberd	NJ8027	57°20·2'	2°19·5'W	X	38
Couternach	Angus	NO4183	56°56·3'	2°57·7'W	X	44
Couters Hill	Orkney	HY4148	59°19·1'	3°1·7'W	H	5
Couthalley Castle	S Lanak	NS9748	55°43·1'	3°37·9'W	A	72
Coutlair Knowe	Scot Bord	NT3311	55°23·6'	3°3·0'W	H	79
Couts Rocks	Aberd	NO8269	56°49·0'	2°17·2'W	X	45
Couttie	Pth & Kin	NO2140	56°33·0'	3°16·7'W	X	53
Cova	Shetld	HU3849	60°13·7'	1°18·3'W	T	3
Covanhill	S Lanak	NS9251	55°44·7'	3°42·8'W	X	65,72
Cove	Arg & Bt	NR7577	55°56·3'	5°35·7'W	X	62
Cove	Arg & Bt	NS2282	56°0·1'	4°50·8'W	T	56
Cove	Cumbr	NY4323	54°36·2'	2°52·5'W	X	90
Cove	Devon	SS9519	50°57·9'	3°29·3'W	T	181
Cove	Hants	SU8555	51°17·5'	0°46·5'W	T	175,186
Cove	Highld	NG8090	57°51·0'	5°42·0'W	T	19
Cove	Scot Bord	NT7771	55°56·1'	2°21·7'W	T	67
Cove Bay	Arg & Bt	NS2182	56°0·1'	4°51·8'W	W	56
Cove Bay	C of Aber	NJ9501	57°6·3'	2°4·5'W	T	38
Cove Bottom	Suff	TM4979	52°21·4'	1°39·8'E	T	156
Cove Burn	S Lanak	NS6132	55°34·0'	4°11·8'W	W	71
Cove Down Fm	Devon	SS9619	50°57·9'	3°28·5'W	FM	181
Covedown Knap	Devon	SS9620	50°58·4'	3°28·5'W	H	181
Cove Fm	Scot Bord	NT7871	55°56·1'	2°20·7'W	FM	67
Covehall Fm	Suff	TM4689	52°26·8'	1°37·6'E	FM	134,156
Cove Harbour	Scot Bord	NT7871	55°56·1'	2°20·7'W	X	67
Covehithe	Suff	TM5281	52°22·4'	1°42·5'E	T	156
Covehithe Broad	Suff	TM5281	52°22·4'	1°42·5'E	W	156
Covehithe Cliffs	Suff	TM5281	52°22·4'	1°42·5'E	X	156
Cove Ho	Devon	SS9519	50°57·9'	3°29·3'W	X	181
Cove Ho	Lancs	SD4575	54°10·3'	2°50·1'W	X	97
Covehouse	Scot Bord	NT6237	55°37·8'	2°35·8'W	X	74
Cove House Fm	Wilts	SU0592	51°37·8'	1°55·3'W	FM	163,173
Covehurst Bay	E Susx	TQ8610	50°51·8'	0°39·0'E	W	199
Covell House Fm	N Yks	SE1270	54°7·8'	1°48·6'W	FM	99
Coven	Staffs	SJ9006	52°39·3'	2°8·5'W	T	127,139
Covenanters' Cave	D & G	NX9573	55°2·7'	3°38·2'W	X	84
Covenanters' Grave	S Lanak	NT0752	55°45·4'	3°28·5'W	X	65,72
Covenanters' Well	Scot Bord	NT5341	55°39·9'	2°44·4'W	W	73
Covenbrook Hall	Essex	TL7824	51°53·4'	0°35·6'E	X	167
Covender	Heref	SO6243	52°5·3'	2°32·9'W	T	149
Coveney	Cambs	TL4882	52°25·2'	0°11·0'E	T	143
Coveney Byall Fen	Cambs	TL4884	52°26·3'	0°11·0'E	X	143
Coveney Sledge Fen	Cambs	TL4981	52°24·6'	0°11·8'E	X	143
Covenham Reservoir	Lincs	TF3496	53°26·9'	0°1·5'E	W	113
Covenham St Bartholomew	Lincs	TF3394	53°25·8'	0°0·5'E	T	113
Covenham St Mary	Lincs	TF3394	53°25·8'	0°0·5'E	T	113
Coven Heath	Staffs	SJ9104	52°38·3'	2°7·6'W	T	127,139
Covenhope	Heref	SO4064	52°16·5'	2°52·4'W	X	137,148,149
Coven Lawn	Staffs	SJ9005	52°38·8'	2°8·5'W	T	127,139
Coventree	Cumbr	SD7186	54°16·4'	2°26·3'W	X	98
Coventry	Cov	SP3378	52°24·2'	1°30·5'W	T	140
Coventry Airport	Warw	SP3574	52°22·0'	1°28·8'W	X	140
Coventry Canal	Staffs	SK1511	52°42·0'	1°46·3'W	W	128
Coventry Canal	Staffs	SK2204	52°38·2'	1°40·1'W	W	139
Coventry Canal	Warw	SP3494	52°32·8'	1°29·5'W	W	140
Coventry Fm	Cambs	TL5657	52°11·6'	0°17·3'E	FM	154
Cove o' Kend	Cumbr	SD1966	54°5·3'	3°13·9'W	X	96
Cove Point	Arg & Bt	NR7107	55°18·5'	5°36·1'W	X	68
Coverack	Corn	SW7818	50°1·5'	5°5·6'W	T	204
Coverack Bridges	Corn	SW6630	50°7·7'	5°16·1'W	T	203
Cover Banks	N Yks	SE1386	54°16·4'	1°47·6'W	X	99
Coverdale	Lancs	SD8446	53°54·8'	2°14·2'W	X	103
Coverdale	N Yks	SE0582	54°14·3'	1°55·0'W	X	98
Coverdale	N Yks	SE0683	54°14·8'	1°54·1'W	X	99
Coverham	N Yks	SE1086	54°16·4'	1°50·4'W	T	99
Cover Head Bents	N Yks	SE0078	54°12·1'	1°59·6'W	X	98
Coverhead Fm	N Yks	SE0078	54°12·1'	1°59·6'W	FM	98
Coveridge Fields	Shrops	SO6081	52°25·8'	2°34·9'W	X	138
Covermill Hill	Leic	SK7920	52°46·5'	0°49·3'W	X	129
Covers Farmhouse	Kent	TQ4353	51°15·7'	0°3·4'E	X	187
Covert Fm	Leic	SK8123	52°48·1'	0°47·5'W	FM	130
Covert Fm	Northnts	SP6568	52°18·6'	1°2·4'W	FM	152
Cover, The	Norf	TF7934	52°52·6'	0°40·0'E	X	132
Coverteside	Ches	SJ5075	53°16·4'	2°44·6'W	X	117
Covert, The	Oxon	SU6684	51°33·3'	1°2·5'W	X	175
Covert Wood	Kent	TR1848	51°11·6'	1°7·6'E	F	179,189
Coverwood	Surrey	TQ0943	51°10·8'	0°26·0'W	X	187
Cove Scar	N Yks	SD9964	54°4·6'	2°0·5'W	X	98
Covesea	Moray	NJ1870	57°43·0'	3°22·1'W	T	28
Covesea Skerries	Moray	NJ1971	57°43·6'	3°21·1'W	X	28
Coves Haven	Northum	NU1344	55°41·6'	1°47·2'W	W	75
Coves House Fm	Durham	NZ0536	54°43·4'	1°54·9'W	FM	92
Coves Resr	Inverc	NS2476	55°56·9'	4°48·7'W	W	63
Coves, The	Arg & Bt	NR7161	55°47·5'	5°38·7'W	X	62
Cove, The	Cumbr	SD2696	54°21·5'	3°7·9'W	X	96,97
Cove, The	I Scilly	SV8807	49°53·2'	6°20·3'W	W	203
Cove, The	Swan	SS4885	51°32·8'	4°11·1'W	W	159
Covet Wood	Kent	TR1748	51°11·6'	1°6·7'E	F	179,189
Covey Hall Fm	N Yks	SE1848	53°55·9'	1°43·1'W	FM	104
Coveyheugh	Scot Bord	NT8662	55°51·3'	2°13·0'W	X	67
Covingham	Swin	SU1985	51°34·1'	1°43·2'W	T	173
Covington	Cambs	TL0570	52°19·3'	0°27·2'W	T	153
Covington	S Lanak	NS9739	55°38·3'	3°37·7'W	T	72
Covin Hill	Arg & Bt	NS0853	55°44·2'	5°3·1'W	X	63
Cowage Brook	Wilts	ST9974	51°28·1'	2°0·5'W	W	173
Cowage Fm	Wilts	ST9085	51°34·1'	2°8·3'W	FM	173
Cowage Grove	Wilts	ST9085	51°34·1'	2°8·3'W	F	173
Cowal	Arg & Bt	NS0884	56°0·9'	5°4·4'W	X	56
Cowall	Staffs	SJ9055	53°5·8'	2°8·6'W	X	118
Cowall Moor	Staffs	SJ9056	53°6·3'	2°8·6'W	X	118
Cowan Bridge	Lancs	SD6376	54°11·0'	2°33·6'W	T	97
Cow and Calf	Brad	SE1246	53°54·8'	1°48·6'W	X	104
Cow and Calf, The	N Yks	SE0858	54°1·3'	1°52·3'W	X	104
Cowan Fell	D & G	NT1603	55°19·1'	3°19·0'W	H	79
Cowans	D & G	NX1039	54°42·9'	4°56·6'W	X	82
Cowan's Croft	Scot Bord	NT2617	55°26·7'	3°9·8'W	H	79
Cowans Fm	D & G	NX8767	54°59·3'	3°45·5'W	FM	84
Cowans Knowe	Scot Bord	NT2825	55°31·1'	3°8·0'W	X	73
Cowans Law	E Ayr	NS5141	55°38·6'	4°21·6'W	X	70
Cowar	D & G	NX8466	54°58·8'	3°48·3'W	X	84
Cowards	Herts	TL3616	51°49·8'	0°1·2'W	X	166
Cow Ark	Lancs	SD6745	53°54·3'	2°29·7'W	T	103
Cowarne Brook	Heref	SO6151	52°9·6'	2°33·8'W	W	149
Cowarne Court	Heref	SO6146	52°6·9'	2°33·8'W	X	149
Cowarne Ho	Heref	SO6148	52°8·0'	2°33·8'W	X	149
Cowbakie Hill	Fife	NO4425	56°25·1'	2°54·0'W	H	54,59
Cow Bank Drain	Lincs	TF5560	53°7·1'	0°19·4'E	W	122
Cowbar	Red & Cl	NZ7718	54°33·3'	0°48·1'W	X	94
Cowbar Nab	Red & Cl	NZ7819	54°33·9'	0°47·2'W	X	94
Cowbeech	E Susx	TQ6114	50°54·4'	0°17·8'E	T	199
Cowbeech Fm	E Susx	TQ6114	50°54·4'	0°17·8'E	FM	199
Cowbeech Hill	E Susx	TQ6113	50°53·9'	0°17·8'E	T	199
Cowberry Hill	Roch	SD9617	53°39·2'	2°3·2'W	X	109
Cowbit	Lincs	TF2618	52°44·9'	0°7·6'W	T	131
Cowbit Ho	Lincs	TF2516	52°43·9'	0°8·5'W	X	131
Cowbit Wash	Lincs	TF2517	52°44·4'	0°8·5'W	X	131
Cowbog	Aberd	NJ8555	57°35·3'	2°14·6'W	X	30
Cowbog	Scot Bord	NT7525	55°31·3'	2°23·3'W	X	74
Cowbound	Cumbr	NY6403	54°25·5'	2°32·9'W	X	91
Cow Br	Cambs	TL5563	52°14·8'	0°16·6'E	X	154
Cow Br	N Yks	SD8256	54°0·2'	2°16·1'W	X	103
Cow Br	Somer	ST5037	51°8·0'	2°42·5'W	X	182,183
Cow Br	Wilts	ST9486	51°34·6'	2°4·8'W	X	173
Cowbraehill	Scot Bord	NT3957	55°48·4'	2°58·0'W	X	66,73
Cow Bridge	E Yorks	SE8430	53°45·8'	0°43·1'W	X	106
Cow Bridge	Lincs	TF2038	52°55·8'	0°12·5'W	X	131
Cowbridge	Lincs	TF3247	53°0·5'	0°1·6'W	T	131
Cowbridge	Somer	SS9542	51°10·3'	3°29·7'W	T	181
Cowbridge Drain	Lincs	TF3446	52°59·9'	0°0·2'E	W	131
Cowbridge Fm	Beds	TL0228	51°56·7'	0°30·6'W	FM	166
Cowbridge / Y Bont-Faen	V of Glam	SS9974	51°27·6'	3°26·8'W	T	170
Cowbrook Fm	Ches	SJ9068	53°12·8'	2°8·6'W	FM	118
Cowburn	D & G	NY2088	55°11·0'	3°15·0'W	X	79
Cow Burn	D & G	NY2189	55°11·6'	3°14·0'W	W	79
Cow Burn	Durham	NZ0037	54°43·9'	1°59·6'W	W	92
Cowburn Rigg	Northum	NY7368	55°0·6'	2°24·9'W	X	86,87
Cowburn Tunnel	Derby	SK0983	53°20·9'	1°51·5'W	X	110
Cowbush Hill	Scot Bord	NT3511	55°23·6'	3°1·1'W	H	79
Cowbyers	Northum	NY9751	54°51·5'	2°2·4'W	X	87
Cowbyers Fell	Northum	NY9552	54°52·0'	2°4·2'W	X	87
Cow & Calf	Corn	SW8370	50°29·6'	5°3·2'W	X	200
Cow & Calf	Corn	SW9680	50°35·3'	4°52·5'W	X	200
Cow & Calf	Devon	SS2227	51°1·1'	4°31·9'W	X	190
Cow & Calf, The	Devon	SS6649	51°13·7'	3°54·8'W	X	180
Cow & Calves	C of Edin	NT2081	56°1·2'	3°16·6'W	X	66
Cow Carr	N Yks	SE8181	54°13·3'	0°45·0'W	X	100
Cow Castle	S Lanak	NT0433	55°35·1'	3°30·9'W	X	72
Cow Castle	Somer	SS7937	51°7·4'	3°43·4'W	A	180
Cow Castle (Fort)	S Lanak	NT0433	55°35·1'	3°30·9'W	A	72
Cowcliffe	Kirk	SE1318	53°39·7'	1°47·8'W	T	110
Cow Close	Durham	NZ0014	54°31·5'	1°59·6'W	X	92
Cow Close	N Yks	SD8873	54°9·4'	2°10·6'W	X	98
Cow Close	N Yks	SD9479	54°12·6'	2°5·1'W	X	98
Cow Close	N Yks	SE1191	54°19·1'	1°49·4'W	X	99
Cow Close Fell	N Yks	SD8973	54°9·4'	2°9·7'W	X	98
Cow Close Fm	Derby	SK2363	53°10·1'	1°38·9'W	FM	119
Cow Close Fm	N Yks	SE2161	54°2·9'	1°40·3'W	FM	99
Cow Close Fm	Rut	SK8911	52°41·6'	0°40·6'W	FM	130
Cowclose Ho	N Yks	NZ2511	54°29·9'	1°36·4'W	X	93
Cow Close Wood	N Yks	SE1568	54°6·7'	1°45·8'W	F	99
Cowcombe Hill	Glos	SO9101	51°42·7'	2°7·4'W	X	163
Cow Common	Cambs	TL4890	52°29·5'	0°11·2'E	X	143
Cow Common	Essex	TL5819	51°51·1'	0°18·0'E	X	167
Cow Common	Lincs	TF0038	52°56·0'	0°30·3'W	X	130
Cow Common	Oxon	SU4392	51°37·7'	1°22·3'W	X	164,174
Cow Common	Oxon	SU5681	51°31·7'	1°11·2'W	X	174
Cow Common	Oxon	SU6490	51°36·5'	1°4·2'W	X	164,175
Cowcorse	D & G	NX9556	54°53·5'	3°37·8'W	X	84
Cowcove Beck	Cumbr	NY2103	54°25·2'	3°12·6'W	W	89,90
Cow Craigs	S Ayr	NX4290	55°11·0'	4°28·5'W	X	77
Cowcroft Fm	Somer	ST4909	50°52·9'	2°43·1'W	FM	193,194
Cowdale	Derby	SK0871	53°14·4'	1°52·4'W	X	119
Cowdale Plantn	E Yorks	SE9057	54°0·3'	0°37·2'W	F	106
Cowdber Fm	Lancs	SD6275	54°10·4'	2°34·5'W	FM	97
Cowdea	Dorset	SY4098	50°46·9'	2°50·7'W	X	193
Cowden	Aberd	NO7582	56°56·0'	2°24·2'W	X	45
Cowden	Dorset	SY6793	50°44·4'	2°27·7'W	X	194
Cowden	Kent	TQ4640	51°8·7'	0°5·6'E	T	188
Cowden	Kent	TQ7528	51°1·7'	0°30·1'E	X	188,199
Cowden	Lancs	SD7333	53°47·8'	2°24·2'W	X	103
Cowden	Northum	NY9179	55°6·6'	2°8·0'W	X	87
Cowden	Pth & Kin	NN7720	56°21·6'	3°59·0'W	T	51,52,57
Cowden	Stir	NS7694	56°7·6'	3°59·3'W	X	57
Cowdenbeath	Fife	NT1691	56°6·5'	3°20·6'W	T	58
Cowdenburn	Scot Bord	NT2052	55°45·5'	3°16·1'W	X	66,73
Cowdenend	Fife	NT1489	56°5·4'	3°22·5'W	X	65
Cowden Fm	Clackm	NS9998	56°10·1'	3°37·2'W	FM	58
Cowden Fm	E Susx	TQ5625	51°0·4'	0°13·8'E	FM	188,199
Cowden Fm	E Susx	TQ6513	50°53·8'	0°21·2'E	FM	199
Cowden Hall	E Susx	TQ5916	50°55·5'	0°16·1'E	X	199
Cowdenhead	W Loth	NS9167	55°53·3'	3°44·1'W	X	65
Cowden Hill	Falk	NS7679	55°59·5'	3°58·8'W	X	64
Cowden Hill	Pth & Kin	NT1196	56°9·2'	3°25·5'W	H	58
Cowdenknowes	Scot Bord	NT5836	55°37·2'	2°39·6'W	A	73,74
Cowdenknowes Mains	Scot Bord	NT5837	55°37·7'	2°39·6'W	X	73,74
Cowdenlaws	Fife	NT3095	56°8·8'	3°7·2'W	X	59
Cowden Magna	E Yorks	TA2141	53°51·3'	0°9·2'W	X	107
Cowdenmoor	E Renf	NS4455	55°46·0'	4°28·8'W	X	64
Cowden Parva	E Yorks	TA2340	53°50·7'	0°7·4'W	X	107
Cowden Pound	Kent	TQ4642	51°9·7'	0°5·7'E	X	188
Cowdens	D & G	NY1677	55°5·1'	3°18·5'W	X	85
Cowdens	Pth & Kin	NN9220	56°21·9'	3°44·4'W	X	52,58
Cowden Sands	E Yorks	TA2442	53°51·8'	0°6·4'W	X	107
Cowden Sta	Kent	TQ4741	51°9·2'	0°6·5'E	X	188
Cowdens Wood	Fife	NO3004	56°13·7'	3°7·3'W	F	59
Cowden Wood	Pth & Kin	NT1196	56°9·2'	3°25·5'W	F	58
Cowdon Burn	E Renf	NS4556	55°46·6'	4°27·8'W	W	64
Cowdon Hill	Dorset	SY6797	50°46·5'	2°27·7'W	X	194
Cow Down	Hants	SU3844	51°11·9'	1°27·0'W	X	185
Cow Down	W Berks	SU4683	51°32·9'	1°19·8'W	X	174
Cow Down	W Berks	SU5178	51°30·1'	1°15·5'W	X	174
Cow Down	Wilts	ST8840	51°9·8'	2°9·9'W	H	183
Cow Down	Wilts	SU2056	51°18·4'	1°42·4'W	X	174
Cow Down	Wilts	SU2251	51°15·7'	1°40·7'W	X	184
Cow Down	Wilts	SU2555	51°17·8'	1°38·1'W	X	174
Cow Down	W Susx	TQ2812	50°53·8'	0°10·4'W	X	198
Cowdown Copse	Hants	SU4448	51°14·0'	1°21·8'W	F	185

Cowdown Farmhouse	Hants	SU3843	51°11·3′	1°27·0′W	X	185
Cowdown Fm	Hants	SU5239	51°9·1′	1°15·0′W	FM	185
Cowdown Fm	W Susx	SU7615	50°56·0′	0°54·7′W	FM	197
Cowdown Hill	Dorset	SY6399	50°47·6′	2°31·1′W	X	194
Cow Down Hill	Wilts	SU0221	50°59·5′	1°57·9′W	X	184
Cowdrait	Scot Bord	NT9660	55°50·2′	2°3·4′W	X	67
Cowdray	W Susx	SU8921	50°59·1′	0°43·5′W	A	197
Cowdray Fm	W Susx	SU8300	50°47·8′	0°48·9′W	FM	197
Cowdray Forest	W Susx	TQ3033	51°5·1′	0°8·2′W	F	187
Cowdray Ho	W Susx	SU9021	50°59·1′	0°42·7′W	X	197
Cowdray Park	W Susx	SU9022	50°59·6′	0°42·7′W	X	197
Cowell's Fm	Lancs	SD5535	53°48·8′	2°40·6′W	FM	102
Cowels Fm	Essex	TL6328	51°55·8′	0°22·6′E	FM	167
Cowend	D & G	NX0454	54°50·8′	5°2·7′W	X	82
Cowen Head	Cumbr	SD4997	54°22·2′	2°46·7′W	T	97
Cowers Lane	Derby	SK3046	53°0·9′	1°32·8′W	T	119,128
Cowes	I of W	SZ4995	50°45·4′	1°17·9′W	T	196
Cowesby	N Yks	SE4689	54°17·9′	1°17·2′W	T	100
Cowesby Moor	N Yks	SE4889	54°17·9′	1°15·3′W	X	100
Cowesby Wood	N Yks	SE4789	54°17·9′	1°16·2′W	F	100
Cowesfield Green	Wilts	SU2523	51°0·6′	1°38·2′W	T	184
Cowesfield House Fm	Wilts	SU2624	51°1·1′	1°37·4′W	FM	184
Cowes Fm	Essex	TQ5897	51°39·2′	0°17·4′E	FM	167,177
Cowes Roads	I of W	SZ5097	50°46·5′	1°17·1′W	W	196
Cowey Green	Essex	TM0925	51°53·3′	1°2·6′E	X	168,169
Cowey Sike	Northum	NY8269	55°1·2′	2°16·5′W	W	86,87
Cow Field	Cumbr	NY0312	54°29·9′	3°29·4′W	H	89
Cowfield	Lancs	SD9038	53°50·5′	2°8·7′W	X	103
Cowfield Fm	Glos	SO9134	52°0·5′	2°7·5′W	FM	150
Cowfield Gould	Lincs	TF3728	52°50·2′	0°2·4′E	X	131
Cowfields Fm	Oxon	SU7381	51°31·6′	0°56·5′W	FM	175
Cowflop Cross	Devon	SS5814	50°54·7′	4°0·8′W	X	180
Cow Fm	Essex	TQ5797	51°39·2′	0°16·6′E	FM	167,177
Cowfold	Cumbr	NY1447	54°48·9′	3°19·9′W	X	85
Cowfold	W Susx	TQ2122	50°59·3′	0°16·2′W	T	198
Cowfold Fm	Darl	NZ2320	54°34·7′	1°38·2′W	FM	93
Cowfold Fm	Hants	SU7256	51°18·1′	0°57·6′W	FM	175,186
Cowfold Grange	N Yks	SE2988	54°17·5′	1°32·8′W	X	99
Cowfold Lodge	W Susx	TQ2121	50°58·8′	0°16·2′W	X	198
Cowford	Aberd	NJ5709	57°10·4′	2°42·2′W	X	37
Cowford	Aberd	NO8999	57°5·2′	2°10·4′W	X	38,45
Cowford	Angus	NO5262	56°45·1′	2°46·6′W	X	44
Cowford	Pth & Kin	NO0432	56°28·5′	3°33·1′W	X	52,53
Cowford	S Lanak	NS9346	55°42·0′	3°41·7′W	X	72
Cowford Cottage	Pth & Kin	NO0432	56°28·5′	3°33·1′W	X	52,53
Cowfords	Aberd	NJ6260	57°38·0′	2°37·7′W	X	29
Cowfords	Aberd	NJ8760	57°38·0′	2°12·6′W	X	30
Cowfords	Aberd	NJ9855	57°35·4′	2°1·5′W	X	30
Cowfords	Moray	NJ3160	57°37·7′	3°8·9′W	X	28
Cowgap	Cumbr	NY7144	54°47·7′	2°26·6′W	X	86,87
Cow Gap	E Susx	TV5995	50°44·2′	0°15·6′E	X	199
Cowgarth Flow	D & G	NY3271	55°2·0′	3°3·4′W	X	85
Cowgask Burn	Pth & Kin	NN9721	56°22·5′	3°39·6′W	W	52,53,58
Cowgate	Cumbr	NY0947	54°48·8′	3°24·5′W	X	85
Cow Gate Fm	N Yks	SE2562	54°3·4′	1°36·7′W	FM	99
Cowgate Slack	N Yks	SE9696	54°21·3′	0°30·9′W	W	94,101
Cowgill	Cumbr	SD7587	54°16·9′	2°22·6′W	T	98
Cow Gill	Lancs	SD8046	53°54·8′	2°17·9′W	X	103
Cowgill	S Lanak	NT0029	55°33·2′	3°34·7′W	X	72
Cow Gill	S Lanak	NT0130	55°33·5′	3°33·7′W	W	72
Cowgill Beck	Cumbr	SD7587	54°16·9′	2°22·6′W	W	98
Cowgill Fm	N Yks	SD6874	54°9·9′	2°29·0′W	FM	98
Cowgill Loch	S Lanak	NT0030	55°33·5′	3°34·7′W	W	72
Cowgill Lower Resr	S Lanak	NT0029	55°32·9′	3°34·7′W	W	72
Cowgill Rig	S Lanak	NT0128	55°32·4′	3°33·7′W	H	72
Cowgill Upper Reservoir	S Lanak	NT0027	55°31·8′	3°34·6′W	W	72
Cowgill Wold Meas	Cumbr	SD7788	54°17·5′	2°20·8′W	X	98
Cow Green	Durham	NY8130	54°40·1′	2°17·3′W	X	91,92
Cow Green	Suff	TM0565	52°14·9′	1°0·6′E	T	155
Cow Green Reservoir	Cumbr	NY8030	54°40·1′	2°18·2′W	W	91,92
Cowgreens	Moray	NJ0251	57°32·6′	3°37·8′W	X	27
Cowgrove	Dorset	SY9899	50°47·7′	2°1·3′W	T	195
Cowgrove	E Ayr	NS5134	55°34·9′	4°21·4′W	X	70
Cow Hayes	Sol	SP1778	52°24·2′	1°44·6′W	X	139
Cow Head	Shetld	HU3060	60°19·6′	1°26·9′W	X	3
Cowheath Wood	Herts	TL3307	51°45·0′	0°4·0′W	F	166
Cowhelm Fms	N Yks	SE5896	54°21·6′	1°6·0′W	FM	100
Cowherd Shute Fm	Dorset	ST8624	51°1·1′	2°11·6′W	FM	183
Cow Hey	Derby	SK1694	53°26·8′	1°45·1′W	X	110
Cow Hey	Lancs	SD7043	53°53·2′	2°27·0′W	X	103
Cowhey Fm	Stock	SJ9790	53°24·6′	2°2·3′W	FM	109
Cowhill	Aberd	NJ7433	57°23·5′	2°25·5′W	X	29
Cowhill	Aberd	NJ9620	57°16·5′	2°3·5′W	X	38
Cowhill	Aberd	NO8190	57°0·3′	2°18·3′W	X	38,45
Cowhill	Derby	SK3546	53°0·8′	1°28·3′W	T	119,128
Cow Hill	Highld	NN1173	56°48·9′	5°5·3′W	H	41
Cow Hill	Lancs	SD5734	53°48·3′	2°38·8′W	T	102
Cow Hill	N Yks	SD8354	53°59·2′	2°15·1′W	X	103
Cow Hill	Oxon	SP3930	51°58·3′	1°25·5′W	X	151
Cowhill	S Glos	ST6091	51°37·2′	2°34·3′W	X	162,172
Cowhill	S Lanak	NS9922	55°29·1′	3°35·5′W	X	72
Cowhill Fold	Lancs	SD7228	53°45·1′	2°25·1′W	X	103
Cowhillock	Angus	NO4361	56°44·5′	2°55·5′W	X	44
Cowhill Plantation	Scot Bord	NT6856	55°48·0′	2°30·2′W	F	67,74
Cowhills	Aberd	NK1042	57°28·3′	1°49·5′W	X	30
Cowhill Tower	D & G	NX9582	55°7·5′	3°38·4′W	X	78
Cowhorn Hill	S Glos	ST6771	51°26·5′	2°28·1′W	T	172
Cowhorse Hill	Durham	NY8142	54°46·6′	2°17·3′W	X	86,87
Cowhouse Bank Fm	N Yks	SE6089	54°17·8′	1°4·3′W	FM	94,100
Cowhouse Bank Wood	N Yks	SE6090	54°18·4′	1°4·3′W	F	94,100
Cow House Fm	Brad	SE0637	53°50·0′	1°54·1′W	FM	104
Cowhouse Fm	Hants	SU4959	51°19·9′	1°17·4′W	FM	174
Cowhouse Fm	Somer	ST5720	50°58·7′	0°55·5′W	FM	197
Cow House Hill	Lancs	SD7949	53°56·4′	2°18·8′W	X	103
Cowhythe	Aberd	NJ6065	57°40·6′	2°39·8′W	X	29
Cowhythe Head	Aberd	NJ6166	57°41·2′	2°38·8′W	X	29
Cowhythe Hill	Aberd	NJ6066	57°41·2′	2°39·8′W	H	29
Cowick	Essex	TL5015	51°49·0′	0°11·0′E	X	167
Cowick Fm	Wilts	SU0074	51°28·1′	1°59·6′W	FM	173
Cowie	Aberd	NO8786	56°58·2′	2°12·4′W	T	45

Cowie	Stir	NS8489	56°5·0′	3°51·4′W	T	65
Cowie Burn	Aberd	NO4188	56°59·0′	2°57·8′W	W	44
Cowie Burn	E Loth	NT5061	55°50·6′	2°47·5′W	W	66
Cowiefauld	Fife	NO1909	56°16·3′	3°18·0′W	X	58
Cowiehall	Stir	NS8489	56°5·0′	3°51·4′W	X	65
Cowie Hill	Aberd	NJ6556	57°35·8′	2°34·7′W	H	29
Cowie Hill	Angus	NO4977	56°53·2′	2°49·8′W	H	44
Cowiehill	Angus	NO5771	56°50·0′	2°41·8′W	X	44
Cowie Ho	Aberd	NO8787	56°58·7′	2°12·4′W	X	45
Cowie Law	Scot Bord	NT8114	55°25·4′	2°17·6′W	X	80
Cowie Moor	S Lanak	NS9927	55°31·8′	3°35·6′W	X	72
Cowiemuir	Moray	NJ3662	57°38·9′	3°3·9′W	X	28
Cowieshill	Aberd	NJ8556	57°35·9′	2°14·6′W	X	30
Cowieshill	Aberd	NO6772	56°50·6′	2°32·0′W	X	45
Cowieslinn	Scot Bord	NT2351	55°45·0′	3°13·2′W	X	66,73
Cowieswells	Aberd	NO8780	56°54·9′	2°12·4′W	X	45
Cowie Water	Aberd	NO8188	56°59·2′	2°18·3′W	W	45
Cowin Grove	Carm	SN3216	51°49·3′	4°25·9′W	X	159
Cowix Fm	Surrey	TQ1938	51°8·0′	0°17·6′W	FM	187
Cowlair	Aberd	NJ9159	57°37·5′	2°8·6′W	X	30
Cowlairs	C of Glas	NS6067	55°52·8′	4°13·8′W	T	64
Cowlake	Durham	NY9826	54°38·0′	2°1·4′W	X	92
Cowlam Manor	E Yorks	SE9665	54°4·6′	0°31·5′W	X	101
Cowlam Village	E Yorks	SE9665	54°4·6′	0°31·5′W	A	101
Cowlands	Corn	SW8240	50°13·4′	5°3·0′W	T	204
Cowlands Fm	Essex	TL6723	51°53·1′	0°26·0′E	FM	167
Cowlas	Devon	SS6219	50°57·5′	3°57·5′W	X	180
Cowlass Hall	Essex	TL6138	52°1·2′	0°21·2′E	X	154
Cowldyke Fm	N Yks	SE7082	54°14·0′	0°55·1′W	FM	100
Cowlease Fm	E Susx	TQ4113	50°54·2′	0°0·7′E	FM	198
Cowlease Grove	Glos	SP0814	51°49·7′	1°52·6′W	F	163
Cowleaze Copse	Oxon	SU6299	51°41·4′	1°5·8′W	F	164,165
Cowleaze Corner	Oxon	SP3002	51°43·2′	1°33·5′W	T	164
Cowleaze Fm	Oxon	SU2487	51°35·1′	1°38·8′W	FM	174
Cowleaze Fm	Oxon	SU2888	51°35·6′	1°35·4′W	FM	174
Cowleaze Wood	Oxon	SU7295	51°39·2′	0°57·2′W	F	165
Cow Lees	Warw	SP3287	52°29·0′	1°31·3′W	X	140
Cowleigh Gate Fm	Heref	SO7547	52°7·5′	2°21·5′W	FM	150
Cowleigh Park Fm	Worcs	SO7647	52°7·5′	2°20·6′W	FM	150
Cowle's Drove	Norf	TL6986	52°27·0′	0°29·6′E	X	143
Cowles Ho	Heref	SO6219	51°52·3′	2°32·7′W	X	162
Cowley	Aberd	NJ6738	57°26·1′	2°32·5′W	X	29
Cowley	Ches	SJ9168	53°12·8′	2°7·7′W	X	118
Cowley	Derby	SK3377	53°17·6′	1°29·9′W	T	119
Cowley	Devon	SX8685	50°39·4′	3°36·4′W	X	191
Cowley	Devon	SX9095	50°44·9′	3°33·2′W	T	192
Cowley	Durham	NZ0625	54°37·5′	1°54·0′W	X	92
Cowley	Glos	SO9614	51°49·7′	2°3·1′W	T	163
Cowley	Hill	TQ0582	51°31·9′	0°28·8′W	T	176
Cowley	Oxon	SP5504	51°44·2′	1°11·8′W	T	164
Cowley	Staffs	SJ8219	52°46·3′	2°15·6′W	X	127
Cowley Bar	Derby	SK3277	53°17·6′	1°30·8′W	X	119
Cowley Br	Devon	SX9095	50°44·9′	3°33·2′W	A	192
Cowley Fm	Bucks	SP6628	51°57·0′	1°2·0′W	FM	164,165
Cowley Head	D & G	NO0102	55°18·4′	3°33·1′W	X	78
Cowley Hill	Staffs	SK1018	52°45·8′	1°50·8′W	X	128
Cowley House Fm	Durham	NZ3827	54°38·4′	1°24·2′W	FM	93
Cowley Lodge	Bucks	SP6727	51°56·5′	1°1·1′W	X	164,165
Cowleymoor	Devon	SS9613	50°54·7′	3°28·4′W	T	181
Cowley Moor Fm	Stock on T	NZ4116	54°32·5′	1°21·6′W	FM	93
Cowley Peachy	Hill	TQ0581	51°31·3′	0°28·8′W	T	176
Cowley's Elm	Glos	SO7412	51°48·6′	2°22·2′W	X	162
Cow Leys Scar	Cumbr	SD1865	54°4·7′	3°14·8′W	X	96
Cowley's Shoff Fm	Lincs	TF1934	52°53·6′	0°13·5′W	FM	130
Cowley Wood	Devon	SS6444	51°11·0′	3°56·4′W	F	180
Cowley Wood	Glos	SO9513	51°49·2′	2°4·0′W	F	163
Cowley Wood	Warw	SP3288	52°29·6′	1°31·3′W	F	140
Cowl Ho	N Yks	SE6196	54°21·6′	1°3·3′W	X	94,100
Cowling	Lancs	SD5917	53°39·1′	2°36·8′W	T	108
Cowling	N Yks	SD9643	53°53·2′	2°3·2′W	T	103
Cowling	N Yks	SE2387	54°16·9′	1°38·4′W	T	99
Cowling Br	Brad	SE0345	53°54·3′	1°56·8′W	X	104
Cowlinge	Suff	TL7154	52°9·7′	0°30·4′E	T	154
Cowlinge Hall	Suff	TL7152	52°8·6′	0°30·3′E	X	154
Cowling Hill	N Yks	SD9644	53°53·8′	2°3·2′W	X	103
Cowling Manor	N Yks	SE2388	54°17·5′	1°38·4′W	X	99
Cowlings Fm	Devon	ST0019	50°57·9′	3°25·1′W	FM	181
Cowlishaw Plantation	Notts	SK6082	53°20·1′	1°5·5′W	F	111,120
Cow Loch	S Ayr	NX2377	55°3·6′	4°45·9′W	W	76
Cowlod	Powys	SO1563	52°15·8′	3°14·3′W	H	148
Cowloe	Corn	SW3426	50°4·7′	5°42·7′W	X	203
Cowloughton	N Yks	SD9641	53°52·2′	2°3·2′W	X	103
Cow Low	Derby	SK0678	53°18·2′	1°54·2′W	A	119
Cow Low	Derby	SK0678	53°18·2′	1°54·2′W	X	119
Cowlow	Derby	SK0972	53°14·9′	1°51·5′W	T	119
Cow Low	Derby	SK1482	53°20·3′	1°47·0′W	X	110
Cowlow	Staffs	SK1059	53°7·9′	1°50·6′W	X	119
Cowlton	Powys	SO2995	52°33·1′	3°2·4′W	X	137
Cowlyers	Cumbr	NY1252	54°51·6′	3°21·8′W	X	85
Cowmes	Kirk	SE1816	53°38·7′	1°43·3′W	T	110
Cowmire Hall	Cumbr	SD4288	54°17·3′	2°53·0′W	X	96,97
Cow Moor	Surrey	SU9257	51°18·5′	0°40·4′W	X	175,186
Cowm Resr	Lancs	SD8719	53°40·3′	2°11·4′W	W	109
Cowms Moor	Derby	SK1290	53°24·6′	1°48·8′W	X	110
Cowms Rocks	Derby	SK1290	53°24·6′	1°48·8′W	X	110
Cow Myers	N Yks	SE2672	54°8·8′	1°35·7′W	X	99
Cown Edge Rocks	Derby	SK0191	53°25·2′	1°58·7′W	X	110
Cown Edge Way	Stock	SJ9692	53°25·7′	2°3·2′W	X	109
Cownham Fm	Glos	SP2128	51°57·2′	1°41·3′W	FM	163
Cownhayne	Devon	SY2593	50°44·1′	3°3·4′W	X	192,193
Coworth Park	Win & Maid	SU9668	51°24·4′	0°36·8′W	X	175,176
Cow Pasture	Lincs	SK9887	53°22·5′	0°31·2′W	X	112,121
Cow Pasture	N Yks	SD8279	54°12·6′	2°16·1′W	X	98
Cow Pasture	N Yks	SD9479	54°12·6′	2°5·1′W	X	98
Cowpasture	Oxon	SP3334	52°0·4′	1°30·8′W	X	151
Cowpasture Fm	Bucks	SP8330	51°58·0′	0°47·1′W	FM	152,165
Cow Pasture Fm	Cambs	TL1384	52°26·8′	0°19·8′W	FM	142
Cow Pasture Fm	Lincs	TF1985	53°21·1′	0°12·3′W	FM	122
Cowpasture Fm	Oxon	SP3335	52°1·0′	1°30·8′W	FM	151
Cowpasture Fm	Suff	TM2936	51°58·7′	1°20·5′E	FM	169

Cowpastures Fm	Leic	SK4103	52°37·6′	1°23·3′W	FM	140
Cowpasture Spinney	Northnts	SP8067	52°17·9′	0°49·2′W	F	152
Cow Pasture Wood	Northnts	SP5653	52°10·6′	1°10·5′W	F	152
Cowpe	Lancs	SD8320	53°40·8′	2°15·0′W	T	103
Cowpe Lowe	Lancs	SD8220	53°40·8′	2°15·9′W	H	103
Cowpe Moss	Lancs	SD8419	53°40·3′	2°14·1′W	X	109
Cowpen	Northum	NZ2981	55°7·6′	1°32·3′W	T	81
Cowpen Bewley	Stock on T	NZ4824	54°36·8′	1°15·0′W	T	93
Cowpen Marsh	Stock on T	NZ4925	54°37·3′	1°14·0′W	X	93
Cowpen Wood	Bucks	SP7634	52°0·2′	0°53·2′W	F	152,165
Cowper Cote	N Yks	SD9258	54°1·3′	2°6·9′W	X	103
Cowpe Resr	Lancs	SD8420	53°40·8′	2°14·1′W	W	103
Cowper Gill	Cumbr	SD7389	54°18·0′	2°24·5′W	X	98
Cowper House Fm	N Yks	NZ3006	54°27·2′	1°31·8′W	FM	93
Cowper's Cross	Brad	SE1045	53°54·3′	1°50·5′W	X	104
Cowpers Oak Lodge	Northnts	SP8553	52°10·4′	0°45·0′W	X	152
Cowper Stone	Derby	SK2583	53°20·8′	1°37·1′W	X	110
Cowper's Wood	Suff	TL9441	52°2·2′	0°50·1′E	F	155
Cowperthwaite	Cumbr	SD6096	54°21·7′	2°36·5′W	X	97
Cowplain	Hants	SU6911	50°53·9′	1°0·7′W	T	197
Cowpool Fm	Dorset	ST5713	50°55·1′	2°36·3′W	FM	194
Cow Pot	Cumbr	SD6680	54°13·1′	2°30·9′W	X	98
Cowpren Point	Cumbr	SD3474	54°9·7′	3°0·2′W	X	96,97
Cowp Scar	Cumbr	SD3473	54°9·2′	3°0·2′W	X	96,97
Cowran	Cumbr	NY5256	54°54·0′	2°44·5′W	X	86
Cowran	Cumbr	SD2576	54°10·7′	3°8·5′W	X	96
Cowran Side	Cumbr	NY5156	54°54·0′	2°45·4′W	X	86
Cow Ridge	N Yks	SE5395	54°21·1′	1°10·7′W	X	100
Cow Ridge	Shrops	SO4394	52°32·7′	2°50·0′W	X	137
Cowrig	Scot Bord	NT7343	55°41·0′	2°25·3′W	X	74
Cowrigg	Cumbr	NY4471	55°2·1′	2°52·1′W	X	85
Cowrigg	D & G	NY0480	55°6·6′	3°29·9′W	X	78
Cow Roast	Herts	SP9510	51°47·1′	0°37·0′W	T	165
Cow Rock	Highld	NG6262	57°35·4′	5°58·5′W	X	24
Cowsden	Worcs	SO9453	52°10·7′	2°4·9′W	X	150
Cowsen Down	Devon	SX5291	50°42·2′	4°5·4′W	X	191
Cowsen Gill	N Yks	SD7262	54°3·4′	2°25·2′W	W	98
Cowshill	Durham	NY8540	54°45·5′	2°13·6′W	T	87
Cowshill Fm	Glos	SO5601	51°42·6′	2°37·8′W	FM	162
Cowship Fm	S Glos	ST7088	51°35·6′	2°25·6′W	FM	162,172
Cowsic Head	Devon	SX5980	50°36·4′	3°59·2′W	W	191
Cowsic River	Devon	SX5977	50°34·8′	3°59·1′W	W	191
Cow Side	Lancs	SD8627	53°44·6′	2°12·3′W	X	103
Cowside	N Yks	SD8466	54°5·6′	2°14·3′W	X	98
Cowside	N Yks	SD9069	54°7·2′	2°8·8′W	X	98
Cow Side	N Yks	SE0278	54°12·1′	1°57·7′W	X	98
Cowside Beck	N Yks	SD8466	54°5·6′	2°14·3′W	W	98
Cowside Beck	N Yks	SD8969	54°7·2′	2°9·7′W	W	98
Cow Sike	N Yks	SE6298	54°22·7′	1°2·3′W	X	94,100
Cowsland	Pemb	SN0908	51°44·5′	4°45·6′W	X	158
Cowsland Fm	Notts	SK7581	53°19·5′	0°52·0′W	FM	120
Cowslaw	Cumbr	NY2544	54°47·4′	3°9·6′W	X	85
Cowslip Fm	Dorset	ST8123	51°0·6′	2°15·9′W	FM	183
Cowslip Fm	Suff	TM1849	52°6·0′	1°11·4′E	FM	169
Cowslip Green	N Som	ST4861	51°21·0′	2°44·4′W	T	172,182
Cowslip Hill	Northum	NU1800	55°17·9′	1°42·6′W	X	81
Cowsmill	Aberd	NJ7456	57°35·9′	2°25·6′W	X	29
Cowsrieve	Aberd	NK0944	57°29·4′	1°50·5′W	X	30
Cow's Snout	D & G	NX8752	54°51·3′	3°45·2′W	X	84
Cowstand	Northum	NZ0774	55°3·9′	1°53·0′W	X	88
Cowstand Burn	Northum	NY9078	55°6·0′	2°9·0′W	W	87
Cowstand Hill	Northum	NY9381	55°7·6′	2°6·2′W	H	80
Cowstead	Kent	TQ8462	51°19·9′	0°38·9′E	X	178,188
Cowstead Fm	Kent	TQ9271	51°24·6′	0°46·0′E	FM	178
Cowstone Gill Ho	N Yks	SE0083	54°14·8′	1°59·6′W	X	98
Cowstrandburn	Fife	NT0390	56°5·8′	3°33·1′W	T	58
Cowsty Knotts	Cumbr	NY4504	54°26·0′	2°50·5′W	X	90
Cowtham Ho	Notts	SK8248	53°1·6′	0°46·2′W	X	130
Cowthat	D & G	NY1875	55°4·0′	3°16·6′W	X	85
Cowthorpe	N Yks	SE4252	53°58·0′	1°21·2′W	T	105
Cowthwaite Plantation	Leeds	SE4239	53°51·0′	1°21·3′W	F	105
Cowton	Aberd	NO8389	56°59·8′	2°16·3′W	W	45
Cowton	Suff	TM4454	52°8·0′	1°34·3′E	X	156
Cowton Burn	Aberd	NO8388	56°59·2′	2°16·3′W	W	45
Cowton Fields Fm	N Yks	NZ3105	54°26·6′	1°30·9′W	FM	93
Cowton Grange	N Yks	NZ2604	54°26·1′	1°35·5′W	X	93
Cowton Moor	N Yks	NZ3005	54°26·6′	1°31·8′W	X	93
Cowton Rocks	E Loth	NT5385	56°3·6′	2°44·8′W	X	66
Cow Tower	Norf	TG2309	52°38·2′	1°18·2′E	X	134
Cow Wath	N Yks	SE5293	54°20·0′	1°11·6′W	X	100
Cow Wold	N Yks	SE8361	54°2·5′	0°43·5′W	X	100
Cow-y-Jack	Corn	SW7719	50°2·0′	5°6·5′W	X	204
Coxall	Heref	SO3774	52°21·9′	2°55·1′W	T	137,148
Coxall	Heref	SO4860	52°14·4′	2°45·3′W	X	137,138,148
Coxall Knoll	Shrops	SO3673	52°21·3′	2°56·0′W	H	137,148
Coxbank	Ches	SJ6541	52°58·2′	2°30·9′W	T	118
Coxbank Fm	Cumbr	SD5584	54°15·2′	2°41·0′W	FM	97
Coxbench	Derby	SK3743	52°59·2′	1°26·5′W	T	119,128
Coxbridge	Somer	ST5436	51°7·5′	2°39·1′W	T	182,183
Coxbury Fm	Glos	SO5307	51°45·8′	2°40·5′W	FM	162
Cox Common	Suff	TM4082	52°23·2′	1°32·0′E	X	156
Coxen Green	Staffs	SK0756	53°6·3′	1°53·3′W	X	119
Coxe's Cliff	Devon	SY1788	50°41·4′	3°10·1′W	X	192
Coxet Hill	Stir	NS7991	56°6·0′	3°56·3′W	X	57
Coxey Hills	Lincs	TF3285	53°21·0′	0°0·6′W	X	122
Coxfield	Beds	TL1258	52°12·8′	0°21·2′W	X	153
Cox Fm	Suff	TL9641	52°2·2′	0°51·9′E	FM	155
Coxford	C of Soton	SU3914	50°55·7′	1°26·3′W	T	196
Coxford	Corn	SX1696	50°44·5′	4°36·1′W	T	190
Coxford	Norf	TF8429	52°49·9′	0°44·3′E	T	132
Coxford Heath	Norf	TF8230	52°50·4′	0°42·5′E	X	132
Coxford Wood	Norf	TF8231	52°51·0′	0°42·6′E	F	132
Cox Green	Bolton	SD7114	53°37·6′	2°25·9′W	T	109
Cox Green	Essex	TQ7195	51°37·9′	0°28·6′E	X	167
Coxgreen	Staffs	SO8086	52°28·5′	2°17·3′W	T	138
Cox Green	Sund	NZ3355	54°53·6′	1°28·7′W	X	88
Cox Green	Surrey	TQ0934	51°5·9′	0°26·2′W	T	187
Cox Green	Win & Maid	SU8779	51°30·4′	0°44·7′W	T	175
Coxhead Bank Common	Powys	SO1671	52°20·1′	3°13·6′W	X	136,148
Coxheath	Kent	TQ7451	51°14·1′	0°29·9′E	T	188

Cox Hill	Beds	TL1749	52°7·8'	0°17·0'W	X	153
Cox Hill	Corn	SW7443	50°14·9'	5°9·8'W	T	204
Cox Hill	Surrey	SU9860	51°20·1'	0°35·2'W	X	175,176,186
Cox Hill	Wilts	SU0590	51°36·8'	1°55·3'W	H	163,173
Coxhill Fm	D & G	NT0904	55°19·6'	3°25·6'W	FM	78
Coxhill Fm	Falk	NS9374	55°57·1'	3°42·4'W	FM	65
Coxhill Fm	Kent	TR2547	51°10·9'	1°13·6'E	FM	179
Coxhill Fm	Norf	TG3709	52°37·8'	1°30·5'E	FM	134
Coxhill Green	Surrey	SU9860	51°20·1'	0°35·2'W	X	175,176,186
Coxhoe	Durham	NZ3136	54°43·3'	1°30·7'W	T	93
Coxhoe	Durham	NZ3235	54°42·8'	1°29·8'W	T	93
Coxhoe East Ho	Durham	NZ3335	54°42·8'	1°28·8'W	X	93
Coxhorne	Glos	SO9719	51°52·4'	2°2·2'W	X	163
Coxlake	Pemb	SN0915	51°48·3'	4°45·8'W	X	158
Coxland	Surrey	TQ0938	51°8·1'	0°26·1'W	X	187
Coxland Cotts	W Susx	SU9621	50°59·0'	0°37·6'W	X	197
Coxland Fm	Devon	SX7793	50°43·7'	3°44·2'W	FM	191
Coxlease Fm	Bucks	SU7488	51°35·4'	0°55·5'W	FM	175
Coxleigh Barton	Devon	SS5835	51°6·0'	4°1·3'W	X	180
Coxley	Somer	ST5343	51°11·3'	2°40·0'W	T	182,183
Coxley	Wakf	SE2717	53°39·2'	1°35·1'W	T	110
Coxley Wick	Somer	ST5243	51°11·3'	2°40·8'W	T	182,183
Coxlodge	N upon Ty	NZ2368	55°0·6'	1°38·0'W	T	88
Coxlow Fm	E Susx	TQ5716	50°55·5'	0°14·4'E	FM	199
Coxmoor	Devon	SX7099	50°46·8'	3°50·3'W	X	191
Cox Moor	Notts	SK5156	53°6·2'	1°13·9'W	T	120
Coxmoor Ho	Notts	SK5256	53°6·2'	1°13·0'W	X	120
Coxmoor Lodge	Notts	SK5156	53°6·2'	1°13·9'W	X	120
Coxmoor Wood	Hants	SU7851	51°15·4'	0°52·5'W	F	186
Coxmore Fm	Glos	SO7325	51°55·6'	2°23·2'W	FM	162
Coxpark	Corn	SX4072	50°31·8'	4°15·1'W	T	201
Cox Pasture Fm	N Yks	SE1692	54°19·6'	1°44·8'W	FM	99
Cox's Creek	Lincs	TF4830	52°51·1'	0°12·3'E	W	131
Cox's Fm	E Susx	TQ4021	50°58·5'	0°0·0'E	FM	198
Cox's Fm	Lincs	TF2811	52°41·1'	0°6·0'W	FM	131,142
Cox's Fm	Somer	ST2746	51°12·7'	3°2·3'W	FM	182
Cox's Fm	Surrey	SU9953	51°16·3'	0°34·5'W	FM	186
Cox's Fm	Wilts	SU1497	51°40·5'	1°47·5'W	FM	163
Cox's Mill	E Susx	TQ6520	50°57·6'	0°21·4'E	X	199
Cox's Walk Fm	Lincs	SK8338	52°56·2'	0°45·5'W	FM	130
Cox's Water	Dorset	ST7412	50°54·6'	2°21·8'W	X	194
Coxtie Green	Essex	TQ5695	51°38·2'	0°15·7'E	T	167,177
Coxton	Aberd	NJ5858	57°36·9'	2°41·7'W	X	29
Coxtontower	Moray	NJ2660	57°37·7'	3°13·9'W	X	28
Coxtor	Devon	SX5276	50°34·1'	4°5·0'W	A	191,201
Cox Tor	Devon	SX5376	50°34·2'	4°4·2'W	H	191,201
Coxwall	Devon	SX4895	50°44·3'	4°8·9'W	X	191
Coxwell	Devon	SS6003	50°48·8'	3°58·9'W	X	191
Coxwold	N Yks	SE5377	54°11·4'	1°10·8'W	T	100
Coxwold Park Ho	N Yks	SE5276	54°10·9'	1°11·8'W	X	100
Coxwood Fm	Wrex	SJ3755	53°5·6'	2°56·0'W	FM	117
Coy	Aberd	NO7498	57°4·6'	2°25·3'W	X	38,45
Coybal	Cered	SN3758	52°12·0'	4°22·7'W	X	145
Coy Br	Lincs	TF3516	52°43·7'	0°0·4'E	X	131
Coychurch	Brig	SS9379	51°30·2'	3°32·1'W	T	170
Coygen	Powys	SO0437	52°1·6'	3°23·6'W	X	160
Coyles of Muick, The	Aberd	NO3291	57°0·6'	3°6·7'W	H	44
Coylton	S Ayr	NS4119	55°26·6'	4°30·4'W	T	70
Coylumbridge	Highld	NH9110	57°10·3'	3°47·7'W	T	36
Coynach	Aberd	NJ4405	57°8·2'	2°55·1'W	T	37
Coynachie	Aberd	NJ4934	57°23·9'	2°50·5'W	X	28,29
Coynant	Carm	SN1525	51°53·8'	4°40·9'W	X	145,158
Coynant	Swan	SN6406	51°44·4'	3°57·8'W	X	159
Coy's Grove	Suff	TL7461	52°13·4'	0°33·2'E	F	155
Coyton	Devon	SX6054	50°22·4'	3°57·8'W	X	202
Coytrahên	Brig	SS8885	51°33·4'	3°36·5'W	T	170
Coytrahen Ho	Brig	SS8985	51°33·4'	3°35·7'W	X	170
Cozen's Fm	Essex	TL5903	51°42·4'	0°18·5'E	FM	167
Craagles Water	Shetld	HU2481	60°31·0'	1°33·3'W	W	3
Craakinish	N Eil	NF9079	57°41·9'	7°11·8'W	X	18
Crabadon	Devon	SX7555	50°23·1'	3°45·1'W	X	202
Crabadon Cross	Devon	SX7554	50°22·6'	3°45·1'W	X	202
Crabart	Swan	SS4086	51°33·3'	4°18·1'W	X	159
Crabba Skerry	Shetld	HU2650	60°14·3'	1°31·3'W	X	3
Crabbe Castle Fm	Norf	TF9039	52°55·1'	0°50·0'E	FM	132
Crabbet Park	W Susx	TQ3037	51°7·3'	0°8·2'W	T	187
Crabbick Fm	Hants	SU6312	50°54·5'	1°5·9'W	FM	196
Crabble	Kent	TR2943	51°8·6'	1°16·8'E	T	179
Crabb's Abbey	Norf	TF6007	52°38·5'	0°22·3'E	X	143
Crabb's Abbey Fm	Norf	TF5806	52°38·0'	0°20·5'E	FM	143
Crabbs Cross	Worcs	SP0364	52°16·7'	1°57·0'W	T	150
Crabb's Fm	Essex	TL8411	51°46·3'	0°40·4'E	FM	168
Crabb's Fm	Essex	TL8517	51°49·5'	0°41·5'E	FM	168
Crabbs Green	Herts	TL4528	51°56·1'	0°7·0'E	T	167
Crabbs Green Fm	Essex	TL5516	51°49·5'	0°15·3'E	FM	167
Crabbs Hill	Dorset	ST4300	50°48·0'	2°48·1'W	X	193
Crab Coppice	Dorset	SY4899	50°47·5'	2°43·9'W	F	193
Crab Fm	Dorset	ST9502	50°49·3'	2°3·9'W	FM	195
Crab Fm	Worcs	SP0441	52°4·3'	1°56·1'W	FM	150
Crabgate	Norf	TG0927	52°48·2'	1°6·4'E	T	133
Crabh Fm	Pemb	SM8007	51°43·4'	5°10·7'W	FM	157
Crabhat Inclosure	Hants	SU3905	50°50·8'	1°26·4'W	F	196
Crabhayne Fm	Devon	SY2792	50°43·6'	3°1·7'W	FM	193
Crab Hill	Oxon	SU4089	51°36·1'	1°25·0'W	X	174
Crabhill Fm	Ches	SJ6150	53°3·0'	2°34·5'W	FM	118
Crab Hill Fm	Surrey	TQ3048	51°13·2'	0°7·9'W	FM	187
Crab Hole	Somer	ST3854	51°17·1'	2°53·0'W	X	182
Crabknowe Spit	Essex	TM2427	51°54·0'	1°15·8'E	X	169
Crablake Fm	Devon	SX9486	50°40·1'	3°29·6'W	FM	192
Crab Ledge	Devon	SY0983	50°38·6'	3°16·8'W	X	192
Crabley Fm	E Yorks	SE9027	53°44·1'	0°37·7'W	FM	106
Crab Mill	Wrex	SJ3242	52°58·5'	3°0·4'W	X	117
Crab Mill	Wrex	SJ4045	53°0·2'	2°53·2'W	X	117
Crabmill Fm	Ches	SJ7260	53°8·4'	2°24·7'W	FM	118
Crab Mill Fm	Flint	SJ3262	53°9·3'	3°0·6'W	FM	117
Crab Mill Fm	Wrex	SJ3739	52°56·9'	2°55·9'W	FM	126
Crabmill Fm	Wrex	SJ3755	53°5·6'	2°56·0'W	FM	117
Crabmoss	Ches	SJ8669	53°13·3'	2°12·2'W	X	118
Crab Orchard	Dorset	SU0806	50°51·4'	1°52·8'W	T	195
Crabrock Point	Devon	SX9253	50°22·3'	3°30·7'W	X	202

Crab Rocks	E Yorks	TA1974	54°9·1'	0°10·3'W	X	101
Crab Rocks	Pemb	SM7304	51°41·6'	5°16·7'W	X	157
Crabs Bay	S Glos	ST5186	51°34·5'	2°42·0'W	W	172
Crab's Cairn	C of Aber	NJ9603	57°7·3'	2°3·5'W	A	38
Crabs Castle Fm	Warw	SP4054	52°11·2'	1°24·5'W	FM	151
Crab's Hole	Lincs	TF4927	52°49·4'	0°13·1'E	W	131
Crabstack	Cumbr	NY6319	54°34·1'	2°33·9'W	X	91
Crabtree	C of Plym	SX5156	50°23·3'	4°5·4'W	T	201
Crabtree	Cumbr	SD5581	54°13·6'	2°41·0'W	X	97
Crabtree	W Susx	TQ2225	51°0·9'	0°15·3'W	T	187,198
Crabtreebeck	Cumbr	NY1321	54°34·9'	3°20·3'W	X	89
Crabtree Cott	Surrey	TQ1552	51°15·6'	0°20·7'W	X	187
Crabtree Cott	Wilts	SU1275	51°28·7'	1°49·2'W	X	173
Crabtree Cottage	Bucks	SP9517	51°50·8'	0°36·9'W	X	165
Crabtree Cotts	Wilts	SU2366	51°23·8'	1°39·8'W	X	174
Crab Tree Earth	Hants	SU2602	50°49·2'	1°37·5'W	X	195
Crabtree Fm	Beds	SP9337	52°1·6'	0°38·3'W	FM	153
Crabtree Fm	Bucks	SP8130	51°58·0'	0°48·9'W	FM	152,165
Crabtree Fm	Ches	SJ4545	53°0·2'	2°48·8'W	FM	117
Crabtree Fm	Ches	SJ5073	53°15·3'	2°44·6'W	FM	117
Crab Tree Fm	Ches	SJ6984	53°21·4'	2°27·5'W	FM	109
Crabtree Fm	Essex	TM1023	51°52·2'	1°3·4'E	FM	168,169
Crabtree Fm	E Susx	TQ4829	51°2·7'	0°7·1'E	FM	188,198
Crabtree Fm	Kent	TQ7934	51°4·9'	0°33·7'E	FM	188
Crabtree Fm	Kent	TR0941	51°9·6'	0°59·7'E	FM	179,189
Crabtree Fm	Lancs	SD4341	53°52·0'	2°51·6'W	FM	102
Crab Tree Fm	Lancs	SD4538	53°50·4'	2°49·7'W	FM	102
Crabtree Fm	N Yks	NZ5005	54°26·5'	1°13·3'W	FM	93
Crabtree Fm	N Yks	NZ5108	54°28·1'	1°12·4'W	FM	93
Crabtree Fm	N Yks	SE3785	54°15·8'	1°25·5'W	FM	99
Crabtree Fm	Oxon	SU2697	51°40·5'	1°37·0'W	FM	163
Crab Tree Fm	Staffs	SK0051	53°3·6'	1°59·6'W	FM	119
Crab Tree Fm	Warw	SP3296	52°33·9'	1°31·3'W	FM	140
Crabtree Fm	York	SE6243	53°53·0'	1°3·0'W	FM	105
Crabtree Green	Wrex	SJ3344	52°59·6'	2°59·5'W	T	117
Crabtreegreen Fm	Ches	SJ5870	53°13·8'	2°37·3'W	FM	117
Crabtree Hall	N Yks	SE5785	54°15·7'	1°7·1'W	X	100
Crabtree Hill	Essex	TQ4894	51°37·7'	0°8·7'E	X	167,177
Crabtree Hill	Glos	SO6313	51°49·1'	2°31·8'W	X	162
Crabtree Ho	Lincs	SK9226	52°49·7'	0°37·7'W	X	130
Crabtree House	N Yks	NZ4906	54°27·1'	1°14·2'W	X	93
Crabtree House Fm	N Yks	NZ1605	54°26·7'	1°44·8'W	FM	92
Crabtree Moss Fm	Ches	SJ3669	53°13·3'	2°12·2'W	FM	118
Crabtree Nook	Lancs	SD5243	53°53·1'	2°43·4'W	X	102
Crabwall Hall	Ches	SJ3869	53°13·3'	2°55·3'W	X	117
Crab Wood	Hants	SU4329	51°3·8'	1°22·8'W	F	185
Crabwood Farm Ho	Hants	SU4429	51°3·7'	1°21·9'W	X	185
Cracalt Ho	Cumbr	SD5188	54°17·4'	2°44·7'W	X	97
Cracaval	N Eil	NB0225	58°7·1'	7°3·2'W	H	13
Crachdy-isaf	Carm	SN5626	51°55·1'	4°5·2'W	X	146
Crachdy-uchaf	Carm	SN5727	51°55·6'	4°4·4'W	X	146
Crach-gelli-fâch	Carm	SN5629	51°56·7'	4°5·3'W	X	146
Crachies	Highld	NH9453	57°33·5'	3°45·8'W	X	27
Crachlwyn	Nth Pt Talb	SN7308	51°45·6'	3°50·0'W	X	160
Crachy Burn	Pth & Kin	NN9932	56°28·4'	3°37·9'W	W	52,53
Crackaig	Arg & Bt	NM3546	56°32·1'	6°18·2'W	X	47,48
Crackaig	Arg & Bt	NR5265	55°49·1'	5°57·1'W	X	61
Crackaig Hill	Arg & Bt	NR5265	55°49·1'	5°57·1'W	H	61
Crackaway Barton	Devon	SS5341	51°9·2'	4°5·7'W	X	180
Cracken Edge	Derby	SK0383	53°20·9'	1°56·9'W	X	110
Crackenedge	Kirk	SE2422	53°41·9'	1°37·8'W	T	104
Crackenthorpe	Cumbr	NY6622	54°35·8'	2°31·2'W	T	91
Crackerpool Burn	Northum	NU1830	55°34·0'	1°42·4'W	W	75
Crack Hill	V of Glam	SS9476	51°28·6'	3°31·2'W	X	170
Cracking Shaw	E Loth	NT6468	55°54·5'	2°34·1'W	X	67
Crackington Haven	Corn	SX1496	50°44·3'	4°37·8'W	T	190
Crackley	Staffs	SJ8350	53°3·1'	2°14·8'W	T	118
Crackley	Warw	SP2973	52°21·5'	1°34·1'W	T	140
Crackleybank	Shrops	SJ7510	52°41·5'	2°21·8'W	T	127
Crackley Wood	Warw	SP2874	52°22·0'	1°34·9'W	F	140
Cracknell Fm	Cambs	TL4174	52°21·0'	0°4·6'E	FM	142,143
Cracknell's Fm	Essex	TQ8194	51°37·2'	0°37·3'E	FM	168,178
Cracknore Hard	Hants	SU4010	50°53·5'	1°25·5'W	X	196
Cracknow Hill	Cambs	TL3850	52°8·1'	0°1·4'E	X	154
Cracknutt Hill	Warw	SP0966	52°17·8'	1°51·7'W	X	150
Crackpot	N Yks	SD9796	54°21·8'	2°2·4'W	T	98
Crackpot Hall	N Yks	NY9000	54°24·0'	2°8·8'W	X	91,92
Crackpot Moor	N Yks	SD9596	54°21·8'	2°4·2'W	X	98
Crackpot Side	N Yks	SD9696	54°21·8'	2°3·3'W	X	98
Crack's Hill	Northnts	SP5973	52°21·3'	1°7·6'W	X	140
Crackstone	Glos	SO8800	51°42·2'	2°10·0'W	X	162
Crackthorn Corner	Suff	TM0378	52°22·0'	0°59·3'E	T	144
Cracoe	Cumbr	NY4724	54°36·8'	2°48·8'W	X	90
Cracoe	N Yks	SD9760	54°2·4'	2°2·3'W	T	98
Cracoe Fell	N Yks	SD9959	54°1·9'	2°0·5'W	X	103
Cracoe Hill	Lancs	SD7754	53°59·1'	2°20·6'W	X	103
Craco Fm	Cumbr	NY8114	54°31·5'	2°17·2'W	FM	91,92
Crac'o'Hill Fm	Heref	SO4631	51°58·7'	2°46·8'W	FM	149,161
Cracow Moss	Staffs	SJ7547	53°1·4'	2°22·0'W	T	118
Cracrop	Cumbr	NY5269	55°1·0'	2°44·6'W	X	86
Craddock	Devon	ST0812	50°54·2'	3°18·1'W	T	181
Craddock Ho	Devon	ST0812	50°54·2'	3°18·1'W	X	181
Craddock Moor	Corn	SX2471	50°31·0'	4°28·6'W	X	201
Craddock's Fm	Somer	ST5829	51°3·8'	2°35·6'W	FM	183
Craddocks Moss	Staffs	SJ7748	53°2·0'	2°20·2'W	F	118
Craddocks Moss Fm	Staffs	SJ7847	53°1·4'	2°19·3'W	FM	118
Cradge Fm	Lincs	TF1615	52°43·4'	0°16·5'W	FM	130
Crâdh Leathad	Arg & Bt	NM6723	56°20·8'	5°45·8'W	X	49
Crâdh Rubha	Arg & Bt	NS0852	55°43·7'	5°3·0'W	X	63,69
Cradle Br	Somer	ST4233	51°5·8'	2°49·3'W	X	182
Cradle Br	Somer	ST4252	51°16·1'	2°49·5'W	X	182
Cradlebridge Fm	Somer	ST4738	51°8·6'	2°45·1'W	FM	182
Cradlebridge Sewer	Kent	TQ9432	51°3·5'	0°46·5'E	W	189
Cradle Edge	Brad	SE0638	53°50·5'	1°54·1'W	T	104
Cradle End	Herts	TL4521	51°52·3'	0°6·8'E	T	167
Cradle Gill Plantn	N Yks	SE1680	54°13·2'	1°44·9'W	F	99
Cradlehall	Highld	NH7044	57°28·3'	4°9·6'W	X	27
Cradle Hall Fm	Norf	TF8039	52°55·3'	0°41·1'E	FM	132
Cradle Head	E Yorks	TA2571	54°7·4'	0°4·8'W	X	101
Cradle Hill	E Susx	TQ5001	50°47·6'	0°8·1'E	X	199

Cradle Hill	Wilts	ST8846	51°13·0'	2°9·9'W	X	183
Cradle Ho	Essex	TL8423	51°52·7'	0°40·8'E	X	168
Cradle House Fm	Oxon	SP3732	51°59·3'	1°27·3'W	FM	151
Cradle Rocks	Powys	SO1147	52°7·1'	3°17·6'W	X	148
Cradle, The	Pemb	SM7823	51°51·9'	5°13·1'W	X	157
Cradley	Dudley	SO9484	52°27·5'	2°4·9'W	T	139
Cradley	Heref	SO7347	52°7·5'	2°23·3'W	T	150
Cradley Brook	Heref	SO7344	52°5·9'	2°23·3'W	W	150
Cradley Hall Fm	Heref	SO6947	52°7·5'	2°26·8'W	FM	149
Cradley Heath	Sand	SO9485	52°28·0'	2°4·9'W	T	139
Cradoc	Powys	SO0130	51°57·8'	3°26·1'W	T	160
Craebreck	Orkney	HY4702	58°54·4'	2°54·7'W	X	6,7
Craeg an Fhithich	N Eil	NB0617	58°2·9'	6°58·5'W	X	13,14
Crae Hill	D & G	NX6569	55°0·1'	4°6·2'W	H	83,84
Craes Hill	D & G	NX7786	55°9·4'	3°55·4'W	X	78
Craflwyn Hall	Gwyn	SH6049	53°1·4'	4°4·8'W	X	115
Crafnant	Gwyn	SH6129	52°50·7'	4°3·4'W	X	124
Crafthole	Corn	SX3654	50°22·0'	4°18·0'W	T	201
Crafton	Bucks	SP8819	51°52·0'	0°42·9'W	T	165
Crafton Stud Fm	Bucks	SP8919	51°52·0'	0°42·0'W	FM	165
Craft Plantn	Norf	TM4097	52°31·3'	1°32·7'E	F	134
Craft Plantn	Suff	TM5283	52°23·4'	1°42·6'E	F	156
Craft's Hill	Cambs	TL3863	52°15·1'	0°1·7'E	X	154
Crafty Webb	Heref	SO3144	52°5·6'	3°0·0'W	X	148,161
Crag	Cumbr	NY1931	54°40·3'	3°14·9'W	X	89,90
Crag	Cumbr	NY7242	54°46·6'	2°25·7'W	X	86,87
Crag	Cumbr	SD3080	54°12·9'	3°4·0'W	X	96,97
Crag	Cumbr	SD3492	54°19·4'	3°0·5'W	X	96,97
Crag	Cumbr	SD4694	54°20·6'	2°49·4'W	X	97
Crag	N Yks	SD9088	54°17·5'	2°8·8'W	X	98
Cragabus Burn	Arg & Bt	NR3345	55°37·8'	6°14·1'W	W	60
Cragaidh	Highld	NC3357	58°28·4'	4°51·3'W	X	9
Cragaig	Arg & Bt	NM4038	56°28·0'	6°12·8'W	X	47,48
Cragan Dubh	Pth & Kin	NN8157	56°41·6'	3°56·1'W	H	52
Craganester	Pth & Kin	NN6638	56°31·2'	4°10·2'W	X	51
Cragan Liath Mór	Pth & Kin	NN7562	56°44·2'	4°2·2'W	H	42
Cragback	Northum	NY9280	55°7·1'	2°7·1'W	X	80
Crag Bank	Lancs	SD4970	54°7·6'	2°46·4'W	T	97
Crag Bank	Scot Bord	NT5907	55°21·6'	2°38·4'W	X	80
Crag Bottom	Brad	SD9837	53°50·0'	2°1·4'W	X	103
Crag Brea	N Yks	SD9880	54°13·2'	2°1·4'W	X	98
Cragcleugh Burn	Northum	NU1223	55°30·3'	1°48·2'W	W	75
Cragdale Allotments	N Yks	SD9283	54°14·8'	2°6·9'W	X	98
Cragdale Moor	N Yks	SD9182	54°14·3'	2°7·9'W	X	98
Cragdale Water	N Yks	SD9184	54°15·3'	2°7·9'W	W	98
Crag End	Lancs	SD5055	53°59·6'	2°45·3'W	X	102
Cragend	Northum	NU0800	55°17·9'	1°52·0'W	X	81
Cragend	Northum	NY7870	55°1·7'	2°20·2'W	X	86,87
Crag End	N Yks	SD9843	53°53·2'	2°1·4'W	X	103
Crag Farm House	Cumbr	NY0815	54°31·6'	3°24·9'W	X	89
Crag Fell	Cumbr	NY0914	54°31·0'	3°23·9'W	H	89
Crag Fm	N Yks	SE2048	53°55·9'	1°41·3'W	FM	104
Crag Fm	N Yks	SE2648	53°55·9'	1°35·8'W	FM	104
Crag Fm	Suff	TM4352	52°7·0'	1°33·4'E	FM	156
Crag Foot	Lancs	SD4873	54°9·3'	2°47·4'W	T	97
Cragg	N Yks	SE6895	54°21·0'	0°56·8'W	X	94,100
Craggach	Highld	NH5744	57°28·1'	4°22·6'W	X	26
Craggan	Aberd	NO3597	57°3·8'	3°3·9'W	X	37,44
Craggan	Highld	NH3498	57°56·7'	4°47·8'W	X	20
Craggan	Moray	NJ1832	57°22·5'	3°21·4'W	X	36
Craggan	Moray	NJ2741	57°27·5'	3°12·5'W	X	28
Craggan	Pth & Kin	NN8117	56°20·1'	3°55·0'W	X	57
Craggan	Stir	NN5823	56°22·9'	4°17·5'W	X	51
Craggan	Stir	NN6635	56°29·5'	4°10·1'W	X	51
Craggan Burn	Highld	NC9821	58°10·2'	3°43·6'W	W	17
Craggan Hill	Aberd	NO3185	56°57·3'	3°7·6'W	X	44
Craggan Hill	Arg & Bt	NR2698	56°8·8'	4°47·6'W	H	56
Cragganmore	Highld	NH4740	57°25·7'	4°32·4'W	X	26
Craggan More	Moray	NJ1634	57°23·6'	3°23·4'W	H	28
Cragganmore	Moray	NJ1636	57°24·7'	3°23·4'W	T	28
Craggan of Clune	Highld	NN7199	57°4·1'	4°7·2'W	X	35
Craggan, The	Highld	NC9016	58°7·4'	3°51·6'W	H	17
Craggan, The	Highld	NC9838	58°19·4'	3°44·0'W	X	11,17
Craggantoul	Pth & Kin	NN6537	56°30·6'	4°11·2'W	X	51
Cragganvallie	Highld	NH5337	57°24·2'	4°26·3'W	X	26
Cragg Brook	Cald	SE0024	53°43·0'	1°59·6'W	W	104
Cragg Cottage	N Yks	SE6895	54°21·0'	0°56·8'W	X	94,100
Craggen Voain	Pth & Kin	NN9132	56°28·3'	3°45·7'W	X	52
Cragg Fm	Cumbr	SD1099	54°23·0'	3°22·7'W	FM	96
Cragg Fm	Cumbr	SD1297	54°21·9'	3°20·8'W	FM	96
Cragg Fm	Cumbr	SD4897	54°22·2'	2°47·6'W	FM	97
Cragg Fm	N Yks	SE1691	54°19·1'	1°44·8'W	FM	99
Cragg Fm, The	Cumbr	SD5693	54°20·1'	2°40·2'W	FM	97
Cragg Hall	Cumbr	SD1887	54°16·6'	3°15·1'W	X	96
Cragg Hall	Lancs	SD6266	54°5·6'	2°34·4'W	X	97
Cragg Hall	N Yks	SE1864	54°4·5'	1°43·1'W	X	99
Cragg Hill	Leeds	SE2437	53°50·0'	1°37·7'W	T	104
Cragghill Fm	N Yks	SD8070	54°7·8'	2°17·9'W	FM	98
Cragg Ho	Cumbr	NY8313	54°31·0'	2°15·3'W	X	91,92
Cragg House Fm	N Yks	SE0354	53°59·2'	1°56·8'W	FM	104
Craggie	Highld	NC3305	58°0·4'	4°49·1'W	X	15
Craggie	Highld	NC8719	58°9·0'	3°54·7'W	X	17
Craggie	Highld	NH7239	57°25·7'	4°7·4'W	X	27
Craggie	Highld	NH9053	57°33·5'	3°49·8'W	X	27
Craggie Beg	Highld	NC7408	58°2·9'	4°7·6'W	X	16
Craggie Burn	Highld	NC8621	58°10·1'	3°55·8'W	W	17
Craggie Burn	Highld	NC8849	58°25·2'	3°54·6'W	W	10
Craggie Burn	Highld	NH7339	57°25·7'	4°6·4'W	W	27
Craggiemore	Highld	NC7308	58°2·8'	4°8·6'W	X	16
Craggiemore	Highld	NH7339	57°25·7'	4°6·4'W	X	27
Craggie Water	Highld	NC8918	58°8·5'	3°52·7'W	W	17
Craggish	Pth & Kin	NN7621	56°22·2'	4°0·0'W	X	51,52,57
Cragg Lot	Lancs	SD5671	54°8·2'	2°40·0'W	H	97
Crag Green	Cumbr	NY8512	54°30·4'	2°13·5'W	X	91,92
Craggs	Lancs	SD6664	54°4·5'	2°30·8'W	X	98
Craggs	Scot Bord	NT5424	55°30·7'	2°43·3'W	X	73
Craggs Hall	Red & Cl	NZ7019	54°33·9'	0°54·6'W	X	94
Craggs Hill	Red & Cl	NZ7018	54°33·4'	0°54·6'W	X	94
Cragg's Hill Ho	Lincs	TF3325	52°48·6'	0°1·2'W	X	131
Craggs Lane Fm	N Yks	SE2094	54°20·7'	1°41·1'W	FM	99

Craggstone	Cumbr	SD6493	54°20·1'	2°32·8'W	X	97
Cragg, The	Northum	NY8885	55°9·8'	2°10·9'W	X	80
Cragg Vale	Cald	SE0022	53°41·9'	1°59·6'W	X	104
Cragg Vale	Cald	SE0023	53°42·4'	1°59·6'W	T	104
Cragg Wood	Durham	NZ1425	54°37·4'	1°46·6'W	F	92
Cragg Wood	Lancs	SD5461	54°2·8'	2°41·7'W	F	97
Craggy	Highld	NC8951	58°26·3'	3°53·6'W	X	10
Cragg Yeat	Cumbr	SD5082	54°14·1'	2°45·6'W	X	97
Craggyhall	Northum	NU0934	55°36·2'	1°51·0'W	X	75
Crag Hall	Ches	SJ9868	53°12·8'	2°1·4'W	X	118
Crag Hall	Lancs	SD4853	53°58·5'	2°47·2'W	X	102
Craghead	Durham	NZ2150	54°50·9'	1°40·0'W	T	88
Crag Head	Northum	NY6194	55°14·6'	2°36·4'W	H	80
Crag Head	Northum	NY7959	54°55·8'	2°19·2'W	X	86,87
Crag Hill	Cumbr	NY1920	54°34·4'	3°14·8'W	H	89,90
Crag Hill	Cumbr	SD6983	54°14·8'	2°28·1'W	H	98
Crag Hill	Durham	NY9916	54°32·6'	2°0·5'W	H	92
Crag Hill	Northum	NU1520	55°28·7'	1°45·3'W	H	75
Crag Hill	N Yks	SE2759	54°1·8'	1°34·9'W	X	104
Crag Ho	Brad	SE0547	53°55·4'	1°55·0'W	X	104
Crag Ho	Cumbr	NY1002	54°24·6'	3°22·8'W	X	89
Crag Ho	Cumbr	SD4396	54°21·6'	2°52·2'W	X	97
Crag Ho	Cumbr	SD5576	54°10·9'	2°41·0'W	X	97
Crag Ho	Lancs	SD6847	53°55·3'	2°28·8'W	X	103
Crag Ho	Northum	NY7586	55°10·3'	2°23·1'W	X	80
Crag Ho	Northum	NY9269	55°1·2'	2°7·1'W	X	87
Crag Ho	N Yks	SE2069	54°7·2'	1°41·2'W	X	99
Craghouse Fm	Ches	SJ7975	53°16·5'	2°18·5'W	FM	118
Crag House Fm	Leeds	SE2441	53°52·1'	1°37·7'W	FM	104
Crag House Fm	N Yks	NZ6806	54°26·9'	0°56·7'W	FM	94
Crag Houses	Cumbr	NY1717	54°32·7'	3°16·6'W	X	89,90
Crag Laithe	N Yks	SD9156	54°0·2'	2°7·8'W	X	103
Crag Lough	Northum	NY7668	55°0·6'	2°22·1'W	W	86,87
Crag Mhòr na Faing	Arg & Bt	NR2756	55°43·5'	6°20·4'W	X	60
Cragmill	Northum	NU1134	55°36·2'	1°49·1'W	X	75
Crag Nook	Cumbr	NY5340	54°45·4'	2°43·4'W	X	86
Crag Nook	N Yks	SD9954	53°59·2'	2°0·5'W	X	103
Crago	N Eil	NG0178	57°41·8'	7°0·7'W	X	18
Crago	N Eil	NG0797	57°52·2'	6°56·0'W	X	14,18
Crag of Blea Moor	N Yks	SD7782	54°14·2'	2°20·8'W	X	98
Crag Point	Northum	NZ3476	55°4·9'	1°27·6'W	X	88
Crag Pond	N Yks	SE6894	54°20·5'	0°56·8'W	W	94,100
Crags	Cumbr	NY3046	54°48·5'	3°4·9'W	X	85
Cragsheilhill Wood	Scot Bord	NT7122	55°29·7'	2°27·1'W	W	74
Cragshield Hope	Northum	NY7383	55°8·7'	2°25·0'W	X	80
Crag Side	Cumbr	SD6983	54°14·8'	2°28·1'W	X	98
Cragside	Northum	NU0702	55°19·0'	1°53·0'W	X	81
Crag Side	N Yks	SD9843	53°53·2'	2°1·4'W	X	103
Crag Stone Rigg	N Yks	SE8397	54°21·9'	0°42·9'W	H	94,100
Crag Stones	Lancs	SD6947	53°55·3'	2°27·9'W	X	103
Crag, The	Lancs	SD5461	54°2·8'	2°41·7'W	X	97
Crag Top	Durham	NZ0723	54°36·4'	1°53·1'W	X	92
Crag Top	N Yks	SD9855	53°59·7'	2°1·4'W	X	103
Crag Top	N Yks	SE0042	53°52·7'	1°59·6'W	X	104
Crag Top	N Yks	SE0146	53°54·9'	1°58·7'W	X	104
Crag Wood	N Yks	SD9555	53°59·7'	2°4·2'W	F	103
Cragwood Ho	Cumbr	NY3900	54°23·8'	2°56·0'W	X	90
Crag y Bwdran	Carm	SN5539	52°2·1'	4°6·4'W	A	146
Crahan	Corn	SW6830	50°7·7'	5°14·4'W	T	203
Crai	Powys	SN8924	51°54·4'	3°36·4'W	T	160
Craibadona	Aberd	NJ9322	57°17·6'	2°6·5'W	X	38
Craibstone	C of Aber	NJ8710	57°11·1'	2°12·4'W	X	38
Craibstone	Moray	NJ4959	57°37·3'	2°50·8'W	X	28,29
Craich	Aberd	NJ6013	57°12·6'	2°39·3'W	X	37
Craichie	Angus	NO5047	56°37·0'	2°48·4'W	T	54
Craichie	D & G	NX7170	55°0·7'	4°0·6'W	X	77,84
Craichie Mill	Angus	NO5046	56°36·4'	2°48·4'W	X	54
Craichmore	D & G	NX0362	54°55·1'	5°4·0'W	X	82
Craig	Arg & Bt	NM5829	56°23·7'	5°54·8'W	X	48
Craig	Arg & Bt	NN0334	56°27·7'	5°11·4'W	X	50
Craig	D & G	NX1761	54°54·9'	4°50·9'W	X	82
Craig	D & G	NX4142	54°45·1'	4°27·8'W	X	83
Craig	D & G	NX5162	54°56·1'	4°19·1'W	X	83
Craig	D & G	NX6875	55°3·4'	4°3·6'W	X	77,84
Craig	D & G	NX6967	54°59·1'	4°2·4'W	X	83,84
Craig	D & G	NX8583	55°7·9'	3°47·8'W	X	78
Craig	D & G	NY0168	55°0·1'	3°32·4'W	X	84
Craig	D & G	NY3488	55°11·2'	3°1·8'W	X	79
Craig	E Ayr	NS6306	55°20·0'	4°9·2'W	X	71,77
Craig	Flint	SJ2073	53°15·1'	3°11·5'W	X	117
Craig	Highld	NG7763	57°36·4'	5°43·5'W	X	19,24
Craig	Highld	NG8233	57°20·4'	5°36·9'W	X	24
Craig	Highld	NH0349	57°29·6'	5°16·8'W	T	25
Craig	I of M	SC3997	54°20·8'	4°28·2'W	X	95
Craig	Northum	NY9399	55°17·4'	2°6·2'W	X	80
Craig	S Ayr	NS2700	55°16·1'	4°42·9'W	X	76
Craig	S Ayr	NS3802	55°17·4'	4°32·6'W	X	77
Craig a Barns	Pth & Kin	NO0143	56°34·4'	3°36·2'W	H	52,53
Craig Abercwmboi	Rho Cyn Taf	ST0398	51°40·6'	3°23·8'W	X	170
Craig Aberserw	Gwyn	SH6926	52°49·2'	3°56·2'W	H	124
Craigadam	D & G	NX8072	55°1·9'	3°52·2'W	X	84
Craig Aderyn	Gwyn	SH6622	52°47·0'	3°58·8'W	H	124
Craig Aderyn	Gwyn	SH7637	52°55·2'	3°50·3'W	X	124
Craig-adwy-wynt	Denb	SJ1253	53°4·3'	3°18·4'W	H	116
Craigag Lodge	Highld	NM9279	56°51·6'	5°24·3'W	X	40
Craigaig Water	Arg & Bt	NR6118	55°24·1'	5°46·1'W	W	68
Craig Airie Fell	D & G	NX2373	55°1·5'	4°45·7'W	H	76
Craigalbert	S Ayr	NX0779	55°4·3'	5°1·0'W	X	76
Craigallian	Stir	NS5377	55°58·1'	4°20·9'W	X	64
Craigallian Loch	Stir	NS5378	55°58·6'	4°20·9'W	W	64
Craig Alltyberau	Carm	SN7746	52°6·2'	3°47·4'W	X	146,147
Craigancash	Angus	NO5877	56°53·2'	2°40·9'W	H	44
Craigan Eich	Pth & Kin	NN8660	56°43·3'	3°51·3'W	X	43
Craigangal	S Ayr	NX0577	55°3·2'	5°2·7'W	X	76
Craigangowan	Angus	NO5878	56°53·7'	2°40·9'W	H	44
Craigangower	Aberd	NO6488	56°59·2'	2°35·1'W	X	45
Craigangower	Angus	NO5375	56°52·1'	2°45·8'W	H	44
Craiganlea Ho	S Ayr	NX0674	55°1·6'	5°1·7'W	X	76
Craigannet	Stir	NS7184	56°2·1'	4°3·8'W	X	57,64
Craigannet Hill	Stir	NS7184	56°2·1'	4°3·8'W	H	57,64
Craiganour Forest	Pth & Kin	NN6064	56°45·1'	4°16·9'W	X	42
Craiganour Lodge	Pth & Kin	NN6159	56°42·4'	4°15·8'W	X	42,51
Craigan Roan	Moray	NJ3964	57°40·0'	3°0·9'W	X	28
Craigans	Arg & Bt	NR9094	56°5·8'	5°22·1'W	X	55
Craig Anthony	D & G	NW9856	54°51·7'	5°8·4'W	X	82
Craigard	Highld	NH2901	57°4·4'	4°48·8'W	X	34
Craigarnhall	Stir	NS7598	56°9·8'	4°0·3'W	X	57
Craig Arthbry	Denb	SJ0345	52°59·9'	3°26·3'W	H	116
Craig Arthur	Denb	SJ2247	53°1·1'	3°9·4'W	X	117
Craigash	E Dunb	NS5676	55°57·6'	4°18·0'W	X	64
Craigathray	Aberd	NJ6554	57°34·7'	2°34·7'W	X	29
Craig Balnafuaran	Moray	NJ1632	57°22·5'	3°23·4'W	X	36
Craigbarnet	E Dunb	NS5979	55°59·3'	4°15·2'W	X	64
Craigbarnet Muir	E Dunb	NS5782	56°0·8'	4°17·2'W	X	64
Craigbea	Pth & Kin	NN9853	56°39·7'	3°39·4'W	X	52,53
Craigbeck	D & G	NT1003	55°19·0'	3°24·7'W	X	78
Craigbeck Hope	D & G	NT1303	55°19·1'	3°21·8'W	X	78
Craig Bedwlwyn	Rho Cyn Taf	SS9899	51°41·1'	3°28·1'W	X	170
Craigbeg	Aberd	NJ6900	57°5·7'	2°30·2'W	X	38
Craigbeg	Aberd	NO7691	57°0·8'	2°23·3'W	H	38,45
Craigbeg	Highld	NN4081	56°53·8'	4°37·2'W	X	34,42
Craig Beinon	Carm	SN7444	52°5·0'	3°49·9'W	X	146,147,160
Craig Ben Lodge	Arg & Bt	NM6425	56°21·8'	5°48·8'W	X	49
Craig Berthlwyd	Merth Tyd	ST0996	51°39·6'	3°18·5'W	T	171
Craig Berwyn	Powys	SJ0733	52°53·4'	3°22·5'W	X	125
Craigbet	Inverc	NS3766	55°51·8'	4°35·8'W	X	63
Craig Bhuilg	Moray	NJ1807	57°9·1'	3°20·9'W	X	36
Craigbill	D & G	NX9369	55°0·5'	3°40·0'W	X	84
Craigbill Hill	D & G	NX9370	55°1·0'	3°40·0'W	H	84
Craig Binning	W Loth	NT0371	55°55·6'	3°32·7'W	X	65
Craigbirnoch	D & G	NX1768	54°58·6'	4°51·1'W	X	82
Craigbirnoch Fell	D & G	NX1768	54°58·6'	4°51·1'W	H	82
Craig Blaen-rhiwarth	Powys	SJ0228	52°50·7'	3°26·9'W	X	125
Craig Blaen-y-cwm	Conwy	SH7448	53°1·1'	3°52·3'W	X	115
Craig Boeth	Powys	SJ0228	52°50·7'	3°26·9'W	X	125
Craig Borenich	Pth & Kin	NN8460	56°43·3'	3°53·3'W	X	43,52
Craigbourach Moss	Moray	NJ5652	57°33·6'	2°43·7'W	X	29
Craigbrack	Arg & Bt	NS1395	56°6·9'	5°0·0'W	X	56
Craigbrae	E Ayr	NS4516	55°25·1'	4°26·5'W	X	70
Craigbrae	S Ayr	NX1984	55°7·3'	4°49·9'W	X	76
Craigbrae Fm	C of Edin	NT1375	55°57·9'	3°23·2'W	FM	65
Craig Branddu	Carm	SN7146	52°6·1'	3°52·6'W	X	146,147
Craigbraneoch Rig	E Ayr	NS6304	55°18·9'	4°9·1'W	H	77
Craig Brawlin	Angus	NO4683	56°56·4'	2°52·8'W	X	44
Craigbreck	Highld	NH6649	57°30·9'	4°13·8'W	X	26
Craigbrex	D & G	NX8456	54°53·4'	3°48·1'W	X	84
Craig Bridge	S Lanak	NS7143	55°40·1'	4°2·6'W	X	71
Craigbrock	D & G	NX5186	55°9·0'	4°19·9'W	X	77
Craigbrock	Stir	NS5481	56°0·2'	4°20·0'W	X	64
Craigbrock Burn	Stir	NS7191	56°5·9'	4°4·0'W	W	57
Craigbrock Hill	S Ayr	NX4295	55°13·7'	4°28·6'W	H	77
Craig Bron-banog	Denb	SJ0151	53°3·1'	3°28·2'W	H	116
Craig Bron-y-cwrt	Carm	SN7744	52°5·1'	3°47·3'W	X	146,147,160
Craig Buarth-glas	Gwyn	SH8215	52°43·4'	3°44·4'W	H	124,125
Craig Buck	Angus	NO4180	56°54·7'	2°57·7'W	H	44
Craigbuie Hill	D & G	NS7500	55°17·0'	3°57·7'W	H	78
Craigbui Wood	Highld	NH7903	57°6·4'	3°59·4'W	F	35
Craigburn	Cumbr	NY4776	55°4·8'	2°49·4'W	X	86
Craigburn	Cumbr	NY5668	55°0·5'	2°40·9'W	X	86
Craig Burn	D & G	NX1661	54°54·8'	4°51·8'W	W	82
Craig Burn	D & G	NY3286	55°10·1'	3°3·6'W	W	79
Craig Burn	E Ayr	NS6405	55°19·5'	4°8·2'W	W	71,77
Craigburn	Scot Bord	NT2354	55°46·6'	3°13·2'W	X	66,73
Craig Burn	Scot Bord	NT6766	55°53·4'	2°31·2'W	W	67
Craig Burn	S Lanak	NS8733	55°34·9'	3°47·1'W	W	71,72
Craig Bwlch-y-moch	Gwyn	SH5740	52°56·4'	4°7·3'W	X	124
Craigbyre	S Ayr	NS4631	55°33·2'	4°26·0'W	X	70
Craig Caerhedyn	Cered	SN7096	52°33·0'	3°54·6'W	H	135
Craig Caerllan	Cered	SN3557	52°11·4'	4°24·4'W	X	145
Craigcaffie	D & G	NX0964	54°56·3'	4°58·5'W	X	82
Craigcannochie Hill	S Ayr	NX2385	55°7·9'	4°46·2'W	H	76
Craig Carnau	Caer	ST2193	51°38·1'	3°8·1'W	H	171
Craig Castle	Aberd	NJ4724	57°18·5'	2°52·3'W	X	37
Craig Cau	Gwyn	SH7112	52°41·7'	3°54·1'W	X	124
Craig-cefn-parc	Swan	SN6702	51°42·3'	3°55·1'W	T	159
Craig Cerrig-gleisiad	Powys	SN9621	51°52·9'	3°30·3'W	X	160
Craig Chaisteil	Arg & Bt	NM9012	56°15·5'	5°23·0'W	X	55
Craigchessie	D & G	NX5190	55°11·2'	4°20·0'W	X	77
Craig Chwefri	Powys	SN9657	52°12·3'	3°30·9'W	H	147
Craig Clangwyn	Cered	SN7747	52°6·7'	3°47·4'W	X	146,147
Craigcleuch	D & G	NY3486	55°10·1'	3°1·7'W	X	79
Craig Clogan	Cered	SN7258	52°12·6'	3°52·0'W	X	146,147
Craig Clwyd	Nth Pt Talb	SN8406	51°44·7'	3°40·4'W	X	160
Craig Clwyd Fechan	Nth Pt Talb	SN8206	51°44·7'	3°42·2'W	X	160
Craig Cnwch	Powys	SN9263	52°15·5'	3°34·5'W	X	147
Craig Cnwch-glas	Cered	SN7649	52°7·8'	3°48·3'W	X	146,147
Craig Coillich	Aberd	NO3795	57°2·8'	3°1·8'W	H	37,44
Craig Cott	Arg & Bt	NS0078	55°57·5'	5°11·8'W	X	62,63
Craig Crane	Angus	NO5179	56°54·2'	2°47·8'W	H	44
Craigcrook Castle	C of Edin	NT2174	55°57·4'	3°15·5'W	A	66
Craigculter	Aberd	NJ9054	57°34·8'	2°9·6'W	X	30
Craig Curyll	Cered	SN6754	52°10·3'	3°56·3'W	X	146
Craig Curyll	Cered	SN6951	52°8·7'	3°54·5'W	X	146
Craig Cwareli	Powys	SO0420	51°52·5'	3°23·3'W	X	160
Craig Cwlwm	Gwyn	SH1524	52°47·2'	4°44·2'W	X	123
Craig Cwm Amarch	Gwyn	SH7011	52°41·1'	3°55·0'W	H	124
Craig Cwmbychan	Gwyn	SH5455	53°4·6'	4°10·4'W	X	115
Craig Cwm-clyd	Powys	SN8962	52°14·9'	3°37·2'W	X	147
Craig Cwm Cynwyn	Powys	SO0220	51°52·5'	3°25·0'W	X	160
Craig Cwm-du	Gwyn	SH8722	52°47·3'	3°40·1'W	H	124,125
Craig Cwm-du	Powys	SN9421	51°52·9'	3°32·0'W	X	160
Craig Cwm-Lloi	Gwyn	SH9015	52°43·5'	3°37·3'W	X	125
Craig Cwm-llwyd	Gwyn	SH6412	52°41·6'	4°0·3'W	X	124
Craig Cwm Maelwg	Nth Pt Talb	SS8187	51°34·4'	3°42·6'W	X	170
Craig Cwmoergwm	Powys	SO0320	51°52·4'	3°24·2'W	X	160
Craig Cwmrhwyddfor	Gwyn	SH7312	52°41·7'	3°52·4'W	H	124
Craig Cwm Sere	Powys	SO0121	51°53·0'	3°25·9'W	X	160
Craig Cwm Silyn	Gwyn	SH5250	53°1·9'	4°12·0'W	H	115
Craig Cwmtinwen	Cered	SN8374	52°21·3'	3°42·7'W	X	135,136,147
Craig Cywarch	Gwyn	SH8418	52°45·1'	3°42·7'W	H	124,125
Craig Dafydd	I of Angl	SH2885	53°20·3'	4°34·6'W	X	114
Craigdallie	Pth & Kin	NO2528	56°26·6'	3°12·5'W	X	53,59
Craigdam	Aberd	NJ8430	57°21·9'	2°15·5'W	T	29,30
Craig Damff	Angus	NO3778	56°53·6'	3°1·6'W	X	44
Craigdarroch	D & G	NS8006	55°20·3'	3°53·1'W	X	71,78
Craigdarroch	D & G	NX7490	55°11·5'	3°58·3'W	X	77
Craigdarroch	E Ayr	NS6306	55°20·0'	4°9·2'W	X	71,77
Craigdarroch	Highld	NH4457	57°34·8'	4°36·1'W	T	26
Craigdarroch Hill	D & G	NX7591	55°12·1'	3°57·4'W	H	78
Craigdarroch Muir	D & G	NS8005	55°19·7'	3°53·1'W	H	71,78
Craigdarroch Water	D & G	NX7390	55°11·5'	3°59·3'W	W	77
Craigdarroch Water	D & G	NX7690	55°11·6'	3°56·4'W	W	78
Craigdasher	D & G	NS7600	55°17·0'	3°56·7'W	H	78
Craigdasher Hill	D & G	NX7982	55°7·3'	3°53·4'W	H	78
Craig David	Aberd	NO8473	56°51·1'	2°15·3'W	X	45
Craig Ddrwg	Gwyn	SH6533	52°52·9'	4°0·0'W	X	124
Craig Ddu	Carm	SN3210	51°46·0'	4°25·7'W	X	159
Craig Ddu	Carm	SN7347	52°6·6'	3°50·9'W	X	146,147
Craig Ddu	Carm	SN7543	52°4·5'	3°49·0'W	X	146,147,160
Craig Ddu	Cered	SN7648	52°7·2'	3°48·3'W	X	146,147
Craig Ddu	Conwy	SH6953	53°3·7'	3°56·9'W	X	115
Craig-ddu	Gwyn	SH6152	53°3·1'	4°4·0'W	X	115
Craig Ddu	Powys	SH9213	52°42·5'	3°35·5'W	H	125
Craig Ddu	Powys	SN9469	52°18·8'	3°32·9'W	X	136,147
Craigddu-isaf	Gwyn	SH6830	52°51·3'	3°57·2'W	X	124
Craig Den	Aberd	NO8083	56°56·5'	2°19·3'W	X	45
Craigden	Pth & Kin	NO1815	56°19·5'	3°19·1'W	X	58
Craig Derlwyn	Carm	SN7215	51°49·4'	3°51·0'W	X	160
Craig Derry	Aberd	NO0498	57°4·0'	3°34·5'W	X	36,43
Craigdews	D & G	NX5072	55°1·4'	4°20·4'W	X	77
Craig Dhu	Aberd	NJ4801	57°6·1'	2°51·0'W	H	37
Craigdhu	Arg & Bt	NM8105	56°11·5'	5°31·3'W	X	55
Craigdhu	D & G	NX3940	54°44·0'	4°29·6'W	X	83
Craigdhu	Highld	NH4440	57°25·7'	4°35·4'W	X	26
Craigdhu	Highld	NJ0332	57°22·3'	3°36·3'W	X	27,36
Craig Dhu	S Ayr	NX4298	55°15·3'	4°28·7'W	H	77
Craig Diferion	Carm	SN7346	52°6·1'	3°50·9'W	X	146,147
Craigdilly	Scot Bord	NT1820	55°28·3'	3°17·4'W	H	72
Craigdimas	Fife	NT1984	56°2·8'	3°17·6'W	X	65,66
Craig Dinas Fach	Powys	SN8550	52°8·4'	3°40·4'W	X	147
Craig Dod	S Lanak	NS9120	55°28·0'	3°43·0'W	H	71,72
Craig Doin	Aberd	NO2290	56°59·9'	3°16·6'W	H	44
Craig Dolfudr	Gwyn	SH8231	52°52·1'	3°44·8'W	X	124,125
Craig Dolwen	Cered	SN7978	52°23·4'	3°46·3'W	X	135,147
Craigdonkey	E Ayr	NS4610	55°21·8'	4°25·4'W	X	70
Craigdoon	D & G	NX6271	55°1·1'	4°9·1'W	X	77
Craig Dorney	Aberd	NJ4035	57°24·3'	2°59·5'W	H	28
Craig Douglas	Scot Bord	NT2924	55°30·5'	3°7·0'W	T	73
Craigdow	S Ayr	NS2705	55°18·8'	4°43·1'W	X	70,76
Craigdow Burn	D & G	NX3356	54°52·5'	4°35·7'W	W	82
Craigdow Loch	S Ayr	NS2606	55°19·3'	4°44·1'W	W	70,76
Craig Dubhaidh	Pth & Kin	NO1373	56°50·7'	3°25·1'W	H	43
Craig Duchrey	Angus	NO4971	56°49·9'	2°49·7'W	H	44
Craigduckie	Fife	NT1091	56°6·5'	3°26·4'W	X	58
Craig Dugwin	Powys	SO0584	52°27·0'	3°23·5'W	X	136
Craig Dullet	Angus	NO4279	56°54·2'	2°56·7'W	X	44
Craigdullyeart Hill	E Ayr	NS6515	55°24·9'	4°7·5'W	H	71
Craig Dunant	Gwyn	SH8516	52°44·0'	3°41·8'W	X	124,125
Craig Dyfnant	Powys	SN8765	52°16·5'	3°39·0'W	X	135,136,147
Craigeach	D & G	NX3156	54°52·5'	4°37·6'W	X	82
Craigeach Fell	D & G	NX3156	54°52·5'	4°37·6'W	H	82
Craigeach Moor	D & G	NX3356	54°52·5'	4°35·7'W	X	82
Craigeam	N Eil	NB1643	58°17·3'	6°50·3'W	X	8,13
Craigearn	Aberd	NJ7214	57°13·2'	2°27·4'W	T	38
Craigeassie	Angus	NO4557	56°42·3'	2°53·4'W	X	54
Craigeazle	D & G	NX4982	55°6·8'	4°21·6'W	H	77
Craigeirig Burn	Scot Bord	NT2023	55°29·9'	3°15·6'W	W	73
Craigellachie	Highld	NH8811	57°10·8'	3°50·7'W	X	35,36
Craigellachie	Moray	NJ2844	57°29·1'	3°11·6'W	T	28
Craigellachie National Nature Reserve	Highld	NH8812	57°11·4'	3°50·7'W	X	35,36
Craigellie	Aberd	NK0260	57°38·1'	1°57·5'W	X	30
Craigelwhan	D & G	NX6563	54°56·9'	4°6·0'W	H	83,84
Craigelwhan	D & G	NX8175	55°3·6'	3°51·4'W	H	84
Craigenally	D & G	NX7467	54°59·2'	3°57·7'W	X	83,84
Craigenbeast	D & G	NX7194	55°13·7'	4°1·3'W	X	77
Craigencallie	S Ayr	NS3801	55°16·8'	4°32·6'W	X	77
Craigencallie Ho	D & G	NX5077	55°4·1'	4°20·5'W	X	77
Craigencallie Lane	D & G	NX5076	55°3·6'	4°20·5'W	W	77
Craigencalt	Fife	NT2587	56°4·5'	3°11·9'W	X	66
Craigencarse	D & G	NX6695	55°14·1'	4°6·0'W	X	77
Craigencat Craigs	Fife	NT1095	56°8·6'	3°26·5'W	X	58
Craigencolon	D & G	NX5096	55°14·4'	4°21·1'W	H	77
Craigencoon	D & G	NX7795	55°14·3'	3°55·6'W	X	78
Craigencorr Hill	D & G	NX6487	55°9·8'	4°7·7'W	X	77
Craigencrosh	D & G	NX0853	54°50·4'	4°59·0'W	X	82
Craigencross	D & G	NX0263	54°55·6'	5°5·0'W	X	82
Craigencrow	Fife	NT0995	56°8·6'	3°27·4'W	X	58
Craigend	Angus	NO5839	56°32·7'	2°40·5'W	T	54
Craigend	Angus	NO5857	56°42·4'	2°40·7'W	X	54
Craigend	C of Edin	NT1275	55°57·9'	3°24·1'W	X	65
Craigend	C of Glas	NS6566	55°52·4'	4°9·0'W	T	64
Craigend	D & G	NX6476	55°3·8'	4°7·3'W	X	77
Craigend	D & G	NX9974	55°3·3'	3°34·4'W	X	84
Craigend	E Renf	NS5357	55°47·3'	4°20·2'W	X	64
Craigend	Falk	NS9072	55°56·0'	3°45·2'W	X	65
Craigend	Falk	NS9375	55°57·6'	3°42·4'W	X	65
Craigend	Fife	NT2099	56°10·9'	3°16·9'W	X	58
Craigend	Moray	NJ1353	57°33·8'	3°26·8'W	X	28
Craigend	Pth & Kin	NN9925	56°24·6'	3°37·8'W	X	52,53,58
Craigend	Pth & Kin	NO0748	56°37·1'	3°30·5'W	X	52,53
Craigend	Pth & Kin	NO0942	56°33·9'	3°28·4'W	X	52,53
Craigend	Pth & Kin	NO1120	56°22·1'	3°26·0'W	X	53,58
Craigend	Renf	NS4570	55°54·1'	4°28·3'W	X	64
Craigend	Scot Bord	NT4545	55°42·0'	2°52·1'W	T	73
Craigend	S Lanak	NS6049	55°43·1'	4°13·3'W	X	64
Craigend	S Lanak	NS8233	55°34·8'	3°51·9'W	X	71,72
Craigend	S Lanak	NS8950	55°44·1'	3°45·6'W	X	65,72
Craigend	Stir	NS6190	56°5·2'	4°13·6'W	X	57

Craigend	Stir	NS7887	56°3·9'	3°57·1'W	T	57
Craigend	W Loth	NS9673	55°56·6'	3°39·5'W	X	65
Craigendarroch	Aberd	NO3696	57°3·3'	3°2·9'W	H	37,44
Craigend Castle	Stir	NS5477	55°58·1'	4°19·9'W	X	64
Craigend Fm	E Dunb	NS5978	55°58·7'	4°15·1'W	FM	64
Craigend Hill	Aberd	NJ4534	57°23·8'	2°54·5'W	X	28,29
Craigend Hill	Scot Bord	NT4446	55°42·5'	2°53·0'W	H	73
Craigendhill	S Lanak	NS6951	55°44·3'	4°4·8'W	X	64
Craigendinnie	Aberd	NO5196	57°3·4'	2°48·0'W	H	37,44
Craigendive	Arg & Bt	NS0583	56°0·3'	5°7·2'W	X	56
Craigend Muir	E Dunb	NS5877	55°58·2'	4°16·1'W	X	64
Craigend of Careston	Angus	NO5460	56°44·0'	2°44·7'W	X	44
Craigendoran	Arg & Bt	NS3181	55°59·8'	4°42·2'W	T	63
Craigendous	D & G	NX3547	54°47·7'	4°33·6'W	X	83
Craigendowie	Angus	NO5269	56°48·9'	2°46·7'W	X	44
Craigends	E Ayr	NS5243	55°39·7'	4°20·7'W	X	70
Craigends	N Lanak	NS7963	55°51·0'	3°55·5'W	X	64
Craigends	Renf	NS4166	55°51·9'	4°32·0'W	T	64
Craigends Dennistoun	Inverc	NS3667	55°52·4'	4°36·8'W	X	63
Craigendunton	E Ayr	NS5145	55°40·8'	4°21·7'W	X	64
Craigendunton Resr	E Ayr	NS5245	55°40·8'	4°20·8'W	W	64
Craigenfaulds Moss	E Ayr	NS5247	55°41·9'	4°20·9'W	X	64
Craigenfeoch	Renf	NS4360	55°48·7'	4°29·9'W	X	64
Craigengall	W Loth	NS9271	55°55·5'	3°43·3'W	X	65
Craigengar	Scot Bord	NT0955	55°47·0'	3°26·6'W	X	65,72
Craigen Gaw	Fife	NO2007	56°15·2'	3°17·0'W	X	58
Craigengelt	Stir	NS7485	56°2·7'	4°0·9'W	X	57
Craigengelt Hill	Stir	NS7286	56°3·2'	4°2·9'W	H	57
Craigengillan	D & G	NX6394	55°13·5'	4°8·8'W	X	77
Craigengillan	E Ayr	NS4702	55°17·6'	4°24·1'W	X	77
Craigengillan Burn	D & G	NX6294	55°13·5'	4°9·7'W	W	77
Craigengillan Hill	D & G	NX6295	55°14·0'	4°9·8'W	H	77
Craigengillan Home Fm	E Ayr	NS4703	55°18·1'	4°24·2'W	FM	77
Craigengour	N Ayr	NS1756	55°46·0'	4°54·6'W	X	63
Craigengower	S Ayr	NS3805	55°17·9'	4°32·7'W	X	77
Craigenhigh	Aberd	NJ6208	57°9·9'	2°37·2'W	X	37
Craigenholly	D & G	NX1858	54°53·7'	4°49·8'W	X	82
Craigenhouses	Arg & Bt	NR5267	55°50·2'	5°57·2'W	T	61
Craigenjig	D & G	NX3882	55°6·6'	4°32·0'W	X	77
Craigenlee	D & G	NX0256	54°51·8'	5°4·7'W	X	82
Craigenlee Croft	D & G	NX0256	54°51·8'	5°4·7'W	X	82
Craigenlee Fell	D & G	NX0257	54°52·4'	5°4·7'W	H	82
Craigenloch Hill	Pth & Kin	NO1669	56°48·6'	3°22·1'W	H	43
Craigenputtock	D & G	NX7782	55°7·3'	3°55·3'W	X	78
Craigenputtock Burn	D & G	NX7681	55°6·7'	3°56·2'W	W	78
Craigenputtock Moor	D & G	NX7783	55°7·8'	3°55·3'W	X	78
Craigenquarroch	D & G	NX0455	54°51·3'	5°2·8'W	X	82
Craigenrae	S Ayr	NX3589	55°10·3'	4°35·0'W	X	77
Craigenreoch	S Ayr	NX3391	55°11·4'	4°37·0'W	H	76
Craigenroan	Moray	NJ4467	57°41·6'	2°55·9'W	X	28
Craigenroy	D & G	NX4074	55°2·3'	4°29·8'W	X	77
Craigens	Arg & Bt	NR2967	55°49·5'	6°19·2'W	X	60
Craigens	E Ayr	NS5818	55°26·4'	4°14·2'W	T	71
Craigens	Pth & Kin	NN9318	56°20·8'	3°41·5'W	X	58
Craigenscore Hill	Aberd	NJ4223	57°17·9'	2°57·3'W	H	37
Craigenseat	Aberd	NJ5538	57°26·1'	2°44·5'W	X	29
Craigenseat	Moray	NJ4653	57°34·1'	2°53·7'W	X	28,29
Craigens Hill	S Ayr	NS2504	55°18·2'	4°45·0'W	X	76
Craigentaggart	Arg & Bt	NM8924	56°21·9'	5°24·5'W	X	49
Craigentaggert Hill	Pth & Kin	NN9005	56°13·7'	3°46·0'W	H	58
Craigentarrie	C of Edin	NT1964	55°52·0'	3°17·2'W	X	65,66
Craigentath	Aberd	NO8797	57°4·1'	2°12·4'W	X	38,45
Craigentinny	C of Edin	NT2974	55°57·5'	3°7·8'W	T	66
Craigenton	S Ayr	NS2305	55°18·7'	4°46·9'W	X	70,76
Craigenveoch	D & G	NX2356	54°52·3'	4°45·1'W	X	82
Craigenveoch Fell	D & G	NX2356	54°52·3'	4°45·1'W	H	82
Craigenvey	D & G	NX7784	55°8·4'	3°55·3'W	X	78
Craigenvey Moor	D & G	NX7783	55°7·8'	3°55·3'W	X	78
Craigenwallie	D & G	NX5491	55°11·8'	4°17·2'W	X	77
Craigerne	Scot Bord	NT2539	55°38·6'	3°11·1'W	T	73
Craig Esgeirydd	Cered	SN7357	52°12·0'	3°51·1'W	X	146,147
Craiget Stone	D & G	NX3879	55°5·0'	4°31·9'W	X	77
Craig-Evan-Leyshan Common	Rho Cyn Taf	ST0893	51°37·9'	3°19·4'W	X	170
Craigeven Bay	Aberd	NO8887	56°58·7'	2°11·4'W	W	45
Craigewan	Aberd	NK1248	57°31·6'	1°47·5'W	X	30
Craigfad	S Ayr	NS3802	55°17·4'	4°32·6'W	X	77
Craigfad Fm	Arg & Bt	NR2355	55°42·8'	6°24·2'W	FM	60
Craig-fadyn	Gwyn	SH5806	52°38·2'	4°5·5'W	X	124
Craig Fan Las	Powys	SO0519	51°51·9'	3°22·4'W	X	160
Craig Fapi	Caer	ST2394	51°38·6'	3°6·4'W	X	171
Craigfarg	Pth & Kin	NO1010	56°16·7'	3°26·8'W	X	58
Craig-fawr	Conwy	SH6965	53°10·2'	3°57·2'W	X	115
Craig Fawr	Powys	SH9007	52°39·2'	3°37·2'W	X	125
Craig Fawr	Powys	SJ1826	52°49·8'	3°12·6'W	X	125
Craig Fawr	Powys	SN8763	52°15·5'	3°38·9'W	H	147
Craig Fell	D & G	NT1103	55°19·0'	3°23·7'W	H	78
Craig Fell	D & G	NT1301	55°18·0'	3°21·8'W	H	78
Craig Fell	D & G	NX1761	54°54·9'	4°50·9'W	H	82
Craig Ferrar	Aberd	NO4999	57°5·0'	2°50·0'W	H	37,44
Craig Filain	Cered	SN2352	52°8·5'	4°34·8'W	X	145
Craigfin	S Ayr	NS2906	55°19·4'	4°41·3'W	X	70,76
Craigfin Wood	S Ayr	NS3005	55°18·9'	4°40·3'W	F	70,76
Craigfionn	E Ayr	NX4491	55°11·6'	4°26·6'W	H	77
Craigfionn	E Ayr	NX4593	55°12·7'	4°25·7'W	X	77
Craig Fm	Carm	SN5514	51°48·6'	4°5·8'W	FM	159
Craig Fm	S Ayr	NX1686	55°8·3'	4°52·8'W	FM	76
Craig Foel-y-ddinas	Gwyn	SH9531	52°52·2'	3°33·2'W	X	125
Craig Fonvuick	Pth & Kin	NN9062	56°44·5'	3°47·5'W	H	43
Craigfoodie	Fife	NO4017	56°20·7'	2°57·8'W	X	59
Craig-For	Powys	SH8810	52°40·8'	3°39·0'W	X	124,125
Craig Formal	Pth & Kin	NN8545	56°35·2'	3°51·9'W	H	52
Craigforth Ho	Stir	NS7794	56°7·6'	3°58·3'W	X	57
Craigforthie	Aberd	NJ8019	57°15·9'	2°19·4'W	X	38
Craigfryn	Powys	SN9598	52°34·4'	3°32·6'W	X	136
Craigfryn	Powys	SO0186	52°28·0'	3°27·0'W	X	136
Craigfryn	Powys	SO0193	52°31·8'	3°27·2'W	X	136
Craig Furnace	Caer	ST2496	51°39·7'	3°5·5'W	X	171
Craig Gamhyll	Powys	SJ1828	52°50·8'	3°12·7'W	X	125
Craig Garth-bwlch	Powys	SJ0218	52°45·3'	3°26·7'W	H	125

Craig Gate	Orkney	ND2097	58°51·4'	3°22·7'W	X	7
Craiggaveral	Fife	NT0894	56°8·0'	3°28·4'W	X	58
Craig Gellidywyll	Powys	SN9576	52°22·6'	3°32·2'W	H	136,147
Craig Gellinudd	Nth Pt Talb	SN7304	51°43·5'	3°49·9'W	X	170
Craig Gibbon	Pth & Kin	NO0137	56°31·1'	3°36·1'W	H	52,53
Craiggie Cat	Aberd	NO8492	57°1·4'	2°15·4'W	T	38,45
Craig Glan-siôn	Caer	ST2296	51°39·7'	3°7·3'W	X	171
Craig Glas	Aberd	NJ4108	57°9·8'	2°58·1'W	H	37
Craigglas	Arg & Bt	NR8490	56°3·5'	5°27·7'W	X	55
Craig Glass Burn	Arg & Bt	NR8388	56°2·4'	5°28·6'W	W	55
Craig-goch	Gwyn	SH8010	52°40·7'	3°46·1'W	X	124,125
Craig Goch Reservoir	Powys	SN8969	52°18·7'	3°37·3'W	W	135,136,147
Craiggowrie	Highld	NH9613	57°12·0'	3°42·8'W	H	36
Craiggowrie Burn	Highld	NH9614	57°12·6'	3°42·8'W	W	36
Craig Gwaun Taf	Powys	SO0020	51°52·4'	3°26·8'W	X	160
Craig Gwent	Newp	ST2599	51°41·3'	3°4·7'W	X	171
Craig Gwladus	Nth Pt Talb	SS7699	51°40·8'	3°47·2'W	X	170
Craiggy Ford	Cumbr	NY4977	55°5·3'	2°47·5'W	X	86
Craig Gyfynys	Gwyn	SH6838	52°55·6'	3°57·4'W	H	124
Craig Hafodwen	Conwy	SH7375	53°15·7'	3°53·8'W	X	115
Craighalbert	N Lanak	NS7475	55°57·3'	4°0·6'W	X	64
Craighall	Aberd	NJ4243	57°28·7'	2°57·6'W	X	28
Craig Hall	Aberd	NJ5229	57°21·2'	2°47·4'W	X	37
Craighall	Fife	NO4010	56°17·0'	2°57·7'W	X	59
Craighall	Pth & Kin	NO0817	56°20·4'	3°28·9'W	X	58
Craighall	Pth & Kin	NO1032	56°28·5'	3°27·2'W	X	53
Craighall	Pth & Kin	NO1748	56°37·2'	3°20·7'W	X	53
Craighall	S Lanak	NS5952	55°44·7'	4°14·3'W	X	64
Craighall Burn	Fife	NO4010	56°17·0'	2°57·7'W	W	59
Craighall Dam	E Renf	NS4755	55°46·1'	4°25·9'W	W	64
Craighall Mains	Fife	NO4011	56°17·5'	2°57·7'W	X	59
Craighalloch Moor	D & G	NX3354	54°51·4'	4°35·7'W	X	82
Craig Hammel	Highld	ND3646	58°24·1'	3°5·2'W	X	12
Craighandle	D & G	NX4771	55°0·9'	4°23·1'W	H	77
Craigharr	Aberd	NJ8221	57°17·0'	2°17·5'W	X	38
Craig Hartle	Fife	NO5814	56°19·2'	2°40·3'W	X	59
Craighat	Stir	NS4984	56°1·8'	4°25·0'W	T	57,64
Craighaugh	D & G	NY2498	55°16·5'	3°11·3'W	X	79
Craig Hd	Fife	NO4228	56°26·7'	2°56·0'W	X	54,59
Craighead	Aberd	NJ4940	57°27·1'	2°50·5'W	T	28,29
Craighead	Aberd	NJ9001	57°6·2'	2°9·5'W	X	38
Craighead	Aberd	NK0837	57°25·7'	1°51·5'W	X	30
Craighead	Aberd	NO7869	56°49·0'	2°21·2'W	X	45
Craighead	Aberd	NO8175	56°52·2'	2°18·3'W	X	45
Craighead	Angus	NO2163	56°45·4'	3°17·1'W	X	44
Craighead	E Ayr	NS4251	55°43·9'	4°30·5'W	X	64
Craighead	E Ayr	NS4832	55°33·7'	4°24·2'W	X	70
Craighead	E Ayr	NS4930	55°32·7'	4°23·2'W	X	70
Craighead	E Dunb	NS6074	55°56·6'	4°14·1'W	X	64
Craighead	Fife	NO6309	56°16·6'	2°35·4'W	X	59
Craighead	Highld	NH7561	57°37·6'	4°5·1'W	X	21,27
Craighead	Highld	NH9653	57°33·6'	3°43·8'W	X	27
Craighead	Moray	NJ1924	57°18·2'	3°20·2'W	X	36
Craighead	Moray	NJ2331	57°22·0'	3°16·4'W	X	36
Craighead	Moray	NJ3451	57°32·9'	3°5·7'W	X	28
Craig Head	Moray	NJ4567	57°41·6'	2°54·9'W	X	28,29
Craighead	N Ayr	NS2848	55°42·0'	4°43·8'W	X	63
Craighead	Pth & Kin	NN8007	56°14·7'	3°55·7'W	X	57
Craighead	Pth & Kin	NO0331	56°27·9'	3°34·0'W	X	52,53
Craighead	Pth & Kin	NO0811	56°17·2'	3°28·7'W	X	58
Craighead	Pth & Kin	NO1255	56°41·0'	3°25·7'W	X	53
Craighead	Pth & Kin	NO1954	56°40·5'	3°18·9'W	X	53
Craig Head	Scot Bord	NT1229	55°33·1'	3°23·3'W	H	72
Craig Head	Scot Bord	NT1721	55°28·8'	3°18·4'W	H	72
Craighead	Scot Bord	NT4139	55°38·7'	2°55·8'W	X	73
Craighead	S Lanak	NS7057	55°47·6'	4°4·0'W	X	64
Craighead	S Lanak	NS8140	55°38·6'	3°53·0'W	X	71,72
Craighead	S Lanak	NS9123	55°29·6'	3°43·1'W	X	71,72
Craighead	Stir	NS6898	56°9·6'	4°7·1'W	X	57
Craighead	W Loth	NS9560	55°49·6'	3°40·1'W	X	65
Craighead Cottage	E Loth	NT5081	56°1·4'	2°47·7'W	X	66
Craighead Fm	Pth & Kin	NO0403	56°12·9'	3°32·4'W	FM	58
Craighead Fm	S Lanak	NS8849	55°43·5'	3°46·6'W	FM	72
Craighead Hill	S Lanak	NS9223	55°29·6'	3°42·1'W	H	71,72
Craighead Plantn	D & G	NX8383	55°7·9'	3°49·7'W	F	78
Craig Hen-gae	Gwyn	SH7510	52°40·6'	3°50·5'W	X	124
Craigherron	D & G	NX5367	54°58·8'	4°17·4'W	X	83
Craig Hill	Aberd	NJ5315	57°13·7'	2°46·3'W	H	37
Craighill	Aberd	NJ5721	57°16·9'	2°42·3'W	X	37
Craighill	Aberd	NJ7247	57°31·0'	2°27·6'W	X	29
Craighill	Aberd	NJ9201	57°6·2'	2°7·5'W	X	38
Craighill	Aberd	NJ9357	57°36·4'	2°6·6'W	X	30
Craighill	Angus	NO4335	56°30·5'	2°55·1'W	X	54
Craig Hill	Angus	NO4366	56°47·2'	2°55·5'W	X	44
Craig Hill	Cumbr	NY5765	54°58·9'	2°39·9'W	H	86
Craig Hill	D & G	NT0206	55°20·5'	3°32·3'W	H	78
Craig Hill	D & G	NX5263	54°56·6'	4°18·2'W	H	83
Craig Hill	D & G	NX6667	54°59·0'	4°5·2'W	H	83,84
Craig Hill	D & G	NX6876	55°3·9'	4°3·5'W	X	77,84
Craig Hill	D & G	NX7569	55°0·2'	3°56·8'W	H	84
Craig Hill	D & G	NY3387	55°10·6'	3°2·7'W	H	79
Craig Hill	Highld	ND3369	58°36·5'	3°8·7'W	X	12
Craig Hill	Pth & Kin	NN8145	56°35·2'	3°55·8'W	H	52
Craig Hill	S Ayr	NS3902	55°17·4'	4°31·7'W	H	77
Craig Hill	S Ayr	NX1687	55°8·8'	4°52·8'W	H	76
Craig Hill	S Ayr	NX2899	55°15·6'	4°42·0'W	X	76
Craig Hill	Scot Bord	NT2415	55°25·6'	3°11·6'W	H	79
Craighill	Scot Bord	NT2614	55°25·1'	3°9·7'W	X	79
Craig Hill	Scot Bord	NT2925	55°31·1'	3°7·0'W	H	73
Craig Hill	Scot Bord	NT3215	55°25·7'	3°4·0'W	H	79
Craig Hill	Scot Bord	NT4433	55°35·5'	2°52·9'W	H	73
Craig Hill	S Lanak	NT0023	55°29·7'	3°34·5'W	H	72
Craighirst	W Dunb	NS4876	55°57·4'	4°25·6'W	X	64
Craighit	D & G	NX5392	55°12·3'	4°18·2'W	H	77
Craighlaw	D & G	NX3061	54°55·1'	4°38·7'W	A	82
Craighlaw Mains	D & G	NX3060	54°54·6'	4°38·7'W	X	82
Craig Ho	Angus	NO7056	56°42·0'	2°28·9'W	X	45
Craig Ho	C of Edin	NT2370	55°55·3'	3°13·5'W	A	66
Craig Ho	E Ayr	NS3737	55°36·2'	4°34·8'W	X	70
Craig Ho	Fife	NT0292	56°6·9'	3°34·1'W	X	58

Craig Ho	Pth & Kin	NO0427	56°25·8'	3°33·0'W	X	52,53,58
Craig Ho	S Ayr	NX1786	55°8·3'	4°51·8'W	X	76
Craighoar Hill	D & G	NT0002	55°18·4'	3°34·1'W	H	78
Craighope	Scot Bord	NT2945	55°41·8'	3°7·3'W	X	73
Craig Hope	Scot Bord	NT3046	55°42·4'	3°6·4'W	X	73
Craighope Burn	Scot Bord	NT2827	55°32·1'	3°8·0'W	W	73
Craighope Burn	Scot Bord	NT3727	55°32·2'	2°59·5'W	W	73
Craighorn	Clackm	NN8800	56°11·0'	3°47·8'W	H	58
Craighouse	Arg & Bt	NR5267	55°50·2'	5°57·2'W	T	61
Craighouse	D & G	NY1884	55°8·9'	3°16·8'W	X	79
Craighouse	D & G	NY2377	55°5·1'	3°12·0'W	X	85
Craighouse	Scot Bord	NT6035	55°36·7'	2°37·7'W	X	74
Craighousesteads Hill	D & G	NY2385	55°9·5'	3°12·1'W	X	79
Craig Hulich	Pth & Kin	NN8937	56°31·0'	3°47·8'W	H	52
Craigie	Aberd	NJ9119	57°16·0'	2°8·5'W	X	38
Craigie	C of Dun	NO4231	56°28·3'	2°56·0'W	T	54
Craigie	D & G	NX3473	55°1·7'	4°35·4'W	X	76
Craigie	Fife	NO4524	56°24·6'	2°53·0'W	X	54,59
Craigie	Pth & Kin	NO1122	56°23·2'	3°26·0'W	T	53,58
Craigie	Pth & Kin	NO1143	56°34·5'	3°26·5'W	T	53
Craigie	S Ayr	NS3421	55°27·5'	4°37·1'W	T	70
Craigie	S Ayr	NS4232	55°33·6'	4°29·9'W	T	70
Craigiebanks	Aberd	NJ9566	57°41·3'	2°4·6'W	X	30
Craigiebeg Hill	Aberd	NJ4915	57°13·6'	2°50·2'W	H	37
Craigiebrae	Aberd	NJ6153	57°34·2'	2°38·7'W	X	29
Craigie Brae	Aberd	NJ8834	57°24·0'	2°11·5'W	X	30
Craigiebuckler	C of Aber	NJ9005	57°8·4'	2°9·5'W	T	38
Craigieburn	D & G	NT1105	55°20·1'	3°23·8'W	X	78
Craigie Burn	D & G	NT1106	55°20·7'	3°23·8'W	W	78
Craigie Burn	D & G	NY0873	55°2·8'	3°26·0'W	W	85
Craigieburn	Falk	NS8578	55°59·1'	3°50·2'W	X	65
Craigieburn Hill	D & G	NT1206	55°20·7'	3°22·8'W	H	78
Craigiedaff	Aberd	NO7994	57°2·5'	2°20·3'W	X	38,45
Craigiedarg	Aberd	NJ7608	57°10·0'	2°23·4'W	X	38
Craigie Doubs	Angus	NO1776	56°52·3'	3°21·2'W	H	43
Craigiefield	Orkney	HY4512	58°59·8'	2°57·0'W	X	6
Craigiefold	Aberd	NJ9265	57°40·7'	2°7·6'W	X	30
Craigieford	Aberd	NJ5660	57°37·9'	2°43·7'W	X	29
Craigieford	Aberd	NJ5930	57°21·8'	2°40·4'W	X	29,37
Craigieford	Aberd	NJ9728	57°20·8'	2°2·5'W	X	38
Craigie Fort	Stir	NS4190	56°4·8'	4°32·9'W	X	56
Craigiehall	C of Edin	NT1675	55°57·9'	3°20·3'W	T	65,66
Craigiehall	S Lanak	NS9949	55°43·7'	3°36·1'W	X	72
Craigiehall Temple	C of Edin	NT1774	55°57·4'	3°19·3'W	X	65,66
Craigie Hill	D & G	NY2893	55°13·8'	3°7·5'W	X	79
Craigie Hill	Fife	NO4424	56°24·6'	2°54·0'W	H	54,59
Craigie Hill	S Ayr	NS4232	55°33·6'	4°29·9'W	H	70
Craigieholm	Pth & Kin	NO1634	56°29·7'	3°21·4'W	X	53
Craigiehowe	Highld	NH6852	57°32·6'	4°11·9'W	H	26
Craigielandshill	D & G	NT0701	55°17·9'	3°27·5'W	X	78
Craigielands Ho	D & G	NT0701	55°17·9'	3°27·5'W	X	78
Craigie Law	Angus	NO2265	56°46·5'	3°16·1'W	H	44
Craigielaw	E Loth	NT4579	56°0·3'	2°52·5'W	T	66
Craigielaw Point	E Loth	NT4480	56°0·8'	2°53·5'W	X	66
Craigie Linn	D & G	NX5865	54°57·8'	4°12·7'W	W	83
Craigieloch	Angus	NO2753	56°40·0'	3°11·0'W	X	53
Craigie Loch	S Ayr	NX2476	55°3·1'	4°44·9'W	W	76
Craigie Mains	S Ayr	NS4031	55°33·0'	4°31·7'W	X	70
Craigiemeg	Angus	NO3067	56°47·6'	3°8·3'W	X	44
Craigiemeg Hill	Angus	NO3068	56°48·2'	3°8·3'W	X	44
Craigierig	Scot Bord	NT2023	55°29·9'	3°15·6'W	T	73
Craigierig Burn	Scot Bord	NT1924	55°30·4'	3°16·5'W	W	72
Craigies	Aberd	NJ8529	57°21·3'	2°14·5'W	X	38
Craigies	Angus	NO4060	56°43·9'	2°58·4'W	X	44
Craigie Sike	Scot Bord	NT6054	55°46·9'	2°37·8'W	W	67,74
Craigie Thieves	Angus	NO2469	56°48·6'	3°14·2'W	H	44
Craigietocher	Aberd	NJ7246	57°30·5'	2°27·6'W	X	29
Craigievar Castle	Aberd	NJ5609	57°10·4'	2°43·2'W	A	37
Craigiewells	Fife	NO5202	56°12·7'	2°46·0'W	X	59
Craig Ifan	Cered	SN6854	52°10·4'	3°55·4'W	X	146
Craigingles Wood	Aberd	NO8799	57°5·2'	2°12·4'W	F	38,45
Craiginmoddie	S Ayr	NX3098	55°15·1'	4°40·0'W	H	76
Craiginour	Aberd	NO7486	56°58·1'	2°25·2'W	H	45
Craig Isallt	Gwyn	SH5345	52°59·2'	4°11·0'W	X	115
Craigisla Ho	Angus	NO2553	56°40·0'	3°13·0'W	X	53
Craig Kipmaclyne	Pth & Kin	NN8726	56°25·0'	3°49·5'W	H	52,58
Craigknowe	S Lanak	NS6859	55°48·6'	4°6·0'W	X	64
Craig Knuckle	D & G	NX5687	55°9·6'	4°15·2'W	X	77
Craig Laggan or Ebbstone		NW9569	54°58·7'	5°11·8'W	X	82
Craiglaigh Hill	S Ayr	NX3489	55°10·3'	4°36·0'W	H	76
Craig Lair	Angus	NO2169	56°48·6'	3°17·2'W	H	44
Craiglands	D & G	NY1876	55°4·6'	3°16·6'W	X	85
Craig Lan-las	Cered	SN7574	52°21·2'	3°49·7'W	X	135,147
Craiglarie Fell	D & G	NX3154	54°51·4'	4°37·5'W	X	82
Craiglarie Moss	D & G	NX3255	54°51·9'	4°36·6'W	X	82
Craig-las	Gwyn	SH6713	52°42·1'	3°57·7'W	H	124
Craig-Lâs	Powys	SJ0324	52°48·5'	3°25·9'W	X	125
Craiglaseithin	Gwyn	SH7333	52°53·0'	3°52·8'W	H	124
Craig Lash	Aberd	NO5792	57°1·3'	2°42·0'W	H	44
Craiglash	Aberd	NO6298	57°4·5'	2°37·2'W	X	37,45
Craiglas Ho	Powys	SO1121	51°53·1'	3°17·2'W	X	161
Craiglatch	Scot Bord	NT4337	55°37·6'	2°53·9'W	X	73
Craig Law	Fife	NO4428	56°26·7'	2°54·1'W	H	54,59
Craiglaw	Pth & Kin	NO0298	56°10·1'	3°34·3'W	X	58
Craig Law	Scot Bord	NT0920	55°28·2'	3°25·9'W	H	72
Craig Lea	Durham	NZ1436	54°43·4'	1°46·5'W	X	92
Craiglea	Highld	NH6056	57°34·6'	4°20·0'W	X	26
Craig Lea	Pth & Kin	NN9432	56°28·4'	3°42·8'W	H	52,53
Craig Leach	Highld	NH6141	57°26·5'	4°18·5'W	X	26
Craiglea Hill	Aberd	NJ4710	57°10·9'	2°52·1'W	H	37
Craiglea Hill	Angus	NO2456	56°41·6'	3°14·0'W	H	53
Craiglearan	D & G	NX7192	55°12·6'	4°1·2'W	X	77
Craiglearan Burn	D & G	NX7092	55°12·6'	4°2·2'W	W	77
Craiglee	D & G	NX4680	55°5·7'	4°24·4'W	H	77
Craiglee	E Ayr	NX4896	55°14·3'	4°23·0'W	H	77
Craig Leek	Aberd	NO1893	57°1·5'	3°20·6'W	H	36,43
Craigleith	Clackm	NS8798	56°9·9'	3°48·7'W	X	58
Craigleith	C of Edin	NT2374	55°57·4'	3°13·6'W	T	66
Craigleith	E Loth	NT5586	56°4·1'	2°42·9'W	X	66
Craigleith	W Dunb	NS4673	55°55·8'	4°27·5'W	X	64

Craiglemine	D & G	NX4039	54°43·5′	4°28·6′W	X	83
Craiglethie	Moray	NJ4952	57°33·6′	2°50·7′W	X	28,29
Craiglethy	Aberd	NO8881	56°55·5′	2°11·4′W	X	45
Craigley	D & G	NX7658	54°54·3′	3°55·6′W	X	84
Craigley	D & G	NX8468	54°59·8′	3°48·4′W	X	84
Craiglich	Aberd	NJ5305	57°8·3′	2°46·1′W	H	37
Craiglin	Arg & Bt	NR7787	56°1·7′	5°34·3′W	X	55
Craiglinscheoch	Inverc	NS3268	55°52·8′	4°40·7′W	X	63
Craiglirian Craig	D & G	NX6992	55°12·5′	4°3·1′W	X	77
Craig Llangiwg	Nth Pt Talb	SN7205	51°44·0′	3°50·8′W	T	160
Craig Llech-gwynt	Carm	SN7242	52°3·9′	3°51·6′W	X	146,147,160
Craig Lledr	Conwy	SH7853	53°3·9′	3°48·8′W	X	115
Craig Llugwy	Conwy	SH6762	53°8·6′	3°58·9′W	X	115
Craig-llwyn	Shrops	SJ2327	52°50·3′	3°8·2′W	T	126
Craig Llys-fedw	Carm	SN7446	52°6·1′	3°50·0′W	X	146,147
Craig Loch	D & G	NX6967	54°59·1′	4°2·4′W	W	83,84
Craig Loch	Orkney	HY4451	59°20·8′	2°58·6′W	W	5
Craig Lochie	Pth & Kin	NN9448	56°37·0′	3°43·2′W	H	52,53
Craiglochie Ho	Pth & Kin	NO2024	56°24·3′	3°17·3′W	X	53,58
Craiglockhart	C of Edin	NT2270	55°55·3′	3°14·4′W	T	66
Craig Lodge	Arg & Bt	NN1727	56°24·2′	4°57·5′W	X	50
Craig Lodge	Arg & Bt	NR9666	55°50·9′	5°15·1′W	X	62
Craig Lodge	Arg & Bt	NS0078	55°57·5′	5°11·8′W	X	62,63
Craig Lodge	D & G	NX2451	54°49·6′	4°44·0′W	X	82
Craig Loisgte	Pth & Kin	NN8056	56°41·1′	3°57·1′W	H	52
Craig Loisgte	Pth & Kin	NO1267	56°47·4′	3°26·0′W	H	43
Craiglowrie	D & G	NX5467	54°58·8′	4°16·5′W	H	83
Craiglowrie Burn	D & G	NX5567	54°58·8′	4°15·5′W	W	83
Craiglug	Aberd	NJ6551	57°33·1′	2°34·6′W	X	29
Craiglug	Aberd	NO8197	57°4·1′	2°18·3′W	X	38,45
Craiglug	C of Aber	NJ8505	57°8·4′	2°14·4′W	X	38
Craiglug	Fife	NO4018	56°21·3′	2°57·8′W	X	59
Craiglug	Moray	NJ3355	57°35·1′	3°6·8′W	X	28
Craiglure	S Ayr	NX4196	55°14·2′	4°29·6′W	H	77
Craigluscar	Fife	NT0690	56°5·9′	3°30·2′W	X	58
Craigluscar Hill	Fife	NT0691	56°6·4′	3°30·2′W	H	58
Craigluscar Resrs	Fife	NT0690	56°5·9′	3°30·2′W	W	58
Craig Lwyd	Gwyn	SH7212	52°41·7′	3°53·2′W	H	124
Craig Lwyd	Pemb	SM9932	51°57·3′	4°55·1′W	X	157
Craig-lwyd-fawr	Powys	SO1420	51°52·6′	3°14·6′W	X	161
Craigmad	Falk	NS9075	55°57·6′	3°45·3′W	X	65
Craigmaddie Ho	E Dunb	NS5776	55°57·6′	4°17·0′W	X	64
Craigmaddie Muir	E Dunb	NS5876	55°57·6′	4°16·0′W	X	64
Craigmaddie Reservior	E Dunb	NS5675	55°57·0′	4°17·9′W	W	64
Craig Maesglase	Gwyn	SH8214	52°42·9′	3°44·4′W	X	124,125
Craig Maes-y-llan	Gwyn	SH6510	52°40·5′	3°59·4′W	X	124
Craigmahandle	Aberd	NO4890	57°0·2′	2°50·9′W	H	44
Craigmaharb	D & G	NX5587	55°9·6′	4°16·1′W	X	77
Craigmaid	Scot Bord	NT0717	55°26·5′	3°27·8′W	H	78
Craigmailing	W Loth	NS9972	55°56·1′	3°36·6′W	X	65
Craigmakerran	Pth & Kin	NO1432	56°28·6′	3°23·3′W	X	53
Craigmalloch	E Ayr	NX4894	55°13·3′	4°22·9′W	X	77
Craigmalloch	S Ayr	NX2894	55°12·9′	4°41·8′W	X	76
Craigman	E Ayr	NS5412	55°23·1′	4°17·8′W	X	70
Craigmancie	Aberd	NJ5946	57°30·4′	2°40·6′W	X	29
Craigmark Hill	E Ayr	NS4708	55°20·8′	4°24·3′W	X	70,77
Craig Marloch	Angus	NO3060	56°43·8′	3°8·2′W	X	44
Craigmarloch	Inverc	NS3471	55°54·5′	4°38·9′W	X	63
Craigmaroinn	Aberd	NO9395	57°3·0′	2°6·5′W	X	38,45
Craig-Marrie Fm	W Loth	NS9169	55°54·4′	3°44·2′W	FM	65
Craigmartin	Aberd	NJ5454	57°34·7′	2°45·7′W	X	29
Craigmasheenie	S Ayr	NX4193	55°12·6′	4°29·5′W	H	77
Craig Maskeldie	Angus	NO3979	56°54·2′	2°59·6′W	H	44
Craigmaud	Aberd	NJ8858	57°37·0′	2°11·6′W	T	30
Craig Maud	Angus	NO2376	56°52·4′	3°15·3′W	X	44
Craigmawhannal	E Ayr	NX4691	55°11·6′	4°24·7′W	H	77
Craigmead	Fife	NO2305	56°14·1′	3°14·1′W	X	58
Craigmeadow	Aberd	NJ6218	57°15·3′	2°37·3′W	X	37
Craig Megen	Aberd	NO3189	56°59·5′	3°7·7′W	H	44
Craigmekie	Angus	NO1969	56°48·6′	3°19·1′W	X	43
Craig Mellon	Angus	NO2676	56°52·4′	3°12·4′W	H	44
Craig-melyn	Rho Cyn Taf	ST0182	51°31·9′	3°25·2′W	X	170
Craig Michael	Angus	NO3685	56°57·4′	3°2·7′W	X	44
Craigmill	Aberd	NJ5411	57°11·5′	2°45·2′W	X	37
Craigmill	Aberd	NJ9047	57°31·0′	2°9·6′W	X	30
Craigmill	Angus	NO5735	56°30·6′	2°41·5′W	T	54
Craigmill	Stir	NS8195	56°8·2′	3°54·5′W	T	57
Craigmillar	C of Edin	NT2871	55°55·9′	3°8·7′W	T	66
Craigmillar Castle	C of Edin	NT2870	55°55·3′	3°8·7′W	A	66
Craigmill Lodge	Moray	NJ1052	57°33·2′	3°29·8′W	X	28
Craigminn	D & G	NX4481	55°6·2′	4°26·3′W	X	77
Craig Minnan	Inverc	NS3264	55°50·7′	4°40·6′W	X	63
Craigmoddie Fell	D & G	NX2472	55°0·9′	4°44·7′W	X	76
Craigmoor Wood	E Loth	NT5781	56°1·5′	2°41·0′W	F	67
Craigmore	Arg & Bt	NS1065	55°50·7′	5°1·7′W	T	63
Craigmore	D & G	NX6971	55°1·2′	4°2·5′W	X	77,84
Craig More	Pth & Kin	NO0446	56°36·0′	3°33·4′W	X	52,53
Craigmore	Stir	NN5102	56°11·5′	4°23·6′W	H	57
Craigmore	Stir	NS5279	55°59·1′	4°21·9′W	X	64
Craigmore Cott	Arg & Bt	NM5641	56°30·1′	5°57·5′W	X	47,48
Craigmore Cott	Stir	NS5279	55°59·1′	4°21·9′W	X	64
Craigmore Hill	D & G	NX9172	55°2·1′	3°41·9′W	H	84
Craigmore Point	D & G	NX5751	54°50·3′	4°13·2′W	X	83
Craigmore Wood	Highld	NJ0222	57°16·9′	3°37·1′W	F	36
Craig Morile	Highld	NH7927	57°19·3′	4°0·1′W	X	35
Craig Moss	D & G	NX9464	54°57·8′	3°38·9′W	X	84
Craigmoston	Aberd	NO6575	56°52·2′	2°34·0′W	X	45
Craigmuie	D & G	NX7386	55°9·4′	3°59·2′W	X	77
Craigmuie Moor	D & G	NX7385	55°8·8′	3°59·1′W	X	77
Craigmuir	Renf	NS4360	55°48·7′	4°29·9′W	X	64
Craigmuir	Renf	NS4469	55°53·6′	4°29·2′W	X	64
Craigmuir	S Lanak	NS7142	55°39·5′	4°2·6′W	X	71
Craigmurchie	D & G	NX3973	55°1·8′	4°30·7′W	H	77
Craig Murrail	Arg & Bt	NR8792	56°4·7′	5°24·9′W	X	55
Craigmyle	Aberd	NJ7416	57°14·3′	2°25·4′W	X	38
Craigmyle Ho	Aberd	NJ6301	57°6·2′	2°36·2′W	X	37
Craig Nabbin	N Ayr	NS1351	55°43·2′	4°58·2′W	X	63,69
Craignacraddoch	D & G	NX3881	55°6·1′	4°31·9′W	X	77
Craignafeoch	Arg & Bt	NR9571	55°53·6′	5°16·3′W	X	62
Craignafeoch Burn	Arg & Bt	NR9571	55°53·6′	5°16·3′W	W	62
Craig na Hash	Pth & Kin	NN9231	56°27·8′	3°44·7′W	H	52
Craignair	D & G	NX8161	54°56·0′	3°51·0′W	X	84
Craignairy	D & G	NX4584	55°7·8′	4°25·4′W	H	77
Craignamoraig	Arg & Bt	NM9616	56°17·8′	5°17·4′W	X	55
Craignane	D & G	NS5804	55°18·8′	4°13·8′W	H	77
Craig nan Sassanach	Arg & Bt	NN0919	56°19·8′	5°4·9′W	H	50,56
Craignant	Gwyn	SH8442	52°58·0′	3°43·2′W	X	124,125
Craignant	Powys	SH9719	52°45·8′	3°31·2′W	X	125
Craignant	Powys	SN9178	52°23·6′	3°35·7′W	X	136,147
Craignant	Shrops	SJ2535	52°54·7′	3°6·5′W	T	126
Craig Nantyfleiddast	Powys	SN8054	52°10·5′	3°44·9′W	X	147
Craignarb	Aberd	NO6799	57°5·1′	2°32·2′W	X	38,45
Craig Narb	Angus	NO5371	56°49·9′	2°45·8′W	X	44
Craignarget	D & G	NX2551	54°49·7′	4°43·0′W	X	82
Craignarget	D & G	NX5170	55°0·4′	4°19·4′W	H	77
Craignarget Burn	D & G	NX2651	54°49·7′	4°42·1′W	W	82
Craignarget Hill	D & G	NX2652	54°50·2′	4°42·1′W	H	82
Craig na Seithe	Pth & Kin	NN7757	56°41·6′	4°0·1′W	X	42,51,52
Craignathro	Angus	NO4648	56°37·5′	2°52·4′W	X	54
Craignathunder	Aberd	NJ6922	57°17·5′	2°30·4′W	X	38
Craignaught Fm	E Ayr	NS4451	55°43·9′	4°28·6′W	FM	64
Craignavar	Pth & Kin	NN8731	56°27·7′	3°49·6′W	X	52
Craignaw	D & G	NX4176	55°3·4′	4°28·9′W	H	77
Craignaw	D & G	NX4583	55°7·3′	4°25·4′W	H	77
Craig Nedd	Nth Pt Talb	SN8203	51°43·0′	3°42·1′W	X	170
Craignee	D & G	NX7590	55°11·6′	3°57·4′W	X	78
Craignee	D & G	NX8194	55°13·8′	3°51·8′W	X	78
Craignee Wood	D & G	NX8294	55°13·8′	3°50·9′W	F	78
Craigneich	Pth & Kin	NN7917	56°20·1′	3°57·0′W	X	57
Craigneil	Aberd	NO7990	57°0·3′	2°20·3′W	H	38,45
Craigneil	S Ayr	NX1485	55°7·7′	4°54·6′W	X	76
Craigneil Hill	S Ayr	NX1484	55°7·2′	4°54·6′W	H	76
Craigneith Castle	S Lanak	NS6655	55°46·4′	4°7·7′W	X	64
Craignelder	D & G	NX5188	55°10·1′	4°19·9′W	X	77
Craignelder Gairy	D & G	NX5189	55°10·6′	4°20·0′W	X	77
Craig Neldricken	D & G	NX4484	55°7·8′	4°26·4′W	X	77
Craignell	D & G	NX5175	55°3·1′	4°19·5′W	X	77
Craignell	D & G	NX5376	55°3·7′	4°17·7′W	X	77
Craigneston Hill	D & G	NX7588	55°10·5′	3°57·3′W	H	78
Craignethan Castle	S Lanak	NS8146	55°41·8′	3°53·2′W	A	72
Craignetherty	Aberd	NJ6448	57°31·5′	2°35·6′W	X	29
Craigneuk	N Lanak	NS7656	55°47·1′	3°58·2′W	T	64
Craigneuk	N Lanak	NS7865	55°52·0′	3°56·5′W	T	64
Craigneuk	Scot Bord	NT4639	55°38·7′	2°51·0′W	X	73
Craigneuk Point	D & G	NX9055	54°52·9′	3°42·5′W	X	84
Craigneuk Wood	Aberd	NJ5324	57°18·5′	2°46·4′W	F	37
Craignine	D & G	NX4566	54°58·1′	4°24·9′W	X	83
Craignish Castle	Arg & Bt	NM7701	56°9·2′	5°35·0′W	A	55
Craignish Point	Arg & Bt	NR7599	56°8·1′	5°36·8′W	X	55
Craignity	Angus	NO2163	56°45·4′	3°17·1′W	X	44
Craigniven	Stir	NS7493	56°7·0′	4°1·2′W	X	57
Craig Nordie	Aberd	NO2394	57°2·1′	3°15·7′W	H	36,44
Craignorth	Pth & Kin	NO1824	56°24·3′	3°19·3′W	X	53,58
Craignorth Hill	D & G	NS8116	55°25·7′	3°52·4′W	H	71,78
Craignuisg	Pth & Kin	NN9551	56°38·6′	3°42·3′W	X	52,53
Craignure	Arg & Bt	NM7136	56°27·9′	5°42·6′W	T	49
Craignure Bay	Arg & Bt	NM7137	56°28·4′	5°42·7′W	W	49
Craig Nyth-y-gigfran	Gwyn	SH6845	52°59·4′	3°57·6′W	X	115
Craigo	Angus	NO6864	56°46·2′	2°31·0′W	T	45
Craigoch	D & G	NX1473	55°1·3′	4°54·1′W	X	76
Craigoch	S Ayr	NS2904	55°18·3′	4°41·2′W	X	76
Craigoch Burn	D & G	NX0167	54°57·7′	5°6·1′W	W	82
Craigoch Burn	D & G	NX1775	55°2·4′	4°51·4′W	W	76
Craigoch Moor	D & G	NX0253	54°50·2′	5°4·6′W	X	82
Craigoch Park Moor	D & G	NX0053	54°50·2′	5°6·4′W	X	82
Craig of Achnabreck	Arg & Bt	NR8691	56°4·1′	5°25·8′W	H	55
Craig of Affrusk	Aberd	NO7093	57°1·9′	2°29·2′W	H	38,45
Craig of Auldallan	Angus	NO3059	56°43·3′	3°8·2′W	H	53
Craig of Balloch	Angus	NO2761	56°44·4′	3°11·2′W	X	44
Craig of Bunzeach	Aberd	NJ3609	57°10·3′	3°3·1′W	H	37
Craig of Cornescorn	Angus	NO5674	56°51·6′	2°42·8′W	X	44
Craig of Dalfro	Aberd	NO6789	56°59·7′	2°32·1′W	H	45
Craig of Dalhastnie	Angus	NO5477	56°53·2′	2°44·8′W	H	44
Craig of Dalwine	S Ayr	NX3496	55°14·1′	4°36·2′W	H	76
Craig of Doune	Angus	NO3983	56°56·3′	2°59·7′W	X	44
Craig of Finnoch	Angus	NO5270	56°49·4′	2°46·7′W	X	44
Craig of Garvock	Aberd	NO7168	56°48·4′	2°28·0′W	X	45
Craig of Gowal	Angus	NO2380	56°54·6′	3°15·4′W	X	44
Craig of Grobdale	D & G	NX6062	54°56·2′	4°10·7′W	H	83
Craig of Knockgray	D & G	NX5794	55°13·4′	4°14·5′W	H	77
Craig of Loinmuie	Aberd	NO3391	57°0·6′	3°5·7′W	H	44
Craig of Neilston	E Renf	NS4755	55°46·1′	4°25·9′W	X	64
Craig of Prony	Aberd	NO3598	57°4·4′	3°3·9′W	H	37,44
Craig of Runavey	Pth & Kin	NO1369	56°48·5′	3°25·0′W	H	43
Craig of Shanno	Angus	NO5575	56°52·1′	2°43·8′W	X	44
Craig of Todholes	Inverc	NS3164	55°50·6′	4°41·5′W	X	63
Craig of Trusta	Angus	NO4865	56°46·7′	2°50·6′W	X	44
Craig Ogwr	Brig	SS9394	51°38·3′	3°32·4′W	X	170
Craigol	Powys	SN9858	52°12·9′	3°29·2′W	X	147
Craigomill	Pth & Kin	NO0905	56°14·0′	3°27·6′W	X	58
Craig Orllwyn	Powys	SJ1626	52°49·7′	3°14·4′W	X	125
Craigoshina	Angus	NO5776	56°52·7′	2°41·9′W	X	44
Craigour	Aberd	NJ6804	57°7·8′	2°31·3′W	H	38
Craigover	Scot Bord	NT6130	55°34·0′	2°36·7′W	X	74
Craigoway Hill	Pth & Kin	NO0914	56°18·8′	3°27·8′W	X	58
Craigower	Pth & Kin	NN9260	56°43·4′	3°45·4′W	H	43
Craigowl Hill	Angus	NO3740	56°33·1′	3°1·0′W	H	54
Craigowmeigle	Pth & Kin	NO0806	56°14·5′	3°28·6′W	X	58
Craigowmill	Pth & Kin	NO0806	56°14·5′	3°28·6′W	X	58
Craig Pant-glas	Caer	ST2496	51°39·7′	3°5·5′W	X	171
Craig Pantshiri	Cered	SN7158	52°12·5′	3°52·9′W	X	146,147
Craigpark	C of Edin	NT1270	55°55·2′	3°24·0′W	X	65
Craig Pen-rhiw-llech	Rho Cyn Taf	SN9702	51°42·7′	3°29·1′W	X	170
Craig Pen-y-buarth	Powys	SJ0327	52°50·2′	3°26·0′W	X	125
Craig Phadrig	Highld	NH6445	57°28·8′	4°15·6′W	H	26
Craig Portas	Gwyn	SH8014	52°42·9′	3°46·2′W	H	124,125
Craigpot Cottage	Aberd	NJ6218	57°15·3′	2°37·3′W	X	37
Craig Pwllfa	Powys	SO0620	51°52·5′	3°21·5′W	X	160
Craig Pysgotwr	Cered	SN7549	52°7·8′	3°49·2′W	X	146,147
Craigquarter	Stir	NS7887	56°3·9′	3°57·1′W	X	57
Craigrae Beg	Aberd	NO4294	57°2·3′	2°56·9′W	H	37,44
Craigrannoch Ho	Highld	NN0559	56°41·2′	5°10·6′W	X	41
Craigraploch	D & G	NX7244	54°46·7′	3°59·0′W	X	83,84
Craigrath	Aberd	NJ6801	57°6·2′	2°31·2′W	H	38
Craigree	D & G	NX3068	54°58·9′	4°39·0′W	X	82
Craig Rennet	Angus	NO2575	56°51·9′	3°13·4′W	X	44
Craigrethill	S Ayr	NS3731	55°33·0′	4°34·6′W	X	70
Craig Rhiwarth	Powys	SJ0526	52°49·6′	3°24·2′W	X	125
Craig Rhiw-ddu	Rho Cyn Taf	SN9801	51°42·1′	3°28·2′W	X	170
Craig Rhosan	Carm	SN7542	52°4·0′	3°49·0′W	X	146,147,160
Craigrie	Clackm	NS9091	56°6·2′	3°45·7′W	X	58
Craig Rig	S Lanak	NS9714	55°24·8′	3°37·2′W	X	78
Craigrine	D & G	NX5087	55°9·5′	4°20·8′W	X	77
Craig River	Highld	NG7963	57°36·4′	5°41·5′W	W	19,24
Craig Roan	D & G	NX8652	54°51·2′	3°46·1′W	X	84
Craig Rock	Fife	NO4304	56°13·8′	2°54·7′W	X	59
Craigronald	D & G	NX5268	54°59·3′	4°18·4′W	X	83
Craigrory	Highld	NH6248	57°30·3′	4°17·7′W	T	26
Craig Rossie	Pth & Kin	NN9812	56°17·6′	3°38·4′W	X	58
Craigrothie	Fife	NO3710	56°17·0′	3°0·6′W	T	59
Craigrothie Burn	Fife	NO3811	56°17·5′	2°59·7′W	W	59
Craigroy	Highld	NH7085	57°50·4′	4°10·9′W	X	21
Craigroy	Highld	NJ0527	57°19·7′	3°34·2′W	X	36
Craigroy	Moray	NJ0451	57°32·6′	3°35·8′W	X	27
Craigroy	Moray	NJ1250	57°32·2′	3°27·7′W	X	28
Craigroy Fm	Moray	NJ1834	57°23·6′	3°21·4′W	FM	28
Craigroy Island	Moray	NJ1839	57°26·3′	3°21·5′W	X	28
Craig Royston	Stir	NN3404	56°12·2′	4°40·1′W	X	56
Craigruadh	Arg & Bt	NR6943	55°37·8′	5°39·7′W	X	62
Craigruie	Stir	NN4920	56°21·2′	4°26·2′W	X	51,57
Craig Ruthven	Highld	NH6227	57°19·0′	4°17·0′W	X	26,35
Craigs	Arg & Bt	NR6823	55°27·0′	5°39·7′W	X	68
Craigs	Cumbr	NY5178	55°5·9′	2°45·6′W	X	86
Craigs	D & G	NX9768	55°0·0′	3°36·2′W	X	84
Craigs	D & G	NY2678	55°5·7′	3°9·1′W	X	85
Craigs	N Lanak	NS7478	55°59·0′	4°0·7′W	X	64
Craigs	S Ayr	NS3733	55°34·1′	4°34·7′W	X	70
Craigs	W Loth	NS9067	55°53·3′	3°45·1′W	X	65
Craigsanquhar	Fife	NO3919	56°21·8′	2°58·8′W	X	59
Craigscorrie	Highld	NH5045	57°28·5′	4°29·6′W	X	26
Craig Selsig	Rho Cyn Taf	SS9197	51°39·9′	3°34·2′W	X	170
Craig's End	Essex	TL7137	52°0·5′	0°29·9′E	T	154
Craigs Farm	D & G	NX9974	55°3·3′	3°34·4′W	FM	84
Craigsford Mains	Scot Bord	NT5638	55°38·3′	2°41·5′W	T	73
Craigs Forest	Highld	NH5392	57°53·9′	4°28·3′W	F	20
Craigs Grain	S Lanak	NS9112	55°23·6′	3°42·8′W	W	71,78
Craigshall	D & G	NX8051	54°50·6′	3°51·7′W	X	84
Craigshannoch	Aberd	NJ6723	57°18·0′	2°32·4′W	X	38
Craigshannoch	Aberd	NJ6905	57°8·3′	2°30·3′W	X	38
Craigshaws	D & G	NY2576	55°4·6′	3°10·1′W	X	85
Craigsheal Burn	Pth & Kin	NO0652	56°39·3′	3°31·5′W	W	52,53
Craigshiel	E Ayr	NS6715	55°24·9′	4°5·6′W	X	71
Craigshield	Northum	NY8077	55°5·5′	2°18·4′W	X	86,87
Craigshields	D & G	NX9892	55°13·0′	3°35·8′W	X	78
Craigs Hill	E Ayr	NS6030	55°32·9′	4°12·7′W	X	71
Craigs Hill	Scot Bord	NT0839	55°38·4′	3°27·3′W	H	72
Craigshill	W Loth	NT0667	55°53·5′	3°29·7′W	T	65
Craigshinnie Burn	D & G	NX5979	55°5·4′	4°12·1′W	W	77
Craigs Ho	Northum	NU1118	55°27·6′	1°49·1′W	X	81
Craig Siarls	Carm	SN7048	52°7·1′	3°53·5′W	H	146,147
Craigside	Aberd	NO7092	57°1·3′	2°29·2′W	X	38,45
Craigside	Conwy	SH8081	53°19·0′	3°47·7′W	X	116
Craigside	Durham	NZ1235	54°42·8′	1°48·4′W	T	92
Craigsimmie	Fife	NO3121	56°22·8′	3°6·6′W	X	53,59
Craigskean	S Ayr	NS2914	55°23·7′	4°41·6′W	X	70
Craigskelly	S Ayr	NX1796	55°13·7′	4°52·2′W	X	76
Craigslave	D & G	NX0057	54°52·3′	5°6·6′W	X	82
Craigs Moss	D & G	NY0173	55°2·8′	3°32·5′W	X	84
Craig Soales	Angus	NO5081	56°55·3′	2°48·8′W	H	44
Craigs of Aultdearg	Moray	NJ1552	57°33·3′	3°24·8′W	X	28
Craigs of Burnfoot	D & G	NX5967	54°58·9′	4°11·8′W	X	83
Craigs of Cuildell	Moray	NJ3355	57°35·1′	3°6·8′W	X	28
Craigs of Inchdowrie	Angus	NO3371	56°49·8′	3°5·4′W	X	44
Craigs of Kyle	S Ayr	NS4215	55°24·5′	4°29·3′W	H	70
Craigs of Lethnot	Angus	NO3665	56°46·6′	3°2·4′W	X	44
Craigs of Loch Wharral	Angus	NO3674	56°51·4′	3°2·5′W	X	44
Craigs of Moniewhitt	Aberd	NJ3113	57°12·4′	3°8·1′W	X	37
Craigs of Sluggan	Moray	NJ1049	57°31·6′	3°29·7′W	H	28
Craigs of Succoth	Aberd	NJ4336	57°24·9′	2°56·5′W	X	28
Craigspark	N Ayr	NS2445	55°40·3′	4°47·5′W	X	63
Craigs Plantation	Fife	NT0684	56°2·6′	3°30·1′W	F	65
Craigstewart	D & G	NX6799	55°16·3′	4°5·2′W	X	77
Craigs, The	Highld	NH4791	57°53·2′	4°34·4′W	X	20
Craigs, The	Scot Bord	NT0714	55°24·9′	3°27·7′W	X	78
Craig Stirling	Aberd	NO9193	57°1·9′	2°8·4′W	X	38,45
Craigston	Aberd	NJ8308	57°10·0′	2°16·4′W	X	38
Craigston	N Eil	NF6601	56°59·0′	7°29·5′W	T	31
Craigston Castle	Aberd	NJ7655	57°35·3′	2°23·6′W	A	29
Craigswalls	Scot Bord	NT8455	55°47·5′	2°14·9′W	X	67,74
Craig Swffryd	Blae Gw	ST2299	51°41·3′	3°7·3′W	X	171
Craigs Windshiel	Scot Bord	NT6961	55°50·7′	2°29·3′W	X	67
Craig Sychtyn	Shrops	SJ2325	52°49·3′	3°8·2′W	X	126
Craigsyke Ford	Cumbr	NY5666	54°59·4′	2°40·8′W	X	86
Craig Talfynydd	Pemb	SN1231	51°57·0′	4°43·8′W	H	145
Craig Tal-y-fan	Brig	SS9286	51°34·0′	3°33·1′W	X	170
Craig Tan-y-bwlch	Conwy	SH7249	53°1·6′	3°54·1′W	X	115
Craigtappock	D & G	NX9460	54°55·7′	3°38·8′W	H	84
Craigtarson	D & G	NS5900	55°16·7′	4°12·8′W	X	77
Craig, The	Aberd	NJ2907	57°9·2′	3°10·0′W	X	37
Craig, The	Aberd	NJ7354	57°34·8′	2°26·6′W	X	29
Craig, The	Aberd	NO7389	56°59·7′	2°26·2′W	H	45
Craig, The	Arg & Bt	NS0679	55°58·1′	5°6·1′W	X	63
Craigthorn	S Lanak	NS7348	55°42·8′	4°0·9′W	X	64
Craigthran	Angus	NO3967	56°47·7′	2°59·5′W	H	44
Craig Tillelet	Angus	NO2669	56°48·7′	3°12·3′W	X	44
Craig Tiribeg	Highld	NH9836	57°24·4′	3°41·4′W	H	27
Craig Tombane	Pth & Kin	NN9341	56°33·2′	3°44·0′W	X	52
Craigton	Aberd	NJ5329	57°21·2′	2°46·4′W	X	37
Craigton	Aberd	NJ5704	57°7·8′	2°42·2′W	X	37
Craigton	Aberd	NJ7100	57°5·7′	2°28·3′W	X	38

Craigton	Angus	NO3250	56°38·5'	3°6·1'W	T	53
Craigton	Angus	NO3961	56°44·5'	2°59·4'W	X	44
Craigton	Angus	NO5138	56°32·1'	2°47·4'W	T	54
Craigton	Clackm	NS9189	56°5·1'	3°44·7'W	X	65
Craigton	C of Aber	NJ8201	57°6·2'	2°17·4'W	X	38
Craigton	C of Glas	NS5464	55°51·1'	4°19·5'W	T	64
Craigton	D & G	NX7960	54°55·5'	3°52·9'W	X	84
Craigton	E Renf	NS4954	55°45·6'	4°24·0'W	X	64
Craigton	Highld	NC6712	58°4·9'	4°14·9'W	X	16
Craigton	Highld	NG9238	57°23·4'	5°27·2'W	X	25
Craigton	Highld	NH6296	57°56·2'	4°19·4'W	X	21
Craigton	Highld	NH6363	57°38·4'	4°17·2'W	X	21
Craigton	Highld	NH6648	57°30·4'	4°13·7'W	T	26
Craigton	N Ayr	NS2162	55°49·3'	4°51·0'W	X	63
Craigton	Pth & Kin	NO0646	56°36·0'	3°31·4'W	X	52,53
Craigton	Pth & Kin	NO1357	56°42·1'	3°24·8'W	X	53
Craigton	Pth & Kin	NT0198	56°10·1'	3°35·2'W	X	58
Craigton	Pth & Kin	NT0999	56°10·8'	3°27·5'W	X	58
Craigton	Renf	NS4470	55°54·1'	4°29·3'W	X	64
Craigton	Stir	NN7804	56°13·0'	3°57·6'W	X	57
Craigton	Stir	NS6286	56°3·1'	4°12·5'W	X	57
Craigton	W Loth	NT0776	55°58·3'	3°29·0'W	X	65
Craigton Burn	E Dunb	NS5276	55°57·5'	4°21·8'W	W	64
Craigton Point	Highld	NH6647	57°29·9'	4°13·7'W	X	26
Craigton Row	D & G	NX7960	54°55·5'	3°52·9'W	X	84
Craigtoun Country Park	Fife	NO4714	56°19·2'	2°51·0'W	X	59
Craigtown	Highld	NC8956	58°29·0'	3°53·7'W	X	10
Craig Trebanos	Nth Pt Talb	SN7003	51°42·9'	3°52·5'W	X	170
Craig Troed-y-rhiw-fer	Carm	SN7545	52°5·6'	3°49·1'W	X	146,147
Craig Turner	Angus	NO4178	56°53·6'	2°57·7'W	X	44
Craigturra	D & G	NX8193	55°13·3'	3°51·8'W	X	78
Craig Twrch	Carm	SN6648	52°7·1'	3°57·0'W	X	146
Craig Tylwch	Powys	SN9680	52°24·7'	3°31·3'W	X	136
Craig Tyn-y-cornel	Gwyn	SH6308	52°39·4'	4°1·1'W	X	124
Craigtype	D & G	NX6161	54°55·7'	4°9·7'W	H	83
Craig Ulatota	Highld	NG5047	57°26·9'	6°9·6'W	H	23,24
Craig Ulian	Arg & Bt	NM7817	56°17·9'	5°34·8'W	H	55
Craig Vallich	Aberd	NO3792	57°1·3'	3°1·8'W	H	44
Craig Varr	Pth & Kin	NN6659	56°42·5'	4°10·9'W	X	42,51
Craigvarren	Highld	NJ1134	57°23·5'	3°28·4'W	X	28
Craig Veann	Moray	NJ1810	57°10·7'	3°20·9'W	H	36
Craigview	N Ayr	NR9522	55°27·2'	5°14·1'W	X	68,69
Craigview	S Ayr	NX0779	55°4·3'	5°1·0'W	X	76
Craig Vinean	Pth & Kin	NN9941	56°33·3'	3°38·1'W	X	52,53
Craigvinean Forest	Pth & Kin	NN9845	56°35·4'	3°39·2'W	F	52,53
Craig Walgan	Aberd	NJ3905	57°8·2'	3°0·0'W	H	37
Craig Walter	Brig	SS8994	51°38·3'	3°35·9'W	X	170
Craig Watch	Moray	NJ3835	57°24·3'	3°1·5'W	H	28
Craigwater Hill	Aberd	NJ4231	57°22·2'	2°57·4'W	H	37
Craigwell	Pth & Kin	NO0703	56°12·9'	3°29·5'W	X	58
Craig-wen	Caer	ST1289	51°35·8'	3°15·8'W	X	171
Craig Wen	Conwy	SH7260	53°7·6'	3°54·4'W	H	115
Craig Wen	Gwyn	SH5950	53°2·0'	4°5·8'W	H	115
Craig Wen	Powys	SJ0229	52°51·2'	3°26·9'W	X	125
Craig Wenallt	Gwyn	SH9741	52°57·6'	3°31·6'W	X	125
Craigwhinnie	D & G	NX5569	54°59·9'	4°15·6'W	H	83
Craigwillie	Aberd	NJ5139	57°26·6'	2°48·5'W	X	29
Craig Wion	Gwyn	SH6632	52°52·4'	3°59·1'W	H	124
Craigwith Fm	Monm	ST3596	51°39·8'	2°56·0'W	FM	171
Craig Wood	Pth & Kin	NO0552	56°39·3'	3°32·5'W	X	52,53
Craig Wood	S Ayr	NX1382	55°6·1'	4°55·4'W	F	76
Craig y Bedw	Swan	SN6204	51°43·3'	3°59·5'W	X	159
Craig y Benglog	Gwyn	SH8024	52°48·3'	3°46·4'W	H	124,125
Craig y Bera	Gwyn	SH5454	53°4·0'	4°10·3'W	X	115
Craig-y-borion	Pemb	SN1509	51°45·2'	4°40·4'W	X	158
Craig-y-bwch	Gwyn	SH6414	52°42·6'	4°0·4'W	X	124
Craig y Bwch	Powys	SN8962	52°14·9'	3°37·2'W	X	147
Craig y-bwla	Powys	SO2620	51°52·7'	3°4·1'W	X	161
Craig y Bwlch	Cered	SN7169	52°18·5'	3°53·1'W	X	135,147
Craig y Bwlch	Gwyn	SH7916	52°43·9'	3°47·1'W	H	124
Craig-y-bwlch	Rho Cyn Taf	SN9403	51°43·2'	3°31·7'W	X	170
Craig y Bychau	Gwyn	SH8235	52°54·2'	3°44·9'W	X	124,125
Craig y Bylfa	Powys	SO0020	51°52·4'	3°26·8'W	X	160
Craig-y-cae	Gwyn	SH7023	52°47·6'	3°55·3'W	H	124
Craig y Castell	Gwyn	SH6917	52°44·3'	3°56·0'W	A	124
Craig y Castell	Powys	SJ0327	52°50·2'	3°26·0'W	X	125
Craig y Castell	Powys	SO1716	51°50·4'	3°11·9'W	X	161
Craig y Cilau	Powys	SO1815	51°49·9'	3°11·0'W	X	161
Craig y Cwm	Pemb	SN0931	51°56·9'	4°46·4'W	X	145
Craig y Cythraul	Denb	SJ2347	53°1·1'	3°8·5'W	X	117
Craig y Ddinas	Rho Cyn Taf	SN9108	51°45·8'	3°34·4'W	X	160
Craig-y-dduallt	Wrex	SJ2239	52°56·8'	3°9·2'W	X	126
Craig-y-Dinas	Gwyn	SH4451	53°2·3'	4°19·2'W	A	115,123
Craig y Dinas	Gwyn	SH6222	52°46·9'	4°2·4'W	A	124
Craig-y-don	Conwy	SH7981	53°19·0'	3°48·6'W	T	115
Craig-y-don	I of Angl	SH5673	53°14·3'	4°9·1'W	X	114,115
Craig-y-dorth	Monm	SO4808	51°46·3'	2°44·8'W	X	161
Craig-y-Duke	Nth Pt Talb	SN7002	51°42·3'	3°52·5'W	T	170
Craig y Dulyn	Conwy	SH6966	53°10·7'	3°57·2'W	X	115
Craigy Edge	D & G	NY3595	55°14·9'	3°0·9'W	X	79
Craig y Fan	Cered	SN7373	52°20·7'	3°51·5'W	H	135,147
Craig y Fan	Powys	SO0719	51°51·9'	3°20·6'W	X	160
Craig y Fan Ddu	Powys	SO0518	51°51·4'	3°22·4'W	X	160
Craigyfedwen	Conwy	SH7576	53°16·2'	3°52·1'W	X	115
Craig y Ffynnon	Gwyn	SH8319	52°45·6'	3°43·6'W	H	124,125
Craig y Fintan	Cered	SN7158	52°12·5'	3°52·9'W	X	146,147
Craig y Foel	Powys	SN9164	52°16·0'	3°35·4'W	X	147
Craig y Foelallt	Cered	SN6755	52°10·9'	3°56·3'W	X	146
Craig y Forwyn	Denb	SJ2347	53°1·1'	3°8·5'W	X	117
Craig y Fro	Powys	SN9620	51°52·4'	3°30·2'W	X	160
Craig y Fron-goch	Cered	SN7766	52°16·9'	3°47·8'W	H	135,147
Craigyfulfran	Cered	SN5882	52°25·3'	4°4·9'W	X	135
Craig y Ganllwyd	Gwyn	SH7025	52°48·7'	3°55·3'W	H	124
Craig-y-garn	Gwyn	SH5144	52°58·6'	4°12·7'W	H	124
Craig y Garn	Gwyn	SH8941	52°57·5'	3°38·7'W	H	124,125
Craig y Geifr	Brig	SS9494	51°38·3'	3°31·5'W	X	170
Craig y Geifr	Gwyn	SH8726	52°49·4'	3°40·2'W	X	124,125
Craig y Gelli	Nth Pt Talb	SS8896	51°39·3'	3°36·8'W	X	170
Craig y Gelli	Wrex	SJ1836	52°55·2'	3°12·8'W	X	125
Craig y Gilwern	Rho Cyn Taf	SS9998	51°40·5'	3°27·3'W	X	170
Craig y Gribin	Powys	SH9721	52°46·8'	3°31·2'W	X	125
Craig y Grut	Gwyn	SH6321	52°46·4'	4°1·5'W	H	124
Craig y Gwbert	Cered	SN1550	52°7·3'	4°41·7'W	X	145
Craig y Gwynt	I of Angl	SH3289	53°22·5'	4°31·1'W	X	114
Craig y Gydros	Gwyn	SH9146	53°0·3'	3°37·1'W	X	116
Craig y Hyrddod	Gwyn	SH8237	52°55·3'	3°44·9'W	H	124,125
Craigy Knowe	Scot Bord	NT6300	55°17·8'	2°34·5'W	X	80
Craig y Llam	Gwyn	SH7412	52°41·7'	3°51·5'W	X	124
Craig y Llan	Gwyn	SH5043	52°58·0'	4°13·6'W	X	124
Craig y Llestri	Gwyn	SH8329	52°51·0'	3°43·8'W	H	124,125
Craig y Lluest	Powys	SN8576	52°22·4'	3°41·0'W	X	135,136,147
Craig-y-llyn	Gwyn	SH6611	52°41·1'	3°58·5'W	X	124
Craig y Llyn	Rho Cyn Taf	SN9103	51°43·1'	3°34·3'W	X	170
Craig y Maes	Powys	SN8794	52°32·2'	3°39·6'W	X	135,136
Craig y March	Cered	SN8088	52°28·8'	3°45·6'W	X	135,136
Craig y Merchant	Newp	ST2591	51°37·0'	3°4·6'W	X	171
Craig y Mwn	Powys	SJ0728	52°50·7'	3°22·5'W	X	125
Craig-y-nos	Powys	SN8315	51°49·5'	3°41·5'W	X	160
Craig-y-nos Country Park	Powys	SN8415	51°49·5'	3°40·6'W	X	160
Craig y Pâl	Swan	SN7000	51°41·3'	3°52·5'W	X	170
Craig y Pandy	Caer	ST2192	51°37·5'	3°8·1'W	X	171
Craig y Pant	Gwyn	SH9122	52°47·3'	3°36·6'W	X	125
Craig y pant	Nth Pt Talb	SN8903	51°43·1'	3°36·0'W	X	170
Craig y parc	Card	ST0980	51°30·9'	3°18·3'W	F	171
Craig-y-parcau	Brig	SS8978	51°29·6'	3°35·6'W	X	170
Craig-y-Penmaen	Gwyn	SH7229	52°50·8'	3°53·6'W	H	124
Craig-y-penrhyn	Cered	SN6592	52°30·8'	3°59·0'W	T	135
Craig y Pistyll	Cered	SN7185	52°27·1'	3°53·5'W	X	135
Craig yr Aber	Nth Pt Talb	SS8586	51°33·9'	3°39·2'W	X	170
Craig yr Aderyn or Birds' Rock	Gwyn	SH6406	52°38·3'	4°0·2'W	H	124
Craig-yr-allt	Monm	SO2906	51°45·1'	3°1·3'W	F	161
Craig yr Allt	Rho Cyn Taf	ST1385	51°33·7'	3°14·9'W	H	171
Craig yr Allt-Ddu	Cered	SN7287	52°28·2'	3°52·7'W	X	135
Craig yr Allt Ddu	Gwyn	SH9632	52°52·8'	3°32·3'W	X	125
Craig-yr-efail	Rho Cyn Taf	ST0797	51°40·1'	3°20·3'W	X	170
Craig yr Eglwys	Cered	SN8089	52°29·4'	3°45·6'W	X	135,136
Craig yr Eryr	Powys	SN9674	52°21·5'	3°31·2'W	X	136,147
Craig-y-Rhacca	Caer	ST1989	51°35·9'	3°9·8'W	T	171
Craig yr Hafdre	Cered	SN8054	52°10·5'	3°44·9'W	X	147
Craig yr Hafod	Gwyn	SH8844	52°59·1'	3°39·7'W	H	124,125
Craig yr Harris	Monm	SO3305	51°44·6'	2°57·8'W	F	161
Craig-y-rhiw	Shrops	SJ2329	52°51·4'	3°8·2'W	X	126
Craig-y-Rhos	Denb	SJ1443	52°58·9'	3°16·5'W	X	125
Craig-yr-hudol	Brig	SS8988	51°35·0'	3°35·7'W	X	170
Craig-yr-hudol	Brig	SS9088	51°35·0'	3°34·9'W	H	170
Craig-yr-Hufen	Caer	ST1191	51°36·9'	3°16·7'W	X	171
Craig-yr-hwch	Powys	SJ2132	52°53·0'	3°10·0'W	H	126
Craig yr Irwch	I of Angl	SH3293	53°24·7'	4°31·3'W	X	114
Craig-yr-iyrchen	Conwy	SH9351	53°3·0'	3°35·4'W	H	116
Craig y Ogof	Gwyn	SH9124	52°48·4'	3°36·6'W	X	125
Craig-y-Ruthin	V of Glam	SS9780	51°30·8'	3°28·7'W	X	170
Craig yr Ysfa	Conwy	SH6963	53°9·1'	3°57·1'W	X	115
Craig-yr-ysgol	Rho Cyn Taf	SN9502	51°42·7'	3°30·8'W	X	170
Craigysgafn	Gwyn	SH6544	52°58·8'	4°0·2'W	X	124
Craig Ysgiog	Gwyn	SH6810	52°40·5'	3°56·7'W	H	124
Craig Ysgwennant	Powys	SJ1931	52°52·5'	3°11·8'W	X	125
Craig Ystradmeurig	Cered	SN7069	52°18·5'	3°54·0'W	X	135,147
Craig y Tân	Gwyn	SH7136	52°54·6'	3°54·7'W	X	124
Craigythorn	D & G	NX6698	55°15·7'	4°6·1'W	X	77
Craig-y-trwyn	Caer	ST1991	51°37·0'	3°9·8'W	X	171
Craig y Trwyn	Caer	ST2396	51°39·7'	3°6·4'W	X	171
Craig y Wenallt	Newp	ST2690	51°36·5'	3°3·7'W	X	171
Craik	Aberd	NJ4625	57°19·0'	2°53·3'W	X	37
Craik	Scot Bord	NT3408	55°21·9'	3°2·0'W	T	79
Craik Cross Hill	D & G	NT3004	55°19·8'	3°5·8'W	H	79
Craik Forest	Scot Bord	NT3409	55°22·5'	3°2·1'W	F	79
Craikhope (Outdoor Centre)	Scot Bord	NT3205	55°20·3'	3°3·9'W	X	79
Craikhow Hall	Cumbr	NY0634	54°41·8'	3°27·1'W	X	89
Craik Moor	Scot Bord	NT3106	55°20·8'	3°4·9'W	X	79
Craik Moor	Scot Bord	NT8118	55°27·6'	2°17·6'W	X	80
Craik Muir	D & G	NT2702	55°18·7'	3°8·6'W	X	79
Craik's Craigs Plantn	D & G	NT0506	55°20·6'	3°29·4'W	F	78
Craiksfold	Angus	NO5354	56°40·8'	2°45·6'W	X	54
Craiksland	S Ayr	NS3531	55°32·9'	4°36·5'W	X	70
Crail	Fife	NO6107	56°15·5'	2°37·3'W	T	59
Crailing	Scot Bord	NT6824	55°30·8'	2°30·0'W	T	74
Crailinghall	Scot Bord	NT6922	55°29·7'	2°29·0'W	T	74
Crailing Ho	Scot Bord	NT6824	55°30·8'	2°30·0'W	X	74
Crailing Tofts	Scot Bord	NT6925	55°31·3'	2°29·0'W	X	74
Crailloch	D & G	NX0458	54°53·0'	5°2·9'W	X	82
Crailloch	D & G	NX3252	54°50·3'	4°36·5'W	X	82
Crailloch Burn	D & G	NX0359	54°53·5'	5°3·9'W	W	82
Crailloch Croft	D & G	NX0458	54°53·0'	5°2·9'W	X	82
Crailloch Hill	D & G	NX0258	54°52·9'	5°4·8'W	H	82
Crailoch	S Ayr	NX1181	55°5·5'	4°57·3'W	X	76
Crailoch Burn	S Ayr	NX1281	55°5·5'	4°56·3'W	W	76
Crailyn	Kent	TQ8737	51°6·3'	0°40·7'E	X	189
Crailzie Hill	Scot Bord	NT1945	55°41·8'	3°16·9'W	H	72
Crain Syke Fm	N Yks	SE2649	53°56·4'	1°35·8'W	FM	104
Craiqievern	Stir	NS4991	56°5·5'	4°25·2'W	X	57
Crairie	Orkney	HY4905	58°56·0'	2°52·7'W	X	6,7
Crairiehill	D & G	NS8503	55°18·7'	3°48·3'W	X	78
Crairieknowe	D & G	NS8303	55°18·7'	3°50·2'W	X	78
Crairiepark	D & G	NS8404	55°19·2'	3°49·3'W	X	78
Crakaig	Highld	NC9510	58°4·3'	3°46·3'W	X	17
Crakaig Crofts	Highld	NC9511	58°4·8'	3°46·4'W	X	17
Crake Bank	N Yks	SE4385	54°15·8'	1°20·0'W	X	99
Crake Dale	E Yorks	SE9868	54°6·2'	0°29·7'W	X	101
Crake Hall	Cumbr	SD5497	54°22·2'	2°42·1'W	X	97
Crake Hall	Cumbr	SD5791	54°19·0'	2°39·2'W	X	97
Crake Hall	N Yks	SE8779	54°12·2'	0°39·6'W	X	101
Crakehill	N Yks	SE4273	54°9·3'	1°21·0'W	T	99
Crake Ho Fm	N Yks	SE1959	54°1·8'	1°42·2'W	FM	104
Crake Low	Derby	SK1753	53°4·7'	1°44·4'W	A	119
Crakemarsh	Staffs	SK0936	52°55·5'	1°51·6'W	T	128
Crake Moor	N Yks	SD8560	54°2·4'	2°13·3'W	X	98
Crakeplace Hall	Cumbr	NY0624	54°36·4'	3°26·9'W	X	89
Crake Scar Fm	Durham	NZ0827	54°38·5'	1°52·1'W	FM	92
Crake Trees	Cumbr	NY6115	54°32·0'	2°35·7'W	X	91
Craketrees	Cumbr	SD5699	54°23·3'	2°40·2'W	X	97
Cralaw	Scot Bord	NT6453	55°46·4'	2°34·0'W	X	67,74
Cralle Place	E Susx	TQ6016	50°55·5'	0°17·0'E	X	199
Cramalt	Scot Bord	NT1923	55°29·9'	3°16·5'W	X	72
Cramalt Burn	Scot Bord	NT1824	55°30·4'	3°17·5'W	W	72
Cramalt Craig	Scot Bord	NT1624	55°30·4'	3°19·4'W	H	72
Crambe	N Yks	SE7364	54°4·2'	0°52·6'W	T	100
Crambeck	N Yks	SE7367	54°5·9'	0°52·6'W	T	100
Crambeck Br	N Yks	SE7367	54°5·9'	0°52·6'W	X	100
Crambe Grange	N Yks	SE7263	54°3·7'	0°53·6'W	X	100
Cramber Tor	Devon	SX5871	50°31·5'	3°59·8'W	X	202
Cramble Cross	N Yks	NZ2704	54°26·1'	1°34·6'W	X	93
Cramer Gutter	Shrops	SO6479	52°24·7'	2°31·4'W	X	138
Cramflat	Pth & Kin	NO0830	56°27·4'	3°29·1'W	X	52,53
Cramhurst	Surrey	SU9440	51°9·3'	0°39·0'W	T	186
Cramie	Angus	NO2967	56°47·6'	3°9·3'W	X	44
Cramie Burn	Angus	NO2969	56°48·7'	3°9·3'W	W	44
Cramla Bank	Aberd	NO7284	56°57·0'	2°27·2'W	X	45
Cramlington	Northum	NZ2676	55°4·9'	1°35·1'W	T	88
Crammag	I of M	SC3788	54°16·0'	4°29·8'W	X	95
Crammag Head	D & G	NX0834	54°40·1'	4°58·2'W	X	82
Crammer Barton	Devon	ST0805	50°50·5'	3°18·0'W	X	192
Crammers	Devon	SX8880	50°36·8'	3°34·6'W	X	192
Crammery Hill	D & G	NX4474	55°2·4'	4°26·1'W	X	77
Crammery Hill	D & G	NX4864	54°57·1'	4°22·0'W	H	83
Cramond	C of Edin	NT1876	55°58·5'	3°18·4'W	T	65,66
Cramond Bridge	C of Edin	NT1775	55°57·9'	3°19·3'W	T	65,66
Cramond Hill	Northum	NT8639	55°38·9'	2°12·9'W	X	74
Cramond Island	C of Edin	NT1978	55°59·5'	3°17·5'W	X	65,66
Crampmoor	Hants	SU3822	51°0·0'	1°27·1'W	T	185
Cramp Pool Fm	Shrops	SJ7608	52°40·4'	2°20·9'W	FM	127
Crampstone	Aberd	NJ4523	57°17·9'	2°54·3'W	X	37
Crampton	Kent	TQ8737	51°6·3'	0°40·7'E	X	189
Crams	Corn	SW6951	50°19·1'	5°14·3'W	W	203
Crams	Corn	SW9078	50°34·1'	4°57·6'W	X	200
Cranachan	Highld	NN2984	56°55·2'	4°48·1'W	X	34,41
Cranage	Ches	SJ7568	53°12·7'	2°22·1'W	T	118
Cranaig	Arg & Bt	NM2160	56°39·2'	6°32·7'W	X	46,47
Cranapool	Devon	SS3808	50°51·2'	4°17·7'W	X	190
Cranberry	Staffs	SJ8235	52°55·0'	2°15·7'W	T	127
Cranberry Brow	Northum	NY7465	54°59·0'	2°23·9'W	X	86,87
Cranberry Carr	N Yks	SE4354	53°59·1'	1°20·2'W	F	105
Cranberry Clough	Sheff	SK1795	53°27·3'	1°44·2'W	X	110
Cranberry Fm	Barns	SE2400	53°30·0'	1°37·9'W	FM	110
Cranberry Fm	D & G	NY3069	55°0·9'	3°5·3'W	FM	85
Cranberry Fm	Lincs	TF4558	53°6·2'	0°10·4'E	FM	122
Cranberry Fm	Wrex	SJ4642	52°58·6'	2°47·8'W	FM	117
Cranberry Ley Fm	Wigan	SD5501	53°30·5'	2°40·3'W	FM	108
Cranberry Moss	Black w Dar	SD7119	53°40·2'	2°25·9'W	X	109
Cranberry Moss	N Yks	SE0966	54°5·6'	1°51·3'W	W	99
Cranberry Pt	D & G	NW9660	54°53·8'	5°10·5'W	X	82
Cranberry Rock	Shrops	SO3698	52°34·8'	2°56·3'W	X	137
Cranberry Rough	Norf	TL9393	52°30·3'	0°51·0'E	F	144
Cranbog	Aberd	NJ8760	57°38·0'	2°12·6'W	X	30
Cranborne	Dorset	SU0513	50°55·2'	1°55·3'W	T	195
Cranborne Chase	Dorset	ST9014	50°55·8'	2°8·2'W	X	195
Cranborne Chase	Wilts	ST9317	50°57·4'	2°5·6'W	X	184
Cranborne Common	Dorset	SU1011	50°54·1'	1°51·1'W	X	195
Cranborne Fm	Dorset	SU0414	50°55·8'	1°56·2'W	FM	195
Cranbourne	Brackn	SU9272	51°26·6'	0°40·2'W	T	175
Cranbourne	Hants	SU6350	51°15·0'	1°5·4'W	X	185
Cranbourne Chase	Win & Maid	SU9372	51°26·6'	0°39·3'W	F	175
Cranbourne Grange	Hants	SU4740	51°9·7'	1°19·3'W	X	185
Cranbourne Tower	Win & Maid	SU9473	51°27·1'	0°38·4'W	X	175
Cranbrook	Devon	SX7488	50°40·9'	3°46·6'W	X	191
Cranbrook	Kent	TQ7736	51°6·0'	0°32·1'E	T	188
Cranbrook	Redbr	TQ4287	51°34·1'	0°3·3'E	T	177
Cranbrook Castle	Devon	SX7389	50°41·4'	3°47·5'W	X	191
Cranbrooke Common	Kent	TQ7838	51°7·0'	0°33·0'E	T	188
Cran Burn	Aberd	NO6684	56°57·0'	2°33·1'W	W	45
Cranbury	Devon	SS3606	50°50·1'	4°19·4'W	X	190
Cranbury Ho	Hants	SU4423	51°0·5'	1°22·0'W	X	185
Cranbury Park	Hants	SU4422	51°0·0'	1°22·0'W	X	185
Crandard, The	Angus	NO3359	56°43·3'	3°5·2'W	H	53
Crandart	Angus	NO1867	56°47·5'	3°20·1'W	X	43
Crandle	Devon	SS8412	50°54·0'	3°38·6'W	X	181
Crandon Br	Somer	ST3339	51°9·0'	2°57·1'W	X	182
Crandon Fm	Bucks	SP7823	51°54·2'	0°51·6'W	FM	165
Crandons Fm	Devon	ST2503	50°49·5'	3°3·5'W	FM	192,193
Crane Castle	Corn	SW6343	50°14·6'	5°19·1'W	A	203
Crane Greave	Barns	SE3000	53°30·0'	1°32·5'W	X	110,111
Craneham	Devon	SS4218	50°56·6'	4°14·6'W	X	180,190
Crane Hill	Cambs	TL2055	52°11·0'	0°14·3'W	X	153
Crane Hill	Devon	SX6268	50°30·0'	3°56·4'W	X	202
Crane Hill	Glos	SO9630	51°58·3'	2°3·1'W	H	150
Cranehow Bottom	N Yks	SE0693	54°20·2'	1°54·0'W	X	99
Crane Islands	Corn	SW6344	50°15·1'	5°19·1'W	X	203
Crane Ledges	Corn	SW6912	49°58·0'	5°12·9'W	X	203
Crane Loch	S Lanak	NT0452	55°45·4'	3°31·3'W	W	65,72
Crane Moor	Barns	SE3001	53°30·5'	1°32·4'W	T	110,111
Cranemoor Lake	W Berks	SU6271	51°26·3'	1°6·1'W	W	175
Crane Moss	Northum	NT9103	55°19·5'	2°8·1'W	W	80
Crane Row	Durham	NZ0927	54°38·5'	1°51·2'W	X	92
Cranes	Essex	TQ7290	51°35·2'	0°29·4'E	F	178
Cranes Copse	Hants	SU6257	51°18·8'	1°6·2'W	F	175
Crane's Corner	Norf	TF9113	52°41·1'	0°50·0'E	T	132
Cranesden	E Susx	TQ5826	51°0·9'	0°15·5'E	X	188,199
Cranesden Fm	E Susx	TQ5825	51°0·4'	0°15·5'E	FM	188,199
Cranes Fm	W Berks	SU3779	51°30·8'	1°27·6'W	FM	174
Crane's Gate Ho	Lincs	TF3323	52°47·5'	0°1·4'W	X	131
Crane's Gate Ho	Lincs	TF3420	52°45·9'	0°0·4'W	X	131
Crane's Hill	Suff	TM2436	51°59·7'	1°16·1'E	X	169
Cranes Moor	Dorset	SY8188	50°41·7'	2°15·8'W	F	194
Cranes Moor	Hants	SU1902	50°49·3'	1°43·4'W	X	195
Crane's Watering Fm	Norf	TM2383	52°24·2'	1°17·1'E	FM	156
Crane Wood Ho	Lancs	SD6645	53°54·2'	2°30·6'W	X	103
Craneydub	Cumbr	NY5249	54°50·3'	2°44·4'W	X	86

Cranfield	Beds	SP9542	52°4·3'	0°36·4'W	T	153
Cranfield Airfield	Beds	SP9442	52°4·3'	0°37·3'W	X	153
Cranford	Devon	SS3421	50°58·1'	4°21·5'W	T	190
Cranford	Houns	TQ1076	51°28·6'	0°24·6'W	T	176
Cranford Cross	Devon	SS5521	50°58·4'	4°3·5'W	X	180
Cranford Fm	S Glos	ST7076	51°29·2'	2°25·5'W	FM	172
Cranford Hall	Barns	SE3905	53°32·7'	1°24·3'W	X	110,111
Cranford Ho	N Yks	SE7480	54°12·9'	0°51·5'W	X	100
Cranford Park	Hill	TQ1077	51°29·1'	0°24·6'W	X	176
Cranford St Andrew	Northnts	SP9277	52°23·2'	0°38·5'W	T	141
Cranford St John	Northnts	SP9276	52°22·7'	0°38·5'W	T	141
Cranford Water	Devon	SS3421	50°58·1'	4°21·5'W	X	190
Cranford Wood	Northnts	SP9379	52°24·3'	0°37·6'W	F	141
Cranham	Devon	SS2219	50°56·8'	4°31·7'W	X	190
Cranham	Glos	SO8912	51°48·6'	2°9·2'W	T	163
Cranham	Hav	TQ5787	51°33·8'	0°16·3'E	T	177
Cranham	Pemb	SM9410	51°45·3'	4°58·7'W	X	157,158
Cranham Common	Glos	SO8912	51°48·6'	2°9·2'W	X	163
Cranham Hall	Hav	TQ5786	51°33·3'	0°16·3'E	X	177
Cranham Place	Hav	TQ5885	51°32·7'	0°17·1'E	X	177
Cranhams, The	Glos	SP0100	51°42·2'	1°58·7'W	X	163
Cranham Wood	Glos	SO9012	51°48·6'	2°8·3'W	F	163
Cranhill	Aberd	NJ8753	57°34·3'	2°12·6'W	X	30
Cran Hill	Aberd	NJ9100	57°5·7'	2°8·5'W	H	38
Cranhill	Aberd	NJ9100	57°5·7'	2°8·5'W	X	38
Cran Hill	Aberd	NO9194	57°2·5'	2°8·4'W	H	38,45
Cranhill	C of Glas	NS6465	55°51·8'	4°9·9'W	T	64
Cranhill	Warw	SP1253	52°10·7'	1°49·1'W	T	150
Cranhill Barn	Glos	SO9301	51°42·7'	2°5·7'W	X	163
Cranhouse Fm	Suff	TL7478	52°22·6'	0°33·8'E	FM	143
Crank	St Hel	SJ5099	53°29·4'	2°44·8'W	T	108
Crankan	Corn	SW4633	50°8·8'	5°33·0'W	X	203
Crankland Fm	Devon	SS9908	50°52·0'	3°25·7'W	FM	192
Crankley	N Yks	SE5168	54°6·6'	1°12·8'W	X	100
Crankley Grange	N Yks	SE5168	54°6·6'	1°12·8'W	X	100
Crankwell Fm	Shrops	SJ2498	52°34·7'	3°6·9'W	FM	137
Crankwood	Wigan	SD6200	53°30·0'	2°34·0'W	T	109
Cranleigh	Surrey	TQ0638	51°8·1'	0°28·7'W	T	187
Cranley	Pth & Kin	NO1441	56°33·4'	3°23·5'W	X	53
Cranley	Suff	TM1572	52°18·5'	1°9·6'E	T	144,156
Cranley Gardens	Hargy	TQ2889	51°35·3'	0°8·7'W	T	176
Cranley Ho	S Lanak	NS9246	55°42·0'	3°42·7'W	X	72
Cranley Manor	Suff	TM1672	52°18·4'	1°10·5'E	X	144,156
Cranley Moss	S Lanak	NS9347	55°42·5'	3°41·7'W	X	72
Cranley Oak	Bucks	SP7437	52°1·8'	0°54·9'W	X	152
Cranloch	Aberd	NJ6238	57°26·1'	2°37·5'W	X	29
Cran Loch	D & G	NY0093	55°13·5'	3°33·9'W	W	78
Cran Loch	Highld	NH9459	57°36·8'	3°46·0'W	W	27
Cranloch	Moray	NJ2858	57°36·6'	3°11·8'W	T	28
Cranmer Bottom	Hants	SU7932	51°5·1'	0°51·9'W	F	186
Cranmere	Shrops	SO7597	52°34·5'	2°21·7'W	X	138
Cranmere Pool Letterbox	Devon	SX6085	50°39·1'	3°58·4'W	X	191
Cranmer Green	Suff	TM0171	52°18·2'	0°57·3'E	T	144,155
Cranmer Hall	Norf	TF8832	52°51·4'	0°48·0'E	X	132
Cranmoor	Staffs	SJ8400	52°36·1'	2°13·8'W	X	127
Cranmoor Lodge Fm	Staffs	SJ8500	52°36·1'	2°12·9'W	FM	127,139
Cranmoor Lots	Cambs	TL4992	52°30·6'	0°12·1'E	X	143
Cranmore	Highld	NH7343	57°27·8'	4°6·6'W	X	27
Cranmore	I of W	SZ3990	50°42·7'	1°26·5'W	T	196
Cranmore	Somer	ST6643	51°11·3'	2°28·8'W	T	183
Cranmore Castle	Devon	SS9511	50°53·6'	3°29·2'W	X	192
Cranmore Castle (Settlement)	Devon	SS9511	50°53·6'	3°29·2'W	A	192
Cranmore Fm	Glos	ST8595	51°39·4'	2°12·6'W	FM	162
Cranmore Fm	Glos	ST8888	51°35·7'	2°10·0'W	FM	162,173
Cranmore Fm	Lincs	TF1709	52°40·2'	0°15·8'W	FM	142
Cranmore Green Fm	Suff	TL8547	52°5·6'	0°42·4'E	FM	155
Cranmore Lodge	Lincs	TF1809	52°40·2'	0°14·9'W	X	142
Cranmore Tower	Somer	ST6745	51°12·4'	2°28·0'W	X	183
Cranmore Wood	Somer	ST6745	51°12·4'	2°28·0'W	F	183
Cranna	Aberd	NJ7335	57°24·5'	2°26·5'W	X	29
Crannabog	Aberd	NJ7334	57°24·0'	2°26·5'W	X	29
Crannach	Arg & Bt	NN3545	56°34·3'	4°40·7'W	X	50
Crannach	Pth & Kin	NO0466	56°46·8'	3°33·8'W	X	43
Crannach Hill	Aberd	NO3899	57°4·9'	3°0·9'W	H	37,44
Crannaford	Devon	SY0196	50°45·5'	3°23·8'W	X	192
Crannag	N Eil	NF7004	57°0·8'	7°25·8'W	X	31
Crannaich	Highld	NH9021	57°16·2'	3°49·0'W	X	36
Crannel Moor	Somer	ST5041	51°10·2'	2°42·5'W	X	182,183
Crannel, The	Angus	NO5773	56°51·0'	2°41·9'W	H	44
Crannich	Arg & Bt	NM5145	56°32·1'	6°2·5'W	X	47,48
Crannich	Highld	NH6476	57°45·5'	4°16·7'W	X	21
Cranniecat Hill	Aberd	NJ5418	57°15·3'	2°45·3'W	H	37
Crannoch	Moray	NJ4954	57°34·7'	2°50·7'W	X	28,29
Crannoch Hill	Aberd	NJ5266	57°41·1'	2°47·8'W	H	29
Crannog	Arg & Bt	NM5152	56°35·9'	6°2·9'W	A	47
Crannog	Arg & Bt	NM5538	56°28·5'	5°58·3'W	A	47,48
Crannog	Arg & Bt	NM9509	56°14·0'	5°18·0'W	X	55
Crannog	Arg & Bt	NR7563	55°48·7'	5°35·0'W	A	62
Crannog	Highld	ND2455	58°28·9'	3°17·7'W	A	11,12
Crannog	Highld	NH4757	57°34·9'	4°33·1'W	X	26
Crannog	Highld	NM7447	56°33·9'	5°40·3'W	A	49
Crannog	S Lanak	NS9041	55°39·3'	3°44·5'W	X	71,72
Cranoe	Leic	SP7595	52°33·1'	0°53·2'W	T	141
Cransford	Suff	TM3164	52°13·8'	1°23·4'E	T	156
Cransford Hall	Suff	TM3265	52°14·3'	1°24·3'E	X	156
Cranshaw Hall	Halton	SJ5188	53°23·4'	2°43·8'W	A	108
Cranshaws	Scot Bord	NT6861	55°50·7'	2°30·2'W	T	67
Cranshaws Fm	Scot Bord	NT6861	55°50·7'	2°30·2'W	FM	67
Cranshaws Hill	Scot Bord	NT6761	55°50·7'	2°31·2'W	H	67
Cranshaws Ho	Scot Bord	NT6861	55°50·7'	2°30·2'W	X	67
Cranslagloan	Arg & Bt	NS0566	55°51·1'	5°6·5'W	X	63
Cranslagmory	Arg & Bt	NS0667	55°51·7'	5°5·6'W	X	63
Cranslagvourity	Arg & Bt	NS0465	55°50·6'	5°7·4'W	X	63
Cransley Lodge	Northnts	SP8176	52°22·8'	0°48·2'W	X	141
Cransley Resr	Northnts	SP8277	52°23·3'	0°47·3'W	W	141
Cransley Wood	Northnts	SP8276	52°22·8'	0°47·3'W	F	141
Cransmill Hill	Aberd	NJ4531	57°22·2'	2°54·4'W	H	29,37
Cranstackie	Highld	NC3555	58°27·4'	4°49·2'W	H	9
Cranstal	I of M	NX4602	54°23·7'	4°21·9'W	T	95
Cranstoun Riddel	Midlo	NT3865	55°52·7'	2°59·0'W	X	66
Cranswick	E Yorks	TA0152	53°57·5'	0°27·2'W	T	106,107
Cranswick Common	E Yorks	TA0451	53°56·9'	0°24·5'W	X	107
Cranswick Grange	E Yorks	TA0552	53°57·4'	0°23·6'W	X	107
Cransworth	Corn	SW9666	50°27·7'	4°52·1'W	X	200
Crantit House	Orkney	HY4409	58°58·1'	2°57·9'W	X	6,7
Crantock	Corn	SW7960	50°24·1'	5°6·2'W	T	200
Crantock Beach	Corn	SW7860	50°24·1'	5°7·1'W	X	200
Cranway Fm	Hants	SU0920	50°59·0'	1°51·9'W	FM	184
Cranway Fm	Somer	ST3307	50°51·8'	2°56·7'W	FM	193
Cranway Fm	Wilts	SU0920	50°59·0'	1°51·9'W	FM	184
Cranwell	Lincs	TF0349	53°1·9'	0°27·4'W	T	130
Cranwell Airfield	Lincs	TF0049	53°2·0'	0°30·1'W	X	130
Cranwell Fms	Bucks	SP7615	51°49·9'	0°53·4'W	FM	165
Cranwich	Norf	TL7894	52°31·1'	0°37·8'E	T	144
Cranwich Heath	Norf	TL7793	52°30·6'	0°36·9'E	F	144
Cranworth	Norf	TF9804	52°36·1'	0°55·8'E	T	144
Cranyke Fm	Leic	SK7525	52°49·3'	0°52·8'W	FM	129
Craobhag	N Eil	NG1599	57°53·6'	6°48·1'W	X	14
Craobhagun	N Eil	NF9375	57°39·9'	7°8·5'W	X	18
Craobh Haven	Arg & Bt	NM7907	56°12·5'	5°33·4'W	T	55
Craobhnaclag	Highld	NH4340	57°25·7'	4°36·4'W	X	26
Craonabhal	N Eil	NF8362	57°32·5'	7°17·4'W	H	22
Craperoch	Arg & Bt	NS3188	56°3·6'	4°42·4'W	X	56
Crapham Down	E Susx	TV5797	50°45·3'	0°13·9'E	X	199
Crapham Hill	E Susx	TV5898	50°45·8'	0°14·8'E	X	199
Crapnell Fm	Somer	ST5945	51°12·4'	2°34·8'W	FM	182,183
Crappich Hill	Pth & Kin	NN7424	56°23·7'	4°2·0'W	H	51,52
Crapstone	Devon	SX5067	50°29·3'	4°6·5'W	T	201
Crapstone Ho	Devon	SX4967	50°29·2'	4°7·3'W	X	201
Crarae	Arg & Bt	NR9897	56°7·6'	5°14·6'W	T	55
Crarae Bay	Arg & Bt	NR9897	56°7·6'	5°14·6'W	W	55
Crarae Burn	Arg & Bt	NR9797	56°7·6'	5°15·5'W	W	55
Crarae Point	Arg & Bt	NR9897	56°7·6'	5°14·6'W	X	55
Craraigh-Mhòr	N Eil	NF8345	57°23·4'	7°16·1'W	X	22
Craro Island	Arg & Bt	NR6247	55°39·8'	5°46·6'W	X	62
Crasg Backlass	Highld	ND0842	58°21·7'	3°33·9'W	H	11,12
Crask	Highld	NC7262	58°31·9'	4°11·4'W	T	10
Crask	Highld	NH6260	57°36·8'	4°18·1'W	X	21
Crask	Highld	NH6633	57°22·3'	4°13·2'W	X	26
Crask	Highld	NH8720	57°15·7'	3°51·9'W	X	35
Crasken	Corn	SW6728	50°6·6'	5°15·2'W	X	203
Craskie	Highld	NH3034	57°22·1'	4°49·2'W	X	26
Crask Inn	Highld	NC5224	58°11·1'	4°30·6'W	X	16
Craskins	Aberd	NJ5106	57°8·8'	2°48·1'W	X	37
Crask of Aigas	Highld	NH4642	57°26·8'	4°33·5'W	T	26
Crask, The	Highld	NC5226	58°12·1'	4°30·6'W	H	16
Crask, The	Highld	NH7292	57°54·2'	4°9·1'W	X	21
Craster	Northum	NU2519	55°28·1'	1°35·8'W	T	81
Craster South Fm	Northum	NU2519	55°28·1'	1°35·8'W	FM	81
Craster Tower	Northum	NU2519	55°28·1'	1°35·8'W	X	81
Craster West Fm	Northum	NU2418	55°27·6'	1°36·8'W	FM	81
Crastock Manor	Surrey	SU9755	51°17·4'	0°36·1'W	X	175,186
Craswall Priory	Heref	SO2737	52°1·8'	3°3·5'W	A	161
Craswell	Heref	SO2934	52°0·2'	3°1·7'W	T	161
Crateford	Shrops	SO7288	52°29·6'	2°24·3'W	T	138
Crateford	Staffs	SJ9009	52°41·0'	2°8·5'W	T	127
Crateman's Fm	W Susx	TQ2121	50°58·8'	0°16·2'W	FM	198
Crate Wood	Dorset	ST7607	50°52·0'	2°20·1'W	F	194
Cratfield	Suff	TM3175	52°19·7'	1°23·8'E	T	156
Cratfield Hall	Suff	TM2976	52°20·3'	1°22·1'E	X	156
Crathes	Aberd	NO7596	57°3·5'	2°24·3'W	T	38,45
Crathes Castle	Aberd	NO7396	57°3·5'	2°26·3'W	A	38,45
Crathie	Aberd	NO2694	57°2·1'	3°12·7'W	T	37,44
Crathie	Highld	NN5894	57°1·2'	4°19·9'W	T	35
Crathie Burn	Aberd	NO2397	57°3·7'	3°15·7'W	W	36,44
Crathienaird	Aberd	NO2595	57°2·7'	3°13·7'W	X	37,44
Crathie Point	Aberd	NJ5467	57°41·7'	2°45·8'W	X	29
Crathorne	N Yks	NZ4407	54°27·6'	1°18·9'W	T	93
Cratt Hill	Wilts	ST9035	51°7·1'	2°8·2'W	X	184
Crauchie	E Loth	NT5678	55°59·8'	2°41·9'W	X	67
Craufurdland Castle	E Ayr	NS4540	55°38·0'	4°27·3'W	A	70
Craufurdland Water	E Ayr	NS4642	55°39·1'	4°26·4'W	W	70
Cravadale	N Eil	NB0013	58°0·6'	7°4·3'W	X	13
Crave Hall Fm	Essex	TL5344	52°4·6'	0°14·4'E	FM	154
Craven Arms	Shrops	SO4382	52°26·2'	2°49·9'W	T	137
Craven Fm	N Yks	SE5870	54°7·6'	1°6·3'W	FM	100
Craven Fm	W Berks	SU4969	51°25·3'	1°17·3'W	FM	174
Craven House	W Berks	SU4166	51°23·7'	1°24·3'W	X	174
Craven Laithe	Lancs	SD8443	53°53·2'	2°14·2'W	X	103
Craven Moor	N Yks	SE0963	54°4·0'	1°51·3'W	X	99
Craven Ridge	N Yks	SD7864	54°4·5'	2°19·8'W	X	98
Cravens	Lancs	SD6936	53°49·4'	2°27·8'W	X	103
Craven's Manor	Suff	TM4478	52°21·0'	1°35·4'E	X	156
Craven View	Lancs	SD5772	54°8·8'	2°39·1'W	X	97
Craw	N Ayr	NR8948	55°41·0'	5°21·0'W	X	62,69
Crawberry Hill	Northum	NY8655	54°53·6'	2°12·7'W	X	87
Crawbutts	Pth & Kin	NO1034	56°29·6'	3°27·3'W	X	53
Crawcraigs	S Lanak	NT0443	55°40·5'	3°31·2'W	X	72
Crawcrook	Ghead	NZ1363	54°57·9'	1°47·4'W	T	88
Crawcwellt	Gwyn	SH6831	52°51·9'	3°57·3'W	X	124
Crawfold Fm	W Susx	TQ0026	51°1·7'	0°34·1'W	FM	186,197
Crawford	Lancs	SD5002	53°31·0'	2°44·8'W	T	108
Crawford	S Lanak	NS9520	55°28·0'	3°39·2'W	T	72
Crawford Br	Dorset	ST9102	50°49·3'	2°7·3'W	A	195
Crawforddyke	S Lanak	NS8549	55°43·5'	3°49·4'W	T	72
Crawford Fm	N Yks	SE3598	54°22·8'	1°27·2'W	FM	99
Crawford Grange	N Yks	SE3697	54°22·3'	1°26·3'W	X	99
Crawford Hill	E Ayr	NS6117	55°25·9'	4°11·4'W	H	71
Crawfordjohn	S Lanak	NS8723	55°29·5'	3°46·9'W	T	71,72
Crawfordjohn Mill Fm	S Lanak	NS8924	55°30·1'	3°45·0'W	FM	71,72
Crawford Priory	Fife	NO3411	56°17·5'	3°3·5'W	X	59
Crawford's Fm	Lincs	TF3440	52°56·7'	0°0·1'E	FM	131
Crawford's Hill	Northum	NZ1278	55°6·0'	1°48·3'W	H	88
Crawfordston	S Ayr	NS3310	55°21·6'	4°37·6'W	X	70
Crawfordston	S Ayr	NS4123	55°28·8'	4°30·5'W	X	70
Crawfordton	D & G	NX7990	55°11·6'	3°55·6'W	T	78
Crawfordton Burn	D & G	NX8088	55°10·6'	3°52·6'W	W	78
Crawfordton Hill	D & G	NX8090	55°11·6'	3°52·7'W	X	78
Crawhead	Aberd	NJ9831	57°22·4'	2°1·5'W	X	30
Crawhill	Fife	NO5504	56°13·8'	2°43·1'W	X	59
Craw Hill	Shetld	HU2956	60°17·5'	1°28·0'W	H	3
Crawhill	W Loth	NS9472	55°56·0'	3°41·4'W	X	65
Crawhin Hill	Inverc	NS2471	55°54·3'	4°48·5'W	X	63
Crawhin Resr	Inverc	NS2470	55°53·7'	4°48·4'W	W	63
Crawick	D & G	NS7711	55°22·9'	3°56·1'W	T	71,78
Crawick Moss	S Lanak	NS8320	55°27·8'	3°50·6'W	X	71,72
Crawick Water	D & G	NS8017	55°26·2'	3°53·4'W	W	71,78
Craw Knowe	Stir	NN3523	56°22·5'	4°39·9'W	H	50
Crawlaw	E Ayr	NS4938	55°37·0'	4°23·4'W	X	70
Crawlaw Rigg	Durham	NY9115	54°32·1'	2°7·9'W	X	91,92
Crawlboys Fm	Wilts	SU2751	51°15·7'	1°36·4'W	FM	184
Crawleas	Durham	NZ2529	54°39·6'	1°36·3'W	X	93
Crawlee Plantn	Scot Bord	NT6946	55°42·6'	2°29·2'W	F	74
Crawless Fm	Glos	ST6999	51°41·6'	2°26·5'W	FM	162
Crawley	Devon	ST2607	50°51·7'	3°2·7'W	T	192,193
Crawley	Glos	ST7899	51°41·6'	2°18·7'W	X	162
Crawley	Hants	SU4234	51°6·5'	1°23·6'W	T	185
Crawley	Oxon	SP3411	51°48·0'	1°30·0'W	T	164
Crawley	W Susx	TQ2736	51°6·8'	0°10·7'W	T	187
Crawley Court	Hants	SU4234	51°6·5'	1°23·6'W	X	185
Crawley Down	Hants	SU4436	51°7·5'	1°21·9'W	F	185
Crawley Down	W Susx	TQ3437	51°7·2'	0°4·7'W	T	187
Crawley End	Essex	TL4440	52°2·6'	0°6·4'E	T	154
Crawley Fm	Bucks	SP7011	51°47·8'	0°58·7'W	FM	165
Crawley Fm	Northum	NU0616	55°26·5'	1°53·9'W	FM	81
Crawley Grange	Mil Key	SP9344	52°5·4'	0°38·2'W	X	153
Crawley Hall Fm	Suff	TL9664	52°14·6'	0°52·7'E	FM	155
Crawleyheath Fm	Beds	SP9634	52°0·0'	0°35·7'W	FM	153,165
Crawley Hill	Surrey	SU8860	51°20·2'	0°43·8'W	T	175,186
Crawley-Hove Link Route	W Susx	TQ2621	50°58·7'	0°11·9'W	X	187,198
Crawley Park	Beds	SP9535	52°0·5'	0°36·6'W	X	153
Crawleyside	Durham	NY9940	54°45·5'	2°0·5'W	T	87
Crawpeel Shore	C of Aber	NJ9500	57°5·7'	2°4·5'W	X	38
Crawshaw	Kirk	SE2313	53°37·0'	1°38·7'W	T	110
Crawshaw	Lancs	SD6951	53°57·5'	2°27·9'W	X	103
Crawshawbooth	Lancs	SD8125	53°43·5'	2°16·9'W	T	103
Crawshaw Fm	Sheff	SK2588	53°23·5'	1°37·0'W	FM	110
Crawshaw Head Ho	Sheff	SK2588	53°23·5'	1°37·0'W	X	110
Crawshaw Moss	Brad	SE0946	53°54·8'	1°51·4'W	X	104
Craw's Knowe	D & G	NY3374	55°3·6'	3°2·5'W	X	85
Craw Stane	Aberd	NJ4926	57°19·6'	2°50·4'W	X	37
Crawston	D & G	NX8985	55°9·1'	3°44·1'W	X	78
Crawston	D & G	NY2076	55°4·6'	3°14·8'W	X	85
Crawston Hill	D & G	NX8885	55°9·1'	3°45·0'W	H	78
Crawter Hill	Somer	SS8945	51°11·8'	3°34·9'W	X	181
Crawthat Hill	D & G	NY2483	55°8·4'	3°11·1'W	H	79
Crawthorne Fm	Dorset	SY7796	50°46·0'	2°19·2'W	FM	194
Crawton	Aberd	NO8779	56°54·4'	2°12·4'W	T	45
Crawton	Shetld	HU2157	60°18·1'	1°36·7'W	T	3
Crawton Bay	Aberd	NO8779	56°54·4'	2°12·4'W	W	45
Crawyn	I of M	SC3496	54°20·2'	4°32·8'W	X	95
Craxton Wood	Ches	SJ3474	53°15·8'	2°59·0'W	X	117
Cray	N Yks	SD9479	54°12·6'	2°5·1'W	T	98
Cray	Pth & Kin	NO1463	56°45·3'	3°23·9'W	T	43
Craya	Orkney	HY2514	59°0·7'	3°17·9'W	X	6
Craycombe Hill	Worcs	SP0047	52°7·5'	1°59·6'W	X	150
Craycombe Ho	Worcs	SP0047	52°7·5'	1°59·6'W	X	150
Craydon	Devon	SX6595	50°44·6'	3°54·4'W	X	191
Crayford	Bexley	TQ5174	51°26·9'	0°10·8'E	T	177
Crayford	Devon	SX7295	50°44·7'	3°48·5'W	X	191
Crayford Marshes	Bexley	TQ5377	51°28·5'	0°12·6'E	X	177
Crayford Ness	Bexley	TQ5378	51°29·0'	0°12·6'E	X	177
Cray Gill	N Yks	SD9378	54°12·1'	2°6·0'W	W	98
Crayke	N Yks	SE5670	54°7·6'	1°8·2'W	T	100
Crayke House Fm	N Yks	TA1081	54°13·0'	0°18·4'W	FM	101
Craykeland Wood	N Yks	SE5677	54°11·4'	1°8·1'W	F	100
Crayke Lodge	N Yks	SE5469	54°7·1'	1°10·0'W	X	100
Crayke Manor	N Yks	SE5671	54°8·1'	1°8·2'W	A	100
Craymere Beck	Norf	TG0630	52°49·9'	1°3·9'E	T	133
Cray Moss	N Yks	SD9381	54°13·7'	2°6·0'W	X	98
Cray Resr	Powys	SN8821	51°52·8'	3°37·2'W	W	160
Crays Fm	W Susx	TQ1117	50°56·7'	0°24·8'W	FM	198
Crays Hall Fm	Essex	TQ7093	51°36·8'	0°27·7'E	FM	178
Crays Hill	Essex	TQ7192	51°36·3'	0°28·6'E	T	178
Cray's Pond	Oxon	SU6380	51°31·2'	1°5·1'W	T	175
Crayston	Cumbr	NY5616	54°32·5'	2°40·4'W	X	90
Cray Tarn	N Yks	SD9281	54°13·7'	2°6·9'W	W	98
Craythorne Fm	Staffs	SK2427	52°50·6'	1°38·2'W	FM	128
Craze Lowman	Devon	SS9814	50°55·2'	3°26·7'W	X	181
Crazies Hill	Wok	SU7980	51°31·0'	0°51·3'W	T	175
Crazy Well Pool	Devon	SX5870	50°31·0'	3°59·8'W	W	202
Creaber	Devon	SX6687	50°40·3'	3°53·4'W	X	191
Creachan an Fhiodha	Highld	NH5082	57°48·4'	4°31·0'W	X	20
Creachan Beag	Arg & Bt	NS0189	56°3·4'	5°11·3'W	X	55
Creachan Beag	Arg & Bt	NS1287	56°2·6'	5°0·7'W	H	56
Creachan Dubh	Arg & Bt	NS0291	56°4·5'	5°10·4'W	X	55
Creachan Hill	Arg & Bt	NS3389	56°4·1'	4°40·5'W	H	56
Creachan Mòr	Arg & Bt	NM4919	56°18·1'	6°3·0'W	H	48
Creachan Mòr	Arg & Bt	NS0190	56°3·9'	5°11·4'W	X	55
Creachan Mòr	Arg & Bt	NS1188	56°3·1'	5°1·7'W	X	56
Creachan Mòr	Arg & Bt	NS1891	56°4·9'	4°55·0'W	H	56
Creachan nan Sgadan	Highld	NH4775	57°44·6'	4°33·8'W	H	20
Creachan Rairigidh	Highld	NH2170	57°41·3'	4°59·7'W	H	20
Creachan Thormaid	Highld	NC3343	58°20·9'	4°50·7'W	H	9
Creachasdal Beag	Arg & Bt	NM1048	56°32·3'	6°42·6'W	X	46
Creachasdal Mòr	Arg & Bt	NM1048	56°32·3'	6°42·6'W	X	46
Creach Beinn	Arg & Bt	NM6427	56°22·8'	5°48·9'W	H	49
Creach Bheinn	Arg & Bt	NM4129	56°23·2'	6°11·3'W	H	48
Creach Bheinn	Arg & Bt	NN0242	56°32·0'	5°12·7'W	H	50
Creach Bheinn	Highld	NM8657	56°39·6'	5°29·1'W	H	49
Creach Bheinn	Highld	NM8657	56°39·6'	5°29·1'W	H	49
Creach Bheinn Bheag	Arg & Bt	NM6326	56°22·3'	5°49·8'W	X	49
Creach Leac	Arg & Bt	NM8225	56°22·3'	5°31·4'W	X	49
Creacombe	Devon	SS8119	50°57·7'	3°41·3'W	T	181
Creacombe Fm	Devon	SX5949	50°19·7'	3°58·5'W	FM	202
Cread Mhosgalaid Mhòr	N Eil	NB3005	57°57·4'	6°33·4'W	X	13,14
Creag a' Bhaca	Highld	NH2029	57°19·2'	4°58·9'W	H	25
Creag a Bhacain	Stir	NN5604	56°12·7'	4°18·9'W	X	57

Creag a' Bhadaidh Daraich	Highld	NC1645	58°21·6'	5°8·2'W	H	9
Creag a' Bhaid Choill	Highld	NC2348	58°23·3'	5°1·2'W	X	9
Creag a' Bhainne	Highld	NH8726	57°18·9'	3°52·1'W	X	35,36
Creag a' Bhaird	Pth & Kin	NN9240	56°32·6'	3°44·9'W	X	52
Creag a' Bhalgain	Highld	NH1121	57°14·7'	5°7·5'W	X	25
Creag a' Bhànain	Highld	NN4291	56°59·3'	4°35·6'W	H	34
Creag a'Bhanan	Arg & Bt	NR7999	56°8·2'	5°33·0'W	H	55
Creag a' Bharra	Highld	NM6254	56°37·3'	5°52·3'W	H	49
Creag a' Bharrain	Highld	NJ1035	57°24·1'	3°29·4'W	H	28
Creag a' Bhata	Highld	NC7202	57°59·6'	4°9·4'W	H	16
Creag a' Bhealaich	Highld	NH6592	57°54·1'	4°16·2'W	H	21
Creag á Bhealaich	Stir	NN4605	56°13·0'	4°28·6'W	X	57
Creag a' Bhealaidh	Highld	NH7826	57°18·8'	4°1·1'W	X	35
Creag a' Bhealaidh	Pth & Kin	NN9244	56°34·8'	3°45·0'W	X	52
Creag a' Bheithe	Highld	NM7866	56°44·2'	5°37·3'W	X	40
Creag a' Bhinnein	Arg & Bt	NN0837	56°29·4'	5°6·7'W	X	50
Creag a' Bhlàir	Highld	NC7300	57°58·5'	4°8·4'W	H	16
Creag a' Bhlàir	Highld	NM8675	56°49·3'	5°30·0'W	X	40
Creag a' Bhòcaidh	Highld	NC6605	58°1·1'	4°15·6'W	H	16
Creag a' Bhocain	Stir	NN3404	56°12·2'	4°40·1'W	H	56
Creag a' Bhodaich	Highld	NC9114	58°6·4'	3°50·5'W	H	17
Creag a' Bhoinne	Highld	NH3949	57°30·4'	4°40·8'W	H	26
Creag a' Bhothain	Highld	NH8738	57°25·4'	3°52·4'W	H	27
Creag a' Bhraighe	Highld	NC1232	58°14·5'	5°11·7'W	H	15
Creag a' Bhruic	Highld	NH2839	57°24·8'	4°51·4'W	X	25
Creag a' Bhuachaille	Stir	NN5331	56°27·2'	4°22·7'W	X	51
Creag a' Bhuairidh	Highld	NG8417	57°11·8'	5°34·1'W	X	33
Creag a' Bhuie	Stir	NN3322	56°21·9'	4°41·8'W	X	50
Creag a' Chadha	Highld	NG8640	57°24·3'	5°33·3'W	X	24
Creag a' Chadha	Highld	NH0393	57°53·2'	5°18·9'W	X	19
Creag a' Chadha Bhriste	Highld	NH0976	57°44·3'	5°12·0'W	X	19
Creag a' Chadha Dhuibh	Moray	NJ1509	57°10·1'	3°23·9'W	X	36
Creag Achadh an Eas	Highld	NH2150	57°30·6'	4°58·8'W	X	25
Creag a' Chàil	Highld	NN1374	56°49·5'	5°3·4'W	X	41
Creag a' Chail	Highld	NN4095	57°1·4'	4°37·7'W	H	34
Creag-a-Chaim	Highld	NG6303	57°3·7'	5°54·1'W	X	32
Creag a' Chàirn Chaoruinn	Highld	NC3849	58°24·2'	4°45·9'W	X	9
Creag a' Chais'	Pth & Kin	NN5266	56°46·0'	4°24·8'W	H	42
Creag a'Chaise	Highld	NG7812	57°9·0'	5°39·8'W	X	33
Creag a' Chaise	Highld	NH1631	57°20·2'	5°3·0'W	X	25
Creag a' Chaise	N Ayr	NR9449	55°41·7'	5°16·2'W	X	62,69
Creag a' Chàise	Pth & Kin	NO0772	56°50·1'	3°31·0'W	H	43
Creag a' Chaisil	Highld	NG9329	57°18·5'	5°25·8'W	X	25,33
Creag a' Chaisteil	Arg & Bt	NM3649	56°33·8'	6°17·4'W	X	47,48
Creag a' Chait	Aberd	NO0788	56°58·7'	3°31·4'W	X	43
Creag a' Chait	Aberd	NO1795	57°2·6'	3°21·6'W	H	36,43
Creag a' Chait	Highld	NG4838	57°22·0'	6°11·0'W	H	23,32
Creag a' Chait	Highld	NH0849	57°29·7'	5°11·8'W	X	25
Creag a' Chait	Highld	NH5498	57°57·1'	4°27·6'W	X	21
Creag a' Chalamain	Highld	NH9605	57°7·7'	3°42·6'W	H	36
Creag a' Chaltuinn	Highld	NM7783	56°53·3'	5°39·2'W	X	40
Creag a'Chanuill	Arg & Bt	NS1184	56°1·0'	5°1·5'W	X	56
Creag a' Chaobh	Highld	NH1941	57°25·7'	5°0·4'W	H	25
Creag a' Chaorainn	Highld	NH0043	57°26·3'	5°19·5'W	X	25
Creag a' Chaorainn	Highld	NH0245	57°27·4'	5°17·6'W	X	25
Creag a' Chaorainn	Highld	NH1222	57°15·3'	5°6·5'W	X	25
Creag a' Chaorainn	Highld	NH1413	57°10·5'	5°4·2'W	X	34
Creag a' Chaorainn	Pth & Kin	NN4444	56°34·0'	4°31·9'W	X	51
Creag a' Chaoruinn	Highld	NH4058	57°35·3'	4°40·1'W	H	26
Creag a'Chapuill	Arg & Bt	NM8502	56°10·0'	5°27·3'W	H	55
Creag a' Charnaich	Highld	NG4355	57°31·0'	6°17·0'W	H	23
Creag a' Chinn Duibh	Highld	NG8562	57°36·1'	5°35·4'W	X	19
Creag a' Chlachain	Highld	NH6533	57°22·3'	4°14·2'W	H	26
Creag a' Chlamhain	Aberd	NO2695	57°2·7'	3°12·7'W	H	37,44
Creag a' Chlàr Locha	Highld	NC2042	58°20·0'	5°4·0'W	H	9
Creag a' Chleirich	Aberd	NO1493	57°1·5'	3°24·5'W	H	36,43
Creag a' Chliabhain	Highld	NH5720	57°15·2'	4°21·8'W	H	26,35
Creag a' Choineachan	Highld	NH5695	57°55·5'	4°25·4'W	H	21
Creag a' Choir Aird	Highld	NH0727	57°17·8'	5°11·7'W	X	25,33
Creag a' Choire	Highld	ND0015	58°7·0'	3°41·4'W	X	17
Creag a' Choire	Pth & Kin	NN9157	56°41·8'	3°46·3'W	X	52
Creag a' Choire Dhuibh	Highld	NH2731	57°20·5'	4°52·0'W	H	25
Creag a' Choire Ghlais	Highld	NC6927	58°13·0'	4°13·3'W	H	16
Creag a' Choire Riabhaich	Highld	NH2167	57°39·7'	4°59·6'W	H	20
Creagach Point	Arg & Bt	NR2847	55°38·7'	6°19·0'W	X	60
Creag a' Chreamha Mór	Arg & Bt	NR5171	55°52·3'	5°58·4'W	X	61
Creag a' Chrionaich	Highld	NC9211	58°4·8'	3°49·4'W	X	17
Creag a Chròcain	Highld	NH8235	57°23·7'	3°57·3'W	X	27
Creag a' Chrochaidh	Pth & Kin	NN9475	56°51·5'	3°43·9'W	X	43
Creag a' Chroisg	Highld	NC2215	58°5·6'	5°0·7'W	H	15
Creag a'Chromain	Arg & Bt	NM8101	56°9·3'	5°31·1'W	H	55
Creag a' Chromain	N Ayr	NR9038	55°35·7'	5°19·5'W	X	68,69
Creag a Chrotha	Arg & Bt	NN0127	56°23·9'	5°13·0'W	H	50
Creag a' Chuilbh	N Eil	NF8441	57°21·3'	7°14·8'W	X	22
Creag a' Chuir	Highld	NN5084	56°55·6'	4°27·4'W	H	42
Creag a' Chumhaing	Highld	NG7940	57°24·1'	5°40·3'W	X	24
Creag a' Ghaill	Arg & Bt	NM4432	56°24·9'	6°8·6'W	X	48
Creag a' Ghamhna	Highld	NG2554	57°29·8'	6°35·0'W	X	23
Creag a' Ghaoirr	Highld	NH4573	57°43·5'	4°35·7'W	H	20
Creag a Ghiubhais	Highld	NH5121	57°15·6'	4°27·8'W	H	26,35
Creag a' Ghiubhais	Highld	NH5528	57°19·4'	4°24·0'W	X	26,35
Creag a' Ghiuthais	Highld	NH9531	57°21·7'	3°44·3'W	H	27
Creag a' Ghlastail	Highld	NH2647	57°29·1'	4°53·7'W	H	25
Creag a' Ghlas-uillt	Aberd	NO2583	56°56·2'	3°13·5'W	X	44
Creag a' Ghlinne	Highld	NM8553	56°37·4'	5°29·8'W	X	49
Creag a' Ghobhair	Highld	NH6594	57°55·2'	4°16·3'W	H	21
Creag a' Ghormlaich	Highld	NH2144	57°27·3'	4°58·6'W	X	25
Creag a' Ghreusaiche	Highld	NH9412	57°11·5'	3°44·8'W	H	36
Creag a' Ghrianain	Highld	NN5991	56°59·6'	4°18·8'W	H	35
Creag a'Ghuail	Arg & Bt	NR8584	56°0·3'	5°26·5'W	X	55
Creag-a' Ghuail	Highld	NG2552	57°28·8'	6°34·8'W	X	23
Creag Aighean	Aberd	NJ2812	57°11·8'	3°11·0'W	X	37
Creagalain	Highld	NG4549	57°27·8'	6°14·7'W	H	23
Creag a' Lain	Highld	NG4658	57°32·7'	6°14·2'W	X	23
Creag Alasdair Mhic Sheumais	Highld	NH5222	57°16·1'	4°26·8'W	X	26,35
Creag Alatair	N Eil	NG0487	57°46·8'	6°58·3'W	X	18
Creag a' Mhadaidh	Aberd	NO1284	56°56·6'	3°26·3'W	H	43
Creag a'Mhadaidh	Arg & Bt	NR7280	55°57·8'	5°38·7'W	X	55
Creag a'Mhadaidh	Arg & Bt	NR8082	55°59·1'	5°31·2'W	H	55
Creag a' Mhadaidh	Highld	NH3514	57°11·5'	4°43·4'W	H	34
Creag a' Mhadaidh	Pth & Kin	NN6365	56°45·6'	4°14·0'W	H	42
Creag a' Mhadaidh	Pth & Kin	NN9145	56°35·3'	3°46·0'W	H	52
Creag a' Mhadaidh	Pth & Kin	NO0459	56°43·0'	3°33·7'W	X	52,53
Creag a' Mhadaidh	Stir	NN5314	56°18·0'	4°22·1'W	X	57
Creag a' Mhadaidh	Stir	NN5816	56°19·2'	4°17·3'W	X	57
Creag a' Mhaigh	Highld	NN4983	56°55·1'	4°28·4'W	H	34,42
Creag a' Mhàil	Highld	NC1445	58°21·5'	5°10·3'W	X	9
Creag a' Mhàim	Highld	NH0807	57°7·1'	5°9·8'W	H	33
Creag a' Mhaol-dhiridh	Arg & Bt	NN1525	56°23·1'	4°59·4'W	X	50
Creag a' Mhill	Highld	NG2450	57°27·6'	6°35·7'W	H	23
Creag a' Mhuilinn	Highld	NH8409	57°9·7'	3°54·6'W	X	35
Creagan	Arg & Bt	NM9744	56°32·9'	5°17·7'W	T	49
Creagan	Stir	NN5617	56°19·7'	4°19·3'W	X	57
Creagan a' Bhuic	Arg & Bt	NN4147	56°35·5'	4°34·9'W	X	51
Creag an Achaidh Mhóir	Highld	NC5245	58°22·4'	4°31·4'W	H	10
Creag an Achaidh Mhóir	Highld	NC6040	58°19·8'	4°23·0'W	X	10
Creagan a' Chaise	Highld	NN3170	56°47·7'	4°45·6'W	H	41
Creagan a' Chaise	Moray	NJ1024	57°18·1'	3°29·2'W	H	36
Creagan a' Chaorainn	Highld	NH2648	57°29·6'	4°53·7'W	H	25
Creagan a' Chaorrainn	Highld	NH2574	57°43·6'	4°55·9'W	X	20
Creagan a' Choin	Highld	NN7095	57°1·9'	4°8·1'W	H	35
Creagan a' Choin Ruaidh	Highld	NH5586	57°50·7'	4°26·1'W	X	21
Creagan a' Choire Etchachan	Aberd	NO0199	57°4·5'	3°37·5'W	X	36,43
Creag an Adhlaic	Arg & Bt	NS1196	56°7·4'	5°2·0'W	X	56
Creag an Airgid	Highld	NM4766	56°43·3'	6°7·7'W	H	47
Creag an Alltan Fheàrna	Highld	NC7432	58°15·8'	4°8·4'W	H	16
Creag an Amalaidh	Highld	NH7597	57°57·0'	4°6·2'W	H	21
Creagan a' Mhuillin	Highld	NN2684	56°55·1'	4°51·1'W	X	34,41
Creagan an Amair	Highld	NN4271	56°48·5'	4°34·8'W	H	42
Creagan an Dìridh	Highld	NC5332	58°15·4'	4°29·8'W	X	16
Creagan an Eich	Arg & Bt	NN1003	56°11·2'	5°3·3'W	H	56
Creagan an Eich Ghlais	Highld	NH3864	57°38·5'	4°42·4'W	H	20
Creagan an Fhithich	Highld	NM7569	56°45·8'	5°40·4'W	X	40
Creagan an Lochain	Pth & Kin	NN6420	56°21·4'	4°11·6'W	X	51,57
Creagan an t-Sagairt	Highld	NM7981	56°52·3'	5°37·1'W	H	40
Creagan an t-Seallaidh	Highld	NN5580	56°53·6'	4°22·4'W	X	42
Creagan an t-Sluichd	Pth & Kin	NN5040	56°31·9'	4°25·9'W	X	51
Creag an Aoineidh	Arg & Bt	NN0527	56°24·0'	5°9·1'W	X	50
Creag an Aonaich	Aberd	NJ2910	57°10·8'	3°10·0'W	H	37
Creag an Ardaich	Highld	NH0748	57°29·1'	5°12·7'W	X	25
Creagan Asdale	Highld	NH7292	57°54·2'	4°9·1'W	H	21
Creagan Beag	Arg & Bt	NR8579	55°57·6'	5°26·2'W	X	62
Creagan Bheithe	Pth & Kin	NO1073	56°50·6'	3°28·1'W	H	43
Creagan Breac	Highld	NN3790	56°58·6'	4°40·5'W	X	34
Creagan Breac	Pth & Kin	NN6761	56°43·6'	4°10·0'W	X	42
Creagan Breaca	Highld	NC2619	58°7·8'	4°56·8'W	H	15
Creagan Breaca	Highld	NG3551	57°28·6'	6°24·8'W	H	23
Creagan Breaca	Highld	NG3839	57°22·2'	6°21·0'W	H	23,32
Creagan Caise	Angus	NO1868	56°48·0'	3°20·1'W	X	43
Creagan Corr	Arg & Bt	NR3774	55°53·5'	6°12·0'W	H	60,61
Creagan Cosach	Highld	ND0821	58°10·4'	3°33·4'W	H	17
Creagan Criche	Arg & Bt	NN3146	56°34·8'	4°44·6'W	X	50
Creagan Crúinn	Arg & Bt	NN3746	56°34·9'	4°38·8'W	X	50
Creag an Dail Bheag	Aberd	NO1498	57°4·2'	3°24·6'W	X	36,43
Creag an Dail Mhor	Aberd	NO1398	57°4·1'	3°25·6'W	X	36,43
Creag an Daimh	Arg & Bt	NN2440	56°31·4'	4°51·2'W	H	50
Creag an Daimh	Highld	NH8344	57°28·5'	3°56·6'W	H	27
Creagandamph	Highld	NC7317	58°7·7'	4°8·9'W	X	16
Creagan Dearga	Highld	NG3156	57°31·1'	6°29·1'W	X	23
Creagan Dearga	Highld	NG7300	57°2·4'	5°44·0'W	X	33
Creagan Dearga	Highld	NG9387	57°49·7'	5°28·7'W	X	19
Creag an Dearg Lochain	Highld	NH5301	57°4·9'	4°25·1'W	X	35
Creag an Dherue	Highld	NC5447	58°23·5'	4°29·4'W	X	10
Creag an Dochdair	Highld	NM7797	57°0·9'	5°39·9'W	X	33,40
Creagan Doire Dhonaich	Highld	NN6377	56°52·1'	4°14·4'W	H	42
Creagan Dubh	Arg & Bt	NR9691	56°4·4'	5°16·2'W	X	55
Creagan Dubh	Arg & Bt	NR9977	55°56·9'	5°12·7'W	X	62
Creagan Dubh	Highld	NC4042	58°20·5'	4°43·5'W	X	9
Creagan Dubh	Highld	NG3524	57°14·1'	6°23·0'W	X	32
Creagan Dubh	Highld	NG5824	57°14·8'	6°0·2'W	X	32
Creagan Dubh	Highld	NG6110	57°7·4'	5°56·5'W	H	32
Creagan Dubh	Highld	NG8814	57°10·3'	5°30·0'W	X	33
Creagan Dubh	Highld	NH4837	57°24·1'	4°31·3'W	X	26
Creagan Dubha	Arg & Bt	NS3692	56°5·8'	4°37·7'W	X	56
Creagan Dubha	Highld	NG8577	57°44·1'	5°36·2'W	X	19
Creagan Dubha	Stir	NN4221	56°21·6'	4°33·0'W	X	51,56
Creagan Dubha	Stir	NS4295	56°7·6'	4°32·1'W	X	56
Creagan Dubha Réidhe Bhig	Highld	NC7544	58°22·3'	4°7·7'W	H	10
Creagan Dubh-choire	Highld	NG7806	57°5·7'	5°39·4'W	X	33
Creag an Dubh-loch	Aberd	NO2382	56°55·6'	3°15·5'W	X	44
Creag an Dubh Shluic	Pth & Kin	NO0968	56°47·9'	3°29·0'W	H	43
Creag an Dubh-thuill	Highld	NH1243	57°26·6'	5°7·5'W	X	25
Creaganducy	Aberd	NO6089	56°59·7'	2°39·0'W	H	45
Creag an Duibh	Pth & Kin	NN9878	56°53·2'	3°40·0'W	H	43
Creag an Duilisg	Highld	NG8333	57°20·4'	5°35·9'W	X	24
Creag an Dùin	Pth & Kin	NN8338	56°31·4'	3°53·7'W	X	52
Creag an Duine	Highld	NH2987	57°50·7'	4°52·4'W	H	20
Creag an Duine Charaich	Highld	NH5496	57°56·0'	4°27·5'W	H	21
Creagandummie	Aberd	NO5494	57°2·3'	2°45·0'W	H	37,44
Creagandunie	Aberd	NO5197	57°3·9'	2°48·0'W	X	37,44
Creagan Eachdarra	Arg & Bt	NN2122	56°21·6'	4°53·4'W	X	50
Creag an Earbaill	Highld	NG8527	57°17·2'	5°33·6'W	H	33
Creag an Eàrra	Pth & Kin	NN6953	56°39·3'	4°7·8'W	H	42,51
Creag an Eich	Highld	NH0582	57°47·4'	5°16·4'W	X	19
Creag an Eich	Highld	NM8385	56°54·6'	5°33·4'W	X	40
Creag an Eich	N Ayr	NR9650	55°42·3'	5°14·4'W	X	62,69
Creag an Eidhein	Highld	NH6226	57°18·5'	4°17·0'W	H	26,35
Creag an Eig	Arg & Bt	NM9037	56°29·0'	5°24·2'W	X	49
Creag an Eighich	Highld	NM7663	56°42·6'	5°39·1'W	X	40
Creag an Eilein	Highld	NG8997	57°55·0'	5°33·3'W	X	19
Creag an Eilein	Highld	NH0047	57°28·4'	5°19·7'W	X	25
Creag an Eilein	Highld	NM7697	57°0·9'	5°40·9'W	X	33,40
Creag an Eilein	N Eil	NF8314	57°6·7'	7°13·8'W	X	31
Creag an Eirionnach	Pth & Kin	NN8962	56°44·4'	3°48·4'W	H	43
Creag an Eòin	Highld	NG5950	57°28·8'	6°0·8'W	X	24
Creag an Eòin	N Eil	NG0994	57°50·7'	6°53·8'W	X	14
Creag an Eunaich	Pth & Kin	NN9743	56°34·3'	3°40·1'W	H	52,53
Creag an Eunan	Aberd	NJ3819	57°15·7'	3°1·2'W	H	37
Creagan Feadaire	Pth & Kin	NN9054	56°40·1'	3°47·2'W	X	52
Creag an Fhàoraich	Pth & Kin	NN5747	56°35·8'	4°19·3'W	X	51
Creag an Fhasgaidh	Arg & Bt	NR9372	55°54·1'	5°18·2'W	X	62
Creag an Fheadain	Pth & Kin	NN4945	56°34·6'	4°27·0'W	H	51
Creag an Fhéidh	Arg & Bt	NM4724	56°20·7'	6°5·2'W	X	48
Creag an Fhireoin	Arg & Bt	NM1756	56°36·9'	6°36·3'W	X	46
Creagan Fhir-eoin	Highld	NG9447	57°28·3'	5°25·7'W	X	25
Creag an Fhir-eòin	Highld	NH1940	57°25·1'	5°0·4'W	X	25
Creag an Fhìr-eòin	Highld	NH4302	57°5·2'	4°35·0'W	X	34
Creag an Fhir-eoin	Highld	NN5999	57°3·9'	4°19·1'W	X	35
Creag an Fhirich	Highld	NN2649	56°36·3'	4°49·6'W	X	50
Creag an Fhirich	Highld	NN2748	56°35·8'	4°48·6'W	X	50
Creag an Fhir-shaighde	Aberd	NO1983	56°56·1'	3°19·4'W	X	43
Creag an Fhithich	Aberd	NO0988	56°58·7'	3°29·4'W	X	43
Creag an Fhithich	Arg & Bt	NM8224	56°21·7'	5°31·3'W	X	49
Creag an Fhithich	Arg & Bt	NM9550	56°36·1'	5°19·9'W	X	49
Creag an Fhithich	Arg & Bt	NN0634	56°27·8'	5°8·5'W	X	50
Creag an Fhithich	Arg & Bt	NN1418	56°19·3'	5°0·0'W	H	50,56
Creag an Fhithich	Arg & Bt	NR7635	55°33·7'	5°32·7'W	X	68,69
Creag an Fhithich	Arg & Bt	NR9573	55°54·6'	5°16·4'W	X	62
Creag an Fhithich	Highld	NC2553	58°26·1'	4°59·4'W	H	9
Creag an Fhithich	Highld	NG2466	57°36·2'	6°36·8'W	X	23
Creag an Fhithich	Highld	NG4846	57°26·3'	6°11·5'W	H	23
Creag an Fhithich	Highld	NG7652	57°30·4'	5°43·9'W	X	24
Creag an Fhithich	Highld	NG8311	57°8·6'	5°34·8'W	X	33
Creag an Fhithich	Highld	NG8567	57°38·8'	5°35·7'W	H	19,24
Creag an Fhithich	Highld	NH5475	57°44·7'	4°26·7'W	X	21
Creag an Fhithich	Highld	NH9321	57°16·3'	3°46·0'W	H	36
Creag an Fhithich	Highld	NM6061	56°41·0'	5°54·7'W	X	40
Creag an Fhithich	Highld	NM6546	56°33·1'	5°49·0'W	X	49
Creag an Fhithich	Pth & Kin	NN6342	56°33·3'	4°13·3'W	H	51
Creag an Fhithich	Pth & Kin	NN6657	56°41·4'	4°10·8'W	H	42,51
Creag an Fhithich	Pth & Kin	NN8756	56°41·2'	3°50·2'W	X	52
Creag an Fhithich	Stir	NN3312	56°16·5'	4°41·4'W	H	50,56
Creag an Fhithic Mór	Highld	NG8591	57°51·7'	5°37·0'W	H	19
Creag an Fhradhairc	Highld	NM6268	56°44·8'	5°53·1'W	H	40
Creag an Fhraoich	Highld	NG8058	57°33·8'	5°40·2'W	X	24
Creag an Fhuarail Bheag	Highld	NH1126	57°17·4'	5°7·7'W	X	25
Creag an Fhuathais	Aberd	NO0983	56°56·0'	3°29·3'W	X	43
Creag an Fhùdair	Pth & Kin	NN7843	56°34·0'	3°58·7'W	H	51,52
Creaganfois	D & G	NX6281	55°6·5'	4°9·4'W	X	77
Creagan Glas	Highld	NC6701	57°59·0'	4°14·5'W	H	16
Creagan Glas	Highld	NH7642	57°27·3'	4°3·5'W	X	27
Creagan Glasa	Highld	NG3056	57°31·1'	6°30·1'W	H	23
Creagan Gorm	Highld	NH9712	57°11·5'	3°41·8'W	H	36
Creag an Iaruinn	Moray	NJ1221	57°16·5'	3°27·1'W	H	36
Creag an Iasgaich	Highld	NM8374	56°48·7'	5°32·8'W	X	40
Creag an-Iarlain	Highld	NH3610	57°9·4'	4°42·2'W	X	
Creagan Leana Muic	N Ayr	NR9634	55°33·7'	5°13·7'W	X	68,69
Creagan Leathan	N Eil	NB0613	58°0·8'	6°58·2'W	H	13,14
Creag an Leinibh	Arg & Bt	NS3192	56°5·7'	4°42·6'W	X	56
Creag an Leth-choin or Lurcher's Crag	Highld	NH9603	57°6·6'	3°42·6'W	H	36
Creagan Liath	Highld	NC9631	58°15·6'	3°45·9'W	X	11,17
Creagan Liatha	Arg & Bt	NN3535	56°29·0'	4°40·3'W	X	50
Creagan Liatha	Highld	NN5490	56°59·0'	4°23·7'W	X	35
Creagan Liatha	N Ayr	NR9632	55°32·6'	5°13·6'W	X	68,69
Creagan Liatha	Stir	NN4221	56°21·6'	4°33·0'W	X	51,56
Creag an Loch	Aberd	NO1984	56°56·7'	3°19·4'W	H	43
Creag an Loch	Pth & Kin	NN7279	56°53·3'	4°5·6'W	X	42
Creag an Loch	Pth & Kin	NN8254	56°40·0'	3°55·1'W	H	52
Creag an Loch	Pth & Kin	NN8740	56°32·6'	3°49·8'W	H	52
Creag an Locha	Highld	NG4155	57°30·9'	6°19·0'W	H	23
Creag an Lochain	Aberd	NO0883	56°56·0'	3°30·3'W	H	43
Creag an Lochain	Highld	NC5728	58°13·3'	4°25·6'W	H	16
Creag an Lochain	Highld	NC7529	58°14·2'	4°7·3'W	H	16
Creag an Lochain	Highld	NN4289	56°58·2'	4°35·5'W	X	34,42
Creag an Lochain	Pth & Kin	NN5840	56°32·1'	4°18·1'W	H	51
Creag an Lochain	Pth & Kin	NN8356	56°41·1'	3°54·2'W	H	52
Creag an Loibein	Highld	NM6767	56°44·4'	5°48·2'W	H	40
Creag an Lòin	Highld	NH6901	57°5·1'	4°9·2'W	H	35
Creagan Loisgte	Arg & Bt	NR4266	55°49·4'	6°6·7'W	X	60,61
Creag-an-Iubhair	Arg & Bt	NR9499	56°8·6'	5°18·5'W	X	55
Creagan Meall Horn	Highld	NC3445	58°22·0'	4°49·8'W	H	9
Creagan Mór	Arg & Bt	NM7129	56°24·1'	5°42·2'W	X	49
Creagan Mór	Highld	NC1914	58°5·0'	5°3·7'W	H	15
Creagan MOR	Highld	NC9108	58°3·1'	3°50·3'W	X	17
Creagan Mór	Highld	ND0819	58°9·3'	3°33·3'W	X	17
Creagan Mór	Highld	NN6180	56°53·7'	4°16·5'W	H	42
Creagan Mór	Highld	NN6998	57°3·5'	4°9·1'W	X	35
Creagan Móra	Arg & Bt	NM0348	56°32·1'	6°49·4'W	X	46
Creagan Mora	Highld	NG3743	57°24·3'	6°22·3'W	H	23
Creagan na Beinne	Highld	NC4858	58°29·3'	4°36·0'W	X	9
Creagan na Beinne	Pth & Kin	NN7437	56°30·8'	4°2·4'W	H	51,52
Creagan na Cailliche	Highld	NH4002	57°5·1'	4°38·0'W	X	34
Creagannacaorach	Highld	NC6808	58°2·8'	4°13·7'W	X	16
Creagan na Còrr	Pth & Kin	NN6054	56°39·7'	4°16·6'W	H	42,51
Creagan na Craoibhe	Highld	NN4371	56°48·5'	4°33·8'W	X	42
Creagan nam Buachaillean	Arg & Bt	NR7998	56°7·7'	5°32·9'W	X	55
Creagan nan Camhna	Highld	NG8822	57°14·6'	5°30·4'W	X	33
Creagan nan Caorach	N Ayr	NR9248	55°41·1'	5°18·1'W	X	62,69
Creagan nan Gabhar	Aberd	NN9992	57°0·7'	3°39·3'W	H	43
Creagan nan Gabhar	Stir	NN6119	56°20·8'	4°14·5'W	X	57
Creagan nan Gobhar	Pth & Kin	NN5246	56°35·2'	4°24·1'W	H	51
Creagan nan Laogh	Highld	NH1561	57°36·3'	5°5·3'W	X	20
Creagan nan Nead	Highld	NN4173	56°49·5'	4°35·9'W	H	42
Creagan nan Sgiath	Stir	NN4914	56°17·9'	4°26·0'W	H	57
Creagan nan Simileirean	Highld	NM8153	56°37·3'	5°33·7'W	X	49
Creagan na Radhairc	Highld	NH2091	57°52·6'	5°1·7'W	X	20
Creagan na Rubhaig Bana	N Eil	NA1504	57°51·8'	8°29·2'W	X	18
Creagan na Sloich	Highld	NH8430	57°21·0'	3°55·2'W	X	27
Creagan na Speireig	Highld	NC4855	58°27·7'	4°35·9'W	H	9
Creagan Odhar	Pth & Kin	NN6260	56°42·9'	4°14·8'W	H	42
Creagan Rainich	Arg & Bt	NR7834	55°33·2'	5°30·8'W	X	68,69
Creagan Reamhar	Highld	NC3427	58°12·3'	4°49·0'W	X	15
Creagan Reamhar	Highld	ND1126	58°13·1'	3°30·4'W	X	17
Creagan Reamhar	Highld	NH6294	57°55·1'	4°19·3'W	X	21
Creagan Reamhar	Highld	NH6894	57°55·2'	4°13·2'W	X	21

Creagan Reamhar	Highld	NN6289	56°58·6′	4°15·8′W	H	42
Creagan Riabhach	Aberd	NO3799	57°4·9′	3°1·9′W	H	37,44
Creagan Ruadha	N Eil	NB0210	57°59·0′	7°2·0′W	X	13
Creagan Ruathair	Pth & Kin	NO0152	56°39·2′	3°36·4′W	H	52,53
Creag an Ruighe	Highld	NG9423	57°15·3′	5°24·5′W	H	25,33
Creag an Sgamhlainn	Highld	NC3632	58°15·0′	4°47·2′W	H	16
Creag an Sgliata	Pth & Kin	NN7639	56°31·9′	4°0·5′W	H	51,52
Creag an Sgor	Aberd	NJ3719	57°15·7′	3°2·2′W	H	37
Creag an Sgriodain	Highld	NC3534	58°16·1′	4°48·3′W	H	15
Creag an Sgrudaidh	Stir	NN5431	56°27·2′	4°21·7′W	X	51
Creagan Sithe	Arg & Bt	NN2700	56°9·9′	4°46·7′W	X	56
Creagan Soilleir	Highld	NN6195	57°1·8′	4°17·0′W	X	35
Creagan Soilleir	Pth & Kin	NN9431	56°27·8′	3°42·8′W	H	52,53
Creagan Soilleir	Stir	NN3325	56°23·5′	4°41·9′W	X	50
Creag an Steallaire	Arg & Bt	NN2444	56°33·6′	4°51·4′W	X	50
Creag an Stùrra	Arg & Bt	NM8214	56°16·4′	5°30·8′W	X	55
Creag' an Taghain	Arg & Bt	NN0822	56°21·3′	5°6·0′W	X	50
Creag an Taghain	Highld	NG8112	57°9·1′	5°36·8′W	X	33
Creag an Tailleir	Arg & Bt	NN2440	56°31·4′	4°51·2′W	H	50
Creag an Tairbh	Highld	NG8625	57°16·2′	5°32·5′W	X	33
Creag an Tairbh	Highld	NH1391	57°52·4′	5°8·7′W	X	19
Creag an Tairbh	Highld	NH1568	57°40·1′	5°5·6′W	X	20
Creag an Tamhaisg	Arg & Bt	NS0782	55°59·8′	5°5·2′W	X	56
Creag an Tarmachain	Highld	NJ1531	57°22·0′	3°24·3′W	X	36
Creaganterve Mhór	Arg & Bt	NM8401	56°9·4′	5°28·3′W	X	55
Creagan Toll an Lochain	Highld	NH1434	57°21·8′	5°5·1′W	X	25
Creag an Torraidh	Angus	NO1871	56°49·7′	3°20·2′W	H	43
Creag an Torra Loisgte	Highld	NH1902	57°4·7′	4°58·7′W	X	34
Creag an t-Sagairt	Highld	NG7909	57°7·4′	5°38·6′W	X	33
Creag an t-Sagairt	N Eil	NF8223	57°11·5′	7°15·4′W	X	22
Creag an t-Samhainich	Highld	NM7173	56°47·8′	5°44·6′W	X	40
Creag an t-Sasunnaich	Stir	NN4726	56°24·3′	4°28·3′W	X	51
Creag an t-Sean-ruigh	Aberd	NO1482	56°55·5′	3°24·3′W	H	43
Creag an t- Seilich	Arg & Bt	NS3394	56°6·8′	4°40·7′W	X	56
Creag an t-Sìthein	Pth & Kin	NO0365	56°46·2′	3°34·8′W	H	43
Creag an t-Sniomha	Highld	NC3029	58°13·3′	4°53·2′W	X	15
Creag an t-Socaich	Highld	NC7630	58°14·7′	4°6·3′W	H	17
Creag an t-Suidheachain	Arg & Bt	NN1203	56°11·2′	5°1·3′W	X	56
Creag an t-Tralghean	Highld	NC5755	58°27·9′	4°26·6′W	X	10
Creag an Tuim Bhig	Highld	NH8227	57°19·4′	3°57·1′W	H	35
Creag an Tùir	Highld	NH4402	57°5·2′	4°34·0′W	X	34
Creag an Tulabhain	Pth & Kin	NN5241	56°32·5′	4°24·0′W	H	51
Creag an Turraich	Highld	NG8848	57°28·6′	5°31·7′W	H	24
Creagan Uaine	Pth & Kin	NO0568	56°47·9′	3°32·9′W	H	43
Creag an Uamhaidh	Pth & Kin	NN9745	56°35·4′	3°40·2′W	H	52,53
Creagan Uilleim	Highld	NH4493	57°54·2′	4°37·5′W	H	20
Creag Aoil	Arg & Bt	NM8011	56°14·7′	5°32·6′W	X	55
Creag Aoil	Highld	NN1877	56°51·2′	4°58·6′W	X	41
Creag a' Phris	Highld	NC1634	58°15·6′	5°7·7′W	H	15
Creag a' Phuill	Arg & Bt	NN1005	56°12·2′	5°3·3′W	X	56
Creag a' Phuirt	Stir	NN4024	56°23·1′	4°35·1′W	X	51
Creag Ard	Pth & Kin	NN6048	56°36·4′	4°16·4′W	H	51
Creag Ard Achaidh	Highld	NH3906	57°7·3′	4°39·1′W	H	34
Creag Ard Mhór	Highld	NH4042	57°26·7′	4°39·5′W	H	26
Creag a' Rubha	N Eil	NB5559	58°27·3′	6°11·5′W	X	8
Creagastrom	N Eil	NF8548	57°25·1′	7°14·4′W	T	22
Creag Bad an t-Seabhaig	Aberd	NO0394	57°1·9′	3°35·4′W	H	43
Creag Bealach na h-Oidhche	Highld	NG8314	57°10·2′	5°34·9′W	X	33
Creag Beinn nan Eun	Pth & Kin	NN7213	56°17·8′	4°3·7′W	X	57
Creag Bhag	Highld	NH1917	57°12·7′	4°59·4′W	X	34
Creag Bhagailteach	Pth & Kin	NN8169	56°48·1′	3°56·5′W	H	43
Creag Bhalg	Aberd	NO0991	57°0·3′	3°29·4′W	H	43
Creag Bhalg	Aberd	NO2096	57°3·1′	3°18·7′W	X	36,44
Creag Bhalg	Highld	NH7603	57°6·3′	4°2·4′W	H	35
Creag Bhalg	Pth & Kin	NN7724	56°23·8′	3°59·1′W	H	51,52
Creag Bhallach	Highld	NH5126	57°18·3′	4°27·9′W	X	26,35
Creag Bhàn	Arg & Bt	NM8427	56°23·4′	5°29·5′W	X	49
Creag Bhàn	Arg & Bt	NN1315	56°17·7′	5°0·9′W	X	50,56
Creag Bhàn	Arg & Bt	NR6450	55°41·4′	5°44·9′W	H	62
Creag Bhàn	Highld	NG4542	57°24·1′	6°14·2′W	H	23
Creag Bhàn	Highld	NM7884	56°53·9′	5°38·3′W	H	40
Creag Bhàn	Highld	NM8481	56°52·5′	5°32·2′W	X	40
Creag Bhàn	Highld	NN1053	56°38·1′	5°5·4′W	X	41
Creag Bhàn Ard	Highld	NM6348	56°34·1′	5°51·0′W	H	49
Creag Bhàn Eigheach	Stir	NN3430	56°26·2′	4°41·1′W	X	50
Creag Bheag	Aberd	NO2294	57°2·1′	3°16·7′W	X	36,44
Creag Bheag	Highld	NH7401	57°5·2′	4°4·3′W	H	35
Creag Bheag	Highld	NH7503	57°6·3′	4°3·4′W	X	35
Creag Bheag	Highld	NH7702	57°5·8′	4°1·4′W	H	35
Creag Bheag	Highld	NM8769	56°46·1′	5°28·7′W	X	40
Creag Bheag	Highld	NN4686	56°56·6′	4°31·4′W	X	34,42
Creag Bheag	Highld	NN4895	57°1·5′	4°29·8′W	H	34
Creag Bheag	Highld	NN8789	56°59·0′	3°51·1′W	X	43
Creag Bheag	Pth & Kin	NN8738	56°31·5′	3°49·8′W	X	52
Creag Bheag	Pth & Kin	NN9842	56°33·8′	3°39·1′W	H	52,53
Creag Bheithe	Highld	NG8504	57°4·9′	5°32·4′W	X	33
Creag Bheithe	Stir	NN6010	56°16·0′	4°15·2′W	X	57
Creagbheitheachain	Highld	NM9868	56°45·9′	5°17·9′W	X	40
Creag Bhile	Highld	NN6394	57°1·3′	4°14·9′W	H	35
Creag Bhinnean	Highld	NH7320	57°15·4′	4°5·9′W	X	35
Creag Bhinnein	Pth & Kin	NO1268	56°48·0′	3°26·0′W	H	43
Creag Bhiórach	Aberd	NO2982	56°55·7′	3°9·5′W	X	44
Creag Bhiorach	Pth & Kin	NN9235	56°29·9′	3°44·8′W	X	52
Creag Bhlair	Stir	NN5308	56°14·8′	4°21·9′W	H	57
Creag Bhlarain	N Eil	NF7276	57°39·5′	7°29·6′W	X	18
Creag Bhocan	Stir	NN3127	56°24·6′	4°43·9′W	X	50
Creag Bhreac	Arg & Bt	NM8400	56°8·9′	5°28·2′W	H	55
Creag Bhreac	Arg & Bt	NR8996	56°6·9′	5°23·2′W	H	55
Creag Bhreac	Highld	NG3735	57°20·0′	6°21·8′W	X	32
Creag Bhreac	Highld	NG3742	57°23·8′	6°22·2′W	H	23
Creag Bhreac	Highld	NH7416	57°13·3′	4°4·7′W	X	35
Creag Bhreac	Highld	NM8569	56°46·0′	5°30·6′W	X	40
Creag Bhreac	Highld	NN0761	56°42·3′	5°8·7′W	X	41
Creag Bhreac	Pth & Kin	NN9461	56°44·0′	3°43·5′W	H	43
Creag Bhreac	Pth & Kin	NO0673	56°50·6′	3°32·0′W	H	43
Creag Bhreac	Pth & Kin	NO0768	56°47·9′	3°30·9′W	H	43
Creag Bhreac	Stir	NN5021	56°21·7′	4°25·2′W	X	51,57
Creag Bhreac Mhór	Highld	NH3773	57°43·3′	4°43·7′W	H	20
Creag Bhreac Mhór	Stir	NN3617	56°19·3′	4°38·7′W	X	50,56

Creag Bhreaig	Highld	NC4553	58°26·5′	4°38·9′W	H	9
Creag Bhrosgan	Arg & Bt	NN2210	56°15·2′	4°52·0′W	X	50,56
Creag Bhuide	Highld	NH6631	57°21·3′	4°13·2′W	X	26
Creag Bhuidhe	Arg & Bt	NN2228	56°24·9′	4°52·7′W	X	50
Creag Bhuidhe	Arg & Bt	NN2930	56°26·1′	4°46·0′W	H	50
Creag Bhuidhe	Highld	NH0659	57°35·0′	5°14·2′W	X	25
Creag Bhuidhe	Highld	NM8081	56°52·4′	5°36·2′W	H	40
Creag Bhuidhe	Highld	NM8268	56°45·4′	5°33·5′W	X	40
Creag Bhuidhe	Highld	NN6192	57°0·2′	4°16·9′W	X	35
Creag Bhuidhe	Pth & Kin	NN3941	56°32·3′	4°36·6′W	X	50
Creag Bhuidhe	Pth & Kin	NN6959	56°42·5′	4°7·9′W	X	42,51
Creag Bracha	Arg & Bt	NN1122	56°21·4′	5°3·1′W	H	50
Creag Braigh an t-Sratha	Highld	NH5678	57°46·4′	4°24·8′W	X	21
Creag Breac	Highld	NC7004	58°0·6′	4°11·5′W	H	16
Creag Breac	Highld	NH1544	57°27·2′	5°4·5′W	H	25
Creag Breac	Pth & Kin	NN9665	56°46·2′	3°41·6′W	H	43
Creag Brimishgan	Arg & Bt	NM4735	56°26·6′	6°5·9′W	X	47,48
Creag Buireinich	Arg & Bt	NR8897	56°7·4′	5°24·2′W	H	55
Creag Bun-Ullidh	Highld	ND0216	58°7·6′	3°39·4′W	H	17
Creag Cairneasair	Highld	NG8978	57°44·8′	5°32·3′W	H	19
Creag Casmul	N Eil	NB1801	57°54·8′	6°45·2′W	X	14
Creag Chailein	Highld	NC8862	58°32·2′	3°54·9′W	H	10
Creag Chaise	Arg & Bt	NR9494	56°5·9′	5°18·3′W	H	55
Creag Chàise	N Eil	NB1909	57°59·2′	6°44·8′W	H	13,14
Creag Chaisean	Pth & Kin	NN8227	56°25·5′	3°54·3′W	X	52
Creag Chaol	Highld	NC5148	58°24·0′	4°32·5′W	H	9
Creag Chaonaig	Arg & Bt	NN1102	56°10·6′	5°2·3′W	X	56
Creag Chaorannach	Stir	NN4313	56°17·3′	4°31·7′W	X	56
Creag Chaoruinneach	Stir	NN5413	56°17·5′	4°21·1′W	X	57
Creag Chathalain	Highld	NN4994	57°1·0′	4°28·8′W	H	34
Creag Chean	Pth & Kin	NN7953	56°39·4′	3°58·0′W	H	42,51,52
Creag Chlachach	Arg & Bt	NM8609	56°13·8′	5°26·7′W	H	55
Creag Chlacharnach	Pth & Kin	NN9867	56°47·3′	3°39·7′W	H	43
Creag Chlachath	Arg & Bt	NM9213	56°16·1′	5°21·1′W	X	55
Creag Chleistir	N Eil	NB1212	58°0·5′	6°52·1′W	H	13,14
Creag Chliabhain	Pth & Kin	NO0366	56°46·8′	3°34·8′W	H	43
Creag Chliostair	N Eil	NB0611	57°59·7′	6°58·1′W	H	13,14
Creag Choic	Highld	NG8085	57°48·3′	5°41·7′W	H	19
Creag Choille	Pth & Kin	NN8540	56°32·5′	3°51·8′W	H	52
Creag Choin Bhàin	Highld	NH4101	57°4·6′	4°36·9′W	X	34
Creag Choinnich	Aberd	NO1691	57°0·4′	3°22·5′W	H	43
Creag-choinnich Lodge	Pth & Kin	NN9170	56°48·8′	3°46·7′W	X	43
Creag Chonochair	Highld	NN3482	56°54·2′	4°43·1′W	H	34,41
Creag Chorcurach	Highld	NH1287	57°50·2′	5°9·5′W	X	19
Creag Chragach	Highld	NG4161	57°34·2′	6°19·4′W	H	23
Creag Chrannach	Pth & Kin	NN5846	56°35·3′	4°18·3′W	X	51
Creag Chraobhach	Highld	NC6227	58°12·9′	4°20·5′W	X	16
Creag Chreagach	Highld	NC7217	58°7·7′	4°9·9′W	H	16
Creag Chrocan	Highld	NN6093	57°0·7′	4°17·9′W	H	35
Creag Chrom	Arg & Bt	NR7439	55°35·8′	5°34·8′W	X	68
Creag Chruachain	Highld	NM8093	56°58·8′	5°36·8′W	H	33,40
Creag Chuinnlean	Pth & Kin	NN9360	56°43·4′	3°44·5′W	H	43
Creag Chumhann	Arg & Bt	NN0817	56°18·7′	5°5·8′W	X	50,56
Creag Clachach	Highld	NH3380	57°47·0′	4°48·1′W	X	20
Creag Clais nan Cruineachd	Highld	NC0627	58°11·6′	5°17·6′W	H	15
Creag Cleap	Highld	NG4766	57°37·0′	6°13·7′W	X	23
Creag Clunie	Aberd	NO1790	56°59·9′	3°21·5′W	X	43
Creag Coir' a' Bhuic	Highld	NH1651	57°31·0′	5°3·9′W	H	25
Creag Coire an Eich	Highld	NC4053	58°26·4′	4°44·0′W	X	9
Creag Coire Doe	Highld	NH4306	57°7·4′	4°35·1′W	H	34
Creag Coire na Feòla	Highld	NH2049	57°30·0′	4°59·8′W	H	25
Creag Coire na Fiar Bhealaich	Highld	NH0404	57°5·4′	5°13·6′W	X	33
Creag Collascard	Highld	NG3966	57°36·8′	6°21·7′W	X	23
Creag Corrag	Highld	NN3692	56°59·7′	4°41·5′W	X	34
Creag Craiggan	Pth & Kin	NN9347	56°36·4′	3°44·1′W	H	52
Creag Cuirn na Laraiche	Highld	NH6525	57°18·0′	4°14·0′W	X	26,35
Creag Dailfeusaig	Highld	NC7011	58°4·4′	4°11·8′W	H	16
Creag Dail na Méine	Highld	NH7199	57°58·0′	4°10·4′W	H	21
Creag Dail nan Gillean	Highld	NC6918	58°8·2′	4°13·0′W	H	16
Creag Dalhorrisgle	Highld	NC7055	58°28·1′	4°13·2′W	H	10
Creag Dallaig	Pth & Kin	NO0875	56°51·7′	3°30·1′W	H	43
Creag Dal-Langal	Highld	NC8921	58°10·1′	3°52·7′W	H	17
Creag Dearg	Aberd	NO3687	56°58·4′	3°2·7′W	H	44
Creag Dhail	N Eil	NB4763	58°29·2′	6°20·0′W	X	8
Creag Dhamh	Stir	NN4607	56°14·1′	4°28·6′W	X	57
Creag Dharach	Highld	NG9231	57°19·6′	5°26·8′W	H	25
Creag Dharaich	Highld	NC0825	58°10·6′	5°15·4′W	H	15
Creag Dhearg	Highld	NC9131	58°15·5′	3°51·0′W	X	17
Creag Dhearg	Highld	NH4520	57°14·9′	4°33·7′W	H	26
Creag Dhearg	Highld	NH5836	57°23·8′	4°21·3′W	X	26
Creag Dhearg	Highld	NH6129	57°20·1′	4°18·1′W	X	26,35
Creag Dhearg	Highld	NM8181	56°52·4′	5°35·2′W	X	40
Creag Dhearg	Highld	NM8499	57°2·2′	5°33·1′W	H	33,40
Creag Dhearg	Pth & Kin	NN5670	56°48·2′	4°21·0′W	X	42
Creag Dhearg	Pth & Kin	NN6948	56°36·6′	4°7·6′W	X	51
Creag Dhearg	Pth & Kin	NN9977	56°52·7′	3°39·0′W	H	43
Creag Dhearg	Pth & Kin	NO0874	56°51·2′	3°30·1′W	X	43
Creag Dhearg	Pth & Kin	NO1173	56°50·7′	3°27·1′W	H	43
Creag Dhonn	Highld	NH2856	57°33·9′	4°52·1′W	X	25
Creag Dhonnaiche	Arg & Bt	NS1086	56°2·0′	5°2·5′W	X	56
Creagdhu	Arg & Bt	NN2604	56°12·1′	4°47·8′W	X	56
Creag Dhubh	Arg & Bt	NM5635	56°26·9′	5°57·1′W	H	47,48
Creag Dhubh	Arg & Bt	NM6834	56°26·7′	5°45·4′W	X	49
Creag Dhubh	Arg & Bt	NM9218	56°18·8′	5°21·3′W	W	55
Creag Dhubh	Arg & Bt	NN0113	56°16·3′	5°12·4′W	X	50,55
Creag Dhubh	Arg & Bt	NN0613	56°16·5′	5°7·6′W	X	50,56
Creag Dhubh	Arg & Bt	NN0808	56°13·8′	5°5·4′W	H	56
Creag Dhubh	Arg & Bt	NN0939	56°30·5′	5°5·8′W	X	50
Creag Dhubh	Arg & Bt	NN1200	56°9·6′	5°1·2′W	X	56
Creag Dhubh	Arg & Bt	NN1304	56°11·8′	5°0·4′W	H	56
Creag Dhubh	Arg & Bt	NN2317	56°19·0′	4°51·3′W	X	50,56
Creag Dhubh	Arg & Bt	NR8793	56°5·2′	5°25·0′W	H	55
Creag Dhubh	Highld	NC1406	58°0·5′	5°8·4′W	X	15
Creag Dhubh	Highld	NC1508	58°1·6′	5°7·5′W	H	15
Creag Dhubh	Highld	NC1940	58°18·9′	5°4·9′W	H	9
Creag Dhubh	Highld	NC6019	58°8·5′	4°22·2′W	H	16
Creag Dhubh	Highld	NC6310	58°3·7′	4°18·9′W	X	16
Creag Dhubh	Highld	NC6549	58°24·8′	4°18·2′W	H	10

Creag Dhubh	Highld	NC6918	58°8·2′	4°13·0′W	H	16
Creag Dhubh	Highld	NC7229	58°14·1′	4°10·3′W	X	16
Creag Dhubh	Highld	NG2650	57°27·7′	6°33·7′W	H	23
Creag Dhubh	Highld	NG3639	57°22·2′	6°23·0′W	X	23,32
Creag Dhubh	Highld	NG7629	57°18·1′	5°42·6′W	X	33
Creag Dhubh	Highld	NG8207	57°6·4′	5°35·5′W	X	33
Creag Dhubh	Highld	NG8220	57°13·4′	5°36·2′W	H	33
Creag Dhubh	Highld	NG9856	57°33·2′	5°22·1′W	H	25
Creag Dhubh	Highld	NH1261	57°36·3′	5°8·3′W	X	19
Creag Dhubh	Highld	NH2176	57°44·5′	5°0·0′W	H	20
Creag Dhubh	Highld	NH2221	57°15·0′	4°56·6′W	H	25
Creag Dhubh	Highld	NH2689	57°51·7′	4°55·5′W	H	20
Creag Dhubh	Highld	NH2851	57°31·3′	4°51·9′W	X	25
Creag Dhubh	Highld	NH3705	57°6·7′	4°41·0′W	H	34
Creag Dhubh	Highld	NH6529	57°20·2′	4°14·1′W	X	26,35
Creag Dhubh	Highld	NH7419	57°14·9′	4°4·8′W	X	35
Creag Dhubh	Highld	NH9004	57°7·1′	3°48·5′W	H	36
Creag Dhubh	Highld	NM6366	56°43·8′	5°52·0′W	H	40
Creag Dhubh	Highld	NM7558	56°39·8′	5°39·9′W	X	49
Creag Dhubh	Highld	NM8472	56°47·6′	5°31·8′W	X	40
Creag Dhubh	Highld	NN1247	56°34·9′	5°3·2′W	X	50
Creag Dhubh	Highld	NN2552	56°37·9′	4°50·7′W	X	41
Creag Dhubh	Highld	NN3282	56°54·2′	4°45·1′W	H	34,41
Creag Dhubh	Highld	NN3777	56°51·6′	4°40·0′W	H	41
Creag Dhubh	Highld	NN5979	56°53·1′	4°18·4′W	X	42
Creag Dhubh	Highld	NN6695	57°1·9′	4°12·0′W	X	35
Creag Dhubh	Highld	NN6797	57°3·0′	4°11·1′W	H	35
Creag Dhubh	Highld	NN8299	57°4·3′	3°56·3′W	H	35,43
Creag Dhubh	Moray	NJ0202	57°6·2′	3°36·6′W	X	36
Creag Dhubh	N Ayr	NR9533	55°33·1′	5°14·6′W	X	68,69
Creag Dhubh	N Ayr	NR9645	55°39·6′	5°14·2′W	X	62,69
Creag Dhubh	Pth & Kin	NN5643	56°33·7′	4°20·1′W	H	51
Creag Dhubh	Pth & Kin	NN5970	56°48·3′	4°18·1′W	H	42
Creag Dhubh	Pth & Kin	NN6647	56°36·0′	4°10·5′W	H	51
Creag Dhubh	Pth & Kin	NN9157	56°41·8′	3°46·3′W	X	52
Creag Dhubh	Pth & Kin	NN9745	56°35·4′	3°40·2′W	H	52,53
Creag Dhubh	Pth & Kin	NO0260	56°43·5′	3°35·6′W	H	43
Creag Dhubh	Pth & Kin	NO0371	56°49·5′	3°34·9′W	H	43
Creag Dhubh	Stir	NN5108	56°14·7′	4°23·8′W	X	57
Creag Dhubh	Stir	NN5402	56°11·6′	4°20·7′W	X	57
Creag Dhubh	Stir	NN6018	56°20·3′	4°15·4′W	X	57
Creag Dhubh a' Bhealaich	Stir	NN2724	56°22·9′	4°47·7′W	X	50
Creag Dhubh Bheag	Highld	NC4732	58°15·3′	4°36·0′W	X	16
Creag Dhubh Bheag	Highld	NG9541	57°25·1′	5°24·4′W	X	25
Creag Dhubh Bheag	Highld	NH1547	57°28·8′	5°4·7′W	H	25
Creag Dhubh Bheag	Highld	NH3982	57°48·2′	4°42·1′W	X	20
Creag Dhubh Bhearraraigh	N Eil	NB0513	58°0·8′	6°59·2′W	H	13,14
Creag Dhubh Coill a' Bhun	Highld	NH1383	57°48·1′	5°8·3′W	X	19
Creag Dhubh Dail nan Gillean	Highld	NC6720	58°9·2′	4°15·1′W	X	16
Creag Dhubh Fannaich	Highld	NH2371	57°41·9′	4°57·7′W	H	20
Creag Dhubh Flichity	Highld	NH6828	57°19·7′	4°11·1′W	H	26,35
Creagdhubh Lodge	Highld	NN6795	57°1·9′	4°11·0′W	X	35
Creag Dhubh Mhór	Highld	NC4533	58°15·8′	4°38·0′W	H	16
Creag Dhubh Mhór	Highld	NG9840	57°24·6′	5°21·3′W	H	25
Creag Dhubh Mhór	Highld	NH1347	57°28·7′	5°6·7′W	H	25
Creag Dhubh Mhór	Highld	NH3881	57°47·6′	4°43·1′W	X	20
Creag Dhubh na h-Airigh	Arg & Bt	NN0817	56°18·7′	5°5·8′W	X	50,56
Creag Dhubh Phollaster	Highld	NG8551	57°30·2′	5°34·9′W	X	24
Creag Dhùghaill	N Eil	NF8735	57°18·2′	7°11·4′W	X	22
Creag Doire na h-Achlaise	Highld	NN6089	56°58·5′	4°17·7′W	H	42
Creag Doire nan Nathrach	Pth & Kin	NN4544	56°34·0′	4°30·9′W	H	51
Creag Druim Gheallogaidh	Highld	NN7597	57°3·1′	4°3·2′W	H	35
Creag Druim nan Rath	Highld	NC9122	58°10·7′	3°50·7′W	X	17
Creag Dubh	Arg & Bt	NN1215	56°17·7′	5°1·8′W	X	50,56
Creag Dubh	Highld	NC2737	58°17·5′	4°56·6′W	X	15
Creag Dubh	Highld	NC3945	58°22·1′	4°44·7′W	X	9
Creag Dubh	Highld	NG7704	57°4·6′	5°40·3′W	X	33
Creag Dubh	Highld	NH0339	57°24·2′	5°16·3′W	X	25
Creag Dubh	Highld	NH1208	57°7·7′	5°5·9′W	X	34
Creag Dubh	Highld	NH1512	57°10·0′	5°3·1′W	X	34
Creag Dubh	Highld	NH1629	57°19·1′	5°2·9′W	X	25
Creag Dubh	Highld	NH1829	57°19·2′	5°0·9′W	X	25
Creag Dubh	Highld	NH1935	57°22·4′	5°0·2′W	H	25
Creag Dubh	Highld	NH7203	57°6·3′	4°6·3′W	H	35
Creag Dubh	Highld	NM7784	56°53·9′	5°39·3′W	X	40
Creag Dubh	Highld	NM7867	56°44·8′	5°37·4′W	X	40
Creag Dubh	N Eil	NB5561	58°28·4′	6°11·6′W	X	8
Creag Dubh-leitir	Pth & Kin	NO0565	56°46·3′	3°32·8′W	H	43
Creag Dubh Tigh an Aitinn	Highld	NH7317	57°13·8′	4°5·8′W	H	35
Creag Each	Pth & Kin	NN7924	56°23·8′	3°57·2′W	H	51,52
Creag Eallaich	Pth & Kin	NN9164	56°45·6′	3°46·5′W	H	43
Creag Ealraich	Highld	NH9430	57°21·2′	3°45·2′W	H	27,36
Creag Eanaiche	Arg & Bt	NR7852	55°42·9′	5°31·6′W	X	62,69
Creag Eas a Chatha	Highld	NH3917	57°13·2′	4°39·5′W	X	34
Creag Easgaidh	Pth & Kin	NO0776	56°52·2′	3°31·1′W	H	43
Creag Eilid	Pth & Kin	NN9250	56°38·0′	3°45·2′W	X	52
Creag Far-leitire	Highld	NH8302	57°5·9′	3°55·4′W	X	35
Creag Feusag	Highld	NH2133	57°21·4′	4°58·1′W	X	25
Creag Feusaige	Highld	NC7446	58°23·3′	4°8·8′W	H	10
Creag Fharsuinn	Stir	NN5112	56°16·9′	4°24·0′W	X	57
Creag Fheargach	Arg & Bt	NR9493	56°5·4′	5°18·2′W	H	55
Creag Fhiaclach	Highld	NH8905	57°7·6′	3°49·6′W	X	35,36
Creag Fhiaclach	Highld	NN3477	56°51·5′	4°42·9′W	X	41
Creag Fhionnlaidh	Highld	NH7218	57°14·4′	4°6·8′W	X	35
Creag Fhraoch	N Eil	NB4215	58°3·2′	6°21·9′W	X	14
Creag Fhraoch	N Eil	NB5142	58°18·0′	6°14·5′W	X	8
Creag Fm	Arg & Bt	NR7963	55°48·8′	5°31·2′W	FM	62
Creag Follais	Highld	NH8904	57°7·1′	3°49·5′W	X	35,36
Creag Gabhar	Highld	NM8372	56°47·6′	5°32·7′W	X	40
Creag Garten	Highld	NH9421	57°16·3′	3°45·0′W	H	36
Creag Ghaineamhach	Highld	NH3153	57°32·4′	4°48·9′W	X	26
Creag Gharbh	Highld	NC7665	58°33·6′	4°7·4′W	X	10
Creag Gharbh	Highld	NH7423	57°17·1′	4°5·0′W	H	35
Creag Gharbh	Pth & Kin	NN7134	56°29·1′	4°5·2′W	X	51,52
Creag Gharbh	Pth & Kin	NO0456	56°41·4′	3°33·6′W	X	52,53
Creag Gharbh	Stir	NN6332	56°27·9′	4°13·0′W	H	51
Creag Gharbh Mhór	Highld	NC2753	58°26·1′	4°57·3′W	X	9
Creag Ghilleaspuig	Highld	NH1803	57°5·2′	4°59·8′W	X	34
Creag Ghiubhais	Aberd	NO3195	57°2·7′	3°7·8′W	H	37,44

Creag Ghiuthsachan	Highld	NN8699	57°4·3′	3°52·4′W	H	35,36,43
Creag Ghlas	Arg & Bt	NN2130	56°26·0′	4°53·7′W	X	50
Creag Ghlas	Arg & Bt	NR8389	56°2·9′	5°28·6′W	H	55
Creag Ghlas	Arg & Bt	NR9688	56°2·7′	5°16·1′W	H	55
Creag Ghlas	Highld	NG2856	57°31·0′	6°32·1′W	X	23
Creag Ghlas	Highld	NG8617	57°11·9′	5°32·1′W	X	33
Creag Ghlas	Highld	NG8644	57°26·4′	5°33·5′W	X	24
Creag Ghlas	Highld	NH0316	57°11·8′	5°15·2′W	X	33
Creag Ghlas	Highld	NH0426	57°17·2′	5°14·7′W	H	25,33
Creag Ghlas	Highld	NH0778	57°45·3′	5°14·2′W	X	19
Creag Ghlas	Highld	NH2454	57°32·8′	4°56·0′W	X	25
Creag Ghlas	Highld	NM8451	56°36·3′	5°30·7′W	X	49
Creag Ghlas	N Ayr	NR9450	55°42·2′	5°16·3′W	X	62,69
Creag Ghlas	N Ayr	NR9845	55°39·6′	5°12·2′W	X	62,69
Creag Ghlas	Stir	NN5226	56°24·4′	4°23·5′W	H	51
Creag Ghlas Bheag	Highld	NH0571	57°41·5′	5°15·8′W	X	19
Creag Ghlas Cuithe	N Ayr	NR9750	55°42·3′	5°13·4′W	X	62,69
Creag Ghlas Laggan	N Ayr	NR9750	55°42·3′	5°13·4′W	X	62,69
Creag Ghlas Mhór	Highld	NH0471	57°41·4′	5°16·8′W	H	19
Creag Ghlasrach	Arg & Bt	NM9123	56°21·5′	5°22·5′W	X	49
Creag Ghleannain	Highld	NH8511	57°10·8′	3°53·7′W	H	35,36
Creag Ghobhar	Highld	NM8581	56°52·5′	5°31·2′W	X	40
Creag Ghobhar	Stir	NN4829	56°26·0.	4°27·5′W	X	51
Creag Ghoraidh	N Eil	NF7948	57°24·8′	7°20·3′W	T	22
Creag Ghorm	Highld	NG7643	57°25·6′	5°43·4′W	X	24
Creag Ghorm	Highld	NH2643	57°26·9′	4°53·5′W	X	25
Creag Ghorm	Highld	NN0358	56°40·6′	5°12·5′W	H	41
Creag Ghorm	N Eil	NB1329	58°9·7′	6°52·3′W	H	13
Creag Ghorm	Pth & Kin	NN9234	56°29·4′	3°44·8′W	X	52
Creag Ghorm a' Bhealaich	Highld	NH2443	57°26·9′	4°55·5′W	H	25
Creag Ghrànda	Arg & Bt	NM9908	56°13·6′	5°14·1′W	X	55
Creag Ghrèinebridh	N Eil	NB1405	57°56·8′	6°49·6′W	H	13,14
Creag Ghrianach	Highld	NH2394	57°54·3′	4°58·8′W	H	20
Creag Ghuanach	Highld	NN3069	56°47·2′	4°46·5′W	H	41
Creag Ghuirm a' Bhaid	N Eil	NG1297	57°52·4′	6°51·0′W	H	14
Creag Glenbrein	Highld	NH4807	57°8·0′	4°30·2′W	X	34
Creag Gownan	Stir	NN5202	56°11·5′	4°22·7′W	X	57
Creag Guir	Pth & Kin	NN9151	56°38·5′	3°46·2′W	X	52
Creag Huristen	N Eil	NF8887	57°46·1′	7°14·4′W	X	18
Creag Iarnlair	Highld	NC3458	58°29·0′	4°50·4′W	X	9
Creag Iasgach	Highld	NM7097	57°0·7′	5°46·8′W	X	33,40
Creagile	Highld	NG3763	57°35·1′	6°23·6′W	X	23
Creag Illie	Highld	NH4382	57°48·3′	4°38·1′W	H	20
Creag Innich	Stir	NN4903	56°12·0′	4°25·6′W	H	57
Creag Innis an Daimh	Highld	NH5826	57°18·4′	4°21·0′W	H	26,35
Creag Innis na Larach	Highld	NH2637	57°23·7′	4°53·3′W	X	25
Creag Innse Chomhraig	Highld	NC6206	58°1·6′	4°19·7′W	H	16
Creag-ira	Highld	NG7500	57°2·4′	5°42·1′W	X	33
Creag Island	Arg & Bt	NM8337	56°28·8′	5°31·0′W	X	49
Creag Iubhair	Stir	NN4328	56°25·3′	4°32·3′W	X	51
Creag Iuchair	Stir	NN4213	56°17·2′	4°32·7′W	X	56
Creag Iucharaidh	Highld	NH2551	57°31·2′	4°54·9′W	H	25
Creag Kynachan	Pth & Kin	NN7657	56°41·6′	4°1·0′W	H	42,51,52
Creag Lamhaich	Pth & Kin	NO0973	56°50·6′	3°29·1′W	H	43
Creaglan	Arg & Bt	NR8784	56°0·4′	5°24·5′W	X	55
Creag Langall	Highld	NG4958	57°32·8′	6°11·2′W	X	23
Creag Laoghain	Pth & Kin	NN5140	56°32·0′	4°24·9′W	H	51
Creag Lathaich	Arg & Bt	NR5781	55°57·9′	5°53·2′W	X	61
Creag Leacach	Angus	NO1574	56°51·2′	3°23·2′W	H	43
Creag Leacagach	Pth & Kin	NO0072	56°50·0′	3°37·9′W	H	43
Creag Leacaidh	Highld	NH0964	57°37·8′	5°11·5′W	X	19
Creag Leachdach	Aberd	NO2081	56°55·1′	3°18·4′W	X	44
Creag Leac nam Fitheach	Highld	NC7307	58°2·3′	4°8·6′W	H	16
Creag Leathan	Highld	NC9863	58°32·9′	3°44·7′W	H	11
Creag Leathan	Highld	NN8598	57°3·8′	3°53·3′W	H	35,36,43
Creag Liaragan	Stir	NN4027	56°24·7′	4°35·2′W	H	51
Creag Liath	Aberd	NO2488	56°58·9′	3°14·6′W	H	44
Creag Liath	Aberd	NO3393	57°1·7′	3°5·8′W	H	37,44
Creag Liath	Arg & Bt	NM9104	56°11·2′	5°21·6′W	X	55
Creag Liath	Arg & Bt	NR9174	55°55·1′	5°20·2′W	X	62
Creag Liath	Arg & Bt	NS1487	56°2·6′	4°58·7′W	X	56
Creag Liath	Highld	NC0731	58°13·8′	5°16·7′W	X	15
Creag Liath	Highld	NC1621	58°8·6′	5°7·1′W	H	15
Creag Liath	Highld	NC2715	58°5·7′	4°55·6′W	X	15
Creag Liath	Highld	NC7430	58°14·7′	4°8·3′W	H	16
Creag Liath	Highld	NG3864	57°35·7′	6°22·6′W	X	23
Creag Liath	Highld	NG9250	57°29·8′	5°27·8′W	X	25
Creag Liath	Highld	NH3029	57°19·5′	4°49·0′W	X	26
Creag Liath	Highld	NH6600	57°4·6′	4°12·2′W	H	35
Creag Liath	Highld	NH7295	57°55·8′	4°9·2′W	H	21
Creag Liath	Highld	NJ0031	57°21·8′	3°39·3′W	H	27,36
Creag Liath	Highld	NN4993	57°0·5′	4°28·7′W	H	34
Creag Liath	Highld	NN6984	56°56·0′	4°8·7′W	H	42
Creag Liath	Highld	NN7686	56°57·2′	4°1·9′W	H	42
Creag Liath	N Ayr	NS0629	55°31·2′	5°4·0′W	X	69
Creag Liath	Pth & Kin	NN7325	56°24·3′	4°3·0′W	H	51,52
Creag Liath	Pth & Kin	NN9033	56°28·8′	3°46·7′W	X	52
Creag Liath	Pth & Kin	NN9837	56°31·1′	3°39·0′W	H	52,53
Creag Liath	Stir	NN4908	56°14·7′	4°25·8′W	X	57
Creag Liath	Stir	NN5008	56°14·7′	4°24·8′W	X	57
Creag Liath a' Bhaid Sgàilich	Highld	NH4579	57°46·7′	4°35·9′W	X	20
Creag Liathad Saoghal	Highld	NG8751	57°30·2′	5°32·9′W	X	24
Creag Liath Bheag	Highld	NM7073	56°47·8′	5°45·5′W	H	40
Creag Liathtais	Highld	NH0906	57°6·6′	5°8·8′W	X	33
Creag Loch nan Dearcag	Highld	NH3356	57°34·1′	4°47·1′W	H	26
Creag Loisgte	Aberd	NJ2909	57°10·2′	3°10·0′W	H	37
Creag Loisgte	Aberd	NO1787	56°58·3′	3°21·5′W	H	43
Creag Loisgte	Arg & Bt	NM8019	56°19·0′	5°33·0′W	H	55
Creag Loisgte	Arg & Bt	NM8421	56°20·2′	5°29·2′W	X	49
Creag Loisgte	Arg & Bt	NR2572	55°52·0′	6°23·3′W	X	60
Creag Loisgte	Highld	NC9913	58°5·9′	3°42·3′W	X	17
Creag Loisgte	Highld	NH2152	57°31·6′	4°58·9′W	X	25
Creag Loisgte	Highld	NH3695	57°55·1′	4°45·7′W	H	20
Creag Loisgte	Highld	NH9910	57°10·4′	3°39·8′W	X	36
Creag Loisgte	Highld	NJ1316	57°13·8′	3°26·0′W	X	36
Creag Loisgte	Highld	NM7369	56°45·7′	5°42·4′W	H	40
Creag Loisgte	Moray	NJ1216	57°13·8′	3°27·0′W	X	36
Creag Loisgte	Moray	NJ1607	57°9·0′	3°22·8′W	X	36
Creag Loisgte	Pth & Kin	NN8066	56°46·5′	3°57·4′W	H	43
Creag Loisgte	Pth & Kin	NN8353	56°39·5′	3°54·1′W	H	52
Creag Loisgte	Pth & Kin	NO0653	56°39·8′	3°31·6′W	X	52,53
Creag Loisgte	Stir	NN3829	56°25·8′	4°37·2′W	X	50
Creag Loisgte	Stir	NN5025	56°23·9′	4°25·4′W	H	51
Creag Loisgte Talatoll	Arg & Bt	NR7554	55°43·9′	5°34·6′W	H	62
Creag Loisk	Pth & Kin	NO0467	56°47·3′	3°33·8′W	X	43
Creag Luaragain Bheag	Arg & Bt	NM8707	56°12·7′	5°25·6′W	H	55
Creag Luaragain Mhór	Arg & Bt	NM8808	56°13·3′	5°24·7′W	H	55
Creag Lundie	Highld	NH1511	57°9·4′	5°3·1′W	H	34
Creag MacRànaich	Stir	NN5425	56°23·9′	4°21·5′W	H	51
Creag Madragil	Highld	NG4154	57°30·4′	6°19·0′W	H	23
Creag Mainnrichean	Highld	NG9648	57°28·8′	5°23·7′W	X	25
Creag Maoile	Arg & Bt	NR9979	55°58·0′	5°12·8′W	X	62
Creag Maoiseach	Pth & Kin	NN9550	56°38·1′	3°42·3′W	H	52,53
Creag Maràil	Highld	ND0116	58°7·6′	3°40·4′W	H	17
Creag Maronaig	Arg & Bt	NN3849	56°36·6′	4°37·9′W	X	50
Creag Martach	Pth & Kin	NN9648	56°37·0′	3°41·2′W	H	52,53
Creag Meadie	Highld	NC7659	58°30·4′	4°7·2′W	X	10
Creag Meagaidh	Highld	NN4287	56°57·1′	4°35·4′W	X	34,42
Creag Meagaidh National Nature Reserve	Highld	NN4688	56°57·7′	4°31·5′W	X	34,42
Creag Meagaidh National Nature Reserve	Highld	NN4688	56°57·7′	4°31·5′W	X	34,42
Creag Meall an Dòmhnaich	Highld	NN6291	56°59·6′	4°15·8′W	X	35
Creag Meggan	Aberd	NO3496	57°3·3′	3°4·8′W	X	37,44
Creag Merkan	Highld	NC4653	58°26·6′	4°37·8′W	X	9
Creag Mhaol	Highld	NG8434	57°21·0′	5°35·0′W	H	24
Creag Mhaol	Highld	NH9180	57°48·0′	3°49·6′W	X	21
Creag Mheadhonach	Arg & Bt	NR9979	55°58·0′	5°12·8′W	X	62
Creag Mheadhonach	Highld	NG4255	57°31·0′	6°18·0′W	H	23
Creag Mheadhonach	Highld	NH9413	57°12·0′	3°44·8′W	X	36
Creag-mheall Beag	Highld	NG9786	57°49·3′	5°24·6′W	H	19
Creag-mheall Meadhonach	Highld	NG9784	57°48·2′	5°24·5′W	H	19
Creag-mheall Mór	Highld	NG9981	57°46·7′	5°22·4′W	H	19
Creag-mheall Mór	Highld	NG9983	57°47·8′	5°22·5′W	H	19
Creag Mhic Chaluim Mhòir	N Eil	NG1594	57°50·9′	6°47·8′W	H	14
Creag Mhic Fhionnlaidh	Arg & Bt	NM5533	56°25·8′	5°58·0′W	X	47,48
Creag Mhigeachaidh	Highld	NH8702	57°6·0′	3°51·5′W	H	35,36
Creag Mholach	Arg & Bt	NS1093	56°5·8′	5°2·8′W	X	56
Creag Mholach	Highld	NH3279	57°46·4′	4°49·0′W	X	20
Creag Mholach	Highld	NN2386	56°56·1′	4°54·1′W	X	34,41
Creag Mholach	Pth & Kin	NO0757	56°42·0′	3°30·7′W	X	52,53
Creag Mhór	Aberd	NO2496	57°3·2′	3°14·7′W	H	36,44
Creag Mhór	Arg & Bt	NM4636	56°27·1′	6°6·9′W	X	47,48
Creag Mhór	Arg & Bt	NM5443	56°31·1′	5°59·5′W	X	47,48
Creag Mhór	Arg & Bt	NM8202	56°9·9′	5°30·2′W	H	55
Creag Mhór	Arg & Bt	NM9223	56°21·5′	5°21·6′W	X	49
Creag Mhór	Arg & Bt	NM9714	56°16·8′	5°16·3′W	H	55
Creag Mhor	Arg & Bt	NM9902	56°10·4′	5°13·8′W	H	55
Creag Mhór	Arg & Bt	NN0304	56°11·5′	5°10·1′W	X	55
Creag Mhòr	Arg & Bt	NN1628	56°24·8′	4°58·5′W	X	50
Creag Mhór	Arg & Bt	NR2162	55°46·5′	6°26·5′W	X	60
Creag Mhór	Arg & Bt	NR2769	55°50·5′	6°21·2′W	X	60
Creag Mhór	Arg & Bt	NR7692	56°4·4′	5°35·5′W	H	55
Creag Mhór	Arg & Bt	NR7963	55°48·8′	5°31·2′W	H	62
Creag Mhór	Arg & Bt	NR8152	55°43·0′	5°28·8′W	X	62,69
Creag Mhór	Arg & Bt	NR9273	55°54·6′	5°19·2′W	H	62
Creag Mhór	Arg & Bt	NR9475	55°55·7′	5°17·4′W	H	62
Creag Mhór	Arg & Bt	NS1684	56°1·1′	4°56·7′W	H	56
Creag Mhór	Highld	NC2026	58°11·4′	5°3·3′W	X	15
Creag Mhór	Highld	NC2255	58°27·1′	5°2·6′W	X	9
Creag Mhór	Highld	NC6924	58°11·4′	4°13·2′W	H	16
Creag Mhór	Highld	NC8752	58°26·8′	3°55·7′W	X	10
Creag Mhór	Highld	NC9962	58°32·3′	3°43·6′W	H	11
Creag Mhór	Highld	NG3638	57°21·6′	6°22·9′W	X	23,32
Creag Mhór	Highld	NG4017	57°10·5′	6°17·6′W	H	32
Creag Mhór	Highld	NG8020	57°13·3′	5°38·2′W	X	33
Creag Mhór	Highld	NG9031	57°19·5′	5°28·8′W	H	25
Creag Mhór	Highld	NG9632	57°20·2′	5°22·9′W	H	25
Creag Mhór	Highld	NH1787	57°50·4′	5°4·5′W	X	20
Creag Mhór	Highld	NH3264	57°38·3′	4°48·4′W	H	20
Creag Mhór	Highld	NH3794	57°54·6′	4°44·6′W	H	20
Creag Mhór	Highld	NH4353	57°32·7′	4°36·9′W	H	26
Creag Mhòr	Highld	NH4530	57°20·3′	4°34·1′W	H	26
Creag Mhór	Highld	NH4817	57°13·4′	4°30·6′W	H	34
Creag Mhor	Highld	NH7302	57°5·7′	4°5·3′W	X	35
Creag Mhór	Highld	NH7904	57°6·9′	3°59·4′W	H	35
Creag Mhór	Highld	NM5799	57°1·4′	5°59·8′W	X	32,39
Creag Mhór	Highld	NM6788	56°55·7′	5°49·3′W	X	40
Creag Mhòr	Highld	NM8152	56°36·8′	5°33·7′W	X	49
Creag Mhór	Highld	NM8497	57°1·1′	5°33·0′W	X	33,40
Creag Mhór	Highld	NN4182	56°54·4′	4°36·2′W	H	34,42
Creag Mhór	Highld	NN4486	56°56·6′	4°33·4′W	X	34,42
Creag Mhór	Highld	NN4997	57°2·6′	4°28·9′W	H	34
Creag Mhór	Highld	NN5399	57°3·8′	4°25·0′W	X	35
Creag Mhór	Moray	NJ0504	57°7·3′	3°33·7′W	H	36
Creag Mhór	N Ayr	NR8936	55°34·6′	5°20·4′W	X	68,69
Creag Mhór	N Ayr	NR9334	55°33·6′	5°16·5′W	X	68,69
Creag Mhòr	N Eil	NB3524	58°7·8′	6°29·6′W	H	14
Creag Mhòr	N Eil	NB4213	58°2·1′	6°21·8′W	X	14
Creag Mhór	N Eil	NF7807	57°2·8′	7°18·2′W	H	31
Creag Mhòr	N Eil	NF8956	57°29·5′	7°11·0′W	H	22
Creag Mhór	N Eil	NL6695	56°55·8′	7°29·0′W	X	31
Creag Mhór	Pth & Kin	NN6856	56°40·9′	4°8·8′W	X	42,51
Creag Mhór	Pth & Kin	NN7148	56°36·6′	4°5·7′W	H	51,52
Creag Mhór	Pth & Kin	NN9143	56°34·2′	3°46·0′W	H	52
Creag Mhór	Pth & Kin	NN9474	56°51·0′	3°43·8′W	X	43
Creag Mhór	Stir	NN3936	56°29·6′	4°36·5′W	H	50
Creag Mhór	Stir	NN5107	56°14·2′	4°23·8′W	X	57
Creag Mhór	Stir	NN5118	56°20·1′	4°24·2′W	H	57
Creag Mhór	Stir	NN5134	56°28·7′	4°24·7′W	H	51
Creag Mhòr Bhatasgeir	N Eil	NB4939	58°16·3′	6°16·4′W	X	8
Creag Mhór Bhrinicoire	Highld	NM7492	56°58·1′	5°42·6′W	H	33,40
Creagmhor Loch	Arg & Bt	NR8091	56°3·9′	5°31·6′W	W	55
Creag Mhór Scòiteis	Highld	NG7501	57°3·0′	5°42·1′W	X	33
Creag Mhór Thollaidh	Highld	NG8677	57°44·2′	5°35·2′W	H	19
Creag Mhuaiteseal	N Eil	NB2806	57°57·9′	6°35·5′W	H	13,14
Creag Mhurchaidh	N Eil	NB2203	57°56·0′	6°41·3′W	X	13,14
Creag Mò	N Eil	NB1709	57°59·1′	6°46·8′W	X	13,14
Creag Moine	Highld	NG4253	57°29·9′	6°17·9′W	H	23
Creag Mòr	N Eil	NF8227	57°13·7′	7°15·7′W	X	22
Creag Mor a' Bhinnein	Highld	NH0478	57°45·2′	5°17·2′W	X	19
Creag Mùigeil	Highld	NH4232	57°21·3′	4°37·1′W	X	26
Creag Mullach	Aberd	NO4195	57°2·8′	2°57·9′W	X	37,44
Creag na Bà	Highld	NG6711	57°8·1′	5°50·6′W	X	32
Creag na Beirighe	N Eil	NB2911	58°0·6′	6°34·8′W	H	13,14
Creag na Botaigeann	Highld	NG9353	57°31·5′	5°27·0′W	X	25
Creag na Bruaich	Highld	NG5843	57°25·0′	6°1·4′W	X	24
Creag na Bruaich	Pth & Kin	NO1467	56°47·5′	3°24·0′W	H	43
Creag na Bunaig	N Eil	NG1899	57°53·7′	6°45·1′W	H	14
Creag na Caillich	Highld	NN1449	56°36·0′	5°1·3′W	X	50
Creag na Caillich	Highld	NN8490	56°59·5′	3°54·1′W	H	35,43
Creag na Caillich	Stir	NN5637	56°30·4′	4°19·9′W	H	51
Creag na Cailliche	Arg & Bt	NS0970	55°53·4′	5°2·8′W	X	63
Creag na Cailliche	Highld	NN4184	56°55·5′	4°36·3′W	H	34,42
Creag na Cathaig	Arg & Bt	NN0343	56°32·5′	5°11·8′W	X	50
Creag na Ceapaich	Highld	NH0889	57°51·2′	5°13·7′W	H	19
Creag na Ceapaich	Highld	NH5589	57°52·3′	4°26·2′W	X	21
Creag na Claise Càrnaich	Highld	NC2952	58°25·6′	4°55·2′W	X	9
Creag na Clibhe	N Eil	NB1714	58°1·8′	6°47·2′W	X	13,14
Creag na Cloiche Gile	Arg & Bt	NN2225	56°23·3′	4°52·6′W	X	50
Creag na Comhla	Arg & Bt	NM4630	56°23·9′	6°6·5′W	X	48
Creag na Còmhla	Arg & Bt	NM5826	56°22·1′	5°54·7′W	X	48
Creag na Creiche	Aberd	NO3098	57°4·3′	3°8·8′W	H	37,44
Creag na Crìche	Highld	NC9151	58°26·3′	3°51·5′W	X	10
Creag na Criche	Pth & Kin	NN9835	56°30·0′	3°39·0′W	H	52,53
Creag na Croiteige	Stir	NN5210	56°15·8′	4°22·9′W	X	57
Creag na Cuinneige	Pth & Kin	NO0364	56°45·7′	3°34·8′W	T	43
Creag na Cuthaige	Highld	NG4157	57°32·0′	6°19·2′W	H	23
Creag na Dalach Móire	Highld	NC7003	58°0·1′	4°11·5′W	H	16
Creag na Dearcaige	Aberd	NO1787	56°58·3′	3°21·5′W	X	43
Creag na Doire	Highld	NG4358	57°32·6′	6°17·2′W	X	23
Creag na Doire Duibhe	Highld	NN6190	56°59·1′	4°16·8′W	H	35
Creag na Dunaich	Arg & Bt	NS1295	56°6·9′	5°1·0′W	X	56
Creag na Faoilinn	Highld	NC3953	58°26·4′	4°45·0′W	H	9
Creag na Feol	Highld	NG9464	57°37·4′	5°26·5′W	X	19
Creag na Feòla	Highld	NH1396	57°55·1′	5°9·0′W	H	19
Creag na Fionndalach	Highld	NC1948	58°23·2′	5°5·3′W	H	9
Creag na Gaibhre	Highld	NN8591	57°0·0′	3°53·1′W	H	35,43
Creag na Gamhna	Aberd	NJ3520	57°16·2′	3°4·2′W	X	37
Creag na Gaoithe	Highld	NG6047	57°27·3′	5°59·6′W	X	24
Creag na Gaoithe	Highld	NH1242	57°26·0′	5°7·5′W	X	25
Creag na Geodha Mòire	N Eil	NB2303	57°56·1′	6°40·3′W	X	13,14
Creag na h-Aire	Highld	NG1841	57°22·6′	6°41·0′W	H	23
Creag na h-Airighe	Stir	NN5310	56°15·8′	4°22·0′W	H	57
Creag na h-Airigh-fraoich	Highld	NG9453	57°31·5′	5°26·0′W	X	25
Creag na h-Eanchainne	Highld	NH2021	57°14·9′	4°58·6′W	X	25
Creag na h-Eige	Highld	NH1427	57°18·0′	5°4·8′W	X	25
Creag na h-Eiginn	Highld	NG4672	57°40·2′	6°15·1′W	X	23
Creag na h-Eilde	Arg & Bt	NN0213	56°16·4′	5°11·4′W	X	50,55
Creag na h-Inghean	Arg & Bt	NR7858	55°46·1′	5°31·9′W	X	62
Creag na h-Inghinn	Highld	NG9052	57°30·8′	5°29·9′W	X	25
Creag na h-Inghinn	Highld	NH1726	57°17·5′	5°1·8′W	X	25
Creag na h-Iolaire	Arg & Bt	NN0702	56°10·6′	5°6·1′W	X	56
Creag na h-Iolaire	Highld	NC1827	58°11·9′	5°5·3′W	H	15
Creag na h-Iolaire	Highld	NC4447	58°23·3′	4°39·6′W	X	9
Creag na h-Iolaire	Highld	NC4803	57°59·7′	4°33·8′W	X	16
Creag na h-Iolaire	Highld	NC5825	58°11·7′	4°24·5′W	X	16
Creag na h-Iolaire	Highld	NC6728	58°13·5′	4°15·4′W	H	16
Creag na h-Iolaire	Highld	NC7846	58°23·4′	4°4·7′W	X	10
Creag na h-Iolaire	Highld	NG4002	57°2·4′	6°16·7′W	X	32,39
Creag na h-Iolaire	Highld	NG7738	57°22·9′	5°42·1′W	X	24
Creag na h-Iolaire	Highld	NG8851	57°30·2′	5°31·9′W	X	24
Creag na h-Iolaire	Highld	NH1398	57°56·2′	5°9·1′W	H	19
Creag na h-Iolaire	Highld	NH1749	57°29·9′	5°2·8′W	H	25
Creag na h-Iolaire	Highld	NH1842	57°26·2′	5°1·5′W	H	25
Creag na h-Iolaire	N Ayr	NR9247	55°40·6′	5°18·0′W	X	62,69
Creag na h-Iolaire	N Eil	NB1234	58°12·3′	6°53·7′W	X	13
Creag na h-Iolaire	N Eil	NB1702	57°55·3′	6°46·3′W	X	14
Creag na h-Iolaire	N Eil	NB2009	57°59·2′	6°43·8′W	X	13,14
Creag na h-Iolaire	N Eil	NF9465	57°34·5′	7°6·7′W	X	18
Creag na h-Iolaire	N Eil	NL6993	56°54·9′	7°25·9′W	H	31
Creag na h-Iolaire	Pth & Kin	NN5267	56°46·5′	4°24·9′W	X	42
Creag na h-Iolaire	Pth & Kin	NN7527	56°25·4′	4°1·1′W	H	51,52
Creag na h'Iolaire	Stir	NN3924	56°23·1′	4°36·0′W	X	50
Creag na h-Iolaire	Stir	NN5611	56°16·4′	4°19·1′W	X	57
Creag na h-Iolair Mhór	Pth & Kin	NN8279	56°53·5′	3°55·8′W	X	43
Creag na h-Iolare	Highld	NH2330	57°19·8′	4°56·0′W	X	25
Creag na h-Iodaire	Arg & Bt	NN2434	56°28·2′	4°51·0′W	X	50
Creag na h-Iolaire	Arg & Bt	NM6129	56°23·8′	5°51·9′W	H	49
Creag na h-Iolaire	Arg & Bt	NM6328	56°23·4′	5°49·9′W	X	49
Creag na h-Iolaire	Arg & Bt	NN0615	56°17·5′	5°7·6′W	X	50,56
Creag na h-Iolaire	Highld	NG9726	57°17·0′	5°21·6′W	X	25,33
Creag na h'Iolaire	Highld	NH5228	57°19·4′	4°27·0′W	X	26,35
Creag na h-Iolaire	Highld	NH8712	57°11·4′	3°51·7′W	X	35,36
Creag na h-Iolaire	Highld	NH9129	57°20·6′	3°48·2′W	H	36
Creag na h-Iolaire	Pth & Kin	NN6520	56°21·4′	4°10·7′W	X	51,57
Creag na h-Iolaire	Pth & Kin	NN7431	56°27·5′	4°2·2′W	X	51,52
Creag na h-Iolaire	Pth & Kin	NO0557	56°42·0′	3°32·6′W	H	52,53
Creag na h-Iolare	Highld	NH6702	57°5·6′	4°11·3′W	H	35
Creag na h-Oisinn	Stir	NN5826	56°24·6′	4°17·6′W	X	51
Creag na h-Uamha	N Eil	NB3015	58°2·8′	6°34·1′W	H	13,14
Creag na h-Uamhaidh	Arg & Bt	NN0740	56°31·0′	5°7·8′W	X	50
Creag na h-Uidhe	Highld	NC3837	58°17·8′	4°45·4′W	H	16
Creag na h-Urbhaird	Highld	NC4656	58°28·2′	4°37·9′W	X	9
Creag na Larach	Pth & Kin	NN9749	56°37·6′	3°40·3′W	H	52,53
Creag na Lubaig	N Eil	NB1413	58°1·1′	6°50·1′W	X	13,14
Creag na Lùibe Bàine	Highld	NC4547	58°23·3′	4°38·6′W	X	9
Creag nam Ban	Aberd	NO2994	57°2·2′	3°9·7′W	H	37,44
Creag nam Bodach	Highld	NN7596	57°2·6′	4°3·2′W	H	35
Creag nam Bodach	Stir	NN4438	56°30·8′	4°31·7′W	X	51
Creag nam Bothan	Stir	NN5640	56°32·1′	4°20·0′W	X	51
Creag nam Brataichean	Pth & Kin	NO1161	56°44·2′	3°26·8′W	H	43
Creag nam Faoileann	Arg & Bt	NN0700	56°9·5′	5°6·0′W	X	56
Creag nam Fiadh	Highld	NC6413	58°5·4′	4°17·9′W	H	16
Creag nam Fiadh	Highld	NC8423	58°11·1′	3°57·9′W	H	17
Creag nam Fiadh	N Eil	NB3033	58°12·5′	6°35·3′W	X	8,13

Creag nam Fiadh Mór	Arg & Bt	NR5981	55°58·0′	5°51·3′W	H	61
Creag nam Fitheach	Arg & Bt	NM4329	56°23·3′	6°9·4′W	X	48
Creag nam Fitheach	Arg & Bt	NM6624	56°21·3′	5°46·8′W	X	49
Creag nam Fitheach	Arg & Bt	NM8304	56°11·0′	5°29·4′W	H	55
Creag nam Fitheach	Arg & Bt	NM8506	56°12·1′	5°27·5′W	X	55
Creag nam Fitheach	Arg & Bt	NN0816	56°18·1′	5°5·8′W	X	50,56
Creag nam Fitheach	Arg & Bt	NS0379	55°58·1′	5°9·0′W	H	63
Creag nam Fitheach	Highld	NM6269	56°45·4′	5°53·2′W	H	40
Creagnam Fitheach	N Ayr	NR9832	55°32·7′	5°11·7′W	X	69
Creag nam Maigheach	Highld	NC9522	58°10·7′	3°46·7′W	X	17
Creag nam Meann	Highld	NG4055	57°30·9′	6°20·0′W	X	23
Creag nam Meann	Highld	NN3177	56°51·5′	4°45·9′W	X	41
Creag nam Meann	N Ayr	NR9439	55°36·3′	5°15·8′W	X	68,69
Creag nam Mial	Pth & Kin	NO0554	56°40·3′	3°32·6′W	H	52,53
Creag nam Peathrain	Highld	NH1811	57°9·5′	5°0·1′W	H	34
Creag nan Abhag	Highld	NH6800	57°4·6′	4°10·2′W	H	35
Creag nan Adhaircean	Highld	NN5886	56°56·9′	4°19·6′W	H	42
Creag nan Aisinnin	Highld	NC3232	58°14·9′	4°51·3′W	H	15
Creag na Nathrach	Highld	NH1506	57°6·7′	5°2·9′W	H	34
Creag nan Caisean	Pth & Kin	NN7760	56°43·2′	4°0·1′W	H	42
Creag nan Calman	Highld	NC1611	58°3·3′	5°6·6′W	H	15
Creag nan Calman	Highld	NH0950	57°30·3′	5°10·8′W	X	25
Creag nan Calman	Highld	NH1920	57°14·4′	4°59·5′W	H	25
Creag nan Calman	Highld	NH4234	57°22·4′	4°37·2′W	H	26
Creag nan Caorach	Highld	NC8731	58°15·5′	3°55·1′W	H	17
Creag nan Caorann	Stir	NN3020	56°20·8′	4°44·6′W	X	50,56
Creag nan Carnach	Arg & Bt	NN1518	56°19·4′	4°59·1′W	X	50,56
Creag nan Clachan Geala	Highld	NH0423	57°15·6′	5°14·5′W	X	25,33
Creag nan Clag	Highld	NH5928	57°19·5′	4°20·0′W	H	26,35
Creag nan Coileach	Arg & Bt	NR9581	55°59·0′	5°16·7′W	H	55
Creag nan Corrachan	Highld	NH3460	57°36·2′	4°46·2′W	H	20
Creag nan Croman	Arg & Bt	NM4757	56°38·4′	6°7·1′W	X	47
Creag nan Cuaran	Arg & Bt	NR2832	56°27·2′	4°47·0′W	X	50
Creag nan Cuilean	Arg & Bt	NM8216	56°17·4′	5°30·9′W	H	55
Creag nan Cuilean	Arg & Bt	NM9517	56°18·3′	5°18·4′W	H	55
Creag nan Cuilean	Arg & Bt	NR6216	55°23·1′	5°45·0′W	H	68
Creag nan Cuilean	Arg & Bt	NR7675	55°55·2′	5°34·7′W	X	62
Creag nan Damh	Highld	NG9811	57°9·0′	5°19·9′W	H	33
Creag nan Dearcag	Highld	NC0910	58°2·5′	5°13·7′W	H	15
Creag nan Dearcag	Highld	NG8953	57°31·3′	5°31·0′W	X	24
Creag nan Eildeag	Pth & Kin	NN6046	56°35·4′	4°16·3′W	H	51
Creag nan Eilid	Highld	NH0129	57°18·8′	5°17·8′W	H	25,33
Creag nan Eun	Highld	NH4317	57°13·3′	4°35·6′W	H	34
Creag nan Eun	Pth & Kin	NN7231	56°27·5′	4°4·2′W	H	51,52
Creag nan Eun	Pth & Kin	NO1275	56°51·7′	3°26·1′W	H	43
Creag-nan-Eun Forest	Highld	NH4519	57°14·4′	4°33·6′W	F	34
Creag-nan-Eun Forest	Highld	NH4721	57°15·5′	4°31·7′W	F	26
Creag nan Gabhar	Aberd	NO1584	56°56·6′	3°23·4′W	H	43
Creag nan Gabhar	Highld	NH8813	57°11·9′	3°50·8′W	X	35,36
Creag nan Gabhar	Pth & Kin	NN6355	56°40·3′	4°13·7′W	H	42,51
Creag nan Gall	Aberd	NO2692	57°1·1′	3°12·7′W	X	44
Creag nan Gall	Highld	NJ0010	57°10·5′	3°38·8′W	H	36
Creag nan Gamhna	Highld	NH7412	57°11·2′	4°4·6′W	X	35
Creag nan Gamhna	N Eil	NF8219	57°9·4′	7°15·1′W	X	31
Creag nan Garadh	Highld	NG8032	57°19·8′	5°38·8′W	H	24
Creag nan Geàrr	Highld	NC9524	58°11·8′	3°46·7′W	H	17
Creag nan Gobhar	Highld	NH1915	57°11·7′	4°59·3′W	X	34
Creag nan Gobhar	Highld	NN3198	57°2·8′	4°46·7′W	H	34
Creag nan Gobhar	Pth & Kin	NN9968	56°47·8′	3°38·8′W	H	43
Creag nan Iallag	Arg & Bt	NR7783	55°59·5′	5°34·1′W	X	55
Creag nan Laogh	Highld	NC6755	58°28·0′	4°16·3′W	X	10
Creag nan Laogh	Highld	NC7041	58°20·6′	4°12·8′W	H	10
Creag nan Leachda	Aberd	NO1788	56°58·8′	3°21·5′W	H	43
Creag nan Lochan	Highld	NM7572	56°47·4′	5°40·6′W	H	40
Creag nan Saighead	N Eil	NB1434	58°12·4′	6°51·7′W	X	13
Creag nan Sailean	Stir	NN4835	56°29·2′	4°27·7′W	X	51
Creag nan Saithean	Highld	NM6056	56°38·3′	5°54·4′W	X	49
Creag nan Seilcheag	Highld	NG8300	57°2·7′	5°34·2′W	X	33
Creag nan Sgarbh	Arg & Bt	NR5163	55°48·0′	5°58·0′W	X	61
Creag nan Sgarbh	Highld	NM5859	56°39·9′	5°56·5′W	X	47
Creag nan Sgarbh	Highld	NM6267	56°44·3′	5°53·1′W	X	40
Creag nan Sgriob	Highld	NM7767	56°44·7′	5°38·4′W	X	40
Creag nan Soithichean	Highld	NH0887	57°50·1′	5°13·6′W	X	19
Creag nan Speireag	Stir	NN4921	56°21·7′	4°26·2′W	H	51,57
Creag nan Suibheag	Highld	NC3829	58°13·5′	4°45·0′W	H	16
Creag nan Uan	Highld	NH2041	57°25·7′	4°59·4′W	X	25
Creag nan Uan	Pth & Kin	NN7928	56°26·0′	3°57·3′W	X	51,52
Creag nan Uan	Stir	NN4429	56°25·9′	4°31·3′W	X	51
Creag nan Ubhal	Pth & Kin	NN6375	56°51·0′	4°14·3′W	X	42
Creag na Rainich	Highld	NC2661	58°30·4′	4°58·7′W	X	9
Creag na Rianaich	Highld	NH0057	57°33·8′	5°20·2′W	X	25
Creag na Sàile	Highld	NH2652	57°31·7′	4°53·9′W	X	25
Creag na Sanais	Highld	NN6592	57°0·2′	4°12·9′W	H	35
Creag na Saobhaidhe	Highld	NG8747	57°28·1′	5°32·6′W	X	24
Creag na Saobhie	Highld	NH0123	57°15·5′	5°17·5′W	X	25,33
Creag na Sgeith	Arg & Bt	NS0083	56°0·2′	5°12·0′W	H	55
Creag na Sgeith	Arg & Bt	NS0292	56°5·0′	5°10·5′W	X	55
Creag na Sgoinne	Highld	NG9882	57°47·2′	5°23·4′W	H	19
Creag na Sgroille	Arg & Bt	NR9392	56°4·8′	5°19·2′W	H	55
Creag na Slabhraidh	Aberd	NO3185	56°57·3′	3°7·6′W	X	44
Creag na Slice	Aberd	NO4695	57°2·8′	2°52·9′W	H	37,44
Creag na Spàine	Aberd	NO2193	57°1·5′	3°17·6′W	H	36,44
Creag na Speireig	Highld	NC6050	58°25·2′	4°23·3′W	X	10
Creag na Speireig	N Eil	NB1106	57°57·2′	6°52·7′W	H	13,14
Creag na Sròine	Highld	NN8496	57°2·7′	3°54·3′W	H	35,43
Creag na Tràighe	N Eil	NB5345	58°19·7′	6°12·7′W	X	8
Creag Nay	Highld	NN5230	57°20·5′	4°27·1′W	H	26
Creag Nearach	Moray	NJ2634	57°23·7′	3°13·4′W	X	28
Creag Neill	N Eil	NB4114	58°2·6′	6°22·9′W	X	14
Creag Nioscar	N Eil	NB0710	57°59·2′	6°57·0′W	H	13,14
Creag Nodha	Highld	NN3462	56°43·5′	4°42·3′W	X	41
Creag Odhar	Pth & Kin	NN7751	56°38·3′	3°59·9′W	H	42,51,52
Creag Odhar	Pth & Kin	NN8763	56°45·0′	3°50·4′W	H	43
Creag of Tulloch	Pth & Kin	NN7762	56°44·3′	4°0·2′W	X	42
Creag Phàdruig	Aberd	NO1785	56°57·2′	3°21·4′W	H	43
Creag Phiobaidh	Aberd	NO3294	57°2·2′	3°6·8′W	H	37,44
Creag Pitridh	Highld	NN4881	56°54·0′	4°29·3′W	H	34,42
Creag Poll-airgh	Highld	NH1202	57°4·5′	5°5·6′W	X	34
Creag Raineach Mór	Highld	NH1974	57°43·4′	5°1·9′W	X	20
Creag Rainich	Highld	NH0975	57°43·7′	5°12·0′W	H	19

Creag Rainich	Highld	NH3176	57°44·8′	4°49·9′W	H	20
Creag Rais	Highld	NH3771	57°42·2′	4°43·7′W	H	20
Creag Raonuill	Arg & Bt	NR7780	55°57·9′	5°34·0′W	X	55
Creag Reamhar	Angus	NO2460	56°43·8′	3°14·1′W	H	44
Creag Réidh Raineach	Highld	NG8925	57°16·3′	5°29·5′W	H	33
Creag Rhuigh à Bhràgdad	Highld	NH0873	57°42·6′	5°12·9′W	H	19
Creag Riabhach	Highld	NC2763	58°31·5′	4°57·8′W	H	9
Creag Riabhach	Highld	NC2858	58°28·8′	4°56·5′W	X	9
Creag Riabhach	Highld	NC4747	58°23·3′	4°36·6′W	X	9
Creag Riabhach	Highld	NC5045	58°22·3′	4°33·4′W	H	9
Creag Riabhach	Highld	NC5330	58°14·3′	4°29·8′W	H	16
Creag Riabhach	Highld	NC6513	58°5·4′	4°16·9′W	X	16
Creag Riabhach	Highld	NC7112	58°5·0′	4°10·8′W	H	16
Creag Riabhach	Highld	NC9311	58°4·8′	3°48·4′W	X	17
Creag Riabhach	Highld	NH3588	57°51·3′	4°46·4′W	H	20
Creag Riabhach	Pth & Kin	NN4447	56°35·6′	4°32·0′W	H	51
Creag Riabhach Bheag	Highld	NC4952	58°26·1′	4°34·7′W	H	9
Creag Riabhach Loch nan Sgaraig	Highld	NC3424	58°10·7′	4°48·9′W	H	15
Creag Riabhach Mhór	Highld	NC5051	58°25·6′	4°33·6′W	H	9
Creag Riabhach na Greighe	Highld	NC6120	58°9·1′	4°21·2′W	H	16
Creag Riasgain	Highld	NC9512	58°5·3′	3°46·4′W	X	17
Creag Righ Tharailt	Highld	NH7905	57°7·5′	3°59·5′W	H	35
Creag Roro	Pth & Kin	NN6345	56°34·9′	4°13·4′W	X	51
Creag Rosa	N Ayr	NR9938	55°35·9′	5°11·0′W	X	69
Creag Ruadh	Highld	NC4862	58°31·4′	4°36·1′W	H	9
Creag Ruadh	Highld	NC6963	58°32·4′	4°14·5′W	X	10
Creag Ruadh	Highld	NG7244	57°26·0′	5°47·5′W	X	24
Creag Ruadh	Highld	NG8211	57°8·6′	5°35·7′W	X	33
Creag Ruadh	Highld	NG8773	57°42·0′	5°34·0′W	H	19
Creag Ruadh	Highld	NH2394	57°54·3′	4°58·8′W	X	20
Creag Ruadh	Highld	NH2753	57°32·3′	4°52·9′W	H	25
Creag Ruadh	Highld	NH4482	57°48·3′	4°37·1′W	H	20
Creag Ruadh	Highld	NH5223	57°16·7′	4°26·8′W	X	26,35,35
Creag Ruadh	Highld	NH5969	57°41·6′	4°23·7′W	X	21
Creag Ruadh	Highld	NN5691	56°59·5′	4°21·8′W	H	35
Creag Ruadh	Highld	NN6192	57°0·2′	4°16·9′W	H	35
Creag Ruadh	Highld	NN6888	56°58·1′	4°9·8′W	H	42
Creag Ruadh	Highld	NN6896	57°2·4′	4°10·1′W	X	35
Creag Ruadh	N Eil	NG1093	57°50·2′	6°52·7′W	X	14
Creag Ruisgte	Arg & Bt	NM9630	56°25·3′	5°18·0′W	H	49
Creag Sail a' Bhàthaich	Highld	NC8537	58°18·7′	3°57·3′W	H	17
Creag Scalabsdale	Highld	NC9724	58°11·8′	3°44·7′W	H	17
Creag Scalan	N Eil	NF9670	57°37·3′	7°5·1′W	X	18
Creag Sgiathan	Highld	NH1751	57°31·0′	5°2·9′W	X	25
Creag Sgoilte	Arg & Bt	NM6123	56°20·6′	5°51·6′W	X	49
Creag Sgoilte	Arg & Bt	NS1597	56°8·1′	4°58·2′W	X	56
Creag Sgoilteach	Highld	NC5724	58°11·2′	4°25·5′W	H	16
Creag Shaodain	Highld	NM7363	56°42·5′	5°42·1′W	X	40
Creag Shiaraidh	Highld	NN6697	57°2·9′	4°12·1′W	H	35
Creag Shocach	N Ayr	NR9534	55°33·7′	5°14·6′W	X	68,69
Creag Shoilleir	Highld	NH6633	57°22·3′	4°13·2′W	X	26
Creag Shoilleir	Highld	NH8117	57°14·0′	3°57·8′W	H	35
Creag Shoilleir	Pth & Kin	NN8340	56°32·5′	3°53·7′W	X	52
Creag Shoiller	Pth & Kin	NO0758	56°42·5′	3°30·7′W	X	52,53
Creag Shomhairle	Highld	NC3850	58°24·8′	4°45·9′W	H	9
Creag Sneosdal	Highld	NG4168	57°37·9′	6°19·9′W	X	23
Creag Spardain	Pth & Kin	NN9665	56°46·2′	3°41·6′W	H	43
Creag Spuir	N Eil	NF8118	57°8·8′	7°16·0′W	X	31
Creag Staonsaid	Highld	NC3847	58°23·2′	4°45·8′W	H	9
Creag Stoirm	Highld	NG4067	57°37·3′	6°20·8′W	X	23
Creag Strollamus	Highld	NG6026	57°16·0′	5°58·4′W	H	32
Creag Stulabhal	N Eil	NB1111	57°59·9′	6°53·0′W	H	13,14
Creag Tamhnachan	Arg & Bt	NS0593	56°5·7′	5°7·6′W	X	56
Creag Thairbhe	Highld	NC4068	58°34·5′	4°44·6′W	X	9
Creag Tharbh	Highld	NG9273	57°42·2′	5°29·0′W	X	19
Creag Tharsuinn	Arg & Bt	NN2807	56°13·7′	4°46·0′W	X	56
Creag Tharsuinn	Arg & Bt	NS0891	56°4·7′	5°4·7′W	X	56
Creag Tharsuinn	Arg & Bt	NS2796	56°7·8′	4°46·6′W	X	56
Creag Tharsuinn	Highld	NN3688	56°57·5′	4°41·4′W	H	34,41
Creag Tharsuinn	Highld	NN4585	56°56·1′	4°32·4′W	X	34,42
Creag Tharsuinn	Highld	NN7184	56°56·0′	4°6·7′W	X	42
Creag Tharsuinn	Pth & Kin	NN7429	56°26·4′	4°2·2′W	X	51,52
Creag Thearlaich	Pth & Kin	NO0561	56°44·1′	3°32·7′W	H	43
Creag Thoraraidh	Highld	ND0418	58°8·7′	3°37·4′W	H	17
Creag Thormaid	Arg & Bt	NR7732	55°32·1′	5°31·6′W	X	68,69
Creag Thulach	Arg & Bt	NN0625	56°22·9′	5°8·1′W	H	50
Creag Thulaichean	Stir	NS4096	56°8·1′	4°34·0′W	X	56
Creag Toll a' Choin	Highld	NH1345	57°27·7′	5°6·6′W	X	25
Creaguaineach Lodge	Highld	NN3068	56°46·6′	4°46·5′W	X	41
Creag Uchdag	Pth & Kin	NN7032	56°28·0′	4°6·2′W	H	51,52
Creag Uilisgeir	N Eil	NB1207	57°57·8′	6°51·7′W	X	13,14
Creag Uilleim	Highld	NN3483	56°54·7′	4°43·1′W	X	34,41
Creag Uird	Stir	NN4837	56°30·3′	4°27·7′W	X	51
Creag Uisge	Pth & Kin	NO0269	56°48·4′	3°35·8′W	H	43
Creag Uisibridh	N Eil	NB0908	57°58·2′	6°54·8′W	H	13,14
Creag Uladail	Highld	NM7250	56°35·5′	5°42·4′W	X	49
Creag Ulladail	Highld	NH4758	57°35·4′	4°33·1′W	H	26
Creag Urbhard	Highld	NC3548	58°23·6′	4°48·9′W	X	9
Creag Urrard	Pth & Kin	NN8467	56°47·1′	3°53·5′W	H	43
Creag Vollan	I of M	SC2281	54°11·9′	4°43·3′W	X	95
Creakers, The	Beds	TL1053	52°10·1′	0°23·1′W	X	153
Creaking Howe	N Yks	SE6888	54°17·2′	0°56·9′W	X	94,100
Creaking Tree	N Yks	NZ2506	54°27·2′	1°36·4′W	X	93
Crealy Barton	Devon	SY0090	50°42·3′	3°24·6′W	X	192
Cream Gorse Fm	Leic	SK7014	52°43·4′	0°57·4′W	FM	129
Cream Lodge	Leic	SK5918	52°45·6′	1°7·1′W	X	129
Creamore Bank	Shrops	SJ5130	52°52·2′	2°43·3′W	T	126
Creamore Fm	Shrops	SJ5130	52°52·2′	2°43·3′W	FM	126
Creampots	Pemb	SM8813	51°46·8′	5°4·0′W	X	157
Creamston	Pemb	SM9815	51°48·1′	4°55·4′W	X	157,158
Crean	Corn	SW3924	50°3·8′	5°38·5′W	T	203
Creanich	Highld	NC4022	58°9·7′	4°42·7′W	X	16
Crear	Arg & Bt	NR7166	55°50·2′	5°39·0′W	X	62
Creara Head	Orkney	ND4384	58°44·7′	2°58·6′W	X	7
Crear Burn	Arg & Bt	NR7166	55°50·2′	5°39·0′W	W	62
Crearhowe	Orkney	HY4902	58°54·4′	2°52·6′W	X	6,7
Crease	Devon	SX4674	50°33·0′	4°10·1′W	X	201
Creaseys Fm	Essex	TQ6493	51°36·9′	0°22·5′E	FM	177

Creason	Devon	SX5280	50°36·3′	4°5·1′W	X	191,201
Creathorne Fm	Corn	SS2102	50°47·6′	4°32·0′W	FM	190
Creaton	Northnts	SP7071	52°20·2′	0°58·0′W	T	141
Creaton Covert	Northnts	SP7172	52°20·7′	0°57·1′W	F	141
Crebana	Denb	SJ0266	53°11·2′	3°27·6′W	X	116
Crebar	Devon	SX5950	50°20·2′	3°58·5′W	X	202
Crebawethan Neck	I Scilly	SV8306	49°52·5′	6°24·4′W	W	203
Crebinicks	I Scilly	SV8005	49°51·8′	6°26·8′W	X	203
Creca	D & G	NY2270	55°1·4′	3°12·8′W	T	85
Creca Hall	D & G	NY2269	55°0·8′	3°12·8′W	X	85
Creddacott Fm	Corn	SX2395	50°43·9′	4°30·1′W	FM	190
Credenhill	Heref	SO4543	52°5·2′	2°47·8′W	T	148,149,161
Credenhill Park Wood	Heref	SO4544	52°5·7′	2°47·8′W	A	148,149,161
Credenhill Park Wood	Heref	SO4544	52°5·7′	2°47·8′W	F	148,149,161
Credis	Corn	SW9172	50°30·9′	4°56·5′W	X	200
Crediton	Devon	SS8300	50°47·5′	3°39·2′W	T	191
Creebank	D & G	NX3476	55°3·3′	4°35·5′W	X	76
Creebank Burn	D & G	NX3481	55°6·0′	4°35·7′W	W	76
Cree Beck	Darl	NZ3012	54°30·4′	1°31·8′W	W	93
Creebridge	D & G	NX4165	54°57·5′	4°28·6′W	T	83
Creech	Dorset	SY9183	50°39·0′	2°7·3′W	T	195
Creechan	D & G	NX1334	54°40·2′	4°53·6′W	X	82
Creechan Park	D & G	NX1234	54°40·2′	4°54·5′W	X	82
Creech Bottom	Dorset	SY9284	50°39·6′	2°6·4′W	T	195
Creech Fm	Hants	SU6310	50°53·4′	1°5·9′W	FM	196
Creech Grange	Dorset	SY9182	50°38·5′	2°7·3′W	A	195
Creech Heath	Dorset	SY9283	50°39·0′	2°6·4′W	X	195
Creech Heathfield	Somer	ST2726	51°2·0′	3°2·1′W	T	193
Creech Hill	Somer	ST6736	51°7·6′	2°27·9′W	H	183
Creech Hill Ho	Dorset	SU0413	50°55·2′	1°56·2′W	X	195
Creech or East Walk	Hants	SU6410	50°53·4′	1°5·0′W	X	196
Creech St Michael	Somer	ST2725	51°1·4′	3°2·1′W	T	193
Creech Woods	Hants	SU6311	50°53·9′	1°5·9′W	F	196
Creed	Corn	SW9347	50°17·4′	4°54·0′W	T	204
Creedholee Fm	Surrey	SU9036	51°7·2′	0°42·5′W	FM	186
Creediknowe	Shetld	HU5565	60°22·2′	0°59·7′W	T	2
Creed, The	Shetld	HU1762	60°20·8′	1°41·0′W	X	3
Creedy Barton	Devon	SX8699	50°47·0′	3°36·6′W	X	191
Creedy Br	Devon	SS8401	50°48·1′	3°38·4′W	X	191
Creedy Park	Devon	SS8301	50°48·0′	3°39·2′W	X	191
Creegbrawse	Corn	SW7443	50°14·9′	5°9·8′W	T	204
Creek	Cambs	TL4298	52°33·9′	0°6·1′E	X	142,143
Creek Beacon	Devon	SX7770	50°31·2′	3°43·7′W	X	202
Creek Fm	Devon	SX7770	50°31·2′	3°43·7′W	FM	202
Creekgall Fen	Cambs	TF4400	52°35·0′	0°7·9′E	X	142,143
Creekmoor	Poole	SZ0093	50°44·4′	1°59·6′W	T	195
Creekmouth	Bark & Dag	TQ4581	51°30·8′	0°5·8′E	T	177
Creeksea	Essex	TQ9396	51°38·0′	0°47·7′E	T	168
Creeksea Hall	Essex	TQ9396	51°38·0′	0°47·7′E	X	168
Creeks End Mill Drain	Norf	TL6290	52°29·3′	0°23·6′E	W	143
Creekside	Devon	SX4764	50°27·6′	4°9·0′W	X	201
Creek Stephen Point	Corn	SW8837	50°11·9′	4°57·9′W	X	204
Creels of Banks	Orkney	ND5199	58°52·8′	2°50·5′W	X	6,7
Creelwell	Aberd	NJ6545	57°29·9′	2°34·6′W	X	29
Creem's	Suff	TL9433	51°57·9′	0°49·8′E	X	168
Creenlorg Hill	E Ayr	NS6504	55°18·9′	4°7·2′W	X	77
Creens Fm	Corn	SW8951	50°19·5′	4°57·5′W	FM	200,204
Creephedge Ho	Essex	TL7800	51°40·5′	0°34·9′E	X	167
Creephole	Glos	ST8187	51°35·1′	2°16·1′W	X	173
Creep Wood	E Susx	TQ7016	50°55·3′	0°25·5′E	F	199
Creeside	S Ayr	NX3080	55°5·4′	4°39·4′W	X	76
Creeting Bottoms	Suff	TM1157	52°10·5′	1°5·6′E	T	155
Creeting Hall	Suff	TM0756	52°10·0′	1°2·0′E	X	155
Creeting St Mary	Suff	TM0956	52°10·0′	1°3·8′E	T	155
Creeting St Peter	Suff	TM0758	52°11·1′	1°2·1′E	X	155
Creeton	Lincs	TF0119	52°45·8′	0°29·8′W	T	130
Creeton Fm	Lincs	TF0121	52°46·9′	0°29·7′W	FM	130
Creetown	D & G	NX4758	54°53·9′	4°22·7′W	T	83
Cregan Gate	Corn	SW9152	50°20·1′	4°55·8′W	X	200,204
Creganterve Beg	Arg & Bt	NM8501	56°9·5′	5°27·3′W	X	55
Creggan	Arg & Bt	NR8656	55°45·3′	5°24·2′W	X	62
Creggan Dubha	Arg & Bt	NN2832	56°27·2′	4°47·0′W	X	50
Creggan Moar	I of M	SC2177	54°9·7′	4°44·1′W	X	95
Creggans	Arg & Bt	NN0802	56°10·6′	5°5·1′W	T	56
Creg Harlot	I of M	SC1870	54°5·9′	4°46·6′W	X	95
Cregiau Eglwyseg	Denb	SJ2244	52°59·5′	3°9·3′W	X	117
Creg Inneen Thalleyr	I of M	SC2866	54°3·9′	4°37·3′W	X	95
Creglea	I of M	SC2179	54°10·8′	4°44·2′W	X	95
Cregneash	I of M	SC1867	54°4·3′	4°46·5′W	T	95
Creg-ny-Baa	I of M	SC3981	54°12·2′	4°27·7′W	X	95
Cregoe	Corn	SW9142	50°14·7′	4°55·5′W	X	204
Cregrina	Powys	SO1252	52°9·8′	3°16·8′W	T	148
Creg, The	I of M	SC3483	54°13·2′	4°32·4′W	H	95
Creg Willey's Hill	I of M	SC3085	54°14·2′	4°36·1′W	H	95
Creg-y-cowin	I of M	SC3784	54°13·8′	4°29·6′W	X	95
Creg y Whullian	I of M	SC3180	54°11·5′	4°35·0′W	H	95
Creich	Arg & Bt	NM3124	56°20·2′	6°20·7′W	T	48
Creich Mains	Highld	NH6488	57°51·9′	4°17·1′W	X	21
Creich Wood	Highld	NH6490	57°53·0′	4°17·1′W	F	21
Creigarestie	W Dunb	NS4475	55°56·8′	4°29·4′W	X	64
Creigau	Monm	ST4899	51°41·5′	2°44·7′W	T	171
Creigen Ddu	Cered	SN7765	52°16·4′	3°47·8′W	H	135,147
Creigh Hill	Angus	NO2658	56°42·7′	3°12·1′W	H	53
Creighton	Staffs	SK0836	52°55·5′	1°52·5′W	T	128
Creighton Park Fm	Staffs	SK0736	52°55·5′	1°53·3′W	FM	128
Creigiau	Card	ST0881	51°31·5′	3°19·2′W	T	170
Creigiau	Conwy	SH8356	53°5·5′	3°44·4′W	X	116
Creigiau	Gwyn	SH9439	52°56·5′	3°34·2′W	X	125
Creigiau	I of Angl	SH2886	53°20·8′	4°34·7′W	X	114
Creigiau	Powys	SO0370	52°19·4′	3°25·0′W	X	136,147
Creigiau Brithion	Gwyn	SH8320	52°46·1′	3°43·7′W	X	124,125
Creigiau Bwlch-Hyddgen	Powys	SN7693	52°31·5′	3°49·3′W	X	135
Creigiau Camddwr	Gwyn	SH8519	52°45·6′	3°41·9′W	H	124,125
Creigiau Cliperau	I of Angl	SH2885	53°20·3′	4°34·6′W	X	114
Creigiau Coed	Cered	SN7967	52°17·5′	3°46·1′W	X	135,147
Creigiau Duon	Powys	SN8254	52°10·5′	3°43·1′W	X	147
Creigiau Duon	Powys	SN8756	52°11·7′	3°38·8′W	X	147
Creigiau Garn-wddog	Gwyn	SH8313	52°42·4′	3°43·5′W	H	124,125
Creigiau Gleision	Conwy	SH7362	53°8·6′	3°53·5′W	H	115
Creigiau Hirion	Powys	SN8659	52°13·3′	3°39·7′W	X	147

Creigiau Ladis	Carm	SN7245	52°5·6′	3°51·7′W	X	146,147
Creigiau Llwydion	Conwy	SH8858	53°6·7′	3°40·0′W	X	116
Creigiau Llwydion	Powys	SN9679	52°24·2′	3°31·3′W	X	136,147
Creigiau-mawr	I of Angl	SH3789	53°22·6′	4°26·6′W	X	114
Creigiau Pennant	Powys	SN8696	52°33·2′	3°40·5′W	X	135,136
Creigiau Rhiwledyn	Conwy	SH8182	53°19·5′	3°46·8′W	H	116
Creigiau'r Hyrddod	Wrex	SJ1337	52°55·6′	3°17·3′W	X	125
Creigiog-isaf	Denb	SJ1955	53°5·4′	3°12·2′W	X	116
Creigiog-Ucha	Denb	SJ2055	53°5·4′	3°11·3′W	X	117
Creigir	Gwyn	SH2928	52°49·6′	4°31·9′W	X	123
Creiglyn Dyfi	Gwyn	SH8622	52°47·3′	3°41·0′W	W	124,125
Creignant	Powys	SN8896	52°33·3′	3°38·7′W	W	135,136
Creignant	Powys	SO2172	52°20·7′	3°9·2′W	X	137,148
Creinch	W Dunb	NS3988	56°3·7′	4°34·7′W	X	56
Creityhall	Stir	NS4590	56°4·9′	4°29·0′W	X	57
Crel	Conwy	SH8667	53°11·5′	3°42·0′W	X	116
Crelevan	Highld	NH3937	57°24·0′	4°40·3′W	X	26
Crelly	Corn	SW6732	50°8·8′	5°15·3′W	T	203
Cremlyn	I of Angl	SH5777	53°16·5′	4°8·3′W	X	114,115
Cremyll	Corn	SX4553	50°21·6′	4°10·4′W	T	201
Crendell	Dorset	SU0813	50°55·2′	1°52·8′W	T	195
Crendle	Dorset	ST6818	50°57·9′	2°27·0′W	X	183
Crendle Down	Corn	SX3465	50°27·9′	4°20·0′W	X	201
Creney Fm	Corn	SX0761	50°25·3′	4°42·6′W	FM	200
Crenver	Corn	SW6333	50°9·2′	5°18·7′W	X	203
Crenver Grove	Corn	SW6333	50°9·2′	5°18·7′W	F	203
Creoch	E Ayr	NS4721	55°27·8′	4°24·8′W	X	70
Creochhill	E Ayr	NS4521	55°27·8′	4°26·7′W	X	70
Creoch Loch	E Ayr	NS5915	55°24·8′	4°13·2′W	W	71
Creochs	D & G	NX7164	54°57·5′	4°0·5′W	X	83,84
Creog nan Gabhar	Pth & Kin	NN6066	56°46·1′	4°17·0′W	H	42
Crepkill	Highld	NG4248	57°27·2′	6°17·6′W	T	23
Crepping Hall	Essex	TL9028	51°55·3′	0°46·2′E	X	168
Crepping Hall	Suff	TM1434	51°58·0′	1°7·3′E	X	169
Creraig	Highld	NH4741	57°26·3′	4°32·5′W	X	26
Cresborough	Pemb	SN0114	51°47·6′	4°52·8′W	X	157,158
Crescent Fm	N upon Ty	NZ1568	55°0·6′	1°45·5′W	FM	88
Creskeld Hall	Leeds	SE2644	53°53·7′	1°35·8′W	X	104
Creslow	Bucks	SP8121	51°53·1′	0°49·0′W	T	165
Crespet Hill	Aberd	NJ3321	57°16·7′	3°6·2′W	H	37
Cressage	Shrops	SJ5904	52°38·2′	2°36·0′W	T	126
Cressage Ho	Shrops	SJ5703	52°37·6′	2°37·7′W	X	126
Cressars	Corn	SW4930	50°7·3′	5°30·3′W	X	203
Cressbrook	Derby	SK1773	53°15·5′	1°44·3′W	T	119
Cresselly	Pemb	SN0606	51°43·4′	4°48·1′W	T	158
Cresselly Big Wood	Pemb	SN0605	51°42·9′	4°48·1′W	F	158
Cressex	Bucks	SU8491	51°36·9′	0°46·8′W	T	175
Cress Green	Glos	SO7804	51°44·3′	2°18·7′W	T	162
Cressing	Essex	TL7820	51°51·2′	0°35·5′E	T	167
Cressing Lodge	Essex	TL7821	51°51·8′	0°35·5′E	X	167
Cressing Sta	Essex	TL7720	51°51·3′	0°34·6′E	X	167
Cressing Temple	Essex	TL7918	51°50·1′	0°36·3′E	X	167
Cresswell	Carm	SN2812	51°47·1′	4°29·2′W	X	158
Cresswell	Northum	NZ2993	55°14·1′	1°32·2′W	T	81
Cresswell	Staffs	SJ9739	52°57·1′	2°2·3′W	T	127
Cresswell Castle	Pemb	SN0407	51°43·9′	4°49·9′W	A	157,158
Cresswell Down Fm	Wilts	ST9054	51°17·3′	2°8·2′W	FM	184
Cresswell Home Fm	Northum	NZ2991	55°13·0′	1°32·2′W	FM	81
Cresswell Quay	Pemb	SN0506	51°43·4′	4°49·0′W	X	158
Cresswell River	Pemb	SN0206	51°43·3′	4°51·6′W	W	157,158
Cresswells Fm	Win & Maid	SU8878	51°29·9′	0°43·5′W	FM	175
Cresswell's Piece	Staffs	SJ9545	53°0·4′	2°4·1′W	F	118
Cressy Hall	Lincs	TF2230	52°51·5′	0°10·9′W	X	131
Crest Hill Fm	Hants	SU7545	51°12·2′	0°55·2′W	FM	186
Crêst Mawr	Denb	SJ0467	53°11·7′	3°25·8′W	F	116
Crest Wood	Shrops	SO2899	52°35·3′	3°3·4′W	F	137
Creswell	Derby	SK5274	53°15·9′	1°12·8′W	T	120
Creswell	Staffs	SJ8925	52°49·6′	2°9·4′W	T	127
Creswell	Staffs	SJ9025	52°49·6′	2°8·5′W	T	127
Creswell Crags	Derby	SK5374	53°15·9′	1°11·9′W	X	120
Creswell Fm	Staffs	SJ8926	52°50·1′	2°9·4′W	FM	127
Creswell Green	Staffs	SK0710	52°41·5′	1°53·4′W	T	128
Crete Hill	Dorset	SY6597	50°46·5′	2°29·4′W	X	194
Creteway Down	Kent	TR2338	51°6·1′	1°11·5′E	X	179,189
Cretingham	Suff	TM2260	52°11·8′	1°15·3′E	T	156
Cretingham Lodge	Suff	TM2262	52°12·9′	1°15·4′E	X	156
Cretlevane	Stir	NS5394	56°7·2′	4°21·4′W	X	57
Cretshengan	Arg & Bt	NR7166	55°50·2′	5°39·0′W	X	62
Cretshengan Bay	Arg & Bt	NR7066	55°50·2′	5°40·0′W	W	61,62
Creuau	Gwyn	SH6541	52°57·2′	4°0·2′W	X	124
Creuch Hill	Inverc	NS2668	55°52·7′	4°46·5′W	H	63
Crew	Cumbr	NY5677	55°5·4′	2°40·9′W	X	86
Crew Castle	Cumbr	NY5677	55°5·4′	2°40·9′W	A	86
Crew Crag	Cumbr	NY5878	55°5·9′	2°39·1′W	X	86
Crewe	Ches	SJ7055	53°5·7′	2°26·5′W	T	118
Crewe-by-Farndon	Ches	SJ4253	53°4·5′	2°51·5′W	T	117
Crewe Fm	Warw	SP3172	52°20·9′	1°32·3′W	FM	140
Crewe Green	Ches	SJ7255	53°5·7′	2°24·7′W	X	118
Crewe Hall	Ches	SJ7353	53°4·7′	2°23·8′W	A	118
Crewe Hill	Ches	SJ4252	53°4·0′	2°51·5′W	X	117
Crewell	Corn	SX0959	50°24·2′	4°40·9′W	X	200
Crewes Ho	Surrey	TQ3559	51°19·1′	0°3·4′W	X	187
Crewgarth	Cumbr	NY6034	54°42·2′	2°36·8′W	T	91
Crewgreen	Powys	SJ3215	52°43·9′	3°0·0′W	T	126
Crewkerne	Somer	ST4409	50°52·9′	2°47·4′W	T	193
Crewkerne Sta	Somer	ST4508	50°52·4′	2°46·5′W	X	193
Crew Moor	Cumbr	NY5677	55°5·4′	2°40·9′W	X	86
Crewood Hall	Ches	SJ5676	53°17·0′	2°39·2′W	X	117
Crews	D & G	NX2354	54°51·2′	4°45·0′W	X	82
Crew's Fm	Wilts	SU0183	51°33·0′	1°58·7′W	FM	173
Crews Hill	Enf	TQ3199	51°40·7′	0°5·9′W	T	166,176,177
Crews Hill	Heref	SO6722	51°54·0′	2°28·4′W	X	162
Crews Hill	Worcs	SO7353	52°10·7′	2°23·3′W	X	150
Crew's Hole	C of Bris	ST6273	51°27·5′	2°32·4′W	T	172
Crewton	C of Derb	SK3733	52°53·8′	1°26·6′W	T	128
Creya	Orkney	HY3824	59°6·2′	3°4·5′W	X	6
Creya	Orkney	HY5807	58°57·2′	2°43·3′W	X	5
Creyke Fm	E Yorks	TA0264	54°3·9′	0°26·1′W	FM	101
Creyke Nest Fm	N Yks	NZ5407	54°27·6′	1°9·6′W	FM	93
Criadhach Mhór	Arg & Bt	NM4755	56°37·4′	6°7·0′W	X	47

Criaendmuir	N Lanak	NS6667	55°52·9′	4°8·1′W	X	64
Criafol	Powys	SO0066	52°17·2′	3°27·6′W	X	136,147
Crianlarich	Stir	NN3825	56°23·6′	4°37·0′W	T	50
Cribach Bay	Cered	SN2552	52°8·6′	4°33·1′W	W	145
Cribarth	Powys	SN8214	51°49·0′	3°42·3′W	H	160
Cribarth	Powys	SN9452	52°9·6′	3°32·6′W	X	147
Cribau Mill	Monm	ST4594	51°38·8′	2°47·3′W	X	171,172
Cribba Head	Corn	SW4022	50°2·7′	5°37·5′W	X	203
Cribba Sound	Shetld	HU3059	60°19·1′	1°26·9′W	W	3
Cribbie	Shetld	HU1562	60°20·8′	1°43·2′W	X	3
Cribbs Causeway	S Glos	ST5780	51°31·3′	2°36·8′W	T	172
Cribb's Fm	N Som	ST4962	51°21·5′	2°43·6′W	FM	172,182
Cribb's Lodge	Leic	SK8918	52°45·4′	0°40·5′W	X	130
Crib Burn	Scot Bord	NY4699	55°17·2′	2°50·6′W	W	79
Crib Cleugh	Scot Bord	NT5159	55°49·6′	2°46·5′W	W	66,73
Cribden Hill	Lancs	SD7924	53°43·0′	2°18·7′W	H	103
Cribden Side	Lancs	SD7924	53°43·0′	2°18·7′W	T	103
Crib-Goch	Gwyn	SH6255	53°4·7′	4°3·2′W	X	115
Crib-House Fm	Dorset	ST8017	50°57·4′	2°16·7′W	FM	183
Cribin Fâch	Gwyn	SH7915	52°43·4′	3°47·1′W	H	124
Cribin Fawr	Gwyn	SH7915	52°43·4′	3°47·1′W	H	124
Crib Law	Scot Bord	NT3309	55°22·5′	3°3·0′W	H	79
Crib Law	Scot Bord	NT5259	55°49·6′	2°45·5′W	H	66,73
Cribog	Pemb	SM6623	51°51·6′	5°23·5′W	X	157
Cribor	Cered	SN4147	52°6·2′	4°18·9′W	X	146
Cribs Hill	Scot Bord	NT4531	55°34·4′	2°51·9′W	H	73
Cribs Hole	Scot Bord	NT5908	55°22·1′	2°38·4′W	X	80
Crib-y-Ddysgl	Gwyn	SH6155	53°4·7′	4°4·1′W	X	115
Cribyn	Cered	SN5251	52°8·5′	4°9·4′W	T	146
Cribyn	Powys	SO0221	51°53·0′	3°25·0′W	X	160
Cribyn Clota	Cered	SN5351	52°8·5′	4°8·5′W	A	146
Cribyn Du	Carm	SN7548	52°7·2′	3°49·2′W	X	146,147
Crib yr Esgair	Cered	SN7984	52°26·7′	3°46·4′W	X	135
Crib-y-rhiw	Gwyn	SH6624	52°48·1′	3°58·9′W	H	124
Criccieth	Gwyn	SH5038	52°55·4′	4°13·5′W	T	124
Criccieth Castle	Gwyn	SH4937	52°54·8′	4°14·3′W	A	123
Criccin	Denb	SJ0477	53°17·1′	3°26·0′W	X	116
Crich	Derby	SK3554	53°5·2′	1°28·2′W	T	119
Crich Carr	Derby	SK3354	53°5·2′	1°30·0′W	T	119
Crich Chase	Derby	SK3452	53°4·1′	1°29·1′W	F	119
Crich Common	Derby	SK3553	53°4·6′	1°28·2′W	X	119
Crichel Down	Dorset	ST9610	50°53·6′	2°3·0′W	X	195
Crichel Ho	Dorset	ST9908	50°52·5′	2°0·5′W	A	195
Crichen	D & G	NX7790	55°11·6′	3°55·9′W	X	78
Crichie	Aberd	NJ7719	57°15·9′	2°22·4′W	X	38
Crichie	Aberd	NJ7835	57°24·5′	2°21·5′W	X	29,30
Crichie Burn	Aberd	NO6476	56°52·7′	2°35·0′W	W	45
Crichie Ho	Aberd	NJ9745	57°30·0′	2°2·5′W	X	30
Crichie Moss	Aberd	NJ9642	57°28·4′	2°3·5′W	X	30
Crichness	Scot Bord	NT6866	55°53·4′	2°30·3′W	X	67
Crichness Hill	Scot Bord	NT6966	55°53·4′	2°29·3′W	X	67
Crichness Law	Scot Bord	NT6866	55°53·4′	2°30·3′W	X	67
Crichneyled	Aberd	NJ7734	57°24·0′	2°22·5′W	X	29,30
Crichope Linn	D & G	NX9195	55°14·5′	3°42·4′W	X	78
Crichton	Midlo	NT3862	55°51·1′	2°59·0′W	T	66
Crichton Castle	Midlo	NT3861	55°50·5′	2°59·0′W	A	66
Crichton Ho	Midlo	NT3962	55°51·1′	2°58·0′W	X	66
Crichton Royal Hospl	D & G	NX9874	55°3·3′	3°35·4′W	X	84
Crichton's Cairn	D & G	NX9598	55°16·2′	3°38·7′W	X	78
Crick	Monm	ST4890	51°36·6′	2°44·7′W	T	171,172
Crick	Northnts	SP5872	52°20·8′	1°8·5′W	T	140
Crickadarn	Powys	SO0842	52°4·4′	3°20·1′W	T	147,160
Crickapit Mill	Corn	SX1461	50°25·4′	4°36·7′W	X	200
Crickchurch Fm	Pemb	SN0503	51°41·8′	4°48·9′W	FM	158
Crick Covert	Northnts	SP5773	52°21·4′	1°9·4′W	F	140
Cricket Court	Somer	ST3611	50°53·9′	2°54·2′W	X	193
Cricket Fm	Somer	ST7443	51°11·4′	2°21·9′W	FM	183
Cricket Hill	Hants	SU8260	51°20·2′	0°49·0′W	T	175,186
Cricket Malherbie	Somer	ST3611	50°53·9′	2°54·2′W	T	193
Cricket St Thomas	Somer	ST3708	50°52·3′	2°53·3′W	T	193
Crickett	Shrops	SJ3634	52°54·2′	2°56·7′W	X	126
Crickham	Somer	ST4349	51°14·5′	2°48·6′W	T	182
Crickheath	Shrops	SJ2922	52°47·7′	3°2·8′W	T	126
Crickheath Hill	Shrops	SJ2723	52°48·2′	3°4·6′W	H	126
Crickheath Wharf	Shrops	SJ2923	52°48·2′	3°2·8′W	T	126
Crickhowell	Powys	SO2118	51°51·5′	3°8·4′W	T	161
Crickie Fm	Powys	SO1429	51°57·4′	3°14·7′W	FM	161
Crickies Chair	Shetld	HP6715	60°49·0′	0°45·6′W	X	1
Cricklade	Wilts	SU0993	51°38·4′	1°51·8′W	T	163,173
Crickleaze Ho	Somer	ST2711	50°53·9′	3°1·9′W	X	193
Crickle Fm	N Yks	SD9150	53°57·0′	2°7·8′W	FM	103
Cricklewood	Brent	TQ2385	51°33·3′	0°13·2′W	T	176
Crickley Barrow Fm	Glos	SP1112	51°48·6′	1°50·0′W	FM	163
Crickley Hill Country Park	Glos	SO9316	51°50·8′	2°5·7′W	X	163
Crick Lodge	Northnts	SP5774	52°21·9′	1°9·4′W	X	140
Crickmarren Fm	Pemb	SR9498	51°38·8′	4°58·4′W	FM	158
Crickmery	Shrops	SJ6729	52°51·7′	2°29·0′W	T	127
Crick's Fm	Cambs	TL6154	52°9·9′	0°21·6′E	FM	154
Crick's Green	Heref	SO6351	52°9·6′	2°32·1′W	T	149
Crickton	Swan	SS5091	51°36·1′	4°9·6′W	X	159
Crick Tunnel	Northnts	SP5971	52°20·3′	1°7·6′W	X	140
Crick Wharf	Northnts	SP5972	52°20·8′	1°7·6′W	X	140
Cricor	Denb	SJ1350	53°2·7′	3°17·5′W	X	116
Criddlestyle	Hants	SU1514	50°55·7′	1°46·8′W	T	195
Criddon	Shrops	SO6691	52°31·2′	2°29·7′W	X	138
Cridling Park	Wakf	SE5122	53°41·8′	1°13·2′W	X	105
Cridling Stubbs	N Yks	SE5221	53°41·2′	1°12·3′W	T	105
Cridmore	I of W	SZ4982	50°38·4′	1°18·0′W	T	196
Criech	Fife	NO3221	56°22·8′	3°5·6′W	T	53,59
Crief	N Yks	SE5580	54°13·0′	1°9·0′W	X	100
Crieff	Angus	NO4057	56°42·3′	2°58·3′W	X	54
Crieff	Pth & Kin	NN8621	56°22·3′	3°50·3′W	T	52,58
Crieff Hill	Pth & Kin	NO0344	56°34·9′	3°34·3′W	H	52,53
Crieffvechter	Pth & Kin	NN8820	56°21·8′	3°48·3′W	X	52,58
Criffel	D & G	NX9562	54°56·7′	3°37·9′W	H	84
Criffel	D & G	NY1495	55°14·8′	3°20·7′W	X	78
Criffell Ho	D & G	NX9759	54°55·2′	3°36·0′W	X	84
Crift	Corn	SX0660	50°24·7′	4°43·5′W	X	200
Crift	Corn	SX3466	50°28·5′	4°20·0′W	X	201
Crift Downs	Corn	SX0659	50°24·2′	4°43·4′W	H	200

Criftin	Shrops	SJ5513	52°43·0′	2°39·6′W	X	126
Criftin Brook	Shrops	SO3992	52°31·6′	2°53·6′W	W	137
Criftin Fm	Notts	SK6349	53°2·3′	1°3·2′W	FM	129
Criftin Ford Br	Heref	SO4172	52°20·8′	2°51·6′W	X	137,148
Criftin Ho	Shrops	SO3791	52°31·0′	2°55·3′W	X	137
Criftins	E Yorks	TA1343	53°52·5′	0°16·5′W	X	107
Criftins	Shrops	SJ3435	52°54·7′	2°58·5′W	X	126
Criftoe	Corn	SW9463	50°26·1′	4°53·7′W	X	200
Crifton Lodge	Notts	SK6459	53°7·7′	1°2·2′W	X	120
Crigdon Hill	Northum	NT8605	55°20·6′	2°12·8′W	H	80
Criggan	Corn	SX0160	50°24·6′	4°47·7′W	T	200
Criggan Moors	Corn	SX0161	50°25·1′	4°47·7′W	X	200
Criggie	Aberd	NO7366	56°47·3′	2°26·1′W	X	45
Criggin	Powys	SO0975	52°22·2′	3°19·8′W	X	136,147
Criggion	Powys	SJ2915	52°43·9′	3°2·7′W	T	126
Crigglestone	Wakf	SE3115	53°38·1′	1°31·5′W	T	110,111
Crimble	Roch	SD8611	53°36·0′	2°12·3′W	T	109
Crimble Dale	N Yks	SE2275	54°10·5′	1°39·4′W	X	99
Crimbles Fm	Sheff	SK2699	53°29·5′	1°36·1′W	FM	110
Crimbourne Fm	W Susx	TQ0223	51°0·1′	0°32·4′W	FM	197
Crimchard	Somer	ST3109	50°52·8′	2°58·5′W	T	193
Crimdon House Fm	Durham	NZ4836	54°43·2′	1°14·9′W	FM	93
Crimdon Park	Durham	NZ4837	54°43·8′	1°14·9′W	T	93
Crimea Fm	Notts	SK6144	52°59·6′	1°5·1′W	FM	129
Crimea Pass or Bwlch y Gorddinan	Conwy	SH7049	53°1·6′	3°55·9′W	X	115
Crime Lake	Oldham	SD9101	53°30·6′	2°7·7′W	W	109
Crime Rigg	Durham	NZ3341	54°46·0′	1°28·8′W	X	88
Crimes Brook	Ches	SJ5259	53°7·8′	2°42·6′W	X	117
Crimond	Aberd	NJ6214	57°13·2′	2°37·3′W	X	37
Crimond	Aberd	NK0556	57°35·9′	1°54·5′W	T	30
Crimondhill	Aberd	NJ8536	57°25·1′	2°14·5′W	X	30
Crimongorth	Aberd	NK0455	57°35·4′	1°55·5′W	X	30
Crimonmogate	Aberd	NK0458	57°37·0′	1°55·5′W	T	30
Crimp	Corn	SS2515	50°54·7′	4°29·0′W	T	190
Crimpiau	Conwy	SH7359	53°7·0′	3°53·5′W	H	115
Crimple	N Yks	SE3354	53°59·1′	1°29·4′W	X	104
Crimple Beck or River Crimple	N Yks	SE3552	53°58·0′	1°27·6′W	W	104
Crimple Head Fm	N Yks	SE2551	53°57·5′	1°36·7′W	FM	104
Crimple Ho	N Yks	SE3153	53°58·6′	1°31·2′W	X	104
Crimplesham	Norf	TF6403	52°36·2′	0°25·7′E	T	143
Crimps Fm	Shrops	SJ4135	52°54·8′	2°52·2′W	FM	126
Crimpton	Lancs	SD6747	53°55·3′	2°29·9′W	T	103
Crim Rocks	I Scilly	SV8009	49°54·0′	6°27·0′W	X	203
Crimscote	Warw	SP2347	52°7·5′	1°39·4′W	T	151
Crimscote Downs	Warw	SP2246	52°6·9′	1°40·3′W	X	151
Crimscote Fields	Warw	SP2246	52°6·9′	1°40·3′W	X	151
Crimsham Manor Fm	W Susx	SU8900	50°47·8′	0°43·8′W	FM	197
Crimson Hill	Somer	ST3121	50°59·3′	2°58·6′W	H	193
Crimsworth Dean	Cald	SD9830	53°46·2′	2°1·4′W	X	103
Crimwellpool Fm	Ches	SJ6079	53°18·6′	2°35·6′W	FM	118
Crina Bottom	N Yks	SD7273	54°9·4′	2°25·3′W	X	98
Crina Bottom Fm	N Yks	SD7468	54°6·7′	2°23·4′W	FM	98
Crinacott	Devon	SS3001	50°47·3′	4°24·3′W	X	190
Crinan	Arg & Bt	NR7894	56°5·5′	5°33·7′W	T	55
Crinan Canal	Arg & Bt	NR8489	56°3·0′	5°27·7′W	W	55
Crinan Ferry	Arg & Bt	NR7993	56°5·0′	5°32·7′W	T	55
Crinan Harbour	Arg & Bt	NR7894	56°5·5′	5°33·7′W	W	55
Crincoed Point	Pemb	SM9540	52°1·5′	4°58·9′W	X	157
Crincombe Bottom	Dorset	ST8003	50°49·8′	2°16·7′W	X	194
Crindau	Newp	ST3189	51°36·0′	2°59·4′W	T	171
Crindledyke	N Lanak	NS8356	55°47·2′	3°51·5′W	T	65,72
Crindledyke Fm	Cumbr	NY5543	54°47·0′	2°41·6′W	FM	86
Crindledykes	Northum	NY7867	55°0·1′	2°20·2′W	X	86,87
Crinei Brook	Pemb	SM9635	51°58·8′	4°57·8′W	W	157
Crinfynydd	Powys	SO1760	52°14·2′	3°12·5′W	H	148
Cringa	Carm	SN2014	51°48·0′	4°36·2′W	X	158
Cringate	Stir	NS6887	56°3·7′	4°6·8′W	X	57
Cringate Law	Stir	NS6888	56°4·3′	4°6·8′W	H	57
Cringate Muir	Stir	NS7087	56°3·7′	4°4·8′W	X	57
Cringie Law	Scot Bord	NT4418	55°27·4′	2°52·7′W	H	79
Cringla Fiold	Orkney	HY2314	59°0·6′	3°20·0′W	X	6
Cringlebarrow Wood	Lancs	SD4975	54°10·3′	2°46·5′W	F	97
Cringlebeck Fm	N Lincs	SE9317	53°38·7′	0°35·2′W	FM	112
Cringleber	Lancs	SD6071	54°8·2′	2°36·3′W	X	97
Cringle Brook	Lincs	SK9229	52°51·3′	0°37·6′W	W	130
Cringlebrooks Fm	Lancs	SD5737	53°49·9′	2°38·8′W	FM	102
Cringle Carr	N Yks	SE5688	54°17·3′	1°8·0′W	X	100
Cringlefield	Orkney	HY4908	58°57·6′	2°52·7′W	X	6,7
Cringle Fm	Lincs	SK9127	52°50·2′	0°38·5′W	FM	130
Cringleford	Norf	TG1905	52°36·1′	1°14·5′E	T	134
Cringle Ho	Northnts	SP8962	52°15·2′	0°41·4′W	X	152
Cringle Moor	N Yks	NZ5302	54°24·9′	1°10·6′W	X	93
Cringle Plantation	I of M	SC2474	54°8·2′	4°41·2′W	F	95
Cringles	Brad	SE0448	53°55·9′	1°55·9′W	T	104
Cringles	Cumbr	NY4452	54°51·8′	2°51·9′W	X	85
Cringletie	Scot Bord	NT2344	55°41·3′	3°13·1′W	T	73
Cringley Hill	N Yks	NZ0000	54°24·0′	1°59·6′W	X	92
Cringoed	Powys	SH8801	52°36·0′	3°38·8′W	X	135,136
Cringraval	N Eil	NF8164	57°33·5′	7°19·6′W	X	18
Crinhayes Fm	Devon	ST2208	50°52·2′	3°6·1′W	FM	192,193
Crinigart	Stir	NS5298	56°9·4′	4°22·5′W	X	57
Crink Law	Scot Bord	NT6608	55°22·1′	2°31·8′W	H	80
Crinkle Crags	Cumbr	NY2505	54°26·3′	3°9·0′W	X	89,90
Crinkle Gill	Cumbr	NY2504	54°25·8′	3°8·9′W	W	89,90
Crinow	Pemb	SN1214	51°47·8′	4°43·2′W	T	158
Crins Hill	E Ayr	NS5444	55°40·3′	4°18·9′W	H	70
Crinshill Moss	E Ayr	NS5544	55°40·3′	4°17·9′W	X	71
Crioch Dhubh	Highld	NH5161	57°37·1′	4°29·2′W	X	20
Criogan	Arg & Bt	NN1502	56°10·7′	4°58·4′W	W	56
Criol Fm	Kent	TQ9738	51°6·7′	0°49·3′E	FM	189
Crionach	Highld	NG3954	57°30·3′	6°21·0′W	X	23
Crionaig	N Eil	NB2806	57°57·9′	6°35·5′W	H	13,14
Crion Larach	Arg & Bt	NM4747	56°33·1′	6°6·6′W	X	47,48
Cripdon Down	Devon	SX7380	50°36·6′	3°47·3′W	H	191
Cripiau Eisteddfa-fach	Powys	SN8084	52°26·7′	3°45·5′W	X	135,136
Cripiau Nantmelyn	Cered	SN8078	52°23·5′	3°45·4′W	X	135,136,147
Crippenden Manor	Kent	TQ4441	51°9·2′	0°3·9′E	A	187
Crippets	Glos	SO9317	51°51·3′	2°5·7′W	X	163

Crippings	Essex	TL6013	51°47·8'	0°19·6'E	X	167
Cripple Corner	Essex	TL8534	51°58·6'	0°42·0'E	T	155
Cripple Hill	Somer	ST4517	50°57·2'	2°46·6'W	X	193
Cripplesease	Corn	SW5036	50°10·5'	5°29·7'W	T	203
Cripplestyle	Dorset	SU0912	50°54·7'	1°51·9'W	T	195
Cripp's Corner	E Susx	TQ7721	50°57·9'	0°31·6'E	T	199
Cripps Fm	Kent	TQ9772	51°25·0'	0°50·4'E	FM	178
Cripp's Fm	Somer	ST3645	51°12·3'	2°54·6'W	FM	182
Cripps Fm	W Berks	SU5970	51°25·8'	1°8·7'W	FM	174
Cripps House Fm	Hill	TQ0492	51°37·3'	0°29·5'W	FM	176
Cripps Manor	E Susx	TQ4031	51°3·9'	0°0·3'E	X	187
Cripps River	Somer	ST3644	51°11·7'	2°54·6'W	W	182
Cripsey Brook	Essex	TL4906	51°44·2'	0°9·9'E	W	167
Cripstone Fm	Corn	SX1663	50°26·5'	4°35·1'W	FM	201
Cripton Cottage	Dorset	SY7086	50°40·6'	2°25·1'W	X	194
Criptor	Devon	SX5572	50°32·0'	4°2·4'W	X	191
Cripwell Fm	Leic	SK6124	52°48·8'	1°5·3'W	FM	129
Cribheinn	N Eil	NF7624	57°11·8'	7°21·4'W	H	22
Crispie	Arg & Bt	NR9171	55°53·5'	5°20·1'W	X	62
Crispins	Essex	TL5307	51°44·7'	0°13·4'E	X	167
Crisp's Fm	Lancs	SD3603	53°31·4'	2°57·5'W	FM	108
Crist	Derby	SK0281	53°19·8'	1°57·8'W	T	110
Cristal Kame	Shetld	HZ2274	59°33·3'	1°36·2'W	X	4
Cristin	Gwyn	SH1121	52°45·5'	4°47·7'W	X	123
Critchell's Green	Hants	SU2926	51°2·2'	1°34·8'W	T	185
Critchill	Somer	ST7647	51°13·5'	2°20·2'W	T	183
Critchill Fm	Somer	ST7547	51°13·5'	2°21·1'W	FM	183
Critchmere	Surrey	SU8833	51°5·6'	0°44·2'W	T	186
Crit Hall	Kent	TQ7833	51°4·3'	0°32·8'E	T	188
Crittenden	Kent	TQ6543	51°10·0'	0°22·0'E	X	188
Criw	I of Angl	SH3892	53°24·2'	4°25·8'W	X	114
Crixhall Court	Kent	TR2655	51°15·2'	1°14·7'E	X	179
Crizeley	Heref	SO4432	51°59·3'	2°48·5'W	T	149,161
Crizeley Wood	Heref	SO4432	51°59·3'	2°48·5'W	F	149,161
Croach Hill	D & G	NX7956	54°53·3'	3°52·8'W	H	84
Croalchapel	D & G	NX9091	55°12·3'	3°43·3'W	X	78
Croan	Corn	SX0271	50°30·6'	4°47·2'W	A	200
Croanford	Corn	SX0371	50°30·6'	4°46·3'W	T	200
Croasdale	Cumbr	NY0917	54°32·7'	3°24·0'W	T	89
Croasdale Beck	Cumbr	NY0817	54°32·6'	3°24·9'W	W	89
Croasdale Brook	Lancs	SD6757	54°0·7'	2°29·8'W	W	103
Croasdale Brook	Lancs	SD7053	53°58·6'	2°27·0'W	W	103
Croasdale Fell	Lancs	SD6756	54°0·2'	2°29·8'W	X	103
Croasdale House	Lancs	SD7055	53°59·7'	2°27·0'W	X	103
Croase Fm	Heref	SO4763	52°16·0'	2°46·2'W	FM	137,138,148
Crobeag	N Eil	NB3921	58°6·3'	6°25·4'W	H	14
Crocadon	Corn	SX3966	50°28·5'	4°15·8'W	X	201
Crocadon Wood	Corn	SX3965	50°28·0'	4°15·7'W	F	201
Crocan a' Chaorainn	Arg & Bt	NM8805	56°11·7'	5°24·6'W	X	55
Crochan Burn	D & G	NX4969	54°59·8'	4°21·2'W	W	83
Crochandoon	N Ayr	NR8931	55°31·9'	5°20·2'W	X	68,69
Crochan Hill	Pth & Kin	NN9533	56°28·9'	3°41·8'W	H	52,53
Crochar	Highld	NH5958	57°35·7'	4°21·1'W	X	26
Crochmore	D & G	NX8670	55°0·9'	3°46·5'W	X	84
Crochmore	D & G	NX8877	55°4·7'	3°44·8'W	X	84
Crochmore Ho	D & G	NX8977	55°4·8'	3°43·9'W	X	84
Crochran	Powys	SO0880	52°24·9'	3°20·8'W	X	136
Crochton	Pth & Kin	NN9767	56°47·2'	3°40·7'W	H	43
Crock	Angus	NO2263	56°45·4'	3°16·1'W	H	44
Crockanord	Highld	NH5441	57°26·4'	4°25·5'W	X	26
Crockenhill	Kent	TQ5067	51°23·2'	0°9·7'E	T	177
Crocker End	Oxon	SU7086	51°34·3'	0°59·0'W	T	175
Crockerhill	Hants	SU5709	50°52·9'	1°11·0'W	T	196
Crockerhill	W Susx	SU9207	50°51·5'	0°41·2'W	T	197
Crockermoor Fm	Dorset	ST5406	50°51·3'	2°38·8'W	FM	194
Crockern Tor	Devon	SX6175	50°33·7'	3°57·4'W	X	191
Crockernwell	Devon	SX7592	50°43·1'	3°45·9'W	T	191
Crockers	Devon	SS5538	51°7·6'	4°3·9'W	T	180
Crocker's Ash	Heref	SO5316	51°50·7'	2°40·5'W	T	162
Crocker's Fm	Devon	ST1511	50°53·8'	3°12·1'W	FM	192,193
Crockers Fm	Dorset	ST7504	50°50·3'	2°20·9'W	FM	194
Crocker's Fm	Dorset	ST8419	50°58·4'	2°13·3'W	FM	183
Crockers Fm	I of W	SZ4892	50°43·8'	1°18·8'W	FM	196
Crockers Hatch Corner	Kent	TQ5338	51°7·5'	0°11·6'E	X	188
Crockers Hele	Devon	SS5206	50°50·3'	4°5·7'W	X	191
Crockerton	Wilts	ST8642	51°10·9'	2°11·6'W	T	183
Crockerton Green	Wilts	ST8642	51°10·9'	2°11·6'W	T	183
Crockerton Hill	Dorset	SU0416	50°56·8'	1°56·2'W	X	184
Crocket Burn	Pth & Kin	NN7808	56°15·2'	3°57·7'W	W	57
Crocketford Ho	D & G	NX8272	55°2·0'	3°50·3'W	X	84
Crocketford or Ninemile Bar	D & G	NX8372	55°2·0'	3°49·4'W	T	84
Crockett	Corn	SX3672	50°31·7'	4°18·5'W	X	201
Crockey Hill	York	SE6246	53°54·6'	1°3·0'W	T	105
Crockford Bridge	Hants	SZ3598	50°47·1'	1°29·8'W	X	196
Crockford's Fm	Cambs	TL4861	52°13·6'	0°24·5'E	FM	154
Crockham Grange	Kent	TQ4449	51°13·5'	0°4·1'E	X	187
Crockham Heath	W Berks	SU4364	51°22·6'	1°22·5'W	T	174
Crockham Hill	Kent	TQ4450	51°14·1'	0°4·2'E	T	187
Crockhamhill Common	Kent	TQ4451	51°14·6'	0°4·2'E	X	187
Crockhamhill Common	Kent	TQ4551	51°14·6'	0°5·0'E	X	188
Crockhurst Street	Kent	TQ6244	51°10·6'	0°19·4'E	T	188
Crock Law	Scot Bord	NT8317	55°27·0'	2°15·7'W	X	80
Crockleford Hall	Essex	TM0327	51°54·5'	0°57·5'E	X	168
Crockleford Heath	Essex	TM0426	51°53·9'	0°58·3'E	T	168
Crockleford Hill	Essex	TM0326	51°54·0'	0°57·4'E	T	168
Crockness	Orkney	ND3192	58°48·9'	3°11·2'W	X	7
Crock Ness	Orkney	ND3293	58°49·4'	3°10·2'W	X	7
Crocknorth	Surrey	TQ1050	51°14·5'	0°25·1'W	X	187
Crock of Gold	Devon	SX6173	50°32·7'	3°57·3'W	X	191
Crock Pits	Devon	SS6849	51°13·7'	3°53·0'W	X	180
Crock Point	Devon	SS6849	51°13·7'	3°53·0'W	X	180
Crockroy	D & G	NS7011	55°22·8'	4°2·7'W	X	71
Crockstead Fm	E Susx	TQ4917	50°56·2'	0°7·6'E	FM	199
Crock Street	Somer	ST3213	50°55·0'	2°57·7'W	T	193
Crockway Fm	Dorset	SY6195	50°45·4'	2°32·8'W	FM	194
Crockwell Fm	Northnts	SP5550	52°9·0'	1°11·4'W	FM	152
Crockwood Fm	Corn	SS2208	50°50·9'	4°31·3'W	FM	190
Crocombe Br	Devon	SX8481	50°37·3'	3°38·0'W	X	191
Crocradie Burn	E Ayr	NS5609	55°21·5'	4°15·9'W	W	71,77

Cro-dubhaig	N Eil	NF8580	57°42·2'	7°16·9'W	X	18
Crò Earraich	Arg & Bt	NR3970	55°51·4'	6°9·8'W	X	60,61
Croe Br	Highld	NG9521	57°14·3'	5°23·4'W	X	25,33
Croesau	Conwy	SH8073	53°14·7'	3°47·5'W	X	116
Croesau Bach	Shrops	SJ2428	52°50·9'	3°7·3'W	T	126
Croesau Hyddgen	Powys	SN7991	52°30·5'	3°46·6'W	X	135
Croes-Bleddyn Fm	Monm	ST4996	51°39·9'	2°43·9'W	FM	162
Croes-Carn-Einion	Newp	ST2585	51°33·8'	3°4·5'W	X	171
Croes-cwtta	V of Glam	SS9174	51°27·5'	3°33·7'W	X	170
Croesdy	Powys	SH9700	52°35·5'	3°30·8'W	X	136
Croesengan Isa	Conwy	SH8472	53°14·2'	3°43·9'W	X	116
Croesengan Ucha	Conwy	SH8372	53°14·2'	3°44·8'W	X	116
Croeserw	Nth Pt Talb	SS8695	51°38·8'	3°38·5'W	T	170
Croes-faen	Gwyn	SH5901	52°35·6'	4°4·5'W	A	135
Croesfoel Fm	Wrex	SJ3048	53°1·7'	3°2·2'W	FM	117
Croesfryn	I of Angl	SH5280	53°18·0'	4°12·8'W	X	114,115
Croes-goch	Pemb	SM8230	51°55·8'	5°9·9'W	T	157
Croes-gwyn	Cered	SN4550	52°7·8'	4°15·5'W	X	146
Croes Howell	Wrex	SJ3457	53°6·6'	2°58·8'W	X	117
Croes-Hywel	Monm	SO3314	51°49·5'	2°57·9'W	T	161
Croes-ifan	Carm	SN2828	51°55·7'	4°29·7'W	X	145,158
Croesiolyn	Denb	SJ2543	52°59·0'	3°6·6'W	X	117
Croes-lan	Cered	SN3844	52°4·5'	4°21·4'W	T	145
Croes Llanfair	Monm	SO3307	51°45·7'	2°57·9'W	T	161
Croesllanfro	Newp	ST2789	51°35·9'	3°2·8'W	X	171
Croes Llwyd	Monm	SO4007	51°45·7'	2°51·8'W	A	161
Croesllwyn	Powys	SN9687	52°28·5'	3°31·5'W	X	136
Croes Lwyd Fach	Powys	SN8248	52°7·3'	3°43·0'W	X	147
Croeslyn	Powys	SN8098	52°34·2'	3°45·8'W	X	135,136
Croesnant	Carm	SN6028	51°56·2'	4°1·8'W	X	146
Croesonen	Conwy	SH8169	53°12·5'	3°46·5'W	X	116
Croesonen	Monm	ST3794	51°38·7'	2°54·2'W	X	171
Croesor	Gwyn	SH6344	52°58·8'	4°2·0'W	T	124
Croesor-fawr	Gwyn	SH6445	52°59·3'	4°1·2'W	X	115
Croespenmaen	Caer	ST1998	51°40·7'	3°9·9'W	T	171
Croes Robert	Monm	SO4805	51°44·7'	2°44·8'W	X	161
Croeswallt or Oswestry	Shrops	SJ2929	52°51·5'	3°2·9'W	T	126
Croeswdig	Pemb	SM7326	51°53·4'	5°17·5'W	X	157
Croeswen	Monm	ST3196	51°39·7'	2°59·5'W	X	171
Croes-wian	Flint	SJ1273	53°15·0'	3°18·7'W	T	116
Croes Wyntoedd	Cered	SN5661	52°13·9'	4°6·1'W	X	146
Croesyceiliog	Torf	ST3096	51°39·7'	3°0·3'W	T	171
Croes-y-ceilog	Carm	SN3115	51°48·7'	4°26·7'W	X	159
Croesyceilog	Carm	SN4016	51°49·4'	4°18·9'W	T	159
Croes y forwyn	Pemb	SN1540	52°1·9'	4°41·4'W	X	145
Croesygiach	Monm	SO3813	51°49·0'	2°53·6'W	X	161
Croes-y-mab	Wrex	SJ3548	53°1·8'	2°57·7'W	X	117
Croes-y-mwyalch	Torf	ST3092	51°37·6'	3°0·3'W	T	171
Croes y pant	Monm	SO3104	51°44·1'	2°59·6'W	T	171
Croesywaun	Gwyn	SH5259	53°6·7'	4°12·3'W	T	115
Croe Water	Arg & Bt	NN2404	56°12·0'	4°49·8'W	W	56
Croffta	Rho Cyn Taf	ST0680	51°30·9'	3°20·9'W	X	170
Crofftau	Cered	SN7564	52°15·8'	3°50·2'W	X	146,147
Crofft-hir Brook	Monm	SO4316	51°50·6'	2°49·3'W	W	161
Crofft-yr-haidd	Rho Cyn Taf	ST0487	51°34·7'	3°22·7'W	X	170
Croford	Somer	ST1027	51°2·4'	3°16·6'W	X	181,193
Croford Ho	Somer	ST1028	51°2·9'	3°16·7'W	X	181,193
Croft	Cumbr	NY5477	55°5·4'	2°42·8'W	X	86
Croft	Devon	SS5600	50°47·1'	4°2·2'W	X	191
Croft	Devon	SX4398	50°45·9'	4°13·2'W	X	190
Croft	Devon	SX7195	50°44·7'	3°49·3'W	X	191
Croft	Devon	SX7345	50°17·7'	3°46·6'W	X	202
Croft	Glos	SO8124	51°55·1'	2°16·2'W	X	162
Croft	Heref	SO4565	52°17·1'	2°48·0'W	T	137,138,148
Croft	Highld	NH8331	57°21·5'	3°56·2'W	X	27
Croft	Highld	NH9009	57°9·8'	3°48·7'W	X	36
Croft	Leic	SP5195	52°33·3'	1°14·5'W	T	140
Croft	Lincs	TF5061	53°7·7'	0°14·9'E	T	122
Croft	Orkney	ND4487	58°46·3'	2°57·6'W	X	7
Croft	Pemb	SM9624	51°52·9'	4°57·5'W	X	157,158
Croft	Pemb	SN1543	52°3·5'	4°41·5'W	X	145
Croft	Warr	SJ6393	53°26·2'	2°33·0'W	T	109
Crofta Fm	V of Glam	ST0178	51°29·8'	3°25·2'W	FM	170
Croft Ambrey	Heref	SO4466	52°17·6'	2°48·9'W	X	137,148,149
Croft Ambrey (Fort)	Heref	SO4466	52°17·6'	2°48·9'W	A	137,148,149
Croftamie	Stir	NS4786	56°2·8'	4°26·9'W	T	57
Croftanrigh	Pth & Kin	NO1832	56°28·6'	3°19·4'W	X	53
Croft-an-Righ	S Lanak	NT0947	55°42·7'	3°26·5'W	X	72
Croftbain	Moray	NJ2124	57°18·2'	3°18·2'W	X	36
Croftcarnoch	Highld	NH7903	57°6·4'	3°59·4'W	X	35
Croftchois	Stir	NN5229	56°26·1'	4°23·6'W	X	51
Croftchuirn	Pth & Kin	NN9558	56°42·4'	3°42·5'W	X	52,53
Croft Closes	N Yks	SD8064	54°4·5'	2°17·9'W	X	98
Croftcrunie	Highld	NH6152	57°32·5'	4°18·9'W	X	26
Croftdavid	Pth & Kin	NN9951	56°38·7'	3°38·4'W	X	52,53
Croftdhu	Highld	NH5624	57°17·3'	4°22·9'W	X	26,35
Croft Dhu	Highld	NH8129	57°20·4'	3°58·2'W	X	35
Croftdow	Highld	NH9722	57°16·9'	3°42·1'W	X	36
Croft Downie	Highld	NH6648	57°30·4'	4°13·7'W	X	26
Croftend	Aberd	NJ5526	57°19·6'	2°44·4'W	X	37
Croft End	Cumbr	SD2491	54°18·8'	3°9·7'W	X	96
Croft End	Lincs	TF4963	53°8·8'	0°14·1'E	X	122
Croft End Fm	Cumbr	NY0117	54°32·6'	3°31·4'W	FM	89
Croftends	Cumbr	NY3462	54°57·1'	3°1·4'W	X	85
Croft Ends	Cumbr	NY6722	54°35·8'	2°30·2'W	X	91
Croft Fm	Hants	SU2738	51°8·7'	1°36·5'W	FM	184
Croft Fm	Lincs	SK8293	53°25·9'	0°45·5'W	FM	112
Croft Fm	Lincs	TF5472	53°13·6'	0°18·8'E	FM	122
Croft Fm	Norf	TF8813	52°41·1'	0°47·3'E	FM	132
Croft Fm	Norf	TG3133	52°50·9'	1°26·2'E	FM	133
Croft Fm	Somer	SS9124	51°0·5'	3°32·8'W	FM	181
Croft Fm	Staffs	SJ9110	52°41·5'	2°7·6'W	FM	127
Croft Fm	Suff	TM2639	52°0·4'	1°18·0'E	FM	169
Croft Fm	Suff	TM3859	52°10·9'	1°29·3'E	FM	156
Croft Fm, The	Oxon	SP3435	52°1·0'	1°29·9'W	FM	151
Croftfoddie	Aberd	NO6593	57°1·9'	2°34·1'W	X	38,45
Croftfoot	C of Glas	NS6060	55°49·0'	4°13·6'W	T	64
Croftfoot	Cumbr	NY0916	54°32·1'	3°24·0'W	X	89
Croft Foot	Cumbr	SD5694	54°20·6'	2°40·2'W	X	97
Croftfoot	E Ayr	NS5326	55°30·6'	4°19·2'W	X	70

Croftfoot	Falk	NS7984	56°2·3'	3°56·1'W	X	57,64
Croftfoot	N Lanak	NS7168	55°53·5'	4°3·3'W	X	64
Croftfoot	S Lanak	NS8750	55°44·1'	3°47·5'W	X	65,72
Croftfoot	S Lanak	NT0035	55°36·2'	3°34·8'W	X	72
Croftgarrow	Pth & Kin	NN7246	56°35·6'	4°4·6'W	X	51,52
Croftgary	Fife	NT1886	56°3·8'	3°18·6'W	X	65,66
Croftglass	Moray	NJ2530	57°21·5'	3°14·3'W	X	37
Croftgloy	Moray	NJ5060	57°37·9'	2°49·8'W	X	29
Croftgowan	Highld	NH8608	57°9·2'	3°52·6'W	X	35,36
Croft Grange	Lincs	TF5561	53°7·6'	0°19·4'E	X	122
Croft Grange	N Yks	NZ2709	54°28·8'	1°34·6'W	X	93
Crofthandy	Corn	SW7342	50°14·3'	5°10·6'W	T	204
Crofthead	Cumbr	NY3870	55°1·5'	2°57·8'W	X	85
Crofthead	Cumbr	NY4141	54°45·9'	2°54·6'W	X	85
Croft Head	Cumbr	NY4501	54°24·3'	2°50·4'W	X	90
Crofthead	D & G	NT1205	55°20·1'	3°22·8'W	X	78
Croft Head	D & G	NT1505	55°20·2'	3°20·0'W	H	79
Crofthead	D & G	NX8268	54°59·8'	3°50·2'W	X	84
Crofthead	E Ayr	NS5018	55°26·2'	4°21·8'W	X	70
Crofthead	E Ayr	NS5326	55°30·6'	4°19·2'W	X	70
Crofthead	E Ayr	NS5431	55°33·3'	4°18·4'W	X	70
Crofthead	E Ayr	NS5518	55°26·3'	4°17·1'W	X	71
Crofthead	Moray	NJ1552	57°33·3'	3°24·8'W	X	28
Crofthead	N Ayr	NS3244	55°39·9'	4°39·8'W	X	63,70
Crofthead	Pth & Kin	NN8109	56°15·8'	3°54·8'W	X	57
Crofthead	Pth & Kin	NN8915	56°19·1'	3°47·2'W	X	58
Crofthead	Pth & Kin	NN9224	56°24·0'	3°44·5'W	X	52,58
Crofthead	S Ayr	NS3620	55°27·0'	4°35·2'W	X	70
Crofthead	S Ayr	NS4328	55°31·5'	4°28·8'W	X	70
Crofthead	S Lanak	NS6540	55°38·3'	4°8·3'W	X	71
Crofthead	S Lanak	NS7548	55°42·8'	3°58·9'W	X	64
Crofthead	S Lanak	NS9751	55°44·7'	3°38·0'W	X	65,72
Crofthead	W Loth	NT0465	55°52·4'	3°31·6'W	X	65
Crofthead Burn	D & G	NT1305	55°20·1'	3°21·9'W	W	78
Croft Head Fm	Cumbr	NY4325	54°37·3'	2°52·5'W	FM	90
Crofthead Hill	D & G	NT1305	55°20·1'	3°21·9'W	H	78
Croftheads	D & G	NY1484	55°8·8'	3°20·5'W	X	78
Croftheads	D & G	NY1766	54°59·2'	3°17·4'W	X	85
Croftheads Cottages	D & G	NY1766	54°59·2'	3°17·4'W	X	85
Croftheads Hill	D & G	NY1584	55°8·8'	3°19·6'W	H	79
Croft Hill	Highld	NG8579	57°45·2'	5°36·3'W	H	19
Crofthill	S Lanak	NS9852	55°45·3'	3°37·1'W	X	65,72
Croft Hills	Cambs	TL5690	52°29·4'	0°18·3'E	X	143
Croft Ho	Cumbr	NY1646	54°48·4'	3°18·0'W	X	85
Croft Ho	Cumbr	NY4563	54°57·8'	2°51·1'W	X	86
Croft Ho	Cumbr	NY5437	54°43·8'	2°42·4'W	X	90
Croft Ho	Hants	SU5015	50°56·2'	1°16·9'W	X	196
Croft Ho	Lincs	TF5260	53°7·2'	0°16·7'E	X	122
Croft Ho	N Lincs	SK7798	53°28·6'	0°50·0'W	X	112
Croft Ho	Norf	TG2918	52°42·9'	1°23·8'E	X	133,134
Croft Ho	N Yks	SE1988	54°17·5'	1°42·1'W	X	99
Croft Ho	Pth & Kin	NO0563	56°45·2'	3°32·8'W	X	43
Croft Ho	Suff	TM2639	52°0·4'	1°18·0'E	X	169
Croft House Fm	Cumbr	NY2538	54°44·1'	3°9·5'W	FM	89,90
Croft House Fm	Norf	TF4900	52°34·9'	0°12·4'E	FM	143
Croft How	N Yks	SE0898	54°22·9'	1°52·2'W	X	99
Croftinloan	Pth & Kin	NN9656	56°41·3'	3°41·4'W	X	52,53
Croftintaggart	Highld	NJ1537	57°25·2'	3°24·5'W	X	28
Croftintaime	Arg & Bt	NN1527	56°24·2'	4°59·4'W	X	50
Croftintygan	Pth & Kin	NN6738	56°31·2'	4°9·3'W	X	51
Croftjames	Highld	NH9722	57°16·9'	3°42·1'W	X	36
Croftjane	D & G	NX8596	55°14·9'	3°48·1'W	X	78
Croftland	Devon	SX8952	50°21·7'	3°33·3'W	X	202
Croftlands	Cumbr	NY0121	54°34·7'	3°31·5'W	X	89
Croftlands	Cumbr	NY1838	54°44·1'	3°16·0'W	X	89,90
Croftlands	Cumbr	SD2876	54°10·7'	3°5·8'W	T	96,97
Croft Lodge	Leic	SP5195	52°33·3'	1°14·5'W	X	140
Croftmalloch	W Loth	NS9464	55°51·7'	3°41·2'W	T	65
Croftmaquien	Highld	NJ0221	57°16·4'	3°37·1'W	X	36
Croft Marsh	Lincs	TF5360	53°7·1'	0°17·6'E	X	122
Croftmill	Pth & Kin	NN8636	56°30·4'	3°50·7'W	X	52
Croft Mitchell	Corn	SW6637	50°11·4'	5°16·3'W	T	203
Croftmoraig	Pth & Kin	NN7947	56°36·2'	3°57·8'W	X	51,52
Croftmore	Moray	NJ3852	57°33·5'	3°1·7'W	X	28
Croftmore	Pth & Kin	NN8868	56°47·7'	3°49·6'W	X	43
Croft-na-Caber	Pth & Kin	NN7744	56°34·6'	3°59·7'W	X	51,52
Croftnacriech	Highld	NH6349	57°30·9'	4°16·8'W	T	26
Croftnahaven	Highld	NH9822	57°16·9'	3°41·1'W	X	36
Croftness	Pth & Kin	NN8548	56°36·8'	3°52·0'W	X	52
Croft of Auchnagorth	Aberd	NJ8355	57°35·3'	2°16·6'W	X	29,30
Croft of Blackcraig	Pth & Kin	NO1151	56°38·8'	3°26·6'W	X	53
Croft of Cortiecram	Aberd	NK0252	57°33·7'	1°57·5'W	X	30
Croft of Cultalonie	Pth & Kin	NO0759	56°43·1'	3°30·7'W	X	52,53
Croft of Dounie	Pth & Kin	NO0859	56°43·1'	3°29·7'W	X	52,53
Croft of Greenbog	Aberd	NJ4912	57°12·0'	2°50·2'W	X	37
Croft of Hardslacks	Aberd	NK0440	57°27·3'	1°55·5'W	X	30
Croft of Tillymaud	Aberd	NK1039	57°26·7'	1°49·5'W	X	30
Croft of Ulaw	Aberd	NJ9429	57°21·3'	2°5·5'W	X	38
Croft of Woodend	Aberd	NJ7340	57°27·2'	2°26·5'W	X	29
Crofton	Brom	TQ4466	51°22·7'	0°4·5'E	T	177
Crofton	Cumbr	NY3050	54°50·6'	3°5·0'W	T	85
Crofton	Essex	TL8600	51°40·3'	0°41·8'E	X	168
Crofton	Lincs	TF0540	52°57·1'	0°25·8'W	X	130
Crofton	Wakf	SE3817	53°39·1'	1°25·1'W	T	110,111
Crofton	Wilts	SU2662	51°21·6'	1°37·2'W	T	174
Crofton Beam Engines	Wilts	SU2662	51°21·6'	1°37·2'W	X	174
Croft-on-Tees	N Yks	NZ2809	54°28·8'	1°33·7'W	T	93
Croft Outerly	Fife	NO2401	56°12·0'	3°13·1'W	T	59
Croftown	Highld	NH1783	57°48·2'	5°4·3'W	X	20
Croft Pascoe	Corn	SW7220	50°2·4'	5°10·7'W	X	204
Croft Pascoe Pool	Corn	SW7319	50°1·9'	5°9·8'W	W	204
Croft Plantn	Scot Bord	NT6509	55°22·7'	2°32·7'W	F	80
Croftronan	Highld	NH9619	57°15·3'	3°43·0'W	X	36
Crofts	Aberd	NJ3517	57°14·6'	3°4·2'W	X	37
Crofts	Angus	NO5743	56°34·9'	2°41·6'W	X	54
Crofts	Cumbr	NY0319	54°33·7'	3°29·6'W	X	89
Crofts	D & G	NX7466	54°58·6'	3°57·7'W	X	83,84
Crofts	D & G	NX7973	55°2·5'	3°53·2'W	X	84
Crofts	Northum	NZ0882	55°8·2'	1°52·0'W	X	81
Crofts Bank	Traf	SJ7595	53°27·3'	2°22·2'W	T	109

Crofts Burn	D & G	NX7872	55°1·9'	3°54·1'W	W	84
Croft School	Warw	SP2354	52°11·3'	1°39·4'W	X	151
Crofts Fm	D & G	NX7874	55°3·0'	3°54·2'W	FM	84
Crofts Fm	Moray	NJ2850	57°32·3'	3°11·7'W	FM	28
Croftside	Northum	NZ1294	55°14·6'	1°48·2'W	X	81
Croftside Park	Stir	NS8088	56°4·4'	3°55·2'W	X	57,65
Croftsike	D & G	NY3374	55°3·6'	3°2·5'W	X	85
Croft Skellioch	Highld	NJ0025	57°18·5'	3°39·1'W	X	36
Crofts Moss	D & G	NX7873	55°2·4'	3°54·1'W	X	84
Croftsmuir	Angus	NO5743	56°34·9'	2°41·6'W	X	54
Crofts of Achimore	Highld	ND0264	58°33·4'	3°40·6'W	X	11,12
Crofts of Benachielt	Highld	ND1838	58°19·6'	3°23·5'W	X	11
Crofts of Brainjohn	Aberd	NJ8535	57°24·6'	2°14·5'W	X	30
Crofts of Brownside	Aberd	NJ6753	57°34·2'	2°32·6'W	X	29
Crofts of Buinach	Moray	NJ1855	57°34·9'	3°21·8'W	X	28
Crofts of Cromlix	Stir	NN7703	56°12·5'	3°58·5'W	X	57
Crofts of Dipple	Moray	NJ3259	57°37·2'	3°7·8'W	T	28
Crofts of Dykeside	Aberd	NJ5242	57°28·2'	2°47·6'W	X	29
Crofts of Haddo	Aberd	NJ8337	57°25·6'	2°16·5'W	T	29,30
Crofts of Hillpark	Highld	ND1755	58°28·8'	3°24·9'W	X	11,12
Crofts of Inverthernie	Aberd	NJ7344	57°29·4'	2°26·6'W	X	29
Crofts of Kingscauseway	Highld	NH7779	57°47·3'	4°3·7'W	T	21
Crofts of Netherthird	Aberd	NJ6839	57°26·7'	2°31·5'W	X	29
Crofts of Pitgair	Aberd	NJ7660	57°38·0'	2°23·7'W	X	29
Crofts of Sallachan	Highld	NM9862	56°42·6'	5°17·6'W	X	40
Crofts of Scalan	Moray	NJ2319	57°15·6'	3°16·1'W	X	36
Crofts of South Dunn	Highld	ND1855	58°28·8'	3°23·9'W	X	11,12
Crofts of Upperthird	Aberd	NJ6739	57°26·7'	2°32·5'W	X	29
Croftspardon	Pth & Kin	NN8950	56°38·0'	3°48·1'W	X	52
Crofts, The	Aberd	NO3594	57°2·2'	3°3·8'W	X	37,44
Crofts, The	E Yorks	TA2170	54°6·9'	0°8·5'W	T	101
Crofts, The	Warw	SP2253	52°10·7'	1°40·3'W	X	151
Croft, The	Carm	SN6036	52°0·5'	4°2·0'W	X	146
Croft, The	Cumbr	NY4955	54°53·5'	2°47·3'W	X	86
Croft, The	Devon	SX6942	50°16·0'	3°49·9'W	X	202
Croft, The	Shrops	SO6894	52°32·8'	2°27·9'W	X	138
Croft, The	Swin	SU2182	51°32·4'	1°41·4'W	X	174
Croftvellick	Pth & Kin	NN6436	56°30·0'	4°12·1'W	X	51
Croftwards	Highld	NH5491	57°53·3'	4°27·3'W	X	21
Croft West	Corn	SW7746	50°16·5'	5°7·4'W	X	204
Croft Wood	N Yks	SE1690	54°18·6'	1°44·8'W	F	99
Crofty	Orkney	HY5106	58°56·6'	2°50·6'W	X	6,7
Crofty	Swan	SS5295	51°38·3'	4°7·9'W	T	159
Croft-y-Bwla	Monm	SO4913	51°49·0'	2°44·0'W	X	162
Croftyperthy	Powys	SO0969	52°18·9'	3°19·7'W	X	136,147
Crogan	N Ayr	NR9948	55°41·3'	5°11·4'W	X	62,69
Crogan Beag	Arg & Bt	NM7025	56°21·9'	5°43·0'W	X	49
Crogan Mór	Arg & Bt	NM7025	56°21·9'	5°43·0'W	X	49
Crogan Ness	Shetld	HP6012	60°47·5'	0°53·4'W	X	1
Crogans	Shetld	HU3792	60°36·8'	1°18·9'W	X	1,2
Crogary Beag	N Eil	NF8773	57°38·6'	7°14·3'W	H	18
Crogary Mór	N Eil	NF8673	57°38·5'	7°15·3'W	H	18
Crogary na Hoe	N Eil	NF9772	57°38·4'	7°4·2'W	H	18
Croga Skerries	Shetld	HP5712	60°47·5'	0°56·7'W	X	1
Crogau	Powys	SN9658	52°12·9'	3°30·9'W	X	147
Crogen	Gwyn	SJ0037	52°55·5'	3°28·9'W	X	125
Crogen Iddon	Wrex	SJ2537	52°55·8'	3°6·5'W	X	126
Crogen Wladys	Wrex	SJ2538	52°56·3'	3°6·6'W	X	126
Cro Geo	Shetld	HU3611	59°53·2'	1°20·9'W	X	4
Crogga	I of M	SC3372	54°7·3'	4°32·9'W	X	95
Croggan	Arg & Bt	NM7027	56°23·0'	5°43·1'W	T	49
Crogga River	I of M	SC3373	54°7·8'	4°32·9'W	W	95
Crog Hill	Oxon	SU3283	51°32·9'	1°31·9'W	X	174
Crog Holm	Shetld	HU3366	60°22·9'	1°23·6'W	X	2,3
Croglin	Cumbr	NY5747	54°49·2'	2°39·7'W	T	86
Croglin Craig	D & G	NX7398	55°15·8'	3°59·5'W	X	77
Croglin Fell	Cumbr	NY6049	54°50·3'	2°36·9'W	X	86
Croglin High Hall	Cumbr	NY5645	54°48·1'	2°40·6'W	X	86
Croglinhurst	Cumbr	SD2189	54°17·7'	3°12·4'W	X	96
Croglin Low Hall	Cumbr	NY5545	54°48·1'	2°41·6'W	A	86
Croglin Water	Cumbr	NY5948	54°49·8'	2°37·9'W	W	86
Crogo Burn	D & G	NX7477	55°4·5'	3°58·0'W	W	77,84
Crogo Mains	D & G	NX7577	55°4·6'	3°57·0'W	X	84
Crogo Mill	D & G	NX7578	55°5·1'	3°57·1'W	X	84
Croham Hurst	Croy	TQ3363	51°21·3'	0°5·0'W	X	176,177,187
Crohans	Corn	SW9340	50°13·7'	4°53·8'W	X	204
Cròic	Highld	ND1047	58°24·4'	3°31·9'W	X	11,12
Croic	N Eil	NF6262	57°31·6'	7°38·4'W	W	22
Cròic a Deas	N Eil	NF7129	57°14·3'	7°26·8'W	W	22
Cròic a Tuath	N Eil	NF7230	57°14·8'	7°25·9'W	W	22
Croic-bheinn	Highld	NG7652	57°30·4'	5°43·9'W	H	24
Croich	Highld	NC4210	58°3·3'	4°40·2'W	X	16
Croich	Highld	NH4591	57°53·2'	4°36·4'W	T	20
Croiche Wood	Highld	NH5243	57°27·5'	4°27·6'W	F	26
Croichley Fold	Bury	SD7614	53°37·6'	2°21·4'W	X	109
Croich na Faoilinn	N Eil	NF7334	57°17·0'	7°25·2'W	W	22
Croick	Highld	NC8954	58°27·9'	3°53·7'W	T	10
Croick Burn	Highld	NC4109	58°2·8'	4°41·2'W	W	16
Croidh-la	Highld	NN7795	57°2·0'	4°1·2'W	H	35
Croig	Arg & Bt	NM4053	56°36·1'	6°13·7'W	X	47
Croig, The	N Eil	NL6599	56°57·9'	7°30·3'W	X	31
Croilburn	E Ayr	NS5344	55°40·3'	4°19·8'W	X	70
Croir	N Eil	NB1539	58°15·1'	6°51·0'W	T	13
Crois an t-sleuchd	N Eil	NF8057	57°29·7'	7°20·0'W	X	22
Crois Bheinn	Highld	NM5855	56°37·7'	5°56·3'W	H	47
Croiscrag	Pth & Kin	NN5456	56°40·6'	4°22·5'W	X	42,51
Croisebrig	Arg & Bt	NM4200	56°7·6'	6°8·7'W	X	61
Crois Mhàraidh Dhubh	Arg & Bt	NM4050	56°34·5'	6°13·5'W	X	47
Crois Mhór	Arg & Bt	NR2970	55°51·1'	6°19·4'W	X	60
Crois Mhór	Highld	NM4985	56°53·6'	6°6·8'W	X	39
Croit Bàgh	Arg & Bt	NR9161	55°48·1'	5°19·6'W	W	62
Croit Bheinn	Highld	NM8177	56°50·2'	5°35·0'W	H	40
Croit e Caley	I of M	SC2267	54°4·3'	4°42·8'W	X	95
Croit nan Sgùlan	Arg & Bt	NM6242	56°30·9'	5°51·7'W	X	49
Croker	Ches	SJ9269	53°13·3'	2°6·8'W	X	118
Croker Hill	Ches	SJ9367	53°12·2'	2°5·9'W	H	118
Croker's Hole	W Berks	SU3281	51°31·9'	1°31·9'W	X	174
Crokna Vord	Shetld	HU2558	60°18·6'	1°32·4'W	H	3
Crom Allt	Highld	NC2406	58°0·8'	4°58·3'W	W	15
Cròm Allt	Highld	NH5503	57°6·0'	4°23·2'W	W	35
Crom Allt	Highld	NJ0214	57°12·6'	3°36·9'W	W	36
Crom Allt	Stir	NN3332	56°27·3'	4°42·1'W	W	50
Cròm-allt Beag	Highld	NC9440	58°20·4'	3°48·2'W	W	11
Cròm-allt Beag	Highld	NH6421	57°15·8'	4°14·8'W	W	26,35
Cròm-allt Mór	Highld	NC9639	58°19·9'	3°46·1'W	W	11,17
Cromal Mount	Highld	NH7855	57°34·4'	4°1·9'W	A	27
Cromalt	Highld	NC2407	58°1·3'	4°58·3'W	X	15
Cromalt Hills	Highld	NC2205	58°0·2'	5°0·3'W	H	15
Cromarty	Aberd	NJ7947	57°31·0'	2°20·6'W	X	29,30
Cromarty	Highld	NH7867	57°40·8'	4°2·3'W	T	21,27
Cromarty Bay	Highld	NH7466	57°40·2'	4°6·3'W	W	21,27
Cromarty Firth	Highld	NH6767	57°40·7'	4°13·4'W	W	21
Cromarty Firth	Highld	NH7067	57°40·7'	4°10·3'W	W	21,27
Cromarty Ho	Highld	NH7967	57°40·9'	4°1·3'W	X	21,27
Cromasaig	Highld	NH0260	57°35·5'	5°18·3'W	X	19
Crombie	Fife	NT0485	56°3·2'	3°32·0'W	T	65
Crombie Burn	Aberd	NJ5951	57°33·1'	2°40·6'W	W	29
Crombie Castle	Aberd	NJ5952	57°33·6'	2°40·7'W	A	29
Crombie Country Park	Angus	NO5240	56°33·2'	2°46·4'W	X	54
Crombie Mill	Angus	NO5240	56°33·2'	2°46·4'W	X	54
Crombie Point	Fife	NO2419	56°21·7'	3°13·4'W	X	59
Crombie Point	Fife	NT0384	56°2·6'	3°33·0'W	X	65
Crombie Reservoir	Angus	NO5240	56°33·2'	2°46·4'W	W	54
Crombie Water	Moray	NJ2224	57°18·3'	3°17·2'W	W	36
Crombleholme Fm	Lancs	SD3843	53°53·0'	2°56·2'W	FM	102
Crombleholme Fold	Lancs	SD5642	53°52·6'	2°39·7'W	X	102
Cromblet	Aberd	NJ7834	57°24·0'	2°21·5'W	X	29,30
Crom Chreag	Pth & Kin	NN8132	56°28·2'	3°55·5'W	X	52
Crom Chreag	Pth & Kin	NN8835	56°29·9'	3°48·7'W	H	52
Cromdale	Highld	NJ0728	57°20·2'	3°32·2'W	T	36
Crom Dhoire	Arg & Bt	NR5573	55°53·5'	5°54·7'W	X	61
Cromer	Herts	TL2928	51°56·4'	0°7·0'W	T	166
Cromer	Norf	TG2142	52°56·0'	1°17·7'E	T	133
Cromer Hill	Staffs	SJ9631	52°52·8'	2°3·2'W	H	127
Cromer-Hyde	Herts	TL2012	51°47·9'	0°15·2'W	T	166
Cromer Point	N Yks	TA0392	54°19·0'	0°24·6'W	X	101
Crome's Broad	Norf	TG3719	52°43·2'	1°31·0'E	W	133,134
Crome's Fm	Norf	TG0227	52°48·4'	1°0·2'E	FM	133
Cromford	Derby	SK2956	53°6·3'	1°33·6'W	T	119
Cromford Canal	Derby	SK3353	53°4·6'	1°30·0'W	W	119
Cromford Moor	Derby	SK3055	53°5·7'	1°32·7'W	F	119
Cromford Sta	Derby	SK3057	53°6·8'	1°32·7'W	X	119
Cromford Wharf	Derby	SK3057	53°6·8'	1°32·7'W	X	119
Cromhall	S Glos	ST6990	51°36·7'	2°26·5'W	T	162,172
Cromhall Common	S Glos	ST6989	51°36·2'	2°26·5'W	T	162,172
Cromhall Fm	Wilts	ST8777	51°29·7'	2°10·8'W	FM	173
Cromie Burn	Angus	NO3153	56°40·1'	3°7·1'W	W	53
Cromiequoy	Highld	ND2656	58°29·4'	3°15·7'W	X	11,12
Crò Mill a' Phealla	N Eil	NB4554	58°24·3'	6°21·4'W	X	8
Cromlabank	Aberd	NK0438	57°26·2'	1°55·5'W	X	30
Cromlech	Gwyn	SH4038	52°55·2'	4°22·4'W	X	123
Cromlet	N Lanak	NS7367	55°53·0'	4°1·4'W	X	64
Cromlet	Pth & Kin	NN7812	56°17·3'	3°57·8'W	H	57
Cromleybank	Aberd	NJ9630	57°21·9'	2°3·5'W	X	30
Cromlix Ho	Stir	NN7806	56°14·1'	3°57·7'W	X	57
Cromlix Home Fm	Stir	NN7706	56°14·1'	3°58·6'W	FM	57
Cromlix Lodge	Stir	NN7706	56°14·1'	3°58·6'W	X	57
Crom Loch	Highld	NH3982	57°48·2'	4°42·1'W	W	20
Crom Mhin	Stir	NN4289	56°4·3'	4°31·9'W	X	56
Cromor	N Eil	NB4021	58°6·4'	6°24·3'W	T	14
Cromps	Essex	TL6416	51°49·3'	0°23·2'E	X	167
Crompton Circuit	Oldham	SD9408	53°34·4'	2°5·0'W	X	109
Crompton Fold	Oldham	SD9409	53°34·9'	2°5·0'W	T	109
Crompton Hall Fm	Flint	SJ3261	53°8·8'	3°0·6'W	FM	117
Crompton Moor	Oldham	SD9610	53°35·4'	2°3·2'W	X	109
Cromrar	Pth & Kin	NN7245	56°35·0'	4°4·6'W	X	51,52
Crom Rig	Scot Bord	NT4206	55°20·9'	2°54·4'W	X	79
Cromrig Burn	Scot Bord	NT4306	55°20·9'	2°53·5'W	W	79
Crom Roinn	Highld	NN0058	56°40·5'	5°15·4'W	X	41
Cromwell	Notts	SK7961	53°8·7'	0°48·7'W	T	120,121
Cromwell Bottom	Cald	SE1222	53°41·9'	1°48·7'W	T	104
Cromwell Fm	Northnts	SP6977	52°23·4'	0°58·8'W	FM	141
Cromwell Lock	Notts	SK8061	53°8·6'	0°47·8'W	X	121
Cromwell Moor	Notts	SK7961	53°8·7'	0°48·7'W	X	120,121
Cromwellpark	Pth & Kin	NO0527	56°25·8'	3°32·0'W	X	52,53,58
Cromwell Plump	N Yks	SE4951	53°57·4'	1°14·8'W	X	105
Cromwellside	Aberd	NJ6728	57°20·7'	2°32·4'W	X	38
Crò na Bà Glaise	Arg & Bt	NM3418	56°17·1'	6°17·4'W	X	48
Cronan	E Ayr	NS5438	55°37·1'	4°18·7'W	X	70
Cronan	Pth & Kin	NO2443	56°34·6'	3°13·8'W	X	53
Cronberry	E Ayr	NS6022	55°28·6'	4°12·5'W	T	71
Crondall	Hants	SU7948	51°13·8'	0°51·7'W	T	186
Crondon	Essex	TL6900	51°40·6'	0°27·1'E	X	167
Crondon Hall	Essex	TL6901	51°41·2'	0°27·1'E	X	167
Crondon Park	Essex	TL6900	51°40·6'	0°27·1'E	X	167
Crong, The	Bucks	SP9008	51°46·0'	0°41·3'W	X	165
Croniarth	Powys	SJ1522	52°47·6'	3°15·2'W	X	125
Cronie	D & G	NX8273	55°2·5'	3°50·4'W	X	84
Cronkbane	I of M	SC3086	54°14·7'	4°36·1'W	X	95
Cronkbane	I of M	SC3474	54°8·4'	4°32·1'W	X	95
Cronkbourne	I of M	SC3677	54°10·0'	4°30·3'W	X	95
Cronk Breck	I of M	SC3381	54°12·1'	4°33·2'W	H	95
Cronkdhoo	I of M	SC3080	54°11·5'	4°35·9'W	X	95
Cronkdoo	I of M	SC3386	54°14·8'	4°33·4'W	X	95
Cronkedooney	I of M	SC2271	54°6·5'	4°43·0'W	X	95
Cronk Fedjag	I of M	SC2375	54°8·7'	4°42·2'W	H	95
Cronkgarroo	I of M	SC4092	54°18·2'	4°27·1'W	X	95
Cronkhill	Shrops	SJ5308	52°40·3'	2°41·3'W	X	126
Cronkley	Durham	NY8628	54°39·1'	2°12·6'W	X	91,92
Cronkley	Northum	NZ0252	54°52·0'	1°57·7'W	X	87
Cronkley Fell	Durham	NY8427	54°38·5'	2°14·5'W	X	91,92
Cronkley Pasture	Durham	NY8529	54°39·6'	2°13·5'W	X	91,92
Cronkley Scar	Durham	NY8329	54°39·6'	2°15·4'W	X	91,92
Cronk ny Arrey	I of M	SC1967	54°4·3'	4°45·6'W	H	95
Cronk ny Arrey Laa	I of M	NX4500	54°22·6'	4°22·8'W	X	95
Cronk ny Arrey Laa	I of M	SC2274	54°8·1'	4°43·1'W	H	95
Cronk ny Arrey Lhaa	I of M	SC3499	54°21·8'	4°32·9'W	A	95
Cronk ny Merriu	I of M	SC3170	54°6·1'	4°34·7'W	H	95
Cronk ny Moghlane	I of M	SC3380	54°11·6'	4°33·2'W	H	95
Cronk-ny-mona	I of M	SC3879	54°11·1'	4°28·5'W	H	95
Cronksbank	D & G	NY3983	55°8·5'	2°57·0'W	X	79
Cronks Fm	Kent	TQ6750	51°13·7'	0°23·9'E	FM	188
Cronkston Grange	Derby	SK1165	53°11·2'	1°49·7'W	X	119
Cronkston Lodge	Derby	SK1165	53°11·2'	1°49·7'W	X	119
Cronkston Low	Derby	SK1166	53°11·7'	1°49·7'W	H	119
Cronk Sumark (Fort)	I of M	SC3994	54°19·2'	4°28·1'W	A	95
Cronk, The	I of M	NX4202	54°23·6'	4°25·6'W	X	95
Cronk, The	I of M	SC3395	54°19·6'	4°33·7'W	T	95
Cronk Urleigh	I of M	SC3289	54°16·4'	4°34·4'W	X	95
Cronk-y-berry Fm	I of M	SC3878	54°10·6'	4°28·5'W	FM	95
Cronk y Cliwe	I of M	NX3500	54°22·4'	4°32·0'W	X	95
Cronk y Garroo	I of M	SC4182	54°12·8'	4°25·9'W	H	95
Cronk y Scottey	I of M	NX3700	54°22·4'	4°30·1'W	X	95
Cronk y Vaare	I of M	SC4086	54°14·9'	4°26·9'W	H	95
Cronk-y-Voddy	I of M	SC3086	54°14·7'	4°36·1'W	H	95
Cronllwyn	Pemb	SM9834	51°58·3'	4°56·1'W	X	157
Cronshaw	Lancs	SD7134	53°48·3'	2°26·0'W	X	103
Cronton	Know	SJ4988	53°23·4'	2°45·6'W	T	108
Croo Back	Orkney	HY3227	59°7·7'	3°10·8'W	X	6
Cro of Ham	Shetld	HU4839	60°8·2'	1°7·7'W	X	4
Crooie Geo	Shetld	HU2861	60°20·2'	1°29·1'W	X	3
Crooie Hill	Shetld	HU2757	60°18·0'	1°30·2'W	H	3
Crooie Hill	Shetld	HU3050	60°14·3'	1°27·0'W	H	3
Crook	Cumbr	NY5172	55°2·7'	2°45·6'W	X	86
Crook	Cumbr	NY5477	55°5·4'	2°42·8'W	X	86
Crook	Cumbr	SD4695	54°21·1'	2°49·4'W	T	97
Crook	Cumbr	SD6693	54°20·1'	2°31·0'W	X	98
Crook	Devon	ST1602	50°48·9'	3°11·2'W	T	192,193
Crook	Durham	NZ1635	54°42·8'	1°44·7'W	T	92
Crook	Highld	NH8854	57°34·0'	3°51·9'W	X	27
Crook	N Yks	SE1448	53°55·9'	1°46·8'W	X	104
Crook	Orkney	HY4022	59°5·1'	3°2·3'W	X	5,6
Crook	Orkney	ND4385	58°45·2'	2°58·6'W	X	7
Crook	Orkney	ND4691	58°48·5'	2°55·6'W	X	7
Crookabeck	Cumbr	NY4015	54°31·9'	2°55·2'W	X	90
Crook-a-dyke	Cumbr	NY4621	54°35·1'	2°49·7'W	X	90
Crook-a-Fleet	Cumbr	NY3633	54°41·5'	2°59·2'W	X	90
Crookahill	Aberd	NJ8860	57°38·0'	2°11·6'W	X	30
Crooka Well	N Yks	SE0172	54°8·9'	1°58·7'W	W	98
Crookbank	Northum	NY7775	55°4·4'	2°21·2'W	F	86,87
Crookbank	Northum	NY7876	55°4·9'	2°20·2'W	X	86,87
Crookbank Fm	Durham	NZ1856	54°54·1'	1°42·7'W	FM	88
Crookbarrow Hill	Worcs	SO8752	52°10·2'	2°11·0'W	H	150
Crook Beck	Durham	NY9918	54°33·7'	2°0·5'W	W	92
Crook Beck	Durham	NZ1524	54°36·9'	1°45·6'W	W	92
Crookboat	S Lanak	NS8939	55°38·2'	3°45·4'W	X	71,72
Crook Brae	E Ayr	NS6817	55°26·0'	4°4·7'W	X	71
Crookburn	Cumbr	NY5078	55°5·9'	2°46·6'W	X	86
Crook Burn	Cumbr	NY7734	54°42·3'	2°21·0'W	W	91
Crook Burn	D & G	NS9804	55°19·4'	3°36·0'W	W	78
Crook Burn	Northum	NY8472	55°2·8'	2°14·6'W	W	86,87
Crook Burn	Scot Bord	NT7057	55°48·6'	2°28·3'W	W	67,74
Crookburn	S Lanak	NS9605	55°19·9'	3°37·9'W	X	78
Crookburn Hill	Cumbr	NY4979	55°6·4'	2°47·5'W	X	86
Crookburn Pike	Cumbr	NY6152	54°51·9'	2°36·0'W	X	86
Crook Cott	Scot Bord	NT2112	55°24·0'	3°14·4'W	X	79
Crook Cottage	Lancs	SD4354	53°59·0'	2°51·7'W	X	102
Crook Crag	Cumbr	SD1998	54°22·5'	3°14·4'W	X	96
Crookdake	Cumbr	NY1943	54°46·8'	3°15·1'W	T	85
Crookdake Hall	Cumbr	NY1944	54°47·3'	3°15·2'W	X	85
Crookdake Mill	Cumbr	NY2044	54°47·3'	3°14·2'W	X	85
Crookdale	Cumbr	NY5306	54°27·1'	2°43·1'W	X	90
Crookdale Beck	Cumbr	NY5306	54°27·1'	2°43·1'W	W	90
Crookdale Crag	Cumbr	NY5505	54°26·6'	2°41·2'W	H	90
Crookdene	Northum	NY9783	55°8·7'	2°2·4'W	X	81
Crookdyke	Cumbr	NY3661	54°56·6'	2°59·5'W	X	85
Crooke	Wigan	SD5507	53°33·7'	2°40·4'W	T	108
Crooke Burnell	Devon	SS6800	50°47·3'	3°52·0'W	X	191
Crooked Bank	S Lanak	NS9010	55°22·6'	3°43·7'W	H	71,78
Crooked Billet	Merton	TQ2370	51°25·2'	0°13·5'W	T	176
Crooked Birch	Cumbr	SD2687	54°16·6'	3°7·8'W	X	96,97
Crooked Braes	Scot Bord	NT3401	55°18·2'	3°1·9'W	H	79
Crooked Clough	Derby	SK0994	53°26·8'	1°51·5'W	X	110
Crooked Dike Barn	N Yks	SD7875	54°10·5'	2°19·8'W	X	98
Crooked Drain	Cambs	TL5877	52°22·3'	0°19·1'E	W	143
Crooked Dyke	Suff	TL7184	52°25·9'	0°31·3'E	W	143
Crooked Edge Hill	Bolton	SD6513	53°37·0'	2°31·3'W	X	109
Crooked End	Glos	SO6217	51°51·3'	2°32·7'W	X	162
Crooked Field	Lancs	SD6842	53°52·6'	2°28·8'W	X	103
Crooked Haven	Aberd	NO8574	56°51·7'	2°14·3'W	W	45
Crookedholm	E Ayr	NS4537	55°36·4'	4°27·2'W	T	70
Crooked Holme	Cumbr	NY5161	54°56·7'	2°45·5'W	X	86
Crooked Hope	Scot Bord	NT7607	55°21·6'	2°22·3'W	X	80
Crooked Loch	Scot Bord	NT3513	55°24·6'	3°1·2'W	W	79
Crookedneuk	Aberd	NK0248	57°31·6'	1°57·5'W	X	30
Crooked Oak	Devon	SS7322	50°59·2'	3°48·2'W	W	180
Crooked Oak	Devon	SS8123	50°59·9'	3°41·4'W	W	181
Crooked Oak	Northum	NZ0549	54°50·4'	1°54·9'W	X	87
Crookedshaws	Scot Bord	NT8025	55°31·4'	2°18·6'W	X	74
Crookedshaws Hill	Scot Bord	NT8024	55°30·8'	2°18·6'W	H	74
Crookedshields	S Lanak	NS6557	55°47·5'	4°8·8'W	X	64
Crookedsike Head	Scot Bord	NT8818	55°27·6'	2°11·0'W	X	80
Crooked Soley	Wilts	SU3172	51°27·0'	1°32·8'W	T	174
Crookedstane	S Lanak	NS9615	55°25·3'	3°38·2'W	X	78
Crookedstane Burn	S Lanak	NS9714	55°24·8'	3°37·2'W	W	78
Crookedstone	S Lanak	NS7249	55°43·3'	4°1·8'W	X	64
Crooked Stone	S Lanak	NS7250	55°43·8'	4°1·9'W	A	64
Crooked Stone	S Lanak	NS9615	55°25·3'	3°38·2'W	A	78
Crookedstonemuir	S Lanak	NS7149	55°43·3'	4°2·8'W	X	64
Crooked Withies	Dorset	SU0505	50°50·9'	1°55·4'W	T	195
Crooked Wood	Moray	NJ2762	57°38·8'	3°12·9'W	F	28
Crooke Gill	N Yks	SD8473	54°9·4'	2°14·3'W	W	98
Crook End	Cumbr	SD4595	54°21·1'	2°50·4'W	X	97
Crookes	Sheff	SK3287	53°23·0'	1°30·7'W	T	110,111
Crooke's Fm	Glos	SO7026	51°56·1'	2°25·8'W	FM	162
Crookesmoor	Sheff	SK3387	53°23·0'	1°29·8'W	T	110,111
Crookestane Rig	S Lanak	NS9714	55°24·8'	3°37·2'W	H	78
Crook Fm	Brad	SE1339	53°51·1'	1°47·7'W	FM	104
Crook Fm	Ches	SJ4555	53°5·6'	2°48·9'W	FM	117
Crook Fm	Cumbr	SD3486	54°16·2'	3°0·4'W	FM	96,97

Crook Fm	Lancs	SD4355	53°59·5′	2°51·7′W	FM	102
Crook Fm	N Yks	SE7687	54°16·6′	0°49·5′W	FM	94,100
Crook Foot	Cumbr	SD4393	54°20·0′	2°52·2′W	X	97
Crookfoot Resr	Hartpl	NZ4331	54°40·6′	1°19·6′W	W	93
Crookford Fm	Notts	SK6775	53°16·3′	0°59·3′W	FM	120
Crookford Hill	Notts	SK6775	53°16·3′	0°59·3′W	X	120
Crookfur	E Renf	NS5356	55°46·8′	4°20·2′W	T	64
Crook Gate	Lancs	SD4042	53°52·5′	2°54·3′W	X	102
Crookgate Bank	Durham	NZ1856	54°54·1′	1°42·7′W	T	88
Crook Gate Resr	Oldham	SD9811	53°36·0′	2°1·4′W	W	109
Crook Gill	N Yks	SD9379	54°12·6′	2°6·0′W	W	98
Crook Hall	Ches	SJ7872	53°14·9′	2°19·4′W	X	118
Crook Hall	Cumbr	SD4594	54°20·6′	2°50·3′W	X	97
Crookhall	Durham	NZ1150	54°50·9′	1°49·3′W	T	88
Crook Hall	Durham	NZ2743	54°47·1′	1°34·4′W	A	88
Crookham	Northum	NT9138	55°38·4′	2°8·1′W	T	74,75
Crookham	W Berks	SU5464	51°22·6′	1°13·1′W	T	174
Crookham Common	W Berks	SU5264	51°22·6′	1°14·8′W	X	174
Crookham Eastfield	Northum	NT9039	55°38·9′	2°9·1′W	X	74,75
Crookham House	W Berks	SU5264	51°22·6′	1°14·8′W	X	174
Crookham Manor	W Berks	SU5365	51°23·1′	1°13·9′W	X	174
Crookham Village	Hants	SU7952	51°15·9′	0°51·7′W	T	186
Crookham Westfield	Northum	NT8838	55°38·4′	2°11·0′W	X	74
Crookhaugh	Scot Bord	NT1026	55°31·4′	3°25·1′W	X	72
Crook Head	Scot Bord	NT1026	55°31·4′	3°25·1′W	H	72
Crookhey Hall	Lancs	SD4751	53°57·4′	2°48·0′W	X	102
Crookhill	Angus	NO5336	56°31·1′	2°45·4′W	X	54
Crook Hill	Derby	SK1886	53°22·5′	1°43·4′W	H	110
Crook Hill	Devon	ST1602	50°48·9′	3°11·2′W	X	192,193
Crook Hill	Dorset	ST4906	50°51·3′	2°43·1′W	H	193,194
Crook Hill	E Ayr	NS5745	55°40·9′	4°16·0′W	X	64
Crookhill	Ghead	NZ1563	54°57·9′	1°45·5′W	T	88
Crook Hill	Roch	SD9219	53°40·3′	2°6·9′W	X	109
Crook Hill	Scot Bord	NT3526	55°31·7′	3°1·3′W	X	73
Crookhill Fm	Derby	SK1886	53°22·5′	1°43·4′W	FM	110
Crookhill Fm	Northum	NZ0565	54°59·0′	1°54·9′W	FM	87
Crook Ho	Wals	SP0596	52°33·9′	1°55·2′W	X	139
Crookholm	D & G	NY4276	55°4·8′	2°54·1′W	X	85
Crook Holme	Cumbr	SD6994	54°20·7′	2°28·2′W	X	98
Crookhorn Wood	Kent	TQ6762	51°20·2′	0°24·2′E	F	177,178,188
Crookhouse	Northum	NT9031	55°34·6′	2°9·1′W	X	74,75
Crookhouse	Scot Bord	NT7626	55°31·9′	2°22·4′W	X	74
Crook House Fm	Barns	SE4006	53°33·2′	1°23·4′W	FM	111
Crook House Fm	N Yks	SE6680	54°12·9′	0°58·9′W	FM	100
Crookhurst	Cumbr	NY0842	54°46·1′	3°25·4′W	X	85
Crookhurst Beck	Cumbr	NY0942	54°46·1′	3°24·4′W	W	85
Crookieden	Aberd	NO7175	56°52·2′	2°28·1′W	X	45
Crook Inn	Scot Bord	NT1126	55°31·4′	3°24·2′W	X	72
Crook Knowes	Scot Bord	NT7219	55°28·1′	2°26·1′W	X	80
Crooklands	Cumbr	NY1847	54°48·9′	3°16·1′W	X	85
Crooklands	Cumbr	SD5383	54°14·7′	2°42·9′W	T	97
Crooklands	N Yks	SD7270	54°7·8′	2°25·3′W	X	98
Crooklands	S Lanak	NS9754	55°46·4′	3°38·1′W	X	65,72
Crookleith Fms	N Yks	SE5597	54°22·2′	1°8·8′W	FM	100
Crooklets Beach	Corn	SS2007	50°50·3′	4°33·0′W	X	190
Crook Moor	N Yks	SE6639	53°50·8′	0°59·4′W	X	105,106
Crookmoor Ash	Glos	SP1615	51°50·2′	1°45·7′W	F	163
Crookmore	Aberd	NJ5818	57°15·3′	2°41·3′W	X	37
Crookmoyle Rock	Corn	SX0382	50°36·5′	4°46·7′W	X	200
Crookna Water	Shetld	HU2881	60°31·0′	1°28·9′W	W	3
Crook Ness	N Yks	TA0293	54°19·6′	0°25·5′W	X	101
Crookness	Orkney	HY4117	59°2·4′	3°1·2′W	X	6
Crook of Baldoon	D & G	NX4452	54°50·6′	4°25·3′W	X	83
Crook of Dee	Ches	SJ4261	53°8·8′	2°51·6′W	W	117
Crook of Devon	Pth & Kin	NO0300	56°11·2′	3°33·3′W	T	58
Crook of Lune	Cumbr	SD6295	54°21·2′	2°34·7′W	X	97
Crook Peak	Somer	ST3855	51°17·7′	2°53·0′W	H	182
Crook Plantn	N Yks	SE9066	54°5·2′	0°37·0′W	F	101
Crookrise	N Yks	SD9956	54°0·2′	2°0·5′W	X	103
Crookrise Wood	N Yks	SD9855	53°59·7′	2°1·4′W	F	103
Crooks	D & G	NX9670	55°1·1′	3°37·2′W	X	84
Crooks	D & G	NY2992	55°13·3′	3°6·5′W	X	79
Crooks	Renf	NS3559	55°48·0′	4°37·5′W	X	63
Crooks	S Ayr	NS3833	55°34·1′	4°33·7′W	X	70
Crooks	Scot Bord	NT8240	55°39·4′	2°16·7′W	X	74
Crooks	Stir	NS5396	56°8·3′	4°21·5′W	X	57
Crook's Altar	Durham	NY9140	54°45·5′	2°8·0′W	X	87
Crooksball	Corn	SX1957	50°23·3′	4°32·4′W	X	201
Crooks Beck	Cumbr	NY7402	54°25·0′	2°23·6′W	X	91
Crooks Beck	Cumbr	SD9186	54°16·4′	2°7·9′W	W	98
Crooksbury Common	Surrey	SU8845	51°12·1′	0°44·0′W	F	186
Crooksbury Hill	Surrey	SU8745	51°12·1′	0°44·9′W	H	186
Crook Seal	N Yks	NY8302	54°25·0′	2°15·3′W	X	91,92
Crooks Hall	Suff	TL7245	52°4·8′	0°31·0′E	X	154
Crookshill Fm	Heref	SO6950	52°9·1′	2°26·8′W	FM	149
Crook's Ho	Durham	NZ0711	54°29·9′	1°53·1′W	X	92
Crooks Ho	Lancs	SD8649	53°56·5′	2°12·4′W	X	103
Crookside Fm	S Ayr	NS3630	55°32·4′	4°35·5′W	FM	70
Crook's Marsh	C of Bris	ST5382	51°32·3′	2°40·3′W	X	172
Crooks Mill	Moray	NJ4051	57°33·0′	2°59·7′W	X	28
Crooks Ness	Orkney	HY6527	59°8·0′	2°36·2′W	X	5
Crooks Plantn	Cumbr	SD5888	54°17·4′	2°38·3′W	F	97
Crooks Pow	D & G	NX9472	55°2·1′	3°39·1′W	W	84
Crookstock	Devon	SS7907	50°51·2′	3°42·8′W	X	191
Crookston	C of Glas	NS5263	55°50·5′	4°21·4′W	T	64
Crookston	E Loth	NT3670	55°55·4′	3°1·0′W	X	66
Crookston	Scot Bord	NT2436	55°37·0′	3°12·0′W	X	73
Crookstone Barn	Derby	SK1587	53°23·0′	1°46·1′W	X	110
Crookstone Hill	Derby	SK1587	53°23·0′	1°46·1′W	X	110
Crookstone Knoll	Derby	SK1488	53°23·6′	1°47·0′W	X	110
Crookston Ho	Scot Bord	NT4251	55°45·2′	2°55·0′W	X	66,73
Crookston Home	C of Glas	NS5261	55°49·4′	4°21·3′W	X	64
Crookston Mains Hill	Scot Bord	NT4154	55°46·8′	2°56·0′W	H	66,73
Crookston North Mains	Scot Bord	NT4253	55°46·3′	2°55·0′W	X	66,73
Crookston Old Ho	Scot Bord	NT4252	55°45·7′	2°55·0′W	X	66,73
Crook, The	Cumbr	SD2094	54°20·4′	3°13·4′W	X	96
Crook, The	Northum	NZ0797	55°16·3′	1°53·0′W	X	81
Crook, The	Orkney	HY7038	59°13·9′	2°31·1′W	X	5
Crook, The	Shetld	HU1957	60°18·1′	1°38·9′W	X	3
Crook, The	Shetld	HU2986	60°33·7′	1°27·8′W	X	1,3

Crooktree	Aberd	NJ6100	57°5·6′	2°38·2′W	X	37
Crookwath	Cumbr	NY3821	54°35·1′	2°57·1′W	X	90
Crookwood Fm	Wilts	SU0158	51°19·5′	1°58·8′W	FM	173
Crookwood Mill Fm	Wilts	SU0258	51°19·5′	1°57·9′W	FM	173
Croom Dale Plantn	E Yorks	SE9467	54°5·7′	0°33·3′W	F	101
Croome Court	Worcs	SO8844	52°5·9′	2°10·1′W	X	150
Croome Fm	E Yorks	SE9366	54°5·1′	0°34·3′W	FM	101
Croome Fm	Worcs	SO8945	52°6·4′	2°9·2′W	FM	150
Croome Ho	E Yorks	SE9365	54°4·6′	0°34·3′W	X	101
Croome Landscape Park	Worcs	SO8744	52°5·9′	2°11·0′W	X	150
Croome Perry Wood	Worcs	SO8946	52°7·0′	2°9·2′W	F	150
Croomes Grove Fm	Glos	ST7997	51°40·5′	2°17·8′W	FM	162
Croome Wold	E Yorks	SE9466	54°5·1′	0°33·4′W	X	101
Croom Hill	E Yorks	TA2037	53°49·2′	0°10·2′W	X	107
Croones Ho	Heref	SO3754	52°11·1′	2°54·9′W	X	148,149
Croop Ho	Cumbr	NY7704	54°26·1′	2°20·9′W	X	91
Croos	Shetld	HU3684	60°32·5′	1°20·1′W	X	1,2,3
Croose Fm	Heref	SO6134	52°0·4′	2°33·7′W	FM	149
Croos, The	Orkney	HY6337	59°13·3′	2°38·4′W	X	5
Croo Stone	Orkney	ND4894	58°50·1′	2°53·6′W	X	7
Croo Taing	Orkney	HY2604	58°55·3′	3°16·6′W	X	6,7
Croo Taing	Orkney	ND4194	58°50·0′	3°0·8′W	X	7
Croo Taing	Shetld	HU3527	60°1·8′	1°21·8′W	X	4
Croo Taing	Shetld	HU4227	60°1·8′	1°14·3′W	X	4
Croo Taing	Shetld	HU4378	60°29·3′	1°12·6′W	X	2,3
Croo Wick	Shetld	HU5263	60°21·1′	1°3·0′W	W	2,3
Cropley Grove	Suff	TL7159	52°12·4′	0°30·6′E	X	154
Cropper	Derby	SK2335	52°55·0′	1°39·1′W	X	128
Cropple How	Cumbr	SD1297	54°21·9′	3°20·8′W	X	96
Cropredy	Oxon	SP4646	52°6·9′	1°19·3′W	T	151
Cropredy Hill	Oxon	SP4547	52°7·4′	1°20·2′W	X	151
Cropredy Lawn	Oxon	SP4548	52°7·9′	1°20·2′W	X	151
Cropshall	Cumbr	NY7342	54°46·6′	2°24·8′W	X	86,87
Cropston	Leic	SK5511	52°41·9′	1°10·8′W	T	129
Cropston Leys	Leic	SK5412	52°42·4′	1°11·6′W	X	129
Cropston Resr	Leic	SK5410	52°41·3′	1°11·7′W	W	129
Cropthorne	Worcs	SO9944	52°5·9′	2°0·5′W	T	150
Cropton	N Yks	SE7589	54°17·7′	0°50·4′W	T	94,100
Cropton Banks Wood	N Yks	SE7487	54°16·6′	0°51·4′W	F	94,100
Cropton Forest	N Yks	SE7994	54°20·4′	0°46·7′W	F	94,100
Cropton Hall	Norf	TG1028	52°48·7′	1°7·4′E	A	133
Cropwell Bishop	Notts	SK6835	52°54·7′	0°58·9′W	T	129
Cropwell Butler	Notts	SK6837	52°55·8′	0°58·9′W	T	129
Cropwell Court	Notts	SK6737	52°55·8′	0°59·8′W	X	129
Cropwell Grove Fm	Notts	SK6838	52°56·3′	0°58·9′W	FM	129
Cropwell Lings	Notts	SK6739	52°56·9′	0°59·8′W	X	129
Cropwell Wolds Fm	Notts	SK6634	52°54·2′	1°0·7′W	FM	129
Crorieshill	S Ayr	NS3312	55°22·7′	4°37·7′W	X	70
Cros	N Eil	NB5061	58°28·2′	6°16·8′W	T	8
Crosben	Highld	NM7254	56°37·6′	5°42·6′W	X	49
Crosbie	N Ayr	NS2149	55°42·3′	4°50·5′W	A	63
Crosbie Hills	N Ayr	NS2351	55°43·5′	4°48·7′W	H	63
Crosbie Ho	S Ayr	NS3430	55°32·4′	4°37·4′W	A	70
Crosbie Resr	N Ayr	NS2150	55°42·9′	4°50·5′W	W	63
Crosbost	N Eil	NB3924	58°7·9′	6°25·6′W	T	14
Crosby	Cumbr	NY0738	54°44·0′	3°26·2′W	T	89
Crosby	I of M	SC3279	54°11·0′	4°34·1′W	T	95
Crosby	I of M	SC4599	54°22·0′	4°22·7′W	X	95
Crosby	N Lincs	SE8711	53°35·5′	0°40·7′W	T	112
Crosby	Sefton	SJ3198	53°28·7′	3°2·0′W	T	108
Crosby Channel		SJ2799	53°29·2′	3°5·6′W	W	108
Crosby Court	N Yks	SE3991	54°19·0′	1°23·6′W	T	99
Crosby Court Grange	N Yks	SE4092	54°19·6′	1°22·7′W	X	99
Crosby East Training Bank	Sefton	SD2800	53°29·8′	3°4·7′W	X	108
Crosby Garrett	Cumbr	NY7209	54°28·8′	2°25·5′W	T	91
Crosby Garrett Fell	Cumbr	NY7007	54°27·7′	2°27·3′W	H	91
Crosby Gill	Cumbr	NY6111	54°29·8′	2°35·7′W	X	91
Crosby Gill	Cumbr	SD1895	54°20·9′	3°15·3′W	W	96
Crosby Grange	N Yks	SE4088	54°17·4′	1°22·7′W	X	99
Crosby Hall	Sefton	SD3201	53°30·3′	3°1·1′W	A	108
Crosby Lodge	Cumbr	NY6212	54°30·4′	2°34·8′W	X	91
Crosby Manor	N Yks	SE4191	54°19·0′	1°21·8′W	X	99
Crosby Moor Fm	N Yks	SE4091	54°19·0′	1°22·7′W	FM	99
Crosby-on-Eden	Cumbr	NY4659	54°55·6′	2°50·1′W	T	86
Crosby Ravensworth	Cumbr	NY6214	54°31·4′	2°34·8′W	T	91
Crosby Ravensworth Fell	Cumbr	NY6010	54°29·3′	2°36·6′W	H	91
Crosbythwaite	Cumbr	SD1994	54°20·4′	3°14·3′W	X	96
Crosby Villa	Cumbr	NY0938	54°44·0′	3°24·4′W	X	89
Crosby Warren	N Lincs	SE9012	53°36·0′	0°38·0′W	X	112
Crosby West Training Bank	Sefton	SJ2898	53°28·7′	3°4·7′W	X	108
Croscombe	Somer	ST5944	51°11·9′	2°34·8′W	T	182,183
Croscombe Barton	Devon	SS6847	51°12·7′	3°53·0′W	X	180
Crosdale Beck	Cumbr	SD6493	54°20·1′	2°32·8′W	W	97
Crosedale	Cumbr	SD6493	54°20·1′	2°32·8′W	X	97
Crosemere	Shrops	SJ4329	52°51·6′	2°50·4′W	T	126
Crose Mere	Shrops	SJ4330	52°52·1′	2°50·4′W	W	126
Croshill Loch	Arg & Bt	NR7119	55°24·9′	5°36·7′W	W	68
Crosland Edge	Kirk	SE1011	53°36·0′	1°50·5′W	T	110
Crosland Hill	Kirk	SE1114	53°37·6′	1°49·6′W	T	110
Crosland Moor	Kirk	SE1115	53°38·1′	1°49·6′W	T	110
Croslands Park	Cumbr	SD2171	54°8·0′	3°12·1′W	T	96
Crosper Fm	N Yks	SE3652	53°58·0′	1°26·7′W	FM	104
Cross	Cumbr	SD1094	54°20·3′	3°22·6′W	X	96
Cross	Devon	SS5439	51°8·0′	4°12·5′W	T	180
Cross	Devon	SS6034	51°5·5′	3°59·6′W	T	180
Cross	Devon	SX7747	50°18·8′	3°43·3′W	X	202
Cross	Lancs	SD7450	53°57·0′	2°23·4′W	X	103
Cross	Monm	SO4123	51°54·4′	2°51·1′W	X	161
Cross	Shrops	SJ3936	52°55·3′	2°54·0′W	T	126
Cross	Somer	ST4154	51°17·2′	2°50·4′W	T	182
Crossags Fm	I of M	SC4493	54°18·8′	4°23·5′W	FM	95
Crossaig	Arg & Bt	NR8351	55°42·5′	5°26·8′W	X	62,69
Crossaig Glen	Arg & Bt	NR8251	55°42·5′	5°27·8′W	X	62,69
Crossal	Highld	NG4531	57°18·2′	6°13·6′W	X	32
Crossapol	Arg & Bt	NL9943	56°29·2′	6°53·0′W	T	46
Crossapol	Arg & Bt	NM1253	56°35·1′	6°41·0′W	X	46
Crossapol Bay	Arg & Bt	NM1352	56°34·6′	6°40·0′W	W	46
Crossapol Point	Arg & Bt	NL9942	56°28·7′	6°52·9′W	X	46

Cross Ash	Monm	SO4019	51°52·2′	2°51·9′W	T	161
Cross-at-Hand	Kent	TQ7846	51°11·4′	0°33·2′E	T	188
Cross Bank	Brad	SE0650	53°57·0′	1°54·1′W	X	104
Cross Bank	Northum	NY6963	54°57·9′	2°28·6′W	X	86,87
Cross Bank	Worcs	SO7473	52°21·5′	2°22·5′W	T	138
Cross Bank Fm	Cambs	TL6485	52°26·5′	0°25·2′E	FM	143
Cross Bank Fm	Ches	SJ7758	53°7·4′	2°20·2′W	FM	118
Cross Bank Fm	Norf	TL6691	52°29·7′	0°27·1′E	FM	143
Crossbank Fm	Suff	TL6580	52°23·8′	0°25·9′E	FM	143
Crossbankhead	D & G	NY2580	55°6·8′	3°10·1′W	X	79
Crossbanks Fm	Ches	SJ6257	53°6·8′	2°33·7′W	FM	118
Cross Bargain Fm	Oxon	SU3389	51°36·2′	1°31·0′W	FM	174
Cross Barn	V of Glam	ST0272	51°26·5′	3°24·2′W	X	170
Crossbarrow	Cumbr	NY0428	54°38·5′	3°28·8′W	X	89
Cross Barton	Devon	SS8002	50°48·5′	3°41·8′W	X	191
Crossbasket	S Lanak	NS6656	55°47·0′	4°7·8′W	X	64
Cross Beck	Cumbr	SD2281	54°13·4′	3°11·4′W	X	96
Cross Belt	Norf	TF7428	52°49·5′	0°35·4′E	F	132
Cross Belt, The	Hants	SU2246	51°13·0′	1°40·7′W	F	184
Crossbog	Angus	NO3862	56°45·0′	3°0·4′W	X	44
Crossbow Hill	Scot Bord	NY4698	55°16·6′	2°50·6′W	H	79
Crossbrae	Aberd	NJ6952	57°33·7′	2°30·6′W	T	29
Crossbrae	Aberd	NJ7551	57°33·2′	2°24·6′W	X	29
Crossbrae	Aberd	NJ9160	57°38·0′	2°8·6′W	X	30
Crossbreck	Highld	NG3636	57°20·5′	6°22·8′W	X	23,32
Crossbrook	Shrops	SJ4702	52°37·0′	2°46·6′W	X	126
Crossburn	E Dunb	NS5374	55°56·5′	4°20·8′W	X	64
Crossburn	Falk	NS8672	55°55·9′	3°49·0′W	T	65
Crossburn	Highld	NC6860	58°30·8′	4°15·5′W	X	10
Crossburn	Moray	NJ4452	57°33·5′	2°55·7′W	X	28
Cross Burn	S Ayr	NX3988	55°9·9′	4°31·2′W	W	77
Cross Burn	Scot Bord	NT6755	55°47·5′	2°31·1′W	W	67,74
Cross Burn Bothy	D & G	NX3887	55°9·3′	4°32·1′W	X	77
Crossburrow Hill	Leic	SP7495	52°33·1′	0°54·1′W	X	141
Crossbury	Devon	SS6730	51°3·5′	3°53·5′W	X	180
Crossbush	E Ayr	NS4334	55°34·7′	4°29·0′W	X	70
Crossbush	W Susx	TQ0306	50°50·9′	0°31·8′W	T	197
Cross Butts Fm	N Yks	NZ8710	54°28·9′	0°39·0′W	FM	94
Crosscanonby	Cumbr	NY0739	54°44·5′	3°26·3′W	T	89
Crosscleuch	Scot Bord	NT2420	55°28·3′	3°11·7′W	X	73
Crosscleuch Burn	Scot Bord	NT2419	55°27·8′	3°11·7′W	W	79
Cross Cleugh	Northum	NT6903	55°19·5′	2°28·9′W	X	80
Crosscliff	N Yks	SE8992	54°19·2′	0°37·5′W	X	94,101
Crosscliff Beck	N Yks	SE8992	54°19·2′	0°37·5′W	W	94,101
Crosscliffe Fm	N Yks	SE8471	54°7·9′	0°42·4′W	FM	100
Crosscliff Wood	N Yks	SE8991	54°18·6′	0°37·5′W	F	94,101
Cross Common	V of Glam	ST1670	51°25·6′	3°12·1′W	X	171
Cross Coombe	Corn	SW7251	50°19·1′	5°11·8′W	T	204
Cross Craigs	Pth & Kin	NN5352	56°38·5′	4°23·4′W	H	42,51
Crosscrake	Cumbr	SD5286	54°16·3′	2°43·8′W	T	97
Crosscryne	Scot Bord	NT0535	55°36·2′	3°30·0′W	H	72
Crosscynon	Powys	SO1273	52°21·1′	3°17·1′W	X	136,148
Crossdale Grains	Lancs	SD6864	54°4·5′	2°28·9′W	X	98
Crossdale Street	Norf	TG2239	52°54·4′	1°18·5′E	T	133
Cross Dike Scar	Cumbr	SD1964	54°4·2′	3°13·9′W	X	96
Cross Dormont	Cumbr	NY4622	54°35·7′	2°49·7′W	X	90
Crossdougal	N Eil	NF7520	57°9·6′	7°22·1′W	X	31
Cross Drain	E Yorks	TA0844	53°53·1′	0°21·0′W	W	107
Cross Drain	Lincs	TF1613	52°42·4′	0°16·6′W	W	130,142
Cross Drains Fm	Norf	TL5892	52°30·4′	0°20·1′E	FM	143
Cross Dyke	I of M	SC3888	54°16·0′	4°28·8′W	A	95
Cross Dyke	Kent	TQ4353	51°15·7′	0°3·4′E	A	187
Cross Dyke	N Yks	SE5289	54°17·9′	1°11·6′W	A	100
Cross Dyke	N Yks	SE5674	54°9·8′	1°8·1′W	A	100
Cross Dyke	Shrops	SO4292	52°31·6′	2°50·9′W	A	137
Cross Dyke	Shrops	SO4394	52°32·7′	2°50·0′W	A	137
Cross Dyke	Shrops	SO4496	52°33·8′	2°49·2′W	A	137
Cross Dyke	Wilts	ST8034	51°6·5′	2°16·8′W	A	183
Crossdykes	D & G	NY2487	55°10·5′	3°11·2′W	X	79
Cross Dykes	Hants	SU6719	50°58·2′	1°2·4′W	A	185
Crossdykes Burn	D & G	NY2488	55°11·1′	3°11·2′W	W	79
Crossdykes Knowe	D & G	NY2589	55°11·6′	3°10·3′W	X	79
Crosse Fm	Devon	SS7423	50°59·8′	3°47·4′W	FM	180
Crosse Fm	Devon	SX7694	50°44·2′	3°45·1′W	FM	191
Cross End	Beds	TL0658	52°12·8′	0°26·5′W	T	153
Cross End	Essex	TL8533	51°58·1′	0°42·0′E	T	168
Cross End	Mil Key	SP9137	52°1·7′	0°40·0′W	T	152
Cross End Fm	Heref	SO3443	52°5·1′	2°57·4′W	FM	148,149,161
Crossens	Sefton	SD3719	53°40·1′	2°56·8′W	T	108
Crossens Marsh	Sefton	SD3621	53°41·1′	2°57·7′W	X	102
Crossens Pool	Sefton	SD3423	53°42·2′	2°59·6′W	W	102
Crosses Fm	Cumbr	NY4100	54°23·8′	2°54·1′W	FM	90
Crosse's Fm	Devon	ST0122	50°59·6′	3°24·3′W	FM	181
Crosses Fm	N Yks	SE9595	54°20·7′	0°31·9′W	FM	94,101
Crosses, The	Derby	SK2314	52°43·6′	1°39·2′W	X	128
Cross Fell	Cumbr	NY6834	54°42·2′	2°29·4′W	H	91
Crossfell Well	Cumbr	NY6834	54°42·2′	2°29·4′W	W	91
Crossfield	Cumbr	NY0114	54°30·9′	3°31·3′W	X	89
Cross Field Fm	N Yks	SE6867	54°5·9′	0°57·2′W	FM	100
Crossfield Ho	E Yorks	SE8840	53°51·2′	0°39·3′W	X	106
Cross Field Knotts	N Yks	SD9163	54°4·0′	2°7·8′W	X	98
Crossfields	Aberd	NJ7453	57°34·2′	2°25·6′W	X	29
Crossflat	Renf	NS3861	55°49·2′	4°34·7′W	X	63
Crossflat Burn	E Ayr	NS7225	55°30·4′	4°1·2′W	W	71
Crossflatt	E Ayr	NS7027	55°31·4′	4°3·1′W	X	71
Crossflatts	Brad	SE1040	53°51·6′	1°50·5′W	T	104
Cross Fm	Corn	SX3961	50°25·8′	4°15·6′W	FM	201
Cross Fm	Devon	SS3609	50°51·7′	4°19·4′W	FM	190
Cross Fm	Devon	SS5912	50°53·7′	3°59·9′W	FM	180
Cross Fm	Devon	SX7290	50°42·0′	3°48·4′W	FM	191
Cross Fm	Heref	SO2852	52°9·9′	3°2·8′W	FM	148
Cross Fm	Heref	SO6357	52°12·8′	2°32·1′W	FM	149
Cross Fm	Herts	TL1512	51°47·9′	0°19·5′W	FM	166
Cross Fm	N Yks	SE6793	54°19·9′	0°57·8′W	FM	94,100
Cross Fm	Oxon	SU6978	51°30·0′	1°0·0′W	FM	175
Cross Fm	Powys	SJ0604	52°37·8′	3°22·9′W	FM	136
Cross Fm	Somer	ST1838	51°8·4′	3°9·9′W	FM	181
Cross Fm	Suff	TM2745	52°3·6′	1°19·1′E	FM	169
Cross Fm	Warr	SJ6383	53°20·8′	2°32·9′W	FM	109
Cross Fm, The	Essex	TL6930	51°56·8′	0°27·9′E	FM	167

Crossfold	Aberd	NJ4902	57°6·6′	2°50·1′W	X	37
Crossfolds	Aberd	NJ5656	57°35·8′	2°43·7′W	X	29
Crossfoot Fm	Powys	SO2245	52°6·1′	3°7·9′W	FM	148
Crossford	D & G	NX8388	55°10·6′	3°49·8′W	X	78
Crossford	Fife	NT0686	56°3·7′	3°30·1′W	T	65
Crossford	Pth & Kin	NO1627	56°25·9′	3°21·3′W	X	53,58
Crossford	S Lanak	NS8246	55°41·8′	3°52·2′W	T	72
Crossford Br	Traf	SJ7993	53°26·2′	2°18·6′W	X	109
Cross Foxes Hotel	Gwyn	SH7616	52°43·9′	3°49·8′W	X	124
Cross Furzes	Devon	SX6966	50°29·0′	3°50·4′W	X	202
Crossgate	Corn	SX3488	50°40·3′	4°20·6′W	T	190
Cross Gate	Cumbr	NY5018	54°33·5′	2°46·0′W	X	90
Cross Gate	Devon	SS6935	51°6·2′	3°51·9′W	X	180
Crossgate	Lincs	TF2426	52°49·3′	0°9·2′W	T	131
Crossgate	Orkney	HY4917	59°2·5′	2°52·8′W	X	6
Crossgate	Staffs	SJ9437	52°56·1′	2°5·0′W	T	127
Cross Gate	W Susx	TQ0413	50°54·7′	0°30·9′W	T	197
Crossgate Fm	Derby	SK1475	53°16·5′	1°47·0′W	FM	119
Crossgate Fm	Lincs	TF2135	52°54·2′	0°11·7′W	FM	131
Crossgatehall	E Loth	NT3669	55°54·8′	3°1·0′W	X	66
Crossgates	Aberd	NO8481	56°55·5′	2°15·3′W	X	45
Cross Gates	Brad	SE0939	53°51·1′	1°51·4′W	T	104
Crossgates	Cumbr	NY0721	54°34·8′	3°25·9′W	T	89
Crossgates	E Ayr	NS3744	55°40·0′	4°35·1′W	X	63,70
Crossgates	Fife	NO3309	56°16·4′	3°4·5′W	X	59
Crossgates	Fife	NO4510	56°17·0′	2°52·9′W	X	59
Crossgates	Fife	NT1488	56°4·9′	3°22·5′W	T	65
Cross Gates	Leeds	SE3534	53°48·3′	1°27·7′W	T	104
Crossgates	N Yks	SE2166	54°5·6′	1°40·3′W	X	99
Crossgates	N Yks	TA0384	54°14·7′	0°24·7′W	T	101
Crossgates	Powys	SO0864	52°16·2′	3°20·5′W	T	147
Crossgates	Pth & Kin	NO0420	56°22·0′	3°32·8′W	X	52,53,58
Crossgates	S Lanak	NS8547	55°42·4′	3°49·4′W	X	72
Crossgates Fm	Lincs	TF2438	52°55·7′	0°8·9′W	FM	131
Cross Geo	Shetld	HP6512	60°47·4′	0°47·9′W	X	1
Crossgerd	Shetld	HU4226	60°1·3′	1°14·3′W	X	4
Cross Gill	Cumbr	NY7339	54°45·0′	2°24·7′W	W	91
Crossgill	Cumbr	NY7440	54°45·5′	2°23·8′W	T	86,87
Crossgill	Lancs	SD5562	54°3·4′	2°40·8′W	T	97
Crossgill Head	Cumbr	NY7235	54°42·8′	2°25·7′W	X	91
Cross Gill Moor	N Yks	SE1065	54°5·1′	1°50·4′W	X	99
Crossgill Pants	Cumbr	NY7235	54°42·8′	2°25·7′W	X	91
Crossgills	D & G	NY0869	55°0·7′	3°25·9′W	X	85
Cross Gills	Lancs	SD6938	53°50·5′	2°27·9′W	X	103
Cross Gill Top	N Yks	SE0994	54°20·7′	1°51·3′W	X	99
Cross Grain	D & G	NY4185	55°9·6′	2°55·1′W	W	79
Cross Green	Devon	SX3888	50°40·4′	4°17·2′W	T	190
Cross Green	Leeds	SE3232	53°47·2′	1°30·4′W	T	104
Cross Green	Newp	ST4293	51°38·2′	2°49·9′W	X	171,172
Cross Green	N Yks	SD9647	53°55·4′	2°3·2′W	X	103
Crossgreen	Shrops	SJ4716	52°44·6′	2°46·7′W	T	126
Cross Green	Staffs	SJ9105	52°38·8′	2°7·6′W	T	127,139
Cross Green	Suff	TL8353	52°8·9′	0°40·9′E	T	155
Cross Green	Suff	TL8955	52°9·9′	0°46·2′E	T	155
Cross Green	Suff	TL9852	52°8·1′	0°54·0′E	T	155
Cross Green	Wrekin	SJ6112	52°42·5′	2°34·2′W	T	127
Cross Green Fm	Suff	TM0078	52°22·0′	0°56·7′E	FM	144
Cross Green Fm	Warw	SP1796	52°33·9′	1°44·6′W	FM	139
Crossgreens	Cumbr	NY5675	55°4·3′	2°40·9′W	X	86
Crosshall	Scot Bord	NT7642	55°40·5′	2°22·5′W	X	74
Cross & Hand	Dorset	ST6303	50°49·8′	2°31·1′W	A	194
Crosshands	Carm	SN1922	51°52·3′	4°37·4′W	T	145,158
Cross Hands	Carm	SN5612	51°47·5′	4°4·9′W	T	159
Crosshands	E Ayr	NS4830	55°32·7′	4°24·1′W	X	70
Cross Hands	Glos	SO6404	51°44·2′	2°30·9′W	X	162
Cross Hands	Pemb	SN0712	51°46·6′	4°47·5′W	T	158
Crosshands Fm	Glos	SO7927	51°56·7′	2°17·9′W	FM	162
Crosshands, The	Monm	SO4303	51°43·6′	2°49·1′W	X	171
Crosshaw Beck	Cumbr	SD6993	54°20·1′	2°28·2′W	W	98
Cross Hayes Ho	Staffs	SK1222	52°48·0′	1°48·9′W	X	128
Cross Heath	Staffs	SJ8447	53°1·4′	2°13·9′W	T	118
Cross Hill	Aberd	NJ4432	57°22·8′	2°55·4′W	H	37
Crosshill	Aberd	NJ8430	57°21·9′	2°15·5′W	X	29,30
Crosshill	Aberd	NJ8647	57°31·0′	2°13·6′W	X	30
Crosshill	Aberd	NJ9332	57°23·0′	2°6·5′W	X	30
Crosshill	Angus	NO6159	56°43·5′	2°37·8′W	X	54
Crosshill	Arg & Bt	NR7119	55°24·9′	5°36·7′W	X	68
Crosshill	C of Glas	NS6863	55°50·8′	4°6·1′W	X	64
Cross Hill	Corn	SX0474	50°32·2′	4°45·6′W	T	200
Crosshill	Cumbr	NY2345	54°47·9′	3°11·4′W	X	85
Crosshill	Cumbr	NY3961	54°56·6′	2°56·7′W	X	85
Crosshill	Cumbr	NY4762	54°57·2′	2°49·2′W	X	86
Crosshill	Cumbr	NY5578	55°5·9′	2°41·9′W	X	86
Cross Hill	Derby	SK4148	53°1·9′	1°22·9′W	T	129
Cross Hill	D & G	NT2507	55°21·3′	3°10·5′W	H	79
Cross Hill	Dorset	ST6201	50°48·7′	2°32·0′W	X	194
Cross Hill	Durham	NY9448	54°49·9′	2°5·2′W	X	87
Crosshill	E Ayr	NS4724	55°29·4′	4°24·9′W	T	70
Crosshill	E Ayr	NS5218	55°26·3′	4°19·9′W	X	70
Crosshill	E Ayr	NS5614	55°24·2′	4°16·0′W	X	71
Crosshill	Falk	NS8772	55°55·9′	3°48·1′W	X	65
Crosshill	Fife	NS9389	56°5·2′	3°42·7′W	X	65
Crosshill	Fife	NT1796	56°9·2′	3°19·7′W	T	58
Cross Hill	Glos	ST5596	51°39·9′	2°38·6′W	T	162
Crosshill	Highld	NH6954	57°33·7′	4°10·9′W	X	26
Crosshill	Moray	NJ1868	57°41·9′	3°22·1′W	X	28
Crosshill	Northum	NU0309	55°22·7′	1°56·7′W	X	81
Cross Hill	N Yks	SE6018	53°39·5′	1°5·1′W	X	111
Crosshill	S Ayr	NS3206	55°19·4′	4°38·4′W	T	70,76
Crosshill	Shrops	SJ4915	52°44·1′	2°44·9′W	X	126
Crosshill	S Lanak	NS6250	55°43·7′	4°11·4′W	X	64
Cross Hill Fm	Lancs	SD4434	53°48·2′	2°50·6′W	FM	102
Crosshill Fm	Lancs	SD5250	53°56·9′	2°43·5′W	FM	102
Cross Hill Ho	N Yks	NZ3705	54°26·6′	1°25·3′W	X	93
Cross Hillocks Fm	Know	SJ4786	53°22·3′	2°47·4′W	FM	108
Cross Hills	Derby	SK5169	53°13·2′	1°13·8′W	X	120
Crosshills	Highld	NH6570	57°42·2′	4°15·5′W	X	21
Cross Hills	N Yks	NZ2501	54°24·5′	1°36·5′W	X	93
Cross Hills	N Yks	SE0044	53°53·8′	1°59·6′W	T	104
Cross Hills	Shrops	SJ7025	52°49·5′	2°26·3′W	X	127
Cross Ho	Cumbr	NY5343	54°47·0′	2°43·4′W	X	86
Cross Ho	Cumbr	SD7286	54°16·4′	2°25·4′W	X	98
Cross Ho	Heref	SO4754	52°11·1′	2°46·1′W	X	148,149
Cross Ho	Lancs	SD4440	53°51·4′	2°50·7′W	X	102
Cross Ho	Lancs	SD5037	53°49·9′	2°45·2′W	X	102
Cross Ho	Lancs	SD5242	53°52·6′	2°43·4′W	X	102
Cross Ho	Lancs	SD5537	53°49·9′	2°40·6′W	X	102
Cross Ho	N Yks	SE0083	54°14·8′	1°59·6′W	X	98
Cross Ho Fm	Ches	SJ4473	53°15·3′	2°50·0′W	FM	117
Cross Holme	N Yks	SE5696	54°21·6′	1°7·9′W	T	100
Cross Holts	Lincs	SK9370	53°13·4′	0°36·0′W	F	121
Cross House	Cumbr	SD1088	54°17·0′	3°22·5′W	X	96
Crosshouse	E Ayr	NS3938	55°36·8′	4°32·9′W	T	70
Crosshouse	Midlo	NT2363	55°51·5′	3°13·4′W	X	66
Crosshouse	S Lanak	NS6051	55°44·2′	4°13·4′W	X	64
Cross House Fm	Lancs	SD4844	53°53·6′	2°47·1′W	FM	102
Cross House Fm	Lancs	SD5337	53°49·9′	2°42·4′W	FM	102
Cross Houses	Cumbr	SD5795	54°21·2′	2°39·3′W	X	97
Crosshouses	Scot Bord	NT2238	55°38·0′	3°13·9′W	X	73
Cross Houses	Shrops	SJ5407	52°39·8′	2°40·4′W	T	126
Cross Houses	Shrops	SO6991	52°31·2′	2°27·0′W	T	138
Crosshow	Cumbr	NY0636	54°42·9′	3°27·1′W	X	89
Cross How	Cumbr	NY6130	54°40·1′	2°35·9′W	X	91
Crossibeg	Arg & Bt	NR7421	55°26·1′	5°33·9′W	X	68
Crossiecrown	Orkney	HY4213	59°0·3′	3°0·1′W	X	6
Crossie Geo	Shetld	HU4326	60°1·3′	1°13·2′W	X	4
Crossing Fm	Suff	TM4263	52°12·9′	1°33·0′E	FM	156
Crossingford Br	Norf	TM2284	52°24·8′	1°16·3′E	X	156
Crossingford Lodge	Norf	TM2184	52°24·8′	1°15·4′E	X	156
Crossings	Cumbr	NY5077	55°5·3′	2°46·6′W	X	86
Cross in Hand	E Susx	TQ5521	50°58·3′	0°12·9′E	T	199
Cross in Hand	Leic	SP5083	52°26·8′	1°15·5′W	X	140
Cross Inn	Carm	SN2912	51°47·1′	4°28·4′W	T	159
Cross Inn	Cered	SN3857	52°11·5′	4°21·8′W	T	145
Cross Inn	Cered	SN5464	52°15·5′	4°8·0′W	T	146
Cross Inn	Rho Cyn Taf	ST0583	51°32·5′	3°21·8′W	T	170
Cross Inn Hall	Carm	SN4538	52°1·4′	4°15·2′W	X	146
Cross Iuran	Highld	NG3339	57°22·1′	6°26·0′W	X	23,32
Crosskeys	Caer	ST2291	51°37·0′	3°7·2′W	T	171
Cross Keys	Cumbr	SD6996	54°21·8′	2°28·2′W	X	98
Cross Keys	Denb	SJ1066	53°11·3′	3°20·4′W	X	116
Cross Keys	Kent	TQ5153	51°15·6′	0°10·2′E	T	188
Cross Keys	Wilts	ST8771	51°26·5′	2°10·8′W	T	173
Crosskirk	Highld	ND0369	58°36·2′	3°39·7′W	T	12
Cross Kirk	Shetld	HP6512	60°47·4′	0°47·9′W	A	1
Cross Kirk	Shetld	HU2178	60°29·4′	1°36·6′W	A	3
Crosskirk Bay	Highld	ND0270	58°36·7′	3°40·7′W	W	12
Crosslace	Monm	SO3806	51°45·2′	2°53·5′W	X	161
Crossland Fosse	Beds	TL0049	52°8·0′	0°32·1′W	X	153
Crosslands	Cumbr	NY7145	54°48·2′	2°26·6′W	X	86,87
Crosslands	Cumbr	SD3489	54°17·8′	3°0·4′W	T	96,97
Crosslands	Devon	SS9910	50°53·1′	3°25·8′W	X	192
Crosslands	D & G	NY2579	55°6·2′	3°10·3′W	X	85
Crosslands Fm	Cumbr	SD5786	54°16·3′	2°39·2′W	FM	97
Crosslands Fm	Devon	SS3111	50°52·7′	4°23·8′W	FM	190
Crossland Sides	Derby	SK1359	53°7·9′	1°47·9′W	X	119
Cross Lane	Ches	SJ6760	53°8·4′	2°29·2′W	T	118
Crosslane	Corn	SX0166	50°27·8′	4°47·9′W	X	200
Cross-lane	Powys	SJ0211	52°41·5′	3°26·6′W	X	125
Cross Lane Br	Lincs	TF0191	53°24·6′	0°28·4′W	X	112
Crosslane Fm	Lincs	TF2126	52°49·3′	0°11·9′W	FM	131
Cross Lane Fm	Notts	SK8250	53°2·7′	0°46·2′W	FM	121
Cross Lane Fm	Powys	SJ1702	52°36·8′	3°13·2′W	FM	136
Crosslane Fm	W Berks	SU6965	51°23·0′	1°0·1′W	FM	175
Cross Lane Head	Shrops	SO7095	52°33·4′	2°26·1′W	T	138
Cross Lanes	Corn	SS2406	50°49·8′	4°29·6′W	X	190
Cross Lanes	Corn	SW6921	50°2·9′	5°13·2′W	T	203
Cross Lanes	Corn	SW7642	50°14·4′	5°8·1′W	X	204
Cross Lanes	Darl	NZ2321	54°35·3′	1°38·2′W	X	93
Cross Lanes	Dorset	ST7602	50°49·3′	2°20·1′W	T	194
Cross Lanes	Durham	NZ0513	54°31·0′	1°54·9′W	X	92
Cross Lanes	N Yks	SE3091	54°19·1′	1°31·9′W	X	99
Cross Lanes	N Yks	SE5265	54°4·9′	1°11·9′W	T	100
Cross Lanes	Oxon	SU6778	51°30·0′	1°1·7′W	T	175
Crosslanes	Oxon	SU7281	51°31·6′	0°57·3′W	X	175
Cross Lanes	Shrops	SJ2733	52°53·6′	3°4·7′W	X	126
Crosslanes	Shrops	SJ3218	52°45·6′	3°0·1′W	T	126
Cross Lanes	Shrops	SJ3536	52°55·3′	2°57·6′W	X	126
Cross Lanes	Wrex	SJ3747	53°1·2′	2°55·9′W	T	117
Crosslanes Fm	Ches	SJ7169	53°13·3′	2°25·7′W	FM	118
Cross Lanes Fm	Ches	SJ7572	53°14·9′	2°22·1′W	FM	118
Cross Lanes Fm	Hants	SU5418	50°57·8′	1°13·5′W	FM	185
Cross Lanes Fm	N Yks	SE1492	54°19·6′	1°46·7′W	FM	99
Cross Lanes Fm	N Yks	SE3091	54°19·1′	1°31·9′W	FM	99
Crosslanes Fm	Shrops	SJ3236	52°55·3′	3°0·3′W	FM	126
Crosslanes Fm	Shrops	SJ3537	52°55·8′	2°57·6′W	FM	126
Cross Lanes Fm	Warw	SP1358	52°13·4′	1°48·2′W	FM	151
Cross Lanes Fm	Wilts	SU1089	51°36·2′	1°50·9′W	FM	173
Crosslar	E Ayr	NS6019	55°26·9′	4°12·4′W	X	71
Cross Law	Northum	NY8689	55°12·0′	2°12·8′W	H	80
Crosslaw	Scot Bord	NT8767	55°54·0′	2°12·0′W	X	67
Cross Law	Scot Bord	NT8768	55°54·5′	2°12·0′W	X	67
Crosslee	Renf	NS4066	55°51·9′	4°33·0′W	T	64
Crosslee	Scot Bord	NT3018	55°27·3′	3°6·0′W	X	79
Crosslee	Scot Bord	NT4539	55°38·7′	2°52·0′W	X	73
Crosslee Burn	Scot Bord	NT3019	55°27·8′	3°6·0′W	W	79
Crosslee Burn	Scot Bord	NT4539	55°38·7′	2°52·0′W	W	73
Crosslee Rig	Scot Bord	NT2919	55°27·8′	3°6·9′W	H	79
Crosslees	E Renf	NS5652	55°44·7′	4°17·2′W	X	64
Cross Lees Fm	Essex	TL5506	51°44·1′	0°15·1′E	FM	167
Crosslees Wood	E Renf	NS5652	55°44·7′	4°17·2′W	F	64
Crosslet	W Dunb	NS4175	55°56·8′	4°32·3′W	X	64
Crossletts Fms	N Yks	NZ5300	54°23·8′	1°10·6′W	FM	93
Crossley	Ches	SJ8965	53°11·2′	2°9·5′W	X	118
Crossley	Kirk	SE2021	53°41·3′	1°41·4′W	X	104
Crossley	Moray	NJ1657	57°36·0′	3°23·9′W	X	28
Crossley	N Yks	NZ7105	54°26·4′	0°53·9′W	X	94
Crossley Gate Fm	N Yks	NZ7106	54°26·9′	0°53·9′W	FM	94
Crossley Hall	Brad	SE1333	53°47·8′	1°47·7′W	T	104
Crossley Hall Fm	Ches	SJ8965	53°11·2′	2°9·5′W	FM	118
Crossley Hill Wood	Notts	SK6083	53°20·7′	1°5·5′W	F	111,120
Crossley House Fm	N Yks	NZ7105	54°26·4′	0°53·9′W	FM	94
Crossley Plantn	Notts	SK4762	53°9·4′	1°17·4′W	F	120
Crossleys	D & G	NX9480	55°6·4′	3°39·3′W	X	78
Cross Leys	Herts	TL4136	52°0·5′	0°3·7′E	X	154
Cross Leys Fm	Peterb	TL0299	52°35·0′	0°29·3′W	FM	141
Crossley's Plantn	Kirk	SE1204	53°32·2′	1°48·7′W	F	110
Cross Llyde	Heref	SO4227	51°56·5′	2°50·2′W	T	161
Cross Lochs, The	Highld	NC8646	58°23·5′	3°56·5′W	W	10
Crosslots	Moray	NJ1767	57°41·4′	3°23·1′W	X	28
Cross Low	Derby	SK1655	53°5·8′	1°45·3′W	A	119
Crosslowbank	Derby	SK1655	53°5·8′	1°45·3′W	X	119
Crossman's Fm	Essex	TM1328	51°54·8′	1°6·2′E	FM	168,169
Crossmere Hill	E Yorks	TA2437	53°49·1′	0°6·6′W	X	107
Crossmichael	D & G	NX7366	54°58·6′	3°58·6′W	T	83,84
Crossmill	E Renf	NS5059	55°48·3′	4°23·2′W	T	64
Cross Mill	Wrex	SJ4041	52°58·0′	2°53·2′W	X	117
Crossmiln	Angus	NO3862	56°45·0′	3°0·4′W	X	44
Cross Moor	Cumbr	SD2676	54°10·7′	3°7·6′W	X	96,97
Crossmoor	Lancs	SD4438	53°50·4′	2°50·6′W	T	102
Crossmoor Fm	Somer	ST2437	51°7·9′	3°4·8′W	FM	182
Crossmount	Pth & Kin	NN7057	56°41·5′	4°6·9′W	X	42,51,52
Crossmyloof	C of Glas	NS5762	55°50·1′	4°16·6′W	T	64
Crossnapend	Lancs	SD5941	53°52·1′	2°37·0′W	X	102
Cross Ness	Bexley	TQ4781	51°30·8′	0°7·5′E	X	177
Crossnish Point	Highld	NG2941	57°23·0′	6°30·1′W	X	23
Cross Oak	Powys	SO1023	51°54·1′	3°18·1′W	T	161
Cross Oaks Fm	Hants	SU2920	50°59·0′	1°34·8′W	FM	185
Crossoaks Fm	Herts	TQ2099	51°40·8′	0°15·5′W	FM	166,176
Cross of Greet	Lancs	SD6860	54°2·3′	2°28·9′W	A	98
Cross of Greet Bridge	Lancs	SD7059	54°1·8′	2°27·1′W	X	103
Cross of Jackston	Aberd	NJ7432	57°22·9′	2°25·5′W	T	29
Cross of Knockando	Moray	NJ1647	57°30·6′	3°23·7′W	X	28
Cross of the Hand	Staffs	SK0822	52°48·0′	1°52·5′W	X	128
Cross of the Tree	Heref	SO3867	52°18·1′	2°54·2′W	X	137,148,149
Cross o'th hands	Derby	SK2846	53°0·9′	1°34·6′W	T	119,128
Cross o' th' Hill	Ches	SJ4947	53°1·3′	2°45·2′W	T	117
Crosspark	Devon	SS3214	50°54·3′	4°23·0′W	X	190
Crossparks	Devon	SS3504	50°49·0′	4°20·2′W	X	190
Crosspark Wood	Corn	SX4163	50°27·0′	4°14·0′W	F	201
Crosspit Burn	Angus	NO5083	56°56·4′	2°48·9′W	W	44
Cross Plain	Somer	ST4155	51°17·7′	2°50·4′W	X	172,182
Cross Plantn	N Yks	SE6793	54°19·9′	0°57·8′W	F	94,100
Crosspost	W Susx	TQ2522	50°59·3′	0°12·8′W	T	198
Crosspost Fm	Corn	SW7438	50°12·2′	5°9·7′W	FM	204
Cross Pot	N Yks	SD8174	54°9·9′	2°17·0′W	X	98
Crossraguel Abbey	S Ayr	NS2708	55°20·4′	4°43·2′W	A	70,76
Cross Rein Wood	N Yks	NZ3102	54°25·0′	1°30·9′W	F	93
Crossridge	Northum	NY8377	55°5·5′	2°15·6′W	X	86,87
Crossridge Fm	S Lanak	NS9237	55°37·1′	3°42·5′W	FM	71,72
Crossrig	Scot Bord	NT8852	55°45·9′	2°11·0′W	X	67,74
Crossrigg	Cumbr	NY1444	54°47·3′	3°19·8′W	X	85
Cross Rigg	Durham	NZ0247	54°49·3′	1°57·7′W	X	87
Crossrigg	N Lanak	NS8368	55°53·7′	3°51·8′W	X	65
Cross Rigg	Northum	NY6461	54°56·8′	2°33·3′W	H	86
Crossrigg Fm	Cumbr	NY6123	54°36·3′	2°35·8′W	FM	91
Crossrigg Hall	Cumbr	NY6024	54°36·8′	2°36·7′W	X	91
Crossroad Fm	Beds	TL2349	52°7·8′	0°11·8′W	FM	153
Crossroads	Aberd	NJ6017	57°14·8′	2°39·3′W	X	37
Crossroads	Aberd	NO7377	56°53·3′	2°26·1′W	X	45
Crossroads	Aberd	NO7594	57°2·4′	2°24·3′W	T	38,45
Cross Roads	Angus	NO5552	56°39·7′	2°43·6′W	X	54
Cross Roads	Brad	SE0437	53°50·0′	1°55·9′W	T	104
Cross Roads	Devon	SX4586	50°39·4′	4°11·2′W	T	201
Crossroads	E Ayr	NS4734	55°34·8′	4°25·2′W	T	70
Crossroads	Fife	NT3699	56°11·0′	3°1·4′W	T	59
Cross Roads	Shrops	SJ7812	52°42·6′	2°19·1′W	X	127
Cross Roads Fm	Bucks	SP7732	51°59·1′	0°52·3′W	FM	152,165
Crossroads Fm	Ches	SJ7084	53°21·4′	2°26·6′W	FM	109
Crossroads Fm	Derby	SK3347	53°1·4′	1°30·1′W	FM	119,128
Crossroads Fm	Leic	SK7728	52°50·9′	0°51·0′W	FM	129
Cross Roads Fm	Lincs	TF2764	53°9·7′	0°5·6′W	FM	122
Crossroads Fm	N Yks	SE4340	53°51·5′	1°20·4′W	FM	105
Cross Roads Fm	Rut	SK9609	52°40·4′	0°34·4′W	FM	141
Cross Roads Lodge	Glos	ST8191	51°37·3′	2°16·1′W	X	162,173
Cross's Grave	Norf	TF8025	52°47·8′	0°40·6′E	X	132
Cross Side	Devon	SS8023	50°59·9′	3°42·2′W	X	181
Cross Slab (Ogham)	Moray	NJ0355	57°34·7′	3°36·9′W	A	27
Cross-slacks	Aberd	NJ8063	57°39·6′	2°19·7′W	X	29,30
Cross Stone	Aberd	NJ9527	57°20·3′	2°4·5′W	X	38
Cross Stone	Cumbr	SD6280	54°13·1′	2°34·5′W	A	97
Cross Street	Suff	TM1876	52°20·5′	1°12·4′E	T	156
Cross Street	Wrex	SJ2644	52°59·5′	3°5·7′W	X	117
Cross, The	Ches	SJ7760	53°8·4′	2°20·2′W	X	118
Cross, The	Durham	NY9720	54°34·8′	2°2·4′W	X	92
Cross, The	Essex	TM0213	51°47·0′	0°56·1′E	X	168
Cross, The	Northum	NY7190	55°12·5′	2°26·9′W	H	80
Cross, The	Powys	SN9881	52°25·3′	3°29·6′W	X	136
Cross, The	Swan	SS4889	51°35·0′	4°11·2′W	X	159
Cross Thorns Barn	N Yks	SE9668	54°6·2′	0°31·5′W	X	101
Cross Thwaite	Cumbr	SD7689	54°18·0′	2°21·7′W	X	98
Crossthwaite Common	Durham	NY9124	54°36·9′	2°7·9′W	X	91,92
Crossthwaite Scars	Durham	NY9225	54°37·5′	2°7·0′W	X	91,92
Crosston	Angus	NO5148	56°37·5′	2°47·5′W	X	54
Crosston	Angus	NO5256	56°41·9′	2°46·6′W	T	54
Cross Town	Ches	SJ7578	53°18·1′	2°22·1′W	T	118
Crosstown	Corn	SS2015	50°54·6′	4°33·2′W	T	190
Crosstown	Devon	SS4083	50°37·7′	4°15·4′W	X	191
Crosstown	V of Glam	ST0469	51°25·0′	3°22·4′W	T	170
Cross-voe-sand	Shetld	HU2379	60°29·9′	1°34·4′W	X	3
Cross Water	S Ayr	NX1979	55°4·6′	4°49·7′W	W	76
Cross Water	S Ayr	NX2280	55°5·2′	4°46·9′W	W	76
Crosswater	Surrey	SU8539	51°8·9′	0°46·7′W	T	186
Cross Water of Luce	D & G	NX1875	55°2·4′	4°50·5′W	W	76
Cross Water of Luce	D & G	NX1967	54°58·1′	4°49·2′W	W	82
Cross Way	Heref	SO3053	52°10·5′	3°1·0′W	X	148
Crossway	Heref	SO3425	51°55·4′	2°57·2′W	X	161
Crossway	Heref	SO6131	51°58·8′	2°33·7′W	T	149
Crossway	Monm	SO3515	51°50·0′	2°56·2′W	X	161
Crossway	Monm	SO4419	51°52·2′	2°48·4′W	T	161

Crossway	Powys	SO0558	52°13·0′	3°23·0′W	T	147
Crossway	Powys	SO1065	52°16·8′	3°18·8′W	X	136,148
Crossway Fm	Powys	SO2145	52°6·1′	3°8·8′W	FM	148
Crossway Green	Monm	ST5294	51°38·8′	2°41·2′W	T	162,172
Crossway Green	Worcs	SO8468	52°18·8′	2°13·7′W	T	138
Crossway Hand Fm	Northnts	SP9992	52°31·2′	0°32·1′W	FM	141
Cross Ways	Bath & NE Somer	ST6459	51°20·0′	2°30·6′W	X	172
Crossways	Derby	SK2646	53°0·9′	1°36·3′W	X	119,128
Crossways	Devon	SX6565	50°28·4′	3°53·8′W	X	202
Crossways	Dorset	SY7788	50°41·7′	2°19·2′W	T	194
Crossways	Essex	TQ5988	51°34·3′	0°18·1′E	X	177
Crossways	Glos	SO5611	51°48·0′	2°37·9′W	X	162
Crossways	Glos	ST7297	51°40·5′	2°23·9′W	X	162
Crossways	Monm	SO3220	51°52·7′	2°58·9′W	T	161
Cross Ways	Norf	TG4901	52°33·2′	1°40·8′E	X	134
Crossways	Powys	SO1473	52°21·1′	3°15·4′W	X	136,148
Crossways	S Glos	ST6590	51°36·7′	2°29·9′W	T	162,172
Crossways	Shrops	SO2085	52°27·7′	3°10·3′W	X	137
Cross Ways	Suff	TL9763	52°14·0′	0°53·5′E	X	155
Crossways	Surrey	SU8538	51°8·3′	0°46·7′W	T	186
Crossways	V of Glam	SS9774	51°27·6′	3°28·6′W	X	170
Crossways Fm	Lincs	TF1152	53°3·5′	0°20·2′W	FM	121
Crossways Fm	Norf	TF6300	52°34·6′	0°24·7′E	FM	143
Crossways Fm	Surrey	TQ1047	51°12·9′	0°25·1′W	FM	187
Crossways Fm	Surrey	TQ2653	51°16·0′	0°11·2′W	FM	187
Crossways Fm	Wilts	ST8858	51°19·5′	2°9·9′W	FM	173
Crossways, The	Hants	SU6613	50°55·0′	1°3·3′W	X	196
Crossways, The	Shrops	SO4079	52°24·6′	2°52·5′W	X	137,148
Crosswell	Pemb	SN1236	51°59·7′	4°43·9′W	T	145
Crosswood	Cered	SN6672	52°20·0′	3°57·6′W	T	135
Crosswoodburn	W Loth	NT0557	55°48·1′	3°30·5′W	X	65,72
Crosswood Burn	W Loth	NT0559	55°49·2′	3°30·5′W	W	65,72
Crosswood Burn	W Loth	NT0656	55°47·5′	3°29·5′W	W	65,72
Crosswoodhill	W Loth	NT0456	55°47·5′	3°31·4′W	X	65,72
Crosswood Reservoir	W Loth	NT0657	55°48·1′	3°29·5′W	W	65,72
Crosswyn	Corn	SW9846	50°17·0′	4°49·8′W	X	204
Crosthwaite	Cumbr	SD4491	54°18·9′	2°51·2′W	T	97
Croston	Lancs	SD4819	53°40·1′	2°46·8′W	T	108
Croston Barn	Lancs	SD4845	53°54·2′	2°47·1′W	X	102
Croston Moss	Lancs	SD4816	53°38·5′	2°46·8′W	X	108
Crostwick	Norf	TG2516	52°41·9′	1°20·2′E	T	133,134
Crostwight	Norf	TG3330	52°49·3′	1°27·9′E	X	133
Crostwight Heath	Norf	TG3430	52°49·2′	1°28·8′E	X	133
Cro Taing	Shetld	HU2977	60°28·8′	1°27·8′W	X	3
Crotia Mill Fm	Ches	SJ7252	53°4·1′	2°24·7′W	FM	118
Crouch	Kent	TQ6155	51°16·5′	0°18·9′E	T	188
Crouch	Kent	TR0558	51°17·3′	0°56·8′E	T	179
Crouch Corner	Essex	TR0194	51°36·8′	0°54·6′E	X	168,178
Crouch End	Hargy	TQ2988	51°34·8′	0°7·9′W	T	176
Crouchers	W Susx	SU8402	50°48·9′	0°48·1′W	T	197
Crouches	Essex	TL6323	51°53·1′	0°22·5′E	X	167
Croucheston	Wilts	SU0625	51°1·7′	1°54·5′W	T	184
Croucheston-Down Fm	Wilts	SU0723	51°0·6′	1°53·6′W	FM	184
Crouch Fm	Brom	TQ4967	51°23·2′	0°8·9′E	FM	177
Crouch Fm	Oxon	SP4338	52°2·6′	1°22·0′W	FM	151
Crouch Fm	W Susx	SU9717	50°56·9′	0°36·8′W	FM	197
Crouch Green	Herts	TL2120	51°52·2′	0°14·2′W	X	166
Crouch Hill	Dorset	ST7010	50°53·6′	2°25·2′W	T	194
Crouch Hill	Herts	TL3137	52°1·2′	0°5·1′W	X	153
Crouch Hill	Oxon	SP4339	52°3·1′	1°22·0′W	H	151
Crouch Hill	Swin	SU1994	51°38·9′	1°43·1′W	H	163,173
Crouch Ho	Essex	TL8137	52°0·3′	0°38·6′E	X	155
Crouch House Fm	Essex	TM0118	51°49·7′	0°55·4′E	FM	168
Crouchhouse Fm	W Susx	SU8523	51°0·2′	0°46·9′W	FM	197
Crouchie Wood	Scot Bord	NT6621	55°29·1′	2°31·8′W	F	74
Crouchland	W Susx	TQ0129	51°3·3′	0°33·1′W	X	186,197
Crouchley Hall Fm	Warr	SJ6886	53°22·4′	2°28·5′W	FM	109
Crouchmans	Essex	TQ9486	51°32·6′	0°48·3′E	X	178
Crouch Moor	Cambs	TL5792	52°30·4′	0°19·2′E	X	143
Crouchmoor Fm	Cambs	TL5791	52°29·9′	0°19·2′E	FM	143
Crouch's Down	Wilts	SU0432	51°5·5′	1°56·2′W	X	184
Crougar	Shetld	HT9640	60°8·9′	2°3·8′W	H	4
Croughly	Moray	NJ1721	57°16·6′	3°22·1′W	X	36
Croughton	Northnts	SP5433	51°59·8′	1°12·4′W	T	152
Croughton Cottage	Ches	SJ4172	53°14·7′	2°52·6′W	X	117
Croulin	Highld	NG7809	57°7·4′	5°39·6′W	X	33
Croulin Burn	Highld	NG7808	57°6·8′	5°39·5′W	W	33
Crousa Common	Corn	SW7720	50°2·5′	5°6·5′W	X	204
Crousa Downs	Corn	SW7618	50°1·4′	5°7·3′W	X	204
Crouse	D & G	NX3655	54°52·0′	4°32·9′W	X	83
Crouse Burn	D & G	NX3554	54°51·5′	4°33·8′W	W	83
Crouse Moor	D & G	NX3554	54°51·5′	4°33·8′W	X	83
Croval	Orkney	HY2408	58°57·4′	3°18·8′W	X	6,7
Croval	Orkney	HY2417	59°2·3′	3°19·0′W	X	6
Crovie	Aberd	NJ8065	57°40·7′	2°19·7′W	T	29,30
Crovie Fm	Aberd	NJ8166	57°41·3′	2°18·7′W	FM	29,30
Crovie Head	Aberd	NJ8066	57°41·3′	2°19·7′W	X	29,30
Crow	Hants	SU1603	50°49·8′	1°46·0′W	T	195
Crowan	Corn	SW6434	50°9·8′	5°17·9′W	T	203
Crowan Beacon	Corn	SW6635	50°10·4′	5°16·3′W	H	203
Cro Water	Shetld	HU4684	60°32·5′	1°9·2′W	W	1,2,3
Cro Waters	Shetld	HU4593	60°37·3′	1°10·2′W	W	1,2
Crowbank	N Lanak	NS8075	55°57·4′	3°54·9′W	X	65
Crow Bar	I Scilly	SV9113	49°56·5′	6°18·1′W	W	203
Crowbeare	Devon	SS5020	50°57·8′	4°7·8′W	X	180
Crowber	Orkney	HY5537	59°13·3′	2°46·8′W	X	5
Crowborough	Devon	SS4639	51°8·0′	4°11·7′W	X	180
Crowborough	E Susx	TQ5130	51°3·2′	0°9·7′E	T	188
Crowborough	Staffs	SJ9057	53°6·8′	2°8·6′W	T	118
Crowborough Common	E Susx	TQ5029	51°2·7′	0°8·8′E	X	188,199
Crowborough Warren	E Susx	TQ5030	51°3·2′	0°8·8′E	T	188
Crowbourne Fm	Kent	TQ7137	51°6·6′	0°27·0′E	FM	188
Crow Brook	Ches	SJ7073	53°15·4′	2°26·6′W	W	118
Crow Burn	Scot Bord	NT2911	55°23·5′	3°6·8′W	W	79
Crow Burn	S Lanak	NS9601	55°17·8′	3°37·8′W	W	78
Crow Chin	Derby	SK2285	53°21·9′	1°39·8′W	X	110
Crowcombe	Somer	ST1336	51°7·2′	3°14·2′W	T	181
Crowcombe Court	Somer	ST1336	51°7·2′	3°14·2′W	X	181
Crowcombe Heathfield	Somer	ST1334	51°6·2′	3°14·2′W	X	181
Crowcombe Park	Somer	ST1437	51°7·8′	3°13·4′W	X	181
Crowcombe Park Gate	Somer	ST1537	51°7·8′	3°12·5′W	X	181
Crow Corner	Essex	TQ9993	51°36·3′	0°52·8′E	X	178
Crow Crags	Northum	NY7971	55°2·2′	2°19·3′W	X	86,87
Crow Craigies	Angus	NO2279	56°54·0′	3°16·4′W	H	44
Crowcroft	Worcs	SO7650	52°9·1′	2°20·7′W	T	150
Crowcroft Bank	Leeds	SE4147	53°55·3′	1°22·1′W	F	105
Crowcrofts	Staffs	SJ8940	52°57·7′	2°9·4′W	X	118
Crow Cwm	Pemb	SM8623	51°52·1′	5°6·1′W	W	157
Crowdecote	Derby	SK1065	53°11·2′	1°50·6′W	T	119
Crowden	Derby	SK0799	53°29·5′	1°53·3′W	T	110
Crowden	Devon	SX4999	50°46·5′	4°8·1′W	T	191
Crowden Brook	Derby	SK1086	53°22·5′	1°50·6′W	W	110
Crowden Great Brook	Derby	SE0601	53°30·6′	1°54·2′W	W	110
Crowden Head	Derby	SK0988	53°23·6′	1°51·5′W	X	110
Crowden Hill	Northum	NZ2391	55°13·0′	1°37·9′W	X	81
Crowden Little Brook	Derby	SE0702	53°31·1′	1°53·3′W	W	110
Crowden Little Moor	Derby	SE0701	53°30·6′	1°53·3′W	X	110
Crowden Meadows	Derby	SE0702	53°31·1′	1°53·3′W	X	110
Crowden Tower	Derby	SK0987	53°23·0′	1°51·5′W	X	110
Crowder Park	Devon	SX7059	50°25·2′	3°49·4′W	T	202
Crowdhill	Hants	SU4920	50°58·9′	1°17·7′W	T	185
Crowdhole	Devon	SS8117	50°56·6′	3°41·3′W	X	181
Crowdieknowe	D & G	NY2580	55°6·8′	3°10·1′W	X	79
Crowdieknowe Hill	D & G	NY2681	55°7·3′	3°9·2′W	H	79
Crowdleham	Kent	TQ5658	51°18·2′	0°14·7′E	T	188
Crowdon	N Yks	SE9997	54°21·8′	0°28·2′W	T	94,101
Crow Down	W Berks	SU3382	51°32·4′	1°31·1′W	X	174
Crowdown Clump	Wilts	SU2157	51°18·9′	1°41·5′W	F	174
Crow Down Springs	Wilts	ST8386	51°34·6′	2°14·3′W	W	173
Crowdundle Beck	Cumbr	NY6531	54°40·6′	2°32·1′W	W	91
Crowdy Hall Fm	N Yks	NZ8909	54°28·4′	0°37·2′W	FM	94
Crowdy Reservoir	Corn	SX1483	50°37·3′	4°37·4′W	W	200
Crow Edge	Barns	SE1804	53°32·2′	1°43·3′W	T	110
Crowe Hall	Norf	TF9013	52°41·1′	0°49·1′E	X	132
Crowe Hall	Suff	TM1534	51°58·0′	1°8·2′E	X	169
Crowell	Oxon	SU7499	51°41·3′	0°55·4′W	T	165
Crowell Fm	W Susx	TQ0819	50°57·8′	0°27·3′W	FM	197
Crowell Hill	Oxon	SU7598	51°40·8′	0°54·5′W	T	165
Crowellhill Fm	Oxon	SU7598	51°40·8′	0°54·5′W	FM	165
Crowellhill Wood	Oxon	SU7598	51°40·8′	0°54·5′W	F	165
Crowell Wood	Oxon	SU7697	51°40·2′	0°53·7′W	F	165
Crowels Ash	Heref	SO6252	52°10·1′	2°32·9′W	X	149
Crowfield	Glos	SO7130	51°58·3′	2°24·9′W	X	149
Crowfield	Monm	SO3216	51°50·5′	2°58·8′W	X	161
Crowfield	Northnts	SP6141	52°4·1′	1°6·2′W	T	152
Crowfield	Suff	TM1457	52°10·4′	1°8·2′E	T	156
Crowfield Fm	Beds	TL0166	52°17·2′	0°30·8′W	FM	153
Crowfield Hall	Suff	TM1357	52°10·4′	1°7·3′E	X	156
Crowfootbank	Scot Bord	NT8248	55°43·8′	2°16·8′W	X	74
Crowfoot's Fm	Suff	TM4484	52°24·2′	1°35·6′E	FM	156
Crowgate Street	Norf	TG3021	52°44·5′	1°24·9′E	T	133,134
Crowgey Fm	Corn	SW7116	50°0·2′	5°11·4′W	FM	203
Crowgey Fm	Corn	SW7130	50°7·8′	5°11·9′W	FM	203
Crowgreaves	Shrops	SO7499	52°35·5′	2°22·6′W	T	138
Crow Green	Essex	TQ5896	51°38·7′	0°17·4′E	T	167,177
Crow Green	Norf	TM2090	52°28·0′	1°14·7′E	F	134
Crowgutter	Staffs	SK0350	53°3·1′	1°56·9′W	X	119
Crow Hall	Lancs	SD5135	53°48·8′	2°44·2′W	X	102
Crow Hall	Lincs	TF2039	52°56·3′	0°12·5′W	X	131
Crowhall	Moray	NH9859	57°36·8′	3°42·0′W	X	27
Crow Hall	Norf	TF8418	52°43·9′	0°43·9′E	X	132
Crow Hall	Norf	TG1422	52°45·4′	1°10·7′E	X	133
Crow Hall	Northum	NZ7964	54°58·5′	2°19·3′W	X	86,87
Crow Hall	Suff	TM0750	52°6·8′	1°1·8′E	X	155
Crow Hall Fm	Cambs	TL5976	52°21·8′	0°20·5′E	FM	143
Crowhall Fm	Cambs	TL6068	52°17·4′	0°21·2′E	FM	154
Crow Hall Fm	Norf	TF8140	52°55·8′	0°42·0′E	FM	132
Crow Hall Fm	N Tyne	NZ3274	55°3·8′	1°29·5′W	FM	88
Crowham Manor	E Susx	TQ8117	50°55·7′	0°34·9′E	X	199
Crow Hill	Cald	SE0122	53°41·9′	1°58·7′W	X	104
Crow Hill	Cumbr	NY7013	54°30·9′	2°27·4′W	X	91
Crowhill	Derby	SK0078	53°18·2′	1°59·6′W	X	119
Crow Hill	Dorset	SY5987	50°41·1′	2°34·4′W	X	194
Crowhill	E Loth	NT7374	55°57·7′	2°25·5′W	X	67
Crowhill	E Renf	NS4951	55°44·0′	4°23·9′W	X	64
Crow Hill	Hants	SU1703	50°49·8′	1°45·1′W	X	195
Crow Hill	Heref	SO6326	51°56·1′	2°31·9′W	T	162
Crow Hill	Lancs	SD9536	53°49·5′	2°4·1′W	X	103
Crowhill	Mil Key	SP8237	52°1·8′	0°47·9′W	T	152
Crow Hill	Norf	TM2893	52°29·5′	1°21·9′E	X	134
Crow Hill	Northnts	SP9571	52°20·0′	0°35·9′W	X	141,153
Crow Hill	Notts	SK6328	52°51·0′	1°3·5′W	X	129
Crow Hill	N Yks	SE1296	54°21·8′	1°48·5′W	X	99
Crow Hill	Pemb	SM9417	51°49·1′	4°58·9′W	X	157,158
Crowhill	Tames	SJ9299	53°29·5′	2°6·8′W	T	109
Crow Hill	V of Glam	ST1271	51°26·1′	3°15·6′W	X	171
Crowhill Fm	Beds	TL0758	52°12·8′	0°25·6′W	FM	153
Crow Hill Fm	Beds	TL0855	52°11·2′	0°24·8′W	FM	153
Crowhill Fm	Notts	SK5047	53°1·3′	1°14·9′W	FM	129
Crowhill Fm	S Lanak	NS8334	55°35·4′	3°51·0′W	FM	71,72
Crow Hill Nook	Cald	SE0127	53°44·6′	1°58·7′W	X	104
Crowhillock	Aberd	NJ7660	57°38·0′	2°23·7′W	X	29
Crowhillock	Aberd	NO8574	56°51·7′	2°14·3′W	X	45
Crow Hill Top	Hants	SU1803	50°49·8′	1°44·3′W	X	195
Crow Ho	N Yks	SE3463	54°4·0′	1°28·4′W	X	99
Crowhole	Derby	SK3375	53°16·5′	1°29·9′W	T	119
Crowhole Bottom	Oxon	SU3584	51°33·5′	1°29·3′W	X	174
Crowhole Resr	Derby	SK3274	53°16·0′	1°30·8′W	W	119
Crowholt	Ches	SJ9067	53°12·2′	2°8·6′W	X	118
Crow Holt	Lincs	TF2195	53°26·5′	0°10·3′W	X	113
Crow Holt	Notts	SK7579	53°18·4′	0°52·1′W	F	120
Crowholt Fm	Halton	SJ6080	53°19·2′	2°35·6′W	FM	109
Crow How	Cumbr	NY3605	54°26·4′	2°58·8′W	X	90
Crowhow End	Cumbr	NY2200	54°23·6′	3°11·7′W	X	89,90
Crowhurst	E Susx	TQ7512	50°53·1′	0°29·7′E	T	199
Crowhurst	Kent	TQ5863	51°20·9′	0°16·5′E	X	177,188
Crowhurst	Surrey	TQ3947	51°12·5′	0°0·2′W	T	187
Crowhurst Bridge Fm	E Susx	TQ6826	51°0·8′	0°24·1′E	FM	188,199
Crowhurst Fm	E Susx	TQ7219	50°56·9′	0°27·3′E	FM	199
Crowhurst Fm	Kent	TQ6055	51°16·5′	0°18·0′E	FM	188
Crowhurst Fm	Kent	TQ6550	51°13·7′	0°22·2′E	FM	188
Crowhurst Ho	Kent	TQ6534	51°5·1′	0°21·7′E	X	188
Crowhurst Lane End	Surrey	TQ3748	51°13·1′	0°1·9′W	T	187
Crowhurst Park	E Susx	TQ7713	50°53·6′	0°31·4′E	X	199
Crowhurst Place	Surrey	TQ3846	51°12·0′	0°1·1′W	A	187
Crowhurst Wood	E Susx	TQ7319	50°56·9′	0°28·2′E	F	199
Crow Hyrne Fm	Norf	TL8198	52°33·2′	0°40·6′E	FM	144
Crow Island	I Scilly	SV8614	49°56·9′	6°22·3′W	X	203
Crow Knowes	D & G	NS7616	55°25·6′	3°57·1′W	X	71,78
Crowland	Lincs	TF2410	52°40·6′	0°9·5′W	T	131,142
Crowland Common	Lincs	TF2212	52°41·7′	0°11·3′W	X	131,142
Crowland Falls	Lincs	TF2413	52°42·3′	0°9·5′W	X	131,142
Crowland Fm	Lincs	SK9845	52°59·8′	0°32·0′W	FM	130
Crowland Fodder Lots	Lincs	TF2312	52°41·7′	0°10·4′W	X	131,142
Crowland High Wash	Lincs	TF2209	52°40·1′	0°11·3′W	X	142
Crow Lane Fm	Lincs	TF1642	52°58·0′	0°16·0′W	FM	130
Crowlas	Corn	SW5133	50°8·9′	5°28·8′W	T	203
Crowle	N Lincs	SE7712	53°36·2′	0°49·8′W	T	112
Crowle	Worcs	SO9256	52°12·4′	2°6·6′W	T	150
Crow Leasow Fm	Shrops	SO5478	52°24·1′	2°40·2′W	FM	137,138
Crowle Common	N Lincs	SE7613	53°36·7′	0°50·7′W	X	112
Crowle Grange	N Lincs	SE7912	53°36·2′	0°48·0′W	X	112
Crowle Green	Worcs	SO9156	52°12·4′	2°7·5′W	T	150
Crowle Hill	N Lincs	SE7713	53°36·7′	0°49·8′W	T	112
Crowle Moors or Waste	N Lincs	SE7515	53°37·8′	0°51·5′W	X	112
Crowle Park	N Lincs	SE7712	53°36·2′	0°49·8′W	T	112
Crowle Sta	N Lincs	SE7811	53°35·6′	0°48·9′W	X	112
Crowle Waste or Moors	N Lincs	SE7515	53°37·8′	0°51·5′W	X	112
Crowley Grange	Ches	SJ6681	53°19·7′	2°30·2′W	X	109
Crowley Hall	Ches	SJ6782	53°20·3′	2°29·3′W	X	109
Crowley Lodge	Ches	SJ6680	53°19·2′	2°30·2′W	X	109
Crowlin Islands	Highld	NG6934	57°20·5′	5°49·9′W	X	24,32
Crowlink	E Susx	TV5497	50°45·4′	0°11·4′E	X	199
Crowlista	N Eil	NB0433	58°11·5′	7°1·8′W	T	13
Crowmallie Ho	Aberd	NJ7025	57°19·1′	2°29·4′W	X	38
Crowmarsh Battle Fm	Oxon	SU6190	51°36·6′	1°6·8′W	FM	164,175
Crowmarsh Fm	Lincs	TF3828	52°50·1′	0°3·3′E	FM	131
Crowmarsh Fm	Oxon	SP5524	51°54·9′	1°11·6′W	FM	164
Crowmarsh Gifford	Oxon	SU6189	51°36·0′	1°6·8′W	T	175
Crowmarsh Hill	Oxon	SU6288	51°35·5′	1°5·9′W	X	175
Crowmere	Cambs	TF4502	52°36·0′	0°8·9′E	X	143
Crowmoor	Heref	SO4644	52°5·7′	2°46·9′W	X	148,149,161
Crow Moss	W Loth	NT0857	55°48·1′	3°27·6′W	X	65,72
Crown	Highld	NH6745	57°28·8′	4°12·6′W	T	26
Crownall Fm	Cambs	TL5865	52°15·9′	0°19·3′E	FM	154
Crown Corner	Suff	TM2570	52°17·1′	1°18·5′E	T	156
Crown Cottages	Brackn	SU9067	51°23·9′	0°42·0′W	X	175
Crowndale	Devon	SX4772	50°31·9′	4°9·2′W	X	191,201
Crown East	Worcs	SO8154	52°11·3′	2°16·3′W	T	150
Crownend Wood	Notts	SK5228	52°51·1′	1°13·3′W	F	129
Crowner Fields Fm	Warw	SP4082	52°26·3′	1°24·3′W	FM	140
Crowness	Aberd	NJ7313	57°12·7′	2°26·4′W	X	38
Crow Ness	Orkney	HY4412	58°59·8′	2°58·0′W	X	6
Crow Nest	Brad	SE1139	53°51·1′	1°49·6′W	T	104
Crow Nest	N Yks	SE5491	54°18·9′	1°9·8′W	X	100
Crownfield	Bucks	SU8099	51°41·3′	0°50·2′W	T	165
Crown Fm	Beds	SP9550	52°8·6′	0°36·3′W	FM	153
Crown Fm	Cambs	TL1162	52°14·9′	0°22·0′W	FM	153
Crown Fm	Ches	SJ6978	53°18·1′	2°27·5′W	FM	118
Crown Fm	E Yorks	TA0839	53°50·4′	0°21·1′W	FM	107
Crown Fm	E Yorks	TA2518	53°38·8′	0°6·1′W	FM	113
Crown Fm	Hants	SU3130	51°4·3′	1°33·1′W	FM	185
Crown Fm	Lincs	TF1210	52°40·8′	0°20·2′W	FM	130,142
Crown Fm	Lincs	TF1256	53°5·6′	0°19·2′W	FM	121
Crown Fm	Lincs	TF3028	52°50·3′	0°3·8′W	FM	131
Crown Fm	Lincs	TF5060	53°7·2′	0°14·9′E	FM	122
Crown Fm	Norf	TF5505	52°37·5′	0°17·8′E	FM	143
Crown Fm	Norf	TG0400	52°33·8′	1°1·0′E	FM	144
Crown Fm	Suff	TM4562	52°12·3′	1°35·6′E	FM	156
Crown Gorse	Scot Bord	NT7941	55°40·0′	2°19·6′W	F	74
Crown Hall Fm	Lincs	TF2122	52°47·2′	0°11·9′W	FM	131
Crown Hall Fm	Lincs	TF3017	52°44·3′	0°4·1′W	FM	131
Crownhead	Aberd	NJ8321	57°17·0′	2°16·5′W	X	38
Crownhill	C of Plym	SX4858	50°24·4′	4°8·0′W	T	201
Crown Hill	Leic	SK7514	52°43·3′	0°53·0′W	X	129
Crown Hill	Warw	SP3462	52°15·5′	1°29·7′W	X	151
Crownhill Down	Devon	SX5660	50°25·6′	4°1·3′W	X	202
Crown Hills	C of Leic	SK6204	52°38·0′	1°4·6′W	T	140
Crown Ho	Norf	TL9998	52°32·8′	0°56·5′E	X	144
Crown Ho	Shrops	SJ2532	52°53·1′	3°6·5′W	X	126
Crownick	Corn	SW8037	50°11·8′	5°4·6′W	X	204
Crowniehillock	Aberd	NJ9242	57°28·3′	2°7·5′W	X	30
Crown Inn (PH)	Cumbr	NY4046	54°48·6′	2°55·6′W	X	85
Crownland	Suff	TM0170	52°17·7′	0°57·3′E	T	144,155
Crownlane Fm	Ches	SJ7473	53°15·4′	2°23·0′W	FM	118
Crown of Scotland	Scot Bord	NT0815	55°25·5′	3°26·8′W	H	78
Crown Park Fm	Essex	TQ4994	51°37·7′	0°9·6′E	FM	167,177
Crownpits	Surrey	SU9743	51°10·8′	0°36·3′W	T	186
Crown Plantn	Scot Bord	NT5910	55°23·2′	2°38·4′W	F	80
Crown Point	Cumbr	NY4137	54°43·7′	2°54·5′W	X	90
Crownpoint	Staffs	SJ9652	53°4·2′	2°3·2′W	X	118
Crown Point Fm	Leic	SK8919	52°45·9′	0°40·5′W	FM	130
Crown Point Ho	Lancs	SD8329	53°45·7′	2°15·1′W	X	103
Crowns, The	Corn	SW3633	50°8·5′	5°41·3′W	X	203
Crownthorpe	Norf	TG0803	52°35·3′	1°4·6′E	T	144
Crowntown	Corn	SW6330	50°7·6′	5°18·6′W	T	203
Crown Wood	Brackn	SU8767	51°23·9′	0°44·6′W	T	175
Crown Wood	Brom	TQ4965	51°22·1′	0°8·8′E	F	177
Crown Wood	E Loth	NT5369	55°55·0′	2°44·7′W	F	66
Crowood Fm	Wilts	SU2873	51°27·5′	1°35·4′W	FM	174
Crowood Ho	Wilts	SU2873	51°27·5′	1°35·4′W	X	174
Crow or Enag Hillock	Highld	ND3464	58°33·8′	3°7·6′W	X	12
Crow Park	Lancs	SD8349	53°56·5′	2°15·1′W	X	103
Crow Park	Notts	SK6772	53°14·7′	0°59·3′W	F	120
Crow Park Fm	Notts	SK7766	53°11·4′	0°50·4′W	FM	120
Crow Plump	N Yks	SE1594	54°20·7′	1°45·7′W	F	99
Crow Point	Devon	SS4631	51°3·7′	4°11·5′W	X	180
Crow Point	I Scilly	SV8913	49°56·4′	6°19·7′W	X	203
Crowpound	Corn	SX1767	50°28·7′	4°34·4′W	A	201

Crowrar	Orkney	HY3922	59°5·1′	3°3·4′W	X	6
Crowrigg Sike	Cumbr	NY6471	55°2·2′	2°33·4′W	W	86
Crow Rock	Devon	SS4531	51°3·7′	4°12·3′W	X	180
Crow Rock	I Scilly	SV9013	49°56·4′	6°18·9′W	X	203
Crow Rock	Pemb	SR8894	51°36·5′	5°3·3′W	X	158
Crows-an-wra	Corn	SW3927	50°5·4′	5°38·6′W	T	203
Crow's Br	Lincs	TF4859	53°6·7′	0°13·1′E	X	122
Crow's Castle	Oxon	SP2315	51°50·2′	1°39·6′W	X	163
Crowsdale Wood	N Yks	SE9475	54°10·0′	0°33·2′W	F	101
Crow's Fm	Essex	TL8141	52°2·5′	0°38·8′E	FM	155
Crow's Green	Essex	TL6925	51°54·1′	0°27·8′E	T	167
Crows Hall	Suff	TM1962	52°13·0′	1°12·8′E	X	156
Crowshall Barn Fm	S Glos	ST7683	51°33·0′	2°20·4′W	FM	172
Crows Hall Fm	W Susx	SU8311	50°53·8′	0°48·8′W	FM	197
Crowshaw Fm	Bolton	SD6011	53°35·9′	2°35·9′W	FM	109
Crowshaw Ho	Lancs	SD6639	53°51·0′	2°30·6′W	X	103
Crowsheath Fm	Essex	TQ7197	51°39·0′	0°28·7′E	FM	167
Crowshill	Norf	TF9406	52°37·3′	0°52·4′E	T	144
Crows Hole Fm	Kent	TQ9550	51°13·2′	0°47·9′E	FM	189
Crowshole Fm	W Susx	SU8422	50°59·7′	0°47·8′W	FM	197
Crowshott	Hants	SU4360	51°20·5′	1°22·6′W	X	174
Crowshouse Moor	Durham	NZ3740	54°45·5′	1°25·1′W	X	88
Crowsley	Oxon	SU7279	51°30·5′	0°57·4′W	T	175
Crowsley Park	Oxon	SU7280	51°31·1′	0°57·3′W	X	175
Crow's Meadow	Norf	TL9395	52°31·3′	0°51·1′E	F	144
Crowsmoor	Shrops	SO4082	52°26·2′	2°52·6′W	X	137
Crow's Nest	Aberd	NO6897	57°4·0′	2°31·2′W	X	38,45
Crow's Nest	Conwy	SH7676	53°16·2′	3°51·2′W	X	115
Crow's Nest	Corn	SX2669	50°29·9′	4°26·8′W	T	201
Crowsnest	Devon	SX3791	50°42·0′	4°18·1′W	X	190
Crow's Nest	D & G	NX2053	54°50·6′	4°47·8′W	X	82
Crow's Nest	Halton	SJ5782	53°20·2′	2°38·3′W	X	108
Crow's Nest	N Yks	TA0883	54°14·1′	0°20·2′W	X	101
Crowsnest	Shrops	SJ3601	52°36·4′	2°56·3′W	T	126
Crow's Nest Bottom	Hants	SU2416	50°56·8′	1°39·1′W	X	184
Crowsnest Dingle	Shrops	SJ3701	52°36·4′	2°55·4′W	F	126
Crow's Nest Fm	Cambs	TL2961	52°14·2′	0°6·3′W	FM	153
Crowsnest Fm	Ches	SJ6683	53°20·8′	2°30·2′W	FM	109
Crow's Nest Fm	Northnts	TL0679	52°24·2′	0°26·1′W	FM	142
Crow's Nest Fm	St Hel	SJ5390	53°24·5′	2°42·0′W	FM	108
Crow's Nest Hill	Cambs	TL0474	52°21·5′	0°28·0′W	X	141
Crow Sound	I Scilly	SV9213	49°56·5′	6°17·2′W	W	203
Crow Stone	Northum	NT8701	55°18·4′	2°11·9′W	X	80
Crow Stone	Sou-on-Sea	TQ8585	51°32·2′	0°40·5′E	X	178
Crow Stones	E Loth	NT6165	55°52·8′	2°37·0′W	A	67
Crow Stones Edge	Sheff	SK1796	53°27·9′	1°44·2′W	X	110
Crow Taing	Orkney	HY4601	58°53·8′	2°55·7′W	X	6,7
Crow Taing	Orkney	HY7446	59°18·2′	2°26·9′W	X	5
Crowtaing	Orkney	ND3490	58°47·8′	3°8·0′W	X	7
Crowther Hall	Powys	SJ2512	52°42·3′	3°6·2′W	X	126
Crowther's Coppice	Powys	SJ2411	52°41·7′	3°7·1′W	F	126
Crowther's Pool	Powys	SO2148	52°7·7′	3°8·9′W	T	148
Crowthorne	Wok	SU8464	51°22·4′	0°47·2′W	T	175,186
Crowthorne Wood	Brackn	SU8565	51°22·9′	0°46·3′W	F	175
Crowthorn School	Black w Dar	SD7418	53°39·7′	2°23·2′W	X	109
Crowton	Ches	SJ5774	53°15·9′	2°38·3′W	T	117
Crow Tor	Devon	SX6078	50°35·3′	3°58·3′W	X	191
Crow Tree	Donc	SE7109	53°34·6′	0°55·2′W	X	112
Crow Tree Fm	Cambs	TL2492	52°30·9′	0°10·0′W	FM	142
Crowtree Fm	Lincs	TF2829	52°50·8′	0°5·6′W	FM	131
Crowtree Fm	N Yks	SE3991	54°19·0′	1°23·6′W	FM	99
Crowtree Fm	Peterb	TF2106	52°38·5′	0°12·3′W	FM	142
Crowtree Fm	Peterb	TF2901	52°35·7′	0°5·3′W	FM	142
Crowtree Ho	N Yks	SE4676	54°10·9′	1°17·3′W	X	100
Crow Trees	Cumbr	SD5476	54°10·9′	2°41·9′W	X	97
Crowtrees	Derby	SK2337	52°56·0′	1°39·1′W	X	128
Crowtrees	Derby	SK2346	53°0·9′	1°39·0′W	X	119,128
Crow Trees	Lancs	SD8640	53°51·6′	2°12·4′W	X	103
Crow Trees	N Yks	SD9297	54°22·4′	2°7·0′W	X	98
Crow Trees	N Yks	SE2257	54°0·8′	1°39·4′W	X	104
Crowtrees	Staffs	SK0445	53°0·4′	1°56·0′W	X	119,128
Crowtrees	Staffs	SK0750	53°3·1′	1°53·3′W	X	119
Crowtrees Fm	Derby	SK3250	53°3·0′	1°31·0′W	FM	119
Crow Trees Fm	Lancs	SD5643	53°53·1′	2°39·8′W	FM	102
Crow Trees Fm	Lancs	SD6041	53°52·1′	2°36·1′W	FM	102,103
Crow Trees Fm	Notts	SK4756	53°6·2′	1°17·5′W	FM	120
Crow Trees Fms	Black w Dar	SD6523	53°42·4′	2°31·4′W	FM	102,103
Crow Trees (PH)	N Yks	SD7855	53°59·7′	2°19·7′W	X	103
Crowville	I of M	SC4791	54°17·8′	4°20·6′W	X	95
Crow Well	N Yks	SE1452	53°58·1′	1°46·8′W	X	104
Crow Wood	Aberd	NJ5342	57°28·2′	2°46·6′W	F	29
Crow Wood	Aberd	NJ6951	57°33·1′	2°30·6′W	F	29
Crow Wood	Donc	SK6797	53°28·2′	0°59·0′W	F	111
Crow Wood	E Yorks	SE9365	54°4·6′	0°34·3′W	F	101
Crow Wood	Halton	SJ5286	53°22·4′	2°42·9′W	T	108
Crow Wood	N Yks	SE3276	54°11·0′	1°30·2′W	F	99
Crow Wood	N Yks	SE5589	54°17·9′	1°8·9′W	F	100
Crow Wood	N Yks	SE8164	54°4·2′	0°45·3′W	F	100
Crow Wood	Powys	SO2492	52°31·5′	3°6·8′W	X	137
Crow Wood Fm	N Yks	NZ5608	54°28·1′	1°7·7′W	FM	93
Crow Wood Hill	Notts	SK5427	52°50·5′	1°11·5′W	X	129
Crow Wood Houses Fm	Lancs	SD8333	53°47·8′	2°15·1′W	FM	103
Croxall	Staffs	SK1913	52°43·1′	1°42·7′W	T	128
Croxby	Lincs	TF1998	53°28·2′	0°12·0′W	T	113
Croxby Pond Plantation	Lincs	TF1999	53°28·7′	0°12·0′W	F	113
Croxby Top	Lincs	TF1698	53°28·2′	0°14·7′W	T	113
Croxdale	Durham	NZ2636	54°43·3′	1°35·4′W	T	93
Croxdale Hall	Durham	NZ2737	54°43·9′	1°34·4′W	X	93
Croxdale Wood Ho	Durham	NZ2738	54°44·4′	1°34·4′W	X	93
Croxden	Staffs	SK0639	52°57·1′	1°54·2′W	T	128
Croxfield Spinney	Leic	SP7294	52°32·6′	0°55·9′W	F	141
Croxley Green	Herts	TQ0696	51°39·4′	0°27·7′W	X	166,176
Croxley Green	Herts	TQ0795	51°38·8′	0°26·8′W	T	166,176
Croxteth	Liv	SJ4096	53°27·7′	2°53·8′W	T	108
Croxteth Country Park	Liv	SJ4094	53°26·6′	2°53·8′W	X	108
Croxton	Cambs	TL2459	52°13·1′	0°10·7′W	T	153
Croxton	N Lincs	TA0912	53°35·8′	0°20·8′W	T	112
Croxton	Norf	TF9831	52°50·6′	0°56·8′E	T	132
Croxton	Norf	TL8786	52°26·6′	0°45·5′E	T	144
Croxton	Staffs	SJ7831	52°52·8′	2°19·2′W	T	127
Croxton	Wrex	SJ4541	52°58·1′	2°48·7′W	X	117
Croxtonbank	Staffs	SJ7832	52°53·3′	2°19·2′W	T	127
Croxton Banks	Leic	SK8330	52°51·9′	0°45·6′W	F	130
Croxton Green	Ches	SJ5452	53°4·0′	2°40·8′W	T	117
Croxton Hall Fm	Ches	SJ6967	53°12·2′	2°27·4′W	FM	118
Croxton Heath	Norf	TL8690	52°28·8′	0°44·7′E	F	144
Croxton Heath	Norf	TL8988	52°27·7′	0°47·3′E	F	144
Croxton Kerrial	Leic	SK8329	52°51·4′	0°45·6′W	T	130
Croxton Lodge	Leic	SK8129	52°51·4′	0°47·4′W	X	130
Croxton Park	Cambs	TL2559	52°13·1′	0°9·8′W	X	153
Croxton Park	Leic	SK8127	52°50·3′	0°47·4′W	X	130
Croxton Park	Norf	TL8588	52°27·7′	0°43·8′E	X	144
Croy	Arg & Bt	NS2585	56°1·8′	4°48·1′W	X	56
Croy	Highld	NH7949	57°31·2′	4°0·8′W	T	27
Croy	Moray	NJ1657	57°36·0′	3°23·9′W	X	28
Croy	N Lanak	NS7275	55°57·3′	4°2·6′W	T	64
Croy Brae (Electric Brae)	S Ayr	NS2513	55°23·0′	4°45·3′W	X	70
Croy Cunningham	Stir	NS5085	56°2·3′	4°24·0′W	X	57
Croyde	Devon	SS4439	51°8·0′	4°13·4′W	T	180
Croyde Bay	Devon	SS4239	51°7·9′	4°15·1′W	W	180
Croyde Bay	Devon	SS4339	51°8·0′	4°14·3′W	T	180
Croyde Hoe	Devon	SS4240	51°8·5′	4°15·1′W	X	180
Croydon	Cambs	TL3149	52°7·7′	0°4·8′W	T	153
Croydon	Croy	TQ3365	51°22·3′	0°5·0′W	T	176,177
Croydon Fm	Cambs	TL2947	52°6·6′	0°6·6′W	FM	153
Croydon Hall School	Somer	ST0138	51°8·2′	3°24·5′W	X	181
Croydon Hill	Cambs	TL3049	52°7·7′	0°5·7′W	X	153
Croydon Hill	Somer	SS9740	51°9·2′	3°28·0′W	H	181
Croydon Hill Fm	Cambs	TL3049	52°7·7′	0°5·7′W	FM	153
Croydon Ho	Somer	SS9640	51°9·2′	3°28·8′W	X	181
Croydon House Fm	Cambs	TL3048	52°7·1′	0°5·7′W	FM	153
Croygorston	Highld	NH7645	57°29·0′	4°3·6′W	X	27
Croy Hill	N Lanak	NS7376	55°57·9′	4°1·6′W	X	64
Croy Hill (Roman Fort)	N Lanak	NS7376	55°57·9′	4°1·6′W	R	64
Croy Ho	S Ayr	NS2412	55°22·5′	4°46·2′W	X	70
Croyle Ho	Devon	ST0609	50°52·6′	3°19·8′W	X	192
Croylet	Moray	NJ5056	57°35·7′	2°49·7′W	X	29
Croys	D & G	NX7767	54°59·2′	3°54·9′W	X	84
Crozen	Heref	SO5748	52°8·0′	2°37·3′W	T	149
Cruach	Arg & Bt	NN3316	56°18·7′	4°41·5′W	H	50,56
Cruach	Arg & Bt	NR3258	55°44·7′	6°15·8′W	X	60
Cruach a' Bhàillidh	Arg & Bt	NR7564	55°49·3′	5°35·1′W	X	62
Cruach a' Bhearraiche	Arg & Bt	NM9201	56°9·6′	5°20·5′W	H	55
Cruach a' Bhuic	Arg & Bt	NS1693	56°5·9′	4°57·1′W	H	56
Cruach Achadh na Craoibhe	Arg & Bt	NN0224	56°22·3′	5°11·9′W	H	50
Cruach Achaidh Ghlais	Arg & Bt	NR7954	55°44·0′	5°30·8′W	H	62
Cruach a' Chaise	Arg & Bt	NS1891	56°4·9′	4°55·0′W	H	56
Cruach a'Cham Loch	Arg & Bt	NR8288	56°2·4′	5°29·5′W	H	55
Cruach a' Choire	Highld	NM6374	56°48·1′	5°52·5′W	X	40
Cruach a' Ghaill	Highld	NM7570	56°46·3′	5°40·5′W	H	40
Cruachain Sgorach	Arg & Bt	NM5628	56°23·1′	5°56·7′W	X	48
Cruach Airde	Arg & Bt	NR7363	55°48·7′	5°36·9′W	H	62
Cruach Airdeny	Arg & Bt	NM9927	56°23·8′	5°15·0′W	H	49
Cruach Airigh an Aon-bhuinn	Highld	NM7175	56°48·9′	5°44·7′W	H	40
Cruachan	Arg & Bt	NM2741	56°29·2′	6°25·6′W	H	46,47,48
Cruachan	Arg & Bt	NM9510	56°14·6′	5°18·1′W	X	55
Cruachan	Arg & Bt	NR6945	55°38·9′	5°39·8′W	X	62
Cruachan	N Eil	NF8014	57°6·6′	7°16·7′W	H	31
Cruachan	Stir	NN3507	56°13·9′	4°39·3′W	H	56
Cruach an Aonaich	Highld	NM7380	56°51·6′	5°43·0′W	H	40
Cruachan Beag	Arg & Bt	NM5733	56°25·9′	5°56·0′W	X	47,48
Cruachan Beinn a' Chearcaill	Highld	NG3546	57°25·9′	6°24·5′W	H	23
Cruachan Buidhe	Highld	NM6158	56°39·4′	5°53·5′W	X	49
Cruachan Ceann a' Ghairbh	Arg & Bt	NM4247	56°32·9′	6°11·4′W	X	47,48
Cruachan Chàrna Dailachreagain	Highld	NM6159	56°40·0′	5°53·6′W	H	49
Cruachan Cruinn	Stir	NN3224	56°23·0′	4°42·8′W	H	50
Cruachan Dearg	Arg & Bt	NM5633	56°25·8′	5°57·0′W	H	47,48
Cruachan Dhùghaill	Highld	NM7692	56°58·2′	5°40·7′W	H	33,40
Cruach an Draghair	Arg & Bt	NS1992	56°5·5′	4°54·1′W	H	56
Cruachan Druim na Croise	Arg & Bt	NM4549	56°34·1′	6°8·6′W	X	47,48
Cruach an Eachlaich	Arg & Bt	NM8606	56°12·2′	5°26·6′W	H	55
Cruach an Earbaige	Arg & Bt	NR8989	56°3·1′	5°22·9′W	H	55
Cruachan Eilgeach	Highld	NG8421	57°14·0′	5°34·3′W	X	33
Cruach an Fhearainn Duibh	Highld	NM7182	56°52·6′	5°45·0′W	H	40
Cruachan Forc Airgid	Arg & Bt	NR9889	56°3·3′	5°14·2′W	X	55
Cruachan-Glen Vic Askill	Highld	NG3546	57°25·9′	6°24·5′W	H	23
Cruach an Locha	Arg & Bt	NR7865	55°49·9′	5°32·3′W	H	62
Cruach an Lochain	Arg & Bt	NN0313	56°16·4′	5°10·5′W	H	50,55
Cruach an Lochain	Arg & Bt	NS0493	56°5·6′	5°8·6′W	H	56
Cruachan Loch Tràth	Arg & Bt	NM4345	56°31·9′	6°10·3′W	H	47,48
Cruachan Meadhon	Highld	NG8522	57°14·6′	5°33·3′W	X	33
Cruachan Min	Arg & Bt	NM4421	56°19·0′	6°7·9′W	H	48
Cruach an Nid	Arg & Bt	NM8514	56°16·4′	5°27·9′W	H	55
Cruachan Odhar	Arg & Bt	NM3846	56°32·2′	6°15·3′W	H	47,48
Cruachan Reservoir	Arg & Bt	NN0828	56°24·6′	5°6·3′W	W	50
Cruach an Sgalaig	Arg & Bt	NR9576	55°56·3′	5°16·5′W	X	62
Cruach an Tailleir	Arg & Bt	NR7469	55°51·9′	5°36·3′W	H	62
Cruach an t-Aon Bhlair	Highld	NM7270	56°46·2′	5°43·4′W	H	40
Cruachan Treshnish	Arg & Bt	NM3447	56°32·6′	6°19·2′W	H	47,48
Cruach an t-Seallaidh	Arg & Bt	NR7764	55°49·3′	5°33·2′W	H	62
Cruach an t-Sidhein	Arg & Bt	NS2796	56°7·8′	4°46·6′W	H	56
Cruach an t-Sorchain	Arg & Bt	NR8765	55°50·1′	5°23·7′W	X	62
Cruach an Uillt Fheàrna	Arg & Bt	NR6290	56°2·9′	5°48·9′W	H	61
Cruach a' Phubuill	Arg & Bt	NR8276	55°55·9′	5°29·0′W	H	62
Cruach Ardrain	Stir	NN4021	56°21·5′	4°34·9′W	H	51,56
Cruach Ardura	Arg & Bt	NM6829	56°24·0′	5°45·1′W	H	49
Cruach Bhiorach	Arg & Bt	NR8361	55°47·9′	5°27·3′W	X	62
Cruach Bhreac	Arg & Bt	NR7550	55°41·7′	5°34·4′W	X	62,69
Cruach Bhreac	Arg & Bt	NR8253	55°43·5′	5°27·9′W	H	62
Cruach Bhreac	Arg & Bt	NR8864	55°49·6′	5°22·6′W	X	62
Cruach Bhreac	Arg & Bt	NR9788	56°2·8′	5°15·1′W	H	55
Cruach Bhreac	Highld	NM6665	56°43·3′	5°49·0′W	H	40
Cruach Bhrochdadail	Highld	NM7176	56°49·4′	5°44·7′W	X	40
Cruach Bhuidhe	Arg & Bt	NS1295	56°6·9′	5°1·0′W	X	56
Cruach Bhuidhe	Highld	NM6374	56°48·1′	5°52·5′W	H	40
Cruach Bhuidhe	Highld	NM8487	56°55·7′	5°32·5′W	H	40
Cruach Breacain	Arg & Bt	NR8186	56°1·3′	5°30·4′W	H	55
Cruach Breac-liath	Arg & Bt	NR9098	56°8·0′	5°22·3′W	H	55
Cruach Brenfield	Arg & Bt	NR8283	55°59·7′	5°29·3′W	H	55
Cruach Camuillt	Arg & Bt	NR9881	55°59·0′	5°13·8′W	X	55
Cruach Chaorainn	Arg & Bt	NR8371	55°53·3′	5°27·8′W	H	62
Cruach Chaorainn	Arg & Bt	NR8556	55°45·2′	5°25·1′W	X	62
Cruach Chaorainn Beaga	Arg & Bt	NR8168	55°51·6′	5°29·5′W	H	62
Cruach Choireadail	Arg & Bt	NM5930	56°24·3′	5°53·9′W	H	48
Cruach Chorrach	Arg & Bt	NR8067	55°51·0′	5°30·4′W	X	62
Cruach Chuilceachan	Arg & Bt	NR9887	56°2·3′	5°14·1′W	H	55
Cruach Clenamacrie	Arg & Bt	NM9329	56°24·7′	5°20·9′W	H	49
Cruach Conchra	Arg & Bt	NS0387	56°2·4′	5°9·3′W	X	55
Cruach Corrach	Highld	NM7093	56°58·5′	5°46·6′W	X	33,40
Cruach Cruinn	Arg & Bt	NR8201	56°9·4′	5°30·2′W	H	55
Cruach Dhubh	Arg & Bt	NS3491	56°5·2′	4°39·6′W	H	56
Cruach Dhubh an Ruidhe Fheàrna	Highld	NM7788	56°56·0′	5°39·5′W	H	40
Cruach Dhubh na Leitreach	Highld	NM7588	56°56·0′	5°41·4′W	H	40
Cruach Doire Léithe	Arg & Bt	NR8863	55°49·1′	5°22·6′W	X	62
Cruach Doire nan Cuilean	Arg & Bt	NM5628	56°23·1′	5°56·7′W	H	48
Cruach Doire n Dòbhrain	Highld	NM6283	56°52·9′	5°53·9′W	H	40
Cruach Eachd	Arg & Bt	NN2132	56°27·0′	4°53·8′W	X	50
Cruach Eighrach	Arg & Bt	NS1792	56°5·4′	4°56·0′W	X	56
Cruach Fasgach	Arg & Bt	NS0293	56°5·6′	5°10·5′W	H	55
Cruach Fhiarach	Arg & Bt	NN2502	56°11·0′	4°48·7′W	X	56
Cruach Gar dhoire	Arg & Bt	NR8368	55°51·6′	5°27·6′W	X	62
Cruach Gharbhachaidh	Arg & Bt	NR8050	55°41·9′	5°29·6′W	X	62,69
Cruach Gille Bheagain	Arg & Bt	NR8271	55°53·2′	5°28·7′W	H	62
Cruach Inagairt	Arg & Bt	NM5623	56°20·4′	5°56·4′W	H	48
Cruach Innse	Highld	NN2776	56°50·9′	4°49·7′W	H	41
Cruach Ionnastail	Arg & Bt	NR6491	56°3·5′	5°47·0′W	H	55,61
Cruach Kames	Arg & Bt	NR9770	55°53·1′	5°14·3′W	H	62
Cruach Kilfinan	Arg & Bt	NR9578	55°57·3′	5°16·6′W	H	62
Cruach Lagain	Arg & Bt	NR7465	55°49·8′	5°36·1′W	H	62
Cruach Lagain	Arg & Bt	NR7865	55°49·9′	5°32·3′W	X	62
Cruach Lagain	Arg & Bt	NR8864	55°49·6′	5°22·6′W	X	62
Cruach Lerags	Arg & Bt	NM8325	56°22·3′	5°30·4′W	H	49
Cruach Lusach	Arg & Bt	NR7883	55°59·6′	5°33·1′W	H	55
Cruach Maolachy	Arg & Bt	NM8914	56°16·3′	5°24·0′W	H	55
Cruach Mhalaig	Highld	NM6997	57°0·6′	5°47·8′W	H	40
Cruach Mheadhonach	Arg & Bt	NR8281	55°58·6′	5°29·2′W	H	55
Cruach Mhic-an t-Saoir	Arg & Bt	NR7442	55°37·4′	5°34·9′W	H	62
Cruach Mhic Choinnich	Arg & Bt	NR7540	55°36·4′	5°33·9′W	X	62,69
Cruach Mhic Eoich	Arg & Bt	NN0311	56°15·3′	5°10·4′W	H	50,55
Cruach Mhic Fhionnlaidh	Arg & Bt	NM9402	56°10·2′	5°18·7′W	H	55
Cruach Mhic Gougain	Arg & Bt	NR7550	55°41·7′	5°34·4′W	H	62,69
Cruach Mhór	Arg & Bt	NN0514	56°17·0′	5°8·6′W	H	50,56
Cruach Mhór	Arg & Bt	NN1421	56°20·9′	5°0·2′W	X	50,56
Cruach Mhór	Arg & Bt	NR3054	55°42·5′	6°17·5′W	X	60
Cruach Mhór	Arg & Bt	NS0386	56°1·8′	5°9·3′W	H	55
Cruach Mhór	Arg & Bt	NS0394	56°6·1′	5°9·6′W	H	55
Cruach Moine-phuill	Arg & Bt	NR9885	56°1·2′	5°14·0′W	H	55
Cruach Muasdale	Arg & Bt	NR6939	55°35·6′	5°39·5′W	H	68
Cruach na Bairness	Highld	NM6576	56°49·2′	5°50·6′W	X	40
Cruach na Caol-bheinn	Arg & Bt	NR8759	55°46·9′	5°23·4′W	X	62
Cruach na Casaich	Arg & Bt	NR7944	55°38·6′	5°30·3′W	H	62,69
Cruach na Cioba	Arg & Bt	NN1401	56°10·2′	4°59·3′W	H	56
Cruach na Cùilidh Bige	Highld	NM6874	56°48·2′	5°47·6′W	H	40
Cruach na Cùilidh Mòire	Highld	NM6774	56°48·2′	5°48·5′W	X	40
Cruach na Gaibhre	Arg & Bt	NR7368	55°51·4′	5°37·2′W	X	62
Cruach na Gearr-choise	Arg & Bt	NN0617	56°18·6′	5°7·7′W	H	50,56
Cruach na h-Airighe	Arg & Bt	NM6925	56°21·9′	5°44·0′W	H	49
Cruach na Machrach	Arg & Bt	NR8963	55°49·1′	5°21·6′W	H	62
Cruach na Maoile	Arg & Bt	NS0780	55°58·7′	5°5·2′W	H	63
Cruach na Maraiche	Highld	NM7974	56°48·6′	5°36·8′W	X	40
Cruach nam Bonnach	Arg & Bt	NR8285	56°0·8′	5°29·4′W	H	55
Cruach nam Broighleag	Arg & Bt	NR9780	55°58·5′	5°14·8′W	H	55
Cruach na Meala	Arg & Bt	NR7369	55°51·9′	5°37·2′W	H	62
Cruach nam Fad	Arg & Bt	NR8068	55°51·6′	5°30·5′W	X	62
Cruach nam Feadan	Highld	NM7474	56°48·4′	5°41·7′W	X	40
Cruach nam Fearna	Arg & Bt	NM8215	56°16·9′	5°30·9′W	H	55
Cruach nam Fiadh	Arg & Bt	NR7376	55°55·7′	5°37·6′W	H	62
Cruach nam Fiadh	Arg & Bt	NR7875	55°55·3′	5°32·7′W	H	62
Cruach nam Fiadh	Arg & Bt	NR8085	56°0·7′	5°31·3′W	H	55
Cruach nam Fiadh	Arg & Bt	NR8256	55°45·2′	5°28·0′W	H	62
Cruach nam Meann	Highld	NM6671	56°46·6′	5°49·4′W	H	40
Cruach nam Miseag	Arg & Bt	NN2806	56°13·2′	4°46·0′W	H	56
Cruach nam Miseag	Arg & Bt	NS1898	56°8·7′	4°55·3′W	H	56
Cruach nam Mult	Arg & Bt	NN1605	56°12·4′	4°57·5′W	H	56
Cruach nam Mult	Arg & Bt	NS0184	56°0·7′	5°11·1′W	X	55
Cruach nan Caorach	Arg & Bt	NR9980	55°58·5′	5°12·8′W	H	55
Cruach nan Caorach	Arg & Bt	NS0781	55°59·2′	5°5·2′W	H	63
Cruach nan Caorach	Highld	NM7973	56°48·0′	5°36·7′W	H	40
Cruach nan Capull	Arg & Bt	NN1405	56°12·3′	4°59·5′W	H	56
Cruach nan Capull	Arg & Bt	NS0797	56°7·9′	5°5·9′W	H	56
Cruach nan Capull	Arg & Bt	NS0979	55°58·2′	5°3·2′W	H	63
Cruach nan Con	Arg & Bt	NM5726	56°22·1′	5°55·6′W	H	48
Cruach nan Cuilean	Arg & Bt	NR8087	56°1·8′	5°31·4′W	H	55
Cruach nan Cuilean	Arg & Bt	NR8273	55°54·3′	5°28·8′W	H	62
Cruach nan Cuilean	Arg & Bt	NS0484	56°0·8′	5°8·2′W	H	55
Cruach nan Duarman	Arg & Bt	NR7363	55°48·7′	5°36·9′W	X	62
Cruach nan Gabhar	Arg & Bt	NR7541	55°36·9′	5°33·9′W	H	62,69
Cruach nan Gearran	Arg & Bt	NR9784	56°0·6′	5°14·9′W	X	55
Cruach nan Lochan	Arg & Bt	NR7578	55°56·8′	5°35·8′W	H	62
Cruach nan Nighean	Arg & Bt	NN2031	56°26·5′	4°54·7′W	X	50
Cruach nan Tarbh	Arg & Bt	NR9782	55°59·5′	5°14·9′W	X	55
Cruach Narrachan	Arg & Bt	NM9115	56°17·1′	5°22·2′W	H	55
Cruach na Seilcheig	Arg & Bt	NM8511	56°14·8′	5°27·8′W	H	55
Cruach na Seilcheig	Arg & Bt	NR6898	56°7·4′	5°43·5′W	H	55,61
Cruach na Seilcheig	Arg & Bt	NR7652	55°42·8′	5°33·5′W	H	62,69
Cruach na Speireig	Arg & Bt	NR8189	56°2·9′	5°30·6′W	X	55
Cruach Neuran	Arg & Bt	NS0882	55°59·8′	5°4·3′W	H	56
Cruach Neuran Burn	Arg & Bt	NS0981	55°59·3′	5°3·3′W	W	63
Cruach Raineachan	Highld	NM8283	56°53·5′	5°34·3′W	X	40

Cruach Rarey	Arg & Bt	NM8116	56°17·4'	5°31·9'W	H	55
Cruach Ruadh	Arg & Bt	NR7845	55°39·1'	5°31·3'W	H	62,69
Cruach Scarba	Arg & Bt	NM6904	56°10·6'	5°42·9'W	H	55
Cruach Sganadail	Arg & Bt	NR5987	56°1·2'	5°51·6'W	X	61
Cruach Sléibhe	Arg & Bt	NM3752	56°35·4'	6°16·6'W	H	47
Cruach Tairbeirt	Arg & Bt	NN3105	56°12·7'	4°43·1'W	H	56
Cruach Tamalabh	Arg & Bt	NR7953	55°43·5'	5°30·7'W	X	62
Cruach Tarsuinn	Arg & Bt	NR8761	55°48·0'	5°23·5'W	X	62
Cruach, The	Arg & Bt	NR9091	56°4·2'	5°22·0'W	H	55
Cruach Thoraraidh	Highld	NM7885	56°54·5'	5°38·3'W	H	40
Cruach Torr an Lochain	Arg & Bt	NM5640	56°29·6'	5°57·4'W	H	47,48
Cruach Tuirc	Arg & Bt	NN2214	56°17·4'	4°52·1'W	H	50,56
Cruaidh-alltan	Highld	NN8885	56°56·8'	3°50·0'W	W	43
Cruaidh Bheinn	Highld	NN3083	56°54·7'	4°47·1'W	X	34,41
Cruaidh Ghleann	Arg & Bt	NR4153	55°42·3'	6°6·9'W	X	60
Cruaidh Ghleann	Arg & Bt	NR5890	56°2·8'	5°52·7'W	X	61
Cruan	Orkney	HY3612	58°59·7'	3°6·3'W	X	6
Cruarg	Highld	NG7045	57°26·5'	5°49·5'W	X	24
Cruats	Moray	NJ4968	57°42·2'	2°50·9'W	X	28,29
Cruban	Orkney	HY2217	59°2·2'	3°21·1'W	X	6
Crùban Beag	Highld	NN6692	57°0·2'	4°11·9'W	H	35
Crùban Mór	Highld	NN6691	56°59·7'	4°11·9'W	H	35
Crubasdale	Arg & Bt	NR6840	55°36·2'	5°40·5'W	X	62
Crubbins Hill	Cumbr	NY5080	55°7·0'	2°46·6'W	X	79
Crubenbeg	Highld	NN6892	57°0·3'	4°9·9'W	X	35
Crubenmore Bridge	Highld	NN6791	56°59·7'	4°10·9'W	X	35
Crubenmore Lodge	Highld	NN6791	56°59·7'	4°10·9'W	X	35
Cruchfield Manor Ho	Win & Maid	SU8774	51°27·7'	0°44·5'W	X	175
Cruchie	Aberd	NJ5842	57°28·2'	2°41·6'W	X	29
Cruckley Fm	E Yorks	TA0854	53°58·5'	0°20·8'W	FM	107
Cruckmeole	Shrops	SJ4309	52°40·8'	2°50·2'W	T	126
Cruckmoor Fm	Shrops	SJ5632	52°53·3'	2°38·8'W	FM	126
Cruckton	Shrops	SJ4310	52°41·3'	2°50·2'W	T	126
Crude Hill	D & G	NY3996	55°15·5'	2°57·2'W	H	79
Cruden Bay	Aberd	NK0936	57°25·1'	1°50·6'W	T	30
Crudgington	Wrekin	SJ6318	52°45·7'	2°32·5'W	T	127
Crudgington Moor	Wrekin	SJ6517	52°45·2'	2°30·7'W	X	127
Crudha' an Eich	Highld	NM7468	56°45·2'	5°41·4'W	X	40
Crudha Ard	Highld	NG8409	57°7·5'	5°33·7'W	X	33
Crudhall Br	E Yorks	SE8045	53°53·9'	0°46·5'W	X	106
Crudie	Aberd	NJ7957	57°36·4'	2°20·6'W	X	29,30
Crudie	Angus	NO6140	56°33·3'	2°37·6'W	X	54
Crudie Acres	Angus	NO6141	56°33·8'	2°37·6'W	X	54
Crudwell	Wilts	ST9592	51°37·8'	2°3·9'W	T	163,173
Crudy	Orkney	HY7142	59°16·1'	2°30·0'W	X	5
Cruereach Hill	D & G	NS7915	55°25·1'	3°54·3'W	H	71,78
Cruetoun	Shetld	HU4942	60°9·8'	1°6·5'W	X	4
Cruffell	D & G	NS6905	55°19·6'	4°3·5'W	H	71,77
Cruft	Devon	SX5396	50°44·9'	4°5·5'W	X	191
Cruft Gate	Devon	SX5396	50°44·9'	4°4·6'W	X	191
Crûg	Carm	SN3924	51°53·7'	4°20·0'W	X	145,159
Crug	Cered	SN6653	52°9·8'	3°57·2'W	H	146
Crug	Powys	SN8551	52°9·0'	3°40·5'W	X	147
Crûg	Powys	SO1972	52°20·6'	3°10·9'W	X	136,148
Cruga Bach	Gwyn	SH2129	52°50·0'	4°39·0'W	X	123
Crugan	Gwyn	SH3332	52°51·8'	4°28·4'W	X	123
Crugan-fawr	Carm	SN4112	51°47·3'	4°17·9'W	X	159
Crugau	Nth Pt Talb	SN8303	51°43·1'	3°41·2'W	X	170
Crugau Wood	Nth Pt Talb	SN8304	51°43·6'	3°41·3'W	F	170
Crug-bach	Carm	SN3931	51°57·5'	4°20·2'W	A	145
Crug-bach	Carm	SN3933	51°58·6'	4°20·3'W	A	145
Crug-bach	Cered	SN3749	52°7·2'	4°22·5'W	X	145
Crug-bach	Pemb	SN2532	51°57·8'	4°32·4'W	X	145
Crug Coe	Cered	SN3050	52°7·6'	4°28·6'W	A	145
Crug Cou	Cered	SN4052	52°8·8'	4°19·9'W	A	146
Crug-du	Cered	SN3850	52°7·7'	4°21·6'W	A	145
Crug Du	Powys	SN9440	52°3·1'	3°32·4'W	H	147,160
Crug-ebolion	Pemb	SN2631	51°57·3'	4°31·5'W	A	145
Crugelwin	Carm	SN2328	51°55·6'	4°34·1'W	A	145,158
Crugeran	Gwyn	SH2432	52°51·6'	4°36·5'W	X	123
Crug Farm	Cered	SN1751	52°7·9'	4°40·0'W	FM	145
Crug Fm	Flint	SJ1764	53°10·2'	3°14·1'W	FM	116
Crug-glas	Carm	SN2931	51°57·3'	4°28·9'W	A	145
Crug-glas	Carm	SN3933	51°58·6'	4°20·3'W	A	145
Crug Glas	Carm	SN6823	51°53·6'	3°54·7'W	X	159
Crug-Glâs Fm	Pemb	SM8129	51°55·2'	5°10·7'W	FM	157
Cruggleton	D & G	NX4843	54°45·8'	4°21·3'W	X	83
Cruggleton or Rigg Bay	D & G	NX4744	54°46·3'	4°22·3'W	W	83
Cruggleton Point	D & G	NX4842	54°45·3'	4°21·3'W	X	83
Crug Gwyn	Carm	SN4032	51°58·0'	4°19·4'W	A	146
Crug Gynon	Cered	SN8064	52°15·9'	3°45·1'W	X	147
Crûg Ho	Gwyn	SH5065	53°9·9'	4°14·2'W	X	114,115
Crug Hywel	Carm	SN2126	51°54·5'	4°35·7'W	A	145,158
Crug hywel (Table Mountain)	Powys	SO2220	51°52·6'	3°7·6'W	A	161
Crugiau	Pemb	SN1241	52°2·4'	4°44·1'W	X	145
Crugiau Cemmaes	Pemb	SN1241	52°2·4'	4°44·1'W	A	145
Crugiau Edryd	Carm	SN5339	52°2·0'	4°8·2'W	A	146
Crugiau Fach	Carm	SN4032	51°58·0'	4°19·4'W	A	146
Crugiau Giar	Carm	SN5037	52°0·9'	4°10·8'W	A	146
Crugiau Merched	Carm	SN7245	52°5·6'	3°51·7'W	A	146,147
Crugiau Rhos-wen	Carm	SN4733	51°58·7'	4°13·3'W	A	146
Crugievan	Carm	SN3131	51°57·4'	4°27·2'W	A	145
Crugiwan	Carm	SN3032	51°57·9'	4°28·1'W	X	145
Crugkern	Corn	SW3830	50°7·0'	5°39·5'W	X	203
Crug Las	Cered	SN3851	52°8·3'	4°21·6'W	A	145
Cruglas	Cered	SN3851	52°8·3'	4°21·6'W	X	145
Cruglas	Cered	SN6965	52°16·3'	3°54·8'W	X	135
Cruglas	Cered	SN7469	52°18·5'	3°50·5'W	X	135,147
Cruglas	Denb	SJ0253	53°4·2'	3°27·4'W	X	116
Cruglwyn	Caer	SO1605	51°44·5'	3°12·6'W	X	161
Crugmaen	Cered	SN4949	52°7·4'	4°11·9'W	X	146
Crug Mawr	Powys	SO2622	51°53·7'	3°4·1'W	H	161
Crugmeer	Corn	SW9076	50°33·0'	4°57·5'W	T	200
Crug-moch	Carm	SN3333	51°58·5'	4°25·5'W	A	145
Crugmore	Cered	SN2047	52°5·8'	4°37·3'W	X	145
Crugnant	Cered	SN7563	52°15·3'	3°49·5'W	W	146,147
Crug Perfa	Carm	SN3534	51°59·0'	4°23·8'W	A	145
Crugsillick Manor	Corn	SW9039	50°13·1'	4°56·3'W	X	204
Crugtarw	Carm	SN3734	51°59·1'	4°22·0'W	A	145
Crugwydd	Powys	SN8751	52°9·0'	3°38·7'W	H	147
Crugwyllt-fawr	Nth Pt Talb	SS7987	51°34·4'	3°44·4'W	X	170
Crugybar	Carm	SN6537	52°1·1'	3°57·7'W	T	146
Crug y Bedw	Carm	SN4935	51°59·8'	4°11·6'W	A	146
Crugybigwrn	Carm	SN3630	51°56·9'	4°22·8'W	A	145
Crug y Biswal	Carm	SN5138	52°1·5'	4°9·9'W	A	146
Crug-y-Bwbach	Powys	SN8432	51°58·7'	3°40·9'W	X	160
Crûg-y-byddar	Powys	SO1581	52°25·5'	3°14·6'W	X	136
Crugyddalfa	Carm	SN3534	51°59·0'	4°23·8'W	A	145
Crugydeirne	Carm	SN2924	51°53·5'	4°28·7'W	X	145,159
Crug-y-deri	Pemb	SN1120	51°51·0'	4°44·3'W	X	145,158
Crug-y-dyrn	Carm	SN2925	51°54·1'	4°28·7'W	A	145
Crug-y-feilog	Cered	SN4758	52°12·2'	4°13·9'W	X	146
Crugygorllwyn	Carm	SN3234	51°59·0'	4°26·4'W	A	145
Crugygorllwyn	Carm	SN3534	51°59·0'	4°23·8'W	A	145
Crugyn	Powys	SN9872	52°20·4'	3°29·4'W	A	136,147
Crugyn Amlwg	Carm	SN4834	51°59·3'	4°12·4'W	A	146
Crugyn Fm	Powys	SO1681	52°25·5'	3°13·7'W	FM	136
Crugyn Gwyddel	Powys	SN9168	52°18·2'	3°35·5'W	A	136,147
Crugyn-llwyd (Cairn)	Powys	SO0279	52°24·3'	3°26·0'W	A	136,147
Crugynnau	Powys	SO1084	52°27·0'	3°19·1'W	X	136
Crugyrafan	Rho Cyn Taf	SS9295	51°38·8'	3°33·3'W	A	170
Crugyreryr	Cered	SN4250	52°7·8'	4°18·1'W	X	146
Crug-yr-hwch	Pemb	SN1732	51°57·6'	4°39·4'W	H	145
Crug yr Wyn	Powys	SN8163	52°15·4'	3°44·2'W	X	147
Crug y Swllt	Pemb	SN1712	51°46·8'	4°38·8'W	A	158
Crug-y-whil	Cered	SN4842	52°3·6'	4°12·6'W	X	146
Cruhill	Orkney	HY5203	58°55·0'	2°49·5'W	X	6,7
Cruib	Arg & Bt	NR5684	55°59·5'	5°54·3'W	H	61
Cruib Lodge	Arg & Bt	NR5682	55°58·4'	5°54·2'W	X	61
Cruichie	D & G	NX6871	55°1·2'	4°3·5'W	X	77,84
Cruick Water	Angus	NO4665	56°46·7'	2°52·6'W	W	44
Cruick Water	Angus	NO5362	56°45·1'	2°45·7'W	W	44
Cruim Leacainn	Highld	NN1680	56°52·8'	5°0·7'W	H	34,41
Cruinn a' Bheinn	Stir	NN3605	56°12·8'	4°38·2'W	H	56
Cruinn Bheinn	Highld	NG4252	57°29·4'	6°17·9'W	H	23
Cruinn Bheinn	Stir	NN4312	56°16·7'	4°31·7'W	H	56
Cruinn Loch	Arg & Bt	NR7479	55°57·3'	5°36·8'W	W	62
Cruise	D & G	NX1762	54°55·4'	4°50·9'W	X	82
Cruise Burn	D & G	NX1763	54°55·9'	4°51·0'W	W	82
Cruise Hill	Worcs	SP0063	52°16·1'	1°59·6'W	T	150
Cruisie Wood	D & G	NX7452	54°51·1'	3°57·3'W	F	83,84
Cruis Taing	Orkney	HY7138	59°13·9'	2°30·0'W	X	5
Cruitir	N Eil	NB1540	58°15·6'	6°51·1'W	X	13
Cruive	Highld	NH4539	57°25·2'	4°34·4'W	X	26
Cruives	Highld	NH5043	57°27·4'	4°29·6'W	X	26
Cruives (ruin)	Highld	ND3352	58°27·3'	3°8·4'W	X	12
Cruivie	Fife	NO4022	56°23·4'	2°57·9'W	X	54,59
Cruivie Castle	Fife	NO4122	56°23·5'	2°56·9'W	A	54,59
Crùlabhig	N Eil	NB1733	58°12·0'	6°48·5'W	T	8,13
Cruland	Orkney	HY2315	59°1·2'	3°20·0'W	X	6
Crumbland	Monm	SO4701	51°42·6'	2°45·6'W	X	171
Crumbland Plantation	Monm	SO4702	51°43·1'	2°45·6'W	F	171
Crumblands	C of Edin	NT1674	55°57·4'	3°20·3'W	X	65,66
Crumbles	E Susx	TQ6402	50°47·9'	0°20·0'E	X	199
Crumblie Hill	Fife	NO4122	56°23·5'	2°56·9'W	H	54,59
Crumbrecks	Orkney	HY3105	58°55·9'	3°11·4'W	X	6,7
Crumhaugh	S Lanak	NS7344	55°40·6'	4°0·7'W	X	71
Crumhaugh Hill	Scot Bord	NT4813	55°24·7'	2°48·8'W	X	79
Crumleyheath Fm	Ches	SJ6277	53°17·6'	2°33·8'W	FM	118
Crumlin	Caer	ST2198	51°40·8'	3°8·2'W	T	171
Crummack	N Yks	SD7771	54°8·3'	2°20·7'W	X	98
Crummack Dale	N Yks	SD7772	54°8·8'	2°20·7'W	X	98
Crumma Ho	N Yks	NZ0907	54°27·7'	1°51·2'W	X	92
Crummiecleuch Rig	Scot Bord	NT4401	55°18·2'	2°52·5'W	X	79
Crummock Bank	Cumbr	NY2145	54°47·9'	3°13·3'W	X	85
Crummock Beck	Cumbr	NY1946	54°48·4'	3°15·2'W	W	85
Crummocksteps	Falk	NS7883	56°1·7'	3°57·0'W	X	57,64
Crummock Water	Cumbr	NY1518	54°33·3'	3°18·4'W	W	89
Crummy Burn	D & G	NX5783	55°7·5'	4°14·1'W	W	77
Crummypark	D & G	NX5884	55°8·1'	4°13·2'W	X	77
Crumpet's Fm	Dorset	SY9696	50°46·0'	2°3·0'W	FM	195
Crumpfield	Worcs	SP0165	52°17·2'	1°58·7'W	X	150
Crumplehorn	Corn	SX2051	50°20·1'	4°31·4'W	T	201
Crump Oak	Heref	SO3454	52°11·1'	2°57·5'W	X	148,149
Crumps	Herts	TL4615	51°49·1'	0°7·5'E	X	167
Crumpsall	Man	SD8402	53°31·1'	2°14·1'W	T	109
Crumpsbrook	Shrops	SO6278	52°24·2'	2°33·1'W	T	138
Crump's Wood	E Susx	TQ4716	50°55·7'	0°5·9'E	F	198
Crump, The	Essex	TL4728	51°56·1'	0°8·7'E	X	167
Crump, The (Earthwork)	Essex	TL4728	51°56·1'	0°8·7'E	A	167
Crumpton Hill	D & G	NY3491	55°12·8'	3°1·8'W	H	79
Crumpton Hill	Heref	SO7648	52°8·0'	2°20·6'W	T	150
Crumpwell	Shrops	SJ3026	52°49·9'	3°1·9'W	X	126
Crumpwood Fm	Staffs	SK0842	52°58·8'	1°52·4'W	FM	119,128
Crumquhill	D & G	NX6959	54°54·8'	4°2·4'W	X	83,84
Crumrig	Scot Bord	NT7244	55°41·6'	2°26·3'W	X	74
Crumside Burn	Scot Bord	NT4341	55°39·8'	2°53·9'W	W	73
Crumside Hill	Scot Bord	NT4240	55°39·3'	2°54·9'W	X	73
Crumstane	Scot Bord	NT8053	55°46·4'	2°18·7'W	X	67,74
Crumstone	Northum	NU2537	55°37·8'	1°35·7'W	X	75
Crumyards	E Renf	NS4656	55°46·6'	4°26·9'W	X	64
Crun a' Bhràghad	Highld	NG2856	57°31·0'	6°32·1'W	X	23
Crundale	Kent	TR0749	51°12·4'	0°58·2'E	T	179,189
Crundale	Pemb	SM9718	51°49·7'	4°56·4'W	T	157,158
Crundale Downs	Kent	TR0848	51°11·8'	0°59·0'E	X	179,189
Crundale Ho	Kent	TR0848	51°11·8'	0°59·0'E	X	179,189
Crundalls Fm	Kent	TQ6642	51°9·4'	0°22·8'E	FM	188
Crundalls Fm	Worcs	SO7876	52°23·1'	2°19·0'W	FM	138
Crungie Clach	Pth & Kin	NN9865	56°46·2'	3°39·7'W	H	43
Crungoed	Powys	SO1971	52°20·1'	3°10·9'W	X	136,148
Crungoed Bank	Powys	SO1871	52°20·1'	3°11·8'W	H	136,148
Crunklaw	Scot Bord	NT7850	55°44·8'	2°20·6'W	X	67,74
Crunkly Gill	N Yks	NZ7507	54°27·4'	0°50·2'W	X	94
Crùn Loch	Highld	NM5855	56°37·7'	5°56·3'W	X	47
Crùn Lochan	Arg & Bt	NM6830	56°24·6'	5°45·2'W	W	49
Crunwear Fm	Pemb	SN1810	51°45·8'	4°37·9'W	FM	158
Crurie	D & G	NY2594	55°14·3'	3°10·3'W	X	79
Crusader Bank	Lancs	SD2930	53°45·9'	3°4·2'W	X	102
Cruss	Shetld	HU6390	60°35·6'	0°50·5'W	X	1,2
Crussa Field	Shetld	HP6110	60°46·4'	0°52·3'W	H	1
Crussa Ness	Shetld	HP5403	60°42·7'	1°0·1'W	X	1
Cruster	Shetld	HU4225	60°0·7'	1°14·3'W	X	4
Crutch Bog	Northum	NU1727	55°32·4'	1°43·4'W	X	75
Crutchenber Fell	Lancs	SD7260	54°2·4'	2°25·2'W	X	98
Crutches Fm	E Susx	TQ8917	50°55·5'	0°41·8'E	FM	189
Crutchfield Fm	Surrey	TQ2644	51°11·1'	0°11·4'W	FM	187
Crutch Fm	Worcs	SO9066	52°17·8'	2°8·4'W	FM	150
Crutch Hill	Worcs	SO9066	52°17·8'	2°8·4'W	X	150
Crutchin Gill Rigg	N Yks	SD7978	54°12·1'	2°18·9'W	X	98
Crutherland Fm	S Lanak	NS6651	55°44·3'	4°7·6'W	FM	64
Cruther's Point	I Scilly	SV9215	49°57·6'	6°17·3'W	X	203
Cruwyshayes	Devon	SS9909	50°52·5'	3°25·8'W	X	192
Cruwys Morchard	Devon	SS8712	50°54·0'	3°36·0'W	T	181
Crux Easton	Hants	SU4256	51°18·3'	1°23·5'W	T	174
Cruxfield	Scot Bord	NT8157	55°48·6'	2°17·8'W	X	67,74
Cruxton	Dorset	SY6096	50°46·0'	2°33·6'W	T	194
Cruys	Angus	NO4275	56°52·0'	2°56·6'W	H	44
Crwbin	Carm	SN4713	51°47·9'	4°12·7'W	T	159
Crwca	Swan	SN6202	51°42·2'	3°59·4'W	X	159
Crya	Orkney	HY3305	58°55·9'	3°9·4'W	X	6,7
Crychan Forest	Carm	SN8440	52°3·0'	3°41·1'W	F	147,160
Crychell	Powys	SO0774	52°21·6'	3°21·5'W	X	136,147
Crychell Brook	Powys	SO0774	52°21·6'	3°21·5'W	W	136,147
Cryers Fm	Ches	SJ4473	53°15·3'	2°50·0'W	FM	117
Cryers Hill	Bucks	SU8796	51°39·6'	0°44·1'W	T	165
Cryfield Grange	Warw	SP2974	52°22·0'	1°34·0'W	X	140
Cryfield Ho	Warw	SP2975	52°22·5'	1°34·0'W	X	140
Crying Taing	Shetld	HU3180	60°30·4'	1°25·6'W	X	1,3
Cryla	Aberd	NJ9350	57°32·7'	2°6·6'W	X	30
Crylla Fm	Corn	SX2370	50°30·4'	4°29·4'W	FM	201
Crymant	Cered	SN3344	52°4·4'	4°25·8'W	X	145
Crymbal Fm	Wrex	SJ3344	52°59·6'	2°59·5'W	FM	117
Crymlyn Manor	Carm	SN6523	51°53·6'	3°57·3'W	X	159
Crymlyn	Gwyn	SH6371	53°13·3'	4°2·7'W	X	115
Crymlyn Bog	Swan	SS6995	51°38·6'	3°53·2'W	W	170
Crymlyn Burrows	Nth Pt Talb	SS7092	51°36·9'	3°52·3'W	X	170
Crymnant	Conwy	SH8546	53°0·2'	3°42·4'W	W	116
Crymych	Pemb	SN1833	51°58·2'	4°38·6'W	T	145
Crynallt	V of Glam	ST0679	51°30·4'	3°20·9'W	X	170
Crynant	Nth Pt Talb	SN7904	51°43·5'	3°44·7'W	T	170
Crynfryn	Carm	SN3625	51°54·2'	4°22·6'W	X	145
Crynfryn	Cered	SN5861	52°14·0'	4°4·4'W	X	146
Crynfrynbychan	Cered	SN6458	52°12·4'	3°59·0'W	X	146
Crynga	Pemb	SN2635	51°59·4'	4°31·7'W	X	145
Cryngae	Carm	SN3539	52°1·7'	4°23·9'W	X	145
Cryngae Mawr	Cered	SN2447	52°5·8'	4°33·8'W	X	145
Crynierth	Gwyn	SH9639	52°56·5'	3°32·5'W	X	125
Crynllwyn	Gwyn	SH5902	52°36·1'	4°4·5'W	X	135
Crynllwyn Mawr	Cered	SN6062	52°14·5'	4°2·6'W	X	146
Crynoch Burn	Aberd	NO8697	57°4·1'	2°13·4'W	W	38,45
Crynos Fm	Shrops	SJ4238	52°56·4'	2°51·4'W	FM	126
Crypt Fm	W Susx	SU8717	50°57·0'	0°45·3'W	FM	197
Crystal Beck	N Yks	SD9174	54°9·9'	2°7·9'W	W	98
Crystal Dairy	Aberd	NO6273	56°51·1'	2°36·9'W	X	45
Crystal Palace	Brom	TQ3470	51°25·0'	0°4·0'W	X	176,177
Crystal Peaks	Sheff	SK4382	53°20·2'	1°20·8'W	X	111,120
Crystal Rig	Scot Bord	NT6667	55°53·9'	2°32·2'W	X	67
Crythan Brook	Nth Pt Talb	SS7695	51°38·6'	3°47·1'W	W	170
Cuaich	Highld	NN6587	56°57·5'	4°12·7'W	X	42
Cuaig	Highld	NG7057	57°32·9'	5°50·2'W	T	24
Cuan	Arg & Bt	NM7514	56°16·2'	5°37·6'W	T	55
Cuan Mór	Arg & Bt	NM4157	56°38·3'	6°13·0'W	W	47
Cuan Point	Arg & Bt	NM7414	56°16·1'	5°38·6'W	X	55
Cuan Sound	Arg & Bt	NM7514	56°16·2'	5°37·6'W	W	55
Cuba Fm	N Yks	SE7965	54°4·7'	0°47·1'W	FM	100
Cubaig	Arg & Bt	NR3386	55°59·8'	6°16·5'W	X	61
Cubben	Cumbr	NY1301	54°24·1'	3°20·0'W	X	89
Cubberley	Heref	SO5822	51°53·9'	2°36·2'W	X	162
Cubbie Roo's Castle	Orkney	HY4426	59°7·3'	2°58·2'W	A	5,6
Cubbigeo	Orkney	HY4843	59°16·5'	2°54·3'W	X	5
Cubbington	Warw	SP3468	52°18·8'	1°29·7'W	T	151
Cubbington Heath Fm	Warw	SP3369	52°19·3'	1°30·6'W	FM	151
Cubbox	D & G	NX6477	55°4·4'	4°7·4'W	X	77
Cubbyhill	Cumbr	NY3473	55°3·1'	3°1·6'W	X	85
Cubeck	N Yks	SD9589	54°18·0'	2°4·2'W	T	98
Cubert	Corn	SW7857	50°22·5'	5°7·0'W	T	200
Cubert Common	Corn	SW7859	50°23·6'	5°7·0'W	X	200
Cubeside	N Ayr	NS2650	55°43·0'	4°45·8'W	X	63
Cubitt Town	T Ham	TQ3879	51°29·8'	0°0·3'W	T	177
Cubley	Barns	SE2402	53°31·1'	1°37·9'W	T	110
Cubley Carr	Derby	SK1636	52°55·5'	1°45·3'W	X	128
Cubley Common	Derby	SK1639	52°57·1'	1°45·3'W	T	128
Cubley Lodge	Derby	SK1636	52°55·5'	1°45·3'W	X	128
Cubley Wood Fm	Derby	SK1640	52°57·7'	1°45·3'W	FM	119,128
Cublington	Bucks	SP8322	51°53·7'	0°47·2'W	T	165
Cublington	Heref	SO4038	52°2·5'	2°52·1'W	X	149,161
Cubrieshaw Hall	N Ayr	NS2147	55°41·3'	4°50·4'W	X	63
Cubstocks	Northum	NY8366	54°59·5'	2°15·5'W	X	86,87
Cuchanlupe	Highld	NJ0016	57°13·7'	3°38·9'W	X	36
Cuckfield	W Susx	TQ3024	51°0·3'	0°8·4'W	T	198
Cuckfield Park	W Susx	TQ2924	51°0·3'	0°9·3'W	A	198
Cuck Hill	Somer	ST4457	51°18·8'	2°47·8'W	X	172,182
Cucklington	Somer	ST7527	51°2·7'	2°21·0'W	T	183
Cuckmere Haven	E Susx	TV5197	50°45·4'	0°8·8'E	W	199
Cuckmere River	E Susx	TQ5610	50°52·3'	0°13·4'E	W	199
Cuckney	Notts	SK5671	53°14·2'	1°9·2'W	T	120
Cuckney Hay Wood	Notts	SK5569	53°13·2'	1°11·1'W	F	120
Cuckold's Combe	Somer	SS9930	51°3·9'	3°26·1'W	X	181
Cuckold's Corner	Kent	TQ9137	51°6·2'	0°44·1'E	X	189
Cuckolds Cross	Herts	TL1719	51°51·7'	0°17·7'W	X	166
Cuckold's Green	Medway	TQ8276	51°27·4'	0°37·6'E	X	178
Cuckold's Green	Suff	TM4882	52°23·0'	1°39·1'E	T	156
Cuckold's Green	Wilts	ST9857	51°19·0'	2°1·3'W	T	173
Cuckold's Holt Fm	Oxon	SP4125	51°55·6'	1°23·8'W	FM	164
Cuckold's Point	Suff	TM4248	52°4·9'	1°32·3'E	X	169
Cuckoo Ball	Devon	SX6658	50°24·6'	3°52·8'W	X	202
Cuckoo Br	Lincs	TF2020	52°46·1'	0°12·9'W	X	131
Cuckoo Brow Wood	Cumbr	SD3796	54°21·6'	2°57·8'W	F	96,97
Cuckoo Bush Fm	Notts	SK5328	52°51·0'	1°12·4'W	FM	129

Cuckoo Fm	Devon	SS8325	51°1·0'	3°39·7'W	FM	181
Cuckoo Fm	Essex	TL9929	51°55·7'	0°54·1'E	FM	168
Cuckoo Fm	Rut	SK9410	52°41·0'	0°36·2'W	FM	130
Cuckoo Fm	Suff	TM3281	52°22·9'	1°24·9'E	FM	156
Cuckoo Green	Suff	TM5199	52°32·1'	1°42·5'E	T	134
Cuckoo Grove	Pemb	SM9216	51°48·5'	5°0·6'W	X	157,158
Cuckoo Hall	Lancs	SD6339	53°51·0'	2°33·3'W	X	102,103
Cuckoo Hill	Leic	SK8016	52°44·4'	0°48·5'W	X	130
Cuckoo Hill	Notts	SK7190	53°24·4'	0°55·5'W	X	112
Cuckoo Hill	Suff	TL7869	52°17·6'	0°37·0'E	X	155
Cuckoo Hill	Surrey	SU9360	51°20·1'	0°39·5'W	X	175,186
Cuckoo Hill (Tumulus)	Suff	TL7869	52°17·6'	0°37·0'E	A	155
Cuckoo Ho	Darl	NZ2418	54°33·6'	1°37·3'W	X	93
Cuckoo Junction Fm	Lincs	TF2221	52°46·6'	0°11·1'W	FM	131
Cuckoo Lodge	Northnts	TF0001	52°36·1'	0°31·0'W	X	141
Cuckoo Lodge	Rut	SK9602	52°36·7'	0°34·5'W	X	141
Cuckoo Nest Fm	E Yorks	SE7151	53°57·3'	0°54·7'W	FM	105,106
Cuckoo Park Fm	Brad	SE0436	53°49·5'	1°55·9'W	FM	104
Cuckoopen Barn Fm	Glos	SO9415	51°50·2'	2°4·8'W	FM	163
Cuckoopen Coppice	Shrops	SO5380	52°25·2'	2°41·1'W	F	137,138
Cuckoo Rock	Devon	SX5868	50°29·9'	3°59·8'W	X	202
Cuckoo Rocks	Ches	SJ9971	53°14·4'	2°0·5'W	X	118
Cuckoo's Corner	Hants	SU7441	51°10·0'	0°56·1'W	T	186
Cuckoo's Corner	Wilts	SU0357	51°19·0'	1°57·0'W	T	173
Cuckoos Fm	Essex	TL7633	51°58·3'	0°34·1'E	FM	167
Cuckoos' Hill	Mil Key	SP7946	52°6·6'	0°50·4'W	X	152
Cuckoo's Knob	Wilts	SU1962	51°21·6'	1°43·2'W	T	173
Cuckoo's Nest	Ches	SJ3760	53°8·2'	2°56·1'W	X	117
Cuckoo Stone	Derby	SK3162	53°9·5'	1°31·8'W	X	119
Cuckoostone Ho	Derby	SK3062	53°9·5'	1°32·7'W	X	119
Cuckoo Tors	Derby	SK0474	53°16·0'	1°56·0'W	X	119
Cuckoo Trail	E Susx	TQ5813	50°53·9'	0°15·2'E	X	199
Cuckoo Tye	Suff	TL8744	52°4·0'	0°44·1'E	T	155
Cuckoo Wood	Brom	TQ4462	51°20·6'	0°4·4'E	F	177,187
Cuckoo Wood	Monm	SO5204	51°44·2'	2°41·3'W	F	162
Cuckoo Wood Fm	Kent	TQ9452	51°14·3'	0°47·1'E	FM	189
Cuckron	Shetld	HU4051	60°14·7'	1°16·2'W	T	3
Cuckseys Fm	Surrey	TQ3348	51°13·2'	0°5·3'W	FM	187
Cuckstool Lane Top	Lancs	SD8337	53°50·0'	2°15·1'W	X	103
Cucumber Corner	Norf	TG3806	52°36·2'	1°31·3'E	T	134
Cucumber Fm	W Susx	SU8713	50°54·8'	0°45·4'W	FM	197
Cucumber Hall	Essex	TL8726	51°54·3'	0°43·5'E	X	168
Cucumber Hall Fm	Herts	TL2706	51°44·5'	0°9·2'W	FM	166
Cucurrian	Corn	SW5034	50°9·4'	5°29·6'W	X	203
Cudana Geo	Orkney	HY6925	59°6·9'	2°32·0'W	X	5
Cudda Stack	Shetld	HP6715	60°49·0'	0°45·6'W	X	1
Cuddenhay Fm	Devon	SS7615	50°55·5'	3°45·5'W	FM	180
Cudden Point	Corn	SW5427	50°5·8'	5°26·0'W	X	203
Cuddesdon	Oxon	SP6003	51°43·6'	1°7·5'W	T	164,165
Cuddesdon Brook	Oxon	SP6004	51°44·1'	1°7·5'W	W	164,165
Cuddesdon Mill	Oxon	SP6102	51°43·0'	1°6·6'W	X	164,165
Cuddies Point	Highld	NG9138	57°23·3'	5°28·2'W	X	25
Cuddie Wood	E Loth	NT4671	55°56·0'	2°51·4'W	F	66
Cuddig	Powys	SJ0116	52°44·2'	3°27·6'W	X	125
Cuddington	Bucks	SP7311	51°47·8'	0°56·1'W	T	165
Cuddington	Ches	SJ5971	53°14·3'	2°36·5'W	T	117
Cuddington Green	Ches	SJ4546	53°0·8'	2°48·8'W	X	117
Cuddington Hall	Ches	SJ4546	53°0·8'	2°48·8'W	X	117
Cuddington Heath	Ches	SJ4746	53°0·8'	2°47·0'W	T	117
Cuddington Mill Fm	Bucks	SP7210	51°47·3'	0°57·0'W	FM	165
Cuddy Hill	Lancs	SD4937	53°49·9'	2°46·1'W	T	102
Cuddy Ho	N Yks	SE6863	54°3·7'	0°57·2'W	X	100
Cuddy's Hall	Cumbr	NY5181	55°7·5'	2°45·7'W	X	79
Cuddy Shaw Reach	N Yks	SE4760	54°2·3'	1°16·5'W	W	100
Cudham	Brom	TQ4459	51°18·9'	0°4·4'E	T	187
Cudham Frith	Brom	TQ4557	51°17·8'	0°5·2'E	X	188
Cudham Grange	Brom	TQ4457	51°17·9'	0°4·3'E	X	187
Cu' Dheis	Arg & Bt	NL9841	56°28·1'	6°53·8'W	X	46
Cud Hill	Glos	SO8512	51°48·6'	2°12·7'W	X	162
Cudleigh Court Fm	Worcs	SO8954	52°11·3'	2°9·3'W	FM	150
Cudlic	Pemb	SM9906	51°43·2'	4°54·2'W	X	157,158
Cudlipptown	Devon	SX5279	50°35·8'	4°5·1'W	T	191,201
Cudmore Fm	Devon	ST0021	50°59·0'	3°25·1'W	FM	181
Cudmore Grove Country Park	Essex	TM0614	51°47·4'	0°59·6'E	X	168
Cudsden's Fm	Bucks	SP9001	51°42·3'	0°41·5'W	FM	165
Cudworth	Barns	SE3808	53°34·3'	1°25·2'W	T	110,111
Cudworth	Somer	ST3710	50°53·4'	2°53·4'W	T	193
Cudworth	Surrey	TQ2141	51°9·6'	0°15·8'W	T	187
Cudworth Common	Barns	SE3907	53°33·7'	1°24·3'W	T	110,111
Cudworth Common	Barns	SE4007	53°33·7'	1°23·4'W	X	111
Cudworthy	Devon	SS5713	50°54·2'	4°1·6'W	X	180
Cudworthy Moor	Devon	SS5813	50°54·2'	4°0·8'W	X	180
Cuerdale Hall	Lancs	SD5729	53°45·6'	2°38·7'W	X	102
Cuerden Green	Lancs	SD5524	53°42·9'	2°40·5'W	T	102
Cuerden Hall	Lancs	SD5623	53°42·3'	2°39·6'W	X	102
Cuerden Valley Country Park	Lancs	SD5623	53°42·3'	2°39·6'W	X	102
Cuerdley Cross	Warr	SJ5487	53°22·9'	2°41·1'W	T	108
Cufaude	Hants	SU6457	51°18·7'	1°4·5'W	T	175
Cuff Burn	S Lanak	NS8731	55°33·8'	3°47·1'W	W	71,72
Cuffern	Pemb	SM8921	51°51·1'	5°3·4'W	T	157,158
Cuffern Mountain	Pemb	SM8922	51°51·6'	5°3·5'W	H	157,158
Cuff Fm	N Ayr	NS3754	55°45·4'	4°35·4'W	FM	63
Cuff Hill	N Ayr	NS3855	55°45·9'	4°34·5'W	X	63
Cuff Hill	S Lanak	NS8631	55°33·8'	3°48·0'W	X	71,72
Cuffhill Resr	N Ayr	NS3855	55°45·9'	4°34·5'W	W	63
Cuffiau	Powys	SN9891	52°30·7'	3°29·8'W	X	136
Cuffley	Herts	TL3003	51°42·9'	0°6·7'W	T	166
Cuffley Brook	Herts	TL3002	51°42·3'	0°6·7'W	W	166
Cuffnell's Fm	Hants	SU2807	50°51·9'	1°35·7'W	FM	195
Cufforth Ho	Leeds	SE4238	53°50·4'	1°21·3'W	X	105
Cuff's Corner	Wilts	ST9768	51°24·9'	2°2·2'W	X	173
Cuffurach	Moray	NJ3961	57°38·3'	3°0·8'W	T	28
Cugley	Glos	SO7123	51°54·5'	2°24·9'W	X	162
Cuhere Wood	Monm	ST4592	51°37·7'	2°47·3'W	F	171,172
Cuidad Rodrigo	Norf	TM1893	52°29·7'	1°13·1'E	X	134
Cuidhe Cròm	Aberd	NO2584	56°56·7'	3°13·5'W	H	44
Cuidhir	N Eil	NB4124	58°8·0'	6°23·5'W	X	14
Cuidhsiadar	N Eil	NB5458	58°26·7'	6°12·5'W	X	8
Cuidhtinis	N Eil	NG0987	57°47·0'	6°53·3'W	T	14
Cuidrach	Highld	NG3759	57°32·9'	6°23·3'W	T	23
Cuidsgeir	N Eil	NB1798	57°53·2'	6°46·0'W	X	14
Cuier	N Eil	NF6703	57°0·1'	7°28·7'W	X	31
Cuiffie Hill	Orkney	HY3515	59°1·3'	3°7·4'W	H	6
Cuiken	Midlo	NT2361	55°50·4'	3°13·3'W	T	66
Cuil	D & G	NX4662	54°56·0'	4°23·8'W	X	83
Cuil	D & G	NX7760	54°55·4'	3°54·7'W	X	84
Cuil	Highld	NM7468	56°45·2'	5°41·4'W	X	40
Cuil	Highld	NM9855	56°38·9'	5°17·2'W	T	49
Cuil	Pth & Kin	NN8550	56°37·9'	3°52·0'W	X	52
Cuilags	Orkney	HY2003	58°54·7'	3°22·9'W	H	7
Cuil-an Daraich	Pth & Kin	NN9652	56°39·2'	3°41·3'W	X	52,53
Cuil-an-duin	Pth & Kin	NN9851	56°38·6'	3°39·3'W	X	52,53
Cuil Bay	Highld	NM9754	56°38·3'	5°18·2'W	W	49
Cuil Burn	D & G	NX9261	54°56·2'	3°40·7'W	W	84
Cuilcheanna Ho	Highld	NN0161	56°42·2'	5°14·6'W	X	41
Cuildarrach	Highld	NM7284	56°53·7'	5°44·2'W	X	40
Cùil Dhubh	Highld	NC2819	58°7·9'	4°54·8'W	X	15
Cuildochart	Stir	NN5932	56°27·8'	4°16·9'W	X	51
Cuilean Rock	Arg & Bt	NM8847	56°34·3'	5°26·6'W	X	49
Cùil Ghlas	Arg & Bt	NN1943	56°32·9'	4°56·2'W	X	50
Cuil Hill	D & G	NX9163	54°57·2'	3°41·7'W	H	84
Cuil Ho	Arg & Bt	NN1711	56°15·6'	4°56·8'W	X	50,56
Cuilimuich	Arg & Bt	NS1895	56°7·0'	4°55·2'W	X	56
Cuillich	Highld	NH6373	57°43·8'	4°17·6'W	X	21
Cuillin Hills	Highld	NG4422	57°13·3'	6°14·0'W	H	32
Cùil Lochain	Highld	NC0616	58°5·7'	5°17·0'W	W	15
Cuiltemhuc	Pth & Kin	NN8171	56°49·2'	3°56·5'W	X	43
Cùil na h-Airigh	Highld	NG5603	57°3·5'	6°1·0'W	X	32,39
Cuil Plantn	D & G	NY3289	55°11·7'	3°3·7'W	F	79
Cùil Rubha	Arg & Bt	NR7274	55°54·6'	5°38·4'W	X	62
Cuilt	Pth & Kin	NN7520	56°21·6'	4°0·9'W	X	51,52,57
Cuilt	Pth & Kin	NN8824	56°24·0'	3°48·4'W	X	52,58
Cuiltaloskin	Pth & Kin	NN7964	56°45·4'	3°58·3'W	X	42
Cuiltballoch	Pth & Kin	NN8319	56°21·2'	3°53·2'W	X	57
Cuilt Brae	Stir	NS5479	55°59·2'	4°20·0'W	X	64
Cuiltburn	Pth & Kin	NN8817	56°20·2'	3°48·3'W	X	58
Cuilt Hill	Angus	NO2663	56°45·4'	3°12·2'W	H	44
Cuil-uaine	Arg & Bt	NM9233	56°26·9'	5°22·0'W	X	49
Cuilvona	Stir	NN4901	56°10·9'	4°25·5'W	X	57
Cuin	Arg & Bt	NM4252	56°35·6'	6°11·7'W	X	47
Cuinabunag	N Eil	NF7652	57°26·8'	7°23·6'W	X	22
Cuingard	Angus	NO1966	56°47·0'	3°19·1'W	H	43
Cuin Geo	Orkney	HY4342	59°15·9'	2°59·5'W	X	5
Cui Parc	Powys	SO1022	51°53·6'	3°18·1'W	X	161
Cùirn Dearga	Highld	NH0091	57°52·1'	5°21·9'W	X	19
Cùirn Mhòra	Arg & Bt	NR3590	56°2·0'	6°14·8'W	X	61
Cuithe Lachlainn	N Eil	NF7974	57°38·8'	7°22·4'W	X	18
Cuithir	Highld	NG4658	57°32·7'	6°14·2'W	X	23
Cuiveg Point	N Eil	NL5679	56°46·8'	7°37·5'W	X	31
Cùl-a-Bhaile	Arg & Bt	NM3120	56°18·0'	6°20·5'W	X	48
Culabhal	N Eil	NB2031	58°11·0'	6°45·3'W	X	8,13
Culabhal Mòr	N Eil	NB2030	58°10·5'	6°45·3'W	H	8,13
Cùl a' Bhogha	Highld	NH1098	57°56·1'	5°12·1'W	X	19
Cùl a' Chaisteil Dhuibh	Highld	NG4762	57°34·9'	6°13·5'W	X	23
Culachy Falls	Highld	NH3705	57°6·7'	4°41·0'W	W	34
Culachy Forest	Highld	NN3999	57°3·5'	4°38·8'W	X	34
Culachy Ho	Highld	NH3706	57°7·2'	4°41·1'W	X	34
Cùlag	Arg & Bt	NS3595	56°7·4'	4°38·8'W	X	56
Culagach	N Eil	NF8227	57°13·7'	7°15·7'W	X	22
Cùl a' Gheata	Arg & Bt	NM4438	56°28·1'	6°8·9'W	X	47,48
Culag Hotel	Highld	NC0922	58°9·0'	5°14·3'W	X	15
Culaird	Highld	NH7850	57°31·7'	4°1·8'W	X	27
Cùl Allt	Moray	NJ2619	57°15·6'	3°13·1'W	W	37
Cùl an Aonaich Oidhir	Pth & Kin	NN5671	56°48·8'	4°21·1'W	X	42
Cùl an Dùin	Highld	NG8117	57°11·8'	5°37·0'W	X	33
Culantuim	Moray	NJ2220	57°16·1'	3°17·1'W	X	36
Culardoch	Aberd	NO1998	57°4·2'	3°19·7'W	H	36,43
Culardoch Bheag	Aberd	NJ1900	57°5·3'	3°19·7'W	X	36
Culbae	D & G	NX3849	54°48·8'	4°30·8'W	X	83
Cùl Beag	Highld	NC1408	58°1·6'	5°8·5'W	H	15
Cùl Beag	Highld	NH4551	57°31·6'	4°34·9'W	H	26
Culbee Moss	D & G	NX0071	54°59·9'	5°7·2'W	X	76,82
Culbeg	Stir	NS6896	56°8·6'	4°7·0'W	X	57
Culbers Cleuch	D & G	NT2604	55°19·7'	3°9·6'W	X	79
Culbhaie	Arg & Bt	NM7705	56°11·4'	5°35·2'W	X	55
Culbie	Highld	NC5907	58°2·1'	4°22·8'W	X	16
Culbin	Highld	NH5663	57°38·3'	4°24·3'W	X	21
Culbin Forest	Moray	NH9862	57°38·4'	3°42·1'W	F	27
Culblair	Highld	NH7751	57°32·2'	4°2·8'W	X	27
Culblean Cotts	Aberd	NJ5103	57°7·2'	2°48·1'W	X	37
Culblean Hill	Aberd	NJ4001	57°6·0'	2°59·0'W	H	37
Culbo	Highld	NH6360	57°36·8'	4°17·1'W	X	21
Culbokie	Highld	NH6059	57°36·2'	4°20·1'W	T	26
Culbokie Wood	Highld	NH6058	57°35·7'	4°20·1'W	F	26
Culbone	Somer	SS8348	51°13·4'	3°40·1'W	X	181
Culbone Hill	Somer	SS8247	51°12·8'	3°41·0'W	H	181
Culbone Wood	Somer	SS8248	51°13·4'	3°41·0'W	F	181
Culbratten	D & G	NX3862	54°55·8'	4°31·3'W	X	83
Culbuie	Arg & Bt	NR2466	55°48·8'	6°23·9'W	X	60
Culbuirg	Arg & Bt	NM2724	56°20·0'	6°24·6'W	X	48
Culburnie	Highld	NH4841	57°26·3'	4°31·5'W	T	26
Culburnie Muir	Highld	NH4841	57°26·3'	4°31·5'W	X	26
Culbyth	Aberd	NJ8255	57°35·3'	2°17·6'W	X	29,30
Culcabock	Highld	NH6844	57°28·3'	4°11·6'W	T	26
Culcaigrie	D & G	NX6558	54°54·2'	4°5·9'W	X	83,84
Culcaigrie Loch	D & G	NX6657	54°53·6'	4°4·9'W	W	83,84
Culcairn	Highld	NH6066	57°40·0'	4°20·4'W	X	21
Culcairn	Highld	NH6771	57°42·8'	4°13·5'W	X	21
Cùl Campay	N Eil	NB1442	58°16·7'	6°52·3'W	X	13
Culcharron	Arg & Bt	NM9139	56°30·1'	5°23·3'W	X	49
Culcharry	Highld	NH8650	57°31·8'	3°53·8'W	T	27
Culcheth	Warr	SJ6595	53°27·3'	2°31·2'W	T	109
Cùl Chreag	N Eil	NB2815	58°2·7'	6°36·1'W	H	13,14
Culchunaig	Highld	NH7344	57°28·4'	4°6·6'W	X	27
Culcombe Fm	Somer	ST0735	51°6·6'	3°19·3'W	FM	181
Culconich	Highld	NG8689	57°50·6'	5°35·9'W	X	19
Culcrae	D & G	NX6960	54°55·4'	4°2·2'W	X	83,84
Culcraggie	Highld	NH6369	57°41·7'	4°17·4'W	X	21
Culcreuch Castle	Stir	NS6287	56°3·6'	4°12·5'W	X	57
Culcrieff	Pth & Kin	NN8623	56°23·4'	3°50·4'W	X	52,58
Culcronchie	D & G	NX5061	54°55·5'	4°20·0'W	X	83
Culcronchie Burn	D & G	NX5062	54°56·1'	4°20·1'W	W	83
Culcronchie Hill	D & G	NX5163	54°56·6'	4°19·1'W	H	83
Culdaremore	Pth & Kin	NN7247	56°36·1'	4°4·7'W	X	51,52
Culdees	Pth & Kin	NN8816	56°19·6'	3°48·2'W	X	58
Culdeesland	Pth & Kin	NO0325	56°24·7'	3°33·9'W	X	52,53,58
Culderry	D & G	NX4746	54°47·4'	4°22·4'W	X	83
Culdi Geo	Orkney	HY4450	59°20·2'	2°58·6'W	X	5
Culdoach	D & G	NX7053	54°51·5'	4°1·1'W	X	83,84
Culdoach	D & G	NX7170	55°0·7'	4°0·6'W	X	77,84
Culdoach Hill	D & G	NX7154	54°52·1'	4°0·2'W	X	83,84
Culdoach Moor	D & G	NX7154	54°52·1'	4°0·2'W	X	83,84
Culdoich	Highld	NH7543	57°27·9'	4°4·6'W	X	27
Cùl Doireachan	Highld	NH0872	57°42·1'	5°12·9'W	X	19
Cùl Doirlinn	Highld	NM6672	56°47·1'	5°49·4'W	X	40
Culdorachmore	Highld	NJ1036	57°24·6'	3°29·4'W	X	28
Culdrain	Aberd	NJ5233	57°23·4'	2°47·5'W	X	29
Culdrain	D & G	NX8663	54°57·2'	3°46·4'W	X	84
Culdrain Ho	Aberd	NJ5133	57°23·3'	2°48·5'W	X	29
Culdrein Fm	Highld	NJ1135	57°24·1'	3°28·4'W	FM	28
Culdrose Airfield	Corn	SW6725	50°5·0'	5°15·1'W	X	203
Culdrose Manor	Corn	SW6626	50°5·5'	5°15·9'W	X	203
Cùl Dubh	Highld	NH2112	57°10·1'	4°57·2'W	X	34
Culduie	Highld	NG7140	57°23·8'	5°48·2'W	T	24
Culduthel	Highld	NH6641	57°26·6'	4°13·5'W	X	26
Culeave	Highld	NH5591	57°53·4'	4°26·3'W	X	21
Culeave Cott	Highld	NH5591	57°53·4'	4°26·3'W	X	21
Culeaze	Dorset	SY8592	50°43·9'	2°12·4'W	X	194
Cùl Eilean	Highld	NC1233	58°15·0'	5°11·7'W	X	15
Culeryin	Shetld	HU2854	60°16·4'	1°29·1'W	W	3
Culevine	Arg & Bt	NS0956	55°45·8'	5°2·2'W	X	63
Culfargie	Pth & Kin	NO1617	56°20·5'	3°21·1'W	X	58
Culfearn	Moray	NJ0043	57°28·2'	3°39·6'W	X	27
Culfern	Highld	NC8958	58°30·0'	3°53·8'W	X	10
Culfoichbeg	Highld	NJ1132	57°22·4'	3°28·3'W	X	36
Culfoichmore Fm	Highld	NJ0832	57°22·4'	3°31·3'W	FM	27,36
Culfoldie	Moray	NJ3355	57°35·1'	3°6·8'W	X	28
Culford	Suff	TL8370	52°18·1'	0°41·4'E	T	144,155
Culfordheath	Suff	TL8574	52°20·2'	0°43·3'E	T	144
Culford Park	Suff	TL8270	52°18·1'	0°40·6'E	X	144,155
Culfork	Aberd	NJ3310	57°10·8'	3°6·0'W	X	37
Culfork	Aberd	NJ4511	57°11·4'	2°54·1'W	X	37
Culfork	Aberd	NJ5315	57°13·7'	2°46·3'W	X	37
Culfosie	Aberd	NJ7307	57°9·4'	2°26·3'W	X	38
Culfuar	Arg & Bt	NR7045	55°38·9'	5°38·9'W	X	62
Culgaith	Cumbr	NY6029	54°39·5'	2°36·8'W	T	91
Culgarie	D & G	NX3748	54°48·3'	4°31·7'W	X	83
Cùl Glas-bheinne	Highld	NN3247	56°35·4'	4°43·7'W	X	50
Culgower	Highld	NC9711	58°4·8'	3°44·3'W	X	17
Culgower Hill	Highld	NC9713	58°5·9'	3°44·4'W	X	17
Culgrange	D & G	NX0856	54°52·0'	4°59·1'W	X	82
Culham	Oxon	SU5095	51°39·3'	1°16·2'W	T	164
Culham Court	Wok	SU7883	51°32·7'	0°52·1'W	X	175
Culham Cut	Oxon	SU5094	51°38·8'	1°16·2'W	W	164,174
Culham Ho	Oxon	SU5095	51°39·3'	1°16·2'W	X	164
Culham Laboratory, The	Oxon	SU5395	51°39·3'	1°13·6'W	X	164
Culham Reach	Oxon	SU4995	51°39·3'	1°17·1'W	W	164
Culham Station	Oxon	SU5295	51°39·3'	1°14·5'W	X	164
Culhawk	Angus	NO3455	56°41·2'	3°4·2'W	X	54
Culhawk Hill	Angus	NO3456	56°41·7'	3°4·2'W	H	54
Culhay	Aberd	NJ5418	57°15·3'	2°45·3'W	X	37
Culhorn Mains	D & G	NX0858	54°53·0'	4°59·2'W	X	82
Culhorn Parks	D & G	NX0759	54°53·6'	5°0·1'W	X	82
Cul Houb	Shetld	HU4668	60°23·9'	1°9·4'W	W	2,3
Culhouse Plantn	N Yks	SD9255	53°59·7'	2°6·9'W	F	103
Culindrach Fm	Arg & Bt	NR9159	55°47·0'	5°19·6'W	FM	62
Culinish	Arg & Bt	NM4041	56°29·6'	6°13·0'W	X	47,48
Culinlongart	Arg & Bt	NR6511	55°20·5'	5°41·9'W	X	68
Culkein	Highld	NC0333	58°14·8'	5°20·9'W	T	15
Culkein Drumbeg	Highld	NC1133	58°15·0'	5°12·8'W	T	15
Culkerton	Glos	ST9395	51°39·5'	2°5·7'W	T	163
Culkiest	D & G	NX8564	54°57·7'	3°47·3'W	X	84
Culla	N Eil	NF7553	57°27·3'	7°24·7'W	W	22
Cullabine Fm	Glos	SP0136	52°1·6'	1°58·7'W	FM	150
Cullach	D & G	NX3765	54°57·4'	4°32·3'W	X	83
Cullachie	Highld	NH9720	57°15·8'	3°42·0'W	X	36
Cullachie of Rymore	Highld	NH9816	57°13·7'	3°40·9'W	X	36
Cullacott	Corn	SX3088	50°40·2'	4°24·0'W	X	190
Cullaford	Devon	SX6897	50°45·7'	3°51·9'W	X	191
Cullaird	Highld	NH6340	57°26·0'	4°16·5'W	X	26
Cul Lairig	Pth & Kin	NN6148	56°36·5'	4°15·4'W	X	51
Cullaloe	Fife	NT1888	56°4·9'	3°18·6'W	X	65,66
Cullaloe Cotts	Fife	NT1988	56°4·9'	3°17·7'W	X	65,66
Cullaloe Hills	Fife	NT1888	56°4·9'	3°18·6'W	X	65,66
Culland Fm	Derby	SK3653	53°4·6'	1°27·4'W	FM	119
Culland Hall	Derby	SK2439	52°57·1'	1°38·2'W	X	128
Culland Mount	Derby	SK2439	52°57·1'	1°38·2'W	X	128
Culla Voe	Shetld	HU1661	60°20·2'	1°42·1'W	W	3
Cùl Leathaid	Highld	NH0454	57°32·3'	5°16·0'W	X	25
Culleave Croft	Highld	NH5591	57°53·4'	4°26·3'W	X	21
Culleigh	Devon	SS4519	50°57·2'	4°12·0'W	X	180,190
Cullen	Moray	NJ5167	57°41·7'	2°48·9'W	T	29
Cullen Bay	Moray	NJ5067	57°41·7'	2°49·9'W	W	29
Cullendoch Hill	D & G	NX5097	55°14·9'	4°21·2'W	H	77
Cullen House	Moray	NJ5066	57°41·1'	2°49·9'W	A	29
Cullenoch	D & G	NX6665	54°58·0'	4°5·2'W	X	83,84
Cullercoats	N Tyne	NZ3670	55°1·6'	1°25·8'W	T	88
Cullerne	Moray	NJ0563	57°39·1'	3°35·0'W	X	27
Cullernie Wood	Highld	NH7446	57°29·5'	4°5·7'W	F	27
Cullernose Point	Northum	NU2618	55°27·6'	1°34·9'W	X	81
Cullever Steps	Devon	SX6092	50°42·9'	3°58·6'W	X	191
Culley's Fm	Wilts	SU1865	51°23·3'	1°44·1'W	FM	173
Cullicudden	Highld	NH6564	57°39·0'	4°15·3'W	T	21
Cullieshangan	Moray	NJ3850	57°32·4'	3°1·7'W	X	28
Culliford Fm	Devon	ST0814	50°55·3'	3°18·2'W	FM	181
Culligart	Stir	NN4208	56°14·6'	4°32·5'W	X	56
Culligart Burn	Stir	NN4207	56°14·0'	4°32·5'W	W	56
Cullig Mires	Shetld	HP4902	60°42·2'	1°5·6'W	W	1

Culligran	Highld	NH3841	57°26·1'	4°41·5'W	X	26
Culligran Falls	Highld	NH3740	57°25·5'	4°42·4'W	W	26
Culligran Wood	Highld	NH3639	57°25·0'	4°43·4'W	F	26
Cullinaw	D & G	NX8059	54°54·9'	3°51·9'W	X	84
Cullinghurst Fm	E Susx	TQ4739	51°8·1'	0°6·5'E	FM	188
Cullingworth	Brad	SE0636	53°49·5'	1°54·1'W	T	104
Cullingworth Moor	Brad	SE0536	53°49·5'	1°55·0'W	X	104
Cullintyre	Highld	NH5016	57°12·9'	4°28·6'W	X	35
Cullipool	Arg & Bt	NM7312	56°15·0'	5°39·4'W	T	55
Cullisse	Highld	NH8275	57°45·2'	3°58·5'W	X	21
Cullister	Shetld	HU4223	59°59·6'	1°14·3'W	X	4
Cullivait	D & G	NX9981	55°7·0'	3°34·6'W	X	78
Culli Voe	Shetld	HP5402	60°42·1'	1°0·1'W	W	1
Cullivoe	Shetld	HP5402	60°42·1'	1°0·1'W	T	1
Culloch	Pth & Kin	NN7817	56°20·0'	3°58·0'W	T	57
Cùl Lochan	Pth & Kin	NN5351	56°37·9'	4°23·3'W	W	42,51
Culloch Burn	D & G	NX8365	54°58·2'	3°49·2'W	W	84
Culloch Hill	D & G	NX8464	54°57·7'	3°48·3'W	H	84
Culloch Knowes	S Ayr	NS3302	55°17·3'	4°37·4'W	X	76
Cullochrig	N Lanak	NS7569	55°54·1'	3°59·5'W	X	64
Cullochy	Highld	NH3404	57°6·1'	4°44·0'W	X	34
Cullochy Lock	Highld	NH3404	57°6·1'	4°44·0'W	X	34
Culloden	Highld	NH7146	57°29·4'	4°8·7'W	T	27
Culloden Fm	Leic	SK3308	52°40·4'	1°30·3'W	FM	128,140
Culloden Forest	Highld	NH7647	57°30·0'	4°3·7'W	F	27
Culloden Ho Hotel	Highld	NH7246	57°29·4'	4°7·7'W	X	27
Culloden Muir	Highld	NH7345	57°28·9'	4°6·6'W	X	27
Culloden Plantn	Notts	SK6164	53°10·4'	1°4·8'W	F	120
Culloden Wood	Highld	NH7345	57°28·9'	4°6·6'W	F	27
Cullompton	Devon	ST0207	50°51·5'	3°23·2'W	T	192
Cullow	Angus	NO3860	56°43·9'	3°0·4'W	X	44
Cull-peppers Dish	Dorset	SY8192	50°43·9'	2°15·8'W	X	194
Culls, The	Glos	SO8406	51°45·4'	2°13·5'W	X	162
Cullurpattie	D & G	NX1062	54°55·2'	4°57·5'W	X	82
Cullyblean	Aberd	NJ5519	57°15·8'	2°44·3'W	X	37
Cullykhan Bay	Aberd	NJ8466	57°41·3'	2°15·6'W	W	29,30
Culmaily	Highld	NC5906	58°1·5'	4°22·8'W	X	16
Culmaily	Highld	NH8099	57°58·1'	4°1·2'W	X	21
Culmaily Burn	Highld	NC7900	57°58·6'	4°2·3'W	W	17
Culmaily Burn	Highld	NH8099	57°58·1'	4°1·2'W	W	21
Culmain Burn	D & G	NX8468	54°59·8'	3°48·4'W	W	84
Culmalzie	D & G	NX3753	54°51·0'	4°31·9'W	X	83
Culmark	D & G	NX6490	55°11·4'	4°7·7'W	X	77
Culmark Hill	D & G	NX6489	55°10·8'	4°7·7'W	X	77
Culmark Moss	D & G	NX6391	55°11·9'	4°8·7'W	X	77
Culm Cross	Devon	SS6400	50°47·3'	3°55·4'W	X	191
Culm Davy	Devon	ST1215	50°55·9'	3°14·8'W	T	181,193
Culm Davy Hill	Devon	ST1215	50°55·9'	3°14·8'W	X	181,193
Culmellie	Aberd	NJ5212	57°12·0'	2°47·2'W	X	37
Culmer	Surrey	SU9439	51°8·8'	0°39·0'W	T	186
Culmers	Kent	TR0562	51°19·4'	0°56·9'E	T	179
Culmhead	Somer	ST2016	50°56·5'	3°7·9'W	X	193
Culmill	Highld	NH5140	57°25·8'	4°28·4'W	X	26
Culmington	Shrops	SO4982	52°26·3'	2°44·6'W	T	137,138
Culmington Manor	Shrops	SO4783	52°26·8'	2°46·4'W	X	137,138
Cul Mor	Highld	NC1611	58°3·3'	5°6·6'W	H	15
Cùl Mór	Highld	NH4551	57°31·6'	4°34·9'W	H	26
Culmore	D & G	NX1452	54°49·9'	4°57·1'W	X	82
Culmore	Stir	NS6796	56°8·5'	4°8·0'W	T	57
Culm Pyne Barton	Devon	ST1314	50°55·4'	3°13·9'W	X	181,193
Culmstock	Devon	ST1013	50°54·8'	3°16·4'W	T	181,193
Culmstock Beacon	Devon	ST1115	50°55·9'	3°15·6'W	H	181,193
Culm Valley	Devon	ST1013	50°54·8'	3°16·4'W	X	181,193
Cùl na Bèinge	Highld	NB9808	58°1·2'	5°24·7'W	X	15
Culnacloich	Pth & Kin	NN9429	56°26·7'	3°42·7'W	X	52,53,58
Culnacnoc	Highld	NG5162	57°35·0'	6°9·5'W	T	23,24
Culnacraig	Highld	NC0603	57°58·7'	5°16·4'W	X	15
Culnacraig	Highld	NH6651	57°32·3'	4°13·8'W	X	26
Cùl na Creige	Stir	NN6229	56°26·2'	4°13·8'W	H	51
Culnadalloch	Arg & Bt	NM9433	56°26·9'	5°20·1'W	X	49
Culnagreine	Stir	NN5604	56°12·7'	4°18·9'W	X	57
Culnaha	Highld	NH8172	57°43·6'	3°59·4'W	X	21
Cul na h-Aird	N Eil	NB1202	57°55·1'	6°51·4'W	X	14
Culnaightrie	D & G	NX7750	54°50·0'	3°54·5'W	X	84
Culnakirk	Highld	NH4930	57°20·4'	4°30·1'W	X	26
Culnamean	Highld	NG4120	57°12·1'	6°16·8'W	X	32
Cul na Muice	N Eil	NF8481	57°42·7'	7°17·9'W	X	18
Cùl nan Creagan	N Ayr	NR9737	55°35·3'	5°12·8'W	H	69
Cùl nan Glas-chlach	Highld	NH1697	57°55·7'	5°6·0'W	X	20
Culnara	Highld	NH6292	57°54·0'	4°19·2'W	X	21
Culnaskeath	Highld	NH5763	57°38·3'	4°23·3'W	X	21
Culnells	Kent	TQ8866	51°21·9'	0°42·4'E	X	178
Cul Ness	Shetld	HU4669	60°24·4'	1°9·4'W	X	2,3
Culnoag	D & G	NX4247	54°47·8'	4°27·0'W	X	83
Culpercy Cott	Aberd	NO7495	57°3·0'	2°25·3'W	X	38,45
Culphin of Park	Aberd	NJ5958	57°36·9'	2°40·7'W	X	29
Culpho	Suff	TM2149	52°5·9'	1°14·0'E	T	169
Culpho Fm	Suff	TM3064	52°13·8'	1°22·5'E	FM	156
Culpho Hall	Suff	TM2048	52°5·4'	1°13·1'E	X	169
Culpho Wood	Suff	TM2049	52°6·0'	1°13·1'E	F	169
Culquha	D & G	NX6958	54°54·2'	4°2·2'W	X	83,84
Culquhasen	D & G	NX2453	54°50·7'	4°44·0'W	X	82
Culquhirk	D & G	NX4256	54°52·7'	4°27·3'W	X	83
Culquoich	Aberd	NJ4113	57°12·5'	2°58·1'W	X	37
Culquoich	Moray	NJ2041	57°27·4'	3°19·5'W	X	28
Culraggie Burn	Moray	NJ2022	57°17·2'	3°19·2'W	W	36
Culrain	Highld	NH5794	57°55·0'	4°24·4'W	T	21
Culra Lodge	Highld	NN5276	56°51·4'	4°25·2'W	X	42
Culraven	D & G	NX6448	54°48·8'	4°6·6'W	X	83
Culreach	Highld	NJ0123	57°17·5'	3°38·1'W	X	36
Culreoch	D & G	NX0658	54°53·0'	5°1·0'W	X	82
Culreoch	D & G	NX5861	54°55·7'	4°12·5'W	X	83
Cùl Riabhach	Aberd	NO1779	56°54·0'	3°21·3'W	X	43
Cùl Riabhach	Pth & Kin	NO1575	56°51·8'	3°23·2'W	H	43
Culrigrein	N Eil	NB4334	58°13·5'	6°22·1'W	T	8
Culross	Fife	NS9885	56°3·1'	3°37·8'W	T	65
Culross Moor	Fife	NS9587	56°4·1'	3°40·8'W	F	65
Culroy	D & G	NX2553	54°50·7'	4°43·1'W	X	82
Culroy	S Ayr	NS3114	55°23·7'	4°39·7'W	T	70
Culscadden	D & G	NX4649	54°49·0'	4°23·4'W	X	83
Culsetter	Shetld	HU3715	59°55·4'	1°19·8'W	X	4
Cùl Sgàthain	Arg & Bt	NL9839	56°27·0'	6°53·7'W	X	46
Culsh	Aberd	NJ4517	57°14·7'	2°54·2'W	X	37
Culsh	Aberd	NJ5005	57°8·2'	2°49·1'W	X	37
Culsh	Aberd	NO3497	57°3·8'	3°4·8'W	X	37,44
Culshabbin	D & G	NX3050	54°49·2'	4°38·3'W	X	82
Culshan	D & G	NX8069	55°0·3'	3°52·1'W	X	84
Culsharg	D & G	NX4182	55°6·7'	4°29·1'W	X	77
Culshaw's Fm	Lancs	SD5119	53°40·2'	2°44·1'W	FM	108
Culswick	Shetld	HU2745	60°11·6'	1°30·3'W	T	4
Cult	W Loth	NS9264	55°51·7'	3°43·1'W	X	65
Cultain	Moray	NJ5362	57°38·9'	2°46·8'W	X	29
Cultalonie	Pth & Kin	NO0858	56°42·5'	3°29·7'W	X	52,53
Cultam Hill	D & G	NX7667	54°59·2'	3°55·8'W	H	84
Cultenhove	Stir	NS7889	56°5·0'	3°57·2'W	X	57
Culter Allers Fm	S Lanak	NT0331	55°34·0'	3°31·9'W	FM	72
Culter Allers House	S Lanak	NT0233	55°35·1'	3°32·9'W	X	72
Culter Cleuch Shank	S Lanak	NT0322	55°29·2'	3°31·7'W	H	72
Cultercullen Fm	Aberd	NJ9124	57°18·6'	2°8·5'W	FM	38
Culter Fell	S Lanak	NT0529	55°33·0'	3°29·9'W	H	72
Culter Field	Shetld	HU4229	60°2·9'	1°14·3'W	X	4
Culter Ho	C of Aber	NJ8401	57°6·2'	2°15·4'W	X	38
Culter Ho	S Lanak	NT0234	55°35·6'	3°32·9'W	X	72
Culter Park	S Lanak	NT0133	55°35·1'	3°33·8'W	X	72
Culter Water	S Lanak	NT0329	55°33·0'	3°31·8'W	W	72
Culter Water	S Lanak	NT0526	55°31·4'	3°29·9'W	W	72
Culter Waterhead	S Lanak	NT0327	55°31·9'	3°31·8'W	X	72
Culteuchar	Pth & Kin	NO0815	56°19·4'	3°28·8'W	X	58
Culteuchar Hill	Pth & Kin	NO0915	56°19·4'	3°27·8'W	H	58
Cultezeoun	S Ayr	NS2809	55°21·0'	4°42·3'W	X	70,76
Culthibert	Aberd	NJ6311	57°11·6'	2°36·3'W	X	37
Cult Hill	Fife	NT0296	56°9·1'	3°34·2'W	H	58
Culthill	Pth & Kin	NO0941	56°33·4'	3°28·4'W	X	52,53
Cultieheldoch	Pth & Kin	NN8415	56°19·1'	3°52·1'W	X	58
Cultie	Highld	NH5220	57°15·1'	4°26·7'W	X	26,35
Cultmill	Fife	NT0394	56°8·0'	3°33·2'W	X	58
Cult Ness	Fife	NT1281	56°1·1'	3°24·3'W	X	65
Cultoquhey	Pth & Kin	NN8923	56°23·4'	3°47·4'W	X	52,58
Cultrig Burr	W Loth	NS9263	55°51·1'	3°43·1'W	W	65
Cults	Aberd	NJ5331	57°22·3'	2°46·4'W	X	29,37
Cults	Aberd	NO6393	57°1·9'	2°36·1'W	X	37,45
Cults	C of Aber	NJ8902	57°6·8'	2°10·4'W	T	38
Cults	D & G	NX1259	54°53·7'	4°55·5'W	X	82
Cults	D & G	NX4643	54°45·8'	4°23·2'W	X	83
Cults	Moray	NJ1619	57°15·5'	3°23·1'W	X	36
Cults Farm	Fife	NO3509	56°16·4'	3°2·5'W	FM	59
Cults Hill	Fife	NO3408	56°15·9'	3°3·5'W	H	59
Cults Loch	D & G	NX1260	54°54·2'	4°55·5'W	W	82
Cults Mill	Fife	NO3410	56°16·9'	3°3·5'W	X	59
Cultsykefoot	W Loth	NS9264	55°51·7'	3°43·1'W	X	65
Cultullich Burn	Pth & Kin	NN8948	56°36·9'	3°48·1'W	W	52
Cultybraggan	Pth & Kin	NN7619	56°21·1'	4°0·0'W	T	57
Cultybraggan Camp	Pth & Kin	NN7619	56°21·1'	4°0·0'W	X	57
Cultybraggan Camp	Pth & Kin	NN7720	56°21·6'	3°59·0'W	X	51,52,57
Culvennan	D & G	NX7364	54°57·5'	3°58·6'W	X	83,84
Culvennan Fell	D & G	NX3165	54°57·3'	4°37·9'W	H	82
Culver	Devon	SX8490	50°42·1'	3°38·2'W	X	191
Culver Cliff	I of W	SZ6385	50°39·9'	1°6·1'W	X	196
Culver Court	Devon	SX8297	50°45·9'	3°40·0'W	X	191
Culver Down	I of W	SZ6385	50°39·9'	1°6·1'W	X	196
Culver Fm	E Susx	TQ4214	50°54·7'	0°1·6'E	FM	198
Culverhayes	Somer	ST1038	51°8·3'	3°16·8'W	X	181
Culverhay Fm	Somer	ST0727	51°2·3'	3°19·2'W	FM	181
Culverhill	Devon	SX4276	50°34·0'	4°13·5'W	X	201
Culverhill Fm	Devon	SS7022	50°59·2'	3°50·7'W	FM	180
Culver Ho	Corn	SW4938	50°11·6'	5°30·6'W	A	203
Culver Hole	Swan	SS4092	51°36·5'	4°18·3'W	A	159
Culver Hole	Swan	SS4684	51°32·3'	4°12·8'W	A	159
Culverhole Point	Devon	SY2789	50°42·0'	3°1·6'W	X	193
Culver Ho, The	Glos	SO6811	51°48·0'	2°27·5'W	X	162
Culverhouse	Corn	SW9871	50°30·5'	4°50·6'W	A	200
Culverlands	Surrey	SU8546	51°12·6'	0°46·6'W	X	186
Culverlands	W Berks	SU6667	51°24·1'	1°2·7'W	X	175
Culverlane	Devon	SX7460	50°25·8'	3°46·1'W	T	202
Culverley Fm	Hants	SU3604	50°50·3'	1°28·9'W	FM	196
Culverslade	S Glos	ST7874	51°28·1'	2°18·6'W	X	172
Culverstone Green	Kent	TQ6362	51°20·2'	0°20·8'E	T	177,188
Culverswell Hill	Surrey	SU8945	51°12·1'	0°43·2'W	X	186
Culverthorpe	Lincs	TF0240	52°57·1'	0°28·5'W	T	130
Culverthorpe Hollow	Lincs	TF0239	52°56·6'	0°28·5'W	X	130
Culverton Manor	Bucks	SP8002	51°42·9'	0°50·1'W	X	165
Culvert's Fm	Essex	TL7609	51°45·3'	0°33·4'E	FM	167
Culverwell	Somer	ST0138	51°8·2'	3°24·5'W	X	181
Culverwood	E Susx	TQ5720	50°57·7'	0°14·5'E	X	199
Culverwood Ho	Herts	TL2908	51°45·6'	0°7·5'W	X	166
Culvery Bridge	Devon	SX8398	50°46·4'	3°39·2'W	X	191
Culvie	Aberd	NJ5953	57°34·2'	2°40·7'W	X	29
Culvie Hill	Aberd	NJ5754	57°34·7'	2°42·7'W	H	29
Culviehill Crofts	Aberd	NJ5754	57°34·7'	2°42·7'W	X	29
Culvie Valley Croft	Aberd	NJ5953	57°34·2'	2°40·7'W	X	29
Culvie Wood	Aberd	NJ5755	57°35·2'	2°42·7'W	X	29
Culwatty Bay	Arg & Bt	NS2781	55°59·7'	4°46·0'W	W	63
Culworth	Northnts	SP5446	52°6·8'	1°12·3'W	T	152
Culworth Grounds	Northnts	SP5345	52°6·3'	1°13·2'W	X	152
Culzean Bay	S Ayr	NS2411	55°21·9'	4°46·2'W	W	70
Culzean Castle	S Ayr	NS2310	55°21·4'	4°47·1'W	A	70
Culzean Country Park	S Ayr	NS2309	55°20·8'	4°47·1'W	X	70,76
Culzie Lodge	Highld	NH5171	57°42·5'	4°29·6'W	X	20
Cumberhead	S Lanak	NS7734	55°35·3'	3°56·7'W	X	71
Cumberhill Fm	Derby	SK3242	52°58·7'	1°31·0'W	FM	119,128
Cumberland Bower	Northum	NT9555	55°47·5'	2°4·3'W	X	67,74,75
Cumberland Cott	Ches	SJ9969	53°13·3'	2°0·6'W	X	118
Cumberland Lodge	Win & Maid	SU9671	51°26·0'	0°36·7'W	X	175,176
Cumberland's Stone	Highld	NH7545	57°28·9'	4°4·6'W	X	27
Cumberley	Shrops	SO5874	52°22·0'	2°36·6'W	X	137,138
Cumberlow Green	Herts	TL3030	51°57·4'	0°6·1'W	T	166
Cumbernauld	N Lanak	NS7674	55°56·8'	3°58·7'W	T	64
Cumbernauld Ho	N Lanak	NS7775	55°57·4'	3°57·8'W	X	64
Cumbernauld Village	N Lanak	NS7676	55°57·9'	3°58·8'W	T	64
Cumber's Bank	Wrex	SJ4439	52°57·0'	2°49·6'W	T	126
Cumber's Fm	W Susx	SU8323	51°0·3'	0°48·6'W	FM	197
Cumberwood Fm	Glos	SO8429	51°57·8'	2°13·6'W	FM	150
Cumberworth	Lincs	TF5073	53°14·2'	0°15·3'E	T	122
Cumberworth Ings	Lincs	TF5072	53°13·7'	0°15·2'E	X	122
Cumblands	Cumbr	SD0897	54°21·9'	3°24·5'W	X	96
Cumbria Coastal Way	Cumbr	SD4480	54°13·0'	2°51·1'W	X	97
Cumbria Cycle Way	Cumbr	NX9822	54°35·2'	3°34·3'W	X	89
Cumbria Cycle Way	Cumbr	NY2859	54°55·5'	3°7·0'W	X	85
Cumbria Cycle Way	Cumbr	NY5352	54°51·9'	2°43·5'W	X	86
Cumbria Cycleway	Cumbr	NY6916	54°32·5'	2°28·3'W	X	91
Cumbrian Mountains	Cumbr	NY2614	54°31·2'	3°8·2'W	H	89,90
Cumbria Way	Cumbr	NY2518	54°33·4'	3°9·2'W	X	89,90
Cumbria Way	Cumbr	NY3745	54°48·0'	2°58·4'W	X	85
Cumbria Way	Cumbr	SD2790	54°18·3'	3°6·9'W	X	96,97
Cumcatch	Cumbr	NY5461	54°56·7'	2°42·7'W	X	86
Cumcrook	Cumbr	NY5074	55°3·7'	2°46·5'W	X	86
Cumdivock	Cumbr	NY3448	54°49·6'	3°1·2'W	T	85
Cum Dulas	Cered	SN6954	52°10·4'	3°54·5'W	X	146
Cumeragh Village	Lancs	SD5636	53°49·3'	2°39·7'W	T	102
Cumery	Devon	SX6649	50°19·8'	3°52·6'W	X	202
Cumha Geodha	N Eil	NB1539	58°15·1'	6°51·0'W	X	13
Cum Hag Wood	N Yks	SE6971	54°8·1'	0°56·2'W	F	100
Cumhang a' Ghlinne	Highld	NG8740	57°24·3'	5°32·3'W	X	24
Cumhann Mór	Arg & Bt	NR5481	55°57·8'	5°56·1'W	W	61
Cuminestown	Aberd	NJ8050	57°32·6'	2°19·6'W	T	29,30
Cuming Fm	Devon	SX7563	50°27·4'	3°45·3'W	FM	202
Cumla	Shetld	HU5894	60°37·8'	0°55·9'W	X	1,2
Cumla Geo	Orkney	ND4583	58°44·1'	2°56·5'W	X	7
Cumlaquoy	Orkney	HY2325	59°6·6'	3°20·2'W	X	6
Cumle	Shetld	HU3263	60°21·3'	1°24·7'W	H	3
Cumledge	Scot Bord	NT7956	55°48·1'	2°19·7'W	T	67,74
Cumledge Mill	Scot Bord	NT7957	55°48·6'	2°19·7'W	X	67,74
Cumlewick	Shetld	HU4222	59°59·1'	1°14·3'W	T	4
Cumlewick Ness	Shetld	HU4222	59°59·1'	1°14·3'W	X	4
Cumleys	D & G	NY0586	55°9·8'	3°29·0'W	X	78
Cumlins	Shetld	HU5279	60°29·7'	1°2·7'W	X	2,3
Cumlodden Cott	Arg & Bt	NS0099	56°8·8'	5°12·7'W	X	55
Cumloden	D & G	NX4167	54°58·6'	4°28·6'W	X	83
Cumloden Deer Parks	D & G	NX4169	54°59·7'	4°28·7'W	X	83
Cummersdale	Cumbr	NY3853	54°52·3'	2°57·5'W	T	85
Cummersdale Grange Fm	Cumbr	NY3853	54°52·3'	2°57·5'W	FM	85
Cummerton	Aberd	NJ7758	57°36·9'	2°22·6'W	X	29,30
Cummerton	Aberd	NJ8463	57°39·7'	2°15·6'W	X	29,30
Cummertrees	D & G	NY1466	54°59·1'	3°20·2'W	T	85
Cummi Howe	Orkney	HY2810	58°58·5'	3°14·7'W	X	6
Cummi Howe (Brock)	Orkney	HY2810	58°58·5'	3°14·7'W	A	6
Cumminess	Orkney	HY2810	58°58·5'	3°14·7'W	X	6
Cumming Carr	Lancs	SD4246	53°54·7'	2°52·6'W	X	102
Cummings Hill	Scot Bord	NT6412	55°24·3'	2°33·7'W	X	80
Cummings Park	C of Aber	NJ9108	57°10·0'	2°8·5'W	T	38
Cummingstown	Moray	NJ1368	57°41·9'	3°27·1'W	T	28
Cummins Fm	Devon	ST2503	50°49·5'	3°3·5'W	FM	192,193
Cummin's Fm	Heref	SO7340	52°3·7'	2°23·2'W	FM	150
Cummins Fm	Worcs	SO8858	52°13·4'	2°10·1'W	FM	150
Cumnock	E Ayr	NS5719	55°26·9'	4°15·2'W	T	71
Cumnock House Fm	E Renf	NS5055	55°46·2'	4°23·0'W	FM	64
Cumnor	Oxon	SP4604	51°44·2'	1°19·6'W	T	164
Cumnor Hill	Oxon	SP4705	51°44·7'	1°18·8'W	T	164
Cumnor Ho (Sch)	E Susx	TQ4028	51°2·3'	0°0·2'E	X	187,198
Cumpstone Ho	Cumbr	NY8315	54°32·0'	2°15·3'W	X	91,92
Cumpston Hill	Cumbr	SD7797	54°22·3'	2°20·8'W	X	98
Cumrack Burn	Highld	NH4611	57°10·1'	4°32·4'W	W	34
Cumrenton	Cumbr	NY4962	54°57·3'	2°47·4'W	X	86
Cumrew	Cumbr	NY5450	54°50·8'	2°42·6'W	T	86
Cumrew Fell	Cumbr	NY5651	54°51·4'	2°40·7'W	H	86
Cumrue	D & G	NY0686	55°9·8'	3°28·1'W	X	78
Cumrue Loch	D & G	NY0686	55°9·8'	3°28·1'W	W	78
Cumstone	D & G	NY1886	55°9·9'	3°16·8'W	X	79
Cumstoun	D & G	NX6853	54°51·5'	4°3·0'W	X	83,84
Cumstoun Mains	D & G	NX6753	54°51·5'	4°3·9'W	X	83,84
Cumwhinton	Cumbr	NY4552	54°51·8'	2°51·0'W	T	86
Cumwhitton	Cumbr	NY5052	54°51·9'	2°46·3'W	T	86
Cundall	N Yks	SE4272	54°8·8'	1°21·0'W	T	99
Cundall Lodge	N Yks	SE4273	54°9·3'	1°21·0'W	X	99
Cundry Mains	S Ayr	NX1490	55°10·4'	4°54·8'W	X	76
Cundy Cross	Barns	SE3706	53°33·2'	1°26·1'W	T	110,111
Cundy Hos	Barns	SK3197	53°28·4'	1°31·6'W	T	110,111
Cunliffe Ho	Derby	SK2182	53°20·3'	1°40·7'W	X	110
Cunliffe Ho Fm	Lancs	SD6934	53°48·3'	2°27·8'W	FM	103
Cunliffe's Fm	Bolton	SD6812	53°36·5'	2°28·6'W	FM	109
Cunmont	Angus	NO4936	56°31·1'	2°49·3'W	X	54
Cunnach Moss	Aberd	NO7599	57°5·1'	2°24·3'W	X	38,45
Cunndal	N Eil	NB5165	58°30·4'	6°16·0'W	W	8
Cunner Law	Fife	NO4806	56°14·9'	2°49·9'W	X	59
Cunnery	Derby	SK3259	53°7·9'	1°30·9'W	X	119
Cunningill Hill	Shetld	HU4367	60°23·3'	1°12·7'W	H	2,3
Cunningar	Aberd	NJ7005	57°8·4'	2°29·3'W	X	38
Cunningar (Motte)	Aberd	NJ7005	57°8·4'	2°29·3'W	A	38
Cunningarth	Cumbr	NY2646	54°48·5'	3°8·7'W	X	85
Cunningar Wood	Aberd	NJ6913	57°12·7'	2°30·3'W	F	38
Cunning Burn	Aberd	NJ6850	57°32·6'	2°31·6'W	W	29
Cunning Dale	Derby	SK0872	53°14·9'	1°52·4'W	X	119
Cunning Garth	Cumbr	NY3547	54°49·1'	3°0·3'W	X	85
Cunning Geo	Shetld	HU3730	60°3·4'	1°19·6'W	X	4
Cunninghame	D & G	NX3855	54°52·1'	4°31·0'W	X	83
Cunninghame	E Ayr	NS4046	55°41·1'	4°32·3'W	X	64
Cunninghame	N Ayr	NS3146	55°40·9'	4°40·8'W	X	63
Cunninghamhead	N Ayr	NS3741	55°38·4'	4°35·0'W	T	70
Cunning Holm	Shetld	HU4855	60°16·8'	1°7·4'W	X	3
Cunning Park	S Ayr	NS3219	55°26·4'	4°38·9'W	X	70
Cunning Point	Cumbr	NX9722	54°35·2'	3°35·2'W	X	89
Cunningsburgh	Shetld	HU4130	60°3·4'	1°15·3'W	X	4
Cunnington's Barn	Norf	TF6808	52°38·8'	0°29·4'E	X	143
Cunnister	Shetld	HU5296	60°38·9'	1°2·4'W	T	1
Cunnoquhie	Fife	NO3115	56°19·6'	3°6·5'W	X	59
Cunnoquhie East Hill Wood	Fife	NO3016	56°20·1'	3°7·5'W	F	59
Cunnoquhie Mill	Fife	NO3116	56°20·1'	3°6·5'W	X	59
Cunnoquhie West Hill Wood	Fife	NO3015	56°19·6'	3°7·5'W	F	59

Cunscough Hall	Sefton	SD4102	53°30·9′	2°53·0′W	X	108
Cunsey Beck	Cumbr	SD3794	54°20·5′	2°57·7′W	W	96,97
Cunsey Wood	Cumbr	SD3793	54°20·0′	2°57·7′W	F	96,97
Cuns Fell	Cumbr	NY6436	54°43·3′	2°33·1′W	H	91
Cunside	Highld	NC5851	58°25·7′	4°25·4′W	X	10
Cunston Cott	Inverc	NS3372	55°55·0′	4°39·9′W	X	63
Cunstone Nab	N Yks	TA1083	54°14·1′	0°18·3′W	X	101
Cunswick Hall	Cumbr	SD4893	54°20·0′	2°47·6′W	X	97
Cunswick Scar	Cumbr	SD4993	54°20·0′	2°46·6′W	X	97
Cunswick Tarn	Cumbr	SD4893	54°20·0′	2°47·6′W	W	97
Cunyan Crags	Northum	NT9718	55°27·6′	2°2·4′W	X	81
Cunzierton Fm	Scot Bord	NT7418	55°27·6′	2°24·2′W	FM	80
Cupar	Fife	NO3714	56°19·1′	3°0·7′W	T	59
Cupar Muir	Fife	NO3613	56°18·6′	3°1·6′W	T	59
Cupernham	Hants	SU3622	51°0·0′	1°28·8′W	T	185
Cupid Green	Herts	TL0709	51°46·4′	0°26·6′W	T	166
Cupid's Hill	Monm	SO4025	51°55·5′	2°52·0′W	T	161
Cuplahills	Fife	NO4120	56°22·4′	2°56·9′W	X	54,59
Cupola	Northum	NY7958	54°55·2′	2°19·2′W	X	86,87
Cupola Fm	Suff	TL6881	52°24·3′	0°28·6′E	FM	143
Cupola, The	Suff	TM4362	52°12·4′	1°33·8′E	X	156
Cuppablack	Orkney	HY3518	59°2·9′	3°7·5′W	X	6
Cuppa Water	Shetld	HU4252	60°15·3′	1°14·0′W	W	3
Cuppers of Vacquoy	Orkney	HY4132	59°10·5′	3°1·4′W	X	5,6
Cuppin	Orkney	HY4950	59°20·3′	2°53·3′W	X	5
Cupping	Orkney	HY3511	58°59·1′	3°7·4′W	X	6
Cupps, The	Shetld	HU2782	60°31·5′	1°30·0′W	X	3
Cuptree	Stir	NS6999	56°10·2′	4°6·2′W	X	57
Cupwith Hill	Kirk	SE0313	53°37·1′	1°56·9′W	X	110
Cupwith Resr	Kirk	SE0314	53°37·6′	1°56·9′W	W	110
Curachan	N Eil	NL7499	56°58·3′	7°21·5′W	X	31
Curbar	Derby	SK2574	53°16·0′	1°37·1′W	T	119
Curbar Edge	Derby	SK2575	53°16·5′	1°37·1′W	X	119
Curborough	Staffs	SK1212	52°42·6′	1°48·9′W	T	128
Curbridge	Hants	SU5211	50°54·0′	1°15·2′W	T	196
Curbridge	Oxon	SP3308	51°46·4′	1°30·9′W	T	164
Curdale	Shrops	SO6675	52°22·6′	2°29·6′W	X	138
Curdale Hill	Shetld	HU3869	60°24·5′	1°18·1′W	H	2,3
Curd Hall Fm	Essex	TL8321	51°51·7′	0°39·9′E	FM	168
Curdiff	Cumbr	NY5857	54°54·6′	2°38·9′W	X	86
Curdlehill Fm	Oxon	SP3223	51°54·5′	1°31·7′W	FM	164
Curdleigh	Somer	ST2117	50°57·1′	3°7·1′W	X	193
Curdridge	Hants	SU5313	50°55·1′	1°14·4′W	T	196
Curds Fm	E Susx	TQ4115	50°55·3′	0°0·8′E	FM	198
Curdworth	Warw	SP1792	52°31·8′	1°44·6′W	T	139
Curefield	Shetld	HU4422	59°59·1′	1°12·2′W	X	4
Cure Water	Shetld	HU3175	60°27·7′	1°25·7′W	W	3
Curf	Cambs	TL3988	52°28·6′	0°3·2′E	X	142,143
Curf Fen	Cambs	TL3988	52°28·6′	0°3·2′E	X	142,143
Curf Fm	Cambs	TL3989	52°29·1′	0°3·2′E	FM	142,143
Curgurrell	Corn	SW8837	50°11·9′	4°57·9′W	T	204
Curham	Devon	SS9911	50°53·6′	3°25·8′W	X	192
Curin	Highld	NH3755	57°33·6′	4°43·0′W	X	26
Cùrlach	Arg & Bt	NR3256	55°43·7′	6°15·7′W	X	60
Curland	Somer	ST2717	50°57·1′	3°2·0′W	T	193
Curland Common	Somer	ST2717	50°57·1′	3°2·0′W	T	193
Curl Brook	Heref	SO3555	52°11·6′	2°56·7′W	W	148,149
Curles Manor	Essex	TL4631	51°57·7′	0°7·9′E	X	167
Curlethney Hill	Aberd	NO8391	57°0·8′	2°16·3′W	H	38,45
Curlew Fm	Lancs	SD4442	53°52·5′	2°50·7′W	FM	102
Curlew Green	Suff	TM3865	52°14·1′	1°29·5′E	T	156
Curlew Lodge	Lincs	TF4824	52°47·8′	0°12·1′E	X	131
Curlews Fm	N Lincs	SE7810	53°35·1′	0°48·9′W	FM	112
Curleys	Angus	NO5242	56°34·3′	2°46·4′W	X	54
Curleywee	D & G	NX4576	55°3·5′	4°25·2′W	H	77
Curlieu Fm	Warw	SP2264	52°16·7′	1°40·3′W	FM	151
Curling Fm	Scot Bord	NT5126	55°31·8′	2°46·1′W	FM	73
Curling Tye Green	Essex	TL8207	51°44·2′	0°38·5′E	T	168
Curload	Somer	ST3428	51°3·1′	2°56·1′W	T	193
Curlusk	Moray	NJ3649	57°31·9′	3°3·7′W	X	28
Curly Burn	Scot Bord	NT3332	55°34·9′	3°3·3′W	W	73
Curnelloch Burn	D & G	NX4980	55°5·7′	4°21·6′W	W	77
Curney	Shrops	SO2084	52°27·1′	3°10·2′W	X	137
Curnix Fm	V of Glam	ST0669	51°25·0′	3°20·7′W	FM	170
Currach Mór	Arg & Bt	NR6111	55°20·4′	5°45·7′W	X	68
Currack Rigg	Durham	NY9918	54°33·7′	2°0·5′W	X	92
Curracksthane	Aberd	NO8196	57°3·5′	2°18·3′W	X	38,45
Curragh a' Ghlinne	Arg & Bt	NR5166	55°49·6′	5°58·1′W	A	61
Curragh Beg	I of M	SC4497	54°20·9′	4°23·6′W	X	95
Curraghs, The	I of M	SC3695	54°19·7′	4°30·9′W	X	95
Curragh, The	S Ayr	NS1901	55°16·5′	4°50·5′W	X	76
Currall Hall	Worcs	SO5965	52°17·1′	2°35·7′W	X	137,138,149
Curra Lochain	Arg & Bt	NS1599	56°9·1′	4°58·3′W	W	56
Currarie	S Ayr	NX1690	55°10·5′	4°52·9′W	X	76
Currarie Fm	S Ayr	NX0678	55°3·8′	5°1·8′W	FM	76
Currarie Glen	S Ayr	NX0678	55°3·8′	5°1·8′W	X	76
Currarie Port	S Ayr	NX0577	55°3·2′	5°2·7′W	W	76
Curr Burn	Scot Bord	NT8324	55°30·8′	2°15·7′W	W	74
Currendon Fm	Dorset	SZ0181	50°38·0′	1°58·8′W	FM	195
Currer Laithe	Brad	SE0840	53°51·6′	1°52·3′W	X	104
Currer Laithe	N Yks	SE0252	53°58·1′	1°57·8′W	X	104
Currer Wood	Brad	SE0244	53°53·8′	1°57·8′W	F	104
Currian Vale	Corn	SW9657	50°22·9′	4°51·8′W	T	200
Currick	Cumbr	NY7338	54°44·4′	2°24·7′W	X	91
Curridge	W Berks	SU4871	51°26·4′	1°18·2′W	T	174
Currie	C of Edin	NT1867	55°53·6′	3°18·2′W	T	65,66
Currie Ho	Midlo	NT3759	55°49·5′	2°59·9′W	X	66,73
Currie Inn Fm	Midlo	NT3758	55°48·9′	2°59·9′W	FM	66,73
Currie Lee	Midlo	NT3862	55°51·1′	2°59·0′W	X	66
Currie Mains	Midlo	NT3759	55°49·5′	2°59·9′W	X	66,73
Currie Rig	D & G	NX5999	55°16·2′	4°12·7′W	X	77
Curries Firth	Orkney	ND3694	58°50·0′	3°6·0′W	W	7
Curriestanes	D & G	NX9575	55°3·8′	3°38·2′W	X	84
Currievale	C of Edin	NT1768	55°54·1′	3°19·2′W	X	65,66
Curriott Hill	Somer	ST4309	50°52·9′	2°48·2′W	X	193
Curriton	Devon	SS7810	50°52·8′	3°43·7′W	X	191
Currochs	Pth & Kin	NN8522	56°22·8′	3°51·3′W	X	52,58
Currock	Cumbr	NY4054	54°52·9′	2°55·7′W	T	85
Currock Hill	Northum	NZ1059	54°55·8′	1°50·2′W	X	88
Curr, The	Scot Bord	NT8523	55°30·3′	2°13·8′W	H	74
Curr Wood	Highld	NH9923	57°17·4′	3°40·1′W	F	36
Curry	Essex	TL9905	51°42·7′	0°53·2′E	X	168
Curry Fm	Kent	TQ4860	51°19·4′	0°7·8′E	FM	177,188
Curry Lane	Corn	SX2993	50°42·9′	4°25·0′W	T	190
Curry Mallet	Somer	ST3221	50°59·3′	2°57·7′W	T	193
Curry Moor	Somer	ST3227	51°2·5′	2°57·8′W	X	193
Currypool Fm	Somer	ST2238	51°8·4′	3°6·5′W	FM	182
Curry Rivel	Somer	ST3925	51°1·5′	2°51·8′W	T	193
Curscombe Fms	Devon	ST1101	50°48·3′	3°15·4′W	FM	192,193
Cursiter	Orkney	HY3712	58°59·7′	3°5·3′W	T	6
Cursneh Hill	Heref	SO4759	52°13·8′	2°46·2′W	X	148,149
Cursta Hill	Shetld	HU2156	60°17·5′	1°36·7′W	H	3
Cursus, The	Wilts	SU1142	51°10·9′	1°50·2′W	A	184
Curteis' Corner	Kent	TQ8539	51°7·4′	0°39·0′E	T	189
Curtis Burn	Northum	NY9281	55°7·6′	2°7·1′W	W	80
Curtisden Green	Kent	TQ7440	51°8·2′	0°29·6′E	T	188
Curtis Fm	Essex	TL4005	51°43·8′	0°2·0′E	FM	167
Curtis Fm	Suff	TL9842	52°2·7′	0°53·6′E	FM	155
Curtishulme Fm	Ches	SJ7364	53°10·6′	2°23·8′W	FM	118
Curtisknowle	Devon	SX7353	50°22·0′	3°46·8′W	T	202
Curtismill Green	Essex	TQ5196	51°38·8′	0°11·3′E	T	167,177
Curwen Hall Fm	Lancs	SD5967	54°6·1′	2°37·2′W	FM	97
Curwen Woods	Cumbr	SD5378	54°12·0′	2°42·8′W	F	97
Curworthy Fm	Devon	SX5697	50°45·5′	4°2·1′W	FM	191
Cury	Corn	SW6721	50°2·8′	5°14·9′W	T	203
Curzon Br	Surrey	SU9256	51°18·0′	0°40·4′W	X	175,186
Curzon Lodge	Derby	SK2356	53°6·3′	1°39·0′W	X	119
Curzon Street Fm	Hants	SU3958	51°19·4′	1°26·0′W	FM	174
Cusa Voe	Shetld	HU3539	60°8·3′	1°21·7′W	W	4
Cusbay	Orkney	HY5537	59°13·3′	2°46·8′W	T	5
Cusbay	Orkney	HY5538	59°13·8′	2°46·8′W	W	5
Cuscas	Derby	SK2544	52°59·8′	1°37·2′W	X	119,128
Cusgarne	Corn	SW7540	50°13·3′	5°8·9′W	T	204
Cushat End	Scot Bord	NT8023	55°30·3′	2°18·6′W	H	74
Cushatgrove	D & G	NX9258	54°54·6′	3°40·7′W	X	84
Cushathill	D & G	NY2275	55°4·1′	3°12·9′W	X	85
Cushat Law	Northum	NT9213	55°24·9′	2°7·2′W	H	80
Cushats, The	S Ayr	NS4121	55°27·7′	4°30·5′W	X	70
Cushat Stiel	Northum	NU2521	55°29·2′	1°35·8′W	X	75
Cushat Wood	D & G	NX9761	54°56·2′	3°36·0′W	F	84
Cushieston	Aberd	NJ7130	57°21·8′	2°28·5′W	X	29
Cushlachie	Aberd	NJ4312	57°12·0′	2°56·1′W	X	37
Cushnie	Aberd	NJ5125	57°19·0′	2°48·4′W	X	37
Cushnie	Aberd	NJ7041	57°27·8′	2°29·5′W	X	29
Cushnie	Aberd	NJ7962	57°39·1′	2°20·7′W	X	29,30
Cushnie	Aberd	NO7578	56°53·8′	2°24·2′W	X	45
Cushnie Burn	Aberd	NJ5211	57°11·5′	2°47·2′W	W	37
Cush Rigg	N Yks	SD8781	54°13·7′	2°11·5′W	X	98
Cushuish	Somer	ST1930	51°4·1′	3°9·0′W	T	181
Cuskayne Fm	Corn	SW8948	50°17·9′	4°57·4′W	FM	204
Cusop	Heref	SO2341	52°4·0′	3°7·0′W	T	148,161
Cusop	Powys	SN9830	51°57·8′	3°28·7′W	X	160
Cusop Dingle	Heref	SO2440	52°3·4′	3°6·1′W	X	148,161
Cusop Hill	Heref	SO2540	52°3·4′	3°5·2′W	H	148,161
Cussacombe Common	Devon	SS8030	51°3·6′	3°42·4′W	X	181
Cussacombe Gate	Devon	SS8030	51°3·6′	3°42·4′W	X	181
Cusse's Gorse	Wilts	SU1637	51°8·2′	1°45·9′W	X	184
Custard Field Fm	Derby	SK1363	53°10·1′	1°47·9′W	FM	119
Custards	Hants	SU2908	50°52·5′	1°34·9′W	T	196
Cust Hall	Essex	TL7336	52°0·0′	0°31·6′E	X	155
Custogion	Powys	SO0579	52°24·3′	3°23·4′W	X	136,147
Custom House	Newham	TQ4181	51°30·8′	0°2·3′E	T	177
Cusveorth Coombe	Corn	SW7643	50°14·9′	5°8·2′W	T	204
Cusworth	Donc	SE5404	53°32·0′	1°10·7′W	T	111
Cusworth Park Country Park	Donc	SE5403	53°31·5′	1°10·7′W	X	111
Cutcare	Corn	SX2767	50°28·9′	4°25·9′W	X	201
Cutcarwood	Scot Bord	NT3225	55°31·1′	3°4·2′W	X	73
Cutchems End	Northnts	SP6852	52°10·0′	0°59·9′W	X	152
Cutcloy	D & G	NX4535	54°41·4′	4°23·9′W	X	83
Cutcombe	Somer	SS9239	51°8·6′	3°32·3′W	T	181
Cutcombe Barrow	Somer	SS9635	51°6·5′	3°28·8′W	A	181
Cut Combe Water	Devon	SX5883	50°38·0′	4°0·1′W	W	191
Cut Dike	Lincs	TF2649	53°1·6′	0°6·9′W	W	131
Cut Dike	Lincs	TF2750	53°2·2′	0°5·9′W	W	122
Cutgate	Roch	SD8614	53°37·6′	2°12·3′W	T	109
Cut Gate	Sheff	SK1996	53°27·9′	1°42·3′W	X	110
Cuthayes Fm	Devon	SY3298	50°46·9′	2°57·5′W	FM	193
Cuthberthope Rig	Scot Bord	NT7814	55°25·4′	2°20·4′W	H	80
Cuthbert Scotts	Wigan	SD5506	53°33·2′	2°40·3′W	X	108
Cuthbert's Hill	Durham	NY9245	54°48·2′	2°7·0′W	X	87
Cuthelton	Falk	NS8281	56°0·7′	3°53·1′W	X	65
Cuthil Brae	Stir	NS7299	56°10·2′	4°3·3′W	X	57
Cuthlie Harbour	Angus	NO7046	56°36·6′	2°28·9′W	X	54
Cut Hill	Devon	SX5982	50°37·5′	3°59·2′W	H	191
Cuthill	E Loth	NT3874	55°57·6′	2°59·1′W	T	66
Cuthill	W Loth	NS9863	55°51·2′	3°37·3′W	X	65
Cuthill Links	Highld	NH7587	57°51·6′	4°5·9′W	X	21
Cuthill Rocks	E Loth	NT3774	55°57·5′	3°0·1′W	X	66
Cuthill Sands	Highld	NH7587	57°51·6′	4°5·9′W	X	21
Cut Hill Stream	Devon	SX6082	50°37·5′	3°58·4′W	W	191
Cuthill Towers	Pth & Kin	NO1508	56°15·7′	3°21·9′W	X	58
Cuthlie	Angus	NO5941	56°33·8′	2°39·6′W	X	54
Cutiau	Gwyn	SH6317	52°44·2′	4°1·4′W	T	124
Cutkive Wood	Corn	SX2967	50°28·9′	4°24·2′W	F	201
Cutland Ho	Devon	SS6817	50°56·5′	3°52·3′W	X	180
Cutler	E Ayr	NS4507	55°20·2′	4°26·2′W	X	70,77
Cutler Brook	Derby	SK2941	52°58·2′	1°33·7′W	W	119,128
Cutlers	Kent	TR0452	51°14·1′	0°55·7′E	X	179,189
Cutler's Fm	Warw	SP1762	52°15·6′	1°44·7′W	FM	151
Cutler's Fm	Worcs	SO8038	52°2·6′	2°17·1′W	FM	150
Cutlers Green	Essex	TL5930	51°57·0′	0°17·2′E	T	167
Cutler's Green	Somer	ST5952	51°16·2′	2°34·9′W	T	182,183
Cutler's Wood	Suff	TM1538	52°0·1′	1°8·3′E	F	169
Cutlinwith	Corn	SX3560	50°25·2′	4°19·0′W	X	201
Cutmadoc	Corn	SX0963	50°26·4′	4°41·0′W	T	200
Cutmaple	Essex	TL7831	51°57·2′	0°35·8′E	X	167
Cutmere	Corn	SX3260	50°25·2′	4°21·5′W	T	201
Cutmill	Glos	SO7330	51°58·3′	2°23·2′W	X	150
Cutmill Fm	Oxon	SP4004	51°44·2′	1°24·9′W	FM	164
Cutnall Green	Worcs	SO8768	52°18·8′	2°11·0′W	T	139
Cut-off Channel	Norf	TL7197	52°32·9′	0°31·7′E	W	143
Cuton Hall	Essex	TL7308	51°44·9′	0°30·8′E	X	167
Cutreoch	D & G	NX4635	54°41·4′	4°22·9′W	X	83
Cutsdean	Glos	SP0830	51°58·3′	1°52·6′W	T	150
Cutsdean Hill	Glos	SP1030	51°58·3′	1°50·9′W	X	150
Cutsey Ho	Somer	ST1820	50°58·6′	3°9·7′W	X	181,193
Cutshaw Fm	Brad	SE0342	53°52·7′	1°56·8′W	FM	104
Cutsyke	Wakf	SE4224	53°42·9′	1°21·4′W	X	105
Cuttacksnest	Aberd	NJ4621	57°16·8′	2°53·3′W	X	37
Cuttenham Fm	Wilts	SU1057	51°19·0′	1°51·0′W	FM	173
Cutten's Hill	Suff	TM4570	52°16·6′	1°35·9′E	X	156
Cutteridge Fm	Devon	SX8792	50°43·2′	3°35·7′W	FM	192
Cutteridge Fm	Wilts	ST8453	51°16·8′	2°13·4′W	FM	183
Cutters Barn	Hants	SU3319	50°58·4′	1°31·4′W	X	185
Cutter's Grove	Suff	TM2657	52°10·1′	1°18·7′E	F	156
Cutter's Pool	D & G	NX6746	54°47·7′	4°3·7′W	W	83,84
Cuttery Fm	Devon	SX7650	50°20·4′	3°44·2′W	FM	202
Cutteslowe	Oxon	SP5010	51°47·4′	1°16·1′W	T	164
Cut, The	Win & Maid	SU8675	51°28·3′	0°45·3′W	W	175
Cut, The	W Susx	TQ0223	51°0·1′	0°32·4′W	F	197
Cut-thorn	Ches	SK0068	53°12·8′	1°59·6′W	X	119
Cutthorn	C of Soton	SU4215	50°56·2′	1°23·7′W	A	196
Cut Thorn	Ghead	NZ1858	54°55·2′	1°42·7′W	X	88
Cutthorne	Somer	SS8938	51°8·1′	3°34·8′W	X	181
Cut-thorn Hill	Ches	SK0068	53°12·8′	1°59·6′W	H	119
Cutthorpe	Derby	SK3473	53°15·4′	1°29·0′W	T	119
Cutthroat Br	Derby	SK2187	53°23·0′	1°40·6′W	X	110
Cuttieburn	Aberd	NJ4625	57°19·0′	2°53·3′W	X	37
Cuttie Burn	D & G	NX5356	54°52·9′	4°17·1′W	W	83
Cuttiemore Burn	D & G	NX5369	54°59·9′	4°17·5′W	W	83
Cuttie Shallow Burn	D & G	NX5371	55°1·0′	4°17·5′W	W	77
Cuttieshillock	Aberd	NO6491	57°0·8′	2°35·1′W	X	45
Cuttiesouter	Aberd	NO7984	56°57·1′	2°20·3′W	X	45
Cuttie's Wood	Aberd	NO6390	57°0·2′	2°36·1′W	F	45
Cuttiford's Door	Somer	ST3210	50°53·4′	2°57·6′W	T	193
Cutting Hill	Herts	TL3122	51°53·1′	0°5·4′W	X	166
Cutting Hole	Suff	TM0267	52°16·1′	0°58·0′E	X	155
Cuttinglye Wood	W Susx	TQ3538	51°7·7′	0°3·8′W	F	187
Cuttivett	Corn	SX3662	50°26·3′	4°18·2′W	X	201
Cuttle Brook	Bucks	SP7603	51°43·5′	0°53·6′W	W	165,165
Cuttle Brook	Oxon	SP7004	51°44·1′	0°58·8′W	W	165
Cuttle Brook	Sol	SP1975	52°22·6′	1°42·9′W	W	139
Cuttlecraigs	Aberd	NJ7526	57°19·7′	2°24·5′W	X	38
Cuttleford	Ches	SJ8359	53°7·9′	2°14·8′W	X	118
Cuttlehill	Fife	NT1589	56°5·4′	3°21·5′W	X	65
Cuttle Hill	Notts	SK6943	52°59·0′	0°57·9′W	X	129
Cuttlesham Fms	Somer	ST6930	51°4·3′	2°26·2′W	FM	183
Cuttlestone Br	Staffs	SJ9113	52°43·1′	2°7·6′W	X	127
Cutt Mill	Dorset	ST7716	50°56·8′	2°19·3′W	X	183
Cutt Mill	Oxon	SU6696	51°39·8′	1°2·4′W	X	164,165
Cutt Mill Ho	Surrey	SU9145	51°12·0′	0°41·5′W	X	186
Cutton	Devon	SX9798	50°46·6′	3°27·3′W	X	192
Cuttpool	Orkney	HY5805	58°56·1′	2°43·3′W	X	6
Cutts	Shetld	HU4038	60°7·7′	1°16·3′W	X	4
Cutt's Wood	Notts	SK6462	53°9·3′	1°2·2′W	F	120
Cuttybridge	Pemb	SM9319	51°50·1′	4°59·9′W	T	157,158
Cuttyhill	Aberd	NK0450	57°32·7′	1°55·5′W	T	30
Cutty Sark	Gren	TQ3877	51°28·7′	0°0·4′W	X	177
Cutty Stubbs	Dorset	SY4096	50°45·9′	2°50·7′W	X	193
Cutwellwalls	Devon	SX7057	50°24·1′	3°49·4′W	X	202
Cuxham	Oxon	SU6695	51°39·2′	1°2·4′W	T	164,165
Cuxton	Medway	TQ7066	51°22·3′	0°26·9′E	T	178
Cuxwold	Lincs	TA1701	53°29·8′	0°13·8′W	T	113
Cwarrau-mawr	Caer	ST1489	51°35·8′	3°14·1′W	X	171
Cwâr y Gigfran	Powys	SO0619	51°51·9′	3°21·5′W	X	160
Cwar yr Hendre	Powys	SO0914	51°49·3′	3°18·8′W	X	161
Cwar-yr-Ystrad	Powys	SO0713	51°48·7′	3°20·6′W	X	160
Cwm	Blae Gw	SO1805	51°44·5′	3°10·9′W	T	161
Cwm	Card	ST1784	51°33·2′	3°11·4′W	X	171
Cwm	Carm	SN2627	51°55·1′	4°31·4′W	X	145,158
Cwm	Carm	SN3222	51°52·5′	4°26·0′W	X	145,159
Cwm	Carm	SN3521	51°52·0′	4°23·4′W	X	145,159
Cwm	Carm	SN4310	51°46·2′	4°16·1′W	X	159
Cwm	Carm	SN4821	51°52·3′	4°12·1′W	X	159
Cwm	Cered	SN2049	52°6·8′	4°37·3′W	X	145
Cwm	Conwy	SH9964	53°10·1′	3°30·2′W	X	116
Cwm	Denb	SJ0539	52°56·6′	3°24·4′W	X	125
Cwm	Denb	SJ0677	53°17·1′	3°24·2′W	T	116
Cwm	Denb	SJ1048	53°1·5′	3°20·1′W	X	116
Cwm	Gwyn	SH4345	52°59·0′	4°19·9′W	X	115,123
Cwm	Nth Pt Talb	SS8094	51°38·2′	3°43·7′W	T	170
Cwm	Powys	SH9701	52°36·1′	3°30·9′W	X	136
Cwm	Powys	SJ0202	52°36·7′	3°26·4′W	X	136
Cwm	Powys	SN9563	52°15·6′	3°31·9′W	X	147
Cwm	Powys	SO0082	52°25·9′	3°27·9′W	X	136
Cwm	Powys	SO0562	52°15·1′	3°23·1′W	X	147
Cwm	Powys	SO0595	52°32·9′	3°23·7′W	T	136
Cwm	Powys	SO0962	52°15·2′	3°19·6′W	X	147
Cwm	Powys	SO1194	52°32·4′	3°18·3′W	X	136
Cwm	Powys	SO1445	52°6·0′	3°14·9′W	X	148
Cwm	Powys	SO1564	52°16·3′	3°14·3′W	X	148
Cwm	Powys	SO1832	51°59·1′	3°11·3′W	X	161
Cwm	Powys	SO2254	52°11·0′	3°8·1′W	X	148
Cwm	Powys	SO2346	52°6·7′	3°7·1′W	X	148
Cwm	Powys	SO2590	52°30·4′	3°5·9′W	T	137
Cwm	Shrops	SO2278	52°23·9′	3°8·4′W	X	137,148
Cwm	Shrops	SO3379	52°24·5′	2°58·7′W	T	137,148
Cwmache	Powys	SO0137	52°1·6′	3°26·2′W	X	160
Cwmafan	Nth Pt Talb	SS7892	51°37·1′	3°45·3′W	T	170
Cwm Afan	Nth Pt Talb	SS8395	51°38·7′	3°41·1′W	X	170
Cwm Afan	Nth Pt Talb	SS8796	51°39·3′	3°37·6′W	X	170
Cwm Afon	Torf	SO2607	51°45·6′	3°3·9′W	X	161
Cwmagol	Carm	SN5621	51°52·4′	4°5·1′W	X	159
Cwmagwr	Cered	SN6976	52°22·2′	3°55·1′W	X	135
Cwmalan	Powys	SJ1119	52°45·9′	3°18·7′W	X	125
Cwmalis	Denb	SJ2441	52°57·9′	3°7·5′W	X	117
Cwm Aman	Carm	SN6913	51°48·3′	3°53·6′W	X	160
Cwmaman	Rho Cyn Taf	ST0099	51°41·1′	3°26·4′W	T	170
Cwm Amarch	Gwyn	SH7110	52°40·6′	3°54·1′W	X	124

Cwmamliw	Powys	SO0655	52°11·4′	3°22·1′W	X	147
Cwmann	Carm	SN5847	52°6·4′	4°4·0′W	T	146
Cwmaran	Powys	SO1467	52°17·9′	3°15·3′W	X	136,148
Cwmarch	Cered	SN2147	52°5·8′	4°36·4′W	X	145
Cwmarch	Cered	SN3949	52°7·2′	4°20·7′W	X	145
Cwmargenau	Carm	SN7234	51°59·6′	3°51·5′W	X	146,160
Cwmarirog	Powys	SO2176	52°22·8′	3°9·2′W	X	137,148
Cwmau	Carm	SN3620	51°51·5′	4°22·5′W	X	145,159
Cwmau Bach	Carm	SN3720	51°51·5′	4°21·6′W	X	145,159
Cwmavon	Torf	SO2706	51°45·1′	3°3·1′W	T	161
Cwmavon Ho	Torf	SO2706	51°45·1′	3°3·1′W	X	161
Cwmbach	Carm	SN2525	51°54·0′	4°32·2′W	T	145,158
Cwmbach	Carm	SN4801	51°41·5′	4°11·6′W	X	159
Cwm-bach	Pemb	SM8322	51°51·5′	5°8·7′W	W	157
Cwmbach	Powys	SO1639	52°2·8′	3°13·1′W	T	161
Cwmbach	Rho Cyn Taf	SO0201	51°42·2′	3°24·7′W	T	170
Cwm Bach	Wrex	SJ1334	52°54·0′	3°17·2′W	X	125
Cwmbach Llechrhyd	Powys	SO0254	52°10·8′	3°25·6′W	T	147
Cwm Banw	Powys	SO2223	51°54·2′	3°7·6′W	X	161
Cwm Bargod	Merth Tyd	SO0801	51°42·3′	3°19·5′W	X	170
Cwm Bargod	Merth Tyd	SO0900	51°41·7′	3°18·6′W	X	171
Cwmbarre	Cered	SN3549	52°7·1′	4°24·2′W	X	145
Cwmbasset	Carm	SN6018	51°50·8′	4°1·6′W	X	159
Cwmbedw	Cered	SN3450	52°7·6′	4°25·1′W	X	145
Cwm-bedw	Cered	SN4359	52°12·7′	4°17·5′W	X	146
Cwmbedw	Powys	SO0569	52°18·9′	3°23·2′W	X	136,147
Cwmbelan	Powys	SN9481	52°25·2′	3°33·1′W	T	136
Cwmberach	Carm	SN6715	51°49·3′	3°55·4′W	X	159
Cwmberllan	Powys	SO2092	52°31·4′	3°10·4′W	X	137
Cwm Bern	Cered	SN2850	52°7·5′	4°30·4′W	X	145
Cwmberwyn	Cered	SN7158	52°12·5′	3°52·9′W	X	146,147
Cwm-berwyn	Powys	SO0754	52°10·8′	3°21·2′W	X	147
Cwm Berwyn Plantation	Cered	SN7256	52°11·5′	3°52·0′W	F	146,147
Cwmbettws	Pemb	SN1639	52°1·4′	4°40·5′W	X	145
Cwm Beusych	Powys	SO2521	51°53·2′	3°5·0′W	X	161
Cwm Big	Blae Gw	SO2003	51°43·4′	3°9·1′W	X	171
Cwmbiga	Powys	SN8589	52°29·5′	3°41·2′W	X	135,136
Cwmbir	Monm	ST3999	51°41·4′	2°52·6′W	X	171
Cwmblaenerw Brook	Powys	SO1051	52°9·2′	3°18·5′W	W	148
Cwm Blaenpelenna	Nth Pt Talb	SS8197	51°39·8′	3°42·8′W	X	170
Cwmbologue	Heref	SO3529	51°57·6′	2°56·4′W	X	149,161
Cwm-brain	Shrops	SO2377	52°23·4′	3°7·5′W	X	137,148
Cwmbran	Carm	SN3337	52°0·6′	4°25·6′W	X	145
Cwm-Brân	Carm	SN7528	51°56·4′	3°48·7′W	X	146,160
Cwmbran	Gwyn	SH4748	53°0·7′	4°16·4′W	X	115,123
Cwmbrân or Cwmbran	Newp	ST2995	51°39·2′	3°1·2′W	T	171
Cwmbran or Cwmbrân	Newp	ST2995	51°39·2′	3°1·2′W	T	171
Cwmbrith	Powys	SO0960	52°14·1′	3°19·6′W	X	147
Cwm-brîth Bank	Powys	SO0860	52°14·1′	3°20·4′W	F	147
Cwm Bromley	Powys	SO2293	52°32·0′	3°8·6′W	X	137
Cwm Brook	Heref	SO3726	51°56·0′	2°54·6′W	W	161
Cwmbrook	Powys	SO1029	51°57·4′	3°18·2′W	X	161
Cwmbrwyn	Carm	SN2512	51°47·0′	4°31·8′W	X	158
Cwmbrwyno	Cered	SN7080	52°24·4′	3°54·3′W	T	135
Cwm Brwynog	Gwyn	SH5955	53°4·7′	4°5·9′W	X	115
Cwmbrynich Fm	Powys	SN9425	51°55·0′	3°32·1′W	FM	160
Cwm Bugail	Powys	SO1779	52°24·4′	3°12·8′W	X	136,148
Cwm Bustach	Powys	SH8502	52°36·5′	3°41·5′W	X	135,136
Cwmbwch	Cered	SN3547	52°6·0′	4°24·2′W	X	145
Cwm-bwch	Monm	SO2619	51°52·1′	3°4·1′W	X	161
Cwm Bwch	Powys	SO1764	52°16·3′	3°12·6′W	X	148
Cwm-bwchel	Monm	SO2827	51°56·4′	3°2·5′W	X	161
Cwm-bwch-fawr	Powys	SO0146	52°6·4′	3°26·3′W	X	147
Cwm-bychan	Carm	SN4334	51°59·2′	4°16·8′W	X	146
Cwmbychan	Cered	SN3647	52°6·1′	4°23·3′W	X	145
Cwmbychan	Cered	SN3852	52°8·8′	4°21·7′W	X	145
Cwm Bychan	Gwyn	SH6046	52°59·8′	4°4·8′W	X	115
Cwm Bychan	Gwyn	SH6431	52°51·8′	4°0·8′W	X	124
Cwm-bychan-bâch	Powys	SH8502	52°36·5′	3°41·5′W	X	135,136
Cwmbychan-mawr	Powys	SH8501	52°35·9′	3°41·5′W	X	135,136
Cwm-byr	Carm	SN6332	51°58·4′	3°59·3′W	X	146
Cwm-byr	Cered	SN6571	52°19·5′	3°58·5′W	X	135
Cwmbyr	Powys	SN7895	52°32·6′	3°47·5′W	X	135
Cwmbyr	Powys	SO0587	52°28·6′	3°23·5′W	X	136
Cwm Cadian	Gwyn	SH7405	52°37·9′	3°51·3′W	X	124
Cwm Cadlan	Rho Cyn Taf	SN9509	51°46·4′	3°30·9′W	X	160
Cwm Cae	Cered	SN6486	52°27·5′	3°59·7′W	X	135
Cwm Cae	Powys	SO2791	52°31·0′	3°4·1′W	X	137
Cwm-cafn	Cered	SN5554	52°10·2′	4°6·8′W	X	146
Cwmcalch Isaf	Powys	SN9199	52°34·9′	3°36·1′W	X	136
Cwm Callan	Powys	SO0614	51°49·2′	3°21·4′W	X	160
Cwm Camlais	Powys	SN9528	51°56·7′	3°31·3′W	X	160
Cwm Camlais-fawr	Powys	SN9526	51°55·6′	3°31·2′W	X	160
Cwmcanol	Carm	SN5942	52°3·7′	4°3·0′W	X	146
Cwm-canol	Carm	SN6421	51°52·5′	3°58·1′W	X	159
Cwm Canol	Conwy	SH8862	53°8·8′	3°40·1′W	X	116
Cwm Canol	Denb	SJ1441	52°57·8′	3°16·4′W	X	125
Cwm Canol	Wrex	SJ1134	52°54·0′	3°19·0′W	X	125
Cwm Capel	Carm	SN4502	51°42·0′	4°14·2′W	T	159
Cwm Caregog	Gwyn	SH5952	53°3·0′	4°5·8′W	X	115
Cwmcarfan Hill	Monm	SO4705	51°44·7′	2°45·7′W	X	161
Cwmcarn	Caer	ST2193	51°38·1′	3°8·1′W	T	171
Cwm-carnedd	Powys	SH9102	52°36·5′	3°36·2′W	X	136
Cwmcarvan	Monm	SO4707	51°45·8′	2°45·7′W	T	161
Cwmcarvan Court	Monm	SO4807	51°45·8′	2°44·8′W	X	161
Cwm-castell	Carm	SN3923	51°53·2′	4°20·0′W	X	145,159
Cwmcathan	Carm	SN4237	52°0·8′	4°17·7′W	X	146
Cwm Cathan	Swan	SN6409	51°46·0′	3°57·9′W	X	159
Cwmcayo Fm	Monm	SO3702	51°43·0′	2°54·3′W	FM	171
Cwm-Cefn-y-Gaer	Powys	SO1269	52°19·0′	3°17·1′W	A	136,148
Cwm-cegyr	Monm	SO2517	51°51·0′	3°4·9′W	X	161
Cwm-ceirw	Cered	SN5676	52°22·0′	4°6·5′W	X	135
Cwm-celli	Carm	SN5527	51°55·6′	4°6·1′W	X	146
Cwm-celyn	Blae Gw	SO2008	51°46·1′	3°9·2′W	T	161
Cwm-celyn	Carm	SN3112	51°47·1′	4°26·6′W	X	159
Cwm-cemrhiw	Powys	SN7696	52°33·1′	3°49·3′W	X	135
Cwm-cenau	Pemb	SN0740	52°1·7′	4°48·4′W	X	145
Cwmcennen	Carm	SN6618	51°50·9′	3°56·3′W	X	159
Cwm Cerddin	Gwyn	SH9120	52°46·2′	3°36·5′W	X	125
Cwm Cerdin	Brig	SS8489	51°35·5′	3°40·1′W	X	170
Cwmcerdinen	Swan	SN6307	51°44·9′	3°58·7′W	T	159
Cwmcerrig	Carm	SN6231	51°57·9′	4°0·1′W	X	146
Cwmcerwyn	Brig	SS8390	51°36·0′	3°41·0′W	X	170
Cwm Cesig	Rho Cyn Taf	SS9694	51°38·4′	3°29·8′W	X	170
Cwm Ceulan	Cered	SN7090	52°29·8′	3°54·5′W	X	135
Cwm Ceunant	Gwyn	SH6263	53°9·0′	4°3·4′W	X	115
Cwm-Cewydd	Gwyn	SH8713	52°42·4′	3°40·0′W	T	124,125
Cwmchwefru	Powys	SN9558	52°12·9′	3°31·8′W	X	147
Cwmcîb	Carm	SN6521	51°52·5′	3°57·3′W	X	159
Cwm-cidy Fm	V of Glam	ST0967	51°23·9′	3°18·1′W	FM	171
Cwm Cilio	Gwyn	SH4244	52°58·5′	4°20·8′W	X	123
Cwm Ciprwth	Gwyn	SH5248	53°0·8′	4°12·0′W	X	115
Cwm Cleisfer	Powys	SO1518	51°51·5′	3°13·7′W	X	161
Cwm Clic	Nth Pt Talb	SN7505	51°44·0′	3°48·2′W	X	160
Cwm Cloch	Gwyn	SH5847	53°0·3′	4°6·6′W	X	115
Cwm Clogwyn	Gwyn	SH5954	53°4·1′	4°5·9′W	X	115
Cwm Clorad	Conwy	SH6855	53°4·8′	3°57·8′W	X	115
Cwm-clorad-isaf	Conwy	SH6856	53°5·3′	3°57·9′W	X	115
Cwm Clwyd	Powys	SN9757	52°12·3′	3°30·0′W	X	147
Cwmclwyd	Wrex	SJ1935	52°54·6′	3°11·9′W	X	125
Cwmclyd	Carm	SN7930	51°57·6′	3°45·3′W	X	146,160
Cwm-clyd	Cered	SN6273	52°20·5′	4°1·1′W	X	135
Cwmclyd	Powys	SO0970	52°19·5′	3°19·7′W	X	136,147
Cwm Clydach	Monm	SO2012	51°48·3′	3°9·2′W	X	161
Cwm-Clydach	Powys	SN8931	51°58·2′	3°36·6′W	X	160
Cwm Clydach	Powys	SN9127	51°56·1′	3°34·7′W	X	160
Cwm Clydach	Rho Cyn Taf	ST0596	51°39·5′	3°22·0′W	X	170
Cwm Clydach	Swan	SN6804	51°43·4′	3°54·3′W	X	159
Cwmclyn	Powys	SN9825	51°55·1′	3°28·6′W	X	160
Cwm Cneifa	Pemb	SN2636	52°0·0′	4°31·7′W	X	145
Cwm Cneifio	Gwyn	SH6258	53°6·3′	4°3·3′W	X	115
Cwm Cnyw	Blae Gw	SO2200	51°41·8′	3°7·3′W	X	171
Cwmcoch	Carm	SN3518	51°50·4′	4°23·3′W	X	159
Cwm-côch	Carm	SN5125	51°54·5′	4°9·6′W	X	146
Cwm-coch	Gwyn	SH6361	53°8·0′	4°2·5′W	X	115
Cwmcoch	Powys	SN9470	52°19·3′	3°32·9′W	X	136,147
Cwmcoched	Heref	SO3226	51°55·9′	2°58·9′W	X	161
Cwmcoedifor	Carm	SN5838	52°1·6′	4°3·8′W	X	146
Cwmcoednerth	Cered	SN3448	52°6·6′	4°25·1′W	T	145
Cwmcoedog	Cered	SN4553	52°9·5′	4°15·6′W	X	146
Cwm Coedycerrig	Monm	SO2921	51°53·2′	3°1·5′W	X	161
Cwm Coeg	Powys	SH8008	52°39·6′	3°46·1′W	X	124,125
Cwm Coel	Powys	SN8963	52°15·5′	3°37·2′W	X	147
Cwm Collo	Shrops	SO2378	52°23·9′	3°7·5′W	X	137,148
Cwm Connell	Pemb	SN1146	52°5·0′	4°45·1′W	X	145
Cwm-coryn Fm	Gwyn	SH4045	52°59·0′	4°22·6′W	FM	115,123
Cwm-Cothi	Merth Tyd	ST0998	51°40·6′	3°18·6′W	X	171
Cwm Cottage Fm	Gwyn	SH9940	52°57·1′	3°29·8′W	FM	125
Cwm-cou	Cered	SN2941	52°2·7′	4°29·2′W	T	145
Cwmcowddu	Carm	SN7231	51°58·0′	3°51·4′W	X	146,160
Cwmcoy	Carm	SN7023	51°53·7′	3°53·0′W	X	160
Cwm-coy	Cered	SN6264	52°15·7′	4°0·9′W	X	146
Cwmcoygen	Carm	SN6636	52°0·6′	3°56·8′W	X	146
Cwmcoynant	Powys	SO2337	52°1·8′	3°6·9′W	X	161
Cwm-cragen	Carm	SN5828	51°56·2′	4°3·5′W	X	146
Cwm Crai	Powys	SN8925	51°55·0′	3°36·4′W	X	160
Cwm Craig Fm	Heref	SO5332	51°59·3′	2°40·7′W	FM	149
Cwmcrawnon	Powys	SO1419	51°52·0′	3°14·6′W	T	161
Cwm Cregan	Nth Pt Talb	SS8497	51°39·8′	3°40·2′W	X	170
Cwmcreigiau-fach	Carm	SN4332	51°58·1′	4°16·7′W	X	146
Cwm Crew	Powys	SO0018	51°51·3′	3°26·7′W	X	160
Cwm Crickadarn	Powys	SO0642	52°4·3′	3°21·9′W	X	147,160
Cwmcringlyn Bank	Powys	SO0772	52°20·5′	3°21·5′W	H	136,147
Cwm Croes	Gwyn	SH8825	52°48·9′	3°39·3′W	X	124,125
Cwm Croesor	Gwyn	SH6445	52°59·3′	4°1·2′W	X	115
Cwmcrwth	Carm	SN5724	51°54·0′	4°4·3′W	X	159
Cwm Cwareli	Powys	SO0521	51°53·0′	3°22·4′W	X	160
Cwm-cwta	Carm	SN5933	51°58·9′	4°2·8′W	X	146
Cwm Cwy	Powys	SO0922	51°53·6′	3°19·0′W	X	161
Cwmcych	Carm	SN2735	51°59·4′	4°30·8′W	T	145
Cwm Cynfal	Gwyn	SH7241	52°57·3′	3°53·9′W	X	124
Cwm Cynffig	Nth Pt Talb	SS8386	51°33·9′	3°40·9′W	X	170
Cwm Cynllwyd	Gwyn	SH9025	52°48·9′	3°37·5′W	X	125
Cwm-cynnar	Swan	SS5294	51°37·8′	4°7·9′W	X	159
Cwm-Cynnen	Carm	SN3722	51°52·6′	4°21·7′W	X	145,159
Cwmcynog	Powys	SN9434	51°59·9′	3°32·2′W	X	160
Cwmcynon	Cered	SN3654	52°9·8′	4°23·5′W	X	145
Cwm Cynwyn	Powys	SO0321	51°53·0′	3°24·2′W	X	160
Cwmcynwyn	Powys	SO0323	51°54·1′	3°24·2′W	X	160
Cwmcynydd Bank	Powys	SO0572	52°20·5′	3°23·3′W	X	136,147
Cwm-cyrnach-uchaf	Swan	SN7100	51°41·3′	3°51·6′W	X	170
Cwm Cywarch	Gwyn	SH8617	52°44·6′	3°40·9′W	X	124,125
Cwm Dâr	Rho Cyn Taf	SS9495	51°38·9′	3°31·5′W	X	170
Cwmdare	Rho Cyn Taf	SN9803	51°43·2′	3°28·2′W	T	170
Cwm-Dawe	Carm	SN6040	52°2·7′	4°2·1′W	X	146
Cwm Ddu	Gwyn	SH8823	52°47·8′	3°39·3′W	X	124,125
Cwm Deildre	Powys	SN9086	52°27·9′	3°36·8′W	X	136
Cwmderw	Powys	SO0378	52°23·7′	3°25·1′W	X	136,147
Cwmderwen	Powys	SH9505	52°38·2′	3°32·7′W	X	125
Cwm-difa	Carm	SN4919	51°51·2′	4°11·2′W	X	159
Cwm Dimbath	Brig	SS9589	51°35·6′	3°30·6′W	X	170
Cwm Dingle	Powys	SJ2506	52°39·0′	3°6·1′W	X	126
Cwm-dirgel	Powys	SO1888	52°29·3′	3°12·1′W	X	136
Cwmdockin	Powys	SO1496	52°33·5′	3°15·7′W	X	136
Cwm Dowlais	Monm	ST3699	51°41·4′	2°55·2′W	X	171
Cwm Dows	Caer	ST2096	51°39·7′	3°9·0′W	T	171
Cwmdu	Carm	SN4122	51°52·7′	4°18·2′W	X	159
Cwm-du	Carm	SN5119	51°51·2′	4°9·4′W	X	159
Cwmdu	Carm	SN6009	51°46·0′	4°1·3′W	X	159
Cwmdu	Carm	SN6330	51°57·3′	3°59·2′W	T	146
Cwm Du	Gwyn	SH5355	53°4·6′	4°11·3′W	X	115
Cwm Du	Nth Pt Talb	SN7306	51°44·5′	3°50·0′W	X	160
Cwmdu	Powys	SO1823	51°54·2′	3°11·1′W	T	161
Cwmdu	Swan	SS6494	51°37·9′	3°57·5′W	T	159
Cwm Du	Torf	SO2502	51°42·9′	3°4·7′W	X	171
Cwmduad	Carm	SN3731	51°57·5′	4°21·9′W	T	145
Cwmduhen	Carm	SN3421	51°52·0′	4°24·3′W	X	145,159
Cwmdu-isaf	Brig	SS8790	51°36·1′	3°37·5′W	X	170
Cwm Dulais	Swan	SN6103	51°42·8′	4°0·3′W	T	159
Cwm Dulais	Swan	SN6204	51°43·3′	3°59·5′W	X	159
Cwmdulas	Powys	SN9356	52°11·8′	3°33·5′W	X	147
Cwmdulas Fm	Heref	SO3530	51°58·1′	2°56·4′W	FM	149,161
Cwmdulla Fm	Powys	SO2896	52°33·7′	3°3·3′W	FM	137
Cwmdwfn	Carm	SN3926	51°54·8′	4°20·1′W	X	145
Cwm Dwfnant	Powys	SN9042	52°4·2′	3°35·9′W	X	147,160
Cwm Dwliwn	Powys	SO1675	52°22·2′	3°13·6′W	X	136,148
Cwmdwr	Carm	SN7032	51°58·5′	3°53·2′W	T	146,160
Cwm Dwr	Powys	SN8431	51°58·2′	3°40·9′W	X	160
Cwm Dwyfor	Gwyn	SH5450	53°1·9′	4°10·2′W	X	115
Cwmdwyfran	Carm	SN4124	51°53·8′	4°18·3′W	X	159
Cwm Dwygo	Powys	SJ0424	52°48·5′	3°25·1′W	X	125
Cwm Dwythwch	Gwyn	SH5657	53°5·7′	4°8·6′W	X	115
Cwm Dyffryn	Nth Pt Talb	SS7890	51°36·0′	3°45·3′W	X	170
Cwm Dyfolog	Brig	SS9689	51°35·7′	3°29·7′W	X	170
Cwm Dyli	Gwyn	SH6454	53°4·2′	4°1·4′W	X	115
Cwmdyllest	Cered	SN4246	52°5·6′	4°18·0′W	X	146
Cwmdylluan	Powys	SN9588	52°29·0′	3°32·4′W	X	136
Cwm Earl	Powys	SO1989	52°29·8′	3°11·2′W	X	136
Cwmearl	Powys	SO1990	52°30·4′	3°11·2′W	X	136
Cwm Ednant	Powys	SN8599	52°34·8′	3°41·4′W	X	135,136
Cwm Edno	Conwy	SH6651	53°2·6′	3°59·5′W	X	115
Cwm Egnant	Powys	SN9338	52°2·0′	3°33·2′W	X	160
Cwmeidrol	Powys	SH8607	52°39·2′	3°40·7′W	X	124,125
Cwm Eigiau	Conwy	SH7063	53°9·1′	3°56·2′W	X	115
Cwmeilath	Carm	SN6833	51°59·0′	3°54·9′W	X	146
Cwm-Einon	Cered	SN4543	52°4·1′	4°15·3′W	X	146
Cwm-Einon-fawr	Carm	SN6339	52°2·2′	3°59·4′W	X	146
Cwm Erchan	Powys	SN9434	51°59·9′	3°32·2′W	X	160
Cwmere	Cered	SN6888	52°28·7′	3°56·2′W	X	135
Cwmerfyn	Cered	SN6982	52°25·5′	3°55·2′W	T	135
Cwmergyr	Cered	SN7982	52°25·6′	3°46·4′W	X	135
Cwmerra	Monm	SO3718	51°51·7′	2°54·5′W	X	161
Cwm Esgyll	Gwyn	SH8818	52°45·1′	3°39·2′W	X	124,125
Cwmfadog	Powys	SN9555	52°11·2′	3°31·8′W	X	147
Cwmfaerdy	Powys	SO0769	52°18·9′	3°21·5′W	X	136,147
Cwm-fagor	Monm	ST4798	51°40·9′	2°45·6′W	X	171
Cwm Farteg	Nth Pt Talb	SS8291	51°36·6′	3°41·9′W	X	170
Cwm fedw	Powys	SJ0622	52°47·5′	3°23·2′W	X	125
Cwmfelin	Brig	SS8689	51°35·5′	3°38·4′W	T	170
Cwmfelin	Merth Tyd	SO0900	51°41·7′	3°18·6′W	T	171
Cwmfelin Boeth	Carm	SN1919	51°50·7′	4°37·3′W	T	158
Cwmfelinfach	Caer	ST1891	51°36·9′	3°10·7′W	T	171
Cwmfelin Mynach	Carm	SN2224	51°53·4′	4°34·8′W	T	145,158
Cwmffernol	Gwyn	SH6700	52°35·1′	3°57·4′W	X	135
Cwmfforch	Powys	SO0037	52°1·6′	3°27·1′W	X	160
Cwmfforest	Powys	SO1829	51°57·4′	3°11·2′W	X	161
Cwm-ffos	Brig	SS8683	51°32·3′	3°38·2′W	X	170
Cwmffrwd	Carm	SN4217	51°50·0′	4°17·2′W	T	159
Cwm-ffrwd	Powys	SO1564	52°16·3′	3°14·3′W	X	148
Cwm-ffrwd	Powys	SO1927	51°56·4′	3°10·3′W	X	161
Cwm Ffrwd	Powys	SO2723	51°54·3′	3°3·3′W	X	161
Cwm Ffrwd	Torf	SO2505	51°44·6′	3°4·8′W	X	161
Cwm Ffrwd-oer	Torf	SO2601	51°42·4′	3°3·9′W	T	171
Cwm Ffrydd	Shrops	SO2586	52°28·2′	3°5·8′W	F	137
Cwm Ffrydyll	Powys	SN9636	52°1·0′	3°30·5′W	X	160
Cwm-Ffynnon	Gwyn	SH8824	52°48·4′	3°39·3′W	X	124,125
Cwm-Ffynnon	Powys	SJ0930	52°51·8′	3°20·7′W	X	125
Cwm-Fields	Torf	SO2800	51°41·9′	3°2·1′W	T	171
Cwm Fm	Carm	SN3808	51°45·1′	4°20·4′W	FM	159
Cwm Fm	Gwyn	SH7341	52°57·3′	3°53·0′W	FM	124
Cwm Fm	Heref	SO2941	52°4·0′	3°1·8′W	FM	148,161
Cwm Fm	Heref	SO3238	52°2·4′	2°59·1′W	FM	161
Cwm Fm	Monm	ST3598	51°40·9′	2°56·0′W	FM	171
Cwm Fm	Powys	SJ1705	52°38·4′	3°13·2′W	FM	125
Cwm Fm	Powys	SJ1814	52°43·3′	3°12·4′W	FM	125
Cwm Fm	Powys	SJ2300	52°35·8′	3°7·8′W	FM	126
Cwm Fm	Powys	SO2323	51°54·3′	3°6·8′W	FM	161
Cwm Fm	V of Glam	ST0476	51°28·7′	3°22·6′W	FM	170
Cwm Fms	Heref	SO3031	51°58·6′	3°0·8′W	FM	161
Cwm Fms	Monm	SO3916	51°50·6′	2°52·7′W	FM	161
Cwm-Fran-fawr	Carm	SN7339	52°2·3′	3°50·7′W	X	146,160
Cwm-fron	Powys	SN9681	52°25·3′	3°31·4′W	X	136
Cwm Garw	Brig	SS9089	51°35·6′	3°34·9′W	X	170
Cwm-garw	Pemb	SN1131	51°57·0′	4°44·6′W	X	145
Cwm Garw Fechan	Brig	SS8991	51°36·7′	3°35·8′W	X	170
Cwm Gast	Powys	SH8509	52°40·2′	3°41·6′W	X	124,125
Cwm Gelli	Caer	ST1798	51°40·7′	3°11·6′W	T	171
Cwmgelli Fm	Carm	SN3136	52°0·0′	4°27·3′W	FM	145
Cwm Gelli-wern	Brig	SS9191	51°36·7′	3°34·1′W	X	170
Cwm-gelynen	Carm	SN6542	52°3·8′	3°57·8′W	X	146
Cwmgest	Carm	SN3226	51°54·7′	4°26·2′W	X	145
Cwmgiedd	Powys	SN7811	51°47·3′	3°45·7′W	T	160
Cwmgigfran	Carm	SN4519	51°51·1′	4°14·6′W	X	159
Cwmgilla	Powys	SO2671	52°20·2′	3°4·8′W	X	137,148
Cwm Glas Mawr	Gwyn	SH6155	53°4·7′	4°4·1′W	X	115
Cwm Glo	Merth Tyd	SO0305	51°44·4′	3°23·9′W	X	160
Cwmgloyne	Pemb	SN1039	52°1·3′	4°45·8′W	X	145
Cwm Gloywfa	Powys	SJ0629	52°51·3′	3°23·4′W	X	125
Cwmgogerddan	Carm	SN6736	52°0·6′	3°55·9′W	X	146
Cwm-golog	Powys	SO1787	52°28·7′	3°12·9′W	X	136
Cwm Gored	Powys	SN9008	51°45·8′	3°35·2′W	X	160
Cwmgors	Nth Pt Talb	SN7010	51°46·7′	3°52·7′W	T	160
Cwm Graig ddu	Powys	SN9647	52°6·9′	3°30·7′W	X	147
Cwm Griffin	Powys	SO1854	52°10·9′	3°11·6′W	X	148
Cwm-gu	Powys	SO1921	51°53·1′	3°10·2′W	X	161
Cwm Gwalley	Powys	SO2158	52°13·1′	3°9·0′W	X	148
Cwmgwared	Gwyn	SH4048	53°0·6′	4°22·7′W	X	115,123
Cwmgwary	Powys	SN9376	52°22·5′	3°33·9′W	X	136,147
Cwm Gwaun	Pemb	SN0034	51°58·4′	4°54·3′W	X	145,157
Cwmgwdi	Powys	SO0225	51°55·1′	3°25·1′W	X	160
Cwm Gwenffrwd	Nth Pt Talb	SS7997	51°39·8′	3°44·6′W	X	170
Cwm Gwenffrwd	Powys	SO2517	51°51·0′	3°4·9′W	X	161
Cwm-Gwengad	Powys	SN9931	51°58·3′	3°27·8′W	X	160
Cwm-gwenyn	Cered	SN6160	52°13·5′	4°1·7′W	X	146
Cwm Gwerin	Cered	SN8088	52°28·8′	3°45·6′W	X	135,136
Cwm Gwernfelen	Carm	SN7933	51°59·2′	3°45·3′W	X	146,160
Cwm-gwernog	Powys	SN9392	52°31·2′	3°34·2′W	X	136
Cwmgwili	Carm	SN4223	51°53·2′	4°17·4′W	X	159
Cwmgwili	Carm	SN5710	51°46·5′	4°4·0′W	T	159
Cwm-Gwilym	Powys	SO0636	52°1·1′	3°21·8′W	X	160

Cwm-Gwilym	Powys	SO1951	52°9·3'	3°10·6'W	X	148
Cwm-gwlaw-fawr	Carm	SN6133	51°58·9'	4°1·1'W	X	146
Cwmgwnen	Powys	SJ0822	52°47·5'	3°21·5'W	X	125
Cwmgwrach	Nth Pt Talb	SN8604	51°43·6'	3°38·6'W	T	170
Cwm Gwrelych	Nth Pt Talb	SN9005	51°44·2'	3°35·2'W	X	160
Cwmgwydd	Powys	SO1899	52°35·2'	3°12·2'W	X	136
Cwm-gwyn	Carm	SN7431	51°58·0'	3°49·7'W	X	146,160
Cwm Gwyn	Gwyn	SH9630	52°51·7'	3°32·3'W	X	125
Cwmgwyn	Powys	SO0862	52°15·1'	3°20·5'W	X	147
Cwm Gwyn	Powys	SO1382	52°26·0'	3°16·4'W	X	136
Cwm Gwyn	Swan	SS6393	51°37·4'	3°58·4'W	T	159
Cwm-gwyn Hall	Powys	SO1382	52°26·0'	3°16·4'W	X	136
Cwm Haffes	Powys	SN8317	51°50·6'	3°41·5'W	X	160
Cwm Hafodyredwydd	Conwy	SH7646	53°0·1'	3°50·5'W	X	115
Cwmharad	Carm	SN5521	51°52·4'	4°6·0'W	X	159
Cwm Harry	Powys	SO1298	52°34·6'	3°17·5'W	X	136
Cwm Head	Shrops	SO4288	52°29·4'	2°50·9'W	T	137
Cwmheisian	Gwyn	SH7427	52°49·8'	3°51·8'W	X	124
Cwmhelig	Powys	SO1145	52°6·0'	3°17·6'W	X	148
Cwm Henog	Powys	SN8347	52°6·8'	3°42·1'W	F	147
Cwm-Henog	Powys	SN8548	52°7·3'	3°40·4'W	X	147
Cwm-hesgen	Gwyn	SH7829	52°50·9'	3°48·3'W	X	124
Cwm Hesgyn	Gwyn	SH8841	52°57·5'	3°39·6'W	X	124,125
Cwmheyope	Powys	SO2174	52°21·7'	3°9·2'W	X	137,148
Cwmhinddu	Powys	SO0347	52°7·0'	3°24·6'W	X	147
Cwmhir	Monm	SO3201	51°42·5'	2°58·7'W	X	171
Cwmhiraeth	Carm	SN3437	52°0·6'	4°24·7'W	T	145
Cwm-hir Bank	Powys	SO0271	52°19·9'	3°25·9'W	H	136,147
Cwm Hirnant	Gwyn	SH9531	52°52·2'	3°33·2'W	X	125
Cwm Hirnant	Powys	SJ0523	52°48·0'	3°24·1'W	X	125
Cwm Howard	Conwy	SH7880	53°18·4'	3°49·5'W	X	115
Cwmhowel	Carm	SN5937	52°1·1'	4°2·9'W	X	146
Cwm-Howell	Carm	SN5407	51°44·8'	4°6·5'W	X	159
Cwm-hwnt	Rho Cyn Taf	SN9105	51°44·2'	3°34·3'W	T	160
Cwmhwplyn	Carm	SN4335	51°59·7'	4°16·8'W	X	146
Cwmhwylog	Cered	SN6177	52°22·6'	4°2·1'W	X	135
Cwmhyar	Cered	SN3845	52°5·0'	4°21·5'W	X	145
Cwmiar	Carm	SN5039	52°2·0'	4°10·8'W	X	146
Cwm Iau	Monm	SO3023	51°54·3'	3°0·7'W	X	161
Cwmifor	Carm	SN6525	51°54·7'	3°57·4'W	T	146
Cwmilward	Powys	SO2366	52°17·4'	3°7·3'W	X	137,148
Cwminkin	Powys	SO2095	52°33·1'	3°10·4'W	X	137
Cwm Irfon	Powys	SN8549	52°7·9'	3°40·4'W	T	147
Cwm Isa	Conwy	SH8862	53°8·8'	3°40·1'W	X	116
Cwm Isaf	Denb	SJ1441	52°57·8'	3°16·4'W	X	125
Cwm Isaf	Gwyn	SH8818	52°45·1'	3°39·2'W	X	124,125
Cwmisfael	Carm	SN4915	51°49·0'	4°11·1'W	T	159
Cwmistir	Gwyn	SH2539	52°55·4'	4°35·8'W	X	123
Cwmithel	Powys	SO2148	52°7·7'	3°8·9'W	X	148
Cwmithig	Powys	SN9970	52°19·4'	3°28·5'W	X	136,147
Cwm Ivy	Swan	SS4393	51°37·1'	4°15·7'W	X	159
Cwm Kesty	Powys	SO1754	52°10·9'	3°12·4'W	X	148
Cwm Iân	Rho Cyn Taf	SS9595	51°38·9'	3°30·7'W	X	170
Cwmlanerch	Conwy	SH7958	53°6·6'	3°48·1'W	X	115
Cwm Lasgarn	Torf	SO2804	51°44·0'	3°2·2'W	X	171
Cwm Lickey	Torf	ST2698	51°40·8'	3°3·8'W	X	171
Cwmlladron	Powys	SO2489	52°29·9'	3°6·8'W	X	137
Cwm-llaethdy	Powys	SN9942	52°4·3'	3°28·0'W	X	147,160
Cwm-llan	Conwy	SH9642	52°58·2'	3°32·5'W	X	125
Cwm Llan	Gwyn	SH6152	53°3·1'	4°4·0'W	X	115
Cwm Llanwenarth	Monm	SO2512	51°48·3'	3°4·9'W	X	161
Cwm Llech	Powys	SJ0224	52°48·5'	3°26·8'W	X	125
Cwm Llech	Powys	SN9233	51°59·3'	3°34·0'W	X	160
Cwm-llechwedd	Cered	SN6671	52°19·5'	3°57·6'W	X	135
Cwmllechwedd	Powys	SO1375	52°22·2'	3°16·3'W	X	136,148
Cwmllecoediog	Powys	SH8209	52°40·2'	3°44·3'W	X	124,125
Cwm Llefrith	Gwyn	SH5546	52°59·7'	4°9·2'W	X	115
Cwmllethryd	Carm	SN5205	51°43·7'	4°8·4'W	X	159
Cwm-llethryd Fm	Carm	SN5104	51°43·1'	4°9·0'W	FM	159
Cwm Lliedi Resr	Carm	SN5103	51°42·6'	4°9·0'W	W	159
Cwm-Llinau	Powys	SH8407	52°39·1'	3°42·5'W	T	124,125
Cwmlliw	Powys	SN9530	51°57·8'	3°31·3'W	X	160
Cwm Lluest	Rho Cyn Taf	SS9199	51°41·0'	3°34·2'W	X	170
Cwm Llusog	Gwyn	SH9328	52°50·6'	3°34·9'W	X	125
Cwm-llwch	Powys	SO0023	51°54·0'	3°26·8'W	X	160
Cwm-Llwchwr	Carm	SN6314	51°48·7'	3°58·9'W	X	159
Cwm-llwm	Denb	SH9962	53°9·0'	3°30·2'W	X	116
Cwm-llwyd	Gwyn	SH6310	52°40·5'	4°1·2'W	X	124
Cwm Llwyd	Powys	SH9700	52°35·5'	3°30·8'W	X	136
Cwm-Llwydd	Gwyn	SH8723	52°47·8'	3°40·2'W	X	124,125
Cwmllwydion	Powys	SO0389	52°29·7'	3°25·3'W	X	136
Cwm Llwydo	Powys	SH8208	52°39·7'	3°44·3'W	X	124,125
Cwmllwynog	Powys	SJ0706	52°38·9'	3°22·1'W	X	125
Cwm-llydan	Cered	SN5153	52°9·6'	4°10·3'W	X	146
Cwm-llydan	Flint	SJ1762	53°9·2'	3°14·1'W	X	116
Cwmllydan Isaf	Carm	SN4729	51°56·5'	4°13·2'W	X	146
Cwmllyfri	Carm	SN3413	51°47·7'	4°24·0'W	X	159
Cwm Llygoed	Gwyn	SH9119	52°45·7'	3°36·5'W	X	125
Cwm-llynfe	Carm	SN6933	51°59·0'	3°54·1'W	X	146,160
Cwmllynfell	Nth Pt Talb	SN7412	51°47·8'	3°49·2'W	T	160
Cwm Llysiog	Merth Tyd	SO0114	51°49·2'	3°25·8'W	X	160
Cwm-Llythin	Powys	SN9335	52°0·4'	3°33·1'W	X	160
Cwm-Llywy-uchaf	Powys	SH8102	52°36·4'	3°45·0'W	X	135,136
Cwm Mabws	Cered	SN5568	52°17·7'	4°7·2'W	X	135
Cwm Maddoc Fm	Heref	SO4720	51°52·8'	2°45·8'W	FM	161
Cwm Maelwg	Nth Pt Talb	SS8087	51°34·4'	3°43·5'W	X	170
Cwm Maen Gwynedd	Powys	SJ1031	52°52·4'	3°19·8'W	X	125
Cwmmaerdy	Powys	SO1358	52°13·0'	3°16·0'W	X	148
Cwm-main	Gwyn	SH9246	53°0·3'	3°36·2'W	X	116
Cwm Main	Gwyn	SH9841	52°57·6'	3°30·7'W	X	125
Cwm-march	Cered	SN4243	52°4·0'	4°17·9'W	X	146
Cwm-march	Cered	SN5461	52°13·9'	4°7·9'W	X	146
Cwm-marchon	Carm	SN6934	51°59·6'	3°54·1'W	X	146,160
Cwmmau Farmhouse	Heref	SO2751	52°9·4'	3°3·6'W	X	148
Cwm Mawan	Powys	SN8935	52°0·4'	3°36·6'W	X	160
Cwm-mawr	Carm	SN5312	51°47·5'	4°7·5'W	T	159
Cwm-mawr	Cered	SN4649	52°7·3'	4°14·6'W	X	146
Cwm-mawr	Cered	SN4657	52°11·6'	4°14·8'W	X	146
Cwm-mawr	Cered	SN5551	52°8·5'	4°6·7'W	X	146
Cwm-mawr	Gwyn	SH6331	52°51·8'	4°1·7'W	X	124

Cwm-mawr	Monm	SO2809	51°46·7'	3°2·2'W	X	161
Cwm-mawr	Pemb	SN0435	51°59·0'	4°50·9'W	X	145,157
Cwm-mawr	Powys	SN8995	52°32·7'	3°37·8'W	X	135,136
Cwm Mawr	Powys	SO2021	51°53·1'	3°9·4'W	X	161
Cwm Mawr	Powys	SO2164	52°16·3'	3°9·1'W	X	137,148
Cwm-mawr	Swan	SS5794	51°37·8'	4°3·6'W	X	159
Cwm Mawr	V of Glam	SS8972	51°26·4'	3°35·4'W	X	170
Cwm Meillionen	Gwyn	SH5648	53°0·8'	4°8·4'W	X	115
Cwm Merddog	Blae Gw	SO1806	51°45·0'	3°10·9'W	X	161
Cwm Merwys	Powys	SO1666	52°17·4'	3°13·5'W	X	136,148
Cwmmeudwy	Cered	SN4041	52°2·9'	4°19·6'W	X	146
Cwm-Meurig	Cered	SN7268	52°18·0'	3°52·2'W	X	135,147
Cwm Milaid	Powys	SO2422	51°53·7'	3°5·9'W	X	161
Cwm-miles	Carm	SN1622	51°52·2'	4°40·0'W	T	145,158
Cwm Moch	Gwyn	SH6636	52°54·5'	3°59·2'W	X	124
Cwm Moch	Shrops	SO2285	52°27·7'	3°8·5'W	X	137
Cwm-mwyn	Powys	SN9245	52°5·8'	3°34·2'W	F	147
Cwm-mwythig	Cered	SN6481	52°24·8'	3°59·6'W	X	135
Cwm-Mynys	Carm	SN7234	51°59·6'	3°51·5'W	X	146,160
Cwmnant	Cered	SN4946	52°5·7'	4°11·9'W	X	146
Cwm-nant	Powys	SO0261	52°14·5'	3°25·7'W	X	147
Cwm-nant	Swan	SS5594	51°37·8'	4°5·3'W	X	159
Cwm Nantcol	Gwyn	SH6426	52°49·1'	4°0·7'W	X	124
Cwm Nant-gam	Monm	SO2012	51°48·3'	3°9·2'W	T	161
Cwm-nant Hopkin	Nth Pt Talb	SN7009	51°46·1'	3°52·7'W	X	160
Cwm-nant-Lleiky	Nth Pt Talb	SN7307	51°45·1'	3°50·0'W	X	160
Cwm Nant-y-Beudy	Carm	SN8030	51°57·6'	3°44·4'W	X	160
Cwm Nant-y-felin	Powys	SO1424	51°54·8'	3°15·4'W	X	161
Cwmnantygelli	Powys	SO1470	52°19·5'	3°15·3'W	X	136,148
Cwm Nant-y-glo	Nth Pt Talb	SS8189	51°35·5'	3°42·7'W	X	170
Cwm Nant-y-groes	Blae Gw	SO2203	51°43·5'	3°7·4'W	X	171
Cwm Nant-y-Meichiaid	Powys	SJ1316	52°44·3'	3°16·9'W	X	125
Cwm Nant-y-moch	Powys	SN9035	52°0·4'	3°35·8'W	X	160
Cwm Nant-y-moel	Brig	SS9293	51°37·8'	3°33·2'W	X	170
Cwmnantyrodyn	Caer	ST1895	51°39·1'	3°10·7'W	T	171
Cwm Nash	V of Glam	SS9070	51°25·3'	3°34·5'W	X	170
Cwm Nedd or Vale of Neath	Nth Pt Talb	SN8303	51°43·1'	3°41·2'W	X	170
Cwmnewidion Isaf	Cered	SN6874	52°21·1'	3°55·9'W	X	135
Cwmnewydion-uchaf	Cered	SN7174	52°21·2'	3°53·2'W	X	135,147
Cwm Newynydd	Powys	SN8622	51°53·3'	3°39·0'W	X	160
Cwm Nofydd	Card	ST1483	51°32·6'	3°14·0'W	X	171
Cwmoerddwr	Conwy	SH9346	53°0·3'	3°35·3'W	X	116
Cwm Oergwm	Powys	SO0421	51°53·0'	3°23·3'W	X	160
Cwm Oergwm	Powys	SO0623	51°54·1'	3°21·6'W	X	160
Cwm-oernant	Carm	SN4121	51°52·1'	4°18·2'W	X	159
Cwm Ogwr Fach	Brig	SS9586	51°34·1'	3°30·5'W	X	170
Cwm Ogwr Fawr	Brig	SS9391	51°36·7'	3°32·3'W	X	170
Cwmole	Powys	SO1149	52°8·2'	3°17·6'W	X	148
Cwm Onnau	Powys	SO1817	51°51·0'	3°11·0'W	X	161
Cwm Orci	Rho Cyn Taf	SS9598	51°40·5'	3°30·7'W	X	170
Cwmorgan	Carm	SN2934	51°58·9'	4°29·0'W	T	145
Cwm Orog	Powys	SJ0427	52°50·2'	3°25·1'W	X	125
Cwm Owen	Powys	SO0243	52°4·8'	3°25·4'W	X	147,160
Cwm Padest	Powys	SN8722	51°53·3'	3°38·1'W	X	160
Cwmparc	Rho Cyn Taf	SS9596	51°39·4'	3°30·7'W	T	170
Cwm Pedol	Carm	SN7016	51°49·9'	3°52·8'W	X	160
Cwm Pelenna	Nth Pt Talb	SS8096	51°39·2'	3°43·7'W	X	170
Cwm Penanner	Gwyn	SH9146	53°0·3'	3°37·1'W	X	116
Cwmpengraig	Carm	SN3436	52°0·1'	4°24·7'W	T	145
Cwm-pen-llydan	Cered	SN7173	52°20·6'	3°53·2'W	X	135,147
Cwm-pen-llydan	Denb	SJ0432	52°52·9'	3°25·2'W	X	125
Cwm Pen Llydan	Powys	SH9206	52°38·7'	3°35·4'W	X	125
Cwm Penmachno	Conwy	SH7547	53°0·6'	3°51·4'W	T	115
Cwm Penmachno	Conwy	SH7547	53°0·6'	3°51·4'W	X	115
Cwm Pennant	Denb	SJ0335	52°54·5'	3°26·1'W	X	125
Cwm Pennant	Gwyn	SH5347	53°0·3'	4°11·0'W	X	115
Cwm Pennant	Powys	SJ0326	52°49·6'	3°26·0'W	X	125
Cwmpennar	Rho Cyn Taf	SO0300	51°41·7'	3°23·8'W	T	170
Cwm Pen-y-gelli	Gwyn	SH9118	52°45·2'	3°36·5'W	X	125
Cwm Perfedd	Gwyn	SH6362	53°8·5'	4°2·5'W	X	115
Cwm Peris	Cered	SN5367	52°17·1'	4°8·9'W	X	135
Cwm Philip	Nth Pt Talb	SS8187	51°34·4'	3°42·6'W	X	170
Cwm-pistyll	Powys	SN9836	52°1·0'	3°28·8'W	X	160
Cwm Plysgog	Pemb	SN1943	52°3·6'	4°38·0'W	T	145
Cwmporth	Powys	SN9213	51°48·6'	3°33·6'W	X	160
Cwmporthman	Cered	SN2749	52°7·0'	4°31·2'W	X	145
Cwm Prysor	Gwyn	SH7436	52°54·6'	3°52·0'W	X	124
Cwm Ratgoed	Gwyn	SH7711	52°41·2'	3°48·8'W	X	124
Cwmrheiddol	Carm	SN4625	51°54·4'	4°13·9'W	X	146
Cwm Rheidol	Cered	SN7178	52°23·3'	3°53·3'W	X	135,147
Cwm Rheidol Reservoir	Cered	SN6979	52°23·8'	3°55·1'W	W	135
Cwm Rhiwarth	Powys	SJ0328	52°50·7'	3°26·0'W	X	125
Cwm-Rhiwiau	Powys	SJ0630	52°51·8'	3°23·4'W	X	125
Cwmrhos	Powys	SO1824	51°54·7'	3°11·1'W	T	161
Cwm-Rhuddan	Carm	SN7632	51°58·6'	3°47·9'W	X	146,160
Cwmrhwyddfor Fm	Gwyn	SH7312	52°41·7'	3°52·4'W	FM	124
Cwmrhybin	Powys	SN9748	52°7·5'	3°29·9'W	X	147
Cwmrhydyceirw	Swan	SS6699	51°40·7'	3°55·9'W	T	159
Cwm Rhyd-y-gau	Nth Pt Talb	SN8805	51°44·2'	3°36·9'W	X	160
Cwm-Ricket	Powys	SN8586	52°27·8'	3°41·2'W	X	135,136
Cwmrisca	Brig	SS8784	51°32·9'	3°37·4'W	X	170
Cwms	Shrops	SO4794	52°32·7'	2°46·5'W	X	137,138
Cwm Saerbren	Rho Cyn Taf	SS9397	51°39·9'	3°32·4'W	X	170
Cwmsaeson	Cered	SN4558	52°12·1'	4°15·7'W	X	146
Cwm-saethe	Carm	SN7743	52°4·5'	3°47·3'W	X	146,147,160
Cwm-sanaham Hill	Shrops	SO2675	52°22·3'	3°4·8'W	H	137,148
Cwm Sawdde Fechan	Carm	SN7620	51°52·1'	3°47·7'W	X	160
Cwm Selsig	Rho Cyn Taf	SS9197	51°39·9'	3°34·2'W	X	170
Cwms Fm	Shrops	SO4793	52°32·2'	2°46·5'W	FM	137,138
Cwm Sian Llwyd	Gwyn	SJ0032	52°52·8'	3°28·8'W	X	125
Cwm-slaid	Cered	SN6690	52°29·7'	3°58·0'W	X	135
Cwm Sorgwm	Powys	SO1627	51°56·3'	3°12·9'W	X	161
Cwm-steps	Heref	SO3032	51°59·2'	3°0·8'W	X	161
Cwm Sychan	Torf	SO2304	51°44·0'	3°6·5'W	X	171
Cwm Sychbant	Brig	SS8490	51°36·1'	3°40·1'W	X	170
Cwmsychbant	Cered	SN4746	52°5·7'	4°13·6'W	X	146
Cwmsyfiog	Caer	SO1502	51°42·9'	3°13·4'W	T	171
Cwmsylltyn	Cered	SN3043	52°3·8'	4°28·4'W	X	145
Cwmsymlog	Cered	SN7083	52°26·0'	3°54·3'W	T	135

Cwm Tâf	Rho Cyn Taf	SO0013	51°48·6'	3°26·6'W	X	160
Cwm Tafolog	Powys	SH8910	52°40·8'	3°38·1'W	X	124,125
Cwm Teigl	Gwyn	SH7243	52°58·4'	3°54·0'W	X	124
Cwmtelmau	Powys	SO0767	52°17·8'	3°21·4'W	X	136,147
Cwm Terwyn	Gwyn	SH8718	52°45·1'	3°40·1'W	X	124,125
Cwm, The	Heref	SO4817	51°51·2'	2°44·9'W	X	161
Cwm, The	Powys	SO1056	52°11·9'	3°18·6'W	X	148
Cwmtillery	Blae Gw	SO2105	51°44·5'	3°8·3'W	T	161
Cwmtillery Resr	Blae Gw	SO2207	51°45·6'	3°7·4'W	W	161
Cwmtirmynach	Gwyn	SH9042	52°58·1'	3°37·9'W	X	125
Cwm Tregalan	Gwyn	SH6053	53°3·6'	4°4·9'W	X	115
Cwm Treweryn	Powys	SN9125	51°55·0'	3°34·7'W	X	160
Cwm Trwsgl	Gwyn	SH5449	53°1·3'	4°10·2'W	X	115
Cwm Tryfan	Conwy	SH6658	53°6·4'	3°59·7'W	X	115
Cwm-twrch	Carm	SN4922	51°52·8'	4°11·2'W	X	159
Cwm Twrch	Cered	SN6850	52°8·2'	3°55·3'W	X	146
Cwm-twrch Isaf	Powys	SN7610	51°46·7'	3°47·5'W	T	160
Cwm-twrch Uchaf	Powys	SN7511	51°47·3'	3°48·3'W	T	160
Cwm-tydi	Denb	SJ1544	52°59·4'	3°15·6'W	X	125
Cwmtydu	Cered	SN3557	52°11·4'	4°24·4'W	X	145
Cwm Tyleri	Blae Gw	SO2206	51°45·1'	3°7·4'W	X	161
Cwm-Tylo	Gwyn	SH8434	52°53·7'	3°43·1'W	X	124,125
Cwm-Tysswg	Blae Gw	SO1307	51°45·5'	3°15·2'W	X	161
Cwm Tyswg	Blae GW	SO1306	51°45·0'	3°15·2'W	X	161
Cwmtywyll	Carm	SN4139	52°1·8'	4°18·7'W	X	146
Cwmwdig Fm	Pemb	SM8030	51°55·7'	5°11·6'W	FM	157
Cwmwdig Water	Pemb	SM8030	51°55·7'	5°11·6'W	T	157
Cwm Wernderi	Nth Pt Talb	SS8090	51°36·0'	3°43·6'W	X	170
Cwm Whitton	Powys	SO2768	52°18·6'	3°3·8'W	X	137,148
Cwmwr isaf	Powys	SJ0623	52°48·0'	3°23·3'W	X	125
Cwmwr Uchaf	Powys	SJ0624	52°48·6'	3°23·3'W	X	125
Cwmwyntell	Pemb	SM9630	51°56·1'	4°57·7'W	X	157
Cwm Wyre	Cered	SN5569	52°18·2'	4°7·2'W	X	135
Cwmwysg	Powys	SN8528	51°56·6'	3°40·0'W	T	160
Cwmwysg-ganol	Powys	SN9329	51°57·2'	3°33·0'W	X	160
Cwm-y-bont	Powys	SO1957	52°12·6'	3°10·7'W	X	148
Cwm-y-Breach	V of Glam	ST0669	51°25·0'	3°20·7'W	X	170
Cwm-y-bwch	Caer	ST1690	51°36·4'	3°12·4'W	X	171
Cwmydalfa	Powys	SO1387	52°28·7'	3°16·5'W	X	136
Cwmydalfa	Powys	SO1487	52°28·7'	3°15·6'W	X	136
Cwm-y-dea	Powys	SO0373	52°21·0'	3°25·1'W	X	136,147
Cwm y Dolau	Gwyn	SH8423	52°47·8'	3°42·8'W	X	124,125
Cwm-Ydw	Carm	SN7831	51°58·1'	3°46·2'W	X	146,160
Cwmydwrgi	Powys	SN7795	52°32·6'	3°48·4'W	X	135
Cwm-y-ffasp	Brig	SS9392	51°37·2'	3°32·3'W	X	170
Cwm-y-fforch	Rho Cyn Taf	SS9598	51°40·5'	3°30·7'W	X	170
Cwmyffynnon	Gwyn	SH5351	53°2·4'	4°11·2'W	X	115
Cwm-y-ffynnon	Powys	SH9105	52°38·2'	3°36·2'W	X	125
Cwm y Fuwch	Brig	SS9490	51°36·2'	3°31·4'W	X	170
Cwm y Gaer	Brig	SS8577	51°29·1'	3°39·0'W	X	170
Cwm-y-gaist	Powys	SO1771	52°20·1'	3°12·7'W	X	136,148
Cwm y Garn	Nth Pt Talb	SS8089	51°35·5'	3°43·5'W	X	170
Cwm-y-geifr	Wrex	SJ1334	52°54·0'	3°17·2'W	X	125
Cwm-y-Gerwyn	Powys	SO1966	52°17·4'	3°10·9'W	X	136,148
Cwm-y-glo	Carm	SN5513	51°48·1'	4°5·8'W	X	159
Cwm-y-glo	Gwyn	SH5562	53°8·4'	4°9·7'W	T	114,115
Cwm y Glyn	Torf	SO2600	51°41·9'	3°3·9'W	X	171
Cwmynace	Powys	SO2053	52°10·4'	3°9·8'W	X	148
Cwmynyscoy	Torf	ST2899	51°41·3'	3°2·1'W	T	171
Cwmyoy	Monm	SO2923	51°54·3'	3°1·5'W	T	161
Cwm yr Aethnen	Gwyn	SH9529	52°51·1'	3°33·2'W	X	125
Cwm-yr-afon	Gwyn	SH6230	52°51·2'	4°2·6'W	X	124
Cwm yr Allt-lwyd	Gwyn	SH7829	52°50·9'	3°48·3'W	X	124
Cwm-yr-annel	Powys	SN9799	52°35·0'	3°30·8'W	X	136
Cwm yr Argoed	Nth Pt Talb	SN8704	51°43·6'	3°37·8'W	X	170
Cwm yr Argoed	Nth Pt Talb	SS8294	51°38·2'	3°41·9'W	X	170
Cwmyrarian	Carm	SN4014	51°48·3'	4°18·9'W	X	159
Cwm yr Ast	Powys	SJ0728	52°50·7'	3°22·5'W	X	125
Cwm-yr-aur	Pemb	SN2332	51°57·7'	4°34·2'W	X	145
Cwm yr Eglwys	Gwyn	SH8315	52°43·4'	3°43·5'W	X	124,125
Cwm-yr-eglwys	Pemb	SN0139	52°1·1'	4°53·6'W	X	145,157
Cwm yr Eithin	Powys	SJ0430	52°51·8'	3°25·2'W	X	125
Cwm-yr-haf	Gwyn	SH4946	52°59·6'	4°14·6'W	X	115,123
Cwm yr Hafod	Powys	SH9620	52°46·3'	3°32·1'W	X	125
Cwm-y-Rhaiadr	Carm	SN7643	52°4·5'	3°48·2'W	F	146,147,160
Cwmyrhaiadr	Powys	SN7596	52°33·1'	3°50·2'W	X	135
Cwm-y-rhinwedd	Conwy	SH9659	53°7·3'	3°32·8'W	X	116
Cwmyrhiwdre	Powys	SO0884	52°27·0'	3°20·8'W	X	136
Cwm-yr-hob	Powys	SO1579	52°24·4'	3°14·6'W	X	136,148
Cwm yr Hom	Powys	SO2427	51°56·4'	3°5·9'W	X	161
Cwmyringel	Powys	SO1878	52°23·9'	3°11·9'W	X	136,148
Cwmyronnen-uchaf	Carm	SN4630	51°57·1'	4°14·1'W	X	146
Cwm yr Wnin	Gwyn	SH7120	52°46·0'	3°54·3'W	X	124
Cwmyrychen	Powys	SN9576	52°22·6'	3°32·2'W	X	136,147
Cwm y Saeson	Powys	SN9377	52°23·1'	3°33·9'W	X	136,147
Cwmysgawen Common	Powys	SO0371	52°20·0'	3°25·0'W	X	136,147
Cwm Ysgiach	Swan	SN6203	51°42·8'	3°59·5'W	X	159
Cwmysgyfarnog	Carm	SN5623	51°53·5'	4°5·2'W	X	159
Cwmystradllyn	Gwyn	SH5644	52°58·7'	4°8·3'W	X	124
Cwm Ystwyth	Cered	SN7773	52°20·7'	3°47·9'W	X	135,147
Cwmystwyth	Cered	SN7874	52°21·3'	3°47·1'W	T	135,147
Cwm-y-wrach	Powys	SO0034	52°0·0'	3°27·0'W	X	160
Cwnburry	Carm	SN3712	51°47·2'	4°21·4'W	X	159
Cwncalch Uchaf	Powys	SN9198	52°34·4'	3°36·1'W	X	136
Cwnd Ho	Shrops	SO3895	52°33·2'	2°54·5'W	X	137
Cwn Eog	Pemb	SN1140	52°1·8'	4°44·9'W	X	145
Cwningar Bodowen	I of Angl	SH3665	53°9·7'	4°26·8'W	X	114
Cwningâr Trefri	I of Angl	SH3667	53°10·7'	4°26·8'W	X	114
Cwnrhapant	Carm	SN4724	51°53·9'	4°13·0'W	X	159
Cwrt	Carm	SN4131	51°57·5'	4°18·5'W	X	146
Cwrt	Carm	SN4538	52°1·4'	4°15·2'W	X	146
Cwrt	Carm	SN5015	51°49·1'	4°10·2'W	X	159
Cwrt	Cered	SN6484	52°26·5'	3°59·7'W	X	135
Cwrt	Gwyn	SH1526	52°48·2'	4°44·3'W	X	123
Cwrt	Gwyn	SH6800	52°35·2'	3°56·5'W	T	135
Cwrt	Gwyn	SH6829	52°50·8'	3°57·2'W	X	124
Cwrt	V of Glam	SS9578	51°29·7'	3°30·4'W	X	170
Cwrtbrynbeirdd	Carm	SN6618	51°50·9'	3°56·3'W	X	159
Cwrt Fm	Cered	SN2046	52°5·2'	4°37·2'W	FM	145
Cwrt Gilbert	Powys	SO0126	51°55·7'	3°26·0'W	X	160

Cwrt-Gwenddwr	Powys	SO0746	52°6·5'	3°21·1'W	X	147
Cwrt Hen	Cered	SN2745	52°4·8'	4°31·1'W	X	145
Cwrt Henllys	Torf	ST2592	51°37·5'	3°4·6'W	X	171
Cwrthyr	Carm	SN3817	51°49·9'	4°20·7'W	X	159
Cwrt Isaf	Gwyn	SH5346	52°59·7'	4°11·0'W	X	115
Cwrt Malle	Carm	SN3717	51°49·9'	4°21·5'W	X	159
Cwrt-mawr	Cered	SN6262	52°14·6'	4°0·9'W	X	146
Cwrt-mawr	Swan	SN6203	51°42·8'	3°59·5'W	X	159
Cwrtnewydd	Cered	SN4847	52°6·3'	4°12·8'W	T	146
Cwrtnewydd	V of Glam	SS9372	51°26·5'	3°32·0'W	X	170
Cwrt Newydd	V of Glam	ST0475	51°28·2'	3°22·5'W	X	170
Cwrt Porth-hir	Rho Cyn Taf	SO3009	51°46·8'	3°0·5'W	X	161
Cwrt-y-bariwns	Nth Pt Talb	SN7108	51°45·6'	3°51·8'W	X	160
Cwrty Brychan	Monm	SO4401	51°42·5'	2°48·2'W	X	171
Cwrt-y-cadno	Carm	SN6944	52°5·0'	3°54·3'W	T	146,160
Cwrt-y-carne	Swan	SN5700	51°41·1'	4°3·7'W	X	159
Cwrt-y-celyn	Rho Cyn Taf	ST1088	51°35·3'	3°17·6'W	X	171
Cwrt-y-defaid	Nth Pt Talb	SS8085	51°33·3'	3°43·5'W	X	170
Cwrt y Gollen	Powys	SO2317	51°51·0'	3°6·7'W	X	161
Cwrt-y-graban	Powys	SO1142	52°4·4'	3°17·5'W	X	148,161
Cwrt-y-Llyn	Conwy	SH9051	53°2·9'	3°38·1'W	X	116
Cwrt-y-prior	Powys	SO1528	51°56·9'	3°13·8'W	X	161
Cwrt-yr-ala	V of Glam	ST1473	51°27·2'	3°13·9'W	X	171
Cwybr	Denb	SJ0279	53°18·2'	3°27·8'W	X	116
Cwyrt	I of Angl	SH4483	53°19·5'	4°20·1'W	X	114,115
Cwyrtai	I of Angl	SH3772	53°13·4'	4°26·1'W	X	114
Cyderhall Fm	Highld	NH7588	57°52·1'	4°6·0'W	FM	21
Cyfannedd	Gwyn	SH6312	52°41·5'	4°1·2'W	X	124
Cyfarthfa Castle (Sch)	Merth Tyd	SO0407	51°45·4'	3°23·1'W	X	160
Cyff	Powys	SN8184	52°26·7'	3°44·7'W	W	135,136
Cyffdy	Conwy	SH8160	53°7·7'	3°46·3'W	X	116
Cyffdy	Gwyn	SH8834	52°53·8'	3°39·5'W	X	124,125
Cyffin	Powys	SJ0313	52°42·6'	3°25·7'W	X	125
Cyffin-fawr	Powys	SJ0314	52°43·1'	3°25·8'W	X	125
Cyffionos	Cered	SN3756	52°10·9'	4°22·7'W	X	145
Cyffredin	Denb	SJ0576	53°16·8'	3°25·1'W	X	116
Cyffylliog	Denb	SJ0557	53°6·3'	3°24·7'W	T	116
Cyfie	Powys	SJ1014	52°43·2'	3°21·3'W	X	125
Cyflymen	Denb	SJ2040	52°57·3'	3°11·0'W	W	117
Cyfnant-Uchaf	Denb	SJ1857	53°6·5'	3°13·1'W	X	116
Cyfronydd	Powys	SJ1407	52°39·5'	3°15·9'W	X	125
Cyfyng	Conwy	SH7753	53°3·9'	3°49·7'W	X	115
Cylchau	Carm	SN7520	51°52·1'	3°48·5'W	X	160
Cyll	Powys	SN9788	52°29·1'	3°30·6'W	X	136
Cyll-y-Felin Fawr	Gwyn	SH1728	52°49·4'	4°42·6'W	X	123
Cymau	Flint	SJ2956	53°6·0'	3°3·2'W	T	117
Cymau Hall	Flint	SJ2955	53°5·5'	3°3·2'W	X	117
Cymbeline's Castle	Bucks	SP8306	51°45·0'	0°47·5'W	A	165
Cymdda	Brig	SS9083	51°32·3'	3°34·8'W	T	170
Cymer	Nth Pt Talb	SS8696	51°39·3'	3°38·5'W	T	170
Cymerau	Cered	SN6996	52°33·0'	3°55·5'W	X	135
Cymerau	Conwy	SH8174	53°15·2'	3°46·6'W	X	116
Cymerau	Gwyn	SH7710	52°40·7'	3°48·8'W	X	124
Cymmer	Rho Cyn Taf	ST0290	51°36·3'	3°24·5'W	T	170
Cymmer Abbey	Gwyn	SH7219	52°45·5'	3°53·4'W	A	124
Cymmer Castle	Gwyn	SH7319	52°45·5'	3°52·5'W	A	124
Cymmo	Denb	SJ1645	53°0·0'	3°14·7'W	X	116
Cymro Gate	Denb	SJ0143	52°58·8'	3°28·1'W	X	116
Cymryd	Conwy	SH7975	53°15·7'	3°48·4'W	A	115
Cymunod	I of Angl	SH3377	53°16·1'	4°29·8'W	X	114
Cymyran Bay	I of Angl	SH2974	53°14·4'	4°33·3'W	W	114
Cynala	Powys	SN9144	52°5·3'	3°35·1'W	X	147,160
Cynant Fm	Carm	SN8144	52°5·1'	3°43·8'W	FM	147,160
Cynant Ganol	Conwy	SH9272	53°14·3'	3°36·7'W	X	116
Cynant Isaf	Conwy	SH9271	53°13·7'	3°36·7'W	X	116
Cynant Ucha	Conwy	SH9171	53°13·7'	3°37·6'W	X	116
Cynarfron	Powys	SJ1530	52°51·9'	3°15·4'W	X	125
Cyncoed	Card	ST1880	51°31·0'	3°10·5'W	T	171
Cyncoed	Cered	SN6780	52°24·4'	3°56·9'W	X	135
Cyncoed Fm	Caer	ST1997	51°40·2'	3°9·9'W	FM	171
Cynefail	Gwyn	SH8342	52°58·0'	3°44·1'W	X	124,125
Cyneiniog	Cered	SN7188	52°28·7'	3°53·6'W	X	135
Cyneiniog	Cered	SN7288	52°28·7'	3°52·7'W	X	135
Cynfal	Gwyn	SH6101	52°35·6'	4°2·7'W	X	135
Cynfal	Gwyn	SH7040	52°56·7'	3°55·7'W	X	124
Cynfal-fawr	Gwyn	SH6700	52°35·1'	3°57·4'W	H	135
Cyn Farch	Carm	SN3436	52°0·1'	4°24·7'W	X	145
Cynffiad	Powys	SN9052	52°9·6'	3°36·1'W	W	147
Cynghordy	Carm	SN6814	51°48·8'	3°54·5'W	X	159
Cynghordy	Swan	SN6603	51°42·8'	3°56·0'W	X	159
Cynghordy Hall	Carm	SN8040	52°3·0'	3°44·6'W	X	147,160
Cynheidre	Carm	SN4907	51°44·7'	4°10·8'W	T	159
Cynhinfa	Powys	SJ0911	52°41·6'	3°20·4'W	X	125
Cynhordy Fm	Brig	SS8889	51°35·6'	3°36·6'W	FM	170
Cyniwyll	Powys	SJ0510	52°41·0'	3°23·9'W	X	125
Cynlas	Gwyn	SH9538	52°56·0'	3°33·3'W	X	125
Cynllaith	Powys	SJ2025	52°49·2'	3°10·8'W	W	126
Cynllaith	Shrops	SJ2329	52°51·4'	3°8·2'W	W	126
Cynllwyd	Conwy	SH7560	53°7·6'	3°51·7'W	X	115
Cynnant Fâch	Powys	SN8245	52°5·7'	3°43·0'W	W	147
Cynnant Fawr	Carm	SN8145	52°5·7'	3°43·8'W	W	147
Cynnull-mawr	Cered	SN6587	52°28·1'	3°58·8'W	X	135
Cynon Brook	Powys	SO2258	52°13·1'	3°8·1'W	W	148
Cynon-fawr	Cered	SN6575	52°21·6'	3°58·6'W	X	135
Cynonville	Nth Pt Talb	SS8295	51°38·7'	3°41·9'W	T	170
Cyntwell	Card	ST1275	51°28·3'	3°15·6'W	T	171
Cynwyd	Denb	SJ0541	52°57·7'	3°24·5'W	T	125
Cynwyd Forest	Denb	SJ0641	52°57·7'	3°23·6'W	F	125
Cynwyl Elfed	Carm	SN3727	51°55·3'	4°21·8'W	T	145
Cynynion	Shrops	SJ2430	52°52·0'	3°7·3'W	X	126
Cynythog	Gwyn	SH8736	52°54·8'	3°40·4'W	X	124,125
Cyplau	Gwyn	SH7627	52°49·8'	3°50·0'W	X	124
Cyrchynan-isaf	Wrex	SJ1531	52°52·4'	3°15·4'W	X	125
Cyrchynan-ucha	Wrex	SJ1431	52°52·4'	3°16·3'W	X	125
Cyrnau	Cered	SN7455	52°11·0'	3°50·2'W	X	146,147
Cyrnau Bach	Cered	SN7575	52°21·8'	3°49·8'W	H	135,147
Cyrniau	Powys	SJ0625	52°49·1'	3°23·3'W	H	125
Cyrniau Nod	Powys	SH9827	52°50·1'	3°30·4'W	H	125
Cyrn-y-Brain	Denb	SJ2149	53°2·2'	3°10·3'W	H	117
Cyrtau	Cered	SN7060	52°13·6'	3°53·8'W	X	146,147

Cysleys Fm	E Susx	TQ4819	50°57·3'	0°6·8'E	FM	198
Cystanog Fm	Carm	SN4620	51°51·7'	4°13·8'W	FM	159
Cystyllen Fawr	Gwyn	SH8633	52°53·2'	3°41·3'W	X	124,125
Cysulog	Conwy	SJ0145	52°59·8'	3°28·1'W	X	116
Cytir	Gwyn	SH8715	52°43·5'	3°40·0'W	X	124,125
Cywarch	Gwyn	SH8518	52°45·1'	3°41·8'W	X	124,125

D

Daaey	Shetld	HU6094	60°37·8'	0°53·7'W	X	1,2
Daal	Shetld	HU4937	60°7·1'	1°6·6'W	X	4
Daal, The	Shetld	HT9538	60°7·9'	2°4·9'W	X	4
Dabshead Hill	Scot Bord	NT5451	55°45·3'	2°43·5'W	H	66,73
Dabshead Hill (Fort)	Scot Bord	NT5451	55°45·3'	2°43·5'W	A	66,73
Dabton	D & G	NX8797	55°15·5'	3°46·3'W	X	78
Dabton Loch	D & G	NX8796	55°15·0'	3°46·2'W	W	78
Daccombe	Devon	SX9068	50°30·3'	3°32·7'W	T	202
Dachray Water	Stir	NS4799	56°9·8'	4°27·4'W	W	57
Dacre	Cumbr	NY4526	54°37·8'	2°50·7'W	T	90
Dacre	N Yks	SE1960	54°2·4'	1°42·2'W	T	99
Dacrebank	Cumbr	NY4527	54°38·4'	2°50·7'W	X	90
Dacre Banks	N Yks	SE1961	54°2·9'	1°42·2'W	T	99
Dacre Beck	Cumbr	NY4526	54°37·8'	2°50·7'W	W	90
Dacre Cottages	Essex	TL6009	51°45·6'	0°19·5'E	X	167
Dacre Lodge	Cumbr	NY4526	54°37·8'	2°50·7'W	X	90
Dacre Pasture	N Yks	SE1860	54°2·4'	1°43·1'W	X	99
Dad Brook	Bucks	SP7310	51°47·3'	0°56·1'W	W	165
Dadbrook Ho	Bucks	SP7310	51°47·3'	0°56·1'W	X	165
Daddry Shield	Durham	NY8937	54°43·9'	2°9·8'W	T	91,92
Daddyhole Cove	Torbay	SX9262	50°27·1'	3°30·9'W	W	202
Dade's Fm	Norf	TG0908	52°38·0'	1°5·7'E	FM	144
Dadford	Bucks	SP6638	52°2·4'	1°1·9'W	T	152
Dà Dhruim Lom	Moray	NJ1404	57°7·4'	3°24·8'W	X	36
Dadlands	Devon	SS5919	50°57·4'	4°0·1'W	X	180
Dadlington	Leic	SP4098	52°34·9'	1°24·2'W	T	140
Dadnor	Heref	SO5626	51°56·1'	2°38·0'W	X	162
Daer Hass	S Lanak	NS9601	55°17·8'	3°37·8'W	X	78
Daerhead	S Lanak	NS9603	55°18·9'	3°37·9'W	X	78
Daer Reservoir	S Lanak	NS9707	55°21·0'	3°37·0'W	W	78
Daerside	S Lanak	NS9609	55°22·1'	3°38·0'W	X	78
Daer Water	S Lanak	NS9512	55°23·7'	3°39·0'W	W	78
Daer Water	S Lanak	NS9604	55°19·4'	3°37·9'W	W	78
Dafadfa-isaf	Carm	SN6821	51°52·6'	3°54·7'W	X	159
Dafadfa Uchaf	Carm	SN6921	51°52·6'	3°53·8'W	X	160
Dafarn-bara-ceirch	Conwy	SH8971	53°13·7'	3°39·4'W	X	116
Dafarn Faig	Gwyn	SH4846	52°59·6'	4°15·5'W	X	115,123
Dafarn-Llefrith	Denb	SJ0173	53°14·9'	3°28·6'W	X	116
Dafen	Carm	SN5201	51°41·5'	4°8·1'W	T	159
Daffaluke	Heref	SO5522	51°53·9'	2°38·8'W	X	162
Daffin	D & G	NX4954	54°51·7'	4°20·7'W	X	83
Daffodil Fm	Staffs	SK0265	53°11·2'	1°57·8'W	FM	119
Daffodil Way	Glos	SO6828	51°57·2'	2°27·5'W	X	149
Daff Resr	Inverc	NS2370	55°53·7'	4°49·4'W	W	63
Daffy Green	Norf	TF9609	52°38·8'	0°54·2'E	T	144
Daft Ann's Steps	Highld	NX8349	54°49·6'	3°48·9'W	X	84
Daftmill Fm	Fife	NO3112	56°18·0'	3°6·5'W	FM	59
Dagdale	Staffs	SK0534	52°54·4'	1°55·1'W	T	128
Dagenham	Bark & Dag	TQ4884	51°32·4'	0°8·4'E	T	177
Dagenham Dock Sta	Bark & Dag	TQ4883	51°31·8'	0°8·4'E	X	177
Dagfa	Carm	SN8032	51°58·7'	3°44·4'W	X	160
Dagfields Fm	Ches	SJ6947	53°1·4'	2°27·3'W	FM	118
Daggers Gate	Dorset	SY8181	50°37·9'	2°15·7'W	X	194
Daggers Hill	Monm	ST4993	51°38·2'	2°43·8'W	X	162,172
Daggons	Dorset	SU1012	50°54·7'	1°51·1'W	T	195
Daglingworth	Glos	SO9905	51°44·9'	2°0·5'W	T	163
Dagnall	Bucks	SP9916	51°50·3'	0°33·4'W	T	165
Dagnall Fm	Bucks	SP9816	51°50·3'	0°34·3'W	FM	165
Dagnall Fm	Northnts	SP7539	52°2·9'	0°54·0'W	FM	152
Dagnam Fm	Medway	TQ8277	51°28·0'	0°37·6'E	FM	178
Dagnam Park	Hav	TQ5593	51°37·1'	0°14·7'E	X	177
Dagnets Fm	Essex	TL7519	51°50·8'	0°32·8'E	FM	167
Dagrum	Moray	NJ0605	57°7·8'	3°32·7'W	X	36
Dagtail End	Worcs	SP0363	52°16·1'	1°57·0'W	T	150
Dagwood Fm	Essex	TQ5898	51°39·7'	0°17·5'E	FM	167,177
Dagworth	Suff	TM0461	52°12·8'	0°59·6'E	T	155
Dagworth Manor	Essex	TL8434	51°58·7'	0°41·1'E	X	155
Daies	Aberd	NJ5628	57°20·7'	2°43·4'W	X	37
Daies	Aberd	NJ6526	57°19·7'	2°34·4'W	X	38
Daiglen Burn	Clackm	NS9098	56°10·0'	3°45·8'W	W	58
Dail	Arg & Bt	NN0539	56°30·4'	5°9·7'W	X	50
Dail a' Chuirn	Highld	NH3105	57°6·6'	4°47·0'W	X	34
Dailbane Hill	Highld	NC7414	58°6·1'	4°7·8'W	H	16
Dail Beag	N Eil	NB2345	58°18·6'	6°43·3'W	T	8
Dail Bhàite	Arg & Bt	NM6042	56°30·8'	5°53·6'W	X	49
Dail bho Dheas	N Eil	NB4861	58°28·1'	6°18·8'W	T	8
Dail bho Thuath	N Eil	NB4961	58°28·2'	6°17·8'W	T	8
Dail-dreaganais	Highld	NG8018	57°12·3'	5°38·1'W	X	33
Daill	Arg & Bt	NR3662	55°48·7'	6°12·2'W	T	60,61
Daill	Arg & Bt	NR8290	56°3·5'	5°29·6'W	T	55
Daill	Highld	NC3568	58°34·4'	4°49·8'W	X	9
Daill Loch	Arg & Bt	NR8189	56°2·9'	5°30·6'W	W	55
Daill River	Highld	NC3467	58°33·8'	4°50·8'W	W	9
Dailly	S Ayr	NS2701	55°16·6'	4°43·0'W	T	76
Dail Mòr	N Eil	NB2144	58°18·0'	6°45·3'W	T	8
Dailnamac	Arg & Bt	NM9732	56°26·5'	5°17·1'W	X	49
Dail na Sneachd	Angus	NO1967	56°47·5'	3°19·1'W	X	43
Daimh-sgeir	Arg & Bt	NR4467	55°50·0'	6°4·9'W	X	60,61
Dainaberg	Shetld	HU4738	60°7·7'	1°8·8'W	X	4
Dainton	Devon	SX8566	50°29·2'	3°36·9'W	T	202

Daintree Fm	Cambs	TL2489	52°29·3'	0°10·0'W	FM	142
Daintree's Fm	Cambs	TL3368	52°17·9'	0°2·6'W	FM	154
Daintry Wood	Beds	SP9931	51°58·3'	0°33·1'W	F	165
Dairies, The	N Yks	SE7170	54°7·5'	0°54·4'W	X	100
Dairsie	Angus	NO3750	56°38·5'	3°1·2'W	X	54
Dairsie	Fife	NO4117	56°20·8'	2°56·8'W	T	59
Dairsie Ho	Fife	NO4015	56°19·7'	2°57·8'W	X	59
Dairsie Mains	Fife	NO4116	56°20·2'	2°56·8'W	X	59
Dairsie or Osnaburgh	Fife	NO4117	56°20·8'	2°56·8'W	T	59
Dairy	Corn	SX0048	50°18·1'	4°48·1'W	X	204
Dairy Barn	Lancs	SD6343	53°53·2'	2°33·4'W	X	102,103
Dairy Byre	Pth & Kin	NN7745	56°35·1'	3°59·7'W	X	51,52
Dairy Farm Ho	Lincs	TF3656	53°5·3'	0°2·3'E	X	122
Dairy Fm	Bucks	SP6730	51°58·1'	1°1·1'W	FM	152,165
Dairy Fm	Ches	SJ6248	53°1·9'	2°33·6'W	FM	118
Dairy Fm	Ches	SJ6860	53°8·4'	2°28·3'W	FM	118
Dairy Fm	Ches	SJ6983	53°20·8'	2°27·5'W	FM	109
Dairy Fm	Ches	SJ7366	53°11·7'	2°23·8'W	FM	118
Dairy Fm	Ches	SJ7880	53°19·2'	2°19·4'W	FM	109
Dairy Fm	Donc	SE7014	53°37·3'	0°56·1'W	FM	112
Dairy Fm	Essex	TQ9299	51°39·6'	0°47·0'E	FM	168
Dairy Fm	Lancs	SD6242	53°52·6'	2°34·3'W	FM	102,103
Dairy Fm	Leic	SK8325	52°49·2'	0°45·7'W	FM	130
Dairy Fm	Leic	SP4998	52°34·9'	1°16·2'W	FM	140
Dairy Fm	Lincs	TF3063	53°9·1'	0°2·9'W	FM	122
Dairy Fm	Mil Key	SP8345	52°6·1'	0°46·9'W	FM	152
Dairy Fm	Monm	SO3911	51°47·9'	2°52·7'W	FM	161
Dairy Fm	Norf	TG0331	52°50·5'	1°1·3'E	FM	133
Dairy Fm	Norf	TG2334	52°51·7'	1°19·2'E	FM	133
Dairy Fm	Norf	TL9281	52°23·8'	0°49·7'E	FM	144
Dairy Fm	Norf	TM0283	52°24·7'	0°58·6'E	FM	144
Dairy Fm	Norf	TM1182	52°23·9'	1°6·5'E	FM	144
Dairy Fm	Norf	TM2199	52°32·9'	1°16·0'E	FM	134
Dairy Fm	Norf	TM2682	52°23·6'	1°19·7'E	FM	156
Dairy Fm	Norf	TM3791	52°28·1'	1°29·8'E	FM	134
Dairy Fm	Notts	SK6453	53°4·5'	1°2·3'W	FM	120
Dairy Fm	N Yks	SD8287	54°16·9'	2°16·2'W	FM	98
Dairy Fm	Suff	TL7359	52°12·3'	0°32·3'E	FM	155
Dairy Fm	Suff	TL9768	52°16·7'	0°53·7'E	FM	155
Dairy Fm	Suff	TL9879	52°22·6'	0°54·9'E	FM	144
Dairy Fm	Suff	TM0076	52°21·0'	0°56·6'E	FM	144
Dairy Fm	Suff	TM0157	52°10·7'	0°56·8'E	FM	155
Dairy Fm	Suff	TM1277	52°21·2'	1°7·2'E	FM	144
Dairy Fm	Suff	TM1565	52°14·7'	1°9·4'E	FM	156
Dairy Fm	Suff	TL2671	52°17·7'	1°19·3'E	FM	156
Dairy Fm	Suff	TM3979	52°21·6'	1°31·0'E	FM	156
Dairy Fm	Swan	SS5789	51°35·1'	4°3·5'W	FM	159
Dairy Fm	Warr	SJ6385	53°21·9'	2°33·0'W	FM	109
Dairy Fm	W Berks	SU4568	51°24·8'	1°20·8'W	FM	174
Dairy Fm	Wilts	ST8337	51°8·2'	2°14·2'W	FM	183
Dairy Fm, The	Shrops	SO6487	52°29·0'	2°31·4'W	FM	138
Dairy Fm, The	Warw	SP2383	52°26·9'	1°39·3'W	FM	139
Dairyground	Stock	SJ9085	53°21·9'	2°8·6'W	X	109
Dairy Hills	Glos	SP1442	52°4·8'	1°47·3'W	X	151
Dairy Ho	Ches	SJ6864	53°10·6'	2°28·3'W	X	118
Dairy Ho	Ches	SJ8783	53°20·9'	2°11·3'W	X	109
Dairy Ho	Dorset	SY8697	50°46·6'	2°11·5'W	X	194
Dairy Ho	Essex	TM1131	51°56·5'	1°4·6'E	X	168,169
Dairy Ho	Essex	TM1819	51°49·8'	1°10·2'E	X	168,169
Dairy Ho	E Yorks	TA2230	53°45·4'	0°8·6'W	X	107
Dairy Ho	Heref	SO3851	52°9·5'	2°54·0'W	X	148,149
Dairy Ho	Kent	TQ7247	51°12·0'	0°28·1'E	X	188
Dairy Ho	Shrops	SJ5530	52°52·2'	2°39·7'W	X	126
Dairy Ho	Shrops	SJ6039	52°57·1'	2°35·3'W	X	127
Dairy Ho	Staffs	SJ9358	53°7·4'	2°5·9'W	X	118
Dairy Ho	Staffs	SJ9846	53°0·9'	2°1·4'W	X	118
Dairy Ho Fm	Staffs	SJ8128	52°51·2'	2°16·5'W	FM	127
Dairy House	Suff	TM1429	51°55·3'	1°7·1'E	X	168,169
Dairyhouse Fm	Cambs	TL3090	52°29·8'	0°4·7'W	FM	142
Dairyhouse Fm	Ches	SJ6050	53°3·0'	2°35·4'W	FM	118
Dairyhouse Fm	Ches	SJ6556	53°6·2'	2°31·0'W	FM	118
Dairy House Fm	Ches	SJ6648	53°1·9'	2°30·0'W	FM	118
Dairyhouse Fm	Ches	SJ6968	53°12·7'	2°27·4'W	FM	118
Dairy House Fm	Ches	SJ7279	53°18·7'	2°24·8'W	FM	118
Dairy House Fm	Ches	SJ7785	53°21·9'	2°20·3'W	FM	109
Dairy House Fm	Ches	SJ8171	53°14·4'	2°16·7'W	FM	118
Dairyhouse Fm	Ches	SJ8265	53°11·1'	2°15·8'W	FM	118
Dairy House Fm	Derby	SK1936	52°55·5'	1°42·6'W	FM	128
Dairy House Fm	Hants	SU5460	51°20·4'	1°13·1'W	FM	174
Dairyhouse Fm	Heref	SO3666	52°17·5'	2°55·9'W	FM	137,148,149
Dairy House Fm	Somer	ST2722	50°59·8'	3°2·0'W	FM	193
Dairy House Fm	Somer	ST2940	51°9·5'	3°0·5'W	FM	182
Dairy House Fm	Somer	ST7951	51°15·7'	2°17·7'W	FM	183
Dairy House Fm	Staffs	SJ9936	52°55·5'	2°0·5'W	FM	127
Dairy House Fm	Traf	SJ7589	53°24·1'	2°22·2'W	FM	109
Dairyhouse Fm	Wilts	ST9255	51°17·9'	2°6·5'W	FM	173
Dairy Houses Fm	Cambs	TL5491	52°29·9'	0°16·5'E	FM	143
Dairy Research Inst	S Ayr	NS3723	55°28·7'	4°34·3'W	X	70
Dairy Wood	Suff	TL8062	52°13·8'	0°38·5'E	F	155
Dairywood Fm	Derby	SK3450	53°3·0'	1°29·2'W	FM	119
Daisy	I Scilly	SV8305	49°51·9'	6°24·3'W	X	203
Daisy Bank	Ches	SJ7657	53°6·8'	2°21·1'W	X	118
Daisy Bank	Derby	SK2056	53°6·3'	1°41·7'W	X	119
Daisy Bank	N Yks	NZ8704	54°25·7'	0°39·1'W	X	94
Daisy Bank	Wals	SP0497	52°34·5'	1°56·1'W	X	139
Daisybank Fm	Ches	SJ7181	53°19·7'	2°25·7'W	FM	109
Daisybank Fm	Ches	SJ7267	53°12·2'	2°24·7'W	FM	118
Daisy Bank Fm	Ches	SJ7653	53°4·7'	2°21·1'W	FM	118
Daisybank Fm	Derby	SK1238	52°56·6'	1°48·9'W	FM	128
Daisy Barn	Lancs	SD5839	53°51·0'	2°37·9'W	X	102
Daisy Green	Essex	TL9325	51°53·6'	0°48·7'E	X	168
Daisy Green	Suff	TM0067	52°16·1'	0°56·3'E	T	155
Daisy Green	Suff	TM0968	52°16·4'	1°4·2'E	T	155
Daisy Hill	Bolton	SD6504	53°32·1'	2°31·3'W	T	109
Daisy Hill	Brad	SE1334	53°48·4'	1°47·7'W	T	104
Daisy Hill	Durham	NZ2348	54°49·8'	1°38·1'W	H	88
Daisy Hill	E Yorks	TA2230	53°45·4'	0°8·6'W	X	107
Daisy Hill	Lancs	SD7145	53°54·3'	2°26·1'W	X	103
Daisy Hill	Leeds	SE2628	53°45·1'	1°35·9'W	T	104
Daisy Hill Fm	Lincs	TF0698	53°28·3'	0°23·8'W	FM	112
Daisy Hill Fm	Warw	SP2459	52°14·0'	1°38·5'W	FM	151

Daisyland	Devon	ST0606	50°51·0′	3°19·7′W	X	192
Daisy Lee Moor	Kirk	SE1404	53°32·2′	1°46·9′W	X	110
Daisymere Fm	Derby	SK0874	53°16·0′	1°52·4′W	FM	119
Daisy Nook	Oldham	SD9100	53°30·0′	2°7·7′W	T	109
Daisy Nook Country Park	Oldham	SD9200	53°30·0′	2°6·8′W	X	109
Dalabheairn	Highld	NH4991	57°53·2′	4°32·3′W	X	20
Dalachy Fm	Fife	NT2086	56°3·9′	3°16·7′W	FM	66
Dalairn	Angus	NO3166	56°47·1′	3°7·3′W	X	44
Dalane Cott	D & G	NX3777	55°3·9′	4°32·7′W	X	77
Dalar Fm	Gwyn	SH5821	52°46·3′	4°5·9′W	FM	124
Dalarwen	Cered	SN7850	52°8·3′	3°46·6′W	X	146,147
Dalavan Bay	D & G	NX5653	54°51·3′	4°14·2′W	W	83
Dalavich	Arg & Bt	NM9612	56°15·7′	5°17·2′W	T	55
Dalavil	Highld	NG5805	57°4·6′	5°59·1′W	X	32,39
Dalawoodie	D & G	NX9579	55°5·9′	3°38·3′W	X	84
Dalbagie	Aberd	NO3496	57°3·3′	3°4·8′W	X	37,44
Dalballoch	Highld	NN6598	57°3·5′	4°13·1′W	X	35
Dalbeath	Fife	NT1491	56°6·5′	3°22·5′W	X	58
Dalbeathie	Pth & Kin	NO0540	56°32·8′	3°32·3′W	X	52,53
Dalbeattie	D & G	NX8361	54°56·1′	3°49·1′W	T	84
Dalbeattie Forest	D & G	NX8558	54°54·5′	3°47·2′W	X	84
Dalbeattie Resr	D & G	NX8061	54°56·0′	3°51·9′W	W	84
Dalbeg	Highld	NH6513	57°11·5′	4°13·6′W	X	35
Dalbeg Bay	N Eil	NB2246	58°19·1′	6°44·4′W	W	8
Dalbhraddan	Arg & Bt	NR6810	55°20·0′	5°39·1′W	X	68
Dalblair	E Ayr	NS6419	55°27·0′	4°8·6′W	T	71
Dalbog	Angus	NO5871	56°50·0′	2°40·8′W	X	44
Dalbrack	Angus	NO4778	56°53·7′	2°51·7′W	X	44
Dalbrack	Stir	NN7405	56°13·5′	4°1·5′W	X	57
Dalbraidie	Aberd	NJ6816	57°14·3′	2°31·4′W	X	38
Dalbreac Lodge	Highld	NH3054	57°32·9′	4°50·0′W	X	26
Dalbreak	Aberd	NO6591	57°0·8′	2°34·1′W	X	38,45
Dalbreck	Highld	NC7416	58°7·2′	4°7·9′W	X	16
Dalbuiack	Highld	NH9223	57°17·4′	3°47·1′W	X	36
Dalbuie	Arg & Bt	NR6913	55°21·7′	5°38·3′W	X	68
Dalbury	Derby	SK2634	52°54·4′	1°36·4′W	T	128
Dalbury Hollow	Derby	SK2634	52°54·4′	1°36·4′W	X	128
Dalby	I of M	SC2179	54°10·8′	4°44·2′W	T	95
Dalby	Lincs	TF4070	53°12·7′	0°6·2′E	T	122
Dalby	N Yks	SE6371	54°8·1′	1°1·7′W	T	100
Dalby Beck	N Yks	SE8587	54°16·5′	0°41·3′W	W	94,100
Dalby Bush Beck	N Yks	SE6471	54°8·1′	1°0·8′W	W	100
Dalby Bush Fm	N Yks	SE6471	54°8·1′	1°0·8′W	FM	100
Dalby Carr	N Yks	SE6470	54°7·6′	1°0·8′W	X	100
Dalby Forest	N Yks	SE8788	54°17·1′	0°39·4′W	F	94,101
Dalby Grange	Lincs	TF4171	53°13·3′	0°7·1′E	X	122
Dalby Hill	Lincs	TF4169	53°12·2′	0°7·1′E	X	122
Dalby Lodge Fm	Leic	SK7312	52°42·3′	0°54·8′W	FM	129
Dalby Mountain	I of M	SC2377	54°9·7′	4°42·3′W	H	95
Dalby Point	I of M	SC2179	54°10·8′	4°44·2′W	X	95
Dalby Wolds	Leic	SK6522	52°47·7′	1°1·8′W	X	129
Dalcairney	E Ayr	NS4604	55°18·6′	4°25·2′W	X	77
Dalcairnie Burn	E Ayr	NS4503	55°18·1′	4°26·1′W	W	77
Dalcataig	Highld	NH4017	57°13·2′	4°38·5′W	X	34
Dalchalloch	Pth & Kin	NN7264	56°45·3′	4°5·2′W	X	42
Dalchalm	Highld	NC9005	58°1·5′	3°51·3′W	T	17
Dalcharn	Highld	NC6258	58°29·6′	4°21·6′W	T	10
Dalcharn	Highld	NC7061	58°31·3′	4°13·5′W	X	10
Dalcharn	Highld	NC8626	58°12·7′	3°55·9′W	X	17
Dalcharn	Highld	NH8145	57°29·0′	3°58·6′W	X	27
Dalchenna	Arg & Bt	NN0706	56°12·7′	5°6·3′W	X	56
Dalchenna Point	Arg & Bt	NN0806	56°12·7′	5°5·3′W	X	56
Dalchiel	Highld	NH7591	57°53·7′	4°6·1′W	X	21
Dalchiorlich	Pth & Kin	NN4841	56°32·4′	4°27·9′W	X	51
Dalchirach	Moray	NJ1934	57°23·6′	3°20·4′W	X	28
Dalchirla	Pth & Kin	NN8215	56°19·0′	3°54·0′W	X	57
Dalchomie	S Ayr	NS2808	55°20·4′	4°42·3′W	X	70,76
Dalchon	Aberd	NJ8628	57°20·8′	2°13·5′W	X	38
Dalchonzie	Pth & Kin	NN7422	56°22·7′	4°2·0′W	X	51,52
Dalchork	Highld	NC5710	58°3·6′	4°24·9′W	X	16
Dalchork Wood	Highld	NC5811	58°4·2′	4°24·0′W	F	16
Dalchosnie	Pth & Kin	NN6757	56°41·4′	4°9·8′W	X	42,51
Dalchreichart	Highld	NH2912	57°10·3′	4°49·2′W	T	34
Dalchroy	Highld	NJ1435	57°24·1′	3°25·4′W	X	28
Dalchruin	Pth & Kin	NN7116	56°19·4′	4°4·7′W	X	57
Dalchully Ho	Highld	NN5993	57°0·7′	4°18·9′W	X	35
Dalclathick	Pth & Kin	NN7117	56°19·9′	4°4·7′W	X	57
Dalcove Mains	Scot Bord	NT6532	55°35·1′	2°32·9′W	X	74
Dalcrag	Highld	NH4917	57°13·4′	4°29·6′W	X	34
Dalcrombie	Highld	NH6128	57°19·5′	4°18·1′W	X	26,35
Dalcross	Highld	NH7748	57°30·6′	4°2·7′W	X	27
Dalcroy Fm	Pth & Kin	NN7759	56°42·7′	4°0·1′W	FM	42,51,52
Dalcrue	Pth & Kin	NO0427	56°25·8′	3°33·0′W	X	52,53,58
Dalcur	S Ayr	NS3107	55°19·9′	4°39·4′W	X	70,76
Dalderby	Lincs	TF2466	53°10·8′	0°8·3′W	T	122
Daldhu	Pth & Kin	NO0270	56°48·9′	3°35·9′W	X	43
Daldilling	E Ayr	NS5726	55°30·7′	4°15·4′W	X	71
Dalditch	Devon	SY0483	50°38·6′	3°21·1′W	X	192
Daldorch	S Ayr	NS4423	55°28·8′	4°27·7′W	X	70
Daldorch Ho (Sch)	E Ayr	NS5326	55°30·6′	4°19·2′W	X	70
Daldorn Fm	Stir	NN6603	56°12·3′	4°9·2′W	FM	57
Daldowie	S Ayr	NX2192	55°11·6′	4°48·3′W	X	76
Daldowie Hill	S Ayr	NX2292	55°11·7′	4°47·4′W	X	76
Daldownie	Aberd	NJ2400	57°5·3′	3°14·8′W	X	36
Daldravaig Fm	Stir	NN5534	56°28·8′	4°20·8′W	FM	51
Dalduff	S Ayr	NS3206	55°19·4′	4°38·4′W	X	70,76
Dale	Cumbr	NY5444	54°47·6′	2°42·5′W	T	86
Dale	Oldham	SD9808	53°34·4′	2°1·4′W	T	109
Dale	Orkney	HY2424	59°6·0′	3°19·1′W	X	6
Dale	Orkney	HY3027	59°7·7′	3°12·9′W	X	6
Dale	Orkney	HY3127	59°7·7′	3°11·8′W	X	6
Dale	Orkney	HY3606	58°56·5′	3°6·2′W	X	6,7
Dale	Orkney	HY3619	59°3·5′	3°6·5′W	X	6
Dale	Orkney	HY5332	59°10·6′	2°48·9′W	X	5,6
Dale	Orkney	HY6524	59°6·4′	2°36·2′W	X	5
Dale	Orkney	ND4390	58°47·9′	2°58·7′W	X	7
Dale	Pemb	SM8005	51°42·3′	5°10·7′W	T	157
Dale	Shetld	HU4168	60°23·9′	1°14·9′W	X	2,3
Dale Abbey	Derby	SK4338	52°56·5′	1°21·2′W	T	129
Dale Abbey Fm	Staffs	SK1047	53°1·5′	1°50·6′W	FM	119,128

Daleacre Hill	Leic	SK4627	52°50·5′	1°18·6′W	X	129
Daleacres	Kent	TR1133	51°3·7′	1°1·1′E	X	179,189
Dalealy	Pth & Kin	NO2521	56°22·8′	3°12·4′W	X	53,59
Dalebank	Derby	SK3661	53°8·9′	1°27·3′W	T	119
Dalebank	S Lanak	NS8322	55°28·9′	3°50·7′W	X	71,72
Dale Bank Fm	Staffs	SK0240	52°57·7′	1°57·8′W	FM	119,128
Dale Barns	Lancs	SD4967	54°6·0′	2°46·4′W	X	97
Dale Beck	Cumbr	NY2937	54°43·6′	3°5·7′W	W	89,90
Dale Beck	Cumbr	NY6336	54°43·3′	2°34·0′W	W	91
Dale Beck	Lancs	SD6560	54°2·3′	2°31·7′W	W	97
Dale Bottom	Cumbr	NY2921	54°35·0′	3°5·5′W	T	89,90
Dale Bottom	Derby	SK2481	53°19·8′	1°38·0′W	X	110
Dale Br	Lincs	TF0490	53°24·0′	0°25·7′W	X	112
Dale Brook	Derby	SK1731	52°52·8′	1°44·4′W	W	128
Dalebrook	Derby	SK1732	52°53·3′	1°44·4′W	X	128
Dale Brook	Derby	SK2275	53°16·5′	1°39·8′W	W	119
Dalebrook Ho	Derby	SK2971	53°14·4′	1°33·5′W	X	119
Dale Brow	Ches	SJ9076	53°17·1′	2°8·6′W	T	118
Dale Burn	Shetld	HU3649	60°13·7′	1°20·5′W	W	3
Dale Cott	E Yorks	SE9236	53°49·0′	0°35·7′W	X	106
Dale Dike Resr	Sheff	SK2491	53°25·2′	1°37·9′W	W	110
Dale End	Cumbr	NY3103	54°25·3′	3°3·4′W	X	90
Dale End	Cumbr	NY3306	54°26·9′	3°1·6′W	X	90
Dale End	Cumbr	NY5100	54°23·8′	2°44·9′W	X	90
Dale End	Derby	SK1459	53°7·9′	1°47·0′W	X	119
Dale End	Derby	SK2161	53°8·9′	1°40·8′W	T	119
Dale End	N Yks	SD9646	53°54·9′	2°3·2′W	T	103
Dale End Fm	Derby	SK1755	53°5·8′	1°44·4′W	FM	119
Dale End Fm	N Yks	NZ8304	54°25·7′	0°42·8′W	FM	94
Dale Fm	Derby	SK1972	53°14·9′	1°42·5′W	FM	119
Dale Fm	Derby	SK2924	52°49·0′	1°33·8′W	FM	128
Dale Fm	Highld	ND1353	58°27·7′	3°29·0′W	FM	11,12
Dale Fm	Kent	TQ5251	51°14·5′	0°11·0′E	FM	188
Dale Fm	Lincs	SK8562	53°9·1′	0°43·3′W	FM	121
Dale Fm	Lincs	TF0451	53°3·0′	0°26·7′W	FM	121
Dale Fm	Northnts	SP7376	52°22·9′	0°55·2′W	FM	141
Dale Fm	N Yks	NZ9107	54°27·3′	0°35·4′W	FM	94
Dale Fm	N Yks	TA1074	54°9·2′	0°18·5′W	FM	101
Dale Fm	Suff	TL9675	52°20·5′	0°53·0′E	FM	144
Dale Fm	Suff	TL9752	52°8·1′	0°53·1′E	FM	155
Dale Fm	Suff	TM1267	52°15·8′	1°6·8′E	FM	155
Dale Fm	Suff	TM3653	52°7·7′	1°27·3′E	FM	156
Dalefoot	Cumbr	NY4920	54°34·6′	2°46·9′W	X	90
Dalefoot	Cumbr	NY7804	54°26·1′	2°19·9′W	X	91
Dale Foot	N Yks	SD9784	54°15·3′	2°2·3′W	X	98
Daleford	Ches	SJ6069	53°13·2′	2°35·5′W	X	118
Daleford Ho	Ches	SJ6275	53°16·5′	2°33·8′W	X	118
Dale Fort Field Centre	Pemb	SM8205	51°42·3′	5°8·9′W	X	157
Dalegarth Hall	Cumbr	NY1600	54°23·6′	3°17·2′W	X	89
Dalegarth Sta	Cumbr	NY1700	54°23·6′	3°16·3′W	X	89,90
Dale Gill	Cumbr	NY7002	54°25·0′	2°27·3′W	W	91
Dale Hall	Essex	TM0931	51°56·5′	1°2·8′E	X	168,169
Dale Hause	Cumbr	NY4719	54°34·1′	2°48·8′W	X	90
Dale Head	Cumbr	NY2215	54°31·7′	3°11·9′W	H	89,90
Dale Head	Cumbr	NY2400	54°23·6′	3°9·8′W	X	89,90
Dale Head	Cumbr	NY4316	54°32·4′	2°52·4′W	X	90
Dalehead	Derby	SK0873	53°15·5′	1°52·4′W	X	119
Dalehead	Derby	SK1084	53°21·4′	1°50·6′W	X	110
Dale Head	Derby	SK1276	53°17·1′	1°48·8′W	X	119
Dalehead	Derby	SK1558	53°7·4′	1°46·1′W	X	119
Dale Head	Durham	NY8034	54°42·3′	2°18·2′W	X	91,92
Dale Head	N Yks	NY9706	54°27·2′	2°2·4′W	X	92
Dale Head	N Yks	NZ6301	54°24·3′	1°1·3′W	X	94
Dale Head	N Yks	NZ6704	54°25·9′	0°57·6′W	X	94
Dale Head	N Yks	NZ7102	54°24·7′	0°53·9′W	X	94
Dale Head	N Yks	SD8471	54°8·3′	2°14·3′W	X	98
Dale Head	N Yks	SD9581	54°13·7′	2°4·2′W	X	98
Dale Head	N Yks	SE4994	54°20·6′	1°14·4′W	X	100
Dale Head Common	N Yks	NY9708	54°28·3′	2°2·4′W	X	92
Dalehead Crags	Cumbr	NY2215	54°31·7′	3°11·9′W	X	89,90
Dale Head Fm	N Yks	SE6899	54°23·2′	0°56·8′W	FM	94,100
Dale Head Fm	N Yks	SE6999	54°23·1′	0°55·8′W	FM	94,100
Dalehead Hall (Hotel)	Cumbr	NY3117	54°32·9′	3°3·6′W	X	90
Dale Hey	Lancs	SD6436	53°49·4′	2°32·4′W	X	102,103
Dale Hill	E Susx	TQ6930	51°2·9′	0°25·1′E	T	188
Dale Hill	E Susx	TQ7030	51°2·9′	0°25·9′E	T	188
Dalehill	Pemb	SM8006	51°42·8′	5°10·7′W	X	157
Dale Hill	Shetld	HU1854	60°16·5′	1°40·0′W	H	3
Dale Ho	Derby	SK3856	53°6·2′	1°25·5′W	X	119
Dale Ho	Highld	ND1252	58°27·1′	3°30·0′W	X	11,12
Dale Ho	Lancs	SD6239	53°51·0′	2°34·2′W	X	102,103
Dale Ho	Lancs	SD7358	54°1·3′	2°24·3′W	X	103
Dale Ho	Northum	NY7850	54°50·9′	2°20·1′W	X	86,87
Dale Ho	N Yks	SD7275	54°10·5′	2°25·3′W	X	98
Dale Hole	Norf	TF8744	52°57·9′	0°47·5′E	X	132
Dalehouse	N Yks	NZ7717	54°32·7′	0°48·2′W	X	94
Dalehouse Fm	Derby	SK1467	53°12·2′	1°47·0′W	FM	119
Dale House Fm	Warw	SP4383	52°26·8′	1°21·6′W	FM	140
Daleigh Fm	Highld	NJ1235	57°24·1′	3°27·4′W	FM	28
Dalelia	Highld	NM7369	56°45·7′	5°42·4′W	T	40
Dalemain	Cumbr	NY4726	54°37·8′	2°48·8′W	A	90
Dale Mill	Cumbr	NY5445	54°48·1′	2°42·5′W	X	86
Dale Mire Barn	N Yks	SD7975	54°10·5′	2°18·9′W	X	98
Dale Moor	Derby	SK4438	52°56·5′	1°20·3′W	T	129
Dalemoor Fm	Derby	SK4438	52°56·5′	1°20·3′W	FM	129
Dalemore	Highld	ND1349	58°25·5′	3°28·9′W	X	11,12
Dale Moss	Highld	ND1351	58°26·6′	3°28·9′W	X	11,12
Dale Mount	Donc	SE7010	53°35·2′	0°56·1′W	X	112
Dale of Corrigall	Orkney	HY3419	59°3·4′	3°8·6′W	X	6
Dale of Helzie	Orkney	HY5607	58°57·1′	2°45·4′W	X	6
Dale of Oddsta	Shetld	HU5893	60°37·2′	0°55·9′W	X	1,2
Dale of Redland	Orkney	HY3617	59°2·4′	3°6·4′W	X	6
Dale of Ure	Shetld	HU2280	60°30·5′	1°35·5′W	X	3
Dale of Walls	Shetld	HU1852	60°15·4′	1°40·0′W	T	3
Dale of Woodwick	Shetld	HP5811	60°46·9′	0°55·6′W	X	1
Dalepark	Shetld	HP6211	60°46·9′	0°51·2′W	X	1
Dale Park	W Susx	SU9709	50°52·6′	0°36·9′W	X	197
Dale Park Beck	Cumbr	SD3592	54°19·4′	2°59·5′W	W	96,97
Dale Plantn	E Yorks	SE9236	53°49·0′	0°35·7′W	F	106
Dale Point	Pemb	SM8205	51°42·3′	5°8·9′W	X	157

Dale Pond	N Yks	SE5972	54°8·7′	1°5·4′W	W	100
Dale Roads	Pemb	SM8105	51°42·3′	5°9·8′W	W	157
Dalesbank Fm	Brad	SE0348	53°55·9′	1°56·8′W	FM	104
Dales Br	Lincs	TF1760	53°7·7′	0°14·7′W	X	121
Dalesbridge Centre	N Yks	SD7667	54°6·1′	2°21·6′W	X	98
Dales Brow	Salf	SD7700	53°30·0′	2°20·4′W	T	109
Dalescord Hill	Shetld	HU3968	60°23·9′	1°17·0′W	H	2,3
Dales Fm	N Yks	NZ3606	54°27·1′	1°26·3′W	FM	93
Dales Fm	Suff	TL8451	52°7·8′	0°41·7′E	FM	155
Dale's Fm	W Susx	SU9730	51°3·9′	0°36·6′W	FM	186
Dalesgap	Staffs	SK1140	52°57·7′	1°49·8′W	X	119,128
Dales Green	Staffs	SJ8556	53°6·3′	2°13·0′W	T	118
Dales Head Dike	Lincs	TF1563	53°9·3′	0°16·4′W	W	121
Dales Ho	Darl	NZ3318	54°33·6′	1°29·0′W	X	93
Dale Side	Cumbr	NY2639	54°44·7′	3°8·5′W	X	89,90
Daleside	N Yks	SE5388	54°17·3′	1°10·7′W	X	100
Daleside Fm	N Yks	NZ6504	54°25·9′	0°59·5′W	FM	94
Dales Lees	Shetld	HU4068	60°23·9′	1°15·9′W	X	2,3
Dalespot	Orkney	HY4506	58°56·5′	2°56·9′W	X	6,7
Daless	Highld	NH8638	57°25·3′	3°53·4′W	X	27
Dales, The	Fife	NT1384	56°2·7′	3°23·4′W	X	65
Dales, The	Lincs	TF1253	53°4·0′	0°19·3′W	X	121
Dales, The	Norf	TG1341	52°55·7′	1°10·5′E	X	133
Dales, The	Staffs	SJ9454	53°5·2′	2°5·0′W	X	118
Dales, The	Wirral	SJ2682	53°20·0′	3°6·3′W	X	108
Dalestie	Moray	NJ1611	57°11·2′	3°22·9′W	X	36
Dalestorth	Notts	SK5060	53°8·3′	1°14·7′W	T	120
Dales Voe	Shetld	HU4270	60°25·0′	1°13·7′W	W	2,3
Dales Voe	Shetld	HU4445	60°11·5′	1°11·9′W	W	4
Dales Way	Brad	SE1048	53°55·9′	1°50·4′W	X	104
Dales Way	Cumbr	SD4296	54°21·6′	2°53·1′W	X	96,97
Dales Way	Cumbr	SD5497	54°22·2′	2°42·1′W	X	97
Dales Way	N Yks	SD8582	54°14·3′	2°13·4′W	X	98
Dales Wood	Falk	NS8185	56°2·8′	3°54·2′W	F	57,65
Dale's Wood	Notts	SK6958	53°7·1′	0°57·7′W	F	120
Daleswood Fm	Worcs	SO9478	52°24·2′	2°4·9′W	FM	139
Dale, The	Ches	SJ3970	53°13·7′	2°54·4′W	X	117
Dale, The	Durham	NY8629	54°39·6′	2°12·6′W	X	91,92
Dale, The	Flint	SJ3260	53°8·2′	3°0·6′W	X	117
Dale, The	Lincs	TF0690	53°24·0′	0°23·9′W	W	112
Dale, The	Norf	TG0935	52°52·5′	1°6·8′E	X	133
Dale, The	Shetld	HU3179	60°29·9′	1°25·6′W	X	3
Dale, The	Shetld	HU5396	60°38·9′	1°1·3′W	X	1
Dale, The	Shetld	HU6189	60°35·1′	0°52·7′W	X	1,2
Dale, The	Staffs	SJ9743	52°59·3′	2°2·3′W	X	118
Dale, The	Staffs	SK0948	53°2·0′	1°51·5′W	X	119
Dale, The	Staffs	SK2308	52°40·4′	1°39·2′W	X	128
Dalethorpe	Essex	TM0433	51°57·7′	0°58·6′E	X	168
Dale Top	Ches	SJ9680	53°19·3′	2°3·2′W	X	109
Dale Town	N Yks	SE5388	54°17·3′	1°10·7′W	X	100
Dale Town Common	N Yks	SE5089	54°17·9′	1°13·5′W	X	100
Dale View	N Yks	NZ6606	54°26·9′	0°58·5′W	X	94
Dale Voe	Shetld	HU3675	60°27·7′	1°20·2′W	W	2,3
Dale Water	Shetld	HU4018	59°57·0′	1°16·5′W	W	4
Dale Wood	Northnts	SP7376	52°22·9′	0°55·2′W	F	141
Dale Wood	N Yks	SE5973	54°9·2′	1°5·4′W	F	100
Dalfaber	Highld	NH9013	57°11·9′	3°48·8′W	T	36
Dalfad	Aberd	NJ3100	57°5·4′	3°7·9′W	X	37
Dalfad	E Ayr	NS6222	55°28·6′	4°10·6′W	X	71
Dalfad Moss	E Ayr	NS6222	55°28·6′	4°10·6′W	X	71
Dalfask	S Ayr	NX2094	55°12·7′	4°49·3′W	X	76
Dalfask Hill	S Ayr	NX2194	55°12·7′	4°48·4′W	H	76
Dalfibble	D & G	NY0486	55°9·8′	3°30·0′W	X	78
Dalfling	Aberd	NJ6919	57°15·9′	2°30·4′W	X	38
Dalfoil	Stir	NS5788	56°4·1′	4°17·4′W	T	57
Dalfouper	Angus	NO6168	56°48·4′	2°37·9′W	X	45
Dalfram	E Ayr	NS6526	55°30·8′	4°7·8′W	X	71
Dalgain	E Ayr	NS5626	55°30·6′	4°16·4′W	X	71
Dalgairn	Fife	NO3715	56°19·6′	3°0·7′W	X	59
Dalganachan	Highld	ND0039	58°20·0′	3°42·0′W	X	11,12,17
Dalgarno's Croft	Aberd	NJ8250	57°32·6′	2°17·6′W	X	29,30
Dalgarven	N Ayr	NS2945	55°40·4′	4°42·7′W	T	63
Dalgety	Angus	NO6059	56°43·5′	2°38·8′W	X	54
Dalgety Bay	Fife	NT1583	56°2·2′	3°21·4′W	T	65
Dalgety Bay	Fife	NT1683	56°2·2′	3°20·4′W	W	65,66
Dalgig	E Ayr	NS5512	55°23·1′	4°16·9′W	X	71
Dalginch	Fife	NO3102	56°12·6′	3°6·3′W	X	59
Dalginross	Pth & Kin	NN7721	56°22·2′	3°59·0′W	T	51,52,57
Dalgonar	D & G	NS7003	55°18·5′	4°2·5′W	X	77
Dalgonar	D & G	NX8684	55°8·5′	3°46·9′W	X	78
Dalgrambich	Highld	NH7847	57°30·1′	4°1·7′W	T	27
Dalguise	Pth & Kin	NN9947	56°36·5′	3°38·3′W	T	52,53
Dalguise Ho	Pth & Kin	NN9947	56°36·5′	3°38·3′W	X	52,53
Dalhabboch	D & G	NX1368	54°58·5′	4°54·9′W	X	82
Dalhally	Angus	NO1970	56°49·1′	3°19·2′W	T	43
Dalham	Suff	TL7261	52°13·4′	0°31·5′E	T	155
Dalham Fm	Medway	TQ7775	51°27·0′	0°33·2′E	FM	178
Dalham Hall	Suff	TL7262	52°14·0′	0°31·5′E	A	154
Dalham Hall Stud	Cambs	TL6560	52°13·0′	0°25·3′E	X	154
Dalhanna	Kent	TQ5163	51°21·0′	0°10·5′E	X	177,188
Dalhanna Fm	E Ayr	NS6110	55°22·1′	4°11·2′W	FM	71
Dalhanna Hill	E Ayr	NS6211	55°22·7′	4°10·2′W	H	71
Dalharrold	Highld	NC6838	58°18·9′	4°14·7′W	X	16
Dalhastnie	Angus	NO5478	56°53·7′	2°44·9′W	X	44
Dalhavaig	Highld	NC8954	58°27·9′	3°53·7′W	T	10
Dalhebity	C of Aber	NJ8703	57°7·3′	2°12·4′W	X	38
Dalhenzean	Pth & Kin	NO1268	56°48·0′	3°26·0′W	T	43
Dalherrick	Aberd	NJ6609	57°10·5′	2°33·3′W	X	38
Dalhousie Burn	Midlo	NT3163	55°51·6′	3°5·7′W	W	66
Dalhousie Castle	Midlo	NT3263	55°51·6′	3°4·7′W	A	66
Dalhousie Chesters	Midlo	NT3063	55°51·6′	3°6·7′W	X	66
Dalhousie Grange	Midlo	NT3163	55°51·6′	3°5·7′W	X	66
Daliburgh	N Eil	NF7521	57°10·1′	7°22·2′W	T	31
Daligan	Arg & Bt	NS3284	56°1·4′	4°41·3′W	X	56
Dalinlongart	Arg & Bt	NS1482	56°0·0′	4°58·5′W	X	56
Dalinlongart Hill	Arg & Bt	NS1481	55°59·4′	4°58·5′W	H	63
Dalintart	Arg & Bt	NM8629	56°24·5′	5°27·7′W	T	49
Dalintober	Arg & Bt	NM9140	56°30·6′	5°23·4′W	X	49
Dalinturuaine	Pth & Kin	NN7569	56°48·0′	4°2·4′W	X	42
Dalivaddy	Arg & Bt	NR6719	55°24·8′	5°40·4′W	X	68

Daljarrock (Hotel)	S Ayr	NX1988	55°9·4'	4°50·0'W	X	76
Daljedburgh	S Ayr	NX3096	55°14·0'	4°40·0'W	X	76
Daljedburgh Hill	S Ayr	NX3196	55°14·0'	4°39·0'W	X	76
Dalkeith	Arg & Bt	NR6636	55°33·9'	5°42·2'W	X	68
Dalkeith	Midlo	NT3467	55°53·8'	3°2·9'W	T	66
Dalkeith	Pth & Kin	NT0198	56°10·1'	3°35·2'W	X	58
Dalkeith House	Midlo	NT3367	55°53·7'	3°3·8'W	A	66
Dalkenneth	Stir	NN6324	56°23·6'	4°12·7'W	X	51
Dalkest	D & G	NX0269	54°58·8'	5°5·2'W	X	82
Dalks Law	Scot Bord	NT8464	55°52·4'	2°14·9'W	H	67
Dall	Highld	ND1644	58°22·8'	3°25·7'W	X	11,12
Dall	Stir	NN6735	56°29·6'	4°9·2'W	X	51
Dallachapple	Highld	NJ0829	57°20·8'	3°31·3'W	X	36
Dallachulish	Arg & Bt	NM9744	56°32·9'	5°17·7'W	X	49
Dallacombe	Devon	SX8049	50°20·0'	3°40·8'W	X	202
Dalladies	Aberd	NO6267	56°47·8'	2°36·9'W	X	45
Dallam	Warr	SJ5990	53°24·6'	2°36·6'W	T	108
Dallam Tower	Cumbr	SD4981	54°13·6'	2°46·5'W	X	97
Dallan Bank	Cumbr	NY5722	54°35·7'	2°39·5'W	X	91
Dallance Ho	Essex	TL3902	51°42·2'	0°1·1'E	X	166
Dallangwell	Highld	NC8259	58°30·5'	4°1·0'W	X	10
Dallars Ho	E Ayr	NS4633	55°34·2'	4°26·1'W	X	70
Dallas	Moray	NJ1252	57°33·2'	3°27·8'W	T	28
Dallasbraughty	Moray	NJ0346	57°29·9'	3°36·7'W	X	27
Dallaschyle	Highld	NH8149	57°31·2'	3°58·7'W	X	27
Dallaschyle Wood	Highld	NH8248	57°30·7'	3°57·7'W	F	27
Dallash	D & G	NX4769	54°59·8'	4°23·1'W	X	83
Dallas Lodge	Moray	NJ1052	57°33·2'	3°29·8'W	X	28
Dallauruach	Highld	NH5535	57°23·2'	4°24·3'W	X	26
Dall Burn	Pth & Kin	NN5754	56°39·6'	4°19·5'W	W	42,51
Dalleagles	E Ayr	NS5710	55°22·0'	4°14·9'W	X	71
Dalleagles Burn	E Ayr	NS5710	55°22·0'	4°14·9'W	W	71
Dalle Crucis Abbey	Denb	SJ2044	52°59·5'	3°11·1'W	A	117
Dallerie	Pth & Kin	NN8521	56°22·3'	3°51·3'W	X	52,58
Dallican Water	Shetld	HU4967	60°23·3'	1°6·2'W	W	2,3
Dallick Ho	Pth & Kin	NN9128	56°26·2'	3°45·6'W	X	52,58
Dallicott	Shrops	SO7794	52°32·8'	2°20·0'W	T	138
Dallimores	I of W	SZ5293	50°44·3'	1°15·4'W	T	196
Dallinghoo	Suff	TM2655	52°9·0'	1°18·6'E	T	156
Dallington	E Susx	TQ6519	50°57·0'	0°21·3'E	T	199
Dallington	Northnts	SP7361	52°14·8'	0°55·4'W	T	152
Dallington Forest	E Susx	TQ6420	50°57·6'	0°20·5'E	F	199
Dallington Heath	Northnts	SP7263	52°15·9'	0°56·3'W	F	152
Dallow	N Yks	SE1971	54°8·3'	1°42·1'W	T	99
Dallowgill	N Yks	SE1871	54°8·3'	1°43·1'W	X	99
Dallowgill Moor	N Yks	SE1671	54°8·3'	1°44·9'W	X	99
Dallowie	E Ayr	NS3910	55°21·7'	4°32·0'W	X	70
Dallow Moor	N Yks	SE1869	54°7·2'	1°43·1'W	X	99
Dally	D & G	NW9768	54°58·2'	5°9·9'W	X	82
Dally Castle (rems of)	Northum	NY7784	55°9·2'	2°21·2'W	A	80
Dalmaca	E Ayr	NS4415	55°24·5'	4°27·4'W	X	70
Dalmacallan	D & G	NX7988	55°10·5'	3°53·6'W	X	78
Dalmacallan Forest	D & G	NX8087	55°10·0'	3°52·6'W	F	78
Dalmacallan Hill	D & G	NX7987	55°10·0'	3°53·5'W	H	78
Dalmacoulter	N Lanak	NS7667	55°53·1'	3°58·5'W	X	64
Dalmadilly	Aberd	NJ7317	57°14·8'	2°26·4'W	X	38
Dalmagarry	Highld	NH7832	57°22·0'	4°1·2'W	X	27
Dalmahoy Country Club	C of Edin	NT1468	55°54·1'	3°22·1'W	X	65
Dalmahoy Hill	C of Edin	NT1366	55°53·0'	3°23·0'W	H	65
Dalmahoy Mains	C of Edin	NT1467	55°53·6'	3°22·1'W	X	65
Dalmaik	Aberd	NO8098	57°4·6'	2°19·3'W	X	38,45
Dalmakerran	D & G	NX8092	55°12·7'	3°52·7'W	X	78
Dalmakethar	D & G	NY1192	55°13·1'	3°23·5'W	X	78
Dalmakethar Burn	D & G	NY1192	55°13·1'	3°23·5'W	W	78
Dalmalin Hill	D & G	NX6259	54°54·7'	4°8·7'W	H	83
Dalmally	Arg & Bt	NN1627	56°24·2'	4°58·5'W	T	50
Dalmally Br	Arg & Bt	NN1627	56°24·2'	4°58·5'W	X	50
Dalmarnock	C of Glas	NS6162	55°50·1'	4°12·7'W	T	64
Dalmarnock	Pth & Kin	NN9945	56°35·4'	3°38·2'W	X	52,53
Dalmary	Stir	NS5195	56°7·7'	4°23·4'W	T	57
Dalmellington	E Ayr	NS4806	55°19·7'	4°23·3'W	T	70,77
Dalmenach	Moray	NJ1933	57°23·1'	3°20·4'W	X	28
Dalmeny	C of Edin	NT1477	55°59·0'	3°22·3'W	T	65
Dalmeny Ho	C of Edin	NT1678	55°59·5'	3°20·4'W	X	65,66
Dalmeny Park	C of Edin	NT1578	55°59·5'	3°21·3'W	X	65
Dalmeny Sta	C of Edin	NT1377	55°58·9'	3°23·2'W	X	65
Dalmichy	Highld	NC5713	58°5·2'	4°25·1'W	X	16
Dalmigavie	Highld	NH7419	57°14·9'	4°4·8'W	X	35
Dalmigavie Lodge	Highld	NH7523	57°17·1'	4°4·0'W	X	35
Dalmilling	S Ayr	NS3622	55°28·1'	4°35·2'W	T	70
Dalminnoch	D & G	NX0864	54°56·3'	4°59·4'W	X	82
Dalmoak Fm	W Dunb	NS3876	55°57·2'	4°35·2'W	FM	63
Dalmoak Ho	W Dunb	NS3877	55°57·8'	4°35·3'W	X	63
Dalmochie	Aberd	NO3796	57°3·3'	3°1·9'W	X	37,44
Dalmonds	Herts	TL3409	51°46·0'	0°3·1'W	X	166
Dalmoney Hill	D & G	NX8263	54°57·1'	3°50·1'W	H	84
Dalmore	Angus	NO5433	56°29·5'	2°44·4'W	T	54
Dalmore	Arg & Bt	NR6910	55°20·0'	5°38·1'W	X	68
Dalmore	Arg & Bt	NR6946	55°39·4'	5°39·9'W	X	62
Dalmore	Highld	NC7103	58°0·1'	4°10·5'W	X	16
Dalmore	Highld	NH5876	57°45·3'	4°22·7'W	X	21
Dalmore	Highld	NH6668	57°41·2'	4°14·4'W	T	21
Dalmore	Highld	NH9153	57°33·5'	3°48·8'W	X	27
Dalmore	S Ayr	NS4323	55°28·8'	4°28·6'W	X	70
Dalmore Craig	Pth & Kin	NN8632	56°28·2'	3°50·6'W	X	52
Dalmore Ho	Highld	NH6569	57°41·7'	4°15·4'W	X	21
Dalmorton	S Ayr	NS3801	55°16·8'	4°32·6'W	X	77
Dalmuir	W Dunb	NS4970	55°54·2'	4°24·5'W	T	64
Dalmunach	Moray	NJ2141	57°27·4'	3°18·5'W	X	28
Dalmunzie House (Hotel)	Pth & Kin	NO0971	56°49·6'	3°29·0'W	X	43
Dalmusternock	E Ayr	NS4541	55°38·5'	4°27·3'W	X	70
Dalnabo	Aberd	NJ3001	57°5·9'	3°8·9'W	X	37
Dalnabo	Pth & Kin	NN9752	56°39·2'	3°40·4'W	X	52,53
Dalnabreck	Highld	NM7069	56°45·6'	5°45·3'W	T	40
Dalnabreck	Pth & Kin	NO0855	56°40·9'	3°29·7'W	X	52,53
Dalnacabaig	Arg & Bt	NM9024	56°22·0'	5°23·6'W	X	49
Dalnacardoch Forest	Pth & Kin	NN6995	56°51·1'	4°10·4'W	X	42
Dalnacardoch Lodge	Pth & Kin	NN7270	56°48·5'	4°5·3'W	X	42
Dalnacarn	Pth & Kin	NO0063	56°45·1'	3°37·7'W	X	43
Dalnacarn Craig	Pth & Kin	NO0061	56°44·1'	3°37·6'W	H	43
Dalnaclach	Highld	NH7376	57°45·6'	4°7·6'W	X	21
Dalnaclairach	Highld	NH7275	57°45·1'	4°8·6'W	X	21
Dalnaclave	Highld	NC3816	58°6·5'	4°44·5'W	X	16
Dalnacloich	Highld	NH6673	57°43·9'	4°14·6'W	X	21
Dalnacroich	Highld	NH3155	57°33·5'	4°49·0'W	X	26
Dalnafree	Highld	NC5664	58°32·7'	4°28·0'W	X	10
Dalnagairn	Pth & Kin	NO0760	56°43·6'	3°30·7'W	X	43
Dalnaglar Castle	Pth & Kin	NO1464	56°45·8'	3°24·0'W	X	43
Dalnaha	Arg & Bt	NM6826	56°22·4'	5°45·0'W	X	49
Dalnaha	Highld	ND0643	58°22·2'	3°35·9'W	X	11,12
Dalnahaitnach	Highld	NH8519	57°15·1'	3°53·9'W	X	35,36
Dalnahasaig	Arg & Bt	NR8293	56°5·1'	5°29·8'W	X	55
Dalnair	Falk	NS8178	55°59·1'	3°54·0'W	X	65
Dalnair	Stir	NS4986	56°2·8'	4°25·0'W	X	57
Dalnair Ho	Stir	NS4886	56°2·8'	4°26·0'W	X	57
Dalnamain	Highld	NH7298	57°57·4'	4°9·3'W	X	21
Dalnamein Forest	Pth & Kin	NN7777	56°52·3'	4°0·6'W	X	42
Dalnamein Forest	Pth & Kin	NN8077	56°52·4'	3°57·7'W	X	43
Dalnamein Lodge	Pth & Kin	NN7569	56°48·0'	4°2·4'W	X	42
Dalnarrow	Arg & Bt	NM7936	56°28·1'	5°34·8'W	X	49
Dalnashean	Arg & Bt	NM9145	56°33·3'	5°23·6'W	X	49
Dalnaspidal Forest	Pth & Kin	NN6074	56°50·4'	4°17·3'W	X	42
Dalnaspidal Lodge	Pth & Kin	NN6472	56°49·4'	4°13·3'W	X	42
Dalnatrat	Highld	NM9653	56°37·7'	5°19·1'W	X	49
Dalnavaid	Pth & Kin	NO0063	56°45·1'	3°37·7'W	X	43
Dalnavert	Highld	NH8506	57°8·1'	3°53·5'W	X	35,36
Dalnavie	Highld	NH6473	57°43·8'	4°16·6'W	X	21
Dalnaw	D & G	NX3276	55°3·3'	4°37·4'W	X	76
Dalnawillan Lodge	Highld	ND0240	58°20·5'	3°40·0'W	X	11,12
Dalnaw Loch	D & G	NX3277	55°3·8'	4°37·4'W	W	76
Dalnean Hill	E Ayr	NS4605	55°19·2'	4°25·2'W	H	70,77
Dal Neich	Highld	NH6372	57°43·3'	4°17·5'W	X	21
Dalneigh	Highld	NH6544	57°28·2'	4°14·6'W	T	26
Dalness	Highld	NN1651	56°37·1'	4°59·5'W	T	41
Dalness	Pth & Kin	NN7317	56°20·0'	4°2·8'W	X	57
Dalnessie	Highld	NC6315	58°6·4'	4°19·0'W	X	16
Dalnigap	D & G	NX1371	55°0·2'	4°55·0'W	X	76
Dalno	Pth & Kin	NN7659	56°42·6'	4°1·1'W	X	42,51,52
Dalnoid	Pth & Kin	NO1461	56°44·2'	3°23·9'W	X	43
Dà Loch an Fhèidh	N Eil	NB3348	58°20·6'	6°33·3'W	W	8
Dà Loch Fhuaimeabhat	N Eil	NB5252	58°23·4'	6°14·1'W	W	8
Da Logat	Shetld	HT9541	60°9·5'	2°4·9'W	X	4
Dalpatrick	Pth & Kin	NN8818	56°20·7'	3°48·3'W	X	58
Dalpeddar	D & G	NS8107	55°20·8'	3°52·2'W	X	71,78
Dalpeddar Hill	D & G	NS8307	55°20·8'	3°50·3'W	H	71,78
Dalphaid	Highld	NC3914	58°5·4'	4°43·4'W	X	16
Dalquat	S Ayr	NS2206	55°19·2'	4°47·9'W	X	70,76
Dalqueich	Pth & Kin	NO0804	56°13·4'	3°28·6'W	T	58
Dalquhairn	D & G	NX8979	55°5·8'	3°43·9'W	X	84
Dalquhairn	S Ayr	NX3296	55°14·0'	4°38·1'W	X	76
Dalquhairn Burn	S Ayr	NX3396	55°14·1'	4°37·1'W	W	76
Dalquhairn Hill	D & G	NX8879	55°5·8'	3°44·9'W	H	84
Dalquhandy	S Lanak	NS7835	55°35·9'	3°55·7'W	X	71
Dalquharran Castle	S Ayr	NS2702	55°17·2'	4°43·0'W	X	76
Dalquharran Mains	S Ayr	NS2702	55°17·2'	4°43·0'W	X	76
Dalrachie	Moray	NJ1729	57°20·9'	3°22·3'W	X	36
Dalrachney Beag	Highld	NH8922	57°16·8'	3°50·0'W	X	35,36
Dalrachney Lodge	Highld	NH9023	57°17·3'	3°49·0'W	X	36
Dalraddie Ho	Aberd	NO3095	57°2·7'	3°8·8'W	X	37,44
Dalraddy	Highld	NH8508	57°9·2'	3°53·6'W	X	35,36
Dalrannoch	Arg & Bt	NM9341	56°31·2'	5°21·5'W	X	49
Dalrannoch	Pth & Kin	NN7619	56°21·1'	4°0·0'W	X	57
Dalrawer	Pth & Kin	NN8148	56°36·8'	3°55·9'W	X	52
Dalreach	Highld	NH4631	57°20·9'	4°33·1'W	X	26
Dalreagle	D & G	NX3755	54°52·0'	4°32·0'W	X	83
Dalreavoch	Highld	NC7508	58°2·9'	4°6·6'W	T	16
Dalreavoch Lodge	Highld	NC7508	58°2·9'	4°6·6'W	X	16
Dalreichmoor	Pth & Kin	NO1827	56°25·9'	3°19·3'W	X	53,58
Dalreoch	Highld	NH6273	57°43·8'	4°18·6'W	X	21
Dalreoch	Pth & Kin	NN9237	56°31·0'	3°44·9'W	X	52
Dalreoch	Pth & Kin	NO0016	56°19·8'	3°36·6'W	X	58
Dalreoch	Pth & Kin	NO0662	56°44·7'	3°31·8'W	X	43
Dalreoch	S Ayr	NX1686	55°8·3'	4°52·8'W	X	76
Dalreoch Br	Pth & Kin	NO0017	56°20·3'	3°36·6'W	X	58
Dalreoch Hill	Pth & Kin	NN9236	56°30·5'	3°44·8'W	H	52
Dalreoch Hill	S Ayr	NX1685	55°7·8'	4°52·7'W	X	76
Dalreoch Wood	Highld	NH6372	57°43·3'	4°17·5'W	F	21
Dalreoich	Highld	NH5776	57°45·3'	4°23·7'W	X	21
Dalrhiw	Powys	SN8860	52°13·8'	3°38·0'W	X	147
Dalriach	Aberd	NJ7114	57°13·2'	2°28·4'W	X	38
Dalriach	Highld	NH6427	57°19·1'	4°15·0'W	X	26,35
Dalriach	Highld	NH7637	57°24·7'	4°3·4'W	X	27
Dalriach	Highld	NJ0831	57°21·9'	3°31·3'W	X	27,36
Dalriach	Moray	NJ3830	57°21·6'	3°1·4'W	X	37
Dalriach	Pth & Kin	NN7459	56°42·6'	4°3·0'W	T	42,51,52
Dalriach Burn	Highld	NH7637	57°24·7'	4°3·4'W	W	27
Dalricket Mill	E Ayr	NS5713	55°23·7'	4°15·0'W	X	71
Dalriech	Pth & Kin	NN7733	56°28·6'	3°59·4'W	X	51,52
Dalrigh	Stir	NN3429	56°25·7'	4°41·1'W	X	50
Dalrioch	Arg & Bt	NR6918	55°24·3'	5°38·5'W	X	68
Dalrossach	Aberd	NJ4014	57°13·0'	2°59·2'W	X	37
Dalroy	Highld	NH7644	57°28·4'	4°3·6'W	X	27
Dalrulzian	Pth & Kin	NO1159	56°43·1'	3°24·8'W	X	53
Dalruscan	D & G	NY0186	55°9·8'	3°32·8'W	X	78
Dalry	C of Edin	NT2372	55°56·3'	3°13·5'W	T	66
Dalry	N Ayr	NS2949	55°42·5'	4°42·9'W	T	63
Dalrymple	E Ayr	NS3614	55°23·8'	4°34·9'W	T	70
Dalrymple Wood	E Ayr	NS3413	55°23·2'	4°36·8'W	F	70
Dalsack	Aberd	NO6091	57°0·8'	2°39·1'W	X	45
Dalsa Field	Shetld	HU5992	60°36·7'	0°54·8'W	X	1,2
Dalsangan	E Ayr	NS4830	55°32·7'	4°24·1'W	X	70
Dalsa Waters	Shetld	HU2355	60°17·0'	1°34·5'W	W	3
Dalscone	D & G	NX9878	55°5·4'	3°35·5'W	X	84
Dalscote	Northnts	SP6854	52°11·0'	0°59·9'W	T	152
Dalserf	S Lanak	NS7950	55°44·0'	3°55·2'W	T	64
Dalsetter	Shetld	HU4016	59°55·9'	1°16·6'W	X	4
Dalsetter	Shetld	HU5099	60°40·5'	1°4·5'W	X	1
Dalshangan	D & G	NX5989	55°10·8'	4°12·4'W	X	77
Dalshannon	N Lanak	NS7372	55°55·7'	4°1·5'W	T	64
Dalskairth	D & G	NX9372	55°2·1'	3°40·0'W	X	84
Dalsmirren	Arg & Bt	NR6413	55°21·5'	5°43·0'W	X	68
Dalsraith	E Ayr	NS4742	55°39·1'	4°25·5'W	X	70
Dalston	Cumbr	NY3650	54°50·7'	2°59·4'W	T	85
Dalston	Hack	TQ3484	51°32·6'	0°3·7'W	T	176,177
Dalston Hall (Hotel)	Cumbr	NY3751	54°51·2'	2°58·5'W	A	85
Dalswinton	D & G	NX9385	55°9·1'	3°40·3'W	T	78
Dalswinton	D & G	NX9484	55°8·6'	3°39·4'W	X	78
Dalswinton Common	D & G	NX9488	55°10·7'	3°39·4'W	X	78
Dalswinton Wood	D & G	NX9486	55°9·7'	3°39·4'W	F	78
Daltamie Ho	D & G	NX4564	54°57·0'	4°24·8'W	X	83
Daltes Fm	Essex	TM1315	51°47·8'	1°5·7'E	FM	168,169
Daltippan	S Ayr	NX1895	55°13·2'	4°51·2'W	X	76
Daltomach	Highld	NH7421	57°16·0'	4°4·9'W	X	35
Dalton	Cumbr	SD5476	54°10·9'	2°41·9'W	T	97
Dalton	D & G	NY1174	55°3·4'	3°23·2'W	T	85
Dalton	Kirk	SE1616	53°38·7'	1°45·1'W	T	110
Dalton	Lancs	SD4908	53°34·2'	2°45·8'W	T	108
Dalton	Northum	NY9158	54°55·2'	2°8·0'W	T	87
Dalton	Northum	NZ1171	55°2·2'	1°49·2'W	T	88
Dalton	N Yks	NZ1108	54°28·3'	1°49·4'W	T	92
Dalton	N Yks	SE4376	54°10·9'	1°20·0'W	T	99
Dalton	Roth	SK4594	53°26·7'	1°18·9'W	T	111
Dalton	S Lanak	NS6658	55°48·1'	4°7·8'W	T	64
Dalton Beck	N Yks	NZ1208	54°28·3'	1°48·5'W	W	92
Dalton Burn	D & G	NY0973	55°2·8'	3°25·0'W	W	85
Dalton Cottage Fm	N Yks	SE4278	54°12·0'	1°21·0'W	FM	99
Dalton Crags	Cumbr	SD5576	54°10·9'	2°41·0'W	X	97
Dalton Fields	N Yks	NZ1109	54°28·8'	1°49·4'W	X	92
Dalton Gates	N Yks	NZ2905	54°26·6'	1°32·7'W	X	93
Dalton Gates Fm	E Yorks	SE8950	53°56·5'	0°38·2'W	FM	106
Dalton Gill	N Yks	NZ1008	54°28·3'	1°50·3'W	W	92
Dalton Grange	N Yks	NZ1209	54°28·8'	1°48·5'W	X	92
Dalton Green	D & G	NY1273	55°2·9'	3°22·2'W	X	85
Dalton Hall	Cumbr	SD5375	54°10·4'	2°42·8'W	X	97
Dalton Hall	E Yorks	SE9545	53°53·8'	0°32·8'W	X	106
Dalton Hillhead	Northum	NZ1072	55°2·8'	1°50·2'W	X	88
Daltonhook	D & G	NY1176	55°4·5'	3°23·2'W	X	85
Dalton-in-Furness	Cumbr	SD2374	54°9·6'	3°10·3'W	T	96
Dalton-le-Dale	Durham	NZ4047	54°49·2'	1°22·2'W	T	88
Dalton Lees	Lancs	SD5008	53°34·2'	2°44·9'W	X	108
Dalton Lodge	N Yks	SE1772	54°8·9'	1°44·0'W	X	99
Dalton Magna	Roth	SK4693	53°26·1'	1°18·0'W	T	111
Dalton Moor	Durham	NZ3948	54°49·8'	1°23·1'W	X	88
Dalton Old Hall Fm	Cumbr	SD5375	54°10·4'	2°42·8'W	FM	97
Dalton-on-Tees	N Yks	NZ2907	54°27·7'	1°32·7'W	T	93
Dalton Park Wood	Cumbr	SD5474	54°9·8'	2°41·9'W	F	97
Dalton Parva	Roth	SK4593	53°26·1'	1°18·9'W	T	111
Dalton Piercy	Hartpl	NZ4631	54°40·6'	1°16·8'W	T	93
Dalton's Point	Swan	SS5396	51°38·9'	4°7·1'W	X	159
Dalton Wood	E Yorks	SE9245	53°53·2'	0°32·9'W	F	106
Daltote	Arg & Bt	NR7583	55°59·5'	5°36·0'W	T	55
Daltote Cott	Arg & Bt	NR7483	55°59·5'	5°37·0'W	X	55
Daltra	Highld	NH9443	57°28·2'	3°45·6'W	X	27
Daltulich	Highld	NH9848	57°30·9'	3°41·7'W	X	27
Daluaine Ho	Moray	NJ2340	57°26·9'	3°16·5'W	X	28
Dalvadie	D & G	NX0851	54°49·3'	4°58·9'W	X	82
Dalvanie	Angus	NO1866	56°47·0'	3°20·1'W	T	43
Dalveallan	Highld	NH6936	57°24·0'	4°10·3'W	X	26
Dalveen	D & G	NS8806	55°20·4'	3°45·5'W	X	71,78
Dalveen Lane	D & G	NS9008	55°21·5'	3°43·7'W	W	71,78
Dalveen Pass	D & G	NS9007	55°20·9'	3°43·7'W	X	71,78
Dalveen Toll Cott	D & G	NS8906	55°20·4'	3°44·6'W	X	71,78
Dalveich	Stir	NN6124	56°23·5'	4°14·7'W	X	51
Dalvennan	E Ayr	NS3810	55°21·7'	4°32·9'W	X	70
Dalvenuan	Moray	NJ1740	57°26·8'	3°22·5'W	X	28
Dalvenvie Fm	Highld	NN1277	56°51·0'	5°4·5'W	FM	41
Dalvey	Pth & Kin	NO0857	56°42·0'	3°29·7'W	X	52,53
Dalvey	Stir	NN6507	56°14·4'	4°10·3'W	X	57
Dalvina Lodge	Highld	NC6943	58°21·6'	4°13·9'W	X	10
Dalvorar Burn	Aberd	NO0488	56°58·7'	3°34·3'W	W	43
Dalvorar Corrie	Aberd	NO0487	56°58·1'	3°34·3'W	X	43
Dalvore	Arg & Bt	NR8294	56°5·6'	5°29·8'W	X	55
Dalvorich	Stir	NN6506	56°13·9'	4°10·2'W	X	57
Dalvourn	Highld	NH6834	57°22·9'	4°11·3'W	X	26
Dalvraid	Highld	NC5663	58°32·1'	4°27·9'W	X	10
Dalvreck	Pth & Kin	NN8522	56°22·8'	3°51·3'W	X	52,58
Dalvuie	Arg & Bt	NM9236	56°28·5'	5°22·2'W	X	49
Dalwearie	Aberd	NJ8015	57°13·8'	2°19·4'W	X	38
Dalwey	Wrekin	SJ6807	52°39·8'	2°28·0'W	T	127
Dalwhat	D & G	NX7393	55°13·1'	3°59·4'W	X	77
Dalwhat Water	D & G	NX7293	55°13·1'	4°0·3'W	W	77
Dalwhat Water	D & G	NX7691	55°12·1'	3°56·5'W	W	78
Dalwhing	Aberd	NO5097	57°3·9'	2°49·0'W	X	37,44
Dalwhinnie	Highld	NN6384	56°55·9'	4°14·6'W	T	42
Dalwhirr	Angus	NO2356	56°41·6'	3°15·0'W	X	53
Dalwood	Devon	ST2400	50°47·9'	3°4·3'W	T	192,193
Dalwood Fm	Devon	ST1014	50°55·3'	3°16·4'W	FM	181,193
Dalwood Hill	Devon	SY2399	50°47·4'	3°5·2'W	X	192,193
Dalwyne	S Ayr	NX3296	55°14·0'	4°38·1'W	X	76
Dalzean	D & G	NS7601	55°17·5'	3°56·7'W	X	78
Dalzean Burn	D & G	NS7501	55°17·5'	3°57·7'W	W	78
Dalzean Snout	D & G	NS7501	55°17·5'	3°57·7'W	X	78
Dalzell House	N Lanak	NS7655	55°46·6'	3°58·2'W	A	64
Dalzell Wood	Stir	NN4900	56°10·4'	4°25·5'W	F	57
Dam	Orkney	ND3593	58°49·4'	3°7·1'W	X	7
Damage Barton	Devon	SS4745	51°11·3'	4°11·0'W	A	180
Damaoidh	Arg & Bt	NR2559	55°45·0'	6°22·5'W	X	60
Damaschool	Orkney	HY3624	59°6·2'	3°6·6'W	X	6
Damas Gill	Lancs	SD5255	53°59·6'	2°43·5'W	W	102
Damas Gill	Lancs	SD5257	54°0·7'	2°43·5'W	X	102
Damask Green	Herts	TL2529	51°57·0'	0°10·5'W	T	166
Dam Br	N Yks	SE5149	53°56·3'	1°13·0'W	X	105
Dambridge Fm	Kent	TR2457	51°16·3'	1°13·1'E	FM	179
Dam Burn	D & G	NX7482	55°7·2'	3°58·1'W	W	77
Dam Cliff	Derby	SK1278	53°18·2'	1°48·8'W	X	119
Dam Close (Earthwork)	Lincs	TF4671	53°13·2'	0°11·6'E	X	122
Dam Dale	Derby	SK1178	53°18·2'	1°49·7'W	X	119
Dam Dike	N Yks	SE5047	53°55·2'	1°13·9'W	W	105
Damdykes	Northum	NZ2574	55°3·8'	1°36·1'W	X	88
Dame Alice Fm	Oxon	SU6992	51°37·6'	0°59·8'W	FM	175

Damehole Point	Devon	SS2226	51°0·6'	4°31·9'W	X	190
Damems	Brad	SE0439	53°51·1'	1°55·9'W	T	104
Damend	Pth & Kin	NO2647	56°36·8'	3°11·9'W	X	53
Damerham	Hants	SU1015	50°56·3'	1°51·1'W	T	184
Damerham Knoll	Hants	SU0918	50°57·9'	1°51·9'W	X	184
Dameron's Fm	Suff	TM1650	52°6·6'	1°9·7'E	FM	156
Damery	Glos	ST7094	51°38·9'	2°25·6'W	T	162,172
Dames Slough Inclosure	Hants	SU2505	50°50·9'	1°38·3'W	F	195
Dameye	Aberd	NJ6715	57°13·7'	2°32·3'W	X	38
Dameye	Angus	NO3952	56°39·6'	2°59·3'W	X	54
Damflask Reservoir	Sheff	SK2790	53°24·6'	1°35·2'W	W	110
Damfolds	Aberd	NJ6449	57°32·0'	2°35·6'W	X	29
Damford Grounds	Lincs	TF1751	53°2·8'	0°14·9'W	X	121
Damgate	Norf	TG4009	52°37·8'	1°33·2'E	T	134
Damgate	Norf	TG4519	52°43·0'	1°38·1'E	T	134
Damgate	Staffs	SK1253	53°4·7'	1°48·8'W	X	119
Dam Green	Norf	TM0585	52°25·7'	1°1·3'E	T	144
Dam Hall	Derby	SK1179	53°18·7'	1°49·7'W	X	119
Damhead	Aberd	NJ6021	57°16·9'	2°39·4'W	X	37
Damhead	Aberd	NJ7326	57°19·7'	2°26·4'W	T	38
Damhead	Aberd	NJ7729	57°21·3'	2°22·5'W	X	38
Damhead	Aberd	NJ8305	57°8·4'	2°16·4'W	X	38
Damhead	Aberd	NJ8625	57°19·2'	2°13·5'W	X	38
Damhead	Aberd	NJ9423	57°18·1'	2°5·5'W	X	38
Damhead	Aberd	NO7698	57°4·6'	2°23·3'W	X	38,45
Dam Head	Cald	SE1027	53°44·6'	1°50·5'W	T	104
Dam Head	D & G	NY0182	55°7·6'	3°32·7'W	X	78
Damhead	E Ayr	NS4645	55°40·7'	4°26·5'W	X	64
Damhead	E Ayr	NS4732	55°33·7'	4°25·1'W	X	70
Dam Head	Lancs	SD5057	54°0·6'	2°45·4'W	X	102
Damhead	Moray	NJ0654	57°34·2'	3°33·8'W	X	27
Damhead	Moray	NJ0862	57°38·6'	3°32·0'W	X	27
Dam Head	N Yks	SD7756	54°0·2'	2°20·6'W	X	103
Damhead	Scot Bord	NT3234	55°35·9'	3°4·3'W	X	73
Damhead	S Lanak	NS9051	55°44·6'	3°44·7'W	X	65,72
Damhead Creek	Medway	TQ8273	51°25·8'	0°37·5'E	W	178
Dam Head Fm	Ches	SJ7979	53°18·7'	2°18·5'W	FM	118
Damhead Ho	E Ayr	NS4135	55°35·2'	4°30·9'W	X	70
Damhead Holdings	Midlo	NT2566	55°53·1'	3°11·5'W	T	66
Damheads	Aberd	NJ5863	57°39·6'	2°41·8'W	X	29
Damhead Shiel	Scot Bord	NT3333	55°35·4'	3°3·3'W	X	73
Dam Hill	Norf	TG0836	52°53·1'	1°5·9'E	X	133
Dam Hill Fm	York	SE6457	54°0·5'	1°1·0'W	FM	105,106
Damhouse	D & G	NW9971	54°59·8'	5°8·1'W	X	76,82
Dam House Fm	Northum	NZ1576	55°4·9'	1°45·5'W	FM	88
Damings Wood	Notts	SK6384	53°21·2'	1°2·8'W	F	111,120
Dam Knowe	D & G	NX0934	54°40·1'	4°57·3'W	X	82
Damley's Cott	Pth & Kin	NO1504	56°13·5'	3°21·8'W	X	58
Dam Loch	Shetld	HP5901	60°41·5'	0°54·7'W	W	1
Dammer Wick	Essex	TQ9696	51°37·9'	0°50·3'E	X	168
Dam Mill	Staffs	SJ8802	52°37·2'	2°10·2'W	T	127,139
Damnaglaur	D & G	NX1235	54°40·8'	4°54·5'W	X	82
Dam of Hoxa	Orkney	ND4294	58°50·0'	2°59·8'W	W	7
Dam of Quoigs	Pth & Kin	NN8306	56°14·2'	3°52·8'W	X	57
Dampton Fm	Renf	NS3863	55°50·2'	4°34·8'W	FM	63
Dams	Clackm	NS8597	56°9·4'	3°50·6'W	X	58
Dams	Orkney	HY3111	58°59·1'	3°11·5'W	X	6
Damsay	Orkney	HY3913	59°0·3'	3°3·2'W	X	6
Dams Bay	V of Glam	ST0765	51°22·8'	3°19·8'W	W	170
Damsbrook Fm	Derby	SK4873	53°15·3'	1°16·4'W	FM	120
Damsells Cross	Glos	SO8710	51°47·5'	2°10·9'W	X	162
Damsfold	Fife	NO3106	56°14·7'	3°6·4'W	X	59
Damside	Angus	NO5257	56°42·4'	2°46·6'W	X	54
Damside	Angus	NO6461	56°44·6'	2°34·9'W	X	45
Damside	Fife	NO3612	56°18·0'	3°1·6'W	X	59
Damside	Fife	NO3717	56°20·7'	3°0·7'W	X	59
Damside	Fife	NO6008	56°16·0'	2°38·3'W	X	59
Dam Side	Lancs	SD4048	53°55·7'	2°54·4'W	T	102
Damside	Pth & Kin	NN9614	56°18·7'	3°40·4'W	X	58
Damside	Pth & Kin	NO1631	56°28·1'	3°21·4'W	X	53
Damside	Pth & Kin	NO1933	56°29·2'	3°18·5'W	X	53
Damside	Scot Bord	NT1648	55°43·3'	3°19·8'W	T	72
Damside Cottages	Angus	NO5749	56°38·1'	2°41·6'W	X	54
Damside Cottages	Pth & Kin	NN9714	56°18·7'	3°39·5'W	X	58
Damside Covert	Notts	SK6260	53°8·2'	1°4·0'W	F	120
Damside Fm	Derby	SK1178	53°18·2'	1°49·7'W	FM	119
Damslane	Staffs	SJ9256	53°6·3'	2°6·8'W	X	118
Dams of Craigie	Aberd	NJ9119	57°16·0'	2°8·5'W	X	38
Dams, The	Cambs	TL4791	52°30·1'	0°10·3'E	X	143
Dams, The	N Yks	TA1078	54°11·4'	0°18·4'W	X	101
Dams, The	V of Glam	ST0765	51°22·8'	3°19·8'W	X	170
Dam, The	D & G	NY1182	55°7·7'	3°23·3'W	X	78
Dam, The	Heref	SO6019	51°52·3'	2°34·5'W	X	162
Dam, The	N Yks	SE5149	53°56·3'	1°13·0'W	W	105
Damwells Fm	Lincs	TF3097	53°27·5'	0°2·1'W	FM	113
Damyon's Fm	Essex	TL9022	51°52·1'	0°46·0'E	FM	168
Danaway	Kent	TQ8662	51°19·8'	0°40·6'E	T	178
Dan Becks	Cumbr	NY3500	54°23·7'	2°59·6'W	X	90
Danbury	Essex	TL7704	51°42·6'	0°34·1'E	A	167
Danbury	Essex	TL7705	51°43·2'	0°34·1'E	T	167
Danbury Common	Essex	TL7804	51°42·6'	0°35·0'E	T	167
Danbury Palace	Essex	TL7604	51°42·7'	0°33·2'E	X	167
Danby	N Yks	NZ7008	54°28·0'	0°54·8'W	T	94
Danby Beacon	N Yks	NZ7309	54°28·5'	0°52·0'W	X	94
Danby Beacon (Tumulus)	N Yks	NZ7309	54°28·5'	0°52·0'W	A	94
Danby Beck	N Yks	NZ6905	54°26·4'	0°55·7'W	W	94
Danby Bottom	N Yks	NZ6904	54°25·8'	0°55·8'W	X	94
Danby Castle	N Yks	NZ7107	54°27·4'	0°53·9'W	A	94
Danby Dale	N Yks	NZ6905	54°26·4'	0°55·7'W	X	94
Danby Grange	N Yks	SE1687	54°16·9'	1°44·8'W	X	99
Danby Grange	N Yks	SE3397	54°22·3'	1°29·1'W	X	99
Danby Hall	N Yks	SE1587	54°16·9'	1°45·8'W	A	99
Danby Head	N Yks	NZ6803	54°25·3'	0°56·7'W	X	94
Danby Head	N Yks	NZ6901	54°24·2'	0°55·8'W	X	94
Danby High Moor	N Yks	NZ6902	54°24·8'	0°55·8'W	X	94
Danby Hill	N Yks	SE3397	54°22·3'	1°29·1'W	X	99
Danby Hill Fm	N Yks	NZ3001	54°24·5'	1°31·8'W	FM	93
Danby Lodge	Glos	SO6408	51°46·4'	2°30·9'W	X	162
Danby Lodge	N Yks	NZ7108	54°28·0'	0°53·9'W	X	94
Danby Low Moor	N Yks	NZ7010	54°29·1'	0°54·7'W	X	94
Danby Park	N Yks	NZ6908	54°28·0'	0°55·7'W	F	94
Danby Rigg	N Yks	NZ7005	54°26·4'	0°54·8'W	H	94
Danby's Fm	Lincs	SK9889	53°23·6'	0°31·2'W	FM	112,121
Danby Wiske	N Yks	SE3398	54°22·8'	1°29·1'W	T	99
Dan Caerlan	Rho Cyn Taf	ST0583	51°32·5'	3°21·8'W	T	170
Dancapel Fm	Carm	SN4038	52°1·3'	4°19·5'W	FM	146
Dance Common	Wilts	SU1092	51°37·8'	1°50·9'W	X	163,173
Dancersend	Bucks	SP9008	51°46·0'	0°41·3'W	X	165
Dancer's Grave	Bucks	SP7633	51°59·6'	0°53·2'W	X	152,165
Dancers Hill	Herts	TQ2399	51°40·8'	0°12·9'W	T	166,176
Dancing Beggars	Devon	SX8748	50°19·5'	3°34·9'W	X	202
Dancing Cross	Somer	ST6726	51°2·2'	2°27·9'W	X	183
Dancing Dicks	Essex	TL7913	51°47·4'	0°36·1'E	X	167
Dancing Green	Heref	SO6320	51°52·9'	2°31·9'W	T	162
Dancing Green Hill	Northum	NU0633	55°35·7'	1°53·9'W	H	75
Dancing Hall	Northum	NU0408	55°22·2'	1°55·8'W	X	81
Dancing Hill	Dorset	ST6315	50°56·2'	2°31·2'W	X	183
Dancing Ledge	Dorset	SY9976	50°35·3'	2°0·5'W	X	195
Dancliff Plantn	N Yks	SD9551	53°57·5'	2°4·2'W	F	103
Dancy Burn	Pth & Kin	NN9939	56°32·2'	3°38·1'W	W	52,53
Dandaleith	Moray	NJ2845	57°29·6'	3°11·6'W	X	28
Dandderwen	Pemb	SN1226	51°54·3'	4°43·6'W	X	145,158
Danderhall	Midlo	NT3069	55°54·8'	3°6·8'W	X	66
Dandies Wood	Fife	NO3823	56°24·0'	2°59·8'W	F	54,59
Dandi Geo	Shetld	HU2964	60°21·8'	1°28·0'W	X	3
Dandra Garth	Cumbr	SD7589	54°18·0'	2°22·6'W	X	98
Dandry Mire	Cumbr	SD7992	54°19·6'	2°19·0'W	X	98
Dand's Pike	Scot Bord	NT6403	55°19·4'	2°33·6'W	X	80
Dandy Birks	Lancs	SD5243	53°53·1'	2°43·4'W	X	102
Dandy Corner	Suff	TM0767	52°16·0'	1°2·4'E	T	155
Dandy Fm	Ches	SJ8980	53°19·2'	2°9·5'W	FM	109
Dandy Fm	Norf	TF9221	52°45·4'	0°51·1'E	FM	132
Dandyford	Shrops	SJ3929	52°51·5'	2°54·0'W	X	126
Dandy's Fm	Warw	SP2589	52°30·1'	1°37·5'W	FM	140
Dandy's Ford	Hants	SU2921	50°59·5'	1°34·8'W	X	185
Dandy's Water	Shetld	HU2583	60°32·1'	1°32·2'W	W	3
Dandy, The	Kent	TQ9133	51°4·1'	0°44·0'E	X	189
Danebank	Ches	SJ9784	53°21·4'	2°2·3'W	T	109
Dane Bank	Tames	SJ9095	53°27·3'	2°8·6'W	T	109
Dane Bottom	Cambs	TL6558	52°12·0'	0°25·3'E	X	154
Dane Bower	Ches	SK0070	53°13·9'	1°59·6'W	X	119
Danebower Hollow	Ches	SK0070	53°13·9'	1°59·6'W	X	119
Danebridge	Ches	SJ9665	53°11·2'	2°3·2'W	T	118
Dane Bridge	Herts	TL4419	51°51·3'	0°5·9'E	X	167
Danebury	Hants	SU3236	51°7·6'	1°32·2'W	X	185
Danebury Down	Hants	SU3237	51°8·1'	1°32·2'W	X	185
Danebury Hill	Hants	SU3237	51°8·1'	1°32·2'W	H	185
Danebury Manor	N Yks	TA0576	54°10·4'	0°23·1'W	X	101
Danebury Ring	Hants	SU3237	51°8·1'	1°32·2'W	A	185
Dane Chantry	Kent	TR1349	51°12·2'	1°3·3'E	X	179,189
Dane Court	Kent	TR0553	51°14·6'	0°56·6'E	X	179,189
Dane Court	Kent	TR2951	51°13·0'	1°17·1'E	X	179
Dane Court	Lincs	TF3493	53°25·2'	0°1·4'E	X	113
Dane End	Herts	TL2727	51°55·8'	0°8·8'W	X	166
Dane End	Herts	TL3321	51°52·5'	0°3·7'W	T	166
Dane End	Herts	TL3435	52°0·1'	0°2·5'W	X	154
Dane End Fm	Herts	TL1010	51°46·9'	0°23·9'W	FM	166
Dane End Tributary	Herts	TL3523	51°53·6'	0°1·9'W	W	166
Dane Fm	Ches	SJ6077	53°17·5'	2°35·6'W	FM	118
Dane Fm	Herts	TL1417	51°50·6'	0°20·3'W	FM	166
Dane Fm	Kent	TR1747	51°11·1'	1°6·7'E	FM	179,189
Danefold Ho	W Susx	TQ1921	50°58·8'	0°17·9'W	X	198
Danegate	E Susx	TQ5633	51°4·7'	0°14·0'E	T	188
Danehill	E Susx	TQ4027	51°1·7'	0°0·2'E	T	187,198
Dane Hill	Oxon	SP4629	51°57·7'	1°19·4'W	X	164
Dane Hill Fm	Beds	TL1650	52°8·4'	0°17·9'W	FM	153
Dane Hill Fm	Cambs	TL6868	52°17·3'	0°28·2'E	FM	154
Danehill Lodge	E Susx	TQ4128	51°2·3'	0°1·1'E	X	187,198
Dane Hill Well	Lancs	SD6855	53°59·6'	2°28·9'W	W	103
Dane Ho	Ches	SJ7167	53°12·2'	2°25·6'W	X	118
Dane Hole	Northnts	SP5259	52°13·8'	1°13·9'W	X	151
Danehurst	E Susx	TQ4026	51°1·2'	0°0·2'E	X	187,198
Dane in Shaw	Ches	SJ8761	53°9·0'	2°11·3'W	T	118
Danemoor Fm	Worcs	SO7941	52°4·3'	2°18·0'W	FM	150
Danemoor Green	Norf	TG0505	52°36·5'	1°2·1'E	T	144
Danemore Park	Kent	TQ5440	51°8·5'	0°12·5'E	X	188
Dane Park	Kent	TR3670	51°23·0'	1°23·9'E	X	179
Danes	Devon	SX8367	50°29·7'	3°38·6'W	X	202
Danesborough	Mil Key	SP9234	52°0·0'	0°39·2'W	A	152,165
Danesborough	Somer	ST2637	51°7·9'	3°3·1'W	X	182
Danes' Bottom	Wilts	ST8336	51°7·6'	2°14·2'W	X	183
Danes Brook	Bucks	SP6011	51°47·9'	1°7·4'W	W	164,165
Dane's Brook	Somer	SS8430	51°3·7'	3°38·9'W	W	181
Danesbrook Fm	Oxon	SP5910	51°47·4'	1°8·3'W	FM	164
Danesbury	Herts	TL2316	51°50·0'	0°12·5'W	T	166
Danesdale	E Yorks	TA0261	54°2·3'	0°26·1'W	X	101
Danes Dike	Fife	NO6309	56°16·6'	2°35·4'W	A	59
Danes' Dyke	E Yorks	TA2171	54°7·5'	0°8·5'W	A	101
Danes Dyke Fm	E Yorks	TA2169	54°6·4'	0°8·5'W	FM	101
Danesfield	Bucks	SU8184	51°33·2'	0°49·5'W	T	175
Danesford	Shrops	SO7291	52°31·2'	2°24·4'W	T	138
Dane's Graves	E Yorks	TA0163	54°3·4'	0°27·0'W	X	101
Dane's Graves (Tumuli)	E Yorks	TA0163	54°3·4'	0°27·0'W	A	101
Danes Hill	Devon	ST2500	50°47·9'	3°3·5'W	H	192,193
Daneshill	Hants	SU6553	51°16·6'	1°3·7'W	T	185,186
Danes Hill	Lincs	TF0215	52°43·6'	0°29·0'W	X	130
Danes Hills	N Yks	SE6437	53°49·8'	1°1·2'W	X	105,106
Danes Hills	N Yks	SE6639	53°50·8'	0°59·4'W	X	105,106
Danes Hills (Tumuli)	N Yks	SE6639	53°50·8'	0°59·4'W	A	105,106
Danes Mill	Devon	ST0703	50°49·4'	3°18·8'W	X	192
Danesmoor	Derby	SK4063	53°10·0'	1°23·7'W	T	120
Danes Moor	Northnts	SP5146	52°6·8'	1°14·9'W	X	151
Danes Moss	Ches	SJ9070	53°13·9'	2°8·6'W	T	118
Danes Stream	Hants	SZ2692	50°43·9'	1°37·5'W	W	195
Danestone	C of Aber	NJ9110	57°11·1'	2°8·5'W	X	38
Dane Street	Kent	TR0553	51°14·6'	0°56·6'E	T	179,189
Dane Street Fm	Beds	TL1320	51°52·3'	0°21·1'W	FM	166
Danes Vale Fm	Essex	TL7230	51°56·7'	0°30·6'E	FM	167
Daneswell	Shrops	SJ5827	52°50·6'	2°37·0'W	X	126
Daneswick	Herts	TL1204	51°43·6'	0°22·3'W	X	166
Danes Wood	Devon	SX9699	50°47·1'	3°28·1'W	F	192
Danethorpe	Notts	SK8458	53°7·0'	0°44·3'W	X	121
Danethorpe Hill	Notts	SK8457	53°6·4'	0°44·3'W	X	121
Danetre Fm	Northnts	SP5471	52°20·3'	1°12·0'W	FM	140
Danevale Park	D & G	NX7365	54°58·1'	3°58·6'W	X	83,84
Dane Villa	Ches	SJ8277	53°17·6'	2°15·8'W	X	118
Daneway	Glos	SO9403	51°43·8'	2°4·8'W	T	163
Daneway Ho	Glos	SO9403	51°43·8'	2°4·8'W	A	163
Danewell Hill	Surrey	TQ0160	51°20·0'	0°32·6'W	X	176,186
Daney's Loch	Shetld	HU2454	60°16·4'	1°33·5'W	W	3
Danford	Shrops	SO8093	52°32·3'	2°17·3'W	X	138
Dangart	S Ayr	NX1786	55°8·3'	4°51·8'W	X	76
Dangerous Corner	Lancs	SD5210	53°35·3'	2°43·1'W	T	108
Dangerous Corner	N Yks	SE2055	53°59·7'	1°41·3'W	X	104
Dangerous Corner	Wigan	SD6503	53°31·6'	2°31·3'W	T	109
Danger Point	Devon	SY0882	50°38·1'	3°17·7'W	X	192
Dangstein	W Susx	SU8224	51°0·8'	0°49·5'W	X	197
Danhill Fm	W Susx	TQ1019	50°57·8'	0°25·6'W	FM	198
Daniel Fm	Ghead	NZ1263	54°57·9'	1°48·3'W	FM	88
Daniel Hartly's Wood	N Yks	SE4534	53°48·3'	1°18·6'W	F	105
Daniel Hayes Fm	Derby	SK3420	52°46·8'	1°29·4'W	FM	128
Danielhill	Ches	SJ8777	53°17·6'	2°11·3'W	X	118
Daniel's Fm	Lancs	SD5935	53°48·8'	2°36·9'W	FM	102
Daniel's Water	Kent	TQ9541	51°8·3'	0°47·6'E	T	189
Daniels Wood	Warw	SP2486	52°28·5'	1°38·4'W	F	139
Dankeith	S Ayr	NS3833	55°34·1'	4°33·7'W	X	70
Dannah Fm	Derby	SK3150	53°3·0'	1°31·8'W	FM	119
Danna na Cloiche	Arg & Bt	NR6977	55°56·1'	5°41·5'W	X	61,62
Dannett	Corn	SX3265	50°27·9'	4°21·7'W	X	201
Dannie's Den	Aberd	NO7163	56°45·7'	2°28·0'W	X	45
Dannonchapel	Corn	SX0382	50°36·5'	4°46·7'W	T	200
Danny	W Susx	TQ2814	50°54·9'	0°10·4'W	A	198
Danny Burn	Pth & Kin	NN8805	56°13·7'	3°48·0'W	W	58
Da Nort Bank	Shetld	HT9440	60°8·9'	2°6·0'W	X	4
Danotty Hall Fm	N Yks	SE3684	54°15·3'	1°26·4'W	FM	99
Dan's Hags	D & G	NY3796	55°15·5'	2°59·0'W	H	79
Dan's Hill	Northum	NY9786	55°10·3'	2°2·4'W	H	81
Danshillock	Aberd	NJ7157	57°36·4'	2°28·7'W	X	29
Danskine	E Loth	NT5667	55°53·9'	2°41·8'W	X	67
Danskine Burn	E Loth	NT5766	55°53·4'	2°40·8'W	W	67
Danskine Loch	E Loth	NT5667	55°53·9'	2°41·8'W	W	67
Danson Hill	Lancs	SD4936	53°49·3'	2°46·1'W	X	102
Danson Park	Bexley	TQ4775	51°27·5'	0°7·4'E	X	177
Danson's Fm	Shrops	SJ5242	52°58·6'	2°42·5'W	FM	117
Danthorpe	E Yorks	TA2432	53°46·4'	0°6·7'W	T	107
Dantzic Ho	N Yks	SE1687	54°16·9'	1°44·8'W	X	99
Danvm (Doncaster)	Donc	SE5702	53°30·9'	1°8·0'W	R	111
Danworth Fm	W Susx	TQ2818	50°57·1'	0°10·3'W	FM	198
Dan-y-banc	Carm	SN4707	51°44·7'	4°12·6'W	X	159
Danybank	Carm	SN4727	51°55·5'	4°13·1'W	X	146
Danycapel	Carm	SN6129	51°56·8'	4°1·0'W	X	146
Dan-y-Capel	Powys	SO2338	52°2·3'	3°7·0'W	X	161
Dan-y-cefn	Powys	SN9428	51°56·7'	3°32·1'W	X	160
Dan-y-cerig	Carm	SN4225	51°54·3'	4°17·4'W	X	146
Danycoed	Pemb	SN0718	51°49·9'	4°47·7'W	X	158
Danydderwen	Carm	SN2229	51°56·1'	4°35·0'W	X	145,158
Dan-y-graig	Brig	SS8478	51°29·6'	3°39·9'W	X	170
Danygraig	Caer	ST2390	51°36·5'	3°6·3'W	T	171
Danygraig	Carm	SN2921	51°51·9'	4°28·6'W	X	145,159
Dan-y-graig	Monm	SO2315	51°49·9'	3°6·7'W	X	161
Dan-y-graig	Monm	SO3820	51°52·7'	2°53·7'W	X	161
Danygraig	Powys	SN8927	51°56·1'	3°36·5'W	X	160
Dan-y-lan	Swan	SS5595	51°38·3'	4°5·3'W	X	159
Danyllan	Powys	SO0433	51°59·5'	3°23·5'W	X	160
Danyparc	Powys	SO1035	52°0·6'	3°18·3'W	X	161
Dan y Parc	Powys	SO2217	51°51·0'	3°7·6'W	X	161
Dan-y-quarry	Carm	SN4706	51°44·2'	4°12·6'W	X	159
Dan-yr-allt	Powys	SO0040	52°3·2'	3°27·1'W	X	147,160
Dan-yr-heol	Monm	SO3008	51°46·2'	3°0·5'W	X	161
Dan-yr-Ogof Caves	Powys	SN8316	51°50·1'	3°41·5'W	X	160
Danywenallt	Powys	SO1020	51°52·5'	3°18·1'W	X	161
Danzey Green	Warw	SP1269	52°19·4'	1°49·0'W	T	139
Dapifers	Essex	TL5725	51°54·3'	0°17·3'E	X	167
Dapple Heath	Staffs	SK0426	52°50·1'	1°56·0'W	T	128
Dappleymoor	Cumbr	NY5074	55°3·7'	2°46·5'W	X	86
Dapsland	E Susx	TQ5626	51°1·0'	0°13·8'E	X	188,199
Daran	Gwyn	SH6413	52°42·1'	4°0·4'W	H	124
Dar Beck	Lincs	SE8901	53°30·1'	0°39·1'W	W	112
Darby Burn	S Lanak	NT0353	55°45·9'	3°32·3'W	W	65,72
Darby End	Dudley	SO9587	52°29·1'	2°4·0'W	T	139
Darby Green	Hants	SU8360	51°20·2'	0°48·1'W	T	175,186
Darby's Corner	Poole	SZ0194	50°45·0'	1°58·8'W	X	195
Darbys Green	Worcs	SO7456	52°12·3'	2°22·4'W	T	150
Darby's Hill	Sand	SO9689	52°30·2'	2°3·1'W	T	139
Darcey Lode	Cambs	TL4789	52°29·0'	0°10·3'E	W	143
Darcey Lode	Cambs	TL4894	52°31·7'	0°11·3'E	X	143
Darcliff Hill	Notts	SK6152	53°3·9'	1°5·0'W	X	120
D'Arcy Gate	Essex	TL9212	51°46·6'	0°47·4'E	X	168
D'Arcy House	Midlo	NT3664	55°52·1'	3°0·9'W	X	66
Darcy Lever	Bolton	SD7308	53°34·3'	2°24·1'W	T	109
Dardarroch	D & G	NX8586	55°9·6'	3°47·9'W	X	78
Darden Burn	Northum	NY8965	54°59·0'	2°9·9'W	W	87
Darden Burn	Northum	NY9696	55°15·7'	2°3·3'W	W	81
Darden Lough	Northum	NY9795	55°15·2'	2°2·4'W	W	81
Darden Rigg	Northum	NY9896	55°15·7'	2°1·5'W	H	81
Dardy	Powys	SO2018	51°51·5'	3°9·3'W	T	161
Daren Cilau	Powys	SO2015	51°49·9'	3°9·3'W	X	161
Darenth	Kent	TQ5671	51°25·2'	0°15·0'E	T	177
Darenthdale	Kent	TQ5162	51°20·4'	0°10·5'E	X	177,188
Darent Ho	E Loth	NT5866	55°53·4'	2°39·9'W	X	67
Darenth Wood	Kent	TQ5772	51°25·7'	0°15·9'E	F	177
Darent Valley Path	Kent	TQ5568	51°23·6'	0°14·1'E	X	177
Daresbury	Halton	SJ5782	53°20·2'	2°38·3'W	T	108
Daresbury Delph	Halton	SJ5782	53°20·2'	2°38·3'W	T	108
Daresbury Firs	Halton	SJ5782	53°20·2'	2°38·3'W	F	108
Dares Fm	Hants	SU8050	51°14·8'	0°50·8'W	FM	186
Dare Valley Country Park	Rho Cyn Taf	SN9802	51°42·7'	3°28·2'W	X	170
Darfash	Aberd	NJ8062	57°39·1'	2°19·6'W	X	29,30
Darfield	Barns	SE4104	53°32·1'	1°22·7'W	T	111
Darfield Fm	Hants	SU3135	51°7·0'	1°33·0'W	FM	185

Darfoulds	Notts	SK5578	53°18·0′	1°10·1′W	T	120
Dargall Lane	D & G	NX4578	55°4·6′	4°25·2′W	W	77
Dargate	Kent	TR0761	51°18·8′	0°58·6′E	T	179
Dargate Common	Kent	TR0861	51°18·8′	0°59·5′E	T	179
Dargate Dikes	N Yks	SE8991	54°18·6′	0°37·5′W	A	94,101
Dargate Ho	Kent	TR0761	51°18·8′	0°58·6′E	X	179
Dargavel Burn	Renf	NS3870	55°54·0′	4°35·0′W	W	63
Dargavel Ho	Renf	NS4369	55°53·6′	4°30·2′W	X	64
Dargill	Pth & Kin	NN8619	56°21·2′	3°50·2′W	T	58
Dargoal Burn	D & G	NX2770	54°59·9′	4°41·9′W	W	76
Dargues	Northum	NY8693	55°14·1′	2°12·8′W	X	80
Dargues Burn	Northum	NY8493	55°14·1′	2°14·7′W	W	80
Dargues Hope	Northum	NY8493	55°14·1′	2°14·7′W	X	80
Darielay Fm	Essex	TL6733	51°58·4′	0°26·3′E	FM	167
Darite	Corn	SX2569	50°29·9′	4°27·7′W	T	201
Dark Gully	Highld	NN5688	56°57·9′	4°21·7′W	X	42
Darkharbour Fm	Somer	ST6824	51°1·1′	2°27·0′W	FM	183
Dark Hill	Glos	SO5908	51°46·4′	2°35·3′W	X	162
Darkhill Wood	Heref	SO4047	52°7·3′	2°52·2′W	F	148,149
Darkland	Moray	NJ2662	57°38·8′	3°13·9′W	T	28
Darklane Fm	Staffs	SK0713	52°43·1′	1°53·4′W	FM	128
Darklass	Moray	NH9858	57°36·3′	3°42·0′W	X	27
Darklaw Hill	Fife	NO3620	56°22·3′	3°1·7′W	H	54,59
Darkley	Heref	SO3647	52°7·3′	2°55·7′W	X	148,149
Darknoll Fm	Dorset	ST8011	50°54·1′	2°16·7′W	FM	194
Dark Slade Wood	Staffs	SJ9716	52°44·7′	2°2·3′W	F	127
Dark Water	Hants	SU4400	50°48·1′	1°22·2′W	W	196
Darland	Medway	TQ7865	51°21·6′	0°33·8′E	X	178
Darland	Wrex	SJ3757	53°6·6′	2°56·1′W	T	117
Darlands, The	Barnet	TQ2494	51°38·1′	0°12·1′W	X	166,176
Darlaston	Wals	SO9797	52°34·5′	2°2·3′W	T	139
Darlaston Grange	Staffs	SJ8834	52°54·4′	2°10·3′W	X	127
Darlaston Green	Wals	SO9797	52°34·5′	2°2·3′W	T	139
Darlaston Park	Staffs	SJ8834	52°54·4′	2°10·3′W	X	127
Darlastonwood Fm	Staffs	SJ8735	52°55·0′	2°11·2′W	FM	127
Darlawhill	D & G	NY2178	55°5·7′	3°13·8′W	X	85
Darlawhill Grain	D & G	NY2179	55°6·2′	3°13·9′W	W	85
Darlees	Northum	NY6764	54°58·4′	2°30·5′W	X	86,87
Darlees Rig	S Lanak	NT0653	55°45·9′	3°29·5′W	H	65,72
Darleith	N Ayr	NS2546	55°40·8′	4°46·6′W	X	63
Darleith Fm	Arg & Bt	NS3480	55°59·3′	4°39·2′W	FM	63
Darleith Muir	W Dunb	NS3482	56°0·4′	4°39·3′W	X	56
Darley	N Yks	SE2059	54°1·8′	1°41·3′W	T	104
Darley	S Ayr	NX2991	55°11·3′	4°40·7′W	X	76
Darley	Shrops	SO6899	52°35·5′	2°27·9′W	T	138
Darley Abbey	C of Derb	SK3538	52°56·5′	1°28·3′W	T	128
Darley Beck	N Yks	SE1859	54°1·8′	1°43·1′W	W	104
Darley Bridge	Derby	SK2661	53°9·0′	1°36·3′W	T	119
Darley Brook	Ches	SJ6164	53°10·5′	2°34·6′W	W	118
Darley Burn	S Ayr	NS3331	55°32·9′	4°38·4′W	W	70
Darley Dale	Derby	SK2663	53°10·0′	1°36·3′W	T	119
Darleyford	Corn	SX2773	50°32·1′	4°26·1′W	T	201
Darley Green	Sol	SP1874	52°22·1′	1°43·7′W	T	139
Darley Hall	Ches	SJ6064	53°10·5′	2°35·5′W	X	118
Darleyhall	Herts	TL1422	51°53·3′	0°20·2′W	T	166
Darley Head	N Yks	SE1959	54°1·8′	1°42·2′W	T	104
Darley Hillside	Derby	SK2763	53°10·0′	1°35·4′W	T	119
Darley Mill Centre	N Yks	SE1959	54°1·8′	1°42·2′W	X	104
Darley Moor	Derby	SK1641	52°58·2′	1°45·3′W	X	119,128
Darley Oakes	Staffs	SK1422	52°48·0′	1°47·1′W	X	128
Darlick Moors	Devon	SS7733	51°5·2′	3°45·0′W	X	180
Darling Fell	Cumbr	NY1222	54°35·4′	3°21·3′W	H	89
Darlingfield	Scot Bord	NT6339	55°38·8′	2°34·8′W	X	74
Darling How	Cumbr	NY1825	54°37·1′	3°15·8′W	X	89,90
Darlingscott	Warw	SP2342	52°4·8′	1°39·5′W	T	151
Darling's Hayes	Staffs	SK0512	52°42·6′	1°55·2′W	F	128
Darling's Hill	Scot Bord	NT5037	55°37·7′	2°47·2′W	H	73
Darling, The	Staffs	SJ9024	52°49·0′	2°8·5′W	W	127
Darlington	Darl	NZ2814	54°31·5′	1°33·6′W	T	93
Darliston	Shrops	SJ5833	52°53·8′	2°37·1′W	T	126
Darloskine Br	D & G	NX2772	55°1·0′	4°41·9′W	X	76
Darlton	Notts	SK7773	53°15·1′	0°50·3′W	T	120
Darlton Field	Notts	SK7772	53°14·6′	0°50·4′W	X	120
Darlton Gaps	Notts	SK7572	53°14·6′	0°52·2′W	X	120
Darmalloch	E Ayr	NS6020	55°27·5′	4°12·4′W	X	71
Darmead Linn	W Loth	NS9156	55°47·4′	3°43·9′W	W	65,72
Darmsden	Suff	TM0953	52°8·4′	1°3·7′E	T	155
Darmule	N Ayr	NS3346	55°41·0′	4°38·9′W	X	63
Darnabo	Aberd	NJ7841	57°27·8′	2°21·5′W	X	29,30
Darnacombe	Devon	SX8044	50°17·3′	3°40·7′W	X	202
Darnaconnar	S Ayr	NX2783	55°6·9′	4°42·3′W	X	76
Darnaford	Devon	SX8689	50°41·6′	3°36·5′W	X	191
Darnagie Hill	D & G	NX2757	54°52·9′	4°41·4′W	H	82
Darnall	Sheff	SK3988	53°23·5′	1°24·4′W	T	110,111
Darnarroch Fell	S Ayr	NX2375	55°2·5′	4°45·8′W	X	76
Darnaw	D & G	NX5176	55°3·6′	4°19·6′W	H	77
Darnaw	D & G	NX5488	55°10·1′	4°17·1′W	X	77
Darnaway Castle	Moray	NH9955	57°34·7′	3°40·9′W	X	27
Darnaway Farm Visitor Centre	Moray	NH9856	57°35·2′	3°41·9′W	X	27
Darnaway Forest	Highld	NH9751	57°32·5′	3°42·8′W	F	27
Darnaw Burn	D & G	NX5276	55°3·6′	4°18·6′W	W	77
Darn Bay	Aberd	NO8573	56°51·1′	2°14·3′W	W	45
Darnbogue	Stir	NS8688	56°4·5′	3°49·5′W	X	65
Darnbrook Beck	N Yks	SD8871	54°8·3′	2°10·6′W	W	98
Darnbrook Fell	N Yks	SD8872	54°8·9′	2°10·6′W	H	98
Darnbrook Ho	N Yks	SD8970	54°7·8′	2°9·7′W	X	98
Darnchester	Scot Bord	NT8142	55°40·5′	2°17·7′W	X	74
Darnchester West Mains	Scot Bord	NT8042	55°40·5′	2°18·6′W	X	74
Darncombe	N Yks	SE9391	54°18·6′	0°33·8′W	X	94,101
Darnconner	E Ayr	NS5723	55°29·0′	4°15·3′W	X	71
Darndaff	Inverc	NS2772	55°54·9′	4°45·6′W	X	63
Darndaff Moor	Inverc	NS2772	55°54·9′	4°45·6′W	X	63
Darnell's Fm	Heref	SO6724	51°55·0′	2°28·4′W	FM	162
Darnell's Lodge	Northnts	SP8488	52°29·2′	0°45·4′W	X	141
Darnet Fort	Medway	TQ8070	51°24·2′	0°35·7′E	X	178
Darney Crag	Northum	NY9187	55°10·9′	2°8·1′W	H	80
Darnfillan	S Lanak	NS8441	55°39·2′	3°50·2′W	X	71,72
Darnford	Aberd	NO7692	57°1·4′	2°23·3′W	X	38,45
Darnford	Shrops	SO4297	52°34·3′	2°50·9′W	X	137
Darnford	Staffs	SK1308	52°40·4′	1°48·1′W	T	128
Darnford Brook	Shrops	SO4197	52°34·3′	2°51·8′W	W	137
Darngaber	S Lanak	NS7250	55°43·8′	4°1·9′W	X	64
Darngaber Burn	S Lanak	NS7150	55°43·8′	4°2·8′W	W	64
Darngae	Gwyn	SH7636	52°54·7′	3°50·2′W	X	124
Darngarroch	D & G	NX6263	54°56·8′	4°8·9′W	X	83
Darngarroch	D & G	NX7981	55°6·8′	3°53·4′W	X	78
Darngarroch Hill	D & G	NX8081	55°6·8′	3°52·5′W	H	78
Darngavel Fm	N Lanak	NS8756	55°47·3′	3°47·7′W	FM	65,72
Darnhall Mains	Scot Bord	NT2448	55°43·4′	3°12·2′W	T	73
Darnhay	E Ayr	NS5229	55°32·2′	4°20·3′W	X	70
Darn Hill	Roch	SD8310	53°35·4′	2°15·0′W	T	109
Darnholm	N Yks	NZ8302	54°24·6′	0°42·8′W	X	94
Darnhunch	E Ayr	NS7428	55°32·0′	3°59·4′W	X	71
Darnick	Scot Bord	NT5334	55°36·1′	2°44·3′W	T	73
Darnlaw	E Ayr	NS5322	55°28·4′	4°19·1′W	X	70
Darnoe	Fife	NO2608	56°15·8′	3°11·2′W	X	59
Darnrigg	Falk	NS8775	55°57·5′	3°48·2′W	X	65
Darnrig Moss	Falk	NS8675	55°57·5′	3°49·1′W	X	65
Darnscaw	D & G	NX5499	55°16·1′	4°17·4′W	X	77
Darntaggart	E Ayr	NS5117	55°25·7′	4°20·8′W	X	70
Darny Burn	Scot Bord	NT4138	55°38·2′	2°55·8′W	W	73
Darnycaip	W Dunb	NS4476	55°57·4′	4°29·5′W	X	64
Darny Rig	Scot Bord	NT4038	55°38·2′	2°56·8′W	X	73
Da Rokness	Shetld	HT9339	60°8·4′	2°7·1′W	X	4
Darowen	Powys	SH8201	52°35·9′	3°44·1′W	T	135,136
Darra	Aberd	NJ7447	57°31·0′	2°25·6′W	X	29
Darrach Hill	Falk	NS7582	56°1·1′	3°59·9′W	H	57,64
Darracott	Corn	SS2711	50°52·6′	4°27·2′W	X	190
Darracott	Corn	SX3092	50°42·4′	4°24·1′W	X	190
Darracott	Devon	SS2317	50°55·8′	4°30·7′W	T	190
Darracott	Devon	SS4739	51°8·0′	4°10·8′W	T	180
Darracott Moor	Devon	SS5121	50°58·4′	4°7·0′W	X	180
Darracott Park	Corn	SX2992	50°42·4′	4°24·9′W	X	190
Darracott Resr	Devon	SS5121	50°58·4′	4°7·0′W	W	180
Darrag	I of M	SC1968	54°4·8′	4°45·6′W	X	95
Darrahill	Aberd	NJ9322	57°17·6′	2°6·5′W	X	38
Darran Wood	Nth Pt Talb	SS7298	51°40·2′	3°50·7′W	F	170
Darras Hall	Northum	NZ1571	55°2·2′	1°45·5′W	T	88
Darrell's Fm	Wilts	SU2770	51°25·9′	1°36·3′W	FM	174
Darren	Monm	SO2924	51°54·8′	3°1·5′W	X	161
Darren	Powys	SN9056	52°11·7′	3°36·2′W	H	147
Darren	Powys	SO2015	51°49·9′	3°9·3′W	X	161
Darren	Powys	SO2121	51°53·2′	3°8·5′W	X	161
Darren	Powys	SO2225	51°55·3′	3°7·7′W	X	161
Darren Ddu	Blae Gw	SO1504	51°43·9′	3°13·5′W	X	171
Darren Ddu	Blae Gw	SO1906	51°45·0′	3°10·0′W	X	161
Darren Ddu	Gwyn	SH8919	52°45·7′	3°38·3′W	H	124,125
Darren Ddu	Nth Pt Talb	SN8699	51°40·9′	3°38·5′W	X	170
Darren Disgwylfa	Monm	SO2114	51°49·4′	3°8·4′W	X	161
Darren Fach	Merth Tyd	SO0210	51°47·0′	3°24·9′W	X	160
Darren Fach	Powys	SO0816	51°50·3′	3°19·7′W	X	160
Darren Fawr	Brig	SS8992	51°37·2′	3°35·8′W	X	170
Darren-fawr	Carm	SN5328	51°56·1′	4°7·9′W	X	146
Darren-fawr	Cered	SN4148	52°6·7′	4°18·9′W	X	146
Darren Fawr	Powys	SO0816	51°50·3′	3°19·7′W	X	160
Darren Goch	Brig	SS9094	51°38·3′	3°35·0′W	X	170
Darren Lwyd	Powys	SO2333	51°59·6′	3°6·9′W	X	161
Darren Wood	Monm	ST4094	51°38·7′	2°51·6′W	F	171,172
Darren y Bannau	Brig	SS8793	51°37·7′	3°37·6′W	X	170
Darrick Wood	Brom	TQ4465	51°22·2′	0°4·5′E	F	177
Darrington	Wakf	SE4820	53°40·7′	1°16·0′W	T	105
Darris	Highld	NH6136	57°23·7′	4°18·3′W	X	26
Darrou	D & G	NX5080	55°5·8′	4°20·6′W	H	77
Darrow Green	Norf	TM2589	52°27·4′	1°19·1′E	T	156
Darrow Wood Fm	Norf	TM1082	52°24·0′	1°5·6′E	FM	144
Darsalloch	D & G	NX6077	55°4·3′	4°11·1′W	X	77
Darsalloch Hill	D & G	NX6076	55°3·8′	4°11·1′W	X	77
Darsdale Fm	Northnts	SP9971	52°19·9′	0°32·4′W	FM	141,153
Darsham	Suff	TM4169	52°16·2′	1°32·3′E	T	156
Darsham Ho	Suff	TM4269	52°16·2′	1°33·2′E	X	156
Darsham's Fm	Suff	TM0064	52°14·5′	0°56·2′E	FM	155
Darsham Sta	Suff	TM4069	52°16·2′	1°31·5′E	X	156
Darshill	Aberd	NJ7762	57°39·1′	2°22·7′W	X	29,30
Darshill	Somer	ST6043	51°11·3′	2°34·0′W	T	183
Dart Br	Devon	SS6613	50°54·3′	3°54·0′W	X	180
Dart Br	Devon	SX7466	50°29·1′	3°46·2′W	X	202
Dartfield	Aberd	NK0157	57°36·4′	1°58·5′W	X	30
Dartford	Kent	TQ5273	51°26·4′	0°11·6′E	T	177
Dartford Heath	Kent	TQ5173	51°26·4′	0°10·8′E	X	177
Dartford Marshes	Kent	TQ5476	51°27·9′	0°13·4′E	X	177
Dartford Tunnel	Kent	TQ5676	51°27·9′	0°15·1′E	X	177
Dartington	Devon	SX7962	50°27·0′	3°41·9′W	T	202
Dartington Hall	Devon	SX7962	50°27·0′	3°41·9′W	A	202
Dartley Fm	Glos	SO9907	51°45·9′	2°0·5′W	FM	163
Dartmeet	Devon	SX6773	50°32·7′	3°52·3′W	T	191
Dartmoor	Devon	SX5880	50°36·4′	4°0·0′W	X	191
Dartmoor Forest	Devon	SX6281	50°37·0′	3°56·7′W	X	191
Dartmoor Wildlife Park	Devon	SX5858	50°24·5′	3°59·5′W	X	202
Dartmouth	Devon	SX8751	50°21·1′	3°34·9′W	T	202
Dartmouth Harbour	Devon	SX8851	50°21·1′	3°34·1′W	W	202
Dartmouth Park	Camden	TQ2886	51°33·7′	0°8·8′W	T	176
Darton	Barns	SE3210	53°35·4′	1°30·6′W	T	110,111
Dart Raffe Fm	Devon	SS7915	50°55·5′	3°42·9′W	FM	180
Dart Raffe Moor	Devon	SS7916	50°56·1′	3°42·9′W	X	180
Dartridge	Devon	SS6713	50°54·3′	3°53·1′W	X	180
Darvel	E Ayr	NS5637	55°36·6′	4°16·7′W	T	71
Darvell	E Susx	TQ7222	50°58·5′	0°27·4′E	X	199
Darvel Moss	E Ayr	NS5540	55°38·2′	4°17·8′W	X	71
Darvillshill	Bucks	SU8299	51°41·3′	0°48·4′W	T	165
Darvole	Somer	ST5512	50°54·6′	2°38·0′W	X	194
Darwell Hill	E Susx	TQ7019	50°56·9′	0°25·6′E	X	199
Darwell Hole	E Susx	TQ6919	50°57·0′	0°24·7′E	T	199
Darwell Resr	E Susx	TQ7121	50°58·0′	0°26·5′E	W	199
Darwell Wood	E Susx	TQ7020	50°57·5′	0°25·6′E	F	199
Darwen	Black w Dar	SD6922	53°41·9′	2°27·8′W	T	103
Darwen Hill	Black w Dar	SD6721	53°41·3′	2°29·6′W	X	103
Darwen Moor	Black w Dar	SD6819	53°40·2′	2°28·7′W	X	109
Darwhilling	E Ayr	NS4842	55°39·1′	4°24·5′W	X	70
Darwonno	Rho Cyn Taf	ST0296	51°39·5′	3°24·6′W	X	170
Darwood Fm	Lincs	TF2066	53°10·9′	0°11·8′W	FM	122
Darzle Fm	Corn	SS2214	50°54·1′	4°31·5′W	FM	190
Da Scrodhurdins	Shetld	HT9339	60°8·4′	2°7·1′W	X	4
Dâs Eithin	Powys	SJ0923	52°48·1′	3°20·6′W	X	125
Daseley's Sand		TF5731	52°51·4′	0°20·3′E	X	131
Daseley's Sled		TF5834	52°53·0′	0°21·3′E	W	131
Dash Beck	Cumbr	NY2532	54°40·9′	3°9·4′W	W	89,90
Dasher	Stir	NS6694	56°7·5′	4°8·9′W	X	57
Dasherhead	Stir	NS7095	56°8·1′	4°5·1′W	X	57
Dash Fm	Cumbr	NY2632	54°40·9′	3°8·4′W	FM	89,90
Dashmonden	Kent	TQ8537	51°6·4′	0°39·0′E	X	189
Dashwellgreen	Cumbr	NY4270	55°1·5′	2°54·0′W	X	85
Dason Court	Heref	SO5326	51°56·1′	2°40·6′W	X	162
Dassels	Herts	TL3927	51°55·7′	0°1·7′E	T	166
Dassel's Hill	Herts	TL3927	51°55·7′	0°1·7′E	X	166
Da Stab	Shetld	HT9339	60°8·4′	2°7·1′W	X	4
Datchet	Win & Maid	SU9877	51°29·2′	0°34·9′W	T	175,176
Datchet Common	Win & Maid	SU9976	51°28·7′	0°34·1′W	T	175,176
Datchworth	Herts	TL2719	51°51·5′	0°8·9′W	T	166
Datchworth Green	Herts	TL2718	51°51·0′	0°9·0′W	T	166
Dauber Gill	N Yks	SE1469	54°7·2′	1°46·7′W	W	99
Daubhill	Bolton	SD7007	53°33·8′	2°26·8′W	T	109
Daubies Fm	Heref	SO6628	51°57·2′	2°29·3′W	FM	149
Daubs	Fife	NO2510	56°16·8′	3°12·2′W	X	59
Dauddyffryn	Gwyn	SN6298	52°34·0′	4°1·8′W	X	135
Daufraich	Pemb	SM6623	51°51·6′	5°23·5′W	X	157
Daugh of Aswanley	Aberd	NJ4339	57°26·5′	2°56·5′W	X	28
Daugh of Cairnborrow	Aberd	NJ4540	57°27·1′	2°54·5′W	X	28,29
Daugh of Carron	Moray	NJ2239	57°26·3′	3°17·5′W	X	28
Daugh of Corinacy	Moray	NJ4031	57°22·2′	2°59·4′W	X	37
Daugh of Edinvillie	Moray	NJ2840	57°26·9′	3°11·5′W	X	28
Daugh of Invermarkie	Aberd	NJ4141	57°27·6′	2°58·5′W	X	28
Daugh of Kinermony	Moray	NJ2441	57°27·4′	3°15·5′W	X	28
Daugleddau	Pemb	SN0006	51°43·3′	4°53·4′W	W	157,158
Dauntsey	Wilts	ST9982	51°32·4′	2°0·5′W	T	173
Dauntsey Lock	Wilts	ST9980	51°31·4′	2°0·5′W	T	173
Dauntsey Park	Wilts	ST9882	51°32·4′	2°1·3′W	X	173
Dauntsey's School	Wilts	ST9953	51°16·8′	2°0·5′W	X	184
Dava	Highld	NJ0038	57°25·5′	3°39·5′W	X	27
Davaar Ho	Arg & Bt	NR7519	55°25·1′	5°32·9′W	X	68,69
Davah	Aberd	NJ7520	57°16·5′	2°24·4′W	X	38
Davan	Aberd	NJ4401	57°6·1′	2°55·0′W	X	37
Davan	Pth & Kin	NO0363	56°45·3′	3°34·7′W	X	43
Davas	Corn	SW8019	50°2·1′	5°4·0′W	X	204
Davencourt	Devon	SX6597	50°45·6′	3°54·5′W	X	191
Davenham	Ches	SJ6570	53°13·8′	2°31·1′W	T	118
Davenholme Burn	D & G	NX1671	55°0·2′	4°52·2′W	W	76
Davenport	Ches	SJ8065	53°11·1′	2°17·6′W	T	118
Davenport	Stock	SJ8987	53°23·0′	2°9·5′W	T	109
Davenport Fm	Warw	SP4267	52°18·2′	1°22·6′W	FM	151
Davenport Green	Ches	SJ8379	53°18·7′	2°14·9′W	T	118
Davenport Green	Traf	SJ8086	53°22·5′	2°17·6′W	T	109
Davenport Hall Fm	Ches	SJ7966	53°11·7′	2°18·5′W	FM	118
Davenport House	Shrops	SO7595	52°33·4′	2°21·7′W	A	138
Davenport Lane Fm	Ches	SJ8368	53°12·8′	2°14·9′W	FM	118
Davenport Wood	Bucks	SU8286	51°34·2′	0°48·6′W	F	175
Daventry	Northnts	SP5762	52°15·4′	1°9·5′W	T	152
Daventry Reservoir	Northnts	SP5763	52°16·0′	1°9·5′W	W	152
Daverneithen	Powys	SO0166	52°17·2′	3°26·7′W	X	136,147
Davey Park Fm	Devon	SX7041	50°15·5′	3°49·1′W	FM	202
Davey's Lodge	Northnts	TL0990	52°30·1′	0°23·3′W	X	142
Daveytown	Devon	SX5473	50°32·5′	4°3·3′W	X	191,201
David Lewis Centre	Ches	SJ8076	53°17·1′	2°17·6′W	X	118
David Livingstone Centre	S Lanak	NS6958	55°48·1′	4°5·0′W	X	64
David Salomon's Ho	Kent	TQ5641	51°9·0′	0°14·2′E	X	188
David's Hill	Dorset	SU1203	50°49·8′	1°49·4′W	X	195
Davidshill	N Ayr	NS3151	55°43·6′	4°41·0′W	X	63
Davidson's Burn	Northum	NT8817	55°27·1′	2°11·0′W	W	80
Davidson's Linn	Northum	NT8815	55°26·0′	2°10·9′W	W	80
Davidson's Mains	C of Edin	NT2075	55°57·9′	3°16·5′W	T	66
David's Pits Covert	Staffs	SJ7819	52°46·3′	2°19·2′W	F	127
Davidston	Angus	NO3139	56°32·5′	3°6·9′W	X	53
Davidston	E Ayr	NS4523	55°28·8′	4°26·7′W	X	70
Davidston	Highld	NH7564	57°39·2′	4°5·2′W	X	21,27
Davidston	N Lanak	NS6770	55°54·5′	4°7·2′W	X	64
Davidston Ho	Moray	NJ4145	57°29·7′	2°58·6′W	A	28
Davidstow	Corn	SX1587	50°39·4′	4°36·7′W	T	190
Davidstow Moor	Corn	SX1583	50°37·3′	4°36·5′W	X	201
Davidstow Woods	Corn	SX1484	50°37·8′	4°37·4′W	F	200
David Street	Kent	TQ6464	51°21·3′	0°21·7′E	T	177,188
David's Well	Powys	SO0577	52°23·2′	3°23·4′W	T	136,147
Davies	Corn	SX3198	50°45·7′	4°23·4′W	X	190
Davie's Burn	S Lanak	NT0338	55°37·8′	3°32·0′W	W	72
Daviesdykes	N Lanak	NS8555	55°46·7′	3°49·6′W	X	65,72
Davies o' the Mill	N Ayr	NS3655	55°45·9′	4°36·4′W	X	63
Davington	D & G	NT2302	55°18·6′	3°12·4′W	T	79
Davington	Kent	TR0061	51°19·0′	0°52·6′E	T	178
Davington Burn	D & G	NT2104	55°19·7′	3°14·3′W	W	79
Daviot	Aberd	NJ7428	57°20·8′	2°25·5′W	T	38
Daviot	Highld	NH7239	57°25·7′	4°7·4′W	T	27
Daviot Wood	Highld	NH7141	57°26·7′	4°8·5′W	F	27
Davishill	Aberd	NJ9224	57°18·6′	2°7·5′W	X	38
Davis's Belt	Suff	TL7873	52°19·8′	0°37·1′E	F	144,155
Davis's Town	E Susx	TQ5217	50°56·2′	0°10·2′E	T	199
Davochbeg	Highld	NC7201	57°59·1′	4°9·4′W	X	16
Davochfin	Highld	NH7789	57°52·7′	4°4·0′W	X	21
Davoch of Grange	Moray	NJ4751	57°33·0′	2°52·7′W	T	28,29
Davoch Plantation	Aberd	NJ4608	57°9·8′	2°53·1′W	F	37
Davo Ho	Aberd	NO7673	56°51·1′	2°23·2′W	X	45
Davo Mains	Aberd	NO7773	56°51·1′	2°22·2′W	X	45
Davy Bank	Cumbr	SD6196	54°21·7′	2°35·6′W	X	97
Davygill	Cumbr	NY5846	54°48·7′	2°38·8′W	X	86
Davyhulme	Traf	SJ7595	53°27·3′	2°22·2′W	T	109
Davy Mea	N Yks	NY8405	54°26·7′	2°14·4′W	X	91,92
Davyshiel	Northum	NY8896	55°15·7′	2°10·9′W	X	80
Davyshiel Common	Northum	NY8997	55°16·3′	2°10·0′W	X	80

Davy's Hill	N Yks	SD9443	53°53·2′	2°5·1′W	X	103
Davy's Round	Cumbr	NY5584	55°9·1′	2°41·9′W	X	80
Daw Cross	N Yks	SE2951	53°57·5′	1°33·1′W	T	104
Dawdles, The	Lincs	TF0391	53°24·6′	0°26·6′W	X	112
Dawdon	Durham	NZ4248	54°49·7′	1°20·3′W	T	88
Daw End	Wals	SK0300	52°36·1′	1°56·9′W	T	139
Dawes Fm	Essex	TL6501	51°41·2′	0°23·6′E	FM	167
Dawes Fm	Pemb	SN1106	51°43·5′	4°43·8′W	FM	158
Dawes Fm	Somer	ST3034	51°6·3′	2°59·6′W	FM	182
Dawesgreen	Surrey	TQ2147	51°12·8′	0°15·7′W	T	187
Dawfields	Ches	SJ7365	53°11·1′	2°23·8′W	X	118
Daw Haw	N Yks	SD8566	54°5·6′	2°13·3′W	X	98
Dawker Hill	N Yks	SE5936	53°49·3′	1°5·8′W	T	105
Dawland Fm	N Yks	SE5518	53°39·6′	1°9·6′W	FM	111
Dawley Bank	Wrekin	SJ6808	52°40·4′	2°28·0′W	T	127
Dawling's Fm	Norf	TG3210	52°38·5′	1°26·2′E	FM	133,134
Dawlish	Devon	SX9676	50°34·7′	3°27·8′W	T	192
Dawlish Warren	Devon	SX9778	50°35·8′	3°26·9′W	T	192
Dawlish Warren	Devon	SX9879	50°36·3′	3°26·1′W	X	192
Dawlish Water	Devon	SX9477	50°35·2′	3°29·5′W	W	192
Dawn	Conwy	SH8672	53°14·2′	3°42·1′W	T	116
Dawna	Corn	SX1461	50°25·4′	4°36·7′W	X	200
Dawney Fm	N Yks	SE5167	54°6·0′	1°12·8′W	FM	100
Dawney's Hill	Surrey	SU9456	51°17·9′	0°38·7′W	X	175,186
Dawns	Cumbr	NY6109	54°28·7′	2°35·7′W	X	91
Dawpool	Wirral	SJ2484	53°21·1′	3°8·1′W	X	108
Dawpool Bank	Wirral	SJ2381	53°19·5′	3°9·0′W	X	108
Daw's Cross	Essex	TL8732	51°57·5′	0°43·7′E	T	168
Daws Fm	Somer	SS9330	51°3·8′	3°31·2′W	FM	181
Daw's Green	Somer	ST1921	50°59·2′	3°8·9′W	T	181,193
Daw's Hall (Wildfowl Farm)	Essex	TL8836	51°59·7′	0°44·7′E	X	155
Dawshaw	Lancs	SD5842	53°52·6′	2°37·9′W	X	102
Daws Heath	Essex	TQ8188	51°33·9′	0°37·1′E	T	178
Daw's Hill	Dorset	ST5700	50°48·1′	2°36·2′W	X	194
Daws Hill	Northum	NT9400	55°17·9′	2°5·2′W	H	80
Dawshill	Worcs	SO8252	52°10·2′	2°15·4′W	T	150
Daws Hill Fm	Bucks	SU7898	51°40·8′	0°51·9′W	FM	165
Daws Hill Ho	Bucks	SU8692	51°37·4′	0°45·1′W	X	175
Dawsholm Park	C of Glas	NS5569	55°53·8′	4°18·7′W	X	64
Daw's House	Corn	SX3182	50°37·0′	4°23·0′W	T	201
Dawsmere	Lincs	TF4430	52°51·1′	0°8·7′E	T	131
Dawsmere Creek	Lincs	TF4731	52°51·6′	0°11·4′E	W	131
Dawsmere Ho	Lincs	TF4430	52°51·1′	0°8·7′E	X	131
Dawson Close	N Yks	SD8673	54°9·4′	2°12·4′W	X	98
Dawson Fm	Ches	SJ9266	53°11·7′	2°6·8′W	FM	118
Dawson Fold	Cumbr	SD4588	54°17·3′	2°50·3′W	X	97
Dawson House	Warr	SJ5588	53°23·5′	2°40·2′W	X	108
Dawson's Fm	Cambs	TL3487	52°28·1′	0°1·2′W	FM	142
Dawson's Wood	Leeds	SE4335	53°48·8′	1°20·4′W	F	105
Dawson's Wood	N Yks	SE7385	54°15·6′	0°52·3′W	F	94,100
Dawson Wood	Brad	SE1839	53°51·1′	1°43·2′W	F	104
Dawston Burn	Scot Bord	NY5798	55°16·7′	2°40·2′W	W	80
Daw Street	Essex	TL6931	51°57·3′	0°28·0′E	X	167
Dawyck House	Scot Bord	NT1635	55°36·3′	3°19·6′W	X	72
Dawyck Mill	Scot Bord	NT1736	55°36·9′	3°18·6′W	X	72
Day Ash	N Yks	SE1858	54°1·3′	1°43·1′W	X	104
Day Brook	C of Nott	SK5643	52°59·1′	1°9·5′W	W	129
Daybrook	Notts	SK5745	53°0·2′	1°8·6′W	T	129
Dayfield Brook	Derby	SK2247	53°1·4′	1°39·9′W	W	119,128
Day Gill Beck	Durham	NZ1226	54°38·0′	1°48·4′W	W	92
Day Green	Ches	SJ7757	53°6·8′	2°20·2′W	T	118
Daygreen Fm	Ches	SJ7857	53°6·8′	2°19·3′W	FM	118
Dayhills	Staffs	SJ9532	52°53·4′	2°4·1′W	T	127
Dayhills Fm	Staffs	SJ9633	52°53·9′	2°3·2′W	FM	127
Day Ho	Heref	SO4462	52°15·4′	2°48·8′W	X	137,148,149
Day Ho	Shrops	SO4898	52°34·9′	2°45·6′W	X	137,138
Day Ho	Shrops	SO6682	52°26·3′	2°29·6′W	X	138
Day Ho	Swin	SU1882	51°32·4′	1°44·0′W	X	173
Day Ho	Wrekin	SJ6619	52°46·3′	2°29·8′W	X	127
Day Ho, The	Shrops	SJ4610	52°41·3′	2°47·5′W	X	126
Dayhouse Bank	Worcs	SO9678	52°24·2′	2°3·1′W	T	139
Day House Fm	Glos	ST7689	51°36·2′	2°20·4′W	FM	162,172
Dayhouse Fm	S Glos	ST6396	51°39·9′	2°31·7′W	FM	162
Day House Fm, The	Heref	SO5855	52°11·7′	2°36·5′W	FM	149
Dayhouse Green Fm	Ches	SJ8160	53°8·4′	2°16·6′W	FM	118
Dayhouse Moor	Wrekin	SJ6518	52°45·8′	2°30·7′W	X	127
Day Houses	Shrops	SO5496	52°33·8′	2°40·3′W	X	137,138
Daylands Fm	W Susx	TQ1516	50°56·1′	0°21·4′W	FM	198
Daylesford	Glos	SP2425	51°55·6′	1°38·7′W	T	163
Daylesford Hill Fm	Glos	SP2526	51°56·2′	1°37·8′W	FM	163
Daylesford Ho	Glos	SP2526	51°56·2′	1°37·8′W	X	163
Dayman's Fm	Corn	SW8867	50°28·1′	4°58·9′W	FM	200
Day Mark	I Scilly	SV9416	49°58·2′	6°15·7′W	X	203
Daymens Hill Fm	Essex	TL8813	51°47·3′	0°43·9′E	FM	168
Daymer Bay	Corn	SW9277	50°33·6′	4°55·8′W	W	200
Dayne Castle	Angus	NO4959	56°43·5′	2°49·6′W	A	54
Daypark	Derby	SK3643	52°59·2′	1°27·4′W	X	119,128
Day Sike	Scot Bord	NY5995	55°15·1′	2°38·3′W	W	80
Day's Lock	Oxon	SU5693	51°38·2′	1°11·1′W	X	164,174
Daywall	Shrops	SJ2933	52°53·6′	3°2·9′W	T	126
Ddalfa	Powys	SN8931	51°58·2′	3°36·6′W	X	160
Dderi	Powys	SN8517	51°50·6′	3°39·8′W	X	160
Dderigôch	Cered	SN5650	52°8·0′	4°5·8′W	X	146
Dderw	Powys	SN9668	52°18·3′	3°31·1′W	X	136,147
Dderw,The	Powys	SO1437	52°1·7′	3°14·8′W	X	161
Dderwyn Goppa	Brig	SS9383	51°32·4′	3°32·2′W	X	170
Ddifed	Powys	SO0195	52°32·9′	3°27·2′W	H	136
Ddôl	Denb	SH9972	53°14·4′	3°30·4′W	X	116
Ddol	Flint	SJ1471	53°14·0′	3°16·9′W	T	116
Ddôl	Powys	SO1179	52°24·3′	3°18·1′W	X	136,148
Ddol	Powys	SO1272	52°20·6′	3°17·1′W	X	136,148
Ddôl	Powys	SO1283	52°26·5′	3°17·3′W	X	136
Ddôl	Shrops	SJ3139	52°56·9′	3°1·2′W	X	126
Ddol	Swan	SS5893	51°37·3′	4°2·7′W	X	159
Ddol	Wrex	SJ3149	53°2·3′	3°1·3′W	X	117
Ddôl	Wrex	SJ3845	53°0·2′	2°55·0′W	X	117
Ddôl Bach	Conwy	SH8473	53°14·7′	3°43·9′W	X	116
Ddôl Cownwy	Powys	SJ0117	52°44·7′	3°27·6′W	T	125
Ddôl-ddu	Denb	SJ1850	53°2·7′	3°13·0′W	X	116

Ddole Fm	Powys	SN9767	52°17·7′	3°30·2′W	FM	136,147
Ddol Fm	Cered	SN3752	52°8·8′	4°22·5′W	FM	145
Ddol Fm	Wrex	SJ3644	52°59·6′	2°56·8′W	FM	117
Ddôl-frwynog	Conwy	SH8757	53°6·1′	3°40·9′W	X	116
Ddol Gwyn Felin	Powys	SJ0100	52°35·6′	3°27·3′W	X	136
Ddôl-hir	Wrex	SJ2036	52°55·2′	3°11·0′W	X	126
Ddolibod	Denb	SJ0672	53°14·4′	3°24·1′W	X	116
Ddol-isaf	Denb	SJ2541	52°57·9′	3°6·6′W	X	117
Ddolwen	Carm	SN3233	51°58·4′	4°26·4′W	X	145
Ddraenen Ddu	Powys	SN9991	52°30·7′	3°28·9′W	X	136
Ddrydwy	I of Angl	SH3674	53°14·5′	4°27·1′W	X	114
Dduallt	Gwyn	SH6741	52°57·2′	3°58·4′W	X	124
Dduallt	Gwyn	SH6742	52°57·8′	3°58·4′W	X	124
Dduallt	Gwyn	SH8127	52°49·9′	3°45·6′W	H	124,125
Dduallt	Pemb	SM7629	51°55·1′	5°15·1′W	X	157
Dduallt	Powys	SN8890	52°30·0′	3°38·6′W	H	135,136
Ddullui Bank	Powys	SO0580	52°24·8′	3°23·4′W	X	136
Ddwy-acer	Denb	SJ0364	53°10·1′	3°26·7′W	X	116
Ddwylig	Denb	SJ0476	53°16·6′	3°26·0′W	X	116
Ddwynant	Powys	SN8367	52°17·6′	3°42·5′W	W	135,136,147
Ddyle	Powys	SO0575	52°22·1′	3°23·3′W	X	136,147
Deabley	Heref	SO6953	52°10·7′	2°26·8′W	X	149
Deacon Hill	Beds	TL1229	51°57·1′	0°21·8′W	H	166
Deaconhill	E Ayr	NS4831	55°33·2′	4°24·1′W	X	70
Deacon Hill	Hants	SU5027	51°2·6′	1°16·8′W	H	185
Deacons	I of W	SZ5889	50°42·1′	1°10·3′W	X	196
Deacons	Somer	ST2028	51°3·0′	3°8·1′W	X	193
Deacons Hill	Herts	TQ1995	51°38·7′	0°16·4′W	T	166,176
Dead Burn	D & G	NT0510	55°22·7′	3°29·5′W	W	78
Dead Burn	Scot Bord	NT1750	55°44·4′	3°18·9′W	W	65,66,72
Dead Burn	Scot Bord	NT3950	55°44·6′	2°57·9′W	W	66,73
Dead Cow Point	Devon	SS1245	51°10·6′	4°41·0′W	X	180
Dead Crags	Cumbr	NY2631	54°40·3′	3°8·4′W	X	89,90
Dead for Cauld	Scot Bord	NT1720	55°28·3′	3°18·3′W	H	72
Dead Friars	Durham	NY9645	54°48·2′	2°3·7′W	X	87
Deadh Choimhead	Arg & Bt	NM9428	56°24·2′	5°19·9′W	H	49
Dead Maids Fm	Wilts	ST8348	51°14·1′	2°14·2′W	FM	183
Deadmanbury Gate	Glos	SP0526	51°56·2′	1°55·2′W	X	163
Deadman Hill	Hants	SU2016	50°56·8′	1°42·5′W	X	184
Deadman's Bay	Pemb	SM7508	51°43·8′	5°15·1′W	W	157
Dead Man's Cave	N Yks	SD8067	54°6·2′	2°17·9′W	X	98
Deadman's Cove	Corn	SW6143	50°14·6′	5°20·8′W	W	203
Deadman's Cross	Beds	TL1141	52°3·6′	0°22·5′W	T	153
Dead Man's Geo	Shetld	HU4752	60°15·2′	1°8·6′W	W	3
Deadman's Gill	D & G	NY0873	55°2·8′	3°26·0′W	W	85
Dead Man's Grave	Norf	TG3032	52°50·4′	1°25·3′E	X	133
Deadman's Grave	Suff	TL7774	52°20·4′	0°36·3′E	X	144
Deadman's Green	Staffs	SK0337	52°56·1′	1°56·9′W	T	128
Deadman's Hill	Beds	TL0739	52°2·6′	0°26·0′W	X	153
Deadman's Hill	Herts	TL2936	52°0·7′	0°6·8′W	X	153
Dead Man's Hill	Norf	TG1243	52°56·8′	1°9·7′E	X	133
Dead Mans Hill	N Yks	SE0578	54°12·1′	1°55·0′W	X	98
Deadman's Hill (Tumuli)	Herts	TL2936	52°0·7′	0°6·8′W	A	153
Deadmans Island	Kent	TQ8972	51°25·2′	0°43·5′E	X	178
Deadman's Oak	Beds	TL1246	52°6·3′	0°21·5′W	X	153
Deadman's Plantation	Norf	TF7704	52°36·5′	0°37·3′E	F	144
Deadman's Point	Corn	SX4254	50°22·1′	4°12·9′W	X	201
Deadman's Point	Essex	TQ7982	51°30·7′	0°35·2′E	X	178
Deadman's Riding Wood	Oxon	SP3822	51°53·9′	1°26·5′W	F	164
Deadmen's Graves (Long Barrows)	Lincs	TF4471	53°13·2′	0°9·8′E	A	122
Deadmoor Common	Dorset	ST7511	50°54·1′	2°20·9′W	F	194
Dead Side	Scot Bord	NT2635	55°36·4′	3°10·0′W	X	73
Dead Side	Scot Bord	NT2718	55°27·3′	3°8·8′W	X	79
Dead Side	S Lanak	NS9415	55°25·3′	3°40·1′W	X	71,78
Dead Stones	Cumbr	NY7939	54°45·0′	2°19·2′W	H	91
Dead Water	Angus	NO2771	56°49·7′	3°11·3′W	W	44
Deadwater	Hants	SU8035	51°6·7′	0°51·0′W	T	186
Deadwater	Northum	NY6096	55°15·6′	2°37·3′W	X	80
Deadwater	Northum	NY6197	55°16·2′	2°36·4′W	X	80
Deadwater Burn	Northum	NY6198	55°16·7′	2°36·4′W	W	80
Deadwater Fell	Northum	NY6297	55°16·2′	2°35·5′W	H	80
Deadwater Moor	Northum	NY6398	55°16·7′	2°34·5′W	X	80
Deadwaters	S Lanak	NS7541	55°39·0′	3°58·8′W	X	71
Dead Wife's Geo	Orkney	HY5214	59°0·9′	2°49·7′W	X	6
Dead Wife's Grave	Scot Bord	NT1835	55°36·3′	3°17·7′W	X	72
Dead Wife's Hillock	Moray	NJ3426	57°19·4′	3°5·3′W	H	37
Dead Wood	Northum	NY8099	55°17·3′	2°18·5′W	F	80
Deaf Heights	Scot Bord	NT3844	55°41·4′	2°58·7′W	H	73
Deaf Hill	Durham	NZ3836	54°43·3′	1°24·2′W	T	93
Deal	Kent	TR3752	51°13·3′	1°24·0′E	T	179
Deal Fm	Norf	TM0883	52°24·6′	1°3·9′E	FM	144
Deal Hall	Essex	TR0197	51°38·4′	0°54·7′E	X	168
Deal Plantn	Suff	TM0763	52°13·8′	1°2·3′E	F	155
Deals, The	Leeds	SE2344	53°53·7′	1°38·6′W	X	104
Deal Tree Fm	Essex	TL5718	51°50·5′	0°17·1′E	FM	167
Deal Wood	Norf	TL8898	52°33·1′	0°46·8′E	F	144
Dean	Cald	SD9626	53°44·1′	2°3·2′W	X	103
Dean	C of Edin	NT2474	55°57·4′	3°12·6′W	T	66
Dean	Cumbr	NY0725	54°36·9′	3°26·0′W	T	89
Dean	Devon	SS6033	51°5·0′	3°59·5′W	X	180
Dean	Devon	SS6245	51°11·5′	3°58·1′W	T	180
Dean	Devon	SS7048	51°13·2′	3°51·3′W	T	180
Dean	Dorset	ST9715	50°56·3′	2°2·2′W	T	184
Dean	Hants	SU4431	51°4·8′	1°21·9′W	T	185
Dean	Hants	SU5619	50°58·3′	1°11·8′W	T	185
Dean	Lancs	SD7937	53°50·0′	2°18·7′W	X	103
Dean	Lancs	SD8525	53°43·5′	2°13·2′W	T	103
Dean	Orkney	HY2504	58°55·3′	3°17·7′W	X	6,7
Dean	Oxon	SP3422	51°54·0′	1°30·0′W	T	164
Dean	Somer	ST6744	51°11·9′	2°28·0′W	X	183
Dean Bank	Durham	NZ2832	54°41·2′	1°33·5′W	T	93
Deanbank Ho	Angus	NO3747	56°36·9′	3°1·1′W	X	54
Dean Bldgs	Oxon	SP3325	51°55·6′	1°30·8′W	X	164
Dean Bottom	Kent	TQ5868	51°23·6′	0°16·7′E	X	177
Dean Bottom	Oxon	SP2514	51°49·7′	1°37·8′W	X	163
Dean Bottom	Somer	ST6644	51°11·9′	2°28·8′W	X	183
Dean Bottom	Wilts	SU1573	51°27·6′	1°46·7′W	X	173
Deanbrae	Scot Bord	NT5314	55°25·3′	2°44·1′W	X	79

Deanbrae Cleuch	Scot Bord	NT7721	55°29·2′	2°21·4′W	W	74
Deanbrae Law	Scot Bord	NT7721	55°29·2′	2°21·4′W	H	74
Dean Bridge Wood	Durham	NZ2730	54°40·1′	1°34·5′W	F	93
Dean Brook	Glos	SO9428	51°57·3′	2°4·8′W	W	150,163
Dean Brook	Lancs	SD6838	53°50·5′	2°28·8′W	W	103
Dean Brook	Worcs	SO9260	52°14·5′	2°6·6′W	W	150
Dean Burn	Midlo	NT4459	55°49·5′	2°53·2′W	W	66,73
Dean Burn	Northum	NT9844	55°41·6′	2°1·5′W	W	75
Dean Burn	Northum	NY8477	55°5·5′	2°14·6′W	W	86,87
Dean Burn	Scot Bord	NT3812	55°24·1′	2°58·3′W	W	79
Dean Burn	Scot Bord	NT5614	55°25·3′	2°41·3′W	W	80
Dean Burn	W Loth	NT1161	55°50·3′	3°24·8′W	W	65
Deanburnhaugh	Scot Bord	NT3911	55°23·6′	2°57·4′W	X	79
Dean Camp	Glos	SP1608	51°46·5′	1°45·7′W	A	163
Dean Castle	E Ayr	NS4339	55°37·4′	4°29·2′W	A	70
Dean Castle Country Park	E Ayr	NS4339	55°37·4′	4°29·2′W	X	70
Dean Clough	Kirk	SE0806	53°33·3′	1°52·3′W	X	110
Dean Clough Head	Brad	SD9938	53°50·5′	2°0·5′W	X	103
Dean Clough Resr	Lancs	SD7133	53°47·8′	2°26·0′W	W	103
Deancombe	Devon	SX7264	50°27·9′	3°47·8′W	X	202
Dean Copse	Hants	SU7046	51°12·8′	0°59·5′W	F	186
Dean Copse	Wilts	SU2528	51°3·3′	1°38·2′W	F	184
Deancorner	Shrops	SJ6600	52°36·0′	2°29·7′W	X	127
Dean Court	Kent	TQ9725	50°59·7′	0°48·8′E	X	189
Dean Court	Kent	TQ9848	51°12·0′	0°50·4′E	X	189
Dean Court	Oxon	SP4705	51°44·7′	1°18·8′W	T	164
Dean Cross	Cumbr	NY0522	54°35·3′	3°27·8′W	X	89
Dean Cross	Devon	SS5042	51°9·7′	4°8·3′W	T	180
Deane	Bolton	SD6807	53°33·8′	2°28·6′W	T	109
Deane	Hants	SU5450	51°15·0′	1°13·2′W	T	185
Deane Down Fm	Hants	SU5551	51°15·6′	1°12·3′W	FM	185
Deanend	Dorset	ST9717	50°57·4′	2°2·2′W	T	184
Deanery Fm	Oxon	SP3104	51°44·3′	1°32·7′W	FM	164
Deanery Fm	Staffs	SK1721	52°47·4′	1°44·5′W	FM	128
Deanery, The	Staffs	SJ9113	52°43·1′	2°7·6′W	X	127
Deane Water	Wilts	SU1961	51°21·1′	1°43·2′W	W	173
Deane Water	Wilts	SU2161	51°21·1′	1°41·5′W	W	174
Dean Fields	Brad	SD9937	53°50·0′	2°0·5′W	X	103
Dean Fm	Bucks	SP8828	51°56·8′	0°42·8′W	FM	165
Dean Fm	Ches	SJ8779	53°18·7′	2°11·3′W	FM	118
Dean Fm	Dorset	ST9606	50°51·4′	2°3·0′W	FM	195
Dean Fm	Dorset	ST9715	50°56·3′	2°2·2′W	FM	184
Dean Fm	E Susx	TQ6417	50°56·0′	0°20·4′E	FM	199
Dean Fm	Glos	SO8917	51°51·3′	2°9·2′W	FM	163
Dean Fm	Glos	SO9528	51°57·3′	2°4·0′W	FM	150,163
Dean Fm	Glos	SP1608	51°46·5′	1°45·7′W	FM	163
Dean Fm	Hants	SU5620	50°58·8′	1°11·7′W	FM	185
Dean Fm	Hants	SU5708	50°52·3′	1°11·0′W	FM	196
Dean Fm	I of W	SZ5277	50°35·7′	1°15·5′W	FM	196
Dean Fm	Kent	TR1246	51°10·7′	1°2·4′E	FM	179,189
Dean Fm	Kent	TR2562	51°19·0′	1°14·1′E	FM	179
Dean Fm	Lancs	SD8926	53°44·1′	2°9·6′W	FM	103
Dean Fm	Medway	TQ6966	51°22·3′	0°26·1′E	FM	177,178
Dean Fm	Shrops	SO6799	52°35·5′	2°28·8′W	FM	138
Dean Fm	Somer	ST1227	51°2·4′	3°14·9′W	FM	181,193
Dean Fm	Surrey	TQ2846	51°12·2′	0°9·7′W	FM	187
Dean Fm	Surrey	TQ2955	51°17·0′	0°8·6′W	FM	187
Dean Fm	Wilts	ST9894	51°38·9′	2°1·3′W	FM	163,173
Dean Fm	Wilts	SU2954	51°17·3′	1°34·7′W	FM	185
Dean Fm	Worcs	SO9260	52°14·5′	2°6·6′W	FM	150
Deanfoot	Scot Bord	NT1552	55°45·5′	3°20·8′W	X	65,72
Deanfoot	Scot Bord	NT5720	55°28·6′	2°40·4′W	X	73,74
Deangarden Wood	Bucks	SU8791	51°36·9′	0°44·2′W	F	175
Dean Gate	Cald	SD9732	53°47·3′	2°2·3′W	X	103
Deangate	Medway	TQ7773	51°25·9′	0°33·2′E	X	178
Dean Grange	Beds	TL0468	52°18·2′	0°28·1′W	X	153
Dean Grange Fm	Leeds	SE2340	53°51·6′	1°38·6′W	FM	104
Dean Green	Ches	SJ8376	53°17·1′	2°14·9′W	X	118
Dean Grove	Oxon	SP3421	51°53·4′	1°30·0′W	F	164
Dean Hall	N Yks	NZ8806	54°26·7′	0°38·2′W	X	94
Dean Hall Fm	Notts	SK7558	53°7·1′	0°52·4′W	FM	120
Dean Head	Barns	SE2600	53°30·0′	1°36·1′W	T	110
Dean Head	Devon	SS6233	51°5·0′	3°57·8′W	X	180
Deanhead	Fife	NT0993	56°7·5′	3°27·4′W	X	58
Deanhead	Kirk	SE0214	53°37·6′	1°57·8′W	X	110
Deanhead	Kirk	SE0415	53°38·1′	1°56·0′W	X	110
Deanhead	S Lanak	NT0447	55°42·7′	3°31·2′W	X	72
Dean Head Hill	Kirk	SE0606	53°33·3′	1°54·2′W	X	110
Deanhead Resr	Kirk	SE0315	53°38·1′	1°56·9′W	W	110
Dean Head Resrs	Cald	SE0230	53°46·2′	1°57·8′W	W	104
Dean Heath Copse	Hants	SU5747	51°13·4′	1°10·6′W	F	185
Dean Hill	Barns	SE2709	53°34·9′	1°35·1′W	X	110
Dean Hill	Bath & NE Somer	ST7166	51°23·8′	2°24·6′W	X	172
Dean Hill	Cambs	TL4085	52°26·9′	0°4·0′E	X	142,143
Dean Hill	Ches	SJ7759	53°7·9′	2°20·2′W	X	118
Dean Hill	Derby	SK1389	53°24·1′	1°47·9′W	X	110
Dean Hill	Dorset	ST9606	50°51·4′	2°3·0′W	X	195
Dean Hill	Dorset	SZ0181	50°38·0′	1°58·8′W	X	195
Dean Hill	Glos	SO6712	51°48·6′	2°28·3′W	X	162
Dean Hill	Surrey	TQ3156	51°17·5′	0°6·9′W	X	187
Dean Hill	Wilts	SU2526	51°2·2′	1°38·2′W	H	184
Deanhill Barn	Wilts	SU2725	51°1·7′	1°36·5′W	X	184
Deanhill Fm	Devon	ST0210	50°53·1′	3°23·2′W	FM	192
Dean Hill Fm	Wilts	SU2325	51°1·7′	1°39·9′W	FM	184
Dean Hills	Beds	SP9634	52°0·0′	0°35·7′W	X	153,165
Dean Ho	Beds	TL0467	52°17·7′	0°28·1′W	X	153
Dean Ho	Hants	SU5925	51°1·5′	1°9·1′W	X	185
Dean Ho	Lancs	SD5435	53°48·8′	2°41·5′W	X	102
Dean Ho	Northum	NU0715	55°26·0′	1°52·9′W	X	81
Dean Ho	Northum	NZ0084	55°9·3′	1°59·6′W	X	81
Dean Hole	Brad	SE0942	53°52·7′	1°51·4′W	X	104
Dean Howl Fm	Durham	NZ0648	54°49·9′	1°54·0′W	FM	87
Deanich Lodge	Highld	NH3683	57°48·7′	4°45·2′W	X	20
Deanie Lodge	Highld	NH3139	57°24·9′	4°48·4′W	X	26
Deanland	Dorset	ST9918	50°57·9′	2°0·5′W	T	184
Deanlands Fm	Hants	SU6954	51°17·1′	1°0·2′W	FM	186
Deanlands Fm	W Susx	TQ3731	51°3·9′	0°2·3′W	FM	187
Deanland Wood	E Susx	TQ5311	50°52·9′	0°10·9′E	F	199
Deanlane End	W Susx	SU7412	50°54·4′	0°56·5′W	T	197

Dean Lane Head	Brad	SE0934	53°48·4′	1°51·4′W	T	104
Dean Lodge Fm	Worcs	SO9751	52°9·7′	2°2·2′W	FM	150
Dean Moor	Cumbr	NY0422	54°35·3′	3°28·7′W	X	89
Dean Moor	Devon	SX6766	50°29·0′	3°52·1′W	X	202
Deanmoor	Northum	NU1708	55°22·2′	1°43·5′W	X	81
Deanoak Brook	Surrey	TQ2244	51°11·2′	0°14·9′W	W	187
Dean Park	Fife	NT1289	56°5·4′	3°24·4′W	X	65
Dean Park	Renf	NS5166	55°52·1′	4°22·4′W	T	64
Dean Park	Shrops	SO5969	52°19·3′	2°35·7′W	X	137,138
Dean Place Fm	Win & Maid	SU8081	51°31·6′	0°50·4′W	FM	175
Dean Plantation	Fife	NT0587	56°4·2′	3°31·1′W	F	65
Dean Plantation	Wilts	ST9894	51°38·9′	2°1·3′W	F	163,173
Dean Plantn	Oxon	SP4725	51°55·5′	1°18·6′W	F	164
Dean Point	Corn	SW8020	50°2·6′	5°4·0′W	X	204
Dean Prior	Devon	SX7263	50°27·4′	3°47·8′W	T	202
Dean Rigg	Northum	NY9752	54°52·0′	2°2·4′W	X	87
Dean Rocks	Oldham	SE0203	53°31·7′	1°57·8′W	X	110
Dean Row	Ches	SJ8681	53°19·8′	2°12·2′W	T	109
Deans	W Loth	NT0268	55°54·0′	3°33·6′W	T	65
Deansbiggin	Cumbr	SD6080	54°13·1′	2°36·4′W	X	97
Deans Bottom	Kent	TQ8660	51°18·7′	0°40·5′E	T	178
Dean's Bottom	Oxon	SU5482	51°32·3′	1°12·9′W	X	174
Dean's Brook	Barnet	TQ2093	51°37·6′	0°15·6′W	W	176
Deanscales	Cumbr	NY0926	54°37·5′	3°24·1′W	T	89
Deans Fm	Ches	SJ8971	53°14·4′	2°9·5′W	FM	118
Dean's Fm	Essex	TL7721	51°51·8′	0°34·6′E	FM	167
Dean's Fm	E Susx	TQ4203	50°48·8′	0°1·3′E	FM	198
Dean's Fm	Lincs	TF3035	52°54·0′	0°3·6′W	FM	131
Dean's Fm	Somer	ST1133	51°5·6′	3°15·9′W	FM	181
Deansgreen	Ches	SJ6985	53°21·9′	2°27·5′W	T	109
Dean's Green	Warw	SP1368	52°18·8′	1°48·2′W	T	139,151
Deans Grove	Dorset	SU0101	50°48·7′	1°58·8′W	X	195
Dean's Hall	Essex	TL8233	51°58·2′	0°39·4′E	X	168
Deanshanger	Northnts	SP7639	52°2·9′	0°53·1′W	T	152
Deanshaugh	Pth & Kin	NN9238	56°31·6′	3°44·9′W	X	52
Dean's Hill	Kent	TQ8654	51°15·5′	0°40·3′E	X	189
Deans Hill	Kent	TQ8660	51°18·7′	0°40·5′E	T	178
Deans Hill	Scot Bord	NT9356	55°48·1′	2°6·3′W	X	67,74,75
Deanshillock	Moray	NJ3056	57°35·6′	3°9·8′W	X	28
Deanside	D & G	NX8774	55°3·1′	3°45·7′W	X	84
Deanside	Highld	NC5955	58°27·9′	4°24·5′W	X	10
Dean Slack	Lancs	SD7351	53°57·5′	2°24·3′W	X	103
Dean Slack Head	Lancs	SD7451	53°57·5′	2°23·4′W	X	103
Deans Leaze Fm	Dorset	ST9706	50°51·4′	2°2·2′W	FM	195
Deansmill	S Ayr	NS2908	55°20·4′	4°41·4′W	X	70,76
Dean's Place	Heref	SO6331	51°58·8′	2°31·9′W	X	149
Deans Rough	Ches	SJ8270	53°13·8′	2°15·8′W	X	118
Deans Slade Fm	Staffs	SK1107	52°39·9′	1°49·8′W	FM	139
Deanston	D & G	NX8672	55°2·0′	3°46·6′W	X	84
Deanston	Stir	NN7101	56°11·3′	4°4·3′W	T	57
Deanston Fm	Stir	NN7001	56°11·3′	4°5·2′W	FM	57
Deanston Loch	D & G	NX8672	55°2·0′	3°46·6′W	W	84
Dean Street	Kent	TQ7452	51°14·7′	0°30·0′E	T	188
Dean, The	Hants	SU6327	51°2·7′	1°5·7′W	X	185
Dean, The	Shrops	SJ6800	52°36·0′	2°27·9′W	X	127
Dean, The	Wilts	SU2475	51°28·6′	1°38·9′W	F	174
Dean Water	Angus	NO3948	56°37·5′	2°59·2′W	W	54
Dean Water	Pth & Kin	NO3146	56°36·3′	3°7·0′W	W	53
Deanwater	Stock	SJ8781	53°19·8′	2°11·3′W	X	109
Dean Wood	Devon	SX7164	50°27·9′	3°48·7′W	F	202
Dean Wood	Oxon	SU6382	51°32·2′	1°5·1′W	F	175
Dean Wood	Wigan	SD5306	53°33·2′	2°42·2′W	F	108
Deanwood Fm	W Berks	SU4468	51°24·8′	1°21·6′W	FM	174
Dearc na Sgeir	N Eil	NA7246	58°17·1′	7°35·4′W	X	13
Dearden Fold	Bolton	SD7510	53°35·4′	2°22·3′W	A	109
Dearden Moor	Lancs	SD8020	53°40·8′	2°17·8′W	X	103
Dearg Abhainn	Arg & Bt	NM9640	56°30·7′	5°18·5′W	W	49
Dearg Allt	Arg & Bt	NR6592	56°4·0′	5°46·1′W	W	55,61
Dearg Allt	Arg & Bt	NR8046	55°39·7′	5°29·4′W	W	62,69
Dearg Allt	Arg & Bt	NR8278	55°57·0′	5°29·1′W	W	62
Dearg Allt	Highld	NH4202	57°5·2′	4°36·0′W	W	34
Dearg Allt	Highld	NM7242	56°31·1′	5°41·9′W	W	49
Dearg Allt	Highld	NM9892	56°58·8′	5°19·0′W	W	33,40
Dearg Bhealach	Arg & Bt	NM4719	56°18·0′	6°4·9′W	X	48
Dearg Choirein	N Ayr	NR9842	55°38·0′	5°12·1′W	X	62,69
Dearg Lochain	Highld	NH4718	57°13·9′	4°31·6′W	W	34
Dearg Lochan	Highld	NH5402	57°5·4′	4°24·1′W	W	35
Dearg Phort	Arg & Bt	NM3025	56°20·7′	6°21·7′W	W	48
Dearg Sgeir	Arg & Bt	NM2915	56°15·3′	6°22·1′W	X	48
Dearg Sgeir	Arg & Bt	NM4026	56°21·6′	6°12·1′W	X	48
Dearg Sgeir	Arg & Bt	NM5945	56°32·4′	5°54·8′W	X	47,48
Dearg Sgeir	Arg & Bt	NM7401	56°9·1′	5°37·9′W	X	55
Dearg Sgeir	Arg & Bt	NM8943	56°32·2′	5°25·4′W	X	49
Dearg Sgeir	Arg & Bt	NR6245	55°38·7′	5°46·5′W	X	62
Dearg Uillt	Highld	NM8348	56°34·7′	5°31·5′W	X	49
Dearham	Cumbr	NY0736	54°42·9′	3°26·2′W	T	89
Dearloves Fm	Cambs	TF3507	52°38·9′	0°0·1′E	FM	142
Dearly Burn	Scot Bord	NT5220	55°28·5′	2°45·1′W	W	73
Dearncomb Beck	N Yks	SE1251	53°57·6′	1°48·6′W	W	104
Dearne	Barns	SE4604	53°32·1′	1°17·9′W	T	111
Dearne Br	Donc	SE4901	53°30·4′	1°15·3′W	X	111
Dearne Head	Kirk	SE1807	53°33·8′	1°43·3′W	X	110
Dearnford Hall	Shrops	SJ5438	52°56·5′	2°40·7′W	X	126
Dearnley	Roch	SD9215	53°38·1′	2°6·8′W	T	109
Dearnsdale	Staffs	SJ8821	52°47·4′	2°10·3′W	X	127
Dearswell	Devon	SX8047	50°18·9′	3°40·8′W	X	202
Deasbreck	Orkney	HY3025	59°6·6′	3°12·9′W	X	6
Deasker	N Eil	NF6466	57°33·8′	7°36·7′W	X	18
Deasland Fm	Worcs	SO7672	52°21·0′	2°20·7′W	FM	138
Debach	Suff	TM2454	52°8·6′	1°16·8′E	X	156
Debach Ho	Suff	TM2455	52°9·1′	1°16·9′E	X	156
de Bathe Fm	Devon	SS6600	50°47·3′	3°53·7′W	FM	191
Debdale	Man	SJ8996	53°27·9′	2°9·5′W	T	109
Debdale Fm	Leic	SK7723	52°48·2′	0°51·1′W	FM	129
Debdale Hill Fm	Notts	SK7657	53°6·5′	0°51·5′W	FM	120
Debdale Lodge	Leic	SK7813	52°42·8′	0°50·3′W	X	129
Debdale Spring Fm	Northnts	SP8763	52°15·7′	0°43·1′W	FM	152
Debdale, The	Lincs	SK8339	52°56·8′	0°45·5′W	F	130
Debdale Wharf	Leic	SP6991	52°31·0′	0°58·6′W	X	141
Debden	Essex	TL5533	51°58·7′	0°15·8′E	T	167
Debden Common	Essex	TL5334	51°59·2′	0°14·1′E	X	154
Debden Court	Kent	TR1352	51°13·9′	1°3·5′E	X	179,189
Debden Fm	Warw	SP2861	52°15·0′	1°35·0′W	FM	151
Debden Green	Essex	TL5732	51°58·1′	0°17·5′E	T	167
Debden Green	Essex	TQ4398	51°40·0′	0°4·5′E	T	167,177
Debden Hall Fm	Essex	TL5533	51°58·7′	0°15·8′E	FM	167
Debden Manor	Essex	TL5534	51°59·2′	0°15·8′E	X	154
Debden Sta	Essex	TQ4496	51°38·9′	0°5·3′E	X	167,177
Debden Top Fm	Cambs	TL2467	52°17·5′	0°10·5′W	FM	153
Debden Water	Essex	TL5334	51°59·2′	0°14·1′E	W	154
Debdhill Fm	Notts	SK7596	53°27·6′	0°51·8′W	FM	112
Debdon	Northum	NU0604	55°20·0′	1°53·9′W	X	81
Debdon Burn	Northum	NU0604	55°20·0′	1°53·9′W	W	81
Debdon Lake	Northum	NU0602	55°19·0′	1°53·9′W	W	81
Debdon Pitt Cott	Northum	NU0704	55°20·0′	1°52·9′W	X	81
Debdon Whitefield	Northum	NU0804	55°20·0′	1°52·0′W	X	81
De Beauvoir Fm	Essex	TQ7295	51°37·9′	0°29·5′E	FM	167
De Beauvoir Town	Hack	TQ3384	51°32·6′	0°4·5′W	T	176,177
Debenham	Suff	TM1763	52°13·6′	1°11·0′E	T	156
Debenham Hall	Suff	TM1662	52°13·1′	1°10·1′E	X	156
Deben Lodge Fm	Suff	TM3038	51°59·8′	1°21·4′E	FM	169
Deblin's Green	Worcs	SO8149	52°8·6′	2°16·3′W	T	150
Debog	S Lanak	NS7728	55°32·1′	3°56·5′W	X	71
Deborah Wood	Durham	NZ1627	54°38·5′	1°44·7′W	F	92
Dechmont	W Loth	NT0470	55°55·1′	3°31·7′W	T	65
Dechmont Fm	S Lanak	NS6657	55°47·5′	4°7·8′W	FM	64
Dechmont Hill	S Lanak	NS6558	55°48·0′	4°8·8′W	H	64
Dechmont Law	W Loth	NT0369	55°54·5′	3°32·7′W	X	65
Dechrode	Stir	NS6185	56°2·5′	4°13·4′W	X	57
Decker Hill	Shrops	SJ7509	52°40·9′	2°21·8′W	X	127
Deckham	Ghead	NZ2661	54°56·8′	1°35·2′W	T	88
Deckler's Cliff	Devon	SX7536	50°12·9′	3°44·7′W	X	202
Deckport Cross	Devon	SS5504	50°49·3′	4°3·1′W	X	191
Deckport Fm	Devon	SS5603	50°48·8′	4°2·3′W	A	191
Decoy	Somer	SS8747	51°12·9′	3°36·7′W	X	181
Decoy	Staffs	SK1801	52°36·6′	1°43·6′W	F	139
Decoy Broad	Norf	TG3216	52°41·7′	1°26·4′E	W	133,134
Decoy Carr	Norf	TG4009	52°37·8′	1°33·2′E	F	134
Decoy Carr	Norf	TG4203	52°34·5′	1°34·7′E	F	134
Decoy Covert	Hants	SU4516	50°56·7′	1°21·2′W	F	185
Decoy Covert	Suff	TL8978	52°22·3′	0°47·0′E	F	144
Decoy Fen	Norf	TL6685	52°26·5′	0°26·9′E	X	143
Decoy Fleet	Medway	TQ7777	51°28·1′	0°33·3′E	W	178
Decoy Fm	Bucks	SP7314	51°49·4′	0°56·1′W	FM	165
Decoy Fm	Cambs	TF4012	52°41·5′	0°4·7′E	FM	131,142,143
Decoy Fm	Ches	SJ3862	53°9·3′	2°55·2′W	FM	117
Decoy Fm	Lincs	TL9508	51°44·4′	0°49·9′E	FM	168
Decoy Fm	E Yorks	SE7121	53°41·1′	0°55·1′W	FM	105,106,112
Decoy Fm	E Yorks	TA0346	53°54·2′	0°25·5′W	FM	107
Decoy Fm	Lincs	SK9371	53°13·9′	0°36·0′W	FM	121
Decoy Fm	Lincs	TF1920	52°46·1′	0°13·8′W	FM	130
Decoy Fm	Lincs	TF2612	52°41·7′	0°7·7′W	FM	131,142
Decoy Fm	Lincs	TF2619	52°45·5′	0°7·6′W	FM	131
Decoy Fm	Lincs	TF4657	53°5·6′	0°11·2′E	FM	122
Decoy Fm	Medway	TQ7877	51°28·1′	0°34·2′E	FM	178
Decoy Fm	Norf	TG4716	52°41·3′	1°39·7′E	FM	134
Decoy Fm	Norf	TG4810	52°38·1′	1°40·3′E	FM	134
Decoy Fm	Norf	TL6494	52°31·4′	0°25·4′E	FM	143
Decoy Fm	Shrops	SJ3428	52°51·0′	2°58·4′W	FM	126
Decoy Fm	Suff	TM5196	52°30·5′	1°42·3′E	FM	134
Decoy Grounds	Suff	TG4800	52°32·7′	1°39·9′E	F	134
Decoy Heath	Dorset	SY9191	50°43·3′	2°7·3′W	X	195
Decoy Ho	E Yorks	TA0649	53°55·8′	0°22·7′W	X	107
Decoy Ho	Lincs	TF1752	53°3·4′	0°14·8′W	X	121
Decoy Ho	Notts	SK6872	53°14·7′	0°58·4′W	X	120
Decoy Plantn	E Yorks	TA1846	53°54·0′	0°11·8′W	F	107
Decoy Plantn	N Yks	SE8264	54°4·2′	0°44·4′W	F	100
Decoy Point	Essex	TL8906	51°43·5′	0°44·6′E	X	168
Decoy Pond	Bucks	SP7207	51°45·7′	0°57·0′W	W	165
Decoy Pond	W Berks	SU6063	51°22·0′	1°7·9′W	W	175
Decoy Pond Fm	Hants	SU3507	50°51·9′	1°29·8′W	FM	196
Decoypond Wood	Bucks	SP6924	51°54·8′	0°59·4′W	F	165
Decoy Pool Fm	Somer	ST4550	51°15·0′	2°46·9′W	FM	182
Decoy Rhyne	Somer	ST4543	51°11·2′	2°46·8′W	W	182
Decoy, The	E Yorks	TA0840	53°50·9′	0°21·1′W	X	107
Decoy, The	Norf	TL6495	52°31·9′	0°25·5′E	F	143
Decoy, The	Staffs	SK2405	52°38·8′	1°38·3′W	X	139
Decoy, The	Warw	SP2383	52°26·9′	1°39·3′W	F	139
Decoy Wood	E Yorks	TA0345	53°53·7′	0°25·5′W	F	107
Decoy Wood	Lincs	TF4657	53°5·6′	0°11·2′E	F	122
Decoy Wood	Norf	TG4820	52°43·5′	1°40·8′E	X	134
Decoy Wood	Suff	TM3951	52°6·6′	1°29·8′E	F	156
Decoy Wood	Suff	TM4158	52°10·3′	1°31·9′E	F	156
Dedda Skerry	Shetld	HU4627	60°1·8′	1°10·0′W	X	4
Deddington	Oxon	SP4631	51°58·8′	1°19·4′W	T	151
Deddington Hill	Warw	SP4147	52°7·4′	1°23·7′W	X	151
Deddington Mill	Oxon	SP4532	51°59·3′	1°20·3′W	X	151
Deddy Combe	Somer	SS8047	51°12·8′	3°42·7′W	X	181
Dedham	Essex	TM0533	51°57·7′	0°59·4′E	T	168
Dedham Heath	Essex	TM0631	51°56·6′	1°0·2′E	T	168
Dedisham	W Susx	TQ1132	51°4·8′	0°24·5′W	X	187
Dedmansey Wood	Beds	TL0316	51°50·2′	0°29·9′W	F	166
Dedra Banks	Cumbr	NY5819	54°34·1′	2°38·6′W	X	91
Dedridge	W Loth	NT0666	55°52·9′	3°29·7′W	T	65
Dedswell Manor Fm	Surrey	TQ0453	51°16·2′	0°30·2′W	FM	186
Dedworth	Win & Maid	SU9476	51°28·7′	0°38·4′W	T	175
Dedwyddfa	Denb	SJ0670	53°13·4′	3°24·1′W	X	116
Deebank	Aberd	NO6995	57°3·0′	2°30·2′W	T	38,45
Dee Bank	Wrex	SJ3642	52°58·5′	2°56·8′W	X	117
Dee Barn	Wilts	ST8435	51°7·1′	2°13·3′W	X	183
Deecastle	Aberd	NO4396	57°3·4′	2°55·9′W	X	37,44
Deek's Fm	Essex	TL7433	51°58·3′	0°32·4′E	FM	167
Deelat, The	Aberd	NJ4417	57°14·7′	2°55·2′W	H	37
Deel's Hill	Northum	NT8010	55°23·3′	2°18·5′W	H	80
Deemshill	Pemb	SM9109	51°44·7′	5°1·3′W	X	157,158
Deemster Manor	Ches	SJ5544	52°59·7′	2°39·8′W	X	117
Deene	Northnts	SP9492	52°31·3′	0°36·5′W	T	141
Deene Park	Northnts	SP9492	52°31·3′	0°36·5′W	X	141
Deenethorpe	Northnts	SP9591	52°30·7′	0°35·6′W	T	141
Deep	Aberd	NO7877	56°53·3′	2°21·2′W	X	45
Deepaller	Devon	SS9015	50°55·7′	3°33·5′W	X	181
Deepburn	Highld	NC6760	58°30·7′	4°16·5′W	X	10
Deepcar	Sheff	SK2897	53°28·6′	1°34·3′W	T	110
Deep Cliff	Brad	SE0738	53°50·5′	1°53·2′W	X	104
Deep Clough	Derby	SK0072	53°14·9′	1°59·6′W	X	119
Deepclough	Derby	SK0497	53°28·4′	1°56·0′W	T	110
Deep Clough	Lancs	SD5862	54°3·4′	2°38·1′W	X	97
Deepcut	Surrey	SU9057	51°18·5′	0°42·1′W	T	175,186
Deepcut Place	Surrey	SU9056	51°18·0′	0°42·2′W	X	175,186
Deepcutting	Powys	SJ2413	52°42·8′	3°7·1′W	X	126
Deepdale	Beds	TL2049	52°7·8′	0°14·4′W	T	153
Deepdale	Cumbr	NY3520	54°34·5′	2°59·9′W	X	90
Deepdale	Cumbr	NY3812	54°30·2′	2°57·0′W	X	90
Deepdale	Cumbr	SD7284	54°15·3′	2°25·4′W	X	98
Deep Dale	Derby	SK0971	53°14·4′	1°51·5′W	X	119
Deep Dale	Derby	SK1669	53°13·3′	1°45·2′W	X	119
Deep Dale	Durham	NY9615	54°32·1′	2°3·2′W	X	91,92
Deep Dale	Durham	NY9715	54°32·1′	2°2·4′W	X	92
Deep Dale	E Yorks	SE8155	53°59·3′	0°45·5′W	X	106
Deep Dale	E Yorks	SE9236	53°49·0′	0°35·7′W	X	106
Deep Dale	Lancs	SD8349	53°56·5′	2°15·1′W	X	103
Deepdale	N Lincs	TA0418	53°39·1′	0°25·2′W	X	112
Deepdale	N Yks	NZ4100	54°23·9′	1°21·7′W	X	93
Deepdale	N Yks	SD8979	54°12·6′	2°9·7′W	T	98
Deep Dale	N Yks	SE8563	54°3·6′	0°41·7′W	X	100
Deep Dale	N Yks	SE9290	54°18·1′	0°34·8′W	X	94,101
Deepdale	Orkney	HY2611	58°59·1′	3°16·8′W	X	6
Deepdale	Orkney	HY4504	58°55·5′	2°56·8′W	X	6,7
Deepdale	Orkney	ND2999	58°52·6′	3°13·4′W	X	6,7
Deep Dale	Shetld	HU1854	60°16·5′	1°40·0′W	X	3
Deepdale Beck	Cumbr	NY3812	54°30·2′	2°57·0′W	W	90
Deepdale Beck	Cumbr	SD7285	54°15·8′	2°25·4′W	W	98
Deepdale Beck	Durham	NY9114	54°31·5′	2°7·9′W	W	91,92
Deepdale Beck	Durham	NZ0216	54°32·6′	1°57·7′W	W	92
Deepdale Common	Cumbr	NY3712	54°30·2′	2°58·0′W	X	90
Deepdale Crag	Cumbr	NY3419	54°34·0′	3°0·8′W	X	90
Deepdale Fm	Cumbr	SD4978	54°12·0′	2°46·5′W	FM	97
Deepdale Fm	Derby	SK4568	53°12·7′	1°19·2′W	FM	120
Deepdale Fm	N Yks	SE4199	54°23·3′	1°21·7′W	FM	99
Deepdale Fm	N Yks	SE9291	54°18·6′	0°34·7′W	FM	94,101
Deepdale Fm	Red & Cl	NZ7219	54°33·9′	0°52·8′W	FM	94
Deepdale Fm	Staffs	SK0853	53°4·7′	1°52·4′W	FM	119
Deepdale Fm	Wrekin	SJ7123	52°48·5′	2°25·4′W	FM	127
Deepdale Gill	N Yks	SD8980	54°13·2′	2°9·7′W	W	98
Deepdale Hall	Cumbr	NY3914	54°31·3′	2°56·1′W	X	90
Deepdale Hause	Cumbr	NY3612	54°30·2′	2°58·9′W	H	90
Deepdale Head	Cumbr	SD7283	54°14·8′	2°25·4′W	X	98
Deep Dale Head	N Yks	SD8255	53°59·7′	2°16·1′W	X	103
Deepdale Head	N Yks	SD9679	54°12·6′	2°3·3′W	X	98
Deepdale Ho	Norf	TF7943	52°57·5′	0°40·3′E	X	132
Deepdale Marsh	Norf	TF8144	52°58·0′	0°42·1′E	X	132
Deepdale Plantn	E Yorks	SE8451	53°57·1′	0°42·8′W	F	106
Deepdale Plantn	E Yorks	SE9540	53°51·1′	0°32·9′W	F	106
Deepdales	Lincs	TF0749	53°1·9′	0°23·9′W	X	130
Deepdale Wood	Durham	NZ0116	54°32·6′	1°58·7′W	F	92
Deep Dean	Heref	SO6120	51°52·9′	2°33·6′W	X	162
Deepdene	Surrey	TQ1749	51°13·9′	0°19·1′W	T	187
Deepdene Station	Surrey	TQ1750	51°14·5′	0°19·0′W	X	187
Deepfields	Dudley	SO9494	52°32·9′	2°4·9′W	T	139
Deep Geo	Shetld	HU3611	59°53·2′	1°20·9′W	X	4
Deep Gill	Cumbr	NY1312	54°30·0′	3°20·2′W	W	89
Deep Gill	Cumbr	NY7700	54°23·9′	2°20·8′W	X	91
Deep Gill	N Eil	NB0112	58°0·1′	7°3·2′W	X	13
Deep Gill	N Yks	SE1484	54°15·3′	1°46·7′W	X	99
Deep Gill Wood	N Yks	SE5487	54°16·8′	1°9·8′W	F	100
Deepgrove Fm	N Yks	NZ8513	54°30·5′	0°40·8′W	FM	94
Deepgrove Wyke	N Yks	NZ8514	54°31·1′	0°40·8′W	W	94
Deepheather	Aberd	NJ9729	57°21·3′	2°2·5′W	X	38
Deepholm Fm	Monm	SO4914	51°49·6′	2°44·0′W	FM	162
Deephope	Scot Bord	NT2713	55°24·6′	3°8·7′W	X	79
Deeping Common	Lincs	TF1611	52°41·3′	0°16·6′W	X	130,142
Deeping Fen	Lincs	TF1816	52°44·0′	0°14·7′W	X	130
Deeping Fen	Lincs	TF2016	52°43·9′	0°13·0′W	X	131
Deeping Fen Fm	Lincs	TF1516	52°44·0′	0°17·4′W	FM	130
Deeping Gate	Peterb	TF1409	52°40·2′	0°18·4′W	T	142
Deeping St James	Lincs	TF1509	52°40·2′	0°17·6′W	T	142
Deeping St Nicholas	Lincs	TF2115	52°43·4′	0°12·1′W	T	131
Deep Lake	Pemb	SM9915	51°48·1′	4°54·5′W	X	157,158
Deepley Fm	N Yks	SE6169	54°7·0′	1°3·6′W	FM	100
Deeply Vale	Lancs	SD8214	53°37·6′	2°15·9′W	X	109
Deepmill Fm	Bucks	SU9099	51°41·2′	0°41·5′W	FM	165
Deep Moor	Devon	SS5221	50°58·5′	4°6·1′W	X	180
Deepmoor Fm	Heref	SO3866	52°17·6′	2°54·1′W	FM	137,148,149
Deepmore Fm	Staffs	SJ9208	52°40·4′	2°6·7′W	FM	127
Deep Nitch	Cald	SD9934	53°48·4′	2°0·5′W	X	103
Deep Point	I Scilly	SV9311	49°55·5′	6°16·3′W	X	203
Deep Rake	Derby	SK2273	53°15·5′	1°39·8′W	X	119
Deep Sike	Scot Bord	NY5388	55°11·3′	2°43·9′W	W	79
Deepslack	Cumbr	SD5798	54°22·8′	2°39·3′W	X	97
Deep Slack	Scot Bord	NT3411	55°23·6′	3°2·1′W	H	79
Deepslack Knowe	Scot Bord	NT2527	55°32·1′	3°10·9′W	H	73
Deep Slade	Swan	SS5686	51°33·5′	4°4·3′W	X	159
Deepslaids (ruin)	Scot Bord	NT4826	55°31·7′	2°49·0′W	X	73
Deeps, The	Lincs	TF4358	53°6·2′	0°8·6′E	F	122
Deeps, The	Shetld	HU3241	60°9·4′	1°24·9′W	W	4
Deepstone	N Ayr	NS3748	55°42·1′	4°35·2′W	X	63
Deep Swincombe	Devon	SX6471	50°31·6′	3°54·7′W	X	202
Deepsyke Forest	Scot Bord	NT1853	55°46·1′	3°18·0′W	X	65,66,72
Deepsykehead	Scot Bord	NT1754	55°46·6′	3°19·0′W	X	65,66,72
Deepthwaite	Cumbr	SD5183	54°14·7′	2°44·7′W	T	97
Deepweir	Monm	ST4887	51°35·0′	2°44·6′W	T	171,172
Deepwood	Heref	SO4674	52°21·9′	2°47·2′W	X	137,138,148
Deer Bank	N Yks	SD7979	54°12·6′	2°18·9′W	X	98
Deerbank, The	Essex	TQ6895	51°37·9′	0°26·0′E	A	167,177
Deer Bields	Cumbr	NY3009	54°28·5′	3°4·4′W	X	90
Deerbolt Hall	Suff	TM1158	52°11·0′	1°5·6′E	X	155
Deer Burn	D & G	NY0096	55°15·1′	3°34·0′W	W	78
Deerbush Burn	Northum	NT8409	55°22·7′	2°14·7′W	W	80
Deerbush Hill	Northum	NT8308	55°22·2′	2°15·7′W	H	80
Deer Clough	Lancs	SD6055	53°59·6′	2°36·2′W	X	102,103

Deercombe	Devon	SS7647	51°12·8'	3°46·1'W	X	180
Deer Craig	Stir	NS5199	56°9·9'	4°23·5'W	H	57
Deer Dyke	Aberd	NO6478	56°53·8'	2°35·0'W	A	45
Deer Dyke Moss	Cumbr	SD3382	54°14·0'	3°1·3'W	X	96,97
Deerfold	Heref	SO3867	52°18·1'	2°54·2'W	X	137,148,149
Deerfold Wood	Worcs	SO9147	52°7·5'	2°7·5'W	F	150
Deer Forest	Cumbr	NY4314	54°31·3'	2°52·4'W	X	90
Deer Gallows Plain	N Yks	SD9955	53°59·7'	2°0·5'W	X	103
Deer Gill	S Lanak	NS9925	55°30·8'	3°35·5'W	W	72
Deerhams Fm	Somer	ST2706	50°51·2'	3°1·8'W	FM	193
Deer Hill	Cumbr	NY6773	55°3·3'	2°30·6'W	X	86,87
Deer Hill	Kirk	SE0711	53°36·0'	1°53·2'W	X	110
Deerhill	Moray	NJ4656	57°35·7'	2°53·7'W	X	28,29
Deer Hill Moss	Kirk	SE0610	53°35·4'	1°54·1'W	X	110
Deerhill Moss	Moray	NJ4656	57°35·7'	2°53·7'W	X	28,29
Deerhillock	Aberd	NO5497	57°4·0'	2°45·1'W	X	37,44
Deer Hill Resr	Kirk	SE0711	53°36·0'	1°53·2'W	W	110
Deer Hills	Cumbr	NY3136	54°43·1'	3°3·8'W	X	90
Deer Holes	Derby	SK1596	53°27·9'	1°46·0'W	X	110
Deerholme Grange	N Yks	SE8079	54°12·3'	0°46·0'W	X	100
Deer Hope	Scot Bord	NT1458	55°48·7'	3°21·9'W	X	65,72
Deerhurst	Glos	SO8729	51°57·8'	2°11·0'W	T	150
Deerhurst Walton	Glos	SO8828	51°57·3'	2°10·1'W	T	150
Deerings Heights	N Yks	SE1461	54°2·9'	1°46·8'W	X	99
Deer Knowl	Derby	SK0998	53°29·0'	1°51·5'W	X	110
Deerland	Pemb	SM9810	51°45·4'	4°55·2'W	T	157,158
Deer Law	Scot Bord	NT2225	55°31·0'	3°13·7'W	H	73
Deerleap Fm	Hants	SU3410	50°53·5'	1°30·6'W	FM	196
Deerleap Inclosure	Hants	SU3409	50°53·0'	1°30·6'W	F	196
Deerleap, The	Shrops	SJ6601	52°36·6'	2°29·7'W	X	127
Deerleap Wood	Surrey	TQ1148	51°13·4'	0°24·2'W	F	187
Deerlee Knowe	Scot Bord	NT7108	55°22·2'	2°27·0'W	X	80
Deerness	Orkney	HY5606	58°56·6'	2°45·4'W	X	6
Deerness Valley Walk	Durham	NZ1739	54°45·0'	1°43·7'W	X	92
Deerness Valley Walk	Durham	NZ2142	54°46·6'	1°40·0'W	X	88
Deer Park	Devon	SS5529	51°2·8'	4°3·7'W	X	180
Deer Park	D & G	NX0959	54°53·6'	4°58·3'W	X	82
Deerpark	D & G	NX5953	54°51·4'	4°11·4'W	X	83
Deer Park	Heref	SO4225	51°55·5'	2°50·2'W	X	161
Deer Park	Highld	NH7056	57°34·8'	4°10·0'W	F	27
Deer Park	Staffs	SK0943	52°59·3'	1°51·6'W	X	119,128
Deer Park Fm	Dorset	SU0410	50°53·6'	1°56·2'W	FM	195
Deer Park Fm	Staffs	SJ9625	52°49·6'	2°3·2'W	FM	127
Deer Park Fm	Warw	SP2668	52°18·8'	1°36·7'W	FM	151
Deer Park Mere	Ches	SJ5450	53°3·0'	2°40·8'W	W	117
Deer Park Wood	Corn	SW8352	50°19·9'	5°2·6'W	F	200,204
Deerpark Wood	Corn	SX2060	50°25·0'	4°31·6'W	F	201
Deerpark Wood	Devon	SS6139	51°8·2'	3°58·8'W	F	180
Deerpark Wood	Essex	TL4003	51°42·7'	0°2·0'E	F	167
Deer Park Wood	N Yks	SE1099	54°23·4'	1°50·3'W	F	99
Deer Play	Northum	NY8490	55°12·5'	2°14·7'W	H	80
Deerplay Moor	Lancs	SD8627	53°44·6'	2°12·3'W	X	103
Deer Rock Hill	Surrey	SU8863	51°21·8'	0°43·8'W	X	175,186
Deer Rudding	Cumbr	NY3637	54°43·7'	2°59·2'W	X	90
Deers Den	D & G	NX5168	54°59·3'	4°19·3'W	X	83
Deer's Green	Essex	TL4631	51°57·7'	0°7·9'E	T	167
Deers Green Fm	Ches	SJ8160	53°8·4'	2°16·6'W	FM	118
Deer's Hill	Aberd	NJ8045	57°29·9'	2°19·6'W	H	29,30
Deer's Howe	S Ayr	NX1176	55°2·8'	4°57·1'W	X	76
Deerslet	Cumbr	SD5275	54°10·4'	2°43·7'W	X	97
Deerson Fm	Kent	TR2359	51°17·4'	1°12·3'E	FM	179
Deer Sound	Orkney	HY5308	58°57·7'	2°48·5'W	W	6,7
Deerstone Moor	Lancs	SD9036	53°49·5'	2°8·7'W	X	103
Deerstones	N Yks	SE0853	53°58·6'	1°52·3'W	T	104
Deerton Street	Kent	TQ9762	51°19·6'	0°50·1'E	T	178
Deer Tower	W Susx	SU9631	51°4·4'	0°37·4'W	X	186
Dee Side Ho	Cumbr	SD7785	54°15·9'	2°20·8'W	X	98
Deeside Ho	Flint	SJ3467	53°12·0'	2°58·9'W	X	117
Dees, The	Orkney	HY6939	59°14·5'	2°32·1'W	X	5
Deeves Hall	Herts	TL2100	51°41·4'	0°14·6'W	X	166
Defaidty	Gwyn	SH9044	52°59·2'	3°37·9'W	X	125
Defaity	I of Angl	SH4875	53°15·3'	4°16·3'W	X	114,115
Deffer Wood	Kirk	SE2608	53°34·3'	1°36·0'W	F	110
Defford	Shrops	SO6790	52°30·7'	2°28·8'W	X	138
Defford	Worcs	SO9143	52°5·4'	2°7·5'W	T	150
Defford Br	Worcs	SO9243	52°5·4'	2°6·6'W	X	150
Defynnog	Powys	SN9227	51°56·1'	3°33·9'W	T	160
Deganwy	Conwy	SH7779	53°17·9'	3°50·3'W	T	115
Deganwy Castle	Conwy	SH7879	53°17·9'	3°49·4'W	A	115
Degar	Rho Cyn Taf	ST0079	51°30·3'	3°26·1'W	T	170
Degembris	Corn	SW8556	50°22·1'	5°1·0'W	X	200
Deggs Leasow	Staffs	SK0635	52°55·0'	1°54·2'W	X	128
Degibna	Corn	SW6525	50°5·0'	5°16·7'W	T	203
Degnish	Arg & Bt	NM7812	56°15·2'	5°34·6'W	X	55
Degnish Point	Arg & Bt	NM7712	56°15·2'	5°35·6'W	X	55
Deheufryn	Conwy	SH8672	53°14·2'	3°42·1'W	X	116
Deheufryn Gorse	Conwy	SH8771	53°13·7'	3°41·2'W	X	116
Deighton	Kirk	SE1619	53°40·3'	1°45·1'W	T	110
Deighton	N Yks	NZ3801	54°24·4'	1°24·5'W	T	93
Deighton	York	SE6244	53°53·5'	1°3·0'W	T	105
Deighton Grange	N Yks	NZ3701	54°24·4'	1°25·4'W	X	93
Deighton Grange	N Yks	SE4051	53°57·5'	1°23·0'W	X	105
Deighton Hills	Norf	TG1415	52°41·6'	1°10·4'E	X	133
Deighton Spring	N Yks	SE3851	53°57·5'	1°24·8'W	F	104
Deildre	Gwyn	SH8530	52°51·6'	3°42·1'W	X	124,125
Deildref	Powys	SN9080	52°24·7'	3°36·6'W	X	136
Deildre Fawr	Powys	SN9086	52°27·9'	3°36·8'W	X	136
Deil Piece	Orkney	HY3949	59°19·6'	3°3·8'W	X	5
Deil's Barn Door	S Lanak	NS9926	55°31·3'	3°35·6'W	X	72
Deil's Caldron	Pth & Kin	NN7623	56°23·2'	4°0·1'W	W	51,52
Deil's Craig Dam	Stir	NS5578	55°58·6'	4°19·0'W	W	64
Deil's Dyke	S Ayr	NS3019	55°26·4'	4°40·8'W	X	70
Deil's Elbow	S Ayr	NS3401	55°16·8'	4°36·4'W	X	76
Deil's Heid,The	Angus	NO6741	56°33·8'	2°31·8'W	X	54
Deil's Jingle	D & G	NY2591	55°12·7'	3°10·3'W	A	79
Deil's Jingle	D & G	NY2593	55°13·8'	3°10·3'W	A	79
Deil's Putting Stone	D & G	NS6200	55°16·7'	4°9·9'W	X	77
Deiniolen	Gwyn	SH5763	53°8·9'	4°7·9'W	T	114,115
Deinol	Cered	SN3048	52°6·5'	4°28·6'W	X	145
Deio	Denb	SJ1648	53°1·6'	3°14·7'W	X	116

Deipkier	Leeds	SE2042	53°52·7'	1°41·3'W	X	104
Deira House	E Yorks	SE8639	53°50·6'	0°41·2'W	X	106
Deishar	Highld	NH9219	57°15·2'	3°46·9'W	T	36
Deith	Orkney	HY3832	59°10·5'	3°4·6'W	X	6
Delab	Aberd	NJ6816	57°14·3'	2°31·4'W	X	38
De La Beche	W Berks	SU5578	51°30·1'	1°12·1'W	X	174
Delabole	Corn	SX0684	50°37·6'	4°44·2'W	T	200
Delabole Point	Corn	SX0282	50°36·5'	4°47·5'W	X	200
Delachule	Moray	NJ1816	57°13·9'	3°21·0'W	X	36
Delachuper	Aberd	NJ2607	57°9·1'	3°12·9'W	X	37
Delacorse	Carm	SN3012	51°47·1'	4°27·5'W	X	159
Delalie	Aberd	NO6375	56°52·2'	2°36·0'W	X	45
Delamas	Essex	TL6300	51°40·7'	0°21·9'E	X	167
Delamere	Ches	SJ5669	53°13·2'	2°39·1'W	T	117
Delamere	Corn	SX0683	50°37·1'	4°44·2'W	X	200
Delamere Forest Park	Ches	SJ5471	53°14·3'	2°40·9'W	F	117
Delamere Ho	Herts	TL2128	51°56·5'	0°14·0'W	A	166
Delamere Lodge	Ches	SJ5769	53°13·2'	2°38·2'W	X	117
Delamere Manor	Ches	SJ5871	53°14·3'	2°37·4'W	X	117
Delamere Park	Ches	SJ5872	53°14·8'	2°37·4'W	X	117
Delameres	Essex	TM0006	51°43·2'	0°54·1'E	X	168
Delamere Sta	Ches	SJ5570	53°13·8'	2°40·0'W	X	117
Delamere Way	Ches	SJ5570	53°13·8'	2°40·0'W	X	117
Delamford	S Ayr	NX2999	55°15·6'	4°41·0'W	X	76
Delamford Hill	S Ayr	NX2998	55°15·0'	4°41·0'W	H	76
Delamore Ho	Devon	SX6059	50°25·1'	3°57·9'W	X	202
De Lank River	Corn	SX1275	50°32·9'	4°38·8'W	W	200
Delaport	Herts	TL1715	51°49·5'	0°17·7'W	X	166
Delapre Abbey	Northnts	SP7559	52°13·7'	0°53·7'W	A	152
Delavals Fm	Cambs	TL3194	52°31·9'	0°3·7'W	FM	142
Delavine	Aberd	NJ2807	57°9·2'	3°11·0'W	X	37
Delavorar	Moray	NJ1615	57°13·3'	3°23·0'W	X	36
Delaware Fm	Kent	TQ4545	51°11·4'	0°4·9'E	FM	188
Delbog	Highld	NH9615	57°13·1'	3°42·9'W	X	36
Delbury Hall	Shrops	SO5085	52°27·9'	2°43·8'W	X	137,138
Delcombe Bottom	Dorset	ST7904	50°50·3'	2°17·5'W	X	194
Delcombe Fm	Dorset	ST7903	50°49·8'	2°17·5'W	FM	194
Delcombe Manor	Dorset	ST7904	50°50·3'	2°17·5'W	X	194
Delcombe Wood	Dorset	ST7805	50°50·9'	2°18·4'W	F	194
Delday	Orkney	HY5604	58°55·5'	2°45·4'W	X	6
Deldow	Highld	NJ1235	57°24·1'	3°27·4'W	X	28
Delegate Hall	Northum	NY9463	54°57·9'	2°5·2'W	X	87
Delf Burn	Northum	NZ0388	55°11·4'	1°56·7'W	W	81
Delfekirk Scar	Cumbr	NY7422	54°35·8'	2°23·7'W	X	91
Delford Br	Corn	SX1175	50°32·9'	4°39·7'W	X	200
Delfrigs	Aberd	NJ9621	57°17·0'	2°3·5'W	X	38
Delfur Lodge	Moray	NJ3252	57°33·4'	3°7·7'W	X	28
Delgarth	Herts	TL1014	51°49·1'	0°23·9'W	X	166
Delgate Fm	Lincs	TF2817	52°44·4'	0°5·8'W	FM	131
Delgatie Castle	Aberd	NJ7550	57°32·6'	2°24·6'W	A	29
Delhandy	Moray	NJ2224	57°18·3'	3°17·2'W	X	36
Deli	Corn	SX0883	50°37·1'	4°42·5'W	X	200
Delight	Northum	NZ0272	55°2·8'	1°57·7'W	X	87
Dell	Highld	NH9011	57°10·9'	3°48·7'W	T	36
Dell	Moray	NJ1627	57°19·8'	3°23·3'W	X	36
Dellacham	Moray	NJ2935	57°24·3'	3°10·4'W	X	28
Delley	Devon	SS5424	51°0·0'	4°4·5'W	X	180
Dell Farm	Highld	NH4816	57°12·8'	4°30·6'W	FM	34
Dell Fm	Glos	SO8709	51°47·0'	2°10·9'W	FM	162
Dell Fm	Hants	SU5751	51°15·5'	1°10·6'W	FM	185
Dell Fm	Notts	SK6727	52°50·4'	0°59·9'W	FM	129
Delliefure	Highld	NJ0730	57°21·3'	3°32·3'W	X	27,36
Dell Lodge	Highld	NH4816	57°12·8'	4°30·6'W	X	34
Dell Lodge	Highld	NJ0119	57°15·3'	3°38·0'W	X	36
Dell of Inshes	Highld	NH6944	57°28·3'	4°10·6'W	X	26
Dell of Killiehuntly, The	Highld	NH7800	57°4·8'	4°0·3'W	X	35
Dell of Morile	Highld	NH8026	57°18·8'	3°59·1'W	X	35
Dell Quay	W Susx	SU8302	50°48·9'	0°48·9'W	T	197
Dell's Fm	Essex	TL5143	52°4·1'	0°12·6'E	FM	154
Dellston	Aberd	NJ9041	57°27·8'	2°9·5'W	X	30
Dell's Wood	Bucks	SU7894	51°38·6'	0°52·0'W	F	175
Dell, The	Glos	SP2526	51°56·2'	1°37·8'W	F	163
Dell, The	Highld	NH6935	57°23·5'	4°10·3'W	X	26
Dell, The	N Yks	NZ7606	54°26·9'	0°49·3'W	X	94
Dell, The	Suff	TM4899	52°32·2'	1°39·8'E	X	134
Delly End	Oxon	SP3513	51°49·1'	1°29·1'W	T	164
Delmerend Fm	Herts	TL0814	51°49·1'	0°25·6'W	FM	166
Delmonden Ho	Kent	TQ7329	51°2·3'	0°28·4'E	X	188,199
Delmonden Manor	Kent	TQ7330	51°2·8'	0°28·5'E	X	188
Delmore	Moray	NJ2442	57°28·0'	3°15·6'W	X	28
Delnabo	Moray	NJ1617	57°14·4'	3°23·1'W	X	36
Delnadamph Lodge	Aberd	NJ2208	57°9·6'	3°16·9'W	X	36
Delnamer	Angus	NO1868	56°48·0'	3°20·1'W	T	43
Delnapot	Moray	NJ1737	57°25·2'	3°22·5'W	X	28
Delny	Highld	NH7372	57°43·5'	4°7·5'W	X	21
Delny Dock	Highld	NH7570	57°42·4'	4°5·4'W	W	21
Delny Muir	Highld	NH7272	57°43·5'	4°8·5'W	X	21
Deloraine Burn	Scot Bord	NT3319	55°27·9'	3°3·1'W	W	79
Deloraineburn	Scot Bord	NT3319	55°27·9'	3°3·1'W	X	79
Delorainehope	Scot Bord	NT3418	55°27·3'	3°2·2'W	X	79
Deloraineshiel	Scot Bord	NT3415	55°25·7'	3°2·1'W	X	79
Delph	Oldham	SD9807	53°33·8'	2°1·4'W	T	109
Delph Bank	Lincs	TF3821	52°46·4'	0°3·1'E	X	131
Delph Bank	Norf	TL9685	52°25·9'	0°53·4'E	X	144
Delph Br	Norf	TL5293	52°31·0'	0°14·8'E	X	143
Delph Dike	Cambs	TL2798	52°34·1'	0°7·2'W	W	142
Delph Fm	Brad	SE0147	53°55·4'	1°58·7'W	FM	104
Delph Fm	Lincs	TF0870	53°13·2'	0°22·5'W	FM	121
Delph Greave	Oldham	SD9808	53°34·4'	2°1·4'W	X	109
Delphorrie	Aberd	NJ4818	57°15·2'	2°51·3'W	X	37
Delph Park	Warr	SJ6092	53°25·6'	2°35·7'W	X	109
Delph Resr	Black w Dar	SD6915	53°38·1'	2°27·7'W	W	109
Delph, The	Suff	TL7080	52°23·7'	0°30·3'E	X	143
Delshangie	Highld	NH4730	57°20·4'	4°32·1'W	X	26
Delshangie Wood	Highld	NH4629	57°19·8'	4°33·0'W	F	26
Delve Fm	Cambs	TL4186	52°27·5'	0°4·9'E	FM	142,143
Delves	Derby	SK3957	53°6·8'	1°24·6'W	X	119
Delves	Durham	NZ1249	54°50·4'	1°48·4'W	T	88
Delves	Kirk	SE1213	53°37·0'	1°48·7'W	X	110

Delves	N Yks	NZ7904	54°25·8'	0°46·5'W	X	94
Delves Fm	E Susx	TQ4316	50°55·8'	0°2·5'E	FM	198
Delves Fm	Warw	SP2498	52°35·0'	1°38·3'W	FM	139
Delve's Grave Cross	Devon	SS5121	50°58·4'	4°7·0'W	X	180
Delves Ridge Ho	N Yks	SE1757	54°0·8'	1°44·0'W	X	104
Delvid	Swan	SS4292	51°36·5'	4°16·5'W	X	159
Delvine	Pth & Kin	NO1240	56°32·9'	3°25·4'W	X	53
Delvine Gardens	Pth & Kin	NO1239	56°32·3'	3°25·4'W	X	53
Delvin End	Essex	TL7535	51°59·4'	0°33·3'E	T	155
Delvyn's Fm	Essex	TL8137	52°0·3'	0°38·6'E	FM	155
Delworthy	Devon	SS5423	50°59·5'	4°4·4'W	X	180
Delyorn	Highld	NJ1136	57°24·6'	3°28·4'W	X	28
Demain Fm	Corn	SW9042	50°14·7'	4°56·4'W	FM	204
Dembert Law	Fife	NO3502	56°12·6'	3°2·4'W	X	59
Dembleby	Lincs	TF0437	52°55·5'	0°26·8'W	T	130
Dembleby Heath Fm	Lincs	TF0337	52°55·5'	0°27·7'W	FM	130
Dembleby Thorns	Lincs	TF0238	52°56·0'	0°28·5'W	F	130
Demelza	Corn	SW9763	50°26·1'	4°51·1'W	T	200
Demesne	Cumbr	NX9714	54°30·9'	3°35·0'W	X	89
Demesne	Cumbr	NY0431	54°40·1'	3°28·9'W	X	89
Demesne	Cumbr	NY3462	54°57·1'	3°1·4'W	X	85
Demesne	Heref	SO4167	52°18·1'	2°51·5'W	X	137,148,149
Demesne	Northum	NU1008	55°22·2'	1°50·1'W	X	81
Demesne Fm	N Yks	NZ9403	54°25·1'	0°32·7'W	FM	94
Demesne Fm	N Yks	SE5361	54°2·8'	1°11·0'W	FM	100
Demesne Ho	Ches	SJ7047	53°1·4'	2°26·4'W	X	118
Demesne, The	Northum	NY9075	55°4·4'	2°9·0'W	X	87
Demesne Wood	Cumbr	NY7307	54°27·7'	2°24·6'W	F	91
Demickmore	Moray	NJ2521	57°16·7'	3°14·2'W	X	37
Demings Moss	Cumbr	NY5506	54°27·1'	2°41·2'W	X	90
Demming Crag	Cumbr	NY2200	54°23·6'	3°11·7'W	X	89,90
Demming Fm	E Yorks	TA1362	54°2·7'	0°16·0'W	FM	101
Demondale	Angus	NO6441	56°33·8'	2°34·7'W	X	54
Demperston	Fife	NO2211	56°17·4'	3°15·2'W	X	58
Dempster Road	D & G	NS8509	55°21·9'	3°48·4'W	X	71,78
Dempsterton	D & G	NX8784	55°8·5'	3°45·9'W	X	78
Denaby Common	Donc	SK4798	53°28·8'	1°17·1'W	X	111
Denaby Main	Donc	SK4999	53°29·4'	1°15·3'W	T	111
Denant	Pemb	SM9113	51°46·8'	5°1·4'W	X	157,158
Denbeath	Fife	NT3598	56°10·5'	3°2·4'W	T	59
Den Beck	N Yks	SE2179	54°12·6'	1°40·3'W	W	99
Denbie	D & G	NY1072	55°2·3'	3°24·1'W	X	85
Denbie Mains	D & G	NY1072	55°2·3'	3°24·1'W	X	85
Denbies	Surrey	TQ1450	51°14·5'	0°21·6'W	X	187
Denbieyett	D & G	NY0970	55°1·2'	3°25·0'W	X	85
Denbigh or Dinbych	Denb	SJ0566	53°11·2'	3°24·9'W	T	116
Denbigh West	Mil Key	SP8634	52°0·1'	0°44·4'W	X	152,165
Denbow Fm	Devon	SY0091	50°42·8'	3°24·6'W	FM	192
Denbrae	Aberd	NJ9146	57°30·5'	2°8·6'W	X	30
Denbrae	Fife	NO3918	56°21·3'	2°58·9'W	X	59
Denbrae Fm	Fife	NO4715	56°19·7'	2°51·0'W	FM	59
Den Brook	Somer	SS9024	51°0·5'	3°33·7'W	W	181
Den Burn	Fife	NO4704	56°13·8'	2°50·9'W	W	59
Denburn Lodge	Aberd	NJ5521	57°16·9'	2°44·3'W	X	37
Denbury	Devon	SX8168	50°30·2'	3°40·3'W	A	202
Denbury	Devon	SX8268	50°30·2'	3°39·5'W	T	202
Denbury Fm	Devon	SX8199	50°46·9'	3°40·9'W	FM	191
Denbury Fm	Somer	ST1429	51°3·5'	3°13·2'W	FM	181,193
Denby	Corn	SX0268	50°28·9'	4°47·1'W	X	200
Denby	Derby	SK3946	53°0·8'	1°24·7'W	T	119,128
Denby Bottles	Derby	SK3846	53°0·8'	1°25·6'W	T	119,128
Denby Common	Derby	SK4147	53°1·4'	1°22·9'W	T	129
Denby Dale	Kirk	SE2208	53°34·3'	1°39·7'W	T	110
Denby Hall	Kirk	SE2408	53°34·3'	1°37·8'W	X	110
Denby Ho	E Yorks	TA0768	54°6·0'	0°21·4'W	X	101
Denby Wood	Kirk	SE2416	53°38·6'	1°37·8'W	F	110
Dencallie	Aberd	NJ9655	57°35·4'	2°3·6'W	X	30
Denchworth	Oxon	SU3891	51°37·2'	1°26·7'W	T	164,174
Dencombe	W Susx	TQ2730	51°3·5'	0°10·9'W	X	187
Den Cottages	Pth & Kin	NO0833	56°29·1'	3°29·2'W	X	52,53
Den Cross	Kent	TQ4444	51°10·8'	0°4·0'E	X	187
Dendles Waste	Devon	SX6162	50°26·7'	3°57·1'W	F	202
Dendoldrum	Aberd	NO8172	56°50·6'	2°18·2'W	X	45
Dendron	Cumbr	SD2470	54°7·5'	3°9·4'W	T	96
Dene Cottage	N Yks	SE2666	54°5·6'	1°35·7'W	X	99
Dene Court	Somer	ST1728	51°3·0'	3°10·7'W	X	181,193
Dene Dip	W Susx	SU9422	50°59·6'	0°39·2'W	X	197
Dene Fm	Kent	TR2455	51°15·2'	1°13·0'E	FM	179
Dene Fm	Surrey	TQ2346	51°12·2'	0°14·0'W	FM	187
Dene Ho	Ches	SJ6677	53°17·6'	2°30·2'W	X	118
Dene Ho	Durham	NZ0943	54°47·2'	1°51·2'W	X	88
Dene Ho	Northum	NU2010	55°23·3'	1°40·6'W	X	81
Dene Ho	Northum	NY8456	54°54·2'	2°14·5'W	X	86,87
Dene House Fm	Durham	NZ3438	54°44·4'	1°27·9'W	FM	93
Dene Leazes	Durham	NZ4338	54°44·4'	1°19·5'W	X	93
Dene Manor	Kent	TQ6665	51°21·8'	0°23·5'E	X	177,178
Dene Mouth	Durham	NZ4540	54°45·4'	1°17·6'W	W	88
Denend	Aberd	NJ6037	57°25·6'	2°39·5'W	X	29
Denend	Aberd	NJ8825	57°19·2'	2°11·5'W	X	38
Denend	Aberd	NK1142	57°28·3'	1°48·5'W	X	30
Denend	Angus	NO3041	56°33·6'	3°7·9'W	X	53
Dene Park	Kent	TQ5950	51°13·8'	0°17·0'E	T	188
Deneridge Fm	Devon	SS7610	50°52·8'	3°45·4'W	FM	191
Deneside	Durham	NZ4148	54°49·8'	1°21·3'W	T	88
Denes, The	Suff	TM5075	52°19·2'	1°40·5'E	X	156
Denes, The	Suff	TM5384	52°23·9'	1°43·6'E	X	156
Dene, The	Durham	NZ1154	54°53·1'	1°49·3'W	T	88
Denfield	Angus	NO6142	56°34·4'	2°37·6'W	X	54
Denfield	Pth & Kin	NN9517	56°20·3'	3°41·5'W	X	58
Denfield Hall Fm	Ches	SJ7383	53°20·8'	2°23·9'W	FM	109
Denfind	Angus	NO5037	56°31·6'	2°48·3'W	X	54
Denfind Brae	Angus	NO5037	56°31·6'	2°48·3'W	X	54
Den Finella	Aberd	NO7667	56°47·9'	2°23·1'W	X	45
Den Fm	Kent	TQ7147	51°12·0'	0°27·3'E	FM	188
Den Fm	Moray	NJ3560	57°37·8'	3°4·8'W	FM	28
Denford	Northnts	SP9976	52°22·6'	0°32·3'W	T	141
Denford	Staffs	SJ9553	53°4·7'	2°4·1'W	T	118
Denford Ash Fm	Northnts	TL0176	52°22·6'	0°30·6'W	FM	141
Denford Manor Fm	W Berks	SU3568	51°24·8'	1°29·4'W	FM	174
Denford North Lodge	Northnts	TL0176	52°22·6'	0°30·6'W	X	141

Denford Park (Training Coll)	W Berks	SU3669	51°25·4'	1°28·5'W	X	174
Denfurlong Fm (Farm Trail)	Glos	SP0610	51°47·6'	1°54·4'W	X	163
Denge Beach	Kent	TR0718	50°55·7'	0°57·1'E	X	189
Denge Marsh	Kent	TR0520	50°56·8'	0°55·5'E	X	189
Dengewell Hall	Essex	TM1627	51°54·2'	1°8·8'E	X	168,169
Denge Wood	Kent	TR0952	51°14·0'	1°0·0'E	F	179,189
Dengie	Essex	TL9801	51°40·6'	0°52·2'E	T	168
Dengie Flat	Essex	TM0404	51°42·1'	0°57·5'E	X	168
Dengie Fm	Essex	TL8112	51°46·9'	0°37·8'E	FM	168
Dengie Marshes	Essex	TM0000	51°40·0'	0°53·9'E	X	168
Den Grove Wood	Kent	TR1760	51°18·1'	1°7·2'E	F	179
Denhall Ho Fm	Ches	SJ2975	53°16·3'	3°3·5'W	FM	117
Denham	Bucks	SP7520	51°52·6'	0°54·2'W	T	165
Denham	Bucks	TQ0486	51°34·0'	0°29·6'W	T	176
Denham	Suff	TL7561	52°13·4'	0°34·1'E	T	155
Denham	Suff	TM1974	52°19·4'	1°13·2'E	T	156
Denham Aerodrome	Bucks	TQ0288	51°35·1'	0°31·3'W	X	176
Denham Br	Devon	SX4767	50°29·2'	4°9·0'W	X	201
Denham Castle	Suff	TL7462	52°13·9'	0°33·3'E	X	155
Denham Corner	Suff	TM1972	52°18·4'	1°13·1'E	T	156
Denham End	Suff	TL7662	52°13·9'	0°35·0'E	T	155
Denham Fm	Bucks	SP7521	51°53·2'	0°54·2'W	FM	165
Denham Green	Bucks	TQ0388	51°35·1'	0°30·4'W	T	176
Denham Hall	Lancs	SD5922	53°41·8'	2°36·8'W	X	102
Denham Hall Fm	Suff	TM1873	52°18·9'	1°12·3'E	FM	156
Denham Mount	Bucks	TQ0286	51°34·0'	0°31·3'W	X	176
Denham Place	Bucks	TQ0387	51°34·6'	0°30·4'W	A	176
Denham Street	Suff	TM1872	52°18·4'	1°12·3'E	X	156
Denhay Fms	Dorset	SY4296	50°45·9'	2°49·0'W	FM	193
Denhay Hill	Dorset	SY4295	50°45·3'	2°49·0'W	H	193
Denhead	Aberd	NJ5903	57°7·2'	2°40·2'W	X	37
Denhead	Aberd	NJ6461	57°38·5'	2°35·7'W	X	29
Denhead	Aberd	NJ7055	57°35·3'	2°29·6'W	X	29
Denhead	Aberd	NJ7120	57°16·4'	2°28·4'W	X	38
Denhead	Aberd	NJ7914	57°13·2'	2°20·4'W	X	38
Denhead	Aberd	NJ9014	57°13·3'	2°9·5'W	X	38
Denhead	Aberd	NJ9061	57°38·6'	2°9·6'W	X	30
Denhead	Aberd	NJ9930	57°21·9'	2°0·5'W	T	30
Denhead	Aberd	NJ9952	57°33·7'	2°0·5'W	X	30
Denhead	Aberd	NJ9959	57°37·5'	2°0·5'W	X	30
Denhead	Aberd	NO8679	56°54·4'	2°13·3'W	X	45
Denhead	Angus	NO3134	56°29·8'	3°6·8'W	X	53
Denhead	Angus	NO3336	56°30·9'	3°4·9'W	X	53
Denhead	Angus	NO4837	56°31·6'	2°50·3'W	X	54
Denhead	Fife	NO3810	56°17·0'	2°59·6'W	X	59
Denhead	Fife	NO4613	56°18·6'	2°51·9'W	T	59
Denhead	Moray	NJ4349	57°31·9'	2°56·7'W	T	28
Denhead Cotts	Angus	NO7062	56°45·2'	2°29·0'W	X	45
Denhead Croft	Aberd	NJ6561	57°38·5'	2°34·7'W	X	29
Denhead of Arbirlot	Angus	NO5742	56°34·3'	2°41·5'W	X	54
Denhead of Gray	C of Dun	NO3431	56°28·2'	3°3·8'W	T	53
Denhill Fm	Aberd	NJ7935	57°24·6'	2°20·5'W	FM	29,30
Denholm	Aberd	NK0845	57°30·0'	1°51·5'W	X	30
Denholm	Scot Bord	NT5618	55°27·5'	2°41·3'W	T	80
Denholm Dean	Scot Bord	NT5617	55°26·9'	2°41·3'W	X	80
Denholme	Brad	SE0634	53°48·4'	1°54·1'W	T	104
Denholme Clough	Brad	SE0732	53°47·3'	1°53·2'W	T	104
Denholme Edge	Brad	SE0634	53°48·4'	1°54·1'W	T	104
Denholme Gate	Brad	SE0732	53°47·3'	1°53·2'W	T	104
Denholme Ho	Brad	SE0733	53°47·8'	1°53·2'W	X	104
Denholmhill	Scot Bord	NT5616	55°26·4'	2°41·3'W	T	80
Denio	Gwyn	SH3735	52°53·5'	4°25·0'W	T	123
Den Knowes	Scot Bord	NT1532	55°34·7'	3°20·5'W	H	72
Den Knowes Head	Scot Bord	NT1631	55°34·2'	3°19·5'W	H	72
Denlethen Wood	Aberd	NO7070	56°49·5'	2°29·0'W	F	45
Denly Hill	Kent	TR0663	51°19·9'	0°57·8'E	X	179
Denman Coll	Oxon	SU4596	51°39·9'	1°20·6'W	X	164
Denman's Fm	Oxon	SP4605	51°44·7'	1°19·6'W	FM	164
Denman's Hill	N Yks	SE0280	54°13·2'	1°57·7'W	X	98
Denmark	Angus	NO5946	56°36·5'	2°39·6'W	X	54
Denmark	Cered	SN5853	52°9·7'	4°4·2'W	X	146
Denmark Bridge	Suff	TM1179	52°22·3'	1°6·4'E	X	144
Denmarkfield	Pth & Kin	NO0928	56°26·4'	3°28·1'W	X	52,53,58
Denmead	Hants	SU6511	50°53·9'	1°4·2'W	T	196
Denmead Mill	Hants	SU6714	50°55·5'	1°2·4'W	X	196
Denmill	Aberd	NJ6013	57°12·6'	2°39·3'W	X	37
Denmill	Aberd	NJ8218	57°15·4'	2°17·4'W	X	38
Denmill	C of Aber	NJ8203	57°7·3'	2°17·4'W	X	38
Denmore	Aberd	NJ9040	57°27·3'	2°9·5'W	T	30
Denmore	C of Aber	NJ9411	57°11·6'	2°5·5'W	T	38
Denmoss	Aberd	NJ6541	57°27·7'	2°34·5'W	X	29
Den Moss	Highld	ND1836	58°18·6'	3°23·5'W	X	11
Denmuir	Fife	NO3018	56°21·2'	3°7·5'W	X	59
Denne	Kent	TR0438	51°6·5'	0°55·3'E	X	179,189
Denne Court	Kent	TR2955	51°15·1'	1°17·3'E	X	179
Denne Fm	W Susx	TQ1436	51°6·9'	0°21·9'W	FM	187
Denne Hill	Kent	TR2249	51°12·0'	1°11·1'E	X	179,189
Denne Hill Fm	Kent	TR2249	51°12·0'	1°11·1'E	FM	179,189
Dennel Hill	Glos	ST5497	51°40·4'	2°39·5'W	X	162
Denne Manor Fm	Kent	TR0453	51°14·6'	0°55·8'E	FM	179,189
Denne Park	W Susx	TQ1629	51°3·1'	0°20·3'W	X	187,198
Denner Hill	Bucks	SP8500	51°41·8'	0°45·8'W	X	165
Dennett's Fm	Somer	ST2907	50°51·7'	3°0·1'W	FM	193
Dennigall Hill	E Ayr	NS7117	55°26·0'	4°1·9'W	X	71
Dennings Plantn	N Yks	SE7760	54°2·1'	0°49·0'W	F	100
Dennington	Devon	SS6129	51°2·8'	3°58·6'W	X	180
Dennington	Suff	TM2867	52°15·5'	1°20·9'E	T	156
Dennington Corner	Suff	TM2865	52°14·4'	1°20·8'E	T	156
Dennington Hall	Suff	TM2968	52°16·0'	1°21·8'E	T	156
Dennington Lodge	Suff	TM2867	52°15·5'	1°20·9'E	X	156
Dennington Place	Suff	TM2666	52°15·0'	1°19·1'E	X	156
Dennington Wood	Suff	TM2967	52°15·4'	1°21·7'E	F	156
Dennis Fm	Corn	SW9463	50°26·1'	4°53·7'W	FM	200
Dennis Fm	Warw	SP3489	52°30·1'	1°29·5'W	FM	140
Dennis Head	Corn	SW7825	50°5·3'	5°5·8'W	X	204
Dennis Head	Orkney	HY7855	59°23·1'	2°22·7'W	X	5
Dennis Hill	Corn	SW9274	50°32·0'	4°55·7'W	X	200
Dennis Knoll	Derby	SK2283	53°20·8'	1°39·8'W	X	110
Dennis Loch	Orkney	HY7855	59°23·1'	2°22·7'W	W	5
Dennis Ness	Orkney	HY7855	59°23·1'	2°22·7'W	X	5
Dennis Point	Corn	SX0486	50°38·7'	4°46·0'W	X	200
Dennistoun	C of Glas	NS6065	55°51·7'	4°13·8'W	T	64
Dennisworth Fm	S Glos	ST6976	51°29·2'	2°26·4'W	FM	172
Dennithorne	Devon	SX5275	50°33·6'	4°5·0'W	X	191,201
Denny	Falk	NS8082	56°1·2'	3°55·1'W	T	57,65
Denny Abbey	Cambs	TL4968	52°17·6'	0°11·5'E	A	154
Denny Bank	Lancs	SD5064	54°4·4'	2°45·4'W	X	97
Denny Bottom	Kent	TQ5639	51°8·0'	0°14·2'E	T	188
Denny End	Cambs	TL4965	52°16·0'	0°11·4'E	T	154
Dennyhill	Cumbr	NY5117	54°33·0'	2°45·0'W	X	90
Denny Hill	Glos	SO7516	51°50·8'	2°21·4'W	X	162
Denny Inclosure	Hants	SU3206	50°51·4'	1°32·3'W	F	196
Denny Island	Bath & NE Somer	ST5760	51°20·5'	2°36·7'W	X	172,182
Denny Island	Monm	ST4581	51°31·7'	2°47·2'W	X	171,172
Dennyloanhead	Falk	NS8080	56°0·1'	3°55·0'W	T	65
Denny Lodge	Cambs	TL4969	52°18·2'	0°11·5'E	X	154
Denny Lodge	Hants	SU3305	50°50·8'	1°31·5'W	X	196
Denny Lodge Inclosure	Hants	SU3304	50°50·3'	1°31·5'W	F	196
Denny Muir	Falk	NS7482	56°1·1'	4°0·8'W	X	57,64
Dennystown	W Dunb	NS3975	55°56·7'	4°34·2'W	T	63
Denny Sutton Hipend	Wilts	SU1557	51°18·9'	1°46·7'W	X	173
Denny Wood	Hants	SU3306	50°51·4'	1°31·5'W	F	196
Den of Altduthrie	Angus	NO2478	56°53·5'	3°14·4'W	X	44
Den of Glasslaw	Aberd	NJ8559	57°37·5'	2°14·6'W	X	30
Den of Lindores	Fife	NO2517	56°20·6'	3°12·4'W	T	59
Den of Morphie	Aberd	NO7165	56°46·8'	2°28·0'W	X	45
Den of Muck	Aberd	NJ8260	57°38·0'	2°17·6'W	X	29,30
Den of Noub	Shetld	HU4686	60°33·6'	1°9·2'W	X	1,2,3
Den of Ogil Reservoir	Angus	NO4361	56°44·5'	2°55·5'W	W	44
Den of Pitlurg	Moray	NJ4345	57°29·8'	2°56·6'W	X	28
Den of Welton	Pth & Kin	NO2049	56°37·8'	3°17·8'W	X	53
Den o'Howie	Aberd	NJ9750	57°32·7'	2°2·5'W	X	30
Den o'Howie	Aberd	NJ9832	57°23·0'	2°1·5'W	X	30
Denoon Law	Angus	NO3544	56°35·3'	3°3·1'W	H	54
Denoon Law (fort)	Angus	NO3544	56°35·3'	3°3·1'W	A	54
Denork	Fife	NO4513	56°18·6'	2°52·9'W	X	59
Denovan	Falk	NS8283	56°1·8'	3°53·2'W	X	57,65
Den Point	Pemb	SS1496	51°38·2'	4°40·9'W	X	158
Dens	Aberd	NJ8642	57°28·3'	2°13·5'W	X	30
Dens	Aberd	NK0744	57°29·4'	1°52·5'W	X	30
Dens Burn	Shetld	HU4794	60°37·9'	1°8·0'W	W	1,2
Dens Fm	E Susx	TQ6428	51°1·9'	0°20·7'E	FM	188,199
Densham	Devon	SS6312	50°53·7'	3°56·5'W	X	180
Densham Fm	Dorset	ST6711	50°54·1'	2°27·8'W	FM	194
Denshaw	Oldham	SD9710	53°35·4'	2°2·3'W	T	109
Denshaw Moor	Oldham	SD9912	53°36·5'	2°0·5'W	X	109
Denside	Aberd	NO7181	56°55·4'	2°28·1'W	X	45
Denside	Aberd	NO8095	57°3·0'	2°19·3'W	T	38,45
Denside	Angus	NO4845	56°35·9'	2°50·4'W	X	54
Denside	Moray	NJ4967	57°41·7'	2°50·9'W	X	28,29
Denside Davo	Aberd	NO7673	56°51·1'	2°23·2'W	X	45
Dens of Crichie	Aberd	NJ9645	57°30·0'	2°3·5'W	X	30
Dens of Muiryhill	Aberd	NJ6457	57°36·4'	2°35·7'W	X	29
Densole	Kent	TR2141	51°7·8'	1°9·9'E	T	179,189
Denspark	Aberd	NJ5849	57°32·0'	2°41·6'W	X	29
Denstead Fm	Kent	TR1057	51°16·6'	1°1·1'E	FM	179
Denstead Wood	Kent	TR0856	51°16·1'	0°59·3'E	F	179
Denston	Suff	TL7652	52°8·5'	0°34·7'E	T	155
Denstone	Staffs	SK0940	52°57·7'	1°51·6'W	T	119,128
Denstone College	Staffs	SK0940	52°57·7'	1°51·6'W	X	119,128
Denstrath	Aberd	NO6369	56°48·9'	2°35·9'W	X	45
Denstroude	Kent	TR1061	51°18·8'	1°1·2'E	T	179
Denstroude Fm	Kent	TR0961	51°18·8'	1°0·3'E	FM	179
Densworth	W Susx	SU8207	50°51·6'	0°49·7'W	X	197
Dent	Cumbr	NY0313	54°30·4'	3°29·5'W	H	89
Dent	Cumbr	SD7086	54°16·4'	2°27·2'W	T	98
Dent Bank	Durham	NY9326	54°38·0'	2°6·1'W	T	91,92
Dent Cottage	Cumbr	NY0212	54°29·9'	3°30·4'W	X	89
Dentdale	Cumbr	SD7186	54°16·4'	2°26·3'W	X	98
Denters Hill	Suff	TM1064	52°14·3'	1°4·9'E	X	155
Dent Fell	Cumbr	SD7886	54°16·4'	2°19·9'W	X	98
Dent Gate Fm	Durham	NZ0722	54°35·8'	1°53·1'W	FM	92
Den, The	Aberd	NJ4515	57°13·6'	2°54·2'W	X	37
Den, The	Aberd	NJ6315	57°13·7'	2°36·3'W	X	37
Den, The	Corn	SX1898	50°45·4'	4°34·4'W	X	190
Den, The	Highld	NH6863	57°38·5'	4°12·2'W	X	21
Den, The	Pth & Kin	NO2430	56°27·6'	3°13·6'W	X	53
Den, The	W Loth	NT0776	55°58·3'	3°29·0'W	X	65
Dent Head Fm	Cumbr	SD7784	54°15·3'	2°20·8'W	FM	98
Dent House Fm	Durham	NZ0413	54°31·0'	1°55·9'W	FM	92
Dentibert Well	E Ayr	NS5632	55°33·9'	4°16·6'W	W	71
Denton	Cambs	TL1487	52°28·4'	0°18·9'W	T	142
Denton	Darl	NZ2118	54°33·7'	1°40·1'W	T	93
Denton	E Susx	TQ4502	50°48·2'	0°3·9'E	T	198
Denton	Kent	TQ6673	51°26·1'	0°23·7'E	T	177,178
Denton	Kent	TR2147	51°11·0'	1°10·1'E	T	179,189
Denton	Lincs	SK8632	52°52·9'	0°42·9'W	T	130
Denton	Norf	TM2788	52°26·8'	1°20·8'E	T	156
Denton	Northnts	SP8358	52°13·1'	0°46·7'W	T	152
Denton	N Yks	SE1448	53°55·9'	1°46·8'W	T	104
Denton	Oxon	SP5902	51°43·0'	1°8·4'W	T	164
Denton	Tames	SJ9295	53°27·3'	2°6·8'W	T	109
Denton Burn	N upon Ty	NZ1965	54°59·0'	1°41·8'W	T	88
Denton Court	Kent	TR2146	51°10·4'	1°10·1'E	X	179,189
Denton Cross Roads	Darl	NZ2118	54°33·7'	1°40·1'W	X	93
Denton Fell	Cumbr	NY6262	54°57·3'	2°35·2'W	X	86
Denton Fm	Cambs	TL1989	52°29·4'	0°14·4'W	FM	142
Denton Foot	Cumbr	NY5762	54°57·3'	2°39·9'W	X	86
Denton Grange	Darl	NZ2119	54°34·2'	1°40·1'W	X	93
Denton Hall	Cumbr	NY5763	54°57·8'	2°39·9'W	A	86
Denton Hill	E Susx	TQ4803	50°48·7'	0°6·4'E	X	198
Denton Ho	Cumbr	NY5862	54°57·3'	2°38·9'W	X	86
Denton Ho	Oxon	SP5902	51°43·0'	1°8·4'W	A	164
Denton Holme	Cumbr	NY4054	54°52·9'	2°55·7'W	T	85
Denton House	Norf	TM2886	52°25·7'	1°21·6'E	X	156
Denton Lodge	Norf	TL7591	52°29·6'	0°35·1'E	X	143
Denton Lodge	Norf	TM2987	52°26·2'	1°22·5'E	X	156
Denton Lodge	Northnts	SP8357	52°12·5'	0°46·7'W	X	152
Denton Lodge Fm	Cambs	TL1688	52°28·9'	0°17·1'W	FM	142
Denton Lodge Fm	Lincs	SK8533	52°53·5'	0°43·8'W	FM	130
Denton Mains	Cumbr	NY6065	54°58·9'	2°37·1'W	X	86
Denton Moor	N Yks	SE1451	53°57·5'	1°46·8'W	X	104
Denton Park	N Yks	SE1448	53°55·9'	1°46·8'W	X	104
Denton Reservoir	Lincs	SK8733	52°53·5'	0°42·0'W	W	130
Denton's Fm	Norf	TF6813	52°41·5'	0°29·6'E	FM	132,143
Denton's Green	St Hel	SJ4996	53°27·7'	2°45·7'W	T	108
Denton Side	Cumbr	NY3540	54°45·3'	3°0·2'W	X	85
Dentonwash Fm	Norf	TM2987	52°26·2'	1°22·5'E	FM	156
Dentonwood Lodge	Northnts	SP8456	52°12·0'	0°45·9'W	X	152
Dent Sta	Cumbr	SD7687	54°16·9'	2°21·7'W	X	98
Denture, The	W Susx	SU9811	50°53·6'	0°36·0'W	X	197
Denver	Norf	TF6101	52°35·2'	0°23·0'E	T	143
Denver Sluice	Norf	TF5901	52°35·2'	0°21·2'E	X	143
Denville Hall	Hill	TQ0791	51°36·7'	0°26·9'W	X	176
Denvilles	Hants	SU7206	50°51·2'	0°58·2'W	T	197
Denwell	Aberd	NJ6209	57°10·5'	2°37·3'W	X	37
Denwell	Aberd	NJ6329	57°21·3'	2°36·4'W	X	37
Denwick	Northum	NU2014	55°25·4'	1°40·6'W	T	81
Denwick	Orkney	HY5708	58°57·7'	2°44·4'W	X	6
Den Wick	Orkney	HY5809	58°58·2'	2°43·3'W	W	6
Denwick Burn	Northum	NU2014	55°25·4'	1°40·6'W	W	81
Denwick Lane End	Northum	NU2116	55°26·5'	1°39·7'W	X	81
Den Wood	Aberd	NJ7436	57°25·1'	2°25·5'W	F	29
Den Wood	Aberd	NJ7756	57°35·9'	2°22·6'W	F	29,30
Den Wood	Aberd	NJ8030	57°21·9'	2°19·5'W	F	29,30
Denyers Barn	Leic	SP5680	52°25·1'	1°10·2'W	X	140
Denzell	Corn	SW8866	50°27·6'	4°58·8'W	X	200
Denzell Downs	Corn	SW9067	50°28·2'	4°57·2'W	H	200
Deopham	Norf	TG0500	52°33·8'	1°1·9'E	T	144
Deopham Green	Norf	TM0499	52°33·3'	1°1·0'E	T	144
Deopham Stalland	Norf	TM0399	52°33·3'	1°0·1'E	T	144
Depden	Suff	TL7757	52°11·2'	0°35·8'E	T	155
Depden Green	Suff	TL7757	52°11·2'	0°35·8'E	T	155
Depedene	Hants	SU4007	50°51·9'	1°25·5'W	X	196
Depperhaugh, The	Suff	TM2076	52°20·5'	1°14·2'E	X	156
Depperhaugh Wood	Suff	TM2175	52°19·9'	1°15·0'E	F	156
Deppers Bridge	Warw	SP3959	52°13·9'	1°25·3'W	T	151
Deptford	Devon	SS2618	50°56·3'	4°28·2'W	X	190
Deptford	Devon	SS6018	50°56·9'	3°59·2'W	X	180
Deptford	Devon	SS6224	51°0·2'	3°57·6'W	X	180
Deptford	Lew	TQ3677	51°28·8'	0°2·1'W	T	177
Deptford	Sund	NZ3857	54°54·6'	1°24·0'W	T	88
Deptford	Wilts	SU0138	51°8·7'	1°58·8'W	T	184
Deptford Down	Wilts	SU0140	51°9·8'	1°58·8'W	X	184
Deptford Field Barn	Wilts	SU0139	51°9·2'	1°58·8'W	X	184
Deptford Fm	Devon	SS8412	50°54·0'	3°38·6'W	FM	181
Deputy Row	Northum	NU0049	55°44·3'	1°59·6'W	X	75
Derachie	Angus	NO4460	56°44·0'	2°54·5'W	X	44
Derbeth	C of Aber	NJ8608	57°10·0'	2°13·4'W	X	38
Derbies Court	Kent	TQ9554	51°15·3'	0°48·1'E	X	189
Derby	C of Derb	SK3535	52°54·9'	1°28·4'W	T	128
Derby	Devon	SS5633	51°4·9'	4°3·0'W	T	180
Derby	Pemb	SM9513	51°46·9'	4°57·9'W	X	157,158
Derby Cycle Route	C of Derb	SK3530	52°52·2'	1°28·4'W	X	128
Derby Fen	Norf	TF7020	52°45·3'	0°31·6'E	X	132
Derby Fort	I of M	SC2967	54°4·5'	4°36·4'W	A	95
Derbyhaven	I of M	SC2867	54°4·5'	4°37·3'W	T	95
Derby Haven	I of M	SC2967	54°4·5'	4°36·4'W	W	95
Derby Hill	Lancs	SD3934	53°48·2'	2°55·2'W	X	102
Derby Hills House Fm	Derby	SK3724	52°49·0'	1°26·7'W	FM	128
Derby Park	Flint	SJ3059	53°7·7'	3°2·4'W	X	117
Derbyshire Br	Derby	SK0171	53°14·4'	1°58·7'W	X	119
Derbyshire Hill	St Hel	SJ5494	53°26·7'	2°41·1'W	T	108
Derclach Loch	S Ayr	NX4499	55°15·9'	4°26·9'W	W	77
Derculich	Pth & Kin	NN8852	56°39·0'	3°49·2'W	X	52
Derculich Burn	Pth & Kin	NN8753	56°39·6'	3°50·2'W	W	52
Deregar	Orkney	ND2797	58°51·5'	3°15·4'W	X	6,7
Dereneneach	N Ayr	NR9333	55°33·1'	5°16·5'W	X	68,69
Dererach	Arg & Bt	NM5129	56°23·5'	6°1·6'W	X	48
Dere Street (Roman Road)	Darl	NZ2116	54°32·6'	1°40·1'W	R	93
Dere Street (Roman Road)	Durham	NZ1448	54°49·8'	1°46·5'W	R	88
Dere Street (Roman Road)	Northum	NY8693	55°14·1'	2°12·8'W	R	80
Dere Street (Roman Road)	Northum	NY9963	54°57·9'	2°0·5'W	R	87
Dere Street (Roman Road)	N Yks	SE3478	54°12·0'	1°28·3'W	R	99
Dere Street (Roman Road)	Scot Bord	NT6425	55°31·3'	2°33·8'W	R	74
Dere Street (Roman Road)	Scot Bord	NT7513	55°24·9'	2°23·2'W	R	80
Dergoals	D & G	NX2459	54°53·9'	4°44·3'W	X	82
Dergoals Burn	D & G	NX2458	54°53·4'	4°44·2'W	W	82
Dergoals Moss	D & G	NX2560	54°54·5'	4°43·4'W	X	82
Dergoed	Denb	SJ2046	53°0·6'	3°11·1'W	X	117
Deri	Caer	SO1201	51°42·3'	3°16·0'W	T	171
Deri	Carm	SN4131	51°57·5'	4°18·5'W	X	146
Deri	Monm	SO2917	51°51·1'	3°1·5'W	X	161
Dericambus	Pth & Kin	NN6647	56°36·0'	4°10·5'W	X	51
Deri-fach	Monm	SO2717	51°51·0'	3°3·2'W	X	161
Deri-Garon	Cered	SN6559	52°13·0'	3°58·2'W	X	146
Deri-isaf	I of Angl	SH4687	53°21·7'	4°18·4'W	X	114
Deri Lodge Wood	Cered	SN5953	52°9·7'	4°3·3'W	F	146
Deri Merddog	Blae Gw	SO1904	51°44·0'	3°10·0'W	X	171
Dering Fm	Kent	TQ8942	51°9·0'	0°42·5'E	FM	189
Dering Wood	Kent	TQ8944	51°10·1'	0°42·6'E	F	189
Deri-Odwyn	Cered	SN6460	52°13·5'	3°59·1'W	X	146
Derllys Court	Carm	SN3520	51°51·5'	4°23·4'W	X	145,159
Derlwyn	Caer	SO1404	51°43·9'	3°14·3'W	X	171
Derlwyn	Carm	SN5544	52°4·8'	4°6·6'W	X	146
Derlwyn	Carm	SN6243	52°4·3'	4°0·4'W	X	146
Derlwyn	Cered	SN4442	52°3·5'	4°16·2'W	X	146
Derlwyn	Cered	SN6359	52°13·0'	3°59·9'W	X	146
Derlwyn	Cered	SN6660	52°13·6'	3°57·3'W	X	146
Derlwyn	Gwyn	SH5858	53°6·3'	4°6·9'W	X	115
Derlwyn	Powys	SN9598	52°34·4'	3°32·6'W	X	136
Derlwyn Fm	Carm	SN4430	51°57·0'	4°15·8'W	FM	146
Derm	Conwy	SH9769	53°12·7'	3°32·1'W	X	116
Dernaglar Loch	D & G	NX2658	54°53·4'	4°42·4'W	W	82
Dern Craig	D & G	NS8907	55°20·9'	3°44·6'W	X	71,78
Derndale	Heref	SO4749	52°8·4'	2°46·1'W	X	148,149
Derndale Hill	Heref	SO4749	52°8·4'	2°46·1'W	X	148,149
Dernford Fm	Cambs	TL4650	52°8·0'	0°8·4'E	FM	154

Dernol	Powys	SN9174	52°21·4′	3°35·6′W	X	136,147
Derrickhill	Suff	TM0749	52°6·3′	1°1·8′E	X	155,169
Derrie	D & G	NX3250	54°49·3′	4°36·5′W	X	82
Derriford	C of Plym	SX4959	50°24·9′	4°7·1′W	T	201
Derril	Devon	SS3003	50°48·3′	4°24·4′W	T	190
Derril Water	Devon	SS3001	50°47·3′	4°24·3′W	W	190
Derrings Beck	N Yks	SE4668	54°6·6′	1°17·4′W	W	100
Derrings Fm	N Yks	SE4568	54°6·6′	1°18·3′W	FM	99
Derrings Fm	N Yks	SE4667	54°6·1′	1°17·4′W	FM	100
Derringstone	Kent	TR2049	51°12·1′	1°9·3′E	T	179,189
Derrington	Shrops	SO6090	52°30·6′	2°35·0′W	T	138
Derrington	Staffs	SJ8922	52°48·0′	2°9·4′W	T	127
Derriton	Devon	SS3303	50°48·4′	4°21·8′W	T	190
Derriton	Devon	SX4176	50°34·0′	4°14·3′W	X	201
Derry	D & G	NX2673	55°1·5′	4°42·9′W	X	76
Derry	Stir	NN6424	56°23·6′	4°11·7′W	X	51
Derryards Fm	Glos	SO9106	51°45·4′	2°7·4′W	FM	163
Derrybeg	Moray	NJ2439	57°26·4′	3°15·5′W	X	28
Derry Brook	Wilts	SU0492	51°37·8′	1°56·1′W	W	163,173
Derry Burn	Aberd	NO0397	57°3·5′	3°35·5′W	W	36,43
Derry Cairngorm	Aberd	NO0198	57°4·0′	3°37·5′W	H	36,43
Derrydaroch	Stir	NN3521	56°21·4′	4°39·8′W	X	50,56
Derrydown Fm	Hants	SU4249	51°14·5′	1°23·5′W	FM	185
Derry Downs	Brom	TQ4767	51°23·2′	0°7·2′E	T	177
Derry Fields	Wilts	SU0493	51°38·4′	1°56·1′W	T	163,173
Derryguaig	Arg & Bt	NM4835	56°26·7′	6°4·9′W	X	47,48
Derry Hall	Carm	SN2917	51°49·8′	4°28·5′W	X	159
Derry Hill	Wilts	ST9570	51°26·0′	2°3·9′W	T	173
Derry Hill Fm	Brad	SE1643	53°53·2′	1°45·0′W	FM	104
Derrylane	Moray	NJ2139	57°26·3′	3°18·5′W	X	28
Derry Lodge	Aberd	NO0493	57°1·3′	3°34·4′W	X	36,43
Derrynaculen	Arg & Bt	NM5629	56°23·7′	5°56·8′W	X	48
Derry Ormond Park	Cered	SN5952	52°9·1′	4°3·3′W	X	146
Derry's Wood	Herts	TL3105	51°43·9′	0°5·8′W	F	166
Derry's Wood	Surrey	TQ0345	51°11·9′	0°31·2′W	F	186
Derrythorpe	N Lincs	SE8208	53°34·0′	0°45·3′W	T	112
Derrythorpe Grange	N Lincs	SE8208	53°34·0′	0°45·3′W	X	112
Derry Wood	Pth & Kin	NN6524	56°23·6′	4°10·8′W	F	51
Derry Woods	Wilts	ST9571	51°26·5′	2°3·9′W	F	173
Dersalloch Hill	S Ayr	NS4203	55°18·0′	4°28·9′W	H	77
Dersingham	Norf	TF6830	52°50·7′	0°30·1′E	T	132
Dersingham Bog	Norf	TF6728	52°49·6′	0°29·1′E	F	132
Dersingham Wood	Norf	TF6929	52°50·1′	0°30·9′E	F	132
Derskelpin	D & G	NX2558	54°53·4′	4°43·3′W	X	82
Dertfords	Wilts	ST8145	51°12·5′	2°15·9′W	T	183
Dertford's Wood	Wilts	ST8144	51°11·9′	2°15·9′W	F	183
Dertley Plain	Wilts	ST8341	51°10·3′	2°14·2′W	X	183
Dervaig	Arg & Bt	NM4352	56°35·6′	6°10·7′W	T	47
Dervaird	D & G	NX2258	54°53·4′	4°46·1′W	X	82
Dervaird Loch	D & G	NX2358	54°53·4′	4°45·2′W	W	82
Derval Fm	Corn	SW4130	50°7·1′	5°37·0′W	FM	203
Derventio Roman Fort	Cumbr	NY1031	54°40·2′	3°23·3′W	R	89
Derwas	Gwyn	SH7017	52°44·3′	3°55·1′W	X	124
Derwen	Brig	SS9182	51°31·8′	3°33·9′W	T	170
Derwen	Carm	SN5914	51°48·7′	4°2·3′W	X	159
Derwen	Denb	SJ0650	53°2·6′	3°23·7′W	T	116
Derwen	Powys	SJ2110	52°41·2′	3°9·7′W	X	126
Derwendeg	Carm	SN8135	52°0·3′	3°43·6′W	X	160
Derwen-dêg	Powys	SJ2229	52°51·4′	3°9·1′W	X	126
Derwendeg Fm	Carm	SN5417	51°50·2′	4°6·8′W	FM	159
Derwen Fawr Fm	Carm	SN6539	52°2·2′	3°57·7′W	FM	146
Derwen Fm	Shrops	SJ3337	52°55·8′	2°59·4′W	FM	126
Derwen Hall	Denb	SJ0951	53°3·2′	3°21·1′W	X	116
Derwenlas	Powys	SN7299	52°34·7′	3°52·9′W	T	135
Derwent	Derby	SK1888	53°23·6′	1°43·4′W	X	110
Derwent Bank	Cumbr	NY2522	54°35·5′	3°9·2′W	X	89,90
Derwent Bay	Cumbr	NY2521	54°35·0′	3°9·2′W	W	89,90
Derwent Br	N Yks	SE7036	53°49·2′	0°55·8′W	X	105,106
Derwent Bridge	Northum	NZ0351	54°51·5′	1°56·8′W	X	87
Derwentcote Steel Furnace	Durham	NZ1356	54°54·2′	1°47·4′W	X	88
Derwent Cottage Fm	N Yks	SE7036	53°49·2′	0°55·8′W	FM	105,106
Derwent Dale	Derby	SK1690	53°24·6′	1°45·1′W	X	110
Derwentdale Fm	N Yks	SE9982	54°13·7′	0°28·5′W	FM	101
Derwent Edge	Derby	SK1988	53°23·5′	1°42·4′W	X	110
Derwent Fells	Cumbr	NY2217	54°32·8′	3°11·9′W	X	89,90
Derwent Fm	N Yks	SE8879	54°12·2′	0°38·6′W	FM	101
Derwentfolds	Cumbr	NY2925	54°37·2′	3°5·6′W	X	89,90
Derwent Grange	Durham	NZ0649	54°50·4′	1°54·0′W	X	87
Derwent House	N Yks	SE9479	54°12·1′	0°33·1′W	X	101
Derwent Isle	Cumbr	NY2622	54°35·5′	3°8·3′W	X	89,90
Derwent Moors	Derby	SK2088	53°23·5′	1°41·5′W	X	110
Derwent Reservoir	Derby	SK1691	53°25·2′	1°45·1′W	W	110
Derwent Reservoir	Durham	NZ0152	54°52·0′	1°58·6′W	W	87
Derwent Walk	Durham	NZ1556	54°54·2′	1°45·5′W	X	88
Derwent Walk Country Park	Ghead	NZ1962	54°57·4′	1°41·8′W	X	88
Derwent Water	Cumbr	NY2521	54°35·0′	3°9·2′W	W	89,90
Derwgoed	Gwyn	SH9738	52°56·0′	3°31·5′W	X	125
Derwin Bach	Gwyn	SH4745	52°59·1′	4°16·3′W	X	115,123
Derwllwydion	Powys	SN9190	52°30·1′	3°35·9′W	X	136
Derwydd	Carm	SN6117	51°50·3′	4°0·7′W	A	159
Derwyn-fawr	Gwyn	SH4746	52°59·6′	4°16·4′W	X	115,123
Derybruich	Arg & Bt	NR9370	55°53·0′	5°18·1′W	X	62
Deryn Castle	Corn	SW9038	50°12·5′	4°56·2′W	A	204
Derz-Fawr	I of Angl	SH4587	53°21·7′	4°19·4′W	X	114
Desborough	Northnts	SP8083	52°26·6′	0°49·0′W	T	141
Desborough Castle	Bucks	SU8493	51°38·0′	0°46·8′W	A	175
Desford	Leic	SK4703	52°37·6′	1°17·9′W	T	140
Deskie	Aberd	NJ4720	57°16·3′	2°52·3′W	X	37
Deskie	Moray	NJ2030	57°21·5′	3°19·3′W	X	36
Deskry	Aberd	NJ3812	57°11·9′	3°1·1′W	X	37
Deskryshiel	Aberd	NJ4010	57°10·9′	2°59·1′W	X	37
Deskry Water	Aberd	NJ4111	57°11·4′	2°58·1′W	W	37
Desmesne Fm	Lancs	SD8352	53°58·1′	2°15·1′W	FM	103
Desnage Lodge	Suff	TL7367	52°16·7′	0°32·6′E	X	155
Desning Hall	Suff	TL7363	52°14·5′	0°32·4′E	X	155
Desoglin	Cumbr	NY5767	55°0·0′	2°39·9′W	X	86
Desolate	Devon	SS7749	51°13·9′	3°45·3′W	X	180

Dess Ho	Aberd	NJ5700	57°5·6′	2°42·1′W	X	37
De Sully Grange	V of Glam	ST1668	51°24·5′	3°12·1′W	X	171
De Tabley Arms (Inn)	Lancs	SD6635	53°48·9′	2°30·6′W	X	103
Detchant	Northum	NU0836	55°37·3′	1°51·9′W	T	75
Detchant Coalhouses	Northum	NU0734	55°36·2′	1°52·9′W	X	75
Detchant Lodge	Northum	NU0936	55°37·3′	1°51·0′W	X	75
Detchant Park	Northum	NU0837	55°37·8′	1°51·9′W	X	75
Detchant Wood	Northum	NU0636	55°37·3′	1°53·8′W	F	75
Dethenydd	Powys	SO0283	52°26·4′	3°26·1′W	X	136
Dethick	Derby	SK3258	53°7·3′	1°30·9′W	X	119
Dethick Common	Derby	SK3359	53°7·9′	1°30·0′W	X	119
Detling	Kent	TQ7958	51°17·8′	0°34·4′E	T	178,188
Detmore Ho	Glos	SO9720	51°52·9′	2°2·2′W	X	163
Detton Hall	Shrops	SO6679	52°24·7′	2°29·6′W	X	138
Deuchar	Angus	NO4662	56°45·0′	2°52·5′W	T	44
Deuchar	Scot Bord	NT3528	55°32·7′	3°1·4′W	X	73
Deuchar Hill	Angus	NO4662	56°45·0′	2°52·5′W	H	44
Deuchar Hill	Scot Bord	NT3628	55°32·7′	3°0·4′W	H	73
Deuchar Law	Scot Bord	NT2829	55°33·2′	3°8·0′W	H	73
Deuchary Hill	Pth & Kin	NO0348	56°37·1′	3°34·4′W	H	52,53
Deucheran Hill	Arg & Bt	NR7644	55°38·5′	5°33·1′W	H	62,69
Deuchny Wood	Pth & Kin	NO1523	56°23·8′	3°22·2′W	F	53,58
Deuchrie	E Loth	NT6271	55°56·1′	2°36·1′W	X	67
Deuchrie Dod	E Loth	NT6272	55°56·7′	2°36·1′W	H	67
Deuchrie Edge	E Loth	NT6370	55°55·6′	2°35·1′W	X	67
Deuchries	Aberd	NJ6919	57°15·9′	2°30·4′W	X	38
Deuchrie Wood	E Loth	NT6371	55°56·1′	2°35·1′W	F	67
Deuddwr	Powys	SJ2417	52°45·0′	3°7·2′W	X	126
Deuddwr Brook	Powys	SO1578	52°23·8′	3°14·6′W	W	136,148
Deudney's Fm	E Susx	TQ6112	50°53·3′	0°17·7′E	FM	199
Deuffrwd	Powys	SN9351	52°9·1′	3°33·4′W	W	147
Deuglawdd	Gwyn	SH1727	52°48·8′	4°42·5′W	X	123
Deunant	Conwy	SH8173	53°14·7′	3°46·6′W	X	116
Deunant-isaf	Conwy	SH9665	53°10·6′	3°33·0′W	X	116
Deunant Uchaf	Conwy	SH9664	53°10·0′	3°32·9′W	X	116
Deuxhill	Shrops	SO6987	52°29·0′	2°27·0′W	T	138
Deva (Chester)	Ches	SJ4066	53°11·5′	2°53·5′W	R	117
Devauden	Monm	ST4898	51°40·9′	2°44·7′W	T	171
Devauden Court	Monm	ST4798	51°40·9′	2°45·6′W	X	171
Devenden	Kent	TQ8230	51°2·7′	0°36·2′E	X	188
Devenish Pitt Fm	Devon	SY1795	50°45·2′	3°10·2′W	FM	192,193
Deveral	Corn	SW5935	50°10·2′	5°22·1′W	T	203
Deverel Down	Dorset	SY8199	50°47·6′	2°15·8′W	X	194
Deverel Fm	Dorset	SY8098	50°47·1′	2°16·6′W	FM	194
Devereux Wootton	Heref	SO3848	52°7·8′	2°54·0′W	X	148,149
Devichoys Wood	Corn	SW7737	50°11·7′	5°7·1′W	F	204
Devilla Forest	Fife	NS9588	56°4·7′	3°40·8′W	F	65
Devilly Burn	Aberd	NO6774	56°51·6′	2°32·0′W	W	45
Devil's Apronful, The	N Yks	SE0759	54°1·9′	1°53·2′W	X	104
Devil's Apronful, The (Cairn)	N Yks	SE0759	54°1·9′	1°53·2′W	A	104
Devil's Arrows	N Yks	SE3966	54°5·5′	1°23·8′W	A	99
Devil's Bank	Liv	SJ3685	53°21·7′	2°57·3′W	X	108
Devils Bed and Bolster, The	Somer	ST8153	51°16·8′	2°16·0′W	A	183
Devil's Beef Tub	D & G	NT0612	55°23·8′	3°28·6′W	H	78
Devil's Bridge	Devon	SX5872	50°32·1′	3°59·8′W	X	191
Devil's Bridge	D & G	NX4634	54°40·9′	4°22·9′W	X	83
Devil's Bridge	Swan	SS3887	51°33·8′	4°19·8′W	X	159
Devil's Bridge (Pontarfynach)	Cered	SN7376	52°22·3′	3°51·5′W	T	135,147
Devil's Brook	Dorset	SY7798	50°47·1′	2°19·2′W	W	194
Devil's Burdens	Fife	NO1906	56°14·6′	3°18·0′W	X	58
Devil's Causeway	N Lincs	SE8924	53°42·5′	0°38·7′W	X	106,112
Devil's Causeway	Northum	NU1201	55°18·4′	1°48·2′W	X	81
Devil's Causeway (Roman Road)	Northum	NU0044	55°41·6′	1°59·6′W	R	75
Devil's Causeway (Roman Road)	Northum	NU0326	55°31·9′	1°56·7′W	R	75
Devil's Causeway (Roman Road)	Northum	NU1201	55°18·4′	1°48·2′W	R	81
Devil's Causeway (Roman Road)	Northum	NZ0478	55°6·0′	1°55·8′W	R	87
Devil's Chair	Shrops	SO3698	52°34·8′	2°56·3′W	X	137
Devil's Chimney	Glos	SO9418	51°51·9′	2°4·8′W	X	163
Devil's Churchyard	Glos	SO8900	51°42·2′	2°9·2′W	F	163
Devils Copse	W Susx	SU7807	50°51·7′	0°53·1′W	F	197
Devil's Den	Kent	TQ4345	51°11·4′	0°3·2′E	X	187
Devil's Den	Kent	TQ7947	51°11·9′	0°34·1′E	X	188
Devil's Den	Staffs	SO8685	52°28·0′	2°12·0′W	X	139
Devil's Den	Surrey	TQ3742	51°9·9′	0°2·0′W	X	187
Devil's Den	Wilts	SU1569	51°25·4′	1°46·7′W	A	173
Devil's Den (Moat)	Kent	TQ4345	51°11·4′	0°3·2′E	A	187
Devil's Dike	Derby	SK0993	53°26·3′	1°51·5′W	W	110
Devil's Ditch	Cambs	TL6062	52°14·2′	0°21·0′E	A	154
Devil's Ditch	Hants	SU3651	51°15·7′	1°28·7′W	A	185
Devil's Ditch	Hants	SU4048	51°14·0′	1°25·2′W	A	185
Devil's Ditch	Herts	TL1208	51°45·8′	0°22·2′W	A	166
Devil's Ditch	Norf	TL9882	52°24·2′	0°55·0′E	A	144
Devil's Ditch	Oxon	SU5682	51°32·3′	1°11·2′W	A	174
Devil's Ditch	Wilts	SU2145	51°12·5′	1°41·6′W	A	184
Devil's Ditch, The	W Susx	SU8708	50°52·1′	0°45·4′W	A	197
Devil's Dressing Room, The	Staffs	SK1603	52°37·7′	1°45·4′W	F	139
Devil's Dyke	Norf	TF7408	52°38·7′	0°34·7′E	A	143
Devil's Dyke	W Susx	TQ2611	50°53·3′	0°12·1′W	X	198
Devil's Dyke Fm	W Susx	TQ2610	50°52·8′	0°12·1′W	FM	198
Devil's Dyke (Fort)	W Susx	TQ2611	50°53·3′	0°12·1′W	A	198
Devil's Elbow	Derby	SK0497	53°28·4′	1°56·0′W	X	110
Devil's Elbow	Derby	SK2434	52°54·4′	1°38·2′W	X	128
Devil's Elbow	Leic	SK4924	52°48·9′	1°16·0′W	X	129
Devil's Elbow	Notts	SK6631	52°52·6′	1°0·8′W	W	129
Devil's Elbow	Pth & Kin	NO1476	56°52·3′	3°24·2′W	X	43
Devil's Frying-pan	Corn	SW7214	49°59·2′	5°10·5′W	X	204
Devil's Gallop	Cumbr	SD3694	54°20·5′	2°58·6′W	X	96,97
Devil's Highway, The (Roman Road)	Wok	SU7863	51°21·9′	0°52·4′W	R	175,186
Devil's Hill	Oxon	SU7089	51°36·0′	0°59·0′W	X	175
Devil's Hill	Suff	TM0158	52°11·2′	0°56·8′E	X	155

Devil's Hill Wood	Suff	TL9652	52°8·1′	0°52·2′E	F	155
Devil's Jump	Corn	SX1079	50°35·0′	4°40·7′W	X	200
Devil's Jumps	W Susx	SU8217	50°57·0′	0°49·6′W	X	197
Devil's Jumps, The	Surrey	SU8639	51°8·9′	0°45·8′W	X	186
Devil's Kitchen or Twll Du	Gwyn	SH6458	53°6·4′	4°1·5′W	X	115
Devil's Lapful	Northum	NY6492	55°13·5′	2°33·5′W	X	80
Devil's Lapful (Long Cairn)	Northum	NY6492	55°13·5′	2°33·5′W	A	80
Devil's Leap	Worcs	SO7456	52°12·3′	2°22·4′W	X	150
Devil's Mouth	Shrops	SO4494	52°32·7′	2°49·1′W	X	137
Devil's Mouthpiece, The	Shrops	SO5282	52°26·3′	2°42·0′W	X	137,138
Devils Point	C of Plym	SX4553	50°21·6′	4°10·4′W	X	201
Devil's Point, The	Aberd	NN9795	57°2·3′	3°41·4′W	H	36,43
Devil's Pulpit	Glos	ST5499	51°41·5′	2°39·5′W	X	162
Devil's Punchbowl	Norf	TL8789	52°28·2′	0°45·6′E	X	144
Devil's Punchbowl	Oxon	SU3584	51°33·5′	1°29·3′W	X	174
Devil's Punch Bowl	Somer	ST5453	51°16·7′	2°39·2′W	X	182,183
Devil's Punch Bowl	Surrey	SU8936	51°7·2′	0°43·3′W	X	186
Devil's Quoit	Pemb	SR9696	51°37·8′	4°56·5′W	X	158
Devil's Quoit (Standing Stone)	Pemb	SR9696	51°37·8′	4°56·5′W	A	158
Devil's Quoit,The	Pemb	SM8800	51°39·8′	5°3·5′W	X	157,158
Devils Quoit,The	Pemb	SR9895	51°37·3′	4°54·7′W	A	158
Devils Quoit,The	Pemb	SR9895	51°37·3′	4°54·7′W	X	158
Devil's Quoit,The (Burial Chamber)	Pemb	SM8800	51°39·8′	5°3·5′W	A	157,158
Devil's Ring and Finger	Staffs	SJ7037	52°56·0′	2°26·4′W	A	127
Devil's Spittleful	Worcs	SO8074	52°22·1′	2°17·2′W	X	138
Devil's Staircase	Highld	NN2157	56°40·5′	4°54·8′W	X	41
Devil's Staircase	Powys	SN8355	52°11·1′	3°42·3′W	X	147
Devil's Staircase	Staffs	SK0049	53°2·5′	1°59·6′W	X	119
Devil's Stone	N Yks	SD9488	54°17·5′	2°5·1′W	X	98
Devil's Thrashing Floor	D & G	NX6647	54°48·3′	4°4·7′W	X	83,84
Devil's Tor	Devon	SX5979	50°35·9′	3°59·2′W	X	191
Devil's Water	Northum	NY9253	54°52·5′	2°7·1′W	W	87
Deviock	Corn	SX1068	50°29·1′	4°40·3′W	X	200
Deviock	Corn	SX3155	50°22·5′	4°22·2′W	X	201
Deviock Wood	Corn	SX1067	50°28·6′	4°40·3′W	F	200
Devitts Green	Warw	SP2790	52°30·7′	1°35·7′W	T	140
Devizes	Wilts	SU0061	51°21·1′	1°59·6′W	T	173
Devoke Water	Cumbr	SD1596	54°21·4′	3°18·1′W	W	96
Devol	Inverc	NS3273	55°55·5′	4°40·9′W	T	63
Devol Moor	Inverc	NS3172	55°54·9′	4°41·8′W	X	63
Devon	Fife	NO3405	56°14·2′	3°3·4′W	X	59
Devonburn	S Lanak	NS8338	55°37·5′	3°51·1′W	X	71,72
Devon Common	Fife	NO3305	56°14·2′	3°4·4′W	X	59
Devon Fm	Cambs	TF3700	52°35·1′	0°1·7′E	FM	142,143
Devon Fm	Notts	SK7747	53°1·1′	0°50·7′W	FM	129
Devonhill	S Lanak	NS6852	55°44·9′	4°5·7′W	X	64
Devonknowes	Clackm	NS9396	56°8·9′	3°42·9′W	X	58
Devon Lodge	Devon	SS5607	50°50·9′	4°2·4′W	X	191
Devonport	C of Plym	SX4555	50°22·7′	4°10·4′W	T	201
Devonport Leat	Devon	SX5670	50°31·0′	4°1·5′W	W	202
Devonport Leat	Devon	SX5975	50°33·7′	3°59·1′W	W	191
Devonshaw Fm	Pth & Kin	NT0098	56°10·1′	3°36·2′W	FM	58
Devonshaw Hill	S Lanak	NS9628	55°32·3′	3°38·4′W	H	72
Devonshire Square	Cumbr	NY4339	54°44·8′	2°52·7′W	X	90
Devonshire Wood	N Yks	SE3570	54°7·7′	1°27·4′W	F	99
Devonshire Wood	N Yks	SE3747	53°55·3′	1°25·8′W	F	104
Devonside	Clackm	NS9296	56°8·9′	3°43·9′W	T	58
Devonside	Fife	NT0193	56°7·4′	3°35·1′W	X	58
Devon, The	Leic	SK8332	52°53·0′	0°45·6′W	X	130
Devonvale	Clackm	NS9296	56°8·9′	3°43·9′W	T	58
Devon Village	Clackm	NS9095	56°8·4′	3°45·8′W	T	58
Devon Wood	Fife	NO3405	56°14·2′	3°3·4′W	F	59
Devoran	Corn	SW7939	50°12·8′	5°5·5′W	T	204
Dewar	Scot Bord	NT3448	55°43·5′	3°2·6′W	X	73
Dewar Burn	Scot Bord	NT3448	55°43·5′	3°2·6′W	W	73
Dewar Hill	Scot Bord	NT3547	55°43·0′	3°1·6′W	H	73
Dewars Fm	Oxon	SP5324	51°55·0′	1°13·4′W	FM	164
Dewars Mill	Fife	NO4715	56°19·7′	2°51·0′W	X	59
Dewartown	Midlo	NT3764	55°52·2′	3°0·0′W	T	66
Dew Bottoms	N Yks	SD9169	54°7·3′	2°7·8′W	X	98
Dewell	Heref	SO3853	52°10·5′	2°54·0′W	X	148,149
Dewersit Well	N Yks	SD9882	54°14·3′	2°1·4′W	W	98
Dewerstone Rock	Devon	SX5363	50°27·1′	4°3·9′W	X	201
Dewes Green	Essex	TL4530	51°57·2′	0°7·0′E	T	167
Deweymeads	Corn	SX1673	50°31·9′	4°35·4′W	X	201
Dew Fm	E Susx	TQ8821	50°57·7′	0°41·0′E	FM	189,199
Dewhill Naze	Derby	SE1001	53°30·6′	1°50·5′W	X	110
Dewhurst House	Lancs	SD6636	53°49·4′	2°30·6′W	X	103
Dewhurst Lodge	E Susx	TQ6133	51°4·6′	0°18·3′E	X	188
Dewi Fawr	Carm	SN2927	51°55·2′	4°28·8′W	W	145
Dewlands Common	Dorset	SU0708	50°52·5′	1°53·6′W	T	195
Dewlands Fm	Somer	ST3826	51°2·0′	2°52·7′W	FM	193
Dewland's Fm	Suff	TM0436	51°59·3′	0°58·7′E	FM	155
Dewlaw	Northum	NZ0271	55°2·3′	1°57·7′W	X	87
Dewley Fell	Northum	NY7052	54°52·0′	2°27·6′W	X	86,87
Dewley Field	Northum	NY7051	54°51·4′	2°27·6′W	X	86,87
Dewley Fm	N upon Ty	NZ1667	55°0·1′	1°44·6′W	FM	88
Dewley Hill	N upon Ty	NZ1568	55°0·6′	1°45·5′W	H	88
Dewlish	Dorset	SY7798	50°47·1′	2°19·2′W	T	194
Dewlish Ho	Dorset	SY7797	50°46·6′	2°19·2′W	A	194
Dewsall Court	Heref	SO4833	51°59·8′	2°45·1′W	X	149,161
Dewsbury	Kirk	SE2422	53°41·9′	1°37·8′W	T	104
Dewsbury Moor	Kirk	SE2222	53°41·9′	1°39·6′W	T	104
Dew's Fm	Suff	TM3871	52°17·4′	1°29·8′E	FM	156
Dewsford	Aberd	NJ7614	57°13·2′	2°23·4′W	X	38
Dewsgreen Burn	Northum	NY7657	54°54·7′	2°22·0′W	W	86,87
Dewshill	N Lanak	NS8564	55°51·6′	3°49·8′W	X	65
Dewstow Ho	Monm	ST4688	51°35·5′	2°46·4′W	X	171,172
Dexbeer	Devon	SS2909	50°51·6′	4°25·4′W	X	190
Dexthorpe	Lincs	TF4071	53°13·3′	0°6·2′E	X	122
Deynes Fm	Essex	TL5533	51°58·7′	0°15·8′E	FM	167
Deystone	Aberd	NJ8114	57°13·2′	2°18·4′W	X	38
Dherue	Highld	NC5446	58°23·0′	4°29·3′W	X	10
Dhiseig	Arg & Bt	NM4935	56°26·7′	6°3·9′W	X	47,48
Dhivach Lodge	Highld	NH4927	57°18·8′	4°30·0′W	X	26
Dhoon	I of M	SC3784	54°13·8′	4°29·6′W	X	95
Dhoon	I of M	SC4586	54°15·0′	4°22·3′W	T	95
Dhoon Bay	I of M	SC4686	54°15·0′	4°21·4′W	W	95

Dhoon Glen	I of M	SC4586	54°15·0'	4°22·3'W	X	95
Dhoor	I of M	SC4496	54°20·4'	4°23·6'W	T	95
D House	Suff	TL8675	52°20·7'	0°44·2'E	X	144
Dhowin	I of M	NX4101	54°23·0'	4°26·5'W	X	95
Dhuallow	Highld	NH6426	57°18·5'	4°15·0'W	X	26,35
Dhuhallow	Highld	NH5522	57°16·2'	4°23·8'W	X	26,35
Dhuloch	Highld	ND3448	58°25·2'	3°7·3'W	X	12
Dhu Loch	Pth & Kin	NO0642	56°33·9'	3°31·3'W	W	52,53
Dhu Loch	S Ayr	NX4298	55°15·3'	4°28·7'W	W	77
Dhurrie	Arg & Bt	NR6822	55°26·5'	5°39·6'W	X	68
Dhustone	Shrops	SO5876	52°23·1'	2°36·6'W	T	137,138
Dhu, The	Stir	NN3813	56°17·2'	4°36·6'W	X	50,56
Diabhal	N Eil	NB4552	58°23·2'	6°21·3'W	H	8
Dial Close	Win & Maid	SU8685	51°33·7'	0°45·2'W	X	175
Dial Fm	Norf	TF5005	52°37·6'	0°13·4'E	FM	143
Dial Fm	N Yks	SE6790	54°18·3'	0°57·8'W	FM	94,100
Dial Fm	Suff	TM1256	52°9·9'	1°6·4'E	FM	155
Dial Fm	Suff	TM2563	52°13·4'	1°18·1'E	FM	156
Dial Green	W Susx	SU9227	51°2·3'	0°40·9'W	T	186,197
Dial Hall Fm	E Yorks	SE7742	53°52·3'	0°49·3'W	FM	105,106
Dial Hill	N Som	ST4072	51°26·9'	2°51·4'W	H	171,172
Dial House Fm	Warw	SP3070	52°19·9'	1°33·2'W	FM	140
Dial House, The	Northnts	SP6262	52°15·4'	1°5·1'W	X	152
Dial Post	W Susx	TQ1519	50°57·8'	0°21·4'W	T	198
Dial Post Fm	W Susx	TQ1936	51°6·9'	0°17·6'W	FM	187
Dial's Green Fm	Somer	ST5634	51°6·5'	2°37·3'W	FM	182,183
Dialstone Fm	N Yks	SE5184	54°15·2'	1°12·6'W	FM	100
Diamond	Corn	SW6646	50°16·3'	5°16·7'W	X	203
Diamond End	Herts	TL1420	51°52·2'	0°20·3'W	X	166
Diamond Fm	Oxon	SP5116	51°50·6'	1°15·2'W	FM	164
Diamond Fm	Somer	ST3056	51°18·2'	2°59·9'W	FM	182
Diamond Hall	Durham	NZ3527	54°38·5'	1°27·0'W	X	93
Diamond Hall Fm	Lancs	SD4824	53°42·8'	2°46·9'W	FM	102
Diamond Hill	Derby	SK0570	53°13·9'	1°55·1'W	X	119
Diamond Hill	N Ayr	NS2154	55°45·0'	4°50·7'W	X	63
Diamond Hill Fm	N Yks	SE2092	54°19·6'	1°41·1'W	FM	99
Diamond Ho	Kent	TQ9233	51°4·1'	0°44·8'E	X	189
Diamond Plantn	N Yks	TA0379	54°12·0'	0°24·8'W	F	101
Diamonds Laggan	D & G	NX7171	55°1·3'	4°0·6'W	X	77,84
Diamond Stone	D & G	NX5975	55°3·2'	4°12·0'W	X	77
Diana Clump	Suff	TL9177	52°21·7'	0°48·7'E	F	144
Diana Field	N Yks	SE5766	54°5·4'	1°7·3'W	X	100
Diana Fountain	Rich	TQ1569	51°24·7'	0°20·4'W	X	176
Dian Ho Fm	Cumbr	NY2049	54°50·0'	3°14·3'W	FM	85
Diar Sgeir	Arg & Bt	NM7211	56°14·5'	5°40·3'W	X	55
Dib	N Yks	SD9867	54°6·2'	2°1·4'W	X	98
Dibberford	Dorset	ST4503	50°49·7'	2°46·5'W	T	193
Dibbin Lane	D & G	NX6996	55°14·7'	4°3·2'W	W	77
Dibbin's Wood	Northnts	SP9491	52°30·8'	0°36·5'W	F	141
Dibble Br	N Yks	NZ6707	54°27·5'	0°57·6'W	X	94
Dibbles Br	N Yks	SE0563	54°4·0'	1°55·0'W	X	98
Dibden	Hants	SU4008	50°52·4'	1°25·5'W	T	196
Dibden	Kent	TQ5153	51°15·6'	0°10·2'E	X	188
Dibden Bottom	Hants	SU3906	50°51·4'	1°26·4'W	X	196
Dibden Hill	Bucks	SU9992	51°37·3'	0°33·8'W	X	175,176
Dibden Inclosure	Hants	SU4005	50°50·8'	1°25·5'W	F	196
Dibden Purlieu	Hants	SU4106	50°51·4'	1°24·7'W	T	196
Dibidal River	Highld	NG2040	57°22·1'	6°39·0'W	W	23
Dibidil	Highld	NM3992	56°57·0'	6°17·1'W	W	39
Dibidil River	Highld	NM3993	56°57·5'	6°17·1'W	W	39
Dibyn Du	Cered	SN7965	52°16·4'	3°46·0'W	H	135,147
Dichindad	Pth & Kin	NT1296	56°9·2'	3°24·6'W	X	58
Dick Brook	Worcs	SO7768	52°18·8'	2°19·8'W	W	138
Dicken-Dyke	N Yks	SE2158	54°1·3'	1°40·4'W	X	104
Dicken Nook	N Yks	SE0856	54°0·2'	1°52·3'W	X	104
Dickens Heath	Sol	SP1076	52°23·2'	1°50·8'W	T	139
Dicken's Lane Plantation	Hants	SU6650	51°14·9'	1°2·9'W	F	185,186
Dicker's Fm	Hants	SU6361	51°20·9'	1°5·3'W	FM	175
Dicker's Wood	Kent	TR0235	51°4·9'	0°53·4'E	F	189
Dicker, The	E Susx	TQ5509	50°51·8'	0°12·5'E	X	199
Dick Hill	Oldham	SE0105	53°32·7'	1°58·7'W	X	110
Dickhurst Ho	W Susx	SU9432	51°5·0'	0°39·1'W	X	186
Dickland	S Lanak	NS8440	55°38·6'	3°50·2'W	X	71,72
Dickleburgh	Norf	TM1682	52°23·8'	1°10·9'E	T	144,156
Dickleburgh Moor	Norf	TM1783	52°24·3'	1°11·8'E	T	156
Dickley Down Fm	Dorset	ST6400	50°48·1'	2°30·3'W	FM	194
Dickley Hall	Essex	TM1129	51°55·4'	1°4·5'E	X	168,169
Dickley Hill	Dorset	ST6500	50°48·1'	2°29·4'W	X	194
Dickley Wood	Kent	TQ8852	51°14·4'	0°42·0'E	F	189
Dickmontlaw	Angus	NO6543	56°34·9'	2°33·7'W	X	54
Dickmont's Den	Angus	NO6641	56°33·8'	2°32·7'W	X	54
Dickon Hills	Lincs	TF4356	53°5·2'	0°8·5'E	T	122
Dickon Howe	N Yks	SE6497	54°22·1'	1°0·5'W	A	94,100
Dick Slack	Cald	SD9816	53°38·7'	2°1·4'W	X	109
Dick's Law	E Ayr	NS5045	55°40·8'	4°22·7'W	X	64
Dick Slee's Cave	Staffs	SJ9919	52°46·4'	2°0·5'W	X	127
Dick's Oldwalls	Northum	NU0734	55°36·2'	1°52·9'W	X	75
Dickstree Cottage	Cumbr	NY3769	55°0·9'	2°58·7'W	X	85
Dicky Edge	N Yks	NZ0803	54°25·6'	1°52·2'W	X	92
Dicky Wood	N Yks	SE1791	54°19·1'	1°43·9'W	F	99
Didbrook	Glos	SP0531	51°58·9'	1°55·2'W	T	150
Didbrook Fields	Glos	SP0431	51°58·9'	1°56·1'W	X	150
Didcot	Oxon	SU5289	51°36·1'	1°14·6'W	T	174
Didcot Fm	Glos	SP0035	52°1·0'	1°59·6'W	FM	150
Didderhowe	N Yks	NZ6807	54°27·5'	0°56·6'W	X	94
Diddersley Hill	N Yks	NZ1708	54°28·3'	1°43·8'W	H	92
Diddies	Corn	SS2306	50°49·8'	4°30·4'W	X	190
Diddington	Cambs	TL1965	52°16·4'	0°15·0'W	T	153
Diddington Brook	Cambs	TL1866	52°17·0'	0°15·8'W	W	153
Diddington Hall	Sol	SP2182	52°26·4'	1°41·1'W	A	139
Diddington Hill	Sol	SP2082	52°26·4'	1°41·9'W	X	139
Diddlebury	Shrops	SO5085	52°27·9'	2°43·8'W	T	137,138
Diddlesfold Manor Fm	W Susx	SU9429	51°3·4'	0°39·1'W	FM	186,197
Diddles Hill	D & G	NX1268	54°58·5'	4°55·8'W	H	82
Diddridge	Durham	NZ1330	54°40·1'	1°47·5'W	X	92
Diddup	N Ayr	NS2644	55°39·8'	4°45·5'W	X	63,70
Diddywell	Devon	SS4529	51°2·6'	4°12·3'W	T	180
Didgemere Hall	Essex	TL4008	51°45·4'	0°2·1'E	X	167
Didham Fm	Devon	SX4867	50°29·2'	4°8·2'W	FM	201
Didley	Heref	SO4532	51°59·3'	2°47·7'W	T	149,161
Didley's Point	I Scilly	SV9017	49°58·6'	6°19·1'W	X	203
Didling	W Susx	SU8318	50°57·6'	0°48·7'W	T	197
Didling Hill	W Susx	SU8317	50°57·0'	0°48·7'W	X	197
Didlington	Dorset	SU0007	50°52·0'	1°59·6'W	X	195
Didlington	Norf	TL7797	52°32·8'	0°37·0'E	T	144
Didmarton	Glos	ST8287	51°35·1'	2°15·2'W	T	173
Didsbury	Man	SJ8491	53°25·2'	2°14·0'W	T	109
Didsbury Intake	Derby	SK0498	53°29·0'	1°56·0'W	X	110
Didworthy	Devon	SX6862	50°26·8'	3°51·2'W	T	202
Diebidale Forest	Highld	NH4584	57°49·4'	4°36·1'W	X	20
Diebidale Lodge	Highld	NH4785	57°50·0'	4°34·1'W	X	20
Diebidale Ridge	Highld	NH4583	57°48·9'	4°36·1'W	X	20
Diebidale River	Highld	NH4583	57°48·9'	4°36·1'W	W	20
Diffin	Orkney	HY5233	59°11·1'	2°49·9'W	X	5,6
Difford Beck	N Yks	SE8778	54°11·7'	0°39·6'W	W	101
Difford Fm	N Yks	SE8777	54°11·1'	0°39·6'W	FM	101
Diffwys	Cered	SN7357	52°12·0'	3°51·1'W	X	146,147
Diffwys	Denb	SJ0257	53°6·3'	3°27·4'W	X	116
Diffwys	Gwyn	SH6623	52°47·5'	3°58·8'W	H	124
Diffwys	Gwyn	SH6635	52°54·0'	3°59·1'W	X	124
Dig a' Bhogha	Highld	NM7167	56°44·6'	5°44·2'W	W	40
Dig an Sgùlain	Highld	NM7267	56°44·6'	5°43·3'W	W	40
Digbeth	Birm	SP0786	52°28·5'	1°53·4'W	T	139
Dig Bhàn	Highld	NM6667	56°44·4'	5°49·1'W	W	40
Dig Bharrain	Arg & Bt	NM8929	56°24·6'	5°24·8'W	W	49
Digby	Lincs	TF0854	53°4·6'	0°22·9'W	T	121
Digby Fen	Lincs	TF1254	53°4·5'	0°19·3'W	X	121
Digby Fm	Leic	SK7304	52°38·0'	0°54·9'W	FM	141
Digby Gorse	Lincs	TF0954	53°4·6'	0°22·0'W	F	121
Digden Bottom	Hants	SU1709	50°53·0'	1°45·1'W	X	195
Digedi Brook	Powys	SO2040	52°3·4'	3°9·6'W	W	148,161
Digedi Brook	Powys	SO2237	52°1·8'	3°7·8'W	W	161
Digg	Highld	NG4669	57°38·6'	6°14·9'W	T	23
Digges Court	Kent	TQ9747	51°11·5'	0°49·6'E	X	189
Digging Wood	Worcs	SO9659	52°14·0'	2°3·1'W	F	150
Diggins Fm	Essex	TL5808	51°45·1'	0°17·7'E	FM	167
Diggle	Oldham	SE0008	53°34·4'	1°59·6'W	T	110
Diggle Green	Warr	SJ6496	53°27·8'	2°32·1'W	X	109
Diggle Resr	Oldham	SE0208	53°34·4'	1°57·8'W	W	110
Diggory's Island	Corn	SW8470	50°29·6'	5°2·4'W	X	200
Diggs	Bucks	SP7308	51°46·2'	0°56·1'W	X	165
Dighills Fm	Ches	SJ8767	53°12·2'	2°11·3'W	FM	118
Dighty	Stir	NS6494	56°7·4'	4°10·8'W	X	57
Dighty Water	C of Dun	NO4532	56°28·9'	2°53·1'W	W	54
Diglake	Lancs	SD3910	53°35·2'	2°54·9'W	X	108
Diglake Fm	Ches	SJ8864	53°10·6'	2°10·4'W	FM	118
Diglane Fm	Ches	SJ6251	53°3·5'	2°33·6'W	FM	118
Diglee	Derby	SJ9982	53°20·3'	2°0·5'W	X	109
Digley Resr	Kirk	SE1007	53°33·8'	1°50·5'W	W	110
Diglis	Worcs	SO8453	52°10·7'	2°13·6'W	T	150
Digmoor	Lancs	SD4904	53°32·1'	2°45·8'W	T	108
Dig na Criche	Highld	NM6967	56°44·5'	5°46·2'W	W	40
Dignash	Kent	TQ9946	51°10·9'	0°51·2'E	X	189
Digoed	Cered	SN5266	52°16·6'	4°9·8'W	X	135
Digro	Orkney	HY4231	59°10·0'	3°0·4'W	X	5,6
Digswell	Herts	TL2515	51°49·4'	0°10·8'W	T	166
Digswell Park	Herts	TL2314	51°48·9'	0°12·5'W	T	166
Digswell Water	Herts	TL2514	51°48·9'	0°10·8'W	T	166
Dihewyd	Cered	SN4855	52°10·6'	4°13·0'W	T	146
Dikehead	Angus	NO5369	56°48·9'	2°45·7'W	X	44
Dikehead Cottages	Aberd	NJ5814	57°13·1'	2°41·3'W	X	37
Dike Ho	Cumbr	NY8313	54°31·0'	2°15·3'W	X	91,92
Dikeneuk	Pth & Kin	NO0645	56°35·5'	3°31·4'W	X	52,53
Dike Nook	Brad	SE0233	53°47·8'	1°57·8'W	X	104
Dikes Fields	N Yks	SE9669	54°6·7'	0°31·5'W	X	101
Dikes Marsh	Donc	SE6816	53°38·4'	0°57·9'W	X	111
Dikes Marsh Fm	Donc	SE6816	53°38·4'	0°57·9'W	FM	111
Dilamore Fm	Cambs	TL5591	52°29·9'	0°17·4'E	FM	143
Dildawn	D & G	NX7259	54°54·8'	3°59·4'W	X	83,84
Dildre	Cered	SN6560	52°13·5'	3°58·2'W	X	146
Diles Lake	Swan	SS4091	51°35·9'	4°18·2'W	W	159
Dilham	Norf	TG3325	52°46·6'	1°27·7'E	T	133,134
Dilham Hall	Norf	TG3326	52°47·1'	1°27·7'E	X	133,134
Dilhorne	Staffs	SJ9743	52°59·3'	2°2·3'W	T	118
Diliw	Cered	SN8377	52°23·0'	3°42·7'W	X	135,136,147
Diliw Fechan	Cered	SN8377	52°23·0'	3°42·7'W	W	135,136,147
Dillacombe	Somer	SS8135	51°6·4'	3°41·6'W	X	181
Dilland	Corn	SX2796	50°44·5'	4°26·7'W	X	190
Dillarburn	S Lanak	NS8241	55°39·1'	3°52·1'W	X	71,72
Dillar Hill	S Lanak	NS8341	55°39·2'	3°51·1'W	H	71,72
Dillars	S Lanak	NS8241	55°39·1'	3°52·1'W	X	71,72
Dillavaird	Angus	NO2950	56°38·4'	3°9·0'W	X	53
Dillay	Glos	SO8908	51°46·5'	2°9·2'W	X	163
Dill Hall	Lancs	SD7429	53°45·6'	2°23·3'W	T	103
Dillicar	Cumbr	SD6888	54°17·4'	2°29·1'W	X	98
Dillicar Common	Cumbr	SD6198	54°22·8'	2°35·6'W	X	97
Dillies Fm, The	Glos	SP0406	51°45·4'	1°56·1'W	FM	163
Dilliner Wood	Notts	SK6860	53°8·2'	0°58·6'W	F	120
Dilliner Wood Fm	Notts	SK6960	53°8·2'	0°57·7'W	FM	120
Dillington	Cambs	TL1365	52°16·5'	0°20·2'W	T	153
Dillington	Somer	ST3715	50°56·1'	2°53·4'W	T	193
Dillington Carr	Norf	TF9715	52°42·0'	0°55·3'E	F	132
Dillington Hall	Norf	TF9714	52°41·5'	0°55·3'E	X	132
Dillington House College	Somer	ST3615	50°56·1'	2°54·3'W	X	193
Dillybrook Fm	Wilts	ST8155	51°17·9'	2°16·0'W	FM	173
Dilly Hill	Aberd	NJ7522	57°17·5'	2°24·4'W	H	38
Dilston	Northum	NY9763	54°57·9'	2°2·4'W	T	87
Dilston Haughs	Northum	NY9764	54°58·5'	2°2·4'W	X	87
Dilston Park	Northum	NY9663	54°57·9'	2°3·3'W	X	87
Dilton	Hants	SU3201	50°48·7'	1°32·4'W	X	196
Dilton Court	Wilts	ST8448	51°14·1'	2°13·4'W	T	183
Dilton Fm	Hants	SU3300	50°48·1'	1°31·5'W	FM	196
Dilton Fm	Surrey	TQ0645	51°11·9'	0°28·6'W	FM	187
Dilton Gardens	Hants	SU3200	50°48·1'	1°32·4'W	X	196
Dilton Marsh	Wilts	ST8449	51°14·6'	2°13·4'W	T	183
Dilty Moss	Angus	NO5142	56°34·3'	2°47·4'W	X	54
Dilworth Ho	Lancs	SD6137	53°49·9'	2°35·1'W	X	102,103
Dilwyn	Heref	SO4154	52°11·2'	2°51·4'W	T	148,149
Dilwyn Common	Heref	SO4255	52°11·7'	2°50·5'W	X	148,149
Dimbols Hall	Essex	TM1731	51°56·3'	1°9·8'E	X	168,169
Dimlands	V of Glam	SS9568	51°24·3'	3°30·2'W	T	170
Dimlington	E Yorks	TA3920	53°39·7'	0°6·6'E	X	107,113
Dimlington High Land	E Yorks	TA3921	53°40·3'	0°6·7'E	X	107,113
Dimma	Corn	SX1997	50°44·9'	4°33·6'W	X	190
Dimmer	Somer	ST6131	51°4·9'	2°33·0'W	T	183
Dimmin Dale	Cald	SE0129	53°45·7'	1°58·7'W	X	104
Dimmingdale Fm	Red & Cl	NZ6811	54°29·6'	0°56·6'W	FM	94
Dimmings Dale	Staffs	SK0543	52°59·3'	1°55·1'W	X	119,128
Dimmock's Cote	Cambs	TL5372	52°19·7'	0°15·1'E	X	154
Dimmock's Moor	Hants	SU5410	50°53·4'	1°13·5'W	X	196
Dimpenley Top	Lancs	SD8238	53°50·5'	2°16·0'W	X	103
Dimple	Bolton	SD7015	53°38·1'	2°26·8'W	T	109
Dimple	Derby	SK2860	53°8·4'	1°34·5'W	T	119
Dimpleknowe	Scot Bord	NT5022	55°29·6'	2°47·0'W	X	73
Dimples	Lancs	SD5044	53°53·6'	2°45·2'W	X	102
Dimples Lees	Scot Bord	NT6855	55°47·5'	2°30·2'W	X	67,74
Dimple, The	S Lanak	NS9534	55°35·6'	3°39·5'W	X	72
Dimple Wells	N Yks	SE4974	54°9·8'	1°14·6'W	X	100
Dimpus Clough	Derby	SK0685	53°22·0'	1°54·2'W	X	110
Dimsdale	Staffs	SJ8448	53°2·0'	2°13·9'W	T	118
Dimsdale Sewer	E Susx	TQ9016	50°55·0'	0°42·6'E	W	189
Dimson	Corn	SX4271	50°31·3'	4°13·4'W	T	201
Dimstone Hill	Dorset	ST5100	50°48·1'	2°41·3'W	X	194
Dinabid Linn	D & G	NS8908	55°21·5'	3°44·6'W	W	71,78
Dinam	Denb	SJ0133	52°53·4'	3°27·9'W	X	125
Dinam	I of Angl	SH3077	53°16·0'	4°32·5'W	X	114
Dinam	I of Angl	SH4568	53°11·4'	4°18·8'W	X	114,115
Dinarth Hall	Conwy	SH8280	53°18·5'	3°45·9'W	X	116
Dinas	Carm	SN2730	51°56·7'	4°30·6'W	T	145
Dinas	Carm	SN7846	52°6·2'	3°46·5'W	H	146,147
Dinas	Cered	SN7482	52°25·5'	3°50·8'W	X	135
Dinas	Conwy	SH8153	53°3·9'	3°46·2'W	X	116
Dinas	Corn	SW9174	50°31·9'	4°56·6'W	T	200
Dinas	Gwyn	SH1631	52°51·0'	4°43·6'W	X	123
Dinas	Gwyn	SH2636	52°53·8'	4°34·8'W	T	123
Dinas	Gwyn	SH4858	53°6·1'	4°15·8'W	T	115,123
Dinas	Gwyn	SH4937	52°54·8'	4°14·3'W	T	123
Dinas	Gwyn	SH5948	53°0·9'	4°5·7'W	X	115
Dinas	Gwyn	SH6129	52°50·7'	4°3·4'W	X	124
Dinas	Gwyn	SH8414	52°42·9'	3°42·6'W	H	124,125
Dinas	I of Angl	SH5082	53°19·1'	4°14·7'W	X	114,115
Dinas	Powys	SN9088	52°29·0'	3°36·8'W	X	136
Dinas	Rho Cyn Taf	ST0091	51°36·8'	3°26·3'W	X	170
Dinas Bach	Carm	SN7740	52°2·9'	3°47·2'W	X	146,147,160
Dinas Bâch	Gwyn	SH1529	52°49·9'	4°44·4'W	X	123
Dinas Bâch	I of Angl	SH3565	53°9·6'	4°27·7'W	X	114
Dinas Cerdin	Cered	SN3846	52°5·6'	4°21·5'W	X	145
Dinas Ceri	Cered	SN3143	52°3·8'	4°27·5'W	X	145
Dinas Cross	Pemb	SN0039	52°1·0'	4°54·5'W	T	145,157
Dinas Dinlle	Gwyn	SH4356	53°4·9'	4°20·2'W	A	115,123
Dinas Dinlle	Gwyn	SH4356	53°4·9'	4°20·2'W	T	115,123
Dinas Dinorwig	Gwyn	SH5465	53°10·0'	4°10·6'W	A	114,115
Dinas Emrys	Gwyn	SH6049	53°1·4'	4°4·8'W	A	115
Dinasfach	Carm	SN2729	51°56·2'	4°30·6'W	X	145,158
Dinas Fach	Pemb	SM8222	51°51·5'	5°9·6'W	X	157
Dinas Fawr	Carm	SN7743	52°4·5'	3°47·3'W	X	146,147,160
Dinas Fawr	Gwyn	SH1529	52°49·9'	4°44·4'W	X	123
Dinas Fawr	Pemb	SM8022	51°51·4'	5°11·3'W	X	157
Dinas Gynfor	I of Angl	SH3995	53°25·9'	4°25·0'W	A	114
Dinas Head	Corn	SW8476	50°32·9'	5°2·6'W	X	200
DINAS HEAD	Pemb	SN0041	52°2·1'	4°54·6'W	X	145,157
Dinas Island	Pemb	SN0040	52°1·6'	4°54·5'W	X	145,157
Dinas-Iwyd	I of Angl	SH3765	53°9·7'	4°25·9'W	X	114
Dinas-Mawddwy	Gwyn	SH8514	52°42·9'	3°41·7'W	T	124,125
Dinas Mawr	Conwy	SH8053	53°3·9'	3°47·0'W	T	116
Dinas Mawr	Gwyn	SH5563	53°8·9'	4°9·7'W	X	114,115
Dinas Mill	Powys	SN8647	52°6·8'	3°39·5'W	X	147
Dinas Mot	Gwyn	SH6256	53°5·2'	4°3·2'W	X	115
Dinas Oleu	Gwyn	SH6115	52°43·1'	4°3·1'W	A	124
Dinas Powis	V of Glam	ST1472	51°26·7'	3°13·9'W	A	171
Dinas Powis	V of Glam	ST1571	51°26·1'	3°13·0'W	T	171
Dinas Reservoir	Cered	SN7482	52°25·5'	3°50·8'W	W	135
Dinas Sitch Tor	Derby	SK1190	53°24·6'	1°49·7'W	X	110
Dinas Trefri	I of Angl	SH3665	53°9·7'	4°26·8'W	X	114
Dinas-y-prif	Gwyn	SH4657	53°5·5'	4°17·6'W	A	115,123
Dinbren Hall	Denb	SJ2143	52°59·0'	3°10·2'W	X	117
Dinbren Isaf	Denb	SJ2144	52°59·5'	3°10·2'W	X	117
Dinbych or Denbigh	Denb	SJ0566	53°11·2'	3°24·9'W	T	116
Dinchall Fm	Heref	SO7034	52°0·5'	2°25·8'W	FM	149
Dinckley	Lancs	SD6835	53°48·9'	2°28·7'W	T	103
Dinckley Grange	Lancs	SD6835	53°48·9'	2°28·7'W	X	103
Dinckley Hall	Lancs	SD6836	53°49·4'	2°28·8'W	X	103
Dinder	Somer	ST5744	51°11·9'	2°36·5'W	T	182,183
Dinder Wood	Somer	ST5845	51°12·4'	2°35·7'W	F	182,183
Dindinnie	D & G	NX0261	54°54·5'	5°4·9'W	X	82
Dindinnie Resr	D & G	NX0260	54°54·0'	5°4·9'W	W	82
Din Dryfol	I of Angl	SH3972	53°13·5'	4°24·3'W	X	114
Dinduff	D & G	NX0264	54°56·1'	5°5·0'W	X	82
Dinedor	Heref	SO5336	52°1·5'	2°40·7'W	T	149
Dinedor Camp	Heref	SO5236	52°1·5'	2°41·6'W	A	149
Dinedor Cross	Heref	SO5235	52°0·9'	2°41·6'W	T	149
Dinedor Hill	Heref	SO5337	52°2·0'	2°40·7'W	H	149
Dinefwr Park	Carm	SN6122	51°53·0'	4°0·8'W	X	159
Dinerth Castle	Cered	SN4962	52°14·4'	4°12·3'W	A	146
Dines Green	Worcs	SO8255	52°11·8'	2°15·4'W	T	150
Dines Hall	Essex	TL7517	51°49·7'	0°32·8'E	X	167
Dineterwood	Heref	SO3827	51°56·5'	2°53·7'W	F	161
Din Fell	Scot Bord	NY4595	55°15·0'	2°51·5'W	H	79
Dingbell Hill	Northum	NY7758	54°55·2'	2°21·1'W	X	86,87
Dingerein Castle	Corn	SW8837	50°11·9'	4°57·9'W	A	204
Dinger Tor	Devon	SX5888	50°40·7'	4°0·2'W	X	191
Dingestow	Monm	SO4510	51°47·4'	2°47·5'W	T	161
Dingestow Court	Monm	SO4509	51°46·9'	2°47·4'W	X	161
Dingford Fm	Somer	ST2914	50°55·5'	3°0·2'W	FM	193
Dinghurst	N Som	ST4459	51°19·9'	2°47·8'W	T	172,182
Dingle	Denb	SJ1451	53°3·2'	3°16·6'W	X	116
Dingle	Liv	SJ3687	53°22·8'	2°57·3'W	T	108
Dingle Br	Shrops	SO2796	52°33·7'	3°4·2'W	X	137
Dingle Brook	Ches	SJ8071	53°14·4'	2°17·6'W	W	118
Dingleden	Kent	TQ8131	51°3·2'	0°35·3'E	T	188

Dingle-du-Bank	Shrops	SO2283	52°26·6'	3°8·5'W	X	137
Dingle Fm	Lancs	SD4531	53°46·6'	2°49·7'W	FM	102
Dingle Fm	Shrops	SJ2910	52°41·2'	3°2·6'W	FM	126
Dingle Fm	Worcs	SO7864	52°16·7'	2°19·0'W	FM	138,150
Dingle Great Hill	Suff	TM4872	52°17·6'	1°38·6'E	X	156
Dingle Leys	Shrops	SO6285	52°27·9'	2°33·2'W	X	138
Dingle Marshes	Suff	TM4771	52°17·1'	1°37·7'E	W	156
Dingle Nook Fm	Suff	TL6979	52°23·2'	0°29·4'E	FM	143
Dingle Resr	Black w Dar	SD6914	53°37·5'	2°27·7'W	W	109
Dinglesden	E Susx	TQ8620	50°57·2'	0°39·3'E	X	189,199
Dingles Fm	Devon	SS5741	51°9·3'	4°2·3'W	FM	180
Dingle Stone Ho	Suff	TM4772	52°17·7'	1°37·7'E	X	156
Dingle, The	I of Angl	SH4576	53°15·7'	4°19·0'W	X	114,115
Dingle, The	Pemb	SN0701	51°40·7'	4°47·1'W	X	158
Dingle, The	Peterb	TF0606	52°38·7'	0°25·6'W	X	142
Dingle, The	Powys	SJ2912	52°42·3'	3°2·6'W	X	126
Dingle, The	Powys	SO1089	52°29·7'	3°19·1'W	X	136
Dingle, The	Shrops	SJ6731	52°52·8'	2°29·0'W	F	127
Dingle, The	Warw	SP2292	52°31·8'	1°40·1'W	X	139
Dingle, The	Worcs	SO9740	52°3·7'	2°2·2'W	X	150
Dingleton	E Loth	NT5378	55°59·8'	2°44·8'W	X	66
Dingleton	Scot Bord	NT5433	55°35·6'	2°43·4'W	T	73
Dingleton Mains	Scot Bord	NT5433	55°35·6'	2°43·4'W	X	73
Dingley	Northnts	SP7787	52°28·8'	0°51·6'W	T	141
Dingley Grange	Northnts	SP7688	52°29·3'	0°52·5'W	X	141
Dingley Hall	Northnts	SP7687	52°28·8'	0°52·5'W	A	141
Dingley Lodge	Northnts	SP7687	52°28·8'	0°52·5'W	X	141
Dingley Wood	Northnts	SP7786	52°28·2'	0°51·6'W	F	141
Dings Rigg	Northum	NY7084	55°9·2'	2°27·8'W	X	80
Dingstopple	Pemb	SN0618	51°49·9'	4°48·5'W	X	158
Dingwall	Highld	NC5700	57°58·2'	4°24·6'W	X	16
Dingwall	Highld	NH5458	57°35·6'	4°26·1'W	T	26
Dingwood Park Fm	Heref	SO7235	52°1·0'	2°24·1'W	FM	149
Dinham	Corn	SW9774	50°32·1'	4°51·5'W	X	200
Dinham's Br	Corn	SX0373	50°31·7'	4°46·4'W	X	200
Dinhill Fm	Somer	ST0426	51°1·8'	3°21·8'W	FM	181
Dinhunlle Isaf	Wrex	SJ3242	52°58·5'	3°0·4'W	X	117
Dinkling Green Fm	Lancs	SD6346	53°54·8'	2°33·4'W	FM	102,103
Dinlabyre	Scot Bord	NY5292	55°13·4'	2°44·8'W	T	79
Din Law	Scot Bord	NT1215	55°25·5'	3°23·0'W	H	78
Dinley	Scot Bord	NY4796	55°15·6'	2°49·6'W	X	79
Dinley Burn	Scot Bord	NY4695	55°15·0'	2°50·5'W	W	79
Dinley Fell	Scot Bord	NY4795	55°15·0'	2°49·6'W	H	79
Dinley Hill	Northum	NY8297	55°5·5'	2°10·9'W	X	87
Dinley Moss	Scot Bord	NY4794	55°14·5'	2°49·6'W	X	79
Din Lligwy	I of Angl	SH4986	53°21·2'	4°15·7'W	A	114
Dinmael	Conwy	SJ0044	52°59·3'	3°29·0'W	T	125
Dinmontlair Knowe	Scot Bord	NY5488	55°11·3'	2°42·9'W	H	79
Dinmont Lairs	Northum	NY6290	55°12·4'	2°35·4'W	X	80
Dinmore Hill	Heref	SO5151	52°9·5'	2°42·6'W	X	149
Dinmore Ho	N Yks	SE2460	54°2·4'	1°37·6'W	X	99
Dinmore Manor	Heref	SO4850	52°9·0'	2°45·2'W	X	148,149
Din Moss	Fife	NT0793	56°7·5'	3°29·3'W	X	58
Din Moss	Scot Bord	NT8031	55°34·6'	2°18·6'W	X	74
Dinmurchie Loch	S Ayr	NX2892	55°11·8'	4°41·7'W	W	76
Dinnabroad	Corn	SX0381	50°36·0'	4°46·7'W	X	200
Dinnance	D & G	NX6764	54°57·4'	4°4·2'W	X	83,84
Dinnans	D & G	NX4740	54°44·2'	4°22·2'W	X	83
Dinnant	Powys	SJ1302	52°36·8'	3°16·7'W	X	136
Dinna Pow	Orkney	HY6716	59°2·1'	2°34·0'W	X	5
Dinnaton Barton	Devon	SS6228	51°2·3'	3°57·7'W	X	180
Dinnet	Aberd	NO4598	57°4·4'	2°54·0'W	T	37,44
Dinnet Ho	Aberd	NO4497	57°3·9'	2°55·0'W	X	37,44
Dinnever Hill	Corn	SX1279	50°35·1'	4°39·0'W	X	200
Dinney Fm	Shrops	SO7186	52°28·5'	2°25·2'W	FM	138
Dinning	D & G	NX8989	55°11·2'	3°44·2'W	X	78
Dinnings Heights	D & G	NY2198	55°16·4'	3°14·2'W	H	79
Dinnings Hill	D & G	NY2197	55°15·9'	3°13·2'W	H	79
Dinnington	N upon Ty	NZ2073	55°3·3'	1°40·8'W	T	88
Dinnington	Roth	SK5285	53°21·8'	1°12·7'W	T	111,120
Dinnington	Somer	ST4012	50°54·5'	2°50·8'W	T	193
Dinnins	D & G	NX4891	55°11·6'	4°22·8'W	X	77
Dinnyhorn	Moray	NJ3246	57°30·2'	3°7·6'W	X	28
Dinorben	Conwy	SH9674	53°15·4'	3°33·1'W	X	116
Dinorwic	Gwyn	SH5961	53°7·9'	4°6·0'W	T	114,115
Dinsdale Park	Darl	NZ3412	54°30·4'	1°28·1'W	X	93
Dinsdale Sta	Darl	NZ3413	54°30·9'	1°28·1'W	X	93
Dinsdale Wood	Darl	NZ3411	54°29·8'	1°28·1'W	F	93
Dinthill	Shrops	SO6171	52°20·4'	2°33·9'W	X	138
Dinthill Hall	Shrops	SJ4212	52°42·4'	2°51·1'W	X	126
Dinting Vale	Derby	SK0194	53°26·8'	1°58·7'W	X	110
Dinton	Bucks	SP7610	51°47·2'	0°53·5'W	T	165
Dinton	Wilts	SU0131	51°4·9'	1°58·8'W	T	184
Dinton Castle	Bucks	SP7611	51°47·8'	0°53·5'W	X	165
Dinvin	D & G	NX0055	54°51·2'	5°6·5'W	X	82
Dinvin (Motte)	S Ayr	NX2093	55°12·2'	4°49·3'W	A	76
Dinwoodie	S Ayr	NS4015	55°24·4'	4°31·2'W	X	70,70
Dinwoodie	Scot Bord	NY4681	55°7·5'	2°50·4'W	X	79
Dinwoodie Green	D & G	NY1088	55°10·9'	3°24·4'W	X	78
Dinwoodie Lodge	D & G	NY1090	55°12·0'	3°24·4'W	X	78
Dinwoodie Mains	D & G	NY1090	55°12·0'	3°24·4'W	X	78
Dinworthy	Devon	SS3115	50°54·8'	4°23·9'W	T	190
Diollaid a' Chairn	Highld	NN4975	56°50·8'	4°27·4'W	X	42
Diollaid a' Mhill Bhric	Highld	NH2382	57°47·8'	4°58·2'W	X	20
Diollaid Bheag	Highld	NM8180	56°51·8'	5°35·1'W	H	40
Diollaid Coire Eindart	Highld	NN8992	57°0·6'	3°49·2'W	X	35,43
Diollaid Mhór	Arg & Bt	NR7367	55°50·8'	5°37·1'W	X	62
Diollaid Mhór	Arg & Bt	NR7739	55°35·9'	5°31·9'W	X	68,69
Diollaid Mhór	Highld	NM8079	56°51·3'	5°36·1'W	H	40
Diollaid nam Fiadh	Arg & Bt	NR4454	55°43·0'	6°4·1'W	X	60
Dions Court	Heref	SO4668	52°18·7'	2°47·1'W	X	137,138,148
Dionscourt Hill	Heref	SO4568	52°18·7'	2°48·0'W	X	137,138,148
Dioraigh	N Eil	NF8343	57°22·3'	7°16·0'W	X	22
Diosg	Powys	SH9101	52°36·0'	3°36·2'W	X	136
Diosg	Powys	SJ0209	52°40·4'	3°26·6'W	X	125
Diosgydd	Conwy	SH7757	53°6·0'	3°49·8'W	X	115
Dipden Bottom	Hants	SU3440	51°9·7'	1°30·4'W	X	185
Dipford	Somer	ST2021	50°59·2'	3°8·0'W	T	193
Dipley	Hants	SU7457	51°18·7'	0°55·9'W	T	175,186

Dippal Burn	E Ayr	NS7032	55°34·1'	4°3·3'W	W	71
Dippal Rig	E Ayr	NS6832	55°34·1'	4°5·2'W	X	71
Dippany	Inverc	NS3169	55°53·3'	4°41·7'W	X	63
Dippen	Arg & Bt	NR7937	55°34·8'	5°29·9'W	X	68,69
Dippen	N Ayr	NS0422	55°27·4'	5°5·6'W	T	69
Dippen Bay	Arg & Bt	NR7936	55°34·3'	5°29·9'W	W	68,69
Dippenhall	Surrey	SU8146	51°12·7'	0°50·0'W	T	186
Dippen Head	N Ayr	NS0522	55°27·4'	5°4·6'W	X	69
Dipper Fm	Corn	SX2695	50°44·0'	4°27·6'W	FM	190
Dippermill	Devon	SS4306	50°50·2'	4°13·4'W	X	190
Dippertown	Devon	SX4284	50°38·3'	4°13·7'W	T	201
Dippin Burn	Arg & Bt	NR8890	56°3·6'	5°23·9'W	W	55
Dipping Stone, The	Derby	SJ9981	53°19·8'	2°0·5'W	A	109
Dippin Lodge	N Ayr	NS0422	55°27·4'	5°5·6'W	X	69
Dipple	Devon	SS3417	50°56·0'	4°21·4'W	T	190
Dipple	Moray	NJ3258	57°36·7'	3°7·8'W	X	28
Dipple	S Ayr	NS2002	55°17·0'	4°49·6'W	T	76
Dipplebrae	Aberd	NK0756	57°35·9'	1°52·5'W	X	30
Dipple Burn	S Lanak	NS6234	55°35·1'	4°10·9'W	W	71
Dipple Wood	Bucks	SU9388	51°35·2'	0°39·1'W	F	175
Dippol Burn	E Ayr	NS5223	55°29·0'	4°20·1'W	W	70
Dippol Burn	E Ayr	NS5623	55°29·0'	4°16·3'W	X	71
Dippool Water	S Lanak	NS9649	55°43·7'	3°38·9'W	W	72
Dippool Water	S Lanak	NS9852	55°45·3'	3°37·1'W	W	65,72
Diprose	Kent	TQ7831	51°3·3'	0°32·8'E	X	188
Diptford	Devon	SX7256	50°23·6'	3°47·7'W	T	202
Diptford Fm	Devon	SS9017	50°56·8'	3°33·6'W	FM	181
Dipton	Durham	NZ1553	54°52·5'	1°45·5'W	T	88
Dipton Cottage	Northum	NY9861	54°56·8'	2°1·4'W	X	87
Dipton Ho	Northum	NY9960	54°56·3'	2°0·5'W	X	87
Diptonmill	Northum	NY9260	54°56·3'	2°7·1'W	T	87
Dipton Wood	Northum	NY9760	54°56·3'	2°2·4'W	F	87
Dipwell	Devon	SX7669	50°30·7'	3°44·6'W	X	202
Dira	Devon	SS8405	50°50·2'	3°38·5'W	X	191
Dirc an Uillt Fhearna	Highld	NN5293	57°0·5'	4°25·8'W	X	35
Dirc Beannain Beaga	Highld	NN4692	56°59·9'	4°31·7'W	H	34
Dirc Creag Chathalain	Highld	NN4894	57°1·0'	4°29·8'W	X	34
Dirc Mhór	Highld	NN5986	56°56·9'	4°18·6'W	X	42
Dirdhu	Highld	NJ0720	57°15·9'	3°32·1'W	X	36
Direadh Beinn	N Eil	NB0928	58°9·0'	6°56·3'W	H	13
Direcleit	N Eil	NG1598	57°53·1'	6°48·0'W	T	14
Diren	N Eil	NG1599	57°53·6'	6°48·1'W	X	14
Dirichurachan	Highld	NH5424	57°17·3'	4°24·9'W	X	26,35
Dirivallan	Highld	NG3333	57°18·8'	6°25·6'W	H	32
Dirk Hatteraick's Cave	D & G	NX5152	54°50·7'	4°18·8'W	X	83
Dirks	Devon	ST3003	50°49·6'	2°59·3'W	X	193
Dirleton	E Loth	NT5183	56°2·5'	2°46·8'W	T	66
Dirleton	E Loth	NT5184	56°3·0'	2°46·8'W	X	66
Dirlot	Highld	ND1248	58°25·0'	3°29·9'W	X	11,12
Dirlot Castle	Highld	ND1248	58°25·0'	3°29·9'W	A	11,12
Dirnanean	Pth & Kin	NO0663	56°45·2'	3°31·8'W	T	43
Dirnean Moss	D & G	NX2557	54°52·9'	4°43·3'W	X	82
Dirneark	D & G	NX2670	54°59·9'	4°42·8'W	X	76
Dirniemow	D & G	NX1770	54°59·7'	4°51·2'W	X	76
Dirniemow Fell	D & G	NX1871	55°0·3'	4°50·3'W	X	76
Dirnow	D & G	NX2965	54°57·3'	4°39·8'W	X	82
Dirr Cott	Highld	NH5934	57°22·7'	4°20·3'W	X	26
Dirrie More	Highld	NH2375	57°44·1'	4°57·9'W	X	20
Dirrington Burn	Scot Bord	NT6854	55°46·9'	2°30·2'W	W	67,74
Dirrington Great Law	Scot Bord	NT6954	55°47·0'	2°29·2'W	H	67,74
Dirrington Hill	Scot Bord	NT6855	55°47·5'	2°30·2'W	H	67,74
Dirrington Little Law	Scot Bord	NT6853	55°46·4'	2°30·2'W	H	67,74
Dirrops	D & G	NY2377	55°5·1'	3°12·0'W	X	85
Dirr Wood	Highld	NH6033	57°22·2'	4°19·2'W	F	26
Dirskelpin Moss	D & G	NX2658	54°53·4'	4°42·4'W	X	82
Dirthope Burn	Scot Bord	NT3509	55°22·5'	3°1·1'W	W	79
Dirtley Wood	Wilts	ST8948	51°14·1'	2°9·1'W	F	184
Dirtlow Fm	Derby	SK1868	53°12·8'	1°43·4'W	FM	119
Dirtlow Rake	Derby	SK1481	53°19·8'	1°47·0'W	X	110
Dirtness Br	N Lincs	SE7409	53°34·6'	0°52·5'W	X	112
Dirtness Levels	N Lincs	SE7411	53°35·7'	0°52·5'W	X	112
Dirt Pit	Durham	NY8929	54°39·6'	2°9·8'W	X	91,92
Dirt Pot	Northum	NY8546	54°48·8'	2°13·6'W	T	87
Dirtup	Cumbr	NY5176	55°4·8'	2°45·6'W	X	86
Dirty Copse	Hants	SU5815	50°56·1'	1°10·1'W	F	196
Dirty Corner	Hants	SU4449	51°14·5'	1°21·8'W	X	185
Dirty Gate	Dorset	ST5101	50°48·6'	2°41·3'W	X	194
Dirty Gutter	Staffs	SK0353	53°4·7'	1°56·9'W	X	119
Dirty Pool	Durham	NY8319	54°34·2'	2°15·4'W	W	92
Dirtywood Fm	Bucks	SP8403	51°43·4'	0°46·6'W	FM	165
Dirvachlie	D & G	NX2470	54°59·9'	4°44·7'W	X	76
Disblair Ho	Aberd	NJ8619	57°15·9'	2°13·5'W	X	38
Discoed	Powys	SO2764	52°16·4'	3°3·8'W	T	137,148
Discove	Somer	ST6933	51°6·0'	2°26·2'W	T	183
Discove Fm	Somer	ST6934	51°6·5'	2°26·2'W	FM	183
Discovery Point	C of Dun	NO4029	56°27·2'	2°58·0'W	X	54,59
Disdow	D & G	NX6156	54°53·0'	4°9·6'W	X	83
Disdow Wood	D & G	NX6057	54°53·5'	4°10·5'W	F	83
Diseworth	Leic	SK4524	52°48·9'	1°19·5'W	T	129
Disgarth Uchaf	Conwy	SH9845	52°59·8'	3°30·8'W	X	116
Disgwilfa	Cered	SN7766	52°16·9'	3°47·8'W	H	135,147
Disgwilfa	Cered	SN7769	52°18·6'	3°47·9'W	H	135,147
Disgwylfa	Cered	SN6889	52°29·2'	3°56·2'W	X	135
Disgwylfa	Powys	SN8117	51°50·6'	3°43·3'W	H	160
Disgwylfa	Carm	SN5009	51°45·8'	4°10·0'W	X	159
Disgwylfa	Carm	SN6229	51°56·8'	4°0·1'W	X	146
Disgwylfa	Cered	SN6974	52°21·1'	3°55·0'W	X	135
Disgwylfa	Powys	SJ0308	52°39·9'	3°25·7'W	H	125
Disgwylfa	Powys	SN8964	52°16·0'	3°37·2'W	H	147
Disgwylfa	Powys	SO2523	51°54·3'	3°5·0'W	X	161
Disgwylfa Fâch	Cered	SN7383	52°26·1'	3°51·7'W	H	135
Disgwylfa Fawr	Cered	SN7384	52°26·6'	3°51·7'W	H	135
Disgwylfa Hill	Powys	SO2251	52°9·4'	3°8·0'W	H	148
Disgwylfa Hill	Shrops	SO3293	52°32·1'	2°59·8'W	H	137
Disgylfa	Rho Cyn Taf	ST0783	51°32·5'	3°19·3'W	X	170
Dishcombe	Devon	SX6593	50°43·5'	3°54·4'W	X	191
Dishes	Orkney	HY6523	59°5·8'	2°36·2'W	T	5
Dishfields Fm	Derby	SK2333	52°53·9'	1°39·1'W	FM	128
Dishforth	N Yks	SE3873	54°9·3'	1°24·7'W	T	99
Dishforth Airfield	N Yks	SE3871	54°8·2'	1°24·7'W	X	99

Dishley	Leic	SK5121	52°47·3'	1°14·2'W	T	129
Disley	Ches	SJ9784	53°21·4'	2°2·3'W	T	109
Disley Tunnel	Stock	SJ9685	53°22·0'	2°3·2'W	X	109
Disputes, The	N Yks	NY9407	54°27·7'	2°5·1'W	X	91,92
Diss	Norf	TM1180	52°22·9'	1°6·4'E	T	144
Disserth	Powys	SO0358	52°12·9'	3°24·8'W	T	147
Dissington East Houses	Northum	NZ1272	55°2·8'	1°48·3'W	X	88
Dissington Hall	Northum	NZ1171	55°2·2'	1°49·2'W	X	88
Dissington Lane Ho	Northum	NZ1369	55°1·2'	1°47·4'W	X	88
Dissington Old Hall	Northum	NZ1270	55°1·7'	1°48·3'W	X	88
Dissington Red Ho	Northum	NZ1172	55°2·8'	1°49·2'W	X	88
Distaff Fm	Stock	SJ9084	53°21·4'	2°8·6'W	FM	109
Distillery Fm	Lincs	TF3425	52°48·6'	0°0·3'W	FM	131
Distington	Cumbr	NY0023	54°35·8'	3°32·4'W	T	89
Distinkhorn	E Ayr	NS5833	55°34·5'	4°14·7'W	H	71
Ditch	Clackm	NS8595	56°8·3'	3°50·6'W	X	58
Ditch Acre Copse	Hants	SU7018	50°57·7'	0°59·8'W	F	197
Ditcham Park Sch	Hants	SU7417	50°57·1'	0°56·4'W	X	197
Ditchampton	Wilts	SU0831	51°4·9'	1°52·8'W	T	184
Ditcham Wood	Oxon	SP3305	51°44·8'	1°30·9'W	F	164
Ditch Cliff	Derby	SK2067	53°12·2'	1°41·6'W	X	119
Ditch Dingle	Shrops	SO2287	52°28·8'	3°8·5'W	X	137
Ditcheat	Somer	ST6236	51°7·6'	2°32·2'W	T	183
Ditcheat Hill	Somer	ST6236	51°7·6'	2°32·2'W	H	183
Ditchedge Lane	Warw	SP3337	52°2·1'	1°30·7'W	X	151
Ditchen	Corn	SX3094	50°43·5'	4°24·1'W	X	190
Ditchend Brook	Hants	SU1714	50°55·7'	1°45·1'W	W	195
Ditchend Brook	Hants	SU1915	50°56·3'	1°43·4'W	W	184
Ditch End Cross	Devon	SS6636	51°6·7'	3°54·5'W	X	180
Ditchend Fm	Oxon	SP6200	51°41·9'	1°5·8'W	FM	164,165
Ditcher Law	Scot Bord	NT5056	55°47·9'	2°47·4'W	X	66,73
Ditches	Cald	SD9121	53°41·4'	2°7·8'W	X	103
Ditches Hall, The	Shrops	SJ4929	52°51·6'	2°45·0'W	X	126
Ditches, The	Shrops	SO2493	52°32·0'	3°6·8'W	X	137
Ditches, The	Shrops	SO5694	52°32·8'	2°38·5'W	H	137,138
Ditches, The (fort)	Shrops	SO5694	52°32·8'	2°38·5'W	A	137,138
Ditchett	Devon	SS8119	50°57·7'	3°41·3'W	X	181
Ditchetts	Devon	SS9312	50°54·1'	3°30·9'W	X	181
Ditchfield	Bucks	SU8091	51°37·0'	0°50·3'W	T	175
Ditch Fm	Cambs	TL5864	52°15·3'	0°19·3'E	FM	154
Ditch Fm	Somer	SS9831	51°4·4'	3°27·0'W	FM	181
Ditchford Bank	Worcs	SO9864	52°16·7'	2°1·4'W	X	150
Ditchford Fm	Warw	SP2339	52°3·2'	1°39·5'W	FM	151
Ditchford Frary	Warw	SP2337	52°2·1'	1°39·5'W	X	151
Ditchford Frary Village	Warw	SP2337	52°2·1'	1°39·5'W	A	151
Ditchford Hill	Glos	SP2136	52°1·6'	1°41·2'W	X	151
Ditch-head	Moray	NJ1151	57°32·7'	3°28·8'W	X	28
Ditchingham	Norf	TM3391	52°28·3'	1°26·2'E	T	134
Ditchingham Lodge	Norf	TM3391	52°28·3'	1°26·2'E	X	134
Ditchingham Park	Norf	TM3292	52°28·8'	1°25·4'E	X	134
Ditchley	Oxon	SP3921	51°53·4'	1°25·6'W	A	164
Ditchley Gate	Oxon	SP4218	51°51·8'	1°23·0'W	X	164
Ditchley Park	Oxon	SP3921	51°53·4'	1°25·6'W	X	164
Ditchling	E Susx	TQ3215	50°55·4'	0°6·9'W	T	198
Ditchling Beacon	E Susx	TQ3313	50°54·3'	0°6·1'W	H	198
Ditchling Beacon (Fort)	E Susx	TQ3313	50°54·3'	0°6·1'W	A	198
Ditch Wood	Suff	TM0851	52°7·3'	1°2·7'E	F	155
Ditchyeld Br	Powys	SO2760	52°14·2'	3°3·7'W	X	137,148
Ditherington	Shrops	SJ5014	52°43·5'	2°44·0'W	T	126
Ditsham	Devon	SX4906	50°50·3'	4°8·3'W	X	191
Ditsworthy Warren	Devon	SX5867	50°29·4'	3°59·7'W	X	202
Ditsworthy Warren Ho	Devon	SX5866	50°28·8'	3°59·7'W	X	202
Ditteridge	Wilts	ST8169	51°25·4'	2°16·0'W	T	173
Dittiscombe	Devon	SX7946	50°18·3'	3°41·6'W	X	202
Dittisham	Devon	SX5370	50°30·9'	4°4·0'W	X	201
Dittisham	Devon	SX8654	50°22·7'	3°35·8'W	T	202
Dittisham Court	Devon	SX8655	50°23·3'	3°35·8'W	X	202
Ditton	E Ayr	NS4034	55°34·7'	4°31·9'W	X	70
Ditton	Halton	SJ4885	53°21·8'	2°46·5'W	T	108
Ditton	Kent	TQ7157	51°17·4'	0°27·5'E	T	178,188
Ditton Brook	Know	SJ4685	53°21·8'	2°48·3'W	W	108
Ditton Brook	Shrops	SO6275	52°22·5'	2°33·1'W	W	138
Ditton Common	Kent	TQ7155	51°16·3'	0°27·5'E	X	178,188
Ditton Enclosure	Shrops	SO5987	52°29·0'	2°35·8'W	F	137,138
Ditton Fm	Heref	SO5324	51°55·0'	2°40·6'W	FM	162
Ditton Green	Cambs	TL6658	52°11·9'	0°26·1'E	T	154
Ditton Ho	Win & Maid	SU8682	51°32·0'	0°45·2'W	X	175
Ditton Park	Win & Maid	SU9977	51°29·2'	0°34·1'W	X	175,176
Ditton Park Wood	Cambs	TL6656	52°10·9'	0°26·1'E	F	154
Ditton Place	W Susx	TQ2829	51°3·0'	0°10·0'W	X	187,198
Ditton Priors	Shrops	SO6089	52°30·1'	2°35·0'W	T	138
Dittons	E Susx	TQ6004	50°49·0'	0°16·7'E	T	199
Ditton Sta	Halton	SJ4884	53°21·3'	2°46·5'W	X	108
Divach	Highld	NH4827	57°18·8'	4°31·0'W	X	26
Divach Burn	Highld	NH4826	57°18·2'	4°30·9'W	W	26
Divach Falls	Highld	NH4927	57°18·8'	4°30·0'W	W	26
Divan Wood	Kent	TQ9654	51°15·0'	0°48·9'E	F	189
Divel Covert	N Yks	SE4658	54°1·2'	1°17·5'W	F	105
Divethill	Northum	NY9879	55°6·6'	2°1·5'W	X	87
Division Moor	Cumbr	NY4528	54°38·9'	2°50·7'W	X	90
Divlyn	Carm	SN7638	52°1·8'	3°48·1'W	X	146,160
Divot Hill	D & G	NX6886	55°9·3'	4°3·9'W	H	77
Dixieland	N Yks	SE7177	54°11·3'	0°54·3'W	X	100
Dixon Carr	Durham	NZ1129	54°39·6'	1°49·3'W	X	92
Dixonfield	Highld	ND1366	58°34·7'	3°29·3'W	X	11,12
Dixons	D & G	NY1579	55°6·1'	3°19·5'W	X	85
Dixon's Covert	Suff	TL8269	52°17·6'	0°40·5'E	F	155
Dixon's Dam	Arg & Bt	NS0959	55°47·5'	5°2·4'W	X	63
Dixon's Fm	W Berks	SU3175	51°28·6'	1°32·8'W	FM	174
Dixon's Gap Br	Herts	SP9014	51°49·3'	0°41·3'W	X	165
Dixon's Wood	Northum	NZ1191	55°13·0'	1°49·2'W	F	81
Dix's Fm	Norf	TG1524	52°46·5'	1°11·7'E	FM	133
Dixter Wood	E Susx	TQ8125	51°0·0'	0°35·2'E	F	188,199
Dixton	E Ayr	NS5821	55°28·0'	4°14·3'W	X	71
Dixton	Glos	SO9830	51°58·3'	2°1·4'W	T	150
Dixton	Monm	SO5113	51°49·0'	2°42·3'W	X	162
Dixton Hill	Glos	SO9830	51°58·3'	2°1·4'W	H	150
Dixton Ho	Glos	SO9830	51°58·3'	2°1·4'W	A	150
Dixton Wood	Glos	SO9731	51°58·9'	2°2·2'W	F	150
Dizzard	Corn	SX1698	50°45·4'	4°36·1'W	T	190

Dizzard Point	Corn	SX1699	50°45·9′	4°36·2′W	X	190
Djuba Voe	Shetld	HU3539	60°8·3′	1°21·7′W	W	4
Djuba Water	Shetld	HU2256	60°17·5′	1°35·6′W	W	3
Djuba Water	Shetld	HU2757	60°18·0′	1°30·2′W	W	3
Djuba Wick	Shetld	HU5593	60°37·3′	0°59·2′W	W	1,2
Djubi Dale	Shetld	HU3479	60°29·9′	1°22·4′W	X	2,3
D'mainholm	Scot Bord	NY4783	55°8·6′	2°49·5′W	X	79
Doach	D & G	NX7957	54°53·8′	3°52·8′W	X	84
Doach Burn	D & G	NX7958	54°54·4′	3°52·8′W	W	84
Doalie	Shetld	HT9636	60°6·8′	2°3·8′W	X	4
Doals	Lancs	SD8625	53°43·5′	2°12·3′W	X	103
Doarlish Ard	I of M	SC2778	54°10·4′	4°38·6′W	X	95
Doarlish-Cashen	I of M	SC2378	54°10·3′	4°42·3′W	X	95
Doatshayne Fm	Devon	SY2895	50°45·2′	3°0·9′W	FM	193
Dobbiner Head	N Yks	NZ8600	54°23·5′	0°40·1′W	X	94
Dobbingstone	S Ayr	NS3000	55°16·1′	4°40·1′W	X	76
Dobbingstone Burn	S Ayr	NS3100	55°16·2′	4°39·2′W	W	76
Dobbin's Wood	Lincs	TF0418	52°45·2′	0°27·1′W	X	130
Dobbin Wood	Cumbr	NY4120	54°34·6′	2°54·3′W	X	90
Dobb's Hall Fm	N Yks	NZ2608	54°28·2′	1°35·5′W	FM	93
Dobb's Moor	Devon	SS6816	50°55·9′	3°52·3′W	X	180
Dobb's Weir	Herts	TL3808	51°45·4′	0°0·4′E	X	166
Dobcross	Oldham	SD9906	53°33·3′	2°0·5′W	T	109
Dobcross Hall	Cumbr	NY3945	54°48·0′	2°56·5′W	X	85
Dobella Fm	E Yorks	SE7021	53°41·1′	0°56·0′W	FM	105,106
Dobella Fm	E Yorks	SE7021	53°41·1′	0°56·0′W	FM	105,106,112
Dob Field	Brad	SE0140	53°51·6′	1°58·7′W	X	104
Dobford	Ches	SJ8967	53°12·2′	2°9·5′W	X	118
Dob Gill	Cumbr	NY3113	54°30·7′	3°3·5′W	W	90
Dobies Grave	Scot Bord	NT4938	55°38·2′	2°48·2′W	X	73
Dobinson's Rush	Darl	NZ2020	54°34·7′	1°41·0′W	F	93
Doble Fm	Somer	ST0422	50°59·6′	3°21·7′W	FM	181
Dobpark	Notts	SK5249	53°2·4′	1°13·1′W	X	129
Dob Park	N Yks	SE1849	53°56·4′	1°43·1′W	X	104
Dobpark Lodge	N Yks	SE1950	53°57·0′	1°42·2′W	A	104
Dobpark Wood	N Yks	SE1950	53°57·0′	1°42·2′W	F	104
Dobroyd Castle School	Cald	SD9223	53°42·4′	2°6·9′W	X	103
Dobrudden Fm	Brad	SE1340	53°51·6′	1°47·7′W	FM	104
Dobs Craig	D & G	NT2107	55°21·3′	3°14·3′W	H	79
Dobs Hill	Flint	SJ3063	53°9·8′	3°2·4′W	T	117
Dobshill Fm	Worcs	SO7831	51°58·9′	2°18·8′W	FM	150
Dob's Hole	Cumbr	SD5996	54°21·7′	2°37·4′W	X	97
Dobson's Bridge	Shrops	SJ4934	52°54·3′	2°45·1′W	T	126
Dobson's Stud	Bucks	SU7586	51°34·3′	0°54·7′W	X	175
Dobwalls	Corn	SX2165	50°27·7′	4°30·9′W	T	201
Doccombe	Devon	SX7786	50°39·9′	3°44·0′W	T	191
Dochanassie	Highld	NN2085	56°55·5′	4°57·0′W	X	34,41
Docharn	Highld	NH9220	57°15·7′	3°47·0′W	X	36
Docharn Craig	Highld	NH9220	57°15·7′	3°47·0′W	H	36
Docherniel	S Ayr	NX2286	55°8·4′	4°47·1′W	X	76
Docherniel Burn	S Ayr	NX2388	55°9·5′	4°46·3′W	W	76
Dochfour Hill	Highld	NH5939	57°25·4′	4°20·4′W	X	26
Dochfour Ho	Highld	NH6039	57°25·5′	4°19·4′W	X	26
Dochgarroch	Highld	NH6140	57°26·0′	4°18·5′W	T	26
Dochlaggie	Highld	NH9319	57°15·2′	3°46·0′W	X	36
Dochlewan	Pth & Kin	NN8511	56°16·9′	3°51·0′W	X	58
Dochnalurig	Highld	NH6140	57°26·0′	4°18·5′W	X	26
Dochrie Hill	Pth & Kin	NO0808	56°15·6′	3°28·7′W	H	58
Dochroyle	S Ayr	NX2379	55°4·7′	4°45·9′W	X	76
Dockber	Lancs	SD7847	53°55·4′	2°19·7′W	X	103
Dockenden	Kent	TQ8135	51°5·4′	0°35·5′E	X	188
Dockeney	Norf	TM3891	52°28·1′	1°30·7′E	T	134
Dockenfield	Surrey	SU8240	51°9·4′	0°49·3′W	T	186
Dockenflat	D & G	NY2377	55°5·1′	3°12·0′W	X	85
Dockens Water	Hants	SU1810	50°53·6′	1°44·3′W	W	195
Dockenwell	Aberd	NJ6910	57°11·0′	2°30·3′W	X	38
Docker	Cumbr	SD5695	54°21·2′	2°40·2′W	X	97
Docker	Lancs	SD5774	54°9·8′	2°39·1′W	T	97
Dockeray Bank Plantn	N Yks	SE2584	54°15·3′	1°36·6′W	F	99
Docker Bridge	Cumbr	SD5696	54°21·7′	2°40·2′W	X	97
Docker Fell	Cumbr	SD5794	54°20·6′	2°39·3′W	H	97
Docker Hall	Lancs	SD5775	54°10·4′	2°39·1′W	X	97
Docker Hill	Kent	TR2863	51°19·4′	1°16·7′E	X	179
Docker Knott	Cumbr	SD6599	54°23·4′	2°31·9′W	H	97
Docker Moor	Lancs	SD5775	54°10·4′	2°39·1′W	H	97
Docker Nook	Cumbr	NY5001	54°24·4′	2°45·8′W	X	90
Docker Park	Lancs	SD5773	54°9·3′	2°39·1′W	X	97
Dockett Pt	Surrey	TQ0665	51°22·7′	0°28·2′W	X	176
Dock Fm	Suff	TM3847	52°4·4′	1°28·8′E	FM	169
Dock Furrows	Lincs	TF0922	52°47·3′	0°22·6′W	X	130
Dockham Bottom	Wilts	ST8823	51°0·6′	2°9·9′W	X	183
Docking	Norf	TF7637	52°54·3′	0°37·4′E	T	132
Docking Common	Norf	TF7935	52°53·2′	0°40·0′E	X	132
Docking Fm	Norf	TG1526	52°47·5′	1°11·7′E	FM	133
Docking Fm	Norf	TM0593	52°30·0′	1°1·6′E	FM	144
Docking Hall	Suff	TM3180	52°22·4′	1°24·0′E	X	156
Docking Lodge	Norf	TF7735	52°53·2′	0°38·3′E	X	132
Docking Slack Plantn	N Yks	NZ3307	54°27·7′	1°29·0′W	F	93
Dockington	Aberd	NJ3815	57°13·6′	3°1·2′W	X	37
Docklow	Heref	SO5657	52°12·8′	2°38·2′W	T	149
Dock of Lingness	Shetld	HU4854	60°16·3′	1°7·4′W	W	3
Dockray	Cumbr	NY2649	54°50·1′	3°8·7′W	X	85
Dockray	Cumbr	NY3921	54°35·1′	2°56·2′W	T	90
Dockraybank	Cumbr	NY2650	54°50·6′	3°8·7′W	X	85
Dockray Hall	Cumbr	NY2750	54°50·6′	3°7·8′W	X	85
Dockray Nook	Cumbr	NY0820	54°34·3′	3°25·0′W	X	89
Dockrayrigg Ho	Cumbr	NY2550	54°50·6′	3°9·7′W	X	85
Dockridding Wood	D & G	NY0768	55°0·1′	3°26·8′W	F	85
Dockroyd	Brad	SE0338	53°50·5′	1°56·9′W	T	104
Docksight Wood	Lincs	TF0115	52°43·6′	0°29·9′W	F	130
Dock Tarn	Cumbr	NY2714	54°31·2′	3°7·2′W	W	89,90
Dockwell Fm	Devon	SX6963	50°27·4′	3°50·4′W	FM	202
Dockwell Gate	Devon	SX6964	50°27·9′	3°50·4′W	X	202
Docton	Devon	SS2421	50°57·9′	4°30·0′W	T	190
Doctor's Barn	Warw	SP3134	52°0·4′	1°32·5′W	X	151
Doctors Coppice	Shrops	SO4278	52°24·1′	2°50·8′W	F	137,148
Doctor's Cotts	Shrops	SO6181	52°25·8′	2°34·0′W	X	138
Doctor's Fm	Devon	ST0111	50°53·6′	3°24·1′W	FM	192
Doctor's Fm	Warw	SP1648	52°8·0′	1°45·6′W	FM	151
Doctor's Gate	Durham	NZ0732	54°41·2′	1°53·1′W	X	92
Doctor's Gate Culvert	Derby	SK0993	53°26·3′	1°51·5′W	X	110
Doctor's Gate (Roman Road)	Derby	SK0893	53°26·3′	1°52·4′W	R	110
Doctor's Pool	Powys	SO1550	52°8·7′	3°14·1′W	W	148
Dod	Scot Bord	NT4705	55°20·4′	2°49·7′W	X	79
Dodavoe	Angus	NO3562	56°45·0′	3°3·3′W	X	44
Dodbrooke	Devon	SX7344	50°17·2′	3°46·6′W	T	202
Dod Burn	Scot Bord	NT4705	55°20·4′	2°49·7′W	W	79
Dodburn	Scot Bord	NT4707	55°21·5′	2°49·7′W	X	79
Dod Burn	Scot Bord	NT8619	55°28·1′	2°12·9′W	W	80
Dodbury	Cumbr	NY7442	54°46·6′	2°23·8′W	X	86,87
Dodcleugh	Scot Bord	NT5257	55°48·5′	2°45·5′W	X	66,73
Dodcott Grange	Ches	SJ6141	52°58·1′	2°34·4′W	X	118
Dod Crag	Cumbr	NY2920	54°34·5′	3°5·5′W	H	89,90
Dodd	Angus	NO4539	56°32·6′	2°53·2′W	X	54
Dodd	Cumbr	NY1615	54°31·6′	3°17·5′W	H	89
Dodd	Cumbr	NY1623	54°36·0′	3°17·6′W	H	89
Dodd	Cumbr	NY2427	54°38·2′	3°10·2′W	H	89,90
Dodd	Cumbr	NY2718	54°33·4′	3°7·3′W	X	89,90
Dodd Bank	Northum	NY7959	54°55·8′	2°19·2′W	X	86,87
Doddenham	Worcs	SO7556	52°12·3′	2°21·6′W	T	150
Doddenhill Fms	Worcs	SO6669	52°19·3′	2°29·5′W	FM	138
Dodder Carr	Red & Cl	NZ7313	54°30·7′	0°51·9′W	X	94
Dodderham Moss	Cumbr	SD7788	54°17·5′	2°20·8′W	F	98
Doddershall Ho	Bucks	SP7120	51°52·7′	0°57·7′W	A	165
Doddershall Wood	Bucks	SP6920	51°52·7′	0°59·5′W	F	165
Dodd Fell	N Yks	SD8484	54°15·3′	2°14·3′W	X	98
Dodd Fell Hill	N Yks	SD8484	54°15·3′	2°14·3′W	H	98
Dodd Hill	Angus	NO4539	56°32·6′	2°53·2′W	H	54
Dodd Hill	D & G	NS5400	55°16·6′	4°17·5′W	H	77
Dodd Hill	D & G	NX5697	55°15·0′	4°15·5′W	H	77
Dodd Hill	D & G	NX6498	55°15·7′	4°8·0′W	H	77
Dodd Hill	N Yks	SE1761	54°2·9′	1°44·0′W	X	99
Doddick	Cumbr	NY3326	54°37·7′	3°1·8′W	X	90
Doddick Fell	Cumbr	NY3327	54°38·3′	3°1·9′W	X	90
Doddick Gill	Cumbr	NY3326	54°37·7′	3°1·8′W	W	90
Doddin	S Lanak	NS9413	55°24·2′	3°40·0′W	H	71,78
Doddinghurst	Essex	TQ5998	51°39·7′	0°18·3′E	T	167,177
Dodding's Fm	Dorset	SY8593	50°44·4′	2°12·4′W	FM	194
Doddington	Cambs	TL3990	52°29·6′	0°3·3′E	T	142,143
Doddington	Kent	TQ9357	51°17·0′	0°46·4′E	T	178
Doddington	Lincs	SK9070	53°13·4′	0°38·7′W	T	121
Doddington	Northum	NT9932	55°35·1′	2°0·5′W	T	75
Doddington	Shrops	SO6176	52°23·1′	2°34·0′W	T	138
Doddington Br	Lincs	SK8347	53°1·1′	0°45·4′W	X	130
Doddington Br	Northum	NT9930	55°34·1′	2°0·5′W	X	75
Doddington Hall	Ches	SJ7046	53°0·9′	2°26·4′W	X	118
Doddington Littlegate	Lincs	SK8747	53°1·0′	0°41·8′W	X	130
Doddington Mill Fm	Ches	SJ7147	53°1·4′	2°25·5′W	FM	118
Doddington Moor	Northum	NU0032	55°35·1′	1°59·6′W	X	75
Doddington Northmoor	Northum	NT9936	55°37·3′	2°0·5′W	X	75
Doddington North Moor	Northum	NU0035	55°36·8′	1°59·6′W	X	75
Doddington Park	Ches	SJ7147	53°1·4′	2°25·5′W	X	118
Doddington Park Fm	Ches	SJ7146	53°0·9′	2°25·5′W	FM	118
Doddington Place	Kent	TQ9457	51°17·0′	0°47·3′E	X	178
Doddiscombe	Devon	SS9823	51°0·1′	3°26·8′W	X	181
Doddiscombsleigh	Devon	SX8586	50°40·0′	3°37·3′W	T	191
Doddle Hill Fm	N Yks	NZ4404	54°26·0′	1°18·9′W	FM	93
Doddlespool Hall	Staffs	SJ7449	53°2·5′	2°22·9′W	X	118
Dodd Resr	Northum	NY8446	54°48·8′	2°14·5′W	W	86,87
Dodd's Bank	E Susx	TQ4526	51°1·1′	0°4·4′E	X	188,198
Dodds Cott	Northnts	SP5254	52°11·1′	1°14·0′W	X	151
Dodd's Fm	Essex	TL5904	51°43·0′	0°18·5′E	FM	167
Dodd's Fm	Essex	TQ6399	51°40·2′	0°21·8′E	FM	167,177
Dodd's Fm	Oxon	SP3213	51°49·1′	1°31·8′W	FM	164
Dodds Fm	Somer	ST2843	51°11·1′	3°1·4′W	FM	182
Dodd's Fm	Suff	TL7655	52°10·1′	0°34·8′E	FM	155
Doddsgreen Fm	Ches	SJ6144	52°59·8′	2°34·5′W	FM	118
Doddshill	Norf	TF6930	52°50·7′	0°31·0′E	T	132
Dodds Howe	Cumbr	SD4391	54°18·9′	2°52·2′W	X	97
Dodd's Wood	Suff	TM3563	52°13·1′	1°26·8′E	F	156
Dodd, The	Cumbr	NY4619	54°34·0′	2°49·7′W	H	90
Dodd, The	Northum	NT9209	55°22·7′	2°7·1′W	H	80
Dodd, The	Northum	NY7392	55°13·5′	2°25·0′W	H	80
Dodd, The	Northum	NY7846	54°48·8′	2°20·1′W	H	86,87
Dodd Wood	Cumbr	NY1424	54°36·5′	3°19·5′W	F	89
Dodd Wood	Cumbr	NY2427	54°38·2′	3°10·2′W	F	89,90
Doddycross	Corn	SX3062	50°26·2′	4°23·2′W	T	201
Dodecote Grange	Shrops	SJ6723	52°48·5′	2°29·0′W	X	127
Dod Fell	D & G	NY3296	55°15·5′	3°3·8′W	H	79
Dod Fell	Scot Bord	NT5800	55°17·8′	2°39·3′W	H	80
Dodford	Northnts	SP6160	52°14·3′	1°6·0′W	T	152
Dodford	Worcs	SO9373	52°21·5′	2°5·8′W	T	139
Dodford Fm	Wilts	ST9780	51°31·4′	2°2·2′W	FM	173
Dodford Fm	Northnts	SP6161	52°14·9′	1°6·0′W	X	152
Dodford Holt	Northnts	SP6061	52°14·9′	1°6·9′W	F	152
Dodford Lodge	Northnts	SP6161	52°14·9′	1°6·0′W	X	152
Dodford Mill	Northnts	SP6159	52°13·8′	1°6·0′W	X	152
Dodge Carr Laithe	N Yks	SD8948	53°55·9′	2°9·6′W	X	103
Dodgen Pot	Cumbr	NY7632	54°41·2′	2°21·9′W	X	91
Dodgsons Fm	N Yks	SD9346	53°54·8′	2°6·0′W	FM	103
Dodgsontown	Cumbr	NY5075	55°4·3′	2°46·6′W	X	86
Dodgson Wood	Cumbr	SD3092	54°19·4′	3°4·2′W	F	96,97
Dodhead	Fife	NT2486	56°3·9′	3°12·8′W	X	66
Dodhead	Scot Bord	NT3619	55°27·9′	3°0·3′W	X	79
Dodhead Burn	Scot Bord	NT3619	55°27·9′	3°0·3′W	W	79
Dodhead Mid Hill	Scot Bord	NT3719	55°27·9′	2°59·4′W	H	79
Dod Hill	Cumbr	NY4105	54°26·5′	2°54·2′W	H	90
Dod Hill	E Loth	NT6263	55°51·8′	2°36·0′W	X	67
Dod Hill	E Loth	NT7267	55°54·0′	2°26·4′W	H	67
Dod Hill	E Renf	NS4953	55°45·1′	4°23·9′W	H	64
Dod Hill	Northum	NT9100	55°17·9′	2°8·1′W	H	80
Dod Hill	Northum	NT9820	55°28·7′	2°1·5′W	H	75
Dod Hill	Scot Bord	NT3232	55°34·9′	3°4·3′W	H	73
Dod Hill	Scot Bord	NT3342	55°40·3′	3°3·5′W	H	73
Dod Hill	Scot Bord	NT4000	55°17·7′	2°56·3′W	H	79
Dod Hill	Scot Bord	NT6912	55°24·3′	2°28·9′W	X	80
Dod Hill	Scot Bord	NT8620	55°28·7′	2°12·9′W	H	74
Dod Hill	Scot Bord	NY4697	55°16·1′	2°50·6′W	H	79
Dod Hill	S Lanak	NT0226	55°31·3′	3°32·7′W	H	72
Dodhill	Somer	ST2128	51°3·0′	3°7·2′W	X	193
Dodholm Fm	N Yks	SE5464	54°4·4′	1°10·1′W	FM	100
Dodholm Wood	N Yks	SE5463	54°3·8′	1°10·1′W	F	100
Dodhurst	Kent	TQ6138	51°7·3′	0°18·4′E	X	188
Dodington	S Glos	ST7480	51°31·3′	2°22·1′W	T	172
Dodington	Somer	ST1740	51°9·4′	3°10·8′W	T	181
Dodington Ash	S Glos	ST7578	51°30·3′	2°21·2′W	X	172
Dodington Ho	S Glos	ST7579	51°30·8′	2°21·2′W	A	172
Dodington Lakes	S Glos	ST7479	51°30·8′	2°22·1′W	W	172
Dodington Manor	S Glos	ST7480	51°31·3′	2°22·1′W	X	172
Dod Law	E Loth	NT5664	55°52·3′	2°41·8′W	H	67
Dod Law	Northum	NU0031	55°34·6′	1°59·6′W	X	75
Dod Law	Scot Bord	NT3750	55°44·6′	2°59·8′W	H	66,73
Dod Law	Scot Bord	NT7716	55°26·5′	2°21·4′W	X	80
Dodleston	Ches	SJ3660	53°8·2′	2°57·0′W	T	117
Dodley	Northum	NZ0769	55°1·2′	1°53·0′W	X	88
Dodley Hill Fm	Bucks	SP7928	51°56·9′	0°50·6′W	FM	165
Dodman Horse	Corn	SX0039	50°13·3′	4°47·9′W	X	204
Dodman Point	Corn	SX0039	50°13·3′	4°47·9′W	X	204
Dodmarsh	Heref	SO5743	52°5·3′	2°37·3′W	T	149
Dod Mill	Scot Bord	NT5848	55°43·7′	2°39·7′W	X	73,74
Dodmoors	Shrops	SJ7206	52°39·3′	2°24·4′W	F	127
Dodnash Priory Fm	Suff	TM1035	51°58·6′	1°3·9′E	FM	155,169
Dodnash Wood	Suff	TM1036	51°59·2′	1°3·9′E	F	155,169
Dodnor Ho	I of W	SZ5091	50°43·2′	1°17·1′W	X	196
Dodovens Fm	Devon	SX5452	50°21·2′	4°2·8′W	FM	201
Dodpen Hill	Dorset	SY3598	50°46·9′	2°54·9′W	X	193
Dod Plantn	Scot Bord	NY4797	55°16·1′	2°49·6′W	F	79
Dodridge Fm	E Loth	NT4164	55°52·2′	2°56·1′W	FM	66
Dod Rig	Scot Bord	NT4602	55°18·8′	2°50·6′W	X	79
Dodrige Law	E Loth	NT4163	55°51·6′	2°56·1′W	H	66
Dods	Scot Bord	NT5847	55°43·1′	2°39·7′W	X	73,74
Dod's Corse Stone	Scot Bord	NT5846	55°42·6′	2°39·7′W	A	73,74
Dodscott	Devon	SS5419	50°57·4′	4°4·3′W	T	180
Dodsdown	Wilts	SU2762	51°21·6′	1°36·3′W	X	174
Dodsey Wood	Lincs	SK9723	52°48·0′	0°33·3′W	F	130
Dodside	E Renf	NS5053	55°45·1′	4°23·0′W	X	64
Dods Leigh	Staffs	SK0134	52°54·4′	1°58·7′W	T	128
Dodsleygate Fm	Ches	SJ5573	53°15·4′	2°40·1′W	FM	117
Dodsley Hall Fm	Ches	SJ5573	53°15·4′	2°40·1′W	FM	117
Dodsley Wood	Hants	SU5438	51°8·6′	1°13·3′W	F	185
Dodsworth Wood	York	SE6849	53°56·2′	0°57·4′W	F	105,106
Dod, The	Cumbr	NY6545	54°48·2′	2°32·2′W	X	86
Dod, The	D & G	NS8114	55°24·6′	3°52·3′W	H	71,78
Dod, The	D & G	NS8114	55°24·6′	3°52·3′W	X	71,78
Dod, The	D & G	NS8117	55°26·2′	3°52·4′W	X	71,78
Dod, The	D & G	NT1100	55°17·4′	3°23·7′W	H	78
Dod, The	D & G	NX9399	55°16·7′	3°40·6′W	X	78
Dod, The	Northum	NT9919	55°28·1′	2°0·5′W	X	81
Dod, The	Scot Bord	NT4121	55°29·0′	2°55·6′W	H	73
Dod, The	Scot Bord	NT5755	55°47·4′	2°40·7′W	X	67,73,74
Dod, The	S Lanak	NS9919	55°27·5′	3°35·4′W	H	78
Dodwell	Warw	SP1654	52°11·3′	1°45·6′W	X	151
Dodworth	Barns	SE3105	53°32·7′	1°31·5′W	T	110,111
Dodworth Bottom	Barns	SE3104	53°32·1′	1°31·5′W	T	110,111
Dodworth Green	Barns	SE3104	53°32·1′	1°31·5′W	T	110,111
Doe Bank	Birm	SP1197	52°34·5′	1°49·9′W	T	139
Doebank Ho	Worcs	SP0362	52°15·6′	1°57·0′W	X	150
Doe Bank Wood	Wals	SP0696	52°33·9′	1°54·3′W	F	139
Doecleuch	Scot Bord	NT4606	55°21·0′	2°50·7′W	X	79
Doeford Br	Lancs	SD6543	53°53·2′	2°31·5′W	X	102,103
Doe Green	Cumbr	NY4219	54°34·0′	2°53·4′W	X	90
Doe Green	Warr	SJ5587	53°22·9′	2°40·2′W	T	108
Doe Hill Fm	Northum	NZ1192	55°13·6′	1°49·2′W	FM	81
Doehill Ho	Derby	SK4159	53°7·8′	1°22·8′W	X	120
Doehole	Derby	SK3558	53°7·3′	1°28·2′W	T	119
Doeholme Fm	Lancs	SD5654	53°59·1′	2°39·8′W	FM	102
Doehouse	Orkney	HY2717	59°2·3′	3°15·8′W	X	6
Doe Lea	Derby	SK4566	53°11·6′	1°19·2′W	T	120
Doe Lea Br	Derby	SK4669	53°13·2′	1°18·3′W	X	120
Doe Park	Brad	SE0734	53°48·4′	1°53·2′W	X	104
Doe Park	Durham	NZ0020	54°34·8′	1°59·6′W	X	92
Doe's Corner	Essex	TL8032	51°57·7′	0°37·6′E	X	168
Does Fm	Essex	TL5102	51°42·0′	0°11·5′E	FM	167
Doesgate Fm	Thurr	TQ6686	51°33·1′	0°24·1′E	FM	177,178
Doe's Hill	D & G	NY2783	55°8·4′	3°8·3′W	H	79
Doeshill Fm	Essex	TQ7392	51°36·2′	0°30·3′E	FM	178
Doeter Common	Devon	SX5384	50°38·5′	4°4·4′W	X	191,201
Doethie Fach	Cered	SN7555	52°11·0′	3°49·3′W	W	146,147
Doethie Fawr	Cered	SN7453	52°9·9′	3°50·1′W	W	146,147
Doe Tor	Devon	SX5484	50°38·5′	4°3·5′W	X	191,201
Doetor Brook	Devon	SX5485	50°39·0′	4°3·5′W	W	191,201
Doffcocker	Bolton	SD6910	53°35·4′	2°27·7′W	T	109
Dog Bank	Pth & Kin	NO3025	56°25·0′	3°7·6′W	X	53,59
Dogberry Plantation	Northum	NU1524	55°30·8′	1°45·3′W	F	75
Dogber Tarn	Cumbr	NY7818	54°33·7′	2°20·0′W	W	91
Dog Bones	Orkney	HY5052	59°21·3′	2°52·3′W	X	5
Dog Burn	D & G	NT0600	55°17·4′	3°28·4′W	W	78
Dogbury	Dorset	ST6605	50°50·8′	2°28·6′W	X	194
Dogbury (Enclosure)	Dorset	ST6605	50°50·8′	2°28·6′W	A	194
Dogbury Gate	Dorset	ST6505	50°50·8′	2°29·4′W	X	194
Dogbush Knowe	Scot Bord	NT6867	55°54·0′	2°30·3′W	X	67
Dog Corner	Norf	TG1226	52°47·6′	1°9·1′E	X	133
Dog Crag	Lancs	SD6156	54°0·2′	2°35·3′W	X	102,103
Dogdean Fm	Wilts	SU1327	51°2·8′	1°48·5′W	FM	184
Dogden Moss	Scot Bord	NT6849	55°44·3′	2°30·1′W	X	74
Dogditch Brook	Shrops	SO5578	52°24·1′	2°39·3′W	W	137,138
Dog & Duck Cott	Shrops	SO2689	52°29·9′	3°5·0′W	X	137
Dogdyke	Lincs	TF2155	53°4·9′	0°11·2′W	T	122
Dog Fall	Highld	NH2828	57°18·9′	4°50·9′W	W	25
Dog Falls	Highld	NN3789	56°58·1′	4°40·4′W	W	34,41
Dog Fm	Beds	TL1049	52°7·9′	0°23·2′W	FM	153
Dogford Wood	Hants	SU6732	51°5·2′	1°2·2′W	F	185,186
Dog Geo	Orkney	HY5317	59°2·5′	2°48·7′W	X	6
Doggerboat	Orkney	HY5337	59°13·3′	2°48·9′W	X	5
Doggett	Suff	TM2274	52°19·4′	1°15·9′E	X	156
Dog & Gun	Liv	SJ3995	53°27·1′	2°54·7′W	T	108
Doghanging Coppice	Worcs	SO7374	52°22·0′	2°23·4′W	F	138
Dog Hill	Cald	SE0017	53°39·2′	1°59·6′W	H	110
Dog Hill	Lincs	TF2178	53°17·3′	0°10·7′W	X	122

Dog Hill	Lincs	TF3476	53°16·1′	0°1·0′E	X	122
Dog Hill	Oldham	SD9509	53°34·9′	2°4·1′W	T	109
Doghillock	Aberd	NJ8952	57°31·3′	2°10·6′W	X	30
Dog Hillock	Angus	NO2879	56°54·1′	3°10·5′W	H	44
Dog Hillock	Angus	NO4270	56°49·3′	2°56·6′W	H	44
Dog Hillock	E Ayr	NS5633	55°34·4′	4°16·6′W	X	71
Doghillock	Falk	NS8283	56°1·8′	3°53·2′W	X	57,65
Doghole Fm	Corn	SX4062	50°26·4′	4°14·8′W	FM	201
Dog Holes	Lancs	SD4873	54°9·3′	2°47·4′W	A	97
Doghouse Fm	Dorset	SY4292	50°43·7′	2°48·9′W	FM	193
Doghouse Hill	Dorset	SY4391	50°43·2′	2°48·1′W	X	193
Dog-in-a-Doublet Fm	Peterb	TL2699	52°34·7′	0°8·0′W	FM	142
Dogingtree Estate	Staffs	SJ9713	52°43·1′	2°2·3′W	T	127
Dog Kennel	Oxon	SP3821	51°53·4′	1°26·5′W	F	164
Dogkennel Cotts	W Susx	SU9515	50°55·8′	0°38·5′W	X	197
Dog Kennel Fm	Bath & NE Somer	ST7958	51°19·5′	2°17·7′W	FM	172
Dog Kennel Fm	E Yorks	TA0041	53°51·6′	0°28·4′W	FM	106,107
Dog Kennel Fm	Herts	TL1225	51°55·0′	0°21·9′W	FM	166
Dog Kennel Fm	Lincs	TF1487	53°22·3′	0°16·8′W	FM	113,121
Dogkennel Green	Surrey	TQ1150	51°14·5′	0°24·2′W	X	187
Dog Kennel Hill	Redbr	TQ4792	51°36·7′	0°7·8′E	H	177
Dog Kennel Pond	Roth	SK4096	53°27·8′	1°23·4′W	W	111
Dog Knowe	Scot Bord	NT5803	55°19·4′	2°39·3′W	H	80
Dog Knowe	Scot Bord	NY4396	55°15·5′	2°53·4′W	X	79
Doglands, The	Staffs	SJ9830	52°52·3′	2°1·4′W	X	127
Doglane Fm	Ches	SJ4545	53°0·2′	2°48·8′W	FM	117
Doglane Fm	Staffs	SK1150	53°3·1′	1°49·7′W	FM	119
Dog Law	Scot Bord	NT6762	55°51·3′	2°31·2′W	X	67
Dogley Lane	Kirk	SE1814	53°37·6′	1°43·3′W	T	110
Dogloitch Wood	Kirk	SE2723	53°42·4′	1°35·0′W	F	104
Dogmersfield	Hants	SU7852	51°15·9′	0°52·5′W	T	186
Dogmersfield Park	Hants	SU7751	51°15·4′	0°53·4′W	X	186
Dog Mills, The	I of M	SC4597	54°21·0′	4°22·7′W	X	95
Dog Rock	Derby	SK0795	53°27·3′	1°53·3′W	X	110
Dogshillock	Aberd	NJ6154	57°34·7′	2°38·7′W	X	29
Dogshillock	Aberd	NJ6255	57°35·3′	2°37·7′W	X	29
Dogsthorpe	Peterb	TF2001	52°35·8′	0°13·9′W	T	142
Dogtail Plantn	Wilts	SU0455	51°17·9′	1°56·2′W	F	173
Dogton	Fife	NT2396	56°9·3′	3°13·9′W	X	58
Dog Village	Devon	SX9896	50°45·5′	3°26·4′W	T	192
Dogwell Fm	Dorset	ST5307	50°51·9′	2°39·7′W	FM	194
Doide	Arg & Bt	NR7076	55°55·6′	5°40·5′W	X	61,62
Doir' a' Bhuilg	Highld	NG4533	57°19·2′	6°13·7′W	X	32
Doir' a' Chatha	Highld	NC5002	57°59·2′	4°31·8′W	X	16
Doir' a' Chrorain	Arg & Bt	NR5876	55°55·2′	5°52·0′W	X	61
Doir' a' Chuilinn	Arg & Bt	NM6731	56°25·1′	5°46·2′W	X	49
Doir a' Mhadaidh	Highld	NH0281	57°46·8′	5°19·3′W	X	19
Doir' a' Mhàim	Arg & Bt	NM6333	56°26·0′	5°50·2′W	X	49
Doir' an Daimh	Highld	NN1697	57°1·9′	5°1·5′W	X	34
Doire a' Chapuill	Highld	NH0360	57°35·5′	5°17·3′W	X	19
Doire an Daimh	Highld	NM7066	56°44·0′	5°45·2′W	X	40
Doireaneighinn	Highld	NM6573	56°47·6′	5°50·4′W	X	40
Doire an Fhùdair	Highld	NC1901	57°58·0′	5°3·1′W	F	15
Doirean na h-Earba	Highld	NN1798	57°2·5′	5°0·5′W	X	34
Doire-aonar	Highld	NG8053	57°31·1′	5°40·0′W	X	24
Doire Asamaidh	Highld	NG8702	57°3·9′	5°30·3′W	X	33
Doire Bàn	Highld	NN0964	56°44·0′	5°6·9′W	H	41
Doire Beithe	Highld	NG9355	57°32·5′	5°27·1′W	X	25
Doire Bhail' Ailein	N Eil	NB2921	58°6·0′	6°35·5′W	F	13,14
Doire Bhraghad	Aberd	NO0790	56°59·8′	3°31·4′W	X	43
Doire Bhuidhe	N Ayr	NR9249	55°41·7′	5°18·1′W	X	62,69
Doire Buidhe	Highld	NM7150	56°35·4′	5°43·3′W	X	49
Doire Chaol	Highld	NG4413	57°8·5′	6°13·4′W	H	32
Doire-chlaigionn	Highld	NG8154	57°31·7′	5°39·0′W	H	24
Doire Chreagach	Arg & Bt	NR7872	55°53·7′	5°32·6′W	X	62
Doire Daimh	Highld	NC2023	58°9·8′	5°3·1′W	X	15
Doire Damh	Highld	NG8750	57°29·7′	5°32·8′W	X	24
Doire Damh	Highld	NH1920	57°14·4′	4°59·5′W	F	25
Doire Darach	Arg & Bt	NN2841	56°32·0′	4°47·4′W	X	50
Doire Daraich	Arg & Bt	NM5738	56°28·5′	5°56·3′W	X	47,48
Doire Daraich	Arg & Bt	NM6739	56°29·4′	5°46·6′W	X	49
Doire Daraich	Highld	NM5366	56°43·5′	6°1·8′W	X	47
Doire Daraich	Highld	NM7440	56°30·1′	5°39·9′W	X	49
Doire Dhamh	Highld	NM8580	56°52·0′	5°31·2′W	X	40
Doire Dhonn	Arg & Bt	NR6589	56°2·4′	5°45·9′W	X	55,61
Doire Dhonn	Highld	NH1109	57°8·2′	5°6·9′W	X	34
Doire Dhubh	Highld	NC1310	58°2·7′	5°9·6′W	X	15
Doire Dhubh	Highld	NH1378	57°45·4′	5°8·1′W	H	19
Doire Donn	Highld	NN0570	56°47·1′	5°11·1′W	X	41
Doire Dorch	Arg & Bt	NM6342	56°30·9′	5°50·7′W	X	49
Doire Driseach	Highld	NN0069	56°46·4′	5°15·9′W	X	41
Doire Dubh	Arg & Bt	NR5575	55°54·6′	5°54·8′W	X	61
Doire Dubh	Highld	NH0901	57°3·9′	5°8·6′W	X	33
Doire Dubh	Highld	NM7366	56°44·1′	5°42·2′W	X	40
Doire Dubh	Highld	NN0190	56°57·8′	5°15·9′W	X	33
Doire Fhada	Arg & Bt	NR7671	55°53·1′	5°34·5′W	X	62
Doire Fhada	Highld	NM6683	56°53·0′	5°50·0′W	X	40
Doire Garbh	Highld	NN1699	57°3·0′	5°1·6′W	X	34
Doire Gharbh	Highld	NH0531	57°19·9′	5°13·9′W	X	25
Doire Giubhais	Highld	NH1163	57°37·3′	5°9·4′W	X	19
Doire Gobhlach	Highld	NH4609	57°9·0′	4°32·3′W	X	34
Doire Leathan	Pth & Kin	NN8155	56°40·6′	3°56·1′W	H	52
Doire Liath	Arg & Bt	NR4057	55°44·5′	6°8·1′W	X	60
Doire Liath	Arg & Bt	NR4466	55°49·4′	6°4·8′W	X	60,61
Doire Meurach	Highld	NH5611	57°10·3′	4°22·4′W	X	35
Doire Mhór	Highld	NG4614	57°9·1′	6°11·5′W	X	32
Doire Mhór	Highld	NH1909	57°8·4′	4°59·0′W	X	34
Doire Mhór	Highld	NH2227	57°18·2′	4°56·8′W	X	25
Doire Mhór	Highld	NH5838	57°24·9′	4°21·4′W	X	26
Doire Mór	Highld	NM9276	56°50·0′	5°24·1′W	X	40
Doire na Gairbhe	Highld	NH0158	57°34·4′	5°19·2′W	X	25
Doire na Guaile	Highld	NG6154	57°31·1′	5°59·0′W	X	24
Doire na h-Achlais	Highld	NG5804	57°4·1′	5°59·1′W	X	32,39
Doire na h-Achlais	Highld	NG6107	57°5·8′	5°56·3′W	X	32
Doire na h-Achlaise	Highld	NH1303	57°5·1′	5°4·7′W	X	34
Doire na h-Achlaise	Highld	NM7786	56°55·0′	5°39·4′W	F	40
Doire na h-Achlaise	Highld	NN2598	57°2·7′	4°52·6′W	X	34
Doire na h-Earbaige	Arg & Bt	NR7335	55°33·6′	5°35·6′W	X	68
Doire na h-Innes	Pth & Kin	NN4357	56°41·0′	4°33·3′W	X	42,51
Doire-nam-bò	Highld	NG4514	57°9·0′	6°12·5′W	X	32
Doire na Muice	Highld	NN0176	56°50·2′	5°15·3′W	X	41
Doire nan Cluainean	Highld	NM9897	57°1·5′	5°19·2′W	X	33,40
Doire nan Damh	Arg & Bt	NM5053	56°36·4′	6°4·0′W	X	47
Doire nan Gad	Highld	NM7757	56°39·4′	5°37·9′W	X	49
Doire nan Taghan	Arg & Bt	NN2341	56°31·9′	4°52·2′W	X	50
Doire na Saor	Arg & Bt	NN0540	56°31·0′	5°9·7′W	X	50
Doire Néill	Highld	NM8584	56°54·1′	5°31·4′W	X	40
Doire Tana	Highld	NH2228	57°18·7′	4°56·9′W	X	25
Doire Thulaichean	Highld	NH3602	57°5·1′	4°41·9′W	X	34
Doirlinn	Highld	NM6058	56°39·4′	5°54·5′W	X	49
Doirlinn a' Chailbhe	Arg & Bt	NM5254	56°37·0′	6°2·1′W	W	47
Doirlinn Head	N Eil	NL6299	56°57·8′	7°33·3′W	X	31
Doirlinn, The	Arg & Bt	NR7419	55°25·0′	5°33·8′W	X	68
Dola	Highld	NC6007	58°2·1′	4°21·8′W	X	16
Dolachddu	Carm	SN7642	52°4·0′	3°48·1′W	X	146,147,160
Doladron	Powys	SJ1013	52°42·7′	3°19·5′W	X	125
Dolaeron	Pemb	SN0620	51°50·9′	4°48·6′W	X	145,158
Dolafallen	Powys	SN9566	52°17·2′	3°32·0′W	X	136,147
Dolalau-isaf	Pemb	SN2136	51°59·9′	4°36·1′W	X	145
Dôl Alice	Monm	SO2728	51°57·0′	3°3·3′W	X	161
Dolanog	Powys	SJ0612	52°42·1′	3°23·1′W	T	125
Dolarddyn	Powys	SJ1506	52°38·9′	3°15·0′W	X	125
Dolassey	Powys	SO2068	52°18·5′	3°10·0′W	X	137,148
Dolau	Cered	SN5143	52°4·2′	4°10·0′W	X	146
Dolau	Cered	SN6281	52°24·8′	4°1·3′W	X	135
Dolau	Conwy	SH8467	53°11·5′	3°43·8′W	X	116
Dolau	Conwy	SH9461	53°8·4′	3°34·7′W	X	116
Dolau	Powys	SH9706	52°38·8′	3°30·9′W	X	125
Dolau	Powys	SJ0405	52°38·3′	3°24·7′W	X	125
Dolau	Powys	SO1467	52°17·9′	3°15·3′W	T	136,148
Dolau	Rho Cyn Taf	ST0082	51°31·9′	3°26·1′W	T	170
Dolau Aeron	Cered	SN5958	52°12·4′	4°3·4′W	X	146
Dolau-bach	Pemb	SN0630	51°56·3′	4°48·9′W	X	145
Dolaucothi Fm	Carm	SN6640	52°2·8′	3°56·8′W	FM	146
Dolau-couon	Cered	SN5460	52°13·4′	4°7·9′W	X	146
Dolaucwmffrwd	Powys	SO0879	52°24·3′	3°20·7′W	X	136,147
Dolau Fm	Carm	SN6926	51°55·3′	3°53·9′W	FM	146,160
Dolaugleision	Carm	SN6435	52°0·0′	3°58·5′W	X	146
Dolaugwyn	Gwyn	SH6203	52°36·7′	4°1·9′W	A	135
Dolau-gwyn	Gwyn	SH6502	52°36·2′	3°59·2′W	X	135
Dolaugwynion	Carm	SN7935	52°0·3′	3°45·4′W	X	146,160
Dolaugwyrddon	Cered	SN5546	52°5·8′	4°6·6′W	X	146
Dolauhirion	Carm	SN7636	52°0·8′	3°48·0′W	X	146,160
Dolau-Ifan-ddu	Brig	SS9387	51°34·5′	3°32·3′W	X	170
Dolau-llannerch	Pemb	SN2335	51°59·4′	4°34·3′W	X	145
Dolaumaen	Pemb	SN1631	51°57·1′	4°40·3′W	X	145
Dolaumeinion	Carm	SN3716	51°49·4′	4°21·5′W	X	159
Dolawen	Gwyn	SH6364	53°9·6′	4°2·5′W	X	115
Dolbachog	Powys	SN8893	52°31·6′	3°38·7′W	X	135,136
Dolbadarn Castle	Gwyn	SH5859	53°6·8′	4°6·9′W	A	115
Dolbantau	Cered	SN4440	52°2·4′	4°16·1′W	X	146
Dolbebin	Gwyn	SH6127	52°49·6′	4°3·4′W	X	124
Dolbedwin	Powys	SO2049	52°8·2′	3°9·7′W	A	148
Dolbelydr	Gwyn	SH7237	52°55·2′	3°53·8′W	X	124
Dolben	Conwy	SJ0170	53°13·3′	3°28·6′W	X	116
Dolbenmaen	Gwyn	SH5043	52°58·0′	4°13·6′W	T	124
Dolberthog	Powys	SO0460	52°14·0′	3°23·9′W	X	147
Dolbeudiau	Cered	SN7166	52°16·9′	3°53·1′W	X	135,147
Dôl-Caradog	Powys	SN7998	52°34·2′	3°46·7′W	X	135
Dol-chenog	Cered	SN7873	52°20·7′	3°47·1′W	X	135,147
Dolcoed	Carm	SN4839	52°2·0′	4°12·6′W	X	146
Dôlcoed	Carm	SN6727	51°55·8′	3°55·7′W	X	146
Dolcoppice	I of W	SZ5079	50°36·7′	1°17·2′W	X	196
Dolcorsllwyn Hall	Powys	SH8409	52°40·2′	3°42·5′W	X	124,125
Dol-cyn-afon	Gwyn	SH7928	52°50·4′	3°47·4′W	X	124
Dolddeuli	Gwyn	SH8223	52°47·7′	3°44·6′W	X	124,125
Dolddinas	Gwyn	SH7337	52°55·2′	3°52·9′W	X	124
Dôl-Deheuwydd	Gwyn	SH6304	52°37·2′	4°1·0′W	X	135
Dolderwen	Powys	SN9451	52°9·1′	3°32·6′W	X	147
Doldowlod Ho	Powys	SN9962	52°15·1′	3°28·4′W	X	147
Doldy Fm	Angus	NO1961	56°44·3′	3°19·0′W	FM	43
Dole	Cered	SN6386	52°27·5′	4°0·6′W	T	135
Dole Bank	N Yks	SE2764	54°4·5′	1°34·8′W	X	99
Dolebolion	Cered	SN7366	52°16·9′	3°51·3′W	X	135,147
Dolebury Warren	N Som	ST4558	51°19·3′	2°47·0′W	H	172,182
Doleham Fm	E Susx	TQ8316	50°55·1′	0°36·6′E	FM	199
Doleham Station	E Susx	TQ8316	50°55·1′	0°36·6′E	X	199
Doleiddan	Carm	SN4921	51°52·3′	4°11·2′W	X	159
Doleinion	Gwyn	SH7211	52°41·1′	3°53·2′W	X	124
Dolellog	Gwyn	SH4858	53°6·1′	4°15·8′W	X	115,123
Dolemeads	Bath & NE Somer	ST7564	51°22·7′	2°21·2′W	T	172
Dolennion	Wrex	SJ4146	53°0·7′	2°52·4′W	X	117
Dolerwydd	Carm	SN2315	51°48·6′	4°33·7′W	X	158
Dole's Ash Fm	Dorset	ST7200	50°48·2′	2°23·5′W	FM	194
Dole's Covert	Suff	TM4590	52°27·4′	1°36·8′E	F	134
Dolesden	Bucks	SU7690	51°36·5′	0°53·8′W	X	175
Doles Fm	Hants	SU3651	51°15·7′	1°28·7′W	FM	185
Doles Fm	Norf	TM2182	52°23·7′	1°15·3′E	FM	156
Dole's Hill Plantation	Dorset	SY7398	50°47·1′	2°22·6′W	F	194
Doles, The	Norf	TG3913	52°39·9′	1°32·5′E	X	133,134
Doles Wood	Hants	SU3852	51°16·2′	1°26·9′W	F	185
Dole Wood	Lincs	TF0916	52°44·1′	0°22·7′W	F	130
Doley	Staffs	SJ7429	52°51·7′	2°22·8′W	T	127
Doleygate	Staffs	SJ8121	52°47·4′	2°16·5′W	X	127
Doley Wood	Suff	TL6952	52°8·7′	0°28·6′E	F	154
Dôl-fach	Gwyn	SH8730	52°51·6′	3°40·3′W	X	124,125
Dolfach	Powys	SH9101	52°36·0′	3°36·2′W	T	136
Dolfach	Powys	SN9177	52°23·1′	3°35·7′W	X	136,147
Dolfallt	Carm	SN7942	52°4·0′	3°45·5′W	X	146,147,160
Dolfan	Powys	SN9252	52°9·6′	3°34·3′W	X	147
Dolfawr	Cered	SN7167	52°17·4′	3°53·1′W	X	135,147
Dolfawr	Gwyn	SH7220	52°46·0′	3°53·4′W	X	124
Dolfawr	Gwyn	SH8830	52°51·6′	3°39·4′W	X	124,125
Dôl Fawr	Powys	SH8806	52°38·7′	3°38·9′W	X	124,125
Dolfawr	Powys	SO0257	52°12·3′	3°25·7′W	X	147
Dolfawr	Powys	SO1826	51°55·8′	3°11·2′W	X	161
Dolfawr Fm	Powys	SO0657	52°12·4′	3°22·1′W	FM	147
Dol-ffanog	Gwyn	SH7210	52°40·6′	3°53·2′W	T	124
Dol-Fonddu	Powys	SH8306	52°38·6′	3°43·4′W	X	124,125
Dolfor	Cered	SN6671	52°19·5′	3°57·6′W	X	135
Dol-fôr	Powys	SH8106	52°38·6′	3°45·1′W	X	124,125
Dolfor	Powys	SO1087	52°28·7′	3°19·1′W	T	136
Dolforgan Hall	Powys	SO1490	52°30·3′	3°15·6′W	X	136
Dolforwyn Castle	Powys	SO1595	52°33·0′	3°14·8′W	A	136
Dolforwyn Hall	Powys	SO1695	52°33·0′	3°13·9′W	X	136
Dolfriog	Gwyn	SH6145	52°59·3′	4°3·8′W	X	115
Dol-friog	Powys	SN9699	52°35·0′	3°31·7′W	X	136
Dôl-frwynog	Gwyn	SH7425	52°48·7′	3°51·8′W	X	124
Dolgadfan	Powys	SH8800	52°35·4′	3°38·8′W	X	135,136
Dolgafros	Carm	SN4828	51°56·0′	4°12·3′W	X	146
Dôl-Gain	Gwyn	SH7230	52°51·4′	3°53·7′W	X	124
Dolgair	Powys	SJ0900	52°35·7′	3°20·2′W	X	136
Dôl-gam	Conwy	SH7457	53°6·0′	3°52·5′W	X	115
Dolgar Brook	Powys	SJ0800	52°35·6′	3°21·1′W	W	136
Dolgarreg	Carm	SN7331	51°58·0′	3°50·5′W	X	146,160
Dolgarrog	Conwy	SH7767	53°11·4′	3°50·1′W	T	115
Dolgau Fm	Cered	SN6486	52°27·5′	3°59·7′W	FM	135
Dolgead Hall	Powys	SJ0808	52°40·0′	3°21·2′W	X	125
Dolgellau	Gwyn	SH7217	52°44·4′	3°53·4′W	T	124
Dolgelynen	Cered	SN2750	52°7·5′	4°31·2′W	X	145
Dolgerdd	Cered	SN4250	52°7·8′	4°18·1′W	T	146
Dolgian	Cered	SN3144	52°4·4′	4°27·6′W	X	145
Dôl-goch	Cered	SN7094	52°31·9′	3°54·6′W	X	135
Dolgoch	Cered	SN7958	52°12·7′	3°45·9′W	X	146,147
Dolgoch	Cered	SN8056	52°11·6′	3°44·9′W	X	147
Dol-goch	Conwy	SH8470	53°13·1′	3°43·8′W	X	116
Dolgoch	Gwyn	SH6504	52°37·3′	3°59·3′W	T	135
Dolgoch Falls	Gwyn	SH6504	52°37·3′	3°59·3′W	W	135
Dolgoed	Gwyn	SH7712	52°41·7′	3°48·8′W	X	124
Dolgors	Cered	SN7474	52°21·2′	3°50·6′W	X	135,147
Dolgoy	Cered	SN3454	52°9·8′	4°25·2′W	X	145
Dolgraian	Conwy	SH8473	53°14·7′	3°43·9′W	X	116
Dolgran	Carm	SN4334	51°59·2′	4°16·8′W	X	146
Dolgrogws Fm	Carm	SN4241	52°2·9′	4°17·9′W	FM	146
Dol-gün	Gwyn	SH7418	52°44·9′	3°51·6′W	X	124
Dolguog Hall	Powys	SH7601	52°35·8′	3°49·4′W	X	135
Dolgwartheg	Cered	SN4661	52°13·8′	4°14·9′W	X	146
Dolgwden	Powys	SN9589	52°29·6′	3°32·4′W	X	136
Dolgwenith	Powys	SN9887	52°28·5′	3°29·7′W	X	136
Dolgwm-Isaf	Carm	SN5545	52°5·3′	4°6·6′W	X	146
Dolgwm-uchaf	Carm	SN5545	52°5·3′	4°6·6′W	X	146
Dolgynglas	Denb	SJ0147	53°0·9′	3°28·1′W	X	116
Dolhafren	Powys	SO0491	52°30·7′	3°24·5′W	X	136
Dol-haidd	Carm	SN3440	52°2·3′	4°24·8′W	X	145
Dôl-haidd	Gwyn	SH7536	52°54·7′	3°51·1′W	X	124
Dolhelfa	Powys	SN9273	52°20·9′	3°34·7′W	T	136,147
Dolhendre	Gwyn	SH8531	52°52·1′	3°42·1′W	T	124,125
Dôl-Hywel	Powys	SH9807	52°39·3′	3°30·1′W	X	125
Dôl-Hywel	Powys	SH9908	52°39·9′	3°29·2′W	X	125
Dolifor	Cered	SN3842	52°3·4′	4°21·4′W	X	145
Dolifor Fm	Powys	SN9565	52°16·6′	3°31·9′W	FM	136,147
Dolish Fm	Devon	ST1706	50°51·1′	3°10·4′W	FM	192,193
Doll	Highld	NC8803	58°0·4′	3°53·2′W	T	17
Dollagh	I of M	SC3494	54°19·1′	4°32·7′W	X	95
Dollagh Mooar	I of M	SC3594	54°19·1′	4°31·8′W	X	95
Dollar	Clackm	NS9698	56°10·1′	3°40·0′W	T	58
Dollarbank	Clackm	NS9598	56°10·0′	3°41·0′W	X	58
Dollarbeg	Clackm	NS9796	56°9·0′	3°39·0′W	X	58
Dollard	D & G	NX9294	55°14·0′	3°41·5′W	X	78
Dollard Hill	D & G	NX9394	55°14·0′	3°40·5′W	H	78
Dollards Fm	Ches	SJ9367	53°12·2′	2°5·9′W	FM	118
Dollarfield	Clackm	NS9697	56°9·5′	3°40·0′W	X	58
Dollar Fm	Bucks	SP8926	51°55·8′	0°41·9′W	FM	165
Dollar Glen	Clackm	NS9698	56°10·1′	3°40·0′W	X	58
Dollar Law	Scot Bord	NT1727	55°32·0′	3°18·5′W	H	72
Dollars Grove Fm	Mil Key	SP9445	52°6·0′	0°37·3′W	FM	153
Dol-lâs	Powys	SJ1900	52°35·7′	3°11·4′W	X	136
Dollaston	Pemb	SN0019	51°50·3′	4°53·8′W	X	157,158
Dollerie House	Pth & Kin	NN9020	56°21·8′	3°46·4′W	X	52,58
Dolleriemuir	Pth & Kin	NN9019	56°21·3′	3°46·4′W	X	58
Dolley Green	Powys	SO2865	52°16·9′	3°2·9′W	T	137,148
Dolling's Fm	Somer	ST1526	51°1·9′	3°12·3′W	FM	181,193
Dollis Hill	Brent	TQ2286	51°33·8′	0°14·0′W	T	176
Dol-llan	Carm	SN4240	52°2·4′	4°17·8′W	X	146
Dol-llugan	Powys	SO2167	52°18·0′	3°9·1′W	X	137,148
Dol-llwyn-hir	Powys	SO0461	52°14·6′	3°24·0′W	X	147
Dol-llys	Powys	SN9585	52°27·4′	3°32·3′W	X	136
Doll, The	Angus	NO2775	56°51·9′	3°11·4′W	X	44
Dollwen	Cered	SN6881	52°24·9′	3°56·1′W	T	135
Dolly Bog Wood	N Yks	SE1688	54°17·5′	1°44·8′W	F	99
Dolly Fm	Fife	NT0692	56°6·9′	3°30·3′W	FM	58
Dollymans Fm	Essex	TQ7792	51°36·2′	0°33·7′E	FM	178
Dollynwydd	Powys	SO0448	52°7·6′	3°23·7′W	X	147
Dolly Rig	Scot Bord	NT3812	55°24·1′	2°58·3′W	X	79
Dollyth Howe	N Yks	SE9167	54°5·7′	0°36·1′W	X	101
Dollywaggon Pike	Cumbr	NY3413	54°30·7′	3°0·7′W	H	90
Dolmaen	Cered	SN4354	52°10·0′	4°17·3′W	X	146
Dolman's Fm	Wilts	ST9890	51°36·8′	2°1·3′W	FM	163,173
Dolman's Hill	Dorset	SY9295	50°45·5′	2°6·4′W	X	195
Dolmeinir	I of Angl	SH4478	53°16·8′	4°20·0′W	X	114,115
Dolmelynllyn	Gwyn	SH7223	52°47·6′	3°53·5′W	X	124
Dolmenyn	Powys	SN9649	52°8·0′	3°30·8′W	X	147
Dolobran	Gwyn	SH8416	52°44·0′	3°42·7′W	X	124,125
Dolobran Hall	Powys	SJ1112	52°42·1′	3°18·6′W	X	125
Dologau	Cered	SN7773	52°20·7′	3°47·9′W	X	135,147
Dolor Point	Corn	SW7818	50°1·5′	5°5·6′W	X	204
Dolpebyll	Powys	SJ0011	52°41·5′	3°28·4′W	X	125
Dolpenanner	Conwy	SH9168	53°12·1′	3°37·5′W	X	116
Dolphenby	Cumbr	NY5731	54°40·6′	2°39·6′W	X	91
Dolphin	Flint	SJ1973	53°15·1′	3°12·4′W	T	116
Dolphin Fm	Norf	TL9582	52°24·3′	0°52·4′E	FM	144
Dolphingstone	E Loth	NT3872	55°56·5′	2°59·1′W	T	66
Dolphinholme	Lancs	SD5153	53°58·5′	2°44·5′W	T	102
Dolphinston	Scot Bord	NT6815	55°25·9′	2°29·9′W	T	80
Dolphin Stones	Northum	NU0941	55°40·0′	1°51·0′W	X	75
Dolphinston Moor	Scot Bord	NT6815	55°25·9′	2°29·9′W	X	80
Dolphinton	S Lanak	NT1046	55°42·2′	3°25·5′W	T	72
Dolpwll	Pemb	SN2135	51°59·3′	4°36·0′W	X	145

Dolrannog	Pemb	SN0636	51°59·6'	4°49·2'W	X	145
Dolrhyd	Gwyn	SH7118	52°44·9'	3°54·3'W	X	124
Dolsdon	Corn	SX2795	50°44·0'	4°26·7'W	X	190
Dolserau	Gwyn	SH7519	52°45·5'	3°50·7'W	X	124
Dolton	Devon	SS5712	50°53·6'	4°1·6'W	T	180
Dolton Beacon	Devon	SS5913	50°54·2'	3°59·9'W	X	180
Dolton's Fm	Beds	SP9433	51°59·5'	0°37·5'W	FM	165
Dol-Twymyn	Powys	SH8204	52°37·5'	3°44·2'W	X	135,136
Dolwallter	Cered	SN4440	52°2·4'	4°16·1'W	X	146
Dolward Fm	Heref	SO3336	52°1·3'	2°58·2'W	FM	149,161
Dolwar Fach	Powys	SJ0614	52°43·2'	3°23·1'W	X	125
Dolwar Hall	Powys	SJ0714	52°43·2'	3°22·2'W	X	125
Dôl-wen	Carm	SN4537	52°0·8'	4°15·1'W	X	146
Dolwen	Cered	SN5045	52°5·2'	4°11·0'W	X	146
Dolwen	Conwy	SH8866	53°11·0'	3°40·2'W	X	116
Dolwen	Conwy	SH8874	53°15·3'	3°40·3'W	T	116
Dolwen	Conwy	SH9344	52°59·2'	3°35·2'W	W	125
Dol-wen	Gwyn	SH8442	52°58·0'	3°43·2'W	X	124,125
Dol-wen	Gwyn	SH9533	52°53·3'	3°33·2'W	X	125
Dolwen	Powys	SH9707	52°39·3'	3°31·0'W	X	125
Dolwen	Powys	SN9985	52°27·5'	3°28·8'W	X	136
Dolwen	Wrex	SJ1433	52°53·5'	3°16·3'W	X	125
Dolwen Point	Carm	SN2307	51°44·3'	4°33·4'W	X	158
Dolwen Resr	Conwy	SH9770	53°13·3'	3°32·2'W	W	116
Dolwerdd	Carm	SN4924	51°53·9'	4°11·3'W	X	159
Dolwgan Isa	Gwyn	SH5143	52°58·1'	4°12·7'W	X	124
Dolwilym	Carm	SN1726	51°54·4'	4°39·2'W	X	145,158
Dolwreiddiog	Gwyn	SH6230	52°51·2'	4°2·6'W	X	124
Dolwyd	Conwy	SH8177	53°16·8'	3°46·7'W	T	116
Dolwyddelan	Conwy	SH7352	53°3·3'	3°53·3'W	T	115
Dôl-y-Bont	Cered	SN6288	52°28·6'	4°1·5'W	T	135
Dôl-y-bont	Powys	SH8407	52°39·1'	3°42·5'W	X	124,125
Dol-y-cae	Gwyn	SH7211	52°41·1'	3°53·2'W	X	124
Dol-y-Cannau	Powys	SO2049	52°8·2'	3°9·7'W	X	148
Dol-y-cannau	Powys	SO2049	52°8·2'	3°9·7'W	T	148
Dol-y-clochydd	Gwyn	SH7321	52°46·5'	3°52·6'W	X	124
Dolydd	Gwyn	SH4757	53°5·5'	4°16·7'W	T	115,123
Dolydd	Powys	SN8790	52°30·0'	3°39·5'W	X	135,136
Dolydd Ceiriog	Wrex	SJ1237	52°55·6'	3°18·1'W	X	125
Dol-y-dre	Powys	SO1067	52°17·9'	3°18·8'W	X	136,148
Dol-y-fan	Powys	SO1972	52°20·6'	3°10·9'W	X	136,148
Dôl-y-fan Hill	Powys	SO0161	52°14·5'	3°26·6'W	H	147
Dolyfelin	Powys	SO2274	52°21·8'	3°8·3'W	X	137,148
Dol-y-fran	Powys	SO1574	52°21·7'	3°14·5'W	X	136,148
Dol-y-gaer	Powys	SN9248	52°7·4'	3°34·3'W	X	147
Dolygaer	Powys	SO0514	51°49·2'	3°22·3'W	X	160
Dolygarn	Powys	SO0878	52°23·8'	3°20·7'W	X	136,147
Dol-y-garreg wen-isaf	Powys	SH9504	52°37·7'	3°32·7'W	X	136
Dôl-y-gaseg	Powys	SH9714	52°43·1'	3°31·1'W	X	125
Dolyhir	Powys	SO2457	52°12·6'	3°6·3'W	T	148
Dol-y-maen	Powys	SH9413	52°42·5'	3°33·7'W	X	125
Dolymelinau	Powys	SO0999	52°35·1'	3°20·2'W	T	136
Dolymynach Resr	Powys	SN9061	52°14·4'	3°36·3'W	W	147
Dolypandy	Cered	SN6579	52°23·8'	3°58·7'W	X	135
Dol-y-penau	Conwy	SJ0044	52°59·3'	3°29·0'W	X	125
Dolyrerw Fm	Powys	SO0153	52°10·2'	3°26·5'W	FM	147
Dolyrychain	Cered	SN7165	52°16·3'	3°53·0'W	X	135,147
Dolywern	Wrex	SJ2137	52°55·7'	3°10·1'W	T	126
Doma	E Susx	TQ4625	51°0·6'	0°5·3'E	X	188,198
Domas	Shrops	SJ5900	52°36·0'	2°35·9'W	X	126
Domellick	Corn	SW9458	50°23·4'	4°53·5'W	X	200
Domen Ddreiniog	Gwyn	SH5905	52°36·6'	4°4·5'W	A	135
Domen-ddu	Powys	SO0178	52°23·7'	3°26·9'W	A	136,147
Domen Fawr	Nth Pt Talb	SN8902	51°42·6'	3°36·0'W	A	170
Domen Gastell	Powys	SJ1819	52°46·0'	3°12·5'W	X	125
Domen-gastell Hill	Powys	SJ1619	52°46·0'	3°14·3'W	H	125
Domen Giw	Powys	SN9081	52°25·2'	3°36·7'W	A	136
Domen Las	Cered	SN6896	52°33·0'	3°56·4'W	A	135
Domen Milwyn	Cered	SN8071	52°19·7'	3°45·3'W	X	135,136,147
Domestic Fowl Trust	Worcs	SP1144	52°5·9'	1°50·0'W	X	150
Dome, The	Essex	TQ8394	51°37·1'	0°39·0'E	X	168,178
Domewood	Surrey	TQ3440	51°8·8'	0°4·7'W	T	187
Domgay	Powys	SJ2819	52°46·1'	3°3·6'W	T	126
Dommett	Somer	ST2814	50°55·5'	3°1·1'W	T	193
Dommett Moor	Somer	ST2714	50°55·5'	3°1·9'W	F	193
Domnaheiche	Pth & Kin	NN7957	56°41·6'	3°58·1'W	X	42,51,52
Domnaheiche	Pth & Kin	NN7958	56°42·1'	3°58·1'W	X	42,51,52
Domons Fm	Devon	SX4791	50°42·1'	4°9·6'W	FM	191
Domsey Brook	Essex	TL8919	51°50·5'	0°45·0'E	W	168
Domvilles	Staffs	SJ7751	53°3·6'	2°20·2'W	X	118
Don	Orkney	HY2210	58°58·5'	3°20·9'W	X	6
Dona Close	Cumbr	NY7111	54°29·9'	2°26·4'W	X	91
Donald Murchison's Monument	Highld	NG7827	57°17·0'	5°40·6'W	X	33
Donald Parks	D & G	NX0760	54°54·1'	5°0·2'W	X	82
Donald Rose Resr	Fife	NO3303	56°13·1'	3°4·4'W	W	59
Donald's Cleuch	Scot Bord	NT1417	55°26·6'	3°21·1'W	X	78
Donald's Cleuch Head	Scot Bord	NT1516	55°26·1'	3°20·2'W	X	79
Donaldson's Lodge	Northum	NT8741	55°40·0'	2°12·0'W	X	74
Donavourd	Pth & Kin	NN9557	56°41·8'	3°42·4'W	X	52,53
Doncaster	Donc	SE5702	53°30·9'	1°8·0'W	T	111
Doncaster Carr	Donc	SE5801	53°30·4'	1°7·1'W	X	111
Doncaster Common	Donc	SE6002	53°30·9'	1°5·3'W	T	111
Doncliffe Hall Fm	Dorset	ST8220	50°59·0'	2°15·0'W	FM	183
Donedge Lodge Fm	Dorset	ST8326	51°2·2'	2°14·2'W	FM	183
Dones Green	Ches	SJ6077	53°17·5'	2°35·6'W	T	118
Dongray Hall	Wrex	SJ4046	53°0·7'	2°53·3'W	X	117
Donhead Clift	Wilts	ST8925	51°1·7'	2°9·0'W	X	184
Donhead Hall	Wilts	ST9023	51°0·6'	2°8·2'W	X	184
Donhead St Andrew	Wilts	ST9124	51°1·2'	2°7·3'W	T	184
Donhead St Mary	Wilts	ST9024	51°1·1'	2°8·2'W	T	184
Donibristle	Fife	NT1688	56°4·9'	3°20·5'W	X	65,66
Donibristle Bay	Fife	NT1682	56°1·7'	3°20·4'W	W	65,66
Donich Water	Arg & Bt	NN2101	56°10·3'	4°52·6'W	W	56
Doniford	Somer	ST0843	51°11·0'	3°18·6'W	T	181
Doniford Stream	Somer	ST0939	51°8·8'	3°17·7'W	W	181
Donington	Lincs	TF2135	52°54·2'	0°11·7'W	T	131
Donington	Shrops	SJ8104	52°38·2'	2°16·4'W	T	127
Donington Eaudike	Lincs	TF2336	52°54·7'	0°9·8'W	T	131
Donington Hall	Leic	SK4226	52°50·0'	1°22·2'W	X	129

Donington High Br	Lincs	TF1735	52°54·2'	0°15·2'W	X	130
Donington Ho	Shrops	SJ8105	52°38·8'	2°16·4'W	X	127
Donington le Heath	Leic	SK4112	52°42·5'	1°23·2'W	T	129
Donington on Bain	Lincs	TF2382	53°19·5'	0°8·8'W	T	122
Donington Park Fm	Leic	SK4125	52°49·5'	1°23·1'W	FM	129
Donington South Ing	Lincs	TF2034	52°53·6'	0°12·6'W	T	131
Donington Westdale	Lincs	TF1836	52°54·7'	0°14·3'W	X	130
Donisthorpe	Leic	SK3114	52°43·6'	1°32·1'W	T	128
Don Johns	Essex	TL8328	51°55·4'	0°40·1'E	T	168
Donkey Street	Kent	TR1032	51°3·2'	1°0·2'E	T	189
Donkey Town	Surrey	SU9360	51°20·1'	0°39·5'W	T	175,186
Donkeywell Fm	Glos	SP1303	51°43·8'	1°48·3'W	FM	163
Donkhill Fm	Derby	SK2115	52°44·2'	1°40·9'W	FM	128
Donkin Rigg	Northum	NZ0389	55°12·0'	1°56·7'W	X	81
Donkins	D & G	NY2373	55°3·0'	3°11·9'W	X	85
Donkins House Fm	Northum	NZ1371	55°2·2'	1°47·4'W	FM	88
Donkleywood	Northum	NY7486	55°10·3'	2°24·1'W	X	80
Donlellan	Pth & Kin	NN7958	56°42·1'	3°58·1'W	X	42,51,52
Donna Nook	Lincs	TF4299	53°28·3'	0°8·8'E	T	113
Donnett	Shrops	SJ3230	52°52·0'	3°0·2'W	X	126
Donnewell	Durham	NZ3628	54°39·0'	1°26·1'W	X	93
Donnington	Glos	SO7033	51°59·9'	2°25·8'W	T	149
Donnington	Glos	SP1928	51°57·2'	1°43·0'W	T	163
Donnington	Shrops	SJ5707	52°39·8'	2°37·7'W	T	126
Donnington	W Berks	SU4668	51°24·8'	1°19·9'W	T	174
Donnington	Wrekin	SJ7013	52°43·1'	2°26·2'W	T	127
Donnington	W Susx	SU8502	50°48·9'	0°47·2'W	T	197
Donnington Hall	Heref	SO7033	51°59·9'	2°25·8'W	X	149
Donnington Holt	W Berks	SU4669	51°25·3'	1°19·9'W	X	174
Donnington Manor	W Susx	SU8502	50°48·9'	0°47·2'W	X	197
Donnington Wood	Wrekin	SJ7012	52°42·5'	2°26·2'W	T	127
Donolly Resr	E Loth	NT5768	55°54·4'	2°40·8'W	W	67
Dons Knowe Ho	D & G	NX7747	54°48·4'	3°54·4'W	X	84
Donwell	Sund	NZ2958	54°55·2'	1°32·4'W	T	88
Donyatt	Somer	ST3314	50°55·5'	2°56·8'W	T	193
Donyland Lodge	Essex	TM0222	51°51·8'	0°56·4'E	X	168
Doocot	Aberd	NJ9265	57°40·7'	2°7·6'W	X	30
Doodfield	Stock	SJ9586	53°22·5'	2°4·1'W	X	109
Doodilmore	Arg & Bt	NR3674	55°53·5'	6°12·9'W	X	60,61
Doodilmore River	Arg & Bt	NR3674	55°53·5'	6°12·9'W	W	60,61
Doo Geo	Orkney	HY7553	59°22·0'	2°25·9'W	X	5
Doolie Ness	Aberd	NO8370	56°49·5'	2°16·3'W	X	45
Doolittle Mill	Beds	SP9920	51°52·4'	0°33·3'W	X	165
Doom Bar, The	Corn	SW9278	50°34·1'	4°55·9'W	X	200
Doomsday Green	W Susx	TQ1929	51°3·1'	0°17·7'W	T	187,198
Doomy	Orkney	HY5534	59°11·7'	2°46·8'W	X	5,6
Doon	D & G	NX4078	55°4·5'	4°29·9'W	X	77
Doon	E Loth	NT6775	55°58·3'	2°31·3'W	X	67
Doon Castle	D & G	NX0644	54°45·5'	5°0·5'W	X	82
Doon Castle (Broch)	D & G	NX0644	54°45·5'	5°0·5'W	A	82
Doone Brae Fm	Herts	TL0716	51°50·2'	0°26·4'W	FM	166
Doone Country	Devon	SS7844	51°11·2'	3°44·4'W	X	180
Doonfoot	S Ayr	NS3218	55°25·9'	4°38·9'W	T	70
Doon Hill	D & G	NX3458	54°53·6'	4°34·9'W	H	82
Doonhill	D & G	NX4146	54°47·3'	4°27·9'W	X	83
Doon Hill	D & G	NX5558	54°54·0'	4°15·3'W	H	83
Doon Hill	D & G	NX5960	54°55·1'	4°11·6'W	H	83
Doon Hill	D & G	NX6856	54°53·1'	4°3·0'W	H	83,84
Doon Hill	D & G	NX7451	54°50·5'	3°57·3'W	H	83,84
Doon Hill	E Loth	NT6875	55°58·3'	2°30·3'W	H	67
Doon Hill	S Ayr	NX2596	55°13·9'	4°44·7'W	X	76
Doonholm	S Ayr	NS3317	55°25·4'	4°37·9'W	X	70
Doonie Point	Aberd	NO9090	57°0·3'	2°9·4'W	X	38,45
Doonies	Angus	NO1962	56°44·8'	3°19·0'W	X	43
Doonies Hill	C of Aber	NJ9603	57°7·3'	2°3·5'W	X	38
Doonies Yawns	C of Aber	NJ9603	57°7·3'	2°3·5'W	W	38
Doon of Carsluith	D & G	NX4954	54°51·7'	4°20·7'W	X	83
Doon of Castramont	D & G	NX5959	54°54·6'	4°11·5'W	H	83
Doon of Culreoch	D & G	NX5863	54°56·7'	4°12·6'W	H	83
Doon of May	D & G	NX2951	54°49·7'	4°39·3'W	A	82
Doon of Urr	D & G	NX7769	55°0·3'	3°55·0'W	X	84
Doon of Waterhead	S Ayr	NX4398	55°15·3'	4°27·8'W	X	77
Doons	D & G	NX8197	55°15·4'	3°51·9'W	H	78
Doonside	D & G	NX8856	54°53·4'	3°44·3'W	X	84
Doons Law	Scot Bord	NT8651	55°45·4'	2°12·9'W	X	67,74
Doons, The	D & G	NX8676	55°4·2'	3°46·7'W	X	84
Doons, The (Earthworks)	D & G	NX8676	55°4·2'	3°46·7'W	A	84
Doons, The (Fort)	D & G	NX8676	55°4·2'	3°46·7'W	A	84
Doon, The	D & G	NX6548	54°48·8'	4°5·6'W	X	83,84
Doon, The	D & G	NX6654	54°52·0'	4°4·9'W	A	83,84
Doon, The	N Ayr	NR8829	55°30·8'	5°21·0'W	X	68,69
Doon, The (Fort)	N Ayr	NR8829	55°30·8'	5°21·0'W	A	68,69
Door of Cairnsmore	D & G	NX5164	54°57·2'	4°19·2'W	X	83
Doorpool	Scot Bord	NT6011	55°23·7'	2°37·5'W	X	80
Doorpool Hill	Scot Bord	NT6211	55°23·7'	2°35·6'W	H	80
Doos' Cove	Shetld	HU4645	60°11·5'	1°9·7'W	X	4
Doralt	Powys	SN8528	51°56·4'	3°40·3'W	X	160
Doran's Bend	I of M	SC2882	54°12·5'	4°37·8'W	X	95
Dora's Green	Hants	SU8148	51°13·8'	0°50·0'W	T	186
Dora's Seat	Durham	NY8832	54°41·2'	2°10·7'W	X	91,92
Dorback Burn	Highld	NJ0517	57°14·3'	3°34·0'W	W	36
Dorback Burn	Moray	NH9942	57°27·7'	3°40·6'W	W	27
Dorback Lodge	Highld	NJ0716	57°13·8'	3°32·0'W	X	36
Dorbshill	Aberd	NJ9932	57°23·0'	2°0·5'W	X	30
Dorcan	Swin	SU1984	51°33·5'	1°43·2'W	T	173
Dorcas Fm	Bucks	SP8629	51°57·4'	0°44·5'W	FM	165
Dorchester	Dorset	SY6890	50°42·8'	2°26·8'W	T	194
Dorchester	Oxon	SU5794	51°38·7'	1°10·2'W	T	164,174
Dordale	Worcs	SO9274	52°22·1'	2°6·7'W	T	139
Dordon	Warw	SK2600	52°36·1'	1°36·6'W	T	140
Dordon Hall Fm	Warw	SK2700	52°36·1'	1°35·7'W	FM	140
Dore	Sheff	SK3181	53°19·7'	1°31·7'W	T	110,111
Dore Head	Cumbr	NY1709	54°28·4'	3°16·4'W	X	89,90
Dore Holm	Shetld	HU2176	60°28·3'	1°36·6'W	X	3
Dore Moor	Sheff	SK2982	53°20·3'	1°33·5'W	X	110
Dores	Highld	NH5934	57°22·8'	4°19·8'W	T	26
Doreshill Fm	I of W	SZ5389	50°42·1'	1°14·6'W	FM	196
Doreward's Hall	Essex	TL7625	51°54·0'	0°33·9'E	A	167
Doreys Fm	Dorset	SY9185	50°40·1'	2°7·3'W	FM	195
Dorfold Dairy Ho	Ches	SJ6351	53°3·5'	2°32·7'W	X	118

Dorfold Hall	Ches	SJ6352	53°4·1'	2°32·7'W	A	118
Dorglwyd	Swan	SN6500	51°41·2'	3°56·8'W	X	159
Dorhall Fm	Worcs	SO8974	52°22·1'	2°9·3'W	FM	139
Dorincourt	Surrey	TQ1558	51°18·8'	0°20·6'W	X	187
Dorket Head	Notts	SK5947	53°1·3'	1°6·8'W	X	129
Dorking	Surrey	TQ1649	51°13·9'	0°19·9'W	T	187
Dorking Tye	Suff	TL9136	51°59·6'	0°47·3'E	T	155
Dor Knap	Worcs	SP1035	52°1·0'	1°50·9'W	X	150
Dorlaithers	Aberd	NJ7047	57°31·0'	2°29·6'W	X	29
Dorlethen	Aberd	NJ6922	57°17·5'	2°30·4'W	X	38
Dorley's Corner	Suff	TM3865	52°14·1'	1°29·5'E	T	156
Dormansland	Surrey	TQ4042	51°9·8'	0°0·5'E	T	187
Dormans Park	Surrey	TQ3940	51°8·8'	0°0·4'W	T	187
Dormans Sta	Surrey	TQ3941	51°9·3'	0°0·4'W	X	187
Dormanstead	Cumbr	NY5070	55°1·6'	2°46·5'W	X	86
Dormanstown	Red & Cl	NZ5823	54°36·2'	1°5·7'W	T	93
Dormer's Wells	Ealing	TQ1380	51°30·7'	0°21·9'W	T	176
Dormestone Fm	Kent	TQ9451	51°13·7'	0°47·1'E	FM	189
Dormieston	E Ayr	NS4421	55°27·7'	4°27·6'W	X	70
Dormington	Heref	SO5840	52°3·6'	2°36·4'W	T	149
Dormont	D & G	NY1174	55°3·4'	3°23·2'W	X	85
Dormston	Worcs	SO9857	52°12·9'	2°1·4'W	T	150
Dormston Manor	Worcs	SO9957	52°12·9'	2°0·5'W	X	150
Dorn	Glos	SP2034	52°0·5'	1°42·1'W	T	151
Dornafield	Devon	SX8368	50°30·2'	3°38·6'W	A	202
Dornaford Park	Devon	SX6099	50°46·7'	3°58·8'W	X	191
Dornal	E Ayr	NS6319	55°27·0'	4°9·5'W	X	71
Dornal	S Ayr	NX2976	55°3·2'	4°40·2'W	X	76
Dornal Hill	S Ayr	NX3079	55°4·8'	4°39·4'W	X	76
Dornal Moss	E Ayr	NS6420	55°27·6'	4°8·6'W	X	71
Dornell	D & G	NX7066	54°58·6'	4°1·4'W	X	83,84
Dornell Loch	D & G	NX7065	54°58·0'	4°1·4'W	W	83,84
Dorney	Bucks	SU9379	51°30·4'	0°39·2'W	T	175
Dorney Common	Bucks	SU9378	51°29·8'	0°39·2'W	X	175
Dorney Court	Bucks	SU9279	51°30·4'	0°40·1'W	A	175
Dorney Reach	Bucks	SU9179	51°30·4'	0°40·9'W	T	175
Dorney Wood	Bucks	SU9384	51°33·1'	0°39·1'W	X	175
Dorn Hill	Glos	SP1934	52°0·5'	1°43·0'W	X	151
Dornie	Highld	NB9810	58°2·3'	5°24·8'W	X	15
Dornie	Highld	NG8826	57°16·8'	5°30·6'W	T	33
Dornoch	Highld	NH8089	57°52·7'	4°0·9'W	T	21
Dornoch Firth	Highld	NH8688	57°52·3'	3°54·8'W	W	21
Dornoch Firth Bridge	Highld	NH7485	57°50·5'	4°6·9'W	X	21
Dornoch Links	Highld	NH7888	57°52·2'	4°2·9'W	X	21
Dornoch Mill	Pth & Kin	NN8818	56°20·7'	3°48·3'W	X	58
Dornoch Point	Arg & Bt	NS1494	56°6·4'	4°59·0'W	X	56
Dornoch Point	Highld	NH8087	57°51·6'	4°0·9'W	X	21
Dornoch Sands	Highld	NH7887	57°51·6'	4°2·9'W	X	21
Dornock	D & G	NY2366	54°59·2'	3°11·8'W	T	85
Dornock	Pth & Kin	NN8818	56°20·7'	3°48·3'W	X	58
Dornockbrow	D & G	NY2365	54°58·7'	3°11·8'W	X	85
Dornock Cottage	D & G	NY2265	54°58·7'	3°12·7'W	X	85
Dornock Mains	D & G	NY2265	54°58·7'	3°12·7'W	X	85
Dorrachan	Highld	NH7174	57°44·5'	4°9·6'W	X	21
Dorra Stack	Shetld	HU3093	60°37·4'	1°26·6'W	X	1
Dorrells Fm	E Susx	TQ7619	50°56·8'	0°30·7'E	FM	199
Dorrel Wood	Hants	SU5556	51°18·3'	1°12·3'W	F	174
Dorrery	Highld	ND0754	58°28·1'	3°35·2'W	T	11,12
Dorridge	Sol	SP1675	52°22·6'	1°45·5'W	T	139
Dorridge Hill	Hants	SU1711	50°54·1'	1°45·1'W	H	195
Dorrington	Lincs	TF0752	53°3·5'	0°23·8'W	T	121
Dorrington	Shrops	SJ4702	52°37·0'	2°46·6'W	T	126
Dorrington	Shrops	SJ7340	52°57·6'	2°23·7'W	X	118
Dorrington Dike	Lincs	TF1253	53°4·0'	0°19·3'W	W	121
Dorrington Fen	Lincs	TF1153	53°4·0'	0°20·2'W	X	121
Dorrington Fm	Essex	TL4506	51°44·3'	0°6·4'E	FM	167
Dorrington Grange	Lincs	TF0853	53°4·0'	0°22·9'W	X	121
Dorrington Grove	Shrops	SJ4802	52°37·0'	2°45·7'W	X	126
Dorrington Hall Fm	Shrops	SJ7241	52°58·2'	2°24·6'W	FM	118
Dorryfield	Cumbr	NY5070	55°1·6'	2°46·5'W	X	86
Dorsell	Aberd	NJ5414	57°13·1'	2°45·2'W	X	37
Dorset Coast Path	Dorset	SZ0176	50°35·3'	1°58·8'W	X	195
Dorset College of Agriculture	Dorset	SY7191	50°43·3'	2°24·3'W	X	194
Dorset Fm	Corn	SX1353	50°21·1'	4°37·3'W	FM	200
Dorset Heavy Horse Centre	Dorset	SU0811	50°54·1'	1°52·8'W	X	195
Dorsetshire Gap	Dorset	ST7403	50°49·8'	2°21·8'W	X	194
Dorsincilly	Aberd	NO3594	57°2·2'	3°3·8'W	X	37,44
Dorsington	Warw	SP1349	52°8·6'	1°48·2'W	T	151
Dorsington Manor	Warw	SP1250	52°9·1'	1°49·1'W	X	150
Dorsley Bank Wood	N Yks	NZ8306	54°26·8'	0°42·8'W	F	94
Dorsley Barton	Devon	SX7760	50°25·9'	3°43·5'W	X	202
Dorsmouth Rock	C of Plym	SX5355	50°22·8'	4°3·7'W	X	201
Dorstone	Heref	SO3141	52°4·0'	3°0·0'W	T	148,161
Dorstone	Heref	SO4455	52°11·7'	2°48·8'W	X	148,149
Dorstone Hill	Heref	SO3242	52°4·6'	2°59·1'W	A	148,161
Dorstone Hill	Heref	SO3242	52°4·6'	2°59·1'W	X	148,161
Dorthgill	Cumbr	NY7538	54°44·4'	2°22·9'W	X	91
Dorton	Bucks	SP6814	51°49·5'	1°0·4'W	T	164,165
Dorton Hill	Bucks	SP6812	51°48·4'	1°0·4'W	X	164,165
Dorton Ho	Kent	TQ5456	51°17·2'	0°12·9'E	X	188
Dorton Park Fm	Bucks	SP6714	51°49·5'	1°1·3'W	FM	164,165
Dorus a' Choilich	Highld	NH1028	57°18·4'	5°8·8'W	X	25
Dorus Beag	N Eil	NB5533	58°13·3'	6°9·9'W	X	8
Dorusduain	Highld	NG9822	57°14·9'	5°20·4'W	X	25,33
Dorus Mór	Arg & Bt	NR7598	56°7·6'	5°36·8'W	W	55
Dorus Mór	Highld	NC1448	58°23·1'	5°10·4'W	X	9
Dorwen	Powys	SN7714	51°48·9'	3°46·7'W	X	160
Dorwen ar Giedd	Powys	SN8015	51°49·5'	3°44·1'W	X	160
Doseley	Wrekin	SJ6706	52°39·3'	2°28·9'W	T	127
Dos Mhucarain	Highld	NH1960	57°35·9'	5°1·3'W	H	20
Dosmuckeran	Highld	NH2060	57°35·9'	5°0·3'W	X	20
Dosthill	Staffs	SK2100	52°36·1'	1°41·0'W	T	139
Dosthill Ho	Staffs	SK2100	52°36·1'	1°41·0'W	X	139
Dothan	Fife	NT2494	56°8·2'	3°12·9'W	X	59
Dothan	I of Angl	SH3774	53°14·5'	4°26·2'W	T	114
Dot Hill	E Yorks	SE9137	53°49·5'	0°36·6'W	X	106
Dothill	Wrekin	SJ6412	52°42·5'	2°31·6'W	T	127
Dotland	Northum	NY9259	54°55·8'	2°7·1'W	X	87

Dotland Park	Northum	NY9360	54°56·3′	2°6·1′W	X	87
Dots & Melons	Essex	TM0004	51°42·2′	0°54·1′E	X	168
Dotterell Hall	Cambs	TL5552	52°8·9′	0°16·3′E	X	154
Dotterill Park	E Yorks	TA0568	54°6·1′	0°23·2′W	X	101
Dottery	Dorset	SY4595	50°45·4′	2°46·4′W	T	193
Dotton Fm	Devon	SY0888	50°41·3′	3°17·8′W	FM	192
Dotton Warren	Devon	SY0788	50°41·3′	3°18·6′W	X	192
Dottrell Ho	Cambs	TL4243	52°4·3′	0°4·7′E	X	154
Douai Abbey & School	W Berks	SU5767	51°24·2′	1°10·4′W	X	174
Double Barrow	Dorset	SY8294	50°45·0′	2°14·9′W	A	194
Doublebois	Corn	SX2064	50°27·1′	4°31·8′W	T	201
Doublebois Ho	Corn	SX1965	50°27·7′	4°32·6′W	X	201
Double Br	Somer	ST3335	51°6·9′	2°57·0′W	X	182
Double Clump	Notts	SK6476	53°16·9′	1°2·0′W	F	120
Double Craigs	Stir	NS6287	56°3·6′	4°12·5′W	X	57
Double Dike	Lincs	TF3474	53°15·0′	0°0·9′E	W	122
Double Dike	N Yks	SE8594	54°20·3′	0°41·1′W	A	94,100
Double Dikes	N Yks	SE5780	54°13·0′	1°7·1′W	A	100
Double Dikes	N Yks	SE6976	54°10·7′	0°56·1′W	W	100
Double Dykes	Bourne	SZ1690	50°42·8′	1°46·0′W	A	195
Doubledykes	Northum	NY6559	54°55·7′	2°32·3′W	X	86
Double Gates	E Yorks	TA2050	53°56·2′	0°9·9′W	X	107
Double Hill	Bath & NE Somer	ST7157	51°18·9′	2°24·6′W	T	172
Double House Fm	Bath & NE Somer	ST5860	51°20·5′	2°35·8′W	FM	172,182
Doublerow Plantn	Norf	TL9093	52°30·3′	0°48·4′E	F	144
Doubler Stones	Brad	SE0746	53°54·8′	1°53·2′W	X	104
Doubler Stones Allotment	Brad	SE0746	53°54·8′	1°53·2′W	X	104
Doubleton Fm	N Som	ST3862	51°21·5′	2°53·0′W	FM	182
Double Waters	Devon	SX4770	50°30·8′	4°9·1′W	W	201
Doubting Castle	N Yks	NZ7110	54°29·1′	0°53·8′W	X	94
Doucegrove	E Susx	TQ8221	50°57·8′	0°35·9′E	X	199
Douchan	Highld	NH5773	57°43·7′	4°23·6′W	X	21
Douchlage	Stir	NS5392	56°6·1′	4°21·4′W	X	57
Dougalshill Fm	Falk	NS8987	56°4·0′	3°46·5′W	FM	65
Dougalston Loch	E Dunb	NS5673	55°56·0′	4°17·9′W	W	64
Douganhill	D & G	NX8056	54°53·3′	3°51·8′W	X	84
Douganstyle	D & G	NX9484	55°8·6′	3°39·4′W	X	78
Dougarie Lodge	N Ayr	NR8837	55°35·1′	5°21·4′W	X	68,69
Dougarie Point	N Ayr	NR8737	55°35·1′	5°22·3′W	X	68,69
Dough Crag	Northum	NY9795	55°15·2′	2°2·4′W	H	81
Doughend Hole	N Ayr	NS1454	55°44·9′	4°57·4′W	X	63
Doughnot Hill	W Dunb	NS4477	55°57·9′	4°29·5′W	H	64
Doughton	Glos	ST8791	51°37·3′	2°10·9′W	T	162,173
Doughton	Norf	TF8729	52°49·8′	0°47·0′E	T	132
Doughty	Lancs	SD8938	53°50·5′	2°9·6′W	W	103
Doughty	S Ayr	NX3297	55°14·6′	4°38·1′W	X	76
Doughty Hill	S Ayr	NX3298	55°15·1′	4°38·2′W	H	76
Dougill Hall	N Yks	SE2061	54°2·9′	1°41·3′W	X	99
Douglas	I of M	SC3875	54°9·0′	4°28·4′W	T	95
Douglas	S Lanak	NS8330	55°33·2′	3°50·9′W	T	71,72
Douglas and Angus	C of Dun	NO4432	56°28·9′	2°54·1′W	T	54
Douglas Bay	I of M	SC3976	54°9·5′	4°27·5′W	W	95
Douglas Burn	Scot Bord	NT2727	55°32·1′	3°9·0′W	W	73
Douglasfield	Pth & Kin	NO0938	56°31·8′	3°28·3′W	X	52,53
Douglashall	D & G	NY1777	55°5·1′	3°17·6′W	X	85
Douglashead	Aberd	NJ8932	57°23·0′	2°10·5′W	X	30
Douglas Head	I of M	SC3874	54°8·4′	4°28·4′W	H	95
Douglas Ho	D & G	NY3069	55°0·9′	3°5·3′W	X	85
Douglaslake Fm	W Susx	TQ0019	50°57·9′	0°34·2′W	FM	197
Douglasmuir	Angus	NO6148	56°37·6′	2°37·7′W	X	54
Douglas Muir	E Dunb	NS5274	55°56·4′	4°21·7′W	X	64
Douglas Pier	Arg & Bt	NS1999	56°9·2′	4°54·4′W	X	56
Douglas Ridge	N Yks	SE5096	54°21·7′	1°13·4′W	H	100
Douglas Rig	S Lanak	NS7424	55°29·9′	3°59·2′W	X	71
Douglas's Cairn	D & G	NX9561	54°56·2′	3°37·9′W	X	84
Douglasshiel Moss	Moray	NJ3854	57°34·6′	3°1·7′W	X	28
Douglastown	Angus	NO4147	56°36·9′	2°57·2′W	T	54
Douglas Water	Arg & Bt	NN0207	56°13·1′	5°11·2′W	W	55
Douglas Water	Arg & Bt	NN0407	56°13·2′	5°9·2′W	W	56
Douglas Water	Arg & Bt	NS3198	56°8·9′	4°42·8′W	W	56
Douglas Water	S Lanak	NS7426	55°30·9′	3°59·3′W	W	71
Douglas Water	S Lanak	NS8736	55°36·5′	3°47·2′W	T	71,72
Douglas Water	S Lanak	NS8737	55°37·1′	3°47·2′W	W	71,72
Douglas West	S Lanak	NS8231	55°33·8′	3°51·8′W	T	71,72
Douievale	D & G	NY0176	55°4·4′	3°32·6′W	X	84
Douky Bottom Cave	N Yks	SD9568	54°6·7′	2°4·2′W	A	98
Doularg	S Ayr	NX2592	55°11·7′	4°44·5′W	X	76
Doularg Hill	S Ayr	NX2692	55°11·8′	4°43·6′W	X	76
Doulin Haugh	Angus	NO3960	56°43·9′	2°59·4′W	X	44
Doulting	Somer	ST6443	51°11·3′	2°30·5′W	T	183
Doulting Sheep Sleight	Somer	ST6341	51°10·3′	2°31·4′W	H	183
Dounalt, The	Angus	NO2476	56°52·4′	3°14·4′W	X	44
Dounan Bay	D & G	NW9668	54°58·1′	5°10·8′W	W	82
Dounan Moor	D & G	NX3454	54°51·4′	4°34·7′W	X	82
Dounby	Orkney	HY2920	59°3·9′	3°13·8′W	T	6
Dùn Chàrlabhaigh	N Eil	NB1841	58°16·3′	6°48·1′W	T	8,13
Dounduff Fm	Moray	NH9949	57°31·5′	3°40·7′W	FM	27
Dounduff Wood	Moray	NH9850	57°32·0′	3°41·8′W	F	27
Doune	Arg & Bt	NN3314	56°17·6′	4°41·5′W	X	50,56
Doune	Arg & Bt	NS3198	56°8·9′	4°42·8′W	X	56
Doune	Highld	NC4400	57°58·0′	4°37·8′W	X	16
Doune	Highld	NG7003	57°3·9′	5°47·2′W	X	33
Doune	Highld	NH8809	57°9·8′	3°50·7′W	T	35,36
Doune	Stir	NN7301	56°11·3′	4°2·3′W	T	57
Doune Cas	Stir	NN7201	56°11·3′	4°3·3′W	A	57
Doune Hill	Arg & Bt	NS2997	56°8·4′	4°44·7′W	H	56
Doune Hill	S Ayr	NX2096	55°13·8′	4°49·4′W	X	76
Doune Lodge	Stir	NN7103	56°12·4′	4°4·3′W	X	57
Doune of Relugas	Moray	NJ0049	57°31·5′	3°39·7′W	X	27
Doune of Relugas (Fort)	Moray	NJ0049	57°31·5′	3°39·7′W	A	27
Dounepark	Aberd	NJ7162	57°39·1′	2°28·7′W	X	29
Douneside	Aberd	NJ4806	57°8·8′	2°51·1′W	X	37
Doun Helzie	Orkney	HY6135	59°12·3′	2°40·5′W	X	5
Dounhurst Fm	W Susx	TQ0327	51°2·2′	0°31·5′W	FM	186,197
Dounie	Arg & Bt	NR7591	56°3·8′	5°36·4′W	X	55
Dounie	Highld	NH5142	57°26·9′	4°28·5′W	X	26
Dounie	Highld	NH5690	57°52·8′	4°25·2′W	T	21
Dounie	Highld	NH6986	57°50·9′	4°12·0′W	T	21
Dounie Cott	Moray	NJ2547	57°30·7′	3°14·7′W	X	28
Dounie Wood	Highld	NH6886	57°50·9′	4°13·0′W	F	21
Dounreay Nuclear Power Development Establishment	Highld	NC9867	58°35·0′	3°44·8′W	X	11
Doup Crag	Cumbr	NY4109	54°28·6′	2°54·2′W	X	90
Doup of Becky	Aberd	NO6790	57°0·3′	2°32·1′W	X	38,45
Doups	Cumbr	NY2526	54°37·7′	3°9·3′W	X	89,90
Doups	Falk	NS7481	56°0·6′	4°0·8′W	X	64
Doura	N Ayr	NS3442	55°38·8′	4°37·8′W	T	63,70
Doura	S Ayr	NS4430	55°32·6′	4°27·9′W	X	70
Doura Mains	N Ayr	NS3442	55°38·8′	4°37·8′W	X	63,70
Dour Hill	Northum	NT7902	55°18·9′	2°19·4′W	H	80
Douri	Shetld	HU4334	60°5·6′	1°13·1′W	X	4
Dourie	D & G	NX3443	54°45·5′	4°34·4′W	X	82
Dour, The	Aberd	NJ8763	57°39·7′	2°12·6′W	W	30
Dousgill Fm	N Yks	NZ0908	54°28·3′	1°51·2′W	FM	92
Dousland	Devon	SX5368	50°29·8′	4°4·0′W	T	201
Douthwaite Dale	N Yks	SE6990	54°18·3′	0°56·0′W	X	94,100
Dova Haw	Cumbr	SD1967	54°5·8′	3°13·9′W	X	96
Dovaston	Shrops	SJ3420	52°46·7′	2°58·3′W	T	126
Dove Bank	Cumbr	SD2384	54°15·0′	3°10·5′W	X	96
Dovebank	Derby	SK1631	52°52·8′	1°45·3′W	X	128
Dove Br	Staffs	SK2328	52°51·2′	1°39·1′W	X	128
Dove Bridge	Staffs	SK1034	52°54·4′	1°50·7′W	A	128
Dove Cave	D & G	NX6046	54°47·6′	4°10·2′W	X	83
Dovecliff Fm	Staffs	SK1140	52°57·7′	1°49·8′W	FM	119,128
Dovecot	Liv	SJ4191	53°25·0′	2°52·9′W	T	108
Dovecot	Northum	NY9778	55°6·0′	2°2·4′W	X	87
Dovecot	Orkney	HY4220	59°4·0′	3°0·2′W	A	5,6
Dovecot	Scot Bord	NT1648	55°43·3′	3°19·8′W	X	72
Dovecote	Cumbr	NY5364	54°58·4′	2°43·6′W	X	86
Dove Cote	Hartpl	NZ4531	54°40·6′	1°17·7′W	X	93
Dove Cote	Lancs	SD6737	53°49·9′	2°29·7′W	X	103
Dovecote Fm	Cambs	TL3681	52°24·8′	0°0·4′E	FM	142
Dovecote Fm	Lincs	TF2149	53°1·7′	0°11·3′W	FM	131
Dovecote Fm	Lincs	TF2944	52°58·9′	0°4·3′W	FM	131
Dovecote Fm	Northum	NZ2081	55°7·6′	1°40·8′W	FM	81
Dovecote Hall Fm	Lincs	TF2753	53°3·8′	0°5·9′W	FM	122
Dovecot Fm	Lincs	TF1735	52°54·2′	0°15·2′W	FM	130
Dovecot Fm	Lincs	TF3758	53°6·3′	0°3·2′E	FM	122
Dovecot Fm	Lincs	TF3954	53°4·1′	0°4·9′E	FM	122
Dovecot Fm	Mil Key	SP9447	52°7·0′	0°37·2′W	FM	153
Dovecothall	E Renf	NS5159	55°48·3′	4°22·2′W	T	64
Dovecot Hall	Scot Bord	NT7670	55°55·6′	2°22·6′W	X	67
Dove Cottage (Mus)	Cumbr	NY3407	54°27·5′	3°0·7′W	A	90
Dovecotwell	D & G	NY0166	54°59·0′	3°32·4′W	X	84
Dove Cove	S Ayr	NX0678	55°3·8′	5°1·8′W	W	76
Dove Crag	Cumbr	NY3710	54°29·1′	2°57·9′W	X	90
Dove Crag	Northum	NZ0398	55°16·8′	1°56·7′W	H	81
Dove Crags	Cumbr	NY5686	55°10·2′	2°41·0′W	X	80
Dovedale	Cumbr	NY3811	54°29·7′	2°57·0′W	X	90
Dovedale	Glos	SP1634	52°0·5′	1°45·6′W	X	151
Dovedale	Staffs	SK1452	53°4·1′	1°47·1′W	X	119
Dovedale Beck	Cumbr	NY3811	54°29·7′	2°57·0′W	W	90
Dovedale Castle	Staffs	SK1451	53°3·6′	1°47·1′W	X	119
Dovedale Fm	Glos	SP1534	52°0·5′	1°46·5′W	FM	151
Dovedale Griff	N Yks	SE8791	54°18·7′	0°39·3′W	W	94,101
Dovedale Wood	Notts	SK4663	53°10·0′	1°18·3′W	F	120
Doveden Hall	Suff	TL8258	52°11·6′	0°40·2′E	X	155
Dovedenhall Wood	Suff	TL8259	52°12·2′	0°40·2′E	F	155
Doveflats	Staffs	SK1140	52°57·7′	1°49·8′W	X	119,128
Dove Ford	Cumbr	SD2384	54°15·0′	3°10·5′W	X	96
Dove Green	Notts	SK4652	53°4·0′	1°18·4′W	T	120
Dove Hall	Brad	SE1439	53°51·1′	1°46·8′W	X	104
Dove Head	Derby	SK0368	53°12·8′	1°56·9′W	X	119
Dovehills, The	Heref	SO6750	52°9·1′	2°28·5′W	X	149
Dove Ho	Essex	TL6227	51°55·3′	0°21·7′E	X	167
Dove Ho	Essex	TM0131	51°56·7′	0°55·9′E	X	168
Dove Ho	Mil Key	SP9448	52°7·6′	0°37·2′W	X	153
Dove Ho	Warw	SP2489	52°30·1′	1°38·4′W	X	139
Dovehole Crag	Northum	NT9636	55°37·3′	2°3·4′W	X	74,75
Dove Holes	Derby	SK0778	53°18·2′	1°53·3′W	T	119
Dove Holes	Derby	SK1453	53°4·7′	1°47·1′W	X	119
Doveholes Dale	Derby	SK0877	53°17·6′	1°52·4′W	X	119
Dove House	K upon H	TA1031	53°46·1′	0°19·5′W	X	107
Dovehouse Fm	Cambs	TL3184	52°26·5′	0°4·0′W	FM	142
Dove House Fm	Ches	SJ7150	53°3·0′	2°25·6′W	FM	118
Dove House Fm	Cumbr	SD5481	54°13·6′	2°41·9′W	FM	97
Dovehouse Fm	Essex	TL6129	51°56·4′	0°20·9′E	FM	167
Dovehouse Fm	Essex	TL8537	52°0·3′	0°42·1′E	FM	155
Dovehouse Fm	Norf	TM1188	52°27·2′	1°6·7′E	FM	144
Dove House Fm	Stock	SJ9685	53°22·0′	2°3·2′W	FM	109
Dovehouse Fm	Suff	TM4266	52°14·2′	1°33·1′E	FM	156
Dovehouse Point	Essex	TM1532	51°56·9′	1°8·1′E	X	168,169
Dovehouse, The	Essex	TL6234	51°59·1′	0°21·9′E	X	154
Dovehouse Wood	Suff	TL9671	52°18·4′	0°52·9′E	F	144,155
Dovelands Plantn	E Yorks	SE7924	53°42·6′	0°47·8′W	F	105,106,112
Dovenanter	N Yks	SD7263	54°4·0′	2°25·3′W	X	98
Dovenby	Cumbr	NY0933	54°41·3′	3°24·3′W	T	89
Dovenby Craggs	Cumbr	NY1032	54°40·8′	3°23·3′W	X	89
Dovenby Mill	Cumbr	NY1033	54°41·3′	3°23·3′W	X	89
Dovendale	Lincs	TF3082	53°19·4′	0°2·5′W	T	122
Dove Nest	Cumbr	NY3802	54°24·8′	2°56·9′W	X	90
Dovenest Crag	Cumbr	NY2511	54°29·6′	3°9·1′W	X	89,90
Dove Point	Suff	TM3946	52°3·9′	1°29·6′E	X	169
Dove Point	Wirral	SJ2390	53°24·3′	3°9·1′W	T	108
Dover	Kent	TR3141	51°7·5′	1°18·5′E	T	179
Dover	Wigan	SD6101	53°30·5′	2°34·9′W	T	109
Dover Beck	Notts	SK6348	53°1·8′	1°3·2′W	W	129
Dovercourt	Essex	TM2531	51°56·1′	1°16·8′E	T	169
Doverdale	Worcs	SO8666	52°17·8′	2°11·9′W	T	150
Doverdale Manor	Worcs	SO8667	52°18·3′	2°11·9′W	X	150
Doverhay	Somer	SS8846	51°12·4′	3°35·8′W	T	181
Doverhay Down	Somer	SS8845	51°11·8′	3°35·8′W	X	181
Dover Hill	Kent	TR2337	51°5·6′	1°11·5′E	X	179,189
Doveridge	Derby	SK1134	52°54·4′	1°49·8′W	T	128
Doverow Hill	Glos	SO8105	51°44·8′	2°16·1′W	H	162
Dovers Fm	Surrey	TQ2547	51°12·7′	0°12·2′W	FM	187
Doversgreen	Surrey	TQ2548	51°13·3′	0°12·2′W	T	187
Dover's Hill	Glos	SP1339	52°3·2′	1°48·2′W	H	151
Dover, The	W Susx	TQ0506	50°50·9′	0°30·1′W	X	197
Dove Scar	N Yks	SE0387	54°17·0′	1°56·8′W	X	98
Dovesdale	S Lanak	NS7746	55°41·8′	3°57·0′W	X	64
Doves Fm	Kent	TQ7834	51°4·9′	0°32·9′E	FM	188
Dove's Fm	Northnts	SP6844	52°5·6′	1°0·0′W	FM	152
Dove's Fm	Suff	TM2160	52°11·9′	1°14·4′E	FM	156
Doves Fm	W Susx	TQ1614	50°55·1′	0°20·6′W	FM	198
Doves Moor	Devon	SS4114	50°54·5′	4°15·3′W	X	180,190
Doves Nest, The	E Susx	TQ4728	51°2·2′	0°6·2′E	X	188,198
Dovestone Clough	Derby	SK1989	53°24·1′	1°42·4′W	X	110
Dove Stone Moss	Oldham	SE0303	53°31·7′	1°56·9′W	X	110
Dovestone Resr	Oldham	SE0103	53°31·7′	1°58·7′W	W	110
Dove Stones	Cald	SD9334	53°48·4′	2°6·0′W	X	103
Dove Stones Moor	Lancs	SD9537	53°50·0′	2°4·1′W	X	103
Dovestone Tor	Derby	SK1989	53°24·1′	1°42·4′W	X	110
Dove Syke	Lancs	SD7345	53°54·3′	2°24·2′W	X	103
Dovetshill	W Loth	NT0363	55°51·3′	3°32·5′W	X	65
Dovey Junc Sta	Powys	SN6998	52°34·1′	3°55·6′W	X	135
Dovey's Fm	Wilts	SU0383	51°33·0′	1°57·0′W	FM	173
Dovey Valley (Dyffryn Dyfi)	Powys	SH7300	52°35·2′	3°52·1′W	X	135
Dowald	Pth & Kin	NN8822	56°22·9′	3°48·4′W	X	52,58
Dowall Hall	Derby	SK0767	53°12·2′	1°53·3′W	X	119
Dowalls	Moray	NJ3046	57°30·2′	3°9·6′W	X	28
Dowally	Pth & Kin	NO0047	56°36·5′	3°37·3′W	X	52,53
Dowally Loch	Pth & Kin	NO0147	56°36·5′	3°36·3′W	W	52,53
Dowalton	D & G	NX4045	54°46·7′	4°28·8′W	X	83
Dowalton Burn	D & G	NX4046	54°47·3′	4°28·9′W	W	83
Dowalty	Aberd	NO7597	57°4·1′	2°24·3′W	X	38,45
Dowan Fm	E Dunb	NS5774	55°56·5′	4°16·9′W	FM	64
Dowanhill	C of Glas	NS5667	55°52·7′	4°17·7′W	T	64
Dow Bank	Cumbr	NY3305	54°26·4′	3°1·6′W	X	90
Dowbiggin	Cumbr	SD6992	54°19·6′	2°28·2′W	X	98
Dowbiggin Foot	Cumbr	SD6892	54°19·6′	2°29·1′W	X	98
Dow Br	Warw	SP5477	52°23·5′	1°12·0′W	X	140
Dowbridge	Lancs	SD4331	53°46·6′	2°51·5′W	T	102
Dow Cave	N Yks	SD9874	54°10·0′	2°1·4′W	X	98
Dow Crag	Cumbr	NY2206	54°26·9′	3°11·8′W	X	89,90
Dow Crag	Cumbr	NY8418	54°33·7′	2°14·4′W	X	91,92
Dow Crag	Cumbr	SD2099	54°23·1′	3°13·5′W	X	96
Dow Crag	Cumbr	SD2698	54°22·6′	3°7·9′W	X	96,97
Dow Craig Hill	D & G	NX6559	54°54·7′	4°5·9′W	H	83,84
Dowde's Fm	Surrey	TQ2251	51°14·9′	0°14·7′W	FM	187
Dowdeswell Reservoir	Glos	SO9919	51°52·4′	2°0·5′W	W	163
Dowdeswell Wood	Glos	SO9920	51°52·9′	2°0·5′W	F	163
Dowd's Fm	Hants	SU4814	50°55·6′	1°18·6′W	FM	196
Dowdyke Grange	Lincs	TF2733	52°53·0′	0°6·3′W	X	131
Doweel Fm	D & G	NX9474	55°3·2′	3°39·1′W	FM	84
Dowe Hill	Norf	TG5016	52°41·3′	1°42·4′E	T	134
Dowel Cave	Derby	SK0767	53°12·2′	1°53·3′W	A	119
Dowells Fm	S Glos	ST6885	51°34·0′	2°27·3′W	FM	172
Dowels, The	Kent	TQ9830	51°2·3′	0°49·9′E	X	189
Dowerfield Fm	Dorset	SY5690	50°42·7′	2°37·0′W	FM	194
Dower Ho	Devon	SX4686	50°39·4′	4°10·3′W	A	201
Dower Ho	Northnts	SP5757	52°12·7′	1°9·5′W	X	152
Dower Ho	Shrops	SO7588	52°29·6′	2°21·7′W	X	138
Dower Ho, The	Devon	ST2404	50°50·1′	3°4·4′W	X	192,193
Dower Ho, The	Hants	SU6848	51°13·9′	1°1·2′W	X	185,186
Dower Ho, The	Norf	TL9685	52°25·9′	0°53·4′E	X	144
Dower House Fm	E Susx	TQ5320	50°57·8′	0°11·1′E	FM	199
Dowgang Hush	Cumbr	NY7742	54°46·6′	2°21·0′W	X	86,87
Dowgas	Corn	SW9651	50°19·7′	4°51·6′W	X	200,204
Dowgill	Cumbr	NY8414	54°31·5′	2°14·4′W	X	91,92
Dowglen Hill	D & G	NX3389	55°11·7′	3°2·7′W	H	79
Dowhill	Pth & Kin	NT1197	56°9·7′	3°25·5′W	X	58
Dowhill	S Ayr	NS2003	55°17·5′	4°49·7′W	X	76
Dow Hill	S Ayr	NX1996	55°13·8′	4°50·3′W	H	76
Dowhill Muir	Pth & Kin	NT1096	56°9·1′	3°26·5′W	X	58
Dowhill Port	S Ayr	NS1903	55°17·5′	4°50·6′W	W	76
Dowhill Sike	Durham	NY8619	54°34·2′	2°12·6′W	W	91,92
Dowiedean Burn	Scot Bord	NT6044	55°41·5′	2°37·7′W	W	74
Dowies	D & G	NX3842	54°45·1′	4°30·6′W	A	83
Dowke Hill	Shrops	SO2280	52°25·0′	3°8·4′W	H	137
Dowlais	Merth Tyd	SO0707	51°45·5′	3°20·5′W	T	160
Dowlais Fm	N Som	ST3969	51°25·2′	2°52·2′W	FM	171,182
Dowlais Top	Merth Tyd	SO0708	51°46·0′	3°20·5′W	T	160
Dowland	Devon	SS5610	50°52·5′	4°2·4′W	T	191
Dowland Moor	Devon	SS5910	50°52·6′	3°59·9′W	X	191
Dowlands	Devon	SY2890	50°42·5′	3°0·8′W	X	193
Dowlands Cliffs and Landslips	Devon	SY2889	50°42·0′	3°0·8′W	X	193
Dowlands Fm	Hants	SU3353	51°16·7′	1°31·2′W	FM	185
Dowlands Fm	Surrey	TQ3241	51°9·4′	0°6·4′W	FM	187
Dowlands, The	N Yks	SE4183	54°14·7′	1°21·8′W	X	99
Dowlass Moss	N Yks	SD7373	54°9·4′	2°24·4′W	X	98
Dowlaw	Scot Bord	NT8570	55°55·6′	2°14·0′W	X	67
Dowlaw Burn	Scot Bord	NT8669	55°55·1′	2°13·0′W	W	67
Dowlaw Dean	Scot Bord	NT8670	55°55·6′	2°13·0′W	X	67
Dowles	Worcs	SO7776	52°23·1′	2°19·9′W	T	138
Dowles Brook	Shrops	SO7476	52°23·1′	2°22·5′W	W	138
Dowlesgreen	Wok	SU8169	51°25·1′	0°49·7′W	T	175
Dowle Street Fm	Kent	TQ9343	51°9·4′	0°46·0′E	FM	189
Dowling's Wood	Bath & NE Somer	ST6060	51°20·5′	2°34·1′W	F	172
Dowlish Brook	Somer	ST3613	50°55·0′	2°54·2′W	W	193
Dowlish Ford	Somer	ST3513	50°55·0′	2°55·1′W	T	193
Dowlish Wake	Somer	ST3712	50°54·5′	2°53·4′W	T	193
Dow Loch	D & G	NX4580	55°5·7′	4°25·3′W	W	77
Dow Loch	D & G	NX4682	55°6·8′	4°24·4′W	W	77
Dow Loch	Pth & Kin	NT0996	56°9·1′	3°27·5′W	W	58
Dow Lochar	D & G	NY0075	55°3·8′	3°33·5′W	W	84
Dow Lochar	D & G	NY0174	55°3·3′	3°32·6′W	W	84
Dow Lochs	D & G	NX3771	55°0·7′	4°32·5′W	W	77
Dowman's Fm	Glos	SO9516	51°50·8′	2°4·0′W	FM	163
Dowmin	Aberd	NJ4942	57°28·2′	2°50·6′W	X	28,29
Down	Devon	SS4113	50°53·9′	4°15·3′W	X	180,190
Down	Devon	SS9220	50°58·4′	3°31·9′W	X	181
Down	Devon	SX7791	50°42·6′	3°44·1′W	X	191
Down	Devon	SX7970	50°31·3′	3°42·0′W	X	202

Downagowan	Pth & Kin	NN8662	56°44·4′	3°51·4′W	X	43
Downall Green	St Hel	SD5500	53°29·9′	2°40·3′W	T	108
Down Ampney	Glos	SU1097	51°40·5′	1°50·9′W	T	163
Down Ampney Ho	Wilts	SU0996	51°40·0′	1°51·8′W	A	163
Downan	Moray	NJ1830	57°21·4′	3°21·3′W	X	36
Downan	S Ayr	NX0780	55°4·9′	5°1·0′W	X	76
Downan Hill	S Ayr	NX0780	55°4·9′	5°1·0′W	H	76
Downan Point	S Ayr	NX0680	55°4·8′	5°1·9′W	X	76
Downans Plantn	Fife	NT1884	56°2·8′	3°18·5′W	F	65,66
Downash	E Susx	TQ6007	50°50·6′	0°16·8′E	X	199
Downash Ho	E Susx	TQ7031	51°3·4′	0°25·9′E	X	188
Downas Valley	Corn	SW7616	50°0·4′	5°7·2′W	X	204
Downatown	Orkney	HY2623	59°5·5′	3°17·0′W	X	6
Down Barn	Oxon	SU3385	51°34·0′	1°31·0′W	X	174
Down Barn	Oxon	SU4484	51°33·4′	1°21·5′W	X	174
Down Barn	Wilts	SU0927	51°2·8′	1°51·9′W	X	184
Down Barn	Wilts	SU1224	51°1·1′	1°49·3′W	X	184
Down Barn	Wilts	SU1369	51°25·4′	1°48·4′W	X	173
Down Barn	Wilts	SU1637	51°8·2′	1°45·9′W	X	184
Down Barn	Wilts	SU2956	51°18·4′	1°34·6′W	X	174
Down Barn Fm	Glos	SO8909	51°47·0′	2°9·2′W	FM	163
Down Barn Fm	Hants	SU5907	50°51·8′	1°9·3′W	FM	196
Downbarn West	Wilts	SU1636	51°7·6′	1°45·9′W	X	184
Down Barton	Kent	TR2566	51°21·1′	1°14·3′E	X	179
Down By Rigg	Cumbr	NY4064	54°58·3′	2°55·8′W	X	85
Downclose Fm	Somer	ST4708	50°52·4′	2°44·8′W	FM	193
Down Copse	W Berks	SU4175	51°28·6′	1°24·2′W	F	174
Down Court	Kent	TQ9257	51°17·0′	0°45·6′E	X	178
Downcourt Fm	I of W	SZ4978	50°36·2′	1°18·1′W	FM	196
Downcraig Ferry	N Ayr	NS1857	55°46·6′	4°53·7′W	X	63
Down Cross	Devon	SS8315	50°55·6′	3°39·5′W	X	181
Downderry	Corn	SW9550	50°19·1′	4°52·4′W	X	200,204
Downderry	Corn	SX3154	50°21·9′	4°22·2′W	T	201
Downderry Fm	Notts	SK7484	53°21·1′	0°52·9′W	FM	120
Downdinner Hill	Red & Cl	NZ7219	54°33·9′	0°52·8′W	X	94
Downe	Brom	TQ4361	51°20·0′	0°3·6′E	T	177,187
Downe	Devon	SS2425	51°0·1′	4°30·1′W	X	190
Downe	Devon	SX7967	50°29·7′	3°42·0′W	X	202
Downe Barns Fm	Ealing	TQ1083	51°32·3′	0°24·4′W	FM	176
Downe Fm	Devon	SS8216	50°56·1′	3°40·4′W	FM	181
Downe Hall	Essex	TL4008	51°45·4′	0°2·1′E	X	167
Downe House (Sch)	W Berks	SU5071	51°26·4′	1°16·4′W	X	174
Downend	Glos	SO7513	51°49·1′	2°21·4′W	X	162
Downend	Glos	ST8398	51°41·1′	2°14·4′W	T	162
Downend	I of W	SZ5387	50°41·0′	1°14·6′W	T	196
Downend	S Glos	ST6477	51°29·7′	2°30·7′W	T	172
Down End	Somer	ST3141	51°10·1′	2°58·8′W	T	182
Downend	W Berks	SU4775	51°28·6′	1°19·0′W	T	174
Downend	Worcs	SO8333	51°59·9′	2°14·5′W	X	150
Downend Fm	Dorset	ST8709	50°53·1′	2°10·7′W	FM	194
Downend Point	Corn	SX2150	50°19·6′	4°30·5′W	X	201
Downes	Devon	SX8599	50°47·0′	3°37·5′W	A	191
Downe's Ground	E Yorks	SE7024	53°42·7′	0°56·0′W	X	105,106,112
Downes Head	Devon	SS8400	50°47·5′	3°38·4′W	X	191
Downes Ho	Devon	SS4721	50°58·3′	4°10·4′W	X	180
Downes Mill Fm	Devon	SX8599	50°47·0′	3°37·5′W	FM	191
Downeycroft	Devon	SX3792	50°42·5′	4°18·1′W	X	190
Downey Hill	D & G	NY2490	55°12·2′	3°11·2′W	H	79
Down Field	Cambs	TL6071	52°19·1′	0°21·2′E	T	154
Downfield	C of Dun	NO3833	56°29·4′	3°0·0′W	T	54
Downfield	Fife	NO3407	56°15·3′	3°3·5′W	X	59
Downfield	Glos	SO9037	52°2·1′	2°8·4′W	X	150
Downfield	Heref	SO3157	52°12·7′	3°0·2′W	X	148
Downfield	Powys	SN9868	52°18·3′	3°29·4′W	X	136,147
Down Field Windmill	Cambs	TL6071	52°19·1′	0°21·2′E	X	154
Down Fm	Bucks	SP9514	51°49·2′	0°36·9′W	FM	165
Down Fm	Carm	SN3311	51°46·6′	4°24·9′W	FM	159
Down Fm	Devon	SS3708	50°51·2′	4°18·6′W	FM	190
Down Fm	Devon	SS4607	50°50·8′	4°10·9′W	FM	190
Down Fm	Devon	SS5712	50°53·6′	4°1·6′W	FM	180
Down Fm	Devon	SS5715	50°55·2′	4°1·7′W	FM	180
Down Fm	Devon	SS6736	51°6·7′	3°53·6′W	FM	180
Down Fm	Devon	SS6821	50°58·6′	3°52·4′W	FM	180
Down Fm	Devon	SS8307	50°51·3′	3°39·4′W	FM	191
Down Fm	Devon	SS9011	50°53·5′	3°33·5′W	FM	192
Down Fm	Devon	SX4565	50°28·1′	4°10·7′W	FM	201
Down Fm	Devon	SX7894	50°44·2′	3°43·4′W	FM	191
Down Fm	Devon	SX8037	50°13·5′	3°40·6′W	FM	202
Down Fm	Dorset	ST9914	50°55·8′	2°0·5′W	FM	195
Down Fm	E Susx	TQ8312	50°52·9′	0°36·5′E	FM	199
Down Fm	Glos	SO8808	51°46·5′	2°10·0′W	FM	162
Down Fm	Glos	ST8590	51°36·8′	2°12·6′W	FM	162,173
Down Fm	Hants	SU0919	50°58·5′	1°51·9′W	FM	184
Down Fm	Hants	SU1319	50°58·4′	1°48·5′W	FM	184
Down Fm	Hants	SU3140	51°9·7′	1°33·0′W	FM	185
Down Fm	Hants	SU3238	51°8·7′	1°32·2′W	FM	185
Down Fm	Hants	SU4426	51°2·1′	1°22·0′W	FM	185
Down Fm	Hants	SU4549	51°14·5′	1°20·9′W	FM	185
Down Fm	Hants	SU4633	51°5·9′	1°20·2′W	FM	185
Down Fm	Hants	SU4754	51°17·2′	1°19·2′W	FM	185
Down Fm	Hants	SU5825	51°1·5′	1°10·0′W	FM	185
Down Fm	Hants	SU6140	51°9·6′	1°7·3′W	FM	185
Down Fm	Hants	SU6849	51°14·4′	1°1·2′W	FM	185,186
Down Fm	Hants	SU7349	51°14·4′	0°56·9′W	FM	186
Down Fm	Oxon	SU5089	51°36·1′	1°16·3′W	FM	174
Down Fm	Oxon	SU6590	51°36·5′	1°3·3′W	FM	164,175
Down Fm	Somer	ST6522	51°0·0′	2°29·5′W	FM	183
Down Fm	W Berks	SU3079	51°30·8′	1°33·7′W	FM	174
Down Fm	Wilts	ST7877	51°29·7′	2°18·6′W	FM	172
Down Fm	Wilts	ST8976	51°29·2′	2°9·1′W	FM	173
Down Fm	Wilts	ST9735	51°7·1′	2°2·2′W	FM	184
Down Fm	Wilts	SU1089	51°36·2′	1°50·9′W	FM	173
Down Fm	Wilts	SU1856	51°18·4′	1°44·1′W	FM	173
Downgate	Corn	SX2871	50°31·0′	4°25·2′W	T	201
Downgate	Corn	SX3672	50°31·7′	4°18·5′W	T	201
Downgate	Kent	TQ7828	51°1·6′	0°32·7′E	X	188,199
Down Hall	Cumbr	NY2852	54°51·7′	3°6·9′W	T	85
Down Hall	Essex	TM0007	51°43·8′	0°54·2′E	X	168
Down Hall	Suff	TL9451	52°7·6′	0°50·5′E	X	155
Down Hall Fm	Cambs	TL3043	52°4·4′	0°5·8′W	FM	153
Down Hall (Hotel)	Essex	TL5213	51°47·9′	0°12·7′E	X	167
Downham	Essex	TQ7295	51°37·9′	0°29·5′E	T	167
Downham	Lancs	SD7844	53°53·7′	2°19·7′W	T	103
Downham	Lew	TQ3971	51°25·5′	0°0·4′E	T	177
Downham	Norf	TG1103	52°35·3′	1°7·3′E	X	144
Downham	Northum	NT8633	55°35·7′	2°12·9′W	T	74
Downham	Pth & Kin	NO2541	56°33·6′	3°12·8′W	X	53
Downham Br	Lancs	SD7845	53°54·3′	2°19·7′W	X	103
Downham Common	Cambs	TL5285	52°26·7′	0°14·6′E	X	143
Downham Green	Lancs	SD7844	53°53·7′	2°19·7′W	X	103
Downham Grove	Norf	TG1203	52°35·2′	1°8·2′E	X	144
Downham Hall	Essex	TQ7395	51°37·9′	0°30·4′E	X	167
Downham Highlodge Warren	Suff	TL8184	52°25·7′	0°40·1′E	F	144
Downham Hill	Glos	ST7798	51°41·1′	2°19·6′W	H	162
Downham Hythe	Cambs	TL4983	52°25·7′	0°11·9′E	X	143
Downham Lodge Fm	Norf	TG1005	52°36·4′	1°6·5′E	FM	144
Downham Market	Norf	TF6103	52°36·3′	0°23·1′E	T	143
Downham Moor	Lancs	SD8042	53°52·7′	2°17·8′W	X	103
Downham Reach	Suff	TM1939	52°0·6′	1°11·9′E	W	169
Downham Road Fm	Cambs	TL5382	52°25·1′	0°15·4′E	FM	143
Downhams Fm	Hants	SU4352	51°16·2′	1°22·6′W	FM	185
Down Hatherley	Glos	SO8622	51°54·0′	2°11·8′W	T	162
Downhayes	Corn	SX3290	50°41·4′	4°22·3′W	X	190
Downhayes	Devon	SX7098	50°46·3′	3°50·2′W	X	191
Downhayne	Devon	SS8306	50°50·7′	3°39·3′W	X	191
Downhayne	Devon	SY2395	50°45·2′	3°5·1′W	X	192,193
Downhead	Corn	SX2384	50°38·0′	4°29·8′W	X	201
Downhead	Somer	ST5625	51°1·6′	2°37·3′W	T	183
Downhead	Somer	ST6945	51°12·4′	2°26·2′W	T	183
Downhead Park	Mil Key	SP8640	52°3·3′	0°44·3′W	T	152
Downhill	Corn	SW8669	50°29·1′	5°0·6′W	T	200
Down Hill	Glos	SO8808	51°46·5′	2°10·0′W	X	162
Down Hill	Northum	NZ2377	55°5·5′	1°37·9′W	H	88
Down Hill	Oxon	SU5491	51°37·1′	1°12·8′W	X	164,174
Downhill	Pth & Kin	NO0930	56°27·5′	3°28·2′W	X	52,53
Downhill	Sund	NZ3559	54°55·7′	1°26·8′W	T	88
Down Hill Fm	Oxon	SP4327	51°56·6′	1°22·1′W	FM	164
Down Hill Fm	S Tyne	NZ3460	54°56·3′	1°27·7′W	FM	88
Downhill Plantn	Norf	TM0186	52°26·3′	0°57·8′E	F	144
Downhills Fm	Devon	SS9921	50°59·0′	3°26·0′W	FM	181
Down Ho	Brom	TQ4361	51°20·0′	0°3·6′E	X	177,187
Down Ho	Devon	SX4586	50°39·4′	4°11·2′W	X	201
Down Ho	Hants	SU3946	51°12·9′	1°26·1′W	X	185
Down Ho	Heref	SO6754	52°11·2′	2°28·6′W	X	149
Down Ho	Wilts	SU1921	50°59·5′	1°43·4′W	X	184
Downholland Brook	Sefton	SD3108	53°34·1′	3°2·1′W	W	108
Downholland Cross	Lancs	SD3606	53°33·0′	2°57·6′W	T	108
Downholland Hall	Lancs	SD3707	53°33·6′	2°56·7′W	A	108
Downholland Moss	Lancs	SD3308	53°34·1′	3°0·3′W	X	108
Downholme	N Yks	SE1197	54°22·3′	1°49·4′W	T	99
Downholme Moor	N Yks	SE1298	54°22·9′	1°48·5′W	X	99
Downholme Park	N Yks	SE1199	54°23·4′	1°49·4′W	X	99
Down Ho, The	Glos	SO7730	51°58·3′	2°19·7′W	X	150
Downhouse	Corn	SX3775	50°33·4′	4°17·7′W	X	201
Downhouse	Devon	SX4180	50°36·1′	4°14·4′W	X	201
Downhouse	Essex	TL7401	51°41·1′	0°31·4′E	X	167
Downhouse Fm	Devon	SX4674	50°33·0′	4°10·1′W	FM	201
Downhouse Fm	Devon	SX8492	50°43·2′	3°38·2′W	FM	191
Down House Fm	Dorset	SY4491	50°43·2′	2°47·2′W	FM	193
Down House Fm	Staffs	SJ8916	52°44·7′	2°9·4′W	FM	127
Downicary	Devon	SX3790	50°41·4′	4°18·1′W	T	190
Downiebank	Angus	NO4941	56°33·7′	2°49·3′W	X	54
Downie Bay	Aberd	NJ8266	57°41·3′	2°17·7′W	W	29,30
Downie Hillock	Angus	NO3468	56°48·2′	3°4·4′W	X	44
Downiehills	Aberd	NK0846	57°30·5′	1°51·5′W	X	30
Downieken	Angus	NO5035	56°30·5′	2°48·3′W	X	54
Downie Mill	Angus	NO5035	56°30·5′	2°48·3′W	X	54
Downie Moor	Angus	NO5041	56°33·8′	2°48·4′W	F	54
Downiepark	Angus	NO4158	56°42·9′	2°57·4′W	X	54
Downie Point	Aberd	NO8885	56°57·6′	2°11·4′W	X	45
Downies	Aberd	NJ6344	57°29·3′	2°36·6′W	X	29
Downies	Aberd	NO9295	57°3·0′	2°7·5′W	T	38,45
Downies Burn	D & G	NX4884	55°7·9′	4°22·6′W	W	77
Downieston	E Ayr	NS4111	55°22·3′	4°30·1′W	X	70
Downing	Flint	SJ1578	53°17·8′	3°16·1′W	X	116
Downing Point	Fife	NT1582	56°1·7′	3°21·4′W	X	65
Downinney	Corn	SX2090	50°41·1′	4°32·5′W	T	190
Down in the Dale	Cumbr	NY1808	54°27·9′	3°15·5′W	X	89,90
Downland Fm	Darl	NZ3621	54°35·2′	1°26·2′W	FM	93
Downland Ho	E Susx	TQ4622	50°59·0′	0°5·2′E	X	198
Downlands	Hants	SU8533	51°5·6′	0°46·8′W	X	186
Down Law	Scot Bord	NT6326	55°31·8′	2°34·7′W	H	74
Downleaze Copse	Hants	SU5921	50°59·4′	1°9·2′W	F	185
Down Level	E Susx	TQ6107	50°50·6′	0°17·6′E	X	199
Downley	Bucks	SU8495	51°39·1′	0°46·8′W	T	165
Downley	Hants	SU7518	50°57·6′	0°55·5′W	X	197
Downley Common	Bucks	SU8495	51°39·1′	0°46·8′W	X	165
Downley Cottage	W Susx	SU8614	50°55·4′	0°46·2′W	X	197
Downmoor Cross	Devon	SS4113	50°53·9′	4°15·3′W	X	180,190
Downoak Fm	E Susx	TQ8115	50°54·6′	0°34·9′E	FM	199
Down Park	W Susx	TQ3338	51°7·8′	0°5·6′W	T	187
Down Park Fm	W Susx	SU7822	50°59·8′	0°52·9′W	FM	197
Down Place	Surrey	SU9549	51°14·2′	0°38·0′W	X	186
Down Place	Win & Maid	SU9277	51°29·3′	0°40·1′W	X	175
Down Place	W Susx	SU7918	50°57·6′	0°52·1′W	X	197
Downrew Fm	Devon	SS5928	51°2·3′	4°0·3′W	FM	180
Downrew Ho	Devon	SS5829	51°2·8′	4°1·2′W	X	180
Down Ridge	Devon	SX6571	50°31·6′	3°53·9′W	X	202
Downrip Fm	Worcs	SP0940	52°3·7′	1°51·7′W	FM	150
Downrow	Corn	SS2500	50°46·6′	4°28·6′W	X	190
Downrow	Corn	SX0687	50°39·3′	4°44·3′W	X	200
Downs	Devon	SS4501	50°47·5′	4°11·6′W	X	190
Downs	V of Glam	SS9570	51°25·4′	3°30·2′W	X	170
Downs	V of Glam	ST1174	51°27·7′	3°16·5′W	T	171
Downs Bank	D & G	NY0078	55°5·4′	3°33·6′W	X	84
Downs Banks	Staffs	SJ9037	52°56·1′	2°8·5′W	X	127
Down's Barn	Mil Key	SP8640	52°3·3′	0°44·3′W	X	152
Downs Barn	Swin	SU2580	51°31·3′	1°38·0′W	X	174
Down's Barn Fm	Corn	SW4124	50°3·8′	5°36·8′W	FM	203
Downs Brake, The	Glos	SP0917	51°51·3′	1°51·8′W	X	163
Downscombe	Somer	SS8439	51°8·5′	3°39·1′W	X	181
Downs Fm	Glos	SP0306	51°45·4′	1°57·0′W	FM	163
Downs Fm	Glos	SP1734	52°0·5′	1°44·7′W	FM	151
Downs Fm	Kent	TQ7051	51°14·2′	0°26·5′E	FM	188
Downs Fm	Norf	TF6839	52°55·6′	0°30·4′E	FM	132
Downs Fm	Oxon	SP2009	51°47·0′	1°42·2′W	FM	163
Downs Fm	S Glos	ST7379	51°30·8′	2°23·0′W	FM	172
Downs Fm	Shrops	SJ6300	52°36·0′	2°32·4′W	FM	127
Down's Fm	Somer	ST7339	51°9·2′	2°22·8′W	FM	183
Downs Fm	Suff	TM2884	52°24·6′	1°21·5′E	FM	156
Downs Fm	V of Glam	ST1669	51°25·1′	3°12·1′W	FM	171
Downs Fm	Warw	SP3442	52°4·8′	1°29·8′W	FM	151
Downs Fm	W Berks	SU4875	51°28·5′	1°18·1′W	FM	174
Downs Fm	W Susx	SU8109	50°52·7′	0°50·5′W	FM	197
Downs Fm	W Susx	TQ0312	50°54·1′	0°31·7′W	FM	197
Downs Fm, The	Surrey	TQ2260	51°19·8′	0°14·5′W	FM	176,187
Downs Gill	N Yks	SD9978	54°12·1′	2°0·5′W	W	98
Downshay Fm	Dorset	SY9879	50°36·9′	2°1·3′W	FM	195
Downs Ho, The	Warw	SP1942	52°4·8′	1°43·0′W	X	151
Downside	Beds	TL0320	51°52·4′	0°29·8′W	T	166
Downside	E Susx	TQ5900	50°46·9′	0°15·7′E	T	199
Downside	N Som	ST4965	51°23·1′	2°43·6′W	T	172,182
Downside	Somer	ST6244	51°11·9′	2°32·2′W	T	183
Downside	Surrey	TQ1058	51°18·9′	0°24·9′W	T	187
Downside	Surrey	TQ1755	51°17·2′	0°18·9′W	T	187
Downside Abbey	Somer	ST6550	51°15·1′	2°29·7′W	X	183
Downside Fm	Somer	ST6450	51°15·1′	2°30·6′W	FM	183
Downside Fm	Surrey	TQ1158	51°18·8′	0°24·0′W	FM	187
Downsland Ho	Hants	SU7950	51°14·8′	0°51·7′W	X	186
Downs Link	Surrey	TQ0242	51°10·3′	0°32·1′W	X	186
Downs Link	W Susx	TQ0932	51°4·8′	0°26·2′W	X	187
Downs Link	W Susx	TQ2017	50°56·6′	0°17·1′W	X	198
Downs Link Cycle Route	W Susx	TQ2017	50°56·6′	0°17·1′W	X	187,198
Downs Lodge	Oxon	SP2615	51°50·2′	1°37·0′W	X	163
Downs Pasture	N Yks	SE0067	54°6·2′	1°59·6′W	X	98
Downs School, The	N Som	ST4973	51°27·5′	2°43·7′W	X	172
Downs, The	Glos	ST8589	51°36·2′	2°12·6′W	X	173
Downs, The	Kent	TR2851	51°13·0′	1°16·3′E	X	179
Downs, The	Norf	TF7943	52°57·5′	0°40·3′E	F	132
Downs, The	Northnts	SP6454	52°11·1′	1°3·4′W	X	152
Downs, The	Oxon	SP5122	51°53·9′	1°15·1′W	X	164
Downs, The	Oxon	SU3985	51°34·0′	1°25·8′W	X	174
Downs, The	Pemb	SR9997	51°38·4′	4°53·9′W	X	158
Downs, The	W Susx	TQ1208	50°51·9′	0°24·1′W	X	198
Down St Mary	Devon	SS7404	50°49·5′	3°47·0′W	T	191
Downstow	Devon	SX6962	50°26·8′	3°50·3′W	X	202
Down Street	E Susx	TQ4424	51°0·1′	0°3·5′E	T	198
Downs View	Surrey	TQ2156	51°17·6′	0°15·5′W	X	187
Downter's Wood	Suff	TL8060	52°12·8′	0°38·5′E	F	155
Down, The	N Som	ST4357	51°18·8′	2°48·7′W	X	172,182
Down, The	Shrops	SO6381	52°25·8′	2°32·3′W	X	138
Down, The	Shrops	SO6890	52°30·7′	2°27·9′W	T	138
Down, The	Somer	ST7750	51°15·2′	2°19·4′W	X	183
Down Thomas	Devon	SX5050	50°20·1′	4°6·1′W	T	201
Downthorns Fm	S Glos	ST7975	51°28·6′	2°17·8′W	FM	172
Downton	Devon	SX8553	50°22·2′	3°36·7′W	X	202
Downton	Hants	SZ2693	50°44·4′	1°37·5′W	T	195
Downton	Powys	SO2360	52°14·2′	3°7·3′W	T	137,148
Downton	Shrops	SJ5412	52°42·5′	2°40·4′W	T	126
Downton	Wilts	SU1821	50°59·5′	1°44·2′W	T	184
Downton Castle	Heref	SO4474	52°21·9′	2°48·9′W	X	137,148
Downton Common	Heref	SO4374	52°21·9′	2°49·8′W	X	137,148
Downton Fms	Glos	SO7704	51°44·3′	2°19·6′W	FM	162
Downton Hall	Shrops	SO5279	52°24·7′	2°41·9′W	X	137,138
Downton on the Rock	Heref	SO4273	52°21·4′	2°50·7′W	X	137,148
Down Tor	Devon	SX5769	50°30·4′	4°0·6′W	X	202
Downtown	Devon	SX5285	50°39·0′	4°5·2′W	X	191,201
Downtown Fm	Devon	SX3789	50°40·9′	4°18·1′W	FM	190
Downtown Hill	Northnts	SP6280	52°25·1′	1°4·9′W	H	140
Downtown Village	Northnts	SP6180	52°25·1′	1°5·8′W	A	140
Downwood	Heref	SO3962	52°15·4′	2°53·2′W	X	137,148,149
Down Wood	Kent	TR0852	51°14·0′	0°59·2′E	F	179,189
Down Wood, The	Dorset	ST9106	50°51·4′	2°7·3′W	F	195
Downy Field	Lancs	SD4259	54°1·7′	2°52·7′W	X	102
Dowran	Corn	SW3830	50°7·0′	5°39·5′W	X	203
Dowrich Br	Devon	SS8204	50°49·6′	3°40·1′W	X	191
Dowrich Ho	Devon	SS8205	50°50·2′	3°40·2′W	X	191
Dowrie Burn	Aberd	NO6671	56°50·0′	2°33·0′W	W	45
Dowrieburn	Aberd	NO6770	56°49·5′	2°32·0′W	X	45
Dowries	Inverc	NS2770	55°53·8′	4°45·6′W	X	63
Dowrog Common	Pemb	SM7726	51°53·5′	5°14·1′W	X	157
Dowry Resr	Oldham	SD9811	53°36·0′	2°1·4′W	W	109
Dowsborough	Somer	ST1639	51°8·9′	3°11·7′W	H	181
Dowsborough (Fort)	Somer	ST1639	51°8·9′	3°11·7′W	A	181
Dow's Burn	S Ayr	NS3528	55°31·3′	4°36·4′W	W	70
Dowsby	Lincs	TF1129	52°51·1′	0°20·7′W	T	130
Dowsby Fen	Lincs	TF1429	52°51·0′	0°18·0′W	X	130
Dowsdale	Lincs	TF2810	52°40·6′	0°6·0′W	T	131,142
Dowse	I of M	SC3082	54°12·6′	4°36·0′W	X	95
Dowse Fm	Lincs	TF3415	52°43·2′	0°0·6′W	FM	131
Dowse Green	Ches	SJ5651	53°3·5′	2°39·0′W	X	117
Dowsett's Fm	Herts	TL3720	51°51·9′	0°0·2′W	FM	166
Dowsgarth	Orkney	HY3310	58°58·6′	3°9·4′W	X	6
Dowsing Fm	Suff	TM2873	52°18·7′	1°21·1′E	FM	156
Dowsland Green	Essex	TL8724	51°53·2′	0°43·4′E	X	168
Dowslands	Somer	ST2322	50°59·8′	3°5·5′W	T	193
Dowson Garth	N Yks	NZ8103	54°25·2′	0°44·7′W	X	94
Dow Spout	D & G	NX4682	55°6·8′	4°24·4′W	W	77
Dowstone Clough	Derby	SK0795	53°27·3′	1°53·3′W	X	110
Dowthorpe Hall	E Yorks	TA1538	53°49·8′	0°14·7′W	X	107
Dowthwaitehead	Cumbr	NY3720	54°34·5′	2°58·1′W	X	90
Dowton on the Rock	Heref	SO4273	52°21·4′	2°50·7′W	X	137,148
Dowyn	I of Angl	SH3176	53°15·5′	4°31·6′W	X	114
Doxey	Staffs	SJ9023	52°48·5′	2°8·5′W	T	127
Doxford Fm	Northum	NU1823	55°30·3′	1°42·5′W	FM	75
Doxford Hall	Northum	NU1824	55°30·8′	1°42·5′W	X	75
Doxford Newhouses	Northum	NU1822	55°29·7′	1°42·5′W	X	75
Doxford Park	Sund	NZ3752	54°51·9′	1°25·0′W	T	88
Doxley Brook	Staffs	SJ8823	52°48·5′	2°10·3′W	W	127

Doyden Point	Corn	SW9680	50°35·3′	4°52·5′W	X	200
Doyley Manor	Hants	SU3955	51°17·8′	1°26·0′W	X	174,185
Doyley Wood	Oxon	SU7289	51°35·9′	0°57·2′W	F	175
Doynton	S Glos	ST7174	51°28·1′	2°24·7′W	T	172
Dozmaryhill	Corn	SX1974	50°32·5′	4°32·9′W	X	201
Dozmary Pool	Corn	SX1974	50°32·5′	4°32·9′W	W	201
Drabber Tor	Staffs	SK1356	53°6·3′	1°47·9′W	X	119
Drabblegate	Norf	TG2028	52°48·5′	1°16·3′E	T	133,134
Drables Hill	Lincs	TA0501	53°29·9′	0°24·6′W	X	112
Drach Law	Aberd	NJ6646	57°30·4′	2°33·6′W	H	29
Drachlaw	Aberd	NJ6647	57°31·0′	2°33·6′W	X	29
Draden Burn	Scot Bord	NT8458	55°49·2′	2°14·9′W	W	67,74
Draen	Powys	SO1232	51°59·0′	3°16·5′W	X	161
Draen Fm	Heref	SO2840	52°3·5′	3°2·6′W	FM	148,161
Draenllwyn-du	Cered	SN7051	52°8·8′	3°53·6′W	X	146,147
Draenog	Carm	SN4302	51°41·9′	4°15·9′W	X	159
Draenogan	Gwyn	SH6035	52°53·9′	4°4·5′W	X	124
Draethen	Caer	ST2287	51°34·8′	3°7·2′W	T	171
Draffan	S Lanak	NS7945	55°41·3′	3°55·0′W	T	64
Draffanmarshill	S Lanak	NS7945	55°41·3′	3°55·0′W	X	64
Draffanmuir	S Lanak	NS7946	55°41·8′	3°55·1′W	X	64
Draffen	E Ayr	NS4245	55°40·6′	4°30·3′W	X	64
Draffin	Angus	NO5144	56°35·4′	2°47·4′W	X	54
Dragdown Hill	Devon	SX6996	50°45·2′	3°51·0′W	X	191
Dragley Beck	Cumbr	SD2977	54°11·3′	3°4·9′W	T	96,97
Dragon	I of Angl	SH5074	53°14·8′	4°14·5′W	X	114,115
Dragonby	N Lincs	SE9014	53°37·1′	0°37·9′W	T	112
Dragon Hall	Ches	SJ4856	53°6·2′	2°46·2′W	X	117
Dragon Hill	Oxon	SU2987	51°35·1′	1°34·5′W	X	174
Dragon Ness	Shetld	HU5164	60°21·7′	1°4·0′W	X	2,3
Dragons Green	W Susx	TQ1423	50°59·9′	0°22·1′W	T	198
Dragon's Hill	Dorset	SY3493	50°44·2′	2°55·7′W	T	193
Dragon's Plantn	Suff	TL6781	52°24·3′	0°27·7′E	F	143
Dragonwyck	Wrex	SJ1938	52°56·2′	3°11·9′W	X	125
Drailes, The	Shrops	SO6588	52°29·6′	2°30·5′W	X	138
Drainage Fm	Lincs	TF1622	52°47·2′	0°16·4′W	FM	130
Drain Bank Plantn	Lincs	TF4258	53°6·2′	0°7·7′E	F	122
Drain Ho	Donc	SE7010	53°35·2′	0°56·1′W	X	112
Drain-llwyn	Gwyn	SH8737	52°55·4′	3°40·4′W	X	124,125
Drainllwynbir	Powys	SO1075	52°22·2′	3°18·9′W	X	136,148
Drainllwynellyn	Powys	SO2193	52°32·0′	3°9·5′W	X	137
Drake Hall (HM Prison)	Staffs	SJ8331	52°52·8′	2°14·8′W	X	127
Drake Ho	Lancs	SD7345	53°54·3′	2°24·2′W	X	103
Drakeholes	Notts	SK7090	53°24·4′	0°56·4′W	X	112
Drakehouse	Sheff	SK4384	53°21·3′	1°20·8′W	T	111,120
Drake Howe	N Yks	NZ5302	54°24·9′	1°10·6′W	A	93
Drakeknowe Plantn	Cumbr	NY4268	55°0·4′	2°54·0′W	F	85
Drakeland Corner	Devon	SX5758	50°24·5′	4°0·4′W	T	202
Drake Law	S Lanak	NS9022	55°29·0′	3°44·0′W	H	71,72
Drakeley Heath Fm	Shrops	SJ6124	52°49·0′	2°34·3′W	FM	127
Drakelow	Worcs	SO8280	52°25·3′	2°15·5′W	T	138
Drakelow Fm	Ches	SJ6970	53°13·8′	2°27·5′W	FM	118
Drakelow Fm	Ches	SJ7371	53°14·4′	2°23·9′W	FM	118
Drakelow Gorse Fm	Ches	SJ7169	53°13·3′	2°25·7′W	FM	118
Drakelow Hall Fm	Ches	SJ7070	53°13·8′	2°26·6′W	FM	118
Drakemire	Cumbr	NY4578	55°5·9′	2°51·3′W	X	86
Drakemire	Scot Bord	NT8061	55°50·8′	2°18·7′W	X	67
Drakemires	Aberd	NJ5960	57°37·9′	2°40·7′W	X	29
Drakemire Strips	Scot Bord	NT7960	55°50·2′	2°19·7′W	F	67
Drakemyre	Aberd	NJ6344	57°29·3′	2°36·6′W	X	29
Drakemyre	Aberd	NJ9639	57°26·7′	2°3·5′W	T	30
Drakemyre	N Ayr	NS2950	55°43·1′	4°42·9′W	T	63
Drakemyre	Scot Bord	NT8062	55°51·3′	2°18·7′W	X	67
Drakenage Fm	Warw	SP2295	52°33·4′	1°40·1′W	FM	139
Drakerous	Highld	ND1158	58°30·3′	3°31·2′W	X	11,12
Drakes Broughton	Worcs	SO9248	52°8·1′	2°6·6′W	T	150
Drakes Cross	Worcs	SP0876	52°23·2′	1°52·5′W	T	139
Drake's Fm	Essex	TL7313	51°47·6′	0°30·9′E	FM	167
Drake's Island	C of Plym	SX4652	50°21·1′	4°9·5′W	X	201
Drake Stone	Northum	NT9204	55°20·0′	2°7·1′W	X	80
Drakestone Green	Suff	TL9945	52°4·3′	0°54·6′E	T	155
Drakestone Point	Glos	ST7397	51°40·5′	2°23·0′W	X	162
Drakewalls	Corn	SX4270	50°30·7′	4°13·3′W	T	201
Dramore Wood	Scot Bord	NT1636	55°36·9′	3°19·6′W	F	72
Drane Fm	Kent	TQ5760	51°19·3′	0°15·6′E	FM	177,188
Dranigower	D & G	NX2065	54°57·1′	4°48·2′W	X	82
Drannandow Fm	D & G	NX3870	55°0·1′	4°31·5′W	FM	77
Drapers Almshouses	Kent	TR3669	51°22·5′	1°23·9′E	X	179
Draper's Fm	Beds	SP9842	52°4·3′	0°33·8′W	FM	153
Draper's Fm	Essex	TL6442	52°3·4′	0°23·9′E	FM	154
Draper's Fm	Essex	TL7121	51°51·9′	0°29·4′E	FM	167
Drapers Mill	Kent	TR3670	51°23·0′	1°23·9′E	X	179
Draughton	Northnts	SP7676	52°22·8′	0°52·6′W	T	141
Draughton	N Yks	SE0352	53°58·1′	1°56·8′W	T	104
Draughton Bottom	N Yks	SE0452	53°58·1′	1°55·9′W	X	104
Draughton Height	N Yks	SE0451	53°57·5′	1°55·9′W	X	104
Draughton Moor	N Yks	SE0450	53°57·0′	1°55·9′W	X	104
Drawback Hill	Oxon	SU7581	51°31·6′	0°54·7′W	X	175
Drawbridge	Corn	SX1665	50°27·6′	4°35·1′W	T	201
Draws Drum	Cered	SN7878	52°23·4′	3°47·2′W	H	135,147
Draw Wood	Corn	SX1664	50°27·1′	4°35·1′W	F	201
Drax	N Yks	SE6726	53°43·8′	0°58·7′W	T	105,106
Drax Abbey Fm	N Yks	SE6728	53°44·9′	0°58·6′W	FM	105,106
Drax Hales	N Yks	SE6725	53°43·3′	0°58·7′W	X	105,106
Draycot	Oxon	SP6405	51°44·6′	1°4·0′W	T	164,165
Draycot Cerne	Wilts	ST9278	51°30·3′	2°6·5′W	T	173
Draycote	Warw	SP4470	52°19·8′	1°20·9′W	T	140
Draycote Hill	Warw	SP4369	52°19·3′	1°21·7′W	X	151
Draycote Hill Fm	Warw	SP4468	52°18·7′	1°20·9′W	FM	151
Draycote Water	Warw	SP4670	52°19·8′	1°19·1′W	W	140
Draycote Water Country Park	Warw	SP4669	52°19·3′	1°19·1′W	X	151
Draycot Fitz Payne	Wilts	SU1462	51°21·6′	1°47·5′W	T	173
Draycot Foliat	Swin	SU1877	51°29·7′	1°44·1′W	T	173
Draycot Hill	Wilts	SU1364	51°22·7′	1°48·4′W	X	173
Draycot Ho	Wilts	ST9378	51°30·3′	2°5·7′W	X	173
Draycott	Derby	SK4433	52°53·8′	1°20·4′W	T	129
Draycott	Glos	SO7402	51°43·2′	2°22·2′W	T	162
Draycott	Glos	SP1835	52°1·0′	1°43·9′W	T	151
Draycott	Shrops	SO8192	52°31·8′	2°16·4′W	T	138
Draycott	Somer	ST4750	51°15·0′	2°45·2′W	T	182
Draycott	Somer	ST5421	50°59·4′	2°38·9′W	T	183
Draycott	Worcs	SO8547	52°7·5′	2°12·8′W	T	150
Draycott Cross	Staffs	SJ9841	52°58·2′	2°1·4′W	X	118
Draycott Fields Fm	Derby	SK4434	52°54·3′	1°20·3′W	FM	129
Draycott Fm	Glos	SO7501	51°42·7′	2°21·3′W	FM	162
Draycott Ho	Derby	SK4334	52°54·3′	1°21·2′W	X	129
Draycott Ho	Staffs	SK1428	52°51·2′	1°47·1′W	X	128
Draycott in the Clay	Staffs	SK1528	52°51·2′	1°46·2′W	T	128
Draycott in the Moors	Staffs	SJ9840	52°57·7′	2°1·4′W	T	118
Draycott Moor	Somer	ST4649	51°14·5′	2°46·0′W	X	182
Draycott Moor Fm	Oxon	SU3999	51°41·5′	1°25·8′W	FM	164
Draydon	Somer	SS8929	51°3·2′	3°34·6′W	X	181
Draydon Knap	Somer	SS8932	51°4·8′	3°34·7′W	X	181
Drayford	Devon	SS7813	50°54·5′	3°43·7′W	T	180
Draynes	Corn	SX2169	50°29·8′	4°31·1′W	X	201
Draynes Common	Corn	SX2170	50°30·4′	4°31·1′W	X	201
Dray's Ditches	Luton	TL0826	51°55·6′	0°25·4′W	A	166
Dray, The	Kent	TQ9369	51°23·5′	0°46·8′E	W	178
Drayton	C of Port	SU6705	50°50·7′	1°2·5′W	T	196
Drayton	Hants	SU6723	51°0·4′	1°2·3′W	X	185
Drayton	Leic	SP8392	52°31·4′	0°46·2′W	T	141
Drayton	Lincs	TF2439	52°56·3′	0°8·9′W	T	131
Drayton	Norf	TG1813	52°40·5′	1°13·9′E	T	133,134
Drayton	Northnts	SP5662	52°15·4′	1°10·4′W	T	152
Drayton	Oxon	SP4241	52°4·2′	1°22·8′W	T	151
Drayton	Oxon	SU4794	51°38·8′	1°18·8′W	T	164,174
Drayton	Somer	ST4024	51°1·0′	2°50·9′W	T	193
Drayton	Somer	ST4515	50°56·1′	2°46·6′W	T	193
Drayton	Warw	SP1655	52°11·8′	1°45·6′W	T	151
Drayton	Worcs	SO9075	52°22·6′	2°8·4′W	T	139
Drayton Barn Fm	Leic	SP3397	52°34·4′	1°30·4′W	FM	140
Drayton Bassett	Staffs	SK1900	52°36·1′	1°42·8′W	T	139
Drayton Beauchamp	Bucks	SP9012	51°48·2′	0°41·3′W	T	165
Drayton Copse	Oxon	SU4593	51°38·3′	1°20·6′W	F	164,174
Drayton Crossroad Fm	Bucks	SP8529	51°57·4′	0°45·4′W	FM	165
Drayton Drewray	Norf	TG1716	52°42·1′	1°13·1′E	X	133,134
Drayton Field Barn	Warw	SP1555	52°11·8′	1°46·4′W	X	151
Drayton Field Fm	Notts	SK7675	53°16·2′	0°51·2′W	FM	120
Drayton Fields Fm	Northnts	SP5564	52°16·5′	1°11·2′W	FM	152
Drayton Gate Fm	Northnts	SP5564	52°16·5′	1°11·2′W	FM	152
Drayton Grange Fm	Leic	SP3497	52°34·4′	1°29·5′W	FM	140
Drayton Ho	Lincs	TF2538	52°55·7′	0°8·0′W	X	131
Drayton Ho	Oxon	SU5996	51°39·8′	1°8·4′W	X	164
Drayton Ho	Worcs	SO9076	52°23·2′	2°8·4′W	X	139
Drayton Ho	W Susx	SU8804	50°50·0′	0°44·6′W	X	197
Drayton House	Northnts	SP9679	52°24·3′	0°34·9′W	A	141
Drayton Lodge	Northnts	SP5561	52°14·9′	1°11·3′W	X	152
Drayton Lodge	Oxon	SP4342	52°4·7′	1°22·0′W	X	151
Drayton Lodge	Shrops	SJ7509	52°40·9′	2°21·8′W	X	127
Drayton Manor	Bucks	SP9010	51°47·1′	0°41·3′W	X	165
Drayton Manor	Staffs	SJ9216	52°44·7′	2°6·7′W	X	127
Drayton Manor Park	Staffs	SK1901	52°36·6′	1°42·8′W	X	139
Drayton Mill	Oxon	SU4893	51°38·3′	1°18·0′W	X	164,174
Drayton Park	Northnts	SP9680	52°24·8′	0°34·9′W	X	141
Drayton Parslow	Bucks	SP8328	51°56·9′	0°47·1′W	T	165
Drayton Resr	Northnts	SP5664	52°16·5′	1°10·4′W	W	152
Drayton St Leonard	Oxon	SU5996	51°39·8′	1°8·4′W	T	164
Drayton Villa Fm	Worcs	SO9076	52°23·2′	2°8·4′W	FM	139
Dreach Seilich	Arg & Bt	NR9890	56°3·9′	5°14·3′W	X	55
Dreadnought	Norf	TL8885	52°26·1′	0°46·3′E	X	144
Dreal's Fm	Kent	TR1944	51°9·4′	1°8·3′E	FM	179,189
Dreamlang Fm	I of M	SC3077	54°9·9′	4°35·8′W	FM	95
Dreavour Fm	Powys	SO1852	52°9·9′	3°11·5′W	FM	148
Drebley	N Yks	SE0559	54°1·9′	1°55·0′W	T	104
Dredgman Hill	Pemb	SM9413	51°46·9′	4°58·8′W	X	157,158
Dreel Burn	Fife	NO5103	56°13·3′	2°47·0′W	W	59
Dreembeary	I of M	SC3183	54°13·1′	4°35·1′W	X	95
Dreemfroy	I of M	SC2974	54°8·3′	4°36·6′W	X	95
Dreemskerry	I of M	SC4791	54°17·8′	4°20·6′W	T	95
Dreem, The	I of M	SC4486	54°15·0′	4°23·3′W	H	95
Dreenhill	Pemb	SM9214	51°47·4′	5°0·6′W	T	157,158
Dreeper Island	Northum	NT8844	55°41·6′	2°11·0′W	X	74
Drefach	Carm	SN2920	51°51·4′	4°28·6′W	T	145,159
Drefach	Carm	SN3538	52°1·2′	4°23·9′W	T	145
Drefach	Carm	SN5213	51°48·0′	4°8·4′W	T	159
Dre-fach	Carm	SN6516	51°49·8′	3°57·2′W	T	159
Dre-fach	Cered	SN5045	52°5·2′	4°11·0′W	T	146
Drefâch	Cered	SN5347	52°6·4′	4°8·4′W	X	146
Drefach Fm	Cered	SN3855	52°10·4′	4°21·8′W	FM	145
Drefaes	Cered	SN5564	52°15·5′	4°7·1′W	X	146
Drefelin	Carm	SN3638	52°1·2′	4°23·0′W	X	145
Drefor Dingle	Powys	SO1788	52°29·3′	3°12·9′W	X	136
Drefor Fm	Powys	SO1689	52°29·8′	3°13·8′W	FM	136
Dreggie	Highld	NJ0228	57°20·2′	3°37·2′W	T	36
Dreghorn	C of Edin	NT2268	55°54·2′	3°14·4′W	T	66
Dreghorn	N Ayr	NS3538	55°36·7′	4°36·7′W	T	70
Dre-gôch	Denb	SJ1068	53°12·3′	3°20·4′W	T	116
Drehir Fm	Nth Pt Talb	SN8202	51°42·5′	3°42·1′W	FM	170
Drellingore	Kent	TR2441	51°7·7′	1°12·5′E	T	179,189
Drem	E Loth	NT5079	56°0·3′	2°47·7′W	T	66
Drem-ddu-fawr	Cered	SN5552	52°9·1′	4°6·8′W	X	146
Drenewydd	Shrops	SJ3130	52°52·0′	3°1·1′W	X	126
Drennick	Corn	SX0347	50°17·6′	4°45·6′W	X	204
Dresden	C of Stoke	SJ9042	52°58·8′	2°8·5′W	T	118
Dressertland	D & G	NX9094	55°13·9′	3°43·4′W	X	78
Dreswick Point	I of M	SC2865	54°3·4′	4°37·3′W	X	95
Dreumasdal	N Eil	NF7637	57°18·8′	7°22·5′W	T	22
Dreva	Scot Bord	NT1435	55°36·3′	3°21·5′W	X	72
Dreva Muirburn	Scot Bord	NT1235	55°36·3′	3°23·4′W	X	72
Dreva Wood	Scot Bord	NT1536	55°36·9′	3°20·5′W	F	72
Drew	Devon	SX6255	50°23·0′	3°56·1′W	X	202
Drewern	Powys	SO1355	52°11·4′	3°16·0′W	X	148
Drewin, The	Powys	SO2690	52°30·4′	3°5·0′W	X	137
Drewitts	W Susx	TQ2324	51°0·4′	0°14·4′W	X	198
Drew's Clieve	Devon	SX9396	50°45·5′	3°30·6′W	X	192
Drews Fm	Glos	SO7322	51°54·0′	2°23·2′W	FM	162
Drews Fm	Glos	SO7723	51°54·5′	2°19·7′W	FM	162
Drews Fm	W Susx	SU7411	50°53·9′	0°56·5′W	FM	197
Drewsland	Devon	SS6404	50°49·4′	3°55·5′W	X	191
Drewsteignton	Devon	SX7391	50°42·5′	3°47·5′W	T	191
Drewston	Devon	SX7287	50°40·4′	3°48·3′W	X	191
Drewstone	Devon	SS7427	51°2·0′	3°47·4′W	X	180
Drewston Ho	Devon	SX7490	50°42·0′	3°46·7′W	X	191
Drewston Wood	Devon	SX7490	50°42·0′	3°46·7′W	F	191
Drewton Fm	E Yorks	SE9132	53°46·8′	0°36·7′W	FM	106
Drewton Manor	E Yorks	SE9233	53°47·3′	0°35·8′W	X	106
Dreybury	Devon	SS4400	50°47·0′	4°12·4′W	X	190
Dreyton	Devon	SX8152	50°21·6′	3°40·0′W	X	202
Driby	Lincs	TF3874	53°14·9′	0°4·5′E	T	122
Driby Top	Lincs	TF4074	53°14·9′	0°6·3′E	X	122
Drid Geo	Shetld	HU2079	60°29·9′	1°37·7′W	X	3
Driemastle	Highld	NH7690	57°53·2′	4°5·0′W	X	21
Driesh	Angus	NO2773	56°50·8′	3°11·4′W	H	44
Driffenbeg	E Renf	NS4851	55°44·0′	4°24·8′W	X	64
Driffield	E Yorks	TA0258	54°0·7′	0°26·2′W	T	106,107
Driffield	Glos	SU0799	51°41·6′	1°53·5′W	T	163
Driffield Canal	E Yorks	TA0556	53°59·6′	0°23·5′W	W	107
Driffield Cross Roads	Glos	SU0698	51°41·1′	1°54·4′W	X	163
Driffield Fm	N Yks	SE5067	54°6·0′	1°13·7′W	FM	100
Driffield Wold	E Yorks	TA0061	54°2·4′	0°28·0′W	X	101
Drift	Corn	SW4328	50°6·0′	5°35·3′W	T	203
Drift Br	Surrey	TQ2360	51°19·8′	0°13·7′W	X	176,187
Drift Fm	Corn	SW7529	50°7·3′	5°8·5′W	FM	204
Drift Resr	Corn	SW4329	50°6·6′	5°35·3′W	W	203
Drigg	Cumbr	SD0698	54°22·4′	3°26·4′W	T	96
Drigg Cross	Cumbr	NY0500	54°23·4′	3°27·4′W	X	89
Drigg Moorside	Cumbr	SD0599	54°22·9′	3°27·3′W	X	96
Drigg Point	Cumbr	SD0795	54°20·8′	3°25·4′W	X	96
Drighlington	Leeds	SE2228	53°45·1′	1°39·6′W	T	104
Drigmorn	D & G	NX4672	55°1·4′	4°24·1′W	X	77
Drigmorn Hill	D & G	NX4774	55°2·5′	4°23·2′W	X	77
Drill Fm	Wilts	SU0586	51°34·6′	1°55·3′W	FM	173
Drim Castle	Pemb	SN0619	51°50·4′	4°48·6′W	A	158
Drimfern	Arg & Bt	NN0814	56°17·0′	5°5·7′W	X	50,56
Drim Fm	Pemb	SN0619	51°50·4′	4°48·6′W	FM	158
Drimlee	Arg & Bt	NN1416	56°18·3′	4°59·9′W	X	50,56
Drimmie	Angus	NO5152	56°39·7′	2°47·5′W	X	54
Drimmies	Aberd	NJ7423	57°18·1′	2°25·4′W	X	38
Drimnagall	Arg & Bt	NR7184	55°59·9′	5°39·9′W	T	55
Drimnatain	Arg & Bt	NM6926	56°22·5′	5°44·0′W	X	49
Drimnin	Highld	NM5554	56°37·1′	5°59·2′W	T	47
Drimnin Ho	Highld	NM5555	56°37·6′	5°59·2′W	X	47
Drimpton	Dorset	ST4105	50°50·7′	2°49·9′W	T	193
Drimsallie Mill	Highld	NM9380	56°52·2′	5°23·3′W	X	40
Drim-Sidinish	N Eil	NF8863	57°33·2′	7°12·5′W	X	18
Drimsynie	Arg & Bt	NN1901	56°10·3′	4°54·5′W	X	56
Drim, The	Pemb	SM9437	51°59·8′	4°59·7′W	X	157
Drimvore	Arg & Bt	NR8394	56°5·6′	5°28·9′W	X	55
Drinan	Highld	NG5415	57°9·9′	6°3·7′W	X	32
Dringhoe	E Yorks	TA1554	53°58·4′	0°14·4′W	T	107
Dringhouses	York	SE5849	53°56·3′	1°6·6′W	T	105
Dringwell	Devon	SX4589	50°41·0′	4°11·3′W	X	190
Drinisiadar	N Eil	NG1794	57°51·0′	6°45·7′W	T	14
Drinkbetween	Fife	NT2688	56°5·0′	3°10·9′W	X	66
Drinkers End	Worcs	SO8130	51°58·3′	2°16·2′W	X	150
Drinkim	Pemb	SS1496	51°38·2′	4°40·9′W	W	158
Drinking Barrow	Dorset	SY9083	50°39·0′	2°8·1′W	A	195
Drinkstone	Scot Bord	NT4817	55°26·9′	2°48·9′W	X	79
Drinkstone	Suff	TL9561	52°13·0′	0°51·7′E	T	155
Drinkstone Green	Suff	TL9660	52°12·4′	0°52·5′E	T	155
Drinkstone Hill	Scot Bord	NT4818	55°27·4′	2°48·9′W	H	79
Drinkstone Park	Suff	TL9461	52°13·0′	0°50·8′E	X	155
Drinkwater's Fm	Worcs	SO8137	52°2·1′	2°16·2′W	FM	150
Drinkwillow Plantn	Suff	TL7669	52°17·7′	0°35·3′E	F	155
Drinliath	Arg & Bt	NS0099	56°8·8′	5°12·7′W	X	55
Drinnick Fm	Corn	SX3079	50°35·4′	4°23·7′W	FM	201
Drinnie's Wood	Aberd	NJ9749	57°32·1′	2°2·5′W	F	30
Drinsey Fm	Lincs	SK8674	53°15·6′	0°42·2′W	FM	121
Drinsey Nook	Notts	SK8774	53°15·6′	0°41·3′W	X	121
Driomor	N Eil	NF7640	57°20·4′	7°22·7′W	X	22
Dripend	Stir	NS7596	56°8·7′	4°0·3′W	X	57
Drip Moss	Stir	NS7595	56°8·1′	4°0·2′W	X	57
Dripshill Ho	Worcs	SO8345	52°6·4′	2°14·5′W	X	150
Drishaig	Arg & Bt	NN1328	56°24·7′	5°1·4′W	X	50
Drishaig	Arg & Bt	NN1328	56°24·7′	5°1·4′W	X	50
Drishaig	Arg & Bt	NN1510	56°15·1′	4°58·7′W	X	50,56
Drissaig	Arg & Bt	NM9415	56°17·2′	5°19·3′W	X	55
Drive End	Dorset	ST5707	50°51·9′	2°36·3′W	T	194
Driver	Somer	SS7340	51°8·9′	3°48·6′W	X	180
Driver's End	Herts	TL2219	51°51·6′	0°13·3′W	T	166
Driver's Fm	Suff	TM2164	52°14·0′	1°14·6′E	FM	156
Drive, The	Shrops	SO7182	52°26·4′	2°25·2′W	X	138
Dr Johnson's Cottage (ruin)	Denb	SJ0365	53°10·6′	3°26·7′W	X	116
Dr Johnson's Head	Corn	SW3425	50°4·2′	5°42·7′W	X	203
Drochaid a' Bhacain	Highld	NN6383	56°55·3′	4°14·6′W	X	42
Drochaid a' Ghiubhais Li	Highld	NH2670	57°41·4′	4°54·7′W	X	20
Drochaid Airigh na Saorach	Highld	NG6820	57°13·0′	5°50·1′W	X	32
Drochaid a' Mhuilinn	Highld	NG6305	57°4·8′	5°54·2′W	X	32
Drochaid an Tuill Easaich	Highld	NH1213	57°10·4′	5°6·1′W	X	34
Drochaid an Uillt Bhig	Highld	NG7443	57°25·5′	5°45·4′W	X	24
Drochaid an Uillt Ghiubhais	Highld	NH0909	57°8·2′	5°8·9′W	X	33
Drochaid Bheag	Arg & Bt	NR3055	55°43·1′	6°17·5′W	X	60
Drochaid Burn	Arg & Bt	NR7544	55°38·5′	5°34·1′W	W	62,69
Drochaid Coire Làir	Highld	NG9950	57°30·0′	5°20·8′W	X	25
Drochaid Coire Mhadaidh	Highld	NH2048	57°29·5′	4°59·7′W	X	25
Drochaid Coire Roill	Highld	NG9051	57°30·3′	5°29·9′W	X	25
Drochaid Ghlas	Arg & Bt	NN0830	56°25·7′	5°6·4′W	X	50
Drochaid Ghriais	N Eil	NB4841	58°17·4′	6°17·5′W	X	8
Drochaid Lusa	Highld	NG6924	57°15·2′	5°49·3′W	X	32
Drochaid Mhór	Highld	NC3560	58°30·1′	4°49·4′W	X	9
Drochaid Mhuilich	Highld	NH1045	57°27·6′	5°9·6′W	X	25
Drochaid na h-Uinneige	Pth & Kin	NN7966	56°46·5′	3°58·3′W	X	42
Drochaid na Luib	Highld	NH2521	57°15·0′	4°53·6′W	X	25
Drochaid nan Uan	Highld	NH1177	57°44·8′	5°21·0′W	X	19
Drochaid Sgainnir	Highld	NM9379	56°51·6′	5°23·3′W	X	40
Drochedlie	Aberd	NJ5561	57°38·5′	2°44·8′W	X	29

Drochil Castle Fm	Scot Bord	NT1643	55°40·6′	3°19·7′W	FM	72
Drochil Hill	Scot Bord	NT1544	55°41·2′	3°20·7′W	H	72
Drodland	Moray	NJ4557	57°36·2′	2°54·8′W	X	28,29
Droichs Burn	Aberd	NJ5413	57°12·6′	2°45·2′W	W	37
Droineath	Arg & Bt	NR7080	55°57·7′	5°40·7′W	X	55,61
Drointon	Staffs	SK0226	52°50·1′	1°57·8′W	T	128
Droitwich	Worcs	SO8963	52°16·1′	2°9·3′W	T	150
Droitwich Canal	Worcs	SO8761	52°15·1′	2°11·0′W	W	150
Droke	W Susx	SU9212	50°54·2′	0°41·1′W	X	197
Drokes	Hants	SZ4098	50°47·0′	1°25·6′W	X	196
Droman	Highld	NC1859	58°29·1′	5°6·8′W	T	9
Dromannan Hundaig	N Eil	NB0302	57°54·8′	7°0·4′W	X	18
Dromedary Lodge	Ches	SJ7669	53°13·3′	2°21·2′W	X	118
Dromenagh	Bucks	TQ0384	51°33·0′	0°30·5′W	X	176
Dromonby Bridge Fm	N Yks	NZ5205	54°26·5′	1°11·5′W	FM	93
Dromonby Fm	N Yks	NZ5305	54°26·5′	1°10·5′W	FM	93
Dromonby Grange Fm	N Yks	NZ5205	54°26·5′	1°11·5′W	FM	93
Dromonby Ho	N Yks	NZ5305	54°26·5′	1°10·5′W	X	93
Dromore	D & G	NX5563	54°56·7′	4°15·4′W	X	83
Dromore	D & G	NX6945	54°47·2′	4°1·8′W	X	83,84
Dron	Pth & Kin	NO1415	56°19·4′	3°23·0′W	T	58
Dron	Pth & Kin	NO2932	56°28·7′	3°8·7′W	X	53
Dronachy Burn	Fife	NT2291	56°6·6′	3°14·8′W	W	58
Drone Hill	Scot Bord	NT8466	55°53·5′	2°14·9′W	X	67
Dronfield	Derby	SK3578	53°18·1′	1°28·1′W	T	119
Dronfield Woodhouse	Derby	SK3378	53°18·1′	1°29·9′W	T	119
Drongan	E Ayr	NS4418	55°26·1′	4°27·5′W	T	70
Drongan Ho	E Ayr	NS4519	55°26·7′	4°26·6′W	X	70
Drongan Mains	E Ayr	NS4517	55°25·6′	4°26·5′W	X	70
Dronger	Shetld	HZ2074	59°33·3′	1°38·3′W	X	4
Drongi Field	Shetld	HU2743	60°10·5′	1°30·3′W	X	4
Drongi Taing	Shetld	HU2743	60°10·5′	1°30·3′W	X	4
Drongs, The	Shetld	HU2575	60°27·7′	1°32·2′W	X	3
Dron Hill	Pth & Kin	NO1214	56°18·9′	3°24·9′W	H	58
Dronley	Angus	NO3435	56°30·4′	3°3·9′W	T	54
Dronley Burn	Angus	NO3136	56°30·9′	3°6·8′W	W	53
Dronley Wood	Angus	NO3436	56°30·9′	3°3·9′W	F	54
Dronner's Dyke	Angus	NO6957	56°42·5′	2°29·9′W	W	54
Dronshiel	Scot Bord	NT7055	55°47·5′	2°28·3′W	X	67,74
Dronshiel Hill	Scot Bord	NT7054	55°47·0′	2°28·3′W	X	67,74
Droop	Dorset	ST7508	50°52·5′	2°20·9′W	T	194
Droop Hill	Aberd	NO7581	56°55·4′	2°24·2′W	H	45
Drooping Point	Shetld	HU4117	59°56·4′	1°15·5′W	X	4
Drop Clough	Kirk	SE0413	53°37·1′	1°56·0′W	X	110
Drope	V of Glam	ST1175	51°28·3′	3°16·5′W	T	171
Drop Fm	Brad	SE0135	53°48·9′	1°58·7′W	FM	104
Dropmore	Bucks	SU9286	51°34·2′	0°40·0′W	X	175
Dropnose Point	I Scilly	SV8908	49°53·7′	6°19·5′W	X	203
Dropping Crag	Cumbr	NY1607	54°27·3′	3°17·3′W	X	89
Dropping Craig	D & G	NX7745	54°47·3′	3°54·4′W	X	84
Droppingstone Fm	Ches	SJ5155	53°5·6′	2°43·5′W	FM	117
Dropping Well	Roth	SK3994	53°26·7′	1°24·4′W	T	110,111
Droppingwells Fm	Worcs	SO8074	52°22·1′	2°17·2′W	FM	138
Dropshort Fm	Beds	TL0028	51°56·7′	0°32·3′W	FM	166
Dropshort Fm	Beds	SP9950	52°8·6′	0°32·8′W	FM	153
Dropshort Fm	Bucks	SP6239	52°3·0′	1°5·4′W	FM	152
Dropshort Lodge	Northnts	SP7878	52°23·9′	0°50·8′W	X	141
Dropswell Fm	Durham	NZ3933	54°41·7′	1°23·3′W	FM	93
Drosgl	Conwy	SH7071	53°13·5′	3°56·4′W	X	115
Drosgl	Gwyn	SH6667	53°11·2′	3°59·9′W	H	115
Drosgol	Cered	SN7587	52°28·2′	3°50·0′W	H	135
Drosgol	Conwy	SH7652	53°3·3′	3°50·6′W	X	115
Droskyn Point	Corn	SW7554	50°20·8′	5°9·4′W	X	200,204
Droslyn	Pemb	SN1315	51°48·4′	4°42·4′W	X	158
Drostre	Powys	SO1030	51°57·9′	3°18·2′W	X	161
Drostre Bank	Powys	SO1031	51°58·5′	3°18·2′W	H	161
Droughduil	D & G	NX1556	54°52·1′	4°52·6′W	X	82
Drought Garden	Rut	SK9008	52°40·0′	0°39·7′W	X	141
Drouk Knowes	Scot Bord	NT8015	55°26·0′	2°18·5′W	X	80
Drove	Somer	ST5837	51°8·1′	2°35·6′W	X	182,183
Drove Cott	Notts	SK8355	53°5·4′	0°45·2′W	X	121
Drove End Fm	Dorset	SU1211	50°54·1′	1°49·4′W	FM	195
Drove Farm Ho	Hants	SU2628	51°3·3′	1°37·4′W	FM	184
Drove Fm	Lincs	TF1553	53°3·9′	0°16·6′W	FM	121
Drove Fm	N Som	ST3560	51°20·4′	2°55·6′W	FM	182
Drove Fm	W Berks	SU3379	51°30·8′	1°31·1′W	FM	174
Drove Fm	Wilts	SU1457	51°18·9′	1°47·6′W	FM	173
Drove Hill	E Dunb	NS6582	56°1·0′	4°9·5′W	X	57,64
Drove Ho	Lincs	TF2749	53°1·6′	0°6·0′W	X	131
Drove Ho, The	Norf	TF7243	52°57·6′	0°34·1′E	X	132
Drove Island	Dorset	SZ0185	50°40·1′	1°58·8′W	X	195
Drove Lane Fm	W Susx	SU9602	50°48·8′	0°37·9′W	FM	197
Drove Park	D & G	NX4258	54°53·8′	4°27·4′W	X	83
Drover Ho	Durham	NZ0942	54°46·6′	1°51·2′W	X	88
Drove Rigg	Northum	NY7085	55°9·8′	2°27·8′W	X	80
Droveroad Plantn	Scot Bord	NT5222	55°29·6′	2°45·2′W	F	73
Drovers	W Susx	SU8714	50°55·4′	0°45·3′W	X	197
Drovers' Arms	Powys	SN9845	52°5·9′	3°29·0′W	X	147
Droversdale Wood	Notts	SK6391	53°25·0′	1°2·7′W	F	111
Droversgate	Cumbr	NY5332	54°41·1′	2°43·3′W	X	90
Drovers Ho	N Yks	SD9997	54°22·4′	2°0·5′W	X	98
Drove Stance	Highld	NH6575	57°44·9′	4°15·6′W	X	21
Drove, The	Norf	TL9183	52°24·9′	0°48·9′E	X	144
Droveway	Swin	SU1594	51°38·9′	1°46·6′W	X	163,173
Droveway Fm	N Som	ST4160	51°20·4′	2°50·4′W	FM	172,182
Droveway Hill	Oxon	SU4386	51°34·5′	1°22·4′W	X	174
Drowndubbs	Angus	NO4942	56°34·3′	2°49·4′W	X	54
Drowning Dubs	Scot Bord	NT2121	55°28·8′	3°14·6′W	X	73
Drowning Flow	Northum	NY7697	55°16·2′	2°22·2′W	W	80
Droxford	Hants	SU6018	50°57·7′	1°8·4′W	T	185
Droylsden	Tames	SJ8998	53°29·0′	2°9·5′W	T	109
Droys Ct	Glos	SO9015	51°50·2′	2°8·3′W	X	163
Droystone	S Ayr	NS4427	55°31·0′	4°27·8′W	X	70
Dr Syntax's Head	Corn	SW3425	50°4·2′	5°42·7′W	X	203
Drub	Kirk	SE1926	53°44·0′	1°42·3′W	T	104
Druce Fm	Dorset	SY7495	50°45·5′	2°21·7′W	FM	194
Druce Higher Barn	Dorset	SY7497	50°46·6′	2°21·7′W	X	194
Druce's Fm	Wilts	ST8453	51°16·8′	2°13·4′W	FM	183
Druchtag	D & G	NX3547	54°47·7′	4°33·6′W	X	83
Druggam	Aberd	NJ7400	57°5·7′	2°25·3′W	X	38

Druggers End	Worcs	SO7938	52°2·6′	2°18·0′W	T	150
Druggon Hill Fm	N Yks	SE1796	54°21·8′	1°43·9′W	FM	99
Druid	Denb	SJ0443	52°58·8′	3°25·4′W	T	125
Druid	Devon	SX7471	50°31·7′	3°46·3′W	X	202
Druid	Pth & Kin	NN9263	56°45·0′	3°45·5′W	X	43
Druidaig Lodge	Highld	NG8724	57°15·7′	5°31·5′W	X	33
Druidale	I of M	SC3688	54°15·9′	4°30·7′W	X	95
Druidale Fm	I of M	SC3688	54°15·9′	4°30·7′W	FM	95
Druid Fm	I of Angl	SH4175	53°15·1′	4°22·6′W	FM	114,115
Druidhall	D & G	NX8198	55°16·0′	3°51·9′W	X	78
Druidhill Burn	D & G	NS8101	55°17·6′	3°52·0′W	W	78
Druid's Combe	Somer	ST0037	51°7·6′	3°25·4′W	X	181
Druidsdale	Aberd	NO8481	56°55·5′	2°15·3′W	X	45
Druidsfield	Aberd	NJ5717	57°14·8′	2°42·3′W	X	37
Druids Grove	Surrey	TQ1553	51°16·1′	0°20·7′W	F	187
Druids Heath Fm	Wals	SK0601	52°36·6′	1°54·3′W	FM	139
Druid's Hill	Corn	SX1261	50°25·4′	4°38·4′W	H	200
Druids Lodge	Swan	SS4490	51°35·5′	4°14·7′W	X	159
Druid's Lodge	Wilts	SU0938	51°8·7′	1°51·9′W	X	184
Druids Moor	Swan	SS4490	51°35·5′	4°14·7′W	X	159
Druids Park	D & G	NX9481	55°7·0′	3°39·3′W	X	78
Druid's Plantn	N Yks	SE1778	54°12·1′	1°43·9′W	F	99
Druids' Seat Wood	Pth & Kin	NO1231	56°28·0′	3°25·3′W	F	53
Druidston	Pemb	SM8616	51°48·3′	5°5·9′W	T	157
Druidstone Ho	Newp	ST2483	51°32·7′	3°5·4′W	X	171
Druidston Haven	Pemb	SM8616	51°48·3′	5°5·9′W	W	157
Druid Temple Fm	Highld	NH6842	57°27·2′	4°11·5′W	FM	26
Druim	Highld	NH9157	57°35·7′	3°49·0′W	X	27
Druim a' Bhealaich	Highld	NM6663	56°42·3′	5°48·9′W	H	40
Druim a' Bhlàir	Arg & Bt	NN2743	56°33·1′	4°48·4′W	X	50
Druim a' Bhotha Chlach	N Eil	NB3038	58°15·1′	6°35·7′W	X	8,13
Druim a' Chaim	Highld	NG2654	57°29·9′	6°34·0′W	X	23
Druim a' Chait	Pth & Kin	NN8971	56°49·3′	3°48·7′W	H	43
Druim a' Chathair	Highld	NH3010	57°9·2′	4°48·2′W	X	34
Druim a' Choilich	Highld	NH2119	57°13·9′	4°57·5′W	H	34
Druim a' Choire Odhair	Highld	NG8304	57°4·8′	5°34·4′W	X	33
Druim a' Choire Rèidh	Highld	NH0011	57°9·0′	5°17·9′W	X	33
Druimachoish	Highld	NN1246	56°34·4′	5°3·2′W	X	50
Druim a' Chracairnie	Highld	ND0653	58°27·6′	3°36·2′W	H	11,12
Druim a' Chuilein	Highld	NH4861	57°37·1′	4°32·2′W	H	20
Druim a' Chuilteir	Arg & Bt	NM9107	56°12·8′	5°21·8′W	X	55
Druim a' Chùirn	Arg & Bt	NR3766	55°49·2′	6°11·5′W	X	60,61
Druim a' Chùirn	Highld	NM8289	56°56·7′	5°34·6′W	H	40
Druim a Chuirn	Highld	NM9694	56°59·8′	5°21·1′W	H	33,40
Druim a' Ghoirtein	Highld	NM8895	57°0·1′	5°29·0′W	H	33,40
Druim Airigh an t-Sluic	Arg & Bt	NR6193	56°4·5′	5°50·0′W	H	61
Druim Airigh na Creige	N Eil	NF8072	57°37·7′	7°21·2′W	H	18
Druim Aladh	Arg & Bt	NR3563	55°47·5′	6°13·2′W	X	60,61
Druim Allt a' Mhuilinn	Highld	NC8268	58°35·3′	4°1·3′W	H	10
Druim Allt Damh Dubh	Pth & Kin	NN8283	56°55·7′	3°55·9′W	H	43
Druim Allt na h-Aire	Highld	NC5532	58°15·4′	4°27·8′W	X	16
Druim an Aoineidh	Arg & Bt	NM2522	56°18·9′	6°26·4′W	H	48
Druim an Aoinidh	Highld	NG8108	57°6·9′	5°36·6′W	X	33
Druim an Aonaich	Highld	NG5842	57°24·5′	6°1·3′W	X	24
Druim an Dubh-leathaid	Highld	NM6684	56°53·6′	5°50·1′W	X	40
Druim an Eilein	Highld	NG7377	57°43·8′	5°48·3′W	H	19
Druim an Fhaillich	Arg & Bt	NM8013	56°15·8′	5°32·7′W	H	55
Druim an Fhasdaidh	Highld	NG8697	57°54·9′	5°36·3′W	H	19
Druim an Fhirich	Highld	NM5962	56°41·5′	5°55·7′W	H	47
Druim an Fhraoich Mhin	Arg & Bt	NM4645	56°32·0′	6°7·4′W	X	47,48
Druim an Fhuarain	Highld	NG5619	57°12·1′	6°1·9′W	X	32
Druim an Iasgair	N Eil	NF8049	57°25·4′	7°19·4′W	X	22
Druim an Iubhair	Highld	NM9361	56°42·0′	5°22·4′W	X	40
Druim an Laoigh	Highld	NM7670	56°46·3′	5°39·5′W	X	40
Druim an Laraidh	Highld	NC9159	58°30·6′	3°51·8′W	H	10
Druimanlochain	Highld	NH8505	57°7·6′	3°53·5′W	X	35,36
Druim an Rubha Bhàin	Highld	NG7479	57°44·9′	5°47·4′W	X	19
Druim an Ruma	Highld	NG4466	57°36·9′	6°16·7′W	H	23
Druim an Scriodain	Highld	NM5469	56°45·1′	6°1·0′W	X	47
Druim an Stuin	Arg & Bt	NR3247	55°38·8′	6°15·1′W	X	60
Druimantavore	Pth & Kin	NN8224	56°23·9′	3°54·3′W	X	52
Druimantorran	Highld	NH5724	57°17·3′	4°21·9′W	X	26,35
Druim an t-Seilich	Highld	NN7589	56°58·8′	4°2·9′W	X	42
Druim an Uisge Fhuair	Arg & Bt	NR3551	55°41·1′	6°12·5′W	X	60
Druimarbin	Highld	NN0871	56°47·7′	5°8·2′W	T	41
Druimavuic	Arg & Bt	NN0044	56°33·0′	5°14·8′W	X	50
Druim Bà	Highld	NH5235	57°23·1′	4°27·3′W	X	26
Druim Bad a' Ghaill	Highld	NC0711	58°3·0′	5°15·8′W	X	15
Druim Baile Fuir	Highld	NC5602	57°59·3′	4°25·7′W	X	16
Druim Baile na Creige	N Eil	NG0088	57°47·1′	7°2·4′W	X	18
Druim Bàn	Highld	NG7011	57°8·2′	5°47·6′W	H	32,33
Druim Barr na Coille	Arg & Bt	NM8315	56°16·9′	5°29·9′W	H	55
Druimbasbie	Highld	NC7763	58°32·5′	4°6·3′W	X	10
Druim Beag	Arg & Bt	NM7702	56°9·8′	5°35·0′W	X	55
Druim Beag	Highld	NN0081	56°52·9′	5°16·5′W	X	41
Druim Beithe	Arg & Bt	NR7699	56°8·1′	5°35·9′W	H	55
Druim Beithe	Pth & Kin	NN4441	56°32·4′	4°31·8′W	X	51
Druim Bhàin	Highld	NG6518	57°11·8′	5°53·0′W	X	32
Druim Bheag	Highld	NH0626	57°17·3′	5°12·7′W	H	25,33
Druim Bhùirich	Aberd	NJ2010	57°10·7′	3°18·9′W	H	36
Druim Breac	Highld	NG8990	57°51·2′	5°32·9′W	X	19
Druim Breac	Highld	NM7970	56°46·4′	5°36·6′W	X	40
Druim Buidhe	Arg & Bt	NM1554	56°35·7′	6°38·1′W	X	46
Druim Buidhe	Arg & Bt	NM5549	56°34·4′	5°58·9′W	X	47,48
Druim Buidhe	Arg & Bt	NM7518	56°18·3′	5°37·8′W	X	55
Druim Buidhe	Arg & Bt	NM8608	56°13·2′	5°26·7′W	H	55
Druim Buidhe	Arg & Bt	NR3560	55°45·9′	6°13·0′W	X	60
Druim Buidhe	Arg & Bt	NR7081	55°58·3′	5°40·7′W	H	55,61
Druim Buidhe	Arg & Bt	NR7378	55°56·7′	5°37·7′W	X	62
Druim Buidhe	Highld	NC6653	58°27·0′	4°17·3′W	H	10
Druim Buidhe	Highld	NH3871	57°42·2′	4°42·7′W	H	20
Druimbuidhe	Highld	NM6057	56°38·9′	5°54·4′W	X	49
Druim Buidhe	Highld	NM9397	57°1·3′	5°24·2′W	H	33,40
Druim Caol	N Eil	NB2202	57°55·5′	6°41·3′W	X	14
Druim Carn nam Muc	Highld	ND0845	58°23·3′	3°33·9′W	X	11,12
Druim Càrn Niall	Highld	NG7988	57°49·9′	5°42·9′W	H	19
Druim Chlachan	Arg & Bt	NR6979	55°57·2′	5°41·6′W	X	61,62
Druim Chòsaidh	Highld	NG9100	57°2·9′	5°26·3′W	X	33
Druim Chuibhe	Highld	NC6961	58°31·3′	4°14·5′W	X	10
Druim Chuilinn	Highld	NM7992	56°58·2′	5°37·7′W	H	33,40

Druim Claigeann Mhicheil	Arg & Bt	NR4047	55°39·1′	6°7·5′W	X	60
Druim Coire a' Bheithe	Highld	NM9386	56°55·4′	5°23·6′W	X	40
Druim Coire an Stangain Bhig	Highld	NN0394	57°0·0′	5°14·2′W	X	33
Druim Coire an Stangain Mhóir	Highld	NN0196	57°1·0′	5°16·2′W	X	33
Druim Coire Mhic-sith	Pth & Kin	NN6674	56°50·5′	4°11·4′W	H	42
Druim Coire nan Eirecheanach	Highld	NH0410	57°8·6′	5°13·9′W	X	33
Druim Coire nan Laogh	Highld	NM8993	56°59·1′	5°27·9′W	X	33,40
Druim Comhnard	Highld	NM7388	56°55·9′	5°43·4′W	H	40
Druim Comhnardaig	Highld	NM7977	56°50·2′	5°36·9′W	X	40
Druim Cùl	Pth & Kin	NO0368	56°47·9′	3°34·8′W	H	43
Druim Dearg	Angus	NO2158	56°42·7′	3°17·0′W	H	53
Druim Dearg	Highld	NC9214	58°6·4′	3°49·5′W	H	17
Druim Dearg	Highld	NG8122	57°14·4′	5°37·3′W	X	33
Druim Dhonn	Highld	NC1430	58°13·4′	5°9·6′W	H	15
Druimdhu	Highld	NH1859	57°35·3′	5°2·2′W	X	25
Druimdhu	Highld	NM6588	56°55·7′	5°51·3′W	X	40
Druim Dhùghaill	Arg & Bt	NM2722	56°19·0′	6°24·5′W	X	48
Druim Donn	Highld	NC1708	58°1·7′	5°5·5′W	H	15
Druim Donn	Highld	NH0193	57°53·2′	5°20·9′W	X	19
Druimdrishaig	Arg & Bt	NR7370	55°52·4′	5°37·3′W	X	62
Druim Dubh	Arg & Bt	NN1417	56°18·8′	5°0·0′W	X	50,56
Druim Dubh	Arg & Bt	NR3467	55°49·6′	6°14·4′W	X	60,61
Druim Dubh	Arg & Bt	NR4247	55°39·1′	6°5·6′W	X	60
Druimdubh	Highld	ND2052	58°27·2′	3°21·8′W	X	11,12
Druim Dubh	Highld	NG5912	57°8·4′	5°58·5′W	H	32
Druim Dubh	Highld	NG9190	57°51·3′	5°30·9′W	H	19
Druim Dubh	Highld	NH1860	57°35·9′	5°2·3′W	X	20
Druim Dubh	Highld	NH1944	57°27·3′	5°0·6′W	H	25
Druim Dubh	Highld	NM6990	56°56·9′	5°47·4′W	H	40
Druim Dubh	N Eil	NB4226	58°9·1′	6°22·6′W	X	8
Druim Dubh	N Eil	NF7369	57°35·8′	7°28·0′W	X	18
Druim Dubh	Pth & Kin	NN8374	56°50·8′	3°54·6′W	X	43
Druim Dubh an Fhuarain	Highld	NH2335	57°22·5′	4°56·2′W	X	25
Druim Eadar Dà Choire	Highld	NG5224	57°14·6′	6°6·2′W	H	32
Druim Ealaidh	Arg & Bt	NM3752	56°35·4′	6°16·6′W	X	47
Druim Eidhbhat	N Eil	NB3743	58°18·1′	6°28·9′W	X	8
Druim Eileasaig	Highld	NG9011	57°8·8′	5°27·8′W	X	33
Druim Fada	Arg & Bt	NM4655	56°37·3′	6°8·0′W	H	47
Druim Fada	Arg & Bt	NM6422	56°20·2′	5°48·6′W	H	49
Druim Fada	Arg & Bt	NR3553	55°42·1′	6°12·6′W	X	60
Druim Fada	Highld	NG8708	57°7·1′	5°30·6′W	H	33
Druim Fada	Highld	NN0782	56°53·6′	5°9·7′W	H	41
Druim Fada	N Eil	NB3529	58°10·5′	6°30·0′W	X	8
Druim Farmolach	Highld	NN0379	56°51·9′	5°13·5′W	X	41
Druim Fearna	Highld	NM9577	56°50·6′	5°21·2′W	X	40
Druim Fèith an t-Seilich	Highld	NM6166	56°43·7′	5°54·0′W	X	40
Druim Fiaclach	Highld	NM7384	56°53·8′	5°43·2′W	H	40
Druim Fiaclach	Highld	NM7979	56°51·3′	5°37·0′W	H	40
Druim Fishaig	Arg & Bt	NM2260	56°39·2′	6°31·7′W	X	46,47
Druim Fuar	Arg & Bt	NR7074	55°54·5′	5°40·4′W	X	61,62
Druim Garbh	Highld	NM6866	56°43·9′	5°47·1′W	H	40
Druim Garbh	Highld	NM8668	56°45·5′	5°29·6′W	X	40
Druim Gealtaig	N Eil	NB4439	58°16·2′	6°21·5′W	X	8
Druimghigha	Arg & Bt	NM4052	56°35·5′	6°13·7′W	X	47
Druim Ghinneabhal	N Eil	NB5455	58°25·1′	6°12·3′W	X	8
Druim Ghlaoidh	Highld	NN2791	56°58·9′	4°50·4′W	H	34
Druim Glac Ealagain	Highld	NM6970	56°46·1′	5°46·4′W	X	40
Druim Glas	Highld	NM8466	56°44·4′	5°31·5′W	H	40
Druim Gleann Laoigh	Highld	NN0685	56°55·2′	5°10·8′W	H	41
Druim Grudaidh	Highld	NG9664	57°37·5′	5°24·5′W	X	19
Druim Hain	Highld	NG4922	57°13·5′	6°9·0′W	X	32
Druim Hallagro	N Eil	NB5458	58°26·7′	6°12·5′W	X	8
Druim Ile Coire	Highld	NM8791	56°57·9′	5°29·8′W	X	33,40
Druimindarroch	Highld	NM6984	56°53·7′	5°47·1′W	T	40
Druimintoul Lodge	Highld	NH9211	57°10·9′	3°46·7′W	X	36
Druim Iosal	Highld	NG8516	57°11·3′	5°33·0′W	X	33
Druim Iriseig	Arg & Bt	NR3547	55°38·9′	6°12·3′W	X	60
Druimkinnerras	Highld	NH4740	57°25·7′	4°32·4′W	X	26
Druim Klibreck	Highld	NC5732	58°15·5′	4°25·8′W	X	16
Druim Lamasaigh	N Eil	NF8332	57°16·4′	7°15·1′W	X	22
Druim Langara	N Eil	NF8165	57°34·0′	7°19·7′W	X	18
Druim Laragan	Highld	NH3503	57°5·6′	4°42·9′W	H	34
Druim Leac a' Sgiathain	Highld	NM8766	56°44·5′	5°28·5′W	X	40
Druim Leac a' Shith	Highld	NM8699	57°2·2′	5°31·2′W	H	33,40
Druim Leathad nam Fias	Highld	NM9570	56°46·8′	5°20·9′W	H	40
Druim Leathann	N Eil	NB4749	58°21·7′	6°19·1′W	X	8
Druim Liath Ard	Highld	NM8462	56°42·2′	5°31·3′W	X	40
Druim Linuisg	N Eil	NB3928	58°10·1′	6°25·8′W	X	8
Druim Loch	Highld	NG4941	57°23·7′	6°10·2′W	W	23
Druim Loch Eilt	Highld	NM8382	56°53·0′	5°33·3′W	X	40
Druim Loch na Gainimh	Highld	NC2655	58°27·2′	4°58·4′W	X	9
Druim Meadhoin	Stir	NN6512	56°17·1′	4°10·4′W	H	57
Druim Meadhonach	Arg & Bt	NR3246	55°38·3′	6°15·1′W	X	60
Druim Meleag	Highld	NC6850	58°25·4′	4°15·1′W	H	10
Druim Min	Highld	NM8963	56°42·9′	5°26·4′W	X	40
Druim Mòr	Angus	NO1977	56°52·9′	3°19·3′W	H	43
Druim Mòr	Arg & Bt	NM7236	56°27·9′	5°41·6′W	H	49
Druim Mòr	Arg & Bt	NM7936	56°28·1′	5°34·8′W	X	49
Druim Mòr	Arg & Bt	NM8428	56°24·0′	5°29·6′W	H	49
Druim Mòr	Arg & Bt	NM9432	56°26·4′	5°20·1′W	H	49
Druim Mòr	Arg & Bt	NR3587	56°0·4′	6°14·6′W	X	61
Druim Mor	Arg & Bt	NR7181	55°58·3′	5°39·8′W	X	55
Druim Mòr	Highld	NG7054	57°31·3′	5°50·0′W	X	24
Druim Mòr	Highld	NM4179	56°50·1′	6°14·3′W	H	39
Druim Mòr	Highld	NM5959	56°39·9′	5°55·5′W	X	47
Druim Mòr	Highld	NN1577	56°51·1′	5°1·6′W	X	41
Druim Mòr	N Eil	NB0436	58°13·1′	7°2·0′W	H	13
Druim Mòr	N Eil	NB5042	58°18·0′	6°15·5′W	X	8
Druim Mòr	Pth & Kin	NN9541	56°33·2′	3°42·0′W	H	52,53
Druim Mòr	Pth & Kin	NN9967	56°47·3′	3°38·7′W	H	43
Druim Mòr	Stir	NN6309	56°15·5′	4°12·3′W	X	57
Druim Mòr Aird na Drochaide	Arg & Bt	NM7331	56°25·3′	5°40·4′W	X	49
Druim Mòr na Buiem	N Eil	NB3039	58°15·7′	6°35·7′W	X	8,13
Druim na Bèiste	Highld	NN5287	56°57·3′	4°25·6′W	H	42
Druim na Birlinn	Highld	NN0364	56°43·8′	5°12·8′W	H	41
Druim na Brein-choille	Highld	NM8882	56°53·1′	5°28·3′W	X	40

Druim na Buainn	Highld	NC2164	58°31·9′	5°4·0′W	H	9
Druim na Cadha Ruaidh	Highld	NM6167	56°44·3′	5°54·0′W	X	40
Druim na Cille	Arg & Bt	NM4147	56°32·9′	6°12·4′W	X	47,48
Druim na Cluain-airighe	Highld	NG7404	57°4·6′	5°43·3′W	H	33
Druim na Coille	Highld	NG4364	57°35·8′	6°17·6′W	H	23
Druim na Cràcaig	Highld	NM5652	56°36·0′	5°58·1′W	X	47
Druim na Criche	Highld	NG4337	57°21·3′	6°15·9′W	H	23,32
Druim na Criche	Highld	NH0656	57°33·4′	5°14·1′W	X	25
Druim na Croise	Arg & Bt	NR3246	55°38·3′	6°15·1′W	X	60
Druimnacroish	Arg & Bt	NM4449	56°34·1′	6°9·6′W	X	47,48
Druim na Cuaich	Aberd	NJ1911	57°11·2′	3°20·0′W	H	36
Druim na Daise	Highld	NG8315	57°10·7′	5°35·0′W	X	33
Druim na Doire Duibhe	Highld	NC2309	58°2·4′	4°59·4′W	X	15
Druim na Dubhaiche	Arg & Bt	NR3762	55°47·0′	6°11·3′W	X	60,61
Druim na Dubh Ghlaic	Arg & Bt	NM7608	56°13·0′	5°36·3′W	H	55
Druim na Fèithe	Highld	NC6243	58°21·5′	4°21·0′W	X	10
Druim na Feuraich	Highld	NN7592	57°0·4′	4°3·0′W	X	35
Druim na Firean	Highld	NG9012	57°9·3′	5°27·9′W	X	33
Druim na Gaibhre	Highld	NH0894	57°53·9′	5°13·9′W	X	19
Druim na Gaoithe	Highld	NH6579	57°47·1′	4°15·8′W	H	21
Druim na Garbh Leachtrach	Highld	NH3912	57°10·5′	4°39·3′W	X	34
Druim na Geàrr Leacainn	Highld	NM4663	56°41·6′	6°8·5′W	H	47
Druim na Geid Salaich	Highld	NN0599	57°2·7′	5°12·4′W	X	33
Druim na Giubhsaich	Highld	NN0788	56°56·8′	5°9·9′W	X	41
Druim na Glaic Mòra	N Eil	NF8150	57°26·0′	7°18·5′W	X	22
Druim na h-Achlaise	Highld	NH1203	57°5·0′	5°5·7′W	X	34
Druim na h-Aibhne	Highld	NH3426	57°17·9′	4°44·8′W	X	26
Druim na h- Aimhne	Highld	NC2546	58°22·3′	4°59·1′W	X	9
Druim na h-Airighe	Arg & Bt	NR3450	55°40·5′	6°13·4′W	X	60
Druim na h-Easgainn	Moray	NJ1414	57°12·8′	3°25·0′W	H	36
Druim na h-Erasaid	Arg & Bt	NR2765	55°48·3′	6°21·0′W	X	60
Druim na h-Imrich	Highld	NC2035	58°16·3′	5°3·7′W	H	15
Druim na h-Iùbhraich	Highld	NM8048	56°34·6′	5°34·5′W	X	49
Druim na h-Uamachd	Highld	NC5414	58°5·7′	4°28·1′W	F	16
Druim na h-Uamha Mòire	Highld	NC2328	58°12·6′	5°0·3′W	X	15
Druim na Leitire	Highld	NG8022	57°14·4′	5°38·3′W	X	33
Druim na Lice	N Eil	NF8449	57°25·5′	7°15·4′W	X	22
Druim na Luibe Dhuibhe	Highld	NN1097	57°1·8′	5°7·4′W	H	34
Druim na Luibe Duibhe	Highld	NN0997	57°1·7′	5°8·4′W	X	33
Druim na Maodalaich	Highld	NM8753	56°37·5′	5°27·9′W	X	49
Druim nam Bad	Highld	NC4737	58°18·0′	4°36·2′W	X	16
Druim nam Bò	Highld	NN8792	57°0·6′	3°51·2′W	H	35,43
Druim nam Feannag	Highld	NH2997	57°56·0′	4°52·8′W	X	20
Druim nam Fiadh	Arg & Bt	NR3164	55°47·9′	6°17·1′W	X	60,61
Druim nam Freumh	Highld	NG8588	57°50·1′	5°36·8′W	H	19
Druim nam Fuath	Highld	NG9993	57°53·1′	5°23·0′W	H	19
Druim nan Bò	Highld	NG8613	57°9·7′	5°31·9′W	X	33
Druim nan Caorach	N Eil	NB1811	58°0·2′	6°45·9′W	X	13,14
Druim nan Caorach	N Eil	NG0389	57°47·8′	6°59·5′W	X	18
Druim nan Carn	Arg & Bt	NM2663	56°41·0′	6°28·0′W	X	46,47
Druim nan Càrn	Arg & Bt	NN0108	56°13·6′	5°12·2′W	X	55
Druim nan Carn	Stir	NN4407	56°14·1′	4°30·6′W	H	57
Druim nan Cleochd	Highld	NG5429	57°17·4′	6°4·5′W	H	32
Druim nan Cliabh	Arg & Bt	NR6698	56°7·3′	5°45·4′W	H	55,61
Druim nan Cliar	Highld	NC5056	58°28·3′	4°33·8′W	X	9
Druim nan Cnaimh	Arg & Bt	NR3348	55°39·4′	6°14·3′W	X	60
Druim nan Cnamh	Highld	NH1207	57°7·2′	5°5·9′W	H	34
Druim nan Colann	Arg & Bt	NR7979	55°57·5′	5°32·0′W	X	62
Druim nan Comhrag	Highld	NC9025	58°12·3′	3°51·8′W	X	17
Druim nan Crann	Arg & Bt	NR2773	55°52·6′	6°21·5′W	X	60
Druim nan Crann Saighde	Pth & Kin	NN6056	56°40·7′	4°16·7′W	X	42,51
Druim nan Damh	Highld	NH5868	57°41·0′	4°22·4′W	X	21
Druim nan Dearcag	N Eil	NF7475	57°39·1′	7°27·5′W	X	18
Druim nan Each	Arg & Bt	NR3252	55°41·5′	6°15·4′W	X	60
Druim nan Eilid	Stir	NN6513	56°17·7′	4°10·4′W	H	57
Druim nan Leargan	N Eil	NB3428	58°9·9′	6°30·9′W	X	8,13
Druim nan Lion	Arg & Bt	NR4574	55°53·8′	6°4·3′W	X	60,61
Druim nan Ramh	Highld	NG4722	57°13·4′	6°11·0′W	H	32
Druim nan Sac	Highld	NN7089	56°58·7′	4°7·9′W	H	42
Druim nan Sgalag	Highld	NM6357	56°38·9′	5°51·5′W	X	49
Druim nan Sgarbh	Highld	NG1449	57°26·7′	6°45·6′W	H	23
Druim nan Sgorach	N Eil	NB3631	58°11·6′	6°29·1′W	X	8
Druim nan Slat	Arg & Bt	NN3447	56°35·4′	4°41·8′W	X	50
Druim nan Sloc	Highld	NM6961	56°41·3′	5°45·9′W	X	40
Druim nan Slochd	Highld	NG4672	57°40·2′	6°15·1′W	H	23
Druim nan Slochd	Highld	NM5750	56°35·0′	5°57·0′W	X	47
Druim nan Uadhag	Highld	NM8995	57°0·1′	5°28·0′W	H	33,40
Druim na Ruaige	Highld	NG5027	57°16·2′	6°8·4′W	X	32
Druim na Saille	Highld	NM9481	56°52·7′	5°22·4′W	X	40
Druim na Saobhaidhe	Highld	NH2285	57°49·4′	4°59·4′W	X	20
Druim na Seilge	Pth & Kin	NN6361	56°43·5′	4°13·9′W	H	42
Druim na Sgriodain	Highld	NM9865	56°44·2′	5°17·7′W	H	40
Druimnashallag	Arg & Bt	NM8916	56°17·6′	5°24·1′W	X	55
Druim na Sròine-Cruime	Arg & Bt	NM4956	56°38·0′	6°5·1′W	H	47
Druimneil Ho	Arg & Bt	NM9044	56°32·7′	5°24·5′W	X	49
Druim Odhar	Aberd	NO2489	56°59·4′	3°14·6′W	X	44
Druim Poll Eòghainn	Highld	NC2009	58°2·3′	5°2·5′W	X	15
Druim Raois	N Eil	NB0028	58°8·6′	7°5·4′W	X	13
Druim Rèidh	Arg & Bt	NM5244	56°31·6′	6°1·5′W	X	47,48
Druim Rèidh	Arg & Bt	NR8180	55°58·0′	5°30·1′W	X	55
Druim Rèidh	Highld	NH1572	57°42·3′	5°5·8′W	X	20
Druim Rèidh	Highld	NH2069	57°40·8′	5°0·7′W	X	20
Druim Reidh-dhalach	Highld	NM4364	56°42·1′	6°11·5′W	H	47
Druim Riabhach	Arg & Bt	NM8224	56°21·7′	5°31·3′W	X	49
Druim Riadh	Highld	NH7121	57°16·0′	4°7·9′W	F	35
Druim Righ	Arg & Bt	NM8306	56°12·1′	5°29·5′W	X	55
Druim Righeanaich	Highld	NM8199	57°2·1′	5°36·1′W	H	33,40
Druim Ruighe Chail	Pth & Kin	NN7574	56°50·7′	4°2·4′W	H	42
Druim Scaraba	Arg & Bt	NR3549	55°40·0′	6°12·4′W	X	60
Druim Scarasta	N Eil	NG0193	57°49·9′	7°1·8′W	X	18
Druim Seasg	Arg & Bt	NR3253	55°42·0′	6°15·5′W	X	60
Druim Sgeilebreac	N Eil	NG0483	57°44·6′	6°58·0′W	X	18
Druim Sgianadail	N Eil	NB2808	57°58·9′	6°35·6′W	X	13,14
Druim Sgurr nan Cabar	Highld	NG9020	57°13·6′	5°28·3′W	H	25,33
Druim Shionnach	Highld	NH0709	57°8·1′	5°10·9′W	X	33
Druimsornaig	Arg & Bt	NM7434	56°26·9′	5°39·6′W	X	49
Druim Speireag	N Eil	NB3531	58°11·6′	6°30·1′W	X	8
Druim Suardalain	Highld	NC1222	58°9·1′	5°11·2′W	X	15
Druim Tarsuinn	Highld	NM8673	56°48·2′	5°29·9′W	X	40
Druim Teamhair	Arg & Bt	NR2268	55°49·8′	6°25·9′W	X	60
Druim Thollaidh	Highld	NH0310	57°8·6′	5°14·9′W	X	33
Druim Thusbaig	N Eil	NB0824	58°6·8′	6°57·0′W	X	13,14
Druim Torc-choire	Highld	NG8400	57°2·7′	5°33·2′W	X	33
Druim Torr nan Cliabh	Highld	NC7612	58°5·0′	4°5·7′W	H	17
Druim Ucsabhat	N Eil	NB3133	58°12·5′	6°34·3′W	H	8,13
Druim Vaine	Highld	NM5949	56°34·5′	5°55·0′W	X	47,48
Druimyeon Bay	Arg & Bt	NR6550	55°41·5′	5°43·9′W	W	62
Druimyeonbeg	Arg & Bt	NR6449	55°40·9′	5°44·8′W	X	62
Druimyeon More	Arg & Bt	NR6550	55°41·5′	5°43·9′W	X	62
Druly Hill Fm	Somer	ST7537	51°8·1′	2°21·1′W	FM	183
Drum	Aberd	NJ4620	57°16·3′	2°53·3′W	X	37
Drum	Aberd	NO6370	56°49·5′	2°35·9′W	X	45
Drum	Angus	NO6658	56°43·0′	2°32·9′W	X	54
Drum	Arg & Bt	NR6725	55°28·1′	5°40·7′W	X	68
Drum	Arg & Bt	NR9376	55°56·2′	5°18·4′W	X	62
Drum	C of Edin	NT3068	55°54·3′	3°6·7′W	T	66
Drum	D & G	NX8574	55°3·1′	3°47·6′W	X	84
Drum	D & G	NX8799	55°16·6′	3°46·3′W	X	78
Drum	D & G	NX8870	55°1·0′	3°44·7′W	X	84
Drum	D & G	NX8885	55°9·1′	3°45·0′W	X	78
Drum	Falk	NS8378	55°59·1′	3°52·1′W	X	65
Drum	Falk	NT0180	56°0·4′	3°34·8′W	X	65
Drum	Gwyn	SH7069	53°12·4′	3°56·4′W	H	115
Drum	Highld	NH6853	57°33·1′	4°11·9′W	X	26
Drum	Moray	NJ4450	57°32·5′	2°55·7′W	X	28
Drum	Powys	SJ0308	52°39·9′	3°25·7′W	X	125
Drum	Pth & Kin	NO0400	56°11·2′	3°32·4′W	T	58
Drum	Stir	NS6395	56°7·9′	4°11·8′W	X	57
Drum	Stir	NS7284	56°2·2′	4°2·8′W	X	57,64
Drumachar	Pth & Kin	NN9729	56°26·8′	3°39·8′W	X	52,53,58
Drumachlie	Angus	NO6060	56°44·1′	2°38·8′W	X	45
Drumachloy	Arg & Bt	NS0367	55°51·6′	5°8·4′W	X	63
Drum à Choire Odhair	Highld	NM9091	56°58·0′	5°26·8′W	X	33,40
Drumacissock	D & G	NX1168	54°58·5′	4°56·8′W	X	82
Drumad	Pth & Kin	NO0532	56°28·5′	3°32·1′W	X	52,53
Drumadoon	N Ayr	NR8929	55°30·8′	5°20·1′W	X	68,69
Drumadoon Bay	N Ayr	NR8827	55°29·7′	5°20·9′W	W	68,69
Drumadoon Point	N Ayr	NR8828	55°30·2′	5°21·0′W	X	68,69
Drumadryland	D & G	NX1268	54°58·5′	4°55·8′W	X	82
Drumaghinier	N Ayr	NR9127	55°29·8′	5°18·1′W	X	68,69
Drumagrain	Moray	NJ1735	57°24·1′	3°22·4′W	X	28
Drumahallan	S Ayr	NX0973	55°1·1′	4°58·8′W	X	76
Drumahallan Burn	S Ayr	NX0873	55°1·1′	4°59·8′W	W	76
Drumahastie	S Ayr	NX1975	55°2·4′	4°49·5′W	X	76
Drumain	Fife	NO2104	56°13·6′	3°16·0′W	X	58
Drumain Resr	Fife	NO2204	56°13·6′	3°15·0′W	W	58
Drumairn	E Dunb	NS6777	55°58·3′	4°7·4′W	X	64
Drumalbin	S Lanak	NS9038	55°37·6′	3°44·4′W	X	71,72
Drumalbin Burn	S Lanak	NS9038	55°37·6′	3°44·4′W	W	71,72
Drumaldrace	N Yks	SD8786	54°16·4′	2°11·6′W	X	98
Drumalea	Arg & Bt	NR6627	55°29·1′	5°41·8′W	X	68
Drumallan	Aberd	NJ3312	57°11·9′	3°6·1′W	X	37
Drumallan	Aberd	NO7997	57°4·1′	2°20·3′W	X	38,45
Drumallan	Stir	NN7905	56°13·6′	3°56·7′W	X	57
Drumanairguid	Highld	NC7306	58°1·8′	4°8·6′W	X	16
Drumancroy	Highld	NH8982	57°49·1′	3°51·6′W	X	21
Drumanee	D & G	NX1572	55°0·7′	4°53·2′W	X	76
Drumanettie	Aberd	NJ3313	57°12·4′	3°6·1′W	X	37
Drumantrae	D & G	NX1046	54°46·6′	4°56·8′W	X	82
Drumantrae Bay	D & G	NX1146	54°46·7′	4°55·9′W	W	82
Drumardoch	Stir	NN6311	56°16·6′	4°12·3′W	X	57
Drumashie	Highld	NH6337	57°24·4′	4°16·4′W	X	26
Drumashie Moor	Highld	NH6236	57°23·9′	4°17·3′W	X	26
Drumatherty	Pth & Kin	NO1141	56°33·4′	3°26·4′W	X	53
Druma Voulin	Arg & Bt	NR6709	55°19·4′	5°39·9′W	X	68
Drumbain	Highld	NH8127	57°19·3′	3°58·1′W	X	35
Drumbain	Moray	NJ2749	57°31·8′	3°12·7′W	X	28
Drumbain	S Ayr	NS2617	55°25·2′	4°44·5′W	X	70
Drumbarton Hill	Aberd	NJ5421	57°16·9′	2°45·3′W	H	37
Drumbauchly	Pth & Kin	NO0126	56°25·2′	3°35·8′W	X	52,53,58
Drum Bay	D & G	NX9862	54°56·8′	3°35·1′W	W	84
Drumbeg	Angus	NO4963	56°45·6′	2°49·6′W	X	44
Drumbeg	D & G	NX3358	54°53·6′	4°35·8′W	X	82
Drumbeg	Highld	NC1232	58°14·5′	5°11·7′W	T	15
Drumbeg	S Ayr	NS2004	55°18·1′	4°49·7′W	X	76
Drumbeg	Stir	NS4788	56°3·9′	4°27·0′W	X	57
Drumbeg	W Loth	NS8768	55°53·8′	3°48·0′W	X	65
Drumbeltie	Pth & Kin	NO1340	56°32·9′	3°24·5′W	X	53
Drumbertnot	Angus	NO6752	56°39·8′	2°31·9′W	X	54
Drumblade	Aberd	NJ5840	57°27·2′	2°41·5′W	T	29
Drumblair	Aberd	NJ6343	57°28·8′	2°36·6′W	X	29
Drumblair	D & G	NX2850	54°49·2′	4°40·2′W	X	82
Drumblair Lodge	Aberd	NJ6342	57°28·3′	2°36·6′W	X	29
Drumblair Moor	D & G	NX2851	54°49·7′	4°40·2′W	X	82
Drumble, The	Shrops	SJ5026	52°50·0′	2°44·1′W	F	126
Drumbo	S Ayr	NX0673	55°1·1′	5°1·6′W	X	76
Drumbow	N Lanak	NS8369	55°54·3′	3°51·8′W	X	65
Drumbowie	E Ayr	NS4615	55°24·5′	4°25·5′W	X	70
Drumbowie	Falk	NS7981	56°0·7′	3°56·0′W	X	64
Drumbowie Burn	E Ayr	NS4715	55°24·6′	4°24·6′W	W	70
Drumbowie Reservoir	Falk	NS7881	56°0·6′	3°57·0′W	W	64
Drumbowie Rig	D & G	NX1476	55°2·9′	4°54·3′W	X	76
Drumboy Fm	S Lanak	NS6138	55°37·2′	4°12·0′W	FM	71
Drumboy Hill	E Ayr	NS5049	55°42·9′	4°22·8′W	X	64
Drumbracken	D & G	NX1475	55°2·3′	4°54·2′W	X	76
Drumbrae	Stir	NS8097	56°9·3′	3°55·5′W	X	57
Drumbreck	D & G	NX6863	54°56·9′	4°3·2′W	X	83,84
Drumbreck	E Dunb	NS6973	55°56·2′	4°5·4′W	X	64
Drumbreck	N Lanak	NS7077	55°58·4′	4°4·5′W	X	64
Drumbreddan	D & G	NX0844	54°45·5′	4°58·6′W	X	82
Drumbreddan Bay	D & G	NX0743	54°44·9′	4°59·5′W	W	82
Drumbreg	D & G	NY0376	55°4·4′	3°30·7′W	X	84
Drumbroider	Falk	NS9274	55°57·1′	3°43·3′W	X	65
Drumbrush Rig	E Ayr	NS5406	55°19·8′	4°17·9′W	X	70,77
Drumbuich Wood	Pth & Kin	NO0027	56°25·7′	3°36·8′W	F	52,53,58
Drumbuie	Arg & Bt	NM3124	56°20·2′	6°20·7′W	X	48
Drumbuie	D & G	NS7410	55°22·3′	3°58·9′W	X	71
Drumbuie	D & G	NX5682	55°6·9′	4°15·0′W	X	77
Drumbuie	D & G	NX9558	54°54·6′	3°37·8′W	H	84
Drumbuie	Highld	NG7731	57°19·2′	5°41·8′W	T	24
Drumbuie	S Ayr	NS3710	55°21·7′	4°33·9′W	X	70
Drumbuie	S Lanak	NS6450	55°43·7′	4°9·5′W	X	64
Drumbuie Hill	D & G	NX5581	55°6·4′	4°15·9′W	H	77
Drumbuie Moorhead	D & G	NS7308	55°21·2′	3°59·8′W	X	71,77
Drumbuie View	Arg & Bt	NM5547	56°33·3′	5°58·8′W	X	47,48
Drumbuie Wood	Pth & Kin	NO0344	56°34·9′	3°34·3′W	F	52,53
Drumbulg	Aberd	NJ4834	57°23·9′	2°51·5′W	X	28,29
Drumburgh	Cumbr	NY2659	54°55·5′	3°8·9′W	T	85
Drumburgh Moss	Cumbr	NY2558	54°54·9′	3°9·8′W	X	85
Drumburle	S Ayr	NS2803	55°17·7′	4°42·1′W	X	76
Drumburn	D & G	NX8854	54°52·3′	3°44·3′W	X	84
Drum Burn	D & G	NX9762	54°56·8′	3°36·1′W	W	84
Drumburn	D & G	NX9861	54°56·2′	3°35·1′W	X	84
Drumburn Hill	D & G	NX9661	54°56·2′	3°37·0′W	H	84
Drumcairn	Angus	NO5368	56°48·3′	2°45·7′W	X	44
Drum Cairn	D & G	NX8790	55°11·7′	3°46·1′W	A	78
Drumcairn	Pth & Kin	NN8807	56°14·8′	3°48·0′W	X	58
Drumcairn	Pth & Kin	NO1714	56°18·9′	3°20·1′W	X	58
Drumcargo	D & G	NX1072	55°0·6′	4°57·9′W	X	76
Drumcarro	Fife	NO4512	56°18·1′	2°52·9′W	X	59
Drumcarrow Craig	Fife	NO4513	56°18·6′	2°52·9′W	X	59
Drum Castle	Aberd	NJ7900	57°5·7′	2°20·3′W	A	38
Drumchapel	C of Glas	NS5270	55°54·3′	4°21·6′W	T	64
Drumchardine	Highld	NH5644	57°28·1′	4°23·6′W	X	26
Drumcharrel	Highld	NH8848	57°30·8′	3°51·7′W	X	27
Drumcharry	Pth & Kin	NN7548	56°36·7′	4°1·8′W	X	51,52
Drumchastle Farm	Pth & Kin	NN6858	56°42·0′	4°8·9′W	FM	42,51
Drumchastle Wood	Pth & Kin	NN6758	56°41·9′	4°9·9′W	F	42,51
Drum Cholzie	Aberd	NO3487	56°58·4′	3°4·7′W	H	44
Drumchork	Highld	NG8788	57°50·1′	5°34·8′W	T	19
Drumchork	Pth & Kin	NN7719	56°21·1′	3°59·0′W	X	57
Drumcleugh Burn	D & G	NX6061	54°55·7′	4°10·7′W	W	83
Drumclog	S Lanak	NS6338	55°37·2′	4°10·1′W	T	71
Drumclune	Angus	NO4156	56°41·8′	2°57·4′W	X	54
Drumclune	Highld	NH4729	57°19·8′	4°32·0′W	X	26
Drumclyer	D & G	NX8878	55°5·3′	3°44·9′W	X	84
Drumcoille Ho	Pth & Kin	NN8512	56°17·4′	3°51·0′W	X	58
Drumcoltran	D & G	NX8768	54°59·9′	3°45·6′W	X	84
Drumcooper	Fife	NT1587	56°4·4′	3°21·5′W	X	65
Drumcork	D & G	NX8897	55°15·5′	3°45·3′W	X	78
Drumcow Burn	D & G	NX9061	54°56·1′	3°42·6′W	W	84
Drumcross	Renf	NS4471	55°54·7′	4°29·3′W	X	64
Drumcross	W Loth	NT0070	55°55·0′	3°35·6′W	X	65
Drumcrosshall	W Loth	NT0170	55°55·0′	3°34·6′W	X	65
Drumcroy Hill	Pth & Kin	NN7262	56°44·2′	4°5·1′W	X	42
Drumcruilton	D & G	NS8802	55°18·2′	3°45·4′W	X	78
Drum Dagwyllton	Powys	SN8460	52°13·8′	3°41·5′W	X	147
Drumdaig	Aberd	NJ5910	57°11·0′	2°40·2′W	X	37
Drum Ddu	Powys	SH9216	52°44·1′	3°35·6′W	X	125
Drum Ddu	Powys	SN9660	52°13·9′	3°31·0′W	H	147
Drum Ddu	Powys	SN9744	52°5·3′	3°29·8′W	H	147,160
Drumdelgie	Aberd	NJ4842	57°28·2′	2°51·6′W	X	28,29
Drumderfit	Highld	NH6551	57°32·0′	4°14·8′W	X	26
Drumderfit Hill	Highld	NH6551	57°32·0′	4°14·8′W	H	26
Drumderg	Pth & Kin	NO1755	56°41·0′	3°20·8′W	H	53
Drumdevan	Highld	NH6541	57°26·6′	4°14·5′W	X	26
Drumdivan	Highld	NH7889	57°52·7′	4°3·0′W	X	21
Drumdivan	Highld	NH8454	57°33·9′	3°55·9′W	X	27
Drumdoch	D & G	NX0957	54°52·5′	4°58·2′W	X	82
Drumdollo	Aberd	NJ5938	57°26·1′	2°40·5′W	T	29
Drumdow	D & G	NW9968	54°58·2′	5°8·0′W	X	82
Drumdow	E Ayr	NS4221	55°27·7′	4°29·5′W	X	70
Drumdow Burn	D & G	NX2957	54°53·0′	4°39·5′W	W	82
Drumdowie	Pth & Kin	NN8613	56°18·0′	3°50·1′W	X	58
Drumdow Moss	D & G	NX2956	54°52·4′	4°39·5′W	X	82
Drumdowns	S Ayr	NX1075	55°2·2′	4°58·0′W	X	76
Drumdreel	Fife	NO2008	56°15·7′	3°17·0′W	X	58
Drumdroch	E Ayr	NS4934	55°34·8′	4°23·3′W	X	70
Drumdruills	Stir	NS7999	56°10·4′	3°56·5′W	X	57
Drumduan	Aberd	NJ4438	57°26·0′	2°55·5′W	X	28
Drumduan	Aberd	NJ5601	57°6·1′	2°43·1′W	X	37
Drumduan	Highld	NH9156	57°35·1′	3°48·9′W	X	27
Drumdurno	Aberd	NJ7024	57°18·6′	2°29·4′W	X	38
Drumdyre	Highld	NH6462	57°37·9′	4°16·2′W	X	21
Drumeldrie	Fife	NO4403	56°13·2′	2°53·7′W	T	59
Drumellan	S Ayr	NS3110	55°21·6′	4°39·5′W	X	70
Drumellie	Pth & Kin	NO1344	56°35·0′	3°24·5′W	X	53
Drumelzie	Aberd	NO7179	56°54·3′	2°28·1′W	X	45
Drumelzier	Falk	NS7983	56°1·7′	3°56·1′W	X	57,64
Drumelzier	Scot Bord	NT1334	55°35·8′	3°22·4′W	T	72
Drumelzier Burn	Scot Bord	NT1532	55°34·7′	3°20·5′W	W	72
Drumelzier Haugh	Scot Bord	NT1434	55°35·8′	3°21·5′W	X	72
Drumelzier Law	Scot Bord	NT1431	55°34·2′	3°21·4′W	H	72
Drumelzier Place	Scot Bord	NT1233	55°35·2′	3°23·3′W	X	72
Drumelzie Wood	Aberd	NO7078	56°53·8′	2°29·1′W	F	45
Drumfad	Arg & Bt	NS3184	56°1·4′	4°42·3′W	X	56
Drumfad	D & G	NX3743	54°45·6′	4°31·6′W	X	83
Drumfad	Pth & Kin	NN9109	56°15·9′	3°45·1′W	X	58
Drumfad	S Ayr	NS3508	55°20·6′	4°35·7′W	X	70,77
Drumfad Burn	D & G	NX0852	54°49·8′	4°58·9′W	W	82
Drumfairn	S Ayr	NS3306	55°19·4′	4°37·5′W	X	70,76
Drumfairn	S Ayr	NX1894	55°12·7′	4°51·2′W	X	76
Drumfearn	Highld	NG6715	57°10·3′	5°50·8′W	T	32
Drumfergue	Aberd	NJ4734	57°23·9′	2°52·5′W	X	28,29
Drumfern	Highld	NM9578	56°51·2′	5°21·3′W	X	40
Drumfern Moss	D & G	NX8662	54°56·6′	3°46·4′W	X	84
Drumfin	Fife	NT0386	56°3·7′	3°33·0′W	X	65
Drumfinn Hill	Pth & Kin	NO0816	56°19·9′	3°28·8′W	H	58
Drumflower	D & G	NX1358	54°53·2′	4°54·5′W	H	82
Drum Fm	Arg & Bt	NR9277	55°56·7′	5°19·4′W	FM	62
Drumfold	Aberd	NJ6829	57°21·3′	2°31·5′W	X	38
Drumforber	Aberd	NO7273	56°51·1′	2°27·1′W	X	45
Drumfork	E Ayr	NS5123	55°28·9′	4°21·0′W	X	70
Drumfork	Pth & Kin	NO1459	56°43·1′	3°23·9′W	X	53
Drumfottie	Aberd	NJ4914	57°13·1′	2°50·2′W	X	37
Drumfours	Aberd	NJ5610	57°11·0′	2°43·2′W	X	37
Drumfrennie	Aberd	NO7298	57°4·6′	2°27·3′W	X	38,45
Drumfurrich	Moray	NJ2944	57°29·1′	3°10·6′W	X	28
Drumgarland	Pth & Kin	NO0504	56°13·4′	3°31·5′W	X	58

Drumgarve	Arg & Bt	NR7226	55°28·7'	5°36·1'W	X	68
Drumgask Fm	Highld	NN6193	57°0·7'	4°16·9'W	FM	35
Drumgelloch	N Lanak	NS7765	55°52·0'	3°57·5'W	T	64
Drumgesk Fm	Aberd	NO5599	57°5·0'	2°44·1'W	FM	37,44
Drumgin	D & G	NX4044	54°46·2'	4°28·8'W	X	83
Drumglas	Pth & Kin	NN6959	56°42·5'	4°7·9'W	X	42,51
Drumglas	Stir	NS4585	56°2·2'	4°28·8'W	X	57
Drumglass	D & G	NX6868	54°59·6'	4°3·4'W	X	83,84
Drumglass	N Lanak	NS7275	55°57·3'	4°2·6'W	X	64
Drumglass	Pth & Kin	NN6840	56°32·3'	4°8·3'W	X	51
Drumglass Hill	D & G	NX6768	54°59·6'	4°4·3'W	H	83,84
Drumgley	Angus	NO4250	56°38·6'	2°56·3'W	T	54
Drumgoudrum Hill	Aberd	NJ4816	57°14·2'	2°51·2'W	H	37
Drumgowan	Aberd	NJ5724	57°18·5'	2°42·4'W	X	37
Drumgrain	Moray	NJ4145	57°29·7'	2°58·6'W	X	28
Drumgrain Plantn	E Ayr	NS4553	55°45·0'	4°27·7'W	F	64
Drumgrange	E Ayr	NS4209	55°21·2'	4°29·1'W	X	70,77
Drumgray Ho	N Lanak	NS7770	55°54·7'	3°57·6'W	X	64
Drumgree Church	D & G	NY0696	55°15·2'	3°28·3'W	A	78
Drumgreen	Angus	NO4778	56°53·7'	2°51·7'W	X	44
Drumguish	Highld	NJ0037	57°25·0'	3°39·4'W	X	27
Drumguish	Highld	NN7999	57°4·2'	3°59·3'W	T	35
Drumharrow	Pth & Kin	NO0230	56°27·4'	3°35·0'W	X	52,53
Drumharvie	Pth & Kin	NN9821	56°22·5'	3°38·6'W	X	52,53,58
Drumhead	Aberd	NJ5046	57°30·3'	2°49·6'W	X	29
Drumhead	Aberd	NJ9518	57°15·4'	2°4·5'W	X	38
Drumhead	Angus	NO5751	56°39·2'	2°41·6'W	X	54
Drumhead	Arg & Bt	NS3379	55°58·8'	4°40·2'W	X	63
Drumhead	Fife	NO4510	56°17·0'	2°52·9'W	X	59
Drumhead	Pth & Kin	NN9008	56°15·4'	3°46·1'W	X	58
Drumhead	Pth & Kin	NO1045	56°35·6'	3°27·5'W	X	53
Drumhead	Pth & Kin	NO1816	56°20·0'	3°19·1'W	X	58
Drumhead	Stir	NS4988	56°3·9'	4°25·1'W	X	57
Drum Hill	Derby	SK3742	52°58·7'	1°26·5'W	H	119,128
Drumhilt	Angus	NO3580	56°54·7'	3°3·6'W	H	44
Drum Hollistan	Highld	NC9264	58°33·3'	3°50·9'W	X	11
Drumhumphry	D & G	NX7775	55°3·5'	3°55·1'W	X	84
Drumhumphry Burn	D & G	NX7875	55°3·5'	3°54·2'W	W	84
Drumhumphry Hill	D & G	NX7876	55°4·1'	3°54·2'W	H	84
Drumin	Moray	NJ1830	57°21·4'	3°21·3'W	X	36
Druminault	Highld	NH7275	57°45·1'	4°8·6'W	X	21
Drumindorsair	Highld	NH4845	57°28·5'	4°31·6'W	X	26
Drumine	Highld	NH7951	57°32·2'	4°0·8'W	X	27
Drumine	Moray	NJ0151	57°32·6'	3°38·8'W	X	27
Drumine Forest	Moray	NJ0251	57°32·6'	3°37·8'W	F	27
Druminnor Castle	Aberd	NJ5126	57°19·6'	2°48·4'W	A	37
Drumjargon	D & G	NX4050	54°49·4'	4°29·0'W	X	83
Drumjoan	E Ayr	NS4617	55°25·6'	4°25·6'W	X	70
Drumjohn	D & G	NX3283	55°7·0'	4°37·6'W	X	76
Drumjohn	D & G	NX5297	55°15·0'	4°19·3'W	X	77
Drumjohn	D & G	NX8767	54°59·3'	3°45·5'W	X	84
Drumkilbo	Pth & Kin	NO3044	56°35·2'	3°7·9'W	X	53
Drumla	N Ayr	NS0221	55°26·8'	5°7·4'W	X	69
Drumlamford Ho	S Ayr	NX2876	55°3·2'	4°41·0'W	X	76
Drumlamford Loch	S Ayr	NX2877	55°3·7'	4°41·2'W	W	76
Drumlane	D & G	NX7064	54°57·5'	4°1·4'W	X	83,84
Drumlang Cott	Arg & Bt	NM5440	56°29·5'	5°59·3'W	X	47,48
Drumlanrig Castle	D & G	NX8599	55°16·6'	3°48·2'W	A	78
Drumlanrig Park	D & G	NS8500	55°17·1'	3°48·2'W	X	78
Drumlanrig Woods	D & G	NS8400	55°17·1'	3°49·2'W	F	78
Drumlanrig Woods	D & G	NX8499	55°16·5'	3°49·1'W	F	78
Drumlassie	Aberd	NJ6405	57°8·3'	2°35·2'W	X	37
Drumlawhinnie Loch	D & G	NX4669	54°59·8'	4°24·0'W	W	83
Drumlea	Highld	NH6730	57°20·7'	4°12·1'W	X	26
Drumlean	Stir	NN4802	56°11·4'	4°26·5'W	X	57
Drumleaning	Cumbr	NY2751	54°51·2'	3°7·8'W	X	85
Drumlemble	Arg & Bt	NR6619	55°24·8'	5°41·4'W	T	68
Drumler Craigs	E Renf	NS4854	55°45·6'	4°24·9'W	X	64
Drumley	D & G	NX1374	55°1·8'	4°55·1'W	X	76
Drumley	D & G	NX2570	54°59·9'	4°43·7'W	X	76
Drumley	Fife	NO2712	56°17·9'	3°10·3'W	X	59
Drumley Fm	S Ayr	NS4025	55°29·8'	4°31·5'W	FM	70
Drumley Ho	S Ayr	NS4025	55°29·8'	4°31·5'W	X	70
Drum Leys	Angus	NO3450	56°38·5'	3°4·1'W	X	54
Drumliah	Highld	NH6093	57°54·5'	4°21·3'W	X	21
Drumligair	Aberd	NJ9016	57°14·3'	2°9·5'W	X	38
Drumlithie	Aberd	NO7880	56°54·9'	2°21·2'W	T	45
Drumlochan	Highld	NH9441	57°27·1'	3°45·5'W	X	27
Drumlochlan Wood	Pth & Kin	NN7422	56°22·7'	4°2·0'W	F	51,52
Drumlochy	Pth & Kin	NN9109	56°15·9'	3°45·1'W	X	58
Drum Loin	Moray	NJ1608	57°9·6'	3°22·9'W	H	36
Drumloist	Stir	NN6806	56°14·0'	4°7·3'W	X	57
Drumly	Fife	NO5510	56°17·1'	2°43·2'W	X	59
Drummad	Pth & Kin	NO1445	56°35·6'	3°23·6'W	X	53
Drum Maen	Powys	SN8684	52°26·8'	3°40·2'W	X	135,136
Drum-Mains	D & G	NX9761	54°56·2'	3°36·0'W	X	84
Drum Mains	N Lanak	NS7173	55°56·2'	4°3·5'W	X	64
Drummaird	Fife	NO3603	56°13·2'	3°1·5'W	X	59
Drummanister	D & G	NX6782	55°7·1'	4°4·7'W	X	77
Drummanmoan	D & G	NX1173	55°1·2'	4°57·0'W	X	76
Drummarkie	Highld	NH7258	57°35·9'	4°8·0'W	X	27
Drummarnock	Stir	NS7487	56°3·8'	4°1·0'W	H	57
Drummaston	D & G	NX4640	54°44·1'	4°23·1'W	X	83
Drum Maw	Scot Bord	NT1747	55°42·8'	3°18·8'W	H	72
Drummawhance	Pth & Kin	NN8814	56°18·6'	3°48·2'W	X	58
Drummels, The	Aberd	NO6289	56°59·7'	2°37·1'W	X	45
Drummer Hill Fm	N Yks	NZ5707	54°27·6'	1°6·8'W	FM	93
Drummersdale	Lancs	SD3913	53°36·8'	2°54·9'W	T	108
Drummick	Pth & Kin	NN9527	56°25·7'	3°41·7'W	X	52,53,58
Drummietermont Fm	Angus	NO5249	56°38·1'	2°46·5'W	FM	54
Drummillan	D & G	NX9767	54°59·5'	3°36·2'W	X	84
Drummilling	N Ayr	NS2049	55°42·3'	4°51·4'W	X	63
Drummin	Highld	NH4695	57°1·5'	4°31·8'W	X	34
Drummin	Pth & Kin	NO0053	56°39·7'	3°37·4'W	X	52,53
Drumminnoch	D & G	NX1465	54°57·0'	4°53·8'W	X	82
Drummochreen	S Ayr	NS2702	55°17·2'	4°43·0'W	A	76
Drummochreen	S Ayr	NS2803	55°17·7'	4°42·1'W	X	76
Drummoddie	D & G	NX3945	54°46·7'	4°29·8'W	X	83
Drummodie Moss	D & G	NX3945	54°46·7'	4°29·8'W	X	83
Drummohr	E Loth	NT3773	55°57·0'	3°0·1'W	X	66
Drummond	Highld	NH5831	57°21·1'	4°21·1'W	X	26
Drummond	Highld	NH6065	57°39·5'	4°20·3'W	T	21
Drummond	Highld	NH6643	57°27·7'	4°13·6'W	T	26
Drummond	Stir	NN6706	56°13·9'	4°8·3'W	X	57
Drummond Castle	Pth & Kin	NN8418	56°20·7'	3°52·2'W	A	58
Drummondernoch	Pth & Kin	NN7920	56°21·7'	3°57·1'W	X	51,52,57
Drummond Hall	Pth & Kin	NO1036	56°30·7'	3°27·3'W	X	53
Drummond Hill	Pth & Kin	NN7546	56°35·6'	4°1·7'W	H	51,52
Drummond Hill Cotts	D & G	NX4344	54°46·2'	4°26·0'W	X	83
Drummond Park	Pth & Kin	NN8518	56°20·7'	3°51·2'W	X	58
Drummond Park	Pth & Kin	NO0130	56°27·4'	3°35·9'W	X	52,53
Drummondreach	Highld	NH5757	57°35·1'	4°23·1'W	X	26
Drummond's Fold	Pth & Kin	NN9510	56°16·5'	3°41·3'W	X	58
Drummonds-hall	Scot Bord	NT5448	55°43·6'	2°43·5'W	X	73
Drummond's Knowe	E Ayr	NS7320	55°27·7'	4°0·1'W	H	71
Drummonie Ho	Pth & Kin	NO1117	56°20·5'	3°25·9'W	X	58
Drummoral	D & G	NX4636	54°42·0'	4°23·0'W	X	83
Drummore	D & G	NX1336	54°41·3'	4°53·7'W	T	82
Drummore	D & G	NX9074	55°3·2'	3°42·9'W	X	84
Drummore	Stir	NN6900	56°10·7'	4°6·2'W	X	57
Drummore Bay	D & G	NX1337	54°41·9'	4°53·7'W	W	82
Drummore Castle	D & G	NX6945	54°47·2'	4°1·8'W	X	83,84
Drummore of Cantray	Highld	NH8045	57°29·0'	3°59·6'W	X	27
Drummore of Clava	Highld	NH7643	57°27·9'	4°3·6'W	X	27
Drummossie Muir	Highld	NH6939	57°25·6'	4°10·4'W	X	26
Drummossie Muir	Highld	NH7142	57°27·3'	4°8·5'W	X	27
Drummournie	Highld	NH8246	57°29·6'	3°57·7'W	X	27
Drummuck	S Ayr	NS2303	55°17·6'	4°46·8'W	X	76
Drummuckloch	D & G	NX0766	54°57·3'	5°0·4'W	X	82
Drummuckloch	D & G	NX5654	54°51·9'	4°14·2'W	X	83
Drummuie	Highld	NH8199	57°58·1'	4°0·2'W	T	21
Drummuir	D & G	NY0474	55°3·3'	3°29·7'W	X	84
Drummuir	Moray	NJ3844	57°29·2'	3°1·6'W	T	28
Drummuir	N Ayr	NS3639	55°37·3'	4°35·8'W	X	70
Drummuir Castle	Moray	NJ3744	57°29·2'	3°2·6'W	X	28
Drummullan	S Ayr	NS3007	55°19·9'	4°40·4'W	X	70,76
Drummullin Burn	D & G	NX4637	54°42·5'	4°23·0'W	W	83
Drummurrie	D & G	NX2863	54°56·2'	4°40·7'W	X	82
Drummurrie Moss	D & G	NX2863	54°56·2'	4°40·7'W	X	82
Drummy	Pth & Kin	NN9323	56°23·5'	3°43·6'W	X	52,58
Drummygar	Angus	NO5543	56°34·9'	2°43·5'W	T	54
Drummy Wood	Aberd	NJ4703	57°7·2'	2°52·1'W	F	37
Drumnabrennan	D & G	NX2967	54°58·4'	4°39·9'W	X	82
Drumnacartle	Aberd	NJ7231	57°22·4'	2°27·5'W	X	29
Drumnadrochit	Highld	NH5029	57°19·9'	4°29·0'W	T	26,35
Drumnadrochit	Highld	NH5030	57°20·4'	4°29·1'W	T	26
Drum na' Feitheachan Odhar	Pth & Kin	NN8381	56°54·6'	3°54·8'W	W	43
Drumnafunner	Aberd	NJ5214	57°13·1'	2°47·2'W	X	37
Drumnagair	Aberd	NO6868	56°48·4'	2°31·0'W	X	45
Drumnagarrachan	Highld	NH4840	57°25·8'	4°31·4'W	X	26
Drumnagesk	Aberd	NO5698	57°4·5'	2°43·1'W	X	37,44
Drumnagoil Burn	Fife	NT1294	56°8·1'	3°24·5'W	W	58
Drumnagorrach	Moray	NJ5252	57°33·6'	2°47·7'W	T	29
Drumnagowan	Pth & Kin	NN8662	56°44·4'	3°51·4'W	X	43
Drumnaheath	Aberd	NJ7512	57°12·1'	2°24·4'W	X	38
Drumnahive	Aberd	NJ4617	57°14·7'	2°53·2'W	X	37
Drumnahoy	Aberd	NJ6911	57°11·6'	2°30·3'W	X	38
Drumnakyle	Pth & Kin	NN7857	56°41·6'	3°59·1'W	X	42,51,52
Drumnamucklach	Arg & Bt	NR6943	55°37·8'	5°39·7'W	X	62
Drum Nantygorlan	Powys	SN8359	52°13·2'	3°42·4'W	X	147
Drum Nantyrhelyg	Powys	SN8159	52°13·2'	3°44·1'W	X	147
Drumnatorran	Highld	NM8262	56°42·2'	5°33·2'W	X	40
Drumneachie	Aberd	NO5496	57°3·4'	2°45·1'W	X	37,44
Drumneil	D & G	NX3547	54°47·7'	4°33·6'W	X	83
Drumneillie Burn	S Ayr	NX2590	55°10·7'	4°44·5'W	W	76
Drumneillie Hill	S Ayr	NX2890	55°10·7'	4°41·6'W	H	76
Drumnescat Loch	D & G	NX3349	54°48·7'	4°35·5'W	W	82
Drumness	D & G	NX5788	55°10·2'	4°14·3'W	X	77
Drumness	Pth & Kin	NN9015	56°19·1'	3°46·3'W	X	58
Drumnessie	N Lanak	NS7380	56°0·0'	4°1·7'W	X	64
Drumniche	Angus	NO4362	56°45·0'	2°55·5'W	X	44
Drumnod	Fife	NO3321	56°22·8'	3°4·7'W	X	53,59
Drumnod Wood	Fife	NO3321	56°22·8'	3°4·7'W	F	53,59
Drumoak	Aberd	NO7898	57°4·6'	2°21·3'W	T	38,45
Drumoak Church	Aberd	NO8198	57°4·6'	2°18·4'W	A	38,45
Drum of Carron	Moray	NJ2139	57°26·3'	3°18·5'W	X	28
Drum of Clashmore	Stir	NS4997	56°8·8'	4°25·4'W	H	57
Drum of Dunnichen	Angus	NO5147	56°37·0'	2°47·5'W	X	54
Drum of Garvock	Pth & Kin	NO0316	56°19·8'	3°33·7'W	X	58
Drum of Kincairney	Pth & Kin	NO0744	56°35·0'	3°30·4'W	X	52,53
Drum of Kinnaird	Falk	NS8785	56°2·9'	3°48·4'W	X	65
Drumore	Aberd	NJ7027	57°20·2'	2°29·4'W	X	38
Drumore	Arg & Bt	NR6632	55°31·8'	5°42·0'W	X	68
Drumore	Arg & Bt	NR7022	55°26·5'	5°37·8'W	X	68
Drumore	Highld	NH5866	57°40·0'	4°22·4'W	X	21
Drumore	Highld	NH6352	57°32·5'	4°16·9'W	X	26
Drumore	Highld	NH9543	57°28·2'	3°44·6'W	X	27
Drumore	Pth & Kin	NO1661	56°44·2'	3°21·9'W	X	43
Drumore	S Ayr	NS3309	55°21·1'	4°37·6'W	X	70,76
Drumore	Stir	NS5186	56°2·9'	4°23·1'W	X	57
Drumore Burn	Arg & Bt	NR6733	55°32·4'	5°41·1'W	W	68
Drumore Loch	Pth & Kin	NO1660	56°43·7'	3°21·9'W	W	43
Drumore Loch	S Ayr	NS3309	55°21·1'	4°37·6'W	W	70,76
Drumore-na-bodach	Arg & Bt	NR6732	55°31·8'	5°41·1'W	X	68
Drumore Wood	Stir	NS4898	56°9·3'	4°26·4'W	F	57
Drumourachie	Highld	NJ0027	57°19·6'	3°39·2'W	X	36
Drumour Fm	Pth & Kin	NN9639	56°32·1'	3°41·0'W	FM	52,53
Drumour Lodge	Pth & Kin	NN9739	56°32·2'	3°40·0'W	X	52,53
Drumpail Burn	D & G	NX2163	54°56·0'	4°47·2'W	W	82
Drumpark	D & G	NX8779	55°5·8'	3°45·8'W	X	84
Drumpark	Pth & Kin	NN9720	56°21·9'	3°39·6'W	X	52,53,58
Drum Peithnant	Cered	SN7785	52°27·2'	3°48·2'W	H	135
Drumpellier	N Lanak	NS7165	55°51·9'	4°3·2'W	T	64
Drumpellier Country Park	N Lanak	NS7165	55°51·9'	4°3·2'W	F	64
Drumphail	D & G	NX2262	54°55·5'	4°46·2'W	X	82
Drumphin	Pth & Kin	NN9322	56°22·9'	3°43·5'W	X	52,58
Drum Point	Arg & Bt	NR9177	55°56·7'	5°20·4'W	X	62
Drumquhill	S Ayr	NS3305	55°18·9'	4°37·5'W	X	70,76
Drumrack	Fife	NO5408	56°16·0'	2°44·1'W	X	59
Drumrae	D & G	NX4043	54°45·6'	4°28·8'W	X	83
Drumraik	D & G	NX4859	54°54·4'	4°21·8'W	X	83
Drumrash	D & G	NX6871	55°1·2'	4°3·5'W	X	77,84
Drumrauck Hall	N Yks	NZ4605	54°26·5'	1°17·0'W	X	93
Drumreach	Highld	NH5644	57°28·1'	4°23·6'W	X	26
Drumreevough	S Lanak	NS6243	55°39·9'	4°11·2'W	X	71
Drumreoch	Arg & Bt	NS0857	55°46·4'	5°3·2'W	X	63
Drumrossie Ho	Aberd	NJ6328	57°20·7'	2°36·4'W	X	37
Drumroy	Highld	NH9633	57°22·8'	3°43·3'W	X	27
Drumruck	D & G	NX5763	54°56·7'	4°13·5'W	X	83
Drumrunie	Highld	NC1605	58°0·0'	5°6·3'W	X	15
Drumrunie Forest	Highld	NC1610	58°2·7'	5°6·6'W	X	15
Drumry	W Dunb	NS5070	55°54·2'	4°23·5'W	T	64
Drums	Aberd	NJ9822	57°17·6'	2°1·5'W	X	38
Drums	Aberd	NK0346	57°30·5'	1°56·5'W	X	30
Drums	Fife	NO2605	56°14·2'	3°11·2'W	X	59
Drums	Renf	NS4071	55°54·6'	4°33·1'W	X	64
Drums	S Lanak	NS8847	55°42·5'	3°46·5'W	X	72
Drums	W Dunb	NS4673	55°55·8'	4°27·5'W	X	64
Drumsallie	Highld	NM9578	56°51·2'	5°21·3'W	X	40
Drum Sands	C of Edin	NT1878	55°59·5'	3°18·4'W	X	65,66
Drumscallan Plantn	D & G	NX3745	54°46·7'	4°31·6'W	X	83
Drumshade	Angus	NO3750	56°38·5'	3°1·2'W	X	54
Drumshade Plantation	Angus	NO2765	56°46·5'	3°11·2'W	F	44
Drumshalloch	Aberd	NO7198	57°4·6'	2°28·2'W	X	38,45
Drumshalloch Loch	D & G	NX2873	55°1·6'	4°41·0'W	W	76
Drumshang	S Ayr	NS2414	55°23·6'	4°46·3'W	X	70
Drumshangan	D & G	NX8284	55°8·4'	3°50·6'W	X	78
Drumshangie	N Lanak	NS7768	55°53·6'	3°57·6'W	X	64
Drumshangie Moss	N Lanak	NS7768	55°53·6'	3°57·6'W	X	64
Drumshang Loch	S Ayr	NS2713	55°23·1'	4°43·4'W	W	70
Drumshinnoch	D & G	NS8700	55°17·1'	3°46·3'W	X	78
Drumshoreland Muir	W Loth	NT0870	55°55·1'	3°27·9'W	X	65
Drumside	Pth & Kin	NN9819	56°21·4'	3°38·6'W	X	58
Drumsinnie	Aberd	NJ7037	57°25·6'	2°29·5'W	X	29
Drumskelly	D & G	NX7365	54°58·1'	3°58·6'W	X	83,84
Drumskeoch	S Ayr	NX1984	55°7·3'	4°49·9'W	X	76
Drumsleed	Aberd	NO7377	56°53·3'	2°26·1'W	X	45
Drumsleet	D & G	NX9474	55°3·2'	3°39·1'W	T	84
Drums Links	Aberd	NJ9922	57°17·6'	2°0·5'W	X	38
Drumsmittal	Highld	NH6449	57°30·9'	4°15·8'W	T	26
Drumsmodden	E Ayr	NS4717	55°25·6'	4°24·6'W	X	70
Drums of Ardgaith	Pth & Kin	NO2223	56°23·8'	3°15·4'W	X	53,58
Drums of Park	Aberd	NJ5557	57°36·3'	2°44·7'W	X	29
Drums, The	Angus	NO3569	56°48·7'	3°3·4'W	X	44
Drumstinchall	D & G	NX8759	54°55·0'	3°45·4'W	H	84
Drumstinchall	D & G	NX8857	54°54·0'	3°44·4'W	X	84
Drumstone	Aberd	NJ8009	57°10·5'	2°19·4'W	X	38
Drum Stone	Aberd	NJ8010	57°11·1'	2°19·4'W	A	38
Drumsturdy	Angus	NO4835	56°30·5'	2°50·2'W	T	54
Drumsuie	S Ayr	NS4317	55°25·6'	4°28·4'W	X	70
Drumsuldry Wood	Pth & Kin	NO2638	56°31·9'	3°11·7'W	F	53
Drumsyniebeg	Arg & Bt	NR1804	56°11·9'	4°55·6'W	X	56
Drumtall	S Lanak	NS6450	55°43·7'	4°9·5'W	X	64
Drumtassie Burn	W Loth	NS8768	55°53·8'	3°48·0'W	W	65
Drumtee	E Ayr	NS4946	55°41·3'	4°23·7'W	X	64
Drumtee Water	E Ayr	NS4946	55°41·3'	4°23·7'W	W	64
Drumtenant	Fife	NO2909	56°16·3'	3°8·3'W	X	59
Drumterlie	D & G	NX3863	54°56·4'	4°31·3'W	X	83
Drum, The	Heref	SO5257	52°12·8'	2°41·8'W	X	149
Drum, The	Moray	NJ1853	57°33·8'	3°21·8'W	X	28
Drumtian	Stir	NS5188	56°4·0'	4°23·2'W	X	57
Drum Tick	Pth & Kin	NO0135	56°30·1'	3°36·1'W	H	52,53
Drumtochty Castle	Aberd	NO6980	56°54·9'	2°30·1'W	X	45
Drumtochty Forest	Aberd	NO6981	56°55·4'	2°30·1'W	F	45
Drumtogle	Pth & Kin	NN9816	56°19·8'	3°38·5'W	X	58
Drumtrissel	Fife	NO3707	56°15·3'	3°0·6'W	X	59
Drumtroddan	D & G	NX3644	54°46·1'	4°32·5'W	X	83
Drumturn Burn	Pth & Kin	NO1557	56°42·1'	3°22·8'W	W	53
Drumuie	Highld	NG4546	57°26·2'	6°14·5'W	T	23
Drumuillie	Highld	NH9420	57°15·8'	3°45·0'W	T	36
Drumvaich	Stir	NN6704	56°12·9'	4°8·2'W	T	57
Drumwall	D & G	NX6155	54°52·5'	4°9·6'W	X	83
Drumwalt	D & G	NX3053	54°50·8'	4°38·4'W	X	82
Drumwhern	Angus	NO3368	56°48·2'	3°5·4'W	X	44
Drumwhindle	Aberd	NJ9236	57°25·1'	2°7·5'W	X	30
Drumwhinnie	D & G	NX8968	54°59·9'	3°43·7'W	X	84
Drumwhirn	D & G	NX7480	55°6·2'	3°58·1'W	X	77
Drumwhirn Cairn	D & G	NX3968	54°59·1'	4°30·5'W	A	83
Drumwhirn Fm	S Ayr	NS2801	55°16·6'	4°42·0'W	FM	76
Drum Wood	Falk	NS8378	55°59·1'	3°52·1'W	F	65
Drum Wood	Moray	NJ2040	57°26·9'	3°19·5'W	F	28
Drum Wood	Stir	NS5198	56°9·3'	4°23·5'W	F	57
Drumyellow	Angus	NO5843	56°34·9'	2°40·6'W	X	54
Drumyocher	Aberd	NO7876	56°52·7'	2°21·2'W	X	45
Drumyork Hill	S Ayr	NS3302	55°17·3'	4°37·4'W	X	76
Drum yr Eira	Powys	SN8559	52°13·3'	3°40·6'W	X	147
Drumcroy	Highld	NH4936	57°23·6'	4°30·3'W	X	26
Drundreggan Reservoir	Highld	NH3515	57°12·0'	4°43·4'W	W	34
Drungans	D & G	NX7850	54°50·1'	3°53·5'W	X	84
Drungans	D & G	NX9166	54°58·9'	3°41·8'W	X	84
Drungans Burn	D & G	NX7750	54°50·0'	3°54·5'W	W	84
Drungewick Manor	W Susx	TQ0630	51°3·8'	0°28·8'W	X	187
Drunkard's Corner	Oxon	SP6108	51°46·3'	1°6·6'W	X	164,165
Drunken Bottom	Oxon	SU6386	51°34·4'	1°5·1'W	X	175
Drunkendub	Angus	NO6646	56°36·5'	2°32·8'W	X	54
Drunken Duck (Inn)	Cumbr	NY3501	54°24·3'	2°59·7'W	X	90
Drun's Hill	Oxon	SP5411	51°47·9'	1°12·6'W	X	164
Drunzie	Pth & Kin	NO1408	56°15·7'	3°22·9'W	X	58
Drunzie Feus	Pth & Kin	NO1308	56°15·6'	3°23·8'W	X	58
Druridge	Northum	NZ2795	55°15·2'	1°34·1'W	X	81
Druridge Bay	Northum	NZ2896	55°15·7'	1°33·1'W	W	81
Druridge Links	Northum	NZ2796	55°15·7'	1°34·1'W	X	81
Drury	Flint	SJ2964	53°10·3'	3°3·3'W	T	117
Drury Lane	D & G	NX4337	54°42·5'	4°25·8'W	X	83
Drurylane	Norf	TF9401	52°34·6'	0°52·2'E	T	144
Drury Lane	Wrex	SJ4642	52°58·6'	2°47·8'W	T	117
Drury Square	Norf	TF9015	52°42·2'	0°49·1'E	T	132
Druxton	Corn	SX3488	50°40·3'	4°20·6'W	X	190
Drws Bach	Gwyn	SH8621	52°46·7'	3°41·0'W	X	124,125

Drws Gwyn	Conwy	SH7959	53°7·1'	3°48·1'W	X	115
Drws-y-buddel	Denb	SJ0259	53°7·4'	3°27·5'W	X	116
Drws-y-coed	Gwyn	SH5453	53°3·5'	4°10·3'W	X	115
Drwsycoed Uchaf	Gwyn	SH5652	53°3·0'	4°8·5'W	X	115
Drws-y-nant-uchaf	Gwyn	SH8426	52°49·4'	3°42·9'W	X	124,125
Drybank Fm	Warw	SP2747	52°7·5'	1°35·9'W	FM	151
Drybarrows	Cumbr	NY4916	54°32·4'	2°46·9'W	X	90
Dry Beck	Cumbr	NY4269	55°1·0'	2°54·0'W	W	85
Drybeck	Cumbr	NY4370	55°1·5'	2°53·1'W	X	85
Dry Beck	Cumbr	NY6514	54°31·5'	2°32·0'W	W	91
Drybeck	Cumbr	NY6615	54°32·0'	2°31·1'W	T	91
Drybeck	Cumbr	SD6186	54°16·3'	2°35·5'W	X	97
Dry Beck	Durham	NY8627	54°38·5'	2°12·6'W	W	91,92
Dry Beck	N Yks	SD8091	54°19·1'	2°18·0'W	W	98
Dry Beck	N Yks	SD8171	54°8·3'	2°17·0'W	X	98
Drybeck Fm	Cumbr	NY5147	54°49·2'	2°45·3'W	FM	86
Drybeck Moor	Cumbr	NY6614	54°31·5'	2°31·1'W	X	91
Drybedd	Cered	SN7783	52°26·1'	3°48·2'W	H	135
Drybrae	Aberd	NJ5013	57°12·6'	2°49·2'W	X	37
Dry Bridge	Devon	SS7545	51°11·7'	3°47·0'W	X	180
Drybridge	Moray	NJ4362	57°38·9'	2°56·8'W	T	28
Drybridge	N Ayr	NS3536	55°35·6'	4°36·7'W	T	70
Drybrook	Glos	SO6417	51°51·3'	2°31·0'W	T	162
Drybrook Ho	Heref	SO5918	51°51·8'	2°35·4'W	X	162
Drybrook Lodge Fm	Leic	SK4516	52°44·6'	1°19·6'W	FM	129
Dryburgh	D & G	NX7866	54°58·7'	3°53·9'W	X	84
Dryburgh	Scot Bord	NT5931	55°34·5'	2°38·6'W	T	73,74
Dryburgh Abbey	Scot Bord	NT5931	55°34·5'	2°38·6'W	A	73,74
Dryburn	Angus	NO3742	56°34·2'	3°1·1'W	X	54
Dry Burn	Cumbr	NY7241	54°46·0'	2°25·7'W	W	86,87
Dryburn	Cumbr	NY7242	54°46·6'	2°25·7'W	X	86,87
Dry Burn	E Loth	NT7174	55°57·7'	2°27·4'W	W	67
Dryburn	Moray	NJ3763	57°39·4'	3°2·9'W	X	28
Dry Burn	Northum	NU0141	55°40·0'	1°58·6'W	W	75
Dry Burn	Northum	NY6793	55°14·1'	2°30·7'W	W	80
Dryburn	Northum	NY7953	54°52·5'	2°19·2'W	X	86,87
Dry Burn	Northum	NY9476	55°5·0'	2°5·2'W	W	87
Dryburn	Scot Bord	NT4540	55°39·3'	2°52·0'W	X	73
Dry Burn	S Lanak	NT0454	55°46·4'	3°31·4'W	W	65,72
Dryburn Moor	Northum	NY7952	54°52·0'	2°19·2'W	X	86,87
Dry Burrows	Pemb	SR9499	51°39·4'	4°58·3'W	X	158
Dry Burrows (Tumuli)	Pemb	SR9499	51°39·4'	4°58·3'W	A	158
Dryby Fm	Lincs	TF4876	53°15·9'	0°13·6'E	FM	122
Dry Cleuch	Scot Bord	NT2524	55°30·5'	3°10·8'W	X	73
Drycleuch Law	Scot Bord	NT2429	55°33·2'	3°11·9'W	H	73
Drycleuchlea	Scot Bord	NT3517	55°26·8'	3°1·2'W	X	79
Drycleuch Rig	Scot Bord	NT2425	55°31·0'	3°11·8'W	X	73
Dryclough	Derby	SK0382	53°20·3'	1°56·9'W	X	110
Dry Corner	Lancs	SD7837	53°50·0'	2°19·6'W	X	103
Dry Cottage	Win & Maid	SU8685	51°33·7'	0°45·2'W	X	175
Dryden	Aberd	NJ4826	57°19·6'	2°51·4'W	X	37
Dryden	Scot Bord	NT4006	55°20·9'	2°56·3'W	X	79
Dryden	Scot Bord	NT4723	55°30·1'	2°49·9'W	T	73
Dryden Fell	Scot Bord	NT3908	55°22·0'	2°57·3'W	H	79
Dryden Greenhill	Scot Bord	NT4824	55°30·7'	2°49·0'W	X	73
Dryden Tower	Midlo	NT2664	55°52·1'	3°10·5'W	X	66
Dryderdale	Durham	NZ0833	54°41·8'	1°52·1'W	X	92
Dryderdale Fm	Durham	NZ0933	54°41·8'	1°51·2'W	FM	92
Dry Doddington	Lincs	SK8546	53°0·5'	0°43·6'W	T	130
Dry Drayton	Cambs	TL3862	52°14·6'	0°1·7'E	T	154
Dryevers	Cumbr	NY6417	54°33·1'	2°33·0'W	X	91
Dryfehead	D & G	NY1699	55°16·9'	3°18·9'W	X	79
Dryfeholm Fm	D & G	NY1183	55°8·3'	3°23·3'W	FM	78
Dryfe Lodge	D & G	NY1893	55°13·7'	3°16·9'W	X	79
Dryfesdalegate	D & G	NY1182	55°7·7'	3°23·3'W	X	78
Dryfesdale Ho	D & G	NY1283	55°8·3'	3°22·4'W	X	78
Dryfe Water	D & G	NY1385	55°9·4'	3°21·5'W	W	78
Dryfe Water	D & G	NY1792	55°13·2'	3°17·9'W	W	79
Drygarn Fach	Powys	SN8457	52°12·2'	3°41·5'W	X	147
Drygarn Fawr	Powys	SN8658	52°12·7'	3°39·7'W	H	147
Drygate	Renf	NS3961	55°49·2'	4°33·8'W	X	63
Dry Gill	Cumbr	SD7291	54°19·1'	2°25·4'W	W	98
Dry Gill	Cumbr	SD7384	54°15·3'	2°24·4'W	W	98
Dry Gill	Durham	NY9108	54°28·3'	2°7·9'W	W	91,92
Dry Gill	N Yks	SE0863	54°4·0'	1°52·2'W	W	99
Drygrange	Scot Bord	NT5735	55°36·7'	2°40·5'W	X	73,74
Drygrange Mains	Scot Bord	NT5735	55°36·7'	2°40·5'W	X	73,74
Drygrove Gill	Cumbr	NY4508	54°28·1'	2°50·5'W	W	90
Drygutter Brae	D & G	NY2986	55°10·0'	3°6·4'W	H	79
Dry Hall	Cumbr	SD2291	54°18·8'	3°11·5'W	X	96
Dryham	E Yorks	SE8732	53°46·9'	0°40·4'W	X	106
Dryhill	Devon	SS9319	50°57·9'	3°31·0'W	X	181
Dry Hill	Hants	SU6536	51°7·4'	1°3·9'W	T	185,186
Dryhill	Kent	TQ4955	51°16·7'	0°8·6'E	T	188
Dryhill	Shrops	SO4397	52°34·3'	2°50·1'W	X	137
Dry Hill	Somer	SS7940	51°9·0'	3°43·4'W	H	180
Dry Hill	Surrey	TQ4341	51°9·2'	0°3·1'E	H	187
Dryhill Fm	Glos	SO9216	51°50·8'	2°6·6'W	FM	163
Dryhill Fm	Shrops	SO4592	52°31·6'	2°48·2'W	FM	137,138
Dry Hill (Fort)	Surrey	TQ4341	51°9·2'	0°3·1'E	A	187
Dryholme	Cumbr	NY1251	54°51·0'	3°21·8'W	X	85
Dryhope	Scot Bord	NT2624	55°30·5'	3°9·9'W	T	73
Dryhope Burn	Scot Bord	NT2625	55°31·0'	3°9·9'W	W	73
Dryhope Hill	Northum	NT9211	55°23·8'	2°7·1'W	H	80
Dryhopehope	Scot Bord	NT2426	55°31·6'	3°11·8'W	X	73
Dryhope Rig	Scot Bord	NT2525	55°31·0'	3°10·8'W	H	73
Dryhowe	Cumbr	NY5202	54°24·9'	2°44·0'W	X	90
Dryhowe Pasture	Cumbr	NY5102	54°24·9'	2°44·9'W	X	90
Dryhurst Fm	Derby	SK3265	53°11·1'	1°30·9'W	FM	119
Dry Know	Aberd	NJ4224	57°18·4'	2°57·3'W	X	37
Dryknowle Fm	Ches	SJ9871	53°14·4'	2°1·4'W	FM	118
Dryland Fm	Kent	TR0153	51°14·7'	0°53·2'E	FM	189
Drylaw	C of Edin	NT2175	55°57·9'	3°15·5'W	T	66
Drylawhill	E Loth	NT5878	55°59·8'	2°40·0'W	X	67
Dryleas Wood	Northnts	SP9294	52°32·4'	0°38·2'W	F	141
Dryleaze Fm	Glos	SU0398	51°41·1'	1°57·0'W	FM	163
Dry Leys Fm	Bucks	SP7321	51°53·2'	0°56·0'W	FM	165
Dryll	Wrex	SJ2646	53°0·6'	3°5·8'W	X	117
Dryll Pool	Powys	SJ1815	52°43·8'	3°12·5'W	W	125
Dryloch	Angus	NO2949	56°37·9'	3°9·0'W	X	53
Dry Loch	D & G	NX4685	55°8·4'	4°24·5'W	W	77
Drym	Corn	SW6233	50°9·2'	5°19·5'W	T	203
Drymeadow Fm	Glos	SO8421	51°53·5'	2°13·6'W	FM	162
Drymen	Stir	NS4788	56°3·9'	4°27·0'W	T	57
Drymen Br	Stir	NS4787	56°3·3'	4°27·0'W	X	57
Drymen Road Cottage	Stir	NS5093	56°6·6'	4°24·3'W	X	57
Drymere	Norf	TF7806	52°37·6'	0°38·2'E	T	144
Drymuir	Aberd	NJ9145	57°30·0'	2°8·6'W	T	30
Drynach	Highld	NH9723	57°17·4'	3°42·1'W	X	36
Drynachan	Highld	NH3202	57°5·0'	4°45·9'W	X	34
Drynachan Lodge	Highld	NH8639	57°25·9'	3°53·5'W	X	27
Drynain	Arg & Bt	NS1789	56°3·8'	4°55·9'W	X	56
Drynain Glen	Arg & Bt	NS1689	56°3·8'	4°56·9'W	X	56
Drynham	Wilts	ST8656	51°18·4'	2°11·7'W	T	173
Drynie	Highld	NH5360	57°36·6'	4°27·2'W	X	20
Drynie Hill	Highld	NM7171	56°46·7'	5°44·5'W	X	40
Drynie Park	Highld	NH5551	57°31·8'	4°24·8'W	T	26
Drynoch	Highld	NG4031	57°18·0'	6°18·5'W	T	32
Dryplaid	Aberd	NO6269	56°48·9'	2°36·9'W	X	45
Drypool Fm	Glos	SP0023	51°54·6'	1°59·6'W	FM	163
Dry Rigg Quarry	N Yks	SD8069	54°7·2'	2°17·9'W	X	98
Dry Sandford	Oxon	SP4600	51°42·0'	1°19·7'W	T	164
Dryscoed	Rho Cyn Taf	ST0984	51°33·1'	3°18·4'W	X	171
Drysgol	Carm	SN6815	51°49·3'	3°54·5'W	X	159
Drysgol	Cered	SN6967	52°17·4'	3°54·8'W	X	135
Drysgol	Cered	SN7069	52°18·5'	3°54·0'W	H	135,147
Drysgol	Gwyn	SH8721	52°46·7'	3°40·1'W	H	124,125
Drysgol	Powys	SN9474	52°21·5'	3°33·0'W	X	136,147
Drysgol-goch	Carm	SN3627	51°55·3'	4°22·7'W	X	145
Drysgol-goch	Pemb	SN2734	51°58·9'	4°30·8'W	X	145
Drysides	Peterb	TL2197	52°33·7'	0°12·5'W	X	142
Dry Sike	Cumbr	NY6276	55°4·9'	2°35·3'W	W	86
Dryslade Fm	Glos	SO5814	51°49·6'	2°36·2'W	FM	162
Dryslwyn	Carm	SN5520	51°51·8'	4°6·0'W	T	159
Dryslwyn	Carm	SN6242	52°3·8'	4°0·4'W	X	146
Drystone Edge	Staffs	SK0268	53°12·8'	1°57·8'W	X	119
Drystone Hill Ho	Oxon	SP3824	51°55·0'	1°26·5'W	X	164
Dry Stones	Staffs	SK0362	53°9·5'	1°56·9'W	X	119
Dry Street	Essex	TQ6986	51°33·1'	0°26·7'E	T	177,178
Dryton	Pth & Kin	NN8722	56°22·9'	3°49·4'W	X	52,58
Dryton	Shrops	SJ5806	52°39·2'	2°36·9'W	T	126
Drywells	Aberd	NJ6556	57°35·8'	2°34·7'W	X	29
Drywells	Moray	NJ3932	57°22·7'	3°0·4'W	X	37
Duachy	Arg & Bt	NM8020	56°19·5'	5°33·1'W	X	49
Duack Burn	Highld	NH9918	57°14·8'	3°40·0'W	W	36
Duag Bridge	Highld	NH3397	57°56·1'	4°48·8'W	X	20
Duaig	Arg & Bt	NM9013	56°16·0'	5°23·0'W	X	55
Duallin	Pth & Kin	NN6840	56°32·3'	4°8·3'W	X	51
Dualt	Stir	NS4983	56°1·2'	4°24·9'W	X	57,64
Dualt Burn	Stir	NS4982	56°0·7'	4°24·9'W	W	57,64
Dualts	Moray	NJ2231	57°22·0'	3°17·4'W	X	36
Duart	Highld	NC1333	58°15·0'	5°10·7'W	X	15
Duart Bay	Arg & Bt	NM7435	56°27·4'	5°39·6'W	W	49
Duartbeg	Highld	NC1639	58°18·3'	5°7·9'W	X	15
Duart Castle	Arg & Bt	NM7435	56°27·4'	5°39·6'W	A	49
Duartmore Bay	Highld	NC1835	58°16·2'	5°5·7'W	W	15
Duartmore Bridge	Highld	NC1937	58°17·3'	5°4·8'W	X	15
Duartmore Forest	Highld	NC1836	58°16·8'	5°5·8'W	F	15
Duartmore Point	Highld	NC1736	58°16·8'	5°6·8'W	X	15
Duart Point	Arg & Bt	NM7435	56°27·4'	5°39·6'W	X	49
Dub Beck	Cumbr	NY0217	54°32·6'	3°30·5'W	W	89
Dubbs	C of Glas	NS5159	55°48·3'	4°22·2'W	X	64
Dubbs	Cumbr	NY6905	54°26·6'	2°28·3'W	X	91
Dubbs	N Ayr	NS2842	55°38·7'	4°43·6'W	X	63,70
Dubbs Cross	Devon	SX3892	50°42·5'	4°17·3'W	T	190
Dubbs Moss	Cumbr	NY1028	54°38·6'	3°23·3'W	X	89
Dubbs Resr	Cumbr	NY4201	54°24·3'	2°53·2'W	W	90
Dubbs, The	Cumbr	NY0928	54°38·6'	3°24·2'W	X	89
Dubbystyle	Aberd	NJ9421	57°17·0'	2°5·5'W	X	38
Dub Cote	N Yks	SD8271	54°8·3'	2°16·1'W	X	98
Dub Cote Scar	N Yks	SD8271	54°8·3'	2°16·1'W	X	98
Dubford	Aberd	NJ7147	57°31·0'	2°28·6'W	X	29
Dubford	Aberd	NJ7963	57°39·6'	2°20·7'W	X	29,30
Dubford	C of Aber	NJ9312	57°12·2'	2°6·5'W	T	38
Dubgarth	N Yks	SD7266	54°5·7'	2°25·3'W	X	98
Dub Hall	Cumbr	NY0420	54°34·2'	3°28·7'W	X	89
Dubh Alltan Beag	Aberd	NO0083	56°55·9'	3°38·1'W	W	43
Dubh-arid	Highld	NG8755	57°32·4'	5°33·1'W	X	24
Dubh Bhealach	Highld	NM6649	56°34·7'	5°48·2'W	X	49
Dubh Bheinn	Arg & Bt	NR4868	55°50·6'	6°1·1'W	H	60,61
Dubh Bheinn	Arg & Bt	NR5888	56°1·7'	5°52·6'W	H	61
Dubh Breac Hill	Aberd	NJ2915	57°13·5'	3°10·1'W	H	37
Dubh-chàrn	Highld	NG4560	57°33·8'	6°15·4'W	X	23
Dubhchladach	Arg & Bt	NR8468	55°51·7'	5°26·7'W	X	62
Dubh Chnoc	Arg & Bt	NN3008	56°14·3'	4°44·1'W	H	56
Dubh Chnoc	Highld	NN1348	56°35·5'	5°2·3'W	H	50
Dubh Chnoc	Stir	NN5606	56°13·7'	4°18·9'W	H	57
Dubh Chnocan	Pth & Kin	NN8063	56°44·9'	3°57·3'W	H	43
Dubh Choille	Highld	NH4068	57°40·7'	4°40·5'W	X	20
Dubh-choire	Aberd	NO1380	56°54·4'	3°25·3'W	H	43
Dubh-choire	Highld	NG7706	57°5·7'	5°40·4'W	X	33
Dubh Choirein	Pth & Kin	NN6149	56°37·0'	4°15·5'W	X	51
Dubh Choirein	Pth & Kin	NN6150	56°37·5'	4°15·5'W	X	42,51
Dubh Choirein	Pth & Kin	NN6416	56°19·3'	4°11·5'W	X	57
Dubh Chreag	Arg & Bt	NR5068	55°50·7'	5°59·2'W	X	61
Dubh Chreag	Arg & Bt	NR7970	55°52·6'	5°31·5'W	H	62
Dubh Chreag	Highld	NM4563	56°41·6'	6°9·4'W	H	47
Dubh-Chlachaich	Arg & Bt	NM8112	56°15·3'	5°31·7'W	W	55
Dubh Dhoire	Highld	NM8058	56°40·0'	5°35·0'W	X	49
Dubheads	Pth & Kin	NN9621	56°22·5'	3°40·6'W	X	52,53,58
Dubh Eas	Stir	NN3020	56°20·8'	4°44·6'W	W	50,56
Dubh Eilean	Arg & Bt	NR3388	56°0·9'	6°16·6'W	X	61
Dubh-fhèith	Arg & Bt	NM7015	56°16·6'	5°42·5'W	X	55
Dubh Ghlac	Arg & Bt	NM7708	56°13·0'	5°35·4'W	X	55
Dubh-ghlac	Highld	NG7003	57°3·7'	5°47·3'W	X	33
Dubh-Ghleann	Aberd	NO0697	57°3·5'	3°32·5'W	X	36,43
Dubh Leathad	Arg & Bt	NM7411	56°14·5'	5°38·6'W	X	55
Dubh Lighe	Highld	NM9381	56°52·7'	5°23·4'W	W	40
Dubh Loch	Aberd	NO2382	56°55·6'	3°15·5'W	W	44
Dubh Loch	Arg & Bt	NM8020	56°19·5'	5°33·1'W	W	49
Dubh Loch	Arg & Bt	NM9101	56°9·6'	5°21·5'W	W	55
Dubh Loch	Arg & Bt	NM9303	56°10·7'	5°19·7'W	W	55
Dubh Loch	Arg & Bt	NM9400	56°9·2'	5°18·6'W	W	55
Dubh Loch	Arg & Bt	NM9402	56°10·2'	5°18·7'W	W	55
Dubh Loch	Arg & Bt	NN0425	56°22·9'	5°10·0'W	W	50
Dubh Loch	Arg & Bt	NN1111	56°15·5'	5°2·6'W	W	50,56
Dubh Loch	Arg & Bt	NR3794	56°4·3'	6°13·1'W	W	61
Dubh Loch	Arg & Bt	NR3977	55°55·2'	6°10·2'W	W	60,61
Dubh Loch	Arg & Bt	NR6287	56°1·3'	5°48·7'W	W	61
Dubh Loch	Arg & Bt	NR7139	55°35·7'	5°37·6'W	W	68
Dubh Loch	Arg & Bt	NR7680	55°57·9'	5°34·9'W	W	55
Dubh Loch	Arg & Bt	NR8087	56°1·8'	5°31·4'W	W	55
Dubh Loch	Highld	NG8470	57°40·3'	5°36·9'W	W	19
Dubh Loch	Highld	NG9876	57°44·0'	5°23·1'W	W	19
Dubh Loch	N Ayr	NR9142	55°37·9'	5°18·8'W	W	62,69
Dubh Loch	N Eil	NB0122	58°5·4'	7°4·0'W	W	13
Dubh Loch	N Eil	NF8254	57°28·1'	7°17·8'W	W	22
Dubh Loch	Pth & Kin	NO0548	56°37·1'	3°32·4'W	W	52,53
Dubh Lochain	Arg & Bt	NN3448	56°35·9'	4°41·8'W	W	50
Dubh Lochain	Arg & Bt	NR5484	55°59·4'	5°56·2'W	W	61
Dubh Lochain	Highld	NG8909	57°7·7'	5°28·7'W	W	33
Dubh Lochain	Highld	NM7161	56°41·3'	5°43·9'W	W	40
Dubh Lochan	Aberd	NO0999	57°4·6'	3°29·6'W	W	36,43
Dubh Lochan	Arg & Bt	NN3216	56°18·7'	4°42·5'W	W	50,56
Dubh-lochan	Highld	NC7463	58°32·5'	4°9·4'W	W	10
Dubh Lochan	Highld	NH4406	57°7·4'	4°34·2'W	W	34
Dubh-lochan	Highld	NH5324	57°17·2'	4°25·9'W	W	26,35
Dubh Lochan	Highld	NH5401	57°4·9'	4°24·1'W	W	35
Dubh Lochan	Highld	NH6330	57°20·7'	4°16·1'W	W	26
Dubh Lochan	Highld	NN2360	56°42·2'	4°53·0'W	W	41
Dubh Lochan	Highld	NN2753	56°38·5'	4°48·8'W	W	41
Dubh Lochan	Highld	NN4676	56°51·3'	4°31·1'W	W	42
Dubh Lochan	Highld	NN4999	57°3·7'	4°29·0'W	W	34
Dubh Lochan	Moray	NJ0302	57°6·2'	3°35·6'W	W	36
Dubh Lochan	N Eil	NF0732	58°11·0'	6°58·6'W	W	13
Dubh-lochan	N Eil	NF7517	57°8·0'	7°21·9'W	W	31
Dubh Lochan	Pth & Kin	NN3953	56°38·7'	4°37·1'W	W	41
Dubh Lochan	Pth & Kin	NN4157	56°40·9'	4°35·3'W	W	42,51
Dubh Lochan	Pth & Kin	NN7167	56°46·9'	4°6·2'W	W	42
Dubh Lochan	Stir	NS3796	56°8·0'	4°36·9'W	W	56
Dubh Lochan na Beinne Boidhich	Pth & Kin	NN5663	56°44·4'	4°20·8'W	W	42
Dubh Loch Beag	Arg & Bt	NM9337	56°29·0'	5°21·3'W	W	49
Dubh Loch Beag	Highld	NC3216	58°6·3'	4°50·6'W	W	15
Dubh Loch Beag	Highld	NC4315	58°6·0'	4°39·4'W	W	16
Dubh Loch Mór	Arg & Bt	NM9438	56°29·6'	5°20·3'W	W	49
Dubh Loch Mór	Highld	NC3118	58°7·4'	4°51·7'W	W	15
Dubh Loch Mór	Highld	NC4313	58°5·0'	4°39·3'W	W	16
Dubh-loch na Beinne	Highld	NC4650	58°24·9'	4°37·7'W	W	9
Dubh-loch na Creige Riabhaich	Highld	NC5050	58°25·0'	4°33·6'W	W	9
Dubh Lochs	Highld	ND2147	58°24·5'	3°20·6'W	W	11,12
Dubh Lochs	Highld	ND2739	58°20·3'	3°14·3'W	W	11,12
Dubh Lochs of Shielton	Highld	ND2048	58°25·0'	3°21·7'W	W	11,12
Dubh Lòn	Highld	NG4445	57°25·7'	6°15·4'W	W	23
Dub How Fm	Cumbr	SD3694	54°20·5'	2°58·6'W	FM	96,97
Dùbhrach Choire	Highld	NC0706	58°0·3'	5°15·5'W	X	15
Dubh Sgeir	Arg & Bt	NM2419	56°17·2'	6°27·2'W	X	48
Dubh Sgeir	Arg & Bt	NM2421	56°18·3'	6°27·3'W	X	48
Dubh Sgeir	Arg & Bt	NM2718	56°16·8'	6°24·2'W	X	48
Dubh Sgeir	Arg & Bt	NM7211	56°14·5'	5°40·3'W	X	55
Dubh Sgeir	Arg & Bt	NM7420	56°19·4'	5°38·9'W	X	49,55
Dubh Sgeir	Arg & Bt	NM7625	56°22·1'	5°37·2'W	X	49
Dubh Sgeir	Arg & Bt	NM8545	56°33·1'	5°29·4'W	X	49
Dubh Sgeir	Arg & Bt	NR6247	55°39·8'	5°46·6'W	X	62
Dubh Sgeir	Arg & Bt	NR6674	55°54·4'	5°44·2'W	X	61,62
Dubh Sgeir	Arg & Bt	NR6678	55°56·5'	5°44·4'W	X	61,62
Dubh Sgeir	Highld	NC1339	58°18·3'	5°11·0'W	X	15
Dubh Sgeir	Highld	NG7757	57°33·2'	5°43·2'W	X	24
Dubh Sgeir	Highld	NM4278	56°49·6'	6°13·3'W	X	39
Dubh Sgeir	Highld	NM4583	56°52·4'	6°10·6'W	X	39
Dubh Sgeir	Highld	NM6169	56°45·3'	5°54·1'W	X	40
Dubh Sgeir	N Eil	NA9828	58°8·5'	7°7·5'W	X	13
Dubh Sgeir	N Eil	NB1744	58°17·9'	6°49·3'W	X	8,13
Dubh Sgeir	N Eil	NG0085	57°45·5'	7°2·2'W	X	18
Dubh-sgeir Bheag	Highld	NC5963	58°32·2'	4°24·8'W	X	10
Dubh Sgeirean	Highld	NC1344	58°20·9'	5°11·3'W	X	9
Dubh Sgeirean	Highld	NC1754	58°26·4'	5°7·6'W	X	9
Dubh Sgeir Lachdunn	N Eil	NA9827	58°8·0'	7°7·4'W	X	13
Dubh Sgeir Leiniger	N Eil	NB2448	58°20·3'	6°42·5'W	X	8
Dubh Sgeir Mhòr	Arg & Bt	NM4332	56°24·9'	6°9·6'W	X	48
Dubh-sgeir Mhòr	Highld	NC5964	58°32·7'	4°24·9'W	X	10
Dubh-sgeir Mhòr	N Eil	NF8423	57°11·6'	7°13·5'W	X	22
Dubh Sgeir nan Sgarbh	Highld	NM3980	56°50·6'	6°16·3'W	X	39
Dubh Thòb	N Eil	NB1836	58°13·6'	6°47·7'W	W	8,13
Dubh Uisge	Arg & Bt	NM9103	56°10·7'	5°21·6'W	W	55
Dubh Uisge	Arg & Bt	NM9512	56°15·6'	5°18·2'W	W	55
Dubh Uisge	Highld	NH2401	57°4·2'	4°53·7'W	W	34
Dubh Uisge	Highld	NN0076	56°50·2'	5°16·3'W	W	41
Dubiton	Aberd	NJ6250	57°32·6'	2°37·6'W	X	29
Dublin	Suff	TM1669	52°16·8'	1°10·4'E	T	156
Dublin Fm	Hants	SU3941	51°10·2'	1°26·1'W	FM	185
Dubmill Point	Cumbr	NY0745	54°47·7'	3°26·4'W	X	85
Dubmill Scar	Cumbr	NY0745	54°47·7'	3°26·4'W	X	85
Dubs Burn	E Ayr	NS5834	55°35·0'	4°14·7'W	W	71
Dubston	Aberd	NJ5420	57°16·4'	2°45·3'W	X	37
Dubston	Aberd	NJ7421	57°17·0'	2°25·4'W	X	38
Dubston	Aberd	NO6292	57°1·3'	2°37·1'W	X	45
Dubthorn	Ches	SJ8461	53°9·0'	2°13·9'W	X	118
Dubton	Aberd	NO6867	56°47·9'	2°31·0'W	X	45
Dubton	Angus	NO5652	56°39·7'	2°42·6'W	X	54
Dubton	Angus	NO5860	56°44·0'	2°40·7'W	X	44
Dubton	Angus	NO6365	56°46·8'	2°35·9'W	X	45
Dubton	Angus	NO7060	56°44·1'	2°29·0'W	X	45
Dubwath	Cumbr	NY1931	54°40·3'	3°14·9'W	T	89,90
Ducat Water	Aberd	NO6973	56°51·1'	2°30·0'W	W	45
Duchal Ho	Inverc	NS3568	55°52·9'	4°37·8'W	X	63
Duchally	Pth & Kin	NN9309	56°15·9'	3°43·2'W	X	58
Duchally Lodge	Highld	NC3817	58°7·0'	4°44·5'W	X	16

Duchal Mains	Inverc	NS3467	55°52·3'	4°38·8'W	X	63
Duchal Moor	Inverc	NS2867	55°52·2'	4°44·5'W	X	63
Duchara Burn	Arg & Bt	NM8811	56°14·9'	5°24·9'W	W	55
Ducharnan	Arg & Bt	NR8693	56°5·2'	5°25·9'W	X	55
Duchery Beg	Aberd	NO5093	57°1·8'	2°49·0'W	H	37,44
Duchess Countess Plantation	Highld	NH7992	57°54·3'	4°2·0'W	F	21
Duchess Fm	Essex	TM1416	51°48·3'	1°6·6'E	FM	168,169
Duchess of Gordon's Monument	Highld	NH8607	57°8·6'	3°52·6'W	X	35,36
Duchess's Drive	Scot Bord	NT3928	55°32·8'	2°57·6'W	X	73
Duchess Walk	Shrops	SO4775	52°22·5'	2°46·3'W	X	137,138,148
Duchies	Surrey	SU9354	51°16·9'	0°39·6'W	X	186
Duchlage	Arg & Bt	NS3487	56°3·1'	4°39·5'W	X	56
Duchlage	Pth & Kin	NN8620	56°21·8'	3°50·3'W	X	52,58
Duchra	D & G	NX0656	54°51·9'	5°1·0'W	X	82
Duchra	S Ayr	NX1384	55°7·2'	4°55·5'W	X	76
Duchrae	D & G	NX6583	55°7·6'	4°6·6'W	X	77
Duchray Burn	Angus	NO1665	56°46·4'	3°22·0'W	W	43
Duchray Castle	Stir	NS4899	56°9·8'	4°26·4'W	X	57
Duchray Hill or Mealna Letter	Pth & Kin	NO1667	56°47·5'	3°22·1'W	H	43
Duchray Ho	Stir	NS4899	56°9·8'	4°26·4'W	X	57
Duchray Water	Stir	NN4200	56°10·2'	4°32·3'W	W	56
Duchrie	Aberd	NO2094	57°2·1'	3°18·6'W	X	36,44
Duchrie Burn	Aberd	NO2399	57°4·8'	3°15·8'W	W	36,44
Duchy Fm	Norf	TL6694	52°31·3'	0°27·2'E	FM	143
Duckaller Fm	Devon	SX9579	50°36·3'	3°28·7'W	FM	192
Duck Bay	W Dunb	NS3783	56°1·0'	4°36·5'W	W	56
Duck Corner	Suff	TM3545	52°3·4'	1°26·1'E	T	169
Duckdubs Burn	D & G	NX0771	55°0·0'	5°0·6'W	W	76
Duck End	Beds	SP9852	52°9·7'	0°33·6'W	T	153
Duck End	Beds	TL0644	52°5·3'	0°26·8'W	T	153
Duck End	Bucks	SP7927	51°56·4'	0°50·6'W	T	165
Duck End	Cambs	TL2464	52°15·8'	0°10·6'W	T	153
Duck End	Essex	TL5122	51°52·8'	0°12·0'E	T	167
Duck End	Essex	TL6526	51°54·7'	0°24·3'E	T	167
Duck End	Essex	TL6833	51°58·4'	0°27·2'E	T	167
Duck End Fm	Essex	TL6428	51°55·8'	0°23·5'E	FM	167
Duckend Green	Essex	TL7223	51°53·0'	0°30·3'E	T	167
Ducketts Fm	Cambs	TL5369	52°18·1'	0°15·0'E	FM	154
Duckett's Fm	Lancs	SD5141	53°52·0'	2°44·3'W	FM	102
Duckham	Devon	SS7210	50°52·8'	3°48·8'W	X	191
Duck Hill	Cald	SD9930	53°46·2'	2°0·5'W	X	103
Duck Hill	Fife	NT0387	56°4·2'	3°33·0'W	X	65
Duck Ho	N Yks	SE6894	54°20·5'	0°56·8'W	X	94,100
Duck Hole	Hants	SU2502	50°49·2'	1°38·3'W	X	195
Duckhole	S Glos	ST6492	51°37·8'	2°30·8'W	T	162,172
Duckhurst Fm	Kent	TQ7744	51°10·3'	0°32·3'E	FM	188
Duckington	Ches	SJ4851	53°3·5'	2°46·1'W	T	117
Duckintree	Cumbr	NY8111	54°29·9'	2°17·2'W	X	91,92
Duckley Plantn	Staffs	SK0625	52°49·6'	1°54·3'W	F	128
Ducklington	Oxon	SP3507	51°45·9'	1°29·2'W	T	164
Duckmanton	Derby	SK4472	53°14·8'	1°20·0'W	T	120
Duckmanton Moor	Derby	SK4270	53°13·8'	1°21·8'W	X	120
Duckmead Ho	Wilts	ST8164	51°22·7'	2°16·0'W	X	173
Duck Nest	E Yorks	SE8437	53°49·6'	0°43·0'W	X	106
Duck Nest	E Yorks	SE8534	53°48·0'	0°42·2'W	X	106
Duckpit Fen	Cambs	TL1884	52°26·7'	0°15·4'W	X	142
Duckpond Plantation	Lincs	TF1885	53°21·2'	0°13·2'W	F	122
Duckpool	Corn	SS1911	50°52·4'	4°34·0'W	W	190
Duck Pool	Denb	SJ2253	53°4·4'	3°9·4'W	W	117
Duckpool Br	Lincs	TF1766	53°10·9'	0°14·5'W	X	121
Duckpool Fm	Oxon	SP3431	51°58·8'	1°29·9'W	FM	151
Duckpuddle Bush	Herts	TL3338	52°1·7'	0°3·3'W	X	154
Ducks Court	Medway	TQ7774	51°26·5'	0°33·2'E	X	178
Duck's Cross	Beds	TL1156	52°11·7'	0°22·2'W	X	153
Ducks Hall	Suff	TL8147	52°5·7'	0°38·9'E	X	155
Duck's Hill	Hill	TQ0790	51°36·1'	0°26·9'W	X	176
Ducks Island	Barnet	TQ2395	51°38·6'	0°12·9'W	T	166,176
Ducksluice Fm	Suff	TL8368	52°17·0'	0°41·4'E	FM	155
Ducksmoor Cottage	Devon	SX7887	50°40·4'	3°43·2'W	X	191
Duck's Nest	Hants	SU1020	50°59·0'	1°51·1'W	X	184
Duck's Nest (Long Barrow)	Hants	SU1020	50°59·0'	1°51·1'W	A	184
Ducks' Pool	Devon	SX6268	50°30·0'	3°56·4'W	W	202
Duckspool	Pemb	SN0418	51°49·8'	4°50·3'W	X	157,158
Ducks' Pool	Somer	ST2132	51°5·1'	3°7·3'W	X	182
Duck Street	Heref	SO3645	52°6·2'	2°55·7'W	X	148,149
Duck Street	N Yks	SE1163	54°4·0'	1°49·5'W	X	99
Duckswich	Worcs	SO8339	52°3·2'	2°14·5'W	T	150
Duckworth	Beds	SP9647	52°7·0'	0°35·5'W	X	153
Duckworth Hall	Lancs	SD7226	53°44·0'	2°25·1'W	X	103
Duckyls	W Susx	TQ3533	51°5·0'	0°4·0'W	X	187
Dudales Hope Fm	Heref	SO5551	52°9·6'	2°39·1'W	FM	149
Dudale's Wood	Heref	SO5652	52°10·1'	2°38·2'W	F	149
Dudbridge	Glos	SO8304	51°44·3'	2°14·4'W	T	162
Dudbrook	Essex	TQ5698	51°39·8'	0°15·7'E	X	167,177
Dudden Hill	Brent	TQ2285	51°33·3'	0°14·0'W	T	176
Duddenhoe End	Essex	TL4636	52°0·4'	0°8·0'E	T	154
Duddenhoe Grange	Essex	TL4435	51°59·9'	0°6·3'E	X	154
Dudderwick	Cumbr	NY4611	54°29·7'	2°49·6'W	X	90
Duddeston Sta	Birm	SP0887	52°29·1'	1°52·5'W	X	139
Dudd Hill	Shetld	HU3552	60°15·3'	1°21·6'W	H	3
Duddingston	C of Edin	NT2972	55°56·4'	3°7·8'W	T	66
Duddingston	W Loth	NT1077	55°58·9'	3°26·1'W	X	65
Duddingston Loch	C of Edin	NT2872	55°56·4'	3°8·7'W	W	66
Duddington	Northnts	SK9800	52°35·6'	0°32·8'W	T	141
Duddin Hill	Shetld	HU3866	60°22·8'	1°18·1'W	H	2,3
Duddle Heath	Dorset	SY7391	50°43·3'	2°22·6'W	X	194
Duddlestone	Somer	ST2321	50°59·2'	3°5·4'W	T	193
Duddleswell	E Susx	TQ4627	51°1·7'	0°5·3'E	T	188,198
Duddleswell Manor	E Susx	TQ4628	51°2·2'	0°5·3'E	X	188,198
Duddlewick	Shrops	SO6583	52°26·9'	2°30·5'W	T	138
Duddo	Northum	NT9342	55°40·5'	2°6·2'W	T	74,75
Duddo Burn	Northum	NZ1779	55°6·6'	1°43·6'W	W	88
Duddo Hill	Northum	NT9242	55°40·5'	2°7·2'W	H	74,75
Duddo Hill	Northum	NZ1980	55°7·1'	1°41·7'W	X	81
Duddon	Ches	SJ5164	53°10·5'	2°43·6'W	T	117
Duddon Bridge	Cumbr	SD1988	54°17·1'	3°14·2'W	T	96

Duddon Channel	Cumbr	SD2081	54°13·4'	3°13·2'W	W	96
Duddon Common	Ches	SJ5265	53°11·0'	2°42·7'W	T	117
Duddon Hall	Cumbr	SD1989	54°17·7'	3°14·3'W	X	96
Duddon Heath	Ches	SJ5065	53°11·0'	2°44·5'W	T	117
Duddon Mill	Ches	SJ5165	53°11·0'	2°43·6'W	X	117
Duddon Mount	Cumbr	SD1882	54°13·9'	3°15·1'W	X	96
Duddon Sands	Cumbr	SD1978	54°11·7'	3°14·1'W	X	96
Duddon Villa	Cumbr	SD1879	54°12·3'	3°15·0'W	X	96
Duddy Bank	Scot Bord	NT6461	55°50·7'	2°34·1'W	H	67
Duddy Hill	Scot Bord	NT7065	55°52·9'	2°28·3'W	X	67
Dudgeley Fm	Shrops	SO4696	52°33·8'	2°47·4'W	FM	137,138
Dudgemore Fm	Wilts	SU1091	51°37·3'	1°50·9'W	FM	163,173
Dudgrove Fm	Glos	SU1998	51°41·1'	1°43·1'W	FM	163
Dudhill	Shrops	SO7887	52°29·1'	2°19·0'W	X	138
Dudland	Lancs	SD8046	53°54·8'	2°17·9'W	X	103
Dudlees	Northum	NT8600	55°17·9'	2°12·8'W	X	80
Dudleston	Shrops	SJ3438	52°56·4'	2°58·5'W	T	126
Dudleston Grove	Shrops	SJ3636	52°55·3'	2°56·7'W	T	126
Dudleston Hall	Shrops	SJ3535	52°54·8'	2°57·6'W	X	126
Dudleston Heath (Criftins)	Shrops	SJ3636	52°55·3'	2°56·7'W	T	126
Dudley	Dudley	SO9390	52°30·7'	2°5·8'W	T	139
Dudley	N Tyne	NZ2673	55°3·3'	1°35·2'W	T	88
Dudley Br	Bucks	SP6733	51°59·7'	1°1·1'W	X	152,165
Dudley Canal	Dudley	SO9785	52°28·0'	2°2·3'W	W	139
Dudley Hill	Brad	SE1831	53°46·7'	1°43·2'W	T	104
Dudley Hill Fm	N Yks	SE6468	54°6·5'	1°0·8'W	FM	100
Dudley Port	Sand	SO9691	52°31·2'	2°3·1'W	T	139
Dudley's Fields	Wals	SJ9801	52°36·6'	2°1·4'W	T	127,139
Dudley Wood	Dudley	SO9486	52°28·6'	2°4·9'W	T	139
Dudley Wood Fm	Warw	SP2793	52°32·3'	1°35·7'W	FM	140
Dudlows Green	Warr	SJ6284	53°21·3'	2°33·8'W	T	109
Dudmaston Hall	Shrops	SO7488	52°29·6'	2°22·6'W	A	138
Dudmire	Cumbr	NY6924	54°36·9'	2°28·4'W	X	91
Dudmoor Fm	Dorset	SZ1596	50°46·0'	1°46·9'W	FM	195
Dudmore Lodge	Wilts	SU2375	51°28·6'	1°39·7'W	X	174
Dudnill	Shrops	SO6474	52°22·0'	2°31·3'W	X	138
Dud of Flamister	Shetld	HU4356	60°17·4'	1°12·8'W	X	2,3
Dudsbury	Dorset	SZ0798	50°47·1'	1°53·7'W	T	195
Dudshill Court	Heref	SO6864	52°16·6'	2°27·7'W	X	138,149
Dudsland Fm	E Susx	TQ5522	50°58·8'	0°12·9'E	FM	199
Dudston	Shrops	SO2497	52°34·2'	3°6·9'W	X	137
Dudswell	Herts	SP9609	51°46·5'	0°36·1'W	T	165
Dudwell Fm	E Susx	TQ6723	50°59·2'	0°23·2'E	FM	199
Dudwell Mountain	Pemb	SM9022	51°51·7'	5°2·6'W	H	157,158
Dudwells	Pemb	SM9021	51°51·1'	5°2·6'W	T	157,158
Dudwell St Mary	E Susx	TQ6825	51°0·2'	0°24·1'E	X	188,199
Dudwick Fm	Norf	TG2122	52°45·2'	1°16·9'E	FM	133,134
Dudwick House	Norf	TG2222	52°45·2'	1°17·8'E	X	133,134
Dudwood Fm	Derby	SK2261	53°9·0'	1°39·9'W	FM	119
Duerdon	Devon	SS3219	50°57·0'	4°23·1'W	T	190
Duerley Beck	N Yks	SD8586	54°16·4'	2°13·4'W	W	98
Duerley Bottom	N Yks	SD8586	54°16·4'	2°13·4'W	X	98
Duesden	Kent	TQ8536	51°5·8'	0°38·9'E	X	189
Dueshill Fm	Northum	NT9601	55°18·4'	2°3·4'W	FM	81
Duffdefiance	Aberd	NJ3016	57°14·0'	3°9·1'W	X	37
Duffergill Burn	Cumbr	NY7338	54°44·4'	2°24·7'W	W	91
Duff House	Aberd	NJ6963	57°39·6'	2°30·7'W	A	29
Duffield	Derby	SK3443	52°59·2'	1°29·2'W	T	119,128
Duffieldbank	Derby	SK3543	52°59·2'	1°28·3'W	T	119,128
Duffryn	Heref	SO4131	51°58·7'	2°51·1'W	X	149,161
Duffryn	Monm	SO3514	51°49·5'	2°56·2'W	X	161
Duffryn	Monm	SO4602	51°43·1'	2°46·5'W	X	171
Duffryn	Newp	ST2784	51°33·2'	3°2·8'W	X	171
Duffryn	Newp	ST2985	51°33·8'	3°1·1'W	T	171
Duffryn	Nth Pt Talb	SS8395	51°38·7'	3°41·1'W	T	170
Duffryn	Shrops	SO2282	52°26·1'	3°8·4'W	T	137
Duffryn Bach Fm	V of Glam	ST0678	51°29·8'	3°20·9'W	FM	170
Duffryn Lloff	V of Glam	ST0577	51°29·3'	3°21·7'W	X	170
Duffryn,The	Monm	SO4515	51°50·1'	2°47·5'W	X	161
Duff's Hill	Aberd	NO9199	57°5·2'	2°8·5'W	T	38,45
Duff's Loch	D & G	NX8556	54°53·4'	3°47·2'W	W	84
Dufftown	Moray	NJ3239	57°26·4'	3°7·5'W	T	28
Duffus	Moray	NJ1668	57°41·9'	3°24·1'W	T	28
Duffushillock	Moray	NJ2159	57°37·1'	3°18·9'W	X	28
Duffushillock	Moray	NJ4860	57°37·9'	2°51·8'W	X	28,29
Duffus House	Moray	NJ1768	57°41·9'	3°23·1'W	X	28
Dufton	Cumbr	NY6825	54°37·4'	2°29·3'W	T	91
Dufton Fell	Cumbr	NY7628	54°39·0'	2°21·9'W	H	91
Dufton Pike	Cumbr	NY6926	54°37·9'	2°28·4'W	H	91
Dufton Wood	Cumbr	NY6823	54°36·3'	2°29·3'W	X	91
Dugdales	Lancs	SD7551	53°57·5'	2°22·4'W	X	103
Dugdales Fm	Wilts	SU0373	51°27·6'	1°57·0'W	FM	173
Duggleby	N Yks	SE8767	54°5·7'	0°39·8'W	T	101
Duggleby Howe	N Yks	SE8866	54°5·2'	0°38·9'W	A	101
Duggleby Wold	N Yks	SE8767	54°5·7'	0°39·8'W	X	101
Duggleby Wold	N Yks	SE8768	54°6·3'	0°39·7'W	X	101
Duggleby Wold Fm	N Yks	SE9673	54°8·9'	0°31·4'W	FM	101
Dugland	D & G	NS6000	55°16·7'	4°11·8'W	H	77
Duglands	Shrops	SJ3517	52°45·0'	2°57·4'W	X	126
Dugmore Fm	Norf	TF8401	52°34·8'	0°43·3'E	FM	144
Dugoed	Conwy	SH8052	53°3·4'	3°47·0'W	X	116
Dugoedydd	Carm	SN7741	52°3·5'	3°47·3'W	X	146,147,160
Dugwm	Powys	SO0585	52°27·5'	3°23·5'W	X	136
Duhonw	Powys	SO0449	52°8·1'	3°23·8'W	W	147
Duhorn	S Ayr	NX1086	55°8·2'	4°58·4'W	X	76
Duiar	Highld	NJ1233	57°23·0'	3°27·4'W	X	28
Duibhe Bheag	Pth & Kin	NN4351	56°37·7'	4°33·1'W	W	42,51
Duibh-eilean	N Eil	NF9157	57°30·1'	7°9·1'W	X	22
Duibh Leitir	Arg & Bt	NM6324	56°21·2'	5°49·7'W	X	49
Duible	Highld	NC9219	58°9·1'	3°49·6'W	X	17
Duich	Arg & Bt	NR3154	55°42·5'	6°16·5'W	X	60
Duich Ho	Highld	NG8921	57°14·1'	5°29·3'W	X	33
Duich Lots	Arg & Bt	NR3354	55°42·6'	6°14·6'W	X	60
Duich River	Arg & Bt	NR3354	55°42·6'	6°14·6'W	W	60
Duiletter	Arg & Bt	NN1530	56°25·8'	4°59·6'W	X	50
Duiletter	Arg & Bt	NS0187	56°2·3'	5°11·2'W	X	55
Duine	Arg & Bt	NM7902	56°9·8'	5°33·1'W	X	55
Duinish	Pth & Kin	NN6167	56°46·7'	4°16·0'W	X	42
Duireaskin	Pth & Kin	NN8749	56°37·4'	3°50·1'W	X	52
Duirinish	Highld	NG7831	57°19·2'	5°40·8'W	T	24

Duirinish Sta	Highld	NG7731	57°19·2'	5°41·8'W	X	24
Duirland	Arg & Bt	NS2987	56°3·0'	4°44·3'W	X	56
Duisdalebeg	Highld	NG6912	57°8·7'	5°48·7'W	T	32
Duisdalemore	Highld	NG7013	57°9·3'	5°47·7'W	T	32,33
Duisgeir	N Eil	NB0804	57°56·0'	6°55·5'W	X	13,14
Duisgeir	N Eil	NB1103	57°55·6'	6°52·4'W	X	13,14
Duisker	Arg & Bt	NR3666	55°49·2'	6°12·4'W	X	60,61
Duisker	N Eil	NA9618	58°3·1'	7°8·7'W	X	13
Duisk River	S Ayr	NX2085	55°7·9'	4°49·0'W	W	76
Duisk River	S Ayr	NX2481	55°5·8'	4°45·1'W	W	76
Duisky	Highld	NN0076	56°50·2'	5°16·3'W	T	41
Duke Br	Warw	SP2188	52°29·6'	1°41·0'W	X	139
Duke End	Warw	SP2188	52°29·6'	1°41·0'W	T	139
Duke End Fm	Warw	SP2287	52°29·1'	1°40·2'W	FM	139
Dukenfield Hall	Ches	SJ7779	53°18·7'	2°20·3'W	X	118
Duke of Gordon's Monument	Highld	NH8708	57°9·2'	3°51·6'W	X	35,36
Duke of Kent School	Surrey	TQ0842	51°10·2'	0°26·9'W	X	187
Duke of Northumberland's River	Hill	TQ0575	51°28·1'	0°28·9'W	W	176
Dukes	Essex	TL6408	51°45·0'	0°22·9'E	X	167
Duke's Boots Wood	Aberd	NJ9427	57°20·3'	2°5·5'W	F	38
Dukes Brake	Wilts	SU0797	51°40·5'	1°53·5'W	F	163
Duke's Chair	Aberd	NN9788	56°58·6'	3°41·2'W	X	43
Duke's Drive, The	Wrekin	SJ6416	52°44·7'	2°31·6'W	X	127
Dukesfield	Northum	NU1734	55°36·2'	1°43·4'W	X	75
Dukesfield	Northum	NY9457	54°54·7'	2°5·2'W	T	87
Duke's Fm	Essex	TL9318	51°49·9'	0°48·5'E	FM	168
Duke's Fm	Monm	SO4120	51°52·8'	2°51·0'W	FM	161
Duke's Fm	Suff	TM3488	52°26·6'	1°27·0'E	FM	156
Dukeshagg Fm	Northum	NZ1060	54°56·3'	1°50·2'W	FM	88
Duke's Head	Norf	TM2499	52°32·8'	1°18·6'E	A	134
Duke's Ho	Northum	NY9563	54°57·9'	2°4·3'W	X	87
Duke's Lane	Win & Maid	SU9571	51°26·0'	0°37·6'W	X	175,176
Duke's Meadows	Houns	TQ2076	51°28·4'	0°15·9'W	X	176
Duke's Oak Fm	Ches	SJ7763	53°10·1'	2°20·2'W	FM	118
Duke's Pass	Stir	NN5103	56°12·0'	4°23·7'W	X	57
Duke's Place	Kent	TQ6452	51°14·8'	0°21·4'E	A	188
Duke's Plantation	Somer	ST1639	51°8·9'	3°11·7'W	F	181
Duke's Ride	Suff	TL8477	52°21·8'	0°42·5'E	X	144
Duke's Strip	Scot Bord	NT6728	55°32·9'	2°30·9'W	F	74
Duke's Table	Blae Gw	SO1114	51°49·3'	3°17·1'W	X	161
Dukes, The	Wrex	SJ4341	52°58·0'	2°50·5'W	X	117
Dukeston of Brux	Aberd	NJ4815	57°13·6'	2°51·2'W	X	37
Dukestown	Blae Gw	SO1310	51°47·2'	3°15·3'W	T	161
Duke's Warren, The	Surrey	TQ1444	51°11·3'	0°21·7'W	X	187
Duke's Wood	Notts	SK7259	53°7·6'	0°55·0'W	F	120
Dukewell	Aberd	NJ5538	57°26·1'	2°44·5'W	X	29
Dukieston	D & G	NX5686	55°9·1'	4°15·2'W	X	77
Dukinfield	Tames	SJ9497	53°28·4'	2°5·0'W	T	109
Dula Burn	Shetld	HU2880	60°30·4'	1°28·9'W	W	3
Dulais	Nth Pt Talb	SN7802	51°42·4'	3°45·6'W	W	170
Dulais	Nth Pt Talb	SN8007	51°45·2'	3°43·9'W	W	160
Dulas	I of Angl	SH4789	53°22·8'	4°17·6'W	T	114
Dulas	Powys	SN9451	52°9·1'	3°32·6'W	W	147
Dulas	Powys	SO1133	51°59·5'	3°17·4'W	W	161
Dulas Bay	I of Angl	SH4989	53°22·8'	4°15·8'W	W	114
Dulas Brook	Heref	SO3530	51°58·1'	2°56·4'W	W	149,161
Dulas Brook	Powys	SO0354	52°10·8'	3°24·7'W	W	147
Dulas Brook	Powys	SO2440	52°3·4'	3°6·1'W	W	148,161
Dulas Court	Heref	SO3729	51°57·6'	2°54·6'W	X	149,161
Dulax	Aberd	NJ3518	57°15·1'	3°4·2'W	X	37
Dulcis Fm	Devon	SY2699	50°47·4'	3°2·6'W	FM	192,193
Dulcote	Somer	ST5644	51°11·8'	2°37·4'W	T	182,183
Dulcote Hill	Somer	ST5644	51°11·8'	2°37·4'W	H	182,183
Duley Dock	N Yks	TA1675	54°9·7'	0°13·0'W	X	101
Dulford	Devon	ST0606	50°51·0'	3°19·7'W	T	192
Dulford Ho	Devon	ST0707	50°51·5'	3°18·9'W	X	192
Dull	Pth & Kin	NN8049	56°37·3'	3°56·9'W	T	52
Dullans	Shetld	HU5991	60°36·1'	0°54·9'W	X	1,2
Dullan Water	Moray	NJ3036	57°24·8'	3°9·5'W	W	28
Dullar Fm	Dorset	SY9498	50°47·1'	2°4·7'W	FM	195
Dullarg Burn	D & G	NX6775	55°3·4'	4°4·5'W	W	77,84
Dullarg Hill	D & G	NX6758	54°54·2'	4°4·0'W	X	83,84
Dullator	Pth & Kin	NN9338	56°31·6'	3°43·9'W	X	52
Dullator Burn	Pth & Kin	NN9336	56°30·5'	3°43·9'W	W	52
Dullatur	N Lanak	NS7476	55°57·9'	4°0·7'W	T	64
Dull Flag	Orkney	HY4953	59°21·9'	2°53·3'W	X	5
Dullingham	Cambs	TL6257	52°11·5'	0°22·6'E	T	154
Dullingham Ho	Cambs	TL6257	52°11·5'	0°22·6'E	X	154
Dullingham Ley	Cambs	TL6456	52°10·9'	0°24·3'E	T	154
Dull's Fm	Norf	TM3594	52°29·8'	1°28·1'E	FM	134
Dull Wood	Pth & Kin	NN7949	56°37·3'	3°57·9'W	F	51,52
Dully Ho	Kent	TQ9361	51°19·1'	0°46·6'E	X	178
Dulnain Bridge	Highld	NH9924	57°18·0'	3°40·1'W	T	36
Duloch	Fife	NT1385	56°3·3'	3°23·4'W	T	65
Duloe	Beds	TL1560	52°13·8'	0°18·6'W	T	153
Duloe	Corn	SX2358	50°24·0'	4°29·1'W	T	201
Duloe Brook	Beds	TL1360	52°13·8'	0°20·3'W	W	153
Duloe Butts	Beds	TL1560	52°13·8'	0°18·6'W	X	153
Dulsie	Highld	NH9341	57°27·1'	3°46·5'W	X	27
Dulsie Wood	Highld	NH9344	57°28·7'	3°46·6'W	X	27
Dulverton	Somer	SS9128	51°2·7'	3°32·9'W	T	181
Dulverton Wood	Worcs	SP1034	52°0·5'	1°50·9'W	F	150
Dulwich	Sthwk	TQ3472	51°26·1'	0°3·9'W	T	176,177
Dulwich Village	Sthwk	TQ3373	51°26·6'	0°4·8'W	T	176,177
Dulyard Brae	Scot Bord	NT1331	55°34·1'	3°22·3'W	H	72
Dulyn Reservoir	Conwy	SH7066	53°10·8'	3°56·3'W	W	115
Dumbadan Burn	E Loth	NT5365	55°52·8'	2°44·6'W	W	66
Dumbain	W Dunb	NS4082	56°0·5'	4°33·5'W	X	56,64
Dumbarnie	Fife	NO4403	56°13·2'	2°53·7'W	X	59
Dumbarrow	Angus	NO5447	56°37·0'	2°44·5'W	X	54
Dumbarrow	Pth & Kin	NO1912	56°17·9'	3°18·1'W	X	58
Dumbarrow Hill	Angus	NO5547	56°37·0'	2°43·5'W	X	54
Dumbarrow Hill	Pth & Kin	NO1913	56°18·4'	3°18·1'W	H	58
Dumbarrow Mains	Angus	NO5546	56°36·5'	2°43·5'W	X	54
Dumbarton	W Dunb	NS4075	55°56·7'	4°33·3'W	T	64
Dumbarton Muir	W Dunb	NS4579	55°59·0'	4°28·6'W	X	64
Dumb Hope	Northum	NT8509	55°22·7'	2°13·8'W	H	80
Dumblar Rigg	Cumbr	NY6070	55°1·6'	2°37·1'W	X	86

Dumbledeer	Somer	ST0040	51°9·3′	3°25·4′W	X	181
Dumble Fm	Warw	SP2388	52°29·6′	1°39·3′W	FM	139
Dumbles, The	Glos	SO7105	51°44·8′	2°24·8′W	W	162
Dumbles, The	Notts	SK4756	53°6·2′	1°17·5′W	X	120
Dumbleton	Glos	SP0136	52°1·6′	1°58·7′W	T	150
Dumbleton Fm	Worcs	SO6969	52°19·3′	2°26·9′W	FM	138
Dumbleton Hill	Glos	SP0035	52°1·0′	1°59·6′W	H	150
Dumbmill	Aberd	NK0050	57°32·7′	1°59·5′W	X	30
Dumbourne	Kent	TQ8930	51°2·5′	0°42·2′E	X	189
Dumbraxhill	S Lanak	NS8240	55°38·6′	3°52·1′W	X	71,72
Dumbreck	C of Glas	NS5663	55°50·6′	4°17·5′W	T	64
Dumbreck	Stir	NS5781	56°0·3′	4°17·2′W	H	64
Dumbrell's Fm	W Susx	TQ2720	50°58·1′	0°11·1′W	FM	198
Dumbretton	D & G	NY2171	55°1·9′	3°13·7′W	X	85
Dumbrock Loch	Stir	NS5578	55°58·6′	4°19·0′W	W	64
Dumbuck	W Dunb	NS4174	55°56·2′	4°32·3′W	X	64
Dumcrieff	D & G	NT1003	55°19·0′	3°24·7′W	T	78
Dumdruff Hill	E Renf	NS5846	55°41·5′	4°15·1′W	H	64
Dumeath	Aberd	NJ4237	57°25·4′	2°57·5′W	X	28
Dumfedling	D & G	NT2401	55°18·1′	3°11·4′W	X	79
Dumfedling Hill	D & G	NT2402	55°18·6′	3°11·4′W	H	79
Dumfedling Knowe	D & G	NT2602	55°18·6′	3°9·5′W	H	79
Dumfin	Arg & Bt	NS3484	56°1·5′	4°39·4′W	X	56
Dumfries	D & G	NX9776	55°4·3′	3°36·4′W	T	84
Dumfries Ho	E Ayr	NS5420	55°27·4′	4°18·1′W	A	70
Dumglow	Pth & Kin	NT0796	56°9·1′	3°29·4′W	X	58
Dumgoyach Fm	Stir	NS5281	56°0·2′	4°22·0′W	FM	64
Dumgoyne	Stir	NS5283	56°1·3′	4°22·0′W	T	57,64
Dumgoyne	Stir	NS5482	56°0·8′	4°20·1′W	H	57,64
Dummah Crag	Cumbr	NY8315	54°32·0′	2°15·3′W	X	91,92
Dummah Hill	Cumbr	NY8215	54°32·0′	2°16·3′W	H	91,92
Dummer	Hants	SU5845	51°12·3′	1°9·8′W	T	185
Dummer Down Fm	Hants	SU5744	51°11·8′	1°10·7′W	FM	185
Dummer Grange	Hants	SU5944	51°11·8′	1°8·9′W	X	185
Dummer Grange Fm	Hants	SU5844	51°11·8′	1°9·8′W	FM	185
Dummiefarline	Pth & Kin	NT0896	56°9·1′	3°28·4′W	X	58
Dummiesholes	Angus	NO5645	56°35·9′	2°42·5′W	X	54
Dummuies	Aberd	NJ5536	57°25·0′	2°44·5′W	X	29
Dumpdon Hill	Devon	ST1704	50°50·0′	3°10·3′W	H	192,193
Dumpdon Hill (Fort)	Devon	ST1704	50°50·0′	3°10·3′W	A	192,193
Dumper's Oak	Hants	SU4035	51°7·0′	1°25·3′W	F	185
Dumpford	W Susx	SU8221	50°59·2′	0°49·5′W	T	197
Dumpford Park Fm	W Susx	SU8221	50°59·2′	0°49·5′W	FM	197
Dump House Fm	Worcs	SP0671	52°20·5′	1°54·3′W	FM	139
Dumpinghill	Devon	SS4408	50°51·3′	4°12·6′W	T	190
Dumpling Castle	Donc	SK6194	53°26·6′	1°4·5′W	X	111
Dumpling Fm	Lincs	SK9426	52°49·6′	0°35·9′W	FM	130
Dumpling Green	Norf	TG0012	52°40·4′	0°57·9′E	T	133
Dumplington	Traf	SJ7697	53°28·4′	2°21·3′W	T	109
Dumpston Mintlaw	Aberd	NK0250	57°32·7′	1°57·5′W	X	30
Dumptilow Fm	Cambs	TL2666	52°16·9′	0°8·8′W	FM	153
Dumpton	Kent	TR3866	51°20·8′	1°25·5′E	T	179
Dumpton Gap	Kent	TR3966	51°20·8′	1°26·3′E	X	179
Dumyat	Stir	NS8397	56°9·3′	3°52·6′W	H	57
Dumyat Fm	Stir	NS8497	56°9·4′	3°51·6′W	FM	58
Dun	Angus	NO6659	56°43·5′	2°32·9′W	T	54
Dun	N Eil	NF1097	57°47·8′	8°33·5′W	X	18
Dùn-aarn	N Eil	NG0280	57°42·9′	6°59·8′W	X	18
Dunach	Arg & Bt	NM8624	56°21·9′	5°27·4′W	X	49
Dunach Fm	Arg & Bt	NM8725	56°22·4′	5°26·5′W	FM	49
Dùn a' Chliabhain (Fort)	Highld	NH4746	57°29·0′	4°32·7′W	A	26
Dùnach Liath	Highld	NH4486	57°50·4′	4°37·2′W	H	20
Dunachton Lodge	Highld	NH8204	57°7·0′	3°56·5′W	X	35
Dunachtonmore Fm	Highld	NH8104	57°7·0′	3°57·5′W	FM	35
Dunacree	Pth & Kin	NN8348	56°36·8′	3°53·9′W	X	52
Dunadd	Arg & Bt	NR8393	56°5·1′	5°28·8′W	X	55
Dunadd (Fort)	Arg & Bt	NR8393	56°5·1′	5°28·8′W	A	55
Dùn Adhamh	Highld	NG4054	57°30·4′	6°20·0′W	X	23
Dùn Adhamh	Highld	NG4154	57°30·4′	6°19·0′W	X	23
Dùn Adhamh (Fort)	Highld	NG4054	57°30·4′	6°20·0′W	A	23
Dùn a' Gheird	Arg & Bt	NM4018	56°17·3′	6°11·6′W	A	48
Dunagoil	Arg & Bt	NS0953	55°44·2′	5°2·1′W	X	63
Dunagoil Bay	Arg & Bt	NS0853	55°44·2′	5°3·1′W	W	63
Dùn a h-Uamha	Arg & Bt	NR2462	55°45·6′	6°23·7′W	A	60
Dùn Ailne	Arg & Bt	NM7804	56°10·9′	5°34·2′W	A	55
Dunaincroy	Highld	NH6441	57°26·6′	4°15·5′W	X	26
Dunain Hill	Highld	NH6243	57°27·6′	4°17·6′W	H	26
Dunain Ho	Highld	NH6242	57°27·1′	4°17·5′W	X	26
Dunain Park	Highld	NH6342	57°27·1′	4°16·5′W	X	26
Dùn Aisgain	Arg & Bt	NM3745	56°31·7′	6°16·2′W	A	47,48
Dùn Alascaig	Highld	NH6586	57°50·9′	4°16·0′W	X	21
Dùn Alascaig (Broch)	Highld	NH6586	57°50·9′	4°16·0′W	A	21
Dunalastair	Pth & Kin	NN7158	56°42·0′	4°6·0′W	T	42,51,52
Dunalastair Water	Pth & Kin	NN6958	56°42·0′	4°7·9′W	W	42,51
Dunalunt	Arg & Bt	NS0464	55°50·0′	5°7·3′W	X	63
Dùn Alva	Arg & Bt	NR9196	56°6·9′	5°21·3′W	H	55
Dunamoddie	S Ayr	NX3696	55°14·1′	4°34·3′W	X	77
Dunamuck	Arg & Bt	NR8492	56°4·6′	5°27·8′W	T	55
Dunamuck Cott	Arg & Bt	NR8491	56°4·0′	5°27·8′W	X	55
Dùnan	Arg & Bt	NR5164	55°48·6′	5°58·0′W	X	61
Dunan	Arg & Bt	NS1678	55°57·8′	4°56·4′W	X	63
Dunan	Heref	SO4637	52°2·0′	2°46·8′W	X	149,161
Dunan	Highld	NG5827	57°16·4′	6°0·4′W	T	32
Dùnan	N Eil	NB3709	57°59·8′	6°26·6′W	X	14
Dunan	Pth & Kin	NN4757	56°41·0′	4°29·4′W	X	42,51
Dunan	Pth & Kin	NN7334	56°29·1′	4°3·3′W	X	51,52
Dùn an Achaidh	Arg & Bt	NM1854	56°35·8′	6°35·2′W	A	46
Dùnan a' Mharcaiche	Arg & Bt	NM4720	56°18·6′	6°5·0′W	X	48
Dunan an Asilidh	Highld	NG5335	57°20·6′	6°5·9′W	A	24,32
Dùnan Beag	Highld	NC2572	58°36·3′	5°0·3′W	H	9
Dunandhu	Aberd	NJ2209	57°10·2′	3°16·9′W	T	36
Dunan Diarmaid	Highld	NG9320	57°13·7′	5°25·3′W	A	25,33
Dùn an Dubh-challa	Arg & Bt	NM8405	56°11·6′	5°28·4′W	X	55
Dùn an Fheurain	Arg & Bt	NM3618	56°17·1′	6°15·5′W	X	48
Dùn an Fhithich	Arg & Bt	NR2744	55°37·0′	6°19·7′W	X	60
Dunanfiew	Aberd	NJ2309	57°10·2′	3°15·9′W	X	36
Dun an Garbh-Shroine	Arg & Bt	NM8008	56°13·1′	5°32·5′W	X	55
Dun an Garbh-Shroine (Fort)	Arg & Bt	NM8008	56°13·1′	5°32·5′W	A	55
Dunan Hill	Pth & Kin	NN7436	56°30·2′	4°2·4′W	H	51,52

Dun an Iarla	Highld	NG2855	57°30·5′	6°32·0′W	H	23
Dùnan Liath	Highld	NH4184	57°49·3′	4°40·2′W	H	20
Dùnan Mór	Arg & Bt	NM3724	56°20·4′	6°14·9′W	X	48
Dùnan Mór	Highld	NC2674	58°37·4′	4°59·3′W	H	9
Dùnan na Marcachd	Arg & Bt	NM5120	56°18·7′	6°1·1′W	X	48
Dùnan na Nighean	Arg & Bt	NR4197	56°6·0′	6°9·5′W	A	61
Dùnan nan Nighean	Arg & Bt	NM4735	56°26·6′	6°5·9′W	H	47,48
Dùnan na Sleaghaich	Highld	NM6548	56°34·2′	5°49·1′W	X	49
Dùn an Oir	Arg & Bt	NS0087	56°2·3′	5°12·2′W	X	55
Dunanrea Bay	D & G	NX0250	54°48·6′	5°4·4′W	W	82
Dùnan Ruadh	Highld	NG7819	57°12·7′	5°40·1′W	X	33
Dùnan Ruadh	N Eil	NF7208	57°3·0′	7°24·1′W	X	31
Dùnan Ruadh	N Eil	NL6187	56°51·3′	7°33·3′W	A	31
Dùn an Ruigh Ruadh	Highld	NH1490	57°51·9′	5°7·7′W	A	20
Dunans	Arg & Bt	NR8090	56°3·4′	5°31·6′W	T	55
Dunans	Arg & Bt	NS0491	56°4·6′	5°8·5′W	X	56
Dunans	Highld	NG4670	57°39·2′	6°15·0′W	X	23
Dùn an Sticer	N Eil	NF8977	57°40·8′	7°12·6′W	A	18
Dùnan Thalasgair	Highld	NM4890	56°56·2′	6°8·1′W	X	39
Dunan Thearna Sgurr	Highld	NG3620	57°11·9′	6°21·8′W	X	32
Dùn an t-Siamain	N Eil	NF8859	57°31·1′	7°12·2′W	A	22
Dun Aorain	Arg & Bt	NM7417	56°17·8′	5°38·7′W	A	55
Dùn Ara	Arg & Bt	NM4257	56°38·3′	6°12·0′W	X	47
Dun Ara (Castle)	Arg & Bt	NM4257	56°38·3′	6°12·0′W	A	47
Dunardry Locks	Arg & Bt	NR8191	56°4·0′	5°30·7′W	X	55
Dùn Ardtreck	Highld	NG3335	57°19·9′	6°25·7′W	A	32
Dùn Arkaig	Highld	NG3542	57°23·7′	6°24·2′W	X	23
Dùn Arkaig (Broch)	Highld	NG3542	57°23·7′	6°24·2′W	A	23
Dùn Arnal	Arg & Bt	NM8203	56°10·4′	5°30·3′W	X	55
Dunaskin Burn	E Ayr	NS4508	55°20·8′	4°26·2′W	W	70,77
Dùn Athad	Arg & Bt	NR2840	55°34·9′	6°18·5′W	A	60
Dùn Auladh	Arg & Bt	NM4052	56°35·5′	6°14·3′W	A	47
Dunaverty	Arg & Bt	NR6807	55°18·4′	5°38·9′W	X	68
Dunaverty Bay	Arg & Bt	NR6807	55°18·4′	5°38·9′W	W	68
Dunbae	D & G	NX0558	54°53·0′	5°2·0′W	X	82
Dunball	Somer	ST3141	51°10·1′	2°58·8′W	T	182
Dunballoch	Highld	NH5244	57°28·0′	4°27·6′W	X	26
Dùn Bàn	Arg & Bt	NM3841	56°29·6′	6°15·0′W	A	47,48
Dùn Bàn	Arg & Bt	NM3845	56°31·7′	6°15·2′W	A	47,48
Dun Bàn	Arg & Bt	NM4056	56°37·7′	6°13·9′W	X	47
Dùn Bàn	Arg & Bt	NR5914	55°21·9′	5°47·8′W	X	68
Dùn Bàn	Highld	NG7010	57°7·7′	5°47·6′W	A	33
Dùn Bàn	Highld	NM4470	56°45·3′	6°10·8′W	X	39,47
Dùn Bàn	Highld	NM5650	56°35·0′	5°58·0′W	X	47
Dùn Bàn	N Eil	NF6300	56°58·4′	7°32·4′W	A	31
Dùn Bàn	N Eil	NF8460	57°31·5′	7°16·3′W	A	22
Dùn Bàn	N Eil	NF8657	57°29·9′	7°14·1′W	A	22
Dùn Bàn (Fort)	Arg & Bt	NM4056	56°37·7′	6°13·9′W	A	47
Dùn Ban (Fort)	Highld	NG7003	57°3·9′	5°47·2′W	A	33
Dùn Ban (Fort)	Highld	NM4470	56°45·3′	6°10·8′W	A	39,47
Dunbar	E Loth	NT6778	55°59·9′	2°31·3′W	T	67
Dunbar Common	E Loth	NT6469	55°55·0′	2°34·1′W	X	67
Dunbarney House	Pth & Kin	NO1118	56°21·0′	3°26·0′W	X	58
Dùn Beag	Highld	NG3338	57°21·5′	6°25·9′W	X	23,32
Dùn Beag	Highld	NG4668	57°38·1′	6°14·9′W	X	23
Dùn Beag	Highld	NG5719	57°12·1′	6°0·9′W	A	32
Dun Beag	Pth & Kin	NN9778	56°53·2′	3°41·0′W	H	43
Dùn Beag (Broch)	Highld	NG3338	57°21·5′	6°25·9′W	A	23,32
Dùn Beag (Fort)	Highld	NG4668	57°38·1′	6°14·9′W	A	23
Dunbeath	Highld	ND1629	58°14·8′	3°25·4′W	T	11,17
Dunbeath Bay	Highld	ND1629	58°14·8′	3°25·4′W	W	11,17
Dunbeath Castle	Highld	ND1528	58°14·2′	3°26·4′W	A	17
Dunbeath Mains	Highld	ND1528	58°14·2′	3°26·4′W	X	17
Dunbeath Water	Highld	ND0234	58°17·3′	3°39·8′W	W	11,17
Dunbeath Water	Highld	ND1331	58°15·8′	3°28·4′W	W	11,17
Dunbeg	Arg & Bt	NM8733	56°26·7′	5°26·9′W	T	49
Dunbeg	D & G	NX6089	55°10·8′	4°11·5′W	X	77
Dùn Beilbt	Highld	NG5604	57°4·0′	6°1·1′W	A	32,39
Dunbennan	Aberd	NJ5040	57°27·1′	2°49·5′W	X	29
Dunbennan Hill	Aberd	NJ4941	57°27·6′	2°50·5′W	H	28,29
Dunberry Hill	Hants	SU1119	50°58·4′	1°50·2′W	X	184
Dùn Bhar-a-chlaom	Arg & Bt	NR2261	55°46·0′	6°25·5′W	A	60
Dùn Bharpa	N Eil	NF6701	56°59·1′	7°28·5′W	X	31
Dùn Bharpa (Chambered Cairn)	N Eil	NF6701	56°59·1′	7°28·5′W	A	31
Dùn Bheolain	Arg & Bt	NR2068	55°49·7′	6°27·8′W	X	60
Dùn Bheolain (Fort)	Arg & Bt	NR2068	55°49·7′	6°27·8′W	A	60
Dùn Bhioramuill	Arg & Bt	NM4338	56°28·1′	6°9·9′W	X	47,48
Dùn Bhlaran	Arg & Bt	NM8224	56°21·7′	5°31·3′W	A	49
Dùn Bhoraraic	Arg & Bt	NR4165	55°48·8′	6°7·6′W	X	60,61
Dùn Bhoraraic (Broch)	Arg & Bt	NR4165	55°48·8′	6°7·6′W	A	60,61
Dùn Bhoraraig	Arg & Bt	NR1757	55°43·7′	6°30·0′W	A	60
Dùn Bhruichlinn	Arg & Bt	NR3663	55°47·5′	6°12·3′W	A	60,61
Dùn Bhuirg	Arg & Bt	NM4226	56°21·6′	6°10·2′W	A	48
Dùn Bhuirgh (Broch)	N Eil	NB4158	58°26·3′	6°25·8′W	A	8
Dùn Bilascleiter	N Eil	NB5657	58°26·3′	6°10·4′W	X	8
Dunblane	Stir	NN7801	56°11·4′	3°57·5′W	T	57
Dunbog	Fife	NO2817	56°20·6′	3°9·4′W	T	59
Dunbog Hill	Fife	NO2816	56°20·1′	3°9·4′W	H	59
Dun Bogs	N Yks	NZ8108	54°27·9′	0°44·6′W	X	94
Dùn Boreraig	Highld	NG1953	57°29·1′	6°40·9′W	T	23
Dùn Boreraig (Broch)	Highld	NG1953	57°29·1′	6°40·9′W	A	23
Dùn Borodale	Highld	NG5536	57°21·2′	6°3·9′W	A	24,32
Dùn Borrafiach	Highld	NG2363	57°34·6′	6°37·6′W	X	23
Dùn Borrafiach (Broch)	Highld	NG2363	57°34·6′	6°37·6′W	A	23
Dùn Borranish	N Eil	NB0533	58°11·5′	7°0·7′W	A	13
Dùn Borve	Highld	NG3452	57°29·1′	6°25·8′W	X	23
Dùn Borve	Highld	NG4547	57°26·8′	6°14·6′W	X	23
Dùn Borve	N Eil	NG0394	57°50·5′	6°59·8′W	A	18
Dùn Borve (Broch)	Highld	NG3452	57°29·1′	6°25·8′W	A	23
Dùn Borve (Broch)	Highld	NG4547	57°26·8′	6°14·6′W	A	23
Dunbrach	Stir	NS6183	56°1·4′	4°13·3′W	X	57,64
Dùn Breac	Arg & Bt	NM5330	56°24·1′	5°59·7′W	X	48
Dùn Breac (Fort)	Arg & Bt	NM5330	56°24·1′	5°59·7′W	A	48
Dunbridge	Hants	SU3126	51°2·2′	1°33·1′W	T	185
Dunbridge Fm	Heref	SO7136	52°1·5′	2°25·0′W	FM	149
Dùn Briste	N Eil	NL5480	56°47·2′	7°39·6′W	X	31
Dùn Briste (Fort)	N Eil	NL5480	56°47·2′	7°39·6′W	A	31
Dùn Buidhe	Arg & Bt	NR8089	56°2·9′	5°31·5′W	A	55
Dùn Buidhe	N Eil	NF7954	57°28·0′	7°20·8′W	A	22

Dunburgh	Norf	TM4091	52°28·1′	1°32·4′E	X	134
Dunburgh Hill	Norf	TM4091	52°28·1′	1°32·4′E	X	134
Dun Burn	Highld	ND0826	58°13·1′	3°33·5′W	W	17
Dunbury	Dorset	ST8103	50°49·8′	2°15·8′W	X	194
Dunbury Fm	Kent	TQ7946	51°11·3′	0°34·1′E	FM	188
Dunbuy	Aberd	NK1137	57°25·6′	1°48·6′W	X	30
Dùn Caan	Highld	NG5739	57°22·9′	6°2·1′W	H	24,32
Duncan Down	Kent	TR1065	51°20·9′	1°1·3′E	X	179
Duncan Gill	S Lanak	NT0026	55°31·3′	3°34·6′W	W	72
Duncangill Head	S Lanak	NT0025	55°30·8′	3°34·6′W	H	72
Duncan Gray's Burn	Aberd	NO0287	56°58·1′	3°36·3′W	W	43
Duncanhaugh	Scot Bord	NT8127	55°32·4′	2°17·6′W	X	74
Duncan Ho	N Yks	SE3890	54°18·5′	1°24·5′W	X	99
Duncanlaw	E Loth	NT5468	55°54·4′	2°43·7′W	X	66
Dùn Canna	Highld	NC1100	57°57·2′	5°11·2′W	X	15
Dùn Canna (Fort)	Highld	NC1100	57°57·2′	5°11·2′W	A	15
Duncannon	Devon	SX8457	50°24·3′	3°37·6′W	X	202
Duncansby Head	Highld	ND4073	58°38·7′	3°1·5′W	X	7,12
Duncansclett	Shetld	HU3630	60°3·5′	1°20·7′W	T	4
Duncan's Fm	Norf	TF5516	52°43·4′	0°18·1′E	FM	131
Duncan's Fm	W Susx	TQ1125	51°1·0′	0°24·7′W	FM	187,198
Duncan's Geo	Orkney	ND2887	58°46·1′	3°14·2′W	X	7
Duncan's Hill	Highld	ND1367	58°35·2′	3°29·3′W	H	11,12
Duncan Sike	D & G	NY4089	55°11·7′	2°56·1′W	W	79
Duncan's Plantn	E Loth	NT5084	56°3·0′	2°47·7′W	F	66
Duncanston	Highld	NH5856	57°34·6′	4°22·0′W	T	26
Duncanstone	Aberd	NJ5726	57°19·6′	2°42·4′W	T	37
Duncanstown	Aberd	NJ5236	57°25·0′	2°47·5′W	X	29
Duncan Wood	Notts	SK6171	53°14·2′	1°4·8′W	F	120
Duncanziemere	E Ayr	NS6121	55°28·0′	4°11·5′W	X	71
Duncarnock Fm	E Renf	NS5055	55°46·2′	4°23·0′W	FM	64
Dunces Arch	Hants	SU3108	50°52·5′	1°33·2′W	X	196
Dunces Hos	Northum	NZ2185	55°9·8′	1°39·8′W	X	81
Dùn Challain	Highld	NM6460	56°40·6′	5°50·7′W	A	40
Dùn Channa	Highld	NG2004	57°2·8′	6°36·6′W	X	39
Dùn Channa (Fort)	Highld	NG2004	57°2·8′	6°36·6′W	A	39
Dùn Chathach	Arg & Bt	NM9633	56°27·0′	5°18·2′W	A	49
Dunchea	Highld	NH5827	57°19·0′	4°21·0′W	X	26,35
Dùn Cheapasaidh Mór	Arg & Bt	NR3866	55°49·2′	6°10·5′W	A	60,61
Dunch Hill	Wilts	SU2148	51°14·1′	1°41·6′W	H	184
Dunch Hill Plantation	Wilts	SU2048	51°14·1′	1°42·4′W	F	184
Dunchideock	Devon	SX8787	50°40·5′	3°35·6′W	T	192
Dùn Chlach	Highld	NG2245	57°24·9′	6°37·3′W	X	23
Dùn Chlif	N Eil	NF6805	57°1·3′	7°27·8′W	A	31
Dùn Choinichean	Arg & Bt	NM4443	56°30·8′	6°9·2′W	A	47,48
Duncholgan	Arg & Bt	NR8785	56°0·9′	5°24·6′W	X	55
Dùn Cholla	Arg & Bt	NR3791	56°2·6′	6°12·9′W	A	61
Dùn Chollapus	Arg & Bt	NR3567	55°49·7′	6°13·5′W	A	60,61
Dùn Chonaill	N Eil	NB2615	58°2·6′	6°38·1′W	H	13,14
Dùn Chonnuill	Arg & Bt	NM6812	56°14·9′	5°44·2′W	X	55
Dùn Chonnuill (Castle)	Arg & Bt	NM6812	56°14·9′	5°44·2′W	A	55
Dunchraigaig	Arg & Bt	NR8396	56°6·7′	5°29·0′W	X	55
Dùn Chroisprig	Arg & Bt	NR2061	55°45·9′	6°27·4′W	A	60
Dunchurch	Warw	SP4871	52°20·3′	1°17·3′W	T	140
Dunchurch Lodge	Warw	SP4871	52°20·3′	1°17·3′W	X	140
Dunchurch Lodge Stud	Cambs	TL6561	52°13·6′	0°25·4′E	X	154
Duncle Ho	Somer	ST1625	51°1·3′	3°11·5′W	X	181,193
Dunclent Fm	Worcs	SO8675	52°22·6′	2°11·9′W	FM	139
Duncliffe Hill	Dorset	ST8222	51°0·1′	2°15·0′W	H	183
Duncliffe Wood	Dorset	ST8222	51°0·1′	2°15·0′W	F	183
Dun Coillich	Pth & Kin	NN7653	56°39·4′	4°0·9′W	H	42,51,52
Dùn Coire Falaich	Highld	NG4353	57°29·9′	6°16·9′W	X	23
Dùn Colbost	Highld	NG2049	57°27·0′	6°39·6′W	T	23
Dùn Colbost (Broch)	Highld	NG2049	57°27·0′	6°39·6′W	A	23
Duncolm	W Dunb	NS4777	55°58·0′	4°26·6′W	H	64
Duncombe	Hants	SU5618	50°57·8′	1°11·8′W	X	185
Duncombe	Lancs	SD5039	53°50·9′	2°45·2′W	T	102
Duncombe Cross	Devon	SX7543	50°16·7′	3°44·9′W	X	202
Duncombe Fm	Bucks	SP9614	51°49·2′	0°36·0′W	FM	165
Duncombe Fm	Hants	SU6721	50°59·3′	1°2·3′W	FM	185
Duncombe Fm	York	SE6361	54°2·7′	1°1·9′W	FM	100
Duncombe Ho	Glos	SP1727	51°56·7′	1°44·8′W	X	163
Duncombe Moor	Durham	NZ3844	54°47·6′	1°24·1′W	X	88
Duncombe Park	N Yks	SE6083	54°14·6′	1°4·3′W	X	100
Duncombe Wood	Bucks	SP9131	51°58·4′	0°40·1′W	F	152,165
Duncombe Wood	York	SE6362	54°3·2′	1°1·8′W	F	100
Dun Connavern	Highld	NG5062	57°35·0′	6°10·5′W	A	23,24
Dunconnel Hill	Renf	NS3259	55°48·0′	4°40·4′W	X	63
Duncorn Hill	Bath & NE Somer	ST7160	51°20·5′	2°24·6′W	H	172
Dùn Corrach	Arg & Bt	NM9308	56°13·4′	5°19·9′W	H	55
Dùn Còrr-bhile	Arg & Bt	NN1010	56°14·9′	5°3·6′W	H	50,56
Dùn Corr Mòr	N Eil	NG1994	57°51·1′	6°43·7′W	X	14
Duncote	Northnts	SP6750	52°8·9′	1°0·9′W	T	152
Duncote Fm	Shrops	SJ5711	52°41·9′	2°37·8′W	FM	126
Duncow	D & G	NX9683	55°8·1′	3°37·5′W	T	78
Duncow Burn	D & G	NX9587	55°10·2′	3°38·5′W	W	78
Duncow Common	D & G	NX9686	55°9·7′	3°37·5′W	X	78
Duncowfold	Cumbr	NY4851	54°51·3′	2°48·2′W	X	86
Duncow Ho	D & G	NX9783	55°8·1′	3°36·5′W	X	78
Dun Cow's Grove	Staffs	SK0466	53°11·7′	1°56·0′W	X	119
Dùn Cragach	Arg & Bt	NR7168	55°51·3′	5°39·1′W	A	62
Duncraggan	Stir	NN5306	56°13·7′	4°21·8′W	X	57
Duncrahill	E Loth	NT4565	55°52·8′	2°52·3′W	X	66
Duncraig Castle College	Highld	NG8133	57°20·4′	5°37·9′W	X	24
Dùn Creich	Highld	NH6588	57°51·9′	4°16·1′W	A	21
Dùn Creich (Fort)	Highld	NH6588	57°51·9′	4°16·1′W	A	21
Duncrievie	Pth & Kin	NO1309	56°16·2′	3°23·8′W	T	58
Duncroft Fm	Hants	SU4759	51°19·9′	1°19·1′W	FM	174
Duncroisk	Stir	NN5236	56°29·8′	4°23·8′W	X	51
Dun Cross	Devon	SX7761	50°26·4′	3°43·6′W	X	202
Duncrub	Pth & Kin	NO0014	56°18·7′	3°36·5′W	X	58
Dùn Cruinn	Highld	NG4151	57°28·8′	6°18·8′W	X	23
Dùn Cruinn (Fort)	Highld	NG4151	57°28·8′	6°18·8′W	A	23
Dùn Crutagain	Arg & Bt	NM7813	56°15·7′	5°34·6′W	H	55
Duncryne	W Dunb	NS4386	56°2·7′	4°30·8′W	H	56
Duncton	W Susx	SU9517	50°56·9′	0°38·5′W	T	197
Duncton Common	W Susx	SU9518	50°57·4′	0°38·5′W	F	197
Duncton Down	W Susx	SU9515	50°55·8′	0°38·5′W	X	197
Duncton Mill	W Susx	SU9616	50°56·4′	0°37·6′W	X	197

Duncuan Island	Arg & Bt	NR8685	56°0·9'	5°25·6'W	X	55
Dùn Cuier	N Eil	NF6603	57°0·1'	7°29·6'W	A	31
Dùn Cuilein	Arg & Bt	NM8240	56°30·4'	5°32·1'W	A	49
Dundaff Hill	Stir	NS7384	56°2·2'	4°1·9'W	H	57,64
Dùn da Ghaoithe	Arg & Bt	NM6736	56°27·8'	5°46·5'W	H	49
Dun-da-Lamh	Highld	NN5892	57°0·1'	4°19·8'W	H	35
Dun-da-lamh (fort)	Highld	NN5892	57°0·1'	4°19·8'W	A	35
Dundale Beck Fm	N Yks	NZ5908	54°28·1'	1°5·0'W	FM	93
Dundale Fm	Kent	TQ6338	51°7·3'	0°20·1'E	FM	188
Dundale Pond	N Yks	SE8291	54°18·7'	0°44·0'W	W	94,100
Dundarg Castle of Fort	Aberd	NJ8964	57°40·2'	2°10·6'W	A	30
Dundarrach	Arg & Bt	NS0275	55°55·9'	5°9·7'W	X	63
Dundas Aqueduct	Wilts	ST7862	51°21·6'	2°18·6'W	A	172
Dundas Castle	C of Edin	NT1176	55°58·4'	3°25·1'W	X	65
Dundas Fm	Kent	TR1143	51°9·1'	1°1·4'E	FM	179,189
Dundas Ho	Orkney	ND4485	58°45·2'	2°57·6'W	X	7
Dundas Loch	C of Edin	NT1176	55°58·4'	3°25·1'W	W	65
Dundas Mains	C of Edin	NT1177	55°58·9'	3°25·1'W	X	65
Dùn Davie	Highld	NH7139	57°25·6'	4°8·4'W	X	27
Dundavie	Highld	NH7139	57°25·6'	4°8·4'W	X	27
Dundavie	Pth & Kin	NN8761	56°43·9'	3°50·4'W	X	43
Dùn Davie (Fort)	Highld	NH7139	57°25·6'	4°8·4'W	A	27
Dùn Deardail	Highld	NN1270	56°47·3'	5°4·2'W	X	41
Dùn Deardail (Fort)	Highld	NN1270	56°47·3'	5°4·2'W	A	41
Dùn Dearduil	Highld	NH5223	57°16·7'	4°26·8'W	X	26,35
Dùn Dearduil (Forts)	Highld	NH5223	57°16·7'	4°26·8'W	A	26,35
Dùn Dearg	Arg & Bt	NR4146	55°38·6'	6°6·5'W	A	60
Dùn Dearg	Highld	NG5164	57°36·1'	6°9·6'W	X	23,24
Dùn Dearg (Fort)	Highld	NG5164	57°36·1'	6°9·6'W	A	23,24
Dundeasal	Highld	NH8947	57°30·2'	3°50·7'W	X	27
Dundee	Aberd	NJ6250	57°32·6'	2°37·6'W	X	29
Dundee	C of Dun	NO3632	56°28·3'	3°1·9'W	T	54
Dundee Law	C of Dun	NO3931	56°28·3'	2°59·0'W	H	54
Dunderave Castle	Arg & Bt	NN1409	56°14·5'	4°59·6'W	A	56
Dunderave Point	Arg & Bt	NN1409	56°14·5'	4°59·6'W	X	56
Dunderhole Point	Corn	SX0488	50°39·8'	4°46·0'W	X	200
Dundeugh	D & G	NX5987	55°9·7'	4°12·4'W	T	77
Dundeugh	D & G	NX6088	55°10·2'	4°11·5'W	X	77
Dundeugh Hill	D & G	NX6089	55°10·8'	4°11·5'W	H	77
Dùn Dhamh	Stir	NS4299	56°9·7'	4°32·2'W	X	56
Dùn Diarmaid (Broch)	Highld	NG3538	57°21·6'	6°23·9'W	A	23,32
Dundock Wood	Scot Bord	NT8239	55°38·9'	2°16·7'W	F	74
Dùn Dòmhnuill	Arg & Bt	NR3589	56°1·5'	6°14·7'W	A	61
Dundon	Somer	ST4732	51°5·3'	2°45·0'W	T	182
Dundonald	Fife	NT2194	56°8·2'	3°15·8'W	T	58
Dundonald	S Ayr	NS3634	55°34·6'	4°35·7'W	T	70
Dundonald Camp	N Ayr	NS3345	55°34·5'	4°38·5'W	X	70
Dundon Hayes	Somer	ST4632	51°5·3'	2°45·9'W	T	182
Dundon Hill	Somer	ST4832	51°5·3'	2°44·2'W	H	182
Dundonnachie	Pth & Kin	NO0041	56°33·3'	3°37·2'W	X	52,53
Dundonnell	Highld	NH0987	57°50·2'	5°12·6'W	T	19
Dundonnell Forest	Highld	NH1181	57°47·0'	5°10·3'W	X	19
Dundonnell Hotel	Highld	NH0888	57°50·7'	5°13·6'W	X	19
Dundonnell House	Highld	NH1185	57°49·1'	5°10·5'W	X	19
Dundonnell River	Highld	NH1284	57°48·6'	5°9·4'W	W	19
Dundonnie	Aberd	NK1341	57°27·8'	1°46·5'W	X	30
Dundoran	D & G	NY1298	55°16·4'	3°22·7'W	H	78
Dùn Dornaigil	Highld	NC4545	58°22·2'	4°38·5'W	X	9
Dun Dornaigil (Broch)	Highld	NC4545	58°22·2'	4°38·5'W	A	9
Dundornie	Pth & Kin	NN7632	56°28·1'	4°0·3'W	X	51,52
Dundraw	Cumbr	NY2149	54°50·0'	3°13·4'W	T	85
Dundream	D & G	NW9972	55°0·4'	5°8·2'W	X	76,82
Dundreggan	Highld	NH3214	57°11·4'	4°46·4'W	X	34
Dundreggan Forest	Highld	NH3217	57°13·0'	4°46·5'W	X	34
Dundreggan Lodge	Highld	NH3214	57°11·4'	4°46·4'W	X	34
Dundreich	Scot Bord	NT2749	55°44·0'	3°9·3'W	H	73
Dundrennan	D & G	NX7447	54°48·4'	3°57·2'W	T	83,84
Dundridge	Devon	SX7858	50°24·8'	3°42·7'W	X	202
Dundridge	Hants	SU5718	50°57·7'	1°10·9'W	T	185
Dundridge Manor	Bucks	SP9106	51°44·9'	0°40·5'W	X	165
Dundriven	Pth & Kin	NO2534	56°29·8'	3°12·6'W	X	53
Dundry	N Som	ST5566	51°23·7'	2°38·4'W	T	172,182
Dùn Dubh	Arg & Bt	NM8604	56°11·1'	5°26·5'W	H	55
Dùn Dubh	Arg & Bt	NR8885	56°0·9'	5°23·6'W	A	55
Dùn Dubh	Arg & Bt	NR8995	56°6·3'	5°23·1'W	H	55
Dùn Dubh	Highld	NG4466	57°36·9'	6°16·7'W	H	23
Dùn Dubh	N Ayr	NS0334	55°33·8'	5°7·0'W	X	69
Dùn Dubh	N Eil	NB5532	58°12·8'	6°9·8'W	X	8
Dùn Dubh	Pth & Kin	NN7219	56°21·0'	4°3·8'W	X	57
Dùn Dubhaich	Arg & Bt	NM8118	56°18·5'	5°32·0'W	H	55
Dunduff	D & G	NS8002	55°18·1'	3°53·0'W	H	78
Dunduff	D & G	NS8002	55°18·1'	3°53·0'W	X	78
Dunduff	Fife	NT0891	56°6·4'	3°28·3'W	X	58
Dunduff	Pth & Kin	NN8211	56°16·9'	3°53·9'W	T	57
Dunduff Castle	S Ayr	NS2716	55°24·7'	4°43·5'W	A	70
Dunduff Fm	S Ayr	NS2616	55°24·7'	4°44·5'W	FM	70
Dùn Dùgan	Highld	NG4746	57°26·3'	6°12·5'W	X	23
Dun Dulan	N Eil	NF7129	57°14·3'	7°26·8'W	A	22
Dundurcas Fm	Moray	NJ2950	57°32·3'	3°10·7'W	FM	28
Dundurn	Pth & Kin	NN6922	56°22·6'	4°6·8'W	X	51
Dundurn	Pth & Kin	NN7023	56°23·1'	4°5·9'W	A	51,52
Dundurn	Pth & Kin	NN7123	56°23·2'	4°4·9'W	X	51,52
Dundyvan	N Lanak	NS7264	55°51·4'	4°2·3'W	T	64
Dunearn	Fife	NT2187	56°4·4'	3°15·7'W	X	66
Dunearn	Highld	NH9341	57°27·1'	3°46·5'W	X	27
Dunearn Lodge	Highld	NH9439	57°26·0'	3°45·5'W	X	27
Duneaton Bridge	S Lanak	NS9124	55°30·1'	3°43·1'W	X	71,72
Duneaton Water	S Lanak	NS7622	55°28·8'	3°57·3'W	W	71
Duneaton Water	S Lanak	NS8722	55°29·0'	3°46·9'W	W	71,72
Duneaves	Pth & Kin	NN7446	56°35·6'	4°2·7'W	X	51,52
Dunecht	Aberd	NJ7509	57°10·5'	2°24·4'W	T	38
Dunecht Ho	Aberd	NJ7507	57°9·4'	2°24·3'W	X	38
Dunedin	Pth & Kin	NN9621	56°22·5'	3°40·6'W	X	52,53,58
Dùn Edinbane (Broch)	Highld	NG3550	57°28·0'	6°24·7'W	A	23
Dùn Eibhinn	Arg & Bt	NR3894	56°4·3'	6°12·2'W	A	61
Dùn Eigheach	Stir	NN3925	56°23·7'	4°36·1'W	X	50
Dùn Eistean	N Eil	NB5365	58°30·5'	6°14·0'W	X	8
Dun Ela	Highld	NG6405	57°4·8'	5°53·2'W	A	32
Dùn Eòrodail	N Eil	NB5463	58°29·4'	6°12·8'W	X	8
Dunesslin	D & G	NX8383	55°7·9'	3°49·7'W	X	78
Dunesslin Moor	D & G	NX8282	55°7·4'	3°50·6'W	X	78
Dùn Eyre	Highld	NG4253	57°29·9'	6°17·9'W	X	23
Dùn Eyre (Fort)	Highld	NG4253	57°29·9'	6°17·9'W	A	23
Dùn Fadaidh	Arg & Bt	NM7712	56°15·2'	5°35·6'W	A	55
Dunfallandy	Pth & Kin	NN9456	56°41·3'	3°43·4'W	X	52,53
Dunfallandy Hill	Pth & Kin	NN9355	56°40·7'	3°44·3'W	X	52
Dunfallandy Ho	Pth & Kin	NN9456	56°41·3'	3°43·4'W	X	52,53
Dunfallandy Stone	Pth & Kin	NN9456	56°41·3'	3°43·4'W	X	52,53
Dunfallandy Stone	Pth & Kin	NN9456	56°41·3'	3°43·4'W	X	52,53
Dùn Feorlig	Highld	NG2942	57°23·5'	6°30·2'W	X	23
Dùn Feorlig (Broch)	Highld	NG2942	57°23·5'	6°30·2'W	A	23
Dunfer Hole	Norf	TF9516	52°42·6'	0°53·6'E	X	132
Dunfermline	Fife	NT1087	56°4·3'	3°26·3'W	T	65
Dùn Fhamhair (Fort)	Highld	NH4847	57°29·5'	4°31·7'W	A	26
Dun Fhinn	Arg & Bt	NR4451	55°41·4'	6°4·0'W	A	60
Dùn Fiadhairt	Highld	NG2350	57°27·6'	6°36·7'W	X	23
Dùn Fiadhairt (Broch)	Highld	NG2350	57°27·6'	6°36·7'W	A	23
Dunfield	Glos	SU1497	51°40·5'	1°47·5'W	T	163
Dunfield	Heref	SO2758	52°13·2'	3°3·7'W	X	148
Dùn Fionn	N Ayr	NS0433	55°33·3'	5°6·0'W	X	69
Dùn Fionn (Fort)	Highld	NH4742	57°26·8'	4°32·5'W	A	26
Dùn Fionn (Fort)	N Ayr	NS0433	55°33·3'	5°6·0'W	A	69
Dùn Flashader	Highld	NG3553	57°29·6'	6°24·9'W	X	23
Dùn Flashader (Broch)	Highld	NG3553	57°29·6'	6°24·9'W	A	23
Dunford	Norf	TL9191	52°29·2'	0°49·2'E	X	144
Dunford Br	Surrey	TQ0161	51°20·6'	0°32·6'W	X	176,186
Dunford Bridge	Barns	SE1502	53°31·1'	1°46·0'W	T	110
Dunford Ho	Leeds	SE4026	53°44·0'	1°23·2'W	X	105
Dunford Ho	W Susx	SU8819	50°58·0'	0°44·4'W	X	197
Dunford's Fm	Somer	ST6648	51°14·0'	2°28·8'W	FM	183
Dunfuinary	Arg & Bt	NM9234	56°27·4'	5°22·1'W	X	49
Dùn Gainmhich	N Eil	NF7955	57°28·6'	7°20·9'W	T	22
Dungairy Knowe	D & G	NY2388	55°11·1'	3°12·1'W	X	79
Dungalston	D & G	NX7690	55°11·6'	3°56·4'W	X	78
Dùn Garbh	Highld	NH5324	57°17·2'	4°25·9'W	H	26,35
Dùn Garbhlaich (Fort)	Highld	NH4646	57°29·0'	4°33·7'W	A	26
Dungarry	D & G	NX7553	54°51·6'	3°56·4'W	H	84
Dungarry (Fort)	D & G	NX7553	54°51·6'	3°56·4'W	A	84
Dùn Garsin	Highld	NG3638	57°21·6'	6°22·9'W	X	23,32
Dùn Garsin (Broch)	Highld	NG3638	57°21·6'	6°22·9'W	A	23,32
Dungarthill	Pth & Kin	NO0541	56°33·3'	3°32·3'W	X	52,53
Dungate	Kent	TQ9159	51°18·1'	0°44·8'E	X	178
Dungate Fm	Cambs	TL5653	52°9·4'	0°17·2'E	FM	154
Dungate Fm	Surrey	SU9932	51°5·0'	0°34·8'W	FM	186
Dungate's Fm	Surrey	TQ2250	51°14·4'	0°14·7'W	FM	187
Dungaval Training Centre	S Lanak	NS6537	55°36·7'	4°8·2'W	X	71
Dungavel Hill	S Lanak	NS6735	55°35·7'	4°6·2'W	H	71
Dungavel Hill	S Lanak	NS9430	55°33·4'	3°40·4'W	H	71,72
Dunge	Wilts	ST8954	51°17·3'	2°9·1'W	T	184
Dùn Gearymore	Highld	NG2364	57°35·1'	6°37·6'W	X	23
Dùn Gearymore (Broch)	Highld	NG2364	57°35·1'	6°37·6'W	A	23
Dunge Brook	Derby	SK2180	53°19·2'	1°40·7'W	W	110
Dungee Barn	Northnts	SP9259	52°13·5'	0°38·8'W	X	152
Dungee Fm	Beds	SP9358	52°13·0'	0°37·9'W	FM	153
Dungee Wood	Beds	SP9359	52°13·5'	0°37·9'W	F	153
Dunge Fm	Ches	SJ9877	53°17·6'	2°1·4'W	FM	118
Dungehill Fm	Leic	SK6223	52°48·3'	1°4·4'W	FM	129
Dungeness	Kent	TR0916	50°54·6'	0°58·8'E	T	189
Dungeon Banks	Ches	SJ4580	53°19·1'	2°49·1'W	X	108
Dungeon Fm	Somer	ST5843	51°11·3'	2°35·7'W	FM	182,183
Dungeon Ghyll Force	Cumbr	NY2806	54°26·9'	3°6·2'W	W	89,90
Dungeon Hill	D & G	NX4685	55°8·4'	4°24·5'W	H	77
Dungeon Hill	Dorset	ST6907	50°51·9'	2°26·0'W	H	194
Dungeon Hill (Fort)	Dorset	ST6907	50°51·9'	2°26·0'W	A	194
Dungeon Lane Fm	Leeds	SE3426	53°44·0'	1°28·7'W	FM	104
Dungeons Fm	Devon	ST0404	50°49·9'	3°21·4'W	FM	192
Dungeon, The	Wirral	SJ2583	53°20·6'	3°7·2'W	F	108
Dùn Gerashader	Highld	NG4845	57°25·8'	6°11·4'W	X	23
Dun Gerashader (Fort)	Highld	NG4845	57°25·8'	6°11·4'W	A	23
Dunge, The	Shrops	SJ6800	52°36·0'	2°27·9'W	X	127
Dungewood Fm	I of W	SZ4680	50°37·3'	1°20·6'W	FM	196
Dùn Ghallain	Arg & Bt	NR3593	56°3·6'	6°15·0'W	A	61
Dùn Ghallain	Arg & Bt	NM6560	56°40·6'	5°49·7'W	A	40
Dùn Glas	Arg & Bt	NM7906	56°12·0'	5°33·3'W	A	55
Dùn Glas	Highld	ND0517	58°8·2'	3°36·3'W	X	17
Dùn Glas an Loin Ghuirm	Arg & Bt	NR2260	55°45·5'	6°25·4'W	A	60
Dunglass	Arg & Bt	NR7009	55°19·5'	5°37·1'W	X	68
Dunglass	E Loth	NT7671	55°56·1'	2°22·6'W	X	67
Dunglass	Highld	NH5354	57°33·4'	4°27·0'W	X	26
Dunglass	Stir	NS5778	55°58·7'	4°17·1'W	H	64
Dunglass Burn	Scot Bord	NT7671	55°56·1'	2°22·6'W	W	67
Dunglass Burn	Scot Bord	NT7671	55°56·1'	2°22·6'W	W	67
Dunglass Church	E Loth	NT7671	55°56·1'	2°22·6'W	A	67
Dunglass Common	Scot Bord	NT7466	55°53·4'	2°24·5'W	X	67
Dunglass Mains	E Loth	NT7672	55°56·7'	2°22·6'W	X	67
Dunglass Wood	Scot Bord	NT8241	55°40·0'	2°16·7'W	F	74
Dungoil	Stir	NS6384	56°2·0'	4°11·5'W	H	57,64
Dungrain Law	S Lanak	NS9112	55°23·6'	3°42·8'W	H	71,78
Dungrianach	Highld	NH5049	57°30·6'	4°29·8'W	X	26
Dùn Grianan	Highld	NG5065	57°36·6'	6°10·7'W	X	23,24
Dùn Grianan	Highld	NG5259	57°33·4'	6°8·3'W	X	23,24
Dùn Grianan (Broch)	Highld	NG5065	57°36·6'	6°10·7'W	A	23,24
Dùn Grianan (Fort)	Highld	NG5259	57°33·4'	6°8·3'W	A	23,24
Dungrove Fm	Bucks	SP9601	51°42·2'	0°36·3'W	FM	165
Dungrove Hill	Dorset	ST9114	50°55·8'	2°7·3'W	X	195
Dùn Grugaig	Highld	NG5312	57°8·2'	6°4·5'W	A	32
Dùn Grugaig	Highld	NG8515	57°10·8'	5°33·0'W	A	33
Dùn Guaidhre	Arg & Bt	NR3864	55°48·2'	6°10·4'W	X	60,61
Dùn Guaidhre (Fort)	Arg & Bt	NR3864	55°48·2'	6°10·4'W	A	60,61
Dunguile Hill	D & G	NX7757	54°53·8'	3°54·7'W	H	84
Dungworth	Sheff	SK2889	53°24·1'	1°34·3'W	T	110
Dungy Head	Dorset	SY8180	50°37·4'	2°15·7'W	X	194
Dùn Hallin	Highld	NG2559	57°32·5'	6°35·3'W	X	23
Dùn Hallin (Broch)	Highld	NG2559	57°32·5'	6°35·3'W	A	23
Dunham Heath	Ches	SJ4871	53°14·3'	2°46·3'W	X	117
Dunham Hill	Norf	TF9824	52°46·9'	0°56·6'E	X	132
Dunham Lodge	Norf	TF8712	52°40·6'	0°46·4'E	X	132
Dunham Massey Hall	Traf	SJ7387	53°23·0'	2°23·9'W	A	109
Dunham on Trent	Notts	SK8174	53°15·6'	0°46·7'W	T	121
Dunham Park	Traf	SJ7487	53°23·0'	2°23·0'W	X	109
Dunhampstead	Worcs	SO9160	52°14·5'	2°7·5'W	T	150
Dunhampton	Worcs	SO8466	52°17·8'	2°13·7'W	T	138,150
Dunhampton Fm	Heref	SO5860	52°14·4'	2°36·5'W	FM	137,138,149
Dunham Rack	Lincs	SK8275	53°16·2'	0°45·8'W	W	121
Dunham Town	Traf	SJ7487	53°23·0'	2°23·0'W	T	109
Dunham Woodhouses	Traf	SJ7288	53°23·5'	2°24·9'W	T	109
Dùn Hanais	Arg & Bt	NL9345	56°30·1'	6°58·9'W	A	46
Dunharberry	D & G	NX5767	54°58·9'	4°13·7'W	X	83
Dunhazles	N Yks	SD8155	53°59·7'	2°17·0'W	X	103
Dùn Heanish	Arg & Bt	NM0343	56°29·4'	6°49·1'W	A	46
Dun Hill	Derby	SE0704	53°32·2'	1°53·3'W	X	110
Dun Hill	D & G	NS5903	55°18·3'	4°12·8'W	H	77
Dun Hill	Northum	NY7255	54°53·6'	2°25·8'W	X	86,87
Dun Hill Moss	D & G	NS5804	55°18·8'	4°13·8'W	X	77
Dun Hillocks	Angus	NO2175	56°51·8'	3°17·3'W	H	44
Dunholme	Lincs	TF0279	53°18·1'	0°27·8'W	T	121
Dunholme Grange	N Yks	SE4463	54°3·9'	1°19·2'W	X	99
Dunholme Lodge	Lincs	TF0078	53°17·6'	0°29·6'W	X	121
Dunhope Burn	Scot Bord	NT2712	55°24·0'	3°8·7'W	W	79
Dunhope Law	Scot Bord	NT2611	55°23·5'	3°9·7'W	H	79
Dunhope Rig	Scot Bord	NT2611	55°23·5'	3°9·7'W	X	79
Dunhope Sike	Scot Bord	NT2711	55°23·5'	3°8·7'W	W	79
Dunhum-On-The-Hill	Ches	SJ4772	53°14·8'	2°47·2'W	T	117
Dunhurst (Sch)	Hants	SU7424	51°0·9'	0°56·3'W	X	197
Dùn I	Arg & Bt	NM2825	56°20·6'	6°23·7'W	H	48
Dùn Iadain	Arg & Bt	NM9124	56°22·0'	5°22·6'W	X	49
Dùn Iadain (Fort)	Arg & Bt	NM9124	56°22·0'	5°22·6'W	A	49
Dùn Ibrig	Arg & Bt	NM0244	56°29·9'	6°50·1'W	A	46
Dunie	Pth & Kin	NN9129	56°26·7'	3°45·6'W	X	52,58
Dunie Burn	Pth & Kin	NN9131	56°27·8'	3°45·7'W	W	52
Duniehinnie	D & G	NX0742	54°44·4'	4°59·5'W	X	82
Duniface	Fife	NO3501	56°12·1'	3°2·4'W	X	59
Duni Fm	Glos	SO7616	51°50·8'	2°20·5'W	FM	162
Dunimarle Castle	Fife	NS9785	56°3·1'	3°38·8'W	X	65
Dunino	Fife	NO5311	56°17·6'	2°45·1'W	T	59
Dunino Burn	Fife	NO5309	56°16·5'	2°45·1'W	W	59
Dunino Law	Fife	NO5411	56°17·6'	2°44·1'W	X	59
Dunion Hill	Scot Bord	NT6218	55°27·5'	2°35·6'W	H	80
Dunipace	Falk	NS8083	56°1·7'	3°55·1'W	T	57,65
Dunira	Pth & Kin	NN7323	56°23·2'	4°3·0'W	T	51,52
Dùn Isagain	Arg & Bt	NM3740	56°29·0'	6°15·9'W	X	47,48
Dunjarg	D & G	NX7865	54°58·1'	3°53·9'W	X	84
Dunjop	D & G	NX7160	54°55·3'	4°0·3'W	X	83,84
Dun Kearstack	Highld	NG5917	57°11·1'	5°58·8'W	A	32
Dunkeld	Pth & Kin	NO0242	56°33·8'	3°35·2'W	T	52,53
Dunkeld End	E Yorks	SE9645	53°53·8'	0°31·9'W	X	106
Dunkenhalgh (Hotel)	Lancs	SD7330	53°46·3'	2°24·2'W	X	103
Dunkenhill Fm	E Yorks	SE9741	53°51·6'	0°31·1'W	FM	106
Dunkenny	Angus	NO3547	56°36·9'	3°3·1'W	T	54
Dunkenshaw	Lancs	SD5755	53°59·6'	2°38·9'W	X	102
Dunkenshaw Fell	Lancs	SD5857	54°0·7'	2°38·0'W	X	102
Dunkerton	Bath & NE					
	Somer	ST7159	51°20·0'	2°24·6'W	T	172
Dunkery Beacon	Somer	SS8941	51°9·7'	3°34·9'W	H	181
Dunkery Gate	Somer	SS8940	51°9·1'	3°34·8'W	X	181
Dunkery Hill	Somer	SS9042	51°10·2'	3°34·0'W	H	181
Dunkessen	Stir	NS6285	56°2·5'	4°12·5'W	X	57
Dunkeswell	Devon	ST1407	50°51·6'	3°12·9'W	T	192,193
Dunkeswell Abbey	Devon	ST1410	50°53·2'	3°13·0'W	A	192,193
Dunkeswell Turbury	Devon	ST1305	50°50·5'	3°13·8'W	X	192,193
Dunkeswell Turbury (Row Barrow)	Devon	ST1305	50°50·5'	3°13·8'W	A	192,193
Dunkeswick	N Yks	SE3046	53°54·8'	1°32·2'W	T	104
Dunkeswick Lodge	N Yks	SE2948	53°55·9'	1°33·1'W	X	104
Dunkeswick Moor	N Yks	SE3047	53°55·3'	1°32·2'W	X	104
Dunkin's Copse	W Berks	SU3570	51°25·9'	1°29·4'W	F	174
Dunkinty	Moray	NJ2361	57°38·2'	3°16·9'W	X	28
Dunkirk	Cald	SE1028	53°45·1'	1°50·5'W	X	104
Dunkirk	Cambs	TL5186	52°27·3'	0°13·7'E	T	143
Dunkirk	Ches	SJ3872	53°14·7'	2°55·3'W	T	117
Dunkirk	C of Nott	SK5538	52°56·4'	1°10·5'W	T	129
Dunkirk	Essex	TL7031	51°57·3'	0°28·8'E	X	167
Dunkirk	Kent	TR0759	51°17·8'	0°58·5'E	T	179
Dunkirk	Lancs	SD7633	53°47·8'	2°21·4'W	X	103
Dunkirk	Norf	TG2027	52°48·0'	1°16·2'E	T	133,134
Dunkirk	Northum	NY9270	55°1·7'	2°7·1'W	X	87
Dunkirk	N Yks	SE1550	53°57·0'	1°45·9'W	X	104
Dunkirk	S Glos	ST7886	51°34·6'	2°18·7'W	T	172
Dunkirk	Staffs	SJ8152	53°4·1'	2°16·6'W	T	118
Dunkirk	Wilts	ST9961	51°21·1'	2°0·5'W	T	173
Dunkirk Fm	Ches	SJ7666	53°11·7'	2°21·2'W	FM	118
Dunkirk Fm	Ghead	NZ2757	54°54·7'	1°34·3'W	FM	88
Dunkirk Fm	N Lincs	TA0714	53°36·9'	0°22·5'W	FM	112
Dunkirk Fm	S Glos	ST7986	51°34·6'	2°17·8'W	FM	172
Dunkirk Park	Pth & Kin	NO1218	56°21·0'	3°25·0'W	X	58
Dunkitterick Cott	D & G	NX5071	55°0·9'	4°20·3'W	X	77
Dunkleys Fm	Warw	SP4872	52°20·9'	1°17·3'W	FM	140
Dun Knowe	Scot Bord	NT3517	55°26·8'	3°1·2'W	H	79
Dun Knowe	Scot Bord	NT6203	55°19·4'	2°35·5'W	X	80
Dunk's Green	Kent	TQ6152	51°14·9'	0°18·8'E	T	188
Dunks, The	Wrex	SJ3450	53°2·8'	2°58·7'W	T	117
Dùn Laeghan	Arg & Bt	NN3747	56°35·5'	4°38·8'W	X	50
Dùn Laigaidh	Highld	NH1491	57°52·5'	5°7·7'W	A	20
Dunlappie	Angus	NO5867	56°47·8'	2°40·8'W	X	44
Dun Law	Scot Bord	NT1725	55°31·0'	3°18·4'W	H	72
Dun Law	Scot Bord	NT3748	55°43·5'	2°59·7'W	X	73
Dun Law	Scot Bord	NT4657	55°48·4'	2°51·3'W	X	66,73
Dun Law	S Lanak	NS9113	55°24·2'	3°42·8'W	H	71,78
Dun Law	S Lanak	NT0125	55°30·8'	3°33·6'W	H	72
Dun Law	S Lanak	NT0217	55°26·5'	3°32·5'W	H	78
Dùn Leacainn	Arg & Bt	NN0301	56°9·9'	5°9·9'W	H	55
Dunlea Fm	Staffs	SK0257	53°6·8'	1°57·8'W	FM	119
Dùn Leathan	Arg & Bt	NM4055	56°37·1'	6°13·8'W	X	47
Dunlee Hill	Scot Bord	NT4142	55°40·3'	2°55·8'W	H	73
Dunlee Hill	Scot Bord	NT4438	55°38·2'	2°52·9'W	H	73
Dunley	Hants	SU4553	51°16·7'	1°20·9'W	T	185
Dunley	Worcs	SO7869	52°19·4'	2°19·0'W	T	138
Dunley Hill Fm	Surrey	TQ1150	51°14·5'	0°24·2'W	FM	187
Dunley Ho	Devon	SX8378	50°35·6'	3°38·8'W	X	191
Dunley Wood	Wilts	ST8581	51°31·9'	2°12·6'W	F	173

Dun Liath	Highld	NG3570	57°38·8′	6°26·0′W	A	23
Dùn Liath	Highld	NG5414	57°9·3′	6°3·6′W	A	32
Dunlichity Lodge	Highld	NH6532	57°21·8′	4°14·2′W	X	26
Dunlop	E Ayr	NS4049	55°42·7′	4°32·4′W	T	64
Dunlop Ho	E Ayr	NS4249	55°42·8′	4°30·5′W	X	64
Dunloskin	Arg & Bt	NS1678	55°57·8′	4°56·4′W	X	63
Dunlossit Ho	Arg & Bt	NR4368	55°50·5′	6°5·9′W	X	60,61
Dun Low	Staffs	SK1149	53°2·5′	1°49·8′W	A	119
Dunlugas Ho	Aberd	NJ6955	57°35·3′	2°30·7′W	X	29
Dunmaglass	Highld	NH3840	57°25·6′	4°41·4′W	X	26
Dunmaglass Lodge	Highld	NH5922	57°16·3′	4°19·8′W	X	26,35
Dunmaglass Mains	Highld	NH6023	57°16·8′	4°18·9′W	X	26,35
Dunmail Raise	Cumbr	NY3211	54°29·6′	3°2·6′W	X	90
Dunman	D & G	NX0933	54°39·6′	4°57·3′W	X	82
Dunman (Fort)	D & G	NX0933	54°39·6′	4°57·3′W	A	82
Dùn Mara	N Eil	NB4963	58°29·2′	6°17·9′W	A	8
Dun Maraig	Highld	NG3759	57°32·9′	6°23·3′W	X	23
Dun Maraig (Fort)	Highld	NG3759	57°32·9′	6°23·3′W	A	23
Dunmay	Pth & Kin	NO1466	56°46·9′	3°24·0′W	X	43
Dùn Meodhonach	Arg & Bt	NR3594	56°4·2′	6°15·0′W	A	61
Dunmere	Corn	SX0467	50°28·4′	4°45·4′W	T	200
Dunmere Wood	Corn	SX0468	50°29·0′	4°45·4′W	F	200
Dùn Merkadale	Highld	NG3930	57°17·4′	6°19·5′W	A	32
Dùn Mhadaidh	Arg & Bt	NM3952	56°35·5′	6°14·6′W	A	47
Dùn Mhic Laitheann	N Eil	NF9773	57°39·0′	7°4·3′W	A	18
Dùn Mhic Leòid	N Eil	NL6499	56°57·9′	7°31·3′W	X	31
Dùn Mhic Raonuill	Arg & Bt	NM8123	56°21·2′	5°32·2′W	A	49
Dùn Mhuilig	Arg & Bt	NM7701	56°9·2′	5°35·0′W	A	55
Dun Mhuirageul	Arg & Bt	NN0130	56°25·5′	5°13·2′W	A	50
Dùn Mhuirich	Arg & Bt	NR7284	55°59·9′	5°39·0′W	A	55
Dùn Mhurchaidh	Highld	NM5370	56°45·6′	6°2·0′W	X	39,47
Dùn Mingulay	N Eil	NL5482	56°48·3′	7°39·7′W	X	31
Dunmoor Burn	Northum	NT9518	55°27·6′	2°4·3′W	W	81
Dunmoor Hill	Northum	NT9618	55°27·6′	2°3·4′W	H	81
Dùn Mór	Arg & Bt	NM0449	56°32·6′	6°48·5′W	X	46
Dùn Mór	Arg & Bt	NM4640	56°29·3′	6°7·1′W	X	47,48
Dùn Mór	Arg & Bt	NM7417	56°17·8′	5°38·7′W	H	55
Dùn Mór	Arg & Bt	NM8340	56°30·4′	5°31·1′W	A	49
Dun Mor	Arg & Bt	NN0132	56°26·6′	5°13·3′W	A	50
Dùn Mór	Arg & Bt	NR7184	55°59·9′	5°39·9′W	X	55
Dùn Mór	Arg & Bt	NR8497	56°7·3′	5°28·1′W	A	55
Dun Mór	Arg & Bt	NS0480	55°58·6′	5°8·0′W	H	63
Dùn Mór	Arg & Bt	NS2199	56°9·3′	4°52·5′W	X	56
Dùn Mór	Highld	NG3339	57°22·1′	6°26·0′W	X	23,32
Dùn Mór	Highld	NG4568	57°38·1′	6°15·9′W	H	23
Dun Mor	Highld	NH5147	57°29·6′	4°28·7′W	A	26
Dùn Mór	Highld	NM5370	56°45·6′	6°2·0′W	X	39,47
Dùn Mór	N Eil	NB5134	58°13·7′	6°14·0′W	X	8
Dùn Mór	N Eil	NF7741	57°21·0′	7°21·8′W	A	22
Dùn Mór	N Eil	NF7862	57°32·3′	7°22·4′W	A	22
Dùn Mór	Pth & Kin	NN9030	56°27·2′	3°46·6′W	H	52
Dùn Mór	Pth & Kin	NN9679	56°53·7′	3°42·0′W	H	43
Dùn Mór a' Chaolais	Arg & Bt	NM0847	56°31·7′	6°44·5′W	X	46
Dùn Mór a' Chaolais (Broch)	Arg & Bt	NM0847	56°31·7′	6°44·5′W	A	46
Dun Morbhaidh	Arg & Bt	NM2363	56°40·9′	6°30·9′W	A	47
Dùn Mór (Broch)	Arg & Bt	NM0449	56°32·6′	6°48·5′W	A	46
Dunmore	Arg & Bt	NR7961	55°47·8′	5°31·1′W	X	62
Dunmore	Arg & Bt	NR8786	56°1·4′	5°24·6′W	X	55
Dunmore	Falk	NS8989	56°5·1′	3°46·6′W	T	65
Dunmore	Fife	NT1798	56°10·3′	3°19·8′W	X	58
Dunmore	Highld	NH5147	57°29·6′	4°28·7′W	T	26
Dunmore	Pth & Kin	NO0641	56°33·4′	3°31·3′W	X	52,53
Dunmore	Stir	NN6007	56°14·4′	4°15·1′W	X	57
Dunmore	Stir	NS6086	56°3·0′	4°14·4′W	H	57
Dunmore Fm	Oxon	SU4899	51°41·5′	1°17·9′W	FM	164
Dunmore (Fort)	Fife	NT1798	56°10·3′	3°19·8′W	A	58
Dunmore Home Fm	Falk	NS8890	56°5·6′	3°47·6′W	FM	58
Dunmore Moss	Falk	NS8689	56°5·1′	3°49·5′W	F	65
Dunmore Park	Falk	NS8889	56°5·1′	3°47·5′W	X	65
Dùn Mór (Fort)	Highld	NG3339	57°22·1′	6°26·0′W	A	23,32
Dùn Mór (Fort)	Highld	NH4545	57°28·4′	4°34·6′W	A	26
Dùn Mór (Fort)	Highld	NH5342	57°26·9′	4°26·5′W	A	26
Dùn Mór (fort)	Pth & Kin	NN9030	56°27·2′	3°46·6′W	A	52
Dùn Mór Ghil	Arg & Bt	NR2744	55°37·0′	6°19·7′W	X	60
Dunmor Ho	Arg & Bt	NM7517	56°17·8′	5°37·7′W	X	55
Dun Moss	Clackm	NS9892	56°6·8′	3°38·0′W	X	58
Dun Moss	D & G	NT1703	55°19·1′	3°18·0′W	H	79
Dun Moss	E Ayr	NS4750	55°43·4′	4°25·7′W	X	64
Dun Moss	Scot Bord	NT7107	55°21·6′	2°27·0′W	X	80
Dun Moss	S Lanak	NS9118	55°26·9′	3°43·0′W	X	71,78
Dun Mount	Aberd	NJ3920	57°16·3′	3°0·2′W	H	37
Dunmow Fm	Essex	TL6424	51°53·6′	0°23·4′E	FM	167
Dùn Mucaig	Arg & Bt	NM7515	56°16·7′	5°37·6′W	A	55
Dunmuck	D & G	NX9258	54°54·6′	3°40·7′W	X	84
Dun Muir	Aberd	NJ2718	57°15·1′	3°12·1′W	H	37
Dun Muir	Pth & Kin	NN9808	56°15·5′	3°38·3′W	X	58
Dunn	Highld	ND1956	58°29·3′	3°22·9′W	X	11,12
Dùn na Ban-òige	Arg & Bt	NM8304	56°11·0′	5°29·4′W	H	55
Dunnabie	D & G	NY2581	55°7·3′	3°10·1′W	X	79
Dunnabridge Fm	Devon	SX6474	50°33·2′	3°54·8′W	FM	191
Dunnabridge Pound	Devon	SX6474	50°33·2′	3°54·8′W	A	191
Dunnaby Hall	E Yorks	SE8934	53°47·9′	0°38·5′W	X	106
Dunnack Burn	S Ayr	NX1479	55°4·5′	4°54·4′W	W	76
Dun na Cuaiche	Arg & Bt	NN0910	56°14·9′	5°4·5′W	A	50,56
Dùn na Dise	N Eil	NF8061	57°31·8′	7°20·4′W	A	22
Dunna Goat	Devon	SX5586	50°39·6′	4°2·7′W	X	191
Dùn na-h-Airde	Highld	NG3455	57°30·7′	6°26·0′W	X	23
Dùn na h-Airde (Fort)	Highld	NG3455	57°30·7′	6°26·0′W	A	23
Dunnairbuck Hill	Inverc	NS2966	55°51·7′	4°43·5′W	X	63
Dùn nam Muc	Stir	NN5305	56°13·2′	4°21·8′W	H	57
Dùn nan Gall	Arg & Bt	NL9340	56°27·4′	6°58·6′W	A	46
Dùn nan Gall	Arg & Bt	NM4053	56°36·1′	6°13·7′W	A	47
Dùn nan Gall	Arg & Bt	NM4343	56°30·8′	6°10·2′W	X	47,48
Dùn nan Gall	Arg & Bt	NR4655	55°43·6′	6°2·3′W	X	60
Dùn nan Gall (Broch)	Arg & Bt	NM4343	56°30·8′	6°10·2′W	A	47,48
Dùn nan Gall (Fort)	Arg & Bt	NR4655	55°43·6′	6°2·3′W	A	60
Dùn na Nighinn	Arg & Bt	NM8402	56°10·0′	5°28·3′W	A	55
Dùn nan Nighean	Arg & Bt	NR2169	55°50·3′	6°26·9′W	A	60
Dunnans Craig	D & G	NX6593	55°13·0′	4°6·9′W	X	77
Dun-neil	Arg & Bt	NM9029	56°24·7′	5°23·8′W	X	49
Dùn Néill	Highld	NG2840	57°22·4′	6°31·0′W	A	23
Dunnerdake Fm	Corn	SX3366	50°28·4′	4°20·8′W	FM	201
Dunnerdale	Cumbr	SD2093	54°19·8′	3°13·4′W	X	96
Dunnerdale Fells	Cumbr	SD2091	54°18·7′	3°13·4′W	X	96
Dunnerdale Fells	Cumbr	SD2393	54°19·9′	3°10·6′W	X	96
Dunner Hill	W Susx	SU8525	51°1·3′	0°46·9′W	H	186,197
Dunnerholme	Cumbr	SD2179	54°12·3′	3°12·3′W	T	96
Dunnet	Highld	ND2271	58°37·5′	3°20·1′W	T	7,12
Dunnet Bay	Highld	ND1970	58°36·9′	3°23·2′W	W	7,12
Dunnet Forest	Highld	ND2269	58°36·4′	3°20·1′W	F	7,12
Dunnet Forest	Highld	ND2269	58°36·4′	3°20·1′W	F	12
Dunnet Head	Highld	ND1974	58°39·0′	3°23·3′W	X	7,12
Dunnet Hill	Highld	ND1973	58°38·5′	3°23·2′W	H	7,12
Dunnett Fm	Somer	ST3954	51°17·1′	2°52·1′W	FM	182
Dunnett's Fm	Suff	TM3174	52°19·1′	1°23·8′E	FM	156
Dunn Hill	Corn	SX3555	50°22·5′	4°18·9′W	X	201
Dunn House Fm	Durham	NZ1019	54°34·2′	1°50·3′W	FM	92
Dunnicaer	Aberd	NO8884	56°57·1′	2°11·4′W	X	45
Dunnichen	Angus	NO5048	56°37·5′	2°48·4′W	T	54
Dunnichen Hill	Angus	NO5049	56°38·1′	2°48·5′W	H	54
Dunniflat	E Ayr	NS4253	55°44·9′	4°30·6′W	X	64
Dunnikier	Fife	NT2694	56°8·2′	3°11·0′W	T	59
Dunnikier Ho	Fife	NT2894	56°8·3′	3°9·1′W	X	59
Dunnimere Fm	Staffs	SK2109	52°40·9′	1°41·0′W	FM	128
Dunninald Castle	Angus	NO7054	56°40·9′	2°28·9′W	X	54
Dunninald Mains	Angus	NO7054	56°40·9′	2°28·9′W	X	54
Dunning	Pth & Kin	NO0214	56°18·8′	3°34·6′W	T	58
Dunning Burn	Pth & Kin	NO0213	56°18·2′	3°34·6′W	W	58
Dunningley	Leeds	SE2826	53°44·0′	1°34·1′W	X	104
Dunnington	E Yorks	TA1552	53°57·3′	0°14·4′W	T	107
Dunnington	Warw	SP0653	52°10·7′	1°54·3′W	T	150
Dunnington	York	SE6652	53°57·8′	0°59·2′W	T	105,106
Dunnington Common	York	SE6650	53°56·8′	0°59·2′W	X	105,106
Dunnington Grange	E Yorks	TA1553	53°57·9′	0°14·4′W	X	107
Dunnington Hall	York	SE6753	53°58·4′	0°58·3′W	X	105,106
Dunnington Heath Fm	Warw	SP0653	52°10·7′	1°54·3′W	FM	150
Dunnington Lodge	York	SE6649	53°56·2′	0°59·3′W	X	105,106
Dunningwell	Cumbr	SD1784	54°14·9′	3°16·0′W	T	96
Dunningworth Hall	Suff	TM3857	52°9·8′	1°29·2′E	X	156
Dunnocks Fold Fm	Ches	SJ7756	53°6·3′	2°20·2′W	FM	118
Dunnockshaw	Lancs	SD8127	53°44·6′	2°16·9′W	T	103
Dunnose	I of W	SZ5878	50°36·2′	1°10·4′W	T	196
Dùn Nosebridge	Arg & Bt	NR3760	55°46·0′	6°11·1′W	A	60
Dunnottar Castle	Aberd	NO8883	56°56·5′	2°11·4′W	A	45
Dunnottar Mains	Aberd	NO8783	56°56·5′	2°12·4′W	X	45
Dunnow Hall	Lancs	SD7051	53°57·5′	2°27·0′W	X	103
Dunnow Syke	Lancs	SD7051	53°57·5′	2°27·0′W	W	103
Dunn's Fm	Corn	SX3191	50°41·9′	4°23·2′W	FM	190
Dunns Fm	Northum	NY9396	55°15·7′	2°6·2′W	FM	80
Dunnsheath	Shrops	SJ4717	52°45·1′	2°46·7′W	T	126
Dunnshill	Derby	SK4138	52°56·5′	1°23·0′W	X	129
Dunns Houses	Northum	NY8692	55°13·6′	2°12·8′W	X	80
Dunns Pitts Fm	Warw	SP2874	52°22·0′	1°34·9′W	FM	140
Dunn Street	Kent	TQ7961	51°19·4′	0°34·5′E	T	178,188
Dunn Street	Kent	TQ9948	51°12·0′	0°51·3′E	T	189
Dunnydeer	Aberd	NJ6128	57°20·7′	2°38·4′W	X	37
Dunnydeer Ho	Aberd	NJ6227	57°20·2′	2°37·4′W	X	37
Dunnyduff Wood	Moray	NJ4449	57°31·9′	2°55·7′W	F	28
Dunnygask	Fife	NT0592	56°6·9′	3°31·2′W	X	58
Dunnymuck	S Ayr	NS2002	55°17·0′	4°49·6′W	X	76
Dunollie	Arg & Bt	NM8531	56°25·6′	5°28·7′W	T	49
Dunollie Beg	Arg & Bt	NM8631	56°25·6′	5°27·8′W	X	49
Dunool	D & G	NX5796	55°14·5′	4°14·5′W	X	77
Dunoon	Arg & Bt	NS1776	55°56·8′	4°55·4′W	T	63
Dùn Ormidale	Arg & Bt	NM8226	56°22·8′	5°31·4′W	X	49
Dùn Ormidale (Fort)	Arg & Bt	NM8226	56°22·8′	5°31·4′W	A	49
Dùn Osdale	Highld	NG2446	57°25·5′	6°35·4′W	X	23
Dùn Osdale (Broch)	Highld	NG2446	57°25·5′	6°35·4′W	A	23
Dùn Othail	N Eil	NB5451	58°23·0′	6°12·0′W	X	8
Dunphail Ho	Moray	NJ0047	57°30·4′	3°39·7′W	X	27
Dunpole Fm	Somer	ST3413	50°55·0′	2°56·0′W	FM	193
Dùn Raghaill	N Eil	NF7737	57°18·8′	7°21·5′W	A	22
Dunragit	D & G	NX1557	54°52·7′	4°52·6′W	T	82
Dunragit House	D & G	NX1558	54°53·2′	4°52·6′W	X	82
Dùn Raisaburgh	Highld	NG5064	57°36·1′	6°10·6′W	X	23,24
Dùn Raisaburgh (Broch)	Highld	NG5064	57°36·1′	6°10·6′W	A	23,24
Dunraven Bay	V of Glam	SS8873	51°26·9′	3°36·3′W	W	170
Dunraven Park	V of Glam	SS8972	51°26·4′	3°35·4′W	X	170
Dunree	S Ayr	NS3412	55°22·7′	4°36·8′W	X	70
Dunridge	Devon	SX5270	50°30·9′	4°4·9′W	X	201
Dun Rig	E Ayr	NS6329	55°32·4′	4°9·8′W	X	71
Dun Rig	E Ayr	NS6708	55°21·1′	4°5·4′W	X	71,77
Dun Rig	Scot Bord	NT1625	55°30·9′	3°19·4′W	H	72
Dun Rig	Scot Bord	NT2531	55°34·3′	3°10·9′W	H	73
Dun Rig	Scot Bord	NT8115	55°26·0′	2°17·6′W	X	80
Dùn Righ	Arg & Bt	NM7901	56°9·3′	5°33·1′W	H	55
Dùn Ringill	Highld	NG5617	57°11·0′	6°1·8′W	A	32
Dunrobin Castle	Highld	NC8500	57°58·7′	3°56·2′W	X	17
Dunrobin Glen	Highld	NC8003	58°0·3′	4°1·4′W	X	17
Dunrobin Mains	Highld	NC8401	57°59·3′	3°57·2′W	X	17
Dunrobin Wood	Highld	NC8502	57°59·8′	3°56·3′W	F	17
Dunrod	Inverc	NS2273	55°55·3′	4°50·5′W	X	63
Dunrod Burn	D & G	NX7044	54°46·7′	4°0·9′W	W	83,84
Dunrod Hill	Inverc	NS2372	55°54·8′	4°49·5′W	H	63
Dunrod Point	D & G	NX6244	54°46·6′	4°8·3′W	X	83
Dùn Rostan	Arg & Bt	NR7380	55°57·8′	5°37·8′W	A	55
Dunrostan	Arg & Bt	NR7381	55°58·4′	5°37·8′W	T	55
Dunruchan	Pth & Kin	NN8016	56°19·5′	3°56·0′W	X	57
Dunruchan Hill	Pth & Kin	NN7916	56°19·5′	3°57·0′W	H	57
Duns	Scot Bord	NT7853	55°46·4′	2°20·6′W	T	67,74
Dunsa	Derby	SK2470	53°13·8′	1°38·0′W	T	119
Dunsall	Northum	NT9839	55°38·9′	2°1·5′W	X	75
Dunsa Manor	N Yks	NZ1309	54°28·8′	1°47·5′W	X	92
Dùn Santavaig	Highld	NG3857	57°31·9′	6°22·2′W	X	23
Dunsapie Loch	C of Edin	NT2873	55°56·9′	3°8·7′W	W	66
Dunsbeare	Devon	SS5113	50°54·1′	4°6·8′W	X	180
Dunsbury	I of W	SZ3884	50°39·5′	1°27·4′W	X	196
Dunsbury Hill Fm	Hants	SU7009	50°52·8′	0°59·9′W	FM	197
Dunsby	Lincs	TF1026	52°49·4′	0°21·6′W	T	130
Dunsby Fen	Lincs	TF1426	52°49·4′	0°18·1′W	X	130
Dunsby Fen Fm	Lincs	TF1627	52°49·9′	0°16·3′W	FM	130
Dunsby House	Lincs	TF0351	53°3·0′	0°27·4′W	X	121
Dunsby Village	Lincs	TF0351	53°3·0′	0°27·4′W	A	121
Dunsby Wood	Lincs	TF0825	52°48·9′	0°23·4′W	F	130
Dunscar	Bolton	SD7114	53°37·5′	2°25·9′W	T	109
Dunscar	Lancs	SD7131	53°46·7′	2°26·0′W	X	103
Dunscar Fm	Derby	SK1483	53°20·9′	1°47·0′W	FM	110
Duns Castle	Scot Bord	NT7754	55°47·0′	2°21·6′W	X	67,74
Duns Castle Nature Reserve	Scot Bord	NT7755	55°47·5′	2°21·6′W	X	67,74
Dùn Scobuill	Arg & Bt	NM4627	56°22·3′	6°6·4′W	A	48
Dunscombe	Devon	SX8698	50°46·5′	3°36·6′W	X	191
Dunscombe	Devon	SY1588	50°41·4′	3°11·8′W	X	192
Dunscombe Cliff	Devon	SY1587	50°40·8′	3°11·8′W	X	192
Dunscombe Fms	Devon	SX8979	50°36·2′	3°33·7′W	FM	192
Dunscore	D & G	NX8684	55°8·5′	3°46·9′W	T	78
Dunscore Hill	D & G	NY1994	55°14·3′	3°16·0′W	H	79
Dunscroft	Aberd	NJ5035	57°24·4′	2°49·5′W	X	29
Dunscroft	Donc	SE6508	53°34·1′	1°0·7′W	T	111
Dùn Scurrival	N Eil	NF6908	57°2·9′	7°27·1′W	A	31
Dunsdale	Ches	SJ5176	53°17·0′	2°43·7′W	X	117
Dunsdale	Kent	TQ4554	51°16·2′	0°5·1′E	X	188
Dunsdale	Northum	NT8923	55°30·3′	2°10·0′W	X	74
Dunsdale	Red & Cl	NZ6018	54°33·5′	1°3·9′W	T	94
Dunsden Green	Oxon	SU7377	51°29·5′	0°56·5′W	T	175
Dun's Dish	Angus	NO6460	56°44·1′	2°34·9′W	W	45
Dunsdon	Devon	SS3008	50°51·0′	4°24·5′W	X	190
Dunsdykes	Aberd	NJ5208	57°9·9′	2°47·2′W	X	37
Dunsfold Common	Surrey	TQ0035	51°6·6′	0°33·9′W	T	186
Dunsfold Green	Surrey	TQ0036	51°7·1′	0°33·9′W	T	186
Dunsfold Ryse	Surrey	SU9834	51°6·0′	0°35·6′W	X	186
Dunsford	Devon	SX8189	50°41·5′	3°40·7′W	T	191
Dunsford	Surrey	TQ0036	51°7·1′	0°33·9′W	T	186
Dunsforth Lodge	N Yks	SE4464	54°4·4′	1°19·2′W	X	99
Dùn Sgalair	Highld	NG4148	57°27·2′	6°18·6′W	H	23
Dunsgreen Fm	Devon	ST1513	50°54·8′	3°12·2′W	FM	181,193
Dùn Shalachain	Highld	NM6048	56°34·0′	5°53·9′W	X	49
Dunshalt	Fife	NO2510	56°16·8′	3°12·2′W	T	59
Dunshay Manor	Dorset	SY9879	50°36·9′	2°1·3′W	A	195
Dunsheugh	Northum	NU2214	55°25·4′	1°38·7′W	X	81
Dùn Shiadair	Arg & Bt	NL9638	56°26·4′	6°55·5′W	A	46
Dunshield	Northum	NY9294	55°14·7′	2°7·1′W	X	80
Dunshill	Worcs	SO8231	51°58·9′	2°15·3′W	X	150
Dun Side	E Loth	NT5963	55°51·8′	2°38·9′W	X	67
Dunside Hill	Scot Bord	NT6357	55°48·5′	2°35·0′W	X	67,74
Dunside Reservoir	S Lanak	NS7437	55°36·9′	3°59·6′W	W	71
Dunside Rig	Scot Bord	NT3113	55°24·6′	3°5·0′W	H	79
Dunside Rig	S Lanak	NS7236	55°36·3′	4°1·5′W	H	71
Dunsill	Notts	SK4661	53°8·9′	1°18·3′W	T	120
Dunsinane Hill	Pth & Kin	NO2131	56°28·1′	3°16·5′W	H	53
Dunsinnan	Pth & Kin	NO1632	56°28·6′	3°21·4′W	X	53
Dunskeath Castle	Highld	NH8068	57°41·4′	4°0·3′W	X	21,27
Dunskeath Castle (Earthwork)	Highld	NH8068	57°41·4′	4°0·3′W	A	21,27
Dunskeig	Arg & Bt	NR7556	55°45·0′	5°34·7′W	X	62
Dùn Skeig	Arg & Bt	NR7557	55°45·5′	5°34·7′W	H	62
Dunskeig Bay	Arg & Bt	NR7556	55°45·0′	5°34·7′W	W	62
Dùn Skeig (Fort & Duns)	Arg & Bt	NR7557	55°45·5′	5°34·7′W	A	62
Dunskellor	N Eil	NF8075	57°39·3′	7°21·5′W	X	18
Dunskellyrig	D & G	NY2772	55°2·5′	3°8·1′W	X	85
Dunskey Castle	D & G	NX0053	54°50·2′	5°6·4′W	A	82
Dunskey Glen	D & G	NW9955	54°51·2′	5°7·5′W	X	82
Dunskey Home Fm	D & G	NX0055	54°51·2′	5°6·5′W	FM	82
Dunskey House	D & G	NX0055	54°51·2′	5°6·5′W	X	82
Dunskiag	Pth & Kin	NN8448	56°36·8′	3°53·0′W	X	52
Dùn Skudiburgh	Highld	NG3764	57°35·6′	6°23·6′W	A	23
Dunslair Heights	Scot Bord	NT2843	55°40·8′	3°8·3′W	H	73
Dunsland Brook	Devon	SS5602	50°48·2′	4°2·2′W	X	191
Dunsland Court	Devon	SS5602	50°48·2′	4°2·2′W	X	191
Dunsland Cross	Devon	SS4003	50°48·5′	4°15·9′W	X	190
Duns Law	Scot Bord	NT7854	55°47·0′	2°20·6′W	H	67,74
Dunslea	Corn	SX2771	50°31·0′	4°26·0′W	T	201
Dunsley	Devon	SS8526	51°1·5′	3°38·0′W	X	181
Dunsley	N Yks	NZ8511	54°29·5′	0°40·8′W	T	94
Dunsley	Staffs	SO8583	52°26·9′	2°12·8′W	T	139
Dunsley Corner	Cambs	TL5260	52°13·3′	0°13·9′E	X	154
Dunsley Hall	Staffs	SO8584	52°27·5′	2°12·8′W	X	139
Duns Mere	Hants	SU4560	51°20·5′	1°20·8′W	W	174
Duns Mill	Scot Bord	NT7852	55°45·9′	2°20·6′W	X	67,74
Dunsmore	Bucks	SP8605	51°44·5′	0°44·9′W	T	165
Dunsmore	Devon	SS9501	50°48·2′	3°29·0′W	X	192
Dunsmore	Warw	SP5476	52°23·0′	1°12·0′W	T	140
Dunsmore Fm	Warw	SP5477	52°23·5′	1°12·0′W	FM	140
Dunsmore Heath	Warw	SP4272	52°20·9′	1°22·6′W	X	140
Dunsmouth Fm	Corn	SS2009	50°51·4′	4°33·1′W	FM	190
Dunsop Bridge	Lancs	SD6550	53°56·9′	2°31·6′W	T	102,103
Dunsop Fell	Lancs	SD6854	53°59·1′	2°28·9′W	X	103
Dunsop Fm	Lancs	SD6954	53°59·1′	2°28·0′W	FM	103
Dun's Pike	Northum	NY7681	55°7·6′	2°22·2′W	H	80
Dun's Stone	Somer	ST0132	51°5·0′	3°24·4′W	X	181
Dunstable	Beds	TL0121	51°52·9′	0°31·6′W	T	166
Dunstable Downs	Beds	TL0019	51°51·9′	0°32·5′W	X	166
Dunstable Fm	Wilts	SU2233	51°6·0′	1°40·8′W	FM	184
Dunstaffnage Bay	Arg & Bt	NM8834	56°27·3′	5°26·0′W	W	49
Dunstaffnage Castle	Arg & Bt	NM8834	56°27·3′	5°26·0′W	A	49
Dunstaffnage Mains Fm	Arg & Bt	NM8733	56°26·7′	5°26·9′W	FM	49
Dunstal	Staffs	SK0726	52°50·1′	1°53·4′W	T	128
Dunstal Brook	Staffs	SK0725	52°49·6′	1°53·4′W	W	128
Dunstall	Staffs	SK1820	52°46·9′	1°43·6′W	T	128
Dunstall Common	Worcs	SO8843	52°5·3′	2°10·1′W	T	150
Dunstall Court	Worcs	SP0062	52°15·6′	1°59·6′W	X	150
Dunstall Fm	Kent	TQ5361	51°19·9′	0°12·2′E	FM	177,188
Dunstall Fm	Notts	SK7966	53°11·3′	0°48·7′W	FM	120,121
Dunstall Fm	Staffs	SK1803	52°37·7′	1°43·6′W	FM	139
Dunstall Green	Suff	TL7460	52°12·9′	0°33·2′E	T	155
Dunstall Hill	Wolv	SJ9000	52°36·1′	2°8·5′W	T	127,139
Dunstall Priory	Kent	TQ5261	51°19·9′	0°11·3′E	X	177,188
Dunstalls, The	Cambs	TL5677	52°22·4′	0°17·9′E	X	143

Dunstall Village	Lincs	SK8993	53°25·8'	0°39·2'W	A	112
Dunstan	Corn	SX3766	50°28·5'	4°17·5'W	X	201
Dunstan	Northum	NU2419	55°28·1'	1°36·8'W	T	81
Dunstanburgh Castle	Northum	NU2521	55°29·2'	1°35·8'W	A	75
Dunstan Fm	Ches	SJ3275	53°16·3'	3°0·8'W	FM	117
Dunstan Fm	Notts	SK7391	53°24·9'	0°53·7'W	FM	112
Dunstan Fm	Sol	SP1782	52°26·4'	1°44·6'W	FM	139
Dunstan Hill	Northum	NU2320	55°28·6'	1°37·7'W	X	75
Dunstan Hills	Leeds	SE3531	53°46·7'	1°27·7'W	X	104
Dunstan Square	Northum	NU2420	55°28·6'	1°36·8'W	X	75
Dunstan Steads	Northum	NU2422	55°29·7'	1°36·8'W	X	75
Dunstaple	Devon	SS3507	50°50·6'	4°20·2'W	X	190
Dunstarn Fm	Leeds	SE2839	53°51·0'	1°34·0'W	FM	104
Dunsteads	Essex	TQ6399	51°40·2'	0°21·8'E	X	167,177
Dunster	Somer	SS9943	51°10·9'	3°26·3'W	T	181
Dunster Beach	Somer	ST0045	51°12·0'	3°25·5'W	X	181
Dunster Fm	Dorset	SY4397	50°46·4'	2°48·1'W	FM	193
Dunster Park	Somer	SS9942	51°10·3'	3°26·3'W	X	181
Dunster Sta	Somer	SS9944	51°11·4'	3°26·3'W	X	181
Duns Tew	Oxon	SP4528	51°57·2'	1°20·3'W	T	164
Dunston	Derby	SK3673	53°15·4'	1°27·2'W	T	119
Dunston	Ghead	NZ2262	54°57·4'	1°39·0'W	T	88
Dunston	Lincs	TF0662	53°8·9'	0°24·5'W	T	121
Dunston	Norf	TG2202	52°34·5'	1°17·0'E	T	134
Dunston	Pemb	SM9017	51°49·0'	5°2·4'W	X	157,158
Dunston	Staffs	SJ9217	52°45·3'	2°6·7'W	T	127
Dunstone	Devon	SX5951	50°20·8'	3°58·5'W	T	202
Dunstone	Devon	SX7175	50°33·9'	3°48·9'W	T	191
Dunstone	Devon	SX7940	50°15·1'	3°41·5'W	T	202
Dun Stone Beck	N Yks	SD8276	54°11·0'	2°16·1'W	W	98
Dunstone Point	C of Plym	SX4852	50°21·1'	4°7·8'W	X	201
Dunston Fen	Lincs	TF1064	53°9·9'	0°20·9'W	X	121
Dunston Grove	Pemb	SM9117	51°49·0'	5°1·6'W	X	157,158
Dunston Heath	Lincs	TF0362	53°8·9'	0°27·2'W	X	121
Dunston Heath	Staffs	SJ9117	52°45·3'	2°7·6'W	T	127
Dunston Hill	E Ayr	NS4212	55°22·8'	4°29·2'W	X	70
Dunston Hill	Ghead	NZ2261	54°56·8'	1°39·0'W	T	88
Dunston Hole Fm	Derby	SK3574	53°15·9'	1°28·1'W	FM	119
Dunston Pillar	Lincs	TF0061	53°8·4'	0°29·9'W	X	121
Dunston's Corner	Suff	TM1353	52°8·3'	1°7·2'E	X	156
Dunstrone (Fort)	Arg & Bt	NS0854	55°44·7'	5°3·1'W	A	63
Dùn Stuigh	N Eil	NB1540	58°15·6'	6°51·1'W	A	13
Dunsty Hill	Bucks	SP6823	51°54·3'	1°0·3'W	X	164,165
Dùn Suladale	Highld	NG3752	57°29·2'	6°22·8'W	X	23
Dùn Suladale (Broch)	Highld	NG3752	57°29·2'	6°22·8'W	A	23
Dunsville	Donc	SE6407	53°33·6'	1°1·6'W	T	111
Dunswater Fm	Heref	SO4235	52°0·9'	2°50·3'W	FM	149,161
Dunswell	Aberd	NJ6403	57°7·2'	2°35·2'W	X	37
Dunswell	E Yorks	TA0735	53°48·3'	0°22·1'W	T	107
Duns Wood	Angus	NO5261	56°44·5'	2°46·6'W	F	44
Duns Wood	Scot Bord	NT7755	55°47·5'	2°21·6'W	F	67,74
Dunsyre	S Lanak	NT0748	55°43·2'	3°28·4'W	T	72
Dunsyre Hill	S Lanak	NT0748	55°43·2'	3°28·4'W	H	72
Dun Tae	Scot Bord	NT6503	55°19·4'	2°32·7'W	X	80
Duntaggart	Pth & Kin	NN8748	56°36·9'	3°50·0'W	X	52
Dùn Taimh	Highld	NG3636	57°20·5'	6°22·8'W	X	23,32
Dùn Taimh (Fort)	Highld	NG3636	57°20·5'	6°22·8'W	A	23,32
Duntanachan	Arg & Bt	NM9628	56°24·3'	5°17·9'W	X	49
Duntanlich	Pth & Kin	NO0424	56°24·2'	3°32·9'W	X	52,53,58
Duntanlich Lochan	Pth & Kin	NN8658	56°42·2'	3°51·3'W	W	52
Duntarvie	W Loth	NT0877	55°58·9'	3°28·0'W	X	65
Duntarvie Castle	W Loth	NT0976	55°58·4'	3°27·0'W	A	65
Duntaylor	Pth & Kin	NN8448	56°36·8'	3°53·0'W	X	52
Dùn Tealfaig	Arg & Bt	NR3898	56°6·4'	6°12·4'W	A	61
Dùn Telve (Broch)	Highld	NG8217	57°11·8'	5°36·1'W	A	33
Duntercleuch	D & G	NS8415	55°25·2'	3°49·5'W	X	71,78
Duntercleuch Rig	D & G	NS8315	55°25·2'	3°50·5'W	H	71,78
Dunter Law	Scot Bord	NT7163	55°51·8'	2°27·4'W	X	67
Dunterlee Plantn	Scot Bord	NT7355	55°47·5'	2°25·4'W	F	67,74
Dunterley	Northum	NY8283	55°8·7'	2°16·5'W	X	80
Dunterton	Devon	SX3779	50°35·5'	4°17·8'W	T	201
Dunterue Wood	Devon	SX3878	50°35·0'	4°16·9'W	F	201
Dunthill	Aberd	NO6867	56°47·9'	2°31·0'W	X	45
Dùn Thomaidh	N Eil	NF7575	57°39·1'	7°26·5'W	A	18
Dunthrop	Oxon	SP3528	51°57·2'	1°29·0'W	T	164
Dunthwaite	Cumbr	NY1732	54°40·8'	3°16·8'W	X	89,90
Duntiglennan Fm	W Dunb	NS4873	55°55·8'	4°25·5'W	FM	64
Duntilland Fm	N Lanak	NS8363	55°51·0'	3°51·7'W	FM	65
Duntilland Hill	N Lanak	NS8364	55°51·6'	3°51·7'W	X	65
Duntisbourne Abbots	Glos	SO9707	51°45·9'	2°2·2'W	T	163
Duntisbourne Common	Glos	SO9506	51°45·4'	2°4·0'W	X	163
Duntisbourne Ho	Glos	SO9506	51°45·4'	2°4·0'W	X	163
Duntisbourne Leer	Glos	SO9707	51°45·9'	2°2·2'W	T	163
Duntisbourne Rouse	Glos	SO9806	51°45·4'	2°1·3'W	T	163
Duntish	Dorset	ST6906	50°51·4'	2°26·0'W	T	194
Duntish Elms Fm	Dorset	ST6907	50°51·9'	2°26·0'W	FM	194
Duntocher	W Dunb	NS4873	55°55·8'	4°25·5'W	T	64
Dùn Toiseach	Arg & Bt	NM8804	56°11·1'	5°24·5'W	A	55
Dunton	Beds	TL2344	52°5·1'	0°11·9'W	T	153
Dunton	Bucks	SP8224	51°54·7'	0°48·1'W	T	165
Dunton	Norf	TF8730	52°50·3'	0°47·0'E	T	132
Dunton Bassett	Leic	SP5490	52°30·5'	1°11·9'W	T	140
Dunton Fen	Beds	TL2245	52°5·6'	0°12·7'W	F	153
Dunton Green	Kent	TQ5157	51°17·7'	0°10·3'E	T	188
Dunton Hall	Essex	TQ6588	51°34·2'	0°23·2'E	X	177,178
Dunton Hall	Lincs	TF4116	52°43·6'	0°5·7'E	X	131
Dunton Hall	Warw	SP1993	52°32·3'	1°42·8'W	X	139
Dunton Hills Fm	Essex	TQ6488	51°34·2'	0°22·4'E	FM	177
Dunton Lodge	Essex	TQ6491	51°35·9'	0°22·5'E	X	177
Dunton Lodge Fm	Beds	TL2542	52°4·0'	0°10·2'W	FM	153
Dunton Manor	Bucks	SP8224	51°54·7'	0°48·1'W	X	165
Dunton Park	Essex	TQ6688	51°34·2'	0°24·1'E	X	177,178
Dunton Patch	Norf	TF8730	52°50·3'	0°47·0'E	T	132
Dunton's Fm	Suff	TL8949	52°6·5'	0°46·0'E	FM	155
Dunton Water	E Ayr	NS5145	55°40·8'	4°21·7'W	W	64
Dunton Wayletts	Essex	TQ6590	51°35·3'	0°23·3'E	X	177,178
Dùn Torvaig	Highld	NG4944	57°25·3'	6°10·4'W	A	23
Duntreath Castle	Stir	NS5381	56°0·2'	4°21·0'W	X	64
Dun Troddan (Broch)	Highld	NG8317	57°11·8'	5°35·1'W	A	33
Duntrune Castle	Arg & Bt	NR7995	56°6·1'	5°32·8'W	A	55
Duntrune Ho	Angus	NO4435	56°30·5'	2°54·1'W	X	54
Duntuim	Pth & Kin	NN8448	56°36·8'	3°53·0'W	X	52
Duntulm	Highld	NG4174	57°41·1'	6°20·3'W	T	23
Duntulm Castle	Highld	NG4074	57°41·1'	6°21·3'W	A	23
Dùn Uabairtich	Arg & Bt	NM8328	56°23·9'	5°30·5'W	X	49
Dun Uamh nan Cradh	Arg & Bt	NM8439	56°29·9'	5°30·1'W	X	49
Dùn Uisealan	N Eil	NF7745	57°23·1'	7°22·1'W	A	22
Dùn Uragaig	Arg & Bt	NR3898	56°6·4'	6°12·4'W	A	61
Dunure	S Ayr	NS2515	55°24·1'	4°45·4'W	T	70
Dunure Mains	S Ayr	NS2514	55°23·6'	4°45·4'W	X	70
Dùn Urgadul	Arg & Bt	NM4955	56°37·4'	6°5·1'W	A	47
Dunval Hall	Shrops	SO7096	52°33·9'	2°26·2'W	A	138
Dùn Vallerain	Highld	NG4669	57°38·6'	6°14·9'W	X	23
Dùn Vallerain (Fort)	Highld	NG4669	57°38·6'	6°14·9'W	A	23
Dunvant	Swan	SS5993	51°37·3'	4°1·8'W	T	159
Dunvegan	Highld	NG2547	57°26·1'	6°34·5'W	T	23
Dunvegan Castle	Highld	NG2449	57°27·1'	6°35·6'W	A	23
Dunvegan Head	Highld	NG1756	57°30·6'	6°43·1'W	X	23
Dunveoch Hill	D & G	NX5881	55°6·4'	4°13·1'W	H	77
Dunveth	Corn	SW9872	50°31·0'	4°50·6'W	T	200
Dun Viden	Highld	NC7251	58°26·0'	4°11·1'W	X	10
Dunviden Burn	Highld	NC7350	58°25·5'	4°10·0'W	W	10
Dunviden Hill	Highld	NC7451	58°26·0'	4°9·0'W	X	10
Dunviden Lochs	Highld	NC7451	58°26·0'	4°9·0'W	W	10
Dun Vlarveg	Highld	NG5137	57°21·6'	6°8·0'W	X	22,23,32
Dun Vlarveg (fort)	Highld	NG5137	57°21·6'	6°8·0'W	A	22,23,32
Dunvournie	Highld	NH5957	57°35·1'	4°21·0'W	X	26
Dunwan Burn	E Renf	NS5649	55°43·0'	4°17·1'W	W	64
Dunwan dam	E Renf	NS5549	55°43·0'	4°18·1'W	W	64
Dunwan Hill	E Renf	NS5448	55°42·5'	4°19·0'W	X	64
Dunwan Hill (Fort)	E Renf	NS5448	55°42·5'	4°19·0'W	A	64
Dunwear	Somer	ST3135	51°6·8'	2°58·8'W	T	182
Dunwell	Devon	SX6754	50°22·5'	3°51·9'W	X	202
Dunwich	Suff	TM4770	52°16·6'	1°37·7'E	T	156
Dunwich Cliffs	Suff	TM4769	52°16·0'	1°37·6'E	X	156
Dunwich Forest	Suff	TM4671	52°17·1'	1°36·8'E	F	156
Dunwich Heath	Suff	TM4768	52°15·5'	1°37·6'E	X	156
Dunwich River	Suff	TM4771	52°17·1'	1°37·7'E	W	156
Dunwood	Heref	SO4151	52°9·5'	2°51·4'W	X	148,149
Dunwood	Staffs	SJ9555	53°5·8'	2°4·1'W	T	118
Dunwood Hall	Staffs	SJ9454	53°5·2'	2°5·0'W	X	118
Dunwood Ho	Staffs	SJ9454	53°5·2'	2°5·0'W	X	118
Dunwood Manor	Hants	SU3122	51°0·0'	1°33·1'W	X	185
Dunyvaig Castle	Arg & Bt	NR4064	55°38·0'	6°7·4'W	A	60
Dupath	Corn	SX3769	50°30·1'	4°17·5'W	X	201
Dupin	S Ayr	NX0875	55°2·2'	4°59·9'W	X	76
Dupin	S Ayr	NX2394	55°12·8'	4°46·5'W	X	76
Dupin Hill	S Ayr	NX0975	55°2·2'	4°58·9'W	X	76
Duporth	Corn	SX0351	50°19·8'	4°45·7'W	X	200,204
Dupple Burn	D & G	NY0099	55°16·8'	3°34·0'W	W	78
Dupplin Castle	Pth & Kin	NO0519	56°21·5'	3°31·8'W	X	58
Dupplin Loch	Pth & Kin	NO0320	56°22·0'	3°33·8'W	W	52,53,58
Dura	N Lanak	NS8655	55°46·7'	3°48·6'W	X	65,72
Dura Den	Fife	NO4114	56°19·1'	2°56·8'W	X	59
Dura Ho	Fife	NO4114	56°19·1'	2°56·8'W	X	59
Dural	Devon	SS2916	50°55·3'	4°25·6'W	X	190
Dura Mains	Fife	NO4014	56°19·1'	2°57·8'W	X	59
Durance	Devon	SX5465	50°28·2'	4°3·1'W	X	201
D'Urban's Fm	Suff	TM2763	52°13·3'	1°19·8'E	FM	156
Durborough Fm	Somer	ST1835	51°6·7'	3°9·9'W	FM	181
Durborough Fm	Somer	ST1941	51°10·0'	3°9·1'W	FM	181
Durbridge Fm	Glos	SO7330	51°58·3'	2°23·2'W	FM	150
Durcha	Highld	NC5002	57°59·2'	4°31·8'W	X	16
Durclawdd	Carm	SN5509	51°45·9'	4°5·7'W	X	159
Durdans, The	Surrey	TQ2059	51°19·3'	0°16·3'W	X	187
Durdar	Cumbr	NY4050	54°50·7'	2°55·6'W	T	85
Durdar Ho	Cumbr	NY4050	54°50·7'	2°55·6'W	X	85
Durdham Down	C of Bris	ST5674	51°28·0'	2°37·6'W	X	172
Durdham Fms	Notts	SK7052	53°3·9'	0°56·9'W	FM	120
Durdle Door	Dorset	SY8080	50°37·4'	2°16·6'W	X	194
Durdle Pier	Dorset	SY7071	50°32·5'	2°25·0'W	X	194
Durdon	Devon	SS6011	50°53·1'	3°59·0'W	X	191
Durdon	Devon	SX5299	50°46·5'	4°5·6'W	X	191
Duredon Fm	Somer	SS7540	51°9·0'	3°46·8'W	FM	180
Dure Down	Somer	SS7540	51°9·0'	3°46·8'W	H	180
Durfold	W Susx	TQ1635	51°6·4'	0°20·2'W	X	187
Durfold Hall Fm	Surrey	SU9933	51°5·5'	0°34·8'W	FM	186
Durfold Wood	Surrey	SU9832	51°5·0'	0°35·7'W	F	186
Durford Abbey Fm	W Susx	SU7723	51°0·3'	0°53·8'W	FM	197
Durford Wood	W Susx	SU7825	51°1·4'	0°52·9'W	F	186,197
Durgan	Corn	SW7727	50°6·3'	5°6·8'W	T	204
Durga Ness	Shetld	HT9738	60°7·9'	2°2·7'W	X	4
Durgates	E Susx	TQ6232	51°4·1'	0°19·1'E	T	188
Durham	Durham	NZ2742	54°46·6'	1°34·4'W	T	88
Durham Bridge Fm	Cumbr	SD4489	54°17·9'	2°51·2'W	FM	97
Durhamfield	Northum	NZ0550	54°50·9'	1°54·9'W	X	87
Durham Fm	Bucks	SP8804	51°43·9'	0°43·1'W	FM	165
Durham Fm	E Susx	TQ4304	50°49·3'	0°2·2'E	FM	198
Durhamhill	D & G	NX7970	55°0·8'	3°53·1'W	X	84
Durham Hill	Durham	NZ1550	54°50·9'	1°45·6'W	X	88
Durham Hill	Notts	SK7381	53°19·5'	0°53·8'W	X	120
Durham Riding	Northum	NZ0961	54°56·9'	1°51·1'W	X	88
Dur Hill Down	Hants	SU1900	50°48·2'	1°43·4'W	X	195
Durie	Aberd	NK0044	57°29·4'	1°59·5'W	X	30
Duriehill	Angus	NO6068	56°48·4'	2°38·9'W	X	45
Durie Ho	Fife	NO3702	56°12·6'	3°0·5'W	X	59
Durie Vale	Fife	NO3400	56°11·5'	3°3·4'W	X	59
Durinemast	Highld	NM6752	56°36·4'	5°47·3'W	X	49
Durisdeer	D & G	NS8903	55°18·8'	3°44·5'W	T	78
Durisdeer Hill	D & G	NS9105	55°19·9'	3°42·7'W	H	71,78
Durisdeermill	D & G	NS8804	55°19·3'	3°45·5'W	T	78
Durisdeer Rig	D & G	NS9004	55°19·3'	3°43·6'W	X	78
Durkar	Wakf	SE3117	53°39·2'	1°31·4'W	T	110,111
Durleigh	Somer	ST2736	51°7·4'	3°2·2'W	T	182
Durleigh Brook	Somer	ST2436	51°7·3'	3°4·8'W	W	182
Durleighmarsh	W Susx	SU7823	51°0·3'	0°52·9'W	T	197
Durleighmarsh Fm	W Susx	SU7823	51°0·3'	0°52·9'W	FM	197
Durleigh Reservoir	Somer	ST2636	51°7·3'	3°3·1'W	W	182
Durlett Fm	Wilts	ST9663	51°22·2'	2°3·1'W	FM	173
Durley	Hants	SU5116	50°56·7'	1°16·1'W	T	185
Durley	Wilts	SU2364	51°22·7'	1°39·8'W	T	174
Durley Fm	Hants	SU3510	50°53·5'	1°29·1'W	FM	196
Durley Hall Fm	Hants	SU5218	50°57·8'	1°15·2'W	FM	185
Durley Manor Fm	Hants	SU5217	50°57·2'	1°15·2'W	FM	185
Durley Mill	Hants	SU5215	50°56·2'	1°15·2'W	X	196
Durley Street	Hants	SU5217	50°57·2'	1°15·2'W	T	185
Durl Head	Torbay	SX9455	50°23·4'	3°29·1'W	X	202
Durlings	Devon	SS7702	50°48·5'	3°44·4'W	X	191
Durlock	Kent	TR2757	51°16·2'	1°15·7'E	T	179
Durlock	Kent	TR3164	51°19·9'	1°19·4'E	X	179
Durlow Common	Heref	SO6339	52°3·1'	2°32·0'W	T	149
Durlston Bay	Dorset	SZ0378	50°36·3'	1°57·1'W	W	195
Durlston Country Park	Dorset	SZ0377	50°35·8'	1°57·1'W	X	195
Durlston Court	Hants	SZ2493	50°44·4'	1°39·2'W	X	195
Durlston Head	Dorset	SZ0377	50°35·8'	1°57·1'W	X	195
Dùr Mór	Highld	NG2803	57°2·5'	6°28·6'W	X	39
Durn	Roch	SD9416	53°38·7'	2°5·0'W	T	109
Durnaford Fm	Corn	SX3466	50°28·5'	4°20·0'W	FM	201
Durnamuck	Highld	NH0192	57°52·7'	5°20·9'W	T	19
Durness	Highld	NC4067	58°34·0'	4°44·6'W	T	9
Durnfield	Somer	ST4920	50°58·9'	2°43·2'W	T	183,193
Durnford Fm	Surrey	TQ0161	51°20·6'	0°32·6'W	FM	176,186
Durn Hill	Aberd	NJ5763	57°39·6'	2°42·8'W	H	29
Durn Ho	Aberd	NJ5865	57°40·6'	2°41·8'W	X	29
Durno	Aberd	NJ7128	57°20·8'	2°28·5'W	T	38
Durno Ho	Aberd	NJ7061	57°38·5'	2°29·7'W	X	29
Durns Town	Hants	SZ2898	50°47·1'	1°35·8'W	T	195
Duror	Highld	NM9854	56°38·3'	5°17·2'W	T	49
Durpley	Devon	SS4213	50°53·9'	4°14·4'W	X	180,190
Durpley Castle	Devon	SS4212	50°53·4'	4°14·4'W	A	180,190
Durra Dale	Shetld	HU4358	60°18·5'	1°12·8'W	X	2,3
Durran	Arg & Bt	NM9507	56°12·9'	5°17·9'W	X	55
Durran	Highld	ND1963	58°33·1'	3°23·0'W	X	11,12
Durrance Fm	Worcs	SO9171	52°20·5'	2°7·5'W	FM	139
Durran Mains	Highld	ND1962	58°32·6'	3°23·0'W	X	11,12
Durrant Green	Kent	TQ8836	51°5·8'	0°41·5'E	T	189
Durrants	Hants	SU7209	50°52·8'	0°58·2'W	T	197
Durrants	I of W	SZ4489	50°42·2'	1°22·2'W	X	196
Durrant's Fm	Essex	TL6802	51°41·7'	0°26·2'E	FM	167
Durrants Fm	E Susx	TQ6216	50°55·5'	0°18·7'E	FM	199
Durrington	Wilts	SU1544	51°11·9'	1°46·7'W	T	184
Durrington	W Susx	TQ1104	50°49·7'	0°25·0'W	T	198
Durrington Down	Wilts	SU1243	51°11·4'	1°49·3'W	X	184
Durrington Hall	Essex	TL4813	51°48·0'	0°9·2'E	X	167
Durrington-on-Sea Sta	W Susx	TQ1203	50°49·2'	0°24·2'W	T	198
Durrington Walls	Wilts	SU1543	51°11·4'	1°46·7'W	A	184
Durris Br	Aberd	NO7595	57°3·0'	2°24·3'W	X	38,45
Durris Cott	Aberd	NO7995	57°3·0'	2°20·3'W	X	38,45
Durrisdale	Orkney	HY3724	59°6·2'	3°5·5'W	T	6
Durris Forest	Aberd	NO7992	57°1·4'	2°20·3'W	F	38,45
Durris Ho	Aberd	NO7996	57°3·5'	2°20·3'W	T	38,45
Durry Loch	Arg & Bt	NR6722	55°26·4'	5°40·6'W	W	68
Dursley	Glos	ST7698	51°41·0'	2°20·4'W	T	162
Dursley	Wilts	ST8654	51°17·3'	2°11·7'W	T	183
Dursley Cross	Glos	SO6920	51°52·9'	2°26·6'W	T	162
Durston	Somer	ST2928	51°3·1'	3°0·4'W	T	193
Durstone Fm	Heref	SO5954	52°11·2'	2°35·6'W	FM	149
Durton Fm	I of W	SZ5288	50°41·6'	1°15·4'W	FM	196
Durtress Burn	Northum	NY8698	55°16·8'	2°12·8'W	W	80
Durval Fm	V of Glam	SS8973	51°26·9'	3°35·5'W	FM	170
Durward's Dike	Angus	NO2654	56°40·6'	3°12·0'W	A	53
Durwards Hall	Essex	TL8416	51°49·0'	0°40·6'E	X	168
Durward's Scalp	Fife	NO2921	56°22·8'	3°8·5'W	X	53,59
Durweston	Dorset	ST8508	50°52·5'	2°12·4'W	T	194
Dur Wood	Hants	SU5523	51°0·5'	1°12·6'W	F	185
Dury	Shetld	HU4560	60°19·6'	1°10·6'W	T	2,3
Duryard	Devon	SX9194	50°44·4'	3°32·3'W	T	192
Dury Fm	Devon	SX6677	50°34·9'	3°53·2'W	FM	191
Dury Voe	Shetld	HU4862	60°20·6'	1°7·3'W	W	2,3
Dury Water	Devon	SX3997	50°45·3'	4°16·6'W	W	190
Dusach	Moray	NH9945	57°29·3'	3°40·6'W	X	27
Duskin Fm	Kent	TR1849	51°12·1'	1°7·6'E	FM	179,189
Dusk Water	N Ayr	NS3448	55°42·1'	4°38·1'W	W	63
Dusk Water	N Ayr	NS3852	55°44·3'	4°34·4'W	W	63
Duslic	Highld	NC2675	58°37·9'	4°59·4'W	X	9
Dussindale Park	Norf	TG2709	52°38·1'	1°21·7'E	X	134
Dustfield Fm	Oxon	SP3819	51°52·3'	1°26·5'W	FM	164
Dust Hill	Northnts	SP6880	52°25·1'	0°59·6'W	X	141
Duston	Northnts	SP7260	52°14·2'	0°56·3'W	T	152
Duston Mill	Northnts	SP7259	52°13·7'	0°56·4'W	X	152
Dusty Drum	Angus	NO5541	56°33·8'	2°43·5'W	X	54
Dustyhall	S Ayr	NS3715	55°24·4'	4°34·0'W	X	70
Dustystile	Staffs	SK0345	53°0·4'	1°56·9'W	X	119,128
Dutch Court Fm	Somer	ST3448	51°13·9'	2°56·3'W	FM	182
Dutch Ho	Hants	SU7556	51°18·1'	0°55·1'W	X	175,186
Dutchlands Fm	Bucks	SP8803	51°43·4'	0°43·2'W	FM	165
Dutchling Common	E Susx	TQ3318	50°57·0'	0°6·0'W	X	198
Dutch Loch	Shetld	HU1660	60°19·7'	1°42·1'W	W	3
Dutchman Bank	Conwy	SH6678	53°17·2'	4°0·2'W	X	115
Dutchman's Cap or Bac Mòr	Arg & Bt	NM2438	56°27·5'	6°28·4'W	X	46,47,48
Dutchman's Island	Kent	TQ9867	51°22·3'	0°51·1'E	X	178
Dutch River	E Yorks	SE7121	53°41·1'	0°55·1'W	W	105,106,112
Dutch Village	Essex	TQ7783	51°31·3'	0°33·5'E	T	178
Duchy Home Fm, The	Corn	SX3574	50°32·8'	4°19·4'W	FM	201
Duthie Park	C of Aber	NJ9304	57°7·9'	2°6·5'W	X	38
Duthieston Ho	Stir	NN7802	56°12·0'	3°57·5'W	X	57
Duthil	Highld	NH9324	57°17·9'	3°46·1'W	T	36
Duthil Burn	Highld	NH9227	57°19·5'	3°47·2'W	W	36
Duthriss Hill	Angus	NO4368	56°48·3'	2°55·6'W	H	44
Dutlas	Powys	SO2177	52°23·4'	3°9·3'W	T	137,148
Dutmoss Woods	Suff	TL8657	52°11·0'	0°43·6'E	F	155
Duton Hill	Essex	TL6026	51°54·8'	0°20·0'E	T	167
Dutson	Corn	SX3485	50°38·7'	4°20·5'W	T	201
Dutton	Ches	SJ5779	53°18·6'	2°38·3'W	T	117
Dutton Hall	Ches	SJ5977	53°17·5'	2°36·5'W	X	117
Dutton Hall	Lancs	SD6636	53°49·4'	2°30·6'W	A	103
Dutton Hollow Fm	Ches	SJ5877	53°17·5'	2°37·4'W	FM	117
Dutton Lodge Fm	Ches	SJ5877	53°17·5'	2°37·4'W	FM	117

Dutton Manor	Lancs	SD6538	53°50·5'	2°31·5'W	X	102,103
Dutton Park Fm	Ches	SJ5777	53°17·5'	2°38·3'W	FM	117
Duttons Fm	Oxon	SP3207	51°45·9'	1°31·8'W	FM	164
Dutton Viaduct	Ches	SJ5876	53°17·0'	2°37·4'W	X	117
Duty Point	Devon	SS6949	51°13·7'	3°52·2'W	X	180
Duvale Barton	Devon	SS9420	50°58·4'	3°30·2'W	X	181
Duver, The	I of W	SZ6389	50°42·1'	1°6·1'W	X	196
Dux	Devon	SS2903	50°48·3'	4°25·2'W	X	190
Duxbury Park	Lancs	SD5815	53°38·0'	2°37·7'W	X	108
Dux Fm	Kent	TQ6054	51°16·0'	0°18·0'E	FM	188
Duxford	Cambs	TL4745	52°5·3'	0°9·1'E	T	154
Duxford	Oxon	SU3699	51°41·5'	1°28·4'W	T	164
Duxford Fm	Oxon	SU3699	51°41·5'	1°28·4'W	FM	164
Duxford Grange Ho	Cambs	TL4544	52°4·7'	0°7·4'E	X	154
Duxhurst	Surrey	TQ2545	51°11·7'	0°12·3'W	X	187
Duxmoor	Devon	SS9213	50°54·6'	3°31·8'W	X	181
Duxmoor	Shrops	SO4477	52°23·5'	2°49·0'W	T	137,148
Duxmore Fm	I of W	SZ5588	50°41·6'	1°12·9'W	FM	196
Dvbris (Dover)	Kent	TR3141	51°7·5'	1°18·5'E	R	179
Dvrnovaria (Dorchester)	Dorset	SY6890	50°42·8'	2°26·8'W	R	194
Dvrobrivae (Rochester)	Medway	TQ7268	51°23·3'	0°28·7'E	R	178
Dvrobrivae (Roman Town)	Peterb	TL1296	52°33·2'	0°20·5'W	R	142
Dvrocobrivis (Dunstable)	Beds	TL0121	51°52·9'	0°31·6'W	R	166
Dvrovernvm (Canterbury)	Kent	TR1457	51°16·5'	1°4·5'E	R	179
Dvrovigvtum (Godmanchester)	Cambs	TL2470	52°19·1'	0°10·4'W	R	153
Dwarfie Hamars	Orkney	HY2400	58°53·1'	3°18·6'W	X	6,7
Dwarfie Stone, The	Orkney	HY2400	58°53·1'	3°18·6'W	A	6,7
Dwarwick Head	Highld	ND2071	58°37·4'	3°22·2'W	X	7,12
Dwelly Fm	Surrey	TQ4146	51°12·0'	0°1·5'E	FM	187
Dwr Llydan	Powys	SN8327	51°56·0'	3°41·7'W	W	160
Dwrnudon	Gwyn	SH8628	52°50·5'	3°41·2'W	X	124,125
Dwygyfylchi	Conwy	SH7377	53°16·7'	3°53·9'W	T	115
Dwylan	Gwyn	SH2927	52°49·1'	4°31·9'W	X	123
Dwyran	I of Angl	SH4466	53°10·3'	4°19·6'W	T	114,115
Dwyrhiw	Powys	SJ0702	52°36·7'	3°22·0'W	T	136
Dyance	Durham	NZ1918	54°33·7'	1°41·9'W	X	92
Dyance Beck	Durham	NZ1918	54°33·7'	1°41·9'W	W	92
Dyce	C of Aber	NJ8812	57°12·2'	2°11·5'W	T	38
Dyche	Somer	ST1641	51°10·0'	3°11·7'W	T	181
Dydon	Staffs	SK1344	52°59·8'	1°48·0'W	X	119,128
Dye Cott	Scot Bord	NT6458	55°49·1'	2°34·0'W	X	67,74
Dye Ho	Surrey	SU8939	51°8·8'	0°43·3'W	X	186
Dye House	Northum	NY9358	54°55·2'	2°6·1'W	T	87
Dye House Fm	Wilts	ST8347	51°13·5'	2°14·2'W	FM	183
Dyemill	D & G	NX1047	54°47·2'	4°56·9'W	X	82
Dyer's Common	S Glos	ST5583	51°32·9'	2°38·5'W	T	172
Dyers Fm	Dorset	ST6104	50°50·3'	2°32·8'W	FM	194
Dyer's Fm	Dorset	ST6509	50°53·0'	2°29·5'W	FM	194
Dyer's Green	Cambs	TL3545	52°5·4'	0°1·4'W	T	154
Dyers Hall	Essex	TL6711	51°46·6'	0°25·6'E	X	167
Dyer's Hall Fm	Beds	TL0429	51°57·2'	0°28·8'W	FM	166
Dyer's Lookout	Devon	SS2225	51°0·1'	4°31·8'W	X	190
Dyers Moor Fm	Devon	SS3720	50°57·6'	4°18·9'W	FM	190
Dyes Fm	Herts	TL2123	51°53·8'	0°14·1'W	FM	166
Dyeshaugh	Scot Bord	NT7059	55°49·7'	2°28·3'W	X	67,74
Dye Water	Scot Bord	NT5858	55°49·1'	2°39·8'W	W	67,73,74
Dye Water	Scot Bord	NT6358	55°49·1'	2°35·0'W	W	67,74
Dyfaenor	Powys	SO0771	52°20·0'	3°21·5'W	A	136,147
Dyfannedd	Denb	SJ0449	53°2·0'	3°25·5'W	X	116
Dyffryd	Shrops	SJ2919	52°46·1'	3°2·7'W	X	126
Dyffryn	Brig	SS8593	51°37·7'	3°39·3'W	T	170
Dyffryn	Brig	SS9581	51°31·3'	3°30·4'W	X	170
Dyffryn	Carm	SN1223	51°52·7'	4°43·5'W	X	145,158
Dyffryn	Carm	SN3122	51°52·5'	4°26·9'W	T	145,159
Dyffryn	Carm	SN5326	51°55·0'	4°7·9'W	X	146
Dyffryn	Cered	SN2246	52°5·3'	4°35·5'W	X	145
Dyffryn	Cered	SN2650	52°7·5'	4°32·1'W	T	145
Dyffryn	Cered	SN4855	52°10·6'	4°13·0'W	X	146
Dyffryn	Cered	SN5850	52°8·0'	4°4·1'W	X	146
Dyffryn	I of Angl	SH5075	53°15·3'	4°14·5'W	X	114,115
Dyffryn	Pemb	SM9437	51°59·8'	4°59·7'W	T	157
Dyffryn	Pemb	SN0628	51°55·2'	4°48·9'W	X	145,158
Dyffryn	Pemb	SN2734	51°58·9'	4°30·8'W	X	145
Dyffryn	Powys	SJ1412	52°42·2'	3°16·0'W	X	125
Dyffryn	Powys	SJ2001	52°36·3'	3°10·5'W	X	126
Dyffryn	Powys	SO2465	52°16·9'	3°6·4'W	X	137,148
Dyffryn	Powys	SO2520	51°52·6'	3°5·0'W	X	161
Dyffryn	Rho Cyn Taf	ST0384	51°33·0'	3°23·6'W	X	170
Dyffryn	V of Glam	ST0971	51°26·1'	3°18·2'W	T	171
Dyffryn	Wrex	SJ2538	52°56·3'	3°6·6'W	X	126
Dyffryn Aled	Conwy	SH9466	53°11·1'	3°34·8'W	X	116
Dyffryn Aled	Conwy	SH9568	53°12·2'	3°33·9'W	X	116
Dyffryn Ardudwy	Gwyn	SH5823	52°47·4'	4°5·9'W	T	124
Dyffryn Ardudwy	Gwyn	SH6022	52°46·9'	4°4·1'W	X	124
Dyffryn Ardudwy Sta	Gwyn	SH5823	52°47·4'	4°5·9'W	X	124
Dyffryn Arth	Cered	SN5462	52°14·5'	4°7·9'W	X	146
Dyffryn-bern	Cered	SN2851	52°8·1'	4°30·4'W	T	145
Dyffryn Brodyn	Carm	SN2226	51°54·5'	4°34·9'W	X	145,158
Dyffryn Cefn Faes	Pemb	SN2335	51°59·4'	4°34·3'W	X	145
Dyffryn Ceidrych	Carm	SN7025	51°54·7'	3°53·0'W	X	146,160
Dyffryn Cellwen	Nth Pt Talb	SN8510	51°46·9'	3°39·6'W	T	160
Dyffryn-Conin	Carm	SN1120	51°51·0'	4°44·3'W	X	145,158
Dyffryn Conwy	Conwy	SH7766	53°10·9'	3°50·0'W	X	115
Dyffryn Court	Newp	ST2786	51°34·3'	3°2·8'W	X	171
Dyffryn Crawnon	Powys	SO1117	51°50·9'	3°17·1'W	H	161
Dyffryn-Dulas	Powys	SN7997	52°33·7'	3°46·7'W	X	135
Dyffryn Dysynni	Gwyn	SH6004	52°37·2'	4°3·7'W	X	135
Dyffryn Dysynni	Gwyn	SH6105	52°37·7'	4°2·8'W	X	124
Dyffryn Edeirnion	Denb	SJ0843	52°58·8'	3°21·8'W	X	125
Dyffryn-ffynnonau	Torf	ST2592	51°37·5'	3°4·6'W	X	171
Dyffryn Fm	Caer	SO1205	51°44·4'	3°16·1'W	FM	161
Dyffryn Fm	Carm	SN5705	51°43·8'	4°3·9'W	FM	159
Dyffryn Fm	Nth Pt Talb	SN7300	51°41·3'	3°49·8'W	FM	170
Dyffryn Fm	Pemb	SN1314	51°47·8'	4°42·3'W	FM	158
Dyffryn Gardens	V of Glam	ST0972	51°26·6'	3°18·2'W	X	171
Dyffryn-glyn-cûl	Gwyn	SN6098	52°34·0'	4°3·5'W	X	135
Dyffryn golwch	V of Glam	ST0872	51°26·6'	3°19·0'W	X	170
Dyffryn golwch	V of Glam	ST0972	51°26·6'	3°18·2'W	X	171
Dyffrynhafod	Carm	SN3917	51°49·9'	4°19·8'W	X	159

Dyffryn-llynod	Cered	SN4045	52°5·1'	4°19·7'W	X	146
Dyffryn Maelor	Denb	SJ0361	53°8·5'	3°26·6'W	X	116
Dyffryn Marlais	Carm	SN2121	51°51·8'	4°35·6'W	X	145,158
Dyffryn-mawr	Monm	SO2515	51°50·0'	3°4·9'W	X	161
Dyffryn Mawr	Pemb	SN0131	51°56·8'	4°53·3'W	X	145,157
Dyffryn Mawr	Pemb	SN1735	51°59·2'	4°39·5'W	X	145
Dyffryn Meifod	Powys	SJ1513	52°42·7'	3°15·1'W	X	125
Dyffryn-Meigan	Pemb	SN1838	52°0·9'	4°38·7'W	X	145
Dyffryn Mymbyr	Conwy	SH6957	53°5·9'	3°57·0'W	X	115
Dyffryn Nantlle	Gwyn	SH5053	53°3·4'	4°13·9'W	X	115
Dyffryn or Valley	I of Angl	SH2979	53°17·1'	4°33·5'W	T	114
Dyffryn Penllyn	Gwyn	SH9735	52°54·4'	3°31·5'W	X	125
Dyffryntrogin	Carm	SN1321	51°51·6'	4°42·6'W	X	145,158
Dyffryn Tywi	Carm	SN6322	51°53·0'	3°59·0'W	X	159
Dyfi Forest	Gwyn	SH8010	52°40·7'	3°46·1'W	F	124,125
Dyfi National Nature Reserve	Cered	SN6094	52°31·8'	4°3·4'W	X	135
Dyfnant	Cered	SN5558	52°12·3'	4°6·9'W	X	146
Dyfnant	Powys	SO0260	52°14·0'	3°25·7'W	W	147
Dyfnant Forest	Powys	SJ0015	52°43·6'	3°28·4'W	F	125
Dyfnia	I of Angl	SH5372	53°13·7'	4°11·7'W	X	114,115
Dyfnog	Denb	SJ0764	53°10·1'	3°23·1'W	X	116
Dyfria	I of Angl	SH3474	53°14·5'	4°28·9'W	X	114
Dygoed	Pemb	SN2637	52°0·5'	4°31·7'W	X	145
Dyke	Cumbr	SD1195	54°20·8'	3°21·7'W	X	96
Dyke	D & G	NT0803	55°19·0'	3°26·6'W	X	78
Dyke	E Ayr	NS5636	55°36·0'	4°16·7'W	X	71
Dyke	E Ayr	NS5639	55°37·7'	4°16·8'W	X	71
Dyke	E Renf	NS4856	55°46·7'	4°25·0'W	X	64
Dyke	Falk	NS8574	55°57·0'	3°50·1'W	X	65
Dyke	Highld	NC8750	58°25·7'	3°55·6'W	X	10
Dyke	Lincs	TF1022	52°47·3'	0°21·7'W	T	130
Dyke	Moray	NH9858	57°36·3'	3°42·0'W	T	27
Dyke	Orkney	HY3626	59°7·2'	3°6·6'W	X	6
Dyke	S Ayr	NS3603	55°17·9'	4°34·6'W	X	77
Dyke	Shetld	HU3568	60°23·9'	1°21·4'W	X	2,3
Dyke	S Lanak	NS8836	55°36·5'	3°46·2'W	X	71,72
Dykebar Hill	Renf	NS4962	55°49·9'	4°24·2'W	X	64
Dykecrofts	Scot Bord	NY5087	55°10·7'	2°46·7'W	X	79
Dykedale	Stir	NN7901	56°11·4'	3°56·5'W	X	57
Dyke-end	Orkney	HY3705	58°55·9'	3°5·2'W	X	6,7
Dyke-end	Orkney	HY4207	58°57·0'	3°0·0'W	X	6,7
Dyke End	Orkney	HY5429	59°9·0'	2°47·8'W	X	5,6
Dyke End	Orkney	ND3884	58°44·6'	3°3·8'W	X	7
Dyke-end	Orkney	ND4792	58°49·0'	2°54·6'W	X	7
Dyke-end Geo	Shetld	HU3527	60°1·8'	1°21·8'W	X	4
Dyke Fen	Lincs	TF1322	52°47·3'	0°19·1'W	X	130
Dyke Fen Fm	Lincs	TF1322	52°47·3'	0°19·1'W	FM	130
Dykefield	E Ayr	NS4929	55°32·1'	4°23·1'W	X	70
Dyke Fm	Cumbr	NY5904	54°26·0'	2°37·5'W	FM	91
Dyke Fm	E Dunb	NS6777	55°58·3'	4°7·4'W	FM	64
Dykefoot	Inverc	NS3071	55°54·4'	4°42·7'W	X	63
Dyke Foot	S Ayr	NX0473	55°1·0'	5°3·5'W	X	76
Dykefoot	S Lanak	NT0252	55°45·3'	3°33·3'W	X	65,72
Dykegatehead	Scot Bord	NT8751	55°45·4'	2°12·0'W	X	67,74
Dykehead	Aberd	NJ2708	57°9·7'	3°12·0'W	X	37
Dykehead	Aberd	NJ5246	57°30·4'	2°47·6'W	X	29
Dykehead	Aberd	NJ5346	57°30·4'	2°46·6'W	X	29
Dykehead	Aberd	NJ5761	57°38·5'	2°42·8'W	X	29
Dykehead	Aberd	NO5099	57°5·0'	2°49·0'W	X	37,44
Dykehead	Aberd	NO6499	57°5·1'	2°35·2'W	X	37,45
Dykehead	Angus	NO2453	56°40·0'	3°14·0'W	X	53
Dykehead	Angus	NO3860	56°43·9'	3°0·4'W	T	44
Dykehead	Cumbr	NY4163	54°57·7'	2°54·9'W	X	85
Dykehead	Cumbr	NY4275	55°4·2'	2°54·1'W	X	85
Dykehead	D & G	NY0993	55°13·6'	3°25·4'W	X	78
Dykehead	Falk	NS8871	55°55·4'	3°47·1'W	X	65
Dykehead	N Ayr	NS2548	55°41·9'	4°46·6'W	X	63
Dykehead	N Ayr	NS3141	55°38·2'	4°40·7'W	X	70
Dykehead	N Lanak	NS6978	55°58·9'	4°5·5'W	X	64
Dykehead	N Lanak	NS7667	55°53·1'	3°58·5'W	X	64
Dykehead	N Lanak	NS8759	55°48·9'	3°47·8'W	T	65,72
Dyke Head	Northum	NU1504	55°20·0'	1°45·4'W	X	81
Dykehead	Northum	NY8398	55°16·8'	2°15·6'W	X	80
Dykehead	Northum	NY8889	55°12·0'	2°10·9'W	X	80
Dyke Head	Northum	NZ0291	55°13·0'	1°57·7'W	X	81
Dykehead	S Lanak	NS6647	55°42·1'	4°7·4'W	X	64
Dykehead	S Lanak	NS7543	55°40·1'	3°58·8'W	X	71
Dykehead	S Lanak	NS7741	55°39·1'	3°56·8'W	X	71
Dykehead	S Lanak	NS8226	55°31·1'	3°51·7'W	X	71,72
Dykehead	S Lanak	NT0354	55°46·4'	3°32·3'W	X	65,72
Dykehead	Stir	NS5997	56°8·9'	4°15·7'W	T	57
Dyke Head Fm	Derby	SK1468	53°12·8'	1°47·0'W	FM	119
Dykehead Fm	S Lanak	NS6156	55°46·9'	4°12·5'W	FM	64
Dykeheads	Cumbr	NY7844	54°47·7'	2°20·1'W	X	86,87
Dyke Heads	N Yks	SD9498	54°22·9'	2°5·1'W	X	98
Dykeheads	Scot Bord	NT5707	55°21·6'	2°40·3'W	X	80
Dyke Hill	E Renf	NS4856	55°46·7'	4°25·0'W	X	64
Dyke Hills	Oxon	SU5793	51°38·2'	1°10·2'W	A	164,174
Dyke Ho	Durham	NY9337	54°43·9'	2°6·1'W	X	91,92
Dyke Ho	Northum	NZ0873	55°3·3'	1°52·1'W	X	88
Dyke Ho	N Yks	SE0398	54°22·9'	1°56·8'W	X	98
Dyke Ho	N Yks	SE7494	54°20·4'	0°51·3'W	X	94,100
Dykehole	S Lanak	NS6648	55°42·7'	4°7·5'W	X	64
Dykelands	Aberd	NO7068	56°48·4'	2°29·0'W	X	45
Dykelands	Cumbr	SD2777	54°11·3'	3°6·7'W	X	96,97
Dykelands	N Yks	SD8960	54°2·4'	2°9·7'W	X	98
Dykelands	N Yks	SE6468	54°6·5'	1°0·8'W	X	100
Dyke Lane Head	N Yks	SE1661	54°2·9'	1°44·9'W	X	99
Dyke Moor	Cambs	TL3689	52°29·1'	0°0·6'E	X	142
Dykend	Angus	NO2557	56°42·2'	3°13·0'W	X	53
Dykend	Angus	NO4160	56°43·9'	2°57·4'W	X	44
Dykend	S Lanak	NS6953	55°45·4'	4°4·8'W	X	64
Dykeneuk	Aberd	NO8493	57°1·9'	2°15·4'W	X	38,45
Dykeneuk	Angus	NO4778	56°53·7'	2°51·7'W	X	44
Dykeneuk	E Ayr	NS5528	55°31·7'	4°17·4'W	X	71
Dykeneuk	Midlo	NT2357	55°48·3'	3°13·3'W	X	66,73
Dykeneuk	S Lanak	NS6150	55°43·7'	4°12·4'W	X	64
Dykeneuk Moss	N Ayr	NS3447	55°41·5'	4°38·0'W	X	63
Dykenook	Aberd	NJ8322	57°17·6'	2°16·5'W	X	38

Dyke Nook	Cumbr	NY2330	54°39·8'	3°11·2'W	X	89,90
Dyke Nook	Cumbr	NY4063	54°57·7'	2°55·8'W	X	85
Dyke Nook	Durham	NZ1147	54°49·3'	1°49·3'W	X	88
Dykenook	Northum	NY9089	55°12·0'	2°9·0'W	X	80
Dykenook	S Lanak	NS6537	55°36·7'	4°8·2'W	X	71
Dykeraw	Scot Bord	NT6308	55°22·1'	2°34·6'W	X	80
Dyke Row	Northum	NY7758	54°55·2'	2°21·1'W	X	86,87
Dyke Row Cottage	Northum	NY8568	55°0·6'	2°13·6'W	X	87
Dykerow Fell	Northum	NY7557	54°54·7'	2°23·0'W	X	86,87
Dykes	E Ayr	NS5318	55°26·3'	4°19·0'W	X	70
Dykes	N Ayr	NS2065	55°50·9'	4°52·1'W	X	63
Dykes	N Ayr	NS2852	55°44·1'	4°43·9'W	X	63
Dykes	Northum	NY7058	54°55·2'	2°27·7'W	X	86,87
Dykes	S Ayr	NS4224	55°29·3'	4°29·6'W	X	70
Dykes	Scot Bord	NT5917	55°27·0'	2°38·5'W	X	80
Dykes	Stir	NS8292	56°6·6'	3°53·4'W	X	57
Dykes Burn	S Lanak	NS6737	55°36·8'	4°6·3'W	W	71
Dykescroft	E Ayr	NS4940	55°38·1'	4°23·5'W	X	70
Dykesfield	Cumbr	NY3059	54°55·5'	3°5·1'W	X	85
Dykes Fm	E Ayr	NS5721	55°28·0'	4°15·3'W	FM	71
Dykes Fm	Somer	ST1117	50°57·0'	3°15·6'W	FM	181,193
Dykes Fm	Somer	ST3527	51°2·6'	2°55·2'W	FM	193
Dykes Ho	N Yks	SE1394	54°20·7'	1°47·6'W	X	99
Dykeside	Aberd	NJ7243	57°28·8'	2°27·6'W	T	29
Dykeside	Aberd	NJ9048	57°31·6'	2°9·6'W	X	30
Dykeside	C of Aber	NJ8608	57°10·0'	2°13·4'W	X	38
Dykeside	Cumbr	NY4261	54°56·7'	2°53·9'W	X	85
Dykeside	Cumbr	NY4365	54°58·8'	2°53·0'W	X	85
Dykeside	D & G	NY3374	55°3·6'	3°2·5'W	X	85
Dykeside	Moray	NJ1159	57°37·0'	3°28·9'W	X	28
Dykeside	Moray	NJ2058	57°36·6'	3°19·9'W	X	28
Dykeside	Moray	NJ3827	57°20·0'	3°1·3'W	X	37
Dykeside	W Loth	NS9670	55°55·0'	3°39·4'W	X	65
Dykes of Fladdabister	Shetld	HU4332	60°4·5'	1°13·1'W	X	4
Dykes Plantation	N Ayr	NS2150	55°42·9'	4°50·5'W	F	63
Dykes Plantn	E Yorks	TA2172	54°8·0'	0°8·5'W	F	101
Dykewood Ho	Norf	TF9115	52°42·2'	0°50·0'E	X	132
Dyland Cotts	Falk	NT0379	55°59·9'	3°32·9'W	X	65
Dylan Thomas's Boathouse	Carm	SN3011	51°46·6'	4°27·5'W	X	159
Dylasau Uchaf	Conwy	SH8351	53°2·9'	3°44·3'W	X	116
Dylife	Powys	SN8694	52°32·2'	3°40·4'W	T	135,136
Dyllcoed Isaf	Carm	SN5615	51°49·1'	4°5·0'W	X	159
Dyll Faen	Cered	SN7784	52°26·7'	3°48·2'W	H	135
Dymchurch	Kent	TR1029	51°1·5'	1°0·1'E	T	189
Dymchurch Redoubt	Kent	TR1232	51°3·1'	1°1·9'E	A	189
Dymchurch Wall	Kent	TR1130	51°2·1'	1°1·0'E	X	189
Dymchwa	I of Angl	SH3791	53°23·7'	4°26·7'W	X	114
Dymock	Glos	SO6931	51°58·8'	2°26·7'W	T	149
Dymock Fm	E Susx	TV5099	50°46·5'	0°8·0'E	FM	199
Dymock's Fm	Oxon	SP5925	51°55·5'	1°8·1'W	FM	164
Dymock's Mill	Wrex	SJ4544	52°59·7'	2°48·8'W	X	117
Dymock Wood	Glos	SO6828	51°57·2'	2°27·5'W	F	149
Dymond's Fm	Devon	SX9892	50°43·4'	3°26·3'W	FM	192
Dynana	Gwyn	SH4839	52°55·9'	4°15·3'W	X	123
Dynaston	Pemb	SN0710	51°45·6'	4°47·4'W	X	158
Dyneley Fm	Lancs	SD8529	53°45·7'	2°13·2'W	FM	103
Dynes Fm	Essex	TL7127	51°55·1'	0°29·6'E	FM	167
Dynes Fm	Kent	TQ9442	51°8·9'	0°46·8'E	FM	189
Dyne's Hall	Essex	TL8033	51°58·2'	0°37·6'E	A	168
Dynevor Home Fm	Carm	SN6122	51°53·0'	4°0·8'W	FM	159
Dynyn	Cered	SN7095	52°32·5'	3°54·6'W	X	135
Dyon Ho	N Yks	SE6933	53°47·6'	0°56·7'W	X	105,106
Dyrah	Cumbr	NY5944	54°47·6'	2°37·8'W	X	86
Dyrham	S Glos	ST7375	51°28·6'	2°22·9'W	T	172
Dyrham Park	Herts	TQ2298	51°40·3'	0°13·7'W	X	166,176
Dyrham Park	S Glos	ST7475	51°28·6'	2°22·1'W	A	172
Dyrham Park Fm	Herts	TQ2299	51°40·8'	0°13·7'W	FM	166,176
Dyrigs Hill	S Lanak	NS7524	55°29·9'	3°58·3'W	H	71
Dyrock Burn	S Ayr	NS3609	55°21·1'	4°34·8'W	W	70,77
Dyrock Hill	S Ayr	NS3610	55°21·7'	4°34·8'W	X	70
Dyrysgol	Gwyn	SH8328	52°50·5'	3°43·8'W	H	124,125
Dyrysgol	Powys	SO0941	52°3·8'	3°19·3'W	X	147,161
Dysart	Fife	NT3093	56°7·7'	3°7·1'W	T	59
Dysart Muir	Fife	NT2995	56°8·8'	3°8·1'W	X	59
Dyscarr Wood	Notts	SK5787	53°22·8'	1°8·2'W	F	111,120
Dysefin	Gwyn	SH6407	52°38·9'	4°0·2'W	X	124
Dyserth	Denb	SJ0579	53°18·2'	3°25·1'W	T	116
Dysgwylfa	Powys	SN8710	51°46·9'	3°37·9'W	X	160
Dyson Ho	N Yks	NZ1011	54°29·9'	1°50·3'W	X	92
Dyson's Fm	Norf	TM1288	52°27·2'	1°7·6'E	FM	144
Dyson's Wood	Oxon	SU7078	51°30·0'	0°59·1'W	F	175
Dysserth	Powys	SJ2105	52°38·5'	3°9·7'W	X	126
Dysyrnant	Gwyn	SN6599	52°34·6'	3°59·1'W	X	135
Dytach	Aberd	NJ5465	57°40·6'	2°45·8'W	X	29
Dytchleys	Essex	TQ5596	51°38·7'	0°14·8'E	X	167,177
Dythel Fm	Carm	SN4603	51°42·5'	4°13·3'W	FM	159
Dyto	Conwy	SH7868	53°12·0'	3°49·2'W	X	115

E

Eabhal	N Eil	NF8859	57°31·1'	7°12·2'W	X	22
Eabost	Highld	NG3139	57°22·0'	6°28·0'W	T	23,32
Eabost West	Highld	NG3140	57°22·5'	6°28·0'W	T	23
Eachcamais	N Eil	NF7859	57°30·7'	7°22·2'W	X	22
Each Donn	Arg & Bt	NM7821	56°20·0'	5°35·0'W	X	49
Each End	Kent	TR3058	51°16·7'	1°18·3'E	T	179
Eachil Rig	E Loth	NT6268	55°54·5'	2°36·0'W	X	67
Each Manor Fm	Kent	TR3058	51°16·7'	1°18·3'E	FM	179
Eachrach, The	Moray	NJ2923	57°17·8'	3°10·2'W	H	37
Eachway	Worcs	SO9876	52°23·2'	2°1·4'W	T	139

Eachwick	Northum	NZ1171	55°2·2′	1°49·2′W	T	88
Eachwick Red Ho	Northum	NZ1071	55°2·3′	1°50·2′W	X	88
Eadar dha Bheinn	Highld	NC1103	57°58·8′	5°11·3′W	W	15
Eades Fm	I of W	SZ4087	50°41·1′	1°25·6′W	FM	196
Eade's Fm	Suff	TM4990	52°27·3′	1°40·3′E	FM	134
Eads Bush	Northum	NY9153	54°52·5′	2°8·0′W	X	87
Eady's Fm	Leic	SK7937	52°55·7′	0°49·1′W	FM	129
Eagamol	Highld	NM3881	56°51·1′	6°17·4′W	X	39
Eagan	Highld	NH0145	57°27·4′	5°18·6′W	H	25
Eag Bheag	Highld	NJ0614	57°12·7′	3°32·9′W	X	36
Eager Fm	Lincs	TF0023	52°47·9′	0°30·6′W	FM	130
Eaglais Bhreagach	Highld	NG5259	57°33·4′	6°8·3′W	X	23,24
Eaglais Breige	Highld	NG5843	57°25·0′	6°1·4′W	W	24
Eaglais Chaluim Chille	N Eil	NB3821	58°6·3′	6°26·4′W	A	14
Eaglais na h-Aoidhe	N Eil	NB4832	58°12·6′	6°16·9′W	A	8
Eagland Hill	Lancs	SD4345	53°54·1′	2°51·6′W	T	102
Eagle	Lincs	SK8767	53°11·8′	0°41·5′W	T	121
Eagle Barnsdale	Lincs	SK8865	53°10·7′	0°40·6′W	T	121
Eagle Crag	Cumbr	NY2712	54°30·1′	3°7·2′W	X	89,90
Eagle Crag	Cumbr	NY3514	54°31·3′	2°59·8′W	X	90
Eagle Down	Devon	SS6212	50°53·7′	3°57·4′W	X	180
Eaglefield	Highld	NH7788	57°52·1′	4°3·9′W	X	21
Eagle Hall	Durham	NZ4145	54°48·1′	1°21·3′W	X	88
Eagle Hall Fm	Lincs	SK8665	53°10·7′	0°42·4′W	FM	121
Eagle Hall Wood	Lincs	SK8665	53°10·7′	0°42·4′W	F	121
Eagle Hill	Notts	SK6380	53°19·0′	1°2·8′W	F	111,120
Eagle Ho	Lincs	TF3222	52°47·0′	0°2·2′W	X	131
Eaglehurst	Hants	SU4700	50°48·1′	1°19·6′W	X	196
Eagle Island	D & G	NX5471	55°1·0′	4°16·6′W	X	77
Eagle Lane Fm	Cambs	TL6258	52°12·0′	0°22·6′E	FM	154
Eagle Lodge	Glos	ST8890	51°36·8′	2°10·0′W	X	162,173
Eagle Moor	Lincs	SK8867	53°11·8′	0°40·6′W	X	121
Eagle Oak	Hants	SU2506	50°51·4′	1°38·3′W	X	195
Eagle Rock	C of Edin	NT1877	55°59·0′	3°18·4′W	X	65,66
Eagle Rock	Highld	NC3316	58°6·4′	4°49·6′W	X	15
Eaglescairnie	E Loth	NT5169	55°54·9′	2°46·6′W	X	66
Eaglescairnie Mains	E Loth	NT5168	55°54·4′	2°46·6′W	X	66
Eaglescliffe	Stock on T	NZ4215	54°32·0′	1°20·6′W	T	93
Eaglesden	Kent	TQ7930	51°2·7′	0°33·6′E	X	188
Eagle's Fall	Arg & Bt	NN2214	56°17·4′	4°52·1′W	W	50,56
Eaglesfield	Cumbr	NY0928	54°38·6′	3°24·2′W	T	89
Eaglesfield	D & G	NY2374	55°3·5′	3°11·9′W	T	85
Eaglesfield Crag	Cumbr	NY0927	54°38·0′	3°24·2′W	X	89
Eaglesham	E Renf	NS5752	55°44·7′	4°16·2′W	T	64
Eagles Nest	Scot Bord	NT3126	55°31·6′	3°5·1′W	X	73
Eagles Rock	Aberd	NO2383	56°56·2′	3°15·5′W	X	44
Eagle's Rock	Pth & Kin	NN8331	56°27·7′	3°53·5′W	X	52
Eagle's Seat	S Ayr	NS0100	55°15·5′	5°7·5′W	X	76
Eagle Stack	Shetld	HP4806	60°44·3′	1°6·7′W	X	1
Eaglestone	Mil Key	SP8637	52°1·7′	0°44·4′W	T	152
Eaglethorpe	Northnts	TL0791	52°30·6′	0°25·0′W	T	142
Eagle Tor	Derby	SK2362	53°9·5′	1°39·0′W	T	119
Eagley	Bolton	SD7113	53°37·0′	2°25·9′W	T	109
Eaglinside	S Lanak	NS7634	55°35·3′	3°57·6′W	X	71
Eag Mhór	Highld	NG7277	57°43·8′	5°49·3′W	X	19
Eag Mhór	Highld	NJ0615	57°13·2′	3°32·9′W	X	36
Eag na Maoile	Arg & Bt	NM2765	56°42·1′	6°27·2′W	X	46,47
Eag, The	Moray	NJ1710	57°10·7′	3°21·9′W	X	36
Eag Uillt	Stir	NN4136	56°29·6′	4°34·5′W	X	51
Eairnyerey	I of M	SC2072	54°7·0′	4°44·8′W	X	95
Eairy	I of M	SC2977	54°9·9′	4°36·7′W	T	95
Eairy Jora	I of M	SC3078	54°10·4′	4°35·9′W	X	95
Eairy Kelly	I of M	SC3078	54°10·4′	4°35·9′W	X	95
Eairy Moar Fm	I of M	SC3084	54°13·7′	4°36·1′W	FM	95
Eairy-ny-suie	I of M	SC3382	54°12·6′	4°33·2′W	X	95
Eaker Hill	Somer	ST5652	51°16·2′	2°37·5′W	H	182,183
Eakley Grange Fm	Mil Key	SP8250	52°8·8′	0°47·7′W	FM	152
Eakley Lanes	Mil Key	SP8150	52°8·8′	0°48·6′W	X	152
Eakring	Notts	SK6762	53°9·3′	0°59·5′W	T	120
Eakring Brail Wood	Notts	SK6660	53°8·2′	1°0·4′W	F	120
Eakring Field Fm	Notts	SK6962	53°9·3′	0°57·7′W	FM	120
Ealaiche Burn	Aberd	NJ4431	57°22·2′	2°55·4′W	W	37
Ealaist	Highld	NG2505	57°3·5′	6°31·7′W	X	39
Ealand	N Lincs	SE7811	53°35·6′	0°48·9′W	T	112
Ealand Grange	N Lincs	SE8011	53°35·6′	0°47·1′W	X	112
Eala Sheadha	N Eil	NB0838	58°14·3′	6°58·1′W	X	13
Ealean a' Gharb-làin	Highld	NG8606	57°6·0′	5°31·5′W	X	33
Ealing	Ealing	TQ1780	51°30·6′	0°18·4′W	T	176
Ealing Common	Ealing	TQ1880	51°30·6′	0°17·6′W	X	176
Ealingham	Northum	NY8480	55°7·1′	2°14·6′W	X	80
Ealingham Rigg	Northum	NY8381	55°7·6′	2°15·6′W	H	80
Ealinghamrigg Common	Northum	NY8282	55°8·2′	2°16·5′W	X	80
Ealinghearth	Cumbr	SD3485	54°15·6′	3°0·4′W	X	96,97
Eallabus	Arg & Bt	NR3363	55°47·5′	6°15·1′W	X	60,61
Eals	Northum	NY6755	54°53·6′	2°30·4′W	T	86,87
Eals	Northum	NY8482	55°8·2′	2°14·6′W	X	80
Eals Burn	Northum	NY8382	55°8·2′	2°15·6′W	X	80
Eals Cleugh	Northum	NY7484	55°9·2′	2°24·1′W	X	80
Eals Fell	Northum	NY6955	54°53·6′	2°28·6′W	X	86,87
Eals, The	Northum	NY7685	55°9·8′	2°22·2′W	T	80
Ealta Choire	N Ayr	NR9640	55°36·9′	5°13·9′W	X	62,69
Eamont Bridge	Cumbr	NY5228	54°38·9′	2°44·2′W	T	90
Earabhig	N Eil	NB5143	58°18·6′	6°14·6′W	X	8
Earadale Point	Arg & Bt	NR5917	55°23·5′	5°47·9′W	X	68
Earby	Lancs	SD9046	53°54·8′	2°8·7′W	T	103
Earby Beck	Lancs	SD9147	53°55·4′	2°7·8′W	W	103
Earby Hall	N Yks	NZ1009	54°28·8′	1°50·3′W	X	92
Earcroft	Black w Dar	SD6824	53°42·9′	2°28·7′W	T	103
Eardington	Shrops	SO7290	52°30·7′	2°24·4′W	T	138
Eardisland	Heref	SO4158	52°13·3′	2°51·4′W	T	148,149
Eardisley	Heref	SO3149	52°8·3′	3°0·1′W	T	148
Eardisley Park	Heref	SO2948	52°7·8′	3°1·8′W	X	148
Eardisley Wootton	Heref	SO3050	52°8·9′	3°1·0′W	X	148
Eardiston	Shrops	SJ3725	52°49·4′	2°55·7′W	T	126
Eardiston	Worcs	SO6968	52°18·8′	2°26·9′W	T	138
Eardley End Fm	Staffs	SJ7952	53°4·1′	2°18·4′W	FM	118
Eardley Grange	Lincs	TF2108	52°39·6′	0°12·3′W	X	142
Eardley Hall	Staffs	SJ8052	53°4·1′	2°17·5′W	X	118
Eardswick Hall	Ches	SJ6759	53°7·9′	2°29·2′W	X	118
Earith	Cambs	TL3874	52°21·0′	0°2·0′E	T	142,143
Earlake Moor	Somer	ST3631	51°4·7′	2°54·4′W	X	182
Earland	Stir	NS6797	56°9·1′	4°8·0′W	X	57
Earl Crag	N Yks	SD9842	53°52·7′	2°1·4′W	X	103
Earldoms Lodge	Wilts	SU2421	50°59·5′	1°39·1′W	X	184
Earle	Northum	NT9826	55°31·9′	2°1·5′W	X	75
Earlehillhead	Northum	NT9726	55°31·9′	2°2·4′W	X	75
Earle Mill	Northum	NT9926	55°31·9′	2°0·5′W	X	75
Earlestown	St Hel	SJ5695	53°27·2′	2°39·3′W	T	108
Earle Whin	Northum	NT9826	55°31·9′	2°1·5′W	H	75
Earley	Wok	SU7571	51°26·2′	0°54·9′W	T	175
Earley Wood	Kent	TR1250	51°12·8′	1°2·5′E	F	179,189
Earl Hall	Lancs	SD9042	53°52·7′	2°8·7′W	X	103
Earl Hall	Lancs	SD9241	53°52·2′	2°6·9′W	X	103
Earlham	Norf	TG1908	52°37·8′	1°14·6′E	T	134
Earlham Hall	Norf	TG1908	52°37·8′	1°14·6′E	X	134
Earl Hill	E Ayr	NS7218	55°26·6′	4°1·0′W	H	71
Earl Hill	E Ayr	NS7327	55°31·5′	4°0·3′W	H	71
Earlish	Highld	NG3861	57°34·1′	6°22·4′W	T	23
Earl Rake	Derby	SK1680	53°19·2′	1°45·2′W	X	110
Earls Barton	Northnts	SP8563	52°15·7′	0°44·9′W	T	152
Earl's Br	Lincs	TF4783	53°19·6′	0°12·8′E	X	122
Earl's Bu	Orkney	HY3304	58°55·3′	3°9·3′W	A	6,7
Earl's Burn	Stir	NS7185	56°2·7′	4°3·8′W	W	57
Earlsburn Reservoirs	Stir	NS7089	56°4·8′	4°4·9′W	W	57
Earls Colne	Essex	TL8528	51°55·4′	0°41·8′E	T	168
Earl's Common	Worcs	SO9559	52°14·0′	2°4·0′W	T	150
Earl's Court	Ham & Ful	TQ2578	51°29·5′	0°11·6′W	T	176
Earlscourt Manor	Swin	SU2185	51°34·0′	1°41·4′W	X	174
Earl's Croome	Worcs	SO8642	52°4·8′	2°11·9′W	T	150
Earl's Cross	Highld	NH8090	57°53·3′	4°1·0′W	A	21
Earlsdale	Shrops	SJ4105	52°38·6′	2°51·9′W	X	126
Earls Ditton	Shrops	SO6275	52°22·5′	2°33·1′W	X	138
Earlsdon	Cov	SP3177	52°23·6′	1°32·3′W	T	140
Earl's Down	E Susx	TQ6419	50°57·0′	0°20·5′E	T	199
Earlseat	Aberd	NK0238	57°26·2′	1°57·5′W	X	30
Earlseat	Highld	NH9554	57°34·1′	3°44·9′W	X	27
Earl Seat	N Yks	SE0758	54°1·3′	1°53·2′W	X	104
Earlseat Burn	E Ayr	NS6506	55°20·0′	4°7·3′W	W	71,77
Earlseat Fm	Fife	NT3197	56°9·9′	3°6·2′W	FM	59
Earlseat Hill	Aberd	NJ4219	57°15·7′	2°57·2′W	H	37
Earl's Eye	Ches	SJ4166	53°11·5′	2°52·6′W	X	117
Earl's Farm Down	Wilts	SU1841	51°10·3′	1°44·2′W	X	184
Earlsferry	Fife	NT4899	56°11·1′	2°49·8′W	T	59
Earlsferry Links	Fife	NT4799	56°11·1′	2°50·8′W	X	59
Earlsfield	Aberd	NJ5528	57°20·7′	2°44·4′W	X	37
Earlsfield	Lincs	SK9035	52°54·5′	0°39·3′W	T	130
Earlsfield	Wan	TQ2673	51°26·7′	0°10·8′W	T	176
Earl's Fm	E Susx	TQ5930	51°3·1′	0°16·5′E	FM	188
Earl's Fm	Herts	TL2100	51°41·4′	0°14·6′W	FM	166
Earls Fm, The	Lincs	TF1820	52°46·1′	0°14·7′W	FM	130
Earlsford	Aberd	NJ8334	57°24·0′	2°16·5′W	X	29,30
Earl's Green	Suff	TM0366	52°15·5′	0°58·9′E	T	155
Earls Hall	Essex	TM1416	51°48·3′	1°6·6′E	X	168,169
Earlshall	Fife	NO4621	56°22·9′	2°52·0′W	A	54,59
Earl's Hall Fm	Suff	TL9053	52°8·8′	0°47·0′E	FM	155
Earlshaugh	Scot Bord	NT0714	55°24·9′	3°27·7′W	X	78
Earlsheaton	Kirk	SE2521	53°41·3′	1°36·9′W	T	104
Earl's Hill	Dorset	ST9014	50°55·8′	2°8·2′W	X	195
Earlshill	Renf	NS3858	55°47·5′	4°34·6′W	X	63
Earl's Hill	Scot Bord	NT2518	55°27·3′	3°10·7′W	H	79
Earl's Hill	Shrops	SJ4004	52°38·1′	2°52·8′W	H	126
Earl's Hill	Stir	NS7188	56°4·3′	4°3·9′W	H	57
Earl's Hill (Fort)	Shrops	SJ4004	52°38·1′	2°52·8′W	A	126
Earl Shilton	Leic	SP4697	52°34·4′	1°18·9′W	T	140
Earlside	Scot Bord	NT5309	55°22·6′	2°44·1′W	X	79
Earl Side	S Lanak	NS9906	55°20·5′	3°35·1′W	H	78
Earl's Kitchen	Dorset	SY8782	50°38·5′	2°10·6′W	X	194
Earls Knoll	Orkney	HY6629	59°9·1′	2°35·2′W	X	5
Earls Knoll (Long Cairn)	Orkney	HY6629	59°9·1′	2°35·2′W	A	5
Earlsmill	Moray	NH9756	57°35·2′	3°42·9′W	X	27
Earls Mill	S Lanak	NS8127	55°31·6′	3°52·7′W	X	71,72
Earl Soham	Suff	TM2363	52°13·4′	1°16·3′E	T	156
Earl Soham Lodge	Suff	TM2363	52°13·4′	1°16·3′E	A	156
Earl's Palace	Orkney	HY2427	59°7·7′	3°19·2′W	A	6
Earl's Seat	Aberd	NJ8761	57°38·6′	2°12·6′W	H	30
Earl's Seat	Northum	NY7192	55°13·5′	2°26·9′W	H	80
Earl's Seat	Stir	NS5683	56°1·4′	4°18·2′W	H	57,64
Earl Sterndale	Derby	SK0967	53°12·2′	1°51·5′W	T	119
Earlston	E Ayr	NS4035	55°35·2′	4°31·9′W	T	70
Earlston	Scot Bord	NT5738	55°38·3′	2°40·6′W	T	73,74
Earlstone Common	Hants	SU4761	51°21·0′	1°19·1′W	T	174
Earl Stoneham	Suff	TM1158	52°11·0′	1°5·6′E	T	155
Earlstone Manor	Hants	SU4759	51°19·9′	1°19·1′W	X	174
Earl Stonham Ho	Suff	TM1059	52°11·6′	1°4·8′E	X	155
Earlston Mains	Scot Bord	NT5739	55°38·8′	2°40·6′W	X	73,74
Earlstoun	D & G	NX6183	55°7·6′	4°10·4′W	X	77
Earlstoun Burn	D & G	NX6384	55°8·1′	4°8·5′W	W	77
Earlstoun Castle	D & G	NX6184	55°8·1′	4°10·4′W	A	77
Earlstoun Linn	D & G	NX6084	55°8·1′	4°11·3′W	W	77
Earlstoun Loch	D & G	NX6183	55°7·6′	4°10·4′W	W	77
Earlsway Fm	Suff	TM3872	52°17·9′	1°29·8′E	FM	156
Earlsway Ho	Staffs	SJ9161	53°9·0′	2°7·7′W	X	118
Earl's Wood	Herts	TL3935	52°0·0′	0°1·9′E	F	154
Earlswood	Monm	ST4495	51°39·3′	2°48·2′W	T	171
Earl's Wood	Northnts	SP6441	52°4·1′	1°3·6′W	F	152
Earlswood	Surrey	TQ2849	51°13·8′	0°9·6′W	T	187
Earlswood	Warw	SP1174	52°22·1′	1°49·9′W	T	139
Earlswood Common	Surrey	TQ2748	51°13·2′	0°10·5′W	X	187
Earlswood Court	Warw	SP1273	52°21·5′	1°49·0′W	X	139
Earlswood Sta	Warw	SP0974	52°22·1′	1°51·7′W	X	139
Earlye Fm	E Susx	TQ5932	51°4·1′	0°16·6′E	FM	188
Early Knowe	Northum	NU0833	55°35·7′	1°51·9′W	X	75
Earlylands	Kent	TQ4349	51°13·6′	0°3·3′E	X	187
Early Ho	N Yks	NZ0910	54°29·4′	1°51·2′W	X	92
Earlypier	Scot Bord	NT2450	55°44·5′	3°12·2′W	X	66,73
Earlyvale	Scot Bord	NT2450	55°44·5′	3°12·2′W	X	66,73
Earlywood	Brackn	SU9266	51°23·4′	0°40·3′W	X	175
Earn	Stir	NN6301	56°11·2′	4°12·0′W	X	57
Earn	Stir	NN7001	56°11·3′	4°5·2′W	X	57
Earncraig Hill	D & G	NS9701	55°17·8′	3°36·9′W	H	78
Earnfold	Moray	NJ3639	57°26·5′	3°3·5′W	X	28
Earnhill	Aberd	NJ8545	57°30·0′	2°14·6′W	X	30
Earnhill Fm	Moray	NJ0160	57°37·4′	3°39·0′W	FM	27
Earnieside	Pth & Kin	NO0105	56°13·9′	3°35·4′W	X	58
Earnknowe	Stir	NN6023	56°23·0′	4°15·6′W	X	51
Earn Law	S Lanak	NS9311	55°23·1′	3°40·9′W	X	71,78
Earnley	W Susx	SZ8196	50°45·7′	0°50·7′W	T	197
Earnley Grange	W Susx	SZ8297	50°46·2′	0°49·8′W	X	197
Earnock	S Lanak	NS6954	55°46·0′	4°4·8′W	T	64
Earnockmuir Fm	S Lanak	NS6952	55°44·9′	4°4·8′W	FM	64
Earnsaig	Highld	NM7496	57°0·3′	5°42·8′W	X	33,40
Earnscleugh	Scot Bord	NT5451	55°45·3′	2°43·5′W	X	66,73
Earnscleugh Rig	Scot Bord	NT5653	55°46·4′	2°41·6′W	X	67,73
Earnscleugh Water	Scot Bord	NT5448	55°43·6′	2°43·5′W	W	73
Earnscleugh Water	Scot Bord	NT5552	55°45·8′	2°42·6′W	W	66,73
Earn's Craig	D & G	NX9662	54°56·8′	3°37·0′W	X	84
Earnsdale Resr	Black w Dar	SD6622	53°41·8′	2°30·5′W	W	103
Earnse Point	Cumbr	SD1669	54°6·8′	3°16·7′W	X	96
Earnshaw Bridge	Lancs	SD5322	53°41·8′	2°42·3′W	T	102
Earnshaw House Fm	Ches	SJ7270	53°13·8′	2°24·8′W	FM	118
Earnsheugh Bay	Aberd	NO9498	57°4·6′	2°5·5′W	W	38,45
Earnshill Ho	Somer	ST3821	50°59·3′	2°52·6′W	X	193
Earnside	Moray	NJ1062	57°38·6′	3°30·0′W	X	28
Earnslaw	Scot Bord	NT8046	55°42·7′	2°18·7′W	X	74
Earnslow Grange	Ches	SJ6270	53°13·8′	2°33·7′W	X	118
Earn Stone	Angus	NO3683	56°56·3′	3°2·7′W	X	44
Earnstrey Hall	Shrops	SO5788	52°29·5′	2°37·6′W	X	137,138
Earn Water	E Renf	NS5453	55°45·2′	4°19·1′W	W	64
Earnwood Copse	Shrops	SO7478	52°24·2′	2°22·5′W	F	138
Earsal	N Eil	NB4153	58°23·6′	6°25·5′W	X	8
Earsary	N Eil	NL7099	56°58·1′	7°25·4′W	T	31
Earsdon	Northum	NZ1993	55°14·1′	1°41·6′W	X	81
Earsdon	N Tyne	NZ3272	55°2·7′	1°29·5′W	T	88
Earsdon Burn	Northum	NZ1994	55°14·6′	1°41·6′W	W	81
Earsdon Hill	Northum	NZ1994	55°14·6′	1°41·6′W	X	81
Earsdon Moor	Northum	NZ1893	55°14·1′	1°42·6′W	X	81
Earshader	N Eil	NB1633	58°11·9′	6°49·6′W	T	13
Earshaig Lake	D & G	NT0501	55°17·9′	3°29·3′W	W	78
Earsham	Norf	TM3289	52°27·2′	1°25·3′E	T	156
Earsham Hall	Norf	TM3089	52°27·3′	1°23·5′E	X	156
Earsham Park Fm	Norf	TM3088	52°26·7′	1°23·5′E	FM	156
Earsham Street	Suff	TM2378	52°21·5′	1°16·9′E	T	156
Earshaw Hill	D & G	NY3482	55°7·9′	3°1·7′W	X	79
Earswick	York	SE6257	54°0·6′	1°2·8′W	T	105
Earswick Grange	York	SE6258	54°1·1′	1°2·8′W	X	105
Earswick Moor	York	SE6357	54°0·5′	1°1·9′W	X	105,106
Eartham	W Susx	SU9309	50°52·6′	0°40·3′W	T	197
Eartham Wood	W Susx	SU9411	50°53·7′	0°39·4′W	F	197
Earthcott Green	S Glos	ST6585	51°34·0′	2°29·9′W	T	172
Earth Holes Wood	Suff	TM4172	52°17·8′	1°32·5′E	F	156
Earthquake Plantn	N Yks	SE8465	54°4·7′	0°42·5′W	F	100
Eary Beg Plantation	I of M	SC2983	54°13·1′	4°36·9′W	F	95
Eary Cushlin	I of M	SC2275	54°8·7′	4°43·1′W	X	95
Eary Fm	I of M	SC3286	54°14·8′	4°34·3′W	FM	95
Earyglass	I of M	SC3184	54°13·7′	4°35·1′W	X	95
Earystane	I of M	SC2372	54°7·1′	4°42·1′W	X	95
Earystane Plantation	I of M	SC2373	54°7·6′	4°42·1′W	F	95
Eary Vane	I of M	SC3381	54°12·1′	4°33·2′W	X	95
Eary Veg	I of M	SC3581	54°12·1′	4°31·4′W	X	95
Eary Ween	I of M	SC3783	54°13·3′	4°29·6′W	X	95
Eas a'Bhacain	Arg & Bt	NM8609	56°13·8′	5°26·7′W	W	55
Eas a' Bhradain	Highld	NG5326	57°15·7′	6°5·3′W	W	32
Eas a' Chais	Arg & Bt	NR8067	55°51·0′	5°30·4′W	W	62
Eas a'Chaorainn	Arg & Bt	NM8110	56°14·2′	5°31·6′W	W	55
Eas a' Chaorainn	Highld	NG7903	57°4·2′	5°38·3′W	W	33
Eas a' Chathaidh	Arg & Bt	NN2433	56°27·6′	4°50·9′W	W	50
Easach Hill	Arg & Bt	NR7229	55°30·4′	5°36·2′W	X	68
Eas a' Choire Dhuibh	Arg & Bt	NN1642	56°32·3′	4°59·1′W	W	50
Eas a' Chraosain	Highld	NH1995	57°54·7′	5°2·8′W	X	20
Eas a' Chrinlet	Arg & Bt	NN0138	56°29·8′	5°13·5′W	W	50
Eas a' Chruisgein	Arg & Bt	NN1802	56°10·8′	4°55·5′W	W	56
Eas a' Chùal Aluinn	Highld	NC2827	58°12·2′	4°55·1′W	W	15
Easa Dubh	Highld	NG7829	57°18·1′	5°40·7′W	W	33
Eas a' Ghaill	Arg & Bt	NN2126	56°23·8′	4°53·6′W	W	50
Eas a' Mhadaidh	Arg & Bt	NN2223	56°22·2′	4°52·5′W	W	50
Eas an Amair	Arg & Bt	NN0112	56°15·8′	5°12·3′W	W	50,55
Easan Bàn	Highld	NH2510	57°9·1′	4°53·1′W	W	34
Easan Buidhe	Highld	NG7803	57°4·1′	5°39·3′W	W	33
Easan Choineas	Highld	NC4144	58°21·6′	4°42·6′W	W	9
Easan Dhonnchaidh	Highld	NG7911	57°8·5′	5°38·7′W	W	33
Easan Dorcha	Highld	NH0152	57°31·1′	5°18·9′W	W	25
Easan Dubh	Highld	NC2320	58°8·3′	4°59·9′W	W	15
Easan Dubh	Highld	NN3069	56°47·2′	4°46·5′W	W	41
Easan Dubha	Arg & Bt	NN2635	56°28·8′	4°49·1′W	W	50
Eas an Duin	Arg & Bt	NR9874	55°55·3′	5°13·5′W	X	62
Eas an Eich Bhain	Arg & Bt	NN1538	56°30·1′	4°59·9′W	W	50
Eas an Eireannaich	Arg & Bt	NM8721	56°20·3′	5°26·3′W	X	49
Eas an Fhaing	Arg & Bt	NM9325	56°22·6′	5°20·7′W	W	49
Eas an Fhithich	Highld	NH3232	57°21·1′	4°47·1′W	W	26
Eas an Fholaich	Highld	NG8003	57°4·2′	5°37·3′W	W	33
Eas Anie	Stir	NN2828	56°25·0′	4°46·9′W	X	50
Easan Mhic Gorraidh	Highld	NG8422	57°14·5′	5°34·3′W	W	33
Eas an Seileachan	Arg & Bt	NM9323	56°21·5′	5°20·6′W	W	49
Eas an Taghainn	Highld	NC2206	58°0·7′	5°0·3′W	W	15
Eas an Teampuill	Highld	NG9542	57°25·6′	5°24·4′W	W	25
Easan Tom Luirg	Arg & Bt	NR7981	55°58·5′	5°32·1′W	W	55
Eas an Torra Bhàin	Highld	NM7266	56°44·1′	5°43·2′W	W	40
Easaval	N Eil	NF7715	57°7·0′	7°19·8′W	H	31
Eas Bàn	Arg & Bt	NR8999	56°8·5′	5°23·3′W	W	55
Eas Bàn	Highld	NG7423	57°14·8′	5°44·3′W	W	33
Eas Bàn	Highld	NG9427	57°17·5′	5°24·7′W	W	25,33
Eas Bàn	Highld	NG9638	57°23·5′	5°23·2′W	W	25
Eas Bàn	Highld	NG9826	57°17·1′	5°20·6′W	W	25,33
Eas Bàn	Highld	NH0977	57°44·8′	5°12·1′W	W	19
Eas Brecks	Shetld	HZ2172	59°32·3′	1°37·2′W	X	4
Eas Buidhe	Arg & Bt	NN2139	56°30·8′	4°54·1′W	X	50
Easby	N Yks	NZ1800	54°24·0′	1°42·9′W	T	92
Easby	N Yks	NZ5708	54°28·1′	1°6·8′W	T	93

Easby Firs	N Yks	NZ5608	54°28·1′	1°7·7′W	X	93
Easby Moor	N Yks	NZ5809	54°28·6′	1°5·9′W	X	93
Easby Wood	N Yks	NZ5809	54°28·6′	1°5·9′W	F	93
Eascairt Point	Arg & Bt	NR8453	55°43·6′	5°26·0′W	X	62
Eas Chia-aig	Highld	NN1789	56°57·6′	5°0·1′W	W	34,41
Eas Coire Odhair	Arg & Bt	NR7973	55°54·2′	5°31·7′W	W	62
Eas Corrach (Waterfall)	Arg & Bt	NM5145	56°32·1′	6°2·5′W	W	47,48
Eas Criche	Arg & Bt	NM9324	56°22·0′	5°20·6′W	W	49
Eas Crom	Highld	NC2307	58°1·3′	4°59·3′W	W	15
Eas Daimh	Arg & Bt	NN2427	56°24·4′	4°50·7′W	W	50
Eas Daimh	Pth & Kin	NN4446	56°35·1′	4°32·0′W	W	51
Eas Dalachulish	Arg & Bt	NM9012	56°15·5′	5°23·0′W	W	55
Easdale	Arg & Bt	NM7317	56°17·7′	5°39·7′W	X	55
Easdale	Arg & Bt	NM7417	56°17·8′	5°38·7′W	T	55
Easdale Sound	Arg & Bt	NM7417	56°17·8′	5°38·7′W	W	55
Eas Daltot	Arg & Bt	NR7582	55°59·0′	5°36·0′W	W	55
Eas Davain	Arg & Bt	NS0791	56°4·6′	5°5·6′W	W	56
Easdon Tor	Devon	SX7282	50°37·7′	3°48·2′W	H	191
Eas Dubh	Arg & Bt	NM4419	56°17·9′	6°7·8′W	W	48
Eas Dubh	Arg & Bt	NN1002	56°10·6′	5°3·2′W	W	56
Eas Dubh	Arg & Bt	NR8075	55°55·3′	5°30·8′W	W	62
Ease Barn Fm	Lancs	SD6635	53°48·9′	2°30·6′W	FM	103
Easebourne	W Susx	SU8922	50°59·7′	0°43·5′W	T	197
Easedale	Cumbr	NY3208	54°28·0′	3°2·5′W	X	90
Easedale Tarn	Cumbr	NY3008	54°28·0′	3°4·4′W	W	90
Easedike	N Yks	SE4745	53°54·2′	1°16·7′W	X	105
Easedike Village	N Yks	SE4745	53°54·2′	1°16·7′W	A	105
Ease Drain	Lincs	SK8341	52°57·8′	0°45·4′W	W	130
Ease Gill	Cumbr	NY8808	54°28·3′	2°10·7′W	W	91,92
Ease Gill	Cumbr	SD6881	54°13·7′	2°29·0′W	W	98
Easegill Force	N Yks	SD7172	54°8·8′	2°26·2′W	W	98
Easegill Head	Cumbr	NY7606	54°27·2′	2°21·8′W	X	91
Ease Gill Kirk	Lancs	SD6680	54°13·1′	2°30·9′W	X	98
Easenhall	Warw	SP4679	52°24·7′	1°19·0′W	T	140
Eas Eoghannan	Pth & Kin	NN4243	56°33·4′	4°33·8′W	W	51
Eas Eonan	Stir	NN3423	56°22·5′	4°40·8′W	W	50
Eas Eunaich	Arg & Bt	NN1430	56°25·8′	5°0·5′W	W	50
Easewell Fm	Devon	SS4645	51°11·2′	4°11·8′W	FM	180
Eas Fhiuran	Pth & Kin	NN3944	56°33·9′	4°36·8′W	X	50
Eas Fionn	Highld	NH2283	57°48·3′	4°59·3′W	W	20
Eas Fors	Arg & Bt	NM4442	56°30·3′	6°9·2′W	W	47,48
Easgach	Aberd	NJ2206	57°8·6′	3°16·9′W	X	36
Eas Garbh	Arg & Bt	NN0042	56°31·9′	5°14·7′W	W	50
Eas Gluta (Waterfall)	Highld	NC9834	58°17·2′	3°43·9′W	W	11,17
Eas Gobhain	Stir	NN6007	56°14·4′	4°15·1′W	X	57
Eashing	Surrey	SU9443	51°10·9′	0°38·9′W	T	186
Eashing Br	Surrey	SU9443	51°10·9′	0°38·9′W	A	186
Eashton Beck	N Yks	SD9454	53°59·2′	2°5·1′W	W	103
Easing Fm	Staffs	SK0157	53°6·9′	1°58·7′W	FM	119
Easington	Bucks	SP6810	51°47·3′	1°0·5′W	T	164,165
Easington	Durham	NZ4143	54°47·1′	1°21·3′W	T	88
Easington	E Yorks	TA3919	53°39·2′	0°6·6′E	T	113
Easington	Lancs	SD7050	53°57·0′	2°27·0′W	T	103
Easington	Northum	NU1234	55°36·2′	1°48·1′W	X	75
Easington	Oxon	SP4539	52°3·1′	1°20·2′W	T	151
Easington	Oxon	SU6697	51°40·3′	1°2·3′W	T	164,165
Easington	Red & Cl	NZ7417	54°32·8′	0°50·9′W	T	94
Easington Beck	N Yks	NZ7516	54°32·3′	0°50·0′W	W	94
Easington Clays	E Yorks	TA3816	53°37·6′	0°5·6′E	X	113
Easington Colliery	Durham	NZ4343	54°47·0′	1°19·5′W	T	88
Easington Demesne	Northum	NU1235	55°36·8′	1°48·1′W	X	75
Easington Fell	Lancs	SD7249	53°56·4′	2°25·2′W	X	103
Easington Grange	Northum	NU1135	55°36·8′	1°49·1′W	X	75
Easington High Moor	Red & Cl	NZ7311	54°29·6′	0°52·0′W	X	94
Easington Lane	Sund	NZ3646	54°48·7′	1°26·0′W	T	88
Easington Woods	Red & Cl	NZ7517	54°32·8′	0°50·0′W	F	94
Easing Villa	Staffs	SK0057	53°6·9′	1°59·6′W	X	119
Easingwold	N Yks	SE5369	54°7·1′	1°11·9′W	T	100
Easingwold Fm	E Yorks	TA0648	53°55·3′	0°22·7′W	FM	107
Easingwold Ho	N Lincs	SE7716	53°38·3′	0°49·7′W	X	112
Easkgill Rig	S Lanak	NS9928	55°32·4′	3°35·6′W	H	72
Easkrigg	D & G	NY1280	55°6·6′	3°22·3′W	X	78
Eas Maol Mhairi	Highld	NH3132	57°21·1′	4°48·1′W	W	26
Eas Mhic Gorraidh	Highld	NG8422	57°14·5′	5°34·3′W	W	33
Eas Mór	Arg & Bt	NM4622	56°19·6′	6°6·1′W	X	48
Eas Mór	Arg & Bt	NM8202	56°9·9′	5°30·2′W	W	55
Eas Mór	Arg & Bt	NM8623	56°21·3′	5°27·4′W	W	49
Eas Mór	Arg & Bt	NM9627	56°23·7′	5°17·9′W	W	49
Eas Mór	Arg & Bt	NS0481	55°59·2′	5°8·1′W	X	63
Eas Mór	Arg & Bt	NS1282	55°59·9′	5°0·4′W	X	56
Eas Mor	Highld	NG8121	57°13·9′	5°37·3′W	W	33
Eas Mór	N Ayr	NS0122	55°27·3′	5°8·4′W	W	69
Eas Mór Chùl an Dùin	Highld	NG8217	57°11·8′	5°36·1′W	W	33
Eas na Buaile	Arg & Bt	NM9326	56°23·1′	5°20·7′W	W	49
Eas na Coille	Highld	NG4637	57°21·4′	6°12·9′W	W	23,32
Eas na Cuingid	Highld	NG8610	57°8·1′	5°31·7′W	W	33
Eas na Fidhle	Highld	NM7950	56°35·7′	5°35·5′W	W	49
Eas na Gaibhre	Highld	NG7864	57°36·9′	5°42·6′W	W	19,24
Eas na Gearr	Arg & Bt	NM9938	56°29·7′	5°15·5′W	W	49
Eas nam Broighleag	Arg & Bt	NR9679	55°57·9′	5°15·7′W	W	62
Eas nam Meirleach	Arg & Bt	NM9431	56°25·8′	5°20·0′W	W	49
Eas nam Meirleach or The Robbers Waterfall	Highld	NN1444	56°33·3′	5°1·1′W	W	50
Eas na Mucaireachd	Highld	NM7349	56°34·9′	5°41·3′W	W	49
Eas nan Aighean	Pth & Kin	NN4243	56°33·4′	4°33·8′W	W	51
Eas nan Cat	Arg & Bt	NR7771	55°53·1′	5°33·5′W	W	62
Eas nan Ceardach	Arg & Bt	NM7916	56°17·4′	5°33·8′W	W	55
Eas nan Damh	Arg & Bt	NM9018	56°18·7′	5°23·3′W	W	55
Eas nan Leacan Mine	Highld	NM8371	56°47·1′	5°32·7′W	X	40
Eas nan Liathanach	Highld	NM8068	56°45·4′	5°35·5′W	W	40
Eas nan Ruadh	Arg & Bt	NN1423	56°22·0′	5°0·2′W	W	50
Easneye	Herts	TL3813	51°48·1′	0°0·5′E	X	166
Eas of Auchness (Waterfall)	Moray	NJ1148	57°31·1′	3°28·7′W	W	28
Eason Mór	Highld	NN3171	56°48·3′	4°45·6′W	W	41
Eason's Green	E Susx	TQ5118	50°56·7′	0°9·4′E	T	199
Eas Riachain	Arg & Bt	NN2112	56°16·3′	4°53·0′W	W	50,56
Eas Ruadh	Arg & Bt	NM8420	56°19·6′	5°29·2′W	W	49
Eas Ruadh	Arg & Bt	NM8921	56°20·3′	5°24·4′W	W	49
Eas Ruadh	Arg & Bt	NM9625	56°22·7′	5°17·8′W	W	49
Eas Ruadh	Arg & Bt	NN2416	56°18·5′	4°50·3′W	W	50,56
Eas Ruadh	Highld	NG4932	57°18·8′	6°9·6′W	W	32
Eas Ruadh	Highld	NM7254	56°37·6′	5°42·6′W	W	49
Eassanee Burn	Highld	NC6755	58°28·0′	4°16·3′W	W	10
Eassie	Angus	NO3345	56°35·8′	3°5·0′W	T	53
Eassie Fm	Angus	NO3447	56°36·9′	3°4·1′W	FM	54
Eassie Mill	Angus	NO3547	56°36·9′	3°3·1′W	X	54
Eas Socach	Highld	NH2822	57°15·6′	4°50·6′W	W	25
East Aberthaw	V of Glam	ST0366	51°23·3′	3°23·3′W	T	170
Eastabist	Orkney	HY3223	59°5·6′	3°10·7′W	X	6
East Acland	Devon	SS5932	51°4·4′	4°0·4′W	X	180
Eastacombe	Devon	SS5329	51°2·7′	4°5·4′W	T	180
Eastacombe	Devon	SS5822	50°59·0′	4°1·0′W	T	180
Eastacombe	Devon	SX3599	50°46·3′	4°20·0′W	X	190
Eastacombe Fm	Devon	SS3703	50°48·5′	4°18·4′W	FM	190
Eastacombe Fm	Devon	SX5498	50°46·0′	4°3·8′W	FM	191
Eastacott	Devon	SS3223	50°59·2′	4°23·2′W	X	190
Eastacott	Devon	SS3915	50°55·0′	4°17·0′W	X	190
Eastacott	Devon	SS5710	50°52·5′	4°1·6′W	X	191
Eastacott	Devon	SS6035	51°6·1′	3°59·6′W	X	180
Eastacott	Devon	SS6223	50°59·6′	3°57·6′W	T	180
Eastacott	Devon	SX8497	50°45·9′	3°38·3′W	X	191
Eastacott Barton	Devon	SX3879	50°35·5′	4°17·0′W	X	201
Eastacott Cross	Devon	SS6223	50°59·6′	3°57·6′W	X	180
Eastacott Fm	Devon	SS8022	50°59·3′	3°42·2′W	FM	181
East Acton	Ealing	TQ2180	51°30·6′	0°15·0′W	T	176
East Adamston	Angus	NO3235	56°30·4′	3°5·8′W	X	53
East Adderbury	Oxon	SP4735	52°0·9′	1°18·5′W	T	151
East Afton	I of W	SZ3686	50°40·6′	1°29·0′W	X	196
East Afton Down	I of W	SZ3686	50°40·6′	1°29·0′W	X	196
Eastalet	Orkney	HY2112	58°59·5′	3°22·0′W	X	6
East Allerdean	Northum	NT9746	55°42·7′	2°2·4′W	X	75
East Allington	Devon	SX7648	50°19·4′	3°44·1′W	T	202
East Almer Fm	Dorset	SY9199	50°47·7′	2°7·3′W	FM	195
East Amat	Highld	NH4891	57°53·2′	4°33·4′W	X	20
East Ancroft	Northum	NU0145	55°42·2′	1°58·6′W	X	75
East Anglian Fm	Norf	TF5922	52°46·6′	0°21·8′E	FM	131
East Angrove	N Yks	NZ5509	54°28·6′	1°8·7′W	X	93
East Anstey	Devon	SS8626	51°1·6′	3°37·2′W	T	181
East Anstey Common	Devon	SS8628	51°2·6′	3°37·2′W	X	181
East Anton	Hants	SU3747	51°13·5′	1°27·8′W	T	185
East Appleton	N Yks	SE2395	54°21·2′	1°38·3′W	T	99
East Ardler	Pth & Kin	NO2641	56°33·6′	3°11·8′W	X	53
East Ardsley	Leeds	SE3025	53°43·5′	1°32·3′W	T	104
East Arnecliff Wood	N Yks	NZ7804	54°25·8′	0°47·4′W	F	94
East Tarsuinn	Arg & Bt	NM8415	56°17·0′	5°28·9′W	W	55
East Ash	Devon	SS3316	50°55·4′	4°22·2′W	X	190
East Ash	Devon	SX6791	50°42·4′	3°52·6′W	X	191
East Ashalls Copse	Northnts	SP7341	52°4·0′	0°55·7′W	F	152
East Ashey Manor Fm	I of W	SZ5888	50°41·6′	1°10·3′W	FM	196
East Ashley	Devon	SS6411	50°53·2′	3°55·6′W	X	191
East Ashling	W Susx	SU8207	50°51·6′	0°49·7′W	T	197
East Aston	Hants	SU4345	51°12·4′	1°22·7′W	T	185
East Auchavaich	Moray	NJ2420	57°16·1′	3°15·2′W	X	36
East Auchronie	Aberd	NJ8109	57°10·5′	2°18·4′W	X	38
Eastaway Manor	Corn	SS2113	50°53·6′	4°32·3′W	X	190
East Axnoller Fm	Dorset	ST4904	50°50·2′	2°43·1′W	FM	193,194
East Ayre	Orkney	ND4497	58°51·7′	2°57·8′W	X	6,7
East Ayton	N Yks	SE9985	54°15·3′	0°28·4′W	T	94,101
Eastbach Court	Glos	SO5815	51°50·2′	2°36·2′W	X	162
East Backs	Arg & Bt	NR6921	55°26·0′	5°38·7′W	X	68
East Backwear	Somer	ST4941	51°10·2′	2°43·4′W	X	182,183
East Badallan	N Lanak	NS9259	55°49·0′	3°43·0′W	X	65,72
East Badworthy	Devon	SS4512	50°53·4′	4°11·9′W	X	180,190
East Balbarton	Fife	NT2491	56°6·6′	3°12·9′W	X	59
East Baldridge Fm	Fife	NT0888	56°4·8′	3°28·3′W	FM	65
East Baldwin	I of M	SC3682	54°12·7′	4°30·5′W	X	95
East Balgray	N Ayr	NS3642	55°38·9′	4°35·9′W	X	63,70
East Balhagarty	Aberd	NO7669	56°49·0′	2°23·1′W	X	45
East Balmirmer	Angus	NO5838	56°32·2′	2°40·5′W	T	54
East Balsdon	Corn	SX2898	50°45·6′	4°25·9′W	X	190
East Balthangie	Aberd	NJ8451	57°33·2′	2°15·6′W	X	29,30
East Banchory	Pth & Kin	NO1940	56°33·0′	3°18·6′W	X	53
East Bangour	W Loth	NT0471	55°55·6′	3°31·7′W	X	65
East Bank	Blae Gw	SO2206	51°45·1′	3°7·4′W	T	161
East Bank	Pth & Kin	NO3129	56°27·1′	3°6·7′W	X	53,59
East Bank Fm	E Yorks	TA2917	53°38·3′	0°2·5′W	FM	113
East Bank Plantn	N Yks	NZ5700	54°23·8′	1°6·9′W	F	93
East Bar	Norf	TG0046	52°58·7′	0°59·1′E	X	133
East Barcloy	D & G	NX8754	54°52·3′	3°45·2′W	X	84
East Barden Dykes	N Yks	SE1394	54°20·7′	1°47·6′W	X	99
East Barkwith	Lincs	TF1681	53°19·0′	0°15·1′W	T	121
East Barming	Kent	TQ7254	51°15·8′	0°28·3′E	T	188
East Barnaigh	Renf	NS3663	55°50·2′	4°36·7′W	X	63
East Barnby	N Yks	NZ8212	54°30·0′	0°43·6′W	T	94
East Barnet	Barnet	TQ2794	51°38·1′	0°9·5′W	T	166,176
East Barnley	Durham	NZ0022	54°35·8′	1°59·6′W	X	92
East Barns	E Loth	NT7176	55°58·8′	2°27·4′W	X	67
East Barr	D & G	NX3347	54°47·7′	4°35·4′W	X	82
East Barsham	Norf	TF9133	52°51·9′	0°50·7′E	T	132
East Barton	Devon	SS5127	51°1·6′	4°7·1′W	X	180
East Barton	Devon	SS8325	51°1·0′	3°39·7′W	X	181
East Barton	Devon	SS9408	50°51·9′	3°30·0′W	X	192
East Barton	Suff	TL9065	52°15·2′	0°47·4′E	T	155
East Batter Law Fm	Durham	NZ4045	54°48·1′	1°22·2′W	FM	88
East Baugh Fell	Cumbr	SD7491	54°19·1′	2°23·6′W	X	98
East Bay	Arg & Bt	NS1776	55°56·8′	4°55·4′W	W	63
East Bay	Pemb	SM7405	51°42·1′	5°15·9′W	W	157
East Beach	W Susx	SZ8794	50°44·6′	0°45·6′W	T	197
East Bearford	E Loth	NT5574	55°57·7′	2°42·8′W	X	66
East Beck	E Yorks	SE8643	53°52·8′	0°41·1′W	W	106
East Beck	N Yks	SE1748	53°55·9′	1°44·0′W	W	104
East Beck	N Yks	SE2548	53°55·9′	1°36·7′W	W	104
East Beckham	Norf	TG1639	52°54·5′	1°13·1′E	T	133
East Bedfont	Houns	TQ0873	51°27·0′	0°26·4′W	T	176
East Beechfield	Northum	NZ0977	55°5·5′	1°51·1′W	X	88
East Bennan	N Ayr	NR9921	55°26·8′	5°10·3′W	T	69
East Benridge	Northum	NZ1787	55°11·0′	1°43·6′W	X	81
East Benton Fm	N upon Ty	NZ2868	55°0·6′	1°33·3′W	FM	88
East Benula Forest	Highld	NH1431	57°20·2′	5°5·0′W	X	25
East Bergholt	Suff	TM0735	51°58·7′	1°1·2′E	T	155,169
East Bexington Dairy Ho	Dorset	SY5585	50°40·0′	2°37·8′W	X	194
East Bexington Fm	Dorset	SY5485	50°40·0′	2°38·7′W	FM	194
East Bierley	Kirk	SE1929	53°45·7′	1°42·3′W	T	104
East Bigging	Orkney	HY2215	59°1·2′	3°21·0′W	X	6
East Biggs	Pth & Kin	NN8606	56°14·2′	3°49·9′W	X	58
East Bight	Orkney	HY5239	59°14·4′	2°50·0′W	W	5
East Bilney	Norf	TF9419	52°44·3′	0°52·8′E	T	132
Eastbister	Orkney	ND3189	58°47·2′	3°11·1′W	X	7
East Blackbyre	E Ayr	NS4944	55°40·2′	4°23·6′W	X	70
East Blackdene	Durham	NY8838	54°44·5′	2°10·8′W	T	91,92
East Blair	Pth & Kin	NO1110	56°16·7′	3°25·8′W	X	58
East Blanerne	Scot Bord	NT8557	55°48·6′	2°13·9′W	X	67,74
East Blatchington	E Susx	TV4899	50°46·5′	0°6·3′E	T	198
East Blean Wood	Kent	TR1864	51°20·2′	1°8·2′E	F	179
East Bloxworth	Dorset	SY8994	50°45·0′	2°9·0′W	T	195
Eastbog	Aberd	NJ8418	57°15·4′	2°15·5′W	X	38
East Bog	Angus	NO4256	56°41·8′	2°56·4′W	X	54
East Boldon	S Tyne	NZ3661	54°56·8′	1°25·9′W	T	88
East Boldre	Hants	SU3700	50°48·1′	1°28·1′W	T	196
East Bolton	Northum	NU1316	55°26·5′	1°47·2′W	X	81
East Bolton Moor	N Yks	SE0194	54°20·7′	1°58·7′W	X	98
East Bonhard	Fife	NT0389	56°5·3′	3°33·1′W	X	65
East Bonhard	Pth & Kin	NO1626	56°25·4′	3°21·3′W	X	53,58
East Bonhard Fm	Falk	NT0279	55°59·9′	3°33·8′W	FM	65
East Boonraw	Scot Bord	NT5018	55°27·4′	2°47·0′W	X	79
Eastbourne	Darl	NZ3014	54°31·5′	1°31·8′W	T	93
Eastbourne	E Susx	TQ5900	50°46·9′	0°15·7′E	T	199
East Bovey Head	Devon	SX6982	50°37·6′	3°50·8′W	W	191
East Bower	Somer	ST3137	51°7·9′	2°58·8′W	T	182
East Bowhill	D & G	NY1470	55°1·3′	3°20·3′W	X	85
Eastbow Hill	Pth & Kin	NN9408	56°15·4′	3°42·2′W	H	58
East Bowley	Devon	SS9103	50°49·2′	3°32·5′W	X	192
East Brachmont	Aberd	NO8195	57°3·0′	2°18·3′W	X	38,45
East Brackley	Pth & Kin	NT1498	56°10·3′	3°22·7′W	X	58
East Brae	Angus	NO5253	56°40·2′	2°46·5′W	X	54
East Brae	Moray	NJ5255	57°35·2′	2°47·7′W	X	29
East Brae	Pth & Kin	NN9152	56°39·1′	3°46·2′W	X	52
East Brae	Stir	NN7103	56°12·4′	4°4·3′W	X	57
East Breary	Leeds	SE2742	53°52·7′	1°34·9′W	X	104
East Brent	Somer	ST3451	51°15·5′	2°56·4′W	T	182
East Bretton	D & G	NY2370	55°1·4′	3°11·8′W	X	85
Eastbridge	Hants	SU7949	51°14·3′	0°51·7′W	X	186
Eastbridge	Suff	TM4566	52°14·5′	1°35·7′E	T	156
East Bridge Fm	Devon	SS4013	50°53·9′	4°16·1′W	FM	180,190
Eastbridge Ho	Kent	TR0731	51°2·7′	0°57·6′E	X	189
East Bridgford	Notts	SK6943	52°59·0′	0°57·9′W	T	129
East Briscoe	Durham	NY9719	54°34·2′	2°2·4′W	T	92
East Brizlee	Northum	NU1515	55°26·0′	1°45·3′W	X	81
East Broadlaw	W Loth	NT0472	55°56·1′	3°31·8′W	X	65
East Broadmoss	E Ayr	NS4546	55°41·2′	4°27·5′W	X	64
East Brockloch	S Ayr	NS2911	55°22·0′	4°41·5′W	X	70
Eastbrocks Ho	Stock on T	NZ3914	54°31·4′	1°23·4′W	X	93
Eastbrook	Somer	ST2122	50°59·8′	3°7·2′W	T	193
Eastbrook	V of Glam	ST1571	51°26·1′	3°13·0′W	T	171
Eastbrook Hay Fm	Herts	TL0610	51°46·9′	0°27·4′W	FM	166
Eastbrook Ho	Devon	ST0717	50°56·9′	3°19·1′W	X	181
East Brora	Highld	NC9004	58°1·0′	3°51·2′W	T	17
East Brora Muir	Highld	NC9004	58°1·0′	3°51·2′W	X	17
East Brow Ho	N Yks	SE8189	54°17·7′	0°44·9′W	X	94,100
East Browncastle	S Lanak	NS6343	55°39·9′	4°10·2′W	X	71
East Brownrigg	Cumbr	NY5237	54°43·8′	2°44·3′W	X	90
East Browns Fm	Devon	SS4414	50°54·5′	4°12·8′W	FM	180,190
East Browson	N Yks	NZ1209	54°28·8′	1°48·5′W	X	92
East Brunton	N upon Ty	NZ2370	55°1·7′	1°38·0′W	X	88
East Buckland	Devon	SS6731	51°4·0′	3°53·5′W	T	180
East Budleigh	Devon	SY0684	50°39·1′	3°19·4′W	T	192
East Budleigh Common	Devon	SY0384	50°39·1′	3°21·9′W	X	192
East Burn	Angus	NO3169	56°48·7′	3°7·4′W	W	44
Eastburn	Brad	SE0144	53°53·8′	1°58·7′W	X	104
Eastburn	E Yorks	SE9955	53°59·1′	0°29·0′W	T	106
East Burn	N Ayr	NS2551	55°43·5′	4°46·8′W	W	63
East Burn	Northum	NT8913	55°24·9′	2°10·0′W	W	80
East Burn	Shetld	HU3477	60°28·8′	1°22·4′W	W	2,3
East Burn	W Loth	NT0958	55°48·7′	3°26·7′W	W	65,72
Eastburn Beck	E Yorks	SE9955	53°59·1′	0°29·0′W	W	106
Eastburn Br	N Yks	SE0244	53°53·8′	1°57·8′W	T	104
East Burnham	Bucks	SU9583	51°32·5′	0°37·4′W	T	175,176
East Burnham Common	Bucks	SU9584	51°33·0′	0°37·4′W	X	175,176
East Burnham Park	Bucks	SU9583	51°32·5′	0°37·4′W	X	175,176
East Burn of Builg	Aberd	NO7085	56°57·6′	2°29·1′W	W	45
East Burn of Glenmoye	Angus	NO4166	56°47·2′	2°57·5′W	W	44
Eastburn Village	E Yorks	SE9955	53°59·1′	0°29·0′W	A	106
Eastburn Warren Fm	E Yorks	SE9856	53°59·7′	0°29·9′W	FM	106
East Burra	Shetld	HU3832	60°4·5′	1°18·5′W	X	4
East Burra Firth	Shetld	HU3557	60°18·0′	1°21·5′W	W	2,3
East Burrafirth	Shetld	HU3657	60°18·0′	1°20·4′W	T	2,3
East Burton	Dorset	SY8386	50°40·6′	2°14·1′W	T	194
Eastbury	Harrow	TQ0992	51°37·2′	0°25·1′W	T	176
Eastbury	W Berks	SU3477	51°29·7′	1°30·2′W	T	174
Eastbury Down	W Berks	SU3479	51°30·8′	1°30·2′W	X	174
Eastbury Farmhouse	Dorset	ST9312	50°54·7′	2°5·6′W	X	195
Eastbury Fields	W Berks	SU3478	51°30·2′	1°30·2′W	X	174
Eastbury Grange	W Berks	SU3579	51°30·8′	1°29·3′W	X	174
Eastbury Ho	Dorset	ST9312	50°54·7′	2°5·6′W	X	195
Eastbury Manor	Surrey	SU9547	51°13·1′	0°38·0′W	X	186
East Butsfield	Durham	NZ1145	54°48·2′	1°49·3′W	X	88
East Butterleigh	Devon	SS9808	50°52·0′	3°26·6′W	T	192
East Butterwick	N Lincs	SE8305	53°32·3′	0°44·4′W	T	112
Eastby	N Yks	SE0154	53°59·2′	1°58·7′W	T	104
Eastby Crag	N Yks	SE0254	53°59·2′	1°57·8′W	X	104
East Bysshe Fm	Surrey	TQ3543	51°10·4′	0°3·7′W	FM	187
East Cairn	Angus	NO3976	56°52·5′	2°59·6′W	X	44
East Cairnbeg	Aberd	NO7076	56°52·7′	2°29·1′W	X	45
East Cairnhill	Aberd	NJ6632	57°22·9′	2°33·5′W	X	29
East Cairn Hill	W Loth	NT1259	55°49·2′	3°23·8′W	H	65,72
East Calder	W Loth	NT0867	55°53·5′	3°27·8′W	T	65
East Camno	Pth & Kin	NO2842	56°34·1′	3°9·9′W	X	53
East Campsie	Pth & Kin	NO2952	56°39·5′	3°9·0′W	X	53
East Cannahars	Aberd	NJ9221	57°17·0′	2°7·5′W	X	38

East Carleton	Norf	TG1701	52°34·0′	1°12·5′E	T	134
East Carlton	E Yorks	TA2239	53°50·2′	0°8·3′W	X	107
East Carlton	Leeds	SE2243	53°53·2′	1°39·5′W	T	104
East Carlton	Northnts	SP8389	52°29·8′	0°46·2′W	T	141
East Carlton Lodge	Northnts	SP8388	52°29·2′	0°46·3′W	X	141
East Carolina	N Yks	SE5068	54°6·6′	1°13·7′W	X	100
East Carr	Scot Bord	NT9661	55°50·8′	2°3·4′W	X	67
East Carr Ho	N Yks	SE9380	54°12·7′	0°34·0′W	X	101
East Carrs Wood	Durham	NZ1519	54°34·2′	1°45·7′W	F	92
East Cassingray	Fife	NO4906	56°14·9′	2°48·9′W	X	59
East Castick	Corn	SX2676	50°33·7′	4°27·0′W	X	201
East Castle	Durham	NZ1452	54°52·0′	1°46·5′W	X	88
East Castle	Wilts	SU0336	51°7·6′	1°57·0′W	A	184
East Cathan	Swan	SS4390	51°35·5′	4°15·6′W	X	159
East Cattie	Aberd	NJ8428	57°20·8′	2°15·5′W	X	38
East Cauldcoats	S Lanak	NS6841	55°38·9′	4°5·4′W	X	71
East Cawledge Farm	Northum	NU2011	55°23·8′	1°40·6′W	FM	81
East Cevidley	Aberd	NJ6018	57°15·3′	2°39·3′W	X	37
East Chaldon or Chaldon Herring	Dorset	SY7983	50°39·0′	2°17·4′W	T	194
East Challoch	D & G	NX1657	54°52·7′	4°51·7′W	X	82
East Challow	Oxon	SU3788	51°35·6′	1°27·6′W	T	174
East Channel	D & G	NX4953	54°51·2′	4°20·7′W	W	83
East Charleton	Devon	SX7642	50°16·1′	3°44·0′W	T	202
East Chase Fm	Warw	SP2773	52°21·5′	1°35·8′W	FM	140
East Chase Fm	Wilts	SU0121	50°59·5′	1°58·8′W	FM	184
East Chelborough	Dorset	ST5505	50°50·8′	2°38·0′W	T	194
East Cheldon Fm	Devon	SS7413	50°54·4′	3°47·1′W	FM	180
East Chevin Fm	Leeds	SE2244	53°53·7′	1°39·5′W	FM	104
East Chiltington	E Susx	TQ3715	50°55·3′	0°2·7′W	T	198
East Chinnock	Somer	ST4913	50°55·1′	2°43·1′W	T	193,194
East Chinnock Hill	Somer	ST5014	50°55·6′	2°42·3′W	H	194
East Chisenbury	Wilts	SU1452	51°16·3′	1°47·6′W	T	184
East Cholderton	Hants	SU2945	51°12·4′	1°34·7′W	T	185
Eastchurch	Devon	SX7395	50°44·7′	3°47·6′W	X	191
Eastchurch	Kent	TQ9871	51°24·4′	0°51·2′E	T	178
Eastchurch Marshes	Kent	TQ9768	51°22·8′	0°50·3′E	X	178
East Clandon	Surrey	TQ0551	51°15·1′	0°29·3′W	T	187
East Claydon	Bucks	SP7325	51°55·4′	0°55·9′W	T	165
East Cleave	Devon	SS6449	51°13·7′	3°56·5′W	X	180
East Clevedon	N Som	ST4171	51°26·3′	2°50·5′W	T	171,172
East Cliff	Cumbr	NY4166	54°59·4′	2°54·9′W	X	85
East Cliff	Dorset	SY4789	50°42·1′	2°44·6′W	X	193
East Cliff	Kent	TR3965	51°20·2′	1°26·3′E	X	179
East Cliff	Kent	TR4068	51°21·8′	1°27·3′E	X	179
East Close	Durham	NZ3828	54°39·0′	1°24·2′W	X	93
East Clough	E Yorks	SE9724	53°42·4′	0°31·4′W	X	106,112
East Clyffe	Wilts	SU0437	51°8·2′	1°56·2′W	X	184
East Clyne	Highld	NC9006	58°2·0′	3°51·3′W	T	17
East Clyth	Highld	ND2939	58°20·3′	3°12·3′W	X	11,12
East Cocklake	Cumbr	NY7546	54°48·7′	2°22·9′W	X	86,87
East Codford Down	Wilts	ST9941	51°10·3′	2°0·5′W	X	184
East Coker	Somer	ST5412	50°54·6′	2°38·9′W	T	194
East Coldcotes	Northum	NZ1575	55°4·4′	1°45·5′W	X	88
East Coldoch	Stir	NS7098	56°9·7′	4°5·2′W	X	57
East Coldside	Northum	NZ1684	55°9·3′	1°44·5′W	X	81
East Collary	E Ayr	NS5043	55°39·7′	4°22·6′W	X	70
East Colliford	Corn	SX1870	50°30·3′	4°33·6′W	X	201
East Comalegy	Aberd	NJ5838	57°26·1′	2°41·5′W	X	29
East Combe	Devon	SS9825	51°1·2′	3°26·9′W	X	181
Eastcombe	Glos	SO8904	51°44·3′	2°9·2′W	T	163
East Combe	Somer	ST1631	51°4·6′	3°11·6′W	T	181
Eastcombe Bottom	Dorset	ST6302	50°49·2′	2°31·1′W	X	194
Eastcombe Wood	Dorset	ST8309	50°53·0′	2°14·1′W	F	194
East Combe Wood	Wilts	ST9922	51°0·1′	2°0·5′W	F	184
East Common	E Yorks	SE7643	53°52·9′	0°50·2′W	X	105,106
East Common	E Yorks	SE8438	53°50·1′	0°43·0′W	X	106
East Common	Norf	TF8737	52°54·1′	0°47·2′E	F	132
East Common	N Yks	SE6231	53°46·5′	1°3·1′W	T	105
East Common Fm	E Yorks	SE7743	53°52·9′	0°49·3′W	FM	105,106
East Compton	Dorset	ST8718	50°57·9′	2°10·7′W	T	183
East Compton	Somer	ST6141	51°10·2′	2°33·1′W	T	183
East Conland	Fife	NO2604	56°13·6′	3°11·2′W	X	59
East Coombe	Corn	SX1750	50°19·5′	4°33·9′W	X	201
East Coombe	Devon	SS8803	50°49·2′	3°35·0′W	X	192
East Copse	Wilts	SU2221	50°59·5′	1°40·8′W	F	184
East Corn Park	Durham	NY9919	54°34·2′	2°0·5′W	X	92
East Cornworthy	Devon	SX8455	50°23·2′	3°37·5′W	T	202
East Corrie Resr	N Lanak	NS6979	55°59·4′	4°5·6′W	W	64
East Cote	Cumbr	NY1155	54°53·2′	3°22·8′W	X	85
Eastcote	Hill	TQ1188	51°35·0′	0°23·5′W	T	176
Eastcote	Northnts	SP6853	52°10·5′	0°59·9′W	T	152
Eastcote	Scot Bord	NT5417	55°26·9′	2°43·2′W	X	79
Eastcote	Sol	SP1979	52°24·8′	1°42·8′W	T	139
Eastcote Village	Hill	TQ1088	51°35·0′	0°24·3′W	T	176
Eastcott	Corn	SS2515	50°54·7′	4°29·0′W	T	190
Eastcott	Corn	SX3195	50°44·0′	4°23·3′W	X	190
Eastcott	Devon	SX4784	50°38·4′	4°9·5′W	X	191,201
Eastcott	Wilts	SU0255	51°17·9′	1°57·9′W	T	173
Eastcottdown Plantn	Devon	SX4685	50°38·9′	4°10·3′W	F	201
Eastcott Fm	Somer	SS8546	51°12·3′	3°38·4′W	FM	181
Eastcott Fms	Somer	SS9934	51°6·0′	3°26·2′W	FM	181
East Cottingwith	E Yorks	SE7042	53°52·4′	0°55·7′W	T	105,106
East Cotton of Kincaldrum	Angus	NO4243	56°34·8′	2°56·2′W	X	54
Eastcotts	Beds	TL0647	52°6·9′	0°26·7′W	T	153
Eastcott Wood	Corn	SX3295	50°44·1′	4°22·5′W	F	190
East Court	Devon	SS9207	50°51·4′	3°31·7′W	X	192
East Court	Kent	TQ7958	51°17·8′	0°34·4′E	X	178,188
East Court	Somer	ST5146	51°12·9′	2°41·7′W	X	182,183
Eastcourt	Wilts	ST9792	51°37·8′	2°2·2′W	T	163,173
Eastcourt	Wilts	SU2361	51°21·1′	1°39·8′W	T	174
East Court	Wok	SU7963	51°21·9′	0°51·5′W	X	175,186
East Court	W Susx	TQ3938	51°7·7′	0°0·4′W	X	187
East Court Fm	Medway	TQ8068	51°23·2′	0°35·6′E	FM	178
Eastcourt Fm	Wilts	SU3164	51°22·7′	1°32·9′W	FM	174
Eastcourt Ho	Wilts	ST9891	51°37·3′	2°1·3′W	X	163,173
East Court Manor	Kent	TQ6872	51°25·5′	0°25·4′E	X	177,178
East Court Wood	Corn	SX1856	50°22·8′	4°33·2′W	F	201
East Cowes	I of W	SZ5095	50°45·4′	1°17·1′W	T	196
East Cowick	E Yorks	SE6621	53°41·1′	0°59·6′W	T	105,106

East Cowton	N Yks	NZ3003	54°25·5′	1°31·8′W	T	93
East Craggyellis	I Scilly	SV9114	49°57·0′	6°18·1′W	X	203
East Crags Wood	E Yorks	TA1468	54°6·0′	0°15·0′W	F	101
East Craig	E Loth	NT5882	56°2·0′	2°40·0′W	X	67
East Craigie	C of Edin	NT1776	55°58·4′	3°19·4′W	X	65,66
East Cramlington	Northum	NZ2876	55°4·9′	1°33·3′W	T	88
East Cranmore	Somer	ST6843	51°11·4′	2°27·1′W	T	183
East Crantum Fm	Lancs	SD3313	53°36·8′	3°0·4′W	FM	108
East Creech	Dorset	SY9282	50°38·5′	2°6·4′W	T	195
East Croachy	Highld	NH6527	57°19·1′	4°14·0′W	T	26,35
Eastcroft	Essex	TL8502	51°41·4′	0°41·0′E	X	168
East Croft Coppice	Wilts	SU2368	51°24·9′	1°39·8′W	F	174
East Croftmore	Highld	NH9519	57°15·2′	3°44·0′W	X	36
East Crosherie	D & G	NX3359	54°54·1′	4°35·9′W	X	82
East Crossley	Aberd	NO8796	57°3·5′	2°12·4′W	X	38,45
East Culkae	D & G	NX4245	54°46·8′	4°27·0′W	X	83
East Cult	Pth & Kin	NO0742	56°33·9′	3°30·4′W	X	52,53
East Culvennan	D & G	NX3065	54°57·3′	4°38·9′W	X	82
East Curry	Corn	SX2993	50°42·9′	4°25·0′W	X	190
East Curthwaite	Cumbr	NY3348	54°49·6′	3°2·1′W	T	85
East Dale	E Yorks	SE9434	53°47·9′	0°34·0′W	X	106
Eastdale	Orkney	HY2525	59°6·6′	3°18·1′W	X	6
Eastdam	Orkney	ND4491	58°48·4′	2°57·7′W	X	7
East Dart Head	Devon	SX6085	50°39·1′	3°58·4′W	W	191
East Dart River	Devon	SX6479	50°35·9′	3°54·9′W	W	191
East Davoch	Aberd	NJ4607	57°9·3′	2°53·1′W	X	37
East Dean	E Susx	TV5598	50°45·9′	0°12·3′E	T	199
East Dean	Glos	SO6520	51°52·9′	2°30·1′W	T	162
East Dean	Hants	SU2726	51°2·2′	1°36·5′W	T	184
East Dean	W Susx	SU9013	50°54·8′	0°42·8′W	T	197
Eastdean Down	E Susx	TV5698	50°45·9′	0°13·1′E	X	199
Eastdean Park	W Susx	SU8911	50°53·7′	0°43·7′W	F	197
East Deanraw	Northum	NY8262	54°57·4′	2°16·4′W	X	86,87
Eastdean Wood	W Susx	SU9015	50°55·9′	0°42·8′W	F	197
East Dene	Roth	SK4493	53°26·2′	1°19·9′W	T	111
East Densham	Devon	SS8209	50°52·3′	3°40·2′W	X	191
East Denside	Angus	NO4738	56°32·1′	2°51·3′W	T	54
East Denton	N upon Ty	NZ2065	54°59·0′	1°40·8′W	T	88
East Dereham	Norf	TF9812	52°40·4′	0°56·1′E	T	132
East Didsbury	Man	SJ8590	53°24·6′	2°13·1′W	T	109
East Ditchburn	Northum	NU1321	55°29·2′	1°47·2′W	X	75
Eastdon	Devon	SX9779	50°36·3′	3°27·0′W	T	192
Eastdon Ho	Devon	SX9779	50°36·3′	3°27·0′W	X	192
East Donyland Hall	Essex	TM0220	51°50·7′	0°56·4′E	X	168
East Down	Devon	SS6041	51°9·3′	3°59·7′W	T	180
East Down	Devon	SX3499	50°46·2′	4°20·9′W	X	190
East Down	Devon	SX4099	50°46·3′	4°15·8′W	X	190
Eastdown	Devon	SX8249	50°20·0′	3°39·1′W	T	202
East Down	Dorset	ST8600	50°48·2′	2°11·5′W	X	194
East Down	Dorset	ST8600	50°48·2′	2°11·5′W	X	194
Eastdown	Kent	TQ5460	51°19·3′	0°13·0′E	X	177,188
East Down	V of Glam	ST0273	51°27·1′	3°24·2′W	X	170
East Down	Wilts	SU0549	51°14·6′	1°55·3′W	X	184
East Down	Wilts	SU3257	51°18·9′	1°32·1′W	X	174
East Downs	Oxon	SP3224	51°55·0′	1°31·7′W	X	164
East Down Wood	Devon	SS7036	51°6·8′	3°51·0′W	F	180
East Draffan	S Lanak	NS7945	55°41·3′	3°55·0′W	X	64
East Drayton	Notts	SK7775	53°16·2′	0°50·3′W	T	120
East Drimmie	Pth & Kin	NO1749	56°37·8′	3°20·7′W	X	53
East Drumlemble	Arg & Bt	NR6619	55°24·8′	5°41·4′W	X	68
East Drumloch	S Lanak	NS6752	55°44·8′	4°6·7′W	X	64
East Drums	Angus	NO5957	56°42·4′	2°39·7′W	X	54
East Dulwich	Sthwk	TQ3474	51°27·2′	0°3·9′W	T	176,177
East Dumer Burn	Aberd	NO7588	56°59·2′	2°24·2′W	W	45
East Dundry	N Som	ST5766	51°23·7′	2°36·7′W	T	172,182
East Dundurn Wood	Pth & Kin	NN7321	56°22·1′	4°2·9′W	F	51,52,57
East Dunley Fm	Wilts	ST8581	51°31·9′	2°12·6′W	FM	173
East Dykes	S Lanak	NS6639	55°37·8′	4°7·3′W	X	71
East Ebb	Dorset	SY4291	50°43·2′	2°48·9′W	X	193
East Ebb Cove	Dorset	SY4391	50°43·2′	2°48·1′W	W	193
East Edington	Northum	NZ1682	55°8·2′	1°44·5′W	X	81
East Ella	K upon H	TA0529	53°45·0′	0°24·0′W	T	107
East Elrington	Northum	NY8663	54°57·9′	2°12·7′W	X	87
East Emlett	Devon	SS8008	50°51·8′	3°41·9′W	X	191
East End	Beds	SP9642	52°4·3′	0°35·6′W	T	153
East End	Beds	TL1055	52°11·2′	0°23·1′W	T	153
East End	Bucks	SP8118	51°51·5′	0°49·0′W	T	165
East End	Dorset	SY9998	50°47·1′	2°0·5′W	T	195
Eastend	Essex	TL4210	51°46·5′	0°3·9′E	T	167
East End	Essex	TM0007	51°43·8′	0°54·2′E	T	168
East End	E Yorks	TA1757	54°0·0′	0°12·5′W	T	107
East End	E Yorks	TA1930	53°45·4′	0°11·3′W	T	107
East End	E Yorks	TA2927	53°43·6′	0°2·3′W	T	107
East End	Glos	SP1500	51°42·1′	1°46·6′W	T	163
East End	Hants	SU4161	51°21·0′	1°24·3′W	T	174
East End	Hants	SU6424	51°0·9′	1°4·9′W	T	185
East End	Hants	SZ3697	50°46·5′	1°29·0′W	T	196
East End	Herts	TL4527	51°55·6′	0°6·9′E	T	167
East End	Kent	TQ8335	51°5·3′	0°37·2′E	T	188
East End	Kent	TQ8543	51°9·6′	0°39·1′E	T	189
East End	Kent	TQ9673	51°25·5′	0°49·6′E	T	178
East End	Mil Key	SP9444	52°5·4′	0°37·3′W	T	153
East End	N Som	ST4870	51°25·8′	2°44·5′W	T	171,172
East End	N Yks	NZ8106	54°26·8′	0°44·6′W	X	94
East End	N Yks	SE2154	53°59·1′	1°40·4′W	X	104
Eastend	Oxon	SP3322	51°54·0′	1°30·8′W	T	164
East End	Oxon	SP3533	51°59·9′	1°29·0′W	T	151
East End	Oxon	SP3914	51°49·6′	1°25·7′W	T	164
East End	Oxon	SP4215	51°50·2′	1°23·0′W	T	164
East End	Oxon	SP4735	52°0·9′	1°18·5′W	T	151
East End	S Glos	ST7873	51°27·6′	2°18·6′W	T	172
Eastend	S Lanak	NS9437	55°37·2′	3°40·6′W	X	71,72
East End	Somer	ST5951	51°15·6′	2°34·9′W	T	182,183
East End	Somer	ST6325	51°1·6′	2°31·3′W	T	183
East End	Somer	ST6746	51°13·0′	2°28·0′W	T	183
East End	Suff	TM1034	51°58·1′	1°3·8′E	T	155,169
East End	Suff	TM1559	52°11·5′	1°9·1′E	T	156
East End Fm	Beds	TL0154	52°10·7′	0°31·0′W	FM	153
Eastend Fm	E Yorks	TA3222	53°40·9′	0°0·3′E	FM	107,113
Eastend Fm	Norf	TM4692	52°28·4′	1°37·7′E	FM	134

East End Fm	Wilts	ST9784	51°33·5′	2°2·2′W	FM	173
East End Fm	W Susx	SU9831	51°4·4′	0°35·7′W	FM	186
East End Fms	Beds	TL0430	51°57·8′	0°28·8′W	FM	166
East End Green	Herts	TL2910	51°46·7′	0°7·4′W	T	166
East End Park	Leeds	SE3233	53°47·8′	1°30·4′W	X	104
East End Vein	N Yks	SE0795	54°21·3′	1°53·1′W	X	99
East Enoch	S Ayr	NS2810	55°21·5′	4°42·4′W	X	70
Easter Aberchalder	Highld	NH5619	57°14·6′	4°22·7′W	T	35
Easter Achnacloich	Highld	NH6673	57°43·9′	4°14·6′W	X	21
Easteraigs Hill	W Loth	NS9068	55°53·8′	3°45·1′W	X	65
Easter Aldie	Pth & Kin	NT0699	56°10·7′	3°30·4′W	X	58
Easter Alemoor	Scot Bord	NT4016	55°26·3′	2°56·5′W	X	79
Easter Anguston	C of Aber	NJ8201	57°6·2′	2°17·4′W	X	38
Easter Aquhorthies	Aberd	NJ7320	57°16·4′	2°26·4′W	X	38
Easter Arboll	Highld	NH8881	57°48·5′	3°52·6′W	X	21
Easter Ardoe	Aberd	NJ9002	57°6·8′	2°9·5′W	X	38
Easter Ardross	Highld	NH6373	57°43·8′	4°17·6′W	T	21
Easter Arr	Highld	NH9352	57°33·0′	3°46·8′W	X	27
Easter Auchallater	Aberd	NO1589	56°59·3′	3°23·5′W	X	43
Easter Aucharnie	Aberd	NJ6441	57°27·7′	2°35·5′W	X	29
Easter Auchinloch	N Lanak	NS6670	55°54·5′	4°8·2′W	X	64
Easter Auchtar	Pth & Kin	NN7245	56°35·0′	4°4·6′W	X	51,52
Easter Auquharney	Aberd	NK0336	57°25·1′	1°56·5′W	X	30
Easter Auquhollie	Aberd	NO8191	57°0·8′	2°18·3′W	X	38,45
Easter Badentyre	Aberd	NJ7752	57°33·7′	2°22·6′W	X	29,30
Easter Balbeggie	Fife	NT2996	56°9·3′	3°8·1′W	X	59
Easter Balcroy	Highld	NH8351	57°32·3′	3°56·8′W	X	27
Easter Baldavie	Aberd	NJ6261	57°38·5′	2°37·7′W	X	29
Easter Balgarvie	Fife	NO3515	56°19·6′	3°2·6′W	X	59
Easter Balgedie	Pth & Kin	NO1703	56°13·0′	3°19·9′W	T	58
Easter Balgillo	Angus	NO4858	56°42·9′	2°50·5′W	X	54
Easter Balgour	Pth & Kin	NO0116	56°19·8′	3°35·6′W	X	58
Easter Balloan	Highld	NH4853	57°32·8′	4°31·9′W	X	26
Easter Balloch	Angus	NO3480	56°54·7′	3°4·6′W	H	44
Easter Ballone	Highld	NH5773	57°43·7′	4°23·6′W	X	21
Easter Balmoral	Aberd	NO2694	57°2·1′	3°12·7′W	T	37,44
Easter Balrymonth	Fife	NO5314	56°19·2′	2°45·2′W	X	59
Easter Bankhead	Pth & Kin	NO0710	56°16·7′	3°29·7′W	X	58
Easter Baton	N Lanak	NS8762	55°50·5′	3°47·8′W	X	65
Easter Bauds	Moray	NJ3059	57°37·2′	3°9·9′W	X	28
Easter Bavelaw	C of Edin	NT1763	55°51·4′	3°19·1′W	X	65,66
Easter Bendochy	Pth & Kin	NO2241	56°33·5′	3°15·7′W	X	53
Easter Binzian	Pth & Kin	NO1269	56°48·5′	3°26·0′W	T	43
Easterbister	Orkney	HY4701	58°53·8′	2°54·7′W	X	6,7
Easter Bleaton	Pth & Kin	NO1458	56°42·6′	3°23·8′W	X	53
Easter Board	E Dunb	NS7175	55°57·3′	4°3·5′W	X	64
Easter Bodilare	Aberd	NJ4140	57°27·0′	2°58·5′W	X	28
Easter Bogbain	Highld	NH7143	57°27·8′	4°8·6′W	X	27
Easter Bogieside	Aberd	NJ5027	57°20·1′	2°49·4′W	X	37
Easter Bogs	Moray	NJ4162	57°38·9′	2°58·8′W	X	28
Easter Bohespic	Pth & Kin	NN7560	56°43·2′	4°2·1′W	X	42
Easter Boleskine	Highld	NH5122	57°16·1′	4°27·8′W	T	26,35
Easter Borland	Stir	NN6400	56°10·7′	4°11·0′W	X	57
Easter Brackland	Stir	NN6608	56°15·0′	4°9·3′W	X	57
Easter Brae	Highld	NH6663	57°38·5′	4°14·2′W	X	21
Easter Brae of Cantray	Highld	NH7948	57°30·6′	4°0·7′W	X	27
Easter Braikie	Angus	NO6351	56°39·2′	2°35·8′W	X	54
Easter Breich	W Loth	NT0165	55°52·3′	3°34·5′W	X	65
Easter Brightmony	Highld	NH9454	57°34·1′	3°45·9′W	X	27
Easter Brogan	Aberd	NK0230	57°21·9′	1°57·5′W	X	30
Easterbrook	Devon	SS5904	50°49·3′	3°59·7′W	X	191
Easterbrook	Devon	SX7297	50°45·7′	3°48·5′W	X	191
Easter Broomhouse	E Loth	NT6876	55°58·8′	2°30·3′W	X	67
Easter Brylack	Moray	NJ0551	57°32·6′	3°34·8′W	X	27
Easterbuchat	Aberd	NJ3915	57°13·6′	3°0·2′W	X	37
Easter Buckieburn	Stir	NS7585	56°2·8′	4°0·0′W	X	57
Easter Bucklyvie	Fife	NT1788	56°4·9′	3°19·6′W	X	65,66
Easter Burn	Angus	NO4284	56°56·9′	2°56·8′W	W	44
Easter Burn	Angus	NO4683	56°56·4′	2°52·8′W	W	44
Easter Burn	Angus	NO5184	56°56·9′	2°47·9′W	W	44
Easter Burn	Scot Bord	NT4016	55°26·3′	2°56·5′W	W	79
Easter Burn	Scot Bord	NT5853	55°46·4′	2°39·7′W	W	67,73,74
Easter Burn of Bouster	Shetld	HU4790	60°35·7′	1°8·0′W	W	1,2
Easter Bush	Heref	SO4869	52°19·2′	2°45·4′W	X	137,138,148
Easter Cairn	Fife	NT0493	56°7·5′	3°32·2′W	X	58
Easter Calcots	Moray	NJ2563	57°39·3′	3°14·9′W	X	28
Easter Caputh	Pth & Kin	NO1139	56°32·3′	3°26·4′W	X	53
Easter Carbeth	Stir	NS5379	55°59·1′	4°20·9′W	X	64
Easter Cardno	Aberd	NJ9764	57°40·2′	2°2·6′W	X	30
Easter Carribber	W Loth	NS9775	55°57·7′	3°38·6′W	X	65
Easter Cash	Fife	NO2309	56°16·3′	3°14·2′W	X	58
Easter Claggan	Moray	NJ2225	57°18·8′	3°17·2′W	X	36
Easter Clatto	Fife	NO4415	56°19·7′	2°53·9′W	X	59
Easter Cloanlawers	Pth & Kin	NN6941	56°32·8′	4°7·4′W	X	51
Easter Cloves	Moray	NJ1461	57°38·1′	3°26·0′W	X	28
Easter Clune	Aberd	NO6191	57°0·8′	2°38·1′W	X	45
Easter Clune	Fife	NT0689	56°5·3′	3°30·2′W	X	65
Easter Clune	Highld	NH9551	57°32·5′	3°44·8′W	X	27
Easter Clunes	Highld	NH5441	57°26·4′	4°25·5′W	X	26
Easter Clunie	Pth & Kin	NO2217	56°20·6′	3°15·3′W	X	58
Easter Coillechat	Stir	NN6803	56°12·3′	4°7·2′W	X	57
Easter Colquhally	Fife	NT1994	56°8·2′	3°17·8′W	X	58
Easter Coltfield	Moray	NJ1164	57°39·7′	3°29·0′W	X	28
Easter Colzie	Fife	NO2313	56°18·4′	3°14·2′W	X	58
Easter Compton	S Glos	ST5782	51°32·4′	2°36·8′W	T	172
Easter Cottage	Ches	SJ9983	53°20·9′	2°0·5′W	X	109
Easter Cotterton	Highld	NH9452	57°33·0′	3°45·8′W	X	27
Easter Cotts	Moray	NJ2659	57°37·2′	3°13·9′W	X	28
Easter Coul	Angus	NO2858	56°42·7′	3°10·1′W	X	53
Easter Coul	Pth & Kin	NN9712	56°17·6′	3°39·4′W	X	58
Easter Cowden	Midlo	NT3667	55°53·8′	3°1·0′W	X	66
Easter Coxton	Moray	NJ2661	57°38·2′	3°13·9′W	X	28
Easter Craggie	Highld	NH7340	57°26·2′	4°6·5′W	X	27
Easter Craig	Angus	NO2652	56°39·5′	3°12·0′W	X	53
Easter Craigfoodie	Fife	NO4118	56°21·3′	2°56·8′W	X	59
Easter Crannich	Highld	NJ0034	57°23·4′	3°39·4′W	X	27
Easter Cringate	Stir	NS7086	56°3·2′	4°4·8′W	X	57
Easter Cringate Cottage	Stir	NS7187	56°3·8′	4°3·9′W	X	57
Easter Crochail	Highld	NH3835	57°22·9′	4°41·2′W	X	26
Eastercroft Ho	N Lanak	NS8366	55°52·6′	3°51·8′W	X	65

Easter Crookies	Moray	NJ1566	57°40·8′	3°25·1′W	X	28
Easter Cruicksfield	Scot Bord	NT8157	55°48·6′	2°17·8′W	X	67,74
Easter Cudrish	Highld	NH5034	57°22·6′	4°29·2′W	X	26
Easter Culbo	Highld	NH6461	57°37·4′	4°16·2′W	X	21
Easter Culbowie	Stir	NS5792	56°6·2′	4°17·5′W	X	57
Easter Culfosie	Aberd	NJ7407	57°9·4′	2°25·3′W	X	38
Easter Cultmalundie	Pth & Kin	NO0422	56°23·1′	3°32·8′W	X	52,53,58
Easter Curr	Highld	NH9924	57°18·0′	3°40·1′W	X	36
Easter Cushnie	Aberd	NJ8062	57°39·1′	2°19·6′W	X	29,30
Easter Dalmeny	C of Edin	NT1477	55°59·0′	3°22·3′W	X	65
Easter Dalnabreck	Pth & Kin	NO0955	56°40·9′	3°28·7′W	X	52,53
Easter Daltullich	Highld	NH7443	57°27·9′	4°5·6′W	X	27
Easter Dalziel	Highld	NH7550	57°31·6′	4°4·8′W	X	27
Easter Darbreich	Moray	NJ4863	57°39·5′	2°51·8′W	X	28,29
Easter Dawyck	Scot Bord	NT1937	55°37·4′	3°16·7′W	X	72
Easter Deans	Scot Bord	NT2253	55°46·1′	3°14·2′W	X	66,73
Easter Delfour	Highld	NH8408	57°9·2′	3°54·6′W	X	35
Easter Delnies	Highld	NH8556	57°35·0′	3°54·9′W	X	27
Easter Deloraine	Scot Bord	NT3320	55°28·4′	3°3·2′W	X	73
Easter Denhead	Pth & Kin	NO2441	56°33·5′	3°13·7′W	X	53
Easter Denoon	Angus	NO3543	56°34·7′	3°3·0′W	X	54
Easter Derry	Angus	NO2354	56°40·5′	3°15·0′W	X	53
Easter Dounie	Pth & Kin	NO0958	56°42·5′	3°28·7′W	X	52,53
Easter Downhill	Pth & Kin	NO0003	56°12·8′	3°36·3′W	X	58
Easterdown Hill	Somer	ST4014	50°55·6′	2°50·8′W	X	193
Easter Drumclair	Falk	NS8671	55°55·4′	3°49·0′W	X	65
Easter Drummond	Highld	NH4714	57°11·7′	4°31·5′W	X	34
Easter Dullater	Stir	NN6006	56°13·8′	4°15·1′W	X	57
Easter Dunsyston	N Lanak	NS8064	55°51·5′	3°54·6′W	X	65
Easter Duthil	Highld	NH9324	57°17·9′	3°46·1′W	X	36
Easter Earshaig	D & G	NT0402	55°18·4′	3°30·3′W	X	78
Easter Echt	Aberd	NJ7606	57°8·9′	2°23·3′W	X	38
Easter Elchies	Moray	NJ2744	57°29·1′	3°12·6′W	X	28
Easter Ellister	Arg & Bt	NR2053	55°41·6′	6°26·9′W	X	60
Easter Erchite	Highld	NH5831	57°21·1′	4°21·1′W	X	26
Easter Eskadale	Highld	NH4640	57°25·7′	4°33·4′W	X	26
Easter Essendy	Pth & Kin	NO1543	56°34·5′	3°22·6′W	T	53
Easter Essenside	Scot Bord	NT4520	55°28·5′	2°51·8′W	X	73
Easter Fannyside	N Lanak	NS8174	55°56·9′	3°53·9′W	X	65
Easter Fearn	Highld	NH6486	57°50·8′	4°17·0′W	X	21
Easter Fearn Burn	Highld	NH6385	57°50·3′	4°18·0′W	W	21
Easter Fearn Point	Highld	NH6487	57°51·4′	4°17·0′W	X	21
Easter Feddal	Pth & Kin	NN8209	56°15·8′	3°53·9′W	X	57
Easter Fernie	Fife	NO3314	56°19·1′	3°4·5′W	X	59
Easterfield	Aberd	NJ6545	57°29·9′	2°34·6′W	X	29
Easterfield	Highld	NH6943	57°27·8′	4°10·6′W	X	26
Easter Filla Burn	Shetld	HU4261	60°20·1′	1°13·9′W	W	2,3
Easter Fodderlee	Scot Bord	NT6114	55°25·4′	2°36·5′W	X	80
Easter Fordel	Pth & Kin	NO1412	56°17·8′	3°22·9′W	X	58
Easter Forret	Fife	NO3921	56°22·9′	2°58·8′W	X	54,59
Easter Fortissat	N Lanak	NS8561	55°50·0′	3°49·7′W	X	65
Easter Fossoway	Pth & Kin	NO0403	56°12·9′	3°32·4′W	X	58
Easter Frew	Stir	NS6996	56°8·6′	4°6·1′W	X	57
Easter Friarton	Fife	NO4326	56°25·6′	2°55·0′W	X	54,59
Easter Gagie	Angus	NO4636	56°31·0′	2°52·2′W	X	54
Easter Galcantray	Highld	NH8148	57°30·7′	3°58·7′W	X	27
Easter Gallovie	Highld	NH9523	57°17·4′	3°44·1′W	X	36
Easter Garden	Stir	NS6095	56°7·9′	4°14·7′W	X	57
Eastergate	W Susx	SU9405	50°50·4′	0°39·5′W	T	197
Easter Gauldwell	Moray	NJ3145	57°29·7′	3°8·6′W	X	28
Easter Gaulrig	Moray	NJ1514	57°12·8′	3°24·0′W	X	36
Easter Gellet	Fife	NT0985	56°3·2′	3°27·2′W	X	65
Easter Geo	Shetld	HU6670	60°24·8′	0°47·6′W	X	2
Easter Glackton	Highld	NH8253	57°33·4′	3°57·9′W	X	27
Easter Glasslie	Fife	NO2305	56°14·1′	3°14·1′W	X	58
Easter Glenboig	Stir	NS6087	56°3·6′	4°14·5′W	X	57
Easter Glen Quoich Burn	Highld	NH0307	57°7·0′	5°14·8′W	W	33
Easter Glentore	N Lanak	NS8171	55°55·3′	3°53·8′W	X	65
Easter Glentore	N Lanak	NS8171	55°55·3′	3°53·8′W	X	65
Easter Glinns	Stir	NS6491	56°5·8′	4°10·7′W	X	57
Easter Gorton	Highld	NJ0128	57°20·2′	3°38·2′W	X	36
Easter Gospetry	Fife	NO1606	56°14·6′	3°20·9′W	X	58
Easter Grangemuir	Fife	NO5404	56°13·8′	2°44·1′W	X	59
Easter Greens	Moray	NJ2368	57°42·0′	3°17·1′W	X	28
Easter Happrew	Scot Bord	NT1939	55°38·5′	3°16·8′W	X	72
Easter Head	Highld	ND2076	58°40·1′	3°22·3′W	X	7,12
Easter Heathfield	Highld	NH7173	57°44·0′	4°9·5′W	X	21
Easter Heog	Shetld	HU3833	60°5·1′	1°18·5′W	H	4
Easter Hevda Wick	Shetld	HU4479	60°29·8′	1°11·4′W	W	2,3
Easter Hill	Devon	SX9681	50°37·4′	3°27·8′W	H	192
Easter Hill	Scot Bord	NT3814	55°25·2′	2°58·3′W	H	79
Easter Hill	Scot Bord	NT3918	55°27·4′	2°57·4′W	H	79
Easter Hill	Scot Bord	NT5337	55°37·7′	2°44·4′W	X	73
Easterhill	Stir	NS5496	56°8·3′	4°20·5′W	X	57
Easterhill Head	Scot Bord	NT3920	55°28·5′	2°57·5′W	H	73
Easter Hill of Dale	Shetld	HU4168	60°23·9′	1°14·9′W	H	2,3
Easter Ho	Shetld	HU5497	60°39·4′	1°0·2′W	X	1
Easter Holland	Orkney	ND4585	58°45·2′	2°56·6′W	X	7
Easterhoull	Shetld	HU4038	60°7·7′	1°16·3′W	X	4
Easterhouse	C of Glas	NS6865	55°51·9′	4°6·1′W	T	64
Easterhouse	S Lanak	NT0154	55°46·4′	3°34·3′W	X	65,72
Easter Housebyres	Scot Bord	NT5337	55°37·7′	2°44·4′W	T	73
Easter Howgate	Midlo	NT2464	55°52·0′	3°12·4′W	T	66
Easter Howlaws	Scot Bord	NT7242	55°40·5′	2°26·3′W	X	74
Easter Inch	W Loth	NS9867	55°53·4′	3°37·4′W	X	65
Easter Inch Moss	W Loth	NS9966	55°52·8′	3°36·4′W	X	65
Easter Jackston	Aberd	NJ7561	57°38·6′	2°24·7′W	X	29
Easter Jawcraig	Falk	NS8475	55°57·5′	3°51·0′W	X	65
Easter Kame	Shetld	HU3788	60°34·7′	1°19·0′W	X	1,2
Easter Keith	Angus	NO2937	56°31·4′	3°8·8′W	X	53
Easter Kelas	Moray	NJ1755	57°34·9′	3°22·8′W	X	28
Easter Kellie	Fife	NO5205	56°14·4′	2°46·0′W	X	59
Easter Kershope	Scot Bord	NT3727	55°32·2′	2°59·5′W	X	73
Easter Kilwhiss	Fife	NO2810	56°16·9′	3°9·3′W	T	59
Easter Kincaple Fm	Fife	NO4717	56°20·8′	2°51·0′W	FM	59
Easter Kinkell	Highld	NH5755	57°34·0′	4°23·0′W	T	26
Easter Kinleith	C of Edin	NT1967	55°53·6′	3°17·3′W	X	65,66
Easter Kinsleith	Fife	NO3318	56°21·2′	3°4·6′W	T	59
Easter Knock	Aberd	NJ9946	57°30·5′	2°0·5′W	X	30
Easterknowe Fm	Scot Bord	NT1837	55°37·4′	3°17·7′W	FM	72
Easter Knowes	Shetld	HU4680	60°30·3′	1°9·2′W	X	1,2,3
Easter Knox	Angus	NO5839	56°32·7′	2°40·5′W	T	54
Easter Laggan	Highld	NJ0025	57°18·5′	3°39·1′W	X	36
Easterlands	Devon	SS9218	50°57·3′	3°31·9′W	X	181
Easterlands	Somer	ST1118	50°57·5′	3°15·7′W	X	181,193
Easter Land Taing	Shetld	HU4480	60°30·3′	1°11·4′W	X	1,2,3
Easter Langlee	Scot Bord	NT5135	55°36·6′	2°46·2′W	T	73
Easter Lathrisk	Fife	NO2808	56°15·8′	3°9·3′W	X	59
Easter Lawrenceton	Moray	NJ0858	57°36·4′	3°31·9′W	X	27
Easter Lednathie	Angus	NO3363	56°45·5′	3°5·3′W	T	44
Easterlee	Shetld	HU5180	60°30·3′	1°3·8′W	X	1,2,3
Easter Lee of Gloup	Shetld	HP5003	60°42·7′	1°4·5′W	X	1
Easter Lennieston	Stir	NN6201	56°11·2′	4°13·0′W	X	57
Easter Letter	Aberd	NJ7511	57°11·6′	2°24·4′W	X	38
Easterley Fm	Lancs	SD7435	53°48·9′	2°23·3′W	FM	103
Easter Limekilns	Highld	NH9936	57°24·5′	3°40·4′W	X	27
Easter Lix	Stir	NN5531	56°27·2′	4°20·7′W	X	51
Easter Loch	Shetld	HP5901	60°41·5′	0°54·7′W	W	1
Easter Lochend	Highld	NH8453	57°33·4′	3°55·9′W	X	27
Easter Lochs	Moray	NJ3163	57°39·4′	3°8·9′W	X	28
Easter Logie	Pth & Kin	NO1246	56°36·1′	3°25·6′W	X	53
Easter Longridge	W Loth	NS9562	55°50·6′	3°40·2′W	X	65
Easter Lovat	Highld	NH5446	57°29·1′	4°25·7′W	X	26
Easter Lumbennie	Fife	NO2316	56°20·1′	3°14·3′W	X	58
Easterly Fm	Lancs	SD7535	53°48·9′	2°22·4′W	FM	103
Easter Mains	Aberd	NJ8408	57°10·0′	2°15·4′W	X	38
Easter Mains	Highld	NH4339	57°25·1′	4°36·4′W	X	26
Easter Manbeen	Moray	NJ1959	57°37·1′	3°20·9′W	X	28
Easter Mandally	Highld	NH2900	57°3·8′	4°48·8′W	X	34
Easter Marcus	Angus	NO5158	56°42·9′	2°47·6′W	X	54
Easter Mause	Pth & Kin	NO1747	56°36·7′	3°20·7′W	X	53
Easter Meathie	Angus	NO4646	56°36·4′	2°52·3′W	T	54
Easter Meiggar	Pth & Kin	NN7618	56°20·5′	3°59·9′W	X	57
Easter Melrose	Aberd	NJ7563	57°39·6′	2°24·7′W	X	29
Easter Milton	Highld	NH4930	57°20·4′	4°30·1′W	X	26
Easter Milton	Highld	NH9553	57°33·6′	3°44·8′W	X	27
Easter Minnonie	Aberd	NJ7860	57°38·0′	2°21·6′W	X	29,30
Easter Moffat	N Lanak	NS7966	55°52·6′	3°55·6′W	X	64
Easter Moffat Fm	N Lanak	NS8066	55°52·6′	3°54·6′W	FM	65
Easter Moncreiffe	Pth & Kin	NO1419	56°21·6′	3°23·1′W	X	58
Easter Moniack	Highld	NH5543	57°27·5′	4°24·6′W	X	26
Easter Montbletton	Aberd	NJ7361	57°38·5′	2°26·7′W	X	29
Easter Moy	Highld	NH4954	57°33·3′	4°31·0′W	X	26
Easter Muirdean	Scot Bord	NT6835	55°36·7′	2°30·0′W	X	74
Easter Muirden	Aberd	NJ7054	57°34·8′	2°29·6′W	X	29
Easter Muirhead	Pth & Kin	NS9995	56°8·5′	3°37·1′W	X	58
Easter Mye	Stir	NS5894	56°7·3′	4°16·6′W	X	57
Eastern Ball	Devon	SS7931	51°4·2′	3°43·2′W	X	180
Eastern Beacon	Devon	SX6658	50°24·6′	3°52·8′W	X	202
Eastern Blackapit	Corn	SX0991	50°41·5′	4°41·9′W	X	190
Eastern Black Rock	Devon	SX9149	50°20·1′	3°31·5′W	X	202
Eastern Breakwater	Swan	SS6691	51°36·4′	3°55·7′W	X	159
Eastern Brockholes	Somer	SS9248	51°13·5′	3°32·4′W	X	181
Eastern Channel	Falk	NS9483	56°1·9′	3°41·6′W	W	65
Eastern Cleddau	Pemb	SN0212	51°46·5′	4°51·8′W	W	157,158
Eastern Cleddau	Pemb	SN1022	51°52·1′	4°45·2′W	W	145,158
Eastern Cliff	Corn	SW7416	50°0·3′	5°8·9′W	X	204
Eastern Craigs	C of Edin	NT2877	55°59·1′	3°8·8′W	X	66
Eastern Docks	Kent	TR3341	51°7·5′	1°20·2′E	X	179
Eastern Down	Devon	SS9102	50°48·7′	3°32·4′W	X	192
Easter Newburn	Fife	NO4404	56°13·8′	2°53·8′W	X	59
Easter Newforres	Moray	NJ0658	57°36·4′	3°33·9′W	X	27
Easter New Moor	Devon	SS8325	51°1·0′	3°39·7′W	X	181
Easter Newton	W Loth	NT1267	55°53·5′	3°24·0′W	X	65
Easternhill Fm	Devon	SX8488	50°41·0′	3°38·1′W	FM	191
Eastern Hill Fm	Warw	SP0462	52°15·6′	1°56·1′W	FM	150
Eastern Isles	I Scilly	SV9414	49°57·1′	6°15·6′W	X	203
Easter Norton	C of Edin	NT1572	55°56·3′	3°21·2′W	X	65
Eastern Tor	Devon	SX5866	50°28·8′	3°59·7′W	X	202
Eastern Wood	Somer	ST0334	51°6·1′	3°22·7′W	F	181
Easter Oathlaw	Angus	NO4756	56°41·8′	2°51·5′W	X	54
Easter Ogil	Angus	NO4561	56°44·5′	2°53·5′W	X	44
Easter Ord	Aberd	NJ8304	57°7·9′	2°16·4′W	X	38
Easter Park	Orkney	HY5001	58°53·9′	2°51·6′W	X	6,7
Easter Park Fm	Glos	SO8101	51°42·7′	2°16·1′W	FM	162
Easter Parkhead	Pth & Kin	NO2144	56°35·1′	3°16·7′W	X	53
Easter Park Hill	Scot Bord	NT4313	55°24·7′	2°53·6′W	H	79
Easter Pettymarcus	Aberd	NK0042	57°28·4′	1°59·5′W	X	30
Easter Pinkerton	E Loth	NT7075	55°58·3′	2°28·4′W	X	67
Easter Pirleyhill	Falk	NS9077	55°58·7′	3°45·3′W	X	65
Easter Pitcorthie	Fife	NO5003	56°13·3′	2°47·9′W	X	59
Easter Pitscottie	Fife	NO4113	56°18·6′	2°56·8′W	X	59
Easter Place	Scot Bord	NT0636	55°36·8′	3°29·1′W	X	72
Easter Poldar	Stir	NS6497	56°9·0′	4°10·9′W	X	57
Easter Quarff	Shetld	HU4235	60°6·1′	1°14·2′W	T	4
Easter Rarichie	Highld	NH8474	57°44·7′	3°56·5′W	X	21
Easter Rattray	Pth & Kin	NO2145	56°35·7′	3°16·7′W	X	53
Easter Reach	Essex	TQ9096	51°38·1′	0°45·1′E	W	168
Easter Rhynd	Pth & Kin	NO1818	56°21·1′	3°19·2′W	X	58
Easter Rigghead	W Loth	NS9070	55°54·9′	3°45·2′W	X	65
Easter Ross	Highld	NH4879	57°46·8′	4°32·9′W	X	20
Easter Ross	Highld	NH6479	57°47·1′	4°16·8′W	X	21
Easter Ross	Stir	NS7295	56°8·1′	4°3·1′W	X	57
Easter Rova Head	Shetld	HU4745	60°11·5′	1°8·7′W	X	4
Easter Row	Stir	NS7599	56°10·3′	4°0·4′W	X	57
Easter Rynaballoch	Highld	NJ1029	57°20·8′	3°29·3′W	X	36
Easter Rynechkra	Highld	NH9830	57°21·2′	3°41·3′W	X	27,36
Easterscord	Shetld	HU4166	60°22·8′	1°14·9′W	X	2,3
Easter Score Holm	Shetld	HU3443	60°10·5′	1°22·7′W	X	4
Easterseat	S Lanak	NS9051	55°44·6′	3°44·7′W	X	65,72
Easter Shenalt	Aberd	NJ2102	57°6·4′	3°17·8′W	W	36
Easter Shennach	Highld	NJ1130	57°21·4′	3°28·3′W	X	36
Easter Shian	Pth & Kin	NN8439	56°32·0′	3°52·7′W	X	52
Easterside	Aberd	NO8783	56°56·5′	2°12·4′W	X	45
Easterside	Midd	NZ5016	54°32·4′	1°13·2′W	T	93
Easterside Fm	N Yks	SE5589	54°17·9′	1°8·9′W	FM	100
Easter Sills Fm	S Lanak	NS9342	55°39·8′	3°41·6′W	FM	71,72
Easter Silverford	Aberd	NJ7763	57°39·6′	2°22·7′W	X	29,30
Easter Skeld	Shetld	HU3144	60°11·0′	1°26·0′W	T	4
Easter Skene Ho	Aberd	NJ7908	57°10·0′	2°20·4′W	X	38
Easter Skerries	Shetld	HU6669	60°24·2′	0°47·6′W	X	2
Easter Sleach	Aberd	NJ2601	57°5·9′	3°12·8′W	X	37
Easter Sluie	Aberd	NO6297	57°4·0′	2°37·1′W	X	37,45
Easter Softlaw	Scot Bord	NT7532	55°35·1′	2°23·4′W	T	74
Easter Sound	Shetld	HU2446	60°12·1′	1°33·5′W	W	4
Easter Stonyfield	Highld	NH6973	57°43·9′	4°11·5′W	X	21
Easter Strath	Highld	NH6758	57°35·8′	4°13·1′W	X	26
Easter Strathkinness	Fife	NO4716	56°20·3′	2°51·0′W	X	59
Easter Strathnoon	Highld	NH7724	57°17·7′	4°2·0′W	X	35
Easter Suddie	Highld	NH6654	57°33·6′	4°13·9′W	X	26
Easter Tarr	Stir	NN6300	56°10·6′	4°12·0′W	X	57
Easter Tillathrowie	Aberd	NJ4734	57°23·9′	2°52·5′W	X	28,29
Easter Tillybo	Aberd	NJ7859	57°37·5′	2°21·6′W	X	29,30
Easter Tofts	S Lanak	NS8635	55°36·0′	3°48·1′W	X	71,72
Easter Tolmauds	Aberd	NJ6207	57°9·4′	2°37·2′W	X	37
Easterton	Aberd	NJ4812	57°12·0′	2°51·2′W	X	37
Easterton	Aberd	NJ7027	57°20·2′	2°29·4′W	X	38
Easterton	Aberd	NJ7631	57°22·4′	2°23·5′W	X	29
Easterton	Aberd	NK0235	57°24·6′	1°57·5′W	X	30
Easterton	Aberd	NK0948	57°31·6′	1°50·5′W	X	30
Easterton	E Dunb	NS6974	55°56·7′	4°5·4′W	X	64
Easterton	Highld	NH6332	57°21·7′	4°16·2′W	X	26
Easterton	Highld	NH9357	57°35·7′	3°46·9′W	X	27
Easterton	Moray	NJ1465	57°40·3′	3°26·0′W	X	28
Easterton	Moray	NJ2156	57°35·5′	3°18·8′W	X	28
Easterton	Moray	NJ3745	57°29·7′	3°2·6′W	X	28
Easterton	Moray	NJ3933	57°23·3′	3°0·4′W	X	28
Easterton	N Lanak	NS8068	55°53·7′	3°54·7′W	X	65
Easterton	Pth & Kin	NN8811	56°17·0′	3°48·1′W	X	58
Easterton	Pth & Kin	NO1211	56°17·3′	3°24·9′W	X	58
Easterton	Stir	NN7402	56°11·9′	4°1·4′W	X	57
Easterton	Stir	NS7284	56°2·2′	4°2·8′W	X	57,64
Easterton	Stir	NS8086	56°3·4′	3°55·2′W	X	57,65
Easterton	Wilts	SU0255	51°17·9′	1°57·9′W	T	173
Easterton of Lenabo	Aberd	NK0242	57°28·4′	1°57·5′W	X	30
Easterton Sands	Wilts	SU0155	51°17·9′	1°58·8′W	T	173
Easter Tor	Northum	NT9128	55°33·0′	2°8·1′W	H	74,75
Eastertoun	Scot Bord	NT4551	55°45·2′	2°52·1′W	X	66,73
Eastertoun Hill	Scot Bord	NT4551	55°45·2′	2°52·1′W	X	66,73
Eastertown	Moray	NJ2026	57°19·3′	3°19·2′W	X	36
Eastertown	S Lanak	NS8622	55°29·0′	3°47·8′W	FM	71,72
Eastertown	S Lanak	NS8737	55°37·1′	3°47·2′W	X	71,72
Eastertown	S Lanak	NS9939	55°38·3′	3°35·8′W	X	72
Eastertown	Somer	ST3454	51°17·1′	2°56·4′W	T	182
Eastertown of Auchleuchries	Aberd	NK0136	57°25·1′	1°58·5′W	X	30
Eastertown of Mayen	Moray	NJ5748	57°31·5′	2°42·6′W	X	29
Easter Tulloch	Aberd	NO7671	56°50·0′	2°23·1′W	X	45
Easter Tulloch	Highld	NH9715	57°13·1′	3°41·9′W	X	36
Eastertyre	Pth & Kin	NN9552	56°39·1′	3°42·3′W	X	52,53
Easter Urray	Highld	NH5152	57°32·3′	4°28·9′W	X	26
Easter Wardmill	Aberd	NJ8101	57°6·2′	2°18·4′W	X	38
Easter Watery Knowe	Angus	NO3579	56°54·1′	3°3·6′W	H	44
Easter Whin	Falk	NS8769	55°54·3′	3°48·0′W	X	65
Easter Whyntie	Aberd	NJ6265	57°40·7′	2°37·8′W	X	29
Easter Wood	Suff	TL7657	52°11·2′	0°34·9′E	F	155
Easter Wooden	Scot Bord	NT7225	55°31·3′	2°26·2′W	X	74
Easterwood Fm	Suff	TL7657	52°11·2′	0°34·9′E	FM	155
Easteryardhouse Hill	S Lanak	NT0151	55°44·8′	3°34·2′W	H	65,72
East Everleigh	Wilts	SU2053	51°16·8′	1°42·4′W	T	184
East Ewell	Surrey	TQ2362	51°20·9′	0°13·6′W	T	176,187
East Farleigh	Kent	TQ7353	51°15·2′	0°29·1′E	T	188
East Farndon	Northnts	SP7185	52°27·7′	0°56·9′W	T	141
East Fauldshope	Scot Bord	NT4126	55°31·7′	2°55·6′W	X	73
East Feal	Pth & Kin	NO2103	56°13·0′	3°16·0′W	X	58
East Feldom	N Yks	NZ1104	54°26·1′	1°49·4′W	X	92
East Fen	Cambs	TL6574	52°20·6′	0°25·7′E	X	143
East Fen	Lincs	TF4055	53°4·7′	0°5·8′E	X	122
East Fen Catchwater Drain	Lincs	TF3458	53°6·4′	0°0·5′E	W	122
East Fen Common	Cambs	TL6073	52°20·1′	0°21·3′E	T	154
East Fenton	E Loth	NT5281	56°1·4′	2°45·8′W	X	66
East Ferry	Lincs	SK8199	53°29·1′	0°46·3′W	T	112
East Fiddie	Aberd	NJ8306	57°8·9′	2°16·4′W	X	38
Eastfield	Aberd	NJ8645	57°30·0′	2°13·6′W	X	30
Eastfield	Angus	NO3437	56°31·5′	3°3·9′W	X	54
Eastfield	Barns	SE2902	53°31·1′	1°33·3′W	T	110
Eastfield	C of Bris	ST5777	51°29·7′	2°36·8′W	T	172
Eastfield	Donc	SK5994	53°26·6′	1°6·3′W	X	111
Eastfield	E Loth	NT6074	55°57·7′	2°38·0′W	X	67
East Field	E Yorks	SE9649	53°55·9′	0°31·9′W	X	106
Eastfield	Falk	NS9087	56°4·0′	3°45·6′W	X	65
Eastfield	Fife	NS9994	56°7·9′	3°37·1′W	X	58
Eastfield	Lincs	TF0380	53°18·6′	0°26·8′W	X	121
Eastfield	N Lanak	NS7474	55°56·8′	4°0·6′W	T	64
Eastfield	N Lanak	NS8368	55°53·7′	3°51·8′W	X	65
Eastfield	N Lanak	NS8964	55°51·6′	3°46·0′W	T	65
Eastfield	N Lincs	SE9421	53°40·9′	0°34·2′W	X	106,112
Eastfield	Northum	NZ2777	55°5·4′	1°34·2′W	T	88
Eastfield	N Yks	TA0484	54°14·7′	0°23·8′W	T	101
Eastfield	Peterb	TL2099	52°34·8′	0°13·3′W	T	142
Eastfield	Pth & Kin	NO0913	56°18·3′	3°27·8′W	X	58
Eastfield	Pth & Kin	NO0918	56°21·0′	3°27·9′W	X	58
Eastfield	Scot Bord	NT5428	55°32·9′	2°43·3′W	T	73
Eastfield	Scot Bord	NT7246	55°42·6′	2°26·3′W	X	74
Eastfield	S Lanak	NS6261	55°49·6′	4°11·7′W	T	64
Eastfield	S Lanak	NS9643	55°40·4′	3°38·8′W	X	72
Eastfield	S Lanak	NT0136	55°36·7′	3°33·9′W	X	72
Eastfield	S Lanak	NT0335	55°36·2′	3°31·9′W	X	72
Eastfield	Somer	ST4814	50°55·6′	2°44·0′W	X	193
East Field	Wilts	SU1162	51°21·6′	1°50·1′W	X	173
Eastfield Cottage	Pth & Kin	NO1329	56°27·0′	3°24·2′W	X	53,58
East Field Fm	Dorset	SY8596	50°46·0′	2°12·4′W	FM	194
Eastfield Fm	E Ayr	NS5535	55°35·5′	4°17·6′W	FM	71
Eastfield Fm	E Yorks	TA0359	54°1·2′	0°25·3′W	FM	107
Eastfield Fm	E Yorks	TA0451	53°56·9′	0°24·5′W	FM	107
Eastfield Fm	E Yorks	TA1152	53°57·4′	0°18·1′W	FM	107
Eastfield Fm	E Yorks	TA1568	54°5·9′	0°14·1′W	FM	101
Eastfield Fm	E Yorks	TA1949	53°55·6′	0°10·8′W	FM	107
Eastfield Fm	Lincs	TA2903	53°30·7′	0°2·9′W	FM	113
Eastfield Fm	Lincs	TF3076	53°16·1′	0°2·6′W	FM	122

Eastfield Fm	Lincs	TF3566	53°10·7′	0°1·6′E	FM	122
Eastfield Fm	Lincs	TF3786	53°21·4′	0°3·9′E	FM	113,122
Eastfield Fm	Lincs	TF3988	53°22·5′	0°5·8′E	FM	113,122
Eastfield Fm	Lincs	TF4184	53°20·3′	0°7·5′E	FM	122
Eastfield Fm	Lincs	TF4187	53°21·9′	0°7·6′E	FM	113,122
Eastfield Fm	Midd	NZ5513	54°30·8′	1°8·6′W	FM	93
East Field Fm	N Lincs	SE9419	53°39·8′	0°34·2′W	FM	112
Eastfield Fm	N Lincs	TA0320	53°40·2′	0°26·0′W	FM	107,112
Eastfield Fm	Norf	TG4323	52°45·2′	1°36·5′E	FM	134
Eastfield Fm	Notts	SK6165	53°11·0′	1°4·8′W	FM	120
Eastfield Fm	Oxon	SU3694	51°38·9′	1°28·4′W	FM	164,174
Eastfield Fm	Oxon	SU6994	51°38·7′	0°59·8′W	FM	175
Eastfield Fm	Pemb	SM7909	51°44·4′	5°11·7′W	FM	157
Eastfield Fm	Pth & Kin	NO1118	56°21·0′	3°26·0′W	FM	58
Eastfield Fm	Rut	SK8713	52°42·7′	0°42·3′W	FM	130
Eastfield Fm	S Lanak	NS9633	55°35·0′	3°38·6′W	FM	72
Eastfield Fm	W Susx	SU7904	50°50·0′	0°52·3′W	FM	197
Eastfield Fm	York	SE5648	53°55·7′	1°8·4′W	FM	105
Eastfield Hall	Northum	NU2206	55°21·1′	1°38·8′W	T	81
Eastfield Hill	Dorset	SY6499	50°47·6′	2°30·3′W	X	194
Eastfield Ho	E Yorks	TA3322	53°40·9′	0°1·2′E	X	107,113
Eastfield Ho	Lincs	TF3198	53°28·0′	0°1·2′W	X	113
Eastfield House Fm	E Yorks	SE7744	53°53·4′	0°49·3′W	FM	105,106
Eastfield House Fm	E Yorks	SE7853	53°58·3′	0°48·2′W	FM	105,106
Eastfield House Fm	N Yks	SE1588	54°17·5′	1°45·8′W	FM	99
Eastfield House Fm	N Yks	SE5925	53°43·3′	1°5·9′W	FM	105
Eastfield of Lempitlaw	Scot Bord	NT7933	55°35·7′	2°19·6′W	X	74
Eastfield of Monaltrie	Aberd	NO3897	57°3·9′	3°0·9′W	X	37,44
Eastfield Plantns	N Yks	NZ3306	54°27·1′	1°29·0′W	F	93
Eastfields	N Yks	NZ3407	54°27·7′	1°28·1′W	X	93
East Fields	N Yks	SE7067	54°5·9′	0°55·4′W	X	100
Eastfields	Staffs	SK1316	52°44·7′	1°48·0′W	X	128
East Fields	W Berks	SU4766	51°23·7′	1°19·1′W	T	174
Eastfields Fm	Beds	TL0466	52°17·2′	0°28·1′W	FM	153
Eastfields Fm	Leic	SK7427	52°50·4′	0°53·7′W	FM	129
Eastfields Fm	Lincs	SK9897	53°27·9′	0°31·0′W	FM	112
Eastfields Fm	N Yks	SE7481	54°13·4′	0°51·5′W	FM	100
Eastfields Fm	Suff	TM0136	51°59·4′	0°56·0′E	FM	155
Eastfield Wood	Norf	TF9021	52°45·4′	0°49·3′E	F	132
East Finchley	Barnet	TQ2689	51°35·4′	0°10·5′W	T	176
East Finglassie	Fife	NT2699	56°10·9′	3°11·1′W	T	59
East Fingle	Devon	SX7491	50°42·5′	3°46·7′W	X	191
East Finnercy	Aberd	NJ7604	57°7·8′	2°23·3′W	X	38
East Firsby	Lincs	TF0085	53°21·4′	0°29·4′W	T	112,121
East Firsby Grange	Lincs	TF0285	53°21·4′	0°27·6′W	X	112,121
East Flashes	Red & Cl	NZ6125	54°37·2′	1°2·9′W	X	94
East Flass Fm	Durham	NZ2043	54°47·1′	1°40·9′W	FM	88
East Flatt	S Lanak	NS6551	55°44·3′	4°8·6′W	X	64
East Fleet	Dorset	SY6379	50°36·8′	2°31·0′W	W	194
East Fleet	Dorset	SY6380	50°37·3′	2°31·0′W	T	194
East Fleet	Norf	TF9344	52°57·7′	0°52·8′E	W	132
East Fleetham	Northum	NU2029	55°33·5′	1°40·5′W	X	75
East Flisk	Fife	NO3222	56°23·4′	3°5·6′W	X	53,59
East Float	Wirral	SJ3190	53°24·4′	3°1·9′W	W	108
East Fm	Cambs	TL3944	52°4·8′	0°2·1′E	FM	154
East Fm	Cumbr	NY1648	54°49·4′	3°18·0′W	FM	85
East Fm	Dorset	ST5815	50°56·2′	2°35·5′W	FM	183
East Fm	Dorset	SY8499	50°47·7′	2°13·2′W	FM	194
East Fm	E Yorks	SE7643	53°52·9′	0°50·2′W	FM	105,106
East Fm	Lincs	TF0985	53°21·3′	0°21·3′W	FM	112,121
East Fm	Lincs	TF3968	53°11·7′	0°5·3′E	FM	122
East Fm	Norf	TF7119	52°44·7′	0°32·4′E	FM	132
East Fm	Norf	TF7736	52°53·8′	0°38·3′E	FM	132
East Fm	Norf	TG2216	52°42·0′	1°17·5′E	FM	133,134
East Fm	Northum	NZ2198	55°16·8′	1°39·7′W	FM	81
East Fm	N Yks	NZ3503	54°25·5′	1°27·2′W	FM	93
East Fm	N Yks	SE2291	54°19·1′	1°39·3′W	FM	99
East Fm	N Yks	SE8167	54°5·8′	0°45·3′W	FM	100
East Fm	N Yks	SE9074	54°9·5′	0°36·9′W	FM	101
East Fm	Suff	TL8778	52°22·3′	0°45·2′E	FM	144
East Fm	Suff	TL9239	52°1·2′	0°48·3′E	FM	155
East Fm	Sund	NZ3951	54°51·4′	1°23·1′W	FM	88
East Fm	Wilts	SU0128	51°3·3′	1°58·8′W	FM	184
East Fm	Wilts	SU1071	51°26·5′	1°51·0′W	FM	173
East Ford	Devon	SX7895	50°44·7′	3°43·4′W	X	191
East Fordun	Pth & Kin	NN9515	56°19·2′	3°41·4′W	X	58
East Foredibban Hill	E Ayr	NS7019	55°27·1′	4°2·9′W	H	71
East Forest	Northum	NZ2095	55°15·2′	1°40·7′W	X	81
East Fortune	E Loth	NT5479	56°0·4′	2°43·8′W	X	66
East Foscote Fm	Wilts	ST8779	51°30·8′	2°10·9′W	FM	173
East Frew	Stir	NS6897	56°9·1′	4°7·1′W	X	57
East Fulton	Renf	NS4265	55°51·4′	4°31·0′W	X	64
East Fulwood	Renf	NS4567	55°52·5′	4°28·2′W	X	64
East Funach	Aberd	NO7694	57°2·4′	2°23·3′W	X	38,45
East Galdenoch	D & G	NX1055	54°51·5′	4°57·2′W	X	82
East Garforth	Leeds	SE4133	53°47·7′	1°22·2′W	T	105
East Garleton	E Loth	NT5076	55°58·7′	2°47·6′W	X	66
East Garston	W Berks	SU3676	51°29·1′	1°28·5′W	T	174
East Garston Down	W Berks	SU3679	51°30·8′	1°28·5′W	X	174
East Garston Woodlands	W Berks	SU3574	51°28·1′	1°29·4′W	X	174
East Gartfarran	Stir	NS5295	56°7·7′	4°22·4′W	X	57
East Garth	N Yks	SD9073	54°9·4′	2°8·8′W	X	98
Eastgate	Durham	NY9538	54°44·5′	2°4·2′W	T	91,92
Eastgate	Norf	TG1423	52°46·0′	1°10·7′E	T	133
Eastgate	Northum	NZ1576	55°4·9′	1°45·5′W	X	88
Eastgate	Peterb	TL2098	52°34·2′	0°13·4′W	T	142
East Gate Barn	I of W	SZ4087	50°41·1′	1°25·6′W	X	196
Eastgate Fm	Norf	TF7311	52°40·4′	0°33·9′E	FM	132,143
Eastgate Fm	Stock on T	NZ3915	54°32·0′	1°23·4′W	FM	93
Eastgate Ho	Norf	TF7321	52°45·8′	0°34·2′E	X	132
East Gateshead	Ghead	NZ2663	54°57·9′	1°35·2′W	T	88
East Gavin	Renf	NS3859	55°48·1′	4°34·6′W	X	63
East Gibseat	Aberd	NJ9442	57°28·4′	2°5·5′W	X	30
East Gill	N Yks	NY9002	54°25·0′	2°8·8′W	W	91,92
East Gill	N Yks	SD8395	54°21·3′	2°15·3′W	W	98
East Gill Head	N Yks	NY9004	54°26·1′	2°8·8′W	X	91,92
East Gilston Mains	Fife	NO4407	56°15·4′	2°53·8′W	X	59
East Ginge	Oxon	SU4486	51°34·5′	1°21·5′W	T	174
East Ginge Down	Oxon	SU4485	51°34·0′	1°21·5′W	X	174
East Girt Hill	N Ayr	NS2762	55°49·5′	4°45·3′W	H	63
East Glasterlaw	Angus	NO6051	56°39·2′	2°38·7′W	X	54
East Glenan Burn	Arg & Bt	NR9371	55°53·5′	5°18·2′W	W	62
East Glenarm	D & G	NX8369	55°0·4′	3°49·3′W	X	84
East Glenquoich Forest	Highld	NH0902	57°4·4′	5°8·6′W	X	33
East Glenquoich Forest	Highld	NH1103	57°5·0′	5°6·7′W	X	34
East Glen River	Lincs	TF0621	52°46·8′	0°25·3′W	W	130
East Glen River	Lincs	TF0813	52°42·5′	0°23·7′W	W	130,142
East Glenshinnoch	Renf	NS4270	55°54·1′	4°31·2′W	X	64
East Goatmilk	Fife	NT2499	56°10·9′	3°13·0′W	X	59
East Gogar	Stir	NS8495	56°8·3′	3°51·6′W	X	58
East Gordon	Scot Bord	NT6643	55°41·0′	2°32·0′W	X	74
East Gores	Essex	TL8823	51°52·7′	0°44·3′E	T	168
East Gormack	Pth & Kin	NO1546	56°36·1′	3°22·6′W	X	53
East Gortleigh	Devon	SS4706	50°50·2′	4°10·0′W	X	191
East Goscote	Leic	SK6413	52°42·9′	1°2·8′W	T	129
East Gowkhill	Aberd	NJ9046	57°30·5′	2°9·6′W	X	30
East Grafton	Wilts	SU2560	51°20·5′	1°38·1′W	T	174
East Grain	Angus	NO4687	56°58·5′	2°52·8′W	W	44
East Grain	Durham	NY8736	54°43·4′	2°11·7′W	W	91,92
East Grain	N Yks	NY9101	54°24·5′	2°7·9′W	W	91,92
East Grain	Scot Bord	NT1811	55°23·4′	3°17·2′W	W	79
East Grain	Scot Bord	NT2312	55°24·0′	3°12·5′W	W	79
East Grain of Badymicks	Aberd	NO5884	56°57·0′	2°41·0′W	W	44
East Grange	Angus	NO4444	56°35·3′	2°54·3′W	X	54
East Grange	Durham	NZ4434	54°42·2′	1°18·6′W	X	93
East Grange	Fife	NT0088	56°4·7′	3°36·0′W	X	65
East Grange	Moray	NJ0961	57°38·0′	3°31·0′W	X	27
East Grange	Northum	NZ1275	55°4·4′	1°48·3′W	X	88
East Grange	N Yks	SE6939	53°50·8′	0°56·7′W	X	105,106
East Grassyards	N Ayr	NS2264	55°50·4′	4°50·1′W	X	63
East Green	Hants	SU7944	51°11·6′	0°51·8′W	T	186
East Green	Inverc	NS3368	55°52·8′	4°39·7′W	X	63
East Green	Suff	TL6853	52°9·2′	0°27·7′E	T	154
East Green	Suff	TM4065	52°14·1′	1°31·3′E	T	156
East Greenland	Highld	ND2466	58°34·8′	3°17·9′W	X	11,12
East Greystone	Durham	NZ1916	54°32·6′	1°42·0′W	X	92
East Grimstead	Wilts	SU2227	51°2·7′	1°40·8′W	T	184
East Grinstead	W Susx	TQ3938	51°7·7′	0°0·4′W	T	187
East Grove Fm	Worcs	SO7964	52°16·7′	2°18·1′W	FM	138,150
Eastgrowths Fm	E Yorks	TA3120	53°39·8′	0°0·6′W	FM	107,113
East Guldeford	E Susx	TQ9321	50°57·6′	0°45·3′E	T	189
East Guldeford Level	E Susx	TQ9421	50°57·6′	0°46·1′E	X	189
East Haddon	Northnts	SP6668	52°18·6′	1°1·5′W	T	152
East Haddon Grange	Northnts	SP6766	52°17·5′	1°0·7′W	X	152
East Haddon Hill	Northnts	SP6566	52°17·5′	1°2·4′W	X	152
East Hagbourne	Oxon	SU5388	51°35·5′	1°13·7′W	T	174
East Hall	Essex	TM0107	51°43·8′	0°55·0′E	X	168
East Hall	Essex	TQ9392	51°35·8′	0°47·6′E	X	178
East Hall	Fife	NO3315	56°19·6′	3°4·6′W	X	59
Easthall	Herts	TL1922	51°53·3′	0°15·9′W	T	166
East Hall	Kent	TQ7849	51°13·0′	0°33·3′E	X	188
East Hall	Kent	TQ9264	51°20·8′	0°45·8′E	X	178
East Hall	Norf	TF7237	52°54·8′	0°33·9′E	X	132
East Hall	Norf	TL7291	52°29·6′	0°32·4′E	X	143
East Hall	N Yks	NZ2205	54°26·6′	1°39·2′W	X	93
Easthall Fm	Herts	TL2021	51°52·7′	0°15·0′W	FM	166
East Halton	N Lincs	TA1319	53°39·6′	0°17·0′W	T	113
East Halton Beck	N Lincs	TA1218	53°39·0′	0°17·9′W	W	113
East Halton Beck	N Lincs	TA1221	53°40·6′	0°17·8′W	W	107,113
East Halton Skitter	N Lincs	TA1422	53°41·2′	0°16·0′W	X	107,113
East Ham	Newham	TQ4283	51°31·9′	0°3·2′E	T	177
East Ham	Shetld	HU4524	60°0·2′	1°11·1′W	W	4
Eastham	Wirral	SJ3580	53°19·0′	2°58·1′W	T	108
Eastham	Worcs	SO6568	52°18·8′	2°30·4′W	T	138
East Hambleton Fm	N Yks	SE8087	54°16·6′	0°45·9′W	FM	94,100
Eastham Br	Worcs	SO6569	52°19·3′	2°30·4′W	X	138
Eastham Country Park	Wirral	SJ3581	53°19·6′	2°58·1′W	X	108
Eastham Ferry	Wirral	SJ3681	53°19·6′	2°57·2′W	T	108
Eastham Grange	Worcs	SO6767	52°18·2′	2°28·6′W	X	138,149
Eastham Hall	Lancs	SD3729	53°45·5′	2°56·9′W	X	102
Eastham Ho	Wirral	SJ3679	53°18·5′	2°57·2′W	X	117
Eastham House Fm	Lancs	SD7139	53°51·0′	2°26·0′W	FM	103
Eastham Locks	Wirral	SJ3780	53°19·0′	2°56·3′W	X	108
Eastham Park	Worcs	SO6567	52°18·2′	2°30·4′W	X	138,149
East Hampnett	W Susx	SU9106	50°51·0′	0°42·1′W	T	197
Easthampstead	Brackn	SU8667	51°24·0′	0°45·4′W	T	175
Easthampstead Park	Brackn	SU8467	51°24·0′	0°47·2′W	X	175
Easthampton	Heref	SO4063	52°16·0′	2°52·4′W	T	137,148,149
Eastham Rake Station	Wirral	SJ3479	53°18·5′	2°59·0′W	X	117
Eastham Sands	Wirral	SJ3981	53°19·6′	2°54·5′W	X	108
East Hanney	Oxon	SU4193	51°38·3′	1°24·1′W	T	164,174
East Hann Fm	N Lincs	TA0821	53°40·7′	0°21·5′W	FM	107,112
East Hanningfield	Essex	TL7701	51°41·0′	0°34·0′E	T	167
East Hanningfield Hall	Essex	TQ7699	51°40·0′	0°33·1′E	X	167
East Hanningfield Lodge	Essex	TQ7699	51°40·0′	0°33·1′E	X	167
East Happas	Angus	NO4441	56°33·7′	2°54·2′W	X	54
East Hardwick	Wakf	SE4618	53°39·6′	1°17·8′W	T	111
East Harlaw	Aberd	NJ7525	57°19·2′	2°24·4′W	X	38
East Harling	Norf	TL9986	52°26·4′	0°56·1′E	T	144
East Harling Common	Norf	TM0087	52°26·9′	0°57·0′E	F	144
East Harling Fen	Norf	TM0087	52°26·9′	0°57·0′E	F	144
East Harling Heath	Norf	TL9983	52°24·8′	0°56·0′E	X	144
East Harlsey	N Yks	SE4299	54°23·3′	1°20·8′W	T	99
East Harptree	Bath & NE Somer	ST5655	51°17·8′	2°37·5′W	T	172,182
East Harptree Woods	Somer	ST5554	51°17·2′	2°38·3′W	F	182,183
East Hartford	Northum	NZ2679	55°6·5′	1°35·1′W	T	88
East Harting	W Susx	SU7919	50°58·1′	0°52·1′W	T	197
East Hartley	Devon	SX8052	50°21·6′	3°40·8′W	X	202
East Harwood	Somer	SS9341	51°9·7′	3°31·4′W	X	181
East Hatch	Wilts	ST9228	51°3·3′	2°6·5′W	T	184
East Hatley	Cambs	TL2850	52°8·2′	0°7·4′W	T	153
Easthaugh	Norf	TG0817	52°42·9′	1°5·2′E	T	133
East Haugh	Pth & Kin	NN9656	56°41·3′	3°41·4′W	X	52,53
East Haugh	W Loth	NT1164	55°51·9′	3°24·9′W	X	65
Easthaugh Hill	Norf	TG0817	52°42·9′	1°5·2′E	X	133
East Hauxwell	N Yks	SE1693	54°20·2′	1°44·8′W	T	99
East Haven	Angus	NO5836	56°31·1′	2°40·5′W	T	54
East Haven Creek	Essex	TQ7685	51°32·4′	0°32·7′E	W	178
East Hawes Fm	Suff	TM2376	52°20·4′	1°16·8′E	FM	156
East Haybogs	Aberd	NJ6111	57°11·5′	2°38·3′W	X	37
Easthay Fm	Dorset	ST3601	50°48·5′	2°54·1′W	FM	193
East Hazeldean	S Lanak	NS7444	55°40·6′	3°59·8′W	X	71
East Head	Aberd	NJ6066	57°41·2′	2°39·8′W	X	29
East Head	W Susx	SZ7699	50°47·4′	0°54·9′W	X	197
East Head of Papa	Shetld	HU3737	60°7·2′	1°19·6′W	X	4
East Heads	E Ayr	NS5338	55°37·1′	4°19·6′W	X	70
East Heath	Kent	TQ7628	51°1·7′	0°31·0′E	X	188,199
Eastheath	Wok	SU8067	51°24·0′	0°50·6′W	T	175
East Heckington	Lincs	TF1944	52°59·0′	0°13·2′W	T	130
East Heddon	Northum	NZ1368	55°0·6′	1°47·4′W	X	88
East Hedleyhope	Durham	NZ1540	54°45·5′	1°45·6′W	T	88
East Helmsdale	Highld	ND0315	58°7·1′	3°38·3′W	T	17
East Hendred	Oxon	SU4588	51°35·6′	1°20·6′W	T	174
East Hendred Down	Oxon	SU4685	51°34·0′	1°19·8′W	X	174
East Hermiston	C of Edin	NT1870	55°55·2′	3°18·3′W	X	65,66
East Herringthorpe	Roth	SK4593	53°26·1′	1°18·9′W	T	111
East Herrington	Sund	NZ3653	54°52·5′	1°25·9′W	T	88
East Heslerton	N Yks	SE9276	54°10·5′	0°35·0′W	T	101
East Heslerton Brow	N Yks	SE9375	54°10·0′	0°34·1′W	X	101
East Heslerton Carr	N Yks	SE9378	54°11·6′	0°34·1′W	X	101
East Heslerton Carr Ho	N Yks	SE9278	54°11·6′	0°35·0′W	X	101
East Heslerton Wold	N Yks	SE9373	54°8·9′	0°34·1′W	X	101
East Heslerton Wold Fm	N Yks	SE9373	54°8·9′	0°34·1′W	FM	101
East Hewish	N Som	ST3964	51°22·5′	2°52·2′W	T	182
East Highridge	Northum	NY8281	55°7·6′	2°16·5′W	X	80
East High Wood	Durham	NZ0823	54°36·4′	1°52·1′W	X	92
Easthill	Aberd	NJ6505	57°8·3′	2°34·2′W	X	38
East Hill	Devon	SS6644	51°11·0′	3°54·7′W	X	180
East Hill	Devon	SX5993	50°43·4′	3°59·5′W	H	191
East Hill	Devon	SY1294	50°44·6′	3°14·5′W	X	192,193
Easthill	D & G	NX9174	55°3·2′	3°41·9′W	X	84
East Hill	Dorset	ST6202	50°49·2′	2°32·0′W	X	194
East Hill	Dorset	ST6404	50°50·3′	2°30·3′W	X	194
East Hill	Dorset	ST7000	50°48·2′	2°25·2′W	X	194
East Hill	Dorset	SY6797	50°46·5′	2°27·7′W	X	194
East Hill	Dorset	SY9682	50°38·5′	2°3·0′W	H	195
East Hill	E Susx	TQ8209	50°51·3′	0°35·5′E	X	199
East Hill	E Yorks	TA2440	53°50·7′	0°6·5′W	X	107
East Hill	Hants	SU7827	51°2·5′	0°52·9′W	X	186,197
East Hill	Kent	TQ5562	51°20·4′	0°13·9′E	T	177,188
East Hill	Kent	TR3746	51°10·1′	1°23·8′E	X	179
East Hill	Northum	NU0316	55°26·5′	1°56·7′W	H	81
East Hill	Orkney	HY2604	58°55·3′	3°16·6′W	H	6,7
East Hill	Pth & Kin	NN9212	56°17·5′	3°44·3′W	X	58
East Hill	Scot Bord	NT5801	55°18·3′	2°39·3′W	H	80
East Hill	Somer	ST6434	51°6·5′	2°30·5′W	H	183
East Hill	Staffs	SK1411	52°42·0′	1°47·2′W	X	128
East Hill	Suff	TM4873	52°18·2′	1°38·7′E	X	156
East Hill Fm	Hants	SZ4499	50°47·6′	1°22·2′W	FM	196
East Hill Fm	Wilts	ST9344	51°11·9′	2°5·6′W	FM	184
East Hillhead	Angus	NO5139	56°32·7′	2°47·4′W	X	54
East Hill of Bellister	Shetld	HU4859	60°19·0′	1°7·4′W	H	2,3
East Hill of Burrafirth	Shetld	HU3658	60°18·5′	1°20·4′W	H	2,3
East Hill of Grunnafirth	Shetld	HU4660	60°19·6′	1°9·5′W	H	2,3
East Hill of Houlland	Shetld	HU3555	60°16·9′	1°21·5′W	H	3
East Hill of Voe	Shetld	HU4061	60°20·1′	1°16·0′W	X	2,3
East Hill of Weisdale	Shetld	HU4053	60°15·8′	1°16·1′W	H	3
Easthills	Aberd	NO7073	56°51·1′	2°29·1′W	X	45
East Hills	Angus	NO5545	56°35·9′	2°43·5′W	X	54
Easthills	Renf	NS3358	55°47·4′	4°39·4′W	X	63
Easthills	S Lanak	NT0448	55°43·2′	3°31·3′W	X	72
East Hills	Swan	SS5492	51°36·7′	4°6·1′W	X	159
Easthills Fm	S Lanak	NS6358	55°48·0′	4°10·7′W	FM	64
East Hill Strips	Devon	SY1293	50°44·0′	3°14·4′W	X	192,193
East Hilltown	Devon	SS7010	50°52·7′	3°50·5′W	X	191
East Ho	Carm	SN3007	51°44·4′	4°27·3′W	X	159
East Ho	Cumbr	NY0926	54°37·5′	3°24·1′W	X	89
East Ho	Cumbr	NY0930	54°39·7′	3°24·2′W	X	89
East Ho	Cumbr	NY1830	54°39·8′	3°15·9′W	X	89,90
East Ho	Cumbr	NY2319	54°33·9′	3°11·0′W	X	89,90
East Ho	Cumbr	SD7793	54°20·2′	2°20·8′W	X	98
East Ho	Durham	NZ0523	54°36·4′	1°54·9′W	X	92
East Ho	Durham	NZ3431	54°40·6′	1°27·9′W	X	93
East Ho	Essex	TM0632	51°57·1′	1°0·3′E	X	168
East Ho	Northum	NU0346	55°42·7′	1°56·7′W	X	75
East Ho	Northum	NU1602	55°19·0′	1°44·4′W	X	81
East Ho	Northum	NU2104	55°20·0′	1°39·7′W	X	81
East Ho	N Yks	NZ2409	54°28·8′	1°37·4′W	X	93
East Ho	Sund	NZ3159	54°55·7′	1°30·5′W	X	88
East Hoathly	E Susx	TQ5216	50°55·6′	0°10·2′E	T	199
East Hoe Manor	Hants	SU6315	50°56·1′	1°5·8′W	X	196
East Hoevdi	Shetld	HT9541	60°9·5′	2°4·9′W	X	4
East Hogaland	Shetld	HU3833	60°5·0′	1°18·5′W	X	4
East Holcombe	Devon	SS9925	51°1·2′	3°26·0′W	X	181
East Holelake Fm	Devon	ST0220	50°58·5′	3°23·4′W	FM	181
East Holme	Dorset	SY8986	50°40·6′	2°9·0′W	T	195
Eastholme Fm	E Yorks	TA2427	53°43·7′	0°6·8′W	FM	107
Eastholme Ho	Cumbr	NY2555	54°53·3′	3°9·7′W	X	85
East Holme Ho	Durham	NZ0218	54°33·7′	1°57·7′W	X	92
East Holmes	E Ayr	NS4736	55°35·9′	4°25·3′W	X	70
East Holton	Dorset	SY9691	50°43·3′	2°3·0′W	T	195
East Holywell	N Tyne	NZ3173	55°3·3′	1°30·5′W	T	88
East Hoo Creek	Medway	TQ8372	51°25·3′	0°38·3′E	W	178
East Hook	Pemb	SM9116	51°48·5′	5°1·5′W	X	157,158
East Hook	Pemb	SM9911	51°45·9′	4°54·4′W	X	157,158
East Hope	Durham	NZ0308	54°28·3′	1°56·8′W	X	92
Easthope	Shrops	SO5695	52°33·3′	2°38·5′W	T	137,138
East Hopes	E Loth	NT5563	55°51·7′	2°42·7′W	X	66
Easthope Wood	Shrops	SO5595	52°33·3′	2°39·4′W	F	137,138
Easthopewood	Shrops	SO5696	52°33·8′	2°38·5′W	T	137,138
East Horndon	Essex	TQ6389	51°34·8′	0°21·5′E	T	177
Easthorpe	Essex	TL9121	51°51·5′	0°46·8′E	T	168
Easthorpe	E Yorks	SE8845	53°53·9′	0°39·2′W	X	106
Easthorpe	Leic	SK8138	52°56·2′	0°47·3′W	T	130
Easthorpe	Notts	SK7053	53°4·4′	0°56·9′W	T	120
Easthorpe Court	Lincs	TF2636	52°54·6′	0°7·2′W	X	131
Easthorpegreen Fm	Essex	TL9021	51°51·5′	0°46·0′E	FM	168
Easthorpe Hall Stud	N Yks	SE7371	54°8·0′	0°52·5′W	X	100
Easthorpe Village	E Yorks	SE8745	53°53·9′	0°40·1′W	A	106

Easthorpe Wold	E Yorks	SE8945	53°53·8'	0°38·3'W	X	106
East Horrington	Somer	ST5846	51°12·9'	2°35·7'W	T	182,183
East Horsley	Surrey	TQ0953	51°16·2'	0°25·9'W	T	187
East Horton	Northum	NU0230	55°34·1'	1°57·7'W	T	75
East Horton Fm	Hants	SU5018	50°57·8'	1°16·9'W	FM	185
East Hotbank	Northum	NY7971	55°2·2'	2°19·3'W	X	86,87
Easthouse	Shetld	HU3845	60°11·5'	1°18·4'W	X	4
East House Fm	N Tyne	NZ2871	55°2·2'	1°33·3'W	FM	88
Easthouses	Midlo	NT3465	55°52·7'	3°2·9'W	T	66
East Howcreek	D & G	NY1165	54°58·6'	3°23·0'W	X	85
East Howe	Bourne	SZ0795	50°45·5'	1°53·7'W	T	195
East Howle Fm	Durham	NZ2933	54°41·7'	1°32·6'W	FM	93
East Howmuir	Angus	NO5058	56°42·9'	2°48·6'W	X	54
East Hoyle Bank	Wirral	SJ2291	53°24·8'	3°10·0'W	X	108
East Huish Fm	Devon	SX8393	50°43·7'	3°39·1'W	FM	191
East Huntow	E Yorks	TA1670	54°7·0'	0°13·1'W	X	101
East Huntspill	Somer	ST3444	51°11·7'	2°56·3'W	T	182
Easthwaite	Cumbr	NY1303	54°25·1'	3°20·0'W	X	89
East Hyde	Beds	TL1217	51°50·6'	0°22·1'W	T	166
East Hyde	Essex	TL9804	51°42·2'	0°52·3'E	X	168
East Idvies	Angus	NO5448	56°37·6'	2°44·5'W	X	54
East Ilkerton	Devon	SS7146	51°12·2'	3°50·4'W	T	180
East Ilsley	W Berks	SU4981	51°31·8'	1°17·2'W	T	174
East Ilsley Down	W Berks	SU5081	51°31·8'	1°16·4'W	X	174
East Inch	Angus	NO3755	56°41·2'	3°1·3'W	X	54
Easting	Orkney	HY7755	59°23·1'	2°23·8'W	T	5
East Ings	N Yks	SE5539	53°50·9'	1°9·4'W	X	105
East Ings	N Yks	SE7067	54°5·9'	0°55·4'W	X	100
Eastington	Devon	SS7409	50°52·2'	3°47·1'W	T	191
Eastington	Devon	SX5596	50°45·0'	4°2·9'W	X	191
Eastington	Glos	SO7705	51°44·8'	2°19·6'W	T	162
Eastington	Glos	SP1213	51°49·2'	1°49·2'W	T	163
Eastington	Pemb	SM9002	51°40·9'	5°1·9'W	X	157,158
Eastington Fm	Dorset	SY9877	50°35·8'	2°1·3'W	FM	195
Eastington Hall	Worcs	SO8352	52°2·6'	2°14·5'W	A	150
Eastington Ho	Glos	SP0801	51°42·7'	1°52·7'W	X	163
East Jeanfield	Angus	NO3736	56°31·0'	3°1·0'W	X	54
East Jordeston	Pemb	SN0701	51°40·7'	4°47·1'W	X	158
East Kame	Shetld	HU4257	60°18·0'	1°13·9'W	H	2,3
East Kames	Arg & Bt	NR9289	56°3·2'	5°20·0'W	X	55
East Keal	Lincs	TF3763	53°9·0'	0°3·3'E	T	122
East Kelt	Falk	NS7980	56°0·1'	3°56·0'W	X	64
East Kennett	Wilts	SU1167	51°24·3'	1°50·1'W	T	173
East Kennett Long Barrow	Wilts	SU1166	51°23·8'	1°50·1'W	A	173
East Kerse Mains	Falk	NS9780	56°0·4'	3°38·7'W	X	65
East Keswick	Leeds	SE3644	53°53·7'	1°26·7'W	T	104
East Ketton	Darl	NZ3020	54°34·7'	1°31·7'W	X	93
East Kielder	Northum	NY6595	55°15·1'	2°32·6'W	X	80
East Kielder Moor	Northum	NY6998	55°16·8'	2°28·9'W	X	80
East Kilbride	Arg & Bt	NS3185	56°1·9'	4°42·3'W	X	56
East Kilbride	N Eil	NF7714	57°6·5'	7°19·7'W	T	31
East Kilbride	S Lanak	NS6354	55°45·9'	4°10·6'W	T	64
East Kimber	Devon	SX4998	50°46·0'	4°8·1'W	T	191
East Kinclune	Angus	NO3156	56°41·7'	3°7·2'W	X	53
East Kingston	W Susx	TQ0802	50°48·7'	0°27·6'W	T	197
East Kinharrachie	Aberd	NJ9231	57°22·4'	2°6·5'W	X	30
East Kinmonth	Aberd	NO7881	56°55·4'	2°21·2'W	X	45
East Kinnear	Fife	NO4023	56°24·0'	2°57·9'W	X	54,59
East Kinnochtry	Pth & Kin	NO2136	56°30·8'	3°16·6'W	X	53
East Kintrockat	Angus	NO5759	56°43·5'	2°41·7'W	X	54
East Kip	Midlo	NT1860	55°49·8'	3°18·1'W	X	65,66
East Kirkby	Lincs	TF3362	53°8·5'	0°0·3'W	T	122
East Kirkby Ho	Lincs	TF3362	53°8·5'	0°0·3'W	X	122
East Kirkcarswell	D & G	NX7549	54°49·5'	3°56·3'W	X	84
East Kirkland	D & G	NX4356	54°52·7'	4°26·4'W	X	83
East Kirkton	Pth & Kin	NN9514	56°18·7'	3°41·4'W	X	58
East Knapton	N Yks	SE8875	54°10·0'	0°38·7'W	T	101
East Knighton	Dorset	SY8185	50°40·1'	2°15·7'W	T	194
East Knitsley Grange	Durham	NZ1248	54°49·8'	1°48·4'W	X	88
East Knock	Angus	NO4876	56°52·6'	2°50·7'W	X	44
East Knock	Sou-on-Sea	TQ9382	51°30·5'	0°47·3'E	X	178
East Knockbrex	D & G	NX3964	54°56·9'	4°30·4'W	X	83
East Knowstone	Devon	SS8323	50°59·9'	3°39·7'W	T	181
East Knoyle	Wilts	ST8830	51°4·4'	2°9·9'W	T	183
East Kyloe	Northum	NU0539	55°38·9'	1°54·8'W	X	75
East Kyo	Durham	NZ1752	54°52·0'	1°43·7'W	T	88
East Laggan	Arg & Bt	NR7325	55°28·2'	5°35·1'W	X	68
Eastlake	Devon	SX6194	50°44·0'	3°57·8'W	X	191
Eastlake	Pemb	SN1608	51°44·7'	4°39·5'W	X	158
Eastlake Fm	Devon	SX4389	50°41·0'	4°13·0'W	FM	190
East Lambrook	Somer	ST4318	50°57·8'	2°48·3'W	T	193
East Lamington	Highld	NH7578	57°46·7'	4°5·7'W	X	21
East Lancs Rly	Lancs	SD7920	53°40·8'	2°18·7'W	X	103
Eastland	Devon	SS8610	50°52·9'	3°36·9'W	X	191
East Land Ends	Northum	NY8363	54°57·9'	2°15·5'W	X	86,87
Eastland Fm	W Susx	SU9531	51°4·5'	0°38·2'W	FM	186
Eastland Fm	W Susx	TQ2327	51°2·0'	0°14·4'W	FM	187,198
Eastland Gate	Hants	SU6712	50°54·4'	1°2·4'W	T	196
East Landing	E Loth	NT6087	56°4·7'	2°38·1'W	X	67
Eastlands	Essex	TM0207	51°43·7'	0°55·9'E	X	168
Eastlands	E Yorks	SE9655	53°59·2'	0°31·7'W	X	106
Eastlands	W Susx	TQ1126	51°1·6'	0°24·6'W	X	187,198
Eastlands Fm	E Susx	TQ7518	50°56·3'	0°29·8'E	FM	199
Eastlands Fm	E Susx	TQ8214	50°54·0'	0°35·7'E	FM	199
Eastlands Fm	Lincs	TF1682	53°19·6'	0°15·1'W	FM	121
Eastlands Fm	Poole	SZ0496	50°46·0'	1°56·2'W	FM	195
Eastlands Fm	Suff	TM0769	52°17·0'	1°2·5'E	FM	155
Eastlands Fm	W Susx	TQ2122	50°59·3'	0°16·2'W	FM	198
Eastlands Ho	D & G	NX8172	55°2·0'	3°51·3'W	X	84
Eastland Wood	Essex	TL8410	51°45·7'	0°40·4'E	F	168
East Lane Fm	Suff	TM3539	52°0·2'	1°25·8'E	FM	169
East Lanegate	D & G	NY0184	55°8·7'	3°32·8'W	X	78
East Lane Ho	N Yks	SD9884	54°15·3'	2°1·4'W	X	98
East Langbank	Renf	NS3972	55°55·1'	4°34·1'W	X	63
East Langdon	Kent	TR3346	51°10·2'	1°20·4'E	T	179
East Langton	E Ayr	NS4051	55°43·8'	4°32·4'W	X	64
East Langton	Leic	SP7292	52°31·5'	0°55·9'W	T	141
East Langwell	Highld	NC7206	58°1·7'	4°9·6'W	T	16
East Lavant	W Susx	SU8608	50°52·1'	0°46·3'W	T	197
East Lavington	W Susx	SU9416	50°56·4'	0°39·3'W	T	197

East Law	Aberd	NJ7027	57°20·2'	2°29·4'W	X	38
East Law	Durham	NZ0954	54°53·1'	1°51·2'W	T	88
Eastlaw	Scot Bord	NT9165	55°52·9'	2°8·2'W	X	67
East Law	S Lanak	NS8251	55°44·5'	3°52·3'W	X	65,72
East Layton	N Yks	NZ1609	54°28·8'	1°44·8'W	T	92
Eastleach Downs Fm	Glos	SP1908	51°46·5'	1°43·1'W	FM	163
East Leach Folly	Glos	SP1706	51°45·4'	1°44·8'W	X	163
Eastleach Martin	Glos	SP2005	51°44·8'	1°42·2'W	T	163
Eastleach Turville	Glos	SP1905	51°44·8'	1°43·1'W	T	163
East Leake	Notts	SK5526	52°50·0'	1°10·6'W	T	129
East Learmouth	Northum	NT8637	55°37·8'	2°12·9'W	T	74
East Learney	Aberd	NJ6303	57°7·2'	2°36·2'W	X	37
East Lease Fm	Somer	ST4810	50°53·5'	2°44·0'W	FM	193
Eastleaze Fm	Wilts	ST8723	51°0·6'	2°10·7'W	FM	183
East Leaze Fm	Wilts	SU2778	51°30·2'	1°36·3'W	FM	174
East Lediken	Aberd	NJ6628	57°20·7'	2°33·4'W	X	38
Eastleigh	Devon	SS4827	51°1·6'	4°9·7'W	T	180
East Leigh	Devon	SS6905	50°50·0'	3°51·2'W	T	191
East Leigh	Devon	SS7312	50°53·8'	3°48·0'W	X	180
East Leigh	Devon	SX6852	50°21·4'	3°51·0'W	T	202
East Leigh	Devon	SX7658	50°24·8'	3°44·3'W	X	202
Eastleigh	Hants	SU4519	50°58·3'	1°21·2'W	T	185
East Leigh Berrys	Corn	SS2406	50°49·8'	4°29·6'W	A	190
Eastleigh Court	Kent	TR1445	51°10·1'	1°4·1'E	X	179,189
Eastleigh Ct	Wilts	ST8943	51°11·4'	2°9·1'W	X	184
East Leigh Ho	Hants	SU7307	50°51·7'	0°57·4'W	X	197
Eastleigh Manor	Devon	SS4828	51°2·1'	4°9·7'W	A	180
Eastleigh Wood	Wilts	ST8842	51°10·9'	2°9·9'W	F	183
East Lendings	Durham	NZ0515	54°32·1'	1°54·9'W	X	92
East Lenham	Kent	TQ9051	51°13·8'	0°43·7'E	X	189
East Lesses	Orkney	HY5640	59°14·9'	2°45·8'W	X	5
East Lexham	Norf	TF8516	52°42·8'	0°44·7'E	T	132
Eastley Copse	W Berks	SU4477	51°29·6'	1°21·6'W	F	174
Eastley Ho	W Berks	SU4477	51°29·6'	1°21·6'W	X	174
East Leys	E Yorks	TA1471	54°7·6'	0°14·9'W	X	101
East Leys Fm	E Yorks	TA1470	54°7·0'	0°14·9'W	FM	101
Eastley Wootton	Hants	SZ2498	50°47·1'	1°39·2'W	X	195
East Lhergydhoo	I of M	SC2784	54°13·6'	4°38·8'W	X	95
East Lilburn	Northum	NU0423	55°30·3'	1°55·8'W	T	75
East Lilling Grange	N Yks	SE6564	54°4·3'	1°0·0'W	X	100
East Lilling Ho	N Yks	SE6562	54°3·2'	1°0·0'W	X	100
East Lilling Village	N Yks	SE6664	54°4·3'	0°59·1'W	A	100
East Linbank	S Lanak	NS6741	55°38·9'	4°6·4'W	X	71
East Linden	Northum	NZ1695	55°15·2'	1°44·5'W	X	81
Eastling	Kent	TQ9656	51°16·4'	0°49·0'E	T	178
East Linga	Shetld	HU6162	60°20·5'	0°53·2'W	X	2
Eastling Down Fm	Kent	TR2947	51°10·8'	1°17·0'E	FM	179
Eastling Wood	Kent	TR3047	51°10·8'	1°17·8'E	F	179
East Linkhall	Northum	NU1721	55°29·2'	1°43·4'W	X	75
East Links	E Loth	NT5585	56°3·6'	2°42·9'W	X	66
East Links	Fife	NT5099	56°11·1'	2°47·9'W	X	59
East Linton	E Loth	NT5977	55°59·3'	2°39·0'W	T	67
East Liss	Hants	SU7827	51°2·5'	0°52·9'W	T	186,197
Eastloch	Scot Bord	NT2651	55°45·1'	3°10·3'W	X	66,73
East Loch of Skaw	Shetld	HU5966	60°22·7'	0°55·3'W	W	2
East Lochran	Pth & Kin	NT1397	56°9·7'	3°23·6'W	X	58
East Loch Tarbert	Arg & Bt	NR8769	55°52·3'	5°23·8'W	W	62
East Lockinge	Oxon	SU4287	51°35·0'	1°23·7'W	T	174
East Lodge	Enf	TQ3099	51°40·7'	0°6·8'W	X	166,176,177
East Lodge	Northnts	SP7752	52°9·9'	0°52·1'W	X	152
East Lodge	N Yks	SE3182	54°14·2'	1°31·0'W	X	99
East Lodge	N Yks	SE3978	54°12·0'	1°23·7'W	X	99
East Lodge	N Yks	SE6840	53°51·3'	0°57·6'W	X	105,106
East Lodge	Shrops	SO5478	52°24·1'	2°40·2'W	X	137,138
East Lodge	Staffs	SK1824	52°49·0'	1°43·6'W	X	128
East Lodge	Stir	NN5905	56°13·3'	4°16·0'W	X	57
East Lodge Fm	Cambs	TL1275	52°21·9'	0°20·9'W	FM	142
East Loftus	Red & Cl	NZ7218	54°33·4'	0°52·7'W	T	94
East Logan	D & G	NX8163	54°57·1'	3°51·1'W	X	84
East Logie Aulton	Aberd	NJ6737	57°25·6'	2°32·5'W	X	29
East Lomond	Fife	NO2406	56°14·7'	3°13·1'W	H	59
East Long Skelly	Aberd	NO8067	56°47·9'	2°19·1'W	X	45
East Looe	Corn	SX2553	50°21·3'	4°27·2'W	T	201
East Looe River	Corn	SX2461	50°25·6'	4°28·3'W	W	201
East Loosemoor	Devon	SS9122	50°59·5'	3°32·8'W	X	181
East Lound	N Lincs	SK7899	53°29·2'	0°49·1'W	T	112
Eastlow Hill	Suff	TL8961	52°13·1'	0°46·4'E	X	155
Eastlow Hill (Tumulus)	Suff	TL8961	52°13·1'	0°46·4'E	R	155
East Low Ho	Northum	NZ1480	55°7·1'	1°46·4'W	X	81
East Lugtonridge	N Ayr	NS3749	55°42·7'	4°35·2'W	X	63
East Lulworth	Dorset	SY8682	50°38·5'	2°11·5'W	T	194
East Lundie	Stir	NN7304	56°13·0'	4°2·4'W	X	57
East Lunna Voe	Shetld	HU4868	60°23·8'	1°7·2'W	W	2,3
East Luscar	Fife	NT0589	56°5·3'	3°31·2'W	X	65
East Lutton	N Yks	SE9469	54°6·7'	0°33·3'W	T	101
East Lydeard	Somer	ST1729	51°3·5'	3°10·7'W	T	181,193
East Lydford	Somer	ST5731	51°4·8'	2°36·4'W	T	182,183
East Lyn	Devon	SS7348	51°13·3'	3°48·7'W	X	180
East Lynch	Somer	SS9246	51°12·4'	3°32·4'W	X	181
East Lyng	Somer	ST3328	51°3·1'	2°57·0'W	T	193
East Lyn River	Devon	SS7748	51°13·3'	3°45·3'W	W	180
East Lynton Fm	E Yorks	SE8028	53°44·8'	0°46·8'W	FM	106
East Mains	Aberd	NJ5529	57°21·2'	2°44·4'W	X	37
East Mains	Aberd	NJ5602	57°6·7'	2°43·1'W	X	37
East Mains	Aberd	NJ7133	57°23·4'	2°28·5'W	X	29
East Mains	Aberd	NJ8564	57°40·2'	2°14·6'W	X	30
East Mains	Aberd	NO6797	57°4·0'	2°32·2'W	T	38,45
East Mains	Angus	NO3337	56°31·5'	3°4·9'W	T	53
East Mains	Angus	NO4946	56°36·4'	2°49·4'W	X	54
East Mains	E Loth	NT4170	55°55·4'	2°56·2'W	X	66
East Mains	E Loth	NT4868	55°54·4'	2°49·5'W	X	66
East Mains	E Loth	NT4871	55°56·0'	2°49·5'W	X	66
East Mains	Pth & Kin	NO0832	56°28·5'	3°29·2'W	X	52,53
East Mains	Scot Bord	NT5647	55°43·1'	2°41·6'W	T	73
East Mains	S Lanak	NS6354	55°45·9'	4°10·6'W	T	64
East mains	S Lanak	NS7446	55°41·7'	3°59·8'W	X	64
East Mains	S Lanak	NS9339	55°38·2'	3°41·6'W	X	71,72
East Mains	S Lanak	NT0334	55°35·7'	3°31·9'W	X	72
East Mains Fm	Pth & Kin	NN9308	56°15·4'	3°43·2'W	FM	58
East Mainshill	S Ayr	NS3411	55°22·2'	4°36·7'W	X	70

East Mains of Barras	Aberd	NO8580	56°54·9'	2°14·3'W	X	45
East Mains of Burnside	Angus	NO5050	56°38·6'	2°48·5'W	T	54
East Mains of Colliston	Angus	NO6146	56°36·5'	2°37·7'W	X	54
East Mains of Craichie	Angus	NO5147	56°37·0'	2°47·5'W	X	54
East Mains of Dumbarrow	Angus	NO5547	56°37·0'	2°43·5'W	X	54
East Mains of Dunnichen	Angus	NO5149	56°38·1'	2°47·5'W	X	54
East Mains of Dysart	Angus	NO6954	56°40·9'	2°29·9'W	X	54
East Mains of Guthrie	Angus	NO5850	56°38·7'	2°40·6'W	X	54
East Mains of Ingliston	C of Edin	NT1472	55°56·3'	3°22·2'W	X	65
East Mains of Keithock	Angus	NO6163	56°45·7'	2°37·8'W	X	45
East Malling	Kent	TQ7057	51°17·4'	0°26·7'E	T	178,188
East Malling Heath	Kent	TQ6955	51°16·4'	0°25·8'E	T	178,188
East Man	Dorset	SY9776	50°35·3'	2°2·2'W	X	195
East Manley	Devon	SS9911	50°53·6'	3°25·8'W	X	192
Eastman's Cairn	D & G	NX4967	54°58·7'	4°21·1'W	X	83
Eastmanton Down	Oxon	SU3384	51°33·5'	1°31·0'W	X	174
East March	Angus	NO4436	56°31·0'	2°54·2'W	T	54
East Marden	W Susx	SU8014	50°55·4'	0°51·3'W	T	197
East Marden Down	W Susx	SU8114	50°55·4'	0°50·5'W	X	197
East Markham	Notts	SK7473	53°15·2'	0°53·0'W	T	120
East Marsh	Carm	SN2808	51°44·9'	4°29·1'W	X	158
East Marsh	Carm	SN2908	51°44·9'	4°28·2'W	X	159
East Marsh	Devon	SS7327	51°1·9'	3°48·3'W	X	180
East Marsh	NE Lincs	TA2710	53°34·5'	0°4·5'W	T	113
East Marsh Fm	N Lincs	TA1224	53°42·3'	0°17·8'W	FM	107,113
Eastmarsh Point	Essex	TM1117	51°48·9'	1°4·1'E	X	168,169
East Martin	Hants	SU0719	50°58·5'	1°53·6'W	T	184
East Marton	N Yks	SD9050	53°57·0'	2°8·7'W	T	103
East Mascalls	W Susx	TQ3625	51°0·7'	0°3·3'W	A	187,198
East Matfen	Northum	NZ0371	55°2·3'	1°56·8'W	X	87
East Matfen Village	Northum	NZ0471	55°2·3'	1°55·8'W	A	87
East Mathers	Aberd	NO7766	56°47·4'	2°22·1'W	X	45
East Mayland	Durham	NZ0829	54°39·6'	1°52·1'W	X	92
Eastmead Fm	Somer	ST4735	51°6·9'	2°45·0'W	FM	182
East Mealour	Pth & Kin	NN6741	56°32·8'	4°9·4'W	X	51
East Melbury	Dorset	ST8820	50°59·0'	2°9·9'W	T	183
East Melginch	Pth & Kin	NO1830	56°27·6'	3°19·4'W	X	53
East Mellwaters	Durham	NY9612	54°30·4'	2°3·3'W	X	91,92
East Memus	Angus	NO4359	56°43·4'	2°55·4'W	X	54
East Meon	Hants	SU6822	50°59·8'	1°1·5'W	T	185
East Mere	Devon	SS9917	50°56·9'	3°25·9'W	T	181
East Mere Ho	Lincs	TF0164	53°10·0'	0°28·9'W	X	121
East Mersea	Essex	TM0514	51°47·4'	0°58·8'E	T	168
East Meur Gorm Craig	Moray	NJ1504	57°7·4'	3°23·8'W	X	36
East Mey	Highld	ND3074	58°39·2'	3°11·9'W	T	7,12
East Middle	Scot Bord	NT5516	55°26·4'	2°42·2'W	X	80
East Middleton	Devon	SS6544	51°11·0'	3°55·5'W	X	180
East Midlands Airport	Leic	SK4525	52°49·5'	1°19·5'W	X	129
East Migvie	Angus	NO4778	56°53·7'	2°51·7'W	X	44
East Mill	Angus	NO2260	56°43·8'	3°16·0'W	X	44
East Mill	Pth & Kin	NO2144	56°35·1'	3°16·7'W	X	53
Eastmill Fm	Pth & Kin	NN9512	56°17·6'	3°41·3'W	FM	58
East Mill Hills	Northum	NY8565	54°59·0'	2°13·6'W	X	87
East Mill Tor	Devon	SX6090	50°41·8'	3°58·6'W	H	191
East Mitchelton Fm	Renf	NS3661	55°49·1'	4°36·6'W	FM	63
East Molesey	Surrey	TQ1467	51°23·7'	0°21·3'W	T	176
East Monar Forest	Highld	NH1742	57°26·2'	5°2·5'W	X	25
East Mondynes	Aberd	NO7779	56°54·4'	2°22·2'W	X	45
East Moneylaws	Northum	NT8735	55°36·8'	2°11·9'W	X	74
East Monteach	Aberd	NJ8740	57°27·3'	2°12·5'W	X	30
Eastmoon Fen	Cambs	TL4089	52°29·1'	0°4·1'E	X	142,143
East Moor	Corn	SX2277	50°34·2'	4°30·4'W	X	201
Eastmoor	Derby	SK3071	53°14·3'	1°32·6'W	X	119
Eastmoor	Norf	TF7303	52°36·1'	0°33·7'E	X	143
East Moor	Northum	NZ2380	55°7·1'	1°37·9'W	X	81
East Moor	N Yks	SE5964	54°4·4'	1°5·5'W	X	100
East Moor	Pemb	SM9509	51°44·8'	4°57·8'W	X	157,158
East Moor	Wakf	SE3421	53°41·3'	1°28·7'W	T	104
East Moor Banks	N Yks	SE7268	54°6·4'	0°53·5'W	F	100
East Moor Cliff	Pemb	SS0497	51°38·5'	4°49·6'W	X	158
Eastmoor Fm	Norf	TG0238	52°54·3'	1°0·6'E	FM	133
East Moor Fm	Northum	NZ2790	55°12·5'	1°34·1'W	FM	81
East Moor Fm	N Yks	SE9485	54°15·4'	0°33·0'W	FM	94,101
East Moorhouse	E Renf	NS5351	55°44·1'	4°20·0'W	X	64
East Moorhouses	Northum	NZ0569	55°1·2'	1°54·9'W	X	87
East Moor Leazes	Durham	NZ2946	54°48·7'	1°32·5'W	X	88
East Moors	Card	ST2075	51°28·3'	3°8·7'W	T	171
East Moors	N Yks	SE6093	54°20·0'	1°4·2'W	X	94,100
East Moor Sch	Leeds	SE2839	53°51·0'	1°34·0'W	X	104
East Moors Fm	Dorset	SU1002	50°49·3'	1°51·1'W	FM	195
East Moor Wood	N Yks	SE6091	54°18·9'	1°4·2'W	F	94,100
East Morden	Dorset	SY9195	50°45·5'	2°7·3'W	T	195
East Morriston	Scot Bord	NT6042	55°40·4'	2°37·7'W	X	74
East Morton	Brad	SE1042	53°52·7'	1°50·5'W	T	104
East Morton	D & G	NS8800	55°17·1'	3°45·4'W	X	78
East Morton Hill	D & G	NS8901	55°17·7'	3°44·5'W	H	78
East Moss	Orkney	HY4603	58°54·9'	2°55·8'W	X	6,7
East Moss-side	Stir	NS6599	56°10·1'	4°10·0'W	X	57
East Moulsecoomb	Bri & Hov	TQ3307	50°51·1'	0°6·2'W	T	198
East Mount Lowther	D & G	NS8710	55°22·5'	3°46·6'W	H	71,78
East Mouse or Ynys Amlwch	I of Angl	SH4494	53°25·4'	4°20·5'W	X	114
East Muchra Hill	Scot Bord	NT2317	55°26·7'	3°12·6'W	H	79
East Muck	Moray	NJ4366	57°41·1'	2°56·9'W	X	28
East Muckcroft	N Lanak	NS6871	55°55·1'	4°6·3'W	X	64
East Mulloch	Aberd	NO7392	57°1·4'	2°26·2'W	X	38,45
East Muntloch	D & G	NX1233	54°39·7'	4°54·5'W	X	82
East Murkle	Highld	ND1768	58°35·8'	3°25·2'W	X	11,12
East Myreriggs	Pth & Kin	NO2142	56°34·1'	3°16·7'W	X	53
East Nancemeer	Corn	SW8555	50°21·6'	5°1·0'W	X	200
East Nappin	I of M	SC3598	54°21·3'	4°31·9'W	X	95
East Neap	Shetld	HU6294	60°37·7'	0°51·5'W	X	1,2
East Ness	Fife	NT1382	56°1·6'	3°23·3'W	X	65
East Ness	N Yks	SE6978	54°11·8'	0°56·1'W	T	100
East Ness	Shetld	HU3679	60°29·9'	1°20·2'W	X	2,3
East Nether Blelock	Pth & Kin	NO0634	56°29·6'	3°31·2'W	X	52,53
East Nevay	Angus	NO3344	56°35·2'	3°5·0'W	T	53
East Newbiggin	Darl	NZ3618	54°33·6'	1°26·2'W	X	93
East Newbiggin	Northum	NT9046	55°42·7'	2°9·1'W	X	74,75
East Newburn	Northum	NT9347	55°43·2'	2°6·3'W	X	74,75

East Newhall	Essex	TM2131	51°56·2′	1°13·3′E	X	169
East Newhall	Fife	NO6010	56°17·1′	2°38·3′W	X	59
East Newham	Northum	NZ1176	55°4·9′	1°49·2′W	X	88
East Newlands	Essex	TL9603	51°41·7′	0°50·6′E	X	168
East Newlands	Essex	TR0394	51°36·7′	0°56·3′E	X	168,178
East Newseat of Tolquhon	Aberd	NJ8829	57°21·3′	2°11·5′W	X	38
East Newton	Aberd	NJ6324	57°18·6′	2°36·4′W	X	37
East Newton	Angus	NO6647	56°37·1′	2°32·8′W	X	54
East Newton	E Ayr	NS5138	55°37·0′	4°21·5′W	X	70
East Newton	E Yorks	TA2637	53°49·1′	0°4·7′W	T	107
East Newton	Fife	NT3397	56°9·9′	3°4·3′W	X	59
East Newton	N Yks	SE6479	54°12·4′	1°0·7′W	T	100
East Newton	Pth & Kin	NO2632	56°28·7′	3°11·6′W	X	53
East Newton	Scot Bord	NT8549	55°44·3′	2°13·9′W	X	74
East Newtonleys	Aberd	NO8684	56°57·1′	2°13·4′W	X	45
Eastney	C of Port	SZ6699	50°47·4′	1°3·4′W	T	196
East Nisbet	Scot Bord	NT6726	55°31·8′	2°30·9′W	X	74
Eastnook	Northum	NY9693	55°14·1′	2°3·3′W	X	81
Eastnor	Heref	SO7337	52°2·1′	2°23·2′W	T	150
Eastnor Castle	Heref	SO7336	52°1·5′	2°23·2′W	X	150
Eastnor Hill	Heref	SO7237	52°2·1′	2°24·1′W	H	149
Eastnor Park	Heref	SO7437	52°2·1′	2°22·3′W	X	150
East Northwood	Devon	SS7709	50°52·3′	3°44·5′W	X	191
East Norton	Leic	SK7800	52°35·8′	0°50·5′W	T	141
East Nubbock	Northum	NY8962	54°57·4′	2°9·9′W	X	87
East Nymph	Devon	SX6896	50°45·2′	3°51·9′W	X	191
East Nynehead	Somer	ST1522	50°59·7′	3°12·3′W	T	181,193
East Oakley	Hants	SU5750	51°15·0′	1°10·6′W	T	185
East of England Showground	Peterb	TL1495	52°32·7′	0°18·7′W	X	142
Eastoft	N Lincs	SE8016	53°38·3′	0°47·0′W	T	112
Eastoft Carr	N Lincs	SE7915	53°37·8′	0°47·9′W	X	112
Eastoft Grange	N Lincs	SE7915	53°37·8′	0°47·9′W	X	112
East Ogwell	Devon	SX8370	50°31·3′	3°38·7′W	T	202
Eastoke	Hants	SZ7398	50°46·8′	0°57·5′W	T	197
East Okement Fm	Devon	SX6091	50°42·3′	3°58·6′W	FM	191
East Okement Head	Devon	SX6088	50°40·7′	3°58·5′W	W	191
East Okement River	Devon	SX6092	50°42·9′	3°58·6′W	W	191
Eastoke Point	Hants	SZ7498	50°46·8′	0°56·6′W	X	197
Easton	Cambs	TL1371	52°19·8′	0°20·1′W	T	153
Easton	C of Bris	ST6174	51°28·1′	2°33·3′W	T	172
Easton	Cumbr	NY2759	54°55·5′	3°7·9′W	T	85
Easton	Cumbr	NY4372	55°2·6′	2°53·1′W	T	85
Easton	Devon	SX6747	50°18·7′	3°51·7′W	T	202
Easton	Devon	SX7188	50°40·9′	3°49·2′W	T	191
Easton	Devon	SX7242	50°16·1′	3°47·4′W	X	202
Easton	Dorset	SY6971	50°32·5′	2°25·9′W	T	194
Easton	Hants	SU5132	51°5·3′	1°15·9′W	T	185
Easton	Heref	SO5464	52°16·6′	2°40·1′W	X	137,138,149
Easton	I of W	SZ3486	50°40·6′	1°30·7′W	T	196
Easton	Lincs	SK9226	52°49·7′	0°37·7′W	T	130
Easton	Norf	TG1310	52°39·0′	1°9·3′E	T	133
Easton	S Lanak	NT0849	55°43·8′	3°27·5′W	X	72
Easton	Somer	ST5147	51°13·4′	2°41·7′W	T	182,183
Easton	Suff	TM2858	52°10·6′	1°20·5′E	T	156
Easton	W Berks	SU4172	51°27·0′	1°24·2′W	T	174
Easton	Wilts	ST8970	51°26·0′	2°9·1′W	T	173
Easton	W Loth	NS9669	55°54·4′	3°39·4′W	X	65
Easton Barton	Devon	SS7406	50°50·6′	3°47·0′W	X	191
Easton Barton	Devon	SX7293	50°43·6′	3°48·4′W	X	191
Easton Bavents	Suff	TM5177	52°20·2′	1°41·5′E	X	156
Easton Broad	Suff	TM5179	52°21·3′	1°41·6′E	W	156
Easton Burn	Scot Bord	NT1737	55°37·4′	3°18·6′W	W	72
Easton Cliffs	Suff	TM5177	52°20·2′	1°41·5′E	X	156
Easton Clump	Wilts	SU2159	51°20·0′	1°41·5′W	F	174
Easton Court	Heref	SO5568	52°18·7′	2°39·2′W	X	137,138
Easton Down	Hants	SU4931	51°4·8′	1°17·6′W	X	185
Easton Down	Wilts	SU0666	51°23·8′	1°54·4′W	X	173
Easton Down	Wilts	SU2335	51°7·1′	1°39·9′W	X	184
Easton Fm	Essex	TL6024	51°53·7′	0°19·9′E	FM	167
Easton Fm	Lincs	SK9326	52°49·6′	0°36·8′W	FM	130
Easton Fm	Suff	TM5078	52°20·8′	1°40·6′E	FM	156
Easton Fm	Wilts	SU0464	51°22·7′	1°56·2′W	FM	173
Easton Fm	W Susx	SZ8396	50°45·7′	0°49·0′W	FM	197
Easton Fm Park	Suff	TM2758	52°10·6′	1°19·6′E	FM	156
Easton Grey	Wilts	ST8887	51°35·1′	2°10·0′W	T	173
Easton Grey Ho	Wilts	ST8787	51°35·1′	2°10·9′W	X	173
Easton Hall	Suff	TM2759	52°11·2′	1°19·7′E	X	156
Easton Hill	Somer	ST6237	51°8·1′	2°32·2′W	X	183
Easton Hill	Wilts	SU0565	51°23·3′	1°55·3′W	X	173
Easton Hill	Wilts	SU2058	51°19·5′	1°42·4′W	H	174
Easton Hillside	Northnts	TF0005	52°38·2′	0°30·9′W	X	141
Easton Hornstocks	Northnts	TF0100	52°35·5′	0°30·1′W	F	141
Easton-in-Gordano	N Som	ST5175	51°28·5′	2°41·9′W	T	172
Easton Lodge	Essex	TL5924	51°53·7′	0°19·0′E	X	167
Easton Lodge	Lincs	SK9327	52°50·2′	0°36·8′W	X	130
Easton Lodge	Northnts	TF0202	52°36·6′	0°29·2′W	X	141
Easton Low	Northnts	SP8958	52°13·0′	0°41·4′W	X	152
Easton Maudit	Northnts	SP8858	52°13·0′	0°42·3′W	T	152
Easton Moor	Devon	SS5322	50°59·0′	4°5·3′W	X	180
Easton Neston Ho	Northnts	SP7049	52°8·3′	0°58·2′W	A	152
Easton Neston Park	Northnts	SP7049	52°8·3′	0°58·2′W	X	152
Easton on the Hill	Northnts	TF0004	52°37·7′	0°30·9′W	T	141
Easton Park	Suff	TM2859	52°11·1′	1°20·5′E	X	156
Easton Park Wood	Hants	SU4254	51°17·2′	1°23·5′W	F	185
Easton Royal	Wilts	SU2060	51°20·6′	1°42·4′W	T	174
Eastontown	Devon	SX5372	50°32·0′	4°4·1′W	X	191,201
Easton Town	Somer	ST5933	51°5·9′	2°34·7′W	T	182,183
Easton Town	Wilts	ST8586	51°34·6′	2°12·6′W	T	173
Easton Wood	Lincs	SK9425	52°49·1′	0°35·9′W	F	130
Easton Wood	Suff	TM5180	52°21·9′	1°41·6′E	F	156
East Orchard	Dorset	ST8317	50°57·4′	2°14·1′W	T	183
East Orchard	Dorset	SY9480	50°37·4′	2°4·7′W	X	195
East or Creech Walk	Hants	SU6410	50°53·4′	1°5·0′W	X	196
East Ord	Northum	NT9951	55°45·4′	2°0·5′W	T	75
Eastover	Somer	ST3037	51°7·9′	2°59·6′W	T	182
Eastover Copse	Hants	SU3242	51°10·8′	1°32·1′W	F	185
Eastover Fm	Hants	SU3242	51°10·8′	1°32·1′W	FM	185
East Overton	S Lanak	NS7045	55°41·1′	4°3·6′W	X	64
East Panson	Devon	SX3692	50°42·5′	4°19·0′W	T	190
East Park	Aberd	NO7998	57°4·6′	2°20·3′W	X	38,45
Eastpark	Devon	SS5708	50°51·5′	4°1·5′W	X	191
East Park	Devon	SX3589	50°40·9′	4°19·8′W	X	190
Eastpark	D & G	NY0565	54°58·5′	3°28·6′W	X	85
East Park	Durham	NY9423	54°36·4′	2°5·2′W	X	91,92
East Park	Durham	NZ1336	54°43·4′	1°47·5′W	X	92
East Park	K upon H	TA1131	53°46·0′	0°18·5′W	X	107
East Park	W Susx	TQ2628	51°2·5′	0°11·8′W	X	187,198
East Parks	Durham	NZ2336	54°43·4′	1°38·2′W	X	93
East Park Wood	Notts	SK7367	53°11·9′	0°54·0′W	F	120
East Parley	Dorset	SZ1097	50°46·6′	1°51·1′W	T	195
East Parley Common	Dorset	SZ1099	50°47·7′	1°51·1′W	X	195
East Pasture Ho	Durham	NZ3135	54°42·8′	1°30·7′W	X	93
East Pastures	Red & Cl	NZ6818	54°33·4′	0°56·5′W	X	94
East Peckham	Kent	TQ6648	51°12·6′	0°23·0′E	T	188
East Peeke	Devon	SX3494	50°43·6′	4°20·7′W	X	190
East Pennard	Somer	ST5937	51°8·1′	2°34·8′W	T	182,183
East Penyllan	Shrops	SO2493	52°32·0′	3°6·8′W	X	137
East Perry	Cambs	TL1566	52°17·0′	0°18·4′W	T	153
East Pickard Bay	Pemb	SM8600	51°39·7′	5°5·3′W	W	157
East Pier	N Yks	NZ9011	54°29·4′	0°36·2′W	X	94
East Pinford	Somer	SS8042	51°10·1′	3°42·6′W	X	181
East Pitcorthie	Fife	NO5707	56°15·5′	2°41·2′W	X	59
East Pitforthie	Angus	NO6160	56°44·1′	2°37·8′W	X	45
East Pitkerro	Angus	NO4634	56°30·0′	2°52·2′W	X	54
East Pitscaff	Aberd	NJ9923	57°18·1′	2°0·5′W	X	38
East Pitscow	Aberd	NK0052	57°33·7′	1°59·5′W	X	30
East Pitton	Devon	SX5854	50°22·4′	3°59·4′W	X	202
Eastplace Burn	Pth & Kin	NN9805	56°13·9′	3°38·3′W	W	58
East Plain Fm	Cumbr	SD3773	54°9·2′	2°57·5′W	FM	96,97
East Plaistow	Devon	SS5838	51°7·7′	4°1·4′W	X	180
East Plantn	E Yorks	SE9536	53°48·9′	0°33·0′W	F	106
East Point	Essex	TL9206	51°43·4′	0°47·2′E	X	168
East Polquhirter	E Ayr	NS6313	55°23·8′	4°9·4′W	X	71
East Pool	Carm	SN2209	51°45·3′	4°34·4′W	X	158
East Port	Devon	SS7825	51°0·9′	3°44·0′W	X	180
East Port	Highld	NJ0729	57°20·8′	3°32·3′W	X	36
East Portlemouth	Devon	SX7438	50°13·9′	3°45·6′W	T	202
East Prawle	Devon	SX7836	50°12·9′	3°42·2′W	T	202
East Preston	D & G	NX9656	54°53·5′	3°36·9′W	T	84
East Preston	W Susx	TQ0702	50°48·7′	0°28·5′W	T	197
East Pulham	Dorset	ST7209	50°53·0′	2°23·5′W	T	194
East Putford	Devon	SS3616	50°55·4′	4°19·6′W	T	190
East Quantoxhead	Somer	ST1343	51°11·0′	3°14·3′W	T	181
East Quoys	Orkney	HY2722	59°5·0′	3°15·9′W	X	6
East Raffles	D & G	NY0872	55°2·3′	3°25·9′W	X	85
East Rainton	Sund	NZ3347	54°49·2′	1°28·8′W	T	88
East Ravendale	NE Lincs	TF2399	53°28·6′	0°8·4′W	T	113
East Raw	Northum	NZ0998	55°16·8′	1°51·1′W	X	81
East Raynham	Norf	TF8825	52°47·6′	0°47·7′E	T	132
Eastrea	Cambs	TL2997	52°33·6′	0°5·4′W	T	142
East Reach Fm	Lincs	TF1914	52°42·9′	0°13·9′W	FM	130
East Redcarr Plantn	E Yorks	TA1255	53°59·0′	0°17·1′W	F	107
East Regwm	Carm	SN2217	51°49·6′	4°34·6′W	X	158
East Reston	Scot Bord	NT9061	55°50·8′	2°9·1′W	X	67
East Reston Mill	Scot Bord	NT8961	55°50·8′	2°10·1′W	X	67
East Revoch	E Renf	NS5650	55°43·6′	4°17·1′W	X	64
East Rhidorroch Lodge	Highld	NH2393	57°53·7′	4°58·7′W	X	20
East Rhyne	Somer	ST3053	51°16·5′	2°59·8′W	W	182
East Riddlesden Hall	Brad	SE0742	53°52·7′	1°53·2′W	A	104
Eastridge Fm	W Susx	TQ2321	50°58·7′	0°14·5′W	FM	198
Eastridge Ho	Wilts	SU3073	51°27·5′	1°33·7′W	X	174
Eastridge Wood	Shrops	SJ3802	52°37·0′	2°54·5′W	F	126
East Rig	E Loth	NT5763	55°51·7′	2°40·8′W	X	67
Eastrig Burn	Pth & Kin	NN9607	56°14·9′	3°40·3′W	W	58
East Rigg	C of Edin	NT1563	55°51·4′	3°21·0′W	X	65
Eastriggs	D & G	NY2466	54°59·2′	3°10·8′W	T	85
East Rigton	Leeds	SE3643	53°53·2′	1°26·7′W	T	104
Eastrington	E Yorks	SE7929	53°45·3′	0°47·7′W	T	105,106
East Ringuinea	D & G	NX0847	54°47·1′	4°58·7′W	X	82
Eastrip	Wilts	ST8271	51°26·5′	2°15·2′W	T	173
East Road	Kent	TR0923	50°58·3′	0°59·0′E	W	189
East Rolstone	N Som	ST3962	51°21·5′	2°52·2′W	T	182
Eastrop	Hants	SU6451	51°15·5′	1°4·6′W	T	185
Eastrop Fm	Swin	SU2192	51°37·8′	1°41·4′W	FM	163,174
Eastrop Grange	Swin	SU2092	51°37·8′	1°42·3′W	X	163,174
East Roughlea	Durham	NZ2731	54°40·6′	1°34·5′W	X	93
East Rounton	N Yks	NZ4203	54°25·5′	1°20·7′W	T	93
East Row	N Yks	NZ8612	54°30·0′	0°39·9′W	X	94
East Row Beck	N Yks	NZ8211	54°29·5′	0°43·6′W	W	94
East Rowden	Devon	SX6599	50°46·7′	3°54·5′W	X	191
East Rowhorne	Devon	SX8794	50°44·3′	3°35·7′W	X	192
East Ruckham	Devon	SS8710	50°52·9′	3°36·0′W	X	192
East Rudham	Norf	TF8228	52°49·4′	0°42·5′E	T	132
East Runton	Norf	TG1942	52°56·1′	1°15·9′E	T	133
East Runton Gap	Norf	TG2042	52°56·0′	1°16·8′E	X	133
East Ruston	Norf	TG3427	52°47·6′	1°28·7′E	T	133,134
East Ruston Allotment	Norf	TG3428	52°48·1′	1°28·7′E	X	133,134
East Ruston Hall	Norf	TG3629	52°48·6′	1°30·5′E	X	133,134
Eastry	Kent	TR3054	51°14·5′	1°18·1′E	T	179
East Saltoun	E Loth	NT4767	55°53·8′	2°50·4′W	T	66
East Sandend	Aberd	NK0833	57°23·5′	1°51·6′W	X	30
East Sands	Fife	NO5116	56°20·3′	2°47·1′W	X	59
East Sanquhar	S Ayr	NS3624	55°29·2′	4°35·3′W	X	70
East Scale Lodge	N Yks	SD9874	54°10·0′	2°1·4′W	X	98
East Scales	D & G	NY2967	54°59·8′	3°6·2′W	X	85
East Scaraben	Highld	ND0827	58°13·6′	3°33·5′W	H	17
East Scrafton	N Yks	SE0884	54°15·3′	1°52·2′W	X	99
East Scrafton Moor	N Yks	SE0882	54°14·3′	1°52·2′W	X	99
East Scryne	Angus	NO5836	56°31·1′	2°40·5′W	X	54
East Seaton	Angus	NO6642	56°34·4′	2°32·8′W	X	54
East Shaftoe Hall	Northum	NZ0581	55°7·6′	1°54·9′W	X	81
East Shag	Torbay	SX9362	50°27·1′	3°30·1′W	X	202
Eastshaw Fm	W Susx	SU8724	51°0·8′	0°45·2′W	FM	197
East Shawhead	N Lanak	NS7362	55°50·3′	4°1·2′W	X	64
East Shaws	Durham	NZ0815	54°32·1′	1°52·2′W	X	92
East Shebster	Highld	ND0263	58°32·9′	3°40·6′W	X	11,12
East Sheen	Rich	TQ2075	51°27·9′	0°16·0′W	T	176
East Sheen Common	Rich	TQ1974	51°27·4′	0°16·8′W	X	176
East Sheep Walk	Suff	TM4874	52°18·7′	1°38·7′E	X	156
East Shefford Ho	W Berks	SU3974	51°28·0′	1°25·9′W	X	174
East Sherford	Devon	SX5554	50°22·3′	4°2·0′W	X	202
East Shethin	Aberd	NJ8931	57°22·4′	2°10·5′W	X	30
Eastshield	S Lanak	NS9650	55°44·2′	3°38·9′W	X	65,72
East Shield Hill	Northum	NZ1988	55°11·4′	1°41·7′W	X	81
East's Hill	Worcs	SP1248	52°8·0′	1°49·1′W	X	150
East Ship Channel	Dorset	SY7076	50°35·2′	2°25·0′W	W	194
East Shittlehopeside	Durham	NZ0038	54°44·5′	1°59·6′W	X	92
Eastshore	Shetld	HU3911	59°53·2′	1°17·7′W	T	4
East Shotton	Durham	NZ1023	54°36·4′	1°50·3′W	X	92
Eastside	Aberd	NJ8105	57°8·4′	2°18·4′W	X	38
Eastside	Aberd	NJ8823	57°18·1′	2°11·5′W	X	38
Eastside	Aberd	NJ9018	57°15·4′	2°9·5′W	X	38
Eastside	Aberd	NO8696	57°3·5′	2°13·4′W	X	38,45
Eastside	D & G	NS8704	55°19·3′	3°46·4′W	X	78
Eastside	Midlo	NT1860	55°49·8′	3°18·1′W	X	65,66
East Side	N Yks	SD8395	54°21·3′	2°15·3′W	X	98
East Side	N Yks	SD8977	54°11·6′	2°9·7′W	X	98
East Side	N Yks	SD8993	54°20·2′	2°9·7′W	X	98
East Side	N Yks	SD9476	54°11·0′	2°5·1′W	X	98
Eastside	Orkney	HY2924	59°6·1′	3°13·9′W	X	6
Eastside	Orkney	ND4691	58°48·5′	2°55·6′W	X	7
Eastside	Scot Bord	NT6150	55°44·8′	2°36·8′W	X	67,74
Eastside Burn	S Lanak	NT0028	55°32·4′	3°34·6′W	W	72
Eastside Heights	Scot Bord	NT3545	55°41·9′	3°1·6′W	H	73
Eastside Knowe	D & G	NT2206	55°20·8′	3°13·4′W	H	79
Eastside Wood	Angus	NO4564	56°46·1′	2°53·5′W	F	44
East Side Wood	N Yks	SE1271	54°8·3′	1°48·6′W	F	99
East Sidewood	S Lanak	NS9752	55°45·3′	3°38·0′W	X	65,72
East Sike	Cumbr	NY6772	55°2·7′	2°30·6′W	W	86,87
East Skears	Durham	NY9827	54°38·5′	2°1·4′W	X	92
East Skelston	D & G	NX8285	55°9·0′	3°50·7′W	T	78
East Skichen	Angus	NO5141	56°33·8′	2°47·4′W	X	54
East Sleekburn	Northum	NZ2883	55°8·7′	1°33·2′W	T	81
East Soar Fm	Devon	SX7237	50°13·4′	3°47·3′W	FM	202
East Sockburn Fm	N Yks	NZ3507	54°27·7′	1°27·2′W	FM	93
East Somerset Railway	Somer	ST6642	51°10·8′	2°28·8′W	X	183
East Somerton	Norf	TG4819	52°42·9′	1°40·7′E	T	134
East Stanley	Durham	NZ2053	54°52·5′	1°40·9′W	T	88
East Statfold	Devon	SS3901	50°47·4′	4°16·7′W	X	190
East Stell	Fife	NT2983	56°2·3′	3°7·9′W	X	66
East Stobswood	Northum	NZ2294	55°14·6′	1°38·8′W	X	81
East Stockwith	Lincs	SK7994	53°26·4′	0°48·2′W	T	112
East Stoke	Dorset	SY8786	50°40·6′	2°10·7′W	T	194
East Stoke	Notts	SK7549	53°2·2′	0°52·5′W	T	129
East Stoke	Somer	ST4817	50°57·2′	2°44·0′W	T	193
East Stone Gill	N Yks	SD9877	54°11·6′	2°1·4′W	W	98
East Stonesdale	N Yks	NY9002	54°25·0′	2°8·8′W	X	91,92
East Stony Keld	Durham	NY9814	54°31·5′	2°1·4′W	X	92
East Stoodleigh Barton	Devon	SS9319	50°57·9′	3°31·0′W	X	181
East Stour	Dorset	ST7922	51°0·1′	2°17·6′W	T	183
East Stour Common	Dorset	ST8123	51°0·6′	2°15·9′W	T	183
East Stour Fm	Kent	TR0752	51°14·0′	0°58·3′E	FM	179,189
East Stourmouth	Kent	TR2662	51°19·0′	1°15·0′E	T	179
East Stour River	Kent	TR0538	51°6·5′	0°56·1′E	W	179,189
East Stowford	Devon	SS6326	51°1·3′	3°56·8′W	T	180
East Stowford Barton	Devon	SS5542	51°9·8′	4°4·0′W	X	180
East Stratton	Hants	SU5439	51°9·1′	1°13·3′W	T	185
East Street	Kent	TR3058	51°16·7′	1°18·3′E	T	179
East Street	Somer	ST5338	51°8·6′	2°39·9′W	T	182,183
East Street	Somer	ST5438	51°8·6′	2°39·1′W	T	182,183
East Studdal	Kent	TR3249	51°11·8′	1°19·6′E	T	179
East Suisnish	Highld	NG5534	57°20·1′	6°3·8′W	T	24,32
East Sutton Park	Kent	TQ8249	51°12·9′	0°36·8′E	X	188
East Swilletts Fm	Dorset	ST4305	50°50·7′	2°48·2′W	FM	193
East Syme	N Yks	SE9894	54°20·2′	0°29·1′W	W	94,101
East Taing	Shetld	HU4470	60°25·0′	1°11·6′W	X	2,3
East Tamana	N Eil	NB0119	58°3·8′	7°3·7′W	X	13
East Tanfield	N Yks	SE2877	54°11·5′	1°33·8′W	X	99
East Tanfield Village	N Yks	SE2878	54°12·1′	1°33·8′W	A	99
East Taphouse	Corn	SX1863	50°26·6′	4°33·4′W	T	201
East Tapps	Devon	SS9023	51°0·0′	3°33·7′W	X	181
East Tarbert Bay	Arg & Bt	NR6652	55°42·6′	5°43·1′W	W	62
East Tarbet	D & G	NX1430	54°38·1′	4°52·5′W	X	82
East Tarns	Cumbr	SD7492	54°19·6′	2°23·6′W	W	98
East-the-Voe	Shetld	HU3556	60°17·5′	1°21·5′W	X	2,3
East-the-Water	Devon	SS4626	51°1·0′	4°11·4′W	T	180,190
East Thickley	Durham	NZ2425	54°37·4′	1°37·3′W	X	93
East Thievesdale Wood	Notts	SK6181	53°19·6′	1°4·6′W	F	111,120
East Thinacremuir	S Lanak	NS7349	55°43·3′	4°0·9′W	X	64
East Third	Pth & Kin	NN9213	56°18·1′	3°44·3′W	X	58
East Third	Scot Bord	NT6436	55°37·2′	2°33·9′W	T	74
East Thirston	Northum	NZ1999	55°17·3′	1°41·6′W	T	81
East Thorn	Northum	NZ1476	55°4·9′	1°46·4′W	X	88
East Thornton	Northum	NZ1187	55°10·9′	1°49·2′W	X	81
East Threave	S Ayr	NS2504	55°18·2′	4°45·0′W	X	76
East Tilbury	Thurr	TQ6878	51°28·8′	0°25·6′E	T	177,178
East Tilbury Marshes	Thurr	TQ6776	51°27·7′	0°24·6′E	X	177,178
East Tillygarmond	Aberd	NO6393	57°1·9′	2°36·1′W	X	37,45
East Tinwald	D & G	NY0481	55°7·1′	3°29·9′W	X	78
East Tisted	Hants	SU7032	51°5·2′	0°59·6′W	T	186
East Todd Sike	Durham	NY9533	54°41·8′	2°4·2′W	W	91,92
East Toe	Orkney	HY5740	59°14·9′	2°44·7′W	X	5
East Toft Dike	N Yks	SE8592	54°19·2′	0°41·2′W	A	94,100
East Toft Fm	Lincs	TF4552	53°3·0′	0°10·2′E	FM	122
East Tor	Devon	SX5389	50°41·2′	4°4·5′W	X	191
East Torphin	W Loth	NT0361	55°50·2′	3°32·5′W	X	65
East Torr	Renf	NS3665	55°51·3′	4°36·8′W	X	63
East Torrie	Stir	NN6504	56°12·8′	4°10·2′W	X	57
East Torrington	Lincs	TF1483	53°20·1′	0°16·9′W	T	121
Easttown	Aberd	NJ4905	57°8·2′	2°50·1′W	X	37
East Town	Somer	ST1032	51°5·1′	3°16·7′W	T	181
East Town	Somer	ST6040	51°9·7′	2°33·9′W	T	183
East Town	Wilts	ST8955	51°17·9′	2°9·1′W	T	173
East Town End Fm	Cumbr	NY0226	54°37·4′	3°30·7′W	FM	89
East Town Fm	Aberd	NO7784	56°57·1′	2°22·2′W	FM	45
East Town Fm	Northum	NZ1275	55°4·4′	1°48·3′W	FM	88
East Town Pasture	Durham	NZ0717	54°33·1′	1°53·1′W	X	92
East Trayne	Devon	SS7022	50°59·2′	3°50·7′W	X	180
East Trewent	Pemb	SS0097	51°38·4′	4°53·0′W	T	158

East Trewick	Northum	NZ1179	55°6·6'	1°49·2'W	X	88
East Trodigal	Arg & Bt	NR6520	55°25·3'	5°42·4'W	X	68
East Trumperton	Angus	NO5349	56°38·1'	2°45·5'W	X	54
East Tuddenham	Norf	TG0811	52°39·6'	1°4·9'E	T	133
East Tullyfergus	Pth & Kin	NO2149	56°37·8'	3°16·8'W	X	53
East Tump	Pemb	SM5909	51°43·9'	5°29·0'W	X	157
East Turnalief	Aberd	NK0938	57°26·2'	1°50·5'W	X	30
East Tytherley	Hants	SU2928	51°3·3'	1°34·8'W	T	185
East Tytherton	Wilts	ST9674	51°28·1'	2°3·1'W	T	173
East Unthank	Northum	NY7363	54°57·9'	2°24·9'W	X	86,87
East Upsall Fm	Red & Cl	NZ5615	54°31·9'	1°7·7'W	FM	93
East Valley Fm	Kent	TR3646	51°10·1'	1°22·9'E	FM	179
East Venn	Devon	SX3997	50°45·3'	4°16·6'W	X	190
East View	Cumbr	NY4146	54°48·6'	2°54·7'W	X	85
East Village	Devon	SS8405	50°50·2'	3°38·5'W	T	191
East Village	V of Glam	SS9974	51°27·6'	3°26·8'W	T	170
Eastville	C of Bris	ST6175	51°28·6'	2°33·3'W	T	172
Eastville	Lincs	TF4056	53°5·2'	0°5·8'E	T	122
Eastville Fm	Lincs	TF4157	53°5·7'	0°6·8'E	FM	122
East Voe of Quarff	Shetld	HU4335	60°6·1'	1°13·1'W	W	4
East Voe of Scalloway	Shetld	HU4038	60°7·7'	1°16·3'W	W	4
East Voe of Skellister	Shetld	HU4754	60°16·3'	1°8·5'W	W	3
East Vows	Fife	NT2888	56°5·0'	3°9·0'W	X	66
East Vows	Fife	NT4899	56°11·1'	2°49·8'W	X	59
East Wall	Shrops	SO5293	52°32·2'	2°42·1'W	T	137,138
East Wall Fm	Staffs	SK0344	52°59·8'	1°56·9'W	FM	119,128
East Wallhouses	Northum	NZ0568	55°0·6'	1°54·9'W	X	87
East Walton	Norf	TF7416	52°43·0'	0°35·0'E	T	132
Eastward	Cumbr	NY5116	54°32·5'	2°45·0'W	X	90
East Ward	Shetld	HU2346	60°12·1'	1°34·6'W	H	4
East Wardlaw	E Ayr	NS4439	55°37·4'	4°28·2'W	X	70
East Ware Fm	Essex	TM0001	51°40·6'	0°54·0'E	FM	168
East Water	Midlo	NT4561	55°50·6'	2°52·3'W	W	66
East Water	S Lanak	NT0118	55°27·0'	3°33·5'W	W	78
East Water	Somer	SS8942	51°10·2'	3°34·9'W	W	181
East Water	Somer	ST5350	51°15·1'	2°40·0'W	T	182,183
Eastway	Devon	SS8213	50°54·5'	3°40·3'W	X	181
Eastways	Lincs	TF3314	52°42·7'	0°1·5'W	X	131
East Wear Bay	Kent	TR2537	51°5·5'	1°13·2'E	W	179
East Weare	Dorset	SY7073	50°33·6'	2°25·0'W	X	194
East Webburn River	Devon	SX7176	50°34·4'	3°48·9'W	W	191
East Week	Devon	SX6692	50°43·0'	3°53·5'W	T	191
Eastwell	Leic	SK7728	52°50·9'	0°51·0'W	T	129
Eastwell	Wilts	ST9957	51°19·0'	2°0·5'W	X	173
East Welland	Devon	SS8023	50°59·9'	3°42·2'W	X	181
Eastwell Court	Kent	TR0046	51°10·9'	0°52·1'E	X	189
East Wellow	Hants	SU3020	50°58·9'	1°34·0'W	T	185
Eastwell Park	Kent	TR0147	51°11·4'	0°53·0'E	T	189
Eastwell Park	Kent	TR0148	51°12·0'	0°53·0'E	X	189
East Wemyss	Fife	NT3396	56°9·4'	3°4·3'W	T	59
East Westacott	Devon	SS6013	50°54·2'	3°59·1'W	X	180
East Wheal Rose Fm	Corn	SW8355	50°21·5'	5°2·7'W	FM	200
East Whitburn	W Loth	NS9665	55°52·3'	3°39·3'W	T	65
East Whitburn Mains	W Loth	NS9664	55°51·7'	3°39·3'W	X	65
East Whiteburn	Aberd	NJ9739	57°26·7'	2°2·5'W	X	30
East Whitefield	Pth & Kin	NO1734	56°29·7'	3°20·3'W	T	53
East Whitelee	E Ayr	NS4648	55°42·3'	4°26·6'W	X	64
East White Sykes	W Loth	NS9961	55°50·2'	3°36·3'W	X	65
East Whorley Hill	Durham	NZ1116	54°32·6'	1°49·4'W	X	92
East Wick	Essex	TR0096	51°37·9'	0°53·8'E	X	168
East Wick	Essex	TR0192	51°35·7'	0°54·5'E	X	178
Eastwick	Herts	TL4311	51°47·0'	0°4·8'E	T	167
Eastwick	Shetld	HU3679	60°29·9'	1°20·9'W	T	2,3
Eastwick	W Berks	SU3860	51°20·5'	1°26·9'W	X	174
Eastwick	Wrex	SJ4841	52°58·1'	2°46·1'W	X	117
Eastwick Fm	Shrops	SJ3737	52°55·8'	2°55·8'W	FM	126
Eastwick Fm	Suff	TM1270	52°17·5'	1°6·9'E	FM	144,155
East Wick Fm	Wilts	SU1863	51°22·2'	1°44·1'W	FM	173
Eastwick Hall Fm	Herts	TL4213	51°48·1'	0°4·0'E	FM	167
East Wickham	Bexley	TQ4677	51°28·6'	0°6·5'E	T	177
Eastwick Head	Essex	TR0291	51°35·1'	0°55·3'E	X	178
Eastwick Lodge Fm	Herts	TL4411	51°47·0'	0°5·7'E	FM	167
East Williamston	Pemb	SN0904	51°42·4'	4°45·5'W	T	158
East Winch	Norf	TF6916	52°43·1'	0°30·5'E	T	132
East Winch Common	Norf	TF7015	52°42·6'	0°31·4'E	F	132
East Winner	Hants	SZ6998	50°46·9'	1°0·9'W	X	197
East Winterslow	Wilts	SU2433	51°6·0'	1°39·0'W	T	184
East Wirren	Angus	NO5373	56°51·0'	2°45·8'W	H	44
East Withy Fm	Somer	ST0131	51°4·4'	3°24·4'W	FM	181
East Wittering	W Susx	SZ8096	50°45·7'	0°51·6'W	T	197
East Witton	N Yks	SE1486	54°16·4'	1°46·7'W	T	99
East Witton Lodge	N Yks	SE1286	54°16·4'	1°48·5'W	X	99
East Witton Row	Durham	NZ1530	54°40·1'	1°45·6'W	X	92
East Wold Fm	N Yks	SE8168	54°6·3'	0°45·3'W	FM	100
East Wolves Fm	W Susx	TQ1316	50°56·2'	0°23·1'W	FM	198
East Wood	Bucks	SU7795	51°39·1'	0°52·8'W	F	165
Eastwood	Cald	SD9625	53°43·5'	2°3·2'W	T	103
East Wood	Corn	SX0568	50°29·0'	4°44·6'W	F	200
Eastwood	Devon	SS4812	50°53·5'	4°9·3'W	X	180
Eastwood	Devon	SS7423	50°59·8'	3°47·4'W	X	180
Eastwood	Devon	SS9724	51°0·6'	3°27·7'W	X	181
Eastwood	Devon	SX8892	50°43·2'	3°34·8'W	X	192
East Wood	Glos	SO5600	51°42·1'	2°37·8'W	F	162
Eastwood	Heref	SO6240	52°3·7'	2°32·9'W	T	149
East Wood	Kent	TQ6937	51°6·7'	0°25·3'E	F	188
Eastwood	Kent	TQ8548	51°12·3'	0°39·3'E	X	189
Eastwood	Midlo	NT3459	55°49·4'	3°2·8'W	X	66,73
Eastwood	N Lincs	SE9609	53°34·4'	0°32·8'W	X	112
East Wood	Norf	TM2987	52°26·2'	1°22·5'E	F	156
East Wood	Northum	NT9630	55°34·1'	2°3·4'W	F	74,75
East Wood	Northum	NY9367	55°0·1'	2°6·1'W	F	87
Eastwood	Notts	SK4646	53°0·8'	1°18·5'W	T	129
East Wood	N Yks	SE1847	53°55·4'	1°43·1'W	F	104
Eastwood	Roth	SK4393	53°26·2'	1°20·8'W	T	111
East Wood	Rut	TF0011	52°41·5'	0°30·8'W	F	130
East Wood	Somer	ST1443	51°11·0'	3°13·4'W	F	181
Eastwood	Sou-on-Sea	TQ8488	51°33·9'	0°39·7'E	T	178
Eastwood	W Loth	NS9361	55°50·1'	3°42·1'W	X	65
East Woodburn	Northum	NY9086	55°10·3'	2°9·0'W	T	80
East Woodburn Common	Northum	NY9287	55°10·9'	2°7·1'W	X	80

Eastwood End	Cambs	TL4293	52°31·2'	0°6·0'E	T	142,143
Eastwood Fm	Bucks	SU7795	51°39·1'	0°52·8'W	FM	165
Eastwood Fm	Notts	SK6649	53°2·3'	1°0·5'W	FM	129
Eastwood Fm	Somer	ST3524	51°0·9'	2°55·2'W	FM	193
Eastwood Fm	Somer	ST6628	51°3·3'	2°28·7'W	FM	183
Eastwood Fm	Suff	TM0154	52°9·1'	0°56·7'E	FM	155
Eastwood Fm	Suff	TM4998	52°31·6'	1°40·7'E	FM	134
Eastwood Grange	Derby	SK3563	53°10·0'	1°28·2'W	X	119
Eastwood Hall	Durham	NZ0812	54°30·4'	1°52·2'W	X	92
Eastwood Hall	Notts	SK4647	53°1·3'	1°18·4'W	T	129
East Woodhay	Hants	SU4061	51°21·0'	1°25·1'W	T	174
East Woodhay Ho	Hants	SU4363	51°22·1'	1°22·5'W	X	174
Eastwood Ho	Northum	NY9959	54°55·8'	2°0·5'W	X	87
East Woodlands	C of Aber	NJ8514	57°13·2'	2°14·4'W	X	38
East Woodlands	Devon	SS5324	51°0·0'	4°5·3'W	X	180
East Woodlands	Somer	ST7844	51°11·9'	2°18·5'W	T	183
Eastwoodlodge Fm	Suff	TM4774	52°18·7'	1°37·8'E	FM	156
Eastwood Manor	Bath & NE Somer	ST5755	51°17·8'	2°36·6'W	X	172,182
Eastwood Park	S Glos	ST6792	51°37·8'	2°28·2'W	X	162,172
East Woodside	Aberd	NJ7402	57°6·8'	2°25·3'W	X	38
East Woodside	Cumbr	NY3149	54°50·1'	3°4·0'W	X	85
Eastwood Trading Estate	Roth	SK4494	53°26·7'	1°19·8'W	X	111
East Worldham	Hants	SU7438	51°8·4'	0°56·1'W	T	186
East Worlington	Devon	SS7713	50°54·4'	3°44·6'W	T	180
East Worsall Fm	N Yks	NZ3907	54°27·7'	1°23·5'W	FM	93
East Worthele	Devon	SX6354	50°22·4'	3°55·2'W	X	202
East Worthing	W Susx	TQ1603	50°49·1'	0°20·8'W	T	198
East Wretham	Norf	TL9190	52°28·7'	0°49·2'E	T	144
East Wretham	Norf	TL9190	52°28·7'	0°49·2'E	T	144
East Wretham Heath	Norf	TL9188	52°27·6'	0°49·1'E	X	144
Eastwrey Barton	Devon	SX7882	50°37·7'	3°43·1'W	X	191
East Wryde Fm	Peterb	TF3104	52°37·3'	0°3·5'W	FM	142
East Wyke Fm	Surrey	SU9050	51°14·8'	0°42·2'W	FM	186
East Wykeham Village	Lincs	TF2288	53°22·7'	0°9·5'W	A	113,122
East Yagland	Devon	SS2919	50°56·9'	4°25·7'W	X	190
East Yarde	Devon	SS4914	50°54·6'	4°8·5'W	X	180
East Yardhouses	S Lanak	NT0051	55°44·8'	3°35·1'W	X	65,72
East Yell	Shetld	HU5284	60°32·4'	1°2·6'W	X	1,2,3
Eastyetts	S Lanak	NT0743	55°40·5'	3°28·3'W	X	72
East Youlstone	Devon	SS2715	50°54·8'	4°27·3'W	T	190
Easty Wood	Suff	TL7948	52°6·3'	0°37·2'E	F	155
Eas Urchaidh	Arg & Bt	NN2432	56°27·1'	4°50·9'W	W	50
Eatenden Wood	E Susx	TQ7218	50°56·4'	0°27·3'E	F	199
Eathie	Arg & Bt	NM8010	56°14·2'	5°32·6'W	X	55
Eathie	Highld	NH7763	57°38·7'	4°3·2'W	X	21,27
Eathie Mains	Highld	NH7763	57°38·7'	4°3·2'W	X	21,27
Eathorne	Corn	SW7431	50°8·4'	5°9·4'W	X	204
Eathorpe	Warw	SP3969	52°19·3'	1°25·3'W	T	151
Eathorpe Park (Hotel)	Warw	SP3969	52°19·3'	1°25·3'W	X	151
Eaton	Ches	SJ5763	53°10·0'	2°38·2'W	T	117
Eaton	Ches	SJ8665	53°11·2'	2°12·2'W	T	118
Eaton	Heref	SO5058	52°13·3'	2°43·5'W	T	149
Eaton	Leic	SK7929	52°51·4'	0°49·2'W	T	129
Eaton	Norf	TF6936	52°53·9'	0°31·2'E	X	132
Eaton	Norf	TG2106	52°36·6'	1°16·3'E	T	134
Eaton	Notts	SK7178	53°17·9'	0°55·7'W	T	120
Eaton	Oxon	SP4403	51°43·7'	1°21·4'W	T	164
Eaton	Shrops	SO3789	52°30·2'	2°55·3'W	T	137
Eaton	Shrops	SO5090	52°30·6'	2°43·8'W	T	137,138
Eaton Bishop	Heref	SO4438	52°2·5'	2°48·6'W	T	149,161
Eaton Br	Heref	SO5058	52°13·3'	2°43·5'W	X	149
Eaton Bray	Beds	SP9720	51°52·4'	0°35·1'W	T	165
Eaton Breck Fm	Notts	SK6977	53°17·4'	0°57·5'W	FM	120
Eaton Brook	Shrops	SO4989	52°30·0'	2°44·7'W	W	137,138
Eaton Camp	Heref	SO4539	52°3·0'	2°47·7'W	A	149,161
Eaton Constantine	Shrops	SJ5906	52°39·3'	2°36·0'W	T	126
Eaton Coppice	Shrops	SO4989	52°30·0'	2°44·7'W	F	137,138
Eaton Dale	Derby	SK1755	53°5·8'	1°44·4'W	X	119
Eaton Dovedale	Derby	SK1037	52°56·1'	1°50·7'W	X	128
Eaton Ford	Cambs	TL1760	52°13·8'	0°16·8'W	T	153
Eaton Grange	Leic	SK8028	52°50·8'	0°48·3'W	X	130
Eaton Hall	Ches	SJ4160	53°8·3'	2°52·5'W	T	117
Eaton Hall Fm	Ches	SJ6470	53°13·8'	2°32·0'W	FM	118
Eaton Hall Fm	Derby	SK1036	52°55·5'	1°50·7'W	FM	128
Eaton Hall Quarry	Ches	SJ8665	53°11·2'	2°12·2'W	X	118
Eaton Hall (Sch)	Notts	SK7178	53°17·9'	0°55·7'W	X	120
Eaton Hastings	Oxon	SU2597	51°40·5'	1°37·9'W	T	163
Eaton Heath	Oxon	SP4403	51°43·7'	1°21·4'W	X	164
Eaton Hill	Derby	SK3642	52°58·7'	1°27·4'W	X	119,128
Eaton Hill	Heref	SO3735	52°0·8'	2°54·7'W	H	149,161
Eaton Hill	Heref	SO5059	52°13·9'	2°43·5'W	X	149
Eaton Ho	Ches	SJ6570	53°13·8'	2°31·1'W	X	118
Eaton Leys Fm	Bucks	SP8832	51°59·0'	0°42·7'W	FM	152,165
Eaton Lodge	Herts	TL0809	51°46·4'	0°25·7'W	X	166
Eaton Lodge	Leic	SK7829	52°51·4'	0°50·1'W	X	129
Eaton Mascott	Shrops	SJ5305	52°38·7'	2°41·3'W	T	126
Eaton Park	Norf	TG2007	52°37·2'	1°15·4'E	X	134
Eatons Fm	W Susx	TQ1816	50°56·1'	0°18·9'W	FM	198
Eaton Socon	Cambs	TL1659	52°13·2'	0°17·7'W	T	153
Eaton upon Tern	Shrops	SJ6523	52°48·4'	2°30·8'W	T	127
Eaton Wood	Derby	SK1036	52°55·5'	1°50·7'W	F	128
Eaton Wood	Notts	SK7277	53°17·3'	0°54·8'W	F	120
Eaton Wood	Oxon	SU2596	51°40·0'	1°37·9'W	F	163
Eau Bank Fm	Lincs	TF4096	53°26·8'	0°6·9'E	FM	113
Eau Bridge Fm	Lincs	TF4195	53°26·2'	0°7·8'E	FM	113
Eau Brink	Norf	TF5816	52°43·3'	0°20·8'E	T	131
Eau End Fm	Lincs	TF1738	52°55·8'	0°15·2'W	FM	130
Eau Well	Lincs	TF1022	52°47·3'	0°21·7'W	W	130
Eau Withington	Heref	SO5442	52°4·7'	2°39·9'W	T	149
Eaval (Eabhal)	N Eil	NF8960	57°31·7'	7°11·3'W	H	22
Eaves	Heref	SO2849	52°8·3'	3°2·7'W	X	148
Eaves Barn	Lancs	SD7832	53°47·3'	2°19·6'W	X	103
Eaves Fm	Lancs	SD4937	53°49·9'	2°46·1'W	FM	102
Eavesford	Staffs	SK0346	53°0·9'	1°56·9'W	X	119,128
Eaves Green	Sol	SP2582	52°26·4'	1°37·5'W	T	140
Eaves Green Fm	Lancs	SD5637	53°49·9'	2°39·7'W	FM	102
Eaves Green Hall	Lancs	SD5637	53°49·9'	2°39·7'W	X	102
Eaves Hall	Derby	SK0679	53°18·7'	1°54·2'W	X	119
Eaves Hall	Lancs	SD7344	53°53·7'	2°24·2'W	X	103

Eaves Ho	Lancs	SD7344	53°53·7'	2°24·2'W	X	103
Eaves Knoll	Derby	SJ9986	53°22·5'	2°0·5'W	X	109
Eaves, The	Glos	SO6106	51°45·3'	2°33·5'W	T	162
Eaves, The	Staffs	SK0141	52°58·2'	1°58·7'W	X	119,128
Eavestone	N Yks	SE2268	54°6·7'	1°39·4'W	T	99
Eavestone Lake	N Yks	SE2267	54°6·1'	1°39·4'W	W	99
Eavestone Moor	N Yks	SE2068	54°6·7'	1°41·2'W	X	99
Eaves Wood	Lancs	SD4676	54°10·9'	2°49·2'W	F	97
Eayres Lodge	Rut	SK9911	52°41·5'	0°31·7'W	X	130
Ebal Rocks	Corn	SW4338	50°11·4'	5°35·7'W	X	203
Ebberly Hill	Devon	SS5719	50°57·4'	4°1·8'W	T	180
Ebberly Ho	Devon	SS5618	50°56·8'	4°2·6'W	X	180
Ebber Rocks	Corn	SW7816	50°0·4'	5°5·5'W	X	204
Ebberston	N Yks	SE8982	54°13·8'	0°37·7'W	T	101
Ebberston Common Fm	N Yks	SE9089	54°17·6'	0°36·6'W	FM	94,101
Ebberston Hall	N Yks	SE8983	54°14·3'	0°37·6'W	X	101
Ebberston Ings	N Yks	SE9081	54°13·2'	0°36·8'W	X	101
Ebberston Low Moor	N Yks	SE9089	54°17·6'	0°36·6'W	X	94,101
Ebbesbourne Wake	Wilts	ST9924	51°1·2'	2°0·5'W	T	184
Ebbing & Flowing Well	Derby	SK0879	53°18·7'	1°52·4'W	W	119
Ebbingford Manor	Corn	SS2005	50°49·2'	4°33·0'W	A	190
Ebblake	Dorset	SU1007	50°52·0'	1°51·1'W	T	195
Ebb of the Riv	Orkney	HY6846	59°18·2'	2°33·2'W	X	5
Ebbor Fm	Somer	ST5247	51°13·4'	2°40·9'W	FM	182,183
Ebbor Gorge	Somer	ST5248	51°14·0'	2°40·9'W	X	182,183
Ebbsfleet	Kent	TR3363	51°19·3'	1°21·0'E	A	179
Ebbsfleet Ho	Kent	TR3362	51°18·8'	1°21·0'E	X	179
Ebbs Ho	Suff	TM0355	52°9·6'	0°58·5'E	X	155
Ebbstone or Craig Laggan		NW9569	54°58·7'	5°11·8'W	X	82
Ebbw Fâch River	Blae Gw	SO2103	51°43·4'	3°8·2'W	W	171
Ebbw River or Afon Ebwy	Caer	ST2193	51°38·1'	3°8·1'W	W	171
Ebbw Vale	Blae Gw	SO1805	51°44·5'	3°10·9'W	X	161
Ebbw Vale	Caer	ST2195	51°39·1'	3°8·1'W	X	171
Ebbw Vale / Glyn Ebwy	Blae Gw	SO1609	51°46·6'	3°12·7'W	T	161
Ebchester	Durham	NZ1055	54°53·6'	1°50·2'W	T	88
Ebdon	N Som	ST3664	51°22·5'	2°54·8'W	T	182
Ebdon Fm	Devon	SY1391	50°43·0'	3°13·6'W	FM	192,193
Ebernoe	W Susx	SU9727	51°2·3'	0°36·6'W	T	186,197
Ebernoe Common	W Susx	SU9726	51°1·7'	0°36·6'W	F	186,197
Ebford	Devon	SX9887	50°40·7'	3°26·2'W	T	192
Ebley	Glos	SO8204	51°44·3'	2°15·2'W	T	162
Ebnal	Ches	SJ4948	53°1·9'	2°45·2'W	T	117
Ebnal Hall	Shrops	SJ3134	52°54·2'	3°1·1'W	X	126
Ebnall	Heref	SO4758	52°13·3'	2°46·2'W	T	148,149
Ebolion	Gwyn	SH1825	52°47·8'	4°41·6'W	X	123
Ebor Ho	N Yks	SE8471	54°7·9'	0°42·4'W	X	100
Ebor Way	Leeds	SE2743	53°53·2'	1°34·9'W	X	104
Ebor Way	N Yks	SE6282	54°14·0'	1°2·5'W	X	100
Ebor Way	York	SE5546	53°54·7'	1°9·3'W	X	105
Ebreywood	Shrops	SJ5417	52°45·2'	2°40·5'W	T	126
Ebreywood Fm	Shrops	SJ5417	52°45·2'	2°40·5'W	FM	126
Ebrie Burn	Aberd	NJ9235	57°24·6'	2°7·5'W	W	30
Ebriehead	Aberd	NJ9044	57°29·4'	2°9·6'W	X	30
Ebrington	Glos	SP1840	52°3·7'	1°43·9'W	T	151
Ebrington Hill	Glos	SP1841	52°4·3'	1°43·8'W	X	151
Ebsbury	Wilts	SU0535	51°7·1'	1°55·3'W	A	184
Ebsbury Copse	Wilts	SU0535	51°7·1'	1°55·3'W	F	184
Ebsbury Hill	Wilts	SU0635	51°7·1'	1°54·5'W	X	184
Ebsley Fm	Somer	ST2136	51°7·3'	3°7·3'W	FM	182
Ebsworthy Moor Fm	Devon	SX4990	50°41·6'	4°7·9'W	FM	191
Ebury Hill	Shrops	SJ5416	52°44·6'	2°40·5'W	X	126
Ebury Hill (Fort)	Shrops	SJ5416	52°44·6'	2°40·5'W	A	126
Ebvracvm (York)	York	SE5951	53°57·3'	1°5·6'W	R	105
Ebworthy	Devon	SX5090	50°41·7'	4°7·1'W	FM	191
E Camps	Fife	NT0588	56°4·8'	3°31·1'W	X	65
Ecchinswell	Hants	SU5059	51°19·9'	1°16·5'W	T	174
Ecclaw	Scot Bord	NT7568	55°54·5'	2°23·6'W	X	67
Ecclaw Hill	Scot Bord	NT7567	55°54·0'	2°23·6'W	H	67
Ecclefechan	D & G	NY1974	55°3·5'	3°15·7'W	T	85
Ecclerigg Hall	Cumbr	SD5989	54°17·9'	2°37·4'W	X	97
Eccle Riggs	Cumbr	SD2186	54°16·1'	3°12·4'W	T	96
Ecclerig Ho	Cumbr	NY3801	54°24·3'	2°56·9'W	X	90
Eccles	D & G	NX8496	55°14·9'	3°49·1'W	X	78
Eccles	Kent	TQ7360	51°19·0'	0°29·3'E	T	178,188
Eccles	Salf	SJ7798	53°28·9'	2°20·4'W	T	109
Eccles	Scot Bord	NT7641	55°40·0'	2°22·5'W	T	74
Ecclesall	Sheff	SK3284	53°21·4'	1°30·7'W	T	110,111
Eccles Alley	Heref	SO3452	52°10·0'	2°57·5'W	X	148,149
Ecclesall Wood	Sheff	SK3282	53°20·3'	1°30·8'W	F	110,111
Ecclesbourne Glen	E Susx	TQ8410	50°51·8'	0°37·3'E	F	199
Eccles Cairn	Scot Bord	NT8527	55°32·4'	2°13·8'W	X	74
Eccles Common	Norf	TM0388	52°27·4'	0°59·7'E	X	144
Ecclesden Fm	W Susx	TQ0804	50°49·8'	0°27·6'W	FM	197
Ecclesden Manor	W Susx	TQ0704	50°49·8'	0°28·5'W	A	197
Ecclesfield	Sheff	SK3594	53°26·7'	1°28·0'W	T	110,111
Eccles Fm	Lancs	SD4812	53°36·4'	2°46·7'W	FM	108
Eccles Fm	Lancs	SD5244	53°53·6'	2°43·4'W	FM	102
Eccles Green	Heref	SO3748	52°7·8'	2°54·8'W	X	148,149
Ecclesgreig	Aberd	NO7365	56°46·8'	2°26·1'W	X	45
Eccles Hall	Norf	TM0289	52°27·9'	0°58·8'E	X	144
Eccleshall	Staffs	SJ8329	52°51·7'	2°14·7'W	T	127
Eccleshall and West Staffs Cycle Way	Staffs	SJ7826	52°50·1'	2°19·2'W	X	127
Eccleshall Road Fm	Staffs	SJ7236	52°55·5'	2°24·6'W	FM	127
Eccles Heath	Norf	TM0189	52°27·9'	0°57·9'E	X	144
Eccleshill	Brad	SE1736	53°49·4'	1°44·1'W	T	104
Eccles Ho	Derby	SK0381	53°19·8'	1°56·9'W	X	110
Eccles Ho	Scot Bord	NT7641	55°40·0'	2°22·5'W	X	74
Ecclesiamagirdle House	Pth & Kin	NO1016	56°19·9'	3°26·9'W	A	58
Ecclesmachan	W Loth	NT0573	55°56·7'	3°30·8'W	T	65
Eccles Newton	Scot Bord	NT7740	55°39·4'	2°21·5'W	X	74
Eccles on Sea	Norf	TG4029	52°48·5'	1°34·1'E	T	134
Eccles Pike	Derby	SK0381	53°19·8'	1°56·9'W	H	110
Eccles Road	Norf	TM0190	52°28·5'	0°58·0'E	T	144
Eccles Tofts	Scot Bord	NT7545	55°42·1'	2°23·4'W	X	74
Eccleston	Ches	SJ4062	53°9·3'	2°53·4'W	T	117
Eccleston	Lancs	SD5117	53°39·1'	2°44·1'W	T	108
Eccleston	St Hel	SJ4895	53°27·2'	2°46·6'W	T	108
Eccleston Hill	Ches	SJ4062	53°9·3'	2°53·4'W	X	117
Eccleston Mere	St Hel	SJ4894	53°26·7'	2°46·6'W	W	108

Eccleston Park	St Hel	SJ4793	53°26·1′	2°47·5′W	T	108
Eccleswall Court	Heref	SO6523	51°54·5′	2°30·1′W	X	162
Eccliffe	Dorset	ST7925	51°1·7′	2°17·6′W	T	183
Eccup	Leeds	SE2842	53°52·6′	1°34·0′W	T	104
Eccup Reservoir	Leeds	SE2941	53°52·1′	1°33·1′W	W	104
Echills	Staffs	SK1016	52°44·7′	1°50·7′W	X	128
Echna Loch	Orkney	ND4796	58°51·2′	2°54·6′W	W	6,7
Echnaloch Bay	Orkney	ND4697	58°51·7′	2°55·7′W	W	6,7
Echo Crags	Northum	NT7404	55°20·0′	2°24·2′W	H	80
Echoes Hill	Shrops	SO7399	52°35·5′	2°23·5′W	X	138
Echt	Aberd	NJ7305	57°8·4′	2°26·3′W	T	38
Eckensfield	W Susx	SU7616	50°56·5′	0°54·7′W	X	197
Eckford	Scot Bord	NT7026	55°31·9′	2°28·1′W	T	74
Eckford Ho	Arg & Bt	NS1484	56°1·0′	4°58·6′W	X	56
Eckfordmoss	Scot Bord	NT7025	55°31·3′	2°28·1′W	T	74
Eckington	Derby	SK4279	53°18·6′	1°21·8′W	T	120
Eckington	Worcs	SO9241	52°4·3′	2°6·6′W	T	150
Eckington Bridge	Worcs	SO9242	52°4·8′	2°6·6′W	A	150
Eckington Corner	E Susx	TQ5109	50°51·9′	0°9·1′E	X	199
Eckington Field Fm	Worcs	SO9240	52°3·7′	2°6·6′W	FM	150
Eckington Hall	Sheff	SK4280	53°19·2′	1°21·8′W	X	111,120
Eckland Lodge Fm	Northnts	SP7884	52°27·1′	0°50·7′W	FM	141
Ecklands	Barns	SE2102	53°31·1′	1°40·6′W	T	110
Eckworthy	Devon	SS4017	50°56·1′	4°16·2′W	T	180,190
Ecton	Northnts	SP8263	52°15·8′	0°47·5′W	T	152
Ecton	Staffs	SK0958	53°7·4′	1°51·5′W	T	119
Ecton Belt	Northnts	SP8164	52°16·3′	0°48·4′W	X	152
Ecton Brook	Northnts	SP8162	52°15·2′	0°48·4′W	T	152
Ecton East Lodge	Northnts	SP8364	52°16·3′	0°46·6′W	X	152
Ecton Hill	Staffs	SK0957	53°6·8′	1°51·5′W	H	119
Ecton Hill	Staffs	SK0957	53°6·8′	1°51·5′W	X	119
Ecton North Lodge	Northnts	SP8265	52°16·9′	0°47·5′W	X	152
Ecton West Lodge	Northnts	SP8164	52°16·3′	0°48·4′W	X	152
Edale	Derby	SK1285	53°21·9′	1°48·8′W	T	110
Edale Cross	Derby	SK0786	53°22·5′	1°53·3′W	A	110
Edale End	Derby	SK1686	53°22·5′	1°45·2′W	T	110
Edale Head	Derby	SK0886	53°22·5′	1°52·4′W	X	110
Edale Moor	Derby	SK1187	53°23·0′	1°49·7′W	X	110
Eday	Orkney	HY5531	59°10·1′	2°46·7′W	X	5,6
Eday Sound	Orkney	HY5833	59°11·2′	2°43·6′W	W	5,6
Edbrook	Somer	SS8938	51°8·1′	3°34·8′W	X	181
Edbrook	Somer	ST2340	51°9·5′	3°5·7′W	T	182
Edbrooke Ho	Somer	SS9134	51°5·9′	3°33·0′W	X	181
Edburton	W Susx	TQ2311	50°53·3′	0°14·7′W	T	198
Edburton Hill	W Susx	TQ2310	50°52·8′	0°14·7′W	H	198
Edbury Fm	Devon	SS8509	50°52·4′	3°37·7′W	FM	191
Edder Acres	Durham	NZ4039	54°44·9′	1°22·3′W	X	93
Edderacres Plantn	Durham	NZ4038	54°44·4′	1°22·3′W	F	93
Edderlick	Aberd	NJ6226	57°19·6′	2°37·4′W	X	37
Edderside	Cumbr	NY1045	54°47·8′	3°23·6′W	T	85
Edderthorpe	Barns	SE4105	53°32·6′	1°22·5′W	X	111
Edderton	Highld	NH7184	57°49·9′	4°9·9′W	T	21
Edderton Burn	Highld	NH7083	57°49·3′	4°10·9′W	W	21
Edderton Fm	Highld	NH7184	57°49·9′	4°9·9′W	FM	21
Edderton Hall	Powys	SJ2302	52°36·9′	3°7·8′W	X	126
Edderton Hill	Highld	NH7182	57°48·8′	4°9·8′W	X	21
Edderton Mains	Highld	NH7183	57°49·3′	4°9·8′W	X	21
Edderton Sands	Highld	NH7384	57°49·9′	4°7·9′W	X	21
Eddington	Kent	TR1867	51°21·8′	1°8·3′E	T	179
Eddington	W Berks	SU3469	51°25·4′	1°30·3′W	T	174
Eddington Ho	W Berks	SU3470	51°25·9′	1°30·3′W	X	174
Eddisbridge	Northum	NZ0351	54°51·5′	1°56·8′W	X	87
Eddisbury Hall	Ches	SJ9373	53°15·5′	2°5·9′W	X	118
Eddisbury Hill	Ches	SJ5569	53°13·2′	2°40·0′W	X	117
Eddisbury Hill (Fort)	Ches	SJ5569	53°13·2′	2°40·0′W	A	117
Eddisbury Lodge	Ches	SJ5370	53°13·7′	2°41·8′W	X	117
Eddisbury Way	Ches	SJ5165	53°11·0′	2°43·6′W	X	117
Eddleston	Scot Bord	NT2447	55°43·2′	3°12·1′W	T	73
Eddleston Water	Scot Bord	NT2345	55°41·8′	3°13·1′W	W	73
Eddlestow Hall Fm	Derby	SK3263	53°10·0′	1°30·9′W	FM	119
Eddlethorpe Hall	N Yks	SE7866	54°5·3′	0°48·0′W	X	100
Eddlewood	S Lanak	NS7153	55°45·4′	4°2·9′W	T	64
Eddrachillis Bay	Highld	NC1336	58°16·6′	5°10·9′W	W	15
Eddy Ho	Cumbr	NY5923	54°36·3′	2°37·7′W	X	91
Eddy's Bridge	Durham	NZ0350	54°50·9′	1°56·8′W	X	87
Eddystone	Corn	SW8968	50°28·7′	4°58·1′W	X	200
Edells	Kent	TQ4742	51°9·7′	0°6·5′E	X	188
Eden	Arg & Bt	NR7110	55°20·1′	5°36·2′W	X	68
Edenbank	Fife	NO4217	56°20·8′	2°55·9′W	X	59
Edenbank	Scot Bord	NT7236	55°37·3′	2°26·2′W	X	74
Edenbank Fm	Cumbr	NY6224	54°36·8′	2°34·9′W	FM	91
Eden Banks	Cumbr	NY4950	54°50·8′	2°47·2′W	X	86
Eden Br	Cumbr	NY5540	54°45·4′	2°41·5′W	X	86
Edenbridge	Kent	TQ4446	51°11·9′	0°4·1′E	T	187
Edenbridge Sta	Kent	TQ4447	51°12·5′	0°4·1′E	X	187
Edenbridge Town Sta	Kent	TQ4446	51°11·9′	0°4·1′E	X	187
Eden Brook	Surrey	TQ3742	51°9·9′	0°2·0′W	W	187
Eden Brook	Surrey	TQ4144	51°10·9′	0°1·4′E	W	187
Eden Brows	Cumbr	NY4949	54°50·2′	2°47·2′W	X	86
Eden Burn	Scot Bord	NT5945	55°42·1′	2°38·7′W	W	73,74
Eden Burn	Scot Bord	NT6045	55°42·1′	2°37·8′W	W	74
Eden Camp (Mus)	N Yks	SE7973	54°9·0′	0°47·0′W	X	100
Edendiack	Aberd	NJ5137	57°25·5′	2°48·5′W	X	29
Edendon Bridge	Pth & Kin	NN7170	56°48·5′	4°6·3′W	X	42
Edendonich	Arg & Bt	NN1627	56°24·2′	4°58·5′W	X	50
Edendon Water	Pth & Kin	NN7175	56°51·2′	4°6·5′W	W	42
Edenfield	Lancs	SD7918	53°39·7′	2°18·7′W	T	109
Edenfields	Cumbr	NY6322	54°35·8′	2°33·9′W	X	91
Eden Flatt	Cumbr	NY7514	54°31·5′	2°22·8′W	X	91
Eden Fm	Devon	SX7263	50°27·4′	3°47·8′W	FM	202
Eden Fm	N Yks	SE7974	54°9·6′	0°47·0′W	FM	100
Eden Gate	Cumbr	NY7415	54°32·0′	2°23·7′W	X	91
Eden Grove	Cumbr	NY4359	54°55·6′	2°52·9′W	X	85
Eden Grove	Cumbr	NY6323	54°36·3′	2°33·9′W	X	91
Edengrove	Fife	NO4216	56°20·2′	2°55·8′W	X	59
Edenhall	Cumbr	NY5632	54°41·1′	2°40·5′W	T	90
Eden Hall	Durham	NZ1031	54°40·7′	1°50·3′W	X	92
Eden Hall	Scot Bord	NT7638	55°38·3′	2°22·4′W	X	74
Eden Hall (Convent)	Kent	TQ4642	51°9·7′	0°5·7′E	X	188
Edenhall Grange	Cumbr	NY5433	54°41·6′	2°42·4′W	X	90
Edenham	Lincs	TF0621	52°46·8′	0°25·3′W	T	130
Eden Hill	Arg & Bt	NR7110	55°20·1′	5°36·2′W	H	68
Eden Hill Fm	Durham	NZ2252	54°52·0′	1°39·0′W	FM	88
Eden Ho	Aberd	NJ6959	57°37·5′	2°30·7′W	X	29
Eden Ho	N Yks	SE7974	54°9·6′	0°47·0′W	X	100
Eden Ho	Suff	TM0460	52°12·3′	0°59·5′E	X	155
Eden Holme	Lancs	SD6633	53°47·8′	2°30·6′W	X	103
Edenhope Hill	Shrops	SO2588	52°29·3′	3°5·9′W	X	137
Eden Lacy	Cumbr	NY5538	54°44·3′	2°41·5′W	X	90
Eden Mount	Cumbr	SD4078	54°11·9′	2°54·8′W	T	96,97
Eden Mouth	Fife	NO5021	56°23·0′	2°48·1′W	W	54,59
Edenmouth	Scot Bord	NT7637	55°37·8′	2°22·4′W	X	74
Eden Park	Brom	TQ3668	51°23·9′	0°2·3′W	T	177
Eden Place	Cumbr	NY7709	54°28·8′	2°20·9′W	X	91
Edenshead Ho	Fife	NO1809	56°16·2′	3°19·0′W	X	58
Eden's Hill	Glos	SO7527	51°56·7′	2°21·4′W	X	162
Edenside	Fife	NO4518	56°21·3′	2°53·0′W	X	59
Edensor	Derby	SK2569	53°13·3′	1°37·1′W	T	119
Edenstown	Fife	NO2910	56°16·9′	3°8·4′W	X	59
Edentaggart	Arg & Bt	NS3293	56°6·3′	4°41·6′W	X	56
Edenthorpe	Donc	SE6106	53°33·1′	1°4·3′W	T	111
Edentown	Cumbr	NY3957	54°54·5′	2°56·7′W	T	85
Edenvale	Corn	SX1281	50°36·1′	4°39·0′W	X	200
Eden Vale	Cumbr	NY7316	54°32·6′	2°24·6′W	X	91
Eden Vale	Durham	NZ4237	54°43·8′	1°20·4′W	T	93
Eden Vale	Wilts	ST8651	51°15·7′	2°11·7′W	T	183
Eden Valley Walk	Kent	TQ4245	51°11·4′	0°2·3′E	X	187
Eden Water	Scot Bord	NT6641	55°39·9′	2°32·0′W	W	74
Edenwood	Fife	NO3511	56°17·5′	3°2·6′W	X	59
Eder Fm	W Susx	TQ1617	50°56·7′	0°20·5′W	FM	198
Ederline	Arg & Bt	NM8702	56°10·0′	5°25·4′W	X	55
Edern	Gwyn	SH2739	52°55·5′	4°34·0′W	T	123
Ederston	Scot Bord	NT2439	55°38·6′	3°12·0′W	X	73
Edeswell Fm	Devon	SX7360	50°25·8′	3°46·9′W	FM	202
Edeys Fm	Essex	TL8037	52°0·4′	0°37·8′E	FM	155
Edfast Plantn	Scot Bord	NT6555	55°47·5′	2°33·1′W	F	67,74
Edford	Somer	ST6748	51°14·0′	2°28·0′W	T	183
Edgair	Orkney	HY2217	59°2·2′	3°21·1′W	X	6
Edgar Burn	Scot Bord	NT6453	55°46·4′	2°34·0′W	W	67,74
Edgar Fm	Norf	TF9138	52°54·6′	0°50·8′E	FM	132
Edgarhope Law	Scot Bord	NT5652	55°45·8′	2°41·6′W	X	67,73
Edgarhope Wood	Scot Bord	NT5549	55°44·2′	2°42·6′W	F	73
Edgarley	Somer	ST5138	51°8·6′	2°41·6′W	T	182,183
Edgar's Cleugh	Scot Bord	NT7762	55°51·3′	2°21·6′W	X	67
Edgarton	D & G	NX6663	54°56·9′	4°5·1′W	X	83,84
Edgarton	D & G	NX9084	55°8·5′	3°43·1′W	X	78
Edgbaston	Birm	SP0584	52°27·5′	1°55·2′W	T	139
Edgbaston Resr	Birm	SP0486	52°28·6′	1°56·1′W	W	139
Edgcote	Northnts	SP5047	52°7·4′	1°15·8′W	T	151
Edgcote Ho	Northnts	SP5047	52°7·4′	1°15·8′W	X	151
Edgcote Lodge Fm	Northnts	SP5146	52°6·8′	1°14·9′W	FM	151
Edgcott	Bucks	SP6722	51°53·8′	1°1·2′W	T	164,165
Edgcott	Somer	SS8438	51°8·0′	3°39·1′W	T	181
Edgcumbe	Corn	SW7233	50°9·4′	5°11·2′W	T	204
Edge	Cumbr	NY5817	54°33·0′	2°38·5′W	X	91
Edge	D & G	NY1472	55°2·4′	3°20·3′W	X	85
Edge	Glos	SO8409	51°47·0′	2°13·5′W	T	162
Edge	Shrops	SJ3908	52°40·2′	2°53·7′W	T	126
Edge Bank	Cumbr	SD2871	54°8·0′	3°5·8′W	X	96,97
Edge Bank	Cumbr	SD5396	54°21·7′	2°43·0′W	X	97
Edgebarrow Woods	Brackn	SU8462	51°21·3′	0°47·2′W	F	175,186
Edge Barton	Devon	SY1889	50°41·9′	3°9·3′W	A	192
Edgebolton	Shrops	SJ5721	52°47·3′	2°37·9′W	T	126
Edgeborough	Surrey	SU8443	51°11·0′	0°47·5′W	X	186
Edgeborough Fm	Somer	ST2028	51°3·0′	3°8·1′W	FM	193
Edgecumbe	Devon	SX3979	50°35·5′	4°16·1′W	X	201
Edge End	Glos	SO5913	51°49·1′	2°35·3′W	T	162
Edge End	Lancs	SD7232	53°47·3′	2°25·1′W	T	103
Edge end	Staffs	SK0057	53°6·9′	1°59·6′W	X	119
Edge End Fm	Cald	SD9725	53°43·5′	2°2·3′W	FM	103
Edge End Moor	Cald	SD9725	53°43·5′	2°2·3′W	H	103
Edgefield	Midlo	NT2866	55°53·2′	3°8·6′W	X	66
Edgefield	Norf	TG0934	52°52·0′	1°6·7′E	T	133
Edgefield Fm	Sheff	SK2591	53°25·2′	1°37·0′W	FM	110
Edgefield Hall	Norf	TG0835	52°52·6′	1°5·9′E	X	133
Edgefield Street	Norf	TG0933	52°51·5′	1°6·7′E	T	133
Edgefield Woods	Norf	TG0836	52°53·1′	1°5·9′E	F	133
Edge Fm	Cumbr	NY6204	54°26·0′	2°34·7′W	FM	91
Edge Fm	Derby	SK3555	53°5·7′	1°28·2′W	FM	119
Edge Fm	Devon	SY1790	50°42·5′	3°10·1′W	FM	192,193
Edge Fm	Glos	SO8510	51°47·5′	2°12·7′W	FM	162
Edge Fm	Lancs	SD4111	53°35·8′	2°53·1′W	FM	108
Edge Fm	Shrops	SO5392	52°31·7′	2°41·2′W	FM	137,138
Edge Fm	S Lanak	NS6553	55°45·3′	4°8·6′W	FM	64
Edge Fold	Black w Dar	SD7218	53°39·7′	2°25·0′W	T	109
Edge Fold	Bolton	SD7006	53°33·2′	2°26·8′W	T	109
Edge Grange	Ches	SJ4751	53°3·5′	2°47·0′W	X	117
Edge Green	Ches	SJ4850	53°2·9′	2°46·1′W	T	117
Edge Green	Norf	TM0485	52°25·7′	1°0·4′E	T	144
Edge Green	Wigan	SJ5999	53°29·4′	2°36·7′W	T	108
Edge Grove	Herts	TQ1498	51°40·4′	0°20·7′W	X	166,176
Edge Hall	Ches	SJ4850	53°2·9′	2°46·1′W	A	117
Edge Head	Fife	NO1806	56°14·6′	3°18·9′W	X	58
Edgehead	Midlo	NT3765	55°52·7′	3°0·0′W	X	66
Edge Hill	Cumbr	SD2875	54°10·2′	3°5·8′W	X	96,97
Edgehill	Derby	SK3542	52°58·7′	1°28·3′W	X	119,128
Edge Hill	Devon	SY2993	50°44·2′	3°0·0′W	H	193
Edge Hill	E Ayr	NS6417	55°25·9′	4°8·5′W	X	71
Edge Hill	Liv	SJ3689	53°23·9′	2°57·3′W	T	108
Edge Hill	Northum	NY6965	54°59·0′	2°28·6′W	X	86,87
Edge Hill	Warw	SP2398	52°35·0′	1°39·2′W	T	139
Edgehill	Warw	SP3549	52°8·5′	1°28·9′W	A	151
Edgehill	Warw	SP3747	52°7·4′	1°27·2′W	T	151
Edge Hill	Warw	SP3847	52°7·4′	1°26·3′W	H	151
Edgehill Country Park	Warw	SP3948	52°8·0′	1°25·4′W	X	151
Edgehill Fm	Warw	SP3646	52°6·9′	1°28·1′W	FM	151
Edge Hills	Glos	SO6615	51°50·2′	2°29·2′W	X	162
Edge Ho	Northum	NY8995	54°55·8′	2°9·9′W	X	87
Edge Ho	Northum	NY9273	55°3·3′	2°7·1′W	X	87
Edge Ho	N Yks	SE0363	54°4·0′	1°56·8′W	X	98
Edgehouse	Northum	NZ0580	55°7·1′	1°54·9′W	X	81
Edge House Fm	Ches	SJ8677	53°17·6′	2°12·2′W	FM	118
Edge Knoll Fm	Durham	NZ1331	54°40·7′	1°47·5′W	FM	92
Edgelaw	Midlo	NT2958	55°48·9′	3°7·5′W	X	66,73
Edgelaw Moor	Midlo	NT2859	55°49·4′	3°8·5′W	X	66,73
Edgelaw Resr	Midlo	NT2958	55°48·9′	3°7·5′W	W	66,73
Edgeley	Shrops	SJ5540	52°57·6′	2°39·8′W	X	117
Edgeley	Stock	SJ8889	53°24·1′	2°10·4′W	T	109
Edgeley Fm	Shrops	SJ5539	52°57·0′	2°39·8′W	FM	126
Edgeley Ho	Shrops	SJ5440	52°57·6′	2°40·7′W	X	117
Edge Mill	Devon	SS4422	50°58·8′	4°13·0′W	X	180,190
Edgemoor	Derby	SK0373	53°15·5′	1°56·9′W	X	119
Edge Moor	Derby	SK3555	53°5·7′	1°28·2′W	X	119
Edgemoor	D & G	NY0792	55°13·1′	3°27·3′W	X	78
Edge Mount	Sheff	SK2793	53°26·2′	1°35·2′W	T	110
Edge Nook	N Yks	SE2162	54°3·5′	1°40·3′W	X	99
Edgerley	Shrops	SJ3418	52°45·6′	2°58·3′W	T	126
Edgerley Fm	Ches	SJ4356	53°6·1′	2°50·7′W	FM	117
Edgerley Hall	Shrops	SJ3419	52°46·1′	2°58·3′W	X	126
Edgerley Stone	Somer	SS7140	51°8·9′	3°50·3′W	X	180
Edgerly Fm	Oxon	SP2602	51°43·2′	1°37·0′W	FM	163
Edgerston	Scot Bord	NT6811	55°23·8′	2°29·9′W	T	80
Edgerston Rig	Scot Bord	NT6711	55°23·8′	2°30·8′W	X	80
Edgerston Tofts	Scot Bord	NT7010	55°23·2′	2°28·0′W	X	80
Edgerton	Kirk	SE1317	53°39·2′	1°47·8′W	T	110
Edgerton Moss	Lancs	SD7322	53°41·9′	2°24·1′W	X	103
Edges Green	Northum	NY7268	55°0·6′	2°25·8′W	X	86,87
Edgeside	Lancs	SD8322	53°41·9′	2°15·0′W	T	103
Edge, The	Derby	SK0889	53°24·1′	1°52·4′W	X	110
Edge, The	Durham	NZ0726	54°38·0′	1°53·1′W	X	92
Edge, The	N Yks	SE0977	54°11·6′	1°51·3′W	X	99
Edgetop	Staffs	SK0466	53°11·7′	1°56·0′W	X	119
Edgetop	Staffs	SK0964	53°10·6′	1°51·5′W	X	119
Edgeview Fm	Ches	SJ8179	53°18·7′	2°16·7′W	FM	118
Edgewell House Fm	Northum	NZ0861	54°56·9′	1°52·1′W	FM	88
Edgeworth	Glos	SO9406	51°45·4′	2°4·8′W	T	163
Edgeworth Mill Fm	Glos	SO9506	51°45·4′	2°4·0′W	FM	163
Edgeworthy	Devon	SS8413	50°54·5′	3°38·6′W	X	181
Edgiford Cross	Devon	SS7214	50°54·9′	3°48·9′W	X	180
Edgington	Devon	SS6521	50°58·6′	3°55·0′W	X	180
Edginswell	Torbay	SX8866	50°29·2′	3°34·4′W	T	202
Edgiock	Worcs	SP0360	52°14·5′	1°57·0′W	T	150
Edgley	N Yks	SE0288	54°17·5′	1°57·7′W	X	98
Edgmond	Wrekin	SJ7219	52°46·3′	2°24·5′W	T	127
Edgmond Common	Wrekin	SJ7121	52°47·4′	2°25·4′W	X	127
Edgmond Ho	Wrekin	SJ7119	52°46·3′	2°25·4′W	X	127
Edgmond Marsh	Wrekin	SJ7120	52°46·8′	2°25·4′W	T	127
Edgton	Shrops	SO3885	52°27·8′	2°54·4′W	T	137
Edgware	Barnet	TQ1992	51°37·1′	0°16·5′W	T	176
Edgwick	Cov	SP3481	52°25·8′	1°29·6′W	T	140
Edgworth	Black w Dar	SD7416	53°38·6′	2°23·2′W	T	109
Edgworth Moor	Black w Dar	SD7418	53°39·7′	2°23·2′W	X	109
Edham	Scot Bord	NT7337	55°37·8′	2°25·3′W	T	74
Edial	Staffs	SK0708	52°40·4′	1°53·4′W	T	128
Edinample	Stir	NN5922	56°22·4′	4°16·5′W	T	51
Edinbanchory	Aberd	NJ4819	57°15·8′	2°51·3′W	X	37
Edinbanchory Hill	Aberd	NJ4920	57°16·3′	2°50·3′W	H	37
Edinbane	Highld	NG3451	57°28·5′	6°25·8′W	T	23
Edinbarnet	W Dunb	NS5074	55°56·4′	4°23·7′W	T	64
Edinbeg	Arg & Bt	NS0567	55°51·7′	5°6·5′W	X	63
Edinbellie	Stir	NS5789	56°4·6′	4°17·4′W	X	57
Edinburgh	C of Edin	NT2773	55°56·9′	3°9·7′W	T	66
Edinburgh Airport	C of Edin	NT1573	55°56·8′	3°21·2′W	X	65
Edinburgh Gate	C of Edin	NT1775	55°57·9′	3°19·3′W	X	65,66
Edinburgh Hill	Kent	TR3242	51°8·0′	1°19·4′E	X	179
Edinchat	Highld	NH8130	57°21·0′	3°58·2′W	X	27
Edinchip	Stir	NN5722	56°22·4′	4°18·5′W	X	51
Edingale	Staffs	SK2112	52°42·6′	1°40·9′W	T	128
Edingale Fields Fm	Staffs	SK2312	52°42·5′	1°39·2′W	FM	128
Edingarioch	Aberd	NJ6224	57°18·6′	2°37·4′W	X	37
Edingham	D & G	NX8362	54°56·6′	3°49·2′W	X	84
Edingham Loch	D & G	NX8363	54°57·1′	3°49·2′W	W	84
Edingham Moss	D & G	NX8462	54°56·6′	3°48·2′W	X	84
Edingight Ho	Moray	NJ5155	57°35·2′	2°48·7′W	X	29
Edingight Wood	Moray	NJ5154	57°34·7′	2°48·7′W	F	29
Edinglassie Ho	Aberd	NJ3212	57°11·9′	3°7·1′W	X	37
Edinglassie Mains	Aberd	NJ4238	57°26·0′	2°57·5′W	X	28
Edingley	Notts	SK6655	53°5·5′	1°0·5′W	T	120
Edingley Hill	Notts	SK6655	53°5·5′	1°0·5′W	X	120
Edingthorpe	Norf	TG3232	52°50·4′	1°27·1′E	T	133
Edingthorpe Green	Norf	TG3131	52°49·8′	1°26·2′E	T	133
Edingthorpe Heath	Norf	TG3031	52°49·9′	1°25·3′E	X	133
Edington	Scot Bord	NT8955	55°47·5′	2°10·1′W	X	67,74
Edington	Somer	ST3839	51°9·0′	2°52·8′W	T	182
Edington	Wilts	ST9253	51°16·8′	2°6·5′W	T	184
Edington Covert	Scot Bord	NT9057	55°48·6′	2°9·1′W	X	67,74,75
Edington Heath	Somer	ST3941	51°10·1′	2°52·0′W	X	182
Edingtonhill	Scot Bord	NT8957	55°48·6′	2°10·1′W	X	67,74
Edington Hill	Wilts	ST9252	51°16·3′	2°6·5′W	H	184
Edington Moor	Somer	ST3941	51°10·1′	2°52·0′W	X	182
Edingworth	Somer	ST3553	51°16·6′	2°55·5′W	T	182
Edin's Hall	Scot Bord	NT7760	55°50·2′	2°21·6′W	X	67
Edin's Hall (Fort & Broch)	Scot Bord	NT7760	55°50·2′	2°21·6′W	A	67
Edintian	Pth & Kin	NN8562	56°44·4′	3°52·4′W	X	43
Edintore	Moray	NJ4246	57°30·3′	2°57·6′W	X	28
Edinvale	Moray	NJ1153	57°33·8′	3°28·8′W	X	28
Edisford Hall	Lancs	SD7241	53°52·1′	2°25·1′W	X	103
Edistone	Devon	SS2421	50°57·9′	4°30·0′W	T	190
Edithmead	Somer	ST3249	51°14·4′	2°58·1′W	T	182
Edith Weston	Rut	SK9305	52°38·3′	0°37·1′W	T	141
Edlaston	Derby	SK1742	52°58·7′	1°44·4′W	T	119,128
Edlesborough	Bucks	SP9719	51°51·9′	0°35·1′W	T	165
Edleston Fm	Ches	SJ6251	53°3·5′	2°33·6′W	FM	118
Edleston Hall	Ches	SJ6350	53°3·0′	2°32·7′W	X	118
Edlingham	Northum	NU1108	55°22·2′	1°49·2′W	T	81
Edlingham Burn	Northum	NU1110	55°23·3′	1°49·2′W	W	81
Edlingham Castle	Northum	NU1109	55°22·7′	1°49·2′W	A	81

Edlingham Woods	Northum	NU1206	55°21·1′	1°48·2′W	F	81
Edlington	Lincs	TF2371	53°13·5′	0°9·0′W	T	122
Edlington Ho	Lincs	TF2371	53°13·5′	0°9·0′W	X	122
Edlington Scrubbs	Lincs	TF2068	53°12·0′	0°11·8′W	F	122
Edlington Wood	Donc	SK5497	53°28·3′	1°10·8′W	F	111
Edmeston	Devon	SX6452	50°21·4′	3°54·3′W	X	202
Edmondbyers Common	Durham	NY9746	54°48·8′	2°2·4′W	X	87
Edmond's Dean	Scot Bord	NT7767	55°54·0′	2°21·6′W	X	67
Edmondsham	Dorset	SU0611	50°54·1′	1°54·5′W	T	195
Edmondsham Ho	Dorset	SU0611	50°54·1′	1°54·5′W	A	195
Edmondsley	Durham	NZ2349	54°50·4′	1°38·1′W	T	88
Edmondstown	Rho Cyn Taf	ST0090	51°36·2′	3°26·2′W	T	170
Edmondthorpe	Leic	SK8517	52°44·9′	0°44·0′W	T	130
Edmondthorpe Lodge	Notts	SK6934	52°54·2′	0°58·0′W	X	129
Edmonston	S Lanak	NT0742	55°40·0′	3°28·3′W	T	72
Edmonstone	C of Edin	NT2970	55°55·3′	3°7·7′W	X	66
Edmonstone	Orkney	HY5220	59°4·1′	2°49·7′W	X	5,6
Edmonton	Corn	SW9672	50°31·0′	4°52·3′W	T	200
Edmonton	Enf	TQ3392	51°36·9′	0°4·3′W	T	176,177
Edmundbyers	Durham	NZ0150	54°50·9′	1°58·6′W	T	87
Edmundbyers Common	Durham	NY9950	54°50·9′	2°0·5′W	X	87
Edmund Hill	Somer	ST5039	51°9·1′	2°42·5′W	X	182,183
Edmund's Hill	Suff	TL7451	52°8·0′	0°32·9′E	X	155
Ednam	Scot Bord	NT7337	55°37·8′	2°25·3′W	X	74
Ednam East Mill	Scot Bord	NT7537	55°37·8′	2°23·4′W	X	74
Ednamhill	D & G	NY2270	55°1·4′	3°12·8′W	X	85
Ednam Hill	Scot Bord	NT7437	55°37·8′	2°24·3′W	H	74
Ednaston	Derby	SK2341	52°58·2′	1°39·0′W	T	119,128
Ednaston Hall	Derby	SK2341	52°58·2′	1°39·0′W	X	119,128
Ednaston Manor	Derby	SK2342	52°58·7′	1°39·0′W	X	119,128
Edney Common	Essex	TL6504	51°42·9′	0°23·7′E	T	167
Edney's Fm	Somer	ST7150	51°15·1′	2°24·5′W	FM	183
Ednie	Aberd	NK0850	57°32·7′	1°51·5′W	X	30
Ednol Fm	Powys	SO2364	52°16·4′	3°7·3′W	FM	137,148
Ednol Hill	Powys	SO2264	52°16·4′	3°8·2′W	X	137,148
Edolphs Fm	Surrey	TQ2442	51°10·1′	0°13·2′W	FM	187
Edra	Stir	NN4510	56°15·7′	4°29·7′W	X	57
Edradour Burn	Pth & Kin	NN9759	56°42·9′	3°40·5′W	W	52,53
Edradour Ho	Pth & Kin	NN9558	56°42·4′	3°42·5′W	X	52,53
Edradynate	Pth & Kin	NN8852	56°39·0′	3°49·2′W	T	52
Edramucky	Pth & Kin	NN6136	56°30·0′	4°15·0′W	X	51
Edrington Castle	Scot Bord	NT9453	55°46·5′	2°5·3′W	A	67,74,75
Edrington Ho	Scot Bord	NT9454	55°47·0′	2°5·3′W	X	67,74,75
Edrington Mains	Scot Bord	NT9454	55°47·0′	2°5·3′W	X	67,74,75
Edrom	Scot Bord	NT8255	55°47·5′	2°16·8′W	T	67,74
Edrom Ho	Scot Bord	NT8255	55°47·5′	2°16·8′W	X	67,74
Edrom Mains	Scot Bord	NT8155	55°47·5′	2°17·7′W	X	67,74
Edrom Newton	Scot Bord	NT8255	55°47·5′	2°16·8′W	X	67,74
Edslee Fm	Corn	SS2111	50°52·5′	4°32·3′W	FM	190
Edstaston	Shrops	SJ5131	52°52·7′	2°43·3′W	T	126
Edston	Scot Bord	NT2239	55°38·6′	3°13·9′W	X	73
Edstone	Warw	SP1761	52°15·0′	1°44·7′W	T	151
Edston Hill	Scot Bord	NT2140	55°39·1′	3°14·9′W	H	73
Edvin Loach	Heref	SO6658	52°13·4′	2°29·5′W	T	149
Edwalton	Notts	SK5935	52°54·8′	1°7·0′W	T	129
Edward's Fm	Suff	TM2962	52°12·7′	1°21·5′E	FM	156
Edwards Green Fm	Herts	TL3209	51°46·1′	0°4·8′W	FM	166
Edwardsrig Plantn	D & G	NY0796	55°15·2′	3°27·4′W	F	78
Edwards's Plantn	Norf	TF8008	52°38·6′	0°40·0′E	F	144
Edwardstone	Suff	TL9442	52°2·8′	0°50·1′E	T	155
Edwardsville	Merth Tyd	ST0896	51°39·6′	3°19·4′W	T	170
Edwicke Fm	Somer	ST5541	51°10·2′	2°38·2′W	FM	182,183
Edwinsford	Carm	SN6334	51°59·5′	3°59·3′W	X	146
Edwin's Hall	Essex	TQ8199	51°39·9′	0°37·4′E	A	168
Edwinstowe	Notts	SK6266	53°11·5′	1°3·9′W	T	120
Edworth	Beds	TL2241	52°3·5′	0°12·8′W	T	153
Edwyn Ralph	Heref	SO6457	52°12·8′	2°31·2′W	T	149
Edzell	Angus	NO6068	56°48·4′	2°38·9′W	T	45
Edzell Airfield	Aberd	NO6368	56°48·4′	2°35·9′W	X	45
Edzell Castle	Angus	NO5869	56°48·9′	2°40·8′W	A	44
Edzell Wood	Angus	NO6067	56°47·8′	2°38·8′W	F	45
Eegittle	Shetld	HP4703	60°42·7′	1°7·8′W	X	1
Eela Water	Shetld	HU3378	60°29·3′	1°23·5′W	W	2,3
Eel Beck	Lancs	SD8247	53°55·4′	2°16·0′W	X	103
Eel Burn	E Loth	NT5184	56°3·0′	2°46·8′W	W	66
Eel Crag	Cumbr	NY1820	54°34·4′	3°15·7′W	H	89,90
Eel Crags	Cumbr	NY2315	54°31·7′	3°11·0′W	X	89,90
Eelfleet Wall	Norf	TG4421	52°44·1′	1°37·3′E	X	134
Eel Ho	Cumbr	SD3693	54°20·0′	2°58·6′W	X	96,97
Eel Hole Fm	Notts	SK5146	53°0·8′	1°14·0′W	FM	129
Eelmire	N Yks	SE1984	54°15·3′	1°42·1′W	X	99
Eelmoor Br	Hants	SU8452	51°15·9′	0°47·4′W	X	186
Eelmoor Hill	Hants	SU8452	51°15·9′	0°47·4′W	X	186
Eel Pie Ho	Notts	SK7174	53°15·7′	0°55·7′W	X	120
Eel Pie Island	Rich	TQ1673	51°26·9′	0°19·4′W	X	176
Eel Point	Pemb	SS1397	51°38·7′	4°41·8′W	X	158
Eel Tarn	Cumbr	NY1801	54°24·1′	3°15·4′W	W	89,90
Eelwell	Northum	NU0040	55°39·5′	1°59·6′W	X	75
Een	Aberd	NJ4744	57°29·2′	2°52·6′W	X	28,29
Eenan Hill	Arg & Bt	NS0167	55°51·6′	5°10·3′W	H	63
Eewpot	N Yks	SE2084	54°15·3′	1°41·2′W	F	99
Efail Blaen Yale	Denb	SJ1346	53°0·5′	3°17·4′W	X	116
Efail-fâch	Nth Pt Talb	SS7895	51°38·7′	3°45·4′W	T	170
Efail Isaf	Rho Cyn Taf	ST0884	51°33·1′	3°19·2′W	T	170
Efailnewydd	Gwyn	SH3535	52°53·5′	4°26·8′W	T	123
Efail-rhyd	Powys	SJ1626	52°49·7′	3°14·4′W	X	125
Efailwen	Carm	SN1325	51°53·8′	4°42·7′W	T	145,158
Efallwag	Powys	SJ1124	52°48·6′	3°18·8′W	X	125
Efenechtyd	Denb	SJ1155	53°5·3′	3°19·3′W	T	116
Efenechtyd	Denb	SJ1643	52°58·9′	3°14·7′W	X	125
Effgill	D & G	NY3092	55°13·3′	3°5·6′W	X	79
Effgill Hill	D & G	NY3093	55°13·8′	3°5·6′W	H	79
Effgill Hope	D & G	NY3193	55°13·8′	3°4·7′W	X	79
Effingham	Surrey	TQ1153	51°16·1′	0°24·1′W	T	187
Effingham Common	Surrey	TQ1055	51°17·2′	0°25·0′W	X	187
Effingham Forest	Surrey	TQ0950	51°14·6′	0°25·9′W	F	187
Effingham Hill Fm	Surrey	TQ1251	51°15·1′	0°23·3′W	FM	187
Effingham Junc Sta	Surrey	TQ1055	51°17·2′	0°25·0′W	X	187
Effingham Park	Surrey	TQ3339	51°8·3′	0°5·5′W	X	187
Effirth	Shetld	HU3152	60°15·3′	1°25·9′W	T	3

Effirth Voe	Shetld	HU3252	60°15·3′	1°24·8′W	W	3
Effledge	Scot Bord	NT5515	55°25·9′	2°42·2′W	T	80
Efflinch	Staffs	SK1917	52°45·3′	1°42·7′W	T	128
Efflins	Corn	SW8570	50°29·7′	5°1·5′W	X	200
Efford	C of Plym	SX5056	50°23·3′	4°6·2′W	T	201
Efford	Devon	SS8901	50°48·1′	3°34·1′W	X	192
Efford Beacon	Corn	SS1905	50°49·2′	4°33·8′W	X	190
Efford Fm	Devon	SX5753	50°21·8′	4°0·3′W	FM	202
Efford Ho	Devon	SX6149	50°19·7′	3°56·8′W	X	202
Efford Ho	Hants	SZ2994	50°44·9′	1°35·0′W	X	196
Efstigarth	Shetld	HU4692	60°36·8′	1°9·1′W	X	1,2
Egbury	Hants	SU4351	51°15·6′	1°22·6′W	A	185
Egbury	Hants	SU4352	51°16·2′	1°22·6′W	T	185
Egbury Castle Fm	Hants	SU4451	51°15·6′	1°21·8′W	FM	185
Egdean	W Susx	SU9920	50°58·5′	0°35·0′W	X	197
Egdon	Worcs	SO9151	52°9·7′	2°7·5′W	T	150
Egerton	Bolton	SD7114	53°37·5′	2°25·9′W	T	109
Egerton	Kent	TQ9047	51°11·7′	0°43·6′E	T	189
Egerton Bank Fm	Ches	SJ5250	53°2·9′	2°42·6′W	FM	117
Egerton Forstal	Kent	TQ8946	51°11·1′	0°42·7′E	T	189
Egerton Green	Ches	SJ5252	53°4·0′	2°42·6′W	T	117
Egerton Hall	Ches	SJ5150	53°2·9′	2°43·5′W	X	117
Egerton Ho	Kent	TQ9047	51°11·7′	0°43·6′E	X	189
Egerton Stud	Cambs	TL6061	52°13·7′	0°21·0′E	X	154
Egerton Village	Shrops	SO6081	52°25·8′	2°34·9′W	A	138
Egford	Somer	ST7548	51°14·1′	2°21·1′W	T	183
Egga Field	Shetld	HU3060	60°19·6′	1°26·9′W	H	3
Egga Field	Shetld	HU3289	60°35·3′	1°24·5′W	X	1
Eggardon Fms	Dorset	SY5394	50°44·9′	2°39·6′W	FM	194
Eggardon Hill	Dorset	SY5494	50°44·9′	2°38·7′W	H	194
Eggardon Hill (Fort)	Dorset	SY5494	50°44·9′	2°38·7′W	A	194
Eggarton Manor	Kent	TR0750	51°12·9′	0°58·2′E	X	179,189
Eggbeare	Corn	SX3388	50°40·3′	4°21·4′W	T	190
Eggborough	N Yks	SE5623	53°42·3′	1°8·7′W	T	105
Eggborough Ings	N Yks	SE5825	53°43·3′	1°6·8′W	X	105
Eggbuckland	C of Plym	SX5057	50°23·9′	4°6·3′W	T	201
Eggerness	D & G	NX4947	54°48·0′	4°20·5′W	X	83
Eggerness Point	D & G	NX4946	54°47·4′	4°20·5′W	X	83
Eggerslack Ho	Cumbr	SD4078	54°11·9′	2°54·8′W	X	96,97
Eggerslack Wood	Cumbr	SD4079	54°12·4′	2°54·8′W	F	96,97
Eggesford Barton	Devon	SS6910	50°52·7′	3°51·3′W	X	191
Eggesford Fourways	Devon	SS6810	50°52·7′	3°52·2′W	X	191
Eggesford Station	Devon	SS6811	50°53·2′	3°52·2′W	T	191
Egg Hill	Worcs	SO9979	52°24·8′	2°0·5′W	H	139
Eggington	Beds	SP9525	51°55·2′	0°36·7′W	T	165
Eggington Ho	Beds	SP9625	51°55·1′	0°35·8′W	A	165
Egginton	Derby	SK2628	52°51·2′	1°36·4′W	T	128
Egginton Common	Derby	SK2729	52°51·7′	1°35·5′W	T	128
Egglesburn	Durham	NY9824	54°36·9′	2°1·4′W	T	92
Egglescliffe	Stock on T	NZ4113	54°30·9′	1°21·6′W	T	93
Eggleshope Ho	Durham	NY9924	54°36·9′	2°0·5′W	X	92
Eggleston	Durham	NZ0023	54°36·4′	1°59·6′W	T	92
Eggleston Bridge	Durham	NY9923	54°36·4′	2°0·5′W	A	92
Eggleston Burn	Durham	NY9826	54°38·0′	2°1·4′W	W	92
Eggleston Common	Durham	NZ0027	54°38·5′	1°59·6′W	X	92
Egglestone Abbey	Durham	NZ0615	54°32·1′	1°54·0′W	A	92
Eggleston Hall	Durham	NY9923	54°36·4′	2°0·5′W	X	92
Eggringe Wood	Kent	TR0950	51°12·9′	0°59·9′E	F	179,189
Eggs Tump	Glos	SO7633	51°59·9′	2°20·6′W	X	150
Egg Well	Staffs	SK0054	53°5·2′	1°59·6′W	A	119
Eggwell Wood	Warw	SP1763	52°16·1′	1°44·7′W	F	151
Eggwood Hill	Somer	ST4313	50°55·1′	2°48·3′W	X	193
Eggworthy Fm	Devon	SX5471	50°31·5′	4°3·2′W	FM	201
Egham	Surrey	TQ0071	51°26·0′	0°33·3′W	T	176
Egham Hythe	Surrey	TQ0270	51°25·4′	0°31·6′W	T	176
Egham Wick	Surrey	SU9870	51°25·5′	0°35·0′W	T	175,176
Egholme Fm	Cumbr	SD6186	54°16·3′	2°35·5′W	FM	97
Egidoch Burn	Arg & Bt	NS0783	56°0·3′	5°5·3′W	W	56
Egilsay	Orkney	HY4729	59°8·9′	2°55·1′W	X	5,6
Egilsay	Shetld	HU3169	60°24·5′	1°25·7′W	X	3
Eglantine Fm	Kent	TQ5667	51°23·1′	0°14·9′E	FM	177
Eglarooze	Corn	SX3454	50°22·0′	4°19·7′W	X	201
Egleton	Rut	SK8707	52°39·5′	0°42·4′W	T	141
Eglingham	Northum	NU1019	55°28·1′	1°50·1′W	T	81
Eglingham Burn	Northum	NU1218	55°27·6′	1°48·2′W	W	81
Eglingham Hill	Northum	NU1119	55°28·1′	1°49·1′W	X	81
Eglingham Moor	Northum	NU1020	55°28·7′	1°50·1′W	X	81
Eglinton Country Park	N Ayr	NS3142	55°38·8′	4°40·7′W	X	63,70
Eglin Lane	D & G	NX4487	55°9·4′	4°26·5′W	W	77
Eglin Lane	E Ayr	NX4591	55°11·6′	4°25·7′W	W	77
Eglinton Castle	N Ayr	NS3242	55°38·8′	4°39·7′W	X	63,70
Eglinton Park Visitor Centre	N Ayr	NS3241	55°38·3′	4°39·7′W	X	70
Eglos Fm	Corn	SW7016	50°0·2′	5°12·2′W	FM	203
Egloshayle	Corn	SX0072	50°31·1′	4°48·9′W	T	200
Egloskerry	Corn	SX2786	50°39·1′	4°26·5′W	T	201
Eglwys-Anne Warren Ffridd	Gwyn	SH9240	52°57·0′	3°36·0′W	X	125
Eglwysbach	Conwy	SH8070	53°13·1′	3°47·4′W	T	116
Eglwys-Brewis	V of Glam	ST0069	51°24·9′	3°25·9′W	T	170
Eglwys Cross	Wrex	SJ4740	52°57·5′	2°46·9′W	T	117
Eglwyseg	Denb	SJ2147	53°1·1′	3°10·3′W	X	117
Eglwyseg Mountain	Denb	SJ2346	53°0·6′	3°8·5′W	H	117
Eglwyseg River	Denb	SJ2045	53°0·0′	3°11·1′W	W	117
Eglwys Fach	Cered	SN6895	52°32·5′	3°56·4′W	T	135
Eglwys Faen	Powys	SO1915	51°49·9′	3°10·1′W	X	161
Eglwys Nunydd	Nth Pt Talb	SS8084	51°32·8′	3°43·4′W	X	170
Eglwys Nunydd Reservoir	Nth Pt Talb	SS7984	51°32·8′	3°44·3′W	W	170
Eglwyswen	Pemb	SN1536	51°59·7′	4°41·3′W	T	145
Eglwyswrw	Pemb	SN1438	52°0·8′	4°42·2′W	T	145
Eglwyswrw Common	Pemb	SN1437	52°0·3′	4°42·2′W	X	145
Egmanton	Notts	SK7368	53°12·5′	0°54·0′W	T	120
Egmanton Common Fm	Notts	SK7468	53°12·5′	0°53·1′W	FM	120
Egmanton Hill Fm	Notts	SK7267	53°11·9′	0°54·9′W	FM	120
Egmanton Wood	Notts	SK7367	53°11·9′	0°54·0′W	F	120
Egmere	Norf	TF9037	52°54·0′	0°49·9′E	T	132
Egmere Fm	Norf	TF9037	52°54·0′	0°49·9′E	FM	132
Egmont Point	Dorset	SY9476	50°35·3′	2°4·7′W	X	195
Egnaig	Highld	NM6574	56°48·2′	5°50·5′W	X	40
Egnaig Hill	Highld	NM6675	56°48·7′	5°49·6′W	H	40

Egno Moss	Angus	NO3552	56°39·6′	3°3·2′W	X	54
Egnyn	Conwy	SJ0163	53°9·5′	3°28·4′W	X	116
Egremont	Cumbr	NY0110	54°28·8′	3°31·3′W	T	89
Egremont	Wirral	SJ3192	53°25·5′	3°1·9′W	T	108
Egrove Fm	Somer	ST0842	51°10·4′	3°18·6′W	FM	181
Egryn Abbey	Gwyn	SH5920	52°45·8′	4°5·0′W	X	124
Egstow Hall	Derby	SK3964	53°10·5′	1°24·6′W	X	119
Egton	N Yks	NZ8006	54°26·8′	0°45·6′W	T	94
Egton Banks	N Yks	NZ7806	54°26·8′	0°47·4′W	X	94
Egton Bridge	N Yks	NZ8005	54°26·3′	0°45·6′W	T	94
Egton Flats	N Yks	NZ8007	54°27·4′	0°45·5′W	X	94
Egton Grange	N Yks	NZ7803	54°25·2′	0°47·5′W	X	94
Egton High Moor	N Yks	NZ7701	54°24·2′	0°48·4′W	X	94
Egton Low Moor	N Yks	NZ8208	54°27·9′	0°43·7′W	X	94
Egton Manor	N Yks	NZ8005	54°26·3′	0°45·6′W	X	94
Egypt	Aberd	NJ9065	57°40·7′	2°9·6′W	X	30
Egypt	Brad	SE0933	53°47·8′	1°51·4′W	T	104
Egypt	Bucks	SU9685	51°33·6′	0°36·5′W	T	175,176
Egypt	Cald	SD9429	53°45·7′	2°5·0′W	X	103
Egypt	Hants	SU4640	51°9·7′	1°20·1′W	T	185
Egypt	W Berks	SU4476	51°29·1′	1°21·6′W	T	174
Egypt Bay	Medway	TQ7779	51°29·2′	0°33·4′E	W	178
Egypt Fm	E Susx	TQ6316	50°55·4′	0°19·5′E	FM	199
Egypt Point	I of W	SZ4896	50°45·9′	1°18·9′W	X	196
Egypts Fm	Essex	TL8020	51°51·2′	0°37·2′E	FM	168
Egypt Woods	Bucks	SU9586	51°34·1′	0°37·4′W	F	175,176
Ehen Hall	Cumbr	NY0113	54°30·4′	3°31·3′W	X	89
E Holling Carr	Durham	NZ3932	54°41·1′	1°23·3′W	X	93
Eich Donna	Arg & Bt	NM7909	56°13·6′	5°33·5′W	X	55
Eidda Fawr	Conwy	SH8249	53°1·8′	3°45·2′W	X	116
Eiden	Highld	NC7300	57°58·5′	4°8·4′W	X	16
Eididh nan Clach Geala	Highld	NH2584	57°48·9′	4°56·3′W	H	20
Eid Low	Staffs	SK0944	52°59·8′	1°51·5′W	A	119,128
Eigg	Highld	NM4686	56°54·0′	6°9·8′W	X	39
Eigg, The	Shetld	HU4495	60°38·4′	1°11·2′W	X	1,2
Eight and Forty	E Yorks	SE8429	53°45·3′	0°43·1′W	X	106
Eight Ash Green	Essex	TL9425	51°53·6′	0°49·6′E	T	168
Eighteen Feet Rhyne	Somer	ST4433	51°5·8′	2°47·6′W	W	182
Eight Elms Fm	Cambs	TL3349	52°7·6′	0°3·0′W	FM	154
Eight Mile Burn	Midlo	NT1959	55°49·3′	3°17·1′W	X	65,66,72
Eight Oaks Fm	Worcs	SO7738	52°2·6′	2°19·7′W	FM	150
Eighton Banks	Ghead	NZ2758	54°55·2′	1°34·3′W	T	88
Eight Riding Tree	Rut	SK8809	52°40·5′	0°41·5′W	F	141
Eight Walks	Wilts	SU2266	51°23·8′	1°40·6′W	X	174
Eigie Links	Aberd	NJ9717	57°14·9′	2°2·5′W	X	38
Eignaig	Highld	NM7943	56°31·9′	5°35·2′W	X	49
Eigneig Bheag	N Eil	NF9260	57°31·8′	7°8·3′W	X	22
Eigneig Mhòr	N Eil	NF9361	57°32·4′	7°7·4′W	X	22
Eign Hill	Heref	SO5239	52°3·1′	2°41·6′W	T	149
Eil	Highld	NH8217	57°14·0′	3°56·8′W	X	35
Eilagadale	Highld	NM5771	56°46·3′	5°58·2′W	X	39,47
Eilanreach	Highld	NG8017	57°11·7′	5°38·0′W	T	33
Eildon	Scot Bord	NT5732	55°35·0′	2°40·5′W	T	73,74
Eildon Hall	Scot Bord	NT5632	55°35·0′	2°41·4′W	X	73
Eildon Hills	Scot Bord	NT5432	55°35·0′	2°43·4′W	H	73
Eildreach	Stir	NN5926	56°24·6′	4°16·7′W	H	51
Eileach an Naoimh	Arg & Bt	NM6409	56°13·2′	5°48·0′W	X	55
Eileach Mhic'ille Riabhaich	Highld	NG9383	57°47·6′	5°28·5′W	W	19
Eileag Burn	Highld	NC8136	58°18·1′	4°1·4′W	W	17
Eileam Creagach	Arg & Bt	NM7809	56°13·6′	5°34·4′W	X	55
Eilean a'Bhealaich	Arg & Bt	NM7107	56°12·3′	5°41·1′W	X	55
Eilean a' Bhàir	N Eil	NB3721	58°6·3′	6°27·4′W	X	14
Eilean a' Bhogha	N Eil	NF8541	57°21·3′	7°13·8′W	X	22
Eilean a' Bhorra	Arg & Bt	NR6386	56°0·8′	5°47·7′W	X	61
Eilean a' Bhreac-achaidh	Highld	NC6835	58°17·3′	4°14·6′W	X	16
Eilean a' Bhreitheimh	Highld	NC1339	58°18·3′	5°11·0′W	X	15
Eilean a'Bhuic	Arg & Bt	NR9170	55°52·9′	5°20·1′W	X	62
Eilean a' Bhuic	Highld	NC1344	58°20·9′	5°11·3′W	X	9
Eilean a' Bhuic	N Eil	NB5452	58°23·5′	6°12·1′W	X	8
Eilean a' Chàise	N Eil	NB5331	58°12·2′	6°11·8′W	X	8
Eilean a' Chait	Highld	NG8034	57°20·9′	5°38·9′W	X	24
Eilean a' Chaoil	Highld	NC5965	58°33·3′	4°24·9′W	X	10
Eilean a' Chaoil	Highld	NG8156	57°32·7′	5°39·1′W	X	24
Eilean a' Chaolais	Highld	NM6980	56°51·5′	5°46·9′W	X	40
Eilean a' Chapuill	Arg & Bt	NR6877	55°56·1′	5°42·4′W	X	61,62
Eilean a' Chapuill	Arg & Bt	NR6974	55°54·5′	5°41·3′W	X	61,62
Eilean a' Chàr	Highld	NB9608	58°1·1′	5°26·8′W	X	15
Eilean a' Charnan	N Eil	NF7644	57°22·5′	7°23·0′W	X	22
Eilean Ach' Dùgraidh	Highld	NH3113	57°10·9′	4°47·3′W	X	34
Eilean a' Chladaich	Arg & Bt	NR3392	56°3·0′	6°16·8′W	X	61
Eilean a' Chlàrsaire	Arg & Bt	NM5629	56°23·7′	5°56·8′W	X	48
Eileanach Lodge	Highld	NH5468	57°41·0′	4°26·5′W	X	21
Eilean a' Choire	Arg & Bt	NM3842	56°30·1′	6°15·0′W	X	47,48
Eilean a' Choire	Highld	NM6273	56°47·5′	5°53·4′W	X	40
Eilean a' Chòmhraidh	Arg & Bt	NN0924	56°22·4′	5°5·1′W	X	50
Eilean a' Chomhraig	Arg & Bt	NR8867	55°51·2′	5°22·8′W	X	62
Eilean a' Chonnaidh	Highld	NC2056	58°27·6′	5°4·7′W	X	9
Eilean a' Chràbhaiche	Arg & Bt	NM5924	56°21·1′	5°53·6′W	X	48
Eilean a' Chrotaich	N Eil	NB5129	58°11·0′	6°13·7′W	X	8
Eilean a'Chùil	Arg & Bt	NR6548	55°40·4′	5°43·8′W	X	62
Eilean a' Chuilinn	Highld	NG8111	57°8·5′	5°36·7′W	X	33
Eilean a' Chuilinn	Highld	NM7362	56°41·9′	5°42·0′W	X	40
Eilean a' Chuirn	Arg & Bt	NR4748	55°39·8′	6°0·9′W	X	60
Eileana Dubha	N Eil	NF9773	57°39·0′	7°4·3′W	X	18
Eilean a' Ghaill	Highld	NM6282	56°52·4′	5°53·9′W	X	40
Eilean a' Ghamhna	Highld	NC2033	58°15·2′	5°3·6′W	X	15
Eilean a' Ghamhna	N Eil	NF7504	57°1·0′	7°20·9′W	X	31
Eilean a' Gheòidh	N Eil	NF7907	57°2·8′	7°17·2′W	X	31
Eilean a' Gheòidh	N Eil	NG1698	57°53·1′	6°47·0′W	X	14
Eilean a' Ghiorr	N Eil	NF8458	57°30·4′	7°16·1′W	X	22
Eilean a' Ghiubhais	Highld	NN0791	56°58·5′	5°10·1′W	X	33
Eilean a' Ghobha	N Eil	NA6946	58°16·9′	7°38·4′W	X	13
Eilean a' Ghobha	N Eil	NF8757	57°30·0′	7°13·1′W	X	22
Eilean a' Ghuail	N Eil	NG1698	57°53·1′	6°47·0′W	X	14
Eileanaigas Ho	Highld	NH4641	57°26·3′	4°33·5′W	X	26
Eilean Aigastan	Highld	NG7408	57°6·7′	5°43·5′W	X	33
Eilean Ailein	N Eil	NF8026	57°13·0′	7°17·6′W	X	22
Eilean Aird Meinish	N Eil	NB0933	58°11·7′	6°56·7′W	X	13
Eilean Aird nan Gobhar	Highld	NG5436	57°21·1′	6°4·9′W	X	24,32
Eilean Aird nan Uan	Highld	NM3980	56°50·6′	6°16·3′W	X	39

Eilean Aird Rainis	N Eil	NG1696	57°52·1′	6°46·9′W	X	14
Eilean Allmha	Highld	NM7589	56°56·5′	5°41·5′W	X	40
Eilean Amalaig	Arg & Bt	NM7029	56°24·1′	5°43·2′W	X	49
Eilean a' Mhadaidh	Arg & Bt	NM7531	56°25·3′	5°38·5′W	X	49
Eilean a' Mhadaidh	Highld	NC1949	58°23·8′	5°5·3′W	X	9
Eilean a' Mhadaidh	N Eil	NF8443	57°22·3′	7°15·0′W	X	22
Eilean a' Mhail	N Eil	NL7099	56°58·1′	7°25·4′W	X	31
Eilean a' Mhal	Highld	NG7428	57°17·5′	5°44·6′W	X	33
Eilean á Mhòrain	N Eil	NF8379	57°41·6′	7°18·8′W	X	18
Eilean a' Mhorair	Highld	NH1201	57°4·0′	5°5·6′W	X	34
Eilean a' Mhuineil	Highld	NG8406	57°5·9′	5°33·5′W	X	33
Eilean a' Mhuirich	Highld	NM8060	56°41·1′	5°35·1′W	X	40
Eilean a' Mhurain	N Eil	NF7072	57°37·3′	7°31·2′W	X	18
Eilean Anabuich	N Eil	NB2005	57°57·0′	6°43·5′W	X	13,14
Eilean an Achaidh	Highld	NC1233	58°15·0′	5°11·7′W	X	15
Eileanan a' Ghille-bheid	N Eil	NG1796	57°52·1′	6°45·9′W	X	14
Eilean an Aigeich	Highld	NC1548	58°23·1′	5°9·4′W	X	9
Eileanan Airde	N Eil	NF8157	57°29·7′	7°19·1′W	X	22
Eileanan an Teampaill	N Eil	NF8854	57°28·4′	7°11·8′W	X	22
Eilean an Aodaich	Arg & Bt	NL9738	56°26·5′	6°54·6′W	X	46
Eileanan Bàna	Arg & Bt	NM5843	56°31·3′	5°55·6′W	X	47,48
Eileanan Chearabhaigh	N Eil	NF8647	57°24·6′	7°13·3′W	X	22
Eileanan Comhlach	Highld	NM8072	56°47·5′	5°35·7′W	X	40
Eileanan Direcleit	N Eil	NG1698	57°53·1′	6°47·0′W	X	14
Eileanan Dubha	Highld	NC1851	58°24·8′	5°6·5′W	X	9
Eileanan Dubha	Highld	NG7626	57°16·4′	5°42·5′W	X	33
Eileanan Dubha	N Eil	NF7807	57°2·8′	7°18·2′W	X	31
Eilean an Duilisg	Arg & Bt	NM3824	56°20·4′	6°13·9′W	X	48
Eilean an Dùin	Arg & Bt	NM7907	56°12·5′	5°33·4′W	X	55
Eilean an Dùnain	Arg & Bt	NR8673	55°54·4′	5°25·0′W	X	62
Eilean an Dùnain	N Eil	NF8979	57°41·9′	7°12·8′W	X	18
Eilean an Eagaill	Arg & Bt	NN1315	56°17·7′	5°0·9′W	X	50,56
Eilean an Easbuig	Arg & Bt	NR5882	55°58·5′	5°52·3′W	X	61
Eilean an Eich Bhàin	Highld	NG9381	57°46·5′	5°28·4′W	X	19
Eilean an Eireannaich	Highld	NC2050	58°24·4′	5°4·4′W	X	9
Eilean an Eoin	Arg & Bt	NR3686	55°59·9′	6°13·6′W	X	61
Eilean an Eòin	Highld	NG7112	57°8·8′	5°46·7′W	X	33
Eilean an Fhèidh	Highld	NM6060	56°40·5′	5°54·6′W	X	40
Eilean an Fheidh	Highld	NM6772	56°47·1′	5°48·4′W	X	40
Eilean an Fhéidh	N Eil	NF9056	57°29·6′	7°10·0′W	X	22
Eilean an Fheòir	Arg & Bt	NM4825	56°21·3′	6°4·3′W	X	48
Eilean an Fhraoich	Highld	NG6153	57°30·5′	5°58·9′W	X	24
Eilean an Fhraoich Miatha	N Eil	NF8541	57°21·3′	7°13·8′W	X	22
Eilean an Fhuarain	Arg & Bt	NM4258	56°38·8′	6°12·1′W	X	47
Eileanan Glasa	Arg & Bt	NM5945	56°32·4′	5°54·8′W	X	47,48
Eileanan Glasa	N Eil	NF8256	57°29·2′	7°18·0′W	X	22
Eileanan Gleann Righ	Arg & Bt	NR5182	55°58·2′	5°59·0′W	X	61
Eileanan Iasgaich	N Eil	NF7818	57°8·7′	7°19·0′W	X	31
Eilean an Inbhire	Highld	NG5442	57°24·4′	6°5·3′W	X	24
Eilean an Inbhire Bhàin	Highld	NG7955	57°32·1′	5°41·1′W	X	24
Eileanan Loisgte	Highld	NM6469	56°45·4′	5°51·2′W	X	40
Eileanan Móra	Arg & Bt	NR2743	55°36·5′	6°19·7′W	X	60
Eileanan na h-Aornan	Arg & Bt	NM2559	56°38·8′	6°28·7′W	X	46,47
Eileanan nan Gad	Highld	NM6468	56°44·9′	5°51·1′W	X	40
Eilean Annraidh	Arg & Bt	NM2926	56°21·2′	6°22·8′W	X	48
Eilean an Righ	Arg & Bt	NM3938	56°28·0′	6°13·8′W	X	47,48
Eilean an Ròin Beag	Highld	NC1658	58°28·6′	5°8·9′W	X	9
Eilean an Ròin Mór	Highld	NC1758	58°28·6′	5°7·8′W	X	9
Eilean an Roin Mór	Highld	NC1858	58°28·6′	5°6·8′W	X	9
Eilean an Rubha	Arg & Bt	NR6486	56°0·8′	5°46·7′W	X	55,61
Eilean an Ruisg	Arg & Bt	NM8423	56°21·3′	5°29·3′W	X	49
Eilean an Sgùirr	N Eil	NF8634	57°17·6′	7°12·3′W	X	22
Eilean an Sgùrra	Highld	NM6782	56°52·5′	5°49·0′W	X	40
Eileanan Stafa	N Eil	NF8246	57°23·9′	7°17·2′W	X	22
Eilean an Stallcair	Arg & Bt	NN2942	56°32·6′	4°46·4′W	X	50
Eilean an Taighe	N Eil	NG4297	57°53·5′	6°20·7′W	X	14
Eilean an Tannais-sgeir	Arg & Bt	NR1863	55°46·9′	6°29·4′W	X	60
Eilean an Tighe	N Eil	NB2230	58°10·5′	6°43·2′W	X	8,13
Eilean an Treogh	Arg & Bt	NM0746	56°31·1′	6°45·4′W	X	46
Eilean an t-Sabhail	Highld	NM6373	56°47·6′	5°52·4′W	X	40
Eilean an t-Sagairt	Arg & Bt	NN0722	56°21·3′	5°7·0′W	X	50
Eilean an t-Sionnaich	Highld	NM7561	56°41·5′	5°40·0′W	X	40
Eilean an t- Sithein	Highld	NC1751	58°24·8′	5°7·5′W	X	9
Eilean an t-Sluic	Arg & Bt	NR4346	55°38·6′	6°4·6′W	X	60
Eilean an t-Snidhe	Highld	NM6281	56°51·8′	5°53·8′W	X	40
Eilean an-t-Sratha	Highld	NG8334	57°21·0′	5°36·0′W	X	24
Eilean an Tuim	Highld	NC2630	58°13·7′	4°57·3′W	X	15
Eilean Aoghainn	Arg & Bt	NR9894	56°6·0′	5°14·4′W	X	55
Eilean Aoidhe	Arg & Bt	NR9367	55°51·4′	5°18·0′W	X	62
Eilean a' Phidhir	Highld	NM7092	56°58·0′	5°46·6′W	X	33,40
Eilean a' Phiòbaire	Highld	NG8308	57°7·0′	5°34·6′W	X	33
Eilean Àrd	Arg & Bt	NR5582	55°58·4′	5°55·2′W	X	61
Eilean Ard	Highld	NC1850	58°24·3′	5°6·4′W	X	9
Eilean Ard an Eoin	N Eil	NF8146	57°23·8′	7°18·2′W	X	22
Eilean Ardgaddan	Arg & Bt	NR9179	55°57·8′	5°20·5′W	X	62
Eilean Arnoil	N Eil	NB3049	58°21·0′	6°36·4′W	X	8
Eilean Arsa	Arg & Bt	NM7807	56°12·5′	5°34·3′W	X	55
Eilean Ascaoineach	Arg & Bt	NM1354	56°35·7′	6°40·1′W	X	46
Eilean Assynt	Highld	NC1925	58°10·9′	5°4·2′W	X	15
Eilean Bailavarkish	N Eil	NF7275	57°39·0′	7°29·5′W	X	18
Eilean Baile Gearraidh	N Eil	NF8752	57°27·3′	7°12·7′W	X	22
Eilean Balnagowan	Highld	NM9553	56°37·7′	5°20·1′W	X	49
Eilean Bàn	Arg & Bt	NM3722	56°19·3′	6°14·8′W	X	48
Eilean Bàn	Arg & Bt	NM3937	56°27·4′	6°13·7′W	X	47,48
Eilean Bàn	Arg & Bt	NM7336	56°27·9′	5°40·7′W	X	49
Eilean Bàn	Highld	NG7427	57°16·9′	5°44·5′W	X	33
Eilean Bàn	Highld	NM6992	56°58·0′	5°47·6′W	X	40
Eilean Bàn-leac	Arg & Bt	NM7319	56°18·8′	5°39·8′W	X	55
Eilean Beag	Arg & Bt	NM6801	56°9·0′	5°43·7′W	X	55,61
Eilean Beag	Arg & Bt	NM8835	56°27·8′	5°26·0′W	X	49
Eilean Beag	Arg & Bt	NR2774	55°53·2′	6°21·5′W	X	60
Eilean Beag	Highld	NG3657	57°31·8′	6°24·2′W	X	23
Eilean Beag	Highld	NG6835	57°21·1′	5°50·9′W	X	24,32
Eilean Beag a' Bhàigh	N Eil	NB2501	57°55·1′	6°38·2′W	X	14
Eilean Beith	Arg & Bt	NN1025	56°23·0′	5°4·2′W	X	50
Eilean Bhàcasaigh	N Eil	NB1836	58°13·6′	6°47·7′W	X	8,13
Eilean Bheirean	N Eil	NF7234	57°17·0′	7°26·2′W	X	22
Eilean Bhinndealaim	N Eil	NB1741	58°16·3′	6°49·1′W	X	8,13
Eilean Bholuim	N Eil	NF8328	57°14·2′	7°14·8′W	X	22
Eilean Bhoramuil	Arg & Bt	NM1150	56°33·4′	6°41·8′W	X	46
Eilean Bhrìde	Arg & Bt	NR4647	55°39·3′	6°1·8′W	X	60
Eilean Bhrìde	Arg & Bt	NR5569	55°51·4′	5°54·5′W	X	61
Eilean Blianais	N Eil	NB1837	58°14·2′	6°47·8′W	X	8,13
Eilean Buidhe	Arg & Bt	NM7720	56°19·5′	5°36·0′W	X	49,55
Eilean Buidhe	Arg & Bt	NM7908	56°13·1′	5°33·4′W	X	55
Eilean Buidhe	Arg & Bt	NR9071	55°53·4′	5°21·1′W	X	62
Eilean Buidhe	Arg & Bt	NR9169	55°52·4′	5°20·0′W	X	62
Eilean Buidhe	Highld	NM7379	56°51·1′	5°42·9′W	X	40
Eilean Buidhe	N Eil	NF8467	57°35·2′	7°16·8′W	X	18
Eilean Buidhe Mór	Arg & Bt	NR6689	56°2·5′	5°45·0′W	X	55,61
Eilean Cam	Arg & Bt	NR1654	55°42·0′	6°30·8′W	X	60
Eilean Camas Drollaman	Highld	NM7669	56°45·8′	5°39·5′W	X	40
Eilean Carrach	Arg & Bt	NM2722	56°19·0′	6°24·5′W	X	48
Eilean Carrach	Arg & Bt	NR8238	55°35·5′	5°27·1′W	X	68,69
Eilean Carrach	Highld	NM4268	56°44·2′	6°12·7′W	X	47
Eilean Ceann Féidh	Highld	NM7284	56°53·7′	5°44·2′W	X	40
Eilean Ceann na Creige	Arg & Bt	NR8162	55°48·4′	5°29·2′W	X	62
Eilean Chalaibrigh	N Eil	NB3822	58°6·8′	6°26·4′W	X	14
Eilean Chalbha	Arg & Bt	NM2826	56°21·1′	6°23·7′W	X	48
Eilean Chalmain	Arg & Bt	NM3017	56°16·4′	6°21·2′W	X	48
Eilean Chaluim Chille	Highld	NG3768	57°37·8′	6°23·9′W	X	23
Eilean Chaluim Chille	N Eil	NB3821	58°6·3′	6°26·4′W	X	14
Eilean Chathastail	Highld	NM4883	56°52·5′	6°7·7′W	X	39
Eilean Chearstaigh	N Eil	NB1933	58°12·0′	6°46·5′W	X	8,13
Eilean Cheòis	N Eil	NB3621	58°6·2′	6°28·4′W	X	14
Eilean Chlamail	Highld	NG7712	57°8·9′	5°40·7′W	X	33
Eilean Choinneich	Highld	NN0659	56°41·2′	5°9·6′W	X	41
Eilean Choinnich	Highld	NG8706	57°6·0′	5°30·5′W	X	33
Eilean Choraidh	Highld	NC4258	58°29·2′	4°42·1′W	X	9
Eilean Chrona	Highld	NC0633	58°14·8′	5°17·9′W	X	15
Eilean Chrossain	N Eil	NF7554	57°27·9′	7°24·8′W	X	22
Eilean Chuaig	Highld	NG6959	57°34·0′	5°51·3′W	X	24
Eilean Chuidhtinis	N Eil	NG0986	57°46·4′	6°53·2′W	X	14
Eilean Clach nan Uamhannan	Arg & Bt	NR7161	55°47·5′	5°38·7′W	X	62
Eilean Clùimhrig	Highld	NC4665	58°33·0′	4°38·3′W	X	9
Eilean Coille	Highld	NM6376	56°49·2′	5°52·6′W	X	40
Eilean Coltair	Arg & Bt	NM8012	56°15·2′	5°32·7′W	X	55
Eilean Craobhach	Arg & Bt	NR4649	55°40·3′	6°1·9′W	X	60
Eilean Creagach	Arg & Bt	NM7809	56°13·6′	5°34·4′W	X	55
Eilean Creagach	Highld	NC5863	58°32·2′	4°25·9′W	X	10
Eilean Creagach	Highld	NG2965	57°35·9′	6°31·7′W	X	23
Eilean Cuithe nam Fiadh	N Eil	NF7847	57°24·2′	7°21·3′W	X	22
Eilean Dà Chuain	Highld	NM6491	56°57·3′	5°52·4′W	X	40
Eilean dà Ghallagain	Arg & Bt	NR8365	55°50·0′	5°27·5′W	X	62
Eilean Dallaig	N Eil	NF6908	57°2·9′	7°27·1′W	X	31
Eilean da Mhèinn	Arg & Bt	NR7894	56°5·5′	5°33·7′W	X	55
Eilean Darach	Highld	NH1087	57°50·2′	5°11·6′W	X	19
Eilean Dearg	Arg & Bt	NS0077	55°56·9′	5°11·7′W	X	62,63
Eilean Dearg	Highld	NG7000	57°2·3′	5°47·0′W	X	33
Eilean Didil	Arg & Bt	NM2624	56°20·0′	6°25·5′W	X	48
Eilean Dioghlum	Arg & Bt	NM3442	56°30·0′	6°18·9′W	X	47,48
Eilean Dìomhain	Arg & Bt	NR5468	55°50·8′	5°55·4′W	X	61
Eilean Donnan	Highld	NG8825	57°16·3′	5°30·5′W	X	33
Eilean Dubh	Arg & Bt	NL9341	56°27·9′	6°58·6′W	X	46
Eilean Dubh	Arg & Bt	NM2819	56°17·4′	6°23·3′W	X	48
Eilean Dubh	Arg & Bt	NM3018	56°16·9′	6°21·3′W	X	48
Eilean Dubh	Arg & Bt	NM3235	56°26·1′	6°20·4′W	X	46,47,48
Eilean Dubh	Arg & Bt	NM4201	56°8·2′	6°8·7′W	X	61
Eilean Dubh	Arg & Bt	NM4749	56°34·1′	6°6·7′W	X	47,48
Eilean Dubh	Arg & Bt	NM7902	56°9·8′	5°33·1′W	X	55
Eilean Dubh	Arg & Bt	NM8338	56°29·3′	5°31·0′W	X	49
Eilean Dubh	Arg & Bt	NM8742	56°31·6′	5°27·3′W	X	49
Eilean Dubh	Arg & Bt	NN0705	56°12·2′	5°6·2′W	X	56
Eilean Dubh	Arg & Bt	NR2456	55°43·4′	6°23·3′W	X	60
Eilean Dubh	Arg & Bt	NR3493	56°3·6′	6°15·9′W	X	61
Eilean Dubh	Arg & Bt	NR7187	56°1·5′	5°40·1′W	X	55
Eilean Dubh	Arg & Bt	NS0075	55°55·8′	5°11·7′W	X	62,63
Eilean Dubh	Highld	NB9703	57°58·5′	5°25·5′W	X	15
Eilean Dubh	Highld	NC2055	58°27·0′	5°4·6′W	X	9
Eilean Dubh	Highld	NC3768	58°34·4′	4°47·7′W	X	9
Eilean Dubh	Highld	NC4361	58°30·8′	4°41·2′W	X	9
Eilean Dubh	Highld	NG2249	57°27·0′	6°37·6′W	X	23
Eilean Dubh	Highld	NG6114	57°9·5′	5°56·7′W	X	32
Eilean Dubh	Highld	NG7833	57°20·3′	5°40·9′W	X	24
Eilean Dubh	Highld	NH1001	57°3·9′	5°7·6′W	X	34
Eilean Dubh	Highld	NM6972	56°47·2′	5°46·5′W	X	40
Eilean Dubh	Highld	NM7481	56°52·2′	5°42·0′W	X	40
Eilean Dubh	Highld	NM8878	56°51·0′	5°28·1′W	X	40
Eilean Dubh	N Eil	NF8215	57°7·2′	7°14·8′W	X	31
Eilean Dubh	N Eil	NF9774	57°39·5′	7°4·4′W	X	18
Eilean Dubh	N Eil	NG1590	57°48·8′	6°47·5′W	X	14
Eilean Dubh	N Eil	NG1698	57°53·1′	6°47·0′W	X	14
Eilean Dubh	N Eil	NG1996	57°52·2′	6°43·9′W	X	14
Eilean Dubh a' Bhàigh	N Eil	NB2500	57°54·5′	6°38·1′W	X	14
Eilean Dubh a'Chumhainn Mhóir	Arg & Bt	NR5581	55°57·8′	5°55·1′W	X	61
Eilean Dubh Beag	Arg & Bt	NM6911	56°14·4′	5°43·2′W	X	55
Eilean Dubh Beag	Highld	NG2149	57°27·0′	6°38·6′W	X	23
Eilean Dubh Chollaim	N Eil	NG1591	57°49·3′	6°47·5′W	X	14
Eilean Dubh Cruinn	Arg & Bt	NM4433	56°25·4′	6°8·6′W	X	47,48
Eilean Dubh Mór	Arg & Bt	NM6910	56°13·8′	5°43·2′W	X	55
Eilean Dubh Mór	N Eil	NF8568	57°35·8′	7°15·9′W	X	18
Eilean Dubh na Ciste	Arg & Bt	NM3025	56°20·7′	6°21·7′W	X	48
Eilean Dubh na Fionndalach Bige	Highld	NC2049	58°23·8′	5°4·3′W	X	9
Eilean Dubh na Muice	N Eil	NF8849	57°25·7′	7°11·5′W	X	22
Eilean Dubh na Sròine	Highld	NG9072	57°41·6′	5°30·9′W	X	19
Eilean Dùghaill	Highld	NG7954	57°31·6′	5°41·0′W	X	24
Eilean Dùin	Arg & Bt	NM7821	56°20·0′	5°35·0′W	X	49
Eilean Duirinnis	Arg & Bt	NN0033	56°27·1′	5°14·3′W	T	50
Eilean Eachainn	Highld	NG9371	57°41·1′	5°27·9′W	X	19
Eilean Eòghainn	Arg & Bt	NR8263	55°48·9′	5°28·3′W	X	62
Eilean Fada	Arg & Bt	NR7575	55°55·2′	5°35·6′W	X	62
Eilean Fada	N Eil	NF8961	57°32·2′	7°11·4′W	X	22
Eilean Fada Mór	Highld	NB9707	58°0·6′	5°25·7′W	X	15
Eilean Feòir	Arg & Bt	NM5338	56°28·4′	6°0·2′W	X	47,48
Eilean Fhianain	Highld	NM7568	56°45·2′	5°40·4′W	X	40
Eilean Fhionnlaidh	Arg & Bt	NR3689	56°1·5′	6°13·8′W	X	61
Eilean Fir Chrothair	N Eil	NB1341	58°16·1′	6°53·2′W	X	13
Eilean Fladday	Highld	NG5850	57°28·8′	6°1·8′W	X	24
Eilean Flodigarry	Highld	NG4871	57°39·8′	6°13·0′W	X	23
Eilean Frachlan	Arg & Bt	NM0951	56°33·9′	6°43·8′W	X	46
Eilean Fraoch	Arg & Bt	NM7513	56°15·6′	5°37·5′W	X	55
Eilean Fraoch	Highld	NG9480	57°46·0′	5°27·3′W	X	19
Eilean Fraoich	Arg & Bt	NR7186	56°1·0′	5°40·0′W	X	55
Eilean Fuam	N Eil	NF9179	57°41·9′	7°10·8′W	X	18
Eilean Furadh Mór	Highld	NG7993	57°52·6′	5°43·2′W	X	19
Eilean Gaineamhach Boreraig	Highld	NG6215	57°10·1′	5°55·8′W	X	32
Eilean Gainimh	Arg & Bt	NM8947	56°34·3′	5°25·6′W	X	49
Eilean Gamhna	Arg & Bt	NM7810	56°14·1′	5°34·5′W	X	55
Eilean Garave	Highld	NG2964	57°35·3′	6°31·6′W	X	23
Eilean Garbh	Arg & Bt	NM4440	56°29·2′	6°9·1′W	X	47,48
Eilean Garbh	Arg & Bt	NR6554	55°43·6′	5°44·1′W	X	62
Eilean Garbh	Highld	NC1440	58°18·8′	5°10·0′W	X	9
Eilean Garbh	Highld	NC7247	58°23·8′	4°10·9′W	X	10
Eilean Garbh	Highld	NG6056	57°32·1′	6°0·1′W	X	24
Eilean Ghamhna	Arg & Bt	NR6775	55°55·0′	5°43·3′W	X	61,62
Eilean Ghaoideamal	Arg & Bt	NR3687	56°0·5′	6°13·7′W	X	61
Eilean Ghòmain	Arg & Bt	NM2820	56°17·9′	6°23·4′W	X	48
Eilean Ghreasamuill	Arg & Bt	NL9344	56°29·5′	6°58·9′W	X	46
Eilean Ghreasamuill	Arg & Bt	NM0849	56°32·8′	6°44·6′W	X	46
Eilean Giubhais	Highld	NM7298	57°1·3′	5°44·9′W	X	33,40
Eilean Glas	Arg & Bt	NM8947	56°34·3′	5°25·6′W	X	49
Eilean Glas	Arg & Bt	NR7994	56°5·5′	5°32·7′W	X	55
Eilean Glas	Highld	NG2149	57°27·0′	6°38·6′W	X	23
Eilean Glas	N Eil	NB4223	58°7·5′	6°22·4′W	X	14
Eilean Glas	N Eil	NF8472	57°37·9′	7°17·2′W	X	18
Eilean Glas	N Eil	NG2494	57°51·3′	6°38·7′W	X	14
Eilean Glas na h-Acarsaid Fhalaich	N Eil	NB2601	57°55·1′	6°37·2′W	X	14
Eilean Gobhlach	Highld	NM7184	56°53·7′	5°45·2′W	X	40
Eilean Gorm	Stir	NN4501	56°10·8′	4°29·4′W	X	57
Eilean Grianain	Arg & Bt	NR8141	55°37·1′	5°28·2′W	X	62,69
Eilean Grianal	Highld	NG2249	57°27·0′	6°37·6′W	X	23
Eilean Grìoda	N Eil	NB4131	58°11·8′	6°24·0′W	X	8
Eilean Halum	Arg & Bt	NM1153	56°35·1′	6°42·0′W	X	46
Eilean Heast	Highld	NG6415	57°10·2′	5°53·8′W	X	32
Eilean Hoan	Highld	NC4467	58°34·1′	4°40·5′W	X	9
Eilean Horrisdale	Highld	NG7874	57°42·3′	5°43·1′W	X	19
Eilean Huilm	N Eil	NB0403	57°55·3′	6°59·5′W	X	13,18
Eilean Iain	N Eil	NF7853	57°27·4′	7°21·7′W	X	22
Eilean Iarmain or Isleornsay	Highld	NG6912	57°8·7′	5°48·7′W	T	32
Eilean Iarmain or Isleornsay	Highld	NG7012	57°8·7′	5°47·7′W	X	32,33
Eilean Ighe	Highld	NM6388	56°55·6′	5°53·2′W	X	40
Eilean Imersay	Arg & Bt	NR4246	55°38·6′	6°5·6′W	X	60
Eilean Inshaig	Arg & Bt	NM8104	56°11·0′	5°31·3′W	X	55
Eilean Iochdrach	N Eil	NF8258	57°30·3′	7°18·1′W	X	22
Eilean Iomallach	Arg & Bt	NM1550	56°33·6′	6°37·9′W	X	46
Eilean Iosal	Arg & Bt	NM7009	56°13·3′	5°42·2′W	X	55
Eilean Iosal	Highld	NC6265	58°33·3′	4°21·8′W	X	10
Eilean Iosal	Highld	NG2865	57°35·8′	6°32·7′W	X	23
Eilean Iubhair	Pth & Kin	NN3753	56°38·7′	4°39·0′W	X	41
Eilean Leac na Gainimh	Highld	NG5933	57°19·7′	5°59·8′W	X	24,32
Eilean Leathan	N Eil	NF7807	57°2·8′	7°18·2′W	X	31
Eilean Leathann	Arg & Bt	NR3290	56°1·9′	6°17·7′W	X	61
Eilean Leathann	N Eil	NF8458	57°30·4′	7°16·1′W	X	22
Eilean Leathann	N Eil	NF8754	57°28·4′	7°12·8′W	X	22
Eilean Leathann	N Eil	NF8961	57°32·2′	7°11·4′W	X	22
Eilean Léim	Arg & Bt	NR6345	55°38·7′	5°45·6′W	X	62
Eilean Leiravay	N Eil	NF9167	57°35·5′	7°9·8′W	X	18
Eilean Liath	Arg & Bt	NM0948	56°32·3′	6°43·6′W	X	46
Eilean Liath	Arg & Bt	NM3440	56°28·9′	6°18·8′W	X	47,48
Eilean Liath	Arg & Bt	NM4739	56°28·8′	6°6·1′W	X	47,48
Eilean Liath	Arg & Bt	NR1859	55°44·8′	6°29·2′W	X	60
Eilean Liath	Arg & Bt	NR4754	55°43·1′	6°1·3′W	X	60
Eilean Liath	Arg & Bt	NR6547	55°39·8′	5°43·8′W	X	62
Eilean Liath	Highld	NG7921	57°13·8′	5°39·2′W	X	33
Eilean Liubhaird	N Eil	NB3809	57°59·8′	6°25·6′W	X	14
Eilean Loain	Arg & Bt	NR7585	56°0·6′	5°36·1′W	X	55
Eilean Loch Oscair	Arg & Bt	NM8645	56°33·2′	5°28·5′W	X	49
Eilean Mairi	N Ayr	NR9620	55°26·1′	5°13·0′W	X	68,69
Eilean Maol	Highld	NG6403	57°3·7′	5°53·1′W	X	32
Eilean Maol	Highld	NM8595	57°0·0′	5°32·0′W	X	33,40
Eilean Maol Mhàrtuin	Arg & Bt	NM2522	56°18·9′	6°26·4′W	X	48
Eilean Maol Mór	Arg & Bt	NM1852	56°34·8′	6°35·1′W	X	46
Eilean Math-ghamhna	Arg & Bt	NS0398	56°8·3′	5°9·8′W	X	55
Eilean Meadhonach	Highld	NG6834	57°20·5′	5°50·9′W	X	24,32
Eilean Meall a' Chaorainn	Highld	NC2248	58°23·3′	5°2·2′W	X	9
Eilean Meall na Suirudhe	Arg & Bt	NR4099	56°7·0′	6°10·5′W	X	61
Eilean Mhànais	N Eil	NG1188	57°47·6′	6°51·3′W	X	14
Eilean Mhàraig	N Eil	NB2006	57°57·6′	6°43·6′W	X	13,14
Eilean Mhartan	Arg & Bt	NR7786	56°1·2′	5°34·3′W	X	55
Eilean Mhiabhaig	N Eil	NB3724	58°7·9′	6°27·6′W	X	14
Eilean Mhic an Fhùlaraich	Highld	NG9371	57°41·1′	5°27·9′W	X	19
Eilean Mhic Caoilte	N Eil	NF8157	57°29·7′	7°19·1′W	X	22
Eilean Mhic Chiarain	Arg & Bt	NM7211	56°14·5′	5°40·3′W	X	55
Eilean Mhic Chrion	Arg & Bt	NM8003	56°10·4′	5°32·2′W	X	55
Eilean Mhic Coinnich	Arg & Bt	NR1652	55°41·0′	6°30·7′W	X	60
Eilean Mhic Dhomhnuill Dhuibh	Highld	NM8172	56°47·5′	5°34·7′W	X	40
Eilean Mhic Fhionnlaidh	N Eil	NG1893	57°50·5′	6°44·7′W	X	14
Eilean Mhic Mhaolmhoire	Arg & Bt	NR4548	55°39·8′	6°2·8′W	X	60
Eilean Mhic Neill	Highld	NM6472	56°47·0′	5°51·4′W	X	40
Eilean Mhogh-sgeir	Highld	NG9007	57°6·6′	5°27·6′W	X	33
Eilean Mhugaig	Arg & Bt	NR3589	56°1·5′	6°14·7′W	X	61
Eilean Mhuire	N Eil	NG4398	57°54·1′	6°19·8′W	X	14
Eilean Mòineseach	Highld	NC0617	58°6·2′	5°17·1′W	X	15
Eilean Molach	Highld	NN3250	56°37·0′	4°43·8′W	X	41
Eilean Molach	N Eil	NA9932	58°10·7′	7°6·8′W	X	13
Eilean Molach or Ellen's Isle	Stir	NN4808	56°14·7′	4°26·7′W	X	57
Eilean Mór	Arg & Bt	NL9538	56°26·4′	6°56·5′W	X	46
Eilean Mór	Arg & Bt	NM2722	56°19·0′	6°24·5′W	X	48
Eilean Mór	Arg & Bt	NM2864	56°41·6′	6°26·1′W	X	46,47
Eilean Mór	Arg & Bt	NM3416	56°16·0′	6°17·3′W	X	48
Eilean Mór	Arg & Bt	NM6124	56°21·1′	5°51·7′W	X	49

Eilean Mór	Arg & Bt	NM6701	56°8·9'	5°44·6'W	X	55,61
Eilean Mór	Arg & Bt	NM8834	56°27·3'	5°26·0'W	X	49
Eilean Mór	Arg & Bt	NR2169	55°50·3'	6°26·9'W	X	60
Eilean Mór	Arg & Bt	NR6675	55°54·9'	5°44·2'W	X	61,62
Eilean Mór	Arg & Bt	NR8883	55°59·8'	5°23·5'W	X	55
Eilean Mór	Highld	NC0517	58°6·2'	5°18·1'W	X	15
Eilean Mór	Highld	NC1213	58°4·2'	5°10·8'W	X	15
Eilean Mór	Highld	NC4550	58°24·9'	4°38·7'W	X	9
Eilean Mór	Highld	NG2248	57°26·5'	6°37·5'W	X	23
Eilean Mór	Highld	NG3557	57°31·8'	6°25·2'W	X	23
Eilean Mór	Highld	NG6934	57°20·5'	5°49·9'W	X	24,32
Eilean Mór	Highld	NG7558	57°33·6'	5°45·2'W	X	24
Eilean Mór	Highld	NG7614	57°10·0'	5°41·8'W	X	33
Eilean Mór	Highld	NM7560	56°40·9'	5°40·0'W	X	40
Eilean Mór	N Ayr	NR8927	55°29·7'	5°20·0'W	X	68,69
Eilean Mór	N Eil	NA7246	58°17·1'	7°35·4'W	X	13
Eilean Mór	N Eil	NB1738	58°14·7'	6°48·9'W	X	8,13
Eilean Mór	N Eil	NB2122	58°6·2'	6°43·7'W	H	13,14
Eilean Mór	N Eil	NB3828	58°10·1'	6°26·8'W	X	8
Eilean Mór	N Eil	NF7665	57°33·8'	7°24·7'W	X	18
Eilean Mór	N Eil	NF7718	57°8·6'	7°20·0'W	X	31
Eilean Mór	N Eil	NF8061	57°31·8'	7°20·4'W	X	22
Eilean Mór	N Eil	NF8456	57°29·3'	7°16·0'W	X	22
Eilean Mór	N Eil	NF8962	57°32·7'	7°11·5'W	X	22
Eilean Mór	N Eil	NL6590	56°53·1'	7°29·6'W	X	31
Eilean Mór	Pth & Kin	NN5556	56°40·7'	4°21·6'W	X	42,51
Eilean Mór a' Bhàigh	N Eil	NB2600	57°54·6'	6°37·1'W	X	14
Eilean Mór Lacasaidh	N Eil	NB3320	58°5·6'	6°31·4'W	X	13,14
Eilean Mór Phabail	N Eil	NB5330	58°11·6'	6°11·7'W	X	8
Eilean mo Shlinneag	Highld	NM7262	56°41·9'	5°43·0'W	X	40
Eilean Mullagrach	Highld	NB9511	58°2·7'	5°27·9'W	X	15
Eilean Munde	Highld	NN0859	56°41·3'	5°7·6'W	X	41
Eilean Musdile	Arg & Bt	NM7835	56°27·6'	5°35·7'W	X	49
Eilean Musimul	Arg & Bt	NM2521	56°18·4'	6°26·3'W	X	48
Eilean na Bà	Highld	NG6938	57°22·7'	5°50·1'W	X	24,32
Eilean na Bà Mór	Highld	NG7934	57°20·8'	5°39·9'W	X	24
Eilean na Bearachd	Highld	NC1439	58°18·3'	5°10·0'W	X	15
Eilean na Beinne	Highld	NG8235	57°21·5'	5°37·0'W	X	24
Eilean na Beithe	Arg & Bt	NM5154	56°37·0'	6°3·1'W	X	47
Eilean na Beithe	Arg & Bt	NR9270	55°53·0'	5°19·1'W	X	62
Eilean na Beitheiche	Highld	NM6146	56°33·0'	5°52·9'W	X	49
Eilean na Bruachain	Arg & Bt	NR7476	55°55·7'	5°36·6'W	X	62
Eilean na Ceardaich	N Eil	NF9981	57°43·3'	7°2·9'W	X	18
Eilean na Cille	Arg & Bt	NR7597	56°7·0'	5°36·7'W	X	55
Eilean na Cille	N Eil	NF8446	57°23·9'	7°15·2'W	X	22
Eilean na Circe	Arg & Bt	NR7689	56°2·7'	5°35·4'W	X	55
Eilean na Cloiche	Arg & Bt	NM8338	56°29·3'	5°31·0'W	X	49
Eilean na Cloiche	N Eil	NF9054	57°28·5'	7°9·9'W	X	22
Eilean na Cloiche	N Eil	NF9179	57°41·9'	7°10·8'W	X	18
Eilean na Cobhair	N Eil	NB4232	58°12·3'	6°23·0'W	X	8
Eilean na Crèadha	Highld	NG7631	57°19·1'	5°42·8'W	X	24
Eilean na Creiche	Arg & Bt	NM3837	56°27·4'	6°14·7'W	X	47,48
Eilean na Creige Duibhe	Highld	NG8233	57°20·4'	5°36·9'W	X	24
Eilean na Gàmhna	Highld	NG7001	57°2·8'	5°47·1'W	X	33
Eilean na Gartaig	Highld	NC2112	58°3·9'	5°1·6'W	X	15
Eilean na Gearrabreac	N Eil	NG1992	57°50·0'	6°43·6'W	X	14
Eilean na Glaschoille	Highld	NG7300	57°2·4'	5°44·0'W	X	33
Eilean na Gualainn	Highld	NM7279	56°51·1'	5°43·9'W	X	40
Eilean na h-Acairseid	Highld	NM5872	56°46·9'	5°57·2'W	X	39,47
Eilean na h-Acairseid	Highld	NM6797	57°0·6'	5°49·8'W	X	40
Eilean na h-Airde	Arg & Bt	NR6452	55°42·5'	5°45·0'W	X	62
Eilean na h-Airde	Highld	NG5211	57°7·6'	6°5·4'W	X	32
Eilean na h-Airigh	N Eil	NF8357	57°29·8'	7°17·1'W	X	22
Eilean na h- Aiteag	Highld	NC1958	58°28·6'	5°5·8'W	X	9
Eilean na h-Aoirinn	Arg & Bt	NR6283	55°59·1'	5°48·5'W	X	61
Eilean na h-Aon Chaorach	Arg & Bt	NM2520	56°17·8'	6°26·3'W	X	48
Eilean na h-Eairne	Arg & Bt	NR7496	56°6·5'	5°37·6'W	X	55
Eilean na h-Oitire	Highld	NM6475	56°48·7'	5°51·5'W	X	40
Eilean na h-Uamha	Arg & Bt	NM4037	56°27·5'	6°12·8'W	X	47,48
Eilean na h-Uamhaidh	Arg & Bt	NR7576	55°55·7'	5°35·7'W	X	62
Eilean na h-Uilinn	Arg & Bt	NR6446	55°39·3'	5°44·7'W	X	62
Eilean nam Bairneach	Highld	NM7279	56°51·1'	5°43·9'W	X	40
Eilean nam Ban	Arg & Bt	NM3024	56°20·1'	6°21·7'W	X	48
Eilean nam Ban	Arg & Bt	NR3594	56°4·2'	6°15·0'W	X	61
Eilean nam Bàn	Highld	NM7269	56°45·7'	5°43·4'W	X	40
Eilean nam Beathach	Arg & Bt	NM7820	56°19·5'	5°35·0'W	X	49
Eilean nam Bò	Arg & Bt	NM2921	56°18·5'	6°22·5'W	X	48
Eilean nam Breaban	Pth & Kin	NN6436	56°30·0'	4°12·1'W	X	51
Eilean nam Breac	Highld	NM7091	56°57·4'	5°46·5'W	X	33,40
Eilean nam Bridianach	N Eil	NG0284	57°45·1'	7°0·1'W	X	18
Eilean nam Caorach	Arg & Bt	NM4624	56°20·7'	6°6·2'W	X	48
Eilean nam Faoileag	Pth & Kin	NN5357	56°41·2'	4°23·5'W	X	42,51
Eilean nam Feannag	N Eil	NB1433	58°11·8'	6°51·6'W	X	13
Eilean nam Freumha	Arg & Bt	NM7820	56°19·5'	5°35·0'W	X	49
Eilean nam Gillean	Highld	NM6460	56°40·6'	5°50·7'W	X	40
Eilean nam Meann	Arg & Bt	NM9711	56°15·1'	5°16·2'W	X	55
Eilean nam Muc	Arg & Bt	NM2457	56°37·7'	6°29·6'W	X	46,47
Eilean nam Muc	Arg & Bt	NM2819	56°17·4'	6°23·3'W	X	48
Eilean nam Muc	Arg & Bt	NR7274	55°54·6'	5°38·4'W	X	62
Eilean nam Mult	N Eil	NF8863	57°33·2'	7°12·5'W	X	18
Eilean na Moil Móire	N Eil	NA9713	58°0·4'	7°7·3'W	X	13
Eilean na Muice Duibhe	Arg & Bt	NR3355	55°43·1'	6°14·7'W	X	60
Eilean nan Cabar	Highld	NM6883	56°53·1'	5°48·0'W	X	40
Eilean nan Caorach	Arg & Bt	NM7431	56°25·3'	5°39·4'W	X	49
Eilean nan Caorach	Arg & Bt	NM9046	56°33·8'	5°24·6'W	X	49
Eilean nan Caorach	Arg & Bt	NR3644	55°37·3'	6°11·2'W	X	60
Eilean nan Caorach	Arg & Bt	NR7357	55°45·4'	5°36·6'W	X	62
Eilean nan Carnan	N Eil	NF8061	57°31·8'	7°20·4'W	X	22
Eilean nan Ceann	Highld	NM7109	56°13·4'	5°41·2'W	X	55
Eilean nan Clach	Highld	NH7734	57°23·1'	4°2·3'W	X	27
Eilean nan Coinean	Arg & Bt	NR7186	56°1·0'	5°40·0'W	X	55
Eilean nan Coinean	Arg & Bt	NR7796	56°6·5'	5°34·7'W	X	55
Eilean nan Coinein	Arg & Bt	NR5468	55°50·8'	5°55·4'W	X	61
Eilean nan Each	Highld	NM3981	56°51·1'	6°16·4'W	X	39
Eilean nan Each	N Eil	NF8751	57°26·7'	7°12·6'W	X	22
Eilean nan Eildean	Highld	NM6158	56°39·4'	5°53·5'W	X	49
Eilean nan Eun	N Eil	NG1389	57°48·2'	6°49·4'W	X	14
Eilean nan Faoileag	N Eil	NF9179	57°41·9'	7°10·8'W	X	18
Eilean nan Gabhar	Arg & Bt	NM7900	56°8·8'	5°33·0'W	X	55
Eilean nan Gabhar	Arg & Bt	NR5367	55°50·2'	5°56·3'W	X	61

Eilean nan Gabhar	Arg & Bt	NR9074	55°55·1'	5°21·2'W	X	62
Eilean nan Gabhar	Highld	NM5553	56°36·6'	5°59·1'W	X	47
Eilean nan Gabhar	Highld	NM6157	56°38·9'	5°53·5'W	X	49
Eilean nan Gall	Highld	NG9420	57°13·7'	5°24·3'W	X	25,33
Eilean nan Gall	Highld	NN0268	56°46·0'	5°13·9'W	X	41
Eilean nan Gamhna	Arg & Bt	NM8130	56°24·9'	5°32·6'W	X	49
Eilean nan Gamhna	Arg & Bt	NM8338	56°29·3'	5°31·0'W	X	49
Eilean nan Gamhna	N Eil	NF8225	57°12·6'	7°15·6'W	X	22
Eilean nan Gamhna	N Eil	NF8345	57°23·4'	7°16·1'W	X	22
Eilean nan Gearr	N Eil	NF8958	57°30·6'	7°11·2'W	X	22
Eilean nan Gobhar	Arg & Bt	NM0343	56°29·4'	6°49·1'W	X	46
Eilean nan Gobhar	Arg & Bt	NR1851	55°40·5'	6°28·7'W	X	60
Eilean nan Gobhar	Highld	NM6979	56°51·0'	5°46·8'W	X	40
Eilean nan Gobhar Mór	Highld	NG7631	57°19·1'	5°42·8'W	X	24
Eilean na Nighinn	Arg & Bt	NM7902	56°9·8'	5°33·1'W	X	55
Eilean nan Leac	Arg & Bt	NR6875	55°55·0'	5°42·3'W	X	61,62
Eilean nan Naomh	Highld	NG7041	57°24·3'	5°49·3'W	X	24
Eilean nan Ron	Arg & Bt	NR3386	55°59·8'	6°16·5'W	X	61
Eilean Nan Ron	Highld	NC6365	58°33·4'	4°20·8'W	X	10
Eilean nan Seachd Seisrichean	Highld	NM4263	56°41·5'	6°12·4'W	X	47
Eilean nan Slat	Arg & Bt	NM2624	56°20·0'	6°25·5'W	X	48
Eilean nan Trom	Highld	NM7279	56°51·1'	5°43·9'W	X	40
Eilean nan Uan	Arg & Bt	NM2363	56°40·9'	6°30·9'W	X	46,47
Eilean nan Uan	Arg & Bt	NR2265	55°48·2'	6°25·7'W	X	60
Eilean nan Uan	Arg & Bt	NR3388	56°0·9'	6°16·6'W	X	61
Eilean nan Uan	Arg & Bt	NR6877	55°56·1'	5°42·4'W	X	61,62
Eilean nan Uan	Highld	NC0935	58°16·0'	5°14·9'W	X	15
Eilean nan Uan	N Eil	NB4630	58°11·4'	6°18·8'W	X	8
Eilean Naomhachd	Arg & Bt	NR6973	55°53·9'	5°41·3'W	X	61,62
Eilean na Praise	N Eil	NG2096	57°52·2'	6°42·9'W	X	14
Eilean na Rainich	Highld	NC1439	58°18·3'	5°10·0'W	X	15
Eilean na Rainich	Highld	NC2234	58°15·8'	5°1·6'W	X	15
Eilean na Roe	N Eil	NF6970	57°36·2'	7°32·1'W	X	18
Eilean na Saille	Highld	NC1753	58°25·9'	5°7·6'W	X	9
Eilean na Seamair	Arg & Bt	NM3117	56°16·4'	6°20·3'W	X	48
Eilean na Sgaite	N Eil	NG1992	57°50·0'	6°43·6'W	X	14
Eilean na Sgioba	Arg & Bt	NR1963	55°47·0'	6°28·5'W	X	60
Eileann Dubh Dhurinish	Highld	NG7732	57°19·7'	5°41·8'W	X	24
Eilean Nòstaig	Arg & Bt	NR2773	55°52·6'	6°21·5'W	X	60
Eilean Odhar	Arg & Bt	NM1255	56°36·2'	6°41·1'W	X	46
Eilean Oighrige	Arg & Bt	NM4424	56°20·6'	6°8·1'W	X	48
Eilean Olmsa	Arg & Bt	NR4196	56°5·5'	6°9·4'W	X	61
Eilean Ona	Arg & Bt	NM7602	56°9·7'	5°36·0'W	X	55
Eilean Orasaidh	N Eil	NB4121	58°6·4'	6°23·3'W	X	14
Eilean Orasaig	Arg & Bt	NM7926	56°22·7'	5°34·3'W	X	49
Eilean Orasaigh	N Eil	NB2132	58°11·6'	6°44·4'W	X	8,13
Eilean Orasaigh	N Eil	NB3625	58°8·4'	6°28·7'W	X	14
Eilean Orasaigh	N Eil	NB4024	58°8·0'	6°24·5'W	X	14
Eilean Ornais	N Eil	NF8538	57°19·7'	7°13·6'W	X	22
Eilean Ornsay	Arg & Bt	NM2255	56°36·5'	6°31·4'W	X	46,47
Eilean Port a' Bhàta	Arg & Bt	NM4137	56°27·5'	6°11·8'W	X	47,48
Eilean Port a' Choit	Highld	NC2148	58°23·3'	5°3·3'W	X	9
Eilean Port nam Murrach	Highld	NM6183	56°52·9'	5°54·9'W	X	40
Eilean Puirt Léithe	Arg & Bt	NR6975	55°55·0'	5°41·4'W	X	61,62
Eilean Raineach	N Eil	NG1997	57°52·7'	6°43·9'W	X	14
Eilean Rainich	Arg & Bt	NM4144	56°31·3'	6°12·2'W	X	47,48
Eilean Rainich	N Eil	NF8357	57°52·5'	6°49·0'W	X	14
Eilean Rairidh	Highld	NC1635	58°16·2'	5°7·8'W	X	15
Eilean Ramsay	Arg & Bt	NM8846	56°33·7'	5°26·6'W	X	49
Eilean Raonuill	Highld	NM6272	56°47·0'	5°53·3'W	X	40
Eilean Ràrsaidh	Highld	NG8111	57°8·5'	5°36·7'W	X	33
Eilean Reamhar	Highld	NG4818	57°11·3'	6°9·8'W	X	32
Eilean Reilean	Arg & Bt	NM4038	56°28·0'	6°12·8'W	X	47,48
Eilean Reinigeadail	N Eil	NB2201	57°55·0'	6°41·2'W	X	14
Eilean Riabhach	Arg & Bt	NM8739	56°30·0'	5°27·2'W	X	49
Eilean Riabhach	Highld	NC1440	58°18·8'	5°10·0'W	X	9
Eilean Righ	Arg & Bt	NM8001	56°9·3'	5°32·1'W	X	55
Eilean Rosaidh	N Eil	NB4120	58°5·9'	6°23·3'W	X	14
Eilean Ruairidh	Highld	NG5912	57°8·4'	5°58·5'W	X	32
Eilean Ruairidh Mór	Highld	NG8973	57°42·1'	5°32·0'W	X	19
Eilean Rubha an Ridire	Highld	NM7240	56°30·1'	5°41·8'W	X	49
Eilean Scarastaigh	N Eil	NB1932	58°11·5'	6°46·4'W	X	8,13
Eilean Sgorach	Highld	NM5599	57°1·3'	6°1·7'W	X	32,39
Eilean Shamadalain	Highld	NM7206	57°5·6'	5°45·4'W	X	33
Eilean Sheumais	N Eil	NF7402	56°59·9'	7°21·7'W	X	31
Eilean Shiphoirt	N Eil	NB2010	57°59·7'	6°43·8'W	X	13,14
Eilean Shona	Highld	NM6473	56°47·6'	5°51·4'W	X	40
Eilean Shona Ho	Highld	NM6573	56°47·6'	5°50·4'W	X	40
Eilean Sionnach	Highld	NG7112	57°8·8'	5°46·7'W	X	33
Eilean Smuaisibhig	N Eil	NB2703	57°56·2'	6°36·3'W	X	13,14
Eilean Stacan	Highld	NG7832	57°19·7'	5°40·8'W	X	24
Eileans, The	N Ayr	NS1654	55°44·9'	4°55·5'W	X	63
Eilean Stocinis	N Eil	NG1390	57°48·7'	6°49·5'W	X	14
Eilean Sùbhainn	Highld	NG9272	57°41·6'	5°28·9'W	X	19
Eilean Sunadale	Arg & Bt	NR8145	55°39·2'	5°28·4'W	X	62,69
Eilean Teinish	N Eil	NB1135	58°12·8'	6°54·8'W	X	13
Eilean Thinngartsaigh	N Eil	NB2702	57°55·7'	6°36·2'W	X	14
Eilean Thòraidh	N Eil	NB4220	58°5·9'	6°22·2'W	X	14
Eilean Thuilm	Highld	NM4891	56°56·8'	6°8·2'W	X	39
Eilean Thuilm	N Eil	NB4430	58°11·3'	6°20·9'W	X	8
Eilean Tigh	Highld	NG6053	57°30·5'	5°59·9'W	X	24
Eilean Tighe	N Eil	NA7246	58°17·1'	7°35·4'W	X	13
Eilean Tioram	Highld	NG7260	57°34·6'	5°48·3'W	X	24
Eilean Tioram	Highld	NG7367	57°38·4'	5°47·7'W	X	19,24
Eilean Tioram	Highld	NG8310	57°8·0'	5°34·7'W	X	33
Eilean Tioram	Highld	NG8726	57°16·8'	5°31·6'W	X	33
Eilean Tioram	Highld	NM8695	57°0·1'	5°31·0'W	X	33,40
Eilean Tomulam	Arg & Bt	NM1452	56°34·6'	6°39·0'W	X	46
Eilean Tràighe	Arg & Bt	NR6880	55°57·7'	5°42·6'W	X	55,61
Eilean Tràighe	Arg & Bt	NR7273	55°54·0'	5°38·4'W	X	62
Eilean Tràighe	Arg & Bt	NR7287	56°1·6'	5°39·1'W	X	55
Eilean Tràighe	Arg & Bt	NR7372	55°53·5'	5°37·4'W	X	62
Eilean Tràighe	Arg & Bt	NR7457	55°45·5'	5°35·7'W	X	62
Eilean Tràighte	Arg & Bt	NM8105	56°11·5'	5°31·3'W	X	55
Eilean Treadhrach	Arg & Bt	NR3888	56°1·1'	6°11·8'W	X	61
Eilean Treunaig	Arg & Bt	NR3486	55°59·8'	6°15·5'W	X	61
Eilean Trianach	Arg & Bt	NM7335	56°27·4'	5°40·6'W	X	49
Eilean Trodday	Highld	NG4378	57°43·4'	6°18·5'W	X	23

Eilean Trosdam	N Eil	NB2132	58°11·6'	6°44·4'W	X	8,13
Eilean Trostain	N Eil	NF6971	57°36·7'	7°32·1'W	X	18
Eilean Uaine	Highld	NM6571	56°46·5'	5°50·3'W	X	40
Eilean Uamh a'Chàise	Arg & Bt	NR6283	55°59·1'	5°48·5'W	X	61
Eilean Uamh Ghuaidhre	Arg & Bt	NM6123	56°20·6'	5°51·6'W	X	49
Eilean Uillne	Highld	NM5456	56°38·1'	6°0·2'W	X	47
Eilean Vialish	N Eil	NF7108	57°3·0'	7°25·1'W	X	31
Eilear na Mola	Highld	NC2058	58°28·7'	5°4·7'W	H	9
Eilein Aoinidh	Highld	NG8725	57°16·2'	5°31·5'W	X	33
Eilein Mór	Highld	NM5861	56°40·9'	5°56·6'W	X	47
Eileraig	Arg & Bt	NM2663	56°41·0'	6°28·0'W	X	46,47
Eilian Ho	I of Angl	SH3175	53°15·0'	4°31·6'W	X	114
Eiligear	Highld	NM6746	56°33·2'	5°47·0'W	X	49
Eilio	Conwy	SH7364	53°9·7'	3°53·6'W	X	115
Eilligan	Arg & Bt	NS1377	55°57·2'	4°59·3'W	H	63
Eilrig	Highld	NN3799	57°3·5'	4°40·8'W	H	34
Eilrig	Scot Bord	NT3708	55°22·0'	2°59·2'W	X	79
Eimisgeir	N Eil	NB2231	58°11·1'	6°43·3'W	X	8,13
Einagraich	N Eil	NB5554	58°24·6'	6°11·2'W	X	8
Eina Stack	Shetld	HU3070	60°25·0'	1°26·8'W	X	3
Eind	Pth & Kin	NN9510	56°16·5'	3°41·3'W	X	58
Einich Cairn	Highld	NN9399	57°4·4'	3°45·4'W	H	36,43
Einig Wood	Highld	NH3598	57°56·7'	4°46·8'W	F	20
Eire	N Eil	NF9979	57°42·3'	7°2·7'W	X	18
Eirianallt	Denb	SJ1942	52°58·4'	3°12·0'W	X	125
Eirianallt	I of Angl	SH4179	53°17·3'	4°22·7'W	X	114,115
Eirianws Fm	Conwy	SH7773	53°14·6'	3°50·2'W	FM	115
Eiridh Gharbh	Highld	NM7081	56°52·1'	5°46·0'W	X	40
Eisgein	N Eil	NB3212	58°1·2'	6°31·8'W	T	13,14
Eisingrug	Gwyn	SH6134	52°53·4'	4°3·6'W	T	124
Eislin Geo	Shetld	HU3893	60°37·4'	1°17·8'W	X	1,2
Eisteddfa	Carm	SN5323	51°53·4'	4°7·8'W	X	159
Eisteddfa	Cered	SN3153	52°9·2'	4°27·8'W	X	145
Eisteddfa	Pemb	SN1035	51°59·1'	4°45·6'W	X	145
Eisteddfa Gurig	Cered	SN7984	52°26·7'	3°46·4'W	X	135
Eithbed	Pemb	SN0828	51°55·3'	4°47·1'W	X	145,158
Eithin	Carm	SN7441	52°3·4'	3°49·9'W	X	146,147,160
Eithindoun-isaf	Carm	SN3023	51°53·0'	4°27·8'W	X	145,159
Eithinduon	Pemb	SN1537	52°0·3'	4°41·3'W	X	145
Eithinduon	Pemb	SN1629	51°56·0'	4°40·2'W	X	145,158
Eithin-duon-uchaf	Carm	SN3023	51°53·0'	4°27·8'W	X	145,159
Eithin-fynydd	Gwyn	SH6021	52°46·4'	4°4·1'W	X	124
Eithinog	Gwyn	SH4552	53°2·8'	4°18·3'W	X	115,123
Eithinog	Powys	SJ1107	52°39·4'	3°18·5'W	X	125
Eithinog-Wen	Gwyn	SH4452	53°2·8'	4°19·2'W	X	115,123
Eitseal	N Eil	NB3030	58°10·8'	6°35·1'W	H	8,13
Eitseal Bheag	N Eil	NB2833	58°12·4'	6°37·4'W	H	8,13
Elam Grange	Brad	SE0643	53°53·2'	1°54·1'W	X	104
Eland Brook	Staffs	SK1426	52°50·1'	1°47·1'W	W	128
Eland Green	Northum	NZ1673	55°3·3'	1°44·5'W	T	88
Eland Hall	Northum	NZ1773	55°3·3'	1°43·6'W	X	88
Eland Lodge	Staffs	SK1427	52°50·7'	1°47·1'W	X	128
Elan Village	Powys	SN9365	52°16·6'	3°33·7'W	T	136,147
Elba	Scot Bord	NT7860	55°50·2'	2°20·6'W	X	67
Elbeckhill	D & G	NY1393	55°13·7'	3°21·6'W	X	78
Elberry Cove	Torbay	SX9057	50°24·4'	3°32·5'W	W	202
Elberry Fm	Torbay	SX8957	50°24·4'	3°33·3'W	FM	202
Elberton	S Glos	ST6088	51°35·6'	2°34·3'W	T	162,172
Elbolton	N Yks	SE0061	54°2·9'	1°59·6'W	H	98
Elbolton Cave	N Yks	SE0061	54°2·9'	1°59·6'W	A	98
Elborough	N Som	ST3759	51°19·8'	2°53·9'W	T	182
Elbourne Ho	W Susx	TQ1212	50°54·0'	0°24·0'W	X	198
Elbow	Fife	NO5628	56°26·8'	2°42·4'W	X	54,59
Elbows	Essex	TL6313	51°47·7'	0°22·2'E	X	167
Elbow Scar	Cumbr	SD2870	54°7·5'	3°5·7'W	X	96,97
Elbows Wood	Kent	TQ6265	51°21·9'	0°20·0'E	F	177
Elbridge	Shrops	SJ3624	52°48·8'	2°56·6'W	T	126
Elbridge	W Susx	SU9102	50°48·8'	0°42·1'W	T	197
Elbridge Ho	Kent	TR2059	51°17·5'	1°9·7'E	X	179
Elbrook Ho	Herts	TL2640	52°2·9'	0°9·4'W	X	153
Elburton	C of Plym	SX5352	50°21·2'	4°3·6'W	T	201
Elbury Fm	Devon	SY0095	50°45·0'	3°24·7'W	FM	192
Elbury Hill	Dorset	ST8618	50°58·1'	2°11·6'W	H	183
Elby Point	I of M	SC2177	54°9·7'	4°44·1'W	X	95
Elcho	Pth & Kin	NO1620	56°22·1'	3°21·1'W	X	53,58
Elcho Castle	Pth & Kin	NO1621	56°22·7'	3°21·2'W	A	53,58
Elcho Park	Pth & Kin	NO1520	56°22·1'	3°22·1'W	X	53,58
Elcock's Brook	Worcs	SP0164	52°16·7'	1°58·7'W	T	150
Elcombe	Glos	SO8007	51°45·9'	2°10·0'W	X	162
Elcombe	Glos	ST7897	51°40·5'	2°18·7'W	T	162
Elcombe	Swin	SU1380	51°31·4'	1°48·4'W	T	173
Elcombe Fm	Dorset	SY4996	50°45·9'	2°43·0'W	FM	193,194
Elcombe Fm	Wilts	ST9722	51°0·1'	2°2·2'W	FM	184
Elcombe Hall	Swin	SU1380	51°31·4'	1°48·4'W	X	173
Elcombe House Fm	Swin	SU1281	51°31·9'	1°49·2'W	FM	173
Elcot	Shrops	SO6878	52°24·2'	2°27·8'W	X	138
Elcot	W Berks	SU3969	51°25·4'	1°26·0'W	T	174
Elcot Park Hotel	W Berks	SU3969	51°25·4'	1°26·0'W	X	174
Eldbotle Wood	E Loth	NT5085	56°3·6'	2°47·7'W	F	66
Eldene	Swin	SU1884	51°33·5'	1°44·0'W	T	173
Elder Beck	Cumbr	NY4723	54°36·2'	2°48·8'W	W	90
Elderbeck	Cumbr	NY4723	54°36·2'	2°48·8'W	X	90
Elderberry Fm	Suff	TL6583	52°25·4'	0°26·0'E	FM	143
Elderden Fm	Kent	TQ7847	51°11·9'	0°33·3'E	FM	188
Elder Fm	E Yorks	SE7434	53°48·1'	0°52·2'W	FM	105,106
Elder Hill	Norf	TL8880	52°23·4'	0°46·2'E	X	144
Elder House	Donc	SE7209	53°34·6'	0°54·3'W	X	112
Elder Lodge	Lincs	TF3721	52°46·4'	0°2·3'E	X	131
Eldernell	Cambs	TL3198	52°34·1'	0°3·6'W	T	142
Eldern Pt	Devon	SS2427	51°1·2'	4°30·2'W	X	190
Elder Park	Devon	SS5613	50°54·1'	4°2·5'W	X	180
Eldersfield	Worcs	SO8031	51°58·9'	2°17·1'W	T	150
Elderslie	Renf	NS4462	55°49·8'	4°29·0'W	T	64
Elder Street	Essex	TL5734	51°59·2'	0°17·6'E	T	154
Elderswell Fm	Beds	SP9551	52°9·2'	0°36·3'W	FM	153
Elderton Clump	Dorset	SY8497	50°46·6'	2°13·2'W	X	194
Elderwood Fm	Cambs	TL4992	52°30·6'	0°12·1'E	FM	143
Eldick Hill	D & G	NX5280	55°5·8'	4°18·7'W	X	77
Eldinhope	Scot Bord	NT2924	55°30·5'	3°7·0'W	X	73
Eldinhope Burn	Scot Bord	NT3023	55°30·0'	3°6·1'W	W	73

Eldinhope Cott	Scot Bord	NT2924	55°30·5'	3°7·0'W	X	73
Eldinhope Knowe	Scot Bord	NT3124	55°30·5'	3°5·1'W	H	73
Eldinhope Middle Hill	Scot Bord	NT3123	55°30·0'	3°5·1'W	X	73
Eldmire	N Yks	SE4274	54°9·8'	1°21·0'W	X	99
Eldmire Cottage	N Yks	SE4374	54°9·8'	1°20·1'W	X	99
Eldmire Fm	N Yks	SE4274	54°9·8'	1°21·0'W	FM	99
Eldmire Hill	N Yks	SE4275	54°10·4'	1°21·0'W	X	99
Eldmire Moor	N Yks	SE4474	54°9·8'	1°19·1'W	X	99
Eldon	Durham	NZ2327	54°38·5'	1°38·2'W	T	93
Eldon Blue Ho	Durham	NZ2428	54°39·0'	1°37·3'W	X	93
Eldon Hill	Derby	SK1181	53°19·8'	1°49·7'W	H	110
Eldon Hill	Durham	NZ2327	54°38·5'	1°38·2'W	X	93
Eldon Ho	Hants	SU3627	51°2·7'	1°28·8'W	X	185
Eldon Hole	Derby	SK1180	53°19·2'	1°49·7'W	X	110
Eldon Lane	Durham	NZ2227	54°38·5'	1°39·1'W	T	93
Eldon Moor Ho	Durham	NZ2626	54°38·0'	1°35·4'W	X	93
Eldon Seat	Dorset	SY9377	50°35·8'	2°5·6'W	X	195
Eldon Wood	Glos	SP0305	51°44·9'	1°57·0'W	F	163
Eldrable	Highld	NC9818	58°8·6'	3°43·5'W	X	17
Eldrable Burn	Highld	NC9717	58°8·1'	3°44·5'W	W	17
Eldrable Hill	Highld	NC9816	58°7·5'	3°43·4'W	H	17
Eldrick	D & G	NX4282	55°6·7'	4°28·2'W	X	77
Eldrick	D & G	NX6795	55°14·1'	4°5·1'W	X	77
Eldrick	S Ayr	NX2881	55°5·9'	4°41·3'W	X	76
Eldrickhill	D & G	NX0654	54°50·8'	5°0·9'W	X	82
Eldrick Hill	S Ayr	NX3692	55°12·0'	4°34·2'W	H	77
Eldrick Hill	S Ayr	NX3797	55°14·7'	4°33·4'W	H	77
Eldridge Hill	S Ayr	NX1581	55°5·6'	4°53·5'W	X	76
Eldrig Fell	D & G	NX2568	54°58·8'	4°43·7'W	H	82
Eldrig Hill	D & G	NX3466	54°57·9'	4°35·2'W	H	82
Eldrig Loch	D & G	NX2569	54°59·3'	4°43·7'W	W	82
Eldrig Moss	D & G	NX2569	54°59·3'	4°43·7'W	X	82
Eldrig Moss	D & G	NX3465	54°57·4'	4°35·1'W	X	82
Eldrig Moss	D & G	NX3565	54°57·4'	4°34·2'W	X	83
Eldroth	N Yks	SD7665	54°5·1'	2°21·6'W	T	98
Eldwick	Brad	SE1240	53°51·6'	1°48·6'W	T	104
Eldwick Crag	Brad	SE1242	53°52·7'	1°48·6'W	X	104
Eldwick Hall	Brad	SE1241	53°52·1'	1°48·6'W	X	104
Eleanor Cross	E Yorks	SE9264	54°4·1'	0°35·2'W	X	101
Eleanor Ho	NE Lincs	TA2012	53°35·7'	0°10·8'W	X	113
Eleanor Wood	Lincs	TF1185	53°21·2'	0°19·5'W	F	121
Elegug Stacks	Pemb	SR9294	51°36·6'	4°59·9'W	X	158
Eleighwater Ho	Somer	ST3310	50°53·4'	2°56·8'W	X	193
Elemore Grange	Durham	NZ3543	54°47·1'	1°26·9'W	X	88
Elemore Hall School	Durham	NZ3544	54°47·6'	1°26·9'W	X	88
Elemore Vale	Sund	NZ3545	54°48·2'	1°26·9'W	T	88
Elephant and Castle Sta	Sthwk	TQ3278	51°29·4'	0°5·5'W	X	176,177
Elephant Rock	Corn	SX1979	50°35·2'	4°33·0'W	X	201
Elephant, The	Cumbr	NY4542	54°46·4'	2°50·9'W	X	86
Eleraig	Arg & Bt	NM8616	56°17·6'	5°27·0'W	H	55
Elerch or Bont-goch	Cered	SN6886	52°27·6'	3°56·2'W	T	135
Eleric	Arg & Bt	NR6108	55°18·7'	5°45·6'W	X	68
Elernion	Gwyn	SH3746	52°59·4'	4°25·3'W	X	123
Eleven Acre Covert	Leic	SP3799	52°35·5'	1°26·8'W	F	140
Eleven Greens	Lincs	TF3990	53°23·5'	0°5·8'E	X	113
Eley's Corner	Suff	TM0445	52°4·2'	0°59·0'E	X	155
Elf Hall	Cumbr	SD1885	54°15·5'	3°15·1'W	X	96
Elf Hill	Aberd	NO7985	56°57·6'	2°20·3'W	X	45
Elfhill	Aberd	NO8085	56°57·6'	2°19·3'W	X	45
Elf Hillock	Angus	NO3470	56°49·3'	3°4·4'W	X	44
Elf Hills	Northum	NZ0185	55°9·8'	1°58·6'W	X	81
Elfhole Fm	N Yks	SE5834	53°48·2'	1°6·7'W	FM	105
Elf House	Moray	NJ2929	57°21·0'	3°10·3'W	X	37
Elfhowe	Cumbr	SD4699	54°23·3'	2°49·5'W	X	97
Elfin Glen	I of M	SC4493	54°18·8'	4°23·5'W	X	95
Elford	Northum	NU1830	55°34·0'	1°42·4'W	X	75
Elford	Staffs	SK1910	52°41·5'	1°42·7'W	T	128
Elford Closes	Cambs	TL5072	52°19·8'	0°12·5'E	T	154
Elford Heath	Staffs	SJ8129	52°51·7'	2°16·5'W	X	127
Elfordlow Fm	Staffs	SK1909	52°40·9'	1°42·7'W	FM	128
Elford Park	Staffs	SK1812	52°42·6'	1°43·6'W	X	128
Elgar	Cered	SN6586	52°27·6'	3°58·8'W	X	135
Elger Wood	Corn	SX3198	50°45·2'	4°23·4'W	F	190
Elgin	Moray	NJ2162	57°38·7'	3°18·9'W	T	28
Elginhaugh	Midlo	NT3167	55°53·7'	3°5·8'W	X	66
Elginshill	Moray	NJ2663	57°39·3'	3°13·9'W	X	28
Elgol	Highld	NG5213	57°8·7'	6°5·5'W	T	32
Elham	Kent	TR1743	51°8·9'	1°6·6'E	T	179,189
Elhampark Wood	Kent	TR1645	51°10·0'	1°5·8'E	F	179,189
Elia Ho	Northum	NY8547	54°49·3'	2°13·6'W	X	87
Elias's Stot Wood	N Yks	SD9398	54°22·9'	2°6·0'W	F	98
Elibank	Scot Bord	NT3936	55°37·1'	2°57·7'W	X	73
Elibank and Traquair Forest	Scot Bord	NT3736	55°37·1'	2°59·6'W	F	73
Elibank Craig	Scot Bord	NT4035	55°36·5'	2°56·7'W	H	73
Elibank Law	Scot Bord	NT3835	55°36·5'	2°58·6'W	H	73
Eliburn	W Loth	NT0367	55°53·4'	3°32·6'W	T	65
Elidir Fach	Gwyn	SH6061	53°7·9'	4°5·2'W	X	115
Elidir Fawr	Gwyn	SH6161	53°7·9'	4°4·3'W	H	115
Elie Ho	Fife	NO4900	56°11·6'	2°48·9'W	X	59
Elie Ness	Fife	NT4999	56°11·1'	2°48·9'W	X	59
Eligar	N Eil	NF8122	57°10·9'	7°16·3'W	H	31
Elilaw	Northum	NT9708	55°22·2'	2°2·4'W	X	81
Elim	I of Angl	SH3584	53°19·9'	4°28·3'W	T	114
Eling	Hants	SU3612	50°54·6'	1°28·9'W	T	196
Eling	W Berks	SU5275	51°28·5'	1°14·7'W	T	174
Eliock	D & G	NS7907	55°20·8'	3°54·1'W	A	71,78
Eliock Br	D & G	NS8008	55°21·3'	3°53·1'W	X	71,78
Eliock Burn	D & G	NS7906	55°20·2'	3°54·0'W	W	71,78
Eliock Grange	D & G	NS8007	55°20·8'	3°53·1'W	X	71,78
Eliock Wood	D & G	NS8305	55°19·8'	3°50·2'W	F	71,78
Eliott's Pike	Northum	NY5987	55°10·8'	2°38·2'W	H	80
Eliseg's Pillar	Denb	SJ2044	52°59·5'	3°11·1'W	A	117
Elisfield Manor	Hants	SU6445	51°12·3'	1°4·6'W	X	185
Elishaw	Northum	NY8695	55°15·2'	2°12·8'W	X	80
Elisheugh Hill	Scot Bord	NT8021	55°29·2'	2°18·6'W	H	74
Elistoun Hill	Clackm	NS9298	56°10·0'	3°43·9'W	X	58
Elizafield	D & G	NY0374	55°3·3'	3°30·7'W	X	84
Eliza Fm	Durham	NZ0945	54°48·2'	1°51·2'W	FM	88
Elkesley	Notts	SK6875	53°16·3'	0°58·4'W	T	120

Elkington	Northnts	SP6276	52°22·9'	1°4·9'W	T	140
Elkington Lodge	Northnts	SP6277	52°23·5'	1°4·9'W	X	140
Elkington Lodge	Northnts	SP6477	52°23·5'	1°3·2'W	X	140
Elkins Green	Essex	TL6001	51°41·3'	0°19·3'E	T	167
Elkstone	Glos	SO9612	51°48·6'	2°3·1'W	T	163
Elkstone Fm	Glos	SO9611	51°48·1'	2°3·1'W	FM	163
Ella	Aberd	NJ6459	57°37·4'	2°35·7'W	X	29
Ellacombe	Torbay	SX9264	50°28·2'	3°30·9'W	T	202
Ellacott	Devon	SX4790	50°41·6'	4°9·6'W	A	191
Ella Dyke	E Yorks	TA0144	53°53·2'	0°27·4'W	W	106,107
Ella Hill	E Yorks	SE9636	53°48·9'	0°32·1'W	X	106
Ella Ho	N Yks	SE5161	54°2·8'	1°12·8'W	X	100
Ellan	Highld	NH8922	57°16·8'	3°50·0'W	T	35,36
Ellanbane	I of M	SC4094	54°19·2'	4°27·2'W	X	95
Elland	Cald	SE1121	53°41·4'	1°49·6'W	T	104
Ellanderroch	Stir	NS3990	56°4·8'	4°34·8'W	X	56
Elland Lower Edge	Cald	SE1221	53°41·4'	1°48·7'W	T	104
Elland Park Wood	Cald	SE1122	53°41·9'	1°49·6'W	F	104
Ellands	Highld	NH9557	57°35·7'	3°44·9'W	X	27
Ellands Fm	Northnts	TL0884	52°26·8'	0°24·3'W	FM	142
Elland Upper Edge	Cald	SE1220	53°40·8'	1°48·7'W	T	104
Ellaneorn	Highld	NJ0119	57°15·3'	3°38·0'W	X	36
Ellan ny Maughot	I of M	SC2282	54°12·4'	4°43·3'W	X	95
Ellan, The	I of M	SC3898	54°21·4'	4°29·2'W	X	95
Ellan Vannin	Highld	NH6463	57°38·4'	4°16·2'W	X	21
Ellar Carr	Brad	SE0637	53°50·0'	1°54·1'W	X	104
Ellarcarr Pike	N Yks	SE1652	53°58·1'	1°45·0'W	X	104
Ellary	Arg & Bt	NR7376	55°55·7'	5°37·6'W	T	62
Ellary Burn	Arg & Bt	NR7477	55°56·2'	5°36·7'W	W	62
Ella's Fm	Leic	SK6323	52°48·3'	1°3·5'W	FM	129
Ellastone	Staffs	SK1143	52°59·3'	1°49·8'W	T	119,128
Ellaway's Barn	Oxon	SU4686	51°34·5'	1°19·8'W	X	174
Ell Barrow	Wilts	SU0751	51°15·7'	1°53·6'W	X	184
Ell Barrow (Long Barrow)	Wilts	SU0751	51°15·7'	1°53·6'W	A	184
Ellbatch Wood	Worcs	SO7366	52°17·7'	2°23·4'W	F	138,149,150
Ellbridge	Corn	SX4063	50°26·9'	4°14·8'W	X	201
Ell Brook	Glos	SO7425	51°55·6'	2°22·3'W	W	162
Ellel	Lancs	SD4856	54°0·1'	2°47·2'W	T	102
Ellel Crag	Lancs	SD5054	53°59·0'	2°45·3'W	X	102
Ellel Grange	Lancs	SD4853	53°58·5'	2°47·2'W	X	102
Ellemford	Scot Bord	NT7260	55°50·2'	2°26·4'W	X	67,74
Ellemford Bridge	Scot Bord	NT7260	55°50·2'	2°26·4'W	X	67,74
Ellemford Covert	Scot Bord	NT7160	55°50·2'	2°27·3'W	F	67,74
Ellem Lodge	Scot Bord	NT7259	55°49·7'	2°26·4'W	X	67
Ellenabeich	Arg & Bt	NM7417	56°17·8'	5°38·7'W	T	55
Ellen Bank	Cumbr	NY2340	54°45·2'	3°11·4'W	X	85
Ellenbank Hall	Cumbr	NY1439	54°44·6'	3°19·8'W	X	89
Ellen Bank (Hotel)	Cumbr	NY0537	54°43·4'	3°28·1'W	X	89
Ellenber Fm	N Yks	SE0252	53°58·1'	1°57·8'W	FM	104
Ellenborough	Cumbr	NY0435	54°42·3'	3°29·0'W	T	89
Ellenbrook	Herts	TL2008	51°45·7'	0°15·3'W	T	166
Ellenbrook	I of M	SC3674	54°8·4'	4°30·2'W	X	95
Ellenbrook	Salf	SD7201	53°30·5'	2°24·9'W	X	109
Ellen Dale	Cumbr	NY1038	54°44·0'	3°23·4'W	X	89
Ellenden Fm	Kent	TQ7632	51°3·8'	0°31·1'E	FM	188
Ellenden Fm	Kent	TR0962	51°19·3'	1°0·4'E	FM	179
Ellenglaze	Corn	SW7757	50°22·5'	5°7·8'W	T	200
Ellenhall	Cumbr	NY1138	54°44·0'	3°22·5'W	X	89
Ellenhall	Staffs	SJ8426	52°50·1'	2°13·8'W	T	127
Ellens	Surrey	TQ1035	51°6·4'	0°25·3'W	X	187
Ellens Geo	Highld	ND3240	58°20·9'	3°9·2'W	X	12
Ellen's Green	Surrey	TQ0935	51°6·5'	0°26·2'W	T	187
Ellen's Twr	I of Angl	SH2081	53°18·0'	4°41·7'W	X	114
Ellenswell	Pemb	SN0517	51°49·3'	4°49·4'W	X	158
Ellenthorpe Hall	N Yks	SE4167	54°6·1'	1°22·0'W	X	99
Ellenthorpe Ings	N Yks	SE4266	54°5·5'	1°21·1'W	X	99
Ellenthorpe Lodge	N Yks	SE4267	54°6·1'	1°21·0'W	X	99
Ellen Villa	Cumbr	NY1340	54°45·1'	3°20·7'W	X	85
Ellenwhorne	E Susx	TQ7921	50°57·9'	0°33·3'E	X	199
Ellenwray	Cumbr	SD5587	54°16·8'	2°41·1'W	X	97
Elleray	Cumbr	SD4198	54°22·7'	2°54·1'W	X	96,97
Ellerbeck	Cumbr	NY0929	54°39·1'	3°24·2'W	X	89
Ellerbeck	Cumbr	SD1196	54°21·4'	3°21·8'W	X	96
Eller Beck	Durham	NY9910	54°29·4'	2°0·5'W	W	92
Eller Beck	N Yks	NZ8302	54°24·6'	0°42·8'W	W	94
Ellerbeck	N Yks	SD7378	54°12·1'	2°24·4'W	X	98
Eller Beck	N Yks	SD9761	54°2·9'	2°2·3'W	W	98
Eller Beck	N Yks	SD9854	53°59·2'	2°1·4'W	W	103
Eller Beck	N Yks	SE1978	54°12·1'	1°42·1'W	W	99
Ellerbeck	N Yks	SE4396	54°21·7'	1°19·9'W	T	99
Eller Beck	N Yks	SE4785	54°15·8'	1°16·3'W	W	100
Eller Beck	N Yks	SE8797	54°21·9'	0°39·2'W	W	94,101
Eller Beck Br	N Yks	SE8598	54°22·5'	0°41·1'W	X	94,100
Ellerbeck Fm	Cumbr	SD4694	54°20·6'	2°49·4'W	FM	97
Ellerbeck Pasture	N Yks	SD7578	54°12·1'	2°22·6'W	X	98
Ellerburn	N Yks	SE8484	54°14·9'	0°42·2'W	T	100
Eller Burn	Scot Bord	NT7660	55°50·2'	2°22·6'W	W	67
Ellerby	N Yks	NZ7914	54°31·1'	0°46·4'W	T	94
Ellerby Bank Top	N Yks	NZ7913	54°30·6'	0°46·4'W	X	94
Ellerby Grange	E Yorks	TA1638	53°49·8'	0°13·8'W	X	107
Ellerby Moor	N Yks	NZ7813	54°30·6'	0°47·3'W	X	94
Eller Carr	N Yks	SD8778	54°12·1'	2°11·5'W	X	98
Eller Carr Moss	N Yks	SD8678	54°12·1'	2°12·5'W	X	98
Ellercow	Cumbr	NY5934	54°42·2'	2°37·8'W	X	91
Ellerdine	Wrekin	SJ6020	52°46·8'	2°35·2'W	T	127
Ellerdine Heath	Wrekin	SJ6122	52°47·9'	2°34·3'W	T	127
Eller Edge Nook	N Yks	SE0961	54°2·9'	1°51·3'W	X	99
Ellergarth	Cumbr	NY3106	54°26·9'	3°3·4'W	X	90
Ellergill	Cumbr	NY6405	54°26·6'	2°32·9'W	X	91
Eller Gill	Cumbr	NY6831	54°40·6'	2°29·4'W	W	91
Ellergill	Cumbr	NY7301	54°24·5'	2°24·5'W	X	91
Ellergill Beck	Cumbr	NY6303	54°25·5'	2°33·8'W	W	91
Ellergill Ho	N Yks	SD9953	53°58·6'	2°0·5'W	X	103
Ellergoffe Knowe	E Ayr	NS6815	55°24·9'	4°4·7'W	X	71
Ellergower Knowe	D & G	NX4780	55°5·7'	4°23·4'W	X	77
Ellergreen	Cumbr	SD4995	54°21·1'	2°46·7'W	X	97
Ellerhayes	Devon	SS9702	50°48·7'	3°27·3'W	T	192
Eller Head	Lancs	SD7850	53°57·0'	2°19·7'W	X	103
Eller Hill	Cumbr	SD7297	54°22·3'	2°25·4'W	X	98
Eller Ho	N Yks	SE6498	54°22·6'	1°0·5'W	X	94,100

Ellerholme Fm	N Lincs	SE7004	53°31·9'	0°56·2'W	FM	112
Eller How	Cumbr	SD4181	54°13·5'	2°53·9'W	X	96,97
Elleric	Arg & Bt	NN0348	56°35·2'	5°12·0'W	X	50
Ellerker	E Yorks	SE9229	53°45·2'	0°35·9'W	T	106
Ellerker North Wold	E Yorks	SE9430	53°45·7'	0°34·0'W	X	106
Ellerkin Scar	N Yks	SD9692	54°19·7'	2°3·3'W	X	144
Eller Mire	Cumbr	SD2385	54°15·5'	3°10·5'W	X	96
Ellermire Fms	N Yks	SE5698	54°22·7'	1°7·9'W	FM	100
Elleron Lodge	N Yks	SE7891	54°18·8'	0°47·6'W	X	94,100
Ellers	Cumbr	NY2417	54°32·8'	3°10·1'W	X	89,90
Ellers	Cumbr	SD5381	54°13·6'	2°42·8'W	X	97
Ellers	N Yks	NY8401	54°24·5'	2°14·4'W	X	91,92
Ellers	N Yks	SE0043	53°53·2'	1°59·6'W	X	104
Ellers	N Yks	SE0899	54°23·4'	1°52·2'W	X	99
Ellers	Red & Cl	NZ6318	54°33·4'	1°1·1'W	X	94
Ellers Burn	Arg & Bt	NS1177	55°57·2'	5°1·2'W	W	63
Ellers Cleuch Rig	Scot Bord	NT1216	55°26·1'	3°23·0'W	H	78
Ellers Cottage	N Lincs	SE7605	53°32·4'	0°50·8'W	X	112
Ellers Fm	Lancs	SD5365	54°5·0'	2°42·7'W	FM	97
Ellers Fm	Lincs	SK8094	53°26·4'	0°47·3'W	FM	112
Ellers Fm	N Yks	NZ7205	54°26·4'	0°53·0'W	FM	94
Ellers Fm	N Yks	SE7257	54°0·5'	0°53·7'W	FM	105,106
Ellershaw Fm	N Yks	SE1976	54°11·0'	1°42·1'W	FM	99
Ellers Hill	Durham	NY9347	54°49·3'	2°6·1'W	X	87
Ellers Ho	N Yks	NZ7305	54°26·4'	0°52·0'W	X	94
Ellershope	Northum	NY8548	54°49·8'	2°13·6'W	X	87
Ellerside	Cumbr	SD3580	54°12·9'	2°59·4'W	H	96,97
Ellerside	Cumbr	SD3586	54°16·2'	2°59·5'W	X	96,97
Ellerside Breast Plantn	Cumbr	SD3579	54°12·4'	2°59·4'W	F	96,97
Ellerside Fm	Cumbr	SD3578	54°11·9'	2°59·4'W	FM	96,97
Ellerside Moss	Cumbr	SD3580	54°12·9'	2°59·4'W	X	96,97
Ellerslee	D & G	NX9785	55°9·2'	3°36·6'W	X	78
Ellerslie Fm	I of M	SC3278	54°10·5'	4°34·0'W	FM	95
Ellers, The	Cumbr	NY3048	54°49·6'	3°5·0'W	X	85
Ellers Wood	N Yks	SE5292	54°19·5'	1°11·6'W	F	100
Ellers Wood	N Yks	SE5589	54°17·9'	1°8·9'W	F	100
Ellerton	E Yorks	SE7039	53°50·8'	0°55·7'W	T	105,106
Ellerton	N Yks	SE2597	54°22·3'	1°36·5'W	T	99
Ellerton	Shrops	SJ7125	52°49·5'	2°25·4'W	T	127
Ellerton Abbey	N Yks	SE0797	54°22·4'	1°53·1'W	X	99
Ellerton Common	E Yorks	SE7040	53°51·3'	0°55·7'W	X	105,106
Ellerton Fm	Shrops	SJ7127	52°50·6'	2°25·4'W	FM	127
Ellerton Grange	Cumbr	NY4446	54°48·6'	2°51·9'W	X	85
Ellerton Grange	Staffs	SJ7225	52°49·5'	2°24·5'W	X	127
Ellerton Grove	Shrops	SJ7126	52°50·1'	2°25·4'W	X	127
Ellerton Hill	N Yks	SE2698	54°22·9'	1°35·6'W	X	99
Ellerton Lodge	N Yks	SE1098	54°22·9'	1°50·3'W	X	99
Ellerton Moor	N Yks	SE0696	54°21·8'	1°54·0'W	X	99
Ellerton Wood	Shrops	SJ7127	52°50·6'	2°25·4'W	F	127
Ellerwood	Cumbr	SD3994	54°20·5'	2°55·9'W	X	96,97
Ellery Grain	Cumbr	NY5680	55°7·0'	2°41·0'W	W	80
Ellery Hill	Arg & Bt	NM8329	56°24·5'	5°30·6'W	H	49
Ellery Hill	N Yks	SE2297	54°22·3'	1°39·3'W	X	99
Ellesborough	Bucks	SP8306	51°45·0'	0°47·5'W	T	165
Ellesmere	Shrops	SJ3934	52°54·2'	2°54·0'W	T	126
Ellesmere	Suff	TM0877	52°21·3'	1°3·7'E	X	144
Ellesmere Fm	Ches	SJ7149	53°2·5'	2°25·5'W	FM	118
Ellesmere Park	Salf	SJ7799	53°29·5'	2°20·4'W	T	109
Ellesmere Port	Ches	SJ4175	53°16·4'	2°52·7'W	T	117
Elley	Devon	SX7799	50°46·9'	3°44·3'W	X	191
Ellfield Ho	Staffs	SK1408	52°40·4'	1°47·2'W	X	128
Ellfoot Ho	Northum	NY8663	54°57·9'	2°12·7'W	X	87
Ellibister	Orkney	HY3821	59°4·6'	3°4·4'W	X	6
Ellicar Fm	Notts	SK7192	53°25·4'	0°55·5'W	FM	112
Ellick	Moray	NJ1722	57°17·1'	3°22·2'W	X	36
Ellick Fm	N Som	ST4958	51°19·4'	2°43·5'W	FM	172,182
Ellicombe	Devon	SS7405	50°50·1'	3°47·0'W	X	191
Ellicombe	Somer	SS9844	51°11·4'	3°27·2'W	T	181
Ellinge	Kent	TR2342	51°8·2'	1°11·7'E	X	179,189
Ellingham	Hants	SU1408	50°52·5'	1°47·7'W	T	195
Ellingham	Norf	TM3692	52°28·7'	1°28·9'E	T	134
Ellingham	Northum	NU1725	55°31·4'	1°43·4'W	T	75
Ellinghurst Fm	S Glos	ST5684	51°33·4'	2°37·7'W	FM	172
Ellingstring	N Yks	SE1783	54°14·8'	1°43·9'W	T	99
Ellingstring Plantn	N Yks	SE1682	54°14·2'	1°44·9'W	F	99
Ellington	Cambs	TL1571	52°19·7'	0°18·3'W	T	153
Ellington	Northum	NZ2791	55°13·0'	1°34·1'W	T	81
Ellington Banks	N Yks	SE2772	54°8·8'	1°34·8'W	X	99
Ellington Firth	N Yks	SE1885	54°15·9'	1°43·0'W	F	99
Ellington Hill	Cambs	TL1570	52°19·2'	0°18·4'W	X	153
Ellington Thorpe	Cambs	TL1570	52°19·2'	0°18·4'W	T	153
Ellin's Tower	I of Angl	SH2082	53°18·5'	4°41·7'W	X	114
Elliot	Angus	NO6139	56°32·7'	2°37·6'W	T	54
Elliothead	Pth & Kin	NO1518	56°21·1'	3°22·1'W	X	58
Elliots Fm	Kent	TR0267	51°22·2'	0°54·5'E	FM	178
Elliots Green	Somer	ST7945	51°12·5'	2°17·7'W	T	183
Elliot's Town	Caer	SO1402	51°42·8'	3°14·3'W	T	171
Elliotts	W Susx	TQ1725	51°1·0'	0°19·5'W	X	187,198
Elliott's Fm	Kent	TQ5343	51°10·2'	0°11·7'E	FM	188
Elliott's Shed	Wilts	ST9120	50°59·0'	2°7·3'W	X	184
Elliot Water	Angus	NO5941	56°33·8'	2°39·6'W	W	54
Ellisade	D & G	NX7576	55°4·0'	3°57·0'W	X	84
Ellis Bank	Ches	SJ9679	53°18·7'	2°3·2'W	X	118
Ellis Barn	Kent	TQ9633	51°4·0'	0°48·2'E	X	189
Ellis Beck	N Yks	SE8978	54°11·6'	0°37·7'W	W	101
Ellis' Close Fm	N Yks	SE9894	54°20·2'	0°29·1'W	FM	94,101
Ellis Crag	Northum	NT7401	55°18·4'	2°24·1'W	X	80
Ellisfield	Hants	SU6346	51°12·8'	1°5·5'W	T	185
Ellis Fm	E Susx	TQ5727	51°1·5'	0°14·7'E	FM	188,199
Ellis Fm	Hants	SU6855	51°17·6'	1°1·1'W	FM	175,185,186
Ellis Fm	Lincs	SK9674	53°15·5'	0°33·2'W	FM	121
Ellis Fm	Norf	TF9639	52°55·0'	0°55·3'E	FM	132
Ellis Gill	N Yks	SD9463	54°4·0'	2°5·1'W	W	98
Ellis Green	Essex	TL6034	51°59·1'	0°20·2'E	X	154
Ellishadder	Highld	NG5065	57°36·6'	6°10·7'W	T	23,24
Ellishayes Fm	Devon	ST1503	50°49·5'	3°12·0'W	FM	192,193
Ellishill	Aberd	NK0948	57°31·6'	1°50·5'W	X	30
Ellis Hill	Staffs	SK1347	53°1·4'	1°48·0'W	X	119,128
Ellis Laithe	Wakf	SE3713	53°37·0'	1°26·0'W	X	110,111
Ellisland Fm	D & G	NX9283	55°8·0'	3°41·2'W	FM	78

Ellismos	Aberd	NJ8012	57°12·2′	2°19·4′W	X	38
Ellismuir Fm	C of Glas	NS6863	55°50·8′	4°6·1′W	FM	64
Ellis of Dumbreck	Aberd	NJ8829	57°21·3′	2°11·5′W	X	38
Ellis's Fm	Glos	SO7612	51°48·6′	2°20·5′W	FM	162
Ellister	Shetld	HU3822	59°59·1′	1°18·6′W	X	4
Elliston	Renf	NS3960	55°48·6′	4°33·7′W	X	63
Elliston	Scot Bord	NT5628	55°32·9′	2°41·4′W	T	73
Ellistown	Leic	SK4311	52°41·9′	1°21·4′W	T	129
Ellis Windmill	Lincs	SK9672	53°14·4′	0°33·3′W	X	121
Ellis Wood	York	SE6261	54°2·7′	1°2·8′W	F	100
Ellivreid	Moray	NJ2632	57°22·6′	3°13·4′W	X	37
Ellmore Fm	Lincs	TA0600	53°29·4′	0°23·7′W	FM	112
Ellon	Aberd	NJ9530	57°21·9′	2°4·5′W	T	30
Ellon	Highld	NJ0617	57°14·3′	3°33·0′W	X	36
Ellonby	Cumbr	NY4235	54°42·6′	2°53·6′W	T	90
Ellough	Suff	TM4486	52°25·3′	1°35·7′E	T	156
Ellough Hill	Suff	TM4389	52°26·9′	1°35·0′E	X	156
Ellough Moor	Suff	TM4488	52°26·3′	1°35·8′E	X	156
Elloughton	E Yorks	SE9427	53°44·1′	0°34·1′W	T	106
Elloughton Dale	E Yorks	SE9528	53°44·6′	0°33·2′W	X	106
Elloughton Hill	E Yorks	SE9527	53°44·1′	0°33·2′W	X	106
Elloughton Wold	E Yorks	SE9528	53°44·6′	0°33·2′W	X	106
Ell Rig	D & G	NX7787	55°10·0′	3°55·4′W	H	78
Ellrig	S Lanak	NS6046	55°41·5′	4°13·2′W	X	64
Ellrig, Loch	Falk	NS8874	55°57·0′	3°47·2′W	W	65
Ellrig Moss	D & G	NX7787	55°10·0′	3°55·4′W	X	78
Ell's Fm	Oxon	SP4237	52°2·0′	1°22·9′W	FM	151
Ell's Knowe	Northum	NT8727	55°32·4′	2°11·9′W	X	74
Ellson Fell	D & G	NY4198	55°16·6′	2°55·3′W	H	79
Ellston Hill	Dorset	ST6301	50°48·7′	2°31·1′W	X	194
Ell Wick	Shetld	HU3468	60°23·9′	1°22·5′W	W	2,3
Ellwood	Glos	SO5908	51°46·4′	2°35·3′W	T	162
Ell Wood	Worcs	SO9679	52°24·8′	2°3·1′W	F	139
Ellwood Ho	Northum	NY9173	55°3·3′	2°8·0′W	X	87
Elly	Angus	NO3862	56°45·0′	3°0·4′W	X	44
Elly Cleugh	E Loth	NT7267	55°54·0′	2°26·4′W	X	67
Ellyhill Fm	Darl	NZ3117	54°33·1′	1°30·8′W	FM	93
Elm	Cambs	TF4706	52°38·1′	0°10·7′E	T	143
Elmbank	Scot Bord	NT7141	55°40·0′	2°27·2′W	X	74
Elm Bottom Cross	Hants	SU6154	51°17·1′	1°7·1′W	X	185
Elm Br	Heref	SO3928	51°57·1′	2°52·9′W	X	149,161
Elmbridge	Glos	SO8519	51°52·4′	2°12·7′W	T	162
Elmbridge	Worcs	SO9067	52°18·3′	2°8·4′W	T	150
Elmbridge Fm	Essex	TL6123	51°53·2′	0°20·8′E	FM	167
Elmbrook Fm	Essex	TQ6698	51°39·6′	0°24·4′E	FM	167,177
Elm Bush	Northum	NU2801	55°18·4′	1°33·1′W	X	81
Elm Clough Wood	Lancs	SD6946	53°54·8′	2°27·9′W	F	103
Elm Corner	Surrey	TQ0757	51°18·3′	0°27·5′W	T	187
Elmcote Fms	Glos	SO7603	51°43·7′	2°20·5′W	FM	162
Elm Cross	Wilts	SU1176	51°29·2′	1°50·1′W	T	173
Elmdon	Essex	TL4639	52°2·0′	0°8·1′E	T	154
Elmdon	Sol	SP1783	52°26·9′	1°44·6′W	T	139
Elmdon Heath	Sol	SP1680	52°25·3′	1°45·5′W	T	139
Elmdon Lee	Essex	TL4838	52°1·5′	0°9·8′E	X	154
Elmdown	Bucks	SU7789	51°35·9′	0°52·9′W	X	175
Elmead	Devon	SX5696	50°45·0′	4°2·1′W	X	191
Elmer	W Susx	SU9800	50°47·7′	0°36·2′W	T	197
Elmerdale	Norf	TG1329	52°49·2′	1°10·1′E	X	133
Elmers Copse	W Susx	SU8528	51°2·9′	0°46·9′W	F	186,197
Elmers End	Brom	TQ3568	51°23·9′	0°3·2′W	T	177
Elmers Green	Lancs	SD4906	53°33·1′	2°45·8′W	T	108
Elmers Marsh	W Susx	SU8628	51°2·9′	0°46·0′W	T	186,197
Elmestree Ho	Glos	ST8791	51°37·3′	2°10·9′W	X	162,173
Elm Farm	Somer	ST6041	51°10·2′	2°33·9′W	FM	183
Elmfield	Corn	SX2290	50°41·2′	4°30·8′W	X	190
Elmfield	I of W	SZ6091	50°43·2′	1°8·6′W	T	196
Elmfield School	Herts	TL1215	51°49·6′	0°22·1′W	X	166
Elm Fm	Cambs	TL2092	52°31·0′	0°13·5′W	FM	142
Elm Fm	Ches	SJ5158	53°7·3′	2°43·5′W	FM	117
Elm Fm	Essex	TL6804	51°42·8′	0°26·3′E	FM	167
Elm Fm	Essex	TL8823	51°52·7′	0°44·3′E	FM	168
Elm Fm	Essex	TM1516	51°48·3′	1°7·5′E	FM	168,169
Elm Fm	Essex	TQ9397	51°38·5′	0°47·8′E	FM	168
Elm Fm	Glos	SO7504	51°44·3′	2°21·3′W	FM	162
Elm Fm	Hants	SU4152	51°16·2′	1°24·3′W	FM	185
Elm Fm	I of W	SZ4288	50°41·6′	1°23·9′W	FM	196
Elm Fm	Kent	TQ8666	51°22·0′	0°40·7′E	FM	178
Elm Fm	Lancs	SD4546	53°54·7′	2°49·8′W	FM	102
Elm Fm	Lincs	TF2211	52°41·2′	0°11·3′W	FM	131,142
Elm Fm	Norf	TG2330	52°49·5′	1°19·0′E	FM	133
Elm Fm	Norf	TM1696	52°31·4′	1°11·4′E	FM	144
Elm Fm	Norf	TM3597	52°31·4′	1°28·3′E	FM	134
Elm Fm	Oxon	SP3637	52°2·0′	1°28·1′W	FM	151
Elm Fm	S Glos	ST6783	51°32·9′	2°28·2′W	FM	172
Elm Fm	Suff	TL7651	52°8·0′	0°34·7′E	FM	155
Elm Fm	Suff	TM0968	52°16·4′	1°4·2′E	FM	155
Elm Fm	Suff	TM1956	52°9·7′	1°12·5′E	FM	156
Elm Fm	Suff	TM3574	52°19·0′	1°27·3′E	FM	156
Elm Fm	Suff	TM5199	52°32·1′	1°42·5′E	FM	134
Elm Gate	Corn	SX3957	50°23·7′	4°15·5′W	X	201
Elmgill	Cumbr	SD7899	54°23·4′	2°19·9′W	X	98
Elm Grange	Darl	NZ2321	54°35·3′	1°38·2′W	X	93
Elm Green Fm	Heref	SO4029	51°57·6′	2°52·0′W	FM	149,161
Elmgreen Fm	Suff	TL9156	52°10·4′	0°48·0′E	FM	155
Elm Grove	Pemb	SN0801	51°40·7′	4°46·2′W	X	158
Elmgrove Fm	E Susx	TQ3516	50°55·9′	0°4·3′W	FM	198
Elmgrove Fm	W Berks	SU4775	51°28·6′	1°19·0′W	FM	174
Elm Grove Ho	Cambs	TL4893	52°31·1′	0°11·3′E	X	143
Elm Hag	N Yks	SE5479	54°12·5′	1°9·9′W	F	100
Elm Hall	Suff	TM2966	52°14·9′	1°21·7′E	X	156
Elm Hall Fm	Essex	TL8116	51°49·0′	0°38·0′E	FM	168
Elmham Ho	Norf	TF9821	52°45·2′	0°56·4′E	X	132
Elm Heads	Red & Cl	NZ7014	54°31·2′	0°54·7′W	X	94
Elm Hill	Dorset	ST8426	51°2·2′	2°13·3′W	T	183
Elm Hill	Worcs	SO8161	52°15·0′	2°16·3′W	X	138,150
Elm Hill Ho	Kent	TQ7330	51°2·8′	0°28·5′E	X	188
Elm Ho	N Yks	NZ6400	54°23·7′	1°0·4′W	X	94
Elm Ho	N Yks	SE0591	54°19·1′	1°55·0′W	X	98
Elm Ho	Staffs	SO8286	52°28·5′	2°15·5′W	X	138
Elm Ho	Suff	TM1877	52°21·1′	1°12·5′E	X	156
Elm Houses	N Yks	SE6195	54°21·1′	1°3·3′W	X	94,100
Elmhow	Cumbr	NY3715	54°31·8′	2°58·0′W	X	90
Elmhurst	Bucks	SP8215	51°49·9′	0°48·2′W	T	165
Elmhurst	Staffs	SJ8959	53°7·9′	2°9·5′W	X	118
Elmhurst	Staffs	SJ9029	52°51·7′	2°8·5′W	X	127
Elmhurst	Staffs	SK1112	52°42·6′	1°49·8′W	T	128
Elmhurst Fm	Kent	TQ6439	51°7·8′	0°21·0′E	FM	188
Elmhurst Fm	Warw	SP1363	52°16·1′	1°48·2′W	FM	151
Elmhurst Fm	Warw	SP4484	52°27·4′	1°20·7′W	FM	140
Elmington Manor Fm	S Glos	ST5581	51°31·8′	2°38·5′W	FM	172
Elmington Top Lodge	Northnts	TL0689	52°29·5′	0°25·9′W	X	142
Elmleaze Barn	Glos	ST8788	51°35·7′	2°10·9′W	X	162,173
Elmley Brook	Worcs	SO8667	52°18·3′	2°11·9′W	W	150
Elmley Castle	Worcs	SO9841	52°4·3′	2°1·4′W	T	150
Elmley Hills	Kent	TQ9267	51°22·4′	0°45·9′E	X	178
Elmley Island	Kent	TQ9368	51°22·9′	0°46·8′E	X	178
Elmley Lovett	Worcs	SO8769	52°19·4′	2°11·0′W	T	139
Elmley Lovett Village	Worcs	SO8669	52°19·4′	2°11·9′W	A	139
Elmley Marshes	Kent	TQ9467	51°22·4′	0°47·6′E	X	178
Elm Leys Fm	Wakf	SE4513	53°36·9′	1°18·8′W	FM	111
Elm Lodge	Northnts	SP6265	52°17·0′	1°5·1′W	X	152
Elm Lodge	Northnts	TL0178	52°23·7′	0°30·5′W	X	141
Elm Lodge	Shrops	SO5076	52°23·0′	2°43·7′W	X	137,138
Elm Lodge	Suff	TM2875	52°19·8′	1°21·2′E	X	156
Elmondbury	Essex	TL4640	52°2·6′	0°8·1′E	X	154
Elmore	Glos	SO7815	51°50·2′	2°18·8′W	T	162
Elmore Back	Glos	SO7716	51°50·8′	2°19·6′W	T	162
Elmore Court	Glos	SO7815	51°50·2′	2°18·8′W	X	162
Elmore Fm	Dorset	ST3601	50°48·5′	2°54·1′W	FM	193
Elmore Hill Fm	Derby	SK1882	53°20·3′	1°43·4′W	FM	110
Elmore Ho	W Berks	SU4567	51°24·2′	1°20·8′W	X	174
Elmorepark Wood	Oxon	SU6381	51°31·7′	1°5·1′W	F	175
Elm Park	Hav	TQ5285	51°32·8′	0°11·9′E	T	177
Elm Pot	Cumbr	SD7298	54°22·8′	2°25·4′W	X	98
Elmridge	Lancs	SD5940	53°51·5′	2°37·0′W	X	102
Elms	Heref	SO6046	52°6·9′	2°34·7′W	X	149
Elmsall Lodge Fm	Wakf	SE4513	53°36·9′	1°18·8′W	FM	111
Elmscleugh	E Loth	NT6971	55°56·1′	2°29·3′W	X	67
Elmscleugh Water	E Loth	NT7072	55°56·7′	2°28·4′W	W	67
Elmscott	Devon	SS2321	50°57·9′	4°30·9′W	T	190
Elmsett	Suff	TM0546	52°4·7′	0°59·9′E	T	155
Elmsett Gate Fm	Suff	TM0645	52°4·1′	1°0·7′E	FM	155
Elmsett Hall Fm	Suff	TM0647	52°5·2′	1°0·8′E	FM	155
Elmsett Park Wood	Suff	TM0646	52°4·7′	1°0·8′E	F	155
Elmsfield Ho	Cumbr	SD5180	54°13·0′	2°44·7′W	X	97
Elms Fm	Beds	TL0851	52°9·0′	0°24·9′W	FM	153
Elms Fm	Cambs	TL2792	52°30·9′	0°7·3′W	FM	142
Elms Fm	Essex	TL5909	51°45·7′	0°18·6′E	FM	167
Elms Fm	Essex	TL6034	51°59·1′	0°20·2′E	FM	154
Elms Fm	Essex	TL6308	51°45·0′	0°22·1′E	FM	167
Elms Fm	Essex	TL6927	51°55·2′	0°27·8′E	FM	167
Elm's Fm	Essex	TL7237	52°0·5′	0°30·8′E	FM	154
Elms Fm	Essex	TL7619	51°50·7′	0°33·7′E	FM	167
Elms Fm	Essex	TL8204	51°42·5′	0°38·5′E	FM	168
Elm's Fm	Essex	TL9132	51°57·4′	0°47·2′E	FM	168
Elms Fm	E Susx	TQ7726	51°0·6′	0°31·8′E	FM	188,199
Elms Fm	E Susx	TQ8815	50°54·5′	0°40·8′E	FM	189,199
Elms Fm	E Yorks	SE6920	53°40·6′	0°56·9′W	FM	105,106
Elms Fm	Heref	SO4026	51°56·0′	2°52·0′W	FM	161
Elms Fm	Leic	SK3107	52°39·8′	1°32·1′W	FM	140
Elms Fm	Leic	SK5003	52°37·6′	1°15·3′W	FM	140
Elms Fm	Leic	SP5297	52°34·3′	1°13·6′W	FM	140
Elms Fm	Lincs	SK9647	53°0·9′	0°33·7′W	FM	130
Elms Fm	Lincs	TF3136	52°54·6′	0°2·7′W	FM	131
Elms Fm	Norf	TM1091	52°28·8′	1°6·0′E	FM	144
Elms Fm	Northnts	SP7949	52°8·2′	0°50·3′W	FM	152
Elms Fm	Oxon	SU4089	51°36·1′	1°25·0′W	FM	174
Elms Fm	Peterb	TF0601	52°36·0′	0°25·7′W	FM	142
Elms Fm	Suff	TL7856	52°10·6′	0°36·6′E	FM	155
Elms Fm	Suff	TL8951	52°7·7′	0°46·1′E	FM	155
Elms Fm	Suff	TM1065	52°14·8′	1°5·0′E	FM	155
Elms Fm	Suff	TM4779	52°21·4′	1°38·1′E	FM	156
Elms Fm	Warw	SP3857	52°12·8′	1°26·2′W	FM	151
Elms Fm	Warw	SP4191	52°31·2′	1°23·3′W	FM	140
Elms Fm, The	Ches	SJ6159	53°7·8′	2°34·6′W	FM	118
Elms Fm, The	Derby	SK4768	53°12·7′	1°17·4′W	FM	120
Elms Fm The	Leic	SP5286	52°28·4′	1°13·7′W	FM	140
Elms Fm, The	Suff	TM4978	52°20·8′	1°39·8′E	FM	156
Elms Fm, The	Thurr	TQ6385	51°32·6′	0°21·4′E	FM	177
Elms Fm, The	Warw	SP4765	52°17·1′	1°18·3′W	FM	151
Elmsgate Ho	Wilts	ST9056	51°18·4′	2°8·2′W	X	173
Elms Green	Heref	SO5056	52°12·2′	2°43·5′W	T	149
Elms Green	Worcs	SO7266	52°17·7′	2°24·2′W	T	138,149
Elms Hall	Essex	TL8329	51°56·0′	0°40·1′E	X	168
Elmshaws Fm	Essex	TQ6693	51°36·9′	0°24·3′E	FM	177,178
Elmslack	Lancs	SD4675	54°10·3′	2°49·2′W	T	97
Elmsleigh Fm	S Glos	ST5780	51°31·3′	2°36·8′W	FM	172
Elmstead	Brom	TQ4270	51°24·9′	0°2·9′E	T	177
Elmstead	Essex	TM0626	51°53·9′	1°0·1′E	T	168
Elmstead Fm	Lincs	TF4865	53°9·9′	0°13·2′E	FM	122
Elmstead Heath	Essex	TM0622	51°51·7′	0°59·9′E	T	168
Elmstead Market	Essex	TM0624	51°52·8′	1°0·0′E	T	168
Elmstead Wood	Brom	TQ4171	51°25·5′	0°2·1′E	F	177
Elmsted	Kent	TR1144	51°9·6′	1°1·5′E	T	179,189
Elms, The	Beds	TL0245	52°5·9′	0°30·3′W	X	153
Elms, The	Ches	SJ3859	53°7·7′	2°55·2′W	X	117
Elms, The	Ches	SJ4648	53°1·8′	2°47·9′W	X	117
Elms, The	Derby	SK3420	52°46·8′	1°29·4′W	X	128
Elms, The	Derby	SK4533	52°53·8′	1°19·5′W	X	129
Elms, The	Donc	SE6715	53°37·9′	0°58·8′W	X	111
Elms, The	Essex	TL5919	51°51·0′	0°18·9′E	X	167
Elms, The	Essex	TL8209	51°45·2′	0°38·6′E	X	168
Elms, The	E Susx	TQ9223	50°58·7′	0°44·5′E	X	189
Elms, The	E Yorks	TA0761	54°2·3′	0°21·5′W	X	101
Elms, The	E Yorks	TA2623	53°41·5′	0°5·1′W	X	107,113
Elms, The	E Yorks	TA2733	53°46·9′	0°3·9′W	X	107
Elms, The	E Yorks	TA2829	53°44·7′	0°3·1′W	X	107
Elms, The	Herts	TL1111	51°47·4′	0°23·0′W	X	166
Elms, The	Leic	SK6516	52°44·5′	1°1·8′W	X	129
Elms, The	Leic	SK7015	52°43·9′	0°57·4′W	X	129
Elms, The	Leic	SK8219	52°46·0′	0°46·7′W	X	130
Elms, The	Leic	SP6392	52°31·6′	1°3·9′W	X	140
Elms, The	Lincs	TF3246	52°59·9′	0°1·6′W	X	131
Elms, The	Lincs	TF5264	53°9·3′	0°16·8′E	X	122
Elms, The	Monm	SO3315	51°50·0′	2°58·0′W	X	161
Elms, The	Monm	SO4208	51°46·3′	2°50·0′W	X	161
Elms, The	N Lincs	SE9021	53°40·9′	0°37·8′W	X	106,112
Elms, The	Norf	TF6018	52°44·4′	0°22·6′E	X	132
Elms, The	Norf	TM4393	52°29·1′	1°35·1′E	A	134
Elms, The	Northnts	SP6251	52°9·5′	1°5·2′W	X	152
Elms, The	Northnts	SP8357	52°12·5′	0°46·7′W	X	152
Elms, The	Oxon	SU5886	51°34·4′	1°9·4′W	X	174
Elms, The	Peterb	TF1305	52°38·1′	0°19·4′W	X	142
Elms, The	Rut	SK9201	52°36·2′	0°38·1′W	X	141
Elms, The	S Glos	ST6693	51°38·3′	2°29·1′W	X	162,172
Elms, The	Somer	ST3348	51°13·9′	2°57·2′W	X	182
Elms, The	Staffs	SO8495	52°33·4′	2°13·8′W	X	138
Elms, The	Suff	TM0948	52°5·7′	1°3·5′E	X	155,169
Elms, The	Suff	TM3382	52°23·4′	1°25·9′E	A	156
Elms, The	Suff	TM3485	52°25·0′	1°26·9′E	X	156
Elms, The	Suff	TM5087	52°25·6′	1°41·0′E	X	156
Elms, The	Wilts	ST8036	51°7·6′	2°16·8′W	X	183
Elms, The	Wilts	SU0090	51°36·8′	1°59·6′W	X	163,173
Elms, The	Worcs	SO7367	52°18·3′	2°23·4′W	X	138,150
Elms, The	Worcs	SO7957	52°12·9′	2°18·0′W	X	150
Elms, The	Worcs	SO8753	52°10·7′	2°11·0′W	X	150
Elms, The	Worcs	SO9634	52°0·5′	2°3·1′W	X	150
Elms, The	Wrex	SJ3654	53°5·0′	2°56·9′W	X	117
Elms, The	W Susx	SZ8496	50°45·7′	0°48·2′W	X	197
Elmsthorpe	Leic	SP4696	52°33·8′	1°18·9′W	T	140
Elmstone	Kent	TQ8538	51°6·9′	0°39·0′E	X	189
Elmstone	Kent	TR2560	51°17·9′	1°14·1′E	T	179
Elmstone Hardwicke	Glos	SO9226	51°56·2′	2°6·6′W	T	163
Elmstone Hole	Kent	TQ8649	51°12·8′	0°40·2′E	X	189
Elmswell	E Yorks	SE9958	54°0·7′	0°28·9′W	T	106
Elmswell	Suff	TL9863	52°14·0′	0°54·4′E	T	155
Elmswell New Hall	Suff	TL9764	52°14·6′	0°53·5′E	X	155
Elmswell Wold	E Yorks	SE9960	54°1·8′	0°28·9′W	X	101
Elmswell Wold Fm	E Yorks	SE9960	54°1·8′	0°28·9′W	FM	101
Elms Wood	Kent	TR2840	51°7·1′	1°15·9′E	F	179
Elmsworth Fm	I of W	SZ4492	50°43·8′	1°22·2′W	FM	196
Elmsworthy Fm	Corn	SS2513	50°53·6′	4°28·9′W	FM	190
Elmton	Derby	SK5073	53°15·3′	1°14·6′W	T	120
Elmton Lodge	Derby	SK4972	53°14·8′	1°15·5′W	X	120
Elmton Park Fm	Derby	SK4972	53°14·8′	1°15·5′W	FM	120
Elm Tree Fm	Ches	SJ5161	53°8·9′	2°43·6′W	FM	117
Elm Tree Fm	Cumbr	SD5482	54°14·1′	2°41·9′W	FM	97
Elm Tree Fm	Essex	TL8431	51°57·0′	0°41·1′E	FM	168
Elmtree Fm	E Yorks	TA2629	53°44·8′	0°4·9′W	FM	107
Elmtree Fm	Glos	SO7803	51°43·8′	2°18·7′W	FM	162
Elmtree Fm	Herts	TL0512	51°48·0′	0°28·2′W	FM	166
Elm Tree Fm	Kent	TR0338	51°6·5′	0°54·4′E	FM	179,189
Elmtree Fm	Kent	TR0743	51°9·1′	0°58·0′E	FM	179,189
Elm Tree Fm	Lancs	SD7524	53°43·0′	2°22·3′W	FM	103
Elm Tree Fm	Lincs	SK8888	53°23·1′	0°40·2′W	FM	112,121
Elmtree Fm	Norf	TM1484	52°24·9′	1°9·2′E	FM	144,156
Elm Tree Fm	Norf	TM1786	52°26·0′	1°11·9′E	FM	156
Elmtree Fm	Norf	TM2188	52°26·9′	1°15·5′E	FM	156
Elm Tree Fm	Northnts	SP5835	52°0·9′	1°8·9′W	FM	152
Elm Tree Fm	N Yks	SE7878	54°11·7′	0°47·8′W	FM	100
Elmtree Fm	S Glos	ST7092	51°37·8′	2°25·6′W	FM	162,172
Elm Tree Fm	Suff	TM1656	52°9·8′	1°9·9′E	FM	156
Elm Tree Fm	Suff	TM2150	52°6·5′	1°14·0′E	FM	156
Elm Tree Fm	Suff	TM2370	52°17·2′	1°16·6′E	FM	156
Elm Tree Ho	E Yorks	SE7527	53°44·3′	0°51·4′W	X	105,106
Elmtree Ho	Lincs	TF4967	53°11·0′	0°14·2′E	X	122
Elm Tree Ho	Norf	TF5313	52°41·8′	0°16·3′E	X	131,143
Elm Vale Fm	Suff	TM1179	52°22·3′	1°6·4′E	FM	144
Elm Wood	Notts	SK6085	53°21·7′	1°5·5′W	F	111,120
Elmwood College Fm	Fife	NO3513	56°18·6′	3°2·6′W	FM	59
Elmwood Fm	Warw	SP2470	52°19·9′	1°38·5′W	FM	139
Elmwood Ho	Oxon	SP2805	51°44·8′	1°35·3′W	X	163
Elnor Lane Fm	Derby	SK0179	53°18·7′	1°58·7′W	FM	119
Elorgarreg	Conwy	SH9653	53°4·1′	3°32·7′W	X	116
Elpha Green	Northum	NY8448	54°49·8′	2°14·5′W	X	86,87
Elphhillock	Aberd	NJ4912	57°12·0′	2°50·2′W	X	37
Elphicks	E Susx	TQ7228	51°1·8′	0°27·6′E	X	188,199
Elphicks	Kent	TQ6937	51°6·7′	0°25·3′E	X	188
Elphicks Fm	Kent	TQ7148	51°12·6′	0°27·3′E	FM	188
Elphin	Aberd	NJ9535	57°24·6′	2°4·5′W	X	30
Elphin	Highld	NC2111	58°3·4′	5°1·5′W	T	15
Elphin Beck	N Yks	SE5276	54°10·9′	1°11·8′W	W	100
Elphinstone	E Loth	NT3970	55°55·4′	2°58·1′W	T	66
Elphinstone Point	Kent	TQ8573	51°25·8′	0°40·1′E	X	178
Elphinstone Tower	E LOTH	NT3969	55°54·9′	2°58·1′W	A	66
Elphinstone Wood	Renf	NS3769	55°53·5′	4°36·0′W	F	63
Elrick	Aberd	NJ5916	57°14·2′	2°40·3′W	X	37
Elrick	Aberd	NJ8206	57°8·9′	2°17·4′W	T	38
Elrick	Aberd	NO8792	57°1·4′	2°12·4′W	X	38,45
Elrick	Moray	NJ4225	57°19·0′	2°57·3′W	X	37
Elrick Burn	Aberd	NJ8817	57°14·9′	2°11·5′W	W	38
Elrick Burn	Highld	NH6712	57°11·0′	4°11·6′W	W	35
Elrick Hill	C of Aber	NJ8410	57°11·1′	2°15·4′W	H	38
Elrick Ho	Aberd	NJ8818	57°15·4′	2°11·5′W	X	38
Elrick More	Pth & Kin	NN9646	56°35·9′	3°41·2′W	H	52,53
Elrick Moss	Aberd	NJ9541	57°27·8′	2°4·5′W	X	30
Elrig	D & G	NX3247	54°47·6′	4°36·4′W	T	82
Elrig	Highld	NH6428	57°19·6′	4°15·1′W	X	26,35
Elrig	Pth & Kin	NN8772	56°49·8′	3°50·7′W	H	43
Elrig	Pth & Kin	NN9169	56°48·2′	3°46·7′W	X	43
Elrig	Pth & Kin	NO0766	56°46·8′	3°30·9′W	H	43
Elrig	Stir	NS3899	56°9·6′	4°36·1′W	X	56
Elrig	Stir	NS4798	56°9·3′	4°27·4′W	X	57
Elrigbeag	Arg & Bt	NN1314	56°17·2′	5°0·8′W	X	50,56
Elrig Fell	D & G	NX3248	54°48·2′	4°36·4′W	X	82
Elrig Fm	D & G	NX3248	54°48·2′	4°36·4′W	FM	82
Elrig Ho	D & G	NX3149	54°48·7′	4°37·4′W	X	82
Elrig'ic an Toisich	Pth & Kin	NN8678	56°53·0′	3°51·8′W	H	43
Elrig Loch	D & G	NX3249	54°48·7′	4°36·4′W	W	82
Elrig na Curigin	Pth & Kin	NN7666	56°46·4′	4°1·3′W	X	42

Elrington	Northum	NY8663	54°57·9′	2°12·7′W	T	87
Elscar	Barns	SE3800	53°30·0′	1°25·2′W	T	110
Elsdon	Heref	SO3254	52°11·0′	2°59·3′W	T	148
Elsdon	Northum	NY9393	55°14·1′	2°6·2′W	T	80
Elsdonburn	Northum	NT8728	55°33·0′	2°11·9′W	X	74
Elsdon Burn	Northum	NT8828	55°33·0′	2°11·0′W	W	74
Elsdon Burn	Northum	NY9192	55°13·6′	2°8·1′W	W	80
Elsdon Burn	Northum	NY9295	55°15·2′	2°7·1′W	W	80
Elsdonburn Shank	Northum	NT8629	55°33·5′	2°12·9′W	X	74
Elsea Wood	Lincs	TF0918	52°45·1′	0°22·7′W	F	130
Elsecar Resr	Barns	SK3899	53°29·4′	1°25·2′W	W	110,111
Elsenham	Essex	TL5326	51°54·9′	0°13·9′E	T	167
Elsenham Sta	Essex	TL5327	51°55·5′	0°13·9′E	T	167
Elses Fm	Kent	TQ5350	51°13·9′	0°11·9′E	FM	188
Elsey Craig	Durham	NZ0007	54°27·7′	1°59·6′W	H	92
Elsfield	Oxon	SP5410	51°47·4′	1°12·6′W	T	164
Elsford Rock	Devon	SX7882	50°37·7′	3°43·1′W	X	191
Elsham	N Lincs	TA0312	53°35·9′	0°26·2′W	T	112
Elsham Carrs	N Lincs	TA0011	53°35·4′	0°28·9′W	X	112
Elsham Hall Country & Wildlife Park	N Lincs	TA0311	53°35·4′	0°26·2′W	X	112
Elsham Hill	N Lincs	TA0213	53°36·5′	0°27·1′W	X	112
Elsham Sta	N Lincs	TA0110	53°34·8′	0°28·1′W	X	112
Elsham Top	N Lincs	TA0511	53°35·3′	0°24·4′W	X	112
Elsham Wolds	N Lincs	TA0513	53°36·4′	0°24·4′W	X	112
Elshieshields	D & G	NY0685	55°9·3′	3°28·1′W	X	78
Elsich Manor	Shrops	SO4984	52°27·3′	2°44·6′W	X	137,138
Elsick Ho	Aberd	NO8994	57°2·5′	2°10·4′W	X	38,45
Elsie Fm	Cambs	TL2590	52°29·8′	0°9·1′W	FM	142
Elsie Moss	Aberd	NO6470	56°49·5′	2°34·9′W	F	45
Elsing	Norf	TG0516	52°42·4′	1°2·5′E	T	133
Elsingbottom Fm	N Yks	SE2248	53°55·9′	1°39·5′W	FM	104
Elsing Hall	Norf	TG0316	52°42·4′	1°0·7′E	A	133
Elsing Lane Fm	Norf	TG0419	52°44·0′	1°1·7′E	FM	133
Elslack	N Yks	SD9249	53°56·5′	2°6·9′W	T	103
Elslack Br	N Yks	SD9249	53°56·5′	2°6·9′W	X	103
Elslack Moor	N Yks	SD9347	53°55·4′	2°6·0′W	X	103
Elslack Resr	N Yks	SD9348	53°55·9′	2°6·0′W	W	103
Els Ness	Orkney	HY6738	59°13·9′	2°34·2′W	X	5
Elsness	Orkney	HY6738	59°13·9′	2°34·2′W	X	5
Elsom Fm	Lincs	TF4873	53°14·2′	0°13·5′E	FM	122
Elson	Hants	SU6001	50°48·6′	1°8·5′W	T	196
Elson	Shrops	SJ3835	52°54·8′	2°54·9′W	T	126
Elsrickle	S Lanak	NT0643	55°40·5′	3°29·2′W	T	72
Elstead	Surrey	SU9043	51°11·0′	0°42·3′W	T	186
Elstead Common	Surrey	SU9042	51°10·4′	0°42·4′W	F	186
Elsted	W Susx	SU8119	50°58·1′	0°50·4′W	T	197
Elsted Marsh	W Susx	SU8320	50°58·6′	0°48·7′W	X	197
Elsted Rough	W Susx	SU8220	50°58·6′	0°49·5′W	F	197
Elsthorpe	Lincs	TF0523	52°47·9′	0°26·2′W	X	130
Elsthorpe Grange	Lincs	TF0624	52°48·4′	0°25·2′W	X	130
Elstob	Durham	NZ3423	54°36·3′	1°28·0′W	T	93
Elstob Hill	Durham	NZ3423	54°36·3′	1°28·0′W	X	93
Elston	Devon	SS7802	50°48·5′	3°43·5′W	T	191
Elston	Devon	SX7045	50°17·7′	3°49·1′W	X	202
Elston	Lancs	SD6032	53°47·2′	2°36·0′W	X	102,103
Elston	Notts	SK7548	53°1·7′	0°52·5′W	T	129
Elston	Wilts	SU0644	51°11·9′	1°54·5′W	T	184
Elstone	Devon	SS6716	50°55·9′	3°53·2′W	T	180
Elston Hill Fm	Wilts	SU0645	51°12·5′	1°54·5′W	FM	184
Elston New Hall	Lancs	SD5932	53°47·2′	2°36·9′W	X	102,103
Elston Towers	Notts	SK7448	53°1·7′	0°53·4′W	X	129
Elstow	Beds	TL0546	52°6·4′	0°27·6′W	T	153
Elstow Hardwick Fm	Beds	TL0445	52°5·8′	0°28·5′W	FM	153
Elstree	Herts	TQ1795	51°38·7′	0°18·1′W	T	166,176
Elstree Aerodrome	Herts	TQ1596	51°39·3′	0°19·9′W	X	166,176
Elstree School	W Berks	SU5767	51°24·2′	1°10·4′W	X	174
Elstree Sta	Herts	TQ1996	51°39·2′	0°16·4′W	X	166,176
Elstronwick	E Yorks	TA2232	53°46·4′	0°8·5′W	T	107
Elswick	Lancs	SD4238	53°50·3′	2°52·5′W	T	102
Elswick	N upon Ty	NZ2263	54°57·9′	1°39·0′W	T	88
Elswick Grange Fm	Lancs	SD4137	53°49·8′	2°53·4′W	FM	102
Elswick Leys	Lancs	SD4237	53°49·8′	2°52·5′W	T	102
Elswick Manor	Lancs	SD4338	53°50·4′	2°51·6′W	X	102
Elsworth	Cambs	TL3163	52°15·2′	0°4·5′W	T	153
Elsworth Lodge	Cambs	TL3063	52°15·2′	0°5·3′W	X	153
Elsworthy	Somer	SS8141	51°9·6′	3°41·7′W	H	181
Elsworthy	Somer	SS9241	51°9·7′	3°32·3′W	X	181
Eltermere	Cumbr	NY3204	54°25·9′	3°2·5′W	X	90
Elterwater	Cumbr	NY3204	54°25·9′	3°2·5′W	T	90
Elter Water	Cumbr	NY3304	54°25·9′	3°1·6′W	W	90
Eltham	Gren	TQ4274	51°27·1′	0°3·0′E	T	177
Eltham Common	Gren	TQ4376	51°28·1′	0°3·9′E	F	177
Eltham Palace	Gren	TQ4273	51°26·5′	0°3·0′E	A	177
Eltham Park	Gren	TQ4375	51°27·6′	0°3·9′E	X	177
Eltisley	Cambs	TL2759	52°13·1′	0°8·1′W	T	153
Eltock Fm	Barns	SE1703	53°31·6′	1°44·2′W	FM	110
Eltofts	Leeds	SE3640	53°51·5′	1°26·7′W	X	104
Elton	Bury	SD7910	53°35·4′	2°18·6′W	T	109
Elton	Cambs	TL0893	52°31·7′	0°24·1′W	T	142
Elton	Ches	SJ4575	53°16·4′	2°49·1′W	T	117
Elton	Derby	SK2260	53°8·4′	1°39·9′W	T	119
Elton	Glos	SO6932	51°49·1′	2°26·6′W	T	162
Elton	Heref	SO4570	52°19·8′	2°48·0′W	T	137,138,148
Elton	Notts	SK7638	52°56·3′	0°51·7′W	T	129
Elton	Stock on T	NZ4017	54°33·0′	1°22·5′W	T	93
Elton Common	Derby	SK2159	53°7·9′	1°40·8′W	X	119
Elton Court	Glos	SO7014	51°49·7′	2°25·7′W	X	162
Elton Fm	Bath & NE Somer	ST5665	51°23·2′	2°37·6′W	FM	172,182
Elton Fm	W Berks	SU3974	51°28·0′	1°25·9′W	FM	174
Elton Furze	Cambs	TL1193	52°31·6′	0°21·4′W	F	142
Elton Green	Ches	SJ4575	53°16·4′	2°49·1′W	T	117
Elton Hall	Ches	SJ7259	53°7·9′	2°24·7′W	X	118
Elton Lane Fm	Stock on T	NZ4019	54°34·1′	1°22·5′W	FM	93
Elton Moor Fm	Stock on T	NZ3918	54°33·6′	1°23·4′W	FM	93
Elton & Orston Sta	Notts	SK7740	52°57·3′	0°50·8′W	X	129
Elton Park	Cambs	TL0893	52°31·7′	0°24·1′W	X	142

Elton Resr	Bury	SD7809	53°34·9′	2°19·5′W	W	109
Elton's Marsh	Heref	SO4943	52°5·2′	2°44·3′W	T	148,149
Elton Wood	W Berks	SU3975	51°28·6′	1°25·9′W	F	174
Eltringham	Northum	NZ0862	54°57·4′	1°52·1′W	T	88
Elva Hill	Cumbr	NY1731	54°40·3′	3°16·8′W	H	89,90
Elvanfoot	S Lanak	NS9517	55°26·4′	3°39·2′W	T	78
Elvan Water	S Lanak	NS9317	55°26·4′	3°41·0′W	W	71,78
Elva Plain	Cumbr	NY1731	54°40·3′	3°16·8′W	X	89,90
Elvaston	Derby	SK4132	52°53·3′	1°23·0′W	T	129
Elvaston Castle Country Park	Derby	SK4032	52°53·3′	1°23·9′W	X	129
Elvastone	Heref	SO5228	51°57·1′	2°41·5′W	X	149
Elveden	Suff	TL8280	52°23·5′	0°40·9′E	T	144
Elveden Forest Holiday Centre	Suff	TL7980	52°23·6′	0°38·2′E	X	144
Elveden Gap	Norf	TL8381	52°24·0′	0°41·8′E	X	144
Elveden Warren	Suff	TL7981	52°24·1′	0°38·3′E	F	144
Elvendon Priory	Oxon	SU6281	51°31·7′	1°6·0′W	X	175
Elverland	Kent	TQ9758	51°17·4′	0°49·9′E	X	178
Elvers Green Fm	Sol	SP1976	52°23·1′	1°42·9′W	FM	139
Elverton	Kent	TQ9862	51°19·6′	0°50·9′E	X	178
Elverway Fm	Devon	SY1990	50°42·5′	3°8·4′W	FM	192,193
Elvetham Fm	Hants	SU7857	51°18·6′	0°52·5′W	FM	175,186
Elvetham Hall	Hants	SU7856	51°18·1′	0°52·5′W	X	175,186
Elvet Hill	Durham	NZ2641	54°46·0′	1°35·3′W	T	88
Elvey Fm	Kent	TQ9145	51°10·6′	0°44·3′E	FM	189
Elvingston	E Loth	NT4674	55°57·6′	2°51·5′W	T	66
Elvington	Kent	TR2750	51°12·5′	1°15·4′E	T	179
Elvington	York	SE7047	53°55·1′	0°55·6′W	T	105,106
Elvington Grange	York	SE6847	53°55·1′	0°57·5′W	X	105,106
Elvington Wood	York	SE6946	53°54·6′	0°56·6′W	F	105,106
Elvister	Shetld	HU2249	60°13·7′	1°35·7′W	X	3
Elvis Voe	Shetld	HU5044	60°10·9′	1°5·4′W	W	4
Elwartlaw	Scot Bord	NT7345	55°42·1′	2°25·3′W	X	74
Elwell	Devon	SS6631	51°4·0′	3°54·4′W	T	180
Elwell	Devon	SX7358	50°24·7′	3°46·9′W	X	202
Elwell	Dorset	SY6684	50°39·5′	2°28·5′W	T	194
Elwell Fm	N Som	ST5566	51°23·7′	2°38·4′W	FM	172,182
Elwell Fms	Dorset	SY4796	50°45·9′	2°44·7′W	FM	193
Elwell Lodge	Dorset	SY4797	50°46·4′	2°44·7′W	X	193
Elwick	Hartpl	NZ4532	54°41·1′	1°17·7′W	T	93
Elwick	Northum	NU1136	55°37·3′	1°49·1′W	T	75
Elwick	Orkney	HY4816	59°1·9′	2°53·9′W	W	6
Elwick	Orkney	HY4816	59°1·9′	2°53·9′W	X	6
Elwick Burn	Northum	NU1037	55°37·8′	1°50·0′W	W	75
Elwill Bay	Devon	SS6348	51°13·1′	3°57·3′W	W	180
Elworth	Ches	SJ7461	53°9·0′	2°22·9′W	T	118
Elworth	Dorset	SY5984	50°39·5′	2°34·4′W	X	194
Elworthy	Devon	SS8515	50°55·6′	3°37·8′W	X	181
Elworthy	Somer	ST0835	51°6·7′	3°18·5′W	T	181
Elworthy Barrows	Somer	ST0733	51°5·6′	3°19·3′W	X	181
Elworthy Barrows (Settlement)	Somer	ST0733	51°5·6′	3°19·3′W	A	181
Elworthy Fm	Somer	ST0820	50°58·6′	3°18·2′W	FM	181
Elwyn	Carm	SN2328	51°55·6′	4°34·1′W	X	145,158
Ely	Cambs	TL5480	52°24·0′	0°16·2′E	T	143
Ely	Card	ST1376	51°28·8′	3°14·8′W	T	171
Ely Brow	Ches	SJ9675	53°16·6′	2°3·2′W	X	118
Ely Court	Kent	TQ7742	51°9·2′	0°32·3′E	X	188
Elygrain	Scot Bord	NT4100	55°17·7′	2°55·3′W	X	79
Ely Grange	E Susx	TQ5936	51°6·3′	0°16·7′E	X	188
Elyhaugh	Northum	NZ1599	55°17·3′	1°45·4′W	X	81
Ely Hill	Suff	TM3647	52°4·5′	1°27·0′E	X	169
Elymains	E Ayr	NS4515	55°24·5′	4°26·5′W	X	70
Ely River	Rho Cyn Taf	ST0284	51°33·0′	3°24·4′W	W	170
Ely River	V of Glam	ST0676	51°28·7′	3°20·8′W	W	170
Ely River or Afon Elái	V of Glam	ST1575	51°28·3′	3°13·0′W	W	171
Ely Valley	V of Glam	ST0579	51°30·4′	3°21·7′W	X	170
Ely Valley	V of Glam	ST1076	51°28·8′	3°17·4′W	X	171
Emanual Pollards	Herts	TL3306	51°44·4′	0°4·0′W	X	166
Emanuel Wood	Essex	TL5341	52°3·0′	0°14·3′E	F	154
Embasy Kirk	N Yks	SE0054	53°59·2′	1°59·6′W	X	104
Embelle Wood	Somer	SS8149	51°13·9′	3°41·9′W	F	181
Ember Combe	Somer	SS8541	51°9·6′	3°38·3′W	X	181
Ember Hill	N Yks	SE5261	54°2·8′	1°11·9′W	X	100
Emberton	Mil Key	SP8849	52°8·2′	0°42·5′W	T	152
Emberton (Country Park)	Mil Key	SP8850	52°8·7′	0°42·4′W	X	152
Embla	Corn	SW4837	50°11·0′	5°31·4′W	X	203
Emblance Downs	Corn	SX1277	50°34·0′	4°38·9′W	X	200
Emble Fm	Somer	ST1133	51°5·6′	3°15·9′W	FM	181
Emblehope	Northum	NY7494	55°14·6′	2°24·1′W	X	80
Emblehope Moor	Northum	NY7495	55°15·2′	2°24·1′W	X	80
Emblem Brae	D & G	NT1713	55°24·5′	3°18·2′W	X	79
Emblestone	Northum	NU2524	55°30·8′	1°35·8′W	X	75
Embleton	Cumbr	NY1730	54°39·7′	3°16·8′W	T	89,90
Embleton	Durham	NZ4129	54°39·5′	1°21·4′W	T	93
Embleton	Northum	NU2322	55°29·7′	1°37·7′W	T	75
Embleton Bay	Northum	NU2423	55°30·3′	1°36·8′W	W	75
Embleton Burn	Northum	NU2322	55°29·7′	1°37·7′W	W	75
Embleton Hall	Northum	NU1301	55°18·4′	1°47·3′W	X	81
Embleton Mill	Northum	NU2221	55°29·2′	1°38·7′W	X	75
Embleton Moor	Northum	NU2123	55°30·3′	1°39·6′W	X	75
Embleton Old Hall	Durham	NZ4131	54°40·6′	1°21·4′W	X	93
Embleton's Bog	Northum	NU1629	55°33·5′	1°44·3′W	X	75
Embleton Steads	Northum	NU1302	55°19·0′	1°47·3′W	X	81
Embleton Terrace	Northum	NZ0897	55°16·3′	1°52·0′W	X	81
Emblett Hill	Devon	SX8470	50°31·3′	3°37·8′W	H	202
Embley	Northum	NY9254	54°53·1′	2°7·1′W	X	87
Embley Fell	Northum	NY9353	54°52·5′	2°6·1′W	X	87
Embley Park School	Hants	SU3220	50°58·9′	1°32·3′W	X	185
Embleys Fm	Essex	TL5507	51°44·6′	0°15·1′E	FM	167
Embley Wood	Hants	SU3218	50°57·9′	1°32·3′W	F	185
Embley Wood	Hants	SU5441	51°10·2′	1°13·3′W	F	185
Embo	Highld	NH8192	57°54·4′	4°0·0′W	T	21
Embo Ho	Highld	NH8092	57°54·3′	4°1·0′W	X	21
Embo Muir	Highld	NH7992	57°54·3′	4°2·0′W	X	21
Emborough	Somer	ST6151	51°15·6′	2°33·1′W	T	183
Emborough Grove	Somer	ST6150	51°15·1′	2°33·1′W	F	183
Embo Street	Highld	NH8091	57°53·8′	4°1·0′W	T	21

Embsay	N Yks	SE0053	53°58·6′	1°59·6′W	T	104
Embsay & Bolton Abbey Steam Railway	N Yks	SE0353	53°58·6′	1°56·8′W	X	104
Embsay Crag	N Yks	SE0055	53°59·7′	1°59·6′W	X	104
Embsay Moor	N Yks	SD9956	54°0·2′	2°0·5′W	X	103
Embsay Moor	N Yks	SE0056	54°0·2′	1°59·6′W	X	104
Embsay Reservoir	N Yks	SD9954	53°59·2′	2°0·5′W	W	103
Embury Beach	Devon	SS2119	50°56·8′	4°32·5′W	X	190
Embury Beacon	Devon	SS2119	50°56·8′	4°32·5′W	A	190
Emeraconart	Arg & Bt	NR3765	55°48·7′	6°11·4′W	X	60,61
Emerald Bank	Cumbr	NY2320	54°34·4′	3°11·0′W	X	89,90
Emerick Fm	Northum	NT9247	55°43·2′	2°7·2′W	FM	74,75
Emer's Isle	D & G	NW9771	54°59·8′	5°10·0′W	X	76,82
Emerson Ho	Durham	NZ1027	54°38·5′	1°50·3′W	X	92
Emerson Park	Hav	TQ5488	51°34·4′	0°13·7′E	T	177
Emerson's Green	S Glos	ST6676	51°29·2′	2°29·0′W	T	172
Emerson Valley	Mil Key	SP8434	52°0·1′	0°46·2′W	T	152,165
Emertley Hill	Northum	NY8359	54°55·8′	2°15·5′W	X	86,87
Emery Down	Hants	SU2808	50°52·5′	1°35·7′W	T	195
Emily Hill	Fife	NO3219	56°21·8′	3°5·6′W	H	59
Emily's Wood	Norf	TL7989	52°28·4′	0°38·5′E	F	144
Emir Cottage	Highld	NH3632	57°21·2′	4°43·1′W	X	26
Emlett Hill	Devon	SS8008	50°51·8′	3°41·9′W	H	191
Emley	Kirk	SE2413	53°37·0′	1°37·8′W	T	110
Emley	Northum	NY7757	54°54·7′	2°21·1′W	X	86,87
Emley Fm	Surrey	SU9037	51°7·7′	0°42·4′W	FM	186
Emley Lodge	Kirk	SE2411	53°35·9′	1°37·8′W	X	110
Emley Moor	Kirk	SE2213	53°37·0′	1°39·6′W	X	110
Emley Old Hall Fm	Kirk	SE2512	53°36·5′	1°36·9′W	FM	110
Emley Park	Kirk	SE2411	53°35·9′	1°37·8′W	X	110
Emlin	Sheff	SK2393	53°26·2′	1°38·8′W	X	110
Emlin Ridge	Sheff	SK2393	53°26·2′	1°38·8′W	X	110
Emly Bank	Midlo	NT2947	55°42·9′	3°7·4′W	H	73
Emlych	Pemb	SM7526	51°53·5′	5°15·8′W	X	157
Emmanuel Head	Northum	NU1343	55°41·1′	1°47·2′W	X	75
Emmaus	Cambs	TL4866	52°16·6′	0°10·6′E	X	154
Emmbrook	Wok	SU7969	51°25·1′	0°51·4′W	T	175
Emmer Green	Read	SU7276	51°28·9′	0°57·4′W	T	175
Emmethill	I of W	SZ4780	50°37·3′	1°19·8′W	X	196
Emmet Law	Northum	NT7806	55°21·1′	2°20·4′W	X	80
Emmets	Lancs	SD5754	53°59·1′	2°38·9′W	X	102
Emmets Post	Devon	SX5663	50°27·2′	4°1·3′W	X	202
Emmett	Devon	SS6025	51°0·7′	3°59·4′W	X	180
Emmett Carr	Derby	SK4577	53°17·5′	1°19·1′W	T	120
Emmetts Garden	Kent	TQ4752	51°15·1′	0°6·8′E	X	188
Emmett's Grange	Somer	SS7536	51°6·8′	3°46·8′W	X	180
Emmetts Hill	Dorset	SY9676	50°35·3′	2°3·0′W	H	195
Emmetts Mill	Surrey	SU9961	51°20·6′	0°34·3′W	X	175,176,186
Emmington	Oxon	SP7402	51°42·9′	0°55·3′W	T	165
Emmock	Angus	NO4035	56°30·5′	2°58·0′W	X	54
Emmotland	E Yorks	TA0851	53°56·9′	0°20·8′W	X	107
Emmott	Lancs	SD9240	53°51·6′	2°6·9′W	X	103
Emmott Moor	Lancs	SD9539	53°51·1′	2°4·1′W	X	103
Emms Hill	Durham	NZ0928	54°39·1′	1°51·2′W	X	92
Emneth	Norf	TF4807	52°38·7′	0°11·7′E	T	143
Emneth Hungate	Norf	TF5107	52°38·6′	0°14·3′E	T	143
Emorsgate	Norf	TF5320	52°45·6′	0°16·5′E	T	131
Empacombe	Corn	SX4452	50°21·1′	4°11·2′W	X	201
Emperor Lake	Derby	SK2670	53°13·8′	1°36·2′W	W	119
Emperor's Hill	Surrey	SU9154	51°16·9′	0°41·3′W	X	186
Emperor Stream	Derby	SK2771	53°14·4′	1°35·3′W	W	119
Empingham	Rut	SK9508	52°39·9′	0°35·3′W	T	141
Empingham Old Wood	Rut	SK9610	52°41·0′	0°34·4′W	F	130
Empleton High Common	Cumbr	NY1627	54°38·1′	3°17·7′W	X	89
Empool Bottom	Dorset	SY7487	50°41·2′	2°21·7′W	X	194
Empool Heath	Dorset	SY7487	50°41·2′	2°21·7′W	X	194
Empshill Fm	Glos	SP1414	51°49·7′	1°47·4′W	FM	163
Empshott	Hants	SU7531	51°4·6′	0°55·4′W	T	186
Empshott Green	Hants	SU7430	51°4·1′	0°56·3′W	T	186
Empsons Fm	Lincs	TF2609	52°40·1′	0°7·8′W	FM	142
Empton Fm	Heref	SO2753	52°10·5′	3°3·7′W	FM	148
Emral Brook	Wrex	SJ4245	53°0·2′	2°51·5′W	W	117
Emral Stud	Wrex	SJ4244	52°59·7′	2°51·4′W	X	117
Emscote	Warw	SP2965	52°17·2′	1°34·1′W	T	151
Em-sger or South Bishop	Pemb	SM6522	51°51·1′	5°24·3′W	X	157
Emstrey	Shrops	SJ5210	52°41·4′	2°42·2′W	T	126
Emsworth	Hants	SU7406	50°51·2′	0°56·5′W	T	197
Emsworth Channel	W Susx	SU7402	50°49·0′	0°56·6′W	W	197
Emsworthy	Devon	SX3789	50°40·9′	4°18·1′W	X	190
Emu Lodge Fm	Notts	SK8452	53°3·8′	0°44·4′W	FM	121
Enaclete	N Eil	NB1228	58°9·1′	6°53·3′W	T	13
Enag or Crow Hillock	Highld	ND3464	58°33·6′	3°7·6′W	X	12
Enard Bay	Highld	NC0316	58°5·6′	5°20·1′W	W	15
Enborne	W Berks	SU4365	51°23·2′	1°22·5′W	T	174
Enborne Copse	W Berks	SU4366	51°23·7′	1°22·5′W	F	174
Enborne Ho	W Berks	SU4566	51°23·7′	1°20·8′W	X	174
Enborne Lodge (Sch)	W Berks	SU4464	51°22·6′	1°21·7′W	X	174
Enborne Row	W Berks	SU4463	51°22·1′	1°21·7′W	T	174
Enborne Street Fm	W Berks	SU4363	51°22·1′	1°22·5′W	FM	174
Encampment Fm	Northum	NT9136	55°37·3′	2°8·1′W	FM	74,75
Enchmarsh	Shrops	SO5096	52°33·8′	2°43·9′W	T	137,138
Encombe Dairy	Dorset	SY9477	50°35·8′	2°4·7′W	X	195
Encombe Ho	Dorset	SY9478	50°36·3′	2°4·7′W	X	195
Endacott	Devon	SX6898	50°46·2′	3°51·9′W	X	191
Endale	Heref	SO5161	52°14·9′	2°42·7′W	X	137,138,149
End Barrow	Dorset	SY8493	50°44·4′	2°13·2′W	A	194
Enderby	Leic	SP5399	52°35·4′	1°12·7′W	T	140
Enderby Hill Fm	Lincs	TF2762	53°8·6′	0°5·7′W	FM	122
Enderby Lodge	Leic	SK5201	52°36·5′	1°13·5′W	X	140
End House Fm	Lincs	TF4863	53°8·8′	0°13·2′E	FM	122
Endicott	Devon	SS9106	50°50·8′	3°32·5′W	X	192
Endlewick Fm	E Susx	TQ5406	50°50·2′	0°11·6′E	FM	199
End Low	Derby	SK1560	53°8·5′	1°46·1′W	H	119
Endmoor	Cumbr	SD5485	54°15·8′	2°42·0′W	T	97
Endmoor	Derby	SK1365	53°11·2′	1°47·9′W	X	119
Endon	Staffs	SJ9253	53°4·7′	2°6·8′W	T	118
Endon Bank	Staffs	SJ9253	53°4·7′	2°6·8′W	T	118
Endon Hall	Ches	SJ9376	53°17·1′	2°5·9′W	X	118
Endon Hall	Worcs	SO9645	52°6·4′	2°3·1′W	X	150
Endon Hays	Staffs	SJ9260	53°8·5′	2°6·8′W	X	118

Endrick Br	Stir	NS5488	56°4·0′	4°20·3′W	X	57
Endrick Mouth	W Dunb	NS4289	56°4·3′	4°31·9′W	W	56
Endrick Water	Stir	NS5788	56°4·1′	4°17·4′W	W	57
Endrick Water	W Dunb	NS4389	56°4·3′	4°30·9′W	W	56
Endsleigh	Devon	SX3978	50°35·0′	4°16·1′W	X	201
Endsleigh Gdns	Devon	SX3978	50°35·0′	4°16·1′W	X	201
Ends Place	W Susx	TQ1433	51°5·3′	0°21·9′W	X	187
Enegars	Orkney	HY2003	58°54·7′	3°22·9′W	X	7
Energlyn	Caer	ST1488	51°35·3′	3°14·1′W	T	171
Enfield	Enf	TQ3396	51°39·0′	0°4·3′W	T	166,176,177
Enfield	Worcs	SP0368	52°18·8′	1°57·0′W	T	139
Enfield Chase	Enf	TQ2898	51°40·2′	0°8·5′W	X	166,176
Enfield Fm	Lincs	SK8667	53°11·8′	0°42·3′W	FM	121
Enfield Highway	Enf	TQ3597	51°39·6′	0°2·5′W	T	166,177
Enfield Lock	Enf	TQ3698	51°40·1′	0°1·6′W	T	166,177
Enfield's Fm	Essex	TL9831	51°56·8′	0°53·3′E	FM	168
Enfield Side	Brad	SE0136	53°49·5′	1°58·7′W	X	104
Enfield Town	Enf	TQ3296	51°39·1′	0°5·1′W	T	166,176,177
Enfield Wash	Enf	TQ3598	51°40·1′	0°2·5′W	T	166,177
Enford	Wilts	SU1351	51°15·7′	1°48·4′W	T	184
Enford Bottom	Dorset	ST8409	50°53·0′	2°13·3′W	X	194
Enford Down	Wilts	SU1049	51°14·6′	1°51·0′W	X	184
Enford Fm	Wilts	SU1250	51°15·2′	1°49·3′W	FM	184
Engal	Highld	ND2337	58°19·2′	3°18·4′W	X	11
Engamoor	Shetld	HU2557	60°18·0′	1°32·4′W	T	3
Engatus, The	Shetld	HU4788	60°34·6′	1°8·0′W	X	1,2
Engedi	I of Angl	SH3676	53°15·6′	4°27·1′W	T	114
Engeham Fm	Kent	TQ9436	51°5·6′	0°46·6′E	FM	189
Engelly	Corn	SW8052	50°19·8′	5°5·1′W	X	200,204
Engine Common	S Glos	ST6984	51°33·5′	2°26·4′W	T	172
Engine Drain	E Yorks	TA0836	53°48·8′	0°21·2′W	W	107
Engine Drain	Lincs	TF1663	53°9·3′	0°15·5′W	W	121
Engine Fm	Cambs	TL2390	52°29·9′	0°10·9′W	FM	142
Engine Fm	Cambs	TL6283	52°25·5′	0°23·4′E	FM	143
Engine Fm	Lincs	TF1163	53°9·4′	0°20·0′W	FM	121
Engine Fm	Lincs	TF1524	52°48·3′	0°17·2′W	FM	130
Engine Fm	Lincs	TF3759	53°6·9′	0°3·2′E	FM	122
Engine House Fm	Donc	SK4798	53°28·8′	1°17·1′W	FM	111
Englands Head	Lancs	SD8452	53°58·1′	2°14·2′W	X	103
England Shelve	Shrops	SO3795	52°33·2′	2°55·4′W	X	137
Englefield	W Berks	SU6272	51°26·8′	1°6·1′W	T	175
Englefield Green	Surrey	SU9971	51°26·0′	0°34·2′W	T	175,176
Englefield Ho	W Berks	SU6271	51°26·3′	1°6·1′W	X	175
Englefield Park	W Berks	SU6271	51°26·3′	1°6·1′W	X	175
Englemere	Win & Maid	SU9168	51°24·5′	0°41·1′W	X	175
Englemere Pond	Brackn	SU9068	51°24·5′	0°42·0′W	W	175
Englesea-brook	Ches	SJ7551	53°3·6′	2°22·0′W	T	118
Englesea Ho	Ches	SJ7454	53°5·2′	2°22·9′W	X	118
Engleton Hall	Staffs	SJ8910	52°41·5′	2°9·4′W	X	127
English and Welsh Grounds		ST3072	51°26·8′	3°0·0′W	X	171
English Bicknor	Glos	SO5815	51°50·2′	2°36·2′W	T	162
Englishcombe	Bath & NE Somer	ST7162	51°21·6′	2°24·6′W	T	172
English Drove Fm	Peterb	TF3006	52°38·4′	0°4·3′W	FM	142
English Fm	Oxon	SU6786	51°34·4′	1°1·6′W	FM	175
English Frankton	Shrops	SJ4529	52°51·6′	2°48·6′W	T	126
English Island	I Scilly	SV9315	49°57·6′	6°16·5′W	X	203
English Kershope	Cumbr	NY5284	55°9·1′	2°44·8′W	X	79
English Lake	S Glos	ST5385	51°34·0′	2°40·3′W	W	172
Englishman's Burn	D & G	NX5058	54°53·9′	4°19·9′W	W	83
English Stones	S Glos	ST5285	51°33·9′	2°41·2′W	X	172
English Strother	Northum	NT8637	55°37·8′	2°12·9′W	X	74
Englishton	Highld	NH6045	57°28·7′	4°19·6′W	X	26
Englishton Muir	Highld	NH6144	57°28·2′	4°18·6′W	X	26
Englishtown	Cumbr	NY3373	55°3·1′	3°2·5′W	X	85
Engollan	Corn	SW8670	50°29·7′	5°0·7′W	T	200
Enham Alamein	Hants	SU3649	51°14·6′	1°28·7′W	T	185
Enholmes Fm	E Yorks	TA3021	53°40·4′	0°1·5′W	FM	107,113
Enholmes Hall	E Yorks	TA2922	53°40·9′	0°2·4′W	X	107,113
Eninteer	Aberd	NJ5412	57°12·0′	2°45·2′W	X	37
Enis	Devon	SS5626	51°1·2′	4°2·8′W	T	180
Enisfirth	Shetld	HU3274	60°27·2′	1°24·6′W	X	3
Enmill Fm	Hants	SU4328	51°3·2′	1°22·8′W	FM	185
Enmore	Somer	ST2435	51°6·8′	3°4·8′W	T	182
Enmore Castle	Somer	ST2335	51°6·8′	3°5·6′W	X	182
Enmore Field	Heref	SO4664	52°16·5′	2°47·1′W	T	137,138,148
Enmore Green	Dorset	ST8523	51°0·6′	2°12·4′W	T	183
Ennerdale Bridge	Cumbr	NY0715	54°31·6′	3°25·8′W	T	89
Ennerdale Fell	Cumbr	NY1313	54°30·5′	3°20·2′W	X	89
Ennerdale Forest	Cumbr	NY1314	54°31·1′	3°20·2′W	F	89
Ennerdale Water	Cumbr	NY1014	54°31·0′	3°23·0′W	W	89
Ennerleigh	Devon	SS9216	50°56·2′	3°31·8′W	X	181
Ennets	Aberd	NJ6006	57°8·8′	2°39·2′W	X	37
Ennim	Cumbr	NY4531	54°40·5′	2°50·8′W	X	90
Ennis Barton	Corn	SW8958	50°23·3′	4°57·7′W	X	200
Enniscaven	Corn	SW9659	50°24·0′	4°51·9′W	T	200
Ennis Fm	Corn	SW8352	50°19·9′	5°2·6′W	FM	200,204
Enniswortgey	Corn	SW9361	50°25·0′	4°54·5′W	X	200
Ennoch Burn	Pth & Kin	NO1261	56°44·2′	3°25·9′W	X	43
Ennochie	Aberd	NO6292	57°1·3′	2°37·1′W	X	45
Ennys	Corn	SW5532	50°8·5′	5°25·4′W	X	203
Enoch	D & G	NS8701	55°17·7′	3°46·3′W	T	78
Enoch	D & G	NX0155	54°51·3′	5°5·6′W	X	82
Enoch	Moray	NJ3337	57°25·4′	3°6·5′W	X	28
Enoch	S Ayr	NX2099	55°15·4′	4°49·5′W	X	76
Enochdhu	Pth & Kin	NO0662	56°44·7′	3°31·8′W	T	43
Enoch Hill	E Ayr	NS5606	55°19·9′	4°15·8′W	H	71,77
Enoch Rock	Corn	SW7010	49°57·0′	5°12·0′W	X	203
Enrick	D & G	NX6154	54°51·9′	4°9·5′W	X	83
Ensay	Arg & Bt	NM3648	56°33·2′	6°17·3′W	X	47,48
Ensay	N Eil	NF9786	57°45·9′	7°5·3′W	X	18
Ensay Bay	N Eil	NF9885	57°45·4′	7°4·2′W	W	18
Ensay Burn	Arg & Bt	NM3647	56°32·7′	6°17·3′W	W	47,48
Ensay House	N Eil	NF9886	57°46·0′	7°4·3′W	X	18
Ensbury	Bourne	SZ0896	50°46·0′	1°52·8′W	T	195
Ensbury Park	Bourne	SZ0794	50°45·0′	1°53·7′W	T	195
Ensdon	Shrops	SJ4016	52°44·5′	2°52·9′W	X	126
Ensdon Ho	Shrops	SJ4117	52°45·1′	2°52·0′W	X	126

Ensfield	Kent	TQ5545	51°11·2′	0°13·5′E	X	188
Enshaw Knoll	Brad	SE0036	53°49·5′	1°59·6′W	X	104
Enslow	Oxon	SP4818	51°51·7′	1°17·8′W	T	164
Enson	Staffs	SJ9428	52°51·2′	2°4·9′W	X	127
Enson Fm	Staffs	SJ9329	52°51·7′	2°5·8′W	FM	127
Enstone	Oxon	SP3724	51°55·0′	1°27·3′W	T	164
Ensworthy	Devon	SX6689	50°41·3′	3°53·4′W	X	191
Enterber	Cumbr	NY7609	54°28·8′	2°21·8′W	X	91
Enterkin Burn	D & G	NS8705	55°19·8′	3°46·4′W	W	71,78
Enterkin Burn	D & G	NS8809	55°22·0′	3°45·6′W	W	71,78
Enterkine	S Ayr	NS4223	55°28·8′	4°29·6′W	X	70
Enterkinfoot	D & G	NS8604	55°19·3′	3°47·4′W	T	78
Enterpen	N Yks	NZ4605	54°26·5′	1°17·0′W	T	93
Entertrona Burn	Scot Bord	NT1807	55°21·3′	3°17·2′W	W	79
Enthorn	D & G	NY3778	55°5·8′	2°58·8′W	X	85
Enthorpe Ho	E Yorks	SE9146	53°54·4′	0°36·5′W	X	106
Enton Green	Surrey	SU9540	51°9·3′	0°38·1′W	T	186
Enton Hall	Surrey	SU9539	51°8·8′	0°38·1′W	X	186
Entrance Channel	Card	ST1973	51°27·2′	3°9·6′W	W	171
Entryfoot	W Loth	NS8767	55°53·2′	3°48·0′W	X	65
Entry Hill	E Susx	TQ5631	51°3·7′	0°14·0′E	X	188
Entwistle Sta	Black w Dar	SD7217	53°39·2′	2°25·0′W	X	109
Enville	Staffs	SO8286	52°28·5′	2°15·5′W	T	138
Enville Common	Staffs	SO8386	52°28·5′	2°14·6′W	X	138
Envilles Fm	Essex	TL5509	51°45·7′	0°15·2′E	FM	167
Enyas Hill	Orkney	HY4020	59°4·0′	3°2·3′W	H	5,6
Enys	Corn	SW7936	50°11·2′	5°5·4′W	X	204
Enys Dodnan	Corn	SW3424	50°3·6′	5°42·6′W	X	203
Enys Head	Corn	SW7214	49°59·2′	5°10·5′W	X	204
Enys, The	Corn	SW3735	50°9·6′	5°40·6′W	X	203
Enys, The	Corn	SW5527	50°5·8′	5°25·2′W	X	203
Enzean	Aberd	NJ6915	57°13·7′	2°30·4′W	X	38
Enzieholm	D & G	NY2891	55°12·7′	3°7·5′W	X	79
Enzieholm Height	D & G	NY2789	55°11·6′	3°8·4′W	H	79
Eoligarry	N Eil	NF7007	57°2·4′	7°26·0′W	T	31
Eoligarry Jetty	N Eil	NF7107	57°2·5′	7°25·0′W	X	31
Eòrabus	Arg & Bt	NM3823	56°19·9′	6°13·9′W	X	48
Eòradal	N Eil	NB5362	58°28·8′	6°13·8′W	X	8
Eorisdale	N Eil	NL6494	56°55·2′	7°30·9′W	X	31
Eòrna Cott	Highld	NM7064	56°42·9′	5°45·1′W	X	40
Europaidh	N Eil	NB5165	58°30·4′	6°16·0′W	T	8
Eorrabus	Arg & Bt	NR3564	55°48·1′	6°13·3′W	X	60,61
Eorsa	Arg & Bt	NM4837	56°27·7′	6°5·0′W	X	47,48
Ephope Law	Scot Bord	NT7309	55°22·7′	2°25·1′W	X	80
Epney	Glos	SO7611	51°48·1′	2°20·5′W	T	162
Epperstone	Notts	SK6548	53°1·8′	1°1·4′W	T	129
Epperstone Park	Notts	SK6349	53°2·3′	1°3·2′W	F	129
Epperstone Park	Notts	SK6350	53°2·8′	1°3·2′W	F	120
Eppie's Taes Bank	Fife	NO2922	56°23·4′	3°8·6′W	X	53,59
Epping	Essex	TL4502	51°42·1′	0°6·3′E	T	167
Epping Forest	Essex	TQ4298	51°40·0′	0°3·6′E	F	167,177
Epping Forest Conservation Centre	Essex	TQ4198	51°40·0′	0°2·7′E	X	167,177
Epping Green	Essex	TL4305	51°43·8′	0°4·6′E	T	167
Epping Green	Herts	TL2906	51°44·5′	0°7·5′W	T	166
Epping Ho	Herts	TL2906	51°44·5′	0°7·5′W	X	166
Epping Long Green	Essex	TL4305	51°43·8′	0°4·6′E	X	167
Epping Upland	Essex	TL4404	51°43·2′	0°5·5′E	T	167
Eppitts	Devon	SY1993	50°44·1′	3°8·5′W	X	192,193
Epple Bay	Kent	TR3070	51°23·2′	1°18·7′E	W	179
Eppleby	N Yks	NZ1713	54°31·0′	1°43·8′W	T	92
Eppleton Hall	Sund	NZ3646	54°48·7′	1°26·0′W	X	88
Eppletons Fm	Devon	SS7503	50°49·0′	3°46·1′W	FM	191
Eppleworth	E Yorks	TA0131	53°46·2′	0°27·6′W	T	106,107
Eppleworth Wood Fm	E Yorks	TA0032	53°46·7′	0°28·5′W	FM	106,107
Epsom	Surrey	TQ2060	51°19·8′	0°16·3′W	T	176,187
Epsom Common	Surrey	TQ1860	51°19·8′	0°18·0′W	X	176,187
Epsom Downs	Surrey	TQ2158	51°18·7′	0°15·4′W	X	187
Epsom Downs Sta	Surrey	TQ2259	51°19·2′	0°14·6′W	X	187
Epwell	Oxon	SP3540	52°3·7′	1°29·0′W	T	151
Epwell Grounds Fm	Oxon	SP3641	52°4·2′	1°28·1′W	FM	151
Epwell Hill	Oxon	SP3541	52°4·2′	1°29·0′W	H	151
Epworth	N Lincs	SE7803	53°31·3′	0°49·0′W	T	112
Epworth Turbary	N Lincs	SE7603	53°31·3′	0°50·8′W	T	112
Erallich Water	Arg & Bt	NN0611	56°15·4′	5°7·5′W	W	50,56
Erasaid	Arg & Bt	NR2965	55°48·4′	6°19·1′W	X	60
Erbetshall	Fife	NO5508	56°16·0′	2°43·1′W	X	59
Erbistock	Wrex	SJ3541	52°58·0′	2°57·7′W	T	117
Erbistock Hall	Wrex	SJ3542	52°58·5′	2°57·7′W	X	117
Erbusaig	Highld	NG7629	57°18·1′	5°42·6′W	T	33
Erbusaig Bay	Highld	NG7529	57°18·0′	5°43·6′W	W	33
Ercall Hall	Wrekin	SJ5917	52°45·2′	2°36·0′W	A	126
Ercall Heath	Shrops	SJ6823	52°48·5′	2°28·1′W	X	127
Ercall Park	Wrekin	SJ5817	52°45·2′	2°36·9′W	X	126
Ercall, The	Wrekin	SJ6409	52°40·9′	2°31·6′W	H	127
Erchite Wood	Highld	NH5831	57°21·1′	4°21·1′W	F	26
Erchless Burn	Highld	NH4141	57°26·2′	4°38·5′W	W	26
Erchless Castle	Highld	NH4040	57°25·6′	4°39·4′W	T	26
Erchless Forest	Highld	NH3944	57°27·7′	4°40·6′W	X	26
Erchless Forest Cottage	Highld	NH4141	57°26·2′	4°38·5′W	X	26
Erddig Country Park	Wrex	SJ3248	53°1·7′	3°0·4′W	X	117
Erddreiniog	I of Angl	SH4680	53°17·9′	4°18·2′W	X	114,115
Erdington	Birm	SP1191	52°31·2′	1°49·9′W	T	139
Eredine	Arg & Bt	NM9609	56°14·0′	5°17·0′W	T	55
Eredine Forest	Arg & Bt	NM9606	56°12·4′	5°16·9′W	F	55
Erens Geo	Orkney	HY2221	59°4·4′	3°21·2′W	X	6
Eresby Ho	Lincs	TF3965	53°10·1′	0°5·2′E	X	122
Erewash Canal	Derby	SK4644	52°59·7′	1°18·5′W	W	129
Erglodd	Cered	SN6590	52°29·7′	3°58·9′W	X	135
Ergyd Isaf	Nth Pt Talb	SS7988	51°34·9′	3°44·4′W	X	170
Ergyd Isaf (Tumuli)	Nth Pt Talb	SS7988	51°34·9′	3°44·4′W	A	170
Ergyd Uchaf	Nth Pt Talb	SS8088	51°34·9′	3°43·5′W	X	170
Ergyd Uchaf (Cairn)	Nth Pt Talb	SS8088	51°34·9′	3°43·5′W	A	170
Eriboll	Highld	NC4356	58°28·1′	4°40·5′W	X	9
Eri Clett	Orkney	HY4731	59°10·1′	2°55·1′W	X	5,6
Eric's Ham	Shetld	HU5487	60°34·0′	1°0·4′W	X	1,2
Eric Stane	D & G	NT0612	55°23·8′	3°28·6′W	X	78
Ericstane	D & G	NT0710	55°22·8′	3°27·6′W	X	78
Eridge Green	E Susx	TQ5535	51°5·8′	0°13·2′E	T	188

Eridge Park	E Susx	TQ5635	51°5·8′	0°14·1′E	X	188
Eridge Sta	E Susx	TQ5434	51°5·3′	0°12·3′E	X	188
Erie Hill	Scot Bord	NT1218	55°27·1′	3°23·1′W	H	78
Eriff	E Ayr	NS5100	55°16·6′	4°20·3′W	X	77
Eriff	E Ayr	NX4999	55°16·0′	4°22·2′W	X	77
Eriff Burn	E Ayr	NS4901	55°17·1′	4°22·2′W	W	77
Eriff Plantation	E Ayr	NS4800	55°16·5′	4°23·1′W	F	77
Erines	Arg & Bt	NR8575	55°55·5′	5°26·0′W	X	62
Erinville	I of M	SC3190	54°16·9′	4°35·3′W	X	95
Erisey Barton	Corn	SW7117	50°0·8′	5°11·4′W	X	203
Erisgeir	Arg & Bt	NM3832	56°24·7′	6°14·4′W	X	48
Eriska	Arg & Bt	NM9042	56°31·6′	5°24·4′W	X	49
Eriskay	N Eil	NF7910	57°4·4′	7°17·4′W	X	31
Eriswell	Suff	TL7278	52°22·6′	0°32·0′E	T	143
Eriswell Hall Fm	Suff	TL7280	52°23·7′	0°32·1′E	FM	143
Eriswell High Warren	Suff	TL7879	52°23·0′	0°37·3′E	X	144
Eriswell Low Warren	Suff	TL7479	52°23·1′	0°33·8′E	X	143
Erith	Bexley	TQ5077	51°28·5′	0°10·0′E	T	177
Erith Marshes	Bexley	TQ4879	51°29·7′	0°8·3′E	X	177
Erith Rands	Hav	TQ5278	51°29·1′	0°11·7′E	W	177
Erith Reach	Hav	TQ5179	51°29·6′	0°10·9′E	W	177
Eriviat-bach	Conwy	SJ0166	53°11·2′	3°28·5′W	X	116
Eriviat Hall	Conwy	SJ0166	53°11·2′	3°28·5′W	X	116
Erkinholme	D & G	NY3685	55°9·6′	2°59·8′W	X	79
Erlas Hall	Wrex	SJ3750	53°2·9′	2°56·0′W	X	117
Erlestoke	Wilts	ST9653	51°16·8′	2°3·1′W	T	184
Erl Wood Manor	Surrey	SU9265	51°22·8′	0°40·3′W	X	175
Erme Head	Devon	SX6266	50°28·9′	3°56·3′W	W	202
Erme Mouth	Devon	SX6147	50°18·6′	3°56·8′W	W	202
Erme Plains	Devon	SX6364	50°27·8′	3°55·4′W	X	202
Erme Pound	Devon	SX6365	50°28·4′	3°55·5′W	A	202
Ermine	Lincs	SK9773	53°14·9′	0°32·4′W	T	121
Ermine Ho	N Lincs	SE9415	53°37·6′	0°33·4′W	X	112
Ermine Lodge	Cambs	TL1687	52°28·3′	0°17·1′W	X	142
Ermine Street Fm	Lincs	SK9429	52°51·3′	0°35·8′W	FM	130
Ermine Street Fm	Lincs	SK9947	53°0·9′	0°31·0′W	FM	130
Ermine Street (Roman Road)	Cambs	TL1591	52°30·5′	0°17·9′W	R	142
Ermine Street (Roman Road)	Cambs	TL2765	52°16·3′	0°7·9′W	R	153
Ermine Street (Roman Road)	Cambs	TL3542	52°3·8′	0°1·4′W	R	154
Ermine Street (Roman Road)	Herts	TL3409	51°46·0′	0°3·1′W	R	166
Ermine Street (Roman Road)	Herts	TL3619	51°51·4′	0°1·1′W	R	166
Ermine Street (Roman Road)	Herts	TL3727	51°55·7′	0°0·1′W	R	166
Ermine Street (Roman Road)	Lincs	SK9330	52°51·8′	0°36·7′W	R	130
Ermine Street (Roman Road)	Lincs	SK9959	53°7·4′	0°30·8′W	R	121
Ermine Street (Roman Road)	Lincs	TF0008	52°39·9′	0°30·9′W	R	141
Ermine Street (Roman Road)	N Lincs	SE9503	53°31·1′	0°33·6′W	R	112
Ermin Fm	Glos	SU0599	51°41·6′	1°55·3′W	FM	163
Ermington	Devon	SX6353	50°21·9′	3°55·2′W	T	202
Ermin Ho	Devon	SX6452	50°21·4′	3°54·3′W	F	202
Ermin Way (Roman Road)	Glos	SO9807	51°45·9′	2°1·3′W	R	163
Ermin Way (Roman Road)	Swin	SU2380	51°31·3′	1°39·7′W	R	174
Ernan Water	Aberd	NJ2812	57°11·8′	3°11·0′W	W	37
Ern Cleuch	Scot Bord	NT3723	55°30·1′	2°59·4′W	X	73
Erncrogo	D & G	NX7468	54°59·7′	3°57·7′W	X	83,84
Erncrogo Loch	D & G	NX7467	54°59·2′	3°57·7′W	W	83,84
Erne Crag	Cumbr	NY3508	54°28·0′	2°59·8′W	X	90
Erneford Ho	Norf	TF8707	52°37·9′	0°46·2′E	X	144
Erne Nest Crag	Cumbr	NY3711	54°29·7′	2°57·9′W	X	90
Ernesettle	C of Plym	SX4459	50°24·8′	4°11·4′W	T	201
Ernespie	D & G	NX7763	54°57·0′	3°54·8′W	X	84
Ernespie Fm	D & G	NX7763	54°57·0′	3°54·8′W	FM	84
Erne's Stack	Shetld	HU1754	60°16·5′	1°41·1′W	X	3
Erne Stack	Shetld	HU3067	60°23·4′	1°26·8′W	X	3
Erne's Ward	Shetld	HU3812	59°53·7′	1°18·8′W	H	4
Ernie Tooin	Orkney	HY3519	59°3·4′	3°7·5′W	X	6
Ernocroft	Stock	SJ9891	53°25·2′	2°1·4′W	X	109
Erns Hamar	Shetld	HP5804	60°43·2′	0°55·7′W	H	1
Ern Stack	Shetld	HU4596	60°39·0′	1°10·1′W	X	1
Erpingham	Norf	TG1931	52°50·1′	1°15·5′E	T	133
Erpingham Ho	Norf	TG2032	52°50·7′	1°16·4′E	X	133
Erracht	Highld	NH8480	57°47·9′	3°56·6′W	X	21
Erraid	Arg & Bt	NM2919	56°17·4′	6°22·3′W	X	48
Erraid Sound	Arg & Bt	NM3020	56°18·0′	6°21·4′W	W	48
Erray Ho	Arg & Bt	NM5056	56°38·0′	6°4·2′W	X	47
Errickstane Hill	S Lanak	NT0214	55°24·9′	3°32·5′W	H	78
Erring Burn	Northum	NY9673	55°3·3′	2°3·3′W	W	87
Erringden Grange	Cald	SD9826	53°44·1′	2°1·4′W	X	103
Erringden Moor	Cald	SD9825	53°43·5′	2°1·4′W	X	103
Errington	Northum	NY9571	55°2·3′	2°4·3′W	X	87
Errington Hill Head	Northum	NY9669	55°1·2′	2°3·3′W	X	87
Errington Red Ho	Northum	NY9771	55°2·3′	2°2·4′W	X	87
Errington Wood	Red & Cl	NZ6220	54°34·5′	1°2·0′W	F	94
Erriottwood	Kent	TQ9359	51°18·1′	0°46·5′E	T	178
Erriwig Fm	Bucks	SP9105	51°44·4′	0°40·5′W	FM	165
Errocht	Highld	NN1482	56°53·8′	5°2·8′W	X	34,41
Errochty Dam	Pth & Kin	NN7165	56°45·8′	4°6·2′W	X	42
Errochty Water	Pth & Kin	NN7563	56°44·8′	4°2·2′W	W	42
Errogie	Highld	NH5522	57°16·2′	4°23·8′W	T	26,35
Errol	Moray	NJ2659	57°37·2′	3°13·9′W	X	28
Errol	Pth & Kin	NO2522	56°23·3′	3°12·4′W	T	53,59
Errollston	Aberd	NK0837	57°25·7′	1°51·5′W	X	30
Errol Park	Pth & Kin	NO2422	56°23·3′	3°13·4′W	X	53,59
Errwood Hall	Derby	SK0074	53°16·0′	1°59·6′W	X	119
Errwood Resr	Derby	SK0175	53°16·6′	1°58·7′W	W	119
Erryd	Carm	SN7538	52°1·8′	3°48·9′W	X	146,160
Erskine	Renf	NS4571	55°54·7′	4°28·4′W	T	64
Erskine Bridge	Renf	NS4672	55°55·2′	4°27·4′W	X	64
Erskine Home Fm	Renf	NS4472	55°55·2′	4°29·3′W	FM	64
Erskine's Knap	Aberd	NO7373	56°51·1′	2°26·1′W	A	45
Ersock Loch	D & G	NX4337	54°42·5′	4°25·8′W	W	83

Erth Barton	Corn	SX3856	50°23·1'	4°16·4'W	X	201
Erth Hill	Corn	SX3855	50°22·6'	4°16·3'W	H	201
Ervadale	Orkney	HY4231	59°10·0'	3°0·4'W	X	5,6
Ervie	D & G	NX0067	54°57·7'	5°7·0'W	X	82
Ervie Moor	D & G	NX6673	55°2·3'	4°5·4'W	X	77,84
Erw	Gwyn	SH5058	53°6·1'	4°14·0'W	X	115
Erwallo	Wrex	SJ2137	52°55·7'	3°10·1'W	X	126
Erwan Fach	Cered	SN3355	52°10·3'	4°26·1'W	X	145
Erwan-fawr	Cered	SN3354	52°9·8'	4°26·1'W	X	145
Erwarton	Suff	TM2134	51°57·9'	1°13·4'E	T	169
Erwarton Bay	Suff	TM2333	51°57·3'	1°15·1'E	W	169
Erwarton Hall	Suff	TM2235	51°58·4'	1°14·3'E	A	169
Erwarton Ness	Suff	TM2133	51°57·3'	1°13·4'E	X	169
Erway Hall	Shrops	SJ3538	52°56·4'	2°57·6'W	X	126
Erw Barfau	Cered	SN7578	52°23·4'	3°49·8'W	H	135,147
Erwbarfe Fm	Cered	SN7478	52°23·4'	3°50·7'W	FM	135,147
Erwbeili	Powys	SN8544	52°5·2'	3°40·3'W	X	147,160
Erwddalen	Powys	SN9955	52°11·3'	3°28·3'W	X	147
Erwddol	Powys	SN9354	52°10·7'	3°33·5'W	X	147
Erw-ddwfr	Gwyn	SH7232	52°52·5'	3°53·7'W	X	124
Erw-Dinmael	Conwy	SH9246	53°0·3'	3°36·2'W	X	116
Erwfaethlon	Gwyn	SN6298	52°34·0'	4°1·8'W	X	135
Erw-fawr	Denb	SJ1853	53°4·3'	3°13·0'W	X	116
Erw-Fawr	Gwyn	SH6043	52°58·2'	4°4·7'W	X	124
Erw Fawr	I of Angl	SH3181	53°18·2'	4°31·8'W	X	114
Erwgerrig Fm	Wrex	SJ1935	52°54·6'	3°11·9'W	FM	125
Erwgilfach	Powys	SO0349	52°8·1'	3°24·6'W	X	147
Erw Goch	Conwy	SH8173	53°14·7'	3°46·6'W	X	116
Erw-gôch	I of Angl	SH3182	53°18·7'	4°31·8'W	X	114
Erwhelm	Powys	SO0349	52°8·1'	3°24·6'W	X	147
Erw-hir	Powys	SO0743	52°4·9'	3°21·0'W	X	147,160
Erw-lon	Pemb	SN0232	51°57·3'	4°52·5'W	X	145,157
Erw Newydd	Gwyn	SH1933	52°52·1'	4°40·9'W	X	123
Erwood	Powys	SO0942	52°4·4'	3°19·3'W	T	147,161
Erw-pwll-y-glo	Gwyn	SH5163	53°8·8'	4°13·3'W	X	114,115
Erw'rhenallt	Powys	SO0645	52°6·0'	3°21·9'W	X	147
Erwsaethau Fm	Nth Pt Talb	SN7500	51°41·3'	3°48·1'W	FM	170
Erwsuran	Gwyn	SH5641	52°57·1'	4°8·2'W	X	124
Erwtomau	Cered	SN7078	52°23·3'	3°54·2'W	X	135,147
Erw-wastad	Carm	SN6008	51°45·4'	4°1·3'W	X	159
Erw-wen	Carm	SN4419	51°51·1'	4°15·5'W	X	159
Eryholme	N Yks	NZ3208	54°28·2'	1°30·0'W	T	93
Eryholme Grange	N Yks	NZ3208	54°28·2'	1°30·0'W	X	93
Eryl-Aran	Gwyn	SH9135	52°54·3'	3°36·8'W	X	125
Eryl Hall	Denb	SJ0372	53°14·4'	3°26·8'W	X	116
Eryrys	Denb	SJ2057	53°6·5'	3°11·3'W	T	117
Esbie	D & G	NY0785	55°9·3'	3°27·1'W	X	78
Escalls	Corn	SW3626	50°4·8'	5°41·0'W	X	203
Escalwen	Pemb	SM9533	51°57·7'	4°58·6'W	X	157
Escart	Arg & Bt	NR8466	55°50·6'	5°26·6'W	X	62
Escart Fm	Arg & Bt	NR8453	55°43·6'	5°26·0'W	FM	62
Escheat Fm	Beds	SP9840	52°3·2'	0°33·8'W	FM	153
Escley Brook	Heref	SO3233	51°59·7'	2°59·0'W	W	161
Esclusham Mountain	Wrex	SJ2550	53°2·8'	3°6·7'W	H	117
Escoe Ho	N Yks	SE0061	54°2·9'	1°59·6'W	X	98
Escomb	Durham	NZ1830	54°40·1'	1°42·8'W	T	92
Escot Park	Devon	SY0898	50°46·7'	3°17·9'W	X	192
Escott	Somer	ST0937	51°7·7'	3°17·6'W	T	181
Escott Fm	Somer	ST0239	51°8·7'	3°23·7'W	FM	181
Escowbeck	Lancs	SD5264	54°4·4'	2°43·6'W	X	97
Escrick	York	SE6342	53°52·5'	1°2·1'W	T	105,106
Escrick Grange Fm	N Yks	SE6141	53°51·9'	1°3·9'W	FM	105
Escrick Park	N Yks	SE6341	53°51·9'	1°2·1'W	X	105,106
Escuan Hall	Gwyn	SN5999	52°34·5'	4°4·4'W	X	135
Escuan Isaf	Gwyn	SN5999	52°34·5'	4°4·4'W	X	135
Escullion	Pth & Kin	NN7718	56°20·6'	3°59·0'W	X	57
Esdale Law	Scot Bord	NT4417	55°26·9'	2°52·7'W	H	79
Esgair	Carm	SN2719	51°50·8'	4°30·3'W	X	158
Esgair	Carm	SN3728	51°55·8'	4°21·9'W	X	145
Esgair	Carm	SN4231	51°57·5'	4°17·6'W	X	146
Esgair	Carm	SN5929	51°56·7'	4°2·7'W	X	146
Esgair	Carm	SN6037	52°1·1'	4°2·0'W	X	146
Esgair	Cered	SN5868	52°17·7'	4°4·5'W	X	135
Esgair	Cered	SN6551	52°8·7'	3°58·0'W	X	146
Esgair	Cered	SN6665	52°16·3'	3°57·4'W	X	135
Esgair	Powys	SH8903	52°37·0'	3°38·0'W	X	135,136
Esgair	Powys	SN7595	52°32·6'	3°50·0'W	H	135
Esgair	Powys	SO0072	52°20·5'	3°27·7'W	X	136,147
Esgair	Powys	SO0372	52°20·5'	3°25·0'W	X	136,147
Esgair	Powys	SO0639	52°2·7'	3°21·8'W	X	160
Esgairadda	Gwyn	SH8816	52°44·0'	3°39·1'W	X	124,125
Esgair Ambor	Cered	SN7559	52°13·1'	3°49·4'W	X	146,147
Esgairannell	Powys	SN9245	52°5·8'	3°34·2'W	X	147
Esgair-Arth	Cered	SN4862	52°14·4'	4°13·2'W	X	146
Esgair Bellaf	Powys	SN8453	52°10·0'	3°41·4'W	X	147
Esgair Berfa	Gwyn	SH6309	52°39·9'	4°1·2'W	H	124
Esgair Berfedd	Carm	SN8145	52°5·7'	3°43·8'W	X	147
Esgair-berfedd	Carm	SN8437	52°1·4'	3°41·0'W	X	160
Esgair Cae	Powys	SN8875	52°21·9'	3°38·3'W	X	135,136,147
Esgair Cerrig	Cered	SN7556	52°11·5'	3°49·3'W	H	146,147
Esgair Cloddiad	Powys	SN8256	52°11·6'	3°43·2'W	X	147
Esgair Cormwg	Powys	SN8570	52°19·2'	3°40·8'W	X	135,136,147
Esgaircorn	Carm	SN6446	52°6·0'	3°58·7'W	X	146
Esgair Crawnllwyn	Powys	SN8769	52°18·7'	3°39·1'W	X	135,136,147
Esgair-crwys	Carm	SN6346	52°6·0'	3°59·6'W	X	146
Esgair Cwmowen	Powys	SJ0000	52°35·6'	3°28·2'W	X	136
Esgair Cywion	Powys	SN8267	52°17·5'	3°43·4'W	X	135,136,147
Esgair Cywion	Powys	SN8770	52°19·2'	3°39·1'W	X	135,136,147
Esgair Dafydd	Powys	SN8345	52°5·7'	3°42·1'W	X	147
Esgair-Dafydd	Powys	SN8444	52°5·2'	3°41·2'W	X	147,160
Esgairdawe	Carm	SN6140	52°2·7'	4°1·2'W	X	146
Esgair-ddedwydd	Carm	SN4447	52°6·2'	4°16·3'W	X	146
Esgair Dderwen	Cered	SN8673	52°20·8'	3°40·0'W	X	135,136,147
Esgairddeugoed	Carm	SN2225	51°53·9'	4°34·8'W	X	145,158
Esgair Ddu	Carm	SN7820	51°52·2'	3°45·9'W	X	160
Esgair Ddu	Powys	SH8710	52°40·8'	3°39·9'W	H	124,125
Esgair Dernol	Powys	SN9075	52°22·0'	3°36·5'W	H	136,147
Esgair Draenllwyn	Powys	SN9294	52°32·2'	3°35·1'W	X	136
Esgair-Ebrill	Conwy	SH8168	53°12·0'	3°46·5'W	X	116
Esgair-Einon	Cered	SN4744	52°4·6'	4°13·6'W	X	146

Esgaireithin	Cered	SN2850	52°7·5'	4°30·4'W	X	145
Esgair Elan	Cered	SN8474	52°21·3'	3°41·8'W	H	135,136,147
Esgair Embor	Cered	SN7670	52°19·1'	3°48·8'W	X	135,147
Esgair Fawr	Cered	SN7458	52°12·6'	3°50·3'W	X	146,147
Esgair-fawr	Powys	SO0573	52°21·1'	3°23·3'W	X	136,147
Esgair Fedwen	Cered	SN7259	52°13·1'	3°52·0'W	X	146,147
Esgair Felen	Gwyn	SH6357	53°5·8'	4°2·4'W	X	115
Esgair Ferchon	Carm	SN7142	52°3·9'	3°52·5'W	H	146,147,160
Esgair Ffosfudr	Cered	SN7388	52°28·8'	3°51·8'W	H	135
Esgair Ffrwd	Cered	SN7557	52°12·1'	3°49·4'W	H	146,147
Esgair-Fochnant	Powys	SN8196	52°33·2'	3°44·9'W	X	135
Esgair Foel-ddu	Cered	SN7092	52°30·9'	3°54·5'W	H	135
Esgair Foel Eirin	Gwyn	SH7404	52°37·4'	3°51·3'W	X	135
Esgair Fraith	Cered	SN7157	52°12·0'	3°52·9'W	X	146,147
Esgair Fraith	Cered	SN7491	52°30·4'	3°51·0'W	X	135
Esgair Fraith	Powys	SN8956	52°11·7'	3°37·0'W	X	147
Esgair-fwyog	Carm	SN8440	52°3·0'	3°41·1'W	X	147,160
Esgair-fynwent	Carm	SN5334	51°59·3'	4°8·1'W	X	146
Esgair Gaeo	Carm	SN7250	52°8·2'	3°51·8'W	X	146,147
Esgair Ganol	Cered	SN7854	52°10·5'	3°46·7'W	H	146,147
Esgair Ganol	Powys	SN8660	52°13·8'	3°39·8'W	X	147
Esgair Ganol	Powys	SN8776	52°22·5'	3°39·2'W	X	135,136,147
Esgairganol	Powys	SN9057	52°12·3'	3°36·2'W	X	147
Esgair-garn	Cered	SN6552	52°9·2'	3°58·0'W	X	146
Esgair Garn	Powys	SN8249	52°7·8'	3°43·0'W	X	147
Esgair Garthen	Powys	SN8364	52°15·9'	3°42·5'W	X	147
Esgair-gawr	Gwyn	SH8122	52°47·2'	3°45·5'W	X	124,125
Esgairgeiliog	Powys	SH7506	52°38·5'	3°50·4'W	T	124
Esgair-geiliog	Powys	SO0076	52°28·1'	3°21·7'W	X	136
Esgair Gelli	Cered	SN7757	52°12·1'	3°47·6'W	H	146,147
Esgair-gelynen	Powys	SH9106	52°38·7'	3°36·3'W	X	125
Esgair Gerwyn	Cered	SN7858	52°12·6'	3°46·7'W	X	146,147
Esgair Geulan	Powys	SN8597	52°33·8'	3°41·4'W	X	135,136
Esgair Gnycog	Powys	SN8462	52°14·9'	3°41·6'W	X	147
Esgair Goch	Cered	SN6752	52°9·3'	3°56·3'W	X	146
Esgair Goch	Cered	SN7085	52°27·1'	3°54·4'W	X	135
Esgair Gorddi	Powys	SN7690	52°29·9'	3°49·3'W	X	135
Esgair Gorlan	Cered	SN7282	52°25·5'	3°52·6'W	H	135
Esgair Gors	Cered	SN7955	52°11·0'	3°45·8'W	X	146,147
Esgair Graflwyn	Powys	SN8396	52°33·2'	3°43·1'W	X	135,136
Esgair Gris	Powys	SN8868	52°18·2'	3°38·2'W	X	135,136,147
Esgair Gul	Powys	SN8856	52°11·7'	3°37·9'W	X	147
Esgair Gwair	Cered	SN7651	52°8·8'	3°48·3'W	X	146,147
Esgair Gwngu	Cered	SN8573	52°20·8'	3°40·9'W	X	135,136,147
Esgair Hendre	Carm	SN6748	52°7·1'	3°56·2'W	H	146
Esgairhendy	Cered	SN6363	52°15·1'	4°0·0'W	X	146
Esgair Hengae	Cered	SN8168	52°18·1'	3°44·3'W	X	135,136,147
Esgairheulog	Conwy	SH7970	53°13·0'	3°48·3'W	X	115
Esgair Hir	Carm	SN7719	51°51·6'	3°46·8'W	X	160
Esgair Hir	Cered	SN6854	52°10·4'	3°55·4'W	X	146
Esgair Hir	Cered	SN7556	52°11·5'	3°49·3'W	X	146,147
Esgair Hir	Cered	SN7855	52°11·0'	3°46·7'W	H	146,147
Esgair-Hir	Powys	SH7804	52°37·4'	3°47·7'W	X	135
Esgair Hir	Powys	SN9093	52°31·7'	3°36·9'W	X	136
Esgairhir-Isaf	Carm	SN3723	51°53·1'	4°21·7'W	X	145,159
Esgair Hirnant	Cered	SN7959	52°13·2'	3°45·9'W	X	146,147
Esgair Inglis	Cered	SN5146	52°5·8'	4°10·1'W	X	146
Esgair Irfon	Powys	SN8454	52°10·6'	3°41·4'W	X	147
Esgairleth	Powys	SN9090	52°30·1'	3°36·8'W	X	136
Esgairliving	Carm	SN5740	52°2·6'	4°4·7'W	X	146
Esgair-llaethdy	Carm	SN7829	51°57·0'	3°46·1'W	X	146,160
Esgair Llethr	Cered	SN7254	52°10·4'	3°51·9'W	H	146,147
Esgair Llewelyn	Powys	SH8008	52°39·6'	3°46·1'W	X	124,125
Esgair Llwyn-gwyn	Powys	SN8879	52°24·1'	3°38·4'W	H	135,136,147
Esgair Llyn-du	Cered	SN7762	52°14·8'	3°47·7'W	X	146,147
Esgair Llys	Powys	SN8682	52°25·7'	3°40·2'W	X	135,136
Esgairlwyd	Powys	SH7807	52°39·1'	3°47·8'W	X	124
Esgair-lygoer	Cered	SN4847	52°6·3'	4°12·8'W	X	146
Esgair-maen	Cered	SN6563	52°15·2'	3°58·3'W	X	146
Esgair Maen	Cered	SN7151	52°8·8'	3°52·7'W	X	146,147
Esgair Maingwynion	Cered	SN8176	52°22·4'	3°44·5'W	X	135,136,147
Esgair Milwyn	Cered	SN7973	52°20·7'	3°46·2'W	H	135,147
Esgair Moel	Powys	SN8845	52°5·8'	3°37·7'W	X	147
Esgairnantau	Powys	SO1762	52°15·2'	3°12·6'W	H	148
Esgair Nantybeddau	Powys	SN8466	52°17·0'	3°41·6'W	H	135,136,147
Esgair Nant-y-brain	Powys	SN8350	52°8·4'	3°42·2'W	X	147
Esgair Nefal	Powys	SN9459	52°13·4'	3°32·7'W	X	147
Esgair Neint	Cered	SN7770	52°19·1'	3°47·9'W	X	135,147
Esgair Neuadd	Cered	SN7086	52°27·6'	3°54·4'W	X	135
Esgaironw-fawr	Cered	SN4353	52°9·4'	4°17·3'W	X	146
Esgair Penygarreg	Powys	SN9168	52°18·2'	3°35·5'W	H	136,147
Esgair Perfedd	Powys	SN9169	52°18·7'	3°35·5'W	X	136,147
Esgair Priciau	Powys	SH9304	52°37·6'	3°34·5'W	X	136
Esgair Rhiwlan	Powys	SN8871	52°19·8'	3°38·2'W	H	135,136,147
Esgair Rudd	Powys	SN8774	52°21·4'	3°39·2'W	X	135,136,147
Esgairsaeson	Cered	SN6364	52°15·7'	4°0·1'W	X	146
Esgair Saeson	Cered	SN7960	52°13·7'	3°45·9'W	X	146,147
Esgair-Tanglwst	Cered	SN3548	52°6·6'	4°24·2'W	X	145
Esgair Tan-lan	Carm	SN6947	52°6·6'	3°54·4'W	H	146
Esgair Uchaf	Gwyn	SH6902	52°36·2'	3°55·7'W	X	135
Esgairuchaf	Powys	SO0979	52°24·3'	3°19·9'W	X	136,147
Esgair-Weddan	Gwyn	SH6800	52°35·2'	3°56·5'W	X	135
Esgair-wen	Carm	SN6045	52°5·4'	4°2·2'W	X	146
Esgair-wen	Cered	SN4552	52°8·9'	4°15·5'W	X	146
Esgair Wen	Cered	SN8166	52°17·0'	3°44·3'W	X	135,136,147
Esgair Wen	Powys	SN8874	52°21·4'	3°38·3'W	X	135,136,147
Esgair-Wian	Powys	SH8106	52°38·6'	3°45·1'W	X	124,125
Esgairwy	Powys	SO0668	52°18·4'	3°22·3'W	X	136,147
Esgair Ychion	Powys	SN8579	52°24·1'	3°41·0'W	X	135,136,147
Esgair y Ffynnon	Powys	SN9357	52°12·3'	3°33·6'W	X	147
Esgair y Gadair	Powys	SN8565	52°16·5'	3°40·7'W	X	135,136,147
Esgair y Garn	Cered	SN7567	52°17·5'	3°49·6'W	H	135,147
Esgair y Graig	Powys	SN9076	52°22·5'	3°36·6'W	X	136,147
Esgair y Groes	Powys	SN9593	52°31·7'	3°32·5'W	X	136
Esgair y Llwyn	Powys	SN8973	52°20·9'	3°37·4'W	X	135,136,147
Esgair y Maen	Powys	SN8185	52°27·2'	3°44·7'W	X	135,136
Esgair y Maes	Powys	SH9611	52°41·4'	3°31·9'W	X	125
Esgair y Maesnant	Powys	SN8386	52°27·8'	3°42·9'W	H	135,136
Esgair yr Adar	Powys	SN8358	52°12·7'	3°42·4'W	X	147
Esgair y Tŷ	Powys	SN8972	52°20·3'	3°37·4'W	X	135,136,147

Esgeiriau	Denb	SJ0532	52°52·9'	3°24·3'W	X	125
Esgeiriau	Gwyn	SH8021	52°46·6'	3°46·3'W	X	124,125
Esger	Cered	SN4251	52°8·3'	4°18·1'W	X	146
Esgerddar	Carm	SN7044	52°5·0'	3°53·4'W	X	146,147,160
Esgereinon	Cered	SN3852	52°8·8'	4°21·7'W	X	145
Esgerfa	Carm	SN3424	51°53·6'	4°24·4'W	X	145,159
Esgerfechan	Carm	SN3723	51°53·1'	4°21·7'W	X	145,159
Esgergraig	Cered	SN3046	52°5·4'	4°28·5'W	X	145
Esgerwen	Carm	SN5939	52°2·1'	4°2·9'W	X	146
Esgors	Essex	TL4605	51°43·7'	0°7·2'E	X	167
Esgyr-fawr	Pemb	SN1347	52°5·6'	4°43·4'W	X	145
Esgyrn	Pemb	SM9634	51°58·3'	4°57·8'W	X	157
Esgyrn Bottom	Pemb	SM9734	51°58·3'	4°56·9'W	X	157
Esgyrn Brook	Powys	SO2438	52°2·4'	3°6·1'W	W	161
Esgyryn	Conwy	SH8078	53°17·4'	3°47·6'W	T	116
Esh	Durham	NZ1944	54°47·7'	1°41·8'W	T	88
Esha Ness	Shetld	HU2279	60°29·9'	1°35·5'W	X	3
Eshber Wood	N Yks	SD9476	54°11·0'	2°5·1'W	F	98
Eshells Moor	Northum	NY8757	54°54·7'	2°11·7'W	X	87
Esher	Surrey	TQ1464	51°22·0'	0°21·3'W	T	176,187
Esher Common	Surrey	TQ1362	51°21·0'	0°22·2'W	X	176,187
Eshiels	Scot Bord	NT2739	55°38·6'	3°9·2'W	T	73
Eshiels Hope	Scot Bord	NT2840	55°39·1'	3°8·2'W	X	73
Esholt	Brad	SE1840	53°51·6'	1°43·2'W	T	104
Esholt Hall	Brad	SE1839	53°51·1'	1°43·2'W	X	104
Eshott	Northum	NZ2097	55°16·3'	1°40·7'W	T	81
Eshott Birnie	Northum	NZ1996	55°15·7'	1°41·6'W	X	81
Eshottheugh	Northum	NZ1997	55°16·3'	1°41·6'W	X	81
Eshton	N Yks	SD9356	54°0·2'	2°6·0'W	T	103
Eshton Br	N Yks	SD9455	53°59·7'	2°5·1'W	X	103
Eshton Ho	N Yks	SD9356	54°0·2'	2°6·0'W	X	103
Eshton Moor	N Yks	SD9157	54°0·8'	2°7·8'W	X	103
Eshton Tarn	N Yks	SD9157	54°0·8'	2°7·8'W	W	103
Esh Winning	Durham	NZ1941	54°46·1'	1°41·9'W	T	88
Eshwood Hall	Durham	NZ2141	54°46·1'	1°40·0'W	X	88
Eskadale	Highld	NH4539	57°25·2'	4°34·4'W	T	26
Eskadale Ho	Highld	NH4641	57°26·3'	4°33·5'W	X	26
Eskadale Moor	Highld	NH4235	57°22·9'	4°37·2'W	X	26
Eskamhorn	N Yks	SE6723	53°42·2'	0°58·7'W	X	105,106
Esk Bank	D & G	NY3876	55°4·7'	2°57·8'W	X	85
Eskbank	Midlo	NT3266	55°53·2'	3°4·8'W	T	66
Esk Boathouse	Cumbr	NY3463	54°57·7'	3°1·4'W	X	85
Eskdale	Cumbr	NY1700	54°23·6'	3°16·3'W	X	89,90
Eskdale	Cumbr	SD1799	54°23·0'	3°16·3'W	X	96
Eskdale	D & G	NY3489	55°11·7'	3°1·8'W	X	79
Esk Dale	N Yks	NZ7407	54°27·4'	0°51·1'W	X	94
Esk Dale	N Yks	NZ8406	54°26·8'	0°41·9'W	X	94
Eskdale Fell	Cumbr	NY1803	54°25·2'	3°15·4'W	X	89,90
Eskdale Green	Cumbr	NY1400	54°23·5'	3°19·1'W	T	89
Eskdale Mill	Cumbr	NY1701	54°24·1'	3°16·3'W	X	89,90
Eskdale Moor	Cumbr	NY1703	54°25·2'	3°16·3'W	X	89,90
Eskdalemuir	D & G	NY2597	55°15·9'	3°10·4'W	T	79
Eskdalemuir Forest	D & G	NT2301	55°18·1'	3°12·3'W	F	79
Eskdale Needle	Cumbr	NY2202	54°24·7'	3°11·7'W	X	89,90
Eskdalerig	D & G	NY1478	55°5·6'	3°20·4'W	X	85
Eske	E Yorks	TA0543	53°52·6'	0°23·8'W	X	107
Eske Boundary Plantn	E Yorks	TA0644	53°53·1'	0°22·8'W	F	107
Eske Carrs	E Yorks	TA0644	53°53·1'	0°22·8'W	X	107
Eskechraggan	Arg & Bt	NS0664	55°50·1'	5°5·4'W	X	63
Eskeleth	N Yks	NY9903	54°25·6'	2°0·5'W	X	92
Eskemore	Moray	NJ2422	57°17·2'	3°15·2'W	X	36
Eskemulloch	Moray	NJ2420	57°16·1'	3°15·2'W	X	36
Eskew Beck Ho	Cumbr	NY5905	54°26·6'	2°37·5'W	X	91
Eske Wood	E Yorks	TA0643	53°52·6'	0°22·8'W	F	107
Esk Hall	N Yks	NZ8607	54°27·3'	0°40·0'W	X	94
Eskham	Lincs	TF3698	53°27·9'	0°3·3'E	T	113
Eskham Ho	Lancs	SD4444	53°53·6'	2°50·7'W	X	102
Esk Hause	Cumbr	NY2308	54°27·9'	3°10·9'W	X	89,90
Eskhill	Angus	NO4356	56°41·8'	2°55·4'W	X	54
Eskhill	Midlo	NT2662	55°51·0'	3°10·5'W	X	66
Esk Ho	N Yks	SE6499	54°23·2'	1°0·4'W	X	94,100
Eskholme	Cumbr	SD6383	54°14·7'	2°33·7'W	X	97
Eskholme	Donc	SE6317	53°39·0'	1°2·4'W	T	111
Eskholme Pike	Cumbr	SD6383	54°14·7'	2°33·7'W	X	97
Eskidal Burn	Highld	NC4648	57°27·3'	6°13·6'W	W	23
Eskielawn	Angus	NO2766	56°47·0'	3°11·2'W	H	44
Eskin	Cumbr	NY1829	54°39·2'	3°15·8'W	X	89,90
Eskishold	Orkney	HY2312	58°59·6'	3°19·9'W	X	6
Esklets Crag	N Yks	NZ6602	54°24·8'	0°58·6'W	X	94
Eskmeals	Cumbr	SD0893	54°19·7'	3°24·5'W	X	96
Eskmeals Ho	Cumbr	SD0993	54°19·7'	3°23·5'W	X	96
Esk Mill	N Yks	NZ6808	54°28·0'	0°56·6'W	X	94
Esknish	Arg & Bt	NR3664	55°48·1'	6°12·3'W	X	60,61
Esk Pike	Cumbr	NY2307	54°27·4'	3°10·8'W	H	89,90
Eskrigg	Cumbr	NY2451	54°51·1'	3°10·6'W	X	85
Eskrigge	Lancs	SD5669	54°7·1'	2°40·0'W	X	97
Eskrigg End	Cumbr	SD5689	54°17·9'	2°40·1'W	X	97
Eskrigg Tarn	Cumbr	SD5788	54°17·4'	2°39·2'W	W	97
Esk Valley	N Yks	NZ8204	54°25·7'	0°43·7'W	T	94
Eslie	Aberd	NO7192	57°1·3'	2°28·2'W	X	38,45
Eslington Highhill	Northum	NU0311	55°23·8'	1°56·7'W	X	81
Eslington Lowhill	Northum	NU0411	55°23·8'	1°55·8'W	X	81
Eslington Park	Northum	NU0412	55°24·4'	1°55·8'W	T	81
Esp Crag	Lancs	SD6458	54°1·2'	2°32·6'W	X	102,103
Esperley Lane Ends	Durham	NZ1324	54°36·9'	1°47·5'W	T	92
Espershields Fm	Northum	NY9954	54°53·1'	2°0·5'W	FM	87
Esperston	Midlo	NT3356	55°47·8'	3°3·7'W	X	66,73
Espersykes	N Yks	SE8174	54°9·6'	0°45·2'W	X	100
Esp Ford	Cumbr	SD4490	54°18·4'	2°51·2'W	X	97
Esp Green	Durham	NZ1449	54°50·4'	1°46·5'W	X	88
Esp Hill	Northum	NY7979	55°6·5'	2°19·3'W	X	86,87
Esp Hill	Wrex	SJ4054	53°5·0'	2°53·3'W	X	117
Esp Ho	N Yks	SE5699	54°23·2'	1°7·8'W	X	100
Espland	Cumbr	NY7218	54°33·6'	2°25·6'W	X	91
Esplandhill	Cumbr	NY6823	54°36·3'	2°29·3'W	X	91
Espley	Shrops	SJ6026	52°50·0'	2°35·2'W	X	127
Espley Hall	Northum	NZ1790	55°12·5'	1°43·5'W	X	81
Esp Mill	Northum	NY8279	55°6·6'	2°16·5'W	X	86,87
Esprick	Lancs	SD4036	53°49·3'	2°54·3'W	T	102
Esp Rigg	N Yks	SE8096	54°21·4'	0°45·7'W	X	94,100

Esps Fm	Cumbr	NY1429	54°39·2′	3°19·6′W	FM	89
Esps Fm	Cumbr	SD2985	54°15·6′	3°5·0′W	FM	96,97
Espsyke Fm	N Yks	NZ8210	54°29·0′	0°43·6′W	FM	94
Esquiebuie	Moray	NJ2440	57°26·9′	3°15·5′W	X	28
Ess	Highld	NH9227	57°19·5′	3°47·2′W	X	36
Essa	Corn	SX1351	50°20·0′	4°37·3′W	X	200
Essan	Highld	NM8181	56°52·4′	5°35·2′W	X	40
Essaquoy	Orkney	HY4331	59°10·0′	2°59·3′W	X	5,6
Esscroft	Brad	SE1547	53°55·4′	1°45·9′W	X	104
Essebeare	Devon	SS8015	50°55·6′	3°42·1′W	X	181
Essendine	Rut	TF0412	52°42·0′	0°27·3′W	T	130
Essendon	Herts	TL2708	51°45·6′	0°9·2′W	T	166
Essendonbury Fm	Herts	TL2709	51°46·1′	0°9·2′W	FM	166
Essendon Place	Herts	TL2707	51°45·1′	0°9·2′W	X	166
Essendy Ho	Pth & Kin	NO1442	56°34·0′	3°23·5′W	X	53
Essenside Head	Scot Bord	NT4320	55°28·5′	2°53·7′W	H	73
Essenside Loch	Scot Bord	NT4520	55°28·5′	2°51·8′W	W	73
Essett Hill	Cumbr	SD5888	54°17·4′	2°38·3′W	H	97
Essex Bridge	Staffs	SJ9922	52°48·0′	2°0·5′W	A	127
Essex Fm	Northnts	SP6884	52°27·2′	0°59·6′W	FM	141
Essex Fm	Oxon	SP6321	51°53·3′	1°4·7′W	FM	164,165
Essex Hall	Essex	TL7239	52°1·6′	0°30·8′E	X	154
Essex Way	Essex	TL6214	51°48·3′	0°21·4′E	X	167
Essex Way	Essex	TL8824	51°53·2′	0°44·3′E	X	168
Essex Way	Essex	TL9830	51°56·2′	0°53·2′E	X	168
Essex Wood	Staffs	SO8185	52°28·0′	2°16·4′W	F	138
Essich	Highld	NH6439	57°25·5′	4°15·4′W	X	26
Essie	Aberd	NJ4627	57°20·1′	2°53·4′W	X	37
Essie	Aberd	NK0853	57°34·3′	1°51·5′W	X	30
Essil	Moray	NJ3363	57°39·4′	3°6·9′W	X	28
Essington	Staffs	SJ9603	52°37·7′	2°3·1′W	T	127,139
Esslemont Ho	Aberd	NJ9330	57°21·9′	2°6·5′W	X	30
Essmitchell	Stir	NN7005	56°13·4′	4°5·4′W	X	57
Ess of Glenlatterach (Waterfall)	Moray	NJ1953	57°33·9′	3°20·8′W	W	28
Essworthy	Devon	SS5402	50°48·2′	4°3·9′W	X	191
Estavarney	Monm	SO3503	51°43·6′	2°56·1′W	X	171
Estcourt Ho	Glos	ST8991	51°37·3′	2°9·1′W	X	163,173
Esthwaite Hall	Cumbr	SD3595	54°21·0′	2°59·6′W	A	96,97
Esthwaite Lodge	Cumbr	SD3596	54°21·6′	2°59·6′W	X	96,97
Esthwaite Water	Cumbr	SD3696	54°21·6′	2°58·7′W	W	96,97
Eston	Red & Cl	NZ5519	54°34·0′	1°8·5′W	T	93
E Stonesdale	N Yks	NY8901	54°24·5′	2°9·7′W	X	91,92
Eston Moor	Red & Cl	NZ5617	54°33·0′	1°7·6′W	X	93
Eston Nab	Red & Cl	NZ5618	54°33·5′	1°7·6′W	H	93
Estover	C of Plym	SX5059	50°24·9′	4°6·3′W	T	201
Estrayer Park	Devon	SX5693	50°43·4′	4°2·0′W	X	191
Estuary Fm	Norf	TF6227	52°49·2′	0°24·7′E	FM	132
Estyn Brook	Powys	SN9957	52°12·4′	3°28·3′W	W	147
Eswick	Shetld	HU4853	60°15·8′	1°7·5′W	T	3
Es Wick	Shetld	HU4954	60°16·3′	1°6·4′W	W	3
Eswick Holm	Shetld	HU4853	60°15·8′	1°7·5′W	X	3
Esworthy	Devon	SS8714	50°55·1′	3°36·1′W	X	181
Etal	Northum	NT9239	55°38·9′	2°7·2′W	T	74,75
Etal Castle	Northum	NT9239	55°38·9′	2°7·2′W	A	74,75
Etal Manor	Northum	NT9239	55°38·9′	2°7·2′W	X	74,75
Etal Moor	Northum	NT9539	55°38·9′	2°4·3′W	X	74,75
Etal Rhodes	Northum	NT9339	55°38·9′	2°6·2′W	X	74,75
Etchden Fm	Kent	TQ9441	51°8·3′	0°46·8′E	FM	189
Etchilhampton	Wilts	SU0460	51°20·6′	1°56·2′W	T	173
Etchilhampton Hill	Wilts	SU0360	51°20·6′	1°57·0′W	H	173
Etchilhampton Water	Wilts	SU0660	51°20·6′	1°54·4′W	W	173
Etchingham	E Susx	TQ7126	51°0·7′	0°26·7′E	T	188,199
Etchinghill	Kent	TR1639	51°6·8′	1°5·6′E	T	179,189
Etchinghill	Staffs	SK0218	52°45·8′	1°57·8′W	T	128
Etchingwood	E Susx	TQ5022	50°58·9′	0°8·6′E	T	199
Eternity Hall Fm	Cambs	TL2086	52°27·8′	0°13·6′W	FM	142
Ethel Point	I of W	SZ6588	50°41·5′	1°4·3′W	X	196
Ether Cleuch	Scot Bord	NT1415	55°25·5′	3°21·1′W	X	78
Etherdwick Grange	E Yorks	TA2337	53°49·1′	0°7·5′W	X	107
Ethergrass	Orkney	HY3810	58°58·6′	3°4·2′W	X	6
Ether Hill	Surrey	TQ0164	51°22·2′	0°32·6′W	X	176,186
Etheridge Fm	Dorset	ST8011	50°54·1′	2°16·7′W	FM	194
Ether Knott	Cumbr	NY2617	54°32·8′	3°8·2′W	X	89,90
Etherley Dene	Durham	NZ1928	54°39·0′	1°41·9′W	T	92
Etherley Fm	Surrey	TQ1241	51°9·7′	0°23·5′W	FM	187
Etherley Grange	Durham	NZ1828	54°39·1′	1°42·8′W	X	92
Etherley Ho	Durham	NZ1116	54°32·6′	1°49·4′W	X	92
Etherow Country Park	Stock	SJ9791	53°25·2′	2°2·3′W	X	109
Ethie Barns	Angus	NO6947	56°37·1′	2°29·9′W	X	54
Ethiebeaton	Angus	NO4734	56°30·0′	2°51·2′W	X	54
Ethie Castle	Angus	NO6846	56°36·5′	2°30·8′W	A	54
Ethie Haven	Angus	NO6948	56°37·6′	2°29·9′W	X	54
Ethie Mains	Angus	NO6948	56°37·6′	2°29·9′W	X	54
Ethnam	Kent	TQ8127	51°1·1′	0°35·2′E	X	188,199
Ethy	Corn	SX1357	50°23·2′	4°37·5′W	A	200
Etling Green	Norf	TG0113	52°40·9′	0°58·8′E	T	133
Etloe	Glos	SO6705	51°44·8′	2°28·3′W	T	162
Etnach	Aberd	NO4191	57°0·6′	2°57·8′W	X	44
Eton	Win & Maid	SU9677	51°29·3′	0°36·6′W	T	175,176
Eton House School	Sou-on-Sea	TQ9187	51°33·2′	0°45·7′E	X	178
Eton Wick	Win & Maid	SU9478	51°29·8′	0°38·4′W	T	175
Etruria	C of Stoke	SJ8647	53°1·4′	2°12·1′W	T	118
Etsell	Shrops	SJ3503	52°37·5′	2°57·2′W	T	126
Etsome Fm	Somer	ST4830	51°4·3′	2°44·1′W	FM	182
Ettenbreck	Aberd	NJ3208	57°9·7′	3°7·0′W	X	37
Etterby	Cumbr	NY3857	54°54·5′	2°57·6′W	T	85
Etteridge	Highld	NN6892	57°0·3′	4°9·9′W	X	35
Ettersgill	Durham	NY8829	54°39·6′	2°10·7′W	T	91,92
Etters Gill Beck	Durham	NY8829	54°39·6′	2°10·7′W	W	91,92
Ettiford Fm	Devon	SS5444	51°10·8′	4°4·9′W	FM	180
Ettiley Heath	Ches	SJ7360	53°8·4′	2°23·8′W	T	118
Ettingley Fm	Warw	SP2551	52°9·6′	1°37·7′W	FM	151
Ettingshall	Wolv	SO9396	52°33·9′	2°5·8′W	T	139
Ettingshall Park	Wolv	SO9295	52°33·4′	2°6·7′W	T	139
Ettington	Warw	SP2648	52°8·0′	1°36·8′W	T	151
Ettington Park (Hotel)	Warw	SP2447	52°7·5′	1°38·6′W	X	151
Etton	E Yorks	SE9843	53°52·7′	0°30·1′W	T	106
Etton	Peterb	TF1406	52°38·6′	0°18·5′W	T	142
Etton Fields Fm	E Yorks	SE9642	53°52·2′	0°32·0′W	FM	106

Etton Gill	N Yks	SE5985	54°15·7′	1°5·2′W	W	100
Etton West Wood	E Yorks	SE9543	53°52·7′	0°32·9′W	F	106
Etton Wold	E Yorks	SE9443	53°52·7′	0°33·8′W	X	106
Ettrick	Scot Bord	NT2714	55°25·1′	3°8·8′W	T	79
Ettrick Bay	Arg & Bt	NS0365	55°50·5′	5°8·3′W	W	63
Ettrickbridge	Scot Bord	NT3824	55°30·6′	2°58·5′W	T	73
Ettrick Burn	Arg & Bt	NS0368	55°52·2′	5°8·5′W	W	63
Ettrick Croft	Aberd	NO4295	57°2·8′	2°56·9′W	X	37,44
Ettrickdale	Arg & Bt	NS0668	55°52·2′	5°5·6′W	X	63
Ettrick Forest	Scot Bord	NT3524	55°30·6′	3°1·3′W	X	73
Ettrick Head	Scot Bord	NT1706	55°20·7′	3°18·1′W	X	79
Ettrickhill	Scot Bord	NT2614	55°25·1′	3°9·7′W	X	79
Ettrick Ho	Scot Bord	NT2514	55°25·1′	3°10·7′W	X	79
Ettrick Pen	D & G	NT1907	55°21·3′	3°16·2′W	H	79
Ettrickshaws Fm	Scot Bord	NT3820	55°28·4′	2°58·4′W	FM	73
Ettrick Water	Scot Bord	NT3018	55°27·3′	3°6·0′W	W	79
Ettrick Water	Scot Bord	NT4125	55°31·2′	2°55·6′W	W	73
Ettridge Fm	Herts	TL3206	51°44·5′	0°4·9′W	FM	166
Etwall	Derby	SK2631	52°52·8′	1°36·4′W	T	128
Etwall Common	Derby	SK2730	52°52·2′	1°35·5′W	T	128
Euchan Cott	D & G	NS7508	55°21·3′	3°57·9′W	X	71,78
Euchan Fall	D & G	NS7708	55°21·3′	3°56·0′W	W	71,78
Euchanhead	D & G	NS6805	55°19·5′	4°4·4′W	X	71,77
Euchan Water	D & G	NS6704	55°19·0′	4°5·3′W	W	77
Euchan Water	D & G	NS7207	55°20·7′	4°0·7′W	W	71,77
Euden Beck	Durham	NZ0429	54°39·6′	1°55·9′W	W	92
Euden Beck Cott	Durham	NZ0630	54°40·1′	1°54·0′W	X	92
Eudinuagain	Highld	NH5826	57°18·4′	4°21·0′W	X	26,35
Eudon Burn	Durham	NY9846	54°48·8′	2°1·4′W	W	87
Eudon Burnell	Shrops	SO6989	52°30·1′	2°27·0′W	T	138
Eudon George	Shrops	SO6888	52°29·6′	2°27·9′W	A	138
Eudon George	Shrops	SO6888	52°29·6′	2°27·9′W	T	138
Eughlam	N Eil	NB1639	58°15·1′	6°50·0′W	X	13
Eunant	Powys	SH9522	52°47·4′	3°33·0′W	W	125
Eunant Fach	Powys	SH9422	52°47·4′	3°33·9′W	W	125
Eunant Fawr	Powys	SH9323	52°47·9′	3°34·8′W	W	125
Eunay Mòr	N Eil	NB1336	58°13·4′	6°52·8′W	X	13
Eun Eilean	Arg & Bt	NR6347	55°39·8′	5°45·7′W	X	62
Eun Loch	Arg & Bt	NM9109	56°13·9′	5°21·9′W	W	55
Eun-tuim	Highld	NM7892	56°58·2′	5°38·7′W	H	33,40
Eurach	Arg & Bt	NM8401	56°9·4′	5°28·3′W	X	55
Euridge Manor Fm	Wilts	ST8372	51°27·0′	2°14·3′W	FM	173
Eurocentral Rail Terminal	N Lanak	NS7461	55°49·8′	4°0·3′W	X	64
Eusan Biorach	Arg & Bt	NS1075	55°56·1′	5°2·1′W	W	63
Eusclaid	N Eil	NB4048	58°20·9′	6°26·1′W	X	8
Eusemere	Cumbr	NY4624	54°36·7′	2°49·7′W	X	90
Euston	Suff	TL8979	52°22·8′	0°47·0′E	T	144
Euston Park	Suff	TL9178	52°22·2′	0°48·7′E	X	144
Euston Sta	Camden	TQ2982	51°31·6′	0°8·0′W	X	176
Euximoor Drove	Cambs	TL4798	52°33·8′	0°10·5′E	X	143
Euximoor Fen	Cambs	TL4799	52°34·4′	0°10·6′E	X	143
Euximoor House Fm	Cambs	TF4900	52°34·9′	0°12·4′E	FM	143
Euxton	Lancs	SD5518	53°39·6′	2°40·4′W	T	108
Evanachan	Arg & Bt	NR9486	56°1·6′	5°17·9′W	X	55
Evancoyd	Powys	SO2663	52°15·9′	3°4·7′W	X	137,148
Evan Howe	N Yks	NZ9201	54°24·0′	0°34·5′W	A	94
Evans' Fm	Lincs	TF1157	53°6·2′	0°20·1′W	FM	121
Evanstown	Brig	SS9789	51°35·7′	3°28·8′W	T	170
Evanton	Highld	NH6066	57°40·0′	4°20·4′W	T	21
Evan Water	D & G	NT0407	55°21·1′	3°30·4′W	W	78
Evattsike	Cumbr	SD5699	54°23·3′	2°40·2′W	X	97
Evedon	Lincs	TF0947	53°0·8′	0°22·1′W	T	130
Evedon Mill	Lincs	TF1047	53°0·8′	0°21·2′W	X	130
Evegate Manor Fm	Kent	TR0639	51°7·0′	0°57·0′E	FM	179,189
Evegate Mill	Kent	TR0638	51°6·5′	0°57·0′E	X	179,189
Eve Hill	Dudley	SO9390	52°30·7′	2°5·8′W	T	139
Evelaw	Scot Bord	NT6652	55°45·9′	2°32·1′W	X	67,74
Eve Law	Scot Bord	NT6653	55°46·4′	2°32·1′W	X	67,74
Evelench Fm	Worcs	SO9057	52°12·9′	2°8·4′W	FM	150
Eveley Fm	Hants	SU3233	51°6·0′	1°32·2′W	FM	185
Evelick	Pth & Kin	NO2025	56°24·9′	3°17·4′W	X	53,58
Evelith	Shrops	SJ7405	52°38·8′	2°22·7′W	X	127
Evelith Manor	Shrops	SJ7404	52°38·2′	2°22·7′W	X	127
Evelix	Highld	NH7690	57°53·2′	4°5·0′W	X	21
Evelix	Highld	NH7691	57°53·7′	4°5·0′W	W	21
Evenall	Shrops	SJ3532	52°53·1′	2°57·6′W	X	126
Evenden Copse	Oxon	SP3317	51°51·3′	1°30·9′W	F	164
Evendine	Heref	SO7541	52°4·2′	2°21·5′W	T	150
Evendons Ho	Wok	SU7966	51°23·5′	0°51·5′W	X	175
Even Hill	Worcs	SO9640	52°3·7′	2°3·1′W	H	150
Evening Hill	Cumbr	NY3249	54°50·1′	3°3·1′W	X	85
Evenjobb	Powys	SO2662	52°15·3′	3°4·7′W	T	137,148
Evenley	Northnts	SP5834	52°0·3′	1°8·9′W	T	152
Evenley Hall	Northnts	SP5835	52°0·9′	1°8·9′W	X	152
Evenley Park	Northnts	SP5835	52°0·9′	1°8·9′W	X	152
Evenlode	Glos	SP2229	51°57·8′	1°40·4′W	T	163
Evenlode Fm	Oxon	SP4210	51°47·5′	1°23·1′W	FM	164
Evenlode Grounds Fm	Glos	SP2327	51°56·7′	1°39·5′W	FM	163
Even Pits	Heref	SO5636	52°1·5′	2°38·1′W	T	149
Even Swindon	Swin	SU1385	51°34·1′	1°48·4′W	T	173
Eventide Home	Aberd	NJ9618	57°15·4′	2°3·5′W	X	38
Evenwood	Durham	NZ1525	54°37·4′	1°45·6′W	T	92
Evenwood	Shrops	SJ5501	52°36·5′	2°39·5′W	X	126
Evenwood Common	Shrops	SJ5402	52°37·1′	2°40·4′W	X	126
Evenwood Gate	Durham	NZ1624	54°36·9′	1°44·7′W	T	92
Everan Hill	Angus	NO3680	56°54·7′	3°2·6′W	X	44
Everard's Fm	Somer	ST5851	51°15·6′	2°35·7′W	FM	182,183
Everbay	Orkney	HY6724	59°6·4′	2°34·1′W	T	5
Everby	Shetld	HU5141	60°9·3′	1°4·4′W	X	4
Evercreech	Somer	ST6438	51°8·6′	2°30·5′W	T	183
Evercreech Park Fm	Somer	ST6337	51°8·1′	2°31·3′W	FM	183
Everdon	Northnts	SP5957	52°12·7′	1°7·8′W	T	152
Everdon Hall	Northnts	SP5958	52°13·3′	1°7·8′W	X	152
Everdon Hill	Northnts	SP5857	52°12·7′	1°8·7′W	H	152
Everdon Hill Fm	Northnts	SP5857	52°12·7′	1°8·7′W	FM	152
Everdon Stubbs	Northnts	SP6056	52°12·2′	1°6·9′W	F	152
Everess Fm	Glos	SO7628	51°57·2′	2°20·6′W	FM	150
Everett's Fm	Norf	TL7899	52°33·8′	0°38·0′E	FM	144
Evergreen	Moray	NJ3061	57°38·3′	3°9·9′W	X	28
Ever Green	Suff	TL6652	52°8·7′	0°26·0′E	X	154

Evergreen Christmas World	Norf	TF5002	52°35·9′	0°13·3′E	X	143
Evergreen Hill	Devon	SY1392	50°43·5′	3°13·6′W	H	192,193
Evergreens, The	Beds	SP9534	52°0·0′	0°36·6′W	F	153,165
Everhoull	Shetld	HU4584	60°32·5′	1°10·3′W	X	1,2,3
Everingham	E Yorks	SE8042	53°52·3′	0°46·6′W	T	106
Everingham Carrs	E Yorks	SE7940	53°51·3′	0°47·5′W	X	105,106
Everingham Park	E Yorks	SE8041	53°51·8′	0°46·6′W	X	106
Everington Ho	W Berks	SU5374	51°28·0′	1°13·8′W	X	174
Everland	Shetld	HU6691	60°36·1′	0°47·2′W	X	1,2
Everlands	Kent	TQ5051	51°14·5′	0°9·3′E	X	188
Everleigh	Wilts	SU2053	51°16·8′	1°42·4′W	T	184
Everleigh Ashes	Wilts	SU1956	51°18·4′	1°43·3′W	F	173
Everleigh Barrows	Wilts	SU1856	51°18·4′	1°44·1′W	A	173
Everleigh Down	Wilts	SU1952	51°16·2′	1°43·3′W	X	184
Everley	Highld	ND3668	58°36·0′	3°5·6′W	X	12
Everley	N Yks	SE9788	54°16·9′	0°30·2′W	X	94,101
Everley Bank Wood	N Yks	SE9789	54°17·5′	0°30·2′W	F	94,101
Everley Fm	Dorset	ST8711	50°54·1′	2°10·7′W	FM	194
Everley Hill Dairy	Dorset	ST8812	50°54·7′	2°9·9′W	X	194
Everor	Shetld	HU2877	60°28·8′	1°28·9′W	X	3
Ever Rigg	Durham	NZ0027	54°38·5′	1°59·6′W	X	92
Eversden Wood	Cambs	TL3453	52°9·8′	0°2·1′W	F	154
Eversfield	Devon	SX4692	50°42·7′	4°10·5′W	X	190
Evershaw Copse	Bucks	SP6438	52°2·4′	1°3·6′W	F	152
Evershaw Fm	Bucks	SP6338	52°2·4′	1°4·5′W	FM	152
Eversheds Fm	Surrey	TQ1438	51°8·0′	0°21·8′W	FM	187
Eversholt	Beds	SP9933	51°59·4′	0°33·1′W	T	165
Evershot	Dorset	ST5704	50°50·3′	2°36·3′W	T	194
Eversley	Cumbr	SD4984	54°15·2′	2°46·5′W	X	97
Eversley	Essex	TQ7488	51°34·1′	0°31·0′E	T	178
Eversley	Hants	SU7762	51°21·3′	0°53·3′W	T	175,186
Eversley Centre	Hants	SU7861	51°20·8′	0°52·4′W	T	175,186
Eversley Common	Hants	SU7959	51°19·7′	0°51·6′W	F	175,186
Eversley Cross	Hants	SU7961	51°20·8′	0°51·5′W	T	175,186
Evers, The	N Yks	SE7360	54°2·1′	0°52·7′W	X	100
Everthorpe	E Yorks	SE9031	53°46·3′	0°37·7′W	T	106
Everthorpe Hall	E Yorks	SE8931	53°46·3′	0°38·6′W	X	106
Everton	Aberd	NJ6123	57°18·0′	2°38·4′W	X	37
Everton	Aberd	NJ6636	57°25·0′	2°33·5′W	X	29
Everton	Beds	TL2051	52°8·9′	0°14·4′W	T	153
Everton	Hants	SZ2994	50°44·9′	1°35·0′W	T	196
Everton	Inverc	NS2171	55°54·2′	4°51·4′W	X	63
Everton	Liv	SJ3592	53°25·5′	2°58·3′W	T	108
Everton	Notts	SK6991	53°24·9′	0°57·3′W	T	111
Everton Carr	Notts	SK6992	53°25·5′	0°57·3′W	X	111
Everton Carr Fm	Notts	SK6993	53°26·0′	0°57·3′W	FM	111
Everton of Auchry	Aberd	NJ7951	57°33·2′	2°20·6′W	X	29,30
Evertown	D & G	NY3576	55°4·7′	3°0·7′W	T	85
Evesbatch	Heref	SO6848	52°8·0′	2°27·7′W	T	149
Eves Corner	Essex	TQ9497	51°38·5′	0°48·6′E	X	168
Evesham	Worcs	SP0343	52°5·4′	1°57·0′W	T	150
Evesham Lodge	Warw	SP0654	52°11·3′	1°54·3′W	X	150
Eves Hill	Norf	TG1121	52°44·9′	1°8·0′E	X	133
Evie	Orkney	HY3525	59°6·7′	3°7·6′W	X	6
Evington	C of Leic	SK6203	52°37·5′	1°4·6′W	T	140
Evington	Kent	TR1045	51°10·2′	1°0·6′E	T	179,189
Evistones	Northum	NY8396	55°15·7′	2°15·6′W	X	80
Evra Houll	Shetld	HU4584	60°32·5′	1°10·3′W	H	1,2,3
Evra Loch	Shetld	HU4897	60°39·5′	1°6·8′W	W	1
Evron Hill	Aberd	NJ4538	57°26·0′	2°54·5′W	X	28,29
Ewan Close	Cumbr	NY5042	54°46·5′	2°46·2′W	X	86
Ewanrigg	Cumbr	NY0335	54°42·3′	3°29·9′W	T	89
Ewanston	D & G	NX6777	55°4·4′	4°4·6′W	X	77,84
Ewanston	D & G	NX7791	55°12·1′	3°55·5′W	X	78
Ewartly Shank	Northum	NT9613	55°24·9′	2°3·4′W	X	81
Ewart Newtown	Northum	NT9631	55°34·6′	2°3·4′W	T	74,75
Ewart Park	Northum	NT9631	55°34·6′	2°3·4′W	X	74,75
Ewden	Sheff	SK2497	53°28·4′	1°37·9′W	X	110
Ewden Beck	Sheff	SK2496	53°27·9′	1°37·9′W	W	110
Ewden Height	Sheff	SK2397	53°28·4′	1°38·8′W	X	110
Ewden Village	Sheff	SK2796	53°27·8′	1°35·2′W	T	110
Ewdness House	Shrops	SO7398	52°35·0′	2°23·5′W	A	138
Ewebank	Cumbr	SD5790	54°18·5′	2°39·2′W	X	97
Ewebank	Durham	NZ0713	54°31·0′	1°53·1′W	X	92
Ewebank Park	Cumbr	NY8510	54°29·4′	2°13·5′W	X	91,92
Ewebrae	Aberd	NJ7846	57°30·5′	2°21·6′W	X	29,30
Ewe Brae	D & G	NX8375	55°3·6′	3°49·5′W	X	84
Ewe Burn	Highld	NC8844	58°22·5′	3°54·4′W	W	10
Eweclose	Cumbr	NY1337	54°43·5′	3°20·6′W	X	89
Ewe Close	Cumbr	NY6013	54°30·9′	2°36·7′W	X	91
Eweclose	Derby	SK2169	53°13·3′	1°40·7′W	X	119
Ewe Close (Settlement)	Cumbr	NY6013	54°30·9′	2°36·7′W	A	91
Ewe Cote	N Yks	NZ8710	54°28·9′	0°39·0′W	X	94
Ewe Cote	N Yks	SE6893	54°19·9′	0°56·8′W	X	94,100
Ewe Cote Fm	N Yks	SE6587	54°16·7′	0°59·7′W	FM	94,100
Ewe Crags	Cumbr	NY4404	54°25·9′	2°51·4′W	X	90
Ewe Craig	D & G	NX7092	55°12·6′	4°2·2′W	H	77
Ewe Dale	Cumbr	SD2478	54°11·8′	3°9·5′W	X	96
Ewefields Fm	Warw	SP3558	52°13·4′	1°28·9′W	FM	151
Ewe Fm	N Yks	NZ7811	54°29·5′	0°47·3′W	FM	94
Ewe Fm	Oxon	SU6195	51°39·3′	1°6·7′W	FM	164,165
Eweford	E Loth	NT6677	55°59·3′	2°32·3′W	X	67
Ewe Gair	S Lanak	NS9504	55°19·4′	3°38·9′W	H	78
Ewe Hill	D & G	NS6500	55°16·8′	4°7·1′W	H	77
Ewe Hill	D & G	NX6164	54°57·3′	4°9·8′W	H	83
Ewe Hill	D & G	NX7086	55°9·3′	4°2·0′W	X	77
Ewe Hill	D & G	NX8296	55°14·9′	3°50·9′W	H	78
Ewe Hill	D & G	NY2887	55°10·6′	3°7·4′W	H	79
Ewe Hill	E Ayr	NS4512	55°22·9′	4°26·4′W	H	70
Ewe Hill	E Ayr	NS5908	55°21·0′	4°13·0′W	X	71,77
Ewe Hill	Northum	NT9649	55°44·3′	2°3·4′W	X	74,75
Ewe Hill	Northum	NT9809	55°22·7′	2°1·5′W	H	81
Ewe Hill	Northum	NT9913	55°24·9′	2°0·5′W	H	81
Ewe Hill	Northum	NU0015	55°26·0′	1°59·6′W	H	81
Ewe Hill	Northum	NU0016	55°26·5′	1°59·6′W	H	81
Ewe Hill	Northum	NU0424	55°30·8′	1°55·8′W	H	75
Ewe Hill	Northum	NY6897	55°16·2′	2°29·8′W	H	80
Ewe Hill	Northum	NZ1976	55°4·9′	1°41·7′W	X	88
Ewe Hill	N Yks	SE5499	54°23·3′	1°9·7′W	X	100

Ewe Hill	N Yks	SE6499	54°23·2′	1°0·4′W	X	94,100
Ewe Hill	Scot Bord	NT0522	55°29·2′	3°29·8′W	H	72
Ewe Hill	Scot Bord	NT2047	55°42·8′	3°16·0′W	H	73
Ewe Hill	Scot Bord	NY4595	55°15·0′	2°51·5′W	H	79
Ewe Hill	S Lanak	NS7921	55°28·3′	3°54·4′W	X	71
Ewe Hill	S Lanak	NS9031	55°33·9′	3°44·2′W	X	71,72
Ewe Hill	S Lanak	NS9826	55°31·3′	3°36·5′W	H	72
Ewe Hill	S Lanak	NT0024	55°30·2′	3°34·6′W	H	72
Ewe Hill	S Lanak	NT0540	55°38·9′	3°30·1′W	H	72
Ewe Hill	W Berks	SU3480	51°31·3′	1°30·2′W	X	174
Ewehurst Wood	Durham	NZ1554	54°53·1′	1°45·5′W	F	88
Ewe Knowe	D & G	NY2696	55°15·4′	3°9·4′W	H	79
Ewe Knowe	Scot Bord	NY5390	55°12·4′	2°43·9′W	X	79
Ewelair Hill	Scot Bord	NT3108	55°21·9′	3°4·9′W	H	79
Ewelairs Hill	D & G	NT1602	55°18·5′	3°19·0′W	H	79
Ewelairs Hill	Scot Bord	NT7165	55°52·9′	2°27·4′W	X	67
Eweleaze	Dorset	SY6487	50°41·1′	2°30·2′W	X	194
Ewell	Surrey	TQ2162	51°20·9′	0°15·4′W	T	176,187
Ewell Fen	Cambs	TL4372	52°19·9′	0°6·3′E	X	154
Ewell Fm	Kent	TR0360	51°18·4′	0°55·1′E	FM	178,179
Ewell Hall	Essex	TL8618	51°50·0′	0°42·4′E	X	168
Ewell Manor	Kent	TQ7152	51°14·7′	0°27·4′E	X	188
Ewell Minnis	Kent	TR2643	51°8·7′	1°14·3′E	T	179
Ewelme	Oxon	SU6491	51°37·1′	1°4·1′W	T	164,175
Ewelme Downs	Oxon	SU6689	51°36·0′	1°2·4′W	X	175
Ewelme Park	Oxon	SU6789	51°36·0′	1°1·6′W	X	175
Ewelock Bank	Cumbr	NY5806	54°27·1′	2°38·4′W	X	91
Ewelock Hill	Cumbr	NY3444	54°47·4′	3°1·2′W	X	85
Ewe Moor	N Yks	SD8864	54°4·6′	2°10·6′W	X	98
Ewen	Glos	SU0097	51°40·5′	1°59·6′W	T	163
Ewenni Down	V of Glam	SS9076	51°28·6′	3°34·6′W	X	170
Ewenni Fach	Rho Cyn Taf	SS9680	51°30·8′	3°29·5′W	W	170
Ewenny	V of Glam	SS9077	51°29·1′	3°34·7′W	T	170
Ewenny Moor	V of Glam	SS9077	51°29·1′	3°34·7′W	X	170
Ewenny Priory	V of Glam	SS9177	51°29·1′	3°33·8′W	A	170
Ewenny River	V of Glam	SS9278	51°29·7′	3°33·0′W	W	170
Ewens Croft	Aberd	NJ6307	57°9·4′	2°36·2′W	X	37
Ewenshope Fell	D & G	NY3899	55°17·1′	2°58·1′W	H	79
Ewe Pens	Glos	SO9902	51°43·2′	2°0·5′W	X	163
Ewerby	Lincs	TF1247	53°0·7′	0°19·4′W	T	130
Ewerby Fen	Lincs	TF1448	53°1·3′	0°17·6′W	X	130
Ewerby Thorpe	Lincs	TF1347	53°0·7′	0°18·5′W	T	130
Ewerby Waithe Common	Lincs	TF1449	53°1·8′	0°17·6′W	X	130
Ewe Rig	D & G	NT2307	55°21·3′	3°12·4′W	H	79
Ewe Rig	D & G	NX4483	55°7·3′	4°26·4′W	X	77
Ewes	D & G	NY3690	55°12·3′	2°59·9′W	X	79
Ewes Castle (rems of)	Scot Bord	NT4344	55°41·4′	2°54·0′W	A	73
Ewes Door	Scot Bord	NY3798	55°16·6′	2°59·1′W	X	79
Ewesdown Fell	D & G	NT3300	55°17·6′	3°2·9′W	H	79
Ewesdown Sike	Scot Bord	NT3401	55°18·2′	3°1·9′W	W	79
Eweslees	D & G	NY3897	55°16·0′	2°58·1′W	X	79
Eweslees Burn	D & G	NY3898	55°16·6′	2°58·1′W	W	79
Eweslees Knowe	D & G	NT3202	55°18·7′	3°3·9′W	H	79
Ewesley	Northum	NZ0692	55°13·6′	1°53·9′W	X	81
Ewesley Burn	Northum	NZ0790	55°12·5′	1°53·0′W	W	81
Ewesley Fell	Northum	NZ0592	55°13·6′	1°54·9′W	X	81
Eweston	Pemb	SM8723	51°52·1′	5°5·3′W	X	157
Ewes Water	D & G	NY3786	55°10·1′	2°58·9′W	W	79
Ewes Water	Scot Bord	NT3845	55°41·9′	2°58·8′W	W	73
Eweton	Pemb	SN0510	51°45·5′	4°49·1′W	X	158
Ewhurst	Surrey	TQ0940	51°9·2′	0°26·1′W	T	187
Ewhurst Green	E Susx	TQ7924	50°59·5′	0°33·4′E	T	199
Ewhurst Green	Surrey	TQ0939	51°8·6′	0°26·1′W	T	187
Ewhurst Ho	Hants	SU5656	51°18·3′	1°11·4′W	X	174
Ewhurst Manor	W Susx	TQ2119	50°57·7′	0°16·2′W	X	198
Ewhurst Park	Hants	SU5757	51°18·8′	1°10·5′W	X	174
Ewhurst Place	Surrey	TQ0841	51°9·7′	0°26·9′W	X	187
Ewich	Stir	NN3627	56°24·7′	4°39·0′W	X	50
Ewieside Hill	Scot Bord	NT7768	55°54·5′	2°21·6′W	H	67
Ewings	Devon	SS9618	50°57·4′	3°28·5′W	X	181
Ewings Fm	Cambs	TF3915	52°43·1′	0°3·9′E	FM	131
Ewingston	E Loth	NT4964	55°52·2′	2°48·5′W	X	66
Ewin's Ash	Devon	ST1405	50°50·5′	3°12·9′W	X	192,193
Ewin's Hill	Wilts	SU2573	51°27·6′	1°38·0′W	X	174
Ewloe	Flint	SJ2966	53°11·4′	3°3·4′W	T	117
Ewloe Green	Flint	SJ2866	53°11·4′	3°4·3′W	T	117
Ewloe Hall	Flint	SJ2865	53°10·9′	3°4·2′W	X	117
Ewnie	Angus	NO3646	56°36·3′	3°2·1′W	X	54
Ewood	Black w Dar	SD6725	53°43·5′	2°29·6′W	T	103
Ewood Bridge	Lancs	SD7920	53°40·8′	2°18·7′W	T	103
Ewood Fm	Surrey	TQ1944	51°11·2′	0°17·4′W	FM	187
Eworthy	Devon	SX4495	50°44·3′	4°12·3′W	T	190
Eworthy Barrow	Devon	SX4495	50°44·3′	4°12·3′W	A	190
Ewshot	Hants	SU8149	51°14·3′	0°50·0′W	T	186
Ewshot Hall	Hants	SU8149	51°14·3′	0°50·0′W	X	186
Ewson's Brook	Essex	TL6304	51°42·9′	0°22·0′E	W	167
Ewson's Fm	Essex	TL6205	51°43·4′	0°21·1′E	FM	167
Ewyas Harold	Heref	SO3828	51°57·1′	2°53·7′W	T	149,161
Ewyas Harold Common	Heref	SO3829	51°57·6′	2°53·7′W	X	149,161
Example Cross	Corn	SX2779	50°35·3′	4°26·3′W	X	201
Exbourne	Devon	SS6002	50°48·3′	3°58·8′W	T	191
Exbury	Hants	SU4200	50°48·1′	1°23·9′W	T	196
Exbury Ho	Hants	SU4200	50°48·1′	1°23·9′W	X	196
Exbury River	Hants	SZ4398	50°47·0′	1°23·0′W	W	196
Exceat	E Susx	TV5199	50°46·5′	0°8·9′E	T	199
Exceat Bridge	E Susx	TV5199	50°46·5′	0°8·9′E	X	199
Exceat New Barn	E Susx	TV5398	50°45·9′	0°10·6′E	X	199
Exe	Corn	SX2294	50°43·2′	4°30·9′W	X	190
Exebridge	Devon	SS9324	51°0·6′	3°31·1′W	T	181
Exe Cleave	Somer	SS7940	51°9·0′	3°43·4′W	X	180
Exe Cleave	Somer	SS8040	51°9·0′	3°42·6′W	X	181
Exe Head	Somer	SS7541	51°9·5′	3°46·9′W	W	180
Exeland	Devon	SS9508	50°52·0′	3°29·1′W	X	192
Exelby	N Yks	SE2986	54°16·4′	1°32·9′W	T	99
Exemoor Fm	Corn	SX2193	50°42·8′	4°31·8′W	FM	190
Exe Plain	Somer	SS7542	51°10·1′	3°46·9′W	X	180
Exeter	Devon	SX9292	50°43·3′	3°31·4′W	T	192
Exeter Airport	Devon	SY0093	50°43·9′	3°24·6′W	X	192
Exeter Canal	Devon	SX9389	50°41·7′	3°30·5′W	W	192
Exeter Hill Cross	Devon	SS8701	50°48·1′	3°35·8′W	X	192
Exeter Wood	Beds	TL1044	52°5·2′	0°23·3′W	F	153
Exe Valley	Devon	SS9416	50°56·3′	3°30·1′W	X	181
Exford	Somer	SS8538	51°8·0′	3°38·2′W	T	181
Exford Common	Somer	SS8540	51°9·1′	3°38·3′W	X	181
Exfords Green	Shrops	SJ4505	52°38·6′	2°48·4′W	T	126
Exhall	Warw	SP1055	52°11·8′	1°50·8′W	T	150
Exhall	Warw	SP3585	52°27·9′	1°28·7′W	T	140
Exhall Grange (School)	Warw	SP3384	52°27·4′	1°30·5′W	X	140
Exhibition Fm	Suff	TL6448	52°6·6′	0°24·1′E	FM	154
Exhibition Site	C of Aber	NJ9410	57°11·1′	2°5·5′W	X	38
Exhurst Manor	Kent	TQ7942	51°9·2′	0°34·0′E	X	188
Exlade Street	Oxon	SU6582	51°32·2′	1°3·4′W	T	175
Exley	Cald	SE0922	53°41·9′	1°51·4′W	T	104
Exley Gate	Kirk	SE2408	53°34·3′	1°37·8′W	X	110
Exley Head	Brad	SE0440	53°51·6′	1°55·9′W	T	104
Exmansworthy	Devon	SS2726	51°0·7′	4°27·6′W	X	190
Exmansworthy Cliff	Devon	SS2727	51°1·2′	4°27·6′W	X	190
Exminster	Devon	SX9487	50°40·6′	3°29·6′W	T	192
Exmoor	Somer	SS7638	51°7·9′	3°46·0′W	X	180
Exmoor Forest	Somer	SS7540	51°9·0′	3°46·8′W	X	180
Exmoor Grange	Cambs	TL4797	52°33·3′	0°10·5′E	X	143
Exmoor Steam Railway	Devon	SS6638	51°7·8′	3°54·5′W	X	180
Exmouth	Devon	SY0081	50°37·4′	3°24·4′W	T	192
Exnaboe	Shetld	HU3912	59°53·7′	1°17·7′W	T	4
Exnalls	Herts	TL4519	51°51·3′	0°6·7′E	X	167
Exning	Suff	TL6165	52°15·8′	0°22·0′E	T	154
Experimental Horticulture Station	Hants	SZ3093	50°44·4′	1°34·1′W	X	196
Exted	Kent	TR1644	51°9·5′	1°5·7′E	T	179,189
Exton	Devon	SX9886	50°40·1′	3°26·2′W	T	192
Exton	Hants	SU6121	50°59·3′	1°7·5′W	T	185
Exton	Pth & Kin	NO2826	56°25·5′	3°9·6′W	X	53,59
Exton	Rut	SK9211	52°41·6′	0°37·9′W	T	130
Exton	Somer	SS9233	51°5·4′	3°32·1′W	T	181
Exton Hill	Somer	SS9334	51°6·0′	3°31·3′W	H	181
Exton Park	Rut	SK9211	52°41·6′	0°37·9′W	X	130
Exton Park	Rut	SK9312	52°42·1′	0°37·0′W	X	130
Extra Fm	Cambs	TL3462	52°14·6′	0°1·8′W	FM	154
Extwistle Hall	Lancs	SD8733	53°47·8′	2°11·4′W	A	103
Extwistle Moor	Lancs	SD9033	53°47·8′	2°8·7′W	X	103
Exwell	Corn	SX3275	50°33·3′	4°21·9′W	X	201
Exwell Barton	Devon	SX9585	50°39·5′	3°28·8′W	X	192
Exwell Hill	Devon	SX9585	50°39·5′	3°28·8′W	X	192
Exwick	Devon	SX9093	50°43·8′	3°33·1′W	T	192
Exwick Barton	Devon	SX9094	50°44·3′	3°33·2′W	X	192
Eyam	Derby	SK2176	53°17·1′	1°40·7′W	T	119
Eyam Edge	Derby	SK2077	53°17·6′	1°41·6′W	X	119
Eyam Moor	Derby	SK2278	53°18·1′	1°39·8′W	X	119
Eyam View Fm	Derby	SK2076	53°17·1′	1°41·6′W	FM	119
Eyarth Hall	Denb	SJ1254	53°4·8′	3°18·4′W	X	116
Eyarth Ho	Denb	SJ1254	53°4·8′	3°18·4′W	X	116
Ey Burn	Aberd	NO0985	56°57·1′	3°29·3′W	W	43
Eycott Hill	Cumbr	NY3829	54°39·4′	2°57·2′W	H	90
Eycot Wood	Glos	SP0010	51°47·6′	1°59·6′W	F	163
Eydon	Northnts	SP5450	52°9·0′	1°12·2′W	T	152
Eydonhill	Northnts	SP5351	52°9·5′	1°13·1′W	X	152
Eye	Heref	SO4963	52°16·0′	2°44·4′W	T	137,138,148
Eye	Peterb	TF2202	52°36·4′	0°11·5′W	T	142
Eye	Suff	TM1473	52°19·0′	1°8·8′E	T	144,156
Eye Brook	Leic	SK7900	52°35·8′	0°49·6′W	W	141
Eyebrook Reservoir	Leic	SP8595	52°33·0′	0°44·4′W	W	141
Eyebroughy	E Loth	NT4986	56°4·1′	2°48·7′W	X	66
Eyebury Fm	Peterb	TF2201	52°35·8′	0°11·5′W	FM	142
Eyecote	Heref	SO4864	52°16·5′	2°45·3′W	X	137,138,148
Eye Fm	Lincs	TF3611	52°41·0′	0°1·1′E	FM	131,142
Eye Fm	Shrops	SJ6005	52°38·7′	2°35·1′W	FM	127
Eye Green	Peterb	TF2203	52°36·9′	0°11·5′W	T	142
Eye Hall Fm	Cambs	TL4963	52°14·9′	0°11·4′E	FM	154
Eye Hill Fm	Cambs	TL5776	52°21·8′	0°18·8′E	FM	143
Eyehorn Hatch Fm	Kent	TQ8762	51°19·8′	0°41·4′E	FM	178
Eye Kettleby Hall	Leic	SK7316	52°44·4′	0°54·7′W	X	129
Eyelids	E Susx	TQ7623	50°59·0′	0°30·8′E	X	199
Eyemouth	Scot Bord	NT9464	55°52·4′	2°5·3′W	T	67
Eye Peninsula (An Rubha)	N Eil	NB5332	58°12·7′	6°11·8′W	X	8
Eyers Down Fm	Hants	SU5110	50°53·5′	1°16·1′W	FM	196
Eyes	S Ayr	NX2479	55°4·7′	4°45·0′W	X	76
Eyes, The	Warr	SJ6488	53°23·5′	2°32·1′W	X	109
Eye Water	Scot Bord	NT7864	55°52·4′	2°20·7′W	W	67
Eyeworth	Beds	TL2445	52°5·6′	0°11·0′W	T	153
Eyeworth Lodge	Hants	SU2214	50°55·7′	1°40·8′W	X	195
Eyeworth Lodge Fm	Beds	TL2544	52°5·0′	0°10·1′W	FM	153
Eyeworth Wood	Hants	SU2215	50°56·3′	1°40·8′W	F	184
Eyford Hill Fm	Glos	SP1325	51°55·6′	1°48·3′W	FM	163
Eyford Knoll	Glos	SP1424	51°55·1′	1°47·4′W	X	163
Eyford Park	Glos	SP1424	51°55·1′	1°47·4′W	X	163
Eyhorne Street	Kent	TQ8354	51°15·6′	0°37·6′E	T	188
Eyhurst Court	Surrey	TQ2655	51°17·0′	0°11·2′W	X	187
Eyhurst Fm	Surrey	TQ2656	51°17·6′	0°11·2′W	FM	187
Eyke	Suff	TM3151	52°6·8′	1°22·8′E	T	156
Eylesbarrow	Devon	SX5968	50°29·9′	3°58·9′W	A	202
Eymore Wood	Worcs	SO7879	52°24·8′	2°19·0′W	F	138
Eynesbury	Cambs	TL1859	52°13·2′	0°16·0′W	T	153
Eynesbury Hardwick	Cambs	TL2056	52°11·6′	0°14·3′W	X	153
Eynesford Castle	Kent	TQ5465	51°22·0′	0°13·1′E	A	177
Eynhallow	Orkney	HY3529	59°8·8′	3°7·7′W	X	6
Eynhallow Sound	Orkney	HY3827	59°7·8′	3°4·5′W	W	6
Eynort	Highld	NG3826	57°15·2′	6°20·2′W	T	32
Eynort River	Highld	NG3828	57°16·3′	6°20·3′W	W	32
Eynsford	Kent	TQ5365	51°22·0′	0°12·3′E	T	177
Eynsham	Oxon	SP4309	51°46·9′	1°22·2′W	T	164
Eynsham Hall	Oxon	SP3912	51°48·5′	1°25·7′W	X	164
Eynsham Park	Oxon	SP3911	51°48·0′	1°25·7′W	X	164
Eyott's Fm	Essex	TQ7996	51°38·3′	0°35·6′E	FM	167
Eype Down	Dorset	SY4392	50°43·7′	2°48·1′W	X	193
Eype's Mouth	Dorset	SY4491	50°43·2′	2°47·2′W	T	193
Eyre	Highld	NG4152	57°29·3′	6°18·9′W	T	23
Eyre	Highld	NG5734	57°20·2′	6°1·8′W	T	24,32
Eyre Burn	D & G	NT0400	55°17·3′	3°30·3′W	W	78
Eyre Point	Highld	NG5834	57°20·2′	6°0·8′W	X	24,32
Eyres Monsell	C of Leic	SP5799	52°35·4′	1°9·1′W	T	140
Eyreswood Fm	Beds	SP9645	52°5·9′	0°35·5′W	FM	153
Eyreton	I of M	SC3279	54°11·0′	4°34·1′W	X	95
Eysey	Wilts	SU1194	51°38·9′	1°50·1′W	X	163,173
Eyston Hall	Essex	TL8342	52°3·0′	0°40·5′E	X	155
Eythorne	Kent	TR2849	51°11·9′	1°16·2′E	T	179
Eythrope	Bucks	SP7714	51°49·4′	0°52·6′W	X	165
Eythrope Park	Bucks	SP7614	51°49·4′	0°53·4′W	X	165
Eythrope Park Fm	Bucks	SP7514	51°49·4′	0°54·3′W	FM	165
Eythrope Village	Bucks	SP7713	51°48·8′	0°52·6′W	A	165
Eyton	Heref	SO4761	52°14·9′	2°46·2′W	T	137,138,148
Eyton	Shrops	SJ3713	52°42·9′	2°55·6′W	T	126
Eyton	Shrops	SJ4422	52°47·8′	2°49·4′W	X	126
Eyton	Shrops	SO3787	52°28·9′	2°55·3′W	T	137
Eyton	Wrex	SJ3444	52°59·6′	2°58·6′W	T	117
Eyton Bank	Wrex	SJ3444	52°59·6′	2°58·6′W	X	117
Eyton Common	Heref	SO4761	52°14·9′	2°46·2′W	T	137,138,148
Eyton Gorse	Shrops	SJ3814	52°43·4′	2°54·7′W	F	126
Eyton Grange	Wrex	SJ3544	52°59·6′	2°57·7′W	X	117
Eyton Hall	Wrekin	SJ6415	52°44·1′	2°31·6′W	X	127
Eyton Hall Fm	Wrex	SJ3644	52°59·6′	2°56·8′W	FM	117
Eyton Moor	Wrekin	SJ6515	52°44·1′	2°30·7′W	X	127
Eyton on Severn	Shrops	SJ5706	52°39·2′	2°37·7′W	T	126
Eyton upon the Weald Moors	Wrekin	SJ6515	52°44·1′	2°30·7′W	T	127
Eywood	Heref	SO3159	52°13·7′	3°0·2′W	X	148

F

Faan Hill	Shetld	HU3480	60°30·4′	1°22·4′W	H	1,2,3
Fabdens	Herts	TL3717	51°50·3′	0°0·3′W	A	166
Faberstown	Hants	SU2750	51°15·1′	1°36·4′W	T	184
Faburn House Fm	N Yks	SE4559	54°1·7′	1°18·4′W	FM	105
Faccombe	Hants	SU3858	51°19·4′	1°26·9′W	T	174
Faccombe Wood	Hants	SU3856	51°18·3′	1°26·9′W	F	174
Faceby	N Yks	NZ4903	54°25·4′	1°14·3′W	T	93
Faceby Beck	N Yks	NZ4903	54°25·4′	1°14·3′W	W	93
Faceby Grange	N Yks	NZ4803	54°25·5′	1°15·2′W	X	93
Faceby Manor	N Yks	NZ4904	54°26·0′	1°14·3′W	X	93
Face of Neeans	Shetld	HU2759	60°19·1′	1°30·2′W	X	3
Fach	I of Angl	SH3576	53°15·6′	4°28·0′W	X	114
Fach	Shrops	SJ3136	52°55·3′	3°1·2′W	X	126
Fachddu	Carm	SN3124	51°53·6′	4°27·0′W	X	145,159
Fachddu	Carm	SN3125	51°54·1′	4°27·0′W	X	145
Fachell	Conwy	SH7566	53°10·8′	3°51·8′W	X	115
Fachell	Conwy	SH9978	53°17·6′	3°30·5′W	X	116
Fachell	Gwyn	SH5466	53°10·5′	4°10·7′W	T	114,115
Fach Fm	Gwyn	SH3129	52°50·2′	4°30·1′W	FM	123
Fach-goch	Gwyn	SH6001	52°35·6′	4°3·6′W	X	135
Fachir	Powys	SO1299	52°35·1′	3°17·5′W	X	136
Fachleidiog	Conwy	SH7875	53°15·7′	3°49·3′W	X	115
Fachlwyd Hall	Denb	SJ0657	53°6·4′	3°23·8′W	X	116
Fachongle	Pemb	SN0837	52°0·1′	4°47·4′W	X	145
Fachrhos	Carm	SN4522	51°52·7′	4°14·7′W	X	159
Fachwen	Denb	SJ0574	53°15·5′	3°25·0′W	X	116
Fachwen	Gwyn	SH5761	53°7·9′	4°7·8′W	T	114,115
Fachwen	Powys	SJ0316	52°44·2′	3°25·8′W	X	125
Fachwen Pool	Powys	SO0893	52°31·9′	3°21·0′W	W	136
Facit	Lancs	SD8819	53°40·3′	2°10·5′W	T	109
Fackley	Notts	SK4761	53°8·9′	1°17·4′W	T	120
Factor's Park Plantation	Moray	NJ5158	57°36·8′	2°48·7′W	F	29
Factory Brook	V of Glam	SS9773	51°27·0′	3°28·6′W	W	170
Factory Fm	Corn	SW6847	50°16·9′	5°15·0′W	FM	203
Factory Fm	Herts	TL3405	51°43·9′	0°3·2′W	FM	166
Facwn	Cered	SN6072	52°19·9′	4°2·9′W	X	135
Fada Beag	N Eil	NB2526	58°8·5′	6°39·9′W	X	8,13
Fada Mòr	N Eil	NB2625	58°8·0′	6°38·8′W	H	13,14
Fàdamull	Arg & Bt	NM0649	56°32·7′	6°46·6′W	X	46
Faddell Rigg	N Yks	SE6890	54°18·3′	0°56·9′W	X	94,100
Fadden	Scot Bord	NT0953	55°46·0′	3°26·6′W	H	65,72
Fadden Hill	Northum	NT9142	55°40·5′	2°8·2′W	H	74,75
Faddiley	Ches	SJ5953	53°4·6′	2°36·3′W	T	117
Faddoch	Highld	NG9528	57°18·1′	5°23·7′W	X	25,33
Fadfa	Cered	SN4249	52°7·2′	4°18·1′W	X	146
Fadhail Losgaintir	N Eil	NG0698	57°52·7′	6°57·1′W	X	14,18
Fadhail Sheileboist	N Eil	NG0697	57°52·2′	6°57·0′W	X	14,18
Fadlydyke	Aberd	NJ9047	57°31·0′	2°9·6′W	X	30
Fadmoor	N Yks	SE6789	54°17·8′	0°57·8′W	T	94,100
Fadog	I of Angl	SH2877	53°16·0′	4°34·3′W	X	114
Fadog	I of Angl	SH3280	53°17·7′	4°30·8′W	X	114
Fadog Frech	I of Angl	SH3186	53°20·9′	4°31·9′W	X	114
Fae	Highld	NJ0917	57°14·3′	3°30·0′W	X	36
Faebait	Highld	NH4850	57°31·1′	4°31·8′W	X	26
Faeldre	Gwyn	SH5824	52°47·9′	4°6·0′W	X	124
Faenog Isaf	Cered	SN4656	52°11·1′	4°14·8′W	X	146
Faenol	Denb	SJ1452	53°3·7′	3°16·6′W	X	116
Faenol Bach	Denb	SH9876	53°16·5′	3°31·4′W	X	116
Faenol-Broper	Denb	SJ0174	53°15·5′	3°28·6′W	X	116
Faenol Fawr	Denb	SJ0076	53°16·5′	3°29·6′W	A	116
Faenor Gaer	Pemb	SN0917	51°49·4′	4°45·9′W	A	158
Faerdre	Gwyn	SH2530	52°50·6′	4°35·5′W	X	123
Faerdre	Swan	SN6901	51°41·8′	3°53·3′W	T	170
Faerdre-fawr	Cered	SN4242	52°3·5′	4°17·9′W	X	146
Faery Knoll	Stir	NN4107	56°14·0′	4°33·5′W	X	56
Faesheallach Burn	Highld	NJ0415	57°13·2′	3°34·9′W	W	36
Faesten Dic	Kent	TQ5071	51°25·3′	0°9·8′E	A	177
Faffernie	Aberd	NO2182	56°55·6′	3°17·4′W	H	44
Fagan Burn	D & G	NX3478	55°4·4′	4°35·6′W	W	76
Fagbury Point	Suff	TM2534	51°57·8′	1°16·9′E	X	169

Faggergill Moor	N Yks	NY9807	54°27·7′	2°1·4′W	X	92
Faggergill Moss	N Yks	NY9908	54°28·3′	2°0·5′W	X	92
Faggot	Northum	NU2526	55°31·9′	1°35·8′W	X	75
Faggoters Fm	Essex	TL5210	51°46·3′	0°12·6′E	FM	167
Fagg's Fm	Kent	TR0335	51°4·9′	0°54·3′E	FM	179,189
Faggs Wood	Kent	TQ9834	51°4·5′	0°50·0′E	F	189
Fagley	Brad	SE1834	53°48·4′	1°43·2′W	T	104
Fagnall Fm	Bucks	SU9394	51°38·5′	0°39·0′W	FM	175
Fagney Clough	Derby	SK1492	53°25·7′	1°46·9′W	X	110
Fagra	D & G	NX7546	54°47·9′	3°56·2′W	X	84
Fagra Hill	D & G	NX7547	54°48·4′	3°56·3′W	H	84
Fagwreinon	Pemb	SN1143	52°3·4′	4°45·0′W	X	145
Fagwr Fawr	Cered	SN7881	52°25·0′	3°47·2′W	X	135
Fagwr Goch	Pemb	SN0432	51°57·4′	4°50·8′W	X	145,157
Fagwyr	Cered	SN6487	52°28·1′	3°59·7′W	X	135
Fagwyr	Swan	SN6702	51°42·3′	3°55·1′W	T	159
Fagwyr-frân	Pemb	SN0031	51°56·7′	4°54·2′W	X	145,157
Fagwyr Goch	Pemb	SN0530	51°56·3′	4°49·8′W	X	145
Fagwyr-Owen	Pemb	SN1127	51°54·8′	4°44·5′W	X	145,158
Fagwyr Wen	Cered	SN8272	52°20·2′	3°43·5′W	X	135,136,147
Fagyad Hill	S Lanak	NS9122	55°29·0′	3°43·1′W	H	71,72
Faichem	Highld	NH2801	57°4·3′	4°49·8′W	T	34
Faichfield Ho	Aberd	NK0646	57°30·5′	1°53·5′W	X	30
Faichfolds	Aberd	NJ7558	57°36·9′	2°24·6′W	X	29
Faich-hill	Aberd	NJ5334	57°23·9′	2°46·5′W	X	29
Faichla	Aberd	NJ3411	57°11·4′	3°5·1′W	X	37
Faidre Fach	Powys	SN9189	52°29·5′	3°35·9′W	X	136
Faifley	W Dunb	NS5072	55°55·3′	4°23·6′W	T	64
Faihore	N Eil	NF9368	57°36·1′	7°7·9′W	X	18
Faikham Rig	S Ayr	NX2698	55°15·0′	4°43·8′W	X	76
Fail	S Ayr	NS4228	55°31·5′	4°29·7′W	X	70
Failand	N Som	ST5271	51°26·4′	2°41·0′W	T	172
Failand Fm	N Som	ST5272	51°26·9′	2°41·1′W	FM	172
Failand Hill Ho	N Som	ST5172	51°26·9′	2°41·9′W	X	172
Failand Ho	N Som	ST5173	51°27·5′	2°41·9′W	X	172
Failand Lodge Fm	N Som	ST5172	51°26·9′	2°41·9′W	FM	172
Failford	S Ayr	NS4626	55°30·5′	4°25·9′W	T	70
Faillie	Highld	NH7138	57°25·1′	4°8·4′W	X	27
Fail Mains	S Ayr	NS4128	55°31·4′	4°30·7′W	X	70
Failsworth	Oldham	SD8901	53°30·6′	2°9·5′W	T	109
Fain	Highld	NH1379	57°46·0′	5°8·2′W	X	19
Fain Bridge	Highld	NH1281	57°47·0′	5°9·3′W	X	19
Fainc Ddu	Cered	SN7887	52°28·3′	3°48·3′W	X	135
Fainc Fawr	Cered	SN7489	52°29·3′	3°50·9′W	X	135
Faindouran Lodge (Bothy)	Moray	NJ0806	57°8·4′	3°30·8′W	X	36
Faingmór	Highld	NG7260	57°34·6′	5°48·3′W	X	24
Faintree Hall	Shrops	SO6688	52°29·6′	2°29·6′W	X	138
Fairbank	Cumbr	NY4836	54°43·2′	2°48·0′W	X	90
Fairbank Fm	Ches	SJ6582	53°20·3′	2°31·1′W	FM	109
Fairbank Fm	Cumbr	SD4597	54°22·2′	2°50·4′W	FM	97
Fair Banks	Derby	SK1496	53°27·9′	1°46·9′W	X	110
Fairbank Wood	Cumbr	NY4736	54°43·2′	2°48·9′W	F	90
Fair Bhan	Highld	NN2046	56°34·5′	4°55·4′W	X	50
Fair Bhuidhe	Pth & Kin	NN8467	56°47·1′	3°53·5′W	H	43
Fairbornes Fm	Hants	SU3724	51°1·1′	1°28·0′W	FM	185
Fairboroughs	Staffs	SJ9560	53°8·5′	2°4·1′W	X	118
Fairbourne	Gwyn	SH6113	52°42·1′	4°3·0′W	T	124
Fairbourne Heath	Kent	TQ8550	51°13·4′	0°39·4′E	T	189
Fairbourne Manor Fm	Kent	TQ8651	51°13·9′	0°40·2′E	FM	189
Fairbourne Railway	Gwyn	SH6114	52°42·6′	4°3·1′W	X	124
Fair Brook	Derby	SK1089	53°24·1′	1°50·6′W	W	110
Fairbrook Fm	Kent	TR0560	51°18·4′	0°56·9′E	FM	179
Fairbrook Naze	Derby	SK0989	53°24·1′	1°51·5′W	X	110
Fairburn	N Yks	SE4727	53°44·5′	1°16·8′W	T	105
Fair Burn	S Lanak	NT0222	55°29·2′	3°32·6′W	W	72
Fairburn Ho	Highld	NH4553	57°32·7′	4°34·9′W	X	26
Fairburn Ings Nature Reserve	Leeds	SE4427	53°44·5′	1°19·6′W	X	105
Fairburn Mains	Highld	NH4753	57°32·7′	4°32·9′W	X	26
Fairburn Rig	S Lanak	NT0122	55°29·2′	3°33·6′W	H	72
Fairburn Tower	Highld	NH4652	57°32·2′	4°33·9′W	A	26
Fairby	Devon	SS9417	50°56·8′	3°30·2′W	X	181
Fairclough Fm	Lancs	SD5941	53°52·1′	2°37·0′W	FM	102
Fairclough Hall Fm	Herts	TL2729	51°56·9′	0°8·7′W	FM	166
Fair Cross	Bark & Dag	TQ4585	51°32·9′	0°5·9′E	T	177
Fair Cross	Corn	SW9547	50°17·5′	4°52·3′W	X	204
Fair Cross	Hants	SU6962	51°21·4′	1°0·2′W	X	175,186
Fair Cross	Somer	ST0539	51°8·8′	3°21·1′W	X	181
Faircross Plantn	W Berks	SU4972	51°26·9′	1°17·3′W	F	174
Fairdean or Farthing Downs	Surrey	TQ2957	51°18·1′	0°8·6′W	H	187
Fàir Dhubh	Highld	NC5263	58°32·1′	4°32·1′W	X	10
Fairdre Fawr	Powys	SN9189	52°29·5′	3°35·9′W	X	136
Fàire Buidhe	Arg & Bt	NM7026	56°22·5′	5°43·0′W	X	49
Fair Edge Hill	Staffs	SJ9561	53°9·0′	2°4·1′W	X	118
Fàire Donn	Highld	NG8624	57°15·7′	5°32·5′W	X	33
Fàire Ghlinne Mhóir	Pth & Kin	NO0375	56°51·6′	3°35·0′W	H	43
Fàire Mhór	Pth & Kin	NN9958	56°42·4′	3°38·5′W	H	52,53
Fàire nan Clach Ruadha	Highld	NC1019	58°7·4′	5°13·1′W	X	15
Fàire na Sgurr	Highld	NM6585	56°54·1′	5°51·1′W	X	40
Fairfax Intrenchment	Brad	SE0839	53°51·1′	1°52·3′W	A	104
Fairfield	Bury	SD8211	53°36·0′	2°15·9′W	T	109
Fairfield	Clackm	NS8994	56°7·8′	3°46·7′W	T	58
Fairfield	Cumbr	NY0121	54°34·7′	3°31·5′W	X	89
Fairfield	Cumbr	NY1526	54°37·6′	3°18·6′W	X	89
Fairfield	Cumbr	NY3511	54°29·7′	2°59·8′W	H	90
Fairfield	Derby	SK0773	53°15·5′	1°53·3′W	T	119
Fairfield	Derby	SK2217	52°45·2′	1°40·0′W	X	128
Fairfield	Derby	SK3470	53°13·8′	1°29·0′W	X	119
Fairfield	Kent	TQ9626	51°0·2′	0°48·0′E	T	189
Fairfield	Liv	SJ3791	53°25·0′	2°56·6′W	T	108
Fairfield	Norf	TF5817	52°43·9′	0°20·8′E	X	131
Fairfield	N Yks	SE3267	54°6·1′	1°30·2′W	X	99
Fairfield	Shetld	HU2978	60°29·3′	1°27·8′W	X	3
Fairfield	Staffs	SK0154	53°5·2′	1°58·7′W	X	119
Fairfield	Stir	NS6395	56°7·9′	4°11·8′W	X	57
Fairfield	Stock on T	NZ4119	54°34·1′	1°21·5′W	T	93
Fairfield	Tames	SJ9097	53°28·4′	2°8·6′W	T	109
Fairfield	Wirral	SJ2982	53°20·1′	3°3·6′W	T	108

Fairfield	Worcs	SO9475	52°22·6′	2°4·9′W	T	139
Fairfield	Worcs	SP0342	52°4·8′	1°57·0′W	T	150
Fairfield	W Susx	SU8619	50°58·1′	0°46·1′W	X	197
Fairfield Common	Derby	SK0774	53°16·0′	1°53·3′W	X	119
Fairfield Cottage	Highld	NG2746	57°25·6′	6°32·4′W	X	23
Fairfield Court	Kent	TQ9726	51°0·2′	0°48·9′E	X	189
Fairfield Court	Worcs	SO9475	52°22·6′	2°4·9′W	X	139
Fairfield Fm	E Yorks	SE7354	53°58·9′	0°52·8′W	FM	105,106
Fairfield Fm	Lancs	SD4542	53°52·5′	2°49·8′W	FM	102
Fairfield Fm	Wilts	SU1761	51°21·1′	1°45·0′W	FM	173
Fairfield Ho	N Yks	SD6766	54°5·6′	2°29·9′W	X	98
Fairfield Hospital	Beds	TL2035	52°0·3′	0°14·7′W	X	153
Fairfield House	Somer	ST1843	51°11·1′	3°10·0′W	A	181
Fairfield Low	Derby	SK0773	53°15·5′	1°53·3′W	A	119
Fairfield Mains	Angus	NO5647	56°37·0′	2°42·6′W	X	54
Fairfield Park	Bath & NE Somer	ST7566	51°23·8′	2°21·2′W	T	172
Fairfields	Ches	SJ8660	53°8·5′	2°12·2′W	X	118
Fairfields	Essex	TL7810	51°45·8′	0°35·2′E	X	167
Fairfields	Glos	SO7432	51°59·4′	2°22·3′W	T	150
Fairfields	I of W	SZ5079	50°36·7′	1°17·2′W	X	196
Fairfields	Kent	TR2263	51°19·6′	1°11·6′E	X	179
Fairfields Fm	Essex	TL9230	51°56·3′	0°48·0′E	FM	168
Fairfields Fm	Stock on T	NZ3716	54°32·5′	1°25·3′W	FM	93
Fairfield Wood	Somer	ST1841	51°10·0′	3°10·0′W	F	181
Fairfold's Fm	Herts	TL1810	51°46·9′	0°17·0′W	FM	166
Fairford	Glos	SP1500	51°42·1′	1°46·6′W	T	163
Fairford Airfield	Glos	SU1498	51°41·1′	1°47·5′W	X	163
Fairgarden Fm	Somer	SS9342	51°10·3′	3°31·4′W	FM	181
Fairgirth	D & G	NX8756	54°53·4′	3°45·3′W	X	84
Fairgirth Hill	D & G	NX8956	54°53·4′	3°43·4′W	H	84
Fairgirth Lane	D & G	NX8756	54°53·4′	3°45·3′W	W	84
Fair Green	Norf	TF6516	52°43·2′	0°27·0′E	T	132
Fairgreen Fm	Oxon	SP2922	51°54·0′	1°34·3′W	FM	164
Fairham Brook	Notts	SK5530	52°52·1′	1°10·6′W	W	129
Fairham Wood	Notts	SK6128	52°51·0′	1°5·2′W	F	129
Fairhaugh	Northum	NT8712	55°24·6′	2°11·9′W	X	80
Fairhaven	E Yorks	SE8442	53°52·3′	0°42·9′W	X	106
Fairhaven	N Ayr	NR9048	55°41·1′	5°20·0′W	X	62,69
Fairhaven	N Ayr	NS1857	55°46·6′	4°53·7′W	X	63
Fairhaven Fm	Devon	SX6892	50°43·0′	3°51·8′W	FM	191
Fairhaven Lake	Lancs	SD3427	53°44·4′	2°59·6′W	W	102
Fairhazel	E Susx	TQ4521	50°58·4′	0°4·3′E	X	198
Fair Head	N Yks	NZ8304	54°25·7′	0°42·8′W	X	94
Fair Hill	Cumbr	NY5031	54°40·5′	2°46·1′W	T	90
Fairhill	Cumbr	NY7145	54°48·2′	2°26·6′W	X	86,87
Fairhill	Cumbr	NY7843	54°47·1′	2°20·1′W	X	86,87
Fair Hill	Cumbr	NY7903	54°25·6′	2°19·0′W	X	91
Fairhill	Kent	TQ5751	51°14·4′	0°15·3′E	X	188
Fair Hill	Lancs	SD7559	54°1·8′	2°22·5′W	X	103
Fairhill	Orkney	HY6523	59°5·8′	2°36·2′W	X	5
Fairhill	S Lanak	NS7153	55°45·4′	4°2·9′W	T	64
Fair Hill Coppy	Lancs	SD7560	54°2·4′	2°22·5′W	X	98
Fair Hill Fm	N Yks	SE5689	54°17·9′	1°8·0′W	FM	100
Fairhills	Renf	NS3359	55°48·0′	4°39·4′W	X	63
Fairholm	D & G	NX8559	55°7·2′	3°22·4′W	X	78
Fairholm	S Lanak	NS7551	55°44·4′	3°59·0′W	X	64
Fairholme	E Yorks	TA1137	53°49·3′	0°18·4′W	X	107
Fairholme	N Yks	SE3289	54°18·0′	1°30·1′W	X	99
Fairholmes	Derby	SK1789	53°24·1′	1°44·2′W	X	110
Fairhouse Fm	Somer	ST2112	50°54·4′	3°7·0′W	FM	193
Fairhurst	Lancs	SD5440	53°51·5′	2°41·5′W	X	102
Fairhurst Hall	Lancs	SD4911	53°35·8′	2°45·8′W	X	108
Fairies Hole	Oxon	SU7483	51°32·7′	0°55·6′W	F	175
Fair Isle	Shetld	HZ2271	59°31·7′	1°36·2′W	X	4
Fairladies Fm	Cumbr	NX9811	54°29·3′	3°34·1′W	FM	89
Fairlands	Essex	TL5511	51°46·8′	0°15·2′E	X	167
Fairlands	Surrey	SU9652	51°15·8′	0°37·1′W	T	186
Fairlands Fm	Surrey	SU9652	51°15·8′	0°37·1′W	FM	186
Fairlands Valley Park	Herts	TL2423	51°53·7′	0°11·5′W	X	166
Fairlaw	Scot Bord	NT8561	55°50·8′	2°13·9′W	X	67
Fairlawne	Kent	TQ5953	51°15·5′	0°17·1′E	X	188
Fairlawne Home Fm	Kent	TQ6052	51°14·9′	0°17·9′E	FM	188
Fairlea	Aberd	NJ5316	57°14·2′	2°46·3′W	X	37
Fairlee	I of W	SZ5090	50°42·7′	1°17·1′W	T	196
Fairley	C of Aber	NJ8607	57°9·5′	2°13·4′W	X	38
Fairley	Northum	NZ0556	54°54·2′	1°54·9′W	X	87
Fairley May	Northum	NZ0456	54°54·2′	1°55·8′W	X	87
Fairlie	N Ayr	NS2055	55°45·6′	4°51·7′W	T	63
Fairliecrevoch	E Ayr	NS3642	55°38·9′	4°35·9′W	X	70
Fairlie Glen	N Ayr	NS2154	55°45·0′	4°50·7′W	X	63
Fairlie Ho	S Ayr	NS3835	55°35·2′	4°33·8′W	A	70
Fairliehope	Scot Bord	NT1556	55°47·6′	3°20·9′W	X	65,72
Fairliehope Burn	Scot Bord	NT1456	55°47·6′	3°21·9′W	W	65,72
Fairlie Mains	S Ayr	NS3835	55°35·2′	4°33·8′W	X	70
Fairlie Moor	N Ayr	NS2255	55°45·6′	4°49·8′W	X	63
Fairlie Roads	N Ayr	NS1854	55°45·0′	4°53·6′W	W	63
Fairlieward	N Ayr	NS2256	55°46·1′	4°49·8′W	X	63
Fairlight	E Susx	TQ8612	50°52·9′	0°39·0′E	T	199
Fairlight Cove	E Susx	TQ8711	50°52·3′	0°39·9′E	T	199
Fairlight Fm	W Susx	TQ4138	51°7·7′	0°1·3′E	FM	187
Fairlight Glen	E Susx	TQ8510	50°51·8′	0°38·1′E	F	199
Fairlight Place	E Susx	TQ8511	50°52·4′	0°38·1′E	X	199
Fairliuch	Devon	SS4737	51°7·0′	4°10·8′W	A	180
Fairloans	Scot Bord	NT7508	55°22·2′	2°23·2′W	X	80
Fairloans	Scot Bord	NY5997	55°16·2′	2°38·3′W	X	80
Fairlop	Redbr	TQ4590	51°35·6′	0°6·0′E	T	177
Fairlop Waters	Redbr	TQ4590	51°35·6′	0°6·0′E	W	177
Fàir Mhór	Highld	NH0695	57°54·4′	5°16·0′W	X	19
Fairmile	Devon	SY0897	50°46·2′	3°17·9′W	T	192
Fairmile	Dorset	SZ1594	50°45·0′	1°46·9′W	T	195
Fair Mile	Oxon	SU7484	51°33·2′	0°55·6′W	X	175
Fairmile	Surrey	TQ1261	51°20·4′	0°23·1′W	T	176,187
Fairmile Beck	Cumbr	SD6397	54°22·3′	2°33·8′W	W	97
Fairmile Bottom	W Susx	SU9809	50°52·6′	0°36·0′W	X	197
Fairmile Common	Surrey	TQ1261	51°20·4′	0°23·1′W	T	176,187
Fairmile Down	Wilts	SU2556	51°18·4′	1°38·1′W	X	174
Fairmile Fm	Dorset	SY6896	50°46·0′	2°26·8′W	FM	194
Fairmile Gate	Cumbr	SD6297	54°22·3′	2°34·7′W	X	97
Fairmilehead	C of Edin	NT2568	55°54·2′	3°11·5′W	T	66

Fair Mile Hospl	Oxon	SU5985	51°33·9′	1°8·5′W	X	174
Fair Mile, The	Oxon	SU5582	51°32·3′	1°12·0′W	X	174
Fair Moor	Northum	NZ1887	55°10·9′	1°42·6′W	T	81
Fairness	Pth & Kin	NN7921	56°22·2′	3°57·1′W	X	51,52,57
Fairney Flat	Northum	NT9653	55°46·5′	2°3·4′W	X	74,75
Fairneyknow	Angus	NO6141	56°33·8′	2°37·6′W	X	54
Fairniehill	W Loth	NT0576	55°58·3′	3°30·9′W	X	65
Fairnieside	Scot Bord	NT9461	55°50·8′	2°5·3′W	X	67
Fairnilee Fm	Scot Bord	NT4532	55°35·0′	2°51·9′W	FM	73
Fairnilee Ho	Scot Bord	NT4533	55°35·5′	2°51·9′W	X	73
Fairnington	Scot Bord	NT6428	55°32·9′	2°33·8′W	X	74
Fairnley	Northum	NZ0088	55°11·4′	1°59·6′W	X	81
Fairnley Burn	Northum	NZ0088	55°11·4′	1°59·6′W	W	81
Fairnylees	Scot Bord	NT4956	55°47·9′	2°48·4′W	X	66,73
Fairoak	Caer	ST1799	51°41·3′	3°11·7′W	T	171
Fair Oak	Devon	ST0218	50°57·4′	3°23·3′W	X	181
Fair Oak	Devon	ST0318	50°57·4′	3°22·5′W	X	181
Fair Oak	Hants	SU4918	50°57·8′	1°17·7′W	T	185
Fair Oak	Hants	SU5561	51°21·0′	1°12·2′W	T	174
Fair Oak	Lancs	SD6446	53°54·8′	2°32·5′W	T	102,103
Fairoak	Staffs	SJ7632	52°53·3′	2°21·0′W	T	127
Fair Oak	W Susx	SU8122	50°59·7′	0°50·4′W	X	197
Fair Oak Fell	Lancs	SD6247	53°55·3′	2°34·3′W	X	102,103
Fair Oak Fm	Card	ST1984	51°33·2′	3°9·7′W	FM	171
Fair Oak Fm	Devon	ST1808	50°52·2′	3°9·5′W	FM	192,193
Fair Oak Fm	Devon	SY0093	50°43·9′	3°24·6′W	FM	192
Fair Oak Fm	E Susx	TQ6226	51°0·9′	0°19·0′E	FM	188,199
Fair Oak Fm	W Susx	TQ1414	50°55·1′	0°22·3′W	FM	198
Fair Oak Green	Hants	SU6760	51°20·3′	1°1·9′W	T	175,186
Fairoak Lodge	Staffs	SK0016	52°44·7′	1°59·6′W	X	128
Fair Oaks	N Yks	SE6127	53°44·4′	1°4·1′W	X	105
Fairoaks Airport	Surrey	TQ0062	51°21·1′	0°33·4′W	X	176,186
Fairoaks Fm	Suff	TM0569	52°17·1′	1°0·7′E	FM	155
Fairoaks Fm	Worcs	SO7637	52°2·1′	2°20·6′W	FM	150
Fair Orchard	Newp	ST3083	51°32·7′	3°0·2′W	X	171
Fair Place	N Yks	SD9842	53°52·7′	2°1·4′W	X	103
Fairplace Fm	E Susx	TQ4328	51°2·2′	0°2·8′E	FM	187,198
Fairplay	Northum	NY7650	54°50·9′	2°22·0′W	X	86,87
Fair Rigg	Cumbr	SD3884	54°15·1′	2°56·7′W	X	96,97
Fair Rosamund's Well	Oxon	SP4316	51°50·7′	1°22·2′W	A	164
Fairseat	Kent	TQ6261	51°19·7′	0°19·9′E	T	177,188
Fairshaw Fm	Northum	NY8873	55°3·3′	2°10·8′W	FM	87
Fairslacks	Scot Bord	NT1554	55°46·6′	3°20·9′W	X	65,72
Fair Snape Fell	Lancs	SD5946	53°54·8′	2°37·0′W	X	102
Fairspear Fm	Oxon	SP3016	51°50·7′	1°33·5′W	FM	164
Fairspring	Northum	NY9974	55°3·9′	2°0·5′W	X	87
Fairstead	Essex	TL7616	51°49·1′	0°33·6′E	T	167
Fairstead	Norf	TF6419	52°44·9′	0°26·2′E	T	132
Fairstead Fm	Suff	TM3879	52°21·7′	1°30·1′E	FM	156
Fairstead Lane Fm	Norf	TM2395	52°30·7′	1°17·6′E	FM	134
Fairstead Lodge	Essex	TL7416	51°49·2′	0°31·9′E	X	167
Fairthorn	Derby	SK0469	53°13·3′	1°56·0′W	X	119
Fairthorne Manor	Hants	SU5112	50°54·5′	1°16·1′W	X	196
Fairthorn Lodge	Sheff	SK2585	53°21·9′	1°37·0′W	X	110
Fairthwaite Park Ho	Lancs	SD6377	54°11·5′	2°33·6′W	X	97
Fairtrough Fm	Brom	TQ4661	51°20·0′	0°6·1′E	FM	177,188
Fair View	Durham	NZ1724	54°36·9′	1°43·8′W	X	92
Fairview	Glos	SO9522	51°54·0′	2°4·0′W	T	163
Fair View	Staffs	SK0453	53°4·7′	1°56·0′W	X	119
Fair View	W Berks	SU3478	51°30·2′	1°30·2′W	X	174
Fairview Fm	Birm	SP1594	52°32·9′	1°46·3′W	FM	139
Fairview Fm	Bucks	SP9716	51°50·3′	0°35·1′W	FM	165
Fair View Fm	Cambs	TL4771	52°19·3′	0°9·8′E	FM	154
Fairview Fm	Derby	SK3223	52°48·5′	1°31·1′W	FM	128
Fairview Fm	Hants	SU3735	51°7·0′	1°27·9′W	FM	185
Fairview Fm	Lincs	SK8936	52°55·1′	0°40·2′W	FM	130
Fair View Fm	N Yks	SE4359	54°1·8′	1°20·2′W	FM	105
Fairview Fm	Somer	ST4124	51°1·0′	2°50·1′W	FM	193
Fairview Ho	Bucks	SU9488	51°35·2′	0°38·2′W	X	175
Fairwarp	E Susx	TQ4626	51°1·1′	0°5·3′E	T	188,198
Fairwater	Card	ST1377	51°29·4′	3°14·8′W	T	171
Fairwater	Devon	SY3499	50°47·4′	2°55·8′W	X	193
Fairwater	Torf	ST2794	51°38·6′	3°2·9′W	T	171
Fairwater Fm	Newp	ST2384	51°33·2′	3°6·2′W	FM	171
Fairwells	S Ayr	NS4431	55°33·1′	4°27·9′W	X	70
Fairwinds Fm	Essex	TL8009	51°45·3′	0°36·9′E	FM	168
Fairwood	Swan	SS5693	51°37·3′	4°4·4′W	X	159
Fairwood	Wilts	ST8451	51°15·7′	2°13·4′W	T	183
Fairwood Common	Swan	SS5692	51°36·7′	4°4·4′W	X	159
Fairwood Corner	Swan	SS5692	51°36·7′	4°4·4′W	X	159
Fairwood Fell	Northum	NT7307	55°21·6′	2°25·1′W	X	80
Fairwood Fm	Wilts	ST8350	51°15·2′	2°14·2′W	FM	183
Fairwood Ho	Wilts	ST8451	51°15·7′	2°13·4′W	X	183
Fairwood Lodge	Swan	SS5892	51°36·8′	4°2·7′W	X	159
Fairy Br	Highld	NG2751	57°28·3′	6°32·8′W	X	23
Fairy Br	I of M	SC3071	54°6·7′	4°35·6′W	X	95
Fairy Cave	Somer	ST6547	51°13·5′	2°29·7′W	X	183
Fairy Cottage	I of M	SC4383	54°13·4′	4°24·1′W	X	95
Fairy Cross	Corn	SX1262	50°25·9′	4°38·5′W	X	200
Fairy Cross	Devon	SS4024	50°59·8′	4°16·4′W	T	180,190
Fairy Cross Plain	N Yks	NZ7205	54°26·4′	0°53·0′W	H	94
Fairydean Burn	Scot Bord	NT2247	55°42·9′	3°14·1′W	W	73
Fairy Dell	N Ayr	NR9452	55°43·3′	5°16·4′W	X	62,69
Fairy Fm	Essex	TL7232	51°57·8′	0°30·6′E	FM	167
Fairy Glen	Conwy	SH8053	53°3·9′	3°47·0′W	X	116
Fairy Glen	N Ayr	NS0134	55°33·8′	5°8·9′W	X	69
Fairy Glen	Staffs	SO8681	52°25·8′	2°12·0′W	F	139
Fairygreen	Pth & Kin	NO2133	56°29·2′	3°16·5′W	X	53
Fairy Haw	N Yks	SD9285	54°15·9′	2°7·0′W	X	98
Fairy Hill	Bath & NE Somer	ST6465	51°23·2′	2°30·7′W	X	172
Fairy Hill	Wakf	SE4624	53°42·9′	1°17·8′W	X	105
Fairyhill (Hotel)	Swan	SS4691	51°36·0′	4°13·0′W	X	159
Fairy Hillock	Highld	ND3451	58°26·8′	3°7·4′W	X	12
Fairy Hole	Herts	TL1029	51°57·1′	0°23·6′W	X	166
Fairyknowe	D & G	NY2675	55°4·1′	3°9·1′W	X	85
Fairy Knowe	Moray	NJ2642	57°28·0′	3°13·6′W	X	28
Fairy Knowe	Stir	NS7998	56°9·8′	3°56·5′W	X	57
Fairy Knowe (Cairn)	Stir	NS7998	56°9·8′	3°56·5′W	A	57

Fairy Steps	Cumbr	SD4878	54°12·0'	2°47·4'W	X	97
Faither,The	Shetld	HU2585	60°33·1'	1°32·1'W	X	3
Fakenham	Norf	TF9230	52°50·2'	0°51·4'E	T	132
Fakenham Common	Norf	TF9329	52°49·7'	0°52·3'E	X	132
Fakenham Heath	Suff	TL8876	52°21·2'	0°46·0'E	X	144
Fakenham Magna	Suff	TL9076	52°21·2'	0°47·8'E	T	144
Fakenham Spinney	Suff	TL8976	52°21·2'	0°46·9'E	F	144
Fakenham Wood	Suff	TL9277	52°21·7'	0°49·6'E	F	144
Fala	Midlo	NT4361	55°50·6'	2°54·2'W	T	66
Fala	Pth & Kin	NO2323	56°23·8'	3°14·4'W	X	53,58
Fala Dam	Midlo	NT4261	55°50·6'	2°55·1'W	X	66
Fala Dam Burn	Midlo	NT4361	55°50·6'	2°54·2'W	W	66
Fala Flow Loch	Midlo	NT4258	55°49·0'	2°55·1'W	W	66,73
Fala Hall	Midlo	NT4461	55°50·6'	2°53·2'W	X	66
Falahill	Scot Bord	NT3956	55°47·9'	2°57·9'W	T	66,73
Fala Mains	Midlo	NT4460	55°50·1'	2°53·2'W	X	66
Fala Moor	Midlo	NT4258	55°49·0'	2°55·1'W	X	66,73
Falbae	D & G	NX5061	54°55·5'	4°20·0'W	X	83
Falbae Burn	D & G	NX4961	54°55·5'	4°21·0'W	W	83
Falbae Loch	D & G	NX7371	55°1·3'	3°58·8'W	W	77,84
Falbae Moor	D & G	NX7272	55°1·8'	3°59·7'W	X	77,84
Falcadon Fm	Devon	SX6599	50°46·7'	3°54·5'W	FM	191
Falcon	Heref	SO6032	51°59·3'	2°34·6'W	T	149
Falcon Clints	Durham	NY8228	54°39·1'	2°16·3'W	X	91,92
Falcon Crag	Cumbr	NY2720	54°34·4'	3°7·3'W	X	89,90
Falcon Crag	Cumbr	NY3512	54°30·2'	2°59·8'W	X	90
Falcon Craig	D & G	NT1212	55°23·9'	3°22·9'W	X	78
Falcondale	Cered	SN5649	52°7·5'	4°5·8'W	X	146
Falconers	W Susx	TQ1220	50°58·3'	0°23·9'W	X	198
Falconers Fm	Worcs	SO8247	52°7·5'	2°15·4'W	FM	150
Falcon Fm	N Yks	NZ6903	54°25·3'	0°55·8'W	FM	94
Falcon Fm	Staffs	SO8385	52°28·0'	2°14·6'W	FM	138
Falconhurst	Kent	TQ4642	51°9·7'	0°5·7'E	X	188
Falconhurst	Kent	TR0734	51°4·3'	0°57·7'E	X	179,189
Falcon Inn	N Yks	SE9798	54°22·3'	0°30·0'W	X	94,101
Falcon Lodge	Birm	SP1496	52°33·9'	1°47·2'W	T	139
Falcons Hall Fm	Essex	TL8909	51°45·1'	0°44·7'E	FM	168
Falcons Hall Fm	Suff	TM0473	52°19·3'	1°0·0'E	FM	144,155
Falcon Stone	Pth & Kin	NO2930	56°27·7'	3°8·7'W	X	53
Falconwood	Bexley	TQ4575	51°27·5'	0°5·6'E	T	177
Falcutt	Northnts	SP5942	52°4·6'	1°7·9'W	T	152
Falcutt Hall	Northnts	SP5941	52°4·1'	1°8·0'W	X	152
Faldarroch	D & G	NX3650	54°49·3'	4°32·7'W	X	83
Faldingworth	Lincs	TF0684	53°20·8'	0°24·1'W	T	121
Faldingworth Grange	Lincs	TF0484	53°20·8'	0°25·9'W	X	121
Faldo Fm	Beds	TL0731	51°58·3'	0°26·1'W	FM	166
Faldonside	Scot Bord	NT5032	55°35·0'	2°47·2'W	T	73
Faldonside Ho	Scot Bord	NT4933	55°35·5'	2°48·1'W	X	73
Falfield	Fife	NO4408	56°15·9'	2°53·8'W	X	59
Falfield	S Glos	ST6893	51°38·3'	2°27·4'W	T	162,172
Falfield Bank	Fife	NO4508	56°15·9'	2°52·8'W	X	59
Falgunzeon	D & G	NX8762	54°56·6'	3°45·4'W	X	84
Falhar	D & G	NX4638	54°43·1'	4°23·0'W	X	83
Falhouse Green	Kirk	SE2117	53°39·2'	1°40·5'W	X	110
Falicon Fm	Lancs	SD6236	53°49·4'	2°34·2'W	FM	102,103
Falkedon	Devon	SX7095	50°44·6'	3°50·2'W	X	191
Falkenham	Suff	TM2939	52°0·4'	1°20·6'E	T	169
Falkenham Creek	Suff	TM3040	52°0·9'	1°21·5'E	W	169
Falkenham Sink	Suff	TM2939	52°0·4'	1°20·6'E	T	169
Falkirk	Falk	NS8880	56°0·2'	3°47·3'W	T	65
Falkland	Fife	NO2507	56°15·2'	3°12·2'W	T	59
Falkland Fm	Hants	SU4563	51°22·1'	1°20·8'W	FM	174
Falkland Memorial	W Berks	SU4664	51°22·6'	1°20·0'W	X	174
Falklandwood	Fife	NO2408	56°15·8'	3°13·2'W	X	59
Falla	Scot Bord	NT7013	55°24·9'	2°28·0'W	X	80
Falla	S Lanak	NS9950	55°44·2'	3°36·1'W	X	65,72
Falla Brae	Scot Bord	NT2840	55°39·1'	3°8·2'W	X	73
Fallady	Angus	NO5648	56°37·6'	2°42·6'W	X	54
Fallady Bank	Angus	NO5548	56°37·6'	2°43·6'W	X	54
Fallago Ridge	Scot Bord	NT5859	55°49·6'	2°39·8'W	X	67,73,74
Fallagoridge Head	E Loth	NT5761	55°50·7'	2°40·8'W	X	67
Falla Knowe	Scot Bord	NT7414	55°25·4'	2°24·2'W	X	80
Falla Moss	Scot Bord	NT0816	55°26·0'	3°26·8'W	X	78
Fallapit Ho (Sch)	Devon	SX7648	50°19·4'	3°44·1'W	X	202
Fallaw	Angus	NO6549	56°38·1'	2°33·8'W	X	54
Fallaws	Angus	NO5140	56°33·2'	2°47·4'W	X	54
Fall Bay	Swan	SS4187	51°33·8'	4°17·3'W	W	159
Fall Beck	Cumbr	SD5686	54°16·3'	2°40·1'W	W	97
Fallburn	S Lanak	NS9637	55°37·2'	3°38·7'W	X	72
Fall Cleuch Wood	S Lanak	NT0023	55°29·7'	3°34·5'W	F	72
Fall Edge Fm	Kirk	SE2206	53°33·2'	1°39·7'W	FM	110
Falleninch	Stir	NS7793	56°7·1'	3°58·3'W	X	57
Fallen Rocks	N Ayr	NS0048	55°41·3'	5°10·5'W	X	63,69
Fallen Yew	Cumbr	SD4692	54°19·5'	2°49·4'W	X	97
Fall Fm	Worcs	SO6965	52°17·2'	2°26·9'W	FM	138,149
Fallford	D & G	NY2680	55°6·8'	3°9·2'W	X	79
Fallgate	Derby	SK3562	53°9·5'	1°28·2'W	T	119
Fall Hill	Derby	SK3562	53°9·5'	1°28·2'W	X	119
Fall Hill	S Lanak	NS9622	55°29·1'	3°38·3'W	H	72
Fallhills	Midlo	NT2558	55°48·8'	3°11·4'W	X	66,73
Fallibroome Fm	Ches	SJ8975	53°16·6'	2°9·5'W	FM	118
Fallin	Stir	NS8391	56°6·1'	3°52·4'W	T	57
Fallinge	Derby	SK2666	53°11·7'	1°36·2'W	T	119
Fallinge Edge	Derby	SK2766	53°11·7'	1°35·3'W	X	119
Falling Foss	N Yks	NZ8803	54°25·1'	0°38·2'W	W	94
Fallings Heath	Wals	SO9896	52°33·9'	2°1·4'W	T	139
Fall Kneesend	S Lanak	NS9816	55°25·9'	3°36·3'W	H	78
Fall Law	Scot Bord	NT2518	55°27·3'	3°10·7'W	H	79
Fallodon Hall	Northum	NU2023	55°30·3'	1°40·6'W	X	75
Fallodon Mill	Northum	NU1924	55°30·8'	1°41·5'W	X	75
Fall of Warness	Orkney	HY5427	59°7·9'	2°47·7'W	W	5,6
Fallow Field	Cumbr	NY3453	54°52·3'	3°1·3'W	X	85
Fallowfield	Durham	NZ3744	54°47·6'	1°25·0'W	X	88
Fallowfield	Man	SJ8593	53°26·3'	2°13·1'W	T	109
Fallowfield	Northum	NY9268	55°0·6'	2°7·1'W	X	87
Fallow Hill	Aberd	NJ6331	57°22·3'	2°36·5'W	H	29,37
Fallow Hill	Cumbr	NY7035	54°42·8'	2°27·5'W	X	91
Fallow Knowes	Northum	NT8507	55°21·7'	2°13·8'W	H	80
Fallowlees	Northum	NZ0194	55°14·7'	1°58·6'W	X	81
Fallowlees Burn	Northum	NZ0092	55°13·6'	1°59·6'W	W	81
Fallowlees Lough	Northum	NZ0194	55°14·7'	1°58·6'W	W	81
Fallows	Angus	NO5640	56°33·3'	2°42·5'W	X	54
Fallows Burn	Angus	NO3636	56°31·0'	3°2·0'W	W	54
Fallows Fm	Notts	SK6453	53°4·5'	1°2·3'W	FM	120
Fallows Hall	Ches	SJ8374	53°16·0'	2°14·9'W	X	118
Fall Rigg	N Yks	SE7690	54°18·2'	0°49·5'W	X	94,100
Falls Fm	Lincs	TF3962	53°8·5'	0°5·1'E	FM	122
Falls Fm, The	Shrops	SO5597	52°34·4'	2°39·4'W	FM	137,138
Fallside	Aberd	NO8182	56°56·0'	2°18·3'W	X	45
Fallside	N Lanak	NS7160	55°49·2'	4°3·1'W	T	64
Fallside	S Lanak	NS9030	55°33·3'	3°44·2'W	X	71,72
Falls of Acharn	Pth & Kin	NN7543	56°34·0'	4°1·6'W	W	51,52
Falls of Balgy	Highld	NG8453	57°31·2'	5°36·0'W	W	24
Falls of Balnaguard	Pth & Kin	NN9351	56°38·6'	3°44·2'W	W	52
Falls of Barvick	Pth & Kin	NN8524	56°23·9'	3°51·3'W	W	52,58
Falls of Bruar, The	Pth & Kin	NN8166	56°46·5'	3°56·4'W	W	43
Falls of Clyde	S Lanak	NS8841	55°39·2'	3°46·4'W	W	71,72
Falls of Cruachan	Arg & Bt	NN0727	56°24·0'	5°7·2'W	W	50
Falls of Damff	Angus	NO3879	56°54·2'	3°0·6'W	W	44
Falls of Dee	Aberd	NN9499	57°4·5'	3°44·5'W	W	36,43
Falls of Dochart	Stir	NN5632	56°27·7'	4°19·8'W	W	51
Falls of Drumly Harry	Angus	NO4562	56°45·0'	2°53·5'W	W	44
Falls of Edinample	Stir	NN6022	56°22·4'	4°15·6'W	W	51
Falls of Falloch	Stir	NN3320	56°20·8'	4°41·7'W	W	50,56
Falls of Feakirk	Moray	NJ0344	57°28·8'	3°36·6'W	W	27
Falls of Garbh Allt	Aberd	NO1989	56°59·4'	3°19·5'W	W	43
Falls of Glomach	Highld	NH0125	57°16·6'	5°17·6'W	W	25,33
Falls of Keltie	Pth & Kin	NN8625	56°24·5'	3°50·4'W	W	52,58
Falls of Keltney	Pth & Kin	NN7749	56°37·3'	3°59·8'W	W	51,52
Falls of Kirkaig	Highld	NC1117	58°6·4'	5°12·0'W	W	15
Falls of Leny	Stir	NN5908	56°14·9'	4°16·1'W	W	57
Falls of Lora	Arg & Bt	NM9134	56°27·4'	5°23·1'W	W	49
Falls of Measach	Highld	NH2078	57°45·6'	5°1·1'W	W	20
Falls of Moness	Pth & Kin	NN8547	56°36·3'	3°52·0'W	W	52
Falls of Monzie	Pth & Kin	NN8826	56°25·0'	3°48·5'W	W	52,58
Falls of Ness	Pth & Kin	NN8815	56°19·1'	3°48·2'W	W	58
Falls of Orrin	Highld	NH4651	57°31·6'	4°33·9'W	W	26
Falls of Pattack	Highld	NN5588	56°57·9'	4°22·6'W	W	42
Falls of Roy	Highld	NN3692	56°59·7'	4°41·5'W	W	34
Falls of Tarf	Pth & Kin	NN9879	56°53·7'	3°40·0'W	W	43
Falls of the Braan	Pth & Kin	NO0041	56°33·3'	3°37·2'W	W	52,53
Falls of Truim	Highld	NN6792	57°0·3'	4°10·9'W	W	35
Falls of Turret	Pth & Kin	NN8324	56°23·9'	3°53·3'W	W	52
Falls of Unich	Angus	NO3880	56°54·7'	3°0·6'W	W	44
Falls, The	Cumbr	SD2980	54°12·9'	3°4·9'W	X	96,97
Falls, The	Pemb	SM8011	51°45·5'	5°10·9'W	X	157
Falls, The	Staffs	SJ8758	53°7·4'	2°11·2'W	X	118
Falmer	E Susx	TQ3508	50°51·6'	0°4·5'W	T	198
Falmer Hill	Bri & Hov	TQ3407	50°51·0'	0°5·4'W	X	198
Falmouth	Corn	SW8032	50°9·1'	5°4·4'W	T	204
Falmouth Bay	Corn	SW8129	50°7·5'	5°3·5'W	W	204
Falnash	Scot Bord	NT3905	55°20·4'	2°57·3'W	T	79
Falnaw Burn	D & G	NX5062	54°56·1'	4°20·1'W	W	83
Falsgrave	N Yks	TA0287	54°16·3'	0°25·6'W	T	101
Falsgrave Moor Fm	N Yks	TA0286	54°15·8'	0°25·6'W	FM	101
Falside	Fife	NO5405	56°14·4'	2°44·1'W	X	59
Falside	Fife	NO5713	56°18·7'	2°41·3'W	X	59
Falside	Scot Bord	NT6411	55°23·7'	2°33·7'W	X	80
Falside	W Loth	NS9668	55°53·9'	3°39·4'W	T	65
Falside Hill	E Loth	NT3871	55°55·9'	2°59·1'W	X	66
Falsidehill	Scot Bord	NT6841	55°39·9'	2°30·1'W	X	74
Falslaff Manor	Suff	TM1137	51°59·7'	1°4·8'E	X	155,169
Falstone	Northum	NY7287	55°10·8'	2°26·0'W	T	80
Fambridge Hall	Essex	TL7818	51°50·2'	0°35·4'E	X	167
Fambridge Sta	Essex	TQ8597	51°38·7'	0°40·8'E	X	168
Fames Wood	Durham	NZ0612	54°30·4'	1°54·0'W	F	92
Family Fm	Oxon	SP5316	51°50·6'	1°13·4'W	FM	164
Famington Fm	Warw	SP2839	52°3·2'	1°35·1'W	FM	151
Famish Hill	Glos	SO9009	51°47·0'	2°8·3'W	X	163
Fan	Carm	SN6731	51°57·9'	3°55·8'W	H	146
Fan	Cered	SN5658	52°12·3'	4°6·0'W	X	146
Fanagmore	Highld	NC1749	58°23·7'	5°7·4'W	T	9
Fanans	Arg & Bt	NN0329	56°25·0'	5°11·2'W	X	50
Fan Bay	Kent	TR3542	51°8·0'	1°21·9'E	W	179
Fan Brycheiniog	Powys	SN8221	51°52·7'	3°42·5'W	H	160
Fan Bwlch Chwyth	Powys	SN9121	51°52·9'	3°34·6'W	H	160
Fancarl Crag	N Yks	SE0662	54°3·5'	1°54·1'W	X	99
Fancarl Ho	N Yks	SE0763	54°4·0'	1°53·2'W	X	99
Fancott	Beds	TL0127	51°56·2'	0°31·5'W	T	166
Fancove Head	Scot Bord	NT9562	55°51·3'	2°4·4'W	X	67
Fancy	Devon	SX6451	50°20·8'	3°54·3'W	X	202
Fan Dringarth	Powys	SN9419	51°51·8'	3°32·0'W	H	160
Fanellan	Highld	NH4842	57°26·8'	4°31·5'W	T	26
Fan Fawr	Powys	SN9619	51°51·8'	3°30·2'W	H	160
Fanfed	Powys	SN9155	52°11·2'	3°35·3'W	X	147
Fan Fm	Carm	SN7931	51°58·1'	3°45·3'W	FM	146,160
Fan Foel	Powys	SN8222	51°53·3'	3°42·5'W	H	160
Fan Fraith	Powys	SN8818	51°51·2'	3°37·2'W	H	160
Fan Frynych	Powys	SN9522	51°53·4'	3°31·2'W	H	160
Fangdale Beck	N Yks	SE5694	54°20·5'	1°7·9'W	T	100
Fang-Dhu	Arg & Bt	NR2943	55°36·6'	6°17·8'W	X	60
Fangfoss	E Yorks	SE7653	53°58·3'	0°50·1'W	T	105,106
Fangfoss Grange	E Yorks	SE7552	53°57·8'	0°51·0'W	X	105,106
Fang nan Each	Highld	NG1653	57°29·0'	6°43·9'W	X	23
Fang Poll a' Chapuill	Arg & Bt	NR2068	55°49·7'	6°27·8'W	W	60
Fangrist Burn	Scot Bord	NT6949	55°44·3'	2°29·2'W	W	74
Fangs Brow Fm	Cumbr	NY1022	54°35·4'	3°23·1'W	FM	89
Fan Gyhirych	Powys	SN8819	51°52·0'	3°37·2'W	H	160
Fanhams Hall	Herts	TL3715	51°49·2'	0°0·3'W	X	166
Fanhaulog	Rho Cyn Taf	ST0494	51°38·4'	3°22·9'W	X	170
Fan Hir	Powys	SN8319	51°51·7'	3°41·6'W	X	160
Fan Hir	Powys	SN8320	51°52·2'	3°41·6'W	H	160
Fanich	Highld	NC8703	58°0·4'	3°54·3'W	X	17
Fankerton	Falk	NS7982	56°1·2'	3°56·0'W	T	57,64
Fan Knowe	Orkney	HY3019	59°3·4'	3°12·7'W	A	6
Fanks	Highld	NG3554	57°30·2'	6°25·0'W	X	23
Fan Llia	Powys	SN9318	51°51·3'	3°32·8'W	H	160
Fanmore	Arg & Bt	NM4144	56°31·3'	6°12·2'W	T	47,48
Fanmore	Highld	NJ1536	57°24·6'	3°24·4'W	X	28
Fanna Bog	Scot Bord	NT5702	55°18·9'	2°40·2'W	X	80
Fannachainglas	Highld	NG7480	57°45·4'	5°47·5'W	X	19
Fanna Hill	Scot Bord	NT5603	55°19·4'	2°41·2'W	H	80
Fanna Rig	Scot Bord	NT5704	55°19·9'	2°40·2'W	X	80
Fan Nedd	Powys	SN9118	51°51·2'	3°34·6'W	H	160
Fanners	E Susx	TQ3420	50°58·1'	0°5·1'W	X	198
Fanner's Green	Essex	TL6712	51°47·1'	0°25·7'E	T	167
Fannich Forest	Highld	NH1969	57°40·7'	5°1·7'W	X	20
Fannich Lodge	Highld	NH2166	57°39·2'	4°59·5'W	X	20
Fanns	Essex	TL5722	51°52·7'	0°17·3'E	X	167
Fanns	Scot Bord	NT4221	55°29·0'	2°54·6'W	X	73
Fanns Burn	Scot Bord	NT4122	55°29·5'	2°55·6'W	W	73
Fann's Fm	Essex	TL6628	51°55·8'	0°25·3'E	FM	167
Fanns Fm	Thurr	TQ5579	51°29·5'	0°14·4'E	FM	177
Fanny Barks (Fox Covert)	Darl	NZ2017	54°33·1'	1°41·0'W	F	93
Fanny Burn	Pth & Kin	NO0006	56°14·4'	3°36·4'W	W	58
Fannyfield	Highld	NH5565	57°39·4'	4°25·3'W	X	21
Fanny Hill	Pth & Kin	NO0006	56°14·4'	3°36·4'W	H	58
Fanny Ho	Lancs	SD4262	54°3·3'	2°52·7'W	X	96,97
Fanny's Cross	Devon	SS8020	50°58·3'	3°42·2'W	X	181
Fanny's Grove	Notts	SK6170	53°13·6'	1°4·8'W	F	120
Fannyside Lochs	N Lanak	NS8073	55°56·4'	3°54·8'W	W	65
Fannyside Mill	N Lanak	NS8073	55°56·4'	3°54·8'W	X	65
Fannyside Muir	N Lanak	NS7974	55°56·9'	3°55·8'W	X	64
Fannyside Muir	N Lanak	NS8074	55°56·9'	3°54·9'W	F	65
Fanolau Fm	Powys	SO0135	52°0·5'	3°26·2'W	FM	160
Fans	Scot Bord	NT6140	55°39·4'	2°36·8'W	T	74
Fanshawe Brook	Ches	SJ8671	53°14·4'	2°12·2'W	W	118
Fanshaw Gate	Derby	SK3078	53°18·1'	1°32·6'W	X	119
Fanshaws	Herts	TL3208	51°45·5'	0°4·8'W	X	166
Fans Hill	Scot Bord	NT6240	55°39·4'	2°35·8'W	H	74
Fanshowe	Ches	SJ8571	53°14·4'	2°13·1'W	T	118
Fans Law	Scot Bord	NT1520	55°28·2'	3°20·2'W	H	72
Fans Loanend	Scot Bord	NT6039	55°38·8'	2°37·7'W	X	74
Fans Loanend Covert	Scot Bord	NT6039	55°38·8'	2°37·7'W	F	74
Fant	Kent	TQ7455	51°16·3'	0°30·1'E	T	178,188
Fant Hill	Warw	SP2940	52°3·7'	1°34·2'W	X	151
Fanthill Fm	Oxon	SP3433	51°59·9'	1°29·9'W	FM	151
Fanthorpe Fm	Lincs	TF3289	53°23·1'	0°0·5'W	FM	113,122
Fanton Hall Fm	Essex	TQ7691	51°35·6'	0°32·9'E	FM	178
Fanville Fm	Oxon	SP3432	51°59·4'	1°29·9'W	FM	151
Fan y big	Powys	SO0320	51°52·4'	3°24·2'W	X	160
Faochag	Highld	NG9512	57°9·4'	5°22·9'W	X	33
Faochag Bay	Highld	NB9717	58°6·0'	5°26·2'W	W	15
Faochaig	Highld	NH0231	57°19·9'	5°16·9'W	H	25
Faodhail a' Chinn Ear	N Eil	NF6362	57°31·6'	7°37·4'W	X	22
Faodhail an Taobh Tuath	N Eil	NF9892	57°49·2'	7°4·7'W	X	18
Faodhail Bhan	Highld	NM6468	56°44·9'	5°51·1'W	W	40
Faodhail Shibhinis	N Eil	NF6262	57°31·6'	7°38·4'W	X	22
Faoilean	Highld	NG5620	57°12·6'	6°2·0'W	X	32
Faoileann	Arg & Bt	NM4022	56°19·4'	6°11·9'W	X	48
Faoileann Ghlas	Arg & Bt	NM6243	56°31·4'	5°51·7'W	X	49
Faolainn	Highld	NG3725	57°14·7'	6°21·1'W	X	32
Fara	Orkney	ND3295	58°50·5'	3°10·2'W	X	7
Faraclett	Orkney	HY4432	59°10·5'	2°58·3'W	X	5,6
Faraclett Head	Orkney	HY4433	59°11·1'	2°58·3'W	H	5,6
Faraday Gill	Cumbr	NY8106	54°27·2'	2°17·2'W	W	91,92
Farafield	Orkney	HY3123	59°5·6'	3°11·8'W	X	6
Farahouse	Orkney	HY5535	59°12·2'	2°46·8'W	X	5,6
Faraid Head	Highld	NC3971	58°36·1'	4°45·8'W	X	9
Far Arnside	Cumbr	SD4476	54°10·9'	2°51·1'W	T	97
Far Askew Gill	Cumbr	SD7193	54°20·2'	2°26·3'W	W	98
Fara, The	Highld	NN5983	56°55·3'	4°18·5'W	H	42
Far Audlands	Cumbr	SD5785	54°15·8'	2°39·2'W	X	97
Faraway	Stir	NS6196	56°8·4'	4°13·8'W	X	57
Faraway Fm	Devon	SY1596	50°45·7'	3°11·9'W	FM	192,193
Faray	Orkney	HY5336	59°12·7'	2°48·9'W	X	5
Far Bank	Cumbr	SD1092	54°19·2'	3°22·6'W	X	96
Far Bank	Donc	SE6413	53°36·8'	1°1·5'W	T	111
Far Banks	Lancs	SD4021	53°41·2'	2°54·1'W	T	102
Far Barn	Heref	SO4276	52°23·0'	2°50·7'W	X	137,148
Far Barn	N Yks	SD8075	54°10·5'	2°18·0'W	X	98
Far Baulker Fm	Notts	SK6154	53°5·0'	1°4·9'W	FM	120
Far Beck	N Yks	SE1867	54°6·2'	1°43·1'W	W	99
Far Bergh	N Yks	SD8676	54°11·0'	2°12·5'W	X	98
Farberry Garth Fm	E Yorks	SE8949	53°56·0'	0°38·2'W	FM	106
Far Black Clough	Derby	SK1298	53°29·0'	1°48·7'W	X	110
Far Bletchley	Mil Key	SP8433	51°59·6'	0°46·2'W	X	152,165
Far Bradshaw	Stock	SJ9990	53°24·6'	2°0·5'W	X	109
Far Broom	Cumbr	NY6623	54°36·3'	2°31·2'W	X	91
Farburn	Aberd	NJ8517	57°14·9'	2°14·5'W	X	38
Far Cairn	D & G	NX2175	55°2·5'	4°47·7'W	H	76
Far Capple Mere	N Yks	SD7997	54°22·3'	2°19·0'W	X	98
Far Cappleside	N Yks	SD8059	54°1·8'	2°17·9'W	X	103
Farcet	Cambs	TL2094	52°32·1'	0°13·4'W	T	142
Farcet Fen	Cambs	TL2392	52°30·9'	0°10·8'W	X	142
Farchwel	Conwy	SH7670	53°13·0'	3°51·0'W	X	115
Farchwel	Powys	SJ0914	52°43·2'	3°20·4'W	X	125
Farchynys	Gwyn	SH6617	52°44·3'	3°58·7'W	X	124
Far Clack Wood	N Yks	SE4497	54°22·2'	1°18·9'W	F	99
Far Close	Cumbr	NY6826	54°37·9'	2°29·3'W	X	91
Far Coombes	Derby	SK0091	53°25·2'	1°59·6'W	X	110
Far Costy Clough	Lancs	SD6859	54°1·8'	2°28·9'W	X	103
Far Cote Gill	Cumbr	SD7696	54°21·8'	2°21·7'W	W	98
Far Coton	Leic	SK3802	52°37·1'	1°25·9'W	T	140
Far Cotton	Northnts	SP7558	52°13·1'	0°53·7'W	T	152
Far Cown Edge Fm	Derby	SK0190	53°24·6'	1°58·7'W	FM	110
Far Cranehow Bottom	N Yks	SE0694	54°20·7'	1°54·0'W	X	99
Far Croft	Warw	SP1670	52°19·9'	1°45·5'W	X	139
Fardalehill	E Ayr	NS4038	55°36·8'	4°32·0'W	X	70
Fardeanside Fm	N Yks	NZ3708	54°28·2'	1°25·3'W	FM	93
Far Deep Clough	Derby	SK1890	53°24·6'	1°43·3'W	X	110
Fardel	Devon	SX6157	50°24·0'	3°57·0'W	X	202
Farden	E Ayr	NS3915	55°24·4'	4°32·1'W	X	70
Farden	E Ayr	NS5811	55°22·6'	4°14·0'W	X	71
Farden	S Ayr	NS2402	55°17·1'	4°45·9'W	X	76
Farden	S Ayr	NX1983	55°6·8'	4°49·8'W	X	76
Farden	Shrops	SO5775	52°22·5'	2°37·5'W	T	137,138
Farden Hill	S Ayr	NX1883	55°6·7'	4°50·8'W	H	76
Fardenreoch	E Ayr	NS5614	55°24·2'	4°16·0'W	X	71
Fardenreoch	S Ayr	NX2086	55°8·4'	4°49·0'W	X	76

Fardens	N Ayr	NS2166	55°51·5'	4°51·2'W	X	63
Fardenwilliam	S Ayr	NS3611	55°22·2'	4°34·8'W	X	70
Fardin	S Ayr	NX3286	55°8·6'	4°37·7'W	X	76
Fardin Burn	S Ayr	NX3287	55°9·2'	4°37·8'W	W	76
Fardingjames	D & G	NX8787	55°10·1'	3°46·0'W	X	78
Fardingmullach	D & G	NS8104	55°19·2'	3°52·1'W	X	78
Fardingmullach Hill	D & G	NS8203	55°18·7'	3°51·1'W	X	78
Fardingmullach Muir	D & G	NS8104	55°19·2'	3°52·1'W	X	78
Farding's Fm	Essex	TL7814	51°48·0'	0°35·3'E	FM	167
Farditch Fm	Derby	SK1069	53°13·3'	1°50·6'W	FM	119
Fardre Fm	Conwy	SH9675	53°16·0'	3°33·2'W	A	116
Far Easedale Gill	Cumbr	NY3109	54°28·5'	3°3·5'W	W	90
Fareham	Hants	SU5606	50°51·3'	1°11·9'W	T	196
Far End	Cumbr	SD1187	54°16·5'	3°21·6'W	X	96
Far End	Cumbr	SD3098	54°22·6'	3°4·2'W	T	96,97
Far End	Derby	SK2672	53°14·9'	1°36·2'W	X	119
Far End	N Yks	SD7969	54°7·2'	2°18·9'W	X	98
Far End Fm	N Yks	SE3791	54°19·0'	1°25·5'W	FM	99
Far End Fm	Stock on T	NZ4110	54°29·3'	1°21·6'W	FM	93
Farewell	Aberd	NJ9437	57°25·7'	2°5·5'W	X	30
Farewell	Durham	NZ0011	54°29·9'	1°59·6'W	X	92
Farewell	Orkney	ND4393	58°49·5'	2°58·7'W	X	7
Farewell	Staffs	SK0811	52°42·0'	1°52·5'W	T	128
Farewell Hall	Durham	NZ2639	54°45·0'	1°35·3'W	X	93
Far Fairholme	N Yks	SE3289	54°18·0'	1°30·1'W	X	99
Far Falls Fm	E Yorks	SE9558	54°0·8'	0°32·6'W	FM	106
Far Fell	N Yks	SD8769	54°7·2'	2°11·5'W	X	98
Farfield	E Ayr	NS4839	55°37·5'	4°24·4'W	X	70
Farfield Corner	Oxon	SP3016	51°50·7'	1°33·5'W	X	164
Farfield Fm	Leeds	SE3445	53°54·2'	1°28·5'W	FM	104
Farfield Fm	Wilts	SU1192	51°37·8'	1°50·1'W	FM	163,173
Farfield Hall	Brad	SE0751	53°57·5'	1°53·2'W	X	104
Farfield Ho	N Yks	SE2890	54°18·5'	1°33·8'W	X	99
Farfield Ho	N Yks	SE7663	54°3·7'	0°49·9'W	X	100
Farfields	N Yks	SE8388	54°17·1'	0°43·1'W	X	94,100
Far Fm	Lincs	TA0801	53°29·9'	0°21·9'W	FM	112
Far Fm	Mil Key	SP8944	52°5·5'	0°41·7'W	FM	152
Far Fm	N Yks	SE5537	53°49·8'	1°9·4'W	FM	105
Far Fold	N Yks	SE0049	53°56·5'	1°59·6'W	X	104
Farford	Devon	SS2723	50°59·1'	4°27·5'W	X	190
Far Forest	Worcs	SO7275	52°22·6'	2°24·3'W	T	138
Farforth	Lincs	TF3178	53°17·2'	0°1·7'W	T	122
Far Foulsyke	Red & Cl	NZ7318	54°33·4'	0°51·9'W	X	94
Far Gearstones	N Yks	SD7880	54°13·2'	2°19·8'W	X	98
Fargen Wen	I of Angl	SH5981	53°18·7'	4°6·6'W	X	114,115
Farglow	Northum	NY6868	55°0·6'	2°29·6'W	X	86,87
Fargo Plantation	Wilts	SU1143	51°11·4'	1°50·2'W	F	184
Far Grange	E Yorks	TA1753	53°57·8'	0°12·6'W	X	107
Far Green	Glos	SO7700	51°42·1'	2°19·6'W	T	162
Far Gulf	Cumbr	NY3163	54°57·7'	3°4·2'W	W	85
Far Hall	Powys	SO1468	52°18·4'	3°15·3'W	X	136,148
Farhead Point	Highld	NC1441	58°19·4'	5°10·1'W	X	9
Far Hearkening Rock	Monm	SO5415	51°50·1'	2°39·7'W	X	162
Far Height	Scot Bord	NT4104	55°19·8'	2°55·4'W	H	79
Far Highfield	Lancs	SD5467	54°6·1'	2°41·8'W	X	97
Farhill	Cumbr	NY3057	54°54·4'	3°5·1'W	X	85
Farhill	Derby	SK3563	53°10·0'	1°28·2'W	T	119
Far Hill	D & G	NX7897	55°15·4'	3°54·7'W	X	78
Far Hill	Scot Bord	NT3834	55°36·0'	2°58·6'W	H	73
Farhill Fm	Glos	SP0919	51°52·4'	1°51·8'W	FM	163
Farhill Fm	Glos	SP1602	51°43·2'	1°45·7'W	FM	163
Farhill Fm	Notts	SK7873	53°15·1'	0°49·4'W	FM	120,121
Farhills	D & G	NX7949	54°49·5'	3°52·6'W	X	84
Far Ho	Cumbr	SD7489	54°18·0'	2°23·6'W	X	98
Far Ho	Lancs	SD7446	53°54·8'	2°23·3'W	X	103
Far Ho	Northum	NY6651	54°51·4'	2°31·4'W	X	86
Far Ho	Staffs	SK0061	53°9·0'	1°59·6'W	X	119
Far Hoarcross	Staffs	SK1322	52°48·0'	1°48·0'W	T	128
Far Hole-edge	Ches	SK0067	53°12·2'	1°59·6'W	X	119
Far Hornsby Gate	Cumbr	NY5249	54°50·3'	2°44·4'W	X	86
Far House Laithe	N Yks	SD9161	54°2·9'	2°7·8'W	X	98
Far Houses	Cumbr	SD2486	54°16·1'	3°9·6'W	X	96
Far Howe	Cumbr	NY3728	54°38·8'	2°58·2'W	X	90
Farigaig Forest	Highld	NH5123	57°16·7'	4°27·8'W	F	26,35
Farindons	Surrey	TQ4041	51°9·3'	0°0·5'E	X	187
Faringdon	Oxon	SU2895	51°39·4'	1°35·3'W	T	163
Faringdon Ho	Oxon	SU2895	51°39·4'	1°35·3'W	X	163
Faringdon Road Down	W Berks	SU3382	51°32·4'	1°31·1'W	X	174
Farington	Lancs	SD5324	53°42·9'	2°42·3'W	T	102
Farington	Lancs	SD5423	53°42·3'	2°41·4'W	T	102
Farington Moss	Lancs	SD5224	53°42·9'	2°43·2'W	T	102
Farkhill	Pth & Kin	NO0435	56°30·1'	3°33·1'W	X	52,53
Far Kiln Bank	Cumbr	SD2193	54°19·8'	3°12·5'W	X	96
Far Kingsley Banks	Staffs	SJ9948	53°2·0'	2°0·5'W	X	118
Far Knotts	Lancs	SD7654	53°59·1'	2°21·5'W	X	103
Far Laches Fm	Staffs	SJ9306	52°39·3'	2°5·8'W	FM	127,139
Farlacombe	Devon	SX7971	50°31·8'	3°42·1'W	X	202
Far Laith	Lancs	SD9340	53°51·6'	2°6·0'W	X	103
Far Laithe Fm	Brad	SE0341	53°52·2'	1°56·8'W	FM	104
Far Laithe Fm	Lancs	SD8939	53°51·1'	2°9·6'W	FM	103
Farlam	Cumbr	NY5558	54°55·1'	2°41·7'W	T	86
Farlam Currick	Cumbr	NY6347	54°49·2'	2°34·1'W	X	86
Farlam Hall (Hotel)	Cumbr	NY5660	54°56·2'	2°40·8'W	X	86
Farland Head	N Ayr	NS1748	55°41·7'	4°54·3'W	X	63
Farland Hill	N Ayr	NS1755	55°45·5'	4°54·6'W	H	63
Farland Point	N Ayr	NS1754	55°44·9'	4°54·5'W	X	63
Farlands Booth	Derby	SK0587	53°23·0'	1°55·1'W	T	110
Farlands Laithe	N Yks	SD9158	54°1·3'	2°7·8'W	X	103
Farlands, The	Heref	SO3668	52°18·6'	2°55·9'W	X	137,148
Farlane Fm	Derby	SK3275	53°16·5'	1°30·8'W	FM	119
Far Langerton	N Yks	SD9961	54°2·9'	2°0·5'W	X	98
Farlary	Highld	NC7705	58°1·3'	4°4·5'W	X	17
Far Laund	Derby	SK3648	53°1·9'	1°27·4'W	T	119
Farleaze Fm	Wilts	ST8783	51°33·0'	2°10·9'W	FM	173
Farleigh	Devon	SS9007	50°51·4'	3°33·4'W	X	192
Farleigh	Devon	SX7553	50°22·1'	3°45·1'W	X	202
Farleigh	N Som	ST4969	51°25·3'	2°43·6'W	T	172,182
Farleigh	Surrey	TQ3760	51°19·6'	0°1·6'W	T	177,187
Farleigh Court	Surrey	TQ3760	51°19·6'	0°1·6'W	T	177,187
Farleigh Green	Kent	TQ7252	51°14·7'	0°28·3'E	T	188

Farleigh Hill	Hants	SU6247	51°13·4'	1°6·3'W	X	185
Farleigh House Sch	Hants	SU6246	51°12·8'	1°6·4'W	X	185
Farleigh Hungerford	Somer	ST8057	51°18·9'	2°16·8'W	T	173
Farleigh Plain	Bath & NE Somer	ST7958	51°19·5'	2°17·7'W	X	172
Farleigh Wallop	Hants	SU6246	51°12·8'	1°6·4'W	T	185
Farleigh Wick	Wilts	ST8064	51°22·7'	2°16·9'W	T	173
Farlesthorpe	Lincs	TF4774	53°14·8'	0°12·6'E	T	122
Farlesthorpe Fen	Lincs	TF4874	53°14·8'	0°13·5'E	X	122
Farleton	Cumbr	SD5381	54°13·6'	2°42·8'W	T	97
Farleton	Lancs	SD5767	54°6·1'	2°39·0'W	T	97
Farleton Fell	Cumbr	SD5480	54°13·1'	2°41·9'W	H	97
Farley	Derby	SK2961	53°9·0'	1°33·6'W	T	119
Farley	Highld	NH4745	57°28·4'	4°32·6'W	X	26
Farley	N Som	ST4274	51°28·0'	2°49·7'W	T	171,172
Farley	Shrops	SJ3807	52°39·7'	2°54·6'W	T	126
Farley	Shrops	SJ6302	52°37·1'	2°32·4'W	T	127
Farley	Staffs	SK0644	52°59·8'	1°54·2'W	T	119,128
Far Ley	Staffs	SO7999	52°35·5'	2°18·2'W	T	138
Farley	Wilts	SU2229	51°3·8'	1°40·8'W	T	184
Farley Court	Wok	SU7564	51°22·4'	0°55·0'W	X	175,186
Farley Down	Hants	SU3928	51°3·2'	1°26·2'W	X	185
Farleyer	Pth & Kin	NN8249	56°37·3'	3°54·9'W	X	52
Farley Fm	Hants	SU3927	51°2·7'	1°26·2'W	FM	185
Farley Fm	Staffs	SK0024	52°49·1'	1°59·6'W	FM	128
Farleygreen	Beds	TL0719	51°51·8'	0°26·4'W	X	166
Farley Green	Suff	TL7353	52°9·1'	0°32·1'E	T	155
Farley Green	Surrey	TQ0645	51°11·9'	0°28·6'W	T	187
Farley Heath	Surrey	TQ0544	51°11·4'	0°29·5'W	X	187
Farley Hill	Beds	TL0720	51°52·3'	0°26·3'W	T	166
Farley Hill	Devon	SS7545	51°11·7'	3°47·0'W	X	180
Farley Hill	Wok	SU7564	51°22·4'	0°55·0'W	T	175,186
Farley Ho	Hants	SU3827	51°2·7'	1°27·1'W	X	185
Farley Mount Country Park	Hants	SU4129	51°3·8'	1°24·5'W	X	185
Farleys	Notts	SK5347	53°1·3'	1°12·2'W	X	129
Farleys End	Glos	SO7715	51°50·2'	2°19·6'W	T	162
Farley's Grave	Devon	SS6804	50°49·5'	3°52·1'W	X	191
Farleys Ho	Notts	SK7070	53°13·6'	0°56·7'W	X	120
Farleys Wood	Notts	SK7071	53°14·1'	0°56·7'W	F	120
Farley Water	Devon	SS7445	51°11·7'	3°47·8'W	W	180
Farley Water Fm	Devon	SS7446	51°12·2'	3°47·8'W	FM	180
Farlie Cotts	Highld	NH5146	57°29·0'	4°28·7'W	X	26
Farlington	C of Port	SU6805	50°50·7'	1°1·7'W	T	196
Farlington	N Yks	SE6167	54°6·0'	1°3·6'W	T	100
Farlington Marshes	C of Port	SU6804	50°50·1'	1°1·7'W	X	196
Farlington Sch	Surrey	TQ1337	51°7·5'	0°22·7'W	X	187
Far Lodge	Lancs	SD5159	54°1·7'	2°44·5'W	X	102
Far Longdon	Warw	SP2240	52°3·7'	1°40·3'W	X	151
Farlow	Shrops	SO6380	52°25·2'	2°32·2'W	T	138
Farlow Brook	Shrops	SO6481	52°25·8'	2°31·4'W	W	138
Farlow Paddocks	Derby	SK2471	53°14·4'	1°38·0'W	X	119
Farmal Sike	Cumbr	NY5969	55°1·1'	2°38·0'W	W	86
Farmanby	Cumbr	NY5937	54°43·8'	2°37·8'W	X	91
Farman's Court	Worcs	SO7571	52°20·4'	2°21·6'W	X	138
Far Marsh Fm	E Yorks	TA2421	53°40·5'	0°7·0'W	FM	107,113
Farmborough	Bath & NE Somer	ST6660	51°20·5'	2°28·9'W	T	172
Farmborough Common	Bath & NE Somer	ST6760	51°20·5'	2°28·0'W	X	172
Farmbridge End	Essex	TL6211	51°46·7'	0°21·3'E	T	167
Farmcote	Glos	SP0628	51°57·3'	1°54·4'W	T	150,163
Farmcote	Shrops	SO7891	52°31·2'	2°19·1'W	T	138
Farmcote Hall	Shrops	SO7892	52°31·8'	2°19·1'W	X	138
Farmcote Wood Fm	Glos	SP0626	51°56·2'	1°54·4'W	FM	163
Farm Cottages	N upon Ty	NZ2571	55°2·2'	1°36·1'W	X	88
Farmersfield	D & G	NX8683	55°7·9'	3°46·9'W	X	78
Farmer's Fm	Suff	TL7344	52°4·3'	0°31·9'E	FM	155
Farmerton	Angus	NO4861	56°44·5'	2°50·6'W	X	44
Farmery	Cumbr	NY0707	54°27·2'	3°25·6'W	X	89
Farmery Mires	N Yks	SE1184	54°15·3'	1°49·5'W	W	99
Farmhall	Pth & Kin	NO0819	56°21·5'	3°28·9'W	X	58
Farm Hall	Shrops	SJ3319	52°46·1'	2°59·2'W	X	126
Farm Hill	Norf	TM1778	52°21·6'	1°11·6'E	X	156
Farm Hill	W Susx	SU9614	50°55·3'	0°37·7'W	H	197
Farmington	Glos	SP1315	51°50·2'	1°48·3'W	T	163
Farmington Fm	Oxon	SP3739	52°3·1'	1°27·2'W	FM	151
Farmington Grove	Glos	SP1516	51°50·8'	1°46·5'W	F	163
Farmington Lodge	Glos	SP1315	51°50·2'	1°48·3'W	X	163
Farm of Place	N Ayr	NS3054	55°45·2'	4°42·1'W	X	63
Far Moor	N Yks	SD7974	54°9·9'	2°18·9'W	X	98
Far Moor	N Yks	SE4999	54°23·3'	1°14·3'W	X	100
Farmoor	Oxon	SP4506	51°45·3'	1°20·5'W	T	164
Farmoor	Staffs	SK0557	53°6·8'	1°55·1'W	X	119
Far Moor	Wigan	SD5304	53°32·1'	2°42·1'W	T	108
Farmoor Reservoir	Oxon	SP4406	51°45·3'	1°21·4'W	W	164
Farm or Further Field	Cambs	TL4366	52°16·6'	0°6·2'E	X	154
Far Moss	Derby	SK0996	53°27·9'	1°51·5'W	X	110
Farm Park	Cered	SN1650	52°7·3'	4°40·9'W	X	145
Farm Park	Corn	SX1065	50°27·5'	4°40·2'W	X	200
Farm Park	Cumbr	NY2032	54°40·9'	3°14·0'W	FM	89,90
Farm Park	Hants	SU3847	51°13·5'	1°27·0'W	X	185
Farm Park	Kent	TQ5674	51°26·8'	0°15·1'E	X	177
Farm Park	Notts	SK5865	53°11·0'	1°7·5'W	FM	120
Farm Park	W Susx	TQ0526	51°1·7'	0°29·8'W	X	187,197
Farms Common	Corn	SW6734	50°9·9'	5°15·4'W	T	203
Farms, The	Shrops	SJ5035	52°54·8'	2°44·2'W	X	126
Farmston	Stir	NN6008	56°14·9'	4°15·1'W	X	57
Farm, The	Arg & Bt	NM9148	56°34·9'	5°23·7'W	X	49
Farm, The	Heref	SO2645	52°6·1'	3°4·4'W	X	148
Farm, The	Heref	SO6848	52°8·0'	2°27·7'W	X	149
Farm, The	Heref	SO6856	52°12·3'	2°27·7'W	X	149
Farm, The	Heref	SO6942	52°4·8'	2°26·7'W	X	149
Farm, The	Monm	SO4319	51°52·2'	2°49·3'W	X	161
Farm, The	Powys	SO0972	52°20·6'	3°19·8'W	X	136,147
Farm, The	Powys	SO1976	52°22·8'	3°11·0'W	X	136,148
Farm, The	Powys	SO2367	52°18·0'	3°7·4'W	X	137,148
Farmton	Aberd	NJ5814	57°13·1'	2°41·3'W	X	37
Farmton	Aberd	NJ5912	57°12·1'	2°40·3'W	X	37
Farmton	Pth & Kin	NN9015	56°19·1'	3°46·3'W	X	58
Farmton Muir	Pth & Kin	NN9014	56°18·6'	3°46·2'W	X	58

Farm Town	Leic	SK3916	52°44·6'	1°24·9'W	T	128
Farmtown	Moray	NJ5051	57°33·0'	2°49·7'W	T	29
Farm View	Leic	SP5688	52°29·5'	1°10·1'W	X	140
Farm Yard	Conwy	SH8363	53°9·3'	3°44·6'W	X	116
Farnah Green	Derby	SK3347	53°1·4'	1°30·1'W	T	119,128
Farnah House Fm	Derby	SK3243	52°59·2'	1°31·0'W	FM	119,128
Farnborough	Brom	TQ4464	51°21·6'	0°4·5'E	T	177,187
Farnborough	Hants	SU8754	51°16·9'	0°44·8'W	T	186
Farnborough	Warw	SP4349	52°8·5'	1°21·9'W	T	151
Farnborough	W Berks	SU4381	51°31·8'	1°22·4'W	T	174
Farnborough Barn	Warw	SP4351	52°9·6'	1°21·9'W	X	151
Farnborough Down	W Berks	SU4182	51°32·4'	1°24·1'W	X	174
Farnborough Down Fm	W Berks	SU4181	51°31·8'	1°24·1'W	FM	174
Farnborough Fields Fm	Warw	SP4450	52°9·0'	1°21·0'W	FM	151
Farnborough Green	Hants	SU8757	51°18·6'	0°44·7'W	T	175,186
Farnborough Park	Hants	SU8755	51°17·5'	0°44·7'W	T	175,186
Farnborough Park	Warw	SP4349	52°8·5'	1°21·9'W	X	151
Farnborough Street	Hants	SU8756	51°18·0'	0°44·7'W	T	175,186
Farnbury	Cumbr	NY7245	54°48·2'	2°25·7'W	X	86,87
Farncombe	Somer	ST6441	51°10·3'	2°30·5'W	X	183
Farncombe	Surrey	SU9745	51°12·0'	0°36·3'W	T	186
Farn Combe	W Berks	SU3177	51°29·7'	1°32·8'W	X	174
Farncombe Down	W Berks	SU2977	51°29·7'	1°34·5'W	X	174
Farncombe Fm	W Berks	SU3178	51°30·2'	1°32·8'W	FM	174
Farncombe Ho	Worcs	SP1138	52°2·7'	1°50·0'W	X	150
Farndale	N Yks	SE6697	54°22·1'	0°58·6'W	X	94,100
Farndale Moor	N Yks	NZ6600	54°23·7'	0°58·6'W	X	94
Farndish	Beds	SP9263	52°15·7'	0°38·7'W	T	152
Farndon	Ches	SJ4154	53°5·0'	2°52·4'W	T	117
Farndon	Notts	SK7752	53°3·8'	0°50·6'W	T	120
Farne Islands	Northum	NU2336	55°37·3'	1°37·7'W	X	75
Farnell	Angus	NO6255	56°41·4'	2°36·8'W	T	54
Farnell Mains	Angus	NO6255	56°41·4'	2°36·8'W	X	54
Farness	Highld	NH7364	57°39·1'	4°7·2'W	X	21,27
Far Newfield Edge	Lancs	SD8545	53°54·3'	2°13·3'W	X	103
Farney Shield	Northum	NY7848	54°49·8'	2°20·1'W	X	86,87
Farneyside	Northum	NY7851	54°51·4'	2°20·1'W	X	86,87
Farnfield Fm	Hants	SU6827	51°2·5'	1°1·4'W	FM	185,186
Farnham	Dorset	ST9515	50°56·3'	2°3·9'W	T	184
Farnham	Essex	TL4724	51°53·9'	0°8·6'E	T	167
Farnham	N Yks	SE3460	54°2·3'	1°28·4'W	T	99
Farnham	Suff	TM3660	52°11·5'	1°27·6'E	T	156
Farnham	Surrey	SU8446	51°12·6'	0°47·5'W	T	186
Farnham Common	Bucks	SU9685	51°33·6'	0°36·5'W	T	175,176
Farnham Green	Essex	TL4625	51°54·5'	0°7·7'E	T	167
Farnham Moor	Northum	NT9703	55°19·5'	2°2·4'W	X	81
Farnham Park	Bucks	SU9683	51°32·5'	0°36·5'W	T	175,176
Farnham Park	Surrey	SU8448	51°13·7'	0°47·4'W	X	186
Farnham Royal	Bucks	SU9683	51°32·5'	0°36·5'W	T	175,176
Farnham Woods	Dorset	ST9315	50°56·3'	2°5·6'W	F	184
Farnhill	N Yks	SE0046	53°54·9'	1°59·6'W	T	104
Farnhill Ings	N Yks	SE0045	53°54·3'	1°59·6'W	X	104
Farnhill Moor	N Yks	SE0047	53°55·4'	1°59·6'W	X	104
Farnicombe	Warw	SP3236	52°1·5'	1°31·6'W	X	151
Farningham	Kent	TQ5466	51°22·6'	0°13·2'E	T	177
Farningham Road Sta	Kent	TQ5569	51°24·2'	0°14·1'E	X	177
Farningham Woods (Nature Reserve)	Kent	TQ5368	51°23·6'	0°12·3'E	X	177
Farnless	Durham	NZ3332	54°41·2'	1°28·9'W	X	93
Farnley	Durham	NZ2032	54°41·2'	1°41·0'W	X	93
Farnley	Leeds	SE2532	53°47·3'	1°36·8'W	T	104
Farnley	Northum	NY9962	54°57·4'	2°0·5'W	X	87
Farnley	N Yks	SE2147	53°55·4'	1°40·4'W	T	104
Farnley Bank	Kirk	SE1613	53°37·0'	1°45·1'W	T	110
Farnley Beck	Leeds	SE2532	53°47·3'	1°36·8'W	W	104
Farnley Lake	N Yks	SE2247	53°55·4'	1°39·5'W	W	104
Farnley Moor	N Yks	SE2049	53°56·4'	1°41·3'W	X	104
Farnley Tyas	Kirk	SE1612	53°36·5'	1°45·1'W	T	110
Farnsfield	Notts	SK6456	53°6·1'	1°2·2'W	T	120
Farnsley Fm	Derby	SK2075	53°16·5'	1°41·6'W	FM	119
Farnsworth Fm	Derby	SK4871	53°14·3'	1°16·4'W	FM	120
Farnton Hill	E Yorks	TA1442	53°51·9'	0°15·6'W	X	107
Farnworth	Bolton	SD7305	53°32·7'	2°24·0'W	T	109
Farnworth	Halton	SJ5187	53°22·9'	2°43·8'W	T	108
Far Oakridge	Glos	SO9203	51°43·8'	2°6·6'W	T	163
Far Old Park Fm	Cumbr	SD2277	54°11·2'	3°11·3'W	FM	96
Far Old Park Wood	Lincs	TF0027	52°50·1'	0°30·5'W	F	130
Far Orrest	Cumbr	NY4100	54°23·8'	2°54·1'W	X	90
Farpark Fm	N Yks	SE5122	53°41·8'	1°13·2'W	FM	105
Far Parks Plantn	N Yks	SE4077	54°11·5'	1°22·8'W	F	99
Far Pasture	Lancs	SD8829	53°45·7'	2°10·5'W	X	103
Far Pasture	Northum	NY7851	54°51·4'	2°20·1'W	X	86,87
Far Pasture Wood	N Yks	SE5192	54°19·5'	1°12·5'W	F	100
Farque	Derby	SK0485	53°22·0'	1°56·0'W	X	110
Farquhar's Point	Highld	NM6272	56°47·0'	5°53·3'W	X	40
Farr	Highld	NC7263	58°32·4'	4°11·5'W	T	10
Farr	Highld	NH6832	57°21·8'	4°11·2'W	X	26
Farr	Highld	NH8203	57°6·4'	3°56·4'W	X	35
Farragon Hill	Pth & Kin	NN8455	56°40·6'	3°53·1'W	H	52
Farraline	Highld	NH5621	57°15·7'	4°22·8'W	T	26,35
Farrants Fm	Devon	SX8389	50°41·6'	3°39·0'W	FM	191
Farrantshayes Fm	Devon	ST0500	50°47·7'	3°20·5'W	FM	192
Farr Bay	Highld	NC7162	58°31·9'	4°12·5'W	W	10
Farr House	Highld	NH6831	57°21·3'	4°11·2'W	X	26
Farringdon	Devon	SY0191	50°42·8'	3°23·8'W	T	192
Farringdon	Somer	ST2731	51°4·7'	3°2·1'W	X	182
Farringdon	Sund	NZ3653	54°52·5'	1°25·9'W	T	88
Farringdon Cross	Devon	SY0090	50°42·3'	3°24·6'W	X	192
Farringdon Hill Fm	Somer	ST2143	51°11·1'	3°7·4'W	FM	182
Farringdon Ho	Devon	SY0191	50°42·8'	3°23·8'W	X	192
Farringford Hotel	I of W	SZ3386	50°40·6'	1°31·6'W	X	196
Farrington	Dorset	ST8415	50°56·3'	2°13·3'W	T	183
Farrington	Powys	SO3070	52°19·7'	3°1·2'W	X	137,148
Farrington Gurney	Bath & NE Somer	ST6355	51°17·8'	2°31·5'W	T	172
Farrmheall	Highld	NC3058	58°28·9'	4°54·5'W	H	9
Farrochill	Pth & Kin	NN8348	56°36·8'	3°53·9'W	X	52
Far Round Plantn	Notts	SK6060	53°8·3'	1°5·8'W	F	120
Farrow Shields	Northum	NY7562	54°57·4'	2°23·0'W	X	86,87
Far Royds	Leeds	SE2631	53°46·7'	1°35·9'W	T	104

Farr Point	Highld	NC7164	58°33·0′	4°12·5′W	X	10
Far Sawrey	Cumbr	SD3795	54°21·0′	2°57·7′W	T	96,97
Far Shields	Cumbr	NY5545	54°48·1′	2°41·6′W	X	86
Far Shires	N Yks	SE5266	54°5·5′	1°11·9′W	X	100
Far Skerr	Northum	NU0348	55°43·8′	1°56·7′W	X	75
Far Slack	Cald	SE0120	53°40·8′	1°58·7′W	X	104
Far Slack	Derby	SK0090	53°24·6′	1°59·6′W	X	110
Farsley	Leeds	SE2135	53°48·9′	1°40·4′W	T	104
Farsley Beck Bottom	Leeds	SE2235	53°48·9′	1°39·5′W	T	104
Far Small Clough	Derby	SK1398	53°29·0′	1°47·8′W	X	110
Farsyde Ho	N Yks	NZ9504	54°25·6′	0°31·7′W	X	94
Farther Howegreen	Essex	TL8401	51°40·9′	0°40·1′E	T	168
Farther Light Ash	Lancs	SD4840	53°51·5′	2°47·0′W	X	102
Fartherwell	Kent	TQ6657	51°17·5′	0°23·2′E	X	178,188
Farthing Common	Kent	TR1340	51°7·4′	1°3·0′E	X	179,189
Farthing Corner	Medway	TQ8163	51°20·5′	0°36·3′E	T	178,188
Farthing Green	Kent	TQ8146	51°11·3′	0°35·8′E	T	188
Farthing Hall	Suff	TL9435	51°59·0′	0°49·9′E	X	155
Farthinghoe	Northnts	SP5339	52°3·0′	1°13·2′W	T	152
Farthinghoe Lodge	Northnts	SP5238	52°2·5′	1°14·1′W	X	151
Farthingloe	Kent	TR2940	51°7·0′	1°16·7′E	T	179
Farthing or Fairdean Downs	Surrey	TQ2957	51°18·1′	0°8·6′W	H	187
Farthing Park	Devon	SS7807	50°51·2′	3°43·6′W	X	191
Farthings Fm	Devon	SY0298	50°46·6′	3°23·0′W	FM	192
Farthing's Fm	Somer	ST1025	51°1·3′	3°16·6′W	FM	181,193
Farthings Hook	Pemb	SN0527	51°54·7′	4°49·7′W	X	145,158
Farthingsole Fm	Kent	TR1646	51°10·6′	1°5·8′E	FM	179,189
Farthingstone	Northnts	SP6154	52°11·1′	1°6·1′W	T	152
Farthingwell	D & G	NX9283	55°8·0′	3°41·2′W	X	78
Farthorpe Fm	Lincs	TF2674	53°15·1′	0°6·3′W	FM	122
Far Thrupp	Glos	SO8603	51°43·8′	2°11·8′W	T	162
Farthwaite	Cumbr	NY0610	54°28·8′	3°26·6′W	X	89
Fartown	Kirk	SE1418	53°39·7′	1°46·9′W	T	110
Far Town	Northum	NY6850	54°50·9′	2°29·5′W	X	86,87
Fartown Fm	Worcs	SO7368	52°18·8′	2°23·4′W	FM	138
Far Upton Wold Fm	Glos	SP1433	52°0·0′	1°47·4′W	FM	151
Farwall	Staffs	SK1051	53°3·6′	1°50·6′W	X	119
Farwath	N Yks	SE8288	54°17·1′	0°44·0′W	X	94,100
Farwath	N Yks	SE8388	54°17·1′	0°43·1′W	X	94,100
Farway	Devon	SY1895	50°45·2′	3°9·4′W	T	192,193
Farway Castle	Devon	SY1695	50°45·1′	3°11·1′W	X	192,193
Farway Castle (Earthwork)	Devon	SY1695	50°45·1′	3°11·1′W	A	192,193
Farway Countryside Park	Devon	SY1894	50°44·6′	3°9·4′W	X	192,193
Farway Hill	Devon	SY1695	50°45·1′	3°11·1′W	X	192,193
Farway Marsh	Devon	ST3004	50°50·1′	2°59·3′W	T	193
Far Wold	E Yorks	SE9531	53°46·2′	0°33·1′W	X	106
Far Wood	N Lincs	SE9510	53°34·9′	0°33·5′W	F	112
Farwood Barton	Devon	SY2095	50°45·2′	3°7·7′W	X	192,193
Fasach	Highld	NG1848	57°26·3′	6°41·5′W	T	23
Fasag	Highld	NG8956	57°33·0′	5°31·1′W	T	24
Fasagrianach	Highld	NH1979	57°46·1′	5°2·1′W	X	20
Fasair-choille	Highld	NG6125	57°15·5′	5°57·3′W	X	32
Fasbourn Hall	Suff	TL9956	52°10·2′	0°55·0′E	X	155
Fascadale	Highld	NM5070	56°45·5′	6°5·0′W	X	39,47
Fascadale Bay	Highld	NM4970	56°45·5′	6°5·9′W	W	39,47
Faschapple	Highld	NH5541	57°26·4′	4°24·5′W	X	26
Faseny Cottage	E Loth	NT6163	55°51·8′	2°36·9′W	X	67
Faseny Water	E Loth	NT6162	55°51·2′	2°36·9′W	W	67
Fasheilach	Aberd	NO3485	56°57·4′	3°4·7′W	H	44
Fashven	Highld	NC3167	58°33·8′	4°53·8′W	H	9
Faside House	E Renf	NS5254	55°45·7′	4°21·1′W	X	64
Faskally	Pth & Kin	NN9160	56°43·4′	3°46·4′W	T	43
Faskally Outdoor Centre	Pth & Kin	NN9159	56°42·9′	3°46·4′W	X	52
Faslane Bay	Arg & Bt	NS2489	56°3·9′	4°49·2′W	W	56
Faslane Port	Arg & Bt	NS2488	56°3·4′	4°49·2′W	T	56
Fasnacloich	Arg & Bt	NN0147	56°34·6′	5°13·9′W	T	50
Fasnadarach	Aberd	NO4698	57°4·5′	2°53·0′W	X	37,44
Fasnagruig	Highld	NH5223	57°16·7′	4°26·8′W	X	26,35
Fasnakyle Forest	Highld	NH2329	57°19·3′	4°55·9′W	X	25
Fasnakyle Ho	Highld	NH3128	57°18·9′	4°47·9′W	X	26
Fasque	Aberd	NO6475	56°52·2′	2°35·0′W	X	45
Fasset Hill	Scot Bord	NT8520	55°28·7′	2°13·8′W	H	74
Fassfern	Highld	NN0278	56°51·3′	5°14·4′W	T	41
Fassis	E Dunb	NS6080	55°59·8′	4°14·2′W	X	64
Fassock	Highld	NH5139	57°25·3′	4°28·4′W	X	26
Fast Castle	Scot Bord	NT8670	55°55·6′	2°13·0′W	A	67
Fast Castle Head	Scot Bord	NT8571	55°56·2′	2°14·0′W	X	67
Fast Geo	Highld	ND3969	58°36·5′	3°2·5′W	X	12
Fastheugh	Scot Bord	NT3928	55°32·8′	2°57·6′W	X	73
Fastheugh Hill	Scot Bord	NT3927	55°32·2′	2°57·6′W	H	73
Fastings Coppice	Shrops	SO7479	52°24·7′	2°22·5′W	F	138
Fatacott	Devon	SS2626	51°0·7′	4°28·4′W	X	190
Fatclose Fm	Durham	NZ3640	54°45·5′	1°26·0′W	FM	88
Fatfield	Sund	NZ3054	54°53·0′	1°31·5′W	T	88
Fatfield Ho	Durham	NZ3144	54°47·6′	1°30·6′W	X	88
Fathan Glinne	Stir	NN4917	56°19·5′	4°26·1′W	X	57
Fatherley Hill	Durham	NZ0239	54°45·0′	1°57·7′W	H	92
Fathgarreg	Cered	SN2651	52°8·0′	4°32·1′W	X	145
Fat Hill	Lancs	SD7649	53°56·4′	2°21·5′W	X	103
Fatholme	Staffs	SK2017	52°45·3′	1°41·8′W	X	128
Fatlips Cas	Scot Bord	NT5820	55°28·6′	2°39·4′W	A	73,74
Fatlips Castle	S Lanak	NS9634	55°35·6′	3°38·6′W	A	72
Fat Rabbit Fm	E Yorks	SE7452	53°57·8′	0°51·9′W	FM	105,106
Fattahead	Aberd	NJ6557	57°36·4′	2°34·7′W	X	29
Fatten Hill Plantn	N Yks	SE2798	54°22·8′	1°34·6′W	F	99
Faucheldean	W Loth	NT0874	55°57·3′	3°28·0′W	T	65
Fauchin House	Shetld	HU3621	59°58·6′	1°20·8′W	X	4
Fauch Moss	Moray	NJ2637	57°25·3′	3°13·5′W	X	28
Faugh	Cumbr	NY5055	54°53·5′	2°46·3′W	T	86
Faugh	S Lanak	NS9312	55°23·7′	3°40·9′W	H	71,78
Faugh Cleugh	Northum	NY6353	54°52·5′	2°34·2′W	X	86
Faugh Head	Cumbr	NY5245	54°48·1′	2°44·4′W	X	86
Faughill	Scot Bord	NT5430	55°33·9′	2°43·3′W	T	73
Faughill Moor	Scot Bord	NT5230	55°33·9′	2°45·2′W	X	73
Faughlin Burn	N Lanak	NS7382	56°1·1′	4°1·8′W	W	57,64
Faughs	Lancs	SD8239	53°51·1′	2°16·0′W	X	103
Fauld	Shetld	HP6200	60°41·0′	0°51·4′W	X	1
Fauld	Staffs	SK1828	52°51·2′	1°43·6′W	T	128
Fauldbog Bay	D & G	NX6444	54°46·6′	4°6·4′W	W	83

Fauld Hall	Staffs	SK1828	52°51·2′	1°43·6′W	X	128
Fauldhead	E Renf	NS4357	55°47·1′	4°29·8′W	X	64
Fauld Hill	D & G	NY1890	55°12·1′	3°16·9′W	H	79
Fauldhouse	W Loth	NS9360	55°49·5′	3°42·0′W	T	65
Fauldhouse Burn	S Lanak	NS8337	55°37·0′	3°51·0′W	W	71,72
Fauldhouse Moor	W Loth	NS9262	55°50·6′	3°43·0′W	F	65
Fauldie	D & G	NY3675	55°4·2′	2°59·7′W	X	85
Fauldiehill	Angus	NO5739	56°32·7′	2°41·5′W	X	54
Fauldingcleuch	D & G	NY2771	55°1·9′	3°8·1′W	X	85
Fauld Mill	Cumbr	NY3767	54°59·9′	2°58·7′W	X	85
Fauld-o'-Wheat	D & G	NX6575	55°3·3′	4°6·4′W	X	77,84
Fauldribbon	S Ayr	NX1997	55°14·3′	4°50·4′W	X	76
Faulds	Cumbr	NY2939	54°44·7′	3°5·8′W	X	89,90
Faulds	Highld	ND2259	58°31·0′	3°19·9′W	X	11,12
Faulds	Inverc	NS3170	55°53·9′	4°41·7′W	X	63
Faulds	Pth & Kin	NN8108	56°15·2′	3°54·8′W	X	57
Faulds	Renf	NS4061	55°49·2′	4°32·8′W	X	64
Faulds Brow	Cumbr	NY2940	54°45·2′	3°5·8′W	H	85
Faulds Fm	E Renf	NS5154	55°45·6′	4°22·0′W	FM	64
Faulds Fm	N Ayr	NS2248	55°41·8′	4°49·5′W	FM	63
Fauldshope	Scot Bord	NT4125	55°31·2′	2°55·6′W	T	73
Fauldshope Burn	Scot Bord	NT4025	55°31·2′	2°56·6′W	W	73
Fauldshope Hill	Scot Bord	NT3926	55°31·7′	2°57·5′W	H	73
Fauldshope West Hill	Scot Bord	NT3925	55°31·1′	2°57·5′W	H	73
Faulds Park	Inverc	NS2176	55°56·9′	4°51·6′W	X	63
Faulds Spring	Cumbr	NY2841	54°45·8′	3°6·7′W	F	85
Fauld, The	Cumbr	NY3766	54°59·3′	2°58·6′W	X	85
Faulkbourne	Essex	TL7917	51°49·6′	0°36·3′E	T	167
Faulkbourne Hall	Essex	TL8016	51°49·0′	0°37·1′E	A	168
Faulkland	Somer	ST7354	51°17·3′	2°22·8′W	T	183
Faulkner Ho	Norf	TF4913	52°41·9′	0°12·7′E	X	131,143
Faulkners	Kent	TQ6249	51°13·3′	0°19·6′E	X	188
Faulkner's Down Fm	Hants	SU4147	51°13·5′	1°24·4′W	FM	185
Faulkners End Fm	Herts	TL1115	51°49·6′	0°23·0′W	FM	166
Faulkners Hill Fm	Kent	TQ5049	51°13·5′	0°9·3′E	FM	188
Fauls	Shrops	SJ5932	52°53·3′	2°36·2′W	T	126
Fauls Fm	Shrops	SJ5832	52°53·3′	2°37·1′W	FM	126
Faulston	Wilts	SU0725	51°1·7′	1°53·6′W	X	184
Faulston Down	Wilts	SU0824	51°1·2′	1°52·8′W	X	184
Faulstone Down Fm	Wilts	SU0823	51°0·6′	1°52·8′W	FM	184
Faunstone Fm	Devon	SX5461	50°26·1′	4°3·0′W	FM	201
Faverdale	Darl	NZ2716	54°32·6′	1°34·5′W	T	93
Faversham	Kent	TR0161	51°19·0′	0°53·5′E	T	178
Favillar	Moray	NJ2734	57°23·7′	3°12·4′W	X	28
Fawber	N Yks	SD8074	54°9·9′	2°18·0′W	X	98
Fawcett	Northum	NY9676	55°5·0′	2°3·3′W	X	87
Fawcett Bank	Cumbr	SD6894	54°20·7′	2°29·1′W	X	98
Fawcett Hill Cottage	Northum	NY9767	55°0·1′	2°2·4′W	X	87
Fawcettlees	Cumbr	NY5673	55°3·2′	2°40·9′W	X	86
Fawcett Mill	Cumbr	NY6306	54°27·1′	2°33·8′W	X	91
Fawcett Moor	N Yks	SD8372	54°8·9′	2°15·2′W	X	98
Fawcett Shank	Northum	NT8823	55°30·3′	2°11·0′W	H	74
Fawcett's Plantn	Lancs	SD7948	53°55·9′	2°18·8′W	F	103
Fawcett Wood	Scot Bord	NT8163	55°51·8′	2°17·8′W	F	67
Fawcliff Village	Northnts	SP5468	52°18·7′	1°12·1′W	A	152
Fawdington	N Yks	SE4372	54°8·8′	1°20·1′W	T	99
Fawdington Ho	N Yks	SE4372	54°8·8′	1°20·1′W	X	99
Fawdon	Northum	NU0315	55°26·0′	1°56·7′W	T	81
Fawdon	N upon Ty	NZ2268	55°0·6′	1°38·9′W	T	88
Fawdon Burn	Northum	NU0315	55°26·0′	1°56·7′W	W	81
Fawdon Dean	Northum	NU0215	55°26·0′	1°57·7′W	X	81
Fawdon Hill	Northum	NY8993	55°14·1′	2°9·9′W	H	80
Fawdon Ho	Northum	NZ2188	55°11·4′	1°39·8′W	X	81
Fawells	Aberd	NJ8221	57°17·0′	2°17·5′W	X	38
Fawe Park	Cumbr	NY2522	54°35·5′	3°9·2′W	X	89,90
Fawfieldhead	Staffs	SK0763	53°10·1′	1°53·3′W	T	119
Faw Head	N Yks	SD8688	54°17·5′	2°12·5′W	X	98
Faw Hill	Scot Bord	NT6313	55°24·8′	2°34·6′W	H	80
Fawhope	Scot Bord	NT7409	55°22·7′	2°24·2′W	X	80
Fawke Common	Kent	TQ5553	51°15·5′	0°13·7′E	F	188
Fawke Farm Ho	Kent	TQ5553	51°15·5′	0°13·7′E	X	188
Fawkham Green	Kent	TQ5865	51°21·9′	0°16·6′E	T	177
Fawkham Manor	Kent	TQ5966	51°22·5′	0°17·5′E	X	177
Fawkners	Hants	SU6042	51°10·7′	1°8·1′W	X	185
Faw Laws	Scot Bord	NT7420	55°28·6′	2°24·2′W	H	74
Fawlaws Burn	Scot Bord	NT7522	55°29·7′	2°23·3′W	W	74
Fawlee Sike	Northum	NY8176	55°4·9′	2°17·4′W	W	86,87
Fawler	Oxon	SP3717	51°51·3′	1°27·4′W	T	164
Fawler	Oxon	SU3188	51°35·6′	1°32·8′W	T	174
Fawley	Bucks	SU7586	51°34·3′	0°54·7′W	T	175
Fawley	Hants	SU4503	50°49·7′	1°21·3′W	T	196
Fawley	W Berks	SU3981	51°31·8′	1°25·9′W	T	174
Fawley Bottom	Bucks	SU7486	51°34·3′	0°55·5′W	T	175
Fawley Chapel	Heref	SO5829	51°57·7′	2°36·3′W	T	149
Fawley Court	Heref	SO5730	51°58·2′	2°37·2′W	A	149
Fawley Court	Oxon	SU7684	51°33·2′	0°53·8′W	A	175
Fawley Court Fm	Bucks	SU7685	51°33·8′	0°53·8′W	FM	175
Fawley Cross	Heref	SO5830	51°58·3′	2°36·3′W	X	149
Fawley Down	Hants	SU5127	51°2·6′	1°16·0′W	X	185
Fawley Fm	Hants	SU6727	51°2·5′	1°2·3′W	FM	185,186
Fawley Fm	Staffs	SK1220	52°46·9′	1°48·9′W	FM	128
Fawley Inclosure	Hants	SU4105	50°50·8′	1°24·7′W	F	196
Faw Mount	Scot Bord	NT1354	55°46·5′	3°22·8′W	X	65,72
Fawnless	Durham	NZ0538	54°44·5′	1°54·9′W	X	92
Fawnless Hall	Durham	NZ0638	54°44·5′	1°54·0′W	X	92
Fawnog	Conwy	SH8574	53°15·3′	3°43·0′W	X	116
Fawnog	Gwyn	SH7210	52°40·6′	3°53·2′W	X	124
Fawnog	Powys	SJ0424	52°48·5′	3°25·1′W	W	125
Fawnog	Powys	SJ2115	52°43·9′	3°9·8′W	X	126
Fawnog	Powys	SJ2122	52°47·6′	3°9·9′W	X	126
Fawnog	Wrex	SJ3149	53°2·3′	3°1·3′W	X	117
Fawnog-fawr	Conwy	SH8558	53°6·7′	3°42·7′W	X	116
Fawnog Fawr	Gwyn	SH8518	52°45·1′	3°41·8′W	X	124,125
Fawnog-figyn	Powys	SJ0718	52°45·3′	3°22·3′W	X	125
Fawnog y Bont	Powys	SN8483	52°26·2′	3°42·0′W	X	135,136
Fawns	Devon	SX6452	50°21·4′	3°54·3′W	X	202
Fawns	Northum	NZ0085	55°9·8′	1°59·6′W	X	81
Fawnspark	W Loth	NT0676	55°58·3′	3°29·9′W	X	65
Fawn Wood	E Loth	NT5268	55°54·4′	2°45·6′W	F	66
Faw Plantn	Scot Bord	NT5536	55°37·2′	2°42·4′W	F	73

Faw Side	D & G	NY3596	55°15·5′	3°0·9′W	H	79
Fawside	Scot Bord	NT6445	55°42·1′	2°33·9′W	X	74
Fawside	Staffs	SK0764	53°10·6′	1°53·3′W	X	119
Faw Side Burn	D & G	NY3496	55°15·5′	3°1·9′W	W	79
Fawside Edge	Staffs	SK0665	53°11·2′	1°54·2′W	X	119
Fawsley Hall	Northnts	SP5656	52°12·2′	1°10·4′W	A	152
Fawsley Park	Northnts	SP5657	52°12·7′	1°10·4′W	X	152
Fawsyde	Aberd	NO8477	56°53·3′	2°15·3′W	X	45
Fawton	Corn	SX1668	50°29·2′	4°35·3′W	X	201
Faxfleet	E Yorks	SE8624	53°42·6′	0°41·4′W	T	106,112
Faxfleet Grange	E Yorks	SE8625	53°43·1′	0°41·4′W	X	106
Faxfleet Ness	E Yorks	SE8623	53°42·0′	0°41·4′W	X	106,112
Faxton	Northnts	SP7875	52°22·3′	0°50·9′W	X	141
Faxton Grange	Northnts	SP7674	52°21·8′	0°52·6′W	X	141
Faygate	Surrey	TQ3647	51°12·6′	0°2·8′W	X	187
Faygate	W Susx	TQ2134	51°5·8′	0°15·9′W	T	187
Fayway	Cambs	TL0678	52°23·6′	0°26·1′W	X	142
Fazakerley	Liv	SJ3896	53°27·7′	2°55·6′W	T	108
Fazeboons	Suff	TM4054	52°8·1′	1°30·8′E	X	156
Fazeley	Staffs	SK2002	52°37·2′	1°41·9′W	T	139
Fea	Orkney	HY2828	59°8·2′	3°15·0′W	X	6
Fea	Orkney	HY3010	58°58·6′	3°12·6′W	X	6
Fea	Orkney	HY3204	58°55·3′	3°10·4′W	X	6,7
Fea	Orkney	HY3410	58°58·6′	3°8·4′W	X	6
Fea	Orkney	HY4408	58°57·6′	2°57·9′W	X	6,7
Fea	Orkney	HY4902	58°54·4′	2°52·6′W	X	6,7
Feabuie	Highld	NH7546	57°29·5′	4°4·7′W	X	27
Feabuie	Highld	NJ0626	57°19·2′	3°33·2′W	X	36
Feadan	Highld	NC0725	58°10·6′	5°16·4′W	X	15
Feadan Diorascail	N Eil	NB0615	58°1·9′	6°58·4′W	H	13,14
Feadan Dubh	Pth & Kin	NN6515	56°18·8′	4°10·5′W	X	57
Feadan Duchairidh	Highld	NH1160	57°35·7′	5°9·3′W	X	19
Feadan Gorm	N Eil	NB3113	58°1·7′	6°32·9′W	W	13,14
Feadan Grassagro	N Eil	NB4959	58°27·1′	6°17·7′W	W	8
Feadan Loch Lochan	N Eil	NB3731	58°11·6′	6°28·1′W	W	8
Feadan Molach	N Eil	NB2632	58°11·8′	6°39·3′W	W	8,13
Feadan Mór	N Eil	NB0829	58°9·5′	6°57·4′W	W	13
Feadan nan Sgarth	N Eil	NB3336	58°14·2′	6°32·5′W	W	8,13
Feadda Ness	Shetld	HU5438	60°7·6′	1°1·2′W	X	4
Fea Fow	Cumbr	SD7794	54°20·7′	2°20·8′W	X	98
Fea Geo	Shetld	HU4437	60°7·2′	1°12·0′W	X	4
Feagour	Highld	NN5690	56°59·0′	4°21·7′W	T	35
Fea Hill	Orkney	HY5309	58°58·2′	2°48·6′W	H	6,7
Fea Hill	Orkney	HY6440	59°15·0′	2°37·4′W	H	5
Feakirk	Moray	NJ0344	57°28·8′	3°36·6′W	X	27
Feal	Shetld	HU6290	60°35·6′	0°51·6′W	X	1,2
Fealar Lodge	Pth & Kin	NO0079	56°53·8′	3°38·0′W	X	43
Feall	Shetld	HP6313	60°48·0′	0°50·0′W	X	1
Feall Bay	Arg & Bt	NM1354	56°35·7′	6°40·1′W	W	46
Fearan nan Cailleach	Highld	NG3738	57°21·7′	6°21·9′W	X	23,32
Fearann Laimhrige	Highld	NM4196	56°59·2′	6°15·4′W	X	39
Fearby	N Yks	SE1981	54°13·7′	1°42·1′W	T	99
Fearby Low Moor Plantn	N Yks	SE1980	54°13·2′	1°42·1′W	F	99
Feardar Burn	Aberd	NO2095	57°2·6′	3°18·7′W	W	36,44
Fearn	Highld	NH8377	57°46·3′	3°57·6′W	T	21
Fearnach Bay	Arg & Bt	NM8313	56°15·9′	5°29·8′W	W	55
Fearnan	Pth & Kin	NN7244	56°34·5′	4°4·6′W	T	51,52
Fearnbeg	Highld	NG7359	57°34·1′	5°47·3′W	T	24
Fearn Fm	Leic	SP8098	52°34·7′	0°48·8′W	FM	141
Fearnhead	Warr	SJ6390	53°24·6′	2°33·0′W	T	109
Fearn Lodge	Highld	NH6387	57°51·4′	4°18·1′W	X	21
Fearnmore	Highld	NG7260	57°34·6′	5°48·3′W	T	24
Fearnoch	Arg & Bt	NM9632	56°26·4′	5°18·1′W	X	49
Fearnoch	Arg & Bt	NR7074	55°54·5′	5°40·4′W	X	61,62
Fearnoch	Arg & Bt	NR8797	56°7·4′	5°25·2′W	X	55
Fearnoch	Arg & Bt	NR9279	55°57·8′	5°19·5′W	X	62
Fearnoch	Arg & Bt	NS0176	55°56·4′	5°10·7′W	X	63
Fearnoch Forest	Arg & Bt	NM9631	56°25·9′	5°18·1′W	F	49
Fearns	Clackm	NS9692	56°6·8′	3°39·9′W	X	58
Fearn Sta	Highld	NH8178	57°46·8′	3°59·6′W	X	21
Fearnville	Leeds	SE3335	53°48·9′	1°29·5′W	T	104
Feastown	Orkney	HY5218	59°3·0′	2°49·7′W	X	6
Featherbed Moss	Derby	SE0400	53°30·0′	1°56·0′W	X	110
Featherbed Moss	Derby	SK0892	53°25·7′	1°52·4′W	X	110
Featherbed Moss	Derby	SK1198	53°29·0′	1°49·6′W	X	110
Feather Bed Moss	N Yks	SE0369	54°7·3′	1°56·8′W	X	98
Featherbed Moss	Sheff	SK1498	53°29·0′	1°46·9′W	X	110
Featherbed Moss	Sheff	SK1994	53°26·8′	1°42·4′W	X	110
Featherbed Rocks	Durham	NZ4349	54°50·3′	1°19·4′W	X	88
Featherbeds	Corn	SW8146	50°16·6′	5°4·1′W	X	204
Featherbed Top	Derby	SK0891	53°25·2′	1°52·4′W	H	110
Feather Hill Fm	N Yks	NZ2600	54°23·9′	1°35·6′W	FM	93
Feather Holme Fm	N Yks	SE5690	54°18·4′	1°7·9′W	FM	100
Featherknowl	Shrops	SO5169	52°19·3′	2°42·7′W	X	137,138
Feathermire	Lancs	SD6168	54°6·6′	2°35·4′W	X	97
Feathers	Aberd	NO8585	56°57·6′	2°14·3′W	X	45
Featherstone	Staffs	SJ9405	52°38·8′	2°4·9′W	T	127,139
Featherstone	Wakf	SE4220	53°40·7′	1°21·4′W	T	105
Featherstone Castle	Northum	NY6760	54°56·3′	2°30·5′W	A	86,87
Featherstone Common	Northum	NY6562	54°57·3′	2°32·4′W	X	86
Featherstone Ho	Stock on T	NZ3712	54°30·4′	1°25·3′W	X	93
Feather Tor	Devon	SX5374	50°33·1′	4°4·1′W	X	191,201
Featherwood	Northum	NT8103	55°19·5′	2°17·5′W	X	80
Feaull	Highld	NG3969	57°38·4′	6°21·9′W	X	23
Feaval	Orkney	HY2528	59°8·2′	3°18·2′W	X	6
Feaval	Orkney	HY2617	59°2·3′	3°16·9′W	X	6
Feawell	Orkney	HY2609	58°58·0′	3°16·7′W	X	6,7
Fechan	N Ayr	NS2357	55°46·7′	4°48·9′W	X	63
Feckenham	Worcs	SP0061	52°15·1′	1°59·6′W	T	150
Feddal Hill	Pth & Kin	NN7909	56°15·7′	3°56·8′W	H	57
Feddan	Moray	NH9656	57°35·2′	3°43·9′W	X	27
Fedden	Highld	NN2094	57°0·4′	4°57·4′W	X	34
Fedderate Resr	Aberd	NJ8652	57°33·7′	2°13·6′W	W	30
Fedderland	N Lanak	NS7772	55°55·8′	3°57·7′W	X	64
Feddinch	Fife	NO4813	56°18·6′	2°50·0′W	X	59
Feddinch Mains	Fife	NO4813	56°18·6′	2°50·0′W	X	59
Fedw	Conwy	SH8159	53°7·1′	3°46·3′W	X	116
Fedw	Conwy	SH8246	53°0·1′	3°45·1′W	X	116
Fedw	Denb	SJ1044	52°59·4′	3°20·0′W	X	125
Fedw	Gwyn	SH9129	52°51·1′	3°36·7′W	X	125

Fedw	Heref	SO3627	51°56·5′	2°55·5′W	X	161
Fedw	I of Angl	SH4786	53°21·2′	4°17·5′W	X	114
Fedw	Merth Tyd	SO0111	51°47·6′	3°25·7′W	X	160
Fedw	Monm	ST4998	51°40·9′	2°43·9′W	X	162
Fedw	Powys	SJ0622	52°47·5′	3°23·2′W	X	125
Fedw	Powys	SN8631	51°58·2′	3°39·2′W	X	160
Fedw	Powys	SN9130	51°57·7′	3°34·8′W	X	160
Fedw	Powys	SN9879	52°24·2′	3°29·6′W	X	136,147
Fedw	Powys	SO1356	52°12·0′	3°16·0′W	X	148
Fedw	Powys	SO1918	51°51·5′	3°10·2′W	X	161
Fedw	Powys	SO2115	51°49·9′	3°8·4′W	X	161
Fedw-arian	Gwyn	SH9136	52°54·9′	3°36·9′W	X	125
Fedw Bach	Gwyn	SH6348	53°1·0′	4°2·1′W	X	115
Fedw-ddu	Powys	SN8591	52°30·5′	3°41·3′W	H	135,136
Fedw Deg	Conwy	SH7853	53°3·9′	3°48·8′W	X	115
Fedw Fawr	Carm	SN8027	51°56·0′	3°44·3′W	H	160
Fedw Fawr	Conwy	SH9464	53°10·0′	3°34·7′W	X	116
Fedw Fawr	I of Angl	SH6081	53°18·7′	4°5·7′W	T	114,115
Fedw Fawr	Monm	SO4906	51°45·3′	2°43·9′W	F	162
Fedw-Lâs Fm	Denb	SJ0858	53°6·9′	3°22·1′W	FM	116
Fedw-Lwyd	Gwyn	SH9036	52°54·9′	3°37·8′W	X	125
Fedw-lwyd	Powys	SH8009	52°40·2′	3°46·1′W	X	124,125
Fedwlydan Fm	Powys	SO1443	52°5·0′	3°14·9′W	FM	148,161
Fedw'r-gog	Conwy	SJ0043	52°58·7′	3°29·0′W	X	125
Fedw'r-gog	Gwyn	SH8939	52°56·5′	3°38·7′W	X	124,125
Fedw Uchaf	Conwy	SH9464	53°10·0′	3°34·7′W	X	116
Fedw Wood	Monm	ST5198	51°41·0′	2°42·1′W	F	162
Feebarrow	Somer	ST5214	50°55·6′	2°40·6′W	X	194
Fee Burn	Angus	NO2475	56°51·9′	3°14·3′W	W	44
Feedale Fm	N Yks	SE3571	54°8·3′	1°27·4′W	FM	99
Feering	Essex	TL8719	51°50·5′	0°43·3′E	T	168
Feeringbury	Essex	TL8621	51°51·6′	0°42·5′E	X	168
Feeshie Burn	S Lanak	NS6938	55°37·3′	4°4·4′W	W	71
Feeshie Moss	S Lanak	NS6937	55°36·8′	4°4·4′W	X	71
Feeshie Rig	S Lanak	NS6837	55°36·8′	4°5·3′W	X	71
Feetham	N Yks	SD9898	54°22·9′	2°1·4′W	T	98
Feetham Pasture	N Yks	SD9899	54°23·4′	2°1·4′W	X	98
Feeze Gill	N Yks	SE9289	54°17·5′	0°34·8′W	W	94,101
Fegg Hayes	C of Stoke	SJ8753	53°4·7′	2°11·2′W	T	118
Fegg, The	Shrops	SO5593	52°32·2′	2°39·4′W	X	137,138
Fegla Fach	Gwyn	SH6315	52°43·2′	4°1·3′W	X	124
Fegla Fawr	Gwyn	SH6214	52°42·6′	4°2·2′W	X	124
Feindallacher Burn	Aberd	NO1986	56°57·7′	3°19·5′W	W	43
Feindallacher Burn	Aberd	NO2088	56°58·8′	3°18·5′W	W	44
Feinne-bheinn Bheag	Highld	NC4246	58°22·7′	4°41·6′W	H	9
Feinne-bheinn Mhór	Highld	NC4346	58°22·7′	4°40·6′W	H	9
Feinn Loch	Arg & Bt	NM8714	56°16·5′	5°26·0′W	W	55
Feinog-uchaf	Cered	SN4754	52°10·0′	4°13·8′W	X	146
Feiriosbhal	N Eil	NB3014	58°2·2′	6°34·0′W	H	13,14
Feith a' Chaoruinn	Highld	NC3061	58°30·5′	4°54·6′W	W	9
Féith a' Chaoruinn	Highld	NC5620	58°9·0′	4°26·3′W	W	16
Féith a' Chicheanais	Highld	NM9794	56°59·8′	5°20·1′W	W	33,40
Féith a' Chreagain	Highld	NC7737	58°18·5′	4°5·5′W	W	17
Féith a' Chùil	Highld	NC5123	58°10·5′	4°31·5′W	W	16
Féith a' Ghiubhais	Highld	NH2429	57°19·3′	4°54·9′W	X	25
Féith a' Mhór-fhir	Highld	NH9531	57°21·7′	3°44·3′W	W	27,36
Féith an Fheòir	Highld	NH0198	57°55·9′	5°21·2′W	W	19
Féith an Laisg	Highld	NC5361	58°31·0′	4°30·9′W	W	10
Féith an Laoigh	Aberd	NO2390	56°59·9′	3°15·6′W	W	44
Féith an Leòthaid	Highld	NC2021	58°8·7′	5°3·0′W	W	15
Féith an Leothaid	Highld	NH0358	57°34·4′	5°17·2′W	W	25
Féith an Lochain	Pth & Kin	NN8977	56°52·5′	3°48·8′W	W	43
Féith Bhàit	Aberd	NJ1908	57°9·6′	3°19·9′W	W	36
Féith Bhàn	Arg & Bt	NM4840	56°29·3′	6°5·2′W	W	47,48
Féith Bhàn	Arg & Bt	NM5541	56°30·1′	5°58·4′W	W	47,48
Féith Bhàn	Arg & Bt	NM5541	56°30·1′	5°58·4′W	X	47,48
Féith Bhàn	Highld	NJ0035	57°23·9′	3°39·4′W	W	27
Féith-bhealach	N Eil	NF8132	57°16·3′	7°17·1′W	X	22
Féith Bhuidhe	Highld	NG8318	57°12·3′	5°35·1′W	X	33
Féith Bhuidhe	Highld	NH6890	57°53·1′	4°13·1′W	F	21
Féith Bhuidhe	Pth & Kin	NN4355	56°39·9′	4°33·3′W	W	42,51
Féith Buidhe	Highld	NC6403	58°0·0′	4°17·6′W	W	16
Féith Buidhe	Moray	NH9901	57°5·6′	3°39·6′W	W	36
Féith Buidhe	Moray	NJ0909	57°10·0′	3°29·8′W	W	36
Féith Chaorunn Mhór	Highld	NC9631	58°15·6′	3°45·9′W	W	11,17
Féith Dubh	Highld	NC6618	58°8·1′	4°16·1′W	W	16
Féithe Bhuidhe	Highld	NH1539	57°24·5′	5°4·3′W	X	25
Féith Fhuaran	Highld	NC9829	58°14·5′	3°43·8′W	W	11,17
Féith Gaineimh Bheag	Highld	NC9434	58°17·2′	3°48·0′W	W	11,17
Féith Gaineimh Mhór	Highld	NC9532	58°16·1′	3°46·9′W	W	11,17
Féith Ghiubhasachain	Moray	NJ0903	57°6·8′	3°29·7′W	W	36
Féith Ghorm Ailleag	Pth & Kin	NN7979	56°53·5′	3°58·7′W	W	42
Féith Ghorm Ailleag	Pth & Kin	NN8080	56°54·0′	3°57·8′W	W	43
Féith Ghrianach	Highld	NH1905	57°6·3′	4°58·9′W	W	34
Feith Hill	Aberd	NJ6543	57°28·8′	2°34·6′W	H	29
Feith Hill	Aberd	NJ6643	57°28·8′	2°33·6′W	X	29
Féith Laoigh	Moray	NJ1703	57°6·9′	3°21·8′W	W	36
Feithlinn	Highld	NH7812	57°11·2′	4°0·7′W	W	35
Féith Loch Ghleadharan	N Eil	NB2441	58°16·5′	6°42·0′W	W	8,13
Féith Mhór	Highld	NH8822	57°16·8′	3°51·0′W	W	35,36
Féith Mhór	Highld	NH9223	57°17·4′	3°47·1′W	W	36
Féith Mhór	Highld	NN8093	57°1·0′	3°58·1′W	W	35,43
Féith Musach	Moray	NJ1921	57°16·6′	3°20·1′W	X	36
Féith na Braclaich	Highld	NN7089	56°58·7′	4°7·9′W	W	42
Féith na Doire	Highld	NH8718	57°14·6′	3°51·9′W	W	35,36
Féith na Leitreach	Highld	NH2220	57°14·4′	4°56·5′W	W	25
Féith na Mad	Pth & Kin	NN7779	56°53·4′	4°0·7′W	W	42
Féith na Sgor	Aberd	NO0291	57°0·2′	3°36·4′W	W	43
Féith na Sithinn	Highld	NC2003	57°59·1′	5°2·2′W	W	15
Féith Odhar Bheag	Pth & Kin	NN8481	56°54·6′	3°53·9′W	W	43
Féith Odhar Mhór	Pth & Kin	NN8381	56°54·6′	3°54·8′W	W	43
Féith Osdail	Highld	NC5914	58°5·8′	4°23·1′W	W	16
Féith Raoicidhdail	Highld	NM9461	56°42·0′	5°21·4′W	W	40
Féith Riabhach	Highld	NC9437	58°18·8′	3°48·1′W	W	11,17
Féith Salach	Highld	NM8571	56°47·1′	5°30·7′W	X	40
Féith Seileach	Highld	NG6710	57°7·6′	5°50·5′W	W	32
Féith Shiol	Highld	NN3582	56°54·3′	4°42·1′W	W	34,41
Féith Talagain	Highld	NN5497	57°2·7′	4°23·9′W	W	35
Féith Thalain	Pth & Kin	NN4545	56°34·5′	4°30·9′W	W	51
Féith Tharsuinn	Highld	NH5393	57°54·4′	4°28·4′W	X	20

Féith Torr a' Bhruic	Highld	NC9726	58°12·9′	3°44·7′W	W	17
Féith Uaine Mhór	Pth & Kin	NN9178	56°53·1′	3°46·9′W	W	43
Feizor	N Yks	SD7967	54°6·2′	2°18·9′W	T	98
Feizor Wood	N Yks	SD7868	54°6·7′	2°19·8′W	F	98
Felagie	Aberd	NO1992	57°1·0′	3°19·6′W	X	43
Felbridge	Surrey	TQ3639	51°8·3′	0°3·0′W	T	187
Felbridge Water	W Susx	TQ3639	51°8·3′	0°3·0′W	W	187
Felbrigg	Norf	TG2039	52°54·4′	1°16·7′E	T	133
Felbury Ho	Surrey	TQ1144	51°11·3′	0°24·3′W	X	187
Felcourt	Surrey	TQ3841	51°9·3′	0°1·2′W	T	187
Feldale	Cambs	TL2998	52°34·1′	0°5·4′W	X	142
Felday	Surrey	TQ1044	51°11·3′	0°25·2′W	X	187
Felden	Herts	TL0405	51°44·3′	0°29·2′W	X	166
Felderland	Kent	TR3256	51°15·6′	1°19·9′E	T	179
Feldom	N Yks	NZ1003	54°25·6′	1°50·3′W	X	92
Feldom Ranges	N Yks	NZ1004	54°26·1′	1°50·3′W	X	92
Feldon Burn	Durham	NY9946	54°48·8′	2°0·5′W	W	87
Feldon Carrs	Durham	NZ0047	54°49·3′	1°59·6′W	X	87
Feldon Plain	Durham	NY9945	54°48·2′	2°0·5′W	X	87
Feldy	Ches	SJ6979	53°18·7′	2°27·5′W	T	118
Feldy Marshes	Essex	TL9913	51°47·0′	0°53·5′E	X	168
Felecia Crags	Northum	NY7277	55°5·4′	2°25·9′W	X	86,87
Felhampton	Heref	SO6426	51°56·1′	2°31·0′W	X	162
Felhampton	Shrops	SO4487	52°28·9′	2°49·1′W	T	137
Felin Bencoed	Gwyn	SH4440	52°56·3′	4°18·9′W	X	123
Felin-Crai	Powys	SN8823	51°53·9′	3°37·3′W	T	160
Felin Cwm	Powys	SO1431	51°58·5′	3°14·7′W	X	161
Felin Cwrt	Carm	SN1421	51°51·6′	4°41·7′W	X	145,158
Felindre	Carm	SN2726	51°54·6′	4°30·5′W	X	145,158
Felindre	Carm	SN3538	52°1·2′	4°23·9′W	T	145
Felindre	Carm	SN4612	51°47·4′	4°13·6′W	T	159
Felindre	Carm	SN5521	51°52·4′	4°6·0′W	T	159
Felindre	Carm	SN5847	52°6·4′	4°4·0′W	X	146
Felindre	Carm	SN6830	51°57·4′	3°54·9′W	X	146
Felindre	Carm	SN7027	51°55·8′	3°53·1′W	X	146,160
Felindre	Cered	SN5455	52°10·7′	4°7·7′W	X	146
Felindre	Gwyn	SH8830	52°51·6′	3°39·4′W	X	124,125
Felindre	Powys	SJ1601	52°36·3′	3°14·0′W	T	136
Felindre	Powys	SO1681	52°25·5′	3°13·7′W	T	136
Felindre	Powys	SO1723	51°54·2′	3°12·0′W	T	161
Felindre	Rho Cyn Taf	SS9781	51°31·3′	3°28·7′W	T	170
Felindre	Swan	SN6302	51°42·2′	3°58·6′W	T	159
Felindre Brook	Powys	SO1836	52°1·2′	3°11·3′W	W	161
Felindre Farchog	Pemb	SN1039	52°1·3′	4°45·8′W	T	145
Felindre Ho	Pemb	SM8131	51°56·3′	5°10·8′W	X	157
Felin Dyffryn	Cered	SN6574	52°21·1′	3°58·5′W	X	135
Felin Dyrnol	Powys	SN9191	52°30·6′	3°36·0′W	X	136
Felinengan	I of Angl	SH5373	53°14·3′	4°11·8′W	X	114,115
Felinfach	Cered	SN5255	52°10·6′	4°9·5′W	T	146
Felin-Fach	I of Angl	SH4372	53°13·6′	4°20·7′W	X	114,115
Felinfach	Powys	SO0833	51°59·5′	3°20·0′W	T	160
Felinfach	Powys	SO0933	51°59·5′	3°19·1′W	T	161
Felin-fawr	Powys	SN9179	52°24·1′	3°35·7′W	X	136,147
Felinfoel	Carm	SN5202	51°42·1′	4°8·1′W	T	159
Felin Gadeg	Conwy	SH9364	53°10·0′	3°35·6′W	X	116
Felinganol	Pemb	SN1642	52°3·0′	4°40·6′W	X	145
Felingelli	Carm	SN4425	51°54·3′	4°15·7′W	X	146
Felingwmisaf	Carm	SN5023	51°53·4′	4°10·4′W	T	159
Felingwmuchaf	Carm	SN5024	51°53·9′	4°10·4′W	T	159
Felin-gythros	Powys	SO0080	52°24·8′	3°27·8′W	X	136
Felin Hên	Denb	SJ0061	53°8·5′	3°29·3′W	X	116
Felin-hên	Gwyn	SH5868	53°11·7′	4°7·1′W	X	114,115
Felin Isaf	Conwy	SH8074	53°15·2′	3°47·5′W	X	116
Felin Isaf	Denb	SJ1064	53°10·2′	3°20·4′W	X	116
Felin Marlais	Carm	SN5131	51°57·7′	4°9·7′W	X	146
Felin Newydd	Carm	SN6638	52°1·7′	3°56·8′W	X	146
Felin Newydd	Powys	SJ2229	52°51·4′	3°9·1′W	X	126
Felin Newydd	Powys	SO1135	52°0·6′	3°17·4′W	T	161
Felin-pandy	Carm	SN3023	51°53·0′	4°27·8′W	X	145,159
Felin Puleston	Wrex	SJ3249	53°2·3′	3°0·4′W	T	117
Felin Rhiw-bwys	Cered	SN5469	52°18·2′	4°8·1′W	X	135
Felin Rhosgerrig	I of Angl	SH4969	53°12·0′	4°15·2′W	X	114,115
Felinrhyd-fawr	Gwyn	SH6439	52°56·1′	4°1·0′W	X	124
Felin Uchaf	Gwyn	SH2028	52°49·4′	4°39·9′W	X	123
Felin-wen	Swan	SN6601	51°41·7′	3°55·9′W	X	159
Felin-Wnda	Cered	SN3246	52°5·5′	4°26·7′W	T	145
Felin Wrdan	Pemb	SN1336	51°59·7′	4°43·0′W	X	145
Felinwynt	Cered	SN2150	52°7·4′	4°36·5′W	X	145
Felin-wynt	Powys	SO1180	52°24·9′	3°18·1′W	X	136
Felin-ysguboriau	Denb	SJ1257	53°6·4′	3°18·5′W	X	116
Felix Fm	Brackn	SU8573	51°27·2′	0°46·2′W	FM	175
Felix Hall	Essex	TL8419	51°50·6′	0°40·7′E	X	168
Felixkirk	N Yks	SE4684	54°15·2′	1°17·2′W	T	100
Felix Place	Essex	TL8418	51°50·0′	0°40·6′E	X	168
Felixstowe	Suff	TM3034	51°57·6′	1°21·3′E	T	169
Felixstowe Ferry	Suff	TM3237	51°59·2′	1°23·1′E	T	169
Felkington	Northum	NT9444	55°41·6′	2°5·3′W	T	74,75
Felkirk	Wakf	SE3812	53°36·4′	1°25·1′W	T	110,111
Fell	D & G	NX7284	55°8·3′	4°0·1′W	X	77
Fellard	D & G	NX9393	55°13·4′	3°40·5′W	X	78
Fellbarrow	Cumbr	NY1324	54°36·5′	3°20·4′W	H	89
Fell Beck	N Yks	SD7573	54°9·4′	2°22·6′W	W	98
Fell Beck	N Yks	SE1966	54°5·6′	1°42·2′W	W	99
Fellbeck Ho	N Yks	SE1965	54°5·1′	1°42·2′W	X	99
Fellborough	Cumbr	SD3894	54°20·5′	2°56·8′W	X	96,97
Fell Briggs Fm	Red & Cl	NZ6121	54°35·1′	1°2·9′W	FM	94
Fell Brook	Lancs	SD7549	53°56·4′	2°22·4′W	W	103
Fell Burn	D & G	NX7484	55°8·3′	3°58·2′W	W	77
Fell Burn	Northum	NY7259	54°55·7′	2°25·8′W	W	86,87
Fellcleugh	Scot Bord	NT7060	55°50·2′	2°28·3′W	X	67,74
Fellcleugh Old Wood	Scot Bord	NT7159	55°49·7′	2°27·3′W	F	67,74
Fell Close	N Yks	SD7674	54°9·9′	2°21·6′W	X	98
Fell Close	N Yks	SD7677	54°11·5′	2°21·7′W	X	98
Fellcot Fm	W Susx	TQ3539	51°8·3′	0°3·8′W	FM	187
Fell Cottage	Cumbr	SD1185	54°15·4′	3°21·6′W	X	96
Fell Cottage	Northum	NY8567	55°0·1′	2°13·6′W	X	87
Fell Cottages	Northum	NY9856	54°54·2′	2°1·4′W	X	87
Fellcroft Loch	D & G	NX7550	54°50·0′	3°56·3′W	W	84
Felldownhead	Devon	SX3780	50°36·1′	4°17·8′W	X	201
Felldyke	Cumbr	NY0819	54°33·7′	3°24·9′W	T	89

Fell Edge	Cumbr	SD4388	54°17·3′	2°52·1′W	X	97
Fell Edge	Cumbr	SD4591	54°18·9′	2°50·3′W	X	97
Fellend	Cumbr	NY0614	54°31·0′	3°26·7′W	X	89
Fell End	Cumbr	NY2234	54°41·9′	3°12·2′W	X	89,90
Fellend	Cumbr	NY4970	55°1·6′	2°47·4′W	X	86
Fellend	Cumbr	NY5351	54°51·3′	2°43·5′W	X	86
Fell End	Cumbr	SD2388	54°17·2′	3°10·6′W	X	96
Fell End	Cumbr	SD3978	54°11·9′	2°55·7′W	X	96,97
Fell End	Cumbr	SD7298	54°22·8′	2°25·4′W	T	98
Fell End	D & G	NX3064	54°56·8′	4°38·8′W	H	82
Fellend	D & G	NX6858	54°54·2′	4°3·1′W	X	83,84
Fellend	D & G	NX9297	55°15·6′	3°41·5′W	X	78
Fell End	Lancs	SD5249	53°56·3′	2°43·5′W	X	102
Fell End	Lancs	SD5546	53°54·7′	2°40·7′W	X	102
Fell End	Lancs	SD6956	54°0·2′	2°28·0′W	X	103
Fell End	Northum	NY6765	54°59·0′	2°30·5′W	X	86,87
Fell End	Northum	NY8481	55°7·6′	2°14·6′W	X	80
Fell End	N Yks	SD7072	54°8·8′	2°27·1′W	X	98
Fell End Clouds	Cumbr	SD7399	54°23·4′	2°24·5′W	X	98
Fell End Fm	Cumbr	SD5078	54°12·0′	2°45·6′W	FM	97
Fell End Fm	Lancs	SD5359	54°1·7′	2°42·6′W	FM	102
Fell End Moor	N Yks	NZ0202	54°25·1′	1°57·7′W	X	92
Felley Priory	Notts	SK4851	53°3·5′	1°16·6′W	A	120
Fell Fm	D & G	NX8370	55°0·9′	3°49·4′W	FM	84
Fell Foot	Cumbr	NY2903	54°25·3′	3°5·2′W	X	89,90
Fellfoot	Cumbr	SD4699	54°23·3′	2°49·5′W	X	97
Fell Foot	Lancs	SD5944	53°53·7′	2°37·0′W	X	102
Fell Foot Park	Cumbr	SD3887	54°16·7′	2°56·7′W	X	96,97
Fellgarth	Cumbr	SD5998	54°22·8′	2°37·5′W	X	97
Fell Garth	Cumbr	SD7086	54°16·4′	2°27·2′W	X	98
Fellgate	Cumbr	NY6142	54°46·5′	2°36·0′W	X	86
Fell Gate	Cumbr	SD2487	54°16·6′	3°9·6′W	X	96
Fell Gate	Cumbr	SD4894	54°20·6′	2°47·6′W	X	97
Fellgate	Cumbr	SD6992	54°19·6′	2°28·2′W	X	98
Fellgate	S Tyne	NZ3262	54°57·3′	1°29·6′W	T	88
Fellgill Fm	N Yks	SE3199	54°23·4′	1°30·9′W	FM	99
Fell Greave	Kirk	SE1520	53°40·8′	1°46·0′W	X	104
Fellgreen	Cumbr	SD1188	54°17·0′	3°21·6′W	X	96
Fell Head	Cumbr	NY6807	54°27·7′	2°29·2′W	X	91
Fell Head	Cumbr	NY6911	54°29·8′	2°28·3′W	X	91
Fell Head	Cumbr	SD6498	54°22·8′	2°32·8′W	H	97
Fellhill	Cumbr	NY3441	54°45·8′	3°1·1′W	X	85
Fell Hill	D & G	NX2865	54°57·3′	4°40·7′W	H	82
Fell Hill	D & G	NX7284	55°8·3′	4°0·1′W	H	77
Fell Hill	D & G	NX8370	55°0·9′	3°49·4′W	H	84
Fell Hill	D & G	NY3092	55°13·3′	3°5·6′W	H	79
Fell Hill	S Ayr	NX1693	55°12·1′	4°53·0′W	H	76
Fell Hill	S Ayr	NX1890	55°10·5′	4°51·1′W	H	76
Fell Hill	S Ayr	NX2990	55°10·7′	4°40·7′W	H	76
Fell Ho	Cumbr	NY7908	54°28·3′	2°19·0′W	X	91
Fell Ho	Cumbr	SD6682	54°14·2′	2°30·9′W	X	98
Fell Ho	Northum	NY7759	54°55·8′	2°21·1′W	X	86,87
Fell Ho	Northum	NY8466	54°59·5′	2°14·6′W	X	86,87
Fell Ho	Northum	NY9576	55°5·0′	2°4·3′W	X	87
Fell Ho	Northum	NZ1569	55°1·2′	1°45·5′W	X	88
Fellhouse Crags	Northum	NY9189	55°12·0′	2°8·1′W	X	80
Fellhouse Fell	Northum	NY7559	54°55·8′	2°23·0′W	H	86,87
Fell House Fm	N upon Ty	NZ1767	55°0·1′	1°43·6′W	FM	88
Felling	Ghead	NZ2761	54°56·8′	1°34·3′W	T	88
Fellingscott	Devon	SS7747	51°12·8′	3°45·3′W	X	180
Felling Shore	Ghead	NZ2763	54°57·9′	1°34·3′W	T	88
Fell Lane	Brad	SE0440	53°51·6′	1°55·9′W	T	104
Fell Lane Fm	Northum	NY9274	55°3·9′	2°7·1′W	FM	87
Fell Loch	D & G	NX3155	54°51·9′	4°37·6′W	W	82
Fell Mill Fm	Warw	SP2641	52°4·2′	1°36·8′W	FM	151
Fellnaw	D & G	NX6757	54°53·7′	4°4·0′W	X	83,84
Fell of Barhullion	D & G	NX3741	54°44·5′	4°31·5′W	H	83
Fell of Barhullion	D & G	NX3742	54°45·0′	4°31·5′W	X	83
Fell of Carleton	D & G	NX3937	54°42·4′	4°29·5′W	H	83
Fell of Eschoncan	D & G	NX4180	55°5·6′	4°29·1′W	X	77
Fell of Fleet	D & G	NX5670	55°0·5′	4°14·7′W	H	77
Fell of Laghead	D & G	NX6161	54°55·7′	4°9·7′W	H	83
Fell of Loch Ronald	D & G	NX2764	54°56·7′	4°41·6′W	X	82
Fell of Talnotry	D & G	NX4872	55°1·4′	4°22·2′W	H	77
Fellonmore	Arg & Bt	NM6827	56°23·0′	5°45·0′W	X	49
Fellowes Fm	Cambs	TL2178	52°23·4′	0°12·9′W	FM	142
Fellowhills	Scot Bord	NT8848	55°43·8′	2°11·0′W	X	74
Fell Plain	Cumbr	SD4596	54°21·6′	2°50·4′W	X	97
Fell Plantation	Northum	NY9455	54°53·6′	2°5·2′W	F	87
Fell Quarries	D & G	NX4956	54°52·8′	4°20·8′W	X	83
Fells	Lancs	SD7553	53°58·6′	2°22·5′W	X	103
Fellsa Moors	Shetld	HU3171	60°25·6′	1°25·7′W	X	3
Fells Fm	Essex	TL7922	51°52·3′	0°36·4′E	FM	167
Fell Shin	S Lanak	NT0329	55°33·0′	3°31·8′W	H	72
Fellside	Cumbr	NY3037	54°43·6′	3°4·8′W	T	90
Fellside	Cumbr	NY6335	54°42·8′	2°34·0′W	X	91
Fellside	Cumbr	SD1188	54°17·0′	3°21·6′W	X	96
Fell Side	Cumbr	SD3584	54°15·1′	2°59·4′W	X	96,97
Fell Side	Cumbr	SD4490	54°18·4′	2°51·2′W	X	97
Fell Side	Cumbr	SD5979	54°12·6′	2°37·3′W	X	97
Fellside	Cumbr	SD6388	54°17·4′	2°33·7′W	X	97
Fellside	D & G	NX8162	54°56·6′	3°51·0′W	X	84
Fellside	Ghead	NZ1959	54°55·8′	1°41·8′W	X	88
Fellside	Ghead	NZ1960	54°56·3′	1°41·8′W	T	88
Fell Side	Lancs	SD5543	53°53·1′	2°40·7′W	X	102
Fell Side	Lancs	SD5641	53°52·0′	2°39·7′W	X	102
Fell Side	Lancs	SD7056	54°0·2′	2°27·0′W	X	103
Fell Side	Lancs	SD7249	53°56·4′	2°25·2′W	X	103
Fell Side	N Yks	SD6775	54°10·4′	2°29·9′W	X	98
Fellside Barn	Lancs	SD6577	54°11·5′	2°31·8′W	X	97
Fellside Brow	Cumbr	NY3036	54°43·1′	3°4·8′W	H	90
Fellside Fm	Cumbr	NY1224	54°36·5′	3°21·3′W	FM	89
Fellside Fm	Ghead	NZ1958	54°55·2′	1°41·8′W	FM	88
Fellside Fm	Lancs	SD5652	53°58·0′	2°39·8′W	FM	102
Fell Side Fm	Lancs	SD6840	53°51·6′	2°28·8′W	FM	103
Fellside Ho	Cumbr	SD2678	54°11·8′	3°7·6′W	X	96,97
Fells Plantn	Leeds	SE2343	53°53·2′	1°38·6′W	F	104
Fell Syke Fm	Durham	NY9118	54°33·7′	2°7·9′W	FM	91,92
Fell, The	D & G	NX7356	54°53·2′	3°58·4′W	H	83,84
Fell, The	Stir	NS7289	56°4·9′	4°3·0′W	X	57

Fell View	Northum	NY8547	54°49·3′	2°13·6′W	X	87
Fell Wood	Lancs	SD8139	53°51·1′	2°16·9′W	F	103
Fell Yeat	Cumbr	SD6379	54°12·6′	2°33·6′W	X	97
Felmersham	Beds	SP9957	52°12·4′	0°32·7′W	T	153
Felmingham	Norf	TG2529	52°48·9′	1°20·7′E	T	133,134
Felmingham Hall (Hotel)	Norf	TG2427	52°47·9′	1°19·8′E	X	133,134
Felmoor Fm	Essex	TL6821	51°52·0′	0°26·8′E	FM	167
Felmore	Essex	TQ7389	51°34·6′	0°30·2′E	T	178
Felon's Oak	Somer	ST0138	51°8·2′	3°24·5′W	X	181
Felpham	W Susx	SU9500	50°47·7′	0°38·7′W	T	197
Felsham	Suff	TL9457	52°10·9′	0°50·7′E	T	155
Felsham Ho	Suff	TL9457	52°10·9′	0°50·7′E	X	155
Felsham Wood	Suff	TL9555	52°9·8′	0°51·5′E	F	155
Felshun	Shetld	HU4959	60°19·0′	1°6·3′W	X	2,3
Felsteads	Essex	TL3904	51°43·3′	0°1·1′E	X	166
Felsted	Essex	TL6720	51°51·4′	0°25·9′E	T	167
Feltham	Houns	TQ1073	51°26·9′	0°24·6′W	T	176
Feltham	Somer	ST2317	50°57·1′	3°5·4′W	T	193
Feltham Fm	Dorset	ST7730	51°4·4′	2°19·3′W	FM	183
Feltham Fm	Somer	ST7846	51°13·0′	2°18·5′W	FM	183
Felthamhill	Surrey	TQ0971	51°25·9′	0°25·5′W	T	176
Felthorpe	Norf	TG1618	52°43·2′	1°12·3′E	T	133
Felthouse	Staffs	SK0753	53°4·7′	1°53·3′W	X	119
Feltimores	Essex	TL4911	51°46·9′	0°10·0′E	X	167
Felton	Heref	SO5748	52°8·0′	2°37·3′W	T	149
Felton	Northum	NU1800	55°17·9′	1°42·6′W	T	81
Felton	N Som	ST5265	51°23·2′	2°41·0′W	T	172,182
Felton	Scot Bord	NT1247	55°42·8′	3°23·6′W	X	72
Felton Butler	Shrops	SJ3917	52°45·1′	2°53·8′W	T	126
Felton Court	Heref	SO5747	52°7·4′	2°37·3′W	X	149
Felton Fence	Northum	NU1500	55°17·9′	1°45·4′W	X	81
Felton Fm	Shrops	SO5076	52°23·0′	2°43·7′W	FM	137,138
Felton Hill	N Som	ST5165	51°23·2′	2°41·9′W	X	172,182
Felton Moor	Shrops	SJ3324	52°48·8′	2°59·2′W	X	126
Felton Park	Northum	NU1700	55°17·9′	1°43·5′W	X	81
Feltons	Suff	TL7663	52°14·4′	0°35·1′E	X	155
Felton's Fm	Surrey	TQ1948	51°13·4′	0°17·4′W	FM	187
Feltwell	Norf	TL7090	52°29·1′	0°30·6′E	T	143
Feltwell Anchor	Norf	TL6589	52°28·7′	0°26·2′E	X	143
Feltwell Common	Norf	TL6791	52°29·7′	0°28·0′E	X	143
Feltwell Lodge	Norf	TL7491	52°29·6′	0°34·2′E	X	143
Feltysitch	Staffs	SK0359	53°7·9′	1°56·9′W	X	119
Felyennan	D & G	NX3546	54°47·2′	4°33·5′W	X	83
Femnock Wood	Highld	NH4940	57°25·8′	4°30·4′W	F	26
Fenacre Fm	Devon	ST0617	50°56·9′	3°19·9′W	FM	181
Fenay Beck	Kirk	SE1814	53°37·6′	1°43·3′W	W	110
Fenay Bridge	Kirk	SE1815	53°38·1′	1°43·3′W	T	110
Fen Beck	N Yks	SD7566	54°5·6′	2°22·5′W	W	98
Fen Bog	N Yks	SE8597	54°21·9′	0°41·1′W	X	94,100
Fen Br	Essex	TM0633	51°57·7′	1°0·3′E	X	168
Fen Br	Lincs	TF4262	53°8·4′	0°7·8′E	X	122
Fen Carr	Norf	TL9590	52°28·6′	0°52·7′E	F	144
Fen Causeway (Roman Road)	Cambs	TL3499	52°34·6′	0°0·9′W	R	142
Fence	Lancs	SD8237	53°50·0′	2°16·0′W	T	103
Fence	Roth	SK4485	53°21·8′	1°19·9′W	X	111,120
Fence Burn	Northum	NZ1489	55°12·0′	1°46·4′W	W	81
Fence Foot	Lancs	SD5038	53°50·4′	2°45·2′W	X	102
Fence Ho	Lancs	SD8137	53°50·0′	2°16·9′W	X	103
Fence Houses	Sund	NZ3250	54°50·9′	1°29·7′W	T	88
Fence of Knockdon	S Ayr	NS4300	55°16·4′	4°27·9′W	X	77
Fences Fm	Mil Key	SP8646	52°6·6′	0°44·3′W	FM	152
Fences Fm	Norf	TF5605	52°37·4′	0°18·7′E	FM	143
Fence Wood	W Berks	SU5171	51°26·4′	1°15·6′W	F	174
Fenchurch St Sta	C of Lon	TQ3380	51°30·4′	0°4·6′W	X	176,177
Fencote Abbey Fm	Heref	SO5959	52°13·9′	2°35·6′W	FM	149
Fencott	Oxon	SP5716	51°50·6′	1°10·0′W	T	164
Fen Croft	Lincs	TF3896	53°26·8′	0°5·1′E	X	113
Fendale Fm	Lincs	TF1653	53°3·9′	0°15·7′W	FM	121
Fenderbridge	Pth & Kin	NN8866	56°46·6′	3°49·5′W	T	43
Fender Burn	Pth & Kin	NN9170	56°48·8′	3°46·7′W	W	43
Fen Ditton	Cambs	TL4860	52°13·3′	0°10·4′E	T	154
Fendoch	Pth & Kin	NN9027	56°25·6′	3°46·6′W	X	52,58
Fendoch Burn	Pth & Kin	NN8828	56°26·1′	3°48·5′W	W	52,58
Fendoch Burn	Pth & Kin	NN9127	56°25·6′	3°45·6′W	W	52,58
Fen Drayton	Cambs	TL3368	52°17·9′	0°2·6′W	T	154
Fendrith Hill	Durham	NY8733	54°41·8′	2°11·7′W	H	91,92
Fenecreich	Highld	NH5118	57°14·0′	4°27·7′W	X	35
Fenemere	Shrops	SJ4422	52°47·8′	2°49·4′W	W	126
Fen End	Lincs	TF2420	52°46·0′	0°9·3′W	T	131
Fen End	Sol	SP2275	52°22·6′	1°40·2′W	T	139
Fen End Fm	Sol	SP2274	52°22·1′	1°40·2′W	FM	139
Fen Farm	Lincs	TF0773	53°14·8′	0°23·4′W	FM	121
Fen Fm	Beds	TL2048	52°7·3′	0°14·4′W	FM	153
Fen Fm	Cambs	TF3508	52°39·4′	0°0·2′E	FM	142
Fen Fm	Cambs	TL3379	52°23·8′	0°2·3′W	FM	142
Fen Fm	Essex	TM0227	51°54·5′	0°56·6′E	FM	168
Fen Fm	Essex	TM0514	51°47·4′	0°58·8′E	FM	168
Fen Fm	Essex	TM0524	51°52·8′	0°59·1′E	FM	168
Fen Fm	Lincs	SK8247	53°1·1′	0°46·2′W	FM	130
Fen Fm	Lincs	SK8650	53°2·7′	0°42·6′W	FM	121
Fen Fm	Lincs	TF0964	53°10·0′	0°21·8′W	FM	121
Fen Fm	Lincs	TF1634	52°53·7′	0°16·1′W	FM	130
Fen Fm	Lincs	TF1922	52°47·2′	0°13·7′W	FM	130
Fen Fm	Lincs	TF2856	53°5·4′	0°4·9′W	FM	122
Fen Fm	Lincs	TF3260	53°7·5′	0°1·2′W	FM	122
Fen Fm	Lincs	TF3316	52°43·7′	0°1·4′W	FM	131
Fen Fm	Lincs	TF3558	53°6·4′	0°1·4′E	FM	122
Fen Fm	Lincs	TF3894	53°25·7′	0°5·0′E	FM	113
Fen Fm	Lincs	TF4020	52°45·8′	0°4·9′E	FM	131
Fen Fm	Mil Key	SP9138	52°2·2′	0°40·0′W	FM	152
Fen Fm	Norf	TF6512	52°41·1′	0°26·9′E	FM	132,143
Fen Fm	Norf	TM0293	52°30·1′	0°59·0′E	FM	144
Fen Fm	Norf	TM3191	52°28·3′	1°24·5′E	FM	134
Fen Fm	Suff	TL7271	52°18·8′	0°31·8′E	FM	154
Fen Fm	Suff	TL9878	52°22·1′	0°54·9′E	FM	144
Fen Fm	Suff	TL9950	52°7·0′	0°54·8′E	FM	155
Fen Fm	Suff	TM1042	52°2·4′	1°4·1′E	FM	155,169
Fen Fm	Suff	TM1043	52°3·0′	1°4·2′E	FM	155,169
Fen Fm	Thurr	TQ6184	51°32·1′	0°19·7′E	FM	177
Fengate	Norf	TG1924	52°46·4′	1°15·2′E	T	133,134
Fengate	Peterb	TL2098	52°34·2′	0°13·4′W	T	142
Fengate Fm	Norf	TL7787	52°27·4′	0°36·7′E	FM	144
Fenham	Northum	NU0840	55°39·5′	1°51·9′W	X	75
Fenham	N upon Ty	NZ2265	54°59·0′	1°38·9′W	T	88
Fenham Burn	Northum	NU0740	55°39·5′	1°52·9′W	W	75
Fenham Flats	Northum	NU1139	55°38·9′	1°49·1′W	X	75
Fenhamhill	Northum	NU0641	55°40·0′	1°53·8′W	X	75
Fenham le Moor	Northum	NU0939	55°38·9′	1°51·0′W	X	75
Fenhampton	Heref	SO3950	52°8·9′	2°53·1′W	X	148,149
Fen Hill	Suff	TM4672	52°17·7′	1°36·9′E	X	156
Fen Ho	Lincs	SK9377	53°17·1′	0°35·9′W	X	121
Fen Ho	Lincs	TF1053	53°4·0′	0°21·1′W	X	121
Fen Ho	N Yks	SE8497	54°21·9′	0°42·0′W	X	94,100
Fen House Fm	Lincs	TF3921	52°46·4′	0°4·0′E	FM	131
Fenhouse Heath	Suff	TL7385	52°26·4′	0°33·1′E	X	143
Fenhouses	Lincs	TF2540	52°56·8′	0°8·0′W	T	131
Feniscliffe	Black w Dar	SD6526	53°44·0′	2°31·4′W	T	102,103
Feniscowles	Black w Dar	SD6525	53°43·5′	2°31·4′W	T	102,103
Feniscowles	Lancs	SD6425	53°43·5′	2°32·3′W	T	102,103
Feniton	Devon	SY0999	50°47·2′	3°17·1′W	T	192
Feniton Court	Devon	SY1099	50°47·2′	3°16·2′W	X	192,193
Fenlake	Beds	TL0648	52°7·4′	0°26·7′W	T	153
Fenland Airfield	Lincs	TF3317	52°44·3′	0°1·4′W	X	131
Fenlands, The	Lincs	TF3820	52°45·8′	0°3·1′E	X	131
Fenlea Fm	Cambs	TL3379	52°23·8′	0°2·3′W	FM	142
Fenleigh Fm	Cambs	TL4569	52°18·2′	0°8·0′E	FM	154
Fen Letch	Northum	NZ2194	55°14·6′	1°39·8′W	W	81
Fen Moor	N Yks	SE8496	54°21·4′	0°42·0′W	X	94,100
Fenmore Fm	Lincs	TF1648	53°1·2′	0°15·8′W	FM	130
Fennachrochan	Arg & Bt	NM8745	56°33·2′	5°27·5′W	X	49
Fenn Creek	Essex	TQ8096	51°38·3′	0°36·5′E	W	168
Fennells Fm	Glos	SO8806	51°45·4′	2°10·0′W	FM	162
Fennemore Fm	Bucks	SP6312	51°48·4′	1°4·8′W	FM	164,165
Fenner's Fm	Norf	TM0781	52°23·5′	1°2·9′E	FM	144
Fennes	Essex	TL7627	51°55·0′	0°34·0′E	X	167
Fenn Fm	Essex	TL8637	52°0·2′	0°43·0′E	FM	155
Fenn Green	Shrops	SO7783	52°26·9′	2°19·9′W	T	138
Fenn Hall Fm	Suff	TL9958	52°11·3′	0°55·1′E	FM	155
Fennie Law	E Loth	NT5663	55°51·7′	2°41·7′W	H	67
Fenning Island	Somer	ST2846	51°12·8′	3°1·5′W	X	182
Fennington	Somer	ST1929	51°3·5′	3°9·0′W	T	181,193
Fennington Weir	Somer	ST1929	51°3·5′	3°9·0′W	X	181,193
Fennis Fields Fm	Warw	SP4677	52°23·6′	1°19·0′W	FM	140
Fenn's Bank	Wrex	SJ5039	52°57·0′	2°44·2′W	T	126
Fenns Fm	Suff	TM0255	52°9·6′	0°57·6′E	FM	155
Fenn's Moss	Wrex	SJ4836	52°55·4′	2°46·0′W	X	126
Fenn's Old Hall	Wrex	SJ5039	52°57·0′	2°44·2′W	X	126
Fenn Street	Medway	TQ7975	51°27·0′	0°35·0′E	T	178
Fenn's Wood	Wrex	SJ4938	52°56·5′	2°45·1′W	F	126
Fenn's Wood	Wrex	SJ5038	52°56·5′	2°44·2′W	X	126
Fenny Bentley	Derby	SK1750	53°3·1′	1°44·4′W	T	119
Fenny Bridges	Devon	SY1198	50°46·7′	3°15·4′W	T	192,193
Fenny Castle Hill (Motte & Bailey)	Somer	ST5043	51°11·3′	2°42·5′W	X	182,183
Fenny Common	Sheff	SK2197	53°28·4′	1°40·6′W	X	110
Fenny Compton	Warw	SP4152	52°10·1′	1°23·6′W	T	151
Fenny Compton Hill	Warw	SP4151	52°9·6′	1°23·6′W	X	151
Fenny Drayton	Leic	SP3596	52°33·9′	1°28·6′W	T	140
Fenny Hill	Northnts	SP6779	52°24·5′	1°0·5′W	H	141
Fenny Rough	Worcs	SO8675	52°22·6′	2°11·9′W	F	139
Fenny Shaw	Brad	SE1143	53°53·2′	1°49·5′W	X	104
Fenny Stratford	Mil Key	SP8834	52°0·1′	0°42·7′W	T	152,165
Fennywood Fm	Ches	SJ6164	53°10·5′	2°34·6′W	FM	118
Fen Place Mill	W Susx	TQ3636	51°6·8′	0°3·0′W	X	187
Fen Plantation	Norf	TM0292	52°29·5′	0°58·9′E	F	144
Fenrother	Northum	NZ1791	55°13·0′	1°43·5′W	X	81
Fenrother Lane	Northum	NZ1691	55°13·0′	1°44·5′W	X	81
Fens	Scot Bord	NT6031	55°34·5′	2°37·6′W	X	74
Fen Side	Cambs	TL5572	52°19·7′	0°16·9′E	X	154
Fenside	Lincs	TF1746	53°0·1′	0°15·0′W	X	130
Fen Side	Lincs	TF3458	53°6·4′	0°0·5′E	T	122
Fenside	Norf	TG3721	52°44·3′	1°31·1′E	X	133,134
Fenside Fm	Lincs	TF0962	53°8·9′	0°21·8′W	FM	121
Fenstanton	Cambs	TL3168	52°17·9′	0°4·3′W	T	153
Fenstead End	Suff	TL8050	52°7·4′	0°38·2′E	T	155
Fens, The	Suff	TM4559	52°10·7′	1°35·4′E	W	156
Fen Street	Norf	TM0680	52°23·0′	1°2·0′E	T	144
Fen Street	Suff	TL9879	52°22·6′	0°54·9′E	T	144
Fen Street	Suff	TM0579	52°22·5′	1°1·1′E	T	144
Fen Street	Suff	TM1862	52°13·0′	1°11·9′E	X	156
Fenterleigh	Corn	SX0788	50°39·8′	4°43·5′W	X	190,200
Fenton	Cambs	TL3179	52°23·8′	0°4·1′W	T	142
Fenton	C of Stoke	SJ8944	52°59·8′	2°9·4′W	T	118
Fenton	Cumbr	NY5056	54°54·0′	2°46·4′W	T	86
Fenton	Lincs	SK8476	53°16·7′	0°44·0′W	T	121
Fenton	Lincs	SK8750	53°2·6′	0°41·7′W	T	121
Fenton	Northum	NT9733	55°35·7′	2°2·4′W	T	75
Fenton	Notts	SK7983	53°20·5′	0°48·4′W	X	120,121
Fenton	Pemb	SM8712	51°46·2′	5°4·8′W	X	157
Fenton	Pemb	SM9817	51°49·1′	4°55·5′W	X	157,158
Fentonadle	Corn	SX0878	50°34·4′	4°42·3′W	T	200
Fenton Barns	E Loth	NT5181	56°1·4′	2°46·7′W	T	66
Fenton Brook	Pemb	SN0017	51°49·2′	4°53·7′W	W	157,158
Fenton Fm	Devon	ST0519	50°58·0′	3°20·8′W	FM	181
Fentongollan	Corn	SW8643	50°15·1′	4°59·7′W	X	204
Fenton Gorse	Notts	SK8083	53°20·5′	0°47·5′W	F	121
Fenton Heights	D & G	NY1992	55°13·2′	3°16·0′W	H	79
Fentonhill	Northum	NT9735	55°36·8′	2°2·4′W	X	75
Fenton Ho	Northum	NT9834	55°36·2′	2°1·5′W	X	75
Fentonladock	Corn	SW8951	50°19·5′	4°57·5′W	X	200,204
Fenton Lane Head	Cumbr	NY5055	54°53·5′	2°46·3′W	X	86
Fenton Lode or Twenty Foot Drain	Cambs	TL3581	52°24·8′	0°0·5′W	W	142
Fenton Low	C of Stoke	SJ8945	53°0·4′	2°9·4′W	T	118
Fenton Manor Fm	Cambs	TL3279	52°23·8′	0°3·2′W	FM	142
Fenton Mill	Northum	NT9634	55°36·2′	2°3·4′W	X	74,75
Fenton Pits	Corn	SX0663	50°26·3′	4°43·6′W	T	200
Fenton's Fm	Essex	TL7122	51°52·4′	0°29·4′E	FM	167
Fenton's Fm	Suff	TM2667	52°15·5′	1°19·1′E	FM	156
Fenton Yet	D & G	NY1993	55°13·7′	3°16·0′W	X	79
Fentrigan	Corn	SX1990	50°41·1′	4°33·4′W	X	190
Fenwick	Cumbr	SD1689	54°17·6′	3°17·0′W	X	96
Fenwick	Donc	SE5916	53°38·5′	1°6·0′W	T	111
Fenwick	E Ayr	NS4643	55°39·6′	4°26·4′W	T	70
Fenwick	Northum	NU0640	55°39·5′	1°53·8′W	T	75
Fenwick	Northum	NZ0572	55°2·8′	1°54·9′W	T	87
Fenwick	Scot Bord	NT4711	55°23·7′	2°49·8′W	X	79
Fenwick Common	Donc	SE5815	53°37·9′	1°7·0′W	X	111
Fenwickfield	Northum	NY8573	55°3·3′	2°13·7′W	X	87
Fenwick Fm	Lincs	TF3813	52°42·1′	0°2·9′E	FM	131,142,143
Fenwick Granary	Northum	NU0740	55°39·5′	1°52·9′W	X	75
Fenwick Grange	Donc	SE6115	53°37·9′	1°4·2′W	X	111
Fenwick Hall	Donc	SE6016	53°38·5′	1°5·1′W	X	111
Fenwick's Close Fm	Northum	NZ3173	55°3·3′	1°30·5′W	FM	88
Fenwick Shield	Northum	NZ0572	55°2·8′	1°54·9′W	X	87
Fenwick Stead	Northum	NU0739	55°38·9′	1°52·9′W	X	75
Fenwick Water	E Ayr	NS4541	55°38·5′	4°27·3′W	W	70
Fenwick Wood	Northum	NU0639	55°38·9′	1°53·8′W	F	75
Feochaig	Arg & Bt	NR7613	55°21·9′	5°31·6′W	X	68,69
Feochan Mhór or River Nell	Arg & Bt	NM8825	56°22·4′	5°25·5′W	W	49
Feoch Bank Wood	S Ayr	NX2682	55°6·4′	4°43·2′W	F	76
Feoch Burn	S Ayr	NX2682	55°6·4′	4°43·2′W	W	76
Feock	Corn	SW8238	50°12·3′	5°2·9′W	T	204
Feodhan Bheag	Arg & Bt	NM9223	56°21·5′	5°21·6′W	W	49
Feoffee Farm	Suff	TM1854	52°8·7′	1°11·6′E	FM	156
Feòirlinn	Arg & Bt	NM5321	56°19·3′	5°59·2′W	X	48
Feolin Ferry	Arg & Bt	NR4469	55°51·0′	6°5·0′W	X	60,61
Feolin Fm	Arg & Bt	NR5269	55°51·3′	5°57·3′W	FM	61
Feolquoy	Orkney	HY2210	58°58·5′	3°20·9′W	X	6
Feolquoy	Orkney	HY3527	59°7·8′	3°7·7′W	X	6
Feolquoy	Orkney	HY3932	59°10·5′	3°3·5′W	X	6
Feorlan	Arg & Bt	NR6307	55°18·3′	5°43·6′W	X	68
Feorlig	Highld	NG2943	57°24·1′	6°30·2′W	T	23
Feorlin	Arg & Bt	NR9597	56°7·6′	5°17·5′W	X	55
Feorlinbreck	Arg & Bt	NS2391	56°5·0′	4°50·2′W	X	56
Feorlin Cott	Arg & Bt	NM5322	56°19·8′	5°59·3′W	X	48
Feorline	Arg & Bt	NS0396	56°7·2′	5°9·7′W	X	55
Feor Wick	Shetld	HU5173	60°26·5′	1°3·9′W	W	2,3
Ferder	Corn	SW9344	50°15·8′	4°53·9′W	X	204
Ferdre	Carm	SN6719	51°51·5′	3°55·5′W	X	159
Feren	Carm	SN5127	51°55·5′	4°9·6′W	X	146
Fereneze Hills	E Renf	NS4859	55°48·3′	4°25·1′W	X	64
Fergus	Angus	NO1968	56°48·0′	3°19·1′W	X	43
Fergushill	Cumbr	NY4266	54°59·4′	2°54·0′W	X	85
Fergushill	E Ayr	NS3940	55°37·9′	4°33·0′W	X	70
Fergushill Hall	N Ayr	NS3446	55°41·0′	4°38·0′W	X	63
Ferguslie Park	Renf	NS4664	55°50·9′	4°27·2′W	T	64
Fergus Loch	S Ayr	NS3918	55°26·0′	4°32·2′W	W	70
Ferindonald	Highld	NG6507	57°5·9′	5°52·3′W	T	32
Ferinquarrie	Highld	NG1750	57°27·4′	6°42·7′W	T	23
Ferley	Powys	SO1973	52°21·2′	3°11·0′W	X	136,148
Ferlochan	Arg & Bt	NM9140	56°30·6′	5°23·4′W	X	49
Ferly Burn	S Ayr	NX3398	55°15·1′	4°37·2′W	W	76
Fermyn Woods	Northnts	SP9685	52°27·5′	0°34·8′W	F	141
Fermyn Woods Hall	Northnts	SP9587	52°28·6′	0°35·7′W	X	141
Fern	Angus	NO4861	56°44·5′	2°50·6′W	T	44
Fern	Bucks	SU8888	51°35·3′	0°43·4′W	T	175
Fern	Shetld	HU4659	60°19·0′	1°9·5′W	X	2,3
Fernaig	Highld	NG8433	57°20·4′	5°34·9′W	X	24
Fernant	Powys	SO0744	52°5·4′	3°21·1′W	W	147,160
Fern Bank	Sol	SP2378	52°24·2′	1°39·3′W	X	139
Fern Bank	Tames	SJ9798	53°29·0′	2°2·3′W	T	109
Fernbank Fm	Kent	TQ5560	51°19·3′	0°13·9′E	FM	177,188
Fern Barrow	Poole	SZ0692	50°43·9′	1°54·5′W	A	195
Fernbeds Down	W Susx	SU7916	50°56·5′	0°52·1′W	X	197
Fernbeds Fm	W Susx	SU7915	50°56·0′	0°52·2′W	FM	197
Fernbrook Fm	Dorset	ST8324	51°1·1′	2°14·2′W	FM	183
Fernchase Manor	Kent	TQ5339	51°8·0′	0°11·6′E	X	188
Fern Dale	Derby	SK1565	53°11·2′	1°46·1′W	X	119
Ferndale	Kent	TQ5940	51°8·5′	0°16·8′E	T	188
Ferndale	Powys	SO2262	52°15·3′	3°8·2′W	X	137,148
Ferndale	Rho Cyn Taf	SS9996	51°39·5′	3°27·2′W	T	170
Fern Den	Angus	NO4861	56°44·5′	2°50·6′W	X	44
Ferndene	Worcs	SO8562	52°15·6′	2°12·8′W	X	150
Ferndown	Dorset	SU0700	50°48·2′	1°53·7′W	T	195
Ferndown Forest	Dorset	SU0306	50°51·4′	1°57·1′W	F	195
Ferne	Wilts	ST9322	51°0·1′	2°5·6′W	T	184
Ferness	Highld	NH9644	57°28·7′	3°43·6′W	T	27
Ferneybeds Fm	Northum	NZ2493	55°14·1′	1°36·9′W	FM	81
Ferneybrae	Aberd	NJ4916	57°14·2′	2°50·2′W	X	37
Ferneycastle	Scot Bord	NT8860	55°50·2′	2°11·1′W	X	67
Ferney Chesters	Northum	NZ0581	55°7·6′	1°54·9′W	X	81
Ferneycleuch	D & G	NY0382	55°7·6′	3°30·8′W	X	78
Ferneyfold	Pth & Kin	NN9721	56°22·5′	3°39·6′W	X	52,53,58
Ferney Green	Cumbr	SD4096	54°21·6′	2°55·0′W	T	96,97
Ferney Hall	Shrops	SO4377	52°23·5′	2°49·9′W	X	137,148
Ferneyhill	Scot Bord	NT7336	55°37·3′	2°25·3′W	X	74
Ferney Hough	Shrops	SJ4127	52°50·5′	2°52·2′W	X	126
Ferneylea	E Loth	NT7469	55°55·1′	2°24·5′W	X	67
Ferney Lees	Ches	SJ5461	53°8·9′	2°40·9′W	X	117
Ferneyrigg Burn	Northum	NY9683	55°8·7′	2°3·3′W	W	81
Ferneystrype	Aberd	NJ7454	57°34·8′	2°25·6′W	X	29
Fernfield	Highld	NG8527	57°17·2′	5°33·6′W	X	33
Fernfield Fm	Bucks	SP8032	51°59·1′	0°49·7′W	FM	152,165
Fern Fm	Ches	SJ8267	53°12·2′	2°15·8′W	FM	118
Fern Fm	Glos	SP2427	51°56·7′	1°38·7′W	FM	163
Fern Fm	Norf	TF5423	52°47·2′	0°17·4′E	FM	131
Fern Fm	Norf	TF6314	52°42·2′	0°25·2′E	FM	132
Fern Fm	Oxon	SU2486	51°34·6′	1°38·8′W	FM	174
Ferngill Crag	Cumbr	NY2909	54°28·5′	3°5·3′W	X	89,90
Fern Glen Fm	Sheff	SK2981	53°19·7′	1°33·5′W	FM	110
Fernhall	Heref	SO2751	52°9·4′	3°3·6′W	X	148
Fernhall Fm	Essex	TL4102	51°42·2′	0°2·8′E	FM	167
Fernham	Devon	SS6736	51°6·7′	3°53·6′W	X	180
Fernham	Oxon	SU2892	51°37·8′	1°35·3′W	T	163,174

Fernham	Oxon	SU2991	51°37·3'	1°34·5'W	T	164,174
Fernham Manor	Oxon	SU2892	51°37·8'	1°35·3'W	X	163,174
Fernhill	Bury	SD8011	53°36·0'	2°17·7'W	T	109
Fernhill	Ches	SJ8574	53°16·0'	2°13·1'W	X	118
Fernhill	C of Aber	NJ8806	57°8·9'	2°11·4'W	X	38
Fernhill	Devon	SX3398	50°45·7'	4°21·7'W	X	190
Fernhill	Devon	SX3687	50°39·8'	4°18·9'W	X	190
Fern Hill	D & G	NX9388	55°10·7'	3°40·4'W	H	78
Fern Hill	Dorset	SY3494	50°44·7'	2°55·7'W	X	193
Fern Hill	Hants	SU7933	51°5·7'	0°51·9'W	X	186
Fernhill	Heref	SO7246	52°6·9'	2°24·1'W	X	149
Fern Hill	Notts	SK6935	52°54·7'	0°58·0'W	X	129
Fern Hill	Oxon	SP4035	52°1·0'	1°24·6'W	X	151
Fern Hill	Oxon	SP5144	52°5·8'	1°14·9'W	X	151
Fern Hill	Pemb	SM9713	51°47·0'	4°56·2'W	X	157,158
Fernhill	Rho Cyn Taf	ST0399	51°41·1'	3°23·8'W	T	170
Fernhill	S Lanak	NS6159	55°48·5'	4°12·6'W	X	64
Fernhill	Staffs	SJ7522	52°47·9'	2°21·8'W	X	127
Fern Hill	Suff	TL8249	52°6·8'	0°39·9'E	T	155
Fernhill	W Susx	TQ3041	51°9·4'	0°8·1'W	T	187
Fernhill Cottage	Essex	TL4507	51°44·8'	0°6·4'E	X	167
Fern Hill Fm	Lancs	SD3646	53°54·6'	2°58·0'W	FM	102
Fern Hill Fm	Northum	NY9567	55°0·1'	2°4·3'W	FM	87
Fernhill Fm	Notts	SK6935	52°54·7'	0°58·0'W	FM	129
Fernhill Fm	S Glos	ST6185	51°34·0'	2°33·4'W	FM	172
Fernhill Fm	Somer	ST5255	51°17·8'	2°40·9'W	FM	172,182
Fernhill Fm	Warw	SP2670	52°19·9'	1°36·7'W	FM	140
Fernhill Fm	Worcs	SP0046	52°7·0'	1°59·6'W	FM	150
Fernhill Gate	Bolton	SD6907	53°33·8'	2°27·7'W	T	109
Fernhill Hall	Shrops	SJ3232	52°53·1'	3°0·2'W	X	126
Fernhill Heath	Worcs	SO8659	52°14·0'	2°11·9'W	T	150
Fernhill Ho	Devon	SX7149	50°19·8'	3°48·4'W	X	202
Fernhill Lodge	Northnts	SP6055	52°11·6'	1°6·9'W	X	152
Fernhill Park	Brackn	SU9272	51°26·6'	0°40·2'W	X	175
Fernhill Wood	Oxon	SP6504	51°44·1'	1°3·1'W	F	164,165
Fern Ho	Derby	SK0571	53°14·4'	1°55·1'W	X	119
Fernhurst	W Susx	SU8928	51°2·9'	0°43·4'W	T	186,197
Fernicombe	Wilts	ST8747	51°13·6'	2°10·8'W	X	183
Fernie	Fife	NO3115	56°19·6'	3°6·5'W	T	59
Fernie	Heref	SO7054	52°11·2'	2°25·9'W	X	149
Ferniebrae	Aberd	NJ7126	57°19·7'	2°28·4'W	X	38
Ferniebrae	Aberd	NJ9957	57°36·4'	2°0·5'W	X	30
Ferniebrae	Aberd	NO8280	56°54·9'	2°17·3'W	X	45
Fernie Castle	Fife	NO3114	56°19·1'	3°6·5'W	A	59
Ferniefiatt	Aberd	NO8577	56°53·3'	2°14·3'W	X	45
Ferniegair	S Lanak	NS7354	55°46·0'	4°1·0'W	T	64
Fernie Grain Sit Burn	Scot Bord	NT3947	55°43·0'	2°57·8'W	W	73
Ferniehall Cotts	Fife	NO3915	56°19·7'	2°58·7'W	X	59
Ferniehaugh	Scot Bord	NT0949	55°43·8'	3°26·5'W	X	72
Ferniehirst	Scot Bord	NT4441	55°39·8'	2°53·0'W	T	73
Ferniehirst Castle	Scot Bord	NT6517	55°27·0'	2°32·8'W	A	80
Ferniehirst Hill	Scot Bord	NT4241	55°39·8'	2°54·9'W	H	73
Fernielea	Moray	NJ0653	57°33·7'	3°33·8'W	X	27
Fernieshaw	N Lanak	NS8159	55°48·8'	3°53·5'W	X	65,72
Fernilea	Highld	NG3634	57°19·5'	6°22·7'W	X	32
Fernilee	Derby	SK0178	53°18·2'	1°58·7'W	T	119
Fernilee Resr	Derby	SK0177	53°17·6'	1°58·7'W	W	119
Fernises Fm	Roch	SD8412	53°36·5'	2°14·1'W	FM	109
Fernking	Moray	NJ4457	57°36·2'	2°55·8'W	X	28
Fernlea Fm	Devon	SS3903	50°48·5'	4°16·7'W	FM	190
Fernlee	Ches	SJ9469	53°13·3'	2°5·0'W	X	118
Fernleigh Fm	Cambs	TL5057	52°11·7'	0°12·1'E	FM	154
Fernleigh Fm	Norf	TM1688	52°27·1'	1°11·1'E	FM	144,156
Fernley Fm	Glos	ST7893	51°38·4'	2°18·7'W	FM	162,172
Fernoch	Arg & Bt	NR8688	56°2·5'	5°25·7'W	X	55
Ferns Fm	Bucks	SP8401	51°42·3'	0°46·7'W	FM	165
Ferns of Cloquhat	Pth & Kin	NO1552	56°39·4'	3°22·7'W	X	53
Fernsplatt	Corn	SW7641	50°13·8'	5°8·1'W	T	204
Ferns, The	Staffs	SK0863	53°10·1'	1°52·4'W	X	119
Fern, The	Shrops	SO6172	52°20·9'	2°34·0'W	X	138
Ferntower	Pth & Kin	NN8723	56°23·4'	3°49·4'W	X	52,58
Ferntown Hill	D & G	NX0557	54°52·4'	5°1·9'W	H	82
Fern Villa	Highld	NG8823	57°15·2'	5°30·4'W	X	33
Fernwood Fm	Warw	SP2570	52°19·9'	1°37·6'W	FM	140
Fernworthy	Devon	SX5187	50°40·1'	4°6·1'W	X	191
Fernworthy Down	Devon	SX5186	50°39·5'	4°6·1'W	X	191,201
Fernworthy Forest	Devon	SX6583	50°38·1'	3°54·2'W	F	191
Fernworthy Reservoir	Devon	SX6684	50°38·7'	3°53·3'W	W	191
Ferny Ball	Somer	SS8035	51°6·3'	3°42·5'W	X	181
Fernybank	Angus	NO5378	56°53·7'	2°45·8'W	X	44
Ferny Barrows	Dorset	SY8681	50°37·9'	2°11·5'W	A	194
Fernybrae	Aberd	NJ7034	57°24·0'	2°29·5'W	X	29
Fernycombe Beach	Devon	SX6146	50°18·1'	3°56·7'W	X	202
Ferny Common	Heref	SO3651	52°9·5'	2°55·7'W	X	148,149
Ferny Crofts	Hants	SU3605	50°50·8'	1°28·9'W	X	196
Fernydale	Derby	SK0867	53°12·2'	1°52·4'W	X	119
Fernyfield	Moray	NJ3064	57°39·9'	3°9·9'W	X	28
Fernyford	Staffs	SK0661	53°9·0'	1°54·2'W	X	119
Ferny Glen	Pemb	SM8822	51°51·6'	5°4·3'W	X	157
Ferny Heys	Ches	SJ6340	52°57·6'	2°32·6'W	X	118
Ferny Hill	Enf	TQ2798	51°40·2'	0°9·4'W	X	166,176
Ferny Hill	Scot Bord	NT1912	55°24·0'	3°16·3'W	H	79
Ferny Hill	Scot Bord	NT5436	55°37·2'	2°43·4'W	X	73
Ferny Hill	Staffs	SK0052	53°4·2'	1°59·6'W	H	119
Ferny Hole	Derby	SK0795	53°27·3'	1°53·3'W	X	110
Fernyhole Point	Devon	SX6738	50°13·9'	3°51·5'W	X	202
Fernyhowe	Aberd	NJ4403	57°7·1'	2°55·0'W	X	37
Ferny Knoll	Lancs	SD4703	53°31·5'	2°47·6'W	X	108
Ferny Knowe	Northum	NY6289	55°11·9'	2°35·4'W	X	80
Fernyknowle	Staffs	SK1062	53°9·5'	1°50·6'W	X	119
Fernyleas	Shrops	SJ5433	52°53·8'	2°40·6'W	X	126
Ferny Ness	E Loth	NT4377	55°59·2'	2°54·4'W	X	66
Fernypits	Pemb	SM9804	51°42·1'	4°55·0'W	X	157,158
Fernyrig	Scot Bord	NT7940	55°39·4'	2°19·6'W	X	74
Fernyrig Cott	Scot Bord	NT7840	55°39·4'	2°20·5'W	X	74
Ferny Side	Derby	SK1291	53°25·2'	1°48·8'W	X	110
Ferrach Burn	D & G	NX3976	55°3·4'	4°30·8'W	W	77
Ferramas	N Eil	NF9369	57°36·7'	7°8·0'W	X	18
Ferrar	Aberd	NO4898	57°4·5'	2°51·0'W	X	37,44
Ferrels Wood	Northnts	SP9394	52°32·4'	0°37·3'W	F	141

Ferrensby	N Yks	SE3660	54°2·3'	1°26·6'W	T	99
Ferrensby Lodge	N Yks	SE3660	54°2·3'	1°26·6'W	X	99
Ferretfold	Aberd	NJ6501	57°6·2'	2°34·2'W	X	38
Ferret of Keith Moor	N Ayr	NS2367	55°52·1'	4°49·3'W	X	63
Ferrets' Hill	Norf	TF6716	52°43·2'	0°28·8'E	X	132
Ferriby Sluice	N Lincs	SE9720	53°40·3'	0°31·5'W	X	106,112
Ferrier Sand	Norf	TF6233	52°52·4'	0°24·8'E	X	132
Ferriers, The	Essex	TL8933	51°58·0'	0°45·5'E	X	168
Ferring	W Susx	TQ0902	50°48·7'	0°26·8'W	T	198
Ferris Court Fm	Glos	SO8805	51°44·8'	2°10·0'W	FM	162
Ferriser	Ches	SJ9770	53°13·9'	2°2·3'W	X	118
Ferrises	W Berks	SU5868	51°24·7'	1°9·6'W	X	174
Ferrowie	Angus	NO3079	56°54·1'	3°8·5'W	H	44
Ferry Br	Dorset	SY6676	50°35·2'	2°28·4'W	X	194
Ferry Br	E Susx	TQ9017	50°55·5'	0°42·6'E	X	189
Ferrybrae	Highld	NH5245	57°28·5'	4°27·6'W	X	26
Ferrybridge	Wakf	SE4724	53°42·9'	1°16·9'W	T	105
Ferrybridge Service Area	Wakf	SE4822	53°41·8'	1°16·0'W	X	105
Ferrybridge Service Area	Wakf	SE4822	53°41·8'	1°16·0'W	X	105
Ferry Burrows	Cambs	TL3882	52°25·3'	0°2·2'E	X	142,143
Ferry Cliff	Suff	TM2748	52°5·2'	1°19·2'E	X	169
Ferryden	Angus	NO7156	56°41·9'	2°28·0'W	T	54
Ferryfield of Carpow	Pth & Kin	NO1918	56°21·1'	3°18·2'W	X	58
Ferry Fm	Cambs	TF4514	52°42·5'	0°9·2'E	FM	131
Ferry Fm	Carm	SN3511	51°46·6'	4°23·1'W	FM	159
Ferry Fm	Ches	SJ4162	53°9·4'	2°52·5'W	FM	117
Ferry Fm	Kent	TQ9428	51°1·3'	0°46·4'E	FM	189
Ferry Fm	Lincs	TF1550	53°2·3'	0°16·7'W	FM	121
Ferry Fm	N Lincs	TA1123	53°41·7'	0°18·7'W	FM	107,113
Ferry Fm	Norf	TF7300	52°34·4'	0°33·6'E	FM	143
Ferry Fm	Norf	TL6193	52°30·9'	0°22·8'E	FM	143
Ferry Fm	Suff	TM4454	52°8·0'	1°34·3'E	FM	156
Ferry Fm	Warw	SP4273	52°21·4'	1°22·6'W	FM	140
Ferrygate	E Loth	NT5284	56°3·0'	2°45·8'W	X	66
Ferry Hill	Cambs	TL3883	52°25·9'	0°2·2'E	T	142,143
Ferryhill	C of Aber	NJ9304	57°7·9'	2°6·5'W	T	38
Ferryhill	Durham	NZ2932	54°41·2'	1°32·6'W	T	93
Ferry Hill	Lincs	TF0871	53°13·7'	0°22·5'W	X	121
Ferry Hill	Pemb	SN0006	51°43·3'	4°53·4'W	X	157,158
Ferryhill Plantn	Renf	NS4072	55°55·1'	4°33·2'W	F	64
Ferry Hills	Fife	NT1281	56°1·1'	3°24·3'W	X	65
Ferryhill Station	Durham	NZ3031	54°40·6'	1°31·7'W	T	93
Ferry Ho	Arg & Bt	NR7558	55°46·0'	5°34·8'W	X	62
Ferry Ho	Peterb	TL1498	52°34·3'	0°18·7'W	X	142
Ferry Ho	W Susx	SZ8596	50°45·7'	0°47·3'W	X	197
Ferry Ho, The	Cumbr	SD3995	54°21·1'	2°55·9'W	X	96,97
Ferry Inn, The	Kent	TR0165	51°21·1'	0°53·6'E	X	178
Ferry Lane Fm	Flint	SJ3766	53°11·5'	2°56·2'W	FM	117
Ferry Lane Fm	Notts	SK8262	53°9·2'	0°46·0'W	FM	121
Ferry Links	Highld	NH8196	57°56·5'	4°0·1'W	X	21
Ferry Marshes	Kent	TQ9069	51°23·5'	0°44·3'E	X	178
Ferry Meadows Country Park	Peterb	TL1497	52°33·8'	0°18·7'W	X	142
Ferrymuir	Fife	NO3613	56°18·6'	3°1·6'W	X	59
Ferry Nab	Cumbr	SD3795	54°21·0'	2°57·7'W	X	96,97
Ferry Point	Highld	NH7385	57°50·5'	4°7·9'W	X	21
Ferry Point	Orkney	HY4014	59°0·8'	3°2·2'W	X	6
Ferryside	Carm	SN3610	51°46·1'	4°22·2'W	T	159
Ferryton	Highld	NH6866	57°40·1'	4°12·3'W	X	21
Ferryton Point	Highld	NH6867	57°40·7'	4°12·3'W	X	21
Fersfield	Norf	TM0683	52°24·6'	1°2·1'E	T	144
Fersfield Common	Norf	TM0684	52°25·1'	1°2·2'E	X	144
Fersfield Hall Fm	Norf	TM0682	52°24·1'	1°2·1'E	FM	144
Fersfield Lodge	Norf	TM0584	52°25·2'	1°1·3'E	X	144
Fersit	Highld	NN3578	56°52·1'	4°42·0'W	T	41
Fersness	Orkney	HY5333	59°11·1'	2°48·9'W	X	5,6
Fers Ness	Orkney	HY5334	59°11·7'	2°48·9'W	X	5,6
Fersness Bay	Orkney	HY5434	59°11·7'	2°47·8'W	W	5,6
Fersness Hill	Orkney	HY5332	59°10·6'	2°48·9'W	H	5,6
Ferter	S Ayr	NX3087	55°9·1'	4°39·7'W	X	76
Fervey	Aberd	NJ8151	57°33·2'	2°18·6'W	X	29,30
Feshiebridge	Highld	NH8504	57°7·0'	3°53·5'W	T	35,36
Festival Gardens	Liv	SJ3686	53°22·3'	2°57·3'W	X	108
Fetcham	Surrey	TQ1455	51°17·2'	0°21·5'W	T	187
Fetcham Downs	Surrey	TQ1554	51°16·6'	0°20·7'W	X	187
Fetch Hill	Shrops	SJ5601	52°36·5'	2°38·6'W	H	126
Fethaland	Shetld	HU3793	60°37·4'	1°18·9'W	X	1,2
Fethan Hill	Scot Bord	NT3032	55°34·9'	3°6·2'W	H	73
Fetlar	Shetld	HU6291	60°36·1'	0°51·6'W	X	1,2
Fetterangus	Aberd	NJ9850	57°32·7'	2°1·5'W	T	30
Fettercairn	Aberd	NO6473	56°51·1'	2°35·0'W	T	45
Fettercairn Ho	Aberd	NO6573	56°51·1'	2°34·0'W	X	45
Fetterdale	Fife	NO4725	56°25·1'	2°51·1'W	X	54,59
Fetteresso Castle	Aberd	NO8485	56°57·6'	2°15·3'W	A	45
Fetteresso Forest	Aberd	NO7787	56°58·7'	2°22·3'W	F	45
Fetterletter	Aberd	NJ8038	57°26·2'	2°19·5'W	X	29,30
Fetterlocks Fm	Worcs	SO7563	52°16·1'	2°21·6'W	FM	138,150
Fetternear Ho	Aberd	NJ7217	57°14·8'	2°27·4'W	X	38
Fetternear House & Bishop's Palace	Aberd	NJ7217	57°14·8'	2°27·4'W	A	38
Fettes	Highld	NH5850	57°31·3'	4°21·8'W	X	26
Feu	Aberd	NK0330	57°21·9'	1°56·6'W	X	30
Feuars Hill	Scot Bord	NT3225	55°31·1'	3°4·2'W	H	73
Feuar's Moor	Scot Bord	NT6956	55°48·0'	2°29·2'W	X	67,74
Feuars Ward	N Ayr	NS2956	55°46·3'	4°43·1'W	X	63
Feuchaw Burn	D & G	NS7205	55°19·6'	4°0·6'W	W	71,77
Feufield	S Lanak	NS9733	55°35·0'	3°37·6'W	X	72
Feur Loch	Arg & Bt	NR7882	55°59·0'	5°33·1'W	W	55
Feur-loch	Highld	NC1306	58°0·5'	5°9·4'W	W	15
Feur-loch	Highld	NC1905	58°0·1'	5°3·3'W	W	15
Feur-loch	Highld	NC1906	58°0·6'	5°3·3'W	W	15
Feur-loch	Highld	NC2004	57°59·6'	5°2·2'W	W	15
Feur Loch	Highld	NC2613	58°4·6'	4°56·6'W	W	15
Feur Loch	Highld	NC2959	58°29·4'	4°55·5'W	W	9
Feur Loch	Highld	NC3731	58°14·5'	4°46·1'W	W	16
Fèur Lochain	Arg & Bt	NR2569	55°50·4'	6°23·1'W	W	60
Feur Lochan	Arg & Bt	NM9011	56°15·0'	5°22·9'W	W	55
Feur Lochan	Arg & Bt	NR7681	55°58·4'	5°35·0'W	W	55
Feur Lochan	Arg & Bt	NR8964	55°49·6'	5°21·7'W	X	62
Feur Lochan	Highld	NC2441	58°19·6'	4°59·9'W	W	9

Feur-lochan	Highld	NG4060	57°33·6'	6°20·4'W	W	23
Feur-lochan	Highld	NH4083	57°48·7'	4°41·1'W	W	20
Feur-lochan	Highld	NH4372	57°42·9'	4°37·7'W	W	20
Feur-lochan	Highld	NH4477	57°45·6'	4°36·9'W	W	20
Feur Lochan	Pth & Kin	NN7068	56°47·4'	4°7·2'W	W	42
Feur Lochanan	Highld	NH1696	57°55·2'	5°5·9'W	W	20
Feur Lochon	Stir	NN5132	56°27·7'	4°24·6'W	W	51
Feur Mór	Highld	NH4282	57°48·3'	4°39·1'W	X	20
Feuside Hill	N Ayr	NS2559	55°47·8'	4°47·1'W	H	63
Fewcott	Oxon	SP5327	51°56·6'	1°13·3'W	T	164
Fewhurst Fm	W Susx	TQ1024	51°0·5'	0°25·5'W	FM	198
Fewler Gate Wood	N Yks	SE9491	54°18·6'	0°32·9'W	F	94,101
Fewling Stones	Cumbr	NY5111	54°29·8'	2°45·0'W	H	90
Fewston	N Yks	SE1954	53°59·1'	1°42·2'W	T	104
Fewston Bents	N Yks	SE1954	53°59·1'	1°42·2'W	T	104
Fewston Reservoir	N Yks	SE1854	53°59·1'	1°43·1'W	W	104
Ffagnallt	Flint	SJ1869	53°12·9'	3°13·3'W	X	116
Ffairfach	Carm	SN6221	51°52·5'	3°59·9'W	T	159
Ffair-Rhos	Cered	SN7468	52°18·0'	3°50·5'W	T	135,147
Ffaldau	Rho Cyn Taf	SS9997	51°40·0'	3°27·2'W	X	170
Ffald Fm	V of Glam	ST0177	51°29·2'	3°25·2'W	FM	170
Ffaldybrenin	Carm	SN6344	52°4·9'	3°59·6'W	T	146
Ffarmers	Carm	SN6544	52°4·9'	3°57·8'W	T	146
Ffarm-fach	Carm	SN3134	51°59·0'	4°27·3'W	X	145
Ffawydden	Powys	SO2525	51°55·3'	3°5·0'W	X	161
Ffawyddog	Brig	SS9189	51°35·6'	3°34·0'W	X	170
Ffawyddog	Powys	SO2018	51°51·5'	3°9·3'W	T	161
Fferam	I of Angl	SH3673	53°14·0'	4°27·0'W	X	114
Fferam	I of Angl	SH5576	53°15·9'	4°10·0'W	X	114,115
Fferam Bailey	I of Angl	SH4170	53°12·4'	4°22·4'W	X	114,115
Fferam-fawr	I of Angl	SH3371	53°12·8'	4°29·7'W	X	114
Fferam Fawr	I of Angl	SH4372	53°13·6'	4°20·7'W	X	114,115
Fferam Paradwys	I of Angl	SH4270	53°12·5'	4°21·5'W	X	114,115
Fferam Rhosydd	I of Angl	SH3972	53°13·5'	4°24·3'W	X	114
Fferam-uchaf	I of Angl	SH3686	53°21·0'	4°27·4'W	X	114
Fferm	Conwy	SH8368	53°12·0'	3°44·7'W	X	116
Fferm	Denb	SJ0176	53°16·5'	3°28·7'W	X	116
Fferm	Denb	SJ1058	53°6·9'	3°20·3'W	X	116
Fferm	Flint	SJ2173	53°15·1'	3°10·6'W	X	117
Fferm	Flint	SJ2760	53°8·2'	3°5·1'W	A	117
Fferm	Powys	SJ1917	52°44·9'	3°11·6'W	X	125
Fferm	Powys	SO1345	52°6·0'	3°15·8'W	X	148
Fferm Felinfach	Carm	SN5646	52°5·9'	4°5·7'W	X	146
Fferm-y-Capel	Pemb	SN1529	51°56·0'	4°41·1'W	X	145,158
Fferm y Cwrt	Cered	SN4948	52°6·8'	4°11·9'W	X	146
Ffernant	Conwy	SH8975	53°15·9'	3°39·4'W	X	116
Ffernant	Powys	SH8301	52°35·9'	3°43·2'W	W	135,136
Fferwd	Conwy	SH9563	53°9·5'	3°33·8'W	X	116
Ffestiniog	Gwyn	SH7041	52°57·3'	3°55·7'W	T	124
Ffestiniog Railway	Gwyn	SH6340	52°56·6'	4°1·9'W	X	124
Ffestiniog Railway	Gwyn	SH6845	52°59·4'	3°57·6'W	X	115
Ffinnant	Carm	SN5019	51°51·2'	4°10·3'W	X	159
Ffinnant	Carm	SN5531	51°57·8'	4°6·2'W	X	146
Ffinnant	Powys	SJ1102	52°36·8'	3°18·5'W	X	136
Ffinnant	Powys	SJ2021	52°47·1'	3°10·8'W	X	126
Ffinnant	Powys	SN9791	52°30·7'	3°30·7'W	X	136
Ffinnant Isaf	Powys	SJ0701	52°36·2'	3°22·0'W	X	136
Ffinnant-isaf	Powys	SN9731	51°58·3'	3°29·6'W	X	160
Fflôs	Powys	SO2198	52°34·7'	3°9·6'W	X	137
Ffoesidoes	Powys	SO2265	52°16·9'	3°8·2'W	X	137,148
Ffoeslaprey	Powys	SO1673	52°21·2'	3°13·6'W	X	136,148
Ffontygari Bay	V of Glam	ST0565	51°22·8'	3°21·5'W	W	170
Fforch Ceulan	Carm	SN7520	51°52·1'	3°48·5'W	X	160
Fforch-dwm	Nth Pt Talb	SS8297	51°39·8'	3°42·0'W	X	170
Fforch EgelFm	Nth Pt Talb	SN7209	51°46·1'	3°50·9'W	X	160
Fforch-orky	Rho Cyn Taf	SS9598	51°40·5'	3°30·7'W	X	170
Fforch-wen	Brig	SS9191	51°36·7'	3°34·1'W	X	170
Ffordd	Carm	SN3412	51°47·2'	4°24·0'W	X	159
Ffordd	Flint	SJ2168	53°12·4'	3°10·6'W	X	117
Ffordd Cotts	V of Glam	ST0975	51°28·2'	3°18·2'W	X	171
Ffordd Ddu	Gwyn	SH6513	52°42·1'	3°59·5'W	X	124
Ffordd Deg	I of Angl	SH5778	53°17·0'	4°8·3'W	X	114,115
Ffordd fawr	Powys	SO1939	52°2·8'	3°10·5'W	X	161
Ffordd Gefn	Powys	SJ0323	52°48·0'	3°25·9'W	X	125
Ffordd Gôch	Powys	SJ0722	52°47·5'	3°22·3'W	X	125
Ffordd-hir	Flint	SJ2164	53°10·3'	3°10·5'W	X	117
Ffordd-las	Conwy	SH9267	53°11·6'	3°36·6'W	X	116
Ffordd-lâs	Denb	SJ0957	53°6·4'	3°21·2'W	X	116
Ffordd-las	Denb	SJ1264	53°10·2'	3°18·6'W	T	116
Ffordd Las	Flint	SJ1276	53°16·7'	3°18·8'W	X	116
Fforddlas	Powys	SO2038	52°2·3'	3°9·6'W	T	161
Ffordd-las Bach Fm	Conwy	SH9575	53°15·9'	3°34·1'W	FM	116
Ffordd-las-fawr	Powys	SO2623	51°54·3'	3°4·1'W	X	161
Ffordd-las Fawr Fm	Conwy	SH9575	53°15·9'	3°34·1'W	FM	116
Ffordd y Bryniau (Ridgeway Walk)	Card	ST1083	51°32·6'	3°17·5'W	X	171
Ffordd y Bryniau (Ridgeway Walk)	Rho Cyn Taf	ST0084	51°33·0'	3°26·1'W	X	170
Ffordd y Bryniau (Ridgeway Walk)	Rho Cyn Taf	ST0085	51°33·5'	3°26·2'W	X	170
Ffordd-y-Dre	Flint	SJ2075	53°16·2'	3°11·6'W	X	117
Ffordd-y-Gyfraith	Brig	SS8684	51°32·8'	3°38·3'W	T	170
Fforest	Carm	SN4214	51°48·4'	4°17·1'W	X	159
Fforest	Carm	SN5804	51°43·2'	4°3·0'W	T	159
Fforest	Carm	SN7638	52°1·8'	3°48·1'W	H	146,160
Fforest	Conwy	SH9462	53°8·9'	3°34·7'W	X	116
Fforest	Pemb	SN0239	52°1·1'	4°52·7'W	X	145,157
Fforest	Powys	SN9252	52°9·6'	3°34·3'W	X	147
Fforest	Powys	SN9490	52°30·1'	3°33·3'W	X	136
Fforest	Powys	SO0541	52°3·8'	3°22·8'W	X	147,160
Fforest Cerdin	Cered	SN3945	52°5·0'	4°20·6'W	X	145
Fforest Fach	Powys	SN9026	51°55·5'	3°35·6'W	H	160
Fforest Fach	Powys	SO1967	52°17·9'	3°10·9'W	F	136,148
Fforest-fach	Swan	SS6295	51°38·5'	3°59·3'W	T	159
Fforest-fawr	V of Glam	ST0179	51°30·3'	3°25·2'W	X	170
Fforest Fm	Carm	SN2216	51°49·1'	4°34·6'W	FM	158
Fforest Fm	Nth Pt Talb	SN7700	51°41·4'	3°46·4'W	FM	170
Fforest Fm	Powys	SO1054	52°10·9'	3°18·6'W	FM	148
Fforest Gôch	Nth Pt Talb	SN7401	51°41·9'	3°49·0'W	T	170
Fforest Gwladys	Caer	ST1299	51°41·2'	3°16·0'W	X	171

Fforest Inn	Powys	SO1758	52°13·1′	3°12·5′W	X	148
Fforest Isaf	Rho Cyn Taf	ST0697	51°40·1′	3°21·2′W	X	170
Fforest-newydd	Swan	SN6301	51°41·7′	3°58·5′W	X	159
Fforest Uchaf	Rho Cyn Taf	ST0788	51°35·2′	3°20·2′W	X	170
Ffos	Brig	SS8791	51°36·6′	3°37·5′W	X	170
Ffos	Cered	SN6867	52°17·4′	3°55·7′W	X	135
Ffosddu	Carm	SN3517	51°49·9′	4°23·3′W	X	159
Ffosddufach	Carm	SN1922	51°52·3′	4°37·4′W	X	145,158
Ffos Dyrysienog	Pemb	SN1034	51°58·6′	4°45·6′W	W	145
Ffos-Esgob	Cered	SN4144	52°4·5′	4°18·8′W	X	146
Ffos-fâch	Carm	SS5599	51°40·5′	4°5·4′W	X	159
Ffosffald	Cered	SN5047	52°6·3′	4°11·0′W	X	146
Ffosgoy	Cered	SN6568	52°17·9′	3°58·4′W	X	135
Ffoshelyg	Carm	SN4427	51°55·4′	4°15·7′W	X	146
Ffoshelyg	Cered	SN4045	52°5·1′	4°19·7′W	X	146
Ffoshelyg	Cered	SN6467	52°17·3′	3°59·2′W	X	135
Ffoshelyg-uchaf	Cered	SN4052	52°8·8′	4°19·9′W	X	146
Ffos-lâs	Cered	SN5675	52°21·5′	4°6·5′W	X	135
Ffoslas	Cered	SN6465	52°16·2′	3°59·2′W	X	135
Ffoslas	Cered	SN6777	52°22·7′	3°56·8′W	X	135
Ffosrhys	Powys	SO1832	51°59·1′	3°11·3′W	X	161
Ffos-Sana	Carm	SN3532	51°58·0′	4°23·7′W	X	145
Ffostrasol	Cered	SN3747	52°6·1′	4°22·4′W	T	145
Ffostyll	Powys	SO1734	52°0·1′	3°12·2′W	X	161
Ffoswinau	Carm	SN2022	51°52·3′	4°36·5′W	X	145,158
Ffos-y-bar	Powys	SN9134	51°59·9′	3°34·9′W	X	160
Ffos-y-bontbren	Cered	SN6173	52°20·5′	4°2·0′W	X	135
Ffos-y-ffin	Cered	SN4460	52°13·2′	4°16·6′W	T	146
Ffos-y-ffin	Cered	SN5948	52°7·0′	4°3·2′W	X	146
Ffos y Ffwdan	Powys	SN8882	52°25·7′	3°38·4′W	X	135,136
Ffosyficar	Pemb	SN2341	52°2·6′	4°34·5′W	X	145
Ffos-y-frân	Merth Tyd	SO0605	51°44·4′	3°21·3′W	T	160
Ffos-y-gaseg	Carm	SN4927	51°55·5′	4°11·4′W	X	146
Ffosygaseg	Cered	SN5153	52°9·6′	4°10·3′W	X	146
Ffosygerwn	Powys	SN9631	51°58·3′	3°30·4′W	X	160
Ffosygest	Carm	SN4424	51°53·8′	4°15·6′W	X	159
Ffos-y-go	Wrex	SJ3054	53°5·0′	3°2·3′W	T	117
Ffosygrafel	Cered	SN6186	52°27·5′	4°2·4′W	X	135
Ffos-y-maen	Carm	SN4127	51°55·4′	4°18·3′W	X	146
Ffosyrhyddod	Powys	SN8949	52°7·9′	3°36·9′W	X	147
Ffos-yr-odyn	Cered	SN6263	52°15·1′	4°0·9′W	X	146
Ffos-y-wern	Powys	SO1014	51°49·3′	3°18·0′W	X	161
Ffrainc	Flint	SJ2355	53°5·4′	3°8·6′W	X	117
Ffridd	Gwyn	SH2732	52°51·7′	4°33·8′W	X	123
Ffridd	Gwyn	SH5152	53°2·9′	4°13·0′W	X	115
Ffridd	Gwyn	SH8211	52°41·3′	3°44·3′W	X	124,125
Ffridd	Powys	SJ0411	52°41·5′	3°24·8′W	X	125
Ffridd	Powys	SO1595	52°33·0′	3°14·8′W	T	136
Ffridd	Powys	SO2871	52°20·2′	3°3·0′W	H	137,148
Ffridd Braich-llwyd	Gwyn	SH9013	52°42·5′	3°37·3′W	X	125
Ffridd Bryn-coch	Gwyn	SH6106	52°38·3′	4°2·9′W	X	124
Ffridd-bryn-côch	Gwyn	SH7028	52°50·3′	3°55·4′W	X	124
Ffridd Bryn-glas	Gwyn	SH6303	52°36·7′	4°1·0′W	X	135
Ffridd Bryn-gogledd	Powys	SJ0317	52°44·8′	3°25·8′W	H	125
Ffridd Brynhelen	Conwy	SH9651	53°3·0′	3°32·7′W	H	116
Ffridd Bwlch-lluan	Powys	SH7806	52°38·5′	3°47·8′W	H	124
Ffridd Cae-penfras	Powys	SJ0014	52°43·1′	3°28·4′W	H	125
Ffridd Cae'rfelin	Powys	SH7907	52°39·1′	3°46·9′W	X	124
Ffridd Cefn-isaf	Gwyn	SN6097	52°33·4′	4°3·5′W	H	135
Ffridd Celynnog	Gwyn	SH8019	52°45·6′	3°46·3′W	X	124,125
Ffridd Cocyn	Gwyn	SH6204	52°37·2′	4°1·9′W	X	135
Ffridd Coed	Gwyn	SH7810	52°40·7′	3°47·9′W	H	124
Ffridd Cwmhesgyn	Gwyn	SH8742	52°58·1′	3°40·6′W	X	124,125
Ffridd Ddu	Gwyn	SH6571	53°13·4′	4°0·9′W	X	115
Ffridd Dôl-y-maen	Powys	SH9314	52°43·0′	3°34·6′W	X	125
Ffridd Dôl-y-moch	Gwyn	SH7733	52°53·1′	3°49·3′W	X	124
Ffridd Fach	Powys	SJ0222	52°47·4′	3°26·8′W	H	125
Ffridd Faldwyn	Powys	SO2197	52°34·1′	3°9·5′W	X	137
Ffridd Faldwyn (Fort)	Powys	SO2197	52°34·1′	3°9·5′W	A	137
Ffridd Fawr	Denb	SJ0560	53°8·0′	3°24·8′W	H	116
Ffriddfawr	Powys	SH8503	52°37·0′	3°41·5′W	X	135,136
Ffridd Fawr	Powys	SH9403	52°37·1′	3°33·5′W	X	136
Ffridd Fawr	Powys	SH9522	52°47·4′	3°33·0′W	X	125
Ffriddfedw	Gwyn	SH6133	52°52·8′	4°3·5′W	X	124
Ffridd Fm	Gwyn	SH6130	52°51·2′	4°3·5′W	FM	124
Ffridd Ganol	Powys	SH9208	52°39·8′	3°35·4′W	X	125
Ffridd-goch	Gwyn	SH2434	52°52·7′	4°36·5′W	X	123
Ffridd-gôch	Gwyn	SH7423	52°47·6′	3°51·7′W	X	124
Ffridd Goch	Powys	SH9510	52°40·9′	3°32·8′W	X	125
Ffridd Gulcwm	Gwyn	SH8314	52°42·9′	3°43·5′W	X	124,125
Ffridd-isaf	Gwyn	SH5752	53°3·0′	4°7·6′W	X	115
Ffridd Isaf	Powys	SO0195	52°32·9′	3°27·2′W	X	136
Ffridd Llamnerch	Powys	SJ1422	52°47·6′	3°16·1′W	X	125
Ffridd Llwydiarth	Powys	SJ0615	52°43·7′	3°23·1′W	X	125
Ffridd Lwyd	Gwyn	SH6834	52°53·5′	3°57·3′W	F	124
Ffridd-lwyd	Gwyn	SH8628	52°50·5′	3°41·2′W	X	124,125
Ffridd Mathrafal	Powys	SJ1110	52°41·1′	3°18·6′W	X	125
Ffridd Newydd	Cered	SN7090	52°29·8′	3°54·5′W	X	135
Ffridd Newydd	Powys	SN8589	52°29·5′	3°41·2′W	X	135,136
Ffriddog	Conwy	SH8560	53°7·7′	3°42·7′W	X	116
Ffridd Rhosfarch	Gwyn	SH6802	52°36·2′	3°56·6′W	X	135
Ffridd Rhosygarreg	Powys	SN8094	52°32·1′	3°45·8′W	X	135,136
Ffridd-Rhyd-Ddu	Powys	SH9603	52°37·1′	3°31·8′W	X	136
Ffridd Trawsgoed	Gwyn	SH8333	52°53·1′	3°43·9′W	X	124,125
Ffridd Ucha	Conwy	SH8265	53°10·4′	3°45·5′W	X	116
Ffridd Uchaf	Gwyn	SH5751	53°2·5′	4°7·6′W	X	115
Ffridd Uchaf	Powys	SH8000	52°35·3′	3°45·9′W	X	135,136
Ffridd-wen	Gwyn	SH2434	52°52·7′	4°36·5′W	X	123
Ffridd Wydd-afon	Powys	SH9524	52°48·4′	3°33·1′W	X	125
Ffridd Wyllt	Powys	SH7900	52°35·3′	3°46·8′W	H	135
Ffridd y Bwlch	Gwyn	SH7048	53°1·1′	3°55·9′W	X	115
Ffridd y Coed	Gwyn	SH8338	52°55·8′	3°44·0′W	X	124,125
Ffridd y Fawnog	Gwyn	SH8538	52°55·9′	3°42·3′W	X	124,125
Ffridd y Fedw	Conwy	SH8346	53°0·2′	3°44·2′W	X	116
Ffridd-y-foel	Conwy	SH8754	53°4·5′	3°40·8′W	H	116
Ffridd-y-foel	Gwyn	SH9036	52°54·9′	3°37·8′W	X	125
Ffridd y Garnedd	Powys	SJ0017	52°44·7′	3°28·5′W	X	125
Ffridd y Graig	Gwyn	SH6117	52°44·2′	4°3·1′W	X	124
Ffridd y Hafod	Gwyn	SH8943	52°58·6′	3°38·8′W	X	124,125
Ffridd y Mynydd	Conwy	SH8275	53°15·8′	3°45·7′W	H	116

Ffrith	Flint	SJ1173	53°15·0′	3°19·6′W	X	116
Ffrith	Flint	SJ1763	53°9·7′	3°14·1′W	X	116
Ffrith	Flint	SJ2855	53°5·5′	3°4·1′W	T	117
Ffrith Bedwyn	Conwy	SH9167	53°11·6′	3°37·5′W	H	116
Ffrith-fedw	Denb	SJ0660	53°8·0′	3°23·9′W	X	116
Ffrith Fm	Ches	SJ5749	53°2·4′	2°38·1′W	FM	117
Ffrith Fm	Denb	SJ0760	53°8·0′	3°23·0′W	FM	116
Ffrith Fm	Flint	SJ2273	53°15·1′	3°9·7′W	FM	117
Ffrith Fm	Flint	SJ2557	53°6·5′	3°6·8′W	FM	117
Ffrith-hall Fm	Ches	SJ5747	53°1·4′	2°38·1′W	FM	117
Ffrith Hen	Conwy	SH8573	53°14·7′	3°43·0′W	X	116
Ffrith Isa	Conwy	SH8165	53°10·4′	3°46·4′W	X	116
Ffrith-lâs	Conwy	SH8165	53°10·4′	3°46·4′W	X	116
Ffrith Lon	Conwy	SH7968	53°12·0′	3°48·3′W	X	115
Ffrith Mountain	Flint	SJ1763	53°9·7′	3°14·1′W	H	116
Ffrithoedd	Conwy	SH9065	53°10·5′	3°38·3′W	X	116
Ffrithuchaf	Conwy	SH8661	53°8·3′	3°41·8′W	H	116
Ffrith-wen	Conwy	SH8374	53°15·3′	3°44·8′W	X	116
Ffrith-y-bont	Conwy	SH7268	53°11·9′	3°54·6′W	X	115
Ffrith y Garreg Wen	Flint	SJ1375	53°16·1′	3°17·9′W	X	116
Ffrwd	Carm	SN4512	51°47·4′	4°14·5′W	X	159
Ffrwd	Carm	SN6127	51°55·7′	4°0·9′W	X	146
Ffrwd	Cered	SN5350	52°8·0′	4°8·5′W	X	146
Ffrwd	Gwyn	SH4556	53°5·0′	4°18·5′W	X	115,123
Ffrwd Brook	Monm	SO3410	51°47·3′	2°57·0′W	W	161
Ffrwd Cynon	Cered	SN6248	52°7·0′	4°0·6′W	W	146
Ffrwd Fawr	Powys	SN8794	52°32·2′	3°39·6′W	W	135,136
Ffrwdgrech	Powys	SO0227	51°56·2′	3°25·1′W	X	160
Ffrwd-isaf	Merth Tyd	SO0207	51°45·4′	3°24·8′W	X	160
Ffrwd Uchaf	Merth Tyd	SO0208	51°46·0′	3°24·8′W	X	160
Ffrwdwen	Carm	SN5928	51°56·2′	4°2·7′W	X	146
Ffrŵd-wen	Powys	SN9745	52°5·9′	3°29·8′W	X	147
Ffrwd-wen	Powys	SO0497	52°34·0′	3°24·6′W	X	136
Ffrwd Wen	Powys	SO0574	52°21·6′	3°23·3′W	W	136,147
Ffrwdwenith	Cered	SN2251	52°8·0′	4°35·7′W	X	145
Ffrwd Wyllt	Nth Pt Talb	SS7990	51°36·0′	3°44·4′W	W	170
Ffrydiau-gwynion	Carm	SN3635	51°59·6′	4°22·9′W	X	145
Ffrydiau Twrch	Carm	SN7616	51°50·0′	3°47·6′W	W	160
Ffyddion Fm	Flint	SJ1276	53°16·7′	3°18·8′W	FM	116
Ffynhonnau	Conwy	SH9275	53°15·9′	3°36·8′W	X	116
Ffynhonnau Fm	Conwy	SH9670	53°13·3′	3°33·1′W	FM	116
Ffynnon	Carm	SN3516	51°49·3′	4°23·3′W	T	159
Ffynnon	Cered	SN2447	52°5·8′	4°33·8′W	X	145
Ffynnon	Pemb	SN1317	51°49·5′	4°42·4′W	X	158
Ffynnon Allgo	I of Angl	SH4984	53°20·1′	4°15·7′W	A	114,115
Ffynnon Arthur	Powys	SJ1015	52°43·8′	3°19·6′W	X	125
Ffynnonau	Carm	SN3211	51°46·6′	4°25·7′W	X	159
Ffynnonau	Cered	SN4740	52°2·5′	4°13·5′W	X	146
Ffynnonau	Powys	SO0529	51°57·3′	3°22·6′W	X	160
Ffynnonau	Powys	SO0953	52°10·3′	3°19·4′W	X	147
Ffynnonau Dyfnant	Carm	SN2228	51°55·6′	4°34·9′W	X	145,158
Ffynnon Bedr	Conwy	SH7668	53°11·9′	3°51·0′W	X	115
Ffynnon Beris	Gwyn	SH6058	53°6·3′	4°5·1′W	A	115
Ffynnon Berw	Cered	SN3252	52°8·7′	4°26·9′W	X	145
Ffynnon Beuno	Gwyn	SH4149	53°1·1′	4°21·8′W	A	115,123
Ffynnon Caradog	Cered	SN6183	52°25·9′	4°2·3′W	X	135
Ffynnon Caseg	Gwyn	SH6764	53°9·6′	3°59·0′W	W	115
Ffynnon Cegin Arthur (Chalybeate)	Gwyn	SH5564	53°9·4′	4°9·7′W	A	114,115
Ffynnoncripil	Cered	SN2545	52°4·8′	4°32·8′W	X	145
Ffynnon Cut-y-geifr	Gwyn	SH9833	52°53·3′	3°30·6′W	W	125
Ffynnoncyll	Carm	SN2014	51°48·0′	4°36·2′W	X	158
Ffynnondafalog	Cered	SN4957	52°11·7′	4°12·2′W	X	146
Ffynnon-dalis	Cered	SN4855	52°10·6′	4°13·0′W	X	146
Ffynnonddeilog	Carm	SN6326	51°55·2′	3°59·1′W	X	146
Ffynnonddofn	Pemb	SN0541	52°2·2′	4°50·2′W	X	145
Ffynnon-ddrain	Carm	SN4021	51°52·1′	4°19·0′W	T	159
Ffynnon Ddygfael	I of Angl	SH3490	53°23·1′	4°29·4′W	A	114
Ffynnon Derfel	Gwyn	SH9737	52°55·5′	3°31·5′W	A	125
Ffynnondici	Pemb	SN0533	51°57·9′	4°49·9′W	X	145
Ffynnon Dogfan	Powys	SH9822	52°47·4′	3°30·4′W	A	125
Ffynnon Drewi (Chalybeate)	Cered	SN6267	52°17·3′	4°1·0′W	W	135
Ffynnon Druidion	Pemb	SM9236	51°59·3′	5°1·4′W	X	157
Ffynnon-dwym	Brig	SS9188	51°35·1′	3°34·0′W	X	170
Ffynnon-dwym	Rho Cyn Taf	ST0596	51°39·5′	3°22·0′W	X	170
Ffynnon Eidda	Gwyn	SH7643	52°58·4′	3°50·4′W	W	124
Ffynnon Eilian	I of Angl	SH4693	53°24·9′	4°18·6′W	A	114
Ffynnon faglan	Gwyn	SH4560	53°7·1′	4°18·6′W	A	114,115
Ffynnon-Fair	Cered	SN2749	52°7·0′	4°31·2′W	X	145
Ffynnon-Fair	Cered	SN3444	52°4·4′	4°24·9′W	X	145
Ffynnon-Fair	Cered	SN5446	52°5·8′	4°7·5′W	X	146
Ffynnon Fair	Denb	SJ0370	53°13·3′	3°26·8′W	X	116
Ffynnon Fair	Gwyn	SH2231	52°51·1′	4°38·2′W	A	123
Ffynnon-fedw	Swan	SN6203	51°42·8′	3°59·5′W	X	159
Ffynnon-felen	Carm	SN2525	51°54·0′	4°32·2′W	X	145,158
Ffynnon-felen	Cered	SN4638	52°1·4′	4°14·3′W	X	146
Ffynnongain	Pemb	SN0622	51°52·0′	4°48·7′W	X	145,158
Ffynnongarreg	Powys	SO0474	52°21·6′	3°24·2′W	X	136,147
Ffynnongog	Cered	SN2946	52°5·4′	4°29·4′W	X	145
Ffynnongollen	Carm	SN5023	51°53·4′	4°10·4′W	X	159
Ffynnon Grasi	Gwyn	SH4042	52°57·3′	4°22·5′W	A	123
Ffynnon Gron	Pemb	SM9026	51°53·8′	5°2·7′W	T	157,158
Ffynnongroyw	Flint	SJ1382	53°19·9′	3°18·0′W	T	116
Ffynnon Gybl	Gwyn	SH4241	52°56·8′	4°20·7′W	A	123
Ffynnon Gynidr	Powys	SO1641	52°3·9′	3°13·1′W	A	148,161
Ffynnon Gynydd	Powys	SO1641	52°3·9′	3°13·1′W	T	148,161
Ffynnon Hywel	Cered	SN5567	52°17·2′	4°7·2′W	X	135
Ffynnon Iago	Carm	SN1423	51°52·7′	4°41·7′W	X	145,158
Ffynnon Illog	Powys	SJ0423	52°48·0′	3°25·0′W	A	125
Ffynnon-lâs	Carm	SN4723	51°53·3′	4°13·0′W	X	159
Ffynnon-Lâs	Carm	SN5034	51°59·3′	4°10·7′W	X	146
Ffynnon-las	Denb	SJ1941	52°57·9′	3°12·0′W	X	125
Ffynnon Las	Gwyn	SH9929	52°51·2′	3°29·6′W	W	125
Ffynnonlefrith	Cered	SN3554	52°9·8′	4°24·4′W	X	145
Ffynnon-lefrith	Swan	SN6404	51°43·3′	3°57·7′W	X	159
Ffynnon-Llewelyn	Cered	SN4445	52°5·1′	4°16·2′W	X	146
Ffynnon Lloer	Conwy	SH6662	53°8·5′	3°59·8′W	W	115
Ffynnon Llugwy Resr	Conwy	SH6962	53°8·6′	3°57·1′W	W	115
Ffynnon Llysiog	Merth Tyd	SO0215	51°49·7′	3°24·9′W	X	160

Ffynnonlwyd	Carm	SN2520	51°51·3′	4°32·1′W	X	145,158
Ffynnon Maen Milgi	Denb	SJ0634	52°54·0′	3°23·4′W	W	125
Ffynnonmeredydd	Cered	SN4556	52°11·1′	4°15·6′W	X	146
Ffynnonoer	Cered	SN4147	52°6·2′	4°18·9′W	X	146
Ffynnon-oer	Cered	SN5353	52°9·6′	4°8·5′W	X	146
Ffynnon Oer	Powys	SO1923	51°54·2′	3°10·3′W	W	161
Ffynnon Samson	Pemb	SN1125	51°53·7′	4°44·4′W	X	145,158
Ffynnon Sarah	Denb	SJ0651	53°3·1′	3°23·7′W	A	116
Ffynnonseiri	Carm	SN3317	51°49·8′	4°25·0′W	X	159
Ffynnon Sulien	Denb	SJ0644	52°59·3′	3°23·6′W	A	125
Ffynnon Tshow	Powys	SO2722	51°53·7′	3°3·3′W	A	161
Ffynnon Tudur	Denb	SJ1249	53°2·1′	3°18·3′W	X	116
Ffynnonwen	Carm	SN1522	51°52·2′	4°40·8′W	X	145,158
Ffynnonwen	Carm	SN2424	51°53·4′	4°33·1′W	X	145,158
Ffynnonwen	Carm	SN2630	51°56·7′	4°31·5′W	X	145
Ffynnonwen	Carm	SN3324	51°53·6′	4°25·2′W	X	145,159
Ffynnonwen	Cered	SN2349	52°6·9′	4°34·7′W	X	145
Ffynnon-wen	Cered	SN3643	52°3·9′	4°23·2′W	X	145
Ffynnonwen	Cered	SN5971	52°19·4′	4°3·7′W	X	135
Ffynnon-wen	Cered	SN6052	52°9·2′	4°2·4′W	X	146
Ffynnon-wen	Cered	SN7279	52°23·9′	3°52·5′W	X	135,147
Ffynnon Wen	Conwy	SH9446	53°0·3′	3°34·4′W	X	116
Ffynnon-wen Rocks	Brig	SS7978	51°29·5′	3°44·2′W	X	170
Ffynnon-y-berth	Denb	SJ1758	53°7·0′	3°14·0′W	X	116
Ffynnon y Capel	Gwyn	SH7522	52°47·1′	3°50·8′W	A	124
Ffynnon-y-drindod	V of Glam	SS9373	51°27·0′	3°32·0′W	A	170
Ffynnon-y-gôg	Rho Cyn Taf	SO0301	51°42·2′	3°23·8′W	X	170
Ffynnon-y-gwyddau	Powys	SN8624	51°54·4′	3°39·0′W	X	160
Ffynnon-y-mab	I of Angl	SH3679	53°17·2′	4°27·2′W	X	114
Ffynnonymenyn	Carm	SN4908	51°45·3′	4°10·9′W	X	159
Ffynnon y Parc	Powys	SO2435	52°0·7′	3°6·0′W	X	161
Ffynoncyff	Cered	SN1950	52°7·4′	4°38·2′W	X	145
Ffynonddewi	Cered	SN3852	52°8·8′	4°21·7′W	X	145
Ffynone	Pemb	SN2438	52°1·0′	4°33·5′W	X	145
Ffynongower	Gwyn	SH8931	52°52·1′	3°38·5′W	X	124,125
Ffynnon Gybi	I of Angl	SH4082	53°18·9′	4°23·7′W	A	114,115
Ffynonrhys	Cered	SN4651	52°8·4′	4°14·6′W	X	146
Ffynonwen	Carm	SN2228	51°55·6′	4°34·9′W	X	145,158
Ffynonwen	Cered	SN2650	52°7·5′	4°32·1′W	X	145
Fiacail Ach Leathanaidh	Pth & Kin	NN7567	56°46·9′	4°2·3′W	X	42
Fiacaill a' Choire Chais	Highld	NH9904	57°7·2′	3°39·6′W	X	36
Fiacail Mhór	Pth & Kin	NN7868	56°47·5′	3°59·4′W	H	42
Fiaclach	Highld	NH4972	57°43·0′	4°31·6′W	X	20
Fiaclan Dearg	Highld	NG5025	57°15·1′	6°8·2′W	X	32
Fiaclan Fuara	Highld	NG8497	57°54·9′	5°38·3′W	X	19
Fiadhach Bhàrr	Arg & Bt	NR8594	56°5·7′	5°26·9′W	H	55
Fiadhairt	Highld	NG2350	57°27·6′	6°36·7′W	X	23
Fiag	Highld	NC4524	58°10·9′	4°37·7′W	X	16
Fiag Bridge	Highld	NC4620	58°8·8′	4°36·5′W	X	16
Fiag Lodge	Highld	NC4528	58°13·1′	4°37·8′W	X	16
Fiag Plantation	Highld	NC4625	58°11·5′	4°36·7′W	F	16
Fianchanis	Highld	NM3694	56°58·0′	6°20·2′W	X	39
Fiarach	Stir	NN3426	56°24·1′	4°40·9′W	H	50
Fiar Allt	N Eil	NB1526	58°8·1′	6°50·1′W	W	13
Fiar Allt	N Eil	NB2630	58°10·7′	6°39·2′W	W	8,13
Fiaray	N Eil	NF7010	57°4·0′	7°26·3′W	X	31
Fiar Chreag	N Eil	NB3607	57°58·7′	6°27·5′W	H	14
Fiarlaid	Highld	NH0558	57°34·5′	5°15·2′W	X	25
Fiar Loch	Highld	NG7251	57°29·8′	5°47·8′W	W	24
Fiart Farm	Arg & Bt	NM8037	56°28·7′	5°33·9′W	FM	49
Fiavig Bàgh	N Eil	NB0235	58°12·4′	7°3·9′W	W	13
Fibden Fm	Worcs	SO8967	52°18·3′	2°9·3′W	FM	150
Fibhig	N Eil	NB2648	58°20·4′	6°40·4′W	X	8
Fibla Fiold	Orkney	HY3621	59°4·5′	3°6·5′W	X	6
Fiblister	Shetld	HU3578	60°29·3′	1°21·3′W	X	2,3
Fice's Well	Devon	SX5775	50°33·7′	4°0·8′W	A	191
Fichlie	Aberd	NJ4513	57°12·5′	2°54·2′W	X	37
Fickleshole	Surrey	TQ3860	51°19·6′	0°0·8′W	T	177,187
Fidden	Arg & Bt	NM3021	56°18·5′	6°21·5′W	X	48
Fiddesbeg	Aberd	NJ9424	57°18·6′	2°5·5′W	X	38
Fiddes Fm	Norf	TM0697	52°32·1′	1°2·7′E	FM	144
Fiddiestown	Aberd	NJ5455	57°35·2′	2°45·7′W	X	29
Fiddington	Glos	SO9230	51°58·3′	2°6·6′W	T	150
Fiddington	Somer	ST2140	51°9·5′	3°7·4′W	T	182
Fiddington Sands	Wilts	SU0154	51°17·3′	1°58·8′W	T	184
Fiddle Clough	Derby	SK1585	53°21·9′	1°46·1′W	X	110
Fiddlecott	Devon	SS7111	50°53·3′	3°49·7′W	X	191
Fiddleford	Dorset	ST8013	50°55·2′	2°16·7′W	T	194
Fiddler Burn	S Lanak	NS8548	55°43·0′	3°49·4′W	W	72
Fiddler' Green	Norf	TM0496	52°31·6′	1°0·8′E	T	144
Fiddler Hall	Cumbr	SD3884	54°15·1′	2°56·7′W	X	96,97
Fiddler Ho	Durham	NY9719	54°34·2′	2°2·4′W	X	92
Fiddlers Bay	Stir	NN6235	56°29·5′	4°14·0′W	X	51
Fiddler's Brook	Herts	TL4416	51°49·7′	0°5·8′E	W	167
Fiddler's Crus	Shetld	HU6192	60°36·7′	0°52·6′W	A	1,2
Fiddler's Dykes	Norf	TM1084	52°25·0′	1°5·7′E	X	144
Fiddler's Elbow	Heref	SO4275	52°22·4′	2°50·7′W	X	137,148
Fiddler's Elbow	Monm	SO5213	51°49·1′	2°41·4′W	X	162
Fiddler's Elbow	Shrops	SO3278	52°24·0′	2°59·6′W	X	137,148
Fiddler's Ferry	Sefton	SD3720	53°40·6′	2°56·8′W	T	102
Fiddler's Ferry	Warr	SJ5586	53°22·4′	2°40·2′W	T	108
Fiddler's Fm	Essex	TL9326	51°54·2′	0°48·7′E	FM	168
Fiddler's Folly	Derby	SK2542	52°58·7′	1°37·3′W	X	119,128
Fiddlers Green	Aberd	NK0459	57°37·5′	1°55·5′W	T	30
Fiddlers Green	Barns	SE1500	53°30·0′	1°46·0′W	X	110
Fiddlers Green	Corn	SW8254	50°21·0′	5°3·5′W	X	200
Fiddlers Green	Glos	SO9122	51°54·0′	2°7·5′W	T	163
Fiddlers Green	Hants	SU5610	50°53·4′	1°11·8′W	F	196
Fiddlers Green	Heref	SO5735	52°0·9′	2°37·2′W	T	149
Fiddler's Green	Norf	TF8216	52°42·9′	0°42·1′E	X	132
Fiddler's Green	N Yks	SE2163	54°4·0′	1°40·3′W	X	99
Fiddler's Hall	Suff	TM3164	52°13·8′	1°23·4′E	X	156
Fiddlers Hamlet	Essex	TL4701	51°41·5′	0°8·0′E	T	167
Fiddler's Hill	Beds	TL1116	51°50·1′	0°22·9′W	X	166
Fiddler's Hill	Norf	TG1020	52°44·4′	1°7·1′E	X	133
Fiddlers Hill	Wilts	SU1175	51°28·7′	1°50·1′W	X	173
Fiddlers Island	Oxon	SP4907	51°45·8′	1°17·0′W	X	164
Fiddlers Moss	D & G	NX7698	55°15·9′	3°56·7′W	X	78
Fiddler's Point	Somer	ST2959	51°19·8′	3°0·8′W	X	182

Fiddler's Reach or St Clement's	Thurr	TQ5976	51°27·9'	0°17·7'E	W	177
Fiddler, The	Corn	SW9368	50°28·8'	4°54·7'W	A	200
Fiddleton	D & G	NY3896	55°15·5'	2°58·1'W	X	79
Fidd, The	Shetld	HP6116	60°49·6'	0°52·2'W	X	1
Fideageo	N Eil	NB5737	58°15·5'	6°8·1'W	X	8
Fidge	Orkney	HY2719	59°3·4'	3°15·9'W	X	6
Fidgeon's Fm	Suff	TM1146	52°4·6'	1°5·1'E	FM	155,169
Fidlar Geo	Shetld	HU1849	60°13·8'	1°40·0'W	X	3
Fidler's Cross	Heref	SO6424	51°55·0'	2°31·0'W	X	162
Fidra	E Loth	NT5186	56°4·1'	2°46·8'W	X	66
Field	Heref	SO3050	52°8·9'	3°1·0'W	T	148
Field	Highld	ND3852	58°27·4'	3°3·3'W	X	12
Field	Shetld	HZ2171	59°31·7'	1°37·2'W	X	4
Field	Somer	ST6142	51°10·8'	2°33·1'W	T	183
Field	Staffs	SK0233	52°53·9'	1°57·8'W	T	128
Field Assarts	Oxon	SP3113	51°49·1'	1°32·6'W	T	164
Field Barn	Dorset	ST8402	50°49·3'	2°13·2'W	X	194
Field Barn	Dorset	SY8298	50°47·1'	2°14·9'W	X	194
Field Barn	Glos	SO9900	51°42·2'	2°0·5'W	X	163
Field Barn	Glos	SP0606	51°45·4'	1°54·4'W	X	163
Field Barn	Glos	SP0931	51°58·9'	1°51·7'W	X	150
Field Barn	Norf	TF8339	52°55·3'	0°43·7'E	X	132
Field Barn	Norf	TF8819	52°44·4'	0°47·5'E	X	132
Field Barn	Norf	TF9239	52°55·1'	0°51·8'E	X	132
Field Barn	Norf	TG0128	52°48·9'	0°59·4'E	X	133
Field Barn	Norf	TL8289	52°28·3'	0°41·2'E	X	144
Field Barn	Oxon	SP4418	51°51·8'	1°21·3'W	X	164
Field Barn	Oxon	SP4732	51°59·3'	1°18·5'W	X	151
Field Barn	Oxon	SU3186	51°34·6'	1°32·8'W	X	174
Field Barn	Oxon	SU3386	51°34·5'	1°31·0'W	X	174
Field Barn	Oxon	SU3585	51°34·0'	1°29·3'W	X	174
Field Barn	Oxon	SU4085	51°34·0'	1°25·0'W	X	174
Field Barn	Suff	TL8775	52°20·7'	0°45·1'E	X	144
Field Barn Buildings	Norf	TG0022	52°45·7'	0°58·3'E	X	133
Field Barn Fm	Hants	SU5157	51°18·8'	1°15·7'W	FM	174
Field Barn Fm	Hants	SU5955	51°17·7'	1°8·8'W	FM	174,185
Field Barn Fm	Norf	TL9084	52°25·5'	0°48·1'E	FM	144
Field Barn Fm	Norf	TL9485	52°25·9'	0°51·6'E	FM	144
Fieldbarn Fm	Northnts	TL0779	52°24·1'	0°25·2'W	FM	142
Field Barn Fm	Oxon	SP5115	51°50·1'	1°15·2'W	FM	164
Field Barn Fm	Oxon	SU4289	51°36·1'	1°23·2'W	FM	174
Field Barn Fm	W Berks	SU6068	51°24·7'	1°7·8'W	FM	175
Field Barn Fm	Wilts	ST8472	51°27·0'	2°13·4'W	FM	173
Field Barns	N Yks	SD8963	54°4·0'	2°9·7'W	X	98
Field Broughton	Cumbr	SD3881	54°13·5'	2°56·6'W	T	96,97
Field Burcote	Northnts	SP6650	52°8·9'	1°1·7'W	X	152
Field Close	Cumbr	SD4697	54°22·2'	2°49·5'W	X	97
Field Common	Surrey	TQ1266	51°23·1'	0°23·0'W	T	176
Field Dairy	Dorset	ST9000	50°48·2'	2°8·1'W	X	195
Field Dairy Fm	Dorset	ST9201	50°48·7'	2°6·4'W	FM	195
Field Dalling	Norf	TG0038	52°54·4'	0°58·9'E	T	133
Field End	Cumbr	NY0802	54°24·6'	3°24·6'W	X	89
Field End	Cumbr	SD3783	54°14·6'	2°57·6'W	X	96,97
Field End	Cumbr	SD5284	54°15·2'	2°43·8'W	X	97
Field End	Cumbr	SD5596	54°21·7'	2°41·1'W	X	97
Fielden Fm	Beds	TL0933	51°59·3'	0°24·4'W	FM	166
Fielden Ho	Beds	TL0933	51°59·3'	0°24·4'W	X	166
Fielder's Fm	Hants	SU7234	51°6·3'	0°57·9'W	FM	186
Field Farm Ho	Oxon	SU7096	51°39·7'	0°58·9'W	X	165
Field Farmhouse	Northnts	SP7887	52°28·8'	0°50·7'W	FM	141
Field Fm	Beds	SP9526	51°55·7'	0°36·7'W	FM	165
Field Fm	Beds	TL0340	52°3·2'	0°29·5'W	FM	153
Field Fm	Bucks	SP6309	51°46·8'	1°4·8'W	FM	164,165
Field Fm	Cambs	TL1288	52°28·9'	0°20·6'W	FM	142
Field Fm	Cambs	TL5471	52°19·2'	0°16·0'E	FM	154
Field Fm	Ches	SJ6362	53°9·5'	2°32·8'W	FM	118
Field Fm	Ches	SJ6756	53°6·3'	2°29·2'W	FM	118
Field Fm	Derby	SK1234	52°54·4'	1°48·9'W	FM	128
Field Fm	Essex	TL5145	52°5·2'	0°12·6'E	FM	154
Field Fm	E Yorks	SE9929	53°45·1'	0°29·5'W	FM	106
Field Fm	Glos	SO7601	51°42·7'	2°20·5'W	FM	162
Field Fm	Glos	ST8199	51°41·6'	2°16·1'W	FM	162
Field Fm	Glos	SU0098	51°41·1'	1°59·6'W	FM	163
Field Fm	Hants	SU7129	51°3·6'	0°58·8'W	FM	186,197
Field Fm	Kent	TQ9048	51°12·2'	0°43·6'E	FM	189
Field Fm	Leic	SK3413	52°43·1'	1°29·4'W	FM	128
Field Fm	Leic	SK4626	52°50·0'	1°18·6'W	FM	129
Field Fm	Leic	SK6124	52°48·8'	1°5·3'W	FM	129
Field Fm	Leic	SP5284	52°27·3'	1°13·7'W	FM	140
Field Fm	Lincs	SK8465	53°10·8'	0°44·2'W	FM	121
Field Fm	Lincs	TF0446	53°0·3'	0°26·6'W	FM	130
Field Fm	Lincs	TF1455	53°5·0'	0°17·5'W	FM	121
Field Fm	Lincs	TF2774	53°15·1'	0°5·4'W	FM	122
Field Fm	Lincs	TF4866	53°10·5'	0°13·2'E	FM	122
Field Fm	Monm	SO3611	51°47·9'	2°55·3'W	FM	161
Field Fm	N Lincs	TA0822	53°41·2'	0°21·5'W	FM	107,112
Field Fm	N Lincs	TA1119	53°39·6'	0°18·8'W	FM	113
Field Fm	Norf	TF7425	52°47·9'	0°35·3'E	FM	132
Field Fm	Norf	TG1115	52°41·7'	1°7·8'E	FM	133
Field Fm	Norf	TL7188	52°28·0'	0°31·4'E	FM	143
Field Fm	Notts	SK5826	52°49·9'	1°7·9'W	FM	129
Field Fm	Notts	SK6628	52°51·0'	1°0·8'W	FM	129
Field Fm	Notts	SK7387	53°22·7'	0°53·7'W	FM	112,120
Field Fm	Notts	SK7552	53°3·8'	0°52·4'W	FM	120
Field Fm	Notts	SK7684	53°21·1'	0°51·1'W	FM	120
Field Fm	Notts	SK7772	53°14·6'	0°50·4'W	FM	120
Field Fm	Oxon	SP2606	51°45·4'	1°37·0'W	FM	163
Field Fm	Oxon	SP3813	51°49·1'	1°26·5'W	FM	164
Field Fm	Oxon	SP3913	51°49·1'	1°25·7'W	FM	164
Field Fm	Oxon	SP4300	51°42·1'	1°22·3'W	FM	164
Field Fm	Oxon	SP6224	51°54·9'	1°5·5'W	FM	164,165
Field Fm	Oxon	SP6704	51°44·1'	1°1·4'W	FM	164,165
Field Fm	Oxon	SU2691	51°37·3'	1°37·1'W	FM	163,174
Field Fm	Oxon	SU5490	51°36·6'	1°12·8'W	FM	164,174
Field Fm	Shrops	SJ7443	52°59·3'	2°22·8'W	FM	118
Field Fm	Suff	TM4882	52°23·0'	1°39·1'E	FM	156
Field Fm	Suff	TM5082	52°23·0'	1°40·8'E	FM	156
Field Fm	Warw	SP0864	52°16·7'	1°52·6'W	FM	150
Field Fm	W Berks	SU6770	51°25·7'	1°1·8'W	FM	175
Field Fm	Wilts	SU0391	51°37·3'	1°57·0'W	FM	163,173
Field Fm	Worcs	SO5567	52°18·2'	2°39·2'W	FM	137,138,149
Field Fm	Worcs	SO6370	52°19·8'	2°32·2'W	FM	138
Field Fm	Worcs	SP0541	52°4·3'	1°55·2'W	FM	150
Field Foot	Cumbr	NY3605	54°26·4'	2°58·8'W	X	90
Fieldgarth	Cumbr	NY5442	54°46·5'	2°42·5'W	X	86
Field Gate	Cumbr	NY5218	54°33·5'	2°44·1'W	X	90
Fieldgate	Essex	TL5227	51°55·5'	0°13·0'E	X	167
Field Gate	N Yks	SD7963	54°4·0'	2°18·8'W	X	98
Fieldgate Fm	Warw	SP4780	52°25·2'	1°18·1'W	FM	140
Field Green	Kent	TQ7829	51°2·2'	0°32·7'E	T	188,199
Field Grove	Dorset	ST8306	50°51·4'	2°14·1'W	F	194
Field Grove Fm	S Glos	ST6769	51°25·4'	2°28·1'W	FM	172
Field Head	Brad	SE0139	53°51·1'	1°58·7'W	X	104
Field Head	Brad	SE0536	53°49·5'	1°55·0'W	X	104
Fieldhead	Ches	SJ9873	53°15·5'	2°1·4'W	X	118
Field Head	Cumbr	NY3727	54°38·3'	2°58·1'W	X	90
Fieldhead	Cumbr	NY4539	54°44·8'	2°50·8'W	X	90
Fieldhead	Cumbr	NY5077	55°5·3'	2°46·6'W	X	86
Field Head	Cumbr	NY5621	54°35·2'	2°40·4'W	X	90
Fieldhead	Cumbr	NY5847	54°49·2'	2°38·8'W	X	86
Field Head	Cumbr	NY8112	54°30·4'	2°17·2'W	X	91,92
Field Head	Cumbr	SD1598	54°22·5'	3°18·1'W	X	96
Field Head	Cumbr	SD3691	54°18·9'	2°58·6'W	X	96,97
Field Head	Durham	NY9128	54°39·1'	2°7·9'W	X	91,92
Field Head	Lancs	SD5661	54°2·8'	2°39·0'W	X	97
Field Head	Lancs	SD7252	53°58·0'	2°25·2'W	X	103
Fieldhead	Leeds	SE3638	53°50·5'	1°26·8'W	X	104
Field Head	Leic	SK4909	52°40·8'	1°16·1'W	T	140
Fieldhead	Moray	NJ4153	57°34·1'	2°58·7'W	X	28
Fieldhead	Northum	NY8086	55°10·3'	2°18·4'W	X	80
Field Head	Northum	NZ0752	54°52·0'	1°53·0'W	X	88
Fieldhead	Northum	NZ1794	55°14·6'	1°43·5'W	X	81
Fieldhead	S Lanak	NS6049	55°43·1'	4°13·3'W	X	64
Field Head	Staffs	SK0861	53°9·0'	1°52·4'W	X	119
Field Head Fm	Brad	SE0236	53°49·5'	1°57·8'W	FM	104
Field Head Fm	Staffs	SK0838	52°56·6'	1°52·5'W	FM	128
Field Head Ho	Cumbr	SD3499	54°23·2'	3°0·6'W	X	96,97
Field Ho	Cumbr	NY3836	54°43·2'	2°57·3'W	X	90
Field Ho	Cumbr	NY4845	54°48·1'	2°48·1'W	X	86
Field Ho	Derby	SK2416	52°44·7'	1°38·3'W	X	128
Field Ho	Durham	NZ1532	54°41·2'	1°45·6'W	X	92
Field Ho	Durham	NZ1817	54°33·1'	1°42·9'W	X	92
Field Ho	E Susx	TQ5510	50°52·3'	0°12·6'E	X	199
Field Ho	E Yorks	SE7620	53°40·5'	0°50·6'W	X	105,106,112
Field Ho	E Yorks	SE8242	53°52·3'	0°44·8'W	X	106
Field Ho	E Yorks	SE8341	53°51·8'	0°43·9'W	X	106
Field Ho	E Yorks	SE9255	53°59·2'	0°35·4'W	X	106
Field Ho	E Yorks	SE9553	53°58·1'	0°32·7'W	X	106
Field Ho	E Yorks	TA0167	54°5·6'	0°26·9'W	X	101
Field Ho	E Yorks	TA0259	54°1·3'	0°26·2'W	X	106,107
Field Ho	E Yorks	TA0358	54°0·7'	0°25·3'W	X	107
Field Ho	E Yorks	TA0667	54°5·5'	0°22·3'W	X	101
Field Ho	E Yorks	TA1052	53°57·4'	0°19·0'W	X	107
Field Ho	E Yorks	TA1344	53°53·0'	0°16·4'W	X	107
Field Ho	E Yorks	TA1634	53°47·6'	0°13·9'W	X	107
Field Ho	E Yorks	TA1730	53°45·4'	0°13·1'W	X	107
Field Ho	E Yorks	TA1870	54°7·0'	0°11·3'W	X	101
Field Ho	Glos	ST8899	51°41·6'	2°10·0'W	X	162
Field Ho	Hants	SU4323	51°0·5'	1°22·8'W	X	185
Field Ho	Leeds	SE3645	53°54·2'	1°26·7'W	X	104
Field Ho	Lincs	SE8800	53°29·6'	0°40·0'W	X	112
Field Ho	Mil Key	SP8143	52°5·0'	0°48·7'W	X	152
Field Ho	N Lincs	TA1121	53°40·7'	0°18·8'W	X	107,113
Field Ho	Norf	TF7841	52°56·4'	0°39·3'E	X	132
Field Ho	Norf	TF9638	52°54·4'	0°55·3'E	X	132
Field Ho	Northum	NU2201	55°18·4'	1°38·8'W	X	81
Field Ho	Northum	NU2413	55°24·9'	1°36·8'W	X	81
Field Ho	Notts	SK4841	52°58·1'	1°16·7'W	X	129
Field Ho	Notts	SK7274	53°15·7'	0°54·8'W	X	120
Field Ho	Notts	SK8459	53°7·5'	0°44·3'W	X	121
Field Ho	N Yks	NZ3806	54°27·1'	1°24·4'W	X	93
Field Ho	N Yks	NZ5307	54°27·6'	1°10·5'W	X	93
Field Ho	N Yks	NZ5407	54°27·6'	1°9·6'W	X	93
Field Ho	N Yks	NZ6907	54°27·5'	0°55·7'W	X	94
Field Ho	N Yks	SE2991	54°19·1'	1°32·8'W	X	99
Field Ho	N Yks	SE6962	54°3·2'	0°56·3'W	X	100
Field Ho	N Yks	SE9078	54°11·6'	0°36·8'W	X	101
Field Ho	Shrops	SJ7402	52°37·1'	2°22·6'W	X	127
Field Ho	Shrops	SO5790	52°30·6'	2°37·6'W	X	137,138
Field Ho	Staffs	SJ7543	52°59·3'	2°21·9'W	X	118
Field Ho	Staffs	SJ9642	52°58·8'	2°3·2'W	X	118
Field Ho	S Tyne	NZ3760	54°56·2'	1°24·9'W	X	88
Field Ho	Thurr	TQ6287	51°33·7'	0°20·6'E	X	177
Field Ho	Worcs	SO9179	52°24·8'	2°7·5'W	X	139
Field Ho Barn	N Yks	SD9371	54°8·3'	2°6·0'W	X	98
Field Ho Fm	E Yorks	SE7352	53°57·8'	0°52·8'W	FM	105,106
Fieldhouse	Cumbr	NY4432	54°41·0'	2°51·7'W	X	90
Field House	Durham	NZ1043	54°47·2'	1°50·2'W	X	88
Fieldhouse	Glos	SO6908	51°46·4'	2°26·6'W	X	162
Fieldhouse Fm	Ches	SJ6974	53°16·0'	2°27·5'W	FM	118
Fieldhouse Fm	Ches	SJ8362	53°9·5'	2°14·8'W	FM	118
Field House Fm	Durham	NZ3246	54°48·7'	1°29·7'W	FM	88
Field House Fm	E Yorks	SE7844	53°53·4'	0°48·4'W	FM	105,106
Field House Fm	E Yorks	SE9035	53°48·4'	0°37·6'W	FM	106
Field House Fm	E Yorks	SE9631	53°46·2'	0°32·2'W	FM	106
Field House Fm	E Yorks	SE9842	53°52·1'	0°30·2'W	FM	106
Field House Fm	Hartpl	NZ4731	54°40·6'	1°15·8'W	FM	93
Field House Fm	Hartpl	NZ4826	54°37·9'	1°15·0'W	FM	93
Field House Fm	Heref	SO6559	52°13·9'	2°30·4'W	FM	149
Fieldhouse Fm	Lincs	TA0502	53°30·5'	0°24·6'W	FM	112
Field House Fm	Lincs	TF0668	53°12·1'	0°24·4'W	FM	121
Field House Fm	Lincs	TF0982	53°19·7'	0°21·4'W	FM	121
Field House Fm	Lincs	TF3148	53°1·0'	0°2·4'W	FM	131
Field House Fm	Lincs	TF5466	53°10·4'	0°18·7'E	FM	122
Field House Fm	N Lincs	SE7102	53°30·8'	0°55·3'W	FM	112
Field House Fm	N Lincs	SE9701	53°30·0'	0°31·8'W	FM	112
Field House Fm	N Lincs	SE9819	53°39·7'	0°30·6'W	FM	112
Field House Fm	N Lincs	TA0017	53°38·6'	0°28·8'W	FM	112
Field House Fm	N Lincs	TA0420	53°40·2'	0°25·1'W	FM	107,112
Fieldhouse Fm	Norf	TG1026	52°47·7'	1°7·3'E	FM	133
Field House Fm	Northum	NZ2283	55°8·7'	1°38·9'W	FM	81
Field House Fm	Notts	SK7242	52°58·5'	0°55·3'W	FM	129
Field House Fm	Notts	SK8252	53°3·8'	0°46·2'W	FM	121
Field House Fm	N Yks	TA0876	54°10·3'	0°20·3'W	FM	101
Field House Fm	Staffs	SK0850	53°3·1'	1°52·4'W	FM	119
Field House Fm	Staffs	SK1258	53°7·4'	1°48·8'W	FM	119
Field House Fm	Stock on T	NZ4011	54°29·8'	1°22·5'W	FM	93
Field House Fm	Warw	SP4466	52°17·7'	1°20·9'W	FM	151
Field Irish	Devon	SS3415	50°54·9'	4°21·3'W	X	190
Fieldlands Fm	W Susx	TQ2218	50°57·1'	0°15·4'W	FM	198
Fieldlane Fm	Glos	SO7300	51°42·1'	2°23·1'W	FM	162
Field of the Mosses	Cald	SD9434	53°48·4'	2°5·1'W	X	103
Fieldon Br	Durham	NZ2026	54°38·0'	1°41·0'W	X	93
Fieldon Br	Warw	SP3099	52°35·5'	1°33·0'W	X	140
Field Place	Surrey	SU9546	51°12·5'	0°38·0'W	X	186
Field Place	Surrey	SU9936	51°7·1'	0°34·7'W	X	186
Field Place	W Susx	TQ1432	51°4·8'	0°22·0'W	A	187
Fieldridge Copse	W Berks	SU3574	51°28·1'	1°29·4'W	F	174
Fields	Lancs	SD7641	53°52·1'	2°21·5'W	X	103
Fields End	Herts	TL0207	51°45·4'	0°30·9'W	T	166
Fields Fm	Bucks	SP8117	51°51·0'	0°49·0'W	FM	165
Fields Fm	Ches	SJ4846	53°0·8'	2°46·1'W	FM	117
Fields Fm	Ches	SJ4945	53°0·2'	2°45·2'W	FM	117
Fields Fm	Ches	SJ5550	53°3·0'	2°39·9'W	FM	117
Fields Fm	Ches	SJ5655	53°5·7'	2°39·0'W	FM	117
Fields Fm	Ches	SJ6451	53°3·5'	2°31·8'W	FM	118
Fields Fm	Ches	SJ6478	53°18·1'	2°32·0'W	FM	118
Fields Fm	Ches	SJ6642	52°58·7'	2°30·0'W	FM	118
Fields Fm	Ches	SJ6747	53°1·4'	2°29·1'W	FM	118
Fields Fm	Ches	SJ6963	53°10·0'	2°27·4'W	FM	118
Fields Fm	Ches	SJ7042	52°58·7'	2°26·4'W	FM	118
Fields Fm	Ches	SJ7162	53°9·5'	2°25·6'W	FM	118
Fields Fm	Ches	SJ7359	53°7·9'	2°23·8'W	FM	118
Fields Fm	Ches	SJ7374	53°16·0'	2°23·9'W	FM	118
Fields Fm	Ches	SJ7662	53°9·5'	2°21·1'W	FM	118
Field's Fm	Ches	SJ8377	53°17·6'	2°14·9'W	FM	118
Fields Fm	Derby	SK2433	52°53·9'	1°38·2'W	FM	128
Fields Fm	Devon	ST1611	50°53·8'	3°11·3'W	FM	192,193
Fields Fm	Dorset	SY8184	50°39·6'	2°15·7'W	FM	194
Field's Fm	Essex	TL6437	52°0·7'	0°23·8'E	FM	154
Field's Fm	Glos	SO9808	51°46·5'	2°1·3'W	FM	163
Field's Fm	Hants	SU4502	50°49·2'	1°21·3'W	FM	196
Fields Fm	Leic	SK4000	52°36·0'	1°24·2'W	FM	140
Fields Fm	Leic	SK4304	52°38·2'	1°21·5'W	FM	140
Fields Fm	Leic	SP4793	52°32·2'	1°18·0'W	FM	140
Fields Fm	Leic	SP5585	52°27·8'	1°11·0'W	FM	140
Fields Fm	Lincs	TF4621	52°46·2'	0°10·3'E	FM	131
Fields Fm	Northnts	SP4855	52°11·7'	1°17·5'W	FM	151
Fields Fm	Notts	SK6427	52°50·4'	1°2·6'W	FM	129
Fields Fm	Notts	SK6738	52°56·3'	0°59·8'W	FM	129
Fields Fm	Shrops	SJ5634	52°54·3'	2°38·8'W	FM	126
Fields Fm	Shrops	SO4799	52°35·4'	2°46·5'W	FM	137,138
Fields Fm	Staffs	SJ7648	53°2·0'	2°21·1'W	FM	118
Fields Fm	Staffs	SJ9355	53°5·8'	2°5·9'W	FM	118
Fields Fm	Warw	SK2900	52°36·1'	1°33·9'W	FM	140
Fields Fm	Warw	SP3666	52°17·7'	1°27·9'W	FM	151
Fields Fm	Warw	SP4060	52°14·4'	1°24·5'W	FM	151
Fields Fm	Wrex	SJ4443	52°59·1'	2°49·6'W	FM	117
Fields Fm	Wrex	SJ4736	52°55·4'	2°46·9'W	FM	126
Fields Fm, The	Ches	SJ7969	53°13·3'	2°18·5'W	FM	118
Fields Fm, The	Shrops	SJ5343	52°59·2'	2°41·6'W	FM	117
Fields Heath	Hants	SU4502	50°49·2'	1°21·3'W	F	196
Fields Ho	Lancs	SD7242	53°52·7'	2°25·1'W	X	103
Fields Ho	Lancs	SD7645	53°54·3'	2°21·5'W	X	103
Fields House, The	Warw	SP4060	52°14·4'	1°24·5'W	X	151
Fieldside	Cumbr	NY1033	54°41·3'	3°23·3'W	X	89
Fieldside	Cumbr	NY2823	54°36·1'	3°6·5'W	X	89,90
Fieldside Fm	Bucks	SP7319	51°52·1'	0°56·0'W	FM	165
Fieldside Fm	Cambs	TL5587	52°27·8'	0°17·3'E	FM	143
Field's Place	Heref	SO4153	52°10·6'	2°51·4'W	T	148,149
Field's Place	Heref	SO4240	52°3·6'	2°50·4'W	X	148,149,161
Fields, The	Shrops	SJ2921	52°47·2'	3°2·8'W	X	126
Fields, The	Shrops	SJ4335	52°54·8'	2°50·5'W	X	126
Fields, The	Shrops	SJ4628	52°51·0'	2°47·7'W	X	126
Fields, The	Shrops	SJ4830	52°52·1'	2°45·9'W	X	126
Fields, The	Staffs	SJ7737	52°56·0'	2°20·1'W	X	127
Fields, The	Staffs	SJ7852	53°4·1'	2°19·3'W	X	118
Fields, The	Wrex	SJ3443	52°59·1'	2°58·6'W	X	117
Fields, The	Wrex	SJ4343	52°59·1'	2°50·5'W	X	117
Field Studies Centre	Wilts	SU3059	51°20·0'	1°33·8'W	X	174
Field, The	Derby	SK4444	52°59·7'	1°20·3'W	X	129
Field, The	Heref	SO4150	52°8·9'	2°51·3'W	X	148,149
Field, The	Heref	SO5438	52°2·5'	2°39·8'W	X	149
Field View	Cumbr	NY3253	54°52·3'	3°3·2'W	X	85
Field View	Lincs	TF3889	53°23·0'	0°4·9'E	X	113,122
Fielnadringa	Shetld	HU3861	60°20·1'	1°18·2'W	X	2,3
Fiendsdale	Lancs	SD5949	53°56·4'	2°37·1'W	X	102
Fiend's Fell	Cumbr	NY6440	54°45·5'	2°33·1'W	H	86
Fiery Furze	Northnts	SP7646	52°6·7'	0°53·0'W	F	152
Fifebanks	Pth & Kin	NO3032	56°28·8'	3°7·7'W	X	53
Fifehead Magdalen	Dorset	ST7821	50°59·5'	2°18·4'W	T	183
Fifehead Neville	Dorset	ST7610	50°53·6'	2°20·1'W	T	194
Fifehead St Quintin	Dorset	ST7710	50°53·6'	2°19·2'W	T	194
Fife Keith	Moray	NJ4250	57°32·4'	2°57·7'W	T	28
Fife Ness	Fife	NO6309	56°16·6'	2°35·4'W	X	59
Fifescar Knowe	Scot Bord	NT1726	55°31·5'	3°18·5'W	H	72
Fifeshill	C of Aber	NJ8505	57°8·4'	2°14·4'W	X	38
Fifield	Oxon	SP2418	51°51·8'	1°38·7'W	T	163
Fifield	Wilts	SU1450	51°15·2'	1°47·6'W	T	184
Fifield	Win & Maid	SU9076	51°28·8'	0°41·8'W	T	175
Fifield Bavant	Wilts	SU0125	51°1·7'	1°58·9'W	T	184
Fifield Down	Wilts	SU0025	51°1·7'	1°59·6'W	X	184
Fifield Heath	Oxon	SP2520	51°52·9'	1°37·8'W	X	163
Fifteen Acre Copse	Somer	ST4338	51°8·5'	2°48·5'W	F	182
Fifteen Acres Fm	S Glos	ST6971	51°26·5'	2°26·4'W	FM	172
Fifthpart	E Ayr	NS4253	55°44·9'	4°30·6'W	X	64
Fifty Acres	Notts	SK6183	53°20·7'	1°4·6'W	F	111,120
Fifty Fm	Suff	TL6575	52°21·1'	0°25·8'E	FM	143
Figgatoch	N Ayr	NS1657	55°46·5'	4°55·6'W	X	63

Figham	E Yorks	TA0538	53°49·9'	0°23·9'W	X	107
Figheldean	Wilts	SU1547	51°13·6'	1°46·7'W	T	184
Figheldean Down	Wilts	SU1849	51°14·6'	1°44·1'W	X	184
Figheldean Field	Wilts	SU1648	51°14·1'	1°45·9'W	X	184
Fighting Cocks Fm	Hants	SU3018	50°57·9'	1°34·0'W	FM	185
Fign Aberbiga	Powys	SN8790	52°30·0'	3°39·5'W	X	135,136
Fign Oer	Gwyn	SH5907	52°38·8'	4°4·7'W	X	124
Figsbury Ring	Wilts	SU1833	51°6·0'	1°44·2'W	A	184
Figtree Fm	Devon	SS9606	50°50·9'	3°28·3'W	FM	192
Figyn Blaenbrefi	Cered	SN7154	52°10·4'	3°52·8'W	X	146,147
Figyn Wood	Powys	SJ1708	52°40·0'	3°13·2'W	F	125
Filands	Wilts	ST9388	51°35·7'	2°5·7'W	T	173
Filby	Norf	TG4613	52°39·8'	1°38·7'E	T	134
Filby Broad	Norf	TG4513	52°39·8'	1°37·8'E	W	134
Filby Heath	Norf	TG4913	52°39·7'	1°41·3'E	T	134
Filchampstead	Oxon	SP4505	51°44·7'	1°20·5'W	T	164
Filching Manor	E Susx	TQ5602	50°48·0'	0°13·2'E	A	199
Filcombe Fm	Devon	SY1291	50°43·0'	3°14·4'W	FM	192,193
Filcombe Fm	Dorset	SY4092	50°43·7'	2°50·6'W	FM	193
Fild, The	Shetld	HP6118	60°50·7'	0°52·2'W	X	1
Filey	N Yks	TA1180	54°12·5'	0°17·5'W	T	101
Filey Bay	N Yks	TA1379	54°11·9'	0°15·6'W	W	101
Filey Brigg	N Yks	TA1381	54°13·0'	0°15·6'W	X	101
Filey Field	N Yks	TA1181	54°13·0'	0°17·4'W	X	101
Filey Sands	N Yks	TA1281	54°13·0'	0°16·5'W	X	101
Filey Spa	N Yks	TA1281	54°13·0'	0°16·5'W	X	101
Filford	Dorset	SY4497	50°46·4'	2°47·3'W	T	193
Filgrave	Mil Key	SP8748	52°7·6'	0°43·3'W	T	152
Filham	Devon	SX6455	50°23·0'	3°54·4'W	T	202
Filkins	Oxon	SP2304	51°44·3'	1°39·6'W	T	163
Filkins Down Fm	Oxon	SP2207	51°45·9'	1°40·5'W	FM	163
Filla	Shetld	HU6668	60°23·7'	0°47·6'W	X	2
Filla Sound	Shetld	HU6668	60°23·7'	0°47·6'W	W	2
Filleigh	Devon	SS6627	51°1·8'	3°54·3'W	T	180
Filleigh	Devon	SS7410	50°52·8'	3°47·1'W	T	191
Filleigh	Devon	SX8780	50°36·8'	3°35·5'W	X	192
Filleigh Moor	Devon	SS4808	50°51·3'	4°9·2'W	X	191
Fillets	Orkney	HY2506	58°56·3'	3°17·7'W	X	6,7
Fillets Fm	Herts	TL4014	51°48·7'	0°2·2'E	FM	167
Filletts	Shrops	SO7885	52°28·0'	2°19·0'W	X	138
Filley Brook	Dorset	ST7524	51°1·1'	2°21·0'W	W	183
Fill Geo	Shetld	HP5708	60°45·3'	0°56·7'W	X	1
Filliberry	Orkney	ND3984	58°44·6'	3°2·8'W	X	7
Filli Field	Shetld	HU3666	60°22·8'	1°20·3'W	X	2,3
Fillingdon Fm	Bucks	SU8094	51°38·6'	0°50·2'W	FM	175
Fillingham	Lincs	SK9485	53°21·4'	0°34·8'W	T	112,121
Fillingham Castle	Lincs	SK9586	53°22·0'	0°33·9'W	X	112,121
Fillingham Grange	Lincs	SK9385	53°21·5'	0°35·7'W	X	112,121
Fillingham Low Wood	Lincs	SK9186	53°22·0'	0°37·5'W	F	112,121
Fillongley	Warw	SP2887	52°29·0'	1°34·9'W	T	140
Fillongley Grange	Warw	SP2986	52°28·5'	1°34·0'W	X	140
Fillongley Hall	Warw	SP2687	52°29·1'	1°36·6'W	X	140
Fillongley Lodge	Warw	SP2788	52°29·6'	1°35·7'W	X	140
Fillongley Mount	Warw	SP2786	52°28·5'	1°35·7'W	X	140
Filloway	Highld	ND2470	58°36·9'	3°18·0'W	X	7,12
Filpoke	Durham	NZ4737	54°43·8'	1°15·8'W	X	93
Filmer Wood	Kent	TQ9255	51°15·9'	0°45·5'E	F	178
Filmore Hill	Hants	SU6627	51°2·5'	1°3·1'W	T	185,186
Filston Fm	Kent	TQ5160	51°19·4'	0°10·4'E	FM	177,188
Filston Hall	Kent	TQ5160	51°19·4'	0°10·4'E	X	177,188
Filton	S Glos	ST6078	51°30·2'	2°34·2'W	T	172
Filton Abbey Wood Station	S Glos	ST6078	51°30·2'	2°34·2'W	X	172
Filton Airfield	S Glos	ST5980	51°31·2'	2°35·1'W	X	172
Filtrick Fm	Corn	SW6839	50°12·6'	5°14·7'W	FM	203
Filwood Park	C of Bris	ST5972	51°25·3'	2°35·0'W	T	172,182
Fimber	E Yorks	SE8960	54°1·9'	0°38·1'W	T	101
Fimber Field Fm	E Yorks	SE9059	54°1·4'	0°37·2'W	FM	106
Finachag	Arg & Bt	NM5321	56°18·3'	5°59·2'W	X	48
Finalty Hill	Angus	NO2175	56°51·8'	3°17·3'W	H	44
Finart Bay	Arg & Bt	NS1888	56°3·3'	4°54·9'W	W	56
Finavon	Angus	NO4957	56°42·4'	2°49·5'W	T	54
Finavon Castle	Angus	NO4956	56°41·8'	2°49·5'W	X	54
Finbracken Hill	Arg & Bt	NS1580	55°58·9'	4°57·5'W	H	63
Fincastle Ho	Pth & Kin	NN8662	56°44·4'	3°51·4'W	X	43
Finchairn	Arg & Bt	NM9003	56°10·7'	5°22·6'W	X	55
Finchale Abbey Training Centre	Durham	NZ2746	54°48·7'	1°34·4'W	X	88
Finchale Banks	Durham	NZ2947	54°49·3'	1°32·5'W	X	88
Finchale Priory	Durham	NZ2947	54°49·3'	1°32·5'W	A	88
Fincham	Liv	SJ4292	53°25·5'	2°52·0'W	T	108
Fincham	Norf	TF6806	52°37·8'	0°29·3'E	T	143
Fincham Fm	Cambs	TL4592	52°30·6'	0°8·6'E	FM	143
Fincham Fm	E Susx	TQ4633	51°4·9'	0°5·5'E	FM	188
Fincham Fm	Norf	TF8222	52°46·1'	0°42·3'E	FM	132
Fincham Hall	Norf	TF6906	52°37·8'	0°30·2'E	A	143
Finchampstead	Wok	SU7963	51°21·9'	0°51·5'W	T	175,186
Fincham's Fm	Norf	TM0283	52°24·7'	0°58·6'E	FM	144
Fincharn Castle	Arg & Bt	NM8904	56°11·2'	5°23·6'W	A	55
Fincharn Loch	Arg & Bt	NM9303	56°10·7'	5°19·7'W	W	55
Fincharn River	Arg & Bt	NM9003	56°10·7'	5°22·6'W	W	55
Finchcocks	Kent	TQ7036	51°6·1'	0°26·1'E	X	188
Finchdean	Hants	SU7312	50°54·4'	0°57·3'W	T	197
Finchden Manor	Kent	TQ9033	51°4·1'	0°43·1'E	X	189
Finches Fm	Herts	TL3023	51°53·7'	0°6·2'W	FM	166
Finch Fm	Know	SJ4584	53°21·2'	2°49·2'W	FM	108
Finch Green	Kent	TQ5041	51°9·1'	0°9·1'E	X	188
Finchingfield	Essex	TL6832	51°57·9'	0°27·1'E	T	167
Finchley	Barnet	TQ2590	51°35·9'	0°11·3'W	T	176
Finchurst Fm	Kent	TQ7240	51°8·2'	0°27·9'E	FM	188
Fin Cop	Derby	SK1770	53°13·8'	1°44·3'W	H	119
Fin Cop (Settlement)	Derby	SK1770	53°13·8'	1°44·3'W	A	119
Fincorrie Fm	Bucks	SP7832	51°59·1'	0°51·5'W	FM	152,165
Fincraigs	Fife	NO3622	56°23·4'	3°1·8'W	T	54,59
Findas	Fife	NO3610	56°16·9'	3°1·6'W	X	59
Findas Bank	Fife	NO3709	56°16·4'	3°0·6'W	X	59
Findas Knowe	Fife	NO3609	56°16·4'	3°1·6'W	X	59
Findatie	Pth & Kin	NT1799	56°10·8'	3°19·8'W	X	58
Finderlie	Pth & Kin	NO0905	56°14·0'	3°27·6'W	X	58
Findern	Derby	SK3030	52°52·2'	1°32·9'W	T	128
Findhorn	Moray	NJ0464	57°39·6'	3°36·1'W	T	27
Findhorn Bay	Moray	NJ0462	57°38·5'	3°36·0'W	W	27
Findhorn Bridge	Highld	NH8027	57°19·3'	3°59·1'W	X	35
Findhorn Foundation	Highld	NH0563	57°37·2'	5°15·4'W	X	27
Findhu Glen	Pth & Kin	NN7215	56°18·9'	4°3·7'W	X	57
Findhuglen	Pth & Kin	NN7215	56°18·9'	4°3·7'W	X	57
Findlater Castle	Aberd	NJ5467	57°41·7'	2°45·8'W	A	29
Findlatree	Aberd	NJ5912	57°12·1'	2°40·3'W	X	37
Findlay Fm	C of Aber	NJ9511	57°11·6'	2°4·5'W	FM	38
Findlay's Rock	Arg & Bt	NM2826	56°21·1'	6°23·7'W	X	48
Findlay's Seat	Moray	NJ2853	57°33·9'	3°11·8'W	X	28
Findlayston	Aberd	NO8488	56°59·2'	2°15·3'W	X	45
Findlayston	E Ayr	NS5020	55°27·3'	4°21·9'W	X	70
Findle Fm	Warw	SP3866	52°17·7'	1°26·2'W	FM	151
Findlins House	Shetld	HU2876	60°28·3'	1°28·9'W	X	3
Findlow Fm	Ches	SJ8678	53°18·2'	2°12·2'W	FM	118
Findochty	Moray	NJ4668	57°42·2'	2°53·9'W	T	28,29
Findo Gask	Pth & Kin	NO0020	56°22·0'	3°36·7'W	T	52,53,58
Findon	Aberd	NJ7963	57°39·6'	2°20·7'W	X	29,30
Findon	Aberd	NO9397	57°4·1'	2°6·5'W	T	38,45
Findon	W Susx	TQ1208	50°51·9'	0°24·1'W	T	198
Findon Mains	Highld	NH6060	57°36·8'	4°20·1'W	X	21
Findon Ness	Aberd	NO9497	57°4·1'	2°5·5'W	X	38,45
Findon Park Fm	W Susx	TQ1309	50°52·4'	0°23·2'W	FM	198
Findon Place	W Susx	TQ1108	50°51·9'	0°25·0'W	X	198
Findon Valley	W Susx	TQ1306	50°50·8'	0°23·3'W	T	198
Findony Fm	Pth & Kin	NO0113	56°18·2'	3°35·6'W	FM	58
Findouran	Moray	NJ3732	57°22·7'	3°2·4'W	X	37
Findowie Hill	Pth & Kin	NN9435	56°30·0'	3°42·9'W	H	52,53
Findowrie	Angus	NO5561	56°44·6'	2°43·7'W	X	44
Findrack Ho	Aberd	NJ6004	57°7·8'	2°39·2'W	X	37
Findrassie	Moray	NJ1965	57°40·3'	3°21·0'W	X	28
Findrassie Wood	Moray	NJ2064	57°39·8'	3°20·0'W	F	28
Findron	Moray	NJ1718	57°15·0'	3°22·1'W	X	36
Findynate Fm	Pth & Kin	NN8953	56°39·6'	3°48·2'W	FM	52
Fine Burn	Durham	NZ0234	54°42·3'	1°57·7'W	W	92
Finechambers Mill	Northum	NY9458	54°55·2'	2°5·2'W	X	87
Finedon	Northnts	SP9172	52°20·5'	0°39·5'W	T	141
Finedonhill Fm	Northnts	SP9169	52°18·9'	0°39·5'W	FM	152
Finegand	Pth & Kin	NO1466	56°46·9'	3°24·0'W	X	43
Fineglen	Arg & Bt	NM9318	56°18·8'	5°20·4'W	X	55
Fine Ho	Northum	NZ0553	54°52·6'	1°54·9'W	X	87
Fine Jane's Fm	Lancs	SD3414	53°37·3'	2°59·5'W	FM	108
Finemerehill Ho	Bucks	SP7122	51°53·8'	0°57·7'W	X	165
Finemere Wood	Bucks	SP7121	51°53·2'	0°57·7'W	F	165
Fineshade Abbey	Northnts	SP9797	52°34·0'	0°33·7'W	X	141
Fine Sike	Durham	NY9636	54°43·4'	2°3·3'W	W	91,92
Fine Street	Heref	SO3339	52°3·0'	2°58·2'W	T	149,161
Fine View	Cumbr	NY4272	55°2·6'	2°54·0'W	X	85
Fineview	D & G	NX1957	54°52·8'	4°48·9'W	X	82
Finfan	Moray	NJ3163	57°39·4'	3°8·9'W	X	28
Fingal's Cave	Arg & Bt	NM3235	56°26·1'	6°20·4'W	X	46,47,48
Fingal Street	Suff	TM2169	52°16·7'	1°14·8'E	T	156
Fingart	E Ayr	NS4352	55°44·4'	4°29·6'W	X	64
Fingask	Aberd	NJ7727	57°20·2'	2°22·5'W	X	38
Fingask	Fife	NO3918	56°21·3'	2°58·8'W	X	59
Fingask	Pth & Kin	NO1619	56°21·6'	3°21·1'W	X	58
Fingask Castle	Pth & Kin	NO2227	56°26·0'	3°15·4'W	A	53,58
Fingask Loch	Pth & Kin	NO1642	56°34·0'	3°21·6'W	W	53
Fingay Hill	N Yks	SE4099	54°23·3'	1°22·6'W	X	99
Fingeo	Orkney	HY6824	59°6·4'	2°33·0'W	X	5
Finger	Conwy	SH9764	53°10·0'	3°32·0'W	X	116
Finger Burn	Northum	NT9142	55°40·5'	2°8·2'W	W	74,75
Finger Cross	Pemb	SM9731	51°56·7'	4°56·8'W	X	157
Finger Farm	Denb	SJ2039	52°56·8'	3°11·0'W	FM	126
Finger Fm	Leic	SK4625	52°49·5'	1°18·6'W	FM	129
Finger Fm	Somer	ST7147	51°13·5'	2°24·5'W	FM	183
Finger Post	Powys	SO1096	52°33·5'	3°19·3'W	X	136
Fingerpost	Worcs	SO7374	52°22·0'	2°23·4'W	T	138
Fingerpost Fm	Ches	SJ7575	53°16·5'	2°22·1'W	FM	118
Fingest	Bucks	SU7791	51°37·0'	0°52·9'W	T	175
Fingest Grove	Bucks	SU7992	51°37·5'	0°51·1'W	X	175
Finghall	N Yks	SE1889	54°18·0'	1°43·0'W	T	99
Finglack	Highld	NH7744	57°28·4'	4°2·6'W	X	27
Fingland	Cumbr	NY2557	54°54·4'	3°9·8'W	T	85
Fingland	D & G	NS7517	55°26·1'	3°58·1'W	X	71,78
Fingland	D & G	NT2304	55°19·7'	3°12·4'W	X	79
Fingland	D & G	NX6790	55°11·4'	4°4·9'W	X	77
Fingland	D & G	NY1394	55°14·2'	3°21·7'W	X	78
Fingland	Scot Bord	NT0519	55°27·6'	3°29·7'W	X	78
Fingland	Scot Bord	NT1947	55°42·8'	3°16·9'W	X	72
Fingland Burn	D & G	NS6003	55°18·3'	4°11·9'W	W	77
Fingland Burn	D & G	NS7417	55°26·1'	3°59·1'W	W	71
Fingland Burn	D & G	NS8012	55°23·5'	3°53·2'W	W	71,78
Fingland Burn	D & G	NT2404	55°19·7'	3°11·4'W	W	79
Fingland Burn	D & G	NX6998	55°15·8'	4°3·3'W	W	77
Fingland Burn	Scot Bord	NT0524	55°30·3'	3°29·8'W	W	72
Fingland Burn	Scot Bord	NT0620	55°28·1'	3°28·8'W	W	72
Fingland Burn	Scot Bord	NT0719	55°27·6'	3°27·8'W	W	78
Fingland Burn	Scot Bord	NT1848	55°43·4'	3°17·9'W	W	72
Fingland Burn	Scot Bord	NT3333	55°35·4'	3°3·3'W	W	73
Fingland Fell	D & G	NY1494	55°14·2'	3°20·7'W	X	78
Finglandfoot	D & G	NS5904	55°18·8'	4°12·9'W	X	77
Fingland Hill	D & G	NX6790	55°11·4'	4°4·9'W	H	77
Fingland Hill	S Lanak	NS7322	55°28·8'	4°0·1'W	H	71
Fingland Lane	D & G	NS7318	55°26·6'	4°0·0'W	W	71
Fingland Lane	D & G	NX6689	55°10·9'	4°5·8'W	W	77
Fingland Moss	Cumbr	NY2557	54°54·4'	3°9·8'W	X	85
Fingland Rig	D & G	NS7919	55°27·2'	3°54·4'W	X	71,78
Fingland Rig	D & G	NS8013	55°24·0'	3°53·3'W	H	71,78
Fingland Rigg	Cumbr	NY2757	54°54·4'	3°7·9'W	X	85
Finglandrigg Wood	Cumbr	NY2756	54°53·9'	3°7·9'W	F	85
Fingland Shoulder	D & G	NS7301	55°17·5'	3°59·6'W	H	77
Finglas Water	Stir	NN4911	56°16·3'	4°25·9'W	W	57
Fingle Br	Devon	SX7489	50°41·5'	3°46·7'W	A	191
Fin Glen	Clackm	NN8802	56°12·1'	3°47·9'W	X	58
Fin Glen	E Dunb	NS5881	56°0·3'	4°16·2'W	X	64
Fin Glen	Pth & Kin	NN6344	56°34·3'	4°13·3'W	X	51
Fin Glen	Pth & Kin	NN6622	56°22·5'	4°9·7'W	X	51
Finglen	Pth & Kin	NN6623	56°23·1'	4°9·8'W	X	51
Finglen Burn	Clackm	NN8801	56°11·6'	3°47·9'W	W	58
Finglen Burn	E Dunb	NS5880	55°59·8'	4°16·2'W	W	64
Finglen Burn	Stir	NN6734	56°29·0'	4°9·1'W	W	51
Finglenny	Aberd	NJ4530	57°21·7'	2°54·4'W	X	29,37
Finglen Rig	Scot Bord	NT1332	55°34·7'	3°22·4'W	H	72
Finglesham	Kent	TR3353	51°13·9'	1°20·7'E	T	179
Fingringhoe	Essex	TM0320	51°50·7'	0°57·2'E	T	168
Fingringhoe Marsh	Essex	TM0318	51°49·6'	0°57·2'E	W	168
Fingringhoe Ranges	Essex	TM0318	51°49·6'	0°57·2'E	X	168
Fingrith Hall	Essex	TL6103	51°42·4'	0°20·2'E	X	167
Finham	Cov	SP3375	52°22·6'	1°30·5'W	T	140
Finham Brook	Warw	SP3173	52°21·5'	1°32·3'W	W	140
Finiskaig	Highld	NM8794	56°59·5'	5°29·9'W	X	33,40
Finiskaig River	Highld	NM8794	56°59·5'	5°29·9'W	W	33,40
Finkel Bottoms	N Yks	NZ7406	54°26·9'	0°51·1'W	X	94
Finkle Holme	N Yks	SE4956	54°0·1'	1°14·7'W	X	105
Finkle Street	Barns	SK3098	53°28·9'	1°32·5'W	T	110,111
Finkley Ho	Hants	SU3848	51°14·0'	1°27·0'W	X	185
Finkley Manor Fm	Hants	SU3848	51°14·0'	1°27·0'W	FM	185
Finlaggan	Arg & Bt	NR3968	55°50·3'	6°9·7'W	X	60,61
Finland Burn	W Dunb	NS4481	56°0·1'	4°29·7'W	W	64
Finlarg Hill	Angus	NO4041	56°33·7'	2°58·1'W	H	54
Finlarig	Highld	NH9925	57°18·5'	3°40·1'W	X	36
Finlarig	Stir	NN5733	56°28·3'	4°18·8'W	X	51
Finlas Water	Arg & Bt	NS3388	56°3·6'	4°40·5'W	W	56
Finlate Hill	Aberd	NJ2917	57°14·6'	3°10·1'W	H	37
Finlaystone	Inverc	NS3673	55°55·6'	4°37·1'W	X	63
Finlet	Angus	NO3164	56°46·0'	3°7·3'W	H	44
Finlet Burn	Angus	NO2267	56°47·5'	3°16·2'W	W	44
Finlets	Aberd	NO5691	57°0·7'	2°43·0'W	X	44
Finley Hill	E Yorks	TA1170	54°7·1'	0°17·7'W	X	101
Finlock Bay	D & G	NX0251	54°49·1'	5°4·5'W	W	82
Finlow Hill Fm	Ches	SJ8676	53°17·1'	2°12·2'W	FM	118
Finmere	Oxon	SP6332	51°59·2'	1°4·6'W	T	152,165
Finmere Grounds	Oxon	SP6433	51°59·7'	1°3·7'W	X	152,165
Finmont Fm	Fife	NT2399	56°10·9'	3°14·0'W	FM	58
Finnart	Pth & Kin	NN5157	56°41·1'	4°25·5'W	X	42,51
Finnart Ho	E Susx	TQ5228	51°2·1'	0°10·5'E	X	188,199
Finnart Lo	Pth & Kin	NN5257	56°41·1'	4°24·5'W	X	42,51
Finnart Point	Arg & Bt	NS0876	55°56·6'	5°4·0'W	X	63
Finnarts Bay	S Ayr	NX0472	55°0·5'	5°3·5'W	W	76
Finnarts Fm,	S Ayr	NX0573	55°1·1'	5°2·6'W	FM	76
Finnarts Hill	S Ayr	NX0574	55°1·6'	5°2·6'W	H	76
Finnarts Point	S Ayr	NX0474	55°1·6'	5°3·6'W	X	76
Finners Hill	Staffs	SK0620	52°46·9'	1°54·3'W	X	128
Finney Green	Ches	SJ8582	53°20·3'	2°13·1'W	T	109
Finney Green	Staffs	SJ7946	53°0·9'	2°18·4'W	T	118
Finney Hill	Leic	SK4618	52°45·7'	1°18·7'W	X	129
Finney Hill	Northum	NY8355	54°53·6'	2°15·5'W	X	86,87
Finney Spring Fm	Leic	SK4617	52°45·2'	1°18·7'W	FM	129
Finn Fm	Kent	TR0138	51°6·6'	0°52·7'E	FM	189
Finnich Blair	Stir	NS4885	56°2·3'	4°25·9'W	X	57
Finnich Glen	Stir	NS4984	56°1·8'	4°25·0'W	X	57,64
Finnich Malise	Stir	NS4785	56°2·3'	4°26·9'W	X	57
Finniebrae	E Renf	NS4356	55°46·6'	4°29·8'W	X	64
Finniegill	D & G	NY1798	55°16·4'	3°18·0'W	X	79
Finniegill Burn	D & G	NY1698	55°16·4'	3°18·9'W	W	79
Finnieston	Angus	NO5150	56°38·6'	2°47·5'W	X	54
Finnigarth	Shetld	HU1950	60°14·3'	1°38·9'W	X	3
Finningham Hall	Suff	TM0570	52°17·6'	1°0·8'E	X	144,155
Finniness	D & G	NX7067	54°59·1'	4°1·5'W	X	83,84
Finningham	Suff	TM0669	52°17·1'	1°1·6'E	T	155
Finningham Lodge Fm	Suff	TM0570	52°17·6'	1°0·8'E	FM	144,155
Finningley Airfield	Donc	SK6698	53°28·7'	0°59·9'W	X	111
Finningly Grange Fm	Donc	SE6800	53°29·8'	0°58·1'W	FM	111
Finnister	Shetld	HU4651	60°14·7'	1°9·7'W	X	3
Finnock Bog Fm	Inverc	NS2070	55°53·6'	4°52·3'W	FM	63
Finnygaud	Aberd	NJ6054	57°34·7'	2°39·7'W	T	29
Finnylost	Aberd	NJ3312	57°12·0'	3°6·1'W	X	37
Finracks	Angus	NO4070	56°49·3'	2°58·5'W	H	44
Finsbay Island	N Eil	NG0985	57°45·9'	6°53·1'W	X	18
Finsbury	Isling	TQ3182	51°31·5'	0°6·3'W	T	176,177
Finsbury Park	Hargy	TQ3187	51°34·2'	0°6·2'W	X	176,177
Finsbury Park	Isling	TQ3086	51°33·7'	0°7·1'W	T	176,177
Finstall	Worcs	SO9870	52°19·9'	2°1·4'W	T	139
Finsthwaite	Cumbr	SD3687	54°16·7'	2°58·6'W	T	96,97
Finsthwaite Heights	Cumbr	SD3688	54°17·3'	2°58·6'W	X	96,97
Finsthwaite Ho	Cumbr	SD3687	54°16·7'	2°58·6'W	X	96,97
Finstock	Oxon	SP3616	51°50·7'	1°28·2'W	T	164
Finstock Sta	Oxon	SP3617	51°51·3'	1°28·2'W	X	164
Finstown	Orkney	HY3513	59°0·2'	3°7·4'W	T	6
Fint	Orkney	HY3629	59°8·8'	3°6·6'W	X	6
Fintalich	Pth & Kin	NN8617	56°20·2'	3°50·2'W	X	58
Fintloch	D & G	NX6379	55°5·4'	4°8·4'W	X	77
Fintray Bay	N Ayr	NS1556	55°46·0'	4°56·5'W	W	63
Fintry	Aberd	NJ7554	57°34·8'	2°24·6'W	T	29
Fintry	C of Dun	NO4133	56°29·4'	2°57·0'W	T	54
Fintry	Stir	NS6186	56°3·1'	4°13·5'W	T	57
Fintry Hills	Stir	NS6488	56°4·2'	4°10·6'W	H	57
Fin Wood	Derby	SK1771	53°14·4'	1°44·3'W	F	119
Finwood	Warw	SP1968	52°18·8'	1°42·9'W	T	139,151
Finzean	Aberd	NO6092	57°1·3'	2°39·1'W	T	45
Finzean Ho	Aberd	NO5993	57°1·8'	2°40·1'W	X	37,44
Fiola an Droma	Arg & Bt	NM7009	56°13·3'	5°42·2'W	X	55
Fiola Meadhonach	Arg & Bt	NM7109	56°13·4'	5°41·2'W	X	55
Fiold	Orkney	HY4449	59°19·7'	2°58·6'W	X	5
Fionchra	Highld	NG3300	57°1·1'	6°23·5'W	H	32,39
Fionn-abhainn	Highld	NG9547	57°28·3'	5°24·7'W	W	25
Fionn-aird	Highld	NM4178	56°49·5'	6°14·3'W	H	39
Fionn Allt	Highld	NC3226	58°11·7'	4°51·0'W	W	15
Fionn Allt Beag	N Eil	NB2836	58°14·0'	6°37·6'W	W	8,13
Fionn Allt Mór	N Eil	NB2935	58°13·5'	6°36·5'W	W	8,13
Fionna Mhàm	Arg & Bt	NM4430	56°23·9'	6°8·5'W	H	48
Fionn Aoineadh	Arg & Bt	NM4027	56°22·1'	6°12·2'W	X	48
Fionnar Choire	Highld	NN8894	57°1·7'	3°50·3'W	X	35,36,43
Fionn Ard	Arg & Bt	NM8637	56°28·9'	5°28·1'W	X	49
Fionn Bhealach	N Ayr	NR9749	55°41·8'	5°13·4'W	H	62,69
Fionn Bheinn	Highld	NH1462	57°36·8'	5°6·4'W	H	20
Fionn Bheinn Bheag	Highld	NC3602	57°58·9'	4°45·9'W	H	16
Fionn Bheinn Mhór	Highld	NC3704	58°0·0'	4°45·0'W	H	16
Fionn Choire	Highld	NG4625	57°15·0'	6°12·2'W	X	32

Fionn Choire	N Ayr	NR9742	55°38·0′	5°13·1′W	X	62,69
Fionn Choirein	Arg & Bt	NN2526	56°23·9′	4°49·7′W	X	50
Fionnghlas an Aird	N Eil	NF7655	57°28·4′	7°23·9′W	X	22
Fionn Ghleann	Highld	NN1254	56°38·7′	5°3·5′W	X	41
Fionn Ghleann	Highld	NN2251	56°37·3′	4°53·6′W	X	41
Fionn Ghleann	Stir	NN3122	56°21·9′	4°43·7′W	X	50
Fionngleann	Highld	NH0518	57°12·9′	5°13·3′W	X	33
Fionn Leirg	Arg & Bt	NN2138	56°30·3′	4°54·1′W	X	50
Fionn Lighe	Highld	NM9682	56°53·3′	5°20·5′W	W	40
Fionn Lighe	Highld	NN0084	56°54·5′	5°16·6′W	W	41
Fionn Loch	Highld	NC1217	58°6·4′	5°11·0′W	W	15
Fionn Loch	Highld	NG9478	57°44·9′	5°27·2′W	W	19
Fionn Loch Beag	Highld	NC3422	58°9·6′	4°48·8′W	W	15
Fionn Loch Mór	Highld	NC3323	58°10·1′	4°49·9′W	W	15
Fionnphort	Arg & Bt	NM3023	56°19·6′	6°21·6′W	T	48
Fionn Phort	Arg & Bt	NM7533	56°26·4′	5°38·6′W	W	49
Fionn Phort	Arg & Bt	NR2857	55°44·1′	6°19·5′W	X	60
Fionn-phort	Arg & Bt	NR4366	55°49·4′	6°5·8′W	W	60,61
Fionn Phort	Arg & Bt	NR9064	55°49·7′	5°20·7′W	W	62
Fionnsabhagh	N Eil	NG0786	57°46·3′	6°55·2′W	T	14,18
Fionn-tom Mór	Highld	NH6306	57°7·7′	4°15·3′W	X	35
Fiorda Taing	Shetld	HU2176	60°28·3′	1°36·6′W	X	3
Fiorloch	Highld	NG7689	57°50·3′	5°46·0′W	W	19
Firbank	Cumbr	NY3864	54°58·3′	2°57·7′W	X	85
Firbank	Cumbr	SD6294	54°20·7′	2°34·7′W	T	97
Firbank Fell	Cumbr	SD6093	54°20·1′	2°36·5′W	H	97
Firbank Fellside	Cumbr	SD6095	54°21·2′	2°36·5′W	X	97
Firbeck	Roth	SK5688	53°23·4′	1°9·1′W	T	111,120
Firbeck Common	Derby	SK5378	53°18·0′	1°11·9′W	X	120
Firbeck Ho	Derby	SK5378	53°18·0′	1°11·9′W	X	120
Fir Bhreugach	Highld	NG4470	57°39·1′	6°17·0′W	H	23
Fir Bog	Aberd	NO4189	56°59·6′	2°57·8′W	X	44
Firbogs	Aberd	NJ6924	57°18·6′	2°30·4′W	X	38
Firbush Point	Stir	NN6033	56°28·4′	4°15·9′W	X	51
Firby	N Yks	SE2686	54°16·4′	1°35·6′W	T	99
Firby	N Yks	SE7466	54°5·3′	0°51·7′W	T	100
Firby Grange	N Yks	SE2586	54°16·4′	1°36·5′W	X	99
Firby Wood	N Yks	SE7467	54°5·9′	0°51·7′W	F	100
Fircone Fm	Worcs	SO9255	52°11·8′	2°6·6′W	FM	150
Firdeal Hill	Notts	SK5423	52°48·3′	1°11·5′W	X	129
Fireach Ard	Highld	NG8626	57°16·7′	5°32·6′W	H	33
Fireach Beag	Moray	NJ1523	57°17·6′	3°24·2′W	H	36
Fireach Dubh	Highld	NM7772	56°47·4′	5°38·6′W	H	40
Fireach na Moine	Arg & Bt	NN2326	56°23·8′	4°51·6′W	X	50
Firebeacon	Devon	SS2420	50°57·4′	4°30·0′W	X	190
Firebeacon	Devon	SS9516	50°56·3′	3°29·3′W	X	181
Fire Beacon Cross	Devon	SS5528	51°2·2′	4°3·7′W	X	180
Firebeacon Hill	Corn	SX0790	50°40·9′	4°43·5′W	X	190
Fire Beacon Hill	Devon	SX8653	50°22·2′	3°35·8′W	X	202
Fire Beacon Point	Corn	SX1092	50°42·0′	4°41·1′W	X	190
Firebrass Hill	Oxon	SU6492	51°37·6′	1°4·1′W	X	164,175
Fireburnmill	Scot Bord	NT8239	55°38·9′	2°16·7′W	X	74
Fire Clay Fm	St Hel	SD4900	53°29·9′	2°45·7′W	FM	108
Fire Hill	Suff	TM2538	51°59·9′	1°17·1′E	X	169
Fire Hills	E Susx	TQ8611	50°52·3′	0°39·0′E	X	199
Firemore	Highld	NG8187	57°49·4′	5°40·8′W	X	19
Firestane Edge	Scot Bord	NT4014	55°25·2′	2°56·4′W	H	79
Firestone Copse	I of W	SZ5591	50°43·2′	1°12·9′W	F	196
Fire Stone Cross	Devon	SX6693	50°43·5′	3°53·5′W	X	191
Firestone Hill	Derby	SK3346	53°0·9′	1°30·1′W	H	119,128
Firfield	Aberd	NJ5462	57°39·0′	2°45·8′W	X	29
Firfield Fm	Lincs	TF0096	53°27·3′	0°29·2′W	FM	112
Firfields	Wilts	SU0333	51°6·0′	1°57·0′W	F	184
Fir Fm	Glos	SP1724	51°55·1′	1°44·8′W	FM	163
Firfolds	Aberd	NJ6559	57°37·4′	2°34·7′W	X	29
Firgo Fm	Hants	SU4644	51°11·8′	1°20·1′W	FM	185
Firgreen Br	Leeds	SE4344	53°53·7′	1°20·3′W	X	105
Firgrove	Denb	SJ1057	53°6·4′	3°20·3′W	X	116
Firgrove	E Susx	TQ5217	50°56·2′	0°10·2′E	X	199
Firgrove	Roch	SD9213	53°37·1′	2°6·8′W	T	109
Fir Grove	Suff	TM4985	52°24·6′	1°40·1′E	F	156
Fir Grove Fm	Dorset	SU1000	50°48·2′	1°51·1′W	FM	195
Firgrove Fm	Lincs	TF2068	53°12·0′	0°11·8′W	FM	122
Firgrove Manor	Hants	SU7960	51°20·2′	0°51·6′W	X	175,186
Firhall	Highld	NH8855	57°34·5′	3°51·9′W	X	27
Firhill	Highld	NH6469	57°41·7′	4°16·4′W	T	21
Fir Hill	Lincs	TF3682	53°19·3′	0°2·9′E	X	122
Fir Hill	Norf	TG2004	52°35·6′	1°15·3′E	X	134
Fir Hill	Stir	NS5396	56°8·3′	4°21·5′W	H	57
Fir Hill	Wilts	SU0029	51°3·9′	1°59·6′W	H	184
Firhills	Angus	NO6345	56°36·0′	2°35·7′W	X	54
Fir Ho	Powys	SJ2704	52°38·0′	3°4·3′W	X	126
Fir I	Cumbr	SD3094	54°20·5′	3°4·2′W	X	96,97
Firkin	Arg & Bt	NN3300	56°10·1′	4°40·9′W	X	56
Firkin Point	Arg & Bt	NN3300	56°10·1′	4°40·9′W	X	56
Fir Knowe	Scot Bord	NT0536	55°36·8′	3°30·1′W	X	72
Firlands	Heref	SO6749	52°8·5′	2°28·5′W	X	149
Firlands	W Berks	SU6466	51°23·6′	1°4·4′W	X	175
Firlands Fm	N Yks	SE3363	54°4·0′	1°29·3′W	FM	99
Firle Beacon	E Susx	TQ4805	50°49·8′	0°6·5′E	H	198
Firle Park	E Susx	TQ4707	50°50·9′	0°5·7′E	X	198
Firle Place	E Susx	TQ4707	50°50·9′	0°5·7′E	A	198
Firle Plantn	E Susx	TQ4706	50°50·3′	0°5·7′E	F	198
Firley Moss	Aberd	NJ7512	57°12·1′	2°24·4′W	F	38
Firmounth Road	Aberd	NO4793	57°1·8′	2°51·9′W	X	37,44
Firmounth Road	Aberd	NO4889	56°59·6′	2°50·9′W	X	44
Firpark	D & G	NY1379	55°6·1′	3°21·4′W	X	85
Firpark	S Lanak	NT0246	55°42·1′	3°33·1′W	X	72
Firpark Plantation	N Ayr	NS2157	55°46·7′	4°50·8′W	F	63
Fir Patch	Norf	TG0732	52°51·0′	1°4·9′E	X	133
Firs	Cumbr	NY1943	54°46·8′	3°15·1′W	X	85
Firs	N Yks	NY8601	54°24·5′	2°12·5′W	X	91,92
Firsby	Lincs	TF4563	53°8·9′	0°10·5′E	T	122
Firsby Clough	Lincs	TF4661	53°7·8′	0°11·3′E	X	122
Firsby Hall Fm	Roth	SK4996	53°27·7′	1°15·3′W	FM	111
Firs Cottage	Aberd	NJ3315	57°13·5′	3°6·1′W	X	37
Firsdon Fm	Devon	SS5815	50°55·3′	4°0·8′W	FM	180
Firsdown	Wilts	SU2133	51°6·0′	1°41·6′W	T	184
Firs Fm	Cambs	TL3058	52°12·5′	0°5·4′W	FM	153
Firs Fm	Derby	SK2145	53°0·4′	1°40·8′W	FM	119,128

Firs Fm	Heref	SO2733	51°59·7′	3°3·4′W	FM	161
Firs Fm	Heref	SO3135	52°0·8′	2°59·9′W	FM	161
Firs Fm	Lincs	SK8478	53°17·8′	0°44·0′W	FM	121
Fir's Fm	Notts	SK5558	53°7·2′	1°10·3′W	FM	120
Firs Fm	Notts	SK6483	53°20·6′	1°1·9′W	FM	111,120
Firs Fm	Notts	SK7745	53°0·0′	0°50·7′W	FM	129
Firs Fm	Staffs	SJ7851	53°3·6′	2°19·3′W	FM	118
Firs Fm	Suff	TM4159	52°10·8′	1°31·9′E	FM	156
Firs Fm	Warw	SP4365	52°17·1′	1°21·8′W	FM	151
Firs Fm	Warw	SP4449	52°8·5′	1°21·0′W	FM	151
Firs Fm	Wrex	SJ3842	52°58·5′	2°55·0′W	FM	117
Firs Fm,The	Norf	TM1486	52°26·0′	1°9·3′E	FM	144,156
Firs Hill	Oxon	SP4236	52°1·5′	1°22·9′W	X	151
Firsland Fm	W Susx	TQ2418	50°57·1′	0°13·7′W	FM	198
Firs Lane	Wigan	SD6400	53°30·0′	2°32·2′W	T	109
First Coast	Highld	NG9291	57°51·9′	5°29·9′W	T	19
First Dale Plantn	E Yorks	SE8550	53°56·6′	0°41·9′W	F	106
Firs, The	Beds	SP9848	52°7·5′	0°33·7′W	X	153
Firs, The	Essex	TM1730	51°55·8′	1°9·8′E	X	168,169
Firs, The	Hants	SU5857	51°18·8′	1°9·7′W	X	174
Firs, The	I of Angl	SH3593	53°24·7′	4°28·5′W	X	114
Firs, The	Kent	TQ9631	51°2·9′	0°48·2′E	X	189
Firs, The	Lincs	SK8642	52°58·3′	0°42·8′W	X	130
Firs, The	Norf	TF6739	52°55·6′	0°29·5′E	X	132
Firs, The	Notts	SK5552	53°4·0′	1°10·3′W	X	120
Firs, The	N Yks	SE8477	54°11·2′	0°42·3′W	X	100
Firs, The	Peterb	TF1904	52°37·5′	0°14·1′W	X	142
Firs, The	S Lanak	NS9324	55°30·1′	3°41·2′W	X	71,72
Firs, The	Sol	SP2475	52°22·6′	1°38·4′W	X	139
Firs, The	Stir	NS5186	56°2·9′	4°23·1′W	X	57
Firs, The	Suff	TM1563	52°13·6′	1°9·3′E	X	156
Firs, The	Suff	TM2166	52°15·1′	1°14·7′E	X	156
Firs, The	Suff	TM3074	52°19·2′	1°22·9′E	X	156
Firs, The	Suff	TM3075	52°19·7′	1°22·9′E	X	156
Firs, The	Suff	TM4353	52°7·5′	1°33·4′E	X	156
Firs, The	Wilts	SU0486	51°34·6′	1°56·1′W	F	173
Firs, The	Wilts	SU0768	51°24·9′	1°53·6′W	X	173
Firs, The	Worcs	SO8851	52°9·7′	2°10·1′W	X	150
Firs, The	Worcs	SO9565	52°17·2′	2°4·0′W	X	150
Firs, The	W Susx	SU9606	50°51·0′	0°37·8′W	X	197
First Hill	Leic	SK7514	52°43·3′	0°53·0′W	X	129
First Inchna Burn	Clackm	NS8598	56°9·9′	3°50·7′W	W	58
First Slips	Suff	TL8078	52°22·5′	0°39·1′E	F	144
Firswood	Traf	SJ8195	53°27·3′	2°16·8′W	T	109
Firth	Angus	NO5340	56°33·2′	2°45·4′W	X	54
Firth	Northum	NU1710	55°23·3′	1°43·5′W	X	81
Firth	Orkney	HY3514	59°0·8′	3°7·4′W	X	6
Firth	Scot Bord	NT5423	55°30·2′	2°43·3′W	T	73
Firth	Shetld	HU4473	60°26·6′	1°11·5′W	X	2,3
Firth Bank	N Yks	SE5792	54°19·5′	1°7·0′W	F	100
Firth Fell	N Yks	SD9375	54°10·5′	2°6·0′W	X	98
Firthfield	Angus	NO5943	56°34·9′	2°39·6′W	X	54
Firthhead	D & G	NX8263	54°57·1′	3°50·1′W	F	84
Firth Hill Plantn	N Yks	SD9663	54°4·0′	2°3·3′W	F	98
Firth Ho	Midlo	NT2561	55°50·4′	3°11·4′W	X	66
Firth Mains	Midlo	NT2560	55°49·9′	3°11·4′W	X	66
Firth Moor	Darl	NZ3013	54°30·9′	1°31·8′W	T	93
Firth Muir of Boysack	Angus	NO5944	56°35·4′	2°39·6′W	T	54
Firth Ness	Shetld	HU4672	60°26·0′	1°9·4′W	X	2,3
Firth of Clyde	Arg & Bt	NS2679	55°58·6′	4°46·9′W	W	63
Firth of Clyde	N Ayr	NS1042	55°38·3′	5°0·7′W	W	63,69
Firth of Forth		NT5789	56°5·8′	2°41·0′W	W	67
Firth of Forth	Fife	NT3685	56°3·5′	3°1·2′W	W	66
Firth of Lorn	Arg & Bt	NM6717	56°17·6′	5°45·5′W	W	55
Firth of Lorn	Arg & Bt	NM7628	56°23·8′	5°37·3′W	W	49
Firth of Tay	C of Dun	NO3928	56°26·7′	2°58·9′W	W	54,59
Firth of Tay	Pth & Kin	NO3024	56°24·4′	3°7·6′W	W	53,59
Firtholme Fm	E Yorks	TA4017	53°38·1′	0°7·5′E	FM	113
Firthope Rig	D & G	NT1515	55°25·5′	3°20·2′W	H	79
Firth Park	Sheff	SK3691	53°25·1′	1°27·1′W	T	110,111
Firth Plantn	E Loth	NT6178	55°59·9′	2°37·1′W	F	67
Firths Voe	Shetld	HU4474	60°27·1′	1°11·5′W	W	2,3
Firth, The	Shetld	HU3450	60°14·2′	1°22·7′W	W	3
Firth Wood	N Yks	SD9475	54°10·5′	2°5·1′W	F	98
Firthybrig Head	Scot Bord	NT1517	55°26·6′	3°20·2′W	H	79
Fir Toll	Kent	TQ9244	51°10·0′	0°45·2′E	T	189
Fir Tree	Durham	NZ1434	54°42·3′	1°46·5′W	T	92
Fir Tree Fm	Bucks	SP7732	51°59·1′	0°52·3′W	FM	152,165
Fir Tree Fm	Ches	SJ5165	53°11·0′	2°43·6′W	FM	117
Firtree Fm	Ches	SJ6682	53°20·3′	2°30·2′W	FM	109
Firtree Fm	Ches	SJ7977	53°17·6′	2°18·5′W	FM	118
Firtree Fm	Ches	SJ8175	53°16·5′	2°16·7′W	FM	118
Fir Tree Fm	Darl	NZ3121	54°35·2′	1°30·8′W	FM	93
Fir Tree Fm	Dorset	ST7307	50°51·9′	2°22·6′W	FM	194
Fir Tree Fm	E Yorks	SE7833	53°47·5′	0°48·5′W	FM	105,106
Fir Tree Fm	Flint	SJ3766	53°11·3′	2°56·2′W	FM	117
Firtree Fm	Hants	SU4817	50°57·3′	1°18·6′W	FM	185
Fir Tree Fm	Kent	TQ8050	51°13·5′	0°35·1′E	FM	188
Fir Tree Fm	Lancs	SD3906	53°33·1′	2°54·8′W	FM	108
Fir Tree Fm	Lancs	SD4341	53°52·0′	2°51·6′W	FM	102
Fir Tree Fm	Lancs	SD4832	53°47·1′	2°46·9′W	FM	102
Fir Tree Fm	Lincs	SK8194	53°26·4′	0°46·4′W	FM	112
Fir Tree Fm	Lincs	TF5367	53°10·9′	0°17·8′E	FM	122
Fir Tree Fm	N Lincs	TA1323	53°41·7′	0°16·9′W	FM	107,113
Fir Tree Fm	Northnts	SP5467	52°18·1′	1°12·1′W	FM	152
Firtree Fm	N Yks	SE3696	54°21·7′	1°26·3′W	FM	99
Fir Tree Fm	N Yks	SE5735	53°48·7′	1°7·6′W	FM	105
Fir Tree Fm	N Yks	SE6635	53°48·7′	0°59·4′W	FM	105,106
Fir Tree Fm	N Yks	SE7580	54°12·9′	0°50·6′W	FM	100
Fir Tree Fm	Oxon	SP4923	51°54·4′	1°16·9′W	FM	164
Fir Tree Fm	Shrops	SJ5841	52°58·1′	2°37·1′W	FM	117
Fir Tree Fm	Somer	ST4244	51°11·8′	2°49·4′W	FM	182
Fir Tree Fm	Somer	ST6028	51°3·2′	2°33·9′W	FM	183
Firtree Fm	Suff	TM3657	52°9·9′	1°27·5′E	FM	156
Fir Tree Fm	Warw	SP2885	52°28·0′	1°34·9′W	FM	140
Fir Tree Fm	Warw	SP4047	52°7·4′	1°24·5′W	FM	151
Fir Tree Fm	York	SE6447	53°55·1′	1°1·1′W	FM	105,106
Fir Tree Grange	Durham	NZ1533	54°41·8′	1°45·6′W	X	92
Firtree Hill	Beds	TL0842	52°4·2′	0°25·1′W	X	153
Firtree Hill	D & G	NY1687	55°10·5′	3°18·7′W	H	79

Fir Tree Ho	N Yks	SE8480	54°12·8′	0°42·3′W	X	100
Firtree Piece	W Susx	SU7511	50°53·8′	0°55·6′W	F	197
Fir Trees	Lancs	SD5639	53°51·0′	2°39·7′W	X	102
Firtrees	Northum	NY8962	54°57·4′	2°9·9′W	X	87
Fir Trees Ho	N Yks	NZ6606	54°26·9′	0°58·5′W	X	94
Fir Vale	Sheff	SK3690	53°24·6′	1°27·1′W	T	110,111
Firwood Fm	Flint	SJ1567	53°11·8′	3°15·9′W	FM	116
Firwood Fold	Bolton	SD7311	53°35·9′	2°24·1′W	T	109
Fiscary	Highld	NC7262	58°31·9′	4°11·4′W	X	10
Fishacre Barton	Devon	SX8164	50°28·1′	3°40·2′W	X	202
Fishacre Wood	Devon	SX4766	50°28·7′	4°9·0′W	F	201
Fish Barn Fm	Lancs	SD6016	53°38·6′	2°35·9′W	FM	109
Fishbeck	Brad	SE0447	53°55·4′	1°55·9′W	X	104
Fishbeck	D & G	NY1084	55°8·8′	3°24·3′W	X	78
Fishbourne	I of W	SZ5592	50°43·7′	1°12·9′W	T	196
Fishbourne	W Susx	SU8304	50°50·0′	0°48·9′W	T	197
Fishburn	Durham	NZ3632	54°41·1′	1°26·1′W	T	93
Fishcombe Point	Torbay	SX9157	50°24·4′	3°31·7′W	X	202
Fishcross	Clackm	NS9095	56°8·4′	3°45·8′W	T	58
Fisher	W Susx	SU8700	50°47·8′	0°45·5′W	X	197
Fisherbriggs	Aberd	NJ9265	57°40·7′	2°7·6′W	X	30
Fisher Crag	Cumbr	NY3016	54°32·3′	3°4·5′W	X	90
Fisherfield Forest	Highld	NH0080	57°46·2′	5°21·3′W	X	19
Fisherford	Aberd	NJ6635	57°24·5′	2°33·5′W	T	29
Fisher Gill	Cumbr	NY2953	54°52·3′	3°6·0′W	X	85
Fisher Gill	Cumbr	NY3218	54°33·4′	3°2·7′W	W	90
Fisherground Fm	Cumbr	NY1500	54°23·6′	3°18·1′W	FM	89
Fisherhills	Angus	NO7262	56°45·2′	2°27·0′W	X	45
Fisherlane Wood	Surrey	SU9832	51°5·0′	0°35·7′W	F	186
Fisherman's Channel	E Yorks	TA2819	53°39·3′	0°3·4′W	W	113
Fishermans Head	Essex	TR0392	51°35·6′	0°56·2′E	X	178
Fishermead	Mil Key	SP8638	52°2·3′	0°44·4′W	T	152
Fishermen's Moss	Aberd	NJ6256	57°35·8′	2°37·7′W	X	29
Fisher Place	Cumbr	NY3118	54°33·4′	3°3·6′W	X	90
Fisherrow	E Loth	NT3473	55°57·0′	3°3·0′W	T	66
Fisherrow Sands	E Loth	NT3373	55°57·0′	3°3·9′W	X	66
Fishers	Suff	TL8050	52°7·4′	0°38·2′E	X	155
Fisher's Brook	Wilts	ST9973	51°27·6′	2°0·5′W	W	173
Fisher's Fm	Essex	TM1222	51°51·6′	1°5·1′E	FM	168,169
Fisher's Fm	Essex	TQ8290	51°35·0′	0°38·0′E	FM	178
Fisher's Fm	E Susx	TQ7024	50°59·6′	0°25·7′E	FM	199
Fisher's Fm	Kent	TQ7844	51°10·3′	0°33·2′E	FM	188
Fisher's Fm	Lancs	SD5239	53°50·9′	2°43·4′W	FM	102
Fisher's Fm	W Berks	SU3573	51°27·5′	1°29·4′W	FM	174
Fisher's Fm	W Berks	SU4970	51°25·8′	1°17·3′W	FM	174
Fisher's Gate	E Susx	TQ4933	51°4·8′	0°8·0′E	X	188
Fishersgate	W Susx	TQ2505	50°50·1′	0°13·1′W	T	198
Fishers Green	Essex	TL3702	51°42·2′	0°0·6′W	X	166
Fishers Green	Herts	TL2226	51°55·4′	0°13·2′W	T	166
Fishersgreen Fm	Ches	SJ5464	53°10·5′	2°40·9′W	FM	117
Fisher Sike	Cumbr	NY7825	54°37·4′	2°20·0′W	W	91
Fisher's Marshes	Norf	TG5006	52°35·9′	1°41·9′E	X	134
Fisher's Pond	Hants	SU4820	50°58·9′	1°18·6′W	T	185
Fisher's Row	Lancs	SD4148	53°55·7′	2°53·5′W	X	102
Fisher Stead	Northum	NT9236	55°37·3′	2°7·2′W	X	74,75
Fishers, The	Oxon	SP4731	51°58·8′	1°18·5′W	X	151
Fisherstreet	W Susx	SU9431	51°4·5′	0°39·1′W	T	186
Fisher Tarn Resr	Cumbr	SD5592	54°19·5′	2°41·1′W	W	97
Fisherton	Devon	SS5728	51°2·3′	4°2·0′W	X	180
Fisherton	Devon	SS5922	50°59·0′	4°0·1′W	X	180
Fisherton	Highld	NH7451	57°32·2′	4°5·8′W	T	27
Fisherton	S Ayr	NS2616	55°24·7′	4°44·5′W	T	70
Fisherton	S Ayr	NS2717	55°25·2′	4°43·6′W	X	70
Fisherton de la Mere	Wilts	SU0038	51°8·7′	1°59·6′W	T	184
Fishertown	Highld	NH8857	57°35·6′	3°52·0′W	X	27
Fisherwick	Staffs	SK1808	52°40·4′	1°43·6′W	T	128
Fisherwick Hall	Staffs	SK1709	52°40·9′	1°44·5′W	X	128
Fishery	Win & Maid	SU8980	51°30·9′	0°42·6′W	T	175
Fishery Cott	C of Edin	NT1579	56°0·0′	3°21·3′W	X	65
Fishery, The	Hants	SU6859	51°19·8′	1°1·0′W	X	175,186
Fish Fm	Highld	NC0713	58°4·1′	5°15·9′W	X	15
Fishfold Fm	Surrey	TQ1339	51°8·6′	0°22·7′W	FM	187
Fishgarth Wood	Cumbr	NY5049	54°50·2′	2°46·3′W	F	86
Fishguard (Abergwaun)	Pemb	SM9537	51°59·9′	4°58·8′W	T	157
Fishguard Bay	Pemb	SM9739	52°1·0′	4°57·1′W	W	157
Fishguard Harbour	Pemb	SM9538	52°0·4′	4°58·8′W	X	157
Fish Hall	Kent	TQ6147	51°12·2′	0°18·7′E	X	188
Fish Hill	Worcs	SP1137	52°2·1′	1°50·0′W	H	150
Fish Holm	Shetld	HU4774	60°27·1′	1°8·2′W	X	2,3
Fish House Moss	Cumbr	SD3382	54°14·0′	3°1·3′W	X	96,97
Fishing Barrow	Dorset	SZ0182	50°38·5′	1°58·8′W	A	195
Fishing Cove	Corn	SW5943	50°14·5′	5°22·4′W	W	203
Fishing Geo	Orkney	HY3630	59°9·4′	3°6·7′W	X	6
Fishing Loch	Arg & Bt	NR6488	56°1·9′	5°46·8′W	W	55,61
Fishing Lodge, The	Fife	NT1291	56°6·5′	3°24·5′W	X	58
Fishing Point	Corn	SX0652	50°20·4′	4°43·2′W	X	200,204
Fishlake	Donc	SE6513	53°36·8′	1°0·6′W	T	111
Fish Lake	Durham	NY8522	54°35·8′	2°13·5′W	W	91,92
Fishleigh	Devon	SS4704	50°49·2′	4°9·9′W	X	191
Fishleigh	Devon	SS5405	50°49·8′	4°4·0′W	T	191
Fishleigh Barton	Devon	SS5824	51°0·1′	4°1·0′W	X	180
Fishleigh Castle	Devon	SS5405	50°49·8′	4°4·0′W	T	191
Fishley	Devon	SX6850	50°20·3′	3°50·9′W	X	202
Fishley	Norf	TG4011	52°38·8′	1°33·3′E	T	134
Fishley	Wals	SK0003	52°37·7′	1°59·6′W	T	139
Fish Locks Ho	Darl	NZ3509	54°28·8′	1°27·2′W	X	93
Fishmere End	Lincs	TF2737	52°55·2′	0°6·3′W	T	131
Fishmoor Resr	Black w Dar	SD6926	53°44·0′	2°27·8′W	W	103
Fishnet Point	Lancs	SD4456	54°0·1′	2°50·8′W	X	102
Fishnish Bay	Arg & Bt	NM6442	56°30·9′	5°49·7′W	W	49
Fishnish Point	Arg & Bt	NM6442	56°30·9′	5°49·7′W	X	49
Fishpits	Essex	TL8733	51°58·1′	0°43·7′E	X	168
Fish Pond	D & G	NX0941	54°43·9′	4°57·6′W	W	82
Fish Pond	Leeds	SE3144	53°53·7′	1°31·3′W	W	104
Fishpond Bottom	Dorset	SY3698	50°46·9′	2°54·1′W	T	193
Fishpond Cottage	Notts	SK6733	52°53·7′	0°59·8′W	X	129
Fish Pond Fm	Lincs	TF0994	53°26·1′	0°21·1′W	FM	112
Fishpond Fm	Somer	ST4639	51°9·1′	2°45·9′W	FM	182
Fishpond Fm	Suff	TM0072	52°18·8′	0°56·5′E	FM	144,155

Fishpond Hill	Notts	SK5161	53°8·9'	1°13·8'W	X	120
Fishponds	C of Bris	ST6375	51°28·6'	2°31·6'W	T	172
Fish Ponds	Pemb	SR9795	51°37·3'	4°55·6'W	W	158
Fishponds Fm	Hants	SU3727	51°2·7'	1°27·9'W	FM	185
Fishponds Fm	Kent	TR0844	51°9·7'	0°58·9'E	FM	179,189
Fishponds Fm	W Berks	SU3963	51°22·1'	1°26·0'W	FM	174
Fish Ponds Wood	E Yorks	TA1467	54°5·4'	0°15·0'W	F	101
Fishpond Wood	E Yorks	SE7738	53°50·2'	0°49·4'W	F	105,106
Fishpond Wood	E Yorks	TA0135	53°48·3'	0°27·6'W	F	106,107
Fishpond Wood	Kent	TR0858	51°17·2'	0°59·4'E	F	179
Fishpond Wood	N Yks	SE1564	54°4·5'	1°45·8'W	F	99
Fishpool	Bury	SD8009	53°34·9'	2°17·7'W	T	109
Fishpool	Glos	SO6629	51°57·7'	2°29·3'W	T	149
Fishpool	N Yks	SE2347	53°55·4'	1°38·6'W	T	104
Fishpool	Powys	SO3195	52°33·1'	3°0·7'W	X	137
Fishpool Brook	Leic	SK5918	52°45·6'	1°7·1'W	W	129
Fishpool Fm	Powys	SO0472	52°20·5'	3°24·2'W	FM	136,147
Fishpool Grange	Leic	SK4519	52°46·2'	1°19·6'W	X	129
Fishpool Hill	Heref	SO6034	52°0·4'	2°34·6'W	X	149
Fishpools	Powys	SO1968	52°18·5'	3°10·9'W	X	136,148
Fishpools, The	Derby	SK3152	53°4·1'	1°31·8'W	X	119
Fishpool Valley	Heref	SO4566	52°17·6'	2°48·0'W	X	137,138,148
Fish's Heath	Suff	TL9569	52°17·3'	0°52·0'E	F	155
Fish, The	Shrops	SO3984	52°27·3'	2°53·5'W	X	137
Fishtoft	Lincs	TF3642	52°57·7'	0°1·9'E	T	131
Fishtoft Drove	Lincs	TF3149	53°1·6'	0°2·4'W	T	131
Fishweir	V of Glam	ST0171	51°26·0'	3°25·1'W	X	170
Fishwick	Lancs	SD5629	53°45·6'	2°39·6'W	T	102
Fishwick	Scot Bord	NT9151	55°45·4'	2°8·2'W	X	67,74,75
Fishwick Mains	Scot Bord	NT9150	55°44·8'	2°8·2'W	X	67,74,75
Fiska Geo	Shetld	HP6115	60°49·1'	0°52·2'W	X	1
Fiskaidly	Aberd	NJ6562	57°39·1'	2°34·7'W	X	29
Fiska Skerry	Shetld	HU4855	60°16·8'	1°7·4'W	X	3
Fiskavaig	Highld	NG3234	57°19·3'	6°26·7'W	T	32
Fiskavaig Bay	Highld	NG3334	57°19·4'	6°25·7'W	W	32
Fiskavaig Burn	Highld	NG3333	57°18·8'	6°25·6'W	W	32
Fiska Wick	Shetld	HP6115	60°49·1'	0°52·2'W	W	1
Fiskerton	Lincs	TF0472	53°14·3'	0°26·1'W	T	121
Fiskerton	Notts	SK7351	53°3·3'	0°54·2'W	T	120
Fiskerton Fen	Lincs	TF0872	53°14·3'	0°22·5'W	X	121
Fiskerton Grange	Notts	SK7250	53°2·8'	0°55·2'W	X	120
Fiskerton Mill	Notts	SK7451	53°3·3'	0°53·3'W	X	120
Fiskerton Moor	Lincs	TF0673	53°14·8'	0°24·3'W	X	121
Fiskerton Sta	Notts	SK7352	53°3·9'	0°54·2'W	X	120
Fisk Hellia	Orkney	HY3328	59°8·3'	3°9·8'W	X	6
Fisk's Fm	Suff	TM3065	52°14·3'	1°22·5'E	FM	156
Fissla Taing	Shetld	HU2976	60°28·3'	1°27·9'W	X	3
Fistard	I of M	SC2067	54°4·3'	4°44·6'W	X	95
Fistral Bay	Corn	SW7962	50°25·2'	5°6·3'W	W	200
Fistral Beach	Corn	SW7962	50°25·2'	5°6·3'W	X	200
Fitch	Shetld	HU3843	60°10·4'	1°18·4'W	X	4
Fitcher Brook	Worcs	SO7958	52°13·4'	2°18·0'W	W	150
Fitches Grange	Durham	NZ1430	54°40·1'	1°46·6'W	X	92
Fitch Way	Essex	TL5721	51°52·2'	0°17·2'E	X	167
Fitful Head	Shetld	HU3413	59°54·3'	1°23·0'W	X	4
Fithie	Angus	NO6353	56°40·8'	2°35·8'W	X	54
Fithie Burn	Angus	NO4236	56°31·0'	2°56·1'W	W	54
Fithie Wood	Angus	NO6353	56°40·3'	2°35·8'W	F	54
Fithlers Hall Fm	Essex	TL6304	51°42·9'	0°22·0'E	FM	167
Fitling	E Yorks	TA2534	53°47·5'	0°5·7'W	T	107
Fitling Hall	E Yorks	TA2533	53°46·9'	0°5·8'W	X	107
Fitties, The	Lincs	TA3800	53°28·9'	0°5·2'E	X	113
Fittleton	Wilts	SU1449	51°14·6'	1°47·6'W	T	184
Fittleworth	W Susx	TQ0119	50°57·9'	0°33·3'W	T	197
Fittleworth Common	W Susx	TQ0118	50°57·4'	0°33·3'W	X	197
Fitton End	Cambs	TF4212	52°41·5'	0°6·5'E	T	131,142,143
Fitton Hall	Norf	TF5913	52°41·7'	0°21·6'E	X	131,143
Fitton Hill	Oldham	SD9302	53°31·1'	2°5·9'W	T	109
Fittontown Fm	Ches	SJ8775	53°16·6'	2°11·3'W	FM	118
Fitty Hill	Orkney	HY4244	59°17·0'	3°0·6'W	H	5
Fitz	Cumbr	NY1640	54°45·1'	3°17·9'W	X	85
Fitz	Shrops	SJ4417	52°45·1'	2°49·4'W	T	126
Fitzandrew's Fm	Essex	TL6914	51°48·2'	0°27·5'E	FM	167
Fitzhall	W Susx	SU8421	50°59·2'	0°47·8'W	X	197
Fitzhead	Somer	ST1128	51°3·2'	3°15·8'W	T	181,193
Fitzjohns	Warw	SP5073	52°21·4'	1°15·5'W	X	140
Fitzjohn's Fm	Essex	TL6713	51°47·7'	0°25·7'E	FM	167
Fitz John's Fm	Essex	TL8132	51°57·6'	0°38·5'E	FM	168
Fitzlea Fm	W Susx	SU9419	50°58·0'	0°39·3'W	FM	197
Fitzleroi Fm	W Susx	TQ0120	50°58·5'	0°33·3'W	FM	197
Fitzroy	Somer	ST1927	51°2·4'	3°8·9'W	X	181,193
Fitz, The	Cumbr	NY1130	54°39·7'	3°22·4'W	X	89
Fitzwalters	Essex	TQ6197	51°39·1'	0°20·0'E	X	167,177
Fitzwilliam	Wakf	SE4115	53°38·0'	1°22·4'W	T	111
Fitzworth Point	Dorset	SY9986	50°40·6'	2°0·5'W	X	195
Fiunary	Highld	NM6146	56°33·0'	5°52·9'W	T	49
Fiurnean	Highld	NG5149	57°28·0'	6°8·7'W	H	23,24
Five Acres	Glos	SO5712	51°48·5'	2°37·0'W	T	162
Five Acres	Somer	ST2712	50°54·4'	3°1·9'W	X	193
Five Ash Down	E Susx	TQ4724	51°0·0'	0°6·1'E	T	198
Five Ashes	Ches	SJ9572	53°14·9'	2°4·1'W	X	118
Five Ashes	E Susx	TQ5525	51°0·4'	0°13·0'E	T	188,199
Five Ashes	Heref	SO5464	52°16·6'	2°40·1'W	X	137,138,149
Five Ash Fm	Hants	SU7229	51°3·6'	0°58·0'W	FM	186,197
Five Barrow Hill	Dorset	SY8784	50°39·6'	2°10·7'W	X	194
Five Barrows	Devon	SS7336	51°6·8'	3°48·5'W	A	180
Five Barrows	I of W	SZ3885	50°40·0'	1°27·4'W	A	196
Five Barrows	I of W	SZ4883	50°38·9'	1°18·9'W	X	196
Five Barrows Cross	Devon	SS7336	51°6·8'	3°48·5'W	X	180
Five Barrows (Earthwork)	I of W	SZ4883	50°38·9'	1°18·9'W	A	196
Five Barrows, The	Northum	NT9502	55°19·0'	2°4·3'W	A	81
Five Beeches	N Yks	SE8473	54°9·0'	0°42·4'W	X	100
Five Bells	Somer	ST0642	51°10·4'	3°20·3'W	T	181
Five Bridges	Dorset	ST7521	50°59·5'	2°21·0'W	X	183
Five Bridges	Heref	SO5740	52°3·6'	2°37·2'W	X	149
Five Bridges	Heref	SO6546	52°6·9'	2°30·3'W	T	149
Five Bridges Fm	Devon	ST0209	50°52·6'	3°23·2'W	FM	192
Five Cairns Hill	Scot Bord	NT1719	55°27·7'	3°18·3'W	H	79
Five Chimneys	E Susx	TQ5224	50°59·9'	0°10·4'E	X	199
Five Clouds	Staffs	SK0062	53°9·5'	1°59·6'W	X	119

Fivecrosses	Ches	SJ5376	53°17·0'	2°41·9'W	T	117
Five Crosses	Devon	SS8414	50°55·1'	3°38·6'W	X	181
Five Cross Way	Devon	SS6937	51°7·3'	3°51·9'W	X	180
Five Cross Way	Somer	ST1719	50°58·1'	3°10·5'W	X	181,193
Five Cross Ways	Devon	SS8728	51°2·7'	3°36·3'W	X	181
Five Cross Ways	Suff	TM1268	52°16·4'	1°6·8'E	X	155
Five Fords	Devon	ST0813	50°54·8'	3°18·1'W	X	181
Five Fords Fm, The	Wrex	SJ3648	53°1·8'	2°56·9'W	A	117
Fivehead	Somer	ST3522	50°59·9'	2°55·2'W	T	193
Fivehead Hill	Somer	ST3523	51°0·4'	2°55·2'W	X	193
Fivehead River	Somer	ST3521	50°59·3'	2°55·2'W	W	193
Five Hillocks,The	Orkney	HY4605	58°56·0'	2°55·8'W	X	6,7
Five Hills Beck	N Yks	NZ2306	54°27·2'	1°38·3'W	W	93
Five Hos	N Yks	NZ4408	54°28·2'	1°18·8'W	X	93
Five Houses	I of W	SZ4287	50°41·1'	1°23·9'W	T	196
Five Hundred Acre Wood	E Susx	TQ4832	51°4·3'	0°7·1'E	F	188
Five Hundred, The	Cambs	TL4689	52°29·0'	0°9·4'E	X	143
Five Knolls	Beds	TL0120	51°52·4'	0°31·6'W	X	166
Five Knolls (Tumuli)	Beds	TL0020	51°52·4'	0°32·4'W	A	166
Five Lane End	Devon	SS4817	50°56·2'	4°9·4'W	X	180
Five Lane Ends	Brad	SE1736	53°49·4'	1°44·1'W	X	104
Fivelane-ends	Ches	SJ9978	53°18·2'	2°0·5'W	X	118
Five Lane Ends	Lancs	SD5053	53°58·5'	2°45·3'W	T	102
Five Lane Ends	Leeds	SE2841	53°52·1'	1°34·0'W	X	104
Five Lane Ends	Notts	SK8873	53°15·0'	0°40·5'W	X	121
Fivelanes	Corn	SX2280	50°35·8'	4°30·5'W	T	201
Five Lanes	Devon	SX8280	50°36·7'	3°39·7'W	X	191
Five Lanes	Devon	SX8763	50°27·6'	3°35·2'W	X	202
Five Lanes	Monm	ST4490	51°36·6'	2°48·1'W	T	171,172
Five Lanes	Wilts	ST9490	51°36·8'	2°4·8'W	X	163,173
Five Lanes End	Hants	SU6950	51°14·9'	1°0·3'W	X	186
Five Lanes Fm	Wilts	ST9758	51°19·5'	2°2·2'W	FM	173
Five Lords	Somer	ST1739	51°8·9'	3°10·8'W	X	181
Five Lord's Burgh	E Susx	TQ4803	50°48·7'	0°6·4'E	X	198
Five Lord's Burgh (Tumulus)	E Susx	TQ4803	50°48·7'	0°6·4'E	A	198
Five Lords Fm	Wilts	ST8250	51°15·2'	2°15·1'W	FM	183
Five Marys	Dorset	SY7884	50°39·5'	2°18·3'W	X	194
Five Marys (Tumuli)	Dorset	SY7884	50°39·5'	2°18·3'W	A	194
Five Mile Bank Fm	N Yks	NZ3501	54°24·4'	1°27·2'W	FM	93
Five Mile Drive	Glos	SP1434	52°0·5'	1°47·4'W	X	151
Five Mile Wood	Pth & Kin	NO0833	56°29·1'	3°29·2'W	F	52,53
Five Oak Green	Kent	TQ6445	51°11·1'	0°21·2'E	T	188
Five Oak Hill Plantation	Staffs	SJ9716	52°44·7'	2°2·3'W	F	127
Five Oaks	W Susx	TQ0928	51°2·7'	0°26·3'W	T	187,198
Five Paths, The	Monm	ST4395	51°39·3'	2°49·0'W	X	171
Five Pikes	Durham	NZ0132	54°41·2'	1°58·6'W	H	92
Five Pits Trail	Derby	SK4264	53°10·5'	1°21·9'W	X	120
Five Roads	Carm	SN4805	51°43·6'	4°11·7'W	T	159
Five Sisters	Highld	NG9717	57°12·2'	5°21·2'W	X	33
Five Sisters, The	Oxon	SP4508	51°46·4'	1°20·5'W	X	164
Fives Lanes Cross	Devon	SS3713	50°53·8'	4°18·7'W	X	190
Five Springs, The	Shrops	SO5985	52°27·9'	2°35·8'W	W	137,138
Five Stones	Scot Bord	NT7516	55°26·5'	2°23·3'W	X	80
Five Stones (Stone Circle)	Scot Bord	NT7516	55°26·5'	2°23·3'W	A	80
Five Thorns Hill	Hants	SU2701	50°48·7'	1°36·6'W	X	195
Five Turnings	Shrops	SO2875	52°22·3'	3°3·1'W	X	137,148
Five Turnings	Shrops	SO3686	52°28·3'	2°56·1'W	X	137
Five Watering Sewer	E Susx	TQ9424	50°59·2'	0°46·2'E	W	189
Five Ways	Birm	SP0585	52°28·0'	1°55·2'W	X	139
Five Ways	Essex	TL9523	51°52·5'	0°50·4'E	X	168
Five Ways	Warw	SP2269	52°19·4'	1°40·2'W	T	139,151
Five Ways	Worcs	SO8780	52°25·3'	2°11·1'W	X	139
Five Wells	S Lanak	NS9401	55°17·8'	3°39·7'W	X	78
Fivewells Fms	Derby	SK1270	53°13·9'	1°48·8'W	FM	119
Five Wents	Kent	TQ8150	51°13·5'	0°35·9'E	T	188
Five Willow Wath Fm	Lincs	TF1846	53°0·1'	0°14·1'W	FM	130
Five Wyches Fm	Devon	SX8078	50°35·6'	3°41·3'W	FM	191
Fixby	Kirk	SE1420	53°40·8'	1°46·9'W	T	104
Flaach, The	Shetld	HU5053	60°15·8'	1°5·3'W	X	3
Flacket Hill	E Ayr	NS5532	55°33·9'	4°17·5'W	X	71
Flackley Ash	E Susx	TQ8723	50°58·8'	0°40·2'E	T	189,199
Flack's Green	Essex	TL7614	51°48·0'	0°33·6'E	T	167
Flackwell Heath	Bucks	SU8989	51°35·8'	0°42·5'W	T	175
Flada Cap	Shetld	HU5136	60°6·6'	1°4·5'W	X	4
Fladbury	Worcs	SO9946	52°7·0'	2°0·5'W	T	150
Fladbury Cross	Worcs	SO9947	52°7·5'	2°0·5'W	T	150
Fladda	Arg & Bt	NM2943	56°30·3'	6°23·8'W	X	46,47,48
Fladda	Arg & Bt	NM7212	56°15·0'	5°40·4'W	X	55
Fladda	Shetld	HU2184	60°32·6'	1°36·5'W	X	3
Fladda	Shetld	HU3684	60°32·5'	1°20·1'W	X	1,2,3
Fladda	Shetld	HU3797	60°39·5'	1°18·9'W	X	1
Fladdabister	Shetld	HU4332	60°4·5'	1°13·1'W	T	4
Fladda-chùain	Highld	NG3681	57°44·7'	6°25·7'W	X	23
Fladday	N Eil	NA9915	58°1·6'	7°5·5'W	X	13
Flae-ass	Shetld	HU3796	60°39·0'	1°18·9'W	X	1
Flaeshans of Rumble	Shetld	HU6061	60°20·0'	0°54·3'W	X	2
Flaeshans of Sandwick	Shetld	HU5361	60°20·0'	1°1·9'W	X	2,3
Flaeshans, The	Shetld	HU5365	60°22·2'	1°1·8'W	X	2,3
Flaeshins, The	Shetld	HU6094	60°37·8'	0°53·7'W	X	1,2
Flaess, The	Shetld	HU3788	60°34·7'	1°19·0'W	X	1,2
Flaga	Orkney	HY2103	58°54·7'	3°21·8'W	X	6,7
Flag Creek	Essex	TM1116	51°48·4'	1°4·0'E	W	168,169
Flag Fen	Cambs	TL2894	52°32·0'	0°6·4'W	X	142
Flag Fen	Peterb	TL2299	52°34·7'	0°11·6'W	X	142
Flag Fen Mus	Peterb	TL2298	52°34·2'	0°11·6'W	X	142
Flagg	Derby	SK1368	53°12·8'	1°47·9'W	T	119
Flagg Moor	Derby	SK1367	53°12·2'	1°47·9'W	X	119
Flaggoners Green	Heref	SO6454	52°11·2'	2°31·2'W	T	149
Flag Head Chine	Poole	SZ0588	50°41·7'	1°55·4'W	X	195
Flag Heath	Norf	TL9194	52°30·8'	0°49·3'E	X	144
Flagmoor	Norf	TF9229	52°49·7'	0°51·4'E	X	132
Flagpond Copse	Hants	SU5409	50°52·9'	1°13·6'W	F	196
Flags Fm	Notts	SK7660	53°8·1'	0°51·4'W	FM	120
Flag Sta	Gwyn	SH8931	52°52·1'	3°38·5'W	X	124,125
Flagstaff	Cumbr	NY1451	54°51·0'	3°19·9'W	X	85
Flags, The	Pemb	SM8611	51°45·7'	5°5·7'W	X	157
Flagstone Fm	Glos	SP1627	51°56·7'	1°45·6'W	FM	163
Flagstone Trail	Highld	ND1968	58°35·8'	3°23·1'W	X	11,12
Flakebridge	Cumbr	NY6604	54°26·1'	2°31·0'W	X	91

Flakebridge	Cumbr	NY7022	54°35·8'	2°27·4'W	X	91
Flakefield	S Lanak	NS6647	55°42·1'	4°7·5'W	X	64
Flake Hill	Scot Bord	NT3610	55°23·0'	3°0·2'W	H	79
Flakiemoss	Orkney	HY4918	59°3·0'	2°52·9'W	X	6
Flambers Hill	N Yks	SD8752	53°58·1'	2°11·5'W	H	103
Flambirds Fm	Essex	TL8100	51°40·4'	0°37·5'E	FM	168
Flamborough	E Yorks	TA2270	54°6·9'	0°7·6'W	T	101
Flamborough Head	E Yorks	TA2570	54°6·9'	0°4·8'W	X	101
Flamborough Maltings	E Yorks	TA1970	54°7·0'	0°10·3'W	X	101
Flamingo Land	N Yks	SE7779	54°12·3'	0°48·8'W	X	100
Flamister	Shetld	HU4455	60°16·9'	1°11·8'W	X	3
Flamstead	Herts	TL0714	51°49·1'	0°26·5'W	T	166
Flamsteadbury Fm	Herts	TL0912	51°48·0'	0°24·8'W	FM	166
Flamstead End	Herts	TL3403	51°42·8'	0°3·2'W	T	166
Flamstead Fm	Bucks	SP9705	51°44·3'	0°35·3'W	FM	165
Flamstead Ho	Derby	SK4046	53°0·8'	1°23·8'W	X	129
Flamstone Fm	Wilts	SU0628	51°3·3'	1°54·5'W	FM	184
Flamstone Pin	N Yks	SE1084	54°15·3'	1°50·4'W	X	99
Flance Acres	N Yks	SE4395	54°21·2'	1°19·9'W	X	99
Flanchford Fm	Surrey	TQ2348	51°13·3'	0°13·9'W	FM	187
Flanders	Corn	SX1596	50°44·3'	4°36·9'W	X	190
Flanders	Cumbr	NY3750	54°50·7'	2°58·4'W	X	85
Flanders Fm	Cambs	TL6285	52°26·6'	0°23·4'E	FM	143
Flanders Green	Herts	TL3228	51°56·3'	0°4·4'W	X	166
Flanders Hall	N Yks	SE0187	54°17·0'	1°58·7'W	X	98
Flanders Hall	Warw	SP2394	52°32·8'	1°39·2'W	X	139
Flanders Moss	Stir	NS5595	56°7·8'	4°19·5'W	F	57
Flanders Moss	Stir	NS6398	56°9·6'	4°11·9'W	X	57
Flanderwell	Roth	SK4792	53°25·6'	1°17·1'W	X	111
Flands Cottages	Essex	TL5909	51°45·7'	0°18·6'E	X	167
Flanesford Priory	Heref	SO5719	51°52·3'	2°37·1'W	A	162
Flangna Field	Shetld	HU2580	60°30·4'	1°32·2'W	X	3
Flangna Field	Shetld	HU3272	60°26·1'	1°24·6'W	X	3
Flannagill	N Yks	SD6667	54°6·1'	2°30·8'W	X	98
Flannan Isles	N Eil	NA7146	58°17·0'	7°36·4'W	X	13
Flannog Fm	Shrops	SJ3240	52°57·4'	3°0·3'W	FM	117
Flansham	W Susx	SU9601	50°48·3'	0°37·9'W	T	197
Flanshaw	Wakf	SE3120	53°40·8'	1°31·4'W	T	104
Flappit Spring	Brad	SE0536	53°49·5'	1°55·0'W	T	104
Flares	Devon	SS4104	50°49·1'	4°15·1'W	X	190
Flasby	N Yks	SD9456	54°0·2'	2°5·1'W	T	103
Flasby Fell	N Yks	SD9656	54°0·2'	2°3·2'W	X	103
Flasby Moor Side	N Yks	SD9557	54°0·8'	2°4·2'W	X	103
Flash	Staffs	SK0267	53°12·2'	1°57·8'W	T	119
Flashader	Highld	NG3452	57°29·1'	6°25·8'W	T	23
Flash Bottom	Staffs	SK0266	53°11·7'	1°57·8'W	X	119
Flashbrook Manor	Staffs	SJ7425	52°49·6'	2°22·7'W	X	127
Flashbrook Wood	Staffs	SJ7424	52°49·0'	2°22·7'W	F	127
Flash Dam	Derby	SK3064	53°10·6'	1°32·7'W	W	119
Flashdown Wood	Devon	SS6710	50°52·7'	3°53·1'W	W	191
Flashers Wood	Lancs	SD6333	53°47·8'	2°33·3'W	F	102,103
Flashes	Orkney	HY2105	58°55·8'	3°21·9'W	X	6,7
Flashes, The	Red & Cl	NZ6125	54°37·2'	1°2·9'W	X	94
Flash Fm	Ches	SJ6580	53°19·2'	2°31·1'W	FM	109
Flash Fm	Ches	SJ7260	53°8·4'	2°24·7'W	FM	118
Flash Fm	Notts	SK7555	53°5·5'	0°52·4'W	FM	120
Flash Fm	Shrops	SJ7243	52°59·3'	2°24·6'W	FM	118
Flash Head	Staffs	SK0367	53°12·2'	1°56·9'W	X	119
Flash Ho	Ches	SJ7753	53°4·7'	2°20·2'W	X	118
Flash Pit Fm	Norf	TG1828	52°48·6'	1°14·5'E	FM	133,134
Flash, The	Wigan	SJ6399	53°29·4'	2°33·1'W	W	109
Flash, The	Wrex	SJ3453	53°4·5'	2°58·7'W	W	117
Flask	Brad	SD9938	53°50·5'	2°0·5'W	X	103
Flask	Cald	SD9332	53°47·3'	2°6·0'W	X	103
Flask	N Yks	SD9069	54°7·2'	2°8·8'W	X	98
Flaska	Cumbr	NY3725	54°37·2'	2°58·1'W	X	90
Flask Brow	N Yks	SE0658	54°1·3'	1°54·1'W	X	104
Flask Edge	Derby	SK2878	53°18·1'	1°34·4'W	X	119
Flask Inn	N Yks	NZ9300	54°23·5'	0°33·6'W	X	94
Flask Wood	D & G	NY3788	55°11·2'	2°58·9'W	F	79
Flass	Cumbr	NY1203	54°25·1'	3°21·0'W	X	89
Flass	Cumbr	NY7402	54°25·1'	2°23·6'W	X	91
Flass	Fife	NO4125	56°25·1'	2°56·9'W	X	54,59
Flass	Lancs	SD7953	53°58·6'	2°18·8'W	X	103
Flass	Lancs	SD9141	53°52·1'	2°7·8'W	X	103
Flass	Scot Bord	NT6251	55°45·3'	2°35·9'W	X	67,74
Flass Bent	Lancs	SD9142	53°52·7'	2°7·8'W	X	103
Flass Brow	N Yks	NZ8602	54°24·6'	0°40·1'W	X	94
Flassen Dale	N Yks	SE5484	54°15·2'	1°9·9'W	X	100
Flass Hall	Durham	NZ2042	54°46·6'	1°40·9'W	X	88
Flass Hill	Scot Bord	NT6152	55°45·8'	2°36·9'W	X	67,74
Flass Ho	Cumbr	NY6215	54°32·0'	2°34·8'W	X	91
Flass Ho	Lancs	SD8546	53°54·8'	2°13·3'W	X	103
Flass Wood	Scot Bord	NT6251	55°45·3'	2°35·9'W	F	67,74
Flass Woodheads	Scot Bord	NT6352	55°45·8'	2°34·9'W	X	67,74
Flasvein	Highld	NG4659	57°33·3'	6°14·3'W	X	23
Flat	Cumbr	NY3155	54°53·7'	3°4·1'W	X	85
Flat	Cumbr	SD5698	54°22·8'	2°40·2'W	X	97
Flat Bank	Cumbr	NY3846	54°48·6'	2°57·5'W	X	85
Flat Barn Fm	Oxon	SP2711	51°48·1'	1°36·1'W	FM	163
Flat Bridge Fm	Cambs	TL4173	52°20·4'	0°4·6'E	FM	154
Flates Barn	N Yks	SD9854	53°59·2'	2°1·4'W	X	103
Flat Fell	Cumbr	NY0513	54°30·4'	3°27·6'W	H	89
Flatfield	Pth & Kin	NO2224	56°24·4'	3°15·4'W	X	53,58
Flatfield	Pth & Kin	NO2440	56°33·0'	3°13·7'W	X	53
Flat Fm	Glos	SO8129	51°57·8'	2°16·2'W	FM	150
Flat Fm	N Yks	SE2960	54°2·4'	1°33·0'W	FM	99
Flat Fm	Suff	TL8758	52°11·5'	0°44·6'E	FM	155
Flatford Mill	Suff	TM0733	51°57·6'	1°1·2'E	A	168,169
Flatford Mill Field Centre	Suff	TM0733	51°57·6'	1°1·2'E	X	168,169
Flat Head	Staffs	SK0962	53°9·5'	1°51·5'W	X	119
Flathill	D & G	NX7448	54°48·9'	3°57·2'W	X	83,84
Flat Holm	V of Glam	ST2264	51°22·4'	3°6·9'W	X	171,182
Flat House Fm	Leic	SP5789	52°30·0'	1°9·2'W	FM	140
Flat Howe	N Yks	NZ6701	54°24·2'	0°57·8'W	A	94
Flat Howe	N Yks	NZ7301	54°24·2'	0°52·1'W	A	94
Flat Howe	N Yks	SE5596	54°21·6'	1°8·8'W	A	100
Flat Howes	N Yks	NZ8504	54°25·7'	0°41·0'W	A	94
Flathurst	W Susx	SU9822	50°59·6'	0°35·8'W	T	197
Flatmeadow Fm	Derby	SK4244	52°59·7'	1°22·0'W	FM	129

Flatmere Plantn	E Yorks	TA2470	54°6·9'	0°5·8'W	F	101
Flat Moor	N Yks	SE1363	54°4·0'	1°47·7'W	X	99
Flat Moss	Durham	NY9014	54°31·5'	2°8·8'W	X	91,92
Flat Moss	N Yks	SE0368	54°6·7'	1°56·8'W	X	98
Flatnadriech	Aberd	NO6173	56°51·1'	2°37·9'W	X	45
Flat Owers	Devon	SX8755	50°23·3'	3°35·0'W	X	202
Flat Point	Devon	SS4947	51°12·4'	4°9·3'W	X	180
Flat Rock or Lead Stone	Torbay	SX9563	50°27·7'	3°28·4'W	X	202
Flats Ho	N Yks	SE3263	54°4·0'	1°30·2'W	X	99
Flats, The	E Yorks	SE7654	53°58·8'	0°50·0'W	X	105,106
Flats, The	Herts	SP9408	51°46·0'	0°37·9'W	X	165
Flats, The	Kent	TQ8977	51°27·8'	0°43·7'E	X	178
Flats, The	Red & Cl	NZ5613	54°30·8'	1°7·7'W	X	93
Flats, The	Suff	TM5074	52°18·6'	1°40·5'E	X	156
Flats, The	V of Glam	SS8575	51°28·0'	3°38·9'W	X	170
Flatt	N Ayr	NS2159	55°47·7'	4°50·9'W	X	63
Flatt	N Yks	SD7470	54°7·8'	2°23·5'W	X	98
Flatt	Scot Bord	NY4783	55°8·6'	2°49·5'W	X	79
Flattenden Fm	E Susx	TQ6328	51°1·9'	0°19·9'E	FM	188,199
Flatt Fm, The	Cumbr	NY5255	54°53·5'	2°44·5'W	FM	86
Flat Top Fm	York	SE5959	54°1·7'	1°5·5'W	FM	105
Flat Top Ho	N Yks	SE8179	54°12·3'	0°45·1'W	X	100
Flat Tor	Devon	SX6081	50°37·0'	3°58·4'W	H	191
Flatts	Cumbr	SD0990	54°18·1'	3°23·5'W	X	96
Flatts	Lancs	SD6945	53°54·3'	2°27·9'W	X	103
Flatts Fm	Durham	NZ2030	54°40·1'	1°41·0'W	FM	93
Flatts Fm	N Lincs	SE8723	53°42·0'	0°40·5'W	FM	106,112
Flatts Fm	Staffs	SK0931	52°52·8'	1°51·6'W	FM	128
Flatts of Cargen	D & G	NX9671	55°1·6'	3°37·2'W	X	84
Flatt, The	Cumbr	NY5678	55°5·9'	2°40·9'W	X	86
Flatt Tops	N Yks	SE6571	54°8·1'	0°59·9'W	X	100
Flat Wood	N Yks	SE1598	54°22·9'	1°45·7'W	F	99
Flat Woods	Cumbr	SD2775	54°10·2'	3°6·7'W	F	96,97
Flaughton Hill	Orkney	HY5532	59°10·6'	2°46·8'W	H	5,6
Flaunden	Herts	TL0100	51°41·6'	0°31·9'W	T	166
Flaunden Bottom	Bucks	TQ0099	51°41·1'	0°32·8'W	X	166,176
Flawborough	Notts	SK7842	52°58·4'	0°49·9'W	T	129
Flawcraig	Pth & Kin	NO2327	56°26·0'	3°14·5'W	X	53,58
Flawford Fm	Notts	SK8554	53°4·8'	0°43·5'W	FM	121
Flawford Ho	Notts	SK6033	52°53·7'	1°6·1'W	X	129
Flawford House Fm	Notts	SK5833	52°53·7'	1°7·9'W	FM	129
Flaw Hill	Shetld	HU4567	60°23·3'	1°10·5'W	H	2,3
Flawith	N Yks	SE4865	54°5·0'	1°15·6'W	T	100
Flawith Beck	E Yorks	SE7356	53°59·9'	0°52·8'W	W	105,106
Flaws	Orkney	HY3725	59°6·7'	3°5·5'W	X	6
Flaws	Orkney	HY5200	58°53·3'	2°49·5'W	X	6,7
Flaws	Orkney	ND4585	58°45·2'	2°56·6'W	X	7
Flawton	Shetld	HU3056	60°17·5'	1°26·9'W	X	3
Flax Bourton	N Som	ST5069	51°25·3'	2°42·8'W	T	172,182
Flaxby	N Yks	SE3957	54°0·7'	1°23·9'W	T	104
Flaxby Covert	N Yks	SE4057	54°0·7'	1°23·0'W	F	105
Flax Dale	N Yks	SE8686	54°16·0'	0°40·4'W	X	94,101
Flaxfields	Hants	SU1612	50°54·7'	1°46·0'W	X	195
Flax Fm	Suff	TL7749	52°6·9'	0°35·5'E	FM	155
Flaxholme	Derby	SK3442	52°58·7'	1°29·2'W	T	119,128
Flaxland	V of Glam	ST0670	51°25·5'	3°20·7'W	X	170
Flaxlands	Norf	TM1093	52°29·9'	1°6·0'E	T	144
Flaxlands Manor Fm	Wilts	SU0684	51°33·5'	1°54·4'W	FM	173
Flaxlands Wood	Wilts	SU0585	51°34·1'	1°55·3'W	F	173
Flaxley	Glos	SO6915	51°50·2'	2°26·6'W	T	162
Flaxley Green	Staffs	SK0216	52°44·7'	1°57·8'W	X	128
Flaxley Lodge	N Yks	SE5933	53°47·6'	1°5·8'W	X	105
Flaxley Woods	Glos	SO6816	51°50·7'	2°27·5'W	F	162
Flaxmere	Ches	SJ5572	53°14·8'	2°40·1'W	X	117
Flax Moss	Lancs	SD7822	53°41·9'	2°19·6'W	T	103
Flaxpool	Somer	ST1435	51°6·7'	3°13·3'W	T	181
Flaxton	N Yks	SE6862	54°3·2'	0°57·3'W	T	100
Flaxton Fm	Norf	TM0795	52°31·0'	1°3·5'E	FM	144
Flaxyard Fm	Ches	SJ5662	53°9·4'	2°39·1'W	FM	117
Flaystones	N Yks	SE0672	54°8·9'	1°54·1'W	X	99
Fleak, The	N Yks	SD9694	54°20·7'	2°3·3'W	X	98
Fleam Dyke	Cambs	TL5454	52°10·0'	0°15·5'E	A	154
Flear Fm	Devon	SX7646	50°18·3'	3°44·1'W	FM	202
Fleasgeir	N Eil	NB1241	58°16·1'	6°54·2'W	X	13
Fleck	Shetld	HU3914	59°54·8'	1°17·7'W	X	4
Flecket Hill	D & G	NT0413	55°24·3'	3°30·5'W	H	78
Fleckney	Leic	SP6493	52°32·1'	1°3·0'W	T	140
Fleckney Grange Fm	Leic	SP6394	52°32·6'	1°3·9'W	FM	140
Fleckney Lodge	Leic	SP6492	52°31·6'	1°3·0'W	X	140
Flecknoe	Warw	SP5163	52°16·0'	1°14·8'W	T	151
Flecknoe Fields Fm	Warw	SP4963	52°16·0'	1°16·5'W	FM	151
Flecknoe House Fm	Warw	SP4964	52°16·6'	1°16·5'W	FM	151
Fledborough	Notts	SK8172	53°14·6'	0°46·8'W	T	121
Fledborough Ho	Notts	SK8071	53°14·0'	0°47·7'W	X	121
Fleecefaulds	Fife	NO4008	56°15·9'	2°57·7'W	X	59
Fleed Fm	Somer	ST0627	51°2·3'	3°20·1'W	FM	181
Fleehope	Northum	NT8823	55°30·3'	2°11·0'W	X	74
Fleehope Burn	Northum	NT8723	55°30·3'	2°11·9'W	W	74
Fleellands	I of W	SZ4290	50°42·7'	1°23·9'W	X	196
Fleemis Gill	N Yks	SE0482	54°14·3'	1°55·9'W	W	98
Fleenasmore	Highld	NH9248	57°30·8'	3°47·7'W	X	27
Fleenasnagael	Highld	NH9150	57°31·9'	3°48·8'W	X	27
Fleensop	N Yks	SE0382	54°14·3'	1°56·8'W	X	98
Fleensop Moor	N Yks	SE0281	54°13·7'	1°57·7'W	X	98
Fleet	Cumbr	SD5880	54°13·1'	2°38·2'W	X	97
Fleet	Dorset	SY6380	50°37·3'	2°31·0'W	T	194
Fleet	Hants	SU7201	50°48·5'	0°58·3'W	T	197
Fleet	Hants	SU8054	51°17·0'	0°50·8'W	T	186
Fleet	Lincs	TF3823	52°47·4'	0°3·2'E	T	131
Fleet	N Yks	SD9542	53°52·7'	2°4·1'W	X	103
Fleet Bank	N Yks	SE5263	54°3·9'	1°11·9'W	X	100
Fleet Bank Fm	N Yks	SE5263	54°3·9'	1°11·9'W	FM	100
Fleet Bay	D & G	NX5652	54°50·8'	4°14·1'W	W	83
Fleet Br	D & G	NX5956	54°53·0'	4°11·5'W	X	83
Fleet Common	Dorset	SY6380	50°37·3'	2°31·0'W	X	194
Fleet Copse	Wok	SU7862	51°21·3'	0°52·4'W	F	175,186
Fleet Dike	Norf	TG3714	52°40·5'	1°30·8'E	W	133,134
Fleet Downs	Kent	TQ5673	51°26·3'	0°15·1'E	T	177
Fleetend	Hants	SU5006	50°51·3'	1°17·0'W	T	196
Fleet Fen	Lincs	TF3619	52°45·3'	0°1·3'E	X	131
Fleet Fm	Kent	TR3060	51°17·8'	1°18·3'E	FM	179
Fleet Fm	N Yks	SE7276	54°10·7'	0°53·4'W	FM	100
Fleet Forest	D & G	NX6055	54°52·5'	4°10·5'W	F	83
Fleet Hall	Essex	TQ8989	51°34·3'	0°44·0'E	X	178
Fleet Hall	Lincs	TF2110	52°40·7'	0°12·2'W	X	131,142
Fleetham Lodge	N Yks	SE2694	54°20·7'	1°35·6'W	X	99
Fleet Hargate	Lincs	TF3924	52°48·0'	0°4·1'E	T	131
Fleet Haven	Lincs	TF4129	52°50·6'	0°6·0'E	W	131
Fleet Haven Outfall	Lincs	TF4433	52°52·7'	0°8·8'E	W	131
Fleet Head	Essex	TQ9489	51°34·2'	0°48·4'E	X	178
Fleethill Fm	Wok	SU7862	51°21·3'	0°52·4'W	FM	175,186
Fleet Ho	Suff	TM3136	51°58·7'	1°22·2'E	X	169
Fleet Holme	Cumbr	SD6296	54°21·7'	2°34·7'W	X	97
Fleetland Fm	Northnts	SP7063	52°15·9'	0°58·1'W	FM	152
Fleetlands	Hants	SU5804	50°50·2'	1°10·2'W	T	196
Fleet Lodge	Lincs	TF3723	52°47·5'	0°2·3'E	X	131
Fleet Marston Fm	Bucks	SP7716	51°50·5'	0°52·5'W	FM	165
Fleet Mill	Devon	SX8258	50°24·8'	3°39·3'W	X	202
Fleet Moss	N Yks	SD8683	54°14·8'	2°12·5'W	W	98
Fleet Moss Tarn	N Yks	SD8783	54°14·8'	2°11·6'W	W	98
Fleet Pond	Hants	SU8255	51°17·5'	0°49·0'W	W	175,186
Fleets	N Yks	SD9660	54°2·4'	2°3·2'W	T	98
Fleet's Corner	Poole	SZ0193	50°44·4'	1°58·8'W	X	195
Fleet Seaves	N Yks	SE1770	54°7·8'	1°44·0'W	X	99
Fleet Service Area	Hants	SU7955	51°17·5'	0°51·6'W	X	175,186
Fleets Ho	N Yks	SE1586	54°16·4'	1°45·8'W	X	99
Fleet Shot	Durham	NZ4335	54°42·7'	1°19·5'W	X	93
Fleet, The	Norf	TG4506	52°36·0'	1°37·5'E	W	134
Fleet, The	Notts	SK8157	53°6·5'	0°47·0'W	W	121
Fleet, The	Notts	SK8263	53°9·7'	0°46·0'W	W	121
Fleetville	Herts	TL1607	51°45·2'	0°18·8'W	T	166
Fleetwith	Cumbr	NY2113	54°30·6'	3°12·8'W	X	89,90
Fleetwith Pike	Cumbr	NY2014	54°31·1'	3°13·7'W	H	89,90
Fleetwood	Lancs	SD3247	53°55·1'	3°1·7'W	T	102
Fleetwood Fm	Lancs	SD3245	53°54·0'	3°1·7'W	FM	102
Flegcroft	Cambs	TL2794	52°32·0'	0°7·3'W	X	142
Fleisirin	N Eil	NB5536	58°19·9'	6°10·1'W	T	8
Fleming Field	Durham	NZ3841	54°46·0'	1°24·1'W	T	88
Fleming Hall	Cumbr	NY0503	54°25·1'	3°27·4'W	X	89
Fleminghill	E Ayr	NS4738	55°36·9'	4°25·3'W	X	70
Fleming Park	Hants	SU4419	50°58·4'	1°22·0'W	X	185
Flemings	Kent	TR2856	51°15·7'	1°16·5'E	T	179
Flemings Fm	Essex	TL6333	51°58·5'	0°22·8'E	FM	167
Flemings Fm	Essex	TQ7496	51°38·4'	0°31·3'E	FM	167
Flemings Fm	Essex	TQ8389	51°34·4'	0°38·8'E	FM	178
Fleming's Hall Fm	Suff	TM1967	52°15·7'	1°13·0'E	FM	156
Flemings Hill Fm	Essex	TL5824	51°53·8'	0°18·2'E	FM	167
Flemingston	V of Glam	ST0170	51°25·5'	3°25·0'W	T	170
Flemingston Moor	V of Glam	ST0270	51°25·5'	3°24·2'W	X	170
Flemington	Angus	NO5255	56°41·3'	2°46·6'W	X	54
Flemington	Pemb	SN0502	51°41·2'	4°48·9'W	X	158
Flemington	Scot Bord	NT1645	55°41·7'	3°19·7'W	X	72
Flemington	Scot Bord	NT9460	55°50·2'	2°5·3'W	X	67
Flemington	S Lanak	NS6559	55°48·6'	4°8·8'W	T	64
Flemington	S Lanak	NS7044	55°40·6'	4°3·6'W	T	71
Flemington Burn	Scot Bord	NT1846	55°42·3'	3°17·9'W	W	72
Flemington Fm	S Lanak	NS6658	55°48·1'	4°7·8'W	FM	64
Flemington Ho	Highld	NH8053	57°33·3'	3°59·9'W	X	27
Flemish Fm	Win & Maid	SU9474	51°27·7'	0°38·4'W	FM	175
Flempton	Suff	TL8169	52°17·6'	0°39·7'E	T	155
Flemyland	N Ayr	NS3045	55°40·4'	4°41·8'W	X	63
Flenders	E Renf	NS5656	55°46·8'	4°17·3'W	X	64
Flenny Bank	Shrops	SO3398	52°34·8'	2°58·9'W	X	137
Fleoideabhagh	N Eil	NG0988	57°47·5'	6°53·4'W	T	14
Fleshbeck	Cumbr	SD6183	54°14·7'	2°35·5'W	X	97
Flesh-house Point	Orkney	HY6327	59°8·0'	2°38·3'W	X	5
Flesh Market	D & G	NX6065	54°57·9'	4°10·8'W	X	83
Flesh Shank	Northum	NT8911	55°23·8'	2°10·0'W	X	80
Fleshwick Bay	I of M	SC2071	54°6·5'	4°44·8'W	W	95
Fleshwick Fm	I of M	SC2071	54°6·5'	4°44·8'W	FM	95
Fless, The	Shetld	HZ2169	59°30·7'	1°37·3'W	X	4
Fletcherfield	Angus	NO4052	56°39·6'	2°58·3'W	X	54
Fletcher Fold Fm	Lancs	SD6432	53°47·2'	2°32·4'W	FM	102,103
Fletcherhill	Derby	SK3761	53°8·9'	1°26·4'W	X	119
Fletchers	W Susx	SZ8499	50°47·3'	0°48·1'W	X	197
Fletchersbridge	Corn	SX1065	50°27·5'	4°40·2'W	T	200
Fletcher's Combe	Devon	SX7656	50°23·7'	3°44·3'W	X	202
Fletchers Fm	Kent	TQ6339	51°7·8'	0°20·2'E	FM	188
Fletchers Fm	Peterb	TF2205	52°38·0'	0°11·4'W	FM	142
Fletcher's Green	Kent	TQ5350	51°13·9'	0°11·9'E	T	188
Fletchers Thorns Inclosure	Hants	SU2704	50°50·3'	1°36·6'W	F	195
Fletchertown	Cumbr	NY2042	54°46·2'	3°14·2'W	T	85
Fletching	E Susx	TQ4223	50°59·6'	0°1·8'E	T	198
Fletching Common	E Susx	TQ4122	50°59·0'	0°0·9'E	T	198
Fletchlaw Burn	Northum	NY7880	55°7·1'	2°20·3'W	W	80
Fletchwood Copse	Hants	SU3310	50°53·5'	1°31·5'W	F	196
Flete	Devon	SX6251	50°20·8'	3°56·0'W	A	202
Flete Fm	Kent	TR3467	51°21·4'	1°22·1'E	FM	179
Flett	Shetld	HU4062	60°20·7'	1°16·0'W	X	2,3
Fletts	Orkney	HY2210	58°58·5'	3°20·9'W	X	6
Fleuchary	Highld	NC7965	58°33·6'	4°4·3'W	X	10
Fleuchary	Highld	NH7591	57°53·7'	4°6·1'W	T	21
Fleuchats	Aberd	NJ3309	57°10·3'	3°6·0'W	X	37
Fleuchlarg	D & G	NX6057	54°53·5'	4°10·5'W	X	83
Fleuchlarg Hill	D & G	NX8588	55°10·6'	3°47·9'W	H	78
Fleughlarg	D & G	NX8587	55°10·1'	3°47·9'W	X	78
Fleuk Hole	D & G	NX3344	54°46·0'	4°35·3'W	W	82
Fleurad	Shetld	HU2051	60°14·8'	1°37·8'W	X	3
Fleur-de-lis	Caer	ST1596	51°39·6'	3°13·3'W	T	171
Fleurs	Scot Bord	NT9165	55°52·9'	2°8·2'W	X	67
Flex	Highld	ND2651	58°26·7'	3°15·6'W	X	11,12
Flex	Scot Bord	NT5012	55°24·2'	2°46·9'W	X	79
Flexbarrow	Somer	SS7838	51°7·9'	3°44·2'W	X	180
Flexbury	Corn	SS2107	50°50·3'	4°32·2'W	T	190
Flexcombe	Hants	SU7627	51°2·5'	0°54·6'W	X	186,197
Flex Ditch	Hants	SU6261	51°20·9'	1°6·2'W	A	175
Flexford	Hants	SU4221	50°59·4'	1°23·7'W	T	185
Flexford	Surrey	SU9250	51°14·7'	0°40·5'W	T	186
Flexford Ho	Hants	SU4359	51°19·9'	1°22·6'W	X	174
Flexford Ho	Surrey	SU9448	51°13·6'	0°38·8'W	X	186
Flexham Park	W Susx	TQ0022	50°59·5'	0°34·1'W	F	197
Flex Hill	Highld	ND2650	58°26·2'	3°15·6'W	X	11,12
Fleydmire	Angus	NO4851	56°39·1'	2°50·4'W	X	54
Flichity Burn	Highld	NH6727	57°19·1'	4°12·1'W	W	26,35
Flichity Ho	Highld	NH6728	57°19·7'	4°12·1'W	X	26,35
Flighthill Fm	Oxon	SP4129	51°57·7'	1°23·8'W	FM	164
Flight Moss	Scot Bord	NY5590	55°12·4'	2°42·0'W	X	80
Flights Fm	Heref	SO6837	52°2·1'	2°27·6'W	FM	149
Flightshott Fm	Kent	TQ6840	51°8·3'	0°24·5'E	FM	188
Flimby	Cumbr	NY0233	54°41·2'	3°30·8'W	T	89
Flimston	Pemb	SN0510	51°45·5'	4°49·1'W	X	158
Flimston	Pemb	SR9295	51°37·2'	4°59·9'W	X	158
Flimston Bay	Pemb	SR9394	51°36·6'	4°59·0'W	W	158
Flimwell	E Susx	TQ7131	51°3·4'	0°26·8'E	T	188
Flimwell Grange	Kent	TQ7032	51°4·0'	0°26·0'E	X	188
Flimworth Hall	Suff	TM1773	52°19·0'	1°11·4'E	X	156
Flingi Geo	Orkney	ND1899	58°52·5'	3°24·8'W	X	7
Flint Barn Fm	Kent	TQ8954	51°15·5'	0°42·9'E	FM	189
Flint Cotts	Herts	TL3931	51°57·8'	0°1·8'E	X	166
Flint Cross	Cambs	TL4042	52°3·7'	0°2·9'E	T	154
Flinter Gill	Cumbr	SD6985	54°15·8'	2°28·1'W	W	98
Flint Fm	Hants	SU3540	51°9·7'	1°29·6'W	FM	185
Flint Fm	Norf	TL9886	52°26·4'	0°55·2'E	FM	144
Flint Fm	Oxon	SU3683	51°32·9'	1°28·5'W	FM	174
Flintford Fm	Somer	ST8047	51°13·5'	2°16·8'W	FM	183
Flint Hall	Bucks	SU7789	51°35·9'	0°52·9'W	X	175
Flint Hall	N Yks	SE7379	54°12·3'	0°52·4'W	X	100
Flint Hall	Warw	SP2956	52°12·3'	1°34·1'W	X	151
Flint Hall Fm	Herts	TL3639	52°2·2'	0°0·6'W	FM	154
Flint Hall Fm	Norf	TM0084	52°25·3'	0°56·9'E	FM	144
Flinthall Fm	Surrey	TQ3653	51°15·8'	0°2·6'W	FM	187
Flintham	Notts	SK7446	53°0·6'	0°53·4'W	T	129
Flintham Grange Fm	Notts	SK7545	53°0·1'	0°52·5'W	FM	129
Flintham Hall	Notts	SK7346	53°0·6'	0°54·3'W	X	129
Flintham Ho	Wilts	ST9893	51°38·4'	2°1·3'W	X	163,173
Flintham Wood	Notts	SK7248	53°1·7'	0°55·2'W	F	129
Flint Hill	Durham	NZ1654	54°53·1'	1°44·6'W	T	88
Flint Hill	Lincs	TF2776	53°16·2'	0°5·3'W	X	122
Flinthill	Northnts	SP6173	52°21·3'	1°5·9'W	X	140
Flint Hill	Notts	SK6428	52°51·0'	1°2·6'W	X	129
Flint Hill	Scot Bord	NT1340	55°39·0'	3°22·5'W	H	72
Flint Hill Fm	Northnts	SP6074	52°21·9'	1°6·7'W	FM	140
Flinthills	Aberd	NJ8335	57°24·6'	2°16·5'W	X	29,30
Flint Ho	Oxon	SU6280	51°31·2'	1°6·0'W	X	175
Flint Ho	Somer	ST6749	51°14·6'	2°28·0'W	X	183
Flint Ho	Surrey	TQ3854	51°16·3'	0°0·9'W	X	187
Flint Howe	Cumbr	SD7498	54°22·9'	2°23·6'W	X	98
Flintloch Hill	D & G	NX6178	55°4·9'	4°10·2'W	X	77
Flint Marsh	Flint	SJ2473	53°15·2'	3°7·9'W	X	117
Flint Mill Grange	Leeds	SE4247	53°55·3'	1°21·2'W	X	105
Flint Mill (Mus)	Staffs	SJ9752	53°4·2'	2°2·3'W	X	118
Flint Mountain	Flint	SJ2470	53°13·5'	3°7·9'W	T	117
Flinton	E Yorks	TA2236	53°48·6'	0°8·4'W	T	107
Flinton Grange	E Yorks	TA2135	53°48·1'	0°9·3'W	X	107
Flinton Hill Fm	Sund	NZ3354	54°53·0'	1°28·7'W	FM	88
Flint or Y Fflint	Flint	SJ2472	53°14·6'	3°7·9'W	T	117
Flints	Cald	SE0121	53°41·4'	1°58·7'W	X	104
Flint Sands	Flint	SJ2573	53°15·2'	3°7·0'W	X	117
Flint's Green	Sol	SP2680	52°25·3'	1°36·7'W	T	140
Flintsham	Heref	SO3158	52°13·2'	3°0·2'W	T	148
Flintsham	Heref	SO3258	52°13·2'	2°59·3'W	X	148
Flinty Cott	Wilts	SU3149	51°14·6'	1°33·0'W	X	185
Flinty Fell	Cumbr	NY7741	54°46·1'	2°21·0'W	H	86,87
Flirum	Highld	NC3970	58°35·6'	4°45·7'W	X	9
Flisaval	N Eil	NF8769	57°36·4'	7°14·0'W	H	18
Flishinghurst	Kent	TQ7537	51°6·6'	0°30·4'E	T	188
Flisk	Fife	NO4216	56°20·2'	2°55·8'W	X	59
Fliskmillan	Fife	NO3021	56°22·8'	3°7·6'W	X	53,59
Fliskmillan Hill	Fife	NO3020	56°22·3'	3°7·6'W	X	53,59
Flisk Point	Fife	NO3122	56°23·4'	3°6·6'W	X	53,59
Flisk Wood	Fife	NO3222	56°23·4'	3°5·6'W	F	53,59
Flisteridge Wood	Wilts	ST9991	51°37·3'	2°0·5'W	F	163,173
Flitcham	Norf	TF7226	52°48·5'	0°33·5'E	T	132
Flitcham Abbey	Norf	TF7326	52°48·5'	0°34·4'E	X	132
Flitcham Hall	Norf	TF7126	52°48·5'	0°32·6'E	X	132
Flitholme	Cumbr	NY7615	54°32·0'	2°21·8'W	T	91
Flitteriss Park Fm	Rut	SK8207	52°39·5'	0°46·9'W	FM	141
Flittermere Fm	Cambs	TL1285	52°27·3'	0°20·7'W	FM	142
Flittogate Fm	Ches	SJ7078	53°18·1'	2°26·6'W	FM	118
Flitton	Beds	TL0535	52°0·4'	0°27·8'W	T	153
Flitton Barton	Devon	SS7130	51°3·5'	3°50·1'W	X	180
Flitton Hills Fm	Northnts	SP6952	52°9·9'	0°59·1'W	FM	152
Flitton Oak	Devon	SS7131	51°4·1'	3°50·1'W	A	180
Flitwick	Beds	TL0334	51°59·9'	0°29·6'W	T	153
Flitwick Manor	Beds	TL0234	51°59·9'	0°30·5'W	A	153
Flitwick Moor (Nature Reserve)	Beds	TL0435	52°0·5'	0°28·7'W	F	153
Flitwick Plantation	Beds	TL0034	52°0·0'	0°32·2'W	F	153
Flitwick Wood	Beds	TL0234	51°59·9'	0°30·5'W	F	153
Fliuchach	Arg & Bt	NR7203	55°16·4'	5°34·9'W	X	68
Flixborough	N Lincs	SE8715	53°37·7'	0°40·7'W	T	112
Flixborough Grange	N Lincs	SE8515	53°37·7'	0°42·5'W	X	112
Flixborough Stather	N Lincs	SE8614	53°37·2'	0°41·6'W	T	112
Flixton	N Yks	TA0379	54°12·0'	0°24·8'W	T	101
Flixton	Suff	TM3186	52°25·6'	1°24·3'E	T	156
Flixton	Traf	SJ7494	53°26·8'	2°23·1'W	T	109
Flixton	Traf	SJ7594	53°26·8'	2°22·2'W	T	109
Flixton Carr Plantn	N Yks	TA0280	54°12·6'	0°25·7'W	F	101
Flixton Decoy	Suff	TM5195	52°29·9'	1°42·3'E	W	134
Flixton Hall	Suff	TM3085	52°25·1'	1°23·3'E	X	156
Flixton Ho	Suff	TM5195	52°29·9'	1°42·3'E	X	134
Flixton Wold	N Yks	TA0377	54°10·9'	0°24·9'W	X	101
Fload	Highld	NH7088	57°52·0'	4°11·0'W	X	21
Floak	E Renf	NS4950	55°43·5'	4°23·8'W	X	64
Float Bay	D & G	NX0647	54°47·1'	5°0·6'W	W	82
Float Bridge	Lancs	SD8936	53°49·5'	2°9·6'W	X	103
Float Fm	E Susx	TQ8818	50°56·1'	0°40·9'E	FM	189,199
Floating Harbour	C of Bris	ST5772	51°27·0'	2°36·7'W	W	172
Flock Hill	D & G	NX7958	54°54·4'	3°52·8'W	H	84
Flockhouse	Pth & Kin	NT1196	56°9·2'	3°25·5'W	X	58

Flocklones	Angus	NO3131	56°28·2'	3°6·8'W	X	53
Flock Mill	Devon	SS9600	50°47·6'	3°28·2'W	X	192
Flockmoor Cott	Hants	SU5943	51°11·2'	1°9·0'W	X	185
Flock Rake	N Yks	SD9268	54°6·7'	2°6·9'W	X	98
Flockton	Kirk	SE2415	53°38·1'	1°37·8'W	T	110
Flockton Green	Kirk	SE2415	53°38·1'	1°37·8'W	T	110
Flockton Moor	Kirk	SE2214	53°37·6'	1°39·6'W	T	110
Flodaigh	N Eil	NF8455	57°28·8'	7°15·9'W	X	22
Flodaigh Beag	N Eil	NF9158	57°30·7'	7°9·2'W	X	22
Flodaigh Mòr	N Eil	NF9157	57°30·1'	7°9·1'W	X	22
Floday	N Eil	NB1033	58°11·7'	6°55·7'W	X	13
Floday	N Eil	NB1241	58°16·1'	6°54·2'W	X	13
Flodda Stack	Shetld	HP5917	60°50·2'	0°54·4'W	X	1
Flodday	N Eil	NF7502	56°59·9'	7°20·7'W	X	31
Flodday	N Eil	NF9469	57°36·7'	7°7·0'W	X	18
Flodday	N Eil	NL6192	56°54·0'	7°33·7'W	X	31
Flodden	Northum	NT9235	55°36·8'	2°7·2'W	X	74,75
Flodden Edge	Northum	NT9135	55°36·8'	2°8·1'W	X	74,75
Flodden Field	Northum	NT8937	55°37·8'	2°10·0'W	A	74
Floddenford Plantation	Northum	NT9335	55°36·8'	2°6·2'W	F	74,75
Flodden Hill	Northum	NT9135	55°36·8'	2°8·1'W	H	74,75
Flodder Hall	Cumbr	SD4587	54°16·8'	2°50·3'W	X	97
Flodigarry	Highld	NG4671	57°39·7'	6°15·1'W	T	23
Flodraskarve Mór	N Eil	NB0429	58°9·3'	7°1·5'W	H	13
Flodravel a Stigh	N Eil	NB0733	58°11·6'	6°58·7'W	H	13
Flod Sgeir	Highld	NM4884	56°53·0'	6°7·8'W	X	39
Floga	Shetld	HU5396	60°38·9'	1°1·3'W	X	1
Flongna Field	Shetld	HP5002	60°42·1'	1°4·5'W	X	1
Flood	Devon	SX7093	50°43·6'	3°50·1'W	X	191
Floodbridge Fm	N Yks	SE2888	54°17·5'	1°33·8'W	FM	99
Flood Fm	Peterb	TF2306	52°38·5'	0°10·5'W	FM	142
Floodgate Burn	Northum	NZ1891	55°13·0'	1°42·6'W	W	81
Floodgate Fm	V of Glam	SS9669	51°24·9'	3°29·3'W	FM	170
Floodgate Fm	W Susx	TQ1621	50°58·8'	0°20·5'W	FM	198
Floodgates	Heref	SO2857	52°12·6'	3°2·8'W	T	148
Floodgates Fm	Glos	ST6798	51°41·0'	2°28·2'W	FM	162
Flood's Drain	Cambs	TL3793	52°31·3'	0°1·6'E	W	142,143
Flood's Ferry	Cambs	TL3593	52°31·3'	0°0·2'W	T	142
Floods Fm	Hants	SU6858	51°19·3'	1°1·1'W	FM	175,186
Flood Street	Hants	SU1417	50°57·4'	1°47·7'W	T	184
Flookburgh	Cumbr	SD3675	54°10·3'	2°58·4'W	T	96,97
Floorey Down	Somer	ST1736	51°7·3'	3°10·8'W	F	181
Floors	Aberd	NO8792	57°1·4'	2°12·4'W	X	38,45
Floors	D & G	NX8594	55°13·9'	3°48·1'W	X	78
Floors	E Renf	NS5554	55°45·7'	4°18·2'W	X	64
Floors	Moray	NJ4952	57°33·6'	2°50·7'W	X	28,29
Floors	N Ayr	NS4042	55°39·0'	4°32·1'W	X	70
Floors Castle	Scot Bord	NT7134	55°36·2'	2°27·2'W	X	74
Floors Craig	Aberd	NO9293	57°1·9'	2°7·5'W	X	38,45
Floors Fm	Aberd	NJ6743	57°28·8'	2°32·6'W	FM	29
Floors Fm	S Lanak	NS7144	55°40·6'	4°2·6'W	FM	71
Floors Home Fm	Scot Bord	NT7034	55°36·2'	2°28·1'W	FM	74
Floors Loch	D & G	NX7761	54°56·0'	3°54·8'W	W	84
Floors, The	Devon	SY0481	50°37·5'	3°21·1'W	X	192
Floral Fm	Norf	TF4511	52°40·9'	0°9·1'E	FM	131,143
Flora Macdonald's Birthplace	N Eil	NF7426	57°12·8'	7°23·6'W	X	22
Flordon	Norf	TM1897	52°31·9'	1°13·3'E	T	134
Flore	Northnts	SP6460	52°14·3'	1°3·4'W	T	152
Flore Fields Fm	Northnts	SP6462	52°15·4'	1°3·3'W	FM	152
Flore Fields Ho	Northnts	SP6462	52°15·4'	1°3·3'W	X	152
Flore Hill Fm	Northnts	SP6360	52°14·3'	1°4·2'W	FM	152
Florence	C of Stoke	SJ9142	52°58·8'	2°7·6'W	T	118
Florence Fm	Ches	SJ8881	53°19·8'	2°10·4'W	FM	109
Florence Terrace	N Yks	SE7098	54°22·6'	0°54·9'W	X	94,100
Florida	Scot Bord	NY5190	55°12·4'	2°45·8'W	X	79
Florie's Fm	Essex	TL8726	51°54·3'	0°43·5'E	FM	168
Florish	Renf	NS4868	55°53·1'	4°25·4'W	X	64
Floriston Hall	Suff	TL7243	52°3·7'	0°30·9'E	X	154
Floristonrigg	Cumbr	NY3564	54°58·2'	3°0·5'W	X	85
Flory Island	Corn	SW8363	50°25·8'	5°3·0'W	X	200
Flosh	D & G	NY1167	54°59·6'	3°23·0'W	X	85
Flosh	D & G	NY2669	55°0·9'	3°9·0'W	X	85
Flosh Burn	Scot Bord	NT5303	55°19·4'	2°44·0'W	W	79
Floshend	D & G	NY3168	55°0·4'	3°4·3'W	X	85
Floshes	Cumbr	NY4051	54°51·3'	2°55·7'W	X	85
Floshes Hill	N Yks	SD8690	54°18·6'	2°12·5'W	X	98
Floshgate	Cumbr	NY4523	54°36·2'	2°50·7'W	X	90
Floshknowe	D & G	NY0076	55°4·4'	3°33·5'W	X	84
Flosh, The	Cumbr	NY5067	55°0·0'	2°46·5'W	X	86
Flosh, The	Cumbr	NY5270	55°1·6'	2°44·6'W	W	86
Flossnan	Highld	NG2337	57°20·6'	6°35·8'W	X	23
Floss, The	Scot Bord	NT4622	55°29·6'	2°50·8'W	X	73
Flossy Groups	Orkney	HY2900	58°53·2'	3°13·4'W	X	6,7
Flossy Knowes	Shetld	HU5864	60°21·6'	0°56·4'W	X	2
Flossy Loch	Shetld	HU4238	60°7·7'	1°14·1'W	W	4
Flothers, The	Northum	NY7076	55°4·9'	2°27·8'W	X	86,87
Flotmanby Carrs	N Yks	TA0780	54°12·5'	0°21·1'W	X	101
Flotta	Orkney	ND3594	58°50·0'	3°7·1'W	X	7
Flotta	Shetld	HU3746	60°12·1'	1°19·5'W	X	4
Flotterton	Northum	NT9902	55°19·0'	2°0·5'W	X	81
Flouch Inn	Barns	SE1901	53°30·6'	1°42·4'W	X	110
Floutern Tarn	Cumbr	NY1217	54°32·7'	3°21·2'W	W	89
Flout Hill	N Yks	SE1067	54°6·2'	1°50·4'W	X	99
Flowdens	D & G	NY2973	55°3·0'	3°6·3'W	X	85
Flowerburn Ho	Highld	NH7360	57°37·0'	4°7·1'W	X	21,27
Flowerburn Mains	Highld	NH7359	57°36·5'	4°7·1'W	X	27
Flowerdale	Pth & Kin	NO1932	56°28·6'	3°18·5'W	X	53
Flowerdale Forest	Highld	NG8967	57°38·9'	5°31·7'W	X	19,24
Flowerdale Ho	Highld	NG8175	57°43·0'	5°40·2'W	X	19
Flowerdale Mains	Highld	NG8175	57°43·0'	5°40·2'W	X	19
Flowerdown Barrows	Hants	SU4531	51°4·8'	1°21·1'W	A	185
Flower Fm	Norf	TF4717	52°44·1'	0°11·0'E	FM	131
Flower Hill	E Yorks	SE9338	53°50·0'	0°34·8'W	X	106
Flower of May	N Yks	SE5174	54°9·8'	1°12·7'W	X	100
Flower's Barrow	Dorset	SY8680	50°37·4'	2°11·5'W	X	194
Flower's Barrow (Fort)	Dorset	SY8680	50°37·4'	2°11·5'W	A	194
Flowers Bottom	Bucks	SU8399	51°41·2'	0°47·6'W	T	165
Flowers Fm	Herts	TL1011	51°47·4'	0°23·9'W	FM	166
Flower's Fm	Wilts	SU0391	51°37·3'	1°57·0'W	FM	163,173
Flowers Green	E Susx	TQ6311	50°52·8'	0°19·4'E	T	199
Flower's Hall	Essex	TL7233	51°58·4'	0°30·6'E	X	167
Flowers Hill	C of Bris	ST6169	51°25·4'	2°33·3'W	X	172
Flowers of May	Fife	NT2399	56°10·9'	3°14·0'W	X	58
Flowery Bank	N Yks	SE7672	54°8·5'	0°49·8'W	X	100
Flowery Field	Tames	SJ9495	53°27·3'	2°5·0'W	T	109
Flow Hill	D & G	NT2900	55°17·6'	3°6·7'W	H	79
Flow Moss	Cumbr	NY5606	54°27·1'	2°40·3'W	X	90
Flow Moss	E Ayr	NS5145	55°40·8'	4°21·7'W	X	64
Flow Moss	E Ayr	NS5244	55°40·3'	4°20·8'W	X	70
Flow Moss	E Ayr	NS5546	55°41·4'	4°18·0'W	X	64
Flow Moss	S Lanak	NS8427	55°31·6'	3°49·8'W	X	71,72
Flow of Airriequhillart	D & G	NX3451	54°49·8'	4°34·6'W	X	82
Flow of Airriequillart	D & G	NX3551	54°49·9'	4°33·7'W	X	83
Flow of Darsnag	D & G	NX3254	54°51·4'	4°36·6'W	X	82
Flow of Dergoals	D & G	NX2358	54°53·4'	4°45·2'W	X	82
Flow of Derrie	D & G	NX3349	54°48·7'	4°35·5'W	X	82
Flow of Drumnescat	D & G	NX3450	54°49·3'	4°34·6'W	X	82
Flow of Elrig	D & G	NX3350	54°49·3'	4°35·5'W	X	82
Flows of Leanas	Highld	ND2648	58°25·1'	3°15·5'W	W	11,12
Flows, The	Highld	ND1949	58°25·6'	3°22·7'W	W	11,12
Flowsware Rig	Scot Bord	NY4795	55°15·0'	2°49·6'W	X	79
Flowton	Suff	TM0846	52°4·6'	1°2·5'E	T	155,169
Flowton Brook	Suff	TM0845	52°4·1'	1°2·5'E	X	155,169
Flubersgerdie	Shetld	HP5712	60°47·5'	0°56·7'W	X	1
Fluchlady	Highld	NH5561	57°37·2'	4°25·2'W	X	21
Fluchter	E Dunb	NS5874	55°56·5'	4°16·0'W	T	64
Fluder	Devon	SX8867	50°29·8'	3°34·4'W	X	202
Fludir, The	Shetld	HU5995	60°38·3'	0°54·8'W	X	1,2
Fluechams	Stir	NS7094	56°7·5'	4°5·0'W	X	57
Flue Taing	Shetld	HP5602	60°42·1'	0°57·9'W	X	1
Fluga Moss	Shetld	HU4884	60°32·5'	1°7·0'W	X	1,2,3
Flugarth	Shetld	HU3690	60°35·8'	1°20·1'W	X	1,2
Flugarth	Shetld	HU4663	60°21·2'	1°9·5'W	T	2,3
Flugarth Hill	Shetld	HU4564	60°21·7'	1°10·6'W	X	2,3
Fluke Hall	Lancs	SD3949	53°56·3'	2°55·3'W	X	102
Fluke Hole	Northum	NU2611	55°23·8'	1°34·9'W	W	81
Flukes Hole	Shetld	HU4679	60°29·8'	1°9·3'W	T	2,3
Flukings Bight	Shetld	HU5866	60°22·7'	0°56·4'W	W	2
Flusco Pike	Cumbr	NY4628	54°38·9'	2°49·8'W	H	90
Flushdyke	Wakf	SE2821	53°41·3'	1°34·1'W	T	104
Flush House	Kirk	SE1107	53°33·8'	1°49·6'W	T	110
Flushiemere Beck	Durham	NY9031	54°40·7'	2°8·9'W	W	91,92
Flushiemere Ho	Durham	NY9030	54°40·1'	2°8·9'W	X	91,92
Flushing	Aberd	NK0546	57°30·5'	1°54·5'W	T	30
Flushing	Corn	SW7825	50°5·3'	5°5·8'W	T	204
Flushing	Corn	SW8033	50°9·6'	5°4·4'W	T	204
Flush Knowes	D & G	NX1271	55°0·1'	4°55·9'W	X	76
Flush Plantn	Scot Bord	NT6106	55°21·0'	2°36·5'W	F	80
Flust	Cumbr	SD7794	54°20·7'	2°20·8'W	X	98
Flutters Hill	Surrey	SU9965	51°22·8'	0°34·3'W	X	175,176
Fluxton	Devon	SY0892	50°43·5'	3°17·8'W	T	192
Flybury Point	Suff	TM3946	52°3·9'	1°29·6'E	X	169
Flyford Flavell	Worcs	SO9854	52°11·6'	2°1·4'W	T	150
Flyingdales Moor	N Yks	NZ9003	54°25·1'	0°36·4'W	X	94
Flying Dingle	Shrops	SJ2804	52°38·0'	3°3·4'W	X	126
Flying Horse Fm	Beds	SP9837	52°1·6'	0°33·9'W	FM	153
Flying Horse Fm	Leeds	SE3838	53°50·5'	1°24·9'W	FM	104
Foadhail Dhubh	Highld	NM6471	56°46·5'	5°51·3'W	W	40
Foage Fm	Corn	SW4637	50°11·0'	5°33·1'W	FM	203
Foal Burn Head	Scot Bord	NT0614	55°24·9'	3°28·7'W	H	78
Foal Cote	N Yks	SE2666	54°5·6'	1°35·7'W	X	99
Foales Arrishes	Devon	SX7375	50°33·9'	3°47·2'W	A	191
Foal Park	N Yks	SE1691	54°19·1'	1°44·8'W	X	99
Foal's Crag	Moray	NJ1709	57°10·1'	3°21·9'W	X	36
Foals Green	Suff	TM2571	52°17·7'	1°18·4'E	T	156
Foal's Well	Highld	NJ0029	57°20·7'	3°39·2'W	X	36
Fobbing	Thurr	TQ7184	51°32·0'	0°28·3'E	T	178
Fobbing Horse	Thurr	TQ7484	51°31·9'	0°30·9'E	X	178
Fobbing Marshes	Thurr	TQ7284	51°31·9'	0°29·2'E	X	178
Fobdown Fm	Hants	SU5734	51°6·4'	1°10·8'W	FM	185
Fober Fm	Lancs	SD6850	53°57·0'	2°28·8'W	FM	103
Fochabers	Moray	NJ3458	57°36·7'	3°5·8'W	T	28
Fochriw	Caer	SO1005	51°44·4'	3°17·8'W	T	161
Fochy Burn	Pth & Kin	NO1005	56°14·0'	3°26·7'W	W	58
Fockbury Fm	Worcs	SO9472	52°21·0'	2°4·9'W	FM	139
Fockerby	N Lincs	SE8419	53°39·9'	0°43·3'W	T	112
Focklesbrook Fm	Surrey	SU9961	51°20·6'	0°34·3'W	FM	175,176,186
Fodder Dike	Lincs	TF4357	53°5·7'	0°8·5'E	W	122
Fodder Fen	Cambs	TL5387	52°27·8'	0°15·5'E	X	143
Fodder Fen	Cambs	TL5980	52°23·9'	0°20·6'E	X	143
Fodder Fen Common	Cambs	TL4893	52°31·2'	0°11·3'E	X	143
Fodderlee Burn	Scot Bord	NT6012	55°24·3'	2°37·5'W	W	80
Fodderletter	Moray	NJ1421	57°16·6'	3°25·1'W	X	36
Fodderstone Gap	Norf	TF6508	52°38·9'	0°26·7'E	T	143
Foddery	Highld	NH5159	57°36·1'	4°29·1'W	T	26
Fodderty Lodge	Highld	NH5159	57°36·1'	4°29·1'W	X	26
Foddington	Somer	ST5829	51°3·8'	2°35·6'W	T	183
Fodens Fm	Ches	SJ9069	53°13·3'	2°8·6'W	FM	118
Fodge Fm	Oxon	SP3435	52°1·0'	1°29·9'W	FM	151
Fodragaigh	N Eil	NF8445	57°23·4'	7°15·1'W	X	22
Fodston	Renf	NS3766	55°51·8'	4°35·8'W	X	63
Fodwen	Wrex	SJ1634	52°54·1'	3°14·5'W	X	125
Foel	Carm	SN3925	51°54·3'	4°20·0'W	X	145
Foel	Carm	SN6711	51°47·2'	3°55·3'W	X	159
Foel	Carm	SN6845	52°5·5'	3°55·2'W	H	146
Foel	Carm	SN8443	52°4·6'	3°41·2'W	X	147,160
Foel	Conwy	SH8270	53°13·1'	3°45·6'W	X	116
Foel	Conwy	SH9466	53°11·1'	3°34·8'W	X	116
Foel	Conwy	SH9863	53°9·5'	3°31·1'W	X	116
Foel	Denb	SJ2042	52°58·4'	3°11·1'W	X	117
Foel	Gwyn	SH4450	53°1·7'	4°19·2'W	H	115,123
Foel	I of Angl	SH2182	53°18·5'	4°40·8'W	X	114
Foel	I of Angl	SH4079	53°17·3'	4°23·6'W	X	114,115
Foel	Powys	SH8006	52°38·6'	3°46·0'W	H	124,125
Foel	Powys	SH9911	52°41·5'	3°29·3'W	T	125
Foel	Powys	SO0679	52°24·3'	3°22·5'W	X	136,147
Foel	Powys	SO1562	52°15·2'	3°14·3'W	X	148
Foelallt	Cered	SN4958	52°12·2'	4°12·2'W	X	146
Foelas	Denb	SJ0449	53°2·0'	3°25·5'W	X	116
Foelasfechan	Conwy	SH8559	53°7·2'	3°42·7'W	H	116
Foel Bach	Gwyn	SH3032	52°51·8'	4°31·1'W	H	123
Foel-bâch	I of Angl	SH3591	53°23·7'	4°28·5'W	X	114
Foel Benddin	Gwyn	SH8516	52°44·0'	3°41·8'W	H	124,125
Foel Boeth	Conwy	SH8047	53°0·7'	3°46·9'W	H	116
Foel Boeth	Gwyn	SH7734	52°53·6'	3°49·3'W	H	124
Foel Boeth	Gwyn	SH8333	52°53·1'	3°43·9'W	H	124,125
Foel-boeth	Gwyn	SH8643	52°58·6'	3°41·5'W	H	124,125
Foel Boethwel	Gwyn	SH6547	53°0·4'	4°0·3'W	X	115
Foel Cae'rberllan	Gwyn	SH6708	52°39·4'	3°57·6'W	H	124
Foel Cae'r-hafotty	Gwyn	SH9130	52°51·6'	3°36·7'W	H	125
Foel Caethle	Gwyn	SN6098	52°34·0'	4°3·5'W	H	135
Foel Caledeiriau	Conwy	SH8366	53°10·9'	3°44·6'W	H	116
Foel Cathau	Conwy	SH8964	53°9·9'	3°39·2'W	X	116
Foel Cedig	Gwyn	SH9828	52°50·6'	3°30·5'W	H	125
Foel Clochydd	Gwyn	SH8920	52°46·2'	3°38·3'W	H	124,125
Foel Coch	Gwyn	SH9429	52°51·1'	3°34·0'W	H	125
Foel Coppice	Powys	SJ2813	52°42·8'	3°3·5'W	F	126
Foel Crochan	Gwyn	SH7610	52°40·7'	3°49·6'W	H	124
Foelcwan	Carm	SN3822	51°52·6'	4°20·8'W	X	145,159
Foel Cwmcerwyn	Pemb	SN0931	51°56·9'	4°46·4'W	H	145
Foel Cwm-Sian Llŵyd	Gwyn	SH9931	52°52·3'	3°29·6'W	H	125
Foel Cynfal	Gwyn	SH7539	52°56·3'	3°51·2'W	X	124
Foel Cynwch	Gwyn	SH7321	52°46·5'	3°52·6'W	H	124
Foel Darw	Powys	SN8225	51°54·9'	3°42·5'W	H	160
Foel Ddu	Conwy	SH8247	53°0·7'	3°45·1'W	H	116
Foel Ddu	Gwyn	SH6328	52°50·2'	4°1·6'W	H	124
Foel Ddu	Gwyn	SH6645	52°59·4'	3°59·4'W	X	115
Foel Ddu	Gwyn	SH6909	52°40·0'	3°55·8'W	H	124
Foel Ddu	Gwyn	SH8124	52°48·3'	3°45·5'W	H	124,125
Foel Ddu	Gwyn	SH8323	52°47·8'	3°43·7'W	H	124,125
Foel Deg	Carm	SN7415	51°49·4'	3°49·3'W	X	160
Foel Deg-arbedd	Carm	SN7015	51°49·4'	3°52·8'W	H	160
Foel-drych	Pemb	SN1630	51°56·5'	4°40·2'W	H	145
Foel Drygarn	Pemb	SN1533	51°58·1'	4°41·2'W	A	145
Foel Dugoed	Gwyn	SH8913	52°42·4'	3°38·2'W	H	124,125
Foel Eryr	Pemb	SN0631	51°56·9'	4°49·0'W	X	145
Foel-fâch	Brig	SS8588	51°35·0'	3°39·2'W	X	170
Foel fâch	Denb	SJ0652	53°3·7'	3°23·8'W	X	116
Foel Fach	Pemb	SN0542	52°2·8'	4°50·2'W	H	145
Foel Fadian	Powys	SN8295	52°32·6'	3°44·0'W	H	135,136
Foel Fawr	Carm	SN7318	51°51·0'	3°50·2'W	X	160
Foel Fawr	Cered	SN6995	52°32·5'	3°55·5'W	H	135
Foel-fawr	Conwy	SH8464	53°9·9'	3°43·7'W	X	116
Foel Fawr	Conwy	SH9768	53°12·2'	3°32·1'W	X	116
Foel Fawr	Denb	SJ0633	52°53·4'	3°23·4'W	H	125
Foel Fawr	Denb	SJ0651	53°3·1'	3°23·7'W	X	116
Foel Fawr	Gwyn	SH3032	52°51·8'	4°31·1'W	X	123
Foel Fawr	Gwyn	SH6805	52°37·8'	3°56·6'W	H	124
Foel Fawr	Gwyn	SH8523	52°47·8'	3°41·9'W	H	124,125
Foel-fawr	I of Angl	SH3591	53°23·7'	4°28·5'W	X	114
Foel Fawr	Nth Pt Talb	SS8595	51°38·8'	3°39·3'W	X	170
Foel Fawr	Pemb	SM7022	51°51·2'	5°20·0'W	X	157
Foel-fawr	Powys	SJ0203	52°37·2'	3°26·5'W	H	136
Foel-fawr	Powys	SO0184	52°26·9'	3°27·0'W	H	136
Foel Feddau	Pemb	SN1032	51°57·5'	4°45·5'W	H	145
Foel Felen	Conwy	SH7652	53°3·3'	3°50·6'W	X	115
Foel Fenlli	Denb	SJ1660	53°8·1'	3°14·9'W	X	116
Foel Fferm	Denb	SJ0677	53°17·1'	3°24·2'W	X	116
Foel Figenau	Gwyn	SH9128	52°50·6'	3°36·7'W	H	125
Foel Fm	Carm	SN2939	52°1·6'	4°29·2'W	FM	145
Foel Fm	Denb	SJ0262	53°9·0'	3°27·5'W	FM	116
Foel Fm	Powys	SJ2120	52°46·6'	3°9·9'W	FM	126
Foel Fodig	Denb	SJ0845	52°59·9'	3°21·8'W	X	116
Foel Fraith	Carm	SN7518	51°51·0'	3°48·5'W	H	160
Foel Fraith	Cered	SN7751	52°8·9'	3°47·5'W	X	146,147
Foel-fras	Gwyn	SH6968	53°11·8'	3°57·3'W	H	115
Foel-fras	Gwyn	SH7248	53°1·1'	3°54·1'W	H	115
Foel fras	Powys	SN7692	52°30·9'	3°49·2'W	X	135
Foel Frech	Conwy	SH8747	53°0·7'	3°40·7'W	H	116
Foel Frech	Denb	SJ0154	53°4·7'	3°28·3'W	H	116
Foel Fynyddau	Nth Pt Talb	SS7893	51°37·6'	3°45·4'W	H	170
Foel Ganol	Denb	SJ0559	53°7·4'	3°24·8'W	H	116
Foel Ganol	Gwyn	SH6665	53°10·2'	3°59·9'W	X	115
Foel-ganol	Gwyn	SH6871	53°13·4'	3°58·2'W	H	115
Foel Gasnach	Denb	SJ0355	53°5·2'	3°26·5'W	H	116
Foel-gastell	Carm	SN5414	51°48·6'	4°6·7'W	T	159
Foel Gasyth	Denb	SJ0262	53°9·0'	3°27·5'W	H	116
Foel Goch	Cered	SN6992	52°30·9'	3°55·4'W	H	135
Foel Goch	Conwy	SH6751	53°2·6'	3°58·6'W	X	115
Foel-goch	Conwy	SH8545	52°59·6'	3°42·4'W	X	116
Foel Goch	Gwyn	SH5756	53°5·2'	4°7·7'W	H	115
Foel-goch	Gwyn	SH6261	53°7·9'	4°3·4'W	H	115
Foel Gôch	Gwyn	SH7202	52°36·3'	3°53·0'W	H	135
Foel Goch	Gwyn	SH9542	52°58·1'	3°33·4'W	H	125
Foel Goch	Pemb	SN0642	52°2·8'	4°49·4'W	X	145
Foel-goch	Powys	SN8784	52°26·8'	3°39·4'W	X	135,136
Foel Goch	Powys	SN9378	52°23·6'	3°34·0'W	H	136,147
Foel Goch	Rho Cyn Taf	SN9300	51°41·6'	3°32·5'W	X	170
Foel Gôch	Wrex	SJ1333	52°53·5'	3°17·2'W	H	125
Foel Gopyn	Conwy	SH8348	53°1·2'	3°44·3'W	X	116
Foel Grach	Gwyn	SH6865	53°10·2'	3°58·1'W	H	115
Foel Grafiau	Powys	SN7592	52°30·9'	3°50·1'W	H	135
Foel Greon	Conwy	SH9763	53°9·5'	3°32·0'W	H	116
Foel Gron	Gwyn	SH5656	53°5·2'	4°8·6'W	X	115
Foel Gron	Gwyn	SH7927	52°49·9'	3°47·4'W	H	124
Foel Gurig	Powys	SN9178	52°23·6'	3°35·7'W	H	136,147
Foel Gwilym Hywel	Brig	SS8892	51°37·2'	3°36·7'W	X	170
Foel Hendre	Pemb	SN1147	52°5·6'	4°45·2'W	H	145
Foel Hill	Powys	SJ2120	52°46·6'	3°9·9'W	H	126
Foel Hill (Fort)	Powys	SJ2120	52°46·6'	3°9·9'W	A	126
Foel Isaf	Denb	SJ0845	52°59·9'	3°21·8'W	X	116
Foel Ispri	Gwyn	SH7020	52°46·0'	3°55·2'W	H	124
Foel Las	Conwy	SH8752	53°3·4'	3°40·8'W	X	116
Foel Lluestbadlon	Gwyn	SH9117	52°44·6'	3°36·5'W	H	125
Foel-llyn	Powys	SJ1028	52°50·8'	3°19·8'W	X	125
Foel Lûs	Conwy	SH7376	53°16·2'	3°53·9'W	H	115
Foel Lwyd	Conwy	SH7272	53°14·0'	3°54·7'W	H	115
Foel Lwyd	Conwy	SH9161	53°8·3'	3°37·4'W	X	116
Foel Mallwyd	Powys	SH8711	52°41·3'	3°39·9'W	H	124,125

Name	County	Grid	Lat	Long	Type	Sheets
Foel Offrwm	Gwyn	SH7520	52°46·0′	3°50·8′W	H	124
Foelortho	Powys	SJ0622	52°47·5′	3°23·2′W	X	125
Foel Penolau	Gwyn	SH6634	52°53·5′	3°59·1′W	H	124
Foel Plantation	Denb	SJ2046	53°0·6′	3°11·1′W	F	117
Foel Rhiwlas	Powys	SJ2032	52°53·0′	3°10·9′W	H	126
Foel Rhudd	Gwyn	SH8924	52°48·4′	3°38·4′W	H	124,125
Foel Rudd	Conwy	SH7645	52°59·5′	3°50·4′W	X	115
Foel Senigl	Gwyn	SH5931	52°51·7′	4°5·3′W	H	124
Foel Trawsnant	Nth Pt Talb	SS8394	51°38·2′	3°41·1′W	X	170
Foel Trefor	Gwyn	SH3031	52°51·2′	4°31·1′W	X	123
Foel Tyn-y-ddôl	Gwyn	SH9341	52°57·6′	3°35·2′W	X	125
Foel-uchaf	Denb	SJ0458	53°6·9′	3°25·7′W	X	116
Foel Uchaf	Denb	SJ0459	53°7·4′	3°25·7′W	H	116
Foel-uchaf	Gwyn	SH4550	53°1·7′	4°18·3′W	X	115,123
Foel Uchaf	Powys	SN8091	52°30·5′	3°45·7′W	H	135,136
Foel-wen	Conwy	SH8143	52°58·5′	3°45·9′W	H	124,125
Foel Wen	Gwyn	SH6327	52°49·6′	4°1·6′W	H	124
Foel Wen	Powys	SJ0933	52°53·4′	3°20·8′W	H	125
Foel Wyddon	Cered	SN7883	52°26·1′	3°47·3′W	H	135
Foel Wylfa	Powys	SJ1933	52°53·5′	3°11·8′W	H	125
Foel Wyllt	Gwyn	SH6304	52°37·2′	4°1·0′W	H	135
Foel y Belan	Powys	SN9993	52°31·8′	3°28·9′W	H	136
Foel y Dyffryn	Brig	SS8494	51°38·2′	3°40·2′W	H	170
Foel-y-Ffridd	Gwyn	SH7402	52°36·3′	3°51·2′W	H	135
Foel-y-ffridd	Gwyn	SH8311	52°41·3′	3°43·5′W	H	124,125
Foel y Geiff	Gwyn	SH7104	52°37·4′	3°53·9′W	H	135
Foel y Geifr	Gwyn	SH9327	52°50·0′	3°34·9′W	H	125
Foel y Gwynt	Denb	SJ1040	52°57·2′	3°20·0′W	X	125
Foel-yr-hydd	Gwyn	SH8716	52°44·0′	3°40·0′W	X	124,125
Fog Close	Cumbr	NY5641	54°46·0′	2°40·6′W	X	86
Fog Close	Cumbr	NY8606	54°27·2′	2°12·5′W	W	91,92
Fog Close	N Yks	NZ5000	54°23·8′	1°13·4′W	X	93
Foggathorpe	E Yorks	SE7537	53°49·7′	0°51·2′W	T	105,106
Foggathorpe Ho	E Yorks	SE7536	53°49·1′	0°51·2′W	X	105,106
Foggathorpe Manor Fm	E Yorks	SE7537	53°49·7′	0°51·2′W	FM	105,106
Foggbrook	Stock	SJ9289	53°24·1′	2°6·8′W	T	109
Fogger	N Yks	SD8955	53°59·7′	2°9·7′W	X	103
Foggieburn	Aberd	NJ5829	57°21·2′	2°41·4′W	X	37
Foggieley	Aberd	NJ5408	57°9·9′	2°45·2′W	X	37
Foggieleys	Fife	NO3806	56°14·8′	2°59·6′W	X	59
Foggiemill	Aberd	NJ3909	57°10·3′	3°0·1′W	X	37
Foggie Moss	Moray	NJ4254	57°34·6′	2°57·7′W	X	28
Foggieton	C of Aber	NJ8603	57°7·3′	2°13·4′W	X	38
Foggit Foot	N Yks	NZ8008	54°27·9′	0°45·5′W	X	94
Fogg's Fm	Ches	SJ6380	53°19·2′	2°32·9′W	FM	109
Foggs Fm	Lancs	SD5343	53°53·1′	2°42·5′W	FM	102
Foggy Gill	Cumbr	SD7298	54°22·8′	2°25·4′W	X	98
Foggy Moss	Moray	NJ4653	57°34·1′	2°53·7′W	X	28,29
Foghanger	Devon	SX4278	50°35·1′	4°13·5′W	X	201
Fogla-lee	Shetld	HU4494	60°37·9′	1°11·2′W	X	1,2
Fogla Skerry	Shetld	HU1461	60°20·2′	1°44·3′W	X	3
Fogla Taing	Shetld	HU4116	59°55·9′	1°15·5′W	X	4
Foglatougs	Shetld	HU3147	60°12·6′	1°25·9′W	X	3
Fogleigh Ho	Wilts	ST8269	51°25·4′	2°15·1′W	X	173
Fogli Stack	Shetld	HZ1970	59°31·2′	1°39·4′W	X	4
Fognam Down	W Berks	SU2980	51°31·3′	1°34·5′W	X	174
Fognam Fm	W Berks	SU2980	51°31·3′	1°34·5′W	FM	174
Fogo	Scot Bord	NT7749	55°44·3′	2°21·5′W	T	74
Fogo Mains	Scot Bord	NT7749	55°44·3′	2°21·5′W	X	74
Fogorig	Scot Bord	NT7748	55°43·7′	2°21·5′W	X	74
Fografiddle	Shetld	HU2742	60°10·0′	1°30·3′W	X	4
Fogrigarth	Shetld	HU2556	60°17·5′	1°32·4′W	T	3
Fogrigg	Northum	NY7666	54°59·5′	2°22·1′W	X	86,87
Fogwatt	Moray	NJ2357	57°36·0′	3°16·8′W	T	28
Foice	Powys	SO1857	52°12·5′	3°11·6′W	X	148
Foich Cottage	Highld	NH1883	57°48·2′	5°3·3′W	X	20
Foich Lodge	Highld	NH1883	57°48·2′	5°3·3′W	X	20
Foinaven	Highld	NC3149	58°24·1′	4°53·0′W	H	9
Foindle	Highld	NC1848	58°23·2′	5°6·3′W	T	9
Foireabhal Bheag	N Eil	NB2210	57°59·8′	6°41·8′W	H	13,14
Foireabhal Mhòr	N Eil	NB2310	57°59·8′	6°40·8′W	H	13,14
Foitealair	N Eil	NB5736	58°15·0′	6°8·0′W	X	8
Foker Grange	Staffs	SJ9657	53°6·8′	2°3·2′W	X	118
Folach	Highld	NG7903	57°4·2′	5°38·3′W	X	33
Fold	N Yks	SD9742	53°52·7′	2°2·3′W	X	103
Folda	Angus	NO1864	56°45·9′	3°20·0′W	T	43
Foldend	Angus	NO2855	56°41·1′	3°10·1′W	X	53
Fold Fm	Herts	TQ2297	51°39·7′	0°13·8′W	FM	166,176
Fold Fm	Staffs	SK1161	53°9·0′	1°49·7′W	FM	119
Fold Garth	Durham	NZ0726	54°38·0′	1°53·1′W	X	92
Fold Gate	Cumbr	SD3596	54°21·6′	2°59·6′W	X	96,97
Foldgate	Shrops	SO5273	52°21·4′	2°41·9′W	X	137,138
Foldgate Fm	Cumbr	SD1191	54°18·7′	3°21·7′W	FM	96
Foldhay	Devon	SS7004	50°49·5′	3°50·4′W	X	191
Fold Head	Lancs	SD8817	53°39·2′	2°10·5′W	T	109
Fold Hill	Lincs	TF4654	53°4·0′	0°11·2′E	T	122
Foldhill Fms	Somer	ST4719	50°58·3′	2°44·9′W	FM	193
Fold Ho	Lancs	SD4047	53°55·2′	2°54·4′W	X	102
Foldrings	Sheff	SK2993	53°26·2′	1°33·4′W	T	110
Folds	Cumbr	SD1791	54°18·7′	3°16·1′W	X	96
Folds Fm	Donc	SK5790	53°24·5′	1°8·1′W	FM	111
Folds Fm	Hants	SU1615	50°56·3′	1°46·0′W	FM	184
Folds of Corhabbie	Moray	NJ2831	57°22·1′	3°11·4′W	X	37
Folds Pasture	Black w Dar	SD6714	53°37·5′	2°29·5′W	X	109
Fold, The	N Yks	SD9546	53°54·9′	2°4·2′W	X	103
Fole	Staffs	SK0437	52°56·1′	1°56·0′W	T	128
Folebank Fm	Staffs	SK0437	52°56·1′	1°56·0′W	FM	128
Fole Hall	Staffs	SK0436	52°55·5′	1°56·0′W	X	128
Foleshill	Cov	SP3582	52°26·3′	1°28·7′W	T	140
Foley Fm	Lancs	SD4664	54°4·4′	2°49·1′W	FM	97
Foley Ho	Essex	TL7727	51°55·0′	0°34·8′E	X	167
Foley Manor	Hants	SU8230	51°4·0′	0°49·4′W	X	186
Foley Park	Worcs	SO8275	52°22·6′	2°15·5′W	T	138
Foliejon Park	Brackn	SU8974	51°27·7′	0°42·7′W	X	175
Folk Burn	D & G	NX5187	55°9·5′	4°19·9′W	W	77
Folke	Dorset	ST6513	50°55·2′	2°29·5′W	T	194
Folkerton Mill	S Lanak	NS8535	55°36·0′	3°49·1′W	X	71,72
Folkes Fm	Hav	TQ5888	51°34·3′	0°17·2′E	FM	177
Folkestone	Kent	TR2136	51°5·1′	1°9·7′E	T	179,189
Folkestone Race Course	Kent	TR1236	51°5·3′	1°2·0′E	X	179,189
Folkeston Hill	Pemb	SM8619	51°50·0′	5°6·0′W	H	157
Folkingham	Lincs	TF0733	52°53·3′	0°24·2′W	T	130
Folkington	E Susx	TQ5503	50°48·6′	0°12·4′E	T	199
Folkington Manor	E Susx	TQ5604	50°49·1′	0°13·3′E	X	199
Folk Moot	Lincs	TF0543	52°58·7′	0°25·8′W	A	130
Folks' Wood	Kent	TR1335	51°4·7′	1°2·8′E	F	179,189
Folksworth	Cambs	TL1489	52°29·5′	0°18·9′W	T	142
Folkton	N Yks	TA0579	54°12·0′	0°23·0′W	T	101
Folkton Brow	N Yks	TA0579	54°12·0′	0°23·0′W	X	101
Folkton Carr	N Yks	TA0580	54°12·5′	0°23·0′W	X	101
Folkton Ho	N Yks	TA0579	54°12·0′	0°23·0′W	X	101
Folkton Manor	N Yks	TA0579	54°12·0′	0°23·0′W	X	101
Folkton Wold Fm	N Yks	TA0578	54°11·5′	0°23·0′W	FM	101
Folla Rule	Aberd	NJ7333	57°23·5′	2°26·5′W	T	29
Follaton Ho (Council Offices)	Devon	SX7860	50°25·9′	3°42·7′W	X	202
Folley	Devon	SS3500	50°46·8′	4°20·1′W	X	190
Folley	Shrops	SO7797	52°34·5′	2°20·0′W	T	138
Follies Fm	Surrey	SU9734	51°6·1′	0°36·5′W	FM	186
Follies, The	Glos	SP2017	51°51·3′	1°42·2′W	X	163
Follies,The	N Lincs	SE9612	53°36·0′	0°32·5′W	F	112
Follifoot	N Yks	SE3452	53°58·0′	1°28·5′W	T	104
Follifoot Ridge	N Yks	SE3252	53°58·0′	1°30·3′W	X	104
Follingsby	Ghead	NZ3060	54°56·3′	1°31·5′W	T	88
Follions	Northum	NU0007	55°21·7′	1°59·6′W	X	81
Followsters	Moray	NJ4254	57°34·6′	2°57·7′W	X	28
Folly	Dorset	ST7203	50°49·8′	2°23·5′W	T	194
Folly	Durham	NZ1028	54°39·1′	1°50·3′W	X	92
Folly	Pemb	SM8619	51°50·0′	5°6·0′W	X	157
Folly	Pemb	SM9220	51°50·6′	5°0·8′W	T	157,158
Folly	Powys	SJ2311	52°41·7′	3°8·0′W	X	126
Folly	Somer	SS8833	51°5·4′	3°35·6′W	X	181
Folly	Staffs	SK0462	53°9·5′	1°56·0′W	X	119
Folly Bank	Shrops	SO2284	52°27·1′	3°8·5′W	X	137
Folly Bank	Shrops	SO2483	52°26·6′	3°6·7′W	W	137
Folly Bank	Shrops	SO4996	52°33·8′	2°44·7′W	X	137,138
Folly Barn	Swin	SU2078	51°30·3′	1°42·3′W	X	174
Folly Br	Leic	SP5993	52°32·1′	1°7·4′W	X	140
Folly Brook	S Glos	ST6878	51°30·2′	2°27·3′W	W	172
Folly Clump	Oxon	SU3584	51°33·5′	1°29·3′W	F	174
Folly Court	Wok	SU7967	51°24·0′	0°51·5′W	X	175
Folly Cove	Corn	SW3522	50°2·6′	5°41·7′W	W	203
Folly Cross	Devon	SS4508	50°51·3′	4°11·8′W	T	190
Folly Dairy	Hants	SU5655	51°17·7′	1°11·4′W	X	174,185
Folly Drain	N Lincs	SE7505	53°32·4′	0°51·7′W	W	112
Folly Drain	N Lincs	SE7909	53°34·5′	0°48·0′W	W	112
Folly Faunts Ho	Essex	TL9009	51°45·1′	0°45·6′E	X	168
Folly Fields Fm	Northnts	SP7440	52°3·4′	0°54·8′W	FM	152
Folly Fm	Beds	TL0435	52°0·5′	0°28·7′W	FM	153
Folly Fm	Bucks	SP7229	51°57·5′	0°56·7′W	FM	165
Folly Fm	Bucks	SP7509	51°46·7′	0°54·4′W	FM	165
Folly Fm	Bucks	SP7918	51°51·5′	0°50·8′W	FM	165
Folly Fm	Cambs	TL5884	52°26·1′	0°19·9′E	FM	143
Folly Fm	Ches	SJ5868	53°12·7′	2°37·3′W	FM	117
Folly Fm	Devon	SX8198	50°46·4′	3°40·9′W	FM	191
Folly Fm	Dorset	ST7723	51°0·6′	2°19·3′W	FM	183
Folly Fm	Essex	TL6121	51°52·1′	0°20·7′E	FM	167
Folly Fm	Glos	SO6618	51°51·8′	2°29·2′W	FM	162
Folly Fm	Glos	SP1220	51°52·9′	1°49·1′W	FM	163
Folly Fm	Glos	SP1314	51°49·7′	1°48·3′W	FM	163
Folly Fm	Glos	ST7590	51°36·7′	2°21·3′W	FM	162,172
Folly Fm	Hants	SU4133	51°5·9′	1°24·7′W	FM	185
Folly Fm	Hants	SU5263	51°22·1′	1°14·8′W	FM	174
Folly Fm	Hants	SU5546	51°12·9′	1°12·4′W	FM	185
Folly Fm	Hants	SU6659	51°19·8′	1°2·8′W	FM	175,186
Folly Fm	Heref	SO4058	52°13·3′	2°52·3′W	FM	148,149
Folly fm	Herts	SP8716	51°50·4′	0°43·8′W	FM	165
Folly Fm	Herts	SP9414	51°49·2′	0°37·8′W	FM	165
Folly Fm	Leic	SP4699	52°35·4′	1°18·9′W	FM	140
Folly Fm	Lincs	TF0508	52°39·8′	0°26·4′W	FM	142
Folly Fm	Mil Key	SP7947	52°7·2′	0°50·4′W	FM	152
Folly Fm	Norf	TM0992	52°29·4′	1°5·1′E	FM	144
Folly Fm	Northnts	SP7370	52°19·6′	0°55·3′W	FM	141
Folly Fm	Northum	NT9855	55°47·5′	2°1·5′W	FM	75
Folly Fm	Northum	NY8258	54°55·2′	2°16·4′W	FM	86,87
Folly Fm	N Yks	NZ5805	54°26·5′	1°5·9′W	FM	93
Folly Fm	Oxon	SP5510	51°47·4′	1°11·8′W	FM	164
Folly Fm	Oxon	SP6223	51°54·4′	1°5·5′W	FM	164,165
Folly Fm	Pemb	SN0512	51°46·6′	4°49·2′W	FM	158
Folly Fm	Pemb	SN1108	51°44·6′	4°43·9′W	FM	158
Folly Fm	Powys	SO3270	52°19·7′	2°59·5′W	FM	137,148
Folly Fm	S Glos	ST8086	51°34·6′	2°16·9′W	FM	173
Folly Fm	Shrops	SJ3817	52°45·1′	2°54·7′W	FM	126
Folly Fm	Shrops	SJ6801	52°36·6′	2°28·0′W	FM	127
Folly Fm	Shrops	SO3686	52°28·3′	2°56·1′W	FM	137
Folly Fm	Somer	ST3017	50°57·1′	2°59·4′W	FM	193
Folly Fm	Somer	ST4308	50°52·4′	2°48·2′W	FM	193
Folly Fm	Somer	ST7038	51°8·7′	2°25·5′W	FM	183
Folly Fm	Suff	TM1235	51°58·6′	1°5·6′E	FM	155,169
Folly Fm	W Berks	SU3469	51°25·4′	1°30·3′W	FM	174
Folly Fm	W Berks	SU4783	51°32·9′	1°18·9′W	FM	174
Folly Fm	Wilts	ST8370	51°26·0′	2°14·3′W	FM	173
Folly Fm	Wilts	ST8677	51°29·7′	2°11·7′W	FM	173
Folly Fm	Wilts	SU0933	51°6·0′	1°51·9′W	FM	184
Folly Fm	Wilts	SU2963	51°22·2′	1°34·6′W	FM	174
Folly Fm	Worcs	SO7554	52°11·3′	2°21·5′W	FM	150
Folly Fm	W Susx	TQ3221	50°58·6′	0°6·8′W	FM	198
Folly Fm Nature Reserve	Bath & NE Somer	ST6060	51°20·5′	2°34·1′W	X	172
Folly Fm, The	Glos	ST8992	51°37·8′	2°9·1′W	FM	163,173
Folly Gate	Devon	SX5797	50°45·5′	4°1·3′W	T	191
Folly Green	Essex	TL8026	51°54·4′	0°37·4′E	T	168
Folly Grove	Suff	TL8672	52°19·1′	0°44·1′E	F	144,155
Folly Hall	Notts	SK6626	52°49·9′	1°0·8′W	X	129
Folly Hall	N Yks	SE1951	53°57·5′	1°42·2′W	X	104
Folly Hall	Staffs	SK1425	52°49·6′	1°47·1′W	X	128
Folly Hall	Suff	TM0170	52°17·7′	0°57·3′E	X	144,155
Folly Hill	Bath & NE Somer	ST6553	51°16·7′	2°29·7′W	X	183
Folly Hill	Dorset	SY6199	50°47·6′	2°32·8′W	X	194
Folly Hill	Hants	SU5533	51°5·8′	1°12·5′W	X	185
Folly Hill	Notts	SK8143	52°58·9′	0°47·2′W	X	130
Folly Hill	Suff	TL6865	52°15·7′	0°28·1′E	X	154
Folly Hill Fm	Kent	TQ7639	51°7·6′	0°31·3′E	FM	188
Folly Ho	Durham	NZ0023	54°36·4′	1°59·6′W	X	92
Folly Ho	Northum	NZ0992	55°13·6′	1°51·1′W	X	81
Folly Ho	Notts	SK8453	53°4·3′	0°44·4′W	X	121
Folly Ho	Suff	TM3549	52°5·6′	1°26·2′E	X	169
Folly Moss	Northum	NY9377	55°5·5′	2°6·2′W	X	87
Folly Plantn	N Yks	NZ1105	54°26·7′	1°49·4′W	F	92
Folly Plantn	Scot Bord	NT5609	55°22·6′	2°41·2′W	F	80
Folly Point	Worcs	SO7878	52°24·2′	2°19·0′W	X	138
Folly Rigg	Cumbr	NY6160	54°56·2′	2°36·1′W	X	86
Follysyke Cotts	Cumbr	NY6160	54°56·2′	2°36·1′W	X	86
Folly, The	Bucks	SP7433	51°59·7′	0°54·9′W	X	152,165
Folly, The	Derby	SK1682	53°20·3′	1°45·2′W	H	110
Folly, The	Dorset	ST8408	50°52·5′	2°13·3′W	X	194
Folly, The	Durham	NZ1223	54°36·4′	1°48·4′W	X	92
Folly, The	Glos	SU0898	51°41·1′	1°52·7′W	F	163
Folly, The	Heref	SO4967	52°18·2′	2°44·5′W	X	137,138,148
Folly, The	Kent	TQ5467	51°23·1′	0°13·2′E	X	177
Folly, The	Norf	TF6728	52°49·6′	0°29·1′E	X	132
Folly, The	Northum	NY9294	55°14·7′	2°7·1′W	X	80
Folly, The	Northum	NZ0980	55°7·1′	1°51·1′W	X	81
Folly, The	Oxon	SU2995	51°39·4′	1°34·5′W	X	164
Folly, The	Powys	SO1858	52°13·1′	3°11·6′W	X	148
Folly, The	Staffs	SJ7136	52°55·5′	2°25·5′W	F	127
Folly, The	Staffs	SJ9650	53°3·1′	2°3·2′W	X	118
Folly, The	Suff	TL8471	52°18·6′	0°42·4′E	X	144,155
Folly, The	Suff	TM2644	52°3·1′	1°18·2′E	X	169
Folly, The	W Berks	SU3765	51°23·2′	1°27·7′W	X	174
Folly, The	Wilts	ST8871	51°26·5′	2°10·0′W	X	173
Folly, The	W Susx	SU9509	50°52·6′	0°38·6′W	X	197
Folly, The (Cromwells Battery)	Oxon	SU2995	51°39·4′	1°34·5′W	A	164
Folly Top	N Yks	SE0359	54°1·9′	1°56·8′W	X	104
Folly Wood	Bath & NE Somer	ST6060	51°20·5′	2°34·1′W	F	172
Folly Wood	Glos	ST7797	51°40·5′	2°19·6′W	F	162
Folsetter	Orkney	HY2624	59°6·1′	3°17·0′W	X	6
Folyats	Essex	TL5505	51°43·6′	0°15·1′E	X	167
Fominoch	D & G	NX6971	55°1·2′	4°2·5′W	X	77,84
Fonaby House Fm	Lincs	TA1103	53°31·0′	0°19·1′W	FM	113
Fonaby Top	Lincs	TA1203	53°30·9′	0°18·2′W	X	113
Fonah	Angus	NO5151	56°39·2′	2°47·5′W	X	54
Fonlief Hir	Gwyn	SH6031	52°51·7′	4°4·4′W	X	124
Fonmon	V of Glam	ST0467	51°23·9′	3°22·4′W	T	170
Fonmon Castle	V of Glam	ST0468	51°24·4′	3°22·4′W	A	170
Fonston	Corn	SX2191	50°41·7′	4°31·7′W	T	190
Fontburn Reservoir	Northum	NZ0493	55°14·1′	1°55·8′W	W	81
Fonthill	Wilts	ST9131	51°4·9′	2°7·3′W	X	184
Fonthill Abbey	Wilts	ST9230	51°4·4′	2°6·5′W	X	184
Fonthill Bishop	Wilts	ST9332	51°5·5′	2°5·6′W	T	184
Fonthill Bushes	Wilts	ST9535	51°7·1′	2°3·9′W	F	184
Fonthill Gifford	Wilts	ST9231	51°4·9′	2°6·5′W	T	184
Fonthill Ho	Wilts	ST9431	51°4·9′	2°4·8′W	X	184
Fontinalis Lochs	Arg & Bt	NM6121	56°19·5′	5°51·5′W	W	49
Font le Roi	Dorset	ST6713	50°55·2′	2°27·8′W	X	194
Fontmell Brook	Dorset	ST8516	50°56·8′	2°12·4′W	W	183
Fontmell Down	Dorset	ST8717	50°57·4′	2°10·7′W	H	183
Fontmell Hill Ho	Dorset	ST8816	50°56·8′	2°9·9′W	X	183
Fontmell Magna	Dorset	ST8616	50°56·8′	2°11·6′W	T	183
Fontmell Parva	Dorset	ST8214	50°55·7′	2°15·0′W	T	194
Fontmell Wood	Dorset	ST8817	50°57·4′	2°9·9′W	F	183
Fontmell Wood	Dorset	ST8917	50°57·4′	2°9·0′W	F	184
Fontmills	E Susx	TQ5814	50°54·5′	0°15·2′E	X	199
Fontridge Manor	E Susx	TQ7024	50°59·6′	0°25·7′E	X	199
Font Stone	Midlo	NT1759	55°49·3′	3°19·0′W	A	65,66,72
Font Stone	Scot Bord	NT1930	55°33·7′	3°16·6′W	X	72
Fontwell	W Susx	SU9407	50°51·5′	0°39·5′W	T	197
Font-y-gary	V of Glam	ST0566	51°23·3′	3°21·5′W	T	170
Fooden	Lancs	SD7949	53°56·4′	2°18·8′W	X	103
Fooden High Wood	Lancs	SD8048	53°55·9′	2°17·9′W	F	103
Fooden Moor	Lancs	SD8050	53°57·0′	2°17·9′W	X	103
Foodie	Fife	NO3817	56°20·7′	2°59·7′W	X	59
Foodieash	Fife	NO3716	56°20·2′	3°0·7′W	T	59
Foodie Cottages	Fife	NO3717	56°20·7′	3°0·7′W	X	59
Foodie Hill	Fife	NO3817	56°20·7′	2°59·7′W	H	59
Foolow	Derby	SK1976	53°17·1′	1°42·5′W	T	119
Foord Ho	Suff	TL7686	52°26·8′	0°35·8′E	X	143
Foord's Fm	E Susx	TQ5917	50°56·1′	0°16·2′E	FM	199
Footabrough	Shetld	HU1949	60°13·8′	1°38·9′W	X	3
Football Hole	Northum	NU2425	55°31·3′	1°36·8′W	W	75
Footbridge	Glos	SP0328	51°57·3′	1°57·0′W	T	150,163
Footdee	C of Aber	NJ9506	57°8·9′	2°4·5′W	X	38
Foothead Garth	E Yorks	TA3228	53°44·1′	0°0·5′E	X	107
Footherley	Staffs	SK1002	52°37·2′	1°50·7′W	T	139
Foot Ho Gate	Lancs	SD8241	53°52·1′	2°16·0′W	X	103
Footie Birness	Aberd	NK0035	57°24·6′	1°59·5′W	X	30
Footland Fm	E Susx	TQ7720	50°57·4′	0°31·6′E	FM	199
Footlands	Devon	SS4821	50°58·3′	4°9·5′W	X	180
Footland Wood	E Susx	TQ7620	50°57·4′	0°30·8′E	F	199
Foot o' Green	Stir	NS7989	56°5·0′	3°56·2′W	X	57
Foot o' Hill	C of Aber	NJ8313	57°12·7′	2°16·4′W	X	38
Footrid	Worcs	SO6870	52°19·9′	2°27·8′W	T	138
Foots Cray	Bexley	TQ4770	51°24·8′	0°7·2′E	T	177
Foot's Hill	Dorset	ST8721	50°59·5′	2°10·7′W	X	183
Foot, The	Orkney	HY5315	59°1·4′	2°48·6′W	X	6
Footway Fm	Kent	TR0522	50°57·9′	0°55·6′E	FM	189
Fopperbeck Burn	S Lanak	NT0114	55°24·8′	3°33·4′W	W	78
Fopston Fm	Pemb	SM7909	51°44·4′	5°11·7′W	FM	157
Fora Dale	Shetld	HU4964	60°21·7′	1°6·2′W	X	2,3
Forage Yard	W Susx	SU8709	50°52·7′	0°45·4′W	X	197
Fora Ness	Shetld	HU3517	59°56·5′	1°21·9′W	X	4
Fora Ness	Shetld	HU3546	60°12·1′	1°21·6′W	X	4
Foraness	Shetld	HU3547	60°12·6′	1°21·6′W	X	3
Fora Ness	Shetld	HU4571	60°25·5′	1°10·5′W	X	2,3
Fora Ness	Shetld	HU4647	60°12·6′	1°9·7′W	X	3
Forbes Place	Inverc	NS1969	55°53·1′	4°53·2′W	X	63

Forbestown	Aberd	NJ3612	57°11·9′	3°3·1′W	T	37
Forbes Villa	Aberd	NJ5617	57°14·8′	2°43·3′W	X	37
Forbridge Hill	Aberd	NJ3810	57°10·9′	3°1·1′W	H	37
Forbury Ho	W Berks	SU3865	51°23·2′	1°26·8′W	X	174
Forcan Ridge	Highld	NG9413	57°10·0′	5°24·0′W	X	33
Force Beck	Cumbr	NY7922	54°35·8′	2°19·1′W	W	91
Force Burn	Cumbr	NY7730	54°40·1′	2°21·0′W	W	91
Force Crag	Cumbr	NY1921	54°34·9′	3°14·8′W	X	89,90
Force Foot	Durham	NY8233	54°41·7′	2°16·3′W	X	91,92
Force Forge	Cumbr	SD3390	54°18·3′	3°1·4′W	T	96,97
Force Garth	Durham	NY8728	54°39·1′	2°11·7′W	X	91,92
Force Gill	N Yks	SD7581	54°13·7′	2°22·6′W	W	98
Force Green	Kent	TQ4455	51°16·8′	0°4·3′E	T	187
Force Ing	N Yks	SD9292	54°19·7′	2°7·0′W	X	98
Forceleap Fm	Northnts	SP5336	52°1·4′	1°13·3′W	FM	152
Force Mills	Cumbr	SD3491	54°18·9′	3°0·5′W	T	96,97
Forcett	N Yks	NZ1712	54°30·4′	1°43·8′W	T	92
Forcett Barns	N Yks	NZ1810	54°29·3′	1°42·9′W	X	92
Forcett Park	N Yks	NZ1712	54°30·4′	1°43·8′W	X	92
Forcett Valley	N Yks	NZ1612	54°30·4′	1°44·8′W	X	92
Forches	Devon	SX9171	50°32·0′	3°31·9′W	X	202
Forches Corner	Somer	ST1817	50°57·0′	3°9·7′W	X	181,193
Forches Cross	Devon	SS7309	50°52·2′	3°47·9′W	X	191
Forches Cross	Devon	SX8473	50°33·0′	3°37·9′W	X	191
Ford	Aberd	NJ5425	57°19·1′	2°45·4′W	X	37
Ford	Arg & Bt	NM8603	56°10·6′	5°26·4′W	T	55
Ford	Bucks	SP7709	51°46·7′	0°52·6′W	T	165
Ford	C of Plym	SX4656	50°23·3′	4°9·6′W	T	201
Ford	Derby	SK4080	53°19·2′	1°23·6′W	T	111,120
Ford	Devon	SS4024	50°59·8′	4°16·4′W	T	180,190
Ford	Devon	SS4213	50°53·9′	4°14·4′W	X	180,190
Ford	Devon	SS7822	50°59·3′	3°43·9′W	X	180
Ford	Devon	SS9703	50°49·3′	3°27·4′W	X	192
Ford	Devon	SS9809	50°52·5′	3°26·6′W	X	192
Ford	Devon	ST2403	50°49·5′	3°4·4′W	T	192,193
Ford	Devon	SX6150	50°20·2′	3°56·8′W	T	202
Ford	Devon	SX7840	50°15·1′	3°42·3′W	T	202
Ford	Devon	SX8390	50°42·1′	3°39·0′W	X	191
Ford	Glos	SP0829	51°57·8′	1°52·6′W	T	150,163
Ford	Heref	SO5155	52°11·7′	2°42·6′W	T	149
Ford	Kent	TR2065	51°20·7′	1°9·9′E	T	179
Ford	Northum	NT9437	55°37·8′	2°5·3′W	T	74,75
Ford	Pemb	SM9108	51°44·1′	5°1·2′W	X	157,158
Ford	Pemb	SM9526	51°53·9′	4°58·4′W	T	157,158
Ford	Sefton	SJ3398	53°28·7′	3°0·2′W	T	108
Ford	Shrops	SJ4113	52°42·9′	2°52·0′W	T	126
Ford	Somer	SS9242	51°10·3′	3°32·3′W	X	181
Ford	Somer	ST0928	51°2·9′	3°17·5′W	T	181
Ford	Somer	ST5953	51°16·7′	2°34·9′W	T	182,183
Ford	Staffs	SK0653	53°4·7′	1°54·2′W	T	119
Ford	Wilts	ST8474	51°28·1′	2°13·4′W	T	173
Ford	Wilts	SU1632	51°5·5′	1°45·9′W	T	184
Ford	W Susx	SU9903	50°49·3′	0°35·3′W	T	197
Ford	W Susx	TQ1717	50°56·7′	0°19·7′W	X	198
Forda	Corn	SS2711	50°52·6′	4°27·2′W	X	190
Forda	Corn	SX2990	50°41·3′	4°24·9′W	X	190
Forda	Devon	SS3800	50°46·9′	4°17·5′W	X	190
Forda	Devon	SS4539	51°8·0′	4°12·5′W	T	180
Forda	Devon	SX5390	50°41·7′	4°4·5′W	T	191
Ford Abbey	Heref	SO5658	52°13·3′	2°38·3′W	X	149
Forda Fm	Devon	SS4405	50°49·6′	4°12·5′W	FM	190
Fordafourie	Aberd	NJ9961	57°38·6′	2°0·5′W	X	30
Ford & Aird	D & G	NX8292	55°12·7′	3°50·8′W	X	78
Forda Mill	Devon	SX3299	50°46·2′	4°22·6′W	X	190
Ford Barton	Devon	SS8712	50°54·0′	3°36·0′W	X	181
Ford Barton	Devon	SS9118	50°57·3′	3°32·7′W	X	181
Ford Br	Devon	ST1803	50°49·5′	3°9·5′W	X	192,193
Ford Bridge	Devon	SS6125	51°0·7′	3°58·5′W	X	180
Fordbridge	Sol	SP1787	52°29·1′	1°44·6′W	T	139
Ford Brook	Devon	SX7996	50°45·3′	3°42·5′W	W	191
Fordbrook	E Susx	TQ5126	51°1·0′	0°9·6′E	X	188,199
Fordcombe	Kent	TQ5240	51°8·6′	0°10·8′E	T	188
Ford Common	Northum	NT9638	55°38·4′	2°3·4′W	X	74,75
Ford Common	Somer	ST3053	51°16·5′	2°59·8′W	X	182
Ford Common Cott	Northum	NT9638	55°38·4′	2°3·4′W	X	74,75
Ford Common (Nature Reserve)	Northum	NT9637	55°37·8′	2°3·4′W	X	74,75
Ford Cross	Devon	SS9202	50°48·7′	3°31·6′W	X	192
Ford Down	Devon	SS8416	50°56·1′	3°38·7′W	X	181
Ford Down Fm	Devon	SS7025	51°0·8′	3°50·8′W	FM	180
Forde Abbey	Dorset	ST3505	50°50·7′	2°55·0′W	A	193
Forde Abbey Fm	Dorset	ST3504	50°50·1′	2°55·0′W	FM	193
Forde Cross	Devon	SS8705	50°50·2′	3°35·9′W	X	192
Forde Grange	Dorset	ST3604	50°50·2′	2°54·2′W	A	193
Forde Hall	Warw	SP1169	52°19·4′	1°49·9′W	X	139
Fordel	Fife	NO4423	56°24·0′	2°54·0′W	X	54,59
Fordel	Pth & Kin	NO1312	56°17·8′	3°23·9′W	T	58
Fordel Dean	Midlo	NT3866	55°53·2′	2°59·0′W	X	66
Fordelhill	Fife	NO4324	56°24·5′	2°55·0′W	X	54,59
Fordell	Fife	NT1588	56°4·9′	3°21·5′W	T	65
Fordell Castle	Fife	NT1485	56°3·3′	3°22·4′W	A	65
Fordel Mains	Midlo	NT3766	55°53·2′	3°0·0′W	X	66
Fordel Parks	Midlo	NT3867	55°53·8′	2°59·0′W	X	66
Forden	Powys	SJ2200	52°35·8′	3°8·7′W	T	126
Ford End	Essex	TL4531	51°57·7′	0°7·0′E	T	167
Ford End	Essex	TL6716	51°49·3′	0°25·8′E	T	167
Ford End Fm	Bucks	SP9416	51°50·3′	0°37·7′W	FM	165
Forder	Corn	SX4158	50°24·3′	4°13·9′W	T	201
Forder	Corn	SX4250	50°20·0′	4°12·8′W	X	201
Forder	Devon	SX6789	50°41·4′	3°52·6′W	X	191
Forder	Devon	SX6966	50°29·0′	3°50·4′W	X	202
Forder	Devon	SX7161	50°26·3′	3°48·6′W	X	202
Forder	Devon	SX7288	50°40·9′	3°48·3′W	X	191
Forder	Devon	SX8149	50°20·0′	3°39·9′W	X	202
Forder Fm	Devon	SX7393	50°43·6′	3°47·6′W	FM	191
Forder Green	Devon	SX7867	50°29·6′	3°42·8′W	T	202
Fordfield Fm	Beds	TL0137	52°1·6′	0°31·3′W	FM	153
Ford Fm	Bucks	SP7709	51°46·7′	0°52·6′W	FM	165
Ford Fm	Ches	SJ4864	53°10·5′	2°46·3′W	FM	117
Ford Fm	Corn	SX0862	50°25·8′	4°41·8′W	FM	200
Ford Fm	Devon	SS5942	51°9·8′	4°0·6′W	FM	180
Ford Fm	Devon	SS7500	50°47·4′	3°46·0′W	FM	191
Ford Fm	Devon	SS8023	50°59·9′	3°42·2′W	FM	181
Ford Fm	Devon	SS8922	50°59·4′	3°34·5′W	FM	181
Ford Fm	Devon	SS9311	50°53·6′	3°30·9′W	FM	192
Ford Fm	Devon	ST0511	50°53·7′	3°20·7′W	FM	192
Ford Fm	Devon	ST2100	50°47·9′	3°6·9′W	FM	192,193
Ford Fm	Devon	SX4077	50°34·5′	4°15·2′W	FM	201
Ford Fm	Devon	SX4684	50°38·4′	4°10·3′W	FM	201
Ford Fm	Devon	SX5855	50°22·9′	3°59·5′W	FM	202
Ford Fm	Devon	SX7997	50°45·8′	3°42·6′W	FM	191
Ford Fm	Devon	SX8693	50°43·8′	3°36·5′W	FM	191
Ford Fm	Devon	SX8897	50°45·9′	3°34·9′W	FM	192
Ford Fm	Devon	SY0186	50°40·1′	3°23·7′W	FM	192
Ford Fm	Devon	SY0394	50°44·5′	3°22·1′W	FM	192
Ford Fm	Essex	TL6322	51°52·6′	0°22·5′E	FM	167
Ford Fm	Essex	TL8218	51°50·1′	0°38·9′E	FM	168
Ford Fm	Essex	TM1130	51°55·9′	1°4·6′E	FM	168,169
Ford Fm	Glos	SO6925	51°55·6′	2°26·7′W	FM	162
Ford Fm	Hants	SU7149	51°14·4′	0°58·6′W	FM	186
Ford Fm	Heref	SO5465	52°17·1′	2°40·1′W	FM	137,138,149
Ford Fm	I of W	SZ5179	50°36·7′	1°16·4′W	FM	196
Ford Fm	Somer	SS9140	51°9·2′	3°33·1′W	FM	181
Ford Fm	Somer	SS9734	51°6·0′	3°27·9′W	FM	181
Ford Fm	Somer	ST1624	51°0·8′	3°11·5′W	FM	181,193
Ford Fm	Somer	ST3638	51°8·5′	2°54·5′W	FM	182
Ford Fm	Staffs	SJ9551	53°3·6′	2°4·1′W	FM	118
Ford Fm	Warw	SP3466	52°17·7′	1°29·7′W	FM	151
Ford Fm	Warw	SP4062	52°15·5′	1°24·4′W	FM	151
Ford Fm	Wilts	ST8363	51°22·2′	2°14·3′W	FM	173
Ford Fm	Wilts	SU2675	51°28·6′	1°37·1′W	FM	174
Ford Fm	Worcs	SO9064	52°16·7′	2°8·4′W	FM	150
Ford Forge	Northum	NT9338	55°38·4′	2°6·2′W	T	74,75
Fordgate	Somer	ST3232	51°5·2′	2°57·9′W	T	182
Fordgate Fm	Somer	ST3232	51°5·2′	2°57·9′W	FM	182
Ford Grange	Staffs	SK0553	53°4·7′	1°55·1′W	X	119
Ford Green	C of Stoke	SJ8850	53°3·1′	2°10·3′W	T	118
Ford Green	Lancs	SD4746	53°54·7′	2°48·0′W	T	102
Ford Hall	Derby	SK0782	53°20·3′	1°53·3′W	X	110
Ford Hall	Suff	TL8748	52°6·1′	0°44·2′E	A	155
Fordhall Fm	Shrops	SJ6432	52°53·3′	2°31·7′W	FM	127
Fordham	Cambs	TL6270	52°18·5′	0°23·0′E	T	154
Fordham	Essex	TL9228	51°55·3′	0°47·9′E	T	168
Fordham	Norf	TL6199	52°34·1′	0°22·9′E	T	143
Fordham Abbey	Cambs	TL6269	52°17·9′	0°22·9′E	A	154
Fordham Fen	Norf	TL6098	52°33·6′	0°22·0′E	X	143
Fordham Fm	E Yorks	SE8257	54°0·4′	0°44·5′W	FM	106
Fordham Heath	Essex	TL9326	51°54·2′	0°48·7′E	T	168
Fordham Ho	Cambs	TL6269	52°17·9′	0°22·9′E	X	154
Fordham Moor	Cambs	TL6371	52°19·0′	0°23·9′E	X	154
Fordham Place	Essex	TL9329	51°55·8′	0°48·8′E	X	168
Fordhayes Fm	Devon	SY2698	50°46·8′	3°2·6′W	FM	192,193
Fordhead	Stir	NS6795	56°8·0′	4°8·0′W	X	57
Ford Heath	Shrops	SJ4011	52°41·8′	2°52·9′W	T	126
Ford Hill	Devon	SS5942	51°9·8′	4°0·6′W	H	180
Ford Hill	Northum	NT9537	55°37·8′	2°4·3′W	T	74,75
Ford Hill	S Ayr	NX1584	55°7·2′	4°53·6′W	H	76
Ford Hill Fm	Glos	SP1130	51°58·3′	1°50·0′W	FM	150
Ford Ho	Cumbr	SD1089	54°17·6′	3°22·5′W	X	96
Ford Ho	Devon	ST2705	50°50·6′	3°1·8′W	X	193
Ford Ho	Devon	SX7291	50°42·5′	3°48·4′W	X	191
Ford Ho	D & G	NX2254	54°51·2′	4°45·9′W	X	82
Fordhouse	Angus	NO6660	56°44·1′	2°32·9′W	X	45
Fordhouse	D & G	NX7765	54°58·1′	3°54·9′W	X	84
Ford House Fm	Glos	SO7327	51°56·7′	2°23·2′W	FM	162
Fordhouses	Wolv	SJ9103	52°37·7′	2°7·6′W	T	127,139
Fordie	Aberd	NJ6401	57°6·2′	2°35·2′W	X	37
Fordie	Pth & Kin	NN7922	56°22·7′	3°57·1′W	T	51,52
Fordingbridge	Hants	SU1414	50°55·7′	1°47·7′W	T	195
Fordington	Lincs	TF4171	53°13·3′	0°7·1′E	T	122
Fordington Down	Dorset	SY6690	50°42·8′	2°28·5′W	X	194
Fordington Lodge	N Yks	SE5363	54°3·9′	1°11·0′W	X	100
Fordington Village	Lincs	TF4171	53°13·3′	0°7·1′E	A	122
Fordington Wood	Lincs	TF4372	53°13·8′	0°8·9′E	F	122
Ford Knowe	D & G	NX8163	54°57·1′	3°51·1′W	X	84
Fordlands	Devon	SS9915	50°55·8′	3°25·9′W	X	181
Fordlands	E Susx	TQ7412	50°53·1′	0°28·8′E	X	199
Fordley	N Tyne	NZ2673	55°3·3′	1°35·2′W	T	88
Fordley Hall	Suff	TM4066	52°14·6′	1°31·3′E	X	156
Fordmill Fm	Devon	SS3217	50°55·9′	4°23·1′W	FM	190
Fordmoor	Devon	ST0503	50°49·4′	3°20·5′W	X	192
Fordmouth	Aberd	NJ6434	57°24·0′	2°35·5′W	X	29
Fordmouth	Aberd	NK0145	57°30·0′	1°58·5′W	X	30
Fordmouth	Angus	NO5153	56°40·2′	2°47·5′W	X	54
Fordmouth	E Ayr	NS5913	55°23·7′	4°13·1′W	X	71
Fordmouth	S Lanak	NS9850	55°44·2′	3°37·0′W	X	65,72
Ford of Pitcur	Pth & Kin	NO2436	56°30·9′	3°13·7′W	X	53
Fordon	E Yorks	TA0475	54°9·9′	0°24·0′W	T	101
Fordoun	Aberd	NO7475	56°52·2′	2°25·1′W	T	45
Fordoun Burn	Aberd	NJ7437	57°25·6′	2°25·5′W	W	29
Fordoun Ho	Aberd	NO7376	56°52·7′	2°26·1′W	X	45
For Down	Hants	SU5255	51°17·7′	1°14·9′W	X	174,185
Ford Park	Devon	SX6786	50°39·7′	3°52·5′W	X	191
Ford Place	Kent	TQ5242	51°9·6′	0°10·8′E	X	188
Ford Place	Thurr	TQ5980	51°30·0′	0°17·8′E	A	177
Ford Point	Pemb	SN0303	51°41·7′	4°50·6′W	X	157,158
Fords Crofts Fm	Somer	ST4210	50°53·4′	2°49·1′W	FM	193
Ford's Fm	Norf	TG4622	52°44·6′	1°39·1′E	FM	134
Ford's Green	E Susx	TQ4427	51°1·7′	0°3·6′E	T	187,198
Ford's Green	Suff	TM0666	52°15·4′	1°1·5′E	T	155
Fordsland Ledge	Devon	SX5788	50°40·7′	4°1·1′W	X	191
Fords of Avon Refuge	Moray	NJ0403	57°6·7′	3°34·7′W	X	36
Fords, The	Shrops	SJ3426	52°49·9′	2°58·4′W	X	126
Fordstreet	Essex	TL9126	51°54·2′	0°47·0′E	T	168
Ford Street	Somer	ST1518	50°57·5′	3°12·2′W	T	181,193
Fords Water	Kent	TR0741	51°8·1′	0°57·9′E	X	179,189
Fordswell	Scot Bord	NT5343	55°40·9′	2°44·4′W	X	73
Fordsyke	Cumbr	NY4563	54°57·8′	2°51·1′W	X	86
Ford, The	Essex	TM0619	51°50·1′	0°59·8′E	X	168
Ford, The	Pth & Kin	NO2431	56°28·2′	3°13·6′W	X	53
Ford, The	Shrops	SO6584	52°27·4′	2°30·5′W	X	138
Fordton Mill	Devon	SX8499	50°47·0′	3°38·4′W	T	191
Fordtown	Aberd	NJ7714	57°13·2′	2°22·4′W	X	38
Fordwater	Devon	ST3102	50°49·0′	2°58·4′W	T	193
Fordwells	Oxon	SP3013	51°49·1′	1°33·5′W	T	164
Ford Westfield	Northum	NT9336	55°37·3′	2°6·2′W	X	74,75
Ford Wetley	Staffs	SK0553	53°4·7′	1°55·1′W	X	119
Fordwich	Kent	TR1859	51°17·5′	1°8·0′E	T	179
Ford Woodhouse	Northum	NT9736	55°37·3′	2°2·4′W	X	75
Fordyce	Aberd	NJ5563	57°39·5′	2°44·8′W	T	29
Fordyce Hill	Aberd	NJ5662	57°39·0′	2°43·8′W	H	29
Forebank	Aberd	NO7064	56°46·3′	2°29·0′W	X	45
Foreberry	Orkney	HY1904	58°55·2′	3°23·9′W	X	7
Forebrae	Pth & Kin	NN9824	56°24·1′	3°38·7′W	X	52,53,58
Fore Brae	S Lanak	NT0220	55°28·1′	3°32·6′W	H	72
Forebridge	Staffs	SJ9222	52°48·0′	2°6·7′W	T	127
Fore Bridge	Wilts	SU2966	51°23·8′	1°34·6′W	X	174
Fore Burn	D & G	NX4976	55°3·6′	4°21·4′W	W	77
Fore Burn	D & G	NY4095	55°15·0′	2°56·2′W	W	79
Fore Burn	Moray	NJ2825	57°18·9′	3°11·3′W	W	37
Fore Burn	Northum	NT9614	55°25·4′	2°3·4′W	W	81
Fore Burn	S Ayr	NX4299	55°15·8′	4°28·8′W	W	77
Fore Burn	Scot Bord	NT4243	55°40·9′	2°54·9′W	W	73
Fore Bush	D & G	NX5486	55°9·1′	4°17·0′W	X	77
Foredale	N Yks	SD8069	54°7·2′	2°17·9′W	T	98
Foredoles Fm	Donc	SK5194	53°26·7′	1°13·5′W	FM	111
Fore Down	Corn	SX2869	50°30·0′	4°25·1′W	X	201
Fore Down	E Susx	TQ5301	50°47·5′	0°10·6′E	X	199
Fore Down	I of W	SZ4483	50°38·9′	1°22·3′W	X	196
Fore Down	Oxon	SU4585	51°34·0′	1°20·7′W	X	174
Fore Down	Wilts	ST9747	51°13·6′	2°2·2′W	X	184
Fore Downs	Corn	SX1369	50°29·7′	4°37·8′W	H	200
Forefield Rake	N Yks	NY9602	54°25·1′	2°3·3′W	X	91,92
Fore Gill	N Yks	NZ0001	54°24·5′	1°59·6′W	W	92
Foregin	Highld	NH8725	57°18·4′	3°52·1′W	T	35,36
Foregirth	D & G	NX9583	55°8·1′	3°38·4′W	X	78
Fore Hareshaw	S Lanak	NS6140	55°38·3′	4°12·1′W	X	71
Forehill	Aberd	NK0945	57°30·0′	1°50·5′W	X	30
Fore Hill	Dorset	SY6097	50°46·5′	2°33·7′W	X	194
Fore Hill	E Susx	TQ4004	50°49·3′	0°0·4′W	X	198
Fore Hill	E Susx	TQ4604	50°49·3′	0°4·8′E	X	198
Forehill	Pemb	SN0524	51°53·1′	4°49·6′W	X	145,158
Forehill	Pth & Kin	NO0940	56°32·8′	3°28·4′W	X	52,53
Forehill	S Ayr	NS3420	55°27·0′	4°37·1′W	T	70
Fore Hill	Wilts	ST9852	51°16·3′	2°1·3′W	X	184
Fore Hill of Glengap	D & G	NX6459	54°54·7′	4°6·9′W	H	83
Fore Hill (Tumuli)	E Susx	TQ4004	50°49·3′	0°0·4′W	A	198
Fore Holm	Shetld	HU3544	60°11·0′	1°21·6′W	X	4
Foreland	I of W	SZ6687	50°41·0′	1°3·6′W	X	196
Foreland Fields	I of W	SZ6587	50°41·0′	1°4·4′W	T	196
Foreland Ho	Arg & Bt	NR2664	55°47·8′	6°21·9′W	X	60
Foreland Point	Devon	SS7551	51°14·9′	3°47·1′W	X	180
Foreland Point	S Ayr	NX0299	55°15·0′	5°6·5′W	X	76
Forelands	Hants	SU6862	51°21·4′	1°1·0′W	X	175,186
Forelands	N Yks	SE0085	54°15·9′	1°59·6′W	X	98
Forelands Rigg	N Yks	SE0185	54°15·9′	1°58·7′W	F	98
Forelands, The	Kent	TR0119	50°56·3′	0°52·0′E	X	189
Foreland, The	Devon	SS7550	51°14·4′	3°47·1′W	H	180
Foreland, The or Handfast Point	Dorset	SZ0582	50°38·5′	1°55·4′W	X	195
Foremannoch	D & G	NX8974	55°3·1′	3°43·8′W	X	84
Foreman's Bridge	Lincs	TF4019	52°45·3′	0°4·9′E	X	131
Foremark	Derby	SK3326	52°50·1′	1°30·2′W	T	128
Foremarke Park Fm	Derby	SK3323	52°48·4′	1°30·2′W	FM	128
Foremark Reservoir	Derby	SK3323	52°48·4′	1°30·2′W	W	128
Fore Marsh	Stock on T	NZ4924	54°36·8′	1°14·1′W	X	93
Fore Moor	D & G	NX5160	54°55·0′	4°19·1′W	X	83
Fore Rogerton	E Ayr	NS5621	55°28·0′	4°16·2′W	X	71
Foreshield	Cumbr	NY7546	54°48·7′	2°22·9′W	X	86,87
Foreshieldgrains	Cumbr	NY7547	54°49·3′	2°22·9′W	X	86,87
Foreside	Aberd	NJ6325	57°19·1′	2°36·4′W	X	37
Foreside	Brad	SE0632	53°47·3′	1°54·1′W	X	104
Foreside	D & G	NX9071	55°1·5′	3°42·8′W	X	84
Foreside	E Renf	NS4657	55°47·2′	4°26·9′W	X	64
Foreside	N Ayr	NS3750	55°43·2′	4°35·3′W	X	63
Foreside Hill	D & G	NX9172	55°2·1′	3°41·9′W	X	84
Foreside of Cairn	Angus	NO4456	56°41·8′	2°54·4′W	X	54
Fore Slack	Cumbr	SD1685	54°15·5′	3°17·0′W	X	96
Forest	N Lanak	NS8566	55°52·7′	3°49·9′W	X	65
Forest	N Yks	NZ2700	54°23·9′	1°34·6′W	X	93
Forest	Pemb	SN1843	52°3·6′	4°38·9′W	X	145
Forest Banks	Staffs	SK1228	52°51·2′	1°48·9′W	F	128
Forest Barn	W Susx	TQ1005	50°50·3′	0°25·9′W	X	198
Forest Becks	Lancs	SD7851	53°57·5′	2°19·7′W	T	103
Forest Buildings	Notts	SK6579	53°18·5′	1°1·1′W	X	120
Forest Burn	Northum	NZ0496	55°15·7′	1°55·8′W	W	81
Forest Burn	Northum	NZ0898	55°16·8′	1°52·0′W	W	81
Forestburn Gate	Northum	NZ0696	55°15·7′	1°53·9′W	X	81
Forest Chapel	Merth Tyd	SO0800	51°41·7′	3°19·5′W	A	170
Forest Coal Pit	Monm	SO2820	51°52·7′	3°2·4′W	T	161
Forest Common	Swan	SS5292	51°36·7′	4°7·9′W	X	159
Forest Cottage	Highld	NH7342	57°27·3′	4°6·5′W	X	27
Forest Cove	Devon	SX8446	50°18·4′	3°37·4′W	W	202
Forest Covert	Staffs	SO8390	52°30·7′	2°14·6′W	F	138
Forestdale	Croy	TQ3662	51°20·7′	0°2·4′W	T	177,187
Forest Edge	Durham	NY8722	54°35·8′	2°11·7′W	X	91,92
Forester's Croft	Aberd	NO8788	56°59·2′	2°12·4′W	X	45
Forester's Croft	Pth & Kin	NN9115	56°19·1′	3°45·3′W	X	58
Foresterseat	Aberd	NJ8616	57°14·3′	2°13·5′W	X	38
Foresterseat	Angus	NO4950	56°38·6′	2°49·4′W	X	54
Foresterseat	Moray	NJ1557	57°36·0′	3°24·9′W	X	28
Foresterseat	Moray	NJ2562	57°38·8′	3°14·9′W	X	28
Forester's Lodge	Durham	NZ0641	54°46·1′	1°54·0′W	X	87
Forester's Lodge	N Yks	NZ7105	54°26·4′	0°53·9′W	X	94
Forester's Lodge Fm	Kent	TR0758	51°17·2′	0°58·5′E	FM	179
Foresters' Oaks	Newp	ST4293	51°38·2′	2°49·9′W	X	171,172
Forest Farm	Card	ST1380	51°31·0′	3°14·8′W	FM	171
Forest Fm	Aberd	NJ7616	57°14·3′	2°23·4′W	FM	38
Forest Fm	Brackn	SU9372	51°26·6′	0°39·3′W	FM	175
Forest Fm	Ches	SJ5666	53°11·6′	2°39·1′W	FM	117

Forest Fm	Cumbr	NY8014	54°31·5′	2°18·1′W	FM	91,92
Forest Fm	Dorset	ST8229	51°3·8′	2°15·0′W	FM	183
Forest Fm	Essex	TL5317	51°50·1′	0°13·6′E	FM	167
Forest Fm	E Susx	TQ4129	51°2·8′	0°1·1′E	FM	187,198
Forest Fm	E Susx	TQ5731	51°3·6′	0°14·8′E	FM	188
Forest Fm	E Yorks	SE8136	53°49·1′	0°45·8′W	FM	106
Forest Fm	Hants	SU5715	50°56·1′	1°10·9′W	FM	196
Forest Fm	Hants	SU6112	50°54·5′	1°7·6′W	FM	196
Forest Fm	I of W	SZ4690	50°42·7′	1°20·5′W	FM	196
Forest Fm	Kent	TQ5943	51°10·1′	0°16·8′E	FM	188
Forest Fm	Mil Key	SP8049	52°8·2′	0°49·5′W	FM	152
Forest Fm	Norf	TG0926	52°47·7′	1°6·4′E	FM	133
Forest Fm	Northnts	SP7341	52°4·0′	0°55·7′W	FM	152
Forest Fm	Notts	SK5255	53°5·6′	1°13·0′W	FM	120
Forest Fm	Notts	SK5751	53°3·4′	1°8·6′W	FM	120
Forest Fm	Notts	SK5848	53°1·8′	1°7·7′W	FM	129
Forest Fm	Notts	SK6257	53°6·6′	1°4·0′W	FM	120
Forest Fm	Notts	SK6284	53°21·2′	1°3·7′W	FM	111,120
Forest Fm	Notts	SK6782	53°20·1′	0°59·2′W	FM	111,120
Forest Fm	N Yks	SE5264	54°4·4′	1°11·9′W	FM	100
Forest Fm	Oxon	SP2815	51°50·2′	1°35·2′W	FM	163
Forest Fm	Oxon	SP5410	51°47·4′	1°12·6′W	FM	164
Forest Fm	Shrops	SJ3108	52°40·2′	3°0·8′W	FM	126
Forest Fm	Staffs	SK1148	53°2·0′	1°49·8′W	FM	119
Forest Fm	Suff	TM4053	52°7·6′	1°30·8′E	FM	156
Forest Fm	Wilts	ST9165	51°23·3′	2°7·4′W	FM	173
Forest Fm	Wilts	ST9371	51°26·5′	2°5·7′W	FM	173
Forest Fm	Wilts	SU0156	51°18·4′	1°58·8′W	FM	173
Forest Fm	Worcs	SO9764	52°16·7′	2°2·2′W	FM	150
Forest Fms	Somer	ST7641	51°10·3′	2°20·2′W	FM	183
Forest Fold Fm	Wigan	SD5308	53°34·2′	2°42·2′W	FM	108
Forestgate	Ches	SJ5472	53°14·8′	2°41·0′W	X	117
Forest Gate	Hants	SU6412	50°54·5′	1°5·0′W	T	196
Forest Gate	Newham	TQ4085	51°33·0′	0°1·5′E	T	177
Forest Gate	Win & Maid	SU9472	51°26·6′	0°38·5′W	X	175
Forest Gate Fm	Wilts	ST9471	51°26·5′	2°4·8′W	FM	173
Forest Glade	Devon	ST1007	50°51·6′	3°16·3′W	X	192,193
Forest Grange School	W Susx	TQ2131	51°4·2′	0°16·0′W	X	187
Forest Green	Glos	SO8400	51°42·1′	2°13·5′W	T	162
Forest Green	Surrey	TQ1241	51°9·7′	0°23·5′W	T	187
Forest Hall	Cumbr	NY2847	54°49·0′	3°6·8′W	X	85
Forest Hall	Cumbr	NY5401	54°24·4′	2°42·1′W	X	90
Forest Hall	Essex	TL5123	51°53·3′	0°12·1′E	X	167
Forest Hall	Essex	TL5317	51°50·1′	0°13·6′E	X	167
Forest Hall	N Tyne	NZ2769	55°1·1′	1°34·2′W	T	88
Forest Hall	Sol	SP2382	52°26·4′	1°39·3′W	X	139
Forest Hall Fm	N Yks	SE5166	54°5·5′	1°12·8′W	FM	100
Forest Hanger	W Susx	SU9015	50°55·9′	0°42·8′W	F	197
Forest Head	Cumbr	NY5857	54°54·6′	2°38·9′W	T	86
Forest Hill	Ches	SJ6171	53°14·3′	2°34·7′W	X	118
Foresthill	Cumbr	NY5134	54°42·2′	2°45·2′W	X	90
Forest Hill	D & G	NX7753	54°51·7′	3°54·6′W	H	84
Foresthill	D & G	NX7853	54°51·7′	3°53·6′W	X	84
Forest Hill	Dorset	SY9696	50°46·0′	2°3·0′W	X	195
Foresthill	Falk	NS7684	56°2·2′	3°59·0′W	X	57,64
Forest Hill	Lew	TQ3573	51°26·6′	0°3·1′W	T	177
Forest Hill	Notts	SK5981	53°19·6′	1°6·4′W	X	111,120
Forest Hill	Oxon	SP5807	51°45·8′	1°9·2′W	T	164
Foresthill	Scot Bord	NT2348	55°43·4′	3°13·1′W	X	73
Forest Hill	Wilts	SU2068	51°24·9′	1°42·4′W	T	174
Forest Hill	Worcs	SO9664	52°16·7′	2°3·1′W	X	150
Forest Hill Fm	York	SE6162	54°3·3′	1°3·7′W	FM	100
Forest Ho	Ches	SJ5367	53°12·1′	2°41·8′W	X	117
Forest Ho	Hants	SU2912	50°54·6′	1°34·9′W	X	196
Forest Ho	Leic	SK4902	52°37·0′	1°16·2′W	X	140
Forest Ho	Wilts	SU3052	51°16·2′	1°33·8′W	X	185
Forest Ho	W Susx	TQ2128	51°2·5′	0°16·0′W	X	187,198
Forest Holme	Lancs	SD8425	53°43·5′	2°14·1′W	T	103
Forest-in-Teesdale	Durham	NY8629	54°39·6′	2°12·6′W	T	91,92
Forest Lane Fm	Derby	SK1578	53°18·2′	1°46·1′W	FM	119
Forest Lane Head	N Yks	SE3356	54°0·2′	1°29·4′W	T	104
Forest Lodge	Arg & Bt	NN2742	56°32·6′	4°48·4′W	X	50
Forest Lodge	Essex	TL5319	51°51·1′	0°13·7′E	X	167
Forest Lodge	Essex	TL7000	51°40·6′	0°27·9′E	X	167
Forest Lodge	Hants	SU4206	50°51·3′	1°23·8′W	X	196
Forest Lodge	Hants	SU8040	51°9·4′	0°51·0′W	X	186
Forest Lodge	Hants	SZ2198	50°47·1′	1°41·7′W	X	195
Forest Lodge	Highld	NJ0216	57°13·7′	3°36·9′W	X	36
Forest Lodge	Northnts	SP8688	52°29·2′	0°43·6′W	X	141
Forest Lodge	Northnts	SP9791	52°30·7′	0°33·8′W	X	141
Forest Lodge	Powys	SN9524	51°54·5′	3°31·2′W	X	160
Forest Lodge	Pth & Kin	NN9374	56°51·0′	3°44·8′W	X	43
Forest Lodge	Scot Bord	NT6028	55°32·9′	2°37·6′W	X	74
Forest Lodge	Somer	ST2618	50°57·6′	3°2·8′W	X	193
Forest Lodge	Suff	TL8171	52°18·7′	0°39·7′E	X	144,155
Forest Lodge	Win & Maid	SU9472	51°26·6′	0°38·5′W	X	175
Forest Lodge	Worcs	SO7775	52°22·6′	2°19·9′W	X	138
Forest Lodge Fm	Dorset	ST8325	51°1·7′	2°14·2′W	FM	183
Forest Lodge Fm	Northnts	SP8151	52°9·3′	0°48·6′W	FM	152
Forest Mere	W Susx	SU8130	51°4·0′	0°50·2′W	X	186
Forest Mill	Clackm	NS9593	56°7·3′	3°40·9′W	T	58
Forest Moor	N Yks	SE2256	54°0·2′	1°39·4′W	X	104
Forest Moor	N Yks	SE3455	53°59·6′	1°28·5′W	T	104
Forest Muir	Angus	NO4254	56°40·7′	2°56·3′W	F	54
Forest Oak	Shrops	SO7490	52°30·7′	2°22·6′W	A	138
Forest of Ae	D & G	NX9992	55°13·0′	3°34·8′W	F	78
Forest of Alyth	Pth & Kin	NO1855	56°41·0′	3°19·9′W	X	53
Forest of Atholl	Pth & Kin	NN7474	56°50·7′	4°3·5′W	X	42
Forest of Atholl	Pth & Kin	NN8674	56°50·9′	3°51·7′W	X	43
Forest of Bere	Hants	SU6611	50°53·9′	1°3·3′W	X	196
Forest of Bere	Hants	SU6911	50°53·9′	1°0·7′W	F	197
Forest of Bere Fm	Hants	SU4029	51°3·8′	1°25·4′W	FM	185
Forest of Birse	Aberd	NO5291	57°0·7′	2°47·0′W	X	44
Forest of Bowland	Lancs	SD6552	53°58·0′	2°31·6′W	F	102,103
Forest of Clunie	Pth & Kin	NO0750	56°38·2′	3°30·5′W	X	52,53
Forest of Dean	Glos	SO6211	51°48·0′	2°32·7′W	F	162
Forest of Deer	Aberd	NJ9650	57°32·7′	2°3·6′W	F	30
Forest of Glenartney	Pth & Kin	NN6918	56°20·4′	4°6·7′W	X	57
Forest of Glenavon	Moray	NJ1105	57°7·9′	3°27·8′W	X	36
Forest of Glen Tanar	Aberd	NO4794	57°2·3′	2°51·9′W	F	37,44
Forest of Harris or Frith na Hearadh	N Eil	NB0609	57°58·6′	6°57·9′W	F	13,14
Forest of Mamlorn	Stir	NN4135	56°29·1′	4°34·5′W	F	51
Forest of Mar	Aberd	NO0591	57°0·3′	3°33·4′W	X	43
Forest of Mewith	N Yks	SD6767	54°6·1′	2°29·9′W	X	98
Forest of Pendle, The	Lancs	SD8238	53°50·5′	2°16·0′W	X	103
Forest of Rossendale	Lancs	SD8425	53°43·5′	2°14·1′W	X	103
Forest of Trawden, The	Lancs	SD9338	53°50·5′	2°6·0′W	X	103
Forest Park	Win & Maid	SU9474	51°27·7′	0°38·4′W	X	175
Forest Plantn	Notts	SK6184	53°21·2′	1°4·6′W	F	111,120
Forestreet	Devon	SS3911	50°52·8′	4°16·9′W	T	190
Forest Row	E Susx	TQ4234	51°5·5′	0°2·1′E	T	187
Forest Side	Cumbr	NY3408	54°28·0′	3°0·7′W	X	90
Forest Side	Durham	NY8721	54°35·3′	2°11·6′W	X	91,92
Forest Side	I of W	SZ4789	50°42·2′	1°19·7′W	T	196
Forestside	W Susx	SU7512	50°54·4′	0°55·6′W	T	197
Forest Side Fm	Dorset	ST8129	51°3·8′	2°15·9′W	FM	183
Forest Stone	Notts	SK5558	53°7·2′	1°10·3′W	A	120
Forest, The	Clackm	NS9493	56°7·3′	3°41·9′W	F	58
Forest, The	Cumbr	NY5303	54°25·5′	2°43·0′W	X	90
Forest, The	D & G	NX4349	54°48·9′	4°26·2′W	F	83
Forest, The	D & G	NX9486	55°9·7′	3°39·4′W	F	78
Forest, The	D & G	NY2675	55°4·1′	3°9·1′W	F	85
Forest, The	Glos	SO9814	51°49·7′	2°1·3′W	F	163
Forest, The	Kent	TQ7832	51°3·8′	0°32·8′E	X	188
Forest, The	Kent	TQ9342	51°8·9′	0°46·0′E	F	189
Forest, The	Monm	ST3497	51°40·3′	2°56·9′W	FM	171
Forest, The	Norf	TL9182	52°24·4′	0°48·9′E	F	144
Forest, The	Powys	SJ1402	52°36·8′	3°15·8′W	F	136
Forest, The	Powys	SO1389	52°29·8′	3°16·5′W	X	136
Forest, The	Powys	SO1828	51°56·9′	3°11·2′W	X	161
Forest, The	Surrey	TQ0955	51°17·2′	0°25·8′W	F	187
Forest, The	Surrey	TQ1760	51°19·8′	0°18·8′W	F	176,187
Forest Thorn	Staffs	SK1720	52°46·9′	1°44·5′W	X	128
Forest Town	Notts	SK5662	53°9·4′	1°9·3′W	T	120
Forest Walks	Lincs	TF0626	52°49·5′	0°25·0′W	X	130
Forest Way	Essex	TL5010	51°46·3′	0°10·8′E	X	167
Forest Way	E Susx	TQ4135	51°6·0′	0°1·2′E	X	187
Forest Way	E Susx	TQ4836	51°6·5′	0°7·2′E	X	188
Forest Wood	Essex	TL6900	51°40·6′	0°27·1′E	F	167
Forest Wood	Heref	SO2554	52°11·0′	3°5·4′W	F	148
Forest Wood	Northum	NZ2096	55°15·7′	1°40·7′W	F	81
Forest Wood	Powys	SO2367	52°18·0′	3°7·4′W	F	137,148
Fore Top	Dorset	ST8818	50°57·9′	2°9·9′W	H	183
Forewick Holm	Shetld	HU1859	60°19·1′	1°39·9′W	X	3
Forewick Ness	Shetld	HU1859	60°19·1′	1°39·9′W	X	3
Fore Wood	E Susx	TQ7513	50°53·6′	0°29·7′E	F	199
Forewoods Common	Wilts	ST8461	51°21·1′	2°13·4′W	T	173
Forfar	Angus	NO4550	56°38·6′	2°53·4′W	T	54
Forgan Church	Fife	NO4425	56°25·1′	2°54·0′W	A	54,59
Forgandenny	Pth & Kin	NO0818	56°21·0′	3°28·9′W	T	58
Forge	Corn	SW6945	50°15·8′	5°14·1′W	T	203
Forge	Powys	SN7699	52°34·7′	3°49·4′W	T	135
Forge Coppice	Shrops	SJ5623	52°48·2′	2°38·8′W	F	126
Forge Fm	Bucks	SP8524	51°54·7′	0°45·5′W	FM	165
Forge Fm	Carm	SN4025	51°54·3′	4°19·2′W	FM	146
Forge Fm	Ches	SJ8058	53°7·4′	2°17·5′W	FM	118
Forge Fm	E Susx	TQ5335	51°5·9′	0°11·5′E	FM	188
Forge Fm	Kent	TQ6552	51°14·8′	0°22·2′E	FM	188
Forge Fm	Kent	TQ7235	51°5·5′	0°27·8′E	FM	188
Forge Fm	Staffs	SK0801	52°36·6′	1°52·5′W	FM	139
Forge Fm	Staffs	SK0822	52°48·0′	1°52·5′W	FM	128
Forge Hammer	Torf	ST2995	51°39·2′	3°1·2′W	T	171
Forge Ho	Cumbr	SD1499	54°23·0′	3°19·0′W	X	96
Forge House	Carm	SN6516	51°49·8′	3°57·2′W	X	159
Forgemill Ho	Ches	SJ7062	53°9·5′	2°26·5′W	X	118
Forge Side	Torf	SO2408	51°46·2′	3°5·7′W	T	161
Forge, The	Cumbr	SD3793	54°20·0′	2°57·7′W	X	96,97
Forge, The	Heref	SO3459	52°13·8′	2°57·6′W	T	148,149
Forge Valley	N Yks	SE9886	54°15·9′	0°29·3′W	X	94,101
Forge Wood	E Susx	TQ5634	51°5·3′	0°14·0′E	F	188
Forgewood	N Lanak	NS7458	55°48·2′	4°0·2′W	T	64
Forge Wood	W Susx	TQ2938	51°7·8′	0°9·0′W	F	187
Forgie	Aberd	NO7870	56°49·5′	2°21·2′W	X	45
Forgie	Moray	NJ3854	57°34·6′	3°1·7′W	X	28
Forgie Hill	Moray	NJ3855	57°35·1′	3°1·8′W	X	28
Forgieston	Aberd	NJ6150	57°32·6′	2°38·6′W	X	29
Forglen House	Aberd	NJ6951	57°33·2′	2°30·6′W	X	29
Forgue	Aberd	NJ6145	57°29·9′	2°38·6′W	T	29
Forgue	Corn	SW8950	50°19·0′	4°57·5′W	X	200,204
Forhill	Worcs	SP0575	52°22·6′	1°55·2′W	T	139
Forhill Ash	Worcs	SP0575	52°22·6′	1°55·2′W	X	139
Fork Cross	Devon	SX7660	50°25·8′	3°44·4′W	X	202
Forkedpond Inclosure	Hants	SU8132	51°5·1′	0°50·2′W	F	186
Forke Fm	Devon	SS8511	50°53·5′	3°37·7′W	FM	191
Forkerleys Fm	E Yorks	TA2028	53°44·3′	0°10·4′W	FM	107
Forkings	E Ayr	NS6829	55°32·5′	4°5·1′W	X	71
Forking Sike	Northum	NY6087	55°10·8′	2°37·3′W	W	80
Forkins	D & G	NX6081	55°6·5′	4°11·3′W	X	77
Forkins	Moray	NJ3844	57°29·2′	3°1·6′W	X	28
Forkins	Scot Bord	NT5809	55°22·6′	2°39·3′W	X	80
Forkin, The	Highld	ND0925	58°12·5′	3°32·4′W	X	17
Forks, The	Northum	NY6388	55°11·3′	2°34·4′W	X	80
Fork, The	Glos	SP1616	51°50·8′	1°45·7′W	X	163
Forlan	Pemb	SN0724	51°53·1′	4°47·9′W	X	145,158
Forley Craig	Aberd	NO8777	56°53·3′	2°12·4′W	X	45
Formakin	Renf	NS4070	55°54·0′	4°33·1′W	X	64
Formal	Angus	NO2554	56°40·6′	3°13·0′W	X	53
Formal Hill	Pth & Kin	NO0033	56°29·0′	3°37·0′W	H	52,53
Formartine and Buchan Way	Aberd	NJ9022	57°17·6′	2°9·5′W	X	38
Formby	Sefton	SD2907	53°33·5′	3°3·9′W	T	108
Formby Bank	Sefton	SD2802	53°30·8′	3°4·7′W	X	108
Formby Hall	Sefton	SD3109	53°34·6′	3°2·1′W	A	108
Formby Hills	Sefton	SD2708	53°34·1′	3°5·7′W	X	108
Formby Point	Sefton	SD2606	53°33·0′	3°6·6′W	X	108
Formby's Fm	Lancs	SD3107	53°33·5′	3°2·1′W	FM	108
Formonthills	Fife	NO2503	56°13·1′	3°12·1′W	X	59
Formosa Ct	Win & Maid	SU9085	51°33·6′	0°41·7′W	X	175
Forms Ho	N Yks	SE3862	54°3·4′	1°24·8′W	X	99
Fornah Gill	N Yks	SD8469	54°7·2′	2°14·3′W	W	98
Forncett End	Norf	TM1493	52°29·8′	1°9·6′E	T	144
Forncett St Mary	Norf	TM1693	52°29·7′	1°11·3′E	X	144
Forncett St Peter	Norf	TM1692	52°29·2′	1°11·3′E	X	144
Forness Point	Kent	TR3871	51°23·5′	1°25·7′E	X	179
Forneth	Pth & Kin	NO0945	56°35·5′	3°28·5′W	X	52,53
Forneth Ho	Pth & Kin	NO1044	56°35·0′	3°27·5′W	X	53
Fornethy Residential School	Angus	NO2455	56°41·1′	3°14·0′W	X	53
Fornety	Aberd	NJ9726	57°19·7′	2°2·5′W	X	38
Forn Geo	Shetld	HP6616	60°49·5′	0°46·7′W	X	1
Fornham All Saints	Suff	TL8367	52°16·5′	0°41·3′E	T	155
Fornham Park	Suff	TL8468	52°17·0′	0°42·3′E	X	155
Fornham St Genevieve	Suff	TL8467	52°16·4′	0°42·2′E	T	155
Fornham St Martin	Suff	TL8567	52°16·4′	0°43·1′E	T	155
Fornighty	Highld	NH9350	57°31·9′	3°46·8′W	X	27
Fornisaig	Arg & Bt	NR2058	55°44·3′	6°27·2′W	X	60
Fornought	Pth & Kin	NN9424	56°24·0′	3°42·6′W	X	52,53,58
Fornside	Cumbr	NY3220	54°34·5′	3°2·7′W	X	90
Forntree	Aberd	NJ6714	57°13·2′	2°32·3′W	X	38
Forrabury	Corn	SX0990	50°40·9′	4°41·8′W	T	190
Forraness Voe	Shetld	HU4547	60°12·6′	1°10·8′W	W	3
Forres	Moray	NJ0358	57°36·4′	3°36·9′W	T	27
Forrest	D & G	NX9285	55°9·1′	3°41·3′W	X	78
Forrestburn	N Lanak	NS8765	55°52·2′	3°47·9′W	X	65
Forrestburn Resr	N Lanak	NS8664	55°51·6′	3°48·8′W	W	65
Forrestburn Water	N Lanak	NS8464	55°51·6′	3°50·8′W	W	65
Forrester Fold	Cumbr	NY2747	54°49·0′	3°7·7′W	X	85
Forresterhill	Aberd	NJ8229	57°21·3′	2°17·5′W	X	38
Forresterquarter	Falk	NS8178	55°59·1′	3°54·0′W	X	65
Forrestfield	N Lanak	NS8567	55°53·2′	3°49·9′W	T	65
Forrest Lane	D & G	NX5588	55°10·2′	4°16·2′W	W	77
Forrest Lodge	D & G	NX5586	55°9·1′	4°16·1′W	X	77
Forrest Slack	Aberd	NJ9858	57°37·0′	2°1·5′W	X	30
Forret Hill	Fife	NO3920	56°22·4′	2°58·8′W	H	54,59
Forret Mill	Fife	NO3921	56°22·9′	2°58·8′W	X	54,59
Forry's Green	Essex	TL7632	51°57·7′	0°34·1′E	T	167
Forsan	Shetld	HU3826	60°1·3′	1°18·6′W	X	4
Forsan	Shetld	HU4029	60°2·9′	1°16·4′W	X	4
Forsay	Highld	NM6877	56°49·5′	5°47·7′W	X	40
Forsay Burn	Highld	NM6977	56°49·5′	5°46·7′W	W	40
Forsbrook	Staffs	SJ9641	52°58·2′	2°3·2′W	T	118
Forse	Highld	ND2134	58°17·5′	3°20·4′W	X	11
Forse	Orkney	HY5300	58°53·4′	2°48·4′W	X	6,7
Forse Burn	Highld	NG2440	57°22·3′	6°35·0′W	W	23
Forse House	Highld	ND2135	58°18·1′	3°20·4′W	X	11
Forse Water	Shetld	HU2954	60°16·4′	1°28·0′W	W	3
Forsgeo	N Eil	NA9922	58°5·3′	7°6·0′W	X	13
Forsham Fm	Kent	TQ8329	51°2·1′	0°37·0′E	FM	188,199
Forshaw Heath	Warw	SP0873	52°21·5′	1°52·6′W	T	139
Forside Hill	S Lanak	NS9126	55°31·2′	3°43·2′W	H	71,72
Forsie	Highld	ND0462	58°32·4′	3°38·5′W	X	11,12
Forsinain Burn	Highld	NC9148	58°24·7′	3°51·5′W	W	10
Forsinain Fm	Highld	NC9148	58°24·7′	3°51·5′W	FM	10
Forsinan Burn	Highld	NC9248	58°24·7′	3°50·4′W	W	11
Forsinard	Highld	NC8943	58°22·0′	3°53·4′W	T	10
Forsinard Lodge	Highld	NC8943	58°22·0′	3°53·4′W	X	10
Forsinard Sta	Highld	NC8942	58°21·4′	3°53·3′W	X	10
Forsnaval	N Eil	NB0635	58°12·6′	6°59·9′W	H	13
Forss Ho (Hotel)	Highld	ND0368	58°35·6′	3°39·7′W	X	11,12
Forss Water	Highld	ND0463	58°32·9′	3°38·5′W	W	11,12
Forstal	Kent	TQ7358	51°17·9′	0°29·3′E	T	178,188
Forstal Fm	E Susx	TQ4835	51°5·9′	0°7·2′E	FM	188
Forstal Fm	E Susx	TQ8923	50°58·7′	0°41·9′E	FM	189
Forstal Fm	Kent	TQ6837	51°6·7′	0°24·4′E	FM	188
Forstal Fm	Kent	TQ7551	51°14·1′	0°30·8′E	FM	188
Forstal Fm	Kent	TQ8932	51°3·6′	0°42·2′E	FM	189
Forstal, The	E Susx	TQ5435	51°5·8′	0°12·4′E	X	188
Forsters Fm	Norf	TM2891	52°28·4′	1°21·8′E	FM	134
Forster's Hill	Northum	NY6570	55°1·6′	2°32·4′W	X	86
Forston	Dorset	SY6695	50°45·4′	2°28·5′W	T	194
Forston Barn	Dorset	SY6796	50°46·0′	2°27·7′W	X	194
Fortacres	S Ayr	NS3934	55°34·6′	4°32·8′W	X	70
Fort Albert	I of W	SZ3289	50°42·2′	1°32·4′W	A	196
Fort Augustus	Highld	NH3709	57°8·8′	4°41·2′W	T	34
Fort Belan	Gwyn	SH4460	53°7·1′	4°19·5′W	A	114,115
Fort Belvedere	Surrey	SU9668	51°24·4′	0°36·8′W	X	175,176
Fort Brockhurst	Hants	SU5902	50°49·1′	1°9·4′W	A	196
Fort Cumberland	C of Port	SZ6899	50°47·4′	1°1·7′W	A	196
Fort Elson	Hants	SU5902	50°49·1′	1°9·4′W	A	196
Fortescue	Devon	SX9299	50°47·1′	3°31·5′W	X	192
Fortescue	Devon	SY1389	50°41·9′	3°13·5′W	X	192
Fortescues	Essex	TL6211	51°46·7′	0°21·3′E	X	167
Forteviot	Pth & Kin	NO0517	56°20·4′	3°31·8′W	T	58
Fort Fareham	Hants	SU5704	50°50·2′	1°11·0′W	X	196
Fort Fm	Cambs	TF3704	52°37·2′	0°1·8′E	FM	142,143
Fort George	Highld	NH7656	57°34·9′	4°4·0′W	T	27
Fort Grange	Hants	SU5900	50°48·0′	1°9·4′W	A	196
Fort Green	Suff	TM4656	52°9·1′	1°36·2′E	X	156
Forth	Aberd	NO7770	56°49·5′	2°22·2′W	X	45
Forth	S Lanak	NS9453	55°45·8′	3°40·9′W	T	65,72
Forthampton	Glos	SO8532	51°59·4′	2°12·7′W	T	150
Forthampton Court	Glos	SO8731	51°58·9′	2°11·0′W	X	150
Forth and Clyde Canal	Falk	NS8480	56°0·2′	3°51·2′W	W	65
Forthar	Fife	NO3006	56°14·7′	3°7·3′W	X	59
Forthar Mill Fm	Fife	NO2805	56°14·2′	3°9·3′W	FM	59
Forthay	Glos	ST7496	51°40·0′	2°22·2′W	T	162
Forth Bridge	C of Edin	NT1379	56°0·0′	3°23·3′W	X	65
Forthburn	Durham	NZ0620	54°34·8′	1°54·0′W	X	92
Forthburn Plantn	Durham	NZ0620	54°34·8′	1°54·0′W	F	92
Forth Cleugh	Northum	NY7476	55°4·9′	2°24·0′W	X	86,87
Forth & Clyde Canal	E Dunb	NS6172	55°55·5′	4°13·0′W	W	64
Fort Henry	Rut	SK9412	52°42·1′	0°36·1′W	X	130
Forth Ho	Cumbr	NY1332	54°40·8′	3°20·5′W	X	89
Forthie Water	Aberd	NO7979	56°54·4′	2°20·2′W	W	45
Forthill	Angus	NO5565	56°46·7′	2°43·7′W	X	44
Fort Hill	N Yks	SE7225	53°43·2′	0°54·1′W	X	105,106
Forth Mains	S Lanak	NS9354	55°46·3′	3°41·9′W	X	65,72
Forth of Lawton	Pth & Kin	NO2035	56°30·3′	3°17·5′W	X	53

Forth Road Bridge	C of Edin	NT1279	56°0·0'	3°24·2'W	X	65
Fortingall	Pth & Kin	NN7347	56°36·1'	4°3·7'W	T	51,52
Fortis Green	Barnet	TQ2789	51°35·4'	0°9·6'W	T	176
Fortissat Ho	N Lanak	NS8561	55°50·0'	3°49·7'W	X	65
Fort Matilda	Inverc	NS2577	55°57·5'	4°47·8'W	T	63
Fort Matilda	Inverc	NS2678	55°58·1'	4°46·8'W	T	63
Fort Monckton	Hants	SZ6197	50°46·4'	1°7·7'W	X	196
Fort Nelson	Hants	SU6007	50°51·8'	1°8·5'W	A	196
Fortnight Fm	Bath & NE Somer	ST7360	51°20·5'	2°22·9'W	FM	172
Forton	Hants	SU4143	51°11·3'	1°24·4'W	T	185
Forton	Hants	SU6000	50°48·0'	1°8·5'W	T	196
Forton	Lancs	SD4851	53°57·4'	2°47·1'W	T	102
Forton	Shrops	SJ4216	52°44·6'	2°51·1'W	T	126
Forton	Somer	ST3307	50°51·8'	2°56·7'W	T	193
Forton	Staffs	SJ7521	52°47·4'	2°21·8'W	T	127
Forton Hall Fm	Lancs	SD4750	53°56·8'	2°48·0'W	FM	102
Forton Heath	Shrops	SJ4317	52°45·1'	2°50·3'W	T	126
Forton Service Area	Lancs	SD5052	53°57·9'	2°45·3'W	X	102
Fortoun Bank	E Loth	NT5679	56°0·4'	2°41·9'W	X	67
Fort Pendlestone	Shrops	SO7294	52°32·8'	2°24·4'W	X	138
Fort Purbrook	C of Port	SU6706	50°51·2'	1°2·5'W	A	196
Fort Putnam	Cumbr	NY4530	54°40·0'	2°50·7'W	X	90
Fortree	Aberd	NJ9429	57°21·3'	2°5·5'W	X	38
Fortrey's Hall	Cambs	TL4482	52°25·2'	0°7·5'E	X	142,143
Fortrie	Aberd	NJ6645	57°29·9'	2°33·6'W	T	29
Fortrie	Aberd	NJ7358	57°36·9'	2°26·7'W	X	29
Fortrie Farm	Aberd	NJ6645	57°29·9'	2°33·6'W	FM	29
Fortrose	Highld	NH7256	57°34·8'	4°8·0'W	T	27
Fort Rowner	Hants	SU5901	50°48·6'	1°9·4'W	A	196
Fortry	Aberd	NK0350	57°32·7'	1°56·5'W	X	30
Fortry	Moray	NJ4953	57°34·1'	2°50·7'W	X	28,29
Fortry Wood	Moray	NJ5053	57°34·1'	2°49·7'W	F	29
Fortshot Ho	Leeds	SE3242	53°52·6'	1°30·4'W	X	104
Fort Southwick	Hants	SU6206	50°51·2'	1°6·8'W	A	196
Fort, The	Gwyn	SH4655	53°4·4'	4°17·5'W	X	115,123
Fortune Fm	Glos	ST7297	51°40·5'	2°23·9'W	FM	162
Fortuneswell	Dorset	SY6873	50°33·6'	2°26·7'W	T	194
Fortunes Wood Fm	Dorset	ST5803	50°49·7'	2°35·4'W	FM	194
Fort Victoria Country Park	I of W	SZ3389	50°42·2'	1°31·6'W	X	196
Fort Wallington	Hants	SU5806	50°51·3'	1°10·2'W	X	196
Fort Widley	C of Port	SU6506	50°51·2'	1°4·2'W	A	196
Fort William	Highld	NN1073	56°48·8'	5°6·3'W	T	41
Forty Acre Cottage	Kent	TR0931	51°2·6'	0°59·3'E	X	189
Forty Acre Fm	Heref	SO6661	52°15·0'	2°29·5'W	FM	138,149
Forty Acre Fm	Lancs	SD6339	53°51·0'	2°33·3'W	FM	102,103
Forty Acre Fm	Lincs	TF0339	52°56·5'	0°27·6'W	FM	130
Forty Acre Plantn	Essex	TQ6996	51°38·5'	0°26·9'E	F	167,177
Forty Acre Plantn	Norf	TF9732	52°51·2'	0°56·0'E	F	132
Forty Acre Plantn	N Yks	NZ3206	54°27·1'	1°30·0'W	F	93
Forty Acres	N Yks	NZ0700	54°24·0'	1°53·1'W	H	92
Forty Acres Fm	Somer	ST5927	51°2·7'	2°34·7'W	FM	183
Forty Acres, The	Staffs	SJ7437	52°56·0'	2°22·8'W	F	127
Forty Acre Wood	Beds	SP9459	52°13·5'	0°37·0'W	F	153
Forty Fm	Suff	TL6579	52°23·3'	0°25·9'E	FM	143
Forty Foot Br	Norf	TF5408	52°39·1'	0°17·0'E	X	143
Forty Foot Fm	Lincs	TF1623	52°47·8'	0°16·4'W	FM	130
Forty Foot Fm	Lincs	TF1631	52°52·1'	0°16·2'W	FM	130
Forty Foot or Vermuden's Drain	Cambs	TL4087	52°28·0'	0°4·1'E	W	142,143
Forty Green	Bucks	SP7603	51°43·5'	0°53·6'W	T	165
Forty Green	Bucks	SU9291	51°36·8'	0°39·9'W	T	175
Forty Hall	Enf	TQ3398	51°40·1'	0°4·2'W	A	166,176,177
Forty Hill	Enf	TQ3397	51°39·6'	0°4·2'W	T	166,176,177
Forty Pence Wood	Red & Cl	NZ6317	54°32·9'	1°1·1'W	F	94
Fortypenny Hill or Low Countam	D & G	NS6800	55°16·8'	4°4·3'W	X	77
Forvie	Aberd	NK0029	57°21·3'	1°59·5'W	X	38
Forvie Centre	Aberd	NK0328	57°20·8'	1°56·6'W	X	38
Forvie Church	Aberd	NK0226	57°19·7'	1°57·6'W	A	38
Forvie National Nature Reserve	Aberd	NK0227	57°20·3'	1°57·6'W	X	38
Forvie Ness or Hackley Head	Aberd	NK0226	57°19·7'	1°57·6'W	X	38
Forward Green	Suff	TM0959	52°11·6'	1°3·9'E	T	155
Forwood	Glos	SO8600	51°42·1'	2°11·8'W	T	162
Forwood Fm	Notts	SK7679	53°18·4'	0°51·2'W	FM	120
Foryd	Gwyn	SH4559	53°6·6'	4°18·5'W	X	115,123
Foryd Bay	Gwyn	SH4459	53°6·6'	4°19·4'W	W	115,123
Fosbury	Wilts	SU3158	51°19·4'	1°32·9'W	T	174
Fosbury	Wilts	SU3256	51°18·4'	1°32·1'W	A	174
Fosbury Fm	Wilts	SU3156	51°18·4'	1°32·9'W	FM	174
Fosbury Ho	Wilts	SU3058	51°19·4'	1°33·8'W	X	174
Foscombe	Glos	SO8026	51°56·2'	2°17·1'W	X	162
Foscot	Oxon	SP2421	51°53·5'	1°38·7'W	T	163
Foscote	Bucks	SP7135	52°0·8'	0°57·5'W	T	152
Foscote	Northnts	SP6647	52°7·3'	1°1·8'W	T	152
Foscote	Wilts	ST8679	51°30·8'	2°11·7'W	T	173
Foscot Fm	Hants	SU5657	51°18·8'	1°11·4'W	FM	174
Fosdyke	Lincs	TF3133	52°52·9'	0°2·8'W	T	131
Fosdyke Bridge	Lincs	TF3132	52°52·4'	0°2·8'W	T	131
Fosdyke Villa	Lincs	TF3234	52°53·5'	0°1·9'W	X	131
Fosdyke Wash	Lincs	TF3635	52°53·9'	0°1·7'E	W	131
Fosfield Fm	N Yks	NZ4305	54°26·6'	1°19·8'W	FM	93
Fosgoy	Powys	SN8543	52°4·6'	3°40·3'W	X	147,160
Fosgrove Fm	Somer	ST2220	50°58·7'	3°6·3'W	FM	193
Foss	Pth & Kin	NN7958	56°42·1'	3°58·1'W	X	42,51,52
Foss Bank	Lancs	SD6665	54°5·0'	2°30·8'W	X	98
Foss Beck	E Yorks	SE7351	53°57·2'	0°52·8'W	W	105,106
Foss Br	Notts	SK6736	52°55·3'	0°59·8'W	X	129
Foss Br	York	SE6260	54°2·2'	1°2·8'W	X	100
Foss Braes	Aberd	NJ7641	57°27·8'	2°23·5'W	F	29
Foss Cross	Glos	SP0609	51°47·0'	1°54·4'W	X	163
Fossdale	N Yks	SD8692	54°19·6'	2°12·5'W	X	98
Fossdale Gill	N Yks	SD8694	54°20·7'	2°12·5'W	W	98
Fossdale Moss	N Yks	SD8595	54°21·3'	2°13·4'W	X	98
Fossdale Pasture	N Yks	SD8593	54°20·2'	2°13·4'W	X	98
Foss Dike	E Yorks	SE7639	53°50·7'	0°50·3'W	W	105,106
Foss Dike	E Yorks	TA2045	53°53·5'	0°10·0'W	W	107
Foss Dike	York	SE5450	53°56·8'	1°10·2'W	W	105

Fossditch	Norf	TL7691	52°29·5'	0°36·0'E	A	143
Fossdyke	Lincs	SK8676	53°16·7'	0°42·2'W	W	121
Fossebridge	Glos	SP0811	51°48·1'	1°52·6'W	T	163
Fosse Fields Fm	Notts	SK7143	52°59·0'	0°56·1'W	FM	129
Fosse Fm	Bath & NE Somer	ST7260	51°20·5'	2°23·7'W	FM	172
Fosse Fm	Glos	SO9610	51°47·6'	2°3·1'W	FM	163
Fosse Fm	Glos	SU0797	51°40·5'	1°53·5'W	FM	163
Fosse Fm	Leic	SP5092	52°31·6'	1°15·4'W	FM	140
Fosse Fm	Warw	SP3663	52°16·1'	1°27·9'W	FM	151
Fosse Fm	Warw	SP3766	52°17·7'	1°27·0'W	FM	151
Fosse Fm	Warw	SP4174	52°22·0'	1°23·5'W	FM	140
Fosse Fm	Warw	SP4484	52°27·4'	1°20·7'W	FM	140
Fosse Fm	Wilts	ST8175	51°28·7'	2°16·0'W	FM	173
Fosse Fm	Wilts	ST9088	51°35·7'	2°8·3'W	FM	173
Fosse Gate	Wilts	ST8479	51°30·8'	2°13·4'W	X	173
Fosse Gate	Wilts	ST9494	51°38·9'	2°4·8'W	X	163,173
Fosse Ho	Leic	SP5295	52°33·3'	1°13·6'W	X	140
Fosse Lodge	Notts	SK6426	52°49·9'	1°2·6'W	X	129
Fosse Lodge	Wilts	ST8582	51°32·4'	2°12·6'W	X	173
Fosses Fm	E Yorks	SE7639	53°50·7'	0°50·3'W	FM	105,106
Fosse, The	Herts	TL1207	51°45·3'	0°22·2'W	R	166
Fosse Tilery Fm	Glos	ST9089	51°36·2'	2°8·3'W	FM	173
Fosseway Ct	Staffs	SK0907	52°39·9'	1°51·6'W	X	139
Fosseway Fm	Glos	SP2031	51°58·9'	1°42·1'W	FM	151
Fosseway Fm	Somer	ST5529	51°3·7'	2°38·1'W	FM	183
Fosse Way (Roman Road)	Bath & NE Somer	ST7261	51°21·1'	2°23·7'W	R	172
Fosse Way (Roman Road)	Notts	SK7751	53°3·3'	0°50·7'W	R	120,121,129
Fosse Way (Roman Road)	Somer	ST5833	51°5·9'	2°35·6'W	A	182,183
Fosse Way (Roman Road)	Somer	ST6344	51°11·9'	2°31·4'W	R	183
Fosse Way (Roman Road)	Warw	SP2951	52°9·6'	1°34·2'W	R	151
Fosse Way (Roman Road)	Wilts	ST8480	51°31·4'	2°13·4'W	R	173
Fosse Wharf Fm	Warw	SP3664	52°16·6'	1°27·9'W	FM	151
Fosse Wood	N Yks	SD9474	54°9·9'	2°5·1'W	F	98
Fosse Wood	Somer	ST5832	51°5·4'	2°35·6'W	F	182,183
Foss Fm	E Yorks	SE7451	53°57·2'	0°51·9'W	FM	105,106
Foss Fm	Notts	SK6839	52°56·9'	0°58·9'W	FM	129
Foss Fm	N Yks	NZ8803	54°25·1'	0°38·2'W	FM	94
Foss Gill	Cumbr	NY7803	54°25·6'	2°19·9'W	W	91
Foss Gill	N Yks	SD9159	54°1·9'	2°7·8'W	W	103
Foss Ho	N Yks	SE6265	54°4·9'	1°2·7'W	X	100
Fossicks	Hants	SU4957	51°18·8'	1°17·4'W	X	174
Fossil Fm	Dorset	SY8084	50°39·6'	2°16·6'W	FM	194
Fossil Tree	Arg & Bt	NM4027	56°22·1'	6°12·2'W	X	48
Foss Plantation	N Yks	NZ8702	54°24·6'	0°39·2'W	F	94
Foss, The	N Yks	SE5044	53°53·6'	1°13·9'W	W	105
Foss, The	N Yks	SE5154	53°59·0'	1°12·9'W	W	105
Foss Walk	N Yks	SE5672	54°8·7'	1°8·1'W	X	100
Foss Way (Roman Road)	Glos	SP0812	51°48·6'	1°52·6'W	R	163
Foss Way (Roman Road)	Lincs	SK8963	53°9·6'	0°39·7'W	R	121
Foss Way (Roman Road)	Notts	SK6530	52°52·0'	1°1·7'W	R	129
Foss Way (Roman Road)	S Glos	ST7970	51°26·0'	2°17·7'W	R	172
Foss Way (Roman Road)	Somer	ST4114	50°55·6'	2°50·0'W	R	193
Foss Way (Roman Road)	Warw	SP4585	52°27·9'	1°19·9'W	R	140
Fostall	Kent	TR0661	51°18·9'	0°57·8'E	T	179
Fosten Green	Kent	TQ8336	51°5·9'	0°37·2'E	T	188
Fosten Ho	Pth & Kin	NO0029	56°26·8'	3°36·9'W	X	52,53,58
Foster Cliffe Fms	Brad	SE0348	53°55·9'	1°56·8'W	FM	104
Foster Flatts Fm	N Yks	SE3564	54°4·5'	1°27·5'W	FM	99
Foster Hill	Durham	NZ0625	54°37·5'	1°54·0'W	X	92
Foster Ho	Darl	NZ3513	54°30·9'	1°27·1'W	X	93
Fosterhouses	Donc	SE6514	53°37·3'	1°0·6'W	T	111
Foster Howes	N Yks	NZ8700	54°23·5'	0°39·2'W	A	94
Foster Howes Rigg	N Yks	NZ8700	54°23·5'	0°39·2'W	X	94
Fosterland Burn	Scot Bord	NT8359	55°49·7'	2°15·8'W	W	67,74
Fostermeadow	D & G	NY1071	55°1·8'	3°24·1'W	X	85
Fostermeadowfoot	D & G	NY1070	55°1·2'	3°24·0'W	X	85
Foster's Booth	Northnts	SP6654	52°11·0'	1°1·7'W	T	152
Foster's Br	Rut	SK9603	52°37·2'	0°34·5'W	X	141
Fosters Fm	Kent	TQ5644	51°10·7'	0°14·3'E	FM	188
Foster's Green	Worcs	SO9765	52°17·2'	2°2·2'W	T	150
Foster's Leap	Lancs	SD9439	53°51·1'	2°5·1'W	X	103
Foster Street	Essex	TL4808	51°45·3'	0°9·1'E	T	167
Fosterton	Fife	NT2596	56°9·3'	3°12·0'W	X	59
Fosterville	Devon	SX8676	50°34·6'	3°36·2'W	X	191
Foston	Derby	SK1831	52°52·8'	1°43·5'W	T	128
Foston	Leic	SP6095	52°33·2'	1°6·5'W	T	140
Foston	Lincs	SK8542	52°58·4'	0°43·6'W	T	130
Foston	N Yks	SE6965	54°4·8'	0°56·3'W	T	100
Foston Beck	Lincs	SK8740	52°57·3'	0°41·9'W	W	130
Foston Brook	Derby	SK1831	52°52·8'	1°43·5'W	W	128
Foston Grange	N Yks	SE6965	54°4·8'	0°56·3'W	X	100
Foston Hall	N Yks	SE7065	54°4·8'	0°55·4'W	X	100
Foston Hall Fm	Leic	SP6095	52°33·2'	1°6·5'W	FM	140
Foston Lodge	N Yks	SE6865	54°4·8'	0°57·2'W	X	100
Foston Lodge Fm	Leic	SP6096	52°33·7'	1°6·5'W	FM	140
Foston Mill Fm	Derby	SK1833	52°53·9'	1°43·5'W	FM	128
Foston on the Wolds	E Yorks	TA1055	53°59·0'	0°18·9'W	T	107
Foston Rectory	N Yks	SE6864	54°4·3'	0°57·2'W	X	100
Foswell Ho	Pth & Kin	NN9610	56°16·5'	3°40·3'W	X	58
Fotherby	Lincs	TF3191	53°24·2'	0°1·4'W	T	113
Fotherby Top	Lincs	TF2991	53°24·2'	0°3·2'W	X	113
Fotherdale	N Yks	SE8360	54°2·0'	0°43·5'W	X	100
Fothergill	Cumbr	NY0234	54°41·7'	3°30·8'W	T	89
Fotheringhams	Stir	NS7396	56°8·6'	4°2·2'W	X	57
Fotheringhay	Northnts	TL0593	52°31·7'	0°26·7'W	T	142
Fotheringhay Lodge	Northnts	TL0794	52°32·2'	0°24·9'W	X	142
Fotherley Buildings	Northum	NZ0357	54°54·7'	1°56·8'W	X	87
Fothringham Hill	Angus	NO4645	56°35·9'	2°52·3'W	H	54
Fothringham Hill Ho	Angus	NO4643	56°34·8'	2°52·3'W	X	54
Fothringham Home Fm	Angus	NO4644	56°35·3'	2°52·3'W	FM	54
Foubister	Orkney	HY5103	58°55·0'	2°50·6'W	X	6,7
Fouchers	Essex	TL6111	51°46·7'	0°20·4'E	X	167
Fouchie Shank	Aberd	NJ5220	57°16·3'	2°47·3'W	X	37
Foufinside	Derby	SK1855	53°5·8'	1°43·5'W	X	119
Fough	Derby	SK0567	53°12·2'	1°55·1'W	X	119
Foul Anchor	Cambs	TF4617	52°44·1'	0°10·2'E	T	131
Foula Wick	Shetld	HU3764	60°21·8'	1°19·3'W	W	2,3
Foulbog	D & G	NT2407	55°21·3'	3°11·5'W	X	79

Foulbog Sike	Cumbr	NY6277	55°5·4'	2°35·3'W	W	86
Foulbridge	Cumbr	NY4148	54°49·7'	2°54·7'W	T	85
Foulbridge	N Yks	SE9179	54°12·2'	0°35·9'W	X	101
Foulbrig	Scot Bord	NT2026	55°31·5'	3°15·6'W	X	73
Foul Burn	Scot Bord	NT7252	55°45·9'	2°26·3'W	W	67,74
Foulburn Gair	Northum	NT9124	55°30·8'	2°8·1'W	H	74,75
Foulby	Wakf	SE3917	53°39·1'	1°24·2'W	T	110,111
Foul Cleugh	Scot Bord	NT6158	55°49·1'	2°36·9'W	X	67,74
Fould	Staffs	SJ9758	53°7·4'	2°2·3'W	X	118
Foulden	Norf	TL7699	52°33·8'	0°36·2'E	T	143
Foulden	Scot Bord	NT9255	55°47·5'	2°7·2'W	T	67,74,75
Foulden Bastle	Scot Bord	NT9155	55°47·5'	2°8·2'W	X	67,74,75
Foulden Common	Norf	TF7500	52°34·4'	0°35·4'E	X	143
Foulden Deans	Scot Bord	NT9355	55°47·5'	2°6·3'W	X	67,74,75
Foulden Hill	Scot Bord	NT9357	55°48·6'	2°6·3'W	X	67,74,75
Foulden New Mains	Scot Bord	NT9156	55°48·1'	2°8·2'W	X	67,74,75
Foulden Newton	Scot Bord	NT9255	55°47·5'	2°7·2'W	X	67,74,75
Fouldshaw House Fm	N Yks	SE1560	54°2·4'	1°45·8'W	FM	99
Foulds House Fm	Lancs	SD8836	53°49·5'	2°10·5'W	FM	103
Foule Crag	Cumbr	NY3228	54°38·8'	3°2·8'W	X	90
Fouledge	Scot Bord	NT4504	55°19·9'	2°51·6'W	X	79
Foul End	Warw	SP2494	52°32·8'	1°38·4'W	T	139
Foulford	Hants	SU1805	50°50·9'	1°44·3'W	T	195
Foulgate Fm	N Yks	SE2175	54°10·5'	1°40·3'W	FM	99
Foul Green	N Yks	NZ6610	54°29·1'	0°58·5'W	X	94
Foulholme Sands	E Yorks	TA1921	53°40·5'	0°11·5'W	X	107,113
Foulis Castle	Highld	NH5864	57°38·9'	4°22·3'W	X	21
Foulis Point	Highld	NH5963	57°38·4'	4°21·3'W	X	21
Foulmartlaw	Northum	NZ0981	55°7·6'	1°51·1'W	X	81
Foulmead Fm	Kent	TR3454	51°14·4'	1°21·5'E	FM	179
Foul Mile	E Susx	TQ6215	50°54·9'	0°18·7'E	T	199
Foulmire Heights	Scot Bord	NY5894	55°14·6'	2°39·2'W	H	80
Foul Moss	Cumbr	SD7181	54°13·7'	2°26·3'W	X	98
Foulnaze	Sefton	SD3022	53°41·6'	3°3·2'W	X	102
Foulness	Norf	TG2341	52°55·4'	1°19·5'E	W	133
Foulness Island	Essex	TR0092	51°35·7'	0°53·7'E	X	178
Foulness Point	Essex	TR0495	51°37·2'	0°57·2'E	X	168,178
Foulness Sands	Essex	TR0696	51°37·7'	0°59·0'E	X	168
Foulney Island	Cumbr	SD2464	54°4·2'	3°9·3'W	X	96
Foulney Twist	Cumbr	SD2463	54°3·7'	3°9·3'W	X	96
Foulpapple	E Ayr	NS5538	55°37·1'	4°17·7'W	X	71
Foulplay Knowe	Northum	NT8900	55°17·9'	2°10·0'W	X	80
Foulpool	Cumbr	NY5250	54°50·8'	2°44·4'W	X	86
Foul Potts	Northum	NY6459	54°55·7'	2°33·3'W	X	86
Foulrice	N Yks	SE6270	54°7·6'	1°2·7'W	X	100
Foulrice Fm	N Yks	SE6168	54°6·5'	1°3·6'W	FM	100
Foulrice Fm	N Yks	SE6170	54°7·6'	1°3·6'W	FM	100
Foulride Green	E Susx	TQ5803	50°48·5'	0°14·9'E	T	199
Foulridge	Lancs	SD8842	53°52·7'	2°10·5'W	T	103
Foulridge Wharf	Lancs	SD8842	53°52·7'	2°10·5'W	X	103
Foulsham	Norf	TG0324	52°46·7'	1°1·0'E	T	133
Foulshaw Moss	Cumbr	SD4682	54°14·1'	2°49·3'W	X	97
Foulshiels	Scot Bord	NY4991	55°12·9'	2°47·7'W	X	79
Foulshiels Fm	Scot Bord	NT4229	55°33·3'	2°54·7'W	FM	73
Foulshiels Hill	Scot Bord	NT4230	55°33·9'	2°54·7'W	H	73
Foulshot Law	Scot Bord	NT7044	55°41·6'	2°28·2'W	X	74
Foul Sike	Cald	SD9434	53°48·4'	2°5·1'W	W	103
Foulsike Fm	N Yks	NZ9102	54°24·6'	0°35·5'W	FM	94
Foul Sike Wham	N Yks	SE1775	54°10·5'	1°44·0'W	W	99
Foulstone Delf	Sheff	SK2190	53°24·6'	1°40·6'W	X	110
Foulstone Moor	Sheff	SK2190	53°24·6'	1°40·6'W	X	110
Foulsyke	Cumbr	NY1421	54°34·9'	3°19·4'W	X	89
Foulsyke	D & G	NY2565	54°58·7'	3°9·9'W	X	85
Foulsyke Fm	Cumbr	NY1349	54°49·9'	3°20·8'W	FM	85
Foulsyke Fm	Cumbr	SD6987	54°16·9'	2°28·2'W	FM	98
Foulsyke Fm	N Yks	TA0091	54°18·5'	0°27·4'W	FM	101
Foulton	S Ayr	NS3927	55°30·9'	4°32·6'W	X	70
Foulton Hall	Essex	TM2229	51°55·1'	1°14·1'E	X	169
Foulwork Burn	Northum	NU1039	55°38·9'	1°50·0'W	W	75
Foulzie	Aberd	NJ7159	57°37·5'	2°28·7'W	X	29
Foumart Knowe	Northum	NU1124	55°30·8'	1°49·1'W	H	75
Foundry	Corn	SW5537	50°11·2'	5°25·6'W	T	203
Foundry Brook	W Berks	SU6965	51°23·0'	1°0·1'W	W	175
Foundry Hill	Norf	TG0928	52°48·8'	1°6·5'E	T	133
Foundry Wood	Glos	SO6610	51°47·5'	2°29·2'W	F	162
Fountain	Brig	SS8883	51°32·3'	3°36·5'W	T	170
Fountainbleau	Aberd	NK1037	57°25·7'	1°49·6'W	X	30
Fountain Dale	Notts	SK5656	53°6·1'	1°9·4'W	X	120
Fountainebleau	Aberd	NJ9725	57°19·2'	2°2·5'W	X	38
Fountain Fm	Essex	TM0329	51°55·6'	0°57·5'E	FM	168
Fountain Fm	Notts	SK7297	53°28·1'	0°54·5'W	FM	112
Fountainhall	E Loth	NT4267	55°53·8'	2°55·2'W	X	66
Fountainhall	Scot Bord	NT4249	55°44·1'	2°55·0'W	T	73
Fountain Head	Durham	NY9915	54°32·1'	2°0·5'W	X	92
Fountain Head	Powys	SO2272	52°20·7'	3°8·3'W	X	137,148
Fountain Hill	Notts	SK7593	53°25·9'	0°51·9'W	X	112
Fountain Hill	Pemb	SN1536	51°59·7'	4°41·3'W	X	145
Fountain Manor	E Yorks	TA0149	53°55·9'	0°27·3'W	X	106,107
Fountains Abbey	N Yks	SE2768	54°6·7'	1°34·8'W	A	99
Fountains Earth Moor	N Yks	SE1472	54°8·9'	1°46·7'W	X	99
Fountains Fell	N Yks	SD8670	54°7·8'	2°12·4'W	H	98
Fountains Fell Tarn	N Yks	SD8671	54°8·3'	2°12·4'W	W	98
Fountain's Fm	W Susx	TQ0227	51°2·2'	0°32·3'W	FM	186,197
Fountainside	Midlo	NT2956	55°47·8'	3°7·5'W	X	66,73
Founthill	E Susx	TQ4220	50°57·9'	0°1·7'E	X	198
Four Acre Belt	Suff	TL7367	52°16·7'	0°32·6'E	F	155
Four Ashes	Bucks	SU8795	51°39·1'	0°44·2'W	T	165
Four Ashes	Dorset	ST4300	50°48·0'	2°48·1'W	X	193
Four Ashes	Sol	SP1575	52°22·6'	1°46·4'W	T	139
Four Ashes	Staffs	SJ9108	52°40·4'	2°7·6'W	T	127
Four Ashes	Staffs	SO8087	52°29·1'	2°17·3'W	T	138
Four Ashes	Suff	TM0070	52°17·7'	0°56·4'E	T	144,155
Four Balls Fm	Cambs	TL5190	52°29·4'	0°13·8'E	FM	143
Four Barrow Hill	Dorset	SY6487	50°41·1'	2°30·2'W	X	194
Four Barrows	Wilts	SU2477	51°29·7'	1°38·9'W	A	174
Four Burrows	Corn	SW7648	50°17·6'	5°8·3'W	A	204
Four Corners	Suff	TL8376	52°21·3'	0°41·6'E	F	144
Four Crosses	Denb	SJ0342	52°57·5'	3°26·3'W	X	125
Four Crosses	Denb	SJ1858	53°7·0'	3°13·1'W	X	116
Four Crosses	Flint	SJ1765	53°10·8'	3°14·1'W	X	116

Four Crosses	I of Angl	SH4189	53°22·7′	4°23·0′W	X	114
Four Crosses	I of Angl	SH5472	53°13·7′	4°10·8′W	X	114,115
Four Crosses	Powys	SJ0508	52°39·9′	3°23·9′W	X	125
Four Crosses	Powys	SJ2718	52°45·5′	3°4·5′W	T	126
Four Crosses	Staffs	SJ9509	52°41·0′	2°4·0′W	T	127
Four Crosses	Wrex	SJ2553	53°4·4′	3°6·8′W	T	117
Four Cross Way	Devon	SS6638	51°7·8′	3°54·5′W	X	180
Four Dell Fm	Hants	SU4524	51°1·0′	1°21·1′W	FM	185
Four Elms	Devon	ST2507	50°51·7′	3°3·6′W	T	192,193
Four Elms	Kent	TQ4648	51°13·0′	0°5·8′E	T	188
Four Elms	Suff	TM1261	52°12·6′	1°6·6′E	X	155
Four Elms	W Berks	SU5174	51°28·0′	1°15·6′W	X	174
Four Elms Fm	Devon	SY1096	50°45·6′	3°16·2′W	FM	192,193
Four Faces	N Yks	SE7368	54°6·4′	0°52·6′W	X	100
Fourfield Close	Surrey	TQ2056	51°17·7′	0°16·3′W	X	187
Four Firs	Devon	SY0286	50°40·2′	3°22·8′W	X	192
Four Foot	Somer	ST5833	51°5·9′	2°35·6′W	T	182,183
Four Forks	Somer	ST2337	51°7·9′	3°5·6′W	T	182
Four Gates	Bolton	SD6407	53°33·7′	2°32·2′W	T	109
Four Gates End	Cald	SD9328	53°45·1′	2°6·0′W	X	103
Four Gotes	Cambs	TF4416	52°43·6′	0°8·3′E	T	131
Fourhole Cross	Corn	SX1774	50°32·5′	4°34·6′W	A	201
Four Houses Corner	W Berks	SU6465	51°23·1′	1°4·4′W	T	175
Four Hundred Fm	Cambs	TL3289	52°29·2′	0°3·0′W	FM	142
Four Hundred Fm	Cambs	TL3291	52°30·3′	0°2·9′W	FM	142
Fourlands Hill	N Yks	SD6671	54°8·3′	2°30·8′W	X	98
Fourlands Ho	N Yks	SD6671	54°8·3′	2°30·8′W	X	98
Four Lane End	Barns	SE2702	53°31·1′	1°35·2′W	T	110
Four Lane Ends	Black w Dar	SD6729	53°45·6′	2°29·6′W	T	103
Four Lane Ends	Brad	SE1333	53°47·8′	1°47·7′W	T	104
Four Lane Ends	Bury	SD7612	53°36·5′	2°21·4′W	T	109
Four Lane Ends	Ches	SJ5561	53°8·9′	2°40·0′W	X	117
Fourlane-ends	Ches	SJ7781	53°19·8′	2°20·3′W	X	109
Four Lane Ends	Cumbr	SD2468	54°6·4′	3°9·3′W	X	96
Four Lane Ends	Cumbr	SD6290	54°18·5′	2°34·6′W	X	97
Fourlane Ends	Derby	SK3855	53°5·7′	1°25·5′W	X	119
Four Lane Ends	Lancs	SD4865	54°4·9′	2°47·3′W	X	97
Four Lane Ends	Lancs	SD5153	53°58·5′	2°44·4′W	X	102
Four Lane Ends	Lancs	SD7126	53°44·0′	2°26·0′W	X	103
Four Lane Ends	Lancs	SD7540	53°51·6′	2°22·4′W	X	103
Four Lane Ends	N Yks	SD6570	54°7·7′	2°31·7′W	X	97
Four Lane Ends	Staffs	SJ8428	52°51·2′	2°13·9′W	X	127
Four Lane Ends	York	SE6751	53°57·3′	0°58·3′W	X	105,106
Four Lanes	Corn	SW6838	50°12·0′	5°14·7′W	T	203
Fourlanes End	Ches	SJ8059	53°7·9′	2°17·5′W	T	118
Four Lanes End	Hants	SU6654	51°17·1′	1°2·8′W	X	185,186
Four Lanes End	Hants	SU7248	51°13·8′	0°57·7′W	X	186
Four Lanes End	Staffs	SJ8720	52°46·9′	2°11·2′W	X	127
Four Lanes End	Wirral	SJ3180	53°19·0′	3°1·7′W	X	108
Four Lanes Ends	N Yks	SE9992	54°19·1′	0°28·3′W	X	94,101
Fourlaws	Northum	NY9082	55°8·2′	2°9·0′W	X	80
Fourlawshill Top	Northum	NY9083	55°8·7′	2°9·0′W	X	80
Fourman Hill	Aberd	NJ5745	57°29·9′	2°42·6′W	H	29
Fourmanhill	Aberd	NJ5845	57°29·9′	2°41·6′W	X	29
Four Marks	Hants	SU6735	51°6·9′	1°2·2′W	T	185,186
Four Meads Fm	Dorset	SY5489	50°42·2′	2°38·7′W	FM	194
Fourmerk	Stir	NS6693	56°6·9′	4°8·9′W	X	57
Fourmerkland	D & G	NX9080	55°6·4′	3°43·0′W	X	78
Fourmerkland	D & G	NY1086	55°9·9′	3°24·3′W	X	78
Fourmerkland Tower	D & G	NX9080	55°6·4′	3°43·0′W	A	78
Four Mile Bar	Lincs	TF2515	52°43·3′	0°8·5′W	X	131
Four Mile Bridge	I of Angl	SH2878	53°16·5′	4°34·4′W	T	114
Four Mile Clump	Wilts	SU1674	51°28·1′	1°45·8′W	F	173
Four Mile Elm	Glos	SO8012	51°48·6′	2°17·0′W	T	162
Four Mile Stable Fm	Cambs	TL5860	52°13·2′	0°19·2′E	FM	154
Fourne Hill Fm	Beds	SP9528	51°56·8′	0°36·7′W	FM	165
Four Oaks	Birm	SP1099	52°35·6′	1°50·7′W	T	139
Four Oaks	Brad	SE0442	53°52·7′	1°55·9′W	X	104
Four Oaks	E Susx	TQ8624	50°59·3′	0°39·4′E	T	189,199
Four Oaks	Glos	SO6928	51°57·2′	2°26·7′W	T	149
Four Oaks	Kent	TQ9862	51°19·6′	0°50·9′E	T	178
Four Oaks	Sol	SP2480	52°25·3′	1°38·4′W	T	139
Four Oaks Park	Birm	SP1198	52°35·0′	1°49·9′W	T	139
Fourpenny	Highld	NH8094	57°55·4′	4°1·1′W	X	21
Fourpenny Plantation	Highld	NH7993	57°54·9′	4°2·1′W	F	21
Four Points	W Berks	SU5578	51°30·1′	1°12·1′W	T	174
Four Pools	Worcs	SP0442	52°4·8′	1°56·1′W	T	150
Four Roads	Carm	SN4409	51°45·7′	4°15·2′W	T	159
Four Roads	I of M	SC2068	54°4·8′	4°44·7′W	T	95
Four Score Acres	Lancs	SD6267	54°6·1′	2°34·5′W	X	97
Four Scores Fm	Norf	TL6391	52°29·8′	0°24·5′E	FM	143
Four Shire Stone, The	Warw	SP2332	51°59·4′	1°39·5′W	X	151
Four Sisters	Suff	TM0636	51°59·3′	1°0·4′E	X	155
Fourstones	Lancs	SD6666	54°5·6′	2°30·8′W	X	98
Fourstones	Northum	NY8967	55°0·1′	2°9·9′W	T	87
Four Stones	Powys	SO2460	52°14·2′	3°6·4′W	A	137,148
Four Stones Rigg	N Yks	SD7377	54°11·5′	2°24·4′W	X	98
Four Stones, The	Worcs	SO9380	52°25·3′	2°5·8′W	X	139
Fourteen Locks	Newp	ST2888	51°35·4′	3°2·0′W	X	171
Fourth Drove	Cambs	TL5286	52°27·3′	0°14·6′E	X	143
Four Throws	Kent	TQ7729	51°2·2′	0°31·9′E	T	188,199
Four Wantz	Essex	TL6111	51°46·7′	0°20·4′E	T	167
Fourways Cross	Devon	SS6107	50°51·0′	3°58·1′W	X	191
Fourways Ho	Devon	ST1434	50°54·8′	3°13·0′W	X	181,193
Four Wents	Kent	TQ6251	51°14·3′	0°19·6′E	X	188
Four Wents	Kent	TQ7537	51°6·6′	0°30·4′E	T	188
Four Wents	Kent	TQ7632	51°3·8′	0°31·1′E	T	188
Four Wheels	Carm	SN2814	51°48·1′	4°29·3′W	X	158
Four Winds Fm	Bucks	SP6015	51°50·1′	1°7·4′W	FM	164,165
Four Winds Fm	Denb	SJ0480	53°18·7′	3°26·0′W	FM	116
Four Winds, The	Devon	SX4678	50°35·1′	4°10·1′W	X	201
Fousley Fm	Ches	SJ7463	53°10·0′	2°22·9′W	FM	118
Fovant	Wilts	SU0029	51°3·9′	1°59·6′W	T	184
Fovant Badges	Wilts	SU0128	51°3·3′	1°58·8′W	X	184
Fovant Down	Wilts	SU0027	51°2·8′	1°59·6′W	X	184
Fovant Hut	Wilts	SU0026	51°2·2′	1°59·6′W	X	184
Fovant Wood	Wilts	SU0030	51°4·4′	1°59·6′W	F	184
Foveran	Aberd	NJ9723	57°18·1′	2°2·5′W	X	38
Foveran	Orkney	HY4208	58°57·6′	3°0·0′W	X	6,7

Foveran Burn	Aberd	NJ9723	57°18·1′	2°2·5′W	W	38
Foveran Ho	Aberd	NJ9924	57°18·7′	2°0·5′W	X	38
Foveran Links	Aberd	NK0023	57°18·1′	1°59·5′W	X	38
Fowberry	Northum	NU1933	55°35·7′	1°41·5′W	X	75
Fowberry Mains	Northum	NU0328	55°33·0′	1°56·7′W	X	75
Fowberrymoor	Northum	NU0127	55°32·5′	1°58·6′W	X	75
Fowberry Moor	Northum	NU0227	55°32·5′	1°57·7′W	X	75
Fowberrypark	Northum	NU0227	55°32·5′	1°57·7′W	X	75
Fowberry Tower	Northum	NU0329	55°33·5′	1°56·7′W	X	75
Fowden	Heref	SO4463	52°16·0′	2°48·8′W	X	137,148,149
Fowelscombe	Devon	SX6955	50°23·1′	3°50·2′W	X	202
Fowey	Corn	SX1251	50°20·0′	4°38·1′W	T	200
Fowgill	N Yks	NZ4401	54°24·4′	1°18·9′W	X	93
Fowgill	N Yks	SD6769	54°7·2′	2°29·9′W	X	98
Fowie	Scot Bord	NT4343	55°40·9′	2°54·0′W	X	73
Fowlbrook Wood	E Susx	TQ7623	50°59·0′	0°30·8′E	F	199
Fowl Craig	Orkney	HY5054	59°22·4′	2°52·3′W	X	5
Fowle Brook	Ches	SJ7356	53°6·3′	2°23·8′W	W	118
Fowle Hall	Kent	TQ6946	51°11·5′	0°25·5′E	X	188
Fowler	E Ayr	NS5028	55°31·6′	4°22·1′W	X	70
Fowler Ho	Darl	NZ2222	54°35·8′	1°39·1′W	X	93
Fowler Rock	C of Dun	NO4130	56°27·8′	2°57·0′W	X	54
Fowler's Arm Chair	Powys	SO0479	52°24·3′	3°24·3′W	A	136,147
Fowlershill	Aberd	NJ9113	57°12·7′	2°8·5′W	X	38
Fowler's Hill	Lancs	SD4847	53°55·2′	2°47·1′W	X	102
Fowler's Laithe	Lancs	SD7050	53°57·0′	2°27·0′W	X	103
Fowler's Park	Kent	TQ7630	51°2·8′	0°31·0′E	X	188
Fowler's Plantation	Norf	TF6724	52°47·5′	0°29·0′E	F	132
Fowler's Plot	Somer	ST3336	51°7·4′	2°57·1′W	T	182
Fowlescombe Gate	Devon	SX6955	50°23·1′	3°50·2′W	X	202
Fowley	Devon	SX5693	50°43·4′	4°2·0′W	X	191
Fowley Common	Warr	SJ6795	53°27·3′	2°29·4′W	T	109
Fowley Cross	Devon	SX5594	50°43·9′	4°2·9′W	X	191
Fowley Island	Hants	SU7404	50°50·1′	0°56·6′W	X	197
Fowley Island	Kent	TQ9765	51°21·2′	0°50·2′E	X	178
Fowl Flag	Orkney	HY5055	59°23·0′	2°52·3′W	X	5
Fowl Ing	Cumbr	SD5293	54°20·1′	2°43·9′W	X	97
Fowlis	Angus	NO3233	56°29·3′	3°5·8′W	T	53
Fowlis Wester	Pth & Kin	NN9224	56°24·0′	3°44·5′W	T	52,58
Fowlmere	Cambs	TL4245	52°5·3′	0°4·8′E	T	154
Fowlstone	Cumbr	SD5680	54°13·1′	2°40·1′W	X	97
Fowlswick Fm	Wilts	ST8875	51°28·7′	2°10·0′W	FM	173
Fowlwood	Moray	NJ5352	57°33·6′	2°46·7′W	X	29
Fownhope	Heref	SO5834	52°0·4′	2°36·3′W	T	149
Fowrass	Cumbr	NY4534	54°42·1′	2°50·8′W	X	90
Fox and Rabbit Fm	N Yks	SE8488	54°17·1′	0°42·2′W	FM	94,100
Foxash Estate	Essex	TM0730	51°56·0′	1°1·1′E	T	168,169
Foxbank Fm	Ches	SJ9369	53°13·3′	2°5·9′W	FM	118
Foxbar	Renf	NS4561	55°49·3′	4°28·0′W	T	64
Fox Barn	Northnts	SP5648	52°7·9′	1°10·5′W	X	152
Foxberry	N Yks	NZ1512	54°30·4′	1°45·7′W	X	92
Foxberry Wood	Oxon	SP3627	51°56·7′	1°28·2′W	F	164
Foxboro Hall	Suff	TM2751	52°6·9′	1°19·3′E	X	156
Foxborough Fm	Essex	TQ7099	51°40·1′	0°27·9′E	FM	167
Fox Brake	Devon	SS8520	50°58·3′	3°37·9′W	F	181
Foxbridge Fm	W Susx	TQ0230	51°3·8′	0°32·3′W	FM	186
Foxburrow Fm	Norf	TF9838	52°54·4′	0°57·1′E	FM	132
Foxburrow Hill	Norf	TF9820	52°44·7′	0°56·4′E	X	132
Foxburrow Plantn	Cambs	TL6567	52°16·8′	0°25·5′E	F	154
Fox Burrows	Redbr	TQ4792	51°36·7′	0°7·8′E	X	177
Foxbury	Brom	TQ4471	51°25·4′	0°4·7′E	T	177
Foxbury Fm	Oxon	SP2808	51°46·4′	1°35·3′W	FM	163
Foxbury Fm	W Berks	SU3380	51°31·3′	1°31·1′W	FM	174
Foxbury Hill	Dorset	SU1100	50°48·2′	1°50·2′W	X	195
Foxbury Ho	Northum	NU2411	55°23·8′	1°36·8′W	X	81
Foxbury Plantation	Hants	SU3017	50°57·3′	1°34·0′W	F	185
Foxbury Point	Hants	SU5904	50°50·2′	1°9·3′W	X	196
Foxbury Wood	Wilts	SU2964	51°22·7′	1°34·6′W	F	174
Foxbury Wood	Wilts	SU3072	51°27·0′	1°33·7′W	F	174
Fox Cairn	Aberd	NJ2802	57°6·5′	3°10·9′W	H	37
Fox Clough	Lancs	SD8938	53°50·5′	2°9·6′W	X	103
Foxcombe	Devon	SX4887	50°40·0′	4°8·9′W	X	191
Foxcombe Fm	W Susx	SU7718	50°57·6′	0°53·8′W	FM	197
Foxcombe Hill	Oxon	SP4901	51°42·6′	1°17·1′W	T	164
Fox Corner	Beds	SP9229	51°57·3′	0°39·3′W	T	165
Fox Corner	Surrey	SU9654	51°16·9′	0°37·0′W	T	186
Foxcote	Glos	SP0118	51°51·9′	1°58·7′W	T	163
Foxcote	Somer	ST7155	51°17·8′	2°24·6′W	T	172
Foxcote	Warw	SP1941	52°4·3′	1°43·0′W	X	151
Foxcote Fm	Dudley	SO9383	52°26·9′	2°5·8′W	FM	139
Foxcote Hill	Glos	SP0117	51°51·3′	1°58·7′W	X	163
Foxcote Hill Fm	Glos	SP0017	51°51·3′	1°59·6′W	FM	163
Foxcote Hill (Tumulus)	Glos	SP0117	51°51·3′	1°58·7′W	A	163
Foxcote Resr	Bucks	SP7136	52°1·3′	0°57·5′W	W	152
Foxcote Wood	Bucks	SP7136	52°1·3′	0°57·5′W	F	152
Foxcotte	Hants	SU3447	51°13·5′	1°30·4′W	T	185
Fox Cotts	Hants	SU4146	51°12·9′	1°24·4′W	X	185
Fox Cove	Corn	SW8573	50°31·3′	5°1·6′W	W	200
Fox Cover Fm	Peterb	TF1308	52°39·7′	0°19·3′W	FM	142
Foxcover Plantn	N Ayr	NS3248	55°42·0′	4°40·0′W	F	63
Fox Covert	Beds	TL0036	52°1·0′	0°32·2′W	F	153
Fox Covert	Bucks	SP7529	51°57·5′	0°54·1′W	X	165
Fox Covert	Bucks	SP8419	51°52·0′	0°46·4′W	F	165
Fox Covert	Bucks	SP8624	51°54·7′	0°44·6′W	F	165
Fox Covert	Ches	SJ6160	53°8·4′	2°34·6′W	F	118
Fox Covert	Ches	SJ7664	53°10·6′	2°21·1′W	F	118
Fox Covert	Donc	SE6008	53°34·1′	1°5·2′W	F	111
Fox Covert	E Yorks	SE8242	53°52·3′	0°44·8′W	F	106
Fox Covert	E Yorks	TA2230	53°45·4′	0°8·6′W	F	107
Fox Covert	E Yorks	TA2828	53°44·2′	0°3·2′W	F	107
Fox Covert	Herts	SP8815	51°49·8′	0°43·0′W	F	165
Fox Covert	Leic	SP6394	52°32·6′	1°3·9′W	F	140
Fox Covert	Lincs	SK8384	53°21·0′	0°44·8′W	F	121
Fox Covert	Lincs	SK9146	53°0·4′	0°38·2′W	F	130
Fox Covert	Lincs	SK9261	53°8·5′	0°37·1′W	F	121
Fox Covert	Lincs	SK9475	53°16·1′	0°35·0′W	F	121
Fox Covert	Lincs	SK9655	53°5·2′	0°33·6′W	F	121
Fox Covert	Lincs	TF0066	53°11·1′	0°29·8′W	F	121
Fox Covert	Lincs	TF0172	53°14·4′	0°28·8′W	F	121
Fox Covert	Lincs	TF1448	53°1·3′	0°17·6′W	F	130

Fox Covert	Lincs	TF2261	53°8·2′	0°10·2′W	F	122
Fox Covert	N Lincs	SE9921	53°40·8′	0°29·7′W	F	106,112
Fox Covert	Norf	TF9121	52°45·4′	0°50·2′E	F	132
Fox Covert	Northnts	SP5746	52°6·8′	1°9·7′W	F	152
Fox Covert	Northnts	SP7264	52°16·4′	0°56·3′W	F	152
Fox Covert	Northnts	SP7752	52°9·9′	0°52·1′W	F	152
Fox Covert	Notts	SK7289	53°23·8′	0°54·6′W	F	112,120
Fox Covert	N Yks	NZ4913	54°30·8′	1°14·2′W	F	93
Fox Covert	N Yks	SE2881	54°13·7′	1°33·8′W	X	99
Fox Covert	N Yks	SE3978	54°12·0′	1°23·7′W	F	99
Fox Covert	N Yks	SE4184	54°15·2′	1°21·8′W	F	99
Fox Covert	N Yks	SE7572	54°8·5′	0°50·7′W	F	100
Fox Covert	N Yks	SE7874	54°9·6′	0°47·9′W	F	100
Fox Covert	Oxon	SP5830	51°58·2′	1°8·9′W	F	152
Fox Covert	Oxon	SP7002	51°43·0′	0°58·8′W	F	165
Fox Covert	Oxon	SU6381	51°31·7′	1°5·1′W	F	175
Fox Covert	Scot Bord	NT5628	55°32·9′	2°41·4′W	F	73
Fox Covert	Scot Bord	NT6433	55°35·6′	2°33·8′W	F	74
Fox Covert	Scot Bord	NT8546	55°42·7′	2°13·9′W	F	74
Fox Covert	Scot Bord	NT9062	55°51·3′	2°9·1′W	F	67
Fox Covert	Shrops	SJ4901	52°36·5′	2°44·8′W	F	126
Fox Covert	Shrops	SJ7802	52°37·2′	2°19·1′W	F	127
Fox Covert	Wilts	SU0244	51°11·9′	1°57·9′W	F	184
Foxcovert Fm	Ches	SJ7664	53°10·6′	2°21·1′W	FM	118
Fox Covert Fm	Derby	SK4130	52°52·2′	1°23·0′W	FM	129
Foxcovert Fm	E Yorks	SE9055	53°59·2′	0°37·2′W	FM	106
Fox Covert Fm	E Yorks	SE9431	53°46·2′	0°34·0′W	FM	106
Fox Covert Fm	Leic	SK4406	52°39·2′	1°20·6′W	FM	140
Foxcovert Fm	Leic	SP3897	52°34·4′	1°26·0′W	FM	140
Fox Covert Fm	N Yks	SE3599	54°23·4′	1°27·2′W	FM	99
Fox Covert Fm	Warw	SP1149	52°8·6′	1°50·0′W	FM	150
Fox Covert Hall	Northnts	SP7566	52°17·5′	0°53·6′W	X	152
Fox Covert Plantn	E Yorks	SE8233	53°47·4′	0°44·9′W	F	106
Fox Covert Plantn	E Yorks	TA1270	54°7·1′	0°16·8′W	F	101
Foxcovert Plantn	Notts	SK5950	53°2·9′	1°6·8′W	F	120
Fox Covert Plantn	N Yks	SE7865	54°4·7′	0°48·0′W	F	100
Fox Covert Rigg	N Yks	SE6180	54°13·0′	1°3·5′W	F	100
Fox Covert Wood	N Yks	NZ1610	54°29·3′	1°44·8′W	F	92
Fox Crags	Cumbr	SD1593	54°19·8′	3°18·0′W	X	96
Fox Craig	D & G	NX6543	54°46·1′	4°5·5′W	X	83,84
Fox Croft	Cumbr	SD1579	54°12·2′	3°17·8′W	X	96
Foxdale	I of M	SC2778	54°10·4′	4°38·6′W	T	95
Foxdale Beck	Lancs	SD5761	54°2·8′	2°39·0′W	W	97
Foxdale Fm	Red & Cl	NZ6215	54°31·8′	1°2·1′W	FM	94
Foxdells Fm	Herts	TL4822	51°52·8′	0°9·4′E	FM	167
Foxdenton Farm	Oldham	SD8904	53°32·2′	2°9·5′W	FM	109
Foxden Wood	Kent	TQ9048	51°12·2′	0°43·6′E	F	189
Foxdon	Devon	SS8214	50°55·0′	3°40·3′W	X	181
Foxdon Hill	Somer	ST3110	50°53·4′	2°58·5′W	H	193
Foxdown	Hants	SU5150	51°15·0′	1°15·8′W	T	185
Foxearth	Essex	TL8344	52°4·1′	0°40·6′E	T	155
Foxearth	Staffs	SJ9546	53°0·9′	2°4·1′W	X	118
Fox Elms	Glos	SO8314	51°49·7′	2°14·4′W	X	162
Foxendown	Kent	TQ6565	51°21·8′	0°22·6′E	T	177,178
Foxen Fm	Kent	TQ9248	51°12·2′	0°45·3′E	FM	189
Foxenhole Lake	Pemb	SN0407	51°43·9′	4°49·9′W	W	157,158
Foxes Bank	E Susx	TQ6330	51°3·0′	0°19·9′E	X	188
Foxes Bank Fm	Ches	SJ6945	53°0·3′	2°27·3′W	FM	118
Foxes' Cross	Devon	SS5022	50°58·9′	4°7·8′W	X	180
Foxes Fm	Suff	TM0453	52°8·5′	0°59·3′E	FM	155
Foxe's Holt	Devon	SX6392	50°42·9′	3°56·1′W	X	191
Foxfield	Cumbr	SD2085	54°15·5′	3°13·3′W	T	96
Foxfield	Cumbr	SD4087	54°16·8′	2°54·9′W	X	96,97
Foxfield Light Railway	Staffs	SJ9643	52°59·3′	2°3·2′W	X	118
Fox Fields	Lancs	SD7038	53°50·5′	2°26·9′W	X	103
Foxfields Fm	Derby	SK2736	52°55·5′	1°35·5′W	FM	128
Fox Fm	E Susx	TQ6927	51°1·3′	0°25·0′E	FM	188,199
Fox Fm	Glos	SP1427	51°56·7′	1°47·4′W	FM	163
Fox Fm	Hants	SU2943	51°11·4′	1°34·7′W	FM	185
Fox Fm	Herts	TL3539	52°2·2′	0°1·5′W	FM	154
Fox Fm	Shrops	SJ5109	52°40·8′	2°43·1′W	FM	126
Fox Fm	W Berks	SU3076	51°29·2′	1°33·7′W	FM	174
Fox Fm	Worcs	SO9580	52°25·3′	2°4·0′W	FM	139
Fox Folly	N Yks	SE5278	54°11·9′	1°11·8′W	X	100
Foxfoot Hay	N Yks	SE5577	54°11·4′	1°9·0′W	X	100
Foxford	Cov	SP3583	52°26·9′	1°28·7′W	T	140
Foxford	Norf	TG0918	52°43·4′	1°6·1′E	X	133
Fox Ghyll	Cumbr	NY3605	54°26·4′	2°58·8′W	X	90
Fox Ghyll	Lancs	SD7849	53°56·4′	2°19·7′W	X	103
Fox Green	Derby	SK5273	53°15·3′	1°12·8′W	X	120
Fox Ground Down	Dorset	ST8603	50°49·8′	2°11·5′W	X	194
Fox Grove	Corn	SW6334	50°9·8′	5°18·7′W	F	203
Foxgrove	W Berks	SU4465	51°23·2′	1°21·7′W	X	174
Fox Hall	Ches	SJ5644	52°59·7′	2°38·9′W	X	117
Foxhall	C of Edin	NT1374	55°57·3′	3°23·2′W	X	65
Foxhall	Denb	SJ0367	53°11·7′	3°26·7′W	X	116
Fox Hall	Shrops	SJ3226	52°49·9′	3°0·2′W	X	126
Foxhall Fm	Bath & NE Somer	ST7168	51°24·9′	2°24·6′W	FM	172
Foxhall Fm	Essex	TL9301	51°40·7′	0°47·9′E	FM	168
Foxhall Fm	Lincs	TF2070	53°13·0′	0°11·8′W	FM	122
Foxhall Fm	N Yks	SE4588	54°17·4′	1°18·1′W	FM	99
Foxhall Hall	Suff	TM2243	52°2·7′	1°14·6′E	X	169
Foxhall Heath	Suff	TM2244	52°3·2′	1°14·7′E	X	169
Foxhall Newydd	Denb	SJ0267	53°11·7′	3°27·6′W	A	116
Foxhalls	Heref	SO6232	51°59·3′	2°32·8′W	X	149
Foxhall Wood	Lincs	TF1173	53°14·8′	0°19·8′W	F	121
Foxham	Wilts	ST9777	51°29·7′	2°2·2′W	T	173
Fox Hatch	Essex	TQ5798	51°39·8′	0°16·6′E	T	167,177
Fox Hill	Bath & NE Somer	ST7562	51°21·6′	2°21·2′W	T	172
Fox Hill	Cambs	TL3651	52°8·7′	0°0·3′W	X	154
Fox Hill	Cambs	TL4853	52°9·6′	0°10·2′E	X	154
Foxhill	Ches	SJ5075	53°16·4′	2°44·6′W	X	117
Fox Hill	Ches	SJ9876	53°17·1′	2°1·4′W	X	118
Fox Hill	Derby	SK4969	53°13·2′	1°15·6′W	X	120
Fox Hill	E Yorks	TA0761	54°2·3′	0°21·5′W	X	101
Fox Hill	Hants	SU3108	50°52·5′	1°33·2′W	X	196
Foxhill	Hants	SU5639	51°9·1′	1°11·6′W	X	185

Fox Hill	Heref	SO6845	52°6·4′	2°27·6′W	T	149
Fox Hill	Herts	TL3931	51°57·8′	0°1·8′E	X	166
Fox Hill	Lincs	TF2262	53°8·7′	0°10·1′W	X	122
Fox Hill	Moray	NJ0140	57°26·6′	3°38·5′W	X	27
Fox Hill	Newp	ST2588	51°35·4′	3°4·6′W	X	171
Fox Hill	Norf	TF6913	52°41·5′	0°30·4′E	X	132,143
Fox Hill	Norf	TG1142	52°56·3′	1°8·8′E	X	133
Fox Hill	Norf	TG3529	52°48·7′	1°29·6′E	X	133,134
Fox Hill	Northnts	SP5761	52°14·9′	1°9·5′W	X	152
Foxhill	Northnts	SP6270	52°19·7′	1°5·0′W	X	140
Fox Hill	Northum	NZ2279	55°6·5′	1°38·9′W	X	88
Fox Hill	Notts	SK5322	52°47·8′	1°12·4′W	X	129
Fox Hill	Notts	SK5327	52°50·5′	1°12·4′W	X	129
Fox Hill	Oxon	SP4721	51°53·4′	1°18·6′W	X	164
Fox Hill	Oxon	SP5230	51°58·2′	1°14·2′W	X	151
Foxhill	Pemb	SN1545	52°4·6′	4°41·6′W	X	145
Fox Hill	Stock on T	NZ3618	54°33·6′	1°26·2′W	X	93
Fox Hill	Surrey	SU9564	51°22·3′	0°37·7′W	X	175,176,186
Fox Hill	Surrey	TQ0358	51°18·9′	0°30·9′W	X	186
Fox Hill	Swin	SU2381	51°31·9′	1°39·7′W	H	174
Foxhill	Swin	SU2381	51°31·9′	1°39·7′W	X	174
Fox Hill	W Berks	SU3764	51°22·7′	1°27·7′W	X	174
Foxhill	W Susx	TQ0022	50°59·5′	0°34·1′W	X	197
Foxhill Fm	Devon	ST1011	50°53·7′	3°16·4′W	FM	192,193
Fox Hill Fm	Glos	SP1418	51°51·9′	1°47·4′W	FM	163
Foxhill Fm	Hants	SU3708	50°52·4′	1°28·1′W	FM	196
Foxhill Fm	Know	SJ4586	53°22·3′	2°49·2′W	FM	108
Foxhill Fm	Leic	SK5719	52°46·2′	1°8·9′W	FM	129
Foxhill Fm	Northnts	SP5549	52°8·4′	1°11·4′W	FM	152
Foxhill Fm	Northnts	SP7969	52°19·0′	0°50·1′W	FM	152
Foxhill Fm	N Yks	TA0877	54°10·9′	0°20·3′W	FM	101
Foxhill Fm	Oxon	SU7376	51°28·9′	0°56·5′W	FM	175
Fox Hill Ho	Birm	SP1498	52°35·0′	1°47·2′W	X	139
Foxhill Manor	Glos	SP1138	52°2·7′	1°50·0′W	X	150
Foxhills	Hants	SU3411	50°54·1′	1°30·6′W	T	196
Fox Hills	Norf	TG2538	52°53·8′	1°21·1′E	H	133
Fox Hills	Surrey	SU9152	51°15·8′	0°41·4′W	X	186
Fox Hills	Surrey	TQ0064	51°22·2′	0°33·4′W	X	176,186
Foxhills Park	N Lincs	SE8813	53°36·6′	0°39·8′W	X	112
Foxhills, The	Staffs	SO8892	52°31·8′	2°10·2′W	X	139
Fox Hill (Tumulus)	E Yorks	TA0761	54°2·3′	0°21·5′W	A	101
Fox Hill West	Surrey	SU9053	51°16·4′	0°42·2′W	X	186
Fox Ho	N Yks	SE8465	54°4·7′	0°42·5′W	X	100
Foxhold	W Berks	SU5163	51°22·1′	1°15·7′W	X	174
Foxhole	Carm	SN2914	51°48·2′	4°28·4′W	X	159
Foxhole	Corn	SW9654	50°21·3′	4°51·7′W	T	200
Foxhole	Corn	SX2596	50°44·5′	4°28·4′W	X	190
Foxhole	Devon	SX4196	50°44·7′	4°14·8′W	X	190
Foxhole	E Susx	TQ6531	51°3·5′	0°21·7′E	X	188
Foxhole	E Susx	TV5298	50°45·9′	0°9·7′E	X	199
Foxhole	Highld	NH5238	57°24·8′	4°27·4′W	X	26
Foxhole	Kent	TQ6542	51°9·4′	0°22·0′E	X	188
Foxhole	Kent	TQ7830	51°2·7′	0°32·8′E	X	188
Foxhole	Norf	TM2197	52°31·8′	1°15·9′E	T	134
Foxhole	Somer	ST2826	51°2·0′	3°1·2′W	X	193
Fox Hole	Swan	SS5587	51°34·0′	4°5·1′W	T	159
Foxhole Bank	Cumbr	SD4392	54°19·5′	2°52·2′W	X	97
Foxhole Barrow	Devon	SX4296	50°44·8′	4°14·0′W	A	190
Fox Hole Cave	Derby	SK0966	53°11·7′	1°51·5′W	X	119
Foxhole Copse	Northnts	SP6843	52°5·1′	1°0·1′W	F	152
Foxhole Cottages	W Susx	TQ2714	50°54·9′	0°11·2′W	X	198
Foxhole Fm	Derby	SK2048	53°2·0′	1°41·7′W	FM	119
Foxhole Fm	Derby	SK4440	52°57·6′	1°20·3′W	FM	129
Foxhole Fm	E Susx	TQ5124	51°0·0′	0°9·5′E	FM	199
Foxhole Fm	E Susx	TQ6223	50°59·2′	0°18·9′E	FM	199
Foxhole Fm	E Susx	TQ7117	50°55·8′	0°26·4′E	FM	199
Foxhole Heath	Suff	TL7377	52°22·0′	0°32·9′E	X	143
Fox Hole Hill	Cambs	TL3281	52°24·9′	0°3·1′W	X	142
Foxhole Point	Corn	SS1800	50°46·5′	4°34·5′W	X	190
Foxhole Pt	Swan	SS4193	51°37·0′	4°17·4′W	X	159
Fox Holes	Cambs	TL2260	52°13·7′	0°12·4′W	X	153
Fox Holes	Derby	SK1087	53°23·0′	1°50·6′W	X	110
Foxholes	Derby	SK3260	53°8·4′	1°30·9′W	X	119
Fox Holes	Durham	NZ4443	54°47·0′	1°18·5′W	X	88
Foxholes	Herts	TL1729	51°57·1′	0°17·5′W	X	166
Foxholes	Herts	TL3230	51°57·4′	0°4·3′W	X	166
Foxholes	Lancs	SD4952	53°57·9′	2°46·2′W	X	102
Fox Holes	Lancs	SD6962	54°3·4′	2°28·0′W	X	98
Foxholes	Northnts	SP5968	52°18·6′	1°7·7′W	X	152
Fox Holes	Notts	SK6660	53°8·2′	1°0·4′W	F	120
Foxholes	N Yks	TA0173	54°8·8′	0°26·8′W	T	101
Foxholes	Oxon	SP2520	51°52·9′	1°37·8′W	X	163
Foxholes	Shrops	SJ5031	52°52·7′	2°44·2′W	X	126
Foxholes	Staffs	SJ8153	53°4·7′	2°16·6′W	X	118
Foxholes	Staffs	SK1627	52°50·7′	1°45·3′W	X	128
Fox Holes	Wilts	ST8641	51°10·3′	2°11·6′W	T	183
Fox Holes Fm	Cambs	TL0976	52°22·5′	0°23·5′W	FM	142
Foxholes Fm	Dorset	SY5888	50°41·6′	2°35·3′W	FM	194
Foxholes Fm	Northnts	TL0478	52°23·6′	0°27·9′W	FM	141
Foxholes Fm	Notts	SK7860	53°8·1′	0°49·6′W	FM	120,121
Foxholes Fm	Wrex	SJ4842	52°58·6′	2°46·1′W	FM	117
Foxhole Slade	Swan	SS4385	51°32·8′	4°15·5′W	X	159
Foxholes Manor	N Yks	TA0073	54°8·8′	0°27·7′W	X	101
Fox Holes Spinney	Leic	SK6806	52°39·1′	0°59·3′W	F	141
Foxholes, The	Shrops	SO6480	52°25·2′	2°31·4′W	T	138
Fox Hollies	Birm	SP1494	52°32·9′	1°47·2′W	X	139
Foxholme	E Yorks	TA0937	53°49·3′	0°20·2′W	X	107
Foxholt	Kent	TR2142	51°8·3′	1°9·9′E	X	179,189
Fox House Fm	Cumbr	NY0633	54°41·2′	3°27·1′W	FM	89
Fox House Inn	Sheff	SK2680	53°19·2′	1°36·2′W	X	110
Foxhouses	Lancs	SD5151	53°57·4′	2°44·4′W	X	102
Fox Howe	N Yks	SE9090	54°18·1′	0°36·6′W	A	94,101
Fox Howl	Ches	SJ5271	53°14·3′	2°42·7′W	X	117
Foxhunt Green	E Susx	TQ5418	50°56·7′	0°11·9′E	T	199
Foxhunting Inclosure	Hants	SU3804	50°50·3′	1°27·2′W	F	196
Fox Lane	Hants	SU8557	51°18·6′	0°46·4′W	T	175,186
Foxlane Fm	Derby	SK2976	53°17·0′	1°33·5′W	FM	119
Foxlease	Hants	SU2907	50°51·9′	1°34·9′W	X	196
Foxley	Heref	SO4146	52°6·8′	2°51·3′W	T	148,149
Foxley	Norf	TG0321	52°45·1′	1°0·9′E	T	133

Foxley	Northnts	SP6451	52°9·4′	1°3·5′W	X	152
Foxley	Staffs	SJ7953	53°4·7′	2°18·4′W	T	118
Foxley	Staffs	SJ8033	52°53·9′	2°17·4′W	X	127
Foxley	Wilts	ST8985	51°34·1′	2°9·1′W	T	173
Foxley Brow Fm	Ches	SJ6479	53°18·6′	2°32·0′W	FM	118
Foxley Corner	Wilts	SU0557	51°19·0′	1°55·3′W	X	173
Foxley Fm	Ches	SJ7753	53°4·7′	2°20·2′W	FM	118
Foxley Fm	Oxon	SP4108	51°46·4′	1°24·0′W	FM	164
Foxley Fm	Warw	SP4868	52°18·7′	1°17·4′W	FM	151
Foxley Fm	Worcs	SO7070	52°19·9′	2°26·0′W	FM	138
Foxley Green	Wilts	ST8985	51°34·1′	2°9·1′W	X	173
Foxley Green Fm	Win & Maid	SU8777	51°29·3′	0°44·4′W	FM	175
Foxley Grove	Wilts	ST8986	51°34·6′	2°9·1′W	F	173
Foxley Henning	Cumbr	NY3744	54°47·5′	2°58·4′W	X	85
Foxley Wood	Norf	TG0522	52°45·6′	1°2·7′E	F	133
Foxlow Fm	Derby	SK0671	53°14·4′	1°54·2′W	FM	119
Foxlydiate	Worcs	SP0167	52°18·3′	1°58·7′W	T	150
Foxon's Corner	Warw	SP4583	52°26·8′	1°19·9′W	X	140
Foxpark	Corn	SX0763	50°26·3′	4°42·7′W	X	200
Fox Park Fm	N Yks	SE2289	54°18·0′	1°39·3′W	FM	99
Fox Pin	Suff	TL8777	52°21·8′	0°45·2′E	F	144
Fox Pitt	Kent	TQ7151	51°14·2′	0°27·4′E	X	188
Fox Plantation	D & G	NX1156	54°52·0′	4°56·3′W	F	82
Fox Plantn	Norf	TF7404	52°36·6′	0°34·6′E	F	143
Fox Plantn	N Yks	SE8465	54°4·7′	0°42·5′W	F	100
Foxpound	Dorset	SY8197	50°46·6′	2°15·8′W	F	194
Fox Royd	Kirk	SE2318	53°39·7′	1°38·7′W	T	110
Foxrush Fm	Red & Cl	NZ5823	54°36·2′	1°5·7′W	FM	93
Fox's Bridge Fm	Cambs	TL3855	52°10·8′	0°1·5′E	FM	154
Fox's Cross	Devon	SS8906	50°50·8′	3°34·2′W	X	192
Fox's Cross	Kent	TR0963	51°19·9′	1°0·4′E	X	179
Fox's Path	Gwyn	SH7113	52°42·2′	3°54·2′W	X	124
Fox's Piece	Derby	SK1692	53°25·7′	1°45·1′W	X	110
Fox Spinney	Suff	TL9069	52°17·4′	0°47·6′E	F	155
Fox's Pulpit	Cumbr	SD6193	54°20·1′	2°35·6′W	X	97
Foxstone Dam	Derby	SK4277	53°17·5′	1°21·8′W	W	120
Fox Street	Essex	TM0227	51°54·5′	0°56·6′E	T	168
Foxt	Staffs	SK0348	53°2·0′	1°56·9′W	T	119
Foxton	Cambs	TL4148	52°7·0′	0°4·0′E	T	154
Foxton	Durham	NZ3624	54°36·8′	1°26·1′W	T	93
Foxton	Fife	NO3916	56°20·2′	2°58·8′W	X	59
Foxton	Leic	SP7089	52°29·9′	0°57·7′W	T	141
Foxton	N Yks	SE4296	54°21·7′	1°20·8′W	T	99
Foxton Burn	Northum	NT9705	55°20·6′	2°2·4′W	W	81
Foxton Hall	Northum	NU2511	55°23·8′	1°35·9′W	X	81
Foxton Wood	Durham	NZ3525	54°37·4′	1°27·1′W	X	93
Foxton Wood	N Yks	SE4196	54°21·7′	1°21·7′W	F	99
Fox Tor	Corn	SX2278	50°34·7′	4°30·5′W	H	201
Fox Tor	Devon	SX6269	50°30·5′	3°56·4′W	X	202
Foxtor Mires	Devon	SX6170	50°31·0′	3°57·3′W	W	202
Fox Tower	Cumbr	NY7816	54°32·6′	2°20·0′W	X	91
Foxtwitchen	Somer	SS8436	51°6·9′	3°39·1′W	X	181
Foxup	N Yks	SD8676	54°11·0′	2°12·5′W	T	98
Foxup Beck	N Yks	SD8676	54°11·0′	2°12·5′W	W	98
Foxup Moor	N Yks	SD8476	54°11·0′	2°14·3′W	X	98
Foxwalks Fm	Worcs	SO9369	52°19·4′	2°5·8′W	FM	139
Foxwarren Park	Surrey	TQ0760	51°20·0′	0°27·5′W	X	176,187
Fox Well	N Yks	NZ1409	54°28·8′	1°46·6′W	X	92
Foxwist Green	Ches	SJ6268	53°12·7′	2°33·7′W	T	118
Foxwold	Kent	TQ4653	51°15·7′	0°5·9′E	X	188
Fox Wood	Notts	SK6148	53°1·8′	1°5·0′W	F	129
Foxwood	Shrops	SO6276	52°23·1′	2°33·1′W	T	138
Foxwood Fm	Ches	SJ7972	53°14·9′	2°18·5′W	FM	118
Foxwood Ho	Notts	SK6248	53°1·8′	1°4·1′W	X	129
Foxworthy	Devon	SX7582	50°37·7′	3°45·7′W	X	191
Foy	Heref	SO5928	51°57·2′	2°35·4′W	T	149
Foyce	Powys	SO2255	52°11·5′	3°8·1′W	X	148
Foyers	Hants	SU3111	50°54·1′	1°33·2′W	X	196
Foyers	Highld	NH4920	57°15·0′	4°29·7′W	T	26
Foyers Bay	Highld	NH4921	57°15·5′	4°29·7′W	W	26
Foyers Hotel	Highld	NH5021	57°15·6′	4°28·8′W	X	26,35
Foyle Fm	Surrey	TQ4049	51°13·6′	0°0·7′E	FM	187
Foyle Riding	Surrey	TQ4049	51°13·6′	0°0·7′E	F	187
Foynesfield	Highld	NH8953	57°33·5′	3°50·8′W	X	27
Foys	Dorset	ST6007	50°51·9′	2°33·7′W	X	194
Fozy Moss	Northum	NY8271	55°2·2′	2°16·5′W	X	86,87
Frachadil	Arg & Bt	NM3851	56°39·3′	6°15·6′W	X	47
Frackersaig	Arg & Bt	NM8240	56°30·4′	5°32·1′W	X	49
Fraddam	Corn	SW5934	50°9·7′	5°22·1′W	T	203
Fraddon	Corn	SW9158	50°23·3′	4°56·0′W	T	200
Fradley	Staffs	SK1613	52°43·1′	1°45·4′W	T	128
Fradley Junction	Staffs	SK1314	52°43·6′	1°48·0′W	T	128
Fradley Wood	Staffs	SK1313	52°43·1′	1°48·0′W	F	128
Fradswell	Staffs	SJ9931	52°52·8′	2°0·5′W	T	127
Fradswell Heath	Staffs	SK0032	52°53·4′	1°59·6′W	X	128
Fragbarrow Fm	W Susx	TQ3217	50°56·5′	0°6·9′W	FM	198
Frainslake Sands	Pemb	SR8897	51°38·2′	5°3·4′W	X	158
Frairdykes Dod	Scot Bord	NT6668	55°54·5′	2°32·2′W	F	67
Fraisthorpe	E Yorks	TA1561	54°2·2′	0°14·2′W	T	101
Fraisthorpe Sands	E Yorks	TA1762	54°2·7′	0°12·4′W	X	101
Framd, The	Shetld	HP6118	60°50·7′	0°52·2′W	X	1
Framedrum	Angus	NO5553	56°40·3′	2°43·6′W	X	54
Frame Fm	Essex	TL8620	51°51·1′	0°42·4′E	FM	168
Frame Fm	Essex	TL9111	51°46·1′	0°46·5′E	FM	168
Frame Heath Inclosure	Hants	SU3403	50°49·8′	1°30·6′W	F	196
Frame Wood	Bucks	SU9884	51°33·0′	0°34·8′W	F	175,176
Frame Wood	Hants	SU3503	50°49·8′	1°29·8′W	F	196
Framfield	E Susx	TQ4920	50°57·8′	0°7·7′E	T	199
Framfield Place	E Susx	TQ4920	50°57·8′	0°7·7′E	X	199
Framgord	Shetld	HP6103	60°42·6′	0°52·4′W	X	1
Framhill	Northum	NU1101	55°18·4′	1°49·2′W	X	81
Framilode	Glos	SO7410	51°47·5′	2°22·2′W	T	162
Framingham Earl	Norf	TG2702	52°34·3′	1°21·4′E	T	134
Framingham Pigot	Norf	TG2703	52°34·9′	1°21·4′E	T	134
Framland Fm	Leic	SK7521	52°47·1′	0°52·9′W	FM	129
Framlingham	Suff	TM2863	52°13·3′	1°20·7′E	T	156
Framlington Gate	Northum	NU1103	55°19·5′	1°49·2′W	X	81
Framlington Villa	Northum	NU1200	55°17·9′	1°48·2′W	X	81
Frampton	Dorset	SY6295	50°45·4′	2°31·9′W	T	194
Frampton	Lincs	TF3239	52°56·2′	0°1·7′W	T	131

Frampton Cotterell	S Glos	ST6681	51°31·8′	2°29·0′W	T	172
Frampton Court	Glos	SO7507	51°45·9′	2°21·3′W	X	162
Frampton Court	Glos	SP0132	51°59·4′	1°58·7′W	X	150
Frampton End	S Glos	ST6781	51°31·9′	2°28·2′W	T	172
Frampton Fm	Glos	SP0133	52°0·0′	1°58·7′W	FM	150
Frampton Ho	Dorset	SY6294	50°44·9′	2°31·9′W	X	194
Frampton Ho	Lincs	TF3039	52°56·2′	0°3·5′W	X	131
Frampton Mansell	Glos	SO9202	51°43·2′	2°6·6′W	T	163
Frampton Marsh	Lincs	TF3538	52°55·6′	0°0·9′E	X	131
Frampton On Severn	Glos	SO7407	51°45·9′	2°22·2′W	T	162
Frampton Sand	Glos	SO7005	51°44·8′	2°25·7′W	X	162
Frampton West End	Lincs	TF3041	52°57·3′	0°3·5′W	T	131
Framsden	Suff	TM2059	52°11·3′	1°13·5′E	T	156
Framside	Highld	ND0862	58°32·4′	3°34·3′W	X	11,12
Framwellgate Moor	Durham	NZ2644	54°47·7′	1°35·3′W	T	88
France	Devon	SS3200	50°46·8′	4°22·6′W	X	190
France	Shrops	SO5378	52°24·1′	2°41·1′W	X	137,138
France	W Dunb	NS4286	56°2·7′	4°31·8′W	X	56
France Down	Dorset	ST8709	50°53·1′	2°10·7′W	X	194
France Firs	Dorset	ST8809	50°53·1′	2°9·9′W	F	194
France Fm	Devon	ST0808	50°52·1′	3°18·1′W	FM	192
France Fm	Surrey	TQ0165	51°22·7′	0°32·5′W	FM	176
France Hill	Devon	SX7090	50°41·9′	3°50·1′W	X	191
France Lynch	Glos	SO9003	51°43·8′	2°8·3′W	T	163
Frances Craig	E Loth	NT6381	56°1·5′	2°35·2′W	X	67
Francesfield	Pth & Kin	NN9629	56°26·8′	3°40·8′W	X	52,53,58
Frances Green	Lancs	SD6236	53°49·4′	2°34·2′W	X	102,103
France Wood	Devon	SX8143	50°16·7′	3°39·8′W	F	202
Franche	Worcs	SO8278	52°24·2′	2°15·5′W	T	138
Franchise	E Susx	TQ6625	51°0·2′	0°22·4′E	X	188,199
Franchise Stone	Heref	SO5338	52°2·5′	2°40·7′W	X	149
Franchises Wood	Wilts	SU2316	50°56·8′	1°40·0′W	F	184
Francil	Roch	SD8710	53°35·4′	2°11·4′W	X	109
Francis Court Fm	Devon	SX9799	50°47·1′	3°27·3′W	FM	192
Francis Fm	Devon	SS5344	51°10·8′	4°5·8′W	FM	180
Francis Fm	Suff	TL8153	52°9·0′	0°39·1′E	FM	155
Francismoor Wood	Cumbr	NY4067	54°59·9′	2°55·8′W	F	85
Francis Wood	Suff	TL7956	52°10·6′	0°37·5′E	F	155
Francombe Wood	Glos	SO9505	51°44·9′	2°4·0′W	F	163
Franderground Fm	Notts	SK4756	53°6·2′	1°17·5′W	FM	120
Frandley	Ches	SJ6379	53°18·6′	2°32·9′W	T	118
Frandley Ho	Ches	SJ6478	53°18·1′	2°32·0′W	X	118
Frandy Burn	Pth & Kin	NN9303	56°12·7′	3°43·1′W	W	58
Frandy Fm	Pth & Kin	NN9404	56°13·3′	3°42·1′W	FM	58
Frangbury	Kent	TQ9356	51°16·4′	0°46·4′E	X	178
Frankaborough	Devon	SX3991	50°42·0′	4°16·4′W	X	190
Frankby	Wirral	SJ2486	53°22·2′	3°8·1′W	T	108
Frank Cliff	N Yks	TA0685	54°15·2′	0°22·0′W	X	101
Frankenbury	Hants	SU1615	50°56·3′	1°46·0′W	A	184
Franker Brook	Derby	SK3047	53°1·4′	1°32·8′W	W	119,128
Frankfield	Kent	TQ5755	51°16·6′	0°15·4′E	X	188
Frank Fm	Flint	SJ2659	53°7·6′	3°6·0′W	FM	117
Frankford	Devon	SX8295	50°44·8′	3°40·0′W	X	191
Frankfort	Norf	TG3024	52°46·1′	1°25·0′E	T	133,134
Frankham	E Susx	TQ5931	51°3·6′	0°16·5′E	X	188
Frankham	Northum	NY8868	55°1·2′	2°10·8′W	X	87
Frankham Fell	Northum	NY8869	55°1·2′	2°10·8′W	X	87
Frankham Fm	Dorset	ST5711	50°54·0′	2°36·3′W	FM	194
Frankham Wood	E Susx	TQ5831	51°3·6′	0°15·7′E	F	188
Frankhill Fm	Devon	SS8219	50°57·7′	3°40·4′W	FM	181
Frankland	Devon	SS6302	50°48·3′	3°56·3′W	X	191
Frankland	Devon	SX8097	50°45·8′	3°41·7′W	X	191
Frankland Fm	Durham	NZ2844	54°47·7′	1°33·4′W	FM	88
Franklands Fm	Devon	SX8381	50°37·3′	3°38·9′W	FM	191
Frankland's Fm	N Yks	NZ7810	54°29·0′	0°47·3′W	FM	94
Franklands Gate	Heref	SO5346	52°6·9′	2°40·8′W	T	149
Frankleigh Fm	Wilts	ST8262	51°21·6′	2°15·1′W	FM	173
Frankley	Birm	SO9978	52°24·2′	2°0·5′W	T	139
Frankley	Worcs	SO9980	52°25·3′	2°0·5′W	T	139
Frankley Beeches	Worcs	SO9979	52°24·8′	2°0·5′W	F	139
Frankley Green	Worcs	SO9980	52°25·3′	2°0·5′W	T	139
Frankley Hill	Worcs	SO9879	52°24·8′	2°1·4′W	T	139
Frankley Lodge Fm	Worcs	SP0079	52°24·8′	1°59·6′W	FM	139
Frankley Resr	Birm	SP0080	52°25·3′	1°59·6′W	W	139
Frankley Service Area	Dudley	SO9881	52°25·9′	2°1·4′W	X	139
Franklin Fm	Hants	SU5720	50°58·8′	1°10·9′W	FM	185
Franklins Fm	Essex	TL4910	51°46·4′	0°10·0′E	FM	167
Franklin's Fm	Surrey	TQ0443	51°10·8′	0°30·3′W	FM	186
Franklin's Fm	Wilts	SU0457	51°19·0′	1°56·2′W	FM	173
Frank Lockwood's Island	Arg & Bt	NM6219	56°18·5′	5°50·4′W	X	49
Franklyden	Pth & Kin	NO2029	56°27·0′	3°17·4′W	X	53,58
Franks	Kent	TQ5567	51°23·1′	0°14·0′E	A	177
Frank's Bridge	Powys	SO1155	52°11·4′	3°17·7′W	T	148
Frank's Fm	Cambs	TL4499	52°34·4′	0°7·9′E	FM	142,143
Franks Fm	Hav	TQ5887	51°33·8′	0°17·2′E	FM	177
Franks Fm	Warr	SJ6794	53°26·7′	2°29·4′W	FM	109
Franks Hall	Kent	TQ5567	51°23·1′	0°14·0′E	A	177
Frank's Point	Pemb	SM7304	51°41·6′	5°16·7′W	X	157
Frankstown Fm	Cumbr	NY3572	55°2·5′	3°0·6′W	FM	85
Frankton	Warw	SP4270	52°19·8′	1°22·6′W	T	140
Frankton Grounds	Warw	SP4169	52°19·3′	1°23·5′W	X	151
Frankwell	Shrops	SJ4813	52°43·0′	2°45·8′W	T	126
Franpton	V of Glam	SS9770	51°25·4′	3°28·5′W	X	170
Frans Green	Norf	TG1014	52°41·2′	1°6·8′E	T	133
Fransgreen Fm	Norf	TG0913	52°40·7′	1°5·9′E	FM	133
Frant	E Susx	TQ5935	51°5·8′	0°16·6′E	T	188
Frant Place	E Susx	TQ5934	51°5·2′	0°16·6′E	X	188
Frant Sta	E Susx	TQ6036	51°6·3′	0°17·5′E	X	188
Fraochaidh	Highld	NN0251	56°36·8′	5°13·1′W	H	41
Fraoch-bheinn	Highld	NM8983	56°53·7′	5°27·4′W	H	40
Fraoch Bheinn	Highld	NM9894	56°59·8′	5°19·1′W	W	33,40
Fraoch Choire	Highld	NH0305	57°5·9′	5°14·7′W	X	33
Fraoch Choire	Highld	NH0525	57°16·7′	5°13·6′W	X	25,33
Fraoch-choire	Highld	NH0918	57°13·0′	5°9·3′W	X	33
Fraoch-choire	Highld	NH2029	57°19·2′	4°58·9′W	X	25
Fraoch-choire	Highld	NN5875	56°50·9′	4°19·2′W	X	42
Fraoch Eilean	Arg & Bt	NM7311	56°14·5′	5°39·4′W	X	55
Fraoch Eilean	Arg & Bt	NN1025	56°23·0′	5°4·2′W	X	50
Fraoch Eilean	Arg & Bt	NS3692	56°5·8′	4°37·7′W	X	56
Fraoch-eilean	Highld	NG7973	57°41·8′	5°42·1′W	X	19

Fraoch Eilean	Highld	NG8706	57°6·0′	5°30·5′W	X	33
Fraoch Eilean Mór	Highld	NG9491	57°51·9′	5°27·9′W	X	19
Fraoch Geal	Pth & Kin	NN9818	56°20·9′	3°38·6′W	X	58
Fraochlan	Highld	NC0518	58°6·7′	5°18·1′W	X	15
Fraoch Mór	Highld	NM9888	56°56·6′	5°18·8′W	X	40
Fraserburgh	Aberd	NJ9967	57°41·8′	2°0·5′W	T	30
Fraserburgh Bay	Aberd	NK0166	57°41·3′	1°58·5′W	W	30
Fraserford	D & G	NX8184	55°8·4′	3°51·6′W	X	78
Frating	Essex	TM0822	51°51·7′	1°1·6′E	T	168,169
Frating Abbey	Essex	TM1020	51°50·6′	1°3·3′E	X	168,169
Frating Green	Essex	TM0923	51°52·2′	1°2·6′E	T	168,169
Frating Lodge	Essex	TM0823	51°52·2′	1°1·7′E	X	168,169
Fratton	C of Port	SU6500	50°48·0′	1°4·3′W	T	196
Fraunch	Devon	SS4502	50°48·0′	4°11·6′W	X	190
Fraw Houll	Shetld	HU3872	60°26·1′	1°18·1′W	H	2,3
Frayes	Essex	TL5811	51°46·7′	0°17·8′E	X	167
Fraysland Fm	E Susx	TQ8514	50°54·0′	0°38·2′E	FM	199
Fray's River	Hill	TQ0582	51°31·9′	0°28·8′W	W	176
Freasley	Warw	SP2499	52°35·5′	1°38·3′W	T	139
Freathingcott Fm	Devon	ST0620	50°58·5′	3°20·0′W	FM	181
Freathy	Corn	SX3952	50°21·0′	4°15·4′W	T	201
Frecheville	Sheff	SK3983	53°20·8′	1°24·4′W	T	110,111
Freckenham	Suff	TL6672	52°19·5′	0°26·6′E	T	154
Freckleton	Lancs	SD4228	53°45·0′	2°52·4′W	T	102
Fredden Hill	Northum	NT9526	55°31·9′	2°4·3′W	H	74,75
Fredley	Surrey	TQ1652	51°15·5′	0°19·9′W	T	187
Fredville Park	Kent	TR2551	51°13·0′	1°13·7′E	X	179
Fred Woolley Ho (Hospl)	Hants	SU4217	50°57·3′	1°23·7′W	X	185
Freebirch	Derby	SK3072	53°14·9′	1°32·6′W	T	119
Freebrough Hill	Red & Cl	NZ6812	54°30·2′	0°56·6′W	H	94
Freeby	Leic	SK8020	52°46·5′	0°48·4′W	T	130
Freeby Lodge	Leic	SK8021	52°47·1′	0°48·4′W	X	130
Freeby View Fm	Leic	SK7923	52°48·2′	0°49·3′W	FM	129
Freeby Wood	Leic	SK8022	52°47·6′	0°48·4′W	F	130
Free Chase	W Susx	TQ2325	51°0·9′	0°14·4′W	X	187,198
Freecroft Wood	Suff	TL9359	52°11·9′	0°49·9′E	F	155
Freedom	Shetld	HU4581	60°30·9′	1°10·3′W	X	1,2,3
Free Down	Dorset	ST8811	50°54·1′	2°9·9′W	X	194
Free Down	Kent	TR3646	51°10·1′	1°22·9′E	X	179
Freedown	Swan	SS4991	51°36·1′	4°10·4′W	X	159
Freefield	Shetld	HU3633	60°5·1′	1°20·7′W	X	4
Freefield Ho	Aberd	NJ6731	57°22·4′	2°32·5′W	X	29
Freefolk	Hants	SU4848	51°14·0′	1°18·4′W	T	185
Freefolk Wood	Hants	SU4944	51°11·8′	1°17·5′W	F	185
Freeford Manor	Staffs	SK1307	52°39·9′	1°48·1′W	X	139
Freegreen Fm	Ches	SJ7574	53°16·0′	2°22·1′W	FM	118
Freegrove Fm	Wilts	SU0277	51°29·7′	1°57·9′W	FM	173
Freehay	Staffs	SK0241	52°58·2′	1°57·8′W	T	119,128
Free Heath	Kent	TQ6534	51°5·1′	0°21·7′E	X	188
Freehold Fm	W Susx	SU9628	51°2·8′	0°37·4′W	FM	186,197
Freeholds Top	Cald	SD9021	53°41·4′	2°8·7′W	H	103
Freeland	Fife	NO1810	56°16·8′	3°19·0′W	X	58
Freeland	Oxon	SP4112	51°48·1′	1°23·9′W	T	164
Freeland	Renf	NS4669	55°53·6′	4°27·3′W	T	64
Freeland Corner	Norf	TG1616	52°42·1′	1°12·2′E	T	133
Freeland Fm	Pth & Kin	NO1018	56°21·0′	3°26·9′W	FM	58
Freelands	Angus	NO5951	56°39·2′	2°39·7′W	X	54
Freelands	Cumbr	NY4764	54°58·3′	2°49·3′W	X	86
Freelands	Northum	NU1912	55°24·3′	1°41·6′W	T	81
Freeman Channel		TF4943	52°58·0′	0°13·5′E	W	131
Freemans Fm	Essex	TL5102	51°42·0′	0°11·5′E	FM	167
Freemans Fm	N Som	ST5166	51°23·7′	2°41·9′W	FM	172,182
Freeman's Gorse	Notts	SK7487	53°22·7′	0°52·8′W	F	112,120
Freemans Hill	Northum	NU1508	55°22·2′	1°45·4′W	X	81
Freeman's Well	Northum	NU1508	55°22·2′	1°45·4′W	X	81
Freemantle	C of Soton	SU4012	50°54·6′	1°25·5′W	T	196
Freemantle Fm	Hants	SU5453	51°16·6′	1°13·2′W	FM	185
Freemantle Park Fm	Hants	SU5256	51°18·3′	1°14·9′W	FM	174
Freemantles Copse	Hants	SU4523	51°0·5′	1°21·1′W	F	185
Freemen's Gap	Northum	NU1613	55°24·9′	1°44·4′W	X	81
Freen's Court	Heref	SO5145	52°6·3′	2°42·5′W	A	149
Freens Court Fm	Heref	SO5245	52°6·3′	2°41·7′W	FM	149
Freeport Village	W Loth	NT0063	55°51·2′	3°35·4′W	T	65
Free Roberts	Essex	TL6436	52°0·1′	0°23·7′E	X	154
Freester	Shetld	HU4553	60°15·8′	1°10·7′W	T	3
Freestone Hall	Pemb	SN0505	51°42·8′	4°49·0′W	X	158
Freestones Lodge	Northnts	SP9572	52°20·5′	0°35·9′W	X	141
Freeth Fm	Wilts	SU0272	51°27·1′	1°57·9′W	FM	173
Freethorpe	Norf	TG4105	52°35·6′	1°33·9′E	T	134
Free Town	Bury	SD8111	53°36·0′	2°16·8′W	T	109
Free Town	Heref	SO6242	52°4·7′	2°32·9′W	X	149
Freevater Forest	Highld	NH3488	57°51·3′	4°47·4′W	X	20
Freewarren Fm	Wilts	SU2561	51°21·1′	1°38·1′W	FM	174
Freewater	Corn	SW9046	50°16·8′	4°56·5′W	X	204
Free Wood	Suff	TL9260	52°12·5′	0°49·0′E	F	155
Freewood Fm	Essex	TL4739	52°2·0′	0°9·0′E	FM	154
Freeze Gill Fm	N Yks	SE9290	54°18·1′	0°34·8′W	FM	94,101
Freezeland Fm	E Susx	TQ7210	50°52·1′	0°27·1′E	FM	199
Freezeland Fm	Wigan	SD6109	53°34·8′	2°34·9′W	FM	109
Freezeland Lodge	Leic	SK7109	52°40·7′	0°56·6′W	X	141
Freezen Hill	Norf	TM0880	52°22·9′	1°3·8′E	X	144
Freezing Hill	S Glos	ST7271	51°26·5′	2°23·8′W	H	172
Freezland	Flint	SJ2260	53°8·1′	3°9·6′W	X	117
Freezy Water	Enf	TQ3699	51°40·6′	0°1·6′W	T	166,177
Freisgill	Highld	NC4965	58°33·1′	4°35·2′W	X	9
Freiston	Lincs	TF3744	52°58·8′	0°2·8′E	T	131
Freiston Br	Lincs	TF3644	52°58·8′	0°1·9′E	X	131
Freiston Low	Lincs	TF4041	52°57·1′	0°5·4′E	X	131
Freiston Shore	Lincs	TF3942	52°57·7′	0°4·6′E	T	131
Freith Fm	Wilts	ST9956	51°18·4′	2°0·5′W	FM	173
Fremington	Cumbr	NY5428	54°38·9′	2°42·4′W	X	90
Fremington	Devon	SS5132	51°4·3′	4°7·2′W	T	180
Fremington	N Yks	SE0499	54°23·4′	1°55·9′W	T	98
Fremington Edge	N Yks	NZ0400	54°24·0′	1°55·9′W	X	92
Fremington Edge	N Yks	SE0599	54°23·4′	1°55·0′W	X	98
Frenchay	S Glos	ST6477	51°29·7′	2°30·7′W	T	172
Frenchay Fm	Kent	TQ9132	51°3·6′	0°43·9′E	FM	189
Frenchbeer	Devon	SX6785	50°39·2′	3°52·5′W	T	191
French Court Fm	E Susx	TQ8614	50°54·0′	0°39·1′E	FM	199
Frenches Close	Ghead	NZ1162	54°57·4′	1°49·3′W	X	88

Frenches Fm	Hants	SU3851	51°15·6′	1°26·9′W	FM	185
Frenches Green	Essex	TL7020	51°51·4′	0°28·5′E	T	167
Frenchfield Fm	Cumbr	NY5329	54°39·5′	2°43·3′W	FM	90
French Fm	Peterb	TF2808	52°39·5′	0°6·0′W	FM	142
French Hill Wood	N Yks	SE4791	54°19·0′	1°16·2′W	X	100
Frenchland	D & G	NT0905	55°20·1′	3°25·6′W	X	78
Frenchland Burn	D & G	NT1005	55°20·1′	3°24·7′W	W	78
Frenchman's Bay	Pemb	SM7903	51°41·2′	5°11·5′W	W	157
Frenchman's Bay	S Tyne	NZ3966	54°59·5′	1°23·0′W	W	88
Frenchman's Pill	Corn	SW7525	50°5·2′	5°8·4′W	X	204
Frenchman's Rock	D & G	NX6646	54°47·7′	4°4·6′W	X	83,84
Frenchman's Rocks	Arg & Bt	NR1554	55°42·0′	6°31·7′W	X	60
Frenchman, The	Corn	SW5329	50°6·8′	5°26·9′W	X	203
French Mill	I of W	SZ5481	50°37·8′	1°13·8′W	X	196
Frenchmoor	Hants	SU2628	51°3·3′	1°37·4′W	T	184
French's Fm	Norf	TM1989	52°27·5′	1°13·8′E	FM	156
French's Fm	Suff	TM0442	52°2·6′	0°58·9′E	FM	155
Frenchstone	Devon	SS7123	50°59·8′	3°49·9′W	X	180
French Street	Kent	TQ4552	51°15·1′	0°5·1′E	T	188
Frenchton	Pth & Kin	NN9529	56°26·7′	3°41·8′W	X	52,53,58
Frenchwood	Lancs	SD5428	53°45·0′	2°41·4′W	T	102
Frendraught Ho	Aberd	NJ6141	57°27·7′	2°38·5′W	X	29
Frenich	Pth & Kin	NN8258	56°42·2′	3°55·2′W	X	52
Frenich	Stir	NN4106	56°13·5′	4°33·4′W	X	56
Frenich Burn	Pth & Kin	NN8257	56°41·6′	3°55·2′W	W	52
Frenich Wood	Pth & Kin	NN8158	56°42·2′	3°56·2′W	F	52
Freni Fawr	Pemb	SN2035	51°59·3′	4°36·9′W	H	145
Frenni Fach	Pemb	SN2234	51°58·8′	4°35·1′W	X	145
Frensham	Surrey	SU8441	51°10·0′	0°47·5′W	T	186
Frensham Common	Surrey	SU8540	51°9·4′	0°46·7′W	X	186
Frensham Great Pond	Surrey	SU8440	51°9·4′	0°47·5′W	W	186
Frensham Heights	Surrey	SU8342	51°10·5′	0°48·4′W	X	186
Frensham Little Pond	Surrey	SU8541	51°9·9′	0°46·7′W	W	186
Frensham Manor	Surrey	SU8340	51°9·4′	0°48·4′W	A	186
Frenze	Norf	TM1380	52°22·8′	1°8·2′E	T	144,156
Frere Hill Wood	Northnts	SP9892	52°31·3′	0°32·9′W	F	141
Fresden Fm	Swin	SU2292	51°37·8′	1°40·5′W	FM	163,174
Fresden Village	Swin	SU2291	51°37·3′	1°40·5′W	A	163,174
Fresgoe	Highld	NC9566	58°34·4′	3°47·8′W	X	11
Freshbrook	Swin	SU1183	51°33·0′	1°50·1′W	T	173
Freshcombe Fm	W Susx	TQ2210	50°52·8′	0°15·6′W	FM	198
Freshfield	Sefton	SD2908	53°34·1′	3°3·9′W	T	108
Freshfield Crossways	W Susx	TQ3825	51°0·7′	0°1·6′W	X	187,198
Freshford	Bath & NE	ST7860	51°20·6′	2°18·6′W	T	172
Freshlands Fm	E Yorks	SE9155	53°59·2′	0°36·3′W	FM	106
Fresh Marshes	Norf	TG0444	52°57·5′	1°2·6′E	X	133
Fresh Moor	Somer	ST2812	50°54·4′	3°1·1′W	X	193
Freshwater	I of W	SZ3486	50°40·6′	1°30·7′W	T	196
Freshwater Bay	Dorset	SY6970	50°32·0′	2°25·9′W	W	194
Fresh Water Bay	I of Angl	SH4892	53°24·4′	4°16·8′W	W	114
Freshwater Bay	I of W	SZ3485	50°40·0′	1°30·7′W	T	196
Freshwater Bay	I of W	SZ3485	50°40·0′	1°30·7′W	W	196
Freshwater East	Pemb	SS0198	51°39·0′	4°52·2′W	T	158
Freshwater East	Pemb	SS0297	51°38·5′	4°51·3′W	W	158
Freshwater Way	I of W	SZ3487	50°41·1′	1°30·7′W	X	196
Fresh Water West	Pemb	SR8899	51°39·2′	5°3·5′W	W	158
Fressingfield	Suff	TM2677	52°20·9′	1°19·5′E	T	156
Freston	Suff	TM1639	52°0·7′	1°9·3′E	T	169
Freston Grove	Suff	TM1737	51°59·6′	1°10·0′E	X	169
Freston Lodge Fm	Suff	TM1639	52°0·7′	1°9·3′E	FM	169
Freston Park	Suff	TM1739	52°0·6′	1°10·1′E	X	169
Freston Reach	Suff	TM1740	52°1·2′	1°10·2′E	W	169
Freswick	Highld	ND3667	58°35·4′	3°5·6′W	T	12
Freswick Bay	Highld	ND3867	58°35·5′	3°3·5′W	W	12
Freswick Ho	Highld	ND3767	58°35·5′	3°4·5′W	X	12
Fretherne	Glos	SO7309	51°47·0′	2°23·1′W	T	162
Frettenham	Norf	TG2417	52°42·5′	1°19·4′E	T	133,134
Freuchan	Stir	NS5197	56°8·8′	4°23·5′W	X	57
Freuchie	Fife	NO2806	56°14·7′	3°9·3′W	T	59
Freuchies	Angus	NO2260	56°43·8′	3°16·0′W	T	44
Freyers	Shetld	HT9641	60°9·5′	2°3·8′W	X	4
Freystrop	Pemb	SM9511	51°45·9′	4°57·9′W	T	157,158
Friarage, The	Stock on T	NZ4212	54°30·3′	1°20·7′W	X	93
Friar Biggins	Cumbr	NY6309	54°28·7′	2°33·8′W	X	91
Friar Cote	Durham	NZ0810	54°29·4′	1°52·2′W	X	92
Friar Dike	N Yks	SE8680	54°12·7′	0°40·5′W	W	101
Friardykes	Scot Bord	NT6668	55°54·5′	2°32·2′W	X	67
Friar Edge	D & G	NY2687	55°10·6′	3°9·3′W	H	79
Friarfold Moor	N Yks	NY9402	54°25·0′	2°5·1′W	X	91,92
Friarfold Rake	N Yks	NY9502	54°25·0′	2°4·2′W	X	91,92
Friar Garth	N Yks	SD9062	54°3·5′	2°8·7′W	X	98
Friar Hill	Cumbr	NY4873	55°3·2′	2°48·4′W	X	86
Friar Hos	Durham	NY8928	54°39·1′	2°9·8′W	X	91,92
Friar Hos	Durham	NY9418	54°33·7′	2°5·1′W	X	91,92
Friarland	S Ayr	NS3719	55°26·5′	4°34·2′W	X	70
Friarminnan	D & G	NS7318	55°26·6′	4°0·0′W	X	71
Friarminnan Burn	D & G	NS7420	55°27·7′	3°59·1′W	W	71
Friarn	Somer	ST1738	51°8·4′	3°10·8′W	T	181
Friar Park	Sand	SP0094	52°32·9′	1°59·6′W	T	139
Friars	Essex	TL5314	51°48·4′	0°13·6′E	X	167
Friars	Herts	TL3132	51°58·5′	0°5·2′W	X	166
Friars	Kent	TQ6541	51°8·9′	0°21·9′E	X	188
Friars Ball Fm	Devon	SX8894	50°44·3′	3°34·9′W	FM	192
Friars' Bay	E Susx	TQ4200	50°47·2′	0°1·3′E	W	198
Friar's Bottom Fm	Cumbr	NY7105	54°26·2′	2°26·4′W	FM	91
Friars Carse	D & G	NX9284	55°8·6′	3°41·2′W	X	78
Friars Cliff	Dorset	SZ1992	50°43·9′	1°43·5′W	T	195
Friar's Court	Glos	SO6631	51°58·8′	2°29·3′W	X	149
Friar's Court	Oxon	SP2800	51°42·1′	1°35·3′W	X	163
Friar's Crag	Cumbr	NY2622	54°35·5′	3°8·3′W	X	89,90
Friarsdykes Dod	Scot Bord	NT6668	55°54·5′	2°32·2′W	X	67
Friar's Fm	Essex	TL6133	51°58·6′	0°21·0′E	FM	167
Friar's Fm	Essex	TL7419	51°50·8′	0°32·0′E	FM	167
Friar's Fm	Oxon	SP4006	51°45·3′	1°24·8′W	FM	164
Friar's Fm	Oxon	SU2290	51°36·7′	1°40·5′W	FM	163,174
Friar's Garth	N Yks	SE2794	54°20·7′	1°34·7′W	X	99
Friar's Gate	E Susx	TQ4933	51°4·8′	0°8·0′E	T	188
Friar's Grange	Essex	TL6014	51°48·3′	0°19·6′E	X	167
Friar's Ground	Cumbr	SD2482	54°13·9′	3°9·5′W	X	96
Friar's Grove	Heref	SO4851	52°9·5′	2°45·2′W	F	148,149

Friars Hall Fm	Suff	TM0142	52°2·6′	0°56·3′E	FM	155
Friarshaw	Scot Bord	NT5225	55°31·2′	2°45·2′W	X	73
Friarshawmuir	Scot Bord	NT5026	55°31·8′	2°47·1′W	X	73
Friars Hayes Fm	Wilts	ST8729	51°3·8′	2°10·7′W	FM	183
Friars Head	N Yks	SD9357	54°0·8′	2°6·0′W	X	103
Friars Hele	Devon	SS5306	50°50·3′	4°4·9′W	X	191
Friar's Hill	E Susx	TQ8513	50°53·4′	0°38·2′E	T	199
Friar's Hill	N Yks	SE7485	54°15·6′	0°51·4′W	X	94,100
Friars Hill	Swin	SU2190	51°36·7′	1°41·4′W	X	163,174
Friar's Hills	Bucks	SP9402	51°42·8′	0°38·0′W	X	165
Friar's Hurst	N Yks	SE2776	54°11·0′	1°34·8′W	X	99
Friarside	Durham	NZ0736	54°43·4′	1°53·1′W	X	92
Friars Ings	N Yks	SE1393	54°20·2′	1°47·6′W	X	99
Friars Moss	Lancs	SD5161	54°2·8′	2°44·5′W	X	97
Friars' Nose	E Loth	NT6662	55°51·3′	2°32·1′W	X	67
Friar's Nose	Scot Bord	NT5059	55°49·6′	2°47·4′W	X	66,73
Friars Point	V of Glam	ST1165	51°22·9′	3°16·3′W	X	171
Friar's Ridge	Derby	SK2583	53°20·8′	1°37·1′W	X	110
Friar's Stones	N Yks	SE0854	53°59·2′	1°52·3′W	X	104
Friars, The	Northum	NU1734	55°36·2′	1°43·4′W	X	75
Friar's Thorne Fm	Norf	TF7939	52°55·3′	0°40·2′E	FM	132
Friar's Wash	Herts	TL0815	51°49·6′	0°25·6′W	X	166
Friar's Well	Northnts	SP5133	51°59·8′	1°15·0′W	W	151
Friars Well	Northum	NU1716	55°26·5′	1°43·4′W	A	81
Friarton	Pth & Kin	NO1121	56°22·6′	3°26·0′W	T	53,58
Friarton	Pth & Kin	NO1430	56°27·5′	3°23·3′W	X	53
Friarton or Moncrieffe Island	Pth & Kin	NO1221	56°22·6′	3°25·1′W	X	53,58
Friar Waddon	Dorset	SY6485	50°40·0′	2°30·2′W	X	194
Friar Waddon Hill	Dorset	SY6485	50°40·0′	2°30·2′W	H	194
Friary Court	Kent	TQ6170	51°24·6′	0°19·3′E	A	177
Friary of St Francis, The	Dorset	ST6304	50°50·3′	2°31·1′W	X	194
Friary Park	Barnet	TQ2792	51°37·0′	0°9·5′W	X	176
Friary Wood	Bath & NE Somer	ST7858	51°19·5′	2°18·6′W	F	172
Fribo Ho	Orkney	HY4445	59°17·5′	2°58·5′W	X	5
Frickley Hall	Donc	SE4608	53°34·2′	1°17·9′W	X	111
Friday Bridge	Cambs	TF4604	52°37·1′	0°9·8′E	T	143
Fridayhill	Aberd	NJ9153	57°34·3′	2°8·6′W	X	30
Friday Hill	Wal F	TQ3993	51°37·3′	0°0·9′E	T	177
Fridays	Essex	TL6513	51°47·7′	0°24·0′E	X	167
Friday Street	Suff	TM2459	52°11·2′	1°17·0′E	X	156
Friday Street	Suff	TM3351	52°6·7′	1°24·6′E	T	156
Friday Street	Suff	TM3760	52°11·5′	1°28·5′E	T	156
Friday Street	Surrey	TQ1245	51°11·8′	0°23·4′W	T	187
Friday Street Fm	Wilts	ST9779	51°30·8′	2°2·2′W	FM	173
Fridaythorpe	E Yorks	SE8759	54°1·4′	0°39·9′W	T	106
Fridaythorpe Field	E Yorks	SE8759	54°1·4′	0°39·9′W	X	106
Fridaywood Fm	Essex	TL9821	51°51·4′	0°52·9′E	FM	168
Fridd Pwll-y-warthol	Powys	SH9303	52°37·1′	3°34·4′W	X	136
Fridd yr Ystrad	Powys	SN9198	52°34·4′	3°36·1′W	X	136
Friden	Derby	SK1660	53°8·5′	1°45·2′W	X	119
Frid Fm	Kent	TQ9341	51°8·4′	0°45·9′E	FM	189
Frid Wood	Kent	TQ8661	51°19·3′	0°40·6′E	F	178
Frienden Fm	Kent	TQ5041	51°9·1′	0°9·1′E	FM	188
Friendlesshead	E Ayr	NS5030	55°32·7′	4°22·2′W	X	70
Friendly	Cald	SE0524	53°43·0′	1°55·0′W	T	104
Friendly Lodge	Northnts	TL0273	52°21·0′	0°29·7′W	X	141,153
Friendship Fm	Devon	SS6541	51°9·4′	3°55·4′W	FM	180
Friern Barnet	Barnet	TQ2892	51°37·0′	0°8·7′W	T	176
Friern Hospital	Barnet	TQ2892	51°37·0′	0°8·7′W	X	176
Friern Manor	Essex	TQ6589	51°34·8′	0°23·3′E	X	177,178
Friesland	Arg & Bt	NM1853	56°35·3′	6°35·2′W	X	46
Friesland Bay	Arg & Bt	NM1853	56°35·3′	6°35·2′W	W	46
Friesland Fm	Cambs	TL3466	52°16·8′	0°1·7′W	FM	154
Friesland Fm	Suff	TL6382	52°24·9′	0°24·2′E	FM	143
Frieslands	W Susx	TQ1211	50°53·5′	0°24·1′W	X	198
Friesthorpe	Lincs	TF0783	53°20·2′	0°23·2′W	T	121
Frieston	Lincs	SK9347	53°1·0′	0°36·4′W	T	130
Frieston Heath Fm	Lincs	SK9747	53°0·9′	0°32·8′W	FM	130
Frieth	Bucks	SU7990	51°36·4′	0°51·2′W	T	175
Frieze Fm	Oxon	SP4911	51°48·0′	1°17·0′W	FM	164
Frieze Fm	Oxon	SU7279	51°30·5′	0°57·4′W	FM	175
Frieze Hall	Essex	TQ5595	51°38·2′	0°14·8′E	X	167,177
Frieze Hill	Somer	ST2125	51°1·4′	3°7·2′W	T	193
Friezeland	Notts	SK4750	53°2·9′	1°17·5′W	T	120
Friezeland Fm	Leic	SK3803	52°37·6′	1°25·9′W	FM	140
Friezingham Fm	Kent	TQ8630	51°2·6′	0°39·6′E	FM	189
Friezley	Kent	TQ7738	51°7·1′	0°32·1′E	X	188
Frigan	I of Angl	SH4883	53°19·6′	4°16·5′W	X	114,115
Frigate Unicorn	C of Dun	NO4030	56°27·8′	2°58·0′W	X	54
Frigidale	N Yks	NZ3204	54°26·1′	1°30·0′W	X	93
Frilford	Oxon	SU4397	51°40·4′	1°22·3′W	T	164
Frilford Heath	Oxon	SU4498	51°41·0′	1°21·4′W	T	164
Frillinghurst Wood	Surrey	SU9234	51°6·1′	0°40·8′W	F	186
Frilsham	W Berks	SU5473	51°27·4′	1°13·0′W	T	174
Frilsham Common	W Berks	SU5573	51°27·4′	1°12·1′W	F	174
Frilsham Park	W Berks	SU5573	51°27·4′	1°12·1′W	X	174
Frimley	Surrey	SU8858	51°19·1′	0°43·8′W	T	175,186
Frimley Green	Surrey	SU8856	51°18·0′	0°43·9′W	T	175,186
Frimley Ridge	Surrey	SU8959	51°19·6′	0°43·0′W	T	175,186
Frindsbury	Medway	TQ7469	51°23·8′	0°30·5′E	T	178
Fring	Norf	TF7334	52°52·8′	0°34·7′E	T	132
Fringford	Oxon	SP6028	51°57·1′	1°7·2′W	T	164,165
Fringford Hill	Oxon	SP6028	51°57·1′	1°7·2′W	X	164,165
Fringford Lodge	Oxon	SP5925	51°55·5′	1°8·1′W	X	164
Fringill	N Yks	SE2058	54°1·3′	1°41·3′W	X	104
Frinningham	Kent	TQ8158	51°17·8′	0°36·2′E	X	178,188
Frinkle Green	Essex	TL7040	52°2·2′	0°29·1′E	T	154
Frinkley Fm	Lincs	SK9143	52°58·8′	0°38·3′W	FM	130
Frinsted	Kent	TQ8957	51°17·1′	0°43·0′E	T	178
Frinton-On-Sea	Essex	TM2319	51°49·7′	1°14·6′E	T	169
Friockheim	Angus	NO5949	56°38·1′	2°39·7′W	T	54
Friock Mains	Angus	NO5849	56°38·1′	2°40·6′W	X	54
Friog	Gwyn	SH6112	52°41·5′	4°3·0′W	T	124
Friog	Gwyn	SH7324	52°48·2′	3°52·6′W	X	124
Frisby	Leic	SK7001	52°36·4′	0°57·6′W	T	141
Frisby Grange	Leic	SK6915	52°43·9′	0°58·3′W	X	129
Frisby Lodge Fm	Leic	SK7201	52°36·4′	0°55·8′W	FM	141
Frisby on the Wreake	Leic	SK6917	52°45·0′	0°58·3′W	T	129

Frisby Village	Leic	SK7001	52°36·4′	0°57·6′W	A	141
Friskney	Lincs	TF4655	53°4·6′	0°11·2′E	T	122
Friskney Eaudyke	Lincs	TF4755	53°4·5′	0°12·1′E	T	122
Friskney Fen	Lincs	TF4456	53°5·1′	0°9·4′E	X	122
Friskney Flats	Lincs	TF5051	53°2·3′	0°14·6′E	X	122
Friskney Low Ground	Lincs	TF4454	53°4·1′	0°9·4′E	X	122
Friskney Tofts	Lincs	TF4654	53°4·0′	0°11·2′E	X	122
Fristling Hall	Essex	TL6700	51°40·7′	0°25·3′E	X	167
Friston	E Susx	TV5598	50°45·9′	0°12·3′E	T	199
Friston	Suff	TM4160	52°11·4′	1°32·0′E	T	156
Friston Forest	E Susx	TV5499	50°46·4′	0°11·4′E	F	199
Friston Hill	E Susx	TV5499	50°46·4′	0°11·4′E	X	199
Friston Ho	Suff	TM4060	52°11·4′	1°31·1′E	X	156
Fristonmoor	Suff	TM4061	52°11·9′	1°31·1′E	X	156
Friston Place	E Susx	TV5498	50°45·9′	0°11·4′E	A	199
Fritchley	Derby	SK3553	53°4·6′	1°28·2′W	T	119
Frith	Kent	TQ9455	51°15·9′	0°47·2′E	T	178
Fritham	Hants	SU2314	50°55·7′	1°40·0′W	T	195
Fritham Cross	Hants	SU2310	50°53·6′	1°40·0′W	X	195
Fritham Ho	Hants	SU2414	50°55·7′	1°39·1′W	X	195
Fritham Lodge	Hants	SU2414	50°55·7′	1°39·1′W	X	195
Fritham Plain	Hants	SU2213	50°55·2′	1°40·8′W	X	195
Frith an Achaidh Mhoir	Highld	NH1429	57°19·1′	5°4·9′W	X	25
Frith Bank	Lincs	TF3147	53°0·5′	0°2·4′W	T	131
Frith Bottom	Staffs	SJ9961	53°9·0′	2°0·5′W	X	118
Frith Common	Worcs	SO6969	52°19·3′	2°26·9′W	T	138
Frith Common Fm	Hants	SU5459	51°19·9′	1°13·1′W	FM	174
Frith Copse	Hants	SU4861	51°21·0′	1°18·3′W	F	174
Frith Copse	Wilts	SU0785	51°34·1′	1°53·5′W	F	173
Frith Copse	Wilts	SU1359	51°20·0′	1°48·4′W	F	173
Frithelstock	Devon	SS4619	50°57·2′	4°11·2′W	T	180,190
Frithelstock Stone	Devon	SS4518	50°56·7′	4°12·0′W	T	180,190
Frithend	Hants	SU8039	51°8·9′	0°51·0′W	T	186
Frithend Ho	Hants	SU8039	51°8·9′	0°51·0′W	X	186
Frithfield	Fife	NO5507	56°15·5′	2°43·1′W	X	59
Frith Fm	Hants	SU5560	51°20·4′	1°12·2′W	FM	174
Frith Fm	Hants	SU5712	50°54·5′	1°11·0′W	FM	196
Frith Fm	Heref	SO7139	52°3·2′	2°25·0′W	FM	149
Frith Fm	Kent	TQ7332	51°3·9′	0°28·5′E	FM	188
Frith Fm	Kent	TR3243	51°8·6′	1°19·4′E	FM	179
Frith Fm	Rut	TF0111	52°41·5′	0°29·9′W	FM	130
Frith Fm	S Glos	ST7187	51°35·1′	2°24·7′W	FM	172
Frith Fm	Somer	ST7327	51°2·7′	2°22·7′W	FM	183
Frithfold Fm	W Susx	SU9828	51°2·8′	0°35·7′W	FM	186,197
Frithgate	Kent	TR0336	51°5·5′	0°54·3′E	X	179,189
Frith Hall	Cumbr	SD1891	54°18·7′	3°15·2′W	X	96
Frith Hall	Derby	SK3370	53°13·8′	1°29·9′W	X	119
Frith Head	Cambs	TL5085	52°26·8′	0°12·8′E	X	143
Frith-hill	Bucks	SP9001	51°42·3′	0°41·5′W	T	165
Frith Hill	Surrey	SU9058	51°19·1′	0°42·1′W	X	175,186
Frith Hill	Surrey	SU9744	51°11·4′	0°36·3′W	T	186
Frith Ho	Dorset	ST7017	50°57·3′	2°25·2′W	X	183
Frith Ho	Somer	ST8147	51°13·5′	2°15·9′W	FM	183
Frithknowle	W Susx	TQ2123	50°59·8′	0°16·2′W	X	198
Frith Manor	W Susx	TQ3839	51°8·2′	0°1·3′W	X	187
Frith Manor Fm	Barnet	TQ2492	51°37·0′	0°12·1′W	FM	176
Frith-Mhellan	Highld	NG9781	57°46·6′	5°24·4′W	X	19
Frith Park	Surrey	TQ2153	51°16·0′	0°15·5′W	X	187
Frithsden	Herts	TL0109	51°46·5′	0°31·8′W	T	166
Frithsden Beeches	Herts	SP9910	51°47·0′	0°33·5′W	F	165
Frith's Fm	Essex	TM1527	51°54·2′	1°7·9′E	FM	168,169
Frith's Fm	E Susx	TQ5314	50°54·5′	0°11·0′E	FM	199
Frith Sgeirean	Arg & Bt	NR3487	56°0·4′	6°15·6′W	X	61
Frith, The	Derby	SK0569	53°13·3′	1°55·1′W	X	119
Frithville	Lincs	TF3150	53°2·1′	0°2·4′W	T	122
Frithwen	Cered	SN6056	52°11·3′	4°2·5′W	X	146
Frith Wood	Bucks	SP9900	51°41·6′	0°33·7′W	F	165
Frith Wood	Bucks	SU9999	51°41·1′	0°33·7′W	F	165,176
Frith Wood	Cumbr	NY5115	54°31·9′	2°45·0′W	F	90
Frith Wood	Hants	SU5452	51°16·1′	1°13·2′W	F	185
Frith Wood	Heref	SO7139	52°3·2′	2°25·0′W	F	149
Frith Wood	Kent	TQ8945	51°10·6′	0°42·6′E	F	189
Frith Wood	Surrey	TQ3761	51°20·1′	0°1·6′W	F	177,187
Frith Wood	W Susx	SU9530	51°3·9′	0°38·3′W	F	186
Frithwood Fm	Derby	SK5272	53°14·8′	1°12·8′W	FM	120
Frithy Wood	Suff	TL8654	52°9·4′	0°43·5′E	F	155
Frittenden	Kent	TQ8141	51°8·6′	0°35·6′E	T	188
Frittiscombe	Devon	SX8043	50°16·7′	3°40·7′W	T	202
Fritton	Norf	TG4018	52°42·6′	1°33·6′E	T	134
Fritton	Norf	TG4600	52°32·8′	1°38·1′E	T	134
Fritton	Norf	TM2292	52°29·1′	1°16·6′E	T	134
Fritton Common	Norf	TM2292	52°29·1′	1°16·6′E	X	134
Fritton Decoy	Suff	TG4800	52°32·7′	1°39·9′E	W	134
Fritton Grange	Norf	TM2294	52°30·1′	1°16·7′E	X	134
Fritton Ho	Norf	TM4699	52°32·2′	1°38·1′E	X	134
Fritton Lake Country Park	Suff	TG4800	52°32·7′	1°39·9′E	X	134
Fritton Marshes	Norf	TG4500	52°32·8′	1°37·2′E	X	134
Fritton Old Hall	Norf	TG4700	52°32·7′	1°39·0′E	A	134
Fritton Warren	Norf	TM4699	52°32·2′	1°38·1′E	F	134
Fritwell	Oxon	SP5229	51°57·7′	1°14·2′W	T	164
Frizenham	Devon	SS4718	50°56·7′	4°10·3′W	X	180
Friz Hill	Warw	SP2953	52°10·7′	1°34·2′W	X	151
Frizinghall	Brad	SE1435	53°48·9′	1°46·8′W	T	104
Frizington	Cumbr	NY0317	54°32·6′	3°29·5′W	T	89
Frizington Hall	Cumbr	NY0117	54°32·6′	3°31·4′W	X	89
Frizington Parks	Cumbr	NY0416	54°32·1′	3°28·6′W	X	89
Frizmore Hill	Warw	SP3462	52°15·5′	1°29·7′W	X	151
Frizzeler's Green	Suff	TL7862	52°13·9′	0°36·8′E	T	155
Frizzleton Fm	Norf	TF8031	52°51·0′	0°40·8′E	FM	132
Fro	Cered	SN5256	52°11·2′	4°9·5′W	X	146
Fro	Powys	SO2319	51°52·1′	3°6·7′W	X	161
Froach-choire	Highld	NG7522	57°14·3′	5°43·3′W	X	33
Frobost	N Eil	NF7325	57°12·2′	7°24·5′W	T	22
Frobury Farm	Hants	SU5159	51°19·9′	1°15·7′W	FM	174
Frocester	Glos	SO7803	51°43·8′	2°18·7′W	T	162
Frocester Court	Glos	SO7802	51°43·2′	2°18·7′W	A	162
Frocester Hill	Glos	SO7901	51°42·7′	2°17·8′W	X	162
Frochas	Gwyn	SH3339	52°55·6′	4°28·7′W	X	123
Frochas	Powys	SJ1908	52°40·1′	3°11·5′W	X	125
Frochas	Powys	SJ2910	52°41·2′	3°2·6′W	T	126
Frochas Fm	Powys	SJ2008	52°40·1′	3°10·6′W	FM	126
Frodaw Height	D & G	NY3797	55°16·0′	2°59·1′W	H	79
Froddle Crook	Cumbr	NY5049	54°50·2′	2°46·3′W	X	86
Frodesley	Shrops	SJ5101	52°36·5′	2°43·0′W	T	126
Frodesley Grange	Shrops	SJ5001	52°36·5′	2°43·9′W	X	126
Frodesley Lane Fm	Shrops	SJ5000	52°36·0′	2°43·9′W	FM	126
Frodesley Lodge	Shrops	SO5199	52°35·4′	2°43·0′W	X	137,138
Frodingham	N Lincs	SE8911	53°35·5′	0°38·9′W	T	112
Frodingham Beck	E Yorks	TA0852	53°57·4′	0°20·8′W	W	107
Frodingham Br	E Yorks	TA0953	53°57·9′	0°19·9′W	X	107
Frodingham Grange	E Yorks	TA1151	53°56·8′	0°18·1′W	X	107
Frodingham Grange	N Lincs	SE8611	53°35·5′	0°41·6′W	X	112
Frodingham Hall	E Yorks	TA3126	53°43·1′	0°0·5′W	X	107
Frodsham	Ches	SJ5277	53°17·5′	2°42·8′W	T	117
Frodsham Marsh	Ches	SJ5078	53°18·0′	2°44·6′W	X	117
Frodsham Marsh Fm	Ches	SJ4979	53°18·6′	2°45·5′W	FM	117
Frodsham Score	Ches	SJ4878	53°18·0′	2°46·4′W	X	117
Froe	Corn	SW8633	50°9·7′	4°59·4′W	X	204
Fro Fm	Monm	SO3209	51°46·8′	2°58·8′W	FM	161
Frogalley Fm	Oxon	SU5186	51°34·5′	1°15·5′W	FM	174
Frogbury	Devon	SS6906	50°50·6′	3°51·3′W	X	191
Frogden	Scot Bord	NT7628	55°33·0′	2°22·4′W	X	74
Frog End	Cambs	TL4052	52°9·1′	0°3·2′E	T	154
Frog End	Cambs	TL5358	52°12·2′	0°14·7′E	T	154
Frog Firle	E Susx	TQ5101	50°47·6′	0°8·9′E	X	199
Frog Fm	W Susx	SU9621	50°59·0′	0°37·6′W	FM	197
Froggatt	Derby	SK2476	53°17·1′	1°38·0′W	T	119
Froggatt Edge	Derby	SK2476	53°17·1′	1°38·0′W	X	119
Froghall	Beds	TL0236	52°1·0′	0°30·4′W	X	153
Frog Hall	Cambs	TL2291	52°30·4′	0°11·7′W	X	142
Frog Hall	Cambs	TL3545	52°5·4′	0°1·4′W	X	154
Frog Hall	Durham	NY8034	54°42·3′	2°18·2′W	X	91,92
Frog Hall	E Yorks	SE7648	53°55·6′	0°50·1′W	X	105,106
Frog Hall	Kent	TR1461	51°18·7′	1°4·6′E	X	179
Froghall	Pemb	SM9923	51°52·4′	4°54·8′W	X	157,158
Froghall	Staffs	SK0247	53°1·5′	1°57·8′W	T	119,128
Frog Hall	Suff	TM0342	52°2·6′	0°58·0′E	X	155
Frog Hall	Suff	TM0545	52°4·1′	0°59·9′E	X	155
Frog Hall	Warw	SP4173	52°21·4′	1°23·5′W	X	140
Froghall Carrs	N Lincs	TA0105	53°32·2′	0°28·2′W	X	112
Froghall Fm	Cambs	TL3285	52°27·0′	0°3·1′W	FM	142
Froghall Fm	E Yorks	TA1731	53°46·0′	0°13·1′W	FM	107
Frog Hall Fm	Leic	SK3000	52°36·1′	1°33·0′W	FM	140
Froghall Fm	N Lincs	TA0205	53°32·1′	0°27·2′W	FM	112
Frog Hall Fm	Norf	TF9934	52°52·2′	0°57·8′E	FM	132
Frog Hall Fm	Worcs	SO9553	52°10·7′	2°4·0′W	FM	150
Frogham	Hants	SU1613	50°55·2′	1°46·0′W	T	195
Frogham	Kent	TR2550	51°12·5′	1°13·7′E	T	179
Frog Hill	Norf	TL8791	52°29·3′	0°45·7′E	X	144
Froghole	Kent	TQ4451	51°14·6′	0°4·2′E	T	187
Froghole	W Susx	SU9919	50°57·9′	0°35·0′W	FM	197
Froghole Fm	E Susx	TQ6225	51°0·3′	0°18·9′E	FM	188,199
Frogholt	Kent	TR1737	51°5·7′	1°6·3′E	T	179,189
Frog Island	Hav	TQ5180	51°30·1′	0°10·9′E	X	177
Frogland Cross	S Glos	ST6483	51°32·9′	2°30·8′W	T	172
Froglands Fm	I of W	SZ4887	50°41·1′	1°18·8′W	FM	196
Froglands Fm	V of Glam	SS9969	51°24·9′	3°26·8′W	FM	170
Froglane Fm	Ches	SJ6978	53°18·1′	2°27·5′W	FM	118
Froglane Fm	Hants	SU6260	51°20·4′	1°6·2′W	FM	175
Froglane Fm	Somer	ST2927	51°2·5′	3°0·4′W	FM	193
Frog Lane Fm	Somer	ST3326	51°2·0′	2°56·9′W	FM	193
Frogmill Fm	Win & Maid	SU8183	51°32·6′	0°49·5′W	FM	175
Frogmire	Devon	SS8201	50°48·0′	3°40·1′W	X	191
Frog Moor	Swan	SS4790	51°35·5′	4°12·1′W	T	159
Frogmore	Aberd	NJ9522	57°17·6′	2°4·5′W	X	38
Frogmore	Corn	SW8548	50°17·8′	5°0·8′W	X	204
Frogmore	Devon	SX7742	50°16·1′	3°43·2′W	T	202
Frogmore	Devon	SX8156	50°23·7′	3°40·1′W	X	202
Frogmore	Hants	SU6822	50°59·8′	1°1·5′W	T	185
Frogmore	Hants	SU8460	51°20·2′	0°47·3′W	T	175,186
Frogmore	Heref	SO6321	51°53·4′	2°31·9′W	X	162
Frogmore	Herts	TL1503	51°43·1′	0°19·7′W	T	166
Frogmore	Herts	TL1723	51°53·8′	0°17·6′W	X	166
Frogmore	Herts	TL2820	51°52·1′	0°8·1′W	X	166
Frogmore	Shrops	SJ5511	52°41·9′	2°39·6′W	X	126
Frogmore	Wilts	ST8752	51°16·3′	2°10·8′W	X	183
Frogmore Creek	Devon	SX7641	50°15·6′	3°44·0′W	W	202
Frogmore Fm	Bucks	SP7801	51°42·4′	0°51·9′W	FM	165
Frogmore Fm	Corn	SX1551	50°20·0′	4°35·6′W	FM	201
Frogmore Fm	Devon	SS6127	51°1·8′	3°58·6′W	FM	180
Frogmore Fm	Devon	SS9900	50°47·7′	3°25·6′W	FM	192
Frogmore Fm	Dorset	SY5697	50°46·5′	2°37·1′W	FM	194
Frogmore Fm	Glos	SP2030	51°58·3′	1°42·1′W	FM	151
Frogmore Fm	N Lincs	TA0917	53°38·5′	0°20·7′W	FM	112
Frogmore Fm	Sol	SP2275	52°22·6′	1°40·2′W	FM	139
Frogmore Fm	Win & Maid	SU8379	51°30·5′	0°47·8′W	FM	175
Frogmore Fm	W Susx	TQ2328	51°2·5′	0°14·3′W	FM	187,198
Frogmore Hall	Herts	TL2820	51°52·1′	0°8·1′W	X	166
Frogmore Hill	Dorset	SY4392	50°43·7′	2°48·1′W	X	193
Frogmore Ho	Win & Maid	SU9776	51°28·7′	0°35·8′W	X	175,176
Frognal	Kent	TQ9463	51°20·2′	0°47·5′E	A	178
Frognal	S Ayr	NS3429	55°31·8′	4°37·4′W	T	70
Frognal Corner	Brom	TQ4571	51°25·4′	0°5·5′E	X	177
Frognall	Kent	TR2259	51°17·4′	1°11·4′E	X	179
Frognall	Lincs	TF1610	52°40·7′	0°16·6′W	T	130,142
Frogpit	Swin	SU1694	51°38·9′	1°45·7′W	X	163,173
Frogpool	Corn	SW7640	50°13·3′	5°8·0′W	T	204
Frog Pool	Worcs	SO7965	52°17·2′	2°18·1′W	T	138,150
Frogs Abbey	Cambs	TL5081	52°24·6′	0°12·7′E	X	143
Frogs' Green	Essex	TL5837	52°0·8′	0°18·5′E	T	154
Frogsgreen Fm	Essex	TL5737	52°0·8′	0°17·7′E	FM	154
Frog's Hall	Norf	TG0215	52°41·9′	0°59·8′E	X	133
Frogshall	Norf	TG2538	52°53·8′	1°21·1′E	T	133
Frogs Hall	Suff	TL7564	52°15·0′	0°34·2′E	X	155
Frog's Hall	Suff	TL9150	52°7·1′	0°47·8′E	X	155
Frogs Hall Fm	Essex	TL5822	51°52·7′	0°18·1′E	FM	167
Frog's Hall Fm	Norf	TM3194	52°29·9′	1°24·6′E	FM	134
Frogs Hill	Kent	TQ8327	51°1·0′	0°36·9′E	X	188,199
Frog's Hole	Kent	TQ7337	51°6·6′	0°28·7′E	X	188
Frogs Hole Fm	Kent	TQ8238	51°7·0′	0°36·4′E	FM	188
Frogs Island Fm	Kent	TR1565	51°20·8′	1°5·6′E	FM	179
Frogsmarsh	Worcs	SO7932	51°59·4′	2°18·0′W	X	150
Frogsnest Fm	Oxon	SP5116	51°50·6′	1°15·2′W	FM	164
Frog Street Fm	Somer	ST3119	50°58·2′	2°58·6′W	FM	193
Frogwell	Corn	SX3468	50°29·5′	4°20·0′W	T	201
Frogwell	Devon	SS9114	50°55·1′	3°32·7′W	X	181
Frogwell	Devon	SX7455	50°23·1′	3°46·0′W	X	202
Frogwell Fm	Somer	SS9627	51°2·2′	3°28·6′W	FM	181
Frolesworth	Leic	SP5090	52°30·6′	1°15·4′W	T	140
Frolic	Northum	NZ0279	55°6·6′	1°57·7′W	X	87
Frome	Somer	ST7747	51°13·5′	2°19·4′W	T	183
Fromebridge	Glos	SO7607	51°45·9′	2°20·5′W	T	162
Fromefield	Somer	ST7848	51°14·1′	2°18·5′W	T	183
Frome Hill	Dorset	SY7189	50°42·2′	2°24·3′W	X	194
Frome Mead	Dorset	SY7590	50°42·8′	2°20·9′W	X	194
Fromes, Hill	Heref	SO6746	52°6·9′	2°28·5′W	T	149
Frome St Quintin	Dorset	ST5902	50°49·2′	2°34·5′W	T	194
Frome Valley Walkway	S Glos	ST6680	51°31·3′	2°29·0′W	X	172
Frome Vauchurch	Dorset	SY5996	50°46·0′	2°34·5′W	X	194
Frome Whitfield	Dorset	SY6991	50°43·3′	2°26·0′W	X	194
Fromington	Heref	SO5347	52°7·4′	2°40·8′W	T	149
Fron	Carm	SN2625	51°54·0′	4°31·4′W	X	145,158
Fron	Carm	SN6832	51°58·5′	3°54·9′W	X	146
Fron	Cered	SN4247	52°6·2′	4°18·0′W	X	146
Fron	Cered	SN6265	52°16·2′	4°1·0′W	X	135
Fron	Conwy	SH8069	53°12·5′	3°47·4′W	X	116
Fron	Conwy	SH9347	53°0·8′	3°35·3′W	X	116
Fron	Conwy	SH9562	53°8·9′	3°33·8′W	X	116
Fron	Conwy	SH9965	53°10·6′	3°30·3′W	X	116
Fron	Denb	SJ0566	53°11·2′	3°24·9′W	T	116
Fron	Denb	SJ0654	53°4·7′	3°23·8′W	X	116
Fron	Denb	SJ0676	53°16·6′	3°24·2′W	X	116
Fron	Flint	SJ1572	53°14·5′	3°16·0′W	X	116
Fron	Flint	SJ2071	53°14·0′	3°11·5′W	X	117
Fron	Flint	SJ2261	53°8·7′	3°9·6′W	X	117
Fron	Flint	SJ2857	53°6·6′	3°4·1′W	X	117
Fron	Gwyn	SH3539	52°55·6′	4°26·9′W	X	123
Fron	Gwyn	SH5154	53°4·0′	4°13·0′W	T	115
Fron	Gwyn	SH6006	52°38·3′	4°3·7′W	H	124
Fron	Gwyn	SH6059	53°6·8′	4°5·1′W	X	115
Fron	Gwyn	SH8734	52°53·7′	3°40·4′W	X	124,125
Fron	Pemb	SN0138	52°0·5′	4°53·6′W	X	145,157
Fron	Pemb	SN1716	51°49·0′	4°38·9′W	X	158
Fron	Powys	SH9200	52°35·5′	3°35·3′W	T	136
Fron	Powys	SJ0206	52°38·8′	3°26·5′W	H	125
Fron	Powys	SJ1729	52°51·4′	3°13·6′W	X	125
Fron	Powys	SJ2127	52°50·3′	3°10·0′W	X	126
Fron	Powys	SJ2203	52°37·4′	3°8·7′W	T	126
Fron	Powys	SN9776	52°22·6′	3°30·4′W	X	136,147
Fron	Powys	SO0557	52°12·4′	3°23·0′W	X	147
Fron	Powys	SO0965	52°16·8′	3°19·6′W	T	136,147
Fron	Powys	SO1078	52°23·8′	3°19·0′W	X	136,148
Fron	Powys	SO1797	52°34·1′	3°13·1′W	T	136
Fron	Powys	SO2195	52°33·1′	3°9·5′W	X	137
Fron	Powys	SO2265	52°16·9′	3°8·2′W	X	137,148
Fron	Shrops	SJ2635	52°54·7′	3°5·6′W	T	126
Fron	Shrops	SO2482	52°26·1′	3°6·7′W	H	137
Fron-Bache	Denb	SJ2141	52°57·9′	3°10·2′W	T	117
Fron Bank	Powys	SO1778	52°23·9′	3°12·8′W	X	136,148
Fron-bellaf	Denb	SJ1461	53°8·6′	3°16·7′W	X	116
Froncysyllte	Denb	SJ2741	52°57·9′	3°4·8′W	T	117
Frondderw	Gwyn	SH9136	52°54·9′	3°36·9′W	X	125
Fronddu	Cered	SN5053	52°9·5′	4°11·2′W	X	146
Fron Ddu	Conwy	SH8251	53°2·8′	3°45·2′W	X	116
Fron Ddu	Denb	SJ0257	53°6·3′	3°27·4′W	X	116
Fronddyrys	Powys	SO1559	52°13·6′	3°14·3′W	X	148
Frondeg	Cered	SN5775	52°21·5′	4°5·6′W	X	135
Frondeg	Powys	SJ1524	52°48·7′	3°15·3′W	X	125
Fron-dêg	Wrex	SJ2748	53°1·7′	3°4·9′W	T	117
Fron-deg Flat	Wrex	SJ2650	53°2·8′	3°5·8′W	X	117
Frondeg Hall	Wrex	SJ2948	53°1·7′	3°3·1′W	X	117
Frondeg Uchaf	I of Angl	SH4467	53°10·9′	4°19·7′W	X	114,115
Fron Dinas	Gwyn	SH4859	53°6·6′	4°15·8′W	X	115,123
Fron-dorddu	Powys	SN9465	52°16·6′	3°32·8′W	X	136,147
Fron-dyffryn	Denb	SJ1366	53°11·3′	3°17·7′W	X	116
Fron-fawnog	Flint	SJ2163	53°9·7′	3°10·5′W	X	117
Fron Fawr	Conwy	SH9570	53°13·2′	3°34·0′W	H	116
Fron-fawr	Denb	SJ0457	53°6·3′	3°25·6′W	X	116
Fron-fawr	Denb	SJ1554	53°4·8′	3°15·7′W	X	116
Fron Fawr	Denb	SJ2044	52°59·5′	3°11·1′W	H	117
Fron Fawr	Gwyn	SH7511	52°41·2′	3°50·6′W	X	124
Fronfedw	Cered	SN4857	52°11·7′	4°13·1′W	X	146
Fronfelan	Cered	SN3251	52°8·1′	4°26·9′W	X	145
Fronfelen	Cered	SN4050	52°7·8′	4°19·9′W	X	146
Fronfelen	Conwy	SH9966	53°11·1′	3°30·3′W	X	116
Fronfelen Hall	Powys	SH7507	52°39·0′	3°50·5′W	X	124
Fronfeuno	Gwyn	SH9135	52°54·3′	3°36·8′W	X	125
Fron Fm	Carm	SN1926	51°54·4′	4°37·5′W	FM	145,158
Fron Fm	Carm	SN7733	51°59·2′	3°47·1′W	FM	146,160
Fron Fm	Conwy	SH8577	53°16·9′	3°43·1′W	FM	116
Fron Fm	Powys	SO0643	52°4·9′	3°21·9′W	FM	147,160
Fronfraith	Cered	SN6181	52°24·8′	4°2·2′W	X	135
Fron-fraith	Gwyn	SH7511	52°41·2′	3°50·6′W	X	124
Fron Fraith Hall	Powys	SO1693	52°31·9′	3°13·9′W	X	136
Fron-Fŷs	Wrex	SJ2137	52°55·7′	3°10·1′W	X	126
Fron Ganol	Denb	SJ1461	53°8·6′	3°16·7′W	X	116
Fron-gastell	Gwyn	SH8731	52°52·1′	3°40·3′W	X	124,125
Frongelyn	Cered	SN5252	52°9·0′	4°9·4′W	X	146
Fron-gelyn	Denb	SJ1267	53°11·8′	3°18·6′W	X	116
Frongoch	Carm	SN4030	51°57·0′	4°19·3′W	X	146
Fron-goch	Cered	SN4056	52°11·0′	4°20·0′W	X	146
Frongoch	Cered	SN7666	52°16·9′	3°48·7′W	X	135,147
Fron Gôch	Conwy	SH7554	53°4·4′	3°51·5′W	X	115
Frongoch	Denb	SJ0439	52°56·6′	3°25·3′W	X	125
Fron Goch	Denb	SJ1448	53°1·6′	3°16·5′W	X	116
Fron-gôch	Gwyn	SH7317	52°44·4′	3°52·5′W	X	124
Fron-gôch	Gwyn	SH8714	52°43·0′	3°40·0′W	X	124,125
Frongoch	Gwyn	SH9039	52°56·5′	3°37·8′W	T	125
Fron-gôch	Gwyn	SN6697	52°33·5′	3°58·2′W	X	135
Fron Goch	I of Angl	SH5279	53°17·5′	4°12·8′W	X	114,115

Frongoch	Pemb	SN0741	52°2·3'	4°48·4'W	X	145
Fron-goch	Powys	SH8101	52°35·9'	3°45·0'W	X	135,136
Fron-gôch	Powys	SH8704	52°37·6'	3°39·8'W	X	135,136
Fron-goch	Powys	SJ0021	52°46·9'	3°28·6'W	X	125
Frongôch	Powys	SJ1225	52°49·2'	3°17·9'W	X	125
Fron-goch	Powys	SJ1623	52°48·1'	3°14·4'W	X	125
Fron-goch	Powys	SO1560	52°14·1'	3°14·3'W	H	148
Fron-goch	Powys	SO2172	52°20·7'	3°9·2'W	X	137,148
Frongoch Fm	Cered	SN6082	52°25·3'	4°3·1'W	FM	135
Frongoch Hall	Powys	SJ0402	52°36·7'	3°24·7'W	X	136
Frongôg	Cered	SN6181	52°24·8'	4°2·2'W	X	135
Frongoy	Cered	SN5263	52°15·0'	4°9·7'W	X	146
Fron Gynnen	Conwy	SH8371	53°13·6'	3°44·8'W	H	116
Fron Hall	Flint	SJ2262	53°9·2'	3°9·6'W	X	117
Fronhaul	Carm	SN1624	51°53·3'	4°40·0'W	X	145,158
Fron-haul	Conwy	SJ0167	53°11·7'	3°28·5'W	X	116
Fron-haul	Denb	SJ1169	53°12·9'	3°19·6'W	X	116
Fron-haul	Denb	SJ1363	53°9·7'	3°17·7'W	X	116
Fron Haul	Denb	SJ2153	53°4·3'	3°10·3'W	X	117
Fron-haul	Flint	SJ1570	53°13·5'	3°16·0'W	X	116
Fron-haul	Powys	SJ0908	52°40·0'	3°20·3'W	X	125
Fron Hên	Denb	SJ1760	53°8·1'	3°14·0'W	H	116
Fron Hen	Denb	SJ1860	53°8·1'	3°13·1'W	X	116
Fron-heulog	Denb	SJ0960	53°8·0'	3°21·2'W	X	116
Fron-heulog	Denb	SJ1759	53°7·5'	3°14·0'W	X	116
Fron-heulog	Gwyn	SH9736	52°54·9'	3°31·5'W	X	125
Fron-heulog	Powys	SH8305	52°38·1'	3°43·3'W	X	124,125
Fronheulog	Powys	SJ0418	52°45·3'	3°24·9'W	X	125
Fron-heulog	Powys	SJ1001	52°36·2'	3°19·3'W	X	136
Fronheulog	Powys	SO1792	52°31·4'	3°13·0'W	X	136
Fronheulog Fm	Gwyn	SH2923	52°46·9'	4°31·7'W	FM	123
Fron Hill	Powys	SO1961	52°14·7'	3°10·8'W	H	148
Fronhir	Powys	SO0362	52°15·1'	3°24·9'W	X	147
Fron Hir	Powys	SO1373	52°21·1'	3°16·2'W	H	136,148
Fron Hydan	Powys	SJ1507	52°39·5'	3°15·0'W	X	125
Fron-isaf	Carm	SN1926	51°54·4'	4°37·5'W	X	145,158
Fron-isaf	Conwy	SH9051	53°2·9'	3°38·1'W	X	116
Fron Isaf	Shrops	SJ2636	52°55·2'	3°5·6'W	X	126
Fron Isaf	Wrex	SJ2740	52°57·4'	3°4·8'W	T	117
Fron-lwyd	Denb	SJ2148	53°1·7'	3°10·3'W	X	117
Fronlas	Carm	SN2928	51°55·7'	4°28·8'W	X	145
Fronlas	Cered	SN2647	52°5·9'	4°32·0'W	X	145
Fronlas	Cered	SN6890	52°29·8'	3°56·3'W	X	135
Fronlas	Pemb	SN1734	51°58·7'	4°39·5'W	X	145
Fron-lâs	Powys	SJ0321	52°46·9'	3°25·9'W	X	125
Fron-las	Powys	SJ1611	52°41·7'	3°14·2'W	X	125
Fron-leppa	Conwy	SH8168	53°12·0'	3°46·5'W	X	116
Fron-Leulog	Denb	SJ1442	52°58·4'	3°16·4'W	X	125
Fronllan Fm	Carm	SN2526	51°54·5'	4°32·3'W	FM	145,158
Fron-Llwyd	Powys	SJ2107	52°39·5'	3°9·7'W	X	126
Fron Llwyd	Wrex	SJ1837	52°55·7'	3°12·8'W	X	125
Fron-newydd	Denb	SJ1045	52°59·9'	3°20·1'W	X	116
Fron Oleu	Gwyn	SH3039	52°55·5'	4°31·3'W	X	123
Fron-oleu	Gwyn	SH4741	52°56·9'	4°16·2'W	X	123
Fron-oleu	Gwyn	SH5741	52°57·1'	4°7·3'W	X	124
Fronoleu	Gwyn	SH7135	52°54·7'	3°54·7'W	X	124
Fronrhydd	Pemb	SM9531	51°56·6'	4°58·6'W	X	157
Fronrhydnewydd	Powys	SO0770	52°19·5'	3°21·5'W	X	136,147
Fron Rocks	Powys	SO1876	52°22·8'	3°11·9'W	X	136,148
Front Bay	D & G	NX3639	54°43·4'	4°32·4'W	W	83
Front Hill	E Susx	TQ4006	50°50·4'	0°0·3'W	X	198
Fronthill	Fife	NO3307	56°15·3'	3°4·4'W	X	59
Fron Top	Powys	SO1179	52°24·3'	3°18·1'W	X	136,148
Fron Ucha	Flint	SJ2161	53°8·7'	3°10·5'W	X	117
Fron Ucha	Powys	SJ1932	52°53·0'	3°11·8'W	X	125
Fron Uchaf	Shrops	SJ2636	52°55·2'	3°5·6'W	X	126
Fron Uchaf	Wrex	SJ2740	52°57·4'	3°4·8'W	X	117
Fronwen	Cered	SN4043	52°4·0'	4°19·7'W	X	146
Fron-wen	Cered	SN4257	52°11·6'	4°18·3'W	X	146
Fron-wen	Conwy	SH8259	53°7·2'	3°45·4'W	X	116
Fron wen	Conwy	SH8668	53°12·1'	3°42·0'W	X	116
Fronwen	Powys	SN9456	52°11·8'	3°32·7'W	X	147
Fron-wen	Powys	SO1766	52°17·4'	3°12·6'W	H	136,148
Fron-Wilym	Cered	SN4357	52°11·6'	4°17·4'W	X	146
Fron-y-Fele	Powys	SJ2111	52°41·7'	3°9·7'W	X	126
Fron-y-gôg	Powys	SH7501	52°35·8'	3°50·3'W	X	135
Fron Yw	Denb	SJ1266	53°11·3'	3°18·6'W	X	116
Fron-yw	Flint	SJ2163	53°9·7'	3°10·5'W	X	117
Froodvale Fm	Carm	SN6438	52°1·7'	3°58·5'W	FM	146
Froskin Burn	Pth & Kin	NN7710	56°16·3'	3°58·7'W	W	57
Frost	Devon	SS7706	50°50·7'	3°44·4'W	T	191
Frostenden	Suff	TM4881	52°22·5'	1°39·0'E	T	156
Frostenden Bottom	Suff	TM4881	52°22·5'	1°39·0'E	F	156
Frostenden Corner	Suff	TM4880	52°21·9'	1°39·0'E	T	156
Frosterley	Durham	NZ0237	54°43·9'	1°57·7'W	T	92
Frosterley Cott	Durham	NZ0137	54°43·9'	1°58·6'W	X	92
Frost Fm	Devon	SX8379	50°36·2'	3°38·8'W	FM	191
Frost Fm	Kent	TR2667	51°21·6'	1°15·2'E	FM	179
Frosthall	Northum	NY8057	54°54·7'	2°18·3'W	X	86,87
Frost Hall	N Yks	SE6498	54°22·6'	1°0·5'W	X	94,100
Frost Hill	N Som	ST4364	51°22·6'	2°48·8'W	T	172,182
Frost Hill Fm	Hants	SU5153	51°16·7'	1°15·7'W	FM	185
Frost Hole	Cumbr	SD4898	54°22·7'	2°47·6'W	X	97
Frostineb	Midlo	NT4260	55°50·0'	2°55·1'W	X	66
Frostland	Devon	SS7804	50°49·6'	3°43·6'W	X	191
Frostlane	Hants	SU4306	50°51·3'	1°23·0'W	T	196
Frostlie Burn	Scot Bord	NT4002	55°18·8'	2°56·3'W	W	79
Frostrow	Cumbr	SD6890	54°18·5'	2°29·1'W	X	98
Frost Row	Norf	TG0002	52°35·0'	0°57·5'E	T	144
Frostrow Fells	Cumbr	SD6890	54°18·5'	2°29·1'W	X	98
Frostrow Fm	Norf	TG0001	52°34·4'	0°57·5'E	FM	144
Frost's Common	Norf	TL9493	52°30·2'	0°51·9'E	F	144
Frost's Corner	Devon	SS5514	50°54·7'	4°3·4'W	X	180
Frost Street	Somer	ST2619	50°58·2'	3°2·9'W	X	193
Frosty Hill	Aberd	NJ4610	57°10·9'	2°53·1'W	H	37
Frostynib	Aberd	NJ9557	57°36·4'	2°4·6'W	X	30
Froswick	Cumbr	NY4308	54°28·1'	2°52·3'W	H	90
Frotoft	Orkney	HY4027	59°7·8'	3°2·4'W	T	5,6
Frowen	Carm	SN1924	51°53·4'	4°37·4'W	X	145,158
Fro-wen	Carm	SN5643	52°4·2'	4°5·7'W	X	146
Frowens Fm	Glos	SO7316	51°50·8'	2°23·1'W	FM	162
Frowick Hall Fm	Essex	TM1218	51°49·4'	1°5·0'E	FM	168,169
Froxfield	Beds	SP9733	51°59·4'	0°34·8'W	T	165
Froxfield	Wilts	SU2968	51°24·8'	1°34·6'W	T	174
Froxfield Green	Hants	SU7025	51°1·4'	0°59·7'W	T	186,197
Froxmere Court	Worcs	SO9355	52°11·8'	2°5·7'W	X	150
Froxton	Corn	SX2599	50°46·1'	4°28·5'W	X	190
Froyle Mill	Hants	SU7642	51°10·6'	0°54·4'W	X	186
Froyz Hall Fm	Essex	TL7928	51°55·5'	0°36·6'E	FM	167
Frozen Fell	Cumbr	NY2833	54°41·5'	3°6·6'W	X	89,90
Fruid	Scot Bord	NT1018	55°27·1'	3°24·9'W	X	78
Fruid Reservoir	Scot Bord	NT0919	55°27·6'	3°25·9'W	W	78
Fruid Resr	Scot Bord	NT0820	55°28·2'	3°26·9'W	W	72
Fruid Water	Scot Bord	NT0821	55°28·7'	3°26·9'W	W	72
Fruid Water	Scot Bord	NT1017	55°26·6'	3°24·9'W	W	78
Fruin Water	Arg & Bt	NS3185	56°1·9'	4°42·3'W	W	56
Fruit Fm, The	Wilts	ST9664	51°22·7'	2°3·1'W	FM	173
Fruix Fm	Pth & Kin	NT1298	56°10·2'	3°24·6'W	FM	58
Frumming Beck	Durham	NY9208	54°28·3'	2°7·0'W	W	91,92
Fru Stack	Shetld	HU5053	60°15·8'	1°5·3'W	X	3
Frustigarth	Orkney	HY5218	59°3·0'	2°49·7'W	X	6
Fryan Fm	Somer	ST0533	51°5·5'	3°21·0'W	FM	181
Fryarne Park	Kent	TR1546	51°10·6'	1°5·0'E	X	179,189
Fryars	Herts	TL4415	51°49·1'	0°5·8'E	X	167
Fryars	I of Angl	SH6077	53°16·5'	4°5·6'W	X	114,115
Fryars Road	I of Angl	SH6177	53°16·6'	4°4·7'W	W	114,115
Frydd	Powys	SN9991	52°30·7'	3°28·9'W	X	136
Fryer Mayne	Dorset	SY7386	50°40·6'	2°22·5'W	X	194
Fryern Court	Hants	SU1416	50°56·8'	1°47·7'W	X	184
Fryern Fm	Surrey	TQ3255	51°17·0'	0°6·0'W	FM	187
Fryern Hall	W Susx	TQ0815	50°55·7'	0°27·4'W	X	197
Fryern Hill	Hants	SU4420	50°58·9'	1°22·0'W	T	185
Fryerning	Essex	TL6400	51°40·7'	0°22·7'E	T	167
Fryerning Wood	Essex	TL6101	51°41·3'	0°20·1'E	F	167
Fryerns	Essex	TQ7289	51°34·6'	0°29·3'E	T	178
Fryer's Br	Dorset	SY7796	50°46·0'	2°19·2'W	X	194
Fryers Fm	Bucks	SU8292	51°37·5'	0°48·5'W	FM	175
Frying Pan Fm	Wilts	ST8963	51°22·2'	2°9·1'W	FM	173
Fry's Fm	Dorset	ST8122	51°0·1'	2°15·9'W	FM	183
Fry's Fm	Somer	ST0926	51°1·8'	3°17·5'W	FM	181
Fry's Hill	Somer	ST4355	51°17·7'	2°48·7'W	X	172,182
Fryster	Highld	ND1863	58°33·1'	3°24·1'W	X	11,12
Fryston Grange	N Yks	SE5230	53°46·1'	1°12·3'W	X	105
Fryston Park	Wakf	SE4625	53°43·4'	1°17·8'W	X	105
Fry's Wood	Somer	ST7438	51°8·7'	2°21·9'W	F	183
Frythens Fm	Corn	SW5433	50°9·0'	5°26·2'W	FM	203
Fryth Wood	Monm	ST5195	51°39·3'	2°42·1'W	F	162
Fryton	N Yks	SE6875	54°10·2'	0°57·1'W	T	100
Fryton Grange	N Yks	SE6875	54°10·2'	0°57·1'W	X	100
Fryton Wood	N Yks	SE6873	54°9·1'	0°57·1'W	F	100
Fryup Hall	N Yks	NZ7204	54°25·8'	0°53·0'W	X	94
Fryup Lodge	N Yks	NZ7203	54°25·3'	0°53·0'W	X	94
Fuam	N Eil	NF9874	57°39·5'	7°3·4'W	X	18
Fuam an Tolla	N Eil	NG2096	57°52·2'	6°42·9'W	X	14
Fuam na h-Ola	N Eil	NF9775	57°40·0'	7°4·4'W	X	18
Fuarain Ghlasa	Highld	NC2816	58°6·2'	4°54·7'W	H	15
Fuaran	Highld	NH0912	57°9·8'	5°9·1'W	X	33
Fuaran Allt nan Uamh	Highld	NC2617	58°6·7'	4°56·7'W	W	15
Fuaran Diotach	Highld	NN9097	57°3·3'	3°48·4'W	W	36,43
Fuaran Mór	Arg & Bt	NN3236	56°29·4'	4°43·3'W	H	50
Fuaran Mòr	Highld	NC4640	58°19·6'	4°37·3'W	X	9
Fuaran Mor	Highld	NG9658	57°34·2'	5°24·2'W	X	25
Fuaran Mor	Highld	NG9765	57°38·0'	5°23·6'W	X	19
Fuaran Mór Chluainidh	Highld	NH0912	57°9·8'	5°9·1'W	X	33
Fuaran na h-Eigin	Highld	NH1449	57°29·8'	5°5·8'W	X	25
Fuaran Riabhachain	Highld	NH1335	57°22·3'	5°6·1'W	X	25
Fuar Bheinn	Highld	NM8556	56°39·0'	5°30·0'W	H	49
Fuar Larach	Arg & Bt	NR8154	55°44·1'	5°28·9'W	H	62
Fuar Loch Beag	Highld	NG9976	57°44·0'	5°22·1'W	W	19
Fuar Loch Mór	Highld	NH0076	57°44·0'	5°21·1'W	W	19
Fuar Mhonadh	Pth & Kin	NN6575	56°51·1'	4°12·4'W	X	42
Fuar Tholl	Highld	NG9748	57°28·9'	5°22·7'W	H	25
Fuar-tholl Beag	Highld	NH1145	57°27·6'	5°8·6'W	X	25
Fuar-tholl Beag	Highld	NH2344	57°27·4'	4°56·6'W	X	25
Fuar-tholl Mór	Highld	NH1245	57°27·6'	5°7·6'W	X	25
Fuchas Las	Gwyn	SH5260	53°7·2'	4°12·3'W	X	114,115
Fuches	Powys	SN8489	52°29·4'	3°42·1'W	X	135,136
Fuches	Powys	SN8683	52°26·2'	3°40·2'W	X	135,136
Fuches	Powys	SN8692	52°31·1'	3°40·4'W	X	135,136
Fuchesgau	Cered	SN7680	52°24·5'	3°49·0'W	X	135
Fuches-wen	Cered	SN7780	52°24·5'	3°48·1'W	X	135
Fuday	N Eil	NF7308	57°3·1'	7°23·2'W	X	31
Fuddlebrook	S Glos	ST7772	51°27·0'	2°19·5'W	X	172
Fuddlebrook Hill	S Glos	ST7773	51°27·6'	2°19·5'W	X	172
Fuel Fm	Norf	TG1033	52°51·4'	1°7·6'E	FM	133
Fuelscot Wood	N Yks	SE7588	54°17·2'	0°50·5'W	F	94,100
Fuffock Hill	D & G	NX6358	54°54·1'	4°7·8'W	H	83
Fuge	Devon	SX8348	50°19·5'	3°38·2'W	X	202
Fugglestone St Peter	Wilts	SU1031	51°4·9'	1°51·0'W	T	184
Fugla Ayre	Shetld	HU3774	60°27·2'	1°19·1'W	X	2,3
Fugla Field	Shetld	HP4901	60°41·6'	1°5·7'W	H	1
Fugla Geo	Shetld	HU4799	60°40·6'	1°7·9'W	X	1
Fugla Ness	Shetld	HU3191	60°36·3'	1°25·5'W	X	1
Fugla Ness	Shetld	HU3635	60°6·1'	1°20·7'W	X	4
Fugla Ness	Shetld	HU3674	60°27·2'	1°20·2'W	H	2,3
Fugla Ness	Shetld	HU4377	60°28·7'	1°12·6'W	X	2,3
Fugla Stack	Shetld	HU3529	60°2·9'	1°21·8'W	X	4
Fugla Water	Shetld	HP4901	60°41·6'	1°5·7'W	W	1
Fugla Water	Shetld	HU5171	60°25·4'	1°3·9'W	W	2,3
Fugsdon Wood	Bucks	SP8505	51°44·5'	0°45·7'W	F	165
Fuiay	N Eil	NF7402	56°59·9'	7°21·7'W	X	31
Fuidge Manor	Devon	SX7094	50°44·1'	3°50·2'W	X	191
Fuidhaigh	N Eil	NF8746	57°24·1'	7°12·2'W	X	22
Fuidhaigh Beag	N Eil	NF8652	57°27·2'	7°13·7'W	X	22
Fulbeck	Lincs	SK9450	53°2·6'	0°35·5'W	T	121
Fulbeck	Northum	NZ1987	55°10·9'	1°41·7'W	T	81
Fulbeck Grange	Lincs	SK9051	53°3·2'	0°39·0'W	X	121
Fulbeck Heath	Lincs	SK9750	53°2·6'	0°32·8'W	X	121
Fulbeck Low Fields	Lincs	SK9250	53°2·6'	0°37·3'W	X	121
Fulbourn	Cambs	TL5156	52°11·1'	0°12·9'E	T	154
Fulbourn Fen	Cambs	TL5158	52°12·2'	0°13·0'E	X	154
Fulbrook	Oxon	SP2613	51°49·1'	1°37·0'W	T	163
Fulbrook Fm	Bucks	SP7422	51°53·7'	0°55·1'W	FM	165
Fulbrook Fm	Northnts	SP6777	52°23·4'	1°0·5'W	FM	141
Fulbrook Gap	Oxon	SP2614	51°49·7'	1°37·0'W	X	163
Fulfen	Staffs	SK0609	52°41·0'	1°54·3'W	X	128
Fulfen Slade	Essex	TL5335	51°59·8'	0°14·1'E	W	154
Fulflood	Hants	SU4729	51°3·7'	1°19·4'W	T	185
Fulford	Devon	SS9115	50°55·7'	3°32·7'W	X	181
Fulford	Midlo	NT2464	55°52·0'	3°12·4'W	X	66
Fulford	Somer	ST2029	51°3·5'	3°8·1'W	T	193
Fulford	Staffs	SJ9537	52°56·1'	2°4·1'W	T	127
Fulford	York	SE6149	53°56·3'	1°3·8'W	T	105
Fulford Dale	Staffs	SJ9338	52°56·6'	2°5·8'W	X	127
Fulford Hall	Sol	SP0975	52°22·6'	1°51·7'W	X	139
Fulford Heath	Sol	SP0974	52°22·1'	1°51·7'W	X	139
Fulfordlees	Scot Bord	NT7669	55°55·1'	2°22·6'W	X	67
Fulfords Fm	W Susx	TQ1329	51°3·2'	0°22·9'W	FM	187,198
Fulford Water	Devon	SS9908	50°52·0'	3°25·7'W	X	192
Fulforth	Durham	NZ2346	54°48·7'	1°38·1'W	X	88
Fulham	Ham & Ful	TQ2476	51°28·4'	0°12·5'W	T	176
Fulham Ho	N Yks	SE5519	53°40·1'	1°9·6'W	X	111
Fulhams, The	Worcs	SO6265	52°17·1'	2°33·0'W	X	138,149
Fulhope	Northum	NT8110	55°23·3'	2°17·6'W	X	80
Fulhope Burn	Northum	NT8108	55°22·2'	2°17·6'W	W	80
Fulhope Edge	Northum	NT8209	55°22·7'	2°16·6'W	H	80
Fulking	W Susx	TQ2411	50°53·3'	0°13·8'W	T	198
Fulking Hill	W Susx	TQ2410	50°52·8'	0°13·9'W	X	198
Fullabrook	Devon	SS5241	51°9·2'	4°6·6'W	T	180
Fullabrook	Devon	SS6725	51°0·8'	3°53·4'W	X	180
Fullabrook Down	Devon	SS5240	51°8·6'	4°6·6'W	H	180
Fullaford	Devon	SS6400	50°47·3'	3°55·4'W	X	191
Fullaford	Devon	SS6838	51°7·8'	3°52·8'W	X	180
Fullaford Down	Devon	SS6938	51°7·8'	3°52·0'W	X	180
Fullamoor	Devon	SX5171	50°31·4'	4°5·7'W	X	201
Fullamoor	Oxon	SU5395	51°39·3'	1°13·6'W	X	164
Fullans	N Yks	SE4774	54°9·8'	1°16·4'W	X	100
Fullarton	C of Glas	NS6463	55°50·7'	4°9·9'W	T	64
Fullarton	Midlo	NT2857	55°48·3'	3°8·5'W	X	66,73
Fullarton	N Ayr	NS3238	55°36·7'	4°39·6'W	T	70
Fullarton	Pth & Kin	NO2944	56°35·2'	3°8·9'W	X	53
Fullarton Ho	S Ayr	NS3430	55°32·4'	4°37·4'W	X	70
Fullarton Water	Midlo	NT2857	55°48·3'	3°8·5'W	W	66,73
Fullbrook	Cered	SN6662	52°14·6'	3°57·4'W	X	146
Full Brook	Monm	SO3618	51°51·7'	2°55·4'W	W	161
Fullbrook Fm	Staffs	SK1112	52°42·6'	1°49·8'W	FM	128
Fullbrook Fm	Surrey	SU9044	51°11·5'	0°42·3'W	FM	186
Fuller's End	Essex	TL5325	51°54·4'	0°13·8'E	T	167
Fullers Fm	Surrey	TQ0750	51°14·6'	0°27·6'W	FM	187
Fullers Gate	Ches	SJ7672	53°14·9'	2°21·2'W	X	118
Fuller's Hay	N Som	ST4958	51°19·4'	2°43·5'W	F	172,182
Fullers Hill	Kent	TQ5656	51°17·1'	0°14·6'E	X	188
Fuller's Hill Fm	Cambs	TL2653	52°9·9'	0°9·1'W	FM	153
Fullers Moor	Ches	SJ4954	53°5·1'	2°45·3'W	T	117
Fullers Slade	Mil Key	SP8039	52°2·8'	0°49·6'W	X	152
Fuller Street	Essex	TL7415	51°48·6'	0°31·8'E	T	167
Fullerton	Angus	NO6755	56°41·4'	2°31·9'W	X	54
Fullerton	Hants	SU3739	51°9·2'	1°27·9'W	T	185
Fullerton Manor	Hants	SU3739	51°9·2'	1°27·9'W	X	185
Fulletby	Lincs	TF2973	53°14·5'	0°3·6'W	T	122
Fulley Wood	Hants	SU5629	51°3·7'	1°11·7'W	F	185
Fullholding Fm	I of W	SZ4288	50°41·6'	1°23·9'W	FM	196
Fullhurst Hall	Ches	SJ6250	53°3·0'	2°33·6'W	X	118
Fullicar Ho	N Yks	SE3897	54°22·3'	1°24·5'W	X	99
Fulling Bridge Fm	Wilts	ST8853	51°16·8'	2°9·9'W	FM	183
Fullingcott Fm	Devon	SS4830	51°3·2'	4°9·7'W	FM	180
Fulling Mill	Northnts	SP6050	52°8·9'	1°7·0'W	X	152
Fulling Mill Fm	Kent	TQ8154	51°15·6'	0°36·0'E	FM	188
Fulling Mill Fm	Oxon	SP4038	52°2·6'	1°24·6'W	FM	151
Fulling Mill Fm	W Susx	TQ3430	51°3·4'	0°4·9'W	FM	187
Fullmoor Lodge	Staffs	SJ9411	52°42·0'	2°4·9'W	X	127
Fullmoor Wood	Staffs	SJ9411	52°42·0'	2°4·9'W	F	127
Fullshaw	Barns	SE2001	53°30·6'	1°41·5'W	T	110
Full Sutton	E Yorks	SE7455	53°59·4'	0°51·9'W	T	105,106
Fullwell Cross	Redbr	TQ4490	51°35·7'	0°5·1'E	T	177
Fullwood	E Ayr	NS4450	55°43·4'	4°28·6'W	T	64
Fullwood	Oldham	SD9408	53°34·4'	2°5·0'W	T	109
Fullwood	S Lanak	NS8846	55°41·9'	3°46·5'W	X	72
Fullwoodhead	N Ayr	NS3654	55°45·4'	4°36·4'W	X	63
Fullwood Hill	D & G	NY2790	55°12·2'	3°8·4'W	X	79
Fullwood Holmes	Derby	SK1685	53°21·9'	1°45·2'W	X	110
Fullwood Stile Fm	Derby	SK1784	53°21·4'	1°44·3'W	FM	110
Fulmer	Bucks	SU9985	51°33·5'	0°33·9'W	T	175,176
Fulmer Br	Suff	TL9369	52°17·3'	0°50·2'E	X	155
Fulmer Chase	Bucks	SU9985	51°33·5'	0°33·9'W	X	175,176
Fulmer Grange	Bucks	SU9984	51°33·0'	0°33·9'W	X	175,176
Fulmer Rise	Bucks	TQ0085	51°33·5'	0°33·1'W	X	176
Fulmodeston	Norf	TF9930	52°50·1'	0°57·7'E	T	132
Fulmodeston Severals	Norf	TG0029	52°49·5'	0°58·5'E	F	133
Fulneck	Leeds	SE2232	53°47·3'	1°39·6'W	T	104
Fulnetby	Lincs	TF0979	53°18·0'	0°21·5'W	T	121
Fulney	Lincs	TF2523	52°47·6'	0°8·4'W	T	131
Fulney Ho	Lincs	TF2722	52°47·1'	0°6·6'W	X	131
Fulready	Warw	SP2846	52°6·9'	1°35·1'W	T	151
Fulsby Wood	Lincs	TF2560	53°7·6'	0°7·5'W	F	122
Fulsby Wood Ho	Lincs	TF2460	53°7·6'	0°8·4'W	X	122
Fulscot Manor	Oxon	SU5488	51°35·5'	1°12·8'W	X	174
Fulsham Rock	Kent	TR3571	51°23·6'	1°23·1'E	X	179
Fulshaw Park	Ches	SJ8480	53°19·2'	2°14·0'W	T	109
Fulshawwood	S Ayr	NS3623	55°28·7'	4°35·3'W	X	70
Fulstone	Kirk	SE1709	53°34·9'	1°44·2'W	T	110
Fulstow	Lincs	TF3297	53°27·4'	0°0·3'W	T	113
Fulstow Mill	Lincs	TF3396	53°26·9'	0°0·6'E	X	113
Fulstow Top	Lincs	TF3198	53°28·0'	0°1·2'W	X	113
Fulthorpe	Stock on T	NZ4124	54°36·8'	1°21·5'W	T	93
Fulton	D & G	NY0086	55°9·7'	3°33·8'W	X	78
Fulton	D & G	NY2477	55°5·1'	3°11·0'W	X	85
Fulton Flow	D & G	NY0399	55°16·8'	3°31·2'W	X	78
Fulton Moor	D & G	NX9986	55°9·7'	3°34·7'W	X	78
Fultons Fm	Essex	TL7800	51°40·5'	0°34·9'E	FM	167

Fulvens Ho	Surrey	TQ0946	51°12·4'	0°26·0'W	X	187
Fulwell	Oxon	SP3723	51°54·5'	1°27·3'W	T	164
Fulwell	Sund	NZ3959	54°55·7'	1°23·1'W	T	88
Fulwell Ho	Oxon	SP6234	52°0·3'	1°5·4'W	X	152,165
Fulwith Mill Fm	N Yks	SE3152	53°58·0'	1°31·2'W	FM	104
Fulwood	Lancs	SD5431	53°46·6'	2°41·5'W	T	102
Fulwood	Renf	NS4367	55°52·5'	4°30·1'W	X	64
Fulwood	Sheff	SK3085	53°21·9'	1°32·5'W	T	110,111
Fulwood	Somer	ST2120	50°58·7'	3°7·1'W	T	193
Fulwood Hall	Sheff	SK2985	53°21·9'	1°33·4'W	X	110
Fulwood Head	Sheff	SK2784	53°21·4'	1°35·3'W	X	110
Fulwood Row	Lancs	SD5632	53°47·2'	2°39·7'W	X	102
Funach Wood	Aberd	NO7595	57°3·0'	2°24·3'W	F	38,45
Funaich Mhór	Arg & Bt	NM7210	56°13·9'	5°40·3'W	X	55
Fundenhall	Norf	TM1596	52°31·4'	1°10·6'E	X	144
Fundenhall Street	Norf	TM1396	52°31·4'	1°8·8'E	T	144
Fungarth	Pth & Kin	NO0343	56°34·4'	3°34·3'W	X	52,53
Funglas	Powys	SO0734	52°0·0'	3°20·9'W	X	160
Fungle Road	Aberd	NO5086	56°58·0'	2°48·9'W	X	44
Fungle Road	Aberd	NO5194	57°2·3'	2°48·0'W	X	37,44
Fungle, The	Aberd	NO5296	57°3·4'	2°47·0'W	X	37,44
Funkirk	N Yks	SD9651	53°57·6'	2°3·2'W	X	103
Funnell's Fm	E Susx	TQ4426	51°1·1'	0°3·6'E	FM	187,198
Funtack Burn	Highld	NH7832	57°22·0'	4°1·2'W	W	27
Funtington	W Susx	SU8008	50°52·2'	0°51·4'W	T	197
Funtington Down Ho	W Susx	SU8008	50°52·2'	0°51·4'W	X	197
Funtley	Hants	SU5608	50°52·4'	1°11·9'W	T	196
Funton	Kent	TQ8867	51°22·5'	0°42·5'E	X	178
Funton Creek	Kent	TQ8768	51°23·0'	0°41·6'E	W	178
Funtulich	Pth & Kin	NN7426	56°24·8'	4°2·1'W	X	51,52
Funzie	Shetld	HU6690	60°35·5'	0°47·2'W	T	1,2
Funzie Bay	Shetld	HU6689	60°35·0'	0°47·2'W	W	1,2
Funzie Girt	Shetld	HU6193	60°37·2'	0°52·6'W	X	1,2
Funzie Ness	Shetld	HU6588	60°34·5'	0°48·3'W	X	1,2
Furda	Corn	SW9445	50°16·4'	4°53·1'W	X	204
Furhouse	Corn	SX1180	50°35·6'	4°39·8'W	X	200
Furland	Somer	ST4211	50°54·0'	2°49·1'W	X	193
Furleigh Cross	Dorset	SY4598	50°47·0'	2°46·4'W	T	193
Furley	Devon	ST2704	50°50·1'	3°1·8'W	T	193
Furlong	Devon	SX7089	50°41·4'	3°50·0'W	X	191
Furlong	Shrops	SO5681	52°25·8'	2°38·4'W	X	137,138
Furlongs	Scot Bord	NT6224	55°30·7'	2°35·7'W	X	74
Furlongs Fm, The	Warw	SP3985	52°27·9'	1°25·2'W	FM	140
Furlongs, The	E Susx	TQ4507	50°50·9'	0°4·0'E	X	198
Furlongs, The	Shrops	SO5676	52°23·1'	2°38·4'W	X	137,138
Furmiston	D & G	NX6092	55°12·4'	4°11·6'W	X	77
Furmiston Craig	D & G	NX6093	55°12·9'	4°11·6'W	X	77
Furmiston Lane	D & G	NX6092	55°12·4'	4°11·6'W	W	77
Furnace	Arg & Bt	NN0200	56°9·4'	5°10·8'W	T	55
Furnace	Carm	SN4300	51°40·8'	4°15·9'W	T	159
Furnace	Carm	SN5001	51°41·5'	4°9·8'W	T	159
Furnace	Cered	SN6895	52°32·5'	3°56·4'W	T	135
Furnace	Highld	NG9570	57°40·7'	5°25·8'W	X	19
Furnace Cott	E Susx	TQ6817	50°55·9'	0°23·8'E	X	199
Furnace End	Warw	SP2491	52°31·2'	1°38·4'W	T	139
Furnace Fm	Kent	TQ4540	51°8·7'	0°4·8'E	FM	188
Furnace Fm	Kent	TQ6635	51°5·6'	0°22·6'E	FM	188
Furnace Fm	Kent	TQ7334	51°5·0'	0°28·6'E	FM	188
Furnace Fm	N Yks	NZ7406	54°26·9'	0°51·1'W	FM	94
Furnace Grange	Staffs	SO8496	52°33·9'	2°13·8'W	X	138
Furnace Green	W Susx	TQ2835	51°6·2'	0°9·9'W	T	187
Furnace Hill	Sheff	SK2589	53°24·1'	1°37·0'W	X	110
Furnace Hillock	Derby	SK4069	53°13·2'	1°23·6'W	X	120
Furnace Ho	Cumbr	NY0527	54°38·0'	3°27·9'W	X	89
Furnace House Fm	Kent	TQ4847	51°12·4'	0°7·5'E	FM	188
Furnace Mill	Kent	TQ6636	51°6·2'	0°22·7'E	X	188
Furnace Place	Surrey	SU9333	51°5·6'	0°39·9'W	X	186
Furnace Pond	Kent	TQ6941	51°8·8'	0°25·4'E	W	188
Furnace Pond	W Susx	TQ2225	51°0·9'	0°15·3'W	W	187,198
Furnace Wood	E Susx	TQ4726	51°1·1'	0°6·1'E	F	188,198
Furnace Wood	Kent	TQ6337	51°6·8'	0°20·1'E	F	188
Furnace Wood	W Susx	TQ3539	51°8·3'	0°3·8'W	T	187
Furneaux Fm	Suff	TM0246	52°4·8'	0°57·3'E	FM	155
Furners Fm	W Susx	TQ2216	50°56·1'	0°15·4'W	FM	198
Furner's Green	E Susx	TQ4026	51°1·2'	0°0·2'E	T	187,198
Furness	Cumbr	SD2790	54°18·3'	3°6·9'W	X	96
Furness Abbey	Cumbr	SD2171	54°8·0'	3°12·1'W	A	96
Furness Fells	Cumbr	NY2800	54°23·7'	3°6·1'W	X	89,90
Furness Fells	Cumbr	NY3000	54°23·7'	3°4·3'W	X	90
Furness Fells	Cumbr	SD3389	54°17·8'	3°1·3'W	X	96,97
Furness Fm	Essex	TL6502	51°41·8'	0°23·6'E	FM	167
Furness Mill Fm	Durham	NZ1933	54°41·7'	1°41·9'W	FM	92
Furness Vale	Derby	SK0083	53°20·9'	1°59·6'W	T	110
Furneux Pelham	Herts	TL4328	51°56·2'	0°5·2'E	T	167
Furnham	Somer	ST3209	50°52·8'	2°57·6'W	T	193
Furnishers, The	Heref	SO3963	52°15·9'	2°53·2'W	X	137,148,149
Furrah Head	Aberd	NK1243	57°28·9'	1°47·5'W	X	30
Furra Stacks	Shetld	HU6688	60°34·5'	0°47·2'W	X	1,2
Furrow Green	Cumbr	NY7704	54°26·1'	2°20·9'W	X	91
Furrows Fm	E Yorks	SE9540	53°51·1'	0°32·9'W	FM	106
Fursan	Orkney	HY3724	59°6·2'	3°5·5'W	X	6
Fursdon	C of Plym	SX5059	50°24·9'	4°6·3'W	X	201
Fursdon	Corn	SX2659	50°24·5'	4°26·6'W	X	201
Fursdon	Corn	SX2767	50°28·9'	4°25·9'W	X	201
Fursdon	Devon	SS5707	50°50·9'	4°1·5'W	X	191
Fursdon	Devon	SS5903	50°48·8'	3°59·7'W	X	191
Fursdon	Devon	SS7106	50°50·6'	3°49·6'W	X	191
Fursdon	Devon	SX4891	50°42·2'	4°8·8'W	X	191
Fursdon	Devon	SX6154	50°22·4'	3°56·9'W	X	202
Fursdon	Devon	SX7294	50°44·1'	3°48·5'W	X	191
Fursdon	Devon	SX7584	50°38·8'	3°45·7'W	X	191
Fursdon	Devon	SX7745	50°17·8'	3°43·2'W	X	202
Fursdon	Devon	SX7864	50°28·0'	3°42·8'W	X	202
Fursdon Ho	Devon	SS9204	50°49·8'	3°31·6'W	X	192
Furse	Orkney	HY3933	59°11·0'	3°3·6'W	X	6
Furse	Shetld	HZ2272	59°32·3'	1°36·2'W	X	4
Furse Barton	Devon	SS5915	50°55·3'	4°0·0'W	X	180
Fursham	Devon	SX7193	50°43·6'	3°49·3'W	X	191
Fursland Fm	Somer	ST3837	51°8·0'	2°52·8'W	FM	182
Furslow Fm	Corn	SX3464	50°27·4'	4°19·9'W	FM	201
Fursnewth	Corn	SX2267	50°28·8'	4°30·2'W	X	201
Furswain	Corn	SX2271	50°30·9'	4°30·3'W	X	201
Further Fen Fm	Norf	TL6095	52°32·0'	0°21·9'E	FM	143
Further Ford End	Essex	TL4532	51°58·3'	0°7·1'E	T	167
Further Hall Fm	Suff	TM2453	52°8·0'	1°16·8'E	FM	156
Further Harrop Fm	Ches	SJ9678	53°18·2'	2°3·2'W	FM	118
Further Hill Fm	Suff	TM3675	52°19·6'	1°28·2'E	FM	156
Further or Farm Field	Cambs	TL4366	52°16·6'	0°6·2'E	X	154
Further Quarter	Kent	TQ8939	51°7·4'	0°42·4'E	T	189
Further Surgill Head	N Yks	SD9544	53°53·8'	2°4·2'W	X	103
Furtho	Northnts	SP7743	52°5·0'	0°52·2'W	T	152
Fur Tor	Devon	SX5883	50°38·0'	4°0·1'W	X	191
Furze	Devon	SS6426	51°1·3'	3°56·0'W	T	180
Furze	Devon	SS6433	51°5·0'	3°56·1'W	X	180
Furze	Devon	SS8800	50°47·6'	3°35·0'W	X	192
Furze	Devon	SS8908	50°51·9'	3°34·3'W	X	192
Furzebeam Hill	Devon	SS4820	50°57·8'	4°9·5'W	H	180
Furze Brake	Oxon	SU5396	51°39·8'	1°13·6'W	F	164
Furzebray	Devon	SS7024	51°0·3'	3°50·8'W	X	180
Furzebrook	Dorset	SY9383	50°39·0'	2°5·6'W	T	195
Furzebrook Ho	Dorset	SY9383	50°39·0'	2°5·6'W	X	195
Furze Closes	Lincs	SK9997	53°27·9'	0°30·1'W	X	112
Furze Closes	Lincs	TF3874	53°14·9'	0°4·5'E	F	122
Furze Common	Suff	TM3988	52°26·5'	1°31·4'E	X	156
Furze Coppice	Wilts	SU2068	51°24·9'	1°42·4'W	X	174
Furze Covert	Norf	TM2181	52°23·2'	1°15·3'E	F	156
Furze Cross	Devon	SS2802	50°47·8'	4°26·1'W	X	190
Furzedown	Hants	SU3629	51°3·8'	1°28·8'W	T	185
Furzedown	Lam	TQ2870	51°25·1'	0°9·2'W	T	176
Furzefield Ho	W Susx	TQ2119	50°57·7'	0°16·2'W	X	198
Furze Fm	Corn	SX2399	50°46·1'	4°30·2'W	FM	190
Furze Fm	Devon	SS4920	50°57·8'	4°8·6'W	FM	180
Furze Fm	Devon	SS8511	50°53·5'	3°37·7'W	FM	191
Furze Fm	Devon	ST0702	50°48·8'	3°18·8'W	FM	192
Furze Fm	Lincs	TF3569	53°12·3'	0°1·7'E	FM	122
Furze Fm	Surrey	SU9359	51°19·6'	0°39·5'W	FM	175,186
Furze Green	Norf	TM2183	52°24·2'	1°15·3'E	X	156
Furze Ground	Oxon	SP2307	51°45·9'	1°39·6'W	F	163
Furze Ground	Oxon	SP6321	51°53·3'	1°4·7'W	X	164,165
Furze Hall	Essex	TL6200	51°40·7'	0°21·0'E	X	167
Furze Heath	Norf	TL8295	52°31·6'	0°41·4'E	F	144
Furze Hill	Cambs	TL5548	52°6·7'	0°16·2'E	X	154
Furzehill	Devon	SS5204	50°49·2'	4°5·7'W	X	191
Furzehill	Devon	SS7244	51°11·1'	3°49·5'W	X	180
Furzehill	Dorset	SU0102	50°49·3'	1°58·8'W	T	195
Furze Hill	Essex	TM1131	51°56·5'	1°4·6'E	X	168,169
Furze Hill	Hants	SU1711	50°54·1'	1°45·1'W	T	195
Furze Hill	Kent	TQ9272	51°25·1'	0°46·1'E	H	178
Furze Hill	Leic	SK7807	52°39·5'	0°50·4'W	H	141
Furze Hill	Lincs	SK9082	53°19·9'	0°38·5'W	X	121
Furze Hill	Lincs	TF1967	53°11·4'	0°12·7'W	X	122
Furzehill	Lincs	TF4877	53°16·4'	0°13·6'E	X	122
Furze Hill	Norf	TF7403	52°36·0'	0°34·6'E	X	143
Furze Hill	Oxon	SU2992	51°37·8'	1°34·5'W	X	164,174
Furze Hill	Pemb	SN0401	51°40·7'	4°49·7'W	X	157,158
Furze Hill	Surrey	SU8953	51°16·4'	0°43·1'W	X	186
Furze Hill	Surrey	SU9256	51°18·0'	0°40·4'W	X	175,186
Furzehill	Swan	SS5490	51°35·6'	4°6·1'W	X	159
Furze Hill	W Berks	SU3269	51°25·4'	1°32·0'W	X	174
Furze Hill	W Berks	SU4268	51°24·8'	1°23·4'W	X	174
Furze Hill	Wilts	SU1165	51°23·3'	1°50·1'W	X	173
Furze Hill	Worcs	SP0039	52°3·2'	1°59·6'W	X	150
Furzehill Common	Devon	SS7344	51°11·1'	3°48·6'W	X	180
Furzehill Fm	Devon	ST3301	50°48·5'	2°56·7'W	FM	193
Furze Hill Fm	Pemb	SM9509	51°44·8'	4°57·8'W	FM	157,158
Furzehills	Lincs	TF2572	53°14·1'	0°7·2'W	X	122
Furzehill Wood	Glos	SP1416	51°50·8'	1°47·4'W	F	163
Furze Knoll	Wilts	SU0366	51°23·8'	1°57·0'W	H	173
Furzeland	Devon	SS7803	50°49·1'	3°43·5'W	X	191
Furzeland	Swan	SS5491	51°36·2'	4°6·1'W	X	159
Furzelands	Devon	SX8086	50°39·9'	3°41·5'W	X	191
Furzeleigh	Devon	SX7467	50°29·6'	3°46·2'W	X	202
Furzeleigh Fm	Devon	SY3197	50°46·3'	2°58·3'W	FM	193
Furzeleigh Ho	Devon	SY3197	50°46·3'	2°58·3'W	X	193
Furzeley Corner	Hants	SU6510	50°53·4'	1°4·2'W	T	196
Furzenfield Fm	Bucks	SP7735	52°0·7'	0°52·3'W	FM	152
Furzen Fm	Bucks	SP7427	51°56·4'	0°55·0'W	FM	165
Furzenhall Fm	Beds	TL1946	52°6·2'	0°15·4'W	FM	153
Furzenhill Fm	Warw	SP3470	52°19·9'	1°29·7'W	FM	140
Furzen Leaze Fm	Glos	SU0198	51°41·1'	1°58·7'W	FM	163
Furze Park	Corn	SW8671	50°30·2'	5°0·7'W	X	200
Furzepark	Devon	SS5810	50°52·6'	4°0·7'W	X	191
Furze Park	Devon	SX8394	50°44·3'	3°39·1'W	X	191
Furze Platt	Oxon	SP4318	51°51·8'	1°22·1'W	X	164
Furze Platt	Win & Maid	SU8782	51°32·0'	0°44·3'W	T	175
Furze, The	E Yorks	TA2932	53°46·3'	0°2·1'W	X	107
Furzewick Down	Oxon	SU3984	51°33·4'	1°25·9'W	X	174
Furzewick Fm	Oxon	SU4085	51°34·0'	1°25·0'W	FM	174
Furzey	Hants	SU2711	50°54·1'	1°36·6'W	X	195
Furzey Barn Fm	Glos	SP1105	51°44·8'	1°50·0'W	FM	163
Furzey Hall Fm	Oxon	SP2306	51°45·4'	1°39·6'W	FM	163
Furzey Hill	Glos	SU1399	51°41·6'	1°48·3'W	X	163
Furzey Island	Dorset	SZ0187	50°41·2'	1°58·8'W	X	195
Furzey Lodge	Hants	SU3602	50°49·2'	1°29·0'W	T	196
Furzley	Hants	SU2816	50°56·8'	1°35·7'W	T	184
Furzley Common	Hants	SU2816	50°56·8'	1°35·7'W	X	184
Furzton	Mil Key	SP8435	52°0·7'	0°46·2'W	T	152
Furzton	Pemb	SR9799	51°39·4'	4°55·7'W	X	158
Furzy Cliff	Dorset	SY6981	50°37·9'	2°25·9'W	X	194
Furzy Knaps	Somer	ST3914	50°55·6'	2°51·7'W	X	193
Furzy Lawn Inclosure	Hants	SU3010	50°53·6'	1°34·0'W	F	196
Furzy Lease	Oxon	SP2713	51°49·1'	1°36·1'W	F	163
Furzy Mount	Pemb	SM9221	51°51·2'	5°0·8'W	X	157,158
Fusedale	Cumbr	NY4418	54°33·5'	2°51·5'W	X	90
Fusedale Beck	Cumbr	NY4418	54°33·5'	2°51·5'W	W	90
Fusethwaite Yeat	Cumbr	NY4101	54°24·3'	2°54·1'W	X	90
Fusilier Plantn	Northum	NZ2276	55°4·9'	1°38·9'W	F	88
Fussells Lodge Fm	Wilts	SU1931	51°4·9'	1°43·3'W	FM	184
Fustyweed	Norf	TG0518	52°43·5'	1°2·6'E	X	133
Fwng	Carm	SN8144	52°5·1'	3°43·8'W	H	147,160
Fwng-uchaf	Carm	SN8043	52°4·6'	3°44·7'W	X	147,160
Fyal	Pth & Kin	NO2150	56°38·4'	3°16·8'W	X	53
Fydell Ho	Lincs	TF3243	52°58·3'	0°1·6'W	X	131
Fyfett	Somer	ST2314	50°55·5'	3°5·4'W	T	193
Fyfield	Essex	TL5606	51°44·1'	0°15·9'E	T	167
Fyfield	Glos	SP2003	51°43·8'	1°42·2'W	T	163
Fyfield	Hants	SU2946	51°13·0'	1°34·7'W	T	185
Fyfield	Oxon	SU4298	51°41·0'	1°23·2'W	T	164
Fyfield	Wilts	SU1468	51°24·9'	1°47·5'W	T	173
Fyfield	Wilts	SU1760	51°20·6'	1°45·0'W	T	173
Fyfield Down	Wilts	SU1470	51°26·0'	1°47·5'W	X	173
Fyfield Down	Wilts	SU1858	51°19·5'	1°44·1'W	X	173
Fyfield Hill	Wilts	SU1469	51°25·4'	1°47·5'W	X	173
Fyfield Manor	Oxon	SU6392	51°37·6'	1°5·0'W	X	164,175
Fyfield Wick	Oxon	SU4196	51°39·9'	1°24·0'W	X	164
Fylands Bridge	Durham	NZ2026	54°38·0'	1°41·0'W	X	93
Fylands' Fm	Norf	TM2695	52°30·6'	1°20·2'E	FM	134
Fyldon	Devon	SS7434	51°5·7'	3°47·6'W	X	180
Fyldon Common	Devon	SS7535	51°6·3'	3°46·7'W	X	180
Fylingdales Moor	N Yks	SE9199	54°22·9'	0°35·5'W	X	94,101
Fyling Hall	N Yks	NZ9304	54°25·6'	0°33·6'W	X	94
Fyling Old Hall	N Yks	NZ9402	54°24·5'	0°32·7'W	X	94
Fyling Park	N Yks	NZ9303	54°25·1'	0°33·6'W	X	94
Fylingthorpe	N Yks	NZ9404	54°25·6'	0°32·6'W	T	94
Fynach Fach	Cered	SN7289	52°29·3'	3°52·7'W	X	135
Fynach Fawr	Cered	SN7289	52°29·3'	3°52·7'W	H	135
Fyndoune Cottage	Durham	NZ2445	54°48·2'	1°37·2'W	X	88
Fyning	W Susx	SU8124	51°0·8'	0°50·3'W	T	197
Fyning Hill	W Susx	SU8125	51°1·3'	0°50·3'W	X	186,197
Fyn Loch	W Dunb	NS4577	55°57·9'	4°28·6'W	W	64
Fynloch Hill	W Dunb	NS4677	55°57·9'	4°27·6'W	X	64
Fynneylane	Staffs	SJ9953	53°4·7'	2°0·5'W	X	118
Fynnon-Deilo	V of Glam	ST0675	51°28·2'	3°20·8'W	A	170
Fynnonfoida	Carm	SN2220	51°51·3'	4°34·7'W	X	145,158
Fynnon Pedr	Nth Pt Talb	SS7986	51°33·8'	3°44·4'W	A	170
Fyrish	Highld	NH6169	57°41·6'	4°19·5'W	X	21
Fyvie	Aberd	NJ7637	57°25·6'	2°23·5'W	T	29
Fyvie Castle	Aberd	NJ7639	57°26·7'	2°23·5'W	A	29

G

Gaada Stack	Shetld	HT9541	60°9·5'	2°4·9'W	X	4
Gaada Stacks	Shetld	HU2345	60°11·6'	1°34·6'W	X	4
Gabalfa	Card	ST1678	51°29·9'	3°12·2'W	T	171
Gabber	Devon	SX5049	50°19·5'	4°6·1'W	X	201
Gabhalach	Arg & Bt	NR7985	56°0·7'	5°32·3'W	H	55
Gabhsann bho Dheas	N Eil	NB4358	58°26·4'	6°23·7'W	T	8
Gabhsann bho Thuath	N Eil	NB4459	58°26·9'	6°22·8'W	T	8
Gable	Shetld	HP5713	60°48·0'	0°56·7'W	X	1
Gable Burn	Highld	NC9037	58°18·7'	3°52·2'W	W	17
Gable Burn	Northum	NT8310	55°23·3'	2°15·7'W	W	80
Gable Fm	N Som	ST5070	51°25·8'	2°42·8'W	FM	172
Gable Fm	Suff	TM3654	52°8·3'	1°27·3'E	FM	156
Gable Head	Hants	SZ7299	50°47·4'	0°58·3'W	T	197
Gable Hook Fm	Kent	TQ9539	51°7·2'	0°47·6'E	FM	189
Gables Clough	Lancs	SD6056	54°0·2'	2°36·2'W	X	102,103
Gables Fm	Glos	SO9118	51°51·9'	2°7·4'W	FM	163
Gables Fm	Leic	SK6717	52°45·0'	1°0·0'W	FM	129
Gables Fm	Suff	TM1756	52°9·8'	1°10·8'E	FM	156
Gables Fm	Suff	TM3988	52°26·5'	1°31·4'E	FM	156
Gables, The	Beds	TL1044	52°5·2'	0°23·3'W	X	153
Gables, The	Essex	TL7701	51°41·0'	0°34·0'E	X	167
Gables, The	Hants	SU4748	51°14·0'	1°19·2'W	X	185
Gables, The	Lincs	TF2731	52°51·9'	0°6·4'W	X	131
Gables, The	Northnts	SP8871	52°20·0'	0°42·1'W	X	141
Gables, The	Somer	ST2137	51°7·8'	3°7·4'W	X	182
Gablon	Highld	NH7191	57°53·7'	4°10·1'W	X	21
Gabriel's Copse	Hants	SU4923	51°0·5'	1°17·7'W	F	185
Gabriel's Manor	Kent	TQ4444	51°10·8'	0°4·0'E	X	187
Gabroc Hill	E Ayr	NS4551	55°43·9'	4°27·7'W	T	64
Gabsnout	D & G	NX1860	54°54·3'	4°49·9'W	X	82
Gadair Fawr	Powys	SO2228	51°56·9'	3°7·7'W	X	161
Gadair-wen	Rho Cyn Taf	ST0780	51°30·9'	3°20·0'W	X	170
Gad Br	Heref	SO4152	52°10·0'	2°51·4'W	X	148,149
Gad Brook	Surrey	TQ2047	51°12·8'	0°16·5'W	W	187
Gadbrook	Surrey	TQ2047	51°12·8'	0°16·5'W	T	187
Gadbrook Fm	Surrey	TQ2048	51°13·3'	0°16·5'W	FM	187
Gadbury Wood	N Lincs	SE9507	53°33·3'	0°33·5'W	F	112
Gadcaisceig	Highld	NH1493	57°53·5'	5°7·8'W	X	20
Gad Cliff	Dorset	SY8879	50°36·9'	2°9·8'W	X	194
Gaddacombe Cross	Devon	SX4390	50°41·5'	4°13·0'W	X	190
Gaddesby	Leic	SK6813	52°42·9'	0°59·2'W	T	129
Gaddesby Lodge	Leic	SK6914	52°43·4'	0°58·3'W	X	129
Gaddesden Hall	Herts	TL0409	51°46·4'	0°29·2'W	X	166
Gaddesden Place	Herts	TL0311	51°47·5'	0°30·0'W	X	166
Gaddesden Row	Herts	TL0512	51°48·0'	0°28·2'W	X	166
Gadding Moor	Barns	SE2505	53°32·7'	1°37·0'W	X	110
Gaddings Dam	Cald	SD9522	53°41·9'	2°4·1'W	W	103
Gaddon	Devon	ST0611	50°53·7'	3°19·8'W	X	192
Gadd's Bottom	Somer	ST2229	51°3·5'	3°6·4'W	X	193
Gadebridge	Herts	TL0408	51°45·9'	0°29·2'W	T	166
Gadfa	I of Angl	SH4589	53°22·8'	4°19·4'W	T	114
Gadfield Elm	Worcs	SO7831	51°58·9'	2°18·8'W	T	150
Gadfly Fm	Beds	SP9846	52°6·4'	0°33·7'W	FM	153
Gadgirth	S Ayr	NS4122	55°28·2'	4°30·5'W	X	70
Gadhole Fm	Ches	SJ8877	53°17·6'	2°10·4'W	FM	118
Gadie Burn	Aberd	NJ5325	57°19·0'	2°46·4'W	W	37
Gadlas	Shrops	SJ3737	52°55·8'	2°55·8'W	T	126
Gadlas Hall	Shrops	SJ3737	52°55·8'	2°55·8'W	X	126
Gadles	Corn	SW7636	50°11·1'	5°7·9'W	X	204
Gadloch	N Lanak	NS6471	55°55·0'	4°10·1'W	W	64

Gadlys	Brig	SS8687	51°34·5'	3°38·3'W	X	170
Gadlys	Brig	SS9587	51°34·6'	3°30·5'W	X	170
Gadlys	Gwyn	SH4857	53°5·6'	4°15·8'W	X	115,123
Gadlys	I of Angl	SH5475	53°15·4'	4°10·9'W	X	114,115
Gadlys	Rho Cyn Taf	SN9902	51°42·7'	3°27·3'W	T	170
Gadshill	Kent	TQ7170	51°24·4'	0°27·9'E	T	178
Gaeddren	Conwy	SH9550	53°2·5'	3°33·6'W	X	116
Gaeilavore Island	Highld	NG3679	57°43·7'	6°25·6'W	X	23
Gaer	Newp	ST2986	51°34·3'	3°1·1'W	T	171
Gaer	Powys	SJ1808	52°40·1'	3°12·4'W	X	125
Gaer	Powys	SO1721	51°53·1'	3°12·0'W	X	161
Gaer	Powys	SO1741	52°3·9'	3°12·3'W	X	148,161
Gaer Bank	Powys	SJ2015	52°43·8'	3°10·7'W	X	126
Gaerddu	Gwyn	SH4541	52°56·9'	4°18·0'W	X	123
Gaer Fach	Cered	SN5351	52°8·5'	4°8·5'W	A	146
Gaer fach	Powys	SO0036	52°1·0'	3°27·0'W	A	160
Gaer Fawr	Cered	SN6571	52°19·5'	3°58·5'W	A	135
Gaer-fawr	Monm	ST4498	51°40·9'	2°48·2'W	T	171
Gaer Fawr	Nth Pt Talb	SS7694	51°38·1'	3°47·1'W	A	170
Gaer Fawr	Powys	SJ2213	52°42·8'	3°8·9'W	A	126
Gaer Fawr	Powys	SO0238	52°2·1'	3°25·3'W	A	160
Gaer-fawr Hill	Powys	SJ2212	52°42·2'	3°8·9'W	H	126
Gaerfechan	Conwy	SH9647	53°0·9'	3°32·6'W	X	116
Gaer Fm	I of Angl	SH4386	53°21·1'	4°21·1'W	FM	114
Gaer Fm	Monm	SO2921	51°53·2'	3°1·5'W	FM	161
Gaer-gerrig	Conwy	SH9944	52°59·3'	3°29·9'W	X	125
Gaergoed	Gwyn	SJ0242	52°58·2'	3°27·2'W	X	125
Gaergywydd	Cered	SN6285	52°27·0'	4°1·4'W	X	135
Gaer-Hill	Monm	ST5197	51°40·4'	2°42·1'W	H	162
Gaer Ho	Monm	SO3623	51°54·3'	2°55·4'W	X	161
Gaerlie	Aberd	NO7083	56°56·5'	2°29·1'W	H	45
Gaerllwydd	Monm	ST4496	51°39·8'	2°48·2'W	T	171
Gaer Maesmynach	Cered	SN5250	52°8·0'	4°9·3'W	A	146
Gaer Stone	Shrops	SO4793	52°32·2'	2°46·5'W	X	137,138
Gaer, The	Powys	SO0166	52°17·2'	3°26·7'W	X	136,147
Gaer, The	Powys	SO2099	52°35·2'	3°10·5'W	X	137
Gaer, The	Powys	SO2551	52°9·4'	3°5·4'W	X	148
Gaer, The (Roman Camp)	Powys	SO0166	52°17·2'	3°26·7'W	R	136,147
Gaer wen	Cered	SN3456	52°10·9'	4°25·3'W	A	145
Gaerwen	Denb	SJ0240	52°57·1'	3°27·1'W	X	125
Gaerwen	Gwyn	SH5057	53°5·6'	4°14·0'W	X	115
Gaerwen	I of Angl	SH3286	53°20·9'	4°31·0'W	X	114
Gaerwen	I of Angl	SH4194	53°25·4'	4°23·2'W	X	114
Gaerwen	I of Angl	SH4871	53°13·1'	4°16·2'W	T	114,115
Gaerwen Fm	Gwyn	SH4542	52°57·4'	4°18·0'W	FM	123
Gaerwen Fm	I of Angl	SH4566	53°10·4'	4°18·7'W	FM	114,115
Gaerwen Isaf	Carm	SN3936	52°0·2'	4°20·3'W	X	145
Gafriw	Cered	SN4754	52°10·0'	4°13·8'W	X	146
Gafrogwy Bach	I of Angl	SH4378	53°16·8'	4°20·9'W	X	114,115
Gage's	Essex	TL8333	51°58·1'	0°40·2'E	X	168
Gages Fms	Surrey	TQ1738	51°8·0'	0°19·3'W	FM	187
Gage's Ho	Essex	TL7841	52°2·6'	0°36·1'E	X	155
Gagie House	Angus	NO4537	56°31·6'	2°53·2'W	A	54
Gagingwell	Oxon	SP4025	51°55·6'	1°24·7'W	T	164
Gagle Brook	Oxon	SP5522	51°53·9'	1°11·6'W	W	164
Gagmansbury Fm	Beds	TL0734	51°59·9'	0°26·1'W	FM	153
Gags Hill	Shrops	SO7590	52°30·7'	2°21·7'W	H	138
Gaich	Highld	NH6831	57°21·3'	4°11·2'W	X	26
Gaich	Highld	NJ0125	57°18·6'	3°38·1'W	T	36
Gaick Forest	Highld	NN7584	56°56·1'	4°2·8'W	X	42
Gaick Lodge	Highld	NN7584	56°56·1'	4°2·8'W	X	42
Gaider, The	Corn	SW7616	50°0·4'	5°7·2'W	X	204
Gaidrew	Stir	NS4886	56°2·8'	4°26·0'W	X	57
Gailes	N Ayr	NS3236	55°35·6'	4°39·5'W	X	70
Gailey	Staffs	SJ9110	52°41·5'	2°7·6'W	T	127
Gailey Lea Fm	Staffs	SJ9310	52°41·5'	2°5·8'W	FM	127
Gailey Wharf	Staffs	SJ9210	52°41·5'	2°6·7'W	T	127
Gain	N Lanak	NS7370	55°54·6'	4°1·5'W	X	64
Gaindykehead	N Lanak	NS7369	55°54·1'	4°1·4'W	X	64
Gaineamh an Openham	Highld	NG7472	57°41·1'	5°47·0'W	X	19
Gaineamh Smo	Highld	NG8188	57°49·9'	5°40·9'W	X	19
Gainerhill	S Lanak	NS6839	55°37·9'	4°5·4'W	X	71
Gaines	Heref	SO7155	52°11·8'	2°25·1'W	X	149
Gaines Hall	Suff	TL7455	52°10·2'	0°33·1'E	X	155
Gainfield	Oxon	SU3495	51°39·4'	1°30·1'W	T	164
Gainfield Fm	Oxon	SU3595	51°39·4'	1°29·2'W	FM	164
Gainford	Durham	NZ1716	54°32·6'	1°43·8'W	T	92
Gainford	E Ayr	NS4444	55°40·1'	4°28·4'W	X	70
Gainford Great Wood	Durham	NZ1618	54°33·7'	1°44·7'W	F	92
Gainhill	E Ayr	NS4443	55°39·6'	4°28·4'W	X	70
Gain Hill	Kent	TQ7046	51°11·5'	0°26·4'E	T	188
Gainsborough	Lincs	SK8189	53°23·7'	0°46·5'W	T	112,121
Gainsborough	Suff	TM1841	52°1·7'	1°11·1'E	T	169
Gainsborough Hill Fm	Staffs	SK0702	52°37·2'	1°53·4'W	FM	139
Gainsford End	Essex	TL7235	51°59·4'	0°30·7'E	T	154
Gainsford Hall	Essex	TL7234	51°58·9'	0°30·7'E	X	154
Gain's Hill	Heref	SO6544	52°5·8'	2°30·3'W	X	149
Gains Law	Northum	NT9528	55°33·0'	2°4·3'W	H	74,75
Gainslaw Hill	Northum	NT9552	55°45·9'	2°4·3'W	H	74
Gainslaw Hill	Northum	NT9552	55°45·9'	2°4·3'W	X	67,74,75
Gainslaw Ho	Northum	NT9552	55°45·9'	2°4·3'W	X	67,74,75
Gainsthorpe Fm	N Lincs	SE9501	53°30·1'	0°33·7'W	FM	112
Gainsthorpe Village	N Lincs	SE9501	53°30·1'	0°33·7'W	A	112
Gair	D & G	NY2676	55°4·6'	3°9·1'W	X	85
Gair	Scot Bord	NT2709	55°22·4'	3°8·7'W	X	79
Gair	S Lanak	NS8652	55°45·1'	3°48·5'W	X	65,72
Gaira	Orkney	ND4488	58°46·8'	2°57·6'W	X	7
Gairalily	Orkney	HY7038	59°13·9'	2°31·1'W	X	5
Gairbeinn	Highld	NN4698	57°3·1'	4°31·9'W	H	34
Gairbh-eilean	N Eil	NF8458	57°30·4'	7°16·1'W	X	22
Gairbh Eilein	Highld	NG2349	57°27·1'	6°36·6'W	X	23
Gairbh-sgeir	Highld	NG3872	57°40·0'	6°23·1'W	X	23
Gair Burn	Northum	NY6279	55°6·5'	2°35·3'W	W	86
Gairdrum	Pth & Kin	NO1629	56°27·0'	3°21·3'W	X	53,58
Gairich	Highld	NN0299	57°2·6'	5°15·4'W	H	33
Gairich Beag	Highld	NN0199	57°2·6'	5°16·4'W	X	33
Gairland Burn	D & G	NX4381	55°6·2'	4°27·2'W	W	77
Gairlaw	Angus	NO3057	56°42·2'	3°8·1'W	X	53
Gairletter	Arg & Bt	NS1884	56°1·1'	4°54·8'W	X	56
Gairletter Point	Arg & Bt	NS1984	56°1·1'	4°53·8'W	X	56

Gairloch	Aberd	NJ7907	57°9·5'	2°20·4'W	X	38
Gairloch	D & G	NY0377	55°4·9'	3°30·7'W	X	84
Gairloch	Highld	NG8076	57°43·5'	5°41·2'W	T	19
Gairlochy	Highld	NN1784	56°54·9'	4°59·9'W	T	34,41
Gairmuir	Scot Bord	NT5952	55°45·8'	2°38·8'W	X	67,73,74
Gairn	C of Aber	NJ8404	57°7·9'	2°15·4'W	X	38
Gairney Bank	Pth & Kin	NT1299	56°10·8'	3°24·6'W	T	58
Gairneybank Fm	Pth & Kin	NT1298	56°10·2'	3°24·6'W	FM	58
Gairneybridge	Pth & Kin	NT1298	56°10·2'	3°24·6'W	X	58
Gairney Burn	Pth & Kin	NT0198	56°10·1'	3°35·2'W	W	58
Gairney Ho	Pth & Kin	NT0898	56°10·2'	3°28·5'W	X	58
Gairney Water	Pth & Kin	NT0799	56°10·7'	3°29·4'W	W	58
Gairney Water	Pth & Kin	NT1198	56°10·2'	3°25·6'W	W	58
Gairnieston	Aberd	NJ7455	57°35·3'	2°25·6'W	X	29
Gairnlea	C of Aber	NJ8504	57°7·9'	2°14·4'W	X	38
Gairnluicht	Highld	NJ0331	57°21·8'	3°36·3'W	X	27,36
Gairnshiel Lodge	Aberd	NJ2900	57°5·4'	3°9·8'W	X	37
Gair Reservoirs	S Lanak	NS8553	55°45·7'	3°49·5'W	W	65,72
Gair Rig	Scot Bord	NT7362	55°51·3'	2°25·4'W	X	67
Gairs	Cumbr	NY5855	54°53·5'	2°38·9'W	X	86
Gairsay	Orkney	HY4422	59°5·1'	2°58·1'W	X	5,6
Gairsay Sound	Orkney	HY4424	59°6·2'	2°58·2'W	W	5,6
Gair Shield	Northum	NY8955	54°53·6'	2°9·9'W	X	87
Gairsna Geo	Orkney	HY7553	59°22·0'	2°25·9'W	X	5
Gairsty	Orkney	HY2323	59°5·5'	3°20·1'W	X	6
Gair, The	Cumbr	NY6573	55°3·3'	2°32·4'W	X	86
Gairy Craig	D & G	NX5590	55°11·2'	4°16·2'W	H	77
Gairy Hill	Orkney	ND4685	58°45·2'	2°55·5'W	X	7
Gairy of Cairnsmore	D & G	NX5998	55°15·6'	4°12·7'W	X	77
Gaiseirnis	N Eil	NF8343	57°22·3'	7°16·0'W	X	22
Gaisgeir	N Eil	NB1541	58°16·2'	6°51·2'W	X	13
Gaisgill	Cumbr	NY6405	54°26·6'	2°32·9'W	T	91
Ga-isker	N Eil	NF9676	57°40·5'	7°5·5'W	X	18
Gaisland	Stir	NS5390	56°5·1'	4°21·3'W	X	57
Gaisty Law	Scot Bord	NT7811	55°23·8'	2°20·4'W	H	80
Gait Barrows (Nature Reserve)	Lancs	SD4877	54°11·4'	2°47·4'W	X	97
Gait Crags	Cumbr	NY2205	54°26·3'	3°11·7'W	X	89,90
Gaitgil	D & G	NX6354	54°52·0'	4°7·7'W	X	83
Gaitkins	Cumbr	NY2503	54°25·3'	3°8·9'W	X	89,90
Gaitnip	Orkney	HY4406	58°56·5'	2°57·9'W	X	6,7
Gaitnip Hill	Orkney	HY4405	58°56·0'	2°57·9'W	X	6,7
Gaitscale Close	Cumbr	NY2402	54°24·7'	3°9·8'W	X	89,90
Gaitscale Gill	Cumbr	NY2503	54°25·3'	3°8·9'W	W	89,90
Gaitsgill	Cumbr	NY3846	54°48·6'	2°57·5'W	T	85
Galabank	Scot Bord	NT4445	55°42·0'	2°53·0'W	X	73
Galabraes	W Loth	NS9870	55°55·0'	3°37·5'W	X	65
Galadean	Scot Bord	NT5643	55°41·0'	2°41·6'W	T	73
Gala Ford	W Loth	NT1061	55°50·3'	3°25·8'W	X	65
Gala Hill	Scot Bord	NT4934	55°36·1'	2°48·1'W	H	73
Gala Lane	D & G	NX4686	55°8·9'	4°24·6'W	W	77
Gala Lane	D & G	NX4791	55°11·6'	4°23·8'W	W	77
Gala Law	E Loth	NT4781	56°1·4'	2°50·6'W	X	66
Gala Law	Scot Bord	NT5016	55°26·4'	2°47·0'W	H	79
Galalaw	Scot Bord	NT6934	55°36·2'	2°29·1'W	X	74
Galalaw Fm	Scot Bord	NT0839	55°38·4'	3°27·3'W	FM	72
Galascaig	Highld	NC2034	58°15·7'	5°3·6'W	X	15
Galashiels	Scot Bord	NT4936	55°37·1'	2°48·2'W	T	73
Galava (Roman Fort)	Cumbr	NY3703	54°25·4'	2°57·8'W	R	90
Gala Water	Scot Bord	NT4153	55°46·3'	2°56·0'W	W	66,73
Gala Water	Scot Bord	NT4541	55°39·8'	2°52·0'W	W	73
Galawhistle Burn	S Lanak	NS7631	55°33·7'	3°57·5'W	W	71
Galchen Fawr	Pemb	SN0928	51°55·3'	4°46·3'W	X	145,158
Galch Hill	Denb	SJ0465	53°10·7'	3°25·8'W	A	116
Galchog	Denb	SJ1156	53°5·9'	3°19·3'W	X	116
Galdenoch	D & G	NW9763	54°55·5'	5°9·7'W	X	82
Galdenoch	D & G	NX1761	54°54·9'	4°50·9'W	X	82
Galdenoch Burn	D & G	NW9663	54°55·0'	5°10·6'W	W	82
Galdenoch Moor	D & G	NW9762	54°54·9'	5°9·6'W	X	82
Galdlys	Flint	SJ2174	53°15·7'	3°10·7'W	T	117
Gale	Devon	SX7971	50°31·8'	3°42·1'W	X	202
Gale	Roch	SD9417	53°39·2'	2°5·0'W	T	109
Gale Bank	N Yks	SE0988	54°17·5'	1°51·3'W	X	99
Gale Brook	Ches	SJ6481	53°19·7'	2°32·0'W	W	109
Gale Carr Fm	E Yorks	SE7843	53°52·9'	0°48·4'W	FM	105,106
Galedrhyd	Powys	SN9366	52°17·1'	3°33·7'W	X	136,147
Gale Fell	Cumbr	NY1316	54°32·2'	3°20·3'W	X	89
Galefield	Cumbr	NY0726	54°37·5'	3°26·0'W	X	89
Gale Fm	E Yorks	SE7348	53°55·6'	0°52·9'W	FM	105,106
Gale Garth	Cumbr	SD6580	54°13·1'	2°31·8'W	X	97
Gale Garth	Cumbr	SD6689	54°18·0'	2°30·9'W	X	98
Galegreen	N Yks	SD6674	54°9·9'	2°30·8'W	X	98
Gale Hall	Cumbr	NY6236	54°43·3'	2°35·0'W	X	91
Gale Hill Rigg	N Yks	SE8196	54°21·4'	0°44·8'W	X	94,100
Gale Ho	Cumbr	NY0225	54°36·9'	3°30·6'W	X	89
Gale Ho	Cumbr	NY6920	54°34·7'	2°28·4'W	X	91
Gale Ho	Northnts	SP6468	52°18·6'	1°3·3'W	X	152
Gale Ho	N Yks	SE5535	53°48·7'	1°9·5'W	X	105
Gale Moss	Ches	SJ6581	53°19·7'	2°31·1'W	X	109
Gales	Denb	SJ1365	53°10·7'	3°17·7'W	X	116
Gales Fm	Suff	TM3568	52°15·8'	1°27·0'E	FM	156
Gale's Ho	N Yks	SE6889	54°17·8'	0°56·9'W	X	94,100
Galesyke	Cumbr	NY1303	54°25·1'	3°20·0'W	X	89
Gale, The	Cumbr	NY1449	54°50·0'	3°19·9'W	X	85
Galewood	Northum	NT9532	55°35·1'	2°4·3'W	X	74,75
Galford	Devon	SX4786	50°39·5'	4°9·5'W	X	191,201
Galford Down	Devon	SX4885	50°38·9'	4°8·6'W	H	191,201
Galgate	Lancs	SD4855	53°59·6'	2°47·2'W	T	102
Galgrie Hill	D & G	NX7958	54°54·4'	3°52·8'W	H	84
Galhampton	Somer	ST6329	51°3·8'	2°31·3'W	T	183
Galilee	Orkney	HY7545	59°17·7'	2°25·8'W	X	5
Gallaber	N Yks	SD6472	54°8·8'	2°32·7'W	X	97
Gallaber	N Yks	SD8456	54°0·2'	2°14·2'W	X	103
Gallaberry	D & G	NX9682	55°7·5'	3°37·4'W	T	78
Gallachan	Arg & Bt	NS0757	55°46·3'	5°4·2'W	X	63
Gallachan Bay	Arg & Bt	NS0656	55°45·8'	5°5·1'W	W	63
Gallachoille	Arg & Bt	NR7689	56°2·7'	5°35·4'W	X	55
Gallahill	D & G	NX0959	54°53·6'	4°58·3'W	X	82
Galla How	Aberd	NJ5518	57°15·3'	2°44·3'W	X	37
Gallahow	Cumbr	NY1842	54°46·2'	3°16·1'W	X	85

Gallamuir	Stir	NS8487	56°4·0'	3°51·4'W	X	65
Gallanach	Arg & Bt	NM2160	56°39·2'	6°32·7'W	X	46,47
Gallanach	Arg & Bt	NM8226	56°22·8'	5°31·4'W	X	49
Gallanach	Arg & Bt	NR7996	56°6·6'	5°32·8'W	X	55
Gallanach	Arg & Bt	NR9799	56°8·7'	5°15·6'W	X	55
Gallanach	Highld	NM4079	56°50·0'	6°15·3'W	X	39
Gallanachbeg	Arg & Bt	NM8327	56°23·4'	5°30·5'W	X	49
Gallanachmore	Arg & Bt	NM8227	56°23·4'	5°31·5'W	X	49
Gallan Beag	N Eil	NB0338	58°14·1'	7°3·2'W	X	13
Gallangad Burn	W Dunb	NS4482	56°0·6'	4°29·7'W	W	57,64
Gallangad Burn	W Dunb	NS4580	55°59·5'	4°28·7'W	W	64
Gallangad Fm	W Dunb	NS4483	56°1·1'	4°29·7'W	FM	57,64
Gallangad Muir	W Dunb	NS4582	56°0·6'	4°28·7'W	X	57,64
Gallan Head	N Eil	NB0539	58°14·7'	7°1·2'W	X	13
Gallansay	Cumbr	NY7111	54°29·9'	2°26·4'W	X	91
Gallant Rock	Devon	SS3125	51°0·2'	4°24·1'W	X	190
Gallantry Bank	Ches	SJ5153	53°4·6'	2°43·5'W	T	117
Gallant's Bower	Devon	SX8850	50°20·6'	3°34·1'W	A	202
Gallant's Fm	Essex	TL8334	51°58·7'	0°40·3'E	FM	155
Gallants Fm	Kent	TQ7252	51°14·7'	0°28·3'E	FM	188
Gallards Fm	Mil Key	SP8646	52°6·6'	0°44·3'W	FM	152
Gallatae	D & G	NT1200	55°17·4'	3°22·7'W	X	78
Gallaton	Aberd	NO8782	56°56·0'	2°12·4'W	X	45
Gallatown	Fife	NT2994	56°8·3'	3°8·1'W	T	59
Gallaven Mire	Devon	SX6388	50°40·8'	3°56·0'W	W	191
Gallery	Angus	NO6765	56°46·8'	2°32·0'W	X	45
Gallery Burn	Angus	NO6764	56°46·2'	2°31·9'W	W	45
Gallewood Common	Essex	TL7002	51°41·7'	0°28·0'E	X	167
Galley Common	Warw	SP3191	52°31·2'	1°32·2'W	T	140
Galley Down	Hants	SU5719	50°58·3'	1°10·9'W	F	185
Galleyend	Essex	TL7203	51°42·2'	0°29·7'E	T	167
Galley Hall	Lancs	SD4871	54°8·2'	2°47·3'W	X	97
Galleyherns Fm	Oxon	SU2688	51°35·6'	1°37·1'W	FM	174
Galley Hill	Beds	TL0927	51°56·1'	0°24·5'W	H	166
Galley Hill	Beds	TL2148	52°7·3'	0°13·6'W	X	153
Galley Hill	Cambs	TL3069	52°18·5'	0°5·2'W	X	153
Galley Hill	Essex	TL4003	51°42·7'	0°2·0'E	X	167
Galley Hill	E Susx	TQ7607	50°50·4'	0°30·4'E	X	199
Galley Hill	Lincs	TF0646	53°0·3'	0°24·8'W	X	130
Galley Hill	Lincs	TF4479	53°17·5'	0°10·0'E	T	122
Galley Hill	Norf	TL9292	52°29·8'	0°50·1'E	F	144
Galley Hill	Oxon	SU2893	51°38·3'	1°35·3'W	X	163,174
Galleyhill Green	Essex	TL4004	51°43·3'	0°2·0'E	F	167
Galleyhill Wood	Essex	TL3903	51°42·7'	0°1·1'E	F	166
Galley Lane Fm	Bucks	SP8932	51°59·0'	0°41·8'W	FM	152,165
Galley Lane Fm	Herts	TQ2297	51°39·7'	0°13·8'W	FM	166,176
Galley Law Fm	Durham	NZ3732	54°41·1'	1°25·1'W	FM	93
Galleypot Fm	Oxon	SP3324	51°55·0'	1°30·8'W	FM	164
Galleywood	Essex	TL7102	51°41·7'	0°28·9'E	T	167
Galleywood Hall	Essex	TL7104	51°42·7'	0°28·9'E	X	167
Gall Fen	Cambs	TL4375	52°21·5'	0°6·4'E	X	142,143
Gall Hill	S Ayr	NS3707	55°20·1'	4°33·8'W	X	70,77
Gallhills	D & G	NY2775	55°4·1'	3°8·2'W	X	85
Gallibar	Cumbr	NY6626	54°37·9'	2°31·2'W	X	91
Gallie Craig	D & G	NX1430	54°38·1'	4°52·5'W	X	82
Galligill	Cumbr	NY7545	54°48·2'	2°22·9'W	T	86,87
Gallihowe	Red & Cl	NZ7419	54°33·9'	0°50·9'W	X	94
Gallin	Pth & Kin	NN5445	56°34·7'	4°22·2'W	T	51
Gallions Reach	Newham	TQ4480	51°30·3'	0°4·9'E	W	177
Gallipot Ho	Worcs	SP0740	52°3·7'	1°53·5'W	X	150
Gall Moss	D & G	NY0281	55°7·1'	3°31·8'W	X	78
Gall Moss of Dirneark	D & G	NX2668	54°58·7'	4°42·7'W	X	82
Gallochoille	Arg & Bt	NR6547	55°39·8'	5°43·8'W	X	62
Gallock Hill	N Yks	SE8293	54°19·8'	0°43·9'W	X	94,100
Gallo Hill	Orkney	HY4246	59°18·1'	3°0·6'W	H	5
Gallon Ho	Somer	SS8139	51°8·5'	3°41·7'W	X	181
Gallop	Wilts	ST9790	51°36·8'	2°2·2'W	X	173
Galloping Bottom	Somer	ST0535	51°6·6'	3°21·0'W	X	181
Galloping Slack	N Yks	SE9669	54°6·7'	0°31·5'W	X	101
Gallops	E Susx	TQ3417	50°56·4'	0°5·2'W	X	198
Gallops Fm	W Susx	TQ1209	50°52·4'	0°24·1'W	FM	198
Gallops,The	Norf	TL9783	52°24·8'	0°54·2'E	X	144
Gallop, The	N Yks	SE2884	54°15·3'	1°33·8'W	F	99
Galloquhine	Aberd	NO7279	56°54·3'	2°27·1'W	X	45
Gallos Brook	Oxon	SP5220	51°52·8'	1°14·3'W	W	164
Gallovie	Highld	NN5589	56°58·4'	4°22·7'W	X	42
Galloward	D & G	NX8883	55°8·0'	3°45·0'W	X	78
Galloway	D & G	NX3466	54°57·9'	4°35·2'W	X	82
Galloway	D & G	NX4866	54°58·2'	4°22·0'W	X	83
Galloway	D & G	NX6566	54°58·5'	4°6·1'W	X	83,84
Galloway Burn	S Ayr	NX0571	55°0·0'	5°2·5'W	W	76
Galloway Deer Museum	D & G	NX5576	55°3·7'	4°15·8'W	X	77
Galloway Gate	Cumbr	SD7888	54°17·5'	2°19·9'W	X	98
Galloway Ho	D & G	NX4745	54°46·8'	4°22·3'W	X	83
Gallowberry	Cumbr	NY5468	55°0·5'	2°42·7'W	X	86
Gallowberry Wood	Scot Bord	NT1243	55°40·6'	3°23·5'W	F	72
Gallowbrae	Aberd	NJ8317	57°14·9'	2°16·4'W	X	38
Gallow Brook	Cambs	TL2262	52°14·8'	0°12·4'W	W	153
Gallow Burn	S Lanak	NS9532	55°34·5'	3°39·5'W	W	72
Gallowfauld	Angus	NO4342	56°34·2'	2°55·2'W	T	54
Gallowfield	Aberd	NJ6106	57°8·9'	2°38·2'W	X	37
Gallowflat	Pth & Kin	NO2021	56°22·7'	3°17·3'W	X	53,58
Gallowgate Fm	Suff	TL8052	52°8·4'	0°38·2'E	FM	155
Gallow Heads	N Yks	SE7583	54°14·5'	0°50·5'W	X	100
Gallowhill	Aberd	NJ5615	57°13·7'	2°43·3'W	X	37
Gallow Hill	Aberd	NJ5926	57°19·6'	2°40·4'W	H	37
Gallow Hill	Aberd	NJ6453	57°34·2'	2°35·7'W	H	29
Gallow Hill	Aberd	NJ7655	57°35·3'	2°23·6'W	X	29
Gallowhill	Aberd	NJ8240	57°27·3'	2°17·5'W	X	29,30
Gallow Hill	Aberd	NO8275	56°52·2'	2°17·3'W	H	45
Gallowhill	Angus	NO3736	56°31·0'	3°1·0'W	X	54
Gallow Hill	Angus	NO3941	56°33·7'	2°59·1'W	H	54
Gallow Hill	Angus	NO4841	56°33·7'	2°50·3'W	H	54
Gallow Hill	Arg & Bt	NS2581	55°59·7'	4°47·9'W	H	63
Gallowhill	Arg & Bt	NS3587	56°3·1'	4°38·5'W	X	56
Gallow Hill	Beds	TL1857	52°12·1'	0°16·0'W	X	153
Gallowhill	C of Glas	NS5957	55°47·4'	4°14·5'W	T	64
Gallow Hill	D & G	NT0806	55°20·6'	3°26·6'W	H	78
Gallowhill	D & G	NX0460	54°54·0'	5°3·0'W	X	82
Gallow Hill	D & G	NX4743	54°45·8'	4°22·3'W	X	83

Gallow Hill	Donc	SK5795	53°27·2′	1°8·1′W	X	111
Gallowhill	Fife	NO3403	56°13·2′	3°3·4′W	X	59
Gallow Hill	Fife	NO3823	56°24·0′	2°59·8′W	X	54,59
Gallow Hill	Highld	NH6954	57°33·7′	4°10·9′W	X	26
Gallow Hill	Highld	NH8066	57°40·3′	4°0·3′W	H	21,27
Gallow Hill	Highld	NH8782	57°49·1′	3°53·7′W	X	21
Gallow Hill	Highld	NJ1336	57°24·6′	3°26·4′W	H	28
Gallow Hill	Leic	SP7189	52°29·9′	0°56·8′W	X	141
Gallowhill	Moray	NJ1928	57°20·4′	3°20·3′W	X	36
Gallow Hill	Moray	NJ4138	57°26·0′	2°58·5′W	X	28
Gallow Hill	Moray	NJ4852	57°33·6′	2°51·7′W	H	28,29
Gallow Hill	Moray	NJ5648	57°31·5′	2°43·6′W	H	29
Gallow Hill	Norf	TF7417	52°43·6′	0°35·0′E	X	132
Gallow Hill	Norf	TF8241	52°56·4′	0°42·9′E	X	132
Gallow Hill	Norf	TF9141	52°56·2′	0°50·9′E	X	132
Gallow Hill	Norf	TG0742	52°56·4′	1°5·2′E	X	133
Gallowhill	Northum	NZ0065	54°59·0′	1°59·6′W	X	87
Gallowhill	Northum	NZ1081	55°7·6′	1°50·2′W	X	81
Gallow Hill	N Yks	SD9845	53°54·3′	2°1·4′W	X	103
Gallow Hill	N Yks	SE3456	54°0·2′	1°28·5′W	X	104
Gallowhill	Orkney	HY4446	59°18·1′	2°58·5′W	X	5
Gallow Hill	Orkney	HY6640	59°15·0′	2°35·3′W	H	5
Gallowhill	Pth & Kin	NO1635	56°30·2′	3°21·4′W	X	53
Gallowhill	Renf	NS4965	55°51·5′	4°24·3′W	T	64
Gallow Hill	Shetld	HP5700	60°41·0′	0°56·9′W	H	1
Gallow Hill	Shetld	HU2551	60°14·8′	1°32·4′W	H	3
Gallow Hill	Shetld	HU3768	60°23·9′	1°19·2′W	H	2,3
Gallow Hill	Shetld	HU3914	59°54·8′	1°17·7′W	H	4
Gallow Hill	Shetld	HU4042	60°9·9′	1°16·3′W	X	4
Gallow Hill	Shetld	HU5991	60°36·1′	0°54·9′W	H	1,2
Gallowhill Croft	Moray	NJ4853	57°34·1′	2°51·7′W	X	28,29
Gallowhill Fm	Pth & Kin	NO1003	56°12·9′	3°26·6′W	FM	58
Gallow Hill Fm	Warw	SP3339	52°3·1′	1°30·7′W	FM	151
Gallow Hill Ho	N Yks	SE3278	54°12·0′	1°30·1′W	X	99
Gallow Hillock	Angus	NO2979	56°54·1′	3°9·5′W	X	44
Gallowhill of Ellon	Aberd	NJ9335	57°24·6′	2°6·5′W	X	30
Gallowhills	Aberd	NK0751	57°33·2′	1°52·5′W	T	30
Gallowhill Sch	Northum	NZ1082	55°8·2′	1°50·2′W	X	81
Gallow Hill (Tumulus)	Norf	TG0742	52°56·4′	1°5·2′E	A	133
Gallowhill Wood	Aberd	NJ6916	57°14·3′	2°30·4′W	W	38
Gallowhill Wood	Highld	NH6049	57°30·8′	4°19·8′W	F	26
Gallow Knowe	Pth & Kin	NO0712	56°17·7′	3°29·7′W	X	58
Gallow Law	Northum	NU0618	55°27·6′	1°53·9′W	X	81
Gallow Law	Northum	NY7582	55°8·2′	2°23·1′W	H	80
Gallow Law	Scot Bord	NT0840	55°38·9′	3°27·3′W	H	72
Gallowleck Plantn	D & G	NX8456	54°53·4′	3°48·1′W	F	84
Gallow Lodge	Leic	SP7290	52°30·4′	0°55·9′W	X	141
Gallowmoor	Northum	NU2120	55°28·6′	1°39·6′W	X	75
Gallowmyre	Pth & Kin	NO1924	56°24·3′	3°18·3′W	X	53,58
Gallowridge	Fife	NS9887	56°4·2′	3°37·9′W	X	65
Gallowridge Hill	Fife	NT0885	56°3·2′	3°28·2′W	X	65
Gallow Rig	D & G	NS6103	55°18·3′	4°11·0′W	X	77
Gallow Rig Moss	D & G	NS5904	55°18·8′	4°12·9′W	X	77
Gallows Barrow	Wilts	SU1548	51°14·1′	1°46·7′W	A	184
Gallows Bridge	Oxon	SU4094	51°38·8′	1°24·9′W	X	164,174
Gallows Brook	Staffs	SP1999	52°35·5′	1°42·8′W	W	139
Gallows Clough	Lancs	SD5454	53°59·0′	2°41·7′W	X	102
Gallowsclough Hill	Ches	SJ5671	53°14·3′	2°39·1′W	H	117
Gallows Corner	Dorset	ST7800	50°48·2′	2°18·3′W	X	194
Gallows Corner	Dorset	ST8314	50°55·7′	2°14·1′W	X	194
Gallows Corner	Hav	TQ5390	51°35·5′	0°12·9′E	T	177
Gallows Dale	Lincs	SK8780	53°18·8′	0°41·2′W	X	121
Gallows Dike	N Yks	SE8494	54°20·3′	0°42·1′W	A	94,100
Gallows Fields	Suff	TM0261	52°12·8′	0°57·8′E	X	155
Gallows Green	Essex	TL6226	51°54·8′	0°21·7′E	T	167
Gallows Green	Essex	TL9226	51°54·2′	0°47·9′E	T	168
Gallows Green	Staffs	SK0741	52°58·2′	1°53·3′W	T	119,128
Gallowsgreen	Torf	SO2606	51°45·1′	3°3·9′W	T	161
Gallows Green	Worcs	SO9362	52°15·6′	2°5·8′W	T	150
Gallowshaw	Northum	NZ1190	55°12·5′	1°49·2′W	X	81
Gallowshieldrigg	Northum	NY7568	55°0·6′	2°23·0′W	X	86,87
Gallows Hill	Aberd	NJ3409	57°10·3′	3°5·0′W	H	37
Gallows Hill	Aberd	NJ4310	57°10·9′	2°56·1′W	H	37
Gallows Hill	Aberd	NJ6041	57°27·7′	2°39·5′W	H	29
Gallows Hill	Aberd	NJ6842	57°28·3′	2°31·6′W	H	29
Gallows Hill	Aberd	NJ7118	57°15·4′	2°28·4′W	H	38
Gallows Hill	Aberd	NK0245	57°30·0′	1°57·5′W	H	30
Gallows Hill	Bucks	SP9717	51°50·8′	0°35·1′W	X	165
Gallows Hill	Corn	SX3185	50°38·6′	4°23·0′W	X	201
Gallows Hill	Dorset	SY8490	50°42·8′	2°13·2′W	X	194
Gallows Hill	Herts	TL3038	52°1·7′	0°5·9′W	H	153
Gallows Hill	Kent	TQ6357	51°17·6′	0°20·7′E	X	188
Gallows Hill	Lancs	SD5960	54°2·3′	2°37·1′W	X	97
Gallows Hill	Lincs	TF1379	53°18·0′	0°17·9′W	X	121
Gallows Hill	Moray	NJ3756	57°35·6′	3°2·8′W	X	28
Gallows Hill	Norf	TG2334	52°51·7′	1°19·2′E	X	133
Gallows Hill	Norf	TL8684	52°25·6′	0°44·5′E	X	144
Gallows Hill	Norf	TM0190	52°28·5′	0°58·0′E	X	144
Gallows Hill	Northum	NT8138	55°38·4′	2°17·7′W	X	74
Gallows Hill	Northum	NZ0289	55°12·0′	1°57·7′W	H	81
Gallows Hill	N Yks	SE9582	54°13·7′	0°32·1′W	X	101
Gallows Hill	Warw	SP2964	52°16·6′	1°34·1′W	X	151
Gallows Hill	Wilts	ST9524	51°1·2′	2°3·9′W	H	184
Gallows Hill	Wilts	SU1321	50°59·5′	1°48·5′W	H	184
Gallows Hill (Tumulus)	Herts	TL3038	52°1·7′	0°5·9′W	A	153
Gallows Inn	Derby	SK4740	52°57·6′	1°17·6′W	T	129
Gallows Knap	Aberd	NO7075	56°52·2′	2°29·1′W	X	45
Gallows Knapp	Heref	SO4530	51°58·2′	2°47·6′W	X	149,161
Gallows Knowe	D & G	NX6078	55°4·7′	4°11·2′W	X	77
Gallows Law	Scot Bord	NT8260	55°50·2′	2°16·8′W	X	67
Gallows Law	Scot Bord	NT8864	55°52·4′	2°11·1′W	X	67
Gallows Moss	Barns	SE1400	53°30·0′	1°46·9′W	X	110
Gallows Outon	D & G	NX4542	54°44·5′	4°24·1′W	X	83
Gallows Point	I of Angl	SH5975	53°15·4′	4°6·4′W	X	114,115
Gallows Pole Hill	Cald	SE0521	53°41·4′	1°55·0′W	X	104
Gallowstree Common	Oxon	SU6880	51°31·1′	1°0·8′W	T	175
Gallowstree Elm	Staffs	SO8484	52°27·5′	2°13·7′W	X	138
Gallox Bridge	Somer	SS9843	51°10·9′	3°27·2′W	A	181
Gallrope Bank	Highld	NH7985	57°50·6′	4°1·8′W	X	21
Galls Fm	Cambs	TL4376	52°22·0′	0°6·4′E	FM	142,143

Galltair	Highld	NG8120	57°13·4′	5°37·2′W	T	33
Gallt Ceiniogau	Gwyn	SH9121	52°46·8′	3°36·6′W	H	125
Galltegfa	Denb	SJ1057	53°6·4′	3°20·3′W	T	116
Galltfaenan Hall	Denb	SJ0269	53°12·8′	3°27·6′W	X	116
Gallt Ffynnon yr Hydd	Gwyn	SH6011	52°41·0′	4°3·9′W	H	124
Gall, The	D & G	NY1790	55°12·1′	3°17·8′W	X	79
Gallt-traeth	Gwyn	SH2430	52°50·6′	4°36·4′W	X	123
Gallt-y-bere	Carm	SN7746	52°6·2′	3°47·4′W	X	146,147
Gallt y Beren	Gwyn	SH3235	52°53·4′	4°29·4′W	X	123
Gallt y Bwlch	Gwyn	SH3443	52°57·8′	4°27·9′W	X	123
Gallt-y-carw	Gwyn	SH7521	52°46·6′	3°50·8′W	X	124
Gallt-y-celyn	Conwy	SH8750	53°2·4′	3°40·7′W	X	116
Gallt-y-cwm	Nth Pt Talb	SS8091	51°36·5′	3°43·6′W	X	170
Gallt-y-foel	Gwyn	SH5862	53°8·4′	4°7·0′W	T	114,115
Gallt y Goedhwch	Powys	SJ1315	52°43·8′	3°16·9′W	H	125
Gallt y Mor	Gwyn	SH2026	52°48·3′	4°39·8′W	X	123
Gallt y Pandy	Conwy	SH8053	53°3·9′	3°47·0′W	X	116
Gallt yr Ancr	Powys	SJ1412	52°42·2′	3°16·0′W	X	125
Galltyrheddwch	Gwyn	SH6919	52°45·4′	3°56·1′W	X	124
Gallt yr Ogof	Conwy	SH6859	53°7·0′	3°57·9′W	X	115
Gallt y Wenallt	Gwyn	SH6453	53°3·7′	4°1·4′W	H	115
Gallt-y-wrach	Shrops	SJ2331	52°52·5′	3°8·2′W	X	126
Gally Bank	Aberd	NO6891	57°0·8′	2°31·2′W	X	38,45
Gallybird Hall	E Susx	TQ4015	50°55·3′	0°0·1′W	X	198
Gally Gap	N Yks	SE7563	54°3·7′	0°50·8′W	X	100
Gally Hills	Donc	SK6594	53°26·6′	1°0·9′W	X	111
Gallypot Street	E Susx	TQ4735	51°6·0′	0°6·4′E	T	188
Galmington	Devon	SS4610	50°52·4′	4°10·9′W	X	190
Galmington	Somer	ST2123	51°0·3′	3°7·2′W	T	193
Galmisdale	Highld	NM4883	56°52·5′	6°7·7′W	T	39
Galmpton	Devon	SX6840	50°14·9′	3°50·7′W	T	202
Galmpton	Torbay	SX8956	50°23·8′	3°33·3′W	T	202
Galmpton Creek	Devon	SX8855	50°23·3′	3°34·2′W	W	202
Galmpton Warborough	Torbay	SX8856	50°23·8′	3°34·2′W	X	202
Galon Uchaf	Merth Tyd	SO0508	51°46·0′	3°22·2′W	T	160
Galowras	Corn	SX0044	50°16·0′	4°48·0′W	X	204
Galphay	N Yks	SE2572	54°8·8′	1°36·6′W	T	99
Galphay Mill	N Yks	SE2672	54°8·8′	1°35·7′W	X	99
Galphay Moor	N Yks	SE2271	54°8·3′	1°39·4′W	X	99
Galphay Wood	N Yks	SE2671	54°8·3′	1°35·7′W	F	99
Galpo	Orkney	HY6826	59°7·4′	2°33·1′W	X	5
Galrigside	S Ayr	NS3835	55°35·2′	4°33·8′W	X	70
Galsey Wood	Beds	TL0360	52°13·9′	0°29·1′W	F	153
Galsham Fm	Devon	SS2422	50°58·5′	4°30·0′W	FM	190
Galson Fm Ho	N Eil	NB4359	58°26·9′	6°23·8′W	X	8
Galson Lodge	N Eil	NB4559	58°27·0′	6°21·8′W	X	8
Galston	E Ayr	NS4936	55°35·9′	4°23·4′W	T	70
Galsworthy	Devon	SS3916	50°55·5′	4°17·1′W	X	190
Galta	Shetld	HU4470	60°25·0′	1°11·6′W	X	2,3
Galta Beag	Highld	NG4673	57°40·8′	6°15·2′W	X	23
Galta Beag	N Eil	NG4098	57°54·0′	6°22·8′W	X	14
Galtachan	N Eil	NG3998	57°54·0′	6°23·8′W	X	14
Galtaha	Orkney	HY5629	59°9·0′	2°45·7′W	X	5,6
Galta Mór	Highld	NG4673	57°40·8′	6°15·2′W	X	23
Galta Stack	Shetld	HU2457	60°18·1′	1°33·4′W	X	3
Galta Water	Shetld	HU2454	60°16·4′	1°33·5′W	W	3
Galtie Rock	Orkney	HY7653	59°22·0′	2°24·8′W	X	5
Galti Geo	Shetld	HU2585	60°33·1′	1°32·1′W	X	3
Galti Stack	Shetld	HU2585	60°33·1′	1°32·1′W	X	3
Galti Stack	Shetld	HU3292	60°36·9′	1°24·4′W	X	1
Galti Stacks	Shetld	HU1559	60°19·2′	1°43·2′W	X	3
Galton	Aberd	NJ4302	57°6·6′	2°56·0′W	X	37
Galton	Dorset	SY7785	50°40·1′	2°19·1′W	X	194
Galtrigill	Highld	NG1854	57°29·6′	6°41·9′W	T	23
Galt Skerry	Orkney	HY4821	59°4·6′	2°53·9′W	X	5,6
Galt, The	Orkney	HY4821	59°4·6′	2°53·9′W	X	5,6
Galtway	D & G	NX7147	54°48·3′	4°0·0′W	X	83,84
Galtway Hill	D & G	NX7148	54°48·9′	4°0·0′W	H	83,84
Gam	Corn	SX0877	50°33·9′	4°42·3′W	T	200
Gamage Hall	Glos	SO7130	51°58·3′	2°24·9′W	A	149
Gamallt	Cered	SN7856	52°11·6′	3°46·7′W	X	146,147
Gamallt	Gwyn	SH6606	52°38·4′	3°58·4′W	H	124
Gamallt	Pemb	SN0738	52°0·7′	4°48·3′W	X	145
Gamallt	Powys	SN8992	52°31·1′	3°37·8′W	H	135,136
Gamallt	Powys	SN9570	52°19·3′	3°32·0′W	H	136,147
Gamas Point	Corn	SX0247	50°17·6′	4°46·4′W	X	204
Gamballs Green	Staffs	SK0367	53°12·2′	1°56·9′W	X	119
Gamber Head	Heref	SO4929	51°57·7′	2°44·1′W	X	149
Gamber's Hall	Essex	TL6532	51°57·9′	0°24·5′E	X	167
Gamber, The	Heref	SO5024	51°55·0′	2°43·2′W	W	162
Gambledown Fm	Hants	SU2924	51°1·1′	1°34·8′W	FM	185
Gamble Hill	Leeds	SE2533	53°47·8′	1°36·8′W	T	104
Gamble Hole Fm	Lancs	SD6851	53°57·5′	2°28·8′W	FM	103
Gamblesby	Cumbr	NY6039	54°44·9′	2°36·9′W	T	91
Gamblesby Fell	Cumbr	NY6441	54°46·0′	2°33·1′W	X	86
Gamble's Green	Essex	TL7614	51°48·0′	0°33·6′E	T	167
Gamblyn Fm	Somer	SS9926	51°1·7′	3°26·0′W	FM	181
Gamboro Plantation	Northnts	SP7274	52°21·8′	0°56·2′W	F	141
Gambra Hill	Glos	SP0909	51°47·0′	1°51·8′W	X	163
Gambuston	Devon	SS6325	51°0·7′	3°56·8′W	X	180
Gameclose Covert	Suff	TL9170	52°17·9′	0°48·5′E	F	144,155
Gamekeeper's Tower	Lancs	SD5471	54°8·2′	2°41·8′W	X	97
Gamelands	E Susx	TQ5715	50°55·0′	0°14·4′E	X	199
Game Lea Fm	Derby	SK3070	53°13·8′	1°32·6′W	FM	119
Gamelsby	Cumbr	NY2552	54°51·7′	3°9·7′W	T	85
Gamelshiel	E Loth	NT6563	55°51·8′	2°33·1′W	X	67
Gamelshiel Castle	E Loth	NT6464	55°52·3′	2°34·1′W	A	67
Gamerigg	D & G	NY0486	55°9·8′	3°30·0′W	X	78
Gamerigg Plantn	D & G	NY0386	55°9·8′	3°30·9′W	F	78
Gamescleuch	Scot Bord	NT2814	55°25·1′	3°7·8′W	X	79
Gamescleuch Hill	Scot Bord	NT2914	55°25·1′	3°6·9′W	H	79
Gameshope	Scot Bord	NT1318	55°27·1′	3°22·1′W	X	78
Gameshope Burn	Scot Bord	NT1318	55°27·1′	3°22·1′W	W	78
Gameshope Loch	Scot Bord	NT1316	55°26·1′	3°22·1′W	W	78
Gameslack Fm	E Yorks	SE9159	54°1·4′	0°36·2′W	FM	106
Gameslack Plantn	E Yorks	SE9060	54°1·9′	0°37·1′W	F	101
Gamesland	E Ayr	NS5538	55°37·1′	4°17·7′W	X	71
Gamesley	Derby	SK0194	53°26·8′	1°58·7′W	T	110
Gamesley Brook	Staffs	SJ8526	52°50·1′	2°13·0′W	W	127
Games Loup	S Ayr	NX1088	55°9·2′	4°58·5′W	X	76

Game Traps	Lincs	TF4471	53°13·2′	0°9·8′E	F	122
Gamhnach Mhór	Arg & Bt	NM5420	56°18·8′	5°58·2′W	X	48
Gamhna Gigha	Arg & Bt	NR6854	55°43·7′	5°41·3′W	X	62
Gamla	Shetld	HU5489	60°35·1′	1°0·4′W	X	1,2
Gamla Vord	Shetld	HU5865	60°22·2′	0°56·4′W	H	2
Gamlers, The	Shetld	HU4653	60°15·8′	1°9·6′W	H	3
Gamlingay	Cambs	TL2352	52°9·4′	0°11·7′W	T	153
Gamlingay Cinques	Cambs	TL2252	52°9·4′	0°12·6′W	T	153
Gamlingay Wood	Cambs	TL2453	52°9·9′	0°10·8′W	F	153
Gamlinghay Great Heath	Cambs	TL2151	52°8·9′	0°13·5′W	T	153
Gamli Stack	Shetld	HP5810	60°46·4′	0°55·6′W	X	1
Gammaton	Devon	SS4825	51°0·5′	4°9·6′W	T	180
Gammaton Moor	Devon	SS4924	51°0·0′	4°8·7′W	T	180
Gammaton Resrs	Devon	SS4825	51°0·5′	4°9·6′W	W	180
Gammersgill	N Yks	SE0582	54°14·3′	1°55·0′W	T	98
Gammersgill Moor	N Yks	SE0283	54°14·8′	1°57·7′W	X	98
Gammon Head	Devon	SX7635	50°12·4′	3°43·9′W	X	202
Gammon's Fm	Kent	TR0631	51°2·7′	0°56·7′E	FM	189
Gammon's Fm	Wilts	SU2755	51°17·8′	1°36·4′W	FM	174
Gammons Hill	Devon	SY2798	50°46·9′	3°1·7′W	X	193
Gammons, The	Aberd	NJ7237	57°25·6′	2°27·5′W	X	29
Gamog	I of Angl	SH3388	53°22·0′	4°30·2′W	X	114
Gamper	Corn	SW3425	50°4·2′	5°42·7′W	W	203
Gamper	Corn	SW4022	50°2·7′	5°37·5′W	W	203
Gam-rhiw	Powys	SN8534	51°59·8′	3°40·1′W	X	160
Gamrie Bay	Aberd	NJ7965	57°40·8′	2°20·7′W	W	29,30
Gamston	Notts	SK6037	52°55·9′	1°6·0′W	T	129
Gamston	Notts	SK7076	53°16·8′	0°56·6′W	T	120
Gamston Wood	Notts	SK7276	53°16·8′	0°54·8′W	F	120
Gamston Wood Fm	Notts	SK7376	53°16·8′	0°53·9′W	FM	120
Gamswell	Cumbr	SD2779	54°12·3′	3°6·7′W	X	96,97
Gamsworth	N Yks	SE0558	54°1·3′	1°55·0′W	X	104
Gamuelston Burn	E Loth	NT5466	55°53·3′	2°43·7′W	W	66
Gana Burn	S Lanak	NS9205	55°19·9′	3°41·7′W	W	71,78
Gana Burn	S Lanak	NS9501	55°17·8′	3°38·8′W	W	78
Gana Hill	D & G	NS9500	55°17·2′	3°38·8′W	H	78
Ganarew	Heref	SO5216	51°50·7′	2°41·4′W	T	162
Ganavan	Arg & Bt	NM8532	56°26·1′	5°28·8′W	X	49
Ganavan Bay	Arg & Bt	NM8532	56°26·1′	5°28·8′W	W	49
Ganavan Hill	Arg & Bt	NM8633	56°26·7′	5°27·9′W	H	49
Ganborough	Glos	SP1729	51°57·8′	1°44·8′W	X	163
Ganbrook Fm	Wilts	ST8564	51°22·7′	2°12·5′W	FM	173
Gandale	N Yks	SE1794	54°20·7′	1°43·9′W	X	99
Ganderbeach	Shrops	SJ3100	52°35·8′	3°0·7′W	X	126
Gander Down	Hants	SU5527	51°2·6′	1°12·5′W	X	185
Ganderdown Fm	Hants	SU5527	51°2·6′	1°12·5′W	FM	185
Gander Fm	N Lincs	SE9902	53°30·6′	0°30·0′W	FM	112
Ganderland	Heref	SO6257	52°12·8′	2°33·0′W	X	149
Ganders Green	Glos	SO7020	51°52·9′	2°25·8′W	T	162
Gandysbrook	Ches	SJ8869	53°13·3′	2°10·4′W	X	118
Gang	Corn	SX3068	50°29·5′	4°23·4′W	T	201
Gang Br	Hants	SU4051	51°15·6′	1°25·2′W	X	185
Ganger Fm	Hants	SU3722	51°0·0′	1°28·0′W	FM	185
Gangies	Herts	TL4515	51°49·1′	0°6·6′E	X	167
Gangsdown Hill	Oxon	SU6787	51°34·9′	1°1·6′W	X	175
Gangsti	Orkney	HY2705	58°55·8′	3°15·6′W	X	6,7
Ganllwyd	Gwyn	SH7223	52°47·6′	3°53·5′W	X	124
Ganllwyd	Gwyn	SH7224	52°48·1′	3°53·5′W	T	124
Gannah Fm	Heref	SO5433	51°59·8′	2°39·8′W	FM	149
Gannaway	Warw	SP2264	52°16·7′	1°40·3′W	X	151
Gannel Burn	Clackm	NS9199	56°10·5′	3°44·9′W	W	58
Gannel, The	Corn	SW8060	50°24·2′	5°5·4′W	W	200
Gannets' Bay	Devon	SS1347	51°11·7′	4°40·2′W	W	180
Gannets' Rock	Devon	SS1347	51°11·7′	4°40·2′W	X	180
Gannetts	Dorset	ST7919	50°58·4′	2°17·6′W	T	183
Gannoch	Aberd	NO4988	56°59·1′	2°49·9′W	H	44
Gannochan	Pth & Kin	NN8509	56°15·8′	3°51·0′W	X	58
Gannochy	Angus	NO5970	56°49·4′	2°39·9′W	X	44
Gannochy	Pth & Kin	NO1224	56°24·3′	3°25·1′W	T	53,58
Gannock Fm	Herts	TL3135	52°0·1′	0°5·1′W	FM	153
Gannocks Castle	Beds	TL1652	52°9·5′	0°17·9′W	A	153
Gannock, The	N Yks	SE7972	54°8·5′	0°47·0′W	X	100
Gannols	Heref	SO3041	52°4·0′	3°0·9′W	X	148,161
Gannow Hill	Shrops	SJ3533	52°53·7′	2°57·6′W	X	126
Gansclet	Highld	ND3344	58°23·0′	3°8·3′W	T	12
Gansey Point	I of M	SC2167	54°4·3′	4°43·7′W	X	95
Ganstead	E Yorks	TA1433	53°47·1′	0°15·8′W	T	107
Ganthorpe	N Yks	SE6870	54°7·5′	0°57·2′W	T	100
Gantocks, The	Arg & Bt	NS1775	55°56·3′	4°55·4′W	X	63
Ganton	N Yks	SE9877	54°11·0′	0°29·5′W	T	101
Ganton Dale	N Yks	TA0075	54°9·9′	0°27·7′W	X	101
Ganton Dale Fm	N Yks	TA0075	54°9·9′	0°27·7′W	FM	101
Gantondale House (Hotel)	N Yks	TA0174	54°9·3′	0°26·8′W	X	101
Ganton Wold	N Yks	SE9975	54°9·9′	0°28·6′W	X	101
Ganton Wold Fm	N Yks	SE9975	54°9·9′	0°28·6′W	FM	101
Gants Hill	Redbr	TQ4388	51°34·6′	0°4·2′E	T	177
Gants Mill	Somer	ST6734	51°6·5′	2°27·9′W	X	183
Ganu Mór	Highld	NC3150	58°24·6′	4°53·1′W	H	9
Ganwick Corner	Herts	TQ2599	51°40·8′	0°11·1′W	T	166,176
Gany of Gersty	Orkney	HY5421	59°4·7′	2°47·7′W	X	5,6
Gaodhail	Arg & Bt	NM6038	56°28·6′	5°53·4′W	X	49
Gaodhail River	Arg & Bt	NM6038	56°28·6′	5°53·4′W	W	49
Gaol, The	N Yks	SE6068	54°6·5′	1°4·5′W	X	100
Gaor Bheinn or Gulvain	Highld	NM9986	56°55·6′	5°17·7′W	X	40
Gaor Bheinn or Gulvain	Highld	NN0089	56°57·2′	5°16·9′W	H	41
Gap	Cumbr	SD6690	54°18·5′	2°30·9′W	X	98
Gap	Northum	NY6466	54°59·5′	2°33·3′W	X	86
Gap Ho	Ches	SJ9980	53°19·3′	2°0·5′W	X	109
Gaping Gill	N Yks	SD7572	54°8·8′	2°22·5′W	X	98
Gappah	Devon	SX8677	50°35·1′	3°36·2′W	T	191
Gappah Brake	Devon	SX8576	50°34·6′	3°37·1′W	F	191
Gap Point	I Scilly	SV9311	49°55·5′	6°16·3′W	X	203
Gapshield	Northum	NY6464	54°58·4′	2°33·3′W	X	86
Gap, The	Arg & Bt	NR5908	55°18·7′	5°47·4′W	X	68
Gap, The	Cumbr	NY1204	54°25·7′	3°21·0′W	X	89
Gapton Marshes	Norf	TG5005	52°35·3′	1°41·9′E	X	134
Gap Wood	Cumbr	NY3569	55°0·9′	3°0·6′W	F	85
Gara	Orkney	HY3405	58°55·9′	3°8·3′W	X	6,7
Garabal	Arg & Bt	NN3117	56°19·2′	4°43·5′W	X	50,56
Garabal Hill	Arg & Bt	NN3017	56°19·2′	4°44·5′W	H	50,56

Gara Br	Devon	SX7253	50°22·0'	3°47·6'W	X	202
Garadhban Forest	Stir	NS4790	56°5·0'	4°27·1'W	F	57
Garadhban Forest	W Dunb	NS4086	56°2·7'	4°33·7'W	F	56
Garadheancal	Highld	NB9907	58°0·7'	5°23·7'W	X	15
Garadh Liath	Arg & Bt	NR8569	55°52·2'	5°25·8'W	X	62
Garadh Mhór	Arg & Bt	NR7979	55°57·5'	5°32·0'W	X	62
Gàradh Ur	N Eil	NF7816	57°7·6'	7°18·8'W	X	31
Gara Fm	N Yks	SE9771	54°7·8'	0°30·5'W	FM	101
Gara Mill	Devon	SX8148	50°19·4'	3°39·9'W	X	202
Gara Point	Devon	SX5246	50°18·0'	4°4·3'W	X	201
Gara Rock	Devon	SX7537	50°13·4'	3°44·8'W	X	202
Gara, The	Devon	SX8148	50°19·4'	3°39·9'W	W	202
Garay Island	Highld	NG2249	57°27·0'	6°37·6'W	X	23
Garbad	Highld	NH6885	57°50·4'	4°12·9'W	X	21
Garbal	Aberd	NJ6846	57°30·4'	2°31·6'W	X	29
Garbat	Highld	NH4167	57°40·2'	4°39·5'W	X	20
Garbat Forest	Highld	NH4368	57°40·7'	4°37·5'W	X	20
Garbeg	Highld	NH5031	57°21·0'	4°29·1'W	X	26
Garbeg Hill	Stir	NS4999	56°9·8'	4°25·5'W	H	57
Garbet Hill	Moray	NJ3634	57°23·8'	3°3·4'W	H	28
Garbethill Ho	N Lanak	NS8175	55°57·5'	3°53·9'W	X	65
Garbethill Muir	N Lanak	NS8275	55°57·5'	3°53·0'W	X	65
Garbett Hall	Shrops	SO2676	52°22·9'	3°4·8'W	X	137,148
Garbett's Hall	Powys	SJ2508	52°40·7'	3°6·1'W	X	126
Garbh	Arg & Bt	NN2400	56°9·9'	4°49·6'W	X	56
Garbh Achadh	Arg & Bt	NN0410	56°14·8'	5°9·4'W	H	50,56
Garbhac Ouartalain	N Eil	NF8159	57°30·8'	7°19·2'W	X	22
Garbh-airde Bheag	Arg & Bt	NR8367	55°51·1'	5°27·6'W	X	62
Garbh-aird Mór	Arg & Bt	NM2664	56°41·5'	6°28·1'W	X	46,47
Garbhal Beag	Highld	NH6224	57°17·4'	4°16·9'W	H	26,35
Garbh Allt	Arg & Bt	NM9624	56°22·1'	5°17·7'W	W	49
Garbh Allt	Arg & Bt	NR8861	55°48·0'	5°22·5'W	W	62
Garbhallt	Arg & Bt	NS0296	56°7·2'	5°10·7'W	T	55
Garbh Allt	Arg & Bt	NS0986	56°2·0'	5°3·5'W	W	56
Garbh Allt	Highld	NC0802	57°58·2'	5°14·3'W	W	15
Garbh Allt	Highld	NC2749	58°24·0'	4°57·1'W	W	9
Garbh Allt	Highld	NC3002	57°58·8'	4°52·0'W	W	15
Garbh Allt	Highld	NC3021	58°9·0'	4°52·8'W	W	15
Garbh Allt	Highld	NC3731	58°14·5'	4°46·1'W	W	16
Garbh Allt	Highld	NC7303	58°0·1'	4°8·5'W	W	16
Garbh-allt	Highld	NC7839	58°19·6'	4°4·5'W	W	17
Garbh-allt	Highld	NC8245	58°22·9'	4°0·6'W	W	10
Garbh Allt	Highld	NC9914	58°6·5'	3°42·4'W	W	17
Garbh Allt	Highld	NG9679	57°45·5'	5°25·3'W	W	19
Garbh Allt	Highld	NH4889	57°52·1'	4°33·3'W	W	20
Garbh Allt	Highld	NJ0204	57°7·3'	3°36·7'W	W	36
Garbh Allt	Highld	NM5969	56°45·3'	5°56·1'W	W	47
Garbh Allt	N Ayr	NR9336	55°34·7'	5°16·6'W	W	68,69
Garbh Allt	N Ayr	NR9738	55°35·9'	5°12·9'W	W	69
Garbh Allt	N Eil	NB2832	58°11·8'	6°37·3'W	W	8,13
Garbh Allt Beag	Arg & Bt	NS0886	56°2·0'	5°4·5'W	W	56
Garbhallt Lochain	Arg & Bt	NS0294	56°6·1'	5°10·6'W	W	55
Garbh-allt Mór	Arg & Bt	NN2012	56°16·2'	4°54·0'W	W	50,56
Garbh Allt Shiel	Aberd	NO1990	56°59·9'	3°19·5'W	T	43
Garbhal-Mòr	Highld	NH6123	57°16·9'	4°17·9'W	H	26,35
Garbhan Beag	Highld	NH5283	57°49·0'	4°29·0'W	X	20
Garbhan Còsach	Highld	NG8023	57°15·0'	5°38·4'W	X	33
Garbhan Mór	Highld	NH5382	57°48·5'	4°28·0'W	H	20
Garbh Ard	Arg & Bt	NM8737	56°28·9'	5°27·1'W	X	49
Garbh-àth Mór	Highld	NJ0829	57°20·8'	3°31·3'W	X	36
Garbh Beinn	Highld	NN1660	56°42·0'	4°59·9'W	H	41
Garbh-bhealach	Highld	NH1526	57°17·5'	5°3·7'W	X	25
Garbh Bhealach	Stir	NN4625	56°23·8'	4°29·3'W	X	51
Garbh-bheinn	Highld	NG5323	57°14·1'	6°5·1'W	H	32
Garbh Bheinn	Highld	NM9062	56°42·4'	5°25·4'W	H	40
Garbh-bheinn	Highld	NN3571	56°48·3'	4°41·7'W	H	41
Garbh Bheirt	Highld	NG5849	57°28·3'	6°1·7'W	X	24
Garbh Bhruthach	Highld	NN4777	56°51·8'	4°30·1'W	X	42
Garbh-chamas	N Eil	NF8537	57°19·1'	7°13·5'W	W	22
Garbh-charn	Highld	NH2941	57°25·9'	4°50·4'W	H	25
Garbh Chioch Bheag	Highld	NM9295	57°0·2'	5°25·1'W	X	33,40
Garbh Chioch Mhór	Highld	NM9096	57°0·7'	5°27·1'W	H	33,40
Garbh Chnapan	Highld	NN3168	56°46·6'	4°45·5'W	H	41
Garbh Chnoc	Highld	NC5753	58°26·8'	4°26·5'W	H	10
Garbh-chnoc Mór	Highld	NC5454	58°27·3'	4°29·6'W	H	10
Garbh-chnoc nan Ealachan	Highld	NC6852	58°26·5'	4°15·2'W	H	10
Garbh-choire	Aberd	NO1778	56°53·4'	3°21·3'W	X	43
Garbh Choire	Arg & Bt	NM5639	56°29·1'	5°57·3'W	X	47,48
Garbh Choire	Highld	NC3019	58°7·9'	4°52·8'W	X	15
Garbh-choire	Highld	NH1735	57°22·4'	5°2·2'W	X	25
Garbh Choire	Highld	NH4301	57°4·7'	4°35·0'W	X	34
Garbh Choire	Highld	NM7658	56°39·9'	5°38·9'W	X	49
Garbh-choire	Highld	NM7762	56°42·1'	5°38·1'W	X	40
Garbh Choire	Highld	NN5071	56°48·6'	4°27·0'W	X	42
Garbh Choire	Moray	NJ1101	57°5·7'	3°27·7'W	X	36
Garbh Choireachan	Highld	NC0803	57°58·8'	5°14·4'W	H	15
Garbh Choirean	Arg & Bt	NN2628	56°25·0'	4°48·8'W	X	50
Garbh-choire Beag	Highld	NN5072	56°49·2'	4°27·0'W	X	42
Garbh-choire Dubh	N Ayr	NR9643	55°38·5'	5°14·1'W	X	62,69
Garbh Choire Mór	Highld	NH0687	57°50·1'	5°15·6'W	X	19
Garbh Choire Mór	Highld	NH2567	57°39·8'	4°55·6'W	X	20
Garbh Chreag	Pth & Kin	NO0450	56°38·2'	3°33·5'W	X	52,53
Garbh Chruach	Arg & Bt	NM9404	56°11·3'	5°18·7'W	X	55
Garbh Coire	N Ayr	NR9645	55°39·6'	5°14·2'W	X	62,69
Garbh Coire Bothy	Aberd	NN9598	57°3·9'	3°43·4'W	X	36,43
Garbh-dhail	Highld	NM4465	56°42·7'	6°10·5'W	X	47
Garbh Dhoire	Arg & Bt	NM7229	56°24·2'	5°41·3'W	X	49
Garbh Dhoire	Highld	NC2123	58°9·8'	5°2·1'W	X	15
Garbh Dhoire	Highld	NH2108	57°7·9'	4°57·0'W	X	34
Garbh Dhoire	Highld	NM6553	56°36·9'	5°49·4'W	H	49
Garbh Eileach	Arg & Bt	NM6611	56°14·3'	5°46·1'W	X	55
Garbh Eilean	Arg & Bt	NM3837	56°27·4'	6°14·7'W	X	47,48
Garbh Eilean	Arg & Bt	NM4018	56°17·3'	6°11·6'W	X	48
Garbh Eilean	Highld	NC2233	58°15·3'	5°1·5'W	X	15
Garbh-eilean	Highld	NC8269	58°35·8'	4°1·3'W	X	10
Garbh Eilean	Highld	NG6153	57°30·5'	5°58·9'W	X	24
Garbh Eilean	Highld	NG9072	57°41·6'	5°30·9'W	X	19
Garbh Eilean	Highld	NH2602	57°4·8'	4°51·8'W	X	34
Garbh Eilean	Highld	NM7461	56°41·4'	5°41·0'W	X	40

Garbh Eilean	N Eil	NB1232	58°11·2'	6°53·6'W	X	13
Garbh Eilean	N Eil	NB3621	58°6·2'	6°28·4'W	X	14
Garbh Eilean	N Eil	NG4198	57°54·0'	6°21·8'W	X	14
Garbh Eilean Mòr	N Eil	NF8855	57°28·9'	7°11·9'W	X	22
Gar Bheinn	N Ayr	NR9929	55°31·1'	5°10·6'W	X	69
Garbh Ghaoir	Pth & Kin	NN4356	56°40·4'	4°33·3'W	W	42,51
Garbhlach Mhór	Highld	NM4165	56°42·6'	6°13·5'W	X	47
Garbh Leachd	Highld	NM8279	56°51·3'	5°34·1'W	X	40
Garbh Leathad	Arg & Bt	NM6531	56°25·0'	5°48·2'W	X	49
Garbh Leathad	Arg & Bt	NR6390	56°2·9'	5°47·9'W	X	61
Garbh Leitir	Arg & Bt	NM7000	56°8·5'	5°41·7'W	X	55,61
Garbh-ling	Highld	NG7729	57°18·1'	5°41·7'W	X	33
Garbh Lingay	N Eil	NF7403	57°0·4'	7°21·8'W	X	31
Garbh Loch	Highld	ND0346	58°23·8'	3°39·1'W	W	11,12
Garbh Lochan	Highld	NN3259	56°41·8'	4°44·2'W	W	41
Garbh Loch Mór	Highld	NC0830	58°13·3'	5°15·7'W	W	15
Garbh-mheall	Highld	NH7807	57°8·5'	4°0·5'W	X	35
Garbh Mheall	Pth & Kin	NN3643	56°33·3'	4°39·6'W	X	50
Garbh Mheall	Pth & Kin	NN5050	56°37·3'	4°26·2'W	H	42,51
Garbh-mheall Mór	Highld	NH8317	57°14·0'	3°55·8'W	H	35
Garbh-mheall Mór	Highld	NN7292	57°0·3'	4°6·0'W	H	35
Garbh Phort	Arg & Bt	NM3325	56°20·8'	6°18·8'W	W	48
Garbh Phort	Arg & Bt	NR5979	55°56·9'	5°51·2'W	W	61
Garbh Phort	Arg & Bt	NR7065	55°49·7'	5°39·9'W	W	61,62
Garbh-phort Caillich	Arg & Bt	NR5977	55°55·8'	5°51·1'W	W	61
Garbh-phort Mór	Arg & Bt	NR5977	55°55·8'	5°51·1'W	W	61
Garbh Rèisa	Arg & Bt	NR7597	56°7·0'	5°36·7'W	X	55
Garbh Rubha	Highld	NM5371	56°46·2'	6°2·1'W	X	39,47
Garbh Sgeir	Highld	NM1596	56°58·3'	6°40·9'W	X	39
Garbh Sgeir	Highld	NM4983	56°52·5'	6°6·7'W	X	39
Garbh-sgeir Mhór	Arg & Bt	NR4447	55°39·2'	6°3·7'W	X	60
Garbh Shlios	Arg & Bt	NM5727	56°22·6'	5°55·7'W	X	48
Garbh Shlios	Highld	NM7642	56°31·3'	5°38·1'W	X	49
Garbh Shròn	Arg & Bt	NM5229	56°23·6'	6°0·7'W	X	48
Garbh Shròn	Arg & Bt	NM8100	56°8·8'	5°31·1'W	H	55
Garbh Shron	Highld	NC2553	58°26·1'	4°59·4'W	X	9
Garbh Thorr	N Ayr	NR9335	55°34·1'	5°16·6'W	H	68,69
Garbh Uisge	Arg & Bt	NR5582	55°58·4'	5°55·2'W	W	61
Garbh-uisge	Highld	NH2139	57°24·6'	4°58·3'W	W	25
Garbh Uisge	Stir	NN5908	56°14·9'	4°16·1'W	W	57
Garbh Uisge Beag	Moray	NH9900	57°5·1'	3°39·5'W	W	36
Garbh Uisge Mór	Moray	NH9900	57°5·1'	3°39·5'W	W	36
Garbh uisge nan Cad	Arg & Bt	NR5992	56°3·9'	5°51·9'W	W	61
Garbity	Moray	NJ3152	57°33·4'	3°8·7'W	X	28
Garblies	Highld	NH9355	57°34·6'	3°46·9'W	X	27
Garb-mheall Beag	Highld	NN7193	57°0·9'	4°7·0'W	H	35
Garbo	Orkney	HY7243	59°16·6'	2°29·0'W	X	5
Garboldisham	Norf	TM0081	52°23·7'	0°56·8'E	T	144
Garboldisham Common	Suff	TL9980	52°23·1'	0°55·9'E	X	144
Garboldisham Heath	Norf	TL9982	52°24·2'	0°55·9'E	X	144
Garboldisham Manor	Norf	TM0082	52°24·2'	0°56·8'E	X	144
Garbole	Highld	NH7524	57°17·6'	4°4·0'W	X	35
Garburn Pass	Cumbr	NY4304	54°25·9'	2°52·3'W	X	90
Garbutt Hill	Northum	NY7158	54°55·2'	2°26·7'W	X	86,87
Garbutts Ghyll	N Yks	SE5374	54°9·8'	1°10·9'W	X	100
Garchell	Stir	NS5494	56°7·2'	4°20·5'W	X	57
Garchew	D & G	NX3375	55°2·7'	4°36·4'W	X	76
Garchew Burn	D & G	NX3376	55°3·3'	4°36·4'W	W	76
Garchory	Aberd	NJ3009	57°10·3'	3°9·0'W	X	37
Garchrie Moss	D & G	NW9964	54°56·1'	5°7·8'W	X	82
Garcrogo	D & G	NX7178	55°5·0'	4°0·8'W	X	77,84
Garcrogo Hill	D & G	NX7279	55°5·6'	3°59·9'W	H	77,84
Gardaness Hill	Shetld	HU4370	60°25·0'	1°12·7'W	H	2,3
Gardden	Powys	SJ0308	52°39·9'	3°25·7'W	X	125
Gardden	Powys	SJ0928	52°50·8'	3°20·7'W	X	125
Gardden Fawr	Powys	SJ1028	52°50·8'	3°19·8'W	X	125
Gardden Hall	Wrex	SJ2945	53°0·1'	3°3·1'W	X	117
Gardden Lodge	Wrex	SJ2944	52°59·6'	3°3·1'W	X	117
Garddfady Fm	Carm	SN8035	52°0·3'	3°44·5'W	FM	160
Garden	Aberd	NJ7964	57°40·2'	2°20·7'W	X	29,30
Garden	Pemb	SN0328	51°55·2'	4°51·5'W	X	145,157,158
Garden	Shetld	HU3252	60°15·3'	1°24·8'W	X	3
Garden	Stir	NS5994	56°7·3'	4°15·6'W	X	57
Gardenburn	D & G	NX8157	54°53·9'	3°50·9'W	X	84
Garden City	Blae Gw	SO1607	51°45·6'	3°12·6'W	T	161
Garden City	Flint	SJ3269	53°13·1'	3°0·7'W	T	117
Garden Copse Fm	Dorset	SU0402	50°49·3'	1°56·2'W	FM	195
Garden Cott	Scot Bord	NT8553	55°46·5'	2°13·9'W	X	67,74
Gardener's Fm	Essex	TL8908	51°44·6'	0°44·7'E	FM	168
Gardeners Green	Wok	SU8266	51°23·5'	0°48·9'W	T	175
Gardenershill	Aberd	NJ9242	57°28·3'	2°7·5'W	X	30
Gardener's Hill	E Susx	TQ4603	50°48·7'	0°4·7'E	X	198
Gardener's Houses Fm	N upon Ty	NZ2074	55°3·9'	1°40·8'W	FM	88
Garden Fm	Cambs	TL1264	52°16·0'	0°21·1'W	FM	153
Gardenhead	Moray	NJ4750	57°32·5'	2°52·7'W	X	28,29
Garden Ho	Darl	NZ3010	54°29·3'	1°31·8'W	X	93
Garden Ho	Durham	NY9649	54°50·4'	2°3·3'W	X	87
Garden Ho	Heref	SO4265	52°17·0'	2°50·6'W	X	137,148,149
Garden Ho	Northum	NZ0887	55°10·9'	1°52·0'W	X	81
Garden Ho	Suff	TM4167	52°15·1'	1°32·3'E	X	156
Gardenholm	D & G	NT0707	55°21·1'	3°27·6'W	X	78
Gardeni	Cered	SN6072	52°19·9'	4°2·9'W	X	135
Garden Lake	Notts	SK5453	53°4·5'	1°11·2'W	W	120
Garden of Maiden Bower	I Scilly	SV8514	49°56·8'	6°23·1'W	X	203
Garden's Hillock	Aberd	NJ8618	57°15·4'	2°13·5'W	X	38
Gardenstone Fm	N Yks	NZ4605	54°26·5'	1°17·0'W	FM	93
Gardenstown	Aberd	NJ8064	57°40·2'	2°19·7'W	T	29,30
Garden Village	Leeds	SE4332	53°47·2'	1°19·5'W	T	105
Garden Village	Sheff	SK2698	53°28·9'	1°36·1'W	T	110
Garden Village	Swan	SS5997	51°39·5'	4°1·9'W	T	159
Garden Village	Wrex	SJ3352	53°3·9'	2°59·6'W	T	117
Garder Hill	Shetld	HU3869	60°24·5'	1°18·1'W	H	2,3
Garderhouse	Shetld	HU2177	60°28·8'	1°36·6'W	X	3
Garderhouse	Shetld	HU3348	60°13·2'	1°23·8'W	T	3
Garderhouse	Shetld	HU5192	60°36·8'	1°3·6'W	X	1,2
Garderhouse Voe	Shetld	HU3347	60°12·6'	1°23·8'W	W	3
Gardham	E Yorks	SE9542	53°52·2'	0°32·9'W	T	106
Gardie	Shetld	HP5910	60°46·4'	0°54·5'W	X	1
Gardie	Shetld	HP6211	60°46·9'	0°51·2'W	T	1
Gardie	Shetld	HU1760	60°19·7'	1°41·0'W	X	3

Gardie	Shetld	HU5091	60°36·2'	1°4·7'W	T	1,2
Gardie Geo	Shetld	HU6066	60°22·7'	0°54·2'W	X	2
Gardie Hill	Shetld	HU4166	60°22·8'	1°14·9'W	H	2,3
Gardie Ho	Shetld	HU4842	60°9·8'	1°7·6'W	X	4
Gardiestaing	Shetld	HU5191	60°36·2'	1°3·6'W	X	1,2
Gardie Taing	Shetld	HU4332	60°4·5'	1°13·1'W	X	4
Gardin	Shetld	HU4865	60°22·2'	1°7·3'W	X	2,3
Gardiner's Fm	Glos	SO8222	51°54·0'	2°15·3'W	FM	162
Gardiner's Hall	Suff	TM1270	52°17·5'	1°6·9'E	X	144,155
Garding Mill Valley	Shrops	SO4494	52°32·7'	2°49·1'W	X	137
Gardins	Shetld	HU4488	60°34·7'	1°11·3'W	X	1,2
Gardner's Barn	Oxon	SP5913	51°49·0'	1°8·2'W	X	164
Gardners End	Herts	TL3227	51°55·8'	0°4·4'W	X	166
Gardners Fm	E Susx	TQ6712	50°53·2'	0°22·8'E	FM	199
Gardner's Fm	Lancs	SD4454	53°59·0'	2°50·8'W	FM	102
Gardners Fm	Wilts	ST8881	51°31·9'	2°10·0'W	FM	173
Gardner's Hall	W Loth	NS9964	55°51·8'	3°36·4'W	X	65
Gardners Hall	W Loth	NS9978	55°59·3'	3°36·7'W	X	65
Gardom's Edge	Derby	SK2773	53°15·4'	1°35·3'W	X	119
Gardrum	E Ayr	NS4644	55°40·2'	4°26·5'W	X	70
Gardrum	Falk	NS9075	55°57·6'	3°45·3'W	X	65
Gardrum Mill	E Ayr	NS4644	55°40·2'	4°26·5'W	X	70
Gardrum Moss	Falk	NS8975	55°57·6'	3°46·2'W	X	65
Gards	Shetld	HU4435	60°6·1'	1°12·0'W	X	4
Gardyne Castle	Angus	NO5748	56°37·6'	2°41·6'W	A	54
Gare	Corn	SW8843	50°15·2'	4°58·1'W	X	204
Gareg Hir	Carm	SN4033	51°58·6'	4°19·4'W	A	146
Gareg Las	Carm	SN7720	51°52·1'	3°46·8'W	X	160
Gareg-lwyd	Carm	SN6419	51°51·4'	3°58·1'W	X	159
Gareg-lwyd	Powys	SN8531	51°58·2'	3°40·1'W	X	160
Gare Hill	Wilts	ST7840	51°9·8'	2°18·5'W	T	183
Gareland	D & G	NS7618	55°26·7'	3°57·2'W	X	71,78
Gareland Burn	D & G	NS7719	55°27·2'	3°56·3'W	W	71,78
Garelet Dod	Scot Bord	NT1217	55°26·6'	3°23·0'W	H	78
Garelet Hill	Scot Bord	NT1220	55°28·2'	3°23·1'W	H	72
Gare Loch	Arg & Bt	NS2585	56°1·8'	4°48·1'W	W	56
Garelochhead	Arg & Bt	NS2391	56°5·0'	4°50·2'W	T	56
Garelochhead Forest	Arg & Bt	NS2187	56°2·8'	4°52·0'W	F	56
Garelochhead Forest	Arg & Bt	NS2482	56°0·2'	4°48·9'W	F	56
Garendon Park	Leic	SK5019	52°46·2'	1°15·1'W	X	129
Garepool Burn	E Ayr	NS6512	55°23·3'	4°7·4'W	W	71
Garey	I of M	SC2579	54°10·9'	4°40·5'W	X	95
Garey	I of M	SC4295	54°19·8'	4°25·4'W	T	95
Garfield	E Ayr	NS5128	55°31·6'	4°21·2'W	X	70
Garfitts	N Yks	NZ5603	54°25·4'	1°7·8'W	X	93
Garford	Oxon	SU4296	51°39·9'	1°23·2'W	T	164
Garford Fm	Heref	SO6043	52°5·3'	2°34·6'W	FM	149
Garforth	Leeds	SE4132	53°47·2'	1°22·2'W	T	105
Garforth Fm	E Yorks	SE8548	53°55·5'	0°41·9'W	FM	106
Garforth Hall	N Yks	SE7775	54°10·1'	0°48·8'W	X	100
Garf Water	S Lanak	NS9332	55°34·4'	3°41·4'W	W	71,72
Gargill	Cumbr	NY5406	54°27·1'	2°42·1'W	X	90
Gargowan	E Ayr	NS4722	55°28·3'	4°24·8'W	X	70
Gargrave	N Yks	SD9354	53°59·2'	2°6·0'W	T	103
Gargrave Ho	N Yks	SD9254	53°59·2'	2°6·9'W	X	103
Gargreave	Cumbr	SD2280	54°12·8'	3°11·3'W	X	96
Gargrie	D & G	NX2852	54°50·3'	4°40·3'W	X	82
Gargrie Moor	D & G	NX2853	54°50·8'	4°40·3'W	X	82
Gargunnock	Stir	NS7094	56°7·5'	4°5·0'W	T	57
Gargunnock Burn	Stir	NS7093	56°7·0'	4°5·0'W	W	57
Gargunnock Hills	Stir	NS6891	56°5·9'	4°6·9'W	H	57
Gargunnock Ho	Stir	NS7194	56°7·5'	4°4·1'W	X	57
Gargus Fm	Corn	SW9547	50°17·5'	4°52·3'W	FM	204
Garguston	Highld	NH5749	57°30·8'	4°22·8'W	X	26
Gargwy Fawr	Powys	SO2226	51°55·9'	3°7·7'W	W	161
Garhallow Burn	Arg & Bt	NS1573	55°55·1'	4°57·2'W	W	63
Garheugh	D & G	NX2750	54°49·2'	4°41·1'W	X	82
Garheugh Fell	D & G	NX2751	54°49·7'	4°41·2'W	X	82
Garheugh Port	D & G	NX2649	54°48·6'	4°42·0'W	W	82
Gariannonum (Roman Fort)	Norf	TG4704	52°34·9'	1°39·2'E	R	134
Gariob	Arg & Bt	NR7889	56°2·8'	5°33·4'W	T	55
Garioch	Aberd	NJ6924	57°18·6'	2°30·4'W	X	38
Gariochsburn	Aberd	NJ6042	57°28·2'	2°39·6'W	X	29
Gariochsford	Aberd	NJ6640	57°27·2'	2°33·5'W	T	29
Garizim	Conwy	SH6975	53°15·6'	3°57·4'W	T	115
Garizle	S Ayr	NX2779	55°4·8'	4°42·2'W	X	76
Garker	Corn	SX0454	50°21·4'	4°45·0'W	T	200
Garlaff	E Ayr	NS5417	55°25·8'	4°18·0'W	X	70
Garland	Moray	NJ3750	57°32·4'	3°2·7'W	X	28
Garland Cross	Devon	SS7118	50°57·1'	3°49·8'W	X	180
Garland Hall	Ches	SJ6681	53°19·7'	2°30·2'W	X	109
Garlandhayes	Devon	ST1715	50°55·9'	3°10·5'W	T	181,193
Garlandhayes Fm	Devon	ST0103	50°49·3'	3°24·0'W	FM	192
Garland Lane Fm	Leic	SK4406	52°39·2'	1°20·6'W	FM	140
Garlandmore	Moray	NJ1742	57°27·9'	3°22·6'W	X	28
Garlands	Cumbr	NY4354	54°52·9'	2°52·9'W	T	85
Garlands	Essex	TL8704	51°42·4'	0°42·8'E	X	168
Garlands	W Susx	TQ0830	51°3·8'	0°27·1'W	X	187
Garlands Fm	Devon	SS4304	50°49·1'	4°13·4'W	FM	190
Garland's Fm	Essex	TL6633	51°58·5'	0°25·4'E	FM	167
Garland's Fm	Essex	TL6842	52°3·3'	0°27·4'E	FM	154
Garland's Fm	Essex	TL8632	51°57·5'	0°42·8'E	FM	168
Garlands Fm	Essex	TL9519	51°50·4'	0°50·2'E	FM	168
Garlands Fm	Oxon	SU3689	51°36·2'	1°28·4'W	FM	174
Garland Stone	Pemb	SM7210	51°44·8'	5°17·8'W	X	157
Garleffan Fm	E Ayr	NS6219	55°27·0'	4°10·5'W	FM	71
Garleffin	S Ayr	NX0881	55°5·4'	5°0·1'W	T	76
Garleffin Fell	S Ayr	NX3599	55°15·7'	4°35·4'W	X	77
Garleffin Hill	S Ayr	NX2486	55°8·3'	4°45·3'W	X	76
Garleigh Moor	Northum	NZ0699	55°17·4'	1°53·9'W	X	81
Garlenick	Corn	SW9450	50°19·1'	4°53·3'W	X	200,204
Garlet	Angus	NO4877	56°53·1'	2°50·8'W	H	44
Garlet Burn	Angus	NO4774	56°51·5'	2°51·7'W	W	44
Garlet Hill	Aberd	NJ4316	57°14·1'	2°56·2'W	H	37
Garleton Fm	E Loth	NT4877	55°59·2'	2°49·6'W	FM	66
Garleton Hills	E Loth	NT5176	55°58·7'	2°46·7'W	H	66
Garleton Walk	E Loth	NT6180	56°0·9'	2°37·1'W	X	67
Garlewood	S Lanak	NS8042	55°39·7'	3°54·0'W	X	71,72
Garlic Flats	N Yks	SE4735	53°48·8'	1°16·8'W	X	105
Garlick Hill	D & G	NX4372	55°1·3'	4°26·9'W	H	77

Garlic Street	Norf	TM2183	52°24·2'	1°15·3'E	T	156
Garlidna Fm	Corn	SW7032	50°8·8'	5°12·8'W	FM	203
Garlies Castle	D & G	NX4269	54°59·7'	4°27·8'W	A	83
Garlies Lodge	D & G	NX3577	55°3·9'	4°34·6'W	X	77
Garlieston	D & G	NX4846	54°47·4'	4°21·4'W	T	83
Garlieston Bay	D & G	NX4946	54°47·4'	4°20·5'W	W	83
Garlies Wood	D & G	NX4268	54°59·1'	4°27·7'W	F	83
Garliford	Devon	SS7525	51°0·9'	3°46·5'W	T	180
Garlinebeg	Moray	NJ1741	57°27·4'	3°22·5'W	X	28
Garline Fm	Moray	NJ1635	57°24·1'	3°23·4'W	FM	28
Garlinge	Kent	TR3369	51°22·6'	1°21·3'E	T	179
Garlinge Green	Kent	TR1152	51°13·9'	1°1·7'E	T	179,189
Garllegan Fach	Carm	SN2822	51°52·4'	4°29·5'W	X	145,158
Garllegan Fawr	Carm	SN2821	51°51·9'	4°29·5'W	X	145,158
Garloch Hill	Stir	NS5583	56°1·3'	4°19·1'W	H	57,64
Garloff	D & G	NX9170	55°1·0'	3°41·9'W	X	84
Garlogie	Aberd	NJ7805	57°8·4'	2°21·4'W	X	38
Garlogs	Hants	SU3035	51°7·0'	1°33·9'W	X	185
Garlot	Aberd	NO3593	57°1·7'	3°3·8'W	H	37,44
Garlot Hill	Aberd	NO6684	56°57·0'	2°33·1'W	X	45
Garlowbank	Angus	NO4054	56°40·7'	2°58·3'W	X	54
Garlyne	Highld	NJ0220	57°15·9'	3°37·0'W	X	36
Garman Carr	N Yks	SE5935	53°48·7'	1°5·8'W	X	105
Garman's Down	Devon	SS5939	51°8·2'	4°0·5'W	X	180
Garmartin	D & G	NX7968	54°59·8'	3°53·1'W	X	84
Garmelow	Staffs	SJ7927	52°50·6'	2°18·3'W	T	127
Garmond	Aberd	NJ8052	57°33·7'	2°19·6'W	T	29,30
Garmondsway	Durham	NZ3334	54°42·2'	1°28·8'W	T	93
Garmony	Arg & Bt	NM6640	56°29·9'	5°47·7'W	X	49
Garmony Burn	Arg & Bt	NM6640	56°29·9'	5°47·7'W	W	49
Garmony Point	Arg & Bt	NM6740	56°29·9'	5°46·7'W	X	49
Garmore	E Dunb	NS6478	55°58·8'	4°10·3'W	X	64
Garmouth	Moray	NJ3364	57°39·9'	3°6·9'W	T	28
Garmsley	Worcs	SO6261	52°15·0'	2°33·0'W	A	138,149
Garmston	Shrops	SJ6006	52°39·3'	2°35·1'W	T	127
Garmus Taing	Shetld	HU3693	60°37·4'	1°20·0'W	X	1,2
Garn	Carm	SN5915	51°49·2'	4°2·4'W	X	159
Garn	Cered	SN6952	52°9·3'	3°54·5'W	H	146
Garn	Denb	SJ0268	53°12·2'	3°27·6'W	X	116
Garn	Gwyn	SH6116	52°43·7'	4°3·1'W	H	124
Garn	Heref	SO3326	51°55·9'	2°58·1'W	X	161
Garn	Pemb	SM9934	51°58·3'	4°55·2'W	X	157
Garn	Powys	SO0173	52°21·0'	3°26·8'W	H	136,147
Garn	Powys	SO1081	52°25·4'	3°19·0'W	T	136
Garn	V of Glam	ST1271	51°26·1'	3°15·6'W	X	171
Garnaburn	S Ayr	NX1586	55°8·3'	4°53·7'W	X	76
Garnacott Fm	Devon	SS5124	51°0·0'	4°7·0'W	FM	180
Garnant	Carm	SN6813	51°48·2'	3°54·5'W	T	159
Garnathwaite	Durham	NZ0309	54°28·8'	1°56·8'W	X	92
Garn Bach	Gwyn	SH2834	52°52·8'	4°33·0'W	H	123
Garn Bank	Shrops	SO2975	52°22·3'	3°2·2'W	X	137,148
Garnbica	Carm	SN6316	51°49·8'	3°58·9'W	X	159
Garn Boduan	Gwyn	SH3139	52°55·6'	4°30·4'W	H	123
Garn Boduan (Fort)	Gwyn	SH3139	52°55·6'	4°30·4'W	A	123
Garn Brys	Conwy	SH8949	53°1·9'	3°38·9'W	X	116
Garn Caws	Powys	SO1216	51°50·4'	3°16·2'W	A	161
Garn Clochdy	Torf	SO2806	51°45·1'	3°2·2'W	X	161
Garn Ddu	Merth Tyd	SO0212	51°48·1'	3°24·9'W	H	160
Garn Ddu	Rho Cyn Taf	SN9511	51°47·5'	3°31·0'W	X	160
Garn Deifog	Pemb	SM9831	51°56·7'	4°56·0'W	X	157
Garndiffaith	Torf	SO2604	51°44·0'	3°3·9'W	T	171
Garndiffaith	Torf	SO2605	51°44·6'	3°3·9'W	T	161
Garndolbenmaen	Gwyn	SH4944	52°58·6'	4°14·5'W	T	123
Garn Dwad	Powys	SN8748	52°7·4'	3°38·6'W	H	147
Garndwyrain	Pemb	SM9431	51°56·6'	4°59·4'W	X	157
Garnedd	Conwy	SH7051	53°2·7'	3°55·9'W	X	115
Garnedd	Conwy	SH8974	53°15·3'	3°39·4'W	X	116
Garnedd	I of Angl	SH5072	53°13·7'	4°14·4'W	X	114,115
Garnedd Fawr	Gwyn	SH9342	52°58·1'	3°35·2'W	A	125
Garnedd-goch	Gwyn	SH5149	53°1·3'	4°12·9'W	A	115
Garnedd-hir	Gwyn	SH5341	52°57·0'	4°10·9'W	X	124
Garnedd Lwyd	Caer	ST1090	51°36·3'	3°17·6'W	A	171
Garnedd Uchaf	Gwyn	SH6866	53°10·7'	3°58·1'W	H	115
Garnedd Ugain	Gwyn	SH6155	53°4·7'	4°4·1'W	H	115
Garnedd-wen	Conwy	SH7473	53°14·6'	3°52·9'W	X	115
Garneddwen	Flint	SJ1770	53°13·5'	3°14·2'W	X	116
Garneddwen	Gwyn	SH7608	52°39·6'	3°49·6'W	X	124
Garneddwen	Powys	SJ1331	52°52·4'	3°17·2'W	H	125
Garner Bank	Cumbr	SD1598	54°22·5'	3°18·1'W	H	96
Garner Ho	Ches	SJ5764	53°10·5'	2°38·2'W	X	117
Garner Ho	Derby	SK2082	53°20·3'	1°41·6'W	X	110
Garness Fm	Carm	SN2108	51°44·8'	4°35·2'W	FM	158
Garness Mill	Pemb	SN1809	51°45·2'	4°37·8'W	X	158
Garnett Bridge	Cumbr	SD5299	54°23·3'	2°43·9'W	T	97
Garnett Ho	Cumbr	SD5095	54°21·1'	2°45·7'W	X	97
Garnetts	Essex	TL6317	51°49·9'	0°22·3'E	T	167
Garnetts Wood	Essex	TL6318	51°50·4'	0°22·4'E	F	167
Garn Fach	Brig	SS9591	51°36·7'	3°30·6'W	A	170
Garn-fâch	Carm	SN5310	51°46·4'	4°7·4'W	X	159
Garn-fâch	Carm	SN6009	51°46·0'	4°1·3'W	X	159
Garnfach	Cered	SN5466	52°16·6'	4°8·0'W	X	135
Garn Fach	Cered	SN5667	52°17·2'	4°6·3'W	X	135
Garn Fach	Nth Pt Talb	SN9003	51°43·1'	3°35·2'W	A	170
Garn Fach	Powys	SO0481	52°25·4'	3°24·3'W	X	136
Garnfadryn	Gwyn	SH2834	52°52·8'	4°33·0'W	T	123
Garn Fawr	Brig	SS9592	51°37·3'	3°30·6'W	A	170
Garn-fawr	Carm	SN3923	51°53·2'	4°20·0'W	A	145,159
Garn Fawr	Carm	SN7147	52°6·6'	3°52·6'W	X	146,147
Garn Fawr	Carm	SN7822	51°53·2'	3°46·0'W	X	160
Garn-fawr	Gwyn	SH4351	53°2·2'	4°20·1'W	X	115,123
Garn-Fawr	Monm	ST3793	51°38·2'	2°54·2'W	X	171
Garn Fawr	Pemb	SM8938	52°0·3'	5°4·1'W	H	157
Garn Fawr	Pemb	SN0036	51°59·4'	4°54·4'W	X	145,157
Garnfawr	Powys	SO1057	52°12·5'	3°18·6'W	X	148
Garn Fechan	Pemb	SM9038	52°0·3'	5°3·2'W	X	157
Garn Felen	Cered	SN7056	52°11·5'	3°53·7'W	A	146,147
Garn-ffrŵd	Carm	SN5014	51°48·5'	4°10·2'W	X	159
Garn Fm	Carm	SN4702	51°42·0'	4°12·5'W	FM	159
Garn Fm	Monm	SO2730	51°58·1'	3°3·4'W	FM	161
Garnfoel	Cered	SN5164	52°15·5'	4°10·6'W	X	146
Garn Folch	Pemb	SM9139	52°0·8'	5°2·4'W	X	157
Garngaled	Powys	SO0027	51°56·2'	3°26·9'W	X	160
Garn Gilfach	Pemb	SM9039	52°0·8'	5°3·2'W	X	157
Garn Goch	Nth Pt Talb	SN8110	51°46·8'	3°43·1'W	A	160
Garn Goch	Nth Pt Talb	SN9001	51°42·1'	3°35·1'W	X	170
Garn Goch	Powys	SO2117	51°51·0'	3°8·4'W	A	161
Garn Gron	Cered	SN7461	52°14·2'	3°50·3'W	H	146,147
Garnhowell	Carm	SN5304	51°43·2'	4°7·3'W	X	159
Garnieland	Renf	NS4869	55°53·7'	4°25·4'W	X	64
Garniemire	D & G	NX5952	54°50·8'	4°11·3'W	X	83
Garn-isaf	Pemb	SM8533	51°57·5'	5°7·4'W	X	157
Garnish Hall	Essex	TL6012	51°47·3'	0°19·6'E	X	167
Garnish Hall	Essex	TQ4799	51°40·5'	0°8·0'E	X	167,177
Garnival's Week Fm	Somer	ST1325	51°1·3'	3°14·0'W	FM	181,193
Garnkirk	N Lanak	NS6768	55°53·5'	4°7·2'W	T	64
Garnkirk Burn	N Lanak	NS6669	55°54·0'	4°8·2'W	W	64
Garn Lâs	Powys	SN8224	51°54·4'	3°42·5'W	X	160
Garn Las	Rho Cyn Taf	SO0203	51°43·3'	3°24·7'W	A	170
Garnless Scar	N Yks	SE0698	54°22·9'	1°54·0'W	X	99
Garnllwyd	V of Glam	ST0571	51°26·0'	3°21·6'W	X	170
Garn Lwyd	Caer	ST1485	51°33·7'	3°14·1'W	X	171
Garn Lwyd	Carm	SN5416	51°49·7'	4°6·7'W	X	159
Garnlwyd	Carm	SN7223	51°53·7'	3°51·2'W	X	160
Garn-lwyd	Cered	SN7054	52°10·4'	3°53·7'W	X	146,147
Garnlwyd	Powys	SN9221	51°52·9'	3°33·8'W	X	160
Garnlydan	Blae Gw	SO1612	51°48·3'	3°12·7'W	T	161
Garnog	I of Angl	SH5090	53°23·4'	4°14·9'W	X	114
Garnons	Essex	TL9433	51°57·9'	0°49·8'E	A	168
Garnons	Heref	SO3943	52°5·2'	2°53·0'W	X	148,149,161
Garnons Hill	Heref	SO3944	52°5·7'	2°53·0'W	H	148,149,161
Garnon Tower	N Lanak	NS7950	55°44·0'	3°55·2'W	X	64
Garn Prys	Conwy	SH8848	53°1·3'	3°39·8'W	H	116
Garn Rock	Shrops	SO2381	52°25·5'	3°7·5'W	X	137
Garnsgate	Lincs	TF4122	52°46·9'	0°5·8'E	T	131
Garnshaw Ho	N Yks	SE0163	54°4·0'	1°58·7'W	X	98
Garnstone Ho	Heref	SO3950	52°8·9'	2°53·1'W	X	148,149
Garnstone Wood	Heref	SO4049	52°8·4'	2°52·2'W	F	148,149
Garn-swllt	Swan	SN6209	51°46·0'	3°59·6'W	T	159
Garnswllt	Swan	SN6209	51°46·0'	3°59·6'W	X	159
Garn, The	Shrops	SO2381	52°25·5'	3°7·5'W	X	137
Garn, The	V of Glam	ST0273	51°27·1'	3°24·2'W	X	170
Garn Turne Rocks	Pemb	SM9727	51°54·5'	4°56·7'W	X	157,158
Garn Uchaf	Powys	SJ0926	52°49·7'	3°20·6'W	X	125
Garn Wen	Brig	SS8492	51°37·1'	3°40·1'W	X	170
Garnwen	Carm	SN4610	51°46·3'	4°13·5'W	X	159
Garnwen	Carm	SN4918	51°50·7'	4°11·1'W	X	159
Garn Wen	Carm	SN7945	52°5·6'	3°45·6'W	A	146,147
Garnwen	Cered	SN6063	52°15·1'	4°2·7'W	X	146
Garn-wen	Cered	SN6884	52°26·5'	3°56·1'W	A	135
Garn-wen	Monm	SO2825	51°55·4'	3°2·4'W	X	161
Garn Wen	Powys	SN8446	52°6·3'	3°41·2'W	H	147
Garn Wen	Powys	SN8736	52°0·9'	3°38·4'W	A	160
Garn Wen	Powys	SN9053	52°10·1'	3°36·1'W	H	147
Garnwen	Powys	SN9221	51°52·9'	3°33·8'W	X	160
Garn Wen	Powys	SN9340	52°3·1'	3°33·2'W	A	147,160
Garn-wen	Torf	SO2804	51°44·0'	3°2·2'W	H	171
Garn-wen (Cairn)	Monm	SO2825	51°55·4'	3°2·4'W	A	161
Garnwen Fm	Carm	SN1728	51°55·5'	4°39·3'W	FM	145,158
Garnwnda	Pemb	SM9339	52°0·9'	5°0·6'W	X	157
Garn Wood	Powys	SO1393	52°31·9'	3°16·6'W	F	136
Garn-yr-erw	Torf	SO2310	51°47·2'	3°6·6'W	T	161
Garpel	E Ayr	NS6227	55°31·3'	4°10·7'W	X	71
Garpel Burn	E Ayr	NX4798	55°15·4'	4°24·0'W	W	77
Garpel Water	E Ayr	NS6924	55°29·8'	4°4·0'W	W	71
Garpin	S Ayr	NS3207	55°20·0'	4°38·5'W	X	70,76
Garpit	Fife	NO4627	56°26·2'	2°52·1'W	X	54,59
Garple Burn	D & G	NX6681	55°6·6'	4°5·6'W	W	77
Garplefoot	D & G	NX6479	55°5·5'	4°7·4'W	X	77
Garpol Spa	D & G	NT0602	55°18·4'	3°28·4'W	W	78
Garpol Water	D & G	NT0304	55°19·5'	3°31·3'W	W	78
Garrabost	N Eil	NB5033	58°13·2'	6°15·0'W	T	8
Garrachan	Highld	NG2447	57°26·0'	6°35·5'W	T	23
Garrachcroit Bàgh	Arg & Bt	NR8044	55°38·2'	5°29·3'W	W	62,69
Garrachoran	Arg & Bt	NS1181	55°59·3'	5°1·4'W	X	63
Garrachra	Arg & Bt	NS0988	56°3·1'	5°3·6'W	X	56
Garrachra Glen	Arg & Bt	NS0990	56°4·1'	5°3·7'W	X	56
Garrack	Aberd	NJ7705	57°8·4'	2°22·3'W	X	38
Garradh	Stir	NN3810	56°15·6'	4°36·5'W	X	50,56
Garradh Mór	Highld	NG3057	57°31·6'	6°30·2'W	X	23
Garra Eallabus	Arg & Bt	NR2870	55°51·0'	6°20·3'W	X	60
Garrafad	Highld	NG4967	57°37·7'	6°11·8'W	T	23
Garralanga	Orkney	HY5004	58°55·5'	2°51·6'W	X	6,7
Garralburn	Moray	NJ4554	57°34·6'	2°54·7'W	X	28,29
Garral Hill	Moray	NJ4455	57°35·2'	2°55·7'W	H	28
Garrallan	E Ayr	NS5418	55°26·3'	4°18·0'W	X	70
Garramarsh	Devon	SS7222	50°59·2'	3°49·0'W	X	180
Garramor	Highld	NM6691	56°57·3'	5°50·5'W	X	40
Garran, The	Aberd	NO8778	56°53·8'	2°12·4'W	X	45
Garrarie	D & G	NX3840	54°44·0'	4°30·5'W	X	83
Garraron	Arg & Bt	NM8009	56°13·6'	5°32·5'W	X	55
Garrary Burn	D & G	NX5280	55°5·8'	4°18·7'W	W	77
Garrary Burn	D & G	NX5379	55°5·3'	4°17·8'W	W	77
Garras	Corn	SW7023	50°4·0'	5°12·5'W	T	203
Garras	Corn	SW8148	50°17·7'	5°4·1'W	X	204
Garrauld	Stir	NS5391	56°5·6'	4°21·3'W	X	57
Garreg	Flint	SJ1377	53°17·2'	3°17·9'W	T	116
Garreg	Gwyn	SH6141	52°57·1'	4°3·7'W	T	124
Garreg Allan	I of Angl	SH5090	53°23·4'	4°14·9'W	X	114
Garreg Bank	Powys	SJ2811	52°41·8'	3°3·5'W	T	126
Garreg Ddu Reservoir	Powys	SN9164	52°16·0'	3°35·4'W	W	147
Garreg-ddu Reservoir	Powys	SN9165	52°16·6'	3°35·5'W	W	136,147
Garregelldrem	Gwyn	SH6143	52°58·2'	4°3·8'W	X	124
Garreg-fawr	Carm	SN7137	52°1·2'	3°52·4'W	X	146,160
Garreg Fawr	Conwy	SH6973	53°14·5'	3°57·4'W	H	115
Garreg Fawr	Gwyn	SH1524	52°47·2'	4°44·2'W	X	123
Garreg Fawr	I of Angl	SH2479	53°17·0'	4°38·0'W	X	114
Garreg Fawr	I of Angl	SH3688	53°22·1'	4°27·5'W	X	114
Garreg-fawr	Powys	SN9313	51°48·6'	3°32·7'W	X	160
Garreg Fawr	Powys	SN9437	52°1·5'	3°32·3'W	H	160
Garregfechan	Carm	SN7136	52°0·7'	3°52·4'W	X	146,160
Garreg Fm	Carm	SN4207	51°44·6'	4°16·9'W	FM	159
Garreg Fraith	Carm	SN7117	51°50·4'	3°52·0'W	X	160
Garreg-Frêch	Gwyn	SH5341	52°57·0'	4°10·9'W	X	124
Garreg-goch	Gwyn	SH5637	52°54·9'	4°8·1'W	X	124
Garreg Goch Ganol	Carm	SN5418	51°50·7'	4°6·8'W	X	159
Garreg Goch Isaf	Carm	SN5318	51°50·7'	4°7·7'W	X	159
Garreg-hir	Powys	SN9997	52°33·9'	3°29·0'W	X	136
Garreg Llwyd	Carm	SN3025	51°54·1'	4°27·9'W	A	145
Garreg Lwyd	Carm	SN7417	51°50·5'	3°49·3'W	H	160
Garreglwyd	Cered	SN7864	52°15·9'	3°46·9'W	X	146,147
Garreg-lwyd	Denb	SJ0059	53°7·4'	3°29·3'W	X	116
Garreg Lwyd	Denb	SJ1757	53°6·5'	3°14·0'W	X	116
Garreg Lwyd	Powys	SN9473	52°20·9'	3°33·0'W	H	136,147
Garreg Lwyd	Powys	SN9512	51°48·0'	3°31·0'W	X	160
Garreg Lydan	Flint	SJ2075	53°16·2'	3°11·6'W	X	117
Garreg-wen	Cered	SN3940	52°2·3'	4°20·5'W	X	145
Garreg-wen	Conwy	SH7363	53°9·2'	3°53·5'W	X	115
Garreg Wen	Gwyn	SH5537	52°54·9'	4°9·0'W	X	124
Garreg Wen	Pemb	SN0428	51°55·2'	4°50·6'W	X	145,157,158
Garreg Wen	Pemb	SN2436	51°59·9'	4°33·4'W	X	145
Garreg Wen	Powys	SH9825	52°49·0'	3°30·4'W	X	125
Garreg y Gwynt	Powys	SN9577	52°23·1'	3°32·2'W	H	136,147
Garrel	D & G	NY0590	55°12·0'	3°29·1'W	X	78
Garrel Burn	N Lanak	NS7080	56°0·0'	4°4·6'W	W	64
Garrelgum	N Yks	SE0460	54°2·4'	1°55·9'W	X	98
Garrel Hill	D & G	NY0488	55°10·9'	3°30·0'W	X	78
Garrel Hill	N Lanak	NS7081	56°0·5'	4°4·7'W	H	64
Garrel Water	D & G	NY0392	55°13·0'	3°31·0'W	W	78
Garren Brook	Heref	SO4725	51°55·5'	2°45·9'W	W	161
Garren Brook	Heref	SO5222	51°53·9'	2°41·5'W	W	162
Garret Hill	Norf	TF9943	52°57·1'	0°58·1'E	X	132
Garret Ho	Cumbr	SD3779	54°12·4'	2°57·5'W	X	96,97
Garrets Green	Birm	SP1485	52°28·0'	1°47·2'W	T	139
Garret Shiels	Northum	NY8693	55°14·1'	2°12·8'W	X	80
Garrets Hill	Northum	NY8452	54°52·0'	2°14·5'W	X	86,87
Garrett Lee	Northum	NZ1096	55°15·7'	1°50·1'W	X	81
Garrett Lee Wood	Northum	NZ1196	55°15·7'	1°49·2'W	F	81
Garretts	Kent	TQ9872	51°25·0'	0°51·2'E	X	178
Garretts Barn	Northnts	SP6666	52°17·5'	1°1·5'W	X	152
Garretts Fm	I of W	SZ5187	50°41·1'	1°16·3'W	FM	196
Garr House Fm	Essex	TL9515	51°48·2'	0°50·1'E	FM	168
Garrick	Pth & Kin	NN8412	56°17·4'	3°52·0'W	X	58
Garrick Burn	Highld	NH7978	57°46·8'	4°1·6'W	W	21
Garrick Fm	E Yorks	SE8544	53°53·4'	0°42·0'W	FM	106
Garrie	D & G	NX0954	54°50·9'	4°58·1'W	X	82
Garrien	Arg & Bt	NR9993	56°5·5'	5°13·4'W	X	55
Garrier Burn	E Ayr	NS4042	55°39·0'	4°32·1'W	W	70
Garrier Burn	N Ayr	NS3739	55°37·3'	4°34·9'W	W	70
Garrieston	D & G	NX8484	55°8·5'	3°48·8'W	X	78
Garriestown	Cumbr	NY3564	54°58·2'	3°0·5'W	X	85
Garrigill	Cumbr	NY7441	54°46·0'	2°23·8'W	T	86,87
Garrigill Bank	Cumbr	NY6236	54°43·3'	2°35·0'W	X	91
Garrimatic	Highld	NH4155	57°33·7'	4°39·0'W	X	26
Garrington Fms	Kent	TR2056	51°15·9'	1°9·6'E	FM	179
Garrion Burn	S Lanak	NS8352	55°45·1'	3°51·4'W	W	65,72
Garrionhaugh	N Lanak	NS7951	55°44·5'	3°55·2'W	X	64
Garrique	Stir	NS6692	56°6·4'	4°8·8'W	X	57
Garrisdale	Highld	NG2105	57°3·4'	6°35·6'W	X	39
Garrisdale Point	Highld	NG2005	57°3·3'	6°36·6'W	X	39
Garrison	Stir	NN3409	56°14·9'	4°40·3'W	X	56
Garrison Point	Kent	TQ9075	51°26·7'	0°44·4'E	X	178
Garrison, The	I Scilly	SV8910	49°54·8'	6°19·6'W	X	203
Garriston	N Yks	SE1592	54°19·6'	1°45·7'W	T	99
Garriston Beck	N Yks	SE1592	54°19·6'	1°45·7'W	W	99
Garristuck	Arg & Bt	NR3115	56°18·1'	4°43·4'W	X	50,56
Garroch	D & G	NX5981	55°6·5'	4°12·2'W	X	77
Garroch	D & G	NX9498	55°16·1'	3°39·7'W	X	78
Garroch Burn	D & G	NX8690	55°11·7'	3°47·0'W	W	78
Garrocher	D & G	NX4959	54°54·4'	4°20·9'W	X	83
Garroch Fell	D & G	NS9300	55°17·2'	3°40·7'W	X	78
Garroch Fm	D & G	NX9475	55°3·7'	3°39·2'W	FM	84
Garroch Head	Arg & Bt	NS0951	55°43·1'	5°2·0'W	X	63,69
Garroch Hill	D & G	NX5981	55°6·5'	4°12·2'W	X	77
Garrochtrie	D & G	NX1138	54°42·3'	4°55·6'W	T	82
Garrochty Fm	Arg & Bt	NS0952	55°43·7'	5°2·1'W	FM	63,69
Garroch Water	D & G	NX9497	55°15·6'	3°39·6'W	W	78
Garrock Burn	D & G	NX5682	55°6·9'	4°15·0'W	W	77
Garrockhill	E Ayr	NS4320	55°27·2'	4°28·5'W	X	70
Garrogie Lodge	Highld	NH5211	57°10·2'	4°26·4'W	X	35
Garrogill	D & G	NT1503	55°19·1'	3°19·9'W	X	79
Garrol Burn	Aberd	NO5890	57°0·2'	2°41·0'W	W	44
Garrold Wood	Aberd	NO6979	56°54·3'	2°30·1'W	F	45
Garrol Hill	Aberd	NO6377	56°53·2'	2°36·0'W	H	45
Garrol Hill	Aberd	NO7290	57°0·3'	2°27·2'W	X	38,45
Garrol, The	Aberd	NO7290	57°0·3'	2°27·2'W	X	38,45
Garrol Wood	Aberd	NO6476	56°52·7'	2°35·0'W	F	45
Garrol Wood	Aberd	NO7290	57°0·3'	2°27·2'W	F	38,45
Garromuir Wood	Aberd	NJ4845	57°29·8'	2°51·6'W	F	28,29
Garron	Pemb	SN0107	51°43·8'	4°52·5'W	X	157,158
Garronhaugh Fm	Moray	NJ5847	57°30·9'	2°41·6'W	FM	29
Garron Pill	Pemb	SN0107	51°43·8'	4°52·5'W	W	157,158
Garron Point	Aberd	NJ5567	57°41·7'	2°44·8'W	X	29
Garron Point	Aberd	NO8987	56°58·7'	2°10·4'W	X	45
Garros	Highld	NG4963	57°35·5'	6°11·5'W	T	23
Garrow	Corn	SX1477	50°34·0'	4°37·2'W	X	200
Garrow	Pth & Kin	NN8240	56°32·5'	3°54·7'W	X	52
Garrowby Hall	E Yorks	SE7957	54°0·4'	0°47·3'W	X	105,106
Garrowby Hill	E Yorks	SE7956	53°59·9'	0°47·3'W	X	105,106
Garrowby Lodge	E Yorks	SE7856	53°59·9'	0°48·2'W	X	105,106
Garrowchorran Hill	Arg & Bt	NS1473	55°55·1'	4°58·2'W	H	63
Garrow Downs	Corn	SX1478	50°34·6'	4°37·2'W	X	200
Garrowhill	C of Glas	NS6764	55°51·3'	4°7·0'W	T	64
Garrow Hill	Pth & Kin	NN8137	56°30·9'	3°55·6'W	H	52
Garrowslack	Moray	NJ1460	57°37·6'	3°25·9'W	X	28
Garrow Tor	Corn	SX1478	50°34·6'	4°37·2'W	H	200
Garry	Pth & Kin	NO0435	56°30·1'	3°33·1'W	X	52,53
Garry Br	Pth & Kin	NN9161	56°43·9'	3°46·4'W	X	43
Garry Burn	Pth & Kin	NO0435	56°30·1'	3°33·1'W	W	52,53
Garry Gaal	N Eil	NF7072	57°37·3'	7°31·2'W	X	18
Garrygall	N Eil	NL6798	56°57·5'	7°28·3'W	T	31

Garrygualach	Highld	NH1700	57°3·5'	5°0·6'W	T	34
Garryheillie	N Eil	NF7522	57°10·7'	7°22·3'W	X	31
Garryhorn	D & G	NX5493	55°12·8'	4°17·3'W	X	77
Garryhorn	S Ayr	NS2913	55°23·1'	4°41·5'W	X	70
Garryhorn Burn	D & G	NX5393	55°12·8'	4°18·2'W	W	77
Garryhorn Rig	D & G	NX5394	55°13·4'	4°18·2'W	X	77
Garrynamonie	N Eil	NF7416	57°7·4'	7°22·8'W	T	31
Garry Point	S Ayr	NX0472	55°0·5'	5°3·5'W	X	76
Garry Skibinish	N Eil	NF8274	57°38·9'	7°19·4'W	X	18
Gars	Cumbr	NY6804	54°26·1'	2°29·2'W	X	91
Gars-bheinn	Highld	NG4618	57°11·2'	6°11·8'W	H	32
Garsdale	Cumbr	SD7389	54°18·0'	2°24·5'W	X	98
Garsdale	Cumbr	SD7489	54°18·0'	2°23·6'W	T	98
Garsdale Common	Cumbr	SD7891	54°19·1'	2°19·9'W	X	98
Garsdale Foot	Cumbr	SD6991	54°19·1'	2°28·2'W	X	98
Garsdale Head	Cumbr	SD7892	54°19·6'	2°19·9'W	T	98
Garsdale Low Moor	Cumbr	SD7892	54°19·6'	2°19·9'W	X	98
Garsdale Rigg	Cumbr	SD6891	54°19·1'	2°29·1'W	X	98
Garsdale Sta	Cumbr	SD7891	54°19·1'	2°19·9'W	X	144
Garsdon	Wilts	ST9687	51°35·1'	2°3·1'W	T	173
Garsdon Wood	Wilts	ST9787	51°35·1'	2°2·2'W	F	173
Garshake Resr	W Dunb	NS4276	55°57·3'	4°31·4'W	W	64
Garshall Green	Staffs	SJ9634	52°54·4'	2°3·2'W	T	127
Garshall Ho	Staffs	SJ9633	52°53·9'	2°3·2'W	X	127
Garshangan	Inverc	NS2971	55°54·4'	4°43·7'W	X	63
Garshill	Cumbr	NY7204	54°26·1'	2°25·5'W	X	91
Garside Hey	Kirk	SE0313	53°37·1'	1°56·9'W	X	110
Garsington	Oxon	SP5802	51°43·1'	1°9·2'W	T	164
Garslade Fm	Somer	ST4942	51°10·7'	2°43·4'W	FM	182,183
Garsley Burn	Highld	NG7902	57°3·6'	5°38·2'W	W	33
Garso	Orkney	HY7755	59°23·1'	2°23·8'W	X	5
Garson	Orkney	HY2403	58°54·7'	3°18·7'W	X	6,7
Garson	Orkney	HY2426	59°7·1'	3°19·2'W	X	6
Garson	Orkney	HY2609	58°58·0'	3°16·7'W	X	6,7
Garson	Orkney	HY2619	59°3·4'	3°16·9'W	X	6
Garson	Orkney	ND2989	58°47·2'	3°13·2'W	X	7
Garsons Fm	Oxon	SU6584	51°33·3'	1°3·4'W	FM	175
Garsons Hill	Oxon	SU6484	51°33·3'	1°4·2'W	X	175
Garso Wick	Orkney	HY7755	59°23·1'	2°23·8'W	W	5
Garstang	Lancs	SD4945	53°54·2'	2°46·2'W	T	102
Garston	Herts	TQ1199	51°41·0'	0°23·3'W	T	166,176
Garston	Liv	SJ4084	53°21·2'	2°53·7'W	T	108
Garston Channel	Liv	SJ3785	53°21·7'	2°56·4'W	W	108
Garston Down	Dorset	SU0018	50°57·9'	1°59·6'W	X	184
Garston Manor	Herts	TL1101	51°42·0'	0°23·2'W	X	166
Garston Park	Surrey	TQ3450	51°14·2'	0°4·4'W	X	187
Garston Rocks	Liv	SJ3983	53°20·7'	2°54·6'W	X	108
Garstons	I of W	SZ4785	50°40·0'	1°19·7'W	X	196
Garstons Down	I of W	SZ4785	50°40·0'	1°19·7'W	X	196
Garston's Fm	W Susx	TQ2521	50°58·7'	0°12·8'W	FM	198
Garswood	St Hel	SJ5599	53°29·4'	2°40·3'W	T	108
Garswood Park	St Hel	SJ5698	53°28·9'	2°39·4'W	X	108
Gart	Stir	NN6406	56°13·9'	4°11·2'W	X	57
Gartacharn	Stir	NS4987	56°3·4'	4°25·1'W	X	57
Gartacharra	Arg & Bt	NR2561	55°46·1'	6°22·6'W	X	60
Gartachoil	Stir	NS5393	56°6·7'	4°21·4'W	X	57
Gartachossan	Arg & Bt	NR3460	55°45·9'	6°14·0'W	X	60
Gartarry	Fife	NS9390	56°5·7'	3°42·8'W	X	58
Gartartan	Stir	NS5398	56°9·4'	4°21·6'W	X	57
Gartartan Castle	Stir	NS5397	56°8·8'	4°21·5'W	A	57
Gartavaich	Arg & Bt	NR8558	55°46·3'	5°25·2'W	X	62
Gart Banks	Orkney	HY6725	59°6·9'	2°34·1'W	X	5
Gartbreck	Arg & Bt	NR2858	55°44·6'	6°19·6'W	X	60
Gartcarron	Stir	NS6685	56°2·6'	4°8·6'W	X	57
Gartcarron Hill	Stir	NS6685	56°2·6'	4°8·6'W	H	57
Gartcharran	Arg & Bt	NM7802	56°9·8'	5°34·1'W	X	55
Gartchonzie	Stir	NN6007	56°14·4'	4°15·1'W	X	57
Gartclach	Stir	NS5194	56°7·2'	4°23·4'W	X	57
Gartcloss Fm	N Lanak	NS7167	55°53·0'	4°3·3'W	FM	64
Gartclush	Stir	NS8289	56°5·0'	3°53·3'W	X	57,65
Gartcosh	N Lanak	NS6968	55°53·5'	4°5·2'W	T	64
Gartcurrachan	Stir	NS5393	56°6·7'	4°21·4'W	X	57
Gartenbeg	Highld	NH9521	57°16·3'	3°44·0'W	X	36
Gartenkeir	Clackm	NS9394	56°7·9'	3°42·9'W	X	58
Gartentruach	Stir	NS5895	56°7·9'	4°16·6'W	X	57
Gartfairn	Stir	NS4390	56°4·9'	4°30·9'W	X	56
Gartfinnan Fm	Clackm	NS9492	56°6·8'	3°41·8'W	FM	58
Gartgreenie	Clackm	NS9593	56°7·3'	3°40·9'W	X	58
Gartgreillan	Arg & Bt	NR7326	55°28·8'	5°35·1'W	X	68
Gartgunnel	Arg & Bt	NR6728	55°29·7'	5°40·9'W	X	68
Garth	Angus	NO4350	56°38·6'	2°55·3'W	X	54
Garth	Brig	SS8690	51°36·1'	3°38·4'W	T	170
Garth	Caer	ST1189	51°35·8'	3°16·7'W	X	171
Garth	Carm	SN6639	52°2·2'	3°56·8'W	X	146
Garth	Carm	SN6744	52°4·9'	3°56·1'W	X	146
Garth	Carm	SN7434	51°59·7'	3°49·7'W	X	146,160
Garth	Cered	SN6455	52°10·8'	3°59·0'W	X	146
Garth	Cered	SN6484	52°26·5'	3°59·7'W	T	135
Garth	Conwy	SH7057	53°5·9'	3°56·1'W	X	115
Garth	Denb	SJ0362	53°9·0'	3°26·6'W	X	116
Garth	Denb	SJ1054	53°4·8'	3°20·2'W	X	116
Garth	Denb	SJ2542	52°58·4'	3°6·6'W	T	117
Garth	Falk	NS7982	56°1·2'	3°56·0'W	X	57,64
Garth	Flint	SJ1381	53°19·4'	3°18·0'W	T	116
Garth	Flint	SJ1564	53°10·2'	3°15·9'W	X	116
Garth	Gwyn	SH5568	53°11·6'	4°9·8'W	X	114,115
Garth	Gwyn	SH5638	52°55·5'	4°8·1'W	X	124
Garth	Gwyn	SH5873	53°14·3'	4°7·3'W	T	114,115
Garth	Gwyn	SH6317	52°44·2'	4°1·4'W	H	124
Garth	Gwyn	SH9839	52°56·6'	3°30·7'W	X	125
Garth	Highld	ND2067	58°35·3'	3°22·1'W	X	11,12
Garth	I of M	SC3177	54°9·9'	4°34·9'W	X	95
Garth	Merth Tyd	SO0609	51°46·5'	3°21·4'W	X	160
Garth	Monm	ST3492	51°37·6'	2°56·8'W	T	171
Garth	Newp	ST2687	51°34·9'	3°3·7'W	T	171
Garth	Nth Pt Talb	SN7007	51°45·0'	3°52·6'W	X	160
Garth	Orkney	HY2310	58°58·5'	3°19·9'W	X	6
Garth	Orkney	HY2413	59°0·1'	3°18·9'W	X	6
Garth	Orkney	HY3117	59°2·3'	3°11·7'W	X	6
Garth	Orkney	HY4607	58°57·1'	2°55·8'W	X	6,7
Garth	Orkney	HY4645	59°17·5'	2°56·4'W	X	5
Garth	Orkney	HY4820	59°4·1'	2°53·9'W	X	5,6
Garth	Orkney	HY5504	58°55·5'	2°46·4'W	X	6
Garth	Orkney	ND4593	58°49·5'	2°56·7'W	X	7
Garth	Powys	SH7501	52°35·8'	3°50·3'W	X	135
Garth	Powys	SJ1323	52°48·1'	3°17·0'W	X	125
Garth	Powys	SJ2110	52°41·2'	3°9·7'W	X	126
Garth	Powys	SN8113	51°48·4'	3°43·2'W	X	160
Garth	Powys	SN9487	52°28·5'	3°33·2'W	X	136
Garth	Powys	SN9549	52°8·0'	3°31·7'W	T	147
Garth	Powys	SN9860	52°14·0'	3°29·2'W	X	147
Garth	Powys	SO0550	52°8·6'	3°22·9'W	H	147
Garth	Powys	SO0642	52°4·3'	3°21·9'W	X	147,160
Garth	Powys	SO2772	52°20·7'	3°3·9'W	T	137,148
Garth	Rho Cyn Taf	ST0282	51°31·9'	3°24·4'W	X	170
Garth	Shetld	HU2157	60°18·1'	1°36·7'W	X	3
Garth	Shetld	HU4754	60°16·3'	1°8·5'W	T	3
Garth	Shrops	SJ2223	52°48·2'	3°9·0'W	X	126
Garthamlock	C of Glas	NS6666	55°52·4'	4°8·1'W	T	64
Garth-Angharad Hospital	Gwyn	SH6616	52°43·7'	3°58·7'W	X	124
Garth Bank	Powys	SN9450	52°8·5'	3°32·5'W	H	147
Garthbanks	Shetld	HU3612	59°53·8'	1°20·9'W	X	4
Garthbeg	Highld	NH5116	57°12·9'	4°27·6'W	X	35
Garthbrengy	Powys	SO0433	51°59·5'	3°23·5'W	T	160
Garth Castle	Pth & Kin	NN7650	56°37·8'	4°0·8'W	A	42,51,52
Garth Choire Mor	Highld	NH0405	57°5·9'	5°13·7'W	X	33
Garth Cott	Pth & Kin	NN7650	56°37·8'	4°0·8'W	X	42,51,52
Garth Cottage	Cumbr	NY1452	54°51·6'	3°20·0'W	X	85
Garth Crook	N Yks	SE1258	54°1·3'	1°48·6'W	X	104
Garthddulwyd	Cered	SN4355	52°10·5'	4°17·4'W	X	146
Garthdee	C of Aber	NJ9103	57°7·3'	2°8·5'W	T	38
Gartheilun	Powys	SJ0810	52°41·0'	3°21·3'W	X	125
Gartheli	Cered	SN5856	52°11·3'	4°4·2'W	X	146
Garthenor	Cered	SN6256	52°11·3'	4°0·7'W	X	146
Gartherley Moor	N Yks	NZ1907	54°27·7'	1°42·0'W	X	92
Gartheryr	Conwy	SH7955	53°5·0'	3°48·0'W	X	115
Gartheryr	Powys	SJ1623	52°48·1'	3°14·4'W	X	125
Garthewin Fm	Conwy	SH9170	53°13·2'	3°37·5'W	FM	116
Garth-fâch	Powys	SJ1112	52°42·1'	3°18·6'W	X	125
Garth Fach	Powys	SN9978	52°23·7'	3°28·7'W	X	136,147
Garth-fawr	Cered	SN6371	52°19·4'	4°0·2'W	X	135
Garth Fawr	Merth Tyd	SO0805	51°44·4'	3°19·6'W	X	160
Garth Fawr	Newp	ST2790	51°36·5'	3°2·9'W	F	171
Garth-Fawr	Powys	SN9979	52°24·2'	3°28·7'W	X	136,147
Garth-fawr	Rho Cyn Taf	ST1084	51°33·1'	3°17·5'W	X	171
Garth Fm	Gwyn	SH5541	52°57·1'	4°9·1'W	FM	124
Garth Fm	York	SE5945	53°54·1'	1°5·7'W	FM	105
Garthfolds	Cumbr	NY5439	54°44·9'	2°42·5'W	X	90
Garth-gell	Gwyn	SH6820	52°45·9'	3°57·0'W	X	124
Garth-gell	Powys	SJ1420	52°46·5'	3°16·1'W	X	125
Garth Goch	Gwyn	SH9535	52°54·4'	3°33·3'W	H	125
Garth-gwyn	Gwyn	SH6740	52°56·7'	3°58·4'W	X	124
Garthgwynion	Powys	SN7397	52°33·6'	3°52·0'W	X	135
Garthgynfawr	Gwyn	SH7515	52°43·3'	3°50·6'W	X	124
Garth Hall	Rho Cyn Taf	ST0994	51°38·5'	3°18·5'W	X	171
Garth Head	Angus	NO2969	56°48·7'	3°9·3'W	X	44
Garth Head	Cumbr	NY5555	54°53·5'	2°41·7'W	X	86
Garth Head	Orkney	ND3188	58°46·7'	3°11·1'W	X	7
Garth Heads	Cumbr	NY4218	54°33·5'	2°53·4'W	X	90
Garth-Heilyn	Powys	SO0986	52°28·1'	3°20·0'W	X	136
Garth Hill	Brig	SS8790	51°36·1'	3°37·5'W	H	170
Garth Hill	Card	ST1083	51°32·6'	3°17·5'W	H	171
Garth Hill	Powys	SO0894	52°32·4'	3°21·0'W	X	136
Garth Hill	Powys	SO2772	52°20·7'	3°3·9'W	H	137,148
Garth Ho	Powys	SN9449	52°8·0'	3°32·5'W	X	147
Garth House	Pth & Kin	NN7547	56°36·2'	4°1·7'W	X	51,52
Garth House	Shetld	HU4074	60°27·1'	1°15·9'W	X	2,3
Garthian	Denb	SJ0336	52°55·0'	3°26·2'W	X	125
Garthionog	Gwyn	SH9013	52°42·5'	3°37·3'W	X	125
Garth Isaf	Gwyn	SH6516	52°43·7'	3°59·6'W	X	124
Garth-isaf	Gwyn	SH8729	52°51·0'	3°40·3'W	X	124,125
Garth-isaf	Powys	SN9034	51°59·9'	3°35·7'W	X	160
Garth-Isaf	Rho Cyn Taf	ST0984	51°33·1'	3°18·4'W	X	171
Garth-iwrch	Conwy	SH7969	53°12·5'	3°48·3'W	X	115
Garthkeen	Highld	NJ0431	57°21·8'	3°35·3'W	X	27,36
Garthland Burn	D & G	NX0655	54°51·4'	5°0·9'W	W	82
Garthland Mains	D & G	NX0755	54°51·4'	5°0·0'W	X	82
Garth-llwyd	Powys	SJ0908	52°40·0'	3°20·3'W	X	125
Garth-lwyd	Carm	SN6243	52°4·3'	4°0·4'W	X	146
Garth-lwyd	Gwyn	SH9937	52°55·5'	3°29·7'W	X	125
Garthmeilio	Conwy	SH9644	52°59·2'	3°32·6'W	X	125
Garthmoel	Carm	SN5539	52°2·1'	4°6·4'W	X	146
Garthmyl	Powys	SO1999	52°35·2'	3°11·3'W	X	136
Garthmyl Ho	Powys	SO1998	52°34·7'	3°11·3'W	X	136
Garthmyn	Conwy	SH7964	53°9·8'	3°48·2'W	X	115
Garthmyn	Conwy	SH8055	53°5·0'	3°47·1'W	X	116
Garthna Geo	Orkney	HY2115	59°1·2'	3°22·1'W	X	6
Garth-obry	Wrex	SJ2538	52°56·3'	3°6·6'W	X	126
Garth of Susetter	Shetld	HU4065	60°22·3'	1°16·0'W	X	2,3
Garthorpe	Leic	SK8320	52°46·5'	0°45·8'W	T	130
Garthorpe	N Lincs	SE8419	53°39·9'	0°43·3'W	T	112
Garthorpe Grange	E Yorks	SE8421	53°41·0'	0°43·3'W	X	106,112
Garthorpe Lodge	Leic	SK8420	52°46·5'	0°44·9'W	X	130
Garth Owen	Powys	SO1090	52°30·3'	3°19·2'W	T	136
Garthpwt	Powys	SN9893	52°31·8'	3°29·8'W	X	136
Garthrow	Cumbr	SD4791	54°19·0'	2°48·5'W	X	97
Garth Row	Cumbr	SD5297	54°22·2'	2°43·9'W	T	97
Garths	Cumbr	SD5489	54°17·9'	2°42·0'W	X	97
Garths	Cumbr	SD6392	54°19·6'	2°33·7'W	X	97
Garths	Shetld	HU3456	60°17·5'	1°22·6'W	X	2,3
Garthside	Cumbr	NY5464	54°58·4'	2°42·7'W	X	86
Garths Ness	Shetld	HU3611	59°53·2'	1°20·9'W	X	4
Garthspool	Shetld	HU4641	60°9·3'	1°9·8'W	X	4
Garths, The	Shetld	HP6615	60°49·0'	0°46·7'W	X	1
Garths Voe	Shetld	HU4073	60°26·6'	1°15·9'W	W	2,3
Garth, The	Monm	SO5213	51°49·1'	2°41·4'W	X	162
Garth, The	Powys	SN9875	52°22·1'	3°29·5'W	X	136,147
Garth, The	Powys	SO1346	52°6·6'	3°15·8'W	X	148
Garth Trevor	Denb	SJ2642	52°58·5'	3°5·7'W	T	117
Garth Uchaf	Powys	SJ0817	52°44·8'	3°21·4'W	X	125
Garth Uchaf	Powys	SN9035	52°0·4'	3°35·8'W	X	160
Garth Wood	Card	ST1182	51°32·0'	3°16·6'W	F	171
Garthydwr	Denb	SJ1643	52°58·9'	3°14·7'W	X	125
Garthyfelin	Powys	SO0249	52°8·1'	3°25·5'W	X	147
Garth-y-neuadd	Denb	SJ1051	53°3·2'	3°20·2'W	X	116
Garthynty	Carm	SN7147	52°6·6'	3°52·6'W	X	146,147
Garth-y-pigau	Conwy	SH8258	53°6·6'	3°45·4'W	X	116
Gartinbantrick	W Dunb	NS4486	56°2·7'	4°29·8'W	X	57
Gartincaber	Stir	NN6900	56°10·7'	4°6·2'W	X	57
Gartincaber	Stir	NS4490	56°4·9'	4°30·0'W	X	57
Gartinstarry	Stir	NS5593	56°6·7'	4°19·5'W	X	57
Gartknowie	Clackm	NS9794	56°7·9'	3°39·0'W	X	58
Gart Law	S Lanak	NS7523	55°29·3'	3°58·3'W	H	71
Gartlea	N Lanak	NS7664	55°51·5'	3°58·4'W	T	64
Gartlea	W Dunb	NS4583	56°1·1'	4°28·8'W	X	57,64
Gartliston Fm	N Lanak	NS7267	55°53·0'	4°2·3'W	FM	64
Gartloaning	Stir	NS5198	56°9·3'	4°23·5'W	X	57
Gartloch	C of Glas	NS6867	55°52·9'	4°6·2'W	T	64
Gartloist	Arg & Bt	NR3360	55°45·8'	6°15·0'W	X	60
Gartloskan Hill	Arg & Bt	NR7013	55°21·7'	5°37·3'W	H	68
Gartlove	Clackm	NS9493	56°7·3'	3°41·9'W	X	58
Gartly	Aberd	NJ5232	57°22·8'	2°47·4'W	T	29,37
Gartly Moor	Aberd	NJ5633	57°23·4'	2°43·5'W	X	29
Gartmain	Arg & Bt	NR3360	55°45·8'	6°15·0'W	X	60
Gartmillan	N Lanak	NS7469	55°54·1'	4°0·5'W	X	64
Gartmore	Stir	NS5297	56°8·8'	4°22·5'W	T	57
Gartmore Ho	Stir	NS5297	56°8·8'	4°22·5'W	X	57
Gartmorn Dam	Clackm	NS9294	56°7·8'	3°43·8'W	W	58
Gartmornhill Fm	Clackm	NS9194	56°7·8'	3°44·8'W	FM	58
Gartnacopaig	Arg & Bt	NR6214	55°22·0'	5°44·9'W	X	68
Gartnafuaran	Stir	NN5420	56°21·2'	4°21·3'W	X	51,57
Gartnagerach Point	Arg & Bt	NR7510	55°20·2'	5°32·4'W	X	68
Gartnagrenach	Arg & Bt	NR7959	55°46·7'	5°31·0'W	T	62
Gartnagrenach Bay	Arg & Bt	NR7960	55°47·2'	5°31·1'W	W	62
Gartnagrenoch	Arg & Bt	NR7890	56°3·3'	5°33·5'W	X	55
Gartnagrenoch (Chambered Cairn)	Arg & Bt	NR7890	56°3·3'	5°33·5'W	A	55
Gartnakeilly	Arg & Bt	NS0764	55°50·1'	5°4·5'W	X	63
Gartnatra	Arg & Bt	NR3260	55°45·8'	6°15·9'W	X	60
Gartnerichnich	Stir	NN4402	56°11·4'	4°30·4'W	X	57
Gartness	N Lanak	NS7864	55°51·5'	3°56·5'W	T	64
Gartness	Stir	NS5086	56°2·9'	4°24·1'W	T	57
Gartness Fm	N Lanak	NS7863	55°50·9'	3°56·5'W	FM	64
Gartocharn	W Dunb	NS4286	56°2·7'	4°31·8'W	T	56
Gartochraggan	W Dunb	NS4287	56°3·2'	4°31·8'W	X	56
Garton	E Yorks	TA2635	53°48·0'	0°4·8'W	T	107
Garton Field	E Yorks	SE9560	54°1·9'	0°32·6'W	X	101
Garton Grange	E Yorks	SE9760	54°1·8'	0°30·7'W	X	101
Garton-on-the-wolds	E Yorks	SE9859	54°1·3'	0°29·8'W	T	106
Garton Wold	E Yorks	SE9861	54°2·4'	0°29·8'W	X	101
Gartree Hill	Leic	SK7614	52°43·3'	0°52·1'W	X	129
Gartrenich	Stir	NS5598	56°9·4'	4°19·6'W	X	57
Gartrenich Moss	Stir	NS5597	56°8·9'	4°19·6'W	X	57
Gartsherrie	N Lanak	NS7166	55°52·5'	4°3·3'W	T	64
Gartsherrie Wood	N Lanak	NS7267	55°53·0'	4°2·3'W	F	64
Gartur	Stir	NS5798	56°9·5'	4°17·7'W	X	57
Gartur	Stir	NS7692	56°6·5'	3°59·2'W	X	57
Gartvaigh	Arg & Bt	NR6708	55°18·9'	5°39·9'W	X	68
Gartwhinnie	Stir	NS8286	56°3·4'	3°53·3'W	X	57,65
Gartwhinzean Feus	Pth & Kin	NT0197	56°9·6'	3°35·2'W	X	58
Garty	Highld	NH7573	57°44·0'	4°5·5'W	X	21
Gartymore	Highld	ND0114	58°6·5'	3°40·3'W	T	17
Garvabeg	Highld	NN5294	57°1·1'	4°25·8'W	X	35
Garva Bridge	Highld	NN5294	57°1·1'	4°25·8'W	X	35
Garvachy	Arg & Bt	NR9797	56°7·6'	5°15·5'W	X	55
Garvald	E Loth	NT5870	55°55·5'	2°39·9'W	T	67
Garvald	Falk	NS7883	56°1·7'	3°57·0'W	X	57,64
Garvald	Scot Bord	NT0949	55°43·8'	3°26·5'W	X	72
Garvald	Scot Bord	NT3551	55°45·1'	3°1·7'W	X	66,73
Garvald Burn	Falk	NS7782	56°1·2'	3°58·0'W	W	57,64
Garvald Burn	S Lanak	NT1048	55°43·3'	3°25·5'W	W	72
Garvald Burn	Stir	NN7108	56°15·1'	4°4·5'W	W	57
Garvald Church	D & G	NY0490	55°11·9'	3°30·1'W	A	78
Garvald Grange	E Loth	NT5871	55°56·1'	2°39·9'W	X	67
Garvald Law	Scot Bord	NT3449	55°44·0'	3°2·6'W	H	73
Garvald Lodge	Scot Bord	NT3550	55°44·6'	3°1·7'W	X	66,73
Garvald Mains	E Loth	NT5869	55°55·0'	2°39·9'W	X	67
Garvald Punks	Scot Bord	NT3247	55°43·0'	3°4·5'W	H	73
Garvalt	Arg & Bt	NR6507	55°18·3'	5°41·7'W	X	68
Garvalt	Arg & Bt	NR7138	55°35·2'	5°37·6'W	X	68
Garvalt Hill	Highld	NC6444	58°22·1'	4°19·0'W	H	10
Garvamore	Highld	NN5294	57°1·1'	4°25·8'W	X	35
Garvan	Highld	NH1882	57°47·7'	5°3·3'W	X	20
Garvan	Highld	NM9777	56°50·7'	5°19·3'W	X	40
Garvard	Arg & Bt	NR3691	56°2·6'	6°13·9'W	T	61
Garvary	Highld	NH5986	57°50·7'	4°22·1'W	X	21
Garvary	Highld	NH6399	57°57·8'	4°18·5'W	X	21
Garvary Burn	Highld	NC7321	58°9·8'	4°9·0'W	W	16
Garvault	Highld	NC3832	58°15·1'	4°45·2'W	H	16
Garvault	Highld	NJ1333	57°23·0'	3°26·4'W	X	28
Garvault Hotel	Highld	NC7838	58°19·1'	4°4·5'W	X	17
Garve	Highld	NH3961	57°36·9'	4°41·3'W	T	20
Garve Bridge	Highld	NH2622	57°15·6'	4°52·6'W	X	25
Garvel	Clackm	NS8394	56°7·7'	3°52·5'W	X	57
Garvelaid	Highld	NH6194	57°55·1'	4°20·3'W	X	21
Garvellachs	Arg & Bt	NM6511	56°14·3'	5°47·1'W	X	55
Garvellan Rocks	D & G	NX5551	54°50·2'	4°15·0'W	X	83
Garvel Point	Inverc	NS2975	55°56·5'	4°43·8'W	X	63
Garvery Hill	Highld	NC9924	58°11·9'	3°42·6'W	X	17
Garvestone	Norf	TG0207	52°37·6'	0°59·5'E	T	144
Garvie	Arg & Bt	NS0390	56°4·0'	5°9·4'W	T	55
Garvie Bay	Highld	NC0413	58°4·0'	5°18·9'W	W	15
Garvie Burn	Arg & Bt	NS0490	56°4·0'	5°8·5'W	W	56
Garvilland	D & G	NX2161	54°55·0'	4°47·1'W	X	82
Garvock	Aberd	NO7470	56°49·5'	2°25·1'W	T	45
Garvock	Inverc	NS2571	55°54·3'	4°47·5'W	X	63
Garvock	Pth & Kin	NO0314	56°18·8'	3°33·6'W	X	58
Garvock Hill	Fife	NT1087	56°4·3'	3°26·3'W	T	65
Garvock Hill	Inverc	NS2569	55°53·2'	4°47·4'W	X	63
Garvoult	Highld	NC7305	58°1·2'	4°8·5'W	X	16

Garwachie Lochs	D & G	NX3468	54°59·0′	4°35·2′W	W	82
Garwachie Moor	D & G	NX3469	54°59·5′	4°35·3′W	X	82
Garwachie Moor	D & G	NX3569	54°59·5′	4°34·3′W	X	83
Garwald	D & G	NT2200	55°17·5′	3°13·3′W	X	79
Garwaldshiels	D & G	NY1998	55°16·4′	3°16·1′W	X	79
Garwald Water	D & G	NT2003	55°19·1′	3°15·2′W	W	79
Garwaldwaterfoot	D & G	NT2400	55°17·5′	3°11·4′W	X	79
Garwall Hill	D & G	NX3483	55°7·1′	4°35·7′W	H	76
Garway	Heref	SO4622	51°53·9′	2°46·7′W	T	161
Garway Common	Heref	SO4622	51°53·9′	2°46·7′W	X	161
Garway Court	Heref	SO4521	51°53·3′	2°47·6′W	X	161
Garway Hill	Heref	SO4425	51°55·5′	2°48·5′W	T	161
Garway Hill Common	Heref	SO4324	51°54·9′	2°49·3′W	X	161
Garw-dyle	Rho Cyn Taf	SN9509	51°46·4′	3°30·9′W	X	160
Garw Fynydd	Gwyn	SH9440	52°57·1′	3°34·3′W	H	125
Garwick	Lincs	TF1744	52°59·1′	0°15·0′W	X	130
Garwick Bay	I of M	SC4381	54°12·3′	4°24·0′W	W	95
Garwick Glen	I of M	SC4381	54°12·3′	4°24·0′W	X	95
Garw-leisiau	Powys	SN8213	51°48·4′	3°42·3′W	X	160
Garwnant Fawr	Rho Cyn Taf	SN9913	51°48·6′	3°27·5′W	W	160
Gasaidh	N Eil	NF8443	57°22·3′	7°15·0′W	X	22
Gasay	N Eil	NF8018	57°8·7′	7°17·0′W	X	31
Gascoigne Fm	N Yks	NZ1903	54°25·6′	1°42·0′W	FM	92
Gascoigne Wood Mine	N Yks	SE5232	53°47·1′	1°12·2′W	X	105
Gasconhall	Pth & Kin	NO2126	56°25·4′	3°16·4′W	X	53,58
Gasdale	Cumbr	NY7422	54°35·8′	2°23·7′W	X	91
Gasgale Crags	Cumbr	NY1721	54°34·9′	3°16·6′W	X	89,90
Gasgale Gill	Cumbr	NY1721	54°34·9′	3°16·6′W	W	89,90
Gashagich	Highld	NH7591	57°53·7′	4°6·1′W	X	21
Gashay Fm	Devon	ST3700	50°48·0′	2°53·3′W	FM	193
Gas Ho	Ches	SJ6439	52°57·1′	2°31·7′W	X	127
Gasi-gya	N Eil	NB0000	57°53·6′	7°3·3′W	W	18
Gask	Aberd	NJ7347	57°31·0′	2°26·6′W	X	29
Gask	Aberd	NJ7906	57°8·9′	2°20·4′W	X	38
Gask	Aberd	NK0840	57°27·3′	1°51·5′W	X	30
Gask	Angus	NO5347	56°37·0′	2°45·5′W	X	54
Gaskan	Highld	NM8072	56°47·5′	5°35·7′W	X	40
Gaskan Wood	Highld	NM8173	56°48·1′	5°34·8′W	F	40
Gaskbeg	Highld	NN6294	57°1·3′	4°15·9′W	X	35
Gaskell Ho	Cumbr	SD5579	54°12·5′	2°41·0′W	X	97
Gasker	N Eil	NA8711	57°58·9′	7°17·3′W	X	13
Gasker Beg	N Eil	NA8810	57°58·5′	7°16·2′W	X	13
Gasketh	Cumbr	SD0998	54°22·4′	3°23·6′W	X	96
Gaskhill Wood	Pth & Kin	NO2334	56°29·8′	3°14·6′W	F	53
Gask Ho	Pth & Kin	NN9918	56°20·9′	3°37·6′W	X	58
Gaskie Hill	Fife	NT1092	56°7·0′	3°26·4′W	X	58
Gaskill's Fm	Glos	SO9509	51°47·0′	2°4·0′W	FM	163
Gaskine Loch	Highld	NM7691	56°57·6′	5°40·6′W	W	33,40
Gask's Fm	Lincs	TF4254	53°4·1′	0°7·6′E	FM	122
Gaskyns	W Susx	TQ1230	51°3·7′	0°23·7′W	X	187
Gason Wood	Surrey	TQ0653	51°16·2′	0°28·4′W	F	187
Gasper	Wilts	ST7633	51°6·0′	2°20·2′W	T	183
Gass	D & G	NX2464	54°56·6′	4°44·4′W	X	82
Gass	D & G	NX3357	54°53·0′	4°35·8′W	X	82
Gass	S Ayr	NS4105	55°19·1′	4°29·9′W	X	70,77
Gass Burn	D & G	NX3358	54°53·6′	4°35·8′W	W	82
Gass Fm	D & G	NX2464	54°56·6′	4°44·4′W	FM	82
Gass Moor	D & G	NX3257	54°53·0′	4°36·7′W	X	82
Gasstown	D & G	NX9976	55°4·3′	3°34·5′W	X	84
Gass Water	E Ayr	NS6521	55°28·1′	4°7·7′W	W	71
Gasswater Head	E Ayr	NS6921	55°28·2′	4°3·9′W	X	71
Gastack Beck	Cumbr	SD7183	54°14·8′	2°26·3′W	W	98
Gastack Beck Bottom	Cumbr	SD7283	54°14·8′	2°25·4′W	X	98
Gastard	Wilts	ST8868	51°24·9′	2°10·0′W	T	173
Gasthorpe	Norf	TL9780	52°23·2′	0°54·1′E	T	144
Gastlings	Beds	TL1342	52°4·1′	0°20·7′W	X	153
Gaston Copse	Hants	SU7148	51°13·8′	0°58·6′W	F	186
Gaston Grange	Hants	SU6539	51°9·0′	1°3·9′W	X	185,186
Gaston Green	Essex	TL4917	51°50·1′	0°10·2′E	T	167
Gaston Green Fm	Wilts	ST9457	51°19·0′	2°4·8′W	FM	173
Gaston Ho	Essex	TL4917	51°50·1′	0°10·2′E	X	167
Gaston's Fm	W Susx	SU9531	51°4·5′	0°38·2′W	FM	186
Gaston Wood	Hants	SU6539	51°9·0′	1°3·9′W	F	185,186
Gatacre	Shrops	SO7990	52°30·7′	2°18·2′W	X	138
Gatacre Park	Shrops	SO7989	52°30·1′	2°18·2′W	T	138
Gat Channel		TF4739	52°55·9′	0°11·6′E	W	131
Gatchell Ho	Somer	ST2122	50°59·8′	3°7·2′W	X	193
Gatcliff Fm	I of W	SZ5280	50°37·3′	1°15·5′W	FM	196
Gatcombe	Glos	SO6705	51°44·8′	2°28·3′W	X	162
Gatcombe	I of W	SZ4885	50°40·0′	1°18·9′W	T	196
Gatcombe Brook	Devon	SX8362	50°27·0′	3°38·5′W	W	202
Gatcombe Fm	Devon	SY2291	50°43·0′	3°5·9′W	FM	192,193
Gatcombe Hill	Wilts	ST8378	51°30·3′	2°14·3′W	X	173
Gatcombe Ho	Devon	SX8262	50°27·0′	3°39·3′W	A	202
Gatcombe Ho	I of W	SZ4984	50°39·4′	1°18·0′W	X	196
Gatcombe Mill	I of W	SZ4985	50°40·0′	1°18·0′W	X	196
Gatcombe Park	Glos	ST8899	51°41·6′	2°10·0′W	X	162
Gatcombe Wood	Glos	ST8799	51°41·6′	2°10·9′W	F	162
Gateacre	Liv	SJ4287	53°22·8′	2°51·9′W	T	108
Gatebarrow	Cumbr	NY0526	54°37·5′	3°27·9′W	H	89
Gatebeck	Cumbr	SD5485	54°15·8′	2°42·0′W	T	97
Gate Burn	Northum	NU1203	55°19·5′	1°48·2′W	W	81
Gate Burton	Lincs	SK8382	53°19·9′	0°44·8′W	X	121
Gatecleuch Hill	Scot Bord	NT2813	55°24·6′	3°7·8′W	H	79
Gate Cott	N Ayr	NR9233	55°33·0′	5°17·4′W	X	68,69
Gate Cottage	E Susx	TQ8521	50°57·7′	0°38·5′E	X	189,199
Gate Court	E Susx	TQ8326	51°0·5′	0°36·9′E	X	188,199
Gate Crag	Cumbr	SD1899	54°23·0′	3°15·3′W	X	96
Gate Croft	Brad	SE0848	53°55·9′	1°52·3′W	X	104
Gate Fm	Donc	SE6603	53°31·4′	0°59·9′W	FM	111
Gate Fm	Essex	TL7219	51°50·8′	0°30·2′E	FM	167
Gate Fm	E Susx	TQ7517	50°55·8′	0°29·8′E	FM	199
Gate Fm	E Susx	TQ7922	50°58·4′	0°33·4′E	FM	199
Gate Fm	E Susx	TQ8522	50°58·3′	0°38·5′E	FM	189,199
Gate Fm	E Yorks	SE7828	53°44·8′	0°48·6′W	FM	105,106
Gate Fm	Lincs	TF2724	52°48·1′	0°6·6′W	FM	131
Gate Fm	S Glos	ST6288	51°35·6′	2°32·5′W	FM	162,172
Gate Fm	Suff	TM0746	52°4·6′	1°1·6′E	FM	155,169
Gateford	Notts	SK5781	53°19·6′	1°8·2′W	T	111,120
Gateford Common	Notts	SK5681	53°19·6′	1°9·1′W	T	111,120
Gateford Hill	Notts	SK5781	53°19·6′	1°8·2′W	X	111,120
Gateford Hill	Notts	SK5881	53°19·6′	1°7·3′W	X	111,120
Gateforth	N Yks	SE5628	53°45·0′	1°8·6′W	T	105
Gateforth Fm	N Yks	SE5729	53°45·5′	1°7·7′W	FM	105
Gateforth Hall	N Yks	SE5529	53°45·5′	1°9·5′W	X	105
Gateforth Wood	N Yks	SE5428	53°45·0′	1°10·5′W	F	105
Gategill	Cumbr	NY3226	54°37·7′	3°2·8′W	X	90
Gategill Fell	Cumbr	NY3126	54°37·7′	3°3·7′W	X	90
Gate Grain	Cumbr	NY5881	55°7·5′	2°39·1′W	W	80
Gateham Fm	Staffs	SK1156	53°6·3′	1°49·7′W	FM	119
Gateham Grange	Staffs	SK1156	53°6·3′	1°49·7′W	X	119
Gatehampton Manor	Oxon	SU6079	51°30·6′	1°7·7′W	X	175
Gate Head	Cald	SE0721	53°41·4′	1°53·2′W	X	104
Gatehead	E Ayr	NS3936	55°35·7′	4°32·9′W	T	70
Gatehead	E Ayr	NS4533	55°34·2′	4°27·1′W	X	70
Gatehead	E Ayr	NS6214	55°24·3′	4°10·3′W	X	71
Gatehead	Renf	NS4170	55°54·1′	4°32·2′W	X	64
Gatehead Fm	N Ayr	NS3752	55°44·3′	4°35·3′W	FM	63
Gate Helmsley	N Yks	SE6955	53°59·4′	0°56·4′W	T	105,106
Gate Helmsley Common	N Yks	SE6955	53°59·4′	0°56·4′W	X	105,106
Gate Hill	N Yks	SE4258	54°1·2′	1°21·1′W	X	105
Gate Ho	Arg & Bt	NR5877	55°55·8′	5°52·0′W	X	61
Gate Ho	Arg & Bt	NR7384	56°0·0′	5°38·0′W	X	55
Gate Ho	Cumbr	SD1184	54°14·9′	3°21·5′W	X	96
Gate Ho	Cumbr	SD6396	54°21·7′	2°33·7′W	X	97
Gate Ho	Essex	TL8915	51°48·3′	0°44·9′E	X	168
Gate Ho	Northum	NY7854	54°53·1′	2°20·2′W	X	86,87
Gate Ho	N Yks	SE7169	54°7·0′	0°54·4′W	X	100
Gate Ho	Shrops	SO4486	52°28·4′	2°49·1′W	X	137
Gate Ho	Staffs	SJ9354	53°5·2′	2°5·9′W	X	118
Gateholm Island	Pemb	SM7607	51°43·3′	5°14·2′W	X	157
Gateholm Stack	Pemb	SM7707	51°43·3′	5°13·3′W	X	157
Gatehopeknowe Burn	Scot Bord	NT3739	55°38·7′	2°59·6′W	W	73
Gatehouse	Derby	SK2283	53°20·8′	1°39·8′W	X	110
Gatehouse	Devon	SS8010	50°52·9′	3°42·0′W	X	191
Gatehouse	Devon	SX9677	50°35·2′	3°27·8′W	X	192
Gatehouse	D & G	NX6764	54°57·4′	4°4·2′W	X	83,84
Gatehouse	Essex	TL6512	51°47·2′	0°23·9′E	X	167
Gatehouse	E Susx	TQ5020	50°57·8′	0°8·6′E	X	199
Gatehouse	Gwyn	SH6170	53°12·8′	4°4·5′W	X	115
Gatehouse	Hants	SU8432	51°5·1′	0°47·7′W	A	186
Gate House	Highld	NH9817	57°14·2′	3°40·9′W	X	36
Gate House	I of Angl	SH3370	53°12·3′	4°29·6′W	X	114
Gatehouse	I of W	SZ5789	50°42·1′	1°11·2′W	X	196
Gatehouse	Northum	NY7888	55°11·4′	2°20·3′W	X	80
Gatehouse	Somer	ST5334	51°6·4′	2°39·9′W	A	182,183
Gate House	Suff	TL7757	52°11·2′	0°35·8′E	X	155
Gate House Br	Lancs	SD5156	54°0·1′	2°44·4′W	X	102
Gatehousecote	Scot Bord	NT5913	55°24·8′	2°38·4′W	X	80
Gatehouse Fm	Essex	TL6724	51°53·6′	0°26·0′E	FM	167
Gatehouse Fm	Essex	TL8526	51°54·3′	0°41·8′E	FM	168
Gatehouse Fm	Essex	TM0229	51°55·6′	0°56·7′E	FM	168
Gatehouse Fm	Essex	TM0819	51°50·1′	1°1·5′E	FM	168,169
Gatehouse Fm	E Yorks	TA0249	53°55·9′	0°26·4′W	FM	106,107
Gatehouse Fm	Kent	TQ7346	51°11·4′	0°28·9′E	FM	188
Gate House Fm	NE Lincs	TA1712	53°35·7′	0°13·5′W	FM	113
Gatehouse Fm	Norf	TG1025	52°47·1′	1°7·3′E	FM	133
Gate House Fm	N Yks	TA0783	54°14·1′	0°21·1′W	FM	101
Gate House Fm	Peterb	TF1503	52°37·0′	0°17·7′W	FM	142
Gate House Fm	Surrey	TQ3643	51°10·4′	0°2·9′W	FM	187
Gatehouse Fm	Worcs	SO6262	52°15·5′	2°33·0′W	FM	138,149
Gatehouse Fm	W Susx	SU8323	51°0·3′	0°48·6′W	FM	197
Gatehouse Fm	W Susx	SU9427	51°2·3′	0°39·2′W	FM	186,197
Gatehouse of Fleet	D & G	NX6056	54°53·0′	4°10·5′W	T	83
Gatehouse Station	D & G	NX5462	54°56·1′	4°16·3′W	X	83
Gatekirk Cave	N Yks	SD7478	54°12·1′	2°23·5′W	X	98
Gatelawbridge	D & G	NX9096	55°15·0′	3°43·4′W	T	78
Gateley	Norf	TF9624	52°46·9′	0°54·8′E	T	132
Gateley Fm	Worcs	SO8868	52°18·8′	2°10·2′W	FM	139
Gateley Green Fm	Ches	SJ8376	53°17·1′	2°14·9′W	FM	118
Gateley Hill	Norf	TF9525	52°47·5′	0°53·9′E	X	132
Gate Lodge Fm	Lincs	SK8445	53°0·0′	0°44·5′W	FM	130
Gately Burn	Scot Bord	NT4244	55°41·4′	2°54·9′W	W	73
Gately Rig	Scot Bord	NT4244	55°41·4′	2°54·9′W	H	73
Gate Manor	Cumbr	SD6689	54°18·0′	2°30·9′W	X	98
Gatenby	N Yks	SE3287	54°16·9′	1°30·1′W	T	99
Gatenby Wood	N Yks	SE3187	54°16·9′	1°31·0′W	F	99
Gatend	N Ayr	NS3550	55°43·2′	4°37·2′W	X	63
Gateon House Fm	Leeds	SE3443	53°53·2′	1°28·5′W	FM	104
Gaterigg	Cumbr	NY3248	54°49·6′	3°3·1′W	X	85
Gaterigghow	Cumbr	NY1003	54°25·1′	3°22·8′W	X	89
Gaterley Hill	Northum	NY8458	54°55·2′	2°14·6′W	X	86,87
Gaterounds Fm	Surrey	TQ1942	51°10·1′	0°17·5′W	FM	187
Gatesbury	Herts	TL3923	51°53·5′	0°1·6′E	X	166
Gatesbury's Fm	Suff	TL7855	52°10·1′	0°36·6′E	FM	155
Gatescarth Pass	Cumbr	NY4709	54°28·7′	2°48·7′W	X	90
Gatesend Hill	Norf	TF8429	52°49·9′	0°44·3′E	X	132
Gates Fm	Ches	SJ6356	53°6·2′	2°32·8′W	FM	118
Gate's Fm	Kent	TQ8939	51°7·4′	0°42·4′E	FM	189
Gates Fm	Wrex	SJ4144	52°59·6′	2°52·3′W	FM	117
Gatesgarth	Cumbr	NY1001	54°24·0′	3°22·8′W	X	89
Gatesgarth	Cumbr	NY1915	54°31·7′	3°14·7′W	T	89,90
Gatesgarthdale Beck	Cumbr	NY2014	54°31·1′	3°13·7′W	W	89,90
Gateshaw	Scot Bord	NT7822	55°29·7′	2°20·5′W	X	74
Gateshawhill	Cumbr	NY5449	54°50·3′	2°42·5′W	X	86
Gateshaw Mill	Cumbr	NY5449	54°50·3′	2°42·5′W	X	86
Gateshaw Rig	D & G	NT1404	55°19·6′	3°20·9′W	X	78
Gateshayes Fm	Devon	SY0397	50°46·1′	3°22·2′W	FM	192
Gateshead	Ghead	NZ2460	54°56·3′	1°37·1′W	T	88
Gateshead Fm	Pth & Kin	NO1541	56°33·5′	3°22·5′W	FM	53
Gatesheath	Ches	SJ4760	53°8·3′	2°47·1′W	T	117
Gateside	Aberd	NJ4716	57°14·2′	2°52·2′W	X	37
Gateside	Aberd	NJ5707	57°9·4′	2°42·2′W	X	37
Gateside	Aberd	NJ6116	57°14·2′	2°38·3′W	X	37
Gateside	Aberd	NJ6630	57°21·8′	2°33·5′W	X	29
Gateside	Aberd	NJ8232	57°22·9′	2°17·5′W	X	29,30
Gateside	Aberd	NJ9422	57°17·6′	2°5·5′W	X	38
Gateside	Aberd	NO6199	57°5·1′	2°38·2′W	X	37,45
Gateside	Aberd	NO6677	56°53·2′	2°33·0′W	X	45
Gateside	Aberd	NO6792	57°1·3′	2°32·2′W	X	38,45
Gateside	Angus	NO4344	56°35·3′	2°55·2′W	T	54
Gateside	Angus	NO5358	56°42·9′	2°45·6′W	X	54
Gateside	C of Aber	NJ8706	57°8·9′	2°12·4′W	X	38
Gateside	Cumbr	SD1483	54°14·4′	3°18·8′W	X	96
Gateside	Cumbr	SD5299	54°23·3′	2°43·9′W	X	97
Gate Side	Cumbr	SD6395	54°21·2′	2°33·7′W	X	97
Gateside	D & G	NS7611	55°22·9′	3°57·0′W	X	71,78
Gateside	D & G	NX8672	55°2·0′	3°46·6′W	X	84
Gateside	D & G	NX9085	55°9·1′	3°43·1′W	X	78
Gateside	D & G	NX9179	55°5·9′	3°42·1′W	X	84
Gateside	D & G	NY1194	55°14·2′	3°23·5′W	T	78
Gateside	E Ayr	NS4233	55°34·2′	4°29·9′W	X	70
Gateside	E Ayr	NS4348	55°42·3′	4°29·5′W	X	64
Gateside	E Ayr	NS4937	55°36·4′	4°23·4′W	X	70
Gateside	E Ayr	NS5640	55°38·2′	4°16·8′W	X	71
Gateside	E Renf	NS4858	55°47·7′	4°25·0′W	T	64
Gateside	Fife	NO1809	56°16·2′	3°19·0′W	T	58
Gateside	Fife	NO2803	56°13·1′	3°9·2′W	X	59
Gateside	Inverc	NS3269	55°53·3′	4°40·7′W	X	63
Gateside	Moray	NJ1061	57°38·1′	3°30·0′W	X	28
Gateside	Moray	NJ3647	57°30·8′	3°3·6′W	X	28
Gateside	N Ayr	NS2845	55°40·3′	4°43·7′W	X	63
Gateside	N Ayr	NS3653	55°44·8′	4°36·3′W	T	63
Gateside	N Lanak	NS7578	55°59·0′	3°59·8′W	X	64
Gateside	Pth & Kin	NO0422	56°23·1′	3°32·8′W	X	52,53,58
Gateside	Pth & Kin	NT0699	56°10·7′	3°30·4′W	X	58
Gateside	S Ayr	NS3721	55°27·6′	4°34·2′W	X	70
Gateside	Shetld	HU2978	60°29·3′	1°27·8′W	X	3
Gateside	S Lanak	NS8330	55°33·2′	3°50·9′W	X	71,72
Gateside	S Lanak	NS8749	55°43·5′	3°47·5′W	X	72
Gateside	S Lanak	NT0235	55°36·2′	3°32·9′W	X	72
Gateside	Stir	NN7904	56°13·0′	3°56·6′W	X	57
Gateside	Stir	NS4888	56°3·9′	4°26·0′W	X	57
Gateside	W Loth	NT0475	55°57·8′	3°31·8′W	X	65
Gateslack	D & G	NS8902	55°18·2′	3°44·5′W	X	78
Gates of Birselawsie, The	Aberd	NJ6406	57°8·9′	2°35·2′W	X	37
Gatestreet Fm	Surrey	TQ0141	51°9·8′	0°32·9′W	FM	186
Gates Wood	Heref	SO4950	52°9·0′	2°44·3′W	F	148,149
Gate, The	I of M	SC2873	54°7·7′	4°37·5′W	X	95
Gatet Hill	D & G	NT0502	55°18·4′	3°29·4′W	H	78
Gate Up Gill	N Yks	SE0566	54°5·6′	1°55·0′W	W	98
Gatewen	Wrex	SJ3151	53°3·4′	3°1·4′W	T	117
Gate Wood End	Donc	SE6704	53°31·9′	0°58·9′W	X	111
Gatewood Hill	Hants	SU4301	50°48·6′	1°23·0′W	X	196
Gatewood House Fm	Lincs	TF2779	53°17·8′	0°5·3′W	FM	122
Gathercauld	Fife	NO4209	56°16·5′	2°55·8′W	X	59
Gatherham Fm	S Glos	ST7174	51°28·1′	2°24·7′W	FM	172
Gatherick	Northum	NT9541	55°40·0′	2°4·3′W	X	74,75
Gathering Cairn	Aberd	NO4288	56°59·0′	2°56·8′W	H	44
Gathering Hill	Derby	SK0894	53°26·8′	1°52·4′W	X	110
Gatherley	Devon	SX3782	50°37·1′	4°17·9′W	T	201
Gatherley Grange	N Yks	NZ2301	54°24·5′	1°38·3′W	X	93
Gatherley Ho	N Yks	NZ2302	54°25·0′	1°38·3′W	X	93
Gatherley Wood	Devon	SX3883	50°37·7′	4°17·1′W	F	201
Gathersnow Hill	Scot Bord	NT0525	55°30·8′	3°29·8′W	H	72
Gatherwynd	Staffs	SJ8012	52°42·6′	2°17·4′W	X	127
Gathurst	Wigan	SD5407	53°33·7′	2°41·3′W	T	108
Gatlas	Newp	ST3492	51°37·6′	2°56·8′W	T	171
Gatley	Stock	SJ8488	53°23·6′	2°14·0′W	T	109
Gatley Barn	Heref	SO4469	52°19·2′	2°48·9′W	X	137,148
Gatley End	Cambs	TL2941	52°3·4′	0°6·7′W	T	153
Gatley Long Coppice	Heref	SO4469	52°19·2′	2°48·9′W	F	137,148
Gatley Park	Heref	SO4468	52°18·7′	2°48·9′W	A	137,148
Gatleyway Fm	Herts	TL3137	52°1·2′	0°5·1′W	FM	153
Gatmore Copse	Wilts	SU2725	51°1·7′	1°36·5′W	F	184
Gatni Geos	Shetld	HU3627	60°1·8′	1°20·7′W	X	4
Gatra	Cumbr	NY0620	54°34·2′	3°26·8′W	X	89
Gat Sand	Lincs	TF4738	52°55·4′	0°11·6′E	X	131
Gat Sand End	Lincs	TF4538	52°55·4′	0°9·8′E	X	131
Gatsford Fm	Heref	SO6126	51°56·1′	2°33·6′W	FM	162
Gattaway	Pth & Kin	NO1916	56°20·0′	3°18·2′W	X	58
Gattax Fm	Warw	SP1066	52°17·8′	1°50·8′W	FM	150
Gatten	Shrops	SO3898	52°34·8′	2°54·5′W	X	137
Gatten Lodge	Shrops	SO3899	52°35·4′	2°54·5′W	X	137
Gatten Plantation	Shrops	SO3798	52°34·8′	2°55·4′W	F	137
Gatteridge Fm	Kent	TR2045	51°9·9′	1°9·2′E	FM	179,189
Gattertop	Heref	SO4853	52°10·6′	2°45·2′W	X	148,149
Gatton	Surrey	TQ2753	51°15·9′	0°10·4′W	T	187
Gatton Hall	Surrey	TQ2752	51°15·4′	0°10·4′W	X	187
Gattons Fm	Medway	TQ7475	51°27·1′	0°30·6′E	FM	178
Gattonside	Scot Bord	NT5435	55°36·6′	2°43·4′W	T	73
Gattonside Ho	Scot Bord	NT5434	55°36·1′	2°43·4′W	X	73
Gattonside Mains	Scot Bord	NT5335	55°36·6′	2°44·3′W	X	73
Gatwick	Glos	SO7313	51°49·1′	2°23·1′W	T	162
Gatwick	Surrey	SU9144	51°11·5′	0°41·5′W	X	186
Gatwick Airport London	W Susx	TQ2740	51°8·9′	0°10·7′W	X	187
Gatwick Fm	Surrey	TQ2554	51°16·5′	0°12·1′W	FM	187
Gatwick Ho	Essex	TQ6893	51°36·9′	0°26·0′E	X	177,178
Gatwick Zoo	Surrey	TQ2340	51°9·0′	0°14·1′W	X	187
Gauber	N Yks	SD7778	54°12·1′	2°20·7′W	X	98
Gauber High Pasture	N Yks	SD7678	54°12·1′	2°21·7′W	X	98
Gauch	Moray	NJ3624	57°18·4′	3°3·3′W	X	37
Gauchalland	E Ayr	NS4935	55°35·4′	4°23·3′W	X	70
Gauch Burn	Moray	NJ3624	57°18·4′	3°3·3′W	W	37
Gauch Hill	Aberd	NJ7815	57°13·8′	2°21·4′W	X	38
Gaucyhillock	Aberd	NJ8719	57°15·9′	2°12·5′W	X	38
Gaudy Ho	N Yks	SD8588	54°17·5′	2°13·4′W	X	98
Gaudywood Park	Shrops	SO6771	52°20·4′	2°28·7′W	F	138
Gaufron	Powys	SN9968	52°18·3′	3°28·5′W	T	136,147
Gau Graig	Gwyn	SH7414	52°42·8′	3°51·5′W	H	124
Gaulby	Leic	SK6900	52°35·8′	0°58·5′W	T	141
Gaulby Lodge	Leic	SP6999	52°35·3′	0°58·5′W	X	141
Gaulden Manor	Somer	ST1131	51°4·5′	3°15·8′W	X	181
Gauldry	Fife	NO3723	56°24·0′	3°0·8′W	T	54,59
Gauldswell	Pth & Kin	NO2051	56°38·9′	3°17·8′W	X	53
Gaulet	Glos	SO6916	51°50·7′	2°26·6′W	X	162
Gaulkthorn	Lancs	SD7526	53°44·0′	2°22·3′W	X	103
Gauls	Pth & Kin	NO0734	56°29·6′	3°30·2′W	X	52,53
Gaulter Gap	Dorset	SY9079	50°36·9′	2°8·1′W	X	195
Gault Hole	Cambs	TL4380	52°24·2′	0°6·5′E	W	142,143

Gaultney Wood	Northnts	SP8283	52°26·6′	0°47·2′W	F	141
Gaumer Hill	Lincs	TF2877	53°16·7′	0°4·4′W	X	122
Gaundle Fm	Somer	ST5017	50°57·2′	2°42·3′W	FM	183
Gaunt Fen	Cambs	TL3684	52°26·5′	0°0·5′E	X	142
Gaunt Fms	Cambs	TL3684	52°26·5′	0°0·5′E	FM	142
Gaunt Ho	Lincs	TF2957	53°5·9′	0°4·0′W	X	122
Gaunt Ho	Oxon	SP4003	51°43·7′	1°24·9′W	X	164
Gauntlet Br	Lincs	TF2139	52°56·3′	0°11·6′W	X	131
Gauntons Bank	Ches	SJ5647	53°1·4′	2°39·0′W	T	117
Gaunt's Common	Dorset	SU0205	50°50·9′	1°57·9′W	T	195
Gaunt's Earthcott	S Glos	ST6384	51°33·5′	2°31·6′W	T	172
Gaunt's End	Essex	TL5425	51°54·4′	0°14·7′E	T	167
Gaunt's Fm	Somer	ST2842	51°10·6′	3°1·4′W	FM	182
Gaunt's Hill	Notts	SK5747	53°1·3′	1°8·6′W	X	129
Gaunt's Ho	Dorset	SU0104	50°50·4′	1°58·8′W	X	195
Gaupieshaugh	Aberd	NO7266	56°47·3′	2°27·1′W	X	45
Gautby	Lincs	TF1772	53°14·2′	0°14·4′W	T	121
Gauter Point	Devon	SS3624	50°59·8′	4°19·8′W	X	190
Gautries Hill	Derby	SK0980	53°19·3′	1°51·5′W	H	110
Gaut Skerries	Shetld	HU3798	60°40·1′	1°18·9′W	X	1
Gauze Brook	Wilts	ST9083	51°33·0′	2°8·3′W	W	173
Gaval	Aberd	NJ9851	57°33·2′	2°1·5′W	X	30
Gavelacre	Hants	SU4142	51°10·8′	1°24·4′W	X	185
Gavel Crag	Cumbr	NY4309	54°28·6′	2°52·4′W	X	90
Gavel Fell	Cumbr	NY1118	54°33·2′	3°22·1′W	H	89
Gavell	N Lanak	NS6977	55°58·3′	4°5·5′W	X	64
Gavells Clough	Lancs	SD6157	54°0·7′	2°35·3′W	X	102,103
Gavelock Hill	Cumbr	NY6872	55°2·7′	2°29·6′W	X	86,87
Gavel Pike	Cumbr	NY3713	54°30·8′	2°58·0′W	H	90
Gavel Rigg	N Yks	SD8272	54°8·9′	2°16·1′W	X	98
Gaverigan Manor	Corn	SW9358	50°23·4′	4°54·4′W	X	200
Gaveston Hall	W Susx	TQ1825	51°1·0′	0°18·7′W	X	187,198
Gaveston's Cross	Warw	SP2867	52°18·3′	1°35·0′W	X	151
Gavieside	W Loth	NT0265	55°52·3′	3°33·5′W	X	65
Gavilmoss	Renf	NS3358	55°47·4′	4°39·4′W	X	63
Gavinburn	W Dunb	NS4573	55°55·8′	4°28·4′W	X	64
Gavin's Glen	N Ayr	NS1658	55°47·1′	4°55·6′W	X	63
Gavinton	Scot Bord	NT7652	55°45·9′	2°22·5′W	T	67,74
Gawber	Barns	SE3207	53°33·8′	1°30·6′W	T	110,111
Gawber Plantn	Lancs	SD8248	53°55·9′	2°16·0′W	F	103
Gawbridge Mill	Somer	ST4419	50°58·3′	2°47·5′W	X	193
Gawburn Nip	Notts	SK7450	53°2·8′	0°53·4′W	W	120
Gawburrow Hill	Northnts	SP6564	52°16·5′	1°2·4′W	X	152
Gawcar House	Lancs	SD7251	53°57·5′	2°25·2′W	X	103
Gawcombe	Glos	SP2121	51°53·5′	1°41·3′W	X	163
Gawcott	Bucks	SP6831	51°58·6′	1°0·2′W	T	152,165
Gawcott Fields Fm	Bucks	SP6832	51°59·2′	1°0·2′W	FM	152,165
Gawdy Hall	Norf	TM2485	52°25·2′	1°18·1′E	X	156
Gawdyhall Big Wood	Norf	TM2585	52°25·2′	1°18·9′E	F	156
Gawen Ho	Durham	NZ0821	54°35·3′	1°52·1′W	X	92
Gaw Glen Burn	E Ayr	NS4802	55°17·6′	4°23·2′W	W	77
Gaw Hill	Lancs	SD3907	53°33·6′	2°54·8′W	H	108
Gawin Moor	D & G	NX9491	55°12·4′	3°39·5′W	X	78
Gawith Field	Cumbr	SD3081	54°13·4′	3°4·0′W	X	96,97
Gawky Hill or Black Hill	S Lanak	NT0432	55°34·6′	3°30·9′W	H	72
Gawlish Cliff	Devon	SS2527	51°1·2′	4°29·3′W	X	190
Gawlish Fm	Devon	SS2526	51°0·6′	4°29·3′W	FM	190
Gawloch	Aberd	NO6367	56°47·8′	2°35·9′W	X	45
Gawnsmoss	Aberd	NJ6358	57°36·9′	2°36·7′W	X	29
Gaws Hill	D & G	NX0750	54°48·7′	4°59·8′W	H	82
Gawstack	Moray	NJ5255	57°35·2′	2°47·7′W	X	29
Gawsworth	Ches	SJ8969	53°13·3′	2°9·5′W	T	118
Gawsworth Common	Ches	SJ9268	53°12·8′	2°6·8′W	X	118
Gawthorpe	Kirk	SE1916	53°38·7′	1°42·3′W	T	110
Gawthorpe	Wakf	SE2722	53°41·9′	1°35·1′W	T	104
Gawthorpe Ho	N Yks	SD9548	53°55·9′	2°4·2′W	X	103
Gawthrop	Cumbr	SD6987	54°16·9′	2°28·2′W	T	98
Gawthwaite	Cumbr	SD2784	54°15·0′	3°6·8′W	T	96,97
Gawthwaite Land	Cumbr	SD2786	54°16·1′	3°6·8′W	X	96,97
Gawton	Devon	SX4568	50°29·7′	4°10·7′W	X	201
Gawton's Well	Staffs	SJ8955	53°5·8′	2°9·5′W	W	118
Gay Bowers	Essex	TL7904	51°42·6′	0°35·9′E	T	167
Gay Bowers Fm	Essex	TL7101	51°41·1′	0°28·8′E	FM	167
Gayclops	N Yks	SD7566	54°5·6′	2°22·5′W	X	98
Gaydon	Warw	SP3654	52°11·2′	1°28·0′W	T	151
Gaydon Hill Fm	Warw	SP3753	52°10·7′	1°27·1′W	FM	151
Gayfield	Orkney	HY4850	59°20·3′	2°54·4′W	X	5
Gayfield Type	D & G	NY1389	55°11·5′	3°21·6′W	X	78
Gay Hill	Worcs	SP0577	52°23·7′	1°55·2′W	X	139
Gayhurst	Mil Key	SP8446	52°6·6′	0°46·0′W	T	152
Gayhurst Ho	Mil Key	SP8446	52°6·6′	0°46·0′W	A	152
Gayhurst Wood	Mil Key	SP8346	52°6·6′	0°46·9′W	F	152
Gayle	N Yks	SD8789	54°18·0′	2°11·6′W	T	98
Gayle Beck	N Yks	SD7880	54°13·2′	2°19·8′W	W	98
Gayle Beck	N Yks	SD8688	54°17·5′	2°12·5′W	W	98
Gayle Moor	N Yks	SD7982	54°14·2′	2°18·9′W	X	98
Gayles	E Susx	TV5397	50°45·4′	0°10·5′E	X	199
Gayles	N Yks	NZ1207	54°27·7′	1°48·5′W	T	92
Gayles Moor	N Yks	NZ0905	54°26·7′	1°51·3′W	X	92
Gaylet Pot	Angus	NO6743	56°34·9′	2°31·8′W	X	54
Gayle Wolds	N Yks	SD8082	54°14·2′	2°18·0′W	X	98
Gaylock Hill	Cumbr	NY5978	55°5·9′	2°38·1′W	X	86
Gaylors Fm	Herts	TL3626	51°55·2′	0°0·9′W	FM	166
Gaynes Lodge Fm	Cambs	TL1565	52°16·5′	0°18·5′W	FM	153
Gaynes Park	Essex	TL4801	51°41·5′	0°8·9′E	X	167
Gays Fm	Devon	SS7804	50°49·6′	3°43·6′W	FM	191
Gaysham Fm	Kent	TQ4355	51°16·8′	0°3·4′E	FM	187
Gays Ho	Win & Maid	SU8977	51°29·3′	0°42·7′W	X	175
Gay Street	W Susx	TQ0820	50°58·4′	0°27·3′W	T	197
Gaythorne Cotts	Cumbr	NY6412	54°30·4′	2°32·9′W	X	91
Gaythorne Hall	Cumbr	NY6413	54°30·9′	2°32·9′W	A	91
Gayton	Heref	SO6226	51°56·1′	2°32·8′W	X	162
Gayton	Norf	TF7219	52°44·7′	0°33·3′E	T	132
Gayton	Northnts	SP7054	52°11·0′	0°58·2′W	T	152
Gayton	Staffs	SJ9828	52°51·2′	2°1·4′W	T	127
Gayton	Wirral	SJ2780	53°19·0′	3°5·3′W	T	108
Gayton Brook	Staffs	SJ9728	52°51·2′	2°2·3′W	W	127
Gayton Cott	Wirral	SJ2680	53°18·9′	3°6·2′W	X	108
Gayton Engine	Lincs	TF4588	53°22·4′	0°11·2′E	T	113,122
Gayton le Marsh	Lincs	TF4284	53°20·3′	0°8·4′E	T	122
Gayton le Marsh Grange	Lincs	TF4586	53°21·3′	0°11·1′E	X	113,122
Gayton le Wold	Lincs	TF2385	53°21·1′	0°8·7′W	T	122
Gayton Sands	Wirral	SJ2478	53°17·9′	3°8·0′W	X	117
Gayton Thorpe	Norf	TF7418	52°44·1′	0°35·0′E	T	132
Gayton Thorpe Common	Norf	TF7317	52°43·6′	0°34·1′E	X	132
Gayton Top	Lincs	TF4183	53°19·7′	0°7·4′E	X	122
Gayton Wilds Ho	Northnts	SP7053	52°10·5′	0°58·2′W	X	152
Gayton Wood Fm	Northnts	SP7153	52°10·5′	0°57·3′W	FM	152
Gaywood	Kent	TQ4348	51°13·0′	0°3·2′E	X	187
Gaywood	Norf	TF6320	52°45·4′	0°25·3′E	T	132
Gaywood River	Norf	TF6720	52°45·3′	0°28·9′E	W	132
Gaza	Shetld	HU3572	60°26·1′	1°21·3′W	X	2,3
Gazeby Hall	Brad	SE1035	53°48·9′	1°50·5′W	X	104
Gazegill	Lancs	SD8246	53°54·8′	2°16·0′W	X	103
Gazeley	Suff	TL7164	52°15·1′	0°30·7′E	T	154
Gazell	Corn	SW4423	50°3·4′	5°34·2′W	X	203
Gazells	Corn	SW4022	50°2·7′	5°37·5′W	X	203
Gazick	Corn	SW3629	50°6·4′	5°41·2′W	X	203
Gazzle	Corn	SW8062	50°25·2′	5°5·5′W	W	200
Geal Charn	Aberd	NJ2810	57°10·8′	3°11·0′W	H	37
Geal Charn	Highld	NH6603	57°6·2′	4°12·3′W	H	35
Geal Charn	Highld	NH7004	57°6·8′	4°8·3′W	H	35
Geal-charn	Highld	NH8801	57°5·4′	3°50·4′W	H	35,36
Geal-charn	Highld	NJ0736	57°24·6′	3°32·4′W	X	27
Geal Charn	Highld	NJ0912	57°11·6′	3°29·9′W	H	36
Geal-charn	Highld	NJ1137	57°25·1′	3°28·4′W	X	28
Geal Charn	Highld	NN1594	57°0·3′	5°2·3′W	H	34
Geal Charn	Highld	NN4498	57°3·1′	4°33·9′W	H	34
Geal-chàrn	Highld	NN4774	56°50·2′	4°30·0′W	H	42
Geal Charn	Highld	NN5081	56°54·0′	4°27·3′W	H	42
Geal Charn	Highld	NN5698	57°3·3′	4°22·0′W	H	35
Geal-charn	Highld	NN5978	56°52·6′	4°18·4′W	H	42
Geal Charn	Moray	NJ1410	57°10·6′	3°24·9′W	H	36
Geal Charn	Moray	NJ3020	57°16·2′	3°9·2′W	X	37
Geal Charn	Pth & Kin	NN6854	56°39·8′	4°8·8′W	H	42,51
Geal Charn	Pth & Kin	NN8533	56°28·8′	3°51·6′W	H	52
Geal Charn	Pth & Kin	NO0383	56°55·9′	3°35·2′W	H	43
Geal-charn Beag	Highld	NH8414	57°12·4′	3°54·8′W	H	35
Geal Charn Beag	Highld	NJ1011	57°11·1′	3°28·9′W	H	36
Geal-charn Mór	Highld	NH8312	57°11·3′	3°55·7′W	H	35
Geallaig Hill	Aberd	NO2998	57°4·3′	3°9·8′W	H	37,44
Gealldruig Mhór	N Eil	HW8131	59°6·8′	5°49·1′W	X	8
Geal Loch	Arg & Bt	NN3116	56°18·6′	4°43·5′W	W	50,56
Gealtaire Beag	N Eil	NA7346	58°17·1′	7°34·3′W	X	13
Gealtaire Mór	N Eil	NA7446	58°17·2′	7°33·3′W	X	13
Geanies Ho	Highld	NH8979	57°47·5′	3°51·6′W	X	21
Gear	Corn	SW4633	50°8·8′	5°33·0′W	X	203
Gear	Corn	SW6136	50°10·8′	5°20·5′W	X	203
Gear	Corn	SW7224	50°4·6′	5°10·8′W	X	204
Gear	Orkney	ND2993	58°49·4′	3°13·3′W	X	7
Gearach	Arg & Bt	NR2259	55°44·9′	6°25·4′W	X	60
Gear Fm	Corn	SW7755	50°21·4′	5°7·7′W	FM	200
Gearnsary	Highld	NC7332	58°15·8′	4°9·4′W	X	16
Gearns Fm	Devon	SS3408	50°51·1′	4°21·1′W	FM	190
Geàrr Abhainn	Arg & Bt	NM5630	56°24·2′	5°56·8′W	W	48
Gearr Abhainn	Arg & Bt	NN1110	56°15·0′	5°2·6′W	W	50,56
Gearradh	Highld	NM9560	56°41·5′	5°20·4′W	X	40
Gearraidh Bhaile-locha	N Eil	NF7472	57°37·5′	7°27·2′W	X	18
Gearraidh Bhailteas	N Eil	NF7326	57°12·7′	7°24·6′W	T	22
Gearraidh Bhaird	N Eil	NB3620	58°5·7′	6°28·3′W	T	14
Gearraidh Choinnich	N Eil	NB2842	58°17·2′	6°38·0′W	X	8,13
Gearraidh Cladach	N Eil	NF8161	57°31·9′	7°19·4′W	X	22
Gearraidh Dubh	N Eil	NF8557	57°29·9′	7°15·1′W	X	22
Gearraidh Hosta	N Eil	NF7372	57°37·4′	7°28·2′W	X	18
Gearraidh Lotaigear	N Eil	NB2101	57°54·9′	6°42·2′W	X	14
Gearraidh Mhurchaidh	N Eil	NB2202	57°55·5′	6°41·3′W	X	14
Gearraidh Mór	Highld	NG1846	57°25·3′	6°41·4′W	X	23
Gearraidh Mór	Highld	NG4651	57°28·9′	6°13·8′W	X	23
Gearraidh na h-Aibhne	N Eil	NB2331	58°11·1′	6°42·3′W	T	8,13
Gearraidh nan Gamhainn	Highld	NG2141	57°22·7′	6°38·1′W	H	23
Gearraidh Siar	N Eil	NF7553	57°27·3′	7°24·7′W	X	22
Gearraidh Thigh'ghearraidh	N Eil	NF7371	57°36·9′	7°28·1′W	X	18
Gearraidh Thoughearraidh	N Eil	NF7371	57°36·9′	7°28·1′W	X	18
Gearran Island	Highld	NG3679	57°43·7′	6°25·6′W	X	23
Geàrr Aonach	Highld	NN1555	56°39·3′	5°0·6′W	X	41
Gearr Chreag	Highld	NM7061	56°41·3′	5°44·9′W	H	40
Gearr Garry	Highld	NH0801	57°3·9′	5°9·5′W	W	33
Gearrgeo	N Eil	NA1506	57°52·9′	8°29·4′W	X	18
Geàrr Leacann	Highld	NN1997	57°2·0′	4°58·5′W	X	34
Geàrr Leacann	Highld	NN3458	56°41·3′	4°42·2′W	X	41
Gearr Leachdann	Highld	NM9772	56°48·0′	5°19·0′W	H	40
Geàrr-leathad	Highld	NH7204	57°4·5′	5°45·3′W	X	33
Gears	Orkney	HY5303	58°55·0′	2°48·5′W	X	6,7
Gear Sands	Corn	SW7655	50°21·4′	5°8·6′W	X	200
Gear's Mill	Dorset	ST8621	50°59·5′	2°11·6′W	X	183
Gearson	Orkney	HY5907	58°57·2′	2°42·3′W	X	6
Gearstones	N Yks	SD7779	54°12·6′	2°20·7′W	X	98
Gear, The	Corn	SW4729	50°6·7′	5°32·0′W	X	203
Gearty Head	Highld	ND3442	58°22·0′	3°7·2′W	X	12
Geary	Highld	NG2661	57°33·6′	6°34·4′W	T	23
Gearymore	Highld	NG3140	57°22·5′	6°28·0′W	T	23
Geary's Heath	Warw	SP2282	52°26·4′	1°40·2′W	X	139
Geasgill Beag	Arg & Bt	NM4237	56°27·5′	6°10·8′W	X	47,48
Geasgill Mór	Arg & Bt	NM4337	56°27·6′	6°9·9′W	X	47,48
Geat Wolford	Warw	SP2434	52°0·5′	1°38·6′W	T	151
Geaylin ny Creggyn	I of M	SC2676	54°9·3′	4°39·5′W	X	95
Gebdykes Quarry	N Yks	SE2382	54°14·2′	1°38·4′W	X	99
Gebro	Orkney	HY4819	59°3·6′	2°53·9′W	X	6
Geddes	Heref	SO5620	51°52·8′	2°38·0′W	X	162
Geddes Ho	Highld	NH8852	57°32·9′	3°51·8′W	X	27
Geddes's Well	Scot Bord	NT1323	55°29·8′	3°22·2′W	X	72
Gedding	Suff	TL9457	52°10·9′	0°50·7′E	T	155
Geddinge Fm	Kent	TR2346	51°10·4′	1°11·8′E	FM	179,189
Gedding Hall	Suff	TL9336	51°59·6′	0°49·1′E	X	155
Gedding Hall	Suff	TL9558	52°11·4′	0°51·6′E	X	155
Geddington	Northnts	SP8983	52°26·5′	0°41·0′W	T	141
Geddington Chase	Northnts	SP9184	52°27·0′	0°39·3′W	F	141
Geddington Grange Fm	Northnts	SP8782	52°26·0′	0°42·8′W	FM	141
Gedges Fm	Kent	TQ6643	51°10·0′	0°22·9′E	FM	188
Gedgrave Hall	Suff	TM4048	52°4·9′	1°30·6′E	T	169
Gedgrave Marshes	Suff	TM4048	52°4·9′	1°30·6′E	X	169
Gedintailor	Highld	NG5235	57°20·5′	6°6·8′W	T	24,32
Gedling	Notts	SK6142	52°58·5′	1°5·1′W	T	129
Gedling Ho	Notts	SK6342	52°58·5′	1°3·3′W	X	129
Gedling Wood Fm	Notts	SK6243	52°59·1′	1°4·2′W	FM	129
Gedloch	Moray	NJ2255	57°35·0′	3°17·8′W	X	28
Gedloch Burn	Moray	NJ2252	57°33·3′	3°17·8′W	W	28
Gedney	Lincs	TF4024	52°48·0′	0°5·0′E	T	131
Gedney Broadgate	Lincs	TF4022	52°46·9′	0°5·0′E	X	131
Gedney Drove End	Lincs	TF4629	52°50·6′	0°10·5′E	T	131
Gedney Dyke	Lincs	TF4126	52°49·0′	0°5·9′E	T	131
Gedney Fen	Lincs	TF3820	52°45·8′	0°3·1′E	X	131
Gedney Hill	Lincs	TF3311	52°41·1′	0°1·5′W	T	131,142
Gedney Marsh	Lincs	TF4429	52°50·6′	0°8·7′E	X	131
Ged Point	D & G	NX6672	55°1·7′	4°5·4′W	X	77,84
Gedrys	Rho Cyn Taf	ST1085	51°33·6′	3°17·5′W	X	171
Ged Strand	D & G	NX6574	55°2·8′	4°6·4′W	W	77,84
Gee Cross	Tames	SJ9593	53°26·3′	2°4·1′W	T	109
Geedon Creek	Essex	TM0417	51°49·1′	0°58·0′E	W	168
Geedon Saltings	Essex	TM0418	51°49·6′	0°58·0′E	W	168
Geen Mill	Corn	SW8747	50°17·3′	4°59·0′W	X	204
Geerings	W Susx	TQ1634	51°5·8′	0°20·2′W	X	187
Geerlane Fm	Derby	SK3980	53°19·2′	1°24·5′W	FM	110,111
Geese Br	Northnts	SP6555	52°11·6′	1°2·5′W	X	152
Gee's Lock	Leic	SP5599	52°35·4′	1°10·9′W	X	140
Geeston	Rut	SK9804	52°37·7′	0°32·7′W	T	141
Gefeiliau Brook	Wrex	SJ3347	53°1·2′	2°59·5′W	W	117
Gefnan	Gwyn	SH6065	53°10·1′	4°5·3′W	X	115
Gefn Blewog	Cered	SN6972	52°20·1′	3°55·0′W	X	135
Gefnir Fm	Gwyn	SH6514	52°42·7′	3°59·5′W	FM	124
Gegan, The	E Loth	NT6084	56°3·1′	2°38·1′W	X	67
Gegin	Wrex	SJ2752	53°3·9′	3°5·0′W	T	117
Geifas	Cered	SN8172	52°20·2′	3°44·4′W	X	135,136,147
Geile Sgeir	N Eil	NB1236	58°13·4′	6°53·8′W	X	13
Geilston	Arg & Bt	NS3477	55°57·7′	4°39·1′W	T	63
Geinas	Denb	SJ0969	53°12·9′	3°21·4′W	T	116
Geirinis	N Eil	NF7741	57°21·0′	7°21·8′W	T	22
Geirisclett	N Eil	NF7675	57°39·2′	7°25·5′W	X	18
Geiris-geo	N Eil	NF8582	57°43·3′	7°17·0′W	X	18
Geirn	I of Angl	SH3881	53°18·3′	4°25·5′W	X	114
Geirum Beag	N Eil	NL5581	56°47·8′	7°38·7′W	X	31
Geirum Mór	N Eil	NL5481	56°47·8′	7°39·6′W	X	31
Geise	Highld	ND1064	58°33·6′	3°32·3′W	X	11,12
Geiselittle	Highld	ND1165	58°34·1′	3°31·3′W	X	11,12
Geisgeil	Highld	NC1741	58°19·4′	5°7·0′W	X	9
Gelder Burn	Aberd	NO2590	57°0·2′	3°13·6′W	W	44
Gelderhouse	Orkney	HY2627	59°7·7′	3°17·1′W	X	6
Gelder Shiel	Aberd	NO2590	57°0·0′	3°13·6′W	X	44
Geldeston	Norf	TM3991	52°28·1′	1°31·5′E	T	134
Geldeston Marshes	Norf	TM3891	52°28·1′	1°30·7′E	X	134
Geldie Burn	Aberd	NN9787	56°58·0′	3°41·2′W	W	43
Geldie Lodge	Aberd	NN9586	56°57·5′	3°43·1′W	X	43
Gelert's Grave	Gwyn	SH5947	53°0·4′	4°5·7′W	X	115
Gelham Hall	Suff	TM2956	52°9·5′	1°21·3′E	X	156
Gell	Conwy	SH8469	53°12·6′	3°43·8′W	T	116
Gell	Conwy	SH8852	53°3·5′	3°39·9′W	X	116
Gell	Gwyn	SH4939	52°55·9′	4°14·4′W	X	123
Gella	Angus	NO3765	56°46·6′	3°1·4′W	X	44
Gellan	Aberd	NO6992	57°1·3′	2°30·2′W	X	38,45
Gellet	Fife	NT0884	56°2·7′	3°28·2′W	X	65
Gell-fain	Powys	SN8432	51°58·7′	3°40·9′W	X	160
Gellfawr	Gwyn	SH6116	52°43·7′	4°3·1′W	X	124
Gell Fm	Flint	SJ2766	53°11·4′	3°5·1′W	FM	117
Gelli	Carm	SN3027	51°55·2′	4°27·9′W	X	145
Gelli	Carm	SN3214	51°48·2′	4°25·8′W	X	159
Gelli	Carm	SN4211	51°46·8′	4°17·0′W	X	159
Gelli	Carm	SN4838	52°1·4′	4°12·5′W	X	146
Gelli	Carm	SN6244	52°4·9′	4°0·4′W	X	146
Gelli	Carm	SN7626	51°55·4′	3°47·8′W	X	146,160
Gelli	Cered	SN4055	52°10·4′	4°20·0′W	X	146
Gelli	Cered	SN5253	52°9·6′	4°9·4′W	X	146
Gelli	Cered	SN7681	52°25·0′	3°49·0′W	X	135
Gelli	Conwy	SH7158	53°6·5′	3°55·2′W	X	115
Gelli	Conwy	SH7663	53°9·2′	3°50·9′W	X	115
Gelli	Denb	SJ1168	53°12·3′	3°19·5′W	X	116
Gelli	Flint	SJ1278	53°17·7′	3°18·8′W	X	116
Gelli	Flint	SJ1768	53°12·4′	3°14·2′W	X	116
Gelli	Flint	SJ2259	53°7·6′	3°9·5′W	X	117
Gelli	Gwyn	SH3736	52°54·0′	4°25·0′W	X	123
Gelli	Gwyn	SH5465	53°10·0′	4°10·6′W	X	114,115
Gelli	Gwyn	SJ0241	52°57·7′	3°27·1′W	X	125
Gelli	Monm	SO3616	51°50·6′	2°55·3′W	X	161
Gelli	Pemb	SM9734	51°58·3′	4°56·9′W	X	157
Gelli	Pemb	SN0819	51°50·4′	4°46·8′W	T	158
Gelli	Pemb	SN1037	52°0·2′	4°45·7′W	X	145
Gelli	Powys	SH7804	52°37·4′	3°47·5′W	X	135
Gelli	Powys	SH8900	52°35·4′	3°37·9′W	X	135,136
Gelli	Powys	SJ0509	52°40·5′	3°23·9′W	X	125
Gelli	Powys	SJ0623	52°48·0′	3°23·3′W	X	125
Gelli	Powys	SJ1407	52°39·5′	3°15·9′W	X	125
Gelli	Powys	SJ2609	52°40·7′	3°5·3′W	X	126
Gelli	Powys	SO0296	52°33·4′	3°26·3′W	X	136
Gelli	Rho Cyn Taf	SS9794	51°38·4′	3°28·9′W	T	170
Gelli	Wrex	SJ1836	52°55·2′	3°12·8′W	X	125
Gelliaraul Fm	V of Glam	SS9577	51°29·2′	3°30·3′W	FM	170
Gelliargwellt Uchaf Fm	Caer	ST1296	51°39·6′	3°15·9′W	FM	171
Gelliau	Gwyn	SH3743	52°57·8′	4°25·2′W	X	123
Gelliau	Powys	SH8604	52°37·6′	3°40·7′W	X	135,136
Gelliau-isaf	Powys	SN9322	51°53·4′	3°32·9′W	X	160
Gelli Aur Country Park	Carm	SN5919	51°51·3′	4°2·5′W	X	159
Gelli-bant	Gwyn	SH6225	52°48·5′	4°2·4′W	X	124
Gelli-bant	Powys	SO1016	51°50·4′	3°18·0′W	X	161
Gelli-benuchel	Nth Pt Talb	SN8005	51°44·1′	3°43·9′W	X	160
Gelli-ben-uchel	Rho Cyn Taf	SN9506	51°44·8′	3°30·9′W	X	160
Gelli-bêr	Newp	ST2582	51°32·2′	3°4·5′W	X	171
Gelli Boeth	Powys	SO2523	51°54·3′	3°5·0′W	X	161
Gelli crugiau	Powys	SN8844	52°5·2′	3°37·7′W	X	147,160
Gellidara	Gwyn	SH3434	52°52·9′	4°27·6′W	X	123
Gelliddewi-Isaf	Carm	SN5744	52°4·8′	4°4·8′W	X	146

Gelli-ddolen	Gwyn	SH9013	52°42·5′	3°37·3′W	X	125
Gelliddu	Carm	SN4315	51°48·9′	4°16·3′W	X	159
Gelli-ddu	Carm	SN5216	51°49·6′	4°8·5′W	X	159
Gelli-ddu-fâch	Rho Cyn Taf	SO0400	51°41·7′	3°22·9′W	X	170
Gellideg	Carm	SN4210	51°46·2′	4°17·0′W	X	159
Gellideg	Cered	SN3149	52°7·1′	4°27·7′W	X	145
Gellideg	Cered	SN5044	52°4·7′	4°10·9′W	X	146
Gelli Deg	Gwyn	SH8438	52°55·9′	3°43·1′W	X	124,125
Gellideg	Merth Tyd	SO0207	51°45·4′	3°24·8′W	T	160
Gelli-deg	Pemb	SN2439	52°1·5′	4°33·5′W	X	145
Gelli-deg	Torf	SO2400	51°41·9′	3°5·6′W	X	171
Gellidoc Fm	Carm	SN5209	51°45·8′	4°8·3′W	FM	159
Gelli Dochllithe	Nth Pt Talb	SN7906	51°44·6′	3°44·8′W	X	160
Gelli-draws	Rho Cyn Taf	ST0588	51°35·2′	3°21·9′W	X	170
Gellidwyll	Powys	SO1452	52°9·8′	3°15·0′W	X	148
Gellidywyll	Powys	SN8898	52°34·3′	3°38·8′W	X	135,136
Gellie	Cered	SN3853	52°9·3′	4°21·7′W	X	145
Gelli Faenog	Powys	SN9254	52°10·7′	3°34·4′W	X	147
Gellifaharen	Cered	SN4143	52°4·0′	4°18·8′W	X	146
Gelli-fanadlog	Caer	ST1290	51°36·4′	3°15·9′W	X	171
Gelli-fanw	Powys	SO2320	51°52·6′	3°6·7′W	X	161
Gelli-fawnen	Carm	SN6514	51°48·7′	3°57·1′W	X	159
Gelli-fawr	Carm	SN4804	51°43·1′	4°11·6′W	X	159
Gelli-fawr	Carm	SN6910	51°46·6′	3°53·5′W	X	160
Gellifawr	Pemb	SN0634	51°58·5′	4°49·1′W	X	145
Gelli Fawr Fm	Torf	ST2792	51°37·6′	3°2·9′W	FM	171
Gelli-feddgaer	Brig	SS9686	51°34·0′	3°29·6′W	X	170
Gelli-felen	Carm	SN7628	51°56·4′	3°47·8′W	X	146,160
Gelli Ffrydiau	Gwyn	SH5253	53°3·5′	4°12·1′W	X	115
Gelli Fm	Carm	SN6110	51°46·5′	4°0·5′W	FM	159
Gelli Fm	Nth Pt Talb	SS8796	51°39·3′	3°37·6′W	FM	170
Gelli Fm	Powys	SJ2319	52°46·0′	3°8·1′W	FM	126
Gelli Fm	Wrex	SJ4643	52°59·1′	2°47·9′W	FM	117
Gellifor	Denb	SJ1262	53°9·1′	3°18·6′W	T	116
Gellifowy	Nth Pt Talb	SN7306	51°44·5′	3°50·0′W	X	160
Gelli-fud	Brig	SS9487	51°34·6′	3°31·4′W	X	170
Gelli-fudr	Powys	SN7596	52°33·1′	3°50·2′W	X	135
Gelligaer	Caer	ST1396	51°39·6′	3°15·1′W	T	171
Gelli-gaer	Nth Pt Talb	SS7694	51°38·1′	3°47·1′W	T	170
Gelligaer Common	Caer	SO0905	51°44·4′	3°18·7′W	X	161
Gelli-gaer Common	Caer	ST1298	51°40·7′	3°16·0′W	X	171
Gelligaer Common	Merth Tyd	SO1004	51°43·9′	3°17·8′W	X	171
Gelligaled	Carm	SN5105	51°43·7′	4°9·1′W	X	159
Gelli-galed	Nth Pt Talb	SN7805	51°44·1′	3°45·6′W	X	160
Gelligarn	V of Glam	SS9578	51°29·7′	3°30·4′W	X	170
Gelligarneddau	Cered	SN6055	52°10·8′	4°2·5′W	X	146
Gelligarn Fm	Powys	SO0260	52°14·0′	3°25·7′W	FM	147
Gelligatrog	Carm	SN4611	51°46·8′	4°13·6′W	X	159
Gelligatti	Carm	SN2941	52°2·7′	4°29·2′W	X	145
Gelli-geiloges	Powys	SO0531	51°58·4′	3°22·6′W	X	160
Gelligemlyn	Gwyn	SH7322	52°47·1′	3°52·6′W	X	124
Gelli Gethin	Powys	SJ0406	52°38·8′	3°24·7′W	X	125
Gelli-gôch	Gwyn	SH7128	52°50·3′	3°54·5′W	X	124
Gelli-gôch	Powys	SN7399	52°34·7′	3°52·1′W	X	135
Gelli-goch	Rho Cyn Taf	SS9497	51°39·9′	3°31·6′W	X	170
Gelligoediog	Caer	SO1702	51°42·9′	3°11·7′W	X	171
Gelli-goll	V of Glam	SS9878	51°29·7′	3°27·8′W	X	170
Gelli-graian	Gwyn	SH6800	52°35·2′	3°56·5′W	X	135
Gelli Grin	Carm	SN5131	51°57·7′	4°9·7′W	X	146
Gelli-grin	Gwyn	SH6339	52°56·1′	4°1·9′W	X	124
Gelli-Grin	Gwyn	SH9434	52°53·8′	3°34·1′W	X	125
Gelligroes	Caer	ST1794	51°38·6′	3°11·6′W	T	171
Gelli-groes	Carm	SN6420	51°52·0′	3°58·1′W	X	159
Gelli Groes	Swan	SS5393	51°37·2′	4°7·0′W	X	159
Gelli-gron	Rho Cyn Taf	ST0088	51°35·2′	3°26·2′W	X	170
Gelli-gwenyn	Cered	SN5752	52°9·1′	4°5·0′W	X	146
Gelli-gwm Rock	Swan	SN6205	51°43·8′	3°59·5′W	X	159
Gelli Gynan	Denb	SJ1854	53°4·9′	3°13·0′W	X	116
Gelli-gynar	Carm	SN3337	52°0·6′	4°25·6′W	X	145
Gelli-hâf	Caer	ST1695	51°39·1′	3°12·5′W	T	171
Gelli-halog	Pemb	SN1510	51°45·7′	4°40·5′W	X	158
Gellihen	Cered	SN4450	52°7·8′	4°16·4′W	X	146
Gelli Hill	Powys	SO0957	52°12·5′	3°19·5′W	H	147
Gelli Hill	Powys	SO0958	52°13·0′	3°19·5′W	H	147
Gellihir	Caer	ST1194	51°38·5′	3°16·8′W	X	171
Gelli Hir	Powys	SO0088	52°29·1′	3°28·0′W	X	136
Gelli-hîr	Swan	SS5693	51°37·3′	4°4·4′W	X	159
Gelli-hîr Wood	Swan	SS5692	51°36·7′	4°4·4′W	F	159
Gelli-isaf	Gwyn	SH9137	52°55·4′	3°36·9′W	X	125
Gelli-lago	Gwyn	SH6348	53°1·0′	4°2·1′W	X	115
Gelli-lâs Fawr	Brig	SS8886	51°33·9′	3°36·6′W	X	170
Gellilefrith	Powys	SN9686	52°28·0′	3°31·5′W	X	136
Gelli-llwyd Fm	Monm	SO3518	51°51·6′	2°56·2′W	FM	161
Gelli Llyn Du	Cered	SN6256	52°11·3′	4°0·7′W	X	146
Gelli-luog	Nth Pt Talb	SN7006	51°44·5′	3°52·6′W	X	160
Gellilwca Fawr	Nth Pt Talb	SN7207	51°45·1′	3°50·9′W	X	160
Gelli-lwch	Rho Cyn Taf	ST0691	51°36·8′	3°21·1′W	X	170
Gellilwyd	Gwyn	SH7016	52°43·8′	3°55·1′W	X	124
Gellilydan	Gwyn	SH6839	52°56·2′	3°57·4′W	T	124
Gelli-march Fm	Nth Pt Talb	SN7600	51°41·3′	3°47·2′W	FM	170
Gellinebwen	Cered	SN6682	52°25·4′	3°57·8′W	X	135
Gelli-newydd	Conwy	SH7763	53°9·2′	3°50·0′W	X	115
Gelliniog	I of Angl	SH4565	53°9·8′	4°18·7′W	X	114,115
Gelliniog Goch	I of Angl	SH4564	53°9·3′	4°18·7′W	X	114,115
Gellinud	Nth Pt Talb	SN7304	51°43·5′	3°49·9′W	T	170
Gellioedd	Conwy	SH9344	52°59·2′	3°35·2′W	X	125
Gellionen	Swan	SN7002	51°42·3′	3°52·5′W	X	170
Gelliorlas	Carm	SN2540	52°2·1′	4°32·7′W	X	145
Gelli'r-haidd	Rho Cyn Taf	SS9987	51°34·6′	3°27·1′W	X	170
Gelli-rhŷdd	Powys	SO0442	52°4·3′	3°23·6′W	X	147,160
Gelli-siriol	Brig	SS8788	51°35·0′	3°37·5′W	X	170
Gelliswick	Pemb	SM8805	51°42·5′	5°3·7′W	X	157
Gelliswick Bay	Pemb	SM8805	51°42·5′	5°3·7′W	W	157
Gellitalgarth	Powys	SN9757	52°12·3′	3°30·0′W	A	147
Gelli, The	Wrex	SJ4643	52°59·1′	2°47·9′W	X	117
Gelli-uchaf	Carm	SN4717	51°50·1′	4°12·8′W	X	159
Gelliwarog	Nth Pt Talb	SN7409	51°46·2′	3°49·2′W	X	160
Gelliwastad	Swan	SN6600	51°41·2′	3°55·9′W	X	159
Gelli-Wen	Rho Cyn Taf	ST0680	51°30·9′	3°20·9′W	X	170
Gelli-wern-ganol	Swan	SN6302	51°42·2′	3°58·6′W	X	159

Gelliwig	Gwyn	SH2530	52°50·6′	4°35·5′W	X	123
Gelli-wion	Rho Cyn Taf	ST0588	51°35·2′	3°21·9′W	X	170
Gelliwion	Rho Cyn Taf	ST0590	51°36·3′	3°21·9′W	X	170
Gelli-wlyb	Powys	SN8824	51°54·4′	3°37·3′W	X	160
Gelli-Wrgan	Rho Cyn Taf	ST0496	51°39·5′	3°22·9′W	X	170
Gell Point	Corn	SW9939	50°13·2′	4°48·7′W	X	204
Gells Fm	Lincs	TF2934	52°53·5′	0°4·5′W	FM	131
Gelly	Carm	SN5739	52°2·1′	4°4·7′W	X	146
Gelly	Pth & Kin	NO0637	56°31·2′	3°31·2′W	X	52,53
Gellybank	Pth & Kin	NO1000	56°11·3′	3°26·6′W	X	58
Gellybanks	Pth & Kin	NO0731	56°28·0′	3°30·1′W	X	52,53
Gellybevan Fm	Carm	SN7020	51°52·0′	3°52·9′W	FM	160
Gellybrae	Aberd	NJ8447	57°31·0′	2°15·6′W	X	29,30
Gelly Burn	Pth & Kin	NO0837	56°31·2′	3°29·3′W	W	52,53
Gellyburn	Pth & Kin	NO0939	56°32·3′	3°28·3′W	X	52,53
Gelly Burn	Pth & Kin	NO1000	56°11·3′	3°26·6′W	W	58
Gelly-ceidrim	Carm	SN6109	51°46·0′	4°0·5′W	X	159
Gellydogin	Carm	SN2021	51°51·8′	4°36·5′W	X	145,158
Gellydywyll	Carm	SN2640	52°2·1′	4°31·8′W	X	145
Gellyeithrym Fm	Swan	SS5895	51°38·4′	4°2·7′W	FM	159
Gellyfeddan	Swan	SN6401	51°41·7′	3°57·7′W	X	159
Gellyfelen	Carm	SN8136	52°0·8′	3°43·6′W	X	160
Gellyfelgaws	Nth Pt Talb	SN7301	51°41·8′	3°49·9′W	X	170
Gelly Fm	Corn	SX1963	50°26·6′	4°32·6′W	FM	201
Gellygen	Gwyn	SH7403	52°36·9′	3°51·3′W	X	135
Gellyglyd	Carm	SN4623	51°53·3′	4°13·9′W	X	159
Gellyglyd	Carm	SN5322	51°52·9′	4°7·8′W	X	159
Gellygron	Carm	SN7723	51°53·8′	3°46·9′W	X	160
Gellygron	Nth Pt Talb	SN7104	51°43·4′	3°51·7′W	T	170
Gellyhill	Aberd	NJ7062	57°39·1′	2°29·7′W	X	29
Gellyolau	Carm	SN0919	51°50·5′	4°46·0′W	X	158
Gellyrhydd	Carm	SN8236	52°0·8′	3°42·8′W	X	160
Gellyrhydd	Powys	SO2419	51°52·1′	3°5·8′W	X	161
Gellywen	Carm	SN2723	51°53·0′	4°30·4′W	T	145,158
Gellywen	Carm	SN5708	51°45·4′	4°3·9′W	X	159
Gellywernen	Carm	SN5305	51°43·7′	4°7·3′W	X	159
Gelmast	Cered	SN7775	52°21·8′	3°48·0′W	X	135,147
Gelscoe Lodge Fm	Leic	SK4322	52°47·9′	1°21·3′W	FM	129
Gelshfield	Highld	ND1858	58°30·4′	3°24·0′W	X	11,12
Gelsmoor	Leic	SK4018	52°45·7′	1°24·0′W	T	129
Gelsthorpe Fm	N Yks	SE4356	54°0·1′	1°20·2′W	FM	105
Gelston	D & G	NX7658	54°54·3′	3°55·6′W	T	84
Gelston	Lincs	SK9145	52°59·9′	0°38·2′W	T	130
Gelston Burn	D & G	NX7759	54°54·9′	3°54·7′W	W	84
Gelston Grange	Lincs	SK8946	53°0·5′	0°40·0′W	X	130
Gelt Burn	Northum	NY6450	54°50·9′	2°33·2′W	W	86
Gelt Ho	Cumbr	NY5059	54°55·6′	2°46·4′W	X	86
Gelt Mill	Cumbr	NY5356	54°54·0′	2°43·6′W	X	86
Geltsdale Ho	Cumbr	NY5653	54°52·4′	2°40·7′W	X	86
Geltsdale Middle	Cumbr	NY6051	54°51·4′	2°37·0′W	X	86
Gelt Side	Cumbr	NY5159	54°55·6′	2°45·5′W	X	86
Gelt Woods	Northum	NY5258	54°55·1′	2°44·5′W	F	86
Gelvan	Pth & Kin	NO0501	56°11·8′	3°31·4′W	X	58
Gelynen	Carm	SN3036	52°0·0′	4°28·2′W	X	145
Gelynog Fms	Rho Cyn Taf	ST0585	51°33·6′	3°21·8′W	FM	170
Gembling	E Yorks	TA1057	54°0·1′	0°18·9′W	T	107
Gembling Ho	E Yorks	TA1156	53°59·5′	0°18·0′W	X	107
Gembling Lane End	E Yorks	TA1056	53°59·5′	0°18·9′W	X	107
Gemini	Warr	SJ5891	53°25·1′	2°37·5′W	T	108
Gemmil	Arg & Bt	NM7805	56°11·4′	5°34·2′W	X	55
Genau-hafod	Powys	SO1087	52°28·7′	3°19·1′W	X	136
Gendros	Swan	SS6395	51°38·5′	3°58·4′W	T	159
Gendrum	Powys	SN8887	52°28·4′	3°38·5′W	H	135,136
Genechal, The or Sean-choille	Aberd	NO2993	57°1·6′	3°9·7′W	X	37,44
General Ross's Cairn	Highld	NM7371	56°46·8′	5°42·5′W	X	40
General's Loch	Highld	NC2653	58°26·1′	4°58·4′W	W	9
General's Pond	Surrey	SU9146	51°12·6′	0°41·4′W	W	186
General Wade's Military Road	Highld	NH3802	57°5·1′	4°39·9′W	X	34
General Wade's Military Road	Highld	NH5326	57°18·3′	4°25·9′W	X	26,35
General Wade's Military Road	Highld	NH5825	57°17·9′	4°20·9′W	X	26,35
General Wade's Military Road	Highld	NH6137	57°24·4′	4°18·4′W	X	26
General Wade's Military Road	Highld	NH7334	57°23·0′	4°6·3′W	X	27
General Wade's Military Road	Highld	NH8422	57°16·7′	3°55·0′W	X	35
General Wade's Military Road	Highld	NN2185	56°55·6′	4°56·0′W	X	34,41
General Wade's Military Road	Highld	NN5893	57°0·6′	4°19·9′W	X	35
General Wade's Military Road	Highld	NN7195	57°1·9′	4°7·1′W	X	35
General Wade's Military Road	Pth & Kin	NN6473	56°50·0′	4°13·3′W	X	42
General Wade's Military Road	Pth & Kin	NN8066	56°46·5′	3°57·4′W	X	43
General Wade's Military Road	Pth & Kin	NN8842	56°33·7′	3°48·9′W	A	52
General Wade's Military Road	Pth & Kin	NN9028	56°26·1′	3°46·6′W	X	52,58
General Wade's Military Road	Pth & Kin	NN9040	56°32·6′	3°46·9′W	X	52
Genesis Green	Suff	TL7457	52°11·3′	0°33·1′E	T	155
Geneva	Cered	SN4557	52°11·6′	4°15·7′W	X	146
Genffordd	Powys	SO1730	51°58·0′	3°12·1′W	X	161
Genie Fea	Orkney	ND2494	58°49·9′	3°18·5′W	H	7
Gennell	Aberd	NO7793	57°1·9′	2°22·3′W	X	38,45
Gennell Ho	N Yks	SE6662	54°3·2′	0°59·1′W	X	100
Gennings Fm	Kent	TQ7250	51°13·6′	0°28·2′E	FM	188
Genoch	S Ayr	NS3901	55°16·9′	4°31·7′W	X	77
Genoch Fm	S Ayr	NS2817	55°25·3′	4°42·6′W	FM	70
Genoch Inner Hill	S Ayr	NS3900	55°16·3′	4°31·6′W	H	77
Genoch Mains	D & G	NX1356	54°52·1′	4°54·4′W	X	82
Genoch Rocks	D & G	NW9670	54°59·2′	5°10·9′W	X	76,82
Gentle Jane	Corn	SW9474	50°32·0′	4°54·0′W	X	200
Gentlemen's Cave	Orkney	HY3948	59°19·1′	3°3·8′W	X	5

Gentlemen's Ha	Orkney	HY5141	59°15·4′	2°51·1′W	X	5
Gentle's Copse	Hants	SU8335	51°6·7′	0°48·5′W	F	186
Gentleshaw	Staffs	SK0511	52°42·0′	1°55·2′W	T	128
Gentleshaw Hill	Staffs	SK0511	52°42·0′	1°55·2′W	X	128
Geo a' Phuinsin	N Eil	NF9794	57°50·2′	7°5·9′W	X	18
Geo Chalum McMhuirich	N Eil	NA0701	57°49·8′	8°36·9′W	X	18
Geo Claver	Shetld	HZ2171	59°31·7′	1°37·2′W	X	4
Geocrab	N Eil	NG1190	57°48·6′	6°51·5′W	T	14
Geo Cuinge	Highld	NC9766	58°34·5′	3°45·8′W	X	11
Geodha an Fhaing	N Eil	NF7274	57°38·5′	7°29·4′W	X	18
Geodha an Leth-roinn	Highld	NC0235	58°15·8′	5°22·0′W	X	15
Geodha an Truillich	N Eil	NB0438	58°14·1′	7°2·1′W	X	13
Geodha an t-Similier	N Eil	NF7274	57°38·5′	7°29·4′W	X	18
Geodha Bàn	N Eil	NF7554	57°27·9′	7°24·8′W	X	22
Geodha Beag	N Eil	NB1100	57°54·0′	6°52·2′W	X	14
Geodh' a' Bhàthaich	Highld	NC4866	58°33·6′	4°36·3′W	X	9
Geodh' a' Bheannaich	N Eil	NB0337	58°13·6′	7°3·1′W	X	13
Geodh' a' Bhrideoin	Highld	NC4867	58°34·1′	4°36·3′W	X	9
Geodha Blàitha Mór	N Eil	HW6130	59°5·7′	6°9·9′W	X	8
Geodha Brat	Highld	NC5567	58°34·3′	4°29·1′W	X	10
Geodha Caol	N Eil	NB0337	58°13·6′	7°3·1′W	X	13
Geodha Caol	N Eil	NB1338	58°14·5′	6°53·0′W	X	13
Geodha Ceann da Aoineadh	Arg & Bt	NM7024	56°21·4′	5°42·9′W	X	49
Geodha Chalmoir	N Eil	NB0937	58°13·8′	6°57·0′W	X	13
Geodhachan	N Eil	NL5681	56°47·9′	7°37·7′W	X	31
Geodh'a'Choin	N Eil	NB1739	58°15·2′	6°49·0′W	X	8,13
Geodh' a' Chruidh	N Eil	NB0117	58°2·7′	7°3·6′W	X	13
Geodha Chruidh	N Eil	NB0337	58°13·6′	7°3·1′W	X	13
Geodh' a' Chuibhrig	N Eil	NB4929	58°11·0′	6°15·7′W	X	8
Geodha Cul an Fraochaidh	Highld	NC2470	58°35·2′	5°1·2′W	X	9
Geodha Daraich	Highld	NG3719	57°11·4′	6°20·7′W	X	32
Geodha Dubh	Highld	NC3571	58°36·0′	4°49·9′W	X	9
Geodha Dubh	Highld	NG3765	57°36·2′	6°23·7′W	X	23
Geodha Dubh	N Eil	NB2200	57°54·4′	6°41·1′W	X	14
Geòdha Dubh	N Eil	NG1891	57°49·4′	6°44·5′W	X	14
Geodha Dubh Caolas Gallan	N Eil	NB0439	58°14·7′	7°2·2′W	X	13
Geòdha Ear	N Eil	NG1891	57°49·4′	6°44·5′W	X	14
Geodha Gaineamhach	N Eil	NB0307	57°57·5′	7°0·8′W	X	13
Geodha Garbh	N Eil	NF7029	57°14·2′	7°27·8′W	X	22
Geodha Ghainmhich	N Eil	NB1538	58°14·6′	6°50·9′W	X	13
Geodha Ghille Mhóire	Arg & Bt	NR2170	55°50·8′	6°27·0′W	W	60
Geodha Glann Neill	N Eil	NF1098	57°48·4′	8°33·6′W	X	18
Geodha Glas	Highld	NC2674	58°37·4′	4°59·3′W	X	9
Geodha Gorm	Arg & Bt	NR3797	56°5·9′	6°13·3′W	X	61
Geodha Gorm	N Eil	NB0638	58°14·2′	7°0·1′W	X	13
Geòdha Gorm	N Eil	NB2605	57°57·3′	6°37·4′W	X	13,14
Geodha Gunna	N Eil	NB0336	58°13·0′	7°3·0′W	X	13
Geodha 'ic Sheòrais	N Eil	NB5537	58°15·5′	6°10·1′W	X	8
Geodha Islaca	N Eil	NA9613	58°0·4′	7°8·3′W	X	13
Geodh' a' Lochaidh	Highld	NC3970	58°35·6′	4°45·7′W	X	9
Geodha Maladale	N Eil	NB0837	58°13·8′	6°58·0′W	X	13
Geodha Meall na Bráthain	N Eil	NF8745	57°23·5′	7°12·2′W	X	22
Geodha Meiril	Highld	NC4862	58°31·4′	4°36·1′W	X	9
Geodha Mhòr an Uillt	N Eil	NB5635	58°14·4′	6°9·0′W	X	8
Geodha Mór	Highld	NC0802	57°58·2′	5°14·3′W	X	15
Geodha Mór	Highld	NG2039	57°21·6′	6°38·9′W	X	23
Geodha Mór	N Eil	NB0539	58°14·7′	7°1·2′W	X	13
Geodha Mòr	N Eil	NB1001	57°54·5′	6°53·3′W	X	14
Geodha Mór	N Eil	NB1139	58°15·0′	6°55·1′W	X	13
Geodha Mór	N Eil	NB1338	58°14·5′	6°53·0′W	X	13
Geodha Mòr	N Eil	NB4636	58°14·6′	6°19·2′W	X	8
Geòdha Mòr	N Eil	NF7130	57°14·8′	7°26·9′W	X	22
Geodha Mór Shleibhte	N Eil	NB1339	58°15·0′	6°53·1′W	X	13
Geòdha na Beairt	N Eil	NB3503	57°56·5′	6°28·2′W	X	14
Geodha na Criche	N Eil	NB1538	58°14·6′	6°50·9′W	X	13
Geodha na h-Aibhne	Highld	NG2541	57°22·8′	6°34·1′W	X	23
Geodha na Mòine	Highld	NG4076	57°42·2′	6°21·4′W	X	23
Geodha nan Aigheann	Highld	NC5368	58°34·8′	4°31·2′W	X	10
Geodha nan Calman	N Eil	NB1339	58°15·0′	6°53·1′W	X	13
Geodha nan Each	Highld	NG1554	57°29·5′	6°44·9′W	X	23
Geodha nan Faochag	Highld	NG2935	57°19·8′	6°29·7′W	X	23
Geodha nan Gall	N Eil	HW8032	59°7·3′	5°50·2′W	X	8
Geodha nan Gobhar	Highld	NG3522	57°13·0′	6°22·9′W	X	32
Geodha nan Gobhar	N Eil	NB4121	58°6·4′	6°23·3′W	X	14
Geòdha nan Nathraichean	N Eil	NB3504	57°57·1′	6°28·3′W	X	14
Geodha nan Sgarbh	N Eil	NB0116	58°2·2′	7°3·5′W	X	13
Geodha nan Sgarbh	N Eil	NB1038	58°14·4′	6°56·0′W	X	13
Geodha Nasavig	N Eil	NB0336	58°13·0′	7°3·0′W	X	13
Geodha na Seamraig	Highld	NC2873	58°36·9′	4°57·2′W	X	9
Geodhan Dubh	N Eil	NB1402	57°55·2′	6°49·3′W	X	14
Geodh'an Eich Bhric	Highld	NG3032	57°18·2′	6°28·5′W	X	32
Geodh' an Fharaidh	N Eil	NA9924	58°6·4′	7°6·2′W	X	13
Geodh' an Fhithich	N Eil	NA9929	58°9·1′	7°6·5′W	X	13
Geodh' an Fhuarain	Highld	NC5765	58°33·2′	4°27·0′W	X	10
Geodh' an Sgadain	Highld	NC4460	58°30·3′	4°40·2′W	X	9
Geodh'an Tairbh	Highld	NG1655	57°30·0′	6°44·0′W	X	23
Geòdh an t-Sil	Arg & Bt	NR6079	55°56·9′	5°50·2′W	X	61,62
Geodha Raineach	Highld	NC4965	58°33·1′	4°35·2′W	X	9
Geodha Roaga	N Eil	NA9811	57°59·4′	7°6·2′W	X	13
Geodha Ruadh	Highld	NC2367	58°33·6′	5°2·1′W	X	9
Geodha Ruadh	N Eil	NB0234	58°11·9′	7°3·9′W	X	13
Geodha Ruadh	N Eil	NB1844	58°17·9′	6°48·3′W	X	8
Geodha Ruadh na Fola	Highld	NC2470	58°35·2′	5°1·2′W	X	9
Geodha Sligeach	Highld	NC3471	58°36·0′	4°50·9′W	X	9
Geodh' a' Storcain	N Eil	NB4009	57°59·9′	6°23·5′W	X	14
Geodh' a' Stoth	N Eil	HW8132	59°7·4′	5°49·1′W	X	8
Geodha Thairinis	N Eil	NB0805	57°56·6′	6°55·6′W	X	13,14
Geodha Toa	N Eil	NB1038	58°14·4′	6°56·0′W	X	13
Geodh' Ghamhainn	Highld	NC7565	58°33·6′	4°8·4′W	X	10
Geodh nam Fitheach	Highld	NC9968	58°35·6′	3°43·8′W	X	11
Geodh nan Cuilean	Arg & Bt	NR2855	55°43·0′	6°19·4′W	X	60
Geodh' nan Sitheanan	N Eil	NB5129	58°11·0′	6°13·7′W	X	8
Geodh' Ruadh	Highld	NC8066	58°34·2′	4°3·3′W	X	10
Geodh' Ruadh	Highld	NC8168	58°35·3′	4°2·3′W	X	10
Geo Ear	N Eil	NA8711	57°58·9′	7°17·3′W	X	13
Geo Eskadale	N Eil	NF9899	57°53·0′	7°5·3′W	X	18
Geo Forse	N Eil	NA9815	58°1·5′	7°6·5′W	X	13
Geo Gharran Buidhe	N Eil	NF0997	57°47·8′	8°34·5′W	X	18

Geo Iar	N Eil	NA8711	57°58·9'	7°17·3'W	X	13
Geo Leinish	N Eil	NF9794	57°50·2'	7°5·9'W	X	18
Geo Lerradale	Shetld	HU2684	60°32·6'	1°31·1'W	X	3
Geo Luon	Orkney	HY5429	59°9·0'	2°47·8'W	X	5,6
Geo Martin	N Eil	NG0396	57°51·6'	7°0·0'W	X	18
Geo na Bà Glaise	N Eil	NF0898	57°48·2'	8°35·6'W	X	18
Geo na Gainmhich	N Eil	NF9694	57°50·2'	7°6·9'W	X	18
Geo na h-Airde	N Eil	NA0800	57°49·3'	8°35·8'W	X	18
Geo na Lashulaich	N Eil	NF0799	57°48·7'	8°36·8'W	X	18
Geo na Tarnanach	N Eil	NA1505	57°52·4'	8°29·3'W	X	18
Geo of Bodista	Shetld	HU4430	60°3·4'	1°12·1'W	X	4
Geo of Bordie	Shetld	HU1562	60°20·8'	1°43·2'W	X	3
Geo of Chival	Orkney	HY5142	59°16·0'	2°51·1'W	X	5
Geo of Clyar	Orkney	HY4852	59°21·3'	2°54·4'W	X	5
Geo of Crowber	Orkney	HY5537	59°13·3'	2°46·8'W	X	5
Geo of Gessan	Orkney	HY6922	59°5·3'	2°32·0'W	X	5
Geo of Ginna Guan	Orkney	HY5142	59°16·0'	2°51·1'W	X	5
Geo of Gunavalla	Shetld	HU3268	60°23·9'	1°24·7'W	X	3
Geo of Hellia	Orkney	HY1904	58°55·2'	3°23·9'W	X	7
Geo of Heuken	Shetld	HP6305	60°43·7'	0°50·2'W	X	1
Geo of Lamar	Shetld	HU3611	59°53·2'	1°20·9'W	X	4
Geo of Lincro	Orkney	HY4938	59°13·8'	2°53·1'W	X	5
Geo of Litlaland	Shetld	HU6588	60°34·5'	0°48·3'W	X	1,2
Geo of Markamouth	Shetld	HP4701	60°41·6'	1°7·9'W	X	1
Geo of Nethertown	Highld	ND3578	58°41·4'	3°6·8'W	X	7,12
Geo of Ockran	Shetld	HU2483	60°32·1'	1°33·3'W	X	3
Geo of Odderaber	Orkney	HY4954	59°22·4'	2°53·4'W	X	5
Geo of Ork	Orkney	HY5422	59°5·2'	2°47·7'W	X	5,6
Geo of Oxen	Orkney	HY5319	59°3·6'	2°48·7'W	X	6
Geo of Rottenloch	Orkney	ND2887	58°46·1'	3°14·2'W	X	7
Geo of Sclaites	Highld	ND4073	58°38·7'	3°1·5'W	X	7,12
Geo of Slough	Shetld	HU3722	59°59·1'	1°19·7'W	X	4
Geo of Steinsa	Orkney	HY5319	59°3·6'	2°48·7'W	X	6
Geo of the Lame	Orkney	ND2097	58°51·4'	3°22·7'W	X	7
Geo of the Light	Orkney	HY1700	58°53·0'	3°25·9'W	X	7
Geo of the Sow	Orkney	HY1801	58°53·6'	3°24·9'W	X	7
Geo of the Uin	Shetld	HU4118	59°57·0'	1°15·5'W	X	4
Geo of the Ward	Shetld	HU2961	60°20·2'	1°28·0'W	X	3
Geo of Toftsness	Orkney	HY7647	59°18·8'	2°24·8'W	X	5
Geo of Ure	Shetld	HU2280	60°30·5'	1°35·5'W	X	3
Geo of Vatsvie	Shetld	HU5242	60°9·8'	1°3·3'W	X	4
Geo of Vigon	Shetld	HP4704	60°43·2'	1°7·8'W	X	1
Geordie's Hill	Scot Bord	NY4396	55°15·5'	2°53·4'W	H	79
Geordie's Holes	Shetld	HU5539	60°8·2'	1°0·1'W	X	4
Geordy's Pike	Northum	NY5985	55°9·7'	2°38·2'W	H	80
Georgefield	D & G	NY2991	55°12·7'	3°6·5'W	X	79
Georgefield	Scot Bord	NT5838	55°38·3'	2°39·6'W	X	73,74
Georgefield	Scot Bord	NT8243	55°41·1'	2°16·7'W	X	74
George Fm	Peterb	TF0305	52°38·2'	0°28·3'W	FM	141
George Green	Bucks	TQ0081	51°31·4'	0°33·1'W	T	176
Georgeham	Devon	SS4639	51°8·0'	4°11·7'W	T	180
Georgemas Junc Sta	Highld	ND1559	58°30·9'	3°27·1'W	X	11,12
George Nympton	Devon	SS7023	50°59·7'	3°50·8'W	T	180
George's Brow	Sefton	SD3524	53°42·7'	2°58·7'W	X	102
George's Scar	N Yks	SD7076	54°11·0'	2°27·2'W	X	98
George's Wood	Norf	TM3994	52°29·7'	1°31·7'E	F	134
George's Wood	Shrops	SJ4134	52°54·3'	2°52·2'W	F	126
George Teign Barton	Devon	SX8583	50°38·4'	3°37·2'W	X	191
Georgeton Burn	Pth & Kin	NT0696	56°9·1'	3°30·3'W	W	58
Georgetown	Blae Gw	SO1408	51°46·1'	3°14·4'W	T	161
Georgetown	D & G	NX9975	55°3·8'	3°34·5'W	T	84
Georgetown	Moray	NJ1938	57°25·8'	3°20·5'W	X	28
George Wood	Beds	TL0727	51°56·1'	0°26·2'W	F	166
George Wood	Beds	TL1119	51°51·7'	0°22·9'W	F	166
George Wood	Scot Bord	NT3848	55°43·5'	2°58·8'W	F	73
Georgia	Corn	SW4836	50°10·5'	5°31·4'W	T	203
Georgia Fm	Hants	SU2941	51°10·3'	1°34·7'W	FM	185
Geo Riva	Shetld	HU3725	60°0·8'	1°19·7'W	X	4
Georth	Orkney	HY3526	59°7·2'	3°7·6'W	X	6
Geo Ruadh	N Eil	NA0702	57°50·3'	8°37·0'W	X	18
Geosetter	Shetld	HU3820	59°58·1'	1°18·7'W	X	4
Geo Sgadain	N Eil	NG1086	57°46·5'	6°52·2'W	X	14
Geos of Conquoy	Orkney	HY4033	59°11·0'	3°2·5'W	X	5,6
Geos of Hovie	Shetld	HU5439	60°8·2'	1°1·2'W	X	4
Geos of the Veng	Shetld	HU5036	60°6·6'	1°5·5'W	X	4
Geostane	Orkney	HY5320	59°4·1'	2°48·7'W	X	5,6
Gerach	Aberd	NO2995	57°2·7'	3°9·8'W	X	37,44
Geraint or Barber's Hill	Denb	SJ2042	52°58·4'	3°11·1'W	H	117
Gerard Hall	Lancs	SD4003	53°31·5'	2°53·9'W	X	108
Gerbestone Manor	Somer	ST1619	50°58·1'	3°11·4'W	A	181,193
Gerda Water	Shetld	HU4966	60°22·8'	1°6·2'W	W	2,3
Gerdden Isa	Conwy	SH9568	53°12·2'	3°33·9'W	X	116
Gerddi Bluog	Gwyn	SH6130	52°51·2'	4°3·5'W	X	124
Gerddi-gleision	Powys	SH8905	52°38·1'	3°38·0'W	X	124,125
Gerdie Loch	Shetld	HU2078	60°29·4'	1°37·7'W	W	3
Gerdiesberg	Shetld	HU6489	60°35·0'	0°49·4'W	X	1,2
Gerdinen Fawr	Swan	SN6307	51°44·9'	3°58·7'W	X	159
Gerdinen isaf	Swan	SN6306	51°44·4'	3°58·7'W	T	159
Gergask	Highld	NN6194	57°1·2'	4°16·9'W	T	35
Gergask Craig	Highld	NN6195	57°1·8'	4°17·0'W	X	35
Gerherda	Shetld	HP4700	60°41·1'	1°7·9'W	X	1
Gerlan	Gwyn	SH6366	53°10·7'	4°2·6'W	T	115
Germains Fm	Essex	TQ5599	51°40·3'	0°14·9'E	FM	167,177
German Hill Wood	Scot Bord	NT1734	55°35·8'	3°18·6'W	F	72
Germansweek	Devon	SX4394	50°43·7'	4°13·1'W	T	190
Germiston	C of Glas	NS6166	55°52·3'	4°12·9'W	T	64
Germoe	Corn	SW5829	50°6·9'	5°22·7'W	T	203
Germonds Fm	V of Glam	ST0175	51°28·2'	3°25·1'W	FM	170
Gerna	Lancs	SD7943	53°53·2'	2°18·8'W	X	103
Gernick	Corn	SW6336	50°10·8'	5°18·8'W	X	203
Gernon Bushes	Essex	TL4702	51°42·1'	0°8·0'E	T	167
Gernos	Pemb	SN0734	51°58·5'	4°48·2'W	X	145
Gernos	Pemb	SN1247	52°5·6'	4°44·3'W	X	145
Gernos Fm	Cered	SN3645	52°5·0'	4°23·2'W	FM	145
Gernos Mountain	Cered	SN3546	52°5·5'	4°24·1'W	H	145
Geroin	Orkney	HY3317	59°2·4'	3°9·6'W	X	6
Gerragarth	Shetld	HP6009	60°45·8'	0°53·4'W	X	1
Gerrans	Corn	SW8735	50°10·8'	4°58·6'W	T	204
Gerrans Bay	Corn	SW9037	50°12·0'	4°56·2'W	W	204
Gerrans Point	Corn	SX0348	50°18·2'	4°45·6'W	X	204
Gerranton	D & G	NX7765	54°58·1'	3°54·9'W	X	84
Gerrard Ho	Cumbr	NY2546	54°48·4'	3°9·6'W	X	85
Gerrard's Bromley	Staffs	SJ7834	52°54·4'	2°19·2'W	T	127
Gerrards Cross	Bucks	SU9987	51°34·6'	0°33·9'W	T	175,176
Gerrard's Fm	Dorset	SY4298	50°47·0'	2°49·0'W	FM	193
Gerrard's Hill	Dorset	ST4501	50°48·6'	2°46·5'W	H	193
Gerra Taing	Orkney	HY7643	59°16·6'	2°24·8'W	X	5
Gerratown	Shetld	HP6412	60°47·4'	0°49·0'W	X	1
Gerrick	Red & Cl	NZ7012	54°30·1'	0°54·7'W	T	94
Gerrick Moor	Red & Cl	NZ7011	54°29·6'	0°54·7'W	X	94
Gerrick Spa	Red & Cl	NZ7012	54°30·1'	0°54·7'W	W	94
Gerrick Wood	Red & Cl	NZ7013	54°30·7'	0°54·7'W	F	94
Gerrieswells	Aberd	NJ5640	57°27·1'	2°43·5'W	X	29
Gerrin's Fm	Norf	TM3196	52°31·0'	1°24·7'E	FM	134
Gerrydown Fm	Devon	SS6108	50°51·5'	3°58·1'W	FM	191
Gersa	Highld	ND2758	58°30·5'	3°14·7'W	X	11,12
Gersfield Water	Shetld	HU2781	60°31·0'	1°30·0'W	W	3
Gerson	Orkney	HY6816	59°2·1'	2°33·0'W	X	5
Gerston	Devon	SX7959	50°25·3'	3°41·8'W	X	202
Gerston	Highld	ND1259	58°30·9'	3°30·2'W	X	11,12
Gerston Fm	Devon	ST0210	50°53·1'	3°23·2'W	FM	192
Gerston Fm	Devon	SX7341	50°15·6'	3°46·5'W	FM	202
Gerston Point	Devon	SX7441	50°15·6'	3°45·7'W	X	202
Ger Tor	Devon	SX5483	50°37·9'	4°3·5'W	X	191,201
Gervally	Moray	NH9848	57°30·9'	3°41·7'W	X	27
Gervally	Moray	NH9948	57°30·9'	3°40·7'W	X	27
Gerwyn-Fechan	Wrex	SJ3745	53°0·2'	2°55·9'W	X	117
Gerwyn Hall	Wrex	SJ3646	53°0·7'	2°56·8'W	X	117
Gesail	Gwyn	SH6406	52°38·3'	4°0·2'W	X	124
Gesail-ddu	Powys	SH9512	52°42·0'	3°32·8'W	X	125
Gesail-fawr	Pemb	SM7428	51°54·5'	5°16·8'W	W	157
Gesail Gyfarch	Gwyn	SH5441	52°57·0'	4°10·0'W	X	124
Geseilfa	Powys	SN9491	52°30·6'	3°33·3'W	T	136
Geshader	N Eil	NB1131	58°10·7'	6°54·5'W	T	13
Gest Ddu	Gwyn	SH6212	52°41·5'	4°2·1'W	X	124
Gestingthorpe	Essex	TL8138	52°0·9'	0°38·7'E	T	155
Gesto Bay	Highld	NG3536	57°20·5'	6°23·8'W	W	23,32
Gesto Ho	Highld	NG3536	57°20·5'	6°23·8'W	X	23,32
Gesyns, The	Suff	TL7356	52°10·7'	0°32·2'E	X	155
Gethsemane	Pemb	SN0742	52°2·8'	4°48·5'W	X	145
Gettern Fm	Lancs	SD3210	53°35·2'	3°1·2'W	FM	108
Geubery Head	Shetld	HU1861	60°20·2'	1°39·9'W	X	3
Geuffordd	Powys	SJ2114	52°43·3'	3°9·8'W	T	126
Geufron	Cered	SN7270	52°19·0'	3°52·3'W	X	135,147
Geufron	Conwy	SH8275	53°15·8'	3°45·7'W	X	116
Geufron	Denb	SJ0342	52°58·2'	3°26·3'W	X	125
Geufron	Denb	SJ2142	52°58·4'	3°10·2'W	T	117
Geufron	Gwyn	SH4140	52°56·3'	4°21·6'W	X	123
Geufron	Powys	SN8885	52°27·3'	3°38·5'W	X	135,136
Geufron	Powys	SN9170	52°19·3'	3°35·6'W	X	136,147
Geulan Las	Nth Pt Talb	SS8088	51°34·9'	3°43·5'W	X	170
Geuos	Gwyn	SH6618	52°44·8'	3°58·7'W	X	124
Geur Rubha	Highld	NG5501	57°2·4'	6°1·9'W	X	32,39
Geusachan Burn	Aberd	NN9693	57°1·2'	3°42·3'W	W	43
Gewans Fm	Corn	SX0251	50°19·8'	4°46·5'W	FM	200,204
Gew Fm	Corn	SW6336	50°10·8'	5°18·8'W	FM	203
Gew-graze	Corn	SW6714	49°59·1'	5°14·7'W	W	203
Gewni	Pemb	SM7923	51°52·0'	5°12·2'W	X	157
Gew, The	Corn	SW7826	50°5·8'	5°5·9'W	X	204
Ghaistrill's Strid	N Yks	SD9964	54°4·6'	2°0·5'W	X	98
Ghenty	Angus	NO3352	56°39·6'	3°5·1'W	X	53
Ghille-mhaoil	Arg & Bt	NR7359	55°46·5'	5°36·7'W	X	62
Ghlas-bheinn	Highld	NC3361	58°30·6'	4°51·5'W	H	9
Ghoirtean Dearg	Highld	NM7045	56°32·7'	5°44·0'W	X	49
Ghyll	Cumbr	NY2625	54°37·1'	3°8·3'W	X	89,90
Ghyllas	Cumbr	SD6892	54°19·6'	2°29·1'W	X	98
Ghyll Bank	Cumbr	NY2320	54°34·4'	3°11·0'W	X	89,90
Ghyll Bank	Cumbr	NY4700	54°23·8'	2°48·6'W	X	90
Ghyll Bank	Cumbr	SD5797	54°22·2'	2°39·3'W	X	97
Ghyll Fm	Cumbr	NX9809	54°28·2'	3°34·0'W	FM	89
Ghyll Fm	Cumbr	NY0611	54°29·4'	3°26·6'W	FM	89
Ghyll Fm	Cumbr	NY0817	54°32·6'	3°24·9'W	FM	89
Ghyll Fm	Cumbr	SD2577	54°11·2'	3°8·5'W	FM	96
Ghyll Fm	Cumbr	SD6192	54°19·6'	2°35·6'W	FM	97
Ghyll Fm	Cumbr	SD6693	54°20·1'	2°31·0'W	FM	98
Ghyll Fm	N Yks	SE0048	53°55·9'	1°59·6'W	FM	104
Ghyll Foot	Cumbr	NY3309	54°28·6'	3°1·6'W	X	90
Ghyll Grange	Brad	SE0645	53°54·3'	1°54·1'W	X	104
Ghyll Hall	N Yks	SE2494	54°20·7'	1°37·4'W	X	99
Ghyllhead	Cumbr	NX9920	54°34·2'	3°33·3'W	X	89
Ghyll Head	Cumbr	SD3992	54°19·4'	2°55·9'W	X	96,97
Ghyll Head Fm	Cumbr	NY3148	54°49·6'	3°4·0'W	FM	85
Ghyllhead Fm	N Yks	SD6670	54°7·7'	2°30·8'W	FM	98
Ghyllheugh	Northum	NZ1397	55°16·3'	1°47·3'W	X	81
Ghyll Ho	Cumbr	NY7044	54°47·6'	2°27·6'W	X	86,87
Ghyll Hos	Cumbr	SD2482	54°13·9'	3°9·5'W	X	96
Ghyll House Fm	Glos	SO5503	51°43·3'	2°38·7'W	FM	162
Ghylls	Lancs	SD7654	53°59·1'	2°21·5'W	X	103
Giant Hill	Dorset	ST6602	50°49·2'	2°28·6'W	H	194
Giant Hill	E Yorks	TA1335	53°48·2'	0°16·6'W	A	107
Giant's Basin	Devon	SX5966	50°28·8'	3°58·9'W	X	202
Giant's Bed	Shetld	HU4227	60°1·8'	1°14·3'W	X	4
Giant's Castle	I Scilly	SV9210	49°54·9'	6°17·1'W	A	203
Giant's Cave	Shrops	SO3199	52°35·3'	3°0·7'W	X	137
Giant's Cave	Wilts	ST8282	51°32·4'	2°15·2'W	X	173
Giant's Cave (Long Barrow)	Wilts	ST8282	51°32·4'	2°15·2'W	A	173
Giant's Chair	Moray	NJ3238	57°25·9'	3°7·5'W	X	28
Giant's Chair, The	Wilts	SU1622	51°0·1'	1°45·9'W	X	184
Giant's Chair, The (Tumulus)	Wilts	SU1622	51°0·1'	1°45·9'W	A	184
Giant's Grave	Corn	SW5032	50°8·4'	5°29·6'W	A	203
Giant's Grave	Dorset	ST7501	50°48·7'	2°20·9'W	A	194
Giant's Grave	Hants	SU1320	50°59·0'	1°48·5'W	X	184
Giant's Grave	I of M	SC2783	54°13·1'	4°38·8'W	X	95
Giant's Grave	N Yks	SD8573	54°9·4'	2°13·4'W	X	98
Giant's Grave	Powys	SO0486	52°28·1'	3°24·4'W	X	136
Giants Grave	Powys	SO1454	52°10·9'	3°15·1'W	X	148
Giant's Grave	Pth & Kin	NN9029	56°26·7'	3°46·6'W	X	52,58
Giant's Grave	Wilts	SU1663	51°22·2'	1°45·8'W	A	173
Giant's Grave	Wilts	SU1858	51°19·5'	1°44·1'W	X	173
Giant's Grave (Long Barrow)	Hants	SU1320	50°59·0'	1°48·5'W	A	184
Giant's Grave (Long Barrow)	Wilts	SU1858	51°19·5'	1°44·1'W	A	173
Giants Graves	N Ayr	NS0424	55°28·5'	5°5·6'W	X	69
Giant's Graves	N Yks	SD9357	54°0·8'	2°6·0'W	X	103
Giant's Grave, The	Wilts	SU1623	51°0·6'	1°45·9'W	X	184
Giant's Grave, The	Wilts	SU2476	51°29·2'	1°38·9'W	A	174
Giant's Grave, The (Long Barrow)	Wilts	SU1623	51°0·6'	1°45·9'W	A	184
Giant's Grave (Tumulus)	N Yks	SD8573	54°9·4'	2°13·4'W	A	98
Giants Grave (Tumulus)	Powys	SO1454	52°10·9'	3°15·1'W	A	148
Giant's Hall	Wigan	SD5607	53°33·7'	2°39·4'W	A	108
Giant's Head	Conwy	SH7854	53°4·4'	3°48·9'W	X	115
Giants Head	Dorset	ST6702	50°49·2'	2°27·7'W	X	194
Giant's Hedge	Corn	SX1657	50°23·3'	4°34·9'W	A	201
Giant's Hedge	Corn	SX1857	50°23·3'	4°33·2'W	A	201
Giant's Hedge	Corn	SX2453	50°21·3'	4°28·1'W	A	201
Giant's Hill	Cambs	TL4368	52°17·7'	0°6·2'E	A	154
Giant's Hill	Devon	SX5966	50°28·8'	3°58·9'W	X	202
Giant's Hills	Lincs	TF4271	53°13·3'	0°8·0'E	X	122
Giant's Hills (Long Barrow)	Lincs	TF4271	53°13·3'	0°8·0'E	A	122
Giant's Hole	Derby	SK1182	53°20·3'	1°49·7'W	X	110
Giant's Knowe	Arg & Bt	NS1277	55°57·2'	5°0·2'W	X	63
Giant's Leg	Shetld	HU5135	60°6·0'	1°4·5'W	X	4
Giant's Quoit	Corn	SW6437	50°11·4'	5°18·0'W	A	203
Giant's Quoits	Corn	SW8021	50°3·1'	5°4·0'W	X	204
Giant's Rock	Corn	SW4538	50°11·5'	5°34·0'W	X	203
Giant's Stone	Shetld	HU2557	60°18·0'	1°32·4'W	A	3
Giants Stones	Shetld	HU2480	60°30·4'	1°33·3'W	A	3
Giant's Stone, The	Glos	SO9106	51°45·4'	2°7·4'W	A	163
Giant, The	Dorset	ST6601	50°48·7'	2°28·6'W	A	194
Giant, The	Shetld	HP6612	60°47·4'	0°46·8'W	X	1
Giar Hill	Highld	ND3670	58°37·1'	3°5·6'W	H	7,12
Giarol	N Eil	NB1324	58°7·0'	6°51·9'W	X	13,14
Gias	Powys	SN8686	52°27·8'	3°40·3'W	H	135,136
Gibberd Garden	Essex	TL4812	51°47·4'	0°9·2'E	X	167
Gibbetdale Wood	Notts	SK5553	53°4·5'	1°10·3'W	F	120
Gibbeter Fm	N Yks	SE0852	53°58·1'	1°52·3'W	FM	104
Gibbet Firs	Dorset	SZ0999	50°47·7'	1°52·0'W	X	195
Gibbet Fm	N Yks	SE3559	54°1·8'	1°27·5'W	FM	104
Gibbet Hill	Cov	SP3074	52°22·0'	1°33·2'W	T	140
Gibbet Hill	Cumbr	SD6299	54°23·4'	2°34·7'W	X	97
Gibbet Hill	Devon	SX5081	50°36·8'	4°6·8'W	H	191,201
Gibbet Hill	Lincs	SK9131	52°52·4'	0°38·5'W	X	130
Gibbet Hill	Lincs	TF0786	53°21·8'	0°23·1'W	X	112,121
Gibbet Hill	Lincs	TF3869	53°12·2'	0°4·4'E	X	122
Gibbet Hill	Norf	TG4717	52°41·9'	1°39·7'E	X	134
Gibbet Hill	Notts	SK6491	53°25·0'	1°1·8'W	X	111
Gibbet Hill	N Yks	SE3559	54°1·8'	1°27·5'W	X	104
Gibbet Hill	Somer	ST7647	51°13·5'	2°20·2'W	H	183
Gibbet Hill	Surrey	SU9035	51°6·7'	0°42·5'W	X	186
Gibbet Hill	Warw	SP5280	52°25·2'	1°13·7'W	T	140
Gibbet Hills	Durham	NZ1433	54°41·8'	1°46·5'W	X	92
Gibbet Mill	Ches	SJ3672	53°14·7'	2°57·1'W	X	117
Gibbet Moor	Derby	SK2870	53°13·8'	1°34·4'W	X	119
Gibbet Oak	Kent	TQ9032	51°3·6'	0°43·1'E	X	189
Gibbet Post Ho	Lincs	TF0288	53°23·0'	0°27·6'W	X	112,121
Gibbets Brow	Somer	ST5455	51°17·8'	2°39·2'W	X	172,182
Gibbet Stone	Aberd	NO5699	57°5·1'	2°43·1'W	A	37,44
Gibbet, The	Wilts	SU0544	51°11·9'	1°55·3'W	X	184
Gibbet Moor Fm	Devon	SS8817	50°56·7'	3°35·3'W	FM	181
Gibbet Tree	Oxon	SP2714	51°49·7'	1°36·1'W	X	163
Gibbet Wood	Staffs	SO8683	52°26·9'	2°12·0'W	F	139
Gibbetwood Fm	Notts	SK8773	53°15·0'	0°41·4'W	FM	121
Gibb Bheinn	Arg & Bt	NM4628	56°22·8'	6°6·4'W	X	48
Gibb Hill	Ches	SJ6478	53°18·1'	2°32·0'W	T	118
Gibb Hill	D & G	NX6750	54°49·9'	4°3·8'W	X	83,84
Gibbie Law's Burn	Shetld	HU2453	60°15·9'	1°33·5'W	W	3
Gibbieston	Pth & Kin	NO0236	56°30·6'	3°35·1'W	X	52,53
Gibblaston	Inverc	NS3565	55°51·3'	4°37·7'W	X	63
Gibbon Br	Lancs	SD6342	53°52·6'	2°33·4'W	X	102,103
Gibbonhill	D & G	NX9869	55°0·6'	3°35·3'W	X	84
Gibbon Hill	N Yks	SE0196	54°21·8'	1°58·7'W	X	98
Gibbon's Bush Fm	Essex	TL4406	51°44·3'	0°5·5'E	FM	167
Gibbons Coppice	Wrekin	SJ6207	52°39·8'	2°33·3'W	F	127
Gibbon's Fm	Bucks	SU7894	51°38·6'	0°52·0'W	FM	175
Gibbons Fm	Lincs	TF4719	52°45·1'	0°11·1'E	FM	131
Gibbons Fm	Somer	ST7538	51°8·7'	2°21·1'W	FM	183
Gibbon's Fm	Suff	TM0654	52°9·0'	1°1·1'E	FM	155
Gibbons Mill	W Susx	TQ0730	51°3·8'	0°28·0'W	X	187
Gibbridge Fm	Shrops	SO5780	52°25·2'	2°37·5'W	FM	137,138
Gibbs	Essex	TL7807	51°44·2'	0°35·1'E	X	167
Gibbs	Lancs	SD6949	53°56·4'	2°27·9'W	X	103
Gibbs Brook	Surrey	TQ3650	51°14·2'	0°2·7'W	W	187
Gibbs Fm	Lincs	TF1412	52°41·9'	0°18·4'W	FM	130,142
Gibbs Hall	Cumbr	SD7386	54°16·4'	2°24·5'W	X	98
Gibbshill	D & G	NX7278	55°5·0'	3°59·9'W	X	77,84
Gibb's Hill	Northum	NU0314	55°25·4'	1°56·7'W	H	81
Gibbs Hill	Northum	NY7469	55°1·1'	2°24·0'W	X	86,87
Gibb's Hole Wood	D & G	NX8352	54°51·2'	3°48·9'W	F	84
Gibbs Marsh Fm	Dorset	ST7519	50°58·4'	2°21·0'W	FM	183
Gibbsneese	Durham	NZ0923	54°36·4'	1°51·2'W	X	92
Gibbsneese Plantn	Durham	NZ0924	54°36·9'	1°51·2'W	F	92
Gibb's Point	Arg & Bt	NS1880	55°59·0'	4°54·6'W	X	63
Gibbs Reed Fm	E Susx	TQ7029	51°2·3'	0°25·9'E	FM	188,199
Gibdale	I of M	SC2874	54°8·2'	4°37·6'W	X	95
Gibdale Point	I of M	SC1566	54°3·7'	4°49·2'W	X	95
Gib Field	Brad	SE1346	53°54·8'	1°47·7'W	X	104
Gibfield Fm	Derby	SK2448	53°2·0'	1°38·1'W	FM	119
Gib Heath	Birm	SP0588	52°29·6'	1°55·2'W	T	139
Gib Hey	Lancs	SD5940	53°51·5'	2°37·0'W	X	102
Gib Hill	Derby	SK1563	53°10·1'	1°46·1'W	X	119
Gib Hill	Somer	ST1933	51°5·7'	3°9·0'W	X	181
Gibigill Burn	Highld	NC9163	58°32·8'	3°51·9'W	W	10
Giblet	Brig	SS9382	51°31·8'	3°32·2'W	X	170
Gibliston	Fife	NO4905	56°14·3'	2°48·9'W	X	59
Gibliston Ho	Fife	NO4904	56°13·8'	2°48·9'W	X	59

Gibraltar	Beds	TL0046	52°6·4′	0°32·0′W	T	153
Gibraltar	Bucks	SP7510	51°47·2′	0°54·4′W	T	165
Gibraltar	Durham	NY9449	54°50·4′	2°5·2′W	X	87
Gibraltar	E Susx	TQ4608	50°51·4′	0°4·9′E	X	198
Gibraltar	Kent	TR2039	51°6·7′	1°9·0′E	T	179,189
Gibraltar	Lincs	TF5558	53°6·0′	0°19·3′E	X	122
Gibraltar	Notts	SK7871	53°14·1′	0°49·5′W	X	120,121
Gibraltar	Oxon	SP4817	51°51·2′	1°17·8′W	X	164
Gibraltar	Suff	TM1954	52°8·7′	1°12·4′E	X	156
Gibraltar Fm	Herts	TL0917	51°50·7′	0°24·7′W	FM	166
Gibraltar Fm	Medway	TQ7763	51°20·5′	0°32·9′E	FM	178,188
Gibraltar Fm	Norf	TG0103	52°35·5′	0°58·5′E	FM	144
Gibraltar Plantn	Notts	SK6071	53°14·2′	1°5·7′W	F	120
Gibraltar Point	Lincs	TF5557	53°5·5′	0°19·3′E	X	122
Gibraltar Rocks	Sheff	SK2490	53°24·6′	1°37·9′W	X	110
Gibralter	Oxon	SP4817	51°51·2′	1°17·8′W	T	164
Gibralter House Fm	Warw	SP4465	52°17·1′	1°20·9′W	FM	151
Gibs de Hall	Ghead	NZ1758	54°55·2′	1°43·7′W	A	88
Gibshiel	Northum	NY8093	55°14·1′	2°18·4′W	X	80
Gibshill	Cumbr	NY4971	55°2·1′	2°47·5′W	X	86
Gibshill	Inverc	NS3074	55°56·0′	4°42·8′W	T	63
Gibside Hillhead	Ghead	NZ1858	54°55·2′	1°42·7′W	X	88
Gibs Knowe	Angus	NO4073	56°50·9′	2°58·6′W	H	44
Gibsley	Clackm	NS9792	56°6·8′	3°38·9′W	X	58
Gibsmere	Notts	SK7148	53°1·7′	0°56·1′W	T	129
Gibson Knott	Cumbr	NY3110	54°29·1′	3°3·5′W	H	90
Gibsons	D & G	NY1579	55°6·1′	3°19·5′W	X	85
Gibsons	Essex	TL5214	51°48·5′	0°12·7′E	X	167
Gibson's Cave	Durham	NY9028	54°39·1′	2°8·9′W	X	91,92
Gibson's Fm	Lancs	SD4744	53°53·6′	2°48·0′W	FM	102
Gibson's Fm	Lancs	SD5158	54°1·2′	2°44·5′W	FM	102
Gibstick Hall	Lancs	SD4547	53°55·2′	2°49·8′W	X	102
Gibston	Aberd	NJ5141	57°27·7′	2°48·5′W	X	29
Gibston	E Ayr	NS4421	55°27·7′	4°27·6′W	X	70
Gibston	Moray	NJ4348	57°31·4′	2°56·6′W	X	28
Gibstown	Cumbr	NY4872	55°2·6′	2°48·4′W	X	86
Gib Torr	Staffs	SK0264	53°10·6′	1°57·8′W	X	119
Gidcott	Devon	SS4009	50°51·7′	4°16·0′W	X	190
Gidcott Mill	Devon	SS4109	50°51·8′	4°15·2′W	X	190
Giddeahall	Wilts	ST8574	51°28·1′	2°12·6′W	T	173
Giddens Cleuch	Scot Bord	NY3699	55°17·1′	3°0·0′W	X	79
Gidding Grove	Cambs	TL1082	52°25·7′	0°22·5′W	X	142
Giddy Green	Dorset	SY8386	50°40·6′	2°14·1′W	T	194
Gidea Park	Hav	TQ5290	51°35·5′	0°12·1′E	T	177
Gideonscleuch	Scot Bord	NT3601	55°18·2′	3°0·1′W	X	79
Gidleigh	Devon	SX6788	50°40·8′	3°52·6′W	T	191
Gidleigh Common	Devon	SX6487	50°40·2′	3°55·1′W	X	191
Gidleigh Tor	Devon	SX6787	50°40·3′	3°52·6′W	H	191
Gidley Br	Devon	SX7063	50°27·4′	3°49·5′W	X	202
Gidley Cross	Devon	SS7717	50°56·6′	3°44·7′W	X	180
Gidley Fm	W Berks	SU4676	51°29·1′	1°19·9′W	FM	174
Giedd Forest	Powys	SN8013	51°48·4′	3°44·0′W	F	160
Gieu-uisg Geo	Highld	ND0169	58°36·1′	3°41·7′W	X	12
Giffard Lodge	Leic	SK7213	52°42·8′	0°55·6′W	X	129
Giffard Park	Mil Key	SP8642	52°4·4′	0°44·3′W	T	152
Giffard's Cross	Staffs	SJ8807	52°39·9′	2°10·2′W	X	127,139
Giffard's Wood	W Susx	TQ3633	51°5·0′	0°3·1′W	F	187
Giffin Ho	N Ayr	NS3449	55°42·6′	4°38·1′W	X	63
Giffnock	E Renf	NS5658	55°47·9′	4°17·4′W	T	64
Gifford	E Loth	NT5367	55°53·9′	2°44·7′W	T	66
Giffordland	N Ayr	NS2648	55°41·9′	4°45·7′W	X	63
Giffords	Devon	SS9921	50°59·0′	3°26·0′W	X	181
Gifford's Fm	Cambs	TL3272	52°20·0′	0°3·4′W	FM	153
Giffords Fm	E Susx	TQ6819	50°57·0′	0°23·9′E	FM	199
Gifford's Hall	Suff	TL7753	52°9·0′	0°35·6′E	X	155
Gifford's Hall	Suff	TL8451	52°7·8′	0°41·7′E	X	155
Gifford's Hall	Suff	TM0137	51°59·9′	0°56·1′E	A	155
Gifford's Hele	Devon	SS5306	50°50·3′	4°4·9′W	X	191
Giffords Hill	Shetld	HU3064	60°21·8′	1°26·9′W	H	3
Giffordtown	Fife	NO2911	56°17·4′	3°8·4′W	T	59
Gifford Vale	E Loth	NT5368	55°54·4′	2°44·7′W	X	66
Gifford Water	E Loth	NT5367	55°53·9′	2°44·7′W	W	66
Gift Hall	Lancs	SD4647	53°55·2′	2°48·9′W	X	102
Gigalum Island	Arg & Bt	NR6445	55°38·7′	5°44·6′W	X	62
Gigg	Bury	SD8109	53°34·9′	2°16·8′W	T	109
Gigger's Island	Dorset	SY9487	50°41·2′	2°4·7′W	X	195
Giggetty	Staffs	SO8692	52°31·8′	2°12·0′W	T	139
Giggleswick	N Yks	SD8164	54°4·5′	2°17·0′W	T	98
Giggleswick Common	N Yks	SD7662	54°3·4′	2°21·6′W	X	98
Giggleswick Scar	N Yks	SD8065	54°5·1′	2°17·9′W	X	98
Giggleswick Sta	N Yks	SD8062	54°3·5′	2°17·9′W	X	98
Giggshill	Surrey	TQ1666	51°23·1′	0°19·6′W	T	176
Gighay	N Eil	NF7604	57°1·1′	7°19·9′W	X	31
Gig Hole	Ches	SJ5770	53°13·8′	2°38·2′W	X	117
Gight	Aberd	NJ7010	57°11·0′	2°29·3′W	X	38
Gight Castle	Aberd	NJ8239	57°26·7′	2°17·5′W	A	29,30
Gight Lodge	Aberd	NJ8139	57°26·7′	2°18·5′W	X	29,30
Gighty Burn	Angus	NO6451	56°39·2′	2°34·8′W	W	54
Gightyburn	Angus	NO6753	56°40·3′	2°31·9′W	X	54
Gightyburn Mill	Angus	NO6250	56°38·7′	2°36·7′W	X	54
Gigley Fm	Oxon	SP3513	51°49·1′	1°29·1′W	FM	164
Gigman Mill	V of Glam	ST0171	51°26·0′	3°25·1′W	X	170
Gignog	Pemb	SM8824	51°52·7′	5°4·4′W	T	157
Gigrin Fm	Powys	SN9767	52°17·7′	3°30·2′W	FM	136,147
Gilandersland	Falk	NS9476	55°58·2′	3°41·5′W	X	65
Gil an Tairbh	N Eil	NB5454	58°24·6′	6°12·2′W	X	8
Gil'an t-Sagairt	N Eil	NB4341	58°17·2′	6°22·6′W	X	8
Gilar	Conwy	SH8849	53°1·8′	3°39·8′W	X	116
Gilberdyke	E Yorks	SE8329	53°45·3′	0°44·1′W	T	106
Gilberdyke Sta	E Yorks	SE8328	53°44·7′	0°44·1′W	X	106
Gilberries	Shrops	SO5193	52°32·2′	2°42·9′W	X	137,138
Gilbert Cott	Heref	SO2753	52°10·5′	3°3·7′W	X	148
Gilbertfield	S Lanak	NS6558	55°48·0′	4°8·8′W	X	64
Gilbertfield (Fort)	S Lanak	NS6558	55°48·0′	4°8·8′W	A	64
Gilbert Hill	Barns	SE2100	53°30·0′	1°40·6′W	X	110
Gilberts Br	Pth & Kin	NN8870	56°48·7′	3°49·6′W	X	43
Gilbert's Coombe	Corn	SW6943	50°14·7′	5°14·0′W	T	203
Gilbert's Cross	Staffs	SO8186	52°28·5′	2°16·4′W	X	138
Gilbert's End	Worcs	SO8242	52°4·8′	2°15·4′W	T	150
Gilbert's Fm	Worcs	SO8051	52°9·7′	2°17·1′W	FM	150
Gilbert's Green	Warw	SP1071	52°20·5′	1°50·8′W	T	139
Gilbert's Hill	Cumbr	NY5974	55°3·8′	2°38·1′W	X	86
Gilbert's Hill Wood	Heref	SO3930	51°58·1′	2°52·9′W	F	149,161
Gilbert's Plot	Lincs	SK9170	53°13·4′	0°37·8′W	F	121
Gilberts Rig	D & G	NT0509	55°22·2′	3°29·5′W	X	78
Gilbertstone	Birm	SP1384	52°27·5′	1°48·1′W	T	139
Gilbert Street	Hants	SU6532	51°5·2′	1°3·9′W	T	185,186
Gilboa Fm	Wilts	ST9290	51°36·8′	2°6·5′W	FM	163,173
Gilboa Wood	Scot Bord	NT5816	55°26·4′	2°39·4′W	F	80
Gilbourn's Fm	Oxon	SU4894	51°38·8′	1°18·0′W	FM	164,174
Gilbrook Wood	Monm	ST4794	51°38·8′	2°45·6′W	F	171,172
Gilbury Hard	Hants	SU4100	50°48·1′	1°24·7′W	X	196
Gilby	Lincs	SK8693	53°25·8′	0°41·9′W	X	112
Gilby Village	Lincs	SK8693	53°25·8′	0°41·9′W	A	112
Gilchester	Northum	NZ0671	55°2·3′	1°53·9′W	X	87
Gilchorn	Angus	NO6447	56°37·1′	2°34·7′W	X	54
Gilchrist	Highld	NH5349	57°30·7′	4°26·8′W	X	26
Gilchristland	D & G	NX9292	55°12·9′	3°41·4′W	X	78
Gilchriston	E Loth	NT4765	55°52·8′	2°50·4′W	T	66
Gil Coltraiseal	N Eil	NB1422	58°5·9′	6°50·8′W	W	13,14
Gilcombe Fm	Somer	ST6936	51°7·6′	2°26·2′W	FM	183
Gilcrux	Cumbr	NY1138	54°44·0′	3°22·5′W	T	89
Gildard Hill	Cumbr	SD6280	54°13·1′	2°34·5′W	X	97
Gildenburgh Water	Cambs	TL2896	52°33·0′	0°6·3′W	W	142
Gilder Beck	N Yks	SE7764	54°4·2′	0°49·0′W	W	100
Gilder Beck	N Yks	SE7960	54°2·0′	0°47·2′W	W	100
Gilderdale Burn	Cumbr	NY6846	54°48·7′	2°29·5′W	W	86,87
Gilderdale Forest	Cumbr	NY6744	54°47·6′	2°30·4′W	X	86,87
Gilderdale Halt	Cumbr	NY7048	54°49·8′	2°27·6′W	X	86,87
Gildersbeck Fm	N Yks	SE0885	54°15·9′	1°52·2′W	FM	99
Gildersber	Brad	SE0648	53°55·9′	1°54·1′W	X	104
Gildersleets	N Yks	SD8062	54°3·5′	2°17·9′W	X	98
Gildersome	Leeds	SE2429	53°45·6′	1°37·7′W	T	104
Gildersome Street	Leeds	SE2428	53°45·1′	1°37·7′W	T	104
Gilder Tofts	N Yks	NZ5707	54°27·6′	1°6·8′W	X	93
Gildiesgreen	Scot Bord	NT3818	55°27·4′	2°58·4′W	X	79
Gildingwells	Roth	SK5585	53°21·8′	1°10·0′W	T	111,120
Gildridge Fm	E Susx	TQ6110	50°52·2′	0°17·7′E	FM	199
Gildwells Cottages	Derby	SK5169	53°13·2′	1°13·8′W	X	120
Giles	Lancs	SD6340	53°51·5′	2°33·3′W	X	102,103
Giles Fm	Kent	TQ9044	51°10·0′	0°43·5′E	FM	189
Gilesgate	Durham	NZ2843	54°47·1′	1°33·5′W	T	88
Gilesgate Moor	Durham	NZ2942	54°46·6′	1°32·5′W	T	88
Giles Great Stone Hags	N Yks	SD9195	54°21·3′	2°7·9′W	X	98
Gileston	V of Glam	ST0167	51°23·8′	3°25·0′W	T	170
Gilestone	Powys	SO1123	51°54·1′	3°17·2′W	X	161
Gilfach	Caer	ST1598	51°40·7′	3°13·4′W	T	171
Gilfach	Carm	SN2523	51°52·9′	4°32·2′W	X	145,158
Gilfach	Carm	SN3116	51°49·3′	4°26·7′W	X	159
Gilfach	Carm	SN3814	51°48·3′	4°20·6′W	X	159
Gilfach	Carm	SN4815	51°49·0′	4°11·9′W	X	159
Gilfach	Carm	SN4822	51°52·8′	4°12·1′W	X	159
Gilfach	Carm	SN5718	51°50·8′	4°4·2′W	X	159
Gilfach	Carm	SN5810	51°46·5′	4°3·1′W	X	159
Gilfach	Carm	SN6643	52°4·4′	3°56·9′W	X	146
Gilfach	Carm	SN7034	51°59·6′	3°53·2′W	X	146,160
Gilfach	Carm	SN7627	51°55·9′	3°47·8′W	X	146,160
Gilfach	Carm	SN8241	52°3·5′	3°42·9′W	X	147,160
Gilfach	Cered	SN3147	52°6·0′	4°27·7′W	X	145
Gilfach	Conwy	SH9263	53°9·4′	3°36·5′W	X	116
Gilfach	Gwyn	SH1828	52°49·4′	4°41·7′W	X	123
Gilfach	Gwyn	SH5246	52°59·7′	4°11·9′W	X	115
Gilfach	Heref	SO3434	52°0·3′	2°57·3′W	T	149,161
Gilfach	Nth Pt Talb	SS7599	51°40·8′	3°48·1′W	X	170
Gilfach	Nth Pt Talb	SS8487	51°34·4′	3°40·0′W	X	170
Gilfach	Powys	SJ1429	52°51·3′	3°16·2′W	X	125
Gilfach	Powys	SN8848	52°7·4′	3°37·8′W	X	147
Gilfach	Powys	SN9671	52°19·9′	3°31·2′W	X	136,147
Gilfach	Powys	SN9895	52°32·8′	3°29·9′W	X	136
Gilfach	Powys	SO0986	52°28·1′	3°20·0′W	X	136
Gilfach	Powys	SO1249	52°8·2′	3°16·8′W	X	148
Gilfach	Powys	SO1426	51°55·8′	3°14·7′W	X	161
Gilfach	Powys	SO2019	51°52·1′	3°9·3′W	X	161
Gilfachafel	Cered	SN5570	52°18·8′	4°7·2′W	X	135
Gilfachau	Cered	SN5671	52°19·3′	4°6·4′W	X	135
Gilfach-chwîth	Cered	SN3842	52°3·4′	4°21·4′W	X	145
Gilfach Cross	Pemb	SN1613	51°47·4′	4°39·7′W	X	158
Gilfachdafydd	Cered	SN4046	52°5·6′	4°19·7′W	X	146
Gilfach-ddofn	Carm	SN1326	51°54·3′	4°42·7′W	X	145,158
Gilfach Ddu Sta	Gwyn	SH5860	53°7·3′	4°6·9′W	X	114,115
Gilfach Fargoed Sta	Caer	ST1599	51°41·2′	3°13·4′W	X	171
Gilfach-fawr	Carm	SN4133	51°58·6′	4°18·5′W	X	146
Gilfach Fm	Pemb	SM8832	51°57·0′	5°4·7′W	FM	157
Gilfach Fm	Pemb	SN1613	51°47·4′	4°39·7′W	FM	158
Gilfachgoch	Cered	SN4960	52°13·3′	4°12·2′W	X	146
Gilfach goch	Cered	SN6477	52°22·7′	3°59·5′W	X	135
Gilfach Goch	Rho Cyn Taf	SS9889	51°35·7′	3°28·0′W	T	170
Gilfachgynyddion	Carm	SN4137	52°0·8′	4°18·6′W	X	146
Gilfach Hill	Powys	SO2766	52°17·5′	3°3·8′W	X	137,148
Gilfach-hîr	Powys	SO0096	52°33·4′	3°28·1′W	X	136
Gilfach-las	Carm	SN3736	52°0·2′	4°22·1′W	X	145
Gilfach-maen	Carm	SN4030	51°57·0′	4°19·3′W	X	146
Gilfach-maen Uchaf	Merth Tyd	ST1199	51°41·2′	3°16·9′W	X	171
Gilfach-Meredydd	Carm	SN5132	51°58·2′	4°9·8′W	X	146
Gilfachreda	Cered	SN4058	52°12·1′	4°20·1′W	T	146
Gilfach Uchaf	Pemb	SN0824	51°53·1′	4°47·0′W	X	145,158
Gilfach-uchaf	Powys	SN9730	51°57·8′	3°29·6′W	X	160
Gilfachwen	Cered	SN4040	52°2·4′	4°19·6′W	X	146
Gilfach-wen	Gwyn	SH7232	52°52·5′	3°53·7′W	X	124
Gilfachwen Fm	Carm	SN2629	51°56·2′	4°31·5′W	FM	145,158
Gilfachwydd	Gwyn	SH7016	52°43·8′	3°55·1′W	X	124
Gilfach-y-Bettws	Carm	SN2728	51°55·7′	4°30·6′W	X	145,158
Gilfachydwn Fawr	Cered	SN7364	52°15·8′	3°51·3′W	X	146,147
Gilfachyfrân	Cered	SN5655	52°10·7′	4°6·0′W	X	146
Gilfachygestin	Carm	SN3229	51°56·3′	4°26·2′W	X	145
Gilfachygwnda	Carm	SN3629	51°56·4′	4°22·8′W	X	145
Gilfach-yr-haidd	Nth Pt Talb	SN7509	51°46·2′	3°48·3′W	X	160
Gilfach-yr-Halen	Cered	SN4361	52°13·7′	4°17·5′W	X	146
Gilfach-yr-heol	Powys	SO2150	52°8·8′	3°8·9′W	X	148
Gilfach-y-rhew	Carm	SN4522	51°52·7′	4°14·7′W	X	159
Gilfach-y-rhiw	Powys	SN9772	52°20·4′	3°30·3′W	X	136,147
Gilfach-y-rhŷd	Rho Cyn Taf	ST0795	51°39·0′	3°20·3′W	X	170
Gilford Clough	Lancs	SD9237	53°50·0′	2°6·9′W	X	103
Gilfumman	Angus	NO4181	56°55·3′	2°57·7′W	X	44
Gilgarran	Cumbr	NY0323	54°35·8′	3°29·7′W	T	89
Gilgerrie	Aberd	NJ5706	57°8·8′	2°42·2′W	X	37
Gilkerscleuch Mains	S Lanak	NS8923	55°29·5′	3°45·0′W	X	71,72
Gilkhorn	Aberd	NJ9245	57°30·0′	2°7·6′W	X	30
Gilkicker Point	Hants	SZ6097	50°46·4′	1°8·6′W	X	196
Gill	Cumbr	NY1205	54°26·2′	3°21·0′W	X	89
Gill	Cumbr	NY3043	54°46·9′	3°4·9′W	X	85
Gill	D & G	NY1168	55°0·2′	3°23·1′W	X	85
Gill	N Ayr	NS2348	55°41·8′	4°48·5′W	X	63
Gill	N Yks	SD9643	53°53·2′	2°3·2′W	T	103
Gill	Orkney	HY4449	59°19·7′	2°58·6′W	X	5
Gill	Orkney	ND4494	58°50·1′	2°57·7′W	X	7
Gill	S Lanak	NS5853	55°45·2′	4°15·3′W	X	64
Gill	S Lanak	NS7844	55°40·7′	3°56·0′W	X	71
Gil Lacasdail	N Eil	NG1097	57°52·4′	6°53·0′W	X	14
Gillahill	C of Aber	NJ8707	57°9·5′	2°12·4′W	X	38
Gillalees	Cumbr	NY5671	55°2·1′	2°40·9′W	X	86
Gillalees Beacon	Cumbr	NY5771	55°2·1′	2°39·9′W	X	86
Gill Allotment	N Yks	SE0565	54°5·1′	1°55·0′W	X	98
Gillamoor	N Yks	SE6889	54°17·8′	0°56·9′W	T	94,100
Gillan	Corn	SW7824	50°4·7′	5°5·8′W	T	204
Gillan Harbour	Corn	SW7825	50°5·3′	5°5·8′W	W	204
Gillard's Fm	Somer	ST1419	50°58·1′	3°13·1′W	FM	181,193
Gillarona	Shetld	HU3262	60°20·7′	1°24·7′W	T	3
Gillar's Green	St Hel	SJ4794	53°26·6′	2°47·5′W	X	108
Gillaval Dubh	N Eil	NB1402	57°55·2′	6°49·3′W	H	14
Gill Avay	N Eil	NB0411	57°59·6′	7°0·1′W	X	13
Gillbank	Cumbr	NY1349	54°49·9′	3°20·8′W	X	85
Gill Bank	Cumbr	NY1801	54°24·1′	3°15·4′W	X	89,90
Gillbank	Cumbr	NY5165	54°58·9′	2°45·5′W	X	86
Gill Bank	Cumbr	NY6234	54°42·2′	2°35·0′W	X	91
Gillbank	Cumbr	NY8313	54°31·0′	2°15·3′W	X	91,92
Gillbank	Cumbr	SD3698	54°22·7′	2°58·7′W	T	96,97
Gill Bank	N Yks	SE7096	54°21·5′	0°54·9′W	X	94,100
Gillbank	S Lanak	NS7042	55°39·5′	4°3·5′W	X	71
Gillbank	S Lanak	NS8249	55°43·5′	3°52·3′W	X	72
Gill Bank	Staffs	SJ8453	53°4·7′	2°13·9′W	X	118
Gill Bay	Orkney	ND4394	58°50·0′	2°58·8′W	W	7
Gill Beck	Brad	SE1640	53°51·6′	1°45·0′W	W	104
Gill Beck	Cumbr	NY3549	54°50·1′	3°0·3′W	W	85
Gill Beck	Cumbr	NY5019	54°34·1′	2°46·0′W	W	90
Gill Beck	Durham	NZ0017	54°33·1′	1°59·6′W	W	92
Gill Beck	Durham	NZ0610	54°29·4′	1°54·0′W	W	92
Gill Beck	Leeds	SE1844	53°53·8′	1°43·2′W	W	104
Gill Beck	Leeds	SE3442	53°52·6′	1°28·6′W	W	104
Gill Beck	N Yks	SD9887	54°17·0′	2°1·4′W	W	98
Gill Beck	N Yks	SE0258	54°1·3′	1°57·8′W	W	104
Gill Beck	N Yks	SE1196	54°21·8′	1°49·4′W	W	99
Gill Beck	N Yks	SE1553	53°58·6′	1°45·9′W	W	104
Gillbeck Br	Durham	NZ0610	54°29·4′	1°54·0′W	X	92
Gill Beck Fm	N Yks	SE1464	54°4·5′	1°46·7′W	FM	99
Gill Beck Head	N Yks	SE0259	54°1·9′	1°57·8′W	X	104
Gillbent	Stock	SJ8684	53°21·4′	2°12·2′W	T	109
Gill Br	Lincs	TF2447	53°0·6′	0°8·7′W	X	131
Gillbrae	D & G	NY1070	55°1·2′	3°24·0′W	X	85
Gillbrow	Cumbr	NY2219	54°33·9′	3°12·0′W	X	89,90
Gill Burn	Highld	ND3468	58°36·0′	3°7·7′W	W	12
Gillburn	S Lanak	NT0343	55°40·5′	3°32·1′W	X	72
Gillcambon	Cumbr	NY4132	54°41·0′	2°54·5′W	X	90
Gillcambon Beck	Cumbr	NY3835	54°42·6′	2°57·3′W	W	90
Gillcar Fm	Kirk	SE2612	53°36·5′	1°36·0′W	FM	110
Gill Cottage	Cumbr	NY3152	54°51·7′	3°4·1′W	X	85
Gill Crag	Cumbr	NY3812	54°30·2′	2°57·0′W	H	90
Gillcroft Fm	N Yks	SE2449	53°56·4′	1°37·6′W	FM	104
Gillean	Highld	NG5808	57°6·2′	5°59·3′W	X	32,39
Gillean Burn	Highld	NG5908	57°6·3′	5°58·3′W	W	32,39
Gill Edge	N Yks	SD9289	54°18·0′	2°7·0′W	X	98
Gillen	Highld	NG2659	57°32·6′	6°34·3′W	T	23
Gillenbie	D & G	NY1885	55°9·4′	3°16·8′W	X	79
Gilleon's Hall	Staffs	SK1022	52°48·0′	1°50·7′W	X	128
Gillercomb	Cumbr	NY2111	54°29·5′	3°12·8′W	X	89,90
Gillercomb Head	Cumbr	NY2111	54°29·5′	3°12·8′W	X	89,90
Gillerthwaite	Cumbr	NY1314	54°31·1′	3°20·2′W	X	89
Gillerthwaite	Cumbr	NY1421	54°34·9′	3°19·4′W	X	89
Gillesbie	D & G	NY1691	55°12·6′	3°18·8′W	T	79
Gillespie	D & G	NX2552	54°50·2′	4°43·1′W	X	82
Gillespie Burn	D & G	NX2553	54°50·7′	4°43·1′W	W	82
Gilletts Fm	Devon	ST2607	50°51·7′	3°2·7′W	FM	192,193
Gill Field	Durham	NY9820	54°34·8′	2°1·4′W	X	92
Gillfield	Highld	ND3453	58°27·9′	3°7·4′W	X	12
Gillfield Wood	N Yks	SE0791	54°19·1′	1°53·1′W	F	99
Gill Fm	Cumbr	NY5807	54°27·6′	2°38·5′W	FM	91
Gill Fm	Kent	TR0134	51°4·4′	0°52·5′E	FM	189
Gill Fm	Kent	TR0338	51°6·5′	0°54·4′E	FM	179,189
Gill Fm	N Yks	SD6371	54°8·3′	2°33·6′W	FM	97
Gillfoot	Cumbr	NY0011	54°29·3′	3°32·2′W	X	89
Gill Foot	Cumbr	SD6186	54°16·3′	2°35·5′W	X	97
Gillfoot	D & G	NX7547	54°48·4′	3°56·3′W	X	84
Gillfoot	D & G	NX9570	55°1·1′	3°38·1′W	X	84
Gillfoot	D & G	NX9755	54°53·0′	3°35·9′W	X	84
Gillfoot Bay	D & G	NX9755	54°53·0′	3°35·9′W	W	84
Gillfoot Cott	D & G	NX9569	55°0·5′	3°38·1′W	X	84
Gill Force (Waterfall)	Cumbr	NY1800	54°23·6′	3°15·4′W	W	89,90
Gill Garbh	N Eil	NB2001	57°54·9′	6°43·2′W	X	14
Gill Garth	N Yks	SD7875	54°10·5′	2°19·8′W	X	98
Gillgarth Beck	N Yks	SD7775	54°10·5′	2°20·7′W	W	98
Gill Gate	N Yks	SD9391	54°19·1′	2°6·0′W	X	98
Gill Gooden	Cumbr	NY1640	54°45·1′	3°17·9′W	W	85
Gill Hag	N Yks	SE6075	54°10·3′	1°4·4′W	F	100
Gillhall	D & G	NY1273	55°2·9′	3°22·2′W	X	85
Gillham	Kent	TQ8741	51°8·5′	0°40·8′E	X	189
Gillha Wood	Aberd	NJ8635	57°24·6′	2°13·5′W	F	30
Gill Head	Brad	SE1245	53°54·3′	1°48·6′W	X	104
Gillhead	Cumbr	NY4453	54°52·4′	2°51·9′W	X	85
Gillhead	Cumbr	NY5019	54°34·1′	2°46·0′W	X	90
Gill Head	Cumbr	SD6985	54°15·8′	2°28·1′W	W	98

Gill Head	Cumbr	SD7392	54°19·6′	2°24·5′W	X	98
Gill Head	N Yks	SD7377	54°11·5′	2°24·4′W	X	98
Gill Head	N Yks	SD9396	54°21·8′	2°6·0′W	X	98
Gill Head	N Yks	SD9747	53°55·4′	2°2·3′W	X	103
Gillhead	S Lanak	NS8253	55°45·6′	3°52·4′W	X	65,72
Gill Head Fm	N Yks	SE2078	54°12·1′	1°41·2′W	FM	99
Gill Hill	N Ayr	NS2449	55°42·4′	4°47·6′W	H	63
Gillhill Wood	Corn	SX2257	50°23·4′	4°29·9′W	F	201
Gill Ho	Cumbr	NY1102	54°24·6′	3°21·9′W	X	89
Gill Ho	Cumbr	NY1745	54°47·8′	3°17·0′W	X	85
Gill Ho	Cumbr	NY4760	54°56·2′	2°49·2′W	X	86
Gill Ho	Cumbr	NY6916	54°32·5′	2°28·3′W	X	91
Gill Ho	Durham	NY9720	54°34·8′	2°2·4′W	X	92
Gill Ho	N Yks	SE0168	54°6·7′	1°58·7′W	X	98
Gill Hole	Cumbr	NY6304	54°26·1′	2°33·8′W	X	91
Gillhope Fm	E Susx	TQ6126	51°0·9′	0°18·1′E	FM	188,199
Gillhouse	Corn	SX1873	50°31·9′	4°33·7′W	X	201
Gill House Beck	Cumbr	SD2482	54°13·9′	3°9·5′W	W	96
Gillhouse Downs	Corn	SX1873	50°31·9′	4°33·7′W	X	201
Gillhouse Fm	Devon	SS7103	50°49·0′	3°49·5′W	FM	191
Gillibrand Hall	Lancs	SD5716	53°38·6′	2°38·6′W	X	108
Gillibrands	Lancs	SD4705	53°32·6′	2°47·6′W	X	108
Gillick Rock	Corn	SW5741	50°13·4′	5°24·0′W	X	203
Gilliehill Clints	Northum	NY7790	55°12·5′	2°21·3′W	X	80
Gilliesellly	Orkney	ND4285	58°45·2′	2°59·7′W	X	7
Gillies Hill	N Ayr	NS3854	55°45·4′	4°34·5′W	X	63
Gillies Hill	Stir	NS7791	56°6·0′	3°58·2′W	H	57
Gilliestongues	Scot Bord	NT6316	55°26·4′	2°34·7′W	X	80
Gillietrang	Orkney	ND4797	58°51·7′	2°54·6′W	X	6,7
Gilligant's Fm	Bolton	SD6713	53°37·0′	2°29·5′W	FM	109
Gilling Beck	N Yks	NZ1904	54°26·1′	1°42·0′W	W	92
Gilling Drove	Kent	TR2365	51°20·6′	1°12·5′E	X	179
Gilling East	N Yks	SE6176	54°10·8′	1°3·5′W	T	100
Gilling Grange	N Yks	NZ1804	54°26·1′	1°42·9′W	X	92
Gillingham	Dorset	ST8026	51°2·2′	2°16·7′W	T	183
Gillingham	Medway	TQ7767	51°22·7′	0°33·0′E	T	178
Gillingham	Norf	TM4191	52°28·0′	1°33·3′E	T	134
Gillingham Marshes	Norf	TM4191	52°28·0′	1°33·3′E	X	134
Gillingham Reach	Medway	TQ7869	51°23·7′	0°33·9′E	W	178
Gillingham Thicks	Norf	TM4193	52°29·1′	1°33·4′E	F	134
Gilling Park	N Yks	SE6076	54°10·8′	1°4·4′W	X	100
Gillingshill	Fife	NO5106	56°14·9′	2°47·0′W	X	59
Gilling West	N Yks	NZ1805	54°26·6′	1°42·9′W	T	92
Gilling Wood	N Yks	NZ1504	54°26·1′	1°45·7′W	F	92
Gillingwood Hall	N Yks	NZ1704	54°26·1′	1°43·9′W	X	92
Gillis Craig	D & G	NX8753	54°51·8′	3°45·2′W	X	84
Gillis Field	Shetld	HU6188	60°34·5′	0°52·7′W	H	1,2
Gillivoan	Highld	ND1934	58°17·5′	3°22·4′W	X	11
Gillkeeket	Scot Bord	NT4427	55°32·3′	2°52·8′W	X	73
Gill Knowe	D & G	NT0006	55°20·5′	3°34·2′W	H	78
Gillmill	E Ayr	NS3945	55°40·6′	4°33·2′W	X	63
Gill Mill	Oxon	SP3706	51°45·3′	1°27·4′W	X	164
Gillmoor	N Yks	SE2464	54°4·5′	1°37·6′W	X	99
Gillmoss	Liv	SJ4096	53°27·7′	2°53·8′W	T	108
Gillock	Highld	ND2159	58°31·0′	3°20·9′W	X	11,12
Gill of Garth	Orkney	HY4707	58°57·1′	2°54·8′W	X	6,7
Gillo Fm	Carm	SN2840	52°2·1′	4°30·1′W	FM	145
Gillot Hey Fm	Derby	SK1489	53°24·1′	1°47·0′W	FM	110
Gillow Heath	Staffs	SJ8858	53°7·4′	2°10·4′W	T	118
Gillow Manor	Heref	SO5325	51°55·5′	2°40·6′W	A	162
Gillows Willows Fm	Norf	TM2387	52°26·3′	1°17·3′E	FM	156
Gill Pier	Orkney	HY4448	59°19·1′	2°58·5′W	X	5
Gill Pike	Northum	NY6183	55°8·6′	2°36·3′W	H	80
Gillridge Fm	E Susx	TQ5132	51°4·3′	0°9·7′E	FM	188
Gillrigg	D & G	NY0687	55°10·4′	3°28·1′W	X	78
Gillroanie	D & G	NX6948	54°48·8′	4°1·9′W	X	83,84
Gillrudding Grange	York	SE6144	53°53·6′	1°3·9′W	X	105
Gills	Highld	ND3272	58°38·1′	3°9·8′W	T	7,12
Gills Bay	Highld	ND3373	58°38·6′	3°8·8′W	W	7,12
Gillscott Fm	Devon	SS7106	50°50·6′	3°49·6′W	FM	191
Gill's Cross	Devon	SX7758	50°24·8′	3°43·5′W	X	202
Gillses	Cumbr	NY8312	54°30·4′	2°15·3′W	X	91,92
Gills Fm	Essex	TL4303	51°42·7′	0°4·6′E	FM	167
Gill's Fm	Kent	TQ5769	51°24·1′	0°15·8′E	FM	177
Gill's Fm	N Yks	SE8459	54°1·4′	0°42·6′W	FM	106
Gill's Green	Kent	TQ7532	51°3·9′	0°30·2′E	T	188
Gillshaw Flow	D & G	NY2772	55°2·5′	3°8·1′W	X	85
Gillshaw Fm	E Susx	TQ8919	50°56·6′	0°41·8′E	FM	189
Gillshaw Wood	D & G	NY2773	55°3·0′	3°8·1′W	F	85
Gill's Hill	Cambs	TL3256	52°11·4′	0°3·7′W	X	153
Gillside	Cumbr	NY3716	54°32·4′	2°58·0′W	X	90
Gillside	Scot Bord	NY4784	55°9·1′	2°49·5′W	X	79
Gills Lap	E Susx	TQ4631	51°3·8′	0°5·4′E	X	188
Gills Law	Northum	NT9409	55°22·7′	2°5·2′W	H	80
Gillsrow	Cumbr	NY3726	54°37·8′	2°58·1′W	X	90
Gillsyard	Renf	NS3359	55°48·0′	4°39·4′W	X	63
Gill Syke	Lincs	TF2347	53°0·6′	0°9·6′W	W	131
Gill, The	Cumbr	NY3548	54°49·6′	3°0·3′W	X	85
Gill, The	Cumbr	NY4164	54°58·3′	2°54·9′W	X	85
Gill, The	Cumbr	NY5580	55°7·0′	2°41·9′W	W	80
Gill, The	Cumbr	NY5679	55°6·5′	2°41·0′W	W	86
Gill Thorn Fm	N Yks	SE2556	54°0·2′	1°36·7′W	FM	104
Gillway	Staffs	SK2004	52°38·2′	1°41·9′W	T	139
Gill Wood	N Yks	SE5675	54°10·3′	1°8·1′W	F	100
Gillwood's Grange	Lincs	TF3882	53°19·2′	0°4·7′E	X	122
Gilly	Corn	SW7023	50°4·0′	5°12·5′W	X	203
Gillybrands	Aberd	NO9094	57°2·5′	2°9·4′W	X	38,45
Gilly Flatts	Darl	NZ3619	54°34·1′	1°26·2′W	X	93
Gilly Fm	Corn	SW7338	50°12·1′	5°10·5′W	FM	204
Gilly Gabben	Corn	SW6825	50°5·0′	5°14·2′W	X	203
Gillylees Wood	N Yks	SE7367	54°5·9′	0°52·6′W	F	100
Gilman Point	Carm	SN2207	51°44·2′	4°34·3′W	X	158
Gilmanscleuch	Scot Bord	NT3321	55°28·9′	3°3·2′W	T	73
Gilmanscleugh Burn	Scot Bord	NT3322	55°29·5′	3°3·2′W	W	73
Gilmartin	D & G	NY2478	55°5·7′	3°11·0′W	X	85
Gil Meodal	N Eil	NG0594	57°50·6′	6°57·8′W	W	14,18
Gilmerston	D & G	NX8584	55°8·5′	3°47·8′W	X	78
Gilmerton	C of Edin	NT2968	55°54·2′	3°7·7′W	T	66
Gilmerton	Pth & Kin	NN8823	56°23·4′	3°48·4′W	T	52,58
Gilmerton Ho	E Loth	NT5477	55°59·3′	2°43·8′W	X	66
Gilmerton Ho	Fife	NO5111	56°17·6′	2°47·1′W	X	59
Gilmilnscroft	E Ayr	NS5525	55°30·1′	4°17·3′W	X	71
Gilmonby	Durham	NY9912	54°30·4′	2°0·5′W	T	92
Gilmonby Moor	Durham	NY9811	54°29·9′	2°1·4′W	X	92
Gilmorton	Aberd	NJ8726	57°19·7′	2°12·5′W	X	38
Gilmorton	Leic	SP5787	52°28·9′	1°9·2′W	T	140
Gilmorton Ho	Leic	SP5787	52°28·9′	1°9·2′W	X	140
Gilmorton Lodge	Leic	SP5786	52°28·4′	1°9·2′W	X	140
Gilmorton Lodge Fm	Leic	SP5689	52°30·0′	1°10·1′W	FM	140
Gilmourton	S Lanak	NS6540	55°38·3′	4°8·3′W	T	71
Gilnow	Bolton	SD7008	53°34·3′	2°26·8′W	T	109
Gilpin Bank	Cumbr	SD4687	54°16·8′	2°49·3′W	X	97
Gilpin Bank	Cumbr	SD5097	54°22·2′	2°45·8′W	X	97
Gilpin Cott	Cumbr	SD4686	54°16·3′	2°49·3′W	X	97
Gilpin Fm	Cumbr	SD4685	54°15·7′	2°49·3′W	FM	97
Gilpin Lodge	Cumbr	SD4295	54°21·1′	2°53·1′W	X	96,97
Gilpin Mill	Cumbr	SD4394	54°20·5′	2°52·2′W	X	97
Gilpinpark Plantation	Cumbr	SD4395	54°21·1′	2°52·2′W	F	97
Gilridge	Kent	TQ4542	51°9·8′	0°4·8′E	X	188
Gilrivie	Angus	NO6859	56°43·6′	2°30·9′W	X	54
Gil Ròisgil Bheag	N Eil	NB1116	58°2·6′	6°53·4′W	X	13,14
Gil Ròisgil Cham	N Eil	NB1117	58°3·1′	6°53·5′W	X	13,14
Gilroyd	Barns	SE3304	53°32·1′	1°29·7′W	T	110,111
Gilsa Water	Shetld	HU3063	60°21·3′	1°26·9′W	W	3
Gilsay	N Eil	NG0179	57°42·3′	7°0·7′W	X	18
Gilscott	Devon	SS3823	50°59·3′	4°18·1′W	X	190
Gilslake	S Glos	ST5683	51°32·9′	2°37·7′W	X	172
Gilsland	Cumbr	NY6366	54°59·5′	2°34·3′W	T	86
Gilsland	E Loth	NT5484	56°3·1′	2°43·9′W	X	66
Gilsland Spa (Hotel)	Cumbr	NY6367	55°0·0′	2°34·3′W	X	86
Gil Slipir	N Eil	NB1310	57°59·5′	6°50·9′W	X	13,14
Gilson	Warw	SP1890	52°30·7′	1°43·7′W	T	139
Gilstead	Brad	SE1239	53°51·1′	1°48·6′W	T	104
Gilstead Hall	Essex	TQ5595	51°38·2′	0°14·8′E	X	167,177
Gilstead Moor	Brad	SE1239	53°51·1′	1°48·6′W	X	104
Gilston	Falk	NS9478	55°59·3′	3°41·5′W	X	65
Gilston	Herts	TL4412	51°47·5′	0°5·7′E	T	167
Gilston	Moray	NJ2066	57°40·9′	3°20·0′W	X	28
Gilston	Scot Bord	NT4456	55°47·9′	2°53·2′W	T	66,73
Gilstone	I Scilly	SV8305	49°51·9′	6°24·3′W	X	203
Gilstone	I Scilly	SV9109	49°54·3′	6°17·9′W	X	203
Gilston Ho	Fife	NO4406	56°14·8′	2°53·8′W	X	59
Gilston Park	Herts	TL4413	51°48·1′	0°5·7′E	T	167
Giltar Point	Pemb	SS1298	51°39·2′	4°42·7′W	X	158
Giltarump	Shetld	HU2741	60°9·4′	1°30·3′W	X	4
Giltbrook	Notts	SK4845	53°0·2′	1°16·7′W	T	129
Gilthwaiterigg	Cumbr	SD5295	54°21·1′	2°43·9′W	X	97
Gilton Hill	Oxon	SU6898	51°40·8′	1°0·6′W	H	164,165
Giltons	Pemb	SM8712	51°46·2′	5°4·8′W	X	157
Gilts	Cumbr	NY6211	54°29·8′	2°34·8′W	X	91
Gilver's Lane	Worcs	SO8141	52°4·3′	2°16·2′W	T	150
Gilwell Park	Essex	TQ3896	51°39·0′	0°0·1′E	T	166,177
Gilwen	Carm	SN7438	52°1·8′	3°49·8′W	X	146,160
Gilwen Fm	Carm	SN3240	52°2·2′	4°26·6′W	FM	145
Gilwern	Cered	SN6974	52°21·1′	3°55·0′W	X	135
Gilwern	Monm	SO2414	51°49·4′	3°5·8′W	T	161
Gilwern	Powys	SN9153	52°10·1′	3°35·2′W	X	147
Gilwern	Powys	SO0858	52°13·0′	3°20·4′W	X	147
Gilwern Brook	Powys	SO1856	52°12·0′	3°11·6′W	W	148
Gilwern Dingle	Powys	SO2156	52°12·0′	3°9·0′W	X	148
Gilwern Hill	Monm	SO2412	51°48·3′	3°5·7′W	X	161
Gilwern Hill	Powys	SO0957	52°12·5′	3°19·5′W	H	147
Gilwyns	Kent	TQ4945	51°11·3′	0°8·3′E	X	188
Gimbers End	Cambs	TL1066	52°17·1′	0°22·8′W	X	153
Gimble Point	I Scilly	SV8816	49°58·0′	6°20·7′W	X	203
Gimblett's Mill	Corn	SX2483	50°37·4′	4°28·9′W	X	201
Gimbro Fm	Leic	SK4425	52°49·5′	1°20·4′W	FM	129
Gimingham	Norf	TG2836	52°52·6′	1°23·7′E	T	133
Gimmenbie	D & G	NY1678	55°5·6′	3°18·5′W	X	85
Gimmer Crag	Cumbr	NY2707	54°27·4′	3°7·1′W	X	89,90
Gimmerscroft	N Lanak	NS7864	55°51·5′	3°56·5′W	X	64
Ginclough	Ches	SJ9576	53°17·1′	2°4·1′W	T	118
Gincox Fm	Surrey	TQ3949	51°13·6′	0°0·2′W	FM	187
Ginge Brook	Oxon	SU4487	51°35·0′	1°21·5′W	W	174
Ginge Ho	Oxon	SU4486	51°34·5′	1°21·5′W	X	174
Gingerland	Devon	SS9905	50°50·4′	3°25·7′W	X	192
Ginger's Green	E Susx	TQ6212	50°53·3′	0°18·6′E	T	199
Gingle Pot	Northum	NY8060	54°56·3′	2°18·3′W	X	86,87
Ginglet	E Loth	NT6274	55°57·7′	2°36·1′W	X	67
Gingling Hole	N Yks	SD8570	54°7·8′	2°13·4′W	X	98
Gin Head	E Loth	NT5985	56°3·6′	2°39·1′W	X	67
Gin Pit	Wigan	SD6801	53°30·5′	2°28·5′W	X	109
Gins	Hants	SZ4198	50°47·0′	1°24·7′W	X	196
Gins Ho	Hants	SZ4197	50°46·5′	1°24·7′W	X	196
Ginst Point	Carm	SN3208	51°45·0′	4°25·6′W	X	159
Giol	Arg & Bt	NR2843	55°36·5′	6°18·7′W	X	60
Giolabhal Glas	N Eil	NB1402	57°55·2′	6°49·3′W	H	14
Giosla	N Eil	NB1225	58°7·5′	6°53·0′W	T	13,14
Gippeswyk Park	Suff	TM1543	52°2·8′	1°8·5′E	X	169
Gipping	Suff	TM0763	52°13·8′	1°2·3′E	T	155
Gipping Fm	Suff	TM0761	52°12·7′	1°2·2′E	FM	155
Gipping Great Wood	Suff	TM0762	52°13·3′	1°2·2′E	F	155
Gipping Lone	Suff	TM0764	52°14·3′	1°2·3′E	X	155
Gippols, The	Shrops	SO5899	52°35·5′	2°36·8′W	X	137,138
Gipp's Fm	E Susx	TQ4319	50°57·4′	0°2·6′E	FM	198
Gipp's Wood	E Susx	TQ4318	50°56·8′	0°2·5′E	F	198
Gipsey Bridge	Lincs	TF2849	53°1·6′	0°5·1′W	T	131
Gipsey Corner	York	SE6648	53°55·7′	0°59·3′W	X	105,106
Gipsey Hole	N Yks	SE1178	54°12·1′	1°49·5′W	X	99
Gipsey Wham	N Yks	SE1278	54°12·1′	1°48·5′W	W	99
Gipsy Bottom	Bucks	SP7115	51°50·0′	0°57·8′W	F	165
Gipsy Castle Fm	Powys	SO2141	52°3·9′	3°8·8′W	FM	148,161
Gipsy Corner	Devon	SS5438	51°7·6′	4°4·8′W	X	180
Gipsy Cross	Devon	ST1210	50°53·2′	3°14·7′W	X	192,193
Gipsy Hall Fm	Warw	SP1558	52°13·4′	1°46·4′W	FM	151
Gipsy Point	D & G	NX6843	54°46·1′	4°2·7′W	X	83,84
Gipsy Row	Suff	TM0738	52°0·3′	1°1·4′E	T	155,169
Gipsy Town	Devon	ST0815	50°55·8′	3°18·2′W	X	181
Gipsyville	E Yorks	TA0127	53°44·0′	0°27·7′W	X	106,107
Gipsyville	K upon H	TA0627	53°44·0′	0°23·2′W	T	107
Gipton	Leeds	SE3335	53°48·9′	1°29·5′W	T	104
Gipton Wood	Leeds	SE3236	53°49·4′	1°30·4′W	T	104
Girdle Burn	S Lanak	NT0232	55°34·6′	3°32·8′W	W	72
Girdle Fell	Northum	NT7000	55°17·8′	2°27·9′W	H	80
Girdle Ness	C of Aber	NJ9705	57°8·4′	2°2·5′W	X	38
Girdle Toll	N Ayr	NS3440	55°37·8′	4°37·8′W	T	63
Girdstingwood	D & G	NX7446	54°47·8′	3°57·2′W	X	83,84
Girdwoodend	S Lanak	NS9951	55°44·8′	3°36·1′W	X	65,72
Girgenti	E Ayr	NS3643	55°39·4′	4°36·0′W	FM	70
Girharrow Burn	D & G	NX7787	55°10·0′	3°55·4′W	W	78
Girharrow Hill	D & G	NX7886	55°9·5′	3°54·5′W	X	78
Girlington	Brad	SE1434	53°48·4′	1°46·8′W	T	104
Girlington Hall	Durham	NZ1213	54°31·0′	1°48·5′W	X	92
Girlsta	Shetld	HU4250	60°14·2′	1°14·0′W	T	3
Girnal	Clackm	NS8496	56°8·8′	3°51·6′W	X	58
Girnick	Scot Bord	NT6337	55°37·8′	2°34·8′W	X	74
Girnigoe	Orkney	HY5221	59°4·7′	2°49·8′W	X	5,6
Girnock Burn	Aberd	NO3294	57°2·2′	3°6·8′W	W	37,44
Girnwood	Scot Bord	NT3811	55°23·6′	2°58·3′W	X	79
Girnwood Loch	Scot Bord	NT3612	55°24·1′	3°0·2′W	W	79
Girrick	Scot Bord	NT6637	55°37·8′	2°32·0′W	X	74
Girron	Pth & Kin	NN9035	56°29·9′	3°46·8′W	X	52
Girron Burn	Pth & Kin	NN9035	56°29·9′	3°46·8′W	W	52
Girron, The	Pth & Kin	NN6925	56°24·2′	4°6·9′W	H	51
Girr Wick	Shetld	HP6613	60°47·9′	0°46·7′W	W	1
Girsa Vird	Shetld	HU2779	60°29·9′	1°30·0′W	X	3
Girsby	Lincs	TF2187	53°22·2′	0°10·5′W	T	113,122
Girsby	N Yks	NZ3508	54°28·2′	1°27·2′W	T	93
Girsby Grange	Lincs	TF2186	53°21·7′	0°10·5′W	X	113,122
Girsby Greens	N Yks	NZ3507	54°27·7′	1°27·2′W	X	93
Girsby Scar	N Yks	NZ3508	54°28·2′	1°27·2′W	X	93
Girsby Top	Lincs	TF2187	53°22·2′	0°10·5′W	X	113,122
Girsby Vale	Lincs	TF2188	53°22·7′	0°10·4′W	X	113,122
Girsie Loch	Shetld	HU4251	60°14·7′	1°14·0′W	W	3
Girsonfield	Northum	NY8993	55°14·1′	2°9·9′W	X	80
Girston	Highld	ND3647	58°24·7′	3°5·2′W	W	12
Girt	Somer	ST6223	51°0·5′	2°32·1′W	T	183
Girt Down	Devon	SS6047	51°12·5′	3°59·9′W	H	180
Girt Fm	Devon	SS5947	51°12·5′	4°0·7′W	FM	180
Girthgate	Scot Bord	NT5043	55°40·9′	2°47·3′W	X	73
Girthhead	D & G	NY1093	55°13·6′	3°24·5′W	X	78
Girthill	N Ayr	NS2646	55°40·8′	4°45·6′W	X	63
Girthon	D & G	NX6053	54°51·4′	4°10·4′W	T	83
Girtley Hill	N Ayr	NS2361	55°48·8′	4°49·1′W	H	63
Girton	Cambs	TL4262	52°14·5′	0°5·2′E	T	154
Girton	Notts	SK8266	53°11·3′	0°46·0′W	T	121
Girton Grange	Notts	SK8268	53°12·4′	0°45·9′W	X	121
Girtridge	S Ayr	NS3636	55°35·7′	4°35·7′W	X	70
Girvan Mains	S Ayr	NX1999	55°15·4′	4°50·5′W	X	76
Girvellan Point	D & G	NX8152	54°51·2′	3°50·8′W	X	84
Girvet's Loch	Shetld	HU2746	60°12·1′	1°30·3′W	W	4
Gisborne's Gorse	Leic	SK4715	52°44·1′	1°17·8′W	F	129
Gisborough Moor	Red & Cl	NZ6212	54°30·2′	1°2·1′W	X	94
Gisburn	Lancs	SD8248	53°55·9′	2°16·0′W	T	103
Gisburn Cotes	Lancs	SD8047	53°55·4′	2°17·9′W	X	103
Gisburne Park	Lancs	SD8249	53°56·5′	2°16·0′W	X	103
Gisburn Forest	Lancs	SD7457	54°0·7′	2°23·4′W	F	103
Gisla River	N Eil	NB1126	58°8·0′	6°54·1′W	W	13
Gisleham	Suff	TM5188	52°26·2′	1°42·0′E	T	156
Gislingham	Suff	TM0771	52°18·1′	1°2·6′E	T	144,155
Gissage Lake	Devon	SS7104	50°49·5′	3°49·5′W	W	191
Gissing	Norf	TM1485	52°25·5′	1°9·3′E	T	144,156
Gissing Fm	Suff	TM1775	52°20·0′	1°11·5′E	FM	156
Gissing's Fm	Suff	TM2977	52°20·8′	1°22·1′E	FM	156
Gistfaen	Cered	SN7471	52°19·6′	3°50·5′W	X	135,147
Gist-Faen	Flint	SJ2257	53°6·5′	3°9·5′W	X	117
Gist Wen	Powys	SO0621	51°53·0′	3°21·6′W	X	160
Gitcombe	Devon	SX8154	50°22·7′	3°40·0′W	X	202
Gittinshay Wood	Shrops	SJ3800	52°35·9′	2°54·5′W	F	126
Gittin Wood	Suff	TM0776	52°20·8′	1°2·8′E	F	144
Gittisham	Devon	SY1398	50°46·7′	3°13·7′W	T	192,193
Gittisham Fm	Devon	SY1298	50°46·7′	3°14·5′W	FM	192,193
Gittisham Hill	Devon	SY1497	50°46·2′	3°12·8′W	X	192,193
Gittisham Hill Ho	Devon	SY1598	50°46·8′	3°12·0′W	X	192,193
Gittshayne	Devon	SY2394	50°44·7′	3°5·1′W	X	192,193
Giùr-bheinn	Arg & Bt	NR3772	55°52·4′	6°11·8′W	X	60,61
Given Dale	N Yks	SE8784	54°14·9′	0°39·5′W	X	101
Given Dale	N Yks	SE8785	54°15·4′	0°39·4′W	X	94,101
Givendale Dike	N Yks	SE8885	54°15·4′	0°38·5′W	A	94,101
Givendale Grange	N Yks	SE3468	54°6·6′	1°28·4′W	X	99
Givendale Head Fm	N Yks	SE8987	54°16·5′	0°37·6′W	FM	94,101
Givendale Wood	N Yks	SE1390	54°18·5′	1°47·6′W	F	99
Givons Grove	Surrey	TQ1754	51°16·6′	0°19·0′W	T	187
Givv, The	Shetld	HP6506	60°44·2′	0°48·0′W	X	1
Gizzen Briggs	Highld	NH8287	57°51·7′	3°58·9′W	X	21
Glac a' Bhodaich	N Eil	NF7939	57°20·0′	7°19·6′W	X	22
Glac a' Chapuill	Highld	NM5557	56°38·7′	5°59·3′W	X	47
Glac a' Chatha	Highld	NH6828	57°19·7′	4°11·1′W	X	26,35
Glac a' Chlaonain	Arg & Bt	NM5641	56°30·1′	5°57·5′W	X	47,48
Glac Airigh-pholl	Arg & Bt	NM3848	56°33·3′	6°15·4′W	X	47,48
Glacan Daraich	Arg & Bt	NR2666	55°48·8′	6°22·0′W	X	60
Glac an Dorchadais	Highld	NM4785	56°53·5′	6°8·8′W	X	39
Glac an Lin	Arg & Bt	NM5242	56°30·5′	6°1·4′W	X	47,48
Glac an Lòin	Highld	NH4911	57°10·2′	4°29·4′W	X	34
Glac an Skulamus	Highld	NG6620	57°12·9′	5°52·1′W	X	32
Glac an Tiadhain	Arg & Bt	NM6321	56°19·6′	5°49·6′W	X	49
Glac an t-Saighdeir	Arg & Bt	NR5072	55°52·8′	5°59·4′W	X	61
Glac Auscar	N Eil	NF7831	57°15·6′	7°20·0′W	X	22
Glacbain	Highld	NC2211	58°3·4′	5°0·5′W	X	15
Glac Bhan a' Bhòcaidh	Highld	NG7781	57°46·1′	5°44·5′W	X	19
Glac Bheag	Arg & Bt	NR8883	55°59·8′	5°23·5′W	W	55
Glac Chaol	Highld	NG9581	57°46·6′	5°26·4′W	X	19
Glac Dhorch	Arg & Bt	NR4964	55°48·5′	5°59·9′W	X	60,61
Glaceriska	Arg & Bt	NM9245	56°33·3′	5°22·6′W	X	49
Glac Fhearna	Highld	NC0732	58°14·3′	5°16·8′W	X	15
Glacgallon	Arg & Bt	NM3740	56°29·0′	6°15·9′W	X	47,48
Glac Gharbh	Arg & Bt	NM9627	56°23·7′	5°17·9′W	X	49
Glac Gharbh	Highld	NM7665	56°43·6′	5°39·2′W	X	40
Glac Gharbh	Highld	NM8975	56°49·4′	5°27·0′W	X	40
Glac Gille Gun Cheann	Arg & Bt	NR4075	55°54·1′	6°9·1′W	X	60,61

Glachavoil	Arg & Bt	NS0275	55°55·9'	5°9·7'W	X	63
Glach-en-ronack	Moray	NJ2938	57°25·9'	3°10·5'W	X	28
Glachog	Flint	SJ2668	53°12·5'	3°6·1'W	X	117
Glack	Aberd	NJ4527	57°20·1'	2°54·4'W	X	37
Glack	Aberd	NJ7311	57°11·6'	2°26·4'W	X	38
Glack	Angus	NO3963	56°45·5'	2°59·4'W	X	44
Glack	Moray	NJ2324	57°18·3'	3°16·2'W	X	36
Glack	Pth & Kin	NO0235	56°30·1'	3°35·1'W	X	52,53
Glackburn	Angus	NO3660	56°43·9'	3°2·3'W	X	44
Glack Harnes	Moray	NJ2836	57°24·8'	3°11·5'W	X	28
Glackmore	Highld	NH6051	57°31·9'	4°19·8'W	T	26
Glackmore	Pth & Kin	NN8764	56°45·5'	3°50·4'W	X	43
Glackmuick	Moray	NJ3642	57°28·1'	3°3·6'W	X	28
Glack of Clunymore	Moray	NJ3641	57°27·5'	3°3·5'W	X	28
Glack of Corraich	Angus	NO3162	56°44·9'	3°7·2'W	X	44
Glack of Glengairney	Pth & Kin	NO1771	56°49·6'	3°21·2'W	H	43
Glack of Kessock	Highld	NH6548	57°30·4'	4°14·7'W	X	26
Glack of Midthird	Moray	NJ3541	57°27·5'	3°4·5'W	X	28
Glack of Newtyle	Angus	NO3040	56°33·1'	3°7·9'W	X	53
Glack of Pitglassie	Moray	NJ3238	57°25·9'	3°7·5'W	X	28
Glackour	Highld	NH1882	57°47·7'	5°3·3'W	X	20
Glacks	Aberd	NJ5112	57°12·0'	2°48·2'W	X	37
Glack's Hill	Aberd	NO6294	57°2·4'	2°37·1'W	H	37,45
Glacks of Balloch	Moray	NJ3534	57°23·8'	3°4·4'W	X	28
Glack, The	Pth & Kin	NO0346	56°36·0'	3°34·3'W	X	52,53
Glack, The	Scot Bord	NT2137	55°37·5'	3°14·8'W	T	73
Glack Wood	Aberd	NJ7310	57°11·1'	2°26·3'W	F	38
Glac Mhór	Arg & Bt	NM4857	56°38·5'	6°6·2'W	X	47
Glac Mhór	Arg & Bt	NR5984	55°59·6'	5°51·4'W	X	61
Glac Mhor	Arg & Bt	NR8666	55°50·6'	5°24·7'W	X	62
Glac Mhór	Arg & Bt	NR8884	56°0·4'	5°23·6'W	W	55
Glac Mhór	Highld	NG4523	57°13·9'	6°13·1'W	X	32
Glac Mhór	Highld	NH1279	57°45·9'	5°9·2'W	X	19
Glac Mhór	Highld	NH9514	57°12·5'	3°43·8'W	X	36
Glac Mhór	Highld	NM7148	56°34·3'	5°43·2'W	X	49
Glac Mhór	Highld	NM7786	56°55·0'	5°39·4'W	X	40
Glac Mhór	N Eil	NF8746	57°24·1'	7°12·2'W	X	22
Glac na Brothaig Airde	Highld	NG3548	57°27·0'	6°24·6'W	X	23
Glac na Ceardaich	Highld	NC3141	58°19·8'	4°52·7'W	X	9
Glac na Criche	Arg & Bt	NR2270	55°50·8'	6°26·1'W	X	60
Glac na Criche Deise	Highld	NG2204	57°2·9'	6°34·6'W	X	39
Glac na Dunaiche	Arg & Bt	NR6286	56°0·7'	5°48·7'W	X	61
Glacna h-Atha	Arg & Bt	NR5488	56°1·6'	5°56·4'W	X	61
Glac na h-Imrich	Highld	NC0825	58°10·6'	5°15·4'W	X	15
Glac na Luachrach	Highld	NG6921	57°13·6'	5°49·2'W	X	32
Glac nam Muileach	Highld	NM4265	56°42·6'	6°12·5'W	X	47
Glac nan Coll	Arg & Bt	NR5683	55°45·9'	6°12·1'W	X	60
Glac nan Cruachan	N Eil	NF8015	57°7·1'	7°16·8'W	X	31
Glac nan Searrach	Highld	NG4551	57°28·9'	6°14·8'W	X	23
Glac nan Sgadan	Highld	NG8208	57°6·9'	5°35·6'W	X	33
Glacour	Highld	NH3354	57°33·0'	4°47·0'W	X	26
Glac Raineach	Highld	NH0904	57°5·5'	5°8·7'W	X	33
Glac Reidh	Arg & Bt	NM4252	56°35·6'	6°11·7'W	X	47
Glac Rheithe	Highld	NH1192	57°52·9'	5°10·8'W	X	19
Glac Ròineach	Arg & Bt	NM3319	56°17·6'	6°18·5'W	H	48
Glac Ruadh	Highld	NM7384	56°53·8'	5°43·2'W	X	40
Glac Ruairidh	N Eil	NF8017	57°8·2'	7°16·9'W	X	31
Glac Smearasmuil	N Eil	NB0807	57°57·7'	6°55·8'W	X	13,14
Glac Tric	Highld	NG7254	57°31·4'	5°48·0'W	X	24
Glac Uamharr	Arg & Bt	NM5251	56°35·4'	6°1·9'W	X	47
Gladder Brook	Worcs	SO7572	52°21·0'	2°21·6'W	W	138
Glade Burn	S Lanak	NS9437	55°37·2'	3°40·6'W	W	71,72
Glade Burn	S Lanak	NS9638	55°37·7'	3°38·7'W	W	72
Glade Fm	Hants	SU7846	51°12·7'	0°52·6'W	FM	186
Glade Fm	N Yks	SE6240	53°51·4'	1°3·0'W	FM	105
Glade How	Cumbr	NY1306	54°26·8'	3°20·1'W	X	89
Gladestry	Powys	SO2355	52°11·5'	3°7·2'W	T	148
Gladestry Brook	Heref	SO2554	52°11·0'	3°5·4'W	W	148
Gladfen Hall	Essex	TL8128	51°55·5'	0°38·3'E	X	168
Gladhayes Fm	Devon	ST1514	50°55·4'	3°12·2'W	FM	181,193
Gladhill	Moray	NJ3265	57°40·4'	3°7·9'W	X	28
Gladhouse	Midlo	NT2954	55°46·7'	3°7·5'W	X	66,73
Gladhouse Cottage	Midlo	NT2951	55°45·1'	3°7·4'W	X	66,73
Gladhouse Mains	Midlo	NT3055	55°47·2'	3°6·5'W	X	66,73
Gladhouse Reservoir	Midlo	NT2953	55°46·2'	3°7·5'W	W	66,73
Gladices	I of W	SZ4779	50°36·8'	1°19·8'W	X	196
Gladsfield	Pth & Kin	NO1435	56°30·2'	3°23·4'W	X	53
Gladshot	E Loth	NT4772	55°56·5'	2°50·5'W	X	66
Gladsmuir	Cumbr	NY4453	54°52·4'	2°51·9'W	X	85
Gladsmuir	E Loth	NT4573	55°57·1'	2°52·4'W	T	66
Gladsmuir Hills	W Loth	NS9256	55°47·4'	3°42·9'W	X	65,72
Gladstone	S Lanak	NT0242	55°40·0'	3°33·0'W	X	72
Gladstone Boreland	S Lanak	NT0343	55°40·5'	3°32·1'W	X	72
Gladstone Fm	Renf	NS3962	55°49·7'	4°33·8'W	FM	63
Gladstone Knott	Cumbr	NY2504	54°25·8'	3°8·9'W	X	89,90
Gladstone Park	Brent	TQ2285	51°33·3'	0°14·0'W	X	176
Gladstone Rock	Gwyn	SH6152	53°3·1'	4°4·0'W	X	115
Gladwin's Mark	Derby	SK3066	53°11·7'	1°32·6'W	X	119
Gladwyns	Essex	TL5114	51°48·5'	0°11·8'E	X	167
Glaic	Arg & Bt	NS0771	55°53·9'	5°4·8'W	X	63
Glaichbea	Highld	NH5139	57°25·3'	4°28·4'W	T	26
Glaichoile	Highld	NH4030	57°20·2'	4°39·0'W	X	26
Glaick	D & G	NW9959	54°53·4'	5°7·6'W	X	82
Glaick	Highld	NG7927	57°17·1'	5°39·6'W	T	33
Glaick	Highld	NH5673	57°43·7'	4°24·6'W	X	21
Glaick	Highld	NH6374	57°44·4'	4°17·6'W	X	21
Glaid Stone	N Ayr	NS1657	55°46·5'	4°55·6'W	X	63
Glaikhead	S Lanak	NS8136	55°36·4'	3°52·9'W	X	71,72
Glais	Swan	SN7000	51°41·3'	3°52·5'W	T	170
Glais Bheinn	Highld	NM7243	56°31·7'	5°42·0'W	H	49
Glaisdale	N Yks	NZ7603	54°25·2'	0°49·3'W	X	94
Glaisdale	N Yks	NZ7705	54°26·3'	0°48·3'W	T	94
Glaisdale Beck	N Yks	NZ7604	54°25·8'	0°49·3'W	W	94
Glaisdale Head Fm	N Yks	NZ7402	54°24·7'	0°51·2'W	FM	94
Glaisdale Moor	N Yks	NZ7201	54°24·2'	0°53·0'W	X	94
Glaisdale Moor	N Yks	NZ7505	54°26·3'	0°50·2'W	X	94
Glaisdale Rigg	N Yks	NZ7303	54°25·3'	0°52·1'W	H	94
Glaisdale Side	N Yks	NZ7504	54°25·8'	0°50·2'W	X	94
Glaisfer	Powys	SO1417	51°50·9'	3°14·5'W	X	161
Glaisgeo	Highld	NC7163	58°32·4'	4°12·5'W	X	10
Glaisnock	E Ayr	NS5717	55°25·8'	4°15·2'W	X	71
Glaisnock Moss	E Ayr	NS5615	55°24·7'	4°16·0'W	X	71
Glaister	E Ayr	NS5838	55°37·1'	4°14·9'W	X	71
Glaister	N Ayr	NR9334	55°33·6'	5°16·5'W	X	68,69
Glaisters	D & G	NX7680	55°6·2'	3°56·2'W	X	78
Glaisters	D & G	NX8865	54°58·3'	3°44·6'W	X	84
Glaisters Br	D & G	NX7580	55°6·2'	3°57·1'W	X	78
Glaisters Burn	D & G	NX8765	54°58·3'	3°45·5'W	W	84
Glaisters Hill	D & G	NX7680	55°6·2'	3°56·2'W	X	78
Glake	S Ayr	NX2287	55°9·0'	4°47·2'W	X	76
Glamaig	Highld	NG5130	57°17·8'	6°7·5'W	H	24,32
Glam Burn	Highld	NG5542	57°24·4'	6°4·3'W	W	24
Glame	Highld	NG5542	57°24·4'	6°4·3'W	X	24
Glamis	Angus	NO3846	56°36·4'	3°0·2'W	T	54
Glamis Castle	Angus	NO3848	56°37·4'	3°0·2'W	A	54
Glan Adda	Gwyn	SH5770	53°12·7'	4°8·1'W	T	114,115
Glan Afon	Gwyn	SH3936	52°54·1'	4°23·2'W	X	123
Glanafon	Pemb	SM9517	51°49·1'	4°58·1'W	T	157,158
Glanafon Fm	Powys	SN8927	51°56·1'	3°36·5'W	FM	160
Glanalders	Powys	SO0269	52°18·9'	3°25·9'W	X	136,147
Glanalwen	Denb	SJ0543	52°58·8'	3°24·5'W	X	125
Glanaman	Carm	SN6713	51°48·2'	3°55·4'W	T	159
Glanau	Monm	SO4907	51°45·8'	2°43·9'W	X	162
Glanbaiden	Monm	SO2614	51°49·4'	3°4·0'W	X	161
Glanbechan	Powys	SO1295	52°33·0'	3°17·5'W	X	136
Glanbidno Isaf	Powys	SN8881	52°25·2'	3°38·4'W	X	135,136
Glanbran	Carm	SN7938	52°1·9'	3°45·4'W	X	146,160
Glanbran	Cered	SN5361	52°13·9'	4°8·8'W	X	146
Glanbrân Ho	Swan	SS7199	51°40·7'	3°51·6'W	X	170
Glan-Brennig	Cered	SN6759	52°13·0'	3°56·4'W	X	146
Glanbrogan Hall	Powys	SJ1818	52°45·4'	3°12·5'W	X	125
Glanbrydan Park	Carm	SN6626	51°55·2'	3°56·5'W	X	146
Glancamddwr	Powys	SN9247	52°6·9'	3°34·2'W	X	147
Glan-carw	Carm	SN4924	51°53·9'	4°11·3'W	X	159
Glan Ceirw	Conwy	SH9646	53°0·3'	3°32·6'W	X	116
Glan-Cennen	Carm	SN6118	51°50·8'	4°0·7'W	X	159
Glan-Cennen Uchaf	Carm	SN6218	51°50·9'	3°59·8'W	X	159
Glanceri	Cered	SN3351	52°8·2'	4°26·0'W	X	145
Glancleddan Fawr	Powys	SN8644	52°5·2'	3°39·4'W	X	147,160
Glancleddau	Pemb	SN0921	51°51·5'	4°46·0'W	X	145,158
Glan-Clwyd	Denb	SJ0573	53°15·0'	3°25·0'W	X	116
Glan-Clwyd	Denb	SJ0968	53°12·3'	3°21·3'W	X	116
Glan Clwyd	Denb	SJ1161	53°8·6'	3°19·4'W	X	116
Glan Conwy	Conwy	SH8352	53°3·4'	3°44·3'W	X	116
Glancorran	Carm	SN2811	51°46·5'	4°29·2'W	X	158
Glancorrwg	Carm	SN4328	51°55·9'	4°16·6'W	X	146
Glancrychan	Carm	SN8037	52°1·3'	3°44·5'W	X	160
Glandeg Fm	Wrex	SJ4347	53°1·3'	2°50·6'W	FM	117
Glan-Denys	Cered	SN5850	52°8·0'	4°4·1'W	X	146
Glanderston Dam	E Renf	NS4956	55°46·7'	4°24·0'W	W	64
Glanderstone	Aberd	NJ5829	57°21·2'	2°41·4'W	X	37
Glanderston Mains	E Renf	NS5056	55°46·7'	4°23·1'W	X	64
Glandfield's Fm	Essex	TL6819	51°50·9'	0°26·7'E	FM	167
Glandford	Norf	TG0441	52°55·9'	1°2·5'E	T	133
Glandovan	Pemb	SN1941	52°2·5'	4°38·0'W	X	145
Glan-Duar	Carm	SN5243	52°4·2'	4°9·2'W	X	146
Glandulais	Carm	SN6527	51°55·7'	3°57·4'W	X	146
Glan-Dulais	Carm	SN7030	51°57·4'	3°53·1'W	X	146,160
Glandulais Fm	Powys	SO0890	52°30·2'	3°20·9'W	FM	136
Glandulas	Carm	SN5521	51°52·4'	4°6·0'W	X	159
Glandulas	Cered	SN3147	52°6·0'	4°27·7'W	X	145
Glandulas	Powys	SN9453	52°10·1'	3°32·6'W	X	147
Glandulas Uchaf	Cered	SN6254	52°10·3'	4°0·7'W	X	146
Glandŵr	Caer	SO2001	51°42·4'	3°9·1'W	T	171
Glandwr	Carm	SN3022	51°52·5'	4°27·8'W	X	145,159
Glandwr	Carm	SN5922	51°53·0'	4°2·5'W	X	159
Glandwr	Cered	SN2851	52°8·1'	4°30·4'W	X	145
Glan-dwr	Cered	SN4449	52°7·3'	4°16·3'W	X	146
Glandwr	Monm	SO3225	51°55·4'	2°58·9'W	X	161
Glan-dŵr	Pemb	SM9825	51°53·5'	4°55·7'W	X	157,158
Glandwr	Pemb	SN0740	52°1·7'	4°48·4'W	X	145
Glandwr	Pemb	SN1928	51°55·5'	4°37·6'W	T	145,158
Glandwr	Powys	SO1330	51°57·9'	3°15·6'W	X	161
Glandwr Fm	Carm	SN8141	52°3·5'	3°43·8'W	FM	147,160
Glandwr Fm	Pemb	SN1344	52°4·0'	4°43·3'W	FM	145
Glandwr Hall	Gwyn	SH6317	52°44·2'	4°1·4'W	X	124
Glandŵr-isaf	Carm	SN1727	51°54·9'	4°39·3'W	X	145,158
Glan Dwyfach	Gwyn	SH4843	52°58·0'	4°15·4'W	T	123
Glandy	Carm	SN1427	51°54·9'	4°41·9'W	X	145,158
Glandy Cross	Carm	SN1426	51°54·3'	4°41·8'W	T	145,158
Glan-Dyfi	Cered	SN6393	52°31·3'	4°0·8'W	X	135
Glandyfi	Cered	SN6996	52°33·0'	3°55·5'W	T	135
Glanedw Fm	Powys	SO1252	52°9·8'	3°16·8'W	FM	148
Glaneirw	Cered	SN2748	52°6·4'	4°31·2'W	X	145
Glan-Elan	Powys	SN9666	52°17·2'	3°31·1'W	X	136,147
Glan-fechan	Gwyn	SH7502	52°36·3'	3°50·4'W	X	135
Glanfedw	Cered	SN7375	52°21·7'	3°51·5'W	X	135,147
Glan Fedwen	Powys	SN8676	52°22·5'	3°40·1'W	H	135,136,147
Glanfeiglo	Powys	SJ1120	52°46·4'	3°18·8'W	X	125
Glanfields	Essex	TM0830	51°56·0'	1°1·9'E	X	168,169
Glanfred	Cered	SN6387	52°28·1'	4°0·6'W	X	135
Glan Frogan Hill	Powys	SJ1818	52°45·4'	3°12·5'W	H	125
Glangeidrych	Carm	SN6824	51°54·2'	3°54·7'W	X	159
Glangors	Cered	SN6459	52°13·0'	3°59·1'W	X	146
Glan Gors	Conwy	SH8475	53°15·8'	3°43·9'W	X	116
Glangors	Gwyn	SH2028	52°49·4'	4°39·9'W	X	123
Glangors	Gwyn	SH4951	53°2·3'	4°14·7'W	X	115,123
Glangors	Gwyn	SH4951	53°2·3'	4°14·7'W	X	115,123
Glan Gors	I of Angl	SH4480	53°17·9'	4°20·0'W	X	114,115
Glan Gors	I of Angl	SH4779	53°17·4'	4°17·3'W	X	114,115
Glangors Ddu	I of Angl	SH4075	53°15·1'	4°23·5'W	X	114,115
Glangorslwyd	Cered	SN7375	52°21·7'	3°51·5'W	X	135,147
Glangrwyney	Powys	SO2416	51°50·5'	3°5·8'W	T	161
Glangwden	Powys	SN9688	52°29·0'	3°31·5'W	X	136
Glangwenlais	Carm	SN7540	52°2·9'	3°49·0'W	X	146,147,160
Glangwesyn	Powys	SN8653	52°10·1'	3°39·6'W	X	147
Glan-Gwili	Carm	SN4322	51°52·7'	4°16·5'W	X	159
Glangwili	Carm	SN4629	51°56·5'	4°14·0'W	X	146
Glan Gwna	Gwyn	SH5062	53°8·3'	4°14·1'W	X	114,115
Glangwy	Powys	SN8778	52°23·5'	3°39·2'W	X	135,136,147
Glangwy	Powys	SN8880	52°24·6'	3°38·4'W	X	135,136
Glangwydderig	Carm	SN7834	51°59·7'	3°46·2'W	X	146,160
Glangwye	Powys	SO1538	52°2·3'	3°14·0'W	X	161
Glanhafon	Powys	SJ0725	52°49·1'	3°22·4'W	X	125
Glan-hafon	Powys	SJ0827	52°50·2'	3°21·5'W	H	125
Glanhafren	Powys	SJ2204	52°37·9'	3°8·8'W	X	126
Glan Hafren	Powys	SO1392	52°31·4'	3°16·5'W	X	136
Glan Hafren	Powys	SO1696	52°33·6'	3°13·9'W	X	136
Glanhafren Hall	Powys	SO0890	52°30·2'	3°20·9'W	X	136
Glanhanog	Powys	SN9499	52°35·0'	3°33·5'W	T	136
Glanhelyg	Cered	SN2144	52°4·2'	4°36·3'W	X	145
Glan Hesbin	Denb	SJ1351	53°3·2'	3°17·5'W	X	116
Glanhirin	Powys	SN8671	52°19·8'	3°40·0'W	X	135,136,147
Glan Honddu	Powys	SO0331	51°58·4'	3°24·3'W	X	160
Glanirfon	Powys	SO0050	52°8·6'	3°27·3'W	X	147
Glanithon	Powys	SO0563	52°15·7'	3°23·1'W	X	147
Glaniwrch	Powys	SJ1425	52°49·2'	3°16·2'W	X	125
Glan-Lerry	Cered	SN6188	52°28·6'	4°2·4'W	X	135
Glanllafar	Gwyn	SH7336	52°54·6'	3°52·9'W	X	124
Glan-Lliw	Swan	SN6100	51°41·1'	4°0·3'W	X	159
Glan Llugwy	Conwy	SH6861	53°8·0'	3°58·0'W	X	115
Glanllyn	Denb	SJ0371	53°13·9'	3°26·8'W	X	116
Glan-llyn	I of Angl	SH4277	53°16·2'	4°21·8'W	X	114,115
Glanllyn	Powys	SN9469	52°18·8'	3°32·9'W	X	136,147
Glanllynan	Cered	SN1947	52°5·7'	4°38·2'W	X	145
Glanllynmawr	Gwyn	SH8816	52°44·0'	3°39·1'W	X	124,125
Glanllynnau	Gwyn	SH4537	52°54·7'	4°17·9'W	X	123
Glanmamog	Carm	SN3036	52°0·0'	4°28·2'W	X	145
Glan-meddyg	Cered	SN6842	52°3·9'	3°55·1'W	X	146
Glan Medeni	Cered	SN2947	52°5·9'	4°29·4'W	X	145
Glanmeryn	Powys	SN7498	52°34·2'	3°51·1'W	X	135
Glanmiheli	Powys	SO1690	52°30·3'	3°13·9'W	X	136
Glanmonnow	Heref	SO4621	51°53·3'	2°46·7'W	X	161
Glanmor	V of Glam	SS8774	51°27·5'	3°37·2'W	X	170
Glanmorfa	I of Angl	SH4367	53°10·9'	4°20·6'W	X	114,115
Glan-Morfa	I of Angl	SH4671	53°13·1'	4°18·0'W	X	114,115
Glanmule	Powys	SO1690	52°30·3'	3°13·9'W	T	136
Glanmwrwg	Carm	SN5501	51°41·6'	4°5·5'W	T	159
Glannau	Powys	SN9065	52°16·6'	3°36·3'W	X	136,147
Glanneaudd	Carm	SN4131	51°57·5'	4°18·5'W	X	146
Glannoventa (Roman Fort)	Cumbr	SD0896	54°21·3'	3°24·5'W	R	96
Glanogeu	Powys	SJ2031	52°52·5'	3°10·9'W	X	126
Glanolmarch	Cered	SN2144	52°4·2'	4°36·3'W	X	145
Glan Peris	Cered	SN5567	52°17·2'	4°7·2'W	X	135
Glanpwllafon	Cered	SN1744	52°4·1'	4°39·8'W	X	145
Glanrafon	Cered	SN6180	52°24·3'	4°2·2'W	T	135
Glanrafon	Cered	SN6790	52°29·7'	3°57·2'W	X	135
Glanrafon	Gwyn	SH2032	52°51·6'	4°40·0'W	X	123
Glanrafon	Gwyn	SH3238	52°55·0'	4°29·5'W	X	123
Glanrafon	Gwyn	SH5264	53°9·4'	4°12·4'W	X	114,115
Glanrafon	I of Angl	SH3671	53°12·9'	4°27·0'W	X	114
Glanrafon	I of Angl	SH4370	53°12·5'	4°20·7'W	X	114,115
Glanrafon bach	Gwyn	SH5160	53°7·2'	4°13·2'W	X	114,115
Glanrafon Fm	I of Angl	SH4269	53°11·9'	4°21·5'W	FM	114,115
Glan Rheidol	Cered	SN6679	52°23·8'	3°57·8'W	X	135
Glanrhocca	Cered	SN6353	52°9·7'	3°59·8'W	X	146
Glanrhos	Cered	SN4153	52°9·4'	4°19·1'W	X	146
Glan-rhos	Cered	SN5774	52°21·0'	4°5·6'W	X	135
Glanrhos	Powys	SN9764	52°16·1'	3°30·2'W	X	147
Glanrhyd	Carm	SN2827	51°55·1'	4°29·7'W	X	145,158
Glanrhyd	Carm	SN3332	51°57·9'	4°25·5'W	X	145
Glanrhyd	Carm	SN4927	51°55·5'	4°11·4'W	X	146
Glanrhyd	Gwyn	SH2838	52°55·0'	4°33·1'W	X	123
Glan-rhŷd	Gwyn	SH4758	53°6·1'	4°16·7'W	X	115,123
Glan-rhyd	Gwyn	SH5666	53°10·5'	4°8·9'W	X	114,115
Glanrhyd	Pemb	SN1442	52°3·0'	4°42·4'W	T	145
Glan-rhyd	Pemb	SN1531	51°57·0'	4°41·1'W	X	145
Glan-rhyd	Powys	SN7709	51°46·2'	3°46·6'W	T	160
Glanrhyd	Powys	SO0693	52°31·8'	3°22·7'W	X	136
Glanrhydsaeson	Carm	SN6826	51°55·3'	3°54·8'W	X	146
Glanrhydw	Carm	SN4313	51°47·9'	4°16·2'W	X	159
Glan-rhyd-y-dre	Cered	SN4248	52°6·7'	4°18·1'W	X	146
Glanrhydypysgod	Cered	SN4640	52°2·5'	4°14·3'W	X	146
Glansevern Hall	Powys	SJ1900	52°35·7'	3°11·4'W	X	136
Glan-Shôn	Caer	ST2295	51°39·1'	3°7·3'W	X	171
Glan Soch	Gwyn	SH2828	52°49·6'	4°32·8'W	X	123
Glantaf	Carm	SN1520	51°51·1'	4°40·8'W	X	145,158
Glantanat Isaf	Powys	SJ1424	52°48·6'	3°16·2'W	X	125
Glan Terrig Fm	Flint	SJ2359	53°7·6'	3°8·6'W	FM	117
Glantlees	Northum	NU1405	55°20·6'	1°46·3'W	T	81
Glantlees Hill	Northum	NU1306	55°21·1'	1°47·3'W	H	81
Glan-Toddeb	Carm	SN7121	51°52·6'	3°52·0'W	X	160
Glanton	Northum	NU0714	55°25·4'	1°52·9'W	T	81
Glanton Hill	Northum	NU0614	55°25·4'	1°53·9'W	H	81
Glanton Pyke	Northum	NU0514	55°25·4'	1°54·8'W	X	81
Glantowy	Carm	SN5321	51°52·3'	4°7·7'W	X	159
Glan-Towy	Carm	SN6724	51°54·2'	3°55·6'W	X	159
Glan-Towy	Carm	SN7029	51°56·9'	3°53·1'W	X	146,160
Glan-Towy	Carm	SN7432	51°58·6'	3°49·7'W	X	146,160
Glantowylan	Carm	SN4621	51°52·2'	4°13·8'W	X	159
Glan-traeth	I of Angl	SH2678	53°16·5'	4°36·2'W	X	114
Glantraeth	I of Angl	SH4169	53°11·9'	4°22·4'W	X	114,115
Glan-Tren	Carm	SN5243	52°4·2'	4°9·2'W	X	146
Glantywyn	I of Angl	SH3374	53°14·5'	4°29·8'W	X	114
Glan-Usk	Monm	SO3110	51°47·3'	2°59·6'W	X	161
Glanusk Park	Powys	SO1919	51°52·1'	3°10·2'W	X	161
Glanville Fm	Devon	SY1897	50°46·2'	3°9·4'W	FM	192,193
Glanvilles Wootton	Dorset	ST6708	50°52·5'	2°27·8'W	T	194
Glanyrnwy Fm	Powys	SJ2220	52°46·6'	3°9·0'W	FM	126
Glanwern	Cered	SN5355	52°10·7'	4°8·6'W	X	146
Glanwern	Cered	SN6188	52°28·6'	4°2·4'W	T	135
Glanwydden	Conwy	SH8180	53°18·5'	3°46·8'W	T	116
Glanwye	Powys	SO0649	52°8·1'	3°22·0'W	X	147
Glan-y-don	Flint	SJ1679	53°18·3'	3°15·2'W	T	116
Glan-y-gors	Conwy	SH9160	53°7·8'	3°37·3'W	X	116
Glan-y-gors	Conwy	SH9349	53°1·9'	3°35·3'W	X	116
Glan-y-gors	Conwy	SH9877	53°17·1'	3°31·4'W	X	116
Glan-y-gors	Denb	SJ2060	53°8·1'	3°11·3'W	X	117
Glan-y-gors	Gwyn	SH3037	52°54·5'	4°31·3'W	X	123
Glan-y-gors	Gwyn	SH5741	52°57·1'	4°7·3'W	X	124

Glan-y-gors	I of Angl	SH3574	53°14·5'	4°28·0'W	X	114
Glan-y-gors	I of Angl	SH3783	53°19·4'	4°26·4'W	X	114
Glan-y-gors	I of Angl	SH3886	53°21·0'	4°25·6'W	X	114
Glan-y-llyn	Rho Cyn Taf	ST1184	51°33·1'	3°16·6'W	T	171
Glan-y-Mawddach	Gwyn	SH6316	52°43·7'	4°1·3'W	X	124
Glan-y-môr	Cered	SN3011	51°46·6'	4°27·5'W	T	159
Glan-y-môr	Cered	SN5884	52°26·4'	4°4·9'W	X	135
Glan-y-mor	Gwyn	SH5834	52°53·3'	4°6·2'W	X	124
Glan-y-Mor	V of Glam	SS9071	51°25·9'	3°34·6'W	X	170
Glan-y-môr Elias	Conwy	SH6674	53°15·0'	4°0·1'W	X	115
Glan-y-morfa	Denb	SH9976	53°16·5'	3°30·5'W	X	116
Glan-y-morfa	Gwyn	SH5540	52°56·5'	4°9·1'W	X	124
Glanymorfa-mawr	Gwyn	SH6005	52°37·7'	4°3·7'W	X	124
Glan-y-môr-isaf	Gwyn	SH6172	53°13·9'	4°4·5'W	X	115
Glan-y-nant	Caer	ST1497	51°40·1'	3°14·2'W	T	171
Glan-y-nant	Powys	SN9384	52°26·9'	3°34·1'W	T	136
Glan-y-pwll	Powys	SJ1616	52°44·3'	3°14·3'W	X	125
Glan-yr-aber	Denb	SJ0651	53°3·1'	3°23·7'W	X	116
Glanyrafon	Carm	SN6121	51°52·5'	4°0·8'W	X	159
Glan-yr-afon	Conwy	SH6974	53°15·1'	3°57·4'W	X	115
Glanyrafon	Conwy	SH8974	53°15·3'	3°39·4'W	X	116
Glan-yr-afon	Denb	SJ0854	53°4·8'	3°22·0'W	X	116
Glan-yr-afon	Denb	SJ2153	53°4·3'	3°10·3'W	X	117
Glan-yr-afon	Flint	SJ1181	53°19·4'	3°19·8'W	T	116
Glanyrafon	Gwyn	SH4450	53°1·7'	4°19·2'W	X	115,123
Glan yr afon	Gwyn	SH5436	52°54·3'	4°9·9'W	X	124
Glan-yr-afon	Gwyn	SH9040	52°57·0'	3°37·8'W	X	125
Glan-yr-afon	Gwyn	SJ0242	52°58·2'	3°27·2'W	T	125
Glan-yr-afon	I of Angl	SH3979	53°17·3'	4°24·5'W	X	114
Glanyrafon	I of Angl	SH5069	53°12·1'	4°14·3'W	X	114,115
Glan-yr-afon	I of Angl	SH6080	53°18·2'	4°5·7'W	T	114,115
Glan-yr-afon	Powys	SH8910	52°40·8'	3°38·1'W	X	124,125
Glan-yr-afon	Powys	SJ0401	52°36·1'	3°24·7'W	X	136
Glan-yr-afon	Powys	SJ2027	52°50·3'	3°10·9'W	X	126
Glan-yr-afon	Powys	SO0681	52°25·4'	3°22·5'W	X	136
Glan-yr-afon	Shrops	SJ2224	52°48·7'	3°9·0'W	T	126
Glan-yr-afon	Swan	SN6306	51°44·4'	3°58·7'W	X	159
Glan-yr-afon-ddu	Cered	SN7059	52°13·1'	3°53·8'W	X	146,147
Glanyrafon Halt	Powys	SN9878	52°23·7'	3°29·5'W	X	136,147
Glan-yr-afon-uchaf	Cered	SN7160	52°13·6'	3°52·9'W	X	146,147
Glanyrannell	Carm	SN6739	52°2·2'	3°56·0'W	X	146
Glan-y-rhyd	Powys	SJ0318	52°45·3'	3°25·8'W	X	125
Glan-y-rhyd	Powys	SJ0514	52°43·2'	3°24·0'W	X	125
Glanyrynys	Carm	SN4614	51°48·4'	4°13·6'W	X	159
Glanyrynys	Carm	SN5015	51°49·1'	4°10·2'W	X	159
Glanystwyth	Cered	SN6475	52°21·6'	3°59·4'W	X	135
Glan-y-wern	Denb	SJ0966	53°11·2'	3°21·3'W	X	116
Glan-y-wern	Gwyn	SH6034	52°53·4'	4°4·5'W	T	124
Glaodhaich	Highld	NH4937	57°24·2'	4°30·3'W	H	26
Glapthorn	Northnts	TL0290	52°30·1'	0°29·4'W	T	141
Glapthorn Cow Pasture	Northnts	TL0090	52°30·2'	0°31·2'W	F	141
Glapwell	Derby	SK4766	53°11·6'	1°17·4'W	T	120
Glaramara	Cumbr	NY2410	54°29·0'	3°10·0'W	H	89,90
Glas-aber	Wrex	SJ1333	52°53·5'	3°17·2'W	X	125
Glasahoile	Stir	NN4608	56°14·6'	4°28·7'W	X	57
Glas Aird	Arg & Bt	NR4094	56°4·3'	6°10·2'W	X	61
Glas Allt	Aberd	NO2683	56°56·2'	3°12·5'W	W	44
Glas Allt Beag	Aberd	NO1595	57°2·6'	3°23·6'W	W	36,43
Glasallt-fawr	Carm	SN7330	51°57·5'	3°50·5'W	X	146,160
Glas Allt Mór	Aberd	NO0499	57°4·6'	3°34·6'W	W	36,43
Glas Allt Mór	Aberd	NO1199	57°4·7'	3°27·6'W	W	43
Glas-allt Shiel	Aberd	NO2782	56°55·7'	3°11·5'W	X	44
Glasath	Moray	NJ0607	57°8·9'	3°32·8'W	W	36
Glasbant	Carm	SN3735	51°59·6'	4°22·1'W	X	145
Glas Bhealach	Arg & Bt	NN2509	56°14·7'	4°49·0'W	X	56
Glas Bhealach	Highld	NH1313	57°10·4'	5°5·1'W	X	34
Glas Bheinn	Arg & Bt	NM6528	56°23·4'	5°48·0'W	H	49
Glas Bheinn	Arg & Bt	NN3247	56°35·4'	4°43·7'W	H	50
Glas Bheinn	Arg & Bt	NR4259	55°45·6'	6°6·3'W	H	60
Glas Bheinn	Arg & Bt	NR5069	55°51·2'	5°59·2'W	H	61
Glas Bheinn	Arg & Bt	NR6795	56°5·7'	5°44·3'W	H	55,61
Glas Bheinn	Highld	NC2526	58°11·6'	4°58·2'W	H	15
Glas Bheinn	Highld	NG3736	57°20·6'	6°21·8'W	H	23,32
Glas Bheinn	Highld	NG9043	57°26·0'	5°29·4'W	H	25
Glas Bheinn	Highld	NM4964	56°42·3'	6°5·6'W	H	47
Glas Bheinn	Highld	NM8357	56°39·5'	5°32·0'W	H	49
Glas Bheinn	Highld	NM9375	56°49·5'	5°23·1'W	H	40
Glas Bheinn	Highld	NN1397	57°1·8'	5°4·4'W	H	34
Glas Bheinn	Highld	NN1791	56°58·7'	5°0·2'W	H	34
Glas Bheinn	Highld	NN2564	56°44·4'	4°51·2'W	H	41
Glas Bheinn	Highld	NN3794	57°0·8'	4°40·6'W	H	34
Glas Bheinn Bheag	Highld	NG5825	57°15·4'	6°0·3'W	H	32
Glas-bheinn Bheag	Highld	NH4523	57°16·5'	4°33·8'W	H	26
Glas Bheinn Chaol	Highld	NN1443	56°32·8'	5°1·1'W	X	50
Glas Bheinn Mhór	Arg & Bt	NN1542	56°32·3'	5°0·1'W	H	50
Glas Bheinn Mhór	Highld	NG5525	57°15·3'	6°3·3'W	H	32
Glas-bheinn Mhór	Highld	NH4323	57°16·5'	4°35·8'W	H	26
Glas Bhienn	Highld	NG8122	57°14·4'	5°37·3'W	H	33
Glas Burn	Angus	NO1774	56°51·3'	3°21·2'W	W	43
Glasbury	Powys	SO1739	52°2·8'	3°12·2'W	T	161
Glasbury Fm	Powys	SO1638	52°2·3'	3°13·1'W	FM	161
Glascairn	Highld	NH6058	57°35·7'	4°20·1'W	X	26
Glascarnoch River	Highld	NH3670	57°41·7'	4°44·6'W	W	20
Glas-charn	Highld	NM8483	56°53·5'	5°32·3'W	H	40
Glas Charn	Highld	NN3597	57°2·3'	4°42·7'W	H	34
Glas Chnoc	Highld	NC1728	58°12·4'	5°6·4'W	H	15
Glaschoil	Highld	NJ0232	57°22·3'	3°37·3'W	X	27,36
Glaschoill	Highld	NH4492	57°53·7'	4°37·4'W	X	20
Glaschoille House	Highld	NG7300	57°2·4'	5°44·0'W	X	33
Glaschoille Loch	Highld	NG7300	57°2·4'	5°44·0'W	W	33
Glaschoine	Arg & Bt	NN1811	56°15·7'	4°55·9'W	X	50,56
Glas Choire	Highld	NG7623	57°14·8'	5°42·3'W	X	33
Glas-choire	Highld	NH6604	57°6·7'	4°12·3'W	X	35
Glas Choire	Highld	NN3586	56°56·4'	4°42·3'W	X	34,41
Glas Choire	Highld	NN3586	56°56·4'	4°42·3'W	X	34,41
Glas Choire	Highld	NN4472	56°49·1'	4°32·9'W	X	42
Glas-choire	Highld	NN5774	56°50·4'	4°20·2'W	X	42
Glas Choire	Pth & Kin	NN5049	56°36·8'	4°26·2'W	X	51
Glas Choire	Pth & Kin	NN7377	56°52·3'	4°4·6'W	X	42
Glas Choirean	Highld	NM8675	56°49·3'	5°30·0'W	X	40

Glas Choirean	Highld	NN2247	56°35·1'	4°53·5'W	X	50
Glas Choire Beag	Highld	NC2917	58°6·8'	4°53·7'W	X	15
Glas-choire Beag	Highld	NC5847	58°23·6'	4°25·3'W	X	10
Glas Choire Bheag	Pth & Kin	NO0676	56°52·2'	3°32·1'W	X	43
Glas Choirein	N Ayr	NR9043	55°38·4'	5°19·8'W	X	62,69
Glas Choirein	N Ayr	NS0026	55°29·5'	5°9·5'W	X	69
Glas Choire Mhór	Pth & Kin	NO0675	56°51·7'	3°32·1'W	X	43
Glas Choire Mór	Highld	NC2917	58°6·8'	4°53·7'W	X	15
Glas Choir Granda	Highld	NC3151	58°25·2'	4°53·1'W	X	9
Glaschul Hill	Aberd	NJ4514	57°13·1'	2°54·2'W	H	37
Glasclune Castle	Pth & Kin	NO1547	56°36·7'	3°22·6'W	A	53
Glascoed	Carm	SN1721	51°51·7'	4°39·1'W	X	145,158
Glascoed	Carm	SN5119	51°51·2'	4°9·4'W	T	159
Glascoed	Carm	SN5219	51°51·2'	4°8·5'W	X	159
Glascoed	Denb	SH9973	53°14·9'	3°30·4'W	T	116
Glascoed	Monm	SO3301	51°42·5'	2°57·8'W	T	171
Glascoed	Powys	SJ1108	52°40·0'	3°18·6'W	X	125
Glascoed	Powys	SJ1412	52°42·2'	3°16·0'W	X	125
Glascoed	Powys	SJ2127	52°50·3'	3°10·0'W	X	126
Glascoed	Powys	SJ2321	52°47·1'	3°8·1'W	X	126
Glascoed	Powys	SO0695	52°32·9'	3°22·8'W	X	136
Glascoed	Powys	SO0888	52°29·2'	3°20·9'W	T	136
Glascoed	Wrex	SJ2754	53°4·9'	3°5·0'W	T	117
Glascoed Fawr	Denb	SJ0271	53°13·9'	3°27·7'W	X	116
Glascoe Fm	I of M	SC4498	54°21·5'	4°23·6'W	FM	95
Glas Coire	Angus	NO4383	56°56·3'	2°55·8'W	X	44
Glascorrie	Aberd	NO4097	57°3·9'	2°58·9'W	X	37,44
Glascorrie	Pth & Kin	NN8020	56°21·7'	3°56·1'W	X	52,57
Glascote	Staffs	SK2202	52°37·2'	1°40·1'W	T	139
Glascwm	Powys	SJ1615	52°43·8'	3°14·2'W	X	125
Glascwm	Powys	SO1553	52°10·4'	3°14·2'W	T	148
Glascwm Hill	Powys	SO1552	52°9·8'	3°14·2'W	H	148
Glas-dhoire	Highld	NN2593	57°0·0'	4°52·4'W	X	34
Glas-Dhoire Mór	Highld	NN2290	56°58·3'	4°55·2'W	X	34
Glas Dhruim	Arg & Bt	NM8645	56°33·2'	5°28·5'W	X	49
Glasdir	Flint	SJ1282	53°19·9'	3°18·9'W	T	116
Glasdir	Gwyn	SH7422	52°47·3'	3°51·7'W	X	124
Glasdir	Pemb	SN0941	52°2·3'	4°46·7'W	X	145
Glasdrum	Arg & Bt	NN0146	56°34·1'	5°13·9'W	X	50
Glas Eilean	Arg & Bt	NM2419	56°17·2'	6°27·2'W	X	48
Glas Eilean	Arg & Bt	NM7311	56°14·5'	5°39·4'W	X	55
Glas Eilean	Arg & Bt	NM8943	56°32·2'	5°25·4'W	X	49
Glas Eilean	Arg & Bt	NR3390	56°2·0'	6°16·7'W	X	61
Glas Eilean	Arg & Bt	NR4465	55°48·9'	6°4·7'W	X	60,61
Glas Eilean	Arg & Bt	NR6972	55°53·4'	5°41·2'W	X	61,62
Glas Eilean	Arg & Bt	NR9185	56°1·0'	5°20·8'W	X	55
Glas Eilean	Highld	NG7000	57°2·3'	5°47·0'W	X	33
Glas Eilean	Highld	NG7811	57°8·4'	5°39·7'W	X	33
Glas Eilean	Highld	NG7975	57°42·9'	5°42·2'W	X	19
Glas Eilean	Highld	NG8425	57°16·1'	5°34·5'W	X	33
Glas Eilean	Highld	NM4862	56°41·2'	6°6·5'W	X	47
Glas Eilean	Highld	NM7560	56°40·9'	5°40·0'W	X	40
Glas Eilean	N Eil	NB0133	58°11·3'	7°4·8'W	X	13
Glas Eilean	N Eil	NB1333	58°11·8'	6°52·6'W	X	13
Glas Eileanan	Arg & Bt	NM7139	56°29·5'	5°42·8'W	X	49
Glas-eileanan	N Eil	NF8641	57°21·3'	7°12·8'W	X	22
Glas-eilean Beag	N Eil	NF7863	57°32·8'	7°22·5'W	X	18
Glas-eilean Mór	N Eil	NF8322	57°11·0'	7°14·4'W	X	22,31
Glas Eilean Mór	N Eil	NF9468	57°36·2'	7°6·9'W	X	18
Glas-eilean na Creige	N Eil	NF8442	57°21·8'	7°14·9'W	X	22
Glas Féith Bheag	Pth & Kin	NN8982	56°55·2'	3°49·0'W	W	43
Glas Féith Mhór	Pth & Kin	NN8882	56°55·2'	3°49·9'W	W	43
Glasffrwd	Cered	SN7465	52°16·4'	3°50·4'W	W	135,147
Glasfield	Highld	NH6057	57°35·1'	4°20·0'W	X	26
Glasfryn	Carm	SN3127	51°55·2'	4°27·1'W	X	145
Glasfryn	Carm	SN3515	51°48·8'	4°23·2'W	X	159
Glasfryn	Conwy	SH8375	53°15·8'	3°44·8'W	X	116
Glasfryn	Conwy	SH9150	53°2·4'	3°37·1'W	T	116
Glasfryn	Denb	SJ0950	53°2·6'	3°21·0'W	X	116
Glasfryn	Gwyn	SH4042	52°57·3'	4°22·5'W	X	123
Glasfryn	Pemb	SM9535	51°58·8'	4°58·7'W	X	157
Glasfynydd Forest	Powys	SN8524	51°54·4'	3°39·9'W	F	160
Glasgoed	Cered	SN3349	52°7·1'	4°26·0'W	T	145
Glasgoed	Gwyn	SH7523	52°47·6'	3°50·8'W	X	124
Glasgoed	Powys	SO0092	52°31·2'	3°28·0'W	X	136
Glasgoed Hall	Gwyn	SH5464	53°9·4'	4°10·6'W	X	114,115
Glasgoforest	Aberd	NJ8112	57°12·2'	2°18·4'W	X	38
Glasgow	C of Glas	NS5965	55°51·7'	4°14·7'W	T	64
Glasgow Airport	Renf	NS4766	55°52·0'	4°26·3'W	X	64
Glasgow Bridge	E Dunb	NS6373	55°56·1'	4°11·1'W	X	64
Glasgow Green	C of Glas	NS6064	55°51·2'	4°13·8'W	X	64
Glasgow Stud	Enf	TL3100	51°41·2'	0°5·9'W	X	166
Glasgow Zoo	C of Glas	NS6862	55°50·2'	4°6·0'W	X	64
Glasgraig Fawr	I of Angl	SH4188	53°22·1'	4°23·0'W	X	114
Glasgrug	Cered	SN6280	52°24·3'	4°1·3'W	X	135
Glasgwm	Gwyn	SH8419	52°45·8'	3°42·7'W	X	124,125
Glasgwm-isaf	Powys	SO0916	51°50·4'	3°18·9'W	X	161
Glasgwn	Powys	SJ0421	52°46·9'	3°25·0'W	X	125
Glasha Burn	Highld	NH3591	57°52·9'	4°46·5'W	W	20
Glas-hirfryn	Powys	SJ1529	52°51·3'	3°15·3'W	X	125
Glashlet Burn	Stir	NN3701	56°10·7'	4°37·1'W	W	56
Glashmore	Aberd	NJ7600	57°5·7'	2°23·3'W	X	38
Glashvin	Highld	NG4768	57°38·1'	6°13·9'W	T	23
Glasinfryn	Gwyn	SH5868	53°11·7'	4°7·1'W	T	114,115
Glas Leac	Highld	NC0721	58°8·3'	5°16·2'W	X	15
Glas Leac	Highld	NC1340	58°18·8'	5°11·1'W	X	9
Glas Leac	Highld	NC1346	58°22·0'	5°11·3'W	X	9
Glas Leac	Highld	NC2055	58°27·0'	5°4·6'W	X	9
Glas-leac Beag	Highld	NB9205	57°59·4'	5°30·7'W	X	15
Glas-leac Mór	Highld	NB9509	58°1·6'	5°27·8'W	X	15
Glas Leathad	Highld	NH2258	57°34·9'	4°58·2'W	X	25
Glas Leathad	Pth & Kin	NN9673	56°50·5'	3°41·8'W	X	43
Glas Leathad a' Chaillich	Highld	NH1371	57°41·7'	5°7·8'W	X	19
Glas-leathad Feshie	Highld	NN8484	56°56·2'	3°59·9'W	H	43
Glas-leathad Lorgaidh	Highld	NN8386	56°57·3'	3°55·0'W	H	43
Glas Leathad Mór	Highld	NH4567	57°40·2'	4°35·5'W	X	20
Glasllwch	Newp	ST2887	51°34·9'	3°2·0'W	T	171
Glas-loch Beag	Highld	NC6620	58°9·2'	4°16·1'W	W	16
Glas-loch Mór	Highld	NC6719	58°8·7'	4°15·1'W	W	16
Glaslyn	Gwyn	SH6154	53°4·2'	4°4·1'W	W	115

Glaslyn	Powys	SJ0406	52°38·8'	3°24·7'W	X	125
Glaslyn	Powys	SN8294	52°32·1'	3°44·0'W	W	135,136
Glaslyn	Powys	SN9765	52°16·7'	3°30·2'W	X	136,147
Glas Maol	Angus	NO1676	56°52·3'	3°22·2'W	H	43
Glas Mheall a' Chumhainn	Pth & Kin	NN5769	56°47·7'	4°20·0'W	H	42
Glas Mheall Beag	Pth & Kin	NN6775	56°51·1'	4°10·4'W	H	42
Glas Mheall Liath	Highld	NH0784	57°48·5'	5°14·4'W	H	19
Glas Mheall Mór	Highld	NH0785	57°49·0'	5°14·5'W	H	19
Glas Mheall Mór	Pth & Kin	NN5667	56°46·6'	4°20·9'W	H	42
GLas Mheall Mór	Pth & Kin	NN6876	56°51·7'	4°9·5'W	H	42
Glasnacardoch	Highld	NM6795	56°59·5'	5°49·7'W	T	40
Glasnacardoch	Highld	NM7080	56°51·5'	5°45·9'W	X	40
Glasnacardoch Bay	Highld	NM6795	56°59·5'	5°49·7'W	W	40
Glasnakille	Highld	NG5313	57°8·8'	6°4·5'W	T	32
Glasnant	Powys	SO1751	52°9·3'	3°12·4'W	W	148
Glasnant	Powys	SO1850	52°8·8'	3°11·5'W	X	148
Glasnock	Highld	NG8545	57°26·9'	5°34·5'W	X	24
Glaspant	Carm	SN2836	52°0·0'	4°29·9'W	X	145
Glasphein	Highld	NG1850	57°27·4'	6°41·7'W	T	23
Glas Phort	Arg & Bt	NM4224	56°20·5'	6°10·1'W	W	48
Glaspits	Aberd	NO5588	56°59·1'	2°44·0'W	X	44
Glaspits Burn	Aberd	NO5689	56°59·7'	2°43·0'W	W	44
Glaspwll	Powys	SN7397	52°33·6'	3°52·0'W	X	135
Glassart Burn	Fife	NO2114	56°19·0'	3°16·2'W	W	58
Glass Brow	Hants	SU7417	50°57·1'	0°56·4'W	X	197
Glassburn	Highld	NH3634	57°22·3'	4°43·2'W	X	26
Glassel	Aberd	NO6599	57°5·1'	2°34·2'W	X	38,45
Glassenbury	Kent	TQ7436	51°6·0'	0°29·5'E	T	188
Glassenbury Ho	Kent	TQ7436	51°6·0'	0°29·5'E	X	188
Glasserton	D & G	NX4238	54°43·0'	4°26·8'W	X	83
Glassert, The	Stir	NN4701	56°10·9'	4°27·5'W	X	57
Glasses Fm	Somer	ST0237	51°7·7'	3°23·6'W	FM	181
Glass Eye Fm	E Susx	TQ8321	50°57·8'	0°36·8'E	FM	199
Glassford	S Lanak	NS7247	55°42·2'	4°1·8'W	T	64
Glas Sgeir	Highld	NG7557	57°33·1'	5°45·2'W	X	24
Glas-sgeir	N Eil	NB0506	57°57·0'	6°58·7'W	X	13,14
Glas-sgeir	N Eil	NB2203	57°56·0'	6°41·3'W	X	13,14
Glas Sgeir	N Eil	NB4220	58°5·9'	6°22·2'W	X	14
Glas Sgeir	N Eil	NG1088	57°47·5'	6°52·4'W	X	14
Glas Sgeir	N Eil	NG1691	57°49·4'	6°46·5'W	X	14
Glassgreen	Moray	NJ2260	57°37·7'	3°17·9'W	X	28
Glasshampton	Worcs	SO7866	52°17·2'	2°19·0'W	X	138,150
Glass Houghton	Wakf	SE4424	53°42·9'	1°19·6'W	T	105
Glasshouse	Glos	SO7021	51°53·4'	2°25·8'W	T	162
Glasshouse Fm	Derby	SK3975	53°16·5'	1°24·5'W	FM	119
Glass House Fm	N Yks	SE1593	54°20·2'	1°45·7'W	FM	99
Glass House Fm	Peterb	TF3303	52°36·7'	0°1·7'W	FM	142
Glasshouse Hill	Glos	SO7020	51°52·9'	2°25·8'W	X	162
Glasshouses	N Yks	SE1764	54°4·5'	1°44·0'W	T	99
Glass Houses	Staffs	SJ7432	52°53·3'	2°22·8'W	X	127
Glas Shròn	Highld	NC3037	58°17·6'	4°53·5'W	H	15
Glassick	Pth & Kin	NN8208	56°15·2'	3°53·8'W	X	57
Glassie	Pth & Kin	NN8550	56°37·9'	3°52·0'W	X	52
Glassingall	Stir	NN7904	56°13·0'	3°56·6'W	X	57
Glasslaw	Aberd	NJ7045	57°29·9'	2°29·6'W	X	29
Glasslaw	Aberd	NO8584	56°57·1'	2°14·3'W	X	45
Glasslet	Angus	NO3668	56°48·2'	3°2·4'W	X	44
Glasslet, The	Angus	NO3078	56°53·5'	3°8·5'W	X	44
Glassliehead	Fife	NT2187	56°4·4'	3°15·7'W	X	66
Glassmonies	Angus	NO5047	56°37·0'	2°48·4'W	X	54
Glass Moor	Cambs	TL2992	52°30·9'	0°5·5'W	X	142
Glassmoor Ho	Cambs	TL2893	52°31·4'	0°6·4'W	X	142
Glassmount	Fife	NT2488	56°5·0'	3°12·8'W	X	66
Glassoch	D & G	NX3369	54°59·5'	4°36·2'W	X	82
Glassoch Br	D & G	NX3369	54°59·5'	4°36·2'W	X	82
Glassoch Burn	D & G	NX3370	55°0·0'	4°36·2'W	W	76
Glassoch Fell	D & G	NX3370	55°0·0'	4°36·2'W	H	76
Glassock	E Ayr	NS4845	55°40·7'	4°24·6'W	X	64
Glasson	Cumbr	NY0336	54°42·8'	3°29·9'W	T	89
Glasson	Cumbr	NY2560	54°56·0'	3°9·8'W	T	85
Glasson	Lancs	SD4456	54°0·1'	2°50·8'W	T	102
Glassonby	Cumbr	NY5738	54°44·4'	2°39·6'W	T	91
Glassonbybeck	Cumbr	NY5739	54°44·9'	2°39·7'W	X	91
Glasson Moss	Cumbr	NY2360	54°56·0'	3°11·7'W	X	85
Glasson Rock	S Ayr	NS2109	55°20·8'	4°49·0'W	X	70,76
Glass Rig	D & G	NX9595	55°14·5'	3°38·7'W	H	78
Glassthorpehill	Northnts	SP6660	52°14·3'	1°1·6'W	X	152
Glassy How Burn	Fife	NO3808	56°15·9'	2°59·6'W	W	59
Glasterim	Moray	NJ3962	57°38·9'	3°0·9'W	X	28
Glasterlaw	Angus	NO5951	56°39·2'	2°39·7'W	X	54
Glas Tholl	Highld	NH0784	57°48·5'	5°14·4'W	X	19
Glas Toll	Highld	NH1733	57°21·3'	5°2·1'W	X	25
Glaston	Rut	SK8900	52°35·7'	0°40·8'W	T	141
Glastonbury	Somer	ST5039	51°9·1'	2°42·5'W	T	182,183
Glastonbury Heath	Somer	ST4739	51°9·1'	2°45·1'W	X	182
Glastonbury Tor	Somer	ST5138	51°8·6'	2°41·6'W	H	182,183
Glaston Hill Ho	Hants	SU7861	51°20·8'	0°52·4'W	X	175,186
Glaston Lodge	Rut	SK9000	52°35·7'	0°39·9'W	X	141
Glastraeth	Gwyn	SH6036	52°54·4'	4°4·5'W	X	124
Glastron	S Ayr	NS3811	55°22·2'	4°33·0'W	X	70
Glas Tulaichean	Pth & Kin	NO0576	56°52·2'	3°33·1'W	H	43
Glastullich	Highld	NH1595	57°54·6'	5°6·9'W	X	20
Glastullich	Highld	NH7976	57°45·7'	4°1·6'W	X	21
Glas Uig	Arg & Bt	NR4751	55°41·4'	6°1·1'W	W	60
Glasvaar	Arg & Bt	NM8801	56°9·5'	5°24·4'W	X	55
Glatting Fm	W Susx	SU9714	50°55·3'	0°36·8'W	FM	197
Glatton	Cambs	TL1586	52°27·8'	0°18·0'W	T	142
Glatton Folly	Cambs	TL1384	52°26·8'	0°19·8'W	F	142
Glatton Lodge	Cambs	TL1385	52°27·3'	0°19·8'W	X	142
Glau Wooar	I of M	SC4686	54°15·0'	4°21·4'W	X	95
Glaze Brook	Devon	SX6859	50°25·2'	3°51·1'W	W	202
Glaze Brook	Salf	SJ6795	53°27·3'	2°29·4'W	W	109
Glazebrook	Warr	SJ6992	53°25·7'	2°27·6'W	T	109
Glazebrook Moss	Warr	SJ6892	53°25·7'	2°28·5'W	X	109
Glazebury	Warr	SJ6797	53°28·4'	2°29·4'W	T	109
Glazeley	Shrops	SO7088	52°29·6'	2°26·1'W	T	138
Glazenwood	Essex	TL8022	51°52·3'	0°37·3'E	X	168
Glazert Burn	E Ayr	NS3847	55°41·6'	4°34·2'W	W	63
Glazert Water	E Dunb	NS6376	55°57·7'	4°11·2'W	W	64
Glazeyfield	Staffs	SJ9139	52°57·1'	2°7·6'W	X	127

Glazier's Copse	Wilts	SU2421	50°59·5′	1°39·1′W	F	184
Glazier's Forge Fm	E Susx	TQ6521	50°58·1′	0°21·4′E	FM	199
Gleadale Ho	Lancs	SD5937	53°49·9′	2°37·0′W	X	102
Gleadless	Sheff	SK3883	53°20·8′	1°25·3′W	T	110,111
Gleadless Valley	Sheff	SK3783	53°20·8′	1°26·2′W	T	110,111
Gleadmoss	Ches	SJ8268	53°12·8′	2°15·8′W	T	118
Gleadscleugh	Northum	NT9529	55°33·5′	2°4·3′W	X	74,75
Gleadsmoss	Ches	SJ8268	53°12·8′	2°15·8′W	X	118
Gleadthorpe Breck Plantn	Notts	SK5970	53°13·7′	1°6·6′W	F	120
Gleadthorpe Grange	Notts	SK5970	53°13·7′	1°6·6′W	X	120
Glean a' Choilich	Highld	NH0925	57°16·8′	5°9·7′W	X	25,33
Glean á Mhill Bhig	Arg & Bt	NN2313	56°16·8′	4°51·1′W	X	50,56
Glean Charnan	Highld	NN1349	56°36·0′	5°2·3′W	X	50
Glean Fithich	Arg & Bt	NR8065	55°49·9′	5°30·3′W	X	62
Glean-leac-na-muidhe	Highld	NN1155	56°39·2′	5°4·5′W	X	41
Glean Lingeadail	N Eil	NB1601	57°54·7′	6°47·2′W	X	14
Gleann a' Chadha Dheirg	Highld	NH2687	57°50·6′	4°55·4′W	X	20
Gleann a' Chaiginn Mhóir	Arg & Bt	NM6126	56°22·2′	5°51·8′W	X	49
Gleann a' Chaimire	N Eil	NG0390	57°48·3′	6°59·5′W	X	18
Gleann a'Chaise	Arg & Bt	NM8027	56°23·3′	5°33·4′W	X	49
Gleann a' Chàm Dhoire	Highld	NN0586	56°55·7′	5°11·8′W	X	41
Gleann a' Chaolais	Highld	NN0457	56°40·1′	5°11·5′W	X	41
Gleann a' Chaolais	N Eil	NG2099	57°53·8′	6°43·1′W	X	14
Gleann a' Chaorainn	Highld	NM9689	56°57·1′	5°20·8′W	X	40
Gleann a' Chapuill Bhàin	Arg & Bt	NR3972	55°52·5′	6°9·9′W	X	60,61
Gleann a' Chàrdaidh	Arg & Bt	NR3166	55°49·0′	6°17·2′W	X	60,61
Gleann a' Chilleine	Pth & Kin	NN7237	56°30·7′	4°4·4′W	X	51,52
Gleann a' Chlachain	Stir	NN3631	56°26·8′	4°39·2′W	X	50
Gleann a' Choilich	Highld	NH1026	57°17·4′	5°8·7′W	X	25
Gleann a' Chroin	Stir	NN6214	56°18·2′	4°13·4′W	X	57
Gleann a' Chrombaidh	Pth & Kin	NN7971	56°49·1′	3°58·5′W	X	42
Gleannagaoidh	Arg & Bt	NR2054	55°42·2′	6°27·0′W	X	60
Gleann a' Ghearraidh	Arg & Bt	NR3145	55°37·7′	6°16·0′W	X	60
Gleann Airigh	Arg & Bt	NR9195	56°6·4′	5°21·2′W	X	55
Gleann Airigh an t-Sluic	Arg & Bt	NR3670	55°51·3′	6°12·7′W	X	60,61
Gleann Airigh Mhic-ceàrra	Arg & Bt	NR6392	56°4·0′	5°48·0′W	X	61
Gleann Airigh na Faing	N Eil	NB3841	58°17·0′	6°27·7′W	X	8
Gleann Airigh na Gile	N Eil	NB3843	58°18·1′	6°27·8′W	X	8
Gleann Airigh na Searsain	Arg & Bt	NM4722	56°19·6′	6°5·1′W	X	48
Gleann Alasgaig	Arg & Bt	NM4921	56°19·2′	6°3·1′W	X	48
Gleann Almagro	N Eil	NB2844	58°18·3′	6°38·1′W	X	8
Gleann Amaind	Arg & Bt	NR2155	55°42·7′	6°26·1′W	X	60
Gleann a' Mhaim	Arg & Bt	NS0781	55°59·2′	5°5·2′W	X	63
Gleann an Dobhrain	Arg & Bt	NR3344	55°37·2′	6°14·0′W	X	60
Gleannan Dorch	Highld	NG8331	57°19·3′	5°35·8′W	X	24
Gleann an Dubh Choirein	Highld	NM8568	56°45·5′	5°30·6′W	X	40
Gleann an Dubh Choirein	Pth & Kin	NN6416	56°19·3′	4°11·5′W	X	57
Gleann an Dubh-Lochain	Highld	NG8200	57°2·6′	5°35·2′W	X	33
Gleann an Fhiodh	Highld	NN0755	56°39·1′	5°8·4′W	X	41
Gleann an Iògain	N Eil	NB2641	58°16·6′	6°40·0′W	X	8,13
Gleann an Lochain Duibh	Highld	NM9070	56°46·7′	5°25·8′W	X	40
Gleann an Lochain Eanaiche	Highld	NM8892	56°58·5′	5°28·8′W	X	33,40
Gleann an Oba	Highld	NH6778	57°46·6′	4°13·7′W	X	21
Gleannan Salach	Highld	NC0823	58°9·5′	5°15·3′W	X	15
Gleannan Salach	Highld	NC1328	58°12·3′	5°10·5′W	X	15
Gleann an t-Slob	Arg & Bt	NR5073	55°53·4′	5°59·5′W	X	61
Gleann an t-Slugain	Aberd	NO1494	57°2·0′	3°24·6′W	X	36,43
Gleann an t-Srath	N Eil	NB2743	58°17·7′	6°39·1′W	X	8
Gleannan t-Suidhe	N Ayr	NR9535	55°34·2′	5°14·7′W	X	68,69
Gleann Aoistail	Arg & Bt	NR6186	56°0·7′	5°49·6′W	X	61
Gleann a' Phuill	Highld	NG1843	57°23·7′	6°41·2′W	X	23
Gleann Ardbhair	Highld	NC1733	58°15·1′	5°6·6′W	X	15
Gleann Asgeamal	Arg & Bt	NR4574	55°53·8′	6°4·3′W	X	60,61
Gleann Astaile	Arg & Bt	NR4871	55°52·2′	6°1·3′W	X	60,61
Gleann Auchreoch	Stir	NN3326	56°24·1′	4°41·9′W	X	50
Gleann Ballach	Highld	NH6401	57°5·1′	4°14·2′W	X	35
Gleann Bàn	Arg & Bt	NM8407	56°12·7′	5°28·5′W	X	55
Gleann Bàn	Arg & Bt	NN1700	56°9·7′	4°56·4′W	X	56
Gleann Bàn	Arg & Bt	NS1282	55°59·9′	5°0·4′W	X	56
Gleann Beag	Arg & Bt	NM6524	56°21·3′	5°47·8′W	X	49
Gleann Beag	Arg & Bt	NM8027	56°23·3′	5°33·4′W	X	49
Gleann Beag	Arg & Bt	NR6999	56°7·9′	5°42·6′W	X	55,61
Gleann Beag	Highld	NG8317	57°11·8′	5°35·1′W	X	33
Gleann Beag	Highld	NH2137	57°23·6′	4°58·3′W	X	25
Gleann Beag	Highld	NH3283	57°48·6′	4°49·2′W	X	20
Gleann Beag	Pth & Kin	NO1273	56°50·7′	3°26·1′W	X	43
Gleann Beag or Hell's Glen	Arg & Bt	NN1706	56°12·9′	4°56·6′W	X	56
Gleann Beinn Dhuibh	N Eil	NG0899	57°53·4′	6°55·2′W	X	14,18
Gleann Bhaidseachan	Arg & Bt	NR6390	56°2·9′	5°47·9′W	X	61
Gleann Bhearraraigh	N Eil	NB0514	58°1·3′	6°59·3′W	X	13,14
Gleann Bhràgair	N Eil	NB3042	58°17·3′	6°35·9′W	X	8,13
Gleann Bhruthadail	N Eil	NB3243	58°17·9′	6°34·0′W	X	8
Gleann Bianasdail	Highld	NH0267	57°39·2′	5°18·6′W	X	19
Gleann Breac-nic	Stir	NN6212	56°17·1′	4°13·3′W	H	57
Gleann Buidhe	Arg & Bt	NR7783	55°59·5′	5°34·1′W	X	55
Gleann Bun an Easa	Arg & Bt	NR2946	55°38·2′	6°17·9′W	X	60
Gleann Cailliche	Pth & Kin	NN3742	56°32·8′	4°38·6′W	X	50
Gleann Camgharaidh	Highld	NM9888	56°56·6′	5°18·8′W	X	40
Gleann Canachadan	Arg & Bt	NN1704	56°11·9′	4°56·5′W	X	56
Gleann Carnach	Pth & Kin	NO1570	56°49·1′	3°23·1′W	X	43
Gleann Carn nan Dobhran	Highld	NM4198	57°0·3′	6°15·5′W	X	39
Gleann Casaig	Stir	NN5410	56°15·9′	4°21·0′W	X	57
Gleann Chàradail	Highld	NM4686	56°54·0′	6°9·8′W	X	39
Gleann Chasdail Mhóir	N Eil	NB3445	58°19·0′	6°32·1′W	X	8
Gleann Chill Donnain	N Eil	NF7427	57°13·3′	7°23·7′W	X	22
Gleann Chinn Eastail	N Eil	NB3911	58°1·0′	6°24·7′W	X	14
Gleann Chlacha Móra	Arg & Bt	NM4328	56°22·7′	6°9·3′W	X	48
Gleann Chliostair	N Eil	NB0711	57°59·8′	6°57·1′W	X	13,14
Gleann Chòinneachain	Highld	NG9922	57°14·9′	5°19·4′W	X	25,33
Gleann Choireadail	Arg & Bt	NR4460	55°46·2′	6°4·5′W	X	60
Gleann Chomhraig	Highld	NN7896	57°2·6′	4°0·2′W	X	35
Gleann Chomraidh	Pth & Kin	NN4854	56°39·4′	4°28·3′W	X	42,51
Gleann Chorainn	Highld	NH2549	57°30·1′	4°54·8′W	X	25
Gleann Chorcaill	Highld	NC9657	58°29·6′	3°46·6′W	X	11
Gleann Chrois	N Eil	NB5060	58°27·7′	6°16·7′W	X	8
Gleann Cia-aig	Highld	NN1890	56°58·2′	4°59·2′W	X	34
Gleann Cinn-locha	Arg & Bt	NR7879	55°57·4′	5°32·9′W	X	62
Gleann Coire Liunndrein	Arg & Bt	NR4458	55°45·1′	6°4·4′W	X	60

Gleann Coradail	N Eil	NF8231	57°15·8′	7°16·0′W	X	22
Gleann Corcadail	N Eil	NB2941	58°16·7′	6°36·9′W	X	8,13
Gleann Cormascoit	N Eil	NF8229	57°14·7′	7°15·9′W	X	22
Gleann Còsaidh	Highld	NG9302	57°4·0′	5°24·4′W	X	33
Gleann Crotha	Stir	NN5020	56°21·2′	4°25·2′W	X	51,57
Gleann Culanach	Arg & Bt	NS2698	56°8·8′	4°47·6′W	X	56
Gleann Cùl an Staca	Highld	NM8588	56°56·3′	5°31·6′W	X	40
Gleann Cùl na Beinne	N Eil	NG2299	57°53·9′	6°41·1′W	X	14
Gleann Dà-Eig	Pth & Kin	NN6045	56°34·8′	4°16·3′W	X	51
Gleann Dà-ghob	Pth & Kin	NN6945	56°35·0′	4°7·5′W	X	51
Gleann Daimh	Pth & Kin	NN4446	56°35·1′	4°32·0′W	X	51
Gleann dà Leirg	Arg & Bt	NR8478	55°57·0′	5°27·1′W	X	62
Gleann Diomhan	N Ayr	NR9346	55°40·1′	5°17·1′W	X	62,69
Gleann Dìridh	Pth & Kin	NN8775	56°51·4′	3°50·7′W	X	43
Gleann Doire Dhubhaig	Arg & Bt	NM4834	56°26·1′	6°4·8′W	X	47,48
Gleann Domhain	Arg & Bt	NM8609	56°13·8′	5°26·7′W	X	55
Gleann Domhanaidh	Highld	NN1577	56°51·1′	5°1·6′W	X	41
Gleann Donn	Highld	NM8784	56°54·2′	5°29·4′W	X	40
Gleann Dorch	Arg & Bt	NR5884	55°59·5′	5°52·4′W	X	61
Gleann Dorch	Arg & Bt	NR6897	56°6·8′	5°43·5′W	X	55,61
Gleann Dorchaidh	N Eil	NF7934	57°17·3′	7°19·2′W	X	22
Gleann Drochaide	Arg & Bt	NR7544	55°38·5′	5°34·1′W	X	62,69
Gleann Droighneach	Arg & Bt	NR2159	55°44·9′	6°26·3′W	X	60
Gleann Dubh	Arg & Bt	NM5330	56°24·1′	5°59·7′W	X	48
Gleann Dubh	Arg & Bt	NM9842	56°31·9′	5°16·6′W	X	49
Gleann Dubh	Arg & Bt	NN0041	56°31·4′	5°14·6′W	W	50
Gleann Dubh	Arg & Bt	NR4277	55°55·3′	6°7·3′W	X	60,61
Gleann Dubh	Arg & Bt	NR4458	55°45·1′	6°4·4′W	X	60
Gleann Dubh	Arg & Bt	NS0898	56°8·4′	5°5·0′W	X	56
Gleann Dubh	Highld	NC2720	58°8·4′	4°55·9′W	X	15
Gleann Dubh	Highld	NC2933	58°15·4′	4°54·4′W	X	15
Gleann Dubh	Highld	NC9957	58°29·6′	3°43·5′W	X	11
Gleann Dubh	Highld	NH1743	57°26·7′	5°2·5′W	X	25
Gleann Dubh	Highld	NM7353	56°37·1′	5°41·5′W	X	49
Gleann Dubh	Highld	NM7377	56°50·0′	5°42·8′W	X	40
Gleann Dubh	N Ayr	NR9647	55°40·7′	5°14·2′W	X	62,69
Gleann Dubh	N Ayr	NR9833	55°33·2′	5°11·7′W	X	69
Gleann Dubh	N Eil	NB0413	58°0·7′	7°0·3′W	X	13
Gleann Dubh	Stir	NN4003	56°11·8′	4°34·3′W	X	56
Gleann Dubh	Stir	NN4915	56°18·5′	4°26·0′W	X	57
Gleann Dubh	Stir	NN5327	56°25·0′	4°22·5′W	X	51
Gleann Dubh Lighe	Highld	NM9482	56°53·3′	5°22·4′W	X	40
Gleann Dubhlinn	N Eil	NG0894	57°50·7′	6°54·8′W	X	14,18
Gleann Dubh Lochain	Highld	NG9010	57°8·2′	5°27·8′W	X	33
Gleann Duibhe	Pth & Kin	NN4554	56°39·4′	4°31·3′W	X	42,51
Gleann Eachach	Highld	NN3494	57°0·7′	4°43·6′W	X	34
Gleann Easan Biorach	N Ayr	NR9548	55°41·2′	5°15·2′W	X	62,69
Gleann Easbuig	N Ayr	NR9536	55°34·7′	5°14·7′W	X	68,69
Gleann Einich	Highld	NH9202	57°6·0′	3°46·5′W	X	36
Gleann Eiracleit	N Eil	NB2638	58°15·0′	6°39·7′W	X	8,13
Gleann Èireraigh	N Eil	NB3249	58°21·1′	6°34·4′W	X	8
Gleann Eoghainn	Highld	NG3047	57°26·2′	6°29·5′W	X	23
Gleann Euscleit	N Eil	NB4147	58°20·4′	6°25·1′W	X	8
Gleann Fada	Highld	NH1616	57°12·1′	5°2·3′W	X	34
Gleann Fearna	Arg & Bt	NM9221	56°20·4′	5°21·5′W	X	49
Gleann Fearnach	Pth & Kin	NO0368	56°47·9′	3°34·8′W	X	43
Gleann Fèith' n Amean	Highld	NM8862	56°42·4′	5°27·4′W	X	40
Gleann Fhaolain	Highld	NN1552	56°37·7′	5°0·5′W	X	41
Gleann Fhiodhaig	Highld	NH1548	57°29·3′	5°4·7′W	X	25
Gleann Fionnlighe	Highld	NM9782	56°53·4′	5°19·5′W	X	40
Gleann Fuar	Arg & Bt	NN2439	56°30·9′	4°51·2′W	X	50
Gleann Gaoithe	Stir	NN3706	56°13·4′	4°37·3′W	X	56
Gleann Gaorsaic	Highld	NH0222	57°15·0′	5°16·5′W	X	25,33
Gleann Geal	Highld	NM7249	56°34·9′	5°42·3′W	X	49
Gleann Ghàireasdail	Arg & Bt	NR4361	55°46·7′	6°5·5′W	X	60
Gleann Gheurasdail	N Eil	NG1098	57°52·9′	6°53·1′W	X	14
Gleann Ghòinean	Pth & Kin	NN6920	56°21·5′	4°6·8′W	X	51,57
Gleann Glas Dhoire	Highld	NN3184	56°55·3′	4°46·1′W	X	34,41
Gleann Gniomhaidh	Highld	NH0519	57°13·5′	5°13·3′W	X	33
Gleann Gniomhaidh	Highld	NH0520	57°14·0′	5°13·4′W	X	25,33
Gleann Goibhre	Highld	NH4248	57°29·9′	4°37·7′W	X	26
Gleann Grunndail	Arg & Bt	NR5271	55°52·4′	5°57·4′W	X	61
Gleann Guid	Arg & Bt	NR6594	56°5·1′	5°46·2′W	X	55,61
Gleann Horavaig	Highld	NG6709	57°7·0′	5°50·5′W	X	32
Gleann Horgaboist	N Eil	NG0595	57°51·1′	6°57·9′W	X	14,18
Gleann Horsa-cleit	N Eil	NG0189	57°47·7′	7°1·5′W	X	18
Gleann Innis an Loichel	Highld	NH1737	57°23·5′	5°2·2′W	X	25
Gleann Ioagro	N Eil	NB3242	58°17·4′	6°33·9′W	X	8,13
Gleann Iolairean	Highld	NN3167	56°46·1′	4°45·5′W	X	41
Gleann Iubharnadeal	Arg & Bt	NR4869	55°51·2′	6°1·1′W	X	60,61
Gleann Labasdail	N Eil	NF7823	57°11·3′	7°19·4′W	X	22
Gleann Lacasdail	N Eil	NB1802	57°55·4′	6°45·3′W	X	14
Gleann Lacasdail	N Eil	NB1803	57°55·9′	6°45·4′W	X	13,14
Gleann Lacasdail	N Eil	NB2707	57°58·4′	6°36·6′W	X	13,14
Gleann Laoigh	Arg & Bt	NR7848	55°40·7′	5°31·4′W	X	62,69
Gleann Laoigh	Arg & Bt	NS0686	56°1·9′	5°6·4′W	X	56
Gleann Laoigh	Highld	NC1609	58°2·2′	5°6·5′W	X	15
Gleann Laragain	Highld	NN1179	56°52·1′	5°5·6′W	X	41
Gleann Lèan	Arg & Bt	NM6235	56°27·1′	5°51·3′W	X	49
Gleann Leireag	Highld	NC1630	58°13·5′	5°7·5′W	X	15
Gleann Leitir	N Eil	NB3139	58°15·7′	6°34·7′W	X	8,13
Gleann Leòra	Arg & Bt	NR4255	55°43·4′	6°6·1′W	X	60
Gleann Liath	Highld	NH5121	57°15·6′	4°27·8′W	X	26,35
Gleann Liathdail	N Eil	NF8230	57°15·3′	7°16·0′W	X	22
Gleann Lichd	Highld	NG9918	57°12·8′	5°19·3′W	X	33
Gleann Lingdail	N Eil	NG1092	57°49·7′	6°52·6′W	X	14
Gleann Lìrein	Arg & Bt	NM6834	56°26·7′	5°45·4′W	X	49
Gleann Loch	Arg & Bt	NR8187	56°1·8′	5°30·5′W	W	55
Gleann Loch an Eilein	N Eil	NB4442	58°17·8′	6°21·7′W	X	8
Gleann Loch Fheòir	N Eil	NB3205	57°57·5′	6°31·4′W	X	13,14
Gleann Màma	Highld	NM7484	56°53·8′	5°42·2′W	X	40
Gleann Maraiche	Arg & Bt	NR3863	55°47·6′	6°10·4′W	X	60,61
Gleann Meadail	Highld	NM8298	57°1·6′	5°35·1′W	X	33,40
Gleann Meadhonach	Highld	NG5905	57°4·6′	5°58·1′W	X	32,39
Gleann Meadhonach	Stir	NS4198	56°9·2′	4°33·1′W	X	56
Gleann Measham	Arg & Bt	NM9616	56°17·8′	5°17·4′W	X	55
Gleann Mèinich	Highld	NH2553	57°32·3′	4°54·9′W	X	25
Gleann Meodal	Highld	NG6610	57°7·5′	5°51·5′W	X	32
Gleann Meran	Pth & Kin	NN3943	56°33·3′	4°36·7′W	X	50
Gleann Mhairc	Pth & Kin	NN8874	56°50·9′	3°49·7′W	X	43

Gleann Mhàirteinn	Highld	NM3979	56°50·0′	6°16·3′W	X	39
Gleann Mhàrtuin	Arg & Bt	NR3766	55°49·2′	6°11·5′W	X	60,61
Gleann Mhiabhaig	N Eil	NB0908	57°58·2′	6°54·8′W	X	13,14
Gleann Mhic Phàil	Highld	NM9167	56°45·1′	5°24·7′W	X	40
Gleann Mhuire	Highld	NH5078	57°46·3′	4°30·8′W	X	20
Gleann Modail	N Eil	NB0512	58°0·2′	6°59·2′W	X	13,14
Gleann Mór	Arg & Bt	NM3521	56°18·7′	6°16·7′W	X	48
Gleann Mór	Arg & Bt	NM8027	56°23·3′	5°33·4′W	X	49
Gleann Mór	Arg & Bt	NM8613	56°15·9′	5°26·9′W	X	55
Gleann Mór	Arg & Bt	NN2106	56°13·0′	4°52·8′W	X	56
Gleann Mór	Arg & Bt	NR2458	55°44·5′	6°23·4′W	X	60
Gleann Mór	Arg & Bt	NR3145	55°37·7′	6°16·0′W	X	60
Gleann Mór	Arg & Bt	NR3166	55°49·0′	6°17·2′W	X	60,61
Gleann Mór	Highld	NH1878	57°45·6′	5°3·1′W	X	20
Gleann Mór	Highld	NH3885	57°49·8′	4°43·2′W	X	20
Gleann Mór	Highld	NH8628	57°20·0′	3°53·2′W	X	35,36
Gleann Mòr	N Eil	NB4757	58°26·0′	6°19·6′W	X	8
Gleann Mòr	N Eil	NF0899	57°48·8′	8°35·7′W	X	18
Gleann Mòr	N Eil	NF8125	57°12·5′	7°16·6′W	X	22
Gleann-Mór	N Eil	NL6490	56°53·0′	7°30·6′W	X	31
Gleann Mór	Pth & Kin	NN7353	56°39·4′	4°3·9′W	X	42,51,52
Gleann Mór	Pth & Kin	NO0176	56°52·2′	3°37·0′W	X	43
Gleann Mòr Bharabhais	N Eil	NB3746	58°19·7′	6°29·1′W	X	8
Gleann Mòr Shiaboist	N Eil	NB2644	58°18·2′	6°40·2′W	X	8
Gleann Muilinn	Pth & Kin	NN7150	56°37·7′	4°5·7′W	X	42,51,52
Gleann na Beinne Fada	Arg & Bt	NM5235	56°26·8′	6°1·0′W	X	47,48
Gleann na Bèiste	Highld	NG7425	57°15·9′	5°44·4′W	X	33
Gleann na Bèiste	N Eil	NF9075	57°39·8′	7°11·5′W	X	18
Gleann na Caillich	Arg & Bt	NR3876	55°54·6′	6°11·1′W	X	60,61
Gleann na Caorainn	Arg & Bt	NS2993	56°6·2′	4°44·5′W	X	56
Gleann na Ciche	Highld	NH1217	57°12·6′	5°6·3′W	X	34
Gleann na Cloiche Sgoilte	Highld	NM8969	56°46·2′	5°26·7′W	X	40
Gleann na Curra	Arg & Bt	NM8128	56°23·9′	5°32·5′W	X	49
Gleann na Gaoithe	Highld	NC0812	58°3·6′	5°14·8′W	X	15
Gleann na Giubhsachan	Highld	NN2866	56°45·5′	4°48·4′W	X	41
Gleann na Guiserein	Highld	NG7703	57°4·1′	5°40·3′W	X	33
Gleann na h-Airigh Riabhaich	N Eil	NB3308	57°59·1′	6°30·6′W	X	13,14
Gleann na h-Iola	Arg & Bt	NM9847	56°34·5′	5°16·9′W	X	49
Gleann nam Feannag	Arg & Bt	NR7032	55°31·9′	5°38·2′W	X	68
Gleann nam Fiadh	Highld	NH1626	57°17·5′	5°2·7′W	X	25
Gleann nam Mèirleach	Arg & Bt	NR3976	55°54·6′	6°10·2′W	X	60,61
Gleann na Muic	Arg & Bt	NM3419	56°17·6′	6°17·5′W	X	48
Gleann na Muic	Highld	NC3713	58°4·8′	4°45·4′W	X	16
Gleann na Muice	Highld	NH0477	57°44·7′	5°17·1′W	X	19
Gleann na Muice	Highld	NH0666	57°38·8′	5°14·6′W	X	19
Gleann na Muice Beag	Highld	NH0378	57°45·2′	5°18·2′W	X	19
Gleann nan Caorach	N Eil	NB4439	58°16·2′	6°21·5′W	X	8
Gleann nan Caorann	Stir	NN3020	56°20·8′	4°44·6′W	X	50,56
Gleann nan Clach Reamhar	Arg & Bt	NR5588	56°1·6′	5°55·5′W	X	61
Gleann nan Eun	Highld	NH4409	57°9·0′	4°34·3′W	X	34
Gleann nan Iomairean	Highld	NM5950	56°35·1′	5°55·0′W	X	47
Gleann nan Laogh	Arg & Bt	NR7667	55°50·9′	5°34·3′W	X	62
Gleann nan Iomairean	Highld	NM6050	56°35·1′	5°54·1′W	X	49
Gleann na Rainich	Arg & Bt	NR1853	55°41·6′	6°28·8′W	X	60
Gleann na Sguaib	Highld	NH2284	57°48·9′	4°59·3′W	X	20
Gleann na Sìga	N Eil	NB4656	58°25·4′	6°20·5′W	X	8
Gleann na Speireig	Highld	NH5064	57°38·7′	4°30·3′W	X	20
Gleann Oraid	Highld	NG3330	57°17·2′	6°25·4′W	X	32
Gleann Oramul	N Eil	NG0188	57°47·2′	7°1·4′W	X	18
Gleann Osamail	Arg & Bt	NR2362	55°46·6′	6°24·6′W	X	60
Gleann Rainich	Highld	NM7230	56°24·7′	5°41·3′W	X	49
Gleann Riabhach	Stir	NN4805	56°13·1′	4°26·6′W	X	57
Gleann Rìgh	Highld	NN0562	56°42·8′	5°10·7′W	X	41
Gleann Sabhail	Arg & Bt	NR7589	56°2·7′	5°36·3′W	X	55
Gleann Salach	Arg & Bt	NM9738	56°29·7′	5°17·4′W	X	49
Gleann Scourie	Highld	NC1744	58°21·0′	5°7·2′W	X	9
Gleann Sèileach	Highld	NH8433	57°22·6′	3°55·3′W	X	27
Gleann Seileach	Highld	NN0463	56°43·3′	5°11·7′W	X	41
Gleann Seilisdeir	Arg & Bt	NM4730	56°23·9′	6°5·6′W	X	48
Gleann Sgaladal	N Eil	NB0220	58°4·4′	7°2·8′W	X	13
Gleann Sheileach	Arg & Bt	NM8528	56°24·0′	5°28·6′W	X	49
Gleann Sheileasdail	N Eil	NF8231	57°15·8′	7°16·0′W	X	22
Gleann Sheileboist	N Eil	NG0695	57°51·1′	6°56·9′W	X	14,18
Gleann Shiadair	N Eil	NB4151	58°22·5′	6°25·3′W	X	8
Gleann Shòrdail	N Eil	NB3849	58°21·3′	6°28·3′W	X	8
Gleann Shranndabhal	N Eil	NG0285	57°45·6′	7°0·2′W	X	18
Gleann Sithidh	Highld	NH0727	57°17·8′	5°11·7′W	X	25,33
Gleann Sleibhte-coire	Arg & Bt	NM6530	56°24·5′	5°48·1′W	X	49
Gleann Speireig	Arg & Bt	NR6395	56°5·6′	5°48·2′W	X	61
Gleann Sròn a' Chreagain	Highld	NN0472	56°48·2′	5°12·2′W	X	41
Gleann Stuladail	N Eil	NB1112	58°0·5′	6°53·1′W	X	13,14
Gleann Suainagadail	N Eil	NB3340	58°16·3′	6°32·7′W	X	8,13
Gleann Sùileag	Highld	NN0181	56°52·9′	5°15·5′W	X	41
Gleann Taitneach	Pth & Kin	NO0874	56°51·2′	3°30·1′W	X	43
Gleann Tanagaidh	Highld	NH0866	57°38·8′	5°12·6′W	X	19
Gleann Taodhail	Highld	NM8589	56°56·8′	5°31·6′W	X	40
Gleann Tarsuinn	Arg & Bt	NR7679	55°57·4′	5°34·9′W	X	62
Gleann Tarsuinn	Highld	NN1793	56°59·8′	5°0·3′W	X	34
Gleann Thagaro	N Eil	NB2746	58°19·3′	6°39·3′W	X	8
Gleann Tholastaidh	N Eil	NB5244	58°19·1′	6°13·6′W	X	8
Gleann Tholastaidh	N Eil	NB5245	58°19·7′	6°13·7′W	X	8
Gleann Tobhtan 'ic Fannan	N Eil	NG0998	57°52·9′	6°54·1′W	X	14
Gleann Torradail	N Eil	NB2940	58°16·2′	6°36·8′W	X	8,13
Gleann Torra-mhichaig	Highld	NG5330	57°17·9′	6°5·6′W	X	24,32
Gleann Trolamaraig	N Eil	NB2001	57°54·9′	6°43·2′W	X	14
Gleann Tuath	Arg & Bt	NR2170	55°50·8′	6°27·0′W	X	60
Gleann Uachdrach	N Eil	NG0090	57°48·2′	7°2·6′W	X	18
Gleann Uaine	Arg & Bt	NN2611	56°15·8′	4°48·1′W	X	50,56
Gleann Udalain	Highld	NG8528	57°17·8′	5°33·7′W	X	33
Gleann Udalain	Highld	NG8730	57°18·9′	5°31·8′W	X	24
Gleann Uisinis	N Eil	NF8333	57°16·9′	7°15·2′W	X	22
Gleann Uisleitir	N Eil	NB1109	57°58·8′	6°52·9′W	X	13,14
Gleann Uisliti r	N Eil	NB1000	57°54·0′	6°53·2′W	X	14
Gleann Ulladail	N Eil	NB0814	58°1·4′	6°56·3′W	X	13,14
Gleann Ullibh	Arg & Bt	NR4666	55°49·5′	6°2·9′W	X	60,61
Gleann Unndalain	Highld	NG8702	57°3·9′	5°30·3′W	X	33
Gleaston	Cumbr	SD2570	54°7·5′	3°8·4′W	T	96

Gleaston Castle	Cumbr	SD2671	54°8·0'	3°7·5'W	A	96,97
Gleaston Park	Cumbr	SD2670	54°7·5'	3°7·5'W	X	96,97
Gleat	Orkney	HY7546	59°18·2'	2°25·9'W	X	5
Glebe	Hants	SU5515	50°56·1'	1°12·6'W	T	196
Glebe	Highld	NH5118	57°14·0'	4°27·7'W	X	35
Glebe	Orkney	HY2628	59°8·2'	3°17·1'W	X	6
Glebe	Shetld	HU4940	60°8·8'	1°6·6'W	T	4
Glebe	Sund	NZ3056	54°54·1'	1°31·5'W	T	88
Glebe Barn	N Yks	SE3091	54°19·1'	1°31·9'W	X	99
Glebe Cliff	Corn	SX0488	50°39·8'	4°46·0'W	X	200
Glebe Cott	E Yorks	TA0371	54°7·7'	0°25·0'W	X	101
Glebe Farm	Birm	SP1387	52°29·1'	1°48·1'W	FM	139
Glebe Fm	Beds	SP9462	52°15·1'	0°37·0'W	FM	153
Glebe Fm	Beds	TL1756	52°11·6'	0°16·9'W	FM	153
Glebe Fm	Bucks	SP6517	51°51·1'	1°3·0'W	FM	164,165
Glebe Fm	Bucks	SP8723	51°54·2'	0°43·7'W	FM	165
Glebe Fm	Cambs	TL0876	52°22·5'	0°24·4'W	FM	142
Glebe Fm	Cambs	TL1274	52°21·4'	0°20·9'W	FM	142
Glebe Fm	Cambs	TL1583	52°26·2'	0°18·1'W	FM	142
Glebe Fm	Cambs	TL3361	52°14·1'	0°2·7'W	FM	154
Glebe Fm	Cambs	TL4371	52°19·3'	0°6·3'E	FM	154
Glebe Fm	Cambs	TL6354	52°9·8'	0°23·4'E	FM	154
Glebe Fm	Ches	SJ5980	53°19·2'	2°36·5'W	FM	108
Glebe Fm	Cumbr	NY1934	54°41·9'	3°15·0'W	FM	89,90
Glebe Fm	Darl	NZ3821	54°35·2'	1°24·3'W	FM	93
Glebe Fm	Derby	SK3928	52°51·1'	1°24·8'W	FM	128
Glebe Fm	Derby	SK4230	52°52·2'	1°22·2'W	FM	129
Glebe Fm	Devon	SS4904	50°49·2'	4°8·2'W	FM	191
Glebe Fm	Devon	ST0801	50°48·3'	3°18·0'W	FM	192
Glebe Fm	Devon	SX5698	50°46·1'	4°2·1'W	FM	191
Glebe Fm	Devon	SX8595	50°44·8'	3°37·4'W	FM	191
Glebe Fm	Dorset	ST7108	50°52·5'	2°24·3'W	FM	194
Glebe Fm	Dorset	ST8903	50°49·8'	2°9·0'W	FM	195
Glebe Fm	Dorset	SY7285	50°40·1'	2°23·4'W	FM	194
Glebe Fm	Durham	NZ1054	54°53·1'	1°50·2'W	FM	88
Glebe Fm	Essex	TL8312	51°46·8'	0°39·6'E	FM	168
Glebe Fm	Essex	TL9902	51°41·1'	0°53·1'E	FM	168
Glebe Fm	E Yorks	SE7338	53°50·2'	0°53·0'W	FM	105,106
Glebe Fm	E Yorks	SE7943	53°52·9'	0°47·5'W	FM	105,106
Glebe Fm	E Yorks	SE7958	54°1·0'	0°47·2'W	FM	105,106
Glebe Fm	E Yorks	SE8240	53°51·2'	0°44·8'W	FM	106
Glebe Fm	E Yorks	SE8633	53°47·4'	0°41·3'W	FM	106
Glebe Fm	E Yorks	SE8755	53°59·3'	0°40·0'W	FM	106
Glebe Fm	E Yorks	SE9848	53°55·4'	0°30·0'W	FM	106
Glebe Fm	E Yorks	TA0836	53°48·8'	0°21·2'W	FM	107
Glebe Fm	E Yorks	TA0844	53°53·1'	0°21·0'W	FM	107
Glebe Fm	E Yorks	TA2932	53°46·3'	0°2·1'W	FM	107
Glebe Fm	Glos	SO5903	51°43·7'	2°35·2'W	FM	162
Glebe Fm	Glos	SO9328	51°57·3'	2°5·7'W	FM	150,163
Glebe Fm	Glos	SP0604	51°44·3'	1°54·4'W	FM	163
Glebe Fm	Glos	SU0096	51°40·0'	1°59·6'W	FM	163
Glebe Fm	Hants	SU1019	50°58·5'	1°51·1'W	FM	184
Glebe Fm	Herts	TL2339	52°2·4'	0°12·0'W	FM	153
Glebe Fm	I of W	SZ4287	50°41·1'	1°23·9'W	FM	196
Glebe Fm	Leic	SK3103	52°37·7'	1°32·1'W	FM	140
Glebe Fm	Leic	SK4314	52°43·6'	1°21·4'W	FM	129
Glebe Fm	Leic	SK4622	52°47·9'	1°18·7'W	FM	129
Glebe Fm	Leic	SK6613	52°42·9'	1°1·0'W	FM	129
Glebe Fm	Leic	SK6914	52°43·4'	0°58·3'W	FM	129
Glebe Fm	Leic	SK7003	52°37·4'	0°57·6'W	FM	141
Glebe Fm	Leic	SK7021	52°47·2'	0°57·3'W	FM	129
Glebe Fm	Leic	SK7303	52°37·4'	0°54·9'W	FM	141
Glebe Fm	Leic	SK7836	52°55·2'	0°50·0'W	FM	129
Glebe Fm	Leic	SK7928	52°50·9'	0°49·2'W	FM	129
Glebe Fm	Leic	SP4497	52°34·4'	1°20·6'W	FM	140
Glebe Fm	Leic	SP5283	52°26·8'	1°13·7'W	FM	140
Glebe Fm	Leic	SP5794	52°32·7'	1°9·2'W	FM	140
Glebe Fm	Leic	SP6297	52°34·3'	1°4·7'W	FM	140
Glebe Fm	Leic	SP6381	52°25·6'	1°4·0'W	FM	140
Glebe Fm	Lincs	SE8501	53°30·2'	0°42·7'W	FM	112
Glebe Fm	Lincs	SK8434	52°54·0'	0°44·7'W	FM	130
Glebe Fm	Lincs	SK8439	52°56·7'	0°44·6'W	FM	130
Glebe Fm	Lincs	SK8694	53°26·4'	0°41·9'W	FM	112
Glebe Fm	Lincs	SK8845	52°59·9'	0°40·9'W	FM	130
Glebe Fm	Lincs	SK9024	52°48·6'	0°39·5'W	FM	130
Glebe Fm	Lincs	SK9252	53°3·7'	0°37·2'W	FM	121
Glebe Fm	Lincs	SK9385	53°21·5'	0°35·7'W	FM	112,121
Glebe Fm	Lincs	SK9878	53°17·6'	0°31·4'W	FM	121
Glebe Fm	Lincs	SK9917	52°44·7'	0°31·6'W	FM	130
Glebe Fm	Lincs	SK9938	52°56·0'	0°31·2'W	FM	130
Glebe Fm	Lincs	SK9941	52°57·7'	0°31·2'W	FM	130
Glebe Fm	Lincs	SK9963	53°9·5'	0°30·8'W	FM	121
Glebe Fm	Lincs	TF0018	52°45·3'	0°30·7'W	FM	130
Glebe Fm	Lincs	TF0069	53°12·8'	0°29·7'W	FM	121
Glebe Fm	Lincs	TF0146	53°0·3'	0°29·3'W	FM	130
Glebe Fm	Lincs	TF0182	53°19·8'	0°28·6'W	FM	121
Glebe Fm	Lincs	TF0190	53°24·1'	0°28·4'W	FM	112
Glebe Fm	Lincs	TF0262	53°9·0'	0°28·1'W	FM	121
Glebe Fm	Lincs	TF0455	53°5·2'	0°26·4'W	FM	121
Glebe Fm	Lincs	TF0692	53°25·1'	0°23·9'W	FM	112
Glebe Fm	Lincs	TF0726	52°49·5'	0°24·3'W	FM	130
Glebe Fm	Lincs	TF0888	53°22·9'	0°22·2'W	FM	112,121
Glebe Fm	Lincs	TF1085	53°21·3'	0°20·4'W	FM	121
Glebe Fm	Lincs	TF1462	53°8·8'	0°17·3'W	FM	121
Glebe Fm	Lincs	TF1636	52°54·8'	0°16·1'W	FM	130
Glebe Fm	Lincs	TF1640	52°56·9'	0°16·0'W	FM	130
Glebe Fm	Lincs	TF1680	53°18·5'	0°15·1'W	FM	121
Glebe Fm	Lincs	TF1846	53°0·1'	0°14·1'W	FM	130
Glebe Fm	Lincs	TF1976	53°16·3'	0°12·5'W	FM	122
Glebe Fm	Lincs	TF2020	52°46·1'	0°12·9'W	FM	131
Glebe Fm	Lincs	TF2154	53°4·4'	0°11·2'W	FM	122
Glebe Fm	Lincs	TF2179	53°17·9'	0°10·7'W	FM	122
Glebe Fm	Lincs	TF2364	53°9·8'	0°9·2'W	FM	122
Glebe Fm	Lincs	TF2465	53°10·3'	0°8·3'W	FM	122
Glebe Fm	Lincs	TF2471	53°13·5'	0°8·1'W	FM	122
Glebe Fm	Lincs	TF2484	53°20·5'	0°7·8'W	FM	122
Glebe Fm	Lincs	TF2574	53°15·1'	0°7·2'W	FM	122
Glebe Fm	Lincs	TF2686	53°21·6'	0°6·0'W	FM	113,122
Glebe Fm	Lincs	TF2872	53°14·0'	0°4·5'W	FM	122
Glebe Fm	Lincs	TF2966	53°10·8'	0°3·8'W	FM	122

Glebe Fm	Lincs	TF3075	53°15·6'	0°2·7'W	FM	122
Glebe Fm	Lincs	TF3275	53°15·6'	0°0·9'W	FM	122
Glebe Fm	Lincs	TF3764	53°9·6'	0°3·4'E	FM	122
Glebe Fm	Lincs	TF3766	53°10·6'	0°3·4'E	FM	122
Glebe Fm	Lincs	TF4145	52°59·3'	0°6·4'E	FM	131
Glebe Fm	Lincs	TF4185	53°20·8'	0°7·5'E	FM	122
Glebe Fm	Lincs	TF4365	53°10·0'	0°8·8'E	FM	122
Glebe Fm	Lincs	TF4566	53°10·5'	0°10·6'E	FM	122
Glebe Fm	Lincs	TF4778	53°16·9'	0°12·7'E	FM	122
Glebe Fm	Mil Key	SP9033	51°59·5'	0°41·0'W	FM	152,165
Glebe Fm	N Lanak	NS8362	55°50·5'	3°51·7'W	FM	65
Glebe Fm	N Lincs	SE8105	53°32·4'	0°46·3'W	FM	112
Glebe Fm	N Lincs	SE9020	53°40·4'	0°37·8'W	FM	106,112
Glebe Fm	N Lincs	TA0421	53°40·7'	0°25·1'W	FM	107,112
Glebe Fm	N Lincs	TA0709	53°34·2'	0°22·6'W	FM	112
Glebe Fm	N Lincs	TA1015	53°37·4'	0°19·8'W	FM	113
Glebe Fm	N Lincs	TA1123	53°41·7'	0°18·7'W	FM	107,113
Glebe Fm	Norf	TG0906	52°36·9'	1°5·6'E	FM	144
Glebe Fm	Norf	TG2022	52°45·3'	1°16·0'E	FM	133,134
Glebe Fm	Norf	TG2134	52°51·7'	1°17·4'E	FM	133
Glebe Fm	Norf	TG4115	52°41·0'	1°34·3'E	FM	134
Glebe Fm	Norf	TM1297	52°32·0'	1°8·0'E	FM	144
Glebe Fm	Northnts	SP5439	52°3·0'	1°12·4'W	FM	152
Glebe Fm	Northnts	SP5748	52°7·9'	1°9·6'W	FM	152
Glebe Fm	Northnts	SP5842	52°4·6'	1°8·8'W	FM	152
Glebe Fm	Northnts	SP6154	52°11·1'	1°6·1'W	FM	152
Glebe Fm	Northnts	SP6372	52°20·8'	1°4·1'W	FM	140
Glebe Fm	Northnts	SP6548	52°7·8'	1°2·6'W	FM	152
Glebe Fm	Northnts	SP6565	52°17·0'	1°2·4'W	FM	152
Glebe Fm	Northnts	SP7065	52°17·0'	0°58·0'W	FM	152
Glebe Fm	Northnts	SP7372	52°20·7'	0°55·3'W	FM	141
Glebe Fm	Northnts	SP7754	52°11·0'	0°52·0'W	FM	152
Glebe Fm	Northnts	SP8479	52°24·4'	0°45·5'W	FM	141
Glebe Fm	Northnts	SP8673	52°21·1'	0°43·8'W	FM	141
Glebe Fm	Northnts	SP9159	52°13·5'	0°39·7'W	FM	152
Glebe Fm	Northnts	SP9279	52°24·3'	0°38·5'W	FM	141
Glebe Fm	Northnts	SP9669	52°18·9'	0°35·1'W	FM	153
Glebe Fm	Northnts	SP9693	52°31·8'	0°34·7'W	FM	141
Glebe Fm	Northum	NZ2583	55°8·7'	1°36·0'W	FM	81
Glebe Fm	Notts	SK5231	52°52·7'	1°13·2'W	FM	129
Glebe Fm	Notts	SK5430	52°52·1'	1°11·5'W	FM	129
Glebe Fm	Notts	SK5826	52°49·9'	1°7·9'W	FM	129
Glebe Fm	Notts	SK6034	52°54·2'	1°6·1'W	FM	129
Glebe Fm	Notts	SK6143	52°59·1'	1°5·1'W	FM	129
Glebe Fm	Notts	SK6333	52°53·7'	1°3·4'W	FM	129
Glebe Fm	Notts	SK6343	52°59·1'	1°3·3'W	FM	129
Glebe Fm	Notts	SK6944	52°59·6'	0°57·9'W	FM	129
Glebe Fm	Notts	SK7044	52°59·6'	0°57·0'W	FM	129
Glebe Fm	Notts	SK7131	52°52·5'	0°56·3'W	FM	129
Glebe Fm	Notts	SK7148	53°1·7'	0°56·1'W	FM	129
Glebe Fm	Notts	SK7276	53°16·8'	0°54·8'W	FM	120
Glebe Fm	Notts	SK7661	53°8·7'	0°51·4'W	FM	120
Glebe Fm	N Yks	NZ2214	54°31·5'	1°39·2'W	FM	93
Glebe Fm	N Yks	NZ4207	54°27·6'	1°20·7'W	FM	93
Glebe Fm	N Yks	SE1787	54°16·9'	1°43·9'W	FM	99
Glebe Fm	N Yks	SE2694	54°20·7'	1°35·6'W	FM	99
Glebe Fm	N Yks	SE7178	54°11·8'	0°54·3'W	FM	100
Glebe Fm	N Yks	SE8367	54°5·8'	0°43·4'W	FM	100
Glebe Fm	Oxon	SP2501	51°42·7'	1°37·9'W	FM	163
Glebe Fm	Oxon	SP2727	51°56·7'	1°36·0'W	FM	163
Glebe Fm	Oxon	SP2819	51°52·4'	1°35·2'W	FM	163
Glebe Fm	Oxon	SP5927	51°56·5'	1°8·1'W	FM	164
Glebe Fm	Peterb	TL2095	52°32·6'	0°13·4'W	FM	142
Glebe Fm	Rut	SK9515	52°43·7'	0°35·2'W	FM	130
Glebe Fm	Shrops	SO6287	52°29·0'	2°33·2'W	FM	138
Glebe Fm	Somer	ST2014	50°55·4'	3°7·9'W	FM	193
Glebe Fm	Suff	TL7458	52°11·8'	0°33·2'E	FM	155
Glebe Fm	Suff	TM0875	52°20·2'	1°3·6'E	FM	144
Glebe Fm	Suff	TM2766	52°14·9'	1°19·9'E	FM	156
Glebe Fm	Suff	TM5288	52°26·1'	1°42·9'E	FM	156
Glebe Fm	Swin	SU1281	51°31·9'	1°49·2'W	FM	173
Glebe Fm	Warw	SP1359	52°14·0'	1°48·2'W	FM	151
Glebe Fm	Warw	SP1449	52°8·6'	1°47·3'W	FM	151
Glebe Fm	Warw	SP3257	52°12·9'	1°31·5'W	FM	151
Glebe Fm	Warw	SP3367	52°18·2'	1°30·6'W	FM	151
Glebe Fm	Warw	SP4355	52°11·7'	1°21·9'W	FM	151
Glebe Fm	Warw	SP4880	52°25·2'	1°17·3'W	FM	140
Glebe Fm	Wilts	SU0492	51°37·8'	1°56·1'W	FM	163,173
Glebe Fm	Wilts	SU0492	51°37·8'	1°56·1'W	FM	163,173
Glebe Fm	Worcs	SO9041	52°4·3'	2°8·4'W	FM	150
Glebe Fm	Wrex	SJ4738	52°56·4'	2°46·9'W	FM	126
Glebe Fm	York	SE5153	53°58·5'	1°12·9'W	FM	105
Glebe Fm	York	SE5847	53°55·2'	1°6·6'W	FM	105
Glebe Fm	York	SE5857	54°0·6'	1°6·5'W	FM	105
Glebefoot	Scot Bord	NT4314	55°25·2'	2°53·6'W	X	79
Glebe Hill	Highld	NM4864	56°42·2'	6°6·6'W	H	47
Glebe Ho	Cumbr	SD1094	54°20·3'	3°22·6'W	X	96
Glebe Ho	Devon	SS4608	50°51·3'	4°10·9'W	X	190
Glebe Ho	Devon	SS7200	50°47·4'	3°48·6'W	X	191
Glebe Ho	Devon	SY2093	50°44·1'	3°7·6'W	X	192,193
Glebe Ho	D & G	NX4756	54°52·8'	4°22·7'W	X	83
Glebe Ho	Essex	TM0018	51°49·7'	0°54·5'E	X	168
Glebe Ho	Essex	TM0332	51°57·2'	0°57·7'E	X	168
Glebe Ho	E Susx	TQ6824	50°59·7'	0°24·0'E	X	199
Glebe Ho	E Susx	TQ8224	50°59·4'	0°36·0'E	X	199
Glebe Ho	E Yorks	SE8249	53°56·1'	0°44·6'W	X	106
Glebe Ho	Northum	NZ1381	55°7·6'	1°47·3'W	X	81
Glebe Ho	Rut	SK9014	52°43·2'	0°39·6'W	X	130
Glebe Ho	Rut	SK9908	52°39·9'	0°31·8'W	X	141
Glebe Ho	Suff	TL6864	52°15·1'	0°28·1'E	X	154
Glebe Ho	Suff	TM3544	52°2·9'	1°26·0'E	X	169
Glebe Ho	Warw	SP2954	52°11·2'	1°34·2'W	X	151
Glebe Ho	Warw	SP3352	52°10·2'	1°30·7'W	X	151
Glebe Ho, The	Suff	TL9438	52°0·6'	0°50·0'E	X	155
Glebe House School	Norf	TF6741	52°56·7'	0°29·5'E	X	132
Glebelands	Cumbr	NY2347	54°49·0'	3°11·5'W	X	85
Glebelands	Cumbr	NY6726	54°37·9'	2°30·3'W	X	91
Glebelands Fm	N Yks	SE4064	54°4·5'	1°22·9'W	FM	99
Glebe Lodge Fm	Leic	SK6114	52°43·4'	1°5·4'W	FM	129
Glebe, The	Cumbr	NY4865	54°58·9'	2°48·3'W	X	86

Glebe, The	Kent	TR0421	50°57·4'	0°54·7'E	X	189
Glebe, The	Pemb	SM8509	51°44·5'	5°6·5'W	X	157
Glebe, The	Shrops	SO5377	52°23·6'	2°41·0'W	X	137,138
Gleckmalloch	D & G	NX3682	55°6·6'	4°33·8'W	X	77
Glecknabae	Arg & Bt	NS0068	55°52·1'	5°11·4'W	X	63
Glecknabae Hill	Arg & Bt	NS0169	55°52·6'	5°10·4'W	H	63
Gleddoch Ho (Hotel)	Renf	NS3872	55°55·1'	4°35·1'W	X	63
Glede Howe	Cumbr	NY5212	54°30·3'	2°44·1'W	X	90
Glede Knowe	Scot Bord	NT3541	55°39·7'	3°1·6'W	H	73
Gledenholm Moor	D & G	NX9887	55°10·3'	3°35·7'W	X	78
Gledfield	Aberd	NJ6155	57°35·3'	2°38·7'W	X	29
Gledfield Ho	Highld	NH5790	57°52·9'	4°24·2'W	X	21
Gled Hill	Wakf	SE3620	53°40·8'	1°26·9'W	X	104
Gledhow	Leeds	SE3136	53°49·4'	1°31·3'W	T	104
Gledlom	Flint	SJ1571	53°14·0'	3°16·0'W	X	116
Gledmein	D & G	NX3651	54°49·9'	4°32·8'W	X	83
Gledpark	D & G	NX6250	54°49·8'	4°8·5'W	X	83
Gledrffordd	Conwy	SH7064	53°9·7'	3°56·3'W	X	115
Gledrid	Shrops	SJ2936	52°55·2'	3°3·0'W	T	126
Gledrydd	Powys	SN8640	52°3·0'	3°39·4'W	X	147,160
Gledsgreen	Aberd	NJ6358	57°36·9'	2°36·7'W	X	29
Gleds Nest	D & G	NX3937	54°42·4'	4°29·5'W	X	83
Gledsnest	Scot Bord	NT4106	55°20·9'	2°55·4'W	X	79
Gledstone Hall	N Yks	SD8851	53°57·5'	2°10·6'W	X	103
Gledswood	Scot Bord	NT5934	55°36·1'	2°38·6'W	X	73,74
Gledwen	Powys	SO0542	52°4·3'	3°22·8'W	X	147,160
Gleedlee	Northum	NY7789	55°11·9'	2°21·3'W	X	80
Gleedon Hill	Shrops	SJ6201	52°36·6'	2°33·3'W	X	127
Gleggs Hall Fm	Ches	SJ4853	53°4·5'	2°46·2'W	FM	117
Gleghornie	E Loth	NT5983	56°2·5'	2°39·0'W	X	67
Gleiniant	Powys	SN9791	52°30·7'	3°30·7'W	T	136
Glemanuilt Glen	Arg & Bt	NR6308	55°18·8'	5°43·7'W	X	68
Glemham Hall	Suff	TM3459	52°11·0'	1°25·8'E	A	156
Glemham Ho	Suff	TM3461	52°12·1'	1°25·9'E	X	156
Glemsford	Suff	TL8248	52°6·2'	0°39·9'E	T	155
Glen	D & G	NX5457	54°53·4'	4°16·2'W	X	83
Glen	D & G	NX8376	55°4·1'	3°49·5'W	X	84
Glen	E Ayr	NS6514	55°24·3'	4°7·5'W	X	71
Glen	N Ayr	NR9550	55°42·3'	5°15·3'W	X	62,69
Glen	Orkney	ND2099	58°52·5'	3°22·8'W	X	7
Glen	Shetld	HU3365	60°22·3'	1°23·6'W	X	2,3
Glenacardoch	Arg & Bt	NR6637	55°34·5'	5°42·3'W	X	68
Glenacardoch Point	Arg & Bt	NR6537	55°34·5'	5°43·2'W	X	68
Glen Achaglachgach	Arg & Bt	NR7963	55°48·8'	5°31·2'W	X	62
Glen Achall	Highld	NH2393	57°53·7'	4°58·7'W	X	20
Glenach Burn	Clackm	NN9101	56°11·6'	3°45·0'W	W	58
Glen Acres	Essex	TL8313	51°47·4'	0°39·6'E	X	168
Glenadale Water	Arg & Bt	NR6311	55°20·4'	5°43·8'W	W	68
Glenae	D & G	NX9984	55°8·7'	3°34·7'W	X	78
Glenae Tower	D & G	NX9890	55°11·9'	3°35·7'W	A	78
Glen Affric	Highld	NH1922	57°15·4'	4°59·6'W	X	25
Glenaffric Forest	Highld	NH0919	57°13·6'	5°9·4'W	X	33
Glenaffric Forest	Highld	NH1119	57°13·6'	5°7·4'W	X	34
Glenaffric Forest	Highld	NH1120	57°14·2'	5°7·4'W	X	25
Glen Afton	E Ayr	NS6308	55°21·1'	4°9·2'W	X	71,77
Glenaggart	D & G	NS9002	55°18·2'	3°43·5'W	X	78
Glenahanty	Arg & Bt	NR6314	55°22·0'	5°44·0'W	X	68
Glenahuil	Arg & Bt	NR9766	55°50·9'	5°14·1'W	X	62
Glenakill	Arg & Bt	NR8568	55°51·7'	5°25·7'W	X	62
Glen Aladale	Highld	NM8176	56°49·7'	5°34·9'W	X	40
Glenaladale	Highld	NM8275	56°49·2'	5°33·9'W	X	40
Glenaladale River	Highld	NM8176	56°49·7'	5°34·9'W	W	40
Glenalbert	Pth & Kin	NN9948	56°37·0'	3°38·3'W	X	52,53
Glen Albyn or Glen Mor	Highld	NH3502	57°5·0'	4°42·9'W	X	34
Glen Albyn or Glen Mor	Highld	NH5426	57°18·3'	4°25·0'W	X	26,35
Glenald	Arg & Bt	NS2390	56°4·5'	4°50·2'W	X	56
Glen Aldie	Highld	NH7679	57°47·3'	4°4·7'W	X	21
Glenaldie Ho	Highld	NH7779	57°47·3'	4°3·7'W	X	21
Glenalla	S Ayr	NS3400	55°16·2'	4°36·3'W	X	76
Glenalla Field	S Ayr	NS3500	55°16·2'	4°35·4'W	X	77
Glen Almond	Pth & Kin	NN9028	56°26·1'	3°46·6'W	X	52,58
Glenalmond	Pth & Kin	NN9527	56°25·7'	3°41·7'W	X	52,53,58
Glen Almond	Pth & Kin	NO0029	56°26·8'	3°36·9'W	X	52,53,58
Glenalmond	S Ayr	NS2813	55°23·1'	4°42·5'W	X	70
Glenalmond College	Pth & Kin	NN9728	56°26·2'	3°39·8'W	X	52,53,58
Glenalmond Ho	Pth & Kin	NN9328	56°26·2'	3°43·7'W	X	52,58
Glen Aln	Northum	NU1212	55°24·4'	1°48·2'W	X	81
Glenamachrie	Arg & Bt	NM9228	56°24·2'	5°21·8'W	X	49
Glenamara Park	Cumbr	NY3815	54°31·8'	2°57·1'W	X	90
Glenamour Loch	D & G	NX4467	54°58·6'	4°25·8'W	W	83
Glen Ample	Stir	NN5918	56°20·3'	4°16·4'W	X	57
Glenample	Stir	NN5920	56°21·3'	4°16·5'W	X	51,57
Glenan	Arg & Bt	NR9270	55°53·0'	5°19·1'W	X	62
Glenan Bay	Arg & Bt	NR9170	55°52·9'	5°20·1'W	W	62
Glenancross	Highld	NM6691	56°57·3'	5°50·5'W	T	40
Glen Andred	E Susx	TQ5235	51°5·9'	0°10·6'E	X	188
Glen Anny	Pth & Kin	NN8704	56°13·2'	3°48·9'W	X	58
Glenapp Castle	S Ayr	NX0980	55°4·9'	4°59·1'W	X	76
Glen Aray	Arg & Bt	NN0814	56°17·0'	5°5·7'W	X	50,56
Glenarder	Moray	NJ1641	57°27·4'	3°23·5'W	X	28
Glen Arklet	Stir	NN3709	56°15·0'	4°37·4'W	X	56
Glenarm	Angus	NO3764	56°46·1'	3°1·4'W	X	44
Glen Arnisdale	Highld	NG8609	57°7·6'	5°31·7'W	X	33
Glen Aros	Arg & Bt	NM5245	56°32·2'	6°1·6'W	X	47,48
Glenaros Cott	Arg & Bt	NM5544	56°31·7'	5°58·6'W	X	47,48
Glenaros Ho	Arg & Bt	NM5544	56°31·7'	5°58·6'W	X	47,48
Glen Arroch	Highld	NG7321	57°13·7'	5°45·2'W	X	33
Glen Artney	Pth & Kin	NN7217	56°19·9'	4°3·8'W	X	57
Glenartney Lodge	Pth & Kin	NN6815	56°18·8'	4°7·6'W	X	57
Glenashdale Burn	N Ayr	NS0324	55°28·5'	5°6·6'W	W	69
Glenashdale Falls	N Ayr	NS0225	55°29·0'	5°7·6'W	W	69
Glenaspet	I of M	SC2681	54°12·0'	4°39·6'W	X	95
Glenastle	Arg & Bt	NR3044	55°37·1'	6°16·9'W	X	60
Glenastle Loch	Arg & Bt	NR2944	55°37·1'	6°17·8'W	W	60
Glenauchie	S Ayr	NS4201	55°16·9'	4°28·8'W	X	77
Glen Auldyn	I of M	SC4292	54°18·2'	4°25·3'W	X	95
Glen Auldyn	I of M	SC4393	54°18·8'	4°24·4'W	T	95
Glen Avon	Moray	NJ1006	57°8·4'	3°28·8'W	X	36
Glenavon	S Lanak	NS7649	55°43·4'	3°58·0'W	X	64
Glenavon	W Loth	NS9877	55°58·8'	3°37·6'W	X	65

Glenaylmer Burn	D & G	NS7315	55°25·0′	3°59·9′W	W	71
Glenbain	Highld	NC2621	58°8·9′	4°56·9′W	X	15
Glenballoch	Highld	NN6799	57°4·0′	4°11·2′W	X	35
Glen Banchor	Highld	NN6698	57°3·5′	4°12·1′W	X	35
Glenbank	Pth & Kin	NN8105	56°13·6′	3°54·7′W	X	57
Glen Banvie	Pth & Kin	NN8468	56°47·6′	3°53·5′W	X	43
Glen Banvie Wood	Pth & Kin	NN8268	56°47·6′	3°55·5′W	F	43
Glenbarr	Arg & Bt	NR6636	55°33·9′	5°42·2′W	T	68
Glenbarr Abbey	Arg & Bt	NR6736	55°34·0′	5°41·3′W	X	68
Glen Barrisdale	Highld	NG8903	57°4·4′	5°28·4′W	X	33
Glenbarry	Aberd	NJ5554	57°34·7′	2°44·7′W	T	29
Glen Batrick	Arg & Bt	NR5178	55°56·1′	5°58·8′W	X	61
Glenbatrick	Arg & Bt	NR5180	55°57·2′	5°58·9′W	X	61
Glenbatrick River	Arg & Bt	NR5178	55°56·1′	5°58·8′W	W	61
Glenbay	S Ayr	NS2813	55°23·1′	4°42·5′W	X	70
Glen Bay or Loch a' Ghlinne	N Eil	NA0800	57°49·3′	8°35·8′W	W	18
Glen Beanie	Angus	NO1767	56°47·5′	3°21·1′W	X	43
Glen Beasdale	Highld	NM7385	56°54·3′	5°43·2′W	X	40
Glen Bee	Pth & Kin	NN9005	56°13·7′	3°46·0′W	X	58
Glen Beg	Aberd	NJ3204	57°7·6′	3°6·9′W	X	37
Glenbeg	Highld	NH3183	57°48·5′	4°50·2′W	X	20
Glenbeg	Highld	NH6325	57°18·0′	4°16·0′W	X	26,35
Glenbeg	Highld	NJ0027	57°19·6′	3°39·2′W	X	36
Glen Beg	Highld	NJ0127	57°19·6′	3°38·2′W	X	36
Glenbeg	Highld	NM5862	56°41·5′	5°56·7′W	X	47
Glenbeg	Moray	NJ4138	57°26·0′	2°58·5′W	X	28
Glenbeg Burn	Aberd	NO1888	56°58·8′	3°20·5′W	W	43
Glenbeg Burn	Highld	NJ0128	57°20·2′	3°38·2′W	W	36
Glenbeich	Stir	NN6124	56°23·5′	4°14·7′W	X	51
Glen Beich	Stir	NN6329	56°26·3′	4°12·9′W	X	51
Glenbeich Lodge	Stir	NN6124	56°23·5′	4°14·7′W	X	51
Glenbenna Burn	Scot Bord	NT3735	55°36·5′	2°59·6′W	W	73
Glen Bernera	Highld	NG8021	57°13·9′	5°38·2′W	X	33
Glen Bernisdale	Highld	NG4048	57°27·1′	6°19·6′W	T	23
Glenbervie	Aberd	NO7680	56°54·9′	2°23·2′W	T	45
Glenbervie	Falk	NS8584	56°2·4′	3°50·3′W	X	65
Glenbervie House	Aberd	NO7680	56°54·9′	2°23·2′W	A	45
Glenbervie Inclosure	Hants	SU8142	51°10·5′	0°50·1′W	F	186
Glenbield	Scot Bord	NT2641	55°39·7′	3°10·1′W	X	73
Glenbogie	Aberd	NJ4824	57°18·5′	2°51·3′W	X	37
Glenboig	N Lanak	NS7268	55°53·5′	4°2·4′W	T	64
Glenboig Fm	N Lanak	NS7269	55°54·1′	4°2·4′W	FM	64
Glen Boltachan	Pth & Kin	NN7125	56°24·2′	4°5·0′W	X	51,52
Glen Boreraig	Highld	NG5917	57°11·1′	5°58·8′W	X	32
Glen Borrodale	Highld	NM6062	56°41·5′	5°54·7′W	X	40
Glenborrodale	Highld	NM6161	56°41·0′	5°53·7′W	T	40
Glenborrodale Bay	Highld	NM6060	56°40·5′	5°54·6′W	W	40
Glen Bracadale	Highld	NG3739	57°22·2′	6°22·0′W	X	23,32
Glenbrae Wood	D & G	NX9285	55°9·1′	3°41·3′W	F	78
Glenbran	Pth & Kin	NO2433	56°29·2′	3°13·6′W	X	53
Glen Branter	Arg & Bt	NS0996	56°7·4′	5°3·9′W	T	56
Glenbranter	Arg & Bt	NS1097	56°7·9′	5°3·0′W	X	56
Glenbranter	Arg & Bt	NS1197	56°8·0′	5°2·0′W	X	56
Glenbranter Forest	Arg & Bt	NS1096	56°7·4′	5°3·0′W	F	56
Glen Breackerie	Arg & Bt	NR6609	55°19·4′	5°40·9′W	X	68
Glenbreck	Scot Bord	NT0521	55°28·7′	3°29·8′W	T	72
Glenbreck Burn	Scot Bord	NT0522	55°29·2′	3°29·8′W	W	72
Glen Brein	Highld	NH4707	57°8·0′	4°31·2′W	X	34
Glenbrein Lodge	Highld	NH4711	57°10·1′	4°31·4′W	X	34
Glen Brerachan	Pth & Kin	NO0263	56°45·2′	3°35·7′W	X	43
Glen Brighty	Angus	NO1673	56°50·7′	3°22·2′W	X	43
Glen Brittle	Highld	NG4123	57°13·7′	6°17·0′W	X	32
Glen Brittle Forest	Highld	NG4026	57°15·3′	6°18·2′W	X	32
Glenbrittle House	Highld	NG4121	57°12·7′	6°16·9′W	X	32
Glen Brittle Hut	Highld	NG4121	57°12·7′	6°16·9′W	X	32
Glenbrock	C of Edin	NT1465	55°52·5′	3°22·0′W	T	65
Glen Brown	Highld	NJ1218	57°14·9′	3°27·0′W	X	36
Glen Bruar	Pth & Kin	NN8272	56°49·7′	3°55·6′W	X	43
Glen Buchat	Aberd	NJ3617	57°14·6′	3°3·2′W	X	37
Glenbuchat Castle	Aberd	NJ3914	57°13·0′	3°0·1′W	A	37
Glenbuchat Lodge	Aberd	NJ3318	57°15·1′	3°6·2′W	X	37
Glenbuck	E Ayr	NS7429	55°32·6′	3°59·4′W	T	71
Glen Buck	Highld	NH3401	57°4·5′	4°43·9′W	X	34
Glenbuck	Highld	NN3399	57°3·4′	4°44·8′W	X	34
Glenbuck Home Fm	E Ayr	NS7529	55°32·6′	3°58·4′W	FM	71
Glen Buckie	Stir	NN5317	56°19·6′	4°22·2′W	X	57
Glenbuck Loch	E Ayr	NS7528	55°32·0′	3°58·4′W	W	71
Glenbuie	Arg & Bt	NR8857	55°45·9′	5°22·3′W	X	62
Glenbuie Burn	D & G	NS8316	55°25·7′	3°50·5′W	W	71,78
Glen Buig	Moray	NJ1705	57°8·0′	3°21·8′W	X	36
Glenbuith	D & G	NX9499	55°16·7′	3°39·7′W	X	78
Glen Burn	Aberd	NJ4738	57°26·0′	2°52·5′W	W	28,29
Glen Burn	D & G	NS7406	55°20·2′	3°58·8′W	W	71,77
Glen Burn	D & G	NX0669	54°58·9′	5°1·5′W	W	82
Glen Burn	D & G	NX5359	54°54·5′	4°17·2′W	W	83
Glen Burn	D & G	NX8476	55°4·1′	3°48·6′W	W	84
Glen Burn	D & G	NX8964	54°57·7′	3°43·6′W	W	84
Glen Burn	D & G	NX9564	54°57·8′	3°38·0′W	W	84
Glen Burn	D & G	NY1268	55°0·2′	3°22·1′W	W	85
Glen Burn	Fife	NO1806	56°14·6′	3°18·9′W	W	58
Glen Burn	Moray	NJ2353	57°33·9′	3°16·8′W	W	28
Glen Burn	Moray	NJ4963	57°39·5′	2°50·8′W	W	28,29
Glen Burn	N Ayr	NS2152	55°44·0′	4°50·6′W	W	63
Glenburn	Renf	NS4761	55°49·3′	4°26·1′W	T	64
Glenburn	Scot Bord	NT4314	55°25·2′	2°53·6′W	X	79
Glenburn	Shetld	HU3151	60°14·8′	1°25·9′W	X	3
Glenburn Hall	Scot Bord	NT6420	55°28·6′	2°33·7′W	X	74
Glenburnie	Aberd	NJ8518	57°15·4′	2°14·5′W	X	38
Glenburnie	Scot Bord	NT5456	55°48·0′	2°43·6′W	X	66,73
Glenburn of Middlehill	Aberd	NJ8349	57°32·1′	2°16·6′W	X	29,30
Glenburn Resr	N Ayr	NS2151	55°43·4′	4°50·6′W	W	63
Glenburn Resr	Renf	NS4760	55°48·8′	4°26·1′W	W	64
Glenburrell	Shrops	SO4186	52°28·4′	2°51·7′W	X	137
Glen Byre	Arg & Bt	NM5724	56°21·0′	5°55·5′W	X	48
Glenbyre	Arg & Bt	NM5823	56°20·5′	5°54·5′W	X	48
Glenbyre Burn	Arg & Bt	NM5724	56°21·0′	5°55·5′W	W	48
Glencadam Ho	Angus	NO6060	56°44·1′	2°38·8′W	X	45
Glencaird	D & G	NX3679	55°5·0′	4°33·7′W	X	77
Glencaird Hill	D & G	NX3580	55°5·5′	4°34·7′W	H	77
Glencairn	Aberd	NJ4821	57°16·9′	2°51·3′W	X	37
Glencairn	Highld	NH9316	57°13·6′	3°45·9′W	X	36
Glencairn Mill	Cumbr	NY4954	54°52·9′	2°47·3′W	X	86
Glen Caladale	Highld	NG3425	57°14·6′	6°24·1′W	X	32
Glen Caladh Fm	Arg & Bt	NS0076	55°56·4′	5°11·7′W	FM	62,63
Glen Callater	Aberd	NO1784	56°56·6′	3°21·4′W	X	43
Glen Callater	Aberd	NO2080	56°54·5′	3°18·4′W	X	44
Glen Callum	Arg & Bt	NS1053	55°44·2′	5°1·2′W	X	63
Glencallum Bay	Arg & Bt	NS1152	55°43·7′	5°0·2′W	W	63,69
Glen Cally	Angus	NO3465	56°46·6′	3°4·4′W	X	44
Glencally	Angus	NO3563	56°45·5′	3°3·3′W	X	44
Glencally Burn	Angus	NO2172	56°50·2′	3°17·2′W	W	44
Glen Calvie	Highld	NH4687	57°51·0′	4°35·2′W	X	20
Glencalvie Forest	Highld	NH4387	57°51·0′	4°38·3′W	X	20
Glencalvie Lodge	Highld	NH4689	57°52·1′	4°35·3′W	X	20
Glencamgarry	Highld	NN0190	56°57·8′	5°15·9′W	X	33
Glencanisp Forest	Highld	NC1619	58°7·6′	5°7·0′W	X	15
Glencanisp Lodge	Highld	NC1122	58°9·1′	5°12·2′W	X	15
Glen Cannel	Arg & Bt	NM5934	56°26·5′	5°54·1′W	X	47,48
Glencannel River	Arg & Bt	NM5935	56°27·0′	5°54·2′W	W	47,48
Glen Cannich	Highld	NH1431	57°20·2′	5°5·0′W	X	25
Glen Cannich	Highld	NH2130	57°19·8′	4°57·9′W	X	25
Glen Cannich	Highld	NH3232	57°21·1′	4°47·1′W	X	26
Glencannich Forest	Highld	NH2333	57°21·5′	4°56·1′W	X	25
Glencaple	D & G	NX9968	55°0·0′	3°34·3′W	T	84
Glencaple	S Lanak	NS9221	55°28·5′	3°42·1′W	X	71,72
Glencaple Burn	S Lanak	NS9220	55°28·0′	3°42·1′W	W	71,72
Glen Carnaig	Stir	NN4520	56°21·1′	4°30·1′W	X	51,57
Glen Carron	Highld	NH0852	57°31·3′	5°11·9′W	X	25
Glencarron and Glenuig Forest	Highld	NH1249	57°29·8′	5°7·8′W	X	25
Glencarron Lodge	Highld	NH0651	57°30·7′	5°13·9′W	X	25
Glen Carse	Pth & Kin	NO1822	56°23·2′	3°19·2′W	X	53,58
Glencarse	Pth & Kin	NO1921	56°22·7′	3°18·3′W	T	53,58
Glencarse Hill	Pth & Kin	NO1822	56°23·2′	3°19·2′W	H	53,58
Glencarse Ho	Pth & Kin	NO1922	56°23·3′	3°18·3′W	X	53,58
Glencartholm	D & G	NY3779	55°6·3′	2°58·8′W	X	85
Glen Cassley	Highld	NC3520	58°8·6′	4°47·7′W	X	15
Glen Cassley	Highld	NC3913	58°4·9′	4°43·4′W	X	16
Glencassley Castle	Highld	NC4407	58°1·8′	4°38·0′W	X	16
Glen Catacol	N Ayr	NR9248	55°41·1′	5°18·1′W	X	62,69
Glencatt	Aberd	NO5493	57°1·8′	2°45·0′W	X	37,44
Glenceitlein	Highld	NN1447	56°34·9′	5°1·3′W	X	50
Glen Ceitlein	Highld	NN1547	56°35·0′	5°0·3′W	X	50
Glen Chalmadale	N Ayr	NR9549	55°41·7′	5°15·3′W	X	62,69
Glenchamber	D & G	NX2363	54°56·1′	4°45·3′W	X	82
Glenchass	I of M	SC1967	54°4·3′	4°45·6′W	T	95
Glen Clachaig	Arg & Bt	NM5635	56°26·9′	5°57·1′W	X	47,48
Glenclach Burn	D & G	NS8510	55°22·5′	3°48·5′W	W	71,78
Glenclair Hill	D & G	NY0179	55°6·0′	3°32·7′W	X	84
Glenclova Forest	Angus	NO2869	56°48·7′	3°10·3′W	F	44
Glen Cloy	N Ayr	NS0035	55°34·3′	5°9·9′W	X	69
Glen Cloy Fm	N Ayr	NS0035	55°34·3′	5°9·9′W	FM	69
Glen Clunie	Aberd	NO1486	56°57·7′	3°24·4′W	X	43
Glen Cochill	Pth & Kin	NN9041	56°33·1′	3°46·9′W	X	52
Glencoe	Aberd	NJ6139	57°26·6′	2°38·5′W	X	29
Glencoe	Highld	NN1058	56°40·8′	5°5·6′W	T	41
Glen Coe	Highld	NN1557	56°40·4′	5°0·7′W	X	41
Glen Coiltie	Highld	NH4727	57°18·7′	4°32·0′W	X	26
Glen Coishletter	N Eil	NG0087	57°46·6′	7°2·3′W	X	18
Glen Colbost	Highld	NG3442	57°23·7′	6°25·2′W	X	23
Glencommon	Aberd	NO6696	57°3·5′	2°33·2′W	X	38,45
Glenconglass	Moray	NJ1722	57°17·1′	3°22·2′W	X	36
Glenconner	E Ayr	NS4919	55°26·8′	4°22·8′W	X	70
Glen Conon	Highld	NG4164	57°35·8′	6°19·6′W	X	23
Glen Convinth	Highld	NH5137	57°24·2′	4°28·3′W	X	26
Glen Coralan	Arg & Bt	NN3435	56°28·9′	4°41·3′W	X	50
Glencorf Burn	D & G	NY3283	55°8·5′	3°3·6′W	W	79
Glencorrie	Moray	NJ3236	57°24·8′	3°7·5′W	X	28
Glencorse	D & G	NX9889	55°11·3′	3°35·7′W	X	78
Glencorse Burn	Midlo	NT2463	55°51·5′	3°12·4′W	W	66
Glencorse Hill	D & G	NX9691	55°12·4′	3°37·6′W	H	78
Glencorse Ho	Midlo	NT2463	55°51·5′	3°12·4′W	X	66
Glencorse Mains	Midlo	NT2362	55°51·0′	3°13·4′W	X	66
Glencorse Resr	Midlo	NT2163	55°51·5′	3°15·3′W	W	66
Glencosie	S Lanak	NS9037	55°37·1′	3°44·4′W	X	71,72
Glencotho	Scot Bord	NT0829	55°33·0′	3°27·1′W	X	72
Glen Cott	Angus	NO2636	56°30·9′	3°11·7′W	X	53
Glen Cott	N Lanak	NS6769	55°54·0′	4°7·2′W	X	64
Glen Cottage	Highld	NC7805	58°1·3′	4°3·2′W	X	17
Glen Cottage	Highld	NG9356	57°33·1′	5°27·1′W	X	25
Glen Cottage	Highld	NM6685	56°54·1′	5°50·1′W	X	40
Glen Cottage	Midlo	NT2263	55°51·5′	3°14·3′W	X	66
Glencoul	Highld	NC2730	58°13·8′	4°56·3′W	X	15
Glen Coul	Highld	NC2829	58°13·2′	4°55·2′W	X	15
Glencoul Mill	Angus	NO4657	56°42·4′	2°52·5′W	X	54
Glen Court	Monm	ST4098	51°40·9′	2°51·7′W	X	171
Glencoyne	Cumbr	NY3618	54°33·4′	2°59·0′W	X	90
Glencoyne	Cumbr	NY3818	54°33·5′	2°57·1′W	X	90
Glencoyne Park	Cumbr	NY3919	54°34·0′	2°56·2′W	X	90
Glencoyne Wood	Cumbr	NY3818	54°33·5′	2°57·1′W	F	90
Glen Craig	D & G	NX9564	54°57·8′	3°38·0′W	H	84
Glencraig	Fife	NT1894	56°8·2′	3°18·7′W	T	58
Glen Craigag	N Ayr	NR9534	55°33·7′	5°14·6′W	X	68,69
Glencraigie Burn	Scot Bord	NT0716	55°26·0′	3°27·8′W	W	78
Glencraigs	Arg & Bt	NR6923	55°27·0′	5°38·8′W	X	68
Glen Crammag	I of M	SC3787	54°15·4′	4°29·7′W	X	95
Glencreggan	Arg & Bt	NR6738	55°35·1′	5°41·4′W	X	68
Glen Creran	Arg & Bt	NN0347	56°34·7′	5°12·0′W	X	50
Glen Creran	Arg & Bt	NN0550	56°36·3′	5°10·2′W	X	41
Glencripesdale	Highld	NM6659	56°40·1′	5°48·7′W	X	49
Glen Cripesdale	Highld	NM6758	56°39·6′	5°47·7′W	X	49
Glencripesdale Burn	Highld	NM6859	56°40·2′	5°46·7′W	W	49
Glen Croe	Arg & Bt	NN2404	56°12·0′	4°49·8′W	X	56
Glencroft	Aberd	NJ9132	57°23·0′	2°8·5′W	X	30
Glencroft	Cumbr	NY4172	55°2·6′	2°55·0′W	X	85
Glencroft	D & G	NY3374	55°3·6′	3°2·5′W	X	85
Glencrosh	D & G	NX7689	55°11·0′	3°56·4′W	X	78
Glencrosh Burn	D & G	NX7489	55°11·0′	3°58·3′W	W	77
Glencrosh Burn	D & G	NX7589	55°11·0′	3°57·4′W	W	78
Glencrosh Hill	D & G	NX7388	55°10·5′	3°59·2′W	H	77
Glencrosh Linn	D & G	NX7689	55°11·0′	3°56·4′W	W	78
Glencruitten	Arg & Bt	NM8729	56°24·6′	5°26·7′W	X	49
Glen Cruitten	Arg & Bt	NM8730	56°25·1′	5°26·8′W	X	49
Glencuie	Aberd	NJ4216	57°14·1′	2°57·2′W	X	37
Glencuilt	Angus	NO3965	56°46·6′	2°59·4′W	X	44
Glencune Burn	Northum	NY6462	54°57·3′	2°33·3′W	W	86
Glendale	Highld	NG1749	57°26·8′	6°42·6′W	T	23
Glen Dale	Highld	NG1848	57°26·3′	6°41·5′W	X	23
Glendale	Northum	NY6965	54°59·0′	2°28·6′W	X	86,87
Glendale	Shetld	HU3937	60°7·2′	1°17·4′W	X	4
Glendale Manor Fm	E Susx	TQ6321	50°58·1′	0°19·7′E	FM	199
Glendalloch	Moray	NJ1831	57°22·0′	3°21·3′W	X	36
Glen Damff	Angus	NO2567	56°47·6′	3°13·2′W	X	44
Glendamff Burn	Angus	NO2465	56°46·5′	3°14·2′W	W	44
Glendams	Pth & Kin	NO2048	56°37·3′	3°17·8′W	W	53
Glendarroch	Arg & Bt	NR8586	56°1·4′	5°26·6′W	X	55
Glendaruel	Arg & Bt	NR9985	56°1·2′	5°13·1′W	X	55
Glendaruel Forest	Arg & Bt	NS0288	56°2·9′	5°10·3′W	F	55
Glendauchan Burn	D & G	NS8307	55°20·8′	3°50·3′W	W	71,78
Glendavan Ho	Aberd	NJ4301	57°6·0′	2°56·0′W	X	37
Glendearg	D & G	NT2305	55°20·2′	3°12·4′W	X	79
Glendearg	Scot Bord	NT5138	55°38·2′	2°46·3′W	T	73
Glendearg Burn	D & G	NT2206	55°20·8′	3°13·4′W	W	79
Glendearg Burn	Scot Bord	NT2110	55°22·9′	3°14·4′W	W	79
Glen Debadel	Arg & Bt	NR6294	56°5·0′	5°49·1′W	X	61
Glendebadel Bay	Arg & Bt	NR6295	56°5·6′	5°49·1′W	W	61
Glen Dee	Aberd	NN9892	57°0·7′	3°40·3′W	X	43
Glen Dee	Aberd	NN9893	57°1·3′	3°40·4′W	X	36,43
Glendelvine Ho	Pth & Kin	NO0941	56°33·4′	3°28·4′W	X	52,53
Glendenholm	D & G	NX9888	55°10·8′	3°35·7′W	X	78
Glenderaterra Beck	Cumbr	NY2927	54°38·2′	3°5·6′W	W	89,90
Glen Derby	Pth & Kin	NO0359	56°43·0′	3°34·6′W	X	52,53
Glen Derry	Aberd	NO0396	57°3·0′	3°35·5′W	X	36,43
Glen Dessarry	Highld	NM9492	56°58·7′	5°22·9′W	X	33,40
Glendessarry	Highld	NM9692	56°58·7′	5°21·0′W	X	33,40
Glendeuglie	Pth & Kin	NO1210	56°16·7′	3°24·8′W	X	58
Glendeven Fm	Fife	NT0785	56°3·2′	3°29·2′W	FM	65
Glen Devon	Pth & Kin	NN9504	56°13·3′	3°41·2′W	X	58
Glendevon	Pth & Kin	NN9904	56°13·3′	3°37·3′W	T	58
Glendevon	W Loth	NT0775	55°57·8′	3°28·9′W	X	65
Glendevon Castle	Pth & Kin	NN9705	56°13·8′	3°39·2′W	A	58
Glendevon Ho	Pth & Kin	NN9704	56°13·3′	3°39·2′W	X	58
Glendey Burn	Pth & Kin	NO0003	56°12·8′	3°36·3′W	W	58
Glendhoo	I of M	SC3491	54°17·5′	4°32·6′W	X	95
Glendhoo	I of M	SC3590	54°17·0′	4°31·7′W	X	95
Glendhoo	I of M	SC3879	54°11·1′	4°28·5′W	X	95
Glen Dhu	Cumbr	NY5585	55°9·7′	2°41·9′W	X	80
Glendhu	Highld	NC2833	58°15·4′	4°55·4′W	X	15
Glendhu	Stir	NN5228	56°25·5′	4°23·5′W	X	51
Glendhu Forest	Highld	NC2834	58°15·9′	4°55·5′W	X	15
Glendhu Hill	Cumbr	NY5686	55°10·2′	2°41·0′W	H	80
Glen Dibidal	Highld	NG2040	57°22·1′	6°39·0′W	X	23
Glen Dibidil	Highld	NM3893	56°57·5′	6°18·1′W	X	39
Glen Diebidale	Highld	NH4583	57°48·9′	4°36·1′W	X	20
Glendinning	D & G	NY2997	55°16·0′	3°6·6′W	X	79
Glendinning Burn	D & G	NY2998	55°16·5′	3°6·6′W	W	79
Glendinning Cleuch	D & G	NX7897	55°15·4′	3°54·7′W	W	78
Glendinning Heights	D & G	NY2899	55°17·0′	3°7·6′W	H	79
Glendinningrigg	Cumbr	NY4475	55°4·2′	2°52·2′W	X	85
Glendivan Burn	D & G	NY3790	55°12·3′	2°59·0′W	W	79
Glen Dochart	Stir	NN4828	56°25·4′	4°27·4′W	X	51
Glen Docherty	Highld	NH0560	57°35·5′	5°15·3′W	X	19
Glen Doe	Highld	NH4107	57°7·8′	4°37·2′W	X	34
Glendoebeg	Highld	NH4109	57°8·9′	4°37·2′W	X	34
Glendoe Forest	Highld	NH4304	57°6·3′	4°35·1′W	X	34
Glendoe Lodge	Highld	NH4009	57°8·9′	4°38·2′W	X	34
Glendoick	Pth & Kin	NO2022	56°23·3′	3°17·3′W	T	53,58
Glendoick Ho	Pth & Kin	NO2023	56°23·8′	3°17·3′W	X	53,58
Glen Doll	Angus	NO2576	56°52·4′	3°13·4′W	X	44
Glendoll Forest	Angus	NO2675	56°51·9′	3°12·4′W	F	44
Glendoll Lodge	Angus	NO2776	56°52·4′	3°11·4′W	X	44
Glendon	Devon	SX6196	50°45·1′	3°57·8′W	X	191
Glendon Hall	Northnts	SP8481	52°25·5′	0°45·5′W	X	141
Glendon Lodge	Northnts	SP8681	52°25·4′	0°43·7′W	X	141
Glendorch	S Lanak	NS8718	55°26·8′	3°46·8′W	X	71,78
Glendorch Burn	D & G	NS8515	55°25·2′	3°48·6′W	W	71,78
Glendorch Burn	S Lanak	NS8719	55°27·4′	3°46·8′W	W	71,78
Glendorch Rig	D & G	NS8614	55°24·7′	3°47·6′W	X	71,78
Glen Douchary	Highld	NH2591	57°52·7′	4°56·6′W	X	20
Glen Douglas	Arg & Bt	NS3098	56°8·9′	4°43·8′W	X	56
Glendouglas	Scot Bord	NT6517	55°27·0′	2°32·8′W	X	80
Glendoune	S Ayr	NX1996	55°13·8′	4°50·3′W	X	76
Glendouran	S Lanak	NS8720	55°27·9′	3°46·8′W	X	71,72
Glendowlin Fm	Cumbr	NY5126	54°37·9′	2°45·1′W	FM	90
Glendown	I of M	SC2068	54°4·8′	4°44·7′W	X	95
Glendowran Burn	S Lanak	NS8720	55°27·9′	3°46·8′W	W	71,72
Glendowran Hill	S Lanak	NS8819	55°27·4′	3°45·8′W	H	71,78
Glendowran Hill	S Lanak	NS8820	55°27·9′	3°45·9′W	H	71,72
Glendow Sike	D & G	NY4196	55°15·5′	2°55·3′W	W	79
Glendrian	Highld	NM4768	56°44·4′	6°7·8′W	X	47
Glendrian Caves	Highld	NM4670	56°45·4′	6°8·9′W	X	39,47
Glendrissaig	S Ayr	NX1994	55°12·7′	4°50·3′W	X	76
Glen Drolla	N Eil	NF7672	57°37·6′	7°25·2′W	X	18
Glen Drolsay	Arg & Bt	NR3365	55°48·5′	6°15·2′W	X	60,61
Glen Dronach	Aberd	NJ6243	57°28·8′	2°37·6′W	X	29
Glen Drynoch	Highld	NG4330	57°17·6′	6°15·5′W	X	32
Glendrynoch Lodge	Highld	NG4131	57°18·0′	6°17·5′W	X	32
Glenduad	Pemb	SN1138	52°0·7′	4°44·9′W	X	145
Glenduckie	Fife	NO2818	56°21·2′	3°9·5′W	T	59
Glenduckie Hill	Fife	NO2819	56°21·7′	3°9·5′W	H	59
Glendue	Northum	NY8865	54°59·0′	2°10·8′W	X	87
Glendue Burn	Northum	NY6556	54°54·1′	2°32·3′W	W	86
Glendue Fell	Northum	NY6455	54°53·6′	2°33·3′W	H	86
Glenduff	I of M	SC4194	54°19·3′	4°26·3′W	X	95
Glen Duian	Highld	NM3397	56°59·5′	6°23·3′W	X	39
Glenduisk	S Ayr	NX2085	55°7·9′	4°49·0′W	X	76
Glendurgan	Corn	SW7727	50°6·3′	5°6·8′W	X	204
Glen Duror	Highld	NN0153	56°37·9′	5°14·2′W	X	41

Glen Dye	Aberd	NO6383	56°56·5'	2°36·0'W	X	45
Glen Dye	Angus	NO2962	56°44·9'	3°9·2'W	X	44
Glendye Lodge	Aberd	NO6486	56°58·1'	2°35·1'W	X	45
Glendyne Burn	D & G	NS8311	55°23·0'	3°50·4'W	W	71,78
Gleneadardacrock	Arg & Bt	NR6115	55°22·5'	5°45·9'W	X	68
Glen Eagles	Pth & Kin	NN9407	56°14·9'	3°42·2'W	X	58
Gleneagles Ho	Pth & Kin	NN9308	56°15·4'	3°43·2'W	X	58
Gleneagles Hotel	Pth & Kin	NN9111	56°17·0'	3°45·2'W	X	58
Gleneagles Old Toll Ho	Pth & Kin	NN9407	56°14·9'	3°42·2'W	X	58
Gleneagles Sta	Pth & Kin	NN9210	56°16·5'	3°44·2'W	X	58
Glenearn	Pth & Kin	NO1016	56°19·9'	3°26·9'W	X	58
Glenearn Ho	Pth & Kin	NO1016	56°19·9'	3°26·9'W	X	58
Glen Ea's Hill	S Lanak	NS9014	55°24·7'	3°43·8'W	H	71,78
Gleneden	Fife	NO2108	56°15·7'	3°16·1'W	X	58
Gleneedle	I of M	SC2679	54°10·9'	4°39·6'W	X	95
Glen Effock	Angus	NO4377	56°53·1'	2°55·7'W	X	44
Gleneffock	Angus	NO4578	56°53·7'	2°53·7'W	X	44
Glenegedale	Arg & Bt	NR3351	55°41·0'	6°14·4'W	T	60
Glenegedale Lots	Arg & Bt	NR3553	55°42·1'	6°12·6'W	X	60
Glenegedalemoor Lots	Arg & Bt	NR3551	55°41·1'	6°12·5'W	X	60
Glenegedale River	Arg & Bt	NR3452	55°41·6'	6°13·5'W	W	60
Glenehervie	Arg & Bt	NR7410	55°20·2'	5°33·4'W	X	68
Glen Einig	Highld	NH3598	57°56·7'	4°46·8'W	X	20
Glen Elchaig	Highld	NG9627	57°17·5'	5°22·7'W	X	25,33
Glenelg	Highld	NG8119	57°12·8'	5°37·2'W	T	33
Glenelg Bay	Highld	NG8019	57°12·8'	5°38·1'W	W	33
Glenericht Ho	Pth & Kin	NO1750	56°38·3'	3°20·7'W	X	53
Glen Ernan	Aberd	NJ3112	57°11·9'	3°8·1'W	X	37
Glenernie	Moray	NJ0146	57°29·9'	3°38·7'W	X	27
Glen Errochty	Pth & Kin	NN7663	56°44·8'	4°1·2'W	X	42
Glen Esk	Angus	NO4778	56°53·7'	2°51·7'W	X	44
Glenesslin	D & G	NX8284	55°8·4'	3°50·6'W	X	78
Glenesslin	D & G	NX8383	55°7·9'	3°49·7'W	X	78
Glenesslin Burn	D & G	NX8284	55°8·4'	3°50·6'W	W	78
Glen Etive	Highld	NN1549	56°36·0'	5°0·4'W	X	50
Glen Etive	Highld	NN1951	56°37·2'	4°56·6'W	X	41
Glenetive Forest	Highld	NN1147	56°34·9'	5°4·2'W	F	50
Glen Euchar	Arg & Bt	NM8419	56°19·1'	5°29·1'W	X	55
Glen Ey	Aberd	NO0985	56°57·1'	3°29·3'W	X	43
Glen Eynort	Highld	NG3828	57°16·3'	6°20·3'W	X	32
Glenfall Ho	Glos	SO9721	51°53·5'	2°2·2'W	X	163
Glen Falloch	Stir	NN3219	56°20·3'	4°42·6'W	X	50,56
Glen Falloch	Stir	NN3622	56°22·0'	4°38·9'W	X	50
Glenfalloch Lodge	Stir	NN3118	56°19·7'	4°43·6'W	X	50
Glenfarg	Pth & Kin	NO1310	56°16·7'	3°23·9'W	T	58
Glen Farg	Pth & Kin	NO1513	56°18·4'	3°22·0'W	X	58
Glenfarg Ho	Pth & Kin	NO1615	56°19·5'	3°21·1'W	X	58
Glenfarg Resr	Pth & Kin	NO1011	56°17·2'	3°26·8'W	W	58
Glenfarquhar Lodge	Aberd	NO7281	56°55·4'	2°27·1'W	X	45
Glen Feardar	Aberd	NO1996	57°3·1'	3°19·7'W	X	36,43
Glen Fender	Pth & Kin	NN8938	56°31·5'	3°47·8'W	X	52
Glen Fender	Pth & Kin	NN9068	56°47·7'	3°47·6'W	X	43
Glenfender Burn	Pth & Kin	NN8938	56°31·5'	3°47·8'W	W	52
Glenfenzie	Aberd	NJ3102	57°6·5'	3°7·9'W	X	37
Glen Fenzie	Aberd	NJ3202	57°6·5'	3°6·9'W	X	37
Glenfenzie Burn	Aberd	NJ3201	57°6·0'	3°6·9'W	W	37
Glenfeochan	Arg & Bt	NM8824	56°21·9'	5°25·5'W	X	49
Glen Feochan	Arg & Bt	NM8924	56°21·9'	5°24·5'W	X	49
Glenfernate Lodge	Pth & Kin	NO0464	56°45·7'	3°33·8'W	X	43
Glenferness Ho	Highld	NH9342	57°27·6'	3°46·6'W	X	27
Glenferness Mains	Highld	NH9443	57°28·2'	3°45·6'W	X	27
Glen Fernisdale	Highld	NN6994	57°1·4'	4°9·0'W	X	35
Glen Feshie	Highld	NN8494	57°1·6'	3°54·2'W	X	35,43
Glenfeshie Forest	Highld	NN8990	56°59·5'	3°49·2'W	X	35,43
Glenfeshie Forest	Highld	NN9190	56°59·6'	3°47·2'W	X	43
Glenfeshie Lodge	Highld	NN8493	57°1·1'	3°54·2'W	X	35,43
Glen Fiag	Highld	NC4524	58°10·9'	4°37·7'W	X	16
Glen Fiddich	Moray	NJ3233	57°23·2'	3°7·4'W	X	28
Glenfiddich Forest	Moray	NJ3030	57°21·6'	3°9·4'W	X	37
Glenfiddich Lodge	Moray	NJ3132	57°22·7'	3°8·4'W	X	37
Glenfield	Leic	SK5405	52°38·6'	1°11·7'W	T	140
Glenfield	Orkney	HY2410	58°58·5'	3°18·8'W	X	6
Glenfield Ho	Worcs	SP0676	52°23·2'	1°54·3'W	X	139
Glen Finart	Arg & Bt	NS1691	56°4·8'	4°57·0'W	X	56
Glen Fincastle	Pth & Kin	NN8661	56°43·9'	3°51·3'W	X	43
Glen Finglas	Stir	NN5011	56°16·3'	4°24·9'W	X	57
Glen Finglas Reservoir	Stir	NN5209	56°15·3'	4°22·9'W	W	57
Glen Finlet	Angus	NO2367	56°47·5'	3°15·2'W	X	44
Glenfinnan	Highld	NM8980	56°52·1'	5°27·3'W	T	40
Glen Finnan	Highld	NM9183	56°53·7'	5°25·4'W	X	40
Glenfinnan Lodge	Highld	NM9184	56°54·3'	5°25·5'W	X	40
Glen Fintaig	Highld	NN2688	56°57·3'	4°51·2'W	X	34,41
Glenfintaig Ho	Highld	NN2086	56°56·1'	4°57·0'W	X	34,41
Glenfintaig Lodge	Highld	NN2286	56°56·1'	4°55·0'W	X	34,41
Glenflosh Hill	D & G	NS7914	55°24·6'	3°54·2'W	H	71,78
Glen Fm	Falk	NS8877	55°58·6'	3°47·3'W	FM	65
Glen Fm	Lincs	TF1722	52°47·2'	0°15·5'W	FM	130
Glen Fm	N Som	ST5373	51°27·5'	2°40·2'W	FM	172
Glen Fm	N Yks	SD9649	53°56·5'	2°3·2'W	FM	103
Glen Fm	Surrey	TQ3442	51°9·9'	0°4·6'W	FM	187
Glenfoot	Clackm	NS9096	56°8·9'	3°45·8'W	X	58
Glenfoot	D & G	NX9285	55°9·1'	3°41·3'W	X	78
Glenfoot	Pth & Kin	NN9804	56°13·3'	3°38·3'W	X	58
Glenfoot	Pth & Kin	NO1815	56°19·5'	3°19·1'W	T	58
Glenfoot	Stir	NS5390	56°5·1'	4°21·3'W	X	57
Glenfoot Ho	N Ayr	NS2145	55°40·2'	4°50·3'W	X	63
Glenforkie	Aberd	NJ5956	57°35·8'	2°40·7'W	X	29
Glen Forsa	Arg & Bt	NM6138	56°28·7'	5°52·4'W	X	49
Glenforslan	Highld	NM7573	56°47·9'	5°40·6'W	X	40
Glen Forslan	Highld	NM7773	56°48·0'	5°38·7'W	X	40
Glenforslan River	Highld	NM7773	56°48·0'	5°38·7'W	W	40
Glen Franka Burn	S Lanak	NS8913	55°24·2'	3°44·7'W	W	71,78
Glen Fruin	Arg & Bt	NS2888	56°3·5'	4°45·3'W	X	56
Glen Fyne	Arg & Bt	NN2216	56°18·4'	4°52·2'W	X	50,56
Glen Fyne	Arg & Bt	NN2321	56°21·2'	4°51·4'W	X	50,56
Glen Fyne	Arg & Bt	NS1172	55°54·5'	5°1·0'W	X	63
Glenfyne Lodge	Arg & Bt	NN2215	56°17·9'	4°52·2'W	X	50,56
Glengaber	Scot Bord	NT2123	55°29·9'	3°14·6'W	X	73
Glengaber	Scot Bord	NT3430	55°33·8'	3°2·4'W	X	73
Glengaber Burn	D & G	NS7418	55°26·6'	3°59·1'W	W	71

Glengaber Burn	Scot Bord	NT2124	55°30·5'	3°14·6'W	W	73
Glengaber Hill	D & G	NS7318	55°26·6'	4°0·0'W	H	71
Glengaber Hill	D & G	NS8413	55°24·1'	3°49·5'W	H	71,78
Glengaber Hill	Scot Bord	NT3429	55°33·3'	3°2·3'W	H	73
Glengainoch Burn	D & G	NX5970	55°0·5'	4°11·9'W	W	77
Glengair	Arg & Bt	NS2385	56°1·8'	4°50·0'W	X	56
Glen Gairn	Aberd	NO3498	57°4·4'	3°4·9'W	X	37,44
Glen Gallain	Arg & Bt	NM8418	56°18·6'	5°29·1'W	X	55
Glengalmadale	Highld	NM8653	56°37·5'	5°28·9'W	X	49
Glen Galmadale	Highld	NM8654	56°38·0'	5°28·9'W	X	49
Glengalmadale River	Highld	NM8654	56°38·0'	5°28·9'W	W	49
Glengap	D & G	NS9102	55°18·3'	3°42·6'W	X	78
Glengap	D & G	NX6559	54°54·7'	4°5·9'W	X	83,84
Glengap Burn	D & G	NS7008	55°21·2'	4°2·6'W	W	71,77
Glengap Burn	D & G	NS7416	55°25·6'	3°59·0'W	W	71
Glengap Burn	D & G	NT1300	55°17·4'	3°21·8'W	W	78
Glengap Burn	D & G	NX6460	54°55·2'	4°6·9'W	W	83
Glengape	D & G	NS7309	55°21·8'	3°59·8'W	X	71,77
Glengap Forest	D & G	NX6360	54°55·2'	4°7·8'W	F	83
Glengap Head	D & G	NT1301	55°18·0'	3°21·8'W	H	78
Glengap Hill	S Ayr	NX3392	55°11·9'	4°37·0'W	X	76
Glengap Rig	D & G	NS9102	55°18·3'	3°42·6'W	X	78
Glengar	D & G	NX8395	55°14·4'	3°50·0'W	X	78
Glengarden	Aberd	NO3497	57°3·8'	3°4·8'W	X	37,44
Glengar Hill	D & G	NX8295	55°14·4'	3°50·9'W	H	78
Glengar Loch	D & G	NX8296	55°14·9'	3°50·9'W	W	78
Glen Garnock	N Ayr	NS3156	55°46·3'	4°41·2'W	X	63
Glengarnock	N Ayr	NS3253	55°44·7'	4°40·2'W	T	63
Glengarnock Castle	N Ayr	NS3157	55°46·9'	4°41·3'W	A	63
Glen Garr	E Ayr	NS5831	55°33·4'	4°14·6'W	X	71
Glen Garr	Pth & Kin	NO0137	56°31·1'	3°36·1'W	X	52,53
Glen Garrisdale	Arg & Bt	NR6496	56°6·2'	5°47·3'W	X	55,61
Glengarrisdale	Arg & Bt	NR6496	56°6·2'	5°47·3'W	X	55,61
Glengarrisdale Bay	Arg & Bt	NR6497	56°6·7'	5°47·3'W	W	55,61
Glengarry	Aberd	NJ5706	57°8·8'	2°42·2'W	X	37
Glen Garry	Highld	NH0900	57°3·4'	5°8·5'W	X	33
Glen Garry	Highld	NH1400	57°3·5'	5°3·6'W	X	34
Glengarry Forest	Highld	NN2296	57°1·5'	4°55·5'W	X	34
Glengarth	N Ayr	NS3157	55°46·9'	4°41·3'W	X	63
Glengarth	N Ayr	NS3257	55°46·9'	4°40·3'W	X	63
Glen Garvan	Highld	NM9675	56°49·6'	5°20·1'W	X	40
Glen Gary	Pth & Kin	NN7270	56°48·5'	4°5·3'W	X	42
Glengavel Reservoir	S Lanak	NS6634	55°35·1'	4°7·1'W	W	71
Glengavel Water	S Lanak	NS6536	55°36·2'	4°8·1'W	W	71
Glengee Wood	S Ayr	NS2902	55°17·2'	4°41·1'W	F	76
Glengeith	S Lanak	NS9416	55°25·8'	3°40·1'W	A	71,78
Glen Gelder	Aberd	NO2491	57°0·5'	3°14·6'W	X	44
Glengelt	Scot Bord	NT4755	55°47·4'	2°50·3'W	X	66,73
Glengennet	S Ayr	NX2895	55°13·4'	4°41·8'W	X	76
Glengenny	D & G	NS8206	55°20·3'	3°51·2'W	X	71,78
Glengenny Burn	D & G	NS8105	55°19·7'	3°52·1'W	W	71,78
Glengenny Muir	D & G	NS8205	55°19·7'	3°51·2'W	X	71,78
Glengeoullie	Highld	NH8547	57°30·2'	3°54·7'W	X	27
Glengep Burn	D & G	NS7515	55°25·0'	3°58·1'W	W	71,78
Glengepp Burn	D & G	NX7998	55°15·9'	3°53·8'W	W	78
Glengerrack	Moray	NJ4552	57°33·5'	2°54·7'W	X	28,29
Glen Geusachan	Aberd	NN9694	57°1·8'	3°42·4'W	X	36,43
Glen Gheallaidh	Highld	NJ1238	57°25·7'	3°27·5'W	X	28
Glen Girnaig	Pth & Kin	NN9466	56°46·7'	3°43·6'W	X	43
Glen Girnock	Aberd	NO3193	57°1·6'	3°7·7'W	X	37,44
Glen Glass	Arg & Bt	NM4139	56°28·6'	6°11·9'W	X	47,48
Glenglass	D & G	NS7006	55°20·1'	4°2·5'W	X	71,77
Glen Glass	Highld	NH5568	57°41·0'	4°25·5'W	X	21
Glenglass Burn	D & G	NS7005	55°19·6'	4°2·5'W	W	71,77
Glen Gloy	Highld	NN2689	56°57·8'	4°51·3'W	X	34,41
Glen Gluitanen	Highld	NM7976	56°49·6'	5°36·9'W	X	40
Glen Golach	Arg & Bt	NR3044	55°37·1'	6°16·9'W	X	60
Glen Golly	Highld	NC4243	58°21·1'	4°41·5'W	X	9
Glengolly	Highld	ND1066	58°34·6'	3°32·4'W	X	11,12
Glen Golly River	Highld	NC4243	58°21·1'	4°41·5'W	W	9
Glengonnar Water	S Lanak	NS8817	55°26·3'	3°45·8'W	W	71,78
Glengonnar Water	S Lanak	NS9121	55°28·5'	3°43·0'W	W	71,72
Glengonnor Hill	Scot Bord	NT0720	55°28·2'	3°27·8'W	H	72
Glen Gorm	Arg & Bt	NM4353	56°36·2'	6°10·8'W	X	47
Glengorm Castle	Arg & Bt	NM4357	56°38·3'	6°11·0'W	X	47
Glen Gorse	Leic	SP6499	52°35·3'	1°2·9'W	F	140
Glengoulandie	Pth & Kin	NN7652	56°38·9'	4°0·9'W	X	42,51,52
Glen Gour	Highld	NM9364	56°43·6'	5°22·6'W	X	40
Glengour	Highld	NN0971	56°47·7'	5°7·2'W	X	41
Glengowan Hill	D & G	NX9798	55°16·2'	3°36·8'W	H	78
Glengower	D & G	NX9382	55°7·5'	3°40·3'W	X	78
Glengrasco	Highld	NG4444	57°25·1'	6°15·4'W	T	23
Glen Grenaugh	I of M	SC3170	54°6·1'	4°34·7'W	X	95
Glen Grenaugh	I of M	SC3171	54°6·7'	4°34·7'W	X	95
Glengruboch Burn	D & G	NX3378	55°4·4'	4°36·5'W	W	76
Glen Grudie	Highld	NG9566	57°38·5'	5°25·6'W	X	19
Glen Grundale	Arg & Bt	NR6190	56°2·9'	5°49·8'W	X	61
Glenguffock Hill	D & G	NS7517	55°26·1'	3°58·1'W	H	71,78
Glen Guirdil	Highld	NG3200	57°1·1'	6°24·5'W	X	32,39
Glengunnoch Hill	D & G	NX7070	55°0·7'	4°1·6'W	H	77,84
Glen Gyle	Stir	NN3614	56°17·7'	4°38·6'W	X	50,56
Glengyle	Stir	NN3813	56°17·2'	4°36·6'W	X	50,56
Glengyle Water	Stir	NN3614	56°17·7'	4°38·6'W	W	50,56
Glen Gynack	Highld	NH7402	57°5·8'	4°4·3'W	X	35
Glengyre	D & G	NW9965	54°56·6'	5°7·2'W	X	82
Glengyron	E Ayr	NS5619	55°26·9'	4°16·2'W	X	71
Glen Hall	D & G	NS6813	55°23·8'	4°4·6'W	X	71
Glenhapple	D & G	NX3771	55°0·7'	4°32·5'W	X	77
Glenhapple Fell	D & G	NX3570	55°0·1'	4°34·4'W	X	77
Glenhapple Moor	D & G	NX3670	55°0·1'	4°33·4'W	X	77
Glen Harris	Highld	NM3595	56°58·5'	6°21·2'W	X	39
Glenharrow Burn	D & G	NS7105	55°19·6'	4°1·6'W	W	71,77
Glenharvie Burn	Scot Bord	NT0629	55°33·0'	3°29·0'W	W	72
Glenhastel Burn	E Ayr	NS5906	55°19·9'	4°12·9'W	W	71,77
Glen Haultin	Highld	NG4451	57°28·9'	6°15·8'W	X	23
Glenhead	Aberd	NJ7517	57°14·8'	2°24·4'W	X	38
Glenhead	Aberd	NO7392	57°1·4'	2°26·2'W	X	38,45
Glenhead	D & G	NX4380	55°5·6'	4°27·2'W	X	77
Glenhead	D & G	NX7652	54°51·1'	3°55·5'W	X	84
Glenhead	D & G	NX8987	55°10·1'	3°44·1'W	X	78

Glenhead	Falk	NS7781	56°0·6'	3°57·9'W	X	64
Glenhead	Falk	NS9176	55°58·1'	3°44·3'W	X	65
Glenhead	N Ayr	NS2145	55°40·2'	4°50·3'W	X	63
Glenhead	N Lanak	NS7480	56°0·0'	4°0·8'W	X	64
Glenhead	N Lanak	NS7975	55°57·4'	3°55·8'W	X	64
Glenhead	Pth & Kin	NO0318	56°20·9'	3°33·7'W	X	58
Glenhead	S Ayr	NS2304	55°18·2'	4°46·9'W	X	76
Glenhead	S Ayr	NS2913	55°23·1'	4°41·5'W	X	70
Glenhead	Stir	NN7501	56°11·4'	4°0·4'W	X	57
Glenhead	Stir	NS7585	56°2·8'	4°0·0'W	X	57
Glenhead	Stir	NS7585	56°2·8'	4°0·0'W	X	64
Glenhead Burn	D & G	NX4478	55°4·6'	4°26·2'W	W	77
Glenhead Cottage	Stir	NN7501	56°11·4'	4°0·4'W	X	57
Glenhead Fm	Angus	NO2562	56°44·9'	3°13·1'W	FM	44
Glenhead Fm	Pth & Kin	NN9505	56°13·8'	3°41·2'W	FM	58
Glenhead Hill	D & G	NX7075	55°3·4'	4°1·7'W	H	77,84
Glenhead Lodge	Angus	NO2664	56°46·0'	3°12·2'W	X	44
Glenhead of Aldouran	D & G	NX0063	54°55·6'	5°6·9'W	X	82
Glenhead Rig	D & G	NX6496	55°14·6'	4°7·9'W	X	77
Glenheath	Moray	NJ3545	57°29·7'	3°4·6'W	X	28
Glen Helen	I of M	SC3084	54°13·7'	4°36·1'W	X	95
Glen Hervie	Arg & Bt	NR7411	55°20·7'	5°33·4'W	X	68
Glenheurie Burn	Scot Bord	NT1325	55°30·9'	3°22·2'W	W	72
Glenheurie Rig	Scot Bord	NT1325	55°30·9'	3°22·2'W	F	72
Glen Heysdal	Highld	NG3044	57°24·6'	6°29·3'W	T	23
Glenhie	D & G	NX0847	54°47·1'	4°58·7'W	X	82
Glenhighton	Scot Bord	NT0831	55°34·1'	3°27·1'W	X	72
Glen Hill	Highld	NC7830	58°14·8'	4°4·2'W	X	17
Glen Hill	Northum	NY8555	54°53·6'	2°13·6'W	X	87
Glen Hill Fm	Northnts	SP8381	52°25·5'	0°46·4'W	FM	141
Glen Hinnisdal	Highld	NG4057	57°32·0'	6°20·2'W	X	23
Glen Ho	Hants	SU5009	50°52·9'	1°17·0'W	X	196
Glen Ho	Lincs	SK9818	52°45·3'	0°32·5'W	X	130
Glen Ho	Scot Bord	NT2933	55°35·4'	3°7·2'W	X	73
Glenhoise	D & G	NX4368	54°59·2'	4°26·8'W	X	83
Glenholm	D & G	NY1376	55°4·5'	3°21·3'W	X	85
Glenholm	Scot Bord	NT1032	55°34·7'	3°25·2'W	X	72
Glenholme	Durham	NZ1030	54°40·1'	1°50·3'W	X	92
Glenholt	C of Plym	SX5060	50°25·5'	4°6·3'W	T	201
Glenhoul	D & G	NX6087	55°9·7'	4°11·4'W	X	77
Glenhoul Glen	D & G	NX6189	55°10·8'	4°10·5'W	X	77
Glen House	Highld	NM9181	56°52·7'	5°25·3'W	X	40
Glenhouses	Aberd	NJ8361	57°38·6'	2°16·6'W	X	29,30
Glenhove	N Lanak	NS7772	55°55·8'	3°57·7'W	X	64
Glenhowan	D & G	NY0166	54°59·0'	3°32·4'W	X	84
Glenhowe	S Ayr	NS3410	55°21·6'	4°36·7'W	X	70
Glenhowl	D & G	NX2059	54°53·9'	4°48·0'W	X	82
Glenhurich	Highld	NM8368	56°45·4'	5°32·5'W	T	40
Glen Hurich	Highld	NM8469	56°46·0'	5°31·6'W	X	40
Glenhurich Forest	Highld	NM8168	56°45·4'	5°34·5'W	F	40
Gleniffer Braes Country Park	Renf	NS4660	55°48·8'	4°27·0'W	X	64
Glenim	D & G	NS8508	55°21·4'	3°48·4'W	X	71,78
Glenimp	D & G	NS9003	55°18·8'	3°43·6'W	X	78
Glenimshaw Burn	D & G	NS8409	55°21·9'	3°49·4'W	W	71,78
Glen Ionadal	Highld	NG1942	57°23·2'	6°40·1'W	X	23
Glen Iorsa	N Ayr	NR9239	55°36·3'	5°17·7'W	X	68,69
Gleniron	D & G	NX1960	54°54·4'	4°49·0'W	X	82
Gleniron Fell	D & G	NX1962	54°55·4'	4°49·0'W	H	82
Glen Isla	Angus	NO1967	56°47·5'	3°19·1'W	X	43
Glenisla House	Angus	NO1864	56°45·9'	3°20·0'W	X	43
Glen Isle	D & G	NX8354	54°52·3'	3°49·0'W	X	84
Glenjaan	D & G	NX7194	55°13·7'	4°1·3'W	X	77
Glenjaan Burn	D & G	NX7095	55°14·2'	4°2·2'W	W	77
Glenjaan Hill	D & G	NX7193	55°13·1'	4°1·2'W	X	77
Glenjorrie	D & G	NX2058	54°53·3'	4°48·0'W	X	82
Glenkeil Hill	D & G	NY3294	55°14·4'	3°3·7'W	X	79
Glen Kendrum	Stir	NN5623	56°22·9'	4°19·5'W	X	51
Glenkens, The	D & G	NX5986	55°9·1'	4°12·3'W	X	77
Glenkerie Burn	Scot Bord	NT0827	55°31·9'	3°27·0'W	W	72
Glen Kerran	Arg & Bt	NR7113	55°21·7'	5°36·4'W	X	68
Glenkerry	Scot Bord	NT2710	55°23·0'	3°8·7'W	X	79
Glenkerry Burn	Scot Bord	NT2610	55°23·0'	3°9·6'W	W	79
Glenkerry Hill	Scot Bord	NT2510	55°22·9'	3°10·6'W	H	79
Glenkiln	D & G	NX8477	55°4·7'	3°48·6'W	X	84
Glenkiln	D & G	NY0191	55°12·5'	3°32·9'W	X	78
Glenkiln	N Ayr	NS0130	55°31·6'	5°8·7'W	X	69
Glenkiln Burn	D & G	NY0088	55°10·8'	3°33·8'W	W	78
Glenkiln Burn	D & G	NY0192	55°13·0'	3°32·9'W	W	78
Glenkiln Hill	D & G	NX8377	55°4·7'	3°49·5'W	X	84
Glenkiln Reservoir	D & G	NX8478	55°5·2'	3°48·6'W	W	84
Glenkilrie	Pth & Kin	NO1360	56°43·7'	3°24·9'W	X	43
Glenkin	Arg & Bt	NS1279	55°58·3'	5°0·3'W	X	63
Glen Kin	Arg & Bt	NS1280	55°58·8'	5°0·4'W	X	63
Glenkin Burn	Arg & Bt	NS1379	55°58·3'	4°59·4'W	W	63
Glenkindie	Aberd	NJ4313	57°12·5'	2°56·2'W	T	37
Glenkindie Ho	Aberd	NJ4214	57°13·0'	2°57·2'W	X	37
Glen Kingie	Highld	NN0497	57°1·6'	5°13·3'W	X	33
Glen Kinglas	Arg & Bt	NN2109	56°14·6'	4°52·9'W	X	56
Glen Kinglass	Arg & Bt	NN1436	56°29·0'	5°0·8'W	X	50
Glenkinglass Lodge	Arg & Bt	NN1638	56°30·1'	4°58·9'W	X	50
Glenkinnon Burn	Scot Bord	NT4233	55°35·5'	2°54·8'W	W	73
Glen Kip	S Lanak	NS8716	55°25·7'	3°46·7'W	X	71,78
Glenkip Burn	S Lanak	NS8617	55°26·3'	3°47·7'W	W	71,78
Glenkirk	Highld	NH8331	57°21·5'	3°56·2'W	X	27
Glenkirk	Scot Bord	NT0729	55°33·0'	3°28·0'W	X	72
Glenkitten Fell	D & G	NX1872	55°0·8'	4°50·4'W	X	76
Glen Knowe	D & G	NX6880	55°6·1'	4°3·7'W	X	77
Glen Kyllachy	Highld	NH7424	57°17·6'	4°5·0'W	X	35
Glenkyllachy Lodge	Highld	NH7523	57°17·1'	4°4·0'W	X	35
Glen Labisdale	N Eil	NF7822	57°10·8'	7°19·3'W	X	31
Glen Laff	Aberd	NJ4319	57°15·7'	2°56·2'W	X	37
Glenlaff Hill	Aberd	NJ4020	57°16·3'	2°59·2'W	H	37
Glenlaggan	D & G	-NX6871	55°1·2'	4°3·5'W	X	77,84
Glenlaggan Hill	D & G	NX7072	55°1·8'	4°1·6'W	H	77,84
Glenlair	D & G	NX7572	55°1·9'	3°56·9'W	X	84
Glenlarie Burn	D & G	NS7306	55°20·2'	3°59·7'W	W	71,77
Glen Latterach	Moray	NJ1951	57°32·8'	3°20·7'W	X	28
Glenlatterach	Moray	NJ1954	57°34·4'	3°20·8'W	X	28
Glenlatterach Reservoir	Moray	NJ1952	57°33·3'	3°20·8'W	W	28

Glen Laudale	Highld	NM7258	56°39·8′	5°42·8′W	X	49
Glenlaugh	D & G	NX8688	55°10·6′	3°47·0′W	X	78
Glen Lealt	Arg & Bt	NR6693	56°4·6′	5°45·2′W	X	55,61
Glenlean	Arg & Bt	NS0883	56°0·3′	5°4·3′W	X	56
Glen Lean	Arg & Bt	NS0982	55°59·8′	5°3·3′W	X	56
Glen Lednock	Pth & Kin	NN7327	56°25·3′	4°3·1′W	X	51,52
Glen Lee	Angus	NO3881	56°55·2′	3°0·7′W	X	44
Glenlee	Angus	NO4179	56°54·2′	2°57·7′W	X	44
Glenlee	D & G	NS6004	55°18·9′	4°11·9′W	X	77
Glenlee	D & G	NX6080	55°5·9′	4°11·2′W	X	77
Glenlee Burn	D & G	NX5780	55°5·9′	4°14·0′W	W	77
Glenlee Hill	D & G	NX5979	55°5·4′	4°12·1′W	H	77
Glenlee Mains	D & G	NX6080	55°5·9′	4°11·2′W	X	77
Glen Leidle	Arg & Bt	NM5224	56°20·9′	6°0·4′W	X	48
Glenleigh Park	E Susx	TQ7308	50°51·0′	0°27·8′E	T	199
Glenleitch	E Ayr	NS4543	55°39·6′	4°27·4′W	X	70
Glenleith Burn	D & G	NS9201	55°17·7′	3°41·6′W	W	78
Glenleith Fell	D & G	NS9202	55°18·3′	3°41·6′W	H	78
Glen Leosaid	N Eil	NB0410	57°59·1′	7°0·0′W	X	13
Glenleraig	Highld	NC1431	58°14·0′	5°9·6′W	X	15
Glenley	Angus	NO4563	56°45·6′	2°53·5′W	X	44
Glenlia Fm	Highld	NH5020	57°15·0′	4°28·7′W	FM	26,35
Glen Libidil	Arg & Bt	NM6622	56°20·2′	5°46·7′W	X	49
Glenlibidil Burn	Arg & Bt	NM6622	56°20·2′	5°46·7′W	W	49
Glenlichorn	Pth & Kin	NN7912	56°17·4′	3°56·8′W	X	57
Glenlicht Ho	Highld	NH0017	57°12·3′	5°18·2′W	X	33
Glen Liever	Arg & Bt	NM9007	56°12·8′	5°22·7′W	X	55
Glen Ling	Highld	NG9432	57°20·2′	5°24·9′W	X	25
Glenling Burn	D & G	NX3251	54°49·8′	4°36·5′W	W	82
Glenling Moss	D & G	NX3251	54°49·8′	4°36·5′W	X	82
Glen Liver	Arg & Bt	NN0835	56°28·3′	5°6·6′W	X	50
Glenliver	Moray	NJ2523	57°17·7′	3°14·2′W	X	37
Glenlivet	Moray	NJ1929	57°20·9′	3°20·3′W	T	36
Glen Livet	Moray	NJ2027	57°19·9′	3°19·3′W	X	36
Glen Loch	Pth & Kin	NN9873	56°50·5′	3°39·9′W	X	43
Glen Lochan	Pth & Kin	NN8335	56°29·8′	3°53·6′W	X	52
Glenlochar	D & G	NX7364	54°57·5′	3°58·6′W	T	83,84
Glenlochar Ho	D & G	NX7364	54°57·5′	3°58·6′W	X	83,84
Glen Lochay	Stir	NN4937	56°30·3′	4°26·8′W	X	51
Glenlochrie	S Ayr	NS2502	55°17·1′	4°44·9′W	X	76
Glen Lochsie	Pth & Kin	NO0572	56°50·0′	3°33·0′W	X	43
Glen Lochsie Burn	Pth & Kin	NO0572	56°50·0′	3°33·0′W	W	43
Glenlochsie Fm	Pth & Kin	NO0871	56°49·5′	3°30·0′W	FM	43
Glenlochsie Lodge	Pth & Kin	NO0672	56°50·1′	3°32·0′W	X	43
Glen Lochy	Arg & Bt	NN2731	56°26·6′	4°47·9′W	X	50
Glen Lochy	Moray	NJ1223	57°17·6′	3°27·2′W	X	36
Glenlochy Crossing	Arg & Bt	NN2529	56°25·5′	4°49·8′W	X	50
Glen Lodge	Highld	NG5636	57°21·2′	6°2·9′W	X	24,32
Glen Lodge	Somer	SS8845	51°11·8′	3°35·8′W	X	181
Glen Lodge Fm	Norf	TG1509	52°38·4′	1°11·1′E	FM	144
Glen Logan	Arg & Bt	NR4262	55°47·2′	6°6·5′W	X	60,61
Glenlogan Ho	E Ayr	NS5626	55°30·6′	4°16·4′W	X	71
Glenlogie	Aberd	NJ5018	57°15·3′	2°49·3′W	X	37
Glenlogie	Aberd	NJ7226	57°19·7′	2°27·4′W	X	38
Glen Logie	Angus	NO3168	56°48·2′	3°7·3′W	X	44
Glenloig	N Ayr	NR9435	55°34·2′	5°15·6′W	X	68,69
Glen Loin	Arg & Bt	NN3006	56°13·2′	4°44·1′W	X	56
Glen Loin	Moray	NJ1409	57°10·1′	3°24·9′W	X	36
Glenloin Ho	Arg & Bt	NN2905	56°12·7′	4°45·0′W	X	56
Glenlomond	Pth & Kin	NO1604	56°13·5′	3°20·8′W	T	58
Glen Lonan	Arg & Bt	NM9427	56°23·7′	5°19·8′W	X	49
Glenlood Hill	Scot Bord	NT0828	55°32·5′	3°27·0′W	H	72
Glenlora	Renf	NS3358	55°47·4′	4°39·4′W	X	63
Glen Lorgasdal	Highld	NG2338	57°21·2′	6°35·9′W	X	23
Glen Lossie	Moray	NJ1347	57°30·6′	3°26·7′W	X	28
Glen Loth	Highld	NC9312	58°5·3′	3°48·4′W	X	17
Glenlough	I of M	SC3478	54°10·5′	4°32·2′W	X	95
Glenloy	D & G	NX9288	55°10·7′	3°41·3′W	X	78
Glen Loy	Highld	NN1084	56°54·8′	5°6·8′W	X	34,41
Glen Loy Lodge (Hotel)	Highld	NN1481	56°53·2′	5°2·7′W	X	34,41
Glenloyne	Highld	NH1305	57°6·1′	5°4·8′W	X	34
Glenluce	D & G	NX1957	54°52·8′	4°48·9′W	T	82
Glenluce Abbey	D & G	NX1858	54°53·3′	4°49·8′W	A	82
Glenlude	Scot Bord	NT3029	55°33·2′	3°6·1′W	X	73
Glenlude Hill	Scot Bord	NT3028	55°32·7′	3°6·1′W	H	73
Glen Lui	Aberd	NO0592	57°0·8′	3°33·4′W	X	43
Glen Luibeg	Aberd	NO0293	57°1·3′	3°36·4′W	X	36,43
Glenluie	Highld	NH2700	57°3·8′	4°50·7′W	X	34
Glenluie	S Ayr	NS2508	55°20·3′	4°45·1′W	X	70,76
Glen Luss	Arg & Bt	NS3293	56°6·3′	4°41·6′W	X	56
Glen Lussa	Arg & Bt	NR7326	55°28·8′	5°35·1′W	X	68
Glenlussa Ho	Arg & Bt	NR7325	55°28·2′	5°35·1′W	X	68
Glenlussa Lodge	Arg & Bt	NR7625	55°28·3′	5°32·2′W	X	68,69
Glenlussa Water	Arg & Bt	NR7425	55°28·3′	5°34·1′W	W	68
Glen Lyon	Pth & Kin	NN5344	56°34·2′	4°23·1′W	X	51
Glenlyon Ho	Pth & Kin	NN7347	56°36·1′	4°3·7′W	X	51,52
Glen Macduff	Pth & Kin	NN8803	56°12·6′	3°47·9′W	X	58
Glenmachrie	Arg & Bt	NR3350	55°40·5′	6°14·4′W	X	60
Glen Machrie	Arg & Bt	NR3351	55°41·0′	6°14·4′W	X	60
Glenmachrie Lots	Arg & Bt	NR3550	55°40·5′	6°12·5′W	X	60
Glenmaddie	D & G	NS7407	55°20·7′	3°58·8′W	X	71,77
Glenmaddie Burn	D & G	NS7507	55°20·7′	3°57·8′W	W	71,78
Glenmaddie Wood	D & G	NS7407	55°20·7′	3°58·8′W	F	71,77
Glenmaddy Burn	D & G	NX9264	54°57·8′	3°40·8′W	W	84
Glenmaid	D & G	NX9789	55°11·3′	3°36·6′W	X	78
Glenmaid Moor	D & G	NX9689	55°11·3′	3°37·6′W	X	78
Glenmallan	Arg & Bt	NS2496	56°7·7′	4°49·5′W	X	56
Glen Mallie	Highld	NN0787	56°56·3′	5°9·9′W	X	41
Glenmallie	Highld	NN0787	56°56·3′	5°9·9′W	X	41
Glenmalloch Hill	D & G	NX4170	55°0·2′	4°28·7′W	H	77
Glen Mama Fm	Highld	NM7384	56°53·8′	5°43·2′W	FM	40
Glenmanna	D & G	NS7601	55°17·5′	3°56·7′W	X	78
Glenmanna Burn	D & G	NS7402	55°18·0′	3°58·7′W	W	77
Glenmanna Burn	D & G	NS7502	55°18·0′	3°57·7′W	W	78
Glenmanuilt	Arg & Bt	NR6407	55°18·3′	5°42·7′W	X	68
Glenmanuilt Hill	Arg & Bt	NR6407	55°18·3′	5°42·7′W	X	68
Glen Mark	Angus	NO3684	56°56·8′	3°2·7′W	X	44
Glenmark	Angus	NO4183	56°56·3′	2°57·7′W	X	44
Glen Markie	Highld	NH5407	57°8·1′	4°24·3′W	X	35
Glen Markie	Highld	NN5897	57°2·8′	4°20·0′W	X	35

Glenmarkie	Moray	NJ3837	57°25·4′	3°1·5′W	X	28
Glenmarkie Burn	Highld	NH5608	57°8·7′	4°22·3′W	W	35
Glenmarkie Lodge	Angus	NO2364	56°45·9′	3°15·1′W	T	44
Glenmarksie	Highld	NH3857	57°34·7′	4°42·1′W	X	26
Glenmassan	Arg & Bt	NS0987	56°2·5′	5°3·5′W	X	56
Glen Massan	Arg & Bt	NS1286	56°2·1′	5°0·6′W	X	56
Glenmavis	N Lanak	NS7567	55°53·1′	3°59·5′W	T	64
Glenmavis	W Loth	NS9869	55°54·5′	3°37·5′W	T	65
Glen Maye	I of M	SC2279	54°10·8′	4°43·2′W	X	95
Glenmaye	I of M	SC2379	54°10·8′	4°42·3′W	T	95
Glenmayne	Scot Bord	NT4933	55°35·5′	2°48·1′W	T	73
Glen Mazeran	Highld	NH7121	57°16·0′	4°7·9′W	X	35
Glenmazeran Lodge	Highld	NH7422	57°16·5′	4°4·9′W	X	35
Glenmead	Scot Bord	NT3636	55°37·1′	3°0·5′W	X	73
Glenmeanie	Highld	NH2852	57°31·8′	4°51·9′W	X	25
Glenmellan	Aberd	NJ6538	57°26·1′	2°34·5′W	X	29
Glenmidge	D & G	NX8987	55°10·1′	3°44·1′W	X	78
Glenmill	Inverc	NS3466	55°51·8′	4°38·7′W	X	63
Glenmillan Ho	Aberd	NJ5905	57°8·3′	2°40·2′W	X	37
Glenmoar Fm	I of M	SC2676	54°9·3′	4°39·5′W	FM	95
Glen Modale	N Eil	NB0021	58°4·9′	7°4·9′W	X	13
Glen Moidart	Highld	NM7573	56°47·9′	5°40·6′W	X	40
Glenmoidart Ho	Highld	NM7472	56°47·3′	5°41·6′W	X	40
Glen Mollochan	Arg & Bt	NS3194	56°6·8′	4°42·6′W	X	56
Glenmollochan	Arg & Bt	NS3294	56°6·8′	4°41·7′W	X	56
Glen Mona	I of M	SC4588	54°16·1′	4°22·4′W	T	95
Glen Mooar	I of M	SC2478	54°10·3′	4°41·4′W	X	95
Glenmooar	I of M	SC2782	54°12·5′	4°38·8′W	X	95
Glen Mooar	I of M	SC3089	54°16·4′	4°36·2′W	X	95
Glen Mooar	I of M	SC4385	54°14·4′	4°24·1′W	X	95
Glen Mor	Highld	NG8540	57°24·2′	5°34·3′W	X	24
Glen More	Arg & Bt	NM5630	56°24·2′	5°56·8′W	X	48
Glen More	Arg & Bt	NM6230	56°24·4′	5°51·0′W	X	49
Glenmore	Arg & Bt	NM8412	56°15·3′	5°28·8′W	X	55
Glen More	Arg & Bt	NS0268	55°52·1′	5°9·4′W	X	63
Glenmore	Arg & Bt	NS0269	55°52·7′	5°9·5′W	X	63
Glenmore	Cumbr	NY0622	54°35·3′	3°26·9′W	X	89
Glenmore	Devon	SS5918	50°56·9′	4°0·1′W	X	180
Glenmore	Highld	NG4340	57°22·9′	6°16·1′W	T	23
Glenmore	Highld	NG8540	57°24·2′	5°34·3′W	X	24
Glen More	Highld	NG8718	57°12·5′	5°31·2′W	X	33
Glenmore	Highld	NH9809	57°9·9′	3°40·7′W	X	36
Glen More	Highld	NM5862	56°41·5′	5°56·7′W	X	47
Glen More	Highld	NM5863	56°42·0′	5°56·7′W	X	47
Glenmore Bay	Highld	NM5961	56°41·0′	5°55·6′W	W	47
Glenmore Bothy	Pth & Kin	NN7152	56°38·8′	4°5·8′W	X	42,51,52
Glenmore Burn	Arg & Bt	NS0270	55°53·2′	5°9·5′W	W	63
Glen More Burn	Highld	NC9637	58°18·8′	3°46·0′W	W	11,17
Glenmore Fm	Cambs	TF4209	52°39·8′	0°6·4′E	FM	142,143
Glenmore Fm	E Susx	TQ4025	51°0·7′	0°0·1′E	FM	187,198
Glen More Forest Park	Highld	NH9710	57°10·4′	3°41·8′W	X	36
Glenmore Hill	Arg & Bt	NS0271	55°53·7′	5°9·6′W	X	63
Glenmore Ho	N Som	ST5264	51°22·6′	2°41·0′W	X	172,182
Glenmore Loch	Highld	NJ0833	57°23·0′	3°31·4′W	W	27
Glenmore Lodge (National Outdoor Training Centre)	Highld	NH9809	57°9·9′	3°40·7′W	X	36
Glenmore River	Highld	NG4339	57°22·4′	6°16·0′W	W	23,32
Glenmore River	Highld	NG8917	57°12·0′	5°29·1′W	W	33
Glenmore River	Highld	NM5863	56°42·0′	5°56·7′W	W	47
Glen Moriston	Highld	NH3113	57°10·9′	4°47·3′W	X	34
Glen Mor or Glen Albyn	Highld	NH3502	57°5·0′	4°42·9′W	X	34
Glen Mor or Glen Albyn	Highld	NH5426	57°18·3′	4°25·0′W	X	26,35
Glenmorven Cott	Highld	NM5651	56°35·5′	5°58·0′W	X	47
Glen Moss	Renf	NS3669	55°53·4′	4°36·9′W	W	63
Glen Moy	Angus	NO3963	56°45·5′	2°59·4′W	X	44
Glenmoy	Angus	NO4064	56°46·1′	2°58·4′W	X	44
Glenmuck	E Ayr	NS5102	55°17·6′	4°20·4′W	X	77
Glenmuck Craig	E Ayr	NS5003	55°18·2′	4°21·3′W	H	77
Glenmuck Height	Scot Bord	NT0724	55°30·3′	3°27·9′W	H	72
Glenmucklach	Arg & Bt	NR7012	55°21·1′	5°37·3′W	X	68
Glen Muick	Aberd	NO3188	56°58·9′	3°7·7′W	X	44
Glenmuick	Highld	NC3912	58°4·3′	4°43·3′W	X	16
Glenmuir	E Ayr	NS6322	55°28·6′	4°9·6′W	X	71
Glenmuir Burn	E Ayr	NS6321	55°28·1′	4°9·6′W	W	71
Glenmuir Hill	E Ayr	NS6920	55°27·6′	4°3·9′W	X	71
Glenmuirshaw	E Ayr	NS6919	55°27·1′	4°3·8′W	X	71
Glenmuirshaw	E Ayr	NS7020	55°27·7′	4°2·9′W	X	71
Glenmuir Water	E Ayr	NS6120	55°27·5′	4°11·5′W	W	71
Glenmuir Water	E Ayr	NS6619	55°27·0′	4°6·7′W	W	71
Glenmullie	Moray	NJ1916	57°13·9′	3°20·0′W	X	36
Glen Nant	Arg & Bt	NN0128	56°24·4′	5°13·1′W	X	50
Glenn App	S Ayr	NX0775	55°2·2′	5°0·8′W	X	76
Glen Neil	Arg & Bt	NS0572	55°54·4′	5°6·7′W	X	63
Glen Nevis	Highld	NN1468	56°46·2′	5°2·2′W	X	41
Glen Nevis Ho	Highld	NN1272	56°48·4′	5°4·3′W	X	41
Glennie	Aberd	NJ5849	57°32·0′	2°41·6′W	X	29
Glennieston	Aberd	NJ5734	57°23·9′	2°42·5′W	X	29
Glenniston	Fife	NT2192	56°7·1′	3°15·8′W	X	58
Glen Nochty	Aberd	NJ3215	57°13·5′	3°7·1′W	X	37
Glennoe	Arg & Bt	NN0534	56°27·7′	5°9·5′W	X	50
Glen Noe	Arg & Bt	NN0733	56°27·2′	5°7·5′W	X	50
Glen Noustapal	N Eil	NF8220	57°9·9′	7°15·2′W	X	31
Glen Oaks	Leic	SP6698	52°34·8′	1°1·2′W	X	141
Glenochar	S Lanak	NS9513	55°24·2′	3°39·1′W	X	78
Glenochar Burn	S Lanak	NS9313	55°24·2′	3°41·0′W	W	71,78
Glen of Balchimmy	Aberd	NJ5011	57°11·5′	2°49·2′W	X	37
Glen of Coachford	Aberd	NJ4646	57°30·3′	2°53·6′W	X	28,29
Glen of Craigo	Angus	NO6762	56°45·2′	2°31·9′W	X	45
Glen of Cushnie	Aberd	NJ4910	57°10·9′	2°50·2′W	X	37
Glen of Drumtochty	Aberd	NO7079	56°54·3′	2°29·1′W	X	45
Glen of Greor	Orkney	HY2203	58°54·7′	3°20·8′W	X	6,7
Glen of Kinpauch	Pth & Kin	NN8906	56°14·3′	3°47·0′W	X	58
Glen of Newmill	Moray	NJ4454	57°34·6′	2°55·7′W	T	28
Glen of Noth	Aberd	NJ5030	57°21·7′	2°49·4′W	X	29,37
Glen of Peat Lochies	Aberd	NJ5203	57°7·2′	2°47·1′W	X	37
Glen of Quarff	Shetld	HU4033	60°5·0′	1°16·4′W	X	4
Glen of Rait	Pth & Kin	NO2127	56°26·0′	3°16·4′W	X	53,58
Glen of Rothes	Moray	NJ2552	57°33·4′	3°14·7′W	X	28
Glen of Rothes	Moray	NJ2651	57°32·8′	3°13·7′W	X	28
Glen of Screel Burn	D & G	NX7854	54°52·2′	3°53·6′W	W	84

Glen of Spottes	D & G	NX8067	54°59·2′	3°52·1′W	X	84
Glen of the Bar	D & G	NX4770	55°0·3′	4°23·1′W	X	77
Glen of the Berry	Orkney	ND2590	58°47·7′	3°17·4′W	X	7
Glen of the Horn	Orkney	HY2303	58°54·7′	3°19·7′W	X	6,7
Glenogil	Angus	NO4463	56°45·6′	2°54·5′W	T	44
Glen Ogil	Angus	NO4465	56°46·6′	2°54·5′W	X	44
Glenogil Reservoir	Angus	NO4464	56°46·1′	2°54·5′W	W	44
Glen Ogilvie	Angus	NO3743	56°34·7′	3°1·1′W	X	54
Glen Ogle	Stir	NN5726	56°24·5′	4°18·6′W	X	51
Glenogle Cotts	Stir	NN5528	56°25·6′	4°20·6′W	X	51
Glenogle Fm	Stir	NN5824	56°23·5′	4°17·6′W	FM	51
Glen Ollisdal	Highld	NG2139	57°21·6′	6°37·9′W	X	23
Glen Orchy	Arg & Bt	NN2433	56°27·6′	4°50·9′W	X	50
Glen Orchy Fm	Arg & Bt	NN2634	56°28·2′	4°49·0′W	FM	50
Glenorkie	Fife	NO3007	56°15·3′	3°7·3′W	X	59
Glenorkney	Orkney	HY4507	58°57·1′	2°56·9′W	X	6,7
Glen Ormidale	N Ayr	NR9834	55°33·7′	5°11·8′W	X	69
Glenormiston Fm	Scot Bord	NT3138	55°38·1′	3°5·3′W	FM	73
Glen Orrin	Highld	NH3849	57°30·4′	4°41·8′W	X	26
Glen Osdale	Highld	NG2344	57°24·4′	6°36·3′W	X	23
Glen Ose	Highld	NG3241	57°23·1′	6°27·1′W	X	23
Glenoul Burn	E Ayr	NS5735	55°35·5′	4°15·7′W	W	71
Glenour	S Ayr	NX1783	55°6·7′	4°51·7′W	X	76
Glenouther Moor	E Ayr	NS4748	55°42·3′	4°25·7′W	F	64
Glenouther Rig	E Ayr	NS4849	55°42·9′	4°24·7′W	X	64
Glenowen	Pemb	SM9505	51°42·6′	4°57·7′W	T	157,158
Glen Oykel	Highld	NC3108	58°2·0′	4°51·3′W	X	15
Glen Oykel	Highld	NC3602	57°58·9′	4°45·9′W	X	16
Glenpark	C of Edin	NT1466	55°53·0′	3°22·1′W	X	65
Glen Park	Renf	NS4860	55°48·8′	4°25·1′W	F	64
Glenparks	S Ayr	NS3618	55°26·0′	4°35·1′W	X	70
Glen Parva	Leic	SP5699	52°35·4′	1°10·0′W	T	140
Glenpatrick	Renf	NS4461	55°49·3′	4°29·0′W	X	64
Glen Pean	Highld	NM9490	56°57·6′	5°22·8′W	X	33,40
Glen Prosen	Angus	NO2967	56°47·6′	3°9·3′W	X	44
Glenprosen Lodge	Angus	NO2968	56°48·1′	3°9·3′W	X	44
Glenprosen Village	Angus	NO3265	56°46·6′	3°6·3′W	T	44
Glenpunty Wood	C of Edin	NT1776	55°58·4′	3°19·4′W	F	65,66
Glen Quaich	Pth & Kin	NN8538	56°31·5′	3°51·7′W	X	52
Glenquaich Lodge	Pth & Kin	NN8637	56°30·9′	3°50·7′W	X	52
Glenquey	Pth & Kin	NN9803	56°12·8′	3°38·2′W	X	58
Glenquey Resr	Pth & Kin	NN9702	56°12·2′	3°39·2′W	W	58
Glen Quharity	Angus	NO2861	56°44·4′	3°10·2′W	X	44
Glenquicken	D & G	NX5159	54°54·5′	4°19·0′W	X	83
Glenquicken Moor	D & G	NX5258	54°53·9′	4°18·1′W	X	83
Glenquiech	Angus	NO4261	56°44·5′	2°56·4′W	X	44
Glenquithle	Aberd	NJ8464	57°40·2′	2°15·6′W	X	29,30
Glen Quoich	Aberd	NO0892	57°0·9′	3°30·5′W	X	43
Glen Quoich	Aberd	NO0893	57°1·4′	3°30·5′W	X	36,43
Glen Quoich	Highld	NH0107	57°6·9′	5°16·7′W	X	33
Glenquoich Forest	Highld	NH0106	57°6·4′	5°16·7′W	X	33
Glenrae Brae	D & G	NS8317	55°26·2′	3°50·5′W	X	71,78
Glenrae Dod	D & G	NS8317	55°26·2′	3°50·5′W	H	71,78
Glenralloch	Arg & Bt	NR8569	55°52·2′	5°25·8′W	X	62
Glenramskill	Arg & Bt	NR7319	55°25·0′	5°34·8′W	X	68
Glenramskill Burn	Arg & Bt	NR7318	55°24·5′	5°34·7′W	W	68
Glenrath	Scot Bord	NT2033	55°35·3′	3°15·7′W	T	73
Glenrath Burn	Scot Bord	NT2132	55°34·8′	3°14·8′W	W	73
Glenrath Heights	Scot Bord	NT2431	55°34·3′	3°11·9′W	H	73
Glenrath Hill	Scot Bord	NT2233	55°35·3′	3°13·8′W	H	73
Glenrathope	Scot Bord	NT2232	55°34·8′	3°13·8′W	X	73
Glenrazie	D & G	NX3668	54°59·0′	4°33·4′W	X	83
Glenrazie Wood	D & G	NX3669	54°59·6′	4°33·4′W	F	83
Glenreasdell	Arg & Bt	NR8260	55°47·3′	5°28·2′W	X	62
Glenreasdell Mains	Arg & Bt	NR8658	55°46·3′	5°24·3′W	X	62
Glenree	N Ayr	NR9425	55°28·8′	5°15·2′W	X	68,69
Glen Remuil	Arg & Bt	NR6312	55°20·9′	5°43·9′W	X	68
Glenrickard	N Ayr	NS0034	55°33·8′	5°9·9′W	X	69
Glenridding	Cumbr	NY3817	54°32·9′	2°57·1′W	T	90
Glenridding Common	Cumbr	NY3516	54°32·4′	2°59·9′W	X	90
Glenridding Dodd	Cumbr	NY3817	54°32·9′	2°57·1′W	H	90
Glen Ridley	Northum	NY8676	55°4·9′	2°12·7′W	X	87
Glenrief	D & G	NY3996	55°15·5′	2°57·2′W	X	79
Glenrief Burn	D & G	NY4097	55°16·1′	2°56·2′W	W	79
Glenrief Rig	D & G	NY4098	55°16·6′	2°56·2′W	H	79
Glenrig	Falk	NS8677	55°58·6′	3°49·2′W	X	65
Glenrigh Forest	Highld	NN0664	56°43·9′	5°9·8′W	F	41
Glen Rinnes	Moray	NJ2834	57°23·7′	3°11·4′W	X	28
Glenrinnes Lodge	Moray	NJ3138	57°25·9′	3°8·5′W	X	28
Glen Risdale	Arg & Bt	NM8018	56°18·5′	5°33·0′W	X	55
Glenroan	D & G	NX7570	55°0·8′	3°56·9′W	X	84
Glen Rock	Highld	NC8003	58°0·3′	4°1·4′W	X	17
Glen Rock Burn	Highld	NC7903	58°0·2′	4°2·4′W	W	17
Glen Rodel	N Eil	NG0484	57°45·1′	6°58·1′W	X	18
Glen Rosa	N Ayr	NR9838	55°35·9′	5°11·9′W	X	69
Glenrosa	N Ayr	NS0037	55°35·4′	5°10·0′W	X	69
Glenrosa Water	N Ayr	NR9838	55°35·9′	5°11·9′W	W	69
Glen Rossal	Highld	NC4604	58°0·2′	4°35·9′W	X	16
Glenrothes	Fife	NO2701	56°12·0′	3°10·2′W	T	59
Glen Roy	Highld	NN3087	56°56·8′	4°47·2′W	X	34,41
Glen Roy	Highld	NN3390	56°58·5′	4°44·4′W	X	34
Glenroy	I of M	SC4083	54°13·3′	4°26·8′W	X	95
Glen Roy	I of M	SC4284	54°13·9′	4°25·0′W	X	95
Glen Roy National Nature Reserve	Highld	NN2888	56°57·3′	4°49·3′W	X	34,41
Glenrusco	Scot Bord	NT1024	55°30·3′	3°25·1′W	X	72
Glenrusco Burn	Scot Bord	NT1124	55°30·4′	3°24·1′W	W	72
Glen Rushen	I of M	SC2476	54°9·2′	4°41·3′W	X	95
Glen Rushen Plantation	I of M	SC2476	54°9·2′	4°41·3′W	F	95
Glenruther	D & G	NX3273	55°1·6′	4°37·3′W	X	76
Glenruther Lodge	D & G	NX3272	55°1·1′	4°37·2′W	X	76
Glensalloch Burn	D & G	NS8214	55°24·6′	3°51·4′W	W	71,78
Glen Sanda	Highld	NM8047	56°34·1′	5°34·4′W	X	49
Glensanda	Highld	NM8246	56°33·6′	5°32·4′W	T	49
Glensanda River	Highld	NM8047	56°34·1′	5°34·4′W	W	49
Glen Sannox	N Ayr	NR9944	55°39·1′	5°11·3′W	X	62,69
Glen Sassunn	Pth & Kin	NN6554	56°39·8′	4°11·7′W	X	42,51
Glen Sassunn Burn	Pth & Kin	NN6553	56°39·2′	4°11·7′W	W	42,51
Glensaugh	Aberd	NO6778	56°53·8′	2°32·1′W	X	45
Glensaugh Lodge	Aberd	NO6677	56°53·2′	2°33·0′W	X	45

Glensax	Scot Bord	NT2634	55°35·9'	3°10·0'W	X	73
Glensax Burn	Scot Bord	NT2634	55°35·9'	3°10·0'W	W	73
Glensaxon Fell	D & G	NY3393	55°13·9'	3°2·8'W	H	79
Glensburgh	Falk	NS9182	56°1·4'	3°44·5'W	T	65
Glen Scaddle	Highld	NM9568	56°45·8'	5°20·8'W	X	40
Glen Scaftigill	N Ayr	NR8939	55°36·2'	5°20·5'W	X	68,69
Glen Scaladal	Highld	NG5216	57°10·3'	6°5·7'W	X	32
Glen Scamadal	Highld	NG4270	57°39·0'	6°19·0'W	X	23
Glenscorrodale Fm	N Ayr	NR9627	55°29·9'	5°13·4'W	FM	68,69
Glensgaich	Highld	NH4560	57°36·5'	4°35·2'W	X	20
Glen Sgionie	Stir	NN4316	56°18·9'	4°31·9'W	X	56
Glensguaib	Highld	NH2085	57°49·4'	5°1·4'W	X	20
Glenshalg	Aberd	NJ5806	57°8·8'	2°41·2'W	X	37
Glenshalloch	D & G	NX4370	55°0·2'	4°26·9'W	X	77
Glenshalloch Burn	D & G	NX4270	55°0·2'	4°27·8'W	W	77
Glenshalloch Burn	E Ayr	NS6007	55°20·5'	4°12·0'W	W	71,77
Glenshalloch Hill	D & G	NX4370	55°0·2'	4°26·9'W	X	77
Glenshalloch Wood	S Ayr	NS2905	55°18·8'	4°41·2'W	F	70,76
Glensham Rock Fm	E Ayr	NS5523	55°29·0'	4°17·2'W	FM	71
Glenshanna	D & G	NY2996	55°15·4'	3°6·6'W	X	79
Glenshanna Burn	D & G	NY3196	55°15·5'	3°4·7'W	W	79
Glenshant Hill	N Ayr	NR9939	55°36·4'	5°11·0'W	H	69
Glenshauch Wood	Pth & Kin	NO0436	56°30·6'	3°33·1'W	F	52,53
Glen Shee	Pth & Kin	NN9734	56°29·5'	3°39·9'W	X	52,53
Glenshee	Pth & Kin	NO1363	56°45·3'	3°24·9'W	X	43
Glenshee Hill	Pth & Kin	NN9735	56°30·0'	3°39·9'W	H	52,53
Glenshee Lodge	Pth & Kin	NO1368	56°48·0'	3°25·0'W	X	43
Glen Shellesder	Highld	NG3301	57°1·6'	6°23·6'W	X	32,39
Glen Shellesder Burn	Highld	NG3301	57°1·6'	6°23·6'W	W	32,39
Glen Shellish	Arg & Bt	NS1094	56°6·3'	5°2·9'W	X	56
Glenshellish Fm	Arg & Bt	NS1197	56°8·0'	5°2·0'W	FM	56
Glenshero Lodge	Highld	NN5493	57°0·6'	4°23·8'W	X	35
Glen Sherup	Pth & Kin	NN9503	56°12·7'	3°41·1'W	X	58
Glensherup Burn	Pth & Kin	NN9503	56°12·7'	3°41·1'W	W	58
Glensherup Resr	Pth & Kin	NN9604	56°13·3'	3°40·2'W	W	58
Glen Shervie	Pth & Kin	NN8135	56°29·8'	3°55·5'W	X	52
Glenshervie Burn	Pth & Kin	NN8134	56°29·2'	3°55·5'W	W	52
Glenshian Lodge Hotel	Highld	NM7782	56°52·8'	5°39·2'W	X	40
Glen Shiel	Highld	NH0310	57°8·6'	5°14·9'W	X	33
Glenshiel	Moray	NH9753	57°33·6'	3°42·8'W	X	27
Glenshiel Banks	Scot Bord	NT2730	55°33·7'	3°9·0'W	X	73
Glen Shieldaig	Highld	NG8250	57°29·5'	5°37·8'W	X	24
Glenshieldaig Forest	Highld	NG8349	57°29·0'	5°36·7'W	X	24
Glenshiel Forest	Highld	NG9414	57°10·5'	5°24·0'W	X	33
Glenshiel Lodge	Highld	NG9318	57°12·6'	5°25·2'W	X	33
Glenshimmeroch	D & G	NX6486	55°9·2'	4°7·6'W	X	77
Glenshimmeroch Hill	D & G	NX6587	55°9·8'	4°6·7'W	H	77
Glen Shira	Arg & Bt	NN1314	56°17·2'	5°0·8'W	X	50,56
Glen Shirra	Highld	NN5391	56°59·5'	4°24·7'W	X	35
Glenshirra Forest	Highld	NN4793	57°0·4'	4°30·7'W	X	34
Glen Shurig	N Ayr	NR9936	55°34·8'	5°10·9'W	X	69
Glenside	D & G	NX0366	54°57·2'	5°4·2'W	X	82
Glenside	E Ayr	NS5321	55°27·9'	4°19·1'W	X	70
Glenside	N Ayr	NS2052	55°43·9'	4°51·6'W	X	63
Glenside	S Ayr	NS2409	55°20·9'	4°46·1'W	X	70,76
Glenside	S Ayr	NS2908	55°20·4'	4°41·4'W	X	70,76
Glenside	S Ayr	NS3708	55°20·6'	4°33·8'W	X	70,77
Glenside	Stir	NS8285	56°2·9'	3°53·2'W	X	65
Glenside Hill	S Ayr	NS3908	55°20·6'	4°31·9'W	X	70,77
Glenskelly Hill	D & G	NX7395	55°14·2'	3°59·4'W	H	77
Glenskible	Arg & Bt	NR8860	55°47·5'	5°22·5'W	X	62
Glenskinnan	Aberd	NO7188	56°59·2'	2°28·2'W	X	45
Glenskinno	Angus	NO6760	56°44·1'	2°31·9'W	X	45
Glenskinno Wood	Angus	NO6761	56°44·6'	2°31·9'W	F	45
Glen Sletdale	Highld	NC9113	58°5·8'	3°50·5'W	X	17
Glen Sligachan	Highld	NG4927	57°16·1'	6°9·3'W	X	32
Glen Sluain	Arg & Bt	NS0999	56°9·0'	5°4·1'W	X	56
Glen Snesdal	Highld	NG4163	57°38·5'	6°19·9'W	X	23
Glens of Foudland	Aberd	NJ6034	57°23·9'	2°39·5'W	X	29
Glens of Kinnaird	Orkney	HY2001	58°53·6'	3°22·8'W	X	7
Glens of Kinnaird	Orkney	HY2101	58°53·6'	3°21·8'W	X	6,7
Glensone	D & G	NX9059	54°55·1'	3°42·5'W	X	84
Glensone	D & G	NX9167	54°59·4'	3°41·8'W	X	84
Glensone Burn	D & G	NX9167	54°59·4'	3°41·8'W	W	84
Glensone Hill	D & G	NX9168	54°59·9'	3°41·8'W	H	84
Glen Spean	Highld	NN3480	56°53·2'	4°43·0'W	X	34,41
Glen Spean	Highld	NN4181	56°53·8'	4°36·2'W	X	34,42
Glenspean Lodge Hotel	Highld	NN2981	56°53·6'	4°48·0'W	X	34,41
Glenstang Burn	E Ayr	NS4423	55°28·8'	4°27·7'W	W	70
Glenstivon Dod	Scot Bord	NT1630	55°33·6'	3°19·5'W	H	72
Glenstockadale	D & G	NX0161	54°54·5'	5°5·8'W	T	82
Glenstockadale Several	D & G	NX0160	54°54·0'	5°5·8'W	X	82
Glenstockdale	Arg & Bt	NM9448	56°35·0'	5°20·8'W	X	49
Glen Stockdale	Arg & Bt	NM9549	56°35·5'	5°19·9'W	X	49
Glenstocken	D & G	NX8653	54°51·8'	3°46·1'W	X	84
Glen Strae	Arg & Bt	NN1631	56°26·4'	4°58·6'W	X	50
Glen Strathfarrar	Highld	NH2939	57°24·8'	4°50·4'W	X	25
Glen Strathfarrar	Highld	NH3439	57°24·9'	4°45·4'W	X	26
Glen Strathfarrar Forest	Highld	NH2337	57°23·6'	4°56·3'W	X	25
Glen Striddle	Arg & Bt	NS3295	56°7·4'	4°41·7'W	X	56
Glenstriven	Arg & Bt	NS0878	55°57·7'	5°4·1'W	X	63
Glenstuart	D & G	NY1267	54°59·6'	3°22·1'W	X	85
Glen Suardal	Highld	NG2551	57°28·2'	6°34·7'W	X	23
Glen Suardal	Highld	NG6420	57°12·9'	5°54·1'W	X	32
Glen Suie	Moray	NJ2826	57°19·4'	3°11·3'W	X	37
Glensulaig (Bothy)	Highld	NN0283	56°54·0'	5°14·6'W	X	41
Glenswinton	D & G	NX7074	55°2·9'	4°1·7'W	X	77,84
Glentaggart	S Lanak	NS8125	55°30·5'	3°52·6'W	X	71,72
Glentaggart Burn	S Lanak	NS8024	55°30·0'	3°53·5'W	W	71,72
Glentaggart Cott	S Lanak	NS8127	55°31·6'	3°52·7'W	X	71,72
Glentairie	Angus	NO3267	56°47·6'	3°6·3'W	X	44
Glen Taitney	Angus	NO2366	56°47·0'	3°15·2'W	X	44
Glentaitney Burn	Angus	NO2466	56°47·0'	3°14·2'W	W	44
Glen Tamanisdale	N Eil	NB0323	58°6·0'	7°2·0'W	X	13
Glen Tanar	Aberd	NO4594	57°2·3'	2°53·9'W	X	37,44
Glen Tanar House	Aberd	NO4795	57°2·8'	2°52·0'W	X	37,44
Glentane Hill	N Ayr	NS2251	55°43·4'	4°49·6'W	H	63
Glentanner Burn	Scot Bord	NT4241	55°39·8'	2°54·9'W	W	73
Glen Tarbert	Highld	NM8660	56°41·2'	5°29·2'W	X	40
Glentarf	Pth & Kin	NN7919	56°21·1'	3°57·0'W	X	57

Glen Tarff	Highld	NH3902	57°5·1'	4°38·9'W	X	34
Glen Tarken	Pth & Kin	NN6626	56°24·7'	4°9·9'W	X	51
Glentarken Wood	Pth & Kin	NN6725	56°24·2'	4°8·9'W	F	51
Glentarkie	Pth & Kin	NO1911	56°17·3'	3°18·1'W	X	58
Glentarroch	Highld	NH9532	57°22·2'	3°44·3'W	X	27,36
Glentarroch Burn	Highld	NH9533	57°22·8'	3°44·3'W	W	27
Glen Tarsan	Arg & Bt	NS0785	56°1·4'	5°5·4'W	X	56
Glentarsan Burn	Arg & Bt	NS0682	55°59·8'	5°6·2'W	W	56
Glen Tealasdale	N Eil	NB0022	58°5·4'	7°5·0'W	X	13
Glentenmont Burn	D & G	NY2983	55°8·4'	3°6·4'W	W	79
Glentenmont Height	D & G	NY2885	55°9·5'	3°7·4'W	H	79
Glentennet	Angus	NO4982	56°55·8'	2°49·8'W	X	44
Glen Tennet	Angus	NO5183	56°56·4'	2°47·9'W	X	44
Glenternie	Scot Bord	NT2136	55°36·9'	3°14·8'W	T	73
Glenterry	D & G	NX6353	54°51·4'	4°7·6'W	X	83
Glentewing	S Lanak	NS8722	55°29·0'	3°46·9'W	X	71,72
Glentham	Lincs	TF0090	53°24·1'	0°29·3'W	T	112
Glentham Cliff	Lincs	SK9890	53°24·1'	0°31·1'W	X	112
Glentham Grange	Lincs	TF0191	53°24·6'	0°28·4'W	X	112
Glen, The	Aberd	NJ7230	57°21·8'	2°27·5'W	X	29
Glen, The	Brad	SE0943	53°53·2'	1°51·4'W	X	104
Glen, The	Cumbr	SD4596	54°21·6'	2°50·4'W	X	97
Glen, The	E Loth	NT5684	56°3·1'	2°41·9'W	X	67
Glen, The	N Ayr	NS2052	55°43·9'	4°51·6'W	X	63
Glen, The	N Eil	NL6798	56°57·5'	7°28·3'W	T	31
Glen, The	Northum	NY9856	54°54·2'	2°1·4'W	X	87
Glen, The	Scot Bord	NT2932	55°34·8'	3°7·1'W	X	73
Glen, The	Scot Bord	NT4148	55°43·6'	2°55·9'W	X	73
Glenthirston Burn	D & G	NT0111	55°23·2'	3°33·3'W	W	78
Glenthorne	Devon	SS7949	51°13·9'	3°43·6'W	X	180
Glenthraig	S Ayr	NX4299	55°15·8'	4°28·8'W	X	77
Glen Tig	S Ayr	NX1482	55°6·1'	4°54·5'W	X	76
Glen Tilt	Pth & Kin	NN9273	56°50·4'	3°45·8'W	X	43
Glentinning Burn	Scot Bord	NT1526	55°31·5'	3°20·4'W	W	72
Glentirranmuir	Stir	NS6594	56°7·4'	4°9·9'W	T	57
Glentisset	S Lanak	NS9442	55°39·9'	3°40·7'W	X	71,72
Glenton	Aberd	NJ6420	57°16·4'	2°35·4'W	X	37
Glenton	S Ayr	NS2804	55°18·3'	4°42·2'W	X	76
Glenton Hill	Aberd	NO8288	56°59·2'	2°17·3'W	H	45
Glenton Hill	N Ayr	NS2349	55°42·4'	4°48·6'W	H	63
Glenton Vale	Cumbr	NY5923	54°36·3'	2°37·7'W	X	91
Glentoo	D & G	NX7062	54°56·4'	4°1·3'W	X	83,84
Glentoo Loch	D & G	NX7062	54°56·4'	4°1·3'W	W	83,84
Glen Torridon	Highld	NG9356	57°33·1'	5°27·0'W	X	25
Glentough	Aberd	NJ6010	57°11·0'	2°39·2'W	X	37
Glentramman	I of M	SC4194	54°19·3'	4°26·3'W	X	95
Glentraugh	I of M	SC3170	54°6·1'	4°34·7'W	X	95
Glentress	Scot Bord	NT2839	55°38·6'	3°8·2'W	T	73
Glentress	Scot Bord	NT3343	55°40·8'	3°3·5'W	X	73
Glentress Burn	Scot Bord	NT3543	55°40·8'	3°1·6'W	W	73
Glentress Forest	Scot Bord	NT2842	55°40·2'	3°8·2'W	F	73
Glentress Rig	Scot Bord	NT3443	55°40·8'	3°2·5'W	H	73
Glentress Water	Scot Bord	NT3343	55°40·8'	3°3·5'W	W	73
Glen Trevie	Moray	NJ0943	57°28·4'	3°30·6'W	X	27
Glen Tromie	Highld	NN7694	57°1·5'	4°2·1'W	X	35
Glentromie Lodge	Highld	NN7796	57°2·6'	4°1·2'W	X	35
Glen Trool	D & G	NX4080	55°5·6'	4°30·0'W	X	77
Glentrool Forest	D & G	NX3683	55°7·1'	4°33·9'W	F	77
Glen Trool Lodge	D & G	NX4080	55°5·6'	4°30·0'W	X	77
Glentrool Village	D & G	NX3578	55°4·4'	4°34·6'W	T	77
Glen Trosdale	Arg & Bt	NR6899	56°7·9'	5°43·6'W	X	55,61
Glentrosdale Bay	Arg & Bt	NM6700	56°8·4'	5°44·6'W	W	55,61
Glen Trothy	Monm	SO3719	51°52·2'	2°54·5'W	X	161
Glentruan	I of M	NX4401	54°23·1'	4°23·7'W	T	95
Glen Truim	Highld	NN6587	56°57·5'	4°12·7'W	X	42
Glen Truim	Highld	NN6790	56°59·2'	4°10·9'W	X	35
Glentruim Ho	Highld	NN6895	57°1·9'	4°10·0'W	X	35
Glen Tulchan	Highld	NJ0936	57°24·6'	3°30·4'W	X	27
Glen Tulchan	Highld	NJ1036	57°24·6'	3°29·4'W	X	28
Glen Tungadal	Highld	NG4238	57°21·8'	6°17·0'W	X	23,32
Glenturk	D & G	NX4257	54°53·2'	4°27·4'W	X	83
Glenturk Moor Croft	D & G	NX4157	54°53·2'	4°28·3'W	X	83
Glen Turret	Highld	NN3393	57°0·1'	4°44·5'W	X	34
Glen Turret	Pth & Kin	NN7930	56°27·1'	3°57·3'W	X	51,52
Glen Turret	Pth & Kin	NN8225	56°24·4'	3°54·3'W	X	52
Glentworth	Lincs	SK9488	53°23·1'	0°34·8'W	T	112,121
Glentworth Cliff Fm	Lincs	SK9587	53°22·5'	0°33·9'W	FM	112,121
Glentworth Fm	Glos	ST8090	51°36·7'	2°16·9'W	FM	173
Glentworth Grange	Lincs	SK9287	53°22·5'	0°36·6'W	X	112,121
Glentworth Ho	Lincs	SK9589	53°23·6'	0°33·9'W	X	112,121
Glentyan Ho	Renf	NS3963	55°50·3'	4°33·8'W	X	63
Glen Tye	Stir	NN8401	56°11·5'	3°51·7'W	X	58
Glentye Cottage	Stir	NN8201	56°11·5'	3°53·6'W	X	57
Glentye Hill	Stir	NN8402	56°12·0'	3°51·7'W	H	58
Glentyrie	Angus	NO5643	56°34·9'	2°42·5'W	X	54
Glenuachdarach	Highld	NG4358	57°32·6'	6°17·2'W	X	23
Glenuaig Lodge	Highld	NH1047	57°28·7'	5°9·7'W	X	25
Glen Uig	Angus	NO3163	56°45·5'	3°7·3'W	X	44
Glenuig	Angus	NO3263	56°45·5'	3°6·3'W	X	44
Glen Uig	Highld	NG4063	57°35·2'	6°20·6'W	X	23
Glen Uig	Highld	NM6775	56°48·8'	5°48·6'W	X	40
Glenuig	Highld	NM6777	56°49·8'	5°48·7'W	T	40
Glenuig Bay	Highld	NM6777	56°49·8'	5°48·7'W	W	40
Glenuig Hill	Highld	NM6876	56°49·3'	5°47·7'W	H	40
Glenure	Arg & Bt	NN0448	56°35·2'	5°11·1'W	X	50
Glen Ure	Arg & Bt	NN0647	56°34·8'	5°9·1'W	X	50
Glen Urlan	Highld	NC9750	58°25·8'	3°45·4'W	X	11
Glen Urquhart	Highld	NH4530	57°20·3'	4°34·1'W	X	26
Glenurquhart	Highld	NH7462	57°38·1'	4°6·2'W	X	21,27
Glenurquhart Forest	Highld	NH4529	57°19·8'	4°34·0'W	F	26
Glenury Viaduct	Aberd	NO8686	56°58·2'	2°13·4'W	X	45
Glen Usk	Monm	ST3692	51°37·6'	2°55·1'W	X	171
Glenvale	Pth & Kin	NO1705	56°14·1'	3°19·9'W	X	58
Glen Vale	Pth & Kin	NO1805	56°14·1'	3°18·9'W	X	58
Glenvalentine	D & G	NS8807	55°20·9'	3°45·5'W	X	71,78
Glenvalley	Scot Bord	NT2932	55°34·8'	3°7·1'W	X	73
Glen Valtos	N Eil	NB0734	58°12·1'	6°58·8'W	X	13
Glen Varragill	Highld	NG4736	57°20·9'	6°11·9'W	X	23,32
Glen Varragill Forest	Highld	NG4736	57°20·9'	6°11·9'W	F	23,32
Glenvarragill Ho	Highld	NG4740	57°23·1'	6°12·1'W	X	23

Glenveg	Scot Bord	NT1025	55°30·9'	3°25·1'W	X	72
Glenvernoch	D & G	NX3475	55°2·8'	4°35·5'W	X	76
Glenvernoch Fell	D & G	NX3374	55°2·2'	4°36·4'W	H	76
Glen Vic Askill	Highld	NG3644	57°24·8'	6°23·3'W	X	23
Glen Vic Askill	Highld	NG3743	57°24·3'	6°22·3'W	X	23
Glen Vidigill	Highld	NG3936	57°20·7'	6°19·8'W	X	23,32
Glenview	Arg & Bt	NN1727	56°24·2'	4°57·5'W	T	50
Glen View	Devon	SX7092	50°43·0'	3°50·1'W	X	191
Glen Village	Falk	NS8878	55°59·2'	3°47·3'W	T	65
Glenville	I of M	SC3879	54°11·1'	4°28·5'W	X	95
Glen Vine	I of M	SC3378	54°10·5'	4°33·1'W	X	95
Glen Vorlich	Pth & Kin	NN6321	56°21·9'	4°12·6'W	X	51,57
Glenward Hill	Renf	NS3261	55°49·0'	4°40·4'W	X	63
Glen Water	Aberd	NJ6134	57°23·9'	2°38·5'W	W	29
Glen Water	E Ayr	NS5741	55°38·7'	4°15·9'W	W	71
Glenwhan Garden	D & G	NX1558	54°53·2'	4°52·6'W	X	82
Glenwhan Lochs	D & G	NX1460	54°54·3'	4°53·6'W	W	82
Glenwhan Moor	D & G	NX1560	54°54·3'	4°52·7'W	X	82
Glenwhappen Burn	Scot Bord	NT0522	55°29·2'	3°29·8'W	W	72
Glenwhappen Dod	Scot Bord	NT0523	55°29·7'	3°29·8'W	H	72
Glenwhappen Rig	Scot Bord	NT0622	55°29·2'	3°28·8'W	H	72
Glenwhappen Rig	Scot Bord	NT0625	55°30·8'	3°28·9'W	H	72
Glenwhargen	D & G	NS7602	55°18·0'	3°56·8'W	X	78
Glenwhargen Burn	D & G	NS7703	55°18·6'	3°55·8'W	W	78
Glenwhargen Craig	D & G	NS7603	55°18·6'	3°56·8'W	H	78
Glenwharrie	D & G	NS7114	55°24·4'	4°1·8'W	X	71
Glenwharrie Burn	D & G	NS7115	55°25·0'	4°1·8'W	W	71
Glenwhask	S Ayr	NX2283	55°6·8'	4°47·0'W	X	76
Glenwhelt	Durham	NY9037	54°43·9'	2°8·9'W	X	91,92
Glenwhern Burn	D & G	NS8003	55°18·6'	3°53·0'W	W	78
Glenwhilk	Stir	NN7403	56°12·4'	4°1·4'W	X	57
Glenwhilly	D & G	NX1771	55°0·3'	4°51·3'W	X	76
Glenwhilt	Scot Bord	NT4930	55°33·9'	2°48·1'W	X	73
Glenwhinnie Hill	Scot Bord	NT3847	55°43·0'	2°58·8'W	H	73
Glenwinnel Burn	Clackm	NS8899	56°10·5'	3°47·8'W	W	58
Glenwood	Aberd	NJ6707	57°9·4'	2°32·3'W	X	38
Glen Wood	Angus	NO6762	56°45·2'	2°31·9'W	F	45
Glenwood Ho	Staffs	SK0048	53°2·0'	1°59·6'W	X	119
Glen Wyllin	I of M	SC3190	54°16·9'	4°35·3'W	X	95
Glenyards	Falk	NS8178	55°59·1'	3°54·0'W	X	65
Glenydd	Cered	SN6275	52°21·6'	4°1·2'W	X	135
Glenyerrock	D & G	NX7956	54°53·3'	3°52·8'W	X	84
Glenzier Beck	D & G	NY3475	55°4·2'	3°1·6'W	W	85
Glenzier Burn	D & G	NY3477	55°5·2'	3°1·6'W	W	85
Glenzierfoot	D & G	NY3673	55°3·1'	2°59·7'W	X	85
Glenzier Garden	D & G	NY3575	55°4·2'	3°0·6'W	X	85
Glenzierhead	D & G	NY3576	55°4·7'	3°0·7'W	X	85
Gleouraich	Highld	NH0305	57°5·9'	5°14·7'W	H	33
Glespin	S Lanak	NS8028	55°32·1'	3°53·7'W	T	71,72
Glespin	S Lanak	NS8127	55°31·6'	3°52·7'W	X	71,72
Glespin Burn	S Lanak	NS8226	55°31·1'	3°51·7'W	W	71,72
Glespin Burn	S Lanak	NS9719	55°27·5'	3°37·3'W	W	78
Glessal Hill	S Ayr	NX1887	55°8·9'	4°50·9'W	X	76
Glessel Burn	E Ayr	NS4602	55°17·5'	4°25·1'W	W	77
Glessel Hill	E Ayr	NS4601	55°17·0'	4°25·1'W	X	77
Gletna Kirk	Shetld	HP5902	60°42·1'	0°54·7'W	A	1
Gletness	Shetld	HU4651	60°14·7'	1°9·7'W	T	3
Glet Ness	Shetld	HU4751	60°14·7'	1°8·6'W	X	3
Gleuch Burn	S Lanak	NS9108	55°21·5'	3°42·7'W	W	71
Glevehouse Fm	Ches	SJ7878	53°18·2'	2°19·4'W	FM	118
Glevering Hall	Suff	TM2957	52°10·0'	1°21·3'E	X	156
Glevvm (Gloucester)	Glos	SO8318	51°51·9'	2°14·4'W	R	162
Glewstone	Heref	SO5522	51°53·9'	2°38·8'W	T	162
Gleyering Hall Fm	Suff	TM2956	52°9·5'	1°21·3'E	FM	156
Glib Cheois	N Eil	NB3621	58°6·2'	6°28·4'W	T	14
Glidden Fm	Hants	SU6615	50°56·1'	1°3·3'W	FM	196
Glien	Carm	SN6627	51°55·8'	3°56·5'W	X	146
Gliffaes-fach	Powys	SO1620	51°52·6'	3°12·8'W	X	161
Glifter	Orkney	HY3928	59°8·3'	3°3·5'W	X	6
Glifters of Lyrawa	Orkney	ND2699	58°52·6'	3°16·5'W	X	6,7
Glifters of Pegal	Orkney	ND2598	58°52·0'	3°17·5'W	X	6,7
Glimps Holm	Orkney	ND4799	58°52·8'	2°54·7'W	X	6,7
Glimpsholm Skerry	Orkney	ND4899	58°52·8'	2°53·6'W	X	6,7
Glims Moss	Orkney	HY3122	59°5·0'	3°11·8'W	X	6
Glingerbank	Cumbr	NY3871	55°2·0'	2°57·8'W	X	85
Glinger Burn	Cumbr	NY3772	55°2·6'	2°58·7'W	X	85
Glinton	Peterb	TF1505	52°38·1'	0°17·6'W	T	142
Glion Gill	I of M	SC3285	54°14·2'	4°34·3'W	X	95
Glion Mooar	I of M	SC2275	54°8·7'	4°43·1'W	X	95
Glithno	Aberd	NO8689	56°59·8'	2°13·4'W	X	45
Glitney Fm	Dorset	SY4398	50°47·0'	2°48·1'W	FM	193
Glitteringstone	Northum	NU0303	55°19·5'	1°56·7'W	X	81
Gloagburn	Pth & Kin	NO0423	56°23·6'	3°32·9'W	X	52,53,58
Globa	Shetld	HU5043	60°10·4'	1°5·4'W	X	4
Globe Fm	Northnts	SP6260	52°14·3'	1°5·1'W	FM	152
Globe, The	Heref	SO3267	52°18·1'	2°59·4'W	H	137,148
Globe Town	T Ham	TQ3582	51°31·5'	0°2·8'W	T	177
Globwll	Powys	SJ1218	52°45·4'	3°17·8'W	X	125
Gloddaeth	Conwy	SH8575	53°15·8'	3°43·0'W	X	116
Gloddaeth Hall (Coll)	Conwy	SH8080	53°18·4'	3°47·7'W	A	116
Gloddaeth-isaf	Conwy	SH8181	53°19·0'	3°46·8'W	X	116
Gloddfa Ganol Slate Mine	Gwyn	SH6946	53°0·0'	3°56·7'W	X	115
Glodwick	Oldham	SD9404	53°32·2'	2°5·0'W	T	109
Glog	Cered	SN7974	52°21·3'	3°46·2'W	X	135,147
Glôg	Rho Cyn Taf	ST0593	51°37·9'	3°22·0'W	X	170
Glog Fach	Cered	SN7554	52°10·4'	3°49·3'W	X	146,147
Glôg Fm	Powys	SO0885	52°27·6'	3°20·8'W	FM	136
Glôg Hill	Powys	SO2269	52°19·1'	3°8·3'W	H	137,148
Glogue	Carm	SN3615	51°48·8'	4°22·4'W	X	159
Glogue	Pemb	SN2132	51°57·7'	4°35·9'W	T	145
Glogue Fm	Pemb	SN2133	51°58·2'	4°36·0'W	FM	145
Glol	Flint	SJ1178	53°17·7'	3°19·7'W	F	116
Glomen	Powys	SO1197	52°34·1'	3°18·4'W	X	136
Gloom Hill	Clackm	NS9699	56°10·6'	3°40·1'W	X	58
Gloon Burn	D & G	NX4283	55°7·2'	4°28·2'W	W	77
Glooston	Leic	SP7595	52°33·1'	0°53·2'W	T	141
Glooston Lodge	Leic	SP7596	52°33·6'	0°53·2'W	X	141
Gloraig a' Chaimbeulaich	N Eil	NG1894	57°51·1'	6°44·7'W	X	14
Gloraig Dhubh	N Eil	NG1894	57°51·1'	6°44·7'W	X	14
Gloraig Iosal	N Eil	NG1894	57°51·1'	6°44·7'W	X	14

Glorat Ho	E Dunb	NS6477	55°58·3'	4°10·3'W	X	64
Glororum	Northum	NU1633	55°35·7'	1°44·3'W	T	75
Glororum	Northum	NZ1982	55°8·2'	1°41·7'W	X	81
Glory Fm	Bucks	SU9394	51°38·5'	0°39·0'W	FM	175
Glory Hill Fm	Bucks	SU9189	51°35·8'	0°40·8'W	FM	175
Glossoms Fm	Leic	SK7722	52°47·6'	0°51·1'W	FM	129
Glossop	Derby	SK0393	53°26·3'	1°56·9'W	T	110
Glossop Low	Derby	SK0696	53°27·9'	1°54·2'W	X	110
Gloster Hill	Northum	NU2504	55°20·0'	1°35·9'W	X	81
Glottenham Manor	E Susx	TQ7222	50°58·5'	0°27·4'E	X	199
Glottenham Stream	E Susx	TQ7222	50°58·5'	0°27·4'E	W	199
Gloucester	Glos	SO8318	51°51·9'	2°14·4'W	T	162
Gloucester and Sharpness Canal, The	Glos	SO7912	51°48·6'	2°17·9'W	W	162
Gloucester Beeches	Glos	SO9504	51°44·3'	2°4·0'W	F	163
Gloucester Beeches	Glos	SO9611	51°48·1'	2°3·1'W	F	163
Gloucester & Cheltenham (Staverton) Airport	Glos	SO8821	51°53·5'	2°10·1'W	X	162
Gloucester Lodge Fm	Northum	NZ3278	55°6·0'	1°29·5'W	FM	88
Gloucester Park	Essex	TQ7089	51°34·7'	0°27·6'E	X	178
Gloucester Road Fm	S Glos	ST6482	51°32·4'	2°30·8'W	FM	172
Gloucestershire & Warwickshire Railway	Glos	SP0431	51°58·9'	1°56·1'W	X	150
Gloup	Orkney	ND4785	58°45·2'	2°54·5'W	X	7
Gloup	Shetld	HP5004	60°43·2'	1°4·5'W	T	1
Gloup Holm	Shetld	HP4806	60°44·3'	1°6·7'W	X	1
Gloup Lochs	Shetld	HP5103	60°42·7'	1°3·4'W	W	1
Gloup Ness	Shetld	HP5005	60°43·8'	1°4·5'W	X	1
Gloup, The	Highld	ND3578	58°41·4'	3°6·8'W	X	7,12
Gloup, The	Orkney	HY5907	58°57·2'	2°42·3'W	X	6
Gloup Voe	Shetld	HP5004	60°43·2'	1°4·5'W	W	1
Glover Fm	Kent	TQ9332	51°3·5'	0°45·6'E	FM	189
Gloversbridge Fm	Kent	TQ8645	51°10·7'	0°40·1'E	FM	189
Glover's Fm	Cambs	TL5986	52°27·2'	0°20·8'E	FM	143
Glovers Fm	Essex	TL4807	51°44·8'	0°9·0'E	FM	167
Glover's Fm	Norf	TF7235	52°53·3'	0°33·8'E	FM	132
Glovershaw	Brad	SE1340	53°51·6'	1°47·7'W	X	104
Glover's Hawes	Kent	TQ4641	51°9·2'	0°5·7'E	X	188
Glover's Wood	Surrey	TQ2240	51°9·0'	0°14·9'W	F	187
Glower	Orkney	HY2525	59°6·6'	3°18·1'W	X	6
Glower O'er Him	Durham	NZ3628	54°39·0'	1°26·1'W	X	93
Gloweth	Corn	SW7944	50°15·5'	5°5·7'W	T	204
Gloyne Fm	Pemb	SN1213	51°47·3'	4°43·2'W	FM	158
Gloyn's	Devon	SS8821	50°58·9'	3°35·4'W	X	181
Gloyw Lyn	Gwyn	SH6429	52°50·7'	4°0·8'W	W	124
Glubhole Fm	Corn	SX2777	50°34·3'	4°26·2'W	FM	201
Gludy	Powys	SO0229	51°57·3'	3°25·2'W	X	160
Glumpsey Wood	Suff	TL7360	52°12·9'	0°32·3'E	F	155
Glùn an Fhuarain	Highld	NM8371	56°47·1'	5°32·7'W	X	40
Glunimore Island	Arg & Bt	NR7405	55°17·5'	5°33·1'W	X	68
Glùn Liath	Highld	NH3690	57°52·4'	4°45·4'W	X	20
Glun Odhar	Highld	NH2544	57°27·4'	4°54·6'W	X	25
Glùn Odhar	Highld	NH2657	57°34·4'	4°54·1'W	X	25
Glusburn Moor	N Yks	SD9845	53°54·3'	2°1·4'W	X	103
Gluss Ayre	Shetld	HU3677	60°28·8'	1°20·2'W	X	2,3
Glussdale Water	Shetld	HU3373	60°26·6'	1°23·5'W	W	2,3
Gluss Isle	Shetld	HU3778	60°29·3'	1°19·1'W	X	2,3
Gluss Voe	Shetld	HU3678	60°29·3'	1°20·2'W	W	2,3
Gluss Water	Shetld	HU2581	60°31·0'	1°32·2'W	W	3
Glusswater Burn	Shetld	HU2582	60°31·5'	1°32·2'W	W	3
Glust	Flint	SJ1868	53°12·4'	3°13·3'W	X	116
Glutt Loch	Highld	NC9937	58°18·9'	3°43·0'W	W	11,17
Glutton	Highld	NH1399	57°56·7'	5°9·1'W	X	19
Glutton Bridge	Derby	SK0866	53°11·7'	1°52·4'W	T	119
Glutton Grange	Derby	SK0867	53°12·2'	1°52·4'W	X	119
Glutt ,The	Highld	NC9936	58°18·3'	3°42·9'W	X	11,17
Glutt Water	Highld	NC9936	58°18·3'	3°42·9'W	W	11,17
Gluvian	Corn	SW8666	50°27·5'	5°0·5'W	X	200
Gluvian	Corn	SW9164	50°26·6'	4°56·2'W	T	200
Glwydgoch Fm	Cered	SN5162	52°14·4'	4°10·5'W	FM	146
Glyder Fâch	Conwy	SH6558	53°6·4'	4°0·6'W	H	115
Glyder Fawr	Gwyn	SH6457	53°5·8'	4°1·5'W	H	115
Glyde's Fm	E Susx	TQ6615	50°54·9'	0°22·1'E	FM	199
Glydwish Hall	E Susx	TQ6923	50°59·1'	0°24·9'E	X	199
Glygyrog-wen	Gwyn	SN6597	52°33·5'	3°59·1'W	X	135
Glyme Fm	Oxon	SP3226	51°56·1'	1°31·7'W	FM	164
Glympton	Oxon	SP4221	51°53·4'	1°23·0'W	T	164
Glympton Assarts Fm	Oxon	SP4119	51°52·3'	1°23·9'W	FM	164
Glympton Heath	Oxon	SP4323	51°54·5'	1°22·1'W	X	164
Glympton Park	Oxon	SP4221	51°53·4'	1°23·0'W	X	164
Glympton Wood	Oxon	SP4120	51°52·9'	1°23·9'W	F	164
Glyn	Conwy	SH7476	53°16·2'	3°53·0'W	X	115
Glyn	Conwy	SH8577	53°16·9'	3°43·1'W	X	116
Glyn	Denb	SJ2147	53°1·1'	3°10·3'W	X	117
Glyn	Gwyn	SH6471	53°13·4'	4°1·8'W	X	115
Glyn	I of Angl	SH5181	53°18·5'	4°13·8'W	X	114,115
Glyn	Monm	ST4796	51°39·9'	2°45·6'W	T	171
Glyn	Pemb	SN1438	52°0·8'	4°42·2'W	X	145
Glyn	Powys	SJ0107	52°39·3'	3°27·4'W	X	125
Glyn	Powys	SJ1203	52°37·3'	3°17·6'W	X	125
Glyn	Powys	SJ1422	52°47·6'	3°16·1'W	X	125
Glyn	Powys	SN9286	52°27·9'	3°35·0'W	T	136
Glyn	Powys	SN9665	52°16·6'	3°31·1'W	X	136,147
Glyn	Powys	SO1398	52°34·6'	3°16·6'W	X	136
Glyn	Rho Cyn Taf	ST0288	51°35·2'	3°24·5'W	X	170
Glyn	Shrops	SJ3011	52°41·8'	3°1·7'W	X	126
Glyn Abbey	Carm	SN4407	51°44·6'	4°15·2'W	X	159
Glynadda	Carm	SN4531	51°57·6'	4°15·0'W	X	146
Glynaeron	Pemb	SN1029	51°55·9'	4°45·4'W	F	145,158
Glynaeron	Pemb	SN1129	51°55·9'	4°44·6'W	X	145,158
Glynarthen	Cered	SN3148	52°6·5'	4°27·7'W	T	145
Glyn Arthur	Denb	SJ1365	53°10·7'	3°17·7'W	X	116
Glyn-bâch	Gwyn	SH9131	52°52·2'	3°36·8'W	X	125
Glynbrochan	Powys	SN9283	52°26·3'	3°34·9'W	T	136
Glyncaerau	Carm	SN5603	51°42·7'	4°4·7'W	X	159
Glyn Castle	Nth Pt Talb	SN8302	51°42·5'	3°41·2'W	T	170
Glyn-Ceirig	Powys	SH8106	52°38·6'	3°45·1'W	X	124,125
Glyn Ceiriog	Wrex	SJ2038	52°56·2'	3°11·0'W	T	126
Glyn Celyn	Powys	SO0832	51°59·0'	3°20·0'W	X	160
Glynch Brook	Glos	SO7632	51°59·4'	2°20·6'W	W	150
Glyn Clawdd Fm	Carm	SN7021	51°52·6'	3°52·9'W	FM	160
Glyn Clydach	Nth Pt Talb	SS7399	51°40·8'	3°49·8'W	X	170
Glyncoch	Carm	SN6017	51°50·3'	4°1·5'W	X	159
Glyncoch	Cered	SN3452	52°8·7'	4°25·2'W	X	145
Glyncoch	Rho Cyn Taf	ST0792	51°37·4'	3°20·2'W	T	170
Glyn-côch	Swan	SN6804	51°43·4'	3°54·3'W	X	159
Glyncoed	Blae Gw	SO1610	51°47·2'	3°12·7'W	T	161
Glyncoed	Gwyn	SH4139	52°55·7'	4°21·5'W	X	123
Glyn Common	Shrops	SJ3011	52°41·8'	3°1·7'W	X	126
Glyn Corrwg	Nth Pt Talb	SS8697	51°39·9'	3°38·5'W	X	170
Glyncorrwg	Nth Pt Talb	SS8799	51°40·9'	3°37·7'W	T	170
Glyn-Cywarch	Gwyn	SH6034	52°53·4'	4°4·5'W	X	124
Glynde	E Susx	TQ4508	50°51·4'	0°4·0'E	T	198
Glyndebourne	E Susx	TQ4510	50°52·5'	0°4·0'E	T	198
Glyndebourne Fm	E Susx	TQ4510	50°52·5'	0°4·0'E	FM	198
Glynde Place	E Susx	TQ4509	50°52·0'	0°4·0'E	A	198
Glynde Reach	E Susx	TQ4609	50°51·9'	0°4·9'E	W	198
Glyn Derw	I of Angl	SH4179	53°17·3'	4°22·7'W	X	114,115
Glyn Dewi	Carm	SN2929	51°56·2'	4°28·9'W	X	145
Glyndley Manor	E Susx	TQ6006	50°50·1'	0°16·7'E	X	199
Glyndon Fm	Somer	ST1618	50°57·6'	3°11·4'W	FM	181,193
Glyndŵr's Way	Powys	SH8604	52°37·6'	3°40·7'W	X	135,136
Glyndŵr's Way	Powys	SJ0713	52°42·6'	3°22·2'W	X	125
Glyndŵr's Way	Powys	SJ1212	52°42·2'	3°17·7'W	X	125
Glyndŵr's Way	Powys	SN8195	52°32·6'	3°44·9'W	X	135,136
Glyndŵr's Way	Powys	SO0775	52°22·2'	3°21·6'W	X	136,147
Glyndŵr's Way	Powys	SO2572	52°20·7'	3°5·7'W	X	137,148
Glyn-Dwyfach	Gwyn	SH4638	52°55·3'	4°17·0'W	X	123
Glyndyfrdwy	Denb	SJ1442	52°58·4'	3°16·4'W	T	125
Glyn Ebwy / Ebbw Vale	Blae Gw	SO1609	51°46·6'	3°12·7'W	T	161
Glyne Gap	E Susx	TQ7708	50°50·9'	0°31·3'E	T	199
Glyneithinog	Carm	SN2638	52°1·0'	4°31·8'W	X	145
Glyneithrym-uchaf	Swan	SN6805	51°43·9'	3°54·3'W	X	159
Glyn Etwy	Blae Gw	SO1709	51°46·6'	3°11·8'W	T	161
Glynfach	Powys	SO0184	52°26·9'	3°27·0'W	X	136
Glyn-Feinion	Powys	SO0183	52°26·4'	3°27·0'W	X	136
Glyn Fm	Conwy	SH7557	53°6·0'	3°51·6'W	FM	115
Glyn Fm	Glos	SO5408	51°46·4'	2°39·6'W	FM	162
Glyn Fm	Monm	SO5209	51°46·9'	2°41·4'W	FM	162
Glyn Fm	Monm	ST4796	51°39·9'	2°45·6'W	FM	171
Glyngarw	Carm	SN2027	51°55·0'	4°36·6'W	X	145,158
Glyn Gower	Gwyn	SH9031	52°52·2'	3°37·7'W	X	125
Glyngwernen	Carm	SN5302	51°42·1'	4°7·2'W	X	159
Glyn-Gwilym Isaf	Nth Pt Talb	SN8201	51°42·0'	3°42·1'W	X	170
Glyn-Gwy	Powys	SN9472	52°20·4'	3°33·0'W	X	136,147
Glyngynwydd	Powys	SN9481	52°25·2'	3°33·1'W	X	136
Glynhafren	Powys	SN8984	52°26·8'	3°37·6'W	T	135,136
Glynhenllan Isaf	Pemb	SN1941	52°2·5'	4°38·0'W	X	145
Glynhir	Carm	SN4709	51°45·8'	4°12·6'W	X	159
Glynhir	Cered	SN4663	52°14·9'	4°15·0'W	X	146
Glynhiriaeth	Powys	SJ0805	52°38·3'	3°21·2'W	X	125
Glynhir Mansion	Carm	SN6315	51°49·3'	3°58·9'W	X	159
Glynhynod	Cered	SN3745	52°5·0'	4°22·3'W	X	145
Glyn Iago	Gwyn	SH7007	52°39·0'	3°54·9'W	X	124
Glynie	Powys	SJ1419	52°45·9'	3°16·1'W	X	125
Glyn Isa	Conwy	SH7672	53°14·1'	3°51·1'W	X	115
Glyn Isaf	Denb	SJ1072	53°14·5'	3°20·5'W	X	116
Glynleigh Level	E Susx	TQ6006	50°50·1'	0°16·7'E	X	199
Glynllan	Brig	SS9487	51°34·6'	3°31·4'W	T	170
Glynllech Uchaf	Powys	SN8412	51°47·9'	3°40·5'W	X	160
Glynllifon Country Park	Gwyn	SH4555	53°4·4'	4°18·4'W	X	115,123
Glynllwyd	Powys	SN9732	51°58·9'	3°29·6'W	X	160
Glynmaen	Pemb	SN1435	51°59·2'	4°42·1'W	X	145
Glyn Mawr	Gwyn	SH9031	52°52·2'	3°37·7'W	H	125
Glynmeherin	Cered	SN4849	52°7·3'	4°12·8'W	X	146
Glynmeirch	Carm	SN6413	51°48·2'	3°58·0'W	X	159
Glyn Morfa	Gwyn	SH5832	52°52·2'	4°6·2'W	X	124
Glynmorlas	Shrops	SJ3137	52°55·8'	3°1·2'W	T	126
Glynmyrddin	Carm	SN4520	51°51·7'	4°14·7'W	X	159
Glynn	Corn	SX1165	50°27·5'	4°39·4'W	X	200
Glyn-nannau	Conwy	SH9546	53°0·3'	3°33·5'W	X	116
Glyn-neath	Nth Pt Talb	SN8706	51°44·7'	3°37·8'W	T	160
Glynogwr	Brig	SS9587	51°34·6'	3°30·5'W	T	170
Glyn Patel	Pemb	SN1214	51°47·8'	4°43·2'W	X	158
Glyn-Pedr	Powys	SO2320	51°52·6'	3°6·7'W	X	161
Glynrhigos	Nth Pt Talb	SN7702	51°42·4'	3°46·4'W	X	170
Glyn Saer	Carm	SN8442	52°4·1'	3°41·1'W	X	147,160
Glynsaithmaen	Pemb	SN1130	51°56·4'	4°44·6'W	X	145
Glyn Sylen	Carm	SN5007	51°44·7'	4°10·0'W	X	159
Glyntaf	Carm	SN1725	51°53·9'	4°39·2'W	X	145,158
Glyntaff	Rho Cyn Taf	ST0889	51°35·8'	3°19·3'W	T	170
Glyn Tarell	Powys	SN9723	51°54·0'	3°29·4'W	X	160
Glyntawe	Powys	SN8416	51°50·1'	3°40·6'W	T	160
Glyn, The	Denb	SJ1408	52°40·0'	3°15·9'W	X	125
Glyn, The	Powys	SO1846	52°6·6'	3°11·5'W	X	148
Glyntwymyn	Powys	SH8403	52°37·0'	3°42·4'W	X	135,136
Glyn Uchaf	Conwy	SH7672	53°14·1'	3°51·1'W	X	115
Glyn-y-bedd	Nth Pt Talb	SN7803	51°43·0'	3°45·6'W	X	170
Glyn-yr-Helyg	Cered	SN4951	52°8·4'	4°12·0'W	X	146
Glyn-yr-henllan	Carm	SN5915	51°49·2'	4°2·4'W	X	159
Gnatham	Devon	SX4664	50°27·6'	4°9·8'W	X	201
Gnatham Barton	Devon	SX5269	50°30·4'	4°4·9'W	X	201
Gnat Hole	Derby	SK0392	53°25·7'	1°56·9'W	X	110
Gnaton Hall	Devon	SX5749	50°19·6'	4°0·2'W	A	202
Gnipe Howe	N Yks	NZ9308	54°27·8'	0°33·5'W	X	94
Gnoc Dubh Mór	Highld	NG2662	57°34·2'	6°34·5'W	X	23
Gnosall	Staffs	SJ8321	52°47·4'	2°14·7'W	T	127
Gnosall Heath	Staffs	SJ8220	52°46·9'	2°15·6'W	T	127
Gnwch Mawr	Cered	SN6853	52°9·8'	3°55·4'W	H	146
Goadby	Leic	SP7598	52°34·7'	0°53·2'W	T	141
Goadby Hall Fm	Leic	SK7726	52°49·8'	0°51·0'W	FM	129
Goadby Marwood	Leic	SK7826	52°49·8'	0°50·1'W	T	129
Goadsbarrow	Cumbr	SD2668	54°6·4'	3°7·5'W	X	96,97
Goal	N Yks	SD8757	54°0·8'	2°11·5'W	X	103
Goal Sike	Cumbr	NY8121	54°35·3'	2°17·2'W	W	91,92
Goal, The	Angus	NO3663	56°45·5'	3°2·4'W	H	44
Goanah Lodges	W Susx	SU9921	50°59·0'	0°35·0'W	X	197
Goatacre	Wilts	SU0177	51°29·7'	1°58·7'W	T	173
Goatacre Fm	Hants	SU6435	51°6·9'	1°4·8'W	FM	185
Goat Burn	D & G	NS8201	55°17·6'	3°51·1'W	W	78
Goat Burn	D & G	NX3179	55°4·9'	4°38·4'W	W	76
Goat Cave	Arg & Bt	NM3235	56°26·1'	6°20·4'W	X	46,47,48
Goatchurch Cavern	N Som	ST4758	51°19·4'	2°45·2'W	X	172,182
Goat Crag	Cumbr	NY1916	54°32·2'	3°14·7'W	X	89,90
Goat Crag	Cumbr	NY2919	54°33·9'	3°5·5'W	X	89,90
Goat Crags	Cumbr	NY2716	54°32·3'	3°7·3'W	X	89,90
Goat Craigs	D & G	NX4989	55°10·6'	4°21·8'W	X	77
Goatend	D & G	NX5957	54°53·5'	4°11·5'W	X	83
Goatfell	N Ayr	NR9941	55°37·5'	5°11·1'W	H	62,69
Goatfield	Arg & Bt	NN0100	56°9·3'	5°11·8'W	T	55
Goat Gap	N Yks	SD7170	54°7·7'	2°26·2'W	X	98
Goat Gill	N Yks	SD7463	54°4·0'	2°23·4'W	W	98
Goatham Green	E Susx	TQ8120	50°57·3'	0°35·0'E	T	199
Goathill	Dorset	ST6717	50°57·3'	2°27·8'W	T	183
Goat Hill	Kirk	SE0415	53°38·1'	1°56·0'W	X	110
Goat Hill	Scot Bord	NT4304	55°19·9'	2°53·5'W	H	79
Goat Hill	Shrops	SO4179	52°24·6'	2°51·6'W	X	137,148
Goat Hill	Somer	SS7240	51°8·9'	3°49·4'W	H	180
Goathland	N Yks	NZ8301	54°24·1'	0°42·9'W	T	94
Goathland Moor	N Yks	SE8598	54°22·5'	0°41·1'W	X	94,100
Goat Ho	Shrops	SO2986	52°28·3'	3°2·3'W	X	137
Goathorn Fm	Dorset	SZ0184	50°39·6'	1°58·9'W	FM	195
Goathorn Plantation	Dorset	SZ0185	50°40·1'	1°58·8'W	F	195
Goathouse Fm	Hants	SU6011	50°53·9'	1°8·4'W	FM	196
Goathurst	Somer	ST2534	51°6·3'	3°3·9'W	T	182
Goathurst Common	Kent	TQ4952	51°15·1'	0°8·5'E	T	188
Goat Island	Devon	SS1343	51°9·6'	4°40·1'W	X	180
Goatlake	Devon	SX8291	50°42·6'	3°39·9'W	X	191
Goatmilk Farm	Fife	NT2499	56°10·9'	3°13·0'W	FM	59
Goatmilk Hills	Fife	NO2400	56°11·4'	3°13·0'W	H	59
Goats	Angus	NO5541	56°33·8'	2°43·5'W	X	54
Goat Scar	Cumbr	NY4706	54°27·0'	2°48·6'W	X	90
Goatscliff	Derby	SK2477	53°17·6'	1°38·0'W	X	119
Goatscrag Hill	Northum	NT9737	55°37·8'	2°2·4'W	H	75
Goatspen Plain	Hants	SU2201	50°48·7'	1°40·9'W	X	195
Goatstones	Northum	NY8474	55°3·9'	2°14·6'W	X	86,87
Goat Strand	D & G	NX5850	54°49·7'	4°12·2'W	W	83
Goat's Water	Cumbr	SD2697	54°22·0'	3°7·9'W	W	96,97
Goat Well Bay	D & G	NX6548	54°48·8'	4°5·6'W	W	83,84
Goauch Wood	Aberd	NO6695	57°2·9'	2°33·2'W	F	38,45
Gob	Conwy	SJ0043	52°58·7'	3°29·0'W	X	125
Gob a'Bharra	Arg & Bt	NR9075	55°55·6'	5°21·2'W	X	62
Gob a' Chairn	Highld	NH2341	57°25·8'	4°56·4'W	X	25
Gob a' Chairn	Highld	NH4374	57°44·0'	4°37·7'W	X	20
Gob a' Champa	N Eil	NB1103	57°55·6'	6°52·4'W	X	13,14
Gob a' Chuaille	Highld	NG8496	57°54·3'	5°38·3'W	X	19
Gob a' Chuilg	N Eil	NB4325	58°8·6'	6°21·6'W	X	14
Gob a' Chùirn	Highld	NH2069	57°40·8'	5°0·7'W	X	20
Gob a' Ghaill	N Eil	NA0501	57°49·7'	8°39·0'W	X	18
Gob a' Gheodha	Highld	NG8394	57°53·2'	5°39·2'W	X	19
Gobagrennan	Arg & Bt	NR7028	55°29·8'	5°38·1'W	X	68
Gob Aird an Tolmachain	N Eil	NB0904	57°56·1'	6°54·5'W	X	13,14
Gob Aird na Cille	N Eil	NG2195	57°51·7'	6°41·8'W	X	14
Gobannivn (Abergavenny)	Monm	SO2914	51°49·4'	3°1·4'W	R	161
Goban Rainich	N Eil	NB2603	57°56·2'	6°37·3'W	X	13,14
Gob an t-Seabhaig	N Eil	NB5547	58°20·9'	6°10·7'W	X	8
Gob a' Phuind	N Eil	NB1003	57°55·6'	6°53·4'W	X	13,14
Gob Ard	Highld	NC1824	58°10·3'	5°5·2'W	X	15
Gobbett, The	Shrops	SO6382	52°26·3'	2°32·3'W	X	138
Gobbs	Aberd	NO8076	56°52·8'	2°19·2'W	X	45
Gob Chaileagadh	N Eil	NB5436	58°14·9'	6°11·1'W	X	8
Gob Dubh	Arg & Bt	NR6385	56°0·2'	5°47·6'W	X	61
Gobe	Powys	SO2254	52°11·0'	3°8·1'W	X	148
Gobe Banks	Powys	SO2255	52°11·5'	3°8·1'W	X	148
Gobernuisgach Lodge	Highld	NC4341	58°20·0'	4°40·4'W	X	9
Gobernuisgeach	Highld	NC9831	58°15·6'	3°43·8'W	X	11,17
Gob Geodha nam Bradan	N Eil	NB0737	58°13·7'	6°59·0'W	X	13
Gob Grutha	N Eil	NB5129	58°11·0'	6°13·7'W	X	8
Gobh-alltan	Highld	NH0829	57°18·9'	5°10·8'W	X	25,33
Gobions Wood	Herts	TL2503	51°42·9'	0°11·0'W	F	166
Goblaen Ho	Powys	SO1747	52°7·1'	3°12·3'W	X	148
Goblands Fm	Kent	TQ6449	51°13·2'	0°21·3'E	FM	188
Gobley Hole	Hants	SU6145	51°12·3'	1°7·2'W	T	185
Gob Lhiack	I of M	SC3471	54°6·7'	4°32·0'W	X	95
Goblin Combe	N Som	ST4765	51°23·1'	2°45·3'W	X	171,172,182
Goblin Ledge	S Glos	ST5386	51°34·5'	2°40·3'W	X	172
Gob Meanais	N Eil	NF8751	57°26·7'	7°12·6'W	X	22
Gob Mór	Highld	NC5936	58°17·7'	4°23·9'W	X	16
Gob na Creige	N Eil	NB5029	58°11·0'	6°14·7'W	X	8
Gobnageay	I of M	SC3881	54°12·2'	4°28·6'W	X	95
Gob na h-Airde	N Eil	NA0801	57°49·9'	8°35·9'W	X	18
Gob na h-Airde Bige	N Eil	NB0118	58°3·3'	7°3·7'W	X	13
Gob na h-Airde Móire	N Eil	NB0117	58°2·7'	7°3·6'W	X	13
Gob na h-Oa	Highld	NG3134	57°19·3'	6°27·7'W	X	32
Gob na Hoe	Highld	NG1542	57°23·0'	6°44·1'W	X	23
Gob na Hoe	Highld	NG1954	57°29·6'	6°40·9'W	X	23
Gob na Lice	Highld	NG8490	57°51·1'	5°37·9'W	X	19
Gob na Miolaid	N Eil	NB4211	58°1·1'	6°21·7'W	X	14
Gob nan Leac	Highld	NC3971	58°36·1'	4°45·8'W	X	9
Gob na Sgeithe Bàine	N Eil	NB4212	58°1·6'	6°21·7'W	X	14
Gob ny Calla	I of M	SC4787	54°15·6'	4°20·5'W	X	95
Gob ny Creggan Glassey	I of M	SC2988	54°15·8'	4°37·1'W	X	95
Gob ny Garvain	I of M	SC4889	54°16·7'	4°19·7'W	X	95
Gob ny How	I of M	SC4788	54°16·1'	4°20·6'W	X	95
Gob ny Portmooar	I of M	SC4990	54°17·3'	4°18·8'W	X	95
Gob ny rona	I of M	SC4793	54°18·8'	4°20·7'W	X	95
Gob ny Strona	I of M	SC4991	54°17·8'	4°18·8'W	X	95
Gobolt's Fm	Essex	TL9214	51°47·5'	0°47·5'E	FM	168
Gobowen	Shrops	SJ3033	52°53·6'	3°2·0'W	T	126
Gob Phursan	N Eil	NA0501	57°49·7'	8°39·0'W	X	18
Gob Rubha Bhalamuis Bhig	N Eil	NB2900	57°54·7'	6°34·1'W	X	14
Gob Rubha Bhatasgeir	N Eil	NB4939	58°16·3'	6°16·4'W	X	8
Gob Rubha Phàil	N Eil	NB0033	58°11·3'	7°5·8'W	X	13
Gob Rubh' Uisinis	N Eil	NB3503	57°56·5'	6°28·2'W	X	14
Gob Scapanish	N Eil	NA1504	57°51·8'	8°29·2'W	X	18
Gob Sgrithir	N Eil	NB1232	58°11·2'	6°53·6'W	X	13
Gobshealach	Highld	NM6470	56°46·0'	5°51·3'W	X	40
Gob Shilldinis	N Eil	NB4631	58°11·9'	6°18·9'W	X	8
Gob Steinis	N Eil	NB4534	58°13·5'	6°20·1'W	X	8

Gob Tanga	N Eil	NB5041	58°17·5′	6°15·5′W	X	8
Gob Thàis	N Eil	NB4940	58°16·9′	6°16·4′W	X	8
Gob Thunisgeir	N Eil	NB5235	58°14·3′	6°13·0′W	X	8
Gob Uisgebrigh	Highld	NG3254	57°30·1′	6°28·0′W	X	23
Gob y Deigan	I of M	SC2887	54°15·2′	4°38·0′W	X	95
Gob yn Ushtey	I of M	SC2175	54°8·6′	4°44·0′W	X	95
Gob y Rheynn	I of M	SC4382	54°12·8′	4°24·0′W	X	95
Gob y Volley	I of M	SC3693	54°18·6′	4°30·8′W	H	95
Gochgarreg	Powys	SN8723	51°53·9′	3°38·1′W	X	160
Gödag	Highld	NM4181	56°51·2′	6°14·4′W	X	39
Godalming	Surrey	SU9643	51°10·9′	0°37·2′W	T	186
Godbolt's Fm	Essex	TL8923	51°52·6′	0°45·1′E	FM	168
Godcott	Corn	SX2990	50°41·3′	4°24·9′W	X	190
Goddard Hill	Lincs	TF1779	53°17·9′	0°14·3′W	X	121
Goddards	Bucks	SU7890	51°36·4′	0°52·0′W	T	175
Goddard's Cleeve	Wilts	SU1054	51°17·3′	1°51·0′W	F	184
Goddard's Corner	Suff	TM2868	52°16·0′	1°20·9′E	T	156
Goddard's Fm	Essex	TL6132	51°58·0′	0°21·0′E	FM	167
Goddards Fm	Hants	SU3450	51°15·1′	1°30·4′W	FM	185
Goddards Fm	Wilts	SU0282	51°32·4′	1°57·9′W	FM	173
Goddard's Green	Kent	TQ7635	51°5·5′	0°31·2′E	X	188
Goddard's Green	Kent	TQ8134	51°4·8′	0°35·4′E	T	188
Goddard's Green	W Berks	SU6666	51°23·6′	1°2·7′W	T	175
Goddards' Green	W Susx	TQ2820	50°58·1′	0°10·2′W	T	198
Godden Green	Kent	TQ5555	51°16·6′	0°13·7′E	T	188
Goddens	Pth & Kin	NO1825	56°24·9′	3°19·3′W	X	53,58
Goddenwick Fm	W Susx	TQ3628	51°2·3′	0°3·2′W	FM	187,198
Godderthwaite	Cumbr	NY0306	54°26·7′	3°29·3′W	X	89
Goddington	Brom	TQ4765	51°22·1′	0°7·1′E	T	177
Goddington	Kent	TQ8653	51°15·0′	0°40·3′E	X	189
Godferhead	Cumbr	NY1421	54°34·9′	3°19·4′W	X	89
Godford Cross	Devon	ST1302	50°48·9′	3°13·7′W	X	192,193
Godford Land Fm	Devon	ST1302	50°48·9′	3°13·7′W	FM	192,193
Godfrey Ho	Kent	TQ8354	51°15·6′	0°37·8′E	A	188
Godfreyhole	Derby	SK2753	53°4·7′	1°35·4′W	X	119
Godfrey's Corner	Somer	ST3131	51°4·7′	2°58·7′W	X	182
Godfrey's Fm	Essex	TL6239	52°1·8′	0°22·1′E	FM	154
Godhams Fm	Somer	ST0028	51°2·8′	3°25·2′W	FM	181
Godington	Oxon	SP6427	51°56·5′	1°3·7′W	X	164,165
Godington Hall	Oxon	SP6326	51°56·0′	1°4·6′W	X	164,165
Godinton	Kent	TQ9843	51°9·3′	0°50·3′E	X	189
Godinton Park	Kent	TQ9842	51°8·8′	0°50·2′E	X	189
Godir-y-bwch	Pemb	SN0542	52°2·8′	4°50·2′W	X	145
Godley	Tames	SJ9595	53°27·3′	2°4·1′W	T	109
Godleybrook	Staffs	SJ9744	52°59·8′	2°2·3′W	T	118
Godley Hill	Tames	SJ9694	53°26·8′	2°3·2′W	T	109
Godleys Green	E Susx	TQ3719	50°57·5′	0°2·6′W	T	198
Godlingston Heath	Dorset	SZ0182	50°38·5′	1°58·8′W	X	195
Godlingston Hill	Dorset	SZ0081	50°38·0′	1°59·6′W	H	195
Godlingston Manor	Dorset	SZ0180	50°37·4′	1°58·8′W	A	195
Godmanchester	Cambs	TL2470	52°19·1′	0°10·4′W	T	153
Godmanstone	Dorset	SY6697	50°46·5′	2°28·6′W	T	194
Godmersham	Kent	TR0650	51°12·9′	0°57·4′E	T	179,189
Godmersham Downs	Kent	TR0550	51°13·0′	0°56·5′E	X	179,189
Godmersham Park	Kent	TR0650	51°12·9′	0°57·4′E	A	179,189
Godminster Fm	Somer	ST6832	51°5·4′	2°27·0′W	FM	183
Godmond Hall	Cumbr	SD4997	54°22·2′	2°46·7′W	X	97
Godney	Somer	ST4842	51°10·7′	2°44·2′W	T	182
Godney Moor	Somer	ST4843	51°11·3′	2°44·3′W	X	182
Godnow Br	N Lincs	SE7611	53°35·6′	0°50·7′W	X	112
Godolphin Cross	Corn	SW6031	50°8·1′	5°21·1′W	T	203
Godolphin Hill	Corn	SW5931	50°8·0′	5°22·0′W	H	203
Godolphin House	Corn	SW6031	50°8·1′	5°21·1′W	A	203
Godor	Powys	SJ0930	52°51·8′	3°20·7′W	H	125
Godor	Powys	SJ2018	52°45·5′	3°10·8′W	X	126
Godor Fm	Carm	SN4923	51°53·3′	4°11·3′W	FM	159
Godredewi	Carm	SN3029	51°56·3′	4°28·0′W	X	145
Godre Fynydd	Gwyn	SH7509	52°40·1′	3°50·5′W	H	124
Godregarreg	Carm	SN6927	51°55·8′	3°53·9′W	X	146,160
Godre'r-graig	Nth Pt Talb	SN7506	51°44·6′	3°48·2′W	T	160
Godre'r-waen	Carm	SN7122	51°53·1′	3°52·1′W	X	160
Godrevy Cove	Corn	SW8020	50°2·6′	5°4·0′W	W	204
Godrevy Island	Corn	SW5743	50°14·5′	5°24·1′W	X	203
Godrevy Point	Corn	SW5743	50°14·5′	5°24·1′W	X	203
Godrevy Towans	Corn	SW5842	50°13·9′	5°23·2′W	X	203
God's Blessing Green	Dorset	SU0303	50°49·8′	1°57·1′W	T	195
God's Bridge	Durham	NY9512	54°30·4′	2°4·2′W	X	91,92
God's Bridge	N Yks	SD7376	54°11·0′	2°24·4′W	X	98
Godsbury	Wilts	SU2157	51°18·9′	1°41·5′W	A	174
Godscroft	Scot Bord	NT7463	55°51·8′	2°24·5′W	X	67
Godscroft Hall	Ches	SJ5076	53°17·0′	2°44·6′W	X	117
God's Cross	Donc	SE6903	53°31·4′	0°57·1′W	X	111
Godsell Fm	Wilts	ST9877	51°29·7′	2°1·3′W	FM	173
Godsfield	Hants	SU6037	51°8·0′	1°8·2′W	X	185
Godsfield Copse	Hants	SU6037	51°8·0′	1°8·2′W	F	185
Godshill	Hants	SU1714	50°55·7′	1°45·1′W	T	195
Godshill	I of W	SZ5281	50°37·8′	1°15·5′W	T	196
God's Hill	Somer	ST6629	51°3·8′	2°28·7′W	X	183
Godshill Inclosure	Hants	SU1716	50°56·8′	1°45·1′W	F	184
Godshill Park	I of W	SZ5381	50°37·8′	1°14·7′W	X	196
Godsmarks Fm	W Susx	TQ1816	50°56·1′	0°18·9′W	FM	198
Godson House Fm	Lancs	SD4835	53°48·8′	2°47·0′W	FM	102
Godstone	Staffs	SK0134	52°54·4′	1°58·7′W	X	128
Godstone	Surrey	TQ3551	51°14·8′	0°3·6′W	T	187
Godstone Fm	Surrey	TQ3551	51°14·8′	0°3·6′W	FM	187
Godstone Sta	Surrey	TQ3648	51°13·1′	0°2·8′W	X	187
Godstow Abbey	Oxon	SP4809	51°46·9′	1°17·9′W	A	164
Godswinscroft	Hants	SZ1996	50°46·0′	1°43·5′W	T	195
Godwell	Devon	SX6455	50°23·0′	3°54·4′W	T	202
Godwick	Norf	TF9022	52°46·0′	0°49·4′E	T	132
Godwick Moor	Norf	TF8922	52°46·0′	0°48·5′E	X	132
Godwick Village	Norf	TF9022	52°46·0′	0°49·4′E	A	132
Godwin's Copse	Oxon	SP6502	51°43·0′	1°3·2′W	F	164,165
Godwin's Place	Suff	TM2558	52°10·7′	1°17·9′E	X	156
Godworthy Fm	Devon	ST2605	50°50·6′	3°2·7′W	FM	192,193
Goedh' nan Uan	Highld	NC0033	58°14·7′	5°24·0′W	X	15
Goelas	Conwy	SH8065	53°10·4′	3°47·3′W	X	116
Goenrounsen	Corn	SW8855	50°21·6′	4°58·5′W	X	200
Goetre	Carm	SN5141	52°3·1′	4°10·0′W	X	146
Goetre	Gwyn	SH5569	53°12·1′	4°9·9′W	X	114,115
Goetre	Gwyn	SH7124	52°48·1′	3°54·4′W	X	124
Goetre	Monm	SO3205	51°44·6′	2°58·7′W	T	161
Goetre	Powys	SJ0109	52°40·4′	3°27·5′W	X	125
Goetre	Powys	SJ1413	52°42·7′	3°16·0′W	X	125
Goetre	Powys	SO1891	52°30·9′	3°12·1′W	X	136
Goetre Fach	Powys	SJ0209	52°40·4′	3°26·6′W	X	125
Goetre Fawr	Carm	SN2522	51°52·4′	4°32·1′W	X	145,158
Goetre Hill	Powys	SO1892	52°31·4′	3°12·1′W	H	136
Goetre-uchaf	Carm	SN2423	51°52·9′	4°33·0′W	X	145,158
Goetre-uchaf	Gwyn	SH6418	52°44·8′	4°0·5′W	X	124
Goetty Mountain	Pemb	SN0629	51°55·8′	4°48·9′W	H	145,158
Gofer	Conwy	SH8472	53°14·2′	3°43·9′W	X	116
Gofer	Conwy	SH9777	53°17·0′	3°32·3′W	X	116
Goferydd	I of Angl	SH2082	53°18·5′	4°41·7′W	T	114
Goffers Knoll	Cambs	TL3942	52°3·8′	0°2·1′E	X	154
Goffers Knoll (Tumulus)	Cambs	TL3942	52°3·8′	0°2·1′E	A	154
Goffin's Fm	Devon	SX9495	50°44·9′	3°29·8′W	FM	192
Goff's Fm	W Susx	SU9528	51°2·8′	0°38·3′W	FM	186,197
Goffsland Fm	W Susx	TQ1423	50°59·9′	0°22·1′W	FM	198
Goffsland Ho	W Susx	TQ1018	50°57·3′	0°25·6′W	X	198
Goff's Oak	Herts	TL3203	51°42·8′	0°5·0′W	T	166
Goff Well Fm	Brad	SE0538	53°50·5′	1°55·0′W	FM	104
Gofton	Northum	NY8375	55°4·4′	2°15·5′W	X	86,87
Gofton Burn	Northum	NY8275	55°4·4′	2°16·5′W	W	86,87
Gofton Fieldhead	Northum	NY8275	55°4·4′	2°16·5′W	X	86,87
Goft's Ho	W Susx	SU9820	50°58·5′	0°35·9′W	X	197
Gofynach	Cered	SN4255	52°10·5′	4°18·2′W	X	146
Gogar	C of Edin	NT1672	55°56·3′	3°20·2′W	T	65,66
Gogar	Stir	NS8396	56°8·8′	3°52·6′W	X	57
Gogarbank Fm	C of Edin	NT1670	55°55·2′	3°20·2′W	FM	65,66
Gogarbank Ho	C of Edin	NT1770	55°55·2′	3°19·2′W	X	65,66
Gogar Burn	C of Edin	NT1573	55°56·8′	3°21·2′W	W	65
Gogar Burn	W Loth	NT1065	55°52·4′	3°25·9′W	W	65
Gogar Mains	C of Edin	NT1573	55°56·8′	3°21·2′W	X	65
Gogar Mount	C of Edin	NT1672	55°56·3′	3°20·2′W	X	65,66
Gogar Park	C of Edin	NT1772	55°56·3′	3°19·3′W	X	65,66
Gogar Stone	C of Edin	NT1572	55°56·3′	3°21·2′W	X	65
Gogarth	Conwy	SH7683	53°20·0′	3°51·3′W	X	115
Gogarth	Gwyn	SN6798	52°34·1′	3°57·3′W	X	135
Gogarth Bay	I of Angl	SH2183	53°19·1′	4°40·8′W	W	114
Goggin, The	Heref	SO4769	52°19·2′	2°46·3′W	X	137,138,148
Goggleby Stone	Cumbr	NY5515	54°31·9′	2°41·3′W	A	90
Gogia	Powys	SO1743	52°5·0′	3°12·3′W	X	148,161
Gogin	Shrops	SO2384	52°27·2′	3°7·6′W	X	137
Goginan	Cered	SN6881	52°24·9′	3°56·1′W	T	135
Goginan-fach	Cered	SN6981	52°24·9′	3°55·2′W	X	135
Goginan-fawr	Cered	SN6882	52°25·4′	3°56·1′W	X	135
Gogland Manor	Devon	SS8513	50°54·5′	3°37·8′W	X	181
Gog Magog Hills	Cambs	TL4954	52°10·1′	0°11·1′E	X	154
Gogo Water	N Ayr	NS2359	55°47·8′	4°49·0′W	W	63
Gogoyan	Cered	SN6354	52°10·3′	3°59·8′W	X	146
Gogwell	Devon	SS9417	50°56·8′	3°30·2′W	X	181
Goile Chròic	N Eil	NB3450	58°21·7′	6°32·4′W	W	8
Goirtean a' Chladaich	Highld	NN0570	56°47·1′	5°11·1′W	X	41
Goirtean Bàn	Arg & Bt	NR3560	55°45·9′	6°13·0′W	X	60
Goirtein Croft	Arg & Bt	NR9589	56°3·3′	5°17·1′W	X	55
Goirtein Driseach	Arg & Bt	NM4724	56°20·7′	6°5·2′W	X	48
Goirtinis	N Eil	NF6463	57°32·2′	7°36·5′W	X	22
Goitre	Carm	SN3723	51°53·1′	4°21·7′W	X	145,159
Goitre	Carm	SN4308	51°45·2′	4°16·1′W	X	159
Goitre	Carm	SN5504	51°43·2′	4°5·6′W	X	159
Goitre	Cered	SN4156	52°11·0′	4°19·2′W	X	146
Goitre	Cered	SN5951	52°8·6′	4°3·2′W	X	146
Goitre	Pemb	SN2040	52°2·0′	4°37·1′W	X	145
Goitre	Powys	SO1791	52°30·9′	3°13·0′W	X	136
Goitre-coed	Rho Cyn Taf	ST0895	51°39·0′	3°19·4′W	X	170
Goitrefach	Carm	SN5604	51°43·2′	4°4·7′W	X	159
Goitre Fm	Carm	SN6529	51°56·8′	3°57·5′W	FM	146
Goitre-wen	Carm	SN5504	51°43·2′	4°5·6′W	X	159
Goit, The	Derby	SK2475	53°16·5′	1°38·0′W	W	119
Goit, The	Lancs	SD6218	53°39·7′	2°34·1′W	W	109
Gokewell Priory Fm	N Lincs	SE9410	53°34·9′	0°34·4′W	FM	112
Golan	Gwyn	SH5242	52°57·5′	4°11·8′W	T	124
Golant	Corn	SX1254	50°21·6′	4°38·2′W	T	200
Golberdon	Corn	SX3271	50°31·1′	4°21·8′W	T	201
Golborne	Wigan	SJ6197	53°28·3′	2°34·8′W	T	109
Golborne Hall	Ches	SJ4559	53°7·8′	2°48·9′W	X	117
Golcar	Kirk	SE1016	53°38·7′	1°50·5′W	T	110
Golcar Fm	Brad	SE1340	53°51·6′	1°47·7′W	FM	104
Golch	Flint	SJ1677	53°17·2′	3°15·2′W	T	116
Goldacre Fm	Devon	SY1895	50°45·2′	3°9·4′W	FM	192,193
Goldborne Brook	Ches	SJ4659	53°7·8′	2°48·0′W	W	117
Goldborne Old Hall	Ches	SJ4659	53°7·8′	2°48·0′W	X	117
Goldborough	Pemb	SM9300	51°39·9′	4°59·2′W	X	157,158
Goldbridge Fm	E Susx	TQ4221	50°58·5′	0°1·7′E	FM	198
Goldburn	Devon	SX5898	50°46·1′	4°0·4′W	X	191
Goldbury Hill	Oxon	SU4488	51°35·6′	1°21·5′W	X	174
Goldcliff	Newp	ST3683	51°32·8′	2°55·0′W	T	171
Gold Cliff	Newp	ST3781	51°31·7′	2°54·1′W	T	171
Goldcliff Pill	Newp	ST3682	51°32·2′	2°55·0′W	W	171
Goldcombe Fm	Dorset	SY6287	50°41·1′	2°31·9′W	FM	194
Gold Corner	Somer	ST3643	51°11·2′	2°54·6′W	X	182
Gold Dike	Peterb	TF3307	52°38·9′	0°1·6′W	W	142
Gold Dike Fm	Peterb	TF3206	52°38·4′	0°2·5′W	FM	142
Golden	Corn	SW9246	50°16·9′	4°54·8′W	X	204
Golden Acre Park and Gardens	Leeds	SE2741	53°52·1′	1°34·9′W	X	104
Golden Ball	I Scilly	SV8817	49°58·5′	6°20·8′W	X	203
Golden Ball Hill	Wilts	SU1263	51°22·2′	1°49·3′W	H	173
Golden Balls	Oxon	SU5597	51°40·4′	1°11·9′W	T	164
Goldenberry	N Ayr	NS1851	55°43·4′	4°53·4′W	X	63
Goldenberry Hill	N Ayr	NS1850	55°42·8′	4°53·4′W	H	63
Golden Cap	Dorset	SY4092	50°43·7′	2°50·6′W	H	193
Golden Chair Fm	Hants	SU7339	51°9·0′	0°57·0′W	FM	186
Golden Clough	Derby	SK1286	53°22·5′	1°48·8′W	X	110
Golden Cross	E Susx	TQ5312	50°53·5′	0°10·9′E	T	199
Golden Cross	E Susx	TQ6310	50°52·2′	0°19·4′E	T	199
Golden Cross	Hants	SU2117	50°57·4′	1°41·7′W	X	184
Golden Cross	Heref	SO4356	52°12·2′	2°49·6′W	X	148,149
Golden Cross (Jacob's Barrow)	Hants	SU2117	50°57·4′	1°41·7′W	A	184
Goldenferry	Essex	TM1428	51°54·8′	1°7·1′E	X	168,169
Golden Flatts	N Yks	SE6467	54°5·9′	1°0·9′W	X	100
Golden Fleece	Cumbr	NY4351	54°51·3′	2°52·8′W	X	85
Golden Gates	Norf	TF9041	52°56·2′	0°50·0′E	X	132
Golden Gates	Wilts	ST9570	51°26·0′	2°3·9′W	X	173
Golden Green	Kent	TQ6348	51°12·7′	0°20·4′E	T	188
Golden Grove	Carm	SN1914	51°48·0′	4°37·1′W	X	158
Golden Grove	Carm	SN5819	51°51·3′	4°3·3′W	T	159
Golden Grove	Flint	SJ0881	53°19·3′	3°22·5′W	A	116
Golden Grove	N Yks	NZ8908	54°27·8′	0°37·2′W	X	94
Golden Grove Ho	Lincs	TF2438	52°55·7′	0°8·9′W	X	131
Golden Groves	N Yks	SE0394	54°20·7′	1°56·8′W	X	98
Goldenhayes	Hants	SU3111	50°54·1′	1°33·2′W	X	196
Golden Hay Fm	Staffs	SJ7849	53°2·5′	2°19·3′W	FM	118
Golden Hill	C of Bris	ST5876	51°29·1′	2°35·9′W	T	172
Goldenhill	C of Stoke	SJ8553	53°4·7′	2°13·0′W	T	118
Golden Hill	E Yorks	TA0556	53°59·6′	0°23·5′W	X	107
Golden Hill	Fife	NO2515	56°19·5′	3°12·3′W	H	59
Golden Hill	Hants	SZ2695	50°45·5′	1°37·5′W	T	195
Golden Hill	Monm	ST4297	51°40·4′	2°49·9′W	H	171
Goldenhill	Northum	NU1632	55°35·1′	1°44·3′W	X	75
Golden Hill	Notts	SK6967	53°12·0′	0°57·6′W	X	120
Golden Hill	Pemb	SM9724	51°52·9′	4°56·6′W	T	157,158
Golden Hill	Pemb	SM9802	51°41·1′	4°54·9′W	T	157,158
Golden Hill	Somer	ST3719	50°58·3′	2°53·5′W	X	193
Golden Hill	Staffs	SK0556	53°6·3′	1°55·1′W	X	119
Golden Hill Fm	N Yks	SE7569	54°6·9′	0°50·7′W	FM	100
Golden Hill Fm	Red & Cl	NZ7113	54°30·7′	0°53·8′W	FM	94
Goldenhill Fm	Staffs	SJ7432	52°53·3′	2°22·8′W	FM	127
Golden Hill Fm	York	SE6160	54°2·2′	1°3·7′W	FM	100
Golden Hill Fort	I of W	SZ3387	50°41·1′	1°31·6′W	A	196
Golden Howe	Cumbr	SD5997	54°22·3′	2°37·4′W	X	97
Goldenhurst	Kent	TR0634	51°4·3′	0°56·8′E	X	179,189
Golden Lands Fm	Surrey	TQ1748	51°13·4′	0°19·1′W	FM	187
Goldenlands Fm	Wilts	SU2259	51°20·0′	1°40·7′W	FM	174
Goldenlea	Renf	NS3965	55°51·3′	4°33·9′W	X	63
Golden Mea	Cumbr	NY7827	54°38·5′	2°20·0′W	X	91
Golden Mill	Corn	SW9246	50°16·9′	4°54·8′W	X	204
Goldenmoor	Northum	NU2014	55°25·4′	1°40·6′W	X	81
Golden Nook	Ches	SJ5970	53°13·8′	2°36·4′W	X	117
Golden Park	Devon	SS2320	50°57·4′	4°30·8′W	T	190
Golden Parsonage	Herts	TL0512	51°48·0′	0°28·2′W	A	166
Golden Pot	Hants	SU7043	51°11·1′	0°59·5′W	T	186
Golden's Fm	Essex	TL7130	51°56·8′	0°29·7′E	FM	167
Golden Slack	Ches	SJ9467	53°12·2′	2°5·0′W	X	118
Golden Springs	Derby	SK0087	53°23·0′	1°59·6′W	X	110
Golden Springs Fm	Dorset	SY7991	50°43·3′	2°17·5′W	FM	194
Golden Square	Devon	ST2203	50°49·5′	3°6·1′W	X	192,192,193
Golden Square	Essex	TL9030	51°56·4′	0°46·2′E	X	168
Golden Square	N Yks	SE6180	54°13·0′	1°3·5′W	X	100
Golden Square	N Yks	SE8077	54°11·2′	0°46·0′W	X	100
Golden Valley	Derby	SK3844	52°59·8′	1°25·6′W	X	119,128
Golden Valley	Derby	SK4251	53°3·5′	1°22·0′W	T	120
Golden Valley	Glos	SO8802	51°43·2′	2°10·0′W	X	162
Golden Valley	Glos	SO9022	51°54·0′	2°8·3′W	T	163
Golden Valley	Heref	SO3636	52°1·4′	2°55·6′W	X	149,161
Golden Valley	Heref	SO6649	52°8·5′	2°29·4′W	T	149
Golden Valley	Highld	NH0147	57°28·4′	5°18·7′W	X	25
Golden Valley	Monm	ST4793	51°38·2′	2°45·6′W	X	171,172
Golden Valley	S Glos	ST6870	51°25·9′	2°27·2′W	X	172
Golden Valley	Worcs	SO7737	52°2·1′	2°19·7′W	X	150
Golden Valley Plantn	E Yorks	SE8651	53°57·1′	0°41·0′W	F	106
Golden Wood	Kent	TR0136	51°5·5′	0°52·6′E	F	189
Golder Field	Heref	SO5661	52°15·0′	2°38·3′W	T	137,138,149
Golder Manor	Oxon	SU6697	51°40·3′	1°2·3′W	X	164,165
Golders Green	Barnet	TQ2488	51°34·9′	0°12·2′W	T	176
Goldfields Fm	Dorset	ST9613	50°55·2′	2°3·0′W	FM	195
Goldfinch Bottom	W Berks	SU5064	51°22·6′	1°16·5′W	T	174
Goldhanger	Essex	TL9008	51°44·5′	0°45·5′E	T	168
Goldhanger Creek	Essex	TL9107	51°44·0′	0°46·4′E	W	168
Goldhayfields	Staffs	SK0918	52°45·8′	1°51·6′W	X	128
Gold Hill	Dorset	ST8213	50°55·2′	2°15·0′W	T	194
Gold Hill	Durham	NY8342	54°46·6′	2°15·4′W	X	86,87
Goldhill	Durham	NZ0547	54°49·3′	1°54·9′W	X	87
Gold Hill	Heref	SO6743	52°5·3′	2°28·5′W	X	149
Gold Hill	Lancs	SD6953	53°58·6′	2°27·9′W	X	103
Gold Hill	Norf	TL5392	52°30·5′	0°15·7′E	X	143
Gold Hill	N Yks	NZ4802	54°24·9′	1°15·2′W	X	93
Gold Hill	W Berks	SU3575	51°28·6′	1°29·4′W	X	174
Gold Hill Fm	Heref	SO7336	52°1·5′	2°23·2′W	FM	150
Goldhill Fm	Kent	TQ6347	51°12·2′	0°20·4′E	FM	188
Goldhill Fm	Notts	SK6855	53°5·5′	0°58·7′W	FM	120
Goldhurst	Staffs	SK0239	52°57·1′	1°57·8′W	X	128
Goldicote Coppice	Warw	SP2452	52°10·2′	1°38·5′W	F	151
Goldicote Ho	Warw	SP2451	52°9·6′	1°38·6′W	X	151
Goldielands	Scot Bord	NT4712	55°24·2′	2°49·8′W	X	79
Goldielea	D & G	NX9373	55°2·7′	3°40·0′W	X	84
Golding	Shrops	SJ5403	52°37·6′	2°40·4′W	X	126
Golding Barn	W Susx	TQ2010	50°52·8′	0°17·3′W	X	198
Goldingham Hall	Essex	TL8340	52°1·9′	0°40·5′E	X	155
Golding Rough	Shrops	SJ5404	52°38·1′	2°40·4′W	F	126
Goldings	Herts	TL3014	51°48·8′	0°6·5′W	X	166
Golding's Fm	Suff	TM4785	52°24·7′	1°38·3′E	FM	156
Goldings, The	W Susx	TQ2029	51°3·1′	0°16·9′W	X	187,198
Golding's Wood	Herts	TL3511	51°47·1′	0°2·2′W	F	166
Goldington	Beds	TL0750	52°8·5′	0°25·8′W	T	153
Goldingtons	Herts	TQ0398	51°40·5′	0°30·2′W	X	166,176
Gold Island	Northum	NY8677	55°5·5′	2°12·7′W	X	87
Goldness Ho	Worcs	SO8472	52°21·0′	2°13·7′W	X	138
Gold Point	Dorset	SY9889	50°42·3′	2°1·3′W	X	195
Goldrill Beck	Cumbr	NY4015	54°31·9′	2°55·2′W	W	90
Goldring	W Susx	SU8126	51°1·9′	0°50·3′W	X	186,197
Goldrings Fm	W Susx	SU8321	50°59·2′	0°48·7′W	FM	197
Goldsand Bridges	Essex	TQ9698	51°39·0′	0°50·4′E	X	168
Goldsborough	N Yks	NZ8314	54°31·1′	0°42·6′W	T	94
Goldsborough	N Yks	SE3856	54°0·2′	1°24·8′W	T	104
Goldsborough Fields	N Yks	SE3856	54°0·2′	1°24·8′W	X	104
Goldsborough Moor	N Yks	SE3956	54°0·2′	1°23·9′W	X	104

Goldsbrorough	Durham	NY9517	54°33·1'	2°4·2'W	X	91,92
Goldscleugh	Northum	NT9123	55°30·3'	2°8·1'W	X	74,75
Gold's Cross	Bath & NE Somer	ST5960	51°20·5'	2°34·9'W	T	172,182
Gold's Fm	Hants	SU6853	51°16·6'	1°1·1'W	FM	185,186
Golds Green	Sand	SO9893	52°32·3'	2°1·4'W	T	139
Goldsitch Ho	Staffs	SK0164	53°10·6'	1°58·7'W	X	119
Goldsitch Moss	Staffs	SK0064	53°10·6'	1°59·6'W	X	119
Goldsithney	Corn	SW5430	50°7·4'	5°26·1'W	T	203
Goldsland	V of Glam	ST1171	51°26·1'	3°16·4'W	X	171
Goldsmith Grange	Leic	SK7723	52°48·2'	0°51·1'W	X	129
Goldsmiths'	Thurr	TQ6785	51°32·6'	0°24·9'E	X	177,178
Goldsmith's Covert	Suff	TM2040	52°1·1'	1°12·8'E	F	169
Goldsticks Fm	Essex	TL7327	51°55·1'	0°31·3'E	FM	167
Goldstone	Shrops	SJ7028	52°51·2'	2°26·3'W	T	127
Goldstone Common	Shrops	SJ6929	52°51·7'	2°27·2'W	X	127
Goldstone Fm	Surrey	TQ1353	51°16·1'	0°22·4'W	FM	187
Goldstones	Essex	TL5941	52°2·9'	0°19·5'E	X	154
Goldstrow	E Susx	TQ4221	50°58·5'	0°1·7'E	X	198
Goldthorn	Shrops	SO6079	52°24·7'	2°34·9'W	X	138
Goldthorn Park	Wolv	SO9196	52°33·9'	2°7·6'W	T	139
Goldthorpe	Barns	SE4604	53°32·1'	1°17·9'W	T	111
Goldthorpe Fm	Notts	SK5987	53°22·8'	1°6·4'W	FM	111,120
Goldwell	Kent	TQ8636	51°5·8'	0°39·8'E	X	189
Goldwell	Kent	TQ9642	51°8·8'	0°48·5'E	X	189
Goldwell Fm	Glos	SP0324	51°55·1'	1°57·0'W	FM	163
Goldwick Fm	Glos	ST7197	51°40·5'	2°24·8'W	FM	162
Goldworthy	Devon	SS3922	50°58·7'	4°17·2'W	T	190
Goleigh Farm Ho	Hants	SU7729	51°3·5'	0°53·7'W	X	186,197
Goleigh Fm	Hants	SU7231	51°4·7'	0°57·9'W	FM	186
Goleigh Manor	Hants	SU7331	51°4·6'	0°57·1'W	A	186
Goleigh Wood	Hants	SU7131	51°4·7'	0°58·8'W	F	186
Goleugell	Conwy	SH8169	53°12·5'	3°46·5'W	X	116
Goleugoed	Carm	SN6637	52°1·2'	3°56·8'W	X	146
Goleugoed	Carm	SN7530	51°57·5'	3°48·8'W	X	146,160
Golfa	Powys	SJ1925	52°49·2'	3°11·7'W	X	125
Golfa Fm	Powys	SJ1906	52°39·0'	3°11·4'W	FM	125
Golf Hill	D & G	NY3489	55°11·7'	3°1·8'W	H	79
Golford	Highld	NH9554	57°34·1'	3°44·9'W	X	27
Golford	Kent	TQ7936	51°5·9'	0°33·8'E	T	188
Golftyn	Flint	SJ2870	53°13·6'	3°4·3'W	T	117
Golgotha	Kent	TR2648	51°11·4'	1°14·5'E	T	179
Golitha Falls	Corn	SX2268	50°29·3'	4°30·2'W	W	201
Gollachy	Moray	NJ3964	57°40·0'	3°0·9'W	T	28
Golland	Devon	SS6515	50°55·4'	3°54·9'W	X	180
Golland	Pth & Kin	NO0504	56°13·4'	3°31·5'W	X	58
Golland Burn	Pth & Kin	NO0404	56°13·4'	3°32·5'W	W	58
Gollanfield	Highld	NH8053	57°33·3'	3°59·9'W	X	27
Gollard Fm	Hants	SU2842	51°10·8'	1°35·6'W	FM	184
Gollawater	Corn	SW7550	50°18·7'	5°9·2'W	T	200,204
Gollick Pk	Devon	ST1614	50°55·4'	3°11·3'W	X	181,193
Gollinglith	N Yks	SE1179	54°12·6'	1°49·5'W	X	99
Gollinglith Foot	N Yks	SE1580	54°13·2'	1°45·8'W	T	99
Gollinglith Ridge	N Yks	SE1280	54°13·2'	1°48·5'W	X	99
Gollings Rough	Shrops	SJ6740	52°57·6'	2°29·1'W	F	118
Golloch Hill	Pth & Kin	NO1008	56°15·6'	3°26·7'W	H	58
Golly	Wrex	SJ3358	53°7·1'	2°59·7'W	T	117
Golly Knapp Fm	Dorset	SY5389	50°42·2'	2°39·6'W	FM	194
Golodd	Gwyn	SH6319	52°45·3'	4°1·4'W	X	124
Golsoncott	Somer	ST0239	51°8·7'	3°23·7'W	T	181
Golspie	Highld	NH8399	57°58·2'	3°58·2'W	T	21
Golspie Burn	Highld	NC8202	57°59·8'	3°59·3'W	W	17
Golspie Links	Highld	NH8197	57°57·1'	4°0·2'W	X	21
Golspie Tower Fm	Highld	NC8300	57°58·7'	3°58·2'W	FM	17
Golta	Orkney	ND3795	58°50·5'	3°5·0'W	X	7
Goltho Grange	Lincs	TF1276	53°16·4'	0°18·8'W	X	121
Goltho Hall	Lincs	TF1176	53°16·4'	0°19·7'W	X	121
Goltho Ho	Lincs	TF1178	53°17·5'	0°19·7'W	X	121
Goltho Village	Lincs	TF1177	53°16·9'	0°19·7'W	A	121
Golticlay	Highld	ND2040	58°20·7'	3°21·5'W	X	11,12
Golt, The	Orkney	ND4494	58°50·1'	2°57·7'W	X	7
Golval	Highld	NC8962	58°32·2'	3°53·9'W	X	10
Golval Hill	Highld	NC9061	58°31·7'	3°52·9'W	H	10
Golynos	Newp	ST2690	51°36·5'	3°3·7'W	X	171
Golynos	Torf	SO2504	51°44·0'	3°4·8'W	T	171
Gomeldon	Wilts	SU1935	51°7·1'	1°43·3'W	T	184
Gomersal	Kirk	SE2026	53°44·0'	1°41·4'W	T	104
Gomershay Fm	Dorset	ST7517	50°57·3'	2°21·0'W	FM	183
Gometra	Arg & Bt	NM3641	56°29·5'	6°16·9'W	X	47,48
Gometra Ho	Arg & Bt	NM3540	56°28·9'	6°17·8'W	X	47,48
Gommerock	Devon	SX8850	50°20·6'	3°34·1'W	A	202
Gommery Hall Fm	E Yorks	TA0044	53°53·2'	0°28·3'W	FM	106,107
Gomshall	Surrey	TQ0847	51°12·9'	0°26·8'W	T	187
Goms Hole	Glos	SP1517	51°51·3'	1°46·5'W	X	163
Gonachan Burn	Stir	NS6084	56°2·0'	4°14·4'W	W	57,64
Gonachan Cottage	Stir	NS6386	56°3·1'	4°11·5'W	X	57
Gonachan Glen	Stir	NS6385	56°2·6'	4°11·5'W	X	57
Gonalston	Notts	SK6747	53°1·2'	0°59·7'W	T	129
Gonamena	Corn	SX2670	50°30·5'	4°26·9'W	T	201
Gonar Burn	Aberd	NJ8758	57°37·0'	2°12·6'W	W	30
Gonarhall	Aberd	NJ8658	57°37·0'	2°13·6'W	X	30
Gonerby Grange	Lincs	SK9040	52°57·2'	0°39·2'W	X	130
Gonerby Hill Foot	Lincs	SK9037	52°55·6'	0°39·3'W	T	130
Gonerby Moor	Lincs	SK8839	52°56·7'	0°41·0'W	X	130
Gon Firth	Shetld	HU3662	60°20·7'	1°20·4'W	W	2,3
Gonfirth	Shetld	HU3761	60°20·1'	1°19·3'W	T	2,3
Gonglass Water	Moray	NJ1621	57°16·6'	3°23·1'W	W	36
Gongl-gam	I of Angl	SH3471	53°12·9'	4°28·8'W	X	114
Gonsal Fm	Shrops	SJ4804	52°38·1'	2°45·7'W	FM	126
Gonsley Green Fm	Ches	SJ7348	53°2·0'	2°23·8'W	FM	118
Gonville Hall	Norf	TG0900	52°33·7'	1°5·4'E	X	144
Gooda	N Yks	SD6673	54°9·3'	2°30·8'W	X	98
Goodacre	Devon	SX4190	50°41·5'	4°14·7'W	X	190
Goodameavy	Devon	SX5364	50°27·7'	4°3·9'W	X	201
Good Bent	Kirk	SE0806	53°33·3'	1°52·3'W	X	110
Goodber Common	Lancs	SD6263	54°3·9'	2°34·4'W	X	97
Goodber Fell	Lancs	SD6262	54°3·4'	2°34·4'W	X	97
Goodbush Hill	S Lanak	NS7134	55°35·2'	4°2·4'W	H	71
Goodcheap Fm	Kent	TR0443	51°9·2'	0°55·4'E	FM	179,189
Goodcop Fm	Donc	SE7308	53°34·0'	0°53·5'W	FM	112
Goodcroft	Cumbr	NY5316	54°32·5'	2°43·2'W	X	90
Good Easter	Essex	TL6212	51°47·2'	0°21·3'E	T	167
Goodedge Fm	Somer	ST7137	51°8·1'	2°24·5'W	FM	183
Goodenbergh Fm	N Yks	SD6370	54°7·7'	2°33·6'W	FM	97
Goodern Manor Fm	Corn	SW7843	50°15·0'	5°6·5'W	FM	204
Gooderstone	Norf	TF7602	52°35·5'	0°36·3'E	T	143
Gooderstone Common	Norf	TF7500	52°34·4'	0°35·4'E	X	143
Gooderstone Warren	Norf	TF7901	52°34·9'	0°38·9'E	X	144
Goodfellows	Essex	TL6025	51°54·3'	0°19·9'E	X	167
Goodhall	Essex	TM0530	51°56·1'	0°59·3'E	X	168
Goodham Gill Rigg	N Yks	SD7795	54°21·2'	2°20·8'W	X	98
Good Hares	Essex	TL8900	51°40·2'	0°44·4'E	X	168
Good Hook	Pemb	SM9816	51°48·6'	4°55·4'W	X	157,158
Goodhope	D & G	NY0792	55°13·1'	3°27·3'W	X	78
Good Hope	Pemb	SM9529	51°55·5'	4°58·5'W	X	157,158
Goodhouses Fm	Notts	SK7571	53°14·1'	0°52·2'W	FM	120
Goodiebank	Stir	NN6697	56°9·1'	4°9·0'W	X	57
Goodiersgreen Fm	Ches	SJ7182	53°20·3'	2°25·7'W	FM	109
Goodie Water	Stir	NN6100	56°10·6'	4°13·9'W	W	57
Goodie Water	Stir	NS6499	56°10·1'	4°11·0'W	W	57
Goodiford Fm	Devon	ST0508	50°52·1'	3°20·6'W	FM	192
Goodings	W Berks	SU3575	51°28·6'	1°29·4'W	X	174
Gooding's Fm	Somer	ST2733	51°5·7'	3°2·2'W	FM	182
Good Intent	N Yks	SE0054	53°59·2'	1°59·6'W	X	104
Goodlands Fm	Suff	TM0439	52°0·9'	0°58·8'E	FM	155
Goodleigh	Devon	SS5934	51°5·5'	4°0·4'W	T	180
Goodleigh	Devon	SS6208	50°51·5'	3°57·3'W	X	191
Goodleigh	Devon	ST1110	50°53·2'	3°15·5'W	X	192,193
Goodley Stock	Kent	TQ4452	51°15·2'	0°4·2'E	T	187
Goodlie Hill	Cumbr	NY6913	54°30·9'	2°28·3'W	X	91
Goodmanham	E Yorks	SE8843	53°52·8'	0°39·3'W	T	106
Goodmanham Grange	E Yorks	SE9044	53°53·3'	0°37·4'W	X	106
Goodmanham Lodge	E Yorks	SE9243	53°52·7'	0°35·6'W	X	106
Goodmanham Wold	E Yorks	SE9043	53°52·8'	0°37·4'W	X	106
Goodmanham Wold Fm	E Yorks	SE9144	53°53·3'	0°36·5'W	FM	106
Goodmans	Devon	ST2605	50°50·6'	3°2·7'W	X	192,193
Goodman's Cairn	D & G	NX1377	55°3·4'	4°55·2'W	X	76
Goodman's Knowe	Moray	NJ3237	57°25·4'	3°7·5'W	X	28
Goodmansleigh	Corn	SX3485	50°38·7'	4°20·5'W	X	201
Goodmayes	Redbr	TQ4686	51°33·5'	0°6·8'E	T	177
Goodmerry Fm	Corn	SX3364	50°27·4'	4°20·8'W	FM	201
Goodnestone	Kent	TR0461	51°18·9'	0°56·0'E	T	178,179
Goodnestone	Kent	TR2554	51°14·7'	1°13·8'E	T	179
Goodnestone Ho	Kent	TR2554	51°14·7'	1°13·8'E	X	179
Goodockhill	N Lanak	NS8161	55°49·9'	3°53·6'W	X	65
Goodrest Fm	Warw	SP2769	52°19·3'	1°35·8'W	FM	151
Goodrest Fm	Worcs	SO9681	52°25·9'	2°3·1'W	FM	139
Goodrich	Heref	SO5719	51°52·3'	2°37·1'W	T	162
Goodrich Castle	Heref	SO5719	51°52·3'	2°37·1'W	A	162
Goodrich Cross	Heref	SO5618	51°51·8'	2°37·9'W	X	162
Goodrington	Torbay	SX8858	50°24·9'	3°34·2'W	T	202
Goodrington Sands	Torbay	SX8959	50°25·5'	3°33·4'W	X	202
Good's Fm	Dorset	ST8120	50°59·0'	2°15·9'W	FM	183
Good's Fm	Somer	ST2034	51°6·2'	3°8·2'W	FM	182
Good's Green	Worcs	SO7881	52°25·8'	2°19·0'W	T	138
Goodshaw	Lancs	SD8125	53°43·5'	2°16·9'W	T	103
Goodshaw Chapel	Lancs	SD8126	53°44·0'	2°16·9'W	T	103
Goodshaw Fold	Lancs	SD8026	53°44·0'	2°17·8'W	T	103
Goodshelter	Devon	SX7638	50°14·0'	3°43·9'W	X	202
Goodshill Fm	Kent	TQ8634	51°4·7'	0°39·7'E	FM	189
Goodstone	Devon	SX7871	50°31·8'	3°42·9'W	T	202
Goodstone Woods	Devon	SX7873	50°32·9'	3°42·9'W	F	191
Goodtrees	C of Edin	NT1565	55°52·5'	3°21·1'W	X	65
Goodwell Field	Durham	NZ2138	54°44·4'	1°40·0'W	X	93
Goodwells Head	Devon	SS6633	51°5·1'	3°54·4'W	X	180
Goodwick Fm	Beds	TL1358	52°12·7'	0°20·4'W	FM	153
Goodwick (Wdig)	Pemb	SM9438	52°0·4'	4°59·7'W	T	157
Goodwin's Fm	Essex	TL9129	51°55·8'	0°47·1'E	FM	168
Goodwood Aerodrome & Motor Racing Circuit	W Susx	SU8707	50°51·6'	0°45·4'W	X	197
Goodwood Country Cycle Route	W Susx	TQ0004	50°49·8'	0°34·4'W	X	197
Goodwood Country Park	W Susx	SU8911	50°53·7'	0°43·7'W	X	197
Goodwood Ho	W Susx	SU8808	50°52·1'	0°44·6'W	A	197
Goodwood Park	W Susx	SU8809	50°52·7'	0°44·6'W	X	197
Goodworth Clatford	Hants	SU3642	51°10·8'	1°28·7'W	T	185
Goodwyns Fm	Suff	TM3470	52°16·9'	1°26·2'E	FM	156
Goody Bridge	Cumbr	NY3308	54°28·0'	3°1·6'W	X	90
Goody Cross	Leeds	SE3930	53°46·1'	1°24·1'W	X	104
Goodyear's Fm	Worcs	SO7965	52°17·2'	2°18·1'W	FM	138,150
Goodyers End	Warw	SP3385	52°28·0'	1°30·5'W	T	140
Goodyhills	Cumbr	NY1046	54°48·3'	3°23·6'W	T	85
Googs Fm	Northnts	SP6953	52°10·5'	0°59·1'W	FM	152
Goole	E Yorks	SE7423	53°42·1'	0°52·3'W	T	105,106,112
Goole Bank Fm	N Yks	SE5837	53°49·8'	1°6·7'W	FM	105
Goole Br	E Yorks	SE7624	53°42·7'	0°50·5'W	X	105,106,112
Goole Dike or River Torne	Donc	SK6095	53°27·1'	1°5·4'W	W	111
Goole Fields	E Yorks	SE7520	53°40·5'	0°51·5'W	X	105,106,112
Goole Fields Fm	E Yorks	SE7519	53°40·0'	0°51·5'W	FM	112
Goole Grange	E Yorks	SE7420	53°40·5'	0°52·4'W	X	105,106,112
Goole Hall	E Yorks	SE7521	53°41·0'	0°51·5'W	X	105,106,112
Goole Moors	E Yorks	SE7317	53°38·9'	0°53·3'W	X	112
Gool Knowe	Scot Bord	NT2021	55°28·8'	3°15·5'W	H	73
Goom's Hill	Worcs	SP0254	52°11·3'	1°57·8'W	T	150
Goonabarn	Corn	SW8954	50°21·1'	4°57·6'W	X	200
Goonabarn	Corn	SW9554	50°21·3'	4°52·5'W	T	200
Goonamarth Fm	Corn	SW9954	50°21·3'	4°49·2'W	FM	200
Goonbell	Corn	SW7249	50°18·1'	5°11·7'W	T	204
Goon Gumpas	Corn	SW7442	50°14·3'	5°9·8'W	T	204
Goonhavern	Corn	SW7853	50°20·3'	5°6·8'W	T	200,204
Goonhilly Downs	Corn	SW7319	50°1·9'	5°9·8'W	X	204
Goonhoskyn	Corn	SW8757	50°22·6'	4°59·4'W	X	200
Goonhusband	Corn	SW6625	50°5·0'	5°15·9'W	T	203
Goonlaze	Corn	SW7137	50°11·6'	5°12·1'W	T	203
Goonown	Corn	SW7250	50°18·6'	5°11·8'W	T	204
Goon Piper	Corn	SW8139	50°12·9'	5°3·8'W	T	204
Goonreeve	Corn	SW7737	50°11·7'	5°7·1'W	X	204
Goonvrea	Corn	SW7049	50°18·0'	5°13·4'W	T	203
Goonzion Downs	Corn	SX1767	50°28·7'	4°34·4'W	X	201
Goorn	Shetld	HZ2271	59°31·7'	1°36·2'W	X	4
Goose Acre Fm	Oxon	SU5298	51°40·9'	1°14·5'W	FM	164
Gooseberry	N Yks	SE2972	54°8·8'	1°32·9'W	X	99
Gooseberry Green	Essex	TQ6795	51°38·0'	0°25·2'E	T	167,177
Gooseberry Hall Fm	Warw	SP2960	52°14·5'	1°34·1'W	FM	151
Goosebradon Fm	Somer	ST3820	50°58·8'	2°52·6'W	FM	193
Goose Brook Fm	Ches	SJ6278	53°18·1'	2°33·8'W	FM	118
Goose Burn	Highld	NH6857	57°35·3'	4°12·0'W	W	26
Goose Common	Norf	TM0098	52°32·8'	0°57·4'E	X	144
Goosecruives	Aberd	NO7583	56°56·5'	2°24·2'W	X	45
Goosedale Fm	Notts	SK5649	53°2·4'	1°9·5'W	FM	129
Goose Dub Fm	Lancs	SD3821	53°41·2'	2°55·9'W	FM	102
Goosedubs	D & G	NX8385	55°9·0'	3°49·7'W	X	78
Goose Eye	Brad	SE0240	53°51·6'	1°57·8'W	T	104
Goose Fm	Kent	TQ6262	51°20·3'	0°19·9'E	FM	177,188
Goose Fm	N Yks	SE5962	54°3·3'	1°5·5'W	FM	100
Gooseford	Corn	SX3867	50°29·1'	4°16·6'W	X	201
Gooseford	Devon	SX6791	50°42·4'	3°52·6'W	T	191
Goosegreen	Cumbr	NY1844	54°47·3'	3°16·1'W	X	85
Goosegreen	Cumbr	NY4123	54°36·2'	2°54·4'W	X	90
Goose Green	Cumbr	SD5484	54°15·2'	2°41·9'W	T	97
Goose Green	Essex	TM1327	51°54·3'	1°6·2'E	T	168,169
Goose Green	Essex	TM1425	51°53·2'	1°7·0'E	T	168,169
Goose Green	Hants	SU3007	50°51·9'	1°34·0'W	X	196
Goose Green	Herts	TL3509	51°46·0'	0°2·2'W	T	166
Goose Green	Kent	TQ6450	51°13·8'	0°21·3'E	T	188
Goose Green	Kent	TQ8437	51°6·4'	0°38·1'E	T	188
Goose Green	Lancs	SD4722	53°41·7'	2°47·8'W	T	102
Goose Green	Lancs	SD4750	53°56·8'	2°48·0'W	X	102
Goose Green	Norf	TM1187	52°26·6'	1°6·7'E	T	144
Goose Green	N Yks	SE1566	54°5·6'	1°45·8'W	X	99
Goose Green	S Glos	ST7183	51°32·9'	2°24·7'W	T	172
Goose Green	Wigan	SD5603	53°31·6'	2°39·4'W	T	108
Goose Green	W Susx	SU7721	50°59·2'	0°53·8'W	T	197
Goose Green	W Susx	SU9905	50°50·4'	0°35·2'W	X	197
Goose Green	W Susx	TQ1118	50°57·4'	0°24·7'W	T	198
Goosegreen	W Susx	TQ1532	51°4·8'	0°21·1'W	X	187
Goose Green Inclosure	Hants	SU8040	51°9·4'	0°51·0'W	F	186
Goose Green	S Glos	ST6774	51°28·1'	2°28·1'W	X	172
Goose Hall	Cambs	TL4867	52°17·1'	0°10·6'E	X	154
Goose Hall	Lancs	SD5734	53°48·3'	2°38·8'W	X	102
Goosehall Fm	Cambs	TL5868	52°17·5'	0°19·4'E	FM	154
Gooseham	Corn	SS2216	50°55·2'	4°31·6'W	T	190
Gooseham Mill	Corn	SS2317	50°55·8'	4°30·7'W	T	190
Goose Hill	Dorset	SY5985	50°40·0'	2°34·4'W	X	194
Goose Hill	Glos	SP2039	52°3·2'	1°42·1'W	X	151
Goose Hill	Hants	SU5362	51°21·5'	1°13·9'W	T	174
Goosehill	S Ayr	NS3608	55°20·6'	4°34·7'W	X	70,77
Goosehill	Somer	ST2119	50°58·1'	3°7·1'W	X	193
Goose Hill	Suff	TM4664	52°13·4'	1°36·5'E	F	156
Goosehill	Wakf	SE3721	53°41·3'	1°26·0'W	T	104
Goosehill Camp	W Susx	SU8212	50°54·3'	0°49·6'W	A	197
Goose Hill Fm	D & G	NS7908	55°21·3'	3°54·1'W	FM	71,78
Goosehill Green	Worcs	SO9361	52°15·1'	2°5·8'W	T	150
Goosehillock	Aberd	NJ7332	57°22·9'	2°26·5'W	X	29
Gooselands	Somer	ST7130	51°4·3'	2°24·5'W	X	183
Gooseley Fm	E Susx	TQ8524	50°59·4'	0°38·6'E	FM	189,199
Gooseley's Fm	Essex	TL7136	52°0·0'	0°29·9'E	FM	154
Goose Loch	Scot Bord	NT3514	55°25·2'	3°1·2'W	W	79
Goosemere Height	N Yks	SD8555	53°59·7'	2°13·3'W	X	103
Goosemoor	Devon	SY0689	50°41·8'	3°19·5'W	T	192
Goosemoor	Somer	SS9535	51°6·5'	3°29·6'W	X	181
Goosemoor	Staffs	SJ8217	52°45·3'	2°15·6'W	T	127
Goosemoor Dyke	Notts	SK7269	53°13·0'	0°54·9'W	W	120
Goosemoor Fm	Devon	SY1291	50°43·0'	3°14·4'W	FM	192,193
Goosemoor Fm	N Yks	SE4351	53°57·4'	1°20·3'W	FM	105
Goosemoor Green	Staffs	SK0611	52°42·0'	1°54·3'W	T	128
Gooseneck	I of M	SC4592	54°18·3'	4°22·5'W	X	95
Goosenford	Somer	ST2427	51°2·5'	3°4·7'W	T	193
Goose Pool	Heref	SO4636	52°1·4'	2°46·8'W	T	149,161
Goose, The	Corn	SW7761	50°24·6'	5°7·9'W	X	200
Goosetree Fm	Cambs	TF3701	52°35·6'	0°1·8'E	FM	142,143
Goosetree Fm	Ches	SJ9169	53°13·3'	2°7·7'W	FM	118
Goosetron Hill	N Ayr	NS2755	55°45·7'	4°45·0'W	X	63
Goosewell	Corn	SX3676	50°33·9'	4°18·6'W	X	201
Goosewell	Devon	SS5547	51°12·5'	4°4·2'W	T	180
Goosewell Fm	Cumbr	NY2923	54°36·1'	3°5·5'W	FM	89,90
Goose Willow	Oxon	SU4592	51°37·7'	1°20·6'W	X	164,174
Goosey	Oxon	SU3591	51°37·2'	1°29·3'W	T	164,174
Goosey Ho	Oxon	SU3592	51°37·8'	1°29·3'W	X	164,174
Goosey's Lodge	Beds	SP9663	52°15·6'	0°35·2'W	X	153
Gooseywick Fm	Oxon	SU3793	51°38·3'	1°27·5'W	FM	164,174
Goosnargh	Lancs	SD5536	53°49·3'	2°40·6'W	T	102
Goosnargh Lane	Lancs	SD5436	53°49·3'	2°41·5'W	X	102
Goosnargh Lodge	Lancs	SD5538	53°50·4'	2°40·6'W	X	102
Goostrey	Ches	SJ7770	53°13·8'	2°20·3'W	T	118
Goostrey Fm	Ches	SJ7569	53°13·3'	2°22·1'W	FM	118
Goostrey Sta	Ches	SJ7869	53°13·3'	2°19·4'W	X	118
Gopa Hill	Swan	SN6003	51°42·7'	4°1·2'W	X	159
Gopa Uchaf	Cered	SN7259	52°13·1'	3°52·0'W	H	146,147
Gopher Wood	Wilts	SU1464	51°22·7'	1°47·5'W	F	173
Gop Hill	Flint	SJ0880	53°18·8'	3°22·4'W	H	116
Goppa Fm	Denb	SJ0265	53°10·6'	3°27·6'W	FM	116
Goppa Fm	Gwyn	SH7036	52°54·6'	3°55·6'W	FM	124
Goppy	Conwy	SH8066	53°10·9'	3°47·3'W	X	116
Gopsall Hall Fm	Leic	SK3506	52°39·3'	1°28·6'W	FM	140
Gopsall House Fm	Leic	SK3405	52°38·7'	1°29·4'W	FM	140
Gopsall Park	Leic	SK3406	52°39·3'	1°29·4'W	X	140
Gopsall Wood	Leic	SK3306	52°39·3'	1°30·3'W	F	140
Gorah Rocks	Devon	SX7936	50°12·9'	3°41·4'W	X	202
Gorbals	C of Glas	NS5964	55°51·2'	4°14·7'W	T	64
Gorbeck	N Yks	SD8565	54°5·1'	2°13·3'W	X	98
Gorbett Bank	Heref	SO4864	52°16·5'	2°45·3'W	X	137,138,148
Gorcock Springs	Northum	NY7946	54°48·8'	2°19·2'W	W	86,87
Gorcombe Fm	Dorset	ST8702	50°49·3'	2°10·7'W	FM	194
Gorcott Hall	Warw	SP0868	52°18·8'	1°52·6'W	A	139
Gorcott Hill	Warw	SP0968	52°18·8'	1°51·7'W	T	139
Gord	Shetld	HU2057	60°18·1'	1°37·8'W	X	3
Gord	Shetld	HU4021	59°58·6'	1°16·5'W	X	4
Gord	Shetld	HU4329	60°2·9'	1°13·2'W	T	4
Gordale Beck	N Yks	SD9164	54°4·6'	2°7·8'W	W	98

Gordale Bridge	N Yks	SD9163	54°4·0'	2°7·8'W	X	98
Gordale Scar	N Yks	SD9164	54°4·6'	2°7·8'W	X	98
Gordano Service Area	N Som	ST5075	51°28·5'	2°42·8'W	X	172
Gorda Water	Shetld	HU1660	60°19·7'	1°42·1'W	W	3
Gorddinan	Conwy	SH7051	53°2·7'	3°55·9'W	X	115
Gorddinog	Gwyn	SH6773	53°14·5'	3°59·2'W	X	115
Gordieston	D & G	NX8583	55°7·9'	3°47·8'W	X	78
Gordi Stack	Shetld	HU2774	60°27·2'	1°30·1'W	X	3
Gordleton	Hants	SZ2996	50°46·0'	1°34·9'W	X	196
Gord of Banks	Orkney	HY4430	59°9·5'	2°58·3'W	X	5,6
Gordon	I of M	SC2380	54°11·4'	4°42·4'W	X	95
Gordon	Scot Bord	NT6443	55°41·0'	2°33·9'W	T	74
Gordon Arms Hotel	Scot Bord	NT3024	55°30·5'	3°6·1'W	X	73
Gordonbank	Scot Bord	NT7243	55°41·0'	2°26·3'W	X	74
Gordon Beck	Durham	NZ1426	54°38·0'	1°46·6'W	W	92
Gordon Boys School	Surrey	SU9461	51°20·6'	0°38·6'W	X	175,186
Gordonbush	Highld	NC8409	58°3·6'	3°57·5'W	T	17
Gordonbush Lodge	Highld	NC8409	58°3·6'	3°57·5'W	X	17
Gordon Castle	Moray	NJ3559	57°37·2'	3°4·8'W	X	28
Gordon East Mains	Scot Bord	NT6543	55°41·0'	2°33·0'W	X	74
Gordonmains Burn	Scot Bord	NT6844	55°41·6'	2°30·1'W	W	74
Gordon Moss Wildlife Reserve	Scot Bord	NT6342	55°40·5'	2°34·9'W	X	74
Gordonsburgh	Moray	NJ4366	57°41·1'	2°56·9'W	T	28
Gordonshall	Fife	NO5306	56°14·9'	2°45·1'W	X	59
Gordon's Lodge	Mil Key	SP7748	52°7·7'	0°52·1'W	X	152
Gordon's Mill	Highld	NH7065	57°39·6'	4°10·3'W	X	21,27
Gordonston	Aberd	NJ5224	57°18·5'	2°47·3'W	X	37
Gordonston	D & G	NX6383	55°7·6'	4°8·5'W	X	77
Gordonstone	Aberd	NJ5901	57°6·1'	2°40·2'W	X	37
Gordonstoun	Moray	NJ1869	57°42·5'	3°22·1'W	A	28
Gordonstown	Aberd	NJ5656	57°35·8'	2°43·7'W	T	29
Gordonstown	Aberd	NJ7138	57°26·1'	2°28·5'W	T	29
Gordonstown	Moray	NJ4853	57°34·1'	2°51·7'W	X	28,29
Gordonstown Hill	Aberd	NJ7139	57°26·7'	2°28·5'W	H	29
Gordonsward	Moray	NJ2564	57°39·8'	3°15·0'W	X	28
Gordontown of Seggat	Aberd	NJ7341	57°27·8'	2°26·5'W	X	29
Gord, The	Shetld	HP6118	60°50·7'	0°52·2'W	X	1
Gord Vats-houll	Shetld	HU5665	60°22·2'	0°58·6'W	X	2
Gore	Dorset	ST5918	50°57·8'	2°34·6'W	T	183
Gore	Kent	TR3055	51°15·1'	1°18·2'E	T	179
Gore	Powys	SO2559	52°13·7'	3°5·5'W	X	148
Gorebridge	Midlo	NT3461	55°50·5'	3°2·8'W	T	66
Gore Common	Cambs	TL2589	52°29·3'	0°9·1'W	X	142
Gore Cott	Somer	ST6251	51°15·6'	2°32·3'W	X	183
Gore Court	Kent	TQ7239	51°7·7'	0°27·9'E	X	188
Gore Court	Kent	TQ7953	51°15·1'	0°34·3'E	X	188
Gore Cove	Dorset	SY6180	50°37·3'	2°32·7'W	W	194
Gore Cross	Wilts	SU0050	51°15·2'	1°59·6'W	X	184
Gored Beuno	Gwyn	SH4150	53°1·7'	4°21·9'W	X	115,123
Goree	Pemb	SM9324	51°52·8'	5°0·1'W	X	157,158
Gore End	Hants	SU4163	51°22·1'	1°24·3'W	T	174
Gorefield	Cambs	TF4111	52°40·9'	0°5·6'E	T	131,142,143
Gore Fm	Ches	SJ6980	53°19·2'	2°27·5'W	FM	109
Gore Fm	Dorset	ST8320	50°59·0'	2°14·1'W	FM	183
Gore Fm	Dorset	ST8918	50°57·9'	2°9·0'W	FM	184
Gore Fm	Kent	TQ8466	51°22·0'	0°39·0'E	FM	178
Gore Fm	Oxon	SU3399	51°41·6'	1°31·0'W	FM	164
Gore Fm	Swin	SU1693	51°38·4'	1°45·7'W	FM	163,173
Gore Green	Kent	TQ7173	51°26·0'	0°28·0'E	X	178
Gore Heath	Dorset	SY9291	50°43·3'	2°6·4'W	F	195
Gore Hill	Bucks	SU9596	51°39·5'	0°37·2'W	X	165,176
Gore Hill	Dorset	ST6303	50°49·8'	2°31·1'W	H	194
Gore Hill	W Berks	SU4883	51°32·9'	1°18·1'W	X	174
Gorehill	W Susx	SU9820	50°58·5'	0°35·9'W	T	197
Gore Hill Fm	Oxon	SU4884	51°33·4'	1°18·1'W	FM	174
Gore Ho	Kent	TQ8465	51°21·5'	0°39·0'E	X	178
Gorehouse	Orkney	HY4430	59°9·5'	2°58·3'W	X	5,6
Gore House Fm	Lancs	SD3504	53°32·0'	2°58·4'W	FM	108
Gorelands	Bucks	TQ0093	51°37·8'	0°32·9'W	X	176
Gore Lane Fm	Wilts	SU2779	51°30·8'	1°36·3'W	FM	174
Goren Fm	Devon	ST2302	50°49·0'	3°5·2'W	FM	192,193
Gore Pit	Essex	TL8719	51°50·5'	0°43·3'E	T	168
Gore Point	Norf	TF7045	52°58·8'	0°32·3'E	X	132
Gore Point	Somer	SS8548	51°13·4'	3°38·4'W	X	181
Gore Saltings	Essex	TL9308	51°44·5'	0°48·1'E	W	168
Gore Sand	Somer	ST2651	51°15·4'	3°3·2'W	X	182
Gores Fm	Derby	SK1690	53°24·6'	1°45·1'W	FM	110
Gores Heights	Derby	SK1690	53°24·6'	1°45·1'W	X	110
Gore's Kirn	Shetld	HU5137	60°7·1'	1°4·4'W	X	4
Gores, The	Peterb	TF2601	52°35·8'	0°8·0'W	X	142
Gore Street	Kent	TR2765	51°20·5'	1°16·0'E	T	179
Gore, The	Devon	SS3424	50°59·7'	4°21·6'W	X	190
Gore, The	Shrops	SO5982	52°26·3'	2°35·8'W	T	137,138
Gore Tree Fm	Cambs	TL2869	52°18·5'	0°6·9'W	FM	153
Gore Water	Midlo	NT3659	55°49·5'	3°0·9'W	W	66,73
Goreys Saddle	Orkney	HY5938	59°13·9'	2°42·6'W	X	5
Gorfen Letch	Northum	NZ1690	55°12·5'	1°44·5'W	X	81
Gorgate Hall	Norf	TF9716	52°42·6'	0°55·4'E	X	132
Gorge Dyke	Notts	SK6766	53°11·4'	0°59·4'W	A	120
Gorgie	C of Edin	NT2272	55°56·3'	3°14·5'W	T	66
Gorhambury	Herts	TL1107	51°45·3'	0°23·1'W	A	166
Gorhambury	Herts	TL1107	51°45·3'	0°23·1'W	T	166
Gorham Wood	Kent	TQ8558	51°17·7'	0°39·6'E	X	178
Goring	Oxon	SU6081	51°31·7'	1°7·7'W	T	175
Goring-by-Sea	W Susx	TQ1103	50°49·2'	0°25·1'W	T	198
Goring Heath	Oxon	SU6579	51°30·6'	1°3·4'W	T	175
Goringlee	W Susx	TQ1122	50°59·4'	0°24·7'W	X	198
Gorlan Tyn-y-waun	Powys	SO0417	51°50·8'	3°23·2'W	X	160
Gorlan-yr-Allt	Powys	SO0615	51°49·8'	3°21·5'W	X	160
Gorless	Northum	NY8293	55°14·1'	2°16·6'W	X	80
Gorleston Cliffs	Norf	TG5302	52°33·6'	1°44·4'E	X	134
Gorleston-on-Sea	Norf	TG5203	52°34·2'	1°43·5'E	T	134
Gorley Hill	Hants	SU1611	50°54·1'	1°46·0'W	X	195
Gorllwyn	Carm	SN3533	51°58·5'	4°23·7'W	X	145
Gorllwyn	Gwyn	SH6216	52°43·7'	4°2·2'W	X	124
Gorllwyn	Powys	SN9159	52°13·3'	3°35·3'W	H	147
Gorllwyn-fâch	Carm	SN7629	51°57·0'	3°47·9'W	X	146,160
Gorllwynuchaf	Gwyn	SH5742	52°57·6'	4°7·3'W	X	124
Gorlofen	Devon	SX5652	50°21·3'	4°1·1'W	X	202

Gormack Burn	Aberd	NJ6904	57°7·8'	2°30·3'W	W	38
Gormack Burn	Aberd	NJ7702	57°6·8'	2°22·3'W	W	38
Gormack Ho	Pth & Kin	NO1446	56°36·1'	3°23·6'W	X	53
Gormal Hill	D & G	NX5671	55°1·0'	4°14·7'W	X	77
Gorman Castle	E Yorks	SE7958	54°1·0'	0°47·2'W	X	105,106
Gorm Chnoc	Highld	NC1528	58°12·4'	5°8·4'W	H	15
Gorm Chnoc	Highld	NC2144	58°21·1'	5°3·1'W	H	9
Gorm Cnoc	Highld	NC2508	58°1·9'	4°57·4'W	X	15
Gormire Lake	N Yks	SE5083	54°14·7'	1°13·5'W	W	100
Gormires Wood	N Yks	SE2458	54°1·3'	1°37·6'W	F	104
Gorm Loch	Highld	NC2144	58°21·1'	5°3·1'W	W	9
Gorm Loch	Highld	NH3379	57°46·4'	4°48·0'W	W	20
Gorm Loch	Highld	NH4093	57°54·1'	4°41·5'W	W	20
Gorm Lochan	Highld	NH1213	57°10·4'	5°6·1'W	W	34
Gorm Loch Beag	Highld	NC1428	58°12·4'	5°9·5'W	W	15
Gorm-loch Beag	Highld	NC7027	58°13·0'	4°12·3'W	W	16
Gorm Loch Beag	Highld	NG9874	57°42·5'	5°23·0'W	W	19
Gorm-loch Fada	Highld	NG8963	57°36·7'	5°31·5'W	W	19,24
Gorm Loch Mór	Highld	NC1429	58°12·9'	5°9·5'W	W	15
Gorm Loch Mór	Highld	NC3124	58°10·6'	4°52·0'W	W	15
Gorm-Loch Mór	Highld	NC7123	58°10·9'	4°11·2'W	W	16
Gorm Loch Mór	Highld	NH0074	57°42·9'	5°21·0'W	W	19
Gorm-loch na Beinne	Highld	NG9063	57°36·8'	5°30·5'W	W	19
Gormol	N Eil	NB3006	57°57·9'	6°33·5'W	H	13,14
Gormul Màraig	N Eil	NB1807	57°58·0'	6°45·7'W	H	13,14
Gormul Mòr	N Eil	NB0912	58°0·4'	6°55·1'W	H	13,14
Gormyre	W Loth	NS9772	55°56·1'	3°38·5'W	X	65
Gorn	Orkney	HY2604	58°55·3'	3°16·6'W	X	6,7
Gorn	Orkney	HY3115	59°1·3'	3°11·6'W	X	6
Gorn	Orkney	HY4018	59°3·0'	3°2·3'W	X	6
Gorn	Orkney	HY5218	59°3·0'	2°49·7'W	X	6
Gornalwood	Dudley	SO9190	52°30·7'	2°7·6'W	T	139
Gorn Hill	Powys	SN9684	52°26·9'	3°31·4'W	H	136
Gornoeth	Powys	SN9557	52°12·3'	3°31·8'W	H	147
Gornogrove	Fife	NO2010	56°16·8'	3°17·1'W	X	58
Goromul	N Eil	NB1702	57°55·3'	6°46·3'W	X	14
Goron	Powys	SO1094	52°32·4'	3°19·2'W	X	136
Goron-ddu	Powys	SO1896	52°33·6'	3°12·2'W	X	136
Gororion	Powys	SN8773	52°20·8'	3°39·1'W	X	135,136,147
Gorphwysfa	Gwyn	SH3636	52°54·0'	4°25·9'W	X	123
Gorphwysfa	Gwyn	SH6455	53°4·7'	4°1·4'W	X	115
Gorple Reservoirs	Cald	SD9331	53°46·8'	2°6·0'W	W	103
Gorpley Resr	Cald	SD9122	53°41·9'	2°7·8'W	W	103
Gorrachie	Aberd	NJ7358	57°36·9'	2°26·7'W	X	29
Gorracott	Corn	SX2290	50°41·2'	4°30·8'W	X	190
Gorran Churchtown	Corn	SW9942	50°14·9'	4°48·8'W	T	204
Gorran Haven	Corn	SX0041	50°14·3'	4°47·9'W	T	204
Gorran High Lanes	Corn	SW9843	50°15·4'	4°49·7'W	T	204
Gorregan	I Scilly	SV8405	49°51·9'	6°23·5'W	X	203
Gorregan Neck	I Scilly	SV8505	49°52·0'	6°22·7'W	W	203
Gorrell Fm	Bucks	SP6638	52°2·4'	1°1·9'W	FM	152
Gorrell Fm	Devon	SS3218	50°56·5'	4°23·1'W	FM	190
Gorrell's Fm	Essex	TL6303	51°42·3'	0°21·9'E	FM	167
Gorrenberry	Scot Bord	NY4697	55°16·1'	2°50·6'W	T	79
Gorrenberry Burn	Scot Bord	NY4598	55°16·6'	2°51·5'W	W	79
Gorrig	Cered	SN4042	52°3·4'	4°19·6'W	T	146
Gorringes	Brom	TQ4362	51°20·6'	0°3·6'E	X	177,187
Gors	Carm	SN3136	52°0·0'	4°27·3'W	X	145
Gors	Carm	SN4427	51°55·4'	4°15·7'W	X	146
Gors	Carm	SN5113	51°48·0'	4°9·3'W	X	159
Gors	Cered	SN3941	52°2·9'	4°20·5'W	X	145
Gors	Cered	SN6377	52°22·7'	4°0·4'W	T	135
Gors	Conwy	SH8961	53°8·3'	3°39·2'W	X	116
Gors	Conwy	SH9778	53°17·6'	3°32·3'W	X	116
Gors	Gwyn	SH1527	52°48·8'	4°44·3'W	X	123
Gors	I of Angl	SH3692	53°24·2'	4°27·6'W	X	114
Gors Bank	Shrops	SO1782	52°26·0'	3°12·9'W	X	136
Gors Cottage	Conwy	SH9778	53°17·6'	3°32·3'W	X	116
Gors-ddalfa	Cered	SN5562	52°14·5'	4°7·0'W	X	146
Gors Dopiog	Conwy	SH8959	53°7·2'	3°39·1'W	X	116
Gors-dyfwch	Powys	SH9902	52°36·6'	3°29·1'W	X	136
Gorsebraehead	E Ayr	NS5936	55°36·1'	4°13·8'W	X	71
Gorse Copse	Wilts	SU0873	51°27·6'	1°52·7'W	F	173
Gorse Covert	Lincs	TF2772	53°14·0'	0°5·4'W	F	122
Gorse Covert	Notts	SK6151	53°3·4'	1°5·6'W	F	120
Gorse Covert	Suff	TL7973	52°19·8'	0°38·0'E	F	144,155
Gorse Covert	Warr	SJ6692	53°25·7'	2°30·3'W	T	109
Gorsedd	Flint	SJ1576	53°16·7'	3°16·1'W	T	116
Gorseddau	Gwyn	SH9041	52°57·5'	3°37·9'W	X	125
Gorsedd Brân	Denb	SH9760	53°7·9'	3°32·0'W	H	116
Gorsedd Grycun	Conwy	SH8359	53°7·2'	3°44·5'W	X	116
Gorsedd-y-penrhyn	I of Angl	SH2781	53°18·1'	4°35·4'W	X	114
Gorsedown Fm	Kent	TR0434	51°4·4'	0°55·1'E	FM	179,189
Gorse Fm	Leic	SK5822	52°47·8'	1°8·0'W	FM	129
Gorse Fm	Lincs	SK9349	53°2·0'	0°36·4'W	FM	130
Gorse Fm	Lincs	TF3073	53°14·5'	0°2·7'W	FM	122
Gorse Fm	Staffs	SK1412	52°42·6'	1°47·2'W	FM	128
Gorse Fm	Staffs	SK2308	52°40·4'	1°39·2'W	FM	128
Gorse Fm	Suff	TM3658	52°10·4'	1°27·5'E	FM	156
Gorse Fm	Worcs	SO9377	52°23·7'	2°5·8'W	FM	139
Gorse Green Fm	Kent	TR0135	51°5·0'	0°52·6'E	FM	189
Gorse Hall	Staffs	SK2019	52°46·3'	1°41·8'W	X	128
Gorse Hall	Wigan	SD5611	53°35·9'	2°39·5'W	X	108
Gorse Hill	Conwy	SH7875	53°15·7'	3°49·3'W	X	115
Gorse Hill	Lincs	TF1039	52°56·5'	0°21·4'W	X	130
Gorse Hill	Notts	SK7356	53°6·0'	0°54·2'W	X	120
Gorse Hill	Oxon	SU2495	51°39·4'	1°38·8'W	X	163
Gorse Hill	Pemb	SM7209	51°44·2'	5°17·8'W	X	157
Gorse Hill	Staffs	SK0721	52°47·4'	1°53·4'W	X	128
Gorse Hill	Swin	SU1586	51°34·6'	1°46·6'W	T	173
Gorse Hill	Traf	SJ8095	53°27·3'	2°17·7'W	T	109
Gorse Hill	Worcs	SO9773	52°21·5'	2°2·2'W	X	139
Gorsehill Abbey Fm	Worcs	SP0839	52°3·2'	1°52·6'W	FM	150
Gorse Hill Covert	Lincs	TF0156	53°5·7'	0°29·1'W	F	121
Gorseinon	Swan	SS5898	51°40·0'	4°2·8'W	T	159
Gorse Lodge	Suff	TM4977	52°20·3'	1°39·5'E	F	156
Gorse Moor	Norf	TF6924	52°47·5'	0°30·8'E	F	132
Gorsendi Geo	Shetld	HU1659	60°19·2'	1°42·1'W	X	3
Gorsendi Geo	Shetld	HU2484	60°32·6'	1°33·2'W	X	3
Gorseness	Orkney	HY4119	59°3·5'	3°1·2'W	T	6

Gorseness Hill	Orkney	HY4020	59°4·0'	3°2·3'W	X	5,6
Gorses Fm	Wigan	SD6109	53°34·8'	2°34·9'W	FM	109
Gorse, The	Norf	TF8834	52°52·5'	0°48·0'E	F	132
Gorse, The	Oxon	SP5124	51°55·0'	1°15·1'W	F	164
Gorse, The	Powys	SO0073	52°21·0'	3°27·7'W	X	136,147
Gorse, The	Shrops	SJ4403	52°37·6'	2°49·2'W	F	126
Gorse Thick	Suff	TM4085	52°24·8'	1°32·2'E	F	156
Gorset Hill	Shetld	HU4797	60°39·5'	1°7·9'W	X	1
Gorsethorpe	Notts	SK5965	53°11·0'	1°6·6'W	T	120
Gorse Wood	Suff	TL8963	52°14·2'	0°46·5'E	F	155
Gorseybank	Derby	SK2953	53°4·6'	1°33·6'W	T	119
Gorsey Bank	Shrops	SJ7812	52°42·6'	2°19·1'W	X	127
Gorsey Bank Fm	Shrops	SJ7142	52°58·7'	2°25·5'W	FM	118
Gorsey Bigbury	Somer	ST4855	51°17·7'	2°44·4'W	X	172,182
Gorsey Bigbury (Henge)	Somer	ST4855	51°17·7'	2°44·4'W	A	172,182
Gorseyknowl	Ches	SJ8270	53°13·8'	2°15·8'W	X	118
Gorsey Leaze	Wilts	ST8984	51°33·5'	2°9·1'W	X	173
Gorsey Leys	Derby	SK3015	52°44·1'	1°32·9'W	X	128
Gorsey Moor Fm	Ches	SJ8666	53°11·7'	2°12·2'W	FM	118
Gorsey Nook	Derby	SK1077	53°17·6'	1°50·6'W	X	119
Gorsfach Fm	Carm	SN4719	51°51·2'	4°12·9'W	FM	159
Gorsfawr	Cered	SN6568	52°17·9'	3°58·4'W	X	135
Gors Fawr	Pemb	SN1329	51°55·9'	4°42·8'W	X	145,158
Gors-fawr	Swan	SN5900	51°41·1'	4°2·0'W	X	159
Gors Fm	Carm	SN2616	51°49·2'	4°31·1'W	FM	158
Gors Fm	Flint	SJ1666	53°11·3'	3°15·0'W	FM	116
Gorsfraith	Pemb	SN1835	51°59·3'	4°38·6'W	X	145
Gors Geo	Shetld	HU6093	60°37·2'	0°53·7'W	X	1,2
Gors-goch	Carm	SN5018	51°50·7'	4°10·3'W	X	159
Gorsgoch	Carm	SN5439	52°2·1'	4°7·3'W	X	146
Gors-goch	Carm	SN5813	51°48·1'	4°3·2'W	X	159
Gorsgoch	Cered	SN4850	52°7·9'	4°12·9'W	T	146
Gors-goch	I of Angl	SH2180	53°17·5'	4°40·7'W	X	114
Gors-goch	Powys	SJ1427	52°50·3'	3°16·2'W	X	125
Gors Goch	Powys	SN8963	52°15·5'	3°37·2'W	W	147
Gors Goch	Powys	SN9393	52°31·7'	3°34·2'W	X	136
Gorsgoed	Swan	SN6001	51°41·7'	4°1·1'W	X	159
Gors Graianog	Gwyn	SH4945	52°59·1'	4°14·6'W	W	115,123
Gorslas	Carm	SN5713	51°48·1'	4°4·0'W	T	159
Gorslas	Cered	SN6171	52°19·4'	4°2·0'W	X	135
Gors-lâs	Conwy	SH8457	53°6·1'	3°43·6'W	H	116
Gorsley	Glos	SO6825	51°55·6'	2°27·5'W	T	162
Gorsley Common	Heref	SO6725	51°55·6'	2°28·4'W	T	162
Gorsley Ley	Staffs	SK0609	52°41·0'	1°54·3'W	T	128
Gorsley Wood	Kent	TR1651	51°13·3'	1°6·0'E	F	179,189
Gors Llwyn	Nth Pt Talb	SN8510	51°46·9'	3°39·6'W	W	160
Gors Lwyd	Cered	SN8575	52°21·9'	3°40·9'W	W	135,136,147
Gorslwyd Fawr	I of Angl	SH4287	53°21·6'	4°22·1'W	X	114
Gors Lydan	Powys	SO1276	52°22·7'	3°17·2'W	X	136,148
Gors Maen-llwyd	Denb	SH9858	53°6·8'	3°31·0'W	X	116
Gorsna Geo	Shetld	HU4116	59°55·9'	1°15·5'W	X	4
Gors Nug	Conwy	SH8952	53°3·5'	3°39·0'W	X	116
Gorsoyffion	Denb	SJ2058	53°7·0'	3°11·3'W	X	117
Gors Penrhiwiau	Conwy	SH9459	53°7·3'	3°34·6'W	X	116
Gorstage	Ches	SJ6172	53°14·9'	2°34·7'W	T	118
Gorstage Hall	Ches	SJ6072	53°14·9'	2°35·6'W	X	118
Gorstain	Arg & Bt	NM9829	56°24·9'	5°16·0'W	X	49
Gorstan	Highld	NH3862	57°37·4'	4°42·3'W	T	20
Gorstanvorran	Highld	NM8071	56°47·0'	5°35·6'W	X	40
Gorst Barn	Shrops	SO4279	52°24·6'	2°50·8'W	X	137,148
Gorstella	Ches	SJ3562	53°9·3'	2°57·9'W	T	117
Gorsten	Arg & Bt	NM7432	56°25·8'	5°39·5'W	X	49
Gorst Hall	Worcs	SO8475	52°22·6'	2°13·7'W	X	138
Gorst Hill	Worcs	SO7472	52°21·0'	2°22·5'W	T	138
Gorsto	Nth Pt Talb	SN7213	51°48·3'	3°51·0'W	X	160
Gorsty	Heref	SO4773	52°21·4'	2°46·3'W	X	137,138,148
Gorstybank	Shrops	SJ3100	52°35·8'	3°0·7'W	X	126
Gorstybirch	Staffs	SJ9540	52°57·7'	2°4·1'W	X	118
Gorsty Common	Heref	SO3655	52°11·6'	2°55·8'W	X	148,149
Gorsty Fields	Derby	SK1934	52°54·4'	1°42·6'W	X	128
Gorstyhill	Ches	SJ7450	53°3·0'	2°22·9'W	T	118
Gorstyhill	Staffs	SK0140	52°57·7'	1°58·7'W	X	119,128
Gorsty Hill	Staffs	SK1029	52°51·7'	1°50·7'W	T	128
Gorsty Hill Fm	Heref	SO5360	52°14·4'	2°40·9'W	FM	137,138,149
Gorsun Geo	Shetld	HP6516	60°49·6'	0°47·8'W	X	1
Gorswen	Carm	SN5117	51°50·1'	4°9·4'W	X	159
Gorswen	Cered	SN5064	52°15·5'	4°11·5'W	X	146
Gorswen	Conwy	SH7571	53°13·5'	3°51·9'W	X	115
Gors-wen	Conwy	SH8362	53°8·8'	3°44·6'W	X	116
Gors-wen	Powys	SN9459	52°13·4'	3°32·7'W	X	147
Gorswgan	Cered	SN5973	52°20·5'	4°3·8'W	X	135
Gorsy Bank	Staffs	SK0615	52°44·2'	1°54·3'W	F	128
Gorsyrhwch	Carm	SN6633	51°59·0'	3°56·7'W	X	146
Gortan	Arg & Bt	NM1753	56°35·3'	6°36·1'W	X	46
Gortan	Arg & Bt	NR2762	55°46·7'	6°20·8'W	X	60
Gortan	Arg & Bt	NR7021	55°26·0'	5°37·7'W	X	68
Gortanansaig Fm	Arg & Bt	NS0970	55°53·4'	5°2·8'W	FM	63
Gortan Cherin	Arg & Bt	NN0538	56°29·9'	5°9·6'W	F	50
Gortanchuirn	Arg & Bt	NR2561	55°46·1'	6°22·6'W	X	60
Gortanilivorrie	Arg & Bt	NR3562	55°47·0'	6°13·2'W	X	60,61
Gortans	Arg & Bt	NS0766	55°51·2'	5°4·6'W	X	63
Gortantaoid	Arg & Bt	NR3373	55°52·8'	6°15·7'W	X	60,61
Gortantaoid Point	Arg & Bt	NR3374	55°53·4'	6°15·8'W	X	60,61
Gortantaoid River	Arg & Bt	NR3472	55°52·3'	6°14·7'W	W	60,61
Gortenachullish	Highld	NM6387	56°55·1'	5°53·2'W	X	40
Gortenanrue	Arg & Bt	NM7227	56°23·1'	5°41·2'W	X	49
Gortenbuie	Arg & Bt	NM5934	56°26·5'	5°54·1'W	X	47,48
Gorteneorn	Highld	NM6367	56°44·3'	5°52·1'W	T	40
Gortenfern	Highld	NM6068	56°44·8'	5°55·1'W	T	40
Gorten Lodge	Arg & Bt	NR7461	55°47·6'	5°35·9'W	X	62
Gorthfield	Aberd	NJ8659	57°37·5'	2°13·6'W	X	30
Gorthleck Ho	Highld	NH5420	57°15·1'	4°24·7'W	X	26,35
Gorthy Wood	Pth & Kin	NN9525	56°24·6'	3°41·7'W	F	52,53,58
Gortinanane	Arg & Bt	NR7047	55°40·0'	5°39·0'W	X	62
Gortnell Common	Somer	ST1617	50°57·0'	3°11·4'W	X	181,193
Gortnell Fm	Somer	ST1518	50°57·5'	3°12·2'W	FM	181,193
Gorton	Arg & Bt	NN3748	56°36·0'	4°38·9'W	X	50
Gorton	Man	SJ8896	53°27·8'	2°10·4'W	T	109
Gortonallister	N Ayr	NS0329	55°31·2'	5°6·8'W	T	69
Gorton Hill	Devon	SS7325	51°0·9'	3°48·2'W	X	180

Gorton Hill	Highld	NJ0129	57°20·7'	3°38·2'W	H	36
Gorton Ho	Midlo	NT2863	55°51·5'	3°8·6'W	X	66
Gortonlee	Midlo	NT2863	55°51·5'	3°8·6'W	X	66
Gorton Lodge	Staffs	SK0712	52°42·6'	1°53·4'W	X	128
Gorton Resrs	Man	SJ9096	53°27·9'	2°8·6'W	W	109
Gortonronach	Arg & Bt	NR9392	56°4·8'	5°19·2'W	T	55
Gorvin Cross	Devon	SS2919	50°56·9'	4°25·7'W	X	190
Gorvin Fm	Devon	SS2919	50°56·9'	4°25·7'W	FM	190
Gorwallt	Powys	SJ0927	52°50·2'	3°20·7'W	X	125
Gorwel	Cered	SN3044	52°4·3'	4°28·4'W	X	145
Gorwel Deg	Powys	SH8305	52°38·1'	3°43·3'W	X	124,125
Gorwelle	Mil Key	SP9449	52°8·1'	0°37·2'W	X	153
Gorwell Fm	Devon	ST1509	50°52·7'	3°12·1'W	FM	192,193
Gorwell Fm	Dorset	SY5787	50°41·1'	2°36·1'W	FM	194
Gorwell Hall	Essex	TL9411	51°46·1'	0°49·1'E	X	168
Gorwood	Devon	SS4119	50°57·1'	4°15·4'W	X	180,190
Gorwydd	Cered	SN5751	52°8·6'	4°5·0'W	X	146
Gorwyn Ho	Devon	SX7893	50°43·7'	3°43·3'W	X	191
Gorwyr	Gwyn	SH7718	52°45·0'	3°48·9'W	X	124
Goryhill	Aberd	NJ4514	57°13·1'	2°54·2'W	X	37
Gosbeck	Suff	TM1555	52°9·3'	1°9·0'E	T	156
Gosbeck's Fm	Essex	TL9722	51°51·9'	0°52·1'E	FM	168
Gosbeck Wood	Suff	TM1455	52°9·3'	1°8·1'E	F	156
Gosberton	Lincs	TF2431	52°52·0'	0°9·1'W	T	131
Gosberton Cheal	Lincs	TF2228	52°50·4'	0°10·9'W	T	131
Gosberton Clough	Lincs	TF1929	52°51·0'	0°13·6'W	T	130
Gosberton Fen	Lincs	TF1928	52°50·4'	0°13·6'W	X	130
Gosberton Fen	Lincs	TF2028	52°50·4'	0°12·7'W	X	131
Gosberton Fen Fm	Lincs	TF1630	52°51·5'	0°16·2'W	FM	130
Gosberton Marsh	Lincs	TF2631	52°51·9'	0°7·3'W	X	131
Goschen	Dorset	SY8799	50°47·7'	2°10·7'W	X	194
Goscote	Wals	SK0201	52°36·6'	1°57·8'W	T	139
Goscott	Corn	SX2396	50°44·4'	4°30·1'W	X	190
Gosdale Fm	Lincs	TF1331	52°52·1'	0°18·9'W	FM	130
Gosden Ho	Surrey	TQ0045	51°12·0'	0°33·7'W	X	186
Goseland Hill	Scot Bord	NT0735	55°36·2'	3°28·1'W	H	72
Goseley Dale	Derby	SK3220	52°46·8'	1°31·1'W	T	128
Gosen	Conwy	SH8267	53°11·5'	3°45·6'W	X	116
Gosenhill Fm	Kent	TQ5167	51°23·1'	0°10·6'E	FM	177
Gosfield	Essex	TL7829	51°56·1'	0°35·8'E	T	167
Gosfield Hall	Essex	TL7729	51°56·1'	0°34·9'E	A	167
Gosfield Lake	Essex	TL7729	51°56·1'	0°34·9'E	W	167
Gosfield Wood	Essex	TL7728	51°55·6'	0°34·9'E	F	167
Gosford	Devon	SY0997	50°46·2'	3°17·0'W	T	192
Gosford	Heref	SO5368	52°18·7'	2°41·0'W	T	137,138
Gosford	Oxon	SP4913	51°49·0'	1°17·0'W	T	164
Gosford Bay	E Loth	NT4478	55°59·8'	2°53·4'W	W	66
Gosford Green	Cov	SP3478	52°24·2'	1°29·6'W	T	140
Gosford Ho	E Loth	NT4578	55°59·8'	2°52·5'W	X	66
Gosford Sands	E Loth	NT4478	55°59·8'	2°53·4'W	X	66
Gosforth	Cumbr	NY0603	54°25·1'	3°26·5'W	T	89
Gosforth	N upon Ty	NZ2368	55°0·6'	1°38·0'W	T	88
Gosforth Crag	Cumbr	NY1609	54°28·4'	3°17·4'W	X	89
Gosforth Lake	N upon Ty	NZ2570	55°1·7'	1°36·1'W	W	88
Gosforth Valley	Derby	SK3478	53°18·1'	1°29·0'W	T	119
Gosforth Wood	N upon Ty	NZ2570	55°1·7'	1°36·1'W	F	88
Goshen	E Loth	NT3672	55°56·5'	3°1·0'W	X	66
Goskiehill	Aberd	NO6676	56°52·7'	2°33·0'W	X	45
Goskins	N Yks	SE2594	54°20·7'	1°36·5'W	X	99
Gosland	Scot Bord	NT0734	55°35·7'	3°28·1'W	X	72
Gosland Green	Ches	SJ5758	53°7·3'	2°38·1'W	X	117
Gosland Green	Suff	TL7650	52°7·4'	0°34·7'E	T	155
Gosling Carr	Notts	SK6672	53°14·7'	1°0·2'W	F	120
Gosling Green	Suff	TL9742	52°2·7'	0°52·8'E	T	155
Gosling Green Fm	N Yks	SE7677	54°11·2'	0°49·7'W	FM	100
Goslingmire	N Yks	NZ4708	54°28·2'	1°16·1'W	X	93
Gosling's Fm	Essex	TL8121	51°51·7'	0°38·1'E	FM	168
Goslington	S Lanak	NS7442	55°39·6'	3°59·7'W	X	71
Gosmere	Kent	TR0257	51°16·8'	0°54·2'E	T	178
Gosmore	Herts	TL1827	51°56·0'	0°16·6'W	T	166
Gospel Ash	Staffs	SO8391	52°31·2'	2°14·6'W	T	138
Gospel Ash Fm	Somer	ST6918	50°57·9'	2°26·1'W	FM	183
Gospel End Village	Staffs	SO8993	52°32·3'	2°9·3'W	T	139
Gospel Green	W Susx	SU9431	51°4·5'	0°39·1'W	T	186
Gospel Hall Fm	Scot Bord	NT6120	55°28·6'	2°36·6'W	FM	74
Gospel Hill Fm	Lincs	TF1977	53°16·8'	0°12·5'W	FM	122
Gospel Oak	Camden	TQ2885	51°33·2'	0°8·8'W	T	176
Gospel Oak	Hants	SU5431	51°4·8'	1°13·4'W	X	185
Gospel Oak	Heref	SO7439	52°3·2'	2°22·4'W	X	150
Gospel Oak	Warw	SP1858	52°13·4'	1°43·8'W	X	151
Gospel Oak	Warw	SP2693	52°32·3'	1°36·6'W	X	140
Gospel Oak Fm	Wilts	SU0588	51°35·7'	1°55·3'W	FM	173
Gospel Pass	Powys	SO2335	52°0·7'	3°6·9'W	X	161
Gospel Well	Donc	SK5697	53°28·2'	1°9·0'W	W	111
Gospenheale	Corn	SX2684	50°38·0'	4°27·3'W	X	201
Gosport	Hants	SU3922	51°0·0'	1°26·3'W	T	185
Gosport	Hants	SU5900	50°48·0'	1°9·4'W	T	196
Gossabrough	Shetld	HU5283	60°31·9'	1°2·6'W	T	1,2,3
Gossaquoy	Orkney	HY4345	59°17·5'	2°59·6'W	X	5
Gossard's Green	Beds	SP9643	52°4·9'	0°35·5'W	T	153
Gossa Water	Shetld	HP5705	60°43·7'	0°56·8'W	W	1
Gossa Water	Shetld	HU2456	60°17·5'	1°33·5'W	W	3
Gossa Water	Shetld	HU3045	60°11·6'	1°27·0'W	W	4
Gossa Water	Shetld	HU4340	60°8·8'	1°13·0'W	W	4
Gossa Water	Shetld	HU4360	60°19·6'	1°12·8'W	W	2,3
Gossa Water	Shetld	HU4684	60°32·5'	1°9·2'W	W	1,2,3
Gossa Water	Shetld	HU4899	60°40·5'	1°6·8'W	W	1
Gossawater Burn	Shetld	HU4361	60°20·1'	1°12·8'W	W	2,3
Gossa Waters	Shetld	HU2583	60°32·1'	1°32·2'W	W	3
Goss Covert	Glos	ST8393	51°38·4'	2°14·3'W	F	162,173
Gosse's Fm	Devon	SS6612	50°53·8'	3°53·9'W	FM	180
Gosse's Fm	Essex	TQ7895	51°37·8'	0°34·7'E	FM	167
Gossesslie	Aberd	NO6570	56°49·5'	2°34·0'W	X	45
Goss Hall	Derby	SK3362	53°9·5'	1°30·0'W	X	119
Goss Hall	Kent	TR3058	51°16·7'	1°18·3'E	X	179
Gossigar	Orkney	ND4385	58°45·2'	2°58·6'W	X	7
Gossigarth	Shetld	HU3630	60°3·5'	1°20·7'W	X	4
Gossington	Glos	SO7302	51°43·2'	2°23·1'W	T	162
Gossington Br	Glos	SO7301	51°42·7'	2°23·1'W	X	162
Goss Moor	Corn	SW9559	50°23·9'	4°52·7'W	X	200

Gossops Green	W Susx	TQ2536	51°6·8'	0°12·5'W	T	187
Goster	Shetld	HU1751	60°14·8'	1°41·1'W	X	3
Gosterwood Manor Fm	Surrey	TQ1340	51°9·1'	0°22·7'W	FM	187
Gostrode Fm	Surrey	SU9533	51°5·5'	0°38·2'W	FM	186
Goswick	Northum	NU0545	55°42·2'	1°54·8'W	X	75
Goswick Sands	Northum	NU0844	55°41·6'	1°51·9'W	X	75
Gote Fm	E Susx	TQ4411	50°53·1'	0°3·2'E	FM	198
Goteley Manor	E Susx	TQ8324	50°59·4'	0°36·8'E	X	199
Gote o' Tram	Highld	ND3647	58°24·7'	3°5·2'W	W	12
Gote, The	E Susx	TQ3413	50°54·3'	0°5·3'W	X	198
Gotham	Derby	SK1858	53°7·4'	1°43·5'W	X	119
Gotham	Devon	SS9208	50°51·9'	3°31·7'W	X	192
Gotham	Dorset	SU0811	50°54·1'	1°52·8'W	T	195
Gotham	E Susx	TQ7009	50°51·6'	0°25·3'E	T	199
Gotham	Notts	SK5330	52°52·1'	1°12·4'W	T	129
Gotham Fm	Oxon	SU5899	51°41·4'	1°9·3'W	FM	164
Gotham Hill	Notts	SK5230	52°52·1'	1°13·2'W	H	129
Gotham Moor	Notts	SK5430	52°52·1'	1°11·5'W	X	129
Gotham Moor Fm	Notts	SK5529	52°51·6'	1°10·6'W	FM	129
Gothelney Green	Somer	ST2537	51°7·9'	3°3·9'W	T	182
Gothelney Hall	Somer	ST2537	51°7·9'	3°3·9'W	A	182
Gotherington	Glos	SO9629	51°57·8'	2°3·1'W	T	150,163
Gotherington Field Fm	Glos	SO9429	51°57·8'	2°4·8'W	FM	150,163
Gotherment	Heref	SO4169	52°19·2'	2°51·5'W	X	137,148
Gothers	Corn	SW9658	50°23·4'	4°51·8'W	T	200
Gothersley Fm	Staffs	SO8586	52°28·5'	2°12·9'W	FM	139
Gothic Fm	Glos	SO9229	51°57·8'	2°6·6'W	FM	150,163
Gothic Fm	Stock	SJ9591	53°25·2'	2°4·1'W	FM	109
Gothic Fm	Suff	TM3372	52°18·0'	1°25·4'E	FM	156
Gothic Ho	Norf	TM1985	52°25·4'	1°13·7'E	X	156
Gothic House Fm	Peterb	TF3008	52°39·5'	0°4·3'W	FM	142
Gothic House Fm	York	SE6545	53°54·1'	1°0·2'W	FM	105,106
Gothigill	Highld	ND1767	58°35·3'	3°25·2'W	X	11,12
Gotleigh Moor	Devon	ST1910	50°53·3'	3°8·7'W	X	192,193
Gotrel Fm	Cered	SN1747	52°5·7'	4°39·9'W	FM	145
Gott	Arg & Bt	NM0346	56°31·0'	6°49·3'W	T	46
Gott	Shetld	HU4328	60°2·3'	1°13·2'W	X	4
Gott	Shetld	HU4346	60°12·0'	1°13·0'W	T	4
Gott Bay	Arg & Bt	NM0546	56°31·1'	6°47·3'W	W	46
Gottenham	Warw	SP3133	51°59·9'	1°32·5'W	X	151
Gotten Leaze	I of W	SZ4285	50°40·0'	1°24·0'W	X	196
Gotten Manor Fm	I of W	SZ4979	50°36·7'	1°18·1'W	FM	196
Gotterbie	D & G	NY1085	55°9·3'	3°24·3'W	X	78
Gotter Water	Inverc	NS3466	55°51·8'	4°38·7'W	W	63
Gott Fm	Shetld	HU4345	60°11·5'	1°13·0'W	FM	4
Gotton	Somer	ST2428	51°3·0'	3°4·7'W	T	193
Gotts Park	Leeds	SE2634	53°48·3'	1°35·9'W	X	104
Gotty Isaf	Pemb	SN0728	51°55·3'	4°48·0'W	X	145,158
Goturm's Hole	Shetld	HP5814	60°48·5'	0°55·5'W	X	1
Gotwick Fm	W Susx	TQ4139	51°8·2'	0°1·3'E	FM	187
Gotwick Manor	E Susx	TQ4239	51°8·2'	0°2·2'E	X	187
Goualit	Cered	SN7553	52°9·9'	3°49·3'W	X	146,147
Goudhurst	Kent	TQ7237	51°6·6'	0°27·8'E	T	188
Goukheads	Orkney	HY4029	59°8·9'	3°2·4'W	X	5,6
Goukhill Fm	Arg & Bt	NS3583	56°1·0'	4°38·4'W	FM	56
Goukmuir	Aberd	NO7577	56°53·3'	2°24·2'W	X	45
Gouknest	E Ayr	NS4047	55°41·7'	4°32·3'W	X	64
Goukstane Burn	D & G	NX9689	55°11·3'	3°37·6'W	W	78
Gouk Stone	C of Aber	NJ8315	57°13·8'	2°16·4'W	A	38
Goukstone	Moray	NJ4856	57°35·7'	2°51·7'W	X	28,29
Goukstyle	Aberd	NO6093	57°1·8'	2°39·1'W	X	37,45
Goukswell	Aberd	NJ6634	57°24·0'	2°33·5'W	X	29
Goukthorn Plantation	D & G	NS8100	55°17·0'	3°52·0'W	F	78
Goukton	Pth & Kin	NO1722	56°23·2'	3°20·2'W	X	53,58
Goulaby Burn	N Eil	NF8876	57°40·2'	7°13·5'W	W	18
Goular	N Eil	NF7070	57°36·2'	7°31·1'W	X	18
Goulceby	Lincs	TF2579	53°17·8'	0°7·1'W	T	122
Gouldings Fm	Hants	SU1406	50°51·4'	1°47·7'W	FM	195
Goulding's Fm	Suff	TL9139	52°1·2'	0°47·4'E	FM	155
Goulds	Devon	SX7863	50°27·5'	3°42·7'W	X	202
Goulds	Essex	TL8734	51°58·6'	0°43·8'E	X	155
Goulds Fm	Devon	SY0198	50°46·6'	3°23·9'W	FM	192
Gould's Fm	Somer	ST7225	51°1·7'	2°23·6'W	FM	183
Goulds Fm	Surrey	TQ3543	51°10·4'	0°3·7'W	FM	187
Gould's Grove Fm	Oxon	SU6489	51°36·0'	1°4·2'W	FM	175
Goule Hall Fm	N Yks	SE6530	53°46·0'	1°0·4'W	FM	105,106
Gouls	Aberd	NJ4134	57°23·8'	2°58·4'W	X	28
Goulton	N Yks	NZ4704	54°26·0'	1°16·1'W	T	93
Goulton Holme	N Yks	NZ4803	54°25·5'	1°15·2'W	X	93
Goultrop Roads	Pemb	SM8412	51°46·1'	5°7·5'W	W	157
Gourach	Arg & Bt	NR7161	55°47·5'	5°38·7'W	X	62
Gourdas	Aberd	NJ7741	57°27·8'	2°22·5'W	X	29,30
Gourdie	C of Dun	NO3532	56°28·8'	3°2·9'W	T	54
Gourdieburn	Aberd	NJ9315	57°13·8'	2°6·5'W	X	38
Gourdiehill	Pth & Kin	NO0232	56°28·5'	3°35·0'W	X	52,53
Gourdie Ho	Pth & Kin	NO1242	56°34·0'	3°25·5'W	X	53
Gourdon	Aberd	NO6670	56°49·5'	2°33·0'W	X	45
Gourdon	Aberd	NO8270	56°49·5'	2°17·2'W	T	45
Gourlaw	Midlo	NT2761	55°50·5'	3°9·5'W	X	66
Gourlay's Burn	Stir	NS6690	56°5·3'	4°8·8'W	W	57
Gourock	Inverc	NS2477	55°57·5'	4°48·7'W	T	63
Gourock Bay	Inverc	NS2477	55°57·5'	4°48·7'W	W	63
Gourt	S Glos	ST7278	51°30·2'	2°23·8'W	X	172
Gourte Fm	Devon	SS8228	51°2·6'	3°40·6'W	FM	181
Gousam	N Eil	NB1033	58°11·7'	6°55·7'W	X	13
Gousman	N Eil	NF9878	57°41·7'	7°3·7'W	X	18
Gouther Crag	Cumbr	NY5112	54°30·3'	2°45·0'W	X	90
Gouthwaite Fm	N Yks	SE1268	54°6·7'	1°48·6'W	FM	99
Gouthwaite Moor	N Yks	SE0968	54°6·7'	1°51·3'W	X	99
Gouthwaite Resr	N Yks	SE1269	54°7·2'	1°48·6'W	W	99
Goutisland	Devon	SS3918	50°56·6'	4°17·1'W	X	190
Goutsford Br	Devon	SX6351	50°20·8'	3°55·2'W	X	202
Goval	Aberd	NJ8815	57°13·8'	2°11·5'W	X	38
Goval Ho	Aberd	NJ8715	57°13·8'	2°12·5'W	X	38
Govals	Aberd	NJ4723	57°18·0'	2°52·3'W	X	37
Govals	Aberd	NJ7325	57°19·1'	2°26·4'W	X	38
Govals	Angus	NO4243	56°34·8'	2°56·2'W	X	54
Govan	C of Glas	NS5565	55°51·6'	4°18·6'W	T	64
Govanhill	Angus	NO6754	56°40·9'	2°31·9'W	X	54
Govanhill	C of Glas	NS5862	55°50·1'	4°15·6'W	T	64

Govel Hill	Aberd	NJ6759	57°37·4'	2°32·7'W	H	29
Gover Fm	Corn	SW7247	50°17·0'	5°11·7'W	FM	204
Gover Hill	Kent	TQ6352	51°14·9'	0°20·5'E	T	188
Goverment Ho	I of M	SC3978	54°10·6'	4°27·6'W	X	95
Governor's Br	I of M	SC3877	54°10·0'	4°28·5'W	X	95
Governs	Corn	SW7845	50°16·0'	5°6·5'W	X	204
Gover's Green	Herts	TL2717	51°50·5'	0°9·0'W	X	166
Goverton	Notts	SK7050	53°2·8'	0°56·9'W	T	120
Gover Valley	Corn	SW9953	50°20·8'	4°49·1'W	X	200,204
Goveton	Devon	SX7546	50°18·3'	3°44·9'W	T	202
Govig	N Eil	NB0109	57°58·5'	7°3·0'W	T	13
Govig Bay	N Eil	NB0008	57°57·9'	7°3·9'W	W	13
Goviley Major	Corn	SW9444	50°15·8'	4°53·1'W	X	204
Goviley Vean	Corn	SW9344	50°15·8'	4°53·9'W	X	204
Govilon	Monm	SO2613	51°48·9'	3°4·0'W	T	161
Gowanbank	Angus	NO4651	56°39·1'	2°52·4'W	T	54
Gowanbank	W Loth	NS9171	55°55·4'	3°44·2'W	X	65
Gowan Bank Fm	Cumbr	SD4498	54°22·7'	2°51·3'W	FM	97
Gowanburn	Northum	NY6491	55°13·0'	2°33·5'W	X	80
Gowanburn	Northum	NY6592	55°13·5'	2°32·6'W	X	80
Gowan Burn	Pth & Kin	NN9831	56°27·9'	3°38·9'W	W	52,53
Gowanfold Rathen	Aberd	NK0364	57°40·2'	1°56·5'W	X	30
Gowan Hall	Lancs	SD5670	54°7·7'	2°40·0'W	X	97
Gowanhead	Angus	NO6156	56°41·9'	2°37·8'W	X	54
Gowan Hill	Aberd	NJ6763	57°39·6'	2°32·7'W	X	29
Gowanhill	Aberd	NK0363	57°39·7'	1°56·5'W	X	30
Gowanhill	C of Edin	NT1668	55°54·1'	3°20·2'W	X	65,66
Gowan Hole	Aberd	NK0465	57°40·7'	1°55·5'W	X	30
Gowan Knowe	Angus	NO3381	56°55·2'	3°5·6'W	X	44
Gowanlea	Aberd	NJ8846	57°30·5'	2°11·6'W	X	30
Gowanlea	N Ayr	NS2851	55°43·6'	4°43·9'W	X	63
Gowanpark	Angus	NO5862	56°45·1'	2°40·8'W	X	44
Gowans	Angus	NO7983	56°56·5'	2°20·3'W	X	45
Gowan's Burn	S Ayr	NX2688	55°9·6'	4°43·4'W	W	76
Gowanside	S Lanak	NS8749	55°43·5'	3°47·5'W	X	72
Gowanwell	Aberd	NJ8841	57°27·8'	2°11·5'W	T	30
Gowany Knowe	Cumbr	NY6675	55°4·3'	2°31·5'W	X	86
Gowbarrow Fell	Cumbr	NY4021	54°35·1'	2°55·3'W	H	90
Gowbarrow Hall	Cumbr	NY4321	54°35·1'	2°52·5'W	X	90
Gowbarrow Park	Cumbr	NY4021	54°35·1'	2°55·3'W	X	90
Gowbusk	N Yks	SE2368	54°6·7'	1°38·5'W	X	99
Gowdall	E Yorks	SE6222	53°41·7'	1°3·2'W	T	105
Gowdall Broach Fm	E Yorks	SE6121	53°41·2'	1°4·2'W	FM	105
Gowdens	Scot Bord	NT7428	55°33·0'	2°24·3'W	X	74
Gowder Crag	Cumbr	NY1410	54°28·9'	3°19·2'W	X	89
Gowdie	Fife	NO2915	56°19·6'	3°8·4'W	X	59
Gowdie Sike	Scot Bord	NT4116	55°26·3'	2°55·5'W	W	79
Gowd Muir	D & G	NY2880	55°6·8'	3°7·3'W	X	79
Gowel Hill	Scot Bord	NT8267	55°54·0'	2°16·8'W	X	67
Gowell Fm	Oxon	SP5623	51°54·4'	1°10·8'W	FM	164
Gowerdale Wood	N Yks	SE5288	54°17·3'	1°11·7'W	F	100
Gower (Gŵyr)	Swan	SS5290	51°35·6'	4°7·8'W	X	159
Gower Hall Fm	N Yks	SE6865	54°4·8'	0°57·2'W	FM	100
Gowers Fm	Essex	TL6018	51°50·5'	0°19·8'E	FM	167
Gower's Fm	Essex	TL8025	51°53·9'	0°37·4'E	FM	168
Gower's Fm	Norf	TM1391	52°28·7'	1°8·6'E	FM	144
Gowerton	Swan	SS5996	51°38·9'	4°1·9'W	T	159
Gowhole	Derby	SK0183	53°20·9'	1°58·7'W	T	110
Gowkesk Rig	D & G	NY2164	54°58·1'	3°13·6'W	X	85
Gowkhall	Fife	NT0589	56°5·3'	3°31·2'W	T	65
Gowk Hill	Cumbr	NY4416	54°32·4'	2°51·5'W	H	90
Gowk Hill	Moray	NJ3848	57°31·3'	3°1·6'W	X	28
Gowk Hill	Northum	NU0904	55°20·0'	1°51·1'W	X	81
Gowkhouse Burn	N Ayr	NS2855	55°45·7'	4°44·0'W	W	63
Gowkley Moss	Midlo	NT2563	55°51·5'	3°11·5'W	X	66
Gowkshaw Burn	E Ayr	NS5544	55°40·3'	4°17·9'W	W	71
Gowkshill Fm	Midlo	NT3363	55°51·6'	3°3·8'W	FM	66
Gowk Stane	Aberd	NJ6725	57°19·1'	2°32·4'W	A	38
Gowkstone	Aberd	NJ8439	57°26·7'	2°15·5'W	X	29,30
Gowk Stone	Fife	NO2305	56°14·1'	3°14·1'W	X	58
Gowk Stone	N Ayr	NS1556	55°46·0'	4°56·5'W	X	63
Gowkthrapple	N Lanak	NS7953	55°45·6'	3°55·3'W	T	64
Gowlands	N Yks	SE4856	54°0·1'	1°15·6'W	X	105
Gowl Burn	Scot Bord	NT6864	55°52·3'	2°30·2'W	W	67
Gowle's Fm	Mil Key	SP9047	52°7·1'	0°40·7'W	FM	152
Gowlie	Pth & Kin	NO1516	56°20·0'	3°22·0'W	X	58
Gowlog	V of Glam	ST0471	51°26·0'	3°22·5'W	X	170
Gowmacmorran	S Lanak	NS9452	55°45·2'	3°40·9'W	X	65,72
Gow Moss	Moray	NJ3853	57°34·0'	3°1·7'W	X	28
Gownfold Fm	W Susx	TQ0125	51°1·2'	0°33·2'W	FM	186,197
Gownie	Moray	NJ2842	57°28·0'	3°11·6'W	X	28
Gownor	Aberd	NJ8128	57°20·8'	2°18·5'W	X	38
Gowrey	Lancs	SD6378	54°12·0'	2°33·6'W	X	97
Gowrie	Aberd	NK0651	57°33·2'	1°53·5'W	X	30
Gowrie	Pth & Kin	NO1031	56°28·0'	3°27·2'W	X	53
Gowston	Stir	NS5692	56°6·2'	4°18·5'W	X	57
Gowthorpe	E Yorks	SE7654	53°58·8'	0°50·0'W	T	105,106
Gowthorpe Beck	E Yorks	SE7755	53°59·4'	0°49·1'W	W	105,106
Gowthorpe House	E Yorks	SE8525	53°43·1'	0°42·3'W	X	106
Gowthorpe Manor	Norf	TG2002	52°34·5'	1°15·2'E	A	134
Gowts Fm	Lincs	TF4593	53°25·1'	0°11·3'E	FM	113
Goxhill	E Yorks	TA1844	53°53·0'	0°11·9'W	T	107
Goxhill	N Lincs	TA1021	53°40·7'	0°19·7'W	T	107,113
Goxhill Haven	N Lincs	TA1225	53°42·8'	0°17·8'W	X	107,113
Goyallt	Cered	SN6159	52°12·9'	4°1·7'W	X	146
Goyden Pot	N Yks	SE1076	54°11·0'	1°50·4'W	X	99
Goyle Hill	Aberd	NO6881	56°55·4'	2°31·1'W	H	45
Goynd	Angus	NO4462	56°45·0'	2°54·5'W	X	44
Goyt Forest	Derby	SJ9977	53°17·6'	2°0·5'W	F	118
Goyt Forest	Derby	SK0077	53°17·6'	1°59·6'W	F	119
Goyt Hall	Stock	SJ9290	53°24·6'	2°6·8'W	A	109
Goytre	Cered	SN3746	52°5·5'	4°22·4'W	X	145
Goytre	Cered	SN5769	52°18·3'	4°5·4'W	X	135
Goytre	Nth Pt Talb	SS7594	51°38·1'	3°48·0'W	X	170
Goytre	Nth Pt Talb	SS7889	51°35·4'	3°45·3'W	T	170
Goytre	Powys	SN9954	52°10·7'	3°28·2'W	X	147
Goytre	Powys	SO2375	52°22·3'	3°7·5'W	X	137,148
Goytre Fm	Monm	ST4397	51°40·4'	2°49·1'W	FM	171
Goytre Hall	Monm	SO3106	51°45·1'	2°59·6'W	X	171
Goytre Ho	Monm	SO3104	51°44·1'	2°59·6'W	X	171

Goytre Wharf	Monm	SO3106	51°45·1'	2°59·6'W	X	161
Goyt's Moss	Derby	SK0172	53°14·9'	1°58·7'W	X	119
Goyt Valley	Derby	SK0177	53°17·6'	1°58·7'W	X	119
Goyt Way	Stock	SJ9690	53°24·6'	2°3·2'W	X	109
Gozzard's Ford	Oxon	SU4698	51°40·1'	1°19·7'W	T	164
Graand,The	Orkney	HY3528	59°8·3'	3°7·7'W	X	6
Graand, The	Orkney	HY4727	59°7·9'	2°55·1'W	X	5,6
Graand, The	Orkney	HY5628	59°8·5'	2°45·7'W	X	5,6
Graand, The	Orkney	HY5739	59°14·4'	2°44·7'W	X	5
Grabbist Hill	Somer	SS9843	51°10·9'	3°27·2'W	X	181
Grabhair	N Eil	NB3715	58°3·0'	6°27·0'W	T	14
Graby	Lincs	TF0929	52°51·1'	0°22·5'W	T	130
Gracca	Corn	SX0159	50°24·1'	4°47·6'W	T	200
Grace Dieu Brook	Leic	SK4520	52°46·8'	1°19·6'W	W	129
Grace Dieu Manor (Sch)	Leic	SK4317	52°45·2'	1°21·4'W	X	129
Grace Dieu Priory	Leic	SK4318	52°45·7'	1°21·4'W	A	129
Gracefield	D & G	NX8789	55°11·2'	3°46·1'W	X	78
Gracefield	Pth & Kin	NO1529	56°27·0'	3°22·3'W	X	53,58
Grace Mire Ho	Lancs	SD4733	53°47·7'	2°47·9'W	X	102
Gracemount	C of Edin	NT2768	55°54·2'	3°9·6'W	T	66
Grace's Cross	Essex	TL7405	51°43·2'	0°31·5'E	X	167
Grace's Walk	Essex	TL7506	51°43·7'	0°32·4'E	X	167
Grach	Powys	SO0179	52°24·2'	3°26·9'W	X	136,147
Gracious Pond Fm	Surrey	SU9863	51°21·7'	0°35·2'W	FM	175,176,186
Gràdaire Leathann	N Eil	NB1336	58°13·4'	6°52·8'W	X	13
Gradbach	Staffs	SJ9965	53°11·2'	2°0·5'W	X	118
Gradbach Hill	Staffs	SJ9965	53°11·2'	2°0·5'W	H	118
Gradbach Hill	Staffs	SK0065	53°11·2'	1°59·6'W	X	119
Graddfa	Caer	ST1492	51°37·5'	3°14·2'W	X	171
Graddoch Burn	D & G	NX4964	54°57·1'	4°21·0'W	W	83
Graddon	Devon	SS4403	50°48·6'	4°12·5'W	X	190
Graddon Moor	Devon	SS4602	50°48·1'	4°10·7'W	X	190
Grade	Corn	SW7114	49°59·2'	5°11·3'W	T	203
Gradeley Green	Ches	SJ5952	53°4·1'	2°36·3'W	X	117
Graden	Scot Bord	NT7930	55°34·0'	2°19·5'W	X	74
Graden Moor	Scot Bord	NT7830	55°34·0'	2°20·5'W	X	74
Gradner Rocks	Devon	SX7880	50°36·7'	3°43·1'W	X	191
Graeanllyn	Conwy	SH8054	53°4·4'	3°47·1'W	X	116
Graemeshall	Orkney	HY4801	58°53·9'	2°53·7'W	X	6,7
Graemeshall Burn	Orkney	HY4804	58°55·5'	2°53·7'W	W	6,7
Graemsay	Orkney	HY2505	58°55·8'	3°17·7'W	X	6,7
Graemshall	Orkney	HY3822	59°5·1'	3°4·4'W	X	6
Graemston	Orkney	ND4484	58°44·7'	2°57·6'W	X	7
Graemston Loch	Orkney	ND4484	58°44·7'	2°57·6'W	W	7
Graffham	W Susx	SU9217	50°56·9'	0°41·0'W	T	197
Graffham Common	W Susx	SU9319	50°58·0'	0°40·1'W	F	197
Graffham Court	W Susx	SU9219	50°58·0'	0°41·0'W	X	197
Graffham Down	W Susx	SU9216	50°56·4'	0°41·0'W	H	197
Graffitoe Fm	N Yks	TA1275	54°9·8'	0°16·7'W	FM	101
Graffridge Wood	Herts	TL2221	51°52·7'	0°13·3'W	F	166
Grafham	Cambs	TL1669	52°18·6'	0°17·5'W	T	153
Grafham	Surrey	TQ0241	51°9·8'	0°32·1'W	T	186
Grafham Grange	Surrey	TQ0141	51°9·8'	0°32·9'W	X	186
Grafham Water	Cambs	TL1468	52°18·1'	0°19·3'W	W	153
Grafiau	Powys	SN8371	52°19·7'	3°42·6'W	X	135,136,147
Grafog	Powys	SO1830	51°58·0'	3°11·2'W	X	161
Grafton	Heref	SO4937	52°2·0'	2°44·2'W	T	149
Grafton	N Yks	SE4163	54°3·9'	1°22·0'W	T	99
Grafton	Oxon	SP2600	51°42·1'	1°37·0'W	T	163
Grafton	Shrops	SJ4318	52°45·6'	2°50·3'W	T	126
Grafton	Worcs	SO5761	52°15·0'	2°37·4'W	X	137,138,149
Grafton	Worcs	SO9837	52°2·1'	2°1·4'W	T	150
Grafton Court	Warw	SP1254	52°11·3'	1°49·1'W	X	150
Grafton Down	Wilts	SU2558	51°19·5'	1°38·1'W	X	174
Grafton Fields	Northnts	SP7545	52°6·1'	0°53·9'W	X	152
Grafton Fields	Wilts	SU2559	51°20·0'	1°38·1'W	X	174
Grafton Flyford	Worcs	SO9656	52°12·4'	2°3·1'W	T	150
Grafton Grange	N Yks	SE4062	54°3·4'	1°22·9'W	X	99
Grafton Hall	Ches	SJ4551	53°3·4'	2°48·8'W	X	117
Grafton Ho	Derby	SK2414	52°43·6'	1°38·3'W	X	128
Grafton Lodge	Northnts	SP7446	52°6·7'	0°54·8'W	X	152
Grafton Lodge	N Yks	SE4263	54°3·9'	1°21·1'W	X	99
Grafton Lodge	Shrops	SJ4318	52°45·6'	2°50·3'W	X	126
Grafton Manor Ho	Worcs	SO9369	52°19·4'	2°5·8'W	A	139
Grafton Oak	Heref	SO4429	51°57·6'	2°48·5'W	X	149,161
Grafton Park Wood	Northnts	SP9381	52°25·4'	0°37·5'W	F	141
Grafton Regis	Northnts	SP7546	52°6·7'	0°53·9'W	T	152
Grafton Underwood	Northnts	SP9280	52°24·8'	0°38·4'W	T	141
Grafton Villa	Heref	SO4936	52°1·4'	2°44·2'W	X	149
Grafton Way	Northnts	SP7046	52°6·7'	0°58·3'W	X	152
Grafton Way	Northnts	SP7444	52°5·6'	0°54·8'W	X	152
Grafton Wood	Worcs	SO9756	52°12·4'	2°2·2'W	F	150
Graft's Fm	Durham	NZ1114	54°31·5'	1°49·4'W	FM	92
Grafty Green	Kent	TQ8748	51°12·3'	0°41·0'E	T	189
Gragareth	N Yks	SD6979	54°12·6'	2°28·1'W	X	98
Graham's Cairn	Stir	NS5582	56°0·8'	4°19·1'W	X	57,64
Graham's Cleugh	Northum	NT8307	55°21·7'	2°15·7'W	X	80
Graham's Folly	Fife	NT3197	56°9·9'	3°6·2'W	F	59
Grahamshill	D & G	NY2870	55°1·4'	3°7·1'W	X	85
Graham's Law	Scot Bord	NT1707	55°21·3'	3°18·1'W	H	79
Grahamslaw	Scot Bord	NT7227	55°32·4'	2°26·2'W	X	74
Graham's Law	Scot Bord	NT7228	55°32·9'	2°26·2'W	H	74
Grahamslaw Plantation	Scot Bord	NT7128	55°32·9'	2°27·1'W	F	74
Graham's Onset	Cumbr	NY5180	55°7·0'	2°45·7'W	X	79
Graham's Point	Arg & Bt	NS1781	55°59·5'	4°55·6'W	X	63
Grahamston	Falk	NS8880	56°0·2'	3°47·3'W	T	65
Grahamstone	Pth & Kin	NO1701	56°11·9'	3°19·8'W	X	58
Graianfryn	I of Angl	SH3284	53°19·8'	4°31·0'W	X	114
Graianog	Gwyn	SH4549	53°1·2'	4°18·2'W	X	115,123
Graianrhyd	Denb	SJ2156	53°6·0'	3°10·4'W	T	117
Graienyn	Gwyn	SH9234	52°53·8'	3°35·9'W	X	125
Graig	Carm	SN4401	51°41·4'	4°15·0'W	T	159
Graig	Cered	SN6954	52°10·4'	3°54·5'W	X	146
Graig	Conwy	SH8071	53°13·6'	3°47·5'W	X	116
Graig	Conwy	SH8074	53°15·2'	3°47·5'W	T	116
Graig	Conwy	SJ0071	53°13·8'	3°29·5'W	X	116
Graig	Denb	SJ0872	53°14·5'	3°22·3'W	T	116
Graig	I of Angl	SH3771	53°12·9'	4°26·1'W	X	114
Graig	Monm	SO2516	51°50·5'	3°4·9'W	F	161
Graig	Pemb	SN1830	51°56·6'	4°38·5'W	X	145
Graig	Powys	SJ1708	52°40·0'	3°13·2'W	X	125
Graig	Powys	SO0082	52°25·9'	3°27·9'W	X	136
Graig	Powys	SO0756	52°11·9'	3°21·2'W	X	147
Graig	Powys	SO0988	52°29·2'	3°20·0'W	X	136
Graig	Powys	SO1258	52°13·0'	3°16·9'W	X	148
Graig	Powys	SO1261	52°14·6'	3°16·9'W	X	148
Graig	Powys	SO1767	52°17·9'	3°12·6'W	X	136,148
Graig	Rho Cyn Taf	ST0689	51°35·8'	3°21·0'W	T	170
Graig	Rho Cyn Taf	ST1385	51°33·7'	3°14·9'W	X	171
Graig	Shrops	SO2575	52°22·3'	3°5·7'W	X	137,148
Graig	V of Glam	SS9978	51°29·8'	3°26·9'W	F	170
Graig	Wrex	SJ2337	52°55·7'	3°8·3'W	T	126
Graig	Wrex	SJ3341	52°58·0'	2°59·5'W	X	117
Graig-Arthur	Flint	SJ0978	53°17·7'	3°21·5'W	X	116
Graig-Arw	Nth Pt Talb	SN7507	51°45·1'	3°48·3'W	X	160
Graig-bâch	Conwy	SH8562	53°8·8'	3°42·8'W	X	116
Graig Cwm Dulyn	Gwyn	SH4949	53°1·3'	4°14·7'W	X	115,123
Graig Ddu	Caer	ST2395	51°39·1'	3°6·4'W	X	171
Graigddu	Cered	SN6552	52°9·2'	3°58·0'W	X	146
Graig Ddu	Cered	SN7574	52°21·2'	3°49·7'W	X	135,147
Graig Ddu	Cered	SN8173	52°20·8'	3°44·4'W	X	135,136,147
Graig Ddu	Denb	SJ1744	52°59·5'	3°13·8'W	X	125
Graig Ddû	Gwyn	SH3544	52°58·3'	4°27·0'W	X	123
Graig Ddu	Gwyn	SH5237	52°54·8'	4°11·7'W	H	124
Graig Ddu	Gwyn	SH7110	52°40·6'	3°54·1'W	X	124
Graig ddu	Gwyn	SH8529	52°51·0'	3°42·1'W	X	124,125
Graig Ddu	Gwyn	SH8842	52°58·1'	3°39·7'W	X	124,125
Graig-ddu	I of Angl	SH4493	53°24·9'	4°20·4'W	X	114
Graig-ddu	Monm	SO2826	51°55·9'	3°2·4'W	X	161
Graig Ddu	Powys	SH7905	52°38·0'	3°46·9'W	X	124
Graig Ddu	Powys	SJ0524	52°48·6'	3°24·2'W	X	125
Graig Ddu	Powys	SN8965	52°16·6'	3°37·2'W	X	135,136,147
Graig Ddu	Torf	SO2501	51°42·4'	3°4·7'W	X	171
Graig-ddu Quarry	Gwyn	SH7245	52°59·5'	3°54·0'W	X	115
Graig Dolfaenog	Powys	SN9166	52°17·1'	3°35·5'W	X	136,147
Graig Fach	Gwyn	SH6408	52°39·4'	4°0·2'W	X	124
Graig-fach	Monm	SO3919	51°52·2'	2°52·8'W	X	161
Graig Fâch	Rho Cyn Taf	SS9395	51°38·9'	3°32·4'W	X	170
Graig Fach-goch	Gwyn	SH6001	52°35·6'	4°3·6'W	X	135
Graig-fael	Gwyn	SH2130	52°50·5'	4°39·1'W	X	123
Graig Fan Ddu	Powys	SO0118	51°51·3'	3°25·9'W	X	160
Graig Fatho	Rho Cyn Taf	ST0185	51°33·5'	3°25·3'W	X	170
Graig Fawr	Blae Gw	SO1902	51°42·9'	3°10·0'W	X	171
Graig-Fawr	Carm	SN6915	51°49·3'	3°53·7'W	X	160
Graig Fawr	Denb	SJ0680	53°18·8'	3°24·2'W	X	116
Graig Fawr	Nth Pt Talb	SS7986	51°33·8'	3°44·4'W	X	170
Graigfawr	Powys	SO1358	52°13·0'	3°16·0'W	X	148
Graig-fawr	Rho Cyn Taf	SS9296	51°39·4'	3°33·3'W	X	170
Graig-Fawr	Swan	SN6004	51°43·3'	4°1·2'W	T	159
Graig Fawr	Swan	SN6106	51°44·4'	4°0·4'W	X	159
Graig Fawr	Wrex	SJ1335	52°54·6'	3°17·2'W	X	125
Graig-fechan	Denb	SJ1454	53°4·8'	3°16·6'W	T	116
Graig Felen	Swan	SN6802	51°42·3'	3°54·2'W	T	159
Graig Fm	Denb	SJ0566	53°11·2'	3°24·9'W	FM	116
Graig Fm	Denb	SJ1555	53°5·4'	3°15·7'W	FM	116
Graig Fm	Denb	SJ2050	53°2·7'	3°11·2'W	FM	117
Graig-goch	Caer	ST1890	51°36·4'	3°10·7'W	X	171
Graig Goch	Cered	SN8074	52°21·3'	3°45·3'W	X	135,136,147
Graig Goch	Conwy	SH8356	53°5·5'	3°44·4'W	X	116
Graig Goch	Gwyn	SH7108	52°39·5'	3°54·0'W	H	124
Graig Goch	Gwyn	SH7544	52°59·0'	3°51·3'W	X	124
Graig-Goch	Nth Pt Talb	SS8186	51°33·9'	3°42·6'W	X	170
Graiggoch Fm	Powys	SN8929	51°57·1'	3°36·5'W	FM	160
Graig Hill	Powys	SO0767	52°17·9'	3°12·6'W	H	136,148
Graig Hill	Powys	SO2568	52°18·5'	3°5·6'W	X	137,148
Graig Hill	Shrops	SO2583	52°26·6'	3°5·8'W	H	137
Graig-hir	Conwy	SH8657	53°6·1'	3°41·8'W	H	116
Graig Iar	Powys	SN9980	52°24·8'	3°28·7'W	H	136
Graig-isaf	Gwyn	SH6325	52°48·6'	4°1·6'W	X	124
Graig Isaf	Nth Pt Talb	SN8803	51°43·1'	3°36·9'W	X	170
Graig-las	Gwyn	SH5249	53°1·3'	4°12·0'W	X	115
Graig-las	Gwyn	SH8340	52°56·9'	3°44·1'W	X	124,125
Graiglas	I of Angl	SH4174	53°14·6'	4°22·6'W	X	114,115
Graig Llanishen	Card	ST1784	51°33·2'	3°11·4'W	X	171
Graiglwyd	Conwy	SH7175	53°15·6'	3°55·6'W	X	115
Graig-lwyd	Denb	SJ0662	53°9·1'	3°23·9'W	X	116
Graig-lwyd	Gwyn	SH5146	52°59·7'	4°12·8'W	X	115
Graig Lwyd	Gwyn	SH6510	52°40·5'	3°59·4'W	H	124
Graig-lwyd	Rho Cyn Taf	ST0283	51°32·5'	3°24·4'W	X	170
Graig Ola	Swan	SN7001	51°41·8'	3°52·5'W	X	170
Graig Olway	Monm	ST3899	51°41·4'	2°53·4'W	X	171
Graigorddle	Powys	SN9993	52°31·8'	3°28·9'W	X	136
Graig Penllyn	V of Glam	SS9777	51°29·2'	3°28·6'W	T	170
Graig Safn-y-coed	Powys	SN9372	52°20·4'	3°33·8'W	X	136,147
Graig Syfyrddin	Monm	SO4022	51°53·8'	2°51·9'W	X	161
Graig, The	Monm	SO5009	51°46·9'	2°43·1'W	X	162
Graig, The	Wrex	SJ3946	53°0·7'	2°54·1'W	X	117
Graig Trewyddfa	Swan	SS6697	51°39·6'	3°55·9'W	T	159
Graig Tŷ-crin	Cered	SN7767	52°17·5'	3°47·8'W	H	135,147
Graig Tŷ-nant	Gwyn	SH8922	52°47·3'	3°38·4'W	H	124,125
Graig Wen	Caer	ST2295	51°39·1'	3°7·3'W	X	171
Graigwen	Cered	SN5254	52°10·1'	4°9·5'W	X	146
Graig Wen	Cered	SN6851	52°8·7'	3°55·4'W	X	146
Graig Wen	Conwy	SH7649	53°1·7'	3°50·5'W	X	115
Graig Wen	Gwyn	SH6906	52°38·4'	3°55·8'W	H	124
Graig Wen	Gwyn	SH7339	52°56·3'	3°53·0'W	X	124
Graig Wen	I of Angl	SH3994	53°25·3'	4°25·0'W	X	114
Graig Wen	Powys	SJ0027	52°50·1'	3°28·7'W	X	125
Graig-wen	Rho Cyn Taf	ST0190	51°36·2'	3°25·4'W	X	170
Graig-wen	Wrex	SJ2336	52°55·2'	3°8·3'W	X	126
Graigwith Ho	Monm	ST3596	51°39·8'	2°56·0'W	X	171
Graigwith Wood	Monm	ST3496	51°39·8'	2°56·9'W	F	171
Graig-Y-Cwm	Monm	SO2809	51°46·7'	3°2·2'W	X	161
Graig-y-gronfa	Powys	SH8611	52°41·3'	3°40·8'W	X	124,125
Graig-y-Master	Monm	ST4196	51°39·8'	2°50·8'W	X	171
Graig-yr-onen	Powys	SO1153	52°10·3'	3°17·7'W	X	148
Graig-y-Saeson	Newp	ST2785	51°33·8'	3°2·8'W	X	171
Grain	Cald	SD9931	53°46·8'	2°0·5'W	X	103
Grain	Medway	TQ8876	51°27·3'	0°42·8'E	T	178
Grain	Orkney	HY3832	59°10·5'	3°4·6'W	X	6
Grain Beck	Cumbr	NY7927	54°38·5'	2°19·1'W	W	91
Grain Beck	N Yks	NZ6205	54°26·4'	1°2·2'W	W	94
Grain Beck	N Yks	SE8893	54°19·7'	0°38·4'W	W	94,101
Grain Burn	D & G	NS7413	55°23·9'	3°58·9'W	W	71
Grainel	Arg & Bt	NR2666	55°48·8'	6°22·0'W	X	60
Grainger Barn	Durham	NZ1421	54°35·3'	1°46·6'W	X	92
Grainger Houses	Cumbr	NY2546	54°48·4'	3°9·6'W	X	85
Grainhall	D & G	NY2178	55°5·7'	3°13·8'W	X	85
Grainhead	Cumbr	NY4867	54°59·9'	2°48·3'W	X	86
Grainhill	Aberd	NJ8443	57°28·9'	2°15·6'W	X	29,30
Grain Hill	Scot Bord	NT4523	55°30·1'	2°51·8'W	H	73
Grain Ho	N Yks	SD7963	54°4·0'	2°18·8'W	X	98
Grainhow	Aberd	NJ8546	57°30·5'	2°14·6'W	X	30
Graining Field	Cumbr	SD6197	54°22·3'	2°35·6'W	X	97
Grainingfold Fm	W Susx	TQ1028	51°2·7'	0°25·5'W	FM	187,198
Grainings	N Yks	SD8982	54°14·3'	2°9·7'W	X	98
Grainings Head	Brad	SE1046	53°54·8'	1°50·5'W	X	104
Grainings Water	Cald	SD9531	53°46·8'	2°4·1'W	W	103
Grain Intakes	N Yks	NZ6105	54°26·4'	1°3·1'W	X	94
Grain Marsh	Medway	TQ8777	51°27·9'	0°41·9'E	X	178
Grains	Cumbr	SD6698	54°22·8'	2°31·0'W	X	98
Grains	D & G	NY1776	55°4·5'	3°17·6'W	X	85
Grains	N Yks	SD8762	54°3·5'	2°11·5'W	X	98
Grains	S Lanak	NT0123	55°29·7'	3°33·6'W	X	72
Grains Bar	Oldham	SD9608	53°34·4'	2°3·2'W	T	109
Grains Burn	Northum	NY5890	55°12·4'	2°39·2'W	W	80
Grains Burn	S Lanak	NT0124	55°30·2'	3°33·6'W	W	72
Grainsby	Lincs	TF2799	53°28·6'	0°4·8'W	T	113
Grainsby Grange	Lincs	TF2698	53°28·1'	0°5·7'W	X	113
Grainsby Healing	Lincs	TA2700	53°29·1'	0°4·7'W	X	113
Grains Fm	Swin	SU1491	51°37·3'	1°47·5'W	FM	163,173
Grains Gill	Cumbr	NY2310	54°29·0'	3°10·9'W	W	89,90
Grainsgill Beck	Cumbr	NY3133	54°41·5'	3°3·8'W	W	90
Grains in the Water	Derby	SK1094	53°26·8'	1°50·6'W	X	110
Grains Moss	Barns	SE1202	53°31·1'	1°48·7'W	X	110
Grains Moss	Derby	SE0604	53°32·2'	1°54·2'W	X	110
Grains of Fetteresso	Aberd	NO8186	56°58·1'	2°18·3'W	X	45
Grains o' th' Beck	Durham	NY8620	54°34·7'	2°12·6'W	X	91,92
Grain Spit	Medway	TQ9077	51°27·8'	0°44·5'E	X	178
Grains, The	N Yks	SD9095	54°21·3'	2°8·8'W	X	98
Grainston	Stir	NN7502	56°11·9'	4°0·4'W	X	57
Grainthorpe	Lincs	TF3897	53°27·3'	0°5·1'E	T	113
Grainthorpe Fen	Lincs	TF3795	53°26·3'	0°4·2'E	T	113
Grainthorpe Haven	Lincs	TA3900	53°28·9'	0°6·1'E	W	113
Grain Tower	Medway	TQ8976	51°27·3'	0°43·6'E	A	178
Grainy Gill Moss	N Yks	SD8696	54°21·8'	2°12·5'W	X	98
Graiselound	N Lincs	SK7798	53°28·6'	0°50·0'W	T	112
Gralisgeir	N Eil	HW6129	59°5·1'	6°9·8'W	X	8
Gramasdail	N Eil	NF8155	57°28·6'	7°18·9'W	T	22
Grambla	Corn	SW6828	50°6·6'	5°14·3'W	X	203
Gramborough Hill	Norf	TG0844	52°57·4'	1°6·2'E	X	133
Grames Ness	Shetld	HU4770	60°24·9'	1°8·3'W	X	2,3
Grammarcombe Wood	Devon	SX9080	50°36·8'	3°32·9'W	F	192
Grammars Hill	Dorset	ST8812	50°54·7'	2°9·9'W	X	194
Grammerby Wood	Devon	SX4876	50°34·1'	4°8·4'W	F	191,201
Grampian Mountains	Aberd	NJ1201	57°5·8'	3°26·7'W	X	36
Grampian Mountains	Aberd	NJ3807	57°9·2'	3°1·0'W	H	37
Grampian Mountains	Highld	NN8790	56°59·5'	3°51·1'W	H	35,43
Grampian Mountains	Pth & Kin	NN3643	56°33·3'	4°39·6'W	H	50
Grampian Mountains	Pth & Kin	NN5670	56°48·2'	4°21·0'W	H	42
Grampound	Corn	SW9348	50°18·0'	4°54·0'W	T	204
Grampound Road	Corn	SW9150	50°19·0'	4°55·8'W	T	200,204
Gramp's Hill	Oxon	SU3784	51°33·5'	1°27·6'W	X	174
Granalaw	I of Angl	SH3685	53°20·4'	4°27·4'W	X	114
Granant	Pemb	SN1247	52°5·6'	4°44·3'W	X	145
Granary	Monm	ST3296	51°39·8'	2°58·6'W	X	171
Granary Fm	N Yks	SE9386	54°15·9'	0°33·9'W	FM	94,101
Granary House Fm	Cambs	TL4693	52°31·1'	0°9·5'E	FM	143
Granary Point	Northum	NU0841	55°40·0'	1°51·9'W	X	75
Granary, The	Lincs	TF0177	53°17·1'	0°28·7'W	X	121
Granary, The	Norf	TF8613	52°41·2'	0°45·5'E	X	132
Granary, The	Northum	NY9260	54°56·3'	2°7·1'W	X	87
Granborough	Bucks	SP7625	51°55·3'	0°53·3'W	T	165
Granby	Notts	SK7536	52°55·2'	0°52·7'W	T	129
Granby Fm	Warw	SP2643	52°5·3'	1°36·8'W	FM	151
Granby Gap	Notts	SK7534	52°54·1'	0°52·7'W	X	129
Granby Lodge	Notts	SK7636	52°55·2'	0°51·8'W	X	129
Granby Lodge	Rut	SK8800	52°35·7'	0°41·6'W	X	141
Granby Wood	Leic	SK8131	52°52·5'	0°47·4'W	F	130
Grandacre Fm	Kent	TR1047	51°11·2'	1°0·7'E	FM	179,189
Grand Avenue	Wilts	SU2167	51°24·3'	1°41·5'W	X	174
Grandborough	Warw	SP4966	52°17·6'	1°16·5'W	T	151
Grandborough Fields	Warw	SP4865	52°17·1'	1°17·4'W	X	151
Grand Br	Oxon	SP4316	51°50·7'	1°22·2'W	X	164
Grandcourt Fm	Norf	TF6816	52°43·2'	0°29·7'E	FM	132
Grandford Ho	Cambs	TL3999	52°34·5'	0°3·5'E	X	142,143
Grandhome Ho	C of Aber	NJ8911	57°11·6'	2°10·5'W	X	38
Grandhome Moss	C of Aber	NJ9112	57°12·2'	2°8·5'W	X	38
Grand Lodge	Staffs	SK0613	52°43·1'	1°54·3'W	X	128
Grandon Lodge	Surrey	TQ1744	51°11·2'	0°19·2'W	X	187
Grandon Manor	Somer	ST8046	51°13·0'	2°16·8'W	X	183
Grandpont	Oxon	SP5105	51°44·7'	1°15·3'W	T	164
Grandsires Green	Ches	SJ6579	53°18·6'	2°31·1'W	X	118
Grandtully	Pth & Kin	NN9152	56°39·1'	3°46·2'W	T	52
Grandtully Castle	Pth & Kin	NN8951	56°38·5'	3°48·2'W	A	52
Grandtully Hill	Pth & Kin	NN9147	56°36·4'	3°46·1'W	H	52
Grandturzel	E Susx	TQ6924	50°59·7'	0°24·9'E	X	199
Grand Union Canal	Ealing	TQ1683	51°32·3'	0°19·3'W	W	176
Grand Union Canal	Herts	TL0702	51°42·6'	0°26·7'W	W	166
Grand Union Canal	Leic	SK5518	52°45·6'	1°10·7'W	W	129
Grand Union Canal	Leic	SP6097	52°34·3'	1°6·5'W	W	140
Grand Union Canal	Leic	SP6990	52°30·4'	0°58·6'W	W	141
Grand Union Canal	Northnts	SP6180	52°25·1'	1°5·8'W	W	140
Grand Union Canal	Northnts	SP7359	52°13·7'	0°55·5'W	W	152
Grand Union Canal	Sol	SP1680	52°25·3'	1°45·5'W	W	139
Grand Union Canal	Warw	SP2266	52°17·7'	1°40·2'W	W	151
Grand Union Canal	Warw	SP3564	52°16·6'	1°28·8'W	W	151
Grand Union Canal (Aylesbury Arm)	Bucks	SP8614	51°49·3'	0°44·7'W	W	165
Grand Union Canal Walk	Warw	SP3564	52°16·6'	1°28·8'W	X	139,151

Grandview	Shetld	HU4345	60°11·5′	1°13·0′W	X	4
Grand Vista	Oxon	SP3417	51°51·3′	1°30·0′W	X	164
Grand Western Canal	Devon	ST0515	50°55·8′	3°20·7′W	W	181
Grandy's Knowe	Northum	NY7867	55°0·1′	2°20·2′W	X	86,87
Grange	Aberd	NO8474	56°51·7′	2°15·3′W	X	45
Grange	Ches	SJ7061	53°9·0′	2°26·5′W	X	118
Grange	Cumbr	NY0310	54°28·8′	3°29·4′W	X	89
Grange	Cumbr	NY2517	54°32·8′	3°9·1′W	T	89,90
Grange	Cumbr	SD1293	54°19·7′	3°20·8′W	X	96
Grange	Denb	SJ1060	53°8·0′	3°20·3′W	X	116
Grange	D & G	NX6847	54°48·3′	4°2·8′W	X	83,84
Grange	Dorset	SU0102	50°49·3′	1°58·8′W	T	195
Grange	E Ayr	NS4137	55°36·3′	4°31·0′W	T	70
Grange	Fife	NO3622	56°23·4′	3°1·8′W	X	54,59
Grange	Fife	NO4700	56°11·6′	2°50·8′W	X	59
Grange	Fife	NT2688	56°5·0′	3°10·9′W	X	66
Grange	Halton	SJ5281	53°19·7′	2°42·8′W	T	108
Grange	Heref	SO4171	52°20·3′	2°51·6′W	X	137,148
Grange	Highld	NH3730	57°20·1′	4°42·0′W	X	26
Grange	I of W	SZ4281	50°37·9′	1°24·0′W	X	196
Grange	Lancs	SD3838	53°50·3′	2°56·1′W	X	102
Grange	Lancs	SD5731	53°46·7′	2°38·7′W	T	102
Grange	Lancs	SD6332	53°47·2′	2°33·3′W	X	102,103
Grange	Leic	SK6012	52°42·4′	1°6·3′W	X	129
Grange	Leic	SP7292	52°31·5′	0°55·9′W	X	141
Grange	Lincs	TF2378	53°17·3′	0°8·9′W	X	122
Grange	Medway	TQ7968	51°23·2′	0°34·7′E	T	178
Grange	NE Lincs	TA2508	53°33·5′	0°6·4′W	T	113
Grange	Norf	TG1009	52°38·5′	1°6·6′E	X	144
Grange	Northum	NZ0459	54°55·8′	1°55·8′W	X	87
Grange	Northum	NZ0970	55°1·7′	1°51·1′W	X	88
Grange	N Yks	SD9391	54°19·1′	2°6·0′W	T	98
Grange	Oldham	SD9808	53°34·4′	2°1·4′W	X	109
Grange	Orkney	HY3629	59°8·8′	3°6·6′W	X	6
Grange	Pth & Kin	NO1420	56°22·1′	3°23·1′W	X	53,58
Grange	Pth & Kin	NO2625	56°24·9′	3°11·5′W	T	53,59
Grange	Shrops	SJ4327	52°50·5′	2°50·4′W	X	126
Grange	S Lanak	NS6845	55°41·1′	4°5·5′W	X	64
Grange	Somer	ST3640	51°9·6′	2°54·5′W	X	182
Grange	Suff	TM4365	52°14·0′	1°33·9′E	X	156
Grange	Warr	SJ6490	53°24·6′	2°32·1′W	T	109
Grange	Wirral	SJ2286	53°22·2′	3°9·9′W	T	108
Grange	W Loth	NT0078	55°59·3′	3°35·7′W	X	65
Grange	W Loth	NT0165	55°52·3′	3°34·5′W	X	65
Grange	York	SE5656	54°0·1′	1°8·3′W	X	
Grange Arch	Dorset	SY9181	50°37·9′	2°7·3′W	X	195
Grange Banks	Scot Bord	NT5922	55°29·7′	2°38·5′W	X	73,74
Grange Barn	Derby	SK2258	53°7·4′	1°39·9′W	X	119
Grange Barn	Dorset	SY9184	50°39·6′	2°7·3′W	X	195
Grange Br	N Yks	SE0245	53°54·3′	1°57·8′W	X	104
Grange Burn	D & G	NX7867	54°59·2′	3°54·0′W	W	84
Grange Burn	Northum	NU2007	55°21·6′	1°40·6′W	W	81
Grangeburn Mill Fm	Northum	NT9653	55°46·5′	2°3·4′W	FM	67,74,75
Grange Chine	I of W	SZ4181	50°37·9′	1°24·8′W	X	196
Grange Cott	Durham	NZ1623	54°36·4′	1°44·7′W	X	92
Grange Cott	Scot Bord	NT8665	55°52·9′	2°13·0′W	X	67
Grange Cottages	Fife	NT2688	56°5·0′	3°10·9′W	X	66
Grange Court	Glos	SO7216	51°50·7′	2°24·0′W	X	162
Grange Cross	Devon	ST0904	50°49·9′	3°17·2′W	X	192
Grange Crossroads	Moray	NJ4754	57°34·6′	2°52·7′W	T	28,29
Grange Dairy	Dorset	SY7883	50°39·0′	2°18·3′W	X	194
Grange de Lings	Lincs	SK9877	53°17·1′	0°31·4′W	X	121
Grange Dell	Midlo	NT2261	55°50·4′	3°14·3′W	X	66
Grange Estate	Dorset	SU1101	50°48·7′	1°50·2′W	T	195
Grange Farm Cotts	Warw	SP1894	52°32·8′	1°43·7′W	X	139
Grange Fell	Cumbr	NY2616	54°32·3′	3°8·2′W	X	89,90
Grange Fell	D & G	NY2481	55°7·3′	3°11·1′W	H	79
Grangefield	Newp	ST3884	51°33·3′	2°53·3′W	X	171
Grange Fields Fm	Derby	SK2537	52°56·0′	1°37·3′W	FM	128
Grange Fm	Beds	SP9458	52°13·0′	0°37·0′W	FM	153
Grange Fm	Beds	SP9626	51°55·7′	0°35·8′W	FM	165
Grange Fm	Beds	SP9649	52°8·1′	0°35·4′W	FM	153
Grange Fm	Beds	SP9731	51°58·4′	0°34·9′W	FM	165
Grange Fm	Beds	TL0366	52°17·2′	0°29·0′W	FM	153
Grange Fm	Beds	TL0464	52°16·1′	0°28·2′W	FM	153
Grange Fm	Beds	TL0531	51°58·3′	0°27·9′W	FM	166
Grange Fm	Beds	TL0755	52°11·2′	0°25·7′W	FM	153
Grange Fm	Beds	TL0766	52°17·1′	0°25·5′W	FM	153
Grange Fm	Beds	TL2647	52°6·6′	0°9·2′W	FM	153
Grange Fm	Bucks	SP6420	51°52·7′	1°3·8′W	FM	164,165
Grange Fm	Bucks	SP7231	51°58·6′	0°56·7′W	FM	152,165
Grange Fm	Bucks	SP7320	51°52·7′	0°56·0′W	FM	165
Grange Fm	Bucks	SU7797	51°40·2′	0°52·8′W	FM	165
Grange Fm	Bucks	SU8099	51°41·3′	0°50·2′W	FM	165
Grange Fm	Bucks	SU8895	51°39·0′	0°43·3′W	FM	165
Grange Fm	Bucks	SU9099	51°41·2′	0°41·5′W	FM	165
Grange Fm	Bucks	SU9883	51°32·5′	0°34·8′W	FM	175,176
Grange Fm	Cambs	TF3503	52°36·7′	0°0·0′E	FM	142
Grange Fm	Cambs	TL0571	52°19·9′	0°27·1′W	FM	153
Grange Fm	Cambs	TL0879	52°24·1′	0°24·3′W	FM	142
Grange Fm	Cambs	TL1278	52°23·5′	0°20·8′W	FM	142
Grange Fm	Cambs	TL1392	52°31·1′	0°19·7′W	FM	142
Grange Fm	Cambs	TL1581	52°25·1′	0°18·1′W	FM	142
Grange Fm	Cambs	TL1981	52°25·1′	0°14·6′W	FM	142
Grange Fm	Cambs	TL2281	52°25·0′	0°12·0′W	FM	142
Grange Fm	Cambs	TL2374	52°21·2′	0°11·2′W	FM	142
Grange Fm	Cambs	TL2577	52°22·8′	0°9·4′W	FM	142
Grange Fm	Cambs	TL3292	52°30·8′	0°2·9′W	FM	142
Grange Fm	Cambs	TL4043	52°4·3′	0°3·0′E	FM	154
Grange Fm	Cambs	TL4162	52°14·5′	0°4·3′E	FM	154
Grange Fm	Cambs	TL4972	52°19·8′	0°11·6′E	FM	154
Grange Fm	Cambs	TL5851	52°8·3′	0°18·9′E	FM	154
Grange Fm	Ches	SJ4257	53°6·7′	2°51·6′W	FM	117
Grange Fm	Ches	SJ4660	53°8·3′	2°48·0′W	FM	117
Grange Fm	Ches	SJ6066	53°11·6′	2°35·5′W	FM	118
Grange Fm	Ches	SJ7965	53°11·1′	2°18·4′W	FM	118
Grange Fm	Cumbr	NY1238	54°44·0′	3°21·6′W	FM	89
Grange Fm	Derby	SK4334	52°54·3′	1°21·2′W	FM	129
Grange Fm	Devon	SS5212	50°53·5′	4°5·9′W	FM	180
Grange Fm	Devon	ST1303	50°49·4′	3°13·7′W	FM	192,193
Grange Fm	D & G	NX7967	54°59·2′	3°53·0′W	FM	84
Grange Fm	Donc	SE6205	53°32·5′	1°3·5′W	FM	111
Grange Fm	Donc	SK4898	53°28·8′	1°16·2′W	FM	111
Grange Fm	Donc	SK5896	53°27·7′	1°7·2′W	FM	111
Grange Fm	Dorset	ST7109	50°53·0′	2°24·4′W	FM	194
Grange Fm	Durham	NZ1438	54°44·5′	1°46·5′W	FM	92
Grange Fm	Essex	TL5818	51°50·5′	0°18·0′E	FM	167
Grange Fm	Essex	TL8422	51°52·2′	0°40·8′E	FM	168
Grange Fm	Essex	TL9302	51°41·2′	0°47·9′E	FM	168
Grange Fm	Essex	TM0102	51°41·1′	0°54·9′E	FM	168
Grange Fm	Essex	TM0830	51°56·0′	1°1·9′E	FM	168,169
Grange Fm	E Yorks	SE7148	53°55·6′	0°54·7′W	FM	105,106
Grange Fm	E Yorks	SE7242	53°52·4′	0°53·9′W	FM	105,106
Grange Fm	E Yorks	SE7437	53°49·7′	0°52·1′W	FM	105,106
Grange Fm	E Yorks	SE7639	53°50·7′	0°50·3′W	FM	105,106
Grange Fm	E Yorks	SE7754	53°58·8′	0°49·1′W	FM	105,106
Grange Fm	E Yorks	SE8134	53°48·0′	0°45·8′W	FM	106
Grange Fm	E Yorks	SE8441	53°51·7′	0°42·9′W	FM	106
Grange Fm	E Yorks	SE9060	54°1·9′	0°37·1′W	FM	101
Grange Fm	E Yorks	SE9641	53°51·6′	0°32·0′W	FM	106
Grange Fm	E Yorks	SE9736	53°48·9′	0°31·2′W	FM	106
Grange Fm	E Yorks	SE9927	53°44·0′	0°29·5′W	FM	106
Grange Fm	E Yorks	SE9939	53°50·5′	0°29·3′W	FM	106
Grange Fm	E Yorks	TA0132	53°46·7′	0°27·6′W	FM	106,107
Grange Fm	Flint	SJ3259	53°7·7′	3°0·6′W	FM	117
Grange Fm	Glos	ST7392	51°37·8′	2°23·0′W	FM	162,172
Grange Fm	Hants	SU5730	51°4·2′	1°10·8′W	FM	185
Grange Fm	Heref	SO4031	51°58·7′	2°52·0′W	FM	149,161
Grange Fm	Kent	TQ6049	51°13·3′	0°17·9′E	FM	188
Grange Fm	Kent	TQ7860	51°18·9′	0°33·6′E	FM	178,188
Grange Fm	Lancs	SD3810	53°35·2′	2°55·8′W	FM	108
Grange Fm	Lancs	SD4428	53°45·0′	2°50·5′W	FM	102
Grange Fm	Lancs	SD5334	53°48·3′	2°42·4′W	FM	102
Grange Fm	Leeds	SE2744	53°53·7′	1°34·9′W	FM	104
Grange Fm	Leic	SK3501	52°36·6′	1°28·6′W	FM	140
Grange Fm	Leic	SK6409	52°40·7′	1°2·8′W	FM	140
Grange Fm	Leic	SK6810	52°41·2′	0°59·2′W	FM	129
Grange Fm	Leic	SK7212	52°42·3′	0°55·7′W	FM	129
Grange Fm	Leic	SK7424	52°48·7′	0°53·7′W	FM	129
Grange Fm	Leic	SK8020	52°46·5′	0°48·4′W	FM	130
Grange Fm	Leic	SP3897	52°34·4′	1°26·0′W	FM	140
Grange Fm	Leic	SP6086	52°28·4′	1°6·6′W	FM	140
Grange Fm	Leic	SP6090	52°30·5′	1°6·6′W	FM	140
Grange Fm	Leic	SP6292	52°31·6′	1°4·8′W	FM	140
Grange Fm	Leic	SP7292	52°31·5′	0°55·9′W	FM	141
Grange Fm	Lincs	SK8335	52°54·6′	0°45·5′W	FM	130
Grange Fm	Lincs	SK8565	53°10·8′	0°43·3′W	FM	121
Grange Fm	Lincs	SK8694	53°26·4′	0°41·9′W	FM	112
Grange Fm	Lincs	SK8897	53°28·0′	0°40·1′W	FM	112
Grange Fm	Lincs	SK9132	52°52·9′	0°38·5′W	FM	130
Grange Fm	Lincs	SK9178	53°17·7′	0°37·7′W	FM	121
Grange Fm	Lincs	SK9328	52°50·7′	0°36·7′W	FM	130
Grange Fm	Lincs	SK9365	53°10·7′	0°36·1′W	FM	121
Grange Fm	Lincs	SK9446	53°0·4′	0°35·5′W	FM	130
Grange Fm	Lincs	SK9783	53°20·3′	0°32·2′W	FM	121
Grange Fm	Lincs	SK9866	53°11·2′	0°31·8′W	FM	121
Grange Fm	Lincs	TA0606	53°32·6′	0°23·6′W	FM	112
Grange Fm	Lincs	TA3401	53°29·6′	0°1·6′E	FM	113
Grange Fm	Lincs	TF0025	52°49·0′	0°30·6′W	FM	130
Grange Fm	Lincs	TF0181	53°19·2′	0°28·6′W	FM	121
Grange Fm	Lincs	TF0343	52°58·7′	0°27·5′W	FM	130
Grange Fm	Lincs	TF0514	52°43·0′	0°26·3′W	FM	130
Grange Fm	Lincs	TF0609	52°40·3′	0°25·5′W	FM	142
Grange Fm	Lincs	TF0613	52°42·5′	0°25·5′W	FM	130,142
Grange Fm	Lincs	TF0736	52°54·9′	0°24·1′W	FM	130
Grange Fm	Lincs	TF0741	52°57·6′	0°24·0′W	FM	130
Grange Fm	Lincs	TF0785	53°21·3′	0°23·1′W	FM	112,121
Grange Fm	Lincs	TF1043	52°58·6′	0°21·3′W	FM	130
Grange Fm	Lincs	TF1128	52°50·5′	0°20·7′W	FM	130
Grange Fm	Lincs	TF1151	53°2·9′	0°20·2′W	FM	121
Grange Fm	Lincs	TF1454	53°4·5′	0°17·5′W	FM	121
Grange Fm	Lincs	TF1489	53°23·4′	0°16·7′W	FM	113,121
Grange Fm	Lincs	TF1581	53°19·0′	0°16·0′W	FM	121
Grange Fm	Lincs	TF1621	52°46·7′	0°16·4′W	FM	130
Grange Fm	Lincs	TF1768	53°12·0′	0°14·5′W	FM	121
Grange Fm	Lincs	TF1769	53°12·5′	0°14·5′W	FM	121
Grange Fm	Lincs	TF1777	53°16·9′	0°14·3′W	FM	121
Grange Fm	Lincs	TF1831	52°52·0′	0°14·4′W	FM	130
Grange Fm	Lincs	TF1973	53°14·7′	0°12·6′W	FM	122
Grange Fm	Lincs	TF1982	53°19·5′	0°12·4′W	FM	122
Grange Fm	Lincs	TF2362	53°8·7′	0°9·2′W	FM	122
Grange Fm	Lincs	TF2485	53°21·1′	0°7·8′W	FM	122
Grange Fm	Lincs	TF2688	53°22·7′	0°5·9′W	FM	113,122
Grange Fm	Lincs	TF2710	52°40·6′	0°6·9′W	FM	131,142
Grange Fm	Lincs	TF2859	53°7·0′	0°4·8′W	FM	122
Grange Fm	Lincs	TF2873	53°14·5′	0°4·5′W	FM	122
Grange Fm	Lincs	TF2890	53°23·7′	0°4·1′W	FM	113
Grange Fm	Lincs	TF2890	53°23·7′	0°4·1′W	FM	113
Grange Fm	Lincs	TF3059	53°7·0′	0°3·0′W	FM	122
Grange Fm	Lincs	TF3065	53°10·2′	0°2·9′W	FM	122
Grange Fm	Lincs	TF3092	53°24·8′	0°2·2′W	FM	113
Grange Fm	Lincs	TF3193	53°25·3′	0°1·3′W	FM	113
Grange Fm	Lincs	TF3274	53°15·0′	0°0·9′W	FM	122
Grange Fm	Lincs	TF3392	53°24·7′	0°0·5′E	FM	113
Grange Fm	Lincs	TF3396	53°26·9′	0°0·6′E	FM	113
Grange Fm	Lincs	TF3758	53°6·3′	0°3·2′E	FM	122
Grange Fm	Lincs	TF3770	53°12·8′	0°3·5′E	FM	122
Grange Fm	Lincs	TF3868	53°11·7′	0°4·4′E	FM	122
Grange Fm	Lincs	TF3891	53°24·1′	0°5·0′E	FM	113
Grange Fm	Lincs	TF4393	53°25·1′	0°9·5′E	FM	113
Grange Fm	Lincs	TF4483	53°19·7′	0°10·1′E	FM	122
Grange Fm	Lincs	TF4570	53°12·7′	0°10·7′E	FM	122
Grange Fm	Lincs	TF4883	53°19·6′	0°13·7′E	FM	122
Grange Fm	Lincs	TF5022	52°46·7′	0°13·8′E	FM	131
Grange Fm	Mil Key	SP8236	52°1·2′	0°47·9′W	FM	152
Grange Fm	Mil Key	SP9046	52°6·5′	0°40·7′W	FM	152
Grange Fm	Mil Key	SP9049	52°8·1′	0°40·7′W	FM	152
Grange Fm	Monm	SO4216	51°50·6′	2°50·1′W	FM	161
Grange Fm	NE Lincs	TA1810	53°34·6′	0°12·7′W	FM	113
Grange Fm	NE Lincs	TA2403	53°30·8′	0°7·4′W	FM	113
Grange Fm	N Lincs	SE8512	53°36·1′	0°42·5′W	FM	112
Grange Fm	N Lincs	SE8606	53°32·9′	0°41·7′W	FM	112
Grange Fm	N Lincs	SE8817	53°38·8′	0°39·7′W	FM	112
Grange Fm	N Lincs	SE9217	53°38·7′	0°36·1′W	FM	112
Grange Fm	N Lincs	SK9499	53°29·0′	0°34·6′W	FM	112
Grange Fm	N Lincs	TA0016	53°38·1′	0°28·8′W	FM	112
Grange Fm	N Lincs	TA0913	53°36·4′	0°20·7′W	FM	112
Grange Fm	Norf	TF4714	52°42·5′	0°11·0′E	FM	131
Grange Fm	Norf	TF5007	52°38·6′	0°13·4′E	FM	143
Grange Fm	Norf	TF6703	52°36·2′	0°28·4′E	FM	143
Grange Fm	Norf	TF8001	52°34·8′	0°39·8′E	FM	144
Grange Fm	Norf	TF8310	52°39·6′	0°42·8′E	FM	132
Grange Fm	Norf	TF9707	52°37·7′	0°55·1′E	FM	144
Grange Fm	Norf	TF9735	52°52·8′	0°56·1′E	FM	132
Grange Fm	Norf	TF9822	52°45·8′	0°56·5′E	FM	132
Grange Fm	Norf	TG0911	52°39·6′	1°5·8′E	FM	133
Grange Fm	Norf	TG1720	52°44·3′	1°13·3′E	FM	133,134
Grange Fm	Norf	TG2315	52°41·4′	1°18·4′E	FM	133,134
Grange Fm	Norf	TG2919	52°43·4′	1°23·9′E	FM	133,134
Grange Fm	Norf	TG3205	52°35·8′	1°25·9′E	FM	134
Grange Fm	Norf	TG3221	52°44·4′	1°26·6′E	FM	133,134
Grange Fm	Norf	TG4317	52°42·0′	1°36·2′E	FM	134
Grange Fm	Norf	TL5096	52°32·7′	0°13·1′E	FM	143
Grange Fm	Norf	TL7088	52°28·0′	0°30·6′E	FM	143
Grange Fm	Norf	TL9687	52°27·0′	0°53·5′E	FM	144
Grange Fm	Norf	TL9791	52°29·1′	0°54·5′E	FM	144
Grange Fm	Norf	TM0380	52°23·0′	0°59·4′E	FM	144
Grange Fm	Norf	TM1387	52°26·6′	1°8·4′E	FM	144,156
Grange Fm	Norf	TM4495	52°30·1′	1°36·1′E	FM	134
Grange Fm	Northnts	SP5753	52°10·6′	1°9·6′W	FM	152
Grange Fm	Northnts	SP5843	52°5·2′	1°8·8′W	FM	152
Grange Fm	Northnts	SP6269	52°19·2′	1°5·0′W	FM	152
Grange Fm	Northnts	SP7085	52°27·7′	0°57·8′W	FM	141
Grange Fm	Northnts	SP7363	52°15·9′	0°55·4′W	FM	152
Grange Fm	Northnts	SP7541	52°4·0′	0°54·0′W	FM	152
Grange Fm	Northnts	SP7670	52°19·6′	0°52·7′W	FM	141
Grange Fm	Northnts	SP7856	52°12·0′	0°51·1′W	FM	152
Grange Fm	Northnts	SP8153	52°10·4′	0°48·5′W	FM	152
Grange Fm	Northnts	SP8181	52°25·5′	0°48·1′W	FM	141
Grange Fm	Notts	SK4757	53°6·7′	1°17·5′W	FM	120
Grange Fm	Notts	SK5323	52°48·4′	1°12·4′W	FM	129
Grange Fm	Notts	SK5450	53°2·9′	1°11·3′W	FM	120
Grange Fm	Notts	SK6655	53°5·5′	1°0·5′W	FM	120
Grange Fm	Notts	SK7168	53°12·5′	0°55·8′W	FM	120
Grange Fm	Notts	SK7536	52°55·2′	0°52·7′W	FM	129
Grange Fm	Notts	SK7967	53°11·9′	0°48·6′W	FM	120,121
Grange Fm	Notts	SK8365	53°10·8′	0°45·1′W	FM	121
Grange Fm	Notts	SK8452	53°3·8′	0°44·4′W	FM	121
Grange Fm	Notts	SK8672	53°14·5′	0°42·3′W	FM	121
Grange Fm	N upon Ty	NZ1665	54°59·0′	1°44·6′W	FM	88
Grange Fm	N Yks	NZ2801	54°24·5′	1°33·7′W	FM	93
Grange Fm	N Yks	NZ3604	54°26·1′	1°26·3′W	FM	93
Grange Fm	N Yks	NZ3608	54°28·2′	1°26·3′W	FM	93
Grange Fm	N Yks	NZ3905	54°26·6′	1°23·5′W	FM	93
Grange Fm	N Yks	SD9278	54°12·1′	2°6·9′W	FM	98
Grange Fm	N Yks	SD9880	54°13·2′	2°1·4′W	FM	98
Grange Fm	N Yks	SE2185	54°15·9′	1°40·2′W	FM	99
Grange Fm	N Yks	SE2289	54°18·0′	1°39·3′W	FM	99
Grange Fm	N Yks	SE2857	54°0·7′	1°33·9′W	FM	104
Grange Fm	N Yks	SE3160	54°2·3′	1°31·2′W	FM	99
Grange Fm	N Yks	SE3690	54°18·5′	1°26·4′W	FM	99
Grange Fm	N Yks	SE5058	54°1·2′	1°13·8′W	FM	105
Grange Fm	N Yks	SE5135	53°48·8′	1°13·1′W	FM	105
Grange Fm	N Yks	SE5420	53°40·7′	1°10·5′W	FM	105
Grange Fm	N Yks	SE5435	53°48·7′	1°10·4′W	FM	105
Grange Fm	N Yks	SE5485	54°15·7′	1°9·8′W	FM	100
Grange Fm	N Yks	SE5861	54°2·7′	1°6·4′W	FM	100
Grange Fm	N Yks	SE6133	53°47·6′	1°4·0′W	FM	105
Grange Fm	N Yks	SE7056	54°0·0′	0°55·5′W	FM	105,106
Grange Fm	N Yks	SE7665	54°4·8′	0°49·9′W	FM	100
Grange Fm	N Yks	SE9695	54°20·7′	0°31·0′W	FM	94,101
Grange Fm	Oxon	SP2518	51°51·8′	1°37·8′W	FM	163
Grange Fm	Oxon	SP2908	51°46·4′	1°34·4′W	FM	164
Grange Fm	Oxon	SP4827	51°56·6′	1°17·7′W	FM	164
Grange Fm	Oxon	SP6122	51°53·8′	1°6·4′W	FM	164,165
Grange Fm	Oxon	SP6427	51°56·5′	1°3·7′W	FM	164,165
Grange Fm	Oxon	SP7405	51°44·6′	0°55·3′W	FM	165
Grange Fm	Peterb	TF2908	52°39·5′	0°5·2′W	FM	142
Grange Fm	Powys	SJ2415	52°43·9′	3°7·1′W	FM	126
Grange Fm	Red & Cl	NZ7318	54°33·4′	0°51·9′W	FM	94
Grange Fm	Roth	SK5079	53°18·6′	1°14·6′W	FM	120
Grange Fm	Rut	TF0212	52°42·0′	0°29·0′W	FM	130
Grange Fm	Shrops	SJ4819	52°46·2′	2°45·8′W	FM	126
Grange Fm	Shrops	SJ6423	52°48·4′	2°31·6′W	FM	127
Grange Fm	Shrops	SJ7504	52°38·2′	2°21·8′W	FM	127
Grange Fm	Sol	SP2377	52°23·7′	1°39·3′W	FM	139
Grange Fm	Staffs	SJ8928	52°51·2′	2°9·4′W	FM	127
Grange Fm	Staffs	SJ9128	52°51·2′	2°7·6′W	FM	127
Grange Fm	Staffs	SJ9840	52°57·7′	2°1·4′W	FM	118
Grange Fm	Staffs	SK0924	52°49·0′	1°51·6′W	FM	128
Grange Fm	Staffs	SK2011	52°42·0′	1°41·8′W	FM	128
Grange Fm	Suff	TL8269	52°17·6′	0°40·5′E	FM	155
Grange Fm	Suff	TL8942	52°2·9′	0°45·8′E	FM	155
Grange Fm	Suff	TL9457	52°10·9′	0°50·7′E	FM	155
Grange Fm	Suff	TL9874	52°19·9′	0°54·8′E	FM	144
Grange Fm	Suff	TM0368	52°16·6′	0°58·9′E	FM	155
Grange Fm	Suff	TM0764	52°14·3′	1°2·3′E	FM	155
Grange Fm	Suff	TM1561	52°12·5′	1°9·2′E	FM	156
Grange Fm	Suff	TM2178	52°21·6′	1°15·1′E	FM	156
Grange Fm	Suff	TM2268	52°16·1′	1°15·6′E	FM	156
Grange Fm	Suff	TM2467	52°15·6′	1°17·3′E	FM	156
Grange Fm	Suff	TM2771	52°17·6′	1°20·1′E	FM	156
Grange Fm	Suff	TM3988	52°26·5′	1°31·4′E	FM	156
Grange Fm	Suff	TM4358	52°10·2′	1°33·6′E	FM	156
Grange Fm	Suff	TM5289	52°26·7′	1°42·9′E	FM	156
Grange Fm	Swin	SU1388	51°35·7′	1°48·3′W	FM	173
Grange Fm	Wals	SK0303	52°37·7′	1°56·9′W	FM	139
Grange Fm	Warw	SP2565	52°17·2′	1°37·6′W	FM	151
Grange Fm	Warw	SP3974	52°22·0′	1°25·2′W	FM	140
Grange Fm	Warw	SP4166	52°17·7′	1°23·5′W	FM	151

Grange Fm	Warw	SP4463	52°16·0'	1°20·9'W	FM	151
Grange Fm	Warw	SP4856	52°12·2'	1°17·5'W	FM	151
Grange Fm	W Berks	SU4870	51°25·8'	1°18·2'W	FM	174
Grange Fm	Wilts	ST7737	51°8·1'	2°19·3'W	FM	183
Grange Fm	Wilts	SU3461	51°21·1'	1°30·3'W	FM	174
Grange Fm	Worcs	SO9067	52°18·3'	2°8·4'W	FM	150
Grange Fm	Worcs	SP0271	52°20·5'	1°57·8'W	FM	139
Grange Fm	W Susx	SZ8694	50°44·6'	0°46·5'W	FM	197
Grange Fm	W Susx	TQ3526	51°1·3'	0°4·1'W	FM	187,198
Grange Fm	York	SE5553	53°58·4'	1°9·3'W	FM	105
Grange Fm	York	SE6349	53°56·2'	1°2·0'W	FM	105,106
Grange Fm	York	SE6649	53°56·2'	0°59·3'W	FM	105,106
Grange Fm	York	SE6657	54°0·5'	0°59·2'W	FM	105,106
Grange Fm	York	SE6846	53°54·6'	0°57·5'W	FM	105,106
Grange Fm, The	Brad	SE0139	53°51·1'	1°58·7'W	FM	104
Grange Fm, The	Essex	TM1721	51°50·9'	1°9·4'E	FM	168,169
Grange Fm, The	Fife	NO5114	56°19·2'	2°47·1'W	FM	59
Grange Fm, The	Hants	SU5536	51°7·5'	1°12·5'W	FM	185
Grange Fm, The	Northnts	SP6876	52°22·9'	0°59·7'W	FM	141
Grange Fm, The	Rut	SK9109	52°40·5'	0°38·8'W	FM	141
Grange Fm, The	Suff	TL7173	52°19·9'	0°31·0'E	FM	154
Grange Fm, The	Suff	TM0940	52°1·4'	1°3·2'E	FM	155,169
Grange Grassings	Cumbr	NY1336	54°42·9'	3°20·6'W	X	89
Grangegreen	Moray	NJ0058	57°36·3'	3°39·9'W	X	27
Grange Green Fm	Warr	SJ5985	53°21·9'	2°36·6'W	FM	108
Grangehall	Aberd	NO6965	56°46·8'	2°30·0'W	X	45
Grange Hall	Cumbr	NY6810	54°29·3'	2°29·2'W	X	91
Grange Hall	Moray	NJ0660	57°37·5'	3°34·0'W	X	27
Grangehall	S Lanak	NS9642	55°39·9'	3°38·8'W	X	72
Grange Head	N Yks	NZ7802	54°24·7'	0°47·5'W	X	94
Grange Heath	Dorset	SY9083	50°39·0'	2°8·1'W	X	195
Grange Hill	Bucks	SP7320	51°52·7'	0°56·0'W	H	165
Grange Hill	Derby	SK3173	53°15·4'	1°31·7'W	H	119
Grange Hill	D & G	NX6947	54°48·3'	4°1·9'W	H	83,84
Grange Hill	Durham	NZ2329	54°39·6'	1°38·2'W	T	93
Grange Hill	Essex	TQ4492	51°36·7'	0°5·2'E	T	177
Grangehill	Fife	NO4700	56°11·6'	2°50·8'W	X	59
Grangehill	Fife	NT2586	56°3·9'	3°11·8'W	X	66
Grange Hill	Moray	NJ0962	57°38·6'	3°31·0'W	H	27
Grangehill	N Ayr	NS3554	55°45·3'	4°37·3'W	X	63
Grange Hill	Scot Bord	NT0721	55°28·7'	3°27·9'W	H	72
Grange Hill	Scot Bord	NT7921	55°29·2'	2°19·5'W	H	74
Grange Hill	Shrops	SJ5601	52°36·5'	2°38·6'W	F	126
Grangehill Fm	Cambs	TF3815	52°43·1'	0°3·0'E	FM	131
Grange Hill Fm	Glos	SP1124	51°55·1'	1°50·0'W	FM	163
Grange Ho	Cumbr	NY5218	54°33·5'	2°44·1'W	X	90
Grange Ho	S Ayr	NS3114	55°23·7'	4°39·7'W	X	70
Grange Ho	York	SE6060	54°2·2'	1°4·6'W	X	100
Grange(Hotel), The	S Glos	ST6382	51°32·4'	2°31·6'W	X	172
Grange House Fm	Ches	SJ8278	53°18·2'	2°15·8'W	FM	118
Grange House Fm	Derby	SK3274	53°16·0'	1°30·8'W	FM	119
Grange Lumb Fm	Derby	SK3174	53°16·0'	1°31·7'W	FM	119
Grange Mains	S Ayr	NS3113	55°23·2'	4°39·6'W	X	70
Grange Manor Fm	E Yorks	SE8541	53°51·7'	0°42·0'W	FM	106
Grange Mill	Angus	NO4444	56°35·3'	2°54·3'W	X	54
Grangemill	Derby	SK2457	53°6·8'	1°38·1'W	T	119
Grange Moor	Kirk	SE2216	53°38·6'	1°39·6'W	T	110
Grangemoor	Northum	NZ0486	55°10·3'	1°55·8'W	X	81
Grange Moor Plantn	N Yks	SE6179	54°12·4'	1°3·5'W	F	100
Grangemount	Pth & Kin	NO2445	56°35·7'	3°13·8'W	X	53
Grangemouth	Falk	NS9381	56°0·9'	3°42·5'W	T	65
Grange Muir	E Ayr	NS5831	55°33·4'	4°14·6'W	X	71
Grangemuir	E Loth	NT6075	55°58·2'	2°38·0'W	X	67
Grangemuir	Fife	NO5304	56°13·8'	2°45·0'W	X	59
Grangeneuk	Falk	NS8273	55°56·4'	3°52·9'W	X	65
Grange of Aberbothrie	Pth & Kin	NO2344	56°35·2'	3°14·8'W	X	53
Grange of Airlie	Angus	NO3151	56°39·0'	3°7·1'W	X	53
Grange of Barry	Angus	NO5334	56°30·0'	2°45·4'W	X	54
Grange of Bladnoch	D & G	NX3657	54°53·1'	4°33·0'W	X	83
Grange of Conon	Angus	NO5844	56°35·4'	2°40·6'W	X	54
Grange of Cree	D & G	NX4559	54°54·4'	4°24·6'W	X	83
Grange of Elcho	Pth & Kin	NO1421	56°22·7'	3°23·1'W	X	53,58
Grange of Lindores	Fife	NO2516	56°20·1'	3°12·3'W	T	59
Grange of Lour	Angus	NO4847	56°37·0'	2°50·4'W	X	54
Grange of Tundergarth	D & G	NY2382	55°7·8'	3°12·0'W	X	79
Grange Outfall	Essex	TM0201	51°40·5'	0°55·7'E	W	168
Grange-Over-Sands	Cumbr	SD4077	54°11·4'	2°54·8'W	T	96,97
Grangepans	Falk	NT0081	56°0·9'	3°35·8'W	T	65
Grange Park	Enf	TQ3195	51°38·5'	0°6·0'W	T	166,176,177
Grange Park	St Hel	SJ4994	53°26·7'	2°45·7'W	T	108
Grange Park	Swin	SU1084	51°33·5'	1°51·0'W	T	
Grange Place	Devon	SX7298	50°46·3'	3°48·5'W	X	191
Grange Plantn	E Yorks	SE7657	54°0·4'	0°50·0'W	F	105,106
Grange Plantn	Scot Bord	NT8664	55°52·4'	2°13·0'W	F	67
Grange (rems of)	Midlo	NT2952	55°45·6'	3°7·4'W	A	66,73
Grangers Fm	Cambs	TL5076	52°21·9'	0°12·6'E	FM	143
Grange Scar	Cumbr	NY6809	54°28·8'	2°29·2'W	X	91
Grangeston	S Ayr	NX2099	55°15·4'	4°49·5'W	X	76
Grange, The	Angus	NO6549	56°38·1'	2°33·8'W	X	54
Grange, The	Beds	TL0255	52°11·3'	0°30·1'W	X	153
Grange, The	Beds	TL0763	52°15·5'	0°25·5'W	X	153
Grange, The	Beds	TL1838	52°1·9'	0°16·4'W	X	153
Grange, The	Bucks	SP8427	51°56·3'	0°46·3'W	X	165
Grange, The	Bucks	SU9492	51°37·4'	0°38·1'W	X	175
Grange, The	Cambs	TL3358	52°12·5'	0°2·8'W	X	154
Grange, The	Cambs	TL3764	52°15·7'	0°0·8'E	X	154
Grange, The	Cambs	TL5250	52°7·9'	0°13·6'E	X	154
Grange, The	Cambs	TL5463	52°14·8'	0°15·8'E	X	154
Grange, The	Cambs	TL5560	52°13·2'	0°16·5'E	X	154
Grange, The	Ches	SJ3477	53°17·4'	2°59·0'W	X	117
Grange, The	Ches	SJ4262	53°9·4'	2°51·6'W	X	117
Grange, The	Ches	SJ5170	53°13·7'	2°43·6'W	X	117
Grange, The	Ches	SJ5354	53°5·1'	2°41·7'W	X	117
Grange, The	Ches	SJ5744	52°59·7'	2°38·0'W	X	117
Grange, The	Ches	SJ6046	53°0·8'	2°35·4'W	X	118
Grange, The	Ches	SJ6349	53°2·5'	2°32·7'W	X	118
Grange, The	Ches	SJ6556	53°6·2'	2°31·0'W	X	118
Grange, The	Ches	SJ6942	52°58·7'	2°27·3'W	X	118
Grange, The	Ches	SJ7446	53°0·9'	2°22·8'W	X	118
Grange, The	Ches	SJ8967	53°12·2'	2°9·5'W	X	118
Grange, The	Derby	SK2713	52°43·1'	1°35·6'W	X	128
Grange, The	Derby	SK2933	52°53·9'	1°33·7'W	X	128
Grange, The	Devon	ST0904	50°49·9'	3°17·2'W	A	192,193
Grange, The	Devon	SX7543	50°16·7'	3°44·9'W	X	202
Grange, The	Devon	SY0295	50°45·0'	3°23·0'W	X	192
Grange, The	Durham	NZ3635	54°42·8'	1°26·0'W	X	93
Grange, The	Essex	TL5623	51°53·2'	0°16·4'E	X	167
Grange, The	Essex	TL5926	51°54·8'	0°19·1'E	X	167
Grange, The	Essex	TL6036	52°0·2'	0°20·3'E	X	154
Grange, The	Essex	TL6400	51°40·7'	0°22·7'E	X	167
Grange, The	Essex	TL6521	51°52·0'	0°24·2'E	X	167
Grange, The	Essex	TL7930	51°56·6'	0°36·7'E	X	167
Grange, The	Essex	TL9332	51°57·4'	0°48·9'E	X	168
Grange, The	Essex	TM1122	51°51·6'	1°4·3'E	X	168,169
Grange, The	Essex	TQ3898	51°40·1'	0°0·1'E	X	166,177
Grange, The	Essex	TQ7395	51°37·9'	0°30·4'E	X	167
Grange, The	E Susx	TQ7821	50°57·9'	0°32·5'E	X	199
Grange, The	E Yorks	SE7345	53°54·0'	0°52·9'W	X	105,106
Grange, The	E Yorks	TA0446	53°54·2'	0°24·6'W	X	107
Grange, The	E Yorks	TA0755	53°59·0'	0°21·7'W	X	107
Grange, The	E Yorks	TA1769	54°6·5'	0°12·2'W	X	101
Grange, The	E Yorks	TA2271	54°7·5'	0°7·6'W	X	101
Grange, The	E Yorks	TA2632	53°46·4'	0°4·9'W	X	107
Grange, The	Flint	SJ1776	53°16·7'	3°14·3'W	X	116
Grange, The	Flint	SJ3361	53°8·8'	2°59·7'W	X	117
Grange, The	Hants	SU3845	51°12·4'	1°27·0'W	X	185
Grange, The	Hants	SU5636	51°7·5'	1°11·6'W	A	185
Grange, The	Hants	SU7556	51°18·1'	0°55·1'W	X	175,186
Grange, The	Heref	SO4626	51°56·0'	2°46·7'W	X	161
Grange, The	Heref	SO7042	52°4·8'	2°25·9'W	X	149
Grange, The	Herts	TL2102	51°42·4'	0°14·5'W	X	166
Grange, The	Herts	TL3639	52°2·2'	0°0·6'W	X	154
Grange, The	Highld	NH6740	57°26·1'	4°12·5'W	X	26
Grange, The	I of M	SC3980	54°11·7'	4°27·7'W	X	95
Grange, The	I of W	SZ5290	50°42·7'	1°15·4'W	X	196
Grange, The	Kent	TQ6538	51°7·3'	0°21·9'E	X	188
Grange, The	Kent	TQ7545	51°10·9'	0°30·6'E	X	188
Grange The	Lancs	SD3645	53°54·1'	2°58·0'W	X	102
Grange, The	Leic	SK6413	52°42·9'	1°2·8'W	X	129
Grange, The	Leic	SK6814	52°43·4'	0°59·2'W	X	129
Grange, The	Leic	SK7710	52°41·2'	0°51·2'W	X	129
Grange, The	Leic	SK7913	52°42·8'	0°49·4'W	X	129
Grange, The	Leic	SK8016	52°44·4'	0°48·5'W	X	130
Grange, The	Leic	SK8318	52°45·4'	0°45·8'W	X	130
Grange, The	Leic	SP6184	52°27·3'	1°5·7'W	X	140
Grange, The	Lincs	SK9068	53°12·3'	0°38·7'W	X	121
Grange, The	Lincs	SK9483	53°20·4'	0°34·9'W	X	121
Grange, The	Lincs	SK9929	52°51·2'	0°31·4'W	X	130
Grange, The	Lincs	TA1602	53°30·3'	0°14·6'W	X	113
Grange, The	Lincs	TF0082	53°19·8'	0°29·5'W	X	121
Grange, The	Lincs	TF0331	52°52·2'	0°27·8'W	X	130
Grange, The	Lincs	TF0779	53°18·1'	0°23·3'W	X	121
Grange, The	Lincs	TF0790	53°24·0'	0°23·0'W	X	112
Grange, The	Lincs	TF0946	53°0·2'	0°22·1'W	X	130
Grange, The	Lincs	TF0994	53°26·1'	0°21·1'W	X	112
Grange, The	Lincs	TF1650	53°2·3'	0°15·8'W	X	121
Grange, The	Lincs	TF1687	53°22·3'	0°15·0'W	X	113,121
Grange, The	Lincs	TF2071	53°13·6'	0°11·7'W	X	122
Grange, The	Lincs	TF2574	53°15·1'	0°7·2'W	X	122
Grange, The	Lincs	TF2763	53°9·2'	0°5·6'W	X	122
Grange, The	Lincs	TF2878	53°17·2'	0°4·4'W	X	122
Grange, The	Lincs	TF3061	53°8·0'	0°3·0'W	X	122
Grange, The	Lincs	TF3065	53°10·2'	0°2·9'W	X	122
Grange, The	Lincs	TF3543	52°58·3'	0°1·0'E	X	131
Grange, The	Lincs	TF3560	53°7·4'	0°1·5'E	X	122
Grange, The	Lincs	TF3595	53°26·3'	0°2·4'E	X	113
Grange, The	Lincs	TF3731	52°51·8'	0°2·5'E	X	131
Grange, The	Lincs	TF4047	53°0·4'	0°5·6'E	X	131
Grange, The	Lincs	TF4068	53°11·7'	0°6·1'E	X	122
Grange, The	Lincs	TF4251	53°2·5'	0°7·5'E	X	122
Grange, The	Lincs	TF4518	52°44·6'	0°9·3'E	X	131
Grange, The	Lincs	TF4665	53°10·0'	0°11·5'E	X	122
Grange, The	Lincs	TF4776	53°15·9'	0°12·7'E	X	122
Grange, The	Lincs	TF5177	53°16·3'	0°16·3'E	X	122
Grange, The	Monm	SO4008	51°46·3'	2°51·8'W	X	161
Grange, The	Monm	SO4113	51°49·0'	2°51·0'W	X	161
Grange, The	Monm	SO4516	51°50·6'	2°47·5'W	X	161
Grange, The	NE Lincs	TA1413	53°36·3'	0°16·2'W	X	113
Grange, The	N Lincs	SE9820	53°40·3'	0°30·6'W	X	106,112
Grange, The	N Lincs	TA1018	53°39·1'	0°19·7'W	X	113
Grange, The	N Lincs	TA1322	53°41·2'	0°16·9'W	X	107,113
Grange, The	Norf	TF6413	52°41·6'	0°26·0'E	X	132,143
Grange, The	Norf	TF8931	52°50·8'	0°48·8'E	X	132
Grange, The	Norf	TF9413	52°41·0'	0°52·6'E	X	132
Grange, The	Norf	TF9712	52°40·4'	0°55·2'E	X	132
Grange, The	Norf	TG1422	52°45·4'	1°10·7'E	T	133
Grange, The	Norf	TG2524	52°46·2'	1°20·5'E	X	133,134
Grange, The	Norf	TG2904	52°35·4'	1°23·3'E	X	134
Grange, The	Norf	TG2908	52°37·5'	1°23·4'E	X	134
Grange, The	Norf	TG3332	52°50·3'	1°28·0'E	X	133
Grange, The	Norf	TG3501	52°33·6'	1°28·4'E	X	134
Grange, The	Norf	TG3826	52°47·0'	1°32·2'E	X	133,134
Grange, The	Norf	TM1480	52°22·8'	1°9·1'E	X	144,156
Grange, The	Norf	TM1588	52°27·1'	1°10·3'E	X	144,156
Grange, The	Norf	TM2080	52°22·7'	1°14·3'E	A	156
Grange, The	Norf	TM2585	52°25·2'	1°18·9'E	X	156
Grange, The	Northnts	SP7856	52°12·0'	0°51·1'W	X	152
Grange, The	Northnts	SP8464	52°16·3'	0°45·7'W	X	152
Grange, The	Northnts	SP8467	52°17·9'	0°45·7'W	X	152
Grange, The	Northnts	SP9077	52°23·2'	0°40·3'W	X	141
Grange, The	Northnts	SP9689	52°29·7'	0°34·8'W	X	141
Grange, The	Northum	NU0513	55°24·9'	1°54·8'W	X	81
Grange, The	Notts	SK6328	52°51·0'	1°3·5'W	X	129
Grange, The	Notts	SK7287	53°22·7'	0°54·6'W	X	112,120
Grange, The	Notts	SK7765	53°10·8'	0°50·5'W	X	120
Grange, The	Notts	SK7948	53°1·6'	0°48·9'W	X	129
Grange, The	N Som	ST3259	51°19·8'	2°58·2'W	X	182
Grange, The	N Yks	NZ2301	54°24·5'	1°38·3'W	X	93
Grange, The	N Yks	NZ5306	54°27·0'	1°10·5'W	X	93
Grange, The	N Yks	NZ5510	54°29·2'	1°8·6'W	X	93
Grange, The	N Yks	NZ6505	54°26·4'	0°59·4'W	X	94
Grange, The	N Yks	NZ7806	54°26·8'	0°47·4'W	X	94
Grange, The	N Yks	SE2390	54°18·5'	1°38·4'W	X	99
Grange, The	N Yks	SE3697	54°22·3'	1°26·3'W	X	99
Grange, The	N Yks	SE3776	54°10·9'	1°25·6'W	X	99
Grange, The	N Yks	SE4076	54°10·9'	1°22·8'W	X	99
Grange, The	N Yks	SE6524	53°42·7'	1°0·5'W	X	105,106
Grange, The	N Yks	SE6863	54°3·7'	0°57·2'W	X	100
Grange, The	N Yks	SE7384	54°15·0'	0°52·4'W	X	100
Grange, The	N Yks	SE7395	54°21·0'	0°52·2'W	X	94,100
Grange, The	Oxon	SP3828	51°57·2'	1°26·4'W	X	164
Grange, The	Oxon	SU2598	51°41·0'	1°37·9'W	X	163
Grange,The	Powys	SO2531	51°58·6'	3°5·1'W	X	161
Grange, The	Rut	SK8607	52°39·5'	0°43·3'W	X	141
Grange, The	Rut	SK9914	52°43·1'	0°31·7'W	X	130
Grange, The	Shrops	SJ3830	52°52·1'	2°54·9'W	X	126
Grange, The	Shrops	SJ3935	52°54·8'	2°54·0'W	X	126
Grange, The	Shrops	SJ4806	52°39·2'	2°45·7'W	X	126
Grange, The	Shrops	SO6199	52°35·5'	2°34·1'W	X	138
Grange, The	Somer	ST2638	51°8·4'	3°3·1'W	X	182
Grange, The	Staffs	SK0249	53°2·5'	1°57·8'W	X	119
Grange, The	Staffs	SK2013	52°43·1'	1°41·8'W	X	128
Grange, The	Suff	TL7169	52°17·8'	0°30·9'E	X	154
Grange, The	Suff	TL9274	52°20·1'	0°49·5'E	X	144
Grange, The	Suff	TL9356	52°10·3'	0°49·7'E	X	155
Grange, The	Suff	TL9761	52°12·9'	0°53·4'E	X	155
Grange, The	Suff	TM0067	52°16·1'	0°56·3'E	X	155
Grange, The	Suff	TM0466	52°15·5'	0°59·7'E	X	155
Grange, The	Suff	TM0935	51°58·7'	1°3·0'E	X	155,169
Grange, The	Suff	TM1077	52°21·3'	1°5·4'E	X	144
Grange, The	Suff	TM1142	52°2·4'	1°5·0'E	X	155,169
Grange, The	Suff	TM1367	52°15·8'	1°7·7'E	X	156
Grange, The	Suff	TM3185	52°25·1'	1°24·2'E	X	156
Grange, The	Suff	TM3465	52°14·2'	1°26·0'E	X	156
Grange, The	Suff	TM4369	52°16·1'	1°34·1'E	X	156
Grange, The	Suff	TM4986	52°25·1'	1°40·1'E	X	156
Grange, The	Surrey	SU8347	51°13·2'	0°48·3'W	X	186
Grange, The	Surrey	SU8741	51°9·9'	0°45·0'W	X	186
Grange, The	Surrey	SU9646	51°12·5'	0°37·2'W	X	186
Grange, The	Surrey	TQ1254	51°16·7'	0°23·3'W	X	187
Grange, The	Surrey	TQ3646	51°12·0'	0°2·8'W	X	187
Grange, The	Surrey	TQ3841	51°9·3'	0°1·2'W	X	187
Grange, The	V of Glam	ST0978	51°29·9'	3°18·3'W	X	171
Grange, The	Warw	SP3748	52°8·0'	1°27·2'W	X	151
Grange, The	Warw	SP4280	52°25·2'	1°22·5'W	X	140
Grange, The	Warw	SP4476	52°23·0'	1°20·8'W	X	140
Grange, The	Win & Maid	SU8885	51°33·6'	0°43·4'W	X	175
Grange, The	Worcs	SO7264	52°16·6'	2°24·2'W	X	138,149
Grange, The	Worcs	SO7948	52°8·0'	2°18·0'W	X	150
Grange, The	Worcs	SO8559	52°14·0'	2°12·8'W	X	150
Grange, The	Worcs	SO9645	52°6·4'	2°3·1'W	X	150
Grange, The	Worcs	SP0937	52°2·1'	1°51·7'W	A	150
Grange, The	Wrekin	SJ6319	52°46·3'	2°32·5'W	X	127
Grange, The	Wrex	SJ4139	52°57·0'	2°52·3'W	X	126
Grange, The	W Susx	TQ2426	51°1·4'	0°13·5'W	X	187,198
Grange, The	W Susx	TQ3437	51°7·2'	0°4·7'W	X	187
Grange, The	York	SE6947	53°55·1'	0°56·5'W	X	105,106
Grangetown	Card	ST1774	51°27·8'	3°11·7'W	T	171
Grangetown	Red & Cl	NZ5520	54°34·6'	1°8·5'W	T	93
Grangetown	Sund	NZ4054	54°53·0'	1°22·2'W	T	88
Grange Villa	Durham	NZ2352	54°52·0'	1°38·1'W	T	88
Grange Village	Glos	SO6712	51°48·6'	2°28·3'W	T	162
Grange Wold Fm	Lincs	TA1607	53°33·0'	0°14·5'W	FM	113
Grange Wood	Derby	SK2714	52°43·6'	1°35·6'W	F	128
Grange Wood	D & G	NX6947	54°48·3'	4°1·9'W	F	83,84
Grange Wood	Northum	NZ2494	55°14·6'	1°36·9'W	F	81
Grange Wood	N Yks	NZ7803	54°25·2'	0°47·5'W	F	94
Grange Wood	N Yks	SE6180	54°13·0'	1°3·5'W	F	100
Grange Wood	N Yks	SE7057	54°0·5'	0°55·5'W	F	105,106
Grange Wood	Shrops	SJ6331	52°52·8'	2°32·6'W	F	127
Grangewood Fm	Derby	SK3174	53°16·0'	1°31·7'W	FM	119
Grangewood Hall	Derby	SK2814	52°43·6'	1°34·7'W	X	128
Grangewood Lodge	Derby	SK2614	52°43·6'	1°36·5'W	X	128
Grange Woods	Dorset	ST6606	50°51·4'	2°28·6'W	F	194
Grang, The	Salf	SJ7499	53°29·5'	2°23·1'W	X	109
Granham Fm	Wilts	SU1767	51°24·3'	1°44·9'W	FM	173
Granham Ho	Lancs	SD6135	53°48·8'	2°35·1'W	X	102,103
Grannock Green	Herts	TL3635	52°0·0'	0°0·7'W	X	154
Grans Barrow	Hants	SU0919	50°58·5'	1°51·9'W	X	184
Grans Barrow (Long Barrow)	Hants	SU0919	50°58·5'	1°51·9'W	A	184
Gransden Lodge	Cambs	TL2853	52°9·9'	0°7·3'W	X	153
Gransden Windmill	Cambs	TL2755	52°10·9'	0°8·1'W	X	153
Gransden Wood	Cambs	TL2655	52°11·0'	0°9·0'W	F	153
Gransmoor	E Yorks	TA1259	54°1·1'	0°17·0'W	T	107
Gransmoor Lodge	E Yorks	TA1359	54°1·1'	0°16·1'W	X	107
Gransmoor Low Ho	E Yorks	TA1159	54°1·1'	0°17·9'W	X	107
Gransmoor Wood	E Yorks	TA1160	54°1·7'	0°17·9'W	F	101
Gransmore Green	Essex	TL6922	51°52·5'	0°27·7'E	T	167
Granston	Pemb	SM8934	51°58·1'	5°3·9'W	T	157
Grant	Pth & Kin	NO1316	56°20·0'	3°24·0'W	X	58
Grantchester	Cambs	TL4355	52°10·7'	0°5·9'E	T	154
Grantfield	Highld	NH7677	57°46·2'	4°4·6'W	X	21
Grantham	Lincs	SK9136	52°55·1'	0°38·4'W	T	130
Grantham Canal	Lincs	SK8634	52°54·0'	0°42·9'W	W	130
Grantham Canal	Notts	SK6830	52°52·0'	0°59·0'W	W	129
Grantham Hall	Kent	TQ6737	51°6·7'	0°23·5'E	X	188
Granthams	Ches	SJ6885	53°21·9'	2°28·4'W	X	109
Grantland	Devon	SS8709	50°52·4'	3°36·0'W	X	192
Grantley Hall	N Yks	SE2469	54°7·2'	1°37·6'W	T	99
Grantlodge	Aberd	NJ7017	57°14·8'	2°29·4'W	X	38
Granton	C of Edin	NT2376	55°58·5'	3°13·6'W	T	66
Granton Harbour	C of Edin	NT2377	55°59·0'	3°13·6'W	X	66
Granton Ho	D & G	NT0709	55°22·2'	3°27·6'W	X	78
Granton Mains	Highld	ND2264	58°33·7'	3°20·0'W	X	11,12
Granton Point	C of Edin	NT2177	55°59·0'	3°15·5'W	X	66
Grantown	Aberd	NJ5754	57°34·7'	2°42·7'W	X	29
Grantown-On-Spey	Highld	NJ0327	57°19·7'	3°36·2'W	T	36
Grantsfield	Fife	NT3399	56°11·0'	3°4·3'W	X	59

Grantsfield	Heref	SO5260	52°14·4′	2°41·8′W	T	137,138,149
Grant's Firs	Wilts	SU1656	51°18·4′	1°45·8′W	F	173
Grant's Fm	Somer	ST1713	50°54·9′	3°10·5′W	FM	181,193
Grant's Fm	Suff	TM2065	52°14·6′	1°13·8′E	FM	156
Grantshouse	Scot Bord	NT8165	55°52·9′	2°17·8′W	T	67
Grants Houses	Durham	NZ4443	54°47·0′	1°18·5′W	X	88
Grantsmuir Fm	Fife	NT2795	56°8·8′	3°10·1′W	FM	59
Grant Thorold	NE Lincs	TA2809	53°34·0′	0°3·6′W	T	113
Granville Country Park	Wrekin	SJ7112	52°42·5′	2°25·4′W	X	127
Graplin	D & G	NX6345	54°47·1′	4°7·4′W	X	83
Grapnells	Essex	TQ9494	51°36·9′	0°48·5′E	X	168,178
Grapnells Fm	Essex	TL8508	51°44·6′	0°41·2′E	FM	168
Grappenhall	Warr	SJ6486	53°22·4′	2°32·1′W	T	109
Grappenhall Heys	Warr	SJ6385	53°21·9′	2°33·0′W	X	109
Grasby	Lincs	TA0804	53°31·5′	0°21·8′W	T	112
Grasby Bottoms	Lincs	TA1006	53°32·6′	0°20·0′W	X	113
Grasby Top	Lincs	TA1006	53°32·6′	0°20·0′W	X	113
Grascott	Devon	SS4610	50°52·4′	4°10·9′W	X	190
Grasmere	Cumbr	NY3306	54°26·9′	3°1·6′W	W	90
Grasmere	Cumbr	NY3307	54°27·5′	3°1·6′W	T	90
Grasmere Common	Cumbr	NY2909	54°28·5′	3°5·3′W	X	89,90
Grasmere Common	Cumbr	NY3009	54°28·5′	3°4·4′W	X	90
Grasmoor	Cumbr	NY1720	54°34·4′	3°16·6′W	H	89,90
Grassavig	N Eil	NB1132	58°11·2′	6°54·6′W	X	13
Grasscroft	Oldham	SD9704	53°32·2′	2°2·3′W	T	109
Grassendale	Liv	SJ3985	53°21·7′	2°54·6′W	T	108
Grassfield	Arg & Bt	NR8160	55°47·3′	5°29·1′W	X	62
Grassfield	Cumbr	NY7744	54°47·7′	2°21·0′W	X	86,87
Grassfield	Scot Bord	NT2050	55°44·5′	3°16·0′W	X	66,73
Grassfield Ho	N Yks	SE1565	54°5·1′	1°45·8′W	X	99
Grassgarth	Cumbr	NY3444	54°47·4′	3°1·2′W	T	85
Grassgarth	Cumbr	SD3582	54°14·0′	2°59·4′W	X	96,97
Grassgarth	Cumbr	SD4499	54°23·3′	2°51·3′W	T	97
Grassgarth	Cumbr	SD4586	54°16·2′	2°50·3′W	X	97
Grassgarth Fm	N Yks	SE1848	53°55·9′	1°43·1′W	FM	104
Grassgate Ho	Norf	TF4711	52°40·8′	0°10·9′E	X	131,143
Grassgill Lodge	Cumbr	NY7212	54°30·4′	2°25·5′W	X	91
Grassgill Rigg	Cumbr	NY7212	54°30·4′	2°25·5′W	X	91
Grassgills	N Yks	SE4261	54°2·8′	1°21·1′W	X	99
Grass Green	Essex	TL7338	52°1·0′	0°31·7′E	T	155
Grassguards	Cumbr	SD2298	54°22·5′	3°11·6′W	X	96
Grasshill Common	Durham	NY8234	54°42·3′	2°16·3′W	X	91,92
Grass Hill Fm	Durham	NY8135	54°42·8′	2°17·3′W	FM	91,92
Grasshill Ho	N Yks	NZ7815	54°31·8′	0°47·3′W	X	94
Grass Holm	Orkney	HY4619	59°3·5′	2°56·0′W	X	6
Grass Holme	Cumbr	SD3892	54°19·4′	2°56·8′W	X	96,97
Grassholme	Durham	NY9221	54°35·3′	2°7·0′W	X	91,92
Grassholme Reservoir	Durham	NY9322	54°35·8′	2°6·1′W	W	91,92
Grassholm Island	Pemb	SM5909	51°43·9′	5°29·0′W	X	157
Grassiehill	Aberd	NJ9052	57°33·7′	2°9·6′W	X	30
Grassieslack	Aberd	NJ7528	57°20·8′	2°24·5′W	X	38
Grassings	Cumbr	NY2453	54°52·2′	3°10·6′W	X	85
Grassington	N Yks	SE0064	54°4·6′	1°59·6′W	T	98
Grassington Moor	N Yks	SE0368	54°6·7′	1°56·8′W	X	98
Grassknop	Cumbr	NY4537	54°43·7′	2°50·8′W	X	90
Grasslands	York	SE5250	53°56·8′	1°12·0′W	X	105
Grasslands Fm	Northnts	SP7180	52°25·0′	0°57·0′W	FM	141
Grasslees	Northum	NY9597	55°16·3′	2°4·3′W	X	81
Grasslees Burn	Northum	NY9598	55°16·8′	2°4·3′W	W	81
Grassmainston	Clackm	NS9292	56°6·8′	3°43·8′W	X	58
Grass Meres	Durham	NY8237	54°43·9′	2°16·3′W	X	91,92
Grassmillees	E Ayr	NS5026	55°30·5′	4°22·1′W	X	70
Grassmillside	E Ayr	NS4240	55°37·9′	4°30·2′W	X	70
Grassmiston	Fife	NO6009	56°16·6′	2°38·3′W	X	59
Grassmoor	Derby	SK4066	53°11·6′	1°23·7′W	T	120
Grass Moor	N Yks	NZ1005	54°26·7′	1°50·3′W	X	92
Grass Paddocks	Cumbr	SD2991	54°18·8′	3°5·1′W	F	96,97
Grass Park	Devon	SS6932	51°4·6′	3°51·8′W	X	180
Grass Point	Arg & Bt	NM7430	56°24·8′	5°39·4′W	X	49
Grassrigg	Cumbr	SD6191	54°19·0′	2°35·6′W	X	97
Grassthorpe	Notts	SK7967	53°11·9′	0°48·6′W	T	120,121
Grassthorpe Holme	Notts	SK8167	53°11·9′	0°46·8′W	X	121
Grassthwaite Howe	Cumbr	NY3816	54°32·4′	2°57·1′W	X	90
Grass Water	Shetld	HU2853	60°15·9′	1°29·1′W	W	3
Grasswell	Sund	NZ3350	54°50·9′	1°28·7′W	T	88
Grass Wood	N Yks	SD9865	54°5·1′	2°1·4′W	F	98
Grassyards	E Ayr	NS4841	55°38·6′	4°24·5′W	X	70
Grassyards	E Ayr	NS5127	55°31·1′	4°21·2′W	X	70
Grassyards Burn	E Ayr	NS4941	55°38·6′	4°23·5′W	W	70
Grassy Cletts	Orkney	ND2887	58°46·1′	3°14·2′W	X	7
Grassy Geos	Orkney	HY5838	59°13·9′	2°43·7′W	X	5
Grassy Nook Fm	Stock on T	NZ4019	54°34·1′	1°22·5′W	FM	93
Graston	Dorset	SY5089	50°42·1′	2°42·1′W	X	194
Grate	Cumbr	SD5089	54°17·9′	2°45·7′W	X	97
Grateley	Hants	SU2741	51°10·3′	1°36·4′W	T	184
Gratnar Fm	Devon	SX7283	50°38·2′	3°48·2′W	FM	191
Gratton	Devon	SS3910	50°52·3′	4°16·9′W	T	190
Gratton	Devon	SS6837	51°7·3′	3°52·8′W	X	180
Gratton	Devon	SX5267	50°29·3′	4°4·8′W	X	201
Gratton	Staffs	SJ9356	53°6·3′	2°5·9′W	X	118
Gratton Dale	Derby	SK2060	53°8·4′	1°41·7′W	X	119
Gratton Hill	Staffs	SK1357	53°6·8′	1°47·9′W	H	119
Gratton Moor	Derby	SK1960	53°8·4′	1°42·6′W	X	119
Gratton Moor Fm	Derby	SK1960	53°8·4′	1°42·6′W	FM	119
Grattons	Devon	SS7301	50°47·9′	3°47·8′W	X	191
Grattons	Devon	SX8062	50°27·0′	3°41·0′W	X	202
Gratwich	Staffs	SK0231	52°52·8′	1°57·8′W	T	128
Gratwicke	W Susx	TQ2120	50°58·2′	0°16·2′W	X	198
Graunt Courts	Essex	TL7022	51°52·5′	0°28·6′E	A	167
Grava Skerries	Shetld	HU1858	60°18·6′	1°40·0′W	X	3
Grave Hill	Powys	SJ1520	52°46·5′	3°15·2′W	H	125
Gravel	Ches	SJ6666	53°11·6′	2°30·1′W	T	118
Gravel	Powys	SO1872	52°20·6′	3°11·8′W	X	136,148
Gravel Bank Fm	Norf	TF5511	52°40·7′	0°18·0′E	FM	131,143
Gravel Bay	Pemb	SM8700	51°39·7′	5°4·4′W	W	157
Gravel Castle	Kent	TR2149	51°12·1′	1°10·2′E	T	179,189
Graveley	Cambs	TL2464	52°15·8′	0°10·6′W	T	153
Graveley	Herts	TL2327	51°55·9′	0°12·3′W	T	166
Gravel Fm	Cambs	TL5273	52°20·3′	0°14·3′E	FM	154
Gravel Fm	Ches	SJ7454	53°5·2′	2°22·9′W	FM	118

Gravel Fm	Glos	SO7212	51°48·6′	2°24·0′W	FM	162
Gravel Hill	Brackn	SU8765	51°22·9′	0°44·6′W	X	175
Gravel Hill	Bucks	TQ0091	51°36·8′	0°33·0′W	T	176
Gravel Hill	Dorset	SY4896	50°45·9′	2°43·9′W	H	193
Gravel Hill	Hants	SU4040	51°9·7′	1°25·3′W	X	185
Gravel Hill	Hants	SU7118	50°57·7′	0°59·0′W	X	197
Gravel Hill	Herts	TL1029	51°57·1′	0°23·6′W	X	166
Gravel Hill	Leic	SP5880	52°25·1′	1°8·4′W	X	140
Gravelhill	Shrops	SJ4813	52°43·0′	2°45·8′W	T	126
Gravel Hill Fm	E Yorks	TA1435	53°48·2′	0°15·7′W	FM	107
Gravel Hill Fm	Lincs	TF0597	53°27·8′	0°24·7′W	FM	112
Gravel Ho	Cambs	TL3197	52°33·5′	0°3·6′W	X	142
Gravel Ho	Cambs	TL4299	52°34·4′	0°6·1′E	X	142,143
Gravel Hole	Oldham	SD9109	53°34·9′	2°7·7′W	T	109
Gravel Hole	Shrops	SJ3636	52°55·3′	2°56·7′W	T	126
Gravelhole Wood	Ches	SJ8772	53°14·9′	2°11·3′W	F	118
Gravelly Bank	Staffs	SK0638	52°56·6′	1°54·2′W	X	128
Gravelly Hill	Birm	SP1090	52°30·7′	1°50·8′W	T	139
Gravelly Hill	Surrey	TQ3353	51°15·9′	0°5·2′W	H	187
Gravelly Way	Staffs	SJ9109	52°41·0′	2°7·6′W	X	127
Gravelpit Copse	Hants	SU6160	51°20·4′	1°7·1′W	F	175
Gravelpit Farm Cotts	Kent	TQ7344	51°10·4′	0°28·9′E	X	188
Gravel Pit Fm	Cambs	TL6064	52°15·3′	0°21·0′E	FM	154
Gravelpit Fm	E Yorks	SE7046	53°54·6′	0°55·6′W	FM	105,106
Gravel Pit Fm	N Yks	SE6858	54°1·1′	0°57·3′W	FM	105,106
Gravelpit Hill	Herts	TL2536	52°0·7′	0°10·3′W	X	153
Gravel Pit Hill	Lincs	TF3669	53°12·3′	0°2·6′E	X	122
Gravelpit Hill	Norf	TF8441	52°56·3′	0°44·7′E	X	132
Gravelpit Hill	Norf	TG0542	52°56·4′	1°3·5′E	X	133
Gravelpit Hill	Norf	TL9695	52°31·3′	0°53·7′E	X	144
Gravelpit Hill	Surrey	SU9051	51°15·3′	0°42·2′W	X	186
Gravelpits	Kent	TQ4846	51°11·9′	0°7·5′E	X	188
Gravel Pit Wood	Notts	SK6180	53°19·0′	1°4·6′W	F	111,120
Gravels	Shrops	SJ3300	52°35·9′	2°59·0′W	T	126
Gravelsbank	Shrops	SJ3300	52°35·9′	2°59·0′W	T	126
Gravels Coppice	Warw	SP2432	51°59·4′	1°38·6′W	F	151
Gravelwalk Plantn	E Yorks	SE9753	53°58·1′	0°30·9′W	F	106
Graven	Shetld	HP4904	60°43·2′	1°5·6′W	X	1
Graven	Shetld	HU4073	60°26·6′	1°15·9′W	X	2,3
Graveney	Kent	TR0562	51°19·4′	0°56·9′E	T	179
Graveney Hill	Kent	TR0563	51°20·0′	0°57·0′E	X	179
Graveney Marshes	Kent	TR0463	51°20·0′	0°56·1′E	X	178,179
Graveney Marshes	Kent	TR0664	51°20·5′	0°57·9′E	X	179
Graven Hill	Oxon	SP5820	51°52·8′	1°9·0′W	H	164
Gravenhunger Moss	Shrops	SJ7342	52°58·7′	2°23·7′W	T	118
Gravesend	Herts	TL4325	51°54·5′	0°5·1′E	T	167
Gravesend	Kent	TQ6574	51°26·7′	0°22·9′E	T	177,178
Gravesend	Powys	SO1067	52°17·9′	3°18·8′W	X	136,148
Graves End	Swan	SS5786	51°33·5′	4°3·4′W	X	159
Gravesend Reach	Thurr	TQ6574	51°26·7′	0°22·9′E	W	177,178
Graves Fm	Lincs	TF3033	52°53·0′	0°3·7′W	FM	131
Grave's Hall	Essex	TL7635	51°59·4′	0°34·2′E	X	155
Graves Park	Sheff	SK3582	53°20·3′	1°28·1′W	X	110,111
Gravestones Fm	Ches	SJ6878	53°18·1′	2°28·4′W	FM	118
Gravetye Manor	W Susx	TQ3634	51°5·6′	0°3·1′W	A	187
Graveyard Fm	Ches	SJ8080	53°19·2′	2°17·6′W	FM	109
Gravity	Orkney	HY7654	59°22·6′	2°24·9′W	X	5
Grawe	I of M	SC4383	54°13·4′	4°24·1′W	X	95
Grawen	Merth Tyd	SO0111	51°47·6′	3°25·7′W	X	160
Grawley	Devon	SS4010	50°52·3′	4°16·1′W	X	190
Gray Bull	Cumbr	NY5309	54°28·7′	2°43·1′W	X	90
Gray Crag	Cumbr	NY4211	54°29·7′	2°53·3′W	X	90
Gray Craig	Arg & Bt	NS0859	55°52·6′	5°10·4′W	X	63
Gray Hill	Monm	ST4393	51°38·2′	2°49·0′W	X	171,172
Gray Hill	Scot Bord	NT4507	55°21·5′	2°51·6′W	H	79
Grayingham	Lincs	SK9396	53°27·4′	0°35·6′W	T	112
Grayingham Cliff	Lincs	SK9495	53°26·8′	0°34·7′W	X	112
Grayingham Grange	Lincs	SK9595	53°26·8′	0°33·8′W	X	112
Grayingham Lodge	Lincs	SK9196	53°27·4′	0°37·4′W	X	112
Graylands	W Susx	TQ1734	51°5·8′	0°19·4′W	X	187
Graymains	Cumbr	SD1195	54°20·8′	3°21·7′W	X	96
Gray Rig	D & G	NY4381	55°7·5′	2°53·2′W	X	79
Grayrigg	Cumbr	SD5797	54°22·2′	2°39·3′W	T	97
Grayrigg Common	Cumbr	SD6099	54°23·3′	2°36·5′W	X	97
Grayrigg Fm	Falk	NS9074	55°57·0′	3°45·3′W	FM	65
Grayrigg Foot	Cumbr	SD5696	54°21·7′	2°40·2′W	X	97
Grayrigg Forest	Cumbr	SD5999	54°23·3′	2°37·5′W	X	97
Grayrigg Head	Cumbr	SD5996	54°21·7′	2°37·4′W	X	97
Grayrigg Pike	Cumbr	SD6099	54°23·3′	2°36·5′W	H	97
Grayrigg Tarn	Cumbr	SD5998	54°22·8′	2°37·5′W	W	97
Grays	N Yks	SE6691	54°18·9′	0°58·7′W	X	94,100
Grays	Thurr	TQ6177	51°28·4′	0°19·5′E	T	177
Graysbridge Fm	Devon	SS6407	50°51·0′	3°55·5′W	FM	191
Grays Fm	Brom	TQ4456	51°17·3′	0°4·3′E	FM	187
Grays Fm	Devon	ST2606	50°51·2′	3°2·7′W	FM	192,193
Gray's Fm	Dorset	ST7418	50°57·9′	2°21·8′W	FM	183
Gray's Fm	Dorset	SY5497	50°46·5′	2°38·8′W	FM	194
Gray's Fm	Essex	TL5501	51°41·4′	0°14·9′E	FM	167
Gray's Fm	Essex	TL6710	51°46·0′	0°25·6′E	FM	167
Gray's Fm	Essex	TL7232	51°57·8′	0°30·6′E	FM	167
Gray's Fm	Essex	TL8010	51°45·8′	0°36·9′E	FM	168
Gray's Fm	Hants	SU6850	51°14·9′	1°1·2′W	FM	185,186
Grays Fm	Kent	TR2267	51°21·7′	1°11·7′E	FM	179
Grays Fm	Lincs	TF1818	52°45·0′	0°14·7′W	FM	130
Gray's Fm	Peterb	TF2306	52°38·5′	0°10·5′W	FM	142
Grayshill	E Dunb	NS7072	55°55·7′	4°4·4′W	X	64
Grayshott	Hants	SU8735	51°6·7′	0°45·0′W	T	186
Grayshott Hall	Hants	SU8535	51°6·7′	0°46·8′W	X	186
Gray Side	S Lanak	NT0027	55°31·8′	3°34·6′W	H	72
Gray's Moor	Cambs	TF4100	52°35·0′	0°5·3′E	X	142,143
Gray's Moor	Devon	SS6407	50°51·0′	3°55·5′W	X	191
Grayson Green	Cumbr	NX9925	54°36·9′	3°33·4′W	T	89
Grayson Ho	Cumbr	NY1248	54°49·4′	3°21·8′W	X	85
Grayson Ho	Fife	NO3621	56°22·9′	3°1·7′W	X	54,59
Grayson's Fm	Lancs	SD4201	53°30·4′	2°52·1′W	FM	108
Graystale	Stir	NS7790	56°5·5′	3°58·2′W	X	57
Graystone	Aberd	NJ5819	57°15·8′	2°41·3′W	X	37
Gray Stone	Aberd	NJ7958	57°36·9′	2°20·6′W	A	29,30
Gray Stone	Northum	NY8290	55°12·5′	2°16·5′W	X	80
Gray Stone	Pth & Kin	NO0211	56°17·1′	3°34·5′W	A	58

Graystone Hill	D & G	NS6705	55°19·5′	4°5·3′W	X	71,77
Graystone Hill	Scot Bord	NY4895	55°15·0′	2°48·7′W	X	79
Graystone Hill	S Lanak	NS6234	55°35·1′	4°10·9′W	X	71
Graystone Hills	N Yks	NZ9104	54°25·6′	0°35·4′W	X	94
Graystone Ho	Cumbr	SD1887	54°16·6′	3°15·1′W	X	96
Graystonelea	W Dunb	NS4384	56°1·6′	4°30·7′W	X	56,64
Graystones	Cumbr	NY1726	54°37·6′	3°16·7′W	H	89,90
Gray Stones	Cumbr	SD1687	54°16·6′	3°17·0′W	X	96
Graystones	Highld	ND3150	58°26·2′	3°10·4′W	X	11,12
Gray Stones	Lancs	SD8339	53°51·1′	2°15·1′W	X	103
Grayston Plain	N Yks	SE2557	54°0·7′	1°36·7′W	X	104
Grayswood	Surrey	SU9134	51°6·1′	0°41·6′W	T	186
Grayswood Common	Surrey	SU9134	51°6·1′	0°41·6′W	X	186
Graythorp	Hartpl	NZ5127	54°38·4′	1°12·2′W	X	93
Graythwaite	Cumbr	NY1123	54°35·9′	3°22·2′W	X	89
Graythwaite Hall	Cumbr	SD3791	54°18·9′	2°57·7′W	X	96,97
Graythwaite Old Hall	Cumbr	SD3790	54°18·4′	2°57·7′W	X	96,97
Gray Wood	E Susx	TQ5316	50°55·6′	0°11·0′E	F	199
Graze Hill Ho	Beds	TL0554	52°10·7′	0°27·5′W	X	153
Grazeley	Wok	SU6966	51°23·6′	1°0·1′W	T	175
Grazeley Court Fm	Wok	SU6967	51°24·1′	1°0·1′W	FM	175
Grazeley Green	W Berks	SU6767	51°24·1′	1°1·8′W	T	175
Grazing Ground Fm	Norf	TM2489	52°27·4′	1°18·2′E	FM	156
Grazing Grounds, The	Norf	TF9107	52°37·9′	0°49·7′E	X	144
Grazing Nook	N Yks	SE2090	54°18·6′	1°41·1′W	X	99
Grèabhal	N Eil	NG0089	57°47·7′	7°2·5′W	H	18
Greadal Fhinn	Highld	NM4764	56°42·2′	6°7·5′W	X	47
Greadal Fhinn (Chambered Cairn)	Highld	NM4764	56°42·2′	6°7·5′W	A	47
Greadon	Devon	SS2917	50°55·9′	4°25·6′W	X	190
Greadow	Corn	SX0658	50°23·6′	4°43·4′W	X	200
Grealin	Highld	NG5061	57°34·5′	6°10·4′W	T	23,24
Greamachary	Highld	NC8539	58°19·7′	3°57·4′W	X	17
Grean	N Eil	NF6703	57°0·1′	7°28·7′W	T	31
Greanamul	N Eil	NF7305	57°1·5′	7°22·9′W	X	31
Greanamul	N Eil	NF8951	57°26·8′	7°10·6′W	X	22
Greanamul	N Eil	NL6189	56°52·4′	7°33·4′W	X	31
Greanamul Deas	N Eil	NF8848	57°25·2′	7°11·4′W	X	22
Greanan	N Eil	NF8888	57°46·6′	7°14·5′W	X	18
Greanascore	N Eil	NF9669	57°36·8′	7°5·0′W	X	18
Greaneclett	N Eil	NF9271	57°37·7′	7°9·1′W	X	18
Greanem	N Eil	NF9277	57°40·9′	7°9·6′W	X	18
Greanem	N Eil	NF9974	57°39·6′	7°2·4′W	X	18
Greasbrough	Roth	SK4195	53°27·2′	1°22·5′W	T	111
Greasby	Wirral	SJ2587	53°22·7′	3°7·2′W	T	108
Greasby Brook	Wirral	SJ2487	53°22·7′	3°8·1′W	W	108
Greasehays Fm	Devon	ST2405	50°50·7′	3°4·4′W	FM	192,193
Greasley	Ches	SJ9466	53°11·7′	2°5·0′W	X	118
Greasley	Notts	SK4947	53°1·3′	1°15·8′W	T	129
Great Abington	Cambs	TL5348	52°6·8′	0°14·5′E	T	154
Great Addington	Northnts	SP9574	52°21·6′	0°35·9′W	T	141
Great Aish	Devon	SX6860	50°25·7′	3°51·1′W	X	202
Great Allan's Plantn	N Yks	NZ2014	54°31·5′	1°41·0′W	F	93
Great Allotment	Durham	NY9515	54°32·1′	2°4·2′W	X	91,92
Great Alne	Warw	SP1259	52°14·0′	1°49·1′W	T	150
Great Altcar	Lancs	SD3206	53°33·0′	3°1·2′W	T	108
Great Ambrook	Devon	SX8265	50°28·6′	3°39·4′W	X	202
Great Amwell	Herts	TL3612	51°47·6′	0°1·3′W	T	166
Great Arming How	Cumbr	SD1899	54°23·0′	3°15·3′W	X	96
Great Arthur	I Scilly	SV9413	49°56·6′	6°15·6′W	X	203
Great Asby	Cumbr	NY6813	54°30·9′	2°29·2′W	T	91
Great Asby Scar	Cumbr	NY6510	54°29·3′	2°32·0′W	X	91
Great Ash	Somer	SS8735	51°6·4′	3°36·5′W	X	181
Great Ashfield	Suff	TL9967	52°16·1′	0°55·4′E	T	155
Great Ash Gill	N Yks	NY8600	54°24·0′	2°12·5′W	W	91,92
Great Ashley	Wilts	ST8162	51°21·6′	2°16·0′W	T	173
Great Ash Moor	Devon	SS8020	50°58·3′	3°42·2′W	X	181
Greatastones	Devon	SX7188	50°40·9′	3°49·2′W	X	191
Great Auclum	W Berks	SU6666	51°23·6′	1°2·7′W	X	175
Great Ayton	N Yks	NZ5611	54°29·7′	1°7·7′W	T	93
Great Ayton Moor	N Yks	NZ5912	54°30·2′	1°4·9′W	X	93
Great Ayton Moor	N Yks	NZ6012	54°30·2′	1°4·0′W	X	94
Great Ayton Sta	N Yks	NZ5710	54°29·2′	1°6·8′W	X	93
Great Baddow	Essex	TL7205	51°43·3′	0°29·8′E	T	167
Great Bailea Fm	Monm	SO4211	51°47·9′	2°50·1′W	FM	161
Great Bainden	E Susx	TQ5926	51°0·9′	0°16·4′E	X	188,199
Great Bangley Fm	Staffs	SK1500	52°36·1′	1°46·3′W	FM	139
Great Bank	Cumbr	NY1401	54°24·1′	3°19·1′W	X	89
Great Bank	Sefton	SD3323	53°42·2′	3°0·5′W	X	102
Great Bardfield	Essex	TL6730	51°56·8′	0°26·2′E	T	167
Great Barford	Beds	TL1252	52°9·5′	0°21·4′W	T	153
Great Barford Ho	Beds	TL1353	52°10·1′	0°20·5′W	X	153
Great Barlington	Devon	SS5616	50°55·8′	4°2·6′W	X	180
Great Barn	Oxon	SU2694	51°38·7′	1°37·1′W	A	163,174
Great Barnets Woods	Monm	ST5194	51°38·8′	2°42·1′W	F	162,172
Great Barnett	Norf	TG0344	52°57·5′	1°1·7′E	W	133
Great Barn Fm	Norf	TF7418	52°44·1′	0°35·0′E	FM	132
Great Barn Fm	W Susx	TQ1412	50°54·0′	0°22·3′W	FM	198
Great Barr	Sand	SP0494	52°32·9′	1°56·1′W	T	139
Great Barrington	Glos	SP2013	51°49·1′	1°42·2′W	T	163
Great Barrow	Ches	SJ4668	53°12·6′	2°48·1′W	T	117
Great Barrow	Cumbr	NY1801	54°24·1′	3°15·4′W	H	89,90
Great Barton	Suff	TL8867	52°16·4′	0°45·7′E	T	155
Great Barton Fm	Devon	SY0399	50°47·2′	3°22·2′W	FM	192
Great Barugh	N Yks	SE7478	54°11·8′	0°51·5′W	T	100
Great Barwick Manor	Herts	TL3818	51°50·8′	0°0·6′E	X	166
Great Batch	Devon	ST2705	50°50·6′	3°1·8′W	X	193
Great Bavington	Northum	NY9880	55°7·1′	2°1·5′W	T	81
Great Bay	Cumbr	NY2519	54°33·9′	3°9·2′W	W	89,90
Great Bayhall	Kent	TQ6239	51°7·9′	0°19·3′E	X	188
Great Bealings	Suff	TM2348	52°5·3′	1°15·7′E	T	169
Great Bear	Somer	ST1638	51°8·3′	3°11·7′W	X	181
Great Bear	W Berks	SU6174	51°27·9′	1°6·9′W	F	175
Great Beard's Wood	Bucks	SU9493	51°37·9′	0°38·1′W	F	175
Great Beccott	Devon	SS6334	51°5·6′	3°57·0′W	X	180
Great Bedwyn	Wilts	SU2764	51°22·7′	1°36·3′W	T	174
Great Beech	E Susx	TQ7216	50°55·3′	0°27·2′E	X	199
Great Beere Fm	Devon	SS6803	50°48·9′	3°52·0′W	FM	191
Great Beere Moor	Devon	SS6902	50°48·4′	3°51·2′W	X	191
Great Beer Fm	Corn	SS2503	50°48·2′	4°28·6′W	FM	190

Great Begbeer	Devon	SX7098	50°46·3′	3°50·2′W	X	191
Great Bell	Cumbr	NY7804	54°26·1′	2°19·9′W	X	91
Great Bells	Kent	TQ9868	51°22·8′	0°51·1′E	X	178
Great Bendysh Wood	Essex	TL6140	52°2·3′	0°21·2′E	F	154
Great Benhams	W Susx	TQ1836	51°6·9′	0°18·5′W	X	187
Great Bentley	Essex	TM1121	51°51·1′	1°4·2′E	T	168,169
Great Bentley Fm	W Susx	TQ3127	51°1·9′	0°7·5′W	FM	187,198
Great Bernera	N Eil	NB1535	58°13·0′	6°50·7′W	X	13
Great Bernera or Beàrnaraigh	N Eil	NB1735	58°13·0′	6°48·7′W	X	8,13
Great Berry	Essex	TQ6787	51°33·7′	0°25·0′E	T	177,178
Great Betley Fm	W Susx	TQ2017	50°56·6′	0°17·1′W	FM	198
Great Bilbo	Heref	SO3529	51°57·6′	2°56·4′W	X	149,161
Great Billing	Northnts	SP8162	52°15·2′	0°48·4′W	T	152
Great Bines	E Susx	TQ6426	51°0·8′	0°20·7′E	X	188,199
Great Bircham	Norf	TF7632	52°51·6′	0°37·3′E	T	132
Great Black Hill	Devon	SS7845	51°11·7′	3°44·4′W	H	180
Great Black Hill	Durham	NY8909	54°28·8′	2°9·8′W	H	92
Great Blackhill Fm	Heref	SO2933	51°59·7′	3°1·7′W	FM	161
Great Blacklaw Hill	Northum	NY6253	54°52·5′	2°35·1′W	H	86
Great Blake Beck	Cumbr	SD7685	54°15·9′	2°21·7′W	W	98
Great Blakenham	Suff	TM1250	52°6·7′	1°6·2′E	T	155
Great Blencow	Cumbr	NY4532	54°41·1′	2°50·8′W	T	90
Great Blowing Gill Beck	N Yks	SE0372	54°8·9′	1°56·8′W	W	98
Great Blunts	Essex	TQ6897	51°39·0′	0°26·1′E	X	167,177
Great Bolas	Wrekin	SJ6421	52°47·4′	2°31·6′W	T	127
Great Bonny Cliff	N Yks	NZ5102	54°24·9′	1°12·4′W	X	93
Great Bookham	Surrey	TQ1354	51°16·7′	0°22·4′W	T	187
Great Bookham Common	Surrey	TQ1256	51°17·8′	0°23·2′W	F	187
Great Borne	Cumbr	NY1216	54°32·1′	3°21·2′W	H	89
Great Bosullow	Corn	SW4133	50°8·7′	5°37·1′W	T	203
Great Bottom	Wilts	ST8133	51°6·0′	2°15·9′W	X	183
Great Bottom	W Susx	SU9712	50°54·2′	0°36·8′W	F	197
Greatbottom Flash	Surrey	SU8953	51°16·4′	0°43·1′W	W	186
Great Bourton	Oxon	SP4545	52°6·3′	1°20·2′W	T	151
Great Bowden	Leic	SP7488	52°29·3′	0°54·2′W	T	141
Great Bowden Hall	Leic	SP7389	52°29·9′	0°55·1′W	X	141
Great Bower	Kent	TR0352	51°14·1′	0°54·9′E	T	179,189
Great Br	Hants	SU3522	51°0·0′	1°29·7′W	X	185
Great Bradford Wood	Wilts	ST8460	51°20·6′	2°13·4′W	F	173
Great Bradley	Devon	SS9013	50°54·6′	3°33·5′W	X	181
Great Bradley	Somer	SS8534	51°5·9′	3°38·2′W	X	181
Great Bradley	Suff	TL6653	52°9·2′	0°26·0′E	T	154
Great Bradley Wood	Wilts	ST7840	51°9·8′	2°18·5′W	F	183
Great Bramingham Fm	Beds	TL0726	51°55·6′	0°26·2′W	FM	166
Great Bramingham Wood	Luton	TL0625	51°55·0′	0°27·1′W	F	166
Great Bramshott Fm	Hants	SU8355	51°17·5′	0°48·2′W	FM	175,186
Great Braxted	Essex	TL8614	51°47·8′	0°42·2′E	T	168
Great Braxted Hall	Essex	TL8514	51°47·9′	0°41·4′E	X	168
Great Breach Wood	Somer	ST5031	51°4·8′	2°42·4′W	F	182,183
Great Bricett	Suff	TM0350	52°6·9′	0°58·3′E	T	155
Great Brickhill	Bucks	SP9030	51°57·9′	0°41·0′W	T	152,165
Great Briddlesford Fm	I of W	SZ5490	50°42·7′	1°13·7′W	FM	196
Great Bridge	Sand	SO9792	52°31·8′	2°2·3′W	T	139
Great Bridgeford	Staffs	SJ8826	52°50·1′	2°10·3′W	T	127
Greatbridge Ho	Hants	SU3522	51°0·1′	1°29·7′W	X	185
Great Brington	Northnts	SP6665	52°17·0′	1°1·5′W	T	152
Great Broadfields	Essex	TL6518	51°50·4′	0°24·1′E	X	167
Great Broadhurst Fm	E Susx	TQ6225	51°0·3′	0°18·9′E	FM	188,199
Great Brockhamhurst	Surrey	TQ1946	51°12·3′	0°17·4′W	X	187
Great Brockhampton Fm	Glos	SP0834	52°0·5′	1°52·6′W	FM	150
Great Brockhurst Fm	W Susx	SU9227	51°2·3′	0°40·9′W	FM	186,197
Great Bromfords	Essex	TQ7391	51°35·7′	0°30·3′E	X	178
Great Bromley	Essex	TM0826	51°53·8′	1°1·8′E	T	168,169
Great Brook	Oxon	SP3401	51°42·6′	1°30·1′W	W	164
Great Brooksend Fm	Kent	TR2968	51°22·1′	1°17·8′E	FM	179
Great Broughton	Cumbr	NY0731	54°40·2′	3°26·1′W	T	89
Great Broughton	N Yks	NZ5406	54°27·0′	1°9·6′W	T	93
Great Brow	D & G	NT2105	55°20·2′	3°14·3′W	H	79
Great Brynhill	V of Glam	ST1070	51°25·5′	3°17·3′W	X	171
Great Brynn Barton	Corn	SW9963	50°26·2′	4°49·5′W	X	200
Great Buckhurst Fm	E Susx	TQ7915	50°54·6′	0°33·2′E	FM	199
Great Buckland	Kent	TQ6663	51°20·7′	0°23·4′E	T	177,178,188
Great Buckstepe	E Susx	TQ6515	50°54·9′	0°21·2′E	X	199
Great Buckster	Northum	NY7172	55°2·7′	2°26·8′W	X	86,87
Great Budbridge Manor	I of W	SZ5283	50°38·9′	1°15·5′W	X	196
Great Budworth	Ches	SJ6677	53°17·6′	2°30·2′W	T	118
Great Bull Hill	Devon	SX9880	50°36·9′	3°26·1′W	X	192
Great Bull Stones	Lancs	SD6757	54°0·7′	2°29·8′W	X	103
Great Burbo Bank	Sefton	SJ2698	53°28·7′	3°6·5′W	X	108
Great Burches Fm	Essex	TQ7889	51°34·5′	0°34·5′E	FM	178
Great Burdon	Darl	NZ3116	54°32·5′	1°30·8′W	T	93
Great Burgh	Surrey	TQ2358	51°18·7′	0°13·7′W	X	187
Great Burney	Cumbr	SD2685	54°15·6′	3°7·7′W	H	96,97
Great Burnt Coppice	Bucks	SU9585	51°33·6′	0°37·4′W	F	175,176
Great Burrow	Devon	SX4991	50°42·2′	4°7·9′W	X	191
Great Burstead	Essex	TQ6892	51°36·3′	0°26·0′E	T	177,178
Great Burwood Fm	Essex	TR0091	51°35·2′	0°53·6′E	FM	178
Great Busby	N Yks	NZ5205	54°26·5′	1°11·5′W	T	93
Great Buscombe	Devon	SS8412	50°54·0′	3°38·6′W	X	180
Great Butts	E Susx	TQ6433	51°4·6′	0°20·9′E	X	188
Great Byards Sale	Northnts	TL0397	52°33·9′	0°28·4′W	F	141
Great Calva	Cumbr	NY2931	54°40·4′	3°5·6′W	H	89,90
Great Campston	Monm	SO3622	51°53·8′	2°55·4′W	X	161
Great Canfield	Essex	TL5918	51°50·5′	0°18·9′E	T	167
Great Canfield Park	Essex	TL5620	51°51·6′	0°16·3′E	X	167
Great Canney	Essex	TL8300	51°40·4′	0°39·2′E	X	168
Great Canon Court	Kent	TQ6854	51°15·8′	0°24·9′E	X	188
Great Cansiron Fm	E Susx	TQ4437	51°7·1′	0°3·8′E	FM	187
Great Cantel	Powys	SO1572	52°20·6′	3°14·5′W	X	136,148
Great Car	E Loth	NT6184	56°3·1′	2°37·1′W	X	67
Great Carlton	Lincs	TF4185	53°20·8′	0°7·5′E	T	122
Great Carr	Suff	TL9372	52°19·0′	0°50·3′E	F	144,155
Great Carr	Suff	TM4690	52°27·4′	1°37·7′E	F	134
Great Carr Ho	N Yks	SE7680	54°12·8′	0°49·7′W	X	100
Great Carrs	Cumbr	NY2600	54°23·7′	3°8·0′W	X	89,90
Great Casterton	Rut	TF0008	52°39·9′	0°30·9′W	T	141
Great Castle	Powys	SO0168	52°18·3′	3°26·7′W	X	136,147
Great Castle Head	Pemb	SM7905	51°42·3′	5°11·5′W	X	157
Great Castle Head	Pemb	SM8405	51°42·4′	5°7·2′W	X	157
Great Cefnyberin	Powys	SO1991	52°30·9′	3°11·2′W	X	136
Great Cellws	Powys	SO0764	52°16·2′	3°21·4′W	T	147
Great Central Railway	Leic	SK5416	52°44·6′	1°11·6′W	X	129
Great Central Rly	C of Leic	SK5809	52°40·8′	1°8·1′W	X	140
Great Chaddington Fm	Wilts	SU1081	51°31·9′	1°51·0′W	FM	173
Great Chalfield	Wilts	ST8663	51°22·2′	2°11·7′W	T	173
Great Chalk Wood	Oxon	SU6280	51°31·2′	1°6·0′W	F	175
Great Chart	Kent	TQ9841	51°8·3′	0°50·2′E	T	189
Great Chattenden Wood	Medway	TQ7473	51°26·0′	0°30·6′E	F	178
Great Chatwell	Staffs	SJ7914	52°43·6′	2°18·3′W	T	127
Great Chell	C of Stoke	SJ8752	53°4·1′	2°11·2′W	T	118
Great Chesterford	Essex	TL5042	52°3·6′	0°11·7′E	T	154
Great Chesters	Northum	NY7066	54°59·5′	2°27·7′W	X	86,87
Great Cheveney	Kent	TQ7342	51°9·3′	0°28·8′E	T	188
Great Cheverell	Wilts	ST9854	51°17·3′	2°1·3′W	T	184
Great Cheverell Hill	Wilts	ST9752	51°16·3′	2°2·2′W	X	184
Great Childerley Village	Cambs	TL3561	52°14·1′	0°1·0′W	A	154
Great Chilton	Durham	NZ2930	54°40·1′	1°32·6′W	T	93
Great Chishill	Cambs	TL4238	52°1·6′	0°4·6′E	T	154
Great Cil-llwch	Monm	SO3813	51°49·0′	2°53·6′W	A	161
Great Clacton	Essex	TM1716	51°48·3′	1°9·3′E	T	168,169
Great Clark's Fm	Essex	TL6332	51°58·0′	0°22·8′E	FM	167
Great Claydons	Essex	TL7602	51°41·6′	0°33·2′E	T	167
Great Cliff	Wakf	SE3016	53°38·6′	1°32·4′W	T	110,111
Great Clifton	Cumbr	NY0429	54°39·1′	3°28·9′W	T	89
Great Cloddiau	Powys	SO1690	52°30·3′	3°13·9′W	X	136
Great Close	N Yks	SD9167	54°6·2′	2°7·8′W	X	98
Great Close Scar	N Yks	SD9066	54°5·6′	2°8·8′W	X	98
Great Clough	Lancs	SD8027	53°44·6′	2°17·8′W	X	103
Great Coates	NE Lincs	TA2310	53°34·6′	0°8·1′W	T	113
Great Cob Island	Essex	TL9811	51°46·0′	0°52·6′E	X	168
Great Cockerhurst	Kent	TQ5063	51°21·0′	0°9·6′E	X	177,188
Great Cocklake	Cumbr	NY7928	54°39·0′	2°19·1′W	X	91
Great Cocklake	Cumbr	NY8028	54°39·0′	2°18·2′W	X	91,92
Great Cocktree	Devon	SX6698	50°46·2′	3°53·6′W	X	191
Great Cockup	Cumbr	NY2733	54°41·5′	3°7·5′W	H	89,90
Great Codham Hall	Essex	TL7328	51°55·6′	0°31·4′E	A	167
Great Coleford	Devon	SS8919	50°57·8′	3°34·5′W	X	181
Great Colemans	Essex	TL5401	51°41·4′	0°14·1′E	X	167
Great Coll Wood	Dorset	SY8899	50°47·7′	2°9·8′W	F	194
Great Comberton	Worcs	SO9542	52°4·8′	2°4·0′W	T	150
Great Common	Norf	TM0382	52°24·1′	0°59·5′E	X	144
Great Common	Somer	SS8829	51°3·2′	3°35·5′W	F	181
Great Common	Suff	TM3787	52°26·0′	1°29·6′E	T	156
Great Common	W Susx	SU8824	51°0·7′	0°44·3′W	F	197
Great Common	W Susx	TQ0127	51°2·2′	0°33·2′W	F	186,197
Great Common Fm	Cambs	TL3359	52°13·0′	0°2·8′W	FM	154
Great Comp Garden	Kent	TQ6356	51°17·0′	0°20·6′E	X	188
Great Conster Fm	E Susx	TQ8420	50°57·2′	0°37·6′E	FM	199
Great Cookshall Wood	Bucks	SU8396	51°39·6′	0°47·6′W	F	165
Great Cooper's Corner Fm	W Susx	TQ2930	51°3·5′	0°9·2′W	FM	187
Great Coop House Fm	Durham	NZ3944	54°47·6′	1°23·2′W	FM	88
Great Coppice	Cumbr	SD3596	54°21·6′	2°59·6′W	F	96,97
Great Copse	Oxon	SU5999	51°41·4′	1°8·4′W	F	164
Great Copt Hall	Suff	TM0049	52°6·4′	0°55·6′E	X	155
Great Corby	Cumbr	NY4754	54°52·9′	2°49·1′W	T	86
Great Cornard	Suff	TL8840	52°1·8′	0°44·8′E	T	155
Great Corras	Heref	SO4124	51°54·9′	2°51·1′W	X	161
Great Coum	Cumbr	SD6099	54°23·3′	2°36·5′W	X	97
Great Coum	Cumbr	SD7083	54°14·8′	2°27·2′W	H	98
Great Coven's Wood	Cambs	TL6253	52°9·3′	0°22·5′E	F	154
Great Covert	Hants	SU4019	50°58·4′	1°25·4′W	F	185
Great Covert	Oxon	SP7403	51°43·5′	0°55·3′W	F	165
Great Cowbridge Grange	Essex	TQ6595	51°38·0′	0°23·4′E	X	167,177
Great Cowden	E Yorks	TA2242	53°51·8′	0°8·3′W	T	107
Great Coxwell	Oxon	SU2693	51°38·3′	1°37·1′W	T	163,174
Great Cozens	Herts	TL3715	51°49·2′	0°0·3′W	X	166
Great Crabbles Wood	Kent	TQ7070	51°24·4′	0°27·1′E	F	178
Great Crag	Cumbr	NY2614	54°31·2′	3°8·2′W	X	89,90
Great Crakehall	N Yks	SE2489	54°18·0′	1°37·5′W	T	99
Great Cransley	Northnts	SP8376	52°22·8′	0°46·4′W	T	141
Great Creaton Lodge	Northnts	SP7072	52°20·7′	0°57·9′W	X	141
Great Crebawethan	I Scilly	SV8307	49°53·0′	6°24·4′W	X	203
Great Creigiau	Powys	SO1963	52°15·8′	3°10·8′W	X	148
Great Cressingham	Norf	TF8501	52°34·7′	0°44·2′E	T	144
Great Cressingham Wood	Norf	TF8402	52°35·3′	0°43·4′E	F	144
Great Crimbles	Lancs	SD4550	53°56·8′	2°49·9′W	X	102
Great Crosby	Sefton	SJ3299	53°29·2′	3°1·1′W	T	108
Great Cross	D & G	NX6750	54°49·9′	4°3·8′W	X	83,84
Great Crosthwaite	Cumbr	NY2624	54°36·6′	3°8·3′W	T	89,90
Great Crwys	Monm	SO4416	51°50·6′	2°48·4′W	X	161
Great Cubley	Derby	SK1638	52°56·6′	1°45·3′W	T	128
Great Cumberwell	Wilts	ST8263	51°22·2′	2°15·1′W	X	173
Great Cumbrae Island	N Ayr	NS1656	55°46·0′	4°55·5′W	X	63
Great Cutts Fm	Herts	TL1317	51°50·6′	0°21·2′W	FM	166
Great Dalby	Leic	SK7414	52°43·3′	0°53·9′W	T	129
Great Dams Fen	Cambs	TL4782	52°25·2′	0°10·1′E	X	143
Great Dams Fm	Cambs	TL4883	52°25·7′	0°11·0′E	FM	143
Great Danegate	E Susx	TQ5632	51°4·2′	0°14·0′E	X	188
Great Danmoor Copse	Hants	SU7360	51°20·3′	0°56·7′W	F	175,186
Great Daux	W Susx	TQ1633	51°5·3′	0°20·2′W	X	187
Great Dawkins	Essex	TL6339	52°1·8′	0°23·0′E	X	154
Great Deane Wood	Hants	SU5552	51°16·1′	1°12·3′W	F	185
Great Deep	W Susx	SU7503	50°49·5′	0°55·7′W	W	197
Great Derwarthy	Devon	SS3611	50°52·8′	4°19·5′W	X	190
Great Dewlands	E Susx	TQ5426	51°1·0′	0°12·1′E	X	188,199
Great Dib	Leeds	SE1944	53°53·8′	1°42·2′W	F	104
Great Dixter	E Susx	TQ8125	51°0·0′	0°35·2′E	A	188,199
Great Dodd	Cumbr	NY3420	54°34·5′	3°0·8′W	H	90
Great Dodd	Cumbr	NY8815	54°32·1′	2°10·7′W	X	91,92
Great Dodd	Northum	NY7992	55°13·6′	2°19·4′W	X	80
Great Doddington	Northnts	SP8864	52°16·3′	0°42·2′W	T	152
Great Domsey	Essex	TL8821	51°51·6′	0°44·2′E	X	168
Great Dorweeke	Devon	SS9506	50°50·9′	3°29·1′W	X	192
Great Douk Cave	N Yks	SD7476	54°11·0′	2°23·5′W	X	98
Great Dour	Northum	NT7903	55°19·5′	2°19·4′W	X	80
Great Doward	Heref	SO5516	51°50·7′	2°38·8′W	T	162
Great Down	W Susx	SU9610	50°53·1′	0°37·7′W	X	197
Great Down Clump	Dorset	ST7801	50°48·7′	2°18·4′W	F	194
Great Downs	Somer	ST1223	51°0·2′	3°14·9′W	X	181,193
Great Downs Fm	Essex	TQ4696	51°38·9′	0°7·0′E	FM	167,177
Great Dudland	Lancs	SD8047	53°55·4′	2°17·9′W	X	103
Great Dummacks	Cumbr	SD6796	54°21·8′	2°30·1′W	X	98
Great Dun Fell	Cumbr	NY7132	54°41·2′	2°26·6′W	H	91
Great Dunham	Norf	TF8714	52°41·7′	0°46·4′E	T	132
Great Dunham Hall	Norf	TF8615	52°42·3′	0°45·6′E	X	132
Great Dunkilns	Glos	SO5703	51°43·7′	2°37·0′W	X	162
Great Dunmow	Essex	TL6122	51°52·6′	0°20·7′E	T	167
Great Durnford	Wilts	SU1338	51°8·7′	1°48·5′W	T	184
Great Early Grove	Beds	TL0953	52°10·1′	0°24·0′W	F	153
Great Easby	Cumbr	NY5362	54°57·3′	2°43·6′W	X	86
Great Easton	Essex	TL6125	51°54·2′	0°20·8′E	T	167
Great Easton	Leic	SP8493	52°31·9′	0°45·3′W	T	141
Great Easton Lodge	Leic	SP8395	52°33·0′	0°46·2′W	X	141
Great East Standen Manor	I of W	SZ5287	50°41·0′	1°15·5′W	X	196
Great Eau	Lincs	TF4384	53°20·2′	0°9·3′E	W	122
Great Ebb	Dorset	SY4391	50°43·2′	2°48·1′W	X	193
Great Eccleston	Lancs	SD4240	53°51·4′	2°52·5′W	T	102
Great Edge	Lancs	SD9142	53°52·7′	2°7·8′W	X	103
Great Edstone	N Yks	SE7084	54°15·1′	0°55·1′W	T	100
Great Eggleshope Beck	Durham	NY9630	54°40·1′	2°3·3′W	W	91,92
Great Ellingham	Norf	TM0197	52°32·2′	0°58·2′E	T	144
Great Elm	Somer	ST7449	51°14·6′	2°22·0′W	T	183
Great Elm Fm	Wilts	ST9887	51°35·1′	2°1·3′W	FM	173
Great End	Cumbr	NY2208	54°27·9′	3°11·8′W	H	89,90
Greatend Crag	Cumbr	NY2517	54°32·8′	3°9·1′W	X	89,90
Great Engeham Manor	Kent	TQ9437	51°6·2′	0°46·7′E	X	189
Great England Hill	E Yorks	TA3227	53°43·6′	0°0·5′E	X	107
Great Englebourne	Devon	SX7756	50°23·7′	3°43·5′W	X	202
Great Enton	Surrey	SU9539	51°8·8′	0°38·1′W	X	186
Great Eppleton	Sund	NZ3648	54°49·8′	1°26·0′W	T	88
Greater Brighter Fm	Corn	SX0476	50°33·3′	4°45·6′W	FM	200
Greater Poston	Shrops	SO5482	52°26·3′	2°40·2′W	X	137,138
Great Ervills Fm	Hants	SU6312	50°54·5′	1°5·9′W	FM	196
Great Eversden	Cambs	TL3653	52°9·7′	0°0·3′W	T	154
Great Ewe Fell	Cumbr	NY7007	54°27·7′	2°27·3′W	H	91
Great Face, The	Arg & Bt	NM3235	56°26·1′	6°20·4′W	X	46,47,48
Great Fairwood Fm	Devon	SX8194	50°44·2′	3°40·8′W	FM	191
Great Farley Wood	Worcs	SO9578	52°24·2′	2°4·0′W	F	139
Great Fen	Cambs	TL6078	52°22·8′	0°21·4′E	X	143
Great Fen	Lincs	TF2744	52°58·9′	0°6·1′W	X	131
Great Fen	Norf	TG3621	52°44·3′	1°30·2′E	W	133,134
Great Fen	Norf	TM0487	52°26·8′	1°0·5′E	X	144
Great Fen	Norf	TM0580	52°23·0′	1°1·1′E	W	144
Great Fencote	N Yks	SE2893	54°20·2′	1°33·7′W	T	99
Great Fern Hill	Cambs	TL3478	52°23·2′	0°1·5′W	X	142
Great Fernhill	Shrops	SJ3132	52°53·1′	3°1·1′W	X	126
Great Ferny Ball	Somer	SS7936	51°6·9′	3°43·3′W	H	180
Greatfield	Wilts	SU0785	51°34·1′	1°53·5′W	T	173
Great Finborough	Suff	TM0157	52°10·7′	0°56·8′E	T	155
Great Fir Covert	Suff	TL8067	52°16·5′	0°38·7′E	F	155
Great Fletchwood Fm	Hants	SU3311	50°54·1′	1°31·5′W	FM	196
Great Force Gill Rigg	Cumbr	SD6797	54°22·3′	2°30·1′W	X	98
Greatford	Lincs	TF0811	52°41·4′	0°23·7′W	T	130,142
Greatford Cut	Lincs	TF1010	52°40·8′	0°22·0′W	W	130,142
Great Fore Down	Wilts	SU0454	51°17·3′	1°56·2′W	X	184
Great Fosters	Surrey	TQ0169	51°24·9′	0°32·5′W	X	176
Great Fox Covert	Leic	SK4605	52°38·7′	1°18·8′W	F	140
Great Framlands	Leic	SK7421	52°47·1′	0°53·8′W	X	129
Great Fransham	Norf	TF8913	52°41·1′	0°48·2′E	T	132
Great Frenches Park	W Susx	TQ3439	51°8·3′	0°4·7′W	X	187
Great Friars' Thornes	Norf	TF7810	52°39·7′	0°38·3′E	X	132
Great Fryup Beck	N Yks	NZ7204	54°25·8′	0°53·0′W	X	94
Great Fryup Dale	N Yks	NZ7304	54°25·8′	0°52·1′W	X	94
Great Fulford	Devon	SX7891	50°42·6′	3°43·3′W	A	191
Great Funtley Fm	Hants	SU5508	50°52·4′	1°12·7′W	FM	196
Great Furze Hill	Suff	TL9180	52°23·3′	0°48·8′E	X	144
Great Furze Ho	Bucks	SP7531	51°58·6′	0°54·1′W	X	152,165
Great Furzenip	Pemb	SR8898	51°38·7′	5°3·5′W	X	158
Great Gable	Cumbr	NY2110	54°29·0′	3°12·7′W	H	89,90
Great Gaddesden	Herts	TL0211	51°47·5′	0°30·9′W	T	166
Great Ganilly	I Scilly	SV9414	49°57·1′	6°15·6′W	X	203
Great Ganinick	I Scilly	SV9313	49°56·5′	6°16·4′W	X	203
Greatgap	Bucks	SP9416	51°50·3′	0°37·7′W	T	165
Great Gargus	Corn	SW9446	50°16·9′	4°53·1′W	X	204
Great Garlands Fm	Thurr	TQ7082	51°30·9′	0°27·4′E	FM	178
Great Gate	Staffs	SK0540	52°57·7′	1°55·1′W	T	119,128
Great Gate Wood	Donc	SE6604	53°31·9′	0°59·8′W	F	111
Greatgate Wood	Staffs	SK0540	52°57·7′	1°55·1′W	F	119,128
Great Gidding	Cambs	TL1183	52°26·3′	0°21·6′W	T	142
Great Gill	N Yks	SD8191	54°19·1′	2°17·1′W	W	98
Great Gimble	Corn	SX2470	50°30·4′	4°28·6′W	X	201
Great Givendale	E Yorks	SE8153	53°58·2′	0°45·5′W	X	106
Great Givendale	N Yks	SE3369	54°7·2′	1°29·3′W	X	99
Great Glemham	Suff	TM3361	52°12·1′	1°25·0′E	T	156
Great Glemham Wood	Suff	TM3360	52°11·6′	1°25·0′E	F	156
Great Glen	Leic	SP6597	52°34·2′	1°2·1′W	T	141
Great Glen Cycle Route	Highld	NH4317	57°13·3′	4°35·6′W	X	34
Great Glen Ho	Leic	SP6697	52°34·2′	1°1·2′W	X	141
Great Gnats' Head	Devon	SX6167	50°29·4′	3°57·2′W	X	202
Great Gobions Fm	Herts	TL2917	51°50·4′	0°7·3′W	FM	166
Great Gonerby	Lincs	SK8938	52°56·2′	0°40·1′W	T	130
Great Gormellick	Corn	SX2462	50°26·1′	4°28·3′W	X	201
Great Gornhay	Devon	SS9713	50°54·7′	3°27·5′W	X	181
Great Gorse	Lincs	TF0834	52°53·8′	0°23·3′W	F	130
Great Goswell Copse	Hants	SU3903	50°49·7′	1°26·4′W	F	196
Great Gott	Monm	SO2918	51°51·6′	3°1·5′W	X	161
Great Goytre	Monm	SO3524	51°54·9′	2°56·3′W	X	161
Great Graces Fm	Essex	TL7606	51°43·7′	0°33·3′E	FM	167
Great Grains Clough	Barns	SE1202	53°31·1′	1°48·7′W	X	110
Great Gransden	Cambs	TL2755	52°10·9′	0°8·1′W	T	153
Great Grassoms	Cumbr	SD1387	54°16·5′	3°19·7′W	X	96
Great Green	Cambs	TL2844	52°5·0′	0°7·5′W	T	153
Great Green	Norf	TM2789	52°27·3′	1°20·9′E	X	156
Great Green	Suff	TL9155	52°9·8′	0°48·0′E	T	155
Great Green	Suff	TL9466	52°15·7′	0°51·0′E	X	155
Great Green	Suff	TM0776	52°20·8′	1°2·8′E	T	144
Great Green	Suff	TM1277	52°21·2′	1°7·2′E	T	144
Great Green Hows	Cumbr	SD3589	54°17·8′	2°59·5′W	X	96,97
Great Gregories Fm	Essex	TL4500	51°41·0′	0°6·2′E	FM	167

Great Greys	Suff	TL9039	52°1·2′	0°46·5′E	X	155
Great Grogley Downs	Corn	SX0167	50°28·4′	4°47·9′W	X	200
Great Ground Fm	Wilts	ST7636	51°7·6′	2°20·2′W	FM	183
Great Ground Hill	Wilts	ST9929	51°3·9′	2°0·5′W	H	184
Great Grove	Suff	TL9375	52°20·6′	0°50·4′E	F	144
Great Grove Fm	Surrey	TQ0364	51°22·2′	0°30·8′W	FM	176,186
Great Grovehurst	Kent	TQ9066	51°21·9′	0°44·2′E	X	178
Great Gutton	Devon	SS8602	50°48·6′	3°36·7′W	X	191
Great Gwern-y-bwch	Powys	SO2351	52°9·4′	3°7·1′W	X	148
Great Habton	N Yks	SE7576	54°10·7′	0°50·6′W	T	100
Great Hagg	Cumbr	SD3586	54°16·2′	2°59·5′W	X	96,97
Great Hagley	Shrops	SO3476	52°22·9′	2°57·8′W	X	137,148
Great Hague	Lancs	SD8943	53°53·2′	2°9·6′W	X	103
Great Haldon	Devon	SX8983	50°38·4′	3°33·8′W	X	192
Great Hale	Lincs	TF1442	52°58·0′	0°17·7′W	T	130
Great Hale Fen	Lincs	TF1843	52°58·5′	0°14·2′W	X	130
Great Halfsbury	Devon	SS6117	50°56·4′	3°58·3′W	X	180
Greathall Gill	Cumbr	NY1403	54°25·2′	3°19·1′W	W	89
Great Hallingbury	Essex	TL5119	51°51·2′	0°11·9′E	T	167
Great Halls	Devon	SY0391	50°42·9′	3°22·1′W	X	192
Greatham	Hants	SU7730	51°4·1′	0°53·7′W	T	186
Greatham	Hartpl	NZ4927	54°38·4′	1°14·0′W	T	93
Greatham	W Susx	TQ0415	50°55·7′	0°30·8′W	T	197
Greatham Bridge	W Susx	TQ0316	50°56·3′	0°31·7′W	X	197
Greatham Common	W Susx	TQ0415	50°55·7′	0°30·8′W	X	197
Great Hameldon	Lancs	SD7928	53°45·1′	2°18·7′W	H	103
Greatham Moor	Hants	SU7830	51°4·1′	0°52·8′W	X	186
Great Hampden	Bucks	SP8401	51°42·3′	0°46·7′W	T	165
Great Hamston	V of Glam	ST0971	51°26·1′	3°18·2′W	X	171
Great Hanging Br	Lancs	SD4617	53°39·0′	2°48·6′W	X	108
Great Hangman	Devon	SS6048	51°13·1′	3°59·9′W	H	180
Great Hardwick	Monm	SO3111	51°47·8′	2°59·6′W	X	161
Great Hares Head	Pemb	SM9918	51°49·7′	4°54·6′W	X	157,158
Great Harlow	N Yks	SD6961	54°2·9′	2°28·0′W	X	98
Great Harrowden	Northnts	SP8770	52°19·5′	0°43·0′W	T	141
Great Harwood	Lancs	SD7332	53°47·3′	2°24·2′W	T	103
Great Haseley	Oxon	SP6401	51°42·5′	1°4·0′W	T	164,165
Great Hasse Fm	Cambs	TL6076	52°21·7′	0°21·4′E	FM	143
Great Hatfield	E Yorks	TA1842	53°51·9′	0°11·9′W	T	107
Great Hautbois	Norf	TG2621	52°44·6′	1°21·3′E	X	133
Great Haw	N Yks	SE0779	54°12·6′	1°53·1′W	H	99
Great Haye Fm	Devon	SX4478	50°35·1′	4°11·8′W	FM	201
Great Hayes	Essex	TQ8398	51°39·3′	0°39·1′E	X	168
Great Hayes Wood	Beds	SP9661	52°14·6′	0°35·2′W	F	153
Great Haywood	Staffs	SK0022	52°48·0′	1°59·6′W	T	128
Great Hazes	Brackn	SU8474	51°27·8′	0°47·1′W	F	175
Great Head Ho	Cumbr	SD3076	54°10·7′	3°3·9′W	X	96,97
Great Headon Plantation	Somer	SS9445	51°11·9′	3°30·6′W	F	181
Great Heale	Devon	SX7597	50°45·8′	3°46·0′W	X	191
Great Heaplaw	Northum	NY6848	54°49·8′	2°29·5′W	X	86,87
Great Heasley	Devon	SS7332	51°4·6′	3°48·4′W	X	180
Great Heath	Cov	SP3480	52°25·3′	1°29·6′W	T	140
Great Heath	Heref	SO5562	52°15·5′	2°39·2′W	X	137,138,149
Great Heath	Norf	TF9722	52°45·8′	0°55·6′E	X	132
Great Heck	N Yks	SE5921	53°41·2′	1°6·0′W	T	105
Greathed Manor	Surrey	TQ4142	51°9·8′	0°1·4′E	X	187
Great Hele Barton	Devon	SS7224	51°0·3′	3°49·1′W	X	180
Great Henny	Essex	TL8637	52°0·2′	0°43·0′E	T	155
Great Heron Wood	Kent	TQ9631	51°2·9′	0°48·2′E	F	189
Great Hetha	Northum	NT8827	55°32·4′	2°11·0′W	H	74
Great Hickle Ho	Essex	TM0631	51°56·6′	1°0·2′E	X	168
Great Hidden Fm	W Berks	SU3570	51°25·9′	1°29·4′W	FM	174
Great Higham	Kent	TQ9257	51°17·0′	0°45·6′E	X	178
Great High Rock	I Scilly	SV8715	49°57·4′	6°21·5′W	X	203
Great Hill	Cumbr	SD3092	54°19·4′	3°4·2′W	X	96,97
Great Hill	D & G	NT0613	55°24·4′	3°28·6′W	H	78
Great Hill	D & G	NX9492	55°12·9′	3°39·5′W	H	78
Great Hill	D & G	NY1991	55°12·6′	3°15·9′W	H	79
Great Hill	D & G	NY3292	55°13·3′	3°3·7′W	H	79
Great Hill	Dorset	SY6487	50°41·1′	2°30·2′W	X	194
Great Hill	Lancs	SD6419	53°40·2′	2°32·3′W	H	109
Great Hill	Lancs	SD9238	53°50·5′	2°6·9′W	X	103
Great Hill	Oldham	SD9812	53°36·5′	2°1·4′W	X	109
Great Hill	Oxon	SU7484	51°33·2′	0°55·6′W	X	175
Great Hill	Scot Bord	NT1126	55°31·4′	3°24·2′W	H	72
Great Hill	Scot Bord	NT1416	55°26·1′	3°21·1′W	H	78
Greathill	S Lanak	NS6943	55°40·0′	4°4·5′W	X	71
Great Hill	S Lanak	NS9314	55°24·7′	3°41·0′W	X	71,78
Great Hill	S Lanak	NS9922	55°29·1′	3°35·5′W	H	72
Great Hill	S Lanak	NT0220	55°28·1′	3°32·6′W	H	72
Great Hill	Somer	ST1536	51°7·3′	3°12·5′W	H	181
Great Hill	Somer	ST2710	50°53·3′	3°1·9′W	X	193
Greathill	Stir	NS7588	56°4·4′	4°0·0′W	X	57
Great Hill	Torbay	SX9167	50°29·8′	3°31·8′W	X	202
Great Hill	Worcs	SO9838	52°2·7′	2°1·4′W	X	150
Great Hill Burrows	Carm	SN2507	51°44·3′	4°31·7′W	X	158
Great Hinton	Wilts	ST9059	51°20·0′	2°8·2′W	T	173
Great Hivings	Bucks	SP9503	51°43·3′	0°37·1′W	T	165
Great Ho	Cald	SD9525	53°43·5′	2°4·1′W	X	103
Great Ho	Cambs	TL4052	52°9·1′	0°3·2′E	A	154
Great Ho	Glos	SO8327	51°56·7′	2°14·4′W	X	162
Great Ho	Lancs	SD7720	53°40·8′	2°20·5′W	X	103
Great Ho	Monm	SO3017	51°51·1′	3°0·6′W	X	161
Great Ho	Monm	SO3311	51°47·9′	2°57·9′W	X	161
Great Ho	Monm	SO3612	51°48·4′	2°55·3′W	X	161
Great Ho	Monm	SO3720	51°52·7′	2°54·5′W	X	161
Great Ho	Monm	SO3900	51°42·0′	2°52·6′W	X	171
Great Ho	Monm	SO4303	51°43·6′	2°49·1′W	X	171
Great Ho	Monm	SO4600	51°42·0′	2°46·5′W	X	171
Great Ho	Monm	ST3793	51°38·2′	2°54·2′W	X	171
Great Ho	Monm	ST4296	51°39·8′	2°49·9′W	X	171
Great Ho	Monm	ST4487	51°35·0′	2°48·1′W	X	171,172
Great Ho	Newp	ST4184	51°33·3′	2°50·7′W	X	171,172
Great Ho	Powys	SO0364	52°16·2′	3°24·9′W	X	147
Great Ho	Powys	SO0944	52°5·5′	3°19·3′W	X	147,161
Great Ho	Powys	SO1748	52°7·7′	3°12·4′W	X	148
Great Ho	Surrey	SU9639	51°8·8′	0°37·3′W	X	186
Great Ho	V of Glam	SS9669	51°24·9′	3°29·3′W	A	170
Great Ho	V of Glam	ST0175	51°28·2′	3°25·1′W	A	170
Great Hockham	Norf	TL9592	52°29·7′	0°52·8′E	T	144
Great Hoggins Fm, The	Glos	SO5704	51°44·2′	2°37·0′W	FM	162
Great Hograh Moor	N Yks	NZ6406	54°27·0′	1°0·4′W	X	94
Great Hogus	Corn	SW5130	50°7·3′	5°28·6′W	X	203
Great Holcombe	Oxon	SU6196	51°39·8′	1°6·7′W	T	164,165
Great Holland	Essex	TM2119	51°49·8′	1°12·8′E	T	169
Great Hollanden Fm	Kent	TQ5650	51°13·9′	0°14·5′E	FM	188
Great Hollands	Brackn	SU8567	51°24·0′	0°46·3′W	T	175
Great Holm	Mil Key	SP8238	52°2·3′	0°47·9′W	T	152
Great Holme	Stock on T	NZ4315	54°31·9′	1°19·7′W	X	93
Great Holt Copse	W Berks	SU4065	51°23·2′	1°25·1′W	F	174
Great Holwell	Somer	ST2134	51°6·2′	3°7·3′W	X	182
Great Home Wood	E Susx	TQ3718	50°56·9′	0°2·6′W	F	198
Great Hook	Kent	TQ9449	51°12·7′	0°47·0′E	X	189
Great Hook	Pemb	SM8625	51°53·2′	5°6·2′W	X	157
Great Horden Fm	Kent	TQ7540	51°8·2′	0°30·5′E	FM	188
Great Horkesley	Essex	TL9730	51°56·2′	0°52·4′E	T	168
Great Hormead	Herts	TL4029	51°56·7′	0°2·6′E	T	167
Great Hormead Bury	Herts	TL3929	51°56·8′	0°1·7′E	X	166
Great Hormead Park	Herts	TL4129	51°56·7′	0°3·5′E	F	167
Great Horringer Hall	Suff	TL8362	52°13·8′	0°41·2′E	X	155
Great Horton	Brad	SE1431	53°46·7′	1°46·8′W	T	104
Great Horton Fm	Worcs	SO8766	52°17·8′	2°11·0′W	FM	150
Great Horwood	Bucks	SP7731	51°58·6′	0°52·3′W	T	152,165
Great Ho, The	Worcs	SO6471	52°20·4′	2°31·3′W	X	138
Great Houghton	Barns	SE4306	53°33·2′	1°20·6′W	T	111
Great Houghton	Northnts	SP7958	52°13·1′	0°50·2′W	T	152
Great Houghton Lodge Fm	Northnts	SP8057	52°12·6′	0°49·4′W	FM	152
Great Houndbeare Fm	Devon	SY0493	50°44·0′	3°21·2′W	FM	192
Great Houndtor	Devon	SX7479	50°36·1′	3°46·5′W	X	191
Greathouse	Wilts	ST9277	51°29·7′	2°6·5′W	X	173
Great House Fm	Dorset	ST8120	50°59·0′	2°15·9′W	FM	183
Greathouse Fm	Essex	TL8533	51°58·1′	0°42·0′E	FM	168
Great House Fm	Monm	SO3104	51°44·1′	2°59·6′W	FM	171
Great House Fm	Monm	SO3925	51°55·4′	2°52·8′W	FM	161
Great House Fm	Powys	SO1242	52°4·4′	3°16·6′W	FM	148,161
Great House Fm	S Glos	ST7483	51°33·0′	2°22·1′W	FM	172
Great House Fm	V of Glam	SS9776	51°28·7′	3°28·6′W	FM	170
Great House Fm	W Susx	TQ1526	51°1·5′	0°21·2′W	FM	187,198
Greathouse Wood	W Berks	SU5973	51°27·4′	1°8·7′W	F	174
Great How	Cumbr	NY1904	54°25·7′	3°14·5′W	H	89,90
Great How	Cumbr	NY3118	54°33·4′	3°3·6′W	H	90
Great Howarth	Roch	SD9015	53°38·1′	2°8·7′W	T	109
Great How Crags	Cumbr	SD2799	54°23·1′	3°7·0′W	X	96,97
Great Howe	Cumbr	NY4806	54°27·1′	2°47·7′W	H	90
Great Howle Fm	Heref	SO6120	51°52·9′	2°33·6′W	FM	162
Great Hucklow	Derby	SK1777	53°17·6′	1°44·3′W	T	119
Great Huish	Devon	SS5217	50°56·2′	4°6·0′W	X	180
Great Huish Fm	Devon	SX8293	50°43·7′	3°39·9′W	FM	191
Great Hulver Hill	Norf	TG0643	52°56·9′	1°4·4′E	X	133
Great Hunters Stone	N Yks	SD9977	54°11·6′	2°0·5′W	X	98
Great Hunt House	Heref	SO3426	51°56·0′	2°57·2′W	X	161
Great Huntley Bank	Hants	SU2705	50°50·9′	1°36·6′W	X	195
Great Hurst Wood	Surrey	TQ2155	51°17·1′	0°15·5′W	F	187
Great Hyde Hall	Herts	TL4915	51°49·1′	0°10·1′E	X	167
Great Innisvouls	I Scilly	SV9514	49°57·1′	6°14·8′W	X	203
Great Intake	Cumbr	NY3002	54°24·8′	3°4·3′W	H	90
Great Intake	Cumbr	SD3493	54°19·9′	3°0·5′W	F	96,97
Great Intake	Derby	SE1001	53°30·6′	1°50·5′W	X	110
Great Isle	Durham	NZ3026	54°37·9′	1°31·7′W	X	93
Great Iwood	E Susx	TQ6318	50°56·5′	0°19·6′E	F	199
Great Job's Cross	Kent	TQ8329	51°2·1′	0°37·0′E	T	188,199
Great Kelk	E Yorks	TA1058	54°0·6′	0°18·9′W	T	107
Great Kellow Fm	Corn	SX2052	50°20·7′	4°31·4′W	FM	201
Great Kendale	E Yorks	TA0160	54°1·8′	0°27·1′W	T	101
Great Kimble	Bucks	SP8205	51°44·5′	0°48·3′W	T	165
Great Kingshill	Bucks	SU8798	51°40·7′	0°44·1′W	T	165
Great Kinmond	Cumbr	NY6709	54°28·8′	2°30·1′W	X	91
Great Kneeset	Devon	SX5985	50°39·1′	3°59·3′W	H	191
Great Knelle Fm (Childrens Fm)	E Susx	TQ8525	50°59·9′	0°38·6′E	FM	189,199
Great Knell Fm	Kent	TR2860	51°17·8′	1°16·6′E	FM	179
Great Knipe	Cumbr	NY8614	54°31·5′	2°12·6′W	H	91,92
Great Knock	Scot Bord	NT1325	55°30·9′	3°22·2′W	H	72
Great Knott	Cumbr	NY2504	54°25·8′	3°8·9′W	X	89,90
Great Knott	Cumbr	SD3391	54°18·9′	3°1·4′W	X	96,97
Great Knoutberry Hill	Cumbr	SD7887	54°16·9′	2°19·9′W	H	98
Great Knowle	Devon	SS3203	50°48·4′	4°22·7′W	X	190
Great Knowl Hill	Hants	SU5359	51°19·9′	1°14·0′W	X	174
Great Ladstones	Cumbr	NY5312	54°30·3′	2°43·1′W	X	90
Great Lake	Notts	SK5773	53°15·3′	1°8·3′W	W	120
Great Lake	N Yks	SE7170	54°7·5′	0°54·4′W	W	100
Greatlake Fm	Surrey	TQ2944	51°11·1′	0°8·9′W	FM	187
Great Landside	Devon	ST0416	50°56·4′	3°21·6′W	X	181
Great Langdale	Cumbr	NY3006	54°26·9′	3°4·4′W	X	90
Great Langdale Beck	Cumbr	NY2906	54°26·9′	3°5·3′W	W	89,90
Great Langdale Beck	Cumbr	NY3006	54°26·9′	3°4·4′W	W	90
Great Langton	N Yks	SE2996	54°21·8′	1°32·8′W	T	99
Great Lanolway	Monm	SO4303	51°43·6′	2°49·1′W	X	171
Great Larkhill Fm	Glos	ST9194	51°38·9′	2°7·4′W	FM	163,173
Greatlaw	Northum	NZ0180	55°7·1′	1°58·6′W	X	81
Great Law	Scot Bord	NT4041	55°39·8′	2°56·8′W	H	73
Great Lawn Wood	N Yks	SE5436	53°49·3′	1°10·4′W	F	105
Great Lawsley	Northum	NY8757	54°54·7′	2°11·7′W	X	87
Great Lea Common	Wok	SU7168	51°24·6′	0°58·4′W	T	175
Great Leasows	Shrops	SO6187	52°29·0′	2°34·1′W	X	138
Great Ledge	Devon	SX6740	50°14·9′	3°51·6′W	X	202
Greatlee Wood	Surrey	TQ1054	51°16·7′	0°25·0′W	F	187
Great Leigh Fm	Devon	SX7996	50°45·3′	3°42·5′W	FM	191
Great Leigh Fm	Devon	SX8485	50°39·4′	3°38·1′W	FM	191
Great Leighs	Essex	TL7217	51°49·7′	0°30·2′E	T	167
Great Lemhill Fm	Glos	SP2001	51°42·7′	1°42·2′W	FM	163
Great Lever	Bolton	SD7207	53°33·8′	2°25·0′W	T	109
Great Lightleigh	Devon	SS6918	50°57·0′	3°51·5′W	X	180
Great Limber	Lincs	TA1308	53°33·6′	0°17·2′W	T	113
Great Limber Grange	Lincs	TA1406	53°32·5′	0°16·4′W	X	113
Great Lindeth	Cumbr	SD3285	54°15·6′	3°2·2′W	X	96,97
Great Lines	Medway	TQ7668	51°23·2′	0°32·2′E	X	178
Great Linford	Mil Key	SP8542	52°4·4′	0°45·2′W	T	152
Great Linford Inclosure	Hants	SU1807	50°52·0′	1°44·3′W	F	195
Great Lingy Hill	Cumbr	NY3133	54°41·5′	3°3·8′W	X	90
Great Links Tor	Devon	SX5586	50°39·6′	4°2·7′W	H	191
Great Litchfield Down	Hants	SU4755	51°17·8′	1°19·2′W	X	174,185
Great Livermere	Suff	TL8871	52°18·5′	0°45·9′E	T	144,155
Great Llanmellin	Monm	ST4592	51°37·7′	2°47·3′W	X	171,172
Great Llanthomas	Monm	SO4606	51°45·2′	2°46·5′W	X	161
Great Llwygy	Monm	SO3221	51°53·2′	2°58·9′W	X	161
Great Llyvos	Monm	SO4018	51°51·7′	2°51·9′W	X	161
Great Lodge	Essex	TL6929	51°56·3′	0°27·9′E	X	167
Great Lodge	Suff	TM2965	52°14·4′	1°21·6′E	X	156
Great Lodge Fm	Essex	TL7936	51°59·8′	0°36·8′E	FM	155
Great Lodge Fm	Wilts	ST9470	51°26·0′	2°4·8′W	FM	173
Great Lodge Fm	Wilts	SU2066	51°23·8′	1°42·4′W	FM	174
Great Lodge Fm	Worcs	SO9763	52°16·1′	2°2·2′W	FM	150
Great Lodge Gill	N Yks	NY8102	54°25·0′	2°17·1′W	W	91,92
Great Lonbrough	Northum	NY8273	55°3·3′	2°16·5′W	X	86,87
Great Longstone	Derby	SK2071	53°14·4′	1°41·6′W	T	119
Great Loveney Hall	Essex	TL8931	51°56·9′	0°45·4′E	X	168
Greatlow	Derby	SK1067	53°12·2′	1°50·6′W	X	119
Great Low	Derby	SK1068	53°12·8′	1°50·6′W	X	119
Great Loyes	Essex	TL7715	51°48·6′	0°34·5′E	X	167
Great Lumley	Durham	NZ2949	54°50·3′	1°32·5′W	T	88
Great Lyth	Shrops	SJ4507	52°39·7′	2°48·4′W	T	126
Great Malgraves	Thurr	TQ6684	51°32·1′	0°24·0′E	T	177,178
Great Malvern	Worcs	SO7846	52°6·9′	2°18·9′W	T	150
Great Manshead Hill	Cald	SE0020	53°40·8′	1°59·6′W	H	104
Great Manson Fm	Monm	SO4915	51°50·1′	2°44·0′W	FM	162
Great Maplestead	Essex	TL8034	51°58·7′	0°37·7′E	T	155
Greatmarsh Fm	Essex	TM1018	51°49·5′	1°3·2′E	FM	168,169
Great Marstow Fm	Glos	SO6018	51°51·8′	2°34·5′W	FM	162
Great Martins	Win & Maid	SU8374	51°27·8′	0°47·9′W	X	175
Great Marton	Blackp	SD3334	53°48·1′	3°0·6′W	T	102
Great Marton Moss	Lancs	SD3331	53°46·5′	3°0·6′W	T	102
Great Mascalls	Essex	TL7303	51°42·2′	0°30·6′E	X	167
Great Massingham	Norf	TF7922	52°46·2′	0°39·6′E	T	132
Great Matridge	Devon	SX8489	50°41·6′	3°38·2′W	X	191
Great Matt's Copse	Hants	SU6644	51°11·7′	1°2·9′W	F	185,186
Great Maytham	Kent	TQ8430	51°2·6′	0°37·9′E	X	188
Great Meadow	I of M	SC2668	54°5·0′	4°39·2′W	X	95
Great Meadow Pond	Win & Maid	SU9670	51°25·5′	0°36·8′W	W	175,176
Great Mell Fell	Cumbr	NY3925	54°37·2′	2°56·3′W	H	90
Great Melton	Norf	TG1306	52°36·8′	1°9·2′E	X	144
Great Merrible Wood	Leic	SP8396	52°33·6′	0°46·1′W	F	141
Great Merrick Ledge	I Scilly	SV9216	49°58·1′	6°17·4′W	X	203
Great Mew Stone	Devon	SX5047	50°18·5′	4°6·0′W	X	201
Great Millstone Sike	Cumbr	NY7527	54°38·5′	2°22·8′W	W	91
Great Milton	Oxon	SP6202	51°43·0′	1°5·8′W	T	164,165
Great Minalto	I Scilly	SV8711	49°55·3′	6°21·3′W	X	203
Great Missenden	Bucks	SP8901	51°42·3′	0°42·3′W	T	165
Great Mis Tor	Devon	SX5676	50°34·2′	4°1·6′W	H	191
Great Mitton	Lancs	SD7138	53°50·5′	2°26·0′W	T	103
Great Moat Fm	Shrops	SO2496	52°33·6′	3°6·9′W	FM	137
Great Moelfre	Powys	SO1275	52°22·2′	3°17·2′W	X	136,148
Great Molleston Fm	Pemb	SN0912	51°46·7′	4°45·7′W	FM	158
Great Mongeham	Kent	TR3451	51°12·8′	1°21·4′E	T	179
Great Monks Wood	Essex	TL8225	51°53·9′	0°39·1′E	F	168
Great Monk Wood	Essex	TQ4298	51°40·0′	0°3·6′E	F	167,177
Greatmoor	Bucks	SP7022	51°53·8′	0°58·6′W	T	165
Great Moor	Devon	SS8615	50°55·6′	3°36·9′W	X	181
Great Moor	Northum	NT9225	55°31·4′	2°7·2′W	X	74,75
Great Moor	Northum	NY8590	55°12·5′	2°13·7′W	H	80
Great Moor	Staffs	SO8398	52°35·0′	2°14·7′W	T	138
Great Moor	Stock	SJ9188	53°23·6′	2°7·7′W	T	109
Greatmoor Hill	Scot Bord	NT4302	55°18·8′	2°53·5′W	H	79
Greatmoor Hill	Scot Bord	NT4800	55°17·7′	2°48·7′W	H	79
Great Moreton	Corn	SS2707	50°50·4′	4°27·1′W	X	190
Great Moreton Hall (Hotel)	Ches	SJ8359	53°7·9′	2°14·8′W	X	118
Great Mornshill Wood	Surrey	TQ1156	51°17·8′	0°24·1′W	F	187
Great Morton Sale	Northnts	TL0397	52°33·9′	0°28·4′W	F	141
Great Moss	Cumbr	NY2205	54°26·3′	3°11·7′W	X	89,90
Great Moss Fen	Norf	TG4226	52°46·9′	1°35·7′E	X	134
Great Moulton	Norf	TM1690	52°28·1′	1°11·2′E	T	144
Great Munden	Herts	TL3524	51°54·1′	0°1·9′W	T	166
Great Musgrave	Cumbr	NY7613	54°31·0′	2°21·8′W	T	91
Great Myles	Essex	TL5601	51°41·4′	0°15·8′E	X	167
Greatness	Kent	TQ5356	51°17·2′	0°12·0′E	T	188
Great Ness	Shrops	SJ3918	52°45·6′	2°53·8′W	T	126
Great Netherton	Glos	SO6832	51°59·4′	2°27·6′W	X	149
Great Newarks	Essex	TL6411	51°46·6′	0°23·0′E	X	167
Great Newra	Newp	ST3684	51°33·3′	2°55·0′W	X	171
Great Newsome Fm	E Yorks	TA3026	53°43·1′	0°1·4′W	FM	107
Great Newton	Carm	SN2612	51°47·0′	4°31·0′W	X	158
Great Nineveh	Kent	TQ7832	51°3·8′	0°32·8′E	X	188
Great Nobury Fm	Worcs	SP0255	52°11·8′	1°57·8′W	FM	150
Great Nodden	Devon	SX5387	50°40·1′	4°4·4′W	X	191
Great Norman Street Fm	Kent	TQ4852	51°15·1′	0°7·6′E	FM	188
Great North Fen	Cambs	TL4468	52°17·7′	0°7·1′E	X	154
Great North Road	Lincs	SK8840	52°57·2′	0°41·0′W	X	130
Great North Road	Notts	SK7177	53°17·3′	0°55·7′W	X	120
Great Norwood	Kent	TQ8766	51°22·0′	0°41·6′E	X	178
Great Notley	Essex	TL7421	51°51·9′	0°32·0′E	T	167
Great Noven Fm	E Susx	TQ3822	50°59·1′	0°1·6′W	FM	198
Great Nunty's Fm	Essex	TL8226	51°54·4′	0°39·1′E	FM	168
Great Nurcott	Somer	SS9036	51°7·0′	3°33·9′W	X	181
Great Oak	Monm	SO3809	51°46·8′	2°53·5′W	T	161
Greatoak	Staffs	SJ8051	53°3·6′	2°17·5′W	X	118
Great Oak Fm	Ches	SJ6885	53°21·9′	2°28·4′W	FM	109
Great Oakley	Essex	TM1927	51°54·1′	1°11·4′E	T	168,169
Great Oakley	Northnts	SP8785	52°27·6′	0°42·8′W	T	141
Great Oakley Hall	Essex	TM2028	51°54·6′	1°12·3′E	X	169
Great Oakley Lodge	Essex	TM1828	51°54·7′	1°10·6′E	X	168,169
Great Oaks	Oxon	SU6380	51°31·2′	1°5·1′W	X	175
Great Oaks Fm	Beds	SP9553	52°10·3′	0°36·3′W	FM	153
Great Oaks Wood	Beds	SP9653	52°10·2′	0°35·4′W	F	153
Great Oakwell Fm	Devon	SS6822	50°59·2′	3°52·5′W	FM	180
Great Oath Hill	Cumbr	SD3179	54°12·4′	3°3·1′W	H	96,97
Great Oddynes	W Susx	TQ3728	51°2·3′	0°2·4′W	X	187,198
Great Oddyns	Essex	TL5920	51°51·6′	0°18·9′E	X	167
Great Odham Moor Plantn	Devon	SS7418	50°57·1′	3°47·2′W	F	180
Great Offley	Herts	TL1426	51°55·5′	0°20·1′W	T	166
Great Old Hay	Kent	TQ6944	51°10·4′	0°25·5′E	X	188

Great Omenden Fm	Kent	TQ8740	51°7·9'	0°40·8'E	FM	189
Great Orcheton Fm	Devon	SX6349	50°19·7'	3°55·1'W	FM	202
Great Orme	Conwy	SH7583	53°20·0'	3°52·2'W	H	115
Great Ormes Head or Pen-y-Gogarth	Conwy	SH7683	53°20·0'	3°51·3'W	X	115
Great Ormside	Cumbr	NY7017	54°33·1'	2°27·4'W	T	91
Greator Rocks	Devon	SX7478	50°35·5'	3°46·4'W	X	191
Great Orton	Cumbr	NY3254	54°52·8'	3°3·2'W	T	85
Great Ote Hall	E Susx	TQ3320	50°58·1'	0°6·0'W	A	198
Great Ouseburn	N Yks	SE4461	54°2·8'	1°19·3'W	T	99
Great Ouseburn Moor	N Yks	SE4160	54°2·3'	1°22·0'W	X	99
Great Ovens Hill	Dorset	SY9290	50°42·8'	2°6·4'W	X	195
Great Oxenbold	Shrops	SO5992	52°31·7'	2°35·9'W	A	137,138
Great Oxendon	Northnts	SP7383	52°26·6'	0°55·2'W	T	141
Great Oxney Green	Essex	TL6606	51°43·9'	0°24·6'E	T	167
Great Pale	Carm	SN2215	51°48·6'	4°34·5'W	X	158
Great Palgrave	Norf	TF8312	52°40·7'	0°42·8'E	X	132
Great Pan Fm	I of W	SZ5088	50°41·6'	1°17·1'W	FM	196
Great Park	Hants	SU6944	51°11·7'	1°0·4'W	F	186
Great Park	Hants	SU7752	51°15·9'	0°53·4'W	X	186
Great Park	I of W	SZ4588	50°41·6'	1°21·4'W	X	196
Great Park	Lincs	TF1671	53°13·6'	0°15·3'W	X	121
Great Park	Monm	SO3420	51°52·7'	2°57·1'W	X	161
Great Park	Oxon	SP4317	51°51·2'	1°22·1'W	X	164
Great Park	Powys	SO0571	52°20·0'	3°23·3'W	X	136,147
Great Park Fm	E Susx	TQ7214	50°54·2'	0°27·2'E	FM	199
Great Park Fm	Oxon	SP4500	51°42·0'	1°20·5'W	FM	164
Great Park Fm	W Berks	SU6864	51°22·5'	1°1·0'W	FM	175,186
Great Park Wood	E Susx	TQ8518	50°56·1'	0°38·4'E	F	189,199
Greatpark Wood	Medway	TQ6763	51°20·7'	0°24·3'E	F	177,178,188
Great Park Wood	W Berks	SU3475	51°28·6'	1°30·2'W	F	174
Great Parlow Close	Cambs	TL2465	52°16·4'	0°10·6'W	X	153
Great Parndon	Essex	TL4308	51°45·4'	0°4·7'E	T	167
Great Pasture	N Yks	SD8385	54°15·9'	2°15·2'W	X	98
Great Pasture	N Yks	SD8777	54°11·6'	2°11·5'W	F	98
Great Pattenden	Kent	TQ7344	51°10·4'	0°28·9'E	T	188
Great Paxton	Cambs	TL2063	52°15·4'	0°14·1'W	T	153
Great Peatling Lodge	Leic	SP6094	52°32·7'	1°6·5'W	X	140
Great Pedding Fm	Kent	TR2657	51°16·3'	1°14·8'E	FM	179
Great Pednor Fm	Bucks	SP9203	51°43·3'	0°39·7'W	FM	165
Great Pelean	Corn	SX0856	50°22·6'	4°41·6'W	X	200
Great Pen	Devon	SY2194	50°44·6'	3°6·8'W	H	192,193
Great Penllan	Heref	SO2752	52°9·9'	3°3·6'W	X	148
Great Pennys Fm	Herts	TL4414	51°48·6'	0°5·7'E	FM	167
Great Pen Wood	Hants	SU4462	51°21·6'	1°21·7'W	F	174
Great Perhaver Beach	Corn	SX0142	50°14·9'	4°47·1'W	X	204
Great Pill	Swan	SS4695	51°38·2'	4°13·1'W	W	159
Great Pinley Fm	Warw	SP2166	52°17·7'	1°41·1'W	FM	151
Great Pinnock	Corn	SX1053	50°21·0'	4°39·9'W	X	200,204
Great Pinseat	N Yks	NY9602	54°25·1'	2°3·3'W	H	91,92
Great Pitford	Devon	SS6111	50°53·1'	3°58·2'W	X	191
Great Pivington Fm	Kent	TQ9152	51°14·3'	0°44·6'E	FM	189
Great Plain	Swan	SS4495	51°38·2'	4°14·9'W	X	159
Great Plantation	Devon	SX8175	50°34·0'	3°40·4'W	F	191
Great Plantation	Dorset	SY8588	50°41·7'	2°12·4'W	F	194
Great Plantation	Norf	TL7497	52°32·8'	0°34·4'E	X	143
Great Plantation	Norf	TL9388	52°27·6'	0°50·9'E	F	144
Great Plantation	Somer	ST1843	51°11·1'	3°10·0'W	F	181
Great Plantn	E Yorks	SE8556	53°59·8'	0°41·8'W	F	106
Great Plantn	N Yks	SE6272	54°8·6'	1°2·6'W	F	100
Great Plantn	Suff	TL7769	52°17·7'	0°36·1'E	F	155
Great Plummerden Fm	W Susx	TQ3626	51°1·3'	0°3·3'W	FM	187,198
Great Plummers Fm	Herts	TL1418	51°51·2'	0°20·3'W	FM	166
Great Plumpton	Lancs	SD3833	53°47·6'	2°56·1'W	T	102
Great Plumstead	Norf	TG3010	52°38·6'	1°24·4'E	T	133,134
Great Pock Stones	N Yks	SE1060	54°2·4'	1°50·4'W	X	99
Great Pond	Derby	SK4563	53°10·0'	1°19·2'W	W	120
Great Pond Fm	Bucks	SP6924	51°54·8'	0°59·4'W	FM	165
Great Ponton	Lincs	SK9230	52°51·8'	0°37·6'W	T	130
Great Pool	I Scilly	SV8914	49°56·9'	6°19·8'W	W	203
Great Pool	Warw	SP2283	52°26·9'	1°40·2'W	W	139
Great Pool	Worcs	SO8763	52°16·1'	2°11·0'W	W	150
Great Pool Hall	Monm	SO3718	51°51·7'	2°54·5'W	X	161
Great Pool, The	Staffs	SJ8000	52°36·1'	2°17·3'W	W	127
Great Pool, The	Staffs	SO8099	52°35·5'	2°17·3'W	W	138
Great Porter's Fm	Essex	TL9327	51°54·7'	0°48·8'E	FM	168
Great Porthamel	Powys	SO1535	52°0·7'	3°13·9'W	X	161
Great Porton	Newp	ST3883	51°32·8'	2°53·3'W	X	171
Great Posbrooke	Hants	SU5305	50°50·8'	1°14·4'W	A	196
Great Postland	Lincs	TF2612	52°41·7'	0°7·7'W	X	131,142
Great Potheridge	Devon	SS5114	50°54·6'	4°6·8'W	X	180
Great Poulders Fm	Kent	TR3157	51°16·1'	1°19·1'E	FM	179
Great Poultney Fm	Leic	SP5785	52°27·8'	1°9·3'W	FM	140
Great Prawls Fm	Kent	TQ9226	51°0·3'	0°44·6'E	FM	189
Great Preston	Leeds	SE4029	53°45·6'	1°23·2'W	T	105
Great Prestons	Essex	TQ7198	51°39·5'	0°28·7'E	X	167
Great Prideaux	Devon	SX5647	50°18·6'	4°1·0'W	X	202
Great Priory Fm	Essex	TL7325	51°54·0'	0°31·3'E	FM	167
Great Puckstone Fm	Kent	TR2060	51°18·0'	1°9·8'E	FM	179
Great Punchard Gill	N Yks	NY9604	54°26·1'	2°3·3'W	W	91,92
Great Punchard Head	N Yks	NY9404	54°26·1'	2°5·1'W	X	91,92
Great Punchardon	Devon	SS6410	50°52·6'	3°55·6'W	X	191
Great Purston	Northnts	SP5139	52°3·1'	1°15·0'W	T	151
Great Queach	Suff	TL9169	52°17·4'	0°48·4'E	F	155
Great Raveley	Cambs	TL2581	52°25·0'	0°9·3'W	T	142
Great Raveley Drain	Cambs	TL2383	52°26·1'	0°11·0'W	W	142
Great Raveley Fen	Cambs	TL2383	52°26·1'	0°11·0'W	X	142
Great Red	Devon	SS7550	51°14·4'	3°47·1'W	X	180
Great Revel End Fm	Herts	TL0811	51°47·5'	0°25·6'W	FM	166
Great Rhos	Powys	SO1862	52°15·2'	3°11·7'W	X	148
Great Ridge	Wilts	ST9236	51°7·6'	2°6·5'W	X	184
Great Ridge Fm	Devon	ST0317	50°56·9'	3°22·5'W	FM	181
Greatridgehall	Scot Bord	NT6532	55°35·1'	2°32·9'W	X	74
Great Rigg	Cumbr	NY3510	54°29·1'	2°59·8'W	H	90
Great Rill Fm	Devon	SS9924	51°0·6'	3°26·0'W	FM	181
Great Rissington	Glos	SP1917	51°51·3'	1°43·1'W	T	163
Great Rock	Cald	SD9526	53°44·1'	2°4·1'W	X	103
Great Rock	Devon	SX8281	50°37·2'	3°39·7'W	X	191
Great Rocks Dale	Derby	SK1073	53°15·5'	1°50·6'W	X	119
Great Rollright	Oxon	SP3231	51°58·8'	1°31·6'W	T	151
Great Rundale Beck	Cumbr	NY7027	54°38·5'	2°27·5'W	W	91
Great Rundale Tarn	Cumbr	NY7328	54°39·0'	2°24·7'W	W	91
Great Rush Plantn	N Yks	SE2292	54°19·6'	1°39·3'W	F	99
Great Rutleigh	Devon	SS5101	50°47·6'	4°6·5'W	X	191
Great Ryburgh	Norf	TF9527	52°48·5'	0°54·0'E	T	132
Great Ryle	Northum	NU0112	55°24·4'	1°58·6'W	X	81
Great Ryton	Shrops	SJ4803	52°37·6'	2°45·7'W	T	126
Great Saling	Essex	TL7025	51°54·1'	0°28·7'E	T	167
Great Salkeld	Cumbr	NY5536	54°43·3'	2°41·5'W	T	90
Great Sampford	Essex	TL6435	51°59·6'	0°23·7'E	T	154
Great Sanders School	E Susx	TQ7719	50°56·8'	0°31·6'E	X	199
Great Sandhurst Wood	Kent	TQ6438	51°7·3'	0°21·0'E	F	188
Great Sankey	Warr	SJ5788	53°23·5'	2°38·4'W	T	108
Great Saredon	Staffs	SJ9508	52°40·4'	2°4·0'W	T	127
Great Sarratt Hall	Herts	TL0300	51°41·6'	0°30·2'W	X	166
Great Saxham	Suff	TL7862	52°13·9'	0°36·8'E	T	155
Great Sca Fell	Cumbr	NY2933	54°41·5'	3°5·7'W	H	89,90
Great Scar	N Yks	SD8664	54°4·5'	2°12·4'W	X	98
Great Scrubbs Wood	Lincs	TF1474	53°15·3'	0°17·1'W	F	121
Great Seabrights	Essex	TL7103	51°42·2'	0°28·9'E	X	167
Great Seabrook	Bucks	SP9216	51°50·3'	0°39·5'W	X	165
Great Seaside	Devon	SY2088	50°41·4'	3°7·6'W	X	192
Great Shacklow Wood	Derby	SK1769	53°13·3'	1°44·3'W	F	119
Great Shack, The	N Yks	SE0959	54°1·9'	1°51·3'W	X	104
Great Shaugh Wood	Devon	SX5260	50°25·5'	4°4·6'W	F	201
Great Shefford	W Berks	SU3875	51°28·6'	1°26·8'W	T	174
Great Shelfin Fm	Devon	SS5245	51°11·3'	4°6·7'W	FM	180
Great Shelford	Cambs	TL4652	52°9·0'	0°8·4'E	T	154
Great Shell Corner	Kent	TR0294	51°36·7'	0°55·5'E	X	168,178
Great Shepcroft Fm	Warr	SJ6182	53°20·3'	2°34·7'W	FM	109
Great Shoddesden	Hants	SU2748	51°14·1'	1°36·4'W	T	184
Great Shoesmiths Fm	E Susx	TQ6234	51°5·2'	0°19·2'E	FM	188
Great Shunner Fell	N Yks	SD8497	54°22·3'	2°14·4'W	H	98
Great Shutter Rock	Devon	SS1343	51°9·6'	4°40·1'W	X	180
Great Sir Hughes	Essex	TL7302	51°41·6'	0°30·6'E	X	167
Great Slab	Cumbr	NY2406	54°26·9'	3°9·9'W	X	89,90
Great Slamseys	Essex	TL7319	51°50·8'	0°31·1'E	X	167
Great Sled Dale	N Yks	NY8500	54°24·0'	2°13·4'W	X	91,92
Great Sleddale Beck	N Yks	NY8500	54°24·0'	2°13·4'W	W	91,92
Great Smeaton	N Yks	NZ3404	54°26·1'	1°28·1'W	T	93
Great Smith	I Scilly	SV8609	49°54·2'	6°22·0'W	X	203
Great Smithcot Fm	Wilts	SU0082	51°32·4'	1°59·6'W	FM	173
Great Snare Hill	Norf	TL8780	52°23·4'	0°45·3'E	X	144
Great Snoring	Norf	TF9434	52°52·3'	0°53·4'E	T	132
Great Somerford	Wilts	ST9682	51°32·4'	2°3·1'W	T	173
Great Southwood Park Fm	Suff	TL7659	52°12·3'	0°34·9'E	FM	155
Great Sowdens Wood	E Susx	TQ8519	50°56·7'	0°38·4'E	F	189,199
Great Stainton	Darl	NZ3321	54°35·2'	1°28·9'W	T	93
Great Stambridge	Essex	TQ9091	51°35·4'	0°45·0'E	T	178
Great Stambridge Hall	Essex	TQ8990	51°34·9'	0°44·1'E	X	178
Great Standrop	Northum	NT9418	55°27·6'	2°5·3'W	H	80
Great Stangate	N Yks	SE0570	54°7·8'	1°55·0'W	X	98
Great Stanks	E Yorks	TA1337	53°49·3'	0°16·6'W	X	107
Great Staughton	Cambs	TL1264	52°16·0'	0°21·1'W	T	153
Great Steeping	Lincs	TF4464	53°9·4'	0°9·6'E	T	122
Great Stent Fm	E Susx	TQ8322	50°58·3'	0°36·8'E	FM	199
Great Stert	Devon	SX5957	50°24·0'	3°58·7'W	A	202
Great Stewardstone	Devon	SX5798	50°46·1'	4°1·3'W	X	191
Great Stickle	Cumbr	SD2191	54°18·8'	3°12·4'W	H	96
Great Stoke	S Glos	ST6280	51°31·3'	2°32·5'W	T	172
Great Stonage Fm	Essex	TL7114	51°48·1'	0°29·2'E	FM	167
Great Stonar	Kent	TR3359	51°17·2'	1°20·9'E	T	179
Great Stone of Fourstones	Lancs	SD6666	54°5·6'	2°30·8'W	X	98
Greatstone-on-Sea	Kent	TR0822	50°57·8'	0°58·1'E	T	189
Great Stony Hill	Durham	NY8236	54°43·4'	2°16·3'W	H	91,92
Great Stony School	Cambs	TL5503	51°42·5'	0°15·0'E	X	167
Great Stour	Kent	TQ9149	51°12·7'	0°44·5'E	W	189
Great Stour	Kent	TR0445	51°10·3'	0°55·5'E	W	179,189
Great Stour	Kent	TR2262	51°19·0'	1°11·5'E	W	179
Great Stowgill	Cumbr	NY8308	54°28·3'	2°15·3'W	W	91,92
Great Stray, The	N Yks	SE1058	54°1·3'	1°50·4'W	X	104
Great Streele	E Susx	TQ4921	50°58·4'	0°7·7'E	X	199
Great Stretton	Leic	SK6500	52°35·9'	1°2·0'W	T	141
Great Strickland	Cumbr	NY5522	54°35·7'	2°41·4'W	T	90
Great Strudgate Fm	W Susx	TQ3333	51°5·1'	0°5·7'W	FM	187
Great Stukeley	Cambs	TL2174	52°21·3'	0°13·0'W	T	142
Great Stukeley Lodge	Cambs	TL2375	52°21·8'	0°11·2'W	X	142
Great Sturton	Lincs	TF2176	53°16·3'	0°10·7'W	T	122
Great Sutton	Ches	SJ3775	53°16·3'	2°56·3'W	T	117
Great Sutton	Shrops	SO5183	52°26·8'	2°42·9'W	T	137,138
Great Swifts	Kent	TQ7836	51°6·0'	0°32·9'E	X	188
Great Swinburne	Northum	NY9375	55°4·4'	2°6·1'W	T	87
Great Swindale	Cumbr	NY6901	54°24·5'	2°28·2'W	X	91
Great Tangley Manor House	Surrey	TQ0246	51°12·5'	0°32·0'W	A	186
Great Tawney Hall	Essex	TQ5098	51°39·9'	0°10·5'E	X	167,177
Great Tew	Oxon	SP3929	51°57·7'	1°25·5'W	T	164
Great Tew Park	Oxon	SP4029	51°57·7'	1°24·7'W	X	164
Great Tey	Essex	TL8925	51°53·7'	0°45·2'E	T	168
Great Thickthorn Fm	Beds	TL0442	52°4·2'	0°28·6'W	FM	153
Great Thirkleby	N Yks	SE4778	54°12·0'	1°16·4'W	T	100
Great Thorndean Fm	W Susx	TQ2725	51°0·8'	0°11·0'W	FM	187,198
Great Thorness	I of W	SZ4592	50°43·8'	1°21·4'W	X	196
Great Thornham Fm	Wilts	ST9359	51°20·0'	2°5·6'W	FM	173
Great Thurlow	Suff	TL6750	52°7·6'	0°26·8'E	T	154
Great Tidnock Fm	Ches	SJ8668	53°12·8'	2°12·2'W	FM	118
Great Tilden	Kent	TQ7447	51°12·0'	0°29·8'E	X	188
Great Todber	Lancs	SD8346	53°54·8'	2°15·1'W	X	103
Great Todham Fm	W Susx	SU9020	50°58·6'	0°42·7'W	FM	197
Great Tomkyns	Hav	TQ5689	51°34·9'	0°15·5'E	A	177
Great Tongue	Cumbr	NY3410	54°29·1'	3°0·7'W	X	90
Great Tongue Rigg	Northum	NT7077	55°5·4'	2°27·8'W	X	86,87
Great Tor	Derby	SK2084	53°21·4'	1°41·6'W	X	110
Great Tor	Swan	SS5387	51°34·0'	4°6·9'W	X	159
Great Torr	Devon	SX6348	50°18·9'	3°55·1'W	X	202
Great Torrington	Devon	SS4919	50°57·3'	4°8·6'W	T	180
Great Tosson	Northum	NU0200	55°17·9'	1°57·7'W	T	81
Great Totham	Essex	TL8511	51°46·2'	0°41·3'E	T	168
Great Totham	Essex	TL8613	51°47·3'	0°42·2'E	T	168
Great Tower Plantation	Cumbr	SD3991	54°18·9'	2°55·8'W	F	96,97
Great Tows	Lincs	TF2290	53°23·8'	0°9·5'W	T	113
Great Tratford	Corn	SX1852	50°20·6'	4°33·1'W	X	201
Great Tree	Corn	SX2655	50°22·4'	4°26·4'W	T	201
Great Tree Hotel	Devon	SX7090	50°41·9'	3°50·1'W	X	191
Great Treffgarne Mountain	Pemb	SM9424	51°52·8'	4°59·2'W	H	157,158
Great Tregassow Wood	Corn	SW8549	50°18·3'	5°0·8'W	F	204
Great Trelanden	Heref	SO3329	51°57·6'	2°58·1'W	X	149,161
Great Tre-Rhew	Monm	SO3717	51°51·1'	2°54·5'W	X	161
Great Trethew	Corn	SX2860	50°25·1'	4°24·9'W	X	201
Great Treverran	Corn	SX0956	50°22·6'	4°40·8'W	X	200
Great Triley	Monm	SO3117	51°51·1'	2°59·7'W	X	161
Great Trippetts Fm	W Susx	SU8226	51°1·9'	0°49·4'W	FM	186,197
Great Trodgers Fm	E Susx	TQ5829	51°2·5'	0°15·6'E	FM	188,199
Great Ulverstone	S Glos	ST5689	51°36·1'	2°37·7'W	X	162,172
Great Up Somborne Wood	Hants	SU4031	51°4·8'	1°25·4'W	F	185
Great Urswick	Cumbr	SD2774	54°9·6'	3°6·7'W	T	96,97
Great Varracombe	Devon	SX6284	50°38·6'	3°56·7'W	X	191
Great Vaynor	Pemb	SN1018	51°49·9'	4°45·1'W	X	158
Great Vintcombe	Somer	SS7239	51°8·4'	3°49·4'W	X	180
Great Wacton	Heref	SO6256	52°12·3'	2°33·0'W	X	149
Great Wadd Fm	Kent	TQ7940	51°8·1'	0°33·9'E	FM	188
Great Wakering	Essex	TQ9487	51°33·1'	0°48·3'E	T	178
Great Waldingfield	Suff	TL9043	52°3·4'	0°46·7'E	T	155
Great Walley Hall	Essex	TL7618	51°50·2'	0°33·7'E	X	167
Great Wallis Fm	E Susx	TQ5828	51°2·0'	0°15·6'E	FM	188,199
Great Walsingham	Norf	TF9437	52°54·0'	0°53·5'E	T	132
Great Waltham	Essex	TL6913	51°47·6'	0°27·4'E	T	167
Great Wanney Crag	Northum	NY9383	55°8·7'	2°6·2'W	H	80
Great Wapses Fm	W Susx	TQ2419	50°57·6'	0°13·7'W	FM	198
Great Warley	Essex	TQ5890	51°35·4'	0°17·2'E	T	177
Great Warley Hall	Essex	TQ5988	51°34·3'	0°18·1'E	X	177
Great Washbourne	Glos	SO9834	52°0·5'	2°1·4'W	T	150
Great Wasketts	Essex	TQ7191	51°35·7'	0°28·5'E	X	178
Great Watch Hill	Northum	NY7075	55°4·4'	2°27·8'W	X	86,87
Great Water	Norf	TG2234	52°51·7'	1°18·3'E	W	133
Great Watersend	Kent	TR2744	51°9·2'	1°15·2'E	X	179
Great Weeke	Devon	SX7187	50°40·3'	3°49·2'W	T	191
Great Wegber	N Yks	SD9991	54°19·1'	2°0·5'W	X	98
Great Well Fm	Devon	SY1195	50°45·1'	3°15·3'W	FM	192,193
Great Welnetham	Suff	TL8759	52°12·1'	0°44·6'E	T	155
Great Wenham	Suff	TM0738	52°0·3'	1°1·4'E	T	155,169
Great West Fen	Norf	TL6097	52°33·1'	0°22·0'E	X	143
Great West Field	Heref	SO4362	52°15·4'	2°49·7'W	X	137,148,149
Great Westfield	Pemb	SM9608	51°44·3'	4°56·9'W	X	157,158
Great West Wood	E Yorks	SE7443	53°52·9'	0°52·0'W	F	105,106
Great Westwood	Herts	TQ0699	51°41·0'	0°27·6'W	X	166,176
Great West Wood	Lincs	TF1076	53°16·4'	0°20·6'W	F	121
Great Whernside	N Yks	SE0074	54°10·0'	1°59·6'W	H	98
Great Whitcombe Manor	I of W	SZ4886	50°40·5'	1°18·9'W	X	196
Great White End	Bucks	SP9900	51°41·6'	0°33·7'W	X	165
Great Whitmans	Essex	TL8300	51°40·4'	0°39·2'E	X	168
Great Whitstone	Devon	SS7718	50°57·1'	3°44·7'W	X	180
Great Whittington	Northum	NZ0070	55°1·7'	1°59·6'W	T	87
Great Widgham Wood	Cambs	TL6655	52°10·3'	0°26·1'E	F	154
Great Wigborough	Essex	TL9615	51°48·2'	0°51·0'E	T	168
Great Wigsell	E Susx	TQ7627	51°1·1'	0°31·0'E	A	188,199
Great Wilbraham	Cambs	TL5457	52°11·6'	0°15·6'E	T	154
Great Wilbraham Hall Fm	Cambs	TL5555	52°10·5'	0°16·4'E	FM	154
Great Wildgoose Wood	W Susx	TQ3535	51°6·1'	0°3·9'W	F	187
Great Wilmores	Essex	TL5109	51°45·8'	0°11·7'E	X	167
Great Wilne	Derby	SK4430	52°52·2'	1°20·4'W	T	129
Great Wilsey Fm	Suff	TL6846	52°5·4'	0°27·5'E	FM	154
Great Wingletang	I Scilly	SV8807	49°53·2'	6°20·3'W	X	203
Great Wishford	Wilts	SU0735	51°7·1'	1°53·6'W	T	184
Great Witchingham	Norf	TG1020	52°44·4'	1°7·1'E	T	133
Great Witchingham Hall	Norf	TG1118	52°43·3'	1°7·9'E	X	133
Great Witcombe	Glos	SO9114	51°49·7'	2°7·4'W	T	163
Great Withy Wood	Wilts	SU0088	51°35·7'	1°59·6'W	F	173
Great Witley	Worcs	SO7566	52°17·7'	2°21·6'W	T	138,150
Great Wold	Cumbr	SD7484	54°15·3'	2°23·5'W	X	98
Great Wold Plantn	E Yorks	SE9432	53°46·8'	0°34·0'W	F	106
Great Wollascott	Shrops	SJ4818	52°45·7'	2°45·8'W	X	126
Great Wood	Bri & Hov	TQ3309	50°52·1'	0°6·2'W	F	198
Great Wood	Bucks	SP7635	52°0·7'	0°53·2'W	F	152
Great Wood	Bucks	SU7687	51°34·8'	0°53·8'W	F	175
Great Wood	Bucks	SU7689	51°35·9'	0°53·8'W	F	175
Greatwood	Corn	SW8136	50°11·2'	5°3·7'W	X	204
Great Wood	Corn	SX0963	50°26·4'	4°41·0'W	F	200
Great Wood	Corn	SX1256	50°22·7'	4°38·3'W	F	200
Great Wood	Cumbr	NY0309	54°28·3'	3°29·4'W	F	89
Great Wood	Cumbr	NY2721	54°35·0'	3°7·3'W	F	89,90
Great Wood	Cumbr	SD3593	54°20·0'	2°59·6'W	F	96,97
Great Wood	Cumbr	SD3686	54°16·2'	2°58·5'W	F	96,97
Great Wood	Devon	SS8820	50°58·3'	3°35·3'W	F	181
Great Wood	Dorset	SY9081	50°37·9'	2°8·1'W	F	195
Great Wood	Durham	NZ0021	54°35·3'	1°59·6'W	F	92
Great Wood	Durham	NZ0919	54°34·2'	1°51·2'W	F	92
Great Wood	Essex	TQ4896	51°38·8'	0°8·7'E	F	167,177
Great Wood	Essex	TQ8287	51°33·4'	0°37·9'E	F	178
Great Wood	E Susx	TQ7615	50°54·7'	0°30·6'E	F	199
Great Wood	Hants	SU3143	51°11·4'	1°33·0'W	F	185
Great Wood	Hants	SU6246	51°12·8'	1°6·4'W	F	185
Great Wood	Heref	SO3435	52°0·8'	2°57·3'W	F	149,161
Great Wood	Herts	TL2804	51°43·4'	0°8·4'W	F	166
Great Wood	Leic	SK4807	52°39·8'	1°17·0'W	F	140
Great Wood	Medway	TQ7068	51°23·4'	0°27·0'E	F	178
Great Wood	Mil Key	SP8452	52°9·8'	0°45·9'W	F	152
Great Wood	Newp	ST3888	51°35·5'	2°53·3'W	F	171
Great Wood	Norf	TF8617	52°43·3'	0°45·7'E	F	132
Great Wood	Norf	TF9109	52°38·9'	0°49·8'E	F	144
Great Wood	Norf	TF9110	52°39·5'	0°49·8'E	F	132
Great Wood	Norf	TF9719	52°44·2'	0°55·5'E	F	132
Great Wood	Norf	TG1621	52°44·8'	1°12·4'E	F	133
Great Wood	Norf	TG1629	52°49·1'	1°12·7'E	F	133
Great Wood	Norf	TG1722	52°45·3'	1°13·4'E	F	133,134
Great Wood	Norf	TG1940	52°55·0'	1°15·9'E	F	133
Great Wood	Norf	TG2334	52°51·7'	1°19·2'E	F	133
Great Wood	Norf	TL8399	52°33·7'	0°42·4'E	F	144
Great Wood	Norf	TM2497	52°31·7'	1°18·5'E	F	134
Great Wood	Norf	TM3190	52°27·8'	1°24·4'E	F	134

Great Wood	Northum	NU0919	55°28·1'	1°51·0'W	F	81
Great Wood	N Yks	SD9356	54°0·2'	2°6·0'W	F	103
Great Wood	N Yks	SE1965	54°5·1'	1°42·2'W	F	99
Great Wood	N Yks	SE2184	54°15·3'	1°40·2'W	F	99
Great Wood	N Yks	SE3855	53°59·6'	1°24·8'W	F	104
Great Wood	N Yks	SE6662	54°3·2'	0°59·1'W	F	100
Great Wood	Somer	ST1736	51°7·3'	3°10·8'W	F	181
Great Wood	Suff	TL7955	52°10·1'	0°37·4'E	F	155
Great Wood	Suff	TL9860	52°12·4'	0°54·3'E	F	155
Great Wood	Suff	TM1963	52°13·5'	1°12·8'E	F	156
Great Wood	Suff	TM2958	52°10·6'	1°21·4'E	F	156
Great Wood	Suff	TM3359	52°11·0'	1°24·9'E	F	156
Great Wood	Suff	TM3985	52°24·9'	1°31·3'E	F	156
Great Wood	Suff	TM4284	52°24·2'	1°33·9'E	F	156
Great Wood	Suff	TM4359	52°10·8'	1°33·7'E	F	156
Great Wood	Swin	SU1789	51°36·2'	1°44·9'W	F	173
Great Wood	Wilts	ST9669	51°25·4'	2°3·1'W	F	173
Great Wood	Wilts	SU0281	51°31·9'	1°57·9'W	F	173
Great Wood	Win & Maid	SU8576	51°28·8'	0°46·2'W	F	175
Great Wood	Wok	SU7365	51°23·0'	0°56·7'W	F	175
Great Wood	W Susx	TQ0828	51°2·7'	0°27·2'W	F	187,197
Great Wood	W Susx	TQ3737	51°7·2'	0°2·2'W	F	187
Greatwood Fm	Devon	SS5412	50°53·6'	4°4·2'W	FM	180
Greatwood Fm	Devon	ST2900	50°47·9'	3°0·1'W	FM	193
Greatwood Fm	Staffs	SJ7731	52°52·8'	2°20·1'W	FM	127
Great Wood Fm	Wilts	SU0281	51°31·9'	1°57·9'W	FM	173
Great Wood Ho	Shrops	SO3595	52°33·2'	2°57·1'W	X	137
Greatwood Lodge	Staffs	SJ7732	52°53·3'	2°20·1'W	X	127
Great Woolcombe	Somer	SS7837	51°7·4'	3°44·2'W	X	180
Great Woolden Hall	Salf	SJ6993	53°26·2'	2°27·6'W	X	109
Great Wootton Wood	Dorset	ST6807	50°51·9'	2°26·9'W	F	194
Great Worge	E Susx	TQ6621	50°58·1'	0°22·2'E	X	199
Great Worm Crag	Cumbr	SD1996	54°21·4'	3°14·4'W	H	96
Greatworth	Northnts	SP5542	52°4·6'	1°11·4'W	T	152
Great Wotton	Devon	SX7598	50°46·3'	3°46·0'W	X	191
Great Wratting	Suff	TL6848	52°6·5'	0°27·6'E	T	154
Great Wrea	Corn	SW8019	50°2·1'	5°4·0'W	X	204
Great Wygill	Cumbr	NY8707	54°27·7'	2°11·6'W	W	91,92
Great Wymondley	Herts	TL2128	51°56·5'	0°14·0'W	T	166
Great Wyrley	Staffs	SJ9907	52°39·9'	2°0·5'W	T	127,139
Great Wytheford	Shrops	SJ5719	52°46·3'	2°37·8'W	T	126
Great Yarlside	Cumbr	NY5207	54°27·6'	2°44·0'W	H	90
Great Yarmouth	Norf	TG5207	52°36·4'	1°43·7'E	T	134
Great Yeldham	Essex	TL7638	52°1·0'	0°34·3'E	T	155
Great Yews	Wilts	SU1123	51°0·6'	1°50·2'W	F	184
Great Ynys	Heref	SO4727	51°56·6'	2°45·9'W	X	161
Great Zawn	Corn	SW4137	50°10·8'	5°37·3'W	W	203
Greave	Arg & Bt	NM2420	56°17·8'	6°27·2'W	X	48
Greave	Lancs	SD8723	53°42·4'	2°11·4'W	T	103
Greave	Stock	SJ9491	53°25·2'	2°5·0'W	T	109
Greave	V of Glam	ST1273	51°27·2'	3°15·6'W	X	171
Greave Clough	Cald	SD9433	53°47·8'	2°5·1'W	X	103
Greave Ho	Derby	SK0477	53°17·6'	1°56·0'W	X	119
Greaveley Fm	Leic	SK4220	52°46·8'	1°22·2'W	FM	129
Greaves	Cumbr	NY4425	54°37·3'	2°51·6'W	X	90
Greaves	Cumbr	SD5588	54°17·4'	2°41·1'W	X	97
Greaves	Lancs	SD7651	53°57·5'	2°21·5'W	X	103
Greaves	Orkney	HY4701	58°53·8'	2°54·7'W	X	6,7
Greaves	Staffs	SK1528	52°51·2'	1°46·2'W	X	128
Greaves End	E Yorks	SE8131	53°46·4'	0°45·8'W	X	106
Greaves Fm	Cumbr	SD3982	54°14·1'	2°55·7'W	FM	96,97
Greaves Fm, The	Shrops	SJ7442	52°58·7'	2°22·8'W	FM	118
Greaves Ground	Cumbr	SD2692	54°19·4'	3°7·8'W	X	96,97
Greave's Piece	Derby	SK2977	53°17·6'	1°33·5'W	X	119
Greaves, The	Ches	SJ4544	52°59·7'	2°48·8'W	X	117
Greaves Wood	Staffs	SK1527	52°50·7'	1°46·2'W	F	128
Grebby	Lincs	TF4368	53°11·6'	0°8·8'E	T	122
Grebe Lake	Bucks	SP6725	51°55·4'	1°1·1'W	W	164,165
Gredenton Hill	Warw	SP4051	52°9·6'	1°24·5'W	X	151
Gredington	Wrex	SJ4438	52°56·4'	2°49·6'W	X	126
Gree	N Ayr	NS3951	55°43·8'	4°33·4'W	X	63
Greeba	I of M	SC3080	54°11·5'	4°35·9'W	X	95
Greeba Br	I of M	SC3081	54°12·0'	4°36·0'W	X	95
Greeba Bridge	I of M	SC3081	54°12·0'	4°36·0'W	X	95
Greeba Castle	I of M	SC3180	54°11·5'	4°35·0'W	X	95
Greeba Mountain	I of M	SC3181	54°12·1'	4°35·0'W	H	95
Greeba Plantation or King's Forest	I of M	SC3181	54°12·1'	4°35·0'W	F	95
Greeba River	I of M	SC3180	54°11·5'	4°35·0'W	W	95
Greeb Point	Corn	SW3936	50°10·2'	5°38·9'W	X	203
Greeb Point	Corn	SW8733	50°9·8'	4°58·6'W	X	204
Greeb Point	Corn	SW9840	50°13·8'	4°49·6'W	X	204
Greeb, The	Corn	SW5329	50°6·8'	5°26·9'W	X	203
Greedy Gut	E Yorks	TA4012	53°35·4'	0°7·3'E	X	113
Greeenways Fm	Sol	SP2580	52°25·3'	1°37·5'W	FM	140
Gree Law	E Ayr	NS4747	55°41·8'	4°25·6'W	X	64
Green	Denb	SJ0568	53°12·3'	3°24·9'W	T	116
Green	D & G	NY2766	54°59·2'	3°8·0'W	X	85
Green	Lancs	SD6467	54°6·1'	2°32·6'W	X	97
Green	Northum	NY7377	55°5·5'	2°25·0'W	X	86,87
Green	Northum	NY7478	55°6·0'	2°24·0'W	X	86,87
Green	N Yks	SD7960	54°2·4'	2°18·8'W	X	98
Green	Orkney	HY2323	59°5·5'	3°20·1'W	X	6
Green	Orkney	HY5728	59°8·5'	2°44·6'W	X	5,6
Green	Pemb	SM9801	51°40·5'	4°54·9'W	T	157,158
Green	Powys	SO2694	52°32·6'	3°5·1'W	T	137
Green	Shrops	SO2479	52°24·5'	3°6·6'W	X	137,148
Greena	Cumbr	NY8116	54°32·6'	2°17·2'W	X	91,92
Greena	Shetld	HU3746	60°12·1'	1°19·5'W	X	4
Greena Ball	Devon	SX5677	50°34·7'	4°1·7'W	X	191
Green Acre	N Yks	SE4478	54°12·0'	1°19·1'W	X	99
Greenacre	Pemb	SN0301	51°40·6'	4°50·6'W	X	157,158
Greenacre Fm	Essex	TQ6997	51°39·0'	0°27·0'E	FM	167,177
Green Acres	Cumbr	NY4161	54°56·7'	2°54·8'W	X	85
Green Acres	Devon	ST0408	50°52·0'	3°21·5'W	X	192
Greenacres	Durham	NZ1442	54°46·6'	1°46·5'W	X	88
Greenacres	Notts	SK7774	53°15·7'	0°50·3'W	X	120
Greenacres	Oldham	SD9405	53°32·7'	2°5·0'W	T	109
Greenacres	Scot Bord	NT2153	55°46·1'	3°15·1'W	X	66,73
Greenacres	Somer	ST5541	51°10·2'	2°38·2'W	X	182,183
Greenacres	Wilts	SU0591	51°37·3'	1°55·3'W	X	163,173
Greenacres	W Susx	TQ2821	50°58·7'	0°10·2'W	X	198
Greenacres Fm	Beds	SP9523	51°54·1'	0°36·8'W	FM	165
Greenacres Fm	Devon	SX4297	50°45·3'	4°14·0'W	FM	190
Greenacres Fm	Norf	TG1010	52°39·0'	1°6·7'E	FM	133
Greenacres Fm	Wilts	SU1023	51°0·6'	1°51·1'W	FM	184
Greenah	Cumbr	NY1545	54°47·8'	3°18·9'W	X	85
Greenah Crag Fm	Cumbr	NY3928	54°38·9'	2°56·3'W	FM	90
Greena Hill	Scot Bord	NY4581	55°7·5'	2°51·3'W	H	79
Greenala Point	Pemb	SS0096	51°37·9'	4°53·0'W	X	158
Greenaleigh Fm	Somer	SS9547	51°13·0'	3°29·8'W	FM	181
Greenaleigh Point	Somer	SS9548	51°13·5'	3°29·8'W	X	181
Green Alley Fm	Warr	SJ6789	53°24·0'	2°29·4'W	FM	109
Greena Moor	Corn	SX2496	50°44·5'	4°29·3'W	X	190
Greenamoor Br	Corn	SX2595	50°43·9'	4°28·4'W	X	190
Greenan	Arg & Bt	NS0663	55°49·5'	5°5·4'W	X	63
Greenan	S Ayr	NS3119	55°26·4'	4°39·9'W	X	70
Greenan Loch	Arg & Bt	NS0664	55°50·1'	5°5·4'W	W	63
Greenan Nev	Orkney	HY5436	59°12·8'	2°47·9'W	X	5
Greenarbour	Essex	TL6127	51°55·3'	0°20·9'E	X	167
Greenas	N Yks	NZ0601	54°24·5'	1°54·0'W	X	92
Greenass Fm	N Yks	SE2574	54°9·9'	1°36·6'W	FM	99
Greenataing	Orkney	HY5217	59°2·5'	2°49·7'W	X	6
Greenaton	S Lanak	NS9947	55°42·6'	3°36·0'W	X	72
Greenaway, The	Corn	SW9378	50°34·1'	4°55·0'W	X	200
Greenawell	Devon	SX7285	50°39·3'	3°48·3'W	X	191
Green Band	Cumbr	NY6534	54°47·6'	2°34·1'W	X	86
Greenbank	Ches	SJ6180	53°19·2'	2°34·7'W	X	109
Greenbank	Ches	SJ6472	53°14·9'	2°32·0'W	T	118
Greenbank	Ches	SJ7261	53°9·0'	2°24·7'W	X	118
Greenbank	Ches	SJ7881	53°19·8'	2°19·4'W	X	109
Green Bank	Cumbr	SD2190	54°18·2'	3°12·4'W	X	96
Green Bank	Cumbr	SD3880	54°13·0'	2°56·6'W	T	96,97
Green Bank	Cumbr	SD5791	54°19·0'	2°39·2'W	X	97
Greenbank	Falk	NS8679	55°59·7'	3°49·2'W	T	65
Green Bank	Lancs	SD5372	54°8·7'	2°42·8'W	X	97
Green Bank	Lancs	SD6561	54°2·9'	2°31·7'W	X	97
Green Bank	Lancs	SD8642	53°52·7'	2°12·4'W	X	103
Greenbank	Moray	NJ4461	57°38·4'	2°55·8'W	X	28
Greenbank	N Yks	NZ1409	54°28·8'	1°46·6'W	X	92
Green Bank	N Yks	SD9051	53°57·5'	2°8·7'W	X	103
Greenbank	Scot Bord	NT1824	55°30·4'	3°17·5'W	H	72
Greenbank	Scot Bord	NT4113	55°24·7'	2°55·5'W	X	79
Greenbank	Shetld	HP5303	60°42·7'	1°1·2'W	T	1
Greenbank	S Lanak	NS6050	55°43·6'	4°13·3'W	X	64
Greenbank	S Lanak	NT0443	55°40·5'	3°31·2'W	X	72
Greenbank Fell	Lancs	SD6460	54°2·3'	2°32·6'W	X	97
Greenbank Fm	Ches	SJ6258	53°7·3'	2°33·7'W	FM	118
Greenbank Fm	Ches	SJ7756	53°6·3'	2°20·2'W	FM	118
Greenbank Fm	Cumbr	NY1229	54°39·2'	3°21·4'W	FM	89
Greenbank Fm	Cumbr	NY3914	54°31·3'	2°56·1'W	FM	90
Greenbank Fm	Cumbr	SD4292	54°19·5'	2°53·1'W	FM	96,97
Greenbank Fm	Lincs	TF2408	52°39·6'	0°9·6'W	FM	142
Greenbank Fm	S Lanak	NS9048	55°43·0'	3°44·6'W	FM	72
Greenbank Gdn	E Renf	NS5656	55°46·8'	4°17·3'W	X	64
Greenbank Hill	Scot Bord	NT4115	55°25·8'	2°55·5'W	X	79
Green Banks	Lancs	SD7545	53°54·3'	2°22·4'W	X	103
Green Banks	Shetld	HU3360	60°19·6'	1°23·6'W	X	2,3
Green Banks	Shrops	SJ4036	52°55·3'	2°53·1'W	X	126
Greenbarn	Ches	SJ9571	53°14·4'	2°4·1'W	X	118
Green Barn	Staffs	SK1202	52°37·2'	1°49·0'W	X	139
Green Barrow	Somer	SS8134	51°5·8'	3°41·6'W	A	181
Green Barrow Fm	Wilts	ST8577	51°29·7'	2°12·6'W	FM	173
Greenbeck	D & G	NY0790	55°12·0'	3°27·2'W	X	78
Green Bell	Cumbr	NY6901	54°24·5'	2°28·2'W	H	91
Green Benan	S Ayr	NX0776	55°2·7'	5°0·8'W	H	76
Greenber Field	Lancs	SD8848	53°55·9'	2°10·6'W	X	103
Greenberry	N Yks	NZ2701	54°24·5'	1°34·6'W	X	93
Greenberry Br	Hants	SU2101	50°48·7'	1°41·7'W	X	195
Greenbog	Moray	NJ4754	57°34·6'	2°52·7'W	X	28,29
Greenbogue	D & G	NY0179	55°6·0'	3°32·7'W	X	84
Greenbog Wood	Pth & Kin	NN8813	56°18·0'	3°48·2'W	F	58
Green Booth	Ches	SJ9877	53°17·6'	2°1·4'W	X	118
Greenbooth Resr	Roch	SD8515	53°38·1'	2°13·2'W	W	109
Greenborough Marshes	Kent	TQ8670	51°24·1'	0°40·8'E	W	178
Green Bottom	Corn	SW7645	50°16·0'	5°8·2'W	T	204
Green Bottom	Glos	SO6715	51°50·2'	2°28·3'W	T	162
Greenbottom Wood	Aberd	NO6773	56°51·1'	2°32·0'W	F	45
Greenbrae	Aberd	NJ7544	57°29·4'	2°24·6'W	X	29
Greenbrae	Aberd	NJ8548	57°31·6'	2°14·6'W	X	30
Greenbrae	Aberd	NJ9244	57°29·4'	2°7·5'W	X	30
Greenbrae	Aberd	NK0246	57°30·5'	1°57·5'W	X	30
Greenbrae	Aberd	NK0535	57°24·6'	1°54·5'W	X	30
Greenbrae	D & G	NX7271	55°1·3'	3°59·7'W	X	77,84
Green Brae	Highld	NH6157	57°35·2'	4°19·0'W	X	26
Greenbraehead	D & G	NY3674	55°3·6'	2°59·7'W	X	85
Green Brough	N Yks	NZ1011	54°29·9'	1°50·3'W	X	92
Green Brow	Aberd	NJ4321	57°16·8'	2°56·3'W	H	37
Greenburn	Aberd	NJ6006	57°8·8'	2°39·2'W	X	37
Greenburn	Aberd	NJ6600	57°5·6'	2°33·2'W	X	38
Greenburn	Aberd	NJ7211	57°11·6'	2°27·3'W	X	38
Greenburn	Aberd	NJ9360	57°38·1'	2°6·6'W	X	30
Greenburn	Angus	NO4839	56°32·7'	2°50·3'W	X	54
Greenburn	Angus	NO5478	56°53·7'	2°44·9'W	X	44
Greenburn	C of Aber	NJ8810	57°11·1'	2°11·5'W	X	38
Green Burn	Cumbr	NY2802	54°24·7'	3°6·1'W	X	89,90
Green Burn	Cumbr	NY7731	54°40·7'	2°21·0'W	W	91
Green Burn	D & G	NW9762	54°54·9'	5°9·6'W	W	82
Green Burn	D & G	NX4672	55°1·4'	4°24·1'W	W	77
Greenburn	D & G	NX4860	54°54·9'	4°21·9'W	X	83
Green Burn	D & G	NX4878	55°4·6'	4°22·4'W	W	77
Green Burn	D & G	NX5395	55°13·9'	4°18·3'W	W	77
Green Burn	D & G	NX5573	55°2·1'	4°15·7'W	W	77
Green Burn	D & G	NX8569	55°0·4'	3°47·5'W	X	84
Green Burn	D & G	NX9266	54°58·9'	3°40·8'W	X	84
Green Burn	D & G	NY0599	55°16·8'	3°29·3'W	W	78
Green Burn	D & G	NY1386	55°9·9'	3°21·5'W	X	78
Green Burn	D & G	NY1387	55°10·4'	3°21·5'W	W	78
Green Burn	D & G	NY3979	55°6·4'	2°56·9'W	X	85
Greenburn	D & G	NY3980	55°6·9'	2°57·0'W	X	79
Greenburn	E Ayr	NS5613	55°23·6'	4°16·0'W	X	71
Green Burn	Moray	NJ2138	57°25·8'	3°18·5'W	W	28
Greenburn	Scot Bord	NT8360	55°50·2'	2°15·8'W	X	67
Green Burn	Scot Bord	NY4586	55°10·2'	2°51·4'W	W	79
Greenburn	Scot Bord	NY4586	55°10·2'	2°51·4'W	X	79
Greenburn	S Lanak	NS7622	55°28·8'	3°57·3'W	X	71
Greenburn	S Lanak	NS7838	55°37·5'	3°55·8'W	X	71
Greenburn	Stir	NN6900	56°10·7'	4°6·2'W	X	57
Green Burn	Stir	NS4684	56°1·7'	4°27·8'W	W	57,64
Green Burn	Stir	NS5094	56°7·2'	4°24·3'W	W	57
Greenburn	W Loth	NS9360	55°49·5'	3°42·0'W	T	65
Green Burn	W Loth	NT0557	55°48·1'	3°30·5'W	W	65,72
Greenburn Beck	Cumbr	NY2902	54°24·8'	3°5·2'W	W	89,90
Greenburn Bottom	Cumbr	NY3110	54°29·1'	3°3·5'W	X	90
Greenburn Fm	S Lanak	NS7444	55°40·6'	3°59·8'W	FM	71
Greenburn Plantation	Scot Bord	NT8361	55°50·8'	2°15·9'W	F	67
Greenburns	Pth & Kin	NO2339	56°32·5'	3°14·7'W	X	53
Greenbury Fm	N Yks	SE2998	54°22·8'	1°32·8'W	FM	99
Greenbury Grange	N Yks	NZ2602	54°25·0'	1°35·5'W	X	93
Greenbush	Angus	NO4282	56°55·8'	2°56·7'W	X	44
Greenbutts Ho	Staffs	SJ7850	53°3·0'	2°19·3'W	X	118
Green Cairn	Aberd	NO6372	56°50·5'	2°35·9'W	X	45
Green Cairn (Fort)	Aberd	NO6372	56°50·5'	2°35·9'W	A	45
Green Carts	Northum	NY8871	55°2·2'	2°10·8'W	X	87
Green Castle	Aberd	NO6676	56°52·7'	2°33·0'W	A	45
Greencastle	Cumbr	NY6939	54°44·9'	2°28·5'W	X	91
Green Castle	Cumbr	NY7131	54°40·6'	2°26·6'W	X	91
Green Castle	E Loth	NT5865	55°52·8'	2°39·8'W	X	67
Green Castle (Castell-moel)	Carm	SN3916	51°49·4'	4°19·8'W	A	159
Green Castle (Fort)	E Loth	NT5865	55°52·8'	2°39·8'W	A	67
Greencastle Tarn	Cumbr	NY6939	54°44·9'	2°28·5'W	W	91
Green Chain Walk	Bexley	TQ4780	51°30·2'	0°7·5'E	X	177
Greenchesters	Northum	NY8794	55°14·6'	2°11·8'W	X	80
Green Cleugh	Scot Bord	NT6057	55°48·5'	2°37·9'W	X	67,74
Greencliff	Devon	SS4026	51°0·9'	4°16·5'W	X	180,190
Greencliffe Hag Wood	N Yks	SE5686	54°16·2'	1°8·0'W	F	100
Greenclose	Cumbr	NY2133	54°41·4'	3°13·1'W	X	89,90
Green Close	Cumbr	NY4226	54°37·8'	2°53·5'W	X	90
Green Close	N Yks	SD7269	54°7·2'	2°25·3'W	T	98
Green Clough	Brad	SE0832	53°47·3'	1°52·3'W	T	104
Green Clough	Derby	SK1592	53°25·7'	1°46·0'W	X	110
Green Combe	Cumbr	NY2714	54°31·2'	3°7·2'W	X	89,90
Green Combe	Cumbr	NY2911	54°29·6'	3°5·3'W	X	89,90
Green Combe	Devon	SX6983	50°38·2'	3°50·8'W	X	191
Green Combs	Durham	NY7934	54°42·3'	2°19·1'W	X	91
Greencomb Sike	Durham	NY7934	54°42·3'	2°19·1'W	W	91
Green Common	Lancs	SD4737	53°49·8'	2°47·9'W	X	102
Greencoombe Fm	Somer	ST3908	50°52·3'	2°51·6'W	FM	193
Green Court	Monm	SO3803	51°43·6'	2°53·5'W	X	171
Green Cowden Fm	Derby	SK1967	53°12·2'	1°42·5'W	FM	119
Green Crag	Cumbr	SD2098	54°22·5'	3°13·5'W	X	96
Green Crag Slack	Brad	SE1345	53°54·3'	1°47·7'W	X	104
Green Craig	D & G	NX7888	55°10·5'	3°54·5'W	H	78
Greencraig	Falk	NS8776	55°58·1'	3°48·2'W	X	65
Green Craig	Fife	NO3221	56°22·8'	3°5·6'W	H	53,59
Greencraig	Moray	NJ4361	57°38·4'	2°56·8'W	X	28
Green Crize	Heref	SO5137	52°2·0'	2°42·5'W	T	149
Greencroft	Aberd	NJ9641	57°27·8'	2°3·5'W	X	30
Green Croft	Cumbr	NY2138	54°44·1'	3°13·2'W	X	89,90
Greencroft	Durham	NZ1651	54°51·5'	1°44·6'W	T	88
Greencroft	N Yks	NZ4603	54°25·5'	1°17·0'W	X	93
Greencroft Park	Durham	NZ1649	54°50·4'	1°44·6'W	X	88
Greencrofts	Essex	TL6021	51°52·1'	0°19·8'E	X	167
Green Cross	Surrey	SU8638	51°8·3'	0°45·9'W	T	186
Greencut Copse	Surrey	SU9349	51°14·2'	0°39·7'W	F	186
Greendale	Ches	SJ8877	53°17·6'	2°10·4'W	T	118
Greendale	Cumbr	NY1405	54°26·2'	3°19·1'W	X	89
Greendale	Devon	SY0089	50°41·8'	3°24·6'W	X	192
Green Dale	N Yks	SE8589	54°17·6'	0°41·2'W	X	94,100
Greendale	Staffs	SK0343	52°59·3'	1°56·9'W	X	119,128
Greendale Barton	Devon	SY0189	50°41·8'	3°23·7'W	X	192
Greendale Oak	Notts	SK5673	53°15·3'	1°9·2'W	F	120
Greendales Fm	Staffs	SK1910	52°41·5'	1°42·7'W	FM	128
Greendale Tarn	Cumbr	NY1407	54°27·3'	3°19·2'W	W	89
Greendams	Aberd	NJ7501	57°6·2'	2°24·3'W	X	38
Greendams	Aberd	NJ8720	57°16·5'	2°12·5'W	X	38
Greendams	Aberd	NO6490	57°0·2'	2°35·1'W	X	45
Green Dean Wood	Oxon	SU6878	51°30·0'	1°0·8'W	F	175
Greenden	Aberd	NJ9519	57°16·0'	2°4·5'W	X	38
Greenden	Aberd	NO8177	56°53·3'	2°18·3'W	X	45
Greenden	Angus	NO6056	56°41·9'	2°38·7'W	X	54
Green Dike	Northum	NY8252	54°52·0'	2°16·4'W	X	86,87
Green Dike	N Yks	NZ9600	54°23·4'	0°30·9'W	A	94
Green Dikes	N Yks	SE4581	54°13·6'	1°18·2'W	X	99
Greendikes	Scot Bord	NT6232	55°35·1'	2°35·7'W	X	74
Green Dikes Plantn	E Yorks	TA0462	54°2·8'	0°24·3'W	F	101
Greenditch Fm	Cambs	TL5748	52°6·7'	0°18·0'E	FM	154
Greenditch Fm	S Glos	ST5886	51°34·5'	2°36·0'W	FM	172
Green Down	Devon	ST2802	50°49·0'	3°0·9'W	T	193
Greendown	Devon	SX7066	50°29·0'	3°49·6'W	X	202
Green Down	Oxon	SU3484	51°33·5'	1°30·2'W	X	174
Greendown	Somer	ST5753	51°16·7'	2°36·6'W	T	182,183
Green Down	V of Glam	ST0672	51°26·6'	3°20·8'W	X	170
Greendown Fm	Devon	SS6524	51°0·2'	3°55·1'W	FM	180
Greendown Fm	Oxon	SU3483	51°32·9'	1°30·2'W	FM	174
Greendowns	Hants	SU5624	51°1·0'	1°11·7'W	X	185
Green Drove Fm	Peterb	TF2807	52°39·0'	0°6·1'W	FM	142
Green Dyke-end Geo	Shetld	HU4012	59°53·7'	1°16·6'W	X	4
Greendykes	Aberd	NJ5955	57°35·3'	2°40·7'W	X	29
Greendykes	Aberd	NO6270	56°49·5'	2°36·9'W	X	45
Green Dykes	Cumbr	SD6094	54°20·6'	2°36·5'W	X	97
Greendykes	E Loth	NT4373	55°57·1'	2°54·3'W	X	66
Greendykes	Northum	NU0628	55°33·0'	1°53·9'W	T	75
Greendykes	W Loth	NT0873	55°56·7'	3°27·9'W	X	65
Greendykeside	N Lanak	NS8170	55°54·8'	3°53·8'W	X	65
Green Edges	Cumbr	SD6788	54°17·4'	2°30·0'W	X	98
Green End	Beds	TL0147	52°7·0'	0°31·1'W	T	153
Green End	Beds	TL0638	52°2·0'	0°26·9'W	T	153
Green End	Beds	TL0764	52°16·1'	0°25·5'W	T	153

Green End	Beds	TL1063	52°15·5'	0°22·9'W	T	153
Green End	Beds	TL1252	52°9·5'	0°21·4'W	T	153
Green End	Bucks	SP9030	51°57·9'	0°41·0'W	T	152,165
Green End	Bucks	SU8095	51°39·1'	0°50·2'W	T	165
Green End	Cambs	TL2274	52°21·3'	0°12·1'W	T	142
Green End	Cambs	TL3856	52°11·3'	0°1·5'E	T	154
Greenend	Cumbr	NY2262	54°57·0'	3°12·6'W	X	85
Greenend	Devon	ST0402	50°48·8'	3°21·4'W	X	192
Greenend	Fife	NT2797	56°9·9'	3°10·1'W	X	59
Green End	Herts	TL0406	51°44·8'	0°29·2'W	T	166
Green End	Herts	TL2630	51°57·5'	0°9·6'W	T	166
Green End	Herts	TL3233	51°59·0'	0°4·3'W	T	166
Green End	Herts	TL3322	51°53·1'	0°3·7'W	T	166
Green End	Herts	TL3925	51°54·6'	0°1·6'E	T	166
Green End	Lancs	SD9046	53°54·8'	2°8·7'W	T	103
Greenend	N Ayr	NS4054	55°45·4'	4°32·5'W	X	64
Greenend	N Lanak	NS7464	55°51·4'	4°0·3'W	T	64
Green End	N Yks	NZ8203	54°25·2'	0°43·8'W	T	94
Green End	Oxon	SP3221	51°53·4'	1°31·7'W	T	164
Greenend	Pth & Kin	NN8424	56°23·9'	3°52·3'W	X	52,58
Greenend	Scot Bord	NT5828	55°32·9'	2°39·5'W	X	73,74
Green End	Warw	SP2686	52°28·5'	1°36·6'W	T	140
Green End Cow Pastures	Cambs	TL4768	52°17·7'	0°9·7'E	X	154
Green End Fm	Cambs	TL5953	52°9·4'	0°19·9'E	FM	154
Greenend Fm	Essex	TL5528	51°56·0'	0°15·7'E	FM	167
Green End Fm	Essex	TM2120	51°50·3'	1°12·9'E	FM	169
Green End Fm	Flint	SJ3462	53°9·3'	2°58·8'W	FM	117
Greenends	Cumbr	NY7744	54°47·7'	2°21·0'W	X	86,87
Greeneye	Aberd	NK0255	57°35·4'	1°57·5'W	X	30
Green Eyes Crags	Northum	NY7388	55°11·4'	2°25·0'W	X	80
Green Face	Highld	NC6622	58°10·3'	4°16·2'W	X	16
Greenfaulds	N Lanak	NS7573	55°56·3'	3°59·6'W	T	64
Green Fell	Cumbr	NY6636	54°43·3'	2°31·2'W	X	91
Green Fell	Cumbr	NY7129	54°39·6'	2°26·5'W	X	91
Green Fell	Durham	NY8825	54°37·4'	2°10·7'W	X	91,92
Greenfell Crag	Cumbr	NY8108	54°28·3'	2°17·2'W	X	91,92
Green Fell End	Durham	NY8726	54°38·0'	2°11·7'W	X	91,92
Greenferns	C of Aber	NJ8807	57°9·5'	2°11·4'W	X	38
Greenfield	Aberd	NJ8246	57°30·5'	2°17·6'W	X	29,30
Greenfield	Angus	NO5344	56°35·4'	2°45·5'W	X	54
Greenfield	Arg & Bt	NS2490	56°4·5'	4°49·2'W	X	56
Greenfield	Beds	TL0534	51°59·9'	0°27·8'W	T	153
Greenfield	C of Glas	NS6464	55°51·3'	4°9·9'W	T	64
Greenfield	Denb	SJ1258	53°7·0'	3°18·5'W	X	116
Greenfield	D & G	NX0459	54°53·5'	5°2·9'W	X	82
Greenfield	Durham	NZ1341	54°46·1'	1°47·5'W	X	88
Green Field	Durham	NZ1728	54°39·1'	1°43·8'W	X	92
Greenfield	E Ayr	NS5634	55°35·0'	4°16·6'W	X	71
Greenfield	E Renf	NS5449	55°43·0'	4°19·0'W	X	64
Greenfield	Flint	SJ2077	53°17·3'	3°11·6'W	T	117
Greenfield	Heref	SO6755	52°11·8'	2°28·6'W	X	149
Greenfield	Highld	NH2000	57°3·6'	4°57·6'W	X	34
Greenfield	Highld	NM9755	56°38·8'	5°18·2'W	X	49
Greenfield	Northum	NY9569	55°1·2'	2°4·3'W	X	87
Greenfield	Oldham	SD9904	53°32·2'	2°0·5'W	T	109
Greenfield	Orkney	HY4512	58°59·8'	2°57·0'W	X	6
Greenfield	Oxon	SU7191	51°37·0'	0°58·1'W	T	175
Greenfield	Pth & Kin	NO0131	56°27·9'	3°36·0'W	X	52,53
Greenfield	Scot Bord	NT9457	55°48·6'	2°5·3'W	X	67,74,75
Green Field	Shetld	HU2679	60°29·9'	1°31·1'W	X	3
Greenfield	Shetld	HU3689	60°35·2'	1°20·1'W	X	1,2
Greenfield	S Lanak	NS6439	55°37·8'	4°9·2'W	X	71
Greenfield	S Lanak	NS8824	55°30·1'	3°46·0'W	X	71,72
Greenfield	Stock on T	NZ4711	54°29·8'	1°16·0'W	X	93
Green Field Beck	N Yks	SD8579	54°12·6'	2°13·4'W	W	98
Greenfield Burn	E Renf	NS5248	55°42·4'	4°20·9'W	W	64
Greenfield Burn	Highld	NN1999	57°3·1'	4°58·6'W	W	34
Greenfield Burn	S Lanak	NT0153	55°45·9'	3°34·2'W	W	65,72
Greenfield Copse	Oxon	SU7092	51°37·6'	0°58·9'W	F	175
Greenfield Fm	Durham	NZ0744	54°47·7'	1°53·0'W	FM	88
Greenfield Fm	Lincs	TF1774	53°15·2'	0°14·4'W	FM	121
Greenfield Fm	Lincs	TF4377	53°16·1'	0°9·1'E	FM	122
Greenfield Fm	Lincs	TF4453	53°3·5'	0°9·3'E	FM	122
Greenfield Ho	N Yks	SE0153	53°58·6'	1°58·7'W	X	104
Greenfield Ho	Pth & Kin	NN9329	56°26·7'	3°43·7'W	X	52,58
Greenfield Ho	S Lanak	NT0156	55°47·5'	3°34·3'W	X	65,72
Greenfield Ho	St Hel	SJ5399	53°29·4'	2°42·1'W	X	108
Greenfield Lodge	Northnts	SP9160	52°14·1'	0°39·6'W	X	152
Greenfield (Maes-Glas)	Flint	SJ1977	53°17·3'	3°12·5'W	T	116
Greenfield Manor Fm	Durham	NZ1728	54°39·1'	1°43·8'W	FM	92
Greenfieldmuir	E Renf	NS4558	55°47·7'	4°27·9'W	X	64
Greenfield Plantns	Scot Bord	NT9458	55°49·2'	2°5·3'W	F	67,74,75
Greenfield Resr	Oldham	SE0205	53°32·7'	1°57·8'W	W	110
Greenfields	Derby	SK2816	52°44·7'	1°34·7'W	X	128
Greenfields	Dorset	SY7296	50°46·0'	2°23·4'W	X	194
Greenfields	Essex	TL6822	51°52·5'	0°26·8'E	X	167
Greenfields	Lancs	SD4321	53°41·2'	2°51·4'W	X	102
Greenfields	Lincs	TF2253	53°3·9'	0°10·4'W	X	122
Greenfields	Northum	NU0615	55°26·0'	1°53·9'W	X	81
Greenfields	Shrops	SJ6126	52°50·0'	2°34·3'W	X	127
Greenfields	Staffs	SJ9249	53°2·5'	2°6·8'W	X	118
Greenfields	W Susx	TQ1812	50°53·9'	0°18·9'W	X	198
Greenfields Fm	Ches	SJ7045	53°0·3'	2°26·4'W	FM	118
Greenfields Fm	Lincs	TF1968	53°12·0'	0°12·7'W	FM	122
Greenfields Fms	Derby	SK2263	53°10·1'	1°39·8'W	FM	119
Greenfield Wood	Highld	NH2000	57°3·6'	4°57·6'W	F	34
Greenfield Wood	Oxon	SU7190	51°36·5'	0°58·1'W	F	175
Green Fm	Beds	SP9423	51°54·1'	0°37·6'W	FM	165
Green Fm	Ches	SJ3670	53°13·6'	2°57·1'W	FM	117
Green Fm	Ches	SJ6952	53°4·1'	2°27·4'W	FM	118
Green Fm	Ches	SJ9582	53°20·3'	2°4·1'W	FM	109
Green Fm	Cumbr	NY5512	54°30·3'	2°41·3'W	FM	90
Green Fm	Derby	SK2257	53°6·8'	1°39·9'W	FM	119
Green Fm	E Susx	TQ5210	50°52·4'	0°10·0'E	FM	199
Green Fm	E Yorks	SE7337	53°49·7'	0°53·0'W	FM	105,106
Green Fm	Heref	SO3748	52°7·8'	2°54·8'W	FM	148,149
Green Fm	Heref	SO4635	52°0·9'	2°46·8'W	FM	149,161
Green Fm	Heref	SO5048	52°7·9'	2°43·4'W	FM	149
Green Fm	I Scilly	SV9212	49°56·0'	6°17·2'W	FM	203
Green Fm	Kent	TQ6972	51°25·5'	0°26·2'E	FM	177,178

Green Fm	Lincs	SK8784	53°21·0'	0°41·2'W	FM	121
Green Fm	Lincs	TF4249	53°1·4'	0°7·4'E	FM	131
Green Fm	Norf	TF9124	52°47·0'	0°50·3'E	FM	132
Green Fm	Norf	TG0239	52°54·9'	1°0·7'E	FM	133
Green Fm	Norf	TG0515	52°41·9'	1°2·4'E	FM	133
Green Fm	Northnts	SP7541	52°4·0'	0°54·0'W	FM	152
Green Fm	N Som	ST4260	51°20·4'	2°49·6'W	FM	172,182
Green Fm	N Yks	SE9482	54°13·7'	0°33·1'W	FM	101
Green Fm	Oxon	SP3909	51°46·9'	1°25·7'W	FM	164
Green Fm	Oxon	SP5329	51°57·6'	1°13·3'W	FM	164
Green Fm	S Glos	ST6894	51°38·9'	2°27·4'W	FM	162,172
Green Fm	Shrops	SJ5005	52°38·7'	2°43·9'W	FM	126
Green Fm	Shrops	SO4999	52°35·4'	2°44·8'W	FM	137,138
Green Fm	Somer	ST3853	51°16·6'	2°52·9'W	FM	182
Green Fm	Somer	ST6845	51°12·4'	2°27·1'W	FM	183
Green Fm	Staffs	SJ8130	52°52·3'	2°16·5'W	FM	127
Green Fm	Suff	TL9365	52°15·2'	0°50·1'E	FM	155
Green Fm	Suff	TM1264	52°14·2'	1°6·7'E	FM	155
Green Fm	Suff	TM1566	52°15·2'	1°9·4'E	FM	156
Green Fm	Suff	TM1770	52°17·3'	1°11·3'E	FM	156
Green Fm	Suff	TM1971	52°17·8'	1°13·1'E	FM	156
Green Fm	Suff	TM2066	52°15·1'	1°13·8'E	FM	156
Green Fm	Suff	TM2358	52°10·7'	1°16·1'E	FM	156
Green Fm	Suff	TM2568	52°16·1'	1°18·3'E	FM	156
Green Fm	Suff	TM3871	52°17·4'	1°29·8'E	FM	156
Green Fm	Suff	TM4270	52°16·7'	1°33·3'E	FM	156
Green Fm	Surrey	SU8738	51°8·3'	0°45·0'W	FM	186
Green Fm	Surrey	TQ3242	51°9·9'	0°6·3'W	FM	187
Green Fm	W Berks	SU6669	51°25·2'	1°2·7'W	FM	175
Green Fm	Worcs	SO8537	52°2·1'	2°12·7'W	FM	150
Green Fm	Worcs	SO9152	52°10·2'	2°7·5'W	FM	150
Green Fm	Worcs	SO9156	52°12·4'	2°7·5'W	FM	150
Green Fm	W Susx	TQ1213	50°54·6'	0°24·0'W	FM	198
Greenfold	Aberd	NJ8225	57°19·2'	2°17·5'W	X	38
Greenfold	Lancs	SD6369	54°7·2'	2°33·5'W	X	97
Greenfold	Moray	NJ6048	57°31·5'	2°39·6'W	X	29
Greenfold	Moray	NJ6049	57°32·0'	2°39·6'W	T	29
Green Folds	Highld	ND2050	58°26·1'	3°21·7'W	X	11,12
Greenfoot	N Lanak	NS7369	55°54·1'	4°1·4'W	T	64
Greenfoot Quarry	Durham	NY9839	54°45·0'	2°1·4'W	X	92
Greenford	Aberd	NJ7331	57°22·4'	2°26·5'W	X	29
Greenford	Angus	NO3439	56°32·6'	3°4·0'W	X	54
Greenford	Angus	NO5640	56°33·3'	2°42·5'W	X	54
Greenford	Ealing	TQ1382	51°31·8'	0°21·9'W	T	176
Green Gable	Cumbr	NY2110	54°29·0'	3°12·7'W	H	89,90
Greengair	D & G	NX6993	55°13·1'	4°3·1'W	X	77
Greengairs	N Lanak	NS7870	55°54·7'	3°56·7'W	T	64
Greengarth Hall	Cumbr	NY0700	54°23·5'	3°25·5'W	T	89
Greengate	Aberd	NK0456	57°35·9'	1°55·5'W	X	30
Greengate	Cumbr	NY7604	54°26·1'	2°21·8'W	X	91
Green Gate	Devon	ST0115	50°55·8'	3°24·1'W	T	181
Green Gate	N Lincs	TA0021	53°40·8'	0°28·7'W	X	106,107,112
Greengate	Norf	TG0116	52°42·5'	0°58·9'E	T	133
Greengate	Roch	SD9115	53°38·1'	2°7·8'W	T	109
Greengate Fm	Ches	SJ4973	53°15·3'	2°45·5'W	FM	117
Greengate Fm	Lincs	SK8961	53°8·6'	0°39·8'W	FM	121
Green Gate Fm	N Yks	SE2794	54°20·7'	1°34·7'W	FM	99
Greengate Head	D & G	NY2194	55°14·3'	3°14·1'W	X	79
Greengatehouse	D & G	NY2277	55°5·1'	3°12·9'W	X	85
Greengate Rig	E Ayr	NS4810	55°21·9'	4°23·5'W	X	70
Green Gates	Brad	SE1145	53°54·3'	1°49·5'W	X	104
Greengates	Brad	SE1936	53°49·4'	1°42·3'W	T	104
Greengates	Durham	NY9323	54°36·4'	2°6·1'W	X	91,92
Greengates	Lancs	SD8349	53°56·5'	2°15·1'W	X	103
Green Gates	Leeds	SE2342	53°52·7'	1°38·6'W	X	104
Greengate Well	Northum	NY6667	55°0·0'	2°31·5'W	X	86
Green Geo	Orkney	HY5000	58°53·3'	2°51·6'W	X	6,7
Greengill	Cumbr	NY1037	54°43·4'	3°23·4'W	T	89
Greengill	Cumbr	NY5336	54°43·3'	2°43·4'W	X	90
Green Gill	Durham	NZ0311	54°29·9'	1°56·8'W	X	92
Greengill Foot	Cumbr	NY5033	54°41·6'	2°46·1'W	X	90
Greengill Head	Cumbr	NY5232	54°41·1'	2°44·2'W	X	90
Greengill Ho	Cumbr	NY5132	54°41·1'	2°45·2'W	X	90
Greengill Syke	Cumbr	NY5922	54°35·7'	2°37·7'W	X	91
Greengore	Lancs	SD6738	53°50·5'	2°29·7'W	X	103
Green Grove	Carm	SN7229	51°56·9'	3°51·4'W	X	146,160
Green Gutter Head	Staffs	SK0165	53°11·2'	1°58·7'W	X	119
Green Hackeber Hill	N Yks	SD8275	54°10·5'	2°16·1'W	X	98
Green Hailey	Bucks	SP8203	51°43·4'	0°48·4'W	T	165
Greenhalgh	Lancs	SD4035	53°48·7'	2°54·3'W	T	102
Greenhall	Carm	SN4409	51°45·7'	4°15·2'W	X	159
Greenhall	Orkney	HY5605	58°56·1'	2°45·4'W	X	6
Green Hall	Powys	SJ1619	52°46·0'	3°14·3'W	X	125
Greenhall	Pth & Kin	NN9320	56°21·9'	3°43·5'W	X	52,58
Greenhall	S Lanak	NS6656	55°47·0'	4°7·8'W	T	64
Greenhall Fm	Aberd	NJ6329	57°21·3'	2°36·4'W	FM	37
Green Hall Fm	Cambs	TL2787	52°28·2'	0°7·4'W	FM	142
Green Hall Hill	Powys	SJ1519	52°46·0'	3°15·2'W	H	125
Green Hall, The	Derby	SK1847	53°1·4'	1°43·5'W	X	119,128
Greenham	Dorset	ST4004	50°50·2'	2°50·7'W	T	193
Greenham	Somer	ST0720	50°58·5'	3°19·1'W	T	181
Greenham	W Berks	SU4865	51°23·2'	1°18·2'W	T	174
Greenham Barton	Somer	ST0819	50°58·0'	3°18·2'W	A	181
Greenham Common Airfield (disused)	W Berks	SU4964	51°22·6'	1°17·4'W	X	174
Greenham Hall	Somer	ST0720	50°58·5'	3°19·1'W	X	181
Greenham Ho	Dorset	ST4004	50°50·2'	2°50·7'W	X	193
Greenham Lodge	W Berks	SU4865	51°23·2'	1°18·2'W	X	174
Green Hammerton	N Yks	SE4556	54°0·1'	1°18·4'W	T	105
Greenhaugh	Aberd	NJ5238	57°26·0'	2°47·5'W	X	29
Greenhaugh	Northum	NY7987	55°10·9'	2°19·4'W	T	80
Greenhaugh	Northum	NY8572	55°2·8'	2°13·7'W	X	87
Green Haume	Cumbr	SD2275	54°10·1'	3°11·3'W	X	96
Green Haw Hill	N Yks	SD9666	54°5·6'	2°3·3'W	X	98
Greenhaw Hut	N Yks	SD9992	54°19·7'	2°0·5'W	X	98
Greenhaw Moor	N Yks	SD8277	54°11·6'	2°16·1'W	X	98
Green Haworth	Lancs	SD7526	53°44·0'	2°22·3'W	T	103
Greenhead	Angus	NO5150	56°38·6'	2°47·5'W	X	54
Green Head	Cumbr	NY2837	54°43·6'	3°6·7'W	X	89,90
Green Head	Cumbr	NY3649	54°50·2'	2°59·4'W	T	85

Greenhead	Cumbr	SD5183	54°14·7'	2°44·7'W	X	97
Green Head	Cumbr	SD5796	54°21·7'	2°39·3'W	X	97
Green Head	Derby	SK1558	53°7·4'	1°46·1'W	X	119
Greenhead	D & G	NS7809	55°21·8'	3°55·1'W	X	71,78
Greenhead	D & G	NX6879	55°5·5'	4°3·7'W	X	77,84
Greenhead	D & G	NX8996	55°15·0'	3°44·3'W	X	78
Greenhead	D & G	NX9082	55°7·5'	3°43·1'W	X	78
Green Head	Durham	NZ1434	54°42·3'	1°46·5'W	X	92
Greenhead	E Ayr	NS4640	55°38·0'	4°26·3'W	X	70
Greenhead	E Loth	NT4667	55°53·8'	2°51·4'W	X	66
Green Head	Lancs	SD8236	53°49·4'	2°16·0'W	X	103
Greenhead	N Ayr	NS2643	55°39·2'	4°45·5'W	X	63,70
Greenhead	N Lanak	NS8054	55°46·1'	3°54·3'W	T	65,72
Greenhead	Northum	NY6665	54°59·0'	2°31·5'W	T	86
Greenhead	Northum	NY8383	55°8·7'	2°15·6'W	X	80
Greenhead	Northum	NZ0551	54°51·5'	1°54·9'W	X	87
Green Head	Orkney	ND3099	58°52·6'	3°12·4'W	X	6,7
Green Head	Orkney	ND4384	58°44·7'	2°58·6'W	X	7
Greenhead	Pth & Kin	NN8821	56°22·3'	3°48·4'W	X	52,58
Greenhead	Pth & Kin	NO1336	56°30·7'	3°24·4'W	X	53
Greenhead	Scot Bord	NT4929	55°33·4'	2°48·1'W	T	73
Greenhead	Scot Bord	NT7731	55°34·6'	2°21·5'W	X	74
Greenhead	Scot Bord	NT8661	55°50·8'	2°13·0'W	X	67
Green Head	Shetld	HU2445	60°11·6'	1°33·5'W	X	4
Green Head	Shetld	HU2546	60°12·1'	1°32·4'W	X	4
Green Head	Shetld	HU4623	59°59·6'	1°10·0'W	X	4
Green Head	Shetld	HU4744	60°10·9'	1°8·7'W	X	4
Green Head	Shetld	HU5138	60°7·7'	1°4·4'W	X	4
Greenhead	S Lanak	NS8741	55°39·2'	3°47·3'W	X	71,72
Greenhead	Staffs	SJ9846	53°0·9'	2°1·4'W	T	118
Greenhead Fm	Durham	NY9739	54°45·0'	2°2·4'W	FM	92
Greenhead Fms	Lancs	SD7846	53°54·8'	2°19·7'W	FM	103
Greenhead Gill	Cumbr	NY3508	54°28·0'	2°59·8'W	W	90
Greenhead of Arnot	Pth & Kin	NO2001	56°11·9'	3°16·9'W	X	58
Greenheads	Aberd	NK0339	57°26·7'	1°56·5'W	X	30
Greenheads	Aberd	NO7481	56°55·4'	2°25·2'W	X	45
Greenheads	Aberd	NO8992	57°1·4'	2°10·4'W	X	38,45
Green Heads	Orkney	ND2392	58°48·8'	3°19·5'W	X	7
Green Heath	Staffs	SJ9913	52°43·1'	2°0·5'W	T	127
Green Heath	Suff	TM5281	52°22·4'	1°42·5'E	X	156
Greenhedge Fm	Notts	SK7541	52°57·9'	0°52·6'W	FM	129
Green Hedges Fm	E Susx	TQ5732	51°4·2'	0°14·8'E	FM	188
Greenheugh Pt	Scot Bord	NT7971	55°56·1'	2°19·7'W	X	67
Greenheys	Salf	SD7004	53°32·2'	2°26·7'W	T	109
Green Heys	Suff	TM3859	52°10·9'	1°29·3'E	X	156
Green Hill	Aberd	NJ3114	57°13·0'	3°8·1'W	H	37
Green Hill	Aberd	NJ4508	57°9·8'	2°54·1'W	H	37
Greenhill	Aberd	NJ5001	57°6·1'	2°49·1'W	X	37
Greenhill	Aberd	NJ5720	57°16·4'	2°42·3'W	X	37
Green Hill	Aberd	NJ6309	57°10·5'	2°36·3'W	H	37
Green Hill	Aberd	NJ6414	57°13·2'	2°35·3'W	H	37
Greenhill	Aberd	NJ9858	57°37·0'	2°1·5'W	X	30
Greenhill	Aberd	NK0145	57°30·0'	1°58·5'W	X	30
Greenhill	Aberd	NK0939	57°26·7'	1°50·5'W	X	30
Green Hill	Angus	NO3475	56°52·0'	3°4·5'W	H	44
Green Hill	Angus	NO4950	56°38·6'	2°49·4'W	X	54
Greenhill	Arg & Bt	NR7934	55°33·2'	5°29·8'W	X	68,69
Green Hill	Bolton	SD6710	53°35·4'	2°29·5'W	X	109
Greenhill	Brad	SE1140	53°51·6'	1°49·6'W	X	104
Green Hill	Ches	SJ6079	53°18·6'	2°35·6'W	X	118
Green Hill	Cumbr	NY2229	54°39·3'	3°12·1'W	H	89,90
Green Hill	Cumbr	NY4020	54°34·5'	2°55·3'W	H	90
Green Hill	Cumbr	SD6886	54°16·4'	2°29·1'W	X	98
Green Hill	Cumbr	SD7081	54°13·7'	2°27·2'W	H	98
Green Hill	Derby	SE0604	53°32·2'	1°54·2'W	X	110
Green Hill	Devon	SX6367	50°29·4'	3°55·5'W	H	202
Greenhill	Devon	SX8373	50°32·9'	3°38·7'W	X	191
Green Hill	Devon	SX8772	50°32·4'	3°35·3'W	X	192,202
Green Hill	D & G	NX6197	55°15·1'	4°10·8'W	X	77
Green Hill	D & G	NX6957	54°53·7'	4°2·1'W	H	83,84
Green Hill	D & G	NX7556	54°53·2'	3°56·5'W	H	84
Green Hill	D & G	NX7853	54°51·7'	3°53·6'W	X	84
Greenhill	D & G	NX8358	54°54·4'	3°49·1'W	X	84
Green Hill	D & G	NX9792	55°12·9'	3°36·7'W	H	78
Green Hill	D & G	NY1079	55°6·1'	3°24·2'W	T	85
Green Hill	D & G	NY2692	55°13·3'	3°9·4'W	H	79
Green Hill	Dorset	ST3703	50°49·6'	2°53·3'W	X	193
Green Hill	Dorset	ST7903	50°49·8'	2°17·5'W	X	194
Green Hill	Dorset	SY6799	50°47·6'	2°27·7'W	X	194
Green Hill	Dorset	SY6984	50°39·5'	2°25·9'W	H	194
Green Hill	Dorset	SY7493	50°44·4'	2°21·7'W	X	194
Green Hill	Durham	NZ3728	54°39·0'	1°25·2'W	X	93
Greenhill	Durham	NZ3947	54°49·2'	1°23·2'W	T	88
Greenhill	E Ayr	NS4039	55°37·4'	4°32·0'W	X	70
Greenhill	E Ayr	NS4107	55°20·1'	4°30·0'W	H	70,77
Greenhill	E Ayr	NS4409	55°21·3'	4°27·2'W	H	70,77
Greenhill	E Ayr	NS4913	55°23·5'	4°22·6'W	X	70
Green Hill	E Ayr	NS5346	55°41·4'	4°19·9'W	X	64
Green Hill	Essex	TL5518	51°50·6'	0°15·4'E	X	167
Greenhill	E Susx	TQ5729	51°2·6'	0°14·8'E	X	188,199
Greenhill	Falk	NS8278	55°59·1'	3°53·0'W	X	65
Greenhill	Falk	NS8372	55°55·9'	3°51·9'W	X	65
Greenhill	Falk	NS8971	55°55·4'	3°46·1'W	X	65
Green Hill	Fife	NO3422	56°23·4'	3°3·7'W	H	54,59
Greenhill	Hants	SU5322	50°59·9'	1°14·3'W	H	185
Greenhill	Harrow	TQ1588	51°35·0'	0°20·0'W	T	176
Greenhill	Heref	SO7148	52°8·0'	2°25·0'W	T	149
Greenhill	Highld	NC9106	58°2·1'	3°50·3'W	X	17
Green Hill	Kent	TQ7954	51°15·6'	0°34·3'E	T	188
Greenhill	Kent	TR1666	51°21·3'	1°6·5'E	T	179
Green Hill	Leeds	SE4337	53°49·9'	1°20·4'W	T	105
Greenhill	Leic	SK4413	52°43·0'	1°20·5'W	T	129
Green Hill	Leic	SK5013	52°43·0'	1°15·2'W	X	129
Green Hill	Leic	SK6923	52°48·2'	0°58·2'W	X	129
Green Hill	Leic	SK7004	52°38·0'	0°57·5'W	H	141
Green Hill	Lincs	SK9036	52°55·1'	0°39·3'W	T	130
Green Hill	Lincs	TF0538	52°56·0'	0°25·9'W	X	130
Greenhill	Moray	NJ2249	57°31·7'	3°17·7'W	H	28
Greenhill	Moray	NJ5159	57°37·4'	2°48·8'W	X	29
Green Hill	Moray	NJ5259	57°37·4'	2°47·8'W	X	29

Green Hill	N Ayr	NS2351	55°43·5'	4°48·7'W	X	63
Green Hill	N Ayr	NS2454	55°45·1'	4°47·8'W	X	63
Green Hill	N Ayr	NS2853	55°44·6'	4°44·0'W	H	63
Green Hill	Norf	TF7421	52°45·7'	0°35·1'E	X	132
Green Hill	Northum	NT9149	55°44·3'	2°8·2'W	X	74,75
Green Hill	Northum	NY6449	54°50·3'	2°33·2'W	X	86
Green Hill	Northum	NY8553	54°52·5'	2°13·6'W	H	87
Green Hill	Northum	NY8647	54°49·3'	2°12·6'W	X	87
Green Hill	Notts	SK6327	52°50·4'	1°3·5'W	X	129
Green Hill	N Som	ST4260	51°20·4'	2°49·6'W	X	172,182
Green Hill	Orkney	HY2502	58°54·2'	3°17·6'W	X	6,7
Green Hill	Orkney	HY4127	59°7·8'	3°1·4'W	X	5,6
Green Hill	Orkney	HY6330	59°9·6'	2°38·3'W	X	5
Greenhill	Orkney	ND2098	58°52·0'	3°22·7'W	X	7
Green Hill	Orkney	ND2888	58°46·7'	3°14·2'W	X	7
Green Hill	Orkney	ND3189	58°47·2'	3°11·1'W	X	7
Greenhill	Pemb	SM9202	51°40·9'	5°0·1'W	X	157,158
Greenhill	Pth & Kin	NN8405	56°13·7'	3°51·8'W	X	58
Greenhill	Pth & Kin	NO0109	56°16·0'	3°35·5'W	X	58
Greenhill	Pth & Kin	NO0123	56°23·6'	3°35·8'W	X	52,53,58
Green Hill	S Ayr	NX2597	55°14·4'	4°44·7'W	H	76
Greenhill	Scot Bord	NT7817	55°27·0'	2°20·4'W	X	80
Green Hill	Scot Bord	NT8016	55°26·5'	2°18·5'W	H	80
Green Hill	S Glos	ST6387	51°35·1'	2°31·7'W	X	172
Greenhill	Sheff	SK3481	53°19·7'	1°29·0'W	T	110,111
Green Hill	Shetld	HU3065	60°22·3'	1°26·9'W	H	3
Green Hill	Shetld	HU4071	60°25·5'	1°15·9'W	H	2,3
Green Hill	Shetld	HU4999	60°40·5'	1°5·7'W	X	1
Green Hill	Shrops	SJ3600	52°35·9'	2°56·3'W	H	126
Green Hill	Shrops	SJ5028	52°51·1'	2°44·1'W	X	126
Greenhill	S Lanak	NS8541	55°39·2'	3°49·2'W	X	71,72
Greenhill	S Lanak	NS9332	55°34·4'	3°41·4'W	X	71,72
Green Hill	S Lanak	NS9333	55°35·0'	3°41·4'W	X	71,72
Greenhill	Stir	NS8186	56°3·4'	3°54·2'W	X	57,65
Greenhill	Stock	SJ9889	53°24·1'	2°1·4'W	X	109
Green Hill	Wilts	SU0686	51°34·6'	1°54·4'W	T	173
Green Hill	Wilts	SU2776	51°29·2'	1°36·3'W	X	174
Greenhill	Worcs	SO8477	52°23·7'	2°13·7'W	T	138
Greenhill	Worcs	SP0445	52°6·4'	1°56·1'W	T	150
Green Hill	W Susx	SU8913	50°54·8'	0°43·7'W	X	197
Greenhill Bank	Shrops	SJ3736	52°55·3'	2°55·8'W	T	126
Green Hill (Broch),	Orkney	HY2502	58°54·2'	3°17·6'W	A	6,7
Greenhill Common Fm	Wilts	SU0581	51°31·9'	1°55·3'W	FM	173
Greenhill Cross	Devon	SS8508	50°51·8'	3°37·7'W	X	191
Greenhill Dod	D & G	NT0411	55°23·3'	3°30·5'W	H	78
Greenhill Down	Oxon	SU3883	51°32·9'	1°26·7'W	X	174
Greenhill Fm	Cumbr	NY2545	54°47·9'	3°9·6'W	FM	85
Greenhill Fm	Devon	SX6394	50°44·0'	3°56·1'W	FM	191
Green Hill Fm	Essex	TL5711	51°46·8'	0°17·0'E	FM	167
Greenhill Fm	Kent	TQ9146	51°11·1'	0°44·4'E	FM	189
Greenhill Fm	Leic	SK6923	52°48·2'	0°58·2'W	FM	129
Greenhill Fm	Leic	SP4099	52°35·5'	1°24·2'W	FM	140
Greenhill Fm	Lincs	SK8195	53°27·0'	0°46·4'W	FM	112
Greenhill Fm	Northnts	SP6166	52°17·6'	1°5·9'W	FM	152
Greenhill Fm	Northum	NU1933	55°35·7'	1°41·5'W	FM	75
Green Hill Fm	Oxon	SP4736	52°1·5'	1°18·5'W	FM	151
Greenhill Fm	Oxon	SP4817	51°51·2'	1°17·8'W	FM	164
Greenhill Fm	Staffs	SJ8729	52°51·7'	2°11·2'W	FM	127
Greenhill Fm	Staffs	SO8792	52°31·8'	2°11·1'W	FM	139
Greenhill Fm	Warw	SP1163	52°16·1'	1°49·9'W	FM	150
Greenhill Fm	Warw	SP3859	52°13·9'	1°26·2'W	FM	151
Greenhill Fms	Wilts	SU0680	51°31·4'	1°54·4'W	FM	173
Greenhillhead	D & G	NY1080	55°6·6'	3°24·2'W	X	78
Greenhill Ho	Arg & Bt	NL9443	56°29·0'	6°57·8'W	X	46
Greenhill Ho	Highld	NH5850	57°31·3'	4°21·8'W	X	26
Green Hill Ho	Lancs	SD5267	54°6·0'	2°43·6'W	X	97
Greenhill Ho	Oxon	SP4736	52°1·5'	1°18·5'W	X	151
Greenhill Ho	Somer	ST5232	51°5·4'	2°40·7'W	X	182,183
Greenhill Lodge	Cambs	TL1092	52°31·1'	0°22·3'W	X	142
Greenhill Lodge Fm	Leic	SK4614	52°43·5'	1°18·7'W	FM	129
Greenhillock	Angus	NO4944	56°35·4'	2°49·4'W	X	54
Greenhillocks	Derby	SK4049	53°2·4'	1°23·8'W	T	129
Greenhill Plantation	Moray	NJ5260	57°37·9'	2°47·8'W	F	29
Greenhill Plantn	D & G	NY1166	54°59·1'	3°23·0'W	F	85
Greenhill Rocks	Northum	NU2033	55°35·7'	1°40·5'W	X	75
Greenhills	Durham	NY8331	54°40·7'	2°15·4'W	X	91,92
Green Hills	Durham	NZ3939	54°44·9'	1°23·2'W	X	93
Greenhills	Lancs	SD4235	53°48·7'	2°52·4'W	X	102
Greenhills	N Ayr	NS3750	55°43·2'	4°35·3'W	X	63
Green Hills	Northum	NY8347	54°49·3'	2°15·5'W	X	86,87
Greenhills	N Yks	NZ3801	54°24·4'	1°24·5'W	X	93
Green Hills	N Yks	SE3390	54°18·5'	1°29·1'W	X	99
Greenhills	S Lanak	NS6252	55°44·8'	4°11·5'W	T	64
Greenhills	Staffs	SJ8602	52°37·2'	2°12·0'W	X	127,139
Greenhills	Staffs	SK0351	53°3·6'	1°56·9'W	X	119
Greenhills	Surrey	SU8741	51°9·9'	0°45·0'W	X	186
Greenhills	Wilts	SU2777	51°29·7'	1°36·3'W	X	174
Greenhills Fm	N Yks	SE4696	54°21·7'	1°17·1'W	FM	100
Greenhills Fm	Red & Cl	NZ6817	54°32·9'	0°56·5'W	FM	94
Green Hills Fm	Worcs	SP0869	52°19·4'	1°52·6'W	FM	139
Greenhillstairs	D & G	NT0410	55°22·7'	3°30·5'W	X	78
Greenhill Wood	Kent	TQ5360	51°19·3'	0°12·1'E	F	177,188
Greenhill Wood	W Susx	SU8829	51°3·4'	0°44·3'W	F	186,197
Green Hippins	N Yks	SD7957	54°0·8'	2°18·8'W	X	103
Greenhirst	N Ayr	NS2749	55°42·5'	4°44·8'W	X	63
Greenhithe	Kent	TQ5875	51°27·3'	0°16·8'E	T	177
Green Ho	Shrops	SO7686	52°28·5'	2°20·8'W	X	138
Green Hole	Cumbr	NY2305	54°26·3'	3°10·8'W	X	89,90
Green Holes	Northum	NT7505	55°20·6'	2°23·2'W	X	80
Greenhole Sike	Northum	NY6468	55°0·6'	2°33·3'W	W	86
Green Hollins	Cumbr	SD6892	54°19·6'	2°29·1'W	X	98
Greenholm	E Ayr	NS5337	55°36·5'	4°19·6'W	T	70
Green Holm	Shetld	HU2958	60°18·6'	1°28·0'W	X	3
Green Holm	Shetld	HU3837	60°7·2'	1°18·5'W	X	4
Green Holm	Shetld	HU4947	60°12·5'	1°6·5'W	X	3
Green Holm	Shetld	HU5178	60°29·2'	1°3·8'W	X	2,3
Greenholme	Cumbr	NY4857	54°54·5'	2°48·2'W	X	86
Greenholme	Cumbr	NY5474	55°3·8'	2°42·8'W	X	86
Greenholme	Cumbr	NY5905	54°26·6'	2°37·5'W	T	91
Greenholme	Cumbr	SD6190	54°18·5'	2°35·5'W	X	97
Greenholme Bank	N Lincs	SE7402	53°30·8'	0°52·6'W	X	112
Greenholme Bank Fm	N Lincs	SE7301	53°30·3'	0°53·5'W	FM	112
Greenholme Fm	Brad	SE1647	53°55·4'	1°45·0'W	FM	104
Greenholme Fm	Cumbr	SD2889	54°17·7'	3°6·0'W	FM	96,97
Greenhope	Scot Bord	NT7361	55°50·7'	2°25·4'W	X	67
Greenhope Burn	Scot Bord	NT7262	55°51·3'	2°26·4'W	W	67
Greenhorn Burn	Clackm	NN8903	56°12·7'	3°46·9'W	W	58
Greenhouse	Scot Bord	NT5523	55°30·2'	2°42·3'W	X	73
Greenhouse	Staffs	SJ9156	53°6·3'	2°7·7'W	X	118
Greenhouse	Staffs	SJ9862	53°9·5'	2°1·4'W	X	118
Greenhouse Court	Glos	SO8708	51°46·5'	2°10·9'W	X	162
Greenhouse Fm	Cambs	TL4959	52°12·8'	0°11·3'E	FM	154
Green House Fm	Ches	SJ8864	53°10·6'	2°10·4'W	FM	118
Greenhouse Fm	E Susx	TQ5631	51°3·7'	0°14·0'E	FM	188
Green Houses	N Yks	NZ7609	54°28·5'	0°49·2'W	X	94
Green How	Cumbr	NY1906	54°26·8'	3°14·5'W	X	89,90
Green How	Cumbr	NY2537	54°43·6'	3°9·5'W	H	89,90
Greenhow	Cumbr	NY6924	54°36·9'	2°28·4'W	X	91
Green How	Cumbr	SD1799	54°23·0'	3°16·3'W	H	96
Green How	Cumbr	SD1898	54°22·5'	3°15·3'W	X	96
Green How	Cumbr	SD2095	54°20·9'	3°13·4'W	X	96,97
Greenhow	N Yks	SE1164	54°4·6'	1°49·5'W	T	99
Greenhow Bank	N Yks	NZ6003	54°25·4'	1°4·1'W	X	94
Greenhowe	Aberd	NJ9200	57°5·5'	2°7·5'W	X	38
Green Howe	Lincs	SK8699	53°29·1'	0°41·8'W	W	112
Green Howe	N Yks	SE3851	53°57·5'	1°24·8'W	A	104
Green Howe	N Yks	SE5398	54°22·7'	1°10·6'W	A	100
Greenhowe Fm	Red & Cl	NZ7313	54°30·7'	0°51·9'W	FM	94
Greenhow Hill	N Yks	NZ5411	54°29·7'	1°9·6'W	X	93
Greenhow Moor	N Yks	NZ5411	54°29·7'	1°9·6'W	X	93
Greenhow Moor	N Yks	NZ6002	54°24·8'	1°4·1'W	X	94
Greenhow Plantn	N Yks	NZ5902	54°24·8'	1°5·0'W	F	93
Greenhow Sike	N Yks	SE1262	54°3·5'	1°48·6'W	W	99
Green Hows Tarn	Cumbr	SD3690	54°18·3'	2°58·6'W	W	96,97
Green Humbleton	Scot Bord	NT8427	55°32·4'	2°14·8'W	H	74
Greenhurst	Cumbr	SD3681	54°13·5'	2°58·5'W	X	96,97
Greenhurst	E Susx	TQ5025	51°0·5'	0°8·7'E	X	188,199
Greenhurst	Shrops	SJ6123	52°48·4'	2°34·3'W	X	127
Greenhurst Hey	Cald	SD9325	53°43·5'	2°6·0'W	X	103
Greenhurth Sike	Durham	NY7832	54°41·2'	2°20·1'W	W	91
Green I	D & G	NX6672	55°1·7'	4°5·4'W	X	77,84
Greenigo	Orkney	HY4007	58°57·0'	3°2·1'W	T	6,7
Greenings	Lancs	SD4015	53°37·9'	2°54·0'W	X	108
Greenings, The	Surrey	TQ2241	51°9·5'	0°14·9'W	X	187
Green Isaf	Denb	SJ0669	53°12·8'	3°24·1'W	X	116
Green Isaf	V of Glam	SS9272	51°26·4'	3°32·8'W	X	170
Green Island	Corn	SW7252	50°19·7'	5°11·8'W	X	204
Green Island	Dorset	SZ0086	50°40·6'	1°59·6'W	X	195
Green Island	Highld	NC0515	58°5·1'	5°18·0'W	X	15
Green Island	I Scilly	SV8812	49°55·8'	6°20·5'W	X	203
Green Isle	Shetld	HU4861	60°20·1'	1°7·3'W	X	2,3
Green Kettle Ho	Lancs	SD3511	53°35·7'	2°58·5'W	X	108
Green Knap	Arg & Bt	NS1178	55°57·7'	5°1·2'W	X	63
Green Knowe	Cumbr	NY5872	55°2·7'	2°39·0'W	H	86
Greenknowe	D & G	NY3574	55°3·6'	3°0·6'W	X	85
Green Knowe	D & G	NY4481	55°7·5'	2°52·3'W	X	79
Green Knowe	Northum	NT9513	55°24·9'	2°4·3'W	X	81
Green Knowe	Orkney	HY4603	58°54·9'	2°55·8'W	X	6,7
Green Knowe	Scot Bord	NT1846	55°42·3'	3°17·9'W	H	72
Green Knowe	Scot Bord	NT2043	55°40·7'	3°15·9'W	X	73
Green Knowe	Scot Bord	NT3631	55°34·4'	3°0·5'W	H	73
Greenknowe	Scot Bord	NT6444	55°41·5'	2°33·9'W	X	74
Green Knowe	Scot Bord	NT8217	55°27·0'	2°16·6'W	X	80
Greenknowe	Scot Bord	NT8249	55°44·3'	2°16·8'W	X	74
Greenknowes	Fife	NT1193	56°7·5'	3°25·5'W	X	58
Green Knowes	Pth & Kin	NN9607	56°14·9'	3°40·3'W	X	58
Green Knowes	Scot Bord	NT2808	55°21·9'	3°7·7'W	X	79
Green Knowes	Scot Bord	NT6809	55°22·7'	2°29·9'W	X	80
Greenknowe Tower	Scot Bord	NT6443	55°41·0'	2°33·9'W	A	74
Green Knowles	Durham	NZ3429	54°39·5'	1°28·0'W	X	93
Greenland	Arg & Bt	NR7323	55°27·2'	5°35·0'W	X	68
Greenland	Cald	SD9429	53°45·7'	2°5·0'W	X	103
Greenland	Dorset	SZ0184	50°39·6'	1°58·8'W	X	195
Greenland	Durham	NZ1844	54°47·7'	1°42·8'W	X	88
Greenland	E Yorks	SE6939	53°39·5'	0°56·9'W	X	111
Greenland	Highld	ND2467	58°35·3'	3°18·0'W	X	11,12
Greenland	Sheff	SK3988	53°23·5'	1°24·4'W	T	110,111
Greenland	Shetld	HU2249	60°13·7'	1°35·7'W	X	3
Greenland	W Dunb	NS4374	55°56·3'	4°30·4'W	X	64
Greenland Fm	E Yorks	SE6720	53°40·6'	0°58·7'W	FM	105,106
Greenland Fm	E Yorks	SE6819	53°40·0'	0°57·8'W	FM	111
Greenland Fm	Lincs	TA1306	53°32·5'	0°17·3'W	FM	113
Greenland Fm	Wilts	SU0943	51°11·4'	1°51·9'W	FM	184
Greenland Fm	W Susx	SU9430	51°3·9'	0°39·1'W	FM	186
Greenland Mains	Highld	ND2467	58°35·3'	3°18·0'W	T	11,12
Greenland Resrs	W Dunb	NS4375	55°56·8'	4°30·4'W	W	64
Greenlands	Aberd	NJ8118	57°15·4'	2°18·4'W	X	38
Greenlands	Bucks	SU7785	51°33·7'	0°53·0'W	T	175
Greenlands	Cumbr	NY0801	54°24·0'	3°24·6'W	X	89
Greenlands	Cumbr	NY1431	54°40·3'	3°19·6'W	X	89
Greenlands	Derby	SK1284	53°21·4'	1°48·8'W	X	110
Greenlands	E Yorks	TA0869	54°6·6'	0°20·5'W	X	101
Greenlands	Somer	SS8441	51°9·6'	3°39·2'W	X	181
Greenlands	Worcs	SP0565	52°17·2'	1°55·2'W	T	150
Greenlands Fm	E Yorks	SE7548	53°55·6'	0°51·1'W	FM	105,106
Greenlands Fm	Lancs	SD6442	53°52·6'	2°32·4'W	FM	102,103
Greenlands Fm	Lincs	TF2416	52°43·9'	0°9·4'W	FM	131
Greenlands Fm	NE Lincs	TA1711	53°35·2'	0°13·5'W	FM	113
Greenlands Fm	N Yks	NZ8303	54°25·2'	0°42·8'W	FM	94
Greenlands Fm	N Yks	SE6168	54°6·5'	1°3·6'W	FM	100
Greenlands Fm	N Yks	TA1672	54°8·1'	0°13·1'W	FM	101
Greenlands Fm	Oxon	SU5882	51°32·3'	1°9·4'W	FM	174
Greenlands Fm	Somer	ST7430	51°4·4'	2°21·9'W	FM	183
Greenlands Howe	N Yks	NZ8603	54°25·1'	0°40·1'W	A	94
Greenland Water	Somer	SS8440	51°9·1'	3°39·1'W	W	181
Green Lane	Cov	SP3275	52°22·6'	1°31·4'W	T	140
Green Lane	Cumbr	NY3649	54°50·2'	2°59·4'W	X	85
Greenlane	Devon	SS4302	50°48·0'	4°13·3'W	X	190
Green Lane	Devon	SX7877	50°35·0'	3°43·0'W	T	191
Green Lane	E Yorks	TA0764	54°3·9'	0°21·5'W	X	101
Green Lane	Heref	SO6245	52°6·4'	2°32·9'W	T	149
Green Lane	Kent	TQ5054	51°16·1'	0°9·4'E	X	188
Green Lane	Powys	SO1795	52°33·0'	3°13·0'W	X	136
Green Lane	Powys	SO1950	52°8·8'	3°10·6'W	X	148
Green Lane	Shrops	SJ6025	52°49·5'	2°35·2'W	X	127
Greenlane	Staffs	SJ9961	53°9·0'	2°0·5'W	X	118
Green Lane	Worcs	SP0664	52°16·7'	1°54·3'W	T	150
Greenlane Coppice	Staffs	SJ7735	52°55·0'	2°20·1'W	F	127
Green Lane Cottage	Lincs	TF2952	53°3·2'	0°4·1'W	X	122
Green Lane End	Devon	SX7750	50°20·5'	3°43·3'W	X	202
Green Lane End	Somer	ST4016	50°56·7'	2°50·9'W	X	193
Greenlane Fm	Derby	SK1342	52°58·7'	1°48·0'W	FM	119,128
Green Lane Fm	Donc	SE6306	53°33·0'	1°2·5'W	FM	111
Green Lane Fm	Essex	TL6407	51°44·5'	0°22·9'E	FM	167
Green Lane Fm	Flint	SJ3363	53°9·8'	2°59·7'W	FM	117
Green Lane Fm	Heref	SO2644	52°5·6'	3°4·4'W	FM	148,161
Green Lane Fm	Heref	SO3261	52°14·8'	2°59·4'W	FM	137,148
Green Lane Fm	Herts	TL0712	51°48·0'	0°26·5'W	FM	166
Green Lane Fm	Kent	TQ9138	51°6·8'	0°44·1'E	FM	189
Green Lane Fm	Kent	TR0050	51°13·1'	0°52·2'E	FM	189
Green Lane Fm	Lancs	SD5239	53°50·9'	2°43·4'W	FM	102
Green Lane Fm	Norf	TF5212	52°41·3'	0°15·3'E	FM	131,143
Green Lane Fm	N Yks	NZ2602	54°25·0'	1°35·5'W	FM	93
Green Lane Fm	N Yks	SE6236	53°49·2'	1°3·1'W	FM	105
Green Lane Fm	Somer	ST6450	51°15·1'	2°30·6'W	FM	183
Green Lane Fm	Suff	TM1258	52°11·0'	1°6·5'E	FM	155
Greenlane Fm	Warr	SJ6383	53°20·8'	2°32·9'W	FM	109
Green Lane Fm	Wilts	ST8757	51°19·0'	2°10·8'W	FM	173
Greenlanes	Devon	SX4483	50°37·8'	4°12·0'W	X	201
Green Lane Wood	Wilts	ST8857	51°19·0'	2°9·9'W	F	173
Green Larg	S Ayr	NX3097	55°14·5'	4°40·0'W	X	76
Green Law	Aberd	NJ6757	57°36·4'	2°32·7'W	X	29
Greenlaw	Aberd	NJ6758	57°36·9'	2°32·7'W	X	29
Greenlaw	D & G	NX7564	54°57·6'	3°56·7'W	X	84
Greenlaw	E Loth	NT4867	55°53·9'	2°49·5'W	X	66
Greenlaw	E Renf	NS5357	55°47·3'	4°20·2'W	X	64
Green Law	Midlo	NT1659	55°49·3'	3°20·0'W	H	65,66,72
Green Law	Northum	NT8011	55°23·2'	2°18·5'W	X	80
Green Law	Pth & Kin	NN9907	56°14·9'	3°37·4'W	H	58
Green Law	Scot Bord	NT1240	55°39·0'	3°23·5'W	H	72
Green Law	Scot Bord	NT6304	55°20·0'	2°34·6'W	H	80
Green Law	Scot Bord	NT6706	55°21·1'	2°30·8'W	X	80
Greenlaw	Scot Bord	NT7146	55°42·6'	2°27·3'W	T	74
Greenlaw	Scot Bord	NT9355	55°47·5'	2°6·3'W	X	67,74,75
Greenlawdean	Scot Bord	NT7046	55°42·6'	2°28·2'W	X	74
Greenlawhill	Angus	NO5434	56°30·0'	2°44·4'W	X	54
Greenlaw Mains	Midlo	NT2461	55°50·4'	3°12·4'W	T	66
Greenlaw Moor	Scot Bord	NT7148	55°43·7'	2°27·3'W	X	74
Greenlaw Rig	Cumbr	NY7602	54°25·0'	2°21·8'W	X	91
Greenlaws Hush	Durham	NY8836	54°43·4'	2°10·8'W	W	91,92
Greenlaw Walls	Northum	NT9341	55°40·0'	2°6·2'W	X	74,75
Greenlea	D & G	NY0375	55°3·9'	3°30·7'W	T	84
Greenlea	N Ayr	NS3646	55°41·0'	4°36·1'W	X	63
Green Lea	Shrops	SO5984	52°27·4'	2°35·8'W	X	137,138
Greenlea Knowe	D & G	NY4188	55°11·2'	2°55·2'W	X	79
Greenleanachs	Highld	NH6158	57°35·7'	4°19·1'W	X	26
Greenlease Fm	W Susx	SZ8694	50°44·6'	0°46·5'W	FM	197
Green Leaze	Dorset	SY5487	50°41·1'	2°38·7'W	X	194
Greenlee	Northum	NY7670	55°1·7'	2°22·1'W	X	86,87
Greenlee Burn	Northum	NY7671	55°2·2'	2°22·1'W	W	86,87
Greenlee Cleugh	Northum	NY7276	55°4·9'	2°25·9'W	X	86,87
Greenlee Lough	Northum	NY7769	55°1·1'	2°21·2'W	W	86,87
Greenlees	Scot Bord	NT6350	55°44·8'	2°34·9'W	X	67,74
Greenlees	Scot Bord	NT7829	55°33·5'	2°20·5'W	X	74
Greenlees	S Lanak	NS6359	55°48·5'	4°10·7'W	X	64
Greenleeshill	S Lanak	NS6358	55°48·0'	4°10·7'W	X	64
Greenleigh Fm	Bath & NE Somer	ST5664	51°22·6'	2°37·5'W	FM	172,182
Greenleighton	Northum	NZ0267	55°0·1'	1°57·7'W	X	87
Greenleighton	Northum	NZ0291	55°13·0'	1°57·7'W	X	81
Greenley	Mil Key	SP8040	52°3·4'	0°49·6'W	T	152
Greenleycleugh	Northum	NY7851	54°51·4'	2°20·1'W	X	86,87
Greenleys	Aberd	NO7971	56°50·2'	2°20·2'W	X	45
Green Lines	Dorset	ST8413	50°55·2'	2°13·3'W	X	194
Greenli Ness	Orkney	HY6221	59°4·7'	2°39·3'W	X	5
Greenloaning	Aberd	NO8898	57°4·6'	2°11·4'W	X	38,45
Greenloaning	Pth & Kin	NN8307	56°14·7'	3°52·8'W	T	57
Greenloch	Aberd	NJ8956	57°35·9'	2°10·6'W	X	30
Green Loch	Highld	NC7139	58°19·5'	4°11·7'W	W	16
Green Lodge	Northnts	SP9683	52°26·4'	0°34·9'W	X	141
Greenlooms	Ches	SJ4763	53°9·9'	2°47·2'W	T	117
Greenlot	Lancs	SD5160	54°2·3'	2°44·5'W	X	97
Greenlow	Cambs	TL3743	52°4·3'	0°0·3'E	X	154
Greenlow Fm	Derby	SK2258	53°7·4'	1°39·9'W	FM	119
Green Lowther	S Lanak	NS9012	55°23·6'	3°43·8'W	H	71,78
Green Man Fm	Lincs	TF0159	53°7·3'	0°29·0'W	FM	121
Greenman's Lane	Wilts	ST9981	51°31·9'	2°0·5'W	T	173
Green Man Wood	Lincs	TF0159	53°7·3'	0°29·0'W	F	121
Green Marsh Fm	E Yorks	TA2025	53°42·7'	0°10·5'W	FM	107,113
Greenmarsh Fm	Norf	TF5521	52°46·1'	0°18·3'E	FM	131
Green Maws	Cumbr	SD6686	54°16·4'	2°30·9'W	X	98
Green Mea	N Yks	SD9592	54°19·7'	2°4·2'W	X	98
Green Meadow	Brig	SS9582	51°31·9'	3°30·4'W	X	170
Greenmeadow	Monm	SO2904	51°44·1'	3°1·3'W	X	171
Greenmeadow	Monm	SO3301	51°42·5'	2°57·8'W	X	171
Greenmeadow	Shetld	HU3156	60°17·5'	1°25·9'W	X	3
Greenmeadow	Swin	SU1487	51°35·1'	1°47·5'W	T	173
Greenmeadow	Torf	ST2795	51°39·2'	3°2·9'W	T	171
Green Meadow Fm	Glos	SP0210	51°47·6'	1°57·9'W	FM	163
Green Meadows Fm	Staffs	SJ9161	53°9·0'	2°7·7'W	FM	118
Greenmeath Sike	Northum	NY6580	55°7·0'	2°32·5'W	W	80
Greenmerse	D & G	NX9770	55°1·1'	3°36·2'W	X	84
Green Mile Fm	Notts	SK6681	53°19·5'	1°0·1'W	FM	111,120
Green Moor	Barns	SK2899	53°29·5'	1°34·3'W	T	110
Green Moor	Cumbr	SD2589	54°17·7'	3°8·7'W	X	96
Greenmoor	Hants	SZ3399	50°47·6'	1°31·5'W	X	196
Green Moor	Newp	ST3985	51°33·9'	2°52·4'W	X	171
Green Moor	N Yks	SE1265	54°5·1'	1°48·6'W	X	99
Greenmoor Arch	Newp	ST4086	51°34·4'	2°51·6'W	X	171,172
Greenmoor Bank	Cumbr	SD5689	54°17·9'	2°40·1'W	X	97

Greenmoor Fm	Newp	ST4085	51°33·9′	2°51·5′W	FM	171,172
Greenmoor Hill	Oxon	SU6481	51°31·7′	1°4·3′W	X	175
Green Moors	Monm	SO3415	51°50·0′	2°57·1′W	X	161
Greenmoor Side	Cumbr	NY0205	54°26·1′	3°30·2′W	X	89
Greenmoss	Aberd	NJ7313	57°12·7′	2°26·4′W	X	38
Greenmoss	Aberd	NJ7912	57°12·2′	2°20·4′W	X	38
Greenmount	Bury	SD7714	53°37·6′	2°20·5′W	T	109
Greenmow	Shetld	HU4428	60°2·3′	1°12·1′W	T	4
Greenmyre	Aberd	NJ7738	57°26·2′	2°22·5′W	X	29,30
Greenmyre	Aberd	NJ8236	57°25·1′	2°17·5′W	X	29,30
Greenmyre	Aberd	NJ8329	57°21·3′	2°16·5′W	X	38
Greenmyre	Aberd	NK0856	57°35·9′	1°51·5′W	X	30
Greenmyre	Angus	NO3154	56°40·6′	3°7·1′W	X	53
Greenness	Aberd	NJ7847	57°31·0′	2°21·6′W	T	29,30
Greenoak	E Yorks	SE8127	53°44·2′	0°45·9′W	T	106
Green Oak Fm	Oldham	SD9908	53°34·4′	2°0·5′W	FM	109
Greenock	Inverc	NS2776	55°57·0′	4°45·8′W	T	63
Greenock	Orkney	HY5007	58°57·1′	2°51·7′W	X	6,7
Greenock Bridge	E Ayr	NS6929	55°32·5′	4°4·1′W	X	71
Greenock Cut	Inverc	NS2474	55°55·9′	4°48·6′W	W	63
Greenock Mains	E Ayr	NS6327	55°31·3′	4°9·8′W	X	71
Greenocks	Stir	NS7696	56°8·7′	3°59·3′W	X	57
Greenock Water	E Ayr	NS6628	55°31·9′	4°7·0′W	W	71
Greenock West	Inverc	NS2676	55°57·0′	4°46·8′W	T	63
Greenodd	Cumbr	SD3182	54°14·0′	3°3·1′W	T	96,97
Greenodd Sands	Cumbr	SD3281	54°13·5′	3°2·2′W	X	96,97
Green of Invermay	Pth & Kin	NO0516	56°19·9′	3°31·7′W	X	58
Green of Keillour	Pth & Kin	NN9725	56°24·6′	3°39·7′W	X	52,53,58
Green Ore	Somer	ST5750	51°15·1′	2°36·6′W	T	182,183
Green Park	Bucks	SP8811	51°47·7′	0°43·0′W	X	165
Green Park	C of West	TQ2980	51°30·5′	0°8·1′W	X	176
Green Parlour	Somer	ST7054	51°17·3′	2°25·4′W	T	183
Green Pike	Lancs	SD7258	54°1·3′	2°25·2′W	X	103
Greenpit Fm	Powys	SO2241	52°4·0′	3°7·9′W	FM	148,161
Green Pits	Northum	NY8447	54°49·3′	2°14·5′W	X	86,87
Green Plantn	N Yks	SE8972	54°8·4′	0°37·8′W	F	101
Green Point	Shetld	HU2958	60°18·6′	1°28·0′W	X	3
Green Point	Shetld	HU3537	60°7·2′	1°21·7′W	X	4
Green Quarter	Cumbr	NY4604	54°26·0′	2°49·5′W	T	90
Green Quarter Fell	Cumbr	NY4703	54°25·4′	2°48·6′W	X	90
Greenridge	Northum	NY8860	54°56·3′	2°10·8′W	X	87
Greenrig	Falk	NS8478	55°59·1′	3°51·1′W	X	65
Green Rig	Scot Bord	NT7748	55°43·7′	2°21·5′W	X	74
Greenrig	S Lanak	NS8542	55°39·7′	3°49·2′W	X	71,72
Greenrigg	Cumbr	NY2248	54°49·5′	3°12·4′W	X	85
Greenrigg	Cumbr	NY2746	54°48·5′	3°7·7′W	X	85
Green Rigg	Cumbr	NY4877	55°5·3′	2°48·5′W	X	86
Green Rigg	Cumbr	NY4979	55°6·4′	2°47·5′W	X	86
Green Rigg	Cumbr	NY6144	54°47·6′	2°36·0′W	X	86
Green Rigg	Cumbr	NY6271	55°2·2′	2°35·2′W	X	86
Green Rigg	Cumbr	SD2693	54°19·9′	3°7·9′W	X	96,97
Greenrigg	D & G	NY3676	55°4·7′	2°59·7′W	X	85
Greenrigg	Northum	NU2111	55°23·8′	1°39·7′W	X	81
Green Rigg	Northum	NY9282	55°8·2′	2°7·1′W	X	80
Greenrigg	W Loth	NS9163	55°51·1′	3°44·0′W	X	65
Greenrigg	W Loth	NS9164	55°51·7′	3°44·1′W	T	65
Greenrigg Ho	Cumbr	NY2938	54°44·2′	3°5·7′W	X	89,90
Greenrigg Moor	Northum	NY8659	54°55·8′	2°12·7′W	X	87
Greenriggs	Cumbr	NY7607	54°27·7′	2°21·8′W	X	91
Greenriggs	Cumbr	SD4791	54°19·0′	2°48·5′W	X	97
Greenriggs	Northum	NY6659	54°55·7′	2°31·4′W	X	86
Greenriggs	Scot Bord	NT8348	55°43·8′	2°15·8′W	X	74
Greenrigg Villa	Cumbr	NY2047	54°48·9′	3°14·3′W	X	85
Greenrigs	Aberd	NJ5861	57°38·5′	2°41·8′W	X	29
Green Road Sta	Cumbr	SD1883	54°14·4′	3°15·1′W	X	96
Green Rock	Corn	SW6521	50°2·8′	5°16·6′W	X	203
Greenrow	Cumbr	NY1052	54°51·5′	3°23·7′W	T	85
Greenrow	Cumbr	NY4124	54°36·7′	2°54·4′W	X	90
Green Royd Fm	Donc	SE6216	53°38·4′	1°3·3′W	FM	111
Greens	Aberd	NJ8346	57°30·5′	2°16·6′W	T	29,30
Greens	Aberd	NJ9755	57°35·4′	2°2·6′W	X	30
Greens	Aberd	NK0650	57°32·7′	1°53·5′W	X	30
Greens	Angus	NO5752	56°39·7′	2°41·6′W	X	54
Greens	Essex	TL5407	51°44·7′	0°14·2′E	X	167
Greens	Orkney	HY5104	58°55·5′	2°50·6′W	X	6,7
Greens	Orkney	HY5303	58°55·0′	2°48·5′W	X	6,7
Greens	Scot Bord	NY4886	55°10·2′	2°48·6′W	T	79
Greens	Staffs	SK0066	53°11·7′	1°59·6′W	X	119
Green Saddle	Corn	SW7416	50°0·3′	5°8·9′W	X	204
Greensand Ridge Walk	Beds	SP9332	51°59·0′	0°38·4′W	X	165
Greensand Ridge Walk	Beds	TL1647	52°6·8′	0°18·0′W	X	153
Greensand Way	Kent	TQ5051	51°14·5′	0°9·3′E	X	188
Greensand Way	Kent	TQ9545	51°10·5′	0°47·8′E	X	189
Greensand Way	Surrey	SU8933	51°5·6′	0°43·4′W	X	186
Greensand Way	Surrey	TQ0141	51°9·8′	0°32·9′W	X	186
Greensand Way	Surrey	TQ2449	51°13·8′	0°13·0′W	X	187
Green's Bridge Fm	Know	SJ4587	53°22·9′	2°49·2′W	FM	108
Green's Burn	Cumbr	NY5769	55°1·1′	2°39·9′W	W	86
Greensburn	Cumbr	NY5769	55°1·1′	2°39·9′W	X	86
Green's Burn	Cumbr	NY5874	55°3·8′	2°39·0′W	W	86
Greens Burn	Pth & Kin	NO1504	56°13·5′	3°21·8′W	W	58
Greensbury Fm	Beds	TL0759	52°13·4′	0°25·6′W	FM	153
Green Scalp	Fife	NO4928	56°26·7′	2°49·2′W	X	54,59
Green Scar	Pemb	SM7922	51°51·4′	5°12·2′W	X	157
Green Scar Mire	N Yks	SD9088	54°17·5′	2°8·8′W	X	98
Green Scar Pasture	N Yks	SD8087	54°16·9′	2°18·0′W	X	98
Green Scar Pasture	N Yks	SD8087	54°16·9′	2°18·0′W	X	98
Green Scar Top	N Yks	SD9282	54°14·3′	2°6·9′W	X	98
Greenscoe Fm	Cumbr	SD2176	54°10·7′	3°12·2′W	FM	96
Green's Combe Fm	Somer	ST6736	51°7·6′	2°27·9′W	FM	183
Greenseat Beck	N Yks	SD8996	54°21·8′	2°9·7′W	W	98
Greensett Craggs	N Yks	SD7481	54°13·7′	2°23·5′W	X	98
Greensett Moss	N Yks	SD7481	54°13·7′	2°23·5′W	X	98
Green's Fell	Northum	NY9175	55°4·4′	2°8·0′W	X	87
Greensfield	Northum	NU1811	55°23·8′	1°42·5′W	X	81
Greensfield Moor Fm	Northum	NU1911	55°23·8′	1°41·6′W	FM	81
Green's Fm	Dorset	ST8322	51°0·1′	2°14·2′W	FM	183
Greens Fm	Essex	TL5007	51°44·7′	0°10·8′E	FM	167
Green's Fm	Essex	TL5608	51°45·2′	0°16·0′E	FM	167
Greens Fm	Essex	TL6215	51°48·8′	0°21·4′E	FM	167

Green's Fm	Suff	TL9436	51°59·5′	0°49·9′E	FM	155
Greens Fm	Suff	TM0872	52°18·6′	1°3·5′E	FM	144,155
Greens Fm	Surrey	TQ1941	51°9·6′	0°17·5′W	FM	187
Greensforge	Staffs	SO8588	52°29·6′	2°12·9′W	T	139
Greensgate	Norf	TG1015	52°41·7′	1°6·9′E	T	133
Greens' Gears	Northum	NY5885	55°9·7′	2°39·1′W	X	80
Greenshaw Plain	Northum	NY8966	54°59·6′	2°9·9′W	X	87
Greensheen Hill	Northum	NU0535	55°36·8′	1°54·8′W	H	75
Greenshieldhouse	S Lanak	NS9949	55°43·7′	3°36·1′W	X	72
Greenshields	S Lanak	NT0243	55°40·5′	3°33·1′W	X	72
Greens Ho	Derby	SK2283	53°20·8′	1°39·8′W	X	110
Green's Houses Fm	N Tyne	NZ2473	55°3·3′	1°37·0′W	FM	88
Green Side	Cumbr	NY3518	54°33·4′	2°59·9′W	X	90
Greenside	Cumbr	NY6060	54°56·2′	2°37·0′W	X	86
Green Side	Cumbr	NY6571	55°2·2′	2°32·4′W	X	86
Greenside	Cumbr	NY7104	54°26·1′	2°26·4′W	T	91
Greenside	Cumbr	SD0699	54°22·9′	3°26·4′W	X	96
Greenside	Cumbr	SD5184	54°15·2′	2°44·7′W	X	97
Greenside	Cumbr	SD5882	54°14·2′	2°38·2′W	X	97
Greenside	Derby	SK3979	53°18·6′	1°24·5′W	T	119
Greenside	E Ayr	NS4640	55°38·0′	4°26·3′W	X	70
Greenside	E Ayr	NS5717	55°25·8′	4°15·2′W	X	71
Greenside	E Ayr	NS6928	55°31·9′	4°4·1′W	X	71
Greenside	E Renf	NS4255	55°46·0′	4°30·7′W	X	64
Greenside	Fife	NO3205	56°14·2′	3°5·4′W	X	59
Greenside	Fife	NO3907	56°15·4′	2°58·6′W	X	59
Greenside	Fife	NO4314	56°19·2′	2°54·8′W	X	59
Greenside	Fife	NO5106	56°14·9′	2°47·0′W	X	59
Greenside	Ghead	NZ1462	54°57·4′	1°46·5′W	T	88
Green Side	Kirk	SE1711	53°36·0′	1°44·2′W	T	110
Greenside	Kirk	SE1716	53°38·7′	1°44·2′W	T	110
Greenside	Lancs	SD5954	53°59·1′	2°37·1′W	X	102
Greenside	Lancs	SD6368	54°6·6′	2°33·5′W	X	97
Green Side	Leeds	SE2732	53°47·3′	1°35·0′W	T	104
Greenside	Moray	NJ2656	57°35·5′	3°13·8′W	X	28
Greenside	N Lanak	NS7673	55°56·3′	3°58·7′W	X	64
Greenside	N Lanak	NS7961	55°49·9′	3°55·5′W	X	64
Greenside	Northum	NY6487	55°10·8′	2°33·5′W	X	80
Greenside	Northum	NZ0686	55°10·3′	1°53·9′W	X	81
Green Side	N Yks	SD8685	54°15·9′	2°12·5′W	X	98
Green Side	N Yks	SD8797	54°22·3′	2°11·6′W	X	98
Greenside	Renf	NS3661	55°49·1′	4°36·6′W	X	63
Greenside	Shetld	HP6108	60°45·3′	0°52·3′W	X	1
Greenside	Tames	SJ9099	53°29·5′	2°8·6′W	T	109
Greenside	Tames	SJ9793	53°26·3′	2°2·3′W	X	109
Greenside Beck	Cumbr	NY7003	54°25·5′	2°27·3′W	W	91
Greenside Cott	Moray	NJ2367	57°41·4′	3°17·0′W	X	28
Greenside Cotts	Scot Bord	NT8747	55°43·2′	2°12·0′W	X	74
Greenside Fm	D & G	NX8482	55°7·4′	3°48·7′W	FM	78
Greenside Fm	Durham	NZ3534	54°42·2′	1°27·0′W	FM	93
Greensidehall	Scot Bord	NT4915	55°25·8′	2°47·9′W	X	79
Greenside Hill	Lancs	SD5855	53°59·6′	2°38·0′W	H	102
Greenside Hill	N Ayr	NS2758	55°47·3′	4°45·1′W	X	63
Greensidehill	Northum	NT9716	55°26·5′	2°2·4′W	X	81
Greenside Hill	Scot Bord	NT8068	55°54·5′	2°18·8′W	X	67
Greenside Law	Scot Bord	NT1925	55°31·0′	3°16·5′W	H	72
Greenside or Courhope	Scot Bord	NT2046	55°42·3′	3°15·9′W	X	73
Greenside Reservoir	W Dunb	NS4775	55°56·9′	4°26·6′W	W	64
Greenside Rigg	Cumbr	NY6060	54°56·2′	2°37·0′W	X	86
Greensides	Derby	SK0668	53°12·8′	1°54·2′W	X	119
Greensides	S Ayr	NX2788	55°9·6′	4°42·5′W	X	76
Greensides	Staffs	SK0950	53°3·1′	1°51·5′W	X	119
Greenside Scalp	Fife	NO4229	56°27·2′	2°56·0′W	X	54,59
Greenside Tarn	Cumbr	NY7103	54°25·5′	2°26·4′W	W	91
Green Side Wood	Northnts	SP9883	52°26·4′	0°33·1′W	F	141
Green Sike	Cumbr	NY6671	55°2·2′	2°31·5′W	W	86
Greensike	Northum	NY7359	54°55·7′	2°24·9′W	W	86,87
Green Sike Rigg	Durham	NY9214	54°31·5′	2°7·0′W	X	91,92
Greensitch	Staffs	SJ9537	52°56·1′	2°4·1′W	X	127
Green Stitches	Derby	SK1891	53°25·2′	1°43·3′W	X	110
Green Skeer	Northum	NZ3182	55°8·1′	1°30·4′W	X	81
Greens Kennels	Moray	NJ0449	57°31·5′	3°35·7′W	X	27
Green Skerry	Orkney	HY7656	59°23·6′	2°24·9′W	X	5
Greenslack	Cumbr	SD2087	54°16·6′	3°13·3′W	X	96
Greenslack	D & G	NX6356	54°53·1′	4°7·7′W	X	83
Greenslade	Devon	SS6400	50°47·3′	3°55·4′W	X	191
Greensland	E Ayr	NS4550	55°43·4′	4°27·6′W	X	64
Greens Landing	Pth & Kin	NO1034	56°29·6′	3°27·3′W	X	53
Greensley Bank	N Yks	SD9289	54°18·0′	2°7·0′W	X	98
Greenslide	Orkney	ND3793	58°49·5′	3°5·0′W	X	7
Greenslinch	Devon	SS9603	50°49·3′	3°28·2′W	X	192
Green's Lodge	Leic	SP5198	52°34·9′	1°14·4′W	X	140
Green's Lodge	Rut	SK8013	52°42·8′	0°48·5′W	X	130
Greens Marsh	Lincs	TF4653	53°3·5′	0°11·1′E	X	122
Greens Norton	Northnts	SP6649	52°8·4′	1°1·7′W	T	152
Green's Norton Park	Northnts	SP6550	52°8·9′	1°2·6′W	X	152
Greens of Afforsk	Aberd	NJ6919	57°15·9′	2°30·4′W	X	38
Greens of Auchmacleddie	Aberd	NJ9258	57°37·0′	2°7·6′W	X	30
Greens of Blairock	Moray	NJ4862	57°39·0′	2°51·8′W	X	28,29
Greens of Bogside	Moray	NJ1956	57°35·5′	3°20·8′W	X	28
Greens of Burgie	Moray	NJ0857	57°35·9′	3°31·9′W	X	27
Greens of Coxton	Moray	NJ2560	57°37·7′	3°14·9′W	T	28
Greens of Gardyne	Angus	NO5751	56°39·2′	2°41·6′W	T	54
Greens of Glenbeg	Moray	NJ4037	57°25·4′	2°59·5′W	X	28
Greens of Middlehill	Aberd	NJ8250	57°32·6′	2°17·6′W	X	29,30
Greens of Savoch	Aberd	NJ9138	57°26·2′	2°8·5′W	X	30
Green's Park	Northnts	SP6247	52°7·3′	1°5·3′W	X	152
Greenspeck	Aberd	NJ8956	57°35·9′	2°10·6′W	X	30
Greensplat	Corn	SW9955	50°21·9′	4°49·2′W	T	200
Greenspot	Aberd	NJ7932	57°22·9′	2°20·5′W	X	29,30
Green Spot	Cumbr	NY0321	54°34·7′	3°29·6′W	X	89
Greenspot	Cumbr	NY2457	54°54·4′	3°10·7′W	X	85
Greenspot	Orkney	HY7653	59°22·0′	2°24·8′W	X	5
Green Stack	Ches	SJ9876	53°17·1′	2°1·4′W	X	118
Greenstead	Essex	TM0225	51°53·4′	0°56·5′E	T	168
Greenstead Green	Essex	TL8228	51°55·5′	0°39·2′E	T	168
Greenstead Hall	Essex	TL8129	51°56·0′	0°38·4′E	X	168
Greensted	Essex	TL5302	51°42·0′	0°13·2′E	T	167
Greensted Green	Essex	TL5203	51°42·5′	0°12·4′E	T	167
Greensted Ho	Essex	TL5203	51°42·5′	0°12·4′E	X	167

Greens, The	Cumbr	NY3742	54°46·4′	2°58·3′W	X	85
Greens, The	Cumbr	NY5755	54°53·5′	2°39·8′W	X	86
Greens, The	Moray	NJ1561	57°38·1′	3°25·0′W	X	28
Greens, The	S Lanak	NT0147	55°42·6′	3°34·1′W	X	72
Greenstone Point or Rubha na Lice Uaine	Highld	NG8598	57°55·4′	5°37·4′W	X	19
Greenstraight	Devon	SX8138	50°14·0′	3°39·7′W	X	202
Greenstrands	S Lanak	NS8739	55°38·1′	3°47·3′W	X	71,72
Green Street	Essex	TQ6299	51°40·2′	0°21·0′E	T	167,177
Green Street	E Susx	TQ7611	50°52·5′	0°30·5′E	T	199
Green Street	Glos	SO7600	51°42·1′	2°20·4′W	T	162
Green Street	Glos	SO8915	51°50·2′	2°9·2′W	T	163
Green Street	Herts	TL4522	51°52·9′	0°6·8′E	T	167
Green Street	Herts	TQ1998	51°40·3′	0°16·3′W	T	166,176
Green Street	Worcs	SO8649	52°8·6′	2°11·9′W	T	150
Green Street	Worcs	SO8740	52°3·7′	2°11·0′W	T	150
Green Street	Worcs	SP0549	52°8·6′	1°55·2′W	X	150
Green Street	W Susx	TQ1422	50°59·4′	0°22·2′W	T	198
Greenstreet Fm	Worcs	SO7959	52°14·0′	2°18·1′W	FM	150
Greenstreet Fms	Bucks	TQ0297	51°40·0′	0°31·1′W	FM	166,176
Green Street Green	Brom	TQ4563	51°21·1′	0°5·3′E	T	177,188
Green Street Green	Kent	TQ5870	51°24·6′	0°16·7′E	T	177
Greenstreet Green	Suff	TM0449	52°6·3′	0°59·1′E	T	155
Greenstyle Fm	Aberd	NJ4516	57°14·1′	2°54·2′W	FM	37
Green Swang	N Yks	SE8999	54°23·0′	0°37·4′W	X	94,101
Greensward, The	Essex	TM2319	51°49·7′	1°14·6′E	X	169
Greenswell	Corn	SX3567	50°29·0′	4°19·2′W	X	201
Greenswood	Devon	SX8350	50°20·5′	3°38·3′W	X	202
Greens Wood	Shrops	SJ7515	52°44·2′	2°21·8′W	F	127
Greensyke	Cumbr	NY3548	54°49·6′	3°0·3′W	X	85
Green Syke	Northum	NY7751	54°51·4′	2°21·1′W	X	86,87
Green Syke Fm	Brad	SE0241	53°52·2′	1°57·8′W	FM	104
Greensykes	D & G	NT3100	55°17·6′	3°4·8′W	X	79
Green Sykes	N Yks	SE6281	54°13·5′	1°2·5′W	F	100
Greentaing	Shetld	HU3464	60°21·8′	1°22·5′W	X	2,3
Greentarn Rigg	Cumbr	NY6061	54°56·8′	2°37·0′W	X	86
Green, The	Aberd	NO7099	57°5·1′	2°29·2′W	X	38,45
Green, The	Arg & Bt	NL9648	56°31·8′	6°56·2′W	X	46
Green, The	Carm	SN3510	51°46·1′	4°23·1′W	X	159
Green, The	Ches	SJ5073	53°15·3′	2°44·6′W	X	117
Green, The	Cumbr	NY4473	55°3·2′	2°52·2′W	X	85
Green, The	Cumbr	NY7202	54°25·0′	2°25·5′W	X	91
Green, The	Cumbr	SD5795	54°21·2′	2°39·3′W	X	97
Green,The	Flint	SJ2468	53°12·5′	3°7·9′W	X	117
Green, The	Glos	SO7123	51°54·5′	2°24·9′W	X	162
Green, The	Hants	SU2729	51°3·8′	1°36·5′W	T	184
Green, The	Heref	SO5717	51°51·2′	2°37·1′W	X	162
Green, The	Heref	SO6254	52°11·2′	2°33·0′W	X	149
Green, The	Northum	NY8579	55°6·6′	2°13·7′W	X	87
Green, The	Notts	SK8174	53°15·6′	0°46·7′W	X	121
Green, The	N Yks	NZ7705	54°26·3′	0°48·3′W	X	94
Green, The	N Yks	NZ8106	54°26·8′	0°44·6′W	X	94
Green, The	N Yks	SE4970	54°7·7′	1°14·6′W	X	100
Green, The	Powys	SJ1202	52°36·8′	3°17·6′W	X	136
Green, The	S Glos	ST6972	51°27·0′	2°26·4′W	X	172
Green, The	Shrops	SO3081	52°25·6′	3°1·4′W	T	137
Green, The	Shrops	SO3893	52°32·1′	2°54·4′W	X	137
Green, The	Shrops	SO4881	52°25·7′	2°45·5′W	X	137,138
Green, The	Wilts	ST8631	51°4·9′	2°11·6′W	T	183
Green, The	Worcs	SO7265	52°17·2′	2°24·2′W	X	138,149
Green Thorn	Lancs	SD6640	53°51·6′	2°30·6′W	X	103
Greenthwaite Grange	N Yks	SE5860	54°2·2′	1°6·4′W	X	100
Greenthwaite Hall	Cumbr	NY4330	54°40·0′	2°52·6′W	A	90
Greentoft	Orkney	HY2525	59°6·6′	3°18·1′W	X	6
Greentoft	Orkney	HY5529	59°9·0′	2°46·7′W	X	5,6
Greentoft	Orkney	HY5607	58°57·1′	2°45·4′W	X	6
Greenton	Shetld	HU2450	60°14·3′	1°33·5′W	X	3
Green Tongue	Cumbr	NY2506	54°26·9′	3°9·0′W	X	89,90
Green Top	D & G	NX2366	54°57·7′	4°45·5′W	H	82
Green Top of Drumwhirn	D & G	NX7380	55°6·1′	3°59·0′W	X	77
Greentop of Margree	D & G	NX6787	55°9·8′	4°4·8′W	X	77
Green Tor	Devon	SX5686	50°39·6′	4°1·9′W	X	191
Green Torr	D & G	NX3979	55°5·0′	4°30·9′W	X	77
Greentowers	S Lanak	NS8745	55°41·4′	3°47·4′W	X	72
Greentree	Staffs	SJ9558	53°7·4′	2°4·1′W	X	118
Green Trees	Cumbr	NY1227	54°38·1′	3°21·4′W	X	89
Greentrees Fm	W Susx	TQ2932	51°4·6′	0°9·1′W	FM	187
Green Tye	Herts	TL4418	51°50·7′	0°5·8′E	T	167
Green Ucha	Denb	SJ0470	53°13·3′	3°25·9′W	X	116
Green Uchaf	V of Glam	SS9272	51°26·4′	3°32·8′W	X	170
Greenup Edge	Cumbr	NY2811	54°29·6′	3°6·3′W	X	89,90
Greenup Gill	Cumbr	NY2812	54°30·1′	3°6·3′W	W	89,90
Greenvale	Highld	ND2472	58°38·0′	3°18·1′W	X	7,12
Greenvale	Orkney	ND4386	58°45·7′	2°58·6′W	X	7
Greenvale	Orkney	ND4696	58°51·1′	2°55·7′W	X	6,7
Greenvale	Shetld	HU3143	60°10·5′	1°26·0′W	X	4
Greenvale Fm	Somer	ST0823	51°0·2′	3°18·3′W	FM	181
Greenvalley	Suff	TM3171	52°17·5′	1°23·7′E	X	156
Green Valley Fm	Mil Key	SP9546	52°6·5′	0°36·4′W	FM	153
Greenwall	Orkney	HY4819	59°3·6′	2°53·9′W	X	6
Greenwall	Orkney	HY5101	58°53·9′	2°50·5′W	X	6,7
Greenwall	Orkney	HY7652	59°21·5′	2°24·8′W	X	5
Greenwall	S Lanak	NS9355	55°46·8′	3°41·9′W	X	65,72
Greenwalls	Ches	SJ3661	53°8·8′	2°57·0′W	X	117
Green Ward	Shetld	HU3274	60°27·2′	1°24·6′W	X	3
Greenwards	Aberd	NK0351	57°33·2′	1°56·5′W	X	30
Greenwards	Aberd	NK0638	57°26·2′	1°53·5′W	X	30
Green Water	Inverc	NS3069	55°53·3′	4°42·7′W	W	63
Greenway	Glos	SO7033	51°59·9′	2°25·8′W	T	149
Greenway	Pemb	SN0630	51°56·3′	4°48·9′W	T	145
Greenway	Powys	SO0926	51°55·7′	3°19·0′W	X	161
Greenway	Somer	ST1628	51°2·9′	3°11·5′W	T	181,193
Greenway	Somer	ST2527	51°2·5′	3°3·8′W	X	193
Greenway	V of Glam	ST0574	51°27·7′	3°21·7′W	T	170
Greenway	Worcs	SO7470	52°19·9′	2°22·5′W	T	138
Greenway Bank	Staffs	SJ8855	53°5·8′	2°10·3′W	X	118
Greenway Cotts	W Berks	SU3980	51°31·3′	1°25·9′W	X	174
Greenway Court	Kent	TQ8554	51°15·5′	0°39·5′E	X	189
Greenway Cross	Shrops	SO4582	52°26·2′	2°48·1′W	X	137,138
Greenway Fm	Bucks	SP7629	51°57·5′	0°53·2′W	FM	165

Greenway Fm	Bucks	SP7730	51°58·0′	0°52·4′W	FM	152,165
Greenway Fm	Heref	SO3439	52°3·0′	2°57·4′W	FM	149,161
Greenway Fm	Heref	SO5417	51°51·2′	2°39·7′W	FM	162
Greenway Fm	S Glos	ST7172	51°27·0′	2°24·7′W	FM	172
Greenway Fm	Somer	ST0728	51°2·9′	3°19·2′W	FM	181
Greenway Fm	Somer	ST2621	50°59·3′	3°2·9′W	FM	193
Greenway Fm	Somer	ST2734	51°6·3′	3°2·2′W	FM	182
Greenway Fm	Suff	TM1556	52°9·8′	1°9·0′E	FM	156
Greenway Fm	Warw	SP4781	52°25·7′	1°18·1′W	FM	140
Greenway Fm	Wilts	SU0478	51°30·3′	1°56·2′W	FM	173
Greenway Forstal	Kent	TQ8553	51°15·0′	0°39·4′E	X	189
Greenwayhead	Shrops	SO5869	52°19·3′	2°36·6′W	X	137,138
Greenway Ho	Devon	SX8754	50°22·7′	3°35·0′W	A	202
Greenway Manor	Devon	ST1605	50°50·5′	3°11·2′W	X	192,193
Greenway Manor	Devon	ST1605	50°50·5′	3°11·2′W	X	192,193
Greenway Nature Trail, The	Warw	SP1650	52°9·1′	1°45·6′W	X	151
Greenways	Cumbr	NY5332	54°41·1′	2°43·3′W	X	90
Greenways	Heref	SO4428	51°57·1′	2°48·5′W	X	149,161
Greenways	Lincs	TF4282	53°19·2′	0°8·3′E	X	122
Greenways Fm	Ches	SJ9773	53°15·5′	2°2·3′W	FM	118
Greenwell	Cumbr	NY5356	54°54·0′	2°43·6′W	T	86
Greenwell	Durham	NY8538	54°44·5′	2°13·6′W	X	91,92
Greenwell	Durham	NZ1037	54°43·9′	1°50·3′W	X	92
Greenwell Fm	Durham	NZ1645	54°48·2′	1°44·6′W	FM	88
Greenwell Ford	Durham	NZ1646	54°48·8′	1°44·6′W	X	88
Greenwellheads	Aberd	NK0655	57°35·4′	1°53·5′W	X	30
Green Well of Scotland	D & G	NX5594	55°13·4′	4°16·3′W	X	77
Greenwells	Falk	NS8876	55°58·1′	3°47·2′W	X	65
Greenwells	Scot Bord	NT5631	55°34·5′	2°41·4′W	T	73
Greenwich	Gren	TQ3977	51°28·7′	0°0·5′E	T	177
Greenwich	Suff	TM1742	52°2·3′	1°10·2′E	T	169
Greenwich	Wilts	ST9232	51°5·5′	2°6·5′W	T	184
Greenwich Park	Gren	TQ3877	51°28·7′	0°0·4′W	X	177
Greenwich Reach	T Ham	TQ3778	51°29·3′	0°1·2′W	W	177
Greenwick	E Yorks	SE8556	53°59·8′	0°41·8′W	X	106
Greenwith Common	Corn	SW7740	50°13·3′	5°7·2′W	T	204
Green Withens Resr	Cald	SD9816	53°38·7′	2°1·4′W	W	109
Green Wood	D & G	NX5761	54°55·6′	4°13·5′W	F	83
Green Wood	Essex	TL4938	52°1·5′	0°10·7′E	F	154
Green Wood	E Susx	TQ6321	50°58·1′	0°19·7′E	F	199
Greenwood	Moray	NJ4447	57°30·8′	2°55·6′W	X	28
Green Wood	Scot Bord	NT8364	55°52·4′	2°15·9′W	F	67
Greenwood	Scot Bord	NT8364	55°52·4′	2°15·9′W	X	67
Greenwood	S Lanak	NT0642	55°40·0′	3°29·2′W	X	72
Green Wood	Surrey	TQ3742	51°9·9′	0°2·0′W	F	187
Greenwood Centre	Gwyn	SH5367	53°11·0′	4°11·6′W	X	114,115
Greenwood Centre	Gwyn	SH5367	53°11·0′	4°11·6′W	X	114,115
Greenwood Fm	Derby	SK2480	53°19·2′	1°38·0′W	FM	110
Greenwood Fm	Hants	SU5017	50°57·2′	1°16·9′W	FM	185
Greenwood Fm	Hants	SU7141	51°10·1′	0°58·7′W	FM	186
Greenwood Fm	Suff	TM1462	52°13·1′	1°8·4′E	FM	156
Greenwood Fm	W Susx	SZ8395	50°45·1′	0°49·0′W	FM	197
Greenwood Gate	E Susx	TQ4830	51°3·2′	0°7·1′E	X	188
Greenwood Haw	Cumbr	SD6789	54°18·0′	2°30·0′W	X	98
Greenwood Ho	Cumbr	NY2848	54°49·6′	3°6·8′W	X	85
Greenwood Law	Northum	NY8999	55°17·3′	2°10·0′W	H	80
Greenwood Lee	Cald	SD9629	53°45·7′	2°3·2′W	X	103
Greenwood Leghe	N Yks	SD7071	54°8·3′	2°27·1′W	X	98
Greenwoods	Essex	TQ6999	51°40·1′	0°27·0′E	T	167,177
Greenwrae	D & G	NY3272	55°2·5′	3°3·4′W	X	85
Greeny	Orkney	HY2822	59°5·0′	3°14·9′W	T	6
Greenyard Fm	V of Glam	ST1370	51°25·6′	3°14·7′W	FM	171
Greenyards	Stir	NN7601	56°11·4′	3°59·4′W	X	57
Greenyards	Stir	NS8189	56°5·0′	3°54·3′W	X	57,65
Greeny Brae	Orkney	HY5836	59°12·8′	2°43·7′W	X	5
Greenybrae Hill	Orkney	HY5737	59°13·3′	2°44·7′W	H	5
Green Yew	Cumbr	SD4193	54°20·0′	2°54·0′W	X	96,97
Greeny Hill	Orkney	HY2923	59°5·5′	3°13·9′W	H	6
Greep	Highld	NG2642	57°23·4′	6°33·2′W	T	23
Greet	Glos	SP0230	51°58·3′	1°57·9′W	T	150
Greet	Kent	TQ9255	51°15·9′	0°45·5′E	T	178
Greeta River or River Creed	N Eil	NB3333	58°12·6′	6°32·3′W	W	8,13
Greete	Shrops	SO5770	52°19·8′	2°37·5′W	T	137,138
Greetham	Lincs	TF3070	53°12·9′	0°2·8′W	T	122
Greetham	Rut	SK9214	52°43·2′	0°37·9′W	T	130
Greetham Ho	Lincs	TF3070	53°12·9′	0°2·8′W	X	122
Greetham Lodge Fm	Rut	SK9415	52°43·7′	0°36·1′W	FM	130
Greetham Wood Far	Rut	SK9514	52°43·2′	0°35·2′W	F	130
Greetham Wood Near	Rut	SK9414	52°43·2′	0°36·1′W	F	130
Greet Ho	Notts	SK7154	53°4·9′	0°56·0′W	X	120
Greetland	Cald	SE0821	53°41·4′	1°52·3′W	T	104
Greetland Wall Nook	Cald	SE0621	53°41·4′	1°54·1′W	T	104
Greeto Br	N Ayr	NS2259	55°47·7′	4°49·9′W	X	63
Greeto Water	N Ayr	NS2361	55°48·8′	4°49·1′W	W	63
Greets Fm	N Yks	SE7367	54°5·9′	0°52·6′W	FM	100
Greets Hill	N Yks	SE0295	54°21·3′	1°57·7′W	X	98
Greets Moss	N Yks	SE0395	54°21·3′	1°56·8′W	X	98
Greetwell	N Lincs	SE9404	53°31·7′	0°34·5′W	T	112
Greetwell Hall	Lincs	TF0171	53°13·8′	0°28·8′W	X	121
Greetwell Hall	N Lincs	SE9304	53°31·7′	0°35·4′W	X	112
Greetwell Hall Fm	N Lincs	SE9304	53°31·7′	0°35·4′W	FM	112
Greety Gate	Cumbr	SD2086	54°16·1′	3°13·3′W	X	96
Greff	Shetld	HP5814	60°48·5′	0°55·5′W	X	1
Gregg Hall	Cumbr	SD4691	54°19·0′	2°49·4′W	X	97
Gregg's Wood	Kent	TQ6041	51°9·0′	0°17·7′E	F	188
Greg Ness	C of Aber	NJ9704	57°7·9′	2°2·5′W	X	38
Gregory Beck	Durham	NZ0409	54°28·8′	1°55·9′W	W	92
Gregory's Fm	Herts	TL3021	51°52·6′	0°6·3′W	FM	166
Gregory's Hill	W Berks	SU6375	51°28·5′	1°5·2′W	X	175
Gregory Spring	Kirk	SE2017	53°39·2′	1°41·4′W	F	110
Greg's Hut	Cumbr	NY6935	54°42·8′	2°28·4′W	X	91
Gregson Lane	Lancs	SD5926	53°44·0′	2°36·9′W	T	102
Gregson's Plantn	Norf	TL9092	52°29·8′	0°48·3′E	F	144
Gregynog	Powys	SO0897	52°34·0′	3°21·0′W	T	136
Greian Head	N Eil	NF6404	57°0·5′	7°31·7′W	X	31
Greidol	Heref	SO3427	51°56·5′	2°57·2′W	X	161
Greig Fm	Monm	SO3722	51°53·8′	2°54·5′W	FM	161
Greigsford	Aberd	NJ9732	57°23·0′	2°2·5′W	X	30
Greigsland	D & G	NY0892	55°13·1′	3°26·3′W	X	78
Greigston House	Fife	NO4411	56°17·5′	2°53·8′W	X	59
Greigwen	Gwyn	SH9242	52°58·1′	3°36·1′W	X	125
Grèinam	N Eil	NB1238	58°14·5′	6°54·0′W	X	13
Grèinam	N Eil	NB1935	58°13·1′	6°46·7′W	X	8,13
Greineam	N Eil	NG2194	57°51·2′	6°41·7′W	X	14
Greineim	N Eil	NA9724	58°6·3′	7°8·2′W	X	13
Greineim	N Eil	NG2495	57°51·8′	6°38·8′W	X	14
Greine Sgeir	N Eil	NB0115	58°1·7′	7°3·4′W	X	13
Greing, The	Shetld	HP5918	60°50·7′	0°54·4′W	X	1
Greinton	Somer	ST4136	51°7·4′	2°50·2′W	T	182
Gremista	Shetld	HU4643	60°10·4′	1°9·8′W	X	4
Grenaby	I of M	SC2672	54°7·1′	4°39·3′W	X	95
Grenaby	I of M	SC4498	54°21·5′	4°23·6′W	X	95
Grenaby Fm	I of M	SC2672	54°7·1′	4°39·3′W	FM	95
Grendisworthy	Devon	SX3899	50°46·3′	4°17·5′W	X	190
Grendon	Northnts	SP8760	52°14·1′	0°43·2′W	T	152
Grendon	Warw	SK2800	52°36·1′	1°34·8′W	T	140
Grendon	Warw	SP2799	52°35·5′	1°35·7′W	T	140
Grendon Bishop	Heref	SO5956	52°12·3′	2°35·6′W	T	149
Grendon Br	Warw	SK2800	52°36·1′	1°34·8′W	X	140
Grendon Common	Warw	SP2798	52°35·0′	1°35·7′W	T	140
Grendon Court	Heref	SO5954	52°11·2′	2°35·6′W	X	149
Grendon Court	Heref	SO6327	51°56·7′	2°31·9′W	X	162
Grendon Fm	Devon	SX4978	50°35·2′	4°7·6′W	FM	191,201
Grendon Fm	Devon	SX6878	50°35·4′	3°51·5′W	FM	191
Grendon Fm	Devon	SX7192	50°43·0′	3°49·3′W	FM	191
Grendon Green	Heref	SO5957	52°12·8′	2°35·6′W	T	149
Grendon Hill Fm	Bucks	SP8216	51°50·4′	0°48·2′W	FM	165
Grendon (HM Prison & Youth Custody Centre	Bucks	SP6822	51°53·8′	1°0·3′W	X	164,165
Grendon Ho Fm	Northnts	SP8861	52°14·6′	0°42·3′W	FM	152
Grendon House Fm	Warw	SK2901	52°36·6′	1°33·9′W	FM	140
Grendons, The	Devon	SS8017	50°56·6′	3°42·1′W	X	181
Grendon Underwood	Bucks	SP6820	51°52·7′	1°0·3′W	T	164,165
Grendon Wood	Bucks	SP6921	51°53·2′	0°59·4′W	F	165
Grenehurst Park	Surrey	TQ1639	51°8·5′	0°20·1′W	X	187
Grenham Bay	Kent	TR2970	51°23·2′	1°17·9′E	W	179
Grenich	Pth & Kin	NN8060	56°43·2′	3°57·2′W	X	43,52
Grenigeo Taing	Orkney	HY5904	58°55·5′	2°42·2′W	X	6
Grenitote	N Eil	NF8275	57°39·4′	7°19·5′W	T	18
Grennan	D & G	NX1239	54°42·9′	4°54·7′W	X	82
Grennan	D & G	NX2461	54°55·0′	4°44·3′W	X	82
Grennan	D & G	NX4145	54°46·7′	4°27·9′W	X	83
Grennan	D & G	NX6379	55°5·4′	4°8·4′W	X	77
Grennan	D & G	NX8494	55°13·8′	3°49·0′W	X	78
Grennan Hill	D & G	NX8554	54°52·3′	3°47·1′W	H	84
Grennan Mill	D & G	NX6480	55°6·0′	4°7·5′W	X	77
Grennan Moss	D & G	NX2561	54°55·0′	4°43·4′W	X	82
Grennan Moss	D & G	NX4045	54°46·7′	4°28·8′W	X	83
Grennan Plantation	D & G	NX1239	54°42·9′	4°54·7′W	F	82
Grennan Point	D & G	NX0743	54°44·9′	4°59·5′W	X	82
Grenofen	Devon	SX4971	50°31·4′	4°7·4′W	T	201
Grenoside	Sheff	SK3393	53°26·2′	1°29·8′W	T	110,111
Grenoven Wood	Corn	SX4173	50°32·3′	4°14·3′W	F	201
Greno Wood	Sheff	SK3295	53°27·3′	1°30·7′W	F	110,111
Grenstein Fm	Norf	TF8919	52°44·4′	0°48·4′E	FM	132
Gren Tor	Devon	SX5587	50°40·1′	4°2·7′W	X	191
Grenville Hall	Hants	SU6317	50°57·2′	1°5·8′W	X	185
Greosabhagh	N Eil	NG1592	57°49·9′	6°47·6′W	T	14
Grere Fell	Cumbr	NY7000	54°23·9′	2°27·3′W	X	91
Gresclett	N Eil	NA9913	58°0·5′	7°5·3′W	H	13
Gresford	Wrex	SJ3554	53°5·0′	2°57·8′W	T	117
Gresford Lo	Wrex	SJ3455	53°5·5′	2°58·7′W	X	117
Gresgarth Hall	Lancs	SD5363	54°3·9′	2°42·7′W	X	97
Gresham	Norf	TG1638	52°54·0′	1°13·1′E	T	133
Gresham Fm	Norf	TG0304	52°36·0′	1°0·3′E	FM	144
Gresham's School	Norf	TG0839	52°54·7′	1°6·0′E	X	133
Greshaw Fm	Suff	TM2983	52°24·0′	1°22·4′E	FM	156
Greshornish	Highld	NG3353	57°29·6′	6°26·9′W	X	23
Greshornish Ho (Hotel)	Highld	NG3354	57°30·1′	6°27·0′W	X	23
Greshornish Point	Highld	NG3456	57°31·2′	6°26·1′W	X	23
Greskine Forest	D & G	NT0308	55°21·6′	3°31·4′W	F	78
Gresley Fm	Suff	TM3343	52°2·4′	1°24·3′E	FM	169
Gressenhall	Norf	TF9616	52°42·6′	0°54·5′E	T	132
Gressingham	Lancs	SD5769	54°7·1′	2°39·1′W	T	97
Grest	I of M	SC4496	54°20·4′	4°23·6′W	X	95
Greta Bridge	Durham	NZ0813	54°31·0′	1°52·2′W	T	92
Gretchveg	I of M	SC4484	54°13·9′	4°23·2′W	X	95
Gretna	D & G	NY3167	54°59·8′	3°4·3′W	T	85
Gretna Green	D & G	NY3168	55°0·4′	3°4·3′W	T	85
Gretnagreen	Pth & Kin	NO1527	56°25·9′	3°22·3′W	X	53,58
Gret Ness	Orkney	HY4342	59°15·9′	2°59·5′W	X	5
Gretton	Glos	SP0030	51°58·3′	1°59·6′W	T	150
Gretton	Northnts	SP8994	52°32·4′	0°40·9′W	T	141
Gretton	Shrops	SO5195	52°33·3′	2°43·0′W	T	137,138
Gretton Fields	Glos	SP0031	51°58·9′	1°59·6′W	T	150
Grevatts	W Susx	SU9124	51°0·7′	0°41·8′W	X	197
Greville Hall Fm	Worcs	SP0340	52°3·7′	1°57·0′W	FM	150
Grevis Field	Shetld	HU3833	60°5·1′	1°18·5′W	X	4
Grevitts Copse	W Susx	SU7913	50°54·9′	0°52·2′W	F	197
Grevodig	Powys	SO1172	52°20·6′	3°18·0′W	X	136,148
Grewburn	Durham	NZ0925	54°37·4′	1°51·2′W	X	92
Grewburn Beck	Durham	NZ1025	54°37·4′	1°50·3′W	W	92
Grewelthorpe	N Yks	SE2376	54°11·0′	1°38·4′W	T	99
Grewelthorpe Moor	N Yks	SE1775	54°10·5′	1°44·0′W	X	99
Grewgrass Fm	Red & Cl	NZ6121	54°35·1′	1°2·9′W	FM	94
Grewshill	Pth & Kin	NO0448	56°37·1′	3°33·4′W	X	52,53
Grexy Cross	Dorset	ST5504	50°50·3′	2°38·0′W	X	194
Grey Abbey Fm	Somer	ST4709	50°52·9′	2°44·8′W	FM	193
Greybearded Man	Shetld	HU5591	60°36·2′	0°59·2′W	X	1,2
Greyber	Cumbr	NY6317	54°33·1′	2°33·9′W	X	91
Grey Burn	D & G	NT0108	55°21·6′	3°33·3′W	W	78
Greybury Fm	Kent	TQ4342	51°9·8′	0°3·1′E	FM	187
Grey Cairn	Highld	ND2356	58°29·4′	3°18·8′W	A	11,12
Grey Cairn	Highld	NH7362	57°38·1′	4°7·2′W	A	21,27
Greycairn	Moray	NJ4454	57°34·6′	2°55·7′W	X	28
Grey Cairn	Pth & Kin	NO1056	56°41·5′	3°27·7′W	A	53
Grey Cairns	Aberd	NO6479	56°54·3′	2°35·0′W	X	45
Grey Cairns of Camster	Highld	ND2644	58°23·0′	3°15·5′W	A	11,12
Grey Corries, The	Highld	NN2473	56°49·2′	4°52·6′W	X	41
Grey Court	Northum	NZ0062	54°57·4′	1°59·6′W	X	87
Grey Crag	Cumbr	NY4907	54°27·6′	2°46·8′W	H	90
Grey Crags	Cumbr	NY1714	54°31·1′	3°16·5′W	X	89,90
Grey Crags	Cumbr	NY2627	54°38·2′	3°8·4′W	X	89,90
Greycrag Tarn	Cumbr	NY4907	54°27·6′	2°46·8′W	W	90
Greycraig	D & G	NY2071	55°1·9′	3°14·7′W	X	85
Grey Craig	Fife	NT0293	56°7·4′	3°34·1′W	X	58
Grey Ditch	Derby	SK1781	53°19·8′	1°44·3′W	A	110
Grey Face	Shetld	HU2777	60°28·8′	1°30·0′W	X	3
Greyfell Common	Cumbr	NY6078	55°5·9′	2°37·2′W	X	86
Greyfield	Bath & NE Somer	ST6458	51°19·4′	2°30·6′W	T	172
Greyfields Court	Staffs	SO8182	52°26·4′	2°16·4′W	X	138
Grey Friar	Cumbr	NY2500	54°23·6′	3°8·9′W	H	89,90
Greyfriars	E Susx	TQ9017	50°55·5′	0°42·6′E	X	189
Greyfriars	Lancs	SD5232	53°47·2′	2°43·3′W	X	102
Grey Friars	Suff	TM4770	52°16·6′	1°37·7′E	X	156
Greyfriars	Surrey	TQ0346	51°12·5′	0°31·1′W	X	186
Greyfriars	W Susx	TQ0813	50°54·6′	0°27·4′W	X	197
Greyfriar's Church	Glos	SO8318	51°51·9′	2°14·4′W	X	162
Grey Gables	Leic	SP5186	52°28·4′	1°14·5′W	X	140
Greygarth	N Yks	SE1872	54°8·9′	1°43·0′W	T	99
Greygarth Monument	N Yks	SE1872	54°8·9′	1°43·0′W	X	99
Greygill Cleuch	D & G	NT1006	55°20·6′	3°24·7′W	X	78
Greygill Head	D & G	NT0908	55°21·7′	3°25·7′W	X	78
Grey Goose Fm	Thurr	TQ6280	51°30·0′	0°20·4′E	FM	177
Grey Green	N Lincs	SE7807	53°33·5′	0°48·9′W	T	112
Grey Head	Orkney	HY5740	59°14·9′	2°44·7′W	X	5
Grey Head	Shetld	HU4839	60°8·2′	1°7·7′W	X	4
Grey Height	Stir	NN3922	56°22·0′	4°35·9′W	H	50
Grey Hill	Cumbr	NY5776	55°4·8′	2°40·0′W	H	86
Grey Hill	D & G	NT2700	55°17·6′	3°8·5′W	H	79
Grey Hill	D & G	NX1372	55°0·7′	4°55·0′W	X	76
Grey Hill	D & G	NX6159	54°54·6′	4°9·7′W	X	83
Grey Hill	D & G	NX6577	55°4·4′	4°6·4′W	X	77,84
Grey Hill	D & G	NX6773	55°2·3′	4°4·4′W	X	77,84
Grey Hill	D & G	NY3194	55°14·4′	3°4·7′W	H	79
Grey Hill	D & G	NY3197	55°16·0′	3°4·7′W	H	79
Grey Hill	Highld	NC8022	58°10·5′	4°1·9′W	X	17
Grey Hill	S Ayr	NX1692	55°11·5′	4°53·0′W	H	76
Grey Hill	Scot Bord	NT3109	55°22·5′	3°4·9′W	H	79
Greyhill Fm	Glos	SO8527	51°56·7′	2°12·7′W	FM	162
Greyhills Fm	Devon	SX7555	50°23·1′	3°45·1′W	FM	202
Grey Ho	Highld	NH1885	57°49·3′	5°3·4′W	X	20
Grey Ho	Newp	ST3991	51°37·1′	2°52·5′W	X	171
Greyhope Bay	C of Aber	NJ9605	57°8·4′	2°5·5′W	W	38
Greyhound Law	Northum	NT7606	55°21·1′	2°22·3′W	H	80
Greyhound Law	Northum	NY6497	55°16·2′	2°33·6′W	X	80
Grey Knotts	Cumbr	NY2112	54°30·1′	3°12·8′W	H	89,90
Greylake	Somer	ST3833	51°5·8′	2°52·7′W	T	182
Greylake Barton	Corn	SX1183	50°37·2′	4°39·9′W	X	200
Greylake Br	Somer	ST3934	51°6·4′	2°51·9′W	X	182
Greylake Fosse	Somer	ST4035	51°6·9′	2°51·0′W	T	182
Greyland	Devon	SS3309	50°51·6′	4°22·0′W	X	190
Grey Leys Fm	York	SE6849	53°56·2′	0°57·4′W	FM	105,106
Grey Mare	Aberd	NK1137	57°25·6′	1°48·6′W	X	30
Grey Mare	D & G	NY0195	55°14·6′	3°33·0′W	H	78
Greymare Fm	Northum	NU0736	55°37·3′	1°52·9′W	FM	75
Grey Mare & her Colts, The	Dorset	SY5887	50°41·1′	2°35·3′W	X	194
Grey Mare & her Colts,The (long Barrow)	Dorset	SY5887	50°41·1′	2°35·3′W	A	194
Greymare Hill	Northum	NY6174	55°3·8′	2°36·2′W	X	86
Greymare Hill	Northum	NZ0455	54°53·6′	1°55·8′W	X	87
Greymare Rigg	Northum	NY8998	55°16·8′	2°10·0′W	X	80
Greymare Rock	Corn	SX2277	50°34·2′	4°30·4′W	X	201
Grey Mare's Currick Crags	Northum	NY6182	55°8·1′	2°36·3′W	H	80
Grey Mares Knowe	Northum	NT6600	55°17·8′	2°31·7′W	H	80
Grey Mare's Tail Burn	D & G	NX4873	55°2·0′	4°22·3′W	W	77
Grey Mare's Tail (Waterfalls)	D & G	NT1814	55°25·0′	3°17·3′W	W	79
Greymoorhill	Cumbr	NY3859	54°55·6′	2°57·6′W	X	85
Greymore	Aberd	NJ7003	57°7·3′	2°29·3′W	H	38
Greymount	Pth & Kin	NO2247	56°36·8′	3°15·8′W	X	53
Grey Nag	Northum	NY6647	54°49·2′	2°31·3′W	H	86
Greynor	Carm	SN5909	51°46·0′	4°2·2′W	T	159
Grey Ridge	N Yks	SE1275	54°10·5′	1°48·6′W	X	99
Greyrigg	D & G	NY0888	55°10·9′	3°26·3′W	T	78
Greyrigg Ho	Cumbr	NY2851	54°51·2′	3°6·9′W	X	85
Greys	Herts	TL3439	52°2·2′	0°2·4′W	X	154
Grey's Br	Dorset	SY7090	50°42·8′	2°25·1′W	A	194
Grey Scar	Cumbr	NY6733	54°41·7′	2°30·3′W	X	91
Grey Scar Fm	Durham	NY9312	54°30·4′	2°6·1′W	FM	91,92
Grey Scars	N Yks	SD7272	54°8·8′	2°25·3′W	X	98
Greys Court	Oxon	SU7283	51°32·7′	0°57·3′W	A	175
Greys Green	Oxon	SU7282	51°32·2′	0°57·3′W	T	175
Greysich Fm	Derby	SK3122	52°47·9′	1°32·0′W	FM	128
Greyside	Northum	NY8668	55°0·6′	2°12·7′W	X	87
Greys Mallory	Warw	SP3061	52°15·0′	1°33·2′W	X	151
Greys Mead	Oxon	SP7004	51°44·1′	0°58·9′W	X	165
Greysouthen	Cumbr	NY0729	54°39·1′	3°26·1′W	T	89
Greys Pike	Northum	NY6593	55°14·0′	2°32·6′W	H	80
Greyspot Hill	Surrey	SU9260	51°20·1′	0°40·4′W	X	175,186
Greystane Geo	Shetld	HU4008	59°51·6′	1°16·7′W	X	4
Greystane Hill	Aberd	NO6487	56°58·6′	2°35·1′W	X	45
Grey Stane of Bonxa	Shetld	HU3927	60°1·8′	1°17·5′W	X	4
Grey Stanes	Shetld	HU4429	60°2·9′	1°12·1′W	X	4
Greystead	Northum	NY7785	55°9·8′	2°21·2′W	T	80
Greystoke	Cumbr	NY4430	54°40·0′	2°51·7′W	T	90
Greystoke Forest	Cumbr	NY3933	54°41·5′	2°56·4′W	F	90
Greystoke Gill	Cumbr	NY4429	54°39·4′	2°51·7′W	T	90
Greystoke Moor	Cumbr	NY4129	54°39·4′	2°54·5′W	X	90
Greystoke Park	Cumbr	NY4231	54°40·5′	2°53·5′W	X	90
Greystoke Pillar	Cumbr	NY4929	54°39·5′	2°47·0′W	X	90
Greystone	Aberd	NJ4341	57°27·6′	2°56·5′W	X	28
Greystone	Aberd	NJ4403	57°7·1′	2°55·3′W	X	37
Greystone	Aberd	NJ5616	57°14·2′	2°43·3′W	X	37
Greystone	Aberd	NJ6535	57°24·5′	2°34·5′W	X	29

Greystone	Aberd	NJ7709	57°10·5'	2°22·4'W	X	38
Greystone	Aberd	NJ7751	57°33·2'	2°22·6'W	X	29,30
Greystone	Aberd	NJ8326	57°19·7'	2°16·5'W	X	38
Greystone	Aberd	NK0237	57°25·7'	1°57·5'W	X	30
Greystone	Aberd	NK0942	57°28·3'	1°50·5'W	X	30
Greystone	Aberd	NO2995	57°2·7'	3°9·8'W	X	37,44
Greystone	Aberd	NO4396	57°3·4'	2°55·9'W	X	37,44
Greystone	Aberd	NO7565	56°46·8'	2°24·1'W	X	45
Greystone	Angus	NO5343	56°34·9'	2°45·5'W	T	54
Greystone	Cumbr	SD5179	54°12·5'	2°44·7'W	T	97
Greystone	Devon	SX7491	50°42·5'	3°46·7'W	X	191
Greystone	D & G	NX6865	54°58·0'	4°3·3'W	X	83,84
Greystone	D & G	NX9776	55°4·3'	3°36·4'W	X	84
Greystone	Highld	NH9749	57°31·4'	3°42·7'W	X	27
Greystone	Lancs	SD8543	53°53·2'	2°13·3'W	X	103
Grey Stone	Leeds	SE3143	53°53·2'	1°31·3'W	X	104
Greystone	Northum	NY7754	54°53·1'	2°21·1'W	X	86,87
Greystone	N Yks	NZ1514	54°31·5'	1°45·7'W	X	92
Grey Stone	N Yks	SE0759	54°1·9'	1°53·2'W	X	104
Greystone	Orkney	ND4484	58°44·7'	2°57·6'W	X	7
Grey Stone	Pth & Kin	NO2221	56°22·7'	3°15·3'W	A	53,58
Greystone	S Lanak	NS8038	55°37·5'	3°53·9'W	X	71,72
Greystone	Stir	NS7499	56°10·3'	4°1·3'W	X	57
Greystone	Stock on T	NZ3922	54°35·7'	1°23·4'W	X	93
Greystone Br	Corn	SX3680	50°36·0'	4°18·7'W	A	201
Greystone Brae	Scot Bord	NT7810	55°23·3'	2°20·4'W	X	80
Greystone Court	Oxon	SP5520	51°52·8'	1°11·7'W	X	164
Greystone Flatts	N Yks	SE4290	54°18·5'	1°20·8'W	X	99
Greystone Fm	Glos	SP1737	52°2·1'	1°44·7'W	FM	151
Greystone Fm	N Yks	NZ8610	54°28·9'	0°39·9'W	FM	94
Greystone Fm	N Yks	SE4592	54°19·5'	1°18·1'W	FM	99
Greystonegill	N Yks	SD6869	54°7·2'	2°29·0'W	T	98
Greystone Hall	Durham	NZ1816	54°32·6'	1°42·9'W	X	92
Grey Stone Hill	Black w Dar	SD7220	53°40·8'	2°25·0'W	H	103
Greystonehill	E Renf	NS4652	55°44·5'	4°26·7'W	X	64
Greystone Ho	Cumbr	NY5522	54°35·7'	2°41·4'W	X	90
Greystone Ho	N Yks	SE3685	54°15·8'	1°26·4'W	X	99
Greystone Knowe	S Ayr	NX1074	55°1·7'	4°57·9'W	X	76
Greystonelees	Scot Bord	NT9560	55°50·2'	2°4·4'W	X	67
Greystoneley	Lancs	SD6445	53°54·2'	2°32·5'W	X	102,103
Greystonerigg	D & G	NY0797	55°15·8'	3°27·4'W	X	78
Greystones	Aberd	NJ5208	57°9·9'	2°47·2'W	X	37
Greystones	Darl	NZ2520	54°34·7'	1°36·4'W	X	93
Grey Stones	Lancs	SD9637	53°50·0'	2°3·2'W	X	103
Greystones	N Yks	NZ2013	54°31·0'	1°41·0'W	X	93
Greystones	N Yks	SE3595	54°21·2'	1°27·3'W	X	99
Grey Stones	N Yks	SE8696	54°21·4'	0°40·2'W	X	94,101
Grey Stones	Orkney	ND5096	58°51·2'	2°51·5'W	X	6,7
Greystones	Oxon	SP3125	51°55·6'	1°32·6'W	X	164
Greystones	Sheff	SK3285	53°21·9'	1°30·7'W	T	110,111
Greystones	Warw	SP0949	52°8·6'	1°51·7'W	T	150
Greystones	Wilts	SU0029	51°3·9'	1°59·6'W	X	184
Greystones Fm	Highld	ND2454	58°28·3'	3°17·7'W	FM	11,12
Greystones Fm	York	SE6458	54°1·1'	1°1·0'W	FM	105,106
Grey Stone, The	Pth & Kin	NO2221	56°22·7'	3°15·3'W	A	53,58
Grey's Well	Durham	NZ1038	54°44·5'	1°50·3'W	X	92
Grey's Wood	Dorset	SY7193	50°44·4'	2°24·3'W	F	194
Greytree	Heref	SO5925	51°55·6'	2°35·4'W	T	162
Grey Valley	Heref	SO4032	51°59·2'	2°52·0'W	X	149,161
Greywell	Hants	SU7151	51°15·5'	0°58·6'W	T	186
Greywell Hill	Hants	SU7151	51°15·5'	0°58·6'W	X	186
Grey Wethers	Devon	SX6383	50°38·1'	3°55·9'W	A	191
Grey Wethers	Wilts	SU1369	51°25·4'	1°48·4'W	X	173
Grey Wethers or Sarsen Stones	Wilts	SU1371	51°26·5'	1°48·4'W	X	173
Grey Yaud Plantn	N Yks	SE1584	54°15·3'	1°45·8'W	F	99
Grey Yauds	Cumbr	NY5448	54°49·7'	2°42·5'W	X	86
Grey Yauds (Stone Circle)	Cumbr	NY5448	54°49·7'	2°42·5'W	A	86
Griag	Powys	SJ1105	52°38·4'	3°18·5'W	X	125
Griamacleit	N Eil	NB2014	58°1·9'	6°44·1'W	H	13,14
Grianabhal Mòr	N Eil	NB3025	58°8·2'	6°34·8'W	H	13,14
Grianaig	Arg & Bt	NM8710	56°14·3'	5°25·8'W	X	55
Grianan	Arg & Bt	NR3347	55°38·8'	6°14·2'W	X	60
Grianan	Highld	NC5652	58°26·2'	4°27·5'W	A	10
Grianan	N Eil	NB4135	58°13·9'	6°24·3'W	T	8
Grianan	N Eil	NF6801	56°59·1'	7°27·5'W	H	31
Grianan a' Choire	Highld	NC3527	58°12·3'	4°48·0'W	H	15
Grianan Mòr	Arg & Bt	NR6395	56°5·6'	5°48·2'W	X	61
Griana-sgeir	Highld	NG5751	57°29·3'	6°2·8'W	X	24
Grianllyn	Conwy	SH8277	53°16·9'	3°45·8'W	X	116
Grian-loch Beag	Highld	NC6456	58°28·5'	4°19·4'W	W	10
Grian-loch Mòr	Highld	NC6455	58°28·0'	4°19·4'W	W	10
Gribb	Dorset	ST3703	50°49·6'	2°53·3'W	T	193
Gribba Point	Corn	SW3530	50°6·9'	5°42·0'W	X	203
Gribbin Head	Corn	SX0949	50°18·8'	4°40·6'W	X	200,204
Gribbleford Bridge	Devon	SS5201	50°47·6'	4°5·6'W	X	191
Gribble Inn	Devon	SS4915	50°55·1'	4°8·5'W	X	180
Gribdae	D & G	NX7350	54°50·0'	3°58·2'W	X	83,84
Gribdae Burn	D & G	NX7250	54°50·0'	3°59·1'W	W	83,84
Gribdale Terrace	N Yks	NZ5811	54°29·7'	1°5·8'W	X	93
Gribin	Conwy	SH8668	53°12·1'	3°42·0'W	X	116
Gribin	Denb	SJ2146	53°0·6'	3°10·2'W	X	117
Gribin	Pemb	SM8024	51°52·5'	5°11·4'W	X	157
Gribin	Powys	SH8506	52°38·6'	3°41·6'W	X	124,125
Gribin	Powys	SJ0007	52°39·3'	3°28·3'W	X	125
Gribin Oernant	Denb	SJ1747	53°1·1'	3°13·8'W	H	116
Gribloch	Stir	NS6391	56°5·8'	4°11·7'W	X	57
Gribloch Ho	Stir	NS6493	56°6·9'	4°10·8'W	X	57
Gribthorpe	E Yorks	SE7635	53°48·6'	0°50·3'W	X	105,106
Gribton	D & G	NX9280	55°6·4'	3°41·1'W	X	78
Gribun	Arg & Bt	NM4534	56°26·0'	6°7·7'W	T	47,48
Gribyn	Powys	SN9153	52°10·1'	3°35·2'W	H	147
Grice Croft	Cumbr	SD1786	54°16·0'	3°16·0'W	X	96
Grice Ness	Orkney	HY6728	59°8·5'	2°34·1'W	X	5
Grickstone Fm	S Glos	ST7782	51°32·4'	2°19·5'W	FM	172
Griesta	Shetld	HU4144	60°11·0'	1°15·2'W	X	4
Grieston Hill	Scot Bord	NT3035	55°36·5'	3°6·2'W	H	73
Grievestead	Northum	NT9345	55°42·2'	2°6·2'W	X	74,75
Grievestead Moor	Northum	NT9245	55°42·2'	2°7·2'W	X	74,75

Griff	Warw	SP3588	52°29·6'	1°28·7'W	T	140
Griffe Grange	Derby	SK2455	53°5·7'	1°38·1'W	X	119
Griffe Grange Fm	Derby	SK2556	53°6·3'	1°37·2'W	FM	119
Griffe Grange Valley	Derby	SK2556	53°6·3'	1°37·2'W	X	119
Griffe Walk Fm	Derby	SK2456	53°6·3'	1°38·1'W	FM	119
Griff Fm	N Yks	SE5883	54°14·6'	1°6·2'W	FM	100
Griffin Fm	N Yks	SE4579	54°12·5'	1°18·2'W	FM	99
Griffin Fm	N Yks	SE4679	54°12·5'	1°17·3'W	FM	100
Griffin Inn, The	Powys	SO0244	52°5·4'	3°25·4'W	X	147,160
Griffin Lloyd	Powys	SO2270	52°19·6'	3°8·3'W	X	137,148
Griffins Barn Fm	Wilts	ST9389	51°36·2'	2°5·7'W	FM	173
Griffin's Fm	Lincs	TF0054	53°4·7'	0°30·0'W	FM	121
Griffin's Fm	W Susx	TQ1721	50°58·8'	0°19·6'W	FM	198
Griffins Hill	Birm	SP0381	52°25·9'	1°57·0'W	T	139
Griffin's Point	Corn	SW8466	50°27·5'	5°2·2'W	X	200
Griffithstown	Torf	ST2999	51°41·4'	3°1·2'W	T	171
Griff Lodge Fm	Warw	SP3588	52°29·6'	1°28·7'W	FM	140
Griff Village	N Yks	SE5883	54°14·6'	1°6·2'W	A	100
Griff Wood	Derby	SK4765	53°11·0'	1°17·4'W	F	120
Griffydam	Leic	SK4118	52°45·7'	1°23·1'W	T	129
Griffyelt	Orkney	HY4006	58°56·5'	3°2·1'W	X	6,7
Grif Skerry	Shetld	HU6362	60°20·5'	0°51·0'W	X	2
Grigadale	Highld	NM4367	56°43·7'	6°11·6'W	X	47
Grigg	Kent	TQ8544	51°10·1'	0°39·2'E	T	189
Grigg's Fm	Essex	TL8322	51°52·2'	0°39·9'E	FM	168
Grigg's Fm	Somer	ST2413	50°54·9'	3°4·5'W	FM	193
Grigg's Fm	W Susx	TQ1529	51°3·2'	0°21·2'W	FM	187,198
Griggs Green	Hants	SU8231	51°4·6'	0°49·4'W	T	186
Grigg, The	Shrops	SJ6821	52°47·4'	2°28·1'W	X	127
Grighay Fm	Dorset	ST3801	50°48·5'	2°52·4'W	FM	193
Grigland	Heref	SO2838	52°2·4'	3°2·6'W	X	161
Grigorhill	Highld	NH9054	57°34·0'	3°49·9'W	X	27
Grike	Cumbr	NY0814	54°31·0'	3°24·9'W	H	89
Grillis	Corn	SW6738	50°12·0'	5°15·5'W	T	203
Grilsay	Aberd	NJ5728	57°20·7'	2°42·4'W	X	37
Grilstone	Devon	SS7324	51°0·3'	3°48·2'W	T	180
Grimbister	Orkney	HY3712	58°59·7'	3°5·3'W	T	6
Grimblethorpe Hall	Lincs	TF2386	53°21·6'	0°8·7'W	X	113,122
Grim Brigs	Aberd	NO9091	57°0·9'	2°9·4'W	X	38,45
Grimbust	Orkney	HY5140	59°14·9'	2°51·1'W	X	5
Grime Fen	Suff	TL7083	52°25·3'	0°30·4'E	X	143
Grimeford Village	Lancs	SD6112	53°36·4'	2°35·0'W	T	109
Grime Lodge Crags	N Yks	SE0466	54°5·6'	1°55·9'W	X	98
Grime Moor	N Yks	SE8692	54°19·2'	0°40·2'W	X	94,101
Grimer's Fm	Glos	SO7732	51°59·4'	2°19·7'W	FM	150
Grimes Brook	Herts	TL2804	51°43·4'	0°8·4'W	W	166
Grimes Gill	N Yks	SE1378	54°12·1'	1°47·6'W	W	99
Grime's Graves	Norf	TL8189	52°28·4'	0°40·3'E	X	144
Grime's Graves (Flint Mines)	Norf	TL8189	52°28·4'	0°40·3'E	A	144
Grimes Hill	Worcs	SP0875	52°22·6'	1°52·5'W	T	139
Grimes Moor	Cumbr	NY6607	54°27·7'	2°31·0'W	X	91
Grimesmoor	Notts	SK6348	53°1·8'	1°3·2'W	X	129
Grimesmoor Ho	Cumbr	NY6507	54°27·7'	2°32·0'W	X	91
Grimesthorpe	Sheff	SK3690	53°24·6'	1°27·1'W	T	110,111
Grimeston	Orkney	HY3114	59°0·7'	3°11·6'W	T	6
Grimethorpe	Barns	SE4109	53°34·8'	1°22·4'W	T	111
Grimethorpe Hall	Barns	SE4009	53°34·8'	1°23·3'W	X	111
Grimgrew	E Ayr	NS5319	55°26·8'	4°19·0'W	X	70
Griminis	N Eil	NF7751	57°26·3'	7°22·6'W	T	22
Griminish	N Eil	NF7575	57°39·1'	7°26·5'W	X	18
Griminish Point	N Eil	NF7276	57°39·5'	7°29·6'W	X	18
Grimister	Shetld	HU4693	60°37·3'	1°9·1'W	T	1,2
Grimley	Worcs	SO8360	52°14·5'	2°14·5'W	T	138,150
Grimley Brook	Worcs	SO8261	52°15·0'	2°15·4'W	W	138,150
Grimley Hall	Worcs	SO9869	52°19·4'	2°1·4'W	X	139
Grimmer, The	Notts	SK7737	52°55·7'	0°50·9'W	W	129
Grimmet	E Ayr	NS4406	55°19·7'	4°27·1'W	X	70,77
Grimmet	S Ayr	NS3210	55°21·6'	4°38·6'W	X	70
Grimmet Hill	E Ayr	NS4305	55°19·1'	4°28·0'W	H	70
Grimness	Orkney	ND4793	58°49·5'	2°54·6'W	X	7
Grim Ness	Orkney	ND4992	58°49·0'	2°52·5'W	X	7
Grimoldby	Lincs	TF3988	53°22·5'	0°5·8'E	T	113,122
Grimoldby Grange	Lincs	TF3888	53°22·5'	0°4·9'E	X	113,122
Grimoldby Ings	Lincs	TF4189	53°23·0'	0°7·6'E	X	113,122
Grimpo	Shrops	SJ3626	52°49·9'	2°56·6'W	T	126
Grimpsey Copse	Northnts	SP8654	52°10·9'	0°44·1'W	F	152
Grimpstone	Devon	SX7952	50°21·6'	3°41·6'W	X	202
Grimpstonleigh	Devon	SX7549	50°19·9'	3°45·0'W	X	202
Grimsacre Fm	Kent	TR1745	51°10·0'	1°6·6'E	FM	179,189
Grimsargh	Lancs	SD5834	53°48·3'	2°37·9'W	T	102
Grimsargh Hall	Lancs	SD5833	53°47·7'	2°37·8'W	X	102
Grimsargh Ho	Lancs	SD5834	53°48·3'	2°37·9'W	X	102
Grimsargh Resrs	Lancs	SD5934	53°48·3'	2°36·9'W	W	102
Grimsay or Griomasaigh	N Eil	NF8656	57°29·4'	7°14·0'W	X	22
Grim's Bank	W Berks	SU6265	51°23·1'	1°6·2'W	A	175
Grimsbury	Oxon	SP4640	52°3·6'	1°19·3'W	T	151
Grimsbury Castle	W Berks	SU5172	51°26·9'	1°15·6'W	X	174
Grimsbury Castle (Fort)	W Berks	SU5172	51°26·9'	1°15·6'W	A	174
Grimsby	NE Lincs	TA2709	53°34·0'	0°4·5'W	T	113
Grimsby Roads		TA2912	53°35·6'	0°2·6'W	W	113
Grimscote	Northnts	SP6553	52°10·5'	1°2·6'W	T	152
Grimscote Heath	Northnts	SP6453	52°10·5'	1°3·4'W	F	152
Grimscott	Corn	SS2606	50°49·9'	4°27·9'W	T	190
Grims Ditch	Bucks	SP8201	51°42·3'	0°48·4'W	A	165
Grims Ditch	Hants	ST0419	50°58·0'	3°21·6'W	A	184
Grim's Ditch	Hants	SU0918	50°57·9'	1°51·9'W	A	184
Grim's Ditch	Harrow	TQ1190	51°36·1'	0°23·4'W	A	176
Grim's Ditch	Harrow	TQ1392	51°37·2'	0°21·7'W	A	176
Grim's Ditch	Herts	SP9309	51°46·5'	0°38·7'W	A	165
Grim's Ditch	Herts	TL0009	51°46·5'	0°32·6'W	A	166
Grims Ditch	Oxon	SP3518	51°51·8'	1°29·1'W	A	164
Grim's Ditch	Oxon	SP4120	51°52·9'	1°23·9'W	A	164
Grim's Ditch	Oxon	SU4284	51°33·4'	1°23·3'W	A	174
Grim's Ditch	Oxon	SU4585	51°34·0'	1°20·7'W	A	174
Grim's Ditch	Oxon	SU4983	51°32·9'	1°17·3'W	A	174
Grim's Ditch	Oxon	SU5383	51°32·8'	1°13·7'W	A	174
Grim's Ditch	Oxon	SU6487	51°34·9'	1°4·2'W	A	175
Grim's Ditch	W Berks	SU4784	51°33·4'	1°18·9'W	A	174
Grim's Ditch	W Berks	SU5678	51°30·1'	1°11·2'W	X	174

Grim's Ditch	W Berks	SU5877	51°29·6'	1°9·5'W	A	174
Grim's Ditch	W Berks	SU5979	51°30·6'	1°8·6'W	A	174
Grimsditch Hall	Ches	SJ6080	53°19·2'	2°35·6'W	X	109
Grimsdyke Fm	Oxon	SP4021	51°53·4'	1°24·7'W	FM	164
Grimshaw	Black w Dar	SD7024	53°42·9'	2°26·9'W	T	103
Grimshaw Cott	Darl	NZ2320	54°34·7'	1°38·2'W	X	93
Grimshaw Green	Lancs	SD4812	53°36·4'	2°46·7'W	T	108
Grimshaw Hall	Sol	SP1877	52°23·7'	1°43·7'W	A	139
Grimshoe	Norf	TL8189	52°28·4'	0°40·3'E	X	144
Grims Lodge Fm	Wilts	SU1023	51°0·6'	1°51·1'W	FM	184
Grims Mound	Lincs	TF2386	53°21·6'	0°8·7'W	A	113,122
Grimspound	Devon	SX7080	50°36·5'	3°49·9'W	A	191
Grimsthorpe	Lincs	TF0423	52°47·9'	0°27·0'W	T	130
Grimsthorpe Castle	Lincs	TF0422	52°47·4'	0°27·1'W	A	130
Grimsthorpe Park	Lincs	TF0320	52°46·3'	0°28·0'W	X	130
Grimston	E Yorks	TA2835	53°48·0'	0°3·0'W	T	107
Grimston	Leic	SK6821	52°47·2'	0°59·1'W	T	129
Grimston	Norf	TF7122	52°46·3'	0°32·5'E	T	132
Grimston	York	SE6451	53°57·3'	1°1·1'W	T	105,106
Grimston Brow	N Yks	SE8366	54°5·2'	0°43·4'W	X	100
Grimston Carr	Norf	TF7222	52°46·3'	0°33·4'E	F	132
Grimstone	Devon	SX5170	50°30·9'	4°5·7'W	X	201
Grimstone	Dorset	SY6494	50°44·9'	2°30·2'W	T	194
Grimstone Down	Dorset	SY6495	50°45·4'	2°30·2'W	X	194
Grimstone End	Suff	TL9369	52°17·3'	0°50·2'E	T	155
Grimston Fields Fm	N Yks	SE8267	54°5·8'	0°44·3'W	FM	100
Grimston Gap	Leic	SK6919	52°46·1'	0°58·2'W	X	129
Grimston Garth	E Yorks	TA2835	53°48·0'	0°3·0'W	X	107
Grimston Grange	N Yks	SE4841	53°52·0'	1°15·8'W	X	105
Grimston Grange	N Yks	SE6073	54°9·2'	1°4·5'W	X	100
Grimston Grange	York	SE6549	53°56·2'	1°0·2'W	X	105,106
Grimston Hall	Suff	TM2636	51°58·8'	1°17·9'E	X	169
Grimston Heath	Norf	TF7622	52°46·2'	0°36·9'E	X	132
Grimston Hill	Notts	SK6865	53°10·9'	0°58·5'W	X	120
Grimston Hill Ho	N Yks	SE8567	54°5·8'	0°41·6'W	X	100
Grimston Hill Ho	York	SE6551	53°57·3'	1°0·2'W	X	105,106
Grimston Lodge	York	SE6451	53°57·3'	1°1·1'W	X	105,106
Grimston Manor Fm	N Yks	SE6175	54°10·3'	1°3·5'W	FM	100
Grimston Moor	N Yks	SE6174	54°9·7'	1°3·5'W	X	100
Grimston Park	N Yks	SE4941	53°52·0'	1°14·9'W	X	105
Grimston Warren	Norf	TF6721	52°45·9'	0°28·9'E	F	132
Grimston Wood	York	SE6649	53°56·2'	0°59·3'W	F	105,106
Grimthorpe Manor	E Yorks	SE8152	53°57·7'	0°45·5'W	X	106
Grimthorpe Wood	E Yorks	SE8152	53°57·7'	0°45·5'W	F	106
Grimwith Fell	N Yks	SE0664	54°4·6'	1°54·1'W	X	99
Grimwith Resr	N Yks	SE0664	54°4·6'	1°54·1'W	W	99
Grinaby	Orkney	HY4843	59°16·5'	2°54·3'W	X	5
Grinacombe	Devon	SX4192	50°42·6'	4°14·7'W	X	190
Grinacombe Moor	Devon	SX4191	50°42·1'	4°14·7'W	T	190
Grinah Stones	Derby	SK1396	53°27·9'	1°47·8'W	X	110
Grind	Orkney	HY5006	58°56·6'	2°51·6'W	X	6,7
Grind	Orkney	HY5504	58°55·5'	2°46·4'W	X	6
Grind	Shetld	HU3364	60°21·8'	1°23·6'W	X	2,3
Grind	Shetld	HU4879	60°29·8'	1°7·1'W	X	2,3
Grindale	E Yorks	TA1371	54°7·6'	0°15·8'W	T	101
Grindale Field	E Yorks	TA1471	54°7·6'	0°14·9'W	X	101
Grindhill	Devon	SX4894	50°43·8'	4°8·8'W	X	191
Grind Hill	Shetld	HU2480	60°30·4'	1°33·3'W	H	3
Grindigar	Orkney	HY5805	58°56·1'	2°43·3'W	X	6
Grinding Burn	Scot Bord	NT5519	55°28·0'	2°42·3'W	W	80
Grindiscol	Shetld	HU4939	60°8·2'	1°6·6'W	T	4
Grindle	Shrops	SJ7503	52°37·7'	2°21·8'W	T	127
Grindle Brook	Devon	SY0090	50°42·3'	3°24·6'W	W	192
Grindle Fm	Suff	TM1145	52°4·0'	1°5·1'E	FM	155,169
Grindleford	Derby	SK2477	53°17·6'	1°38·0'W	T	119
Grindleford Sta	Derby	SK2578	53°18·1'	1°37·1'W	X	119
Grindleforge	Shrops	SJ7503	52°37·7'	2°21·8'W	X	127
Grindlesgrain Tor	Derby	SK1292	53°25·7'	1°48·8'W	X	110
Grindleton	Lancs	SD7545	53°54·3'	2°22·4'W	T	103
Grindleton Fell	Lancs	SD7447	53°55·4'	2°23·3'W	X	103
Grindley	Orkney	ND4485	58°45·2'	2°57·6'W	X	7
Grindley	Staffs	SK0329	52°51·7'	1°56·9'W	T	128
Grindley Brook	Shrops	SJ5242	52°58·6'	2°42·5'W	T	117
Grindley Brook Fm	Shrops	SJ5243	52°59·2'	2°42·5'W	FM	117
Grindlow	Derby	SK1877	53°17·6'	1°43·4'W	T	119
Grind Low	Derby	SK2067	53°12·2'	1°41·6'W	A	119
Grind of the Navir	Shetld	HU2180	60°30·5'	1°36·6'W	X	3
Grindon	Northum	NT9144	55°41·6'	2°8·2'W	T	74,75
Grindon	Northum	NY8269	55°1·2'	2°16·5'W	X	86,87
Grindon	Staffs	SK0854	53°5·2'	1°52·4'W	T	119
Grindon	Stock on T	NZ3925	54°37·4'	1°23·3'W	T	93
Grindon	Sund	NZ3554	54°53·0'	1°26·8'W	T	88
Grindon Green	Northum	NY7373	55°3·3'	2°24·9'W	X	86,87
Grindon Hill	Northum	NY8268	55°0·6'	2°16·5'W	X	86,87
Grindon Lough	Northum	NY8067	55°0·1'	2°18·3'W	W	86,87
Grindon Mill Hills	Northum	NY8068	55°0·6'	2°18·3'W	X	86,87
Grindon Moor	Staffs	SK0655	53°5·8'	1°54·2'W	X	119
Grindonmoor Gate	Staffs	SK0754	53°5·2'	1°53·3'W	X	119
Grindonrigg	Northum	NT9243	55°41·1'	2°7·2'W	X	74,75
Grinds Brook	Derby	SK1187	53°23·0'	1°49·7'W	W	110
Grindsbrook Booth	Derby	SK1286	53°22·5'	1°48·8'W	T	110
Grindslow Ho	Derby	SK1286	53°22·5'	1°48·8'W	X	110
Grindslow Knoll	Derby	SK1086	53°22·5'	1°50·6'W	X	110
Grindstone Burn	Scot Bord	NT7608	55°22·2'	2°22·3'W	W	80
Grindstone Cleugh	Durham	NY9146	54°48·8'	2°8·0'W	X	87
Grindstone Crook	N Yks	SE3596	54°21·7'	1°27·3'W	X	99
Grindstonehill	Beds	SP9551	52°9·2'	0°36·3'W	X	153
Grindstonelaw	Northum	NZ0073	55°3·3'	1°59·6'W	X	87
Grindstone Law	Scot Bord	NT7607	55°21·6'	2°22·3'W	H	80
Grindstone Rig	E Ayr	NS7223	55°29·3'	4°1·1'W	X	71
Grindybrecks	Shetld	HU3044	60°11·0'	1°27·1'W	X	4
Gringley Carr	Notts	SK7293	53°26·0'	0°54·6'W	X	112
Gringley Grange	Notts	SK7481	53°19·5'	0°52·9'W	X	120
Gringley Grange	Notts	SK7590	53°24·3'	0°51·9'W	X	112
Gringley on the Hill	Notts	SK7390	53°24·3'	0°53·7'W	T	112
Grinkle Park	Red & Cl	NZ7314	54°31·2'	0°51·9'W	X	94
Grinllwm	Conwy	SH7762	53°8·7'	3°49·9'W	H	115
Grin Low	Derby	SK0571	53°14·4'	1°55·1'W	X	119
Grinsdale	Cumbr	NY3658	54°55·0'	2°59·5'W	T	85

Grinshill	Shrops	SJ5223	52°48·4'	2°42·3'W	T	126
Grinstead Hill	Suff	TM0954	52°8·9'	1°3·7'E	T	155
Grinstone Hill Ho	N Yks	SE1171	54°8·3'	1°49·5'W	X	99
Grinton	N Yks	SE0498	54°22·9'	1°55·9'W	T	98
Grinton Gill	N Yks	SE0497	54°22·4'	1°55·9'W	W	98
Grinton Lodge	N Yks	SE0497	54°22·4'	1°55·9'W	X	98
Grinton Moor	N Yks	SE0495	54°21·3'	1°55·9'W	X	98
Griomarstadh	N Eil	NB2130	58°10·5'	6°44·3'W	X	8,13
Griomasaigh	N Eil	NF8347	57°24·4'	7°16·3'W	T	22
Griomaval	N Eil	NB0122	58°5·4'	7°4·0'W	H	13
Griomsidar	N Eil	NB4025	58°8·5'	6°24·6'W	T	14
Griosamol	N Eil	NB1729	58°9·8'	6°48·3'W	H	8,13
Griosamul	N Eil	NB1415	58°2·2'	6°50·3'W	H	13,14
Grip	Cered	SN5870	52°18·8'	4°4·6'W	X	135
Grip Heath	Dorset	SY9787	50°41·2'	2°2·2'W	X	195
Gripper's Hill	Devon	SX6865	50°28·4'	3°51·2'W	H	202
Gripp-fawr	Carm	SN6319	51°51·4'	3°59·0'W	X	159
Gripps Fm	Red & Cl	NZ6919	54°33·9'	0°55·5'W	FM	94
Grip Shank	S Lanak	NT0121	55°28·6'	3°33·5'W	H	72
Grisa Lee	Shetld	HP6215	60°49·0'	0°51·1'W	X	1
Grisdale	Cumbr	SD7793	54°20·2'	2°20·8'W	T	98
Grisdale Beck	Cumbr	NY3614	54°31·3'	2°58·9'W	W	90
Grisdale Pike	Cumbr	SD7592	54°19·6'	2°22·6'W	X	98
Griseburn	Cumbr	NY7112	54°30·4'	2°26·5'W	X	91
Grisedale	Cumbr	NY3715	54°31·8'	2°58·0'W	X	90
Grisedale	Cumbr	NY5501	54°24·4'	2°41·2'W	X	90
Grisedale	Lancs	SD4874	54°9·8'	2°47·4'W	X	97
Grisedale Beck	Cumbr	SD7793	54°20·2'	2°20·8'W	W	98
Grisedale Bridge	Cumbr	NY3916	54°32·4'	2°56·1'W	X	90
Grisedale Brow	Cumbr	NY3615	54°31·8'	2°58·9'W	X	90
Grisedale Forest	Cumbr	NY3513	54°30·7'	2°59·8'W	X	90
Grisedale Gill	Cumbr	NY2023	54°36·0'	3°13·9'W	W	89,90
Grisedale Hause	Cumbr	NY3411	54°29·7'	3°0·7'W	X	90
Grisedale Pike	Cumbr	NY1922	54°35·5'	3°14·8'W	H	89,90
Grisedale Tarn	Cumbr	NY3412	54°30·2'	3°0·7'W	W	90
Grisedale Wood	Lancs	SD4874	54°9·8'	2°47·4'W	F	97
Grishipoll	Arg & Bt	NM1959	56°38·6'	6°34·6'W	T	46
Grishipoll Bay	Arg & Bt	NM1860	56°39·1'	6°35·6'W	W	46
Grishipoll Point	Arg & Bt	NM1859	56°38·5'	6°35·5'W	X	46
Griskerry	Shetld	HU3622	59°59·1'	1°20·8'W	X	4
Grisling Common	E Susx	TQ4321	50°58·5'	0°2·6'E	T	198
Grist Ho	Shrops	SO3985	52°27·8'	2°53·5'W	X	137
Gristhorpe	N Yks	TA0882	54°13·6'	0°20·2'W	T	101
Gristhorpe Cliff	N Yks	TA0983	54°14·1'	0°19·2'W	X	101
Gristhorpe Cliff Fm	N Yks	TA0982	54°13·6'	0°19·3'W	FM	101
Gristhwaite Fm	N Yks	SE4278	54°12·0'	1°21·0'W	FM	99
Griston	Norf	TL9499	52°33·5'	0°52·1'E	T	144
Griswolds Fm	Warw	SP2060	52°14·5'	1°42·0'W	FM	151
Grit Fell	Lancs	SD5558	54°1·2'	2°40·8'W	H	102
Grit Fm	Worcs	SO7749	52°8·6'	2°19·8'W	FM	150
Grit Hill	D & G	NX9799	55°16·7'	3°36·9'W	X	78
Grithill	Heref	SO4234	52°0·3'	2°50·3'W	X	149,161
Grit Hill	Shrops	SO3398	52°34·8'	2°58·9'W	X	137
Grithill Fm	Worcs	SO6461	52°15·0'	2°31·2'W	FM	138,149
Gritley	Orkney	HY5604	58°55·5'	2°45·4'W	X	6
Gritnam	Hants	SU2806	50°51·4'	1°35·7'W	X	195
Gritnam Wood	Hants	SU2806	50°51·4'	1°35·7'W	F	195
Grit Ness	Orkney	HY3626	59°7·2'	3°6·6'W	X	6
Grits, The	N Yks	SE9676	54°10·5'	0°31·3'W	X	101
Gritstone Trail	Ches	SJ9473	53°15·5'	2°5·0'W	X	118
Gritstone Trail	Ches	SJ9682	53°20·3'	2°3·2'W	X	109
Grittenham	Wilts	SU0382	51°32·4'	1°57·0'W	X	173
Grittenham Fm	W Susx	SU9421	50°59·1'	0°39·3'W	FM	197
Grittlesend	Heref	SO7249	52°8·6'	2°24·2'W	T	149
Grittleton	Wilts	ST8580	51°31·4'	2°12·6'W	T	173
Grittleton Ho (Sch)	Wilts	ST8680	51°31·4'	2°11·7'W	X	173
Gritts Fm	N Yks	SE8560	54°2·0'	0°41·7'W	FM	100
Grives, The	Notts	SK5054	53°5·1'	1°14·8'W	X	120
Grizebeck	Cumbr	SD2385	54°15·5'	3°10·5'W	T	96
Grizedale	Cumbr	SD3394	54°20·5'	3°1·4'W	T	96,97
Grize Dale	Lancs	SD5148	53°55·8'	2°44·4'W	X	102
Grizedale Barn	Lancs	SD5656	54°0·1'	2°39·9'W	X	102
Grizedale Beck	Cumbr	SD3393	54°19·9'	3°1·4'W	W	96,97
Grizedale Br	Lancs	SD5655	53°59·6'	2°39·9'W	X	102
Grizedale Fell	Lancs	SD5550	53°56·9'	2°40·7'W	X	102
Grizedale Forest	Cumbr	SD3394	54°20·5'	3°1·4'W	F	96,97
Grizedale Head	Lancs	SD5650	53°56·9'	2°39·8'W	X	102
Grizedale Head	Lancs	SD5658	54°1·2'	2°39·9'W	X	102
Grizedale Lea Resr	Lancs	SD5348	53°55·8'	2°42·5'W	W	102
Grizedale Resr	Lancs	SD5248	53°55·8'	2°43·4'W	W	102
Grizedales	N Yks	SD8764	54°4·5'	2°11·5'W	X	98
Grizedale Tarn	Cumbr	SD3494	54°20·5'	3°0·5'W	W	96,97
Grizelrig	Scot Bord	NT7842	55°40·5'	2°20·6'W	X	74
Grizzlefield	Scot Bord	NT5839	55°38·8'	2°39·6'W	X	73,74
Grizzle Field Ho	N Yks	SE4483	54°14·7'	1°19·1'W	X	99
Gro	Powys	SJ0611	52°41·6'	3°23·1'W	X	125
Gro	Powys	SJ2420	52°46·6'	3°7·2'W	X	126
Groalpans	Moray	NJ4455	57°35·2'	2°55·7'W	X	28
Groam	Highld	NH5646	57°29·1'	4°23·7'W	X	26
Groam of Annat	Highld	NH5143	57°27·4'	4°28·6'W	X	26
Groan	Pth & Kin	NO0030	56°27·4'	3°36·9'W	X	52,53
Groatay	N Eil	NF9773	57°39·0'	7°4·3'W	X	18
Groat Haugh	Northum	NT8845	55°42·1'	2°11·0'W	X	74
Groat Hill	N Yks	SE6296	54°21·6'	1°2·3'W	X	94,100
Groat's Loch	Highld	ND3140	58°20·8'	3°10·3'W	W	11,12
Groatster	Orkney	HY4906	58°56·6'	2°52·7'W	X	6,7
Groay	N Eil	NG0079	57°42·3'	7°1·7'W	X	18
Grob a' Chuthaich	Arg & Bt	NM7227	56°23·1'	5°41·2'W	X	49
Groban	Highld	NH0970	57°41·0'	5°11·8'W	H	19
Groba nan Each	Highld	NG4560	57°33·8'	6°15·4'W	H	23
Groban na Sgeire	Highld	NG2255	57°30·3'	6°38·0'W	X	23
Gròb Bàgh	Arg & Bt	NR6346	55°39·2'	5°45·6'W	W	62
Grobdale Lane	D & G	NX6167	54°58·9'	4°9·9'W	W	83
Grobdale of Balmaghie	D & G	NX6264	54°57·3'	4°8·9'W	X	83
Grobdale of Girthon	D & G	NX6264	54°57·3'	4°8·9'W	X	83
Grobister	Orkney	HY6524	59°6·4'	2°36·2'W	T	5
Grobolls	Arg & Bt	NR3359	55°45·3'	6°14·9'W	X	60
Grobridh	N Eil	NB4010	58°0·5'	6°23·6'W	W	14
Grobs Ness	Shetld	HU3663	60°21·2'	1°20·4'W	X	2,3
Grobsness	Shetld	HU3763	60°21·2'	1°19·3'W	T	2,3

Grobust	Orkney	HY4249	59°19·7'	3°0·7'W	X	5
Groby	Leic	SK5207	52°39·7'	1°13·5'W	T	140
Groby Fm	Ches	SJ7157	53°6·8'	2°25·6'W	FM	118
Groby Lodge Fm	Leic	SK5007	52°39·7'	1°15·2'W	FM	140
Groby Park Fm	Leic	SK5008	52°40·3'	1°15·2'W	FM	140
Groby Pool	Leic	SK5208	52°40·3'	1°13·5'W	W	140
Grochall	Corn	SW6914	49°59·1'	5°13·0'W	X	203
Grochlie Geo	Orkney	HY6520	59°4·2'	2°36·1'W	X	5
Groddie	Aberd	NJ4005	57°8·2'	2°59·0'W	X	37
Grodwell Burn	Clackm	NN9102	56°12·1'	3°45·0'W	W	58
Grodwell Hill	Clackm	NN9101	56°11·6'	3°45·0'W	X	58
Groemeshall Burn	Orkney	HY4704	58°55·5'	2°54·7'W	W	6,7
Groes	Cered	SN6651	52°8·7'	3°57·1'W	X	146
Groes	Conwy	SJ0064	53°10·1'	3°29·4'W	T	116
Groes	Nth Pt Talb	SS7986	51°33·8'	3°44·4'W	X	170
Groes	Powys	SJ0718	52°45·3'	3°22·3'W	X	125
Groes	Wrex	SJ3845	53°0·2'	2°55·0'W	X	117
Groes Bryn-llwyd	Powys	SN8170	52°19·2'	3°44·4'W	X	135,136,147
Groes-ddu	Powys	SJ0911	52°41·6'	3°20·4'W	X	125
Groes Efa	Denb	SJ1165	53°10·7'	3°19·5'W	T	116
Groes-faen	Rho Cyn Taf	ST0681	51°31·4'	3°20·9'W	T	170
Groes-faen Fm	Caer	SO1300	51°41·8'	3°15·1'W	FM	171
Groes Fawr	Cered	SN7359	52°13·1'	3°51·2'W	W	146,147
Groes-fawr	Denb	SJ1265	53°10·7'	3°18·6'W	T	116
Groesffordd	Conwy	SH7775	53°15·7'	3°50·2'W	X	115
Groesffordd	Conwy	SH9867	53°11·7'	3°31·2'W	X	116
Groesffordd	Gwyn	SH2739	52°55·5'	4°33·7'W	T	123
Groesffordd	Powys	SO0728	51°56·8'	3°20·8'W	T	160
Groesffordd Marli	Denb	SJ0073	53°14·9'	3°29·5'W	X	116
Groes Fm	Flint	SJ2269	53°13·0'	3°9·7'W	FM	117
Groes Fm	V of Glam	SS8774	51°27·5'	3°37·2'W	FM	170
Groes-lâs	Gwyn	SH5729	52°50·6'	4°7·0'W	X	124
Groeslon	Gwyn	SH4755	53°4·5'	4°16·6'W	T	115,123
Groeslon	Gwyn	SH5260	53°7·2'	4°12·3'W	T	114,115
Groes-lwyd	Denb	SJ0645	52°59·9'	3°23·6'W	X	116
Groeslwyd	Denb	SJ1743	52°58·9'	3°13·8'W	X	125
Groeslwyd	Gwyn	SH7417	52°44·4'	3°51·6'W	X	124
Groes-lwyd	Monm	SO3222	51°53·8'	2°58·9'W	T	161
Groes-lwyd	Powys	SJ2111	52°41·7'	3°9·7'W	T	126
Groespluan	Powys	SJ2108	52°40·1'	3°9·7'W	T	126
Groesuchaf	Powys	SN8956	52°11·7'	3°37·0'W	X	147
Groesvaen	Powys	SO1546	52°6·6'	3°14·1'W	X	148
Groes-wen	Caer	ST1286	51°34·2'	3°15·8'W	T	171
Groes-wen	Powys	SO0443	52°4·9'	3°23·7'W	X	147,160
Groes y Forwyn	Powys	SJ0220	52°46·4'	3°26·8'W	X	125
Groffa Crag	Cumbr	SD2783	54°14·5'	3°6·8'W	X	96,97
Grofft	Powys	SH8104	52°37·5'	3°45·1'W	X	135,136
Grogan Dubh	Arg & Bt	NM8341	56°30·9'	5°31·2'W	X	49
Grogarth Fm	Corn	SW9145	50°16·3'	4°55·6'W	FM	204
Grogport	Arg & Bt	NR8044	55°38·6'	5°29·3'W	T	62,69
Gro Hill	Powys	SN9262	52°15·0'	3°34·5'W	H	147
Groigearraidh	N Eil	NF7639	57°19·8'	7°22·6'W	X	22
Gromford	Suff	TM3858	52°10·4'	1°29·2'E	T	156
Gromlech	I of Angl	SH2676	53°15·4'	4°36·1'W	X	114
Grommond	Shetld	HU4693	60°37·3'	1°9·1'W	X	1,2
Gronant	Flint	SJ0983	53°20·4'	3°21·6'W	T	116
Gronant	I of Angl	SH3285	53°20·4'	4°31·0'W	X	114
Gronataing	Shetld	HU2446	60°12·1'	1°33·5'W	X	4
Grona Taing	Shetld	HU3671	60°25·5'	1°20·3'W	X	2,3
Gronfoel	Flint	SJ1665	53°10·8'	3°15·0'W	X	116
Gron-gaer	Carm	SN5721	51°52·4'	4°4·2'W	A	159
Grongaer	Swan	SS5594	51°37·8'	4°5·3'W	A	159
Groni Field	Shetld	HU3053	60°15·9'	1°27·0'W	H	3
Gronwen	Shrops	SJ2726	52°49·8'	3°4·6'W	T	126
Gronwen	Wrex	SJ3240	52°57·4'	3°0·3'W	X	117
Grood, The	Shetld	HU4334	60°5·6'	1°13·1'W	X	4
Groombridge	E Susx	TQ5336	51°6·4'	0°11·5'E	T	188
Groombridge Place	Kent	TQ5337	51°6·9'	0°11·5'E	A	188
Groom House Fm	Somer	ST2939	51°9·0'	3°0·5'W	FM	182
Grooms Fm	Hants	SU8139	51°8·9'	0°50·1'W	FM	186
Groose, The	Swan	SS4494	51°37·6'	4°14·8'W	X	159
Groot Ness	Shetld	HU3528	60°2·4'	1°21·8'W	X	4
Groot,The	Shetld	HU5059	60°19·0'	1°5·2'W	W	2,3
Groove Beck	Cumbr	NY3621	54°35·1'	2°59·0'W	W	90
Groove Gill	N Yks	SE0467	54°6·2'	1°55·9'W	W	98
Grory	Orkney	HY3629	59°8·8'	3°6·6'W	X	6
Grory	Orkney	HY4531	59°10·0'	2°57·2'W	X	5,6
Grosa Cleit	N Eil	NG1393	57°50·3'	6°49·7'W	H	14
Grose	Corn	SW9059	50°23·8'	4°56·9'W	X	200
Grosefield	Angus	NO5862	56°45·1'	2°40·8'W	X	44
Grosmont	Monm	SO4024	51°54·9'	2°51·9'W	T	161
Grosmont	N Yks	NZ8205	54°26·3'	0°43·7'W	T	94
Grosmont Castle	Monm	SO4024	51°54·9'	2°51·9'W	A	161
Grosmont Fm	N Yks	NZ8306	54°26·8'	0°42·8'W	FM	94
Grosmont Manor	N Yks	NZ8105	54°26·3'	0°44·6'W	X	94
Grosmont Wood Fm	Monm	SO3921	51°53·3'	2°52·8'W	FM	161
Gross Gill Dike	N Yks	SE1065	54°5·1'	1°50·4'W	W	99
Gross Green	Warw	SP3857	52°12·8'	1°26·2'W	T	151
Grosvenor Br	Wan	TQ2877	51°28·9'	0°9·0'W	X	176
Grosvenor House Fm	Suff	TL6483	52°25·4'	0°25·1'E	FM	143
Grosvenor House Sch	N Yks	SE2359	54°1·8'	1°38·5'W	X	104
Grotaig	Highld	NH4923	57°16·6'	4°29·8'W	X	26
Grotaig Burn	Highld	NH4823	57°16·6'	4°30·8'W	W	26
Gro Taing	Shetld	HU2277	60°28·8'	1°35·5'W	X	3
Groton	Shrops	SJ2901	52°36·4'	3°2·5'W	X	126
Groton	Suff	TL9541	52°2·2'	0°51·0'E	T	155
Groton Ho	Suff	TL9642	52°2·7'	0°51·9'E	X	155
Groton Pl	Suff	TL9542	52°2·7'	0°51·0'E	X	155
Groton Wood (Nature Reserve)	Suff	TL9743	52°3·2'	0°52·8'E	F	155
Grottics Geo	Orkney	HY5739	59°14·4'	2°44·7'W	X	5,6
Grottington Fm	Northum	NY9769	55°1·2'	2°2·4'W	FM	87
Grotto Copse	Hants	SU4357	51°18·9'	1°22·6'W	F	174
Grotto Hill	Shrops	SJ5729	52°51·6'	2°37·9'W	X	126
Grotto Ho	Ches	SJ7873	53°15·5'	2°19·4'W	X	118
Grotton	Oldham	SD9604	53°32·2'	2°3·2'W	T	109
Grotton Hall	Oldham	SD9704	53°32·2'	2°2·3'W	A	109
Grotto, The	Cumbr	NY5128	54°38·9'	2°45·1'W	X	90
Grotto, The	Derby	SK2669	53°13·3'	1°36·2'W	X	119
Grotto, The	N Yks	SE1592	54°19·6'	1°45·7'W	X	99

Grotto, The	W Berks	SU5979	51°30·6'	1°8·6'W	X	174
Gro Tump	Powys	SO1292	52°31·4'	3°17·4'W	A	136
Groubear Fm	Devon	SS9011	50°53·5'	3°33·5'W	FM	192
Gröudd Hall	Conwy	SH9548	53°1·4'	3°33·5'W	X	116
Groudle Glen	I of M	SC4178	54°10·6'	4°25·8'W	X	95
Groud, The	Shetld	HU1652	60°15·4'	1°42·2'W	X	3
Grougar Mains	E Ayr	NS4638	55°36·9'	4°26·3'W	X	70
Grougfoot	Falk	NT0278	55°59·4'	3°33·8'W	X	65
Groundhills Fm	Red & Cl	NZ6616	54°32·3'	0°58·4'W	FM	94
Groundistone	Scot Bord	NT4919	55°28·0'	2°48·0'W	X	79
Grounds Fm	Bucks	SP6535	52°0·8'	1°2·8'W	FM	152
Grounds Fm	Oxon	SP3632	51°59·4'	1°28·1'W	FM	151
Grounds Fm	Warw	SP1695	52°33·4'	1°45·4'W	FM	139
Grounds Fm	Warw	SP2771	52°20·4'	1°35·8'W	FM	140
Grounds Fm	Warw	SP4074	52°22·0'	1°24·4'W	FM	140
Grounds Fm	Warw	SP4685	52°27·9'	1°19·0'W	FM	140
Grounds Fm	Worcs	SO7839	52°3·2'	2°18·9'W	FM	150
Groundslow Fields	Staffs	SJ8637	52°56·1'	2°12·1'W	X	127
Groundwater	Orkney	HY3708	58°57·5'	3°5·2'W	X	6,7
Groundwell Fm	Swin	SU1589	51°36·2'	1°46·6'W	FM	173
Groundy Croft	Cumbr	SD0699	54°22·9'	3°26·4'W	X	96
Groups Hollows	Cumbr	NY7009	54°28·8'	2°27·4'W	X	91
Grousecrag	Northum	NY9188	55°11·4'	2°8·1'W	X	80
Grouse Hall	Cumbr	SD7790	54°18·6'	2°20·8'W	X	98
Grouse Hall	N Yks	SE6990	54°18·3'	0°56·0'W	X	94,100
Grouse Hill	S Lanak	NS7235	55°35·8'	4°1·4'W	X	71
Grouse Ho	Northum	NY9053	54°52·5'	2°8·9'W	X	87
Grouselands	W Susx	TQ2230	51°3·6'	0°15·2'W	X	187
Grouse Lodge	Shrops	SJ2333	52°53·6'	3°8·3'W	X	126
Grouse, The (PH)	Derby	SK0390	53°24·6'	1°56·9'W	X	110
Grove	Bucks	SP9122	51°53·6'	0°40·3'W	T	165
Grove	Corn	SS2603	50°48·3'	4°27·8'W	X	190
Grove	Corn	SX3757	50°23·7'	4°17·2'W	X	201
Grove	Devon	SX3790	50°41·4'	4°18·1'W	X	190
Grove	Dorset	SY6972	50°33·0'	2°25·9'W	T	194
Grove	Heref	SO6144	52°5·8'	2°33·8'W	T	149
Grove	Kent	TR2361	51°18·5'	1°12·4'E	T	179
Grove	Notts	SK7379	53°18·4'	0°53·9'W	T	120
Grove	Oxon	SU4090	51°36·7'	1°24·9'W	T	164,174
Grove	Pemb	SM9800	51°40·0'	4°54·9'W	T	158
Grove Ash Fm	Oxon	SP4131	51°58·8'	1°23·8'W	FM	151
Grovebeck	N Yks	SE0396	54°21·8'	1°56·8'W	X	98
Grovebridge Fm	E Susx	TQ5915	50°55·0'	0°16·1'E	FM	199
Grovebury Fm	Beds	SP9223	51°54·1'	0°39·4'W	FM	165
Grove Cliff	Dorset	SY7071	50°32·5'	2°25·0'W	X	194
Grove Cott	Shrops	SO3891	52°31·0'	2°54·4'W	X	137
Grove Dale	N Yks	SE2475	54°10·5'	1°37·5'W	X	99
Grove End	Birm	SP1695	52°33·4'	1°45·4'W	T	139
Grove End	Kent	TQ8961	51°19·2'	0°43·1'E	T	178
Grove End	N Yks	SD9778	54°12·1'	2°2·3'W	X	98
Grove End	Warw	SP3039	52°3·1'	1°33·4'W	T	151
Grove End Fm	Bucks	SP7107	51°45·7'	0°57·9'W	FM	165
Grove-end Fm	Ches	SJ8782	53°20·3'	2°11·3'W	FM	109
Grove Ferry	Kent	TR2363	51°19·6'	1°12·4'E	X	179
Grove Fields	Warw	SP2659	52°13·9'	1°36·8'W	X	151
Grove Fm	Beds	TL0126	51°55·6'	0°31·5'W	FM	166
Grove Fm	Bucks	SP7936	52°1·2'	0°50·5'W	FM	152
Grove Fm	Bucks	SP8308	51°46·1'	0°47·4'W	FM	165
Grove Fm	Bucks	SP9418	51°51·4'	0°37·7'W	FM	165
Grove Fm	Bucks	SP9804	51°43·8'	0°34·5'W	FM	165
Grove Fm	Bucks	SU8292	51°37·5'	0°48·5'W	FM	175
Grove Fm	Bucks	SU9891	51°36·8'	0°34·7'W	FM	175,176
Grove Fm	Cambs	TL3549	52°7·6'	0°1·3'W	FM	154
Grove Fm	Cambs	TL6271	52°19·0'	0°23·0'E	FM	154
Grove Fm	Ches	SJ3871	53°14·2'	2°55·3'W	FM	117
Grove Fm	Ches	SJ9473	53°15·5'	2°5·0'W	FM	118
Grove Fm	Cumbr	SD3882	54°14·0'	2°56·7'W	FM	96,97
Grove Fm	Derby	SK2036	52°55·5'	1°41·7'W	FM	128
Grove Fm	Derby	SK2318	52°45·8'	1°39·1'W	FM	128
Grove Fm	Derby	SK3269	53°13·3'	1°30·8'W	FM	119
Grove Fm	Derby	SK4538	52°56·5'	1°19·4'W	FM	129
Grove Fm	Essex	TL7502	51°41·6'	0°32·3'E	FM	167
Grove Fm	Essex	TL8737	52°0·2'	0°43·9'E	FM	155
Grove Fm	Essex	TL8813	51°47·3'	0°43·9'E	FM	168
Grove Fm	Essex	TM0623	51°52·3'	0°59·9'E	FM	168
Grove Fm	E Yorks	SE7344	53°53·5'	0°52·9'W	FM	105,106
Grove Fm	E Yorks	SE8245	53°53·9'	0°44·7'W	FM	106
Grove Fm	Glos	SO6915	51°50·2'	2°26·6'W	FM	162
Grove Fm	Glos	SO7727	51°56·7'	2°19·7'W	FM	162
Grove Fm	Glos	SP1319	51°52·4'	1°48·3'W	FM	163
Grove Fm	Glos	ST9196	51°40·0'	2°7·4'W	FM	163
Grove Fm	Hants	SU6436	51°7·4'	1°4·7'W	FM	185
Grove Fm	Hants	SU7952	51°15·9'	0°51·7'W	FM	186
Grove Fm	Heref	SO2756	52°12·1'	3°3·7'W	FM	148
Grove Fm	Heref	SO3135	52°0·8'	2°59·9'W	FM	161
Grove Fm	Heref	SO3425	51°55·4'	2°57·2'W	FM	161
Grove Fm	Heref	SO3659	52°13·8'	2°55·8'W	FM	148,149
Grove Fm	Heref	SO4931	51°58·7'	2°44·2'W	FM	149
Grove Fm	Herts	TL0713	51°48·6'	0°26·5'W	FM	166
Grove Fm	Herts	TL0717	51°50·7'	0°26·4'W	FM	166
Grove Fm	Herts	TL1621	51°52·8'	0°18·5'W	FM	166
Grove Fm	Kent	TQ5866	51°22·5'	0°16·6'E	FM	177
Grove Fm	Kent	TQ9336	51°5·7'	0°45·8'E	FM	189
Grove Fm	Kent	TR1938	51°6·2'	1°8·1'E	FM	179,189
Grove Fm	Leeds	SE2843	53°53·2'	1°34·0'W	FM	104
Grove Fm	Lincs	SK8659	53°7·5'	0°42·5'W	FM	121
Grove Fm	Lincs	SK8887	53°22·6'	0°40·2'W	FM	112,121
Grove Fm	Lincs	TF1237	52°55·4'	0°19·6'W	FM	130
Grove Fm	Lincs	TF1781	53°19·0'	0°14·2'W	FM	121
Grove Fm	Lincs	TF2575	53°15·7'	0°7·1'W	FM	122
Grove Fm	Lincs	TF3293	53°25·3'	0°0·4'W	FM	113
Grove Fm	Lincs	TF3491	53°24·2'	0°1·3'E	FM	113
Grove Fm	Lincs	TF3887	53°21·9'	0°4·9'E	FM	113,122
Grove Fm	Lincs	TF4193	53°25·1'	0°7·7'E	FM	113
Grove Fm	Lincs	TF4522	52°46·8'	0°9·4'E	FM	131
Grove Fm	Midlo	NT3264	55°52·1'	3°4·8'W	FM	66
Grove Fm	NE Lincs	TA2504	53°31·3'	0°6·5'W	FM	113
Grove Fm	NE Lincs	TA2704	53°31·3'	0°4·6'W	FM	113
Grove Fm	Norf	TF9031	52°50·8'	0°49·7'E	FM	132
Grove Fm	Norf	TF9341	52°56·1'	0°52·7'E	FM	132

Grove Fm	Norf	TG0003	52°35·5'	0°57·6'E	FM	144
Grove Fm	Norf	TG2137	52°53·3'	1°17·5'E	FM	133
Grove Fm	Norf	TG2317	52°42·5'	1°18·5'E	FM	133,134
Grove Fm	Norf	TG2621	52°44·6'	1°21·3'E	FM	133,134
Grove Fm	Norf	TG3517	52°42·2'	1°29·1'E	FM	133,134
Grove Fm	Norf	TL9099	52°33·6'	0°48·6'E	FM	144
Grove Fm	Norf	TM0285	52°25·8'	0°58·7'E	FM	144
Grove Fm	Norf	TM1585	52°25·5'	1°10·1'E	FM	144,156
Grove Fm	Norf	TM1779	52°22·2'	1°11·7'E	FM	156
Grove Fm	Norf	TM2080	52°22·7'	1°14·3'E	FM	156
Grove Fm	Norf	TM2188	52°26·9'	1°15·5'E	FM	156
Grove Fm	Norf	TM2295	52°30·7'	1°16·7'E	FM	134
Grove Fm	Norf	TM2888	52°26·8'	1°21·7'E	FM	156
Grove Fm	Norf	TM4094	52°29·7'	1°32·5'E	FM	134
Grove Fm	Northnts	SP5669	52°19·2'	1°10·3'W	FM	152
Grove Fm	Northnts	SP6370	52°19·7'	1°4·1'W	FM	140
Grove Fm	Notts	SK6830	52°52·0'	0°59·0'W	FM	129
Grove Fm	Notts	SK8553	53°4·3'	0°43·5'W	FM	121
Grove Fm	Oxon	SP2430	51°58·3'	1°38·6'W	FM	151
Grove Fm	Oxon	SP3009	51°47·0'	1°33·5'W	FM	164
Grove Fm	Oxon	SP5117	51°51·2'	1°15·2'W	FM	164
Grove Fm	Oxon	SU5187	51°35·0'	1°15·4'W	FM	174
Grove Fm	Oxon	SU6182	51°32·2'	1°6·8'W	FM	175
Grove Fm	Powys	SO2352	52°9·9'	3°7·2'W	FM	148
Grove Fm	Powys	SO2871	52°20·2'	3°3·0'W	FM	137,148
Grove Fm	S Glos	ST6487	51°35·1'	2°30·8'W	FM	172
Grove Fm	Shrops	SJ4805	52°38·7'	2°45·7'W	FM	126
Grove Fm	Sol	SP1778	52°24·2'	1°44·6'W	FM	139
Grove Fm	Somer	ST1131	51°4·5'	3°15·8'W	FM	181
Grove Fm	Somer	ST5110	50°53·5'	2°41·4'W	FM	194
Grove Fm	Somer	ST5753	51°16·7'	2°36·6'W	FM	182,183
Grove Fm	Somer	ST6431	51°4·9'	2°30·5'W	FM	183
Grove Fm	Somer	ST7026	51°2·2'	2°25·3'W	FM	183
Grove Fm	Staffs	SJ9547	53°1·5'	2°4·1'W	FM	118
Grove Fm	Staffs	SK1254	53°5·2'	1°48·8'W	FM	119
Grove Fm	Staffs	SO8087	52°29·1'	2°17·3'W	FM	138
Grove Fm	Stock on T	NZ4209	54°28·7'	1°20·7'W	FM	93
Grove Fm	Suff	TL8247	52°5·7'	0°39·8'E	FM	155
Grove Fm	Suff	TL9275	52°20·6'	0°49·5'E	FM	144
Grove Fm	Suff	TL9454	52°9·2'	0°50·6'E	FM	155
Grove Fm	Suff	TL9464	52°14·6'	0°50·9'E	FM	155
Grove Fm	Suff	TL9965	52°15·1'	0°55·3'E	FM	155
Grove Fm	Suff	TM0674	52°19·7'	1°1·8'E	FM	144
Grove Fm	Suff	TM0839	52°0·8'	1°2·3'E	FM	155,169
Grove Fm	Suff	TM0847	52°5·2'	1°2·6'E	FM	155,169
Grove Fm	Suff	TM0856	52°10·0'	1°2·9'E	FM	155
Grove Fm	Suff	TM1064	52°14·3'	1°4·9'E	FM	155
Grove Fm	Suff	TM1070	52°17·5'	1°5·2'E	FM	144,155
Grove Fm	Suff	TM1137	51°59·7'	1°4·8'E	FM	155,169
Grove Fm	Suff	TM1461	52°12·6'	1°8·3'E	FM	156
Grove Fm	Suff	TM1646	52°4·4'	1°9·5'E	FM	169
Grove Fm	Suff	TM1872	52°18·4'	1°12·3'E	FM	156
Grove Fm	Suff	TM2063	52°13·5'	1°13·7'E	FM	156
Grove Fm	Suff	TM2070	52°17·3'	1°13·9'E	FM	156
Grove Fm	Suff	TM2264	52°14·0'	1°15·5'E	FM	156
Grove Fm	Suff	TM2354	52°8·6'	1°16·0'E	FM	156
Grove Fm	Suff	TM2360	52°11·8'	1°16·2'E	FM	156
Grove Fm	Suff	TM2779	52°21·9'	1°20·5'E	FM	156
Grove Fm	Suff	TM2855	52°9·0'	1°20·4'E	FM	156
Grove Fm	Suff	TM2975	52°19·7'	1°22·1'E	FM	156
Grove Fm	Suff	TM3071	52°17·6'	1°22·8'E	FM	156
Grove Fm	Suff	TM3378	52°21·3'	1°25·7'E	FM	156
Grove Fm	Suff	TM3460	52°11·5'	1°25·8'E	FM	156
Grove Fm	Suff	TM3471	52°17·5'	1°26·3'E	FM	156
Grove Fm	Suff	TM3586	52°25·5'	1°27·8'E	FM	156
Grove Fm	Suff	TM3757	52°9·8'	1°28·3'E	FM	156
Grove Fm	Suff	TM3764	52°13·6'	1°28·6'E	FM	156
Grove Fm	Suff	TM3771	52°17·4'	1°28·9'E	FM	156
Grove Fm	Suff	TM3778	52°21·1'	1°29·2'E	FM	156
Grove Fm	Suff	TM3781	52°22·8'	1°29·3'E	FM	156
Grove Fm	Suff	TM3868	52°15·7'	1°29·7'E	FM	156
Grove Fm	Suff	TM4072	52°17·8'	1°31·6'E	FM	156
Grove Fm	Suff	TM4187	52°25·9'	1°33·1'E	FM	156
Grove Fm	Surrey	TQ2345	51°11·7'	0°14·0'W	FM	187
Grove Fm	Swan	SN5801	51°41·6'	4°2·9'W	FM	159
Grove Fm	Swin	SU1290	51°36·8'	1°49·2'W	FM	163,173
Grove Fm	Warw	SP2549	52°8·6'	1°37·7'W	FM	151
Grove Fm	Warw	SP2571	52°20·4'	1°37·6'W	FM	140
Grove Fm	Warw	SP3162	52°15·6'	1°32·4'W	FM	151
Grove Fm	Warw	SP4271	52°20·4'	1°22·6'W	FM	140
Grove Fm	Warw	SP4487	52°29·0'	1°20·7'W	FM	140
Grove Fm	Wilts	ST8776	51°29·2'	2°10·8'W	FM	173
Grove Fm	Wilts	ST9476	51°29·2'	2°4·8'W	FM	173
Grove Fm	Wilts	ST9482	51°32·4'	2°4·8'W	FM	173
Grove Fm	Wilts	SU0287	51°35·1'	1°57·9'W	FM	173
Grove Fm	Wilts	SU0382	51°32·4'	1°57·0'W	FM	173
Grove Fm	Wilts	SU0492	51°37·8'	1°56·1'W	FM	163,173
Grove Fm	Wilts	SU2269	51°25·4'	1°40·6'W	FM	174
Grove Fm	Worcs	SO7868	52°18·8'	2°19·0'W	FM	138
Grove Fm	Worcs	SO8254	52°11·3'	2°15·4'W	FM	150
Grove Fm	Worcs	SO9551	52°9·7'	2°4·0'W	FM	150
Grove Fm	Worcs	SO9951	52°9·7'	2°0·5'W	FM	150
Grove Fm	Worcs	SP0060	52°14·5'	1°59·6'W	FM	150
Grove Fm	Worcs	SP1244	52°5·9'	1°49·1'W	FM	150
Grove Fm	Wrekin	SJ7318	52°45·8'	2°23·6'W	FM	127
Grovefoot Fm	Cumbr	NY4325	54°37·3'	2°52·5'W	FM	90
Grove Green	Kent	TQ7856	51°16·7'	0°33·5'E	T	178,188
Grove Hall	Wakf	SE4821	53°41·2'	1°16·0'W	X	105
Grove Hall, The	Denb	SJ1069	53°12·9'	3°20·5'W	X	116
Grove Head	N Yks	SD8183	54°14·8'	2°17·1'W	X	98
Grove Hill	Devon	SX9688	50°41·2'	3°28·0'W	X	192
Grovehill	D & G	NX8695	55°14·4'	3°47·1'W	X	78
Grove Hill	Dorset	SY6388	50°41·7'	2°31·0'W	X	194
Grove Hill	E Susx	TQ6014	50°54·4'	0°16·9'E	T	199
Grovehill	E Susx	TQ7326	51°0·7'	0°28·4'E	X	188,199
Grovehill	E Yorks	TA0439	53°50·4'	0°24·7'W	T	107
Grove Hill	Glos	SO9905	51°44·9'	2°0·5'W	X	163
Grovehill	Herts	TL0609	51°46·4'	0°27·4'W	T	166
Grove Hill	Kent	TR2360	51°17·9'	1°12·3'E	T	179
Grove Hill	Staffs	SK0703	52°37·7'	1°53·4'W	X	139

Grovehill Fm	Bucks	SP6036	52°1·4'	1°7·1'W	FM	152
Grovehill Fm	Bucks	SP6633	51°59·7'	1°1·9'W	FM	152,165
Grovehill Fm	Oxon	SP7404	51°44·0'	0°55·3'W	FM	165
Grove Hill Ho	Norf	TM2383	52°24·2'	1°17·1'E	X	156
Grove Ho	Ches	SJ5465	53°11·0'	2°40·9'W	X	117
Grove Ho	Ches	SJ6850	53°3·0'	2°28·2'W	X	118
Grove Ho	Donc	SE7111	53°35·7'	0°55·2'W	X	112
Grove Ho	Essex	TQ5095	51°38·3'	0°10·5'E	X	167,177
Grove Ho	E Susx	TQ6809	50°51·6'	0°23·6'E	X	199
Grove Ho	Glos	SO7333	51°59·9'	2°23·2'W	X	150
Grove Ho	Heref	SO4356	52°12·2'	2°49·6'W	X	148,149
Grove Ho	Lincs	SE8301	53°30·2'	0°44·5'W	X	112
Grove Ho	Lincs	SK9450	53°2·6'	0°35·5'W	X	121
Grove Ho	Norf	TG3528	52°48·1'	1°29·6'E	X	133,134
Grove Ho	N Yks	SE8191	54°18·7'	0°44·9'W	X	94,100
Grove Ho	Shrops	SJ3928	52°51·0'	2°53·9'W	X	126
Grove Ho	Suff	TM1247	52°5·1'	1°6·1'E	X	155,169
Grove Ho	Suff	TM3745	52°3·4'	1°27·8'E	X	169
Grove Ho	Wan	TQ2174	51°27·3'	0°15·1'W	X	176
Grove House Fm	Ches	SJ8466	53°11·7'	2°14·0'W	FM	118
Grove House Fm	Lincs	TF4863	53°8·8'	0°13·2'E	FM	122
Grove House Fm	N Yks	SE8076	54°10·7'	0°46·0'W	FM	94,100
Grove House Fm	Suff	TM0579	52°22·5'	1°1·1'E	FM	144
Grove House Fm	Worcs	SO8045	52°6·4'	2°17·1'W	FM	150
Grovehurst	Kent	TQ7140	51°8·2'	0°27·1'E	X	188
Grovehurst Fm	E Susx	TQ5027	51°1·2'	0°8·7'E	FM	188,199
Grovelands	V of Glam	ST0770	51°25·5'	3°19·9'W	X	170
Grovelands	W Susx	TQ2319	50°57·7'	0°14·5'W	X	198
Grovelands Copse	Hants	SU4227	51°2·7'	1°23·7'W	F	185
Grovelands Fm	W Susx	TQ3631	51°4·0'	0°3·2'W	FM	187
Groveleys	Glos	SP0331	51°58·9'	1°57·0'W	X	150
Grove Lock	Bucks	SP9123	51°54·1'	0°40·2'W	X	165
Grovely Castle	Wilts	SU0435	51°7·1'	1°56·2'W	A	184
Grovelye Fm	E Susx	TQ6418	50°56·5'	0°20·5'E	FM	199
Grovely Fm	Worcs	SP0276	52°23·2'	1°57·8'W	FM	139
Grovely Hill	Wilts	SU0732	51°5·5'	1°53·6'W	X	184
Grovely Lodge	Wilts	SU0433	51°6·0'	1°56·2'W	X	184
Grovely Wood	Wilts	SU0534	51°6·5'	1°55·3'W	F	184
Grove Manor Fm	Kent	TR3156	51°15·6'	1°19·1'E	FM	179
Grove Mill, The	Herts	TQ0898	51°40·5'	0°25·9'W	X	166,176
Grove Moor Fm	Notts	SK7580	53°18·9'	0°52·0'W	FM	120
Grove Park	Corn	SS2205	50°49·8'	4°31·3'W	X	190
Grovepark	Devon	SX6850	50°20·3'	3°50·9'W	X	202
Grove Park	E Susx	TQ5914	50°54·4'	0°16·1'E	X	199
Grove Park	Houns	TQ2077	51°29·0'	0°15·9'W	T	176
Grove Park	Lew	TQ4172	51°26·0'	0°2·1'E	T	177
Grove Park	Notts	SK7379	53°18·4'	0°53·9'W	X	120
Grove Park	Suff	TM3968	52°15·7'	1°30·5'E	X	156
Grove Park	Warw	SP2364	52°16·7'	1°39·4'W	X	151
Grove Place (Sch)	Hants	SU3616	50°56·8'	1°28·9'W	X	185
Groveridge Hill	Glos	SO9312	51°48·6'	2°5·7'W	X	163
Grover's Fm	E Susx	TQ4423	50°59·5'	0°3·5'E	FM	198
Grovers Fm	Surrey	SU8045	51°12·1'	0°50·9'W	FM	186
Groves	Durham	NZ0922	54°35·8'	1°51·2'W	X	92
Groves	E Susx	TQ8621	50°57·7'	0°39·3'E	X	189,199
Groves	I of M	SC3578	54°10·5'	4°31·3'W	X	95
Groves	Kent	TR2657	51°16·3'	1°14·8'E	T	179
Grovesend	Heref	SO6938	52°2·6'	2°26·7'W	X	149
Grovesend	S Glos	ST6589	51°36·2'	2°29·9'W	X	162,172
Grovesend	Swan	SN5900	51°41·1'	4°2·0'W	T	159
Groves Fm	E Yorks	SE7426	53°43·7'	0°52·3'W	FM	105,106
Groves Fm	Kent	TQ9770	51°23·9'	0°50·3'E	FM	178
Groves Fm	Wrex	SJ3541	52°58·0'	2°57·7'W	FM	117
Groves Fm	W Susx	SU9002	50°48·9'	0°43·0'W	FM	197
Grove Stall Fm	Dorset	SY5899	50°47·6'	2°35·4'W	FM	194
Groves, The	Shrops	SJ5621	52°47·3'	2°38·7'W	X	126
Groves, The	Wrex	SJ3345	53°0·1'	2°59·5'W	X	117
Grove, The	Brig	SS8279	51°30·1'	3°41·6'W	X	170
Grove, The	Bucks	SU9488	51°35·2'	0°38·2'W	F	175
Grove, The	Carm	SN2517	51°49·7'	4°32·0'W	X	158
Grove, The	Carm	SN5122	51°52·8'	4°9·5'W	X	159
Grove, The	Ches	SJ4072	53°14·7'	2°53·5'W	X	117
Grove, The	Ches	SJ6179	53°18·6'	2°34·7'W	X	118
Grove, The	Cumbr	SD0896	54°21·3'	3°24·5'W	X	96
Grove, The	Cumbr	SD4283	54°14·6'	2°53·0'W	X	96,97
Grove, The	Derby	SK1947	53°1·4'	1°42·6'W	X	119,128
Grove, The	Derby	SK3271	53°14·3'	1°30·8'W	X	119
Grove, The	D & G	NX9178	55°5·3'	3°42·0'W	X	84
Grove, The	D & G	NX9878	55°5·4'	3°35·5'W	X	84
Grove, The	Durham	NZ0629	54°39·6'	1°54·0'W	X	92
Grove, The	Essex	TL3909	51°46·0'	0°1·3'E	F	166
Grove, The	Essex	TL6629	51°56·3'	0°25·3'E	X	167
Grove, The	Essex	TL7304	51°42·7'	0°30·6'E	X	167
Grove, The	Essex	TM0532	51°57·1'	0°59·4'E	X	168
Grove, The	Glos	SO5308	51°46·4'	2°40·5'W	X	162
Grove, The	Glos	SO6813	51°49·1'	2°27·5'W	X	162
Grove, The	Glos	SO7421	51°53·5'	2°22·3'W	X	162
Grove, The	Glos	SP1206	51°45·4'	1°49·2'W	F	163
Grove, The	Hants	SU2611	50°53·8'	1°37·6'W	F	195
Grove, The	Heref	SO5219	51°52·3'	2°41·4'W	X	162
Grove, The	Herts	TL1513	51°48·5'	0°19·5'W	X	166
Grove, The	Kent	TQ5142	51°9·7'	0°10·0'E	X	188
Grove, The	Kent	TQ5556	51°17·1'	0°13·8'E	X	188
Grove, The	Leeds	SE2043	53°53·2'	1°41·3'W	X	104
Grove, The	Leic	SK7710	52°41·2'	0°51·2'W	X	129
Grove, The	Lincs	TF3827	52°49·6'	0°3·5'E	X	131
Grove, The	Norf	TF6505	52°37·3'	0°26·7'E	X	143
Grove, The	Norf	TG0405	52°36·5'	1°1·2'E	X	144
Grove, The	Norf	TG1221	52°44·9'	1°8·9'E	X	133
Grove, The	Norf	TG2837	52°53·1'	1°23·7'E	X	133
Grove, The	Norf	TG3009	52°38·0'	1°24·3'E	X	134
Grove, The	Norf	TG3826	52°47·0'	1°32·2'E	X	133,134
Grove, The	Norf	TM1686	52°26·0'	1°11·1'E	X	144,156
Grove, The	Norf	TM1792	52°29·2'	1°12·2'E	X	134
Grove, The	Norf	TM1981	52°23·2'	1°13·5'E	F	156
Grove, The	Norf	TM4594	52°29·6'	1°37·0'E	X	134
Grove, The	Notts	SK6737	52°55·8'	0°59·8'W	X	129
Grove, The	N Som	ST4663	51°22·0'	2°46·2'W	X	172,182
Grove, The	Oxon	SU7484	51°33·2'	0°55·6'W	X	175
Grove, The	Pemb	SN0912	51°46·7'	4°45·7'W	X	158

Grove, The	Powys	SJ2101	52°36·3'	3°9·6'W	X	126
Grove, The	Roth	SK5490	53°24·5'	1°10·9'W	X	111
Grove, The	Shrops	SJ3705	52°38·6'	2°55·5'W	T	126
Grove, The	Shrops	SJ7040	52°57·6'	2°26·4'W	X	118
Grove, The	Shrops	SO4384	52°27·3'	2°49·9'W	T	137
Grove, The	Staffs	SJ9349	53°2·5'	2°5·9'W	X	118
Grove, The	Staffs	SJ9834	52°54·4'	2°1·4'W	X	127
Grove, The	Suff	TL7759	52°12·3'	0°35·8'E	X	155
Grove, The	Suff	TL9443	52°3·3'	0°50·2'E	X	155
Grove, The	Suff	TL9765	52°15·1'	0°53·6'E	F	155
Grove, The	Suff	TM0070	52°17·7'	0°56·4'E	X	144,155
Grove, The	Suff	TM0778	52°21·9'	1°2·8'E	X	144
Grove, The	Suff	TM1677	52°21·1'	1°10·7'E	F	144,156
Grove, The	Suff	TM2347	52°4·8'	1°15·7'E	X	169
Grove, The	Suff	TM2569	52°16·6'	1°18·3'E	X	156
Grove, The	Suff	TM2861	52°12·2'	1°20·6'E	X	156
Grove, The	Suff	TM3341	52°1·3'	1°24·2'E	F	169
Grove, The	Suff	TM3462	52°12·6'	1°25·9'E	F	156
Grove, The	Suff	TM4381	52°22·6'	1°34·6'E	X	156
Grove, The	Suff	TM4665	52°13·9'	1°36·6'E	F	156
Grove, The	Suff	TM4781	52°22·5'	1°38·1'E	F	156
Grove, The	Thurr	TQ5984	51°32·2'	0°18·0'E	X	177
Grove, The	Worcs	SO6363	52°16·1'	2°32·1'W	X	138,149
Grove, The	Worcs	SO8640	52°3·7'	2°11·9'W	T	150
Grove, The	W Susx	TQ3235	51°6·2'	0°6·5'W	X	187
Grove, The (Cheshire Home)	Norf	TG1801	52°34·0'	1°13·4'E	X	134
Grovetown	Corn	SX3188	50°40·3'	4°23·1'W	X	190
Grove Town	Wakf	SE4621	53°41·2'	1°17·8'W	T	105
Grove Vale	Sand	SP0394	52°32·9'	1°56·9'W	T	139
Groveway Fm	Bucks	SP8218	51°51·5'	0°48·2'W	FM	165
Grove Wharf	N Lincs	SE8412	53°36·1'	0°43·4'W	X	112
Grove Wick Fm	Oxon	SU4091	51°37·2'	1°24·9'W	FM	164,174
Grove Wold Fm	Lincs	TA1706	53°32·5'	0°13·6'W	FM	113
Grove Wood	Bucks	SP6915	51°50·0'	0°59·5'W	W	165
Grove Wood	Oxon	SU2996	51°40·0'	1°34·4'W	F	164
Grove Wood	Oxon	SU7497	51°40·2'	0°55·4'W	F	165
Grove Wood	Suff	TM4161	52°11·9'	1°32·0'E	F	156
Growen Fm	Devon	ST0008	50°52·0'	3°24·9'W	FM	192
Grower Rock	Corn	SX0890	50°40·9'	4°42·7'W	X	190
Grow Sike	Durham	NY8720	54°34·7'	2°11·6'W	W	91,92
Grow Sike Rigg	Durham	NY8619	54°34·2'	2°12·6'W	X	91,92
Groyne Point	Corn	SW7426	50°5·7'	5°9·2'W	X	204
Gruagach	N Eil	NF6910	57°4·0'	7°27·2'W	X	31
Gruaidhean	N Eil	NB1401	57°54·7'	6°49·3'W	X	14
Grubbins Point	Cumbr	SD3791	54°18·9'	2°57·7'W	X	96,97
Grubbins Wood	Cumbr	SD4478	54°11·9'	2°51·1'W	F	97
Grubbit Law	Scot Bord	NT7923	55°30·3'	2°19·5'W	H	74
Grubb's Fm	Cambs	TL5390	52°29·4'	0°15·6'E	FM	143
Grubb Street	Kent	TQ5869	51°24·1'	0°16·7'E	T	177
Grub Low	Staffs	SK0752	53°4·2'	1°53·3'W	A	119
Grub's Copse	Northnts	SP6451	52°9·4'	1°3·5'W	F	152
Grub Street	Staffs	SJ7825	52°49·6'	2°19·2'W	T	127
Grud Burn	Shetld	HU3182	60°31·5'	1°25·6'W	W	1,3
Grudgehouse	Highld	ND3248	58°25·2'	3°9·4'W	X	12
Grudie	Highld	NC3663	58°31·7'	4°48·5'W	X	9
Grudie	Highld	NH3062	57°37·2'	4°50·3'W	T	20
Grudie Burn	Highld	NC5305	58°0·9'	4°28·8'W	W	16
Grudie River	Highld	NC3362	58°31·1'	4°51·6'W	W	9
Grud Waters	Shetld	HP4801	60°41·6'	1°6·8'W	W	1
Grueldykes	Scot Bord	NT7752	55°45·9'	2°21·6'W	X	67,74
Gruf Hill	Orkney	HY3206	58°56·4'	3°10·4'W	H	6,7
Grugar	Orkney	HY3526	59°7·2'	3°7·6'W	X	6
Grugar	Orkney	HY4730	59°9·5'	2°55·1'W	X	5,6
Grugfryn	Conwy	SH8273	53°14·7'	3°45·7'W	X	116
Gruggy	S Glos	ST5186	51°34·5'	2°42·0'W	X	172
Grug Hill	Shrops	SJ3723	52°48·3'	2°55·7'W	X	126
Gruglwyn	Powys	SN9055	52°11·2'	3°36·1'W	X	147
Grugmor	I of Angl	SH3088	53°21·9'	4°32·9'W	X	114
Grugor-bach	I of Angl	SH3773	53°14·0'	4°26·1'W	X	114
Grugwith	Corn	SW7520	50°2·5'	5°8·2'W	X	204
Gruids	Highld	NC5604	58°0·4'	4°25·7'W	T	16
Gruids Wood	Highld	NC5603	57°59·8'	4°25·7'W	F	16
Gruinard Bay	Highld	NG9293	57°52·9'	5°30·0'W	W	19
Gruinard House	Highld	NG9592	57°52·5'	5°26·9'W	X	19
Gruinard Island	Highld	NG9494	57°53·5'	5°28·1'W	X	19
Gruinard River	Highld	NG9789	57°50·9'	5°24·8'W	W	19
Gruinards	Highld	NH5490	57°52·8'	4°27·3'W	X	21
Gruinards Lodge	Highld	NH5292	57°53·8'	4°29·4'W	X	20
Gruinart	Arg & Bt	NR2866	55°48·9'	6°20·1'W	X	60
Gruinart Flats	Arg & Bt	NR2966	55°48·9'	6°19·1'W	X	60
Gruinart Fm	Arg & Bt	NR2768	55°49·9'	6°21·2'W	FM	60
Grukalty Pier	Orkney	HY4617	59°2·5'	2°56·0'W	X	6
Grula	Highld	NG3826	57°15·2'	6°20·2'W	X	32
Grulinbeg	Arg & Bt	NR2468	55°49·8'	6°24·0'W	X	60
Gruline	Arg & Bt	NM5440	56°29·5'	5°59·3'W	T	47,48
Gruline Ho	Arg & Bt	NM5539	56°29·0'	5°58·3'W	X	47,48
Grulin Iochdrach	Highld	NM4484	56°52·9'	6°11·7'W	X	39
Grulinmore	Arg & Bt	NR2466	55°48·8'	6°23·9'W	X	60
Grulin Uachdrach	Highld	NM4683	56°52·4'	6°9·7'W	X	39
Grumack Hill	Aberd	NJ4233	57°23·3'	2°57·4'W	H	28
Grumbeg	Highld	NC6338	58°18·8'	4°19·8'W	X	16
Grumbla	Corn	SW4029	50°6·5'	5°37·8'W	T	203
Grumby	Highld	NC7109	58°3·3'	4°10·7'W	X	16
Grumby Rock	Highld	NC7010	58°3·9'	4°11·7'W	H	16
Grummore	Highld	NC6036	58°17·7'	4°22·8'W	X	16
Grummore Burn	Highld	NC5937	58°18·2'	4°23·9'W	W	16
Grumply Hill	Cumbr	NY6731	54°40·6'	2°30·3'W	X	91
Gruna	Shetld	HU2859	60°19·1'	1°29·1'W	X	3
Grunagary	Highld	NG4030	57°17·5'	6°18·5'W	X	32
Gruna Stack	Shetld	HU2886	60°33·7'	1°28·9'W	X	1,3
Grunavi Head	Orkney	HY6239	59°14·4'	2°39·5'W	X	5
Gruna Water	Shetld	HU6691	60°36·1'	0°47·2'W	W	1,2
Grunay	Shetld	HU6971	60°25·3'	0°44·3'W	X	2
Grundcruie	Pth & Kin	NO0026	56°25·2'	3°36·8'W	X	52,53,58
Grundisburgh	Suff	TM2250	52°6·4'	1°14·9'E	T	156
Grundisburgh Hall	Suff	TM2249	52°5·9'	1°14·9'E	A	169
Grundle Fm	Suff	TM0173	52°19·3'	0°57·4'E	FM	144,155
Grundle, The	Suff	TL9772	52°18·9'	0°53·8'E	X	144,155
Grundle, The	Suff	TM0173	52°19·3'	0°57·4'E	X	144,155

Grundsound	Shetld	HU3733	60°5·1′	1°19·6′W	T	4
Grundy House Fm	Derby	SK1677	53°17·6′	1°45·2′W	FM	119
Grune	Cumbr	NY1356	54°53·7′	3°21·0′W	X	85
Grune Cast	Cumbr	NY1357	54°54·3′	3°21·0′W	X	85
Grune Point	Cumbr	NY1456	54°53·7′	3°20·0′W	X	85
Grunewald	Scot Bord	NT9256	55°48·1′	2°7·2′W	X	67,74,75
Gruney	Shetld	HU3896	60°39·0′	1°17·8′W	X	1
Grunivoe	Shetld	HU2548	60°13·2′	1°32·4′W	X	3
Grunka Hellier	Shetld	HP5815	60°49·1′	0°55·5′W	X	1
Grunna Taing	Shetld	HU4475	60°27·6′	1°11·5′W	X	2,3
Grunna Taing	Shetld	HU4856	60°17·4′	1°7·4′W	X	2,3
Grunnavoe	Shetld	HU2150	60°14·3′	1°36·7′W	X	3
Grunnavoe	Shetld	HU4475	60°27·6′	1°11·5′W	X	2,3
Grunna Voe	Shetld	HU4767	60°23·3′	1°8·3′W	W	2,3
Grunna Water	Shetld	HU4554	60°16·3′	1°10·7′W	W	3
Grunn Taing	Shetld	HU3779	60°29·8′	1°19·1′W	X	2,3
Grunsagill	Lancs	SD7854	53°59·1′	2°19·7′W	T	103
Grunta Beach	Devon	SS4544	51°10·7′	4°12·7′W	X	180
Grunta Pool	Devon	SS4544	51°10·7′	4°12·7′W	W	180
Grun, The	Northum	NY6699	55°17·3′	2°31·7′W	X	80
Gruntley Beck	Cumbr	NY8108	54°28·3′	2°17·2′W	W	91,92
Gruntly Burn	Scot Bord	NT3931	55°34·4′	2°57·6′W	W	73
Grunton	N Yks	NZ2211	54°29·9′	1°39·2′W	X	93
Grunty Fen Drain	Cambs	TL5180	52°24·1′	0°13·6′E	W	143
Grunty Fen Fm	Cambs	TL4876	52°22·0′	0°10·8′E	FM	143
Gruskham	N Yks	SD6866	54°5·6′	2°28·9′W	X	98
Grusterwick Geo	Shetld	HU2964	60°21·8′	1°28·0′W	X	3
Grut Fea	Orkney	HY1901	58°53·6′	3°23·9′W	X	7
Grutha	Orkney	ND4794	58°50·1′	2°54·6′W	X	7
Grutha Point	Orkney	ND4894	58°50·1′	2°53·6′W	X	7
Gruti Field	Shetld	HU3958	60°18·5′	1°17·2′W	H	2,3
Grutin	Shetld	HU4068	60°23·9′	1°15·9′W	X	2,3
Gruting	Shetld	HU2849	60°13·7′	1°29·2′W	T	3
Gruting Voe	Shetld	HU2647	60°12·7′	1°31·4′W	W	3
Grut Ness	Shetld	HU3491	60°36·3′	1°22·2′W	X	1,2
Grutness	Shetld	HU4009	59°52·1′	1°16·7′W	T	4
Grut Ness	Shetld	HU6591	60°36·1′	0°48·3′W	X	1,2
Grutness Voe	Shetld	HU4010	59°52·7′	1°16·6′W	W	4
Grut Wells	Shetld	HU3285	60°33·1′	1°24·5′W	X	1,3
Grut Wick	Shetld	HU3841	60°9·4′	1°18·4′W	W	4
Grut Wick	Shetld	HU5070	60°24·9′	1°5·0′W	W	2,3
Grut Wick	Shetld	HU5138	60°7·7′	1°4·4′W	W	4
Gruund Loch	Arg & Bt	NR2857	55°44·1′	6°19·5′W	W	60
Grwnamlwg	Powys	SJ1515	52°43·8′	3°15·1′W	X	125
Grwn-oer	Powys	SJ0218	52°45·3′	3°26·7′W	X	125
Grwyne Fawr	Monm	SO2822	51°53·8′	3°2·4′W	W	161
Grwyne Fawr	Powys	SO2131	51°58·6′	3°8·6′W	W	161
Grwyne Fawr	Powys	SO2429	51°57·5′	3°6·0′W	X	161
Grwyne Fawr Reservoir	Powys	SO2230	51°58·0′	3°7·7′W	W	161
Grwyne Fechan	Powys	SO2226	51°55·9′	3°7·7′W	W	161
Gryce Hall	Kirk	SE2112	53°36·5′	1°40·5′W	X	110
Gryfe Resrs	Inverc	NS2871	55°54·3′	4°44·7′W	W	63
Gryfe Water	Inverc	NS2670	55°53·8′	4°46·5′W	W	63
Gryfe Water	Inverc	NS3270	55°53·9′	4°40·8′W	W	63
Gryffe	Renf	NS3866	55°51·9′	4°34·9′W	X	63
Gryffeside	Inverc	NS3370	55°53·9′	4°39·8′W	X	63
Gryffe Wraes	Renf	NS3966	55°51·9′	4°33·9′W	X	63
Gryliss	Powys	SO1659	52°13·6′	3°13·4′W	X	148
Gryme's Dyke	Essex	TL9624	51°53·0′	0°51·3′E	A	168
Grymsdyke	Bucks	SU8299	51°41·3′	0°48·4′W	X	165
Gryn Goch	Gwyn	SH4048	53°0·6′	4°22·7′W	T	115,123
Gryphon Lodge Fm	Wilts	SU0490	51°36·8′	1°56·1′W	FM	163,173
Grysedale Ho	N Yks	SD9763	54°4·0′	2°2·3′W	X	98
Gt Agill Head	N Yks	SE0759	54°1·9′	1°53·2′W	X	104
Gt Appleford Fm	I of W	SZ5080	50°37·3′	1°17·2′W	FM	196
Gt Dowles Fm	Kent	TR1246	51°10·7′	1°2·4′E	FM	179,189
Gt Everden Fm	Kent	TR2342	51°8·2′	1°11·7′E	FM	179,189
Gt Furzefield Wood	Herts	TL1005	51°44·2′	0°24·0′W	F	166
Gt Hougham Court Fm	Kent	TR2739	51°6·5′	1°15·0′E	FM	179
Gt Shuttlesfield Fm	Kent	TR1741	51°7·8′	1°6·5′E	FM	179,189
Gt Wheatley Fm	Essex	TQ7990	51°35·0′	0°35·4′E	FM	178
Guaineamol	N Eil	NB2613	58°1·6′	6°38·0′W	H	13,14
Guala Achadh nan Each	Arg & Bt	NM5246	56°32·7′	6°1·6′W	X	47,48
Guala a' Choire Mhóir	Highld	NG3822	57°13·1′	6°19·9′W	X	32
Gúala an Tùir	Highld	NM7446	56°33·4′	5°40·2′W	X	49
Guala Buidhe	Arg & Bt	NM5540	56°29·6′	5°58·4′W	F	47,48
Gualachaolish	Arg & Bt	NM7128	56°23·6′	5°42·2′W	X	49
Gualachulain	Highld	NN1145	56°33·8′	5°4·1′W	X	50
Guala Dhubh	Arg & Bt	NR4270	55°51·5′	6°6·9′W	X	60,61
Gual' a' Mhairbh	Arg & Bt	NM5723	56°20·5′	5°55·5′W	X	48
Gual' a' Mheoraich	Arg & Bt	NM7136	56°27·9′	5°42·6′W	X	49
Guala Mhór	Arg & Bt	NN4046	56°35·0′	4°35·9′W	X	51
Guala Mhór	N Eil	NF9165	57°34·4′	7°9·7′W	X	18
Gualan	N Eil	NF7747	57°24·2′	7°22·2′W	X	22
Guala na h-Imrich	N Eil	NF7969	57°36·1′	7°22·0′W	X	18
Guala na Leitreach	Arg & Bt	NM6342	56°30·9′	5°50·7′W	X	49
Gualan Dhubh	Arg & Bt	NM5351	56°35·4′	6°0·9′W	H	47
Gualann	Stir	NS4594	56°7·1′	4°29·1′W	H	57
Gualann an Sgairbh	Arg & Bt	NR4176	55°54·7′	6°8·2′W	X	60,61
Gualann Mhór	Highld	NG8687	57°49·6′	5°35·8′W	X	19
Gualann na Faing	Pth & Kin	NN8928	56°26·1′	3°47·6′W	X	52,58
Gualann nam Fiadh	Highld	NG5724	57°14·8′	6°1·2′W	X	32
Gualann nam Osna	Highld	NM9887	56°56·1′	5°18·8′W	X	40
Gualann nan Carn	Arg & Bt	NR7169	55°51·8′	5°39·2′W	X	62
Gualann na Pairce	Highld	NM3396	56°58·9′	6°23·2′W	H	39
Gualann Sheileach	Pth & Kin	NN6165	56°45·6′	4°16·0′W	H	42
Guala Riabhach	N Ayr	NR8941	55°37·3′	5°20·6′W	X	62,69
Gualin Ho	Highld	NC3056	58°27·8′	4°54·4′W	X	9
Guallann Mhór	Arg & Bt	NR9062	55°48·6′	5°20·6′W	H	62
Guanock Fm	Lincs	TF3712	52°41·5′	0°2·0′E	FM	131,142,143
Guanock Ho	Lincs	TF3714	52°42·6′	0°2·1′E	X	131
Guardbridge	Fife	NO4519	56°21·9′	2°53·0′W	T	59
Guard Ho	Cumbr	NY2358	54°54·9′	3°11·6′W	X	85
Guard House	Brad	SE0441	53°52·2′	1°55·9′W	T	104
Guardhouse	Cumbr	NY3325	54°37·2′	3°1·8′W	X	90
Guards Hill	Cumbr	NY5367	55°0·0′	2°43·7′W	X	86
Guards, The	Cumbr	NY2439	54°44·7′	3°10·4′W	X	89,90
Guards, The	Cumbr	SD2279	54°12·3′	3°11·3′W	X	96
Guards, The	Ghead	NZ1161	54°56·9′	1°49·3′W	X	88
Guardswell	Pth & Kin	NO2429	56°27·1′	3°13·5′W	X	53,59
Guard, The	Aberd	NO5195	57°2·9′	2°48·0′W	X	37,44
Guarlford	Worcs	SO8145	52°6·4′	2°16·2′W	T	150
Guarsay Mór	N Eil	NL5484	56°49·4′	7°39·9′W	X	31
Guay	Pth & Kin	NN9949	56°37·6′	3°38·3′W	T	52,53
Gubbergill	Cumbr	SD0899	54°22·9′	3°24·6′W	X	96
Gubberhill Fm	Glos	SO8737	52°2·1′	2°11·0′W	FM	150
Gubbin's Hole	Bucks	SP6622	51°53·8′	1°2·1′W	X	164,165
Gubbins Hole Fm	Bucks	SP6622	51°53·8′	1°2·1′W	FM	164,165
Gubbion's Green	Essex	TL7317	51°49·7′	0°31·0′E	T	167
Gubbion's Hall	Essex	TL7317	51°49·7′	0°31·0′E	X	167
Gubblecote	Herts	SP9014	51°49·3′	0°41·3′W	T	165
Gubbs Fm	Devon	SS6531	51°4·0′	3°55·2′W	FM	180
Gubeon Plantns	Northum	NZ1782	55°8·2′	1°43·6′W	F	81
Gubeon, The	Northum	NZ1783	55°8·7′	1°43·6′W	X	81
Gubhill	D & G	NX9792	55°12·9′	3°36·7′W	X	78
Gubhill Rig	D & G	NX9693	55°13·5′	3°37·7′W	H	78
Gudder	Powys	SO2420	51°52·6′	3°5·9′W	X	161
Gudge Copse	Hants	SU3926	51°2·2′	1°26·2′W	F	185
Gudna Lee	Shetld	HU6493	60°37·2′	0°49·3′W	X	1,2
Gudon	Shetld	HU5283	60°31·9′	1°2·6′W	X	1,2,3
Gue	Orkney	HY3829	59°8·9′	3°4·5′W	X	6
Gue	Shetld	HP6010	60°46·4′	0°53·4′W	X	1
Guelt	E Ayr	NS6319	55°27·0′	4°9·5′W	X	71
Guelt Water	E Ayr	NS6716	55°25·4′	4°5·7′W	W	71
Guerness Gill	Cumbr	NY4813	54°30·8′	2°47·8′W	W	90
Guerness Wood	Cumbr	NY4813	54°30·8′	2°47·8′W	F	90
Guesachan	Highld	NM8877	56°50·4′	5°28·1′W	X	40
Guesdale Water	Arg & Bt	NR7534	55°33·1′	5°33·6′W	W	68,69
Guesses Fm	W Susx	TQ1514	50°55·1′	0°21·4′W	FM	198
Guessgate Fm	W Susx	TQ1514	50°55·1′	0°21·4′W	FM	198
Guestling Green	E Susx	TQ8513	50°53·4′	0°38·2′E	T	199
Guestling Thorn	E Susx	TQ8515	50°54·5′	0°38·3′E	T	189,199
Guestling Wood	E Susx	TQ8614	50°54·0′	0°39·1′E	F	199
Guestwick	Norf	TG0627	52°48·3′	1°3·8′E	T	133
Guestwick Green	Norf	TG0526	52°47·8′	1°2·9′E	T	133
Guffock Hill	D & G	NS7414	55°24·5′	3°59·0′W	X	71
Guffogland	D & G	NX8062	54°56·5′	3°52·0′W	X	84
Gugh	I Scilly	SV8908	49°53·7′	6°19·5′W	X	203
Guibean Ulavailt	Arg & Bt	NM5531	56°24·7′	5°57·9′W	X	48
Guide	Black w Dar	SD7025	53°43·5′	2°26·9′W	T	103
Guidebest	Highld	ND1835	58°18·0′	3°23·5′W	X	11
Guide Bridge	Tames	SJ9298	53°29·0′	2°6·8′W	T	109
Guide House, The	N Yks	NZ8005	54°26·3′	0°45·6′W	X	94
Guide Post	Northum	NZ2585	55°9·8′	1°36·0′W	T	81
Guide Post Fm	Essex	TM0429	51°55·5′	0°58·4′E	FM	168
Guidepost Fm	Lincs	TF2435	52°54·1′	0°9·0′W	FM	131
Guidfa	Powys	SO0965	52°16·8′	3°19·6′W	X	136,147
Guifron Fm	Shrops	SO2281	52°25·5′	3°8·4′W	FM	137
Guilcaugh, The	I of M	SC3998	54°21·4′	4°28·2′W	X	95
Guildables Wood	Kent	TQ4349	51°13·6′	0°3·3′E	F	187
Guildacre Fm	Cambs	TL5084	52°26·2′	0°12·8′E	FM	143
Guilden Down	Shrops	SO3082	52°26·1′	3°1·4′W	X	137
Guildenhurst Manor	W Susx	TQ0625	51°1·1′	0°28·9′W	X	187,197
Guilden Morden	Cambs	TL2743	52°4·5′	0°8·4′W	T	153
Guilden Sutton	Ches	SJ4468	53°12·6′	2°49·9′W	T	117
Guildford	Surrey	SU9949	51°14·1′	0°34·5′W	T	186
Guildford Fm	I of W	SZ5589	50°42·1′	1°12·9′W	FM	196
Guildford Park	Surrey	SU9849	51°14·1′	0°35·4′W	T	186
Guildhall	C of Aber	NJ8514	57°13·2′	2°14·4′W	X	38
Guild Hall	C of Lon	TQ3281	51°31·0′	0°5·5′W	A	176,177
Guild Hall	Essex	TL5841	52°2·9′	0°18·6′E	A	154
Guildhouse	S Lanak	NS9552	55°45·3′	3°39·9′W	X	65,72
Guildiehaugh	W Loth	NS9867	55°53·4′	3°37·4′W	T	65
Guildie Howes	Midlo	NT3558	55°48·9′	3°1·8′W	X	66,73
Guild of Monks	Staffs	SJ7820	52°46·9′	2°19·2′W	X	127
Guildtown	Pth & Kin	NO1331	56°28·0′	3°24·3′W	T	53
Guildy	Angus	NO5239	56°32·7′	2°46·4′W	T	54
Guildyden	Angus	NO5238	56°32·1′	2°46·4′W	X	54
Guile Hass	Scot Bord	NY4396	55°15·5′	2°53·4′W	X	79
Guile Point	Northum	NU1240	55°39·5′	1°48·1′W	X	75
Guileshill Fm	Surrey	TQ0656	51°17·8′	0°28·4′W	FM	187
Guilford	Pemb	SM9809	51°44·8′	4°55·2′W	T	157,158
Guilford	Pemb	SM9909	51°44·9′	4°54·3′W	T	157,158
Guillamon Island	Highld	NG6327	57°16·6′	5°55·4′W	X	32
Guillyburn	D & G	NX9785	55°9·2′	3°36·6′W	X	78
Guillyhill	D & G	NX9678	55°5·4′	3°37·3′W	X	84
Guilmire	Cumbr	SD7387	54°16·9′	2°24·5′W	X	98
Guilsborough	Northnts	SP6773	52°21·3′	1°0·6′W	T	141
Guilsfield Brook	Powys	SJ2212	52°42·2′	3°8·9′W	W	126
Guilsfield or Cegidfa	Powys	SJ2211	52°41·7′	3°8·8′W	T	126
Guilthwaite	Roth	SK4589	53°24·0′	1°19·0′W	T	111,120
Guilton	Kent	TR2858	51°16·7′	1°16·6′E	T	179
Guiltreehill	S Ayr	NS3510	55°21·6′	4°35·8′W	X	70
Guiltree Hill	S Ayr	NS3511	55°22·2′	4°35·8′W	H	70
Guilyknowes	Moray	NJ4252	57°33·5′	2°57·7′W	X	28
Guinea Fm	Derby	SK2030	52°52·3′	1°41·8′W	FM	128
Guineaford	Devon	SS5437	51°7·1′	4°4·8′W	T	180
Guinea Wiggs Fm	Suff	TL9434	51°58·5′	0°49·9′E	FM	155
Guirasdeal	Arg & Bt	NM6907	56°12·2′	5°43·0′W	X	55
Guirdil	Highld	NG3201	57°1·6′	6°24·5′W	X	32,39
Guirdil Bay	Highld	NG3101	57°1·6′	6°25·5′W	W	32,39
Guisachan	Highld	NH3026	57°17·8′	4°48·8′W	X	26
Guisachan Fall	Highld	NH2924	57°16·7′	4°49·7′W	W	25
Guisachan Forest	Highld	NH2219	57°13·9′	4°56·5′W	F	34
Guisachan Forest	Highld	NH2921	57°15·1′	4°49·6′W	X	25
Guisachan Ho	Highld	NH2825	57°17·3′	4°50·8′W	X	25
Guisborough	Red & Cl	NZ6115	54°31·8′	1°3·0′W	T	94
Guisborough Woods	Red & Cl	NZ6214	54°31·3′	1°2·1′W	F	94
Guise	Aberd	NJ5813	57°12·6′	2°41·3′W	X	37
Guise Cliff	N Yks	SE1663	54°4·0′	1°44·9′W	X	99
Guisecliff Wood	N Yks	SE1663	54°4·0′	1°44·9′W	F	99
Guiseley	Leeds	SE1942	53°52·7′	1°42·2′W	T	104
Guiseley Moor	Leeds	SE1943	53°53·2′	1°42·2′W	X	104
Guislich Farm	Highld	NH9111	57°10·9′	3°47·7′W	FM	36
Guisnes Court	Essex	TL9411	51°46·1′	0°49·1′E	X	168
Guist	Norf	TF9925	52°47·4′	0°57·5′E	T	132
Guist Bottom	Norf	TF9826	52°47·9′	0°56·6′E	X	132
Guist Hall	Norf	TG0026	52°47·9′	0°58·4′E	X	133
Guist Hill	Norf	TF9925	52°47·4′	0°57·5′E	X	132
Guith	Orkney	HY5536	59°12·8′	2°46·8′W	T	5
Guitinghill Fm	Glos	SP1329	51°57·8′	1°48·3′W	FM	163
Guiting Power	Glos	SP0924	51°55·1′	1°51·8′W	T	163
Guiting Stud	Glos	SP1024	51°55·1′	1°50·9′W	X	163
Guiting Wood	Glos	SP0726	51°56·2′	1°53·5′W	F	163
Gulberwick	Shetld	HU4338	60°7·7′	1°13·1′W	T	4
Gulber Wick	Shetld	HU4438	60°7·7′	1°12·0′W	W	4
Guldeford Lane Corner	E Susx	TQ9522	50°58·1′	0°47·0′E	X	189
Gulf of Corryvreckan	Arg & Bt	NM6901	56°9·0′	5°42·7′W	W	55,61
Gulf Rock	I Scilly	SV8714	49°56·9′	6°21·4′W	X	203
Gulf Scrubs, The	Glos	SP0113	51°49·2′	1°58·7′W	F	163
Gullacoombe	Corn	SX3376	50°33·8′	4°21·1′W	X	201
Gullaford	Devon	SX7767	50°29·6′	3°43·7′W	X	202
Gulland	Somer	SS9026	51°1·6′	3°33·7′W	X	181
Gulland Rock	Corn	SW8779	50°34·6′	5°0·1′W	X	200
Gullane	E Loth	NT4882	56°1·9′	2°49·6′W	T	66
Gullane Bay	E Loth	NT4783	56°2·5′	2°50·6′W	W	66
Gullane Bents	E Loth	NT4783	56°2·5′	2°50·6′W	X	66
Gullane Links	E Loth	NT4782	56°1·9′	2°50·6′W	X	66
Gullane Point	E Loth	NT4683	56°2·5′	2°51·6′W	X	66
Gullane Sands	E Loth	NT4581	56°1·4′	2°52·5′W	X	66
Gullastem	Corn	SX0589	50°40·3′	4°45·2′W	X	200
Gull Cove	Devon	SX5947	50°18·6′	3°58·4′W	W	202
Gull Craig	D & G	NX6548	54°48·8′	4°5·6′W	X	83,84
Gullege	W Susx	TQ3638	51°7·7′	0°3·0′W	A	187
Guller's End	Worcs	SO8535	52°1·0′	2°12·7′W	T	150
Gullet Fm	Devon	SX7639	50°14·5′	3°44·0′W	FM	202
Gullet, The	Cambs	TL4178	52°23·1′	0°4·7′E	X	142,143
Gullet, The	Heref	SO7637	52°2·1′	2°20·6′W	F	150
Gullet, The	Northnts	SP7344	52°5·6′	0°55·7′W	X	152
Gullet, The	Surrey	TQ3056	51°17·5′	0°7·7′W	F	187
Gull Fm	Suff	TM1763	52°13·6′	1°11·0′E	FM	156
Gull House Fm	Lincs	TF2414	52°42·8′	0°9·5′W	FM	131
Gullielands	D & G	NY2068	55°0·3′	3°14·6′W	X	85
Gullielands Burn	D & G	NY2068	55°0·3′	3°14·6′W	W	85
Gulliford	Devon	SX9479	50°36·3′	3°29·5′W	X	192
Gulliford Fm	Devon	SX9985	50°39·6′	3°25·4′W	FM	192
Gulliland	S Ayr	NS3634	55°34·6′	4°35·7′W	X	70
Gulling Green	Suff	TL8256	52°10·6′	0°40·1′E	T	155
Gull Island	Corn	SX0451	50°19·8′	4°44·9′W	X	200,204
Gulliver's Fm	Dorset	SU0703	50°49·8′	1°53·7′W	FM	195
Gullivers Kingdom	Derby	SK2957	53°6·8′	1°33·6′W	X	119
Gulliver's Kingdom	Derby	SK2958	53°7·3′	1°33·6′W	X	119
Gull Loch	Highld	NC6743	58°21·6′	4°15·9′W	W	10
Gull Nest	Moray	NJ2150	57°32·3′	3°18·7′W	X	28
Gull Nook	E Yorks	TA2272	54°8·0′	0°7·5′W	X	101
Gullom Holme	Cumbr	NY6528	54°39·0′	2°32·1′W	T	91
Gull or Carter's Rocks	Corn	SW7559	50°23·5′	5°9·6′W	X	200
Gull Point	N Ayr	NS1450	55°42·7′	4°57·2′W	X	63,69
Gull Ponds	N Lincs	SE9305	53°32·2′	0°35·4′W	W	112
Gull Rock	Corn	SS2017	50°55·7′	4°33·3′W	X	190
Gull Rock	Corn	SW6445	50°15·7′	5°18·3′W	X	203
Gull Rock	Corn	SW6813	49°58·6′	5°13·8′W	X	203
Gull Rock	Corn	SW9236	50°11·5′	4°54·5′W	X	204
Gull Rock	Corn	SX0386	50°38·7′	4°46·8′W	X	200
Gull Rock	Corn	SX1193	50°42·6′	4°40·2′W	X	190
Gull Rock	Devon	SS1446	51°11·2′	4°39·3′W	X	180
Gull Rock	Devon	SS2120	50°57·3′	4°32·5′W	X	190
Gull's Fm	Essex	TL8724	51°53·2′	0°43·4′E	FM	168
Gull's Walk	N Ayr	NS1952	55°43·9′	4°52·5′W	X	63
Gull, The	Suff	TM1954	52°8·7′	1°12·4′E	W	156
Gull, The	Suff	TM3464	52°13·7′	1°26·0′E	W	156
Gull, The	Suff	TM3568	52°15·8′	1°27·0′E	W	156
Gull, The	Suff	TM4147	52°4·4′	1°31·4′E	W	169
Gullyhill	E Ayr	NS5436	55°36·0′	4°18·6′W	X	70
Gullylane Fm	Devon	ST1708	50°52·2′	3°10·4′W	FM	192,193
Gullyn Rock	Corn	SW6747	50°16·9′	5°15·9′W	X	203
Gulpher	Suff	TM3036	51°58·7′	1°21·3′E	X	169
Gulsons	Essex	TL9933	51°57·8′	0°54·2′E	X	168
Gulvain or Gaor Bheinn	Highld	NM9986	56°55·6′	5°17·7′W	X	40
Gulvain or Gaor Bheinn	Highld	NN0089	56°57·2′	5°16·9′W	H	41
Gulval	Corn	SW4831	50°7·8′	5°31·2′W	T	203
Gulworthy	Devon	SX4472	50°31·9′	4°11·7′W	T	201
Gumber Fm	W Susx	SU9611	50°53·7′	0°37·7′W	FM	197
Gumbland	Devon	SS9422	50°59·5′	3°30·2′W	X	181
Gumbrills Fm	Mil Key	SP9245	52°6·0′	0°39·0′W	FM	152
Gumersam Bheag	N Eil	NG0281	57°43·5′	6°59·9′W	X	18
Gumersam Mhór	N Eil	NG0181	57°43·4′	7°0·9′W	X	18
Gumfreston	Pemb	SN1001	51°40·8′	4°44·5′W	T	158
Gumley	Leic	SP6890	52°30·5′	0°59·5′W	T	141
Gumley Covert	Leic	SP6789	52°29·9′	1°0·4′W	F	141
Gumley Lodge	Leic	SP6789	52°29·9′	1°0·4′W	X	141
Gumley Wood	Leic	SP6890	52°30·5′	0°59·5′W	F	141
Gumma	Powys	SO2865	52°16·9′	3°2·9′W	X	137,148
Gummershaye Fm	Dorset	SY3798	50°46·9′	2°53·2′W	FM	193
Gummer's How	Cumbr	SD3988	54°17·3′	2°55·8′W	H	96,97
Gummow	Corn	SW8848	50°17·9′	4°58·2′W	X	204
Gummow's Shop	Corn	SW8657	50°22·7′	5°0·2′W	T	200
Gumpick	Orkney	HY5408	58°57·7′	2°47·5′W	X	6,7
Gump of Spurness	Orkney	HY6035	59°12·3′	2°41·5′W	H	5,6
Gum Slade	Birm	SP1098	52°35·0′	1°50·7′W	F	139
Gun	Staffs	SJ9761	53°9·0′	2°2·3′W	H	118
Gunamul	N Eil	NL5482	56°48·3′	7°39·7′W	X	31
Gunboro Wood	Lincs	TF0623	52°47·9′	0°25·3′W	F	130
Gunby	E Yorks	SE7035	53°48·6′	0°55·8′W	T	105,106
Gunby	Lincs	SK9121	52°47·0′	0°38·6′W	T	130
Gunby	Lincs	TF4666	53°10·5′	0°11·5′E	T	122
Gunby Gorse	Lincs	SK8920	52°46·4′	0°40·4′W	F	130
Gunce's Fm	Essex	TL7438	52°1·0′	0°32·5′E	FM	155
Gundale Wood	N Yks	SE7987	54°16·6′	0°46·8′W	F	94,100
Gundenham	Somer	ST1222	50°59·7′	3°14·9′W	T	181,193
Gundleton	Hants	SU6133	51°5·8′	1°7·3′W	T	185
Gun End Fm	Staffs	SJ9662	53°9·5′	2°3·2′W	FM	118
Gun End Ho	Staffs	SJ9662	53°9·5′	2°3·2′W	X	118
Gunfleet Sand	Essex	TM2712	51°45·9′	1°17·8′E	X	169
Gun Fm	Stock	SK0090	53°24·6′	1°59·6′W	FM	110
Gungeon	Angus	NO5663	56°45·6′	2°42·7′W	X	44
Gun Green	Kent	TQ7730	51°2·7′	0°31·9′E	T	188
Gungrog Hall	Powys	SJ2308	52°40·1′	3°7·9′W	X	126

Gungstie	Shetld	HU4120	59°58·0′	1°15·4′W	X	4
Gungstie	Shetld	HU5341	60°9·3′	1°2·2′W	X	4
Gunhill	Aberd	NJ7425	57°19·1′	2°25·4′W	X	38
Gun Hill	E Susx	TQ5614	50°54·5′	0°13·5′E	T	199
Gun Hill	I of W	SZ4781	50°37·8′	1°19·7′W	X	196
Gun Hill	Norf	TF8545	52°58·5′	0°45·7′E	X	132
Gun Hill	Warw	SP2889	52°30·1′	1°34·8′W	X	140
Gunhill Cliff	Suff	TM5075	52°19·2′	1°40·5′E	X	156
Gun Hill Fm	Essex	TL8007	51°44·2′	0°36·8′E	FM	168
Gunhill Fm	Thurr	TQ6577	51°28·3′	0°22·9′E	FM	177,178
Gun Hill Pl	Essex	TM0333	51°57·7′	0°57·7′E	X	168
Gun Hills	Derby	SK3144	52°59·8′	1°31·9′W	X	119,128
Gunley Hall	Powys	SJ2601	52°36·3′	3°5·2′W	X	126
Gunley Wood	Powys	SJ2602	52°36·9′	3°5·2′W	F	126
Gunn	Devon	SS6333	51°5·0′	3°57·0′W	T	180
Gunna	Arg & Bt	NM1051	56°33·9′	6°42·8′W	X	46
Gunnacott	Devon	SX3497	50°45·2′	4°20·8′W	X	190
Gunnamanning	Corn	SW8951	50°19·5′	4°57·5′W	X	200,204
Gunna Sound	Arg & Bt	NM0950	56°33·4′	6°43·7′W	W	46
Gunnerby	NE Lincs	TF2199	53°28·7′	0°10·2′W	X	113
Gunnerfleet Fm	N Yks	SD7579	54°12·6′	2°22·6′W	FM	98
Gunners	I Scilly	SV8209	49°54·0′	6°25·4′W	X	203
Gunner's Box	Northum	NY9892	55°13·6′	2°1·5′W	A	81
Gunnersbury	Houns	TQ1978	51°29·5′	0°16·8′W	T	176
Gunnersbury Park	Houns	TQ1879	51°30·1′	0°17·6′W	X	176
Gunner's Hall	Cambs	TL5451	52°8·4′	0°15·4′E	X	154
Gunnerside	N Yks	SD9598	54°22·9′	2°4·2′W	T	98
Gunnerside Gill	N Yks	NY9301	54°24·5′	2°6·1′W	W	91,92
Gunnerside Gill	N Yks	SD9499	54°23·4′	2°5·1′W	W	98
Gunnerside Moor	N Yks	SD9302	54°25·0′	2°6·1′W	X	91,92
Gunnerside Pasture	N Yks	SD9399	54°23·4′	2°6·0′W	X	98
Gunnersvale Fm	Hartpl	NZ4429	54°39·5′	1°18·7′W	FM	93
Gunnerthwaite	Lancs	SD5573	54°9·3′	2°40·9′W	X	97
Gunnerton	Northum	NY9075	55°4·4′	2°9·0′W	T	87
Gunnerton Burn	Northum	NY9176	55°4·9′	2°8·0′W	W	87
Gunnerton Fell	Northum	NY9077	55°5·5′	2°9·0′W	X	87
Gunness	N Lincs	SE8411	53°35·6′	0°43·4′W	T	112
Gunnice	Worcs	SO8535	52°1·0′	2°12·7′W	X	150
Gunnislake	Corn	SX4371	50°31·3′	4°12·5′W	T	201
Gunnislake Station	Corn	SX4270	50°30·7′	4°13·3′W	X	201
Gunnista	Shetld	HU5043	60°10·4′	1°5·4′W	T	4
Gunnistay Waters	Shetld	HU4592	60°36·8′	1°10·2′W	W	1,2
Gunnister	Shetld	HP5804	60°43·2′	0°55·7′W	X	1
Gunnister	Shetld	HU3274	60°27·2′	1°24·6′W	X	3
Gunnister Voe	Shetld	HU3174	60°27·2′	1°25·7′W	W	3
Gunnocks	Pth & Kin	NN8411	56°16·9′	3°52·0′W	X	58
Gunn's Croft	Highld	NC9865	58°33·9′	3°44·7′W	X	11
Gunn's Plantn	Highld	NC5906	58°1·5′	4°22·8′W	F	16
Gunoak Wood	Corn	SX3876	50°33·9′	4°16·9′W	F	201
Gun Point	Corn	SW9176	50°33·0′	4°56·6′W	X	200
Gun Rock	Northum	NU2337	55°37·8′	1°37·6′W	X	75
Gunsgreenhill	Scot Bord	NT9463	55°51·9′	2°5·3′W	X	67
Gunshall	Cumbr	NY5864	54°58·4′	2°38·9′W	X	86
Gunshaw Hall	Norf	TM2382	52°23·7′	1°17·1′E	X	156
Gunshill	E Ayr	NS3947	55°41·6′	4°33·3′W	X	63
Gunshot Common	W Susx	TQ0428	51°2·7′	0°30·6′W	F	186,197
Gunside	Staffs	SJ9860	53°8·5′	2°1·4′W	X	118
Gunson Height	Cumbr	SD2582	54°13·9′	3°8·6′W	X	96
Gunstone	Staffs	SJ8704	52°38·3′	2°11·1′W	T	127,139
Gunstone Ho	Devon	SX8098	50°46·4′	3°41·7′W	X	191
Gunstone Mill	Devon	SX8098	50°46·4′	3°41·7′W	X	191
Guns Village	Sand	SO9991	52°31·2′	2°0·5′W	T	139
Gunters	Essex	TL5536	52°0·3′	0°15·9′E	X	154
Gunter's Bridge	W Susx	SU9723	51°0·1′	0°36·7′W	T	197
Gunter's Grove	Somer	ST2144	51°11·6′	3°7·4′W	X	182
Gunter Wood	Leeds	SE4146	53°54·8′	1°22·1′W	F	105
Gun, The	Shetld	HU4421	59°58·6′	1°12·2′W	X	4
Gunthorpe	N Lincs	SK8196	53°27·5′	0°47·3′W	T	112
Gunthorpe	Norf	TG0134	52°52·2′	0°59·6′E	T	133
Gunthorpe	Notts	SK6844	52°59·6′	0°58·8′W	T	129
Gunthorpe	Peterb	TF1802	52°36·4′	0°15·0′W	T	142
Gunthorpe	Rut	SK8605	52°38·4′	0°43·3′W	T	141
Gunthorpe Fm	Lincs	TF4718	52°44·6′	0°11·1′E	FM	131
Gunthorpe Park	Norf	TG0034	52°52·2′	0°58·7′E	X	133
Gunthwaite Hall	Barns	SE2306	53°33·2′	1°38·8′W	X	110
Gunton	Suff	TM5495	52°29·8′	1°44·9′E	T	134
Gunton Hall	Suff	TM5396	52°30·4′	1°44·1′E	X	134
Gunton Park	Norf	TG2333	52°51·1′	1°19·1′E	X	133
Gunton Sta	Norf	TG2535	52°52·1′	1°21·0′E	X	133
Gunvenna	Corn	SW9678	50°34·2′	4°52·5′W	X	200
Gunver Head	Corn	SW8977	50°33·5′	4°58·4′W	X	200
Gunville	I of W	SZ4789	50°42·2′	1°19·7′W	T	196
Gunville Down	Dorset	ST9012	50°54·7′	2°8·1′W	X	195
Gunwalloe	Corn	SW6522	50°3·7′	5°16·6′W	T	203
Gunwalloe Fishing Cove	Corn	SW6522	50°3·3′	5°16·6′W	T	203
Gupe Craig	D & G	NT1514	55°25·0′	3°20·1′W	X	79
Guphill	Devon	SS8428	51°2·6′	3°38·9′W	X	181
Gupton Burrows	Pemb	SR8999	51°39·3′	5°2·6′W	X	158
Gupton Fm	Pemb	SR8998	51°38·7′	5°2·6′W	FM	158
Gupworthy	Somer	SS9635	51°6·5′	3°28·8′W	T	181
Gupworthy Fm	Somer	SS9940	51°9·3′	3°26·3′W	FM	181
Gurdon's Fm	Bucks	SU7597	51°40·2′	0°54·5′W	FM	165
Gurgedyke Croft	Aberd	NJ8636	57°25·1′	2°13·5′W	X	30
Gurland Fm	Corn	SW3628	50°5·8′	5°41·1′W	FM	203
Gurl	Pth & Kin	NN9964	56°45·7′	3°38·7′W	H	43
Gurl, The	Orkney	HY4643	59°16·5′	2°56·4′W	X	5
Gurlyn	Corn	SW5632	50°8·5′	5°24·5′W	X	203
Gurnadee	Orkney	HY4128	59°8·4′	3°1·4′W	X	5,6
Gurnal Dubs	Cumbr	SD5099	54°23·3′	2°45·8′W	W	97
Gurnard	I of W	SZ4795	50°45·4′	1°19·6′W	T	196
Gurnard Bay	I of W	SZ4795	50°45·4′	1°19·6′W	W	196
Gurnard Ledge	I of W	SZ4694	50°44·9′	1°20·5′W	X	196
Gurnard Pines	I of W	SZ4794	50°44·8′	1°19·6′W	X	196
Gurnard's Fm	Essex	TQ6992	51°36·3′	0°26·8′E	FM	177,178
Gurnard's Head	Corn	SW4338	50°11·4′	5°35·7′W	X	203
Gurnett	Ches	SJ9271	53°14·4′	2°6·8′W	T	118
Gurney Slade	Somer	ST6249	51°14·6′	2°32·3′W	T	183
Gurney's Manor	Norf	TG0101	52°34·4′	0°58·4′E	X	144
Gurnhams	Essex	TM1223	51°52·1′	1°5·2′E	X	168,169
Gurnos	Carm	SN6823	51°53·6′	3°54·7′W	X	159

Gurnos	Merth Tyd	SO0407	51°45·4′	3°23·1′W	T	160
Gurnos	Powys	SN7709	51°46·2′	3°46·6′W	T	160
Gurnos	Powys	SN9257	52°12·3′	3°34·4′W	X	147
Gurrington Ho	Devon	SX7869	50°30·7′	3°42·9′W	X	202
Gurshill Fm	Glos	SO6504	51°44·3′	2°30·0′W	FM	162
Gurston Down	Wilts	SU0126	51°2·2′	1°58·8′W	X	184
Gurston Fm	Wilts	SU0225	51°1·7′	1°57·9′W	FM	184
Gurtla	Corn	SX0460	50°24·7′	4°45·1′W	X	200
Gurtof Beck	N Yks	SE4985	54°15·7′	1°14·4′W	W	100
Gurtof Wood	N Yks	SE4888	54°17·4′	1°15·3′W	F	100
Gurtons Fm	Essex	TL6112	51°47·2′	0°20·5′E	FM	167
Guscar Rocks	Glos	ST6098	51°41·0′	2°34·3′W	X	162
Guscott	Devon	SS5023	50°59·4′	4°7·9′W	X	180
Gushmere	Kent	TR0457	51°16·8′	0°55·9′E	T	178,179
Gussage All Saints	Dorset	SU0010	50°53·6′	1°59·6′W	T	195
Gussage Hill	Dorset	ST9913	50°55·2′	2°0·5′W	H	195
Gussage St Andrew	Dorset	ST9714	50°55·8′	2°2·2′W	T	195
Gussage St Michael	Dorset	ST9811	50°54·1′	2°1·3′W	T	195
Gusselton	Shetld	HU3916	59°55·9′	1°17·6′W	X	4
Gusset	Derby	SK1990	53°24·6′	1°42·4′W	X	110
Gusset	Northum	NZ0897	55°16·3′	1°52·0′W	X	81
Gussetts Wood	Bucks	SU7688	51°35·4′	0°53·8′W	F	175
Gustard Wood	Herts	TL1716	51°50·0′	0°17·7′W	T	166
Gusted Hall	Essex	TQ8390	51°35·0′	0°38·9′E	X	178
Gusti Vean	Corn	SW8461	50°24·8′	5°2·0′W	X	200
Gusti Veor	Corn	SW8361	50°24·8′	5°2·9′W	X	200
Guston	Kent	TR3244	51°9·1′	1°19·4′E	T	179
Guston Fm	Kent	TR3060	51°17·8′	1°18·3′E	FM	179
Gutch Common	Wilts	ST8925	51°1·7′	2°9·0′W	X	184
Gutch Common	Wilts	ST8925	51°1·7′	2°9·0′W	X	184
Gutcher	Shetld	HU5499	60°40·5′	1°0·2′W	T	1
Gutcher's Isle	D & G	NX8652	54°51·2′	3°46·1′W	X	84
Gutchpool Fm	Dorset	ST8328	51°3·3′	2°14·2′W	FM	183
Gutherscale	Cumbr	NY2421	54°35·0′	3°10·1′W	X	89,90
Guther's Island	I Scilly	SV9114	49°57·0′	6°18·1′W	X	203
Guthram Gowt	Lincs	TF1722	52°47·2′	0°15·5′W	T	130
Guthrie	Angus	NO5650	56°38·6′	2°42·6′W	T	54
Guthrie Castle	Angus	NO5650	56°38·6′	2°42·6′W	X	54
Guthrie Hill	Angus	NO5551	56°39·2′	2°43·6′W	H	54
Guthrie's Memorial	I of M	SC4391	54°17·7′	4°24·3′W	X	95
Guttald	Shetld	HU5661	60°20·0′	0°58·6′W	X	2
Gutta Wood	N Yks	SE4688	54°17·4′	1°17·2′W	F	100
Gutt Br	Corn	SW9775	50°32·6′	4°51·5′W	X	200
Gutterby	Cumbr	SD1084	54°14·9′	3°22·5′W	X	96
Gutterby Spa	Cumbr	SD1084	54°14·9′	3°22·5′W	W	96
Gutter Fm	Shrops	SO4993	52°32·2′	2°44·7′W	FM	137,138
Gutter Fm	Staffs	SK0551	53°3·6′	1°55·1′W	FM	119
Gutterford Burn	Midlo	NT1558	55°48·7′	3°20·9′W	W	65,72
Gutteridge Fm	Herts	TL0008	51°45·9′	0°32·7′W	FM	166
Gutteridge Fm	Wilts	SU2434	51°6·5′	1°39·0′W	FM	184
Gutteridge Hall	Essex	TM1421	51°51·0′	1°6·8′E	X	168,169
Gutteridge Wood	Hill	TQ0984	51°32·9′	0°25·3′W	F	176
Gutterpool	Orkney	HY4603	58°54·9′	2°55·8′W	X	6,7
Gutters	Durham	NZ0410	54°29·4′	1°55·9′W	X	92
Gutter Sound	Orkney	ND3196	58°51·0′	3°11·3′W	W	6,7
Gutter Tor	Devon	SX5766	50°28·6′	4°0·6′W	H	202
Guttle Hole	Pemb	SM8501	51°40·2′	5°6·2′W	X	157
Guval Downs	Corn	SW4834	50°9·4′	5°31·3′W	X	203
Guy Hill	Lancs	SD6368	54°6·6′	2°33·5′W	X	97
Guyhirn	Cambs	TF4003	52°36·6′	0°4·5′E	T	142,143
Guyhirn Corner	Cambs	TF3802	52°36·1′	0°2·7′E	X	142,143
Guyhirn Gull	Cambs	TF3904	52°37·2′	0°3·6′E	T	142,143
Guy Ho	Kent	TQ8638	51°6·9′	0°39·8′E	X	189
Guynd	Angus	NO5641	56°33·8′	2°42·5′W	X	54
Guys	Lancs	SD5051	53°57·4′	2°45·3′W	X	102
Guy's Cleugh	Northum	NY6450	54°50·9′	2°33·2′W	X	86
Guy's Cliffe	Warw	SP2866	52°17·7′	1°35·0′W	T	151
Guy's Close	Durham	NY9739	54°45·0′	2°2·4′W	X	92
Guy's Fen	Peterb	TF2703	52°36·8′	0°7·0′W	X	142
Guy's Head	Lincs	TF4825	52°48·4′	0°12·1′E	T	131
Guy's Hill	Bath & NE Somer	ST6164	51°22·7′	2°33·2′W	X	172
Guy's Marsh	Dorset	ST8420	50°59·0′	2°13·3′W	T	183
Guyzance	Northum	NU2103	55°19·5′	1°39·7′W	T	81
Guyzance Lee	Northum	NU1803	55°19·5′	1°42·5′W	X	81
Guzzle Down	Torbay	SX9054	50°22·8′	3°32·5′W	X	202
Gwaelod	Powys	SJ1416	52°44·3′	3°16·0′W	X	125
Gwaelod-y-garth	Card	ST1183	51°32·6′	3°16·6′W	T	171
Gwaelod-y-maes	Carm	SN5526	51°55·1′	4°6·1′W	X	146
Gwaelod-y-rhos	Powys	SN9066	52°17·1′	3°36·4′W	X	136,147
Gwaen Cerrig Llwydion	Powys	SO0519	51°51·9′	3°22·4′W	X	160
Gwaenfynydd	I of Angl	SH3476	53°15·5′	4°28·9′W	X	114
Gwaentrebeddau	Powys	SO1198	52°34·6′	3°18·4′W	X	136
Gwaenydd	Powys	SJ0003	52°37·0′	3°28·2′W	X	136
Gwaenynog Bach	Denb	SJ0265	53°10·6′	3°27·6′W	X	116
Gwaenysgor	Flint	SJ0781	53°19·3′	3°23·4′W	T	116
Gwahan	Pemb	SM7026	51°53·3′	5°20·2′W	X	157
Gwaithla	Powys	SO2156	52°12·0′	3°9·0′W	X	148
Gwalchmai	I of Angl	SH3975	53°15·1′	4°24·4′W	T	114
Gwalchmai Uchaf	I of Angl	SH3975	53°15·1′	4°24·4′W	T	114
Gwalciau'r Cwm	Powys	SO0619	51°51·9′	3°21·5′W	X	160
Gwalia	Wrex	SJ3640	52°57·5′	2°56·8′W	X	117
Gwallon	Corn	SW5231	50°7·9′	5°27·8′W	T	203
Gwal y Filiast	Carm	SN1725	51°53·9′	4°39·2′W	X	145,158
Gwal y Filiast (Burial Chamber)	Carm	SN1725	51°53·9′	4°39·2′W	A	145,158
Gwal-yr-hŵch	Carm	SN5807	51°44·9′	4°3·0′W	X	159
Gwanas-fawr	Gwyn	SH7716	52°43·9′	3°48·9′W	X	124
Gwarafog Ho	Powys	SN9548	52°7·5′	3°31·6′W	X	147
Gwarallt	Carm	SN4738	52°1·4′	4°13·4′W	X	146
Gwarallt	Cered	SN5458	52°12·3′	4°7·8′W	X	146
Gwarallt	Cered	SN6479	52°23·6′	3°59·5′W	X	135
Gwarallt	Powys	SO0049	52°8·1′	3°27·3′W	X	147
Gwar-allt	Powys	SO1251	52°9·3′	3°16·8′W	X	148
Gwaralltyfaerdre	Cered	SN4349	52°7·2′	4°17·2′W	X	146
Gwaralltyryn	Cered	SN4347	52°6·2′	4°17·1′W	X	146
Gwarcae	Powys	SO0632	51°59·0′	3°21·7′W	X	160
Gwarcaeau	Cered	SN5969	52°18·3′	4°3·7′W	X	135
Gwar-caeau	Cered	SN7568	52°18·0′	3°49·6′W	X	135,147
Gwar-castell	Cered	SN7260	52°13·6′	3°52·1′W	X	146,147

Gwarcoed	Carm	SN5940	52°2·7′	4°3·0′W	X	146
Gwar-coed	Cered	SN5548	52°6·9′	4°6·7′W	X	146
Gwarcoed-Einon	Cered	SN4644	52°4·6′	4°14·4′W	X	146
Gwarcwm	Carm	SN4432	51°58·1′	4°15·9′W	X	146
Gwarcwm	Carm	SN4840	52°2·5′	4°12·6′W	X	146
Gwarcwm	Cered	SN4245	52°5·1′	4°18·0′W	X	146
Gwar-cwm	Cered	SN6791	52°30·3′	3°57·2′W	X	135
Gwardafolog	Cered	SN4348	52°6·7′	4°17·2′W	X	146
Gwarder	Corn	SW7835	50°10·6′	5°6·2′W	X	204
Gwardolau	Powys	SN9668	52°18·3′	3°31·1′W	X	136,147
Gwarfelin	Powys	SN9937	52°1·6′	3°27·9′W	X	160
Gwarffynnon	Cered	SN5750	52°8·0′	4°5·0′W	X	146
Gwarffynnon	Cered	SN6450	52°8·1′	3°58·8′W	X	146
Gwargraig	Carm	SN5142	52°3·6′	4°10·0′W	X	146
Gwar-henallt	Powys	SO0648	52°7·6′	3°22·0′W	X	147
Gwarllwyn	Carm	SN8234	51°59·8′	3°42·7′W	X	160
Gwarllwyn	Pemb	SN1829	51°56·0′	4°38·5′W	X	145,158
Gwarllwyneidos	Cered	SN4147	52°6·2′	4°18·9′W	X	146
Gwarllyn	Cered	SN5963	52°15·1′	4°3·5′W	X	146
Gwarmacwydd	Carm	SN1620	51°51·1′	4°39·9′W	X	145,158
Gwarnick	Corn	SW8148	50°17·7′	5°4·1′W	X	204
Gwarnoethle	Carm	SN6740	52°2·8′	3°56·0′W	X	146
Gwarthlow	Shrops	SO2495	52°33·1′	3°6·9′W	X	137
Gwarwenallt	Carm	SN3219	51°50·9′	4°26·0′W	X	159
Gwar-y-coed	Pemb	SM8024	51°52·5′	5°11·4′W	X	157
Gwar-y-coed	Pemb	SN0326	51°54·1′	4°51·4′W	X	145,157,158
Gwaryfelin	Cered	SN5979	52°23·7′	4°3·9′W	X	135
Gwar-y-felin	Powys	SN9335	52°0·4′	3°33·1′W	X	160
Gwar-y-gorof	Carm	SN6539	52°2·2′	3°57·7′W	X	146
Gwar y Tŷ	Powys	SN8974	52°21·4′	3°37·4′W	X	135,136,147
Gwastad	Blae Gw	SO2305	51°44·5′	3°6·5′W	H	161
Gwastad	Pemb	SN0424	51°53·0′	4°50·5′W	T	145,157,158
Gwastad	Powys	SJ1119	52°45·9′	3°18·7′W	X	125
Gwastad	Powys	SN9374	52°21·5′	3°33·9′W	X	136,147
Gwastadannas	Gwyn	SH6553	53°3·7′	4°0·5′W	X	115
Gwastadcoed	Powys	SO0087	52°28·5′	3°27·9′W	X	136
Gwastadfryn	Gwyn	SH6709	52°40·0′	3°57·6′W	X	124
Gwastadgoed	Gwyn	SH5910	52°40·4′	4°4·7′W	T	124
Gwastad-mawr	Newp	ST2989	51°36·0′	3°1·1′W	X	171
Gwastadnant	Gwyn	SH6157	53°5·8′	4°4·2′W	T	115
Gwastadros	Gwyn	SH8935	52°54·3′	3°38·6′W	X	124,125
Gwastedyn Hill	Powys	SN9866	52°17·2′	3°29·3′W	H	136,147
Gwastedyn	Cered	SN5656	52°11·2′	4°6·0′W	X	146
Gwastod mawr	Carm	SN4031	51°57·5′	4°19·3′W	X	146
Gwaun-arlwyddes	Caer	ST1398	51°40·7′	3°15·1′W	X	171
Gwaun Bryn-bwch	Powys	SN9111	51°47·5′	3°34·4′W	X	160
Gwaun-Cae-Gurwen	Nth Pt Talb	SN7011	51°47·2′	3°52·7′W	T	160
Gwaun Cefnygarreg	Powys	SN9413	51°48·6′	3°31·9′W	X	160
Gwaunceste Hill	Powys	SO1555	52°11·4′	3°14·2′W	H	148
Gwaun Crew	Powys	SN9917	51°50·8′	3°27·6′W	X	160
Gwaundylo	Gwyn	SH8534	52°53·7′	3°42·2′W	X	124,125
Gwaunfelen	Torf	SO2509	51°46·7′	3°4·8′W	X	161
Gwaun-Leision	Nth Pt Talb	SN7012	51°47·7′	3°52·7′W	T	160
Gwaun Llanhari	Rho Cyn Taf	ST0081	51°31·4′	3°26·1′W	X	170
Gwaun Meisgyn	Rho Cyn Taf	ST0684	51°33·1′	3°21·0′W	X	170
Gwaun Nant-ddu	Powys	SO0017	51°50·8′	3°26·7′W	X	160
Gwaun Perfedd	Powys	SO0220	51°52·4′	3°25·0′W	X	160
Gwaun Rhys	Nth Pt Talb	SS8997	51°39·9′	3°35·9′W	X	170
Gwaun Sanau	Powys	SN8361	52°14·3′	3°42·4′W	X	147
Gwaun Taf	Powys	SO0120	51°52·4′	3°25·9′W	X	160
Gwaun-y-bara	Caer	ST1887	51°34·8′	3°10·6′W	X	171
Gwaunydd	Pemb	SN0638	52°0·6′	4°49·2′W	X	145
Gwaun-y-gwiail	Gwyn	SH6366	53°10·7′	4°2·6′W	X	115
Gwaun-y-maglau	Powys	SJ0101	52°36·1′	3°27·3′W	X	136
Gwaunynog	Powys	SJ0811	52°41·6′	3°21·3′W	X	125
Gwaun y Pynt	Powys	SO0315	51°49·8′	3°24·1′W	H	160
Gwavas	Corn	SW6529	50°7·1′	5°16·9′W	T	203
Gwavas	Corn	SW7113	49°58·6′	5°11·3′W	T	203
Gwavas Lake	Corn	SW4728	50°6·1′	5°31·9′W	W	203
Gwaves, The	Aberd	NO5191	57°0·7′	2°48·0′W	X	44
Gwaynynog	Denb	SJ0365	53°10·6′	3°26·7′W	X	116
Gwbert	Cered	SN1649	52°6·8′	4°40·8′W	T	145
Gwddw Llanddwyn	I of Angl	SH3963	53°8·6′	4°24·0′W	X	114
Gweal	I Scilly	SV8615	49°57·4′	6°22·3′W	X	203
Gwealavellan	Corn	SW5941	50°13·4′	5°22·4′W	X	203
Gwealeath	Corn	SW6922	50°3·4′	5°13·3′W	X	203
Gwedna	Corn	SW6032	50°8·6′	5°21·2′W	T	203
Gweek	Corn	SW7026	50°5·6′	5°12·6′W	T	203
Gwehelog	Monm	SO3804	51°44·1′	2°53·5′W	T	171
Gweinion	Gwyn	SH8712	52°41·9′	3°39·9′W	X	124,125
Gweirglodd-gilfach	Gwyn	SH8926	52°49·4′	3°38·4′W	X	124,125
Gweirthdy	I of Angl	SH5376	53°15·9′	4°11·8′W	X	114,115
Gwely'r Misgl	Brig	SS7880	51°30·6′	3°45·1′W	X	170
Gwempa	Carm	SN4311	51°46·8′	4°16·2′W	X	159
Gwenddwr	Powys	SO0643	52°4·9′	3°21·9′W	T	147,160
Gwendra	Corn	SW9038	50°12·5′	4°56·2′W	X	204
Gwendraeth	Carm	SN3706	51°44·0′	4°21·2′W	W	159
Gwendraeth Fach	Carm	SN4312	51°47·3′	4°16·2′W	W	159
Gwendraeth Fawr	Carm	SN4810	51°46·3′	4°11·8′W	W	159
Gwendra Point	Corn	SX0349	50°18·7′	4°45·6′W	X	204
Gwendreath Fm	Corn	SW7316	50°0·3′	5°9·7′W	FM	204
Gwenfrwd	Carm	SN7446	52°6·1′	3°50·0′W	W	146,147
Gwenfrwd	Cered	SN5960	52°13·5′	4°3·5′W	W	146
Gwenfrwd	Powys	SO0331	51°58·4′	3°24·3′W	X	160
Gwenfro Isaf	I of Angl	SH5079	53°17·5′	4°14·6′W	X	114,115
Gwenfro Uchaf	I of Angl	SH4978	53°16·9′	4°15·5′W	X	114,115
Gwenhafdre Isaf	Cered	SN6767	52°17·3′	3°56·6′W	X	135
Gwenherrion Fm	Heref	SO5018	51°51·7′	2°43·2′W	FM	162
Gwenlais-fâch	Swan	SN6101	51°41·7′	4°0·3′W	X	159
Gwenlais-fawr	Swan	SN6001	51°41·7′	4°1·1′W	X	159
Gwenlais-uchaf	Swan	SN6101	51°41·7′	4°0·3′W	X	159
Gwenlas	Powys	SO1180	52°24·9′	3°18·1′W	X	136
Gwenlas Brook	Powys	SO1079	52°24·3′	3°19·0′W	W	136,148
Gwennap	Corn	SW7340	50°13·2′	5°10·6′W	T	204
Gwennap Head	Corn	SW3621	50°2·1′	5°40·8′W	X	203
Gwennap Pit	Corn	SW7141	50°13·7′	5°12·3′W	X	203
Gwennymoor	Corn	SW9967	50°28·3′	4°49·6′W	X	200
Gwenter	Corn	SW7417	50°0·9′	5°8·9′W	T	204
Gwerclas	Denb	SJ0542	52°58·3′	3°24·5′W	X	125
Gwerddon	Carm	SN7934	51°59·7′	3°45·4′W	X	146,160

Gwern	Powys	SJ1819	52°46·0′	3°12·5′W	X	125
Gwernaffel	Powys	SO2670	52°19·6′	3°4·8′W	X	137,148
Gwernaffield-y-Waun	Flint	SJ2064	53°10·3′	3°11·4′W	T	117
Gwernafon	Powys	SN9290	52°30·1′	3°35·1′W	T	136
Gwernalltcwm	Powys	SO0848	52°7·6′	3°20·2′W	X	147
Gwernalway	Powys	SO1843	52°5·0′	3°11·4′W	X	148,161
Gwernan Lake Hotel	Gwyn	SH7015	52°43·3′	3°55·1′W	X	124
Gwernant Fm	Pemb	SN0820	51°51·0′	4°46·9′W	FM	145,158
Gwernant Home Fm	Cered	SN3346	52°5·5′	4°25·9′W	FM	145
Gwernau	Caer	ST1593	51°38·0′	3°13·3′W	X	171
Gwernau	Powys	SN9292	52°31·2′	3°35·1′W	X	136
Gwernbere	Powys	SH8302	52°36·4′	3°43·3′W	X	135,136
Gwernbiseg	Gwyn	SH8636	52°54·8′	3°41·3′W	X	124,125
Gwernblaedda	Powys	SN9009	51°46·4′	3°35·3′W	X	160
Gwern Borter	Conwy	SH7673	53°14·6′	3°51·1′W	X	115
Gwern-brain	Denb	SJ1748	53°1·6′	3°13·8′W	X	116
Gwern-bwys	Conwy	SH8265	53°10·4′	3°45·5′W	X	116
Gwerncynydd	Powys	SO0264	52°16·2′	3°25·8′W	X	147
Gwernddu	Monm	ST3997	51°40·3′	2°52·5′W	X	171
Gwern-Ddu Hill	Monm	ST4097	51°40·4′	2°51·7′W	X	171
Gwern-dyfnant	Powys	SO2356	52°12·1′	3°7·2′W	X	148
Gwern-eiddig	Monm	SO4106	51°45·2′	2°50·9′W	X	161
Gwern Einion	Gwyn	SH5928	52°50·1′	4°5·2′W	X	124
Gwerneirin	Powys	SO0289	52°29·6′	3°26·2′W	T	136
Gwerneirin	Powys	SO1880	52°25·0′	3°11·9′W	T	136
Gwernesney	Monm	SO4101	51°42·5′	2°50·8′W	T	171
Gwern Estyn	Flint	SJ3157	53°6·6′	3°1·4′W	X	117
Gwernewydd	Powys	SO1691	52°30·9′	3°13·9′W	X	136
Gwernfach	Powys	SO1056	52°11·9′	3°18·6′W	X	148
Gwern feifod	Powys	SJ0928	52°50·8′	3°20·7′W	X	125
Gwern-feistrol	Gwyn	SH8936	52°54·8′	3°38·6′W	X	124,125
Gwernfelen	Carm	SN7933	51°59·2′	3°45·3′W	X	146,160
Gwernfythen	Powys	SO2044	52°5·6′	3°9·7′W	X	148,161
Gwern Gof Isaf	Conwy	SH6860	53°7·5′	3°58·0′W	X	115
Gwern Gof Uchaf	Conwy	SH6760	53°7·5′	3°58·9′W	X	115
Gwerngraig	Gwyn	SH7515	52°43·3′	3°50·6′W	X	124
Gwern Hall	Flint	SJ2454	53°4·9′	3°7·7′W	X	117
Gwernhefin	Gwyn	SH8932	52°52·7′	3°38·6′W	X	124,125
Gwern-hywaid	Powys	SO1440	52°3·3′	3°14·9′W	X	148,161
Gwernhywel-ganol	Conwy	SH8650	53°2·4′	3°41·6′W	X	116
Gwern Hywel Uchaf	Conwy	SH8649	53°1·8′	3°41·6′W	X	116
Gwerni	Denb	SJ0651	53°3·1′	3°23·7′W	H	116
Gwernigron Fm	Denb	SJ0275	53°16·0′	3°27·8′W	FM	116
Gwern-illa	Powys	SO2153	52°10·4′	3°8·9′W	X	148
Gwernleyshon	Caer	ST2386	51°34·3′	3°6·3′W	X	171
Gwernllertai	Powys	SN9424	51°54·5′	3°32·1′W	X	160
Gwernllwyd Fm	Powys	SO1733	51°59·6′	3°12·1′W	FM	161
Gwernllwyn	Brig	SS9087	51°34·5′	3°34·9′W	X	170
Gwernogle	Carm	SN5334	51°59·3′	4°8·1′W	T	146
Gwernol	Denb	SJ2052	53°3·8′	3°11·2′W	T	117
Gwern-owddwy	Powys	SJ2818	52°45·5′	3°3·6′W	X	126
Gwernpwll	Carm	SN7842	52°4·0′	3°46·4′W	X	146,147,160
Gwern Rhiw	Flint	SJ2258	53°7·1′	3°9·5′W	X	117
Gwern Sebon	Powys	SJ1126	52°49·7′	3°18·9′W	X	125
Gwernto Fm	Flint	SJ2555	53°5·5′	3°6·8′W	FM	117
Gwern-vale	Powys	SO2119	51°52·1′	3°8·5′W	X	161
Gwern y brenin	Shrops	SJ3026	52°49·9′	3°1·9′W	T	126
Gwernybuarth	Powys	SO1893	52°32·0′	3°12·1′W	X	136
Gwern-y-bwlch	Powys	SH8504	52°37·5′	3°41·5′W	X	135,136
Gwern-y-bwlch	Powys	SH8704	52°37·6′	3°39·8′W	X	135,136
Gwern-y-bwtler	Powys	SO2219	51°52·1′	3°7·6′W	X	161
Gwern-y-Ciliau	Conwy	SH9273	53°14·8′	3°36·7′W	X	116
Gwernydd	Powys	SJ0802	52°36·7′	3°21·1′W	T	136
Gwern-y-domen	Caer	ST1787	51°34·8′	3°11·5′W	X	171
Gwernyfed	Powys	SO1829	51°57·4′	3°11·2′W	X	161
Gwernyfed Park	Powys	SO1737	52°1·8′	3°12·2′W	X	161
Gwern-y-gadfa	Denb	SJ0559	53°7·4′	3°24·8′W	X	116
Gwern-y-Gae	V of Glam	ST0777	51°29·3′	3°20·0′W	X	170
Gwern-y-gedrych	V of Glam	ST0778	51°29·8′	3°20·0′W	X	170
Gwern-y-go	Powys	SJ2817	52°45·0′	3°3·6′W	X	126
Gwern-y-go	Powys	SO2291	52°30·9′	3°8·6′W	X	137
Gwern-y-go Wood	Powys	SO2091	52°30·9′	3°10·3′W	F	137
Gwern-y-marl	Flint	SJ2268	53°12·4′	3°9·7′W	X	117
Gwern-y-mynach	Powys	SN9656	52°11·8′	3°30·9′W	X	147
Gwernymynydd	Flint	SJ2162	53°9·2′	3°10·5′W	T	117
Gwern-y-pwll	Powys	SO0395	52°32·9′	3°25·4′W	X	136
Gwernyrargllwydd Fm	Powys	SO1559	52°13·6′	3°14·3′W	FM	148
Gwern-yr-ewig	Gwyn	SH9631	52°52·2′	3°32·3′W	X	125
Gwern-y-Steeple	V of Glam	ST0775	51°28·2′	3°20·0′W	T	170
Gwersyll	Rho Cyn Taf	SO0204	51°43·8′	3°24·8′W	A	170
Gwersyll Glanllyn	Gwyn	SH8831	52°52·1′	3°39·4′W	X	124,125
Gwersyllt	Wrex	SJ3253	53°4·4′	3°0·5′W	T	117
Gwespyr	Flint	SJ1183	53°20·4′	3°19·8′W	T	116
Gwestydd	Powys	SO1193	52°31·9′	3°18·3′W	X	136
Gwgia	Powys	SO0597	52°34·0′	3°23·7′W	W	136
Gwili Railway	Carm	SN4124	51°53·8′	4°18·3′W	X	159
Gwili Rly	Carm	SN4125	51°54·3′	4°18·3′W	X	146
Gwili Steam Railway	Carm	SN3926	51°54·8′	4°20·1′W	X	145
Gwills	Corn	SW6720	50°2·3′	5°14·9′W	X	203
Gwills	Corn	SW8259	50°23·7′	5°3·7′W	T	200
Gwindra	Corn	SW9552	50°20·2′	4°52·5′W	X	200,204
Gwindy	Gwyn	SH4643	52°58·0′	4°17·2′W	X	123
Gwinear	Corn	SW5937	50°11·3′	5°22·2′W	T	203
Gwinear Downs	Corn	SW6034	50°9·7′	5°21·3′W	T	203
Gwineas or Gwinges	Corn	SX0342	50°14·9′	4°45·4′W	X	204
Gwinges	Corn	SW8221	50°3·2′	5°2·4′W	X	204
Gwinges or Gwineas	Corn	SX0342	50°14·9′	4°45·4′W	X	204
Gwithian	Corn	SW5841	50°13·4′	5°23·2′W	T	203
Gwithian Towans	Corn	SW5741	50°13·4′	5°24·0′W	X	203
Gwlybycoed	I of Angl	SH4689	53°22·8′	4°18·5′W	X	114
Gwndir	Denb	SJ0848	53°1·5′	3°21·9′W	X	116
Gwndwn	Carm	SN4737	52°0·9′	4°13·4′W	X	146
Gwndwn	Pemb	SN1639	52°1·4′	4°40·5′W	X	145
Gwndwn	Pemb	SN1740	52°1·9′	4°39·7′W	X	145
Gwndwn	Pemb	SN1832	51°57·6′	4°38·6′W	X	145
Gwndwn	Powys	SO1623	51°54·2′	3°12·9′W	X	161
Gwndwngwyn	Pemb	SM9027	51°54·4′	5°2·8′W	X	157,158
Gwndwnwal Fm	Powys	SO1129	51°57·4′	3°17·3′W	FM	161
Gwnhingar	I of Angl	SH4164	53°9·2′	4°22·3′W	X	114,115
Gwninger	Conwy	SH8156	53°5·5′	3°46·2′W	X	116

Gwnodl Bach	Denb	SJ0440	52°57·2′	3°25·3′W	X	125
Gwnodl Fawr	Denb	SJ0440	52°57·2′	3°25·3′W	X	125
Gworlodith	Heref	SO3432	51°59·2′	2°57·3′W	X	149,161
Gwrach ddu	I of Angl	SH5068	53°11·5′	4°14·3′W	X	114,115
Gwrachen	Powys	SH9609	52°40·4′	3°31·9′W	X	125
Gŵr-bach	Gwyn	SH6403	52°36·7′	4°0·1′W	X	135
Gwredog	I of Angl	SH4086	53°21·0′	4°23·8′W	T	114
Gwredog	I of Angl	SH4190	53°23·2′	4°23·0′W	X	114
Gwreiddiau	Powys	SJ0419	52°45·8′	3°25·0′W	X	125
Gwreiddyn	Conwy	SH9474	53°15·4′	3°34·9′W	X	116
Gwrhay	Caer	ST1899	51°41·3′	3°10·8′W	T	171
Gwrhyd	Blae Gw	SO2206	51°45·1′	3°7·4′W	X	161
Gwrhyd	Nth Pt Talb	SN7308	51°45·6′	3°50·0′W	X	160
Gwrhyd Mawr	Pemb	SM7627	51°54·0′	5°15·0′W	X	157
Gwrid	Shrops	SO1884	52°27·1′	3°12·0′W	X	136
Gwrlodde	Powys	SO1631	51°58·5′	3°13·0′W	X	161
Gwrthwynt-uchaf	Cered	SN5358	52°12·3′	4°8·7′W	X	146
Gwrych Bedw	Denb	SJ1048	53°1·5′	3°20·1′W	X	116
Gwrych Castle	Conwy	SH9277	53°17·0′	3°36·8′W	X	116
Gwryd	Powys	SN9339	52°2·6′	3°33·2′W	H	160
Gwter Siani	Wrex	SJ2449	53°2·2′	3°7·6′W	X	117
Gwyddel	Gwyn	SH1425	52°47·7′	4°45·1′W	X	123
Gwyddelfynydd	Gwyn	SH6103	52°36·7′	4°2·8′W	X	135
Gwyddelwern	Denb	SJ0746	53°0·4′	3°22·8′W	T	116
Gwyddfan	Carm	SN6315	51°49·3′	3°58·9′W	W	159
Gwŷddfor	I of Angl	SH3378	53°16·6′	4°29·9′W	X	114
Gwyddfryniau	Gwyn	SH5904	52°37·2′	4°4·6′W	X	135
Gwyddgrug	Carm	SN4635	51°59·8′	4°14·2′W	T	146
Gwyddgwion	Gwyn	SN6298	52°34·0′	4°1·8′W	X	135
Gwydir	Gwyn	SH3747	53°0·0′	4°25·3′W	X	123
Gwydir Castle	Conwy	SH7961	53°8·2′	3°48·1′W	X	115,116
Gwydir Uchaf Chapel	Conwy	SH7960	53°7·7′	3°48·1′W	A	116
Gwydre	Carm	SN7827	51°55·9′	3°46·1′W	X	146,160
Gwydryn Newydd	I of Angl	SH4968	53°11·5′	4°15·2′W	X	114,115
Gwydyr Uchaf	Conwy	SH7960	53°7·7′	3°48·1′W	X	115
Gwylfa	Gwyn	SH3443	52°57·8′	4°27·9′W	X	123
Gwylfa Hiraethog	Conwy	SH9459	53°7·3′	3°34·6′W	X	116
Gwylwyr Carreglefain	Gwyn	SH3241	52°56·7′	4°29·6′W	X	123
Gwynant	Powys	SO0883	52°26·5′	3°20·8′W	X	136
Gwyndy	Gwyn	SH2235	52°53·2′	4°38·3′W	X	123
Gwyndy	I of Angl	SH3979	53°17·3′	4°24·5′W	X	114
Gwyndy	I of Angl	SH5273	53°14·3′	4°12·7′W	X	114,115
Gwyndy Fm	Pemb	SN1616	51°49·0′	4°39·8′W	FM	158
Gwyndy-isaf	Conwy	SH8873	53°14·8′	3°40·3′W	X	116
Gwyndy-newydd	Conwy	SH7349	53°1·6′	3°53·2′W	X	115
Gwyndy-uchaf	Conwy	SH8873	53°14·8′	3°40·3′W	X	116
Gwynfaen	Swan	SS5799	51°40·5′	4°3·7′W	X	159
Gwynfan	Powys	SN7799	52°34·7′	3°48·5′W	X	135
Gwynfan	Powys	SO0364	52°16·2′	3°24·9′W	X	147
Gwynfryn	Cered	SN4955	52°10·6′	4°12·1′W	X	146
Gwynfryn	Gwyn	SH3635	52°53·5′	4°25·9′W	X	123
Gwynfryn	Wrex	SJ2552	53°3·8′	3°6·7′W	T	117
Gwynfryn Plâs	Gwyn	SH4639	52°55·8′	4°17·1′W	X	123
Gwyn-fynydd	Gwyn	SH7328	52°50·3′	3°52·7′W	X	124
Gwynfynydd	Powys	SO0393	52°31·8′	3°25·4′W	X	136
Gwyngoed	Cered	SN6756	52°11·4′	3°56·3′W	X	146
Gwyniasa	Gwyn	SH3541	52°56·7′	4°26·9′W	X	123
Gwynnant	Cered	SN4459	52°12·7′	4°16·6′W	X	146
Gwynne's Hill	Heref	SO6530	51°58·3′	2°30·2′W	X	149
Gwynt Fm	Wrex	SJ4043	52°59·1′	2°53·2′W	FM	117
Gwynus	Gwyn	SH3441	52°56·7′	4°27·8′W	X	123
Gwysaney Hall	Flint	SJ2266	53°11·4′	3°9·6′W	A	117
Gwys Fach	Powys	SN7815	51°49·5′	3°45·8′W	W	160
Gwys Fawr	Powys	SN7917	51°50·5′	3°45·0′W	W	160
Gwystre	Powys	SO0665	52°16·7′	3°22·3′W	T	136,147
Gwytherin	Conwy	SH8761	53°8·3′	3°41·0′W	T	116
Gwythrian	Gwyn	SH1627	52°48·8′	4°43·4′W	X	123
Gybhouse Fm	Worcs	SO7273	52°21·5′	2°24·3′W	FM	138
Gydros	Gwyn	SH9046	53°0·2′	3°38·0′W	X	116
Gyfeile	Cered	SN4145	52°5·1′	4°18·8′W	X	146
Gyfelan	Gwyn	SH1932	52°51·5′	4°40·9′W	X	123
Gyfelia	Wrex	SJ3245	53°0·1′	3°0·4′W	T	117
Gyfelog	Gwyn	SH4547	53°0·1′	4°18·2′W	X	115,123
Gyffin	Conwy	SH7776	53°16·2′	3°50·3′W	T	115
Gyffylog	Conwy	SH8170	53°13·1′	3°46·5′W	X	116
Gyfylchau	Powys	SJ0409	52°40·5′	3°24·8′W	X	125
Gyfylchi	Nth Pt Talb	SS8195	51°38·7′	3°42·8′W	X	170
Gyfynys	I of Angl	SH6078	53°17·1′	4°5·6′W	X	114,115
Gylched	I of Angl	SH4876	53°15·8′	4°16·3′W	X	114,115
Gylchedd	Conwy	SH8544	52°59·1′	3°42·4′W	X	124,125
Gylen Castle	Arg & Bt	NM8026	56°22·8′	5°33·4′W	A	49
Gylen Park	Arg & Bt	NM8026	56°22·8′	5°33·4′W	X	49
Gyles Croft	Bucks	SP9306	51°44·9′	0°38·8′W	X	165
Gyllyngvase Beach	Corn	SW8031	50°8·5′	5°4·4′W	X	204
Gypsey Race	E Yorks	TA0968	54°6·0′	0°19·6′W	W	101
Gyran	Orkney	HY2415	59°1·2′	3°18·9′W	H	6
Gyratesmyre Fm	Aberd	NO7879	56°54·4′	2°21·2′W	FM	45
Gyre	Orkney	HY3403	58°54·8′	3°8·3′W	X	6,7
Gyrehouse	Orkney	HY3410	58°58·6′	3°8·4′W	X	6
Gyrn	Denb	SJ1658	53°7·0′	3°14·9′W	T	116
Gyrn	Gwyn	SH6468	53°11·7′	4°1·7′W	H	115
Gyrn	Gwyn	SH8829	52°51·1′	3°39·4′W	X	124,125
Gyrn	Shrops	SJ2633	52°53·6′	3°5·6′W	X	126
Gyrn Castle	Flint	SJ1181	53°19·4′	3°19·8′W	X	116
Gyrn Ddu	Gwyn	SH4046	52°59·5′	4°22·6′W	H	115,123
Gyrn Goch	Gwyn	SH4047	53°0·0′	4°22·7′W	H	115,123
Gyrn-goch	Gwyn	SH5043	52°58·0′	4°13·6′W	X	124
Gyrn Moelfre	Powys	SJ1829	52°51·4′	3°12·7′W	H	125
Gyrnos	Powys	SO0543	52°4·9′	3°22·8′W	X	147,160
Gyrnos Fm	Merth Tyd	SO0408	51°46·0′	3°23·1′W	FM	160
Gyrn Wigau	Gwyn	SH6567	53°11·2′	4°0·8′W	H	115

H

Ha	Orkney	HY3705	58°55·9′	3°5·2′W	X	6,7
Haa	Shetld	HZ2070	59°31·2′	1°38·3′W	X	4
Haa Buttons	Shetld	HU4561	60°20·1′	1°10·6′W	X	2,3
Haaf Gruney (Nature Reserve)	Shetld	HU6398	60°39·9′	0°50·3′W	X	1
Haafs Hellia	Orkney	HY3130	59°9·3′	3°11·9′W	X	6
Haa Geo	Shetld	HU4481	60°30·9′	1°11·4′W	X	1,2,3
Haa Ness	Shetld	HU5461	60°20·0′	1°0·8′W	X	2
Haa of Aywick	Shetld	HU5386	60°33·5′	1°1·5′W	X	1,2,3
Haa of Houlland	Shetld	HP5304	60°43·2′	1°1·2′W	T	1
Haa of Stong	Shetld	HU2985	60°33·1′	1°27·8′W	X	1,3
Haa of Stova	Shetld	HU4015	59°55·3′	1°16·6′W	X	4
Haa of Udhouse	Shetld	HU5294	60°37·8′	1°2·5′W	X	1,2
Haarwell	Shetld	HU3355	60°16·9′	1°23·7′W	X	3
Haas, The	Shetld	HU3729	60°2·9′	1°19·6′W	X	4
Haa, The	Shetld	HP6516	60°49·6′	0°47·8′W	X	1
Haa, The	Shetld	HU4523	59°59·6′	1°11·1′W	X	4
Haa, The	Shetld	HU5460	60°19·5′	1°0·8′W	X	2
Habber Gallows Hill	Oxon	SP2416	51°50·8′	1°38·7′W	X	163
Habberley	Shrops	SJ3903	52°37·5′	2°53·7′W	T	126
Habberley	Worcs	SO8077	52°23·7′	2°17·2′W	T	138
Habbershaw	Aberd	NJ8023	57°18·1′	2°19·5′W	X	38
Habbie's Howe	Midlo	NT1756	55°47·7′	3°19·0′W	X	66
Haben Fm	W Susx	SU8022	50°59·7′	0°51·2′W	FM	197
Haber	Cumbr	NY6014	54°31·4′	2°36·7′W	X	91
Haberdasher's Aske's School, The	Herts	TQ1696	51°39·3′	0°19·0′W	X	166,176
Haberfield Park Fm	N Som	ST5374	51°28·0′	2°40·2′W	FM	172
Habergham	Lancs	SD8133	53°47·8′	2°16·9′W	T	103
Habertoft	Lincs	TF5069	53°12·0′	0°15·2′E	T	122
Habholme Dike	N Yks	SE5332	53°47·1′	1°11·3′W	W	105
Habin	W Susx	SU8022	50°59·7′	0°51·2′W	T	197
Habitancvm (Roman Fort)	Northum	NY8986	55°10·3′	2°9·9′W	R	80
Habrough	NE Lincs	TA1413	53°36·3′	0°16·2′W	T	113
Habton Grange Fm	N Yks	SE7477	54°11·2′	0°51·5′W	FM	100
Haca	N Eil	NF8352	57°27·1′	7°16·7′W	X	22
Hacche Barton	Devon	SS7127	51°1·9′	3°50·0′W	X	180
Hacche Moor	Devon	SS7127	51°1·9′	3°50·0′W	X	180
Haccombe	Devon	SX8970	50°31·4′	3°33·6′W	T	202
Haccombe Ho	Devon	SX8970	50°31·4′	3°33·6′W	X	202
Haceby	Lincs	TF0236	52°54·9′	0°28·6′W	T	130
Haceby Lodge	Lincs	TF0236	52°54·9′	0°28·6′W	X	130
Hacheston	Suff	TM3059	52°11·1′	1°22·3′E	T	156
Hacienda Fun Park	Donc	SE6214	53°37·4′	1°3·3′W	X	111
Hackbridge	Sutton	TQ2865	51°22·4′	0°9·3′W	T	176
Hackensall Hall	Lancs	SD3447	53°55·1′	2°59·9′W	X	102
Hackenthorpe	Sheff	SK4183	53°20·8′	1°22·6′W	T	111,120
Hacker Gill	Cumbr	SD7485	54°15·8′	2°23·5′W	W	98
Hacket	Cumbr	NY3203	54°25·3′	3°2·5′W	X	90
Hackett	Pemb	SN0908	51°44·5′	4°45·6′W	X	158
Hack Fall	N Yks	SE2377	54°11·5′	1°38·4′W	X	99
Hack Field	Shetld	HU1756	60°17·5′	1°41·1′W	X	3
Hack Fm	Wilts	ST9365	51°23·3′	2°5·6′W	FM	173
Hackford	Norf	TG0602	52°34·8′	1°2·8′E	T	144
Hackford	Northum	NY9154	54°53·1′	2°8·0′W	X	87
Hackford Fm	Northum	NY8964	54°58·5′	2°9·9′W	FM	87
Hackford Hall	Norf	TG0722	52°45·6′	1°4·5′E	X	133
Hackforth	N Yks	SE2493	54°20·2′	1°37·4′W	T	99
Hack Green	Ches	SJ6448	53°1·9′	2°31·8′W	T	118
Hack Hall	N upon Ty	NZ2172	55°2·8′	1°39·9′W	X	88
Hack House	Ches	SJ6448	53°1·9′	2°31·8′W	A	118
Hackhurst Downs	Surrey	TQ0948	51°13·5′	0°26·0′W	X	187
Hackhurst Fm	Surrey	TQ0948	51°13·5′	0°26·0′W	FM	187
Hackhurst Stud	E Susx	TQ5612	50°53·4′	0°13·5′E	X	199
Hackingbag	Cumbr	NY4346	54°48·6′	2°52·8′W	X	85
Hacking Hall	Lancs	SD7036	53°49·4′	2°26·9′W	A	103
Hackland	Orkney	HY2719	59°3·4′	3°15·9′W	X	6
Hackland	Orkney	HY3920	59°4·0′	3°3·3′W	T	6
Hackland Fm	Devon	ST0405	50°50·4′	3°21·4′W	FM	192
Hackland Hill	Orkney	HY4021	59°4·6′	3°2·3′W	X	5,6
Hacklete	N Eil	NB1534	58°12·4′	6°50·7′W	T	13
Hackleton	Northnts	SP8055	52°11·5′	0°49·4′W	T	152
Hackley Bay	Aberd	NK0327	57°20·3′	1°56·6′W	W	38
Hackley Brook	Heref	SO6353	52°10·7′	2°32·1′W	W	149
Hackley Fm	Heref	SO6353	52°10·7′	2°32·1′W	FM	149
Hackley Head or Forvie Ness	Aberd	NK0226	57°19·7′	1°57·6′W	X	38
Hacklinge	Kent	TR3454	51°14·4′	1°21·5′E	T	179
Hackman's Gate	Worcs	SO8977	52°23·7′	2°9·3′W	T	139
Hackmarsh	Corn	SS2416	50°55·2′	4°29·9′W	X	190
Hackmead Fm	Somer	ST6851	51°15·7′	2°27·1′W	FM	183
Hacknell	Devon	SS6318	50°56·9′	3°56·6′W	X	180
Hackness	N Yks	SE9790	54°18·0′	0°30·1′W	T	94,101
Hackness	Orkney	ND3390	58°47·8′	3°9·1′W	X	7
Hackness	Somer	ST3345	51°12·3′	2°57·2′W	T	182
Hackness Fm	Somer	ST3445	51°12·3′	2°56·3′W	FM	182
Hackney	Hack	TQ3484	51°32·6′	0°3·7′W	T	176,177
Hackney Cross	Heref	SO7245	52°6·4′	2°24·1′W	X	149
Hackney Marsh	Hack	TQ3686	51°33·6′	0°1·9′W	X	177
Hackney Wick	T Ham	TQ3784	51°32·5′	0°1·1′W	T	177
Hackpen Barton	Devon	ST0911	50°53·7′	3°17·3′W	X	192
Hackpen Fm	Swin	SU1477	51°29·7′	1°47·5′W	FM	173
Hackpen Hill	Devon	ST1112	50°54·3′	3°15·6′W	H	181,193
Hackpen Hill	Oxon	SU3585	51°34·0′	1°29·3′W	X	174
Hackpen Hill	Wilts	SU1274	51°28·1′	1°49·2′W	H	173
Hacks Ness	Orkney	HY6134	59°11·7′	2°40·5′W	X	5
Hacks of Auchenmade	N Ayr	NS3448	55°42·1′	4°38·1′W	X	63
Hackthorn	Lincs	SK9982	53°19·8′	0°30·4′W	T	121
Hackthorn	Wilts	SU1545	51°12·5′	1°46·7′W	T	184
Hackthorne	Corn	SS2402	50°47·7′	4°29·5′W	X	190

Hackthorne Fm	Somer	ST7420	50°59·0'	2°21·8'W	FM	183
Hackthorn Hill	Dorset	ST5001	50°48·6'	2°42·2'W	H	194
Hackthorpe	Cumbr	NY5423	54°36·3'	2°42·3'W	T	90
Hackwood	Northum	NY9363	54°57·9'	2°6·1'W	X	87
Hackwood Copse	Hants	SU3949	51°14·6'	1°26·1'W	F	185
Hackwood Fm	C of Derb	SK3036	52°55·5'	1°32·8'W	FM	128
Hackwood Fm	Hants	SU6649	51°14·4'	1°2·9'W	FM	185,186
Hackwood Ho	Hants	SU6449	51°14·4'	1°4·6'W	X	185
Hackwood Park	Hants	SU6549	51°14·4'	1°3·7'W	X	185,186
Hackwoods Fm	E Susx	TQ7224	50°59·6'	0°27·5'E	FM	199
Hackworthy	Devon	SX8093	50°43·7'	3°41·6'W	X	191
Hackworthy Brakes	Devon	SX8192	50°43·2'	3°40·8'W	F	191
Hackworthy Fm	Devon	SX8794	50°44·3'	3°35·7'W	FM	192
Haclait	N Eil	NF8148	57°24·9'	7°18·3'W	T	22
Hà-cleit	N Eil	NG0387	57°46·7'	6°59·3'W	X	18
Ha Cleuch	D & G	NS8505	55°19·8'	3°48·3'W	X	71,78
Haconby	Lincs	TF1025	52°48·9'	0°21·7'W	T	130
Haconby Fen	Lincs	TF1425	52°48·9'	0°18·1'W	X	130
Haco's Ness	Orkney	HY5214	59°0·9'	2°49·7'W	X	6
Hacton	Hav	TQ5484	51°32·3'	0°13·6'E	T	177
Hadborough	Somer	SS9628	51°2·8'	3°28·6'W	X	181
Hadd	Shetld	HU3689	60°35·2'	1°20·1'W	X	1,2
Haddacott	Devon	SS5024	51°0·0'	4°7·9'W	T	180
Hadden	Scot Bord	NT7836	55°37·3'	2°20·5'W	T	74
Hadden	Wilts	SU0634	51°6·5'	1°54·5'W	X	184
Haddenham	Bucks	SP7408	51°46·2'	0°55·3'W	T	165
Haddenham	Cambs	TL4675	52°21·4'	0°9·0'E	T	143
Haddenham and Thame Parkway	Bucks	SP7208	51°46·2'	0°57·0'W	X	165
Haddenham End Field	Cambs	TL4676	52°22·0'	0°9·1'E	T	143
Haddenham Low	Bucks	SP7510	51°47·2'	0°54·4'W	X	165
Haddenham Pastures	Cambs	TL4775	52°21·4'	0°9·9'E	X	143
Hadden Hill	Oxon	SU5490	51°36·6'	1°12·8'W	X	164,174
Hadden Hill	Wilts	SU0734	51°6·5'	1°53·6'W	X	184
Hadderdale	Cumbr	NY6815	54°32·0'	2°29·2'W	X	91
Haddieweel	Orkney	HY4405	58°56·0'	2°57·9'W	X	6,7
Haddington	E Loth	NT5173	55°57·1'	2°46·6'W	T	66
Haddington	Lincs	SK9163	53°9·6'	0°37·9'W	T	121
Haddington Hill	Bucks	SP8809	51°46·6'	0°43·1'W	X	165
Haddiport	Devon	SS4510	50°52·4'	4°11·8'W	X	190
Haddiscoe	Norf	TM4496	52°30·7'	1°36·2'E	T	134
Haddiscoe Marshes	Norf	TM4598	52°31·7'	1°37·1'E	X	134
Haddiscoe Sta	Norf	TM4598	52°31·7'	1°37·1'E	X	134
Haddo	Aberd	NJ6146	57°30·4'	2°38·6'W	X	29
Haddo	Aberd	NJ8238	57°26·2'	2°17·5'W	X	29,30
Haddo	Aberd	NK0129	57°21·3'	1°58·5'W	X	38
Haddo	Aberd	NK0757	57°36·4'	1°52·5'W	X	30
Haddo	Aberd	NO7473	56°51·1'	2°25·1'W	X	45
Haddoch	Aberd	NJ5344	57°29·3'	2°46·6'W	X	29
Haddoch	Moray	NJ3927	57°20·0'	3°0·3'W	X	37
Haddock Low	Derby	SK0980	53°19·3'	1°51·5'W	X	110
Haddock Sands	Shetld	HU3443	60°10·5'	1°22·7'W	W	4
Haddocks, The	N Yks	SE4565	54°5·0'	1°18·3'W	X	99
Haddockston	Renf	NS3970	55°54·0'	4°34·1'W	X	63
Haddockstones	N Yks	SE2765	54°5·1'	1°34·8'W	X	99
Haddockstones Fm	N Yks	SE2048	53°55·9'	1°41·3'W	FM	104
Haddo Ho	Aberd	NJ8634	57°24·0'	2°13·5'W	X	30
Haddon	Cambs	TL1392	52°31·1'	0°19·7'W	T	142
Haddon	Staffs	SJ9760	53°8·5'	2°2·3'W	X	118
Haddon End Fm	Somer	SS9927	51°2·2'	3°26·1'W	FM	181
Haddon Fields	Derby	SK2165	53°11·1'	1°40·7'W	X	119
Haddon Fm	Ches	SJ9569	53°13·3'	2°4·1'W	FM	118
Haddon Fm	Somer	SS9528	51°2·7'	3°29·5'W	FM	181
Haddon Fm	Somer	ST2631	51°4·6'	3°3·0'W	FM	182
Haddon Grove	Derby	SK1766	53°11·7'	1°44·3'W	X	119
Haddon Hall	Derby	SK2366	53°11·7'	1°38·9'W	A	119
Haddon Hall	Suff	TM2747	52°4·7'	1°19·2'E	X	169
Haddon Hall Fm	Ches	SJ3175	53°16·3'	3°1·7'W	FM	117
Haddon Hill	Devon	ST2803	50°49·6'	3°1·0'W	X	193
Haddon Hill	Shrops	SO4395	52°33·2'	2°50·0'W	H	137
Haddon Hill	Somer	SS9728	51°2·8'	3°27·8'W	H	181
Haddon Hill	Wilts	ST8731	51°4·9'	2°10·7'W	H	183
Haddon Ho	Derby	SK2267	53°12·2'	1°39·8'W	X	119
Haddon Lodge	Dorset	ST7016	50°56·8'	2°25·2'W	X	183
Haddon Lodge Fm	Cambs	TL1393	52°31·6'	0°19·7'W	FM	142
Haddon Park Fm	Derby	SK2367	53°12·2'	1°38·9'W	FM	119
Haddon Pasture	Notts	SK5974	53°15·8'	1°6·5'W	F	120
Hade Edge	Kirk	SE1405	53°32·7'	1°46·9'W	T	110
Hademore	Staffs	SK1708	52°40·4'	1°44·5'W	T	128
Haden Cross	Sand	SO9685	52°28·0'	2°3·1'W	T	139
Hades Hill	Roch	SD9020	53°40·8'	2°8·7'W	H	103
Hadfast	Midlo	NT3868	55°54·3'	2°59·1'W	X	66
Hadfield	Derby	SK0196	53°27·9'	1°58·7'W	T	110
Hadfold Fm	W Susx	TQ0723	51°0·0'	0°28·1'W	FM	197
Hadham Cross	Herts	TL4218	51°50·8'	0°4·1'E	T	167
Hadham Ford	Herts	TL4322	51°52·9'	0°5·1'E	T	167
Hadham Hall (School)	Herts	TL4522	51°52·9'	0°6·8'E	A	167
Hadham Mill	Herts	TL4217	51°50·2'	0°4·1'E	X	167
Hadham Park	Herts	TL4622	51°52·9'	0°7·7'E	X	167
Hadleigh	Essex	TQ8187	51°33·4'	0°37·1'E	T	178
Hadleigh	Suff	TM0242	52°2·6'	0°57·1'E	T	155
Hadleigh Fm	Suff	TM0641	52°2·0'	1°0·6'E	FM	155
Hadleigh Heath	Suff	TL9941	52°2·1'	0°54·5'E	T	155
Hadleigh Marsh	Essex	TQ8085	51°32·3'	0°36·1'E	X	178
Hadleigh Railway Walk	Suff	TM0440	52°1·5'	0°58·8'E	X	155
Hadleigh Ray	Essex	TQ8184	51°31·8'	0°37·0'E	W	178
Hadler's Hole	Norf	TL8786	52°26·6'	0°45·5'E	X	144
Hadley	Barnet	TQ2496	51°39·2'	0°12·1'W	T	166,176
Hadley	Shrops	SJ5141	52°58·1'	2°43·4'W	X	117
Hadley	Worcs	SO8663	52°16·1'	2°11·9'W	T	150
Hadley	Wrekin	SJ6712	52°42·5'	2°28·9'W	T	127
Hadley Brook	Worcs	SO8664	52°16·7'	2°11·9'W	W	150
Hadley Castle	Wrekin	SJ6712	52°42·5'	2°28·9'W	T	127
Hadley End	Staffs	SK1320	52°46·9'	1°48·0'W	T	128
Hadley Hall	Ches	SJ5546	53°0·8'	2°39·8'W	X	117
Hadleys, The	Shrops	SO7584	52°27·4'	2°21·7'W	X	138
Hadley Wood	Enf	TQ2697	51°39·7'	0°10·3'W	T	166,176
Hadlow	Kent	TQ6350	51°13·8'	0°20·5'E	T	188
Hadlow Down	E Susx	TQ5324	50°59·9'	0°11·2'E	T	199
Hadlow Ho	E Susx	TQ5424	50°59·9'	0°12·1'E	X	199

Hadlow Place Fm	Kent	TQ6248	51°12·7'	0°19·6'E	FM	188
Hadlow Stair	Kent	TQ6047	51°12·2'	0°17·8'E	T	188
Hadman's Place	Kent	TQ8642	51°9·0'	0°40·0'E	X	189
Hadnall	Shrops	SJ5220	52°46·8'	2°42·3'W	T	126
Hadnock Court	Monm	SO5314	51°49·6'	2°40·5'W	X	162
Hadodty Newydd	Gwyn	SH5857	53°5·7'	4°6·8'W	X	115
Hadrian Stud	Cambs	TL6561	52°13·6'	0°25·4'E	X	154
Hadrian's Wall	Cumbr	NY2361	54°56·5'	3°11·7'W	R	85
Hadrian's Wall	Cumbr	NY3359	54°55·5'	3°2·3'W	R	85
Hadrian's Wall	Northum	NY8471	55°2·2'	2°14·6'W	R	86,87
Hadrian's Wall	Northum	NY9669	55°1·2'	2°3·3'W	R	87
Hadrian's Wall	Northum	NZ1267	55°0·1'	1°48·3'W	R	88
Hadspen	Somer	ST6532	51°5·4'	2°29·6'W	T	183
Hadspen Ho	Somer	ST6631	51°4·9'	2°28·7'W	X	183
Hadstock	Essex	TL5544	52°4·6'	0°16·1'E	T	154
Hadstock Common	Essex	TL5543	52°4·0'	0°16·1'E	X	154
Hadston	Northum	NZ2599	55°17·3'	1°36·0'W	T	81
Hadston Carrs	Northum	NU2800	55°17·8'	1°33·1'W	X	81
Hadwin's Close	Northum	NU1510	55°23·3'	1°45·4'W	X	81
Hadworth Fm	W Susx	SU9914	50°55·2'	0°35·1'W	FM	197
Hady	Derby	SK3970	53°13·8'	1°24·5'W	T	119
Hadyard Hill	S Ayr	NX2799	55°15·5'	4°42·9'W	H	76
Hadzor	Worcs	SO9162	52°15·6'	2°7·5'W	T	150
Hadzor Hall	Worcs	SO9162	52°15·6'	2°7·5'W	X	150
Hael	Swan	SS5687	51°34·0'	4°4·3'W	X	159
Haelfaes	V of Glam	ST0975	51°28·2'	3°18·2'W	X	171
Haelfron	Powys	SJ0008	52°39·9'	3°28·3'W	X	125
Hael Woods	Monm	SO5307	51°45·8'	2°40·5'W	F	162
Haerie	Shetld	HU5155	60°16·8'	1°4·2'W	X	3
Hafan	Powys	SJ0410	52°41·0'	3°24·8'W	X	125
Haffenden Fm	Kent	TQ8736	51°5·8'	0°40·6'E	FM	189
Haffenden Fm	Kent	TR0628	51°1·1'	0°56·6'E	FM	189
Haffenden Quarter	Kent	TQ8840	51°7·9'	0°41·6'E	T	189
Haffield	Heref	SO7233	51°59·9'	2°24·1'W	X	149
Hafna Mine (dis)	Conwy	SH7860	53°7·6'	3°49·0'W	X	115
Hafnant	Conwy	SH8046	53°0·1'	3°46·9'W	W	116
Hafod	Carm	SN2122	51°52·3'	4°35·6'W	X	145,158
Hafod	Carm	SN3029	51°56·3'	4°28·0'W	X	145
Hafod	Carm	SN4423	51°53·3'	4°15·6'W	X	159
Hafod	Carm	SN5134	51°59·3'	4°9·8'W	X	146
Hafod	Carm	SN5924	51°54·0'	4°2·6'W	X	159
Hafod	Carm	SN6126	51°55·2'	4°0·9'W	X	146
Hafod	Cered	SN1850	52°7·3'	4°39·1'W	X	145
Hafod	Cered	SN2546	52°5·3'	4°32·9'W	X	145
Hafod	Cered	SN5463	52°15·0'	4°7·9'W	X	146
Hafod	Conwy	SH8058	53°6·6'	3°47·2'W	X	116
Hafod	Conwy	SH8963	53°9·4'	3°39·2'W	X	116
Hafod	Conwy	SH9746	53°0·3'	3°31·7'W	X	116
Hafod	Conwy	SJ0068	53°12·2'	3°29·4'W	X	116
Hafod	Flint	SJ2163	53°9·7'	3°10·5'W	X	117
Hafod	Flint	SJ2172	53°14·6'	3°10·6'W	X	117
Hafod	Flint	SJ2959	53°7·6'	3°3·3'W	X	117
Hafod	Gwyn	SH3743	52°57·8'	4°25·2'W	X	123
Hafod	Gwyn	SH5361	53°7·8'	4°11·4'W	X	114,115
Hafod	I of Angl	SH4479	53°17·3'	4°20·0'W	X	114,115
Hafod	Nth Pt Talb	SS8089	51°35·5'	3°43·5'W	X	170
Hafod	Pemb	SN1941	52°2·5'	4°38·0'W	X	145
Hafod	Pemb	SN2635	51°59·4'	4°31·6'W	X	145
Hafod	Powys	SH9807	52°39·3'	3°30·1'W	X	125
Hafod	Powys	SJ0214	52°43·1'	3°26·7'W	X	125
Hafod	Powys	SJ0919	52°45·9'	3°20·5'W	X	125
Hafod	Powys	SJ1020	52°46·4'	3°19·6'W	X	125
Hafod	Powys	SJ1427	52°50·3'	3°16·2'W	X	125
Hafod	Powys	SJ2032	52°53·0'	3°10·9'W	X	126
Hafod	Powys	SN9495	52°32·8'	3°33·4'W	X	136
Hafod	Powys	SN9793	52°31·8'	3°30·7'W	X	136
Hafod	Powys	SO0687	52°28·6'	3°22·6'W	X	136
Hafod	Swan	SS6694	51°38·0'	3°55·8'W	T	159
Hafod	V of Glam	SS9966	51°23·3'	3°26·7'W	X	170
Hafod Adams	Wrex	SJ1633	52°53·5'	3°14·5'W	X	125
Hafodau	Cered	SN6980	52°24·4'	3°55·2'W	X	135
Hafod-bach	Conwy	SH8464	53°9·9'	3°43·7'W	X	116
Hafod Bilston	Denb	SJ2051	53°3·3'	3°11·2'W	X	117
Hafod-boeth	Gwyn	SH6441	52°57·2'	4°1·1'W	X	124
Hafod Br	Carm	SN6936	52°0·7'	3°54·1'W	X	146,160
Hafod-Caradoc	Denb	SH9859	53°7·3'	3°31·1'W	X	116
Hafod-Dafydd	Conwy	SH9762	53°9·0'	3°32·0'W	X	116
Hafod Dafydd Mynydd	Conwy	SH9459	53°7·3'	3°34·6'W	X	116
Hafod-ddu	Pemb	SN0928	51°55·3'	4°46·3'W	X	145,158
Hafod-dew	Flint	SJ1573	53°15·1'	3°16·0'W	X	116
Hafod-Dinbych	Conwy	SH8953	53°4·0'	3°39·0'W	X	116
Hafod Dre Uchaf	Conwy	SH8852	53°3·5'	3°39·9'W	X	116
Hafod Dwyryd	Conwy	SH7949	53°1·7'	3°47·9'W	A	115
Hafod-dywyll	Gwyn	SH6815	52°43·2'	3°56·9'W	X	124
Hafod-Eddig	Conwy	SH8649	53°1·8'	3°41·6'W	X	116
Hafod Fawr	Carm	SN8131	51°58·1'	3°43·5'W	X	160
Hafod-fawr	Conwy	SH8463	53°9·3'	3°43·7'W	X	116
Hafod-fawr	Gwyn	SH7240	52°56·8'	3°53·9'W	X	124
Hafodfeddgar	Powys	SN8785	52°27·3'	3°39·4'W	X	135,136
Hafod-ferched	Pemb	SM9333	51°57·7'	5°0·4'W	X	157
Hafod Feredydd	Gwyn	SH7822	52°47·2'	3°48·1'W	X	124
Hafod Fm	Carm	SN3220	51°51·4'	4°26·0'W	FM	145,159
Hafod Fm	Carm	SN6621	51°52·5'	3°56·4'W	FM	159
Hafod Fm	Wrex	SJ2444	52°59·5'	3°7·5'W	FM	117
Hafod Fm	Wrex	SJ2551	53°3·3'	3°6·7'W	FM	117
Hafod Fraith	Gwyn	SH7427	52°49·8'	3°51·8'W	X	124
Hafod-fraith	Powys	SN9278	52°23·6'	3°34·8'W	X	136,147
Hafod Fudr	Powys	SH9621	52°46·8'	3°32·1'W	X	125
Hafod Garregog	Gwyn	SH6044	52°58·7'	4°4·7'W	X	124
Hafod-gau	Conwy	SH9062	53°8·9'	3°38·3'W	X	116
Hafod Grove	Pemb	SN1244	52°4·0'	4°44·2'W	T	145
Hafodgwenllian	Conwy	SH7150	53°2·1'	3°55·0'W	X	115
Hafodheulog	Nth Pt Talb	SS8484	51°32·8'	3°40·0'W	X	170
Hafod Hir	Carm	SN4819	51°51·2'	4°12·0'W	X	159
Hafodhir	Cered	SN5561	52°13·9'	4°7·0'W	X	146
Hafod Hir	Powys	SJ0128	52°50·7'	3°27·8'W	H	125
Hafod-hir-isaf	Cered	SN5562	52°14·5'	4°7·0'W	X	146
Hafod Ho	Cered	SN7068	52°17·9'	3°54·0'W	X	135,147
Hafod Ho	Wrex	SJ3146	53°0·7'	3°1·3'W	X	117
Hafod Ifan	Conwy	SH8348	53°1·2'	3°44·3'W	X	116

Hafodig	Powys	SJ2131	52°52·5'	3°10·0'W	X	126
Hafod Ithel	Cered	SN6167	52°17·3'	4°1·9'W	H	135
Hafodiwan	Cered	SN3854	52°9·9'	4°21·7'W	T	145
Hafodlas	Cered	SN5969	52°18·3'	4°3·7'W	X	135
Hafodlas	Cered	SN6757	52°12·0'	3°56·4'W	X	146
Hafod Las	Cered	SN7350	52°8·3'	3°50·9'W	H	146,147
Hafod-las	Conwy	SH7855	53°4·9'	3°48·9'W	X	115
Hafod Las	Conwy	SH8347	53°0·7'	3°44·2'W	X	116
Hafodlas	Conwy	SH8357	53°6·1'	3°44·4'W	X	116
Hafodlas	Gwyn	SH5361	53°7·8'	4°11·4'W	X	114,115
Hafodllin	I of Angl	SH4091	53°23·7'	4°24·0'W	X	114
Hafod-llwyn	Denb	SJ0177	53°17·1'	3°28·7'W	X	116
Hafod-lom	Conwy	SH8571	53°13·7'	3°43·0'W	X	116
Hafod-lom	Conwy	SH8967	53°11·6'	3°39·3'W	X	116
Hafod-lom	Powys	SJ0300	52°35·6'	3°25·5'W	X	136
Hafodlon	Gwyn	SH3939	52°55·7'	4°23·3'W	X	123
Hafod-lwyd	Denb	SJ1848	53°1·6'	3°13·0'W	X	116
Hafodneddyn	Carm	SN5824	51°54·0'	4°3·4'W	X	159
Hafod-newydd	Cered	SN7563	52°15·3'	3°49·5'W	X	146,147
Hafod-oer	Gwyn	SH7615	52°43·4'	3°49·8'W	X	124
Hafodol	I of Angl	SH4089	53°22·7'	4°23·9'W	X	114
Hafod Onnen	I of Angl	SH4291	53°23·8'	4°22·2'W	X	114
Hafodonnen	I of Angl	SH4291	53°23·8'	4°22·2'W	X	114
Hafod-Owen	Gwyn	SH6248	53°0·9'	4°3·0'W	X	115
Hafodowen	Powys	SH9202	52°36·5'	3°35·3'W	X	136
Hafod-Peris	Cered	SN5567	52°17·2'	4°7·2'W	X	135
Hafod Rhisgl	Gwyn	SH6552	53°3·1'	4°0·4'W	X	115
Hafod-rhŷd	Cered	SN7264	52°15·8'	3°52·1'W	X	146,147
Hafodrisclawdd	Caer	SO1801	51°42·3'	3°10·8'W	X	171
Hafod Ruffydd	Gwyn	SH5749	53°1·4'	4°7·5'W	X	115
Hafod Ruffydd Isaf	Gwyn	SH5750	53°1·9'	4°7·5'W	X	115
Hafodrwynos	Carm	SN5536	52°0·5'	4°6·4'W	X	146
Hafod-tafolog	Carm	SN7036	52°0·7'	3°53·3'W	X	146,160
Hafod Tan-y-graig	Gwyn	SH6350	53°2·0'	4°2·2'W	X	115
Hafod-tridrws	Carm	SN5134	51°59·3'	4°9·8'W	X	146
Hafodty	Conwy	SH7575	53°15·7'	3°52·0'W	X	115
Hafodty	Conwy	SH7969	53°12·5'	3°48·3'W	X	115
Hafodty	Conwy	SH8563	53°9·3'	3°42·8'W	X	116
Hafodty	Conwy	SH8571	53°13·7'	3°43·0'W	X	116
Hafodty	Conwy	SH9769	53°12·7'	3°32·1'W	X	116
Hafodty	Gwyn	SH7301	52°35·8'	3°52·1'W	X	135
Hafodty	Powys	SJ2029	52°51·4'	3°10·9'W	X	126
Hafod Ty Ddu	Denb	SJ0159	53°7·4'	3°28·4'W	X	116
Hafodty Fm	Conwy	SH8378	53°17·4'	3°44·9'W	FM	116
Hafodty Gwyn	Conwy	SH8452	53°3·4'	3°43·4'W	X	116
Hafodty-hendre	Gwyn	SH7627	52°49·8'	3°50·0'W	X	124
Hafodty Wen	Denb	SJ1046	53°0·5'	3°20·1'W	X	116
Hafod Uchaf	Gwyn	SH6343	52°58·3'	4°2·0'W	X	124
Hafod-uchaf	Gwyn	SH6521	52°46·4'	3°59·7'W	X	124
Hafod-uchel	Gwyn	SH9833	52°53·3'	3°30·6'W	X	125
Hafodunos Hall	Conwy	SH8667	53°11·5'	3°42·0'W	X	116
Hafod-wen	Carm	SN3918	51°50·5'	4°19·8'W	X	159
Hafod-wen	Cered	SN2043	52°3·6'	4°37·2'W	X	145
Hafod-wen	Conwy	SH9850	53°2·5'	3°30·9'W	X	116
Hafodwen	Denb	SH9859	53°7·3'	3°31·1'W	X	116
Hafod-wen	Gwyn	SH7335	52°54·1'	3°52·9'W	X	124
Hafod-wen	Gwyn	SH8441	52°57·5'	3°43·2'W	X	124,125
Hafodwen	Powys	SN9199	52°34·9'	3°36·1'W	X	136
Hafod-wen	Rho Cyn Taf	SN9800	51°41·6'	3°28·2'W	X	170
Hafod-Wen	Wrex	SJ2749	53°2·2'	3°4·9'W	X	117
Hafod Wennol Fm	Nth Pt Talb	SN6709	51°46·1'	3°55·3'W	FM	159
Hafod-weunog	Cered	SN6670	52°18·9'	3°57·6'W	X	135
Hafodwnog	Cered	SN5565	52°16·1'	4°7·1'W	X	135
Hafodwnog	Powys	SN7693	52°31·5'	3°49·3'W	X	135
Hafod Wood	Conwy	SJ0068	53°12·2'	3°29·4'W	F	116
Hafodwynog	Carm	SN3948	52°6·7'	4°20·7'W	X	145
Hafod-y-Brenhin	Gwyn	SH6724	52°48·1'	3°58·0'W	X	124
Hafod-y-bryn	Gwyn	SH5826	52°49·0'	4°6·0'W	X	124
Hafod-y-Bryn	Gwyn	SH9143	52°58·6'	3°37·0'W	X	125
Hafod-y-bwch	Wrex	SJ3147	53°1·2'	3°1·3'W	X	117
Hafod-y-calch	Denb	SJ0542	52°58·3'	3°24·5'W	X	125
Hafod-y-cefn-plâs-onn	Conwy	SH9861	53°8·4'	3°31·1'W	X	116
Hafod-y-coed	Denb	SJ0772	53°14·5'	3°23·2'W	X	116
Hafod-y-coed	Gwyn	SH5927	52°49·6'	4°5·2'W	X	124
Hafod-y-cwm	Flint	SJ1468	53°12·4'	3°16·9'W	X	116
Hafod-y-dafal	Blae Gw	SO2003	51°43·4'	3°9·1'W	X	171
Hafodydd Brithion	Gwyn	SH6449	53°1·5'	4°1·3'W	X	115
Hafod-y-fedw	Gwyn	SH7221	52°46·5'	3°53·5'W	X	124
Hafod-y-foel	Powys	SH9201	52°36·0'	3°35·3'W	X	136
Hafod-y-garreg	Conwy	SH7367	53°11·3'	3°53·6'W	X	115
Hafod y Garreg	Conwy	SH8752	53°3·4'	3°40·8'W	X	116
Hafod y garreg	Gwyn	SH8637	52°55·3'	3°41·3'W	X	124,125
Hafod-y-garreg	Powys	SN7299	52°34·7'	3°52·9'W	X	135
Hafodygarreg	Powys	SO1041	52°3·8'	3°18·4'W	X	148,161
Hafod-y-garreg	Wrex	SJ1836	52°55·2'	3°12·8'W	X	125
Hafod-y-gôg	Conwy	SH9066	53°11·0'	3°38·4'W	X	116
Hafod-y-gors	Cered	SN5560	52°13·4'	4°7·0'W	X	146
Hafodygors-wen	Conwy	SH7367	53°11·3'	3°53·6'W	X	115
Hafod-y-Green	Denb	SJ0471	53°13·9'	3°25·9'W	T	116
Hafod-y-grugyn	Carm	SN5129	51°56·6'	4°9·7'W	X	146
Hafod-y-llan	Gwyn	SH6251	53°2·6'	4°3·1'W	X	115
Hafod-y-llan Isaf	Conwy	SH9553	53°4·1'	3°33·6'W	X	116
Hafod-y-llyn	Gwyn	SH5929	52°50·6'	4°5·3'W	W	124
Hafod-y-llyn	Gwyn	SH5944	52°58·7'	4°5·6'W	X	124
Hafodymaidd	Carm	SN6340	52°2·7'	3°59·5'W	X	146
Hafod-y-meirch	Gwyn	SH7615	52°43·4'	3°49·8'W	X	124
Hafod-y-mŷn	I of Angl	SH4185	53°20·5'	4°22·9'W	X	114
Hafod-y-pant	Carm	SN8043	52°4·6'	3°44·7'W	X	147,160
Hafod-y-porth	Gwyn	SH6049	53°1·4'	4°4·8'W	X	115
Hafod-y-pwll	Carm	SN2128	51°55·5'	4°35·8'W	X	145,158
Hafod-yr-Abad	Denb	SJ1848	53°1·6'	3°13·0'W	X	116
Hafod-yr-ancr	Powys	SN9853	52°10·2'	3°29·1'W	X	147
Hafodyredwydd	Conwy	SH7645	52°59·5'	3°50·4'W	X	115
Hafod-yr-Esgob	Gwyn	SH9043	52°58·6'	3°37·9'W	X	125
Hafod-yr-Haf	Gwyn	SH5569	53°12·1'	4°9·9'W	X	114,115
Hafod-yr-haidd	Wrex	SJ2138	52°56·3'	3°10·1'W	X	126
Hafod-y-rhiw	Conwy	SH7264	53°9·7'	3°54·5'W	X	115
Hafod-yr-ŵyn	Cered	SN4851	52°8·4'	4°12·9'W	X	146
Hafodyrynys	Caer	ST2299	51°41·3'	3°7·3'W	T	171
Hafod-y-wern	Gwyn	SH4149	53°1·1'	4°21·8'W	X	115,123

Hafotty	I of Angl	SH5678	53°17·0′	4°9·2′W	X	114,115
Hafotty Bach	Denb	SJ0357	53°6·3′	3°26·5′W	X	116
Hafotty Bennett	Conwy	SH8369	53°12·6′	3°44·7′W	X	116
Hafotty-boeth	Denb	SJ0749	53°2·1′	3°22·8′W	X	116
Hafotty Cerrig	Conwy	SH9346	53°0·3′	3°35·3′W	X	116
Hafotty Covert	I of Angl	SH5677	53°16·5′	4°9·2′W	F	114,115
Hafotty-fâch	Gwyn	SH6613	52°42·1′	3°58·6′W	X	124
Hafotty Fawr	Conwy	SH8259	53°7·2′	3°45·4′W	X	116
Hafotty-Garthmeilio	Conwy	SH9545	52°59·8′	3°33·5′W	X	116
Hafotty Gwastadfryn	Gwyn	SH6712	52°41·6′	3°57·7′W	X	124
Hafotty Hendre	Conwy	SJ0051	53°3·1′	3°29·1′W	X	116
Hafotty Isaf	Gwyn	SH9742	52°58·2′	3°31·6′W	X	125
Hafotty Newydd	Conwy	SJ0054	53°4·7′	3°29·2′W	X	116
Hafotty Wen	Conwy	SH9752	53°3·6′	3°31·8′W	X	116
Hafoty	Conwy	SH8365	53°10·4′	3°44·6′W	X	116
Hafoty Cedig	Powys	SH9925	52°49·0′	3°29·5′W	X	125
Hafoty Foel	Denb	SJ0347	53°0·9′	3°26·4′W	X	116
Hafoty Gwyn	Conwy	SH7370	53°13·0′	3°53·7′W	X	115
Hafoty Llechwedd	Conwy	SH9750	53°2·5′	3°31·8′W	X	116
Hafoty'r Bwlch	Gwyn	SH9116	52°44·1′	3°36·5′W	X	125
Hafoty Siôn Llwyd	Denb	SH9856	53°5·7′	3°31·0′W	X	116
Hafoty Wen	Gwyn	SJ0038	52°56·0′	3°28·9′W	X	125
Hafrena	Powys	SN9551	52°9·1′	3°31·7′W	W	147
Hafren Forest	Powys	SN8487	52°28·4′	3°42·1′W	F	135,136
Hafryn	Shrops	SJ2124	52°48·7′	3°9·9′W	X	126
Hafton Ho	Arg & Bt	NS1779	55°58·4′	4°55·5′W	X	63
Hag Bank	Northum	NY7961	54°56·8′	2°19·2′W	X	86,87
Hagbourne Hill	Oxon	SU4986	51°34·5′	1°17·2′W	H	174
Hagbourne Mill Fm	Oxon	SU5387	51°35·0′	1°13·7′W	FM	174
Hagbrae	Midlo	NT3761	55°50·5′	2°59·9′W	X	66
Hagdale	Shetld	HP6410	60°46·3′	0°49·0′W	X	1
Hagdales Ness	Shetld	HP5708	60°45·3′	0°56·7′W	X	1
Hag Dike	N Yks	SD9873	54°9·4′	2°1·4′W	X	98
Hagdon	Northum	NU1122	55°29·7′	1°49·1′W	X	75
Hag End	Cumbr	SD4397	54°22·2′	2°52·2′W	X	97
Hag Fold	Wigan	SD6704	53°32·1′	2°29·5′W	T	109
Hagg	Cumbr	SD2189	54°17·7′	3°12·4′W	X	96
Hagg	D & G	NY3779	55°6·3′	2°58·8′W	X	85
Hagg	Northum	NT8635	55°36·8′	2°12·9′W	X	74
Hagg	N Yks	SD8978	54°12·1′	2°9·7′W	X	98
Haggaback	N Yks	NZ6608	54°28·0′	0°58·5′W	X	94
Haggard's Lodge	Norf	TF8737	52°54·1′	0°47·2′E	X	132
Haggas Hall	N Yks	SE2947	53°55·3′	1°33·1′W	X	104
Haggate	Lancs	SD8735	53°48·9′	2°11·4′W	T	103
Haggate	Oldham	SD9107	53°33·8′	2°7·7′W	T	109
Haggaton	Devon	SS3104	50°48·9′	4°23·6′W	X	190
Haggbeck	Cumbr	NY4773	55°3·2′	2°49·4′W	X	86
Hagg Beck	N Yks	SD9078	54°12·1′	2°8·8′W	W	98
Hagg Br	E Yorks	SE7145	53°54·0′	0°54·7′W	X	105,106
Haggburn Gate	Northum	NY8253	54°52·5′	2°16·4′W	X	86,87
Hagg Bush	N Yks	SE6027	53°44·4′	1°5·0′W	X	105
Hagg Common	N Yks	SE6391	54°18·9′	1°1·5′W	X	94,100
Hagg Dean	Northum	NU1627	55°32·4′	1°44·4′W	X	75
Hagge Farm	Derby	SK4176	53°17·0′	1°22·7′W	FM	120
Hagg End	N Yks	SE5792	54°19·5′	1°7·0′W	X	100
Hagg End Fm	N Yks	SE6892	54°19·4′	0°56·8′W	FM	94,100
Haggerleases Fm	Durham	NZ1126	54°38·0′	1°49·4′W	FM	92
Haggersta	Shetld	HU3847	60°12·6′	1°18·4′W	T	3
Haggerston	Hack	TQ3383	51°32·0′	0°4·6′W	T	176,177
Haggerston	Northum	NU0443	55°41·1′	1°55·7′W	T	75
Haggerston Burn	Northum	NU0443	55°41·1′	1°55·7′W	X	75
Hagg Farms	N Yks	SE6787	54°16·7′	0°57·8′W	FM	94,100
Hagg Fm	Ches	SJ9482	53°20·3′	2°5·0′W	FM	109
Hagg Fm	Derby	SK1688	53°23·6′	1°45·2′W	FM	110
Hagg Fm	Durham	NZ2333	54°41·7′	1°38·2′W	FM	93
Hagg Fm	Northum	NZ1064	54°58·5′	1°50·2′W	FM	88
Hagg Fm	Notts	SK6749	53°2·3′	0°59·6′W	FM	129
Hagg Fm	N Yks	SD9854	53°59·2′	2°1·4′W	FM	103
Hagg Fm	N Yks	SE6271	54°8·1′	1°2·6′W	FM	100
Hagg Fm	Red & Cl	NZ6719	54°33·9′	0°57·4′W	FM	94
Hagg Fm	York	SE6752	53°57·8′	0°58·3′W	FM	105,106
Hagg Fms	Derby	SK4239	52°57·0′	1°22·1′W	FM	129
Hagg Foot	Cumbr	SD4997	54°22·2′	2°46·7′W	X	97
Hagg Gill	Cumbr	NY4207	54°27·6′	2°53·3′W	W	90
Hagg Hall	N Yks	SE5684	54°15·2′	1°8·0′W	X	100
Hagg Hill	Derby	SK4066	53°11·6′	1°23·7′W	X	120
Hagg Hill	D & G	NY3679	55°6·3′	2°59·8′W	X	85
Hagg Hill	Ghead	NZ1861	54°56·8′	1°42·7′W	X	88
Hagg Hill	Notts	SK5774	53°15·8′	1°8·3′W	X	120
Hagg Ho	Derby	SK4161	53°8·9′	1°22·8′W	X	120
Hagg Ho	Durham	NZ1356	54°54·2′	1°47·4′W	X	88
Hagg Ho	N Yks	NZ8808	54°27·8′	0°38·1′W	X	94
Hagg Ho	N Yks	SE4179	54°12·5′	1°21·9′W	X	99
Hagg Ho	N Yks	SE5429	53°45·5′	1°10·4′W	X	105
Hagg Ho	N Yks	SE5897	54°22·2′	1°6·0′W	X	100
Hagg Ho	N Yks	SE8183	54°14·4′	0°45·0′W	X	100
Hagg House	Northum	NZ2692	55°13·5′	1°35·0′W	X	81
Hagg House Fm	N Yks	SE5293	54°20·0′	1°11·6′W	FM	100
Hagg House Fm	York	SE5449	53°56·3′	1°10·2′W	FM	105
Hagg House Moor	N Yks	SE5898	54°22·7′	1°6·0′W	X	100
Haggie Knowe	Scot Bord	NT6301	55°18·4′	2°34·5′W	H	80
Haggieshall	Aberd	NJ5244	57°29·3′	2°47·6′W	X	29
Haggieshaw Wood	Moray	NJ3542	57°28·1′	3°4·6′W	F	28
Hagginton Hill	Devon	SS5547	51°12·5′	4°4·2′W	T	180
Haggis Fm	Cambs	TL4156	52°11·3′	0°4·2′E	FM	154
Haggis Hill	S Ayr	NX3292	55°11·9′	4°37·9′W	H	76
Haggis Side	Scot Bord	NY3698	55°16·6′	3°0·0′W	H	79
Haggitt Hill	N Yks	NZ4204	54°26·0′	1°20·7′W	X	93
Hagg Lane Fm	N Yks	SE6732	53°47·0′	0°58·6′W	FM	105,106
Haggle Rigg	Northum	NY8374	55°3·9′	2°15·5′W	X	86,87
Haggmuir Fm	N Lanak	NS7368	55°53·6′	4°1·4′W	FM	64
Haggrister	Shetld	HU3470	60°25·0′	1°22·5′W	T	2,3
Haggs	Falk	NS7978	55°59·0′	3°55·9′W	T	64
Haggs	S Lanak	NS7146	55°41·7′	4°2·7′W	X	64
Haggs Cas	C of Glas	NS5662	55°50·0′	4°17·5′W	A	64
Haggs Fm	C of Edin	NT1367	55°53·6′	3°23·0′W	FM	65
Haggs Fm	E Yorks	TA0331	53°46·1′	0°25·8′W	FM	107
Haggs Fm	Notts	SK4750	53°2·9′	1°17·5′W	FM	120
Haggs Fm	N Yks	SE3351	53°57·5′	1°29·4′W	FM	104
Hagg's Hall	Lancs	SD6732	53°47·2′	2°29·6′W	X	103
Hagg Side	Derby	SK1788	53°23·6′	1°44·3′W	X	110
Haggs, The	York	SE6852	53°57·8′	0°57·4′W	X	105,106
Hagg, The	Cumbr	NY4973	55°3·2′	2°47·5′W	X	86
Hagg, The	Northum	NY8353	54°52·5′	2°15·5′W	X	86,87
Hagg The	N Yks	SE0598	54°22·9′	1°55·0′W	X	98
Hagg Wood	Cumbr	SD4677	54°11·4′	2°49·2′W	F	97
Hagg Wood	N Yks	SE4493	54°20·1′	1°19·0′W	F	99
Hagg Wood	N Yks	SE6787	54°16·7′	0°57·8′W	F	94,100
Hagg Wood	York	SE5545	53°54·1′	1°9·4′W	F	105
Hagg Wood	York	SE6852	53°57·8′	0°57·4′W	F	105,106
Haggwood Fm	York	SE6746	53°54·6′	0°58·4′W	FM	105,106
Haggy Hill	D & G	NY2885	55°9·5′	3°7·4′W	H	79
Haghill	C of Glas	NS6265	55°51·8′	4°11·9′W	T	64
Hag Hill	Kirk	SE2512	53°36·5′	1°36·9′W	X	110
Hag Hill	Wilts	ST8959	51°20·0′	2°9·1′W	X	173
Hag Ho	Durham	NZ2746	54°48·7′	1°34·4′W	X	88
Hag Ho	N Yks	SE4484	54°15·2′	1°19·1′W	X	99
Hag House Fm	Durham	NZ2043	54°47·1′	1°40·9′W	FM	88
Hag Law	Scot Bord	NT1847	55°42·8′	3°17·9′W	H	72
Hagley	Heref	SO5641	52°4·2′	2°38·1′W	T	149
Hagley	Shrops	SO2797	52°34·2′	3°4·2′W	X	137
Hagley	Worcs	SO9181	52°25·9′	2°7·5′W	T	139
Hagley Bridge Fm	Somer	ST0523	51°0·1′	3°20·9′W	FM	181
Hagleyhill Fm	Worcs	SO9281	52°25·9′	2°6·7′W	FM	139
Hagley Hill Fm	Worcs	SO9376	52°23·2′	2°5·8′W	FM	139
Hagley Park	Worcs	SO9280	52°25·3′	2°6·7′W	X	139
Hagley's Dumble	Notts	SK6961	53°8·7′	0°57·7′W	W	120
Hagley Wood	Worcs	SO9381	52°25·9′	2°5·8′W	F	139
Hagloe	Glos	SO6806	51°45·3′	2°27·4′W	T	162
Hagloe Ho	Glos	SO6806	51°45·3′	2°27·4′W	X	162
Hagmark Hill	Shetld	HU3150	60°14·3′	1°25·9′W	H	3
Hagmark Stack	Shetld	HP6612	60°47·4′	0°46·8′W	X	1
Hag Mark Stone	Shetld	HU3958	60°18·5′	1°17·2′W	X	2,3
Hag Moor	N Yks	SE4669	54°7·1′	1°17·4′W	X	100
Hagmore Green	Suff	TL9539	52°1·1′	0°50·9′E	T	155
Hagmuir	Angus	NO5151	56°39·2′	2°47·5′W	X	54
Hagnaby	Lincs	TF3462	53°8·5′	0°0·6′E	T	122
Hagnaby	Lincs	TF4879	53°17·5′	0°13·6′E	T	122
Hagnaby Lock	Lincs	TF3359	53°6·9′	0°0·4′W	T	122
Hagnaby Priory	Lincs	TF3462	53°8·5′	0°0·6′E	X	122
Hag Plantn	Scot Bord	NT6518	55°27·5′	2°32·8′W	F	80
Hags Gill Plantn	N Yks	SE0696	54°21·8′	1°54·0′W	F	99
Hagshaw Burn	S Lanak	NS7932	55°34·3′	3°54·7′W	W	71
Hagshaw Hill	S Lanak	NS7830	55°33·2′	3°55·6′W	H	71
Hag Sike	Northum	NY6973	55°3·3′	2°28·7′W	W	86,87
Hags of Borgan	D & G	NX4076	55°3·4′	4°29·9′W	X	77
Hags Wood	N Yks	SE5683	54°14·6′	1°8·0′W	F	100
Hag, The	Cumbr	NY5326	54°37·9′	2°43·3′W	X	90
Hagthorpe Hall	N Yks	SE7030	53°45·9′	0°55·9′W	X	105,106
Hague	Lancs	SD7748	53°55·9′	2°20·6′W	X	103
Hague Bar	Derby	SJ9885	53°22·0′	2°1·4′W	T	109
Hague Ho	Lancs	SD9043	53°53·2′	2°8·7′W	X	103
Haguelands Fm	Kent	TR1030	51°2·1′	1°0·1′E	FM	189
Hague, The	Derby	SK4477	53°17·5′	1°20·0′W	X	120
Hag Wood	Durham	NZ1943	54°47·1′	1°41·8′W	F	88
Hag Wood	Durham	NZ2149	54°50·4′	1°40·0′W	F	88
Hag Wood	Northum	NY6758	54°55·2′	2°30·5′W	F	86,87
Hag Wood	N Yks	NZ1301	54°24·5′	1°47·6′W	F	92
Hag Wood	N Yks	SD9597	54°22·4′	2°4·2′W	F	98
Hag Wood	Scot Bord	NT9157	55°48·6′	2°8·2′W	F	67,74,75
Hagworm Hall	Durham	NY9317	54°33·1′	2°6·1′W	X	91,92
Hagworm Hill	Durham	NY8624	54°36·9′	2°12·6′W	X	91,92
Hagworm Hill	N Yks	TA0087	54°16·4′	0°27·4′W	A	101
Hagworthingham	Lincs	TF3469	53°12·3′	0°0·8′E	T	122
Hagworthingham Grange	Lincs	TF3370	53°12·9′	0°0·1′W	X	122
Ha' Hill	D & G	NX2270	54°59·8′	4°46·5′W	X	76
Ha Houll	Shetld	HP5201	60°41·6′	1°2·4′W	X	1
Haie, The	Glos	SO6710	51°47·5′	2°28·3′W	X	162
Haigh	Barns	SE2912	53°36·5′	1°33·3′W	T	110
Haigh	Wigan	SD6009	53°34·8′	2°35·8′W	T	109
Haigh End	N Yks	SE5619	53°40·1′	1°8·7′W	X	111
Haigh Hall Country Park	Wigan	SD5908	53°34·3′	2°36·7′W	X	108
Haigh Moor	Leeds	SE2824	53°42·9′	1°34·1′W	T	104
Haighton Green	Lancs	SD5634	53°48·3′	2°39·7′W	T	102
Haighton Hall	Lancs	SD5735	53°48·8′	2°38·8′W	X	102
Haighton Ho	Lancs	SD5633	53°47·7′	2°39·7′W	X	102
Haighton Top	Lancs	SD5534	53°48·3′	2°40·6′W	T	102
Haigsfield	Scot Bord	NT8040	55°39·4′	2°18·7′W	X	74
Hail Br	Cambs	TL1761	52°14·3′	0°16·8′W	X	153
Hailcombe Barn Fm	Oxon	SP3932	51°59·3′	1°25·5′W	FM	151
Haile	Cumbr	NY0308	54°27·7′	3°29·4′W	T	89
Haile Hall	Cumbr	NY0309	54°28·3′	3°29·4′W	X	89
Hailes	Glos	SP0430	51°58·3′	1°56·1′W	T	150
Haile Sand Fort	Lincs	TA3406	53°32·2′	0°1·7′E	X	113
Hailes Castle	E Loth	NT5775	55°58·2′	2°40·9′W	A	67
Hailes Wood	Glos	SP0530	51°58·3′	1°55·2′W	F	150
Hailey	Herts	TL3710	51°46·5′	0°0·5′W	T	166
Hailey	Oxon	SP3512	51°48·6′	1°29·1′W	T	164
Hailey	Oxon	SU6485	51°33·8′	1°4·2′W	T	175
Haileybury College	Herts	TL3510	51°46·6′	0°2·2′W	X	166
Hailey Copse	W Berks	SU4678	51°30·2′	1°19·8′W	F	174
Hailey Fm	Glos	SO9501	51°42·7′	2°4·0′W	FM	163
Hailey Wood	Glos	SO9500	51°42·2′	2°3·9′W	F	163
Hailey Wood	Oxon	SU2783	51°32·9′	1°36·2′W	F	174
Hailey Wood	Oxon	SU7496	51°39·7′	0°55·4′W	F	165
Hailforth	Cumbr	NY0846	54°48·3′	3°25·5′W	X	85
Hailsham	E Susx	TQ5909	50°51·7′	0°16·0′E	T	199
Hailstone Fm	Glos	SP1633	51°59·9′	1°45·6′W	FM	151
Hailstone Hill	Wilts	SU0894	51°38·9′	1°52·7′W	T	163,173
Hail Storm Hill	Roch	SD8418	53°39·7′	2°14·1′W	X	109
Hailthorpe	N Yks	NZ7513	54°30·6′	0°50·1′W	X	94
Hail Weston	Cambs	TL1662	52°14·9′	0°17·6′W	T	153
Hailwood's Rise	I of M	SC3986	54°14·9′	4°27·9′W	X	95
Haimer	Highld	ND1467	58°35·2′	3°28·3′W	X	11,12
Haim The	Powys	SJ3216	52°44·5′	3°0·0′W	X	126
Haimwood	Powys	SJ3116	52°44·5′	3°0·9′W	T	126
Haimwood Fm	Powys	SJ3117	52°45·0′	3°0·9′W	FM	126
Hainault	Redbr	TQ4591	51°36·2′	0°6·0′E	T	177
Hainault Fm	Redbr	TQ4690	51°35·6′	0°6·9′E	FM	177
Hainault Forest (Country Park)	Redbr	TQ4793	51°37·2′	0°7·8′E	F	177
Haind Park Wood	Glos	SO6830	51°58·3′	2°27·6′W	F	149
Haine	Kent	TR3566	51°20·9′	1°22·9′E	T	179
Haine Fm	Kent	TR3567	51°21·4′	1°22·9′E	FM	179
Haines Ash Bottom	Glos	SO9703	51°43·8′	2°2·2′W	F	163
Haines Fm	Hants	SU6360	51°20·4′	1°5·3′W	FM	175
Haines Hill	Wok	SU8174	51°27·8′	0°49·6′W	X	175
Haine's Mill	Powys	SO2060	52°14·2′	3°9·9′W	X	137,148
Haine's Rock	Corn	SW9136	50°11·5′	4°55·3′W	X	204
Hainey Fm	Cambs	TL5575	52°21·3′	0°17·0′E	FM	143
Hainey Hill	Cambs	TL5575	52°21·3′	0°17·0′E	X	143
Hainford	Norf	TG2218	52°43·1′	1°17·6′E	T	133,134
Haining	Northum	NY7375	55°4·4′	2°24·9′W	X	86,87
Haining	Northum	NY9292	55°13·6′	2°7·1′W	X	80
Haining	Sund	NZ3550	54°50·9′	1°26·9′W	X	88
Haining Burn	Cumbr	NY6459	54°55·7′	2°33·3′W	W	86
Haining Hall	Northum	NY7859	54°55·8′	2°20·2′W	X	86,87
Haininghead	S Lanak	NS9152	55°45·2′	3°43·8′W	X	65,72
Haining Ho	Cumbr	NY6459	54°55·7′	2°33·3′W	X	86
Haining Mains	E Ayr	NS4535	55°35·3′	4°27·1′W	X	70
Haining Place	E Ayr	NS4534	55°34·8′	4°27·1′W	X	70
Hainingrigg	Northum	NY8484	55°9·3′	2°14·6′W	X	80
Hainings Ho	Cumbr	NY5266	54°59·4′	2°44·6′W	X	86
Haining, The	Falk	NS9477	55°58·7′	3°41·5′W	X	65
Haining, The	Northum	NY7575	55°4·4′	2°23·1′W	X	86,87
Haining, The	Northum	NY8356	54°54·2′	2°15·5′W	X	86,87
Haining, The	Scot Bord	NT4627	55°32·3′	2°50·9′W	X	73
Hains	Dorset	ST7719	50°58·4′	2°19·3′W	T	183
Hainses	Glos	SO6801	51°42·6′	2°27·4′W	X	162
Hains Fm	N Lincs	SE7310	53°35·1′	0°53·4′W	FM	112
Hainslack	Lancs	SD9343	53°53·2′	2°6·0′W	FM	103
Hainstone	Heref	SO3841	52°4·1′	2°53·9′W	X	148,149,161
Hainton	Lincs	TF1884	53°20·6′	0°13·2′W	T	122
Hainton Hall	Lincs	TF1784	53°20·6′	0°14·1′W	X	121
Hainton Walk Fm	Lincs	TF1886	53°21·7′	0°13·2′W	FM	113,122
Hainworth	Brad	SE0638	53°50·5′	1°54·1′W	T	104
Hainworth Shaw	Brad	SE0639	53°51·1′	1°54·1′W	T	104
Hairdrigg	Cumbr	SD5896	54°21·7′	2°38·4′W	X	97
Hairlaw	S Lanak	NS6847	55°42·2′	4°5·6′W	X	64
Hairmyres	S Lanak	NS6053	55°45·3′	4°13·4′W	T	64
Hairpin	I of M	SC4493	54°18·8′	4°23·5′W	X	95
Hairshaw	E Ayr	NS4548	55°42·3′	4°27·6′W	X	64
Hairy Craig	E Loth	NT5775	55°58·2′	2°40·9′W	X	67
Hairyhillock	Aberd	NO8497	57°4·1′	2°15·4′W	X	38,45
Hairy Ness	Scot Bord	NT9465	55°52·9′	2°5·3′W	X	67
Hairy Side	Northum	NZ0054	54°53·1′	1°59·6′W	X	87
Haiselman's Fm	E Susx	TQ7525	51°0·1′	0°30·0′E	FM	188,199
Haist	Orkney	HY2301	58°53·6′	3°19·7′W	X	6,7
Haisthorpe	E Yorks	TA1264	54°3·8′	0°16·9′W	T	101
Haisthorpe Field	E Yorks	TA1265	54°4·4′	0°16·9′W	X	101
Haithwaite	Cumbr	NY4477	55°5·3′	2°52·2′W	X	85
Hakeford	Devon	SS6135	51°6·1′	3°58·7′W	T	180
Hakerley Bridge	Lincs	TF3252	53°3·2′	0°1·4′W	X	122
Hakes	Devon	ST2904	50°50·1′	3°0·1′W	X	193
Hake's Fm	Cambs	TL3495	52°32·4′	0°1·0′W	FM	142
Hakin	Pemb	SM8905	51°42·5′	5°2·9′W	T	157,158
Hakin Point	Pemb	SN0304	51°42·3′	4°50·7′W	X	157,158
Halabezack	Corn	SW7034	50°9·9′	5°12·9′W	T	203
Halabhal Bheag or Macleod's Table South	Highld	NG2242	57°23·3′	6°37·1′W	H	23
Halam	Notts	SK6754	53°5·0′	0°59·6′W	T	120
Halaman Bay	N Eil	NF6400	56°58·4′	7°31·4′W	W	31
Halamanning	Corn	SW5631	50°8·0′	5°24·5′W	T	203
Halam Mill	Notts	SK6755	53°5·5′	0°59·6′W	I	120
Halangy Point	I Scilly	SV9012	49°55·9′	6°18·8′W	X	203
Halanoweth Fm	Corn	SW7225	50°5·1′	5°10·9′W	FM	204
Halbeath	Fife	NT1288	56°4·9′	3°24·4′W	T	65
Halberry Head	Highld	ND3037	58°19·2′	3°11·2′W	X	11
Halberton	Devon	ST0012	50°54·2′	3°24·9′W	T	181
Halcombe	Wilts	ST9286	51°34·6′	2°6·5′W	X	173
Halcombe Fm	E Susx	TQ4202	50°48·2′	0°1·3′E	FM	198
Halcon	Somer	ST2425	51°1·4′	3°4·6′W	T	193
Halcro	Highld	ND2360	58°31·5′	3°18·9′W	X	11,12
Halcro	Orkney	ND4685	58°45·2′	2°55·5′W	X	7
Halcro Head	Orkney	ND4785	58°45·2′	2°54·5′W	X	7
Haldenby Grange	N Lincs	SE8217	53°38·8′	0°45·2′W	X	112
Haldenby Hall Fm	N Lincs	SE8218	53°39·4′	0°45·1′W	FM	112
Haldenby Ness	N Lincs	SE8215	53°37·7′	0°45·2′W	X	112
Haldenby Park	N Lincs	SE8216	53°38·3′	0°45·2′W	X	112
Halden Lane Fm	Kent	TQ8432	51°3·7′	0°37·9′E	FM	188
Halden Place	Kent	TQ8433	51°4·2′	0°38·0′E	X	188
Halden Place	Kent	TQ8533	51°4·2′	0°38·8′E	X	189
Haldens	Herts	TL2414	51°48·9′	0°11·7′W	T	166
Haldish Fm	Surrey	TQ0444	51°11·4′	0°30·3′W	FM	186
Haldon Belvedere	Devon	SX8786	50°40·0′	3°35·6′W	X	192
Hale	Cumbr	SD5078	54°12·0′	2°45·6′W	T	97
Hale	Halton	SJ4682	53°20·2′	2°48·2′W	T	108
Hale	Hants	SU1919	50°58·4′	1°43·4′W	T	184
Hale	Kent	TR2867	51°21·6′	1°16·9′E	T	179
Hale	Medway	TQ7765	51°21·6′	0°32·9′E	T	178
Hale	Somer	ST7527	51°2·7′	2°21·0′W	T	183
Hale	Surrey	SU8448	51°13·7′	0°47·4′W	T	186
Hale	Traf	SJ7686	53°22·5′	2°21·2′W	T	109
Hale	W Susx	TQ0631	51°4·3′	0°28·8′W	X	187
Haleacre Wood	Bucks	SU9198	51°40·6′	0°40·6′W	F	165
Hale Bank	Halton	SJ4883	53°20·7′	2°46·5′W	T	108
Halebank Fm	Man	SJ7984	53°21·4′	2°18·5′W	FM	109
Halebarns	Traf	SJ7985	53°21·9′	2°18·5′W	T	109
Halebourne Fm	Surrey	SU9461	51°20·6′	0°38·6′W	FM	175,186
Halebourne Ho	Surrey	SU9562	51°21·2′	0°37·8′W	X	175,176,186
Halecat Ho	Cumbr	SD4383	54°14·6′	2°52·1′W	X	97
Hale Common	I of W	SZ5484	50°39·4′	1°13·8′W	X	196
Halecommon	W Susx	SU8024	51°0·8′	0°51·2′W	T	197
Hale Coombe	N Som	ST4256	51°18·2′	2°49·5′W	T	172,182
Hale Court Fm	E Susx	TQ5037	51°7·0′	0°9·0′E	FM	188
Hale End	Wal F	TQ3891	51°36·3′	0°0·0′W	T	177
Hale Fen	Cambs	TL4781	52°24·7′	0°10·1′E	X	143
Halefield Fm	Cumbr	NY6326	54°37·9′	2°34·0′W	FM	91

Halefield Lodge	Northnts	TL0293	52°31·8′	0°29·4′W	X	141
Hale Fields	Cambs	TL3777	52°22·7′	0°1·2′E	X	142,143
Hale Fm	Bucks	SP8516	51°50·4′	0°45·6′W	FM	165
Hale Fm	Devon	ST1700	50°47·9′	3°10·3′W	FM	192,193
Hale Fm	Hants	SU6844	51°11·7′	1°1·2′W	FM	185,186
Hale Fm	Hants	SU6954	51°17·1′	1°0·2′W	FM	186
Hale Fm	Kent	TQ5148	51°12·9′	0°10·1′E	FM	188
Hale Fm	Kent	TQ7361	51°19·5′	0°29·4′E	FM	178,188
Hale Fm	Oxon	SU3390	51°36·7′	1°31·0′W	FM	164,174
Hale Fm	Oxon	SU6192	51°37·6′	1°6·7′W	FM	164,175
Hale Fm	Powys	SJ1915	52°43·8′	3°11·6′W	FM	125
Hale Fm	W Susx	SZ8098	50°46·8′	0°51·5′W	FM	197
Halegate Fm	Halton	SJ4782	53°20·2′	2°47·3′W	FM	108
Hale Grange	Cumbr	NY6327	54°38·5′	2°34·0′W	X	91
Hale Green	Cumbr	SD5078	54°12·0′	2°45·6′W	X	97
Hale Green	E Susx	TQ5514	50°54·5′	0°12·7′E	T	199
Hale Hall	Lancs	SD4535	53°48·7′	2°49·7′W	X	102
Hale Head	Halton	SJ4781	53°19·6′	2°47·3′W	X	108
Hale Hill Fm	E Susx	TQ5918	50°56·6′	0°16·2′E	FM	199
Hale House	Surrey	TQ1337	51°7·5′	0°22·7′W	X	187
Hale Manor Fm	I of W	SZ5484	50°39·4′	1°13·8′W	FM	196
Hale Mills	Corn	SW7542	50°14·3′	5°9·0′W	T	204
Hale Moss	Cumbr	SD5077	54°11·4′	2°45·6′W	X	97
Hale Nook	Lancs	SD3943	53°53·0′	2°55·3′W	T	102
Hale Oak Fm	Kent	TQ5149	51°13·4′	0°10·1′E	FM	188
Hale Park	Hants	SU1818	50°57·9′	1°44·2′W	A	184
Hale Purlieu	Hants	SU2018	50°57·9′	1°42·5′W	X	184
Hales	E Yorks	SE6919	53°40·0′	0°56·9′W	X	111
Hales	Norf	TM3897	52°31·4′	1°30·9′E	T	134
Hales	Staffs	SJ7134	52°54·4′	2°25·5′W	T	127
Hales Bank	Heref	SO6150	52°9·1′	2°33·8′W	T	149
Hales Br	Surrey	TQ2143	51°10·6′	0°15·7′W	X	187
Hales Castle	Somer	ST7944	51°11·9′	2°17·6′W	A	183
Hales Cott	Bucks	SU9286	51°34·2′	0°40·0′W	X	175
Halesend	Heref	SO7348	52°8·0′	2°23·3′W	X	150
Halesend Wood	Heref	SO7349	52°8·6′	2°23·3′W	F	150
Halesfield	Wrekin	SJ7104	52°38·2′	2°25·3′W	T	127
Hales Fm	Essex	TL5812	51°47·3′	0°17·8′E	FM	167
Hale's Fm	Essex	TL6020	51°51·6′	0°19·8′E	FM	167
Hale's Fm	Essex	TL8413	51°47·3′	0°40·5′E	FM	168
Hale's Fm	Essex	TL8601	51°40·8′	0°41·8′E	FM	168
Hale's Fm	N Som	ST4772	51°26·9′	2°45·4′W	FM	171,172
Hales Fm	Shrops	SO6183	52°26·9′	2°34·0′W	FM	138
Halesgate	Lincs	TF3226	52°49·2′	0°2·1′W	T	131
Hales Green	Derby	SK1841	52°58·2′	1°43·5′W	T	119,128
Hales Green	Norf	TM3796	52°30·8′	1°30·0′E	T	134
Hales Hall	Lancs	SD3943	53°53·0′	2°55·3′W	X	102
Hales Hall	Norf	TM3696	52°30·9′	1°29·1′E	A	134
Hales Hall	Staffs	SK0244	52°59·8′	1°57·8′W	A	119,128
Hales Hill Fm	N Yks	SE5842	53°52·5′	1°6·7′W	FM	105
Halesowen	Dudley	SO9583	52°26·9′	2°4·0′W	T	139
Hales Park	Worcs	SO7775	52°22·6′	2°19·9′W	T	138
Hales Pasture	Ches	SJ7570	53°13·8′	2°22·1′W	X	118
Hales Place	Kent	TR1459	51°17·6′	1°4·6′E	T	179
Hales Street	Norf	TM1587	52°26·5′	1°10·2′E	T	144,156
Hale Street	Kent	TQ6749	51°13·2′	0°23·9′E	T	188
Hales Wood	Essex	TL5740	52°2·4′	0°17·7′E	F	154
Hales Wood	Heref	SO6030	51°58·3′	2°34·5′W	T	149
Hales Wood	Norf	TM3795	52°30·3′	1°29·9′E	F	134
Halesworth	Suff	TM3877	52°20·6′	1°30·1′E	T	156
Hale, The	Bucks	SP8907	51°45·5′	0°42·2′W	X	165
Hale Wood	Bucks	SP8907	51°45·5′	0°42·2′W	F	165
Hale Wood	Bucks	SU7493	51°38·1′	0°55·5′W	F	175
Halewood	Know	SJ4485	53°21·8′	2°50·1′W	T	108
Hale Wood	Monm	ST4796	51°39·9′	2°45·6′W	F	171
Hale Wood	W Susx	SU7616	50°56·5′	0°54·7′W	F	197
Hale Woods	Worcs	SO5100	51°42·0′	2°42·2′W	F	162
Haley Hill	Herts	TL3728	51°56·2′	0°0·0′W	X	166
Halezy	Corn	SW9151	50°19·5′	4°55·8′W	X	200,204
Half Acre	Kent	TQ8370	51°24·2′	0°38·3′E	W	178
Half Acre Fm	Cambs	TL5576	52°21·8′	0°17·0′E	FM	143
Halfen	Powys	SJ0914	52°43·2′	3°20·4′W	X	125
Halferne	D & G	NX7566	54°58·6′	3°56·8′W	X	84
Halferne Cottages	D & G	NX7667	54°59·2′	3°55·8′W	X	84
Halfkey	Worcs	SO7649	52°8·6′	2°20·6′W	X	150
Halfland Barns	E Loth	NT5884	56°3·1′	2°40·0′W	X	67
Halflaw Kiln	Midlo	NT3859	55°49·5′	2°58·9′W	X	66,73
Half Mark	D & G	NX0062	54°55·0′	5°6·8′W	X	82
Halfmark	D & G	NX7182	55°7·2′	4°0·9′W	X	77
Halfmark Burn	D & G	NX5491	55°11·8′	4°17·2′W	W	77
Halfmark Rig	S Ayr	NS3800	55°16·3′	4°32·6′W	X	77
Halfmerk	S Ayr	NX3079	55°4·8′	4°39·4′W	X	76
Half Merk Burn	S Ayr	NX2785	55°8·0′	4°42·4′W	W	76
Halfmerk Hill	D & G	NS7016	55°25·5′	4°2·8′W	H	71
Halfmerkland	S Lanak	NS7736	55°36·4′	3°56·7′W	X	71
Half Merk Loch	S Ayr	NX2785	55°8·0′	4°42·4′W	W	76
Half Moon Bay	Lancs	SD4060	54°2·2′	2°54·6′W	W	96,97
Half Moon Common	Hants	SU2916	50°56·8′	1°34·8′W	X	185
Half Moon Fm	Ches	SJ7248	53°2·0′	2°24·6′W	FM	118
Half Moon Plantation	Glos	SP1031	51°58·9′	1°50·9′W	F	150
Half Moon Village	Devon	SX8997	50°46·0′	3°34·1′W	T	192
Halford	Devon	SX8174	50°33·5′	3°40·4′W	X	191
Halford	Shrops	SO4383	52°26·8′	2°49·9′W	T	137
Halford	Warw	SP2645	52°6·4′	1°36·8′W	T	151
Halford Hill Fm	Warw	SP2644	52°5·9′	1°36·8′W	FM	151
Halford Manor	Devon	SX6497	50°45·6′	3°55·3′W	X	191
Halford Moor	Devon	SX6497	50°45·6′	3°55·3′W	X	191
Halforth	Cumbr	SD4783	54°14·6′	2°48·4′W	X	97
Halfpenny	Cumbr	SD5387	54°16·8′	2°42·9′W	T	97
Halfpenny Furze	Carm	SN2713	51°47·6′	4°30·1′W	T	158
Halfpenny Gate Cott	E Yorks	SE9935	53°48·3′	0°29·4′W	X	106
Halfpenny Green	Staffs	SO8291	52°31·2′	2°15·5′W	T	138
Halfpenny Green Airport	Staffs	SO8291	52°31·2′	2°15·5′W	X	138
Halfpenny Hill	Glos	SO9908	51°46·5′	2°0·5′W	X	163
Halfpenny Ho	N Yks	SE1295	54°21·3′	1°48·5′W	X	99
Halfpenny House	Cumbr	NY7607	54°27·7′	2°21·8′W	X	91
Halfpenny House Moor	N Yks	SE1297	54°22·3′	1°48·5′W	X	99
Halfpenny Houses	N Yks	SE2284	54°15·3′	1°39·3′W	X	99
Halfridge	Heref	SO6950	52°9·1′	2°26·8′W	X	149
Halfridge Wood	Oxon	SU7186	51°34·3′	0°58·1′W	F	175
Halftide Ledges	I Scilly	SV8709	49°54·2′	6°21·2′W	X	203
Half Tide Rock		NS2729	55°31·7′	4°44·0′W	X	70
Halftide Rock	Devon	SS1244	51°10·1′	4°41·0′W	X	180
Half Tide Rock	Pemb	SM7422	51°51·3′	5°16·5′W	X	157
Halfway	Carm	SN5200	51°41·0′	4°8·1′W	T	159
Halfway	Carm	SN6430	51°57·4′	3°58·4′W	X	146
Halfway	Carm	SN8232	51°58·7′	3°42·7′W	T	160
Halfway	Pth & Kin	NO0235	56°30·1′	3°35·1′W	X	52,53
Halfway	Sheff	SK4381	53°19·7′	1°20·9′W	T	111,120
Halfway	W Berks	SU4068	51°24·8′	1°25·1′W	T	174
Halfway	Wilts	ST8747	51°13·6′	2°10·8′W	T	183
Halfway	W Susx	TQ3014	50°54·9′	0°8·7′W	X	198
Halfway Br	Glos	SO7518	51°51·8′	2°21·4′W	X	162
Halfway Br	Gwyn	SH6068	53°11·7′	4°5·3′W	X	115
Halfway Bridge	W Susx	SU9321	50°59·1′	0°40·1′W	T	197
Halfway Bush	Kent	TR0719	50°56·2′	0°57·2′E	X	189
Halfway Bush Fm	Wilts	ST8487	51°35·1′	2°13·5′W	FM	173
Halfway Cottages	Suff	TM4662	52°12·3′	1°36·4′E	X	156
Half Way Firs	Wilts	ST8570	51°26·0′	2°12·6′W	T	173
Halfway Fm	Cambs	TL2287	52°28·3′	0°11·8′W	FM	142
Half Way Fm	Herts	TL2534	51°59·7′	0°10·4′W	FM	153
Halfway Fm	Somer	ST4652	51°16·1′	2°46·1′W	FM	182
Halfway Fm	Wilts	ST9166	51°23·8′	2°7·4′W	FM	173
Halfway Forest	Carm	SN8434	51°59·8′	3°41·0′W	F	160
Halfway Hill	Herts	TL1628	51°56·5′	0°18·3′W	X	166
Halfway Ho	Cambs	TL1990	52°29·9′	0°14·4′W	X	142
Halfway Ho	Denb	SJ1559	53°7·5′	3°15·8′W	X	116
Halfway Ho	D & G	NX3061	54°55·1′	4°38·7′W	X	82
Halfway Ho	Dorset	ST6016	50°56·8′	2°33·8′W	X	183
Halfway Ho	Essex	TL6119	51°51·0′	0°20·7′E	X	167
Halfway Ho	E Yorks	TA0436	53°48·8′	0°24·8′W	X	107
Halfway Ho	E Yorks	TA0536	53°48·8′	0°23·9′W	X	107
Halfway Ho	Gwyn	SH5956	53°5·2′	4°5·9′W	X	115
Halfway Ho	Heref	SO6252	52°10·1′	2°32·9′W	X	149
Halfway Ho	Herts	TL4012	51°47·6′	0°2·2′E	X	167
Halfway Ho	Lancs	SD6372	54°8·8′	2°33·6′W	X	97
Halfway Ho	Lincs	TF3686	53°21·4′	0°3·0′E	X	113
Halfway Ho	Northnts	SP8082	52°26·0′	0°49·0′W	X	141
Halfway Ho	Northum	NY9367	55°0·1′	2°6·1′W	X	87
Halfway Ho	N Yks	SE0973	54°9·4′	1°51·3′W	X	99
Halfway Ho	N Yks	SE3695	54°21·2′	1°26·3′W	X	99
Halfway Ho	N Yks	SE5470	54°7·6′	1°10·0′W	X	100
Halfway Ho	Shrops	SJ5607	52°39·8′	2°38·6′W	X	126
Halfway Ho	Shrops	SO5077	52°23·6′	2°43·7′W	X	137,138
Halfway Ho	W Loth	NT0759	55°49·2′	3°28·6′W	X	65,72
Halfway House	Essex	TQ6389	51°34·8′	0°21·5′E	X	177
Half Way House	Pth & Kin	NO2246	56°36·2′	3°15·8′W	X	53
Halfwayhouse	Scot Bord	NT8427	55°32·4′	2°14·8′W	X	74
Halfway House	Shrops	SJ3411	52°41·8′	2°58·2′W	T	126
Halfway House Fm	Bucks	SP9401	51°42·2′	0°38·0′W	FM	165
Halfway House Fm	Essex	TQ5794	51°37·6′	0°16·5′E	FM	167,177
Halfway House Fm	Somer	ST4819	50°58·3′	2°44·1′W	FM	193
Halfway Houses	Bury	SD7609	53°34·9′	2°21·3′W	T	109
Halfway Houses	Kent	TQ9373	51°25·6′	0°47·0′E	T	178
Halfway Houses	Lincs	SK8863	53°9·6′	0°40·6′W	X	121
Halfway Houses	Mil Key	SP7947	52°7·2′	0°50·4′W	X	152
Halfway Houses	N Yks	SE6825	53°43·3′	0°57·8′W	X	105,106
Half Way Hut	Aberd	NO4393	57°1·7′	2°55·9′W	X	37,44
Half Way Inn	Devon	SY0490	50°42·3′	3°21·2′W	X	192
Halfway Reach	Bexley	TQ4881	51°30·7′	0°8·4′E	W	177
Halfway Rock	Pemb	SM8011	51°45·5′	5°10·9′W	X	157
Halfway Sta	Gwyn	SH5957	53°5·7′	4°5·9′W	X	115
Half Way Stone	D & G	NX5177	55°4·2′	4°19·6′W	X	77
Halfway Street	Kent	TR2547	51°10·9′	1°13·6′E	T	179
Halfwaywell	Cumbr	NY5335	54°42·7′	2°43·3′W	X	90
Halgabron	Corn	SX0788	50°39·8′	4°43·5′W	T	190,200
Halgarrack Fm	Corn	SW6337	50°11·4′	5°18·9′W	FM	203
Halgavor Moor	Corn	SX0765	50°27·4′	4°42·8′W	X	200
Halgavor Plantn	Corn	SX0864	50°26·9′	4°41·9′W	F	200
Halghton Hall	Wrex	SJ4142	52°58·6′	2°52·3′W	A	117
Halghton Lane Fm	Wrex	SJ4242	52°58·6′	2°51·4′W	FM	117
Halghton Lodge	Wrex	SJ4143	52°59·1′	2°52·3′W	X	117
Halghton Mill	Wrex	SJ4143	52°59·1′	2°52·3′W	X	117
Halghton Villa	Wrex	SJ4440	52°57·5′	2°49·6′W	X	117
Halgoss	Corn	SW6542	50°14·1′	5°17·4′W	X	203
Halhead Hall	Cumbr	SD4894	54°20·6′	2°47·6′W	X	97
Halhill	Fife	NO2813	56°18·5′	3°9·4′W	X	59
Halidean Mill	Scot Bord	NT5934	55°36·1′	2°38·6′W	X	73,74
Halidon Hill	Northum	NT9654	55°47·0′	2°3·4′W	H	74,75
Halifax	Cald	SE0925	53°43·5′	1°51·4′W	T	104
Halifax Fm	Leic	SK4505	52°38·7′	1°19·7′W	FM	140
Halk Burn	Scot Bord	NT4740	55°39·3′	2°50·1′W	W	73
Halkburn	Scot Bord	NT4740	55°39·3′	2°50·1′W	T	73
Halkerston	Midlo	NT3458	55°48·9′	3°2·8′W	X	66,73
Halkerton	Angus	NO4448	56°37·5′	2°54·3′W	X	54
Halket	E Ayr	NS4252	55°44·4′	4°30·6′W	T	64
Halket Leathes	D & G	NX7963	54°57·1′	3°52·9′W	X	84
Halkirk	Highld	ND1359	58°30·9′	3°29·1′W	T	11,12
Halkyn Mountain	Flint	SJ1971	53°14·0′	3°12·4′W	H	116
Halkyn Mountain	Flint	SJ2070	53°13·5′	3°11·5′W	T	117
Halkyn or Helygain	Flint	SJ2171	53°14·1′	3°10·6′W	T	117
Hall	Devon	SS6934	51°5·7′	3°51·9′W	X	180
Halladale River	Highld	NC8953	58°27·3′	3°53·7′W	W	10
Hallagather	Corn	SX1495	50°43·7′	4°37·8′W	X	190
Halla-gya	N Eil	NA9900	57°53·5′	7°4·3′W	W	18
Hallaig	Highld	NG5938	57°22·4′	6°0·1′W	X	24,32
Hallam	Highld	ND0367	58°35·1′	3°39·6′W	X	11,12
Hallam Fields	Derby	SK4739	52°57·0′	1°17·6′W	T	129
Hallamhall Fm	Halton	SJ5881	53°19·7′	2°37·4′W	FM	108
Hallam Moors	Sheff	SK2486	53°22·5′	1°37·9′W	X	110
Hallam Moors	Sheff	SK2684	53°21·4′	1°36·2′W	X	110
Hallams Fm	Notts	SK5255	53°5·6′	1°13·0′W	FM	120
Hallams, The	Surrey	TQ0345	51°11·9′	0°31·2′W	X	186
Halland	E Susx	TQ5016	50°55·7′	0°8·5′E	T	199
Halland Park Fm	E Susx	TQ5115	50°55·1′	0°9·3′E	FM	199
Hallands Fm	N Lincs	TA0820	53°40·2′	0°21·5′W	FM	107,112
Hallane	Corn	SX0348	50°18·2′	4°45·6′W	X	204
Hallan Hill	N Yks	SD9742	53°52·7′	2°2·3′W	X	103
Hallard's Fen	Cambs	TL5767	52°16·9′	0°18·5′E	X	154
Hallas Br	Brad	SE0736	53°49·5′	1°53·2′W	X	104
Hallas Cote Fm	Brad	SE0736	53°49·5′	1°53·2′W	FM	104
Hallas Rough Park	Brad	SE0535	53°48·9′	1°55·0′W	X	104
Hallaton	Leic	SP7896	52°33·6′	0°50·6′W	T	141
Hallaton Manor	Leic	SP7895	52°33·1′	0°50·6′W	X	141
Hallaton Spinneys	Leic	SP7798	52°34·7′	0°51·4′W	F	141
Hallaton Wood	Leic	SP7697	52°34·2′	0°52·3′W	F	141
Hallatrow	Bath & NE Somer	ST6357	51°18·9′	2°31·5′W	T	172
Hall Bank	Cald	SE0125	53°43·5′	1°58·7′W	X	104
Hall Bank	Cumbr	NY1241	54°45·6′	3°21·6′W	X	85
Hall Bank	Cumbr	NY2441	54°45·7′	3°10·4′W	X	85
Hall Bank	Cumbr	SD1782	54°13·9′	3°16·0′W	X	96
Hall Bank	Cumbr	SD5790	54°18·5′	2°39·2′W	X	97
Hallbank	Cumbr	SD6891	54°19·1′	2°29·1′W	X	98
Hallbank	Cumbr	SD7187	54°16·9′	2°26·3′W	X	98
Hallbank	D & G	NY1781	55°7·2′	3°17·7′W	X	79
Hall Bank Fm	N Yks	SE5560	54°2·2′	1°9·2′W	FM	100
Hallbankgate	Cumbr	NY5859	54°55·7′	2°38·9′W	T	86
Hall Barn	Bucks	SU9489	51°35·7′	0°38·2′W	X	175
Hall Barn Fm	Lancs	SD6938	53°50·5′	2°27·9′W	FM	103
Hall Barns	Northum	NY8773	55°3·3′	2°11·8′W	X	87
Hallbarns Fm	E Ayr	NS3737	55°36·2′	4°34·8′W	FM	70
Hall Bay	Aberd	NO8989	56°59·8′	2°10·4′W	W	45
Hall Beck	Cumbr	NY4700	54°23·8′	2°48·6′W	W	90
Hallbeck	Cumbr	SD6288	54°17·4′	2°34·6′W	X	97
Hallbeck Ho	Cumbr	SD1484	54°14·9′	3°18·8′W	X	96
Hall Bolton	Cumbr	NY0803	54°25·1′	3°24·6′W	X	89
Hallborough	Kent	TQ5441	51°9·1′	0°12·5′E	X	188
Hallbottom Fm	Bucks	SU7697	51°40·2′	0°53·7′W	FM	165
Hall Bower	Kirk	SE1414	53°37·6′	1°46·9′W	T	110
Hallbrae	N Lanak	NS7471	55°55·2′	4°0·5′W	X	64
Hallbreck	Orkney	ND4894	58°50·1′	2°53·6′W	X	7
Hall Broad Fm	Essex	TL8415	51°48·4′	0°40·5′E	FM	168
Hall Broom	Sheff	SK2789	53°24·1′	1°35·2′W	T	110
Hall Burn	Cumbr	NY3968	55°0·4′	2°56·8′W	W	85
Hall Burn	D & G	NS7702	55°18·1′	3°55·8′W	W	78
Hallburn	D & G	NY1279	55°6·1′	3°22·3′W	X	85
Hall Burn	D & G	NY3279	55°6·3′	3°3·5′W	W	85
Hall Burn	N Ayr	NS3447	55°41·5′	4°38·0′W	W	63
Hall Burn	Scot Bord	NT6257	55°48·5′	2°35·9′W	W	67,74
Hall Burn	Scot Bord	NT6859	55°49·6′	2°30·2′W	W	67,74
Hall Burn	Scot Bord	NT8120	55°28·7′	2°17·6′W	W	74
Hallburn	S Lanak	NS6540	55°38·3′	4°8·3′W	X	71
Hallburncroft	Cumbr	NY4169	55°1·0′	2°54·9′W	X	85
Hall Carleton	Cumbr	SD0797	54°21·9′	3°25·5′W	X	96
Hall Carr	Norf	TF7504	52°36·6′	0°35·5′E	F	143
Hallcliff Fm	Derby	SK3170	53°13·8′	1°31·7′W	FM	119
Hall Close	Derby	SK3042	52°58·7′	1°32·8′W	X	119,128
Hall Close	N Yks	SE4557	54°0·7′	1°18·4′W	X	105
Hall Close Wood	N Yks	SD9451	53°57·5′	2°5·1′W	F	103
Hall Common	Norf	TG3817	52°42·1′	1°31·8′E	X	133,134
Hall Coppice	Shrops	SO4986	52°28·4′	2°44·7′W	F	137,138
Hall Copse	Hants	SU3220	50°58·9′	1°32·3′W	F	185
Hall Court	Hants	SU5413	50°55·1′	1°13·5′W	X	196
Hall Court	Heref	SO6435	52°1·0′	2°31·1′W	X	149
Hall Court	Heref	SO6448	52°8·0′	2°31·2′W	X	149
Hall Court Fm	E Susx	TQ4909	50°51·9′	0°7·4′E	FM	199
Hallcourt Fm	W Berks	SU5667	51°24·2′	1°11·3′W	FM	174
Hallcraig	S Lanak	NS8350	55°44·0′	3°51·4′W	X	65,72
Hallcroft	D & G	NX7574	55°2·9′	3°57·0′W	X	84
Hallcroft	Fife	NT0295	56°8·5′	3°34·2′W	X	58
Hallcroft Hall	Brad	SE0849	53°56·5′	1°52·3′W	X	104
Hallcroft Moor	D & G	NX7575	55°3·5′	3°57·0′W	X	84
Hallcrofts	D & G	NY3583	55°8·5′	3°0·8′W	X	79
Hall Cross	Devon	SX6259	50°25·1′	3°56·2′W	X	202
Hall Cross	Lancs	SD4230	53°46·0′	2°52·4′W	T	102
Hall Dale	Derby	SK2864	53°10·6′	1°34·5′W	X	119
Hall Dale	Staffs	SK1453	53°4·7′	1°47·1′W	X	119
Hall Dike	Kirk	SE1111	53°36·0′	1°49·6′W	W	110
Hall Down	Carm	SN2812	51°47·1′	4°29·2′W	X	158
Hall Downs	Corn	SX1564	50°27·0′	4°36·0′W	X	201
Hall Downs	Kent	TR1845	51°10·0′	1°7·5′E	X	179,189
Halldrine Cove	Corn	SW4137	50°10·8′	5°37·3′W	W	203
Hall Dunnerdale	Cumbr	SD2195	54°20·9′	3°12·5′W	T	96
Halldykes	D & G	NY1582	55°7·8′	3°19·6′W	X	79
Halleaths	D & G	NY0982	55°7·7′	3°25·2′W	X	78
Hallees	Cumbr	NY4372	55°2·6′	2°53·1′W	X	85
Hallegan	Corn	SW6436	50°10·9′	5°18·0′W	X	203
Hallen	S Glos	ST5580	51°31·3′	2°38·5′W	T	172
Hall End	Beds	TL0045	52°5·9′	0°32·0′W	T	153
Hall End	Beds	TL0737	52°1·5′	0°26·0′W	T	153
Hall End	Bucks	SP8210	51°47·2′	0°48·3′W	X	165
Hall End	Lincs	TF4350	53°1·9′	0°8·4′E	T	122
Hall End	S Glos	ST7086	51°34·6′	2°25·6′W	T	172
Hall End	Warw	SK2500	52°36·1′	1°37·5′W	T	140
Hallend	Warw	SP1367	52°18·3′	1°48·2′W	T	151
Hallend Fm	Heref	SO6436	52°1·5′	2°31·1′W	FM	149
Hall End Skear	Lancs	SD4255	53°59·5′	2°52·7′W	X	102
Hallen Marsh	C of Bris	ST5480	51°31·3′	2°39·4′W	X	172
Hallew	Corn	SX0059	50°24·0′	4°48·5′W	T	200
Halleykeld Rigg	N Yks	SE9386	54°15·9′	0°33·9′W	X	94,101
Halley Moor	Northum	NY7649	54°50·4′	2°22·0′W	X	86,87
Halleypike Lough	Northum	NY8071	55°2·2′	2°18·3′W	W	86,87
Halleywell	Northum	NY8849	54°50·4′	2°10·8′W	X	87
Halleywell Fell	Northum	NY8848	54°49·8′	2°10·8′W	X	87
Hall Farm	Suff	TM3986	52°25·4′	1°31·3′E	FM	156
Hall Farm Ho	Norf	TL9398	52°33·0′	0°51·2′E	X	144
Hall Fell	N Yks	SD9858	54°1·3′	2°1·4′W	X	103
Hall Fen	Cambs	TL4982	52°25·2′	0°11·9′E	X	143
Hall Fen	Norf	TG3620	52°43·8′	1°30·1′E	W	133,134
Hall Field	Cumbr	NY3638	54°44·2′	2°59·2′W	X	90
Hallfield	Cumbr	NY5151	54°51·3′	2°45·4′W	X	86
Hallfield	Durham	NZ4044	54°47·6′	1°22·2′W	X	88
Hallfield	E Yorks	TA2129	53°44·8′	0°9·5′W	X	107
Hallfield	Sheff	SK2391	53°25·2′	1°38·8′W	X	110
Hallfield	S Lanak	NS6440	55°38·3′	4°9·2′W	X	71
Hallfield Fm	Sheff	SK2980	53°19·2′	1°33·5′W	FM	110
Hallfield Gate	Derby	SK3958	53°7·3′	1°24·6′W	T	119
Hall Flat	Worcs	SO9773	52°21·5′	2°2·2′W	T	139
Hall Flatt	Cumbr	NY4663	54°57·8′	2°50·2′W	X	86

Hall Fm	Beds	SP9450	52°8·6'	0°37·2'W	FM	153
Hall Fm	Bucks	SP9420	51°52·5'	0°37·7'W	FM	165
Hall Fm	Bucks	SP9814	51°49·2'	0°34·3'W	FM	165
Hall Fm	Cambs	TL1388	52°28·9'	0°19·8'W	FM	142
Hall Fm	Cambs	TL5461	52°13·8'	0°15·7'E	FM	154
Hall Fm	Cambs	TL6152	52°8·8'	0°21·6'E	FM	154
Hall Fm	Cambs	TL6160	52°13·1'	0°21·8'E	FM	154
Hall Fm	Cambs	TL6374	52°20·6'	0°24·0'E	FM	143
Hall Fm	Cambs	TL6453	52°9·3'	0°24·2'E	FM	154
Hall Fm	Cambs	TL7060	52°12·9'	0°29·7'E	FM	154
Hall Fm	Ches	SJ7468	53°12·7'	2°23·0'W	FM	118
Hall Fm	Ches	SJ8470	53°13·8'	2°14·0'W	FM	118
Hall Fm	Corn	SX1352	50°20·5'	4°37·3'W	FM	200
Hall Fm	Derby	SK3145	53°0·3'	1°31·9'W	FM	119,128
Hall Fm	Devon	SS7748	51°13·3'	3°45·3'W	FM	180
Hall Fm	Devon	SX3982	50°37·2'	4°16·2'W	FM	201
Hall Fm	Devon	SX5083	50°37·9'	4°6·9'W	FM	191,201
Hall Fm	Devon	SX6359	50°25·1'	3°55·3'W	FM	202
Hall Fm	Essex	TL5022	51°52·8'	0°11·2'E	FM	167
Hall Fm	Essex	TL5108	51°45·2'	0°11·7'E	FM	167
Hall Fm	Essex	TL5119	51°51·2'	0°11·9'E	FM	167
Hall Fm	Essex	TL7616	51°49·1'	0°33·6'E	FM	167
Hall Fm	Essex	TL8205	51°43·1'	0°38·5'E	FM	168
Hall Fm	Essex	TL9203	51°41·8'	0°47·1'E	FM	168
Hall Fm	Essex	TQ7498	51°39·5'	0°31·3'E	FM	167
Hall Fm	E Yorks	SE8224	53°42·6'	0°45·0'W	FM	106,112
Hall Fm	E Yorks	TA0842	53°52·0'	0°21·0'W	FM	107
Hall Fm	E Yorks	TA3028	53°44·2'	0°1·3'W	FM	107
Hall Fm	Glos	SO6907	51°45·9'	2°26·6'W	FM	162
Hall Fm	Lancs	SD4835	53°48·8'	2°47·0'W	FM	102
Hall Fm	Lancs	SD5666	54°5·5'	2°39·9'W	A	97
Hall Fm	Leic	SK3817	52°45·2'	1°25·8'W	FM	128
Hall Fm	Leic	SK4319	52°46·2'	1°21·4'W	FM	129
Hall Fm	Leic	SK4814	52°43·5'	1°17·0'W	FM	129
Hall Fm	Leic	SK6117	52°45·1'	1°5·4'W	FM	129
Hall Fm	Leic	SK6913	52°42·8'	0°58·3'W	FM	129
Hall Fm	Leic	SK7212	52°42·3'	0°55·7'W	FM	129
Hall Fm	Leic	SK7327	52°50·4'	0°54·6'W	FM	129
Hall Fm	Leic	SK7728	52°50·9'	0°51·0'W	FM	129
Hall Fm	Leic	SK7902	52°36·8'	0°49·6'W	FM	141
Hall Fm	Leic	SK8320	52°46·5'	0°45·8'W	FM	130
Hall Fm	Leic	SK8521	52°47·0'	0°44·0'W	FM	130
Hall Fm	Leic	SK8717	52°44·8'	0°42·3'W	FM	130
Hall Fm	Lincs	SK8373	53°15·1'	0°44·9'W	FM	121
Hall Fm	Lincs	SK8589	53°23·7'	0°42·9'W	FM	112,121
Hall Fm	Lincs	SK8597	53°28·0'	0°42·8'W	FM	112
Hall Fm	Lincs	SK8792	53°25·3'	0°41·0'W	FM	112
Hall Fm	Lincs	SK9048	53°1·5'	0°39·1'W	FM	130
Hall Fm	Lincs	SK9488	53°23·1'	0°34·8'W	FM	112,121
Hall Fm	Lincs	SK9521	52°46·9'	0°35·1'W	FM	130
Hall Fm	Lincs	SK9761	53°8·5'	0°32·6'W	FM	121
Hall Fm	Lincs	TF0450	53°2·5'	0°26·5'W	FM	121
Hall Fm	Lincs	TF0462	53°8·9'	0°26·3'W	FM	121
Hall Fm	Lincs	TF0582	53°19·7'	0°25·0'W	FM	121
Hall Fm	Lincs	TF0694	53°26·2'	0°23·8'W	FM	112
Hall Fm	Lincs	TF1179	53°18·0'	0°19·7'W	FM	121
Hall Fm	Lincs	TF1346	53°0·2'	0°18·6'W	FM	130
Hall Fm	Lincs	TF1544	52°59·1'	0°16·8'W	FM	130
Hall Fm	Lincs	TF1943	52°58·5'	0°13·3'W	FM	130
Hall Fm	Lincs	TF2071	53°13·6'	0°11·7'W	FM	122
Hall Fm	Lincs	TF2366	53°10·8'	0°9·2'W	FM	122
Hall Fm	Lincs	TF3064	53°9·7'	0°2·9'W	FM	122
Hall Fm	Lincs	TF3067	53°11·3'	0°2·9'W	FM	122
Hall Fm	Lincs	TF3267	53°11·3'	0°1·1'W	FM	122
Hall Fm	Lincs	TF3471	53°13·4'	0°0·8'E	FM	122
Hall Fm	Lincs	TF4147	53°0·3'	0°6·5'E	FM	131
Hall Fm	Lincs	TF4363	53°8·9'	0°8·7'E	FM	122
Hall Fm	Lincs	TF4468	53°11·6'	0°9·7'E	FM	122
Hall Fm	Lincs	TF4688	53°22·4'	0°12·1'E	FM	113
Hall Fm	Lincs	TF4688	53°22·4'	0°12·1'E	FM	122
Hall Fm	Lincs	TF5156	53°5·0'	0°15·7'E	FM	122
Hall Fm	NE Lincs	TA2501	53°29·7'	0°6·5'W	FM	113
Hall Fm	NE Lincs	TA2806	53°32·3'	0°3·7'W	FM	113
Hall Fm	Norf	TF6726	52°48·6'	0°29·1'E	FM	132
Hall Fm	Norf	TF6923	52°46·9'	0°30·8'E	FM	132
Hall Fm	Norf	TF7004	52°36·7'	0°31·1'E	FM	143
Hall Fm	Norf	TF7712	52°40·8'	0°37·5'E	FM	132
Hall Fm	Norf	TF8604	52°36·3'	0°45·2'E	FM	144
Hall Fm	Norf	TF8709	52°39·0'	0°46·3'E	FM	144
Hall Fm	Norf	TF9226	52°48·1'	0°51·3'E	FM	132
Hall Fm	Norf	TF9506	52°37·2'	0°53·3'E	FM	144
Hall Fm	Norf	TF9615	52°42·1'	0°54·5'E	FM	132
Hall Fm	Norf	TF9636	52°53·4'	0°55·2'E	FM	132
Hall Fm	Norf	TG0102	52°34·9'	0°58·4'E	FM	144
Hall Fm	Norf	TG0415	52°41·9'	1°1·6'E	FM	133
Hall Fm	Norf	TG0606	52°37·0'	1°3·0'E	FM	144
Hall Fm	Norf	TG0729	52°49·4'	1°4·7'E	FM	133
Hall Fm	Norf	TG0800	52°33·7'	1°4·5'E	FM	144
Hall Fm	Norf	TG1206	52°36·8'	1°8·3'E	FM	144
Hall Fm	Norf	TG1235	52°52·5'	1°9·4'E	FM	133
Hall Fm	Norf	TG1400	52°33·6'	1°9·8'E	FM	144
Hall Fm	Norf	TG1534	52°51·9'	1°12·1'E	FM	133
Hall Fm	Norf	TG1635	52°52·4'	1°13·0'E	FM	133
Hall Fm	Norf	TG2126	52°47·4'	1°17·1'E	FM	133,134
Hall Fm	Norf	TG2226	52°47·4'	1°18·0'E	FM	133,134
Hall Fm	Norf	TG2331	52°50·0'	1°19·0'E	FM	133
Hall Fm	Norf	TG2520	52°44·1'	1°20·4'E	FM	133,134
Hall Fm	Norf	TG2520	52°44·1'	1°20·4'E	FM	133,134
Hall Fm	Norf	TG2736	52°52·6'	1°22·8'E	FM	133
Hall Fm	Norf	TG2807	52°37·0'	1°22·5'E	FM	134
Hall Fm	Norf	TG2934	52°51·5'	1°24·5'E	A	133
Hall Fm	Norf	TG3333	52°50·9'	1°28·0'E	FM	133
Hall Fm	Norf	TG3521	52°44·4'	1°29·3'E	FM	133,134
Hall Fm	Norf	TG3912	52°39·4'	1°32·4'E	FM	133,134
Hall Fm	Norf	TG4203	52°34·5'	1°34·7'E	FM	134
Hall Fm	Norf	TG4219	52°43·1'	1°35·4'E	FM	134
Hall Fm	Norf	TL7294	52°31·2'	0°32·5'E	FM	143
Hall Fm	Norf	TL7497	52°32·8'	0°34·4'E	FM	143
Hall Fm	Norf	TL8786	52°26·6'	0°45·5'E	FM	144
Hall Fm	Norf	TL8798	52°33·1'	0°45·9'E	FM	144

Hall Fm	Norf	TL8991	52°29·3'	0°47·4'E	FM	144
Hall Fm	Norf	TL9585	52°25·9'	0°52·5'E	FM	144
Hall Fm	Norf	TL9797	52°32·3'	0°54·7'E	FM	144
Hall Fm	Norf	TL9982	52°24·2'	0°55·9'E	FM	144
Hall Fm	Norf	TL9991	52°29·1'	0°56·3'E	FM	144
Hall Fm	Norf	TM0291	52°29·0'	0°58·9'E	FM	144
Hall Fm	Norf	TM0481	52°23·6'	1°0·3'E	FM	144
Hall Fm	Norf	TM1687	52°26·5'	1°11·1'E	FM	144,156
Hall Fm	Norf	TM1992	52°29·1'	1°13·9'E	FM	134
Hall Fm	Norf	TM1994	52°30·2'	1°14·0'E	FM	134
Hall Fm	Norf	TM2888	52°26·8'	1°21·7'E	FM	156
Hall Fm	Norf	TM3090	52°27·8'	1°23·6'E	FM	134
Hall Fm	Norf	TM3293	52°29·4'	1°25·4'E	FM	134
Hall Fm	Norf	TM3599	52°32·5'	1°28·3'E	FM	134
Hall Fm	Norf	TM3794	52°29·8'	1°29·9'E	FM	134
Hall Fm	Norf	TM3992	52°28·6'	1°31·6'E	FM	134
Hall Fm	Norf	TM4197	52°31·3'	1°33·6'E	FM	134
Hall Fm	Norf	TM4893	52°28·9'	1°39·6'E	FM	134
Hall Fm	Northnts	SP5770	52°19·7'	1°9·4'W	FM	140
Hall Fm	Northnts	SP5839	52°3·0'	1°8·9'W	FM	152
Hall Fm	Northnts	SP8071	52°20·1'	0°49·2'W	FM	141
Hall Fm	Northnts	SP8083	52°26·6'	0°49·0'W	FM	141
Hall Fm	Notts	SK6134	52°54·2'	1°5·2'W	FM	129
Hall Fm	Notts	SK6538	52°56·4'	1°1·6'W	FM	129
Hall Fm	Notts	SK6831	52°52·6'	0°59·0'W	FM	129
Hall Fm	Notts	SK7036	52°55·2'	0°57·1'W	FM	129
Hall Fm	Notts	SK7168	53°12·5'	0°55·8'W	FM	120
Hall Fm	Notts	SK7232	52°53·1'	0°55·4'W	FM	129
Hall Fm	Notts	SK7744	52°59·5'	0°50·8'W	FM	129
Hall Fm	Notts	SK7887	53°22·7'	0°49·2'W	FM	112,120,121
Hall Fm	N Yks	NZ3400	54°23·9'	1°28·2'W	FM	93
Hall Fm	N Yks	NZ4706	54°27·1'	1°16·1'W	FM	93
Hall Fm	N Yks	SE0262	54°3·5'	1°57·8'W	FM	98
Hall Fm	N Yks	SE3757	54°0·7'	1°25·7'W	FM	104
Hall Fm	N Yks	SE4591	54°19·0'	1°18·1'W	FM	99
Hall Fm	N Yks	SE5236	53°49·3'	1°12·2'W	FM	105
Hall Fm	N Yks	SE5560	54°2·2'	1°9·2'W	FM	100
Hall Fm	N Yks	SE6698	54°22·6'	0°58·6'W	FM	94,100
Hall Fm	N Yks	SE6937	53°49·7'	0°56·7'W	FM	105,106
Hall Fm	N Yks	SE7482	54°13·9'	0°51·5'W	FM	100
Hall Fm	Oxon	SP4613	51°49·1'	1°19·6'W	FM	164
Hall Fm	Powys	SO2416	51°50·5'	3°5·8'W	FM	161
Hall Fm	Rut	SK9112	52°42·1'	0°38·8'W	FM	130
Hall Fm	Shrops	SJ4120	52°46·7'	2°52·1'W	FM	126
Hall Fm	Shrops	SO5279	52°24·7'	2°41·9'W	FM	137,138
Hall Fm	Shrops	SO5689	52°30·1'	2°38·5'W	FM	137,138
Hall Fm	Shrops	SO6987	52°29·0'	2°27·0'W	FM	138
Hall Fm	Staffs	SJ7627	52°50·6'	2°21·0'W	FM	127
Hall Fm	Staffs	SJ9327	52°50·7'	2°5·8'W	FM	127
Hall Fm	Staffs	SJ9534	52°54·4'	2°4·1'W	FM	127
Hall Fm	Staffs	SK1112	52°42·6'	1°49·8'W	FM	128
Hall Fm	Staffs	SK1355	53°5·8'	1°47·9'W	FM	119
Hall Fm	Suff	TL6547	52°6·0'	0°24·9'E	FM	154
Hall Fm	Suff	TL7173	52°19·9'	0°31·0'E	FM	154
Hall Fm	Suff	TL7270	52°18·3'	0°31·8'E	FM	154
Hall Fm	Suff	TL7957	52°11·2'	0°37·5'E	FM	155
Hall Fm	Suff	TL8667	52°16·4'	0°44·0'E	FM	155
Hall Fm	Suff	TL8861	52°13·1'	0°45·5'E	FM	155
Hall Fm	Suff	TL9059	52°12·0'	0°47·2'E	FM	155
Hall Fm	Suff	TL9559	52°11·9'	0°51·6'E	FM	155
Hall Fm	Suff	TL9680	52°23·2'	0°53·2'E	FM	144
Hall Fm	Suff	TL9967	52°16·1'	0°55·4'E	FM	155
Hall Fm	Suff	TM0577	52°21·4'	1°1·0'E	FM	144
Hall Fm	Suff	TM0878	52°21·9'	1°3·7'E	FM	144
Hall Fm	Suff	TM0974	52°19·7'	1°4·4'E	FM	144
Hall Fm	Suff	TM1273	52°19·1'	1°7·0'E	FM	144,155
Hall Fm	Suff	TM2056	52°9·7'	1°13·4'E	FM	156
Hall Fm	Suff	TM2172	52°18·3'	1°14·9'E	FM	156
Hall Fm	Suff	TM2553	52°8·0'	1°17·7'E	FM	156
Hall Fm	Suff	TM2772	52°18·2'	1°20·2'E	FM	156
Hall Fm	Suff	TM3259	52°11·0'	1°24·0'E	FM	156
Hall Fm	Suff	TM3363	52°13·2'	1°25·1'E	FM	156
Hall Fm	Suff	TM3972	52°17·9'	1°30·7'E	FM	156
Hall Fm	Suff	TM4374	52°18·8'	1°34·3'E	FM	156
Hall Fm	Suff	TM4483	52°23·7'	1°35·6'E	FM	156
Hall Fm	Suff	TM4589	52°26·9'	1°36·7'E	FM	134,156
Hall Fm	Suff	TM4589	52°26·9'	1°36·7'E	FM	156
Hall Fm	Suff	TM4986	52°25·1'	1°40·1'E	FM	156
Hall Fm	Suff	TM5183	52°23·5'	1°41·7'E	FM	156
Hall Fm	Suff	TM5187	52°25·6'	1°41·9'E	FM	156
Hall Fm	Tames	SK0097	53°28·4'	1°59·6'W	FM	110
Hall Fm	Warw	SP2389	52°30·1'	1°39·3'W	FM	139
Hall Fm	Wilts	ST8373	51°27·6'	2°14·3'W	FM	173
Hall Fm	Wok	SU7568	51°24·6'	0°54·9'W	FM	175
Hall Fm	Wok	SU8162	51°21·3'	0°49·8'W	FM	175,186
Hall Fm	Worcs	SO6462	52°15·5'	2°31·2'W	FM	138,149
Hall Fm	Worcs	SO9453	52°10·7'	2°4·9'W	FM	150
Hall Fm	Worcs	SO9742	52°4·8'	2°2·2'W	FM	150
Hall Fms	Norf	TG4517	52°41·9'	1°38·0'E	FM	134
Hall Fm, The	Shrops	SO6088	52°29·5'	2°34·9'W	FM	138
Hall Fm, The	Staffs	SJ8317	52°45·3'	2°14·7'W	FM	127
Hall Fm, The	Warw	SP4552	52°10·1'	1°20·1'W	FM	151
Hallfoot	Cumbr	NY4667	54°59·9'	2°50·2'W	X	86
Hall Foot	Lancs	SD7742	53°52·7'	2°20·6'W	X	103
Hall Forest	Aberd	NJ7715	57°13·8'	2°22·4'W	F	38
Hallforest	Aberd	NJ7715	57°13·8'	2°22·4'W	X	38
Hallgarden	Corn	SX1689	50°40·5'	4°35·9'W	X	190
Hall Garth	Cumbr	NY7713	54°31·0'	2°20·9'W	X	91
Hallgarth	Durham	NZ3343	54°47·1'	1°28·8'W	T	88
Hall Garth	E Yorks	SE9946	53°54·3'	0°29·2'W	X	106
Hall Garth	E Yorks	TA0945	53°53·6'	0°20·1'W	X	107
Hall Garth	Lancs	SD5170	54°7·7'	2°44·6'W	X	97
Hall Garth	N Yks	NZ5401	54°24·3'	1°9·7'W	X	93
Hall Garth	N Yks	SE2873	54°9·4'	1°33·9'W	A	99
Hall Garth	N Yks	SE4833	53°47·7'	1°15·9'W	A	105
Hall Garth	York	SE6751	53°57·3'	0°58·3'W	T	105,106
Hallgarth Fm	Lincs	TF2369	53°12·5'	0°9·1'W	FM	122
Hallgarth Ho	Worcs	SO9449	52°8·6'	2°4·9'W	X	150
Hall Garth (Hotel)	Darl	NZ2920	54°34·7'	1°32·7'W	X	93
Hall Garth Ponds	N Yks	SE3174	54°9·9'	1°31·1'W	W	99

Hallgate Fm	Lincs	TF3615	52°43·2'	0°1·2'E	FM	131
Hallgate Fm	W Susx	SU9820	50°58·5'	0°35·9'W	FM	197
Hall Gill	Lancs	SD5452	53°58·0'	2°41·7'W	W	102
Hallglen	Falk	NS8978	55°59·2'	3°46·3'W	T	65
Hallgreen	Aberd	NJ4947	57°30·9'	2°50·6'W	X	28,29
Hall Green	Birm	SP1181	52°25·8'	1°49·9'W	T	139
Hall Green	Ches	SJ8356	53°6·3'	2°14·8'W	T	118
Hall Green	Cov	SP3582	52°26·3'	1°28·7'W	T	140
Hall Green	Essex	TL7838	52°0·9'	0°36·0'E	T	155
Hall Green	Lancs	SD4624	53°42·8'	2°48·7'W	T	102
Hall Green	Lancs	SD5105	53°32·6'	2°44·0'W	T	108
Hall Green	Norf	TF9315	52°42·1'	0°51·8'E	X	132
Hall Green	Sand	SP0094	52°32·9'	1°59·6'W	T	139
Hall Green	Wakf	SE3115	53°38·1'	1°31·5'W	T	110,111
Hall Green	Wrex	SJ4942	52°58·6'	2°45·2'W	T	117
Hallgreen Castle	Aberd	NO8372	56°50·6'	2°16·3'W	A	45
Hall Green Fm	Cambs	TL3168	52°17·9'	0°4·3'W	FM	153
Hallgreen Mains	Aberd	NO8271	56°50·1'	2°17·2'W	X	45
Hall Grove	Herts	TL2511	51°47·2'	0°10·9'W	T	166
Hall Grove Fm	Surrey	SU9164	51°22·3'	0°41·2'W	FM	175,186
Hall Guards	Cumbr	NY5866	54°59·5'	2°39·0'W	X	86
Hallhays	Devon	ST1017	50°57·0'	3°16·5'W	X	181,193
Hall Heads	Durham	NZ2531	54°40·7'	1°36·3'W	X	93
Hall Heath	Suff	TL7969	52°17·6'	0°37·9'E	X	155
Hall Heath	Suff	TL8077	52°21·9'	0°39·0'E	X	144
Hallhill	Aberd	NO5972	56°50·5'	2°39·9'W	X	44
Hallhill	Aberd	NO8676	56°52·8'	2°13·3'W	X	45
Hall Hill	Ches	SJ9277	53°17·6'	2°6·8'W	X	118
Hall Hill	Cumbr	SD7799	54°23·4'	2°20·8'W	X	98
Hallhill	D & G	NX9079	55°5·8'	3°43·0'W	X	84
Hallhill	E Loth	NT6777	55°59·3'	2°31·3'W	X	67
Hallhill	Pth & Kin	NO0503	56°12·9'	3°31·5'W	X	58
Hallhill	Renf	NS4160	55°48·7'	4°31·8'W	X	64
Hallhill	S Lanak	NS8244	55°40·8'	3°52·2'W	X	71,72
Hallhill	Staffs	SK0763	53°10·1'	1°53·3'W	X	119
Hallhill Burn	S Lanak	NS8144	55°40·8'	3°53·1'W	W	71,72
Hall Hill Fm	Durham	NZ1243	54°47·2'	1°48·4'W	FM	88
Hall Hills	Cumbr	NY4767	54°59·9'	2°49·3'W	X	86
Hallhills	D & G	NY1488	55°11·0'	3°20·6'W	X	78
Hall Hills	Norf	TG1112	52°40·1'	1°7·6'E	X	133
Hall Hills Fm	Cumbr	NY3845	54°48·0'	2°57·4'W	FM	85
Hallhills Loch	D & G	NY1688	55°11·0'	3°18·7'W	W	79
Hall Ho	Cumbr	SD5591	54°19·0'	2°41·1'W	X	97
Hall Ho	Devon	SS5416	50°55·7'	4°4·3'W	X	180
Hall Ho	Kent	TQ7529	51°2·2'	0°30·2'E	X	188,199
Hallhole	Pth & Kin	NO1839	56°32·4'	3°19·6'W	X	53
Hall House Fm	Heref	SO7135	52°1·0'	2°25·0'W	FM	149
Halliagarry Burn	Highld	NC8521	58°10·0'	3°56·8'W	W	17
Halliagarry Hill	Highld	NC8422	58°10·6'	3°57·9'W	X	17
Halliburton	Scot Bord	NT4836	55°37·1'	2°49·1'W	T	73
Halliburton	Scot Bord	NT6748	55°43·7'	2°31·1'W	X	74
Hallicks Fm	Somer	ST2841	51°10·1'	3°1·4'W	FM	182
Hallidayhill	D & G	NX8986	55°9·6'	3°44·1'W	X	78
Hallidayhill	D & G	NY0974	55°3·4'	3°25·0'W	X	85
Halliday Hill	Lincs	TA1106	53°32·6'	0°19·1'W	F	113
Hallidays Fm	Lancs	SD4938	53°50·4'	2°46·1'W	FM	102
Hallifirs	Lincs	SK9675	53°16·0'	0°33·2'W	F	121
Halligarth	Shetld	HP6209	60°45·8'	0°51·2'W	X	1
Halligye	Corn	SW7123	50°4·0'	5°11·6'W	X	203
Halligill	Cumbr	NY6613	54°30·9'	2°31·1'W	X	91
Hallikeld Fm	N Yks	SE3996	54°21·7'	1°23·6'W	FM	99
Hallilee	Shetld	HU3921	59°58·6'	1°17·6'W	H	4
Halliloo Fm	Surrey	TQ3557	51°18·0'	0°3·4'W	FM	187
Halliman Skerries	Moray	NJ2172	57°44·1'	3°19·1'W	X	28
Hallin	Highld	NG2558	57°32·0'	6°35·2'W	T	23
Hallin Bank	Cumbr	NY4319	54°34·0'	2°52·5'W	X	90
Hallin Fell	Cumbr	NY4319	54°34·0'	2°52·5'W	H	90
Halling	Medway	TQ7064	51°21·2'	0°26·9'E	T	178,188
Hallingbury Park	Essex	TL5119	51°51·2'	0°11·9'E	X	167
Hallingbury Street	Essex	TL5219	51°51·2'	0°12·8'E	T	167
Hallings Fm	Somer	ST0625	51°1·2'	3°20·0'W	FM	181
Hallington	Lincs	TF3085	53°21·0'	0°2·4'W	T	122
Hallington	Northum	NY9875	55°4·4'	2°1·5'W	T	87
Hallington High Fm	Northum	NY9977	55°5·5'	2°0·5'W	FM	87
Hallington New Ho	Northum	NY9976	55°5·0'	2°0·5'W	X	87
Hallington Reservoirs	Northum	NY9776	55°5·0'	2°2·4'W	W	87
Hallington Top	Lincs	TF2886	53°21·6'	0°4·2'W	X	113,122
Hall i' th' Wood	Bolton	SD7211	53°35·9'	2°25·0'W	T	109
Hallival	Highld	NM3996	56°59·2'	6°17·3'W	H	39
Hallivick	Corn	SW9353	50°20·7'	4°54·2'W	X	200,204
Halliwell	Bolton	SD7010	53°35·4'	2°26·8'W	T	109
Halliwell Beck	Darl	NZ2322	54°35·8'	1°38·2'W	W	93
Halliwell Ho	Durham	NY8640	54°45·5'	2°12·6'W	X	87
Hall Lands Ho	Hants	SU4919	50°58·3'	1°17·7'W	X	185
Hall-lane Fm	Halton	SJ5882	53°20·2'	2°37·4'W	FM	108
Hall Leys	Derby	SK5476	53°16·9'	1°11·0'W	X	120
Hallmanor	Scot Bord	NT2035	55°36·4'	3°15·8'W	X	73
Hallmanor Burn	Scot Bord	NT1934	55°35·8'	3°16·7'W	W	72
Hall Meadow Fm	Warw	SP3339	52°3·1'	1°30·7'W	FM	151
Hallmill	Shrops	SJ3110	52°41·2'	3°0·8'W	X	126
Hall Moor	Darl	NZ2415	54°32·0'	1°37·3'W	X	93
Hall Moor	N Yks	NY9102	54°25·0'	2°7·9'W	X	91,92
Hall Moor	York	SE5758	54°1·1'	1°7·4'W	X	105
Hall Moor Fm	Derby	SK3464	53°10·6'	1°29·1'W	FM	119
Hallmoss	Aberd	NK0463	57°39·7'	1°55·5'W	X	30
Hallmoss	Aberd	NK1048	57°31·6'	1°49·5'W	X	30
Hall Moss	Stock	SJ8883	53°20·9'	2°10·4'W	X	109
Hallmuir	D & G	NY1279	55°6·1'	3°22·3'W	X	85
Hall o'Coole	Ches	SJ6245	53°0·3'	2°33·6'W	X	118
Hall of Aberuthven	Pth & Kin	NN9714	56°18·7'	3°39·5'W	X	58
Hall of Auchincross	E Ayr	NS5814	55°24·2'	4°14·1'W	X	71
Hall of Barnweill	S Ayr	NS4129	55°32·0'	4°30·7'W	X	70
Hall of Clestrain	Orkney	HY2907	58°56·9'	3°13·6'W	X	6,7
Hall of Drumpark	D & G	NX8779	55°5·8'	3°45·8'W	X	84
Hall of Hammonds Fm	Shrops	SO7278	52°24·2'	2°24·3'W	FM	138
Hall of Herston	Orkney	ND4190	58°47·9'	3°0·8'W	X	7
Hall of Kype	S Lanak	NS7041	55°39·0'	4°3·5'W	X	71
Hall of Mansfield	E Ayr	NS6314	55°24·3'	4°9·4'W	X	71
Hall of Rendall	Orkney	HY4220	59°4·0'	3°0·2'W	X	5,6
Hall of Tankerness	Orkney	HY5208	58°57·7'	2°49·6'W	X	6,7

Hall of the Forest	Shrops	SO2083	52°26·6′	3°10·2′W	X	137
Hall of Yenstay	Orkney	HY5009	58°58·2′	2°51·7′W	X	6,7
Hall o' Lee	Ches	SJ8456	53°6·3′	2°13·9′W	X	118
Hallon	Shrops	SO7596	52°33·9′	2°21·7′W	T	138
Hallonsford	Shrops	SO7596	52°33·9′	2°21·7′W	T	138
Hall Orchard Fm	Shrops	SO6880	52°25·3′	2°27·8′W	FM	138
Hall o'the Heath	Ches	SJ7555	53°5·7′	2°22·0′W	X	118
Hall o'th Hey	Ches	SJ5575	53°16·4′	2°40·1′W	X	117
Hall o' th' Hill	Lancs	SD6014	53°37·5′	2°35·9′W	X	109
Hall o'th' Wood	Staffs	SJ7650	53°3·0′	2°21·1′W	A	118
Halloughton	Notts	SK6851	53°3·4′	0°58·7′W	T	120
Halloughton Dumble	Notts	SK6850	53°2·8′	0°58·7′W	W	120
Halloughton Grange	Warw	SP2293	52°32·3′	1°40·1′W	X	139
Halloughton Wood	Notts	SK6751	53°3·4′	0°59·6′W	F	120
Halloughton Wood Fm	Notts	SK6751	53°3·4′	0°59·6′W	FM	120
Hall Out Pasture	N Yks	NY9001	54°24·5′	2°8·8′W	X	91,92
Hallow	Worcs	SO8258	52°13·4′	2°15·4′W	T	150
Hallow Bank	Cumbr	NY4605	54°26·5′	2°49·5′W	X	90
Hallow Burn	Scot Bord	NT0623	55°29·8′	3°28·8′W	W	72
Hallow Burn	Scot Bord	NT0823	55°29·8′	3°26·9′W	W	72
Hallowchapel	S Ayr	NX1987	55°8·9′	4°50·0′W	X	76
Hallowes	Derby	SK3577	53°17·6′	1°28·1′W	T	119
Hallow Heath	Worcs	SO8259	52°14·0′	2°15·4′W	T	150
Hallowkiln Wood	E Yorks	TA1466	54°4·9′	0°15·0′W	F	101
Hallow Park	Worcs	SO8357	52°12·9′	2°14·5′W	X	150
Hallowsgate	Ches	SJ5267	53°12·1′	2°42·7′W	T	117
Hallowshean	S Ayr	NS2405	55°18·7′	4°46·0′W	X	70,76
Hall Park	Devon	SS7524	51°0·3′	3°46·5′W	X	180
Hall Park	N Yks	NZ7707	54°27·4′	0°48·3′W	X	94
Hall Park	N Yks	TA0976	54°10·3′	0°19·4′W	X	101
Hall Parks Fm	Leeds	SE4448	53°55·8′	1°19·4′W	FM	105
Hall Pastures Fm	Derby	SK3232	52°53·3′	1°31·1′W	FM	128
Hallpeat Moss	Northum	NY7265	54°59·0′	2°25·8′W	X	86,87
Hall Place	Bexley	TQ5074	51°26·9′	0°9·9′E	A	177
Hall Place	Bucks	SU9691	51°36·8′	0°36·4′W	X	175,176
Hall Place	Hants	SU3626	51°2·2′	1°28·8′W	X	185
Hall Place	Kent	TQ5446	51°11·8′	0°12·6′E	X	188
Hall Place	Kent	TQ5655	51°16·6′	0°14·6′E	X	188
Hall Place	Kent	TQ7154	51°15·8′	0°27·5′E	X	188
Hall Place	Kent	TR1258	51°17·1′	1°2·8′E	X	179
Hall Place	Oxon	SU3487	51°35·1′	1°30·2′W	X	174
Hall Place	Surrey	TQ0237	51°7·6′	0°32·2′W	X	186
Hall Place	Win & Maid	SU8381	51°31·5′	0°47·8′W	X	175
Hall Place Fm	W Berks	SU5967	51°24·2′	1°8·7′W	FM	174
Hall Pool	Warw	SP2183	52°26·9′	1°41·1′W	W	139
Hall Pt	Suff	TM2038	52°0·0′	1°12·7′E	X	169
Hall Quarter	Stir	NS7886	56°3·3′	3°57·1′W	X	57
Hallrig	S Ayr	NS4227	55°30·9′	4°29·7′W	X	70
Hallrigg	Cumbr	NY4837	54°43·8′	2°48·0′W	X	90
Hall Rings	Corn	SX2155	50°22·3′	4°30·7′W	A	201
Hall Road Sta	Sefton	SD3000	53°29·8′	3°2·9′W	X	108
Hallroom	Pth & Kin	NO1332	56°28·6′	3°24·3′W	X	53
Hallrule	Scot Bord	NT5914	55°25·3′	2°38·4′W	X	80
Hallrule Mill	Scot Bord	NT5913	55°24·8′	2°38·4′W	X	80
Halls	Corn	SS2209	50°51·4′	4°31·4′W	X	190
Halls	E Loth	NT6572	55°56·6′	2°33·2′W	X	67
Hallsands	Devon	SX8138	50°14·0′	3°39·7′W	T	202
Hallsannery	Devon	SS4524	50°59·9′	4°12·2′W	X	180,190
Hall Santon	Cumbr	NY1001	54°24·0′	3°22·8′W	T	89
Hall's Burn	S Lanak	NS6736	55°36·2′	4°6·2′W	W	71
Hallscaur	D & G	NS7701	55°17·5′	3°55·8′W	X	78
Hallscaur Craig	D & G	NS7701	55°17·5′	3°55·8′W	X	78
Hall's Close	E Susx	TQ6809	50°51·6′	0°23·6′E	T	199
Halls Cross	Devon	SS6241	51°9·3′	3°58·0′W	X	180
Hallsdown Fm	Devon	SS6341	51°9·3′	3°57·2′W	FM	180
Hall Senna	Cumbr	NY0601	54°24·0′	3°26·5′W	X	89
Hallsenna Moor	Cumbr	NY0600	54°23·5′	3°26·4′W	X	89
Hall's Fell	Cumbr	NY3226	54°37·7′	3°2·8′W	X	90
Hallsfell Top	Cumbr	NY3227	54°38·3′	3°2·8′W	H	90
Halls Fm	Cambs	TF3603	52°36·7′	0°0·9′E	FM	142
Hall's Fm	Hants	SU5260	51°20·4′	1°14·8′W	FM	174
Hall's Fm	Hants	SU7462	51°21·4′	0°55·8′W	FM	175,186
Halls Fm	Midlo	NT2358	55°48·8′	3°13·3′W	FM	66,73
Hall's Fm	Norf	TG4007	52°36·7′	1°33·1′E	FM	134
Hall's Fm	Worcs	SO7877	52°23·7′	2°19·0′W	FM	138
Hallsford	Cumbr	NY4772	55°2·6′	2°49·3′W	X	86
Hallsford Bridge	Essex	TL5602	51°41·9′	0°15·8′E	T	167
Halls Green	Essex	TL4108	51°45·4′	0°3·0′E	T	167
Hall's Green	Herts	TL2728	51°56·4′	0°8·7′W	T	166
Hall's Green	Kent	TQ5249	51°13·4′	0°11·0′E	T	188
Hall's Grove	Glos	SO9811	51°48·1′	2°1·3′W	X	163
Hall's Hill	Lincs	SK9235	52°54·5′	0°37·5′W	X	130
Hallshill	Northum	NY8988	55°11·4′	2°9·9′W	X	80
Hall's Hill	Warw	SP4250	52°9·0′	1°22·8′W	X	151
Hallside	S Lanak	NS6660	55°49·1′	4°7·9′W	X	64
Hallslake	Devon	SS7448	51°13·3′	3°47·9′W	X	180
Hallsmead Ait	Oxon	SU7677	51°29·4′	0°53·9′W	X	175
Halls of Duncanstone	Aberd	NJ5826	57°19·6′	2°41·4′W	X	37
Hallsoven	Cumbr	NY4673	55°3·2′	2°50·3′W	X	86
Hallspill	Devon	SS4723	50°59·4′	4°10·4′W	T	180
Hall's Place	Kent	TQ9453	51°14·8′	0°47·2′E	X	189
Hallstack Fm	N Yks	SD8057	54°0·8′	2°17·9′W	FM	103
Hallstead	Cumbr	SD2484	54°15·0′	3°9·6′W	X	96
Hall's Tenement	Cumbr	NY5251	54°51·3′	2°44·4′W	X	86
Hallsworth Fold Fm	Lancs	SD6015	53°38·0′	2°35·9′W	FM	109
Hall, The	Cambs	TL4238	52°1·6′	0°4·6′E	X	154
Hall, The	Cambs	TL5857	52°11·5′	0°19·1′E	X	154
Hall, The	Cambs	TL6355	52°10·4′	0°23·4′E	X	154
Hall, The	Cambs	TL7068	52°17·3′	0°30·0′E	X	154
Hall The	Ches	SJ4468	53°12·6′	2°49·9′W	X	117
Hall, The	Ches	SJ7954	53°5·2′	2°18·4′W	X	118
Hall, The	Cumbr	NY4758	54°55·1′	2°49·2′W	X	86
Hall, The	Derby	SK0972	53°14·9′	1°51·5′W	X	119
Hall, The	Derby	SK1335	52°55·0′	1°48·0′W	A	128
Hall, The	Derby	SK1971	53°14·4′	1°42·5′W	A	119
Hall, The	Derby	SK2329	52°51·7′	1°39·1′W	X	128
Hall, The	Derby	SK3728	52°51·1′	1°26·6′W	X	128
Hall, The	Essex	TL4435	51°59·9′	0°6·3′E	X	154
Hall, The	Essex	TL4926	51°55·0′	0°10·4′E	X	167
Hall, The	Essex	TL5431	51°57·6′	0°14·9′E	X	167
Hall, The	Essex	TL5917	51°50·0′	0°18·9′E	X	167
Hall, The	E Susx	TQ8512	50°52·9′	0°38·2′E	X	199
Hall, The	E Yorks	TA1545	53°53·5′	0°14·6′W	X	107
Hall, The	Heref	SO5026	51°56·1′	2°43·2′W	X	162
Hall, The	Kent	TQ8442	51°9·1′	0°38·3′E	X	188
Hall, The	Kent	TR0842	51°8·6′	0°58·8′E	X	179,189
Hall, The	Kirk	SE2518	53°39·7′	1°36·9′W	A	110
Hall, The	Leic	SK6309	52°40·7′	1°3·7′W	X	140
Hall, The	Leic	SK7913	52°42·8′	0°49·4′W	X	129
Hall, The	Leic	SP6484	52°27·2′	1°3·1′W	X	140
Hall, The	Leic	SP7196	52°33·7′	0°56·8′W	X	141
Hall, The	Lincs	SK8857	53°6·4′	0°40·7′W	X	121
Hall, The	N Lincs	SK8099	53°29·1′	0°47·2′W	X	112
Hall, The	Norf	TF7016	52°43·1′	0°31·4′E	X	132
Hall, The	Norf	TG2525	52°46·8′	1°20·6′E	X	133,134
Hall, The	Norf	TG3810	52°38·4′	1°31·5′E	X	133,134
Hall, The	Norf	TG4226	52°46·9′	1°35·7′E	X	134
Hall, The	Norf	TG4326	52°46·8′	1°36·6′E	A	134
Hall, The	Norf	TG4522	52°44·6′	1°38·2′E	X	134
Hall, The	Norf	TM0082	52°24·2′	0°56·8′E	X	144
Hall, The	Norf	TM1878	52°21·6′	1°12·5′E	X	156
Hall, The	Norf	TM2185	52°25·3′	1°15·4′E	X	156
Hall, The	Norf	TM3395	52°30·4′	1°26·4′E	X	134
Hall, The	Norf	TM3794	52°29·8′	1°29·9′E	X	134
Hall, The	Norf	TM3893	52°29·2′	1°30·7′E	X	134
Hall, The	Norf	TM3996	52°30·8′	1°31·7′E	A	134
Hall, The	Northnts	SP9771	52°19·9′	0°34·2′W	X	141,153
Hall, The	Northum	NZ0878	55°6·0′	1°52·0′W	X	88
Hall, The	Notts	SK5580	53°19·1′	1°10·1′W	X	111,120
Hall, The	Notts	SK5829	52°51·6′	1°7·9′W	A	129
Hall, The	Notts	SK6239	52°56·9′	1°4·2′W	X	129
Hall, The	Notts	SK6854	53°5·0′	0°58·7′W	X	120
Hall, The	Notts	SK7142	52°58·5′	0°56·2′W	X	129
Hall, The	Notts	SK7149	53°2·2′	0°56·1′W	X	129
Hall, The	Notts	SK7154	53°4·9′	0°56·0′W	X	120
Hall, The	Notts	SK7339	52°56·8′	0°54·4′W	X	129
Hall, The	Notts	SK7890	53°24·3′	0°49·2′W	X	112
Hall, The	Notts	SK7958	53°7·0′	0°48·8′W	X	120,121
Hall, The	Notts	SK8271	53°14·0′	0°45·9′W	X	121
Hall, The	N Som	ST4156	51°18·2′	2°50·4′W	X	172,182
Hall, The	N Yks	SE3181	54°13·7′	1°31·1′W	A	99
Hall, The	N Yks	SE7366	54°5·3′	0°52·6′W	X	100
Hall, The	Orkney	ND4487	58°46·3′	2°57·6′W	X	7
Hall, The	Pemb	SM8602	51°40·8′	5°5·3′W	X	157
Hall, The	Powys	SJ2915	52°43·9′	3°2·7′W	X	126
Hall, The	Powys	SO0571	52°20·0′	3°23·3′W	X	136,147
Hall, The	Powys	SO1164	52°16·3′	3°17·9′W	X	148
Hall, The	Shetld	HU6098	60°39·9′	0°53·6′W	X	1
Hall, The	Shrops	SJ5834	52°54·3′	2°37·1′W	X	126
Hall, The	Shrops	SJ6625	52°49·5′	2°29·9′W	X	127
Hall, The	Shrops	SJ7028	52°51·2′	2°26·3′W	X	127
Hall, The	Shrops	SJ7907	52°39·9′	2°18·2′W	X	127
Hall, The	Staffs	SO8494	52°32·9′	2°13·8′W	X	138
Hall, The	Suff	TL6267	52°16·9′	0°22·9′E	X	154
Hall, The	Suff	TM2356	52°9·7′	1°16·0′E	X	156
Hall, The	Wrekin	SJ6319	52°46·3′	2°32·5′W	X	127
Hallthwaites	Cumbr	SD1885	54°15·5′	3°15·1′W	T	96
Hall Torbane Fm	W Loth	NS9566	55°52·8′	3°40·3′W	FM	65
Halltown	Cumbr	NY3463	54°57·7′	3°1·4′W	X	85
Hall Treasses	Fife	NO4109	56°16·4′	2°56·7′W	X	59
Halltree	Scot Bord	NT4152	55°45·7′	2°56·0′W	X	66,73
Hall Trees Fm	Lancs	SD6042	53°52·6′	2°36·1′W	FM	102,103
Hall Villa	Donc	SE5608	53°34·2′	1°8·9′W	X	111
Hall Waberthwaite	Cumbr	SD1095	54°20·8′	3°22·7′W	T	96
Hallwith Fm	N Yks	SE1488	54°17·5′	1°46·7′W	FM	99
Hall Wood	Corn	SX2155	50°22·3′	4°30·7′W	F	201
Hall Wood	Cumbr	NY4503	54°25·4′	2°50·4′W	F	90
Hall Wood	Cumbr	SD3393	54°19·9′	3°1·4′W	F	96,97
Hall Wood	Derby	SK2652	53°4·1′	1°36·3′W	F	119
Hall Wood	Essex	TL7606	51°43·7′	0°33·3′E	F	167
Hall Wood	Essex	TQ6293	51°37·0′	0°20·8′E	F	177
Hall Wood	Kent	TQ6261	51°19·7′	0°19·9′E	F	177,188
Hall Wood	Leeds	SE4246	53°54·7′	1°21·2′W	F	105
Hall Wood	N Yks	SE1779	54°12·6′	1°43·9′W	F	99
Hall Wood	Suff	TL9444	52°3·8′	0°50·2′E	F	155
Hallwood Fm	Ches	SJ3475	53°16·3′	2°59·0′W	FM	117
Hallwood Fm	Devon	SS5108	50°51·4′	4°6·6′W	FM	191
Hallwood Green	Glos	SO6733	51°59·9′	2°28·4′W	T	149
Hallworthy	Corn	SX1887	50°39·5′	4°34·1′W	T	190
Hallyards	Aberd	NJ5462	57°39·0′	2°45·8′W	X	29
Hallyards	C of Edin	NT1273	55°56·8′	3°24·1′W	X	65
Hallyards	Northum	NZ0761	54°56·9′	1°53·0′W	X	88
Hallyards	Pth & Kin	NO2746	56°36·3′	3°10·9′W	X	53
Hallyards	S Ayr	NS3533	55°33·9′	4°36·6′W	X	70
Hallyards	Scot Bord	NT2137	55°37·5′	3°14·8′W	T	73
Hallyards Castle	Fife	NT2191	56°6·6′	3°15·8′W	A	58
Hall Yards Fm	Lincs	TF1668	53°12·0′	0°15·4′W	FM	121
Hallyburton Ho	Pth & Kin	NO2438	56°31·9′	3°13·7′W	X	53
Hallydown	Scot Bord	NT9264	55°52·4′	2°7·2′W	X	67
Hallyholm	D & G	NX1238	54°42·4′	4°54·7′W	X	82
Hallyne	Scot Bord	NT1940	55°39·1′	3°16·8′W	T	72
Hallytreeholme	E Yorks	TA0849	53°55·8′	0°20·9′W	X	107
Hallywell Hill	Scot Bord	NT5019	55°28·0′	2°47·0′W	X	79
Hallywell Rig	Scot Bord	NT6953	55°46·4′	2°29·2′W	X	67,74
Halmadarie Burn	Highld	NC6930	58°14·6′	4°13·4′W	W	16
Halmer End	Staffs	SJ7949	53°2·5′	2°18·4′W	T	118
Halmerend Hall	Staffs	SJ7849	53°2·5′	2°19·3′W	X	118
Halmond's Frome	Heref	SO6747	52°7·5′	2°28·5′W	T	149
Halmore	Glos	SO6902	51°43·2′	2°26·5′W	T	162
Halmpstone Manor	Devon	SS5928	51°2·3′	4°0·3′W	X	180
Halmyre	D & G	NX7659	54°54·9′	3°55·6′W	X	84
Halmyre	D & G	NX8166	54°58·7′	3°51·1′W	X	84
Halmyre	D & G	NX9376	55°4·3′	3°40·1′W	X	84
Halmyre Deans	Scot Bord	NT1748	55°43·4′	3°18·8′W	X	72
Halmyre Ho	Scot Bord	NT1749	55°43·9′	3°18·9′W	X	72
Halmyre Mains	Scot Bord	NT1749	55°43·9′	3°18·9′W	T	72
Halnaby Grange	N Yks	NZ2605	54°26·6′	1°35·5′W	X	93
Halnaby Hall	N Yks	NZ2606	54°27·2′	1°35·5′W	X	93
Halnaker	W Susx	SU9008	50°52·1′	0°42·9′W	T	197
Halnaker Hill	W Susx	SU9109	50°52·6′	0°42·0′W	H	197
Halnaker Ho	W Susx	SU9008	50°52·1′	0°42·9′W	A	197
Halnaker Park	W Susx	SU9009	50°52·6′	0°42·9′W	X	197
Halsall	Lancs	SD3610	53°35·2′	2°57·6′W	T	108
Halsall Moss	Lancs	SD3511	53°35·7′	2°58·5′W	X	108
Halsall's Lodge Fm	Lancs	SD4408	53°34·2′	2°50·3′W	FM	108
Halsary	Highld	ND1849	58°25·6′	3°23·8′W	X	11,12
Halsbeer Fm	Devon	ST0809	50°52·6′	3°18·1′W	FM	192
Halsbury Barton	Devon	SS4121	50°58·2′	4°15·5′W	X	180,190
Halscombe	Devon	SX8889	50°41·6′	3°34·8′W	X	192
Halscombe	Somer	SS7738	51°7·9′	3°45·1′W	X	180
Halscombe Allotment	Somer	SS8133	51°5·3′	3°41·6′W	X	181
Halscombe Fm	Somer	SS9130	51°3·8′	3°32·9′W	FM	181
Halsdon Barton	Devon	SS3805	50°49·6′	4°17·6′W	X	190
Halsdon Ho	Devon	SS5512	50°53·6′	4°3·3′W	X	180
Halsdon Ho	Devon	ST1804	50°50·0′	3°9·5′W	X	192,193
Halsdown Fm	Somer	ST0425	51°1·2′	3°21·7′W	FM	181
Halse	Devon	SS7711	50°53·4′	3°44·5′W	X	191
Halse	Northnts	SP5640	52°3·6′	1°10·6′W	T	152
Halse	Somer	ST1427	51°2·4′	3°13·2′W	T	181,193
Halse Copse	Northnts	SP5741	52°4·1′	1°9·7′W	F	152
Halsecopse Fm	Northnts	SP5641	52°4·1′	1°10·6′W	FM	152
Halse Fm	Devon	SS6700	50°47·3′	3°52·8′W	FM	191
Halse Fm	Somer	SS8934	51°5·9′	3°34·7′W	FM	181
Halsegate Cross	Devon	SS6700	50°47·3′	3°52·8′W	X	191
Halse Moor	Devon	SS6700	50°47·3′	3°52·8′W	X	191
Halsetown	Corn	SW5038	50°11·6′	5°29·8′W	T	203
Halse Water	Somer	ST1527	51°2·4′	3°12·4′W	W	181,193
Halsewood	Devon	SS9806	50°50·9′	3°26·6′W	X	192
Halseycross Fm	Somer	ST2038	51°8·4′	3°8·2′W	FM	182
Halsey's Fm	W Susx	SZ8697	50°46·2′	0°46·4′W	FM	197
Halsey Wood	Beds	SP9961	52°14·5′	0°32·6′W	F	153
Halsfordwood	Devon	SX8793	50°43·8′	3°35·7′W	T	192
Halsgrove	Somer	SS8436	51°6·9′	3°39·1′W	X	181
Halsham	E Yorks	TA2727	53°43·7′	0°4·1′W	T	107
Halsham Grange	E Yorks	TA2628	53°44·2′	0°5·0′W	X	107
Halshanger	Devon	SX7573	50°32·8′	3°45·5′W	X	191
Halshanger Common	Devon	SX7474	50°33·4′	3°46·3′W	X	191
Halshayne Manor Fm	Devon	SY2298	50°46·8′	3°6·0′W	FM	192,193
Halsinger	Devon	SS5138	51°7·6′	4°7·4′W	T	180
Halsinger Down	Devon	SS5139	51°8·1′	4°7·4′W	X	180
Halstead	Essex	TL8130	51°56·6′	0°38·4′E	T	168
Halstead	Kent	TQ4861	51°20·0′	0°7·9′E	T	177,188
Halstead	Leic	SK7505	52°38·5′	0°53·1′W	T	141
Halstead Fell	Lancs	SD7360	54°2·4′	2°24·3′W	X	98
Halstead Hall	Lincs	TF1866	53°10·9′	0°13·6′W	X	122
Halstead Ho	Leic	SK7505	52°38·5′	0°53·1′W	X	141
Halsteads	Lancs	SD7444	53°53·7′	2°23·3′W	X	103
Halsteads	N Yks	SD6873	54°9·4′	2°29·0′W	X	98
Halsteads Fm	Lancs	SD7459	54°1·8′	2°23·4′W	FM	103
Halsteads Fm	Lancs	SD8046	53°54·8′	2°17·9′W	FM	103
Halstead Wood	Lincs	TF1965	53°10·4′	0°12·8′W	F	122
Halstock	Dorset	ST5308	50°52·4′	2°39·7′W	T	194
Halston	Shrops	SJ4107	52°39·7′	2°51·9′W	X	126
Halston Hall	Shrops	SJ3431	52°52·6′	2°58·4′W	A	126
Halstow	Devon	SX8292	50°43·2′	3°39·9′W	X	191
Halstow Creek	Kent	TQ8668	51°23·1′	0°40·8′E	W	178
Halstow Marshes	Medway	TQ7778	51°28·6′	0°33·3′E	X	178
Halsway	Somer	ST1237	51°7·8′	3°15·1′W	T	181
Halsway Manor	Somer	ST1238	51°8·3′	3°15·1′W	X	181
Halswell	Devon	SX7867	50°29·6′	3°42·8′W	X	202
Halswell Fm	Devon	SS6724	51°0·2′	3°53·4′W	FM	180
Halswell House	Somer	ST2533	51°5·7′	3°3·9′W	A	182
Halsworthy	Devon	SX7568	50°30·2′	3°45·4′W	X	202
Haltadans	Shetld	HU6292	60°36·7′	0°51·5′W	A	1,2
Haltcliff Bridge	Cumbr	NY3636	54°43·1′	2°59·2′W	T	90
Haltcliff Hall	Cumbr	NY3637	54°43·7′	2°59·2′W	X	90
Haltcliff Ho	Cumbr	NY3536	54°43·1′	3°0·1′W	X	90
Haltcliff View	Cumbr	NY3535	54°42·6′	3°0·1′W	X	90
Haltemprice Fm	E Yorks	TA0430	53°45·6′	0°24·9′W	FM	107
Halter Burn	Scot Bord	NT8427	55°32·4′	2°14·8′W	W	74
Halterburn	Scot Bord	NT8427	55°32·4′	2°14·8′W	X	74
Halterworth	Hants	SU3721	50°59·5′	1°28·0′W	T	185
Halt Fm	Oxon	SP3230	51°58·3′	1°31·7′W	FM	151
Haltham	Lincs	TF2463	53°9·2′	0°8·3′W	T	122
Haltham Beck	Lincs	TF2564	53°9·7′	0°7·4′W	W	122
Haltham Wood	Lincs	TF2663	53°9·2′	0°6·5′W	F	122
Haltoft End	Lincs	TF3645	52°59·3′	0°2·0′E	T	131
Halton	Bucks	SP8710	51°47·1′	0°43·9′W	T	165
Halton	Halton	SJ5381	53°19·7′	2°41·9′W	T	108
Halton	Lancs	SD5064	54°4·4′	2°45·4′W	T	97
Halton	Leeds	SE3433	53°47·8′	1°28·6′W	T	104
Halton	Northum	NY9967	55°0·1′	2°0·5′W	T	87
Halton	Wrex	SJ3039	52°56·9′	3°2·1′W	T	126
Halton Barton	Corn	SX4065	50°28·0′	4°14·9′W	X	201
Halton Br	Lincs	TF4264	53°9·5′	0°7·8′E	X	122
Halton Br	N Yks	SD8555	53°59·7′	2°13·3′W	X	103
Halton Brook	Halton	SJ5282	53°20·2′	2°42·8′W	X	108
Halton Camp	Bucks	SP8809	51°46·6′	0°43·1′W	X	165
Halton Drain	N Lincs	SE9121	53°40·9′	0°36·9′W	W	106,112
Halton East	N Yks	SE0453	53°58·6′	1°55·9′W	T	104
Halton Fenside	Lincs	TF4263	53°8·9′	0°7·8′E	T	122
Halton Fm	Wrex	SJ3039	52°56·9′	3°2·1′W	FM	126
Halton Gill	N Yks	SD8876	54°11·0′	2°10·6′W	T	98
Halton Green	Lancs	SD5165	54°5·0′	2°44·5′W	T	97
Halton Green	N Yks	SE0354	53°59·2′	1°56·8′W	X	104
Halton Height	N Yks	SE0355	53°59·7′	1°56·8′W	X	104
Halton Hill	Fife	NO2416	56°20·1′	3°13·3′W	X	59
Halton Holegate	Lincs	TF4165	53°10·0′	0°7·0′E	T	122
Halton Holegate Fen	Lincs	TF4261	53°7·9′	0°7·8′E	X	122
Halton Lea	Northum	NY6558	54°55·2′	2°32·3′W	X	86
Haltonlea Fell	Northum	NY6457	54°54·6′	2°33·3′W	X	86
Halton Lea Gate	Northum	NY6558	54°55·2′	2°32·3′W	T	86
Halton Marshes	N Lincs	TA1521	53°40·6′	0°15·1′W	X	107,113
Halton Moor	Leeds	SE3433	53°47·8′	1°28·6′W	T	104
Halton Moor	N Yks	SE0355	53°59·7′	1°56·8′W	X	104
Halton Moss	Halton	SJ5684	53°21·3′	2°39·3′W	X	108
Halton Park	Lancs	SD5265	54°5·0′	2°43·6′W	X	97
Halton Place	N Yks	SD8554	53°59·2′	2°13·3′W	X	103
Halton Quay	Corn	SX4165	50°28·0′	4°14·1′W	X	201
Halton Red House	Northum	NZ0068	55°0·6′	1°59·6′W	X	87

Halton Shields	Northum	NZ0168	55°0·6′	1°58·6′W	T	87
Halton View	Halton	SJ5286	53°22·4′	2°42·9′W	T	108
Halton West	N Yks	SD8454	53°59·2′	2°14·2′W	T	103
Halton Wood	Bucks	SP8808	51°46·1′	0°43·1′W	F	165
Halton Wood	Wrex	SJ3040	52°57·4′	3°2·1′W	F	117
Haltosh Point	N Eil	NF8886	57°45·6′	7°14·3′W	X	18
Haltwhistle	Northum	NY7064	54°58·4′	2°27·7′W	T	86,87
Haltwhistle Burn	Northum	NY7065	54°59·0′	2°27·7′W	W	86,87
Haltwhistle Common	Northum	NY7065	54°59·0′	2°27·7′W	X	86,87
Halvana	Corn	SX2178	50°34·7′	4°31·3′W	X	201
Halvana Plantn	Corn	SX2078	50°34·7′	4°32·2′W	F	201
Halvergate	Norf	TG4206	52°36·1′	1°34·8′E	T	134
Halvergate Marshes	Norf	TG4607	52°36·5′	1°38·4′E	X	134
Halvose	Corn	SW7525	50°5·2′	5°8·4′W	X	204
Halvosso	Corn	SW7433	50°9·5′	5°9·5′W	X	204
Halwell	Corn	SX3076	50°33·8′	4°23·6′W	X	201
Halwell	Devon	SX5352	50°21·2′	4°3·6′W	X	201
Halwell	Devon	SX7753	50°22·1′	3°43·4′W	T	202
Halwell Camp	Devon	SX7853	50°22·1′	3°42·6′W	A	202
Halwell Fm	Devon	SX8268	50°30·2′	3°39·5′W	FM	202
Halwell Ho	Devon	SX7640	50°15·1′	3°44·0′W	X	202
Halwill	Devon	SX4299	50°46·4′	4°14·1′W	T	190
Halwill Barton	Corn	SX1288	50°39·9′	4°39·2′W	X	190,200
Halwill Junction	Devon	SS4400	50°47·0′	4°12·4′W	T	190
Halwill Mill	Devon	SX4298	50°45·8′	4°14·0′W	X	190
Halwill Moor Plantation	Devon	SS4300	50°46·9′	4°13·2′W	F	190
Halwin	Corn	SW6933	50°9·4′	5°13·7′W	T	203
Halwinnick Butts	Corn	SX3074	50°32·7′	4°23·6′W	X	201
Halwyn	Corn	SW4626	50°5·0′	5°32·7′W	X	203
Halwyn	Corn	SW7823	50°4·2′	5°5·8′W	X	204
Halwyn	Corn	SW8038	50°12·3′	5°4·6′W	X	204
Halwyn	Corn	SW9373	50°31·4′	4°54·9′W	X	200
Halymyres	Aberd	NO8683	56°56·5′	2°13·4′W	X	45
Halzephron Cliff	Corn	SW6521	50°2·8′	5°16·6′W	X	203
Halzephron Cove	Corn	SW6521	50°2·8′	5°16·6′W	W	203
Ham	C of Plym	SX4657	50°23·8′	4°9·6′W	T	201
Ham	Devon	ST2301	50°48·4′	3°5·2′W	T	192,193
Ham	Glos	SO9721	51°53·5′	2°2·2′W	T	163
Ham	Glos	ST6898	51°41·0′	2°27·4′W	T	162
Ham	Highld	ND2373	58°38·5′	3°19·1′W	T	7,12
Ham	Kent	TR3254	51°14·5′	1°19·8′E	T	179
Ham	Rich	TQ1772	51°26·3′	0°18·6′W	T	176
Ham	Shetld	HT9739	60°8·4′	2°2·7′W	T	4
Ham	Shetld	HU4939	60°8·2′	1°6·6′W	X	4
Ham	Somer	SS9040	51°9·2′	3°34·0′W	X	181
Ham	Somer	ST1521	50°59·2′	3°12·3′W	T	181,193
Ham	Somer	ST2825	51°1·4′	3°1·2′W	T	193
Ham	Somer	ST2913	50°55·0′	3°0·2′W	T	193
Ham	Somer	ST3251	51°15·5′	2°58·1′W	X	182
Ham	Somer	ST6748	51°14·0′	2°28·0′W	T	183
Ham	V of Glam	SS9877	51°29·2′	3°27·8′W	X	170
Ham	Wilts	SU3362	51°21·6′	1°31·2′W	T	174
Hamalan	N Eil	NF1097	57°47·8′	8°33·5′W	X	18
Hamar	Orkney	HY5336	59°12·7′	2°48·9′W	X	5
Hamar	Shetld	HP6409	60°45·8′	0°49·0′W	X	1
Hamar	Shetld	HT9438	60°7·9′	2°6·0′W	X	4
Hamar	Shetld	HU3176	60°28·3′	1°25·7′W	T	3
Hamar	Shetld	HU4863	60°21·2′	1°7·3′W	X	2,3
Hamar	Shetld	HU5136	60°6·6′	1°4·5′W	X	4
Hamara Field	Shetld	HU3190	60°35·8′	1°25·5′W	X	1
Hamara Field	Shetld	HU6093	60°37·2′	0°53·7′W	H	1,2
Hamaramore	Highld	NG1649	57°26·8′	6°43·6′W	T	23
Hamara Neap	Shetld	HU5966	60°22·7′	0°55·3′W	X	2
Hamara River	Highld	NG1847	57°25·8′	6°41·5′W	W	23
Hamara Scord	Shetld	HU3376	60°28·2′	1°23·5′W	X	2,3
Hamaraverin	Highld	NG1649	57°26·8′	6°43·6′W	T	23
Hamarberg	Shetld	HP5803	60°42·6′	0°55·7′W	X	1
Hamarfiold	Orkney	HY3833	59°11·0′	3°4·6′W	X	6
Hamarhill	Orkney	HY5736	59°12·8′	2°44·7′W	T	5,6
Hamari Field	Shetld	HU4127	60°1·8′	1°15·4′W	H	4
Hamarigrind	Shetld	HU4061	60°20·1′	1°16·0′W	X	2,3
Hamarigrind Scord	Shetld	HU4060	60°19·6′	1°16·0′W	X	2,3
Hamari Water	Shetld	HU2555	60°17·0′	1°32·4′W	W	3
Hamars	Orkney	HY5141	59°15·4′	2°51·1′W	X	5
Hamars	Shetld	HU4064	60°21·7′	1°16·0′W	T	2,3
Hamars Ness	Shetld	HU5894	60°37·8′	0°55·9′W	X	1,2
Hamars of Burraland, The	Shetld	HU3375	60°27·7′	1°23·5′W	H	2,3
Hamars of Houlland	Shetld	HU5080	60°30·3′	1°4·9′W	X	1,2,3
Hamars, The	Shetld	HP5910	60°46·4′	0°54·5′W	X	1
Hamars, The	Shetld	HU3926	60°1·3′	1°17·5′W	X	4
Hamars, The	Shetld	HU4446	60°12·0′	1°11·9′W	X	4
Hamars, The	Shetld	HU4524	60°0·2′	1°11·1′W	H	4
Hamar, The	Shetld	HU1849	60°13·8′	1°40·0′W	X	3
Hamar, The	Shetld	HU1948	60°13·2′	1°38·9′W	H	3
Hamarty Hill	D & G	NS9802	55°18·3′	3°36·0′W	H	78
Hamar Voe	Shetld	HU3076	60°28·3′	1°26·8′W	W	3
Hamatethy	Corn	SX0978	50°34·5′	4°41·5′W	X	200
Ham Barn	Glos	SU1797	51°40·5′	1°44·9′W	X	163
Hamberhayne	Devon	SY2195	50°45·2′	3°6·8′W	X	192,193
Hamberlins Fm	Herts	SP9609	51°46·5′	0°36·1′W	FM	165
Ham Berry	Highld	ND2473	58°38·6′	3°18·1′W	X	7,12
Hamberts Fm	Essex	TQ8098	51°39·3′	0°36·5′E	FM	168
Hamblecliff Ho	Hants	SU4607	50°51·9′	1°20·4′W	X	196
Hamble Common	Hants	SU4806	50°51·3′	1°18·7′W	X	196
Hambleden	Bucks	SU7886	51°34·3′	0°52·1′W	T	175
Hambledon	Hants	SU6414	50°55·5′	1°5·0′W	T	196
Hambledon	Surrey	SU9638	51°8·2′	0°37·3′W	T	186
Hambledon Hill	Dorset	ST8412	50°54·7′	2°13·3′W	X	194
Hambledon Hill (Neolithic Camp)	Dorset	ST8412	50°54·7′	2°13·3′W	A	194
Hambledon Hurst	Surrey	SU9637	51°7·7′	0°37·3′W	F	186
Hamble-le-Rice	Hants	SU4706	50°51·3′	1°19·6′W	T	196
Hamble Spit	Hants	SU4804	50°50·2′	1°18·7′W	X	196
Hambleton	Lancs	SD3742	53°52·5′	2°57·1′W	T	102
Hambleton	N Yks	SE0553	53°58·6′	1°55·0′W	T	104
Hambleton	N Yks	SE5530	53°46·0′	1°9·5′W	T	105
Hambleton Fold Fm	Stock	SJ9989	53°24·1′	2°0·5′W	FM	109
Hambleton Hill	Lincs	SK9241	52°57·7′	0°37·4′W	X	130
Hambleton Hill	N Yks	SE1473	54°9·4′	1°46·7′W	X	99
Hambleton Hills, The	N Yks	SE5187	54°16·8′	1°12·6′W	H	100
Hambleton Ho	N Yks	SE5283	54°14·6′	1°11·7′W	X	100
Hambleton Hough	N Yks	SE5529	53°45·5′	1°9·5′W	F	105
Hambleton House Fm	N Yks	SE2051	53°57·5′	1°41·3′W	FM	104
Hambleton Inn	N Yks	SE5282	54°14·1′	1°11·7′W	X	100
Hambleton Moss Side	Lancs	SD3842	53°52·5′	2°56·2′W	T	102
Hambleton Wood	Rut	SK9007	52°39·4′	0°39·8′W	F	141
Ham Br	Leic	SK8018	52°45·5′	0°48·5′W	X	130
Ham Br	W Berks	SU4967	51°24·2′	1°17·3′W	X	174
Hambridge	Somer	ST3921	50°59·3′	2°51·8′W	T	193
Ham Bridge	Worcs	SO7361	52°15·0′	2°23·3′W	X	138,150
Ham Brook	Glos	SO9019	51°52·4′	2°8·3′W	W	163
Hambrook	S Glos	ST6478	51°30·2′	2°30·7′W	T	172
Hambrook	W Susx	SU7806	50°51·1′	0°53·1′W	T	197
Hambrook Ho	W Susx	SU7907	50°51·7′	0°52·3′W	X	197
Ham Burn	Northum	NY9058	54°55·2′	2°8·9′W	W	87
Hamburn Hall	Northum	NY9058	54°55·2′	2°8·9′W	X	87
Hambury Tout	Dorset	SY8180	50°37·4′	2°15·7′W	H	194
Ham Common	Dorset	ST8125	51°1·7′	2°15·9′W	T	183
Ham Common	Rich	TQ1871	51°25·8′	0°17·8′W	X	176
Ham Copse	Hants	SU7547	51°13·3′	0°55·2′W	F	186
Ham Copse	W Berks	SU6171	51°26·3′	1°7·0′W	F	175
Ham Court	Oxon	SP3003	51°43·7′	1°33·5′W	A	164
Ham Court	Worcs	SO8538	52°2·6′	2°12·7′W	X	150
Ham Creek	Suff	TM4257	52°9·7′	1°32·7′E	W	156
Hamden	Kent	TQ8940	51°7·9′	0°42·5′E	X	189
Hamdown Ho	Somer	ST4327	51°2·6′	2°48·4′W	X	193
Hameldon	Lancs	SD8932	53°47·3′	2°9·6′W	X	103
Hameldon Hill	Lancs	SD8128	53°45·1′	2°16·9′W	H	103
Hamel Down	Devon	SX7179	50°36·0′	3°49·0′W	H	191
Hameldown Beacon	Devon	SX7078	50°35·5′	3°49·8′W	X	191
Hameldown Tor	Devon	SX7080	50°36·5′	3°49·9′W	H	191
Hamels Park	Herts	TL3724	51°54·1′	0°0·1′W	X	166
Hamera Head	Shetld	HU4862	60°20·6′	1°7·3′W	X	2,3
Hamer Bridge	N Yks	SE7497	54°22·0′	0°51·2′W	X	94,100
Hameringham	Lincs	TF3167	53°11·3′	0°2·0′W	T	122
Hameringham Top	Lincs	TF3166	53°10·7′	0°2·0′W	X	122
Hamer Moor	N Yks	SE7598	54°22·6′	0°50·3′W	X	94,100
Hamersay	N Eil	NF9368	57°36·1′	7°7·9′W	X	18
Hamerton	Cambs	TL1379	52°24·1′	0°19·9′W	T	142
Hamerton	N Yks	SD8056	54°0·2′	2°17·9′W	X	103
Hamerton Grove	Cambs	TL1279	52°24·1′	0°20·8′W	F	142
Hamerton Hill Syke	N Yks	SD9662	54°3·5′	2°3·3′W	W	98
Hame's Hall	Cumbr	NY1131	54°40·2′	3°22·4′W	X	89
Hametoun	Shetld	HT9637	60°7·3′	2°3·8′W	T	4
Ham Farm Ho	Hants	SU5659	51°19·9′	1°11·4′W	X	174
Hamfield Fm	Glos	ST6699	51°41·6′	2°29·1′W	FM	162
Ham Fields	Win & Maid	SU9975	51°28·1′	0°34·1′W	X	175,176
Ham Fm	Bucks	SP7018	51°51·6′	0°58·6′W	FM	165
Ham Fm	Bucks	SU8094	51°38·6′	0°50·2′W	FM	175
Ham Fm	Corn	SS2213	50°53·6′	4°31·5′W	FM	190
Ham Fm	Devon	SS5324	51°0·0′	4°5·3′W	FM	180
Ham Fm	Devon	SS5711	50°53·1′	4°1·6′W	FM	191
Ham Fm	Devon	SX5262	50°26·6′	4°4·7′W	FM	201
Ham Fm	Devon	SX6999	50°46·8′	3°51·1′W	FM	191
Ham Fm	Devon	SX7249	50°19·9′	3°47·5′W	FM	202
Ham Fm	E Susx	TQ4313	50°54·1′	0°2·4′E	FM	198
Ham Fm	E Susx	TQ5137	51°7·0′	0°9·8′E	FM	188
Ham Fm	Glos	SO7800	51°42·1′	2°18·7′W	FM	162
Ham Fm	Kent	TQ9929	51°1·8′	0°50·7′E	FM	189
Ham Fm	Kent	TR0162	51°19·5′	0°53·5′E	FM	178
Ham Fm	Kent	TR1849	51°12·1′	1°7·6′E	FM	179,189
Ham Fm	N Som	ST3866	51°23·6′	2°53·1′W	FM	171,182
Ham Fm	N Som	ST4167	51°24·2′	2°50·5′W	FM	171,172,182
Ham Fm	Somer	ST3055	51°17·6′	2°59·9′W	FM	182
Ham Fm	Warw	SP3566	52°17·7′	1°28·8′W	FM	151
Ham Fm	Worcs	SO7359	52°13·9′	2°23·3′W	FM	150
Ham Fm	W Susx	SZ8395	50°45·1′	0°49·0′W	FM	197
Ham Fm	W Susx	TQ1613	50°54·5′	0°20·6′W	FM	198
Ham Fms	Somer	ST6044	51°11·9′	2°34·0′W	FM	183
Hamford Water	Essex	TM2225	51°53·0′	1°13·9′E	W	169
Ham Geo	Orkney	ND4683	58°44·1′	2°55·5′W	X	7
Ham Green	Bucks	SP6918	51°51·6′	0°59·5′W	T	165
Ham Green	Hants	SU4330	51°4·3′	1°22·8′W	T	185
Ham Green	Heref	SO7444	52°5·9′	2°22·4′W	T	150
Ham Green	Kent	TQ8468	51°23·1′	0°39·1′E	T	178
Ham Green	Kent	TQ8926	51°0·4′	0°42·0′E	T	189
Ham Green	N Som	ST5375	51°28·6′	2°40·2′W	T	172
Ham Green	Wilts	ST8561	51°21·1′	2°12·5′W	T	173
Ham Green	Worcs	SP0163	52°16·1′	1°58·7′W	T	150
Ham Hall	N Yks	SE2991	54°19·1′	1°32·8′W	X	99
Ham Hill	Glos	SO9821	51°53·5′	2°1·3′W	X	163
Ham Hill	Kent	TQ7060	51°19·0′	0°26·8′E	T	178,188
Ham Hill	Wilts	SU3361	51°21·1′	1°31·2′W	X	174
Ham Hill	Worcs	SO8252	52°10·2′	2°15·4′W	X	150
Ham Hill Country Park	Somer	ST4716	50°56·7′	2°44·9′W	X	193
Ham Ho	Rich	TQ1773	51°26·9′	0°18·6′W	A	176
Hamildean	Scot Bord	NT1841	55°39·6′	3°17·8′W	X	72
Hamildean Hill	Scot Bord	NT1841	55°39·6′	3°17·8′W	H	72
Hamilton	C of Leic	SK6307	52°39·7′	1°3·7′W	T	140
Hamilton	S Lanak	NS7255	55°46·5′	4°2·0′W	T	64
Hamilton Fm	Hants	SU5625	51°1·5′	1°11·7′W	FM	185
Hamilton Grounds	Leic	SK6407	52°39·7′	1°2·8′W	X	140
Hamiltonhall	Scot Bord	NT1548	55°43·3′	3°20·8′W	X	72
Hamilton High Parks	S Lanak	NS7352	55°44·9′	4°1·0′W	X	64
Hamilton Hill	Lincs	TF1290	53°23·9′	0°18·5′W	H	113
Hamilton Hill	Notts	SK5258	53°7·2′	1°13·0′W	X	120
Hamilton Hill	Scot Bord	NT2342	55°40·2′	3°13·0′W	H	73
Hamiltonhill Fm	E Yorks	TA1660	54°1·6′	0°13·3′W	FM	101
Hamilton Isle	N Ayr	NS0532	55°32·8′	5°5·0′W	X	69
Hamilton Lodge	Essex	TM0825	51°53·3′	1°1·8′E	X	168,169
Hamilton Service Area	S Lanak	NS7256	55°47·1′	4°2·0′W	X	64
Hamilton Stud	Suff	TL6264	52°15·2′	0°22·8′E	X	154
Hamilton Village	Leic	SK6407	52°39·7′	1°2·8′W	A	140
Hamilton Wood	Fife	NO5304	56°13·8′	2°45·0′W	F	59
Hamish Park	Heref	SO7153	52°10·7′	2°25·1′W	X	149
Hamister	Shetld	HU5463	60°21·1′	1°0·8′W	T	2
Ham Lake	Hants	SU3018	50°57·9′	1°34·0′W	W	185
Ham Lees Fm	Kent	TR0032	51°3·4′	0°51·6′E	FM	189
Hamlet	Devon	SY1499	50°47·3′	3°12·8′W	T	192,193
Hamlet	Dorset	ST5908	50°52·4′	2°34·6′W	T	194
Hamley	N Yks	SE7488	54°17·2′	0°51·4′W	X	94,100
Hamley Hagg	N Yks	SE7488	54°17·2′	0°51·4′W	X	94,100
Hamley Ho	Staffs	SK0521	52°47·4′	1°55·1′W	X	128
Ham Little	Shetld	HT9738	60°7·9′	2°2·7′W	W	4
Hamly Br	E Susx	TQ5513	50°54·0′	0°12·6′E	X	199
Hamly Hill	Orkney	HY4903	58°54·9′	2°52·7′W	H	6,7
Hamlyns Fm	Devon	SX8782	50°37·8′	3°35·5′W	FM	192
Ham Manor	W Susx	TQ0503	50°49·2′	0°30·2′W	X	197
Hammarhill	Orkney	HY5636	59°12·8′	2°45·8′W	T	5
Hammars	Orkney	HY4344	59°17·0′	2°59·5′W	X	5
Ham Marshes	Kent	TR0263	51°20·0′	0°54·4′E	X	178
Hammars Hill	Orkney	HY3822	59°5·1′	3°4·4′W	H	6
Hammenden Fm	W Susx	TQ3629	51°2·9′	0°3·2′W	FM	187,198
Hammer	W Susx	SU8732	51°5·1′	0°45·1′W	T	186
Hammer Bottom	Hants	SU8632	51°5·1′	0°45·9′W	T	186
Hammerbrake	Orkney	HY6740	59°15·0′	2°34·2′W	X	5
Hammerden	E Susx	TQ6627	51°1·3′	0°22·4′E	X	188,199
Hammer Dyke	Kent	TQ6346	51°11·6′	0°20·4′E	W	188
Hammerfield	Herts	TL0407	51°45·4′	0°29·2′W	T	166
Hammer Fm	N Yks	SE1584	54°15·3′	1°45·8′W	FM	99
Hammer Fm	W Susx	TQ1420	50°58·3′	0°22·2′W	FM	198
Hammerhall	Scot Bord	NT8357	55°48·6′	2°15·8′W	X	67,74
Hammer Head	Scot Bord	NT1338	55°37·9′	3°22·5′W	H	72
Hammer Hill	Beds	TL0943	52°4·7′	0°24·2′W	X	153
Hammer Hill	W Susx	TQ2827	51°1·9′	0°10·1′W	X	187,198
Hammerhill Fm	Beds	TL0942	52°4·2′	0°24·2′W	FM	153
Hammer Hill Fm	Essex	TL6029	51°56·4′	0°20·1′E	FM	167
Hammerley Down	S Glos	ST7191	51°37·3′	2°24·7′W	X	162,172
Hammermill Hill	Shrops	SO6069	52°19·3′	2°34·8′W	X	138
Hammer Pond	Surrey	SU9140	51°9·3′	0°41·5′W	W	186
Hammer Pond	W Susx	TQ2229	51°3·1′	0°15·2′W	W	187,198
Hammerpot	W Susx	TQ0605	50°50·3′	0°29·3′W	T	197
Hammershield	Northum	NY8447	54°49·3′	2°14·5′W	X	86,87
Hammerside Point	Cumbr	SD3177	54°11·3′	3°3·0′W	X	96,97
Hammersmith	Derby	SK3951	53°3·5′	1°24·7′W	T	119
Hammersmith	Ham & Ful	TQ2279	51°30·0′	0°14·1′W	T	176
Hammersmith Bottom	Glos	SP1804	51°44·3′	1°44·0′W	X	163
Hammersmith Br	Rich	TQ2278	51°29·5′	0°14·2′W	X	176
Hammer Stream	Kent	TQ8239	51°7·5′	0°36·4′E	W	188
Hammer Stream	W Susx	SU8325	51°1·3′	0°48·6′W	W	186,197
Hammerton Hall	Lancs	SD7153	53°58·6′	2°26·1′W	A	103
Hammerton Knowl Fm	Ches	SJ9667	53°12·2′	2°3·2′W	FM	118
Hammerton Mere	Lancs	SD7354	53°59·1′	2°24·3′W	X	103
Hammerton Moss	Ches	SJ9666	53°11·7′	2°3·2′W	X	118
Hammerwich	Staffs	SK0607	52°39·9′	1°54·3′W	T	139
Hammerwood	E Susx	TQ4339	51°8·2′	0°3·0′E	T	187
Hammer Wood	Kent	TQ8237	51°6·4′	0°36·4′E	F	188
Hammer Wood	W Susx	SU8424	51°0·8′	0°47·8′W	F	197
Hammerwood Ho	W Susx	SU8523	51°0·2′	0°46·9′W	X	197
Hammerwood Park	E Susx	TQ4438	51°7·6′	0°3·9′E	X	187
Hammett	Corn	SX3265	50°27·9′	4°21·7′W	X	201
Hammett Down	Corn	SX3366	50°28·4′	4°20·8′W	X	201
Hammett's Fm	Dorset	ST8908	50°52·5′	2°9·0′W	FM	195
Ham Mill	Corn	SX3487	50°39·8′	4°20·6′W	X	190
Hammill	Kent	TR2955	51°15·1′	1°17·3′E	T	179
Hammill Court	Kent	TR2855	51°15·1′	1°16·4′E	X	179
Ham Mill Fm	Kent	TR0031	51°2·8′	0°51·6′E	FM	189
Hammiton Fm	Dorset	SY5191	50°43·2′	2°41·3′W	FM	194
Hammond Beck	Lincs	TF1836	52°54·7′	0°14·3′W	W	130
Hammond Beck	Lincs	TF2038	52°55·8′	0°12·5′W	W	131
Hammonds	Suff	TL8459	52°12·1′	0°42·0′E	X	155
Hammonds Barn	Warw	SP4153	52°10·7′	1°23·6′W	X	151
Hammond's Copse	Surrey	TQ2144	51°11·2′	0°15·7′W	F	187
Hammonds Corner	Kent	TR0524	50°59·0′	0°55·6′E	X	189
Hammonds Eau	Cambs	TL3980	52°24·2′	0°3·0′E	W	142,143
Hammonds End Fm	Herts	TL1212	51°48·0′	0°22·1′W	FM	166
Hammond's Fm	Essex	TL7507	51°44·3′	0°32·5′E	FM	167
Hammond's Fm	Essex	TL9129	51°55·8′	0°47·1′E	FM	168
Hammonds Fm	Essex	TQ4996	51°38·8′	0°9·6′E	FM	167,177
Hammonds Fm	Glos	SO8506	51°45·4′	2°12·6′W	FM	162
Hammonds Fm	Hants	SU3118	50°57·9′	1°33·1′W	FM	185
Hammonds Fm	Herts	TL1432	51°58·7′	0°20·0′W	FM	166
Hammonds Fm	Herts	TL1811	51°47·3′	0°17·0′W	FM	166
Hammond's Fm	Oxon	SU6583	51°32·8′	1°3·4′W	FM	175
Hammonds Fm	Somer	ST3023	51°0·4′	2°59·5′W	FM	193
Hammond's Fm	W Susx	TQ3723	50°59·6′	0°2·5′W	FM	198
Hammond's Green	E Susx	TQ4920	50°57·8′	0°7·7′E	X	199
Hammondshall Fm	Bucks	SP8903	51°43·3′	0°42·3′W	FM	165
Hammonds, The	E Susx	TQ8819	50°56·6′	0°41·0′E	X	189,199
Hammond Street	Herts	TL3304	51°43·4′	0°4·1′W	T	166
Hammond Street Fm	Dorset	ST7306	50°51·4′	2°22·6′W	FM	194
Hammonhead	N Yks	SD7167	54°6·1′	2°26·2′W	X	98
Hammoon	Dorset	ST8114	50°55·7′	2°15·8′W	T	194
Ham Moor	Surrey	TQ0664	51°22·1′	0°28·2′W	T	176,187
Hammouth Hill	Glos	ST7889	51°36·2′	2°18·7′W	X	162,172
Hamna Dale	Shetld	HU5065	60°22·2′	1°5·1′W	X	2,3
Hamnafield	Shetld	HT9539	60°8·4′	2°4·9′W	X	4
Hamnavoe	Orkney	HY2509	58°58·0′	3°17·8′W	W	6,7
Hamna Voe	Shetld	HU1659	60°19·2′	1°42·1′W	W	3
Hamna Voe	Shetld	HU2380	60°30·4′	1°34·4′W	W	3
Hamnavoe	Shetld	HU2380	60°30·4′	1°34·4′W	T	3
Hamna Voe	Shetld	HU3636	60°6·7′	1°20·6′W	W	4
Hamnavoe	Shetld	HU3735	60°6·1′	1°19·6′W	T	4
Hamna Voe	Shetld	HU4879	60°29·8′	1°7·1′W	W	2,3
Hamna Voe	Shetld	HU4971	60°25·5′	1°6·1′W	W	2,3
Hamnavoe	Shetld	HU4971	60°25·5′	1°6·1′W	X	2,3
Hamnavoe	Shetld	HU4980	60°30·3′	1°6·0′W	T	1,2,3
Hamner's Lodge Fm	Leic	SK7206	52°39·1′	0°55·7′W	FM	141
Ham Ness	Shetld	HP6301	60°41·5′	0°50·3′W	X	1
Hamnish Clifford	Heref	SO5359	52°13·9′	2°40·9′W	T	149
Hamoaze	C of Plym	SX4455	50°22·7′	4°11·3′W	W	201
Ham of Muness	Shetld	HP6301	60°41·5′	0°50·3′W	W	1
Ham Ooze	Kent	TQ8470	51°24·2′	0°39·1′E	X	178
Hamp	Somer	ST3036	51°7·4′	2°59·6′W	T	182
Hampage Fm	Hants	SU5430	51°4·2′	1°13·4′W	FM	185
Hampage Wood	Hants	SU5430	51°4·2′	1°13·4′W	F	185
Hamp Brook	Somer	ST2835	51°6·8′	3°1·3′W	W	182
Hampden Bottom Fm	Bucks	SP8503	51°43·4′	0°45·8′W	FM	165
Hampden Common	Bucks	SP8401	51°42·3′	0°46·7′W	F	165
Hampden Fm	Kent	TR0033	51°3·9′	0°51·7′E	FM	189

Hampden Hall (College)	Bucks	SP8411	51°47·7′	0°46·5′W	X	165
Hampden Ho	Bucks	SP8402	51°42·9′	0°46·7′W	A	165
Hampdenleaf Wood	Bucks	SP8604	51°43·9′	0°44·9′W	F	165
Hampden Park	C of Glas	NS5961	55°49·6′	4°14·6′W	X	64
Hampden Park	E Susx	TQ6002	50°47·9′	0°16·6′E	T	199
Hampden's Mon	Oxon	SU6497	51°40·3′	1°4·1′W	X	164,165
Hampen	Glos	SP0519	51°52·4′	1°55·2′W	T	163
Hampen Fm	Glos	SP0520	51°52·9′	1°55·2′W	FM	163
Hamperden End	Essex	TL5730	51°57·0′	0°17·5′E	T	167
Hamperley	Shrops	SO4189	52°30·0′	2°51·7′W	T	137
Hampers	Essex	TL8233	51°58·2′	0°39·4′E	X	168
Hampers Green	W Susx	SU9722	50°59·6′	0°36·7′W	T	197
Hampeth	Northum	NU1707	55°21·7′	1°43·5′W	T	81
Hampeth Burn	Northum	NU1607	55°21·7′	1°44·4′W	W	81
Hampnett	Glos	SP0915	51°50·2′	1°51·8′W	T	163
Ham Point	Devon	SX7541	50°15·6′	3°44·8′W	X	202
Hampole	Donc	SE5010	53°35·3′	1°14·3′W	T	111
Hampole Grange	Donc	SE5109	53°34·7′	1°13·4′W	X	111
Hampole Wood	Donc	SE5008	53°34·2′	1°14·3′W	F	111
Hampreston	Dorset	SZ0598	50°47·1′	1°55·4′W	T	195
Hampsfield	Cumbr	SD4080	54°13·0′	2°54·8′W	T	96,97
Hampsfield Fell	Cumbr	SD3979	54°12·4′	2°55·7′W	H	96,97
Hampsfield Hall	Cumbr	SD3980	54°13·0′	2°55·7′W	A	96,97
Hampshire Gap	Hants	SU2440	51°9·8′	1°39·0′W	X	184
Hampshire Gate	Hants	SU3254	51°17·3′	1°32·1′W	X	185
Hampsley Hollow	Wilts	SU0066	51°23·8′	1°59·6′W	X	173
Hampson	Devon	SS7101	50°47·9′	3°49·5′W	X	191
Hampson Green	Lancs	SD4954	53°59·0′	2°46·2′W	T	102
Hampsons	Black W Dar	SD6914	53°37·5′	2°27·7′W	X	109
Hampstead	Camden	TQ2685	51°33·2′	0°10·6′W	T	176
Hampstead	Northum	NY9865	54°59·0′	2°1·4′W	X	87
Hampstead Fm	Oxon	SU7477	51°29·5′	0°55·7′W	FM	175
Hampstead Garden Suburb	Barnet	TQ2688	51°34·8′	0°10·5′W	T	176
Hampstead Heath	Camden	TQ2686	51°33·8′	0°10·5′W	X	176
Hampstead Norreys	W Berks	SU5276	51°29·1′	1°14·7′W	T	174
Hampsthwaite	N Yks	SE2658	54°1·3′	1°35·8′W	T	104
Hampston Hill	E Yorks	TA0537	53°49·4′	0°23·9′W	X	107
Hampt	Corn	SX3874	50°32·8′	4°16·8′W	X	201
Hampton	Devon	SY2696	50°45·8′	3°2·6′W	T	192,193
Hampton	Kent	TR0743	51°9·1′	0°58·0′E	X	179,189
Hampton	Kent	TR1667	51°21·9′	1°6·6′E	T	179
Hampton	Rich	TQ1370	51°25·3′	0°22·1′W	T	176
Hampton	Shrops	SO7486	52°28·5′	2°22·6′W	T	138
Hampton	Surrey	SU9046	51°12·6′	0°42·3′W	X	186
Hampton	Swin	SU1892	51°37·8′	1°44·0′W	T	163,173
Hampton	Worcs	SP0243	52°5·4′	1°57·9′W	T	150
Hampton Bank	Shrops	SJ4534	52°54·3′	2°48·7′W	T	126
Hampton Barns	Essex	TQ9091	51°35·4′	0°45·0′E	X	178
Hampton Beech	Shrops	SJ3005	52°38·5′	3°1·7′W	T	126
Hampton Bishop	Heref	SO5538	52°2·6′	2°39·0′W	T	149
Hampton Coppice	Sol	SP1681	52°25·8′	1°45·5′W	F	139
Hampton Court	Heref	SO5252	52°10·1′	2°41·7′W	A	149
Hampton Court	I of M	SC3473	54°7·8′	4°32·0′W	X	95
Hampton Court Park	Rich	TQ1668	51°24·2′	0°19·5′W	X	176
Hampton Fields	Glos	ST8899	51°41·6′	2°10·0′W	T	162
Hampton Fm	Worcs	SO8866	52°17·8′	2°10·2′W	FM	150
Hampton Gay	Oxon	SP4816	51°50·7′	1°17·8′W	T	164
Hampton Gorse	Oxon	SP5115	51°50·1′	1°15·2′W	F	164
Hampton Gorse	Warw	SP2458	52°13·4′	1°38·5′W	F	151
Hampton Green	Ches	SJ5149	53°2·4′	2°43·4′W	T	117
Hampton Hall	Shrops	SJ3105	52°38·5′	3°0·8′W	X	126
Hamptonhayes	Shrops	SJ3206	52°39·1′	2°59·9′W	X	126
Hampton Heath	Ches	SJ4949	53°2·4′	2°45·2′W	T	117
Hampton Hill	Rich	TQ1471	51°25·8′	0°21·2′W	T	176
Hampton House Fm	Lincs	TF4049	53°1·4′	0°5·7′E	FM	131
Hampton House Fm	Shrops	SJ4335	52°54·8′	2°50·5′W	FM	126
Hampton in Arden	Sol	SP2081	52°25·3′	1°42·0′W	T	139
Hampton Lane Fm	Sol	SP1880	52°25·3′	1°43·7′W	FM	139
Hampton Loade	Shrops	SO7486	52°28·5′	2°22·6′W	T	138
Hampton Lodge	Warw	SP2563	52°16·1′	1°37·6′W	X	151
Hampton Lovett	Worcs	SO8865	52°17·2′	2°10·2′W	T	150
Hampton Lucy	Warw	SP2557	52°12·9′	1°37·6′W	T	151
Hampton Magna	Warw	SP2665	52°17·2′	1°36·7′W	T	151
Hampton Manor Homes	Sol	SP2080	52°25·3′	1°42·0′W	X	139
Hampton Meadow	Heref	SO5639	52°3·1′	2°38·1′W	X	149
Hampton on the Hill	Warw	SP2564	52°16·6′	1°37·6′W	T	151
Hampton Park	C of Soton	SU4315	50°56·2′	1°22·9′W	T	196
Hampton Park	Heref	SO5339	52°3·1′	2°40·7′W	T	149
Hampton Park	Surrey	SU9046	51°12·6′	0°42·3′W	X	186
Hampton Park Cottages Fm	Heref	SO5254	52°11·2′	2°41·7′W	FM	149
Hampton Post	Ches	SJ5049	53°2·4′	2°44·3′W	X	117
Hampton Poyle	Oxon	SP5015	51°50·1′	1°16·1′W	T	164
Hampton Ridge	Hants	SU1813	50°55·2′	1°44·2′W	X	195
Hamptons	Kent	TQ6252	51°14·9′	0°19·7′E	T	188
Hampton Valley	Staffs	SO8486	52°28·5′	2°13·7′W	X	138
Hampton Wafre Fm	Heref	SO5757	52°12·8′	2°37·4′W	FM	149
Hampton Wick	Rich	TQ1769	51°24·7′	0°18·7′W	T	176
Hampton Wood	Shrops	SJ4337	52°55·9′	2°50·5′W	X	126
Hampton Wood	Warw	SP2559	52°14·0′	1°37·6′W	F	151
Hampton Wood Hall	Shrops	SJ4237	52°55·9′	2°51·4′W	X	126
Hamptworth	Wilts	SU2419	50°58·4′	1°39·1′W	T	184
Hamptworth Common	Wilts	SU2418	50°57·9′	1°39·1′W	X	184
Hamptworth Lodge	Wilts	SU2219	50°58·4′	1°40·8′W	X	184
Hamrow	Norf	TF9124	52°47·0′	0°50·3′E	T	132
Hams	W Susx	SU9602	50°48·8′	0°37·9′W	X	197
Hams Barton	Devon	SX8780	50°36·8′	3°35·5′W	X	192
Hamsell Manor	E Susx	TQ5533	51°4·7′	0°13·2′E	X	188
Hamsell Wood Fm	E Susx	TQ5435	51°5·8′	0°12·4′E	FM	188
Hamsey	E Susx	TQ4112	50°53·6′	0°0·7′E	T	198
Hamsey Green	Surrey	TQ3559	51°19·1′	0°3·4′W	T	187
Hamsey Ho	E Susx	TQ4112	50°53·6′	0°0·7′E	X	198
Hamseyplace Fm	E Susx	TQ4112	50°53·6′	0°0·7′E	FM	198
Hams Hall	Warw	SP2192	52°31·8′	1°41·0′W	X	139
Hamshill	Glos	SO7701	51°42·7′	2°19·6′W	T	162
Hamshill Ditches	Wilts	SU0533	51°6·0′	1°55·3′W	A	184
Hamslade Ho	Devon	SS9121	50°58·9′	3°32·8′W	X	181
Ham Spray Ho	Wilts	SU3463	51°22·1′	1°30·3′W	X	174
Hamstall Hall	Staffs	SK1019	52°46·3′	1°50·7′W	A	128

Hamstall Ridware	Staffs	SK1019	52°46·3′	1°50·7′W	T	128
Hamstead	I of W	SZ3991	50°43·3′	1°26·5′W	X	196
Hamstead	Sand	SP0493	52°32·3′	1°56·1′W	T	139
Hamstead Holt Fm	W Berks	SU3966	51°23·7′	1°26·0′W	FM	174
Hamstead Marshall	W Berks	SU4165	51°23·2′	1°24·3′W	T	174
Hamstead Park	W Berks	SU4266	51°23·7′	1°23·4′W	X	174
Hamstead Sta	Birm	SP0492	52°31·8′	1°56·1′W	X	139
Hamstead Trail	I of W	SZ3887	50°41·1′	1°27·3′W	X	196
Hamsteels Hall	Durham	NZ1744	54°47·7′	1°43·7′W	X	88
Hamsterley	Durham	NZ1131	54°40·7′	1°49·3′W	T	92
Hamsterley	Durham	NZ1156	54°54·2′	1°49·3′W	T	88
Hamsterley Common	Durham	NZ0531	54°40·7′	1°54·9′W	X	92
Hamsterley Forest	Durham	NZ0428	54°39·1′	1°55·9′W	F	92
Hamsterley Hall	Durham	NZ1455	54°53·6′	1°46·5′W	X	88
Hamsterley Mill	Durham	NZ1456	54°54·2′	1°46·5′W	X	88
Hamsts, The	Notts	SK6642	52°58·5′	1°0·6′W	X	129
Ham Stone	Devon	SX6936	50°12·8′	3°49·8′W	X	202
Ham Stone	Devon	SX7636	50°12·9′	3°43·9′W	X	202
Hamstone Gill	Lancs	SD5966	54°5·5′	2°37·2′W	X	97
Hamstreet	Kent	TR0033	51°3·9′	0°51·7′E	T	189
Ham Street	Somer	ST5534	51°6·4′	2°38·2′W	T	182,183
Hamswell Ho	S Glos	ST7371	51°26·5′	2°22·9′W	X	172
Hamsworthy	Devon	SS3108	50°51·0′	4°23·7′W	X	190
Ham, The	Oxon	SU3987	51°35·1′	1°25·8′W	X	174
Ham, The	Wilts	ST8652	51°16·3′	2°11·7′W	T	183
Hamtops Low	Staffs	SK1352	53°4·1′	1°48·0′W	A	119
Ham Voe	Shetld	HT9738	60°7·9′	2°2·7′W	W	4
Ham Wood	Hants	SU7343	51°11·1′	0°56·9′W	F	186
Hamwood	N Som	ST3757	51°18·8′	2°53·8′W	X	182
Ham Wood	Oxon	SU5681	51°31·7′	1°11·2′W	F	174
Hamwood Fm	Somer	ST1921	50°59·2′	3°8·9′W	FM	181,193
Ham Woods	Somer	ST6045	51°12·4′	2°34·0′W	F	183
Hamworthy	Poole	SY9991	50°43·3′	2°0·5′W	T	195
Hanbury	Staffs	SK1727	52°50·7′	1°44·5′W	T	128
Hanbury	Worcs	SO9663	52°16·1′	2°3·1′W	T	150
Hanbury Grange	Staffs	SK1527	52°50·7′	1°46·2′W	X	128
Hanbury Hall	Worcs	SO9463	52°16·1′	2°4·9′W	A	150
Hanbury Hill	Staffs	SK1728	52°51·2′	1°44·4′W	X	128
Hanbury Park	Staffs	SK1725	52°49·6′	1°44·5′W	X	128
Hanbury Woodend	Staffs	SK1626	52°50·1′	1°45·3′W	T	128
Hanby	Lincs	TF0231	52°52·2′	0°28·7′W	T	130
Hanchet End	Suff	TL6546	52°5·5′	0°24·9′E	T	154
Hanchet Hall	Suff	TL6445	52°5·0′	0°24·0′E	X	154
Hanch Hall	Staffs	SK1013	52°43·1′	1°50·7′W	X	128
Hanch Resr	Staffs	SK1013	52°43·1′	1°50·7′W	W	128
Hanchurch	Staffs	SJ8441	52°58·2′	2°13·9′W	T	118
Hanchurch Hills	Staffs	SJ8340	52°57·7′	2°14·8′W	X	118
Hanchurch Hills	Staffs	SJ8439	52°57·1′	2°13·9′W	H	127
Hancock's Fm	Hants	SU7951	51°15·4′	0°51·7′W	FM	186
Hancock's Fm	Kent	TQ7835	51°5·4′	0°32·9′E	FM	188
Hancock's Well	Wilts	ST8484	51°33·5′	2°13·5′W	W	173
Hancox	E Susx	TQ7619	50°56·8′	0°30·7′E	X	199
Handa Island	Highld	NC1348	58°23·1′	5°11·4′W	X	9
Handale	Red & Cl	NZ7215	54°31·8′	0°52·8′W	X	94
Hand and Pen	Devon	SY0495	50°45·0′	3°21·3′W	T	192
Handborough Sta	Oxon	SP4314	51°49·6′	1°22·2′W	X	164
Handbridge	Ches	SJ4165	53°11·0′	2°52·6′W	T	117
Handcock's Bottom	Dorset	ST8912	50°54·7′	2°9·0′W	X	195
Handcock's Fm	Kent	TQ9638	51°6·7′	0°48·4′E	FM	189
Handcross	W Susx	TQ2629	51°3·0′	0°11·8′W	T	187,198
Handcross Park	W Susx	TQ2630	51°3·6′	0°11·7′W	X	187
Hand Dale	Derby	SK1461	53°9·0′	1°47·0′W	X	119
Handen Fm	Kent	TR0537	51°6·0′	0°56·1′E	FM	179,189
Handfast Point or The Foreland	Dorset	SZ0582	50°38·5′	1°55·4′W	X	195
Handfield Fm	Ches	SJ8162	53°9·5′	2°16·6′W	FM	118
Handford	Devon	SS6217	50°56·4′	3°57·5′W	X	180
Handforth	Ches	SJ8583	53°20·9′	2°13·1′W	T	109
Handgate Fm	Worcs	SP0249	52°8·6′	1°57·8′W	FM	150
Hand Green	Ches	SJ5460	53°8·4′	2°40·9′W	T	117
Hand Lake	Cumbr	NY6400	54°23·9′	2°32·9′W	H	91
Hand Leasow Wood	Staffs	SK0230	52°52·3′	1°57·8′W	F	128
Handless	Shrops	SO3990	52°30·5′	2°53·5′W	T	137
Handley	Ches	SJ4657	53°6·7′	2°48·0′W	T	117
Handley	Derby	SK3761	53°8·9′	1°26·4′W	T	119
Handley	Northnts	SP6747	52°7·3′	1°0·9′W	X	152
Handleybarn	Ches	SJ9881	53°19·8′	2°1·4′W	X	109
Handley Barn	Northnts	SP6646	52°6·7′	1°1·8′W	X	152
Handley Barns	Essex	TL6401	51°41·3′	0°22·8′E	X	167
Handley Bottom	Derby	SK2370	53°13·8′	1°38·9′W	X	119
Handley Common	Dorset	ST9818	50°57·9′	2°1·3′W	X	184
Handley Down	Dorset	SU0016	50°56·8′	1°59·6′W	X	184
Handley Down	Dorset	SU0116	50°56·8′	1°58·8′W	X	184
Handley Fm	Devon	ST0324	51°0·7′	3°22·6′W	FM	181
Handley Fold Fm	Ches	SJ9880	53°19·3′	2°1·4′W	FM	109
Handley Green	Essex	TL6501	51°41·2′	0°23·6′E	T	167
Handley Lodge	Derby	SK3762	53°9·5′	1°26·4′W	X	119
Handley Park	Ches	SJ5546	53°0·8′	2°39·8′W	X	117
Handley Plain	Oxon	SP2713	51°49·1′	1°36·1′W	X	163
Handley's Br	Cumbr	SD7097	54°22·3′	2°27·3′W	X	98
Handley's Corner	I of M	SC3186	54°14·8′	4°35·2′W	X	95
Handley's Cross	Heref	SO4140	52°3·6′	2°51·2′W	X	148,149,161
Handley Wood	Derby	SK3248	53°1·9′	1°31·0′W	F	119
Handleywood Fm	Derby	SK4075	53°16·5′	1°23·6′W	FM	120
Handlye Fm	E Susx	TQ4115	50°55·3′	0°0·8′E	FM	198
Handmore Fm	Heref	SO3545	52°6·2′	2°56·5′W	FM	148,149
Handsacre	Staffs	SK0916	52°44·7′	1°51·6′W	T	128
Handsel Fm	E Susx	TQ7722	50°58·4′	0°31·7′E	FM	199
Hand's Fm	Essex	TL6104	51°42·9′	0°20·2′E	FM	167
Handsford	Devon	SS6404	50°49·4′	3°55·5′W	X	191
Handsford Fm	Devon	SS7210	50°52·8′	3°48·8′W	FM	191
Handside	Herts	TL2312	51°47·8′	0°12·6′W	T	166
Handsmooth	Oxon	SU6585	51°33·8′	1°3·3′W	X	175
Handsworth	Birm	SP0390	52°30·7′	1°56·9′W	T	139
Handsworth	Sheff	SK4086	53°22·4′	1°23·5′W	T	111,120
Handsworth Wood	Birm	SP0590	52°30·7′	1°55·2′W	T	139
Hand, The	Monm	ST3997	51°40·3′	2°52·5′W	X	171
Handwell Hill	Durham	NZ1350	54°50·9′	1°47·4′W	H	88
Handy Cross	Bucks	SU8590	51°36·4′	0°46·0′W	T	175
Handy Cross	Hants	SU2007	50°52·0′	1°42·6′W	X	195

Handy Cross	Somer	ST1231	51°4·5′	3°15·0′W	T	181
Handy Cross Plain	Hants	SU1907	50°52·0′	1°43·4′W	X	195
Handywater Fm	Oxon	SP3538	52°2·6′	1°29·0′W	FM	151
Hanfield	Staffs	SJ9652	53°4·2′	2°3·2′W	X	118
Hanford	C of Stoke	SJ8742	52°58·8′	2°11·2′W	T	118
Hanford	Dorset	ST8411	50°54·1′	2°13·3′W	T	194
Hanford House (Sch)	Dorset	ST8411	50°54·1′	2°13·3′W	A	194
Hanga	Orkney	HY4503	58°54·9′	2°56·8′W	X	6,7
Hanger Down	Devon	SX6258	50°24·6′	3°56·2′W	X	202
Hanger Fm	Bucks	SU7891	51°37·0′	0°52·0′W	FM	175
Hanger Fm	Devon	ST1106	50°51·0′	3°15·5′W	FM	192,193
Hanger Fm	Wilts	ST9181	51°31·9′	2°7·4′W	FM	173
Hanger Hill	Notts	SK5968	53°12·6′	1°6·6′W	X	120
Hanger Lane Sta	Ealing	TQ1882	51°31·7′	0°17·5′W	X	176
Hanger Lodge	Northnts	SP7541	52°4·0′	0°54·0′W	X	152
Hanger Park Fm	Wilts	ST9874	51°28·1′	2°1·3′W	FM	173
Hangershell Rock	Devon	SX6559	50°25·2′	3°53·6′W	X	202
Hangersley	Hants	SU1706	50°51·4′	1°45·1′W	T	195
Hangers, The	Hants	SU5619	50°58·3′	1°11·8′W	F	185
Hanger Wood	Beds	SP9949	52°8·1′	0°32·8′W	F	153
Hanger Wood	Bucks	SU7792	51°37·5′	0°52·9′W	F	175
Hang Gill	D & G	NT1309	55°22·3′	3°21·9′W	X	78
Hang Goose Fm	Brad	SE0647	53°55·4′	1°54·1′W	FM	104
Hangie Bay	Orkney	HY5410	58°58·7′	2°47·5′W	W	6
Hangie Head	Orkney	HY7138	59°13·9′	2°30·0′W	X	5
Hanging Bank	Kent	TQ4851	51°14·6′	0°7·6′E	T	188
Hanging Banks	Derby	SK3866	53°11·6′	1°25·5′W	X	119
Hanging Br	Staffs	SK1545	53°0·4′	1°46·2′W	A	119,128
Hanging Fall	E Yorks	SE9263	54°3·5′	0°35·3′W	X	101
Hangingfolds	Moray	NJ2154	57°34·4′	3°18·8′W	X	28
Hanginggate Fm	Ches	SJ9268	53°12·8′	2°6·8′W	FM	118
Hanging Grimston Wold	N Yks	SE8061	54°2·6′	0°46·3′W	X	100
Hanging Grove Fm	N Som	ST5366	51°23·7′	2°40·1′W	FM	172,182
Hanging Heaton	Kirk	SE2523	53°42·4′	1°36·9′W	T	104
Hanging Hill	Leic	SK3116	52°44·7′	1°32·0′W	X	128
Hanging Hill	S Glos	ST7170	51°25·9′	2°24·6′W	X	172
Hanging Hill Plantn	Notts	SK6970	53°13·6′	0°57·6′W	F	120
Hanging Houghton	Northnts	SP7573	52°21·2′	0°53·5′W	T	141
Hanging Knotts	Cumbr	NY2407	54°27·4′	3°9·9′W	X	89,90
Hanging Langford	Wilts	SU0337	51°8·2′	1°57·0′W	T	184
Hanging Langford Camp	Wilts	SU0135	51°7·1′	1°58·8′W	A	184
Hanging Lund	Cumbr	SD7898	54°22·9′	2°19·9′W	X	98
Hanging Moor	N Yks	SE1657	54°0·8′	1°44·9′W	X	104
Hangingmyre Fm	Fife	NO2405	56°14·1′	3°13·1′W	FM	59
Hanging Rock	Derby	SK0276	53°17·1′	1°57·8′W	X	119
Hanging Seal	Cumbr	NY8022	54°35·8′	2°18·2′W	X	91,92
Hangingshaw	Cumbr	NY6821	54°35·2′	2°29·3′W	X	91
Hangingshaw	D & G	NY1089	55°11·5′	3°24·4′W	T	78
Hanging Shaw	Durham	NY8630	54°40·1′	2°12·6′W	X	91,92
Hanging Shaw	Northum	NY6652	54°51·9′	2°31·4′W	X	86
Hangingshaw	Scot Bord	NT3930	55°33·8′	2°57·6′W	T	73
Hangingshaw	Scot Bord	NT4153	55°46·3′	2°56·0′W	X	66,73
Hangingshaw	S Lanak	NS9147	55°42·5′	3°43·6′W	X	72
Hangingshaw Burn	Scot Bord	NT3931	55°34·4′	2°57·6′W	W	73
Hangingshaw Hill	D & G	NT0004	55°19·4′	3°34·1′W	H	78
Hangingshaw Hill	D & G	NY0394	55°14·1′	3°31·1′W	H	78
Hangingshaw Hill	Scot Bord	NT4215	55°25·8′	2°54·6′W	H	79
Hangingshaw Hill	Scot Bord	NT7613	55°24·9′	2°22·3′W	H	80
Hangingshields Rigg	Northum	NY6867	55°0·0′	2°29·6′W	X	86,87
Hanging Stone	Durham	NZ1551	54°51·5′	1°45·6′W	X	88
Hanging Stone	Lancs	SD9738	53°50·5′	2°2·3′W	A	103
Hanging Stone	Northum	NY8861	54°56·9′	2°10·8′W	X	87
Hanging Stone	N Yks	SE4494	54°20·6′	1°19·0′W	X	99
Hanging Stone	Wilts	SU0960	51°20·6′	1°51·9′W	X	173
Hangingstone Crag	Cumbr	NY5881	55°7·5′	2°39·1′W	X	80
Hangingstone Fm	Staffs	SJ9765	53°11·2′	2°2·3′W	FM	118
Hangingstone Hill	Ches	SJ5469	53°13·2′	2°40·9′W	H	117
Hangingstone Hill	Devon	SX6186	50°39·7′	3°57·6′W	H	191
Hangingstone Hills	Leic	SK5215	52°44·0′	1°13·4′W	X	129
Hangingstone Scar	Cumbr	SD7999	54°23·4′	2°19·0′W	X	98
Hanging Tar	Pemb	SR8896	51°37·6′	5°3·4′W	X	158
Hanging, The	Dorset	ST8507	50°52·0′	2°12·4′W	F	194
Hangington Clough Br	Lancs	SD5854	53°59·1′	2°38·0′W	X	102
Hanging Walls of Mark Anthony	Cumbr	NY6532	54°41·2′	2°32·2′W	X	91
Hanging Walls of Mark Anthony (Cultivation Terraces)	Cumbr	NY6532	54°41·2′	2°32·2′W	A	91
Hanging Wells	Durham	NY9440	54°45·5′	2°5·2′W	X	87
Hangingwells Common	Durham	NY9240	54°45·5′	2°7·0′W	X	87
Hanging Wood	Bucks	SU7487	51°34·8′	0°55·5′W	F	175
Hanging Wood	N Som	ST5061	51°21·0′	2°42·7′W	F	172,182
Hanglam	N Eil	NF7168	57°35·2′	7°29·9′W	X	18
Hangland Fm	Oxon	SP5044	52°5·8′	1°15·8′W	FM	151
Hangleton	Bri & Hov	TQ2606	50°50·6′	0°12·2′W	T	198
Hangleton	W Susx	TQ0803	50°49·2′	0°27·6′W	T	197
Hangley Cleave	Somer	SS7536	51°6·8′	3°46·8′W	X	180
Hangman Hill	Northum	NY8952	54°52·0′	2°9·9′W	H	87
Hangman Point	Devon	SS5848	51°13·1′	4°1·6′W	X	180
Hangman's Barrow	Corn	SW6736	50°10·9′	5°15·5′W	A	203
Hangman's Corner	Peterb	TF2706	52°38·4′	0°7·0′W	X	142
Hangman's Cross	Swan	SS4886	51°33·4′	4°11·2′W	X	159
Hangman's Hall	Leic	SP4299	52°35·5′	1°22·4′W	X	140
Hangman's Hall Fm	Glos	SP1536	52°1·6′	1°46·5′W	FM	151
Hangman's Hill	Devon	SS5929	51°2·8′	4°0·3′W	H	180
Hangman's Hill	Surrey	SU9154	51°16·9′	0°41·3′W	X	186
Hangman's Hill	Worcs	SO7639	52°3·2′	2°20·6′W	H	150
Hangman's Hill Cross	Devon	SS9220	50°58·4′	3°31·9′W	X	181
Hangman's Land	Northum	NT9148	55°43·8′	2°8·2′W	X	74,75
Hangman's Stone	Devon	SY2090	50°42·5′	3°7·6′W	X	192,193
Hangman's Stone	Glos	SP0815	51°50·2′	1°52·6′W	X	163
Hangman's Stone	W Berks	SU3181	51°31·9′	1°32·8′W	X	174
Hangman's Stone	W Berks	SU4374	51°28·0′	1°22·5′W	A	174
Hango Hill	I of M	SC2767	54°4·4′	4°38·2′W	X	95
Hangour Hill	Norf	TF7508	52°38·7′	0°35·6′E	X	143
Hangour Hill (Tumulus)	Norf	TF7508	52°38·7′	0°35·6′E	A	143
Hang Rock	N Som	ST4375	51°28·5′	2°48·9′W	X	171,172
Hangsman Hill	Donc	SE6714	53°37·3′	0°58·5′W	T	111
Hangs, The	Norf	TG0642	52°56·4′	1°4·3′E	X	133
Hangs, The	Norf	TG0841	52°55·8′	1°6·1′E	F	133

Hangstone Davey	Pemb	SM8914	51°47·3′	5°3·2′W	A	157,158
Hang Thorn	Stock on T	NZ3616	54°32·5′	1°26·2′W	X	93
Hangthwaite	Donc	SE5507	53°33·6′	1°9·8′W	X	111
Hangwell Law	Northum	NU1224	55°30·8′	1°48·2′W	H	75
Hang Wood	Hants	SU7052	51°16·0′	0°59·4′W	F	186
Hang Yeat	Lancs	SD4853	53°58·5′	2°47·2′W	X	102
Hanham	S Glos	ST6472	51°27·0′	2°30·7′W	T	172
Hanham Court	S Glos	ST6470	51°25·9′	2°30·7′W	A	172
Hanham Green	S Glos	ST6470	51°25·9′	2°30·7′W	T	172
Hanham Ho	Bath & NE Somer	ST6557	51°18·9′	2°29·7′W	X	172
Hanicombe Wood	Devon	SX7389	50°41·4′	3°47·5′W	F	191
Haningshaw Hill	Scot Bord	NT4154	55°46·8′	2°56·0′W	H	66,73
Hanjague	I Scilly	SV9515	49°57·7′	6°14·8′W	X	203
Hankelow	Ches	SJ6745	53°0·3′	2°29·1′W	T	118
Hankelow Hall	Ches	SJ6646	53°0·9′	2°30·0′W	X	118
Hankerton	Wilts	ST9790	51°36·8′	2°2·2′W	T	163,173
Hankerton Field Fm	Wilts	ST9591	51°37·3′	2°3·9′W	FM	163,173
Hankford Barton	Devon	SS3815	50°54·9′	4°17·9′W	X	190
Hankham	E Susx	TQ6105	50°49·6′	0°17·5′E	T	199
Hankills	Red & Cl	NZ6915	54°31·8′	0°55·6′W	X	94
Hankin Fm	Derby	SK3254	53°5·2′	1°30·9′W	FM	119
Hankins Heys	Ches	SJ6941	52°58·2′	2°27·3′W	X	118
Hankinson Ho	Lancs	SD5036	53°49·3′	2°45·2′W	X	102
Hankinson's Fm	Lancs	SD3945	53°54·1′	2°55·3′W	FM	102
Hankley Common	Surrey	SU8841	51°9·9′	0°44·1′W	X	186
Hankley Cott	Surrey	SU8943	51°11·0′	0°43·2′W	X	186
Hankley Fm	Surrey	SU8943	51°11·0′	0°43·2′W	FM	186
Hanley	C of Stoke	SJ8847	53°1·4′	2°10·3′W	T	118
Hanley Castle	Worcs	SO8341	52°4·3′	2°14·5′W	T	150
Hanley Child	Worcs	SO6565	52°17·2′	2°30·4′W	T	138,149
Hanley Court	Heref	SO4135	52°0·9′	2°51·2′W	X	149,161
Hanley Court	Worcs	SO6766	52°17·7′	2°28·6′W	X	138,149
Hanley Hall	Shrops	SJ3524	52°48·8′	2°57·5′W	X	126
Hanley Hall	Worcs	SO8141	52°4·3′	2°16·2′W	X	150
Hanley Hayes	Staffs	SJ9247	53°1·5′	2°6·8′W	X	118
Hanley Ho	Glos	ST5696	51°39·9′	2°37·8′W	X	162
Hanley Park	C of Stoke	SJ8846	53°0·9′	2°10·3′W	X	118
Hanley Swan	Worcs	SO8142	52°4·8′	2°16·2′W	T	150
Hanley William	Worcs	SO6765	52°17·2′	2°28·6′W	T	138,149
Hanlith	N Yks	SD9061	54°2·9′	2°8·7′W	T	98
Hanlith Moor	N Yks	SD9162	54°3·5′	2°7·8′W	X	98
Hanmer	Wrex	SJ4539	52°57·0′	2°48·7′W	T	126
Hanmer Hall Fm	Wrex	SJ4640	52°57·5′	2°47·8′W	FM	117
Hanmer Mere	Wrex	SJ4539	52°57·0′	2°48·7′W	W	126
Hanmer Mill Fm	Wrex	SJ4540	52°57·5′	2°48·7′W	FM	117
Hannaborough	Devon	SS5202	50°48·2′	4°5·6′W	X	191
Hannaford	Devon	SS6029	51°2·8′	3°59·5′W	T	180
Hannaford Manor	Devon	SX7070	50°31·2′	3°49·7′W	X	202
Hannafore	Corn	SX2552	50°20·8′	4°27·2′W	T	201
Hannafore Point	Corn	SX2552	50°20·8′	4°27·2′W	X	201
Hannah	Lincs	TF5079	53°17·4′	0°15·4′E	T	122
Hannahfield	C of Edin	NT1566	55°53·0′	3°21·1′W	X	65
Hannah Law	Renf	NS3061	55°49·0′	4°42·4′W	H	63
Hannah Moor	Cumbr	NX9414	54°30·9′	3°37·8′W	X	89
Hannah Park	Notts	SK5977	53°17·4′	1°6·5′W	X	120
Hannahston	E Ayr	NS4419	55°26·7′	4°27·5′W	X	70
Hannakin	Cumbr	SD3597	54°22·1′	2°59·6′W	X	96,97
Hannam's Copse	Hants	SU7949	51°14·3′	0°51·7′W	F	186
Hannam's Hall	Essex	TM1524	51°52·6′	1°7·8′E	X	168,169
Hannaston	D & G	NX5982	55°7·0′	4°12·2′W	X	77
Hannaston Wood	D & G	NX5982	55°7·0′	4°12·2′W	F	77
Hannath Hall	Cambs	TF4417	52°44·1′	0°8·4′E	X	131
Hannatoft	Orkney	HY5016	59°2·0′	2°51·8′W	X	6
Hannayston Hill	D & G	NX5983	55°7·5′	4°12·2′W	X	77
Hannel	Scot Bord	NT3330	55°33·8′	3°3·3′W	X	73
Hannel Bog	Scot Bord	NT3330	55°33·8′	3°3·3′W	X	73
Hann Fm	N Lincs	TA0822	53°41·2′	0°21·5′W	FM	107,112
Hannibal's Carn	Corn	SW4336	50°10·3′	5°35·6′W	X	203
Hannigarth	Shetld	HP6101	60°41·5′	0°52·5′W	X	1
Hanni Geo	Highld	ND3038	58°19·8′	3°11·2′W	X	11
Hanningfield Reservoir	Essex	TQ7398	51°39·5′	0°30·5′E	W	167
Hanningfields Green	Suff	TL8754	52°9·4′	0°44·4′E	T	155
Hannington	Hants	SU5455	51°17·7′	1°13·1′W	T	174,185
Hannington	Northnts	SP8171	52°20·1′	0°48·3′W	T	141
Hannington	Swin	SU1793	51°38·4′	1°44·9′W	T	163,173
Hannington Br	Glos	SU1796	51°40·0′	1°44·9′W	X	163
Hannington Grange	Northnts	SP8271	52°20·1′	0°47·4′W	X	141
Hannington Wick	Swin	SU1795	51°39·4′	1°44·9′W	T	163
Hanns Hall Fm	Ches	SJ3177	53°17·4′	3°1·7′W	FM	117
Hanny Combe	Somer	SS9141	51°9·7′	3°33·1′W	X	181
Hanover	Highld	NH9653	57°33·6′	3°43·8′W	X	27
Hanover	Orkney	HY4330	59°9·4′	2°59·3′W	X	5,6
Hanover Cove	Corn	SW7353	50°20·2′	5°11·0′W	W	204
Hanover Fm	Bucks	SP7529	51°57·5′	0°54·1′W	FM	165
Hanover Hill	Bucks	SU7991	51°37·0′	0°51·1′W	X	175
Hanover Hill	Dorset	ST6816	50°56·8′	2°26·9′W	H	183
Hanover Ho	N Yks	SE5471	54°8·2′	1°10·0′W	X	100
Hanover Lodge	Leic	SK6116	52°44·5′	1°5·4′W	X	129
Hanover Point	I of W	SZ3783	50°39·0′	1°28·2′W	X	196
Hanover Wood	Somer	ST6817	50°57·3′	2°27·0′W	F	183
Hanscombe End	Beds	TL1133	51°59·3′	0°22·6′W	T	166
Hansdale	Aberd	NJ7055	57°35·3′	2°29·6′W	X	29
Hansel	Devon	SX8247	50°18·9′	3°39·1′W	T	202
Hansell Fm	Warw	SP1754	52°11·3′	1°44·7′W	FM	151
Hansel Village	S Ayr	NS3830	55°32·5′	4°33·6′W	T	70
Hans Fm	Kent	TR0332	51°3·3′	0°54·2′E	FM	189
Hansford Barton	Devon	SS6615	50°55·4′	3°54·0′W	X	180
Hansford Cross	Devon	SS6414	50°54·8′	3°55·7′W	X	180
Hans Hill Fm	Glos	SP1629	51°57·8′	1°45·6′W	FM	163
Hanslett's Ho	Kent	TQ9859	51°18·0′	0°50·8′E	X	178
Hansley Cross	Staffs	SK0642	52°58·8′	1°54·2′W	T	119,128
Hanslope	Mil Key	SP8046	52°6·6′	0°49·5′W	T	152
Hanslope Lodge	Mil Key	SP8144	52°5·5′	0°48·7′W	X	152
Hanslope Park	Mil Key	SP8145	52°6·1′	0°48·6′W	X	152
Hansnett Wood	Heref	SO6542	52°4·8′	2°30·2′W	F	149
Hanson Grange	Derby	SK1453	53°4·7′	1°47·1′W	X	119
Hanson Ho	Ches	SJ7981	53°19·8′	2°18·5′W	X	109
Hansons	Lancs	SD7346	53°54·8′	2°24·2′W	X	103
Hanstead Stud	Bucks	SP8116	51°50·4′	0°49·1′W	X	165
Hantergantick	Corn	SX1075	50°32·9′	4°40·5′W	X	200
Hanter Hill	Powys	SO2557	52°12·6′	3°5·5′W	H	148
Hantertavis	Corn	SW7433	50°9·5′	5°9·5′W	X	204
Hanthorpe	Lincs	TF0824	52°48·4′	0°23·5′W	T	130
Hanton Fm	Pemb	SM9714	51°47·5′	4°56·2′W	FM	157,158
Hanway Common	Shrops	SO4870	52°19·8′	2°45·4′W	X	137,138,148
Hanwell	Ealing	TQ1580	51°30·7′	0°20·2′W	T	176
Hanwell	Oxon	SP4343	52°5·3′	1°21·9′W	T	151
Hanwell Fields	Oxon	SP4442	52°4·7′	1°21·1′W	X	151
Hanwood	Shrops	SJ4409	52°40·8′	2°49·3′W	T	126
Hanwood Bank	Shrops	SJ4410	52°41·3′	2°49·3′W	T	126
Hanworth	Brackn	SU8666	51°23·4′	0°45·4′W	T	175
Hanworth	Houns	TQ1271	51°25·8′	0°22·9′W	T	176
Hanworth	Norf	TG1935	52°52·3′	1°15·7′E	T	133
Hanworth Cross	Norf	TG2134	52°51·7′	1°17·4′E	X	133
Hanworth Hall	Norf	TG1935	52°52·3′	1°15·7′E	A	133
Hanworth Park	Houns	TQ1172	51°26·4′	0°23·8′W	X	176
Hanyards	Staffs	SJ9624	52°49·0′	2°3·2′W	X	127
Ha' of Durran	Highld	ND1963	58°33·1′	3°23·0′W	X	11,12
Ha'penny Bridge	Swin	SU2199	51°41·6′	1°41·4′W	A	163
Hapland	D & G	NS8603	55°18·7′	3°47·3′W	X	78
Hapland	E Ayr	NS4149	55°42·8′	4°31·4′W	X	64
Haplandmuir	E Ayr	NS4150	55°43·3′	4°31·5′W	X	64
Happendon	S Lanak	NS8533	55°34·9′	3°49·0′W	X	71,72
Happendon Wood	S Lanak	NS8534	55°35·4′	3°49·1′W	F	71,72
Happerton Fms	N Som	ST5274	51°28·0′	2°41·1′W	FM	172
Happertutie Burn	Scot Bord	NT2016	55°26·1′	3°15·4′W	W	79
Happisburgh	Norf	TG3830	52°49·1′	1°32·3′E	T	133
Happisburgh Common	Norf	TG3729	52°48·6′	1°31·4′E	T	133,134
Happyhillock	Aberd	NJ9365	57°40·7′	2°6·6′W	X	30
Happyland Fm	Beds	SP9830	51°57·8′	0°34·0′W	FM	165
Happylands Fm	Lincs	TF0795	53°26·7′	0°22·9′W	FM	112
Happy Valley	Conwy	SH7883	53°20·0′	3°49·5′W	X	115
Happy Valley	Northum	NT9924	55°30·8′	2°0·5′W	X	75
Happy Valley (Cwm Maethlon)	Gwyn	SN6398	52°34·0′	4°0·9′W	X	135
Happy Valley Fm	Oxon	SP4234	52°0·4′	1°22·9′W	FM	151
Hapsford	Ches	SJ4774	53°15·9′	2°47·3′W	T	117
Hapsford	Somer	ST7549	51°14·6′	2°21·1′W	T	183
Hapstead	W Susx	TQ3429	51°2·9′	0°4·9′W	X	187,198
Hapstead Camphill	Devon	SX7166	50°29·0′	3°48·7′W	X	202
Hapton	Lancs	SD7931	53°46·7′	2°18·7′W	T	103
Hapton	Norf	TM1796	52°31·3′	1°12·3′E	T	134
Hapton Park	Lancs	SD8029	53°45·7′	2°17·8′W	X	103
Hapturnell Burn	S Lanak	NS9810	55°22·7′	3°36·2′W	W	78
Ha'quoy	Orkney	HY5321	59°4·7′	2°48·7′W	X	5,6
Harabreck	Orkney	HY3707	58°57·0′	3°5·2′W	X	6,7
Haranish	N Eil	NB0113	58°0·6′	7°3·3′W	X	13
Harbarrow	Cumbr	SD2571	54°8·0′	3°8·5′W	X	96
Harber	N Yks	SD8072	54°8·9′	2°18·0′W	X	98
Harber Scar	N Yks	SD8173	54°9·4′	2°17·0′W	X	98
Harberton	Devon	SX7758	50°24·8′	3°43·5′W	T	202
Harbertonford	Devon	SX7856	50°23·7′	3°42·6′W	T	202
Harberwain	Cumbr	NY6014	54°31·4′	2°36·7′W	X	91
Harbin's Fm	Dorset	ST6809	50°53·0′	2°26·9′W	FM	194
Harbin's Park	Dorset	ST9013	50°55·2′	2°8·2′W	X	195
Harbin's Park Fm	Dorset	ST9013	50°55·2′	2°8·2′W	FM	195
Harbledown	Kent	TR1358	51°17·1′	1°3·7′E	T	179
Harborne	Birm	SP0284	52°27·5′	1°57·8′W	T	139
Harboro	I of W	SZ4084	50°39·5′	1°25·7′W	X	196
Harboro Fm	Leic	SK4620	52°46·8′	1°18·7′W	FM	129
Harboro' Rocks	Derby	SK2455	53°5·7′	1°38·1′W	X	119
Harboro (Tumuli)	I of W	SZ4084	50°39·5′	1°25·7′W	A	196
Harborough	Kent	TQ4847	51°12·4′	0°7·5′E	X	188
Harborough Banks	Warw	SP1870	52°19·9′	1°43·8′W	A	139
Harborough Fields Fm	Warw	SP5080	52°25·2′	1°15·5′W	FM	140
Harborough Hall Fm	Essex	TL9018	51°49·9′	0°45·9′E	FM	168
Harborough Hill	Northnts	SP9094	52°32·4′	0°40·0′W	X	141
Harborough Hill	Worcs	SO8879	52°24·8′	2°10·2′W	H	139
Harborough Magna	Warw	SP4779	52°24·7′	1°18·1′W	T	140
Harborough Parva	Warw	SP4778	52°24·1′	1°18·2′W	T	140
Harborough Plantation	Northum	NU0222	55°29·8′	1°57·7′W	F	75
Harbottle	Northum	NT9304	55°20·0′	2°6·2′W	T	80
Harbottle Crag	Northum	NT9202	55°19·0′	2°7·1′W	X	80
Harbottle Grange	Northum	NT9605	55°20·6′	2°3·4′W	X	81
Harbottle Hills	Northum	NT9204	55°20·0′	2°7·1′W	H	80
Harbour	Highld	NG7012	57°8·7′	5°47·7′W	W	32,33
Harbour	I of M	SC4077	54°10·1′	4°26·6′W	W	95
Harbour	Powys	SO1851	52°9·3′	3°11·5′W	X	148
Harbour Channel	Norf	TF7245	52°58·7′	0°34·1′E	W	132
Harbour Cove	Corn	SW9177	50°33·6′	4°56·7′W	W	200
Harbour Craig	Scot Bord	NT1855	55°47·1′	3°18·0′W	X	65,66,72
Harbour Flatt	Cumbr	NY7223	54°36·3′	2°25·6′W	X	91
Harbour Fm	I of W	SZ6388	50°41·5′	1°6·1′W	FM	196
Harbourgill	Cumbr	SD7686	54°16·4′	2°21·7′W	X	98
Harbour Heights	E Susx	TQ4300	50°47·1′	0°2·1′E	T	198
Harbour Hill	C of Edin	NT2065	55°52·5′	3°16·3′W	H	66
Harbour Hill	Heref	SO6944	52°5·8′	2°26·8′W	X	149
Harbour Hill	Warw	SP1946	52°7·0′	1°43·0′W	X	151
Harbour House Fm	Durham	NZ2848	54°49·8′	1°33·4′W	FM	88
Harbourland	Kent	TQ7757	51°17·3′	0°32·7′E	T	178,188
Harbour Lodge	Brad	SD9935	53°48·9′	2°0·5′W	X	103
Harbourneford	Devon	SX7162	50°26·9′	3°48·6′W	T	202
Harbourne Head	Devon	SX6965	50°28·4′	3°50·4′W	W	202
Harbourne River	Devon	SX7460	50°25·8′	3°46·1′W	W	202
Harbourne River	Devon	SX8056	50°23·7′	3°40·9′W	W	202
Harbour Shields	Aberd	NO8374	56°51·7′	2°16·3′W	X	45
Harbours Hill	Worcs	SO9565	52°17·2′	2°4·0′W	T	150
Harbour,The	Northum	NU1241	55°40·0′	1°48·1′W	W	75
Harbour, The	Shetld	HU3626	60°1·3′	1°20·8′W	W	4
Harbour Village	Pemb	SM9438	52°0·4′	4°59·7′W	T	157
Harboury House	Bucks	SP8128	51°56·9′	0°48·9′W	X	165
Harbridge	Hants	SU1410	50°53·6′	1°47·7′W	T	195
Harbridge Green	Hants	SU1410	50°53·6′	1°47·7′W	T	195
Harbrough Fm	N Yks	SE4496	54°21·7′	1°19·0′W	FM	99
Harburn	W Loth	NT0460	55°49·7′	3°31·5′W	X	65
Harburn	W Loth	NT0461	55°50·2′	3°31·5′W	T	65
Harburnhead	W Loth	NT0460	55°49·7′	3°31·5′W	X	65
Harburnhead Hill	W Loth	NT0357	55°48·0′	3°32·4′W	X	65,72
Harbury	Warw	SP3759	52°13·9′	1°27·1′W	T	151
Harbury Fields	Warw	SP3560	52°14·5′	1°28·8′W	X	151
Harbut Law	Cumbr	NY7047	54°49·3′	2°27·6′W	X	86,87
Harbut Lodge	Cumbr	NY7147	54°49·3′	2°26·7′W	X	86,87
Harby	Leic	SK7431	52°52·5′	0°53·6′W	T	129
Harby	Notts	SK8770	53°13·4′	0°41·4′W	T	121
Harbybrow	Cumbr	NY1941	54°45·7′	3°15·1′W	X	85
Harby Hills	Leic	SK7628	52°50·9′	0°51·9′W	X	129
Harby Lodge Fm	Leic	SK7331	52°52·5′	0°54·5′W	FM	129
Harcamlow Way	Cambs	TL5752	52°8·9′	0°18·1′E	X	154
Harcamlow Way	Essex	TL4927	51°55·5′	0°10·4′E	X	167
Harcamlow Way	Essex	TL5320	51°51·7′	0°13·7′E	X	167
Harcamlow Way	Herts	TL3718	51°50·9′	0°0·3′W	X	166
Harcarse	Scot Bord	NT8148	55°43·8′	2°17·7′W	X	74
Harcarse Hill	Scot Bord	NT8148	55°43·8′	2°17·7′W	X	74
Harcles Hill	Bury	SD7717	53°39·2′	2°20·5′W	X	109
Harcombe	Devon	SX8881	50°37·3′	3°34·6′W	T	192
Harcombe	Devon	SY1590	50°42·4′	3°11·8′W	T	192,193
Harcombe	Hants	SU6330	51°4·2′	1°5·7′W	X	185
Harcombe Bottom	Devon	SY3395	50°45·3′	2°56·6′W	T	193
Harcombe Bottom	Glos	SO9514	51°49·7′	2°4·0′W	F	163
Harcombe Fm	Glos	SO9511	51°48·1′	2°4·0′W	FM	163
Harcombe Fm	S Glos	ST7775	51°28·6′	2°19·5′W	FM	172
Harcombe Hill	Devon	SY1591	50°43·0′	3°11·9′W	X	192,193
Harcourt	Corn	SW8137	50°11·8′	5°3·7′W	T	204
Harcourt	Shrops	SJ5624	52°48·9′	2°38·8′W	X	126
Harcourt Fm	Cambs	TL2670	52°19·0′	0°8·7′W	FM	153
Harcourt Hill	Oxon	SP4904	51°44·2′	1°17·0′W	T	164
Harcourt Hill	Oxon	SU6689	51°36·0′	1°2·4′W	X	175
Harcourt Mill	Shrops	SJ5524	52°48·9′	2°39·7′W	X	126
Harcus	Scot Bord	NT2448	55°43·4′	3°12·2′W	X	73
Hardaberg	Shetld	HP6511	60°46·9′	0°47·9′W	X	1
Hardacres	Scot Bord	NT7442	55°40·5′	2°24·4′W	X	74
Hardale Head	N Yks	NZ7511	54°29·6′	0°50·1′W	X	94
Hardbedlam	Aberd	NJ8745	57°30·0′	2°12·6′W	X	30
Hardberry Fm	Durham	NY9327	54°38·5′	2°6·1′W	FM	91,92
Hardberry Gutter	Durham	NY9328	54°39·1′	2°6·1′W	X	91,92
Hardberry Hill	Durham	NY9328	54°39·1′	2°6·1′W	X	91,92
Hardbreck	Orkney	HY4602	58°54·4′	2°55·8′W	X	6,7
Hardcake Hall	Cumbr	NY3051	54°51·2′	3°5·0′W	X	85
Hardcastle Crags	Cald	SD9630	53°46·2′	2°3·2′W	X	103
Hardcastle Garth	N Yks	SE2260	54°2·4′	1°39·4′W	X	99
Hardcastle Moor	N Yks	SE1065	54°5·1′	1°50·4′W	X	99
Hard Crag	Cumbr	SD3683	54°14·6′	2°58·5′W	X	96,97
Hard Crag	Cumbr	SD3779	54°12·4′	2°57·5′W	X	96,97
Hardcroft	D & G	NX1864	54°56·5′	4°50·1′W	X	82
Hardeicke	Glos	SO8012	51°48·6′	2°17·0′W	T	162
Harden	Barns	SE1503	53°31·6′	1°46·0′W	T	110
Harden	Brad	SE0838	53°50·5′	1°52·3′W	T	104
Harden	Kent	TQ5142	51°9·7′	0°10·0′E	X	188
Harden	Scot Bord	NT4514	55°25·3′	2°51·7′W	A	79
Harden	Wals	SK0101	52°36·6′	1°58·7′W	T	139
Harden Beck	Brad	SE0837	53°50·0′	1°52·3′W	W	104
Harden Br	N Yks	SD7667	54°6·1′	2°21·6′W	X	98
Harden Burn	Northum	NT9609	55°22·7′	2°3·4′W	W	81
Harden Burn	Scot Bord	NT4415	55°25·8′	2°52·7′W	W	79
Harden Clough	Barns	SE1403	53°31·6′	1°46·9′W	X	110
Hardendale	Cumbr	NY5814	54°31·4′	2°38·5′W	T	91
Hardendale Fell	Cumbr	NY5712	54°30·3′	2°39·4′W	X	91
Hardendale Nab	Cumbr	NY5814	54°31·4′	2°38·5′W	X	91
Harden Edge	Northum	NT7807	55°21·6′	2°20·4′W	H	80
Harden Gill Beck	N Yks	SE1059	54°1·9′	1°50·4′W	W	104
Harden Grange	Brad	SE0938	53°50·5′	1°51·4′W	X	104
Hardengreen	Midlo	NT3265	55°52·7′	3°4·8′W	X	66
Harden Hill	Kirk	SE1008	53°34·4′	1°50·5′W	H	110
Harden Hill	Northum	NT9709	55°22·7′	2°2·4′W	H	81
Harden Hill	Scot Bord	NY5288	55°11·3′	2°44·8′W	H	79
Hardenhuish Park	Wilts	ST9174	51°28·1′	2°7·4′W	X	173
Harden Mains	Scot Bord	NT7019	55°28·1′	2°28·0′W	X	80
Harden Moor	Barns	SK1698	53°28·9′	1°45·1′W	X	110
Harden Moor	Brad	SE0738	53°50·5′	1°53·2′W	X	104
Harden Moor	Lancs	SD8116	53°38·7′	2°16·8′W	X	109
Harden Moss	Scot Bord	NY5289	55°11·8′	2°44·8′W	X	79
Harden Moss Fm	Kirk	SE0908	53°34·4′	1°51·4′W	FM	110
Harden Old Ho	Lancs	SD9244	53°53·8′	2°6·9′W	X	103
Harden Park	Ches	SJ8479	53°18·7′	2°14·0′W	T	118
Hardenpeel	Scot Bord	NT6819	55°28·1′	2°29·9′W	X	80
Harden's Fm	Wilts	ST9373	51°27·6′	2°5·7′W	FM	173
Harden's Gap	Lincs	TF3574	53°15·0′	0°1·8′E	X	122
Hardens Hill	Scot Bord	NT7354	55°47·0′	2°25·4′W	X	67,74
Hardenside	D & G	NY4181	55°7·4′	2°55·1′W	X	79
Hardens, The	Scot Bord	NT7554	55°47·0′	2°23·5′W	X	67,74
Hardford	Aberd	NJ8234	57°24·0′	2°17·5′W	X	29,30
Hard Gap	N Yks	SE0773	54°9·4′	1°53·2′W	X	99
Hardgate	Aberd	NJ7801	57°6·2′	2°21·3′W	T	38
Hardgate	Aberd	NJ8653	57°34·3′	2°13·6′W	X	30
Hardgate	D & G	NX8166	54°58·7′	3°51·1′W	T	84
Hardgate	N Yks	SE2662	54°3·4′	1°35·8′W	T	99
Hardgate	W Dunb	NS5072	55°55·3′	4°23·6′W	T	64
Hardgate Hall	Derby	SK1175	53°16·6′	1°49·7′W	X	119
Hardgatehead	Scot Bord	NT1250	55°44·4′	3°23·7′W	X	65,72
Hardgatehead	S Lanak	NS9853	55°45·8′	3°37·1′W	X	65,72
Hardgatewall	Derby	SK1175	53°16·6′	1°49·7′W	T	119
Hardgrove	D & G	NY1170	55°1·2′	3°23·1′W	X	85
Hardgroves Hill	N Yks	SE1958	54°1·3′	1°42·2′W	X	104
Hardham	W Susx	TQ0317	50°56·8′	0°31·6′W	T	197
Hardham Priory	W Susx	TQ0317	50°56·8′	0°31·6′W	A	197
Hard Head	Corn	SX1571	50°30·8′	4°36·2′W	X	201
Hard Head	Corn	SX2050	50°19·6′	4°31·4′W	X	201
Hardhead	Lancs	SD4649	53°56·3′	2°48·9′W	X	102
Hard Head Fm	N Yks	SD7958	54°1·3′	2°18·8′W	FM	103
Hard Heugh	Northum	NU0506	55°21·1′	1°54·8′W	H	81
Hardhill	Aberd	NK0738	57°26·2′	1°52·5′W	X	30
Hard Hill	Angus	NO4182	56°55·8′	2°57·7′W	H	44
Hard Hill	Cumbr	NY7333	54°41·7′	2°24·7′W	X	91
Hard Hill	D & G	NX9599	55°16·7′	3°38·7′W	H	78
Hardhill	Highld	NH7848	57°30·6′	4°1·7′W	X	27
Hardhill	Orkney	HY3911	58°59·2′	3°3·2′W	X	6
Hardhillock	Aberd	NO8296	57°3·5′	2°17·4′W	X	38,45
Hardhillock	Moray	NJ1561	57°38·1′	3°25·0′W	X	28

Hard Hill Top	Lancs	SD6657	54°0·7'	2°30·7'W	X	103
Hard Ho Fm	Lancs	SD8246	53°54·8'	2°16·0'W	FM	103
Hardhorn	Lancs	SD3538	53°50·3'	2°58·9'W	T	102
Hardhurst	Cumbr	NY5466	54°59·4'	2°42·7'W	X	86
Hardhurst Fm	Derby	SK2952	53°4·1'	1°33·6'W	FM	119
Hardhurst Howes	N Yks	SE9797	54°21·8'	0°30·0'W	A	94,101
Hardicott Fm	Devon	SX4077	50°34·5'	4°15·2'W	FM	201
Hardiesmill Place	Scot Bord	NT6640	55°39·4'	2°32·0'W	X	74
Hardilands	Falk	NS9284	56°2·5'	3°43·6'W	X	65
Hard Ing	Cumbr	NY5919	54°34·1'	2°37·6'W	X	91
Hard Ing	N Yks	SE1256	54°0·2'	1°48·6'W	X	104
Hardinge	Wilts	ST9480	51°31·4'	2°4·8'W	X	173
Harding Fm	Wilts	SU2962	51°21·6'	1°34·6'W	FM	174
Hardingham	Norf	TG0403	52°35·4'	1°1·1'E	T	144
Hardingland	Ches	SJ9572	53°14·9'	2°4·1'W	X	118
Harding Plantn	N Yks	SE8078	54°11·7'	0°46·0'W	F	100
Hardings	Ches	SJ9570	53°13·9'	2°4·1'W	X	118
Hardings	Durham	NY9920	54°34·8'	2°0·5'W	X	92
Hardings	Herts	TL4515	51°49·1'	0°6·6'E	X	167
Hardings Booth	Staffs	SK0664	53°10·6'	1°54·2'W	T	119
Hardings Down	Swan	SS4390	51°35·5'	4°15·6'W	X	159
Hardingsdown	Swan	SS4491	51°36·0'	4°14·8'W	X	159
Hardings Fm	Dorset	ST7624	51°1·1'	2°20·1'W	FM	183
Harding's Fm	Essex	TL6401	51°41·3'	0°22·8'E	FM	167
Harding's Fm	Notts	SK7766	53°16·8'	0°50·3'W	FM	120
Harding's Fm	Suff	TL9865	52°15·1'	0°54·4'E	FM	155
Harding's Fm	W Susx	SU8500	50°47·8'	0°47·2'W	FM	197
Hardings Hill	Pemb	SM8701	51°40·3'	5°4·4'W	X	157
Hardingshute Fm	I of W	SZ5988	50°41·5'	1°9·5'W	FM	196
Hardings, The	Lincs	TF1084	53°20·7'	0°20·4'W	X	121
Hardingstone	Northnts	SP7657	52°12·6'	0°52·9'W	T	152
Hardingstone Lodge	Northnts	SP7857	52°12·6'	0°51·1'W	X	152
Hardings Wood	Staffs	SJ8354	53°5·2'	2°14·8'W	T	118
Harding, The	Lincs	TF1250	53°2·4'	0°19·4'W	X	121
Hardington	Somer	ST7452	51°16·2'	2°22·0'W	T	183
Hardington Ho	S Lanak	NS9630	55°33·4'	3°38·5'W	X	72
Hardington Mains	S Lanak	NS9731	55°34·0'	3°37·6'W	X	72
Hardington Mandeville	Somer	ST5111	50°54·0'	2°41·4'W	T	194
Hardington Marsh	Somer	ST5009	50°52·9'	2°42·3'W	T	194
Hardington Moor	Somer	ST5112	50°54·6'	2°41·4'W	T	194
Hardiston	Pth & Kin	NT0697	56°9·6'	3°30·4'W	X	58
Hardiston	Stir	NS6194	56°7·4'	4°13·7'W	X	57
Hardiston Hill	Pth & Kin	NT0596	56°9·1'	3°31·3'W	H	58
Hardisty Hill	N Yks	SE1756	54°0·2'	1°44·0'W	X	104
Hardistys	N Yks	SE0951	53°57·5'	1°51·4'W	X	104
Hardisworthy	Devon	SS2220	50°57·4'	4°31·7'W	T	190
Hardiwick	Staffs	SJ9432	52°53·4'	2°4·9'W	X	127
Hardiwick	Staffs	SJ9544	52°59·8'	2°4·1'W	X	118
Hardiwick Fm	Staffs	SJ9431	52°52·8'	2°4·9'W	FM	127
Hardiwick Grove	Staffs	SJ9432	52°53·4'	2°4·9'W	X	127
Hard Knott	Cumbr	NY2302	54°24·7'	3°10·8'W	H	89,90
Hardknott Castle	Cumbr	NY2101	54°24·1'	3°12·6'W	X	89,90
Hardknott Pass	Cumbr	NY2301	54°24·2'	3°10·8'W	X	89,90
Hard Knowe	D & G	NX7499	55°16·4'	3°58·6'W	H	77
Hard Knowe	Shetld	HU4553	60°15·8'	1°10·7'W	X	3
Hardlawbank	D & G	NX9578	55°5·4'	3°38·3'W	X	84
Hardlee Flow	Scot Bord	NT6003	55°19·4'	2°37·4'W	X	80
Hard Level Gill	N Yks	NY9601	54°24·5'	2°3·3'W	W	91,92
Hard Lewis Rocks	I Scilly	SV9515	49°57·7'	6°14·8'W	X	203
Hardley	Hants	SU4304	50°50·3'	1°23·0'W	T	196
Hardley Cross	Norf	TG4001	52°33·5'	1°32·8'E	A	134
Hardley Flood	Norf	TM3899	52°32·4'	1°31·0'E	W	134
Hardley Hall	Norf	TG3800	52°33·0'	1°31·0'E	A	134
Hardley Hill	Derby	SK2434	52°54·4'	1°38·2'W	X	128
Hardley Marshes	Norf	TG3801	52°33·5'	1°31·1'E	X	134
Hardley Street	Norf	TG3801	52°33·5'	1°31·1'E	T	134
Hardman Rock	I of W	SZ4081	50°37·9'	1°25·7'W	X	196
Hardmead	Mil Key	SP9347	52°7·0'	0°38·1'W	T	153
Hardmuir	Highld	NH9557	57°35·7'	3°44·9'W	X	27
Hard Nab	Northum	NU0508	55°22·2'	1°54·8'W	X	81
Hard Nese	Brad	SE0234	53°48·4'	1°57·8'W	X	104
Hardown Hill	Dorset	SY4094	50°44·8'	2°50·6'W	H	193
Hardraw	N Yks	SD8691	54°19·1'	2°12·5'W	T	98
Hardraw Force	N Yks	SD8691	54°19·1'	2°12·5'W	W	98
Hardridge Fm	Inverc	NS3268	55°52·8'	4°40·7'W	FM	63
Hardridge Hill	Inverc	NS3067	55°52·2'	4°42·6'W	X	63
Hardriding	Northum	NY7563	54°57·9'	2°23·0'W	X	86,87
Hardriding	W Susx	TQ2633	51°5·2'	0°11·7'W	X	187
Hard Rigg	Cumbr	NY1905	54°26·3'	3°14·5'W	X	89,90
Hard Rigg	Cumbr	NY7448	54°49·8'	2°23·9'W	H	86,87
Hard Rigg Edge	Cumbr	NY6538	54°44·4'	2°32·2'W	X	91
Hardrigg Gill	Cumbr	NY1905	54°26·3'	3°14·5'W	W	89,90
Hardrigg Hall	Cumbr	NY4236	54°43·2'	2°53·6'W	X	90
Hardrigg Lodge	D & G	NY2167	54°59·7'	3°13·7'W	X	85
Hardriggs	Northum	NY6865	54°59·0'	2°29·6'W	X	86,87
Hardrig Head	S Lanak	NS9926	55°31·3'	3°35·6'W	H	72
Hards Fm	Cumbr	NY1347	54°48·9'	3°20·8'W	FM	85
Hardslacks	Aberd	NK0439	57°26·7'	1°55·5'W	X	30
Hardstoft	Derby	SK4463	53°10·0'	1°20·1'W	T	120
Hardstoft Common	Derby	SK4363	53°10·0'	1°21·0'W	T	120
Hardstone Fm	Devon	SX3679	50°35·5'	4°18·6'W	FM	201
Hardstones Fm	Stock on T	NZ3615	54°32·0'	1°26·2'W	FM	93
Hardsworthy	Devon	SS2816	50°55·3'	4°26·5'W	X	190
Hard, The	Fife	NO2318	56°21·1'	3°14·3'W	X	58
Hard, The	Fife	NO2319	56°21·7'	3°14·3'W	X	58
Hardthorn	D & G	NX9477	55°4·8'	3°39·2'W	X	84
Hard to Find Fm	Bucks	SU8790	51°36·4'	0°44·2'W	FM	175
Hardwall	Shetld	HU3770	60°25·0'	1°19·2'W	X	2,3
Hardway	Hants	SU6001	50°48·6'	1°8·5'W	T	196
Hardway	Somer	ST7134	51°6·5'	2°24·5'W	T	183
Hardwell Fm	Oxon	SU2887	51°35·1'	1°35·4'W	FM	174
Hardwick	Bucks	SP8019	51°52·1'	0°49·9'W	T	165
Hardwick	Cambs	TL1868	52°18·1'	0°15·8'W	T	153
Hardwick	Cambs	TL3759	52°13·0'	0°0·7'E	T	154
Hardwick	Derby	SK3364	53°10·6'	1°30·0'W	X	119
Hardwick	Kent	TQ5749	51°13·3'	0°15·3'E	X	188
Hardwick	Lincs	SK8675	53°16·1'	0°42·2'W	X	121
Hardwick	Norf	TM2289	52°27·5'	1°16·5'E	T	156
Hardwick	Northnts	SP8569	52°19·0'	0°44·8'W	T	152
Hardwick	Oxon	SP3806	51°45·3'	1°26·6'W	T	164
Hardwick	Oxon	SP4441	52°4·2'	1°21·1'W	T	151
Hardwick	Oxon	SP5729	51°57·6'	1°9·8'W	T	164
Hardwick	Roth	SK4886	53°22·4'	1°16·3'W	T	111,120
Hardwick	Shrops	SJ3734	52°54·2'	2°55·8'W	X	126
Hardwick	Shrops	SO3690	52°30·5'	2°56·2'W	T	137
Hardwick	Stock on T	NZ4121	54°35·2'	1°21·5'W	T	93
Hardwick	Wals	SP0799	52°35·6'	1°53·4'W	T	139
Hardwicke	Glos	SO9027	51°56·7'	2°8·3'W	T	163
Hardwicke	Heref	SO2643	52°5·1'	3°4·4'W	T	148,161
Hardwicke	Shrops	SO6682	52°26·3'	2°29·6'W	X	138
Hardwicke Brook	Heref	SO2444	52°5·6'	3°6·2'W	W	148,161
Hardwicke Court	Glos	SO7811	51°48·1'	2°18·8'W	X	162
Hardwicke Fm	Cambs	TL2857	52°12·0'	0°7·2'W	FM	153
Hardwicke Fm	Glos	SO7813	51°49·1'	2°18·8'W	FM	162
Hardwicke Lodge Fm	Leic	SP5298	52°34·9'	1°13·6'W	FM	140
Hardwicke Manor	Heref	SO6455	52°11·8'	2°31·2'W	X	149
Hardwick Fm	Beds	SP9756	52°11·9'	0°34·4'W	FM	153
Hardwick Fm	C of Plym	SX5355	50°22·8'	4°3·7'W	FM	201
Hardwick Fm	Lincs	SK8676	53°16·7'	0°42·2'W	FM	121
Hardwick Fm	Monm	ST4589	51°36·1'	2°47·3'W	FM	171,172
Hardwick Fm	N Yks	SE9595	54°20·7'	0°31·9'W	FM	94,101
Hardwick Fm	Oxon	SP4542	52°4·7'	1°20·2'W	FM	151
Hardwick Fm	Rut	SK9612	52°42·1'	0°34·4'W	FM	130
Hardwick Fm	Warw	SP3447	52°7·4'	1°29·8'W	FM	151
Hardwickforge	Shrops	SO6581	52°25·8'	2°30·5'W	X	138
Hardwick Grange	Lincs	TF2542	52°57·9'	0°7·9'W	X	131
Hardwick Grange Fm	Lincs	SE8300	53°29·6'	0°44·5'W	FM	112
Hardwick Green	Worcs	SO8132	51°59·4'	2°16·2'W	T	150
Hardwick Hall	Derby	SK4663	53°10·0'	1°18·3'W	A	120
Hardwick Hall Country Park	Derby	SK4563	53°10·0'	1°19·2'W	X	120
Hardwick Hall Country Park	Durham	NZ3429	54°39·5'	1°28·0'W	X	93
Hardwick Hall Fm	Durham	NZ4539	54°44·9'	1°17·6'W	FM	93
Hardwick Hill	Lincs	SK8399	53°29·1'	0°44·5'W	H	112
Hardwick Ho	Oxon	SU6577	51°29·5'	1°3·4'W	A	175
Hardwick Ho	Warw	SP0864	52°16·7'	1°52·6'W	X	150
Hardwick Ho	Worcs	SO9135	52°1·0'	2°7·5'W	X	150
Hardwick Industrial Estate	Norf	TF6318	52°44·3'	0°25·3'E	X	132
Hardwick Lodge	Northnts	SP8370	52°19·5'	0°46·5'W	X	141
Hardwick Manor	Suff	TL8462	52°13·8'	0°42·1'E	X	155
Hardwick Stud Fm	Oxon	SU6577	51°29·5'	1°3·4'W	FM	175
Hardwick Village	Notts	SK6375	53°16·3'	1°2·9'W	T	120
Hardwick Wood	Cambs	TL3557	52°11·9'	0°1·1'W	F	154
Hardwick Wood	Derby	SK3765	53°11·1'	1°26·4'W	F	119
Hardwick Wood	Northnts	SP8270	52°19·5'	0°47·4'W	F	141
Hardwick Wood	Notts	SK6376	53°16·9'	1°2·9'W	F	120
Hardwick Wood Fm	Lincs	SK8775	53°16·1'	0°41·3'W	FM	121
Hardyards	Aberd	NJ9950	57°32·7'	2°0·5'W	X	30
Hardybarn	Derby	SK0875	53°16·6'	1°52·4'W	X	119
Hardy Gang Wood	Lincs	TF0974	53°15·3'	0°21·6'W	F	121
Hardy Monument	Dorset	SY6187	50°41·1'	2°32·7'W	X	194
Hardy's Birthplace	Dorset	SY7292	50°43·8'	2°23·4'W	X	194
Hardy's Green	Essex	TL9320	51°50·9'	0°48·5'E	T	168
Hare	Somer	ST2915	50°56·0'	3°0·2'W	T	193
Hare and Hounds Corner	Suff	TM1753	52°8·2'	1°10·7'E	X	156
Hare Appletree	Lancs	SD5358	54°1·2'	2°42·6'W	T	102
Hare Appletree Fell	Lancs	SD5458	54°1·2'	2°41·7'W	X	102
Harebarrow Fm	Ches	SJ8876	53°17·1'	2°10·4'W	FM	118
Hareburn	Falk	NS9073	55°56·5'	3°45·2'W	X	65
Hare Burn	Midlo	NT2157	55°48·2'	3°15·2'W	W	66,73
Hare Burn	Scot Bord	NT0826	55°31·6'	3°27·0'W	W	72
Hare Bushes	Glos	SP0302	51°43·2'	1°57·0'W	F	163
Harebutt Bank	Wrekin	SJ6420	52°46·8'	2°31·6'W	X	127
Hareby	Lincs	TF3365	53°10·2'	0°0·2'W	T	122
Hareby Ho	Lincs	TF3365	53°10·2'	0°0·2'W	X	122
Hare Cairn	Aberd	NJ9517	57°14·9'	2°4·5'W	A	38
Hare Cairn	Aberd	NO3787	56°58·5'	3°1·7'W	X	44
Hare Cairn	Angus	NO2462	56°44·9'	3°14·1'W	H	44
Hare Cairn	Angus	NO4577	56°53·1'	2°53·7'W	H	44
Harecairn	Angus	NO4840	56°33·2'	2°50·3'W	X	54
Hare Cairn	Angus	NO4841	56°33·7'	2°50·3'W	X	54
Hare Cairn	Northum	NY8898	55°16·8'	2°10·9'W	A	80
Harecairns	S Lanak	NT0443	55°40·5'	3°31·2'W	X	72
Hare Carr	N Yks	SE1656	54°0·2'	1°44·9'W	X	104
Harecastle Fm	Staffs	SJ8352	53°4·1'	2°14·8'W	FM	118
Harecastle Tunnels	Staffs	SJ8452	53°4·1'	2°13·9'W	X	118
Harecleuch	S Lanak	NT0019	55°27·5'	3°34·5'W	X	78
Hare Cleuch Head	Scot Bord	NT0318	55°27·0'	3°31·6'W	X	78
Hare Cleugh	E Loth	NT6161	55°50·7'	2°36·9'W	X	67
Harecleugh Forest	Scot Bord	NT6153	55°46·4'	2°36·9'W	F	67,74
Hare Clough	Lancs	SD7045	53°54·3'	2°27·0'W	X	103
Hare Clough	Lancs	SD7621	53°41·3'	2°21·4'W	X	103
Hare Clough Barn	Lancs	SD7046	53°54·8'	2°27·0'W	X	103
Hare Clough Beck	Lancs	SD7057	54°0·7'	2°27·1'W	W	103
Harecops	Staffs	SK1158	53°7·4'	1°49·7'W	X	119
Hare Crag	Cumbr	NY2829	54°39·3'	3°6·5'W	X	89,90
Hare Crag	Northum	NU1022	55°29·7'	1°50·1'W	X	75
Hare Crags	Cumbr	SD2795	54°21·0'	3°7·0'W	X	96,97
Hare Craig	Aberd	NK1240	57°27·3'	1°47·5'W	X	30
Harecraig	Aberd	NO8793	57°1·9'	2°12·4'W	X	38,45
Hare Craig	E Ayr	NS7431	55°33·6'	3°59·4'W	X	71
Harecramp Cotts	Bucks	SU7692	51°37·5'	0°53·7'W	X	175
Harecroft	Brad	SE0835	53°48·9'	1°52·3'W	T	104
Harecroft Hall (School)	Cumbr	NY0702	54°24·5'	3°25·6'W	X	89
Hareden	Aberd	NO8078	56°53·8'	2°19·2'W	X	45
Hareden	Lancs	SD6450	53°56·9'	2°32·5'W	X	102,103
Hareden Brook	Lancs	SD6249	53°56·4'	2°34·3'W	W	102,103
Haredene	Northum	NZ1392	55°13·6'	1°47·3'W	X	81
Haredene Wood	Wilts	ST9628	51°3·3'	2°3·0'W	F	184
Hareden Fell	Lancs	SD6249	53°56·4'	2°34·3'W	H	102,103
Hare Edge	Derby	SK3072	53°14·9'	1°32·6'W	T	119
Harefaulds	Scot Bord	NT5750	55°44·7'	2°40·7'W	X	67,73,74
Harefaulds (Fort & Settlement)	Scot Bord	NT5750	55°44·7'	2°40·7'W	A	67,73,74
Hare Fen	Norf	TG3712	52°39·5'	1°30·7'E	X	133,134
Harefield	C of Soton	SU4613	50°55·1'	1°20·3'W	T	196
Harefield	Devon	SY0084	50°39·1'	3°24·5'W	X	192
Harefield	Hill	TQ0590	51°36·2'	0°28·6'W	T	176
Harefield Fm	Kent	TR0356	51°16·2'	0°55·0'E	FM	178,179
Harefield Grove	Hill	TQ0591	51°36·7'	0°28·6'W	T	176
Harefield Ho	Ches	SJ8479	53°18·7'	2°14·0'W	X	118
Harefield Plantation	Hants	SU1109	50°53·1'	1°50·2'W	F	195
Hare Fm	E Susx	TQ8318	50°56·2'	0°36·7'E	FM	199
Hare Fm	Somer	ST3015	50°56·0'	2°59·4'W	FM	193
Hareford Burn	Scot Bord	NT6442	55°40·5'	2°33·9'W	W	74
Haregate	Staffs	SJ9957	53°6·9'	2°0·5'W	T	118
Hare Gill	Cumbr	SD1698	54°22·5'	3°17·2'W	X	96
Hare Gill	N Yks	SD7681	54°13·7'	2°21·7'W	W	98
Haregill Lodge	N Yks	SE1883	54°14·8'	1°43·0'W	X	99
Haregills	D & G	NY1877	55°5·1'	3°16·6'W	X	85
Haregrain Burn	D & G	NY3198	55°16·5'	3°4·7'W	W	79
Haregrain Edge	Scot Bord	NT3605	55°20·3'	3°0·1'W	H	79
Haregrain Rig	D & G	NY1899	55°17·0'	3°17·0'W	H	79
Haregrain Rig	Scot Bord	NY4594	55°14·5'	2°51·5'W	X	79
Hare Green	Essex	TM0924	51°52·7'	1°2·6'E	T	168,169
Haregrove	Brig	SS8581	51°31·2'	3°39·1'W	X	170
Hare Hall	Cumbr	SD2192	54°19·3'	3°12·5'W	X	96
Hare Hall	Oxon	SU6393	51°38·2'	1°5·0'W	X	164,175
Hare Hatch	Wok	SU8077	51°29·4'	0°50·5'W	T	175
Harehaugh	Northum	NY9799	55°17·4'	2°2·4'W	X	81
Harehaugh Hill	Northum	NY9699	55°17·4'	2°3·3'W	H	81
Harehead	Scot Bord	NT4228	55°32·8'	2°54·7'W	X	73
Harehead	Scot Bord	NT6963	55°51·8'	2°29·3'W	X	67
Harehead Hill	Scot Bord	NT4328	55°32·8'	2°53·8'W	H	73
Hare Heads	N Yks	SE2165	54°5·1'	1°40·3'W	H	99
Hareheugh Craigs	Scot Bord	NT6940	55°39·4'	2°29·1'W	X	74
Hare Hill	Aberd	NO6787	56°58·6'	2°32·1'W	X	45
Hare Hill	Brad	SE0038	53°50·5'	1°59·6'W	X	104
Hare Hill	Ches	SJ8776	53°17·1'	2°11·3'W	X	118
Harehill	C of Aber	NJ9414	57°13·3'	2°5·5'W	X	38
Hare Hill	Cumbr	NY5664	54°58·4'	2°40·8'W	X	86
Hare Hill	Cumbr	SD4085	54°15·7'	2°54·8'W	X	96,97
Harehill	Derby	SK1735	52°55·0'	1°44·4'W	T	128
Hare Hill	E Ayr	NS6509	55°21·6'	4°7·4'W	H	71,77
Hare Hill	Midlo	NT1762	55°50·9'	3°19·1'W	H	65,66
Hare Hill	Notts	SK7062	53°9·3'	0°56·8'W	X	120
Hare Hill	S Lanak	NS9053	55°45·7'	3°44·7'W	H	65,72
Hare Hill	Tames	SE0001	53°30·6'	1°59·6'W	X	110
Harehill Fm	Durham	NZ3741	54°46·0'	1°25·1'W	FM	88
Harehills	Leeds	SE3234	53°48·3'	1°30·4'W	T	104
Hare Hills Fm	Lincs	TF4062	53°8·4'	0°6·0'E	FM	122
Hare Holes Fm	Staffs	SK1827	52°50·6'	1°43·6'W	FM	128
Hare Holme Fm	Durham	NZ2142	54°46·6'	1°40·0'W	FM	88
Hare Holt	E Susx	TQ6226	51°0·9'	0°19·0'E	X	188,199
Harehope	Durham	NZ0335	54°42·8'	1°56·8'W	X	92
Harehope	Northum	NU0920	55°28·7'	1°51·0'W	X	75
Harehope	Scot Bord	NT2044	55°41·2'	3°15·9'W	T	73
Harehope Burn	Northum	NU0821	55°29·2'	1°52·0'W	W	75
Harehope Burn	Scot Bord	NT2144	55°41·2'	3°15·0'W	W	73
Harehope Hall	Durham	NZ0149	54°50·4'	1°58·6'W	X	87
Harehope Hall	Northum	NU0820	55°28·7'	1°52·0'W	X	75
Harehope Hill	Durham	NZ0147	54°49·3'	1°58·6'W	X	87
Harehope Hill	E Loth	NT5263	55°51·7'	2°45·6'W	X	66
Harehope Hill	Northum	NT9528	55°33·0'	2°4·3'W	H	74,75
Harehope Hill	Northum	NU0820	55°28·7'	1°52·0'W	H	75
Harehope Hill	Scot Bord	NT1944	55°41·2'	3°16·9'W	H	72
Hare Lane Fm	Dorset	SU0812	50°54·7'	1°52·8'W	FM	195
Hare Law	Durham	NY9739	54°45·0'	2°2·4'W	X	92
Hare Law	Durham	NZ0537	54°43·9'	1°54·9'W	X	92
Harelaw	Durham	NZ1652	54°52·0'	1°44·6'W	T	88
Harelaw	E Loth	NT4476	55°58·7'	2°53·4'W	X	66
Harelaw	E Renf	NS4654	55°45·5'	4°26·8'W	X	64
Hare Law	Fife	NO4428	56°26·7'	2°54·1'W	H	54,59
Harelaw	Fife	NT1996	56°9·2'	3°17·8'W	X	58
Harelaw	Inverc	NS3172	55°54·9'	4°41·8'W	X	63
Harelaw	Midlo	NT3169	55°54·8'	3°5·8'W	X	66
Harelaw	N Ayr	NS2957	55°46·8'	4°43·2'W	X	63
Harelaw	Northum	NT8430	55°34·1'	2°14·8'W	X	74
Hare Law	Northum	NT8530	55°34·1'	2°13·8'W	X	74
Hare Law	Northum	NT9026	55°31·9'	2°9·1'W	H	74,75
Hare Law	Northum	NT9819	55°28·1'	2°1·5'W	X	81
Harelaw	Northum	NY7677	55°5·5'	2°22·1'W	X	86,87
Harelaw	Northum	NZ0082	55°8·2'	1°59·6'W	X	81
Harelaw	Northum	NZ1591	55°13·0'	1°45·4'W	X	81
Harelaw	Pth & Kin	NT0399	56°10·7'	3°33·3'W	X	58
Harelaw	Renf	NS3863	55°50·2'	4°34·8'W	X	63
Harelaw	Renf	NS4960	55°48·8'	4°24·2'W	X	64
Harelaw	S Ayr	NS4133	55°34·1'	4°30·9'W	X	70
Hare Law	Scot Bord	NT3732	55°34·9'	2°59·5'W	H	73
Harelaw	Scot Bord	NT5323	55°30·2'	2°44·2'W	X	73
Hare Law	Scot Bord	NT6448	55°43·7'	2°34·0'W	X	74
Hare Law	Scot Bord	NT7518	55°27·6'	2°23·3'W	H	80
Harelaw	Scot Bord	NT8757	55°48·6'	2°12·0'W	X	67,74
Harelaw	S Lanak	NS6048	55°42·6'	4°13·3'W	X	64
Harelaw	S Lanak	NS9147	55°42·5'	3°43·6'W	X	72
Hare Law	S Lanak	NT0049	55°43·7'	3°35·1'W	H	72
Harelaw	S Lanak	NT0050	55°44·2'	3°35·1'W	X	65,72
Harelaw Burn	E Loth	NT5463	55°51·7'	2°43·7'W	W	66
Harelaw Burn	Northum	NT9819	55°28·1'	2°1·5'W	W	81
Harelaw Cairn	Northum	NT9126	55°31·9'	2°8·1'W	X	74,75
Harelawcraigs Plantn	Scot Bord	NT7655	55°47·5'	2°22·5'W	F	67,74
Harelaw Dam	E Renf	NS4753	55°45·0'	4°25·8'W	W	64
Harelawhagg	D & G	NY4378	55°5·8'	2°53·2'W	X	85
Harelawhill	D & G	NY4278	55°5·8'	2°54·1'W	X	85
Harelawhole	D & G	NY4278	55°5·8'	2°54·1'W	X	85
Harelaw Mill	D & G	NY4478	55°5·8'	2°52·2'W	X	85
Harelaw Moor	Scot Bord	NT6548	55°43·7'	2°33·0'W	X	74
Harelaw Moor	Scot Bord	NT6549	55°44·2'	2°33·0'W	X	74
Harelaw Pike	D & G	NY4279	55°6·4'	2°54·1'W	H	85
Harelaw Resr	E Renf	NS4859	55°48·3'	4°25·1'W	W	64
Harelaw Resr	Inverc	NS3173	55°55·5'	4°41·9'W	W	63
Harelawside	Scot Bord	NT8165	55°52·9'	2°17·8'W	X	67
Harelawslack	D & G	NY4478	55°5·8'	2°52·2'W	X	85
Harelea Hill	E Ayr	NS6038	55°37·2'	4°13·0'W	X	71
Hareleeshill	S Lanak	NS7750	55°43·9'	3°57·1'W	T	64
Hare Leys Fm	Oxon	SP6224	51°54·9'	1°5·5'W	FM	164,165
Haremere Hall	E Susx	TQ7226	51°0·7'	0°27·5'E	X	188,199
Haremire	Aberd	NJ5229	57°21·2'	2°47·4'W	X	37

Haremire Ho	N Yks	SE0790	54°18·6'	1°53·1'W	X	99
Haremoor Fm	Oxon	SU3096	51°40·0'	1°33·6'W	FM	164
Haremoss	Aberd	NJ6443	57°28·8'	2°35·6'W	X	29
Haremoss	Aberd	NJ7849	57°32·1'	2°21·6'W	X	29,30
Haremoss	Aberd	NO8396	57°3·5'	2°16·4'W	X	38,45
Hare Moss	Aberd	NO9099	57°5·2'	2°9·4'W	X	38,45
Hare Moss	Durham	NY9516	54°32·6'	2°4·2'W	X	91,92
Hare Moss	Midlo	NT2056	55°47·7'	3°16·1'W	X	66,73
Haremoss Loch	Aberd	NJ6844	57°29·4'	2°31·6'W	W	29
Hare Moss Wood	W Loth	NS9265	55°52·2'	3°43·1'W	F	65
Haremuir	Aberd	NO7971	56°50·1'	2°20·2'W	X	45
Hare Myre	Pth & Kin	NO1841	56°33·5'	3°19·6'W	W	53
Hare Ness	C of Aber	NO9599	57°5·2'	2°4·5'W	X	38,45
Hare Park	Cambs	TL5859	52°12·6'	0°19·2'E	X	154
Hare Park	Wakf	SE3717	53°39·1'	1°26·0'W	X	110,111
Hare Park Fm	Herts	TL2836	52°0·7'	0°7·7'W	FM	153
Harepath	Devon	SS5514	50°54·7'	4°3·4'W	X	180
Harepath	Devon	SX7192	50°43·0'	3°49·3'W	X	191
Harepath Fm	Wilts	SU0664	51°22·7'	1°54·4'W	FM	173
Harepie Cross	Devon	SS5527	51°1·7'	4°3·7'W	X	180
Harepit Way	Wilts	SU0768	51°24·9'	1°53·6'W	A	173
Hareplain	Kent	TQ8339	51°7·5'	0°37·3'E	T	188
Haresbrook	Worcs	SO5867	52°18·2'	2°36·6'W	X	137,138,149
Harescough	Cumbr	NY6042	54°46·5'	2°36·9'W	T	86
Harescough Fell	Cumbr	NY6343	54°47·1'	2°34·1'W	X	86
Harescombe	Glos	SO8310	51°47·5'	2°14·4'W	T	162
Harescombe Grange	Glos	SO8410	51°47·5'	2°13·5'W	X	162
Haresdean	W Susx	TQ2912	50°53·8'	0°9·5'W	X	198
Hares Down	Devon	SS8421	50°58·8'	3°38·8'W	X	181
Hare's Down	Devon	SX8591	50°42·7'	3°37·4'W	X	191
Hares Down Cross	Devon	SS8420	50°58·3'	3°38·7'W	X	181
Haresfield	Glos	SO8110	51°47·5'	2°16·1'W	T	162
Haresfield	Swin	SU2093	51°38·4'	1°42·3'W	T	163,174
Haresfield Beacon	Glos	SO8108	51°46·5'	2°16·1'W	X	162
Haresfield Court	Glos	SO8109	51°47·0'	2°16·1'W	X	162
Haresfield Hill	Glos	SO8209	51°47·0'	2°15·3'W	X	162
Haresfinch	St Hel	SJ5197	53°28·3'	2°43·9'W	T	108
Hares Fm	Devon	ST2607	50°51·7'	3°2·7'W	FM	192,193
Hares Fm	Hants	SU7657	51°18·7'	0°54·2'W	FM	175,186
Haresfoot	Herts	SP9806	51°44·9'	0°34·4'W	X	165
Haresfoot Fm	Herts	SP9806	51°44·9'	0°34·4'W	FM	165
Hares Green Fm	Powys	SO3067	52°18·0'	3°1·2'W	FM	137,148
Hares Grove	Norf	TM3695	52°30·3'	1°29·1'E	F	134
Hare Shaw	Cumbr	NY4913	54°30·8'	2°46·8'W	H	90
Hare Shaw	Cumbr	NY6201	54°24·4'	2°34·7'W	H	91
Hare Shaw	Cumbr	SD6797	54°22·3'	2°30·1'W	X	98
Hareshaw	E Ayr	NS4843	55°39·7'	4°24·5'W	X	70
Hareshaw	N Ayr	NS3151	55°43·6'	4°41·0'W	X	63
Hareshaw	N Lanak	NS8160	55°49·4'	3°53·5'W	T	65
Hareshaw	S Lanak	NS6241	55°38·8'	4°11·1'W	X	71
Hareshaw Burn	Northum	NY8485	55°9·8'	2°14·6'W	W	80
Hareshaw Burn	S Lanak	NS7339	55°37·9'	4°0·6'W	W	71
Hareshaw Cleugh	Northum	NT9214	55°25·4'	2°7·2'W	X	80
Hareshaw Common	Northum	NY8286	55°10·3'	2°16·5'W	X	80
Hareshaw Head	Northum	NY8588	55°11·4'	2°13·7'W	X	80
Hareshawhead	S Lanak	NS7339	55°37·9'	4°0·6'W	X	71
Hareshawhead Plantation	Scot Bord	NT4842	55°40·4'	2°49·2'W	F	73
Hareshaw Hill	D & G	NY3887	55°10·7'	2°58·0'W	X	79
Hareshaw Hill	E Ayr	NS5245	55°40·8'	4°20·8'W	X	64
Hareshaw Hill	E Ayr	NS7629	55°32·6'	3°57·5'W	H	71
Hareshaw Hill	Scot Bord	NT4332	55°35·0'	2°53·8'W	H	73
Hareshawhill	S Lanak	NS6040	55°38·3'	4°13·0'W	X	71
Hareshaw Ho	Northum	NY8487	55°10·9'	2°14·6'W	X	80
Hareshaw Knowe	E Loth	NT6161	55°50·7'	2°36·9'W	X	67
Hareshaw Knowe	Scot Bord	NT6809	55°22·7'	2°29·9'W	X	80
Hareshaw Linn	Northum	NY8485	55°9·8'	2°14·6'W	H	80
Hareshawmuir	E Ayr	NS5043	55°39·7'	4°22·6'W	X	70
Hareshawmuir Water	E Ayr	NS5143	55°39·7'	4°21·7'W	W	70
Hareshaw Rig	D & G	NY0198	55°16·2'	3°33·1'W	H	78
Hares Hill Fm	Roch	SD8409	53°34·9'	2°14·1'W	FM	109
Hareshowe	Aberd	NJ8851	57°33·2'	2°11·6'W	X	30
Hareslade Fm	Swan	SS5887	51°34·1'	4°2·5'W	FM	159
Haresnape's Fm	Lancs	SD4454	53°59·0'	2°50·8'W	FM	102
Harestanes	E Dunb	NS6774	55°56·7'	4°7·3'W	T	64
Harestanes	Fife	NT2197	56°9·8'	3°15·9'W	X	58
Harestanes Heights	D & G	NS9901	55°17·8'	3°35·0'W	H	78
Harestanes Woodland Centre	Scot Bord	NT6424	55°30·8'	2°33·8'W	X	74
Haresteads Fm	Ches	SJ9582	53°20·3'	2°4·1'W	FM	109
Harestock	Hants	SU4631	51°4·8'	1°20·2'W	T	185
Harestone	Aberd	NJ6224	57°18·6'	2°37·4'W	X	37
Harestone	Aberd	NO7397	57°4·1'	2°26·3'W	X	38,45
Hare Stone	Devon	SX8138	50°14·0'	3°39·7'W	X	202
Harestone Hill	E Loth	NT5662	55°51·2'	2°41·7'W	H	67
Harestone Moss	Aberd	NJ9319	57°16·0'	2°6·5'W	X	38
Hareston Fm	Devon	SX5653	50°21·8'	4°1·1'W	A	202
Harestonhill	N Lanak	NS8254	55°46·2'	3°52·4'W	X	65,72
Hare Street	Essex	TL4309	51°45·9'	0°4·7'E	T	167
Hare Street	Herts	TL3128	51°56·3'	0°5·3'W	T	166
Hare Street	Herts	TL3829	51°56·8'	0°0·9'E	T	166
Hare Street Fm	Wilts	ST9776	51°29·2'	2°2·2'W	FM	173
Hares Wood	Aberd	NJ7400	57°5·7'	2°25·3'W	F	38
Hare Syke	Lancs	SD6057	54°0·7'	2°36·2'W	W	102,103
Hare Tor	Devon	SX5584	50°38·5'	4°2·7'W	X	191
Harewalls	Northum	NY9286	55°10·3'	2°7·1'W	X	80
Hare Warren	Wilts	SU0928	51°3·3'	1°51·9'W	F	184
Hare Warren	Wilts	SU2147	51°13·5'	1°41·6'W	X	184
Hare Warren	W Susx	SU7510	50°53·3'	0°55·6'W	F	197
Hare Warren Fm	Hants	SU4854	51°17·2'	1°18·3'W	FM	185
Hareway Fm	Warw	SP2861	52°15·0'	1°35·0'W	FM	151
Harewell Hall	N Yks	SE1863	54°4·0'	1°43·1'W	A	99
Harewell Ho	N Yks	SE1863	54°4·0'	1°43·1'W	X	99
Hare Wood	Cambs	TL6247	52°6·1'	0°22·3'E	F	154
Harewood	Corn	SX4469	50°30·2'	4°11·6'W	X	201
Harewood	Cumbr	SD5599	54°23·3'	2°41·2'W	X	97
Harewood	Leeds	SE3245	53°54·3'	1°30·4'W	T	104
Harewood	Shrops	SO6086	52°28·5'	2°34·9'W	F	138
Harewood	Win & Maid	SU9469	51°25·0'	0°38·5'W	X	175
Harewood Burn	D & G	NY2798	55°16·5'	3°8·5'W	W	79
Harewood Castle	Leeds	SE3245	53°54·3'	1°30·4'W	A	104
Harewood Downs Ho	Bucks	SU9895	51°38·9'	0°34·6'W	X	165,176
Harewood End	Heref	SO5227	51°56·6'	2°41·5'W	T	162
Harewood Fm	Somer	SS9630	51°3·8'	3°28·7'W	FM	181
Harewood Forest	Hants	SU4044	51°11·9'	1°25·3'W	F	185
Harewood Glen	Scot Bord	NT4229	55°33·3'	2°54·7'W	X	73
Harewood Grange	Derby	SK3168	53°12·7'	1°31·7'W	X	119
Harewood Hall Fm	Staffs	SK0044	52°59·8'	1°59·6'W	FM	119,128
Harewood Hill	Brad	SE0438	53°50·5'	1°55·9'W	T	104
Harewood Ho	Surrey	TQ3346	51°12·1'	0°5·4'W	X	187
Harewood House	Leeds	SE3144	53°53·7'	1°31·3'W	A	104
Harewood House Fm	Derby	SK3268	53°12·7'	1°30·8'W	FM	119
Harewood Moor	Derby	SK3167	53°12·2'	1°31·7'W	X	119
Harewood Park	Heref	SO5228	51°57·1'	2°41·5'W	X	149
Harewood Park	Staffs	SK0044	52°59·8'	1°59·6'W	X	119,128
Harewood Peak	Hants	SU4046	51°12·9'	1°25·2'W	F	185
Harewood Whin	York	SE5452	53°57·9'	1°10·2'W	X	105
Harfa Bank Fm	N Yks	SE4999	54°23·3'	1°14·3'W	FM	100
Harfa Ho	N Yks	NZ4900	54°23·8'	1°14·3'W	X	93
Harfield	Hants	SU5130	51°4·3'	1°15·9'W	X	185
Harfields Fm	Hants	SU5315	50°56·1'	1°14·4'W	FM	196
Harford	Carm	SN6343	52°4·3'	3°59·5'W	X	146
Harford	Devon	SS6031	51°3·9'	3°59·5'W	T	180
Harford	Devon	SX6359	50°25·1'	3°55·3'W	T	202
Harford	Devon	SX8196	50°45·3'	3°40·8'W	X	191
Harford Br	Devon	SX5076	50°34·1'	4°6·7'W	X	191,201
Harford Br	Glos	SP1222	51°54·0'	1°49·1'W	X	163
Harford Br	Norf	TG2204	52°35·5'	1°17·1'E	X	134
Harford Fm	Norf	TG2204	52°35·5'	1°17·1'E	FM	134
Harford Hill	Worcs	SO8662	52°15·6'	2°11·9'W	X	150
Harford Hill Fm	Glos	SP1422	51°54·0'	1°47·4'W	FM	163
Harford Moor	Devon	SX6462	50°26·8'	3°54·6'W	X	202
Hargate	Norf	TM1191	52°28·8'	1°6·8'E	T	144
Hargate Forest	E Susx	TQ5736	51°6·3'	0°14·9'E	F	188
Hargate Hill	Barns	SE4308	53°34·2'	1°20·6'W	X	111
Hargate Hill	Derby	SK0193	53°26·3'	1°58·7'W	T	110
Hargate Manor	Derby	SK2530	52°52·3'	1°37·3'W	X	128
Hargham Hall	Norf	TM0292	52°29·5'	0°58·9'E	X	144
Hargham Heath	Norf	TM0392	52°29·5'	0°59·8'E	F	144
Hargill Beck	Durham	NY8622	54°35·8'	2°12·6'W	W	91,92
Hargill Br	Durham	NY8821	54°35·3'	2°10·7'W	X	91,92
Hargill Hill	Durham	NZ1532	54°41·2'	1°45·6'W	X	92
Hargill Ho	Northum	NY7059	54°55·7'	2°27·7'W	X	86,87
Hargill Ho	N Yks	SE0083	54°14·8'	1°59·6'W	X	98
Harglodd	Pemb	SM7726	51°53·5'	5°14·1'W	X	157
Hargrave	Ches	SJ4862	53°9·4'	2°46·3'W	T	117
Hargrave	Northnts	TL0370	52°19·3'	0°28·9'W	T	141,153
Hargrave	Suff	TL7759	52°12·3'	0°35·8'E	T	155
Hargrave Bank	Shrops	SJ3109	52°40·7'	3°0·8'W	H	126
Hargrave Fm	Ches	SJ4862	53°9·4'	2°46·3'W	FM	117
Hargrave Hall	Suff	TL7660	52°12·8'	0°35·0'E	X	155
Hargrave Hall Fm	Wirral	SJ3279	53°18·5'	3°0·8'W	FM	117
Hargrave House Fm	Wirral	SJ3379	53°18·5'	2°59·9'W	FM	117
Hargrave Riding Centre	Northnts	TL0170	52°19·4'	0°30·7'W	X	141,153
Hargreaves	Shrops	SJ3110	52°41·2'	3°0·8'W	X	126
Hargreaves Wood	Staffs	SJ8541	52°58·2'	2°13·0'W	F	118
Hargrove	Lancs	SD7934	53°48·3'	2°18·7'W	X	103
Hargrove Barn	Glos	SO9300	51°42·2'	2°5·7'W	X	163
Hargrove Fm	Dorset	ST7415	50°56·3'	2°21·8'W	FM	183
Hargrove Fm	Shrops	SO4992	52°31·6'	2°44·7'W	FM	137,138
Hariff Lane Fm	E Yorks	TA2327	53°43·7'	0°7·7'W	FM	107
Haring's Fm	Beds	TL0263	52°15·6'	0°29·9'W	FM	153
Harker	Cumbr	NY3960	54°56·1'	2°56·7'W	T	85
Harkera Gill	N Yks	SE0479	54°12·6'	1°55·9'W	W	98
Harker Gates	N Yks	SE5291	54°19·0'	1°11·6'W	X	100
Harker Grange	Cumbr	NY3960	54°56·1'	2°56·7'W	X	85
Harker Hill	N Yks	NZ5010	54°29·2'	1°13·3'W	X	93
Harker Ho	N Yks	NY8602	54°25·0'	2°12·5'W	X	91,92
Harker Marsh	Cumbr	NY0634	54°41·8'	3°27·1'W	T	89
Harkers	Lancs	SD7055	53°59·7'	2°27·0'W	X	103
Harkers Hill	Scot Bord	NT7416	55°26·5'	2°24·2'W	H	80
Harkerside Moor	N Yks	SE0397	54°22·4'	1°56·8'W	X	98
Harkerside Place	N Yks	SE0298	54°22·9'	1°57·7'W	X	98
Harker Springs	Durham	NY9421	54°35·3'	2°5·1'W	X	91,92
Harkess Rocks	Northum	NU1735	55°36·7'	1°43·4'W	X	75
Hark Hill Nook	N Yks	SE2560	54°2·4'	1°36·7'W	X	99
Harkland	Shetld	HU4489	60°35·2'	1°11·3'W	T	1,2
Harknett's Gate	Essex	TL4206	51°44·3'	0°3·8'E	T	167
Harkstead	Suff	TM1834	51°57·9'	1°10·8'E	T	169
Harkstead Hall Fm	Suff	TM1935	51°58·4'	1°11·7'E	FM	169
Harlakenden Fm	Kent	TQ9538	51°6·7'	0°47·5'E	FM	189
Harlam Hill	Lincs	TF0194	53°26·2'	0°28·4'W	X	112
Harland	Highld	ND1967	58°35·3'	3°23·1'W	X	11,12
Harland	Highld	ND3253	58°27·9'	3°9·5'W	X	12
Harland	N Yks	SE6693	54°19·9'	0°58·7'W	X	94,100
Harland Beck	N Yks	SE6692	54°19·4'	0°58·7'W	W	94,100
Harland Beck Fm	N Yks	SE6791	54°18·9'	0°57·8'W	FM	94,100
Harland Edge	Derby	SK2968	53°12·7'	1°33·5'W	X	119
Harland Hill	N Yks	NZ5508	54°28·1'	1°8·7'W	X	93
Harland Hill	N Yks	SE0284	54°15·3'	1°57·7'W	H	98
Harland Moor	N Yks	SE6792	54°19·4'	0°57·8'W	X	94,100
Harland Sick	Derby	SK2968	53°12·7'	1°33·5'W	W	119
Harlaston	Staffs	SK2110	52°41·5'	1°41·0'W	T	128
Harlaw	Aberd	NJ7424	57°18·6'	2°25·4'W	X	38
Harlaw	Scot Bord	NT7440	55°39·4'	2°24·4'W	X	74
Harlaw Fm	C of Edin	NT1765	55°52·5'	3°19·2'W	FM	65,66
Harlaw Hill	Northum	NU2115	55°26·0'	1°39·7'W	X	81
Harlaw Ho	Aberd	NJ7424	57°18·6'	2°25·4'W	X	38
Harlaw Muir	Scot Bord	NT1855	55°47·1'	3°18·0'W	X	65,66,72
Harlawmuir	Scot Bord	NT1855	55°47·1'	3°18·0'W	X	65,66,72
Harlawmuir Burn	Scot Bord	NT1754	55°46·6'	3°19·0'W	W	65,66,72
Harlaw Resr	C of Edin	NT1864	55°52·0'	3°18·2'W	W	65,66
Harlaxton	Lincs	SK8832	52°52·9'	0°41·1'W	T	130
Harlaxton Lower Lodge	Lincs	SK8934	52°54·0'	0°40·2'W	X	130
Harlaxton Manor	Lincs	SK8932	52°52·9'	0°40·2'W	X	130
Harleburn Head	S Lanak	NT0017	55°26·5'	3°34·4'W	H	78
Harlech	Gwyn	SH5831	52°51·7'	4°6·2'W	T	124
Harlech Point	Gwyn	SH5635	52°53·8'	4°8·0'W	X	124
Harlequin	Notts	SK6539	52°56·9'	1°1·5'W	T	129
Harle Rigging	Midlo	NT4061	55°50·6'	2°57·1'W	X	66
Harlescott	Shrops	SJ5115	52°44·1'	2°43·1'W	T	126
Harlesden	Brent	TQ2183	51°32·2'	0°14·9'W	T	176
Harlesford Fm	Oxon	SP6800	51°41·9'	1°0·6'W	FM	164,165
Harlesford Ho	Oxon	SP6801	51°42·4'	1°0·6'W	X	164,165
Harlesthorpe	Derby	SK4976	53°17·0'	1°15·5'W	T	120
Harleston	Devon	SX7945	50°17·8'	3°41·6'W	T	202
Harleston	Norf	TM2483	52°24·2'	1°18·0'E	T	156
Harleston	Suff	TM0160	52°12·3'	0°56·9'E	T	155
Harlestone	Northnts	SP7064	52°16·4'	0°58·0'W	T	152
Harlestone Heath	Northnts	SP7163	52°15·9'	0°57·2'W	F	152
Harleswynd	Fife	NO4110	56°17·0'	2°56·7'W	X	59
Harle Syke	Lancs	SD8635	53°48·9'	2°12·3'W	T	103
Harley	Roth	SK3698	53°28·9'	1°27·0'W	T	110,111
Harley	Shrops	SJ5901	52°36·6'	2°35·9'W	T	126
Harley Brook	Shrops	SJ5900	52°36·0'	2°35·9'W	W	126
Harley Bushes	Oxon	SU2781	51°31·9'	1°36·3'W	X	174
Harley Dingle	Powys	SO1963	52°15·8'	3°10·8'W	X	148
Harley Down	Dorset	SU0013	50°55·2'	1°59·6'W	X	195
Harley Fm	Wilts	SU0067	51°24·4'	1°59·6'W	FM	173
Harleyford Manor	Bucks	SU8284	51°33·2'	0°48·6'W	X	175
Harley Grange	Derby	SK0868	53°12·8'	1°52·4'W	X	119
Harley Hill	N Yks	SE1997	54°22·3'	1°42·0'W	X	99
Harley Hill	Shrops	SJ6000	52°36·0'	2°35·0'W	H	127
Harleyholm	S Lanak	NS9238	55°37·7'	3°42·5'W	X	71,72
Harleyrigg	D & G	NX9883	55°8·1'	3°35·6'W	X	78
Harley's Hill	Powys	SO2964	52°16·4'	3°2·0'W	H	137,148
Harley Shute	E Susx	TQ7809	50°51·7'	0°32·1'E	T	199
Harley's Mountain	Heref	SO3468	52°18·6'	2°57·7'W	H	137,148
Harley Thorns	Staffs	SJ8338	52°56·6'	2°14·8'W	F	127
Harley Way	Northnts	SP9685	52°27·5'	0°34·8'W	X	141
Harleywood	Glos	ST8498	51°41·1'	2°13·5'W	T	162
Harlica Fm	Suff	TL7151	52°8·1'	0°30·3'E	FM	154
Harling Fm	Norf	TM0087	52°26·9'	0°57·0'E	FM	144
Harling Road	Norf	TL9787	52°26·9'	0°54·3'E	T	144
Harlington	Beds	TL0330	51°57·8'	0°29·7'W	T	166
Harlington	Donc	SE4802	53°31·0'	1°16·2'W	T	111
Harlington	Hill	TQ0877	51°29·1'	0°26·3'W	T	176
Harlington Wood End	Beds	TL0131	51°58·3'	0°31·4'W	X	166
Harlock	Cumbr	SD2580	54°12·9'	3°8·6'W	X	96
Harlock Hill	Cumbr	SD2579	54°12·3'	3°8·6'W	H	96
Harlock Resr	Cumbr	SD2479	54°12·3'	3°9·5'W	W	96
Harlock's Fm	Cambs	TL5677	52°22·4'	0°17·9'E	FM	143
Harlosh	Highld	NG2841	57°23·0'	6°31·1'W	T	23
Harlosh Island	Highld	NG2739	57°21·8'	6°32·0'W	X	23
Harlosh Point	Highld	NG2840	57°22·4'	6°31·0'W	X	23
Harlosh Skerry	Highld	NG2740	57°22·4'	6°32·0'W	X	23
Harlow	Essex	TL4509	51°45·9'	0°6·5'E	T	167
Harlowbank	Northum	NY7857	54°54·7'	2°20·2'W	X	86,87
Harlow Bower	Northum	NY7856	54°54·1'	2°20·2'W	X	86,87
Harlowbury	Essex	TL4712	51°47·5'	0°8·3'E	X	167
Harlow Carr	N Yks	SE2854	53°59·1'	1°34·0'W	T	104
Harlow Common	Essex	TL4708	51°45·3'	0°8·2'E	X	167
Harlow Field	Northum	NY8061	54°56·8'	2°18·3'W	X	86,87
Harlow Fm	Staffs	SK1446	53°0·9'	1°47·1'W	FM	119,128
Harlow Green	Ghead	NZ2658	54°55·2'	1°35·2'W	T	88
Harlow Hill	Northum	NZ0768	55°0·6'	1°53·0'W	T	88
Harlow Hill	N Yks	SE2854	53°59·1'	1°34·0'W	T	104
Harlow Mill Sta	Essex	TL4712	51°47·5'	0°8·3'E	X	167
Harlow Park	Essex	TL4707	51°44·8'	0°8·2'E	F	167
Harlow Town Sta	Essex	TL4411	51°47·0'	0°5·7'E	X	167
Harlow Tye	Essex	TL5010	51°46·3'	0°10·8'E	X	167
Harlow Wood	Notts	SK5557	53°6·7'	1°10·3'W	F	120
Harlow Wood Fm	Notts	SK6445	53°0·1'	1°2·4'W	FM	129
Harlsey Beck	N Yks	SE4099	54°23·3'	1°22·6'W	W	99
Harlsey Castle	N Yks	SE4198	54°22·8'	1°21·7'W	A	99
Harlsley Grange	N Yks	SE4098	54°22·8'	1°22·6'W	X	99
Harlthorpe	E Yorks	SE7437	53°49·7'	0°52·1'W	T	105,106
Harlton	Cambs	TL3852	52°9·2'	0°1·4'E	T	154
Harlyn	Corn	SW8775	50°32·4'	5°0·0'W	T	200
Harlyn Bay	Corn	SW8775	50°32·4'	5°0·0'W	W	200
Harlyn House	Corn	SW8775	50°32·4'	5°0·0'W	A	200
Harman's Corner	Kent	TQ8862	51°19·8'	0°42·3'E	T	178
Harman's Cross	Dorset	SY9880	50°37·4'	2°1·3'W	T	195
Harman's Hill	Worcs	SO9560	52°14·5'	2°4·0'W	X	150
Harmansole Fm	Kent	TR1352	51°13·9'	1°3·5'E	FM	179,189
Harmans Water	Brackn	SU8768	51°24·5'	0°44·6'W	T	175
Harmas Fm	Essex	TL7628	51°55·6'	0°34·0'E	FM	167
Harmby	N Yks	SE1289	54°18·0'	1°48·5'W	T	99
Harmby Moor Ho	N Yks	SE1391	54°19·1'	1°47·6'W	X	99
Harmer Green	Herts	TL2516	51°49·9'	0°10·8'W	T	166
Harmergreen Wood	Herts	TL2517	51°50·5'	0°10·7'W	F	166
Harmer Hill	Shrops	SJ4822	52°47·8'	2°45·9'W	T	126
Harmer Moss Plantation	Shrops	SJ4822	52°47·8'	2°45·9'W	F	126
Harmes Fm	Essex	TQ4794	51°37·8'	0°7·8'E	FM	167,177
Harmeston	Pemb	SM9208	51°44·2'	5°0·4'W	X	157,158
Harmire	N Yks	SE2798	54°22·8'	1°34·6'W	X	99
Harmondsworth	Hill	TQ0577	51°29·2'	0°28·9'W	T	176
Harmston	Lincs	SK9762	53°9·0'	0°32·6'W	T	121
Harmston Field	Lincs	SK9561	53°8·5'	0°34·4'W	X	121
Harmston Heath	Lincs	SK9962	53°9·0'	0°30·8'W	X	121
Harnage	Shrops	SJ5604	52°38·2'	2°38·6'W	T	126
Harnage Grange	Shrops	SJ5602	52°37·1'	2°38·6'W	X	126
Harnage Ho	Shrops	SJ5604	52°38·2'	2°38·6'W	X	126
Harnalie	Shetld	HT9439	60°8·4'	2°6·0'W	X	4
Harness Grove	Notts	SK5578	53°18·0'	1°10·1'W	X	120
Harnham	Northum	NZ0780	55°7·1'	1°53·0'W	T	81
Harnham	Wilts	SU1328	51°3·3'	1°48·5'W	T	184
Harnham Buildings	Northum	NZ0680	55°7·1'	1°53·9'W	X	81
Harnham Fm	Somer	ST1725	51°1·3'	3°10·6'W	FM	181,193
Harnhill	Glos	SP0700	51°42·2'	1°53·5'W	T	163
Harnisha Hill	Durham	NY9632	54°41·2'	2°3·3'W	X	91,92
Harold Court	Hav	TQ5591	51°36·0'	0°14·7'E	X	177
Harold Hill	Hav	TQ5492	51°36·6'	0°13·8'E	T	177
Harold Park	Hav	TQ5591	51°36·0'	0°14·7'E	T	177
Harold's Br	Cambs	TF3811	52°41·0'	0°2·9'E	X	131,142,143
Haroldsfield Fm	Glos	ST7489	51°36·2'	2°22·1'W	FM	162,172
Harolds Fm	Warw	SP2142	52°4·8'	1°41·2'W	FM	151
Haroldsgarth	Orkney	HY5115	59°1·4'	2°50·7'W	X	6
Harold's Park Fm	Essex	TL4104	51°43·2'	0°2·9'E	FM	167
Harold's Stones	Monm	SO4905	51°44·7'	2°43·9'W	A	162
Haroldston Chins	Pemb	SM8516	51°48·3'	5°6·7'W	X	157

Harold Stone	Pemb	SM8614	51°47·3′	5°5·8′W	A	157
Harold Stone	Pemb	SR9695	51°37·3′	4°56·4′W	A	158
Haroldston West	Pemb	SM8615	51°47·8′	5°5·8′W	T	157
Harold's Tower	Highld	ND1369	58°36·3′	3°29·4′W	X	12
Haroldswick	Shetld	HP6312	60°47·4′	0°50·1′W	T	1
Harold's Wick	Shetld	HP6411	60°46·9′	0°49·0′W	W	1
Harold Wood	Hav	TQ5490	51°35·5′	0°13·8′E	T	177
Harome	N Yks	SE6481	54°13·5′	1°0·7′W	T	100
Harome Fox Covert	N Yks	SE6681	54°13·5′	0°58·9′W	F	100
Harome Heads Fm	N Yks	SE6483	54°14·6′	1°0·7′W	FM	100
Haropgreen	Ches	SJ8270	53°13·8′	2°15·8′W	X	118
Harpa Skerry	Shetld	HU3842	60°9·9′	1°18·4′W	X	4
Harpenden	Herts	TL1314	51°49·0′	0°21·2′W	T	166
Harpenden Common	Herts	TL1313	51°48·5′	0°21·3′W	T	166
Harper Burn	Northum	NY7193	55°14·1′	2°26·9′W	W	80
Harper Crag	Northum	NY7093	55°14·1′	2°27·9′W	X	80
Harpercroft	S Ayr	NS3632	55°33·5′	4°35·6′W	X	70
Harperdean	E Loth	NT5074	55°57·6′	2°47·6′W	X	66
Harperfield	S Lanak	NS8939	55°38·2′	3°45·4′W	X	71,72
Harper Fm	Leeds	SE2531	53°46·7′	1°36·8′W	FM	104
Harper Green	Bolton	SD7206	53°33·2′	2°24·9′W	T	109
Harperhall	S Lanak	NT0543	55°40·5′	3°30·2′W	X	72
Harperhill	Aberd	NJ6248	57°31·5′	2°37·6′W	X	29
Harper Hill	Cumbr	NY5071	55°2·1′	2°46·5′W	X	86
Harper Hill	Derby	SK3568	53°12·7′	1°28·1′W	X	119
Harper Hill	N Yks	SE1970	54°7·8′	1°42·1′W	X	99
Harper Hills	Cumbr	NY5114	54°31·4′	2°45·0′W	H	90
Harperland	S Ayr	NS3735	55°35·1′	4°34·7′W	X	70
Harperleas	Pth & Kin	NO2005	56°14·1′	3°17·0′W	X	58
Harperleas Reservoir	Fife	NO2105	56°14·1′	3°16·0′W	W	58
Harperley	Durham	NZ1753	54°52·5′	1°43·7′W	T	88
Harperley Hall	Durham	NZ1234	54°42·3′	1°48·4′W	X	92
Harper Rash	N Yks	SE4639	53°51·0′	1°17·6′W	F	105
Harper Ridge	Northum	NT8741	55°40·0′	2°12·0′W	X	74
Harperrig	W Loth	NT1061	55°50·3′	3°25·8′W	X	65
Harperrig Reservoir	W Loth	NT0961	55°50·3′	3°26·7′W	W	65
Harper's	Bucks	SU7899	51°41·3′	0°51·9′W	X	165
Harper's Brook	Northnts	SP8585	52°27·6′	0°44·5′W	W	141
Harper's Brook	Northnts	SP9583	52°26·4′	0°35·7′W	W	141
Harpersend	Staffs	SK0162	53°9·5′	1°58·7′W	X	119
Harpers Fm	Somer	ST1919	50°58·1′	3°8·8′W	FM	181,193
Harper's Gate	Staffs	SJ9557	53°6·8′	2°4·1′W	T	118
Harper's Green	Norf	TF9422	52°45·9′	0°52·9′E	T	132
Harper's Hill	Devon	SX7959	50°25·3′	3°41·8′W	X	202
Harper's Hill	Leic	SP3894	52°32·8′	1°26·0′W	X	140
Harper's Hill	Leic	SP4298	52°34·9′	1°22·4′W	X	140
Harper's Hill	Suff	TL9634	51°58·4′	0°51·6′E	X	155
Harperstone	Pth & Kin	NN8404	56°13·1′	3°51·8′W	X	58
Harpertoun	Scot Bord	NT7439	55°38·9′	2°24·4′W	X	74
Harpfields Fm	Shrops	SO5770	52°19·8′	2°37·5′W	FM	137,138
Harp Fm	Kent	TQ7759	51°18·4′	0°32·8′E	FM	178,188
Harpford	Devon	SY0990	50°42·4′	3°16·9′W	T	192
Harpford Common	Devon	SY0690	50°42·4′	3°19·5′W	X	192
Harpford Common	Devon	SY1190	50°42·4′	3°15·2′W	X	192,193
Harpford Fm	Somer	ST1021	50°59·1′	3°16·6′W	FM	181,193
Harpford Ho	Devon	SY0990	50°42·4′	3°16·9′W	X	192
Harpford Wood	Devon	SY1090	50°42·4′	3°16·1′W	F	192,193
Harpham	E Yorks	TA0961	54°2·2′	0°19·7′W	T	101
Harpham Field	E Yorks	TA0763	54°3·3′	0°21·5′W	X	101
Harpham Grange	E Yorks	TA0962	54°2·8′	0°19·7′W	X	101
Harpham Moor	E Yorks	TA1060	54°1·7′	0°18·8′W	X	101
Harpham Plump	E Yorks	TA0864	54°3·9′	0°20·6′W	X	101
Harp Ho	Shrops	SO2983	52°26·7′	3°2·3′W	X	137
Harpington Hill	Durham	NZ3326	54°37·9′	1°28·9′W	X	93
Harplaw	N Ayr	NS2161	55°48·8′	4°51·0′W	X	63
Harpley	Norf	TF7825	52°47·8′	0°38·8′E	T	132
Harpley	Worcs	SO6861	52°15·0′	2°27·7′W	T	138,149
Harpley Common	Norf	TF7627	52°48·9′	0°37·1′E	X	132
Harpley Common	Norf	TF8024	52°47·2′	0°40·6′E	X	132
Harpley Dams	Norf	TF7725	52°47·8′	0°37·9′E	X	132
Harpley Dams Ho	Norf	TF7526	52°48·4′	0°36·2′E	X	132
Harplow	Staffs	SJ9942	52°58·8′	2°0·5′W	X	118
Harpole	Kent	TQ7858	51°17·8′	0°33·6′E	X	178,188
Harpole	Northnts	SP6960	52°14·3′	0°59·0′W	T	152
Harpole Covert	Northnts	SP6761	52°14·8′	1°0·7′W	F	152
Harpole Grange	Northnts	SP6961	52°14·8′	0°59·0′W	X	152
Harpole Hill Fm	Northnts	SP6761	52°14·8′	1°0·7′W	FM	152
Harpridge	Devon	SS9314	50°55·2′	3°31·0′W	X	181
Harprigg	Cumbr	SD6087	54°16·9′	2°36·4′W	X	97
Harpsdale	Highld	ND1356	58°29·3′	3°29·1′W	X	11,12
Harpsden	Oxon	SU7680	51°31·1′	0°53·9′W	T	175
Harpsden Bottom	Oxon	SU7580	51°31·1′	0°54·8′W	T	175
Harpsden Court	Oxon	SU7680	51°31·1′	0°53·9′W	A	175
Harpsden Wood	Oxon	SU7680	51°31·1′	0°53·9′W	F	175
Harps Fm	Essex	TL5220	51°51·7′	0°12·8′E	FM	167
Harp's Hall	Norf	TF5011	52°40·8′	0°13·5′E	X	131,143
Harps Oak	Surrey	TQ2854	51°16·5′	0°9·5′W	X	187
Harpson Fm	Devon	SS8122	50°59·3′	3°41·4′W	FM	181
Harpsquoy	Orkney	HY2326	59°7·1′	3°20·2′W	X	6
Harp Stone	Dorset	SY9280	50°37·4′	2°6·4′W	A	195
Harpswell	Lincs	SK9389	53°23·6′	0°35·7′W	T	112,121
Harpswell Grange	Lincs	SK9190	53°24·2′	0°37·5′W	X	112
Harpswell Wood	Lincs	SK9088	53°23·1′	0°38·4′W	F	112,121
Harpswood	Kent	TQ8454	51°15·5′	0°38·6′E	X	188
Harpswood	Shrops	SO6891	52°31·2′	2°27·9′W	X	138
Harpton	Powys	SO2359	52°13·7′	3°7·2′W	T	148
Harpton Court	Powys	SO2359	52°13·7′	3°7·2′W	X	148
Harptree Court	Bath & NE Somer	ST5655	51°17·8′	2°37·5′W	X	172,182
Harptree Hill Fm	Somer	ST5455	51°17·8′	2°39·2′W	FM	172,182
Harptree Lodge	Somer	ST5352	51°16·1′	2°40·0′W	X	182,183
Harpurhey	Man	SD8601	53°30·6′	2°12·3′W	T	109
Harpur Hill	Derby	SK0671	53°14·4′	1°54·2′W	T	119
Harpur's Downs	Corn	SX1179	50°35·0′	4°39·8′W	X	200
Harpy Taing	Orkney	HY4217	59°2·4′	3°0·2′W	X	6
Harrabrough Head	Orkney	ND4190	58°47·9′	3°0·8′W	X	7
Harraby	Cumbr	NY4254	54°52·9′	2°53·8′W	T	85
Harracles Hall	Staffs	SJ9557	53°6·8′	2°4·1′W	X	118
Harracott	Devon	SS5526	51°1·1′	4°3·7′W	T	180
Harra Ebb	Orkney	HY2114	59°0·6′	3°22·0′W	X	6
Harragrove	Devon	SX5176	50°34·1′	4°5·9′W	X	191,201
Harram Bottom	Suff	TL8359	52°12·2′	0°41·1′E	X	155
Harram Hill	Suff	TL8360	52°12·7′	0°41·1′E	X	155
Harran Hill	Fife	NT1696	56°9·2′	3°20·7′W	H	58
Harran Plantation	Angus	NO2764	56°46·0′	3°11·2′W	F	44
Harrapool	Highld	NG6523	57°14·5′	5°53·2′W	T	32
Harras	Cumbr	NX9818	54°33·1′	3°34·2′W	T	89
Harras, The	Cumbr	NY5346	54°48·6′	2°43·5′W	X	86
Harraton	Devon	SX6750	50°20·3′	3°51·8′W	X	202
Harraton	Sund	NZ2954	54°53·0′	1°32·5′W	T	88
Harratt Grange	Derby	SK0980	53°19·3′	1°51·5′W	X	110
Harray	Orkney	HY3218	59°2·9′	3°10·6′W	X	6
Harridens Fm	Hants	SU5359	51°19·9′	1°14·0′W	FM	174
Harridge	Tames	SJ9999	53°29·5′	2°0·5′W	X	109
Harridge Wood	Somer	ST6548	51°14·0′	2°29·7′W	F	183
Harrier	Shetld	HT9540	60°8·9′	2°4·9′W	X	4
Harriet Air Fm	N Yks	SE5785	54°15·7′	1°7·1′W	FM	100
Harrietfield	Pth & Kin	NN9829	56°26·8′	3°38·8′W	T	52,53,58
Harrietfield	Scot Bord	NT7036	55°37·3′	2°28·1′W	X	74
Harriet Plantation	Highld	NH7693	57°54·8′	4°5·1′W	F	21
Harrietsfield	Scot Bord	NT6226	55°31·8′	2°35·7′W	X	74
Harriets Fm	Essex	TL5506	51°44·1′	0°15·1′E	FM	167
Harrietsham	Kent	TQ8752	51°14·4′	0°41·1′E	T	189
Harri Garth	Orkney	HY6629	59°9·1′	2°35·2′W	X	5
Harriington Field Fm	Oxon	SP6502	51°43·0′	1°3·2′W	FM	164,165
Harriman's Fm	Peterb	TF3101	52°35·7′	0°3·6′W	FM	142
Harringay	Hargy	TQ3188	51°34·8′	0°6·2′W	T	176,177
Harringe Brooks Wood	Kent	TR1036	51°5·3′	1°0·3′E	F	179,189
Harringe Court	Kent	TR0937	51°5·9′	0°59·5′E	X	179,189
Harrington	Cumbr	NX9825	54°36·8′	3°34·3′W	T	89
Harrington	Lincs	TF3671	53°13·3′	0°2·6′E	T	122
Harrington	Northnts	SP7780	52°25·0′	0°51·7′W	T	141
Harrington Hall	Shrops	SJ7402	52°37·1′	2°22·6′W	X	127
Harrington Hall Fm	Lincs	TF3824	52°48·0′	0°3·2′E	FM	131
Harrington Hill	Lincs	TF3672	53°13·9′	0°2·7′E	X	122
Harrington Ling Fm	Cumbr	NY4643	54°47·0′	2°50·0′W	FM	86
Harrington Lodge	Northnts	SP7878	52°23·9′	0°50·8′W	X	141
Harrington Parks	Cumbr	NX9824	54°36·3′	3°34·3′W	X	89
Harringworth	Northnts	SP9197	52°34·0′	0°39·0′W	T	141
Harringworth Lodge	Northnts	SP9395	52°32·9′	0°37·3′W	X	141
Harriot's Hayes	Shrops	SJ8305	52°38·8′	2°14·7′W	X	127
Harriott's End Fm	Herts	SP9805	51°44·3′	0°34·4′W	FM	165
Harris	Highld	NM3395	56°58·4′	6°23·2′W	X	39
Harris	N Eil	NG1198	57°52·9′	6°52·1′W	X	14
Harris Br	Leic	SK3503	52°37·7′	1°28·6′W	X	140
Harris Close	Staffs	SK1162	53°9·5′	1°49·7′W	X	119
Harris Croft	Wilts	SU0882	51°32·4′	1°52·7′W	X	173
Harriseahead	Staffs	SJ8656	53°6·3′	2°12·1′W	T	118
Harrisend Fell	Lancs	SD5350	53°56·9′	2°42·6′W	X	102
Harris Fms	Suff	TL6682	52°24·9′	0°26·9′E	FM	143
Harris Green	Norf	TM2389	52°27·4′	1°17·3′E	X	156
Harrison's Fm	Lancs	SD5835	53°48·8′	2°37·9′W	FM	102
Harrison's Fm	Warw	SP1470	52°19·9′	1°47·3′W	FM	139
Harrison's Rocks	E Susx	TQ5335	51°5·9′	0°11·5′E	X	188
Harrison Stickle	Cumbr	NY2807	54°27·4′	3°6·2′W	X	89,90
Harris or Na Hearadh	N Eil	NB1405	57°56·8′	6°49·6′W	X	13,14
Harris or Na Hearadh	N Eil	NG0693	57°50·1′	6°56·7′W	X	14,18
Harris Side	Cumbr	NY0918	54°33·2′	3°24·0′W	X	89
Harri Stack	Shetld	HU3066	60°22·9′	1°26·9′W	X	3
Harriston	Cumbr	NY1641	54°45·7′	3°17·9′W	T	85
Harrock Hall	Lancs	SD5012	53°36·4′	2°44·9′W	X	108
Harrock Hill	Lancs	SD5113	53°36·9′	2°44·0′W	X	108
Harrocks Wood	Herts	TQ0697	51°39·9′	0°27·6′W	F	166,176
Harrods Fm	Warw	SP2945	52°6·4′	1°34·2′W	FM	151
Harrogate	N Yks	SE3055	53°59·7′	1°32·1′W	T	104
Harrogate Ho	N Yks	SE3894	54°20·6′	1°24·5′W	X	99
Harrogate & Knaresborough Ringway Footpath	N Yks	SE3454	53°59·1′	1°28·5′W	X	104
Harrold	Beds	SP9456	52°11·9′	0°37·1′W	T	153
Harrold Lodge Fm	Beds	SP9355	52°11·4′	0°38·0′W	FM	153
Harrold Park Fm	Beds	SP9258	52°13·0′	0°38·8′W	FM	152
Harrolds	Pemb	SN0704	51°42·3′	4°47·2′W	X	158
Harrop Brook	Ches	SJ9578	53°18·2′	2°4·1′W	W	118
Harrop Brow	Ches	SJ9480	53°19·3′	2°5·0′W	X	109
Harrop Dale	Oldham	SE0008	53°34·4′	1°59·6′W	T	110
Harrop Edge	Brad	SE0934	53°48·4′	1°51·4′W	X	104
Harrop Edge	Oldham	SD9908	53°34·4′	2°0·5′W	X	109
Harrop Edge	Tames	SJ9796	53°27·9′	2°2·3′W	X	109
Harrop Fell	Lancs	SD7349	53°56·4′	2°24·3′W	X	103
Harrop Fm	Derby	SK1685	53°21·9′	1°45·2′W	FM	110
Harrop Fold	Lancs	SD7449	53°56·4′	2°23·4′W	X	103
Harrop Fold Fm	Ches	SJ9678	53°18·2′	2°3·2′W	FM	118
Harrop Green Fm	Ches	SJ9279	53°18·7′	2°6·8′W	FM	118
Harrop Hall	Lancs	SD7351	53°57·5′	2°24·3′W	X	103
Harrop House Fm	Ches	SJ9778	53°18·2′	2°2·3′W	FM	118
Harrop Lane	Brad	SE0835	53°48·9′	1°52·3′W	X	104
Harrop Lodge	Lancs	SD7450	53°57·0′	2°23·4′W	X	103
Harrop Moss	Derby	SK0796	53°27·9′	1°53·3′W	X	110
Harrop Pike	Cumbr	NY5007	54°27·6′	2°45·9′W	H	90
Harrop Tarn	Cumbr	NY3113	54°30·7′	3°3·5′W	W	90
Harros	Corn	SX0161	50°25·1′	4°47·7′W	X	200
Harrot	Cumbr	NY1527	54°38·1′	3°18·6′W	H	89
Harrow	Harrow	TQ1488	51°35·0′	0°20·9′W	T	176
Harrow	Highld	ND2874	58°39·1′	3°14·0′W	X	7,12
Harrow	Scot Bord	NT1737	55°37·4′	3°18·6′W	X	72
Harroway Fm	Hants	SU7121	50°59·4′	0°58·9′W	FM	197
Harrowbarrow	Corn	SX3969	50°30·2′	4°15·8′W	T	201
Harrowbeer	Devon	SX5168	50°29·8′	4°5·7′W	T	201
Harrowbridge	Corn	SX2074	50°32·5′	4°32·1′W	X	201
Harrowbridge Hill Fm	Corn	SX2073	50°32·0′	4°32·0′W	FM	201
Harrow Brook	Warw	SP3992	52°31·7′	1°25·1′W	W	140
Harrowby Hall	Lincs	SK9335	52°54·5′	0°36·6′W	X	130
Harrowden	Beds	TL0647	52°6·9′	0°26·7′W	T	153
Harrowdown Hill	Oxon	SP3800	51°42·1′	1°26·6′W	H	164
Harrowfield	Pth & Kin	NO0437	56°31·2′	3°33·2′W	X	52,53
Harrow Fm	Leic	SK6121	52°47·2′	1°5·3′W	FM	129
Harrow Fm	Wilts	SU2767	51°24·3′	1°36·3′W	FM	174
Harrowgate Hill	Darl	NZ2916	54°32·5′	1°32·7′W	T	93
Harrowgate Village	Darl	NZ2817	54°33·1′	1°33·6′W	T	93
Harrow Green	Suff	TL8554	52°9·4′	0°42·7′E	T	155
Harrow Hill	Ches	SJ5567	53°12·1′	2°40·0′W	X	117
Harrow Hill	Essex	TL7236	52°0·0′	0°30·7′E	X	154
Harrow Hill	Glos	SO6416	51°50·7′	2°31·0′W	T	162
Harrow Hill	Warw	SP2833	51°59·9′	1°35·1′W	X	151
Harrow Hill	W Susx	TQ0809	50°52·4′	0°27·5′W	H	197
Harrow Hill (Enclosure)	W Susx	TQ0805	50°50·3′	0°27·6′W	A	197
Harrow Hope	Scot Bord	NT1539	55°38·5′	3°20·6′W	X	72
Harrowick	Beds	TL0568	52°18·2′	0°27·2′W	X	153
Harrow Law	Scot Bord	NT7722	55°29·7′	2°21·4′W	H	74
Harrow Lodge	Hants	SZ1997	50°46·6′	1°43·4′W	X	195
Harrow Lodge Park	Hav	TQ5286	51°33·4′	0°12·0′E	X	177
Harrow on the Hill	Harrow	TQ1586	51°33·9′	0°20·1′W	T	176
Harrow's Beck	Cumbr	NY6167	55°0·0′	2°36·2′W	W	86
Harrow School	Harrow	TQ1587	51°34·4′	0°20·0′W	X	176
Harrow Slack	Cumbr	SD3896	54°21·6′	2°56·8′W	X	96,97
Harrows Law	S Lanak	NT0553	55°45·9′	3°30·4′W	X	65,72
Harrowsley Green Fm	Surrey	TQ3043	51°10·5′	0°8·0′W	FM	187
Harrow Street Fm	Suff	TL9637	52°0·0′	0°51·7′E	FM	155
Harrow Weald	Harrow	TQ1590	51°36·1′	0°20·0′W	T	176
Harrow Weald Common	Harrow	TQ1493	51°37·7′	0°20·8′W	X	176
Harry Burn	Scot Bord	NT5148	55°43·6′	2°46·4′W	W	73
Harry Burn	S Lanak	NS9318	55°26·9′	3°41·1′W	W	71,78
Harryburn Brae	S Lanak	NS9318	55°26·9′	3°41·1′W	H	71,78
Harryburn Ho	Scot Bord	NT5248	55°43·6′	2°45·4′W	X	73
Harry Crofts	Roth	SK5282	53°20·2′	1°12·7′W	X	111,120
Harry Fold	Bolton	SD7413	53°37·0′	2°23·2′W	X	109
Harry Furlough's Rocks	I of Angl	SH3394	53°25·2′	4°30·4′W	X	114
Harry Guards Wood	Cumbr	NY3200	54°23·7′	3°2·4′W	F	90
Harry Hut	Derby	SK0490	53°24·6′	1°56·0′W	X	110
Harry Place Fm	Cumbr	NY3106	54°26·9′	3°3·4′W	FM	90
Harry's Park Wood	Northnts	SP9487	52°28·6′	0°36·6′W	F	141
Harry's Pike	Northum	NT7504	55°20·0′	2°23·2′W	H	80
Harry's Pund	Shetld	HU2677	60°28·8′	1°31·1′W	X	3
Harry Stoke	S Glos	ST6278	51°30·2′	2°32·5′W	T	172
Harry's Walls	I Scilly	SV9010	49°54·8′	6°18·7′W	A	203
Harry's Wood	Northum	NY9792	55°13·6′	2°2·4′W	F	81
Harry's Wood	W Susx	TQ2630	51°3·6′	0°11·7′W	F	187
Harsfold Manor	W Susx	TQ0424	51°0·6′	0°30·7′W	X	197
Harsgeir	N Eil	NB1040	58°15·5′	6°56·2′W	X	13
Harsgeir Beag	N Eil	NA9723	58°5·8′	7°8·1′W	X	13
Harsgeir Mór	N Eil	NA9723	58°5·8′	7°8·1′W	X	13
Harsley Grove	N Yks	NZ4000	54°23·9′	1°22·6′W	X	93
Harsondale	Northum	NY8061	54°56·8′	2°18·3′W	X	86,87
Harston	Cambs	TL4251	52°8·6′	0°4·9′E	T	154
Harston	Leic	SK8331	52°52·4′	0°45·6′W	T	130
Harston Hill	Cambs	TL4350	52°8·0′	0°5·8′E	X	154
Harswell	E Yorks	SE8240	53°51·2′	0°44·8′W	T	106
Hart	Hartpl	NZ4735	54°42·7′	1°15·8′W	T	93
Hartabreck	N Eil	NF8214	57°6·7′	7°14·7′W	H	31
Harta Corrie	Highld	NG4723	57°13·9′	6°11·1′W	X	32
Hartamul	N Eil	NF8311	57°5·1′	7°13·5′W	X	31
Hartavagh	N Eil	NF8315	57°7·3′	7°13·8′W	W	31
Hartaval	Highld	NG4855	57°31·2′	6°12·1′W	H	23
Hartaval	N Eil	NF6800	56°58·6′	7°27·4′W	H	31
Hartbarrow	Cumbr	SD4090	54°18·4′	2°54·9′W	T	96,97
Hartburn	D & G	NX7353	54°51·6′	3°58·3′W	X	83,84
Hart Burn	Northum	NZ0486	55°10·3′	1°55·8′W	W	81
Hartburn	Northum	NZ0886	55°10·3′	1°52·0′W	T	81
Hartburn	Stock on T	NZ4218	54°33·6′	1°20·6′W	T	93
Hartburn Beck	Stock on T	NZ4217	54°33·0′	1°20·6′W	W	93
Hartburn Grange	Northum	NZ0686	55°10·3′	1°53·9′W	X	81
Hartburn Grange Fm	Stock on T	NZ4118	54°33·6′	1°21·5′W	FM	93
Hartbush	D & G	NY0083	55°8·1′	3°33·7′W	X	78
Hart Bushes Hall	Durham	NZ4134	54°42·2′	1°21·4′W	X	93
Hartchyside	Northum	NY6451	54°51·4′	2°33·2′W	H	86
Hartcliffe	C of Bris	ST5867	51°24·3′	2°35·8′W	T	172,182
Hartcliff Fm	Dorset	ST8010	50°53·6′	2°16·7′W	FM	194
Hartcliff Hill	Barns	SE2201	53°30·6′	1°39·7′W	X	110
Hart Common	Bolton	SD6305	53°32·7′	2°33·1′W	T	109
Hart Crag	Cumbr	NY3611	54°29·7′	2°58·9′W	H	90
Hart Crag	Cumbr	NY4017	54°32·9′	2°55·2′W	X	90
Hart Crag	Cumbr	NY4108	54°28·1′	2°54·2′W	X	90
Harten Hill	S Lanak	NS9326	55°31·2′	3°41·3′W	H	71,72
Harterbeck	Lancs	SD6163	54°3·9′	2°35·3′W	X	97
Harter Fell	Cumbr	NY4609	54°28·7′	2°49·6′W	H	90
Harter Fell	Cumbr	NY7200	54°23·9′	2°25·5′W	H	91
Harter Fell	Cumbr	SD2199	54°23·1′	3°12·6′W	H	96
Harter Fell	Durham	NY9223	54°36·4′	2°7·3′W	X	91,92
Harter's Hill	Somer	ST5342	51°10·8′	2°40·0′W	X	182,183
Hartest	Suff	TL8352	52°8·4′	0°40·9′E	T	155
Hartest Hill	Suff	TL8352	52°8·4′	0°40·9′E	T	155
Hart Fell	D & G	NT1113	55°24·4′	3°23·9′W	H	78
Hart Fell	D & G	NY2389	55°11·6′	3°12·1′W	H	79
Hartfell Craig	D & G	NT1213	55°24·4′	3°23·0′W	X	78
Hartfell Rig	Scot Bord	NT1214	55°25·0′	3°23·0′W	H	78
Hartfell Spa	D & G	NT0911	55°23·3′	3°25·8′W	W	78
Hartfield	D & G	NY0692	55°13·1′	3°28·2′W	X	78
Hartfield	E Susx	TQ4735	51°6·0′	0°6·4′E	T	188
Hartfield	Highld	NH7781	57°48·4′	4°3·7′W	X	21
Hartfield	N Lanak	NS8557	55°47·8′	3°49·6′W	X	65,72
Hartfield	Renf	NS4258	55°47·6′	4°30·8′W	X	64
Hartfield (Adventure School)	Highld	NG7246	57°27·1′	5°47·6′W	X	24
Hartfield Lodge	Leic	SK6908	52°40·2′	0°58·4′W	X	141
Hartfield Moss	Renf	NS4156	55°46·5′	4°31·7′W	H	64
Hart Fm	Wilts	SU0481	51°31·9′	1°56·1′W	FM	173
Hartford	Cambs	TL2572	52°20·1′	0°9·5′W	T	153
Hartford	Ches	SJ6371	53°14·3′	2°32·9′W	T	118
Hartford	Somer	SS9529	51°3·3′	3°29·5′W	T	181
Hartfordbeach	Ches	SJ6372	53°14·9′	2°32·9′W	T	118
Hartford Bottom	Somer	SS9529	51°3·3′	3°29·5′W	F	181
Hartford Br	Ches	SJ6471	53°14·3′	2°32·0′W	X	118
Hartfordbridge	Hants	SU7757	51°18·6′	0°53·3′W	T	175,186
Hartford Bridge	Northum	NZ2479	55°6·5′	1°37·0′W	X	88
Hartford Bridge Flats	Hants	SU8058	51°19·2′	0°50·7′W	X	175,186
Hartford End	Essex	TL6817	51°49·8′	0°26·7′E	T	167
Hartford Hall	Northum	NZ2480	55°7·1′	1°37·0′W	X	81
Hartford Heath	Hants	SU3904	50°50·3′	1°26·4′W	F	196
Hartford Hill	Cambs	TL2773	52°20·7′	0°7·7′W	X	153

Hartford Hill Fm	Cambs	TL2674	52°21·2′	0°8·6′W	FM	142
Hartforth	N Yks	NZ1706	54°27·2′	1°43·8′W	T	92
Hartforth Grange	N Yks	NZ1607	54°27·7′	1°44·8′W	X	92
Hartforth Wood	N Yks	NZ1606	54°27·2′	1°44·8′W	F	92
Hartgrove	Dorset	ST8418	50°57·9′	2°13·3′W	T	183
Hart Grove Fm	Devon	SY2994	50°44·7′	3°0·0′W	FM	193
Hart Hall	N Yks	NZ7704	54°25·8′	0°48·4′W	X	94
Harthall	Shrops	SO5870	52°19·8′	2°36·6′W	X	137,138
Hart Hall Fm	Herts	TL0904	51°43·7′	0°24·9′W	FM	166
Hartham	Herts	TL3213	51°48·2′	0°4·7′W	T	166
Hartham Common	Herts	TL4330	51°57·2′	0°5·3′E	X	167
Hartham Park	Wilts	ST8672	51°27·0′	2°11·7′W	X	173
Harthill	Aberd	NJ6825	57°19·1′	2°31·4′W	X	38
Harthill	Ches	SJ5055	53°5·6′	2°44·4′W	T	117
Hart Hill	Ches	SJ5671	53°14·3′	2°39·1′W	X	117
Hart Hill	Cumbr	NY4618	54°33·5′	2°49·7′W	X	90
Harthill	Derby	SK0189	53°24·1′	1°58·7′W	X	110
Hart Hill	E Dunb	NS6082	56°0·9′	4°14·3′W	X	57,64
Hart Hill	Glos	SO5502	51°43·1′	2°38·7′W	X	162
Hart Hill	Kent	TQ9450	51°13·2′	0°47·1′E	X	189
Hart Hill	Luton	TL1022	51°53·4′	0°23·7′W	T	166
Hart Hill	Moray	NJ2354	57°34·4′	3°16·8′W	H	28
Harthill	N Lanak	NS9064	55°51·7′	3°45·0′W	T	65
Harthill	Roth	SK4980	53°19·1′	1°15·5′W	T	111,120
Hart Hill	S Lanak	NS6031	55°33·4′	4°12·7′W	H	71
Hart Hill	Stir	NS6988	56°4·3′	4°5·8′W	H	57
Hart Hill	Wilts	ST8442	51°10·9′	2°13·3′W	X	183
Harthill Castle	Aberd	NJ6825	57°19·1′	2°31·4′W	A	38
Harthill Court	Glos	SO5602	51°43·1′	2°37·8′W	X	162
Hart Hill Down	Hants	SU3558	51°19·4′	1°29·5′W	X	174
Harthill Field	Roth	SK4979	53°18·6′	1°15·5′W	X	120
Hart Hill Fm	Wilts	ST8625	51°1·7′	2°11·6′W	FM	183
Harthill Moor Fm	Derby	SK2262	53°9·5′	1°39·9′W	FM	119
Harthill Resr	Roth	SK4880	53°19·1′	1°16·4′W	W	111,120
Harthills	Aberd	NJ7514	57°13·2′	2°24·4′W	X	38
Harthill Service Area	N Lanak	NS9064	55°51·7′	3°45·0′W	X	65
Harthills Plantn	Aberd	NJ7614	57°13·2′	2°23·4′W	F	38
Hart Holes	N Yks	NZ0006	54°27·2′	1°59·6′W	X	92
Harthope	D & G	NT0312	55°23·8′	3°31·5′W	X	78
Harthope	Durham	NZ0634	54°42·3′	1°54·0′W	X	92
Harthope Bank	D & G	NT0311	55°23·3′	3°31·4′W	X	78
Harthope Beck	Durham	NY8632	54°41·2′	2°12·6′W	W	91,92
Harthope Beck	Durham	NZ0933	54°41·8′	1°51·2′W	W	92
Harthope Burn	D & G	NT0211	55°23·2′	3°32·4′W	W	78
Harthope Burn	Northum	NT9522	55°29·8′	2°4·3′W	W	74,75
Harthope Linn	Northum	NT9220	55°28·7′	2°7·2′W	X	74,75
Harthope Moor	Durham	NY8635	54°42·8′	2°12·6′W	X	91,92
Harthope Moss	Durham	NY8634	54°42·3′	2°12·6′W	X	91,92
Hart Horn	Cumbr	NY6475	55°4·3′	2°33·4′W	X	86
Harthorn Hill	E Ayr	NS5104	55°18·7′	4°20·4′W	X	77
Harthurstfield Fm	Glos	SO9022	51°54·0′	2°8·3′W	FM	163
Harting Combe	W Susx	SU8126	51°1·9′	0°50·3′W	X	186,197
Harting Downs	W Susx	SU7918	50°57·6′	0°52·1′W	H	197
Harting Hill	W Susx	SU7917	50°57·0′	0°52·1′W	H	197
Harting Pond	W Susx	SU7721	50°59·2′	0°53·8′W	W	197
Harting Rig	S Lanak	NS6936	55°36·3′	4°4·3′W	X	71
Hartington	Derby	SK1260	53°8·5′	1°48·8′W	T	119
Hartington Hall	Northum	NZ0288	55°11·4′	1°57·7′W	X	81
Hartington-moor Fm	Derby	SK1461	53°9·0′	1°47·0′W	FM	119
Hartlake	Kent	TQ6347	51°12·2′	0°20·4′E	X	188
Hartlake Br	Somer	ST5141	51°10·2′	2°41·7′W	X	182,183
Hartlake Fm	Somer	ST5340	51°9·7′	2°39·9′W	FM	182,183
Hartlakes	N Yks	NY9000	54°24·0′	2°8·8′W	X	91,92
Hartland	Devon	SS2524	50°59·6′	4°29·2′W	T	190
Hartland Abbey	Devon	SS2424	50°59·5′	4°30·1′W	X	190
Hartland Moor	Dorset	SY9485	50°40·1′	2°4·7′W	X	195
Hartland Point	Devon	SS2227	51°1·1′	4°31·9′W	X	190
Hartland Quay	Devon	SS2224	50°59·5′	4°31·8′W	X	190
Hartland's Hill	Glos	SO7515	51°50·2′	2°21·4′W	X	162
Hartland Stud	Dorset	SY9384	50°39·6′	2°5·6′W	X	195
Hartland Tor	Devon	SX6479	50°35·9′	3°54·9′W	H	191
Hartland View	Devon	SS5839	51°8·2′	4°1·4′W	X	180
Hartlaw	Cumbr	NY1353	54°52·1′	3°20·9′W	X	85
Hart Law	Northum	NT9812	55°24·4′	2°1·5′W	H	81
Hart Law	Northum	NU2006	55°21·1′	1°40·6′W	X	81
Hartle	Worcs	SO9276	52°23·2′	2°6·7′W	T	139
Hartleap	Scot Bord	NT2821	55°28·9′	3°7·9′W	X	73
Hartlebury	Shrops	SO7497	52°34·5′	2°22·6′W	T	138
Hartlebury	Worcs	SO8370	52°19·9′	2°14·6′W	T	138
Hartlebury Common	Worcs	SO8270	52°19·9′	2°15·5′W	T	138
Hartlebury Sta	Worcs	SO8570	52°19·9′	2°12·8′W	X	139
Hartleigh Barton	Devon	SS5008	50°51·4′	4°7·5′W	X	191
Hartlemoor Fm	Derby	SK1680	53°19·2′	1°45·2′W	FM	110
Hartlepool	Hartpl	NZ5032	54°41·1′	1°13·0′W	T	93
Hartlepool Bay	Hartpl	NZ5232	54°41·1′	1°11·2′W	W	93
Hartleton	Heref	SO6425	51°55·6′	2°31·0′W	X	162
Hartley	Cald	SD9226	53°44·1′	2°6·9′W	X	103
Hartley	C of Plym	SX4857	50°23·8′	4°7·9′W	T	201
Hartley	Cumbr	NY7808	54°28·3′	2°19·9′W	T	91
Hartley	Kent	TQ6067	51°23·0′	0°18·4′E	T	177
Hartley	Kent	TQ7534	51°4·9′	0°30·3′E	T	188
Hartley	Northum	NZ3375	55°4·3′	1°28·6′W	X	88
Hartley Bottom	Glos	SO9517	51°51·3′	2°4·0′W	F	163
Hartley Burn	Northum	NY6559	54°55·7′	2°32·3′W	W	86
Hartleyburn Common (North Side)	Northum	NY6461	54°56·8′	2°33·3′W	X	86
Hartleyburn Common (South Side)	Northum	NY6557	54°54·6′	2°32·3′W	X	86
Hartley Castle	Cumbr	NY7808	54°28·3′	2°19·9′W	X	91
Hartleycleugh	Northum	NY8048	54°49·8′	2°18·3′W	X	86,87
Hartley Court	Wok	SU7068	51°24·6′	0°59·2′W	X	175
Hartley Fell	Cumbr	NY8007	54°27·7′	2°18·1′W	X	91,92
Hartley Fm	Bath & NE Somer	ST7570	51°25·9′	2°21·2′W	FM	172
Hartley Fm	Flint	SJ1074	53°15·6′	3°20·5′W	FM	116
Hartley Fm	Glos	SO9517	51°51·3′	2°4·0′W	FM	163
Hartley Fm	Lincs	TF4031	52°51·7′	0°5·2′E	FM	131
Hartley Fold	Cumbr	NY7809	54°28·8′	2°20·0′W	X	91
Hartley Green	Kent	TQ6067	51°23·0′	0°18·4′E	T	177
Hartley Green	Staffs	SJ9729	52°51·7′	2°2·3′W	T	127

Hartley Ground	Cumbr	SD2189	54°17·7′	3°12·4′W	X	96
Hartley Hill	Glos	SO9518	51°51·9′	2°4·0′W	H	163
Hartley Ho	Hants	SU6959	51°19·8′	1°0·2′W	X	175,186
Hartley Ho	Kent	TQ7534	51°4·9′	0°30·3′E	X	188
Hartley Manor Fm	Dorset	ST6406	50°51·4′	2°30·3′W	FM	194
Hartley Mauditt	Hants	SU7436	51°7·3′	0°56·2′W	T	186
Hartley Mauditt Village	Hants	SU7436	51°7·3′	0°56·2′W	A	186
Hartley Moor	Northum	NY8148	54°49·8′	2°17·3′W	H	86,87
Hartley Park	Hants	SU7436	51°7·3′	0°56·2′W	X	186
Hartley Park	N Yks	SE0997	54°22·3′	1°51·3′W	X	99
Hartley Park Fm	Hants	SU7335	51°6·8′	0°57·0′W	FM	186
Hartleys Fm	Lancs	SD7655	53°59·7′	2°21·5′W	FM	103
Hartley Wespall	Hants	SU6958	51°19·2′	1°0·2′W	T	175,186
Hartley West Fm	Northum	NZ3375	55°4·3′	1°28·6′W	FM	88
Hartley Wintney	Hants	SU7656	51°18·1′	0°54·2′W	T	175,186
Hartley Wood	Essex	TM1517	51°48·8′	1°7·6′E	F	168,169
Hartley Wood	Kent	TQ6168	51°23·5′	0°19·2′E	F	177
Hartleywood Fm	Essex	TM1418	51°49·4′	1°6·7′E	FM	168,169
Hartlington	N Yks	SE0361	54°2·9′	1°56·8′W	T	98
Hartlington Pasture	N Yks	SE0564	54°4·6′	1°55·0′W	X	98
Hartlip	Kent	TQ8364	51°21·0′	0°38·1′E	T	178,188
Hartlip Hill	Kent	TQ8465	51°21·5′	0°39·0′E	X	178
Hartlip Place	Kent	TQ8364	51°21·0′	0°38·1′E	X	178,188
Hartly Wood	Devon	SX4184	50°38·3′	4°14·5′W	F	201
Hartly Wood	Leeds	SE4533	53°47·7′	1°18·6′W	F	105
Hartmanor (Hotel)	D & G	NY2596	55°15·4′	3°10·4′W	X	79
Hartmires	N Yks	SE2347	53°55·4′	1°38·6′W	X	104
Hartmoor	Dorset	ST7624	51°1·1′	2°20·1′W	T	183
Hartmoor Fm	Dorset	ST7009	50°53·0′	2°25·2′W	FM	194
Hart Moor Fm	Hartpl	NZ4534	54°42·2′	1°17·7′W	FM	93
Hartmoor Wood	Bucks	SU7594	51°38·6′	0°54·6′W	F	175
Hartmount	Highld	NH7577	57°46·2′	4°5·6′W	T	21
Hartnoll Barton	Devon	SS5540	51°8·7′	4°4·0′W	X	180
Hartnoll Fm	Devon	SS9912	50°54·2′	3°25·8′W	FM	181
Hart Nooking	N Yks	SE6339	53°50·8′	1°2·1′W	X	105,106
Hartoft Beck	N Yks	SE7594	54°20·4′	0°50·4′W	W	94,100
Hartoft End	N Yks	SE7492	54°19·3′	0°51·3′W	T	94,100
Hartoft Moor	N Yks	SE7496	54°21·5′	0°51·3′W	X	94,100
Hartoft Rigg	N Yks	SE7495	54°20·9′	0°51·3′W	X	94,100
Harton	N Yks	SE7061	54°2·7′	0°55·4′W	T	100
Harton	Shrops	SO4888	52°29·5′	2°45·6′W	T	137,138
Harton	S Tyne	NZ3764	54°58·4′	1°24·9′W	T	88
Harton Crag	Cumbr	NY8516	54°32·6′	2°13·5′W	X	91,92
Harton Lodge Fm	N Yks	SE6961	54°2·7′	0°56·4′W	FM	100
Harton Lodge Plantn	N Yks	SE6961	54°2·7′	0°56·4′W	F	100
Harton Manor	N Yks	SE7061	54°2·7′	0°55·4′W	X	100
Hart on the Hill	Hartpl	NZ4631	54°40·6′	1°16·8′W	X	93
Harton Wood	Shrops	SO4888	52°29·5′	2°45·6′W	F	137,138
Hartor Tors	Devon	SX6067	50°29·4′	3°58·0′W	X	202
Hartpiece	Devon	SS5735	51°6·0′	4°2·2′W	X	180
Hartpury	Glos	SO7925	51°55·6′	2°17·9′W	T	162
Hartpury Ho (College of Agriculture)	Glos	SO7822	51°54·0′	2°18·8′W	X	162
Hartree Hills	Scot Bord	NT0635	55°36·2′	3°29·1′W	H	72
Hartree Mill	Scot Bord	NT0436	55°36·7′	3°31·0′W	X	72
Hartridge	Devon	ST1706	50°51·1′	3°10·4′W	X	192,193
Hartridge Fm	W Berks	SU5777	51°29·6′	1°10·3′W	FM	174
Hartridge Ho	Kent	TQ7739	51°7·6′	0°32·2′E	X	188
Hartridge Manor Fm	Kent	TQ7739	51°7·6′	0°32·2′E	FM	188
Hartrigg	Cumbr	NY4506	54°27·0′	2°50·5′W	X	90
Hartrigge	Scot Bord	NT6621	55°29·1′	2°31·8′W	X	74
Hartriza Point	Corn	SW9439	50°13·1′	4°52·9′W	X	204
Hartrow Manor	Somer	ST0934	51°6·1′	3°17·6′W	X	181
Harts	Devon	SX3983	50°37·7′	4°16·2′W	X	201
Harts	S Glos	ST6185	51°34·0′	2°33·4′W	X	172
Hartsdown Park	Kent	TR3470	51°23·1′	1°22·2′E	X	179
Hart's Fm	Dorset	SU0913	50°55·2′	1°51·9′W	FM	195
Harts Fm	I of W	SZ5083	50°38·9′	1°17·2′W	FM	196
Hart's Fm	Norf	TG1201	52°34·2′	1°8·1′E	FM	144
Hart's Fm	Staffs	SK0923	52°48·5′	1°51·6′W	FM	128
Hart's Fm	Staffs	SK1026	52°50·1′	1°50·7′W	FM	128
Hart's Fm	W Susx	SU8102	50°48·9′	0°50·6′W	FM	197
Hartsgarth	Scot Bord	NY4992	55°13·4′	2°47·7′W	X	79
Hartsgarth Burn	Scot Bord	NY4792	55°13·4′	2°49·6′W	W	79
Hartsgarth Fell	Scot Bord	NY4594	55°14·5′	2°51·5′W	H	79
Hartsgarth Flow	Scot Bord	NY4994	55°14·5′	2°47·7′W	X	79
Hartsgreen	Shrops	SO7983	52°26·9′	2°18·1′W	T	138
Hart's Green	Suff	TL8755	52°9·9′	0°44·5′E	T	155
Hartshall Fm	Suff	TM0270	52°17·7′	0°58·1′E	FM	144,155
Hartshead	Kirk	SE1822	53°41·9′	1°43·2′W	T	104
Hartshead Green	Tames	SD9601	53°30·6′	2°3·2′W	T	109
Hartshead Moor Service Area	Cald	SE1624	53°43·0′	1°45·0′W	X	104
Hartshead Moor Side	Kirk	SE1724	53°43·0′	1°44·1′W	T	104
Hartshead Moor Top	Cald	SE1625	53°43·5′	1°45·0′W	T	104
Hartshead Pike	Tames	SD9602	53°31·1′	2°3·2′W	T	109
Hartsheath	Flint	SJ2860	53°8·2′	3°4·2′W	X	117
Harts Heath Fm	Kent	TQ7541	51°8·7′	0°30·5′E	FM	188
Hartshill	C of Stoke	SJ8645	53°0·4′	2°12·1′W	T	118
Hart's Hill	Dudley	SO9288	52°29·6′	2°6·7′W	T	139
Hartshill	Warw	SP3293	52°32·3′	1°31·3′W	T	140
Hart's Hill	W Berks	SU5368	51°24·7′	1°13·9′W	X	174
Harts Hill Fm	W Berks	SU5268	51°24·7′	1°14·7′W	FM	174
Hartshill Green	Warw	SP3294	52°32·8′	1°31·3′W	T	140
Hartshill Hayes Country Park	Warw	SP3194	52°32·8′	1°32·2′W	X	140
Hartshole Fm	Devon	SX4670	50°30·8′	4°10·0′W	FM	201
Hartsholme Country Park	Lincs	SK9469	53°12·8′	0°35·1′W	X	121
Hartshorne	Derby	SK3221	52°47·4′	1°31·1′W	T	128
Hartshorn Pike	Scot Bord	NT6201	55°18·3′	2°35·5′W	H	80
Hartshurst Fm	Surrey	TQ1342	51°10·2′	0°22·6′W	FM	187
Hart Side	Cumbr	NY3519	54°34·0′	2°59·9′W	H	90
Hartside	E Loth	NT6572	55°56·6′	2°33·2′W	X	67
Hartside	Northum	NT9716	55°26·5′	2°2·4′W	X	81
Hartside	Northum	NY9182	55°8·2′	2°8·0′W	X	80
Hartside	Northum	NY9287	55°10·9′	2°7·1′W	X	80
Hart Side	Northum	NY9288	55°11·4′	2°7·1′W	H	80
Hartside	Scot Bord	NT1555	55°47·1′	3°20·9′W	X	65,72
Hartside	Scot Bord	NT4653	55°46·3′	2°51·2′W	X	66,73
Hartside	S Lanak	NS9629	55°32·9′	3°38·5′W	X	72

Hartside Burn	S Lanak	NS9728	55°32·3′	3°37·5′W	W	72
Hartside Cafe	Cumbr	NY6441	54°46·0′	2°33·1′W	X	86
Hartside Cottages	Cumbr	NY6943	54°47·1′	2°28·5′W	X	86,87
Hartside Fm	Durham	NZ2545	54°48·2′	1°36·2′W	FM	88
Hartside Height	Cumbr	NY6542	54°46·5′	2°32·2′W	X	86
Hartside Hill	Northum	NT9815	55°26·0′	2°1·5′W	H	81
Hartside Hill	Scot Bord	NT4454	55°46·8′	2°53·1′W	H	66,73
Hartsland	Kent	TQ5141	51°9·1′	0°9·9′E	X	188
Hartsmailing	Stir	NS8291	56°6·1′	3°53·4′W	X	57
Hartsop	Cumbr	NY4013	54°30·8′	2°55·2′W	T	90
Hartsop above How	Cumbr	NY3812	54°30·2′	2°57·0′W	X	90
Hartsop Dodd	Cumbr	NY4111	54°29·7′	2°54·2′W	H	90
Hartsop Hall	Cumbr	NY3912	54°30·2′	2°56·1′W	X	90
Hart Station	Hartpl	NZ4836	54°43·2′	1°14·9′W	T	93
Hartstone Fm	Devon	SX5361	50°26·1′	4°3·8′W	FM	201
Hartswell	Devon	SX4785	50°38·9′	4°9·5′W	X	191,201
Hartswell	Somer	ST0827	51°2·3′	3°18·4′W	T	181
Hartswell Fm	Notts	SK6454	53°5·0′	1°2·3′W	FM	120
Hart's Wood	Essex	TQ6092	51°36·5′	0°19·0′E	F	177
Hartswood Manor	Surrey	TQ2447	51°12·7′	0°13·1′W	X	187
Hart Tor	Devon	SX5872	50°32·1′	3°59·8′W	H	191
Hart Warren	Hartpl	NZ4935	54°42·7′	1°13·9′W	X	93
Hartwell	Devon	SX4175	50°33·4′	4°14·3′W	X	201
Hartwell	E Susx	TQ4736	51°6·5′	0°6·4′E	X	188
Hartwell	Northnts	SP7850	52°8·8′	0°51·2′W	T	152
Hartwell	Staffs	SJ9139	52°57·1′	2°7·6′W	T	127
Hartwell Clear Copse	Northnts	SP7951	52°9·3′	0°50·3′W	F	152
Hartwell End Ho	Northnts	SP7949	52°8·2′	0°50·3′W	X	152
Hartwell Fm	Glos	SP1104	51°44·3′	1°50·0′W	FM	163
Hartwellhall Fm	Staffs	SJ9038	52°56·6′	2°8·5′W	FM	127
Hartwell Hill Fm	Bucks	SP8123	51°54·2′	0°49·0′W	FM	165
Hartwell Ho	Bucks	SP7912	51°48·3′	0°50·9′W	A	165
Hartwith	N Yks	SE2161	54°2·9′	1°40·3′W	T	99
Hartwith Mill	N Yks	SE2260	54°2·4′	1°39·4′W	X	99
Hartwith Moor	N Yks	SE2162	54°3·5′	1°40·3′W	X	99
Hart Wood	Corn	SX0964	50°26·9′	4°41·0′W	F	200
Hartwood	D & G	NY0778	55°5·5′	3°27·0′W	X	85
Hartwood	Lancs	SD5819	53°40·2′	2°37·7′W	T	108
Hartwood	N Lanak	NS8459	55°48·9′	3°50·6′W	T	65,72
Hart Wood	Suff	TL6652	52°8·7′	0°26·0′E	F	154
Hartwoodburn	Scot Bord	NT4726	55°31·7′	2°49·9′W	T	73
Hartwood Burn	S Lanak	NS8024	55°30·0′	3°53·5′W	W	71,72
Hartwood Hill	D & G	NY0678	55°5·5′	3°27·9′W	X	85
Hartwood Hill	S Lanak	NS7924	55°29·9′	3°54·5′W	H	71
Hartwood Ho	W Loth	NT0161	55°50·2′	3°34·4′W	X	65
Hartwoodmyres	Scot Bord	NT4324	55°30·6′	2°53·7′W	X	73
Harty Marshes	Kent	TR0268	51°22·7′	0°54·6′E	X	178
Harty Marshes	Kent	TR0368	51°22·7′	0°55·4′E	X	178,179
Harvard Fm	Dorset	ST5409	50°53·0′	2°38·9′W	FM	194
Harvel	Kent	TQ6463	51°20·8′	0°21·7′E	T	177,188
Harvenna Fm	Corn	SW9058	50°23·3′	4°56·9′W	FM	200
Harvester Fm	N Lincs	SE7402	53°30·8′	0°52·6′W	FM	112
Harvestgate Fm	Hants	SU6220	50°58·8′	1°6·6′W	FM	185
Harvest Hill	Cov	SP2882	52°26·4′	1°34·9′W	T	140
Harvesthill	W Susx	TQ2922	50°59·2′	0°9·3′W	X	198
Harvest Slade Bottom	Hants	SU2106	50°51·4′	1°41·7′W	X	195
Harvestwood Fm	Devon	ST2008	50°52·2′	3°7·8′W	FM	192,193
Harvey Gate	Staffs	SK0256	53°6·3′	1°57·8′W	X	119
Harvey Hill	Durham	NZ0335	54°42·8′	1°56·8′W	X	92
Harvey's Fm	Essex	TL9816	51°48·7′	0°52·7′E	FM	168
Harvey's Fm	Essex	TM0228	51°55·1′	0°56·6′E	FM	168
Harveyshill Fm	Herts	TL2929	51°56·9′	0°7·0′W	FM	166
Harvieston	Aberd	NO8578	56°53·8′	2°14·3′W	X	45
Harvieston	Highld	NC8431	58°15·4′	3°58·1′W	X	17
Harvieston	Stir	NS5989	56°4·6′	4°15·5′W	X	57
Harvieston Ho	Midlo	NT3460	55°50·0′	3°2·8′W	X	66
Harvieston Mains	Midlo	NT3460	55°50·0′	3°2·8′W	X	66
Harviestoun Home Fm	Clackm	NS9397	56°9·5′	3°42·9′W	FM	58
Harvills Hawthorn	Sand	SO9893	52°32·3′	2°1·4′W	T	139
Harvington	Worcs	SO8774	52°22·1′	2°11·1′W	T	139
Harvington	Worcs	SP0549	52°8·6′	1°55·2′W	T	150
Harvington Birch Fm	Staffs	SJ8508	52°40·4′	2°12·9′W	FM	127
Harvington Hill	Worcs	SP0449	52°8·6′	1°56·1′W	X	150
Harwarton	Kent	TQ5541	51°9·1′	0°13·4′E	X	188
Harwell	Notts	SK6891	53°24·9′	0°58·2′W	T	111
Harwell	Oxon	SU4989	51°36·1′	1°17·2′W	T	174
Harwell Field	Oxon	SU4887	51°35·0′	1°18·0′W	X	174
Harwell Laboratory	Oxon	SU4786	51°34·5′	1°18·9′W	X	174
Harwich	Essex	TM2431	51°56·2′	1°15·9′E	T	169
Harwich Harbour	Essex	TM2633	51°57·2′	1°17·7′E	W	169
Harwod Fields	Roch	SD8212	53°36·5′	2°15·9′W	X	109
Harwood	Bolton	SD7511	53°35·9′	2°22·3′W	T	109
Harwood	Durham	NY8233	54°41·7′	2°16·3′W	T	91,92
Harwood	Northum	NZ0090	55°12·5′	1°59·6′W	X	81
Harwood	Scot Bord	NT5608	55°22·1′	2°41·2′W	X	80
Harwood	W Loth	NT0162	55°50·7′	3°34·4′W	X	65
Harwood Beck	Durham	NY8232	54°41·2′	2°16·3′W	W	91,92
Harwood Burn	E Ayr	NS6729	55°32·5′	4°6·0′W	W	71
Harwood Burn	Northum	NY9890	55°12·5′	2°1·5′W	W	81
Harwood Burn	Scot Bord	NT5103	55°19·4′	2°45·9′W	W	79
Harwood Common	Durham	NY7935	54°42·8′	2°19·1′W	X	91
Harwood Dale	N Yks	SE9695	54°20·7′	0°31·0′W	T	94,101
Harwood Dale Forest	N Yks	SE9697	54°21·8′	0°30·9′W	F	94,101
Harwood Dale Moor	N Yks	SE9598	54°22·4′	0°31·8′W	X	94,101
Harwood Fm	Somer	ST0730	51°3·9′	3°19·3′W	FM	181
Harwood Fm	Somer	ST6742	51°10·8′	2°27·9′W	FM	183
Harwood Forest	Northum	NY9894	55°14·7′	2°1·5′W	F	81
Harwood Gate	Northum	NZ0189	55°12·0′	1°58·6′W	X	81
Harwoodgate Fm	S Glos	ST7482	51°32·4′	2°22·1′W	FM	172
Harwood Hall	Hav	TQ5684	51°32·2′	0°15·4′E	X	177
Harwood Head	Northum	NY9790	55°12·5′	2°2·4′W	X	81
Harwood Lee	Bolton	SD7412	53°36·5′	2°23·2′W	T	109
Harwood Lodge	Hants	SU4262	51°21·6′	1°23·4′W	X	174
Harwoodmill	Scot Bord	NT5809	55°22·6′	2°39·3′W	X	80
Harwood Moss	Scot Bord	NT5505	55°20·5′	2°42·1′W	X	80
Harwood on Teviot	Scot Bord	NT4409	55°22·6′	2°52·6′W	T	79
Harwood Rig	Scot Bord	NT4404	55°19·9′	2°52·5′W	H	79
Harwoods	W Susx	TQ1915	50°55·6′	0°18·0′W	X	198
Harwoods Green	W Susx	TQ0320	50°58·4′	0°31·6′W	X	197
Harwood Shield	Northum	NY9051	54°51·5′	2°8·9′W	X	87

Harwoodshield Fell	Northum	NY8950	54°50·9′	2°9·9′W	X	87
Harwoods House Fm	Warw	SP3358	52°13·4′	1°30·6′W	FM	151
Harwood Water	W Loth	NT0262	55°50·7′	3°33·5′W	W	65
Harworth	Notts	SK6191	53°25·0′	1°4·5′W	T	111
Hasbury	Dudley	SO9583	52°26·9′	2°4·0′W	T	139
Hascombe	Surrey	TQ0039	51°8·7′	0°33·8′W	T	186
Hascombe Hill	Surrey	TQ0038	51°8·2′	0°33·9′W	H	186
Hascombe Hill (Fort)	Surrey	TQ0038	51°8·2′	0°33·9′W	A	186
Hascombe Stud	Cambs	TL6962	52°14·0′	0°28·9′E	X	154
Hascosay	Shetld	HU5592	60°36·7′	0°59·2′W	X	1,2
Hascosay Sound	Shetld	HU5492	60°36·7′	1°0·3′W	W	1,2
Hascot Hill Fm	Suff	TM0653	52°8·4′	1°1·0′E	FM	155
Haselbech	Northnts	SP7177	52°23·4′	0°57·0′W	T	141
Haselbech Grange	Northnts	SP7277	52°23·4′	0°56·1′W	X	141
Haselbech Hill	Northnts	SP7176	52°22·9′	0°57·0′W	X	141
Haselbury Park Fm	Somer	ST4808	50°52·4′	2°44·0′W	FM	193
Haselbury Plucknett	Somer	ST4710	50°53·5′	2°44·8′W	T	193
Haselden Fm	E Susx	TQ6719	50°57·0′	0°23·0′E	FM	199
Haselden Wood	E Susx	TQ6718	50°56·5′	0°23·0′E	F	199
Haseley	Warw	SP2367	52°18·3′	1°39·4′W	T	151
Haseley Brook	Oxon	SP6500	51°41·9′	1°3·2′W	W	164,165
Haseley Court	Oxon	SP6400	51°41·9′	1°4·0′W	X	164,165
Haseley Green	Warw	SP2369	52°19·4′	1°39·4′W	T	139,151
Haseley Hall	Warw	SP2369	52°19·4′	1°39·4′W	X	139,151
Haseley Knob	Warw	SP2371	52°20·4′	1°39·3′W	T	139
Haseley Manor	I of W	SZ5485	50°40·0′	1°13·8′W	X	196
Haseley Wood	Oxon	SP6301	51°42·5′	1°4·9′W	F	164,165
Hasell Hedge	Beds	TL1850	52°8·4′	0°16·1′W	X	153
Haselor	Warw	SP1257	52°12·9′	1°49·1′W	T	150
Haselor Fm	Worcs	SP0142	52°4·8′	1°58·7′W	FM	150
Haselor Hill	Worcs	SP0042	52°4·8′	1°59·6′W	X	150
Haselor Lodge	Warw	SP1356	52°12·4′	1°48·2′W	X	151
Haselour Hall	Staffs	SK2010	52°41·5′	1°41·8′W	X	128
Haselour Ho	Staffs	SK2010	52°41·5′	1°41·8′W	X	128
Hasfield	Glos	SO8227	51°56·7′	2°15·3′W	T	162
Hasfield Court	Glos	SO8227	51°56·7′	2°15·3′W	X	162
Hasfield Ham	Glos	SO8426	51°56·2′	2°13·6′W	X	162
Hasgill	Lancs	SD7257	54°0·7′	2°25·2′W	X	103
Hasgill Beck	Lancs	SD7258	54°1·3′	2°25·2′W	W	103
Hasgill Fell	Lancs	SD7159	54°1·8′	2°26·1′W	X	103
Hasguard	Pemb	SM8509	51°44·5′	5°6·5′W	X	157
Hasguard Cross	Pemb	SM8410	51°45·1′	5°7·4′W	X	157
Hasguard Hall	Pemb	SM8510	51°45·1′	5°6·5′W	X	157
Hasham Copse	W Berks	SU3778	51°30·2′	1°27·6′W	F	174
Hasholme Garth	E Yorks	SE8332	53°46·9′	0°44·0′W	X	106
Hasholme Grange	E Yorks	SE8233	53°47·4′	0°44·9′W	X	106
Hasholme Hall	E Yorks	SE8233	53°47·4′	0°44·9′W	X	106
Hasholme Heavy Horses	E Yorks	SE8334	53°48·0′	0°44·0′W	X	106
Hashy Gill	Cumbr	NY7400	54°23·9′	2°23·6′W	W	91
Haskayne	Lancs	SD3508	53°34·1′	2°58·5′W	T	108
Haske	Devon	SS8502	50°48·6′	3°37·6′W	X	191
Haskeir Eagach	N Eil	NF5980	57°41·1′	7°42·9′W	X	18
Haskeir Island	N Eil	NF6181	57°41·7′	7°41·0′W	X	18
Hasker Fm	Derby	SK2652	53°4·1′	1°36·3′W	FM	119
Hasketon	Suff	TM2450	52°6·4′	1°16·7′E	T	156
Hasketon Grange	Suff	TM2449	52°5·9′	1°16·6′E	X	169
Hasketon Hall	Suff	TM2351	52°7·0′	1°15·8′E	X	156
Hasketon Manor	Suff	TM2650	52°6·3′	1°18·4′E	X	156
Haskew Beck	Cumbr	NY5112	54°30·3′	2°45·0′W	W	90
Haskew Tarn	Cumbr	NY5211	54°29·8′	2°44·0′W	W	90
Haskhaw Gill	Cumbr	SD7593	54°20·2′	2°22·7′W	W	98
Haskie Taing	Orkney	HY7653	59°22·0′	2°24·8′W	X	5
Haskins Fm	Devon	ST0802	50°48·8′	3°18·0′W	FM	192
Haskin's Fm	S Glos	ST7486	51°34·6′	2°22·1′W	FM	172
Hàslam	Highld	NG2404	57°2·9′	6°32·6′W	X	39
Haslam Park	Lancs	SD5130	53°46·1′	2°44·2′W	X	102
Haslams Fm	N Lincs	SE7500	53°29·7′	0°51·8′W	FM	112
Hasland	Derby	SK3969	53°13·2′	1°24·5′W	T	119
Hasland Fm	Devon	ST2701	50°48·5′	3°1·8′W	FM	193
Hasland Green	Derby	SK3969	53°13·2′	1°24·5′W	X	119
Haslands	W Susx	SU9715	50°55·8′	0°36·8′W	X	197
Haslar Royal Naval Hospital	Hants	SZ6198	50°46·9′	1°7·7′W	X	196
Haslemere	Surrey	SU8932	51°5·1′	0°43·4′W	T	186
Haslett Copse	W Susx	SU7912	50°54·4′	0°52·2′W	F	197
Haslett Fm	I of W	SZ4682	50°38·4′	1°20·6′W	FM	196
Hasley Inclosure	Hants	SU1912	50°54·7′	1°43·4′W	F	195
Haslingbourne	W Susx	SU9820	50°58·5′	0°35·9′W	T	197
Haslingden	Lancs	SD7823	53°42·4′	2°19·6′W	T	103
Haslingden Grane	Lancs	SD7522	53°41·9′	2°22·3′W	X	103
Haslingden Moor	Lancs	SD7624	53°43·0′	2°21·4′W	X	103
Haslingfield	Cambs	TL4052	52°9·1′	0°3·2′E	T	154
Hasling Hall Fm	N Yks	SE2246	53°54·8′	1°39·5′W	FM	104
Haslington	Ches	SJ7355	53°5·7′	2°23·8′W	T	118
Haslington Ho	Ches	SJ7457	53°6·8′	2°22·9′W	X	118
Hasluck's Green	Sol	SP1078	52°24·2′	1°50·8′W	T	139
Has of Queyfirth	Shetld	HU3582	60°31·5′	1°21·2′W	X	1,2,3
Haspielaw	S Lanak	NS6951	55°44·3′	4°4·8′W	X	64
Hass	D & G	NX7653	54°51·6′	3°55·5′W	X	84
Hass	D & G	NY2477	55°5·1′	3°11·0′W	X	85
Hass	Orkney	HY2924	59°6·1′	3°13·9′W	X	6
Hass	S Lanak	NS9015	55°25·2′	3°43·8′W	X	71,78
Hassage	Somer	ST7555	51°17·8′	2°21·1′W	X	172
Hassall	Ches	SJ7657	53°6·8′	2°21·1′W	T	118
Hassall Green	Ches	SJ7858	53°7·4′	2°19·3′W	T	118
Hassall Moss	Ches	SJ7658	53°7·4′	2°21·1′W	X	118
Hass Burn	D & G	NX7752	54°51·1′	3°54·5′W	W	84
Hassell Street	Kent	TR0846	51°10·7′	0°59·0′E	T	179,189
Hassendean	Scot Bord	NT5420	55°28·6′	2°43·2′W	T	73
Hassendean Bank	Scot Bord	NT5618	55°27·5′	2°41·3′W	X	80
Hassendean Burn	Scot Bord	NT5219	55°28·0′	2°45·1′W	W	79
Hassendean Common	Scot Bord	NT5220	55°28·5′	2°45·1′W	X	73
Hasse, The	Cambs	TL6175	52°21·2′	0°22·2′E	X	143
Hassiehillock	Moray	NJ5549	57°32·0′	2°44·6′W	X	29
Hassiewells	Aberd	NJ6540	57°27·2′	2°34·5′W	T	29
Hassingham	Norf	TG3605	52°35·7′	1°29·5′E	T	134
Hassington	Scot Bord	NT7341	55°40·0′	2°25·3′W	X	74
Hassington East Mains	Scot Bord	NT7341	55°40·0′	2°25·3′W	X	74
Hassington West Mains	Scot Bord	NT7340	55°39·4′	2°25·3′W	X	74
Hassness	Cumbr	NY1815	54°31·7′	3°15·6′W	X	89,90

Hassocks	Angus	NO5846	56°36·5′	2°40·6′W	X	54
Hassocks	W Susx	TQ3015	50°55·4′	0°8·6′W	T	198
Hass of Goustie	Orkney	HY4228	59°8·4′	3°0·3′W	X	5,6
Hassop	Derby	SK2272	53°14·9′	1°39·8′W	T	119
Hassop Common	Derby	SK2273	53°15·5′	1°39·8′W	X	119
Hassop Park	Derby	SK2171	53°14·4′	1°40·7′W	X	119
Hass Sike	Scot Bord	NT5705	55°20·5′	2°40·2′W	W	80
Hass, The	D & G	NY1483	55°8·3′	3°20·5′W	H	78
Hassy The	Aberd	NK1058	57°37·0′	1°49·5′W	X	30
Haste Hill	Surrey	SU9132	51°5·0′	0°41·7′W	X	186
Haster	Highld	ND3250	58°26·2′	3°9·4′W	X	12
Haster	Highld	ND3251	58°26·8′	3°9·4′W	X	12
Ha's, The	Aberd	NJ8120	57°16·5′	2°18·4′W	X	38
Hasthorpe	Lincs	TF4869	53°12·1′	0°13·4′E	T	122
Hastigrow	Highld	ND2561	58°32·1′	3°16·8′W	X	11,12
Hastingford Fm	E Susx	TQ5225	51°0·5′	0°10·4′E	FM	188,199
Hasting Hill	Sund	NZ3554	54°53·0′	1°26·8′W	T	88
Hastingleigh	Kent	TR0944	51°9·6′	0°59·7′E	T	179,189
Hastings	E Susx	TQ7415	50°54·7′	0°28·9′E	A	199
Hastings	E Susx	TQ8110	50°51·9′	0°34·7′E	T	199
Hastings	Somer	ST3116	50°56·6′	2°58·5′W	T	193
Hastings House Fm	Durham	NZ3443	54°47·1′	1°27·9′W	FM	88
Hastingwood	Essex	TL4807	51°44·8′	0°9·0′E	T	167
Hastoe	Herts	SP9109	51°46·6′	0°40·5′W	T	165
Hastoe Hill	Herts	SP9109	51°46·6′	0°40·5′W	X	165
Haston	Shrops	SJ5120	52°46·8′	2°43·2′W	T	126
Haston Grove	Shrops	SJ5020	52°46·8′	2°44·1′W	X	126
Hasty Bank	N Yks	NZ5603	54°25·4′	1°7·8′W	X	93
Hasty Bank Fm	N Yks	NZ5603	54°25·4′	1°7·8′W	FM	93
Hasty Bank Fm	N Yks	SE6288	54°17·3′	1°2·4′W	FM	94,100
Hasty Leys Fm	Warw	SP3238	52°2·6′	1°31·6′W	FM	151
Haswalls	Shetld	HZ2171	59°31·7′	1°37·2′W	X	4
Haswell	Devon	SX7157	50°24·2′	3°48·5′W	X	202
Haswell	Durham	NZ3743	54°47·1′	1°25·1′W	T	88
Haswell Grange	N Yks	NZ3105	54°26·6′	1°30·9′W	X	93
Haswell Lodge	Durham	NZ3643	54°47·1′	1°26·0′W	X	88
Haswell Moor	Durham	NZ3841	54°46·0′	1°24·1′W	T	88
Haswell Moor Fm	Durham	NZ3542	54°46·5′	1°26·9′W	FM	88
Haswell Plough	Durham	NZ3742	54°46·5′	1°25·1′W	T	88
Haswellsykes	Scot Bord	NT2039	55°38·5′	3°15·8′W	T	73
Hatch	Beds	TL1547	52°6·8′	0°18·8′W	T	153
Hatch	Devon	SX7146	50°18·2′	3°48·3′W	T	202
Hatch	Hants	SU6752	51°16·0′	1°2·0′W	T	185,186
Hatch	Kent	TQ9634	51°4·5′	0°48·3′E	X	189
Hatch-a-Way	Derby	SK0867	53°12·2′	1°52·4′W	X	119
Hatchbank	Pth & Kin	NT1198	56°10·2′	3°25·6′W	X	58
Hatch Beauchamp	Somer	ST3020	50°58·7′	2°59·4′W	T	193
Hatch Bottom	Hants	SU4714	50°55·6′	1°19·5′W	T	196
Hatch Court	Somer	ST3021	50°59·3′	2°59·5′W	A	193
Hatchednize	Scot Bord	NT8041	55°40·0′	2°18·6′W	X	74
Hatch End	Beds	TL0761	52°14·4′	0°25·6′W	T	153
Hatch End	Harrow	TQ1291	51°36·6′	0°22·6′W	T	176
Hatchery Ho	Suff	TL7664	52°15·0′	0°35·1′E	X	155
Hatches Fm	Essex	TQ6692	51°36·4′	0°24·2′E	FM	177,178
Hatches Fm	E Susx	TQ5610	50°52·3′	0°13·4′E	FM	199
Hatches Fm	Herts	TL0313	51°48·6′	0°30·0′W	FM	166
Hatchet Flat	Notts	SK6381	53°19·6′	1°2·8′W	F	111,120
Hatchet Gate	Hants	SU3701	50°48·7′	1°28·1′W	T	196
Hatchet Green	Hants	SU1919	50°58·4′	1°43·4′W	T	184
Hatchet Moor	Hants	SU3500	50°48·1′	1°29·8′W	X	196
Hatchet Pond	Hants	SU3601	50°48·7′	1°29·0′W	W	196
Hatchetts	Surrey	TQ2042	51°10·1′	0°16·6′W	X	187
Hatchetts Fm	Worcs	SO9866	52°17·8′	2°1·4′W	FM	150
Hatchet Wood	Bucks	SU7889	51°35·9′	0°52·0′W	F	175
Hatch Farm Hill	W Susx	SU9029	51°3·4′	0°42·6′W	T	186,197
Hatchfield Fm	Suff	TL6465	52°15·7′	0°24·6′E	FM	154
Hatch Fm	Essex	TQ6190	51°35·4′	0°19·8′E	FM	177
Hatch Fm	Thurr	TQ6385	51°32·6′	0°21·4′E	FM	177
Hatch Fm	W Susx	SU8429	51°3·5′	0°47·7′W	FM	186,197
Hatch Fm Ho	W Berks	SU6165	51°23·1′	1°7·0′W	X	175
Hatchford Park	Surrey	TQ0958	51°18·9′	0°25·8′W	X	187
Hatchgate Fm	W Berks	SU5168	51°24·8′	1°15·6′W	FM	174
Hatch Gate Fm	Wok	SU7972	51°26·7′	0°51·4′W	FM	175
Hatchgate Ho	Wok	SU7881	51°31·6′	0°52·1′W	X	175
Hatch Green	Somer	ST3019	50°58·2′	2°59·4′W	T	193
Hatch Hill	Kent	TQ6765	51°21·8′	0°24·3′E	H	177,178
Hatch-hill Fm	Bucks	SP6940	52°3·5′	0°59·2′W	FM	152
Hatch-hill Wood	Bucks	SP6941	52°4·0′	0°59·2′W	F	152
Hatch Ho	Wilts	ST9028	51°3·3′	2°8·2′W	X	184
Hatch House Fm	W Berks	SU4062	51°21·6′	1°25·1′W	FM	174
Hatching Green	Herts	TL1312	51°47·9′	0°21·3′W	T	166
Hatching Hill	Oxon	SP3216	51°50·7′	1°31·7′W	X	164
Hatchlands	Dorset	SY4798	50°47·0′	2°44·7′W	X	193
Hatchlands	Surrey	TQ0652	51°15·7′	0°28·5′W	X	187
Hatchlands Fm	Kent	TQ5151	51°14·5′	0°10·2′E	FM	188
Hatchley	Staffs	SJ9845	53°0·4′	2°1·4′W	X	118
Hatchmead Fm	Bucks	SP8105	51°44·5′	0°49·2′W	FM	165
Hatchmere	Ches	SJ5571	53°14·3′	2°40·0′W	T	117
Hatch Mere	Ches	SJ5572	53°14·8′	2°40·1′W	W	117
Hatch Mill	Devon	SX4768	50°29·7′	4°9·1′W	X	201
Hatch Moor	Devon	SS5119	50°57·3′	4°6·9′W	X	180
Hatch Park	Kent	TR0640	51°7·6′	0°57·0′E	X	179,189
Hatch Park	Somer	ST2920	50°58·7′	3°0·3′W	X	193
Hatchpen	Herts	TL3637	52°1·1′	0°0·7′W	X	154
Hatch, The	Wrekin	SJ6408	52°40·4′	2°31·5′W	X	127
Hatch The	W Susx	TQ2321	50°58·7′	0°14·5′W	X	198
Hatch Warren	Hants	SU6048	51°13·9′	1°8·0′W	T	185
Hatch Warren Fm	Hants	SU6148	51°13·9′	1°7·2′W	FM	185
Hatchwell Fm	Devon	SX7077	50°34·9′	3°49·8′W	FM	191
Hatchwell's Covert	Staffs	SJ7821	52°47·4′	2°19·2′W	F	127
Hatch Wood	Devon	SX4371	50°31·3′	4°12·5′W	F	201
Hatchwood	Devon	SX4372	50°31·8′	4°12·5′W	X	201
Hatchwood Fm	Lancs	SD6026	53°44·0′	2°36·0′W	FM	102,103
Hatchwood Ho	Hants	SU7451	51°15·4′	0°56·0′W	X	186
Hatcliffe	NE Lincs	TA2100	53°29·2′	0°10·2′W	T	113
Hatcliffe Top	NE Lincs	TA2301	53°29·7′	0°8·3′W	X	113
Hateley Heath	Sand	SP0093	52°32·3′	1°59·6′W	T	139
Hatfield	Donc	SE6609	53°34·6′	0°59·8′W	T	111
Hatfield	Heref	SO5959	52°13·9′	2°35·6′W	T	149
Hatfield	Herts	TL2207	51°45·1′	0°13·6′W	T	166

Hatfield	Worcs	SO8750	52°9·1′	2°11·0′W	T	150
Hatfield Aerodrome	Herts	TL2008	51°45·7′	0°15·3′W	X	166
Hatfield Broad Oak	Essex	TL5416	51°49·5′	0°14·5′E	T	167
Hatfield Chase	Donc	SE7110	53°35·1′	0°55·2′W	T	112
Hatfield Court	Heref	SO5759	52°13·9′	2°37·4′W	X	149
Hatfield Fm	Wilts	SU0559	51°20·0′	1°55·3′W	FM	173
Hatfield Forest	Essex	TL5320	51°51·7′	0°13·7′E	F	167
Hatfield Garden Village	Herts	TL2109	51°46·2′	0°14·4′W	T	166
Hatfield Grange	Essex	TL5414	51°48·4′	0°14·4′E	X	167
Hatfield Grange	E Yorks	TA1942	53°51·9′	0°11·0′W	X	107
Hatfield Grange	Notts	SK5771	53°14·2′	1°8·3′W	X	120
Hatfield Heath	Essex	TL5215	51°49·0′	0°12·7′E	T	167
Hatfield Ho	Herts	TL2308	51°45·7′	0°12·7′W	A	166
Hatfield Hyde	Herts	TL2411	51°47·3′	0°11·7′W	T	166
Hatfield Moors	Donc	SE7006	53°33·0′	0°56·2′W	X	112
Hatfield Park	Essex	TL5520	51°51·6′	0°15·5′E	X	167
Hatfield Peverel	Essex	TL7911	51°46·4′	0°36·1′E	T	167
Hatfield Place	Essex	TL7811	51°46·4′	0°35·2′E	X	167
Hatfield Plantn	Notts	SK5770	53°13·7′	1°8·4′W	F	120
Hatfield Regis Grange	Essex	TL5618	51°50·6′	0°16·3′E	X	167
Hatfield Waste Drain	N Lincs	SE7510	53°35·1′	0°51·6′W	W	112
Hatfield Wick	Essex	TL7712	51°46·9′	0°34·4′E	X	167
Hatfield Woodhouse	Donc	SE6808	53°34·1′	0°58·0′W	T	111
Hat Fm	Leic	SK5401	52°36·5′	1°11·8′W	FM	140
Hatford	Oxon	SU3394	51°38·9′	1°31·0′W	T	164,174
Hat Gate Cottage	Wilts	SU2164	51°22·7′	1°41·5′W	X	174
Hathenshaw Fm	N Yks	SE1350	53°57·0′	1°47·7′W	FM	104
Hatherden	Hants	SU3450	51°15·1′	1°30·4′W	T	185
Hatherden Ho	Hants	SU3450	51°15·1′	1°30·4′W	X	185
Hatherden Manor	Hants	SU3450	51°15·1′	1°30·4′W	X	185
Hatherland	Devon	SS9316	50°56·2′	3°31·0′W	X	181
Hatherleigh	Devon	SS5404	50°49·3′	4°4·0′W	T	191
Hatherleigh Fm	Suff	TM3063	52°13·3′	1°22·4′E	FM	156
Hatherleigh Fms	Somer	ST7027	51°2·7′	2°25·3′W	FM	183
Hatherley	Glos	SO9221	51°53·5′	2°6·6′W	T	163
Hatherley Brook	Glos	SO8622	51°54·0′	2°11·8′W	W	162
Hatherley Ho	Suff	TM2251	52°7·0′	1°15·0′E	X	156
Hatherly Fm	Dorset	ST7505	50°50·9′	2°20·9′W	FM	194
Hathern	Leic	SK5022	52°47·8′	1°15·1′W	T	129
Hatherop	Glos	SP1505	51°44·8′	1°46·6′W	T	163
Hathersage	Derby	SK2381	53°19·8′	1°38·9′W	T	110
Hathersage Booths	Derby	SK2480	53°19·2′	1°38·0′W	T	110
Hathersage Moor	Sheff	SK2581	53°19·8′	1°37·1′W	X	110
Hathersham Fm	Surrey	TQ3044	51°11·1′	0°8·0′W	FM	187
Hathershaw	Oldham	SD9203	53°31·7′	2°6·8′W	T	109
Hatherton	Ches	SJ6947	53°1·4′	2°27·3′W	T	118
Hatherton	Devon	SX6199	50°46·7′	3°57·9′W	X	191
Hatherton	Staffs	SJ9510	52°41·5′	2°4·0′W	T	127
Hatherton Fm	Ches	SJ6848	53°1·9′	2°28·2′W	FM	118
Hatherton Ho	Ches	SJ6748	53°1·9′	2°29·1′W	X	118
Hatherton Lodge	Ches	SJ6947	53°1·4′	2°27·3′W	X	118
Hatherton Lodge Fm	Ches	SJ6947	53°1·4′	2°27·3′W	FM	118
Hatherton Manor	Ches	SJ6746	53°0·9′	2°29·1′W	X	118
Hatherwood Point	I of W	SZ3086	50°40·6′	1°34·1′W	X	196
Hat Hill	W Susx	SU8613	50°54·8′	0°46·2′W	H	197
Hatley Fm	Ches	SJ5376	53°17·0′	2°41·9′W	FM	117
Hatley Park	Cambs	TL2750	52°8·2′	0°8·3′W	A	153
Hatley's Fm	Cambs	TL5165	52°16·0′	0°13·2′E	FM	154
Hatley St George	Cambs	TL2851	52°8·8′	0°7·4′W	T	153
Hatling Bigni	Cered	SN2052	52°8·5′	4°37·4′W	X	145
Ha' Tower	Pth & Kin	NO0414	56°18·8′	3°32·7′W	A	58
Hatsford	Heref	SO6436	52°1·5′	2°31·1′W	X	149
Hatson	Orkney	HY4312	58°59·7′	2°59·0′W	T	6
Hatt	Corn	SX3961	50°25·8′	4°15·6′W	T	201
Hatt Common	Hants	SU4263	51°22·1′	1°23·4′W	X	174
Hatterell	W Susx	TQ1719	50°57·7′	0°19·6′W	X	198
Hatteringill Head	Cumbr	NY1324	54°36·5′	3°20·4′W	X	89
Hatterrall Hill	Monm	SO3025	51°55·4′	3°0·7′W	H	161
Hatters Br	Lancs	SD8844	53°53·8′	2°10·5′W	X	103
Hatterseat	Aberd	NJ9821	57°17·0′	2°1·5′W	X	38
Hatter's Hall	N Yks	NZ4005	54°26·6′	1°22·6′W	X	93
Hattersley	Tames	SJ9894	53°26·8′	2°1·4′W	T	109
Hattersley Sta	Tames	SJ9794	53°26·8′	2°2·3′W	X	109
Hatt Hill	Hants	SU3126	51°2·2′	1°33·1′W	T	185
Hatt Ho	Corn	SX3962	50°26·4′	4°15·7′W	X	201
Hatt Ho	Wilts	ST8367	51°24·3′	2°14·3′W	X	173
Hattingley	Hants	SU6437	51°8·0′	1°4·7′W	T	185
Hatton	Aberd	NJ9200	57°5·7′	2°7·5′W	X	38
Hatton	Aberd	NJ9616	57°14·3′	2°3·5′W	X	38
Hatton	Aberd	NK0537	57°25·7′	1°54·5′W	T	30
Hatton	Aberd	NO6767	56°47·9′	2°32·0′W	X	45
Hatton	Angus	NO3040	56°33·1′	3°7·9′W	X	53
Hatton	Angus	NO4642	56°34·3′	2°52·3′W	X	54
Hatton	Angus	NO4653	56°40·2′	2°52·4′W	X	54
Hatton	Derby	SK2130	52°52·3′	1°40·9′W	T	128
Hatton	Fife	NT2287	56°4·4′	3°14·7′W	X	66
Hatton	Houns	TQ0975	51°28·0′	0°25·5′W	T	176
Hatton	Lincs	TF1776	53°16·3′	0°14·3′W	T	121
Hatton	Moray	NJ0964	57°39·7′	3°31·0′W	X	27
Hatton	Moray	NJ1253	57°33·8′	3°27·8′W	X	28
Hatton	Moray	NJ2741	57°27·5′	3°12·5′W	X	28
Hatton	Pth & Kin	NO0244	56°34·9′	3°35·3′W	X	52,53
Hatton	Pth & Kin	NO1737	56°31·3′	3°20·5′W	X	53
Hatton	Pth & Kin	NO1816	56°20·0′	3°19·1′W	X	58
Hatton	Pth & Kin	NO1847	56°36·7′	3°19·7′W	X	53
Hatton	Renf	NS4072	55°55·1′	4°33·2′W	X	64
Hatton	Shrops	SO4690	52°30·6′	2°47·3′W	T	137,138
Hatton	Warr	SJ5982	53°20·2′	2°36·5′W	T	108
Hatton	Warw	SP2367	52°18·3′	1°39·4′W	T	151
Hatton Bank Fm	Warw	SP2358	52°13·4′	1°39·4′W	FM	151
Hattonburn	Aberd	NJ7100	57°5·7′	2°28·3′W	X	38
Hattonburn	Arg & Bt	NS2484	56°1·3′	4°49·0′W	X	56
Hattonburn	Pth & Kin	NO1205	56°14·0′	3°24·7′W	X	58
Hatton Cairn	Angus	NO4741	56°33·7′	2°51·3′W	A	54
Hatton Castle	Aberd	NJ7546	57°30·5′	2°24·6′W	X	29
Hatton Cott	Warr	SJ5983	53°20·8′	2°36·5′W	X	108
Hatton Country World	Warw	SP2366	52°17·7′	1°39·4′W	X	151
Hattoncrook	Aberd	NJ8424	57°18·6′	2°15·5′W	X	38
Hatton Fields	Derby	SK2232	52°53·3′	1°40·0′W	X	128
Hatton Fm	Angus	NO5837	56°31·6′	2°40·5′W	FM	54

Hatton Fm	Ches	SJ4662	53°9·4′	2°48·0′W	FM	117
Hatton Fm	Fife	NO4004	56°13·7′	2°57·6′W	FM	59
Hatton Fm	Oxon	SU2897	51°40·5′	1°35·3′W	FM	163
Hatton Grange	Shrops	SJ7604	52°38·2′	2°20·9′W	T	127
Hattongrove Fm	Shrops	SO4689	52°30·0′	2°47·3′W	FM	137,138
Hatton Hall	Ches	SJ4761	53°8·9′	2°47·1′W	X	117
Hatton Heath	Ches	SJ4561	53°8·8′	2°48·9′W	T	117
Hattonheath Fm	Ches	SJ4560	53°8·3′	2°48·9′W	FM	117
Hatton Hill	Angus	NO3140	56°33·1′	3°6·9′W	H	53
Hattonhill	E Loth	NT4763	55°51·7′	2°50·4′W	X	66
Hatton Hill	Surrey	SU9364	51°22·3′	0°39·4′W	T	175,186
Hatton Hill Fm	Shrops	SJ7705	52°38·8′	2°20·0′W	FM	127
Hatton Ho	Angus	NO5936	56°31·1′	2°39·5′W	X	54
Hatton Ho	Ches	SJ4661	53°8·8′	2°48·0′W	X	117
Hatton Ho	C of Edin	NT1268	55°54·1′	3°24·0′W	X	65
Hatton Ho	Derby	SK2231	52°52·8′	1°40·0′W	X	128
Hatton Ho	Warw	SP2367	52°18·3′	1°39·4′W	X	151
Hatton House Fm	N Yks	SE2463	54°4·0′	1°37·6′W	FM	99
Hattonknowe	Scot Bord	NT2346	55°42·3′	3°13·1′W	T	73
Hatton Lane Fm	Warr	SJ6082	53°20·2′	2°35·6′W	FM	109
Hattonlaw	Fife	NO4003	56°13·2′	2°57·6′W	X	59
Hatton Lodge	Ches	SJ4562	53°9·4′	2°48·9′W	X	117
Hatton Lodge	Leic	SK6924	52°48·8′	0°58·2′W	X	129
Hatton Mains	C of Edin	NT1469	55°54·6′	3°22·1′W	X	65
Hatton Manor	Aberd	NJ7042	57°28·3′	2°29·6′W	X	29
Hatton Mill	Angus	NO6150	56°38·7′	2°37·7′W	X	54
Hatton of Ardoyne	Aberd	NJ6526	57°19·7′	2°34·4′W	X	38
Hatton of Eassie	Angus	NO3546	56°36·3′	3°3·1′W	X	54
Hatton of Fintray	Aberd	NJ8416	57°14·3′	2°15·4′W	T	38
Hatton of Ogilvie	Angus	NO3844	56°35·3′	3°0·1′W	T	54
Hatton Park	Northnts	SP8868	52°18·4′	0°42·2′W	T	152
Hatton Rock	Warw	SP2357	52°12·9′	1°39·4′W	X	151
Hatton's Fm	Suff	TM3581	52°22·8′	1°27·6′E	FM	156
Hattonslap	Aberd	NJ8133	57°23·5′	2°18·5′W	X	29,30
Hatton Sta	Warw	SP2266	52°17·7′	1°40·2′W	X	151
Hatton Wood	Lincs	TF1674	53°15·3′	0°15·3′W	F	121
Hattrick Fm	Inverc	NS3567	55°52·3′	4°37·8′W	FM	63
Hatts Barn	Dorset	ST9018	50°57·9′	2°8·2′W	X	184
Hatts Fm	Wilts	ST8725	51°1·7′	2°10·7′W	FM	183
Hatway Hill	Devon	SY1492	50°43·5′	3°12·7′W	X	192,193
Haud Yauds	Scot Bord	NT8368	55°54·5′	2°15·9′W	X	67
Haugh	Aberd	NO5697	57°4·0′	2°43·1′W	X	37,44
Haugh	Angus	NO4579	56°54·2′	2°53·7′W	X	44
Haugh	C of Edin	NT1172	55°56·2′	3°25·0′W	X	65
Haugh	E Ayr	NS4925	55°30·0′	4°23·0′W	T	70
Haugh	Lincs	TF4175	53°15·4′	0°7·2′E	T	122
Haugh	Northum	NT9336	55°37·3′	2°6·2′W	X	74,75
Haugh	Roch	SD9411	53°36·0′	2°5·0′W	T	109
Haugham	Lincs	TF3381	53°18·8′	0°0·2′E	T	122
Haugham Pasture	Lincs	TF3482	53°19·3′	0°1·1′E	F	122
Haugham Slates	Lincs	TF3481	53°18·8′	0°1·1′E	X	122
Haugham Wood	Lincs	TF3581	53°18·8′	0°2·0′E	F	122
Haugh Burn	W Loth	NT0275	55°57·7′	3°33·8′W	W	65
Haugh Corner	Norf	TM0888	52°27·2′	1°4·1′E	X	144
Haugh Cott	Clackm	NS8493	56°7·2′	3°51·5′W	X	58
Haughead	Angus	NO4462	56°45·0′	2°54·5′W	X	44
Haughead	Orkney	HY4010	58°58·6′	3°2·1′W	X	6
Haughend	Aberd	NO5991	57°0·8′	2°40·1′W	X	44
Haughend	Angus	NO5774	56°51·6′	2°41·9′W	X	44
Haughend	Pth & Kin	NO0214	56°18·8′	3°34·6′W	X	58
Haughend	Pth & Kin	NO0342	56°33·9′	3°34·3′W	X	52,53
Haughend	Pth & Kin	NO2946	56°36·3′	3°8·9′W	X	53
Haugh Field	N Yks	SD8754	53°59·2′	2°11·5′W	X	103
Haugh Fm	Durham	NY9624	54°36·9′	2°3·3′W	FM	91,92
Haugh Fm	Norf	TM0889	52°27·8′	1°4·1′E	FM	144
Haugh Fm	Suff	TM0362	52°13·3′	0°58·7′E	FM	155
Haugh Fm	Wilts	ST8062	51°21·6′	2°16·8′W	FM	173
Haughhead	Aberd	NO6872	56°50·6′	2°31·0′W	X	45
Haughhead	E Dunb	NS6079	55°59·3′	4°14·2′W	X	64
Haugh Head	Northum	NU0026	55°31·9′	1°59·6′W	T	75
Haugh-head	Scot Bord	NT3436	55°37·0′	3°2·4′W	T	73
Haughhead	S Lanak	NS7354	55°46·0′	4°1·0′W	X	64
Haughhead	S Lanak	NT1047	55°42·7′	3°25·5′W	X	72
Haughhead Fm	C of Edin	NT1365	55°52·5′	3°23·0′W	FM	65
Haugh Head Ho	Midlo	NT4261	55°50·6′	2°55·1′W	X	66
Haugh Hill	Stir	NS6884	56°2·1′	4°6·7′W	X	57,64
Haugh Island	Moray	NJ3253	57°34·0′	3°7·7′W	X	28
Haughland	Orkney	HY5217	59°2·5′	2°49·7′W	X	6
Haughley	Suff	TM0262	52°13·4′	0°57·8′E	T	155
Haughley Bushes	Suff	TM0160	52°12·3′	0°56·9′E	X	155
Haughley Green	Suff	TM0264	52°14·4′	0°57·9′E	T	155
Haughley New Street	Suff	TM0162	52°13·4′	0°57·0′E	T	155
Haughley Park	Suff	TM0061	52°12·9′	0°56·1′E	X	155
Haughmond Abbey	Shrops	SJ5415	52°44·1′	2°40·5′W	A	126
Haughmond Fm	Shrops	SJ5415	52°44·1′	2°40·5′W	FM	126
Haughmond Hill	Shrops	SJ5414	52°43·5′	2°40·5′W	X	126
Haughmuir	Angus	NO5859	56°43·5′	2°40·7′W	X	54
Haugh of Aberuthven	Pth & Kin	NN9817	56°20·3′	3°38·6′W	X	58
Haugh of Ballechin	Pth & Kin	NN9452	56°39·1′	3°43·3′W	X	52,53
Haugh of Blackgrange	Clackm	NS8492	56°6·7′	3°51·5′W	X	58
Haugh of Glass	Moray	NJ4239	57°26·5′	2°57·5′W	T	28
Haugh of Kercock	Pth & Kin	NO1339	56°32·4′	3°24·4′W	X	53
Haugh of Kilmorich	Pth & Kin	NN9950	56°38·1′	3°38·3′W	X	52,53
Haugh of Kilnmaichlie	Moray	NJ1833	57°23·1′	3°21·4′W	X	36
Haugh OF Maggie	Aberd	NJ6648	57°31·5′	2°33·6′W	X	29
Haugh of Sluie	Aberd	NO6296	57°3·5′	2°37·1′W	X	37,45
Haugh of Urr	D & G	NX8066	54°58·7′	3°52·1′W	T	84
Haugh Rigg	N Yks	SE8088	54°17·1′	0°45·8′W	X	94,100
Haugh Rigg	N Yks	SE8089	54°17·7′	0°45·8′W	X	94,100
Haughs	Aberd	NJ6838	57°26·1′	2°31·5′W	X	29
Haughs	Moray	NJ2747	57°30·7′	3°12·6′W	X	28
Haughs	Moray	NJ4151	57°33·0′	2°58·7′W	X	28
Haughs Bay	Aberd	NO8168	56°48·4′	2°18·2′W	W	45
Haughs End	Norf	TG3116	52°41·8′	1°25·5′E	X	133,134
Haughs of Airth	Falk	NS9186	56°3·5′	3°44·6′W	X	65
Haughs of Ashogle	Aberd	NJ7052	57°33·7′	2°29·6′W	X	29
Haughs of Ballinshoe	Angus	NO4253	56°40·2′	2°56·3′W	X	54
Haughs of Benholm	Aberd	NO8168	56°48·4′	2°18·2′W	X	45
Haughs of Clinterty	C of Aber	NJ8311	57°11·6′	2°16·4′W	X	38
Haughs of Cossans	Angus	NO4049	56°38·0′	2°58·2′W	X	54
Haughs of Cromdale	Highld	NJ0927	57°19·7′	3°30·2′W	X	36
Haughs of Finavon	Angus	NO5057	56°42·4′	2°48·6′W	X	54
Haughs of Grange	Moray	NJ4850	57°32·5′	2°51·7′W	X	28,29
Haughs of Kinnaird	Angus	NO6457	56°42·5′	2°34·8′W	X	54
Haughs of Pittentian	Pth & Kin	NN8719	56°21·2′	3°49·3′W	X	58
Haughs,The	Aberd	NJ5049	57°32·0′	2°49·6′W	X	29
Haughs, The	Aberd	NO8273	56°51·1′	2°17·3′W	X	45
Haughstrother Wood	Northum	NY7563	54°57·9′	2°23·0′W	F	86,87
Haughterslaw	Northum	NU1323	55°30·3′	1°47·2′W	X	75
Haugh, The	Aberd	NO4396	57°3·4′	2°55·9′W	X	37,44
Haugh, The	Derby	SK0183	53°20·9′	1°58·7′W	X	110
Haugh, The	Moray	NJ2643	57°28·5′	3°13·6′W	X	28
Haugh, The	Pth & Kin	NO2343	56°34·6′	3°14·8′W	X	53
Haughton	Aberd	NJ4612	57°12·0′	2°53·2′W	X	37
Haughton	Aberd	NJ7520	57°16·5′	2°24·4′W	X	38
Haughton	Notts	SK6772	53°14·7′	0°59·3′W	T	120
Haughton	Powys	SJ3018	52°45·5′	3°1·8′W	T	126
Haughton	Shrops	SJ3726	52°49·9′	2°55·7′W	T	126
Haughton	Shrops	SJ5516	52°44·6′	2°39·6′W	T	126
Haughton	Shrops	SJ7408	52°40·4′	2°22·7′W	T	127
Haughton	Shrops	SO6795	52°33·3′	2°28·8′W	T	138
Haughton	Staffs	SJ8620	52°46·9′	2°12·1′W	T	127
Haughton Castle	Northum	NY9172	55°2·8′	2°8·0′W	A	87
Haughton Common	Northum	NY8072	55°2·8′	2°18·4′W	X	86,87
Haughtondale	Staffs	SJ8721	52°47·4′	2°11·2′W	X	127
Haughton Fm	Powys	SJ3017	52°45·0′	3°1·8′W	FM	126
Haughton Fm	Shrops	SJ4035	52°54·8′	2°53·1′W	FM	126
Haughton Fm	Shrops	SJ7308	52°40·4′	2°23·6′W	FM	127
Haughtongreen	Northum	NY7871	55°2·2′	2°20·2′W	X	86,87
Haughton Green	Tames	SJ9393	53°26·3′	2°5·9′W	T	109
Haughton Hall Fm	Notts	SK6873	53°15·2′	0°58·4′W	FM	120
Haughton Hall School	Shrops	SJ7408	52°40·4′	2°22·7′W	X	127
Haughtonhill Fm	Shrops	SJ7409	52°40·9′	2°22·7′W	FM	127
Haughton Ho	Aberd	NJ5816	57°14·2′	2°41·3′W	X	37
Haughton Ho	Staffs	SJ8719	52°46·3′	2°11·2′W	X	127
Haughton Le Skerne	Darl	NZ3116	54°32·5′	1°30·8′W	T	93
Haughton Mains	Northum	NY9221	55°2·3′	2°7·1′W	X	87
Haughton Moss	Ches	SJ5756	53°6·2′	2°38·1′W	T	117
Haughton Park Ho	Notts	SK6873	53°15·2′	0°58·4′W	X	120
Haughton Pasture	Northum	NY9072	55°2·8′	2°9·0′W	X	87
Haughton Strother	Northum	NY8973	55°3·3′	2°9·9′W	X	87
Haughton Warren	Notts	SK6772	53°14·7′	0°59·3′W	X	120
Haughurst Hill	Hants	SU5762	51°21·5′	1°10·5′W	T	174
Haugh Wood	Heref	SO5936	52°1·5′	2°35·5′W	F	149
Haugh Wood	N Yks	SE7687	54°16·6′	0°49·5′W	F	94,100
Haugh Wood	N Yks	SE8086	54°16·0′	0°45·9′W	F	94,100
Haughyett	E Ayr	NS4926	55°30·5′	4°23·0′W	X	70
Haulfryn	Carm	SN4724	51°53·9′	4°13·0′W	X	159
Hault Fm	Kent	TR1149	51°12·3′	1°1·6′E	FM	179,189
Haulton Ring	Wrex	SJ4637	52°55·9′	2°47·8′W	X	126
Haulton Ring (Moat)	Wrex	SJ4637	52°55·9′	2°47·8′W	A	126
Haultwick	Herts	TL3323	51°53·6′	0°3·6′W	T	166
Haulwen	Pemb	SM9937	51°59·9′	4°55·3′W	X	157
Haun	N Eil	NF7911	57°4·9′	7°17·5′W	T	31
Haunches, The	D & G	NY4284	55°9·1′	2°54·2′W	X	79
Haunn	Arg & Bt	NM3347	56°32·6′	6°20·2′W	X	47,48
Haunton	Staffs	SK2310	52°41·5′	1°39·2′W	T	128
Haupland Muir	N Ayr	NS2347	55°41·3′	4°48·5′W	X	63
Hauplands	N Ayr	NS2246	55°40·7′	4°49·4′W	X	63
Hause	Cumbr	NY1109	54°28·4′	3°22·0′W	X	89
Hause Fm	Cumbr	NY4319	54°34·0′	2°52·5′W	FM	90
Hause Fm	Cumbr	NY5811	54°29·8′	2°38·5′W	FM	91
Hause Foot	Cumbr	NY5505	54°26·6′	2°41·2′W	X	90
Hause Gill	Cumbr	NY2313	54°30·6′	3°10·9′W	W	89,90
Hause in the Scar	Cumbr	NY6338	54°44·4′	2°34·1′W	X	91
Hause Point	Cumbr	NY1618	54°33·3′	3°17·5′W	X	89
Hause Point	Cumbr	NY3115	54°31·8′	3°3·6′W	X	90
Hause, The	Cumbr	NY4817	54°33·0′	2°47·8′W	X	90
Hautboyes	W Susx	TQ2914	50°54·9′	0°9·5′W	X	198
Hautville's Quoit	Bath & NE Somer	ST6063	51°22·1′	2°34·1′W	A	172
Hauxley Fm	Darl	NZ3221	54°35·2′	1°29·5′W	FM	93
Hauxley Haven	Northum	NU2902	55°18·9′	1°32·2′W	W	81
Hauxton	Cambs	TL4352	52°9·1′	0°5·8′E	T	154
Hauxwell Moor	N Yks	SE1595	54°21·3′	1°45·7′W	X	99
Havannah	Ches	SJ8764	53°10·6′	2°11·3′W	T	118
Havannah	Shrops	SJ7909	52°40·9′	2°18·2′W	X	127
Havannah Fm	Beds	TL2346	52°6·1′	0°11·9′W	FM	153
Havant	Hants	SU7106	50°51·2′	0°59·1′W	T	197
Havant Thicket	Hants	SU7110	50°53·3′	0°59·0′W	F	197
Havelock Ho	Lancs	SD5471	54°8·2′	2°41·8′W	X	97
Haven	Heref	SO4054	52°11·1′	2°52·3′W	T	148,149
Haven	Heref	SO4645	52°6·3′	2°46·9′W	X	148,149
Haven	Heref	SO5849	52°8·5′	2°36·4′W	T	149
Haven Ball	Devon	SY2590	50°42·5′	3°3·4′W	X	192,193
Haven Bank	Lincs	TF2352	53°3·3′	0°9·5′W	T	122
Havenbeach Marshes	Suff	TM5075	52°19·2′	1°40·5′E	X	156
Haven Cliff	Devon	SY2689	50°42·0′	3°2·5′W	X	192,193
Havenfields	Bucks	SP8902	51°42·8′	0°42·3′W	X	165
Haven Fm	Heref	SO3966	52°17·6′	2°53·3′W	FM	137,148,149
Havengore Head	Essex	TQ9888	51°33·6′	0°51·8′E	X	178
Havengore Island	Essex	TQ9789	51°34·1′	0°51·0′E	X	178
Haven Hill	Derby	SK2151	53°3·6′	1°40·8′W	H	119
Havenhills	Shrops	SJ7302	52°37·1′	2°23·5′W	X	127
Haven Ho	Suff	TM4758	52°10·1′	1°37·1′E	X	156
Havenhouse Fm	Derby	SK1237	52°56·1′	1°48·9′W	FM	128
Havenhouse Sta	Lincs	TF5259	53°6·6′	0°16·7′E	X	122
Haven Point	Essex	TQ9787	51°33·1′	0°50·9′E	X	178
Haven Point	Pemb	SM7509	51°44·3′	5°15·1′W	X	157
Havenstreet	I of W	SZ5690	50°42·6′	1°12·0′W	T	196
Haven, The	Highld	ND2574	58°39·1′	3°17·1′W	W	7,12
Haven, The	Highld	ND3543	58°22·5′	3°6·3′W	W	12
Haven, The	Lincs	TF3639	52°56·1′	0°1·8′E	W	131
Haven, The	Orkney	ND3985	58°45·2′	3°2·8′W	W	7
Haven, The	Suff	TM4758	52°10·1′	1°37·1′E	X	156
Haverah Park Top	N Yks	SE2254	53°59·1′	1°39·5′W	X	104
Haverbrack	Cumbr	SD4880	54°13·0′	2°47·4′W	X	97
Haver Close	N Yks	SE0976	54°11·0′	1°51·3′W	X	99
Havercroft	Cumbr	NY0722	54°35·3′	3°25·9′W	X	89
Havercroft	Wakf	SE3913	53°37·0′	1°24·2′W	T	110,111
Haverdale Ho	N Yks	SD9797	54°22·4′	2°2·4′W	X	98
Haverdale Ho	N Yks	SE9370	54°7·3′	0°34·2′W	X	101
Haverfield Ho	E Yorks	TA3321	53°40·3′	0°1·2′E	X	107,113
Haverfield Ho	N Yks	SE7476	54°10·7′	0°51·6′W	X	100
Haverflatts	Cumbr	SD5082	54°14·1′	2°45·6′W	X	97
Haverfordwest (Hwlffordd)	Pemb	SM9515	51°48·0′	4°58·0′W	T	157,158
Havergate Island Nature Reserve	Suff	TM4147	52°4·4′	1°31·4′E	X	169
Haverhill	Pemb	SM9823	51°52·4′	4°55·7′W	X	157,158
Haverhill	Suff	TL6645	52°4·9′	0°25·8′E	T	154
Haverhill Dale Brook	Derby	SK2152	53°4·1′	1°40·8′W	W	119
Haverhill Hall	Suff	TL6644	52°4·4′	0°25·7′E	X	154
Haverholme Ho	N Lincs	SE9512	53°36·0′	0°33·5′W	X	112
Haverholme Priory	Lincs	TF1049	53°1·9′	0°21·2′W	X	130
Haverigg	Cumbr	SD1578	54°11·7′	3°17·8′W	T	96
Haverigg Haws	Cumbr	SD1478	54°11·7′	3°18·7′W	X	96
Haverigg Holme	Cumbr	SD2691	54°18·8′	3°7·8′W	X	96,97
Haverigg Point	Cumbr	SD1477	54°11·1′	3°18·7′W	X	96
Haverigg Pool	Cumbr	SD1579	54°12·2′	3°17·8′W	W	96
Haveriggs	Cumbr	SD5597	54°22·2′	2°41·1′W	X	97
Haverigg Spit	Cumbr	SD1375	54°10·1′	3°19·5′W	X	96
Havering-atte-Bower	Hav	TQ5193	51°37·2′	0°11·3′E	T	177
Havering Country Park	Hav	TQ5093	51°37·2′	0°10·4′E	X	177
Havering Fm	Surrey	SU9954	51°16·8′	0°34·4′W	FM	186
Haveringland Hall	Norf	TG1521	52°44·9′	1°11·5′E	X	133
Havering Plain	Essex	TQ5494	51°37·6′	0°13·9′E	X	167,177
Haverland Fm	N Yks	SE5842	53°52·5′	1°6·7′W	FM	105
Haverlands Fm	Devon	ST2606	50°51·2′	3°2·7′W	FM	192,193
Haverlands Ho	Cumbr	NY2856	54°53·9′	3°6·9′W	X	85
Haverley Ho	Durham	NZ3848	54°49·8′	1°24·1′W	X	88
Haverscroft Ho	Norf	TM0393	52°30·0′	0°59·9′E	X	144
Haversham	Mil Key	SP8243	52°5·0′	0°47·8′W	T	152
Haversheaf Hall	Cumbr	NY5528	54°39·0′	2°41·4′W	X	90
Haverthwaite	Cumbr	SD3483	54°14·6′	3°0·3′W	T	96,97
Haverton Hill	Stock on T	NZ4822	54°35·7′	1°15·0′W	T	93
Haverwitz Fm	N Yks	SE5470	54°7·6′	1°10·0′W	FM	100
Haviker Street	Kent	TQ7246	51°11·5′	0°28·1′E	T	188
Havyatt	Somer	ST5237	51°8·0′	2°40·8′W	T	182,183
Havyatt Fm	N Som	ST4761	51°21·0′	2°45·3′W	FM	172,182
Havyatt Green	N Som	ST4760	51°20·4′	2°45·3′W	T	172,182
Hawarden Airport	Flint	SJ3465	53°10·9′	2°58·9′W	X	117
Hawarden Br	Flint	SJ3069	53°13·1′	3°2·5′W	X	117
Hawarden Bridge Sta	Flint	SJ3169	53°13·1′	3°1·6′W	X	117
Hawarden Castle	Flint	SJ3265	53°10·9′	3°0·6′W	X	117
Hawarden or Penarlâg	Flint	SJ3165	53°10·9′	3°1·5′W	T	117
Haw Beck	N Yks	SD9887	54°17·0′	2°1·4′W	W	98
Haw Beck	N Yks	SE0153	53°58·6′	1°58·7′W	W	104
Haw Birren	D & G	NY2292	55°13·2′	3°13·1′W	X	79
Haw Birren (Fort)	D & G	NY2292	55°13·2′	3°13·1′W	A	79
Haw Br	Glos	SO8427	51°56·8′	2°13·6′W	X	162
Hawbridge	Worcs	SO9049	52°8·6′	2°8·4′W	T	150
Hawbridge Fm	Hants	SU7441	51°10·0′	0°56·1′W	FM	186
Haw Burn	S Ayr	NX2277	55°3·6′	4°46·8′W	W	76
Haw Burn	S Lanak	NS9433	55°35·0′	3°40·5′W	W	71,72
Hawbushes Fm	Bucks	SU8897	51°40·1′	0°43·3′W	FM	165
Hawbush Fm	Herts	TL0611	51°47·5′	0°27·4′W	FM	166
Hawbush Fm	Suff	TL7252	52°8·6′	0°31·2′E	FM	154
Hawbush Green	Essex	TL7820	51°51·2′	0°35·5′E	T	167
Hawcoat	Cumbr	SD2071	54°8·0′	3°13·0′W	T	96
Hawcocks Fm	Shrops	SJ3407	52°39·6′	2°58·1′W	FM	126
Hawcroft Fm	Kent	TR1761	51°18·6′	1°7·2′E	FM	179
Hawcross	Glos	SO7530	51°58·3′	2°21·4′W	T	150
Hawddamor	Gwyn	SH6819	52°45·4′	3°57·0′W	T	124
Hawden Fm	Kent	TQ5747	51°12·3′	0°15·2′E	FM	188
Hawdin's Wood	Lincs	SK8760	53°8·0′	0°41·6′W	F	121
Hawdref-fawr	Nth Pt Talb	SS7794	51°38·1′	3°46·3′W	X	170
Hawe Fm	Kent	TR1966	51°21·3′	1°9·1′E	FM	179
Hawell	Orkney	HY5106	58°56·6′	2°50·6′W	X	6,7
Hawen	Cered	SN3446	52°5·5′	4°25·0′W	T	145
Hawerby Hall	NE Lincs	TF2697	53°27·5′	0°5·7′W	X	113
Hawerby Hall Fm	NE Lincs	TF2598	53°28·1′	0°6·6′W	FM	113
Hawes	Cumbr	NY0717	54°32·6′	3°25·8′W	X	89
Hawes	Cumbr	SD2190	54°18·2′	3°12·4′W	X	96
Hawes	Cumbr	SD5088	54°17·4′	2°45·7′W	X	97
Hawes	N Yks	SD8789	54°18·0′	2°11·6′W	T	98
Hawes End	Cumbr	NY2421	54°35·0′	3°10·1′W	X	89,90
Hawes Fm	Kent	TR1544	51°9·5′	1°4·9′E	FM	179,189
Hawes' Green	Norf	TM2399	52°32·8′	1°17·7′E	T	134
Hawes Ho	Lancs	SD3636	53°49·2′	2°57·9′W	X	102
Hawes Ho	Lancs	SD5662	54°3·4′	2°39·9′W	X	97
Hawesrew Fm	Surrey	TQ1845	51°11·7′	0°18·3′W	FM	187
Hawes Side	Blackp	SD3234	53°48·1′	3°1·5′W	T	102
Hawes, The	Cumbr	SD0986	54°15·9′	3°23·4′W	X	96
Hawes Water	Lancs	SD4776	54°10·9′	2°48·3′W	W	97
Haweswater Beck	Cumbr	NY5216	54°32·5′	2°44·1′W	W	90
Haweswater Reservoir	Cumbr	NY4814	54°31·4′	2°47·8′W	W	90
Hawe's Wood	Essex	TQ8199	51°39·9′	0°37·4′E	F	168
Hawes Wood	Kent	TQ8666	51°22·0′	0°40·7′E	F	178
Haw Fell	N Yks	SD9274	54°9·9′	2°6·9′W	X	98
Hawfield	Glos	SO6707	51°45·9′	2°28·3′W	X	162
Haw Fm	N Yks	SE0083	54°14·8′	1°59·6′W	FM	98
Haw Fm	W Berks	SU5477	51°29·6′	1°12·9′W	FM	174
Hawford	Worcs	SO8460	52°14·5′	2°13·7′W	T	138,150
Hawford Burn	E Ayr	NS4612	55°22·9′	4°25·4′W	W	70
Hawford Ho	Worcs	SO8459	52°14·0′	2°13·7′W	X	150
Hawgreen	Shrops	SJ6225	52°49·5′	2°33·4′W	T	127
Hawhaw, The	Bath & NE Somer	ST6462	51°21·6′	2°30·6′W	X	172
Haw Head	N Yks	SD9786	54°16·4′	2°2·3′W	X	98
Hawhill	N Ayr	NS2951	55°43·6′	4°42·9′W	X	63
Hawhills Fm	Beds	TL0540	52°3·1′	0°27·7′W	FM	153
Ha Wick	Orkney	ND2489	58°47·2′	3°18·4′W	W	7
Hawick	Scot Bord	NT5015	55°25·8′	2°47·0′W	T	79
Hawick Crags	Northum	NY9682	55°8·2′	2°3·3′W	H	81
Hawick Fm	Northum	NY9682	55°8·2′	2°3·3′W	FM	81
Hawickshiel	Scot Bord	NT5442	55°40·4′	2°43·4′W	X	73
Hawkadon	Devon	SX3689	50°40·9′	4°18·9′W	X	190
Hawk Aller	Devon	SS9706	50°50·9′	3°27·4′W	X	192
Hawkbarrow Fm	Cumbr	NY0904	54°25·6′	3°23·7′W	FM	89

Hawkbatch Valleys	Worcs	SO7677	52°23·7'	2°20·8'W	X	138
Hawk Burn	Northum	NT7504	55°20·0'	2°23·2'W	W	80
Hawkchurch	Devon	ST3400	50°48·0'	2°55·8'W	T	193
Hawkcliffe Fm	Brad	SE0444	53°53·8'	1°55·9'W	FM	104
Hawk Combe	Somer	SS8745	51°11·8'	3°36·7'W	F	181
Hawkcombe	Somer	SS8846	51°12·4'	3°35·8'W	T	181
Hawkcombe Head	Somer	SS8445	51°11·8'	3°39·2'W	X	181
Hawk Conservancy, The	Hants	SU3045	51°12·4'	1°33·8'W	X	185
Hawk Crag	Cumbr	NY4116	54°32·4'	2°54·3'W	X	90
Hawk Craig	Stir	NN3823	56°22·6'	4°37·0'W	X	50
Hawkcraig Point	Fife	NT2084	56°2·8'	3°16·6'W	X	66
Hawkdown	Devon	SS5710	50°52·5'	4°1·6'W	X	191
Hawke Channel		TA3612	53°35·4'	0°3·7'E	W	113
Hawkedon	Suff	TL7952	52°8·5'	0°37·4'E	T	155
Hawkedon Ho	Suff	TL7953	52°9·0'	0°37·4'E	X	155
Hawkenbury	Kent	TQ5938	51°7·4'	0°16·7'E	T	188
Hawkenbury	Kent	TQ8045	51°10·8'	0°34·9'E	T	188
Hawkeridge	Wilts	ST8653	51°16·8'	2°11·7'W	T	183
Hawkerland	Devon	SY0588	50°41·3'	3°20·3'W	T	192
Hawkerland Valley	Devon	SY0589	50°41·8'	3°20·3'W	X	192
Hawker's Cove	Corn	SW9177	50°33·6'	4°56·7'W	W	200
Hawker's Fm	Dorset	ST8121	50°59·5'	2°15·9'W	FM	183
Hawker's Fm	Glos	SO8329	51°57·8'	2°14·5'W	FM	150
Hawker's Hill Fm	Norf	TF8142	52°56·9'	0°42·1'E	FM	132
Hawker's Hut	Corn	SS1915	50°54·6'	4°34·1'W	X	190
Hawkersland Cross	Heref	SO5347	52°7·4'	2°40·8'W	T	149
Hawkes Ball	Devon	SX7769	50°30·7'	3°43·7'W	X	202
Hawkesbury	S Glos	ST7686	51°34·6'	2°20·4'W	T	172
Hawkesbury	Warw	SP3684	52°27·4'	1°27·8'W	T	140
Hawkesbury Common	S Glos	ST7587	51°35·1'	2°21·3'W	X	172
Hawkesbury Knott	S Glos	ST7687	51°35·1'	2°20·4'W	X	172
Hawkesbury Upton	S Glos	ST7886	51°34·6'	2°18·7'W	T	172
Hawkesdown Hill	Devon	SY2691	50°43·1'	3°2·5'W	X	192,193
Hawkesdown Hill (Fort)	Devon	SY2691	50°43·1'	3°2·5'W	A	192,193
Hawkes End	Cov	SP2982	52°26·3'	1°34·0'W	T	140
Hawkes Fm	Essex	TL6535	51°59·6'	0°24·6'E	FM	154
Hawke Sike	Durham	NY9143	54°47·2'	2°8·0'W	W	87
Hawkesley	Birm	SP0477	52°23·7'	1°56·1'W	T	139
Hawkeswell Fm	Warw	SP2187	52°29·1'	1°41·0'W	FM	139
Hawkfield	Cumbr	SD2573	54°9·1'	3°8·5'W	X	96
Hawk Fm	Essex	TM1423	51°52·1'	1°6·9'E	FM	168,169
Hawk Green	Stock	SJ9587	53°23·0'	2°4·1'W	T	109
Hawkhall	Aberd	NJ6241	57°27·7'	2°37·5'W	X	29
Hawkham Hollow	Shrops	SO4397	52°34·3'	2°50·1'W	X	137
Hawkhass	Scot Bord	NT4802	55°18·8'	2°48·7'W	X	79
Hawkhill	Aberd	NJ9356	57°35·9'	2°6·6'W	X	30
Hawkhill	Angus	NO6851	56°39·2'	2°30·5'W	X	54
Hawk Hill	Cumbr	NY0029	54°39·0'	3°32·6'W	T	89
Hawkhill	Fife	NS9288	56°4·6'	3°43·7'W	X	65
Hawkhill	N Ayr	NS2742	55°38·7'	4°44·5'W	X	63,70
Hawkhill	Northum	NU2212	55°24·3'	1°38·7'W	T	81
Hawk Hill	Oxon	SP4230	51°58·2'	1°22·9'W	X	151
Hawkhill	S Ayr	NX2299	55°15·4'	4°47·6'W	X	76
Hawk Hill	Scot Bord	NT4802	55°18·8'	2°48·7'W	H	79
Hawkhill Fm	Aberd	NO7580	56°54·9'	2°24·2'W	FM	45
Hawkhill Inclosure	Hants	SU3502	50°49·2'	1°29·8'W	F	196
Hawkhillock	Aberd	NJ8029	57°21·3'	2°19·5'W	X	38
Hawk Hills	Staffs	SK1422	52°48·0'	1°47·1'W	X	128
Hawkhills Beck	N Yks	SE5467	54°6·0'	1°10·0'W	W	100
Hawkhills, The	N Yks	SE5367	54°6·0'	1°11·0'W	X	100
Hawk Hirst	Northum	NY8079	55°6·5'	2°18·4'W	X	86,87
Hawkhope	Northum	NY7188	55°11·4'	2°26·9'W	T	80
Hawkhope	Northum	NY7189	55°11·9'	2°26·9'W	X	80
Hawkhope Burn	Northum	NY7191	55°13·0'	2°26·9'W	W	80
Hawkhope Hill	Northum	NY7288	55°11·4'	2°26·0'W	X	80
Hawkhouse Green	Donc	SE6013	53°36·8'	1°5·2'W	X	111
Hawkhurst	Heref	SO6054	52°11·2'	2°34·7'W	X	149
Hawkhurst	Kent	TQ7630	51°2·8'	0°31·0'E	T	188
Hawkhurst Common	E Susx	TQ5218	50°56·7'	0°10·2'E	T	199
Hawkhurst Common Wood	E Susx	TQ5319	50°57·2'	0°11·1'E	F	199
Hawkhurst Court	W Susx	TQ0223	51°0·1'	0°32·4'W	X	197
Hawkhurst Head	Derby	SJ9981	53°19·8'	2°0·5'W	X	109
Hawking Craig	N Ayr	NS1750	55°42·8'	4°54·3'W	X	63
Hawking Down	Wilts	ST9033	51°6·0'	2°8·2'W	X	184
Hawkinge	Kent	TR2140	51°7·2'	1°9·9'E	T	179,189
Hawking Grove	Shrops	SO6596	52°33·9'	2°30·6'W	F	138
Hawking Hall	Cumbr	SD6185	54°15·8'	2°35·5'W	X	97
Hawking Sopers	W Susx	TQ1515	50°55·6'	0°21·4'W	X	198
Hawkington	Somer	SS8939	51°8·6'	3°34·8'W	X	181
Hawkins Fm	Bucks	SU8288	51°35·3'	0°48·6'W	FM	175
Hawkins Fm	Dorset	ST6813	50°55·2'	2°26·9'W	FM	194
Hawkins Fm	Suff	TM0964	52°14·3'	1°4·1'E	FM	155
Hawkins Hall Fm	Herts	TL2718	51°51·0'	0°9·0'W	FM	166
Hawkin's Harvest	Essex	TL7030	51°56·8'	0°28·8'E	X	167
Hawkin's Hill	Essex	TL6633	51°58·5'	0°25·4'E	T	167
Hawkin's Point	E Yorks	TA2816	53°37·9'	0°4·3'W	X	113
Hawkins Pond	W Susx	TQ2129	51°3·1'	0°16·0'W	W	187,198
Hawkins, The	Heref	SO6851	52°9·6'	2°27·7'W	X	149
Hawkins Wood	Hants	SU7444	51°11·7'	0°56·1'W	F	186
Hawkins Wood	Herts	TL3334	51°59·5'	0°3·4'W	F	154
Hawk Knowe	Northum	NY7194	55°14·6'	2°26·9'W	X	80
Hawk Lake	Shrops	SJ5730	52°52·2'	2°37·9'W	W	126
Hawklaw	Fife	NO3715	56°19·6'	3°0·7'W	X	59
Hawklawtongues	Scot Bord	NT5604	55°19·9'	2°41·2'W	X	80
Hawkley	Hants	SU7429	51°3·6'	0°56·3'W	T	186,197
Hawkley	Wigan	SD5703	53°31·6'	2°38·5'W	T	108
Hawkley Fm	Worcs	SO7469	52°19·3'	2°22·5'W	FM	138
Hawkley Hurst	Hants	SU7530	51°4·1'	0°55·4'W	X	186
Hawk Mill Fm	Cambs	TL5358	52°12·2'	0°14·7'E	FM	154
Hawkmoor House Fm	Devon	SX4373	50°32·4'	4°12·6'W	FM	201
Hawknest Rig	D & G	NY4193	55°13·9'	2°55·2'W	X	79
Hawkridge	Somer	SS8630	51°3·7'	3°37·2'W	T	181
Hawkridge Barton	Devon	SS6125	51°0·7'	3°58·5'W	X	180
Hawkridge Brook	Devon	SS6125	51°0·7'	3°58·5'W	W	180
Hawkridge Common	Somer	SS8531	51°4·2'	3°38·1'W	H	181
Hawkridge Common	Somer	ST2035	51°6·8'	3°8·2'W	X	182
Hawkridge Fm	Devon	SS6909	50°52·3'	3°51·3'W	FM	191
Hawkridge Fm	W Berks	SU5472	51°26·9'	1°13·0'W	FM	174
Hawkridge Ho	W Berks	SU5372	51°26·9'	1°13·8'W	X	174
Hawkridge Plain	Somer	SS8332	51°4·8'	3°39·8'W	X	181
Hawkridge Resr	Somer	ST2036	51°7·3'	3°8·2'W	W	182
Hawkridge Ridge	Somer	SS8630	51°3·7'	3°37·2'W	X	181
Hawkridge Wood	W Berks	SU5472	51°26·9'	1°13·0'W	F	174
Hawkrigg	Cumbr	NY6520	54°34·7'	2°32·1'W	X	91
Hawkrigg	Cumbr	SD5591	54°19·0'	2°41·1'W	X	97
Hawkrigg	Cumbr	SD5982	54°14·2'	2°37·3'W	X	97
Hawkrigg Ho	Cumbr	NY2346	54°48·4'	3°11·5'W	X	85
Hawksdale	Cumbr	NY3648	54°49·6'	2°59·3'W	T	85
Hawksdale Hall	Cumbr	NY3747	54°49·1'	2°58·4'W	X	85
Hawksdale Pasture	Cumbr	NY3647	54°49·1'	2°59·3'W	X	85
Hawksden Park Wood	E Susx	TQ6126	51°0·9'	0°18·1'E	F	188,199
Hawksford	W Susx	SU8928	51°2·9'	0°43·4'W	X	186,197
Hawks Geo	Shetld	HU6688	60°34·5'	0°47·2'W	X	1,2
Hawks Green	Staffs	SJ9910	52°41·5'	2°0·5'W	T	127
Hawksground	Corn	SX1883	50°37·3'	4°34·0'W	X	201
Hawks Grove	Wilts	SU2328	51°3·3'	1°39·9'W	F	184
Hawkshaw	Bury	SD7515	53°38·1'	2°22·3'W	T	109
Hawkshaw	Scot Bord	NT0722	55°29·2'	3°27·9'W	X	72
Hawkshaw Burn	Scot Bord	NT0719	55°27·6'	3°27·8'W	W	78
Hawkshaw Burn	Scot Bord	NT0720	55°28·2'	3°27·8'W	W	72
Hawkshaw Gill Wood	N Yks	SE1863	54°4·0'	1°43·1'W	F	99
Hawkshead	Cumbr	SD3598	54°22·6'	2°59·6'W	T	96,97
Hawkshead	Lancs	SD5265	54°5·0'	2°43·6'W	X	97
Hawkshead	Lancs	SD5362	54°3·4'	2°42·7'W	X	97
Hawkshead	Lancs	SD6360	54°2·3'	2°33·5'W	H	97
Hawkshead Hall Park	Cumbr	SD3397	54°22·1'	3°1·5'W	F	96,97
Hawkshead Hill	Cumbr	SD3398	54°22·6'	3°1·5'W	T	96,97
Hawkshead Moor	Cumbr	SD3496	54°21·6'	3°0·5'W	X	96,97
Hawksheads	Lancs	SD4968	54°6·6'	2°46·4'W	X	97
Hawkshead Wood	Herts	TL2202	51°42·4'	0°13·7'W	F	166
Hawks Heath Fm	N Yks	SD7165	54°5·1'	2°26·2'W	FM	98
Hawkshill	Aberd	NJ8716	57°14·3'	2°12·5'W	X	38
Hawks Hill	Bucks	SU9086	51°34·2'	0°41·7'W	T	175
Hawk's Hill	Surrey	TQ1555	51°17·2'	0°20·7'W	T	187
Hawkshill Down	Kent	TR3749	51°11·7'	1°23·9'E	X	179
Hawkshole	D & G	NY3776	55°4·7'	2°58·8'W	X	85
Hawkshutts, The	Staffs	SJ8509	52°40·9'	2°12·9'W	X	127
Hawk Side	Northum	NY7972	55°2·8'	2°19·3'W	X	86,87
Hawk Sikes	Durham	NY9643	54°47·2'	2°3·3'W	W	87
Hawksland	Corn	SW9571	50°30·4'	4°53·1'W	X	200
Hawksland	Devon	SS6106	50°50·4'	3°58·1'W	X	191
Hawksland	S Lanak	NS8439	55°37·3'	3°50·1'W	X	71,72
Hawkslaw	Scot Bord	NT8143	55°41·1'	2°17·7'W	X	74
Hawkslee	Ches	SJ9365	53°11·2'	2°5·9'W	X	118
Hawksley Fm	Notts	SK7475	53°16·2'	0°53·0'W	FM	120
Hawksley Hill	Durham	NZ0321	54°35·3'	1°56·8'W	X	92
Hawk's Leys	Suff	TL8155	52°10·0'	0°39·2'E	X	155
Hawks Low	Derby	SK1756	53°6·3'	1°44·4'W	A	119
Hawkslow Fm	Derby	SK1756	53°6·3'	1°44·4'W	FM	119
Hawksmoor	Shrops	SJ6640	52°57·6'	2°30·0'W	X	118
Hawk's Moor	Somer	ST2216	50°56·5'	3°6·2'W	X	193
Hawksmoor Wood	Staffs	SK0344	52°59·8'	1°56·9'W	F	119,128
Hawksneet Copse	Oxon	SP3416	51°50·7'	1°30·0'W	F	164
Hawks Ness	Shetld	HU4648	60°13·1'	1°9·7'W	X	3
Hawks Ness	Shetld	HU6097	60°39·4'	0°53·6'W	X	1
Hawk's Nest	Hants	SU5814	50°55·6'	1°10·1'W	X	196
Hawk's Nest	Kent	TQ9551	51°13·7'	0°48·0'E	X	189
Hawk's Nest	Northum	NT9501	55°18·4'	2°4·3'W	X	81
Hawksnest	N Yks	SE4099	54°23·3'	1°22·6'W	X	99
Hawksnest	Scot Bord	NT4941	55°39·8'	2°48·2'W	X	73
Hawk's Nest	Staffs	SK0167	53°12·2'	1°58·7'W	X	119
Hawk's Nest Wood	Leeds	SE4134	53°48·3'	1°22·2'W	F	105
Hawk's Nib	Arg & Bt	NS1153	55°44·3'	5°0·2'W	X	63
Hawkspur Green	Essex	TL6532	51°57·9'	0°24·5'E	T	167
Hawks Stones	Cald	SD9227	53°44·6'	2°6·9'W	T	103
Hawksteel	Northum	NY8055	54°53·6'	2°18·3'W	X	86,87
Hawk Stone	Oxon	SP3323	51°54·5'	1°30·8'W	A	164
Hawkstone Abbey Fm	Shrops	SJ5730	52°52·2'	2°37·9'W	FM	126
Hawkstone Fm	Leeds	SE1741	53°52·1'	1°44·1'W	FM	104
Hawkstone Hall	Shrops	SJ5829	52°51·7'	2°37·0'W	A	126
Hawkstone Hall (Pastoral Centre)	Shrops	SJ5829	52°51·7'	2°37·0'W	X	126
Hawkstone Park	Shrops	SJ5729	52°51·6'	2°37·9'W	X	126
Hawk's Tor	Corn	SX1475	50°32·9'	4°37·2'W	H	200
Hawk's Tor	Corn	SX2576	50°33·7'	4°27·9'W	H	201
Hawks' Tor	Devon	SX5562	50°26·6'	4°2·2'W	X	202
Hawkstor Downs	Corn	SX1475	50°32·9'	4°37·2'W	X	200
Hawk's Tor Fm	Corn	SX1374	50°32·4'	4°38·0'W	FM	200
Hawkswell	Cumbr	SD2783	54°14·5'	3°6·8'W	X	96,97
Hawkswell Fm	Beds	SP9856	52°11·8'	0°33·6'W	FM	153
Hawkswick	N Yks	SD9570	54°7·8'	2°4·2'W	T	98
Hawkswick Clowder	N Yks	SD9468	54°6·7'	2°5·1'W	X	98
Hawkswick Cote	N Yks	SD9470	54°7·8'	2°5·1'W	X	98
Hawkswick Moor	N Yks	SD9571	54°8·3'	2°4·2'W	X	98
Hawkswick Wood	N Yks	SD9471	54°8·3'	2°5·1'W	F	98
Hawk's Wood	Bucks	TQ0186	51°34·1'	0°32·2'W	F	176
Hawk's Wood	Kent	TQ5544	51°10·7'	0°13·4'E	F	188
Hawks Wood	Roth	SK5281	53°19·6'	1°12·7'W	F	111,120
Hawkswood	Shrops	SO6984	52°27·4'	2°27·0'W	X	138
Hawkswood Fm	Heref	SO2543	52°5·1'	3°5·3'W	FM	148,161
Hawkswood Fm	Shrops	SJ3729	52°51·5'	2°55·7'W	FM	126
Hawksworth	Leeds	SE1641	53°52·1'	1°45·0'W	T	104
Hawksworth	Leeds	SE2537	53°50·0'	1°36·8'W	T	104
Hawksworth	Notts	SK7543	52°59·0'	0°52·6'W	T	129
Hawksworth Moor	Leeds	SE1443	53°53·2'	1°46·8'W	X	104
Hawksworth Shaw	Leeds	SE1443	53°53·2'	1°46·8'W	X	104
Hawk, The	Cumbr	SD2492	54°19·3'	3°9·7'W	X	96
Hawktree Moors	Somer	SS8725	51°1·0'	3°36·3'W	X	181
Hawkuplee	Northum	NY7851	54°51·4'	2°20·1'W	X	86,87
Hawkwell	Devon	SS3511	50°52·7'	4°20·3'W	X	190
Hawkwell	Essex	TQ8591	51°35·5'	0°40·6'E	T	178
Hawkwell	Northum	NZ0771	55°2·3'	1°53·0'W	X	88
Hawkwell Cross	Devon	SS8725	51°1·0'	3°36·3'W	X	181
Hawkwell Fm	Kent	TQ6343	51°10·0'	0°20·3'E	FM	188
Hawkwell Fm	Oxon	SP5624	51°54·9'	1°10·8'W	FM	164
Hawkwell Fm	Somer	SS8725	51°1·0'	3°36·3'W	FM	181
Hawkwell Hall Fm	Essex	TQ8691	51°35·5'	0°41·5'E	FM	178
Hawkwell Head	Durham	NY8737	54°43·9'	2°11·7'W	X	91,92
Hawkwillow Burn	Scot Bord	NT7508	55°22·2'	2°23·2'W	W	80
Hawkwood	Brom	TQ4469	51°24·3'	0°4·6'E	X	177
Hawkwood	Glos	SO8506	51°45·4'	2°12·6'W	X	162
Hawkwood	S Lanak	NS6839	55°37·9'	4°5·4'W	X	71
Hawkwood Head	Durham	NZ0032	54°41·2'	1°59·6'W	X	92
Hawkwood Hill	S Lanak	NS6838	55°37·3'	4°5·3'W	H	71
Hawkwood Hill	S Lanak	NS9624	55°30·2'	3°38·4'W	H	72
Hawkwoods	Essex	TL7631	51°57·2'	0°34·1'E	X	167
Hawley	Hants	SU8558	51°19·1'	0°46·4'W	T	175,186
Hawley	Kent	TQ5471	51°25·2'	0°13·3'E	T	177
Hawley Bottom	Devon	ST2300	50°47·9'	3°5·2'W	T	192,193
Hawley Common	Hants	SU8458	51°19·1'	0°47·3'W	X	175,186
Hawley Hill	Hants	SU8458	51°19·1'	0°47·3'W	X	175,186
Hawley Ho	Hants	SU5961	51°20·9'	1°8·8'W	X	174
Hawley Lake	Hants	SU8457	51°18·6'	0°47·3'W	W	175,186
Hawley Lane	Hants	SU8657	51°18·6'	0°45·6'W	T	175,186
Hawley Park	Hants	SU8558	51°19·1'	0°46·4'W	X	175,186
Hawley's Corner	Brom	TQ4356	51°17·3'	0°3·4'E	X	187
Hawling	Glos	SP0623	51°54·6'	1°54·4'W	T	163
Hawling Lodge	Glos	SP0823	51°54·6'	1°52·6'W	X	163
Hawlk Hill	E Ayr	NS7326	55°30·9'	4°0·2'W	X	71
Haw Moss	D & G	NY0598	55°16·3'	3°29·3'W	X	78
Hawn	Orkney	HY4426	59°7·3'	2°58·2'W	X	5,6
Hawnby	N Yks	SE5489	54°17·9'	1°9·8'W	T	100
Hawnby Moor	N Yks	SE5392	54°19·5'	1°10·7'W	X	100
Hawne	Dudley	SO9684	52°27·5'	2°3·1'W	T	139
Haworth	Brad	SE0337	53°50·0'	1°56·9'W	T	104
Haworth Moor	Brad	SE0035	53°48·9'	1°59·6'W	X	104
Haw Park	N Yks	SE0152	53°58·1'	1°58·7'W	X	104
Haw Park	Wakf	SE3615	53°38·1'	1°26·9'W	F	110,111
Hawpark Fm	Glos	ST7592	51°37·8'	2°21·3'W	FM	162,172
Haw Pike	N Yks	SE0652	53°58·1'	1°54·1'W	H	104
Hawpike Fm	N Yks	SE0652	53°58·1'	1°54·1'W	FM	104
Hawridge Common	Bucks	SP9406	51°44·9'	0°37·9'W	X	165
Hawridge Court	Bucks	SP9405	51°44·4'	0°37·9'W	X	165
Haws	N Yks	SD9544	53°53·8'	2°4·2'W	X	103
Haws Bank	Cumbr	SD2262	54°3·1'	3°11·1'W	X	96
Haws Bank	Cumbr	SD3096	54°21·5'	3°4·2'W	T	96,97
Haws Bed	Cumbr	SD2162	54°3·1'	3°12·0'W	X	96
Hawse Burn	D & G	NX5185	55°8·5'	4°19·8'W	W	77
Hawse Fm	Newp	ST2882	51°32·2'	3°1·9'W	FM	171
Hawsen Burn	Northum	NT9423	55°30·3'	2°5·3'W	W	74,75
Hawse of Halla	Shetld	HU6493	60°37·2'	0°49·3'W	X	1,2
Hawset	N Yks	SE1873	54°9·4'	1°43·0'W	X	99
Haws Gill Wheel	N Yks	SD7478	54°12·1'	2°23·5'W	X	98
Hawshaw Moor	N Yks	SD9444	53°53·8'	2°5·1'W	X	103
Haw's Hill	Essex	TL5645	52°5·1'	0°17·0'E	X	154
Haws Hill	Worcs	SO6065	52°17·1'	2°34·8'W	X	138,149
Haws Hill Fm	Win & Maid	SU8975	51°28·2'	0°42·7'W	FM	175
Haws Ho	Cumbr	SD1883	54°14·4'	3°15·1'W	X	96
Hawsker Bottoms	N Yks	NZ9407	54°27·2'	0°32·6'W	X	94
Hawsker Hall Fm	N Yks	NZ9207	54°27·2'	0°34·4'W	FM	94
Hawson Court	Devon	SX7168	50°30·1'	3°48·8'W	X	202
Hawson Hills	Suff	TL7162	52°14·0'	0°30·6'E	X	154
Haws Point	Cumbr	SD2362	54°3·1'	3°10·2'W	X	96
Haws Scar	Cumbr	SD2263	54°3·7'	3°11·1'W	X	96
Hawstead	Suff	TL8559	52°12·1'	0°42·8'E	T	155
Hawstead Fm	Hants	SU4223	51°0·5'	1°23·7'W	FM	185
Hawstead Green	Suff	TL8658	52°11·6'	0°43·7'E	T	155
Hawstead Hall	Suff	TL8659	52°12·1'	0°43·6'E	X	155
Hawstead Lodge	Suff	TL8460	52°12·7'	0°42·0'E	X	155
Hawstead Place	Suff	TL8459	52°12·1'	0°42·0'E	X	155
Haws Wood	Cumbr	SD3890	54°18·4'	2°56·8'W	F	96,97
Haws Wood	Suff	TL8156	52°10·6'	0°39·2'E	F	155
Haw, The	Glos	SO8427	51°56·7'	2°13·6'W	X	162
Hawthorn	Durham	NZ4145	54°48·1'	1°21·3'W	T	88
Hawthorn	Hants	SU6733	51°5·8'	1°2·2'W	T	185,186
Hawthorn	Heref	SO5163	52°16·0'	2°42·7'W	X	137,138,149
Hawthorn	N Yks	SD9888	54°17·5'	2°1·4'W	X	98
Hawthorn	Rho Cyn Taf	ST0988	51°35·2'	3°18·4'W	T	171
Hawthorn	Scot Bord	NT4033	55°35·5'	2°56·7'W	X	73
Hawthorn	Wilts	ST8469	51°25·4'	2°13·4'W	X	173
Hawthorn Burn	Durham	NZ4245	54°48·1'	1°20·4'W	W	88
Hawthorn Bush	Worcs	SO7774	52°22·1'	2°19·9'W	X	138
Hawthorn Clough	Derby	SE1200	53°30·0'	1°48·7'W	X	110
Hawthorn Corner	Kent	TR0223	50°58·5'	0°53·0'E	X	189
Hawthorn Corner	Kent	TR2167	51°21·8'	1°10·9'E	T	179
Hawthorndale Fm	N Yks	NZ8609	54°28·4'	0°40·0'W	FM	94
Hawthornden	Midlo	NT2963	55°51·6'	3°7·6'W	X	66
Hawthornden Castle	Midlo	NT2863	55°51·5'	3°8·6'W	A	66
Hawthorn Dingle	Shrops	SO6497	52°34·4'	2°31·5'W	X	138
Hawthorn Fm	Bucks	SP9301	51°42·2'	0°38·9'W	FM	165
Hawthorn Fm	Ches	SJ6358	53°7·3'	2°32·8'W	FM	118
Hawthorn Fm	Lincs	TF1732	52°52·6'	0°15·3'W	FM	130
Hawthorn Fm	Lincs	TF3710	52°40·5'	0°2·0'E	FM	131,142,143
Hawthorn Fm	Norf	TG0910	52°39·1'	1°5·8'E	FM	133
Hawthorn Fm	N Yks	NZ7914	54°31·1'	0°46·4'W	FM	94
Hawthorn Fm	Oxon	SP3704	51°44·2'	1°27·5'W	FM	164
Hawthorn Fm	Shrops	SO6596	52°33·9'	2°30·6'W	FM	138
Hawthorn Fm	Somer	ST0624	51°0·7'	3°19·9'W	FM	181
Hawthorn Fm	Suff	TM4266	52°14·6'	1°33·1'E	FM	156
Hawthorn Hill	Brackn	SU8774	51°27·7'	0°44·5'W	T	175
Hawthorn Hill	Lincs	TF2155	53°4·9'	0°11·2'W	T	122
Hawthorn Hill	N Yks	NZ8302	54°24·6'	0°42·8'W	X	94
Hawthorn Hill	Powys	SO2867	52°18·0'	3°3·0'W	H	137,148
Hawthorn Hive	Durham	NZ4446	54°48·7'	1°18·5'W	W	88
Hawthorn Ho	Durham	NZ2425	54°37·4'	1°37·3'W	X	93
Hawthorn Ho	N Yks	NZ6505	54°26·4'	0°59·4'W	X	94
Hawthorn Lodge	Norf	TG0513	52°40·8'	1°2·4'E	X	133
Hawthorns	Staffs	SJ8045	53°0·4'	2°17·5'W	T	118
Hawthornside	Scot Bord	NT5611	55°23·7'	2°41·2'W	X	80
Hawthorns, The	Glos	SO8030	51°58·3'	2°17·1'W	X	150
Hawthornsyke	W Loth	NT0678	55°59·4'	3°30·0'W	X	65
Hawthornthwaite	Lancs	SD5653	53°58·5'	2°39·8'W	X	102
Hawthornthwaite Fell	Lancs	SD5751	53°57·4'	2°38·9'W	X	102
Hawthornthwaite Fell Top	Lancs	SD5751	53°57·4'	2°38·9'W	H	102
Hawthorn Vale	Pth & Kin	NT1299	56°10·8'	3°24·6'W	X	58
Hawthorn Wood	N Yks	SE9888	54°16·9'	0°29·3'W	F	94,101
Hawthorpe	Lincs	TF0427	52°50·1'	0°27·0'W	T	130
Hawton	Notts	SK7851	53°3·3'	0°49·8'W	T	120,121
Hawton Fm	Warw	SP2630	51°58·3'	1°36·9'W	FM	151
Hawton Ho	Notts	SK7951	53°3·3'	0°48·9'W	X	120,121

Haw Top	Wakf	SE3112	53°36·5′	1°31·5′W	X	110,111
Haw Wood	S Glos	ST5579	51°30·7′	2°38·5′W	F	172
Haw Wood	Suff	TM4272	52°17·8′	1°33·4′E	F	156
Haw Wood	Wilts	SU2663	51°22·2′	1°37·2′W	F	174
Haw Wood Fm	Suff	TM4271	52°17·2′	1°33·3′E	FM	156
Haxby	York	SE6057	54°0·6′	1°4·7′W	T	105
Haxby Gates	York	SE6056	54°0·0′	1°4·7′W	X	105
Haxby Grange Fm	York	SE6059	54°1·6′	1°4·6′W	FM	105
Haxby Landing	York	SE6158	54°1·1′	1°3·7′W	X	105
Haxby Lodge Fm	York	SE6160	54°2·2′	1°3·7′W	FM	100
Haxby Moor	York	SE6060	54°2·2′	1°4·6′W	X	100
Haxby Plantn	E Yorks	SE7346	53°54·5′	0°52·9′W	F	105,106
Haxby Plantn	N Yks	NZ9005	54°26·2′	0°35·3′W	F	94
Haxells Fm	Essex	TL9917	51°49·2′	0°53·6′E	FM	168
Haxey	N Lincs	SK7699	53°29·2′	0°50·9′W	T	112
Haxey Carr	N Lincs	SE7501	53°30·3′	0°51·7′W	T	112
Haxey Grange	N Lincs	SK7397	53°28·1′	0°53·6′W	X	112
Haxey Turbary	N Lincs	SE7401	53°30·3′	0°52·6′W	X	112
Haxland Pits	Hants	SZ4399	50°47·6′	1°23·0′W	F	196
Haxmoor Fm	Wilts	SU0990	51°36·8′	1°51·8′W	FM	163,173
Haxted	Surrey	TQ4245	51°11·4′	0°2·3′E	T	187
Haxton	Devon	SS6436	51°6·7′	3°56·2′W	X	180
Haxton	Wilts	SU1449	51°14·6′	1°47·6′W	T	184
Haxton Down	Devon	SS6536	51°6·7′	3°55·3′W	X	180
Haxton Down	Wilts	SU2050	51°15·2′	1°42·4′W	X	184
Haxton O	Wilts	SU1950	51°15·2′	1°43·3′W	F	184
Hay	Corn	SW8651	50°19·4′	5°0·0′W	X	200,204
Hay	Corn	SW9552	50°20·2′	4°52·5′W	X	200,204
Hay	Corn	SW9770	50°29·9′	4°51·4′W	T	200
Hay	Corn	SX0148	50°18·1′	4°47·3′W	X	204
Hay	Devon	SS4308	50°51·2′	4°13·5′W	X	190
Hay-a-Park	N Yks	SE3758	54°1·2′	1°25·7′W	X	104
Haybanks	Cumbr	NY6715	54°32·0′	2°30·2′W	X	91
Hay Barton Fm	Corn	SW9243	50°15·3′	4°54·7′W	FM	204
Haybays	Ches	SJ6352	53°4·1′	2°32·7′W	X	118
Hayber	N Yks	SD8552	53°58·1′	2°13·3′W	X	103
Hayber Beck	Cumbr	NY7518	54°33·6′	2°22·8′W	W	91
Haybergill	Cumbr	NY7516	54°32·6′	2°22·8′W	X	91
Hayberries	Durham	NY9822	54°35·8′	2°1·4′W	X	92
Hay Bluff	Powys	SO2436	52°1·3′	3°6·1′W	X	161
Hayborough	Cumbr	NY0535	54°42·3′	3°28·0′W	X	89
Haybrake	Orkney	ND3094	58°49·9′	3°12·3′W	X	7
Haybrake	Orkney	ND4593	58°49·5′	2°56·7′W	X	7
Haybridge	Shrops	SO6473	52°21·5′	2°31·3′W	T	138
Haybridge	Somer	ST5346	51°12·9′	2°40·0′W	T	182,183
Haybridge	Wrekin	SJ6711	52°42·0′	2°28·9′W	T	127
Hay Bridge Fm	N Yks	SE9779	54°12·1′	0°30·4′W	FM	101
Haybridge Mill Fm	E Yorks	SE7657	54°0·4′	0°50·0′W	FM	105,106
Hay Brow	N Yks	TA0090	54°18·0′	0°27·4′W	X	101
Hayburn Beck Fm	N Yks	SE9997	54°21·8′	0°28·2′W	FM	94,101
Hayburn Wyke	N Yks	TA0197	54°21·7′	0°26·3′W	W	101
Hayburn Wyke Hotel	N Yks	TA0096	54°21·2′	0°27·3′W	X	101
Hay Carr	Lancs	SD4853	53°58·5′	2°47·2′W	X	102
Hay Castle	Powys	SO2342	52°4·5′	3°7·0′W	A	148,161
Hay Close	Cumbr	NY4441	54°45·9′	2°51·8′W	X	85
Hayclose	Cumbr	SD5390	54°18·5′	2°42·9′W	X	97
Haycock	Cumbr	NY1410	54°28·9′	3°19·2′W	H	89
Haycocks	Essex	TM0214	51°47·5′	0°56·1′E	X	168
Haycocks	I Scilly	SV8509	49°54·1′	6°22·9′W	X	203
Haycock Spinney	Rut	SK8205	52°38·4′	0°46·9′W	F	141
Haycombe Hill Fm	Wilts	ST8940	51°9·8′	2°9·1′W	FM	184
Hay Copse	Northnts	SP8553	52°10·4′	0°45·0′W	F	152
Haycrock	Corn	SW9669	50°29·4′	4°52·2′W	X	200
Haycroft	Ches	SJ5557	53°6·7′	2°39·9′W	X	117
Haycroft Bottom	Glos	SP1515	51°50·2′	1°46·5′W	F	163
Haycroft Fm	Devon	SS5221	50°58·4′	4°6·1′W	FM	180
Haycroft Hill	W Berks	SU3476	51°29·1′	1°30·2′W	X	174
Haycroft Ho	Glos	SP1515	51°50·2′	1°46·5′W	X	163
Haycross Fm	Kent	TQ9234	51°4·6′	0°44·9′E	FM	189
Haydah	Corn	SX2398	50°45·5′	4°30·2′W	X	190
Hay Dale	Derby	SK1276	53°17·1′	1°48·8′W	X	119
Hayden	Glos	SO9023	51°54·6′	2°8·3′W	T	163
Hayden Fm	Glos	SO7312	51°48·6′	2°23·1′W	FM	162
Hayden Fm	Oxon	SU6886	51°34·4′	1°0·7′W	FM	175
Haydens	Essex	TL6314	51°48·3′	0°22·3′E	X	167
Haydens	Essex	TL6523	51°53·1′	0°24·2′E	X	167
Hay Dike	N Yks	SE4645	53°54·2′	1°17·6′W	W	105
Haydock	St Hel	SJ5696	53°27·8′	2°39·4′W	T	108
Haydock Park	St Hel	SJ5897	53°28·3′	2°37·6′W	X	108
Haydock Park Fm	St Hel	SJ5897	53°28·3′	2°37·6′W	FM	108
Haydon	Bath & NE Somer	ST6853	51°16·7′	2°27·1′W	T	183
Haydon	Corn	SX2998	50°45·6′	4°25·1′W	X	190
Haydon	Devon	SS9016	50°56·2′	3°33·6′W	X	181
Haydon	Dorset	ST6715	50°56·2′	2°27·8′W	T	183
Haydon	Dorset	ST7512	50°54·6′	2°21·0′W	X	194
Haydon	Northum	NY8465	54°59·0′	2°14·6′W	X	86,87
Haydon	Somer	ST2523	51°0·3′	3°3·8′W	T	193
Haydon	Somer	ST5848	51°14·0′	2°35·7′W	T	182,183
Haydon	Swin	SU1288	51°35·7′	1°49·2′W	T	173
Haydon Bridge	Northum	NY8464	54°58·5′	2°14·6′W	T	86,87
Haydon Common	Devon	SX9383	50°38·4′	3°30·4′W	F	192
Haydon Dean	Northum	NT9743	55°41·1′	2°2·4′W	X	75
Haydon Down	Dorset	SY5492	50°43·8′	2°38·7′W	X	194
Haydon Fell	Northum	NY8466	54°59·5′	2°14·6′W	X	86,87
Haydon Fm	Devon	SS8908	50°51·9′	3°34·3′W	FM	192
Haydon Fm	Dorset	ST7611	50°54·1′	2°20·1′W	FM	194
Haydon Grange	Somer	ST5254	51°17·2′	2°40·9′W	X	182,183
Haydon Hill	Dorset	SY6694	50°44·9′	2°28·5′W	X	194
Haydon Hill	Herts	TQ1294	51°38·2′	0°22·5′W	X	166,176
Haydon Letch	Northum	NZ2789	55°11·9′	1°34·1′W	W	81
Haydon Mill Fm	Bucks	SP7914	51°49·4′	0°50·8′W	FM	165
Haydon Moor Plantns	Corn	SX2897	50°45·1′	4°25·9′W	F	190
Haydon Way Fm	Warw	SP0762	52°15·6′	1°53·4′W	FM	150
Haydon Wick	Swin	SU1387	51°35·1′	1°48·4′W	T	173
Haydown Hill	Wilts	SU3156	51°18·4′	1°32·9′W	H	174
Haye	Corn	SX3263	50°26·8′	4°21·6′W	X	201
Haye	Corn	SX3469	50°30·1′	4°20·1′W	T	201
Haye	Corn	SX3655	50°22·6′	4°18·0′W	X	201
Haye	Corn	SX4166	50°28·6′	4°14·1′W	X	201
Haye	Corn	SX4263	50°27·0′	4°13·2′W	X	201
Haye Barton	Corn	SX2967	50°28·9′	4°24·2′W	X	201
Haye Fm	C of Plym	SX5254	50°22·3′	4°4·5′W	FM	201
Haye Fm	Corn	SX1355	50°22·1′	4°37·4′W	FM	200
Haye Fm	Devon	SX3999	50°46·3′	4°16·6′W	FM	190
Haye Fm	Devon	SX6048	50°19·2′	3°57·6′W	FM	202
Haye Fm	Devon	SY2792	50°43·6′	3°1·7′W	FM	193
Haye Fm	Essex	TM0119	51°50·2′	0°55·5′E	FM	168
Haye Fm	Worcs	SO8564	52°16·7′	2°12·8′W	FM	150
Haye Ho	Shrops	SO7389	52°30·1′	2°23·5′W	X	138
Hayend Wood	Staffs	SK0919	52°46·3′	1°51·6′W	F	128
Haye Park Ho	Heref	SO4871	52°20·3′	2°45·4′W	X	137,138,148
Haye Park Wood	Heref	SO4972	52°20·9′	2°44·5′W	F	137,138,148
Hayes	Brom	TQ4066	51°22·8′	0°1·1′E	T	177
Hayes	Devon	SS6113	50°54·2′	3°58·2′W	X	180
Hayes	Glos	SO6506	51°45·3′	2°30·0′W	X	162
Hayes	Hants	SU4062	51°21·6′	1°25·1′W	X	174
Hayes	Hill	TQ0980	51°30·7′	0°25·4′W	T	176
Hayes	Shrops	SJ3515	52°44·0′	2°57·4′W	X	126
Hayes	Staffs	SJ7848	53°2·0′	2°19·3′W	X	118
Hayes	Staffs	SK0860	53°8·5′	1°52·4′W	T	119
Hayes Barton	Devon	SS5800	50°47·2′	4°0·5′W	X	191
Hayes Barton	Devon	SX9697	50°46·0′	3°28·1′W	X	192
Hayes Barton	Devon	SY0485	50°39·6′	3°21·1′W	A	192
Hayes Castle	Cumbr	NY0022	54°35·2′	3°32·4′W	A	89
Hayes Common	Brom	TQ4065	51°22·2′	0°1·1′E	F	177
Hayes Coppice	Monm	SO5214	51°49·6′	2°41·4′W	F	162
Haye's Down	W Susx	SU8610	50°53·2′	0°46·3′W	X	197
Hayes End	Hill	TQ0882	51°31·8′	0°26·2′W	T	176
Hayes Fm	Derby	SK4042	52°58·7′	1°23·9′W	FM	129
Hayes Fm	Devon	SX9994	50°44·4′	3°25·5′W	FM	192
Hayes Fm	Dorset	ST8019	50°58·4′	2°16·7′W	FM	183
Hayes Fm	Essex	TQ7995	51°37·7′	0°35·6′E	FM	167
Hayes Fm	E Susx	TQ8520	50°57·2′	0°38·4′E	FM	189,199
Hayes Fm	Glos	SO7229	51°57·8′	2°24·1′W	FM	149
Hayes Fm	Glos	SO8310	51°47·5′	2°14·4′W	FM	162
Hayes Fm	Kent	TQ9129	51°1·9′	0°43·8′E	FM	189
Hayes Fm	Northnts	SP6545	52°6·2′	1°2·7′W	FM	152
Hayes Fm	S Glos	ST7581	51°31·9′	2°21·2′W	FM	172
Hayes Fm	Worcs	SO5666	52°17·7′	2°38·3′W	FM	137,138,149
Hayes Fms	Somer	ST4631	51°4·8′	2°45·9′W	FM	182
Hayes Gate	Monm	ST5091	51°37·2′	2°42·9′W	X	162,172
Hayesgate	Staffs	SK0959	53°7·9′	1°51·5′W	X	119
Hayeshead	Staffs	SK0859	53°7·9′	1°52·4′W	X	119
Hayes Hill Fm	Essex	TL3803	51°42·8′	0°0·2′E	FM	166
Hayes Ho	Staffs	SK0434	52°54·4′	1°56·0′W	X	128
Hayes Knoll	Wilts	SU1090	51°36·8′	1°50·9′W	T	163,173
Hayes Lodge	Northnts	SP8165	52°16·9′	0°48·4′W	X	152
Hayes Oak Fm	Wilts	SU1090	51°36·8′	1°50·9′W	FM	163,173
Hayes Point	V of Glam	ST1467	51°24·0′	3°13·8′W	X	171
Hayes, The	Derby	SK3024	52°49·0′	1°32·9′W	X	128
Hayes, The	Derby	SK4152	53°4·1′	1°22·9′W	X	120
Hayes, The	Shrops	SJ2830	52°52·0′	3°3·8′W	X	126
Hayes, The	Shrops	SJ4521	52°47·3′	2°48·5′W	X	126
Hayes, The	Staffs	SJ9135	52°55·0′	2°7·6′W	X	127
Hayes, The	Wilts	ST8765	51°23·3′	2°10·8′W	X	173
Hayes Town	Hill	TQ1080	51°30·7′	0°24·5′W	T	176
Hayeswater	Cumbr	NY4312	54°30·3′	2°52·4′W	W	90
Hayeswater Gill	Cumbr	NY4213	54°30·8′	2°53·3′W	W	90
Hayes Wood	Devon	SY0484	50°39·1′	3°21·1′W	F	192
Hayes Wood	Staffs	SK0444	52°59·8′	1°56·0′W	F	119,128
Hay Fell	Cumbr	SD5594	54°20·6′	2°41·1′W	H	97
Hayfellside	Cumbr	SD5390	54°18·5′	2°42·9′W	X	97
Hayfield	Arg & Bt	NN0723	56°21·9′	5°7·0′W	X	50
Hayfield	Derby	SK0387	53°23·0′	1°56·9′W	T	110
Hayfield	D & G	NX8996	55°15·0′	3°44·3′W	X	78
Hayfield	D & G	NY2871	55°1·9′	3°7·2′W	X	85
Hay Field	Donc	SK6499	53°29·3′	1°1·7′W	T	111
Hayfield	Fife	NT2792	56°7·2′	3°10·0′W	T	59
Hayfield	Highld	ND1966	58°34·7′	3°23·1′W	X	11,12
Hayfield Fm	Beds	SP9437	52°1·6′	0°37·4′W	FM	153
Hayfield Knowe	D & G	NX9265	54°58·3′	3°40·8′W	X	84
Hayfield Lodge	Northnts	SP9076	52°22·7′	0°40·3′W	X	141
Hay Fm	Aberd	NK0734	57°24·0′	1°52·6′W	FM	30
Hay Fm	Devon	ST2406	50°51·1′	3°4·4′W	FM	192,193
Hay Fm	Glos	SO6922	51°54·0′	2°26·6′W	FM	162
Hay Fm	Glos	SO7525	51°55·6′	2°21·4′W	FM	162
Hay Fm	Kent	TR3254	51°14·5′	1°19·8′E	FM	179
Hay Fm	Northum	NT9438	55°38·4′	2°5·3′W	FM	74,75
Hay Fm	Staffs	SO8088	52°29·6′	2°17·3′W	FM	138
Hayford Fm	Shrops	SJ3610	52°41·3′	2°56·4′W	FM	126
Hayford Hall	Devon	SX6867	50°29·5′	3°51·3′W	X	202
Hay Forest	Powys	SO1936	52°1·2′	3°10·4′W	F	161
Haygarth	Cumbr	SD5694	54°20·6′	2°40·2′W	X	97
Haygate	Wrekin	SJ6410	52°41·4′	2°31·6′W	T	127
Haygill Fm	Brad	SE0350	53°57·0′	1°56·8′W	FM	104
Hay Grange	Derby	SK4337	52°56·0′	1°21·2′W	X	129
Haygrass	Somer	ST2321	50°59·2′	3°5·4′W	T	193
Hay Green	Essex	TL6000	51°40·8′	0°19·3′E	T	167
Hay Green	Herts	TL3436	52°0·6′	0°2·5′W	T	154
Hay Green	Norf	TF5418	52°44·5′	0°17·3′E	T	131
Haygreen Fm	Suff	TL8058	52°11·7′	0°38·4′E	FM	155
Hayhead Fm	Wals	SP0498	52°35·0′	1°56·1′W	FM	139
Hayheath	W Susx	TQ3136	51°6·7′	0°7·3′W	X	187
Hayhill	E Ayr	NS4616	55°25·1′	4°25·5′W	T	70
Hayhill	S Lanak	NS5953	55°45·2′	4°14·4′W	X	64
Hay Hill	Somer	ST5244	51°11·8′	2°40·8′W	H	182,183
Hayhill	Staffs	SJ8757	53°6·8′	2°11·2′W	X	118
Hayhillock	Aberd	NJ9233	57°23·5′	2°7·5′W	X	30
Hayhillock	Angus	NO5242	56°34·3′	2°46·4′W	T	54
Hay Hills Fms	Brad	SE0347	53°55·4′	1°56·8′W	FM	104
Hay Ho	Devon	SX9898	50°46·6′	3°26·4′W	X	192
Hay Ho	Staffs	SJ9017	52°45·3′	2°8·5′W	X	127
Hayhope	Scot Bord	NT8227	55°32·4′	2°16·7′W	X	74
Hay House Fm	Essex	TL8528	51°55·4′	0°41·8′E	FM	168
Hay Knott	Cumbr	NY3036	54°43·1′	3°4·8′W	X	90
Hayknowes	D & G	NY1765	54°58·6′	3°17·4′W	X	85
Hay Lake	Corn	SX3263	50°26·8′	4°21·6′W	W	201
Haylake	Devon	SX7892	50°43·1′	3°43·3′W	X	191
Hayland Fm	W Susx	SU9117	50°56·9′	0°41·9′W	FM	197
Haylands	I of W	SZ5891	50°43·2′	1°10·3′W	T	196
Haylands Bank	N Yks	SE1675	54°10·5′	1°44·9′W	X	99
Haylands Fm	Kent	TQ8542	51°9·1′	0°39·1′E	FM	189
Hayle	Corn	SW5537	50°11·2′	5°25·6′W	T	203
Hayleazes	Northum	NY8056	54°54·1′	2°18·3′W	X	86,87
Hayle Bay	Corn	SW9379	50°34·7′	4°55·1′W	W	200
Hayle Fm	Corn	SX0177	50°33·8′	4°48·2′W	FM	200
Hayle Fm	Kent	TQ6839	51°7·8′	0°24·5′E	FM	188
Hayle Fm	Wilts	SU0269	51°25·4′	1°57·9′W	FM	173
Hayleigh Fm	E Susx	TQ3415	50°55·4′	0°5·2′W	FM	198
Hayle Kimbro Pool	Corn	SW6916	50°0·2′	5°13·1′W	W	203
Hayle Place	Kent	TQ7553	51°15·2′	0°30·9′E	X	188
Haylett	Pemb	SM9413	51°46·9′	4°58·8′W	X	157,158
Hayley Dingle	Worcs	SO7553	52°10·7′	2°21·5′W	F	150
Hayley Green	Dudley	SO9482	52°26·4′	2°4·9′W	T	139
Hayleys Manor Fm	Essex	TL4504	51°43·2′	0°6·3′E	FM	167
Hayley Wood	Cambs	TL2952	52°9·3′	0°6·5′W	F	153
Haylie Resr	N Ayr	NS2158	55°47·2′	4°50·8′W	W	63
Hayling Bay	Hants	SZ7198	50°46·9′	0°59·2′W	W	197
Hayling Island	Hants	SU7201	50°48·5′	0°58·3′W	X	197
Hayling Wood	Hants	SU6525	51°1·5′	1°4·0′W	F	185,186
Haylot Fell	Lancs	SD5861	54°2·8′	2°38·1′W	X	97
Haylot Fm	Lancs	SD5962	54°3·4′	2°37·2′W	FM	97
Haymains	W Loth	NT0461	55°50·2′	3°31·5′W	X	65
Hayman's Fm	Ches	SJ8576	53°17·1′	2°13·1′W	FM	118
Haymans Fm	W Susx	SU9731	51°4·4′	0°36·5′W	FM	186
Haymans Hill Fm	Kent	TQ7141	51°8·8′	0°27·1′E	FM	188
Haymarket Sta	C of Edin	NT2373	55°56·9′	3°13·5′W	X	66
Haymead Hill	Herts	TL3329	51°56·8′	0°3·5′W	X	166
Haymes	Glos	SO9726	51°56·2′	2°2·2′W	X	163
Hay Mill	Heref	SO4373	52°21·4′	2°49·8′W	X	137,148
Hay Mills	Birm	SP1184	52°27·5′	1°49·9′W	T	139
Hay Moor	Somer	ST3126	51°2·0′	2°58·7′W	X	193
Hay Moor	Somer	ST3233	51°5·8′	2°57·9′W	X	182
Hay Moor	Somer	ST4525	51°1·5′	2°46·7′W	X	193
Haymoor End	Somer	ST3025	51°1·4′	2°59·5′W	T	193
Haymoor Green	Ches	SJ6850	53°3·0′	2°28·2′W	T	118
Haymoor Old Rhyne	Somer	ST3226	51°2·0′	2°57·8′W	W	193
Haymore Fm	Shrops	SO6285	52°27·9′	2°33·2′W	FM	138
Haymount	Scot Bord	NT6733	55°35·6′	2°31·0′W	X	74
Haynall	Heref	SO5467	52°18·2′	2°40·1′W	X	137,138,149
Hayne	Devon	SS4505	50°49·7′	4°11·7′W	X	190
Hayne	Devon	SS5829	51°2·8′	4°1·2′W	X	180
Hayne	Devon	SS7103	50°49·0′	3°49·5′W	X	191
Hayne	Devon	SS8807	50°51·3′	3°35·1′W	T	192
Hayne	Devon	SS9515	50°55·7′	3°29·3′W	X	181
Hayne	Devon	SX4286	50°39·4′	4°13·7′W	X	201
Hayne	Devon	SX7685	50°39·3′	3°44·9′W	X	191
Hayne	Somer	ST2317	50°57·1′	3°5·4′W	X	193
Hayne Barton	Devon	SS3702	50°47·9′	4°18·4′W	X	190
Hayne Barton	Devon	SS6416	50°55·9′	3°55·7′W	X	180
Hayne Barton	Devon	SS9824	51°0·6′	3°26·9′W	X	181
Hayne Barton	Devon	ST0308	50°52·0′	3°22·3′W	X	192
Hayne Barton	Devon	SX8693	50°43·8′	3°36·5′W	X	191
Hayne Barton	Devon	SX8999	50°47·0′	3°34·1′W	X	192
Hayne Barton	Devon	SY0991	50°42·9′	3°17·0′W	X	192
Hayne Down	Devon	SX7480	50°36·6′	3°46·5′W	H	191
Hayne Fm	Devon	SS6709	50°52·1′	3°53·0′W	FM	191
Hayne Fm	Devon	SS9525	51°1·1′	3°29·4′W	FM	181
Hayne Fm	Devon	ST0502	50°48·8′	3°20·5′W	FM	192
Hayne Fm	Devon	ST1110	50°53·2′	3°15·5′W	FM	192,193
Hayne Fm	Devon	ST1904	50°50·0′	3°8·6′W	FM	192,193
Hayne Fm	Devon	SX8897	50°45·9′	3°34·9′W	FM	192
Hayne Fm	Somer	SS9929	51°3·3′	3°26·1′W	FM	181
Hayne Fm	Somer	ST2318	50°57·6′	3°5·4′W	FM	193
Hayne Ho	Devon	SS9601	50°48·2′	3°28·2′W	X	192
Hayne Ho	Devon	ST0502	50°48·8′	3°20·5′W	X	192
Hayneholme	N Yks	SE0452	53°58·1′	1°55·9′W	X	104
Haynemoor Wood	Devon	SS9923	51°0·1′	3°26·0′W	F	181
Hayne Oak	Devon	SS9807	50°51·4′	3°26·6′W	X	192
Haynes	Beds	TL0942	52°4·2′	0°24·2′W	T	153
Haynes Church End	Beds	TL0841	52°3·6′	0°25·1′W	T	153
Haynes Down Fm	Somer	SS9826	51°1·7′	3°26·9′W	FM	181
Haynes Fm	Glos	SO7322	51°54·0′	2°23·2′W	FM	162
Haynes Fm	Kent	TR2748	51°11·4′	1°15·3′E	FM	179
Hayne's Fm	Peterb	TF2403	52°36·9′	0°9·7′W	FM	142
Haynes Green	Essex	TL9017	51°49·5′	0°45·8′E	X	168
Haynes West End	Beds	TL0640	52°3·1′	0°26·8′W	T	153
Haynetown Fm	Devon	SS6421	50°58·6′	3°55·9′W	FM	180
Hayne Valley	Devon	SS6710	50°52·7′	3°53·1′W	X	191
Hayog Fm	Pemb	SM9725	51°53·4′	4°56·6′W	FM	157,158
Hay-on-Wye / Y Gelli Gandryll	Powys	SO2242	52°4·5′	3°7·9′W	T	148,161
Hay Place	Hants	SU7740	51°9·5′	0°53·5′W	X	186
Hayrake	Northum	NY8347	54°49·3′	2°15·5′W	X	86,87
Hay Rake	Northum	NY8552	54°52·0′	2°13·6′W	X	87
Hayreed	E Susx	TQ5506	50°50·2′	0°12·5′E	X	199
Hayridge Fm	Derby	SK1389	53°24·1′	1°47·9′W	FM	110
Hayrigg	Cumbr	NY1250	54°50·5′	3°21·8′W	X	85
Hayrigg	D & G	NY1380	55°6·7′	3°21·4′W	X	78
Hayring	Cumbr	NY7644	54°47·7′	2°22·0′W	X	86,87
Hays	Pemb	SM9312	51°46·3′	4°59·6′W	X	157,158
Hays	Pemb	SN0401	51°40·7′	4°49·7′W	X	157,158
Hays	Staffs	SJ9260	53°8·5′	2°6·8′W	X	118
Hays	Wilts	ST8728	51°3·3′	2°10·7′W	X	183
Hay's Br	Oxon	SP4847	52°7·4′	1°17·5′W	X	151
Hays Bridge Fm	Surrey	TQ3544	51°11·0′	0°3·7′W	FM	187
Hayscastle	Pemb	SM8925	51°53·3′	5°3·6′W	T	157,158
Hayscastle Tump	Pemb	SM9024	51°52·7′	5°2·7′W	A	157,158
Hays Fm	Notts	SK5151	53°3·5′	1°13·9′W	FM	120
Haysford	Pemb	SM9221	51°51·2′	5°0·8′W	T	157,158
Hayshaw Fell	Lancs	SD5450	53°56·9′	2°41·6′W	X	102
Hayshead	Angus	NO6442	56°34·4′	2°34·7′W	T	54
Hayside	Scot Bord	NT4818	55°27·4′	2°48·9′W	X	79
Hay Sike	Scot Bord	NT3008	55°21·9′	3°5·8′W	W	79
Haysike	Scot Bord	NT4712	55°24·2′	2°49·8′W	X	79
Haysmuir	E Ayr	NS3743	55°39·4′	4°35·0′W	X	63,70
Haystack	Fife	NT1782	56°1·7′	3°19·5′W	X	65,66
Hay Stacks	Cumbr	NY1913	54°30·6′	3°14·6′W	X	89,90
Hays, The	Oxon	SP3615	51°50·2′	1°28·3′W	X	164

Hayston	E Dunb	NS6473	55°56·1'	4°10·2'W	T	64
Hayston	Fife	NO4120	56°22·4'	2°56·9'W	X	54,59
Hayston	Pemb	SR9396	51°37·7'	4°59·1'W	X	158
Hayston Hall	Pemb	SM9308	51°44·2'	4°59·5'W	X	157,158
Hayston Hill	Angus	NO4144	56°35·3'	2°57·2'W	X	54
Hayston Mill	Pemb	SM9308	51°44·2'	4°59·5'W	X	157,158
Haystoun	Scot Bord	NT2538	55°38·0'	3°11·0'W	T	73
Hay Street	Herts	TL3926	51°55·1'	0°1·7'E	T	166
Hay, The	Shrops	SO6489	52°30·1'	2°31·4'W	X	138
Haythorne	Dorset	SU0307	50°52·0'	1°57·1'W	T	195
Haythwaite	Cumbr	NY3745	54°48·0'	2°58·4'W	X	85
Haythwaite	Durham	NZ0509	54°28·8'	1°54·9'W	X	92
Hayton	C of Aber	NJ9308	57°10·0'	2°6·5'W	T	38
Hayton	Cumbr	NY1041	54°45·6'	3°23·5'W	T	85
Hayton	Cumbr	NY5057	54°54·6'	2°46·4'W	T	86
Hayton	E Yorks	SE8245	53°53·9'	0°44·7'W	T	106
Hayton	Notts	SK7284	53°21·1'	0°54·7'W	T	120
Hayton Brow	Cumbr	NY1344	54°47·3'	3°20·8'W	X	85
Hayton Castle Fm	Notts	SK7486	53°22·2'	0°52·9'W	FM	112,120
Hayton Castle (Hotel)	Cumbr	NY4958	54°55·1'	2°47·3'W	X	86
Hayton Field Fm	E Yorks	SE8044	53°53·4'	0°46·5'W	FM	106
Haytongate	Cumbr	NY5564	54°58·4'	2°41·8'W	X	86
Hayton Grange	E Yorks	SE8145	53°53·9'	0°45·6'W	X	106
Hay Tongue Fm	N Yks	SD9873	54°9·4'	2°1·4'W	FM	98
Hayton Ho	N Yks	SE4538	53°50·4'	1°18·6'W	X	105
Hayton Manor	Kent	TR1238	51°6·3'	1°2·1'E	X	179,189
Hayton Moss	Cumbr	NY5255	54°53·5'	2°44·5'W	F	86
Hayton's Bent	Shrops	SO5180	52°25·2'	2°42·8'W	T	137,138
Hayton Wood	N Yks	SE4438	53°50·4'	1°19·5'W	F	105
Hay Top	Derby	SK1772	53°14·9'	1°44·3'W	X	119
Haytor Down	Devon	SX7677	50°35·0'	3°44·7'W	H	191
Haytor Rocks	Devon	SX7577	50°35·0'	3°45·6'W	H	191
Haytor Vale	Devon	SX7777	50°35·0'	3°43·9'W	T	191
Haytown	Devon	SS3814	50°54·4'	4°17·9'W	T	190
Hayward Br	Dorset	ST8212	50°54·7'	2°15·0'W	X	194
Hayward Rock	Glos	ST6498	51°41·0'	2°30·9'W	X	162
Haywards	Essex	TL8321	51°51·7'	0°39·9'E	X	168
Haywards	E Susx	TQ5328	51°2·1'	0°11·3'E	X	188,199
Haywards Fm	Hants	SZ3299	50°47·6'	1°32·4'W	FM	196
Hayward's Fm	S Glos	ST6487	51°35·1'	2°30·8'W	FM	172
Haywards Heath	W Susx	TQ3324	51°0·2'	0°5·9'W	T	198
Haywards Water	Somer	ST1520	50°58·6'	3°12·3'W	W	181,193
Hayway Fm	Worcs	SP0939	52°3·2'	1°51·7'W	FM	150
Haywold Fm	E Yorks	SE9254	53°58·7'	0°35·4'W	FM	106
Hay Wood	Beds	SP9734	52°0·0'	0°34·8'W	F	153,165
Haywood	Corn	SX0373	50°31·7'	4°46·4'W	X	200
Hay Wood	Derby	SK3141	52°58·2'	1°31·9'W	F	119,128
Haywood	Devon	SS6326	51°1·3'	3°56·8'W	X	180
Haywood	Donc	SE5812	53°36·3'	1°7·0'W	T	111
Hay Wood	Glos	SO6827	51°56·7'	2°27·5'W	F	162
Hay Wood	Hants	SU5553	51°16·6'	1°12·3'W	F	185
Haywood	Heref	SO4834	52°0·4'	2°45·1'W	X	149,161
Haywood	Kent	TQ9362	51°19·7'	0°46·6'E	X	178
Hay Wood	N Som	ST3458	51°19·3'	2°56·4'W	F	182
Hay Wood	S Glos	ST6089	51°36·1'	2°34·3'W	F	162,172
Haywood	S Lanak	NS9754	55°46·4'	3°38·1'W	T	65,72
Hay Wood	Suff	TL8057	52°11·1'	0°38·4'E	F	155
Hay Wood	Warw	SP2071	52°20·4'	1°42·0'W	F	139
Haywood Common	Heref	SO2756	52°12·1'	3°3·7'W	X	148
Haywood Fm	Devon	ST0505	50°50·4'	3°20·6'W	FM	192
Haywood Fm	Shrops	SJ3007	52°39·6'	3°1·7'W	FM	126
Haywood Fm	Shrops	SJ7030	52°52·2'	2°26·3'W	FM	127
Haywood Fm	Somer	ST7153	51°16·8'	2°24·6'W	FM	183
Haywood Lodge	Heref	SO4836	52°1·4'	2°45·1'W	X	149,161
Haywood Oaks	Notts	SK6055	53°5·6'	1°5·8'W	T	120
Haywood Park	Staffs	SJ9920	52°46·9'	2°0·5'W	X	127
Haywood Slade	Staffs	SJ9919	52°46·4'	2°0·5'W	X	127
Haywood, The	Derby	SK2577	53°17·6'	1°37·1'W	X	119
Haywood Warren	Staffs	SJ9919	52°46·4'	2°0·5'W	F	127
Hazard	Devon	SX7559	50°25·3'	3°45·2'W	X	202
Hazard's Green	E Susx	TQ6812	50°53·2'	0°23·7'E	T	199
Hazeland Fm	Wilts	ST9772	51°27·1'	2°2·2'W	FM	173
Haze Law	Scot Bord	NT2911	55°23·5'	3°6·8'W	H	79
Hazelaw Knowe	Scot Bord	NT2811	55°23·5'	3°7·8'W	H	79
Hazelbank	Arg & Bt	NN0904	56°11·7'	5°4·3'W	X	56
Hazel Bank	Cumbr	NY2615	54°31·7'	3°8·2'W	X	89,90
Hazelbank	D & G	NX4448	54°48·4'	4°25·2'W	X	83
Hazelbank	D & G	NY0894	55°14·2'	3°26·4'W	X	78
Hazelbank	D & G	NY1392	55°13·1'	3°21·6'W	X	78
Hazelbank	Moray	NJ1055	57°34·8'	3°29·8'W	X	28
Hazel Bank	N Yks	SE1963	54°4·0'	1°42·2'W	X	99
Hazelbank	S Lanak	NS8345	55°41·3'	3°51·2'W	T	72
Hazelbank Fm	E Ayr	NS4352	55°44·4'	4°29·6'W	FM	64
Hazel Bank Fm	E Yorks	SE6722	53°41·6'	0°58·7'W	FM	105,106
Hazelbank Plantn	D & G	NY0794	55°14·1'	3°27·3'W	F	78
Hazel Barrow	Staffs	SK0163	53°10·1'	1°58·7'W	X	119
Hazelbeach	Pemb	SM9404	51°42·1'	4°58·5'W	T	157,158
Hazelberry	D & G	NY1880	55°6·7'	3°16·7'W	X	79
Hazelberry Plantn	Wilts	SU2353	51°16·8'	1°39·8'W	F	184
Hazelborough Wood	Northnts	SP6543	52°5·1'	1°2·7'W	F	152
Hazel Bottom Gill	Cumbr	SD7683	54°14·8'	2°21·7'W	W	98
Hazel Bridge	Surrey	SU9634	51°6·1'	0°37·3'W	X	186
Hazelbrow	Derby	SK3344	52°59·8'	1°30·1'W	X	119,128
Hazel Burn	Angus	NO5381	56°55·3'	2°45·9'W	W	44
Hazelbury Bryan	Dorset	ST7408	50°52·5'	2°21·8'W	T	194
Hazelbury Manor	Wilts	ST8368	51°24·9'	2°14·3'W	X	173
Hazelbush	York	SE6657	54°0·5'	0°59·2'W	X	105,106
Hazelbush Hill	S Lanak	NT0316	55°26·0'	3°31·5'W	H	78
Hazelby Ho	Hants	SU4063	51°22·1'	1°25·1'W	X	174
Hazel Close	N Yks	SE0973	54°9·4'	1°51·3'W	X	99
Hazel Court	Heref	SO6238	52°2·6'	2°32·8'W	X	149
Hazel Ct	E Susx	TQ8112	50°53·0'	0°34·8'E	X	199
Hazeldean	S Lanak	NS7344	55°40·6'	4°0·7'W	X	71
Hazeldean Ho	E Renf	NS5353	55°45·1'	4°20·1'W	X	64
Hazeldene	C of Plym	SX5353	50°21·7'	4°3·6'W	X	201
Hazeldene	Northum	NZ2183	55°8·7'	1°39·8'W	X	81
Hazeldene Fm	Bucks	SP9403	51°43·3'	0°38·0'W	FM	165
Hazeldene Fm	Durham	NZ1226	54°38·0'	1°48·4'W	FM	92
Hazeldene Fm	Kent	TQ8947	51°11·7'	0°42·7'E	FM	189
Hazelden Fm	Kent	TQ7638	51°7·1'	0°31·3'E	FM	188
Hazelden Fm	W Susx	TQ3736	51°6·6'	0°2·2'W	FM	187
Hazeldine Coppice	Shrops	SO4987	52°29·0'	2°44·7'W	F	137,138
Hazeldon	Devon	SX4975	50°33·6'	4°7·5'W	X	191,201
Hazeldon	Wilts	ST9327	51°2·8'	2°5·6'W	X	184
Hazel Down	Hants	SU3639	51°9·2'	1°28·7'W	X	185
Hazeldown Fm	Hants	SU3638	51°8·6'	1°28·7'W	FM	185
Hazeleigh	Essex	TL8203	51°42·0'	0°38·4'E	T	168
Hazeleigh Hall	Essex	TL8303	51°42·0'	0°39·3'E	X	168
Hazel End	Essex	TL4924	51°53·9'	0°10·3'E	T	167
Hazeley	Hants	SU7459	51°19·7'	0°55·9'W	T	175,186
Hazeley Bottom	Hants	SU7557	51°18·7'	0°55·0'W	T	175,186
Hazeley Down	Hants	SU5025	51°1·6'	1°16·8'W	X	185
Hazeley Fm	Hants	SU5024	51°1·0'	1°16·8'W	FM	185
Hazeley Heath	Hants	SU7558	51°19·2'	0°55·0'W	T	175,186
Hazeley Lea	Hants	SU7459	51°19·7'	0°55·9'W	T	175,186
Hazelfield Ho	D & G	NX7749	54°49·5'	3°54·5'W	X	84
Hazel Fm	Dorset	ST5805	50°50·8'	2°35·4'W	FM	194
Hazel Fm	Heref	SO7036	52°1·5'	2°25·8'W	FM	149
Hazel Fm	Herts	TL2720	51°52·1'	0°8·9'W	FM	166
Hazel Fm	S Glos	ST6187	51°35·1'	2°33·4'W	FM	172
Hazel Fm	Somer	ST5356	51°18·3'	2°40·1'W	FM	172,182
Hazelford	Derby	SK2380	53°19·2'	1°38·9'W	X	110
Hazelford Ferry	Notts	SK7249	53°2·2'	0°55·2'W	X	129
Hazel Gap	Notts	SK5971	53°14·2'	1°6·6'W	X	120
Hazel Gap Wood	Notts	SK5971	53°14·2'	1°6·6'W	F	120
Hazelgarth Rigg	Durham	NY9319	54°34·2'	2°6·1'W	X	91,92
Hazel Gill	Cumbr	NY3341	54°45·8'	3°2·1'W	X	85
Hazelgill	Cumbr	NY5547	54°49·2'	2°41·6'W	X	86
Hazel Gill	Cumbr	NY6275	55°4·3'	2°35·3'W	W	86
Hazelgill	Cumbr	SD7799	54°23·4'	2°20·8'W	X	98
Hazel Gill Combe	Cumbr	SD6984	54°15·3'	2°28·1'W	X	98
Hazelgill Crag	Cumbr	NY5975	55°4·3'	2°38·1'W	X	86
Hazelgill Knott	Cumbr	SD6799	54°23·4'	2°30·1'W	H	98
Hazel Green	N Yks	SE6091	54°18·9'	1°4·2'W	X	94,100
Hazel Grove	Carm	SN2011	51°46·4'	4°36·2'W	X	158
Hazelgrove	Notts	SK5348	53°1·8'	1°12·2'W	T	129
Hazel Grove	Red & Cl	NZ6521	54°35·0'	0°59·2'W	X	94
Hazel Grove	Stock	SJ9286	53°22·5'	2°6·8'W	T	109
Hazel Grove Fm	Lancs	SD5076	54°10·9'	2°45·5'W	FM	97
Hazelgrove Ho	Somer	ST5926	51°2·1'	2°34·7'W	X	183
Hazel Hall	Surrey	TQ0845	51°11·9'	0°26·9'W	X	187
Hazel Hall Fm	N Yks	SE9082	54°13·8'	0°36·7'W	FM	101
Hazelhanger Fm	W Berks	SU4674	51°28·0'	1°19·9'W	FM	174
Hazel Hanger Wood	Glos	SO9112	51°48·6'	2°7·4'W	F	163
Hazel Head	Cumbr	NY2748	54°49·5'	3°7·8'W	X	85
Hazel Head	Cumbr	SD1994	54°20·4'	3°14·3'W	X	96
Hazel Head	N Yks	SE8099	54°23·1'	0°45·7'W	X	94,100
Hazelhead Moor	N Yks	SE8694	54°20·3'	0°40·2'W	X	94,101
Hazel Head Wood	N Yks	SE5392	54°19·5'	1°10·7'W	F	100
Hazel Hedge	Oxon	SP4832	51°59·3'	1°17·7'W	X	151
Hazel Hill	Glos	SO6616	51°50·7'	2°29·2'W	X	162
Hazel Hill	N Yks	SE5467	54°6·0'	1°10·0'W	X	100
Hazel Hill	Pemb	SN0501	51°40·7'	4°48·8'W	X	158
Hazel Ho	Barns	SE2507	53°33·8'	1°36·9'W	X	110
Hazel Ho	N Yks	SD8187	54°16·9'	2°17·1'W	X	98
Hazel Ho	N Yks	SE5566	54°5·5'	1°9·1'W	X	100
Hazel Ho	N Yks	SE6696	54°21·6'	0°58·6'W	X	94,100
Hazel Ho	N Yks	SE7774	54°9·6'	0°48·8'W	X	100
Hazel Holme	Cumbr	NY0314	54°31·0'	3°29·5'W	X	89
Hazel Holt	Hants	SU5819	50°58·3'	1°10·0'W	X	185
Hazelhope Burn	Scot Bord	NT3804	55°19·8'	2°58·2'W	W	79
Hazelhope Hill	Scot Bord	NT3705	55°20·4'	2°59·2'W	H	79
Hazel Hurn	Norf	TF9702	52°35·0'	0°54·9'E	F	144
Hazelhurst	Bury	SD7815	53°38·1'	2°19·6'W	T	109
Hazelhurst	Cumbr	NY3628	54°38·8'	2°59·1'W	X	90
Hazelhurst	Hants	SZ2796	50°46·0'	1°36·6'W	X	195
Hazelhurst	Lancs	SD5647	53°55·3'	2°39·8'W	X	102
Hazelhurst	Salf	SD7501	53°30·5'	2°22·2'W	T	109
Hazelhurst	Tames	SD9600	53°30·0'	2°3·2'W	T	109
Hazelhurst Fell	Lancs	SD5647	53°55·3'	2°39·8'W	X	102
Hazelhurst Fm	Ches	SJ7980	53°19·2'	2°18·5'W	FM	109
Hazelhurst Fm	Derby	SK0377	53°17·6'	1°56·9'W	FM	119
Hazelhurst Fm	E Susx	TQ6832	51°4·0'	0°24·3'E	FM	188
Hazelhurst Point	Cumbr	SD3379	54°12·4'	3°1·2'W	X	96,97
Hazel Knoll Fm	Stock	SJ9487	53°23·0'	2°5·0'W	FM	109
Hazells	Kent	TQ6271	51°25·1'	0°20·2'E	X	177
Hazells Hall	Beds	TL1850	52°8·4'	0°16·1'W	X	153
Hazelly Burn	E Loth	NT6266	55°53·4'	2°36·0'W	W	67
Hazelly Burn	Northum	NT9424	55°30·8'	2°5·3'W	W	74,75
Hazelmere	E Yorks	TA1439	53°50·3'	0°15·6'W	X	107
Hazelmere	Lancs	SD5233	53°47·7'	2°43·3'W	X	102
Hazelmere Fm	Derby	SK5174	53°15·9'	1°13·7'W	FM	120
Hazel Moor	Cumbr	NY6111	54°29·8'	2°35·7'W	X	91
Hazel Mount	Cumbr	NY0940	54°45·1'	3°24·4'W	X	85
Hazel Mount	Cumbr	SD1886	54°16·0'	3°15·1'W	X	96
Hazelpits Fm	Kent	TQ8344	51°10·2'	0°37·5'E	FM	188
Hazel Rig	Scot Bord	NT3114	55°25·2'	3°5·0'W	H	79
Hazelrig Fm	D & G	NX9983	55°8·1'	3°34·6'W	FM	78
Hazel Rigg	Cumbr	NY6140	54°45·5'	2°35·9'W	X	86
Hazelrigg	Cumbr	SD3784	54°15·1'	2°57·6'W	X	96,97
Hazelrigg	Lancs	SD4957	54°0·6'	2°46·3'W	X	102
Hazelrigg Beck	Cumbr	NY5839	54°44·9'	2°38·7'W	W	91
Hazelrigg Beck	Cumbr	NY6040	54°45·4'	2°36·9'W	W	86
Hazelrigg Mill	Northum	NU0433	55°35·7'	1°55·8'W	X	75
Hazels	Ches	SJ9667	53°12·2'	2°3·2'W	X	118
Hazelseat	Cumbr	SD3692	54°19·4'	2°58·6'W	X	96,97
Hazelshaw Fm	Barns	SK3197	53°28·4'	1°31·6'W	FM	110,111
Hazelshaw Fm	Ches	SJ7864	53°10·6'	2°19·3'W	FM	118
Hazelshaw Hill	D & G	NY0676	55°4·4'	3°27·9'W	H	85
Hazelshaw Ho	N Yks	SE5493	54°20·0'	1°9·8'W	X	100
Hazelside	S Lanak	NS8128	55°32·1'	3°52·7'W	X	71,72
Hazel Sike	Cumbr	SD6782	54°14·2'	2°30·0'W	W	98
Hazelslack	Cumbr	SD4778	54°11·9'	2°48·3'W	T	97
Hazelslade	Staffs	SK0212	52°42·6'	1°57·8'W	T	128
Hazelsprings Fm	Cumbr	NY2943	54°46·9'	3°5·8'W	FM	85
Hazels The	Shrops	SJ3106	52°39·1'	3°0·8'W	X	126
Hazel Street	Kent	TQ6939	51°7·7'	0°25·3'E	T	188
Hazel Street	Kent	TQ8559	51°18·2'	0°39·6'E	T	178
Hazel Stub	Suff	TL6544	52°4·4'	0°24·9'E	T	154
Hazelton	Glos	SP0718	51°51·9'	1°53·5'W	T	163
Hazelton Clump	Staffs	SK1249	53°2·5'	1°48·9'W	F	119
Hazelton Covert	Glos	ST9299	51°41·6'	2°6·6'W	F	163
Hazelton Grove	Glos	SP0718	51°51·9'	1°53·5'W	F	163
Hazeltongue Fm	Leic	SK7325	52°49·3'	0°54·6'W	FM	129
Hazelton Manor Fm	Glos	ST9298	51°41·1'	2°6·6'W	FM	163
Hazeltonrig	Northum	NT9810	55°23·3'	2°1·5'W	X	81
Hazeltonrig Burn	Northum	NT9610	55°23·3'	2°3·4'W	W	81
Hazeltonrig Hill	Northum	NT9611	55°23·8'	2°3·4'W	H	81
Hazelton Walls	Fife	NO3322	56°23·4'	3°4·7'W	T	53,59
Hazelton Wood	Essex	TL7518	51°50·2'	0°32·8'E	F	167
Hazel Tor	Devon	SX6937	50°13·3'	3°49·8'W	X	202
Hazelwall	Ches	SJ8671	53°14·4'	2°12·2'W	X	118
Hazelwall Fm	Staffs	SJ9946	53°0·9'	2°0·5'W	FM	118
Hazel Warren Fm	Somer	ST5156	51°18·3'	2°41·8'W	FM	172,182
Hazelwells	Shrops	SO7384	52°27·4'	2°23·4'W	X	138
Hazel Wood	Brom	TQ4461	51°20·0'	0°4·4'E	F	177,187
Hazelwood	Brom	TQ4461	51°20·0'	0°4·4'E	T	177,187
Hazelwood	Derby	SK3246	53°0·9'	1°31·0'W	T	119,128
Hazelwood	Devon	SX7252	50°21·5'	3°47·6'W	T	202
Hazelwood	Devon	SX8280	50°36·7'	3°39·7'W	X	191
Hazelwood	Devon	SY2089	50°41·9'	3°7·6'W	X	192
Hazel Wood	Glos	ST8698	51°41·1'	2°11·8'W	F	162
Hazelwood	Moray	NJ3144	57°29·1'	3°8·6'W	X	28
Hazel Wood	Suff	TL9544	52°3·8'	0°51·1'E	F	155
Hazelwood Castle	N Yks	SE4439	53°51·0'	1°19·5'W	X	105
Hazelwood Castle	N Yks	SE4539	53°51·0'	1°18·5'W	X	105
Hazelwood Common	Suff	TM4358	52°10·2'	1°33·6'E	X	156
Hazelwood Fm	Norf	TF9225	52°47·5'	0°51·3'E	FM	132
Hazelwood Hall Fm	Derby	SK3345	53°0·3'	1°30·1'W	FM	119,128
Hazelwood Hill	Somer	ST3706	50°51·2'	2°53·3'W	X	193
Hazely Hill	Northum	NT9540	55°39·5'	2°4·3'W	X	74,75
Hazely Law	Northum	NT8714	55°25·4'	2°11·9'W	H	80
Hazely Peat Moor	N Yks	SE0386	54°16·4'	1°56·8'W	X	98
Hazelyside	Scot Bord	NY4893	55°14·0'	2°48·6'W	X	79
Hazelyside Hill	Scot Bord	NY4588	55°11·2'	2°51·4'W	H	79
Hazelyside Rig	Scot Bord	NY4793	55°14·0'	2°49·6'W	H	79
Hazlebadge Hall	Derby	SK1780	53°19·2'	1°44·3'W	X	110
Hazlebarrow Fm	Derby	SK3681	53°19·7'	1°27·2'W	FM	110,111
Hazlecote Fm	Glos	ST8395	51°39·4'	2°14·4'W	FM	162
Hazle Fm	Worcs	SO7470	52°19·9'	2°22·5'W	FM	138
Hazle Hall	N Yks	SD7268	54°6·7'	2°25·3'W	X	98
Hazlehead	Barns	SE1902	53°31·1'	1°42·4'W	T	110
Hazlehead	C of Aber	NJ8905	57°8·4'	2°10·5'W	X	38
Hazlehurst	Derby	SK2642	52°58·7'	1°36·4'W	X	119,128
Hazlehurst Fm	Derby	SK3881	53°19·7'	1°25·4'W	FM	110,111
Hazle Manor	Glos	SO9109	51°47·0'	2°7·4'W	X	163
Hazlemere	Bucks	SU8995	51°39·0'	0°42·4'W	T	165
Hazler	Shrops	SO4693	52°32·2'	2°47·4'W	T	137,138
Hazler Hill	Shrops	SO4692	52°31·6'	2°47·4'W	H	137,138
Hazlerigg	N upon Ty	NZ2371	55°2·2'	1°38·0'W	T	88
Hazles	Staffs	SK0047	53°1·5'	1°59·6'W	T	119,128
Hazlescross	Staffs	SK0047	53°1·5'	1°59·6'W	T	119,128
Hazles Fm	Shrops	SJ5923	52°48·4'	2°36·1'W	FM	126
Hazlet Ho	Durham	NZ1641	54°46·1'	1°44·7'W	X	88
Hazlewood	N Yks	SE0853	53°58·6'	1°52·3'W	T	104
Hazlewood Hall	Suff	TM4358	52°10·2'	1°33·6'E	X	156
Hazlewood Moor	N Yks	SE0956	54°0·2'	1°51·3'W	X	104
Hazleyshaw	Clackm	NS9592	56°6·8'	3°40·9'W	X	58
Hazliebank	S Lanak	NS6940	55°38·4'	4°4·4'W	X	71
Hazliebrae	D & G	NY0585	55°9·3'	3°29·0'W	X	78
Hazlieburn	Scot Bord	NT1553	55°46·0'	3°20·9'W	X	65,72
Hazlie Green	D & G	NX3864	54°56·9'	4°31·3'W	X	83
Hazon	Northum	NU1904	55°20·0'	1°41·6'W	T	81
Hazon Burn	Northum	NU1903	55°19·5'	1°41·6'W	W	81
Hazon High Houses	Northum	NU1905	55°20·6'	1°41·6'W	X	81
Hazon Lee	Northum	NU1804	55°20·0'	1°42·5'W	X	81
Heacham	Norf	TF6737	52°54·5'	0°29·4'E	T	132
Heacham Bottom Fm	Norf	TF6835	52°53·4'	0°30·2'E	FM	132
Heacham Harbour	Norf	TF6635	52°53·4'	0°28·5'E	W	132
Heacham River	Norf	TF6937	52°54·5'	0°31·2'E	W	132
Head	Orkney	HY2105	58°55·8'	3°21·9'W	X	6,7
Head	Orkney	ND4587	58°46·3'	2°56·6'W	X	7
Head	Orkney	ND4892	58°49·0'	2°53·5'W	X	7
Headagee	Northum	NZ3091	55°13·0'	1°31·3'W	X	81
Headal	N Eil	NG0386	57°46·2'	6°59·2'W	X	18
Headborough	Pemb	SM8811	51°45·7'	5°3·9'W	X	157
Headbourne Worthy	Hants	SU4832	51°5·3'	1°18·5'W	T	185
Headbrook	Heref	SO3056	52°12·1'	3°1·1'W	T	148
Headcorn	Kent	TQ8344	51°10·2'	0°37·5'E	T	188
Head Dike	Lincs	TF1846	53°0·1'	0°14·1'W	W	130
Head Down	I of W	SZ5077	50°35·7'	1°17·2'W	X	196
Head Down Plantation	Hants	SU7319	50°58·2'	0°57·2'W	F	197
Head Drain	Roch	SD9618	53°39·7'	2°3·2'W	W	109
Head Dyke Lane	Lancs	SD3947	53°55·2'	2°55·3'W	X	102
Head-dykes	Pth & Kin	NN8304	56°13·1'	3°52·8'W	X	57
Headed Stone	D & G	NX4878	55°4·6'	4°22·4'W	X	77
Headfen Fm	Cambs	TL5188	52°28·4'	0°13·8'E	FM	143
Head Fm	E Yorks	TA2570	54°6·9'	0°4·8'W	FM	101
Headfoldswood Fm	W Susx	TQ0330	51°3·8'	0°31·4'W	FM	186
Headgate	Cumbr	NY5277	55°5·4'	2°44·7'W	X	86
Headgate	Devon	SS7830	51°3·6'	3°44·1'W	X	180
Headgoe	Orkney	HY5421	59°4·7'	2°47·7'W	X	5,6
Head Green	Kirk	SE0315	53°38·1'	1°56·9'W	X	110
Head Hag	N Yks	SE7271	54°8·0'	0°53·5'W	F	100
Head Ho	Cumbr	SD3982	54°14·1'	2°55·7'W	X	96,97
Head Ho	N Yks	NZ7306	54°26·9'	0°52·0'W	X	94
Head Ho	N Yks	SE5397	54°22·2'	1°10·6'W	X	100
Head Ho	N Yks	SE7694	54°20·4'	0°49·4'W	X	94,100
Headhone Fm	W Susx	SU9303	50°49·4'	0°40·4'W	FM	197
Head House Fm	Derby	SK4442	52°58·6'	1°20·3'W	FM	129
Head House Fm	N Yks	SE6698	54°22·6'	0°58·6'W	FM	94,100
Headinch	Aberd	NO4196	57°3·3'	2°57·9'W	X	37,44
Headingley	Leeds	SE2836	53°49·4'	1°34·1'W	T	104
Headington	Oxon	SP5407	51°45·8'	1°12·7'W	T	164
Headington Hill	Oxon	SP5306	51°45·2'	1°13·5'W	T	164
Headin Haw	Cumbr	SD2167	54°5·8'	3°12·1'W	X	96
Headiton	Aberd	NJ5930	57°21·8'	2°40·4'W	X	29,37
Headiton	Aberd	NJ7363	57°39·6'	2°26·7'W	X	29
Headiton	Aberd	NJ8653	57°34·3'	2°13·6'W	X	30
Headitown	Aberd	NJ6047	57°30·9'	2°39·6'W	X	29

Headlam	Durham	NZ1819	54°34·2'	1°42·9'W	T	92
Headland	Heref	SO3954	52°11·1'	2°53·1'W	X	148,149
Headland Fm	Pemb	SM9925	51°53·5'	4°54·9'W	FM	157,158
Headland Ho	Leic	SK7012	52°42·3'	0°57·4'W	X	129
Headlands Fm	Wilts	SU1092	51°37·8'	1°50·9'W	FM	163,173
Headland Warren	Devon	SX6881	50°37·1'	3°51·6'W	X	191
Headless Cross	Cumbr	SD3878	54°11·9'	2°56·6'W	T	96,97
Headless Cross	Devon	SX7787	50°40·4'	3°44·1'W	X	191
Headless Cross	Lancs	SD6113	53°37·0'	2°35·0'W	X	109
Headless Cross	N Lanak	NS9158	55°48·4'	3°43·9'W	X	65,72
Headless Cross	Worcs	SP0365	52°17·2'	1°57·0'W	T	150
Headless Knowe	D & G	NY4296	55°15·5'	2°54·3'W	X	79
Headley	Hants	SU5162	51°21·5'	1°15·7'W	T	174
Headley	Hants	SU8236	51°7·3'	0°49·3'W	T	186
Headley	Surrey	TQ2054	51°16·6'	0°16·4'W	T	187
Headley Bar	N Yks	SE4541	53°52·0'	1°18·5'W	X	105
Headley Court	Surrey	TQ1955	51°17·1'	0°17·2'W	X	187
Headley Down	Hants	SU8336	51°7·3'	0°48·5'W	T	186
Headley Grove	Surrey	TQ2053	51°16·0'	0°16·4'W	X	187
Headley Hall	Leeds	SE4441	53°52·0'	1°19·4'W	X	105
Headley Heath	Surrey	TQ2053	51°16·0'	0°16·4'W	X	187
Headley Heath	Worcs	SP0676	52°23·2'	1°54·3'W	T	139
Headley Mill Fm	Hants	SU8135	51°6·7'	0°50·2'W	FM	186
Headley Park	C of Bris	ST5769	51°25·3'	2°36·7'W	T	172,182
Headley Park	Hants	SU8138	51°8·4'	0°50·1'W	X	186
Headley Park	Surrey	TQ2055	51°17·1'	0°16·4'W	X	187
Headley Stud	Hants	SU5162	51°21·5'	1°15·7'W	X	174
Headley Wood Fm	Hants	SU8137	51°7·8'	0°50·2'W	FM	186
Headlow Fields	Derby	SK1642	52°58·7'	1°45·3'W	X	119,128
Head Mark Lane	E Ayr	NS5011	55°22·5'	4°21·6'W	W	70
Headmark Moss	E Ayr	NS4809	55°21·3'	4°23·4'W	X	70,77
Head Mill	Devon	SS6618	50°57·0'	3°54·1'W	X	180
Headmore Fm	Hants	SU6833	51°5·8'	1°1·3'W	FM	185,186
Headnook Fm	Lancs	SD5038	53°50·4'	2°45·2'W	FM	102
Head o'da Taing	Shetld	HT9739	60°8·4'	2°2·7'W	X	4
Head of Balglass	Stir	NS5887	56°3·5'	4°16·4'W	X	57
Head of Berg	Shetld	HU5363	60°21·1'	1°1·9'W	X	2,3
Head of Black Burn	Aberd	NO3987	56°58·5'	2°59·8'W	H	44
Head of Bratta	Shetld	HU4799	60°40·6'	1°7·9'W	X	1
Head of Bresdale	Shetld	HU5989	60°35·1'	0°54·9'W	X	1,2
Head of Brough	Shetld	HU4484	60°32·5'	1°11·4'W	X	1,2,3
Head of Calsta	Shetld	HU3787	60°34·2'	1°19·0'W	X	1,2
Head of Crees	Highld	ND3174	58°39·2'	3°10·9'W	X	7,12
Head of Cumla	Shetld	HU6792	60°36·6'	0°46·1'W	X	1,2
Head of Garbh Choire	Aberd	NO3990	57°0·1'	2°59·8'W	H	44
Head of Garness	Aberd	NJ7465	57°40·7'	2°25·7'W	X	29
Head of Geo	Orkney	HY4325	59°6·8'	2°59·2'W	X	5,6
Head of Greenock Water	E Ayr	NS6931	55°33·6'	4°4·2'W	X	71
Head of Gutcher	Shetld	HU5599	60°40·5'	0°59·1'W	X	1
Head of Haile	Cumbr	NY0409	54°28·3'	3°28·5'W	X	89
Head of Hevdagarth	Shetld	HU5291	60°36·2'	1°2·5'W	H	1,2
Head of Holland	Orkney	HY4812	58°59·8'	2°53·8'W	X	6
Head of Hosta	Shetld	HU6791	60°36·1'	0°46·1'W	X	1,2
Head of Lambhoga	Shetld	HU6287	60°34·0'	0°51·6'W	X	1,2
Head of Lee	Lancs	SD6538	53°50·5'	2°31·5'W	X	102,103
Head of Man	Highld	ND2071	58°37·4'	3°22·2'W	X	7,12
Head of Moclett	Orkney	HY4949	59°19·7'	2°53·3'W	X	5
Head of Moulin	Pth & Kin	NN9932	56°28·4'	3°37·9'W	X	52,53
Head of Muir	Falk	NS8181	56°0·7'	3°54·1'W	T	65
Head of Mula	Shetld	HU5699	60°40·5'	0°58·0'W	X	1
Head of Onibery	Shetld	HU2458	60°18·6'	1°33·4'W	X	3
Head of Pernealy	Orkney	HY5839	59°14·4'	2°43·7'W	X	5
Head of Row	Highld	ND3240	58°20·9'	3°9·2'W	X	12
Head of Skennif	Shetld	HU5365	60°22·2'	1°1·8'W	X	2,3
Head of Stanshi	Shetld	HU2180	60°30·5'	1°36·6'W	X	3
Head of the Holm	Shetld	HU3709	59°52·1'	1°19·9'W	X	4
Head of Tind	Shetld	HZ1969	59°30·7'	1°39·4'W	X	4
Head of Trent	C of Stoke	SJ8952	53°4·1'	2°9·4'W	W	118
Head of Virdibreck	Shetld	HU3891	60°36·3'	1°17·9'W	X	1,2
Head of Work	Orkney	HY4713	59°0·3'	2°54·9'W	X	6
Headon	Corn	SX1994	50°43·3'	4°33·5'W	X	190
Headon	Devon	SS3602	50°47·9'	4°19·3'W	T	190
Headon	Notts	SK7477	53°17·3'	0°53·0'W	T	120
Headon Barrow	Corn	SX1994	50°43·3'	4°33·5'W	A	190
Headon Cross	Devon	SS3602	50°47·9'	4°19·3'W	X	190
Headon Cross	Somer	SS9345	51°11·9'	3°31·5'W	X	181
Headon Down	Devon	SX5860	50°25·6'	3°59·6'W	X	202
Headon Fm	Devon	SS3007	50°50·5'	4°24·5'W	FM	190
Headon Warren	I of W	SZ3185	50°40·1'	1°33·3'W	X	196
Headon Wood	Notts	SK7477	53°17·3'	0°53·0'W	F	120
Head o'th Moor	Lancs	SD6541	53°52·1'	2°31·5'W	X	102,103
Headroom	Aberd	NJ9565	57°40·7'	2°4·6'W	X	30
Headrooms	Aberd	NJ9858	57°37·0'	2°1·5'W	X	30
Heads	D & G	NX8571	55°1·5'	3°47·5'W	X	84
Heads	Lancs	SD3545	53°54·1'	2°58·9'W	X	102
Heads	S Lanak	NS7247	55°42·2'	4°1·8'W	T	64
Heads	W Loth	NS9363	55°51·2'	3°42·1'W	X	65
Head Scar	Cumbr	SD2265	54°4·7'	3°11·1'W	X	96
Head's Fm	W Berks	SU5063	51°22·1'	1°16·5'W	FM	174
Headshaw	Scot Bord	NT4622	55°29·6'	2°50·8'W	T	73
Headshaw	Scot Bord	NT4955	55°47·4'	2°48·4'W	X	66,73
Headshaw Burn	Scot Bord	NT4857	55°48·5'	2°49·3'W	W	66,73
Headshaw Hill	Scot Bord	NT4856	55°47·9'	2°49·3'W	H	66,73
Headshaw Loch	Scot Bord	NT4523	55°30·1'	2°51·8'W	W	73
Heads Hill	Pth & Kin	NO0507	56°15·0'	3°31·5'W	H	58
Head's Hill	W Berks	SU5063	51°22·1'	1°16·5'W	X	174
Heads Hope	Durham	NZ4137	54°43·8'	1°21·4'W	X	93
Headshope	Northum	NY9399	55°17·4'	2°6·2'W	X	80
Headsmuir Fm	S Lanak	NS8649	55°43·5'	3°48·5'W	FM	72
Heads Nook	Cumbr	NY4955	54°53·5'	2°47·3'W	T	86
Heads Nook Hall	Cumbr	NY4954	54°52·9'	2°47·3'W	X	86
Heads of Ayr	S Ayr	NS2818	55°25·8'	4°41·7'W	X	70
Heads of Grocken	Shetld	HU2677	60°28·8'	1°31·1'W	X	3
Heads of Peitron	Shetld	HZ2273	59°32·8'	1°36·2'W	X	4
Heads of Skelmuir	Aberd	NJ9742	57°28·4'	2°2·5'W	X	30
Headson	Devon	SX4490	50°41·6'	4°12·1'W	X	190
Headson Cross	Devon	SX4490	50°41·6'	4°12·1'W	X	190
Heads Plantn	E Yorks	SE9744	53°53·2'	0°31·0'W	F	106
Heads, The	Cumbr	NY2946	54°48·5'	3°5·9'W	X	85
Headstone	Harrow	TQ1389	51°35·5'	0°21·7'W	T	176

Head Stone	Sheff	SK2587	53°23·0'	1°37·0'W	X	110
Headstone Lane Sta	Harrow	TQ1390	51°36·1'	0°21·7'W	X	176
Heads Wood	Cumbr	NY5063	54°57·8'	2°46·4'W	X	86
Headswood Ho	Falk	NS8282	56°1·2'	3°53·1'W	X	57,65
Head, The	Pemb	SM7204	51°41·5'	5°17·6'W	X	157
Head, The	Shetld	HU4490	60°35·7'	1°11·3'W	H	1,2
Headtown	Aberd	NJ6158	57°36·9'	2°38·7'W	X	29
Headwell	Fife	NT0988	56°4·8'	3°27·3'W	T	65
Head Wood	Devon	SS6518	50°57·0'	3°54·9'W	F	180
Heady Hill	Roch	SD8410	53°35·4'	2°14·1'W	T	109
Heage	Derby	SK3750	53°3·0'	1°26·5'W	T	119
Heage Common Fm	Derby	SK3550	53°3·0'	1°28·3'W	FM	119
Heage Firs	Derby	SK3550	53°3·0'	1°28·3'W	X	119
Heag Sound	Shetld	HU2458	60°18·6'	1°33·4'W	W	3
Heag,The	Shetld	HU2458	60°18·6'	1°33·4'W	X	3
Heag, The	Shetld	HU2860	60°19·7'	1°29·1'W	X	3
Heakley Hall Fm	C of Stoke	SJ9051	53°3·6'	2°8·5'W	FM	118
Healabhal Mhor or Macleod's Table North	Highld	NG2144	57°24·3'	6°38·3'W	H	23
Healam Ho	N Yks	SE3283	54°14·7'	1°30·1'W	X	99
Healaugh	N Yks	SE0199	54°23·4'	1°58·7'W	T	98
Healaugh	N Yks	SE4947	53°55·2'	1°14·8'W	T	105
Healaugh Beck	N Yks	SE5147	53°55·2'	1°13·0'W	W	105
Healaugh Grange	N Yks	SE4948	53°55·8'	1°14·8'W	X	105
Healaugh Manor Fm	N Yks	SE4747	53°55·3'	1°16·6'W	FM	105
Healaugh Priory	N Yks	SE4846	53°54·7'	1°15·7'W	A	105
Healaval	Highld	NG2564	57°35·2'	6°35·6'W	X	23
Heald Brow	Lancs	SD4674	54°9·8'	2°49·2'W	X	97
Heald Brow Pasture	Cumbr	SD3194	54°20·5'	3°3·3'W	F	96,97
Heald Fm	Lancs	SD5145	53°54·2'	2°44·3'W	FM	102
Heald Fm	Monm	SO3920	51°52·8'	2°52·8'W	FM	161
Heald Green	Stock	SJ8585	53°21·9'	2°13·1'W	T	109
Heald Moor	Lancs	SD8826	53°44·1'	2°10·5'W	X	103
Healds Green	Oldham	SD8907	53°33·8'	2°9·6'W	T	109
Heald, The	Ches	SJ5848	53°1·9'	2°37·2'W	X	117
Heald Wood	Cumbr	SD3898	54°22·7'	2°56·9'W	F	96,97
Heale	Devon	SS6446	51°12·1'	3°56·4'W	X	180
Heale	Devon	SX3686	50°39·3'	4°18·8'W	X	201
Heale	Somer	ST2419	50°58·2'	3°4·6'W	T	193
Heale	Somer	ST3825	51°1·5'	2°52·7'W	T	193
Heale	Somer	ST6844	51°11·9'	2°27·1'W	T	183
Heale Down	Devon	SS6546	51°12·1'	3°55·6'W	H	180
Heale Fm	Devon	SS6114	50°54·8'	3°58·3'W	FM	180
Heale Ho	Devon	SS4423	50°59·4'	4°13·0'W	X	180,190
Heale Ladder	Somer	ST7044	51°11·9'	2°25·4'W	X	183
Heale Town	Devon	SS5621	50°58·5'	4°2·7'W	X	180
Healey	Kirk	SE2224	53°43·0'	1°39·6'W	T	104
Healey	Northum	NU0900	55°17·9'	1°51·1'W	X	81
Healey	Northum	NZ0158	54°55·2'	1°58·6'W	T	87
Healey	N Yks	SE1880	54°13·2'	1°43·0'W	T	99
Healey	Roch	SD8815	53°38·1'	2°10·5'W	T	109
Healey	Wakf	SE2719	53°40·2'	1°35·1'W	T	110
Healey Cote	Northum	NU1100	55°17·9'	1°49·2'W	T	81
Healey Croft Fm	Leeds	SE2925	53°43·5'	1°33·2'W	FM	104
Healey Dell Nature Reserve	Roch	SD8716	53°38·7'	2°11·4'W	X	109
Healeyfield	Durham	NZ0648	54°49·9'	1°54·0'W	T	87
Healey Hall	Northum	NZ0057	54°54·7'	1°59·6'W	T	87
Healey Mill	Northum	NY9958	54°55·2'	2°0·5'W	X	87
Healey Mill	Northum	NZ0892	55°13·6'	1°52·0'W	X	81
Healey Nab	Lancs	SD6018	53°39·7'	2°35·9'W	F	109
Healey Riggend	Northum	NZ0056	54°54·2'	1°59·6'W	X	87
Healey Whins	Northum	NZ0056	54°54·2'	1°59·6'W	X	87
Healeywood	Northum	NZ2284	55°9·2'	1°38·9'W	X	81
Healing	NE Lincs	TA2110	53°34·6'	0°9·9'W	T	113
Healing Covert	NE Lincs	TA2010	53°34·6'	0°10·8'W	F	113
Healis Scars	N Som	ST4966	51°23·7'	2°43·6'W	X	172,182
Healthwaite Hall	N Yks	SE2947	53°55·3'	1°33·1'W	X	104
Healthwaite Hill	N Yks	SE2948	53°55·9'	1°33·1'W	H	104
Healy Hill	D & G	NY3281	55°7·4'	3°3·5'W	H	79
Heamies	Staffs	SJ8531	52°52·8'	2°13·0'W	X	127
Heamoor	Corn	SW4631	50°7·7'	5°32·9'W	T	203
Hean Cas	Pemb	SN1305	51°43·0'	4°42·0'W	X	158
Heane Fm	Devon	SS5204	50°49·2'	4°5·7'W	FM	191
Heaning	Cumbr	SD4399	54°23·2'	2°52·2'W	T	97
Heaning	Lancs	SD6850	53°57·0'	2°28·8'W	X	103
Heanings Fm	Cumbr	NY7713	54°31·0'	2°20·9'W	FM	91
Heanish	Arg & Bt	NM0343	56°29·4'	6°49·1'W	T	46
Heanley Fm	Warw	SP2596	52°33·9'	1°37·5'W	FM	140
Heanor	Derby	SK4346	53°0·8'	1°21·1'W	T	129
Heanor Gate	Derby	SK4245	53°0·3'	1°22·0'W	T	129
Heanton Barton	Devon	SS5010	50°52·4'	4°7·5'W	X	191
Heanton Punchardon	Devon	SS5035	51°5·9'	4°8·2'W	T	180
Heanton Satchville	Devon	SS5311	50°53·0'	4°5·0'W	X	191
Heap Bridge	Roch	SD8210	53°35·4'	2°15·9'W	T	109
Heapey	Lancs	SD6020	53°40·7'	2°35·9'W	X	102,103
Heapham	Lincs	SK8788	53°23·1'	0°41·1'W	T	112,121
Heapham Grange	Lincs	SK8988	53°23·1'	0°39·3'W	X	112,121
Heard's Fm	Essex	TQ6097	51°39·2'	0°19·2'E	FM	167,177
Heards Fm	Hants	SU7231	51°4·7'	0°57·9'W	FM	186
Hearlake	Somer	SS7339	51°8·4'	3°48·5'W	X	180
Hearn	Hants	SU8337	51°7·8'	0°48·4'W	T	186
Hearnden Green	Kent	TQ8246	51°11·3'	0°36·7'E	T	188
Hearne	N Yks	SD8495	54°21·3'	2°14·4'W	X	98
Hearne Beck	N Yks	SD8594	54°20·7'	2°13·4'W	W	98
Hearne Fm	Devon	ST0121	50°59·0'	3°24·2'W	FM	181
Hearne Ho	Somer	ST5641	51°10·2'	2°37·4'W	X	182,183
Hearne, The	Shrops	SJ6129	52°51·7'	2°34·4'W	X	127
Hearn Fm	Devon	ST0605	50°50·4'	3°19·7'W	FM	192
Hearn Fm	Somer	ST1534	51°6·2'	3°12·5'W	FM	181
Hearnton Wood	Bucks	SU8296	51°39·6'	0°48·5'W	F	165
Hearsall Common	Cov	SP3178	52°24·2'	1°32·3'W	X	140
Hearse Wood	Suff	TL7862	52°13·9'	0°38·6'E	F	155
Hearson	Devon	SS6029	51°2·8'	3°59·5'W	X	180
Hearson Hill	Devon	SS6029	51°2·8'	3°59·5'W	H	180
Hearthstane	Scot Bord	NT1126	55°31·4'	3°24·2'W	X	72
Hearthstane Burn	Scot Bord	NT1225	55°30·9'	3°23·2'W	W	72
Hearthstone	Derby	SK3058	53°7·3'	1°32·7'W	T	119
Heart in Hand	Kent	TR2066	51°21·2'	1°10·0'E	X	179
Heart Law	Scot Bord	NT7166	55°53·4'	2°27·4'W	X	67

Heartleap Well	N Yks	SE1396	54°21·8'	1°47·6'W	X	99
Heart Loch	Arg & Bt	NN2031	56°26·5'	4°54·7'W	W	50
Heart Moss	D & G	NX7647	54°48·4'	3°55·3'W	W	84
Heart of Arden Walk	Warw	SP1466	52°17·8'	1°47·3'W	X	151
Heart of England Way	Warw	SP1745	52°6·4'	1°44·7'W	X	151
Hearts Delight	Kent	TQ8862	51°19·8'	0°42·3'E	T	178
Heart's Delight	Kent	TR1949	51°12·1'	1°8·5'E	X	179,189
Heartsease	Powys	SO1369	52°19·0'	3°16·2'W	X	136,148
Heartsease	Powys	SO3472	52°20·8'	2°57·7'W	X	137,148
Hearts Toe, The	Northum	NT7606	55°21·1'	2°22·3'W	X	80
Hearty Gate Fm	Somer	ST5440	51°9·7'	2°39·1'W	FM	182,183
Hearty Moor	Somer	ST5439	51°9·1'	2°39·1'W	X	182,183
Heaselands	W Susx	TQ3122	50°59·2'	0°7·6'W	X	198
Heasley Mill	Devon	SS7332	51°4·6'	3°48·4'W	T	180
Heastabhal	N Eil	NB2219	58°4·6'	6°42·5'W	H	13,14
Heaste	Highld	NG6417	57°11·2'	5°53·9'W	T	32
Heatenthorn Fm	W Susx	TQ2417	50°56·6'	0°13·7'W	FM	198
Heath	Card	ST1779	51°30·5'	3°11·4'W	T	171
Heath	Derby	SK4466	53°11·6'	1°20·1'W	T	120
Heath	Devon	SX3997	50°45·3'	4°16·6'W	X	190
Heath	Devon	SX6997	50°45·7'	3°51·1'W	X	191
Heath	Devon	SX7049	50°19·8'	3°49·2'W	X	202
Heath	Devon	SX9896	50°45·5'	3°26·4'W	X	192
Heath	Halton	SJ5081	53°19·7'	2°44·6'W	T	108
Heath	Powys	SO2075	52°22·3'	3°10·1'W	X	137
Heath	Powys	SO2075	52°22·3'	3°10·1'W	X	137,148
Heath	Wakf	SE3520	53°40·8'	1°27·8'W	X	104
Heatham	Corn	SS2412	50°53·1'	4°29·8'W	X	190
Heath and Reach	Beds	SP9227	51°56·3'	0°39·3'W	T	165
Heathayne	Devon	SY2394	50°44·7'	3°5·1'W	X	192,193
Heath Barn	Glos	SP2029	51°57·8'	1°42·1'W	X	163
Heath Barn	W Berks	SU4578	51°30·2'	1°20·7'W	X	174
Heathbarn Down	W Susx	SU8412	50°54·3'	0°47·9'W	X	197
Heath Barn Fm	Suff	TL7867	52°16·6'	0°37·0'E	FM	155
Heath Barton	Devon	SX8494	50°44·3'	3°38·3'W	X	191
Heath Bottom	Dorset	ST7905	50°50·9'	2°17·5'W	X	194
Heath Br	Devon	SS8404	50°49·7'	3°38·4'W	X	191
Heath Br	Oxon	SP6320	51°52·7'	1°4·7'W	X	164,165
Heathbrook	Shrops	SJ6228	52°51·1'	2°33·5'W	X	127
Heath Charnock	Lancs	SD5914	53°37·5'	2°36·8'W	T	108
Heath Common	Shrops	SO5192	52°31·7'	2°42·9'W	X	137,138
Heath Common	Wakf	SE3519	53°40·2'	1°27·8'W	X	110,111
Heath Common	W Susx	TQ1114	50°55·1'	0°24·9'W	T	198
Heathcot	Aberd	NJ8901	57°6·2'	2°10·4'W	X	38
Heathcote	Aberd	NJ5505	57°8·3'	2°44·2'W	X	37
Heathcote	Derby	SK1460	53°8·5'	1°47·0'W	T	119
Heathcote	Shrops	SJ6528	52°51·1'	2°30·8'W	T	127
Heathcote	Warw	SP3063	52°16·1'	1°33·2'W	T	151
Heathcote Fm	Warw	SP2958	52°13·4'	1°34·1'W	FM	151
Heathcote Hill Fm	Warw	SP2964	52°16·6'	1°34·1'W	FM	151
Heath Cottage	E Ayr	NS6128	55°31·8'	4°11·7'W	X	71
Heath Cottages	Suff	TL9276	52°21·1'	0°49·6'E	X	144
Heath Cottages	Suff	TM2541	52°1·5'	1°17·2'E	X	169
Heath Covert	Suff	TL8773	52°19·6'	0°45·1'E	F	144,155
Heathcroft Fm	Ches	SJ4363	53°9·9'	2°50·8'W	FM	117
Heathcroft Fm	Hants	SU6839	51°9·0'	1°1·3'W	FM	185,186
Heath Cross	Devon	SX7097	50°45·7'	3°50·2'W	T	191
Heath Cross	Devon	SX8494	50°44·3'	3°38·3'W	T	191
Heathencote	Northnts	SP7147	52°7·2'	0°57·4'W	X	152
Heath End	Bucks	SP9506	51°44·9'	0°37·0'W	T	165
Heath End	Bucks	SU8898	51°40·7'	0°43·2'W	T	165
Heath End	Ches	SJ7856	53°6·3'	2°19·3'W	X	118
Heath End	Hants	SU4162	51°21·6'	1°24·3'W	T	174
Heath End	Hants	SU5862	51°21·5'	1°9·6'W	T	174
Heath End	Leic	SK3621	52°47·4'	1°27·6'W	T	128
Heath End	Oxon	SU6686	51°34·4'	1°2·5'W	X	175
Heath End	Oxon	SU6782	51°32·2'	1°1·6'W	X	175
Heath End	S Glos	ST6989	51°36·2'	2°26·5'W	T	162,172
Heath End	Surrey	SU8449	51°14·3'	0°47·4'W	T	186
Heath End	Wals	SK0202	52°37·2'	1°57·8'W	T	139
Heath End	Warw	SP2360	52°14·5'	1°39·4'W	T	151
Heath End	W Susx	SU9618	50°57·4'	0°37·6'W	T	197
Heather	Leic	SK3810	52°41·4'	1°25·9'W	T	128
Heather Bank	Cumbr	NY0741	54°45·6'	3°26·3'W	X	85
Heather Bank	Cumbr	NY1051	54°51·0'	3°23·7'W	X	85
Heather Centre	Highld	NH9722	57°16·9'	3°42·1'W	X	36
Heathercombe	Devon	SX7181	50°37·1'	3°49·0'W	T	191
Heathercote	Durham	NY9721	54°35·3'	2°2·4'W	X	92
Heather Cottage	Stir	NN5529	56°26·1'	4°20·7'W	X	51
Heather Cotts	Northum	NU1635	55°36·7'	1°44·3'W	X	75
Heatherdeep	Highld	ND2656	58°29·4'	3°15·7'W	X	11,12
Heatherden	E Susx	TQ5621	50°58·3'	0°13·7'E	X	199
Heather Dene	N Yks	SE1894	54°20·7'	1°43·0'W	X	99
Heatherfield	Highld	NG4841	57°23·6'	6°11·2'W	T	23
Heather Fm	Bath & NE Somer	ST7267	51°24·3'	2°23·8'W	FM	172
Heather Fm	Lancs	SD3410	53°35·2'	2°59·4'W	FM	108
Heather Fm	Surrey	SU9960	51°20·1'	0°34·3'W	FM	175,176,186
Heather Hill	Cald	SD9535	53°48·9'	2°4·1'W	X	103
Heather Ho	Cumbr	NY5375	55°4·3'	2°43·7'W	X	86
Heatherhope	Scot Bord	NT8016	55°26·5'	2°18·5'W	X	80
Heatherhope Burn	Scot Bord	NT8017	55°27·0'	2°18·5'W	W	80
Heatherhouse	Arg & Bt	NR4269	55°51·3'	6°6·9'W	X	60,61
Heatherhouse	Orkney	HY5311	58°59·3'	2°48·6'W	X	6
Heather House Fm	N Yks	SE2556	54°0·2'	1°36·7'W	FM	104
Heatheridge	Northum	NY9072	55°2·8'	2°9·0'W	X	87
Heatherinch	Fife	NO3009	56°16·4'	3°7·4'W	X	59
Heather Knowe	Scot Bord	NT6100	55°17·8'	2°36·4'W	X	80
Heatherlands	N Yks	SE2270	54°7·8'	1°39·4'W	X	99
Heatherlands	W Loth	NT1164	55°51·9'	3°24·9'W	X	65
Heather Law	Northum	NU1038	55°38·4'	1°50·0'W	X	75
Heather Lea	Cumbr	NY0318	54°33·1'	3°29·6'W	X	89
Heatherlea	Durham	NY9725	54°37·5'	2°2·4'W	X	92
Heatherlea	Highld	NJ1535	57°24·1'	3°24·4'W	T	28
Heatherley	Surrey	TQ3340	51°8·9'	0°5·5'W	X	187
Heathermount	Win & Maid	SU9467	51°23·9'	0°38·5'W	X	175
Heatherquoy	Orkney	HY4709	58°58·2'	2°54·8'W	X	6,7
Heather Row	Hants	SU7152	51°15·9'	0°58·5'W	T	186
Heatherside	Surrey	SU9059	51°19·6'	0°42·1'W	T	175,186
Heatherslaw	Northum	NT9338	55°38·4'	2°6·2'W	X	74,75

Heatherslaw	Northum	NZ0874	55°3·9'	1°52·1'W	X	88
Heatherslaw Light Railway	Northum	NT9238	55°38·4'	2°7·2'W	X	74,75
Heatherslaw Light Railway	Northum	NT9238	55°38·4'	2°7·2'W	X	74,75
Heatherstacks	Angus	NO4552	56°39·7'	2°53·4'W	X	54
Heather Stone	Devon	SX7279	50°36·0'	3°48·1'W	X	191
Heatherton Park Fm	Somer	ST1622	50°59·7'	3°11·4'W	FM	181,193
Heathertown	Shetld	HU3050	60°14·3'	1°27·0'W	X	3
Heatherway Fm	Lancs	SD5743	53°53·1'	2°38·8'W	FM	102
Heatherwick	Aberd	NJ8018	57°15·4'	2°19·4'W	X	38
Heatherwick	Northum	NY8992	55°13·6'	2°9·9'W	X	80
Heatherwold	Hants	SU4761	51°21·0'	1°19·1'W	X	174
Heatherwood Park	Highld	NH8091	57°53·8'	4°1·0'W	X	21
Heatherybanks	Aberd	NJ7744	57°29·4'	2°22·6'W	X	29,30
Heatherybraes	Aberd	NJ6837	57°25·6'	2°31·5'W	X	29
Heatheryburn	Northum	NY9049	54°50·4'	2°8·9'W	X	87
Heatheryburn Moor	Northum	NY9048	54°49·9'	2°8·9'W	X	87
Heathery Carr	Scot Bord	NT8969	55°55·1'	2°10·1'W	X	67
Heathery Dam	D & G	NX9193	55°13·4'	3°42·4'W	W	78
Heathery Edge	Northum	NZ0366	54°59·6'	1°56·8'W	X	87
Heatheryfield	Aberd	NJ4644	57°29·2'	2°53·6'W	X	28,29
Heatheryford	Pth & Kin	NO1002	56°12·4'	3°26·6'W	X	58
Heatheryhall	Northum	NU0229	55°33·5'	1°57·7'W	X	75
Heathery Hall	Northum	NY7889	55°11·9'	2°20·3'W	X	80
Heatheryhall	S Lanak	NS9740	55°38·8'	3°37·8'W	X	72
Heatheryhaugh	Aberd	NO6586	56°58·1'	2°34·1'W	X	45
Heatheryhaugh	D & G	NT0906	55°20·6'	3°25·7'W	X	78
Heatheryhaugh	Pth & Kin	NO1751	56°38·9'	3°20·8'W	X	53
Heathery Hill	Aberd	NO6786	56°58·1'	2°32·1'W	H	45
Heathery Hill	D & G	NS7703	55°18·6'	3°55·8'W	X	78
Heathery Howes	Orkney	HY4706	58°56·5'	2°54·8'W	X	6,7
Heatheryknowe	Cumbr	NY4072	55°2·6'	2°55·9'W	X	85
Heatheryleys	Pth & Kin	NO0912	56°17·8'	3°27·8'W	X	58
Heatherytops	Northum	NT9950	55°44·9'	2°0·5'W	X	75
Heathfield	Aberd	NJ6138	57°26·1'	2°38·5'W	X	29
Heathfield	Aberd	NO9098	57°4·6'	2°9·4'W	X	38,45
Heathfield	Cambs	TL4546	52°5·8'	0°7·4'E	T	154
Heathfield	Ches	SJ5766	53°11·6'	2°38·2'W	X	117
Heathfield	Ches	SJ6847	53°1·4'	2°28·2'W	X	118
Heathfield	Croy	TQ3563	51°21·2'	0°3·3'W	X	177,187
Heathfield	Cumbr	NY1743	54°46·8'	3°17·0'W	X	85
Heathfield	Devon	SS9100	50°47·6'	3°32·4'W	X	192
Heathfield	Devon	SX4679	50°35·7'	4°10·2'W	X	201
Heathfield	Devon	SX8376	50°34·6'	3°38·8'W	T	191
Heathfield	D & G	NX9182	55°7·5'	3°42·1'W	X	78
Heathfield	D & G	NY2067	54°59·7'	3°14·6'W	X	85
Heathfield	E Susx	TQ5630	51°3·1'	0°13·9'E	T	188
Heathfield	E Susx	TQ5821	50°58·2'	0°15·4'E	T	199
Heathfield	Glos	ST7098	51°41·0'	2°25·6'W	T	162
Heathfield	Hants	SU5506	50°51·3'	1°12·7'W	T	196
Heathfield	Hants	SZ2098	50°47·1'	1°42·6'W	X	195
Heathfield	Highld	ND1066	58°34·6'	3°32·4'W	X	11,12
Heathfield	Highld	ND2473	58°38·6'	3°18·1'W	X	7,12
Heathfield	Highld	NH8050	57°31·7'	3°59·8'W	X	27
Heathfield	Highld	NJ0328	57°20·2'	3°36·2'W	X	36
Heathfield	Lincs	TF1193	53°25·6'	0°19·4'W	T	113
Heathfield	N Lanak	NS6868	55°53·5'	4°6·2'W	X	64
Heathfield	N Yks	SE1367	54°6·2'	1°47·7'W	T	99
Heathfield	Orkney	HY4110	58°58·7'	3°1·1'W	X	6
Heathfield	Renf	NS3262	55°49·6'	4°40·5'W	X	63
Heathfield	S Ayr	NS3523	55°28·6'	4°36·2'W	T	70
Heathfield	Somer	ST1626	51°1·9'	3°11·5'W	T	181,193
Heathfield	Somer	ST1633	51°5·6'	3°11·6'W	T	181
Heathfield	Surrey	TQ2349	51°13·8'	0°13·9'W	X	187
Heathfield Barton	Devon	SX7152	50°21·5'	3°48·4'W	X	202
Heathfield Fm	Ches	SJ7555	53°5·7'	2°22·0'W	FM	118
Heathfield Fm	Corn	SX3966	50°28·5'	4°15·8'W	FM	201
Heathfield Fm	Devon	SX8169	50°30·8'	3°40·3'W	FM	202
Heathfield Fm	Devon	SX9989	50°41·7'	3°25·4'W	FM	192
Heathfield Fm	Devon	SY2891	50°43·1'	3°0·8'W	FM	193
Heathfield Fm	I of W	SZ5192	50°43·8'	1°16·3'W	FM	196
Heathfield Fm	Pemb	SM9230	51°56·0'	5°1·2'W	FM	157
Heathfield Fm	Somer	ST1335	51°6·7'	3°14·2'W	FM	181
Heathfield Ho	E Susx	TQ5920	50°57·7'	0°16·2'E	X	199
Heathfield Lo	Devon	SX4777	50°34·6'	4°9·3'W	X	191,201
Heathfield Manor	Devon	SX6850	50°20·3'	3°50·9'W	X	202
Heathfield Moor	D & G	NY0789	55°11·4'	3°27·2'W	X	78
Heathfield Moor	N Yks	SE1167	54°6·2'	1°49·5'W	X	99
Heathfield Nook	Derby	SK0770	53°13·9'	1°53·3'W	X	119
Heathfield Park	E Susx	TQ5920	50°57·7'	0°16·2'E	X	199
Heathfield Village	Oxon	SP5216	51°50·6'	1°14·3'W	T	164
Heath Fm	Cambs	TL2178	52°23·4'	0°12·9'W	FM	142
Heath Fm	Cambs	TL3841	52°3·2'	0°1·2'E	FM	154
Heath Fm	Cambs	TL4344	52°4·8'	0°5·6'E	FM	154
Heath Fm	Cambs	TL4853	52°9·6'	0°10·2'E	FM	154
Heath Fm	Cambs	TL5253	52°9·5'	0°13·7'E	FM	154
Heath Fm	Ches	SJ3275	53°16·3'	3°0·8'W	FM	117
Heath Fm	Ches	SJ3973	53°15·3'	2°54·5'W	FM	117
Heath Fm	Ches	SJ4073	53°15·3'	2°53·6'W	FM	117
Heath Fm	Ches	SJ4472	53°14·8'	2°49·9'W	FM	117
Heath Fm	Ches	SJ7251	53°3·6'	2°24·7'W	FM	118
Heath Fm	Ches	SJ7252	53°4·1'	2°24·7'W	FM	118
Heath Fm	Ches	SJ7472	53°14·9'	2°23·0'W	FM	118
Heath Fm	Derby	SK1077	53°17·6'	1°50·6'W	FM	119
Heath Fm	Derby	SK3520	52°46·8'	1°28·5'W	FM	128
Heath Fm	Devon	SS3215	50°54·8'	4°23·0'W	FM	190
Heath Fm	Devon	SS6310	50°52·6'	3°56·5'W	FM	191
Heath Fm	Devon	SS7918	50°57·2'	3°43·0'W	FM	180
Heath Fm	Devon	SX5199	50°46·5'	4°6·4'W	FM	191
Heath Fm	E Susx	TQ3618	50°56·9'	0°3·4'W	FM	198
Heath Fm	Glos	SP1135	52°1·0'	1°50·0'W	FM	150
Heath Fm	Heref	SO6762	52°15·5'	2°28·6'W	FM	138,149
Heath Fm	Herts	TL3037	52°1·2'	0°5·9'W	FM	153
Heath Fm	Herts	TL3739	52°2·2'	0°0·2'E	FM	154
Heath Fm	Lancs	SD7657	54°0·8'	2°21·6'W	FM	103
Heath Fm	Leic	SK4606	52°39·2'	1°18·8'W	FM	140
Heath Fm	Leic	SK8428	52°50·8'	0°44·8'W	FM	130
Heath Fm	Lincs	SK9435	52°54·5'	0°35·7'W	FM	130
Heath Fm	Lincs	SK9436	52°55·0'	0°35·7'W	FM	130
Heath Fm	Lincs	SK9749	53°2·0'	0°32·8'W	FM	130
Heath Fm	Lincs	SK9824	52°48·5'	0°32·4'W	FM	130
Heath Fm	Lincs	SK9854	53°4·7'	0°31·8'W	FM	121
Heath Fm	Lincs	SK9887	53°22·5'	0°31·2'W	FM	112,121
Heath Fm	Lincs	SK9936	52°55·0'	0°31·3'W	FM	130
Heath Fm	Lincs	TF0157	53°6·3'	0°29·1'W	FM	121
Heath Fm	Lincs	TF0247	53°0·9'	0°28·4'W	FM	130
Heath Fm	Lincs	TF0456	53°5·7'	0°26·4'W	FM	121
Heath Fm	Norf	TF6609	52°39·4'	0°27·7'E	FM	143
Heath Fm	Norf	TF9325	52°47·5'	0°52·2'E	FM	132
Heath Fm	Norf	TF9430	52°50·2'	0°53·2'E	FM	132
Heath Fm	Norf	TF9723	52°46·3'	0°55·6'E	FM	132
Heath Fm	Norf	TG0714	52°41·3'	1°4·2'E	FM	133
Heath Fm	Norf	TG0938	52°54·2'	1°6·9'E	FM	133
Heath Fm	Norf	TG2017	52°42·6'	1°15·8'E	FM	133,134
Heath Fm	Norf	TG2238	52°53·8'	1°18·4'E	FM	133
Heath Fm	Norf	TG3012	52°39·6'	1°24·5'E	FM	133,134
Heath Fm	Norf	TG3032	52°50·4'	1°25·3'E	FM	133
Heath Fm	Norf	TG3921	52°44·2'	1°32·8'E	FM	133,134
Heath Fm	Norf	TG4027	52°47·5'	1°34·0'E	FM	134
Heath Fm	Norf	TG4913	52°39·7'	1°41·3'E	FM	134
Heath Fm	Norf	TM0887	52°26·7'	1°4·0'E	FM	144
Heath Fm	Norf	TM0988	52°27·2'	1°5·0'E	FM	144
Heath Fm	Northnts	SP6152	52°10·0'	1°6·1'W	FM	152
Heath Fm	Northnts	SP6156	52°12·2'	1°6·0'W	FM	152
Heath Fm	Northnts	SP7062	52°15·3'	0°58·1'W	FM	152
Heath Fm	Oxon	SP2619	51°52·4'	1°36·9'W	FM	163
Heath Fm	Oxon	SP3931	51°58·8'	1°25·5'W	FM	151
Heath Fm	Oxon	SP4223	51°54·5'	1°23·0'W	FM	164
Heath Fm	Oxon	SP4328	51°57·2'	1°22·1'W	FM	164
Heath Fm	Oxon	SP5731	51°58·7'	1°9·8'W	FM	152
Heath Fm	Oxon	SP6403	51°43·6'	1°4·0'W	FM	164,165
Heath Fm	Oxon	SU2496	51°40·0'	1°38·8'W	FM	163
Heath Fm	Shrops	SJ3711	52°41·8'	2°55·5'W	FM	126
Heath Fm	Shrops	SJ5836	52°55·4'	2°37·1'W	FM	126
Heath Fm	Shrops	SJ6126	52°50·0'	2°34·3'W	FM	127
Heath Fm	Sol	SP1885	52°28·0'	1°43·7'W	FM	139
Heath Fm	Sol	SP2381	52°25·8'	1°39·3'W	FM	139
Heath Fm	Staffs	SJ9309	52°41·0'	2°5·8'W	FM	127
Heath Fm	Suff	TL6970	52°18·4'	0°29·1'E	FM	154
Heath Fm	Suff	TL7566	52°16·1'	0°34·3'E	FM	155
Heath Fm	Suff	TL8673	52°19·6'	0°44·2'E	FM	144,155
Heath Fm	Suff	TL9070	52°17·9'	0°47·6'E	FM	144,155
Heath Fm	Suff	TL9478	52°22·2'	0°51·4'E	FM	144
Heath Fm	Suff	TM2886	52°25·7'	1°21·6'E	FM	156
Heath Fm	Suff	TM5388	52°26·1'	1°43·7'E	FM	156
Heath Fm	Surrey	TQ2054	51°16·6'	0°16·4'W	FM	187
Heath Fm	Warw	SP1168	52°18·8'	1°49·9'W	FM	139
Heath Fm	Warw	SP2252	52°10·2'	1°40·3'W	FM	151
Heath Fm	Warw	SP3455	52°11·8'	1°29·8'W	FM	151
Heath Fm	Warw	SP4371	52°20·4'	1°21·7'W	FM	140
Heath Fm	Warw	SP4374	52°22·0'	1°21·7'W	FM	140
Heath Fm	Warw	SP5280	52°25·2'	1°13·7'W	FM	140
Heath Fms	Cambs	TL5655	52°10·5'	0°17·3'E	FM	154
Heath Fms	Norf	TM0989	52°27·8'	1°5·0'E	FM	144
Heathgates	Shrops	SJ5734	52°54·3'	2°38·0'W	X	126
Heath Grange	Lincs	TF0461	53°8·4'	0°26·3'W	X	121
Heath Green	Hants	SU6337	51°8·0'	1°5·6'W	T	185
Heath Green	Worcs	SP0771	52°20·5'	1°53·4'W	T	139
Heathhall	D & G	NX9979	55°6·0'	3°34·5'W	T	84
Heathhall	D & G	NY0889	55°11·5'	3°26·3'W	X	78
Heath Hall	Surrey	SU9138	51°8·3'	0°41·6'W	X	186
Heath Hall Fm	Ches	SJ6177	53°17·6'	2°34·7'W	FM	118
Heath Hanger Copse	W Berks	SU3670	51°25·9'	1°28·5'W	F	174
Heath Hay	Staffs	SJ9059	53°7·9'	2°8·6'W	X	118
Heath Hayes	Staffs	SK0110	52°41·5'	1°58·7'W	T	128
Heath-Hill	Aberd	NJ9663	57°39·7'	2°3·6'W	X	30
Heath Hill	Devon	SS6010	50°52·6'	3°59·0'W	X	191
Heath Hill	Glos	SP1822	51°54·0'	1°43·9'W	X	163
Heath Hill	Shrops	SJ7614	52°43·6'	2°20·9'W	T	127
Heath Hill	Wilts	SU0733	51°6·0'	1°53·6'W	X	184
Heath Hill	W Susx	SU9314	50°55·3'	0°40·2'W	X	197
Heath Hill Fm	Worcs	SO8437	52°2·1'	2°13·6'W	FM	150
Heath Ho	Derby	SK2132	52°53·3'	1°40·9'W	X	128
Heath Ho	Hants	SU3935	51°7·0'	1°26·2'W	X	185
Heath Ho	Heref	SO3876	52°23·0'	2°54·3'W	X	137,148
Heath Ho	Lincs	TF0160	53°7·9'	0°29·0'W	X	121
Heath Ho	Norf	TF9933	52°51·7'	0°57·8'E	X	132
Heath Ho	Norf	TG0737	52°53·7'	1°5·0'E	X	133
Heath Ho	Shrops	SJ5924	52°49·0'	2°36·1'W	X	126
Heath Ho	Shrops	SO4796	52°33·8'	2°46·5'W	X	137,138
Heath Ho	Shrops	SO5585	52°27·9'	2°39·3'W	X	137,138
Heath Ho	Staffs	SJ8601	52°36·6'	2°12·0'W	X	127,139
Heath Ho	Staffs	SJ9458	53°7·4'	2°5·0'W	X	118
Heath Ho	Staffs	SJ9651	53°3·6'	2°3·2'W	X	118
Heath Ho	Staffs	SK0239	52°57·1'	1°57·8'W	X	128
Heath Ho	Staffs	SK0758	53°7·4'	1°53·3'W	X	119
Heath Ho	Staffs	SK0864	53°10·6'	1°52·4'W	X	119
Heath Ho	Surrey	TQ2054	51°16·6'	0°16·4'W	X	187
Heath Ho	Warw	SP4274	52°22·0'	1°22·6'W	X	140
Heath House	Orkney	HY3009	58°58·0'	3°12·6'W	X	6,7
Heath House	Somer	ST4246	51°12·9'	2°49·4'W	T	182
Heath House Fm	Norf	TF7630	52°50·6'	0°37·2'E	FM	132
Heath House Fm	Norf	TM0787	52°26·7'	1°3·2'E	FM	144
Heath House Fm	Shrops	SJ7702	52°37·2'	2°20·0'W	FM	127
Heath House Fm	Somer	ST8147	51°13·5'	2°15·9'W	FM	183
Heath Lake	Wok	SU8265	51°22·9'	0°48·9'W	W	175
Heathland	S Lanak	NS9455	55°46·9'	3°41·0'W	X	65,72
Heathlands	Cumbr	NY3761	54°56·6'	2°58·6'W	X	85
Heathlands	Devon	SY0692	50°43·4'	3°19·5'W	X	192
Heathlands	Staffs	SO8385	52°28·0'	2°14·6'W	X	138
Heathlands	Wok	SU8265	51°22·9'	0°48·9'W	T	175
Heathlands Fm	Traf	SJ7190	53°24·6'	2°25·8'W	FM	109
Heathlands Fm	W Susx	SU8720	50°58·6'	0°45·3'W	FM	197
Heath Lanes	Wrekin	SJ6121	52°47·3'	2°34·3'W	T	127
Heathley Fm	Staffs	SK1800	52°36·1'	1°43·7'W	FM	139
Heath Lodge	Bucks	TQ0281	51°31·3'	0°31·4'W	X	176
Heath Lodge	Ches	SJ6176	53°17·0'	2°34·7'W	X	118
Heath Mill	W Susx	TQ0717	50°56·8'	0°28·2'W	X	197
Heath Moor	Devon	SX5198	50°46·0'	4°6·4'W	X	191
Heathmount	Highld	NH7679	57°47·3'	4°4·7'W	X	21
Heathmount	Highld	NH8852	57°32·9'	3°51·8'W	X	27
Heath Mynd	Shrops	SO3394	52°32·6'	2°58·9'W	H	137
Heath Paddocks	Shrops	SJ5638	52°56·5'	2°38·9'W	X	126
Heath Park	Devon	SX4490	50°41·6'	4°12·1'W	X	190
Heath Park	Hav	TQ5288	51°34·4'	0°12·0'E	T	177
Heath Place	Thurr	TQ6480	51°29·9'	0°22·2'E	X	177
Heath Plantn	Cambs	TL6869	52°17·8'	0°28·2'E	F	154
Heath Pond	Hants	SU7522	50°59·8'	0°55·5'W	W	197
Heathpool Common	Scot Bord	NT2544	55°41·3'	3°11·1'W	X	73
Heath Poult Cross	Somer	SS9436	51°7·0'	3°30·5'W	X	181
Heath Road House Fm	Shrops	SJ5539	52°57·0'	2°39·8'W	FM	126
Heathrow Airport London	Hill	TQ0775	51°28·1'	0°27·2'W	X	176
Heathryfauld	Aberd	NK0144	57°29·4'	1°58·5'W	X	30
Heathryfold	C of Aber	NJ9008	57°10·0'	2°9·5'W	T	38
Heath Side	Kent	TQ5172	51°25·8'	0°10·7'E	T	177
Heathside	Shrops	SJ6724	52°49·0'	2°29·0'W	X	127
Heathstock	Devon	ST2403	50°49·5'	3°4·4'W	T	192,193
Heath Stone	Devon	SX6783	50°38·1'	3°52·5'W	A	191
Heath, The	Ches	SJ7478	53°18·1'	2°23·0'W	X	118
Heath, The	Glos	SO7630	51°58·3'	2°20·6'W	X	150
Heath, The	Heref	SO5355	52°11·7'	2°40·9'W	X	149
Heath, The	Heref	SO6451	52°9·6'	2°31·2'W	X	149
Heath, The	Lincs	TF0114	52°43·1'	0°29·9'W	F	130
Heath, The	Oxon	SP5225	51°55·5'	1°14·2'W	F	164
Heath, The	Powys	SO0498	52°34·5'	3°24·6'W	X	136
Heath, The	Shrops	SO6586	52°28·5'	2°30·5'W	X	138
Heath, The	Worcs	SO8076	52°23·1'	2°17·2'W	X	138
Heathton	Shrops	SO8192	52°31·8'	2°16·4'W	T	138
Heathtop	Derby	SK2032	52°53·3'	1°41·8'W	T	128
Heath Town	Wolv	SO9299	52°35·6'	2°6·7'W	T	139
Heath View Fm	Somer	ST4441	51°10·2'	2°47·7'W	FM	182
Heath Village	Shrops	SO5584	52°27·4'	2°39·3'W	A	137,138
Heathwaite	Cumbr	SD2996	54°21·5'	3°5·1'W	X	96,97
Heathwaite	Cumbr	SD4197	54°22·2'	2°54·1'W	X	96,97
Heathwaite	Cumbr	SD4476	54°10·9'	2°51·1'W	X	97
Heathwaite	N Yks	NZ4801	54°24·4'	1°15·2'W	T	93
Heathwaite Fm	Cumbr	SD2486	54°16·1'	3°9·6'W	FM	96
Heathwaite Moss	Cumbr	SD2487	54°16·6'	3°8·7'W	X	96
Heath Warren	Hants	SU7660	51°20·3'	0°54·1'W	F	175,186
Heath Wood	Bucks	SU8087	51°34·8'	0°50·3'W	F	175
Heath Wood	Heref	SO3854	52°11·1'	2°54·0'W	F	148,149
Heath Wood	Herts	TQ0899	51°41·0'	0°25·9'W	F	166,176
Heath Wood	Wilts	SU0733	51°6·0'	1°53·6'W	F	184
Heathy Brow	E Susx	TQ3212	50°53·8'	0°7·0'W	X	198
Heathy Close	Derby	SK2036	52°55·5'	1°41·7'W	X	128
Heathydale Ward	Derby	SK1474	53°16·0'	1°47·0'W	X	119
Heathy Park	Heref	SO3571	52°20·2'	2°56·8'W	X	137,148
Heathy Roods	Staffs	SK0857	53°6·8'	1°52·4'W	X	119
Heatley	Ches	SJ6246	53°0·8'	2°33·6'W	X	118
Heatley	Staffs	SK0627	52°50·7'	1°54·3'W	T	128
Heatley	Warr	SJ7088	53°23·5'	2°26·7'W	T	109
Heaton	Bolton	SD6909	53°34·8'	2°27·7'W	T	109
Heaton	Brad	SE1335	53°48·9'	1°47·7'W	T	104
Heaton	Devon	SS5828	51°2·3'	4°1·1'W	X	180
Heaton	Lancs	SD4460	54°2·2'	2°50·9'W	T	97
Heaton	N upon Ty	NZ2766	54°59·5'	1°34·3'W	T	88
Heaton	Staffs	SJ9562	53°9·5'	2°4·1'W	T	118
Heaton Chapel	Stock	SJ8892	53°25·7'	2°10·4'W	T	109
Heaton Covert	Northum	NT9039	55°38·9'	2°9·1'W	F	74,75
Heaton Hall	Lancs	SD4459	54°1·7'	2°50·9'W	X	102
Heaton Hall	Man	SD8304	53°32·2'	2°15·0'W	A	109
Heaton Ho	N Yks	SE4164	54°4·5'	1°22·0'W	X	99
Heaton Ho	Staffs	SJ9462	53°9·5'	2°5·0'W	X	118
Heatonlow	Staffs	SJ9563	53°10·1'	2°4·1'W	X	118
Heaton Mersey	Stock	SJ8691	53°25·2'	2°12·2'W	T	109
Heaton Mill Ho	Northum	NT9042	55°40·5'	2°9·1'W	X	74,75
Heaton Moor	Northum	NT9040	55°39·5'	2°9·1'W	X	74,75
Heaton Moor	Stock	SJ8791	53°25·2'	2°11·3'W	T	109
Heaton Norris	Stock	SJ8890	53°24·6'	2°10·4'W	T	109
Heaton Park	Man	SD8204	53°32·2'	2°15·9'W	X	109
Heaton Park Resr	Man	SD8204	53°32·2'	2°15·9'W	W	109
Heaton Royds	Brad	SE1336	53°49·4'	1°47·7'W	T	104
Heaton's Bridge	Lancs	SD4011	53°35·8'	2°54·0'W	T	108
Heaton Shay	Brad	SE1336	53°49·4'	1°47·7'W	X	104
Heaton's Wood	Lincs	SK9086	53°22·0'	0°38·4'W	F	112,121
Heatree Ho	Devon	SX7280	50°36·6'	3°48·2'W	X	191
Heaval	N Eil	NL6799	56°58·0'	7°28·3'W	H	31
Heave Coppice	Dorset	SY6997	50°46·5'	2°26·0'W	F	194
Heaven Fm (Mus)	E Susx	TQ4026	51°1·2'	0°0·2'E	X	187,198
Heaven Gate	Wrekin	SJ6308	52°40·3'	2°32·4'W	X	127
Heaven Gate (Fort)	Wrekin	SJ6308	52°40·3'	2°32·4'W	A	127
Heavenly Valley Fm	Cambs	TL4874	52°20·9'	0°10·8'E	FM	143
Heaven's Door	Somer	ST6021	50°59·5'	2°33·8'W	T	183
Heaven's Gate	Wilts	ST8242	51°10·8'	2°15·1'W	X	183
Heavens, The	Glos	SO8604	51°44·3'	2°11·8'W	X	162
Heaven Wood	Essex	TL8341	52°2·5'	0°40·5'E	F	155
Heaverham	Kent	TQ5758	51°18·2'	0°15·5'E	T	188
Heaves Fm	Dorset	SY6997	50°46·5'	2°26·0'W	FM	194
Heaviley	Stock	SJ9088	53°23·6'	2°8·6'W	T	109
Heavitree	Devon	SX9492	50°43·3'	3°29·7'W	T	192
Heavy Hill	Essex	TL5040	52°2·5'	0°11·6'E	X	154
Heavyland Wood	Suff	TM3185	52°25·1'	1°24·2'E	F	156
Heavyside	Scot Bord	NT7720	55°28·6'	2°21·4'W	X	74
Heavyside	S Lanak	NT0537	55°37·3'	3°30·1'W	X	72
Heawood Hall	Ches	SJ8375	53°16·5'	2°14·9'W	X	118
Heazille Barton	Devon	SS9500	50°47·6'	3°29·0'W	X	192
Heazle Fm	Devon	ST1516	50°56·5'	3°12·2'W	FM	181,193
Hebberdens	I of W	SZ4389	50°42·2'	1°23·1'W	X	196
Hebble Brook	Cald	SE0627	53°44·6'	1°54·1'W	W	104
Hebblethwaite Hall	Cumbr	SD6993	54°20·1'	2°28·2'W	X	98
Hebblethwaites	Cumbr	SD6391	54°19·0'	2°33·7'W	X	97
Hebburn	S Tyne	NZ3164	54°58·4'	1°30·5'W	T	88
Hebburn Colliery	S Tyne	NZ3165	54°59·0'	1°30·5'W	T	88
Hebburn New Town	S Tyne	NZ3064	54°58·4'	1°31·5'W	T	88
Hebden	N Yks	SE0263	54°4·6'	1°57·7'W	T	98
Hebden Beck	N Yks	SE0264	54°4·6'	1°57·7'W	W	98
Hebden Bridge	Cald	SD9827	53°44·6'	2°1·4'W	T	103
Hebden Fm	Wilts	ST8282	51°32·4'	2°15·2'W	FM	173
Hebden Green	Ches	SJ6265	53°11·1'	2°33·7'W	T	118
Hebden Moor	N Yks	SE0465	54°5·1'	1°55·9'W	X	98
Hebden Water	Cald	SD9631	53°46·8'	2°3·2'W	W	103

Hebden Wood	N Yks	SE2465	54°5·1′	1°37·6′W	F	99
Hebden Wood Ho	N Yks	SE2465	54°5·1′	1°37·6′W	X	99
Heberdens	Hants	SU7314	50°55·5′	0°57·3′W	X	197
Heber Hill	Lancs	SD6476	54°11·0′	2°32·7′W	X	97
Heber Moss	Brad	SE0946	53°54·8′	1°51·4′W	X	104
Heber's Ghyll	Brad	SE0947	53°55·4′	1°51·4′W	F	104
Hebing End	Herts	TL3122	51°53·1′	0°5·4′W	T	166
Hebron	Carm	SN1827	51°54·9′	4°38·4′W	T	145,158
Hebron	Carm	SN4135	51°59·7′	4°18·6′W	X	146
Hebron	I of Angl	SH4584	53°20·1′	4°19·3′W	T	114,115
Hebron	Northum	NZ1989	55°11·9′	1°41·7′W	T	81
Hebron Hill	Northum	NZ1890	55°12·5′	1°42·6′W	X	81
Hebron Sta	Gwyn	SH5858	53°6·3′	4°6·9′W	X	115
Heck	D & G	NY0980	55°6·6′	3°25·2′W	T	78
Heckbarley	Cumbr	NY0714	54°31·0′	3°25·8′W	X	89
Heck Brow	N Yks	SD9685	54°15·9′	2°3·3′W	X	98
Heck Crag	Cumbr	NY4214	54°31·3′	2°53·3′W	X	90
Heck Dale	N Yks	SE8686	54°16·0′	0°40·4′W	X	94,101
Heckdyke	Notts	SK7996	53°27·5′	0°48·2′W	T	112
Hecken	Highld	ND2661	58°32·1′	3°15·8′W	X	11,12
Heckfield	Hants	SU7260	51°20·3′	0°57·6′W	T	175,186
Heckfield Green	Suff	TM1875	52°20·0′	1°12·4′E	T	156
Heckfield Heath	Hants	SU7261	51°20·8′	0°57·6′W	F	175,186
Heckfield Heath Ho	Hants	SU7261	51°20·8′	0°57·6′W	X	175,186
Heckfield Place	Hants	SU7361	51°20·8′	0°56·7′W	X	175,186
Heckfordbridge	Essex	TL9421	51°51·5′	0°49·4′E	T	168
Heck Gill Fm	N Yks	SE2058	54°1·3′	1°41·3′W	FM	104
Heckgill Mire	Cumbr	NY7502	54°25·0′	2°22·7′W	W	91
Heck Hall Fm	N Yks	SE5920	53°40·6′	1°6·0′W	FM	105
Heckies Hole	E Loth	NT6379	56°0·4′	2°35·2′W	X	67
Heckingham	Norf	TM3898	52°31·9′	1°31·0′E	T	134
Heckington	Lincs	TF1444	52°59·1′	0°17·7′W	T	130
Heckington Eau	Lincs	TF1545	52°59·6′	0°16·8′W	W	130
Heckington Fen	Lincs	TF1845	52°59·6′	0°14·1′W	X	130
Heckington Fen	Lincs	TF2045	52°59·6′	0°12·3′W	X	131
Heckington Sta	Lincs	TF1443	52°58·6′	0°17·7′W	X	130
Hecklebirnie	S Lanak	NS8938	55°37·6′	3°45·3′W	X	71,72
Heckley Fence	Northum	NU1817	55°27·0′	1°42·5′W	X	81
Heckley High Ho	Northum	NU1815	55°26·0′	1°42·5′W	X	81
Heckley Ho	Northum	NU1816	55°26·5′	1°42·5′W	X	81
Heckmondwike	Kirk	SE2123	53°42·4′	1°40·5′W	T	104
Heckney Hill	D & G	NY1995	55°14·8′	3°16·0′W	H	79
Heckpen	Devon	SS6409	50°52·1′	3°55·6′W	X	191
Heckwood	Devon	SX5473	50°32·5′	4°3·3′W	X	191,201
Heckwood Tor	Devon	SX5373	50°32·5′	4°4·1′W	X	191,201
Hecla	N Eil	NL5582	56°48·3′	7°38·8′W	H	31
Hecla Point	N Eil	NL5782	56°48·4′	7°36·8′W	X	31
Hecla (Thacla)	N Eil	NF8234	57°17·4′	7°16·3′W	H	22
Hector's Hill	Highld	NC7918	58°8·3′	4°2·8′W	X	17
Hedchester Law	Northum	NZ1079	55°6·6′	1°50·2′W	X	88
Hedderwick	E Loth	NT6377	55°59·3′	2°35·1′W	X	67
Hedderwick Hill	E Loth	NT6478	55°59·9′	2°34·2′W	X	67
Heddeswell	Devon	SX7043	50°16·6′	3°49·1′W	X	202
Heddington	Wilts	ST9966	51°23·8′	2°0·5′W	T	173
Heddington Wick	Wilts	ST9866	51°23·8′	2°1·3′W	T	173
Heddle	Orkney	HY3512	58°59·7′	3°7·4′W	T	6
Heddlicliff	Shetld	HT9737	60°7·3′	2°2·7′W	X	4
Hedd o'da Baa	Shetld	HT9738	60°7·9′	2°2·7′W	X	4
Heddon	Devon	SS3610	50°52·2′	4°19·5′W	X	190
Heddon	Devon	SS6528	51°2·4′	3°55·2′W	T	180
Heddon	Northum	NU0317	55°27·1′	1°56·7′W	X	81
Heddon Banks Fm	Northum	NZ1366	54°59·6′	1°47·4′W	FM	88
Heddon Birks	Northum	NZ1468	55°0·6′	1°46·4′W	X	88
Heddon Hall	Northum	NZ1466	54°59·5′	1°46·4′W	X	88
Heddon Hill	Northum	NU0020	55°28·7′	1°59·6′W	H	75
Heddon Ho	Northum	NZ1268	55°0·6′	1°48·3′W	X	88
Heddon Law	Northum	NZ1469	55°1·2′	1°46·4′W	A	88
Heddon Laws Fm	Northum	NZ1469	55°1·2′	1°46·4′W	FM	88
Heddon Mill	Northum	NZ1267	55°0·1′	1°48·3′W	X	88
Heddon Oak	Somer	ST1137	51°7·8′	3°15·9′W	X	181
Heddon-on-the-Wall	Northum	NZ1366	54°59·6′	1°47·4′W	T	88
Heddon's Mouth	Devon	SS6549	51°13·7′	3°55·6′W	X	180
Heddon's Mouth Cleave	Devon	SS6549	51°13·7′	3°55·6′W	X	180
Heddon Steads	Northum	NZ1168	55°0·6′	1°49·3′W	X	88
Heddon Wood	Northum	NU0021	55°29·2′	1°59·6′W	F	75
Hedenham	Norf	TM3193	52°29·4′	1°24·6′E	T	134
Hedenham Hall	Norf	TM3192	52°28·8′	1°24·5′E	A	134
Hedenham Hall Fm	Norf	TM3193	52°29·4′	1°24·6′E	FM	134
Hedenham Park	Norf	TM3193	52°29·4′	1°24·6′E	X	134
Hedenham Wood	Norf	TM3194	52°29·9′	1°24·6′E	F	134
Hedge Barton	Devon	SX7378	50°35·5′	3°47·3′W	X	191
Hedgecock Hill	Somer	ST4817	50°57·2′	2°44·0′W	X	193
Hedgecourt	Surrey	TQ3540	51°8·8′	0°3·8′W	X	187
Hedgecourt Lake	Surrey	TQ3540	51°8·8′	0°3·8′W	W	187
Hedge Cross	Devon	SX4885	50°38·9′	4°8·6′W	X	191,201
Hedge End	Dorset	ST8206	50°51·4′	2°15·0′W	T	194
Hedge End	Hants	SU4912	50°54·6′	1°17·8′W	T	196
Hedge-end Island	Essex	TM2424	51°52·4′	1°15·6′E	X	169
Hedge End Sta	Hants	SU4915	50°56·2′	1°17·8′W	X	196
Hedgefields	Oxon	SP3201	51°42·6′	1°31·8′W	X	164
Hedge Fms	Somer	ST6139	51°9·2′	2°33·1′W	FM	183
Hedgehog Bridge	Lincs	TF2546	53°0·0′	0°7·8′W	T	131
Hedgeholme	Durham	NZ1416	54°32·6′	1°46·6′W	X	92
Hedgehope Hill	Northum	NT9419	55°28·1′	2°5·3′W	H	80
Hedge House Fm	Heref	SO6859	52°13·9′	2°27·7′W	FM	149
Hedgeland	Devon	SS9005	50°50·3′	3°33·4′W	X	192
Hedgeley Hall	Northum	NU0717	55°27·1′	1°52·9′W	X	81
Hedgeley Moor 1464	Northum	NU0419	55°28·1′	1°55·8′W	A	81
Hedgemoor Copse	Hants	SU2631	51°4·9′	1°37·3′W	F	184
Hedge Nook	N Yks	SE2073	54°9·4′	1°41·2′W	X	99
Hedgerley	Bucks	SU9687	51°34·6′	0°36·5′W	T	175,176
Hedgerley Green	Bucks	SU9787	51°34·6′	0°35·6′W	T	175,176
Hedgerley Hill	Bucks	SU9786	51°34·1′	0°35·6′W	T	175,176
Hedgerley Park	Bucks	SU9786	51°34·1′	0°35·6′W	X	175,176
Hedge Rock	I Scilly	SV9015	49°57·5′	6°19·0′W	X	203
Hedge's Fm	Herts	TL1311	51°47·4′	0°21·3′W	FM	166
Hedges Fm	Herts	TL1504	51°43·6′	0°19·7′W	FM	166
Hedges Fm	Norf	TF9809	52°38·8′	0°56·0′E	FM	144
Hedgestocks	Somer	ST6837	51°8·1′	2°27·1′W	X	183
Hedge Wood	Suff	TL9157	52°10·9′	0°48·0′E	F	155
Hedging	Somer	ST3029	51°3·6′	2°59·5′W	T	193
Hedley Burn	Scot Bord	NT3405	55°20·3′	3°2·0′W	W	79
Hedley Grange Fm	Northum	NZ0758	54°55·2′	1°53·0′W	FM	88
Hedley Hall Fm	Ghead	NZ2256	54°54·1′	1°39·0′W	FM	88
Hedley Hill	Durham	NZ1541	54°46·1′	1°45·6′W	T	88
Hedley Hill Fm	Durham	NZ1541	54°46·1′	1°45·6′W	FM	88
Hedleyhope Burn	Durham	NZ1643	54°47·1′	1°44·6′W	W	88
Hedley on the Hill	Northum	NZ0759	54°55·8′	1°53·0′W	T	88
Hedley Park Fm	Northum	NZ0859	54°55·8′	1°52·1′W	FM	88
Hedley's Wood	Durham	NZ2045	54°48·2′	1°40·9′W	F	88
Hedley West House Fm	Ghead	NZ2056	54°54·1′	1°40·9′W	FM	88
Hedley Wood	Northum	NZ1497	55°16·3′	1°46·3′W	X	81
Hednesford	Staffs	SK0012	52°42·6′	1°59·6′W	T	128
Hedon	E Yorks	TA1928	53°44·3′	0°11·3′W	T	107
Hedon Haven	E Yorks	TA1727	53°43·8′	0°13·2′W	W	107
Hedon Howe	N Yks	SE7866	54°5·3′	0°48·0′W	A	100
Hedre-fawr	Gwyn	SH3745	52°58·9′	4°25·3′W	X	123
Hedrick Grange	Durham	NZ0521	54°35·3′	1°54·9′W	X	92
Hedrick Rigg	Durham	NZ0521	54°35·3′	1°54·9′W	X	92
Hedsor	Bucks	SU9187	51°34·7′	0°40·8′W	T	175
Hedsor Court	Bucks	SU9186	51°34·2′	0°40·8′W	X	175
Hedsor Ho	Bucks	SU9085	51°33·6′	0°41·7′W	X	175
Hedsor Priory	Bucks	SU9086	51°34·2′	0°41·7′W	X	175
Hedsor Wharf	Bucks	SU9086	51°34·2′	0°41·7′W	X	175
Hedworth	S Tyne	NZ3363	54°57·9′	1°28·6′W	T	88
Heelands	Mil Key	SP8339	52°2·8′	0°47·0′W	T	152
Heeley	Sheff	SK3584	53°21·3′	1°28·0′W	T	110,111
Heel Fm	Kent	TQ9753	51°14·7′	0°49·8′E	FM	189
Heelors, The	Shetld	HZ2270	59°31·2′	1°36·2′W	X	4
Heely Dod	Northum	NY9298	55°16·8′	2°7·1′W	H	80
Heesom Green Fm	Ches	SJ7474	53°16·0′	2°23·0′W	FM	118
Heet Fm	Bucks	SP6420	51°52·7′	1°3·8′W	FM	164,165
Hegdale	Cumbr	NY5317	54°33·0′	2°43·2′W	X	90
Hegdon Hill	Heref	SO5853	52°10·7′	2°36·5′W	X	149
Heggadon	Devon	SX3798	50°45·8′	4°18·3′W	X	190
Heggatt Hall	Norf	TG2718	52°42·9′	1°22·1′E	X	133,134
Heggerscales	Cumbr	NY8210	54°29·3′	2°16·3′W	X	91,92
Hegg Hill Fm	Kent	TQ8743	51°9·6′	0°40·9′E	FM	189
Hegglehead	Cumbr	NY3734	54°42·1′	2°58·2′W	X	90
Heggle Lane	Cumbr	NY3635	54°42·6′	2°59·2′W	T	90
Hegglie Ber	Orkney	HY6037	59°13·3′	2°41·6′W	X	5
Heglibister	Shetld	HU3851	60°14·8′	1°18·3′W	T	3
Heidagul River	N Eil	NB2242	58°17·0′	6°44·1′W	W	8,13
Heiferlaw Bank	Northum	NU1818	55°27·6′	1°42·5′W	X	81
Heiferlaw Tower	Northum	NU1817	55°27·0′	1°42·5′W	A	81
Heiffers	Devon	SS8218	50°57·2′	3°40·4′W	X	181
Heigh	Northum	NT9111	55°23·8′	2°8·1′W	X	80
Heigham Br	Norf	TG4118	52°42·6′	1°34·5′E	A	134
Heigham Holmes	Norf	TG4420	52°43·6′	1°37·2′E	X	134
Heigham Sound	Norf	TG4320	52°43·6′	1°36·3′E	W	134
Heigh Head	N Yks	SD7166	54°5·6′	2°26·2′W	X	98
Heighington	Darl	NZ2422	54°35·8′	1°37·3′W	T	93
Heighington	Lincs	TF0369	53°12·7′	0°27·0′W	T	121
Heighington Fen	Lincs	TF0770	53°13·2′	0°23·4′W	X	121
Heighington Sta	Durham	NZ2722	54°35·8′	1°34·5′W	X	93
Heighley	Staffs	SJ7747	53°1·4′	2°20·2′W	T	118
Heighley Gate	Northum	NZ1789	55°11·9′	1°43·5′W	X	81
Heigholme Hall	E Yorks	TA0946	53°54·2′	0°20·0′W	X	107
Height	Cumbr	SD4084	54°15·1′	2°54·8′W	X	96,97
Height	N Yks	SD9168	54°6·7′	2°7·8′W	X	98
Height End	Lancs	SD7923	53°42·4′	2°18·7′W	T	103
Height Fm	Cald	SD9625	53°43·5′	2°3·2′W	FM	103
Heigh, The	Northum	NY9057	54°54·7′	2°8·9′W	X	87
Heightington	Worcs	SO7671	52°20·4′	2°20·7′W	T	138
Height Lathe	N Yks	SD9564	54°4·6′	2°4·2′W	X	98
Heightley	Shrops	SO2798	52°34·7′	3°4·2′W	X	137
Height of Hazely	N Yks	SE0385	54°15·9′	1°56·8′W	H	98
Height of Winder	Cumbr	SD6393	54°20·1′	2°33·7′W	X	97
Heighton	D & G	NX0272	55°0·4′	5°5·4′W	X	76,82
Heighton Hill	E Susx	TQ4703	50°48·7′	0°5·6′E	X	198
Height o' th' Hill	Lancs	SD3545	53°54·1′	2°58·9′W	X	102
Heights	Cumbr	NY7014	54°31·5′	2°27·4′W	X	91
Heights	Cumbr	SD6086	54°16·3′	2°36·4′W	X	97
Heights	N Yks	SD9698	54°22·9′	2°3·3′W	X	98
Heights	Oldham	SD9808	53°34·4′	2°1·4′W	T	109
Heights	Stir	NS5893	56°6·8′	4°16·6′W	X	57
Heights	W Loth	NS9069	55°54·3′	3°45·1′W	X	65
Heights Castle	Cumbr	NY6915	54°32·0′	2°28·3′W	X	91
Heights Fm	Lancs	SD5362	54°3·4′	2°42·7′W	FM	97
Heights Fm	N Yks	SD9949	53°56·5′	2°0·5′W	FM	103
Height Side	Black w Dar	SD6821	53°41·3′	2°28·7′W	X	103
Heights of Abraham	Derby	SK2858	53°7·3′	1°34·5′W	X	119
Heights of Brae	Highld	NH5161	57°37·1′	4°29·2′W	X	20
Heights of Dochcarty	Highld	NH5261	57°37·1′	4°28·2′W	X	20
Heights of Fodderty	Highld	NH5160	57°36·6′	4°29·2′W	X	20
Heights of Keppoch	Highld	NH5060	57°36·6′	4°30·2′W	X	20
Heights of Kinlochewe	Highld	NH0664	57°37·7′	5°14·5′W	T	19
Heights of Olnesfirth	Shetld	HU3177	60°28·8′	1°25·7′W	X	3
Heights of Ramnageo	Shetld	HU5280	60°30·3′	1°2·7′W	H	1,2,3
Heights Plantn	N Yks	SE7964	54°4·2′	0°47·1′W	F	100
Heights Quarry	Durham	NY9239	54°45·0′	2°7·0′W	X	91,92
Heights, The	Brad	SE1140	53°51·6′	1°49·6′W	X	104
Heights, The	Cumbr	SD4088	54°17·3′	2°54·9′W	X	96,97
Heights,The	Cumbr	SD4599	54°23·3′	2°50·4′W	X	97
Heights, The	N Yks	SE1561	54°2·9′	1°45·8′W	X	99
Heights, The	N Yks	SE4474	54°9·8′	1°19·1′W	X	99
Height, The	Brad	SD9936	53°49·5′	2°0·5′W	X	103
Height, The	Brad	SE0743	53°53·2′	1°53·2′W	X	104
Height, The	Cumbr	NY3141	54°45·8′	3°3·9′W	X	85
Height, The	Cumbr	NY3147	54°49·0′	3°4·0′W	X	85
Height, The	Cumbr	NY6168	55°0·6′	2°36·2′W	X	86
Heilam	Highld	NC4560	58°30·3′	4°39·1′W	X	9
Heilasbhal Beag	N Eil	NG0794	57°50·6′	6°55·8′W	X	14,18
Heild End Fm	Ches	SJ9867	53°12·2′	2°1·4′W	FM	118
Heileasbhal Mòr	N Eil	NG0792	57°49·6′	6°55·7′W	H	14,18
Heilem	N Eil	NF7300	56°58·8′	7°22·5′W	X	31
Heilia Brune	Shetld	HP5904	60°43·2′	0°54·6′W	X	1
Heilia Water	Shetld	HU2753	60°15·9′	1°30·2′W	W	3
Heilinabretta	Shetld	HU6791	60°36·1′	0°46·1′W	X	1,2
Heill Head	Shetld	HU2860	60°19·7′	1°29·1′W	X	3
Heillia	Shetld	HU2684	60°32·6′	1°31·1′W	X	3
Heimar Water	Shetld	HP5812	60°47·5′	0°55·6′W	W	1
Heinish	N Eil	NF7809	57°3·8′	7°18·3′W	X	31
Heip Hill	Scot Bord	NT4915	55°25·8′	2°47·9′W	H	79
Heisgeir	N Eil	NB5547	58°20·9′	6°10·7′W	W	8
Heishival Beag	N Eil	NL6396	56°56·2′	7°32·0′W	H	31
Heishival Mór	N Eil	NL6296	56°56·2′	7°33·0′W	H	31
Heisinish	N Eil	NF8009	57°3·9′	7°16·3′W	X	31
Heisker	N Eil	NG0080	57°42·8′	7°1·8′W	X	18
Heisker or Monach Islands(Theisgeir no na h-Eileanan Monach)	N Eil	NF6262	57°31·6′	7°38·4′W	X	22
Heithat	D & G	NY1988	55°11·0′	3°15·9′W	X	79
Heithat Burn	D & G	NY1989	55°11·6′	3°15·9′W	W	79
Heithatpark	D & G	NY1889	55°11·6′	3°16·9′W	X	79
Heiton	Scot Bord	NT7130	55°34·0′	2°27·2′W	T	74
Heiton Mill	Scot Bord	NT7031	55°34·6′	2°28·1′W	X	74
Helbeck	Cumbr	NY7915	54°32·0′	2°19·1′W	T	91
Helbeck Fell	Cumbr	NY8119	54°34·2′	2°17·2′W	X	91,92
Helbeck Hall	Cumbr	NY7915	54°32·0′	2°19·1′W	X	91
Helbeck Intake	Cumbr	NY7916	54°32·6′	2°19·1′W	X	91
Helbeck Wood	Cumbr	NY7816	54°32·6′	2°20·0′W	F	91
Heldale	Orkney	ND2891	58°48·3′	3°14·3′W	X	7
Heldale Water	Orkney	ND2592	58°48·8′	3°17·4′W	W	7
Heldon Hill	Moray	NJ1358	57°36·5′	3°26·9′W	H	28
Heldonside	Moray	NJ1759	57°37·1′	3°22·9′W	X	28
Heldon Wood	Moray	NJ1257	57°35·9′	3°27·9′W	F	28
Heldre Hill	Powys	SJ2809	52°40·7′	3°3·5′W	H	126
Held, The	Powys	SO0326	51°55·7′	3°24·3′W	X	160
Hele	Corn	SS2104	50°48·7′	4°32·1′W	X	190
Hele	Devon	SS4219	50°57·2′	4°14·6′W	X	180,190
Hele	Devon	SS5347	51°12·4′	4°5·9′W	T	180
Hele	Devon	SS6620	50°58·1′	3°54·1′W	X	180
Hele	Devon	SS9902	50°48·8′	3°25·6′W	T	192
Hele	Devon	SX3391	50°41·9′	4°21·5′W	T	190
Hele	Devon	SX5262	50°26·6′	4°4·7′W	X	201
Hele	Devon	SX7470	50°31·2′	3°46·3′W	T	202
Hele	Somer	ST1824	51°0·8′	3°9·8′W	T	181,193
Hele	Torbay	SX9065	50°28·7′	3°32·6′W	T	202
Hele Almhouses	Devon	SX5249	50°19·6′	4°4·4′W	A	201
Hele Barton	Corn	SX2197	50°44·9′	4°31·9′W	X	190
Hele Barton	Devon	SS5106	50°50·3′	4°6·6′W	X	191
Hele Barton	Devon	SS7911	50°53·4′	3°42·8′W	X	191
Hele Bay	Devon	SS5348	51°13·0′	4°5·9′W	W	180
Hele Br	Somer	SS9327	51°2·2′	3°31·2′W	X	181
Helebridge	Corn	SS2103	50°48·2′	4°32·0′W	T	190
Hele Bridge	Devon	SS5406	50°50·3′	4°4·0′W	X	191
Hele Cross	Devon	SX6161	50°26·2′	3°57·1′W	X	202
Hele Fm	Devon	SS7108	50°51·7′	3°49·6′W	FM	191
Hele Fm	Devon	SX4274	50°32·9′	4°13·4′W	FM	201
Hele Fm	Devon	SX7284	50°38·7′	3°48·2′W	FM	191
Hele Fm	Somer	ST0424	51°0·7′	3°21·7′W	FM	181
Hele Fm	Somer	ST0631	51°4·5′	3°20·1′W	FM	181
Hele Hill	Somer	ST1824	51°0·8′	3°9·8′W	X	181,193
Hele Lane	Devon	SS7910	50°52·8′	3°42·8′W	X	191
Hele Manor	Somer	ST1824	51°0·8′	3°9·8′W	X	181,193
Hele Manor Fm	Somer	SS9224	51°0·6′	3°32·0′W	FM	181
Helenamore	Aberd	NJ8662	57°39·1′	2°13·6′W	X	30
Helensburgh	Arg & Bt	NS2982	56°0·3′	4°44·1′W	T	56
Helensfield	Clackm	NS9192	56°6·8′	3°44·7′W	X	58
Helen's Stone	D & G	NX4383	55°7·2′	4°27·3′W	X	77
Helenston	Angus	NO5847	56°37·0′	2°40·6′W	X	54
Helenton	S Ayr	NS3930	55°32·5′	4°32·7′W	X	70
Helentongate	S Ayr	NS3931	55°33·0′	4°32·7′W	X	70
Helenton Mains	S Ayr	NS3930	55°32·5′	4°32·7′W	X	70
Hele Park	Devon	SX8372	50°32·4′	3°38·7′W	X	191
Hele Payne	Devon	SS9902	50°48·8′	3°25·6′W	X	192
Hele Wood	Devon	SS6620	50°58·1′	3°54·1′W	F	180
Heley Ho	Durham	NZ3526	54°37·9′	1°27·0′W	X	93
Helfa	Gwyn	SH5857	53°5·7′	4°6·8′W	X	115
Helford	Corn	SW7526	50°5·7′	5°8·4′W	T	204
Helford Passage	Corn	SW7626	50°5·7′	5°7·6′W	T	204
Helford River	Corn	SW7626	50°5·7′	5°7·6′W	W	204
Helga Water	Shetld	HU2778	60°29·4′	1°30·0′W	W	3
Helham Green	Herts	TL3915	51°49·2′	0°1·4′E	T	166
Helhoughton	Norf	TF8626	52°48·2′	0°46·0′E	T	132
Helhoughton Common	Norf	TF8627	52°48·7′	0°46·0′E	F	132
Heligan	Corn	SW9946	50°17·0′	4°48·9′W	X	204
Heligar Pike	N Yks	SE1352	53°58·1′	1°47·7′W	X	104
Helions	Essex	TL6441	52°2·8′	0°23·9′E	X	154
Helions Bumpstead	Essex	TL6541	52°2·8′	0°24·8′E	T	154
Helks	N Yks	SE1271	54°8·3′	1°48·6′W	X	99
Helks Bank Fm	Lancs	SD6464	54°4·5′	2°32·6′W	FM	97
Hellabrick's Wick	Shetld	HT9636	60°6·8′	2°3·8′W	W	4
Hellaby	Roth	SK5092	53°25·6′	1°14·4′W	T	111
Helladale River	Highld	NC9238	58°19·3′	3°50·2′W	W	11,17
Hellam	Shetld	HU4868	60°23·8′	1°7·2′W	X	2,3
Helland	Corn	SX0770	50°30·1′	4°42·9′W	T	200
Helland	Somer	ST3224	51°0·9′	2°57·8′W	T	193
Helland Barton	Corn	SW9049	50°18·5′	4°56·6′W	X	204
Helland Barton	Corn	SX0782	50°36·6′	4°43·3′W	X	200
Hellandbridge	Corn	SX0671	50°30·6′	4°43·8′W	T	200
Helland Ho	Corn	SW7531	50°8·4′	5°8·6′W	X	204
Helland Meads	Somer	ST3224	51°0·9′	2°57·8′W	X	193
Helland Mill	Corn	SW7531	50°8·4′	5°8·6′W	X	204
Helland Wood	Corn	SX0769	50°29·6′	4°42·9′W	F	200
Hellangove Fm	Corn	SW4834	50°9·4′	5°31·3′W	FM	203
Hella Point	Corn	SW3721	50°2·1′	5°40·0′W	X	203
Hell Bank Plantn	Derby	SK2868	53°12·7′	1°34·4′W	F	119
Hell Bay	I Scilly	SV8715	49°57·4′	6°21·5′W	W	203
Hell Beck	Cumbr	NY5457	54°54·6′	2°42·6′W	W	86
Hell Brake	Warw	SP2943	52°5·3′	1°34·2′W	F	151
Hell Brook	Derby	SK3231	52°52·8′	1°31·1′W	W	128
Hell Clough	Staffs	SK0336	52°55·5′	1°56·9′W	F	128
Hell Coppice	Bucks	SP6010	51°47·4′	1°7·4′W	F	164,165
Hell Corner	Dorset	ST6006	50°51·4′	2°33·7′W	X	194
Hell Corner	W Berks	SU3864	51°22·7′	1°26·9′W	T	174
Hellenge Hill	N Som	ST3457	51°18·7′	2°56·4′W	H	182
Hellen's	Essex	TL9220	51°51·0′	0°47·7′E	X	168

Hellens	Heref	SO6633	51°59·9'	2°29·3'W	A	149
Hellescott	Corn	SX2888	50°40·2'	4°25·7'W	X	190
Hellescott Bridge	Corn	SX2887	50°39·7'	4°25·6'W	X	190
Hellesdon	Norf	TG2012	52°39·9'	1°15·6'E	T	133,134
Hellesveor	Corn	SW5040	50°12·7'	5°29·9'W	T	203
Hell Gate	Wrekin	SJ6308	52°40·3'	2°32·4'W	X	127
Hell Gill	Cumbr	NY2505	54°26·3'	3°9·0'W	X	89,90
Hellgill	Cumbr	SD7896	54°21·8'	2°19·9'W	X	98
Hell Gill Beck	N Yks	SD7997	54°22·3'	2°19·0'W	W	98
Hell Gill Br	N Yks	SD7896	54°21·8'	2°19·9'W	X	98
Hellgill Plantn	Cumbr	SD5583	54°14·7'	2°41·0'W	F	97
Hell Hole	Norf	TG1437	52°53·5'	1°11·3'E	X	133
Hell Hole	N Yks	SE3651	53°57·5'	1°26·7'W	X	104
Hell Hole	Shrops	SO3086	52°28·3'	3°1·4'W	X	137
Hell Hole	Staffs	SJ8022	52°48·0'	2°17·4'W	F	127
Hell Hole	Staffs	SK0019	52°46·4'	1°59·6'W	X	128
Hell Hole	Warw	SP3054	52°11·2'	1°33·3'W	X	151
Hellia	Orkney	HY1904	58°55·2'	3°23·9'W	X	7
Hellia	Orkney	HY4207	58°57·0'	3°0·0'W	X	6,7
Hellia	Shetld	HU4528	60°2·3'	1°11·0'W	X	4
Hellia	Shetld	HU4640	60°8·8'	1°9·8'W	X	4
Helliack	Orkney	ND3288	58°46·7'	3°10·1'W	X	7
Helliack, The	Shetld	HU4677	60°28·7'	1°9·3'W	X	2,3
Helliack, The	Shetld	HU5386	60°33·5'	1°1·5'W	X	1,2,3
Hellia Cluve	Shetld	HU5340	60°8·7'	1°2·2'W	X	4
Helliar Holm	Orkney	HY4815	59°1·4'	2°53·9'W	X	6
Helliasour	Orkney	HY3934	59°11·6'	3°3·6'W	X	6
Hellia Spur	Orkney	HY3734	59°11·5'	3°5·7'W	X	6
Hellidon	Northnts	SP5158	52°13·3'	1°14·8'W	T	151
Hellie	Orkney	ND4688	58°46·8'	2°55·6'W	X	7
Helliehow	Orkney	HY6945	59°17·7'	2°32·2'W	X	5
Helliers Ness	Shetld	HU6087	60°34·0'	0°53·8'W	X	1,2
Helliers Water	Shetld	HP6104	60°43·1'	0°52·4'W	W	1
Hellifield	N Yks	SD8556	54°0·2'	2°13·3'W	T	103
Helli Field	Shetld	HP5301	60°41·6'	1°1·3'W	X	1
Hellifield Green	N Yks	SD8556	54°0·2'	2°13·3'W	T	103
Hellifield Moor	N Yks	SD8658	54°1·3'	2°12·4'W	H	103
Hellifield Peel	N Yks	SD8555	53°59·7'	2°13·3'W	X	103
Helligan Barton	Corn	SX0672	50°31·2'	4°43·8'W	X	200
Helligan Wood	Corn	SX0872	50°31·2'	4°42·1'W	F	200
Helligill Burn	Shetld	HU3870	60°25·0'	1°18·1'W	W	2,3
Helligoblo	Shetld	HU1065	60°22·4'	1°48·6'W	X	3
Hellinaquhida	Shetld	HU4790	60°35·7'	1°8·0'W	X	1,2
Helli Ness	Shetld	HU4628	60°2·3'	1°10·0'W	X	4
Hellinghayes Fm	Devon	SS7815	50°55·5'	3°43·8'W	FM	180
Hellingly	E Susx	TQ5812	50°53·4'	0°15·2'E	T	199
Hellings Fm	Somer	ST4509	50°52·9'	2°46·5'W	FM	193
Hellington	Norf	TG3103	52°34·8'	1°25·0'E	T	134
Hellington Corner	Norf	TG3102	52°34·2'	1°24·9'E	X	134
Hellingtown	Devon	SX5066	50°28·7'	4°6·5'W	X	201
Hellir	Shetld	HU3892	60°36·8'	1°17·8'W	X	1,2
Hellisay	N Eil	NF7504	57°1·0'	7°20·9'W	X	31
Hellister	Shetld	HU3849	60°13·7'	1°18·3'W	T	3
Hellman's Cross	Essex	TL5818	51°50·5'	0°18·0'E	T	167
Hellmoor Loch	Scot Bord	NT3816	55°26·3'	2°58·4'W	W	79
Hellot Scales Barn	Cumbr	SD6680	54°13·1'	2°30·9'W	X	98
Hell Peak	Heref	SO3266	52°17·5'	2°59·4'W	H	137,148
Hell's Glen or Gleann Beag	Arg & Bt	NN1706	56°12·9'	4°56·6'W	X	56
Hell's Hole	Scot Bord	NT5807	55°21·6'	2°39·3'W	X	80
Hell's Lum	Aberd	NJ8366	57°41·3'	2°16·6'W	X	29,30
Hell's Mouth	Corn	SW6043	50°14·5'	5°21·6'W	W	203
Hells Mouth	Orkney	HY6921	59°4·8'	2°32·0'W	X	5
Hell's Mouth or Porth Cynfor	I of Angl	SH3995	53°25·9'	4°25·0'W	W	114
Hell's Mouth or Porth Neigwl	Gwyn	SH2626	52°48·5'	4°34·5'W	W	123
Hell Stone	Dorset	SY6086	50°40·6'	2°33·6'W	X	194
Hell Stone (Long Barrow)	Dorset	SY6086	50°40·6'	2°33·6'W	A	194
Hellweathers	I Scilly	SV8607	49°53·1'	6°21·9'W	X	203
Helm	Cumbr	NY7015	54°32·0'	2°27·4'W	X	91
Helm	Northum	NZ1896	55°15·7'	1°42·6'W	X	81
Helm	N Yks	SD9391	54°19·1'	2°6·0'W	T	98
Helman Head	Highld	ND3646	58°24·1'	3°5·2'W	X	12
Helman Tor	Corn	SX0661	50°25·2'	4°43·5'W	H	200
Helm Beck	Cumbr	NY7014	54°31·5'	2°27·4'W	W	91
Helm Beck Cott	Cumbr	NY7114	54°31·5'	2°26·5'W	X	91
Helmburn	Scot Bord	NT3924	55°30·6'	2°57·5'W	T	73
Helmburn Hill	Scot Bord	NT3923	55°30·1'	2°57·5'W	H	73
Helm Crag	Cumbr	NY3209	54°28·6'	3°2·5'W	H	90
Helmdon	Northnts	SP5843	52°5·2'	1°8·8'W	T	152
Helme	Kirk	SE0911	53°36·0'	1°51·4'W	T	110
Helme Lodge	Cumbr	SD5190	54°18·4'	2°44·8'W	X	97
Helm End	Cumbr	SD5388	54°17·4'	2°42·9'W	X	97
Helme Park	Durham	NZ1236	54°43·4'	1°48·4'W	X	92
Helme Park Wood	Durham	NZ1235	54°42·8'	1°48·4'W	F	92
Helmersdale	N Yks	SE3892	54°19·6'	1°24·5'W	X	99
Helmesley	Ches	SJ9866	53°11·7'	2°1·4'W	X	118
Helmeth Hill	Shrops	SO4693	52°32·2'	2°47·4'W	H	137,138
Helm Ho	N Yks	SE5693	54°20·0'	1°7·9'W	X	100
Helm House Wood	N Yks	SE5693	54°20·0'	1°7·9'W	F	100
Helming	N Yks	SE1986	54°16·4'	1°42·1'W	X	99
Helmingham	Suff	TM1857	52°10·3'	1°11·7'E	T	156
Helmingham Park	Suff	TM1857	52°10·3'	1°11·7'E	X	156
Helmington Hall	Durham	NZ1833	54°41·7'	1°42·8'W	X	92
Helmington Row	Durham	NZ1835	54°42·8'	1°42·8'W	T	92
Helmsdale	Highld	ND0215	58°7·1'	3°39·3'W	T	17
Helmshore	Lancs	SD7821	53°41·3'	2°19·6'W	T	103
Helmside	Cumbr	NY3309	54°28·6'	3°1·6'W	X	90
Helmside	Cumbr	SD6888	54°17·4'	2°29·1'W	T	98
Helmside Fm	Cumbr	SD5389	54°17·9'	2°42·9'W	FM	97
Helms Knott	Cumbr	SD6889	54°18·0'	2°29·1'W	H	98
Helmsley	N Yks	SE6184	54°15·1'	1°3·4'W	T	100
Helmsley Fm	Leeds	SE4245	53°54·2'	1°21·2'W	FM	105
Helmsley Moor	N Yks	SE5991	54°18·9'	1°5·2'W	X	100
Helm, The	Cumbr	SD5389	54°17·9'	2°42·9'W	H	97
Helmydd	Conwy	SH8368	53°12·0'	3°44·7'W	X	116
Helperby	N Yks	SE4369	54°7·1'	1°20·1'W	T	99
Helperby Moor	N Yks	SE4570	54°7·7'	1°18·3'W	X	99
Helperby Moor	N Yks	SE4670	54°7·7'	1°17·3'W	X	100

Helperthorpe	N Yks	SE9570	54°7·3'	0°32·4'W	T	101
Helperthorpe Pasture	N Yks	SE9668	54°6·2'	0°31·5'W	X	101
Helpestons Manor	Essex	TL7020	51°51·4'	0°28·5'E	X	167
Helpot Fm	Cumbr	SD4792	54°19·5'	2°48·5'W	FM	97
Helpringham	Lincs	TF1340	52°57·0'	0°18·7'W	T	130
Helpringham Fen	Lincs	TF1638	52°55·8'	0°16·0'W	X	130
Helpston	Peterb	TF1205	52°38·1'	0°20·3'W	T	142
Helsay	Northum	NU2505	55°20·2'	1°35·9'W	X	81
Helsbury Castle	Corn	SX0879	50°35·0'	4°42·4'W	A	200
Helsbury Fm	Corn	SX0879	50°35·0'	4°42·4'W	FM	200
Helsby	Ches	SJ4875	53°16·4'	2°46·4'W	T	117
Helsby Hill	Ches	SJ4975	53°16·4'	2°45·5'W	H	117
Helsby Hill (Fort)	Ches	SJ4975	53°16·4'	2°45·5'W	A	117
Helsby Marsh	Ches	SJ4876	53°16·9'	2°46·4'W	X	117
Helscott	Corn	SS2102	50°47·6'	4°32·0'W	T	190
Helsdon's Fm	Norf	TG2135	52°52·2'	1°17·4'E	FM	133
Helsett	Corn	SX1490	50°41·0'	4°37·6'W	X	190
Helsey	Lincs	TF5172	53°13·6'	0°16·1'E	T	122
Helsfell	Cumbr	SD4993	54°20·0'	2°46·6'W	X	97
Helshaw Grange	Shrops	SJ6329	52°51·7'	2°32·6'W	X	127
Helshetter	Highld	NC9662	58°32·3'	3°46·7'W	X	11
Helsington Barrows	Cumbr	SD4990	54°18·4'	2°46·6'W	X	97
Helsington Laithes	Cumbr	SD5090	54°18·4'	2°45·7'W	X	97
Helson	Corn	SX2387	50°39·6'	4°29·9'W	X	190
Helsthorpe Fm	Bucks	SP8819	51°52·0'	0°42·9'W	FM	165
Helston	Corn	SW6627	50°5·1'	5°16·0'W	T	203
Helston Downs	Corn	SW6726	50°5·5'	5°15·1'W	X	203
Helstone	Corn	SX0881	50°36·1'	4°42·4'W	T	200
Helston Fm	Devon	SX4367	50°29·1'	4°12·4'W	FM	201
Helston Water	Corn	SW7841	50°13·9'	5°6·4'W	T	204
Helton	Cumbr	NY5122	54°35·7'	2°45·1'W	T	90
Heltondale	Cumbr	NY4920	54°34·6'	2°46·9'W	X	90
Heltondale Beck	Cumbr	NY4920	54°34·6'	2°46·9'W	W	90
Helton Fell	Cumbr	NY4720	54°34·6'	2°48·8'W	X	90
Heltonhead	Cumbr	NY5021	54°35·2'	2°46·0'W	X	90
Helton Tarn	Cumbr	SD4184	54°15·1'	2°53·9'W	W	96,97
Heltor	Devon	SX7987	50°40·4'	3°42·4'W	X	191
Heltor Rock	Devon	SX7987	50°40·4'	3°42·4'W	X	191
Helvellyn	Cumbr	NY3415	54°31·8'	3°0·8'W	H	90
Helvellyn Gill	Cumbr	NY3216	54°32·3'	3°2·6'W	W	90
Helvellyn Screes	Cumbr	NY3215	54°31·8'	3°2·6'W	X	90
Helwath Beck	N Yks	SE9498	54°22·4'	0°32·8'W	W	94,101
Helwell Fm	Devon	SX9482	50°37·9'	3°29·6'W	FM	192
Helwith	N Yks	NZ0703	54°25·6'	1°53·1'W	X	92
Helwith Bridge	N Yks	SD8169	54°7·2'	2°17·0'W	T	98
Helyg	Cered	SN2751	52°8·1'	4°31·3'W	X	145
Helyg	Conwy	SH6960	53°7·5'	3°57·1'W	X	115
Helyg	Powys	SO1352	52°9·8'	3°15·9'W	X	148
Helygain or Halkyn	Flint	SJ2171	53°14·1'	3°10·6'W	T	117
Helygog	Gwyn	SH7819	52°45·5'	3°48·1'W	X	124
Helzie	Orkney	HY5040	59°14·9'	2°52·1'W	X	5
Helziegetha	Orkney	HY4428	59°8·4'	2°58·2'W	X	5,6
Hem	Powys	SJ2300	52°35·8'	3°7·8'W	X	126
Hemble Hill	Red & Cl	NZ5615	54°31·9'	1°7·7'W	X	93
Hemblesgate	Cumbr	NY5360	54°56·2'	2°43·6'W	X	86
Hemblington	Norf	TG3411	52°39·0'	1°28·0'E	T	133,134
Hemblington Corner	Norf	TG3311	52°39·0'	1°27·1'E	T	133,134
Hemborough	Devon	SX8352	50°21·6'	3°38·3'W	X	202
Hemborough Post	Devon	SX8352	50°21·6'	3°38·3'W	X	202
Hembridge	Somer	ST5936	51°7·5'	2°34·8'W	T	182,183
Hembury	Devon	ST1103	50°49·4'	3°15·4'W	A	192,193
Hembury Castle	Devon	SS4217	50°56·1'	4°14·5'W	A	180,190
Hembury Castle	Devon	SX7268	50°30·1'	3°47·9'W	A	202
Hembury Fort Ho	Devon	ST1102	50°48·9'	3°15·4'W	X	192,193
Hembury Hill	Somer	ST5044	51°11·8'	2°42·5'W	H	182,183
Hemel Fm	Northum	NZ1899	55°17·3'	1°42·6'W	FM	81
Hemel Hempstead	Herts	TL0607	51°45·3'	0°27·5'W	T	166
Hemels	Cumbr	NY7115	54°32·0'	2°26·5'W	X	91
Hemelspeth	Northum	NZ1899	55°17·3'	1°42·6'W	X	81
Hemerdon	Devon	SX5657	50°23·9'	4°1·2'W	T	202
Hemerdon Ball	Devon	SX5758	50°24·5'	4°0·4'W	X	202
Hem Fm	Powys	SJ2200	52°35·8'	3°8·7'W	FM	126
Hem Fm	Shrops	SJ3506	52°39·1'	2°57·3'W	FM	126
Hem Fm	Shrops	SO6998	52°35·0'	2°27·1'W	FM	138
Hemford	Shrops	SJ3200	52°35·9'	2°59·8'W	T	126
Hem Gill Shaw	N Yks	SD9976	54°11·0'	2°0·5'W	X	98
Hem Heath	C of Stoke	SJ8841	52°58·2'	2°10·3'W	T	118
Hemhill	Heref	SO5541	52°4·2'	2°39·0'W	X	149
Hem Hill	S Lanak	NS9508	55°21·5'	3°38·9'W	X	78
Hem Ho	Wrex	SJ3855	53°5·6'	2°55·1'W	X	117
Hemholme Br	Lincs	TF4058	53°6·3'	0°5·9'E	X	122
Hemingbrough	N Yks	SE6730	53°46·0'	0°58·6'W	T	105,106
Hemingbrough Grange	N Yks	SE6829	53°45·4'	0°57·7'W	X	105,106
Hemingby	Lincs	TF2374	53°15·2'	0°9·0'W	T	122
Heminge Fm	Kent	TR1140	51°7·4'	1°1·3'E	FM	179,189
Hemingfield	Barns	SE3901	53°30·5'	1°24·3'W	T	110,111
Hemingford Abbots	Cambs	TL2770	52°19·0'	0°7·0'W	T	153
Hemingford Grey	Cambs	TL2970	52°19·0'	0°6·0'W	T	153
Hemingford Ho	Warw	SP2356	52°12·3'	1°39·4'W	X	151
Hemingford Park	Cambs	TL2771	52°19·6'	0°7·8'W	X	153
Hemingstone	Suff	TM1553	52°8·2'	1°8·9'E	T	156
Hemington	Leic	SK4528	52°51·1'	1°19·5'W	T	129
Hemington	Northnts	TL0985	52°27·4'	0°23·3'W	T	142
Hemington	Somer	ST7253	51°16·8'	2°23·7'W	T	183
Hemington Fields Ho	Leic	SK4630	52°52·2'	1°18·6'W	X	129
Hemington Ho	Northnts	TL1085	52°27·3'	0°22·5'W	X	142
Hemington Lodge	Northnts	TL0984	52°26·8'	0°23·4'W	X	142
Hemlaw Knowes	Scot Bord	NT5705	55°20·5'	2°40·2'W	X	80
Hemley	Suff	TM2842	52°2·0'	1°19·8'E	T	169
Hemley Copse	W Berks	SU4378	51°30·2'	1°22·4'W	F	174
Hemley Hall	Suff	TM2843	52°2·5'	1°19·9'E	X	169
Hemley Hill	Bucks	SP8001	51°42·4'	0°50·1'W	X	165
Hemlingford Ho	Warw	SP2095	52°33·4'	1°41·9'W	X	139
Hemlington	Midd	NZ4914	54°31·4'	1°14·2'W	T	93
Hemlington Hall	Midd	NZ4814	54°31·4'	1°15·1'W	X	93
Hemlock Fm	Dorset	ST5404	50°50·3'	2°38·8'W	FM	194
Hemmel Hill	Northum	NY9993	55°14·1'	2°0·5'W	H	81
Hemmel Ho	Northum	NU0615	55°26·0'	1°53·9'W	X	81
Hemmel Rigg	Northum	NY8171	55°2·2'	2°17·4'W	X	86,87
Hemmick Beach	Corn	SW9940	50°13·8'	4°48·7'W	X	204

Hem Mill	Shrops	SJ7205	52°38·8'	2°24·4'W	X	127
Hemming's Fm	Bucks	SP9904	51°43·8'	0°33·6'W	FM	165
Hemming Syke Wood	N Yks	SE2960	54°2·4'	1°33·0'W	F	99
Hem Moor	Powys	SJ2400	52°35·8'	3°6·9'W	X	126
Hemner Hill	W Susx	SU7719	50°58·1'	0°53·8'W	H	197
Hemp Green	Suff	TM3769	52°16·3'	1°28·8'E	T	156
Hemphill	E Ayr	NS4940	55°38·1'	4°23·5'W	X	70
Hemphole Plantn	Northum	NU1230	55°34·1'	1°48·1'W	F	75
Hempholme	E Yorks	TA0850	53°56·3'	0°20·9'W	X	107
Hemp Knoll	Wilts	SU0766	51°23·8'	1°53·6'W	X	173
Hempland Hill	D & G	NY0280	55°6·5'	3°31·7'W	H	78
Hemplands	D & G	NY0279	55°6·0'	3°31·7'W	X	84
Hemplands	Norf	TL6896	52°32·4'	0°29·0'E	X	143
Hemplands Fm	Suff	TM3181	52°22·9'	1°24·1'E	FM	156
Hemploe Lodge Fm	Northnts	SP6278	52°24·0'	1°4·9'W	FM	140
Hemplow Hills	Northnts	SP6279	52°24·6'	1°4·9'W	X	140
Hempnall	Norf	TM2494	52°30·1'	1°18·4'E	T	134
Hempnall Green	Norf	TM2493	52°29·6'	1°18·4'E	T	134
Hempnall Ho	Norf	TM2492	52°29·0'	1°18·3'E	X	134
Hempnalls Hall	Suff	TM0867	52°15·9'	1°3·3'E	X	155
Hempriggs	Moray	NJ1063	57°39·1'	3°30·0'W	X	28
Hempriggs Ho	Highld	ND3547	58°24·7'	3°6·3'W	X	12
Hempsals Fen	Cambs	TL4370	52°18·8'	0°6·3'E	X	154
Hemp's Green	Essex	TL9129	51°55·8'	0°47·1'E	T	168
Hemps Hill	Herts	TL2802	51°42·4'	0°8·5'W	H	166
Hempshill Vale	C of Nott	SK5244	52°59·7'	1°13·1'W	T	129
Hemp Stack	Orkney	HY4406	58°56·5'	2°57·9'W	X	6,7
Hempstall's Fm	Essex	TM1327	51°54·3'	1°6·2'E	FM	168,169
Hempstead	Essex	TL6338	52°1·2'	0°22·9'E	T	154
Hempstead	E Susx	TQ4821	50°58·4'	0°6·9'E	X	198
Hempstead	Medway	TQ7964	51°21·0'	0°34·6'E	T	178,188
Hempstead	Norf	TG1037	52°53·6'	1°7·7'E	T	133
Hempstead	Norf	TG4028	52°48·0'	1°34·0'E	T	134
Hempstead Fm	E Susx	TQ5710	50°52·3'	0°14·3'E	FM	199
Hempstead Hall	Essex	TL6639	52°1·7'	0°25·6'E	X	154
Hempstead Heath	Norf	TG4027	52°47·5'	1°34·0'E	X	134
Hempstead Marshes	Norf	TG4127	52°47·4'	1°34·9'E	X	134
Hempstead Wood	Essex	TL6538	52°1·2'	0°24·7'E	F	154
Hempsted	Glos	SO8116	51°50·8'	2°16·2'W	T	162
Hempster Fm	Devon	SS5544	51°10·8'	4°4·1'W	FM	180
Hempstones Point	Halton	SJ5384	53°21·3'	2°42·0'W	X	108
Hempsyke Hall	N Yks	NZ8805	54°26·2'	0°38·2'W	X	94
Hempton	Norf	TF9129	52°49·7'	0°50·5'E	T	132
Hempton	Oxon	SP4431	51°58·8'	1°21·2'W	T	151
Hempton Fm	Kent	TR1340	51°7·4'	1°3·0'E	FM	179,189
Hempton Wainhill	Oxon	SP7601	51°42·4'	0°53·6'W	T	165
Hemsby	Norf	TG4917	52°41·8'	1°41·5'E	T	134
Hemsby Hole	Norf	TG5217	52°41·7'	1°44·2'E	W	134
Hemscott Hill	Northum	NZ2795	55°15·2'	1°34·1'W	X	81
Hemsford	Devon	SX8163	50°27·5'	3°40·2'W	X	202
Hemsted	Kent	TR1441	51°7·9'	1°3·9'E	T	179,189
Hemsted Forest	Kent	TQ8135	51°5·4'	0°35·5'E	F	188
Hemswell	Lincs	SK9291	53°24·7'	0°36·5'W	T	112
Hemswell Cliff	Lincs	SK9491	53°24·7'	0°34·7'W	X	112
Hemswell Cliff	Lincs	SK9589	53°23·6'	0°33·9'W	T	112,121
Hemswell Grange	Lincs	SK9090	53°24·2'	0°38·4'W	X	112
Hemsworth	Dorset	ST9605	50°50·9'	2°3·0'W	T	195
Hemsworth	Sheff	SK3683	53°20·8'	1°27·1'W	T	110,111
Hemsworth	Wakf	SE4213	53°37·0'	1°21·5'W	T	111
Hemsworthy Gate	Devon	SX7476	50°34·4'	3°46·4'W	X	191
Hemyock	Devon	ST1313	50°54·8'	3°13·9'W	T	181,193
Hemyock Common	Devon	ST1111	50°53·7'	3°15·6'W	X	192,193
Henacroft	Devon	SS5908	50°51·5'	3°59·8'W	X	191
Henaford	Devon	SS2418	50°56·3'	4°29·9'W	T	190
Hen Allt	Powys	SJ1621	52°47·0'	3°14·3'W	H	125
Henallt	Powys	SO0648	52°7·6'	3°22·0'W	X	147
Hen and Chickens	Glos	ST5590	51°36·7'	2°38·6'W	X	162,172
Henbant	Cered	SN4150	52°7·8'	4°19·0'W	X	146
Henbant	Cered	SN4442	52°3·5'	4°16·1'W	X	146
Henbant	Cered	SN5961	52°14·0'	4°3·5'W	X	146
Henbant	Powys	SN8646	52°6·3'	3°39·5'W	X	147
Hen-Bant	Powys	SO2420	51°52·6'	3°5·9'W	X	161
Henbarc	Gwyn	SH6267	53°11·2'	4°3·5'W	X	115
Henbarc	Pemb	SN1530	51°56·5'	4°41·1'W	X	145
Henbarns	Shrops	SJ3826	52°49·9'	2°54·8'W	X	126
Hen Bentref Llandegfan	I of Angl	SH5674	53°14·9'	4°9·1'W	H	114,115
Hen Bentref Llandegfan	I of Angl	SH5674	53°14·9'	4°9·1'W	T	114,115
Henbere	Devon	SS9506	50°52·0'	3°29·1'W	X	192
Henberrow	Glos	SO6934	52°0·5'	2°26·7'W	X	149
Henblas	Conwy	SH8262	53°8·8'	3°45·5'W	X	116
Henblas	Conwy	SH9277	53°17·0'	3°36·8'W	X	116
Henblas	Conwy	SH9444	52°59·2'	3°34·3'W	X	125
Henblas	Denb	SJ0871	53°13·9'	3°22·3'W	X	116
Hen-blas	Gwyn	SH9837	52°55·5'	3°30·6'W	X	125
Henblas	I of Angl	SH4272	53°13·5'	4°21·6'W	X	114,115
Henblas	I of Angl	SH4692	53°24·4'	4°18·6'W	X	114
Henblas	Powys	SJ1623	52°48·1'	3°14·4'W	X	125
Hen Bont	Carm	SN7423	51°53·7'	3°49·5'W	X	160
Henborough Fm	Devon	ST0914	50°55·3'	3°17·3'W	FM	181
Hen Borth	Gwyn	SH1524	52°47·2'	4°44·2'W	W	123
Hen Borth	I of Angl	SH3193	53°24·7'	4°32·2'W	W	114
Hen Brook	Cambs	TL2058	52°12·7'	0°14·2'W	W	153
Henbrook	Worcs	SO9266	52°17·8'	2°6·6'W	T	150
Henbury	Ches	SJ8873	53°15·5'	2°10·4'W	T	118
Henbury	C of Bris	ST5678	51°30·2'	2°37·6'W	T	172
Henbury	Dorset	SY9598	50°47·1'	2°3·9'W	T	195
Henbury	Kent	TR1944	51°9·4'	1°8·3'E	X	179,189
Henbury Barrow	Dorset	SY9498	50°47·1'	2°4·7'W	A	195
Henbury Hall	Ches	SJ8672	53°14·9'	2°12·2'W	X	118
Henbury Moss	Ches	SJ8672	53°14·9'	2°12·2'W	X	118
Henbury Plantation	Dorset	SY9697	50°46·6'	2°3·0'W	F	195
Hen-bwll	Gwyn	SH9114	52°43·0'	3°36·4'W	X	125
Hen Caer	Cered	SN6384	52°26·5'	4°0·5'W	A	135
Hen Capel Lligwy	I of Angl	SH4986	53°21·2'	4°15·7'W	A	114
Hen Castell	Powys	SO2116	51°50·5'	3°8·4'W	A	161
Henceford	Devon	SS8211	50°53·4'	3°40·3'W	X	191
Henceford Moor	Devon	SS8212	50°54·0'	3°40·3'W	X	181
Hen & Chickens	Devon	SS1348	51°12·3'	4°40·2'W	X	180
Hen Cloud	Staffs	SK0061	53°9·0'	1°59·6'W	H	119
Hen Comb	Cumbr	NY1318	54°33·2'	3°20·3'W	H	89

Hencott	Shrops	SJ4815	52°44·0'	2°45·8'W	X	126
Hencott Pool	Shrops	SJ4916	52°44·6'	2°44·9'W	W	126
Hen Crag	Cumbr	NY2800	54°23·7'	3°6·1'W	X	89,90
Hen Croft	Cumbr	SD2390	54°18·2'	3°10·6'W	X	96
Hendai	Carm	SN5946	52°5·9'	4°3·1'W	X	146
Hên-dai	Powys	SJ0401	52°36·1'	3°24·7'W	X	136
Hendai Fm	Caer	ST1197	51°40·1'	3°16·8'W	FM	171
Hendale Wood	Lincs	TA0907	53°33·1'	0°20·9'W	F	112
Hendale Wood	Lincs	TA1007	53°33·1'	0°20·0'W	F	113
Hendal Fm	E Susx	TQ5136	51°6·4'	0°9·8'E	FM	188
Hendall	E Susx	TQ4725	51°0·6'	0°6·1'E	X	188,198
Hendall Wood	E Susx	TQ4724	51°0·0'	0°6·1'E	F	198
Hen Ddinbych	Denb	SH9956	53°5·7'	3°30·1'W	A	116
Henden Manor	Kent	TQ4850	51°14·0'	0°7·6'E	X	188
Hender Barrow	Devon	SX4597	50°45·4'	4°11·5'W	A	190
Henderbarrow Corner	Devon	SX4498	50°45·9'	4°12·3'W	X	190
Henderbarrow Fm	Devon	SX4498	50°45·9'	4°12·3'W	FM	190
Hendergrove	Corn	SX2168	50°29·3'	4°31·0'W	X	201
Henderland	D & G	NX8774	55°3·1'	3°45·7'W	X	84
Henderland	Scot Bord	NT2323	55°29·9'	3°12·7'W	X	73
Henderland Hill	Scot Bord	NT2324	55°30·5'	3°12·7'W	H	73
Hendersick Fm	Corn	SX2352	50°20·7'	4°28·9'W	FM	201
Henderson's Ho	Durham	NZ1022	54°35·8'	1°50·3'W	X	92
Henderson's Rock	Arg & Bt	NM7415	56°16·7'	5°38·6'W	X	55
Henderston	Angus	NO3240	56°33·1'	3°5·9'W	X	53
Henderston Hill	Angus	NO3341	56°33·6'	3°5·0'W	H	53
Hendersyde Fm	Scot Bord	NT7436	55°37·3'	2°24·3'W	FM	74
Hendersyde Park	Scot Bord	NT7435	55°36·7'	2°24·3'W	X	74
Hendham	Devon	SX7450	50°20·4'	3°45·9'W	X	202
Hendir-uchaf	Brig	SS9783	51°32·4'	3°28·7'W	X	170
Hendom	Denb	SJ1342	52°58·3'	3°17·3'W	X	125
Hendom	Powys	SO1942	52°4·5'	3°10·5'W	X	148,161
Hen Domen	Powys	SO2198	52°34·7'	3°9·6'W	A	137
Hendomen	Powys	SO2198	52°34·7'	3°9·6'W	T	137
Hendon	Barnet	TQ2389	51°35·4'	0°13·1'W	T	176
Hendon	Sund	NZ4055	54°53·5'	1°22·2'W	T	88
Hendon Fm	Oxon	SP4728	51°57·1'	1°18·6'W	FM	164
Hendon Moor	Devon	SS2518	50°56·3'	4°29·1'W	X	190
Hendra	Corn	SW3629	50°6·4'	5°41·2'W	X	203
Hendra	Corn	SW5927	50°5·9'	5°21·8'W	T	203
Hendra	Corn	SW6931	50°8·3'	5°13·6'W	T	203
Hendra	Corn	SW7017	50°0·8'	5°12·3'W	T	203
Hendra	Corn	SW7237	50°11·6'	5°11·3'W	T	204
Hendra	Corn	SW7855	50°21·4'	5°6·9'W	X	200
Hendra	Corn	SW8360	50°24·2'	5°2·9'W	X	200
Hendra	Corn	SW9557	50°22·9'	4°52·6'W	T	200
Hendra	Corn	SW9651	50°19·7'	4°51·6'W	X	200,204
Hendra	Corn	SW9864	50°26·7'	4°50·3'W	T	200
Hendra	Corn	SX0275	50°32·7'	4°47·3'W	X	200
Hendra	Corn	SX0381	50°36·0'	4°46·7'W	X	200
Hendra	Corn	SX0673	50°31·7'	4°43·9'W	X	200
Hendra	Corn	SX0983	50°37·2'	4°41·6'W	T	200
Hendra	Corn	SX1186	50°38·8'	4°40·0'W	X	200
Hendra	Corn	SX1388	50°39·9'	4°38·4'W	X	190,200
Hendra	Corn	SX1954	50°21·7'	4°32·3'W	X	201
Hendra	Corn	SX2079	50°35·2'	4°32·3'W	X	201
Hendra	Corn	SX2091	50°41·7'	4°32·5'W	X	190
Hendra	Corn	SX3355	50°22·5'	4°20·5'W	X	201
Hendrabridge	Corn	SX2665	50°27·8'	4°26·7'W	T	201
Hendraburnick	Corn	SX1287	50°39·4'	4°39·2'W	T	190,200
Hendraburnick Down	Corn	SX1387	50°39·4'	4°38·4'W	X	190,200
Hendra Croft	Corn	SW7955	50°21·4'	5°6·1'W	T	200
Hendra Downs	Corn	SX1979	50°35·2'	4°33·0'W	X	201
Hendra Fm	Corn	SW8553	50°20·5'	5°0·9'W	FM	200,204
Hendragreen	Corn	SX2886	50°39·1'	4°25·6'W	X	201
Hendravossan	Corn	SW7755	50°21·4'	5°7·7'W	X	200
Hendrawalls	Corn	SX1285	50°38·3'	4°39·2'W	X	200
Hendraws	Cered	SN3247	52°6·0'	4°26·8'W	X	145
Hendre	Brig	SS9381	51°31·3'	3°32·1'W	X	170
Hendre	Carm	SN3213	51°47·7'	4°25·8'W	X	159
Hendre	Cered	SN3453	52°9·3'	4°25·2'W	X	145
Hendre	Conwy	SH7360	53°7·6'	3°53·5'W	X	115
Hendre	Conwy	SH7776	53°16·2'	3°50·3'W	X	115
Hendre	Conwy	SH8862	53°8·8'	3°40·1'W	X	116
Hendre	Denb	SJ0247	53°0·9'	3°27·2'W	X	116
Hendre	Denb	SJ0438	52°56·1'	3°25·3'W	X	125
Hendre	Denb	SJ0747	53°1·0'	3°22·8'W	X	116
Hendre	Denb	SJ0852	53°3·7'	3°22·0'W	X	116
Hendre	Denb	SJ0870	53°13·4'	3°22·3'W	X	116
Hendre	Denb	SJ2045	53°0·0'	3°11·1'W	X	117
Hendre	Flint	SJ1967	53°11·9'	3°12·3'W	T	116
Hendre	Gwyn	SH1827	52°48·8'	4°41·6'W	X	123
Hendre	Gwyn	SH2739	52°55·5'	4°34·0'W	X	123
Hendre	Gwyn	SH3137	52°54·5'	4°30·4'W	X	123
Hendre	Gwyn	SH3435	52°53·5'	4°27·7'W	X	123
Hendre	Gwyn	SH5909	52°39·9'	4°4·7'W	T	124
Hendre	Gwyn	SH6705	52°37·8'	3°57·5'W	H	124
Hendre	Gwyn	SH6706	52°38·4'	3°57·5'W	X	124
Hendre	Gwyn	SH7626	52°49·3'	3°50·0'W	X	124
Hendre	Gwyn	SH9539	52°56·5'	3°33·4'W	X	125
Hendre	Gwyn	SH9741	52°57·6'	3°31·6'W	X	125
Hendre	Heref	SO5523	51°54·5'	2°38·9'W	X	162
Hendre	I of Angl	SH4274	53°14·6'	4°21·7'W	X	114,115
Hendre	I of Angl	SH4679	53°17·4'	4°18·2'W	X	114,115
Hendre	Monm	SO3520	51°52·7'	2°56·3'W	X	161
Hendre	Nth Pt Talb	SN9001	51°42·1'	3°35·1'W	X	170
Hendre	Pemb	SM7827	51°54·1'	5°13·2'W	X	157
Hendre	Pemb	SN1020	51°51·0'	4°45·1'W	X	145,158
Hendre	Pemb	SN1136	51°59·7'	4°44·8'W	X	145
Hendre	Pemb	SN1247	52°5·6'	4°44·3'W	X	145
Hendre	Pemb	SN1617	51°49·5'	4°39·8'W	X	158
Hendre	Powys	SJ0214	52°43·1'	3°26·7'W	X	125
Hendre	Powys	SJ0709	52°40·5'	3°22·1'W	X	125
Hendre	Powys	SJ1120	52°46·5'	3°18·8'W	X	125
Hendre	Powys	SN8796	52°33·2'	3°39·6'W	X	135,136
Hendre	Powys	SN9799	52°35·0'	3°30·8'W	T	136
Hendre	Powys	SN9950	52°8·6'	3°28·2'W	X	147
Hendre	Powys	SO0847	52°7·1'	3°20·2'W	X	147
Hendre	Powys	SO1582	52°26·0'	3°14·6'W	X	136
Hendre-Aled	Conwy	SH9262	53°8·9'	3°36·5'W	X	116

Hendre Arddwyfaen	Conwy	SH9646	53°0·3'	3°32·6'W	X	116
Hendreaur	Powys	SN9579	52°24·2'	3°32·2'W	X	136,147
Hendre-bach	Conwy	SH9549	53°1·9'	3°33·5'W	X	116
Hendre-bach	Conwy	SH9676	53°16·5'	3°33·2'W	X	116
Hendre-bach	Gwyn	SH9142	52°58·1'	3°37·0'W	X	125
Hendre-bolon	Powys	SN9211	51°47·5'	3°33·6'W	X	160
Hendre Bryn Cyffo	Denb	SJ0646	53°0·4'	3°23·7'W	X	116
Hendrecaradog	Nth Pt Talb	SN7504	51°43·5'	3°48·2'W	X	170
Hendre Cennin	Gwyn	SH4543	52°58·0'	4°18·1'W	X	123
Hendre Cymru	Pemb	SN2535	51°59·4'	4°32·5'W	X	145
Hendre-ddu	Conwy	SH8766	53°11·0'	3°41·1'W	T	116
Hendre-ddu Cottages	Gwyn	SH8012	52°41·8'	3°46·1'W	X	124,125
Hendredenny Park	Caer	ST1387	51°34·7'	3°14·9'W	T	171
Hendred Ho	Oxon	SU4688	51°35·6'	1°19·8'W	X	174
Hendre-Einon	Powys	SO0653	52°10·3'	3°22·1'W	X	147
Hendre Eynon	Pemb	SM7728	51°54·6'	5°14·1'W	X	157
Hendref	Gwyn	SH8714	52°43·0'	3°40·0'W	X	124,125
Hendrefach	Pemb	SM9233	51°57·6'	5°1·3'W	X	157
Hendre-Fadog	Carm	SN5332	51°58·3'	4°8·0'W	X	146
Hendre Fechan	Gwyn	SH5921	52°46·3'	4°5·0'W	X	124
Hendrefeinws	Gwyn	SH3839	52°55·7'	4°24·2'W	X	123
Hendre-felen	Cered	SN7269	52°18·5'	3°52·3'W	X	135,147
Hendref Fawr	I of Angl	SH3191	53°23·6'	4°32·1'W	X	114
Hendre Fm	Carm	SN2918	51°50·3'	4°28·5'W	FM	159
Hendre Fm	Flint	SJ1968	53°12·4'	3°12·4'W	FM	116
Hendre Fm	I of Angl	SH5177	53°16·4'	4°13·7'W	FM	114,115
Hendre Fm	Monm	SO4512	51°48·5'	2°47·5'W	FM	161
Hendre Fm	Powys	SJ2918	52°45·5'	3°2·7'W	FM	126
Hendre Fm	Wrex	SJ1834	52°54·1'	3°12·7'W	FM	125
Hendrefoelas	Denb	SJ2159	53°7·6'	3°10·4'W	X	117
Hendrefor	Gwyn	SH1831	52°51·0'	4°41·8'W	X	123
Hendrefor	I of Angl	SH5477	53°16·4'	4°11·0'W	X	114,115
Hendreforfydd	Denb	SJ1245	52°59·9'	3°18·3'W	X	116
Hendreforgan	Rho Cyn Taf	SS9888	51°35·1'	3°27·9'W	T	170
Hendreforwydd	Powys	SO1819	51°52·1'	3°11·1'W	X	161
Hendrefydd	Powys	SN9008	51°45·8'	3°35·2'W	X	160
Hendre Gadog	I of Angl	SH4569	53°12·0'	4°18·8'W	X	114,115
Hendre Garthmeilio	Conwy	SH9444	52°59·2'	3°34·3'W	X	125
Hendregenny	Powys	SO2569	52°19·1'	3°5·6'W	X	137,148
Hendre Glan Alwen	Conwy	SH9850	53°2·5'	3°30·9'W	X	116
Hendre Glyn Fm	Monm	SO2807	51°45·7'	3°2·2'W	FM	161
Hendre Gyfeiliad	Gwyn	SH7518	52°45·0'	3°50·7'W	X	124
Hendrehedog	Carm	SN4423	51°53·3'	4°15·6'W	X	159
Hendre-hên	Powys	SJ2012	52°42·2'	3°10·6'W	X	126
Hendre Ho	Conwy	SH8158	53°6·6'	3°46·3'W	X	116
Hendre Ho	Pemb	SM8327	51°54·2'	5°8·9'W	X	157
Hendre-Isa	Denb	SJ0749	53°2·1'	3°22·8'W	X	116
Hendre Isaf	Conwy	SH8551	53°2·9'	3°42·5'W	X	116
Hendre Isaf	Monm	SO3207	51°45·7'	2°58·7'W	X	161
Hendre-ladis	Powys	SN8010	51°46·8'	3°44·0'W	X	160
Hendrelas	Cered	SN5455	52°10·7'	4°7·7'W	X	146
Hendrelas	Nth Pt Talb	SN7503	51°42·9'	3°48·2'W	X	170
Hendrellwyn-y-maen	Conwy	SH8967	53°11·6'	3°39·3'W	X	116
Hendre Owen	Rho Cyn Taf	ST0182	51°31·9'	3°25·2'W	X	170
Hendre Penprys	Gwyn	SH3439	52°55·6'	4°27·8'W	X	123
Hendre-post	Brig	SS9385	51°33·5'	3°32·2'W	X	170
Hendrerwydd	Denb	SJ1263	53°9·7'	3°18·6'W	T	116
Hendrescythan	Rho Cyn Taf	ST0783	51°32·5'	3°20·1'W	X	170
Hendreseifion	Powys	SH7602	52°36·3'	3°49·5'W	X	135
Hendre-ucha	Conwy	SH9445	52°59·8'	3°34·4'W	X	116
Hendre Ucha	Flint	SJ2361	53°8·7'	3°8·7'W	X	117
Hendre-uchaf	Conwy	SH9576	53°16·5'	3°34·1'W	X	116
Hendrewallog	Gwyn	SH6806	52°38·4'	3°56·6'W	X	124
Hendrewen	Pemb	SM9234	51°58·2'	5°1·3'W	X	157
Hendrewen	Swan	SN6107	51°44·9'	4°0·4'W	T	159
Hendre Wen Fm	Conwy	SH8178	53°17·4'	3°46·7'W	FM	116
Hendrew Fm	Newp	ST3991	51°37·1'	2°52·5'W	FM	171
Hendryd	Cered	SN5448	52°6·9'	4°7·5'W	X	146
Hendry's Corse	W Loth	NS9758	55°48·5'	3°38·2'W	F	65,72
Hendry's Holes	Orkney	HY1802	58°54·1'	3°24·9'W	X	7
Hendwick Hall Fm	York	SE6954	53°58·9'	0°56·5'W	FM	105,106
Hendwr	Denb	SJ0338	52°56·1'	3°26·2'W	X	125
Hen Dŵr	Denb	SJ0736	52°55·0'	3°22·6'W	X	125
Hendy	Carm	SN2938	52°1·1'	4°29·1'W	X	145
Hendy	Carm	SN3814	51°48·3'	4°20·6'W	X	159
Hendy	Carm	SN5803	51°42·7'	4°2·9'W	T	159
Hen-dy	Conwy	SH7575	53°15·7'	3°52·0'W	X	115
Hendy	Denb	SJ1944	52°59·5'	3°12·0'W	X	125
Hen-dŷ	Gwyn	SH2432	52°51·6'	4°36·5'W	X	123
Hendy	Gwyn	SH4761	53°7·7'	4°16·8'W	X	114,115
Hendy	Gwyn	SH5825	52°48·5'	4°6·0'W	X	124
Hen-dy	Gwyn	SH5901	52°35·6'	4°4·5'W	X	135
Hen-dy	I of Angl	SH3091	53°23·6'	4°33·0'W	X	114
Hendy	I of Angl	SH4366	53°10·3'	4°20·5'W	X	114,115
Hendy	Powys	SO0374	52°21·6'	3°25·1'W	X	136,147
Hendy	Powys	SO0646	52°6·5'	3°22·0'W	X	147
Hendy	Powys	SO1258	52°13·0'	3°16·9'W	X	148
Hendy	Rho Cyn Taf	ST0481	51°31·4'	3°22·6'W	X	170
Hendy	Swan	SS5595	51°38·3'	4°5·3'W	X	159
Hendy Fm	Denb	SJ0172	53°14·4'	3°28·6'W	FM	116
Heneage Ct	S Glos	ST6893	51°38·3'	2°27·4'W	X	162,172
Hen Efail	Conwy	SH7773	53°14·6'	3°50·2'W	X	115
Hên-efail	Denb	SJ0663	53°9·6'	3°23·9'W	T	116
Hen-efail	Powys	SJ0608	52°39·9'	3°23·0'W	X	125
Henegar	Devon	ST0917	50°57·0'	3°17·3'W	X	181
Heneglwys	I of Angl	SH4276	53°15·7'	4°21·7'W	T	114,115
Heneglwys Fm	Pemb	SM9329	51°55·5'	5°0·2'W	FM	157,158
Heneward	Corn	SX1180	50°35·6'	4°39·8'W	X	200
Henfache	Powys	SJ1227	52°50·2'	3°18·0'W	X	125
Henfaes	Carm	SN5042	52°3·6'	4°10·9'W	X	146
Henfaes	Flint	SJ1568	53°12·4'	3°16·0'W	X	116
Henfaes	Gwyn	SH8021	52°46·6'	3°46·3'W	X	124,125
Henfaes	Powys	SN8980	52°24·6'	3°37·5'W	X	135,136
Henfaes	Powys	SO1197	52°34·1'	3°18·4'W	X	136
Henfeddau Fawr	Pemb	SN2431	51°57·2'	4°33·3'W	X	145
Henfford	Gwyn	SH6572	53°13·9'	4°0·9'W	X	115
Henffrith	Conwy	SH8263	53°9·3'	3°45·5'W	X	116
Henfield	Scot Bord	NT7411	55°23·8'	2°24·2'W	X	80
Henfield	S Glos	ST6779	51°30·8'	2°28·1'W	T	172
Henfield	W Susx	TQ2116	50°56·1'	0°16·3'W	T	198

Henfield Wood	W Susx	TQ3624	51°0·2'	0°3·3'W	F	198
Hen Flatts	N Yks	SE7689	54°17·7'	0°49·5'W	X	94,100
Henfold	Surrey	TQ1843	51°10·7'	0°18·3'W	X	187
Henford	Devon	SX3694	50°43·6'	4°19·0'W	T	190
Henford Moor	Devon	SX3694	50°43·6'	4°19·0'W	X	190
Henfords Marsh	Wilts	ST8743	51°11·4'	2°10·8'W	T	183
Henford Water	Devon	SX3897	50°45·2'	4°17·4'W	W	190
Henford Wood	Devon	SX3793	50°43·1'	4°18·2'W	F	190
Henfron	Powys	SN8746	52°6·3'	3°38·6'W	X	147
Henfron	Powys	SN9064	52°16·0'	3°36·3'W	X	147
Henfron	Powys	SO1896	52°33·6'	3°12·2'W	X	136
Henfryn	Carm	SN4029	51°56·4'	4°19·3'W	X	146
Henfryn	Conwy	SH8669	53°12·6'	3°42·0'W	X	116
Henfryn	Denb	SH9960	53°7·9'	3°30·2'W	X	116
Henfryn	Powys	SO0768	52°18·4'	3°21·4'W	X	136,147
Henfryn Hall	Flint	SJ0779	53°18·2'	3°23·3'W	X	116
Hengae	Carm	SN3837	52°0·7'	4°21·2'W	X	145
Hen-gae	Gwyn	SH7511	52°41·2'	3°50·6'W	X	124
Hen Gaerau	Pemb	SN2834	51°58·9'	4°29·9'W	A	145
Hengar	Corn	SX0876	50°33·4'	4°42·3'W	X	200
Hen Gastell	Gwyn	SH4757	53°5·5'	4°16·7'W	A	115,123
Henge	Aberd	NJ4430	57°21·7'	2°55·4'W	A	37
Henge	Wilts	SU2052	51°16·2'	1°42·4'W	A	184
Hengefn	Powys	SJ0805	52°38·3'	3°21·2'W	X	125
Hen-gefn	Powys	SO1970	52°19·6'	3°10·9'W	X	136,148
Hen Gerrig	Powys	SH9518	52°45·2'	3°32·9'W	X	125
Hengherst	Kent	TQ9536	51°5·6'	0°47·5'E	X	189
Hengil-Isaf	Carm	SN4524	51°53·8'	4°14·8'W	X	159
Hen Gill	Lancs	SD8052	53°58·1'	2°17·9'W	X	103
Hengiluchaf	Carm	SN4525	51°54·4'	4°14·8'W	X	146
Hengistbury Head	Bourne	SZ1790	50°42·8'	1°45·2'W	X	195
Hen Glanllyn	Gwyn	SH8832	52°52·7'	3°39·5'W	X	124,125
Hengoed	Caer	ST1495	51°39·1'	3°14·2'W	T	171
Hengoed	Carm	SN4410	51°46·3'	4°15·3'W	X	159
Hengoed	Carm	SN5103	51°42·6'	4°9·0'W	X	159
Hengoed	Denb	SJ0858	53°6·5'	3°22·1'W	T	116
Hengoed	Heref	SO2451	52°9·4'	3°6·3'W	X	148
Hengoed	Pemb	SN0121	51°51·4'	4°53·0'W	X	145,157,158
Hengoed	Powys	SO2253	52°10·4'	3°8·0'W	T	148
Hengoed	Shrops	SJ2833	52°53·6'	3°3·8'W	T	126
Hen Graig	Powys	SJ1730	52°51·9'	3°13·6'W	H	125
Hen Grain	D & G	NX9998	55°16·2'	3°34·9'W	W	78
Hengrave	Norf	TG1319	52°43·8'	1°9·7'E	T	133
Hengrave	Suff	TL8268	52°17·0'	0°40·5'E	T	155
Hengrave Hall	Suff	TL8268	52°17·0'	0°40·5'E	A	155
Hengrove	C of Bris	ST6068	51°24·8'	2°34·1'W	T	172
Hengrove Fm	Kent	TR3368	51°22·0'	1°21·2'E	X	179
Hengrove Park	C of Bris	ST5968	51°24·8'	2°35·0'W	T	172,182
Hengwm	Gwyn	SH4346	52°59·5'	4°19·9'W	X	115,123
Hengwm	Gwyn	SH5921	52°46·3'	4°5·0'W	X	124
Hengwm	Gwyn	SH8619	52°45·6'	3°41·0'W	X	124,125
Hengwm	Powys	SJ1506	52°38·9'	3°15·0'W	X	125
Hengwm-cyfeiliog	Powys	SN7894	52°32·1'	3°47·5'W	X	135
Hengwm-fawr	Powys	SO0447	52°7·0'	3°23·7'W	X	147
Hengwm Hill	Powys	SO2868	52°18·6'	3°3·0'W	X	137,148
Hengwrt	Gwyn	SH7118	52°44·9'	3°54·3'W	X	124
Hengwrt Hall	Gwyn	SH7921	52°46·6'	3°47·2'W	X	124
Hen-hafod	Cered	SN6694	52°31·9'	3°58·1'W	X	135
Henhafod	Cered	SN7684	52°26·6'	3°49·1'W	X	135
Hen-hafod	Gwyn	SH9437	52°55·4'	3°34·2'W	X	125
Hen Hafod Fm	Wrex	SJ1636	52°55·1'	3°14·6'W	FM	125
Henham	Essex	TL5428	51°56·0'	0°14·8'E	T	167
Henhambridge Brook	Somer	ST7852	51°16·2'	2°18·5'W	W	183
Henham Lodge	Essex	TL5429	51°56·5'	0°14·8'E	X	167
Henham Park	Suff	TM4577	52°20·4'	1°36·2'E	X	156
Hen Heads Fm	Lancs	SD7826	53°44·0'	2°19·6'W	FM	103
Hen Hill	Aberd	NO6083	56°56·4'	2°39·0'W	H	45
Hen Hill	Cumbr	NY6073	55°3·2'	2°37·1'W	X	86
Hen Hill	Cumbr	NY6375	55°4·3'	2°34·3'W	X	86
Hen Hill	D & G	NY2786	55°10·0'	3°8·3'W	H	79
Henhill	Northum	NU1628	55°33·0'	1°44·4'W	X	75
Hen Hole	Northum	NT8820	55°28·7'	2°11·0'W	X	74
Hen Holme	Cumbr	SD3997	54°22·1'	2°55·9'W	X	96,97
Henhow	Cumbr	NY4317	54°33·0'	2°52·5'W	X	90
Henhullbridge Fm	Ches	SJ6354	53°5·2'	2°32·7'W	FM	118
Henhull Hall	Ches	SJ6453	53°4·6'	2°31·8'W	X	118
Henhurst	Kent	TQ6669	51°24·0'	0°23·6'E	X	177,178
Henhurst Fm	Kent	TQ7842	51°9·2'	0°33·1'E	FM	188
Heniarth	Powys	SJ1208	52°40·0'	3°17·7'W	T	125
Henilyn	Powys	SO1046	52°6·5'	3°18·5'W	W	148
Hening Wood	Durham	NZ0511	54°29·9'	1°54·9'W	F	92
Heniton Hill	Somer	ST0321	50°59·0'	3°22·5'W	H	181
Hen Knowes	D & G	NY2298	55°16·5'	3°13·2'W	H	79
Henlade	Somer	ST2623	51°0·3'	3°2·9'W	T	193
Henlade Ho	Somer	ST2723	51°0·3'	3°2·0'W	X	193
Henlake Down	Devon	SX6357	50°24·0'	3°55·3'W	X	202
Henland Fms	Devon	ST0807	50°51·5'	3°18·0'W	FM	192
Henlaw Fm	Northum	NU0529	55°33·5'	1°54·8'W	FM	75
Henlaw Wood	Scot Bord	NT7154	55°47·0'	2°27·3'W	F	67,74
Henleaze	C of Bris	ST5876	51°29·1'	2°35·9'W	T	172
Henless Beck	N Yks	SE0568	54°6·7'	1°55·0'W	W	98
Henley	Dorset	ST6904	50°50·3'	2°26·0'W	T	194
Henley	Glos	SO9016	51°50·8'	2°8·3'W	T	163
Henley	Shrops	SO4588	52°29·5'	2°48·2'W	X	137,138
Henley	Shrops	SO5476	52°23·0'	2°40·2'W	T	137,138
Henley	Somer	ST4307	50°51·8'	2°48·2'W	X	193
Henley	Somer	ST4332	51°5·3'	2°48·4'W	T	182
Henley	Suff	TM1551	52°7·2'	1°8·8'E	T	156
Henley	Wilts	ST8267	51°24·3'	2°15·1'W	T	173
Henley	Wilts	SU3259	51°20·0'	1°32·1'W	T	174
Henley	W Susx	SU8925	51°1·3'	0°43·5'W	T	186,197
Henley Common	Shrops	SO4588	52°29·5'	2°48·2'W	X	137,138
Henley Common	W Susx	SU8826	51°1·8'	0°44·3'W	T	186,197
Henley Corner	Somer	ST4332	51°5·3'	2°48·4'W	X	182
Henley Fm	Glos	SO9309	51°47·0'	2°5·7'W	FM	163
Henley Fm	Shrops	SO6894	52°32·8'	2°27·9'W	FM	138
Henley Fm	W Berks	SU3978	51°30·2'	1°25·9'W	FM	174
Henley Green	Cov	SP3681	52°25·8'	1°27·8'W	T	140
Henley Grove Fm	Somer	ST6837	51°8·1'	2°27·1'W	FM	183
Henley Hill	S Glos	ST6089	51°36·1'	2°34·3'W	X	162,172

Henley Hill	S Glos	ST7471	51°26·5'	2°22·1'W	H	172
Henley Hill	S Glos	ST7872	51°27·0'	2°18·6'W	X	172
Henleyhill	Shrops	SO5679	52°24·7'	2°38·4'W	X	137,138
Henley Hill	Somer	ST5246	51°12·9'	2°40·8'W	H	182,183
Henleyhill Wood	Bucks	SU7688	51°35·4'	0°53·8'W	F	175
Henley Ho	Lincs	TF3153	53°3·7'	0°2·3'W	X	122
Henley-in-Arden	Warw	SP1565	52°17·2'	1°46·4'W	T	151
Henley Knapp	Oxon	SP3722	51°54·0'	1°27·3'W	F	164
Henley-on-Thames	Oxon	SU7682	51°32·1'	0°53·9'W	T	175
Henley Park	Oxon	SU7584	51°33·2'	0°54·7'W	X	175
Henley Park	Surrey	SU9352	51°15·8'	0°39·6'W	X	186
Henleypark Fm	Surrey	SU9252	51°15·8'	0°40·5'W	FM	186
Henleypark Lake	Surrey	SU9353	51°16·3'	0°39·6'W	W	186
Henley Reach	Oxon	SU7684	51°33·2'	0°53·8'W	W	175
Henley's Down	E Susx	TQ7312	50°53·1'	0°28·0'E	T	199
Henley Square	Suff	TM1652	52°7·7'	1°9·7'E	X	156
Henley Street	Kent	TQ6667	51°22·9'	0°23·5'E	T	177,178
Henley Tyning Fm	S Glos	ST7571	51°26·5'	2°21·2'W	FM	172
Henley Wood	E Susx	TQ6034	51°5·2'	0°17·5'E	F	188
Henllan	Cered	SN3540	52°2·3'	4°23·9'W	T	145
Henllan	Denb	SJ0268	53°12·2'	3°27·6'W	T	116
Henllan	Monm	SO2925	51°55·4'	3°1·6'W	X	161
Henllan	Pemb	SN1238	52°0·8'	4°44·0'W	X	145
Henllan	Pemb	SN1316	51°48·9'	4°42·4'W	X	158
Henllan	Powys	SJ1308	52°40·0'	3°16·8'W	X	125
Henllan	Powys	SN7798	52°34·2'	3°48·5'W	X	135
Henllan Amgoed	Carm	SN1819	51°50·6'	4°38·1'W	T	158
Henllan Amgoed	Carm	SN1820	51°51·2'	4°38·2'W	T	145,158
Henllan Fm	Carm	SN1820	51°51·2'	4°38·2'W	FM	145,158
Henlle	Shrops	SJ3233	52°53·7'	3°0·2'W	T	126
Henlle Hall	Shrops	SJ3035	52°54·7'	3°2·1'W	X	126
Henllwyn	Gwyn	SH1120	52°44·9'	4°47·6'W	W	123
Henllys	Carm	SN7536	52°0·7'	3°48·9'W	X	146,160
Henllys	Cered	SN6388	52°28·6'	4°0·6'W	X	135
Henllys	Conwy	SH9069	53°12·6'	3°38·4'W	X	116
Henllys	Gwyn	SH3132	52°51·8'	4°30·2'W	X	123
Henllys	Monm	SO4110	51°47·4'	2°50·9'W	X	161
Henllys	Pemb	SM8131	51°56·3'	5°10·8'W	X	157
Henllys	Pemb	SN1039	52°1·3'	4°45·8'W	X	145
Henllys	Powys	SJ1103	52°37·3'	3°18·5'W	X	136
Henllys	Swan	SS4589	51°35·0'	4°13·8'W	X	159
Henllys	Torf	ST2693	51°38·1'	3°3·8'W	T	171
Henllys-fawr	I of Angl	SH3570	53°12·3'	4°27·8'W	X	114
Henllys Vale	Torf	ST2792	51°37·6'	3°2·9'W	T	171
Henlow	Beds	TL1738	52°1·9'	0°17·3'W	T	153
Henlow Airfield	Beds	TL1636	52°0·8'	0°18·2'W	X	153
Henlow Fm	Cambs	TF3608	52°39·4'	0°1·0'E	FM	142
Henmead Hall	W Susx	TQ2825	51°0·8'	0°10·1'W	X	187,198
Henmoor	Derby	SK3763	53°10·0'	1°26·4'W	X	119
Henmoor Hill	Shrops	SO5997	52°34·4'	2°35·9'W	X	137,138
Henmore Brook	Derby	SK2047	53°1·4'	1°41·7'W	W	119,128
Hen Moss Fm	Cumbr	NY3655	54°53·4'	2°59·4'W	FM	85
Henmuir Burn	D & G	NX7650	54°50·0'	3°55·4'W	W	84
Henna Cliff	Corn	SS1915	50°54·6'	4°34·1'W	X	190
Hennah Hall	Cumbr	NY0733	54°41·3'	3°26·1'W	X	89
Henne	Pemb	SN0127	51°54·6'	4°53·2'W	X	145,157,158
Hennel Bottom	S Glos	ST7888	51°35·7'	2°18·7'W	X	162,172
Hennerton Ho	Wok	SU7880	51°31·0'	0°52·2'W	X	175
Hennerwood Fm	Heref	SO5653	52°10·6'	2°38·2'W	FM	149
Hennett	Corn	SX1391	50°41·6'	4°38·5'W	X	190
Hennhill	Pth & Kin	NO0417	56°20·4'	3°32·7'W	X	58
Henning Hill	Dorset	ST7601	50°48·7'	2°20·1'W	H	194
Hennock	Devon	SX8381	50°37·3'	3°38·9'W	T	191
Hennor	Heref	SO5358	52°13·3'	2°40·9'W	X	149
Henny Street	Essex	TL8738	52°0·8'	0°43·9'E	T	155
Hen of Gairsay	Orkney	HY4521	59°4·6'	2°57·1'W	X	5,6
Henon	Corn	SX0980	50°35·5'	4°41·5'W	X	200
Hen Parc	Swan	SS5991	51°36·3'	4°1·8'W	X	159
Hen Poo	Scot Bord	NT7754	55°47·0'	2°21·6'W	W	67,74
Henrhiw	Monm	SO3502	51°43·0'	2°56·1'W	X	171
Henrhiw Isaf	Conwy	SH7851	53°2·8'	3°48·8'W	X	115
Henrhyd	Carm	SN6710	51°46·6'	3°55·3'W	X	160
Henrhyd	Conwy	SH8170	53°13·1'	3°46·5'W	X	116
Henrhyd	Powys	SJ0922	52°47·5'	3°20·6'W	X	125
Henrhyd Falls	Powys	SN8512	51°47·9'	3°39·7'W	W	160
Henridding	Cumbr	SD5475	54°10·4'	2°41·9'W	X	97
Henrie's Burn	D & G	NY2292	55°13·2'	3°13·1'W	W	79
Henrietta Park	Highld	NH6865	57°39·6'	4°12·3'W	X	21
Henrietta Reef	Arg & Bt	NR7305	55°17·5'	5°34·1'W	X	68
Henryd	Conwy	SH7774	53°15·2'	3°50·2'W	T	115
Henry's Grove	Notts	SK6570	53°13·6'	1°1·2'W	F	120
Henry's Hill	Cumbr	NY4567	54°59·9'	2°51·2'W	X	86
Henry's Hill	S Lanak	NS7931	55°33·7'	3°54·7'W	X	71
Henry's Loch	Shetld	HU4335	60°6·1'	1°13·1'W	W	4
Henry's Moat	Pemb	SN0427	51°54·7'	4°50·6'W	T	145,157,158
Henry's Scorth	Aberd	NO8880	56°54·9'	2°11·4'W	X	45
Henryton	E Ayr	NS5738	55°37·1'	4°15·8'W	X	71
Hensall	N Yks	SE5923	53°42·2'	1°6·0'W	T	105
Hensall Ings	N Yks	SE6024	53°42·8'	1°5·0'W	X	105
Hensbarrow Downs	Corn	SW9957	50°22·9'	4°49·3'W	H	200
Hensborough Fm	Warw	SP4668	52°18·7'	1°19·1'W	FM	151
Hensborough Hill	Warw	SP4669	52°19·3'	1°19·1'W	H	151
Henscath	Corn	SW6618	50°1·2'	5°15·6'W	X	203
Hen's Cliff	Glos	ST7991	51°37·3'	2°17·8'W	X	162,172
Henscott	Devon	SS4108	50°51·2'	4°15·2'W	X	190
Henscott Plantns	Devon	SX5183	50°37·9'	4°6·0'W	F	191,201
Hense Moor	Devon	ST1707	50°51·6'	3°10·4'W	X	192,193
Hensford	Devon	SX9579	50°36·3'	3°28·7'W	X	192
Hens Grove	Oxon	SP2913	51°49·1'	1°34·4'W	F	164
Henshaw	Leeds	SE2040	53°51·6'	1°41·3'W	T	104
Henshaw	Northum	NY7664	54°58·5'	2°22·1'W	T	86,87
Henshaw Burn	Scot Bord	NT1358	55°48·7'	3°22·9'W	W	65,72
Henshaw Common	Northum	NY7573	55°3·3'	2°23·1'W	F	86,87
Henshaw Fm	Surrey	TQ3148	51°13·2'	0°7·1'W	FM	187
Henshaw Green Fm	Ches	SJ7175	53°16·5'	2°25·7'W	FM	118
Henshaw Hall Fm	Ches	SJ8670	53°13·9'	2°12·2'W	FM	118
Henshaw Hill	S Lanak	NT0654	55°46·5'	3°29·5'W	H	65,72
Henshaw Law	Scot Bord	NT7916	55°26·5'	2°19·5'W	X	80
Henshilwood	S Lanak	NS9451	55°44·7'	3°40·9'W	X	65,72
Hensill Ho	Kent	TQ7530	51°2·8'	0°30·2'E	X	188

Hensingham	Cumbr	NX9816	54°32·0'	3°34·2'W	T	89
Hensington	Oxon	SP4516	51°50·7'	1°20·4'W	T	164
Hensleigh Fm	Devon	SS9211	50°53·5'	3°31·8'W	FM	192
Hensleigh Ho	Devon	SS9312	50°54·1'	3°30·9'W	X	181
Hensley	Devon	SS7613	50°54·4'	3°45·4'W	X	180
Hensley Hill	N Yks	SD7859	54°1·8'	2°19·7'W	X	103
Hensol	V of Glam	ST0479	51°30·3'	3°22·6'W	X	170
Hensol Forest	V of Glam	ST0476	51°28·7'	3°22·6'W	F	170
Hensol Ho	D & G	NX6769	55°0·1'	4°4·3'W	X	83,84
Hensol Lake	V of Glam	ST0478	51°29·8'	3°22·6'W	W	170
Henspark	Devon	SS8627	51°2·1'	3°37·2'W	X	181
Henstaffe Court	Card	ST0780	51°30·9'	3°20·0'W	X	170
Henstead	Suff	TM4985	52°24·6'	1°40·1'E	T	156
Henstill	Devon	SS8003	50°49·1'	3°41·8'W	X	191
Hensting	Hants	SU4921	50°59·1'	1°17·7'W	T	185
Hensting Fm	Hants	SU4922	50°59·9'	1°17·7'W	FM	185
Henstone Band Side	N Yks	SE0569	54°7·3'	1°55·0'W	X	98
Hen Stones	N Yks	SE0859	54°1·9'	1°52·3'W	X	104
Henstown	Somer	SS9930	51°3·9'	3°26·1'W	X	181
Henstridge	Devon	SS5844	51°10·9'	4°1·5'W	T	180
Henstridge	Somer	ST7219	50°58·4'	2°23·5'W	T	183
Henstridge Ash	Somer	ST7220	50°59·0'	2°23·5'W	T	183
Henstridge Bowden	Somer	ST6920	50°58·9'	2°26·1'W	T	183
Henstridge Marsh	Somer	ST7420	50°59·0'	2°21·8'W	T	183
Hens Wood	Wilts	SU2468	51°24·9'	1°38·9'W	F	174
Henthitchen	Devon	SS7138	51°7·8'	3°50·2'W	X	180
Hentig Plantn	E Yorks	SE8144	53°53·4'	0°45·6'W	F	106
Hentland	Heref	SO5426	51°56·1'	2°39·8'W	X	162
Hen Toe Burn	Scot Bord	NT7559	55°49·7'	2°23·5'W	W	67,74
Henton	Oxon	SP7602	51°42·9'	0°53·6'W	T	165
Henton	Somer	ST4945	51°12·4'	2°43·4'W	T	182,183
Henton Fm	Newp	ST3583	51°32·8'	2°55·9'W	FM	171
Hen Tor	Devon	SX5965	50°28·3'	3°58·8'W	X	202
Hentor Warren	Devon	SX5965	50°28·3'	3°58·8'W	X	202
Hentshill Fm	Somer	ST7337	51°8·1'	2°22·8'W	FM	183
Hen Voelas	Conwy	SH8752	53°3·4'	3°40·8'W	X	116
Henwick Hall	N Yks	SE6129	53°45·5'	1°4·1'W	X	105
Henwick Manor	W Berks	SU4968	51°24·8'	1°17·3'W	X	174
Henwood	Corn	SX2673	50°32·1'	4°26·9'W	T	201
Hen Wood	Hants	SU6622	50°59·8'	1°3·2'W	F	185
Hen Wood	Hants	SU6647	51°13·3'	1°2·9'W	F	185,186
Henwood	Oxon	SP4602	51°43·1'	1°19·7'W	T	164
Henwood Down	Hants	SU6621	50°59·3'	1°3·2'W	X	185
Henwood Fm	Heref	SO4155	52°11·6'	2°51·4'W	FM	148,149
Henwood Fm	Oxon	SP4702	51°43·1'	1°18·8'W	FM	164
Henwood Green	Kent	TQ6340	51°8·4'	0°20·2'E	T	188
Henwood Hall Fm	Sol	SP1878	52°24·2'	1°43·7'W	FM	139
Henwood Hill	Dorset	SY4294	50°44·8'	2°48·9'W	X	193
Hên Wrych	Conwy	SH9278	53°17·5'	3°36·8'W	X	116
Henzie Burn	Pth & Kin	NN8433	56°28·7'	3°52·6'W	W	52
Heock Ness	Shetld	HU2547	60°12·7'	1°32·4'W	X	3
Heog	Shetld	HU4971	60°25·5'	1°6·1'W	X	2,3
Heogals, The	Shetld	HU5281	60°30·8'	1°2·7'W	X	1,2,3
Heogan	Shetld	HU4743	60°10·4'	1°8·1'W	T	4
Heoga Neap	Shetld	HU3591	60°36·3'	1°21·1'W	X	1,2
Heoga Ness	Shetld	HU5379	60°29·7'	1°1·6'W	X	2,3
Heogel of the Moor	Shetld	HU3391	60°36·3'	1°23·3'W	X	1,2
Heogel, The	Shetld	HU3180	60°30·4'	1°25·6'W	X	1,3
Heog, The	Shetld	HU3482	60°31·5'	1°22·3'W	H	1,2,3
Heog, The	Shetld	HU6289	60°35·0'	0°51·6'W	X	1,2
Heog, The	Shetld	HU6590	60°35·6'	0°48·3'W	X	1,2
Heolcwn	Cered	SN1849	52°6·8'	4°39·1'W	X	145
Heol-ddu	Carm	SN4603	51°42·5'	4°13·3'W	T	159
Heol-ddu	Carm	SN5315	51°49·1'	4°7·6'W	X	159
Heol-ddu	Swan	SS6498	51°40·1'	3°57·6'W	T	159
Heol-draw	Powys	SO1820	51°52·6'	3°11·1'W	X	161
Heol-Einon	Powys	SO0738	52°2·2'	3°21·0'W	X	160
Heolfanog	Powys	SO0125	51°55·1'	3°26·0'W	X	160
Heol-fawr	Carm	SN5319	51°51·3'	4°7·7'W	X	159
Heol-feinog	Cered	SN4446	52°5·7'	4°16·2'W	X	146
Heolgerrig	Merth Tyd	SO0306	51°44·9'	3°23·9'W	T	160
Heol-laethog	Brig	SS9384	51°32·9'	3°32·2'W	T	170
Heol-las	Brig	SS9382	51°31·8'	3°32·2'W	T	170
Heol-lâs	Rho Cyn Taf	SN9409	51°46·4'	3°31·8'W	X	160
Heol Las	Swan	SS6998	51°40·2'	3°53·3'W	T	159
Heol-las Fm	Powys	SO1423	51°54·2'	3°14·6'W	FM	161
Heol Llygoden	Powys	SO1729	51°57·4'	3°12·1'W	X	161
Heol Senni	Powys	SN9223	51°53·9'	3°33·8'W	T	160
Heol-y-cawl	Rho Cyn Taf	ST0887	51°34·7'	3°19·3'W	X	170
Heol-y-Cefn	Powys	SO1430	51°57·9'	3°14·7'W	X	161
Heol-y-Cyw	Brig	SS9484	51°32·9'	3°31·3'W	T	170
Heol-y-gaer	Powys	SO1939	52°2·8'	3°10·5'W	T	161
Heol-y-mynydd	V of Glam	SS8874	51°27·5'	3°36·3'W	T	170
Heolyrhedyn Fm	Powys	SN9314	51°49·1'	3°32·8'W	FM	160
Hepburn	Northum	NU0624	55°30·8'	1°53·9'W	T	75
Hepburn Bell	Northum	NU0523	55°30·3'	1°54·8'W	X	75
Hepburn Moor	Northum	NU0824	55°30·8'	1°52·0'W	X	75
Hepburn Wood	Northum	NU0723	55°30·3'	1°52·9'W	F	75
Hepden Burn	Northum	NT8714	55°25·4'	2°11·9'W	W	80
Hephill	Heref	SO5540	52°3·6'	2°39·0'W	X	149
Hepnalls	Derby	SK2633	52°53·9'	1°36·4'W	X	128
Hepple	Northum	NT9800	55°17·9'	2°1·5'W	T	81
Hepple Heugh	Northum	NY9284	55°9·3'	2°7·1'W	H	80
Hepple Whitefield	Northum	NY9899	55°17·4'	2°1·5'W	H	81
Hepplewoodside	Northum	NY9798	55°16·8'	2°2·4'W	X	81
Hepscott	Northum	NZ2284	55°9·2'	1°38·9'W	T	81
Hepscott Manor	Northum	NZ2182	55°8·2'	1°39·8'W	X	81
Hepscott Manor Fm	Northum	NZ2183	55°8·7'	1°39·8'W	FM	81
Hepscott Park	Northum	NZ2282	55°8·2'	1°38·9'W	X	81
Hepscott Red Ho	Northum	NZ2284	55°9·2'	1°38·9'W	X	81
Hepshaw	Barns	SE1705	53°32·7'	1°44·2'W	X	110
Hepste fawr	Powys	SN9512	51°48·0'	3°31·0'W	X	160
Hepste-fechan	Powys	SN9613	51°48·6'	3°30·1'W	X	160
Hepthorne Lane	Derby	SK4064	53°10·5'	1°23·7'W	T	120
Heptonstall	Cald	SD9728	53°45·1'	2°2·3'W	T	103
Heptonstall Moor	Cald	SD9330	53°46·2'	2°6·0'W	X	103
Hepwell Br	Corn	SX3064	50°27·3'	4°23·3'W	X	201
Hepwood Lodge Fm	Suff	TM2273	52°18·1'	1°15·8'E	FM	156
Hepworth	Kirk	SE1606	53°33·3'	1°45·1'W	T	110
Hepworth	Suff	TL9874	52°19·9'	0°54·8'E	T	144

Hepworth Hall	Essex	TL8032	51°57·7'	0°37·6'E	X	168
Hepworth Hall Fm	Suff	TL9874	52°19·9'	0°54·8'E	FM	144
Hepworth Ho	Suff	TL9875	52°20·5'	0°54·8'E	X	144
Hepworth South Common	Suff	TL9974	52°19·9'	0°55·6'E	X	144
Herberdeg	Carm	SN4707	51°44·7'	4°12·6'W	X	159
Herberts	Essex	TL5436	52°0·3'	0°15·0'E	X	154
Herbertshaw Fm	Midlo	NT2557	55°48·3'	3°11·4'W	FM	66,73
Herbert's Heath	Oxon	SP2419	51°52·4'	1°38·7'W	X	163
Herbert's Hill	Heref	SO5221	51°53·4'	2°41·5'W	X	162
Herberts Hole	Bucks	SP9302	51°42·8'	0°38·8'W	X	165
Herbert's Lodge	Swan	SS5887	51°34·1'	4°2·5'W	X	159
Herbertsmoor	Pemb	SS0098	51°39·0'	4°53·1'W	X	158
Herbrandston	Pemb	SM8607	51°43·5'	5°5·5'W	T	157
Herbury	Dorset	SY6180	50°37·3'	2°32·7'W	X	194
Hercocks Fm	Lincs	TF1242	52°58·1'	0°19·5'W	FM	130
Hercules Wood	Norf	TG1628	52°48·6'	1°12·7'E	F	133
Herdacott	Corn	SS2512	50°53·1'	4°28·9'W	X	190
Herdborough House Fm	N Yks	TA0282	54°13·7'	0°25·7'W	FM	101
Herders Inn (PH)	Lancs	SD9439	53°51·1'	2°5·1'W	X	103
Herd Fm	Leeds	SE3142	53°52·6'	1°31·3'W	FM	104
Herd Hill	Aberd	NO6176	56°52·7'	2°37·9'W	X	45
Herdhill	Angus	NO3753	56°40·1'	3°1·2'W	X	54
Herd Hill	Cumbr	NY1759	54°55·4'	3°17·3'W	X	85
Herd Hill	Cumbr	NY2162	54°57·0'	3°13·6'W	X	85
Herd Hill	Warw	SP3247	52°7·5'	1°31·6'W	X	151
Herd Hill Fm	Warw	SP3248	52°8·0'	1°31·6'W	FM	151
Herdhillmuir	Angus	NO3653	56°40·1'	3°2·2'W	X	54
Herdhill Scar	Cumbr	NY2162	54°57·0'	3°13·6'W	X	85
Herd House Moss	Cumbr	SD2184	54°15·0'	3°12·3'W	X	96
Herd Howe	Red & Cl	NZ7011	54°29·6'	0°54·7'W	A	94
Herdicott	Devon	SX3399	50°46·2'	4°21·7'W	X	190
Herding Hill	Northum	NY7065	54°59·0'	2°27·7'W	X	86,87
Herdlaw	Northum	NY9498	55°16·8'	2°5·2'W	X	80
Herdmans Close Fm	Derby	SK1848	53°2·0'	1°43·5'W	FM	119
Herdmanston Mains	E Loth	NT4770	55°55·5'	2°50·5'W	X	66
Herd Naze	D & G	NS7100	55°16·9'	4°1·4'W	X	77
Herd Sand	S Tyne	NZ3767	55°0·0'	1°24·9'W	X	88
Herd's Hill	E Ayr	NX4698	55°15·4'	4°25·0'W	X	77
Herd's Hill	E Loth	NT6162	55°51·2'	2°36·9'W	X	67
Herdship	Durham	NY8133	54°41·7'	2°17·3'W	X	91,92
Herdship Fell	Durham	NY7933	54°41·7'	2°19·1'W	H	91
Herd's Ho	Northum	NY7652	54°52·0'	2°22·0'W	X	86,87
Herds Law	Northum	NY8654	54°53·1'	2°12·7'W	X	87
Herdswick Farm	Wilts	SU1875	51°28·7'	1°44·1'W	FM	173
Herdus	Cumbr	NY1116	54°32·1'	3°22·1'W	X	89
Herdwick	Devon	SS6507	50°51·0'	3°54·7'W	X	191
Herdwick Croft	Cumbr	NY1932	54°40·8'	3°15·0'W	X	89,90
Herdwicke	Devon	SS3504	50°49·0'	4°20·2'W	X	190
Herebere	Devon	SX8071	50°31·8'	3°41·2'W	X	202
Hereford	Heref	SO5140	52°3·6'	2°42·5'W	T	149
Herefordshire Beacon	Heref	SO7539	52°3·2'	2°21·5'W	H	150
Hereliving	Somer	SS7938	51°7·9'	3°43·4'W	X	180
Hereward Way	Norf	TL8387	52°27·2'	0°42·0'E	X	144
Hereward Way	Suff	TL6584	52°26·0'	0°26·0'E	X	143
Hereward Way	Suff	TL8087	52°27·3'	0°39·4'E	X	144
Hergan	Shrops	SO2685	52°27·7'	3°5·0'W	H	137
Hergest	Powys	SO1249	52°8·2'	3°16·8'W	X	148
Hergest Court	Heref	SO2855	52°11·6'	3°2·8'W	X	148
Hergest Croft Gardens	Heref	SO2856	52°12·1'	3°2·8'W	X	148
Hergest Ridge	Heref	SO2556	52°12·1'	3°5·5'W	H	148
Heribost	Highld	NG2745	57°25·1'	6°32·4'W	T	23
Heribusta	Highld	NG4070	57°39·0'	6°21·0'W	T	23
Heriot	Scot Bord	NT4053	55°46·3'	2°56·9'W	T	66,73
Heriot Cleugh	Scot Bord	NT3754	55°46·8'	2°59·8'W	X	66,73
Heriot Ho	Scot Bord	NT4054	55°46·8'	2°57·0'W	X	66,73
Heriot Mill	Scot Bord	NT3952	55°45·7'	2°57·9'W	X	66,73
Heriot's Dyke	Scot Bord	NT7148	55°43·7'	2°27·3'W	A	74
Heriot Toun Fm	Scot Bord	NT4053	55°46·3'	2°56·9'W	FM	66,73
Heriot Town Hill	Scot Bord	NT3953	55°46·2'	2°57·9'W	X	66,73
Heriot Water	Scot Bord	NT3651	55°45·1'	3°0·7'W	W	66,73
Heriot Water	Scot Bord	NT7668	55°54·5'	2°22·6'W	W	67
Heriot-Watt University	C of Edin	NT1769	55°54·7'	3°19·2'W	X	65,66
Herishader	Highld	NG5162	57°35·0'	6°9·5'W	X	23,24
Heritage Motor Centre	Warw	SP3554	52°11·2'	1°28·9'W	X	151
Heritage, The	Scot Bord	NT8550	55°44·8'	2°13·9'W	X	67,74
Heritage Trail	I of M	SC3180	54°11·5'	4°35·0'W	X	95
Herive Burn	Stir	NN3625	56°23·6'	4°39·0'W	W	50
Herkstead Hall Fm	Essex	TL6738	52°1·1'	0°26·4'E	FM	154
Hermand	W Loth	NT0263	55°51·3'	3°33·5'W	X	65
Herma Ness	Shetld	HP5918	60°50·7'	0°54·4'W	X	1
Hermaness Hill	Shetld	HP6017	60°50·1'	0°53·3'W	H	1
Herman Law	Scot Bord	NT2115	55°25·6'	3°14·5'W	H	79
Hermeston Hall	Notts	SK5888	53°23·4'	1°7·3'W	X	111,120
Hermetray	N Eil	NF9874	57°39·5'	7°3·4'W	X	18
Hermisgarth	Orkney	HY6642	59°16·1'	2°35·3'W	X	5
Hermiston	C of Edin	NT1770	55°55·2'	3°19·2'W	T	65,66
Hermiston	Scot Bord	NT5123	55°30·2'	2°46·1'W	X	73
Hermiston Ho	C of Edin	NT1770	55°55·2'	3°19·2'W	X	65,66
Hermitage	Ches	SJ7668	53°12·8'	2°21·2'W	X	118
Hermitage	D & G	NX8068	54°59·8'	3°52·1'W	X	84
Hermitage	Dorset	ST6407	50°51·9'	2°30·3'W	T	194
Hermitage	N Yks	NZ7909	54°28·5'	0°46·4'W	X	94
Hermitage	N Yks	NZ8311	54°29·5'	0°42·7'W	X	94
Hermitage	N Yks	SE7965	54°4·7'	0°47·1'W	X	100
Hermitage	Powys	SO2225	51°55·3'	3°7·7'W	X	161
Hermitage	Scot Bord	NY5095	55°15·0'	2°46·8'W	T	79
Hermitage	Staffs	SK0247	53°1·5'	1°57·8'W	X	119,128
Hermitage	W Berks	SU5173	51°27·5'	1°15·6'W	T	174
Hermitage	W Susx	SU7505	50°50·6'	0°55·7'W	T	197
Hermitage Castle	Scot Bord	NY4996	55°15·6'	2°47·7'W	A	79
Hermitage Cottage	Scot Bord	NY5095	55°15·0'	2°46·8'W	X	79
Hermitage Fm	Cambs	TL4075	52°21·5'	0°3·8'E	FM	142,143
Hermitage Fm	Hants	SU6617	50°57·1'	1°3·2'W	FM	185
Hermitage Fm	Hants	SU7029	51°3·6'	0°59·7'W	FM	186,197
Hermitage Fm	Kent	TQ7256	51°16·9'	0°28·4'E	FM	178,188
Hermitage Fm	Leic	SK7312	52°42·3'	0°54·8'W	FM	129
Hermitage Fm	Lincs	SK9389	53°23·6'	0°35·7'W	FM	112,121
Hermitage Fm	Lincs	TF2551	53°2·7'	0°7·7'W	FM	122
Hermitage Fm	Mil Key	SP8940	52°3·3'	0°41·7'W	FM	152
Hermitage Fm	Northum	NU2406	55°21·1'	1°36·9'W	FM	81

Hermitage Fm	Shrops	SJ5727	52°50·6'	2°37·9'W	FM	126
Hermitage Fm	Somer	ST3115	50°56·1'	2°58·5'W	FM	193
Hermitage Fm	Suff	TL7746	52°5·3'	0°35·4'E	FM	155
Hermitage Fm	Worcs	SO8848	52°8·0'	2°10·1'W	FM	150
Hermitage Green	Warr	SJ6094	53°26·7'	2°35·7'W	T	109
Hermitage Hill	Scot Bord	NY4997	55°16·1'	2°47·7'W	H	79
Hermitage Low Fm	Lincs	SK9288	53°23·1'	0°36·6'W	FM	112,121
Hermitage of Braid	C of Edin	NT2570	55°55·3'	3°11·6'W	X	66
Hermitage, The	Derby	SK4338	52°56·5'	1°21·2'W	A	129
Hermitage, The	Devon	SS2118	50°56·3'	4°32·5'W	X	190
Hermitage, The	Durham	NZ2649	54°50·4'	1°35·3'W	X	88
Hermitage, The	E Susx	TQ8721	50°57·7'	0°40·2'E	X	189,199
Hermitage, The	Heref	SO4647	52°7·4'	2°46·9'W	X	148,149
Hermitage, The	I of W	SZ4978	50°36·2'	1°18·1'W	X	196
Hermitage, The	Kent	TQ6249	51°13·3'	0°19·6'E	X	188
Hermitage, The	Kent	TQ6857	51°17·5'	0°25·0'E	X	178,188
Hermitage, The	Lincs	TF1071	53°13·7'	0°20·7'W	X	121
Hermitage, The	Northnts	SP7885	52°27·7'	0°50·7'W	X	141
Hermitage, The	Northum	NY9365	54°59·0'	2°6·1'W	X	87
Hermitage, The	Northum	NY9374	55°3·9'	2°6·1'W	X	87
Hermitage, The	N Yks	SE2285	54°15·9'	1°39·3'W	X	99
Hermitage, The	Shrops	SO7293	52°32·3'	2°24·4'W	A	138
Hermitage, The	Somer	ST7438	51°8·7'	2°21·9'W	X	183
Hermitage, The	Suff	TM4780	52°22·0'	1°38·1'E	X	156
Hermitage, The	Surrey	TQ2253	51°16·0'	0°14·7'W	X	187
Hermitage, The	York	SE6557	54°0·5'	1°0·1'W	X	105,106
Hermitage Water	Scot Bord	NY5092	55°13·4'	2°46·7'W	W	79
Hermitage Wood	Cambs	TL1977	52°22·9'	0°14·7'W	F	142
Hermitage Wood	Northnts	SP7885	52°27·7'	0°50·7'W	F	141
Hermit Dam	Lincs	SK8486	53°22·1'	0°43·8'W	F	112,121
Hermit Hill	Barns	SE3200	53°30·0'	1°30·6'W	T	110,111
Hermit Hole	Brad	SE0539	53°51·1'	1°55·0'W	T	104
Hermits Cave	Derby	SK2262	53°9·5'	1°39·9'W	A	119
Hermit's Cave	Glos	ST8794	51°38·9'	2°10·9'W	X	162,173
Hermit's Cell	S Glos	ST8183	51°33·0'	2°16·1'W	X	173
Hermit Seat	Aberd	NJ6422	57°17·5'	2°35·4'W	H	37
Hermit's Well	Fife	NO5905	56°14·4'	2°39·2'W	X	59
Hermit Well	Northum	NY7499	55°17·3'	2°24·1'W	X	80
Hermon	Carm	SN3630	51°56·9'	4°22·8'W	T	145
Hermon	Carm	SN6728	51°56·3'	3°55·7'W	X	146
Hermon	I of Angl	SH3868	53°11·3'	4°25·1'W	T	114
Hermon	Pemb	SN2031	51°57·1'	4°36·8'W	T	145
Hermongers	W Susx	TQ1034	51°5·9'	0°25·4'W	X	187
Hernaford	Devon	SX7855	50°23·2'	3°42·6'W	X	202
Hern Clough	Derby	SK0994	53°26·8'	1°51·5'W	X	110
Herne	Devon	ST0011	50°53·6'	3°24·9'W	X	192
Herne	Kent	TR1866	51°21·3'	1°8·3'E	T	179
Herne Bay	Kent	TR1767	51°21·9'	1°7·4'E	T	179
Herne Bay	Kent	TR1769	51°22·9'	1°7·5'E	W	179
Herne Common	Cambs	TL2488	52°28·8'	0°10·0'W	X	142
Herne Common	Kent	TR1765	51°20·8'	1°7·4'E	T	179
Herne Fm	Beds	SP9829	51°57·3'	0°34·0'W	FM	165
Herne Grange	Beds	SP9929	51°57·3'	0°33·2'W	X	165
Herne Green Fm	Beds	SP9930	51°57·8'	0°33·1'W	FM	165
Herne Hill	Somer	ST3513	50°55·0'	2°55·1'W	H	193
Herne Hill	Sthwk	TQ3274	51°27·2'	0°5·6'W	T	176,177
Hernehill Down	W Berks	SU4582	51°32·3'	1°20·7'W	X	174
Herne Hill Fm	Norf	TF9710	52°39·3'	0°55·2'E	FM	132
Herne Hill Fm	Suff	TM3677	52°20·6'	1°28·3'E	FM	156
Herne Ho	Kent	TR0333	51°3·8'	0°54·2'E	X	179,189
Herne Manor Fm	Beds	SP9929	51°57·3'	0°33·2'W	FM	165
Herne Poplar Fm	Beds	SP9928	51°56·7'	0°33·2'W	FM	165
Herne Pound	Kent	TQ6554	51°15·9'	0°22·3'E	T	188
Herner	Devon	SS5826	51°1·2'	4°1·1'W	X	180
Hernes	Oxon	SU7482	51°32·2'	0°55·6'W	X	175
Herne's Barrow	Somer	SS8536	51°6·9'	3°38·2'W	A	181
Herne, The	Cambs	TL2490	52°29·9'	0°10·0'W	X	142
Herne Willow Fm	Beds	SP9930	51°57·8'	0°33·1'W	FM	165
Hern Head Ho	N Yks	SE9187	54°16·5'	0°35·7'W	X	94,101
Hernhill	Kent	TR0660	51°18·3'	0°57·7'E	T	179
Hernhill Copse	Devon	SX8464	50°28·1'	3°37·7'W	F	202
Herniss	Corn	SW7334	50°10·0'	5°10·4'W	T	204
Hern Point Rock	Devon	SY0985	50°39·7'	3°16·9'W	X	192
Hernsey Wood	Suff	TM3467	52°15·3'	1°26·1'E	F	156
Hernsey Wood Fm	Suff	TM3466	52°14·8'	1°26·1'E	FM	156
Hern Stones	Derby	SK0995	53°27·3'	1°51·5'W	X	110
Herod Down	Corn	SX3564	50°27·4'	4°19·1'W	X	201
Herod Fm	Derby	SK0292	53°25·7'	1°57·8'W	FM	110
Herodhill	Aberd	NJ6456	57°35·8'	2°35·7'W	X	29
Herodsfoot	Corn	SX2160	50°25·0'	4°30·8'W	T	201
Herod Wood	Corn	SX3564	50°27·4'	4°19·1'W	F	201
Heronbridge	Ches	SJ4064	53°10·4'	2°53·5'W	X	117
Heronbrook Ho	Warw	SP1874	52°22·1'	1°43·7'W	X	139
Heron Crag	Cumbr	NY2203	54°25·2'	3°11·7'W	X	89,90
Heron Crag	Cumbr	NY2712	54°30·1'	3°7·2'W	X	89,90
Heron Cross	C of Stoke	SJ8943	52°59·3'	2°9·4'W	T	118
Heronden	Kent	TQ7949	51°12·9'	0°34·2'E	X	188
Heronden	Kent	TR2954	51°14·6'	1°17·3'E	T	179
Heronden Fm	Kent	TQ8227	51°1·0'	0°36·1'E	FM	188,199
Heronden Hall	Kent	TQ8732	51°3·6'	0°40·5'E	X	189
Heronfield	Sol	SP1975	52°22·6'	1°42·9'W	X	139
Heronfield Ho	Sol	SP1974	52°22·1'	1°42·9'W	X	139
Heron Fm	Cambs	TL5168	52°17·6'	0°13·3'E	FM	154
Heron Fm	Norf	TM0895	52°31·0'	1°4·3'E	FM	144
Herongate	Essex	TQ6291	51°35·9'	0°20·7'E	T	177
Heron Grove	Dorset	SY9597	50°46·6'	2°3·9'W	F	195
Heron Hall	Essex	TQ6391	51°35·9'	0°21·6'E	X	177
Heron Holt	N Lincs	SE9510	53°34·9'	0°33·5'W	F	112
Heron Pike	Cumbr	NY3508	54°28·0'	2°59·8'W	H	90
Heron Pike	Cumbr	NY3717	54°32·9'	2°58·0'W	X	90
Heron's Bank	Devon	ST0209	50°52·6'	3°23·2'W	X	192
Heron's Close	Northum	NZ1790	55°12·5'	1°43·5'W	X	81
Heron's Court	Stir	NS5386	56°2·9'	4°21·2'W	X	57
Heronsdale	Kent	TQ8945	51°10·6'	0°42·6'E	X	189
Heronsdale Manor	E Susx	TQ5418	50°56·7'	0°11·9'E	X	199
Heron's Fm	Devon	ST0006	50°50·9'	3°24·9'W	FM	192
Herons Fm	Essex	TL5605	51°43·5'	0°15·9'E	FM	167
Herons Fm	Essex	TL8221	51°51·7'	0°39·0'E	FM	168
Herons Fm	Essex	TL8525	51°53·8'	0°41·7'E	FM	168
Herons Fm	W Berks	SU6074	51°27·9'	1°7·8'W	FM	175

Heronsford	S Ayr	NX1183	55°6·6'	4°57·4'W	T	76
Heronsgate	Herts	TQ0294	51°38·4'	0°31·2'W	T	166,176
Heron's Ghyll	E Susx	TQ4826	51°1·1'	0°7·0'E	T	188,198
Herons Green	Bath & NE Somer	ST5559	51°19·9'	2°38·4'W	T	172,182
Heronshaw Hall	Lincs	TF4049	53°1·4'	0°5·7'E	X	131
Heronston	V of Glam	SS9178	51°29·7'	3°33·8'W	T	170
Heronswood Fm	Lancs	SD4656	54°0·1'	2°49·0'W	FM	102
Heronswood Mere	Surrey	TQ2953	51°15·9'	0°8·7'W	W	187
Herontye	W Susx	TQ3937	51°7·1'	0°0·4'W	X	187
Heron Wood	N Yks	SE6141	53°51·9'	1°3·9'W	F	105
Herra	Shetld	HU4865	60°22·2'	1°7·3'W	X	2,3
Herra	Shetld	HU6091	60°36·1'	0°53·8'W	T	1,2
Herra, The	Shetld	HU4593	60°37·3'	1°10·2'W	H	1,2
Herraval	N Eil	NB0000	57°53·6'	7°3·3'W	H	18
Herriard	Hants	SU6645	51°12·3'	1°2·9'W	T	185,186
Herriard Common	Hants	SU6544	51°11·7'	1°3·8'W	F	185,186
Herriard Grange	Hants	SU6545	51°12·3'	1°3·8'W	X	185,186
Herriard Ho	Hants	SU6646	51°12·8'	1°2·9'W	X	185,186
Herriard Park	Hants	SU6646	51°12·8'	1°2·9'W	X	185,186
Herricks	Moray	NJ4356	57°35·7'	2°56·8'W	X	28
Herricks Moss	Moray	NJ4356	57°35·7'	2°56·8'W	X	28
Herridge Fm	Dorset	ST3403	50°49·6'	2°55·8'W	FM	193
Herridge Stud Fm	Wilts	SU2654	51°17·3'	1°37·2'W	FM	184
Herriesdale	D & G	NX8164	54°57·6'	3°51·1'W	X	84
Herringay Hill	Norf	TL7097	52°32·9'	0°30·8'E	X	143
Herringby Hall	Norf	TG4410	52°38·2'	1°36·8'E	X	134
Herringdean Wood	W Susx	SU8815	50°55·9'	0°44·5'W	F	197
Herringfleet	Suff	TM4897	52°31·1'	1°39·7'E	T	134
Herringfleet Hall	Suff	TM4899	52°32·2'	1°39·8'E	X	134
Herringfleet Hills	Suff	TM4698	52°31·7'	1°38·0'E	X	134
Herring Gorse	Leic	SK8627	52°50·3'	0°43·0'W	X	130
Herring Hill	Lincs	TF4037	52°55·0'	0°5·3'E	X	131
Herrings Fm	E Susx	TQ5723	50°59·3'	0°14·6'E	FM	199
Herrings Fm	E Susx	TQ6618	50°56·5'	0°22·2'E	FM	199
Herring's Green	Beds	TL0844	52°5·3'	0°25·0'W	T	153
Herring's Ho	Cambs	TL5356	52°11·1'	0°14·7'E	X	154
Herring's Lodge Fm	Lincs	SK8927	52°50·2'	0°40·3'W	FM	130
Herringston	Dorset	SY6888	50°41·7'	2°26·8'W	A	194
Herringston Barrow	Dorset	SY6888	50°41·7'	2°26·8'W	A	194
Herringston Fm	Dorset	SY6887	50°41·1'	2°26·8'W	FM	194
Herringswell	Suff	TL7169	52°17·8'	0°30·9'E	T	154
Herringthorpe	Roth	SK4492	53°25·6'	1°19·9'W	T	111
Herrington Hill Ho	Sund	NZ3452	54°51·9'	1°27·8'W	X	88
Herriot's Fm	Hants	SU6761	51°20·9'	1°1·9'W	FM	175,186
Herriotshiels	Scot Bord	NT4953	55°46·3'	2°48·3'W	X	66,73
Herriotts Br	Bath & NE Somer	ST5758	51°19·4'	2°36·6'W	X	172,182
Herrison Hospl	Dorset	SY6794	50°44·9'	2°27·7'W	X	194
Herris's	Lancs	SD7647	53°55·4'	2°21·5'W	X	103
Herrock Hill	Heref	SO2759	52°13·7'	3°3·7'W	H	148
Herrockside	Moray	NJ4548	57°31·4'	2°54·6'W	X	28,29
Herrod's Hill	Notts	SK4660	53°8·3'	1°18·3'W	X	120
Herscha Hill	Aberd	NO7380	56°59·4'	2°26·2'W	H	45
Hersden	Kent	TR2062	51°19·1'	1°9·8'E	T	179
Hersedd	Flint	SJ1869	53°12·9'	3°13·3'W	X	116
Hersham	Corn	SS2507	50°50·4'	4°28·8'W	T	190
Hersham	Surrey	TQ1164	51°22·1'	0°23·9'W	T	176,187
Hersham Fm	Surrey	TQ0065	51°22·7'	0°33·4'W	FM	176
Herstmonceux	E Susx	TQ6312	50°53·3'	0°19·4'E	T	199
Herstmonceux Castle	E Susx	TQ6410	50°52·2'	0°20·2'E	A	199
Herstmonceux Place	E Susx	TQ6311	50°52·8'	0°19·4'E	X	199
Herston	Dorset	SZ0178	50°36·3'	1°58·8'W	T	195
Herston	Orkney	ND4191	58°48·4'	3°0·8'W	X	7
Herston Head	Orkney	ND4191	58°48·4'	3°0·8'W	X	7
Herston Taing	Orkney	ND4192	58°49·0'	3°0·8'W	X	7
Hertford	Herts	TL3212	51°47·7'	0°4·8'W	T	166
Hertford Dale	N Yks	SE9980	54°12·6'	0°28·5'W	X	101
Hertford Heath	Herts	TL3511	51°47·1'	0°2·2'W	T	166
Hertfordshire Ho	Bucks	SU9494	51°38·4'	0°38·1'W	X	175
Hertingfordbury	Herts	TL3012	51°47·7'	0°6·5'W	T	166
Herton	Devon	SS5532	51°4·4'	4°3·8'W	X	180
Hesbert Hall	Lancs	SD7557	54°0·7'	2°22·5'W	X	103
Hescombe	Orkney	HY6725	59°6·9'	2°34·1'W	X	5
Hescott Fm	Devon	SS2824	50°59·6'	4°26·7'W	FM	190
Heselton Fm	N Yks	SE1991	54°19·1'	1°42·1'W	FM	99
Heshie Ber	Orkney	HY4333	59°11·1'	2°59·4'W	X	5,6
Hesket Fm	Cumbr	NY4426	54°37·8'	2°51·6'W	FM	90
Hesketh	Lancs	SD4322	53°41·7'	2°51·4'W	X	102
Hesketh Bank	Lancs	SD4323	53°42·3'	2°51·4'W	T	102
Hesketh Dike	N Yks	SE5187	54°16·8'	1°12·6'W	A	100
Hesketh End	Lancs	SD6141	53°52·1'	2°35·2'W	A	102,103
Hesketh Grange	N Yks	SE5086	54°16·3'	1°13·5'W	X	100
Hesketh Hall	Cumbr	SD2290	54°18·2'	3°11·5'W	X	96
Hesketh Ho	N Yks	SE0653	53°58·6'	1°54·1'W	X	104
Hesketh House Fm	Lancs	SD8447	53°55·4'	2°14·2'W	FM	103
Hesketh Lane	Lancs	SD6141	53°52·1'	2°35·2'W	T	102,103
Hesketh Moss	Lancs	SD4322	53°41·7'	2°51·4'W	T	102
Hesketh New Marsh	Lancs	SD4324	53°42·8'	2°51·4'W	X	102
Hesketh Out Marsh	Lancs	SD4225	53°43·3'	2°52·3'W	X	102
Hesketh Sands	Lancs	SD3925	53°43·3'	2°55·1'W	X	102
Hesket Newmarket	Cumbr	NY3338	54°44·2'	3°2·0'W	T	90
Hesk Fell	Cumbr	SD1794	54°20·3'	3°16·2'W	H	96
Heskin	Conwy	SH9566	53°11·1'	3°33·9'W	X	116
Heskin Green	Lancs	SD5315	53°38·0'	2°42·2'W	T	108
Heskin Hall	Lancs	SD4109	53°34·7'	2°53·1'W	X	108
Heskin Old Hall	Lancs	SD5115	53°38·0'	2°44·1'W	X	108
Heskyn Mill	Corn	SX3459	50°24·7'	4°19·8'W	A	201
Hesleden	Durham	NZ4438	54°44·3'	1°18·6'W	T	93
Hesleden Beck	N Yks	SD8874	54°9·9'	2°10·6'W	W	98
Hesleden Bergh	N Yks	SD8775	54°10·5'	2°11·5'W	X	98
Hesleden High Bergh	N Yks	SD8675	54°10·5'	2°12·5'W	X	98
Hesledon East House	Durham	NZ4347	54°49·2'	1°19·4'W	X	88
Hesledon Moor East	Durham	NZ3946	54°48·7'	1°23·2'W	X	88
Heslerton Grange	N Yks	SE9376	54°10·5'	0°34·1'W	X	101
Heslett Wood	N Yks	SE2478	54°12·1'	1°37·5'W	F	99
Hesley	Cumbr	NY5823	54°36·3'	2°38·6'W	X	91
Hesley	N Yks	SD7859	54°1·8'	2°19·7'W	X	103
Hesley Hall	N Yks	SD7959	54°1·8'	2°18·8'W	X	103
Hesley Hall School	Donc	SK6195	53°27·1'	1°4·5'W	X	111

Hesleyside	Northum	NY8183	55°8·7'	2°17·5'W	X	80
Hesleyside Mill	Northum	NY8084	55°9·2'	2°18·4'W	X	80
Hesleywell	Northum	NY7750	54°50·9'	2°21·1'W	X	86,87
Hesleywell	Northum	NY9152	54°52·0'	2°8·0'W	X	87
Hesleywell Moor	Northum	NY7647	54°49·3'	2°22·0'W	X	86
Heslington	York	SE6250	53°56·8'	1°2·9'W	T	105
Heslington Common	York	SE6348	53°55·7'	1°2·0'W	X	105,106
Heslin's Barn Fm	Lincs	SK8927	52°50·2'	0°40·3'W	FM	130
Hesp Alyn	Flint	SJ1865	53°10·8'	3°13·2'W	X	116
Hespeck Raise	Cumbr	NY5553	54°52·4'	2°41·7'W	X	86
Hespin Wood	Cumbr	NY3663	54°57·7'	2°59·5'W	F	85
Hessacott	Corn	SX3190	50°41·3'	4°23·2'W	X	190
Hessaford Fm	Corn	SS2509	50°51·5'	4°28·8'W	FM	190
Hessay	York	SE5253	53°58·5'	1°12·0'W	T	105
Hessenford	Corn	SX3057	50°23·5'	4°23·1'W	T	201
Hessett	Suff	TL9361	52°13·0'	0°49·9'E	T	155
Hessett Ho	Suff	TL9462	52°13·5'	0°50·8'E	X	155
Hessilhead	N Ayr	NS3852	55°44·3'	4°34·4'W	X	63
Hessle	E Yorks	TA0326	53°43·4'	0°25·9'W	T	107
Hessle	Wakf	SE4317	53°39·1'	1°20·6'W	T	111
Hessle Haven	E Yorks	TA0325	53°42·9'	0°25·9'W	W	107
Hessle Mount	E Yorks	TA0227	53°44·0'	0°26·8'W	X	106,107
Hessleskew	E Yorks	SE9240	53°51·1'	0°35·7'W	X	106
Hessleskew Gare	E Yorks	SE9239	53°50·6'	0°35·7'W	X	106
Hestaford	Shetld	HU2751	60°14·8'	1°30·2'W	T	3
Hesta Geo	Orkney	HY2528	59°8·2'	3°18·2'W	X	6
Hestam	N Eil	NF9174	57°39·3'	7°10·4'W	X	18
Hesta Mires	Shetld	HU4994	60°37·8'	1°5·8'W	W	1,2
Hestam Stromay	N Eil	NF9474	57°39·4'	7°7·4'W	X	18
Hesta Ness	Shetld	HU6692	60°36·6'	0°47·2'W	X	1,2
Hestan Island	D & G	NX8350	54°50·1'	3°48·9'W	X	84
Hestan Rack	D & G	NX8350	54°50·1'	3°48·9'W	X	84
Hesta Rock	Orkney	ND4687	58°46·3'	2°55·5'W	X	7
Hesta Taing	Shetld	HU3557	60°18·0'	1°21·5'W	X	2,3
Hest Bank	Lancs	SD4766	54°5·5'	2°48·2'W	T	97
Hestem	N Eil	NF9982	57°43·9'	7°3·0'W	X	18
Hestercombe Ho	Somer	ST2428	51°3·0'	3°4·7'W	X	193
Hesters Copse	Hants	SU7346	51°12·7'	0°56·9'W	F	186
Hester's Way	Glos	SO9223	51°54·6'	2°6·6'W	T	163
Hesterworth	Shrops	SO3982	52°26·2'	2°53·4'W	X	137
Hestham Hall Fm	Cumbr	SD1579	54°12·2'	3°17·8'W	FM	96
Hestholme	N Yks	SE0288	54°17·5'	1°57·7'W	X	98
Hesti Geo	Orkney	HY4207	58°57·0'	3°0·0'W	X	6,7
Hesti Geo	Orkney	ND3388	58°46·7'	3°9·0'W	X	7
Hesti Geo	Shetld	HT9736	60°6·8'	2°2·7'W	X	4
Hesti Geo	Shetld	HU1755	60°17·0'	1°41·1'W	X	3
Hesti Geo	Shetld	HU3881	60°30·9'	1°18·0'W	X	1,2,3
Hestingott	Shetld	HU3812	59°53·7'	1°18·8'W	T	4
Hestinsetter	Shetld	HU2945	60°11·6'	1°28·1'W	T	4
Hestley Green	Suff	TM1567	52°15·8'	1°9·4'E	X	156
Hestley Hall	Suff	TM1468	52°16·3'	1°8·6'E	X	156
Heston	Houns	TQ1277	51°29·1'	0°22·8'W	T	176
Heston Service Area	Houns	TQ1177	51°29·1'	0°23·7'W	X	176
Hestor	Orkney	HY2404	58°55·3'	3°18·7'W	X	6,7
Hestow Barton	Devon	SX8876	50°34·6'	3°34·5'W	X	192
Hestwall	Orkney	HY2516	59°1·7'	3°17·9'W	T	6
Hestwall	Orkney	HY4702	58°54·4'	2°54·7'W	X	6,7
Heswall	Wirral	SJ2683	53°20·6'	3°6·3'W	T	108
Hesworth Common	W Susx	TQ0019	50°57·9'	0°34·2'W	F	197
Het	Orkney	HY3806	58°56·5'	3°4·2'W	X	6,7
Het Burn	Northum	NT9518	55°27·6'	2°4·3'W	W	81
Hetchell Wood	Leeds	SE3742	53°52·6'	1°25·8'W	F	104
Hetha Burn	Northum	NT8727	55°32·4'	2°11·9'W	W	74
Hethe	E Susx	TQ4739	51°8·1'	0°6·5'E	X	188
Hethe	Oxon	SP5929	51°57·6'	1°8·1'W	T	164
Hethe Brede	Oxon	SP5828	51°57·1'	1°9·0'W	X	164
Hethel	Norf	TG1700	52°33·5'	1°12·5'E	T	134
Hethelpit Cross	Glos	SO7729	51°57·8'	2°19·7'W	T	150
Hetherbank	Cumbr	NY4666	54°59·4'	2°50·2'W	X	86
Hether Burn	Cumbr	NY4967	54°59·9'	2°47·4'W	W	86
Hetherington	Northum	NY8278	55°6·0'	2°16·5'W	X	86,87
Hethersett	Norf	TG1504	52°35·7'	1°10·9'E	T	144
Hethersgill	Cumbr	NY4767	54°59·9'	2°49·3'W	T	86
Hetherside	Cumbr	NY4366	54°59·4'	2°53·0'W	T	85
Hetherson Green	Ches	SJ5249	53°2·4'	2°42·5'W	T	117
Hethfelton	Dorset	SY8588	50°41·7'	2°12·4'W	X	194
Het Hill	Northum	NT9614	55°25·4'	2°3·4'W	H	81
Hethpool	Northum	NT8928	55°33·0'	2°10·0'W	X	74
Hetland Hall Hotel	D & G	NY0972	55°2·3'	3°25·0'W	X	85
Hetlandhill	D & G	NY0972	55°2·3'	3°25·0'W	X	85
Hett	Durham	NZ2836	54°43·3'	1°33·5'W	T	93
Hett Hills	Durham	NZ2351	54°51·4'	1°38·1'W	X	88
Hett Moor	Durham	NZ2835	54°42·8'	1°33·5'W	X	93
Hetton	N Yks	SD9658	54°1·3'	2°3·2'W	T	103
Hetton Burn	Northum	NU0431	55°34·6'	1°55·8'W	W	75
Hetton Common	N Yks	SD9462	54°3·5'	2°5·1'W	X	98
Hetton Common Beck	N Yks	SD9461	54°2·9'	2°5·1'W	W	98
Hetton Downs	Sund	NZ3548	54°49·8'	1°26·9'W	T	88
Hetton Hall	Northum	NU0333	55°35·7'	1°56·7'W	X	75
Hetton Ho	Northum	NU0429	55°33·5'	1°55·8'W	X	75
Hetton House Fm	Northum	NU0430	55°34·1'	1°55·8'W	FM	75
Hetton Law	Northum	NU0234	55°36·2'	1°57·7'W	X	75
Hetton-le-Hill	Sund	NZ3545	54°48·2'	1°26·9'W	T	88
Hetton-Le-Hole	Sund	NZ3547	54°49·2'	1°26·9'W	T	88
Hetton Lime Works Fm	Northum	NU0235	55°36·8'	1°57·7'W	FM	75
Hetton North Fm	Northum	NU0236	55°37·3'	1°57·7'W	FM	75
Hetton Steads	Northum	NU0335	55°36·8'	1°56·7'W	X	75
Hetty Pegler's Tump	Glos	SO7800	51°42·1'	2°18·7'W	X	162
Hetty Pegler's Tump (Long Barrow)	Glos	SO7800	51°42·1'	2°18·7'W	A	162
Heugg, The	Shetld	HU3429	60°2·9'	1°22·9'W	X	4
Heugh	Aberd	NJ4401	57°6·1'	2°55·0'W	X	37
Heugh	Durham	NZ1842	54°46·6'	1°42·8'W	X	88
Heugh	Northum	NY8780	55°7·1'	2°11·8'W	X	80
Heugh	Northum	NZ0873	55°3·3'	1°52·1'W	T	88
Heugh	N Yks	SD9691	54°19·1'	2°3·3'W	X	98
Heugh Brae	Cumbr	NY5667	55°0·0'	2°40·8'W	X	86
Heughead	Aberd	NJ6117	57°14·8'	2°38·3'W	X	37
Heugh Fm	E Loth	NT5684	56°3·1'	2°41·9'W	FM	67
Heugh Fm	N Yks	SE0154	53°59·2'	1°58·7'W	FM	104

Heugh Hall Fm	Durham	NZ3138	54°44·4'	1°30·7'W	FM	93
Heugh Hall Row	Durham	NZ3137	54°43·9'	1°30·7'W	X	93
Heugh-head	Aberd	NJ3811	57°11·4'	3°1·1'W	T	37
Heugh-head	Aberd	NO5098	57°4·5'	2°49·0'W	X	37,44
Heugh-head	Aberd	NO5899	57°5·1'	2°41·1'W	X	37,44
Heugh-head	Aberd	NO6892	57°1·3'	2°31·2'W	X	38,45
Heugh-head	Angus	NO5537	56°31·6'	2°43·4'W	X	54
Heugh-head	Angus	NO5850	56°38·7'	2°40·6'W	X	54
Heugh Head	Scot Bord	NT8762	55°51·3'	2°12·0'W	X	67
Heugh Hill	Scot Bord	NT5649	55°44·2'	2°41·6'W	H	73
Heughmill	S Ayr	NS4030	55°32·5'	4°31·7'W	X	70
Heugh Mill Fm	Northum	NZ0971	55°2·3'	1°51·1'W	FM	88
Heughscar Hill	Cumbr	NY4823	54°36·2'	2°47·9'W	H	90
Heughs of Laggan	D & G	NX8955	54°52·9'	3°43·4'W	X	84
Heughs, The	Northum	NU2520	55°28·6'	1°35·8'W	X	75
Heugh, The	Cumbr	NY5365	54°58·9'	2°43·6'W	X	86
Heuksland	D & G	NS7810	55°22·4'	3°55·1'W	X	71,78
Heulah Cottage	N Yks	NZ8510	54°28·9'	0°40·9'W	X	94
Heulah Fm	N Yks	NZ8510	54°28·9'	0°40·9'W	FM	94
Heulog Fm	Flint	SJ2656	53°6·0'	3°5·9'W	FM	117
Hevda	Shetld	HP6417	60°50·1'	0°48·9'W	X	1
Hevda	Shetld	HU5661	60°20·0'	0°58·6'W	X	2
Hevda	Shetld	HU6690	60°35·5'	0°47·2'W	X	1,2
Hevdadale Head	Shetld	HU3089	60°35·3'	1°26·6'W	X	1
Hevdadale Water	Shetld	HU3189	60°35·3'	1°25·5'W	W	1
Hevda Hill	Shetld	HP5810	60°46·4'	0°55·6'W	H	1
Hevda Skerries	Shetld	HU6872	60°25·8'	0°45·4'W	X	2
Hevda Skerry	Shetld	HP5711	60°46·9'	0°56·7'W	X	1
Hevda Skerry	Shetld	HU5054	60°16·3'	1°5·3'W	X	3
Hevden Ness	Shetld	HU3565	60°22·3'	1°21·4'W	X	2,3
Hevdi	Shetld	HU4838	60°7·7'	1°7·7'W	X	4
Heveningham	Suff	TM3372	52°18·0'	1°25·4'E	T	156
Heveningham Hall	Suff	TM3573	52°18·5'	1°27·2'E	X	156
Hever	Kent	TQ4744	51°10·8'	0°6·6'E	T	188
Hever Castle Fm	Kent	TQ4746	51°11·9'	0°6·6'E	FM	188
Hevershan	Cumbr	SD4983	54°14·7'	2°46·5'W	T	97
Hever Sta	Kent	TQ4644	51°10·8'	0°5·7'E	X	188
Heverswood	Kent	TQ4654	51°16·2'	0°6·0'E	X	188
Hever Warren	Kent	TQ4643	51°10·3'	0°5·7'E	X	188
Hevingham	Norf	TG1921	52°44·8'	1°15·1'E	T	133,134
Hevingham Park	Norf	TG1920	52°44·2'	1°15·0'E	F	133,134
Hewan	Orkney	HY4918	59°3·0'	2°52·9'W	X	6
Hewarths Fm, The	Derby	SK4636	52°55·4'	1°18·5'W	FM	129
Hewas	Corn	SW9153	50°20·6'	4°55·9'W	X	200,204
Hewas Water	Corn	SW9649	50°18·6'	4°51·5'W	T	204
Hewdon Fm	Bucks	SP7609	51°46·7'	0°53·5'W	FM	165
Hew Down	Devon	SX6386	50°39·7'	3°55·9'W	X	191
Hewell Grange	Worcs	SP0068	52°18·8'	1°59·6'W	X	139
Hewell Kennels	Worcs	SP0168	52°18·8'	1°58·7'W	X	139
Hewells Fm	W Susx	TQ1636	51°6·9'	0°20·2'W	FM	187
Hewelsfield	Glos	SO5602	51°43·1'	2°37·8'W	T	162
Hewelsfield Common	Glos	SO5402	51°43·1'	2°39·6'W	T	162
Hewenden	Brad	SE0736	53°49·5'	1°53·2'W	X	104
Hewenstreet Fm	E Susx	TQ3915	50°55·3'	0°1·0'W	FM	198
Hewer Hill	Cumbr	NY3738	54°44·2'	2°58·3'W	T	90
Hew Green	N Yks	SE2358	54°1·3'	1°38·5'W	T	104
Hewin	Orkney	HY3327	59°7·7'	3°9·8'W	X	6
Hewing	Orkney	HY3616	59°1·8'	3°6·4'W	X	6
Hewins Wood Fm	W Berks	SU6073	51°27·4'	1°7·8'W	FM	175
Hewisbridge Cottage	Scot Bord	NY5393	55°14·0'	2°43·9'W	X	79
Hewish	N Som	ST4064	51°22·5'	2°51·3'W	T	172,182
Hewish	Somer	ST4208	50°52·3'	2°49·1'W	T	193
Hewish Barton	Devon	SS5541	51°9·2'	4°4·0'W	X	180
Hewish Down	Devon	SS5640	51°8·7'	4°3·1'W	H	180
Hewish Fm	Dorset	ST8000	50°48·2'	2°16·6'W	FM	194
Hewish Fm	Dorset	SY6484	50°39·5'	2°30·2'W	FM	194
Hewish Hill	Dorset	SY6483	50°39·0'	2°30·2'W	X	194
Hewits	Cumbr	NY8220	54°34·7'	2°16·3'W	X	91,92
Hewitson Hill Fm	N Yks	SE2999	54°23·4'	1°32·8'W	FM	99
Hewitts	Aberd	NJ5231	57°22·3'	2°47·4'W	X	29,37
Hewitts	Brom	TQ4863	51°21·0'	0°7·9'E	X	177,188
Hewitts	Essex	TL8935	51°59·1'	0°45·5'E	X	155
Hewitts Fm	N Yks	SD9546	53°54·9'	2°4·2'W	FM	103
Hewke	D & G	NY1488	55°11·0'	3°20·6'W	X	78
Hewke Burn	D & G	NY1588	55°11·0'	3°19·7'W	W	79
Hewland House Fm	Leeds	SE2844	53°53·7'	1°34·0'W	FM	104
Hewletts Fm	Dorset	ST7517	50°57·3'	2°21·0'W	FM	183
Hewletts, The	Glos	SO9822	51°54·0'	2°1·4'W	X	163
Hewood	Dorset	ST3502	50°49·1'	2°55·0'W	T	193
Heworth	Ghead	NZ2861	54°56·8'	1°33·3'W	T	88
Heworth	York	SE6152	53°57·9'	1°3·8'W	T	105
Heworth Ho	Durham	NZ2923	54°36·3'	1°32·6'W	X	93
Heworth Village	Durham	NZ2923	54°36·3'	1°32·6'W	A	93
Hewrigg Fm	Cumbr	NY0801	54°24·0'	3°24·6'W	FM	89
Hewshott Ho	Hants	SU8532	51°5·1'	0°46·8'W	X	186
Hewstown	Cumbr	NY4770	55°1·6'	2°49·3'W	X	86
Hewthwaite	Cumbr	SD6689	54°18·0'	2°30·9'W	X	98
Hewthwaite Hall	Cumbr	NY1532	54°40·8'	3°18·7'W	A	89
Hewton	Devon	SX4365	50°28·1'	4°12·4'W	X	201
Hewton	Devon	SX5092	50°42·7'	4°7·1'W	X	191
Hexden Channel	Kent	TQ8328	51°1·6'	0°37·0'E	W	188,199
Hexden Fm	Kent	TQ8228	51°1·6'	0°36·1'E	FM	188,199
Hexdown	Devon	SX6644	50°17·1'	3°52·5'W	X	202
Hexgreave Park	Notts	SK6558	53°7·1'	1°1·3'W	X	120
Hexham	Northum	NY9363	54°57·9'	2°6·1'W	T	87
Hexhamshire Common	Northum	NY8753	54°52·5'	2°11·7'W	H	87
Hexpath	Scot Bord	NT6646	55°42·6'	2°32·0'W	X	74
Hextable	Kent	TQ5170	51°24·8'	0°10·7'E	T	177
Hextall	Staffs	SJ8524	52°49·0'	2°13·0'W	X	127
Hextall Court	Kent	TQ6650	51°13·7'	0°23·0'E	X	188
Hext Hill	Somer	ST4328	51°3·1'	2°48·4'W	X	193
Hexthorpe	Donc	SE5602	53°30·9'	1°8·9'W	T	111
Hexton	Herts	TL1030	51°57·7'	0°23·5'W	T	166
Hexton Common	Herts	TL1131	51°58·2'	0°22·7'W	X	166
Hexton Manor	Herts	TL1030	51°57·7'	0°23·5'W	X	166
Hextons Fm	Worcs	SO7582	52°26·4'	2°21·7'W	FM	138
Hexworthy	Corn	SX3680	50°36·0'	4°18·7'W	X	201
Hexworthy	Devon	SX6572	50°32·2'	3°53·9'W	T	191
Hey	Lancs	SD7646	53°54·8'	2°21·5'W	X	103
Hey	Lancs	SD8843	53°53·2'	2°10·5'W	T	103

Heybridge	Essex	TL8508	51°44·6'	0°41·2'E	T	168
Heybridge	Essex	TQ6398	51°39·7'	0°21·8'E	T	167,177
Heybridge Basin	Essex	TL8707	51°44·1'	0°42·9'E	T	168
Heybridge Hall	Essex	TL8507	51°44·1'	0°41·2'E	X	168
Heybrook Bay	Devon	SX4948	50°19·0'	4°6·9'W	T	201
Hey Clough	Derby	SE0801	53°30·6'	1°52·4'W	X	110
Hey Clough	Kirk	SE0906	53°33·3'	1°51·4'W	X	110
Heyden Br	Derby	SE0900	53°30·0'	1°51·4'W	X	110
Heyden Brook	Derby	SE0902	53°31·1'	1°51·4'W	W	110
Heyden Head	Derby	SE0804	53°32·2'	1°52·3'W	X	110
Heyden Moor	Derby	SE0902	53°31·1'	1°51·4'W	X	110
Heydon	Cambs	TL4340	52°2·6'	0°5·5'E	T	154
Heydon	Norf	TG1127	52°48·2'	1°8·2'E	T	133
Heydon Common	Somer	ST0228	51°2·8'	3°23·5'W	X	181
Heydon Grange	Cambs	TL4142	52°3·7'	0°3·8'E	X	154
Heydon Hill	Beds	TL0038	52°2·1'	0°32·1'W	X	153
Heydon Hill	Somer	ST0327	51°2·3'	3°22·6'W	H	181
Heydour	Lincs	TF0039	52°56·6'	0°30·3'W	T	130
Heydour Lodge Fm	Lincs	SK9937	52°55·5'	0°31·2'W	FM	130
Heydour Southings	Lincs	TF0137	52°55·5'	0°29·4'W	F	130
Heydour Warren	Lincs	SK9840	52°57·1'	0°32·1'W	X	130
Hey Edge	Derby	SE0800	53°30·0'	1°52·4'W	X	110
Heyesmere	Ches	SJ6271	53°14·3'	2°33·8'W	X	118
Hey Farm	Somer	ST3806	50°51·2'	2°52·5'W	A	193
Heyfields	Staffs	SJ8737	52°56·1'	2°11·2'W	X	127
Heyfields Fm	Ches	SJ6441	52°58·1'	2°31·8'W	FM	118
Hey Fm	Warr	SJ6493	53°26·2'	2°32·1'W	FM	109
Hey Fold	Lancs	SD8843	53°53·2'	2°10·5'W	X	103
Heyford Hills	Northnts	SP6557	52°12·7'	1°2·5'W	X	152
Heyford Sta	Oxon	SP4824	51°55·0'	1°17·7'W	X	164
Heygate Fm	N Yks	SE7296	54°21·5'	0°53·1'W	FM	94,100
Heygates	Northnts	SP6173	52°21·3'	1°5·9'W	X	140
Hey Green	Kirk	SE0312	53°36·5'	1°56·9'W	T	110
Heyheads	Tames	SD9801	53°30·6'	2°1·4'W	T	109
Hey Ho	Staffs	SJ7743	52°59·3'	2°20·2'W	X	118
Hey House	Bury	SD7715	53°38·1'	2°20·5'W	A	109
Hey House Fm	Lancs	SD7944	53°53·7'	2°18·8'W	FM	103
Hey Houses	Lancs	SD3429	53°45·4'	2°59·7'W	T	102
Heyhouses	Lancs	SD7837	53°50·0'	2°19·6'W	X	103
Hey Hurst	Lancs	SD6736	53°49·4'	2°29·7'W	X	103
Heylee	Derby	SK0377	53°17·6'	1°56·9'W	X	119
Heylipol	Arg & Bt	NL9743	56°29·2'	6°54·9'W	T	46
Heylor	Shetld	HU2881	60°31·0'	1°28·9'W	X	3
Hey Moss	Derby	SE0700	53°30·0'	1°53·3'W	X	110
Heyop	Powys	SO2374	52°21·8'	3°7·5'W	T	137,148
Hey Ridge	Derby	SK1390	53°24·6'	1°47·9'W	X	110
Heyrod	Tames	SJ9799	53°29·5'	2°2·3'W	T	109
Heyrose Fm	Ches	SJ7079	53°18·7'	2°26·6'W	FM	118
Heyroyd	Lancs	SD9040	53°51·6'	2°8·7'W	X	103
Heys Fm	Lancs	SD7334	53°48·3'	2°24·2'W	FM	103
Heysham	Lancs	SD4161	54°2·7'	2°53·6'W	T	96,97
Heysham Lake	Lancs	SD3857	54°0·6'	2°56·3'W	W	102
Heysham Moss	Lancs	SD4261	54°2·7'	2°52·7'W	X	96,97
Heysham Sands	Lancs	SD4062	54°3·3'	2°54·6'W	X	96,97
Heyshaw	N Yks	SE1761	54°2·9'	1°44·0'W	T	99
Heyshaw Moor	N Yks	SE1562	54°3·5'	1°45·8'W	X	99
Heyshott	W Susx	SU8918	50°57·5'	0°43·6'W	T	197
Heyshott Down	W Susx	SU8916	50°56·4'	0°43·6'W	X	197
Heyshott Green	W Susx	SU8918	50°57·5'	0°43·6'W	T	197
Heyside	Oldham	SD9307	53°33·8'	2°5·9'W	T	109
Hey Slack Allotment	N Yks	SE1259	54°1·9'	1°48·6'W	X	104
Heyspan	Orkney	ND3495	58°50·5'	3°8·1'W	X	7
Hey Sprink	Staffs	SJ7842	52°58·7'	2°19·3'W	F	118
Heys, The	Derby	SK0485	53°22·0'	1°56·0'W	X	110
Heystones Fm	N Yks	NZ8307	54°27·3'	0°42·8'W	FM	94
Heyswood Ho	Devon	SS6711	50°53·2'	3°53·1'W	X	191
Heytesbury	Wilts	ST9242	51°10·9'	2°6·5'W	T	184
Heytesbury Fm	Hants	SU5709	50°53·0'	1°11·0'W	FM	196
Heytesbury Ho	Wilts	ST9342	51°10·9'	2°5·6'W	X	184
Hey, The	Lancs	SD6752	53°58·0'	2°29·8'W	X	103
Heythrop	Oxon	SP3527	51°56·7'	1°29·1'W	T	164
Heythrop Park	Oxon	SP3626	51°56·1'	1°28·2'W	X	164
Hey Wood	Kirk	SE1512	53°36·5'	1°46·0'W	F	110
Heywood	Roch	SD8510	53°35·4'	2°13·2'W	T	109
Heywood	Shrops	SO6282	52°26·3'	2°33·1'W	X	138
Heywood	Somer	ST1323	51°0·2'	3°14·0'W	X	181,193
Heywood	Surrey	TQ1162	51°21·0'	0°24·0'W	X	176,187
Heywood	Wilts	ST8753	51°16·8'	2°10·8'W	T	183
Heywood Fm	Ches	SJ6441	52°58·1'	2°31·8'W	FM	118
Heywood Fm	Wilts	ST8976	51°29·2'	2°9·1'W	FM	173
Heywood Fm	Win & Maid	SU8678	51°29·9'	0°45·3'W	FM	175
Heywood Grange	Staffs	SJ9645	53°0·4'	2°3·2'W	X	118
Heywood Hall	Norf	TM1286	52°26·1'	1°7·5'E	X	144
Heywood Ho	Wilts	ST8753	51°16·8'	2°10·8'W	X	183
Heywood Manor	Norf	TM1187	52°26·6'	1°6·7'E	X	144
Heywoods	Devon	SS6403	50°48·9'	3°55·5'W	X	191
Heywood's Fm	Hants	SU6860	51°20·3'	1°1·0'W	FM	175,186
Heywood, The	Norf	TM1283	52°24·5'	1°7·4'E	X	144
Heywood Wood	Devon	SS6712	50°53·8'	3°53·1'W	F	180
Hiam Fm	Cambs	TL2974	52°21·2'	0°6·0'W	FM	142
Hiam's Fm	Cambs	TL4282	52°25·3'	0°5·7'E	FM	142,143
Hibaldstow	N Lincs	SE9702	53°30·6'	0°31·8'W	T	112
Hibaldstow Br	N Lincs	TA0001	53°30·0'	0°29·1'W	X	112
Hibaldstow Grange	N Lincs	SE9602	53°30·6'	0°32·7'W	X	112
Hibb's Green	Suff	TL8753	52°8·8'	0°44·4'E	T	155
Hibernian, The	I of M	SC4591	54°17·7'	4°22·5'W	X	95
Hich Holm	Shetld	HU3521	59°58·6'	1°21·9'W	X	4
Hickaton Hill	Devon	SX6766	50°29·0'	3°52·1'W	X	202
Hickbush	Essex	TL8737	52°0·2'	0°43·9'E	X	155
Hickerage, The	Essex	TL6607	51°44·5'	0°24·7'E	X	167
Hickford Hill	Essex	TL7844	52°4·2'	0°36·2'E	T	155
Hicklam Ho	Leeds	SE4336	53°49·3'	1°20·4'W	X	105
Hickleton	Donc	SE4805	53°32·6'	1°16·1'W	T	111
Hickley Fm	Hants	SU4713	50°55·1'	1°19·5'W	FM	196
Hickley Plain	Devon	SX6662	50°26·8'	3°52·9'W	X	202
Hickling	Norf	TG4123	52°45·3'	1°34·7'E	T	134
Hickling	Notts	SK6929	52°51·5'	0°58·1'W	T	129
Hickling Broad	Norf	TG4121	52°44·2'	1°34·6'E	W	134
Hickling Green	Norf	TG4023	52°45·3'	1°33·8'E	T	134
Hickling Heath	Norf	TG4022	52°44·8'	1°33·8'E	T	134

Hickling Pastures	Notts	SK6628	52°51·0'	1°0·8'W	T	129
Hickling Standard	Notts	SK6727	52°50·4'	0°59·9'W	X	129
Hickling Wall	Norf	TG4324	52°45·8'	1°36·5'E	X	134
Hickman's Fm	Kent	TQ5340	51°8·6'	0°11·6'E	FM	188
Hickmans Green	Kent	TR0658	51°17·3'	0°57·7'E	T	179
Hickman's Hill	Herts	TL2631	51°58·0'	0°9·6'W	X	166
Hicknaham Fm	Bucks	SU9387	51°34·7'	0°39·1'W	FM	175
Hicks Common	S Glos	ST6580	51°31·3'	2°29·9'W	X	172
Hicks Forstal	Kent	TR1863	51°19·7'	1°8·1'E	T	179
Hicks Gate	Bath & NE Somer	ST6369	51°25·4'	2°31·5'W	T	172
Hick's Mill	Corn	SW7640	50°13·3'	5°8·0'W	T	204
Hicks Mill	Corn	SX2682	50°36·9'	4°27·2'W	X	201
Hicks's Fm	Heref	SO3369	52°19·1'	2°58·6'W	FM	137,148
Hick's Park Wood	Somer	ST7438	51°8·7'	2°21·9'W	F	183
Hicks's Plantn	Suff	TL9735	51°58·9'	0°52·5'E	F	155
Hickstead	W Susx	TQ2620	50°58·2'	0°11·9'W	T	198
Hidcote Bartrim	Glos	SP1742	52°4·8'	1°44·7'W	T	151
Hidcote Boyce	Glos	SP1741	52°4·3'	1°44·7'W	T	151
Hidcote Combe	Glos	SP1843	52°5·3'	1°43·8'W	X	151
Hidcote House	Glos	SP1742	52°4·8'	1°44·7'W	A	151
Hideaway, The	Oxon	SU3296	51°39·9'	1°31·8'W	X	164
Hides Close	Hants	SU3803	50°49·7'	1°27·2'W	X	196
Hides Fm	Lincs	TF2110	52°40·7'	0°12·2'W	FM	131,142
Hidmore	Shrops	SO2079	52°24·4'	3°10·2'W	X	137,148
Hield Ho	Ches	SJ6777	53°17·6'	2°29·3'W	X	118
Hield Ho	Durham	NY8927	54°38·5'	2°9·8'W	X	91,92
Hifnal	Shrops	SO7099	52°35·5'	2°26·2'W	T	138
Higford	Shrops	SJ7500	52°36·1'	2°21·7'W	X	127
Higger Tor	Sheff	SK2582	53°20·3'	1°37·1'W	X	110
Higging Head	Cumbr	SD5281	54°13·6'	2°43·8'W	X	97
Higginsfield Ho	Ches	SJ5552	53°4·0'	2°39·9'W	X	117
Higginshaw	Oldham	SD9306	53°33·3'	2°5·9'W	T	109
Higgins' Neuk	Falk	NS9187	56°4·1'	3°44·6'W	X	65
High Abbothill	S Ayr	NS3718	55°26·0'	4°34·1'W	X	70
High Ackworth	Wakf	SE4417	53°39·1'	1°19·6'W	T	111
Higha Clett	Orkney	HY5429	59°9·0'	2°47·8'W	X	5,6
High Acres	Heref	SO6058	52°13·4'	2°34·7'W	X	149
High Acton Currick	Durham	NZ0328	54°39·1'	1°56·8'W	X	92
High Actonmill	Northum	NY9753	54°52·6'	2°2·4'W	X	87
High Agra	N Yks	SE1581	54°13·7'	1°45·8'W	X	99
High Aird	E Ayr	NS4725	55°29·9'	4°24·9'W	X	70
High Airyolland	D & G	NX1562	54°55·4'	4°52·8'W	X	82
High Aketon	Cumbr	NY2043	54°46·8'	3°14·2'W	X	85
High Alderstocks	S Lanak	NS6144	55°40·4'	4°12·2'W	X	71
High Allers	Durham	NY8440	54°45·5'	2°14·5'W	X	86,87
Highall Wood	Lincs	TF2165	53°10·3'	0°11·0'W	F	122
High Altercannoch	S Ayr	NX2580	55°5·3'	4°44·1'W	X	76
Higham	Barns	SE3107	53°33·8'	1°31·5'W	T	110,111
Higham	Derby	SK3959	53°7·8'	1°24·6'W	T	119
Higham	Fife	NO2718	56°21·2'	3°10·4'W	X	59
Higham	Fife	NO4609	56°16·5'	2°51·9'W	X	59
Higham	Kent	TQ7171	51°25·0'	0°27·9'E	T	178
Higham	Lancs	SD8036	53°49·4'	2°17·8'W	T	103
Higham	Suff	TL7465	52°15·6'	0°33·4'E	T	155
Higham	Suff	TM0335	51°58·8'	0°57·8'E	T	155
Higham Bury	Beds	TL0532	51°58·8'	0°27·9'W	X	166
Higham Common	Barns	SE3106	53°33·2'	1°31·5'W	T	110,111
Higham Creek	Kent	TQ7076	51°27·7'	0°27·2'E	W	178
Higham Cross	Mil Key	SP7847	52°7·2'	0°51·2'W	X	152
Higham Dykes	Northum	NZ1375	55°4·4'	1°47·4'W	X	88
Higham Ferrers	Northnts	SP9668	52°18·3'	0°35·1'W	T	153
Higham Fields	Leic	SP3896	52°33·9'	1°26·0'W	X	140
Higham Fm	E Susx	TQ6135	51°5·7'	0°18·3'E	FM	188
Higham Fm	Kent	TQ9731	51°2·9'	0°49·0'E	FM	189
Higham Fm	Kent	TR1959	51°17·5'	1°8·9'E	FM	179
Higham Gobion	Beds	TL1032	51°58·8'	0°23·5'W	T	166
Higham Grange	E Yorks	SE8628	53°44·7'	0°41·3'W	X	106
Higham Grange (Hospl)	Leic	SP3994	52°32·8'	1°25·1'W	X	140
Higham Hall	Cumbr	NY1831	54°40·3'	3°15·9'W	X	89,90
Higham Hall	Kent	TQ7172	51°25·5'	0°28·0'E	X	178
Higham Hall	Suff	TM0335	51°58·8'	0°57·8'E	X	155
Higham Heath	Suff	TL7668	52°17·1'	0°35·2'E	X	155
Higham Hill	Suff	TM0337	51°59·9'	0°57·8'E	X	155
Higham Hill	Wal F	TQ3690	51°35·8'	0°1·8'W	T	177
Higham Ho	E Susx	TQ7524	50°59·5'	0°30·0'E	X	199
Higham Lodge	Suff	TM0335	51°58·8'	0°57·8'E	X	155
Higham Marshes	Kent	TQ7175	51°27·1'	0°28·1'E	X	178
Higham on the Hill	Leic	SP3895	52°33·3'	1°26·0'W	T	140
Higham Park	Northnts	SP9764	52°16·2'	0°34·3'W	X	153
Highampton	Devon	SS4804	50°49·2'	4°9·1'W	T	191
Highams	W Susx	TQ2037	51°7·4'	0°16·7'W	X	187
Higham Saltings	Kent	TQ7075	51°27·1'	0°27·2'E	W	178
Higham's Fm	Essex	TL6033	51°58·6'	0°20·2'E	FM	167
Highams Fm	Essex	TL9109	51°45·0'	0°46·4'E	FM	168
Higham's Hill	Brom	TQ4061	51°20·1'	0°1·0'E	X	177,187
Higham Side	Lancs	SD4637	53°49·8'	2°48·8'W	X	102
Highams Park	Wal F	TQ3791	51°36·3'	0°0·9'W	T	177
Higham Sta	Kent	TQ7172	51°25·5'	0°28·0'E	X	178
Higham Wood	Kent	TQ6048	51°12·7'	0°17·8'E	T	188
High and Over	E Susx	TQ5000	50°47·0'	0°8·1'E	X	199
High Angerton	Northum	NZ0985	55°9·8'	1°51·1'W	T	81
High Ardley	Northum	NY9059	54°55·8'	2°8·9'W	X	87
High Ardwell	D & G	NX0071	55°0·0'	5°7·2'W	X	76,82
High Ardwell	D & G	NX0745	54°46·0'	4°59·6'W	T	82
High Arkland	D & G	NX7357	54°53·7'	3°58·4'W	X	83,84
High Armsheugh	N Ayr	NS3441	55°38·3'	4°37·8'W	X	70
High Arnsgill Fm	N Yks	SE5296	54°21·7'	1°11·6'W	FM	100
High Arrow	D & G	NX4436	54°41·9'	4°24·8'W	X	83
High Ash	Ches	SJ5144	52°59·7'	2°43·4'W	X	117
High Ash	Ches	SJ5754	53°5·1'	2°38·1'W	X	117
High Ash	Staffs	SK0465	53°11·2'	1°56·0'W	X	119
High Ash Bank	N Yks	SE2587	54°16·9'	1°36·5'W	X	99
High Ashes Fm	Derby	SK3466	53°11·6'	1°29·1'W	FM	119
High Ashes Fm	Surrey	TQ1243	51°10·7'	0°23·5'W	FM	187
High Ash Fm	Ches	SJ9870	53°13·9'	2°1·4'W	FM	118
Highash Fm	Norf	TG1402	52°34·6'	1°9·9'E	FM	144
Highash Fm	Norf	TG2403	52°34·9'	1°18·8'E	FM	134
High Ash Fm	Warw	SP2583	52°26·9'	1°37·5'W	FM	140

High Ashgill	Cumbr	NY7639	54°45·0'	2°21·9'W	X	91
High Ash Head	N Yks	SE1375	54°10·5'	1°47·6'W	X	99
High Ash Head Moor	N Yks	SE1275	54°10·5'	1°48·6'W	X	99
Highash Hill	Norf	TL8097	52°32·7'	0°39·7'E	X	144
High Ashurst	Surrey	TQ1953	51°16·0'	0°17·3'W	X	187
High Askew	N Yks	SE7491	54°18·8'	0°51·3'W	X	94,100
High Auchenlarie	D & G	NX5353	54°51·3'	4°17·0'W	X	83
High Auchenree	D & G	NX0158	54°52·9'	5°5·7'W	X	82
High Auchneel	D & G	NW9665	54°56·5'	5°10·7'W	X	82
High Auldgirth	D & G	NX9287	55°10·2'	3°41·3'W	X	78
High Austby	N Yks	SE1049	53°56·5'	1°50·4'W	X	104
High Balantyre	Arg & Bt	NN0711	56°15·4'	5°6·5'W	X	50,56
High Balcray	D & G	NX4538	54°43·0'	4°24·0'W	X	83
High Balernock	Arg & Bt	NS2588	56°3·4'	4°48·2'W	X	56
High Ballevain	Arg & Bt	NR6626	55°28·6'	5°41·7'W	X	68
High Ballochdowan	S Ayr	NX0776	55°2·7'	5°0·8'W	X	76
High Balsarroch	S Ayr	NS3616	55°24·9'	4°35·0'W	X	70
High Baltersan	D & G	NX4161	54°55·4'	4°28·4'W	X	83
High Balyett	D & G	NX0862	54°55·2'	4°59·3'W	X	82
High Band	Durham	NZ0407	54°27·7'	1°55·9'W	X	92
High Bank	Cumbr	SD7798	54°22·9'	2°20·8'W	X	98
High Bank	N Yks	SD8780	54°13·2'	2°11·5'W	X	98
Highbank Fm	Ches	SJ6058	53°7·3'	2°35·5'W	FM	118
High Bankhill	Cumbr	NY5642	54°46·5'	2°40·6'W	T	86
High Bank Ho	Cumbr	SD2381	54°13·4'	3°10·4'W	X	96
High Banks	D & G	NX7049	54°49·4'	4°1·0'W	X	83,84
Highbanks	S Lanak	NS8239	55°38·1'	3°52·0'W	X	71,72
High Bank Side	Cumbr	SD3677	54°11·3'	2°58·4'W	X	96,97
High Banniscue	N Yks	SE5491	54°18·9'	1°9·8'W	X	100
High Banton	N Lanak	NS7480	56°0·0'	4°0·8'W	T	64
High Barcaple	D & G	NX6758	54°54·2'	4°4·0'W	X	83,84
High Barcheskie	D & G	NX7345	54°47·3'	3°58·1'W	X	83,84
High Barlay	D & G	NX6158	54°54·1'	4°9·6'W	X	83
High Barn	Cald	SD9224	53°43·0'	2°6·9'W	X	103
Highbarn	Cumbr	NY5728	54°39·0'	2°39·6'W	X	91
High Barn	Cumbr	NY5732	54°41·1'	2°39·6'W	X	91
High Barn	Cumbr	NY6711	54°29·8'	2°30·2'W	X	91
High Barn	Cumbr	SD5898	54°22·8'	2°38·4'W	X	97
High Barn	Durham	NZ0211	54°29·9'	1°57·7'W	X	92
High Barn	E Susx	TQ5409	50°51·8'	0°11·7'E	X	199
High Barn	E Yorks	TA1870	54°7·0'	0°11·3'W	X	101
High Barn	Lincs	TF3664	53°9·6'	0°2·5'E	T	122
High Barn	Norf	TF8138	52°54·8'	0°41·9'E	X	132
High Barn	Northum	NY7763	54°57·9'	2°21·1'W	X	86,87
High Barn	N Yks	SD8561	54°2·9'	2°13·3'W	X	98
High Barn	N Yks	SE9371	54°7·8'	0°34·2'W	X	101
High Barn	Surrey	TQ1252	51°15·6'	0°23·3'W	X	187
High Barnaby Fm	Red & Cl	NZ5717	54°32·9'	1°6·7'W	FM	93
Highbarn Cottage	Cumbr	NY5630	54°40·0'	2°40·5'W	X	90
High Barnes	N Tyne	NZ2574	55°3·8'	1°36·1'W	X	88
High Barness	D & G	NX3854	54°51·5'	4°31·0'W	X	83
High Barnet	Barnet	TQ2496	51°39·2'	0°12·1'W	T	166,176
High Barnet Sta	Barnet	TQ2596	51°39·2'	0°11·2'W	X	166,176
High Barn Fm	Beds	TL0262	52°15·0'	0°29·9'W	FM	153
High Barn Fm	E Yorks	SE8654	53°58·7'	0°40·9'W	FM	106
High Barn Fm	Kent	TQ5748	51°12·8'	0°15·3'E	FM	188
High Barn Fm	Leic	SK4324	52°48·9'	1°21·3'W	FM	129
High Barn Fm	Leic	SK6611	52°41·8'	1°1·0'W	FM	129
High Barn Fm	Lincs	TF3877	53°16·6'	0°4·6'E	FM	122
High Barn Fm	Norf	TG4818	52°42·4'	1°40·7'E	FM	134
High Barn Fm	N Yks	SE3294	54°20·7'	1°30·0'W	FM	99
Highbarn Hall	Essex	TL8027	51°55·0'	0°37·4'E	X	168
High Barns	Beds	TL1354	52°10·6'	0°20·4'W	X	153
High Barns	Cumbr	SD5085	54°15·7'	2°45·6'W	X	97
High Barns	Hartpl	NZ4432	54°41·1'	1°18·6'W	X	93
High Barns	Northum	NY7563	54°57·9'	2°23·0'W	X	86,87
High Barns	Northum	NY9267	55°0·1'	2°7·1'W	X	87
High Barns	Northum	NZ0163	54°57·9'	1°58·6'W	X	87
High Barns	Northum	NZ0865	54°59·0'	1°52·1'W	X	88
High Barnultoch	D & G	NX0857	54°52·5'	4°59·1'W	X	82
High Barrow	Devon	SS3409	50°51·6'	4°21·1'W	A	190
High Baswick	E Yorks	TA0647	53°54·7'	0°22·8'W	X	107
High Batscombe	Somer	ST0325	51°1·2'	3°22·6'W	X	181
High Baulk	Northum	NZ0070	55°1·7'	1°59·6'W	X	87
High Baxton's Fm	N Yks	SE5987	54°16·8'	1°5·2'W	FM	100
High Beach	Essex	TQ4097	51°39·5'	0°1·8'E	T	167,177
High Beara	Devon	SX7566	50°29·1'	3°45·3'W	X	202
High Beaumont Hill Fm	Darl	NZ2819	54°34·2'	1°33·6'W	FM	93
High Beck	Cumbr	NY1512	54°30·0'	3°18·3'W	W	89
High Beck Head	Durham	NY8830	54°40·1'	2°10·7'W	X	91,92
High Beech	E Susx	TQ7812	50°53·0'	0°32·2'E	X	199
High Beeches	Monm	SO2816	51°50·5'	3°2·3'W	X	161
Highbeeches Forest	W Susx	TQ2731	51°4·1'	0°10·9'W	F	187
High Beley	Fife	NO5310	56°17·1'	2°45·1'W	X	59
High Bellmanear	N Yks	SE8670	54°7·4'	0°40·6'W	X	101
High Belthorpe	E Yorks	SE7854	53°58·8'	0°48·2'W	X	105,106
High Bent	S Lanak	NS6743	55°40·0'	4°6·4'W	X	71
High Bentham	N Yks	SD6669	54°7·2'	2°30·8'W	T	98
High Bergh	N Yks	SD8775	54°10·5'	2°11·5'W	X	98
Highberries	Cumbr	NY4664	54°58·3'	2°50·2'W	X	86
Highberries Beck	Cumbr	NY4763	54°57·8'	2°49·2'W	W	86
High Bethecar	Cumbr	SD3089	54°17·8'	3°4·1'W	X	96,97
High Bewaldeth	Cumbr	NY2234	54°41·9'	3°12·2'W	X	89,90
High Bickington	Devon	SS5920	50°58·0'	4°0·1'W	T	180
High Biggins	Cumbr	SD6078	54°12·0'	2°36·4'W	T	97
High Billinge House	Ches	SJ5566	53°11·6'	2°40·0'W	X	117
High Billinghurst Fm	Surrey	TQ0236	51°7·1'	0°32·2'W	FM	186
High Birch	Essex	TM1419	51°49·9'	1°6·8'E	X	168,169
High Birchclose	Cumbr	NY4125	54°37·3'	2°54·4'W	X	90
High Birk	Cumbr	SD3193	54°19·9'	3°3·2'W	F	96,97
High Birkby	N Yks	SE2772	54°8·8'	1°34·8'W	X	99
High Birk Hat	Durham	NY9318	54°33·7'	2°6·1'W	X	91,92
High Birks	Cumbr	SD4290	54°18·4'	2°53·1'W	X	96,97
High Birks	N Yks	SD7364	54°4·5'	2°24·3'W	X	98
High Birkwith	N Yks	SD8076	54°11·0'	2°18·0'W	X	98
High Birstwith	N Yks	SE2258	54°1·3'	1°39·4'W	T	104
High Bishopley	Durham	NZ0135	54°42·8'	1°58·6'W	X	92
High Bishopside	N Yks	SE1667	54°6·2'	1°44·9'W	X	99
High Blaeberry Craigs	N Ayr	NS2856	55°46·3'	4°44·1'W	X	63
High Blaithwaite	Cumbr	NY2244	54°47·3'	3°12·4'W	X	85
High Blakey Moor	N Yks	SE6699	54°23·2'	0°58·6'W	X	94,100
High Blansby	N Yks	SE8287	54°16·6'	0°44·0'W	X	94,100
High Blantyre	S Lanak	NS6856	55°47·0'	4°5·9'W	X	64
High Blayshaw	N Yks	SE0972	54°8·9'	1°51·3'W	X	99
High Bleakhope	Northum	NT9215	55°26·0'	2°7·2'W	X	80
High Blean	N Yks	SD9287	54°17·0'	2°7·0'W	X	98
High Bogany	Arg & Bt	NS0963	55°49·6'	5°2·5'W	X	63
High Bogside	N Ayr	NS3755	55°45·9'	4°35·4'W	X	63
High Bohemia	N Yks	SE5662	54°3·3'	1°8·3'W	X	100
High Bolham	Devon	SS9022	50°59·4'	3°33·7'W	X	181
High Bonnybridge	Falk	NS8379	55°59·6'	3°52·1'W	T	65
High Bonwick	E Yorks	TA1652	53°57·3'	0°13·5'W	X	107
High Boreland	D & G	NX0858	54°53·0'	4°59·2'W	X	82
High Boreland	D & G	NX1858	54°53·3'	4°49·8'W	X	82
High Borgue	D & G	NX6451	54°50·4'	4°6·6'W	X	83
High Borland	S Ayr	NS4332	55°33·6'	4°28·9'W	X	70
Highborough Fm	Norf	TG1140	52°55·2'	1°8·7'E	FM	133
High Borrans	Cumbr	NY4300	54°23·8'	2°52·3'W	X	90
High Borrow Br	Cumbr	NY5504	54°26·0'	2°41·2'W	X	90
High Borrowdale	Cumbr	NY5702	54°24·9'	2°39·3'W	X	91
High Botaurnie	Stir	NN4836	56°29·8'	4°27·7'W	X	51
High Bottom	Cumbr	SD2564	54°4·2'	3°8·4'W	X	96
High Bottom	Cumbr	SD2664	54°4·2'	3°7·4'W	X	96,97
High Bottom	N Yks	SD6668	54°6·7'	2°30·8'W	X	98
High Bottom	N Yks	SE0150	53°57·0'	1°58·7'W	X	104
High Bowhill	E Ayr	NS5240	55°38·1'	4°20·6'W	X	70
High Boydstone	N Ayr	NS2245	55°40·2'	4°49·4'W	X	63
High Br	Dorset	ST7922	51°0·1'	2°17·6'W	X	183
High Br	Lincs	TF2241	52°57·4'	0°10·6'W	X	131
High Br	Norf	TF6613	52°41·6'	0°27·8'E	X	132,143
High Br	Staffs	SK0916	52°44·7'	1°51·6'W	X	128
High Br	Wilts	SU0593	51°38·4'	1°55·3'W	X	163,173
High Bracken Hill Fm	Brad	SE0248	53°55·9'	1°57·8'W	FM	104
High Bradfield	Sheff	SK2692	53°25·7'	1°36·1'W	T	110
High Bradley	Durham	NZ1253	54°52·5'	1°48·4'W	X	88
High Bradley	N Yks	SE0049	53°56·5'	1°59·6'W	T	104
High Bradley Moor	N Yks	SE0150	53°57·0'	1°58·7'W	X	104
High Bradshaw Hill	Northum	NY7253	54°52·5'	2°25·8'W	H	86,87
High Bradup	Brad	SE0844	53°53·8'	1°52·3'W	X	104
High Brae of Camps	Orkney	HY4128	59°8·4'	3°1·4'W	X	5,6
High Bramley Grange	N Yks	SE2077	54°11·5'	1°41·2'W	X	99
High Branchal	Inverc	NS3366	55°51·8'	4°39·7'W	X	63
High Bransholme	K upon H	TA1135	53°48·2'	0°18·5'W	X	107
High Bray	Devon	SS6934	51°5·7'	3°51·9'W	T	180
High Brettenham	Norf	TL9284	52°25·4'	0°49·8'E	X	144
High Bride Stones	N Yks	NZ8504	54°25·7'	0°41·0'W	A	94
Highbridge	Cumbr	NY3943	54°46·9'	2°56·5'W	T	85
Highbridge	Hants	SU4721	50°59·4'	1°19·4'W	T	185
Highbridge	Highld	NN1981	56°53·4'	4°57·8'W	T	34,41
High Bridge	N Lincs	SE8215	53°37·7'	0°45·2'W	X	112
High Bridge	Somer	ST0841	51°9·9'	3°18·6'W	X	181
Highbridge	Somer	ST3247	51°13·3'	2°58·0'W	T	182
Highbridge	Wals	SK0204	52°38·3'	1°57·8'W	T	139
Highbridge Fm	Cambs	TL5465	52°15·9'	0°15·8'E	FM	154
Highbridge Fm	Somer	ST6235	51°7·0'	2°32·2'W	FM	183
High Bridge Ho	Lincs	TF3792	53°24·7'	0°4·1'E	X	113
High Bridge of Ken	D & G	NX6190	55°11·3'	4°10·6'W	X	77
High Bridgham	Norf	TL9486	52°26·5'	0°51·7'E	X	144
High Broadrayne	Cumbr	NY3309	54°28·6'	3°1·6'W	X	90
High Brockabank	Brad	SE0748	53°55·9'	1°53·2'W	X	104
High Brockholme	N Yks	SE3297	54°22·3'	1°30·0'W	X	99
Highbrook	Flint	SJ1777	53°17·3'	3°14·3'W	X	116
Highbrook	W Susx	TQ3630	51°3·4'	0°3·2'W	T	187
Highbrooks Fm	Somer	ST4925	51°1·6'	2°43·2'W	FM	183,193
High Brooms	Kent	TQ5941	51°9·0'	0°16·8'E	T	188
High Brotheridge	Glos	SO8913	51°49·2'	2°9·2'W	T	163
High Brow	Cumbr	NY3621	54°35·1'	2°59·0'W	H	90
High Brow	Cumbr	SD1883	54°14·4'	3°15·1'W	X	96
High Brow	Lancs	SD3821	53°41·2'	2°55·9'W	X	102
High Brown Hill Pasture	N Yks	SD7178	54°12·1'	2°26·3'W	X	98
High Brown Knoll	Cald	SE0130	53°46·2'	1°58·7'W	X	104
High Brownmuir	S Lanak	NS7047	55°42·2'	4°3·7'W	X	64
High Bucker Ho	N Yks	SD9462	54°3·5'	2°5·1'W	X	98
High Buildings	Cumbr	NY3839	54°44·8'	2°57·4'W	X	90
High Buildings Fm	W Susx	SU9826	51°1·7'	0°35·8'W	FM	186,197
High Bullen	Devon	SS5320	50°57·9'	4°5·2'W	T	180
High Bullen Fm	Devon	SS7430	51°3·6'	3°47·5'W	FM	180
Highbullen (Hotel)	Devon	SS6520	50°58·1'	3°55·0'W	X	180
High Burncrooks	S Ayr	NS2807	55°19·9'	4°42·3'W	X	70,76
High Burnham	N Lincs	SE7801	53°30·2'	0°49·0'W	X	112
Highburn Ho	Northum	NT9828	55°33·0'	2°1·5'W	X	75
High Burnhopeside	Durham	NZ1846	54°48·8'	1°42·8'W	X	88
High Burnlea	Durham	NZ1133	54°41·8'	1°49·3'W	X	92
High Burnside	E Ayr	NS5617	55°25·8'	4°16·1'W	X	71
High Burnside	Renf	NS4259	55°48·2'	4°30·8'W	X	64
High Burnthwaite	Cumbr	NY4048	54°49·6'	2°55·6'W	X	85
High Burntoff	Hartpl	NZ4427	54°38·4'	1°18·7'W	X	93
Highburton	Kirk	SE1913	53°37·0'	1°42·4'W	T	110
High Burton	N Yks	SE2282	54°14·2'	1°39·3'W	X	99
Highbury	C of Port	SU6604	50°50·1'	1°3·4'W	T	196
Highbury	Glos	SO6203	51°43·7'	2°32·6'W	X	162
Highbury	Isling	TQ3185	51°33·1'	0°6·2'W	T	176,177
Highbury	Somer	ST6949	51°14·6'	2°26·3'W	T	183
Highbury Fm	Glos	SO5309	51°46·9'	2°40·5'W	FM	162
Highbury Hill	Bath & NE Somer	ST6358	51°19·4'	2°31·5'W	H	172
Highbury Vale	C of Nott	SK5444	52°59·7'	1°11·3'W	T	129
High Buston	Northum	NU2308	55°22·2'	1°37·8'W	T	81
High Butterby Fm	Durham	NZ2838	54°44·4'	1°33·5'W	FM	93
High Button	Surrey	SU9036	51°7·2'	0°42·5'W	X	186
High Byre	Durham	NY8341	54°46·1'	2°15·4'W	X	86,87
High Cairn	D & G	NS6610	55°22·2'	4°6·4'W	X	71
High Cairn	D & G	NS6812	55°23·3'	4°4·6'W	X	71
Highcairn Plantation	Northum	NU0126	55°31·9'	1°58·6'W	F	75
High Callerton	Northum	NZ1670	55°1·7'	1°44·6'W	T	88
High Callis Wold	E Yorks	SE8356	53°59·8'	0°43·6'W	X	106
High Camer Wood	D & G	NX3673	55°1·7'	4°33·5'W	F	77
High Camilty	W Loth	NT0660	55°49·7'	3°29·6'W	X	65
High Canfold Stud	Surrey	TQ0741	51°9·7'	0°27·8'W	X	187
High Cank	Dorset	ST6503	50°49·8'	2°29·4'W	H	194
High Canons	Herts	TQ2099	51°40·8'	0°15·5'W	X	166,176
High Cantle	Northum	NT9216	55°26·5'	2°7·2'W	H	80
High Cap	Cumbr	NY6634	54°42·2'	2°31·2'W	X	91
High Cape	Norf	TF9046	52°58·9'	0°50·2'E	X	132
High Capon Edge	Northum	NY7478	55°6·0'	2°24·0'W	H	86,87
High Cark	Cumbr	SD3882	54°14·0'	2°56·7'W	T	96,97
High Carl	N Yks	SE0095	54°21·3'	1°59·6'W	H	98
High Carlbury	Darl	NZ2117	54°33·1'	1°40·1'W	X	93
High Carlingcraig	E Ayr	NS5639	55°37·7'	4°16·8'W	X	71
High Carlingill	Cumbr	NY6100	54°23·9'	2°35·6'W	X	91
High Carnduff	S Lanak	NS6645	55°41·1'	4°7·4'W	X	64
High Carr	N Yks	SE5963	54°3·8'	1°5·5'W	X	100
High Carr	N Yks	SE7683	54°14·5'	0°49·6'W	X	100
High Carr	Staffs	SJ8350	53°3·1'	2°14·8'W	X	118
High Carrick	Northum	NY9296	55°15·7'	2°7·1'W	X	80
High Carriteth	Northum	NY7983	55°8·7'	2°19·3'W	X	80
High Carr Plantn	N Yks	SE8477	54°11·2'	0°42·3'W	F	100
High Carry Ho	Northum	NY8679	55°6·6'	2°12·7'W	X	87
High Carse	Arg & Bt	NR7462	55°48·2'	5°35·9'W	X	62
High Carseduchan	D & G	NX3648	54°48·3'	4°32·7'W	X	83
High Carston	E Ayr	NS5118	55°26·2'	4°20·9'W	X	70
High Casterton	Cumbr	SD6278	54°12·0'	2°34·5'W	T	97
High Castle Wood	Kent	TQ5662	51°20·4'	0°14·8'E	F	177,188
High Cattadale	Arg & Bt	NR6710	55°20·0'	5°40·0'W	X	68
High Catton	E Yorks	SE7153	53°58·3'	0°54·6'W	T	105,106
High Catton Grange	E Yorks	SE7254	53°58·9'	0°53·7'W	X	105,106
High Caythorpe	E Yorks	TA1169	54°6·5'	0°17·7'W	X	101
High Cayton	N Yks	SE2863	54°4·0'	1°33·9'W	X	99
High Cell Ho	Lincs	TF1570	53°13·1'	0°16·2'W	X	121
High Challoch	D & G	NX0262	54°55·1'	5°4·9'W	X	82
High Chambers	Kirk	SE2312	53°36·5'	1°38·7'W	X	110
High Chang Hill	E Ayr	NS5607	55°20·4'	4°15·8'W	H	71,77
High Changue	S Ayr	NX2993	55°12·4'	4°40·8'W	X	76
High Chapel	Cumbr	SD7286	54°16·4'	2°25·4'W	X	98
High Chapelton	D & G	NX6247	54°48·2'	4°8·4'W	X	83
High Chart, The	Surrey	TQ4352	51°15·2'	0°3·3'E	F	187
Highchesters	Scot Bord	NT4514	55°25·3'	2°51·7'W	X	79
Highchesters Hill	Scot Bord	NT4514	55°25·3'	2°51·7'W	H	79
High Chibburn	Northum	NZ2697	55°16·1'	1°35·0'W	X	81
High Chimney Fm	Kent	TR1547	51°11·1'	1°5·0'E	FM	179,189
High Chimneys	Warw	SP2168	52°18·8'	1°41·1'W	X	139,151
High Church	D & G	NX9797	55°15·6'	3°36·8'W	X	78
High Church	Northum	NZ1985	55°9·8'	1°41·7'W	T	81
Highchurch Fm	Somer	ST7453	51°16·8'	2°22·0'W	FM	183
High Clachaig	Arg & Bt	NR6940	55°36·2'	5°39·6'W	X	62
High Clachan	D & G	NX0269	54°58·8'	5°5·2'W	X	82
High Clachan	D & G	NX6955	54°52·6'	4°2·1'W	X	83,84
High Clachanmore	D & G	NX0846	54°46·6'	4°58·7'W	X	82
High Clandon	Surrey	TQ0650	51°14·6'	0°28·5'W	X	187
High Clay Ho	N Yks	NZ5401	54°24·3'	1°9·7'W	X	93
Highclear	Northum	NY9657	54°54·7'	2°3·3'W	X	87
Highclear	Shrops	SO6393	52°32·3'	2°32·3'W	X	138
High Clear Plantation	Wilts	SU2376	51°29·2'	1°39·7'W	F	174
Highclere	Hants	SU4360	51°20·5'	1°22·6'W	T	174
Highclere Castle	Hants	SU4458	51°19·4'	1°21·7'W	X	174
Highclere Fm	Hants	SU4359	51°19·9'	1°22·6'W	FM	174
Highclere Park	Hants	SU4459	51°19·9'	1°21·7'W	X	174
Highclere Stud	Hants	SU4457	51°18·9'	1°21·7'W	X	174
High Cleughearn Fm	S Lanak	NS6248	55°42·6'	4°11·4'W	FM	64
High Clews	E Ayr	NS5124	55°29·5'	4°21·1'W	X	70
High Cliff	Ches	SJ9476	53°17·1'	2°5·0'W	X	118
High Cliff	Corn	SW7929	50°7·4'	5°5·1'W	X	204
High Cliff	Corn	SX1294	50°43·2'	4°39·4'W	X	190
High Cliff	Pemb	SS1497	51°37·7'	4°40·9'W	X	158
High Cliff	Stock	SJ9886	53°22·5'	2°1·4'W	X	109
Highcliffe	Derby	SK2177	53°17·6'	1°40·7'W	T	119
Highcliffe	Dorset	SZ2193	50°44·4'	1°41·8'W	T	195
High Cliffe	Durham	NZ1316	54°32·6'	1°47·5'W	X	92
Highcliffe	Northum	NU0051	55°45·4'	1°59·6'W	X	75
Highcliffe Castle	Dorset	SZ2093	50°44·4'	1°42·6'W	X	195
Highcliffe Fm	Brad	SE0537	53°50·0'	1°55·0'W	FM	104
Highcliffe Fm	Red & Cl	NZ6013	54°30·8'	1°4·0'W	FM	94
Highcliff Nab	Red & Cl	NZ6113	54°30·8'	1°3·0'W	X	94
Highcliff Plantn	E Yorks	SE8550	53°56·6'	0°41·9'W	F	106
High Clifton Fm	Northum	NZ2082	55°8·2'	1°40·7'W	FM	81
High Close	Cumbr	NY1438	54°44·0'	3°19·7'W	X	89
High Close	Cumbr	NY3305	54°26·4'	3°1·6'W	X	90
High Close	Cumbr	NY5557	54°54·6'	2°41·7'W	X	86
High Close	Durham	NZ1715	54°32·1'	1°43·8'W	X	92
High Close Fm	Warw	SP2359	52°14·0'	1°39·4'W	FM	151
High Close Ho	Northum	NZ1165	54°59·0'	1°49·3'W	X	88
High Clove Hill	Durham	NY8419	54°34·2'	2°14·4'W	X	91,92
High Clows	Worcs	SO7171	52°20·4'	2°25·1'W	X	138
High Clump	Notts	SK6782	53°20·1'	0°59·2'W	F	111,120
High Coalsgarth	N Yks	NZ1403	54°25·6'	1°46·6'W	X	92
High Cocklaw	Northum	NT9554	55°47·0'	2°4·3'W	X	67,74,75
High Cogges	Oxon	SP3709	51°46·9'	1°27·4'W	T	164
High Cold Knot	Durham	NZ1335	54°42·8'	1°47·5'W	X	92
High Coldstream	S Lanak	NS6947	55°42·2'	4°4·6'W	X	64
High Coledale	Cumbr	NY2222	54°35·5'	3°12·0'W	X	89,90
Highcomb Bottom	Surrey	SU8937	51°7·7'	0°43·3'W	F	186
High Combs	N Yks	SE1153	53°58·6'	1°49·5'W	X	104
High Common	Norf	TF9905	52°36·6'	0°56·8'E	T	144
High Common	Norf	TM1781	52°23·3'	1°11·7'E	X	156
High Common	Suff	TM3888	52°26·5'	1°30·5'E	X	156
High Common Fm	N Yks	SE3072	54°8·8'	1°32·0'W	FM	99
High Common Ho	Northum	NZ1884	55°9·2'	1°42·6'W	X	81
High Coniscliffe	Darl	NZ2215	54°32·0'	1°39·2'W	T	93
High Copelaw	Durham	NZ2924	54°36·9'	1°32·6'W	X	93
High Coppice	N Yks	SE7586	54°16·1'	0°50·5'W	X	94,100
High Copse	W Berks	SU5572	51°26·9'	1°12·1'W	F	174
High Copse Fm	Wok	SU7267	51°24·1'	0°57·5'W	FM	175
High Corby Knowe	N Ayr	NS2761	55°48·9'	4°45·2'W	X	63
High Corner Inn	Hants	SU1910	50°53·6'	1°42·6'W	X	195
High Corney	Cumbr	SD1292	54°19·2'	3°20·8'W	X	96
High Corrie	N Ayr	NS0242	55°38·1'	5°8·3'W	X	63,69
High Corrie	Stir	NS4795	56°7·7'	4°27·3'W	X	57
High Cote	Cumbr	SD4878	54°12·0'	2°47·4'W	X	97
High Cote Fm	N Yks	SE1781	54°13·7'	1°43·9'W	FM	99
High Cote Moor	N Yks	SD9269	54°7·3'	2°6·9'W	X	98
High Countam	D & G	NS6900	55°16·9'	4°3·3'W	X	77

High Countess Park	Northum	NY8680	55°7·1′	2°12·7′W	X	80
High Cove	Corn	SW8468	50°28·6′	5°2·3′W	W	200
High Cove	Corn	SW8471	50°30·2′	5°2·4′W	W	200
High Cow Ho	N Yks	SD9460	54°2·4′	2°5·1′W	X	98
High Coxlease Ho	Hants	SU2906	50°51·4′	1°34·9′W	X	196
High Crag	Cumbr	NY1814	54°31·1′	3°15·6′W	H	89,90
High Crag	Cumbr	NY2713	54°30·7′	3°7·2′W	X	89,90
High Crag	Cumbr	NY3413	54°30·7′	3°0·7′W	X	90
High Crag	Cumbr	NY3500	54°23·7′	2°59·6′W	H	90
High Crag	Durham	NY8323	54°36·4′	2°15·4′W	X	91,92
High Crag	Durham	NY9915	54°32·1′	2°0·5′W	X	92
High Crag	Northum	NY8186	55°10·3′	2°17·5′W	X	80
High Crag	N Yks	SE0962	54°3·5′	1°51·3′W	H	99
High Crag	N Yks	SE1662	54°3·5′	1°44·9′W	X	99
High Crags	Cumbr	NY2117	54°32·8′	3°12·9′W	X	89,90
High Crags	Cumbr	NY2319	54°33·9′	3°11·0′W	X	89,90
High Crags	Cumbr	NY3314	54°31·3′	3°1·7′W	X	90
High Crag Wood	Cumbr	SD4485	54°15·7′	2°51·2′W	F	97
High Craig	N Yks	NZ6803	54°25·3′	0°56·7′W	X	94
High Craigcaffie	D & G	NX0964	54°56·3′	4°58·5′W	H	82
High Craigeazle	D & G	NX5270	55°0·4′	4°18·4′W	X	77
High Craighead	S Ayr	NS2201	55°16·5′	4°47·7′W	X	76
High Craigton	E Dunb	NS5276	55°57·5′	4°21·8′W	X	64
High Crankley Fm	N Yks	SE5168	54°6·6′	1°12·8′W	FM	100
High Creagan	Pth & Kin	NN5935	56°29·4′	4°17·0′W	X	51
High Creoch	D & G	NX6059	54°54·6′	4°10·6′W	X	83
High Creoch Burn	D & G	NX6159	54°54·6′	4°9·7′W	W	83
High Crewburn	S Lanak	NS6642	55°39·4′	4°7·4′W	X	71
High Crindledike	Cumbr	NY3860	54°56·1′	2°57·6′W	X	85
High Cringle Fell	Cumbr	NY8410	54°29·4′	2°14·4′W	X	91,92
High Croach	D & G	NX0768	54°58·4′	5°0·5′W	X	82
High Croft	Cumbr	NY0725	54°36·9′	3°26·0′W	X	89
Highcroft	Kent	TQ5066	51°22·6′	0°9·7′E	X	177
Highcroft	Staffs	SK0046	53°0·9′	1°59·6′W	X	119,128
Highcroft Copse	W Berks	SU3869	51°25·4′	1°26·8′W	F	174
Highcroft Fm	Somer	ST6248	51°14·0′	2°32·3′W	FM	183
Highcroft Fm	Somer	ST7744	51°11·9′	2°19·4′W	FM	183
High Croft Ho	Durham	NZ3539	54°44·9′	1°27·0′W	X	93
Highcroft Lodge Fm	Leic	SP6385	52°27·8′	1°4·0′W	FM	140
High Crompton	Oldham	SD9209	53°34·9′	2°6·8′W	T	109
Highcrook	Northum	NY7963	54°57·9′	2°19·3′W	X	86,87
High Cross	Cambs	TL4259	52°12·9′	0°5·1′E	T	154
High Cross	Corn	SW7428	50°6·8′	5°9·3′W	T	204
Highcross	Cumbr	NY1321	54°34·9′	3°20·3′W	X	89
High Cross	Cumbr	SD3398	54°22·6′	3°1·5′W	X	96,97
High Cross	E Ayr	NS4046	55°41·1′	4°32·3′W	X	64
High Cross	E Susx	TQ4918	50°56·8′	0°7·7′E	X	199
High Cross	E Susx	TQ5628	51°2·0′	0°13·9′E	T	188,199
High Cross	Glos	SO9613	51°49·2′	2°3·1′W	X	163
High Cross	Hants	SU7126	51°2·0′	0°58·9′W	T	186,197
High Cross	Herts	TL3618	51°50·9′	0°1·1′W	T	166
High Cross	Herts	TQ1498	51°40·4′	0°20·7′W	T	166,176
High Cross	Newp	ST2888	51°35·4′	3°2·0′W	T	171
High Cross	Norf	TG0023	52°46·3′	0°58·3′E	X	133
High Cross	Northnts	SP6240	52°3·5′	1°5·3′W	X	152
High Cross	N Yks	SE0063	54°4·0′	1°59·6′W	X	98
High Cross	N Yks	SE7388	54°17·2′	0°52·3′W	A	94,100
High Cross	Scot Bord	NT5547	55°43·1′	2°42·5′W	X	73
High Cross	Staffs	SK0255	53°5·8′	1°57·8′W	X	119
High Cross	Warw	SP1967	52°18·3′	1°42·9′W	T	151
High Cross	W Susx	TQ2417	50°56·6′	0°13·7′W	T	198
High Crossett	N Yks	SE5794	54°20·5′	1°7·0′W	X	100
High Cross Fm	E Susx	TQ4818	50°56·8′	0°6·8′E	FM	198
Highcross Fm	Glos	SO7817	51°51·3′	2°18·8′W	FM	162
High Cross Fm	Notts	SK7050	53°2·8′	0°56·9′W	FM	120
High Crosshill	Cumbr	NY2345	54°47·9′	3°11·4′W	X	85
High Crosshill	S Lanak	NS6160	55°49·1′	4°12·7′W	T	64
High Cross Moor	Lancs	SD5556	54°0·1′	2°40·8′W	X	102
High Cross Moor Fm	Brad	SE0246	53°54·9′	1°57·8′W	FM	104
High Croxdale	Durham	NZ2837	54°43·9′	1°33·5′W	X	93
High Culgroat	D & G	NX0951	54°49·3′	4°58·0′W	X	82
High Cullis	Heref	SO4769	52°19·2′	2°46·3′W	X	137,138,148
High Cummersdale	Cumbr	NY3953	54°52·3′	2°56·6′W	X	85
High Cunsey	Cumbr	SD3894	54°20·5′	2°56·8′W	T	96,97
High Cup Gill	Cumbr	NY7325	54°37·4′	2°24·7′W	X	91
High Cup Nick	Cumbr	NY7426	54°38·0′	2°23·7′W	X	91
High Cup Plain	Cumbr	NY7426	54°38·0′	2°23·7′W	X	91
High Curley	Surrey	SU9161	51°20·7′	0°41·2′W	T	175,186
High Currochtrie	D & G	NX1136	54°41·3′	4°55·5′W	X	82
High Dalblair	E Ayr	NS6719	55°27·1′	4°5·7′W	X	71
High Dalby Ho	N Yks	SE8588	54°17·1′	0°41·2′W	X	94,100
High Dale	Derby	SK1571	53°14·4′	1°46·1′W	X	119
High Dalebanks	Cumbr	NY6013	54°30·9′	2°36·7′W	X	91
High Dale Cott	N Yks	TA0883	54°14·1′	0°20·2′W	X	101
Highdale Fm	N Yks	NZ7303	54°25·3′	0°52·1′W	FM	94
High Dale Fm	N Yks	SE9672	54°8·3′	0°31·4′W	FM	101
High Dale Park	Cumbr	SD3593	54°20·0′	2°59·6′W	X	96,97
High Dales	N Yks	SE9492	54°19·1′	0°32·9′W	X	94,101
Highdales Fm	N Yks	SE9492	54°19·1′	0°32·9′W	FM	94,101
High Dalloy	E Ayr	NS5336	55°36·0′	4°19·6′W	X	70
High Dam	Cumbr	SD3688	54°17·3′	2°58·6′W	W	96,97
High Dam	D & G	NY0182	55°7·6′	3°32·7′W	W	78
High Dam	E Renf	NS5550	55°43·6′	4°18·1′W	W	64
High Dar Wood	Lincs	TF2066	53°10·9′	0°11·8′W	F	122
High Dean & Chapter	Cumbr	NY3936	54°43·2′	2°56·4′W	X	90
High Deepdale	N Yks	TA0485	54°15·2′	0°23·8′W	X	101
High Dell Fm	Hants	SU6234	51°6·3′	1°6·5′W	FM	185
Highden	Wilts	SU0976	51°29·2′	1°51·8′W	X	173
Highden Barn	W Susx	TQ1110	50°53·0′	0°24·9′W	X	198
Highden Fm	Oxon	SU2794	51°38·9′	1°36·2′W	FM	174,163,174
Highden Fm	Oxon	SU2795	51°39·4′	1°36·2′W	FM	163
Highden Hill	W Susx	TQ1111	50°53·5′	0°24·9′W	X	198
Highden Ho	W Susx	TQ1111	50°53·5′	0°24·9′W	X	198
High Denton Fm	N Yks	SE1350	53°57·0′	1°47·7′W	FM	104
High Dike	Lincs	SK9537	52°55·6′	0°34·8′W	X	130
High Dike	Lincs	SK9952	53°3·6′	0°31·0′W	X	121
High Dodd	Cumbr	NY4118	54°33·5′	2°54·3′W	H	90
Highdole Hill	E Susx	TQ3904	50°49·4′	0°1·2′W	X	198
High Dolphin Seat	Cumbr	NY8208	54°28·3′	2°16·2′W	X	91,92
High Dolphinsty	Cumbr	NY7600	54°23·9′	2°21·8′W	X	91

Highdon	Dorset	ST7501	50°48·7′	2°20·9′W	X	194
High Dougarie	N Ayr	NR8837	55°35·1′	5°21·4′W	X	68,69
High Down	Devon	SS6429	51°2·9′	3°56·0′W	H	180
Highdown	Devon	ST0104	50°49·9′	3°24·0′W	X	192
High Down	Devon	SX5284	50°38·5′	4°5·2′W	X	191,201
High Down	W Susx	SU9113	50°54·8′	0°41·9′W	H	197
Highdown Cottages	Devon	SS2825	51°0·2′	4°26·7′W	X	190
Highdown Fm	Herts	TL1430	51°57·6′	0°20·1′W	FM	166
Highdown Fm	Warw	SP3261	52°15·0′	1°31·5′W	FM	151
Highdown Hill	W Susx	TQ0904	50°49·7′	0°26·7′W	X	198
High Down House	Herts	TL1430	51°57·6′	0°20·1′W	A	166
Highdown Tower	W Susx	TQ0904	50°49·7′	0°26·7′W	X	198
High Drumclog	S Lanak	NS6239	55°37·8′	4°11·1′W	X	71
High Drumdow	S Ayr	NS2105	55°18·6′	4°48·8′W	X	70,76
High Drumlamford	S Ayr	NX2778	55°4·2′	4°42·1′W	X	76
High Drummore	D & G	NX1335	54°40·8′	4°53·6′W	X	82
High Drumskeog	D & G	NX3445	54°46·6′	4°34·4′W	X	82
High Dubmire	Sund	NZ3249	54°50·3′	1°29·7′W	T	88
High Dubwath	Cumbr	NY4669	55°1·0′	2°50·2′W	X	86
High Dunashry	Arg & Bt	NR7047	55°40·0′	5°39·0′W	X	62
High Duncryne	W Dunb	NS4385	56°2·2′	4°30·8′W	X	56
High Dyke	Cumbr	NY1026	54°37·5′	3°23·2′W	X	89
High Dyke	Cumbr	NY4732	54°41·1′	2°48·9′W	H	90
High Dyke	Durham	NY9525	54°37·5′	2°4·2′W	T	91,92
High Dyke	N Yks	SD8094	54°20·7′	2°18·0′W	X	98
High Dyke	S Lanak	NS7240	55°38·5′	4°1·6′W	X	71
Highdyke Fm	Lincs	SK9428	52°50·7′	0°35·9′W	FM	130
High Dyke Fm	Lincs	SK9951	53°3·1′	0°31·0′W	FM	121
High Dyke Fm	S Lanak	NS7241	55°39·0′	4°1·6′W	FM	71
High Dykes	S Lanak	NS6638	55°37·3′	4°7·2′W	X	71
Highdykes	W Dunb	NS4078	55°58·4′	4°33·4′W	X	64
High Dyon Side	Cumbr	NY0222	54°35·3′	3°30·6′W	X	89
High Easter	Essex	TL6214	51°48·3′	0°21·4′E	T	167
High Easton Fm	E Yorks	TA1569	54°6·5′	0°14·0′W	FM	101
High East Quarter	S Lanak	NS7347	55°42·2′	4°0·8′W	X	64
High Edge	Brad	SE0250	53°57·0′	1°57·8′W	X	104
High Edge	Derby	SK0668	53°12·8′	1°54·2′W	H	119
High Edge	N Yks	SE0450	53°57·0′	1°55·9′W	X	104
High Eggborough	N Yks	SE5722	53°41·7′	1°7·8′W	T	105
High Eldrig	D & G	NX2469	54°59·3′	4°44·6′W	X	82
High Ellington	N Yks	SE1983	54°14·8′	1°42·1′W	T	99
High Elm Fm	Norf	TG0400	52°33·8′	1°1·0′E	FM	144
High Elm Fm	Suff	TM1356	52°9·9′	1°7·3′E	FM	156
High Elm Fm	Suff	TM1759	52°11·4′	1°10·9′E	FM	156
High Elms	Staffs	SJ9535	52°55·0′	2°4·1′W	X	127
High Elms Country Park	Brom	TQ4463	51°21·1′	0°4·5′E	X	177,187,188
High Elms Fm	Suff	TL7153	52°9·2′	0°30·4′E	FM	154
Highend	Scot Bord	NT5710	55°23·2′	2°40·3′W	X	80
Highenden Ho	Norf	TF5118	52°44·5′	0°14·6′E	X	131
High Entercommon	N Yks	NZ3305	54°26·6′	1°29·0′W	X	93
Higher Agden	Lancs	SD8053	53°58·6′	2°17·9′W	X	103
Higher Alham	Somer	ST6741	51°10·3′	2°27·9′W	T	183
Higher Ansty	Dorset	ST7603	50°49·8′	2°20·1′W	T	194
Higher Argal	Corn	SW7632	50°9·0′	5°7·8′W	X	204
Higher Ashton	Devon	SX8584	50°38·9′	3°37·2′W	T	191
Higher Audley	Black w Dar	SD6927	53°44·6′	2°27·8′W	T	103
Higher Aylescott	Devon	SS5242	51°9·7′	4°6·6′W	X	180
Higher Bagmores Fm	Devon	SX9987	50°40·7′	3°25·4′W	FM	192
Higher Bal	Corn	SW7050	50°18·5′	5°13·4′W	T	203
Higher Ballam	Lancs	SD3530	53°46·0′	2°58·8′W	T	102
Higher Barker	Lancs	SD5540	53°51·5′	2°40·6′W	X	102
Higher Barn	Ches	SJ9870	53°13·9′	2°1·4′W	X	118
Higher Barn Fm	Ches	SJ5466	53°11·6′	2°40·9′W	FM	117
Higher Barn Fm	Essex	TM1526	51°53·7′	1°7·9′E	FM	168,169
Higher Barns	Wrex	SJ4743	52°59·1′	2°47·0′W	X	117
Higher Bartle	Lancs	SD5033	53°47·7′	2°45·1′W	T	102
Higher Barton	Devon	SX8585	50°39·4′	3°37·2′W	X	191
Higher Basil	Corn	SX1883	50°37·3′	4°34·0′W	X	201
Higher Beara	Devon	SX7161	50°26·3′	3°48·6′W	X	202
Higher Bebington	Wirral	SJ3185	53°21·7′	3°1·8′W	T	108
Higher Beer	Devon	SS6629	51°2·9′	3°54·3′W	X	180
Higher Beesley	Lancs	SD5639	53°51·0′	2°39·7′W	X	102
Higher Berry	Devon	SX7995	50°44·8′	3°42·5′W	X	191
Higher Berrycourt	Wilts	ST9221	50°59·5′	2°6·5′W	X	184
Higher Berry End	Beds	SP9834	52°0·0′	0°34·0′W	T	153,165
Higher Besley Fm	Devon	ST0418	50°57·4′	3°21·6′W	FM	181
Higher Blackley	Man	SD8404	53°32·2′	2°14·1′W	T	109
Higher Blackpool Fm	Devon	SS6825	51°0·8′	3°52·5′W	FM	180
Higher Blakelow Fm	Ches	SJ9372	53°14·9′	2°5·9′W	FM	118
Higher Boarshaw	Roch	SD8706	53°33·3′	2°11·4′W	T	109
Higher Bockhampton	Dorset	SY7292	50°43·8′	2°23·4′W	T	194
Higher Boden	Corn	SW7623	50°4·1′	5°7·4′W	X	204
Higher Bodinnar	Corn	SW4132	50°8·1′	5°37·1′W	X	203
Higher Boscaswell	Corn	SW3834	50°9·1′	5°39·7′W	T	203
Higher Bowden	Devon	SX5591	50°42·3′	4°2·8′W	X	191
Higher Bowerhay	Devon	SS8209	50°52·3′	3°40·2′W	X	191
Higher Bridmore Fm	Wilts	ST9620	50°59·0′	2°3·0′W	FM	184
Higher Brixham	Torbay	SX9255	50°23·3′	3°30·8′W	T	202
Higher Broadwood	Lancs	SD6266	54°5·6′	2°34·4′W	X	97
Higher Brockholes	Lancs	SD5831	53°46·7′	2°37·8′W	X	102
Higher Brock Mill	Lancs	SD5744	53°53·7′	2°38·8′W	X	102
Higher Broomfield	Lancs	SD5972	54°8·8′	2°37·2′W	X	97
Higher Broughton	Salf	SD8200	53°30·0′	2°15·9′W	T	109
Higher Brownstone Fm	Devon	SX9050	50°20·6′	3°32·4′W	FM	202
Higher Bruckland Fm	Devon	SY2893	50°44·2′	3°0·8′W	FM	193
Higher Burnt Hill	Lancs	SD9244	53°53·8′	2°6·9′W	X	103
Higher Burrow	Somer	ST4020	50°58·8′	2°50·9′W	T	193
Higher Burrowtown	Devon	SY0097	50°46·1′	3°24·7′W	T	192
Higher Burton Fm	Dorset	SY6992	50°43·8′	2°26·0′W	FM	194
Higher Burwardsley	Ches	SJ5256	53°6·2′	2°42·6′W	T	117
Higher Bury	Devon	SX7995	50°44·8′	3°42·5′W	A	191
Higher Bushey Fm	Dorset	SY9783	50°39·0′	2°2·2′W	FM	195
Higher Bussow Fm	Corn	SW4938	50°11·6′	5°30·6′W	FM	203
Higher Cadshaw	Lancs	SD6634	53°48·3′	2°30·6′W	X	103
High Ercall	Wrekin	SJ5917	52°45·2′	2°36·0′W	T	126
Higher Callestick Fm	Corn	SW7649	50°18·1′	5°8·4′W	FM	204
Higher Came Fm	Dorset	SY6987	50°41·1′	2°25·9′W	FM	194
Higher Campscott	Devon	SS4944	51°10·8′	4°9·2′W	X	180
Higher Carblake	Corn	SX1170	50°30·2′	4°39·5′W	X	200

Higher Carden	Ches	SJ4652	53°4·0′	2°47·9′W	X	117
Higher Carr Fm	N Yks	SE1948	53°55·9′	1°42·2′W	FM	104
Higher Chalmington	Dorset	ST5901	50°48·7′	2°34·5′W	T	194
Higher Change	Lancs	SD8823	53°42·4′	2°10·5′W	X	103
Higher Chapeltown	Devon	SS9006	50°50·8′	3°33·4′W	X	192
Higher Charlwood Fm	Devon	SX9178	50°35·7′	3°32·0′W	FM	192
Higher Cheriton	Devon	ST1000	50°47·8′	3°16·2′W	T	192,193
Higher Chieflowman	Devon	ST0015	50°55·8′	3°25·0′W	X	181
Higher Chillington	Somer	ST3810	50°53·4′	2°52·5′W	T	193
Higher Chisworth	Derby	SJ9991	53°25·2′	2°0·5′W	T	109
Higher City Fm	Dorset	SY6499	50°47·6′	2°30·3′W	FM	194
Higher Clapton Fm	Somer	ST6727	51°2·7′	2°27·9′W	FM	183
Higher Clatcombe Fm	Dorset	ST6319	50°58·4′	2°31·2′W	FM	183
Highercliff	Corn	SX2457	50°23·4′	4°28·2′W	T	201
Higher Cliviger	Lancs	SD8630	53°46·2′	2°12·3′W	H	103
Higher Clough	Lancs	SD7358	54°1·3′	2°24·3′W	X	103
Higher Clough	Lancs	SD8545	53°54·3′	2°13·3′W	X	103
Higher Clovelly	Devon	SS3123	50°59·1′	4°24·1′W	T	190
Higher Clowne	Corn	SX1660	50°24·9′	4°35·0′W	X	201
Higher Coltscombe	Devon	SX8045	50°17·8′	3°40·7′W	X	202
Higher Colvannick	Corn	SX1271	50°30·8′	4°38·7′W	X	200
Higher Combe	Somer	SS8638	51°8·0′	3°37·4′W	X	181
Highercombe	Somer	SS9030	51°3·8′	3°33·8′W	X	181
Higher Comberoy Fm	Devon	ST0100	50°47·7′	3°23·9′W	FM	192
Higher Comeytrowe Fm	Somer	ST1922	50°59·7′	3°8·9′W	FM	181,193
Higher Compton Barton	Devon	SX8764	50°28·1′	3°35·2′W	X	202
Higher Condurrow	Corn	SW6639	50°12·5′	5°16·4′W	T	203
Higher Cookworthy	Devon	SX3986	50°39·3′	4°16·3′W	X	201
Higher Coombe	Devon	SS9004	50°49·7′	3°33·3′W	X	192
Higher Coombe	Devon	SX8379	50°36·2′	3°38·8′W	X	191
Higher Coombe	Dorset	SY5391	50°43·2′	2°39·6′W	X	194
Higher Core	Lancs	SD5944	53°53·7′	2°37·0′W	X	102
Higher Corrie Fm	Devon	ST2400	50°47·9′	3°4·3′W	FM	192,193
Higher Cowley	Devon	SS6345	51°11·5′	3°57·3′W	X	180
Higher Cowlings	Somer	SS9630	51°3·8′	3°28·7′W	X	181
Higher Crabdown	Devon	SS6115	50°55·3′	3°58·3′W	X	180
Higher Crackington	Corn	SX1595	50°43·7′	4°36·9′W	T	190
Higher Crannow	Corn	SX1697	50°44·8′	4°36·1′W	X	190
Higher Cransworth	Corn	SW9668	50°28·8′	4°52·2′W	T	200
Higher Croft	Black w Dar	SD6826	53°44·0′	2°28·7′W	T	103
Higher Cross	Devon	ST0814	50°55·3′	3°18·2′W	X	181
Higher Dairy	Dorset	ST8803	50°49·8′	2°9·8′W	X	194
Higher Dairy	Dorset	ST9309	50°53·1′	2°5·6′W	X	195
Higher Danbank	Stock	SJ9488	53°23·6′	2°5·0′W	X	109
Higher Darracott Fm	Devon	SS5021	50°58·4′	4°7·8′W	FM	180
Higher Deer Ho	Lancs	SD6739	53°51·0′	2°29·7′W	X	103
Higher Den Fm	Ches	SJ7347	53°1·4′	2°23·7′W	FM	118
Higher Denham	Bucks	TQ0287	51°34·6′	0°31·3′W	T	176
Higher Densham	Devon	SS8109	50°52·3′	3°41·1′W	X	191
Higher Dinnicombe	Devon	SX8153	50°22·1′	3°40·0′W	X	202
Higher Dinting	Derby	SK0294	53°26·8′	1°57·8′W	T	110
Higher Disley	Ches	SJ9784	53°21·4′	2°2·3′W	T	109
Higher Doles Fm	Ches	SJ9279	53°18·7′	2°6·8′W	FM	118
Higher Down	Devon	SS6742	51°9·9′	3°53·8′W	X	180
Higher Down	Dorset	ST6801	50°48·7′	2°26·9′W	X	194
Higher Downs	Corn	SW5530	50°7·4′	5°25·3′W	T	203
Higher Durston	Somer	ST2828	51°3·0′	3°1·2′W	T	193
Higher Edge	Lancs	SD7452	53°58·0′	2°23·4′W	X	103
Higher Edgecumbe	Devon	SX4079	50°35·6′	4°15·3′W	X	201
Higher Eggbeer	Devon	SX7692	50°43·1′	3°45·0′W	X	191
Higher Elker	Lancs	SD7135	53°48·9′	2°26·0′W	X	103
Higher Elms	Ches	SJ6661	53°8·9′	2°30·1′W	X	118
Higher Elsford Fm	Devon	SX7983	50°38·3′	3°42·3′W	FM	191
Higher End	Wigan	SD5203	53°31·5′	2°43·0′W	T	108
Higherend Fm	Hants	SU1817	50°57·4′	1°44·2′W	FM	184
Higher Eype	Dorset	SY4492	50°43·7′	2°47·2′W	T	193
Higher Fair Snape	Lancs	SD5845	53°54·2′	2°37·9′W	X	102
Higher Farleigh	Devon	SS9313	50°54·6′	3°30·9′W	X	181
Higherfence	Ches	SJ9373	53°15·5′	2°5·9′W	X	118
Higher Fence Wood	Lancs	SD6347	53°55·3′	2°33·4′W	F	102,103
Higher Ferry Ho	Flint	SJ3665	53°10·9′	2°57·1′W	X	117
Higher Fingle	Devon	SX7491	50°42·5′	3°46·7′W	X	191
Higher Flass	Lancs	SD7953	53°58·6′	2°18·8′W	X	103
Higher Fm	Ches	SJ7267	53°12·2′	2°24·7′W	FM	118
Higher Fm	Devon	ST2601	50°48·5′	3°2·6′W	FM	192,193
Higher Fm	Devon	SX4779	50°35·7′	4°9·3′W	FM	191,201
Higher Fm	Dorset	ST6213	50°55·1′	2°32·1′W	FM	194
Higher Fm	Dorset	ST9610	50°53·6′	2°3·0′W	FM	195
Higher Fm	Somer	ST3711	50°53·9′	2°53·4′W	FM	193
Higher Fm	Somer	ST5426	51°2·1′	2°39·0′W	FM	183
Higher Fm	Somer	ST6029	51°3·8′	2°33·9′W	FM	183
Higherfold Fm	Derby	SK0189	53°24·1′	1°58·7′W	FM	110
Higher Folds	Wigan	SD6800	53°30·0′	2°28·5′W	T	109
Higherford	Lancs	SD8640	53°51·6′	2°12·4′W	T	103
Higher Foxhanger Fm	Somer	SS9432	51°4·9′	3°30·4′W	FM	181
Higher Gabwell	Devon	SX9269	50°30·9′	3°31·0′W	T	202
Higher Ghylls	Lancs	SD7655	53°59·7′	2°21·5′W	X	103
Higher Gills	Lancs	SD8244	53°53·8′	2°16·0′W	X	103
Higher Godsworthy	Devon	SX5277	50°34·7′	4°5·0′W	X	191,201
Higher Gorhuish	Devon	SX5297	50°45·5′	4°5·5′W	X	191
Higher Gorsley Fm	Ches	SJ8469	53°13·3′	2°14·0′W	FM	118
Higher Grange	Shrops	SJ3935	52°54·8′	2°54·0′W	X	126
Higher Grants Fm	Devon	SS9324	51°0·6′	3°31·1′W	FM	181
Higher Green	Wigan	SD7000	53°30·0′	2°26·7′W	T	109
Higher Greendale	Devon	SY0289	50°41·8′	3°22·9′W	X	192
Higher Green Nook	Lancs	SD5936	53°49·4′	2°37·0′W	X	102
Higher Greenway	Devon	SX8854	50°22·7′	3°34·1′W	X	202
Higher Hall	Ches	SJ4950	53°2·9′	2°45·2′W	X	117
Higher Hall	Wrex	SJ4149	53°2·3′	2°52·4′W	X	117
Higher Halstock	Devon	SX6092	50°42·9′	3°58·6′W	X	191
Higher Halstock Leigh	Dorset	ST5107	50°51·9′	2°41·4′W	T	194
Higher Halwyn	Corn	SW9373	50°31·4′	4°54·9′W	X	200
Higher Harlyn	Corn	SW8774	50°31·9′	5°0·0′W	X	200
Higher Hawkerland Fm	Devon	SY0490	50°42·3′	3°21·2′W	FM	192
Higher Haye	Devon	SX4478	50°35·1′	4°11·8′W	X	201
Higher Healey	Lancs	SD6018	53°39·7′	2°35·9′W	A	109
Higher Heathcombe Fm	Somer	ST2333	51°5·7′	3°5·6′W	FM	182
Higher Heathfield	Devon	SX7947	50°18·9′	3°41·6′W	X	202

Higher Heights	Lancs	SD7648	53°55·9′	2°21·5′W	X	103
Higher Heights Fm	Brad	SE0638	53°50·5′	1°54·1′W	FM	104
Higher Hey	Lancs	SD7827	53°44·6′	2°19·6′W	X	103
Higher Heysham	Lancs	SD4160	54°2·2′	2°53·6′W	T	96,97
Higher Higson	Lancs	SD8143	53°53·2′	2°16·9′W	X	103
Higher Hill	Black w Dar	SD6522	53°41·8′	2°31·4′W	X	102,103
Higher Hill	Dorset	ST7202	50°49·2′	2°23·5′W	X	194
Higher Hill	Lancs	SD8318	53°39·7′	2°15·0′W	X	109
Higher Hill Bottom	Dorset	SY6599	50°47·6′	2°29·4′W	X	194
Higher Hill Fm	Corn	SX1367	50°28·6′	4°37·8′W	FM	200
Higher Hill Fm	Somer	ST1542	51°10·5′	3°12·6′W	FM	181
Higher Hill Ho	Lancs	SD4836	53°49·3′	2°47·0′W	X	102
Higher Ho	Devon	SS5724	51°0·1′	4°1·9′W	X	180
Higher Ho	Flint	SJ3064	53°10·4′	3°2·4′W	X	117
Higher Ho	Lancs	SD4230	53°46·0′	2°52·4′W	X	102
Higher Ho	Somer	SS8839	51°8·6′	3°35·7′W	X	181
Higher Hodder	Lancs	SD6941	53°52·1′	2°27·9′W	X	103
Higher Hogshead	Lancs	SD8822	53°41·9′	2°10·5′W	T	103
Higher Holbrook Fm	Somer	ST6829	51°3·8′	2°27·0′W	FM	183
Higher Holnest	Dorset	ST6408	50°52·5′	2°30·3′W	X	194
Higher Holton	Somer	ST6827	51°2·7′	2°27·0′W	T	183
Higher Honeybrook Fm	Dorset	SU0002	50°49·3′	1°59·6′W	FM	195
Higher Hopcott	Somer	SS9645	51°11·9′	3°28·9′W	X	181
Higher Horrells	Devon	SX8788	50°41·1′	3°35·6′W	X	192
Higher Horslett	Devon	SX3297	50°45·1′	4°22·5′W	X	190
Higher Houghton Fm	Dorset	ST8004	50°50·3′	2°16·7′W	FM	194
Higher House Fm	Bury	SD7515	53°38·1′	2°22·3′W	FM	109
Higher House Fm	Ches	SJ8575	53°16·5′	2°13·1′W	FM	118
Higher House Fm	Ches	SJ8778	53°18·2′	2°11·3′W	FM	118
Higher House Fm	Ches	SJ9481	53°19·8′	2°5·0′W	FM	109
Higher House Fm	Lancs	SD5938	53°50·4′	2°37·0′W	FM	102
Higher House Fm	N Yks	SE0149	53°56·5′	1°58·7′W	FM	104
Higherhouse Fm	Warr	SJ6686	53°22·4′	2°30·3′W	FM	109
Higher Houses	Lancs	SD8252	53°58·1′	2°16·0′W	X	103
Higher Hurdsfield	Ches	SJ9374	53°16·0′	2°5·9′W	T	118
Higher Huxley Hall	Ches	SJ4961	53°8·9′	2°45·3′W	X	117
Higher Hyde Heath	Dorset	SY8590	50°42·8′	2°12·4′W	X	194
Higher Intake	Brad	SD9940	53°51·6′	2°0·5′W	X	103
Higher Kennelands	Devon	SS4104	50°49·1′	4°15·1′W	X	190
Higher Kerrowe	Corn	SW4536	50°10·4′	5°33·9′W	X	203
Higher Kingcombe	Dorset	SY5499	50°47·6′	2°38·8′W	T	194
Higher Kingston Fm	Dorset	SY7192	50°43·8′	2°24·3′W	FM	194
Higher Kinnerton	Flint	SJ3261	53°8·8′	3°0·6′W	T	117
Higher Kitcott	Devon	SS7519	50°57·6′	3°46·4′W	X	180
Higherland	Corn	SX3773	50°32·3′	4°17·6′W	X	201
Higher Lanes Bank	Wrex	SJ4843	52°59·2′	2°46·1′W	X	117
Higher Lanes Fm	Wrex	SJ4842	52°58·6′	2°46·1′W	FM	117
Higher Langdon	Corn	SX2073	50°32·0′	4°32·0′W	X	201
Higher Langdon	Dorset	ST5002	50°49·2′	2°42·2′W	X	194
Higher Lanherne	Corn	SW8868	50°28·6′	4°58·9′W	X	200
Higher Lanner	Corn	SW6426	50°5·5′	5°17·6′W	X	203
Higher Lath Fm	Cumbr	SD2780	54°12·9′	3°6·7′W	FM	96,97
Higher Leah Fm	Corn	SW4027	50°5·4′	5°37·7′W	FM	203
Higher Ledge	I Scilly	SV9114	49°57·0′	6°18·1′W	X	203
Higher Lees Fm	Lancs	SD6644	53°53·7′	2°30·6′W	FM	103
Higher Lench	Lancs	SD8221	53°41·4′	2°15·9′W	X	103
Higher Ley	Devon	SS7528	51°2·5′	3°46·6′W	X	180
Higher Ley	Devon	SX8245	50°17·8′	3°39·0′W	W	202
Higher Lodge Fm	Devon	SY3299	50°47·4′	2°57·5′W	FM	193
Higher Longbeak	Corn	SS1903	50°48·1′	4°33·7′W	X	190
Higher Ludbrook	Devon	SX6653	50°21·9′	3°52·7′W	X	202
Higher Lugsland	Devon	SS8812	50°54·0′	3°35·2′W	X	181
Higher Manaton	Corn	SX3373	50°32·2′	4°21·0′W	X	201
Higher Marsh	Somer	ST7320	50°59·0′	2°22·7′W	T	183
Higher Marsh Fm	Somer	ST7425	51°1·7′	2°21·9′W	FM	183
Higher Matley Hall	Tames	SJ9795	53°27·3′	2°2·3′W	X	109
Higher Melcombe	Dorset	ST7402	50°49·2′	2°21·8′W	A	194
Higher Melcombe	Dorset	ST7402	50°49·2′	2°21·8′W	T	194
Higher Menadew	Corn	SX0359	50°24·1′	4°46·0′W	T	200
Higher Mere Park	Wilts	ST8429	51°3·8′	2°13·3′W	X	183
Higher Mere Syke	N Yks	SD7955	53°59·7′	2°18·8′W	X	103
Higher Metcombe	Devon	SY0692	50°43·4′	3°19·5′W	T	192
Higher Minnend	Ches	SJ9364	53°10·6′	2°5·9′W	X	118
Higher Molland	Devon	SS7033	51°5·1′	3°51·0′W	T	180
Higher Moor Head	Lancs	SD5456	54°0·1′	2°41·7′W	X	102
Higher Moors	I Scilly	SV9210	49°54·9′	6°17·1′W	X	203
Higher Morrey	Shrops	SJ6239	52°57·1′	2°33·5′W	X	127
Higher Muddiford	Devon	SS5538	51°7·6′	4°3·9′W	T	180
Higher Munty	Somer	ST1912	50°54·3′	3°8·7′W	X	181,193
Higher Mutlow	Ches	SJ8667	53°12·2′	2°12·2′W	X	118
Higher Nabbs	Ches	SJ9768	53°12·8′	2°2·3′W	X	118
Higher Netley	Shrops	SJ4601	52°36·5′	2°47·4′W	X	126
Higher Newham	Corn	SW8243	50°15·0′	5°3·1′W	X	204
Higher Noss Point	Devon	SX8753	50°22·2′	3°35·0′W	X	202
Higher Nyland	Dorset	ST7322	51°0·0′	2°22·7′W	T	183
Higher Oak	Wrex	SJ3948	53°1·8′	2°54·2′W	X	117
Higher Oaken Head	Lancs	SD5541	53°52·0′	2°40·6′W	X	102
Higher Oakley Fm	Somer	ST5221	50°59·4′	2°40·7′W	FM	183
Higher Overton	Staffs	SJ8961	53°9·0′	2°9·5′W	X	118
Higher Park	Devon	SS6908	50°51·6′	3°51·3′W	X	191
Higher Park	Devon	SS8511	50°53·5′	3°37·7′W	X	191
Higher Park	Lancs	SD8845	53°54·3′	2°10·5′W	X	103
Higher Park Fm	Dorset	ST4403	50°49·7′	2°47·3′W	FM	193
Higher Park Fm	Dorset	SY3998	50°46·9′	2°51·5′W	FM	193
Higher Parkhead	Staffs	SK0449	53°2·5′	1°56·0′W	X	119
Higher Penstroda	Corn	SX1172	50°31·3′	4°39·6′W	X	200
Higher Pentire	Corn	SW6524	50°4·4′	5°16·7′W	X	203
Higher Penwartha	Corn	SW7549	50°18·1′	5°9·2′W	X	204
Higher Penwortham	Lancs	SD5128	53°45·0′	2°44·2′W	T	102
Higher Pertwood	Wilts	ST8835	51°7·1′	2°9·9′W	T	183
Higher Pigsdon Fm	Corn	SS2809	50°51·5′	4°26·3′W	FM	190
Higher Piles	Devon	SX6461	50°26·2′	3°54·5′W	X	202
Higher Pimbo	Lancs	SD5103	53°31·5′	2°43·9′W	X	108
Higher Pitt	Devon	SX8391	50°42·6′	3°39·0′W	X	191
Higher Pitt Fm	Devon	SS9108	50°51·9′	3°32·6′W	FM	192
Higher Pitts Fm	Somer	ST5349	51°14·5′	2°40·0′W	FM	182,183
Higher Platts Fm	N Yks	SE1361	54°2·9′	1°47·7′W	FM	99
Higher Porthpean	Corn	SX0250	50°19·2′	4°46·5′W	T	200,204
Higher Poynton	Ches	SJ9483	53°20·9′	2°5·0′W	T	109

Higher Prestacott	Devon	SX3996	50°44·7′	4°16·5′W	T	190
Higher Radnidge Moor	Devon	SS8525	51°1·0′	3°38·0′W	X	181
Higher Rads End	Beds	SP9932	51°58·9′	0°33·1′W	T	165
Higher Radway Fm	Devon	SX9074	50°33·6′	3°32·8′W	FM	192
Higher Relowas	Corn	SW7223	50°4·0′	5°10·8′W	X	204
Higher Ridge	Shrops	SJ3533	52°53·7′	2°57·6′W	T	126
Higher Ridgegate	Ches	SJ9571	53°14·4′	2°4·1′W	X	118
Higher Rill Fm	Devon	SY1194	50°44·6′	3°15·3′W	FM	192,193
Higher Rocombe Barton	Devon	SX9168	50°30·3′	3°31·9′W	T	202
Higher Row	Dorset	SU0404	50°50·4′	1°56·2′W	T	195
Higher Rowden	Devon	SS3925	51°0·3′	4°17·3′W	X	190
Higher Row Mires	N Yks	SE7596	54°21·5′	0°50·3′W	X	94,100
Higher Runcorn	Halton	SJ5182	53°20·2′	2°43·7′W	T	108
Higher Salter Close	Lancs	SD6261	54°2·9′	2°34·4′W	X	97
Higher Sandford	Dorset	ST6220	50°58·9′	2°32·1′W	T	183
Higher Sandy Sike	Lancs	SD7556	54°0·2′	2°22·5′W	X	103
Higher Scarsick	Corn	SX2088	50°40·1′	4°32·5′W	X	190
Higher Sharpnose Point	Corn	SS1914	50°54·1′	4°34·1′W	X	190
Higher Shaw Fm	Know	SJ4889	53°24·0′	2°46·5′W	FM	108
Higher Shelf Stones	Derby	SK0994	53°26·8′	1°51·5′W	X	110
Higher Shilstone	Devon	SX6690	50°41·9′	3°53·5′W	A	191
Higher Shotton	Flint	SJ3067	53°12·0′	3°2·5′W	T	117
Higher Shurlach	Ches	SJ6772	53°14·9′	2°29·3′W	T	118
Higher Shutehanger	Devon	ST0313	50°54·7′	3°22·4′W	X	181
Higher Shutscombe	Devon	SS6834	51°5·6′	3°52·7′W	X	180
Higher Sigford	Devon	SX7874	50°33·4′	3°43·0′W	X	191
Higher Silcock	Lancs	SD4841	53°52·0′	2°47·0′W	X	102
Higher Skippet Fm	Dorset	SY6391	50°43·3′	2°31·1′W	FM	194
Higher Slade	Devon	SS5046	51°11·9′	4°8·4′W	T	180
Higher Smallwood	Ches	SJ8159	53°7·9′	2°16·6′W	X	118
Higher Snab Fm	Ches	SJ5448	53°1·9′	2°40·8′W	FM	117
Higher Snab Fm	Lancs	SD5568	54°6·6′	2°40·9′W	FM	97
High Ersock	D & G	NX4437	54°42·5′	4°24·9′W	X	83
Higher Southcombe Fm	Dorset	ST6800	50°48·2′	2°26·9′W	FM	194
Higher Southey Fm	Somer	ST1911	50°53·8′	3°8·7′W	FM	192,193
Higher Spargo	Corn	SW7532	50°9·0′	5°8·6′W	X	204
Higher Spreacombe	Devon	SS4841	51°9·1′	4°10·0′W	X	180
Higher Spriddlescombe	Devon	SX6854	50°22·5′	3°51·0′W	X	202
Higher Spring	Devon	SX4980	50°36·2′	4°7·7′W	X	191,201
Higher Stanbear	Corn	SX2672	50°31·6′	4°26·9′W	X	201
Higher Standen	Lancs	SD7540	53°51·6′	2°22·4′W	X	103
Higher Stavordale Fm	Somer	ST7232	51°5·4′	2°23·6′W	FM	183
Higher Stiniel	Devon	SX7085	50°39·2′	3°50·0′W	X	191
Higher Stony Clough	Lancs	SD6656	54°0·2′	2°30·7′W	X	103
Higher Stout Fm	Devon	ST2310	50°53·3′	3°5·3′W	FM	192,193
Higher Street	Somer	ST1342	51°10·5′	3°14·3′W	T	181
Higher Sturthill Fm	Dorset	SY5192	50°43·8′	2°41·3′W	FM	194
Higher Sweetcombe Fm	Devon	SY1692	50°43·5′	3°11·0′W	FM	192,193
Higher Tale	Devon	ST0601	50°48·3′	3°19·7′W	T	192
Higher Thorn Fm	Somer	ST6130	51°4·3′	2°33·0′W	FM	183
Higher Thornhill	Staffs	SJ7645	53°0·3′	2°21·1′W	X	118
Higher Thornton Fm	Devon	SX9283	50°38·4′	3°31·3′W	FM	192
Higher Thrushgill	Lancs	SD6562	54°3·4′	2°31·7′W	X	97
Higher Tideford	Devon	SX8254	50°22·7′	3°39·2′W	X	202
Higher Tolcarne	Corn	SW8865	50°27·0′	4°58·8′W	T	200
Higher Tor	Devon	SX6191	50°42·4′	3°57·7′W	H	191
Higher Totnell	Dorset	ST6208	50°52·4′	2°32·0′W	T	194
Highertown	Corn	SW8044	50°15·5′	5°4·8′W	T	204
Higher Town	Corn	SX0061	50°25·1′	4°48·6′W	T	200
Highertown	Corn	SX1281	50°36·1′	4°39·0′W	T	200
Higher Town	Devon	SS8627	51°2·1′	3°37·2′W	X	181
Higher Town	I Scilly	SV9215	49°57·6′	6°17·3′W	T	203
Higher Town	Somer	SS9646	51°12·5′	3°28·9′W	T	181
Higher Trapp Hotel	Lancs	SD7735	53°48·9′	2°20·5′W	X	103
Higher Tregantle Fm	Corn	SX3952	50°21·0′	4°15·4′W	FM	201
Higher Trelean	Corn	SW9847	50°17·5′	4°49·8′W	X	204
Higher Trelease Fm	Corn	SW8440	50°13·5′	5°1·3′W	FM	204
Higher Tremail Fm	Corn	SX1585	50°38·4′	4°36·6′W	FM	201
Higher Tremarcoombe	Corn	SX2569	50°29·9′	4°27·7′W	T	201
Higher Trenhouse	N Yks	SD8766	54°5·6′	2°11·5′W	X	98
Higher Trenower	Corn	SW7423	50°4·1′	5°9·1′W	X	204
Higher Trenoweth	Corn	SW9064	50°26·5′	4°57·1′W	X	200
Higher Trenoweth	Corn	SW9561	50°25·0′	4°52·8′W	X	200
Higher Trethake	Corn	SX2769	50°30·0′	4°26·0′W	X	201
Higher Trethern Fm	Corn	SX0885	50°38·2′	4°42·5′W	FM	200
Higher Trevilgan	Corn	SW6925	50°5·0′	5°13·4′W	X	203
Higher Trevilmick	Corn	SX0661	50°25·2′	4°43·5′W	X	200
Higher Turnshaw Fm	Brad	SE0138	53°50·5′	1°58·7′W	FM	104
Higher Turtley	Devon	SX6958	50°24·7′	3°50·2′W	X	202
Higher Tynes	Corn	SX0582	50°36·5′	4°45·0′W	X	200
Higher Upcott	Devon	SX5796	50°45·0′	4°1·2′W	X	191
Higher Upton	Devon	SS8108	50°51·8′	3°41·1′W	X	191
Higher Venn	Devon	SS7805	50°50·1′	3°43·6′W	X	191
Higher Vexford	Somer	ST1035	51°6·7′	3°16·8′W	T	181
Higher Walreddon	Devon	SX4871	50°31·4′	4°8·3′W	X	201
Higher Walton	Lancs	SD5727	53°44·5′	2°38·7′W	T	102
Higher Walton	Warr	SJ5985	53°21·9′	2°36·6′W	T	108
Higher Wambrook	Somer	ST2908	50°52·3′	3°0·2′W	T	193
Higher Warcombe	Devon	SS4745	51°11·3′	4°11·0′W	T	180
Higher Waterhouse	Devon	SS8808	50°51·9′	3°35·1′W	X	192
Higher Waterston	Dorset	SY7295	50°45·5′	2°23·4′W	X	194
Higher Way	Devon	SS8914	50°55·1′	3°34·4′W	X	181
Higher Weaver	Devon	ST0504	50°49·9′	3°20·6′W	T	192
Higher Week	Devon	SS7204	50°49·5′	3°48·7′W	X	191
Higher Week Fm	Devon	SS6243	51°10·4′	3°58·1′W	FM	180
Higher Westwater	Devon	SY2799	50°47·4′	3°1·8′W	X	193
Higher Whatcombe	Dorset	ST8301	50°48·7′	2°14·1′W	T	194
Higher Wheathead	Lancs	SD8442	53°52·7′	2°14·2′W	X	103
Higher Wheelton	Lancs	SD6122	53°41·8′	2°35·0′W	T	102,103
Higher Whiteleigh	Corn	SX2494	50°43·4′	4°29·2′W	X	190
Higher Whiteleigh	Devon	SS4202	50°48·0′	4°14·2′W	X	190
Higher Whitemore Fm	Staffs	SJ8860	53°8·5′	2°10·4′W	FM	118
Higher White Tor	Devon	SX6178	50°35·3′	3°57·4′W	H	191
Higher Whitewell	Lancs	SD6547	53°55·3′	2°31·6′W	X	102,103
Higher Whitley	Ches	SJ6180	53°19·2′	2°34·7′W	T	109
Higher Willyards	Devon	SY0197	50°46·1′	3°23·9′W	X	192
Higher Wincham	Ches	SJ6876	53°17·0′	2°28·4′W	T	118
Higher Wiscombe Fm	Devon	SY1893	50°44·1′	3°9·3′W	FM	192,193
Higher Withins	Lancs	SD7927	53°44·6′	2°18·7′W	X	103
Higher Wood Br	Dorset	ST7012	50°54·6′	2°25·2′W	X	194

Higher Woodhill	Bury	SD7912	53°36·5′	2°18·6′W	X	109
Higher Wood Ho	Lancs	SD6954	53°59·1′	2°28·0′W	X	103
Higher Woodsford	Dorset	SY7689	50°42·2′	2°20·0′W	T	194
Higher Worthyvale	Corn	SX0986	50°38·8′	4°41·7′W	X	200
Higher Wraxall	Dorset	ST5601	50°48·6′	2°37·1′W	T	194
Higher Wych	Ches	SJ4943	52°59·2′	2°45·2′W	T	117
Higher Yarde Fm	Somer	ST2027	51°2·4′	3°8·1′W	FM	193
Higher Yewards Fm	Ches	SJ8978	53°18·2′	2°9·5′W	FM	118
High Eshells	Northum	NY8957	54°54·7′	2°9·9′W	X	87
High Eskholme	Cumbr	SD1197	54°21·9′	3°21·8′W	X	96
High Etherley	Durham	NZ1628	54°39·1′	1°44·7′W	T	92
High Ewebank	Cumbr	NY8409	54°28·8′	2°14·4′W	X	91,92
High Ewecote	N Yks	SE5795	54°21·1′	1°7·0′W	X	100
High Faggergill	N Yks	NY9806	54°27·2′	2°1·4′W	X	92
High Fairbank	Cumbr	SD4497	54°22·2′	2°51·3′W	X	97
High Fall	Cumbr	NY3606	54°27·0′	2°58·8′W	W	90
High Farm Cottages	N Yks	SE2379	54°12·6′	1°38·4′W	X	99
High Farnham	Northum	NT9602	55°19·0′	2°3·4′W	X	81
High Farthingbank	D & G	NS8401	55°17·6′	3°49·2′W	X	78
High Farthingwell	D & G	NX9282	55°7·5′	3°41·2′W	X	78
High Faverdale Fm	Darl	NZ2717	54°33·1′	1°34·5′W	FM	93
High Fawes	Cumbr	SD6991	54°19·1′	2°28·2′W	X	98
High Fawr	Shrops	SJ2729	52°51·5′	3°4·7′W	X	126
High Fea	Orkney	HY2001	58°53·6′	3°22·8′W	X	7
High Fell	Cumbr	NY1608	54°27·9′	3°17·3′W	X	89
Highfell	Cumbr	NY5758	54°55·1′	2°39·8′W	X	86
High Fell	Cumbr	SD2899	54°23·1′	3°6·1′W	H	96,97
High Fell End	Cumbr	SD4383	54°14·6′	2°52·1′W	X	97
High Fell Gate	Cumbr	SD3977	54°11·4′	2°55·7′W	X	96,97
High Fell Ho	Cumbr	SD5885	54°15·8′	2°38·3′W	X	97
High Fells	Cumbr	NY3319	54°34·0′	3°1·8′W	X	90
High Fen	Cambs	TL1885	52°27·2′	0°15·4′W	X	142
High Fen	Norf	TL7097	52°32·9′	0°30·8′E	X	143
High Fen	Suff	TL7179	52°23·2′	0°31·2′E	X	143
Highfen Fm	Cambs	TL5368	52°17·6′	0°15·0′E	FM	154
High Fen Fm	Cambs	TL5472	52°19·7′	0°16·0′E	FM	154
High Fen Fm	Suff	TL7285	52°26·4′	0°32·2′E	FM	143
High Ferry	Lincs	TF3549	53°1·5′	0°1·2′E	T	131
Highfield	Aberd	NJ5664	57°40·1′	2°43·8′W	X	29
Highfield	Arg & Bt	NR6551	55°42·0′	5°44·0′W	X	62
Highfield	Bolton	SD7105	53°32·7′	2°25·8′W	T	109
Highfield	C of Soton	SU4214	50°55·7′	1°23·8′W	T	196
Highfield	Corn	SX3090	50°41·3′	4°24·0′W	X	190
Highfield	Cumbr	NY5125	54°37·3′	2°45·1′W	X	90
Highfield	Cumbr	NY5343	54°47·0′	2°43·4′W	X	86
Highfield	Cumbr	NY5862	54°57·3′	2°38·9′W	X	86
High Field	Cumbr	NY6021	54°35·2′	2°36·7′W	X	91
Highfield	Cumbr	NY6514	54°31·5′	2°32·0′W	X	91
Highfield	Darl	NZ3414	54°31·5′	1°28·1′W	X	93
Highfield	Derby	SK1085	53°21·9′	1°50·6′W	X	110
High Field	Derby	SK1672	53°14·9′	1°45·2′W	H	119
Highfield	Derby	SK3576	53°17·0′	1°28·1′W	X	119
Highfield	E Ayr	NS5049	55°42·9′	4°22·8′W	X	64
Highfield	E Loth	NT5483	56°2·5′	2°43·9′W	X	66
Highfield	Essex	TL9705	51°42·8′	0°51·5′E	X	168
Highfield	E Susx	TQ7718	50°56·3′	0°31·5′E	X	199
Highfield	E Yorks	SE7236	53°49·2′	0°54·0′W	T	105,106
Highfield	E Yorks	SE9661	54°2·4′	0°31·6′W	X	101
Highfield	Ghead	NZ1458	54°55·2′	1°46·5′W	T	88
Highfield	Glos	SO6403	51°43·7′	2°30·9′W	T	162
Highfield	Hants	SU6425	51°1·5′	1°4·9′W	X	185
Highfield	Herts	TL0608	51°45·9′	0°27·4′W	T	166
Highfield	Highld	NH5251	57°31·8′	4°27·8′W	X	26
Highfield	Kent	TQ5460	51°19·3′	0°13·0′E	X	177,188
High Field	Lancs	SD7252	53°58·0′	2°25·2′W	T	103
Highfield	Lincs	TF0660	53°7·8′	0°24·5′W	X	121
Highfield	Lincs	TF1051	53°2·9′	0°21·1′W	X	121
Highfield	N Ayr	NS3050	55°43·1′	4°41·9′W	T	63
Highfield	Northum	NY7391	55°13·0′	2°25·0′W	X	80
Highfield	Northum	NY7590	55°12·5′	2°23·1′W	X	80
Highfield	Northum	NZ0655	54°53·6′	1°54·0′W	X	87
High Field	N Yks	SE0583	54°14·8′	1°55·0′W	X	98
Highfield	N Yks	SE1367	54°6·2′	1°47·7′W	X	99
Highfield	N Yks	SE3785	54°15·8′	1°25·5′W	X	99
High Field	N Yks	SE9567	54°5·6′	0°32·4′W	X	101
Highfield	Oxon	SP5723	51°54·4′	1°9·9′W	T	164
Highfield	S Ayr	NS3724	55°29·2′	4°34·4′W	X	70
Highfield	Sheff	SK3585	53°21·9′	1°28·0′W	T	110,111
Highfield	Shrops	SO4697	52°34·3′	2°47·4′W	X	137,138
Highfield	S Lanak	NT0133	55°35·1′	3°33·8′W	X	72
Highfield	Wigan	SD5503	53°31·5′	2°40·3′W	T	108
Highfield Burn	Northum	NY7491	55°13·0′	2°24·1′W	W	80
Highfield Cottages	Cambs	TL3141	52°3·3′	0°5·0′W	X	153
Highfield Fm	Beds	SP9638	52°2·2′	0°35·6′W	FM	153
Highfield Fm	Beds	TL1651	52°8·9′	0°17·9′W	FM	153
Highfield Fm	Brad	SE0651	53°57·5′	1°54·1′W	FM	104
Highfield Fm	Cambs	TF4009	52°39·9′	0°4·6′E	FM	142,143
Highfield Fm	Cambs	TL1666	52°17·0′	0°17·6′W	FM	153
Highfield Fm	Cambs	TL2055	52°11·0′	0°14·3′W	FM	153
Highfield Fm	Cambs	TL2742	52°3·9′	0°8·4′W	FM	153
Highfield Fm	Cambs	TL3240	52°2·8′	0°4·1′W	FM	153
Highfield Fm	Cambs	TL3442	52°3·8′	0°2·3′W	FM	154
Highfield Fm	Cambs	TL3559	52°13·0′	0°1·0′W	FM	154
Highfield Fm	Cambs	TL3767	52°17·3′	0°0·9′E	FM	154
Highfield Fm	Cambs	TL3857	52°11·9′	0°1·6′E	FM	154
Highfield Fm	Cambs	TL5686	52°27·2′	0°18·2′E	FM	143
Highfield Fm	Ches	SJ4355	53°5·6′	2°50·7′W	FM	117
Highfield Fm	Ches	SJ5951	53°3·5′	2°36·3′W	FM	117
Highfield Fm	Ches	SJ7271	53°14·4′	2°24·8′W	FM	118
Highfield Fm	Essex	TL9429	51°55·8′	0°49·7′E	FM	168
Highfield Fm	E Yorks	TA0053	53°58·0′	0°28·1′W	FM	106,107
Highfield Fm	E Yorks	TA0170	54°7·2′	0°26·9′W	FM	
Highfield Fm	Glos	SO8928	51°57·3′	2°9·2′W	FM	150,163
Highfield Fm	Glos	ST8994	51°38·9′	2°9·1′W	FM	163,173
Highfield Fm	Hants	SU5519	50°58·3′	1°12·6′W	FM	185
Highfield Fm	Leeds	SE4036	53°49·4′	1°23·1′W	FM	105
Highfield Fm	Leic	SK3001	52°36·6′	1°33·0′W	FM	140
Highfield Fm	Leic	SK7208	52°40·1′	0°55·7′W	FM	141
Highfield Fm	Leic	SK7328	52°50·9′	0°54·6′W	FM	129
Highfield Fm	Leic	SP5783	52°26·8′	1°9·3′W	FM	140

Highfield Fm	Leic	SP6298	52°34·8′	1°4·7′W	FM	140
Highfield Fm	Lincs	SK8968	53°12·3′	0°39·6′W	FM	121
Highfield Fm	Lincs	SK9890	53°24·1′	0°31·1′W	FM	112
Highfield Fm	Lincs	TA0901	53°29·9′	0°21·0′W	FM	112
Highfield Fm	Lincs	TF0063	53°9·5′	0°29·9′W	FM	121
Highfield Fm	Lincs	TF0399	53°28·9′	0°26·5′W	FM	112
Highfield Fm	Lincs	TF0895	53°26·7′	0°22·0′W	FM	112
Highfield Fm	Lincs	TF1582	53°19·6′	0°16·0′W	FM	121
Highfield Fm	Lincs	TF2393	53°25·4′	0°8·5′W	FM	113
Highfield Fm	Lincs	TF2675	53°15·7′	0°6·3′W	FM	122
Highfield Fm	Lincs	TF2877	53°16·7′	0°4·4′W	FM	122
Highfield Fm	Lincs	TF3269	53°12·3′	0°1·0′W	FM	122
Highfield Fm	Lincs	TF3565	53°10·1′	0°1·6′E	FM	122
Highfield Fm	Lincs	TF3689	53°23·1′	0°3·1′E	FM	113,122
Highfield Fm	Lincs	TF4569	53°12·1′	0°10·7′E	FM	122
Highfield Fm	N Lincs	SE8505	53°32·3′	0°42·6′W	FM	112
Highfield Fm	N Lincs	SE9416	53°38·2′	0°34·3′W	FM	112
Highfield Fm	Norf	TF9304	52°36·2′	0°51·4′E	FM	144
Highfield Fm	Norf	TF9427	52°48·6′	0°53·1′E	FM	132
Highfield Fm	Norf	TG3712	52°39·5′	1°30·7′E	FM	133,134
Highfield Fm	Northnts	SP5358	52°13·3′	1°13·0′W	FM	152
Highfield Fm	Northum	NY8258	54°55·2′	2°16·4′W	FM	86,87
Highfield Fm	Notts	SK7388	53°23·3′	0°53·7′W	FM	112,120
Highfield Fm	Notts	SK7592	53°25·4′	0°51·9′W	FM	112
Highfield Fm	Notts	SK7637	52°55·7′	0°51·8′W	FM	129
Highfield Fm	Notts	SK7838	52°56·3′	0°50·0′W	FM	129
Highfield Fm	Notts	SK8267	53°11·9′	0°45·9′W	FM	121
Highfield Fm	N Yks	SE2095	54°21·3′	1°41·1′W	FM	99
Highfield Fm	N Yks	SE2162	54°3·5′	1°40·3′W	FM	99
Highfield Fm	N Yks	SE2450	53°57·0′	1°37·6′W	FM	104
Highfield Fm	N Yks	SE3484	54°15·3′	1°28·3′W	FM	99
Highfield Fm	N Yks	SE3696	54°21·7′	1°26·3′W	FM	99
Highfield Fm	N Yks	SE4054	53°59·1′	1°23·0′W	FM	105
Highfield Fm	N Yks	SE4675	54°10·4′	1°17·3′W	FM	100
Highfield Fm	N Yks	SE7281	54°13·4′	0°53·3′W	FM	100
Highfield Fm	S Glos	ST7785	51°34·0′	2°19·5′W	FM	172
Highfield Fm	Staffs	SK0739	52°57·1′	1°53·3′W	FM	128
Highfield Fm	Suff	TL7248	52°6·4′	0°31·1′E	FM	154
Highfield Fm	Suff	TM3685	52°24·9′	1°28·6′E	FM	156
Highfield Fm	Surrey	TQ3543	51°10·4′	0°3·7′W	FM	187
Highfield Fm	V of Glam	SS9376	51°28·6′	3°32·1′W	FM	170
Highfield Fm	Warw	SP4270	52°19·8′	1°22·6′W	FM	140
Highfield Fm	Wigan	SJ6196	53°27·8′	2°34·8′W	FM	109
Highfield Fm	Wok	SU7979	51°30·5′	0°51·3′W	FM	175
Highfield Fm	York	SE6145	53°54·1′	1°3·9′W	FM	105
Highfield Hall	Flint	SJ2568	53°12·5′	3°7·0′W	X	117
Highfield Hall	Herts	TL1805	51°44·1′	0°17·1′W	X	166
Highfield Hall	Staffs	SJ9757	53°6·8′	2°2·3′W	X	118
High Field Head Fm	Derby	SK1984	53°21·4′	1°42·5′W	FM	110
Highfield Ho	Bath & NE Somer	ST5762	51°21·6′	2°36·7′W	X	172,182
Highfield Ho	Brad	SE0650	53°57·0′	1°54·1′W	X	104
Highfield Ho	Ches	SJ9265	53°11·2′	2°6·8′W	X	118
Highfield Ho	Cumbr	NY0925	54°37·0′	3°24·1′W	X	89
Highfield Ho	Cumbr	SD3498	54°22·6′	3°0·5′W	X	96,97
Highfield Ho	Derby	SK1476	53°17·1′	1°47·0′W	X	119
Highfield Ho	Derby	SK3725	52°49·5′	1°26·6′W	X	128
Highfield Ho	Glos	SO7708	51°46·4′	2°19·6′W	X	162
Highfield Ho	Hants	SU4254	51°17·2′	1°23·5′W	X	185
Highfield Ho	Hants	SU7260	51°20·3′	0°57·6′W	X	175,186
Highfield Ho	Kirk	SE2414	53°37·6′	1°37·8′W	X	110
Highfield Ho	Leic	SP6384	52°27·3′	1°4·0′W	X	140
Highfield Ho	Lincs	SK9968	53°12·2′	0°30·7′W	X	121
Highfield Ho	Lincs	TA0300	53°29·4′	0°26·4′W	X	112
Highfield Ho	Lincs	TA3103	53°30·7′	0°1·1′W	X	113
Highfield Ho	Lincs	TF0638	52°56·0′	0°25·0′W	X	130
Highfield Ho	Lincs	TF2476	53°16·2′	0°8·0′W	X	122
Highfield Ho	Notts	SK6886	53°22·2′	0°58·3′W	X	111,120
Highfield Ho	Notts	SK7461	53°8·7′	0°53·2′W	X	120
Highfield Ho	Notts	SK7691	53°24·9′	0°51·0′W	X	112
High Field Ho	N Yks	SE1978	54°12·1′	1°42·1′W	X	99
Highfield Ho	N Yks	SE2484	54°15·3′	1°37·5′W	X	99
Highfield Ho	N Yks	SE2664	54°4·5′	1°35·7′W	X	99
Highfield Ho	N Yks	SE5073	54°9·3′	1°13·6′W	X	100
Highfield Ho	N Yks	SE6878	54°11·8′	0°57·0′W	X	100
Highfield Ho	N Yks	SE8069	54°6·9′	0°46·2′W	X	100
Highfield Ho	W Berks	SU4376	51°29·1′	1°22·5′W	X	174
Highfield Ho	Wilts	SU2454	51°17·3′	1°39·0′W	X	184
Highfield Ho Fm	Warw	SP3286	52°28·5′	1°31·3′W	FM	140
High Field House	Lincs	SK9643	52°58·8′	0°33·8′W	X	130
Highfield House Fm	Lincs	TF0056	53°5·7′	0°30·0′W	FM	121
Highfield House Fm	Suff	TM2551	52°6·9′	1°17·6′E	FM	156
Highfieldmoor	Cumbr	NY4561	54°56·7′	2°51·1′W	X	86
Highfield Moss	Wigan	SJ6195	53°27·3′	2°34·8′W	X	109
Highfield Park	Highld	NH5553	57°32·9′	4°24·9′W	X	26
Highfield Plantation	Lincs	TF0399	53°28·9′	0°26·5′W	F	112
Highfields	Arg & Bt	NS3285	56°2·0′	4°41·3′W	X	56
Highfields	Cambs	TL3558	52°12·4′	0°1·1′W	T	154
Highfields	C of Leic	SK6004	52°38·1′	1°6·4′W	T	140
High Fields	Derby	SK2174	53°16·0′	1°40·7′W	X	119
Highfields	Derby	SK4265	53°11·1′	1°21·9′W	T	120
Highfields	Donc	SE5306	53°33·1′	1°11·6′W	T	111
Highfields	Essex	TL8422	51°52·2′	0°40·8′E	X	168
Highfields	Essex	TL8617	51°49·5′	0°42·3′E	T	168
Highfields	E Susx	TQ4938	51°7·5′	0°8·1′E	X	188
Highfields	Glos	ST7697	51°40·5′	2°20·4′W	T	162
Highfields	Lincs	SK9957	53°6·3′	0°30·9′W	X	121
Highfields	Northum	NT9954	55°47·0′	2°0·5′W	T	75
Highfields	Notts	SK5827	52°50·5′	1°7·9′W	X	129
Highfields	N Yks	NZ3909	54°28·7′	1°23·5′W	X	93
High Fields	N Yks	SE8283	54°14·4′	0°44·1′W	X	100
Highfields	Shrops	SJ6740	52°57·6′	2°29·1′W	A	118
High Fields	Shrops	SO5397	52°34·4′	2°41·2′W	X	137,138
Highfields	Staffs	SJ9121	52°47·4′	2°7·6′W	T	127
Highfields	Staffs	SJ9648	53°2·0′	2°3·2′W	X	118
Highfields	Staffs	SK2408	52°40·4′	1°38·3′W	X	128
Highfields	Warw	SP4577	52°23·6′	1°19·9′W	X	140
Highfield Sch	W Susx	SU8530	51°4·0′	0°46·8′W	X	186
Highfields Fm	Ches	SJ6558	53°7·3′	2°31·0′W	FM	118
Highfields Fm	Ches	SJ6741	52°58·2′	2°29·1′W	FM	118
Highfields Fm	Derby	SK2275	53°16·5′	1°39·8′W	FM	119
Highfields Fm	Derby	SK2633	52°53·9′	1°36·4′W	FM	128
Highfields Fm	Derby	SK3132	52°53·3′	1°32·0′W	FM	128
Highfields Fm	E Susx	TQ6030	51°3·0′	0°17·4′E	FM	188
Highfields Fm	E Yorks	SE7919	53°39·9′	0°47·8′W	FM	112
Highfields Fm	Leic	SK4621	52°47·3′	1°18·7′W	FM	129
Highfields Fm	Leic	SK7216	52°44·4′	0°55·6′W	FM	129
Highfields Fm	Lincs	TF1342	52°58·0′	0°18·6′W	FM	130
Highfields Fm	Monm	SO3304	51°44·1′	2°57·8′W	FM	171
Highfields Fm	Red & Cl	NZ7316	54°32·3′	0°51·9′W	FM	94
Highfields Fm	Staffs	SJ9938	52°56·6′	2°0·5′W	FM	127
High-Fields Fm	Staffs	SK0459	53°7·9′	1°56·0′W	FM	119
Highfields Fm	Suff	TL9068	52°16·9′	0°47·5′E	FM	155
Highfields Fm	Worcs	SO7254	52°11·2′	2°24·2′W	FM	149
Highfields Fm	W Susx	TQ2917	50°56·5′	0°9·4′W	FM	198
Highfields Hall	Staffs	SK0732	52°53·4′	1°53·4′W	X	128
Highfields Ho	Northnts	SP5950	52°8·9′	1°7·9′W	X	152
Highfield Stile Fm	Essex	TL7624	51°53·4′	0°33·9′E	FM	167
Highfield Wood	Herts	TL3408	51°45·5′	0°3·1′W	F	166
High Finnich	Stir	NS4983	56°1·2′	4°24·9′W	X	57,64
High Finnock Plantn	Inverc	NS1970	55°53·6′	4°53·2′W	F	63
Highflat Fm	S Lanak	NS6156	55°46·9′	4°12·5′W	FM	64
High Flats	Durham	NZ2652	54°52·0′	1°35·3′W	X	88
High Flatt Fm	Cumbr	NY1237	54°43·5′	3°21·6′W	FM	89
High Flatts	Kirk	SE2107	53°33·8′	1°40·6′W	T	110
High Flust	Cumbr	SD7694	54°20·7′	2°21·7′W	X	98
Highflyer's Fm	Cambs	TL5582	52°25·1′	0°17·2′E	FM	143
High Fm	Cambs	TL2840	52°2·8′	0°7·6′W	FM	153
High Fm	Ches	SJ6759	53°7·9′	2°29·2′W	FM	118
High Fm	Cumbr	SD3082	54°14·0′	3°4·0′W	FM	96,97
High Fm	Cumbr	SD4078	54°11·9′	2°54·8′W	FM	96,97
High Fm	Durham	NY9343	54°47·2′	2°6·1′W	FM	87
High Fm	Durham	NZ1534	54°42·3′	1°45·6′W	FM	92
High Fm	E Yorks	TA0943	53°52·5′	0°20·1′W	FM	107
High Fm	Hartpl	NZ4332	54°41·1′	1°19·6′W	FM	93
High Fm	Leic	SP8199	52°35·2′	0°47·9′W	FM	141
High Fm	Lincs	TF3475	53°15·5′	0°0·9′E	FM	122
High Fm	Norf	TF6831	52°51·2′	0°30·1′E	FM	132
High Fm	Norf	TF9107	52°37·9′	0°49·7′E	FM	144
High Fm	N Tyne	NZ2872	55°2·7′	1°33·3′W	FM	88
High Fm	N Yks	NZ4902	54°24·9′	1°14·3′W	FM	93
High Fm	N Yks	NZ5808	54°28·1′	1°5·9′W	FM	93
High Fm	N Yks	SE4272	54°8·8′	1°21·0′W	FM	99
High Fm	N Yks	SE4358	54°1·2′	1°20·2′W	FM	105
High Fm	N Yks	SE5973	54°9·2′	1°5·4′W	FM	100
High Fm	N Yks	SE6389	54°17·8′	1°1·5′W	FM	94,100
High Fm	N Yks	SE7593	54°19·9′	0°50·4′W	FM	94,100
High Fm	N Yks	SE7760	54°2·1′	0°49·0′W	FM	100
High Fm	N Yks	SE7769	54°6·9′	0°48·9′W	FM	100
High Fm	Peterb	TF0902	52°36·5′	0°23·0′W	FM	142
High Fm	Staffs	SK0637	52°56·1′	1°54·2′W	FM	128
High Fm	Stock on T	NZ4812	54°30·3′	1°15·1′W	FM	93
High Fm,The	Cumbr	SD4390	54°18·4′	2°52·1′W	FM	97
High Fm, The	Lancs	SD5673	54°9·3′	2°40·0′W	FM	97
High Fog Close	Cumbr	NY5740	54°45·4′	2°39·7′W	X	86
Highfold Fm	Glos	SO8510	51°47·5′	2°12·7′W	FM	162
High Force	Cumbr	NY4020	54°34·5′	2°55·3′W	W	90
High Force	Durham	NY8828	54°39·1′	2°10·7′W	W	91,92
High Force	N Yks	SD9387	54°17·0′	2°6·0′W	X	98
Highford	Northum	NY9163	54°57·9′	2°8·0′W	X	87
Highford Beck	Cumbr	SD1897	54°22·0′	3°15·3′W	W	96
Highford Fm	Devon	SS2923	50°59·1′	4°25·8′W	FM	190
High Fordon Fm	E Yorks	TA0375	54°9·9′	0°24·9′W	FM	101
High Forest	Staffs	SJ9865	53°11·2′	2°1·4′W	X	118
High Forge	Durham	NZ2254	54°53·1′	1°39·0′W	T	88
High Fosham	E Yorks	TA2039	53°50·2′	0°10·2′W	X	107
High Fotherley	Northum	NZ0257	54°54·7′	1°57·7′W	X	87
High Foulshaw	Cumbr	SD4683	54°14·6′	2°49·3′W	X	97
High Foxton	N Yks	NZ4608	54°28·2′	1°17·0′W	X	93
High Friarside	Durham	NZ1656	54°54·2′	1°44·6′W	T	88
High Frith	Cumbr	SD3380	54°12·9′	3°1·2′W	X	96,97
High Frith	N Yks	NY8903	54°25·6′	2°9·8′W	X	91,92
Highfure	W Susx	TQ0922	50°59·4′	0°26·4′W	X	198
High Furze	Warw	SP2437	52°2·1′	1°38·6′W	X	151
High Gale	Lancs	SD6376	54°11·0′	2°33·6′W	X	97
High Gallowberry	E Ayr	NS4248	55°42·2′	4°31·1′W	X	64
High Gallowhill	E Dunb	NS6472	55°55·6′	4°10·2′W	T	64
High Gameshill	E Ayr	NS4148	55°42·2′	4°31·4′W	X	64
High Gardham	E Yorks	SE9440	53°51·1′	0°33·8′W	X	106
High Garford	Durham	NZ0420	54°34·8′	1°55·9′W	X	92
High Garleffan	E Ayr	NS6217	55°25·9′	4°10·4′W	X	71
High Garnshaw Ho	N Yks	SE0164	54°4·6′	1°58·7′W	X	98
High Garphar	S Ayr	NS3505	55°18·9′	4°35·6′W	X	70,77
High Garrett	Essex	TL7726	51°54·5′	0°34·8′E	T	167
High Garth	E Yorks	SE8337	53°49·6′	0°43·9′W	X	106
Highgate	Barns	SE4503	53°31·5′	1°18·9′W	T	111
Highgate	Birm	SP0785	52°28·0′	1°53·4′W	T	139
High Gate	Cald	SD9628	53°45·1′	2°3·2′W	X	103
Highgate	Camden	TQ2887	51°34·3′	0°8·8′W	T	176
Highgate	Carm	SN3332	51°57·9′	4°25·5′W	X	145
Highgate	Corn	SX1555	50°22·2′	4°35·7′W	X	201
Highgate	Denb	SJ0946	53°0·5′	3°21·0′W	X	116
Highgate	D & G	NY3375	55°4·1′	3°2·5′W	X	85
Highgate	E Susx	TQ4234	51°5·5′	0°2·1′E	T	187
Highgate	E Yorks	SE8237	53°49·6′	0°44·8′W	X	106
Highgate	Kent	TQ7630	51°2·8′	0°31·0′E	T	188
Highgate	Lincs	TF1139	52°56·4′	0°20·5′W	X	130
High Gate	Lincs	TF4686	53°21·3′	0°12·0′E	X	113,122
Highgate	N Ayr	NS3952	55°44·3′	4°33·4′W	X	63
Highgate	N Yks	SE5918	53°39·5′	1°6·0′W	X	111
Highgate	Pemb	SN0610	51°45·5′	4°48·3′W	X	158
Highgate	Powys	SO1195	52°33·0′	3°18·4′W	T	136
Highgate	Staffs	SJ9658	53°7·4′	2°3·2′W	X	118
Highgate Cemy	Camden	TQ2887	51°34·3′	0°8·8′W	X	176
Highgateclose	Cumbr	NY3525	54°37·2′	3°0·0′W	X	90
Highgate Country Park	Staffs	SO8389	52°30·2′	2°14·6′W	X	138
Highgate Fm	Cumbr	NY4427	54°38·3′	2°51·6′W	FM	90
Highgate Fm	Cumbr	NY6022	54°35·7′	2°36·7′W	FM	91
Highgate Fm	E Susx	TQ5530	51°3·1′	0°13·1′E	FM	188
Highgate Fm	Glos	SO9512	51°48·6′	2°4·0′W	FM	163
Highgate Fm	Leic	SK6115	52°44·0′	1°5·4′W	FM	129
Highgate Fm	N Yks	SD9554	53°59·2′	2°4·2′W	FM	103
Highgate Fm	Staffs	SO8390	52°30·7′	2°14·6′W	FM	138
Highgate Fm	Wilts	SU0484	51°33·5′	1°56·1′W	FM	173
Highgate Hall	E Yorks	TA0053	53°58·0′	0°28·1′W	X	106,107
Highgate Head	Derby	SK0486	53°22·5′	1°56·0′W	X	110
Highgate Hill	Powys	SO0995	52°33·0′	3°20·1′W	H	136
Highgate Hill	Powys	SO2059	52°13·6′	3°9·9′W	H	148
Highgate Ho	Northnts	SP7071	52°20·2′	0°58·0′W	X	141
Highgate Howe	N Yks	NZ9110	54°28·9′	0°35·3′W	X	94
Highgate Lodge Fm	Leic	SP4794	52°32·7′	1°18·0′W	FM	140
Highgate Ponds	Camden	TQ2786	51°33·7′	0°9·7′W	W	176
High Gaterley	N Yks	SE7369	54°6·9′	0°52·6′W	X	100
Highgates	Essex	TL6332	51°58·0′	0°22·8′E	X	167
High Gateside Fm	Cumbr	SD3781	54°13·5′	2°57·6′W	FM	96,97
Highgate Wood	Hargy	TQ2888	51°34·8′	0°8·8′W	F	176
High Gatherley	N Yks	NZ2201	54°24·5′	1°39·2′W	X	93
High Gayle	N Yks	SD7881	54°13·7′	2°19·8′W	X	98
High Genoch	S Ayr	NS3800	55°16·3′	4°32·6′W	X	77
High Gill	N Yks	SD9888	54°17·5′	2°1·4′W	X	98
High Gill Beck	N Yks	NZ7502	54°24·7′	0°50·2′W	X	94
High Gillbrea	Cumbr	NY1526	54°37·6′	3°18·6′W	X	89
High Gillespie	D & G	NX2552	54°50·2′	4°43·1′W	X	82
High Gill Moor	N Yks	SE2364	54°4·5′	1°38·5′W	X	99
High Gingerfield Lodge	N Yks	NZ1502	54°25·0′	1°45·7′W	X	92
High Girsby Grange	N Yks	NZ3607	54°27·7′	1°26·3′W	X	93
High Glasnick	D & G	NX3562	54°55·8′	4°34·1′W	X	83
High Glenadale	Arg & Bt	NR6211	55°20·4′	5°44·8′W	X	68
High Glencoy	N Ayr	NS0035	55°34·3′	5°9·9′W	X	69
High Glencroe	Arg & Bt	NN2306	56°13·1′	4°50·8′W	X	56
High Glenling	D & G	NX3151	54°49·8′	4°37·4′W	X	82
High Glenmuir	E Ayr	NS6220	55°27·5′	4°10·5′W	X	71
High Glenramskill	Arg & Bt	NR7318	55°24·5′	5°34·7′W	X	68
High Glentriplock	D & G	NX3546	54°47·2′	4°33·5′W	X	83
High Gooseloan	N Ayr	NS3246	55°41·0′	4°39·9′W	X	63
High Goosepool Fm	Darl	NZ3614	54°31·4′	1°26·2′W	FM	93
High Gordon	Durham	NZ1326	54°38·0′	1°47·5′W	X	92
High Gosforth Park	N upon Ty	NZ2470	55°1·7′	1°37·0′W	X	88
High Grain	N Yks	SD7463	54°4·0′	2°23·4′W	X	98
High Grains	Cumbr	NY5875	55°4·3′	2°39·0′W	X	86
Highgrains Waste	Cumbr	NY6076	55°4·9′	2°37·2′W	X	86
High Grange	Durham	NZ1731	54°40·7′	1°43·8′W	T	92
High Grange	Durham	NZ2939	54°45·0′	1°32·5′W	X	93
High Grange	N Yks	NZ1708	54°28·3′	1°43·8′W	X	92
High Grange	N Yks	SE2986	54°16·4′	1°32·9′W	X	99
High Grange	N Yks	SE4193	54°20·1′	1°21·7′W	X	99
High Grange	N Yks	SE7484	54°15·0′	0°51·4′W	X	100
High Grange	S Ayr	NS3012	55°22·6′	4°40·6′W	X	70
High Grange	York	SE6060	54°2·2′	1°4·6′W	X	100
High Grantley	N Yks	SE2369	54°7·2′	1°38·5′W	T	99
High Greave	Cald	SD9932	53°47·3′	2°0·5′W	X	103
High Greave	Sheff	SK2981	53°19·7′	1°33·5′W	X	110
High Greaves	Cumbr	SD2678	54°11·8′	3°7·6′W	X	96,97
High Greenbury	N Yks	NZ2602	54°25·0′	1°35·5′W	X	93
High Green	Cumbr	NY4103	54°25·4′	2°54·1′W	T	90
High Green	Cumbr	NY6017	54°33·0′	2°36·7′W	X	91
High Green	Cumbr	SD6286	54°16·3′	2°34·6′W	X	97
High Green	Kirk	SE1914	53°37·6′	1°42·4′W	T	110
High Green	Norf	TF9214	52°41·6′	0°50·9′E	T	132
High Green	Norf	TF9307	52°37·8′	0°51·5′E	T	144
High Green	Norf	TG1305	52°36·3′	1°9·1′E	T	144
High Green	N Yks	NZ0002	54°25·1′	1°59·6′W	X	92
High Green	Sheff	SK3397	53°28·4′	1°29·8′W	T	110,111
High Green	Shrops	SO7083	52°26·9′	2°26·1′W	T	138
High Green	Suff	TL8560	52°12·7′	0°42·9′E	T	155
High Green	Worcs	SO8745	52°6·4′	2°11·0′W	T	150
High Greenan	S Ayr	NS3118	55°25·9′	4°39·8′W	X	70
High Greenbank Fm	E Ayr	NS5737	55°36·6′	4°15·8′W	FM	71
High Greenfield	Durham	NY8541	54°46·1′	2°13·6′W	X	87
High Green Field	N Yks	SD8279	54°12·6′	2°16·1′W	X	98
High Green Field Knott	N Yks	SD8478	54°12·1′	2°14·3′W	H	98
High Green Fm	Suff	TM0076	52°21·0′	0°56·6′E	FM	144
High Green Hill	Cumbr	NY5269	55°1·0′	2°44·6′W	X	86
Highgreen Manor	Northum	NY8091	55°13·0′	2°18·4′W	X	80
High Greenrigg	Cumbr	SD7499	54°23·4′	2°23·6′W	X	98
High Greenrigg Ho	Cumbr	NY2837	54°43·6′	3°6·7′W	X	89,90
High Greenwood Fm	Cald	SD9630	53°46·2′	2°3·2′W	FM	103
High Grindon	Durham	NZ3224	54°36·9′	1°29·8′W	X	93
Highground	Cumbr	NY5527	54°38·4′	2°41·4′W	X	90
High Ground	Cumbr	SD1798	54°22·5′	3°16·2′W	X	96
High Ground	Cumbr	SD2895	54°21·0′	3°6·0′W	X	96,97
High Ground	N Yks	SD8755	53°59·7′	2°11·5′W	X	103
High Grounds	Derby	SK1442	52°58·7′	1°47·1′W	X	119,128
High Grounds Fm	Derby	SK1837	52°56·0′	1°43·5′W	FM	128
Highgrove	Ches	SJ8077	53°17·6′	2°17·6′W	X	118
Highgrove	Devon	SX7471	50°31·7′	3°46·3′W	X	202
High Grove	Essex	TM1417	51°48·9′	1°6·7′E	F	168,169
High Grove	Norf	TF9207	52°37·8′	0°50·6′E	F	144
High Grove	Norf	TM3994	52°29·7′	1°31·7′E	F	134
Highgrove	Powys	SO0927	51°56·3′	3°19·0′W	X	161
High Grove	Suff	TM3362	52°12·6′	1°25·0′E	F	156
High Grove Fm	Dorset	ST8123	51°0·6′	2°15·9′W	FM	183
Highgrove Fm	Glos	SO5703	51°43·7′	2°37·0′W	FM	162
Highgrove Fm	Staffs	SO8582	52°26·4′	2°12·8′W	FM	139
Highgrove Fm	Worcs	SO9550	52°9·1′	2°4·0′W	FM	150
Highgrove Ho	Glos	ST8791	51°37·3′	2°10·9′W	X	162,173
Highgrove House (Hotel)	S Ayr	NS3432	55°33·5′	4°37·5′W	X	70
High Grundon Fm	N Yks	SE8380	54°12·8′	0°43·2′W	FM	100
High Haden Fm	Cambs	TL1486	52°27·8′	0°18·9′W	FM	142
High Halden	Kent	TQ8937	51°6·3′	0°42·4′E	T	189
High Hall	Corn	SX2385	50°38·5′	4°29·8′W	X	201
High Hall	Cumbr	NY2743	54°46·8′	3°7·7′W	X	85
High Hall	Cumbr	SD7087	54°16·9′	2°27·2′W	X	98
High Hall	Dorset	SU0002	50°49·3′	1°59·6′W	X	195
High Hall	Essex	TL9113	51°47·2′	0°46·6′E	X	168
High Hall	E Yorks	SE9843	53°52·7′	0°30·1′W	X	106
High Hall	N Yks	SD7995	54°21·3′	2°19·0′W	X	98
High Hall	N Yks	SD9390	54°18·6′	2°6·0′W	X	98
High Hall	Staffs	SJ8111	52°42·0′	2°16·5′W	X	127

High Hall	Suff	TM0271	52°18·2′	0°58·2′E	X	144,155
High Hall	Suff	TM0850	52°6·8′	1°2·7′E	X	155
High Halstead	Lancs	SD8833	53°47·8′	2°10·5′W	X	103
High Halstow	Medway	TQ7875	51°27·0′	0°34·1′E	T	178
High Ham	Somer	ST4231	51°4·8′	2°49·3′W	T	182
Highhams	Essex	TL5914	51°48·3′	0°18·8′E	X	167
High Handenhold	Durham	NZ2353	54°52·5′	1°38·1′W	T	88
High Hangers	N Yks	SD9596	54°21·8′	2°4·2′W	X	98
High Harker Hill	N Yks	SE0297	54°22·4′	1°57·7′W	X	98
High Harrington	Cumbr	NY0025	54°36·9′	3°32·5′W	T	89
High Harrogate	N Yks	SE3155	53°59·6′	1°31·2′W	T	104
High Hartsop Dodd	Cumbr	NY3910	54°29·1′	2°56·1′W	H	90
High Haswell	Durham	NZ3643	54°47·1′	1°26·0′W	T	88
High Hatfield	Notts	SK5771	53°14·2′	1°8·3′W	X	120
High Hatton	Shrops	SJ6124	52°49·0′	2°34·3′W	T	127
High Haume Fm	Cumbr	SD2275	54°10·1′	3°11·3′W	FM	96
High Hauxley	Northum	NU2703	55°19·5′	1°34·0′W	T	81
High Havens Farm	Oxon	SP3932	51°59·3′	1°25·5′W	FM	151
High Hawkhope	Northum	NY7188	55°11·4′	2°26·9′W	X	80
High Haw Leas	N Yks	SE2579	54°12·6′	1°36·6′W	X	99
High Hawsker	N Yks	NZ9207	54°27·2′	0°34·4′W	T	94
High Hay Bridge	Cumbr	SD3387	54°16·7′	3°1·3′W	X	96,97
High Hayden Fm	Northnts	SP9767	52°17·8′	0°34·3′W	FM	153
High Head	Lancs	SD7655	53°59·7′	2°21·5′W	X	103
High Head Castle	Cumbr	NY4043	54°46·9′	2°55·6′W	X	85
High Head Fm	Cumbr	NY4043	54°46·9′	2°55·6′W	FM	85
High Heads	Cumbr	SD4687	54°16·8′	2°49·3′W	X	97
High Heath	Birm	SP1497	52°34·5′	1°47·2′W	X	139
High Heath	Shrops	SJ6827	52°50·6′	2°28·1′W	T	127
High Heath	Wals	SK0302	52°37·2′	1°56·9′W	T	139
High Heath Fm	Herts	TL2018	51°51·1′	0°15·1′W	FM	166
High Heavens Wood	Bucks	SU8389	51°35·9′	0°47·7′W	F	175
High Hedley Hope	Durham	NZ1440	54°45·5′	1°46·5′W	X	88
High Hermitage	Durham	NZ0942	54°46·6′	1°51·2′W	X	88
High Heron Rock	S Glos	ST5994	51°38·8′	2°35·2′W	X	162,172
High Hesket	Cumbr	NY4744	54°47·5′	2°49·0′W	T	86
High Hesleden	Durham	NZ4538	54°44·3′	1°17·6′W	T	93
High Highlaws	Northum	NZ1789	55°11·9′	1°43·5′W	X	81
High Hill	Bri & Hov	TQ3704	50°49·4′	0°2·9′W	X	198
High Hill	Cumbr	NY2523	54°36·0′	3°9·2′W	T	89,90
High Hill	Norf	TG3527	52°47·6′	1°29·5′E	X	133,134
High Hill	Northum	NU1628	55°33·0′	1°44·4′W	X	75
High Hill	N Yks	SE1670	54°7·8′	1°44·9′W	X	99
High Hill	Worcs	SP0376	52°23·2′	1°57·0′W	X	139
Highhill Cott	E Renf	NS5750	55°43·6′	4°16·2′W	X	64
High Hill Ho	Durham	NZ2732	54°41·2′	1°34·4′W	X	93
High Hills	Norf	TF8537	52°54·1′	0°45·5′E	X	132
High Ho	Brad	SE0748	53°55·9′	1°53·2′W	X	104
High Ho	Ches	SJ6872	53°14·9′	2°28·4′W	X	118
High Ho	Cumbr	NX9514	54°30·9′	3°36·9′W	X	89
High Ho	Cumbr	NX9712	54°29·8′	3°35·0′W	X	89
High Ho	Cumbr	NY0524	54°36·4′	3°27·8′W	X	89
High Ho	Cumbr	NY1951	54°51·1′	3°15·3′W	X	85
High Ho	Cumbr	NY4300	54°23·8′	2°52·3′W	X	90
High Ho	Cumbr	NY4700	54°23·8′	2°48·6′W	X	90
High Ho	Cumbr	NY5001	54°24·4′	2°45·8′W	X	90
High Ho	Cumbr	NY6065	54°58·9′	2°37·1′W	X	86
High Ho	Cumbr	SD4494	54°20·6′	2°51·3′W	X	97
High Ho	Cumbr	SD4989	54°17·9′	2°46·6′W	X	97
High Ho	Cumbr	SD5387	54°16·8′	2°42·9′W	X	97
High Ho	Cumbr	SD6195	54°21·2′	2°35·6′W	X	97
High Ho	Cumbr	SD6986	54°16·4′	2°28·1′W	X	98
High Ho	Darl	NZ3022	54°35·8′	1°31·7′W	X	93
High Ho	Devon	SX7443	50°16·6′	3°45·7′W	X	202
High Ho	Durham	NY9548	54°49·9′	2°4·2′W	X	87
High Ho	Durham	NY9741	54°46·1′	2°2·4′W	X	87
High Ho	Durham	NZ0320	54°34·8′	1°56·8′W	X	92
High Ho	Durham	NZ0820	54°34·8′	1°52·2′W	X	92
High Ho	Durham	NZ1226	54°38·0′	1°48·4′W	X	92
High Ho	Essex	TL5523	51°53·3′	0°15·5′E	X	167
High Ho	Essex	TQ7795	51°37·8′	0°33·8′E	X	167
High Ho	Essex	TQ9188	51°33·7′	0°45·7′E	X	178
High Ho	Heref	SO6864	52°16·6′	2°27·7′W	X	138,149
High Ho	Lancs	SD5976	54°10·9′	2°37·3′W	X	97
High Ho	Lancs	SD6338	53°50·5′	2°33·3′W	X	102,103
High Ho	Lancs	SD7935	53°48·9′	2°18·7′W	X	103
High Ho	Lincs	TF0485	53°21·3′	0°25·8′W	X	112,121
High Ho	Lincs	TF2476	53°16·2′	0°8·0′W	X	122
High Ho	Norf	TF7918	52°44·0′	0°39·5′E	X	132
High Ho	Norf	TF8521	52°45·5′	0°44·9′E	X	132
High Ho	Norf	TF9310	52°39·4′	0°51·6′E	X	132
High Ho	Norf	TF9810	52°39·3′	0°56·1′E	X	132
High Ho	Norf	TG0307	52°37·6′	1°0·4′E	X	144
High Ho	Norf	TM0781	52°23·5′	1°2·9′E	X	144
High Ho	Northum	NY8566	54°59·5′	2°13·6′W	X	87
High Ho	Northum	NZ0569	55°1·2′	1°54·9′W	X	87
High Ho	Northum	NZ1174	55°3·9′	1°49·2′W	X	88
High Ho	Notts	SK7886	53°22·1′	0°49·3′W	FM	112,120,121
High Ho	N Yks	NZ6403	54°25·3′	1°0·4′W	X	94
High Ho	N Yks	SE5299	54°23·3′	1°11·5′W	X	100
High Ho	Suff	TM2154	52°8·6′	1°14·2′E	X	156
High Ho	Thurr	TQ6579	51°29·4′	0°23·0′E	X	177,178
High Hockley Fm	Kent	TQ9733	51°4·0′	0°49·1′E	FM	189
High Hoes	W Susx	SU9919	50°57·9′	0°35·0′W	X	197
High Hogg Hill	Scot Bord	NT0419	55°27·6′	3°30·7′W	H	78
High Holborn	Heref	SO2650	52°8·8′	3°4·5′W	X	148
High Holborn	Notts	SK6626	52°49·9′	1°0·8′W	X	129
High Holborn	Shrops	SJ8205	52°38·8′	2°15·6′W	X	127
High Holborn Fm	Bucks	SP8208	51°46·1′	0°48·3′W	FM	165
High Holborn Fm	Cambs	TL2681	52°25·0′	0°8·4′W	FM	142
High Holborn Fm	Northnts	TL1286	52°27·9′	0°20·7′W	FM	142
High Holborn Hill	Cambs	TL1682	52°25·7′	0°17·2′W	X	142
High Hollows	Cumbr	NY3524	54°36·7′	3°0·0′W	X	90
Highholm	Fife	NT1190	56°5·9′	3°25·4′W	X	58
High Holme Ho	N Yks	SE1369	54°7·2′	1°47·6′W	X	99
High Holms	Northum	NY9257	54°54·7′	2°7·1′W	X	87
High Hook	S Lanak	NS6745	55°41·1′	4°6·5′W	X	64
High Hope	Heref	SO6721	51°53·4′	2°28·4′W	X	162
High Hos	Northum	NU0309	55°22·7′	1°56·7′W	X	81
High Houghall	Durham	NZ2739	54°45·0′	1°34·4′W	X	93
High House	Cumbr	NY5304	54°26·0′	2°43·1′W	X	90
High House	Durham	NY8438	54°44·4′	2°14·5′W	X	91,92
High House	Essex	TQ9398	51°39·1′	0°47·8′E	X	168
High House	E Yorks	TA0636	53°48·8′	0°23·0′W	X	107
High House	Monm	SO4012	51°48·4′	2°51·8′W	X	161
High House	N Yks	NZ2412	54°30·4′	1°37·3′W	X	93
High House	S Lanak	NT0742	55°40·0′	3°28·3′W	A	72
High House Bank	Cumbr	NY5404	54°26·0′	2°42·1′W	H	90
High House Fell	Cumbr	NY5106	54°27·1′	2°44·9′W	H	90
High House Fm	Brom	TQ4061	51°20·1′	0°1·0′E	FM	177,187
High House Fm	Cumbr	NY0121	54°34·7′	3°31·5′W	FM	89
High House Fm	Cumbr	NY0410	54°28·8′	3°28·5′W	FM	89
High House Fm	Cumbr	NY0701	54°24·0′	3°25·5′W	FM	89
High House Fm	Cumbr	NY4444	54°47·5′	2°51·8′W	FM	85
High House Fm	Cumbr	SD4193	54°20·0′	2°54·0′W	FM	96,97
High House Fm	Derby	SK4367	53°12·1′	1°21·0′W	FM	120
High House Fm	Durham	NZ1040	54°45·5′	1°50·3′W	FM	88
High House Fm	Essex	TL9702	51°41·2′	0°51·4′E	FM	168
High House Fm	Essex	TQ5095	51°38·3′	0°10·5′E	FM	167,177
High House Fm	E Susx	TQ4118	50°56·9′	0°0·8′E	FM	198
High House Fm	Kent	TQ9129	51°1·9′	0°43·8′E	FM	189
High House Fm	Lancs	SD5342	53°52·6′	2°42·5′W	FM	102
High House Fm	Lancs	SD7635	53°48·9′	2°21·5′W	FM	103
High House Fm	Norf	TF7837	52°54·3′	0°39·2′E	FM	132
High House Fm	Norf	TF8719	52°44·4′	0°46·6′E	FM	132
High House Fm	Norf	TF8920	52°44·9′	0°48·4′E	FM	132
High House Fm	Norf	TF9717	52°43·1′	0°55·4′E	FM	132
High House Fm	Norf	TG0021	52°45·2′	0°58·2′E	FM	133
High House Fm	Norf	TG1307	52°37·4′	1°9·2′E	FM	144
High House Fm	Norf	TM1499	52°33·0′	1°9·8′E	FM	144
High House Fm	Norf	TM3998	52°31·9′	1°31·8′E	FM	134
High House Fm	N Yks	SE1280	54°13·2′	1°48·5′W	FM	99
High House Fm	N Yks	SE1361	54°2·9′	1°47·7′W	FM	99
High House Fm	N Yks	SE4878	54°12·0′	1°15·4′W	FM	100
High House Fm	N Yks	SE5284	54°15·2′	1°11·7′W	FM	100
High House Fm	N Yks	SE6997	54°22·1′	0°55·9′W	FM	94,100
High House Fm	N Yks	SE8591	54°18·7′	0°41·2′W	FM	94,100
High House Fm	Shrops	SJ8303	52°37·7′	2°14·7′W	FM	127
High House Fm	S Tyne	NZ3161	54°56·8′	1°30·5′W	FM	88
High House Fm	Suff	TL9550	52°7·1′	0°51·3′E	FM	155
High House Fm	Suff	TM1450	52°6·6′	1°7·9′E	FM	156
High House Fm	Suff	TM2653	52°8·0′	1°18·5′E	FM	156
High House Fm	Suff	TM2960	52°11·7′	1°21·4′E	FM	156
High House Fm	Suff	TM3253	52°7·8′	1°23·8′E	FM	156
High House Fm	Suff	TM3264	52°13·7′	1°24·2′E	FM	156
High House Fm	Suff	TM3268	52°15·9′	1°24·4′E	FM	156
High House Fm	Suff	TM3273	52°18·6′	1°24·6′E	FM	156
High House Fm	Suff	TM3439	52°0·2′	1°25·0′E	FM	169
High House Fm	Suff	TM3470	52°16·9′	1°26·2′E	FM	156
High House Fm	Suff	TM3662	52°12·6′	1°27·7′E	FM	156
High House Fm	Suff	TM3780	52°22·2′	1°29·3′E	FM	156
High House Fm	Suff	TM4352	52°7·0′	1°33·4′E	FM	156
High House Fm	Wakf	SE3013	53°37·0′	1°32·4′W	FM	110,111
High House Fm	Warw	SP2587	52°29·1′	1°37·5′W	FM	140
High House Fm	Warw	SP2987	52°29·0′	1°34·0′W	FM	140
High House Fm	Warw	SP4864	52°16·6′	1°17·4′W	FM	151
High House Fm	Wilts	ST8145	51°12·5′	2°15·9′W	FM	183
High House Fm	Worcs	SO9968	52°18·8′	2°0·5′W	FM	139
High House Fm	Worcs	SP0969	52°19·4′	1°51·7′W	FM	139
High Houses	Cumbr	NY2137	54°43·6′	3°13·2′W	X	89,90
High Houses	Essex	TL6813	51°47·6′	0°26·6′E	T	167
High Houses	N Yks	SD8387	54°16·9′	2°15·2′W	X	98
High House Tarn	Cumbr	NY2409	54°28·5′	3°9·9′W	W	89,90
High-house Waste	Devon	SX6162	50°26·7′	3°57·1′W	X	202
High Hoyland	Barns	SE2710	53°35·4′	1°35·1′W	T	110
High Hundybridge	Cumbr	NY7342	54°46·6′	2°24·8′W	X	86,87
High Hunsley	E Yorks	SE9535	53°48·4′	0°33·0′W	T	106
High Hunsley Circuit	E Yorks	SE9731	53°46·2′	0°31·3′W	X	106
High Hunsley Circuit	E Yorks	TA0034	53°47·8′	0°28·5′W	X	106,107
High Huntow Fm	E Yorks	TA1572	54°8·1′	0°14·0′W	FM	101
High Hurst	Cumbr	SD2094	54°20·4′	3°13·4′W	X	96
High Hurst	Durham	NY8526	54°38·0′	2°13·5′W	X	91,92
High Hurstwood	E Susx	TQ4926	51°1·1′	0°7·9′E	T	188,199
High Hutton	N Yks	SE7568	54°6·4′	0°50·8′W	T	100
High Ingram Grange	N Yks	NZ3903	54°25·5′	1°23·5′W	X	93
High Inhams	N Yks	SE5965	54°4·9′	1°5·5′W	X	100
High Intack	Cumbr	NY2737	54°43·6′	3°7·6′W	X	89,90
High Intake	N Yks	SE2173	54°9·4′	1°40·3′W	X	99
High Ireby	Cumbr	NY2237	54°43·6′	3°12·2′W	T	89,90
High Jervaulx	N Yks	SE1784	54°15·3′	1°43·9′W	X	99
High Jofless	Durham	NZ0540	54°45·5′	1°54·9′W	X	87
High Kays Lea	Durham	NZ0828	54°39·1′	1°52·1′W	X	92
High Keil	Arg & Bt	NR6708	55°18·9′	5°39·9′W	X	68
High Keillor	Pth & Kin	NO2739	56°32·5′	3°10·8′W	X	53
High Kelling	Norf	TG1040	52°55·2′	1°7·8′E	T	133
Highkettle Fm	W Susx	SU9003	50°49·4′	0°42·9′W	FM	197
High Kilburn	N Yks	SE5179	54°12·5′	1°12·7′W	T	100
High Kildonan	D & G	NX1236	54°41·3′	4°54·6′W	X	82
High Killerby	N Yks	TA0683	54°14·1′	0°22·0′W	X	101
High Kiln Bank Fm	Cumbr	SD2194	54°20·4′	3°12·5′W	FM	96
High Kilphin	S Ayr	NX1080	55°4·9′	4°58·2′W	X	76
High Kilroy	D & G	NX9183	55°8·0′	3°42·2′W	X	78
High Kingthorpe	N Yks	SE8486	54°16·0′	0°42·2′W	X	94,100
High Kisdon	N Yks	SD9198	54°22·9′	2°7·9′W	X	98
High Kitty Crag	Durham	NY9038	54°44·5′	2°8·9′W	X	91,92
High Knells	Cumbr	NY4161	54°56·7′	2°54·8′W	X	85
High Knipe	Cumbr	NY5219	54°34·1′	2°44·1′W	X	90
Highknock Channel	Kent	TQ9426	51°0·3′	0°46·3′E	W	189
High Knockrioch	Arg & Bt	NR7019	55°24·9′	5°37·6′W	X	68
High Knott	Cumbr	NY2512	54°30·1′	3°9·1′W	H	89,90
High Knoweglass Fm	S Lanak	NS6449	55°43·2′	4°9·5′W	FM	64
High Knowes	Northum	NT9612	55°24·4′	2°3·4′W	H	81
High Knowes	S Lanak	NS9707	55°21·0′	3°37·0′W	X	78
High Knowle	N Yks	SE1878	54°12·1′	1°43·0′W	X	99
High Knypes	D & G	NS7316	55°25·5′	4°0·0′W	H	71
High Kop	Cumbr	NY4515	54°31·9′	2°50·6′W	H	90
High Lad Ridge	Sheff	SK2386	53°22·5′	1°38·8′W	X	110
High Laithe	Lancs	SD6555	53°59·6′	2°31·6′W	X	102,103
Highland	D & G	NX9196	55°15·0′	3°42·5′W	X	78
Highland	Heref	SO3361	52°14·8′	2°58·5′W	X	137,148,149
Highland	Powys	SJ1823	52°48·1′	3°12·6′W	X	125
Highland Boath	Highld	NH8844	57°28·6′	3°51·6′W	T	27
Highland Court Fm	Kent	TR1953	51°14·3′	1°8·6′E	FM	179,189
Highlander, The	I of M	SC3180	54°11·5′	4°35·0′W	X	95
Highland Fm	Durham	NZ3332	54°41·2′	1°28·9′W	FM	93
Highland Lodge	Glos	SP1432	51°59·4′	1°47·4′W	X	151
Highlandman's Rig	D & G	NX3383	55°7·1′	4°36·7′W	X	76
Highlandman's Wood	Arg & Bt	NS2884	56°1·3′	4°45·1′W	F	56
High Land of Orcombe	Devon	SY0279	50°36·4′	3°22·7′W	X	192
Highlands	Aberd	NJ8717	57°14·9′	2°12·5′W	X	38
Highlands	Angus	NO5745	56°36·0′	2°41·6′W	X	54
Highlands	Bath & NE Somer	ST5260	51°20·5′	2°41·0′W	X	172,182
Highlands	Beds	TL1137	52°1·4′	0°22·5′W	X	153
Highlands	Dorset	SY4591	50°43·2′	2°46·4′W	T	193
Highlands	Dorset	SY6998	50°47·1′	2°26·0′W	X	194
High Lands	Durham	NZ1225	54°37·4′	1°48·4′W	X	92
Highlands	Essex	TL4830	51°57·2′	0°9·6′E	X	167
Highlands	Essex	TL9301	51°40·7′	0°47·9′E	X	168
Highlands	E Susx	TQ4921	50°58·4′	0°7·7′E	X	199
Highlands	Kent	TQ6357	51°17·6′	0°20·7′E	X	188
High Lands	Peterb	TF2803	52°36·8′	0°6·2′W	X	142
Highlands	Suff	TM0834	51°58·2′	1°2·1′E	X	155,169
Highlands	Wok	SU7066	51°23·6′	0°59·2′W	X	175
Highlands	W Susx	TQ2623	50°59·8′	0°11·9′W	X	198
Highlands Dairy Fm	Somer	ST4108	50°52·3′	2°49·9′W	FM	193
Highlands Fm	Beds	TL1346	52°6·3′	0°20·6′W	FM	153
Highlands Fm	Devon	SS5842	51°9·8′	4°1·5′W	FM	180
Highlands Fm	Essex	TQ7699	51°40·0′	0°33·1′E	FM	167
Highlands Fm	E Susx	TQ5314	50°54·5′	0°11·0′E	FM	199
Highlands Fm	E Susx	TQ5708	50°51·2′	0°14·2′E	FM	199
Highlands Fm	Kent	TQ5269	51°24·2′	0°11·5′E	FM	177
Highlands Fm	Kent	TQ9534	51°4·6′	0°47·4′E	FM	189
Highlands Fm	Oxon	SU5791	51°37·1′	1°10·2′W	FM	164,174
Highlands Fm	Oxon	SU7481	51°31·6′	0°55·6′W	FM	175
Highlands Fm	Shrops	SJ5500	52°36·0′	2°39·5′W	FM	126
Highlands Fm	Suff	TL9648	52°6·0′	0°52·1′E	FM	155
Highlands Fm	Suff	TM4788	52°26·3′	1°38·5′E	FM	156
Highlands Fm	Surrey	TQ1855	51°17·1′	0°18·1′W	FM	187
Highlandshiels Burn	Scot Bord	NT2834	55°35·9′	3°8·1′W	W	73
Highlands Park	Staffs	SK1921	52°47·4′	1°42·7′W	X	128
Highlands, The	Shrops	SO6785	52°28·0′	2°28·7′W	X	138
High Lands,The	Somer	ST6840	51°9·7′	2°27·1′W	X	183
Highland Water	Hants	SU2607	50°51·9′	1°37·4′W	W	195
Highland Water Inclosure	Hants	SU2509	50°53·0′	1°38·3′W	F	195
Highland Wood	Oxon	SU6978	51°30·0′	1°0·0′W	F	175
Highlane	Ches	SJ8868	53°12·8′	2°10·4′W	T	118
Highlane	Derby	SK4082	53°20·2′	1°23·5′W	T	111,120
High Lane	Derby	SK4342	52°58·7′	1°21·2′W	X	129
High Lane	Heref	SO6760	52°14·5′	2°28·6′W	T	138,149
High Lane	Staffs	SJ8148	53°2·0′	2°16·6′W	X	118
High Lane	Stock	SJ9585	53°22·0′	2°4·1′W	T	109
High Lanes	Corn	SW5637	50°11·2′	5°24·7′W	T	203
Highlanes	Corn	SW9072	50°30·8′	4°57·4′W	T	200
Highlanes	Staffs	SJ7932	52°53·3′	2°18·3′W	T	127
Highlanes Fm	Staffs	SJ8032	52°53·3′	2°17·4′W	FM	127
High Langber	N Yks	SD8561	54°2·9′	2°13·3′W	X	98
High Langdale End	N Yks	SE9295	54°20·8′	0°34·7′W	X	94,101
High Langmuir	E Ayr	NS3941	55°38·4′	4°33·0′W	X	70
High Langside	S Ayr	NS4231	55°33·1′	4°29·8′W	X	70
High Latch	E Loth	NT5263	55°51·7′	2°45·6′W	X	66
High Lathe	Cumbr	SD7692	54°19·6′	2°21·7′W	X	98
High Laver	Essex	TL5208	51°45·2′	0°12·5′E	T	167
High Laver Grange	Essex	TL5209	51°45·8′	0°12·6′E	X	167
High Law	Aberd	NK0633	57°23·5′	1°53·6′W	H	30
Highlaw	D & G	NY1378	55°5·6′	3°21·4′W	X	85
High Laws	Cumbr	NY1449	54°50·0′	3°19·9′W	X	85
Highlaws	Cumbr	NY1449	54°50·0′	3°19·9′W	T	85
Highlaws	Northum	NZ0783	55°8·7′	1°53·0′W	X	81
Highlaws	Scot Bord	NT9363	55°51·9′	2°6·3′W	X	67
Highlawside	S Lanak	NS7248	55°42·8′	4°1·8′W	X	64
Highlea	E Loth	NT4664	55°52·2′	2°51·3′W	X	66
Highleadon	Glos	SO7623	51°54·5′	2°20·5′W	T	162
Highleadon Court	Glos	SO7724	51°55·1′	2°19·7′W	X	162
High Lea Fm	Devon	ST2801	50°48·5′	3°0·9′W	FM	193
High Lea Fm	Dorset	SU0005	50°50·9′	1°59·6′W	FM	195
Highleam	Northum	NY8887	55°10·9′	2°10·9′W	X	80
High Learchild	Northum	NU0910	55°23·3′	1°51·0′W	X	81
High Leas	Lincs	TF3982	53°19·2′	0°5·6′E	X	122
High Leas	N Yks	NZ7606	54°26·9′	0°49·3′W	X	94
High Leas	N Yks	NZ8212	54°30·0′	0°43·6′W	X	94
High Leas Fm	Derby	SK3157	53°6·8′	1°31·8′W	FM	119
High Leas Fm	Leic	SK7829	52°51·4′	0°50·1′W	FM	129
High Leaze Fm	Somer	ST5116	50°56·7′	2°41·5′W	FM	183
High Lee	Barns	SE2603	53°31·6′	1°36·1′W	X	110
High Lee	Ches	SJ9568	53°12·8′	2°4·1′W	X	118
High Lee	Staffs	SJ9262	53°9·5′	2°6·8′W	X	118
Highlee Hill	Scot Bord	NT6108	55°22·1′	2°36·5′W	X	80
Highlees	Ches	SJ8674	53°16·0′	2°12·2′W	X	118
Highlees	S Ayr	NS3633	55°34·0′	4°35·6′W	X	70
Highlees	S Lanak	NS7652	55°45·0′	3°58·1′W	X	64
High Lees Fm	Kent	TQ6846	51°11·5′	0°24·6′E	FM	188
High Legh	Ches	SJ7083	53°20·8′	2°26·6′W	T	109
High Legh Ho	Ches	SJ6983	53°20·8′	2°27·5′W	X	109
Highleigh	Devon	SS9123	51°0·0′	3°32·8′W	X	181
High Leigh	Herts	TL3608	51°45·5′	0°1·4′W	X	166
Highleigh	W Susx	SZ8498	50°46·8′	0°48·1′W	T	197
High Letham	Northum	NT9653	55°46·5′	2°3·4′W	X	74,75
High Letterpin	S Ayr	NX1991	55°11·1′	4°50·1′W	X	76
High Lettre	Stir	NS5284	56°1·8′	4°22·1′W	X	57,64
High Levels	Donc	SE7110	53°35·1′	0°55·2′W	X	112
High Leven	Stock on T	NZ4412	54°30·3′	1°18·8′W	T	93
Highley	Devon	SS6743	51°10·5′	3°53·8′W	X	180
Highley	Shrops	SO7483	52°26·9′	2°22·6′W	T	138
Highley Fm	Devon	ST2209	50°52·7′	3°6·1′W	FM	192,193
Highley Hill	Herts	TL2837	52°1·2′	0°7·7′W	X	153
Highley Hill (Tumulus)	Herts	TL2837	52°1·2′	0°7·7′W	A	153
Highley Manor	W Susx	TQ3031	51°4·0′	0°8·3′W	X	187
High Leys	Cumbr	SD4593	54°20·0′	2°50·3′W	X	97
High Leys	Leic	SK8132	52°53·0′	0°47·4′W	X	130

High Leys	N Yks	SD7171	54°8·3′	2°26·2′W	X	98
High Leys	N Yks	SE5375	54°10·3′	1°10·9′W	X	100
High Leys Fm	Cambs	TL0996	52°33·3′	0°23·1′W	FM	142
High Leys Fm	Leic	SK8031	52°52·5′	0°48·3′W	FM	130
High Leys Fm	N Yks	SE5885	54°15·7′	1°6·2′W	FM	100
High Leys Fm	Shrops	SO5582	52°26·3′	2°39·3′W	FM	137,138
High Leys Nature Reserve	Cumbr	NY0519	54°33·7′	3°27·7′W	X	89
High Lickbarrow	Cumbr	SD4197	54°22·2′	2°54·1′W	X	96,97
High Lighthouse	Angus	NO5331	56°28·4′	2°45·3′W	X	54
Highlightley Fm	Derby	SK3276	53°17·0′	1°30·8′W	FM	119
High Lindrick	N Yks	SE2770	54°7·8′	1°34·8′W	X	99
High Ling Close	Durham	NZ3942	54°46·5′	1°23·2′W	X	88
High Linn	Northum	NU0902	55°19·0′	1°51·1′W	X	81
High Lions Lodge	N Yks	SE5775	54°10·3′	1°7·2′W	X	100
High Littleton	Bath & NE Somer	ST6458	51°19·4′	2°30·6′W	T	172
High Lochenbreck	D & G	NX6465	54°57·9′	4°7·0′W	X	83
High Lode	Cambs	TL2886	52°27·6′	0°6·6′W	W	142
High Lodge	Oxon	SP3217	51°51·3′	1°31·7′W	X	164
High Lodge	Oxon	SP4315	51°50·1′	1°22·2′W	X	164
High Lodge	Oxon	SU5196	51°39·9′	1°15·4′W	X	164
High Lodge	Staffs	SO8882	52°26·4′	2°10·2′W	X	139
High Lodge	Suff	TL7679	52°23·1′	0°35·6′E	X	143
High Lodge Fm	Derby	SK4537	52°55·9′	1°19·4′W	FM	129
High Lodge Fm	Oxon	SP2517	51°51·3′	1°37·8′W	FM	163
High Lodore	Cumbr	NY2618	54°33·4′	3°8·2′W	X	89,90
High Lofthouse	N Yks	SE1073	54°9·4′	1°50·4′W	X	99
High Loft Wood	Cumbr	SD4086	54°16·2′	2°54·9′W	F	96,97
High London Fm	Norf	TM0985	52°25·6′	1°4·8′E	FM	144
High Long Ho	Northum	NY6086	55°10·3′	2°37·2′W	X	80
High Longmire	Cumbr	SD3287	54°16·7′	3°2·2′W	X	96,97
High Long Ridge	N Yks	SD9465	54°5·1′	2°5·1′W	X	98
High Longthwaite	Cumbr	NY2546	54°48·4′	3°9·6′W	T	85
High Lorton	Cumbr	NY1625	54°37·0′	3°17·6′W	T	89
High Lossit	Arg & Bt	NR6319	55°24·7′	5°44·2′W	X	68
High Lovelynch	Somer	ST1024	51°0·7′	3°16·6′W	X	181,193
High Low	Derby	SK1568	53°12·8′	1°46·1′W	X	119
Highlow Brook	Derby	SK2179	53°18·7′	1°40·7′W	W	119
Highlow Fm	Derby	SK1465	53°11·2′	1°47·0′W	FM	119
High Low Hall	Cumbr	NX9915	54°31·5′	3°33·2′W	X	89
Highlow Hall	Derby	SK2180	53°19·2′	1°40·7′W	X	110
High Lowscales	Cumbr	SD1682	54°13·9′	3°16·9′W	X	96
Highlows, The	Staffs	SJ8633	52°53·9′	2°12·1′W	X	127
High Loxley	Surrey	TQ0137	51°7·6′	0°33·0′W	X	186
High Luckens	Cumbr	NY5072	55°2·6′	2°46·5′W	X	86
High Lugtonridge	N Ayr	NS3648	55°42·1′	4°36·2′W	X	63
High Machriemore	Arg & Bt	NR6909	55°19·5′	5°38·1′W	X	68
High Magdalen	N Yks	NZ3305	54°26·6′	1°29·0′W	X	93
High Mains	D & G	NX4439	54°43·6′	4°24·9′W	X	83
High Mains	D & G	NX9192	55°12·9′	3°42·4′W	X	78
High Mains	S Ayr	NS2603	55°17·7′	4°44·0′W	X	76
High Mains	S Lanak	NS6256	55°46·9′	4°11·6′W	X	64
High Mains	Stir	NS4489	56°4·4′	4°29·9′W	X	57
Highmains Fm	D & G	NY0167	54°59·5′	3°32·4′W	FM	84
High Mains Fm	N Yks	SE2183	54°14·8′	1°40·2′W	FM	99
Highmains Hill	D & G	NY0168	55°0·1′	3°32·4′W	H	84
High Malsis	N Yks	SD9944	53°53·8′	2°0·5′W	X	103
High Man	Cumbr	SD3296	54°21·5′	3°2·4′W	X	96,97
High Marishes	N Yks	SE8178	54°11·7′	0°45·1′W	T	100
High Mark	D & G	NW9664	54°56·0′	5°10·6′W	X	82
High Mark	D & G	NX1370	54°59·6′	4°55·0′W	X	76
High Mark	N Yks	SD9267	54°6·2′	2°6·9′W	X	98
High Marnham	Notts	SK8070	53°13·5′	0°47·7′W	T	121
High Marriforth	N Yks	SE1987	54°16·9′	1°42·1′W	X	99
High Mathernock	Inverc	NS3271	55°54·4′	4°40·8′W	X	63
High McGownston	S Ayr	NS2203	55°17·6′	4°47·8′W	X	76
Highmead	Monm	SO3407	51°45·7′	2°57·0′W	X	161
Highmead Fm	Monm	SO3112	51°48·4′	2°59·7′W	FM	161
High Meadow	Northum	NY8065	54°59·0′	2°18·3′W	X	86,87
High Meadow	Powys	SO1418	51°51·5′	3°14·5′W	X	161
High Meadow Fm	Glos	SO5510	51°47·4′	2°38·8′W	FM	162
Highmeadow Woods	Glos	SO5513	51°49·1′	2°38·8′W	F	162
High Melton	Donc	SE5001	53°30·4′	1°14·4′W	T	111
High Melwood	N Lincs	SE7902	53°30·8′	0°48·1′W	X	112
High Merebeck	Cumbr	NY0314	54°31·0′	3°29·5′W	X	89
High Mere Beck	Cumbr	SD2279	54°12·3′	3°11·3′W	X	96
High Mere Greave	Cumbr	NY4307	54°27·6′	2°52·3′W	X	90
High Merrybent	N Yks	NZ2006	54°27·2′	1°41·1′W	X	93
High Merryton	S Lanak	NS7552	55°45·0′	3°59·1′W	X	64
High Metham	E Yorks	SE8025	53°43·2′	0°46·8′W	X	106
High Mickley	Northum	NZ0761	54°56·9′	1°53·0′W	T	88
High Midton	S Ayr	NS3215	55°24·3′	4°38·8′W	X	70
High Mill	Cumbr	NY1525	54°37·0′	3°18·6′W	X	89
High Mill	Cumbr	SD4194	54°20·5′	2°54·0′W	X	96,97
High Mill	Cumbr	SD5897	54°22·3′	2°38·4′W	X	97
High Mill Burn	D & G	NX3581	55°6·0′	4°34·7′W	W	77
Highmilldown	D & G	NX1275	55°2·3′	4°56·1′W	X	76
High Mill Fm	N Yks	SE9676	54°10·5′	0°31·3′W	FM	101
High Mill Hill	Norf	TG3918	52°42·6′	1°32·7′E	X	133,134
High Mill Ho	Surrey	SU8547	51°13·2′	0°46·6′W	X	186
High Millmore	S Ayr	NX0975	55°2·2′	4°58·9′W	H	76
High Milndovan	Arg & Bt	NS3579	55°58·8′	4°38·2′W	X	63
High Milton	D & G	NX3147	54°47·6′	4°37·3′W	X	82
High Milton	S Ayr	NS3013	55°23·1′	4°40·6′W	X	70
High Mindork	D & G	NX3058	54°53·5′	4°38·6′W	X	82
Highmoat	Cumbr	NY3973	55°3·1′	2°56·9′W	X	85
High Moncur	N Ayr	NS3243	55°39·3′	4°39·8′W	X	63,70
High Moor	Brad	SE0845	53°54·3′	1°52·3′W	F	104
High Moor	Ches	SJ9670	53°13·9′	2°3·2′W	H	118
High Moor	Corn	SX1680	50°35·7′	4°35·6′W	X	201
Highmoor	Cumbr	NY2547	54°49·0′	3°9·6′W	T	85
High Moor	Derby	SK4680	53°19·1′	1°18·2′W	T	111,120
High Moor	Derby	SK4680	53°19·1′	1°18·2′W	T	111,120
High Moor	D & G	NX2949	54°48·7′	4°39·2′W	X	82
High Moor	Lancs	SD3836	53°49·2′	2°56·1′W	X	102
High Moor	Lancs	SD5011	53°35·8′	2°44·9′W	T	108
High Moor	Lancs	SD5445	53°54·2′	2°41·6′W	X	102
Highmoor	Northum	NZ1597	55°16·3′	1°45·4′W	X	81
High Moor	N Yks	NZ1304	54°26·1′	1°47·6′W	X	92
High Moor	N Yks	NZ6711	54°29·6′	0°57·5′W	X	94
High Moor	N Yks	NZ7202	54°24·7′	0°53·0′W	X	94
High Moor	N Yks	SE2166	54°5·6′	1°40·3′W	X	99
High Moor	N Yks	SE9298	54°22·4′	0°34·6′W	X	94,101
High Moor	Oldham	SD9706	53°33·3′	2°2·3′W	X	109
Highmoor	Oxon	SU7085	51°33·8′	0°59·0′W	T	175
High Moor	Red & Cl	NZ6513	54°30·7′	0°59·3′W	X	94
High Moor	Red & Cl	NZ6811	54°29·6′	0°56·6′W	X	94
High Moor	York	SE5254	53°59·0′	1°12·0′W	X	105
Highmoor Brook	Oxon	SP3004	51°44·3′	1°33·5′W	W	164
Highmoor Copse	Swin	SU2191	51°37·3′	1°41·4′W	F	163,174
Highmoor Cross	Oxon	SU6984	51°33·3′	0°59·9′W	T	175
High Moor Dyke	Cumbr	NY3738	54°44·2′	2°58·3′W	X	90
High Moor Fm	N Yks	SE2455	53°59·7′	1°37·6′W	FM	104
High Moor Fm	N Yks	SE2649	53°56·4′	1°35·8′W	FM	104
High Moor Fm	N Yks	SE2651	53°57·5′	1°35·8′W	FM	104
Highmoor Fm	Rut	SK9310	52°41·0′	0°37·1′W	FM	130
Highmoorhead	Cumbr	NY4169	55°1·0′	2°54·9′W	X	85
Highmoor Hill	Monm	ST4689	51°36·1′	2°46·4′W	T	171,172
High Moor Ho	Durham	NZ1621	54°35·3′	1°44·7′W	X	92
High Moor of Killiemore	D & G	NX3660	54°54·7′	4°33·1′W	X	83
High Moorside	Cumbr	NY0701	54°24·0′	3°25·5′W	X	89
High Moorsley	Sund	NZ3345	54°48·2′	1°28·8′W	T	88
Highmoor Trench	Oxon	SU7085	51°33·8′	0°59·0′W	X	175
Highmoor Wood	Heref	SO3152	52°10·0′	3°0·1′W	F	148
High Moralee	Northum	NY8476	55°4·9′	2°14·6′W	X	86,87
High Moss	Cumbr	NY2021	54°34·9′	3°13·8′W	X	89,90
High Mossend	D & G	NX4148	54°48·4′	4°28·0′W	X	83
High Mossthorn	Cumbr	NY5173	55°3·2′	2°45·6′W	X	86
High Mount	E Ayr	NS5314	55°24·1′	4°18·9′W	H	70
High Mowthorpe	N Yks	SE8868	54°6·3′	0°38·8′W	X	101
High Mowthorpe Plantns	N Yks	SE8868	54°6·3′	0°38·8′W	F	101
High Mowthorpe Plantns	N Yks	SE8869	54°6·8′	0°38·8′W	F	101
High Muffles	N Yks	SE7793	54°19·8′	0°48·5′W	X	94,100
High Muir	D & G	NY2777	55°5·2′	3°8·2′W	X	85
High Mulberry	Durham	NZ1521	54°35·3′	1°45·7′W	X	92
High Murber	Cumbr	NY5818	54°33·6′	2°38·5′W	X	91
High Murdonochee	D & G	NX1775	55°2·4′	4°51·4′W	H	76
High Mye	D & G	NX0954	54°50·9′	4°58·1′W	X	82
Highnam	Glos	SO7919	51°52·4′	2°17·9′W	T	162
Highnam Copse	Hants	SU7445	51°12·2′	0°56·1′W	F	186
Highnam Court	Glos	SO7919	51°52·4′	2°17·9′W	A	162
Highnam Fm	Heref	SO6139	52°3·1′	2°33·7′W	FM	149
Highnam Green	Glos	SO7920	51°52·9′	2°17·9′W	T	162
Highnam Woods	Glos	SO7719	51°52·4′	2°19·7′W	F	162
High Nash	Glos	SO5710	51°47·5′	2°37·0′W	T	162
High Neb	Derby	SK2285	53°21·9′	1°39·8′W	H	110
High Needham	Derby	SK1165	53°11·2′	1°49·7′W	X	119
High Nentsberry	Cumbr	NY7645	54°48·2′	2°22·0′W	X	86,87
High Ness	Aberd	NJ8545	57°30·0′	2°14·6′W	X	30
Highness Fm	N Yks	SE3383	54°14·7′	1°29·2′W	FM	99
High Newlands	S Ayr	NS2704	55°18·2′	4°43·1′W	X	76
High Newstead	N Yks	SE1684	54°15·3′	1°44·8′W	X	99
High Newton	Cumbr	SD4082	54°14·1′	2°54·8′W	T	96,97
High Newton	E Ayr	NS5936	55°36·1′	4°13·8′W	X	71
High Newton	Northum	NY7984	55°9·2′	2°19·3′W	X	80
High Newton-by-the-Sea	Northum	NU2325	55°31·3′	1°37·7′W	T	75
High Nibthwaite	Cumbr	SD2989	54°17·7′	3°5·0′W	T	96,97
High Nook Fm	Cumbr	NY1220	54°34·3′	3°21·3′W	FM	89
Highnoon Fm	Norf	TG3408	52°37·4′	1°27·8′E	FM	134
High Noon Fm	Suff	TL6648	52°6·5′	0°25·8′E	FM	154
Highnoons Fm	W Susx	SU9828	51°2·8′	0°35·7′W	FM	186,197
High-no-place	N Yks	SE3099	54°23·4′	1°31·9′W	X	99
High Normanby	N Yks	NZ9306	54°26·7′	0°33·5′W	X	94
High North Fm	N Yks	SE2165	54°5·1′	1°40·3′W	FM	99
High Northolme Fm	N Yks	SE7080	54°12·9′	0°55·2′W	FM	100
High Northsceugh	Cumbr	NY5348	54°49·7′	2°43·5′W	X	86
High Nova Fm	N Yks	SE7888	54°17·1′	0°47·7′W	FM	94,100
High Nun Ho	Cumbr	SD7185	54°15·8′	2°26·3′W	X	98
High Nunton	D & G	NX6449	54°49·3′	4°6·6′W	X	83
Highoak	Norf	TG0700	52°33·7′	1°3·6′E	T	144
High Oak Fm	Kent	TQ9438	51°6·7′	0°46·7′E	FM	189
High Oak Fm	Worcs	SO7771	52°20·4′	2°19·9′W	FM	138
High Oaks	Cumbr	NY4740	54°45·4′	2°49·0′W	X	86
High Oaks	Cumbr	SD6291	54°19·0′	2°34·6′W	T	97
High Oaks Fm	Norf	TM1586	52°26·0′	1°10·2′E	FM	144,156
High Offley	Staffs	SJ7826	52°50·1′	2°19·2′W	T	127
High Old Shields	Northum	NY6767	55°0·0′	2°30·5′W	X	86,87
High Ongar	Essex	TL5603	51°42·5′	0°15·9′E	T	167
High Onn	Staffs	SJ8216	52°44·7′	2°15·6′W	T	127
High Onn Wharf	Staffs	SJ8316	52°44·7′	2°14·7′W	T	127
High Onn Wood	Staffs	SJ8116	52°44·7′	2°16·5′W	F	127
High Onset	Cumbr	NY5578	55°5·9′	2°41·9′W	X	86
Highoredish Fm	Derby	SK3559	53°7·9′	1°28·2′W	FM	119
High Osgoodby Grange	N Yks	SE4980	54°13·0′	1°14·5′W	X	100
High Oustley	Northum	NY8156	54°54·1′	2°17·4′W	X	86,87
Highover Fm	Herts	TL1930	51°57·6′	0°15·7′W	FM	166
High Overmuir	E Ayr	NS5744	55°40·4′	4°16·0′W	X	71
High Oxque	N Yks	SE0998	54°22·9′	1°51·3′W	X	99
High Oxspring	Barns	SE2603	53°31·6′	1°36·1′W	X	110
High Pale Fm	Suff	TL9035	51°59·1′	0°46·4′E	FM	155
High Paley Green	N Yks	SD7964	54°4·5′	2°18·8′W	X	98
High Paradise Fm	N Yks	SE5088	54°17·4′	1°13·5′W	FM	100
High Park	Arg & Bt	NR6925	55°28·1′	5°38·8′W	X	68
High Park	Cumbr	NY0421	54°34·8′	3°28·7′W	H	89
Highpark	Cumbr	NY1420	54°34·3′	3°19·4′W	X	89
High Park	Cumbr	NY5571	55°2·1′	2°41·8′W	X	86
High Park	Cumbr	SD5390	54°18·5′	2°42·9′W	T	97
High Park	Devon	SS4224	50°59·9′	4°14·7′W	X	180,190
Highpark	D & G	NX6476	55°3·8′	4°7·3′W	X	77
High Park	E Ayr	NS6212	55°23·2′	4°10·3′W	X	71
High Park	Lancs	SD6478	54°12·0′	2°32·7′W	X	97
High Park	Northum	NU2001	55°18·4′	1°40·7′W	X	81
High Park	Notts	SK5756	53°6·1′	1°8·5′W	X	120
High Park	N Yks	SE0998	54°22·9′	1°51·3′W	X	99
High Park	S Ayr	NS2205	55°18·7′	4°47·9′W	X	70,76
Highpark	S Ayr	NS4019	55°26·6′	4°31·3′W	X	70
High Park	Sefton	SD3617	53°39·0′	2°57·7′W	T	108
High Park	Shrops	SO4397	52°34·3′	2°50·1′W	X	137
High Park	Staffs	SJ8100	52°36·1′	2°16·4′W	X	127
Highpark	Surrey	TQ0637	51°7·6′	0°28·7′W	X	187
High Park	Worcs	SO8762	52°15·6′	2°11·0′W	X	150
High Park Fm	Cambs	TL1269	52°18·7′	0°21·0′W	FM	153
High Park Fm	E Susx	TQ3311	50°53·2′	0°6·2′W	FM	198
High Park Fm	Lincs	TF0729	52°51·1′	0°24·3′W	FM	130
Highpark Fm	Norf	TM1295	52°30·9′	1°7·9′E	FM	144
High Park Fm	Notts	SK8561	53°8·6′	0°43·3′W	FM	121
High Park Fm	N Yks	SE3449	53°56·4′	1°28·5′W	FM	104
High Park Fm	N Yks	SE6988	54°17·2′	0°56·0′W	FM	94,100
High Park Fm	N Yks	SE8984	54°14·9′	0°37·6′W	FM	101
High Park Fm	Staffs	SO8784	52°27·5′	2°11·1′W	FM	139
High Parkfoot	Cumbr	NY5073	55°3·2′	2°46·5′W	X	86
High Park Ho	N Yks	SE4196	54°21·7′	1°21·7′W	X	99
High Park Ho	Shrops	SO4497	52°34·3′	2°49·2′W	X	137
High Park Wall	Durham	NZ0319	54°34·2′	1°56·8′W	X	92
High Park Wood	Ghead	NZ2258	54°55·2′	1°39·0′W	F	88
High Park Wood	Notts	SK4849	53°2·4′	1°16·6′W	F	129
High Pasture	N Yks	SD8881	54°13·7′	2°10·6′W	X	98
High Pasture	N Yks	SD9380	54°13·2′	2°6·0′W	X	98
High Pasture	N Yks	SE0377	54°11·6′	1°56·8′W	X	98
High Pasture Hill	E Yorks	SE7557	54°0·5′	0°50·9′W	X	105,106
High Pastures	Suff	TM0266	52°15·5′	0°58·0′E	X	155
High Peacockbank	E Ayr	NS4244	55°40·1′	4°30·3′W	X	70
High Peak	Derby	SK1288	53°23·6′	1°48·8′W	H	110
High Peak	Devon	SY1085	50°39·7′	3°16·0′W	X	192
High Peak (Fort)	Devon	SY1085	50°39·7′	3°16·0′W	A	192
Highpeak Junction	Derby	SK3155	53°5·7′	1°31·8′W	X	119
High Peak Trail	Derby	SK1760	53°8·5′	1°44·3′W	X	119
High Penhowe	N Yks	SE7764	54°4·2′	0°49·0′W	X	100
High Peninver	Arg & Bt	NR7525	55°28·3′	5°33·2′W	X	68,69
High Pennard	Swan	SS5787	51°34·1′	4°3·4′W	X	159
High Penn Fm	Wilts	SU0172	51°27·1′	1°58·7′W	FM	173
High Pike	Cumbr	NY3135	54°42·6′	3°3·8′W	H	90
High Pike	Cumbr	NY3708	54°28·1′	2°57·9′W	H	90
High Pike	Cumbr	NY6509	54°28·8′	2°32·0′W	X	91
High Pike	Cumbr	SD7182	54°14·2′	2°26·3′W	H	98
High Pike	Durham	NY8835	54°42·8′	2°10·8′W	X	91,92
High Pike Hill	Cumbr	NY8003	54°25·6′	2°18·1′W	X	91,92
High Pikehow	Cumbr	NY1409	54°28·4′	3°19·2′W	X	89
High Pinmore	S Ayr	NS3115	55°24·2′	4°39·7′W	X	70
High Pitfold Fm	Surrey	SU8734	51°6·1′	0°45·1′W	FM	186
High Plains	Cumbr	NY4274	55°3·7′	2°54·1′W	X	85
High Plains	Cumbr	NY6614	54°31·5′	2°31·1′W	X	91
High Plains	Cumbr	NY7243	54°47·1′	2°25·7′W	X	86,87
High Plains	Northum	NZ0160	54°56·3′	1°58·6′W	X	87
High Plantn	Durham	NY9022	54°35·8′	2°8·9′W	F	91,92
High Plantn	Durham	NZ0743	54°47·2′	1°53·0′W	F	88
High Plantn	E Yorks	SE8345	53°53·9′	0°43·8′W	F	106
High Plantn	E Yorks	SE8844	53°53·3′	0°39·2′W	F	106
High Plantn	Norf	TF8403	52°35·8′	0°43·4′E	F	144
High Plantn	N Yks	SE6198	54°22·7′	1°3·2′W	F	94,100
High Plewland	S Lanak	NS6534	55°35·1′	4°8·1′W	X	71
High Plyde	E Ayr	NS4817	55°25·7′	4°23·7′W	X	70
High Point	Corn	SW9939	50°13·2′	4°48·7′W	X	204
High Point	Pemb	SM7609	51°44·3′	5°14·3′W	X	157
High Pole Fm	N Yks	SE0041	53°52·2′	1°59·6′W	FM	104
High Polquheys	E Ayr	NS6216	55°25·4′	4°10·4′W	X	71
High Polquhirter	E Ayr	NS6312	55°23·2′	4°9·3′W	X	71
High Pond Ho	N Yks	SE2187	54°16·9′	1°40·2′W	X	99
High Post	Wilts	SU1536	51°7·6′	1°46·8′W	X	184
High Post Fm	Suff	TL6678	52°22·7′	0°26·7′E	FM	143
High Pow	Cumbr	NY2543	54°46·8′	3°9·5′W	X	85
High Pow	Cumbr	NY3948	54°49·6′	2°56·5′W	X	85
High Prestwick Fm	Surrey	SU9334	51°6·1′	0°39·9′W	FM	186
High Quebec	N Yks	NZ8604	54°25·7′	0°40·0′W	X	94
High Rails Fm	N Yks	SE2660	54°2·4′	1°35·8′W	FM	99
High Raise	Cumbr	NY2809	54°28·5′	3°6·2′W	H	89,90
High Raise	Cumbr	NY4413	54°30·8′	2°51·5′W	H	90
High Raise	Cumbr	NY7746	54°48·7′	2°21·0′W	X	86,87
High Rake	Derby	SK1677	53°17·6′	1°45·2′W	X	119
High Rake	Derby	SK2073	53°15·5′	1°41·6′W	H	119
High Ranachan	Arg & Bt	NR7024	55°27·6′	5°37·9′W	X	68
High Ray Carr	N Yks	SE2072	54°8·8′	1°41·2′W	X	99
High Red Hos	Northum	NZ1385	55°9·8′	1°47·3′W	X	81
High Rews Fm	Bucks	SU8388	51°35·3′	0°47·7′W	FM	175
High Ridehalgh	Lancs	SD8935	53°48·9′	2°9·6′W	X	103
Highridge	C of Bris	ST5669	51°25·3′	2°37·6′W	T	172,182
Highridge	Devon	SS7120	50°58·1′	3°49·9′W	X	180
High Ridge	Leic	SP5687	52°28·9′	1°10·1′W	X	140
Highridge	N Som	ST5667	51°24·3′	2°37·6′W	T	172,182
Highridge	Staffs	SJ9764	53°10·6′	2°2·3′W	X	118
Highridge Fm	Lincs	TF2066	53°10·9′	0°11·8′W	FM	122
High Ridge Fm	Surrey	TQ4049	51°13·6′	0°0·7′E	FM	187
Highridgehall	Scot Bord	NT7638	55°38·3′	2°22·4′W	X	74
Highridges	Staffs	SK0338	52°56·6′	1°56·9′W	X	128
High Rid Resr	Bolton	SD6610	53°35·4′	2°30·4′W	W	109
High Rigg	Cumbr	NY3021	54°35·0′	3°4·6′W	X	90
Highrigg	Cumbr	NY4437	54°43·7′	2°51·8′W	X	90
High Rigg	Durham	NY8538	54°44·5′	2°13·6′W	X	91,92
High Rigg	Durham	NY8737	54°43·9′	2°11·7′W	X	91,92
High Rigg	Northum	NY9796	55°15·7′	2°2·4′W	X	81
High Rigg Fm	N Yks	SE8688	54°17·1′	0°40·3′W	FM	94,101
High Riggs	N Yks	SE0774	54°9·9′	1°53·1′W	X	99
High Risby	N Lincs	SE9114	53°37·1′	0°37·0′W	T	112
High Road Fm	Norf	TF5911	52°40·6′	0°21·5′E	FM	131,143
Highroad Well Moor	Cald	SE0626	53°44·1′	1°54·1′W	T	104
High Roans Ho	N Yks	SE6262	54°3·3′	1°2·8′W	X	100
High Rochester	Northum	NY8398	55°16·8′	2°15·6′W	X	80
High Rock	Shrops	SO7294	52°32·8′	2°24·4′W	X	138
High Rockliffe	Darl	NZ2909	54°28·8′	1°32·7′W	X	93
High Rocks	E Susx	TQ5638	51°7·4′	0°14·1′E	X	188
High Rocks	Notts	SK5763	53°9·9′	1°8·4′W	X	120
High Roding	Essex	TL6017	51°49·9′	0°19·7′E	T	167
High Rodingbury Fm	Essex	TL5916	51°49·4′	0°18·8′E	FM	167
High Rotherhope	Cumbr	NY7142	54°46·6′	2°26·6′W	X	86,87
High Rouchan	D & G	NX4138	54°43·0′	4°27·7′W	X	83
High Rougham	Suff	TL9262	52°13·6′	0°49·1′E	T	155
High Row	Cumbr	NY3535	54°42·6′	3°0·1′W	T	90
High Row	Cumbr	NY3721	54°35·1′	2°58·1′W	T	90
High Row Fm	Cumbr	NY3125	54°37·2′	3°3·7′W	FM	90
Highrow Wood	Suff	TM1958	52°10·8′	1°12·6′E	F	156

High Royds Hall	Leeds	SE1642	53°52·7'	1°45·0'W	X	104
High Ruckles	N Yks	SE1668	54°6·7'	1°44·9'W	X	99
High Saddle	Cumbr	NY2912	54°30·1'	3°5·4'W	X	89,90
High Salter	Lancs	SD6062	54°3·4'	2°36·2'W	X	97
High Salvington	W Susx	TQ1206	50°50·8'	0°24·2'W	T	198
High Sand Creek	Norf	TF9546	52°58·8'	0°54·7'E	W	132
High Santon Fm	N Lincs	SE9411	53°35·5'	0°34·4'W	FM	112
High Scald Fell	Cumbr	NY7128	54°39·0'	2°26·5'W	X	91
High Scale	Cumbr	SD7891	54°19·1'	2°19·9'W	X	98
High Scale	N Yks	SD8255	53°59·7'	2°16·1'W	X	103
High Scales	Cumbr	NY1845	54°47·8'	3°16·1'W	T	85
High Scales	Cumbr	NY5906	54°27·1'	2°37·5'W	X	91
High Scales	N Yks	NZ1604	54°26·1'	1°44·8'W	X	92
High Scamridge	N Yks	SE8987	54°16·5'	0°37·6'W	X	94,101
High Scar	N Yks	SD9584	54°15·3'	2°4·2'W	X	98
High Scarth Crag	Cumbr	NY2103	54°25·2'	3°12·6'W	H	89,90
High Scathwaite	Cumbr	SD2983	54°14·5'	3°5·0'W	X	96,97
High Scawdel	Cumbr	NY2315	54°31·7'	3°11·0'W	H	89,90
High Scroggs Ho	N Yks	SE2488	54°17·5'	1°37·5'W	X	99
High Scrubs	Herts	SP9208	51°46·0'	0°39·6'W	F	165
High Seat	Cumbr	NY2818	54°33·4'	3°6·4'W	H	89,90
High Seat	Cumbr	NY8001	54°24·5'	2°18·1'W	H	91,92
High Seat	Northum	NZ1067	55°0·1'	1°50·2'W	X	88
High Seat	N Yks	SE9396	54°21·3'	0°33·7'W	X	94,101
High Seat	Scot Bord	NT4009	55°22·5'	2°56·4'W	H	79
High Sellafield	Cumbr	NY0204	54°25·6'	3°30·2'W	T	89
High Sharpley	Durham	NZ3749	54°50·3'	1°25·0'W	X	88
High Sharpley	Leic	SK4416	52°44·6'	1°20·5'W	X	129
High Shaw	Northum	NY9185	55°9·8'	2°8·0'W	X	80
High Shaw	Northum	NY9498	55°16·8'	2°5·2'W	X	80
High Shaw	N Yks	SD8691	54°19·1'	2°12·5'W	T	98
Highshaw Clough	Derby	SK2187	53°23·0'	1°40·6'W	X	110
High Sheen Fm	Staffs	SK1162	53°9·5'	1°49·7'W	FM	119
High Shield	Northum	NY6548	54°49·8'	2°32·3'W	X	86
High Shield	Northum	NY7667	55°0·1'	2°22·1'W	X	86,87
High Shield	Northum	NY8545	54°48·2'	2°13·6'W	X	87
High Shield	Northum	NY9263	54°57·9'	2°7·1'W	X	87
High Shields	S Tyne	NZ3666	54°59·5'	1°25·8'W	T	88
High Shilford	Northum	NZ0260	54°56·3'	1°57·7'W	X	87
High Shincliffe	Durham	NZ2940	54°45·5'	1°32·5'W	T	88
High Shipley	Durham	NZ0121	54°35·3'	1°58·6'W	X	92
High Shipley	Durham	NZ1133	54°41·8'	1°49·3'W	X	92
Highshutt	Staffs	SK0343	52°59·3'	1°56·9'W	X	119,128
High Side	Cumbr	NY1626	54°37·6'	3°17·6'W	X	89
High Side	Cumbr	NY1628	54°38·7'	3°17·7'W	X	89
High Side	Cumbr	NY2330	54°39·8'	3°11·2'W	T	89,90
Highside	Cumbr	SD6790	54°18·5'	2°30·0'W	X	98
Highside	E Ayr	NS5839	55°37·7'	4°14·9'W	X	71
Highside	Northum	NY6561	54°56·8'	2°32·4'W	X	86
Highside	Northum	NY9064	54°58·5'	2°8·9'W	X	87
High Side	N Yks	SD8561	54°2·9'	2°13·3'W	X	98
High Side	N Yks	SE1291	54°19·1'	1°48·5'W	X	99
Highside	Scot Bord	NT7926	55°31·9'	2°19·5'W	H	74
High Side Bank	Darl	NZ2322	54°35·8'	1°38·2'W	X	93
Highside Hill	E Loth	NT6673	55°57·2'	2°32·2'W	H	67
High Sikes	N Yks	SE1173	54°9·4'	1°49·5'W	X	99
High Skelding	N Yks	SE2169	54°7·2'	1°40·3'W	X	99
High Skelghyll	Cumbr	NY3902	54°24·8'	2°56·0'W	X	90
High Skelgill	Cumbr	NY7346	54°48·7'	2°24·8'W	X	86,87
High Skeog	D & G	NX4539	54°43·6'	4°24·0'W	X	83
High Skibeden Fm	N Yks	SE0252	53°58·1'	1°57·8'W	FM	104
High Skirlington	E Yorks	TA1852	53°57·3'	0°11·7'W	X	107
High Skydes	Cumbr	NY7342	54°46·6'	2°24·8'W	X	86,87
High Skyreholme	N Yks	SE0760	54°2·4'	1°53·2'W	X	99
High Slack	Cumbr	NY6631	54°40·6'	2°31·2'W	X	91
High Sleights Fm	N Yks	SE7860	54°2·0'	0°48·1'W	FM	100
High Slock	D & G	NX1034	54°40·2'	4°56·4'W	X	82
High Smerby	Arg & Bt	NR7523	55°27·2'	5°33·1'W	X	68,69
High's Mill	Norf	TG4219	52°43·1'	1°35·4'E	X	134
High Smithston	S Ayr	NS3212	55°22·7'	4°38·7'W	X	70
High Smithstone	N Ayr	NS2845	55°40·3'	4°43·7'W	X	63
High Snab	Cumbr	NY2218	54°33·3'	3°11·9'W	X	89,90
High Snab Bank	Cumbr	NY2118	54°33·3'	3°12·9'W	X	89,90
High Snape	N Yks	SE3150	53°57·0'	1°31·2'W	X	104
High Snowden	N Yks	SE1752	53°58·1'	1°44·0'W	X	104
High Sockburn	Darl	NZ3408	54°28·2'	1°28·1'W	X	93
High Sourmire	N Yks	SE1479	54°12·6'	1°46·7'W	X	99
High Southwick	Sund	NZ3859	54°55·7'	1°24·0'W	T	88
High Spelder Banks	N Yks	SE2081	54°13·7'	1°41·2'W	X	99
High Spen	Ghead	NZ1359	54°55·8'	1°47·4'W	T	88
High Springs	N Yks	SD7981	54°13·7'	2°18·9'W	W	98
High Spy	Cumbr	NY2316	54°32·3'	3°11·0'W	H	89,90
High Stacks	E Yorks	TA2570	54°6·9'	0°4·8'W	W	101
High Staindale	N Yks	SE8890	54°18·1'	0°38·4'W	X	94,101
High Staindrop Field Ho	Durham	NZ1624	54°36·9'	1°44·7'W	X	92
High Stakesby	N Yks	NZ8810	54°28·9'	0°38·1'W	T	94
High Stand	Cumbr	NY4849	54°50·2'	2°48·2'W	X	86
High Stand Plantation	Cumbr	NY4848	54°49·7'	2°48·1'W	F	86
High Stanerigg	Falk	NS8675	55°57·5'	3°49·1'W	X	65
High Starlings	Norf	TM0487	52°26·8'	1°0·5'E	X	144
High Staward	Northum	NY8059	54°55·8'	2°18·3'W	X	86,87
Highstead	Devon	SS4105	50°49·6'	4°15·1'W	X	190
Highstead	Kent	TR2166	51°21·2'	1°10·8'E	T	179
Highstead Ash	Cumbr	NY5969	55°1·1'	2°38·0'W	X	86
Highstead Hill	Northum	NY8585	55°9·8'	2°13·7'W	H	80
High Steads	Northum	NZ2490	55°12·5'	1°36·9'W	X	81
Highsted	Kent	TQ9161	51°19·2'	0°44·9'E	T	178
High Stennerley	Cumbr	SD2785	54°15·6'	3°6·8'W	X	96,97
High Stenries	D & G	NY2976	55°4·7'	3°6·3'W	X	85
High Stephen's Head	Lancs	SD6060	54°2·3'	2°36·2'W	X	97
High Stile	Cumbr	NY1614	54°31·1'	3°17·4'W	H	89
High Stittenham	N Yks	SE6767	54°5·9'	0°58·1'W	X	100
High Stobhill Fm	Northum	NZ2084	55°9·2'	1°40·7'W	FM	81
High Stone	Red & Cl	NZ6125	54°37·2'	1°2·9'W	X	94
High Stonehills	E Yorks	TA1460	54°1·6'	0°15·2'W	X	101
Highstone Rocks	Derby	SK0699	53°29·5'	1°54·2'W	X	110
High Stones Hill	Cald	SE0123	53°42·4'	1°58·7'W	X	104
High Stony Bank	N Yks	SD9166	54°5·6'	2°7·8'W	X	98
High Stoop	Durham	NZ1040	54°45·5'	1°50·3'W	T	88
High Stotfold	Hartpl	NZ4430	54°40·0'	1°18·6'W	X	93

High Stott Park	Cumbr	SD3788	54°17·3'	2°57·6'W	X	96,97
High Stoy	Dorset	ST6405	50°50·8'	2°30·3'W	X	194
High Straggleton Fm	N Yks	NZ8711	54°29·5'	0°39·0'W	FM	94
High Stream Head Fm	Brad	SE0834	53°48·4'	1°52·3'W	FM	104
High Street	Corn	SW9653	50°20·7'	4°51·7'W	T	200,204
High Street	Cumbr	NY4411	54°29·7'	2°51·5'W	H	90
High Street	Kent	TQ7430	51°2·8'	0°29·3'E	T	188
Highstreet	Kent	TR0862	51°19·4'	0°59·5'E	T	179
High Street	Lincs	TF1791	53°24·4'	0°14·0'W	X	113
High Street	Lincs	TF2275	53°15·7'	0°9·8'W	X	122
High Street	Suff	TM3684	52°24·4'	1°28·6'E	T	156
High Street	Suff	TM4170	52°16·7'	1°32·4'E	T	156
High Street	Suff	TM4355	52°8·6'	1°33·5'E	T	156
High Street Fm	Cambs	TL1178	52°23·6'	0°21·7'W	FM	142
High Street Fm	Lincs	TF1889	53°23·3'	0°13·1'W	FM	113,122
High Street Fm	Suff	TL8747	52°5·6'	0°44·2'E	FM	155
High Street Fm	Suff	TM0049	52°6·4'	0°55·6'E	FM	155
Highstreet Green	Essex	TL7634	51°58·8'	0°34·2'E	T	155
High Street Green	Suff	TM0055	52°9·6'	0°55·8'E	T	155
Highstreet Green	Surrey	SU9835	51°6·6'	0°35·6'W	T	186
High Street Ho	Lincs	TF2086	53°21·7'	0°11·4'W	X	113,122
High Street (Roman Road)	Cumbr	NY4515	54°31·9'	2°50·6'W	R	90
High Strip	Scot Bord	NT7061	55°50·7'	2°28·3'W	F	67
High Struthers	Northum	NY8555	54°53·6'	2°13·6'W	X	87
High Studdon	Northum	NY8453	54°52·5'	2°14·5'W	X	86,87
High Sunderland	Scot Bord	NT4731	55°34·4'	2°50·0'W	T	73
High Sutton	N Yks	SE2082	54°14·2'	1°41·2'W	X	99
High Swainston	Durham	NZ4028	54°39·0'	1°22·4'W	X	93
High Sweden Bridge	Cumbr	NY3706	54°27·0'	2°57·9'W	X	90
Hightae	D & G	NX7561	54°55·9'	3°56·6'W	X	84
Hightae	D & G	NY0978	55°5·5'	3°25·1'W	T	85
Hightae Mill Loch (Nature Reserve)	D & G	NY0880	55°6·6'	3°26·1'W	W	78
High Tarbeg	E Ayr	NS4820	55°27·3'	4°23·8'W	X	70
High Tarn Green	Cumbr	SD4185	54°15·7'	2°53·9'W	X	96,97
Highter's Heath	Birm	SP0879	52°24·8'	1°52·5'W	T	139
High, The	Cumbr	NY0020	54°34·2'	3°32·4'W	X	89
High Thoresby	N Yks	SE0290	54°18·6'	1°57·7'W	X	98
Highthorn	Northum	NZ2693	55°14·1'	1°35·0'W	X	81
High Thornborough	N Yks	SE3892	54°19·6'	1°24·5'W	X	99
Highthorne	N Yks	SE5174	54°9·8'	1°12·7'W	X	100
High Thorneyburn	Northum	NY7686	55°10·3'	2°22·2'W	X	80
Highthorn Fm	Leic	SK6323	52°48·3'	1°3·5'W	FM	129
Highthorn Fm	Notts	SK5428	52°51·0'	1°11·5'W	FM	129
High Thornhope	Northum	NY6750	54°50·9'	2°30·4'W	X	86,87
Highthorns	E Yorks	TA1150	53°56·3'	0°18·1'W	X	107
High Thorpe	Notts	SK6738	52°56·3'	0°59·8'W	X	129
High Threaber Fm	N Yks	SD6673	54°9·3'	2°30·8'W	FM	98
High Threave	D & G	NX3759	54°54·2'	4°32·1'W	X	83
High Three Mark	D & G	NX0751	54°49·3'	4°59·8'W	X	82
High Throston	Hartpl	NZ4833	54°41·6'	1°14·9'W	T	93
High Thurney Fm	Leic	SK6610	52°41·3'	1°1·0'W	FM	129
High Tilberthwaite	Cumbr	NY3001	54°24·2'	3°4·3'W	X	90
High Tilt	Kent	TQ8136	51°5·9'	0°35·5'E	X	188
High Tipalt	Northum	NY6968	55°0·6'	2°28·7'W	X	86,87
High Tirfergus	Arg & Bt	NR6518	55°24·2'	5°42·3'W	X	68
High Toch	Pemb	SN0514	51°47·7'	4°49·3'W	X	158
High Todhill	E Ayr	NS4343	55°39·6'	4°29·3'W	X	70
Highton	I of M	SC3778	54°10·6'	4°29·4'W	X	95
High Tongue	Cumbr	SD2397	54°22·0'	3°10·7'W	X	96
High Tor	Derby	SK2959	53°7·9'	1°33·6'W	H	119
High Tor	Swan	SS5587	51°34·0'	4°5·1'W	X	159
High Tor Fm	Leic	SK4515	52°44·1'	1°19·6'W	FM	129
High Tove	Cumbr	NY2816	54°32·3'	3°6·3'W	X	89,90
Hightown	Ches	SJ8762	53°9·5'	2°11·3'W	T	118
Hightown	C of Soton	SU4311	50°54·0'	1°19·5'W	T	196
Hightown	D & G	NY0283	55°8·2'	3°31·8'W	X	78
Hightown	Hants	SU1604	50°50·3'	1°46·0'W	T	195
Hightown	Kirk	SE1824	53°43·0'	1°43·2'W	T	104
High Town	Luton	TL0921	51°52·8'	0°24·6'W	T	166
High Town	Northum	NY9762	54°57·4'	2°2·4'W	X	87
Hightown	Sefton	SD2903	53°31·4'	3°3·8'W	T	108
High Town	Shrops	SO7193	52°32·3'	2°25·3'W	T	138
High Town	Staffs	SJ9812	52°42·6'	2°1·4'W	T	127
Hightown	Wrex	SJ3349	53°2·3'	2°59·6'W	T	117
High Town Fm	Northum	NU1200	55°17·9'	1°48·2'W	FM	81
Hightown Green	Suff	TL9756	52°10·2'	0°53·3'E	T	155
High Townhead	D & G	NX9385	55°9·1'	3°40·3'W	X	78
Hightown Heights	Kirk	SE1724	53°43·0'	1°44·1'W	T	104
Hightown Hill	D & G	NY0383	55°8·2'	3°30·9'W	H	78
Hightown of Craigs	D & G	NY0072	55°2·2'	3°33·5'W	X	84
High Toynton	Lincs	TF2869	53°12·4'	0°4·6'W	T	122
High Toynton Lodge	Lincs	TF2970	53°12·9'	0°3·7'W	X	122
High Tralorg	S Ayr	NX2396	55°13·8'	4°46·6'W	X	76
High Tranmire Fm	N Yks	NZ7611	54°29·6'	0°49·2'W	FM	94
Hightree Copse	W Berks	SU3965	51°23·2'	1°26·0'W	F	174
High Tree Fm	Suff	TM0148	52°5·9'	0°56·5'E	FM	155
Hightrees	Heref	SO5634	52°0·4'	2°38·1'W	X	149
High Trees	Wilts	SU2067	51°24·3'	1°42·4'W	X	174
Hightrees Cottages	Shrops	SJ6134	52°54·4'	2°34·4'W	X	127
High Trees Fm	Essex	TL6016	51°49·4'	0°19·7'E	FM	167
High Trees Fm	Herts	TL3521	51°52·5'	0°1·9'W	FM	166
High Trees Fm	Staffs	SK0828	52°51·2'	1°52·5'W	FM	128
High Trees Fm	Suff	TL9839	52°1·1'	0°53·5'E	FM	155
Hightrees Fm	Worcs	SO8083	52°26·9'	2°17·3'W	FM	138
High Tree, The	Angus	NO2568	56°48·1'	3°13·2'W	X	44
High Trewhitt	Northum	NU0005	55°20·6'	1°59·6'W	T	81
High Trewhitt	Northum	NU0005	55°20·6'	1°59·6'W	X	81
High Trewitley	Northum	NZ1291	55°13·0'	1°48·3'W	X	81
High Troweir	S Ayr	NX2295	55°13·3'	4°47·5'W	X	76
Hights of Inchvannie	Highld	NH4960	57°36·5'	4°31·2'W	X	20
High Tunstall	Hartpl	NZ4832	54°41·1'	1°14·9'W	X	93
High Tunstall Fm	N Yks	NZ5312	54°30·3'	1°10·5'W	FM	93
High Ugadale	Arg & Bt	NR7829	55°30·5'	5°30·5'W	X	68,69
High Underbrow	Cumbr	SD5197	54°22·2'	2°44·8'W	X	97
High Unthank	S Lanak	NS6744	55°40·5'	4°6·5'W	X	71
High Urpeth	Durham	NZ2353	54°52·5'	1°38·1'W	T	88
High Valleyfield	Fife	NT0086	56°3·6'	3°35·9'W	T	65
Highveer Point	Devon	SS6549	51°13·7'	3°55·6'W	X	180
Highview	D & G	NY0973	55°2·8'	3°25·0'W	X	85

High Vinnalls	Heref	SO4772	52°20·8'	2°46·3'W	H	137,138,148
High Volts Fm	Hartpl	NZ4534	54°42·2'	1°17·7'W	FM	93
High Waitgate	N Yks	NZ0805	54°26·7'	1°52·2'W	X	92
High Walls Fm	N Yks	NZ7408	54°28·0'	0°51·1'W	FM	94
Highwall Spinney	Warw	SP2939	52°3·2'	1°34·2'W	F	151
High Walton	Cumbr	NX9812	54°29·8'	3°34·1'W	T	89
High Walton	E Renf	NS4854	55°45·6'	4°24·9'W	X	64
High Walton	Shrops	SO4778	52°24·1'	2°46·3'W	X	137,138,148
High Warden	Northum	NY9167	55°0·1'	2°8·0'W	T	87
High Wardneuk	S Ayr	NS3928	55°31·4'	4°32·6'W	X	70
High Warren	Warr	SJ6184	53°21·3'	2°34·7'W	X	109
High Warren Fm	N Yks	SE2857	54°0·7'	1°33·9'W	FM	104
High Warren Fm	N Yks	SE6074	54°9·7'	1°4·4'W	FM	100
High Waskerley	Northum	NZ0853	54°52·5'	1°52·1'W	X	88
High Water Head	Cumbr	SD3198	54°22·6'	3°3·3'W	T	96,97
High Waterside	Cumbr	NY0415	54°31·5'	3°28·6'W	X	89
High Wathcote	N Yks	NZ1902	54°25·0'	1°42·0'W	X	92
High Waupley	Red & Cl	NZ7214	54°31·2'	0°52·8'W	X	94
Highway	Corn	SW7143	50°14·8'	5°12·4'W	T	203
Highway	Corn	SX1996	50°44·4'	4°33·5'W	X	190
Highway	Heref	SO4549	52°8·4'	2°47·8'W	T	148,149
High Way	N Yks	SD7995	54°21·3'	2°19·0'W	X	98
Highway	Somer	ST4620	50°58·8'	2°45·8'W	T	193
Highway	Staffs	SJ7944	52°59·8'	2°18·4'W	X	118
Highway	Swan	SS5588	51°34·6'	4°5·2'W	X	159
Highway	Wilts	SU0474	51°28·1'	1°56·2'W	T	173
Highway	Win & Maid	SU8681	51°31·5'	0°45·2'W	T	175
Highway Fm	Hill	TQ0688	51°35·1'	0°27·8'W	FM	176
Highway Fm	Shrops	SJ6323	52°48·4'	2°32·5'W	FM	127
Highway Hill	Wilts	SU0474	51°28·1'	1°56·2'W	X	173
Highway Ho	Hants	SU7643	51°11·1'	0°54·4'W	X	186
Highweek	Devon	SS4405	50°49·6'	4°12·5'W	X	190
Highweek	Devon	SX8472	50°32·4'	3°37·8'W	T	191
Highweek Wood	Devon	SS4506	50°50·2'	4°11·7'W	F	190
High Weetslade	N Tyne	NZ2572	55°2·8'	1°36·1'W	X	88
High Weldon	Northum	NZ1499	55°17·3'	1°46·3'W	X	81
High Well Ho	Northum	NY9774	55°3·9'	2°2·4'W	X	87
High West Scar	Cumbr	NY1861	54°56·5'	3°16·4'W	X	85
High West Thickley	Durham	NZ2125	54°37·4'	1°40·1'W	X	93
High Westwood	Durham	NZ1155	54°53·6'	1°49·3'W	T	88
High Wether Hill	Durham	NZ1328	54°39·1'	1°47·5'W	X	92
High Wether Howe	Cumbr	NY5110	54°29·2'	2°45·0'W	H	90
High Wexford	S Ayr	NS3630	55°32·4'	4°35·5'W	X	70
High Wham	Durham	NZ1126	54°38·0'	1°49·4'W	X	92
High Wheeldon	Derby	SK1066	53°11·7'	1°50·6'W	X	119
High Whinholme	N Yks	NZ3101	54°24·5'	1°30·9'W	X	93
High Whinnow	Cumbr	NY3051	54°51·2'	3°5·0'W	T	85
High Whitber	Cumbr	NY6220	54°34·7'	2°34·9'W	X	91
High Whitefarland	N Ayr	NR8641	55°37·2'	5°23·5'W	X	62,69
High White Stones	Cumbr	NY2709	54°28·5'	3°7·2'W	X	89,90
High Whittaker Fm	Lancs	SD8035	53°48·9'	2°17·8'W	FM	103
High Wigsell	E Susx	TQ7626	51°0·6'	0°30·9'E	X	188,199
High Willhays	Devon	SX5889	50°41·2'	4°0·2'W	H	191
High Wind Bank	N Yks	SD9769	54°7·3'	2°2·3'W	X	98
High Winder	Cumbr	NY4923	54°36·2'	2°46·9'W	X	90
High Windhill	N Yks	SD9544	53°53·8'	2°4·2'W	X	103
High Wind Hill	N Yks	SE7595	54°20·9'	0°50·3'W	X	94,100
High Winsley	N Yks	SE2462	54°3·4'	1°37·6'W	X	99
High Wiserley	Durham	NZ0736	54°43·4'	1°53·1'W	X	92
High Wold Fm	E Yorks	SE9041	53°51·7'	0°37·5'W	FM	106
High Wood	Barns	SE2810	53°35·4'	1°34·2'W	F	110
High Wood	Corn	SX2365	50°27·7'	4°29·3'W	F	201
High Wood	Cumbr	NY1204	54°25·7'	3°21·0'W	F	89
High Wood	Cumbr	NY4853	54°52·4'	2°48·2'W	F	86
High Wood	Cumbr	SD2989	54°17·7'	3°5·0'W	F	96,97
High Wood	Derby	SK4678	53°18·1'	1°18·2'W	F	120
Highwood	Derby	SK5176	53°16·9'	1°13·7'W	X	120
Highwood	Devon	ST1406	50°51·1'	3°12·9'W	T	192,193
High Wood	D & G	NX6276	55°3·8'	4°9·2'W	F	77
High Wood	Dorset	SU1112	50°54·7'	1°50·2'W	F	195
Highwood	Dorset	SY8685	50°40·1'	2°11·5'W	T	194
High Wood	Dorset	SY9397	50°46·6'	2°5·6'W	F	195
High Wood	E Ayr	NS6525	55°30·3'	4°7·8'W	X	71
High Wood	E Loth	NT6871	55°56·1'	2°30·3'W	F	67
High Wood	Essex	TL4536	52°0·4'	0°7·2'E	F	154
High Wood	Essex	TL6021	51°52·1'	0°19·8'E	F	167
High Wood	E Susx	TQ4424	51°0·1'	0°3·5'E	F	198
High Wood	E Susx	TQ6618	50°56·5'	0°22·2'E	F	199
High Wood	E Susx	TQ6622	50°58·6'	0°22·3'E	F	199
High Wood	E Susx	TQ7117	50°55·8'	0°26·4'E	F	199
High Wood	E Yorks	SE8449	53°56·1'	0°42·8'W	F	106
High Wood	E Yorks	SE9553	53°58·1'	0°32·7'W	F	106
High Wood	E Yorks	TA1566	54°4·9'	0°14·1'W	F	101
High Wood	Glos	SO7535	52°1·0'	2°21·5'W	F	150
High Wood	Glos	ST5499	51°41·5'	2°39·5'W	F	162
High Wood	Glos	ST8399	51°41·6'	2°14·4'W	F	162
Highwood	Hants	SU1707	50°52·0'	1°45·1'W	T	195
High Wood	Hants	SU5422	50°59·9'	1°13·4'W	F	185
High Wood	Hants	SU6344	51°11·7'	1°5·5'W	F	185
High Wood	Hants	SU6844	51°11·7'	1°1·2'W	F	185,186
High Wood	Herts	TL2823	51°53·7'	0°8·0'W	F	166
High Wood	Highld	NH7648	57°30·6'	4°3·7'W	F	27
High Wood	I of W	SZ4487	50°41·1'	1°22·2'W	F	196
High Wood	Kent	TQ8555	51°16·1'	0°39·5'E	F	178
High Wood	Kent	TQ8758	51°17·6'	0°41·3'E	F	178
High Wood	Lincs	SK8677	53°17·2'	0°42·2'W	X	121
High Wood	Lincs	TF0146	53°0·3'	0°29·3'W	F	130
High Wood	Moray	NH9959	57°36·8'	3°41·0'W	F	27
High Wood	N Lincs	SE9405	53°32·2'	0°34·5'W	F	112
High Wood	Norf	TF9825	52°47·4'	0°56·6'E	F	132
High Wood	Northnts	SP5854	52°11·1'	1°8·7'W	F	152
High Wood	Northum	NT9640	55°39·5'	2°3·4'W	F	74,75
High Wood	Northum	NY9164	54°58·5'	2°8·0'W	F	87
High Wood	Notts	SK7363	53°9·8'	0°54·1'W	F	120
High Wood	N Yks	SD9555	53°59·7'	2°4·2'W	F	103
High Wood	N Yks	SD9582	54°14·3'	2°4·2'W	F	98
High Wood	N Yks	SE4773	54°9·3'	1°16·4'W	F	100
High Wood	N Yks	SE5897	54°22·2'	1°6·0'W	F	100
High Wood	N Yks	SE6072	54°8·7'	1°4·5'W	F	100
High Wood	N Yks	SE8588	54°17·1'	0°41·2'W	F	94,100

High Wood	Oxon	SU7579	51°30·5′	0°54·8′W	F	175
High Wood	Oxon	SU7597	51°40·2′	0°54·5′W	F	165
High Wood	Shrops	SO7082	52°26·3′	2°26·1′W	F	138
Highwood	Staffs	SK0931	52°52·8′	1°51·6′W	X	128
High Wood	Stir	NN7005	56°13·4′	4°5·4′W	F	57
High Wood	Suff	TL9242	52°2·8′	0°48·4′E	F	155
High Wood	Surrey	TQ4136	51°6·6′	0°1·2′E	F	187
High Wood	W Berks	SU4769	51°25·3′	1°19·1′W	F	174
High Wood	Wilts	ST8042	51°10·8′	2°16·8′W	F	183
Highwood	Worcs	SO6566	52°17·7′	2°30·4′W	T	138,149
High Woodale	N Yks	SE0777	54°11·6′	1°53·1′W	X	99
High Woodbank	Cumbr	NY4152	54°51·8′	2°54·7′W	X	85
High Woodend	Cumbr	NY6104	54°26·0′	2°35·7′W	X	91
Highwood Fm	Devon	SS9918	50°57·4′	3°25·9′W	FM	181
Highwood Fm	Glos	ST7390	51°36·7′	2°23·0′W	FM	162,172
High Wood Fm	N Lincs	TA0612	53°35·9′	0°23·5′W	FM	112
Highwood Fm	Northum	NY9165	54°59·0′	2°8·0′W	FM	87
Highwood Fm	Notts	SK6896	53°27·6′	0°58·1′W	FM	111
Highwood Fm	W Berks	SU3862	51°21·6′	1°26·9′W	FM	174
Highwood Hall Fm	Herts	TL0905	51°44·2′	0°24·9′W	FM	166
High Wood Head	Brad	SE0643	53°53·2′	1°54·1′W	X	104
Highwood Heath	Dorset	SY8785	50°40·1′	2°10·7′W	X	194
Highwood Hill	Barnet	TQ2293	51°37·6′	0°13·9′W	T	176
Highwood Ho	Heref	SO4565	52°17·1′	2°48·0′W	X	137,138,148
High Woodifield	Durham	NZ1435	54°42·8′	1°46·5′W	X	92
High Wood Meadows	Durham	NY8937	54°43·9′	2°9·8′W	X	91,92
High Woodnook	Cumbr	NY1940	54°45·2′	3°15·1′W	X	85
Highwood Pasture	N Yks	SD7376	54°11·0′	2°24·4′W	X	98
High Woods	Essex	TL6302	51°41·8′	0°21·9′E	X	167
Highwoods	E Susx	TQ7109	50°51·5′	0°26·2′E	F	199
High Woods	N Yks	SE2064	54°4·5′	1°41·2′W	X	99
High Woods	N Yks	SE5679	54°12·5′	1°8·1′W	X	100
Highwoods	W Berks	SU6667	51°24·1′	1°2·7′W	X	175
High Woods Country Park	Essex	TM0026	51°54·0′	0°54·8′E	X	168
Highwood's Fm	Essex	TL7929	51°56·1′	0°36·6′E	FM	167
High Woodston	S Ayr	NS3912	55°22·8′	4°32·0′W	X	70
High Woof Howe	N Yks	SE8996	54°21·3′	0°37·4′W	A	94,101
High Woolaston	Glos	ST5799	51°41·5′	2°36·9′W	T	162
High Wooley	Durham	NZ1739	54°45·0′	1°43·7′W	X	92
High Worsall	N Yks	NZ3809	54°28·7′	1°24·4′W	T	93
High Worsall Moor	N Yks	NZ3807	54°27·7′	1°24·4′W	X	93
Highworth	Swin	SU2092	51°37·8′	1°42·3′W	T	163,174
Highworth Fm	Surrey	TQ2342	51°10·1′	0°14·1′W	FM	187
Highworthy	Devon	SS3122	50°58·6′	4°24·1′W	X	190
Highworthy	Devon	SS4408	50°51·3′	4°12·6′W	T	190
High Wray	Cumbr	SD3799	54°23·2′	2°57·8′W	T	96,97
High Wray Bay	Cumbr	NY3700	54°23·7′	2°57·8′W	W	90
High Wreay	Cumbr	NY4348	54°49·7′	2°52·8′W	X	85
High Wrong Corner	Norf	TL8282	52°24·6′	0°41·0′E	F	144
High Wych	Herts	TL4614	51°48·6′	0°7·5′E	T	167
High Wycombe	Bucks	SU8693	51°38·0′	0°45·0′W	T	175
High Wykehurst	Surrey	TQ0740	51°9·2′	0°27·8′W	X	187
High Yarridge	Northum	NY9162	54°57·4′	2°8·0′W	X	87
High Yedmandale	N Yks	SE9786	54°15·9′	0°30·2′W	X	94,101
High Yewdale	Cumbr	SD3199	54°23·2′	3°3·3′W	X	96,97
Higney Grange	Cambs	TL2083	52°26·1′	0°13·7′W	X	142
Hilborough	Norf	TF8200	52°34·3′	0°41·5′E	T	144
Hilbre	Cumbr	NY4576	55°4·8′	2°51·3′W	X	86
Hilbre Island	Wirral	SJ1887	53°22·7′	3°13·6′W	X	108
Hilcombe Fm	Somer	ST7435	51°7·1′	2°21·9′W	FM	183
Hilcop Bank	Shrops	SJ5427	52°50·6′	2°40·6′W	X	126
Hilcot	Glos	SO9916	51°50·8′	2°0·5′W	T	163
Hilcot Brook	Glos	SO9914	51°49·7′	2°0·5′W	W	163
Hilcote	Derby	SK4558	53°7·3′	1°19·2′W	T	120
Hilcote Fm	Staffs	SJ8430	52°52·3′	2°13·9′W	FM	127
Hilcote Hall	Staffs	SJ8429	52°51·7′	2°13·9′W	X	127
Hilcot End	Glos	SP0702	51°43·2′	1°53·5′W	T	163
Hilcott	Wilts	SU1158	51°19·5′	1°50·1′W	T	173
Hilcot Wood	Glos	SO9816	51°50·8′	2°1·3′W	F	163
Hildasay	Shetld	HU3540	60°8·8′	1°21·7′W	X	4
Hilda Wood	N Yks	SE9791	54°18·6′	0°30·1′W	F	94,101
Hildenborough	Kent	TQ5648	51°12·8′	0°14·4′E	T	188
Hilden Brook	Kent	TQ5848	51°12·8′	0°16·1′E	W	188
Hildenley Home Fm	N Yks	SE7470	54°7·5′	0°51·6′W	FM	100
Hildenley Wood	N Yks	SE7570	54°7·5′	0°50·7′W	F	100
Hilden Park	Kent	TQ5747	51°12·3′	0°15·2′E	T	188
Hilders	Kent	TQ4347	51°12·5′	0°3·2′E	X	187
Hilder's Court	E Susx	TQ5415	50°55·1′	0°11·8′E	X	199
Hilders Fm	Kent	TQ4848	51°12·9′	0°7·5′E	FM	188
Hilders Fm	W Susx	TQ2822	50°59·2′	0°10·2′W	FM	198
Hildersham	Cambs	TL5448	52°6·8′	0°15·3′E	T	154
Hildersley	Heref	SO6124	51°55·0′	2°33·6′W	T	162
Hilderstone	Lancs	SD5176	54°10·9′	2°44·6′W	X	97
Hilderstone	Staffs	SJ9434	52°54·4′	2°4·9′W	T	127
Hilderston Fm	W Loth	NS9671	55°55·5′	3°39·4′W	FM	65
Hilderthorpe	E Yorks	TA1765	54°4·3′	0°12·3′W	T	101
Hilderthorpe Village	E Yorks	TA1765	54°4·3′	0°12·3′W	A	101
Hildrew	Devon	SS5626	51°1·2′	4°2·8′W	X	180
Hile	N Yks	SD7857	54°0·8′	2°19·7′W	X	103
Hile, The	Lancs	SD8523	53°42·4′	2°13·2′W	X	103
Hilfield	Dorset	ST6304	50°50·3′	2°31·1′W	T	194
Hilfield Castle	Herts	TQ1596	51°39·3′	0°19·9′W	X	166,176
Hilfield Manor	Dorset	ST6306	50°51·4′	2°31·2′W	X	194
Hilfield Park Resr	Herts	TQ1595	51°38·7′	0°19·9′W	W	166,176
Hilgay	Norf	TL6298	52°33·6′	0°23·8′E	T	143
Hilgay Fen	Norf	TL5895	52°32·0′	0°20·2′E	X	143
Hilgay Fen	Norf	TL6398	52°33·6′	0°24·7′E	X	143
Hill	Birm	SP1199	52°35·6′	1°49·9′W	T	139
Hill	Corn	SX1494	50°43·2′	4°37·7′W	X	190
Hill	Cumbr	NY4023	54°36·2′	2°55·3′W	X	90
Hill	Cumbr	SD0799	54°22·9′	3°25·5′W	X	96
Hill	Cumbr	SD3679	54°12·4′	2°58·5′W	X	96,97
Hill	Devon	SS6237	51°7·2′	3°57·9′W	X	180
Hill	Devon	SS6926	51°1·3′	3°51·7′W	X	180
Hill	Devon	ST0019	50°57·9′	3°25·1′W	X	181
Hill	D & G	NX6578	55°4·9′	4°6·5′W	X	77,84
Hill	D & G	NX7260	54°55·4′	3°59·4′W	X	83,84
Hill	D & G	NX8671	55°1·5′	3°46·6′W	H	84
Hill	E Ayr	NS5418	55°26·3′	4°18·0′W	X	70
Hill	E Ayr	NS5535	55°35·5′	4°17·6′W	X	71

Hill	Falk	NS9473	55°56·6′	3°41·4′W	X	65
Hill	Inverc	NS2071	55°54·2′	4°52·3′W	X	63
Hill	Pemb	SN1311	51°46·2′	4°42·2′W	X	158
Hill	S Glos	ST6495	51°39·4′	2°30·8′W	T	162
Hill	S Lanak	NS7848	55°42·9′	3°56·1′W	X	64
Hill	Warw	SP4567	52°18·2′	1°20·0′W	T	151
Hill	Worcs	SO9848	52°8·1′	2°1·4′W	X	150
Hilla Green Fm	N Yks	SE9490	54°18·1′	0°32·9′W	FM	94,101
Hillam	Lancs	SD4552	53°57·9′	2°49·9′W	X	102
Hillam	N Yks	SE5028	53°45·0′	1°14·1′W	T	105
Hilland Fm	W Susx	TQ0926	51°1·6′	0°26·4′W	FM	187,198
Hillands Fm	W Susx	SZ8399	50°47·3′	0°49·0′W	FM	197
Hill Ash	Glos	SO7032	51°59·4′	2°25·8′W	X	149
Hill Ash Fm	Devon	SS4314	50°54·5′	4°13·6′W	FM	180,190
Hill Ash Fm	W Susx	SU7821	50°59·2′	0°52·9′W	FM	197
Hillbank	D & G	NY0580	55°6·6′	3°28·9′W	X	78
Hill Barn	Dorset	SY6498	50°47·1′	2°30·3′W	X	194
Hill Barn	Dorset	SY6993	50°44·4′	2°26·0′W	X	194
Hill Barn	Dorset	SY7995	50°45·5′	2°17·5′W	X	194
Hill Barn	Glos	SO9514	51°49·7′	2°4·0′W	X	163
Hill Barn	Glos	SP0518	51°51·9′	1°55·2′W	X	163
Hill Barn	Glos	SP0916	51°50·8′	1°51·8′W	X	163
Hill Barn	Glos	SP1911	51°48·1′	1°43·1′W	X	163
Hill Barn	Hants	SU4540	51°9·7′	1°21·0′W	X	185
Hill Barn	Heref	SO4164	52°16·5′	2°51·5′W	X	137,148,149
Hillbarn	Monm	SO3213	51°48·9′	2°58·8′W	X	161
Hill Barn	Oxon	SP2415	51°50·2′	1°38·7′W	X	163
Hillbarn	Oxon	SP4632	51°59·3′	1°19·4′W	X	151
Hill Barn	Oxon	SU3385	51°34·0′	1°31·0′W	X	174
Hill Barn	Oxon	SU3991	51°37·2′	1°25·8′W	X	164,174
Hill Barn	Oxon	SU5583	51°32·8′	1°12·0′W	X	174
Hill Barn	Powys	SO1480	52°24·9′	3°15·5′W	X	136
Hill Barn	Swin	SU2080	51°31·3′	1°42·3′W	X	174
Hill Barn	W Berks	SU5079	51°30·7′	1°16·4′W	X	174
Hillbarn	W Susx	SU8114	50°55·4′	0°50·5′W	X	197
Hill Barn	W Susx	SU8716	50°56·4′	0°45·3′W	X	197
Hill Barn Fm	Glos	SP1033	52°0·0′	1°50·9′W	FM	150
Hill Barn Fm	Oxon	SP3131	51°58·8′	1°32·5′W	FM	151
Hill Barn Fm	Oxon	SP3818	51°51·8′	1°26·5′W	FM	164
Hill Barn Fm	Somer	ST3907	50°51·8′	2°51·6′W	FM	193
Hillbarn Fm	Wilts	SU2861	51°21·1′	1°35·5′W	FM	174
Hillbarns	Angus	NO5357	56°42·4′	2°45·6′W	X	54
Hillbarns	Pth & Kin	NO1645	56°35·6′	3°21·6′W	X	53
Hill Barton	Devon	SS5546	51°11·9′	4°4·1′W	X	180
Hill Barton	Devon	SS6604	50°49·4′	3°53·8′W	X	191
Hill Barton	Devon	SS7608	50°51·7′	3°45·3′W	X	191
Hill Barton	Devon	SX5998	50°46·1′	3°59·6′W	FM	191
Hill Barton Fm	Devon	SY0090	50°42·3′	3°24·6′W	FM	192
Hillberry	I of M	SC3879	54°11·1′	4°28·5′W	T	95
Hillblock	Pemb	SN0015	51°48·1′	4°53·7′W	T	157,158
Hillborough	Kent	TR2067	51°21·8′	1°10·0′E	T	179
Hillborough	Warw	SP1252	52°10·2′	1°49·1′W	X	150
Hillborough Manor	Warw	SP1252	52°10·2′	1°49·1′W	A	150
Hillborough Village	Warw	SP1251	52°9·7′	1°49·1′W	A	150
Hill Bottom	Oxon	SU6479	51°30·6′	1°4·3′W	T	175
Hillbourne	Poole	SZ0094	50°45·0′	1°59·6′W	T	195
Hillbrae	Aberd	NJ6047	57°30·9′	2°39·6′W	X	29
Hillbrae	Aberd	NJ6532	57°22·9′	2°34·5′W	X	29
Hillbrae	Aberd	NJ6824	57°18·6′	2°31·4′W	X	38
Hillbrae	Aberd	NJ7923	57°18·1′	2°20·5′W	X	38
Hillbrae	Aberd	NJ8334	57°24·0′	2°16·5′W	X	29,30
Hillbrae Croft	Aberd	NJ8335	57°24·6′	2°16·5′W	X	29,30
Hillbrae Fm	Aberd	NJ9021	57°17·0′	2°9·5′W	FM	38
Hill Bridge	Devon	SX5380	50°36·3′	4°4·3′W	X	191,201
Hill Brook	Devon	SS6648	51°13·2′	3°54·7′W	W	180
Hillbrook	Somer	ST2022	50°59·7′	3°8·0′W	X	193
Hill Brow	Hants	SU7926	51°1·9′	0°52·0′W	T	186,197
Hillbrow Fm	Dorset	ST4902	50°49·2′	2°43·1′W	FM	193,194
Hillbrow Fm	Suff	TM1849	52°6·0′	1°11·4′E	FM	169
Hill Buildings	Oxon	SP2716	51°50·7′	1°36·1′W	X	163
Hill Burn	Scot Bord	NT5520	55°28·6′	2°42·3′W	W	73
Hillbutts	Dorset	ST9901	50°48·7′	2°0·5′W	T	195
Hillcairnie	Fife	NO3618	56°21·3′	3°1·7′W	X	59
Hillcarr Wood	Derby	SK2563	53°10·0′	1°37·2′W	F	119
Hill Chorlton	Staffs	SJ7939	52°57·1′	2°18·4′W	T	127
Hillcliffe	Warr	SJ6185	53°21·9′	2°34·8′W	T	109
Hillcliffiane	Derby	SK2947	53°1·4′	1°33·7′W	T	119,128
Hill Climb	Worcs	SO7162	52°15·6′	2°25·1′W	X	138,149
Hill Clumps	Warw	SP2742	52°4·8′	1°36·0′W	F	151
Hill & Coles Fm	Herts	TL0815	51°49·6′	0°25·6′W	FM	166
Hillcombe Coppice	Dorset	ST8308	50°52·5′	2°14·1′W	F	194
Hill Common	Norf	TG4122	52°44·7′	1°34·7′E	T	134
Hillcommon	Somer	ST1426	51°1·9′	3°13·2′W	T	181,193
Hillcoose	Corn	SW8850	50°18·9′	4°58·3′W	X	200,204
Hill Corner	Somer	ST8048	51°14·1′	2°16·8′W	T	183
Hill Corner	W Berks	SU5876	51°29·0′	1°9·5′W	X	174
Hill Cott	Wilts	SU0065	51°23·3′	1°59·6′W	X	173
Hill Cottage	Shetld	HU3871	60°25·5′	1°18·1′W	X	2,3
Hill Cottages	N Yks	SE7197	54°22·1′	0°54·0′W	X	94,100
Hillcourt	Glos	ST8789	51°36·2′	2°10·9′W	X	162,173
Hill Court	Heref	SO5721	51°53·4′	2°37·1′W	A	162
Hill Court	Kent	TQ4747	51°12·4′	0°6·7′E	X	188
Hill Court	S Glos	ST6595	51°39·4′	2°30·0′W	X	162
Hill Court	Worcs	SO8334	52°0·5′	2°14·5′W	X	150
Hill Court	Worcs	SO9557	52°12·9′	2°4·0′W	X	150
Hill Court Fm	Worcs	SO7932	51°59·4′	2°18·0′W	FM	150
Hill Covert	Suff	TM4675	52°19·3′	1°37·0′E	F	156
Hillcrest	Cumbr	SD2872	54°8·6′	3°5·7′W	X	96,97
Hill Crest	Durham	NZ0039	54°45·0′	1°59·6′W	X	92
Hillcrest	Flint	SJ2768	53°12·5′	3°5·2′W	X	117
Hillcrest	Heref	SO5929	51°57·7′	2°35·4′W	X	149
Hillcrest	N Lincs	TA1116	53°38·0′	0°18·9′W	X	113
Hill Crest	Northum	NU1929	55°33·5′	1°41·5′W	X	75
Hill Crest	N Yks	SE1888	54°17·5′	1°43·0′W	X	99
Hillcrest Fm	Devon	SS5442	51°9·8′	4°4·9′W	FM	180
Hillcrest Fm	Leic	SK7116	52°44·5′	0°56·5′W	FM	129
Hillcroft	Essex	TL6407	51°44·5′	0°22·9′E	X	167
Hillcroft	Highld	NG3740	57°22·7′	6°22·1′W	X	23
Hill Croft Fm	N Yks	SE3547	53°55·3′	1°27·6′W	FM	104
Hillcroft Fm	Oxon	SP5515	51°50·1′	1°11·7′W	FM	164

Hillcroft Open Fm	Highld	NG3739	57°22·2′	6°22·0′W	FM	23
Hill Crofts	Cambs	TL6152	52°8·8′	0°21·6′E	F	154
Hill Croome	Worcs	SO8840	52°3·7′	2°10·1′W	T	150
Hillcross	C of Derb	SK3333	52°53·8′	1°30·2′W	T	128
Hill Cross	Heref	SO6858	52°13·4′	2°27·7′W	X	149
Hillcross Fm	I of W	SZ4591	50°43·2′	1°21·4′W	FM	196
Hill Dairy	Dorset	ST9101	50°48·7′	2°7·3′W	X	195
Hill Dale	Lancs	SD4912	53°36·4′	2°45·8′W	T	108
Hilldavale	Orkney	HY4247	59°18·6′	3°0·6′W	X	5
Hill Deverill	Wilts	ST8640	51°9·8′	2°11·6′W	T	183
Hill Deverill Village	Wilts	ST8640	51°9·8′	2°11·6′W	A	183
Hilldown	Devon	SX7299	50°46·8′	3°48·6′W	X	191
Hilldrop	Wilts	SU2672	51°27·0′	1°37·2′W	X	174
Hilldrop Fm	W Berks	SU3275	51°28·6′	1°32·0′W	FM	174
Hilldyke	Lincs	TF3447	53°0·4′	0°0·2′E	T	131
Hill Em	Kent	TQ7072	51°25·5′	0°27·1′E	X	178
Hillend	Aberd	NJ4144	57°29·2′	2°58·6′W	X	28
Hillend	Aberd	NJ5561	57°38·5′	2°44·8′W	X	29
Hillend	Angus	NO4848	56°37·5′	2°50·4′W	T	54
Hillend	Clackm	NS9193	56°7·3′	3°44·8′W	X	58
Hill End	Cumbr	SD1483	54°14·4′	3°18·8′W	X	96
Hillend	D & G	NS5603	55°18·3′	4°15·7′W	X	77
Hillend	D & G	NS6808	55°21·2′	4°4·5′W	X	71,77
Hillend	D & G	NY1865	54°58·6′	3°16·4′W	X	85
Hill End	Durham	NY8629	54°39·6′	2°12·6′W	X	91,92
Hill End	Durham	NZ0135	54°42·8′	1°58·6′W	T	92
Hillend	Falk	NS8473	55°56·4′	3°51·0′W	X	65
Hillend	Falk	NS9172	55°56·0′	3°44·2′W	X	65
Hill End	Fife	NT0395	56°8·5′	3°33·2′W	T	58
Hillend	Fife	NT1483	56°2·2′	3°22·4′W	T	65
Hillend	Glos	SO8430	51°58·3′	2°13·6′W	X	150
Hill End	Glos	SO9037	52°2·1′	2°8·4′W	T	150
Hill End	Heref	SO5741	52°4·2′	2°37·2′W	X	149
Hill End	Heref	SO6335	52°1·0′	2°32·0′W	X	149
Hillend	Heref	SO7436	52°1·5′	2°22·3′W	X	150
Hill End	Hill	TQ0491	51°36·7′	0°29·5′W	T	176
Hill End	Lancs	SD8838	53°50·5′	2°10·5′W	X	103
Hillend	Midlo	NT2566	55°53·1′	3°11·5′W	X	66
Hillend	N Ayr	NS2948	55°42·0′	4°42·8′W	X	63
Hillend	N Ayr	NS4054	55°45·4′	4°32·5′W	X	64
Hillend	N Lanak	NS8267	55°53·2′	3°52·8′W	T	65
Hill End	Northum	NZ0689	55°12·0′	1°53·9′W	X	81
Hillend	N Som	ST3758	51°19·3′	2°53·9′W	T	182
Hill End	N Yks	SE0954	53°59·2′	1°51·3′W	T	104
Hill End	N Yks	SE7383	54°14·5′	0°52·4′W	X	100
Hill End	Scot Bord	NT0621	55°28·7′	3°28·8′W	H	72
Hillend	Scot Bord	NT4436	55°37·1′	2°52·9′W	X	73
Hillend	Scot Bord	NT5621	55°29·1′	2°41·3′W	X	73
Hillend	Scot Bord	NT8663	55°51·8′	2°13·0′W	X	67
Hillend	Scot Bord	NY4883	55°8·6′	2°48·5′W	X	79
Hillend	Shetld	HU5090	60°35·7′	1°4·7′W	X	1,2
Hill End	Shrops	SO5094	52°32·7′	2°43·8′W	H	137,138
Hillend	Shrops	SO8094	52°32·8′	2°17·3′W	T	138
Hillend	S Lanak	NS9427	55°31·8′	3°40·3′W	X	71,72
Hillend	S Lanak	NT0438	55°37·8′	3°31·1′W	X	72
Hill End	Somer	ST5011	50°54·0′	2°42·3′W	T	194
Hillend	Staffs	SK0663	53°10·1′	1°54·2′W	X	119
Hill End	Staffs	SK1062	53°9·5′	1°50·6′W	X	119
Hillend	Swan	SS4191	51°36·0′	4°17·4′W	T	159
Hillend	W Loth	NT0673	55°56·7′	3°29·9′W	X	65
Hill End	Worcs	SO9063	52°16·1′	2°8·4′W	T	150
Hillend Burrows	Swan	SS4190	51°35·4′	4°17·3′W	X	159
Hillend Court	Worcs	SO8037	52°2·1′	2°17·1′W	X	150
Hill End Fm	Bucks	SP8406	51°45·0′	0°46·6′W	FM	165
Hillend Fm	Devon	ST1807	50°51·6′	3°9·5′W	FM	192,193
Hill End Fm	Hants	SU6257	51°18·8′	1°6·2′W	FM	175
Hill End Fm	Herts	TL1006	51°44·7′	0°24·0′W	FM	166
Hillend Fm	Herts	TL1611	51°47·4′	0°18·7′W	FM	166
Hill End Fm	Herts	TL1923	51°53·8′	0°15·8′W	FM	166
Hillend Fm	Herts	TL2509	51°46·2′	0°10·9′W	FM	166
Hill End Fm	N Yks	SE5796	54°21·6′	1°6·9′W	FM	100
Hillend Fm	Shrops	SO3987	52°28·9′	2°53·5′W	FM	137
Hill-End Fm	Shrops	SO4785	52°27·9′	2°46·4′W	FM	137,138
Hillend Fm	Staffs	SK1348	53°2·0′	1°48·0′W	FM	119
Hillend Fm	Worcs	SO7460	52°14·5′	2°22·5′W	FM	138,150
Hillend Fms	Heref	SO6346	52°6·9′	2°32·0′W	FM	149
Hillend Green	Glos	SO7028	51°57·2′	2°25·8′W	T	149
Hillend Hill	E Ayr	NS5705	55°19·4′	4°14·8′W	X	71,77
Hill End Ho	N Yks	SE5390	54°18·4′	1°10·7′W	X	100
Hillend Reservoir	N Lanak	NS8367	55°53·2′	3°51·8′W	W	65
Hill Ends	Cumbr	NY4946	54°48·6′	2°47·2′W	X	86
Hilleraye	Fife	NO5709	56°16·5′	2°41·2′W	X	59
Hillersdon Ho	Devon	SS9907	50°51·5′	3°25·7′W	X	192
Hillersland	Glos	SO5614	51°49·6′	2°37·9′W	T	162
Hillerton	Devon	SX7298	50°46·3′	3°48·5′W	T	191
Hillesden	Bucks	SP6828	51°57·0′	1°0·2′W	T	164,165
Hillesden Hamlet	Bucks	SP6730	51°58·1′	1°1·1′W	T	152,165
Hillesden House	Bucks	SP6828	51°57·0′	1°0·2′W	X	164,165
Hilles Ho Fm	Glos	SO8511	51°48·1′	2°12·7′W	FM	162
Hillesley	Glos	ST7689	51°36·2′	2°20·4′W	T	162,172
Hilley Fm	Shrops	SJ3717	52°45·1′	2°55·6′W	FM	126
Hill Farm	Hants	SZ2099	50°47·6′	1°42·6′W	FM	195
Hill Farm	Lincs	TA0803	53°31·0′	0°21·9′W	FM	112
Hill Farm Estate	Northnts	SP9672	52°20·5′	0°35·0′W	X	141
Hill Farm Ho	Beds	TL0829	51°57·2′	0°25·3′W	X	166
Hill Farms	Heref	SO4740	52°3·6′	2°46·0′W	FM	148,149,161
Hillfarrance	Somer	ST1624	51°0·8′	3°11·5′W	T	181,193
Hillfarrance Brook	Somer	ST1424	51°0·8′	3°13·2′W	W	181,193
Hill Fell	Cumbr	SD3399	54°23·2′	3°1·5′W	H	96,97
Hillfield	Cumbr	NY5265	54°58·9′	2°44·6′W	X	86
Hillfield	Devon	SX8351	50°21·1′	3°38·3′W	T	202
Hill Field	E Yorks	TA1669	54°6·5′	0°13·1′W	X	101
Hillfield	Sol	SP1478	52°24·2′	1°47·3′W	T	139
Hill Field Fm	Leic	SP5493	52°32·2′	1°11·8′W	FM	140
Hillfield Hall	Sol	SP1578	52°24·2′	1°46·4′W	A	139
Hillfield Ho	Worcs	SO8130	51°58·3′	2°16·2′W	X	150
Hillfields	C of Bris	ST6475	51°28·6′	2°30·7′W	T	172
Hillfields	Cov	SP3479	52°24·7′	1°29·6′W	T	140
Hillfields	Warw	SP3254	52°11·2′	1°31·5′W	X	151
Hillfields	W Berks	SU6667	51°24·1′	1°2·7′W	X	175

Hill Fields Fm	Cov	SP2782	52°26·4′	1°35·8′W	FM	140
Hillfields Fm	Warw	SP3980	52°25·2′	1°25·2′W	FM	140
Hill Fields Fm	W Berks	SU6078	51°30·1′	1°7·7′W	FM	175
Hillfields Ho	Worcs	SO7881	52°25·8′	2°19·0′W	X	138
Hill Fm	Beds	SP9430	51°57·9′	0°37·5′W	FM	165
Hill Fm	Beds	SP9525	51°55·2′	0°36·7′W	FM	165
Hill Fm	Beds	SP9628	51°56·8′	0°35·8′W	FM	165
Hill Fm	Beds	SP9648	52°7·5′	0°35·5′W	FM	153
Hill Fm	Beds	SP9656	52°11·9′	0°35·3′W	FM	153
Hill Fm	Beds	SP9742	52°4·3′	0°34·7′W	FM	153
Hill Fm	Beds	TL0026	51°55·6′	0°32·3′W	FM	166
Hill Fm	Beds	TL0216	51°50·2′	0°30·8′W	FM	166
Hill Fm	Beds	TL1248	52°7·4′	0°21·4′W	FM	153
Hill Fm	Beds	TL1741	52°3·5′	0°17·2′W	FM	153
Hill Fm	Beds	TL1938	52°1·9′	0°15·5′W	FM	153
Hill Fm	Brackn	SU8572	51°26·7′	0°46·2′W	FM	175
Hill Fm	Bucks	SP6435	52°0·8′	1°3·7′W	FM	152
Hill Fm	Bucks	SP7014	51°49·4′	0°58·7′W	FM	165
Hill Fm	Bucks	SP7139	52°2·9′	0°57·5′W	FM	152
Hill Fm	Bucks	SP7321	51°53·2′	0°56·0′W	FM	165
Hill Fm	Bucks	SP7328	51°57·0′	0°55·9′W	FM	165
Hill Fm	Bucks	SP7837	52°1·8′	0°51·4′W	FM	152
Hill Fm	Bucks	SP9320	51°52·5′	0°38·5′W	FM	165
Hill Fm	Bucks	SP9506	51°44·9′	0°37·0′W	FM	165
Hill Fm	Bucks	SU9182	51°32·0′	0°40·9′W	FM	175
Hill Fm	Cambs	TL1294	52°32·2′	0°20·5′W	FM	142
Hill Fm	Cambs	TL1469	52°18·7′	0°19·3′W	FM	153
Hill Fm	Cambs	TL2754	52°10·4′	0°8·2′W	FM	153
Hill Fm	Cambs	TL2763	52°15·3′	0°8·0′W	FM	153
Hill Fm	Cambs	TL2882	52°25·5′	0°6·7′W	FM	142
Hill Fm	Cambs	TL3765	52°16·2′	0°0·9′E	FM	154
Hill Fm	Cambs	TL3869	52°18·3′	0°1·8′E	FM	154
Hill Fm	Cambs	TL4286	52°27·4′	0°5·8′E	FM	142,143
Hill Fm	Cambs	TL4647	52°6·4′	0°8·3′E	FM	154
Hill Fm	Cambs	TL6248	52°6·6′	0°22·3′E	FM	154
Hill Fm	Cambs	TL6858	52°11·9′	0°27·9′E	FM	154
Hill Fm	Ches	SJ3771	53°14·2′	2°56·2′W	FM	117
Hill Fm	Ches	SJ4844	52°59·7′	2°46·1′W	FM	117
Hill Fm	Ches	SJ5563	53°10·0′	2°40·0′W	FM	117
Hill Fm	Ches	SJ5861	53°8·9′	2°37·3′W	FM	117
Hill Fm	Ches	SJ5878	53°18·1′	2°37·4′W	FM	117
Hill Fm	Ches	SJ6247	53°1·4′	2°33·6′W	FM	118
Hill Fm	Ches	SJ7159	53°7·9′	2°25·6′W	FM	118
Hill Fm	Ches	SJ7466	53°11·7′	2°22·9′W	FM	118
Hill Fm	C of Bris	ST5967	51°24·3′	2°35·0′W	FM	172,182
Hill Fm	Cumbr	NY1226	54°37·5′	3°21·4′W	FM	89
Hill Fm	Cumbr	NY1236	54°42·9′	3°21·5′W	FM	89
Hill Fm	Cumbr	NY3158	54°55·0′	3°4·2′W	FM	85
Hill Fm	Cumbr	SD0789	54°17·5′	3°25·3′W	FM	96
Hill Fm	Cumbr	SD4498	54°22·7′	2°51·3′W	FM	97
Hill Fm	Derby	SK2929	52°51·7′	1°33·8′W	FM	128
Hill Fm	Derby	SK3024	52°49·0′	1°32·9′W	FM	128
Hill Fm	Derby	SK3927	52°50·6′	1°24·9′W	FM	128
Hill Fm	Derby	SK4046	53°0·8′	1°23·8′W	FM	129
Hill Fm	Devon	SS5123	50°59·5′	4°7·0′W	FM	180
Hill Fm	Devon	SS5520	50°57·9′	4°3·5′W	FM	180
Hill Fm	Devon	SS5806	50°50·4′	4°0·6′W	FM	191
Hill Fm	Devon	SS5831	51°3·9′	4°1·2′W	FM	180
Hill Fm	Devon	SS5926	51°1·2′	4°0·2′W	FM	180
Hill Fm	Devon	SS6417	50°56·4′	3°55·8′W	FM	180
Hill Fm	Devon	SS8426	51°1·5′	3°38·9′W	FM	181
Hill Fm	Devon	SS8510	50°52·9′	3°37·7′W	FM	191
Hill Fm	Devon	ST0117	50°56·9′	3°24·2′W	FM	181
Hill Fm	Devon	ST1516	50°56·5′	3°12·2′W	FM	181,193
Hill Fm	Devon	SX7394	50°44·1′	3°47·6′W	FM	191
Hill Fm	Devon	SX8490	50°42·1′	3°38·2′W	FM	191
Hill Fm	Devon	SX8986	50°40·0′	3°33·9′W	FM	192
Hill Fm	Dorset	ST5003	50°49·7′	2°42·2′W	FM	194
Hill Fm	Dorset	ST7706	50°51·4′	2°19·2′W	FM	194
Hill Fm	Dorset	ST8221	50°59·5′	2°15·0′W	FM	183
Hill Fm	Dorset	ST8814	50°55·8′	2°9·9′W	FM	194
Hill Fm	E Ayr	NS4939	55°37·5′	4°23·5′W	FM	70
Hill Fm	Essex	TL5414	51°48·4′	0°14·4′E	FM	167
Hill Fm	Essex	TL6115	51°48·9′	0°20·5′E	FM	167
Hill Fm	Essex	TL6409	51°45·6′	0°23·0′E	FM	167
Hill Fm	Essex	TL6434	51°59·0′	0°23·7′E	FM	154
Hill Fm	Essex	TL7139	52°1·6′	0°30·0′E	FM	154
Hill Fm	Essex	TL7236	52°0·0′	0°30·7′E	FM	154
Hill Fm	Essex	TL7500	51°40·5′	0°32·3′E	FM	167
Hill Fm	Essex	TL8104	51°42·6′	0°37·6′E	FM	168
Hill Fm	Essex	TL8239	52°1·4′	0°39·6′E	FM	155
Hill Fm	Essex	TL8736	51°59·7′	0°43·8′E	FM	155
Hill Fm	Essex	TL8817	51°49·4′	0°44·1′E	FM	168
Hill Fm	Essex	TL8934	51°58·6′	0°45·5′E	FM	155
Hill Fm	Essex	TL9211	51°46·1′	0°47·4′E	FM	168
Hill Fm	Essex	TL9520	51°50·9′	0°50·3′E	FM	168
Hill Fm	Essex	TL9702	51°41·2′	0°51·4′E	FM	168
Hill Fm	Essex	TM0132	51°57·2′	0°55·9′E	FM	168
Hill Fm	Essex	TM0731	51°56·6′	1°1·1′E	FM	168,169
Hill Fm	Essex	TM1323	51°52·1′	1°6·0′E	FM	168,169
Hill Fm	Essex	TQ4797	51°39·4′	0°7·9′E	FM	167,177
Hill Fm	E Susx	TQ6907	50°50·5′	0°24·4′E	FM	199
Hill Fm	E Susx	TQ7016	50°55·3′	0°25·5′E	FM	199
Hill Fm	E Yorks	SE6221	53°41·1′	1°3·3′W	FM	105
Hill Fm	E Yorks	TA0973	54°8·7′	0°19·5′W	FM	101
Hill Fm	E Yorks	TA1236	53°48·7′	0°17·5′W	FM	107
Hill Fm	E Yorks	TA1359	54°1·1′	0°16·1′W	FM	107
Hill Fm	E Yorks	TA1926	53°43·2′	0°11·4′W	FM	107
Hill Fm	Glos	SO6604	51°44·3′	2°29·2′W	FM	162
Hill Fm	Glos	SO7618	51°51·8′	2°20·5′W	FM	162
Hill Fm	Glos	SO7901	51°42·7′	2°17·8′W	FM	162
Hill Fm	Glos	SO8024	51°55·1′	2°17·1′W	FM	162
Hill Fm	Glos	SO8127	51°56·7′	2°16·2′W	FM	162
Hill Fm	Glos	SP0034	52°0·5′	1°59·6′W	FM	150
Hill Fm	Glos	SP2022	51°54·0′	1°42·2′W	FM	163
Hill Fm	Glos	ST8898	51°41·1′	2°10·0′W	FM	162
Hill Fm	Hants	SU4337	51°8·1′	1°22·7′W	FM	185
Hill Fm	Hants	SU5115	50°56·2′	1°16·1′W	FM	196
Hill Fm	Hants	SU5124	51°1·0′	1°16·0′W	FM	185
Hill Fm	Hants	SU5314	50°55·6′	1°14·4′W	FM	196
Hill Fm	Hants	SU7327	51°2·5′	0°57·1′W	FM	186,197
Hill Fm	Hants	SU8045	51°12·1′	0°50·9′W	FM	186
Hill Fm	Hants	SU8259	51°19·7′	0°49·0′W	FM	175,186
Hill Fm	Heref	SO3728	51°57·1′	2°54·6′W	FM	161
Hill Fm	Heref	SO3738	52°2·4′	2°54·7′W	FM	149,161
Hill Fm	Heref	SO3932	51°59·2′	2°52·9′W	FM	149,161
Hill Fm	Heref	SO4545	52°6·3′	2°47·8′W	FM	148,149
Hill Fm	Heref	SO4920	51°52·8′	2°44·1′W	FM	162
Hill Fm	Heref	SO4932	51°59·3′	2°44·2′W	FM	149
Hill Fm	Heref	SO5518	51°51·8′	2°38·8′W	FM	162
Hill Fm	Heref	SO6022	51°53·9′	2°34·5′W	FM	162
Hill Fm	Heref	SO6337	52°2·0′	2°32·0′W	FM	149
Hill Fm	Heref	SO7046	52°6·9′	2°25·9′W	FM	149
Hill Fm	Heref	SO7238	52°2·6′	2°24·1′W	FM	149
Hill Fm	Herts	SP9710	51°47·0′	0°35·2′W	FM	165
Hill Fm	Herts	TL0514	51°49·1′	0°28·2′W	FM	166
Hill Fm	Herts	TL0617	51°50·7′	0°27·3′W	FM	166
Hill Fm	Herts	TL1009	51°46·4′	0°23·9′W	FM	166
Hill Fm	Herts	TL1417	51°50·6′	0°20·3′W	FM	166
Hill Fm	Herts	TL1500	51°41·4′	0°19·8′W	FM	166
Hill Fm	Herts	TL2016	51°50·0′	0°15·1′W	FM	166
Hill Fm	Herts	TL3621	51°52·5′	0°1·1′W	FM	166
Hill Fm	I of W	SZ3388	50°41·7′	1°31·6′W	FM	196
Hill Fm	I of W	SZ5685	50°39·9′	1°12·1′W	FM	196
Hill Fm	I of W	SZ6188	50°41·5′	1°7·8′W	FM	196
Hill Fm	Kent	TQ5367	51°23·1′	0°12·3′E	FM	177
Hill Fm	Kent	TQ7050	51°13·7′	0°26·5′E	FM	188
Hill Fm	Kent	TQ8550	51°13·4′	0°39·4′E	FM	189
Hill Fm	Kent	TR0334	51°4·4′	0°54·3′E	FM	179,189
Hill Fm	Kent	TR3647	51°10·6′	1°23·0′E	FM	179
Hill Fm	Lancs	SD5464	54°4·4′	2°41·8′W	FM	97
Hill Fm	Lancs	SD6738	53°50·5′	2°29·7′W	FM	103
Hill Fm	Leic	SK3010	52°41·4′	1°33·0′W	FM	128
Hill Fm	Leic	SK3203	52°37·7′	1°31·2′W	FM	140
Hill Fm	Leic	SK3314	52°43·6′	1°30·3′W	FM	128
Hill Fm	Leic	SK3714	52°43·6′	1°26·7′W	FM	128
Hill Fm	Leic	SK4306	52°39·2′	1°21·5′W	FM	140
Hill Fm	Leic	SK4814	52°43·5′	1°17·0′W	FM	129
Hill Fm	Leic	SK7527	52°50·4′	0°52·8′W	FM	129
Hill Fm	Leic	SK7903	52°37·4′	0°49·6′W	FM	141
Hill Fm	Leic	SK8036	52°55·2′	0°48·2′W	FM	130
Hill Fm	Leic	SP3498	52°35·0′	1°29·5′W	FM	140
Hill Fm	Leic	SP3597	52°34·4′	1°28·6′W	FM	140
Hill Fm	Leic	SP4989	52°30·0′	1°16·3′W	FM	140
Hill Fm	Leic	SP4999	52°35·4′	1°16·2′W	FM	140
Hill Fm	Leic	SP5381	52°25·7′	1°12·8′W	FM	140
Hill Fm	Leic	SP5581	52°25·7′	1°11·1′W	FM	140
Hill Fm	Leic	SP5784	52°27·3′	1°9·3′W	FM	140
Hill Fm	Lincs	SK8546	53°0·5′	0°43·6′W	FM	130
Hill Fm	Lincs	SK9820	52°46·4′	0°32·4′W	FM	130
Hill Fm	Lincs	TF0553	53°4·1′	0°25·6′W	FM	121
Hill Fm	Lincs	TF0681	53°19·2′	0°24·1′W	FM	121
Hill Fm	Lincs	TF2170	53°13·0′	0°10·9′W	FM	122
Hill Fm	Lincs	TF3173	53°14·5′	0°1·8′W	FM	122
Hill Fm	Lincs	TF4463	53°8·9′	0°9·6′E	FM	122
Hill Fm	Mil Key	SP8343	52°5·0′	0°46·9′W	FM	152
Hill Fm	Mil Key	SP9044	52°5·5′	0°40·8′W	FM	152
Hill Fm	Monm	SO3705	51°44·6′	2°54·4′W	FM	161
Hill Fm	Monm	SO4605	51°44·7′	2°46·5′W	FM	161
Hill Fm	Monm	ST4597	51°40·4′	2°47·3′W	FM	171
Hill Fm	NE Lincs	TA1514	53°36·8′	0°15·3′W	FM	113
Hill Fm	Newp	ST4192	51°37·7′	2°50·8′W	FM	171,172
Hill Fm	N Lanak	NS8965	55°52·2′	3°46·0′W	FM	65
Hill Fm	Norf	TF5806	52°38·0′	0°20·5′E	FM	143
Hill Fm	Norf	TF7105	52°37·2′	0°32·0′E	FM	143
Hill Fm	Norf	TF7924	52°47·3′	0°39·7′E	FM	132
Hill Fm	Norf	TF8415	52°42·3′	0°43·8′E	FM	132
Hill Fm	Norf	TF8907	52°37·9′	0°48·0′E	FM	144
Hill Fm	Norf	TF9613	52°41·0′	0°54·4′E	FM	132
Hill Fm	Norf	TF9625	52°47·4′	0°54·8′E	FM	132
Hill Fm	Norf	TG0907	52°37·5′	1°5·7′E	FM	144
Hill Fm	Norf	TG0926	52°47·7′	1°6·4′E	FM	133
Hill Fm	Norf	TG1311	52°39·5′	1°9·4′E	FM	133
Hill Fm	Norf	TG2236	52°52·8′	1°18·4′E	FM	133
Hill Fm	Norf	TG3319	52°43·3′	1°27·4′E	FM	133,134
Hill Fm	Norf	TL5499	52°34·2′	0°16·7′E	FM	143
Hill Fm	Norf	TL7298	52°33·4′	0°32·6′E	FM	143
Hill Fm	Norf	TM0491	52°29·0′	1°0·7′E	FM	144
Hill Fm	Norf	TM0682	52°24·1′	1°2·1′E	FM	144
Hill Fm	Norf	TM1490	52°28·2′	1°9·4′E	FM	144
Hill Fm	Norf	TM1799	52°33·0′	1°12·4′E	FM	134
Hill Fm	Norf	TM1892	52°29·2′	1°13·1′E	FM	134
Hill Fm	Norf	TM2085	52°25·3′	1°14·5′E	FM	156
Hill Fm	Norf	TM2693	52°29·5′	1°20·2′E	FM	134
Hill Fm	Norf	TM3092	52°28·9′	1°23·6′E	FM	134
Hill Fm	Norf	TM3190	52°27·8′	1°24·4′E	FM	134
Hill Fm	Norf	TM3898	52°31·9′	1°31·0′E	FM	134
Hill Fm	Norf	TM4292	52°28·6′	1°34·2′E	FM	134
Hill Fm	Northnts	SP5055	52°11·7′	1°15·7′W	FM	151
Hill Fm	Northnts	SP5245	52°6·3′	1°14·0′W	FM	151
Hill Fm	Northnts	SP5255	52°11·7′	1°14·0′W	FM	151
Hill Fm	Northnts	SP5639	52°3·0′	1°10·6′W	FM	152
Hill Fm	Northnts	SP6647	52°7·3′	1°1·8′W	FM	152
Hill Fm	Northnts	SP7057	52°12·6′	0°58·1′W	FM	152
Hill Fm	Northnts	SP8055	52°11·5′	0°49·4′W	FM	152
Hill Fm	Northnts	TL0883	52°26·3′	0°24·3′W	FM	142
Hill Fm	Notts	SK5825	52°49·4′	1°8·0′W	FM	129
Hill Fm	Notts	SK5934	52°54·2′	1°7·0′W	FM	129
Hill Fm	Notts	SK6429	52°51·5′	1°2·6′W	FM	129
Hill Fm	Notts	SK6431	52°52·6′	1°2·5′W	FM	129
Hill Fm	Notts	SK6544	52°59·6′	1°1·5′W	FM	129
Hill Fm	Notts	SK6549	53°2·3′	1°1·4′W	FM	129
Hill Fm	Notts	SK6728	52°51·0′	0°59·9′W	FM	129
Hill Fm	Notts	SK6849	53°2·3′	0°58·7′W	FM	129
Hill Fm	Notts	SK7440	52°57·4′	0°53·5′W	FM	129
Hill Fm	Notts	SK7446	53°0·6′	0°53·4′W	FM	129
Hill Fm	Notts	SK7763	53°9·7′	0°50·5′W	FM	120
Hill Fm	Notts	SK8353	53°4·3′	0°45·3′W	FM	121
Hill Fm	Notts	SK8363	53°9·7′	0°45·1′W	FM	121
Hill Fm	N Yks	SE2195	54°21·2′	1°40·2′W	FM	99
Hill Fm	N Yks	SE6041	53°51·9′	1°4·8′W	FM	105
Hill Fm	N Yks	SE6639	53°50·8′	0°59·4′W	FM	105,106
Hill Fm	N Yks	TA0976	54°10·3′	0°19·4′W	FM	101
Hill Fm	Oxon	SP2417	51°51·3′	1°38·7′W	FM	163
Hill Fm	Oxon	SP2528	51°57·2′	1°37·8′W	FM	163
Hill Fm	Oxon	SP3542	52°4·7′	1°29·0′W	FM	151
Hill Fm	Oxon	SP3810	51°47·5′	1°26·5′W	FM	164
Hill Fm	Oxon	SP4031	51°58·8′	1°24·7′W	FM	151
Hill Fm	Oxon	SP4220	51°52·9′	1°23·0′W	FM	164
Hill Fm	Oxon	SP4529	51°57·7′	1°20·3′W	FM	164
Hill Fm	Oxon	SP5804	51°44·1′	1°9·2′W	FM	164
Hill Fm	Oxon	SP5900	51°42·0′	1°8·4′W	FM	164
Hill Fm	Oxon	SP6020	51°52·8′	1°7·3′W	FM	164,165
Hill Fm	Oxon	SP6703	51°43·5′	1°1·4′W	FM	164,165
Hill Fm	Oxon	SU4690	51°36·6′	1°19·7′W	FM	164,174
Hill Fm	Oxon	SU5292	51°37·7′	1°14·5′W	FM	164,174
Hill Fm	Oxon	SU6197	51°40·3′	1°6·7′W	FM	164,165
Hill Fm	Oxon	SU7296	51°39·7′	0°57·1′W	FM	165
Hill Fm	Oxon	SU7497	51°40·2′	0°55·4′W	FM	165
Hill Fm	Pemb	SM9014	51°47·4′	5°2·3′W	FM	157,158
Hill Fm	Pemb	SR9999	51°39·5′	4°54·0′W	FM	158
Hill Fm	Pemb	SS0797	51°38·6′	4°47·0′W	FM	158
Hill Fm	Peterb	TF2205	52°38·0′	0°11·4′W	FM	142
Hill Fm	Peterb	TF2406	52°38·5′	0°9·6′W	FM	142
Hill Fm	Peterb	TF2702	52°36·3′	0°7·1′W	FM	142
Hill Fm	Powys	SJ3214	52°43·4′	3°0·0′W	FM	126
Hill Fm	Powys	SO2338	52°2·3′	3°7·0′W	FM	161
Hill Fm	Powys	SO2352	52°9·9′	3°7·2′W	FM	148
Hill Fm	S Ayr	NS4730	55°32·6′	4°25·1′W	FM	70
Hill Fm	S Glos	ST7371	51°26·5′	2°22·9′W	FM	172
Hill Fm	Shrops	SJ3010	52°41·2′	3°1·7′W	FM	126
Hill Fm	S Lanak	NS6741	55°38·9′	4°6·4′W	FM	71
Hill Fm	Somer	SS8340	51°9·1′	3°40·0′W	FM	181
Hill Fm	Somer	SS8432	51°4·8′	3°39·0′W	FM	181
Hill Fm	Somer	SS9631	51°4·4′	3°28·7′W	FM	181
Hill Fm	Somer	ST0621	50°59·1′	3°20·0′W	FM	181
Hill Fm	Somer	ST2429	51°3·6′	3°4·7′W	FM	193
Hill Fm	Somer	ST2442	51°10·6′	3°4·8′W	FM	182
Hill Fm	Somer	ST2520	50°58·7′	3°3·7′W	FM	193
Hill Fm	Somer	ST3911	50°53·9′	2°51·7′W	FM	193
Hill Fm	Somer	ST4155	51°17·7′	2°50·4′W	FM	172,182
Hill Fm	Somer	ST5837	51°8·1′	2°35·6′W	FM	182,183
Hill Fm	Staffs	SJ8431	52°52·8′	2°13·9′W	FM	127
Hill Fm	Staffs	SK1410	52°41·5′	1°47·2′W	FM	128
Hill Fm	Staffs	SK1701	52°36·6′	1°44·5′W	FM	139
Hill Fm	Suff	TL6875	52°21·1′	0°28·4′E	FM	143
Hill Fm	Suff	TL7149	52°7·0′	0°30·3′E	FM	154
Hill Fm	Suff	TL7468	52°17·2′	0°33·5′E	FM	155
Hill Fm	Suff	TL8059	52°12·2′	0°38·5′E	FM	155
Hill Fm	Suff	TL9141	52°2·3′	0°47·5′E	FM	155
Hill Fm	Suff	TL9347	52°5·5′	0°49·4′E	FM	155
Hill Fm	Suff	TL9352	52°8·2′	0°49·6′E	FM	155
Hill Fm	Suff	TL9360	52°12·5′	0°49·9′E	FM	155
Hill Fm	Suff	TL9534	51°58·4′	0°50·7′E	FM	155
Hill Fm	Suff	TL9557	52°10·8′	0°51·5′E	FM	155
Hill Fm	Suff	TL9660	52°12·4′	0°52·5′E	FM	155
Hill Fm	Suff	TL9751	52°7·6′	0°53·1′E	FM	155
Hill Fm	Suff	TL9858	52°11·3′	0°54·2′E	FM	155
Hill Fm	Suff	TM0049	52°6·4′	0°55·6′E	FM	155
Hill Fm	Suff	TM0155	52°9·6′	0°56·7′E	FM	155
Hill Fm	Suff	TM0241	52°2·1′	0°57·1′E	FM	155
Hill Fm	Suff	TM0452	52°7·9′	0°59·2′E	FM	155
Hill Fm	Suff	TM0648	52°5·7′	1°0·8′E	FM	155
Hill Fm	Suff	TM0746	52°4·6′	1°1·6′E	FM	155,169
Hill Fm	Suff	TM0766	52°15·4′	1°2·4′E	FM	155
Hill Fm	Suff	TM0857	52°10·5′	1°2·9′E	FM	155
Hill Fm	Suff	TM0863	52°13·8′	1°3·1′E	FM	155
Hill Fm	Suff	TM1044	52°3·5′	1°4·2′E	FM	155,169
Hill Fm	Suff	TM1270	52°17·5′	1°6·9′E	FM	144,155
Hill Fm	Suff	TM1548	52°5·5′	1°8·7′E	FM	169
Hill Fm	Suff	TM1554	52°8·8′	1°8·9′E	FM	156
Hill Fm	Suff	TM1652	52°7·7′	1°9·7′E	FM	156
Hill Fm	Suff	TM1863	52°13·5′	1°11·9′E	FM	156
Hill Fm	Suff	TM1946	52°4·4′	1°12·1′E	FM	169
Hill Fm	Suff	TM2179	52°22·1′	1°15·2′E	FM	156
Hill Fm	Suff	TM2249	52°5·9′	1°14·9′E	FM	169
Hill Fm	Suff	TM2252	52°7·5′	1°15·0′E	FM	156
Hill Fm	Suff	TM2358	52°10·7′	1°16·1′E	FM	156
Hill Fm	Suff	TM2381	52°23·1′	1°17·0′E	FM	156
Hill Fm	Suff	TM2646	52°4·2′	1°18·3′E	FM	169
Hill Fm	Suff	TM2665	52°14·4′	1°19·0′E	FM	156
Hill Fm	Suff	TM2761	52°12·2′	1°19·7′E	FM	156
Hill Fm	Suff	TM2762	52°12·8′	1°19·8′E	FM	156
Hill Fm	Suff	TM3072	52°18·1′	1°22·8′E	FM	156
Hill Fm	Suff	TM3165	52°14·3′	1°23·4′E	FM	156
Hill Fm	Suff	TM3172	52°18·1′	1°23·7′E	FM	156
Hill Fm	Suff	TM3187	52°26·1′	1°24·3′E	FM	156
Hill Fm	Suff	TM3271	52°17·5′	1°24·5′E	FM	156
Hill Fm	Suff	TM3363	52°13·2′	1°25·1′E	FM	156
Hill Fm	Suff	TM3368	52°15·9′	1°25·3′E	FM	156
Hill Fm	Suff	TM3373	52°18·6′	1°25·5′E	FM	156
Hill Fm	Suff	TM3466	52°14·8′	1°26·1′E	FM	156
Hill Fm	Suff	TM3479	52°21·8′	1°26·6′E	FM	156
Hill Fm	Suff	TM3486	52°25·5′	1°26·9′E	FM	156
Hill Fm	Suff	TM3575	52°19·6′	1°27·3′E	FM	156
Hill Fm	Suff	TM3586	52°25·5′	1°27·8′E	FM	156
Hill Fm	Suff	TM3658	52°10·4′	1°27·5′E	FM	156
Hill Fm	Suff	TM3668	52°15·8′	1°27·9′E	FM	156
Hill Fm	Suff	TM3770	52°16·8′	1°28·9′E	FM	156
Hill Fm	Suff	TM3952	52°7·1′	1°29·9′E	FM	156
Hill Fm	Suff	TM3961	52°11·9′	1°30·3′E	FM	156
Hill Fm	Suff	TM3970	52°16·8′	1°30·6′E	FM	156
Hill Fm	Suff	TM3977	52°20·6′	1°30·9′E	FM	156
Hill Fm	Suff	TM4177	52°20·5′	1°32·7′E	FM	156
Hill Fm	Suff	TM4255	52°8·6′	1°32·6′E	FM	156
Hill Fm	Suff	TM4264	52°13·5′	1°33·0′E	FM	156
Hill Fm	Suff	TM4286	52°25·3′	1°34·0′E	FM	156
Hill Fm	Suff	TM4383	52°23·7′	1°34·7′E	FM	156
Hill Fm	Suff	TM4464	52°13·4′	1°34·8′E	FM	156
Hill Fm	Suff	TM4587	52°25·8′	1°36·6′E	FM	156

Hill Fm	Suff	TM4678	52°20·9′	1°37·1′E	FM	156
Hill Fm	Warw	SK3007	52°39·8′	1°33·0′W	FM	140
Hill Fm	Warw	SP1260	52°14·5′	1°49·1′W	FM	150
Hill Fm	Warw	SP1369	52°19·4′	1°48·2′W	FM	139,151
Hill fm	Warw	SP1662	52°15·6′	1°45·5′W	FM	151
Hill Fm	Warw	SP1697	52°34·5′	1°45·4′W	FM	139
Hill Fm	Warw	SP2348	52°8·0′	1°39·4′W	FM	151
Hill Fm	Warw	SP2391	52°31·2′	1°39·3′W	FM	139
Hill Fm	Warw	SP2488	52°29·6′	1°38·4′W	FM	139
Hill Fm	Warw	SP2489	52°30·1′	1°38·4′W	FM	139
Hill Fm	Warw	SP3054	52°11·2′	1°33·3′W	FM	151
Hill Fm	Warw	SP3091	52°31·2′	1°33·1′W	FM	140
Hill Fm	Warw	SP3292	52°31·7′	1°31·3′W	FM	140
Hill Fm	Warw	SP3367	52°18·2′	1°30·6′W	FM	151
Hill Fm	Warw	SP3463	52°16·1′	1°29·7′W	FM	151
Hill Fm	Warw	SP3870	52°19·8′	1°26·1′W	FM	140
Hill Fm	Warw	SP3990	52°30·6′	1°25·1′W	FM	140
Hill Fm	Warw	SP4255	52°11·7′	1°22·7′W	FM	151
Hill Fm	Warw	SP4277	52°23·6′	1°22·6′W	FM	140
Hill Fm	Warw	SP4470	52°19·8′	1°20·9′W	FM	140
Hill Fm	W Berks	SU4464	51°22·6′	1°21·7′W	FM	174
Hill Fm	Wilts	ST8860	51°20·6′	2°9·9′W	FM	173
Hill Fm	Wilts	ST9923	51°0·6′	2°0·5′W	FM	184
Hill Fm	Wilts	SU0840	51°9·8′	1°52·7′W	FM	184
Hill Fm	Wilts	SU1133	51°6·0′	1°50·2′W	FM	184
Hill Fm	Wilts	SU2433	51°6·0′	1°39·0′W	FM	184
Hill Fm	Worcs	SO5863	52°16·1′	2°36·5′W	FM	137,138,149
Hill Fm	Worcs	SO6166	52°17·7′	2°33·9′W	FM	138,149
Hill Fm	Worcs	SO7060	52°14·5′	2°26·0′W	FM	138,149
Hill Fm	Worcs	SO7778	52°24·2′	2°19·9′W	FM	138
Hill Fm	Worcs	SO7959	52°14·0′	2°18·1′W	FM	150
Hill Fm	Worcs	SO8666	52°17·8′	2°11·9′W	FM	150
Hill Fm	Worcs	SO9760	52°14·5′	2°2·2′W	FM	150
Hill Fm	Worcs	SO9956	52°12·4′	2°0·5′W	FM	150
Hill Fm	Worcs	SP0671	52°20·5′	1°54·3′W	FM	139
Hill Fm	Wrex	SJ4437	52°55·9′	2°49·6′W	FM	126
Hill Fm	W Susx	TQ2123	50°59·8′	0°16·2′W	FM	198
Hill Fm Ho	Bucks	SU9794	51°38·4′	0°35·5′W	X	175,176
Hill Fms	Cambs	TL4954	52°10·1′	0°11·1′E	FM	154
Hill Fm, The	Cumbr	NY1550	54°50·5′	3°19·0′W	FM	85
Hill Fm,The	Heref	SO4820	51°52·8′	2°44·9′W	FM	161
Hill Fm, The	Staffs	SK0810	52°41·5′	1°52·5′W	FM	128
Hill Fm, The	Worcs	SO9068	52°18·8′	2°8·4′W	FM	139
Hill Fm, The	Worcs	SP0359	52°14·0′	1°57·0′W	FM	150
Hillfold	Aberd	NJ7016	57°14·3′	2°29·4′W	X	38
Hillfolds	Aberd	NJ5655	57°35·2′	2°43·7′W	X	29
Hillfoot	Aberd	NJ9756	57°35·9′	2°2·6′W	X	30
Hill Foot	Lancs	SD8144	53°53·8′	2°16·9′W	X	103
Hillfoot	Leeds	SE2033	53°47·8′	1°41·4′W	T	104
Hillfoot	Pth & Kin	NO2235	56°30·3′	3°15·6′W	X	53
Hillfoot End	Beds	TL1234	51°59·8′	0°21·7′W	T	153
Hillfoot Fm	Beds	TL0733	51°59·3′	0°26·1′W	FM	166
Hillfoot Fm	Warr	SJ6085	53°21·9′	2°35·7′W	FM	109
Hillfoot Fm	W Berks	SU5670	51°25·8′	1°11·3′W	FM	174
Hillfoot Hill	Clackm	NN9600	56°11·1′	3°40·1′W	H	58
Hillford Croft	Aberd	NJ6624	57°18·6′	2°33·4′W	X	38
Hill Furze	Worcs	SO9948	52°8·1′	2°0·5′W	T	150
Hill Garth Fm	N Lincs	TA1114	53°36·9′	0°18·9′W	FM	113
Hill Gate	Heref	SO4927	51°56·6′	2°44·1′W	T	162
Hillgate Fm	Kent	TQ8529	51°2·1′	0°38·7′E	FM	189,199
Hill Gill Fm	Durham	NY9319	54°34·2′	2°6·1′W	FM	91,92
Hill Grange	Somer	ST5453	51°16·7′	2°39·2′W	X	182,183
Hill Green	Essex	TL4832	51°58·2′	0°9·7′E	T	167
Hill Green	Kent	TQ8362	51°19·9′	0°38·0′E	T	178,188
Hillgreen	W Berks	SU4576	51°29·1′	1°20·7′W	T	174
Hill Green Fm	Beds	SP9644	52°5·4′	0°35·5′W	FM	153
Hill Green Fm	Ches	SJ9184	53°21·4′	2°7·7′W	FM	109
Hill Green Fm	Herts	SP9410	51°47·1′	0°37·8′W	FM	165
Hillgreen Fm	Oxon	SU5887	51°35·0′	1°9·4′W	FM	174
Hillgreen Fm	Suff	TM0072	52°18·8′	0°56·5′E	FM	144,155
Hill Ground	Powys	SO1174	52°21·7′	3°18·0′W	X	136,148
Hillgrounds	Devon	ST2205	50°50·6′	3°6·1′W	X	192,193
Hill Grove	Somer	ST5749	51°14·5′	2°36·6′W	X	182,183
Hillgrove	W Susx	SU9428	51°2·8′	0°39·2′W	T	186,197
Hill Grove Fm	Oxon	SP3310	51°47·5′	1°30·9′W	FM	164
Hillgrove Fm	Win & Maid	SU8885	51°33·6′	0°43·4′W	FM	175
Hill Hall	Essex	TL6532	51°57·9′	0°24·5′E	X	167
Hill Hall	Essex	TQ4899	51°40·4′	0°8·8′E	A	167,177
Hillhall	Moray	NJ2645	57°29·6′	3°13·6′W	X	28
Hill Halton	Shrops	SO4875	52°22·5′	2°45·4′W	X	137,138,148
Hillhampton	Heref	SO5847	52°7·4′	2°36·4′W	T	149
Hillhampton Fm	Worcs	SO7765	52°17·2′	2°19·8′W	FM	138,150
Hill Harling	Norf	TM0085	52°25·8′	0°56·9′E	X	144
Hillhead	Aberd	NJ5006	57°8·8′	2°49·1′W	X	37
Hillhead	Aberd	NJ5226	57°19·6′	2°47·4′W	X	37
Hillhead	Aberd	NJ5600	57°5·6′	2°43·1′W	X	37
Hillhead	Aberd	NJ5735	57°24·5′	2°42·5′W	X	29
Hillhead	Aberd	NJ5801	57°6·1′	2°41·1′W	X	37
Hillhead	Aberd	NJ5827	57°20·2′	2°41·4′W	X	37
Hillhead	Aberd	NJ6005	57°8·3′	2°39·2′W	X	37
Hillhead	Aberd	NJ6452	57°33·7′	2°35·6′W	X	29
Hillhead	Aberd	NJ6958	57°36·9′	2°30·7′W	X	29
Hillhead	Aberd	NJ7007	57°9·4′	2°29·3′W	X	38
Hillhead	Aberd	NJ7511	57°11·6′	2°24·4′W	X	38
Hillhead	Aberd	NJ7527	57°20·2′	2°24·5′W	X	38
Hillhead	Aberd	NJ7738	57°26·2′	2°22·5′W	X	29,30
Hillhead	Aberd	NJ7910	57°11·1′	2°20·4′W	T	38
Hillhead	Aberd	NJ7924	57°18·6′	2°20·5′W	X	38
Hillhead	Aberd	NJ7931	57°22·4′	2°20·5′W	X	29,30
Hillhead	Aberd	NJ8021	57°17·0′	2°19·4′W	T	38
Hillhead	Aberd	NJ8553	57°34·3′	2°14·6′W	X	30
Hillhead	Aberd	NJ9216	57°14·3′	2°7·5′W	X	38
Hillhead	Aberd	NJ9361	57°38·6′	2°6·6′W	X	30
Hillhead	Aberd	NJ9434	57°24·0′	2°5·5′W	X	30
Hillhead	Aberd	NJ9521	57°17·0′	2°4·5′W	X	38
Hillhead	Aberd	NJ9553	57°34·3′	2°4·6′W	X	30
Hillhead	Aberd	NK0234	57°24·0′	1°57·5′W	X	30
Hillhead	Aberd	NK0253	57°34·3′	1°57·5′W	X	30
Hillhead	Aberd	NK0363	57°39·7′	1°56·5′W	X	30
Hillhead	Aberd	NO4796	57°3·4′	2°52·0′W	X	37,44

Hillhead	Angus	NO3854	56°40·7′	3°0·3′W	X	54
Hillhead	Angus	NO5345	56°35·9′	2°45·5′W	X	54
Hillhead	C of Aber	NJ8602	57°6·8′	2°13·4′W	X	38
Hillhead	C of Aber	NJ8803	57°7·3′	2°11·4′W	X	38
Hillhead	C of Aber	NJ8904	57°7·9′	2°10·4′W	X	38
Hillhead	C of Aber	NJ9113	57°12·7′	2°8·5′W	X	38
Hillhead	C of Aber	NJ9300	57°5·7′	2°6·5′W	X	38
Hillhead	Corn	SX0960	50°24·8′	4°40·9′W	T	200
Hillhead	Cumbr	NY5080	55°7·0′	2°46·6′W	X	79
Hill Head	Cumbr	NY5165	54°58·9′	2°45·5′W	X	86
Hill Head	Devon	SS6718	50°57·0′	3°53·2′W	X	180
Hillhead	Devon	SX9053	50°22·2′	3°32·4′W	T	202
Hillhead	D & G	NS6814	55°24·4′	4°4·7′W	X	71
Hillhead	D & G	NX3853	54°51·0′	4°31·0′W	X	83
Hillhead	D & G	NX7891	55°12·1′	3°54·6′W	X	78
Hillhead	D & G	NX8574	55°3·1′	3°47·6′W	X	84
Hillhead	D & G	NX8820	55°10·1′	3°45·1′W	X	78
Hillhead	D & G	NX9372	55°2·1′	3°40·0′W	X	84
Hillhead	D & G	NY0697	55°15·7′	3°28·3′W	X	78
Hillhead	D & G	NY2769	55°0·9′	3°8·1′W	X	85
Hillhead	D & G	NY4176	55°4·7′	2°55·0′W	X	85
Hillhead	E Ayr	NS4238	55°36·9′	4°30·1′W	T	70
Hillhead	E Ayr	NS4928	55°31·6′	4°23·1′W	X	70
Hillhead	E Ayr	NS4942	55°39·1′	4°23·6′W	X	70
Hillhead	E Ayr	NS5117	55°25·7′	4°20·8′W	X	70
Hillhead	E Ayr	NS5625	55°30·1′	4°16·4′W	X	71
Hillhead	E Ayr	NS6121	55°28·0′	4°11·5′W	X	71
Hillhead	E Dunb	NS6074	55°56·6′	4°14·1′W	X	64
Hillhead	E Loth	NT3769	55°54·9′	3°0·0′W	X	66
Hillhead	Falk	NS8673	55°56·4′	3°49·1′W	X	65
Hillhead	Fife	NO5714	56°19·2′	2°41·3′W	X	59
Hillhead	Fife	NT0891	56°6·4′	3°28·3′W	X	58
Hillhead	Hants	SU4801	50°48·6′	1°18·7′W	X	196
Hill Head	Hants	SU5402	50°49·1′	1°13·6′W	T	196
Hillhead	Heref	SO4064	52°16·5′	2°52·4′W	X	137,148,149
Hillhead	Highld	ND1759	58°30·9′	3°25·0′W	X	11,12
Hillhead	Highld	ND2371	58°37·5′	3°19·1′W	H	7,12
Hillhead	Highld	ND2535	58°18·1′	3°16·3′W	X	11
Hillhead	Highld	ND3751	58°26·8′	3°4·3′W	X	12
Hillhead	Highld	NH7750	57°31·7′	4°2·8′W	X	27
Hillhead	Moray	NJ0759	57°36·9′	3°32·9′W	X	27
Hillhead	Moray	NJ1640	57°26·8′	3°23·5′W	X	28
Hillhead	Moray	NJ2058	57°36·6′	3°19·9′W	X	28
Hillhead	Moray	NJ2332	57°22·6′	3°16·4′W	X	36
Hillhead	Moray	NJ4354	57°34·6′	2°56·7′W	X	28
Hillhead	N Ayr	NS2743	55°39·2′	4°44·5′W	X	63,70
Hillhead	N Ayr	NS3942	55°38·9′	4°33·1′W	X	63,70
Hillhead	N Lanak	NS7663	55°50·9′	3°58·4′W	X	64
Hillhead	N Lanak	NS8669	55°54·3′	3°49·0′W	X	65
Hill Head	Northum	NU1010	55°23·3′	1°50·1′W	X	81
Hillhead	Northum	NU1908	55°22·2′	1°41·6′W	X	81
Hill Head	Northum	NY6163	54°57·9′	2°36·1′W	X	86
Hill Head	Northum	NY8976	55°4·9′	2°9·9′W	X	87
Hill Head	Northum	NY9369	55°1·2′	2°6·1′W	X	87
Hillhead	Northum	NY9391	55°13·0′	2°6·2′W	X	80
Hillhead	Northum	NZ0479	55°6·6′	1°55·8′W	X	87
Hill Head	Northum	NZ1266	54°59·6′	1°48·3′W	X	88
Hill Head	Northum	NZ1482	55°8·2′	1°46·4′W	X	81
Hillhead	Orkney	HY4408	58°57·6′	2°57·9′W	X	6,7
Hillhead	Orkney	HY7243	59°16·6′	2°29·0′W	X	5
Hill Head	Orkney	ND2689	58°47·2′	3°16·3′W	X	7
Hillhead	Pth & Kin	NN8613	56°18·0′	3°50·1′W	X	58
Hillhead	S Ayr	NS4219	55°26·6′	4°29·4′W	T	70
Hillhead	S Ayr	NS4424	55°29·4′	4°27·7′W	X	70
Hill Head	Scot Bord	NT3501	55°18·2′	3°1·0′W	H	79
Hillhead	Shetld	HU4235	60°6·1′	1°14·2′W	X	4
Hillhead	S Lanak	NS6641	55°38·9′	4°7·3′W	X	71
Hillhead	S Lanak	NS8650	55°44·1′	3°48·5′W	X	65,72
Hillhead	S Lanak	NS9652	55°45·3′	3°39·0′W	X	65,72
Hillhead	S Lanak	NS9740	55°38·8′	3°37·8′W	X	72
Hillhead	Stir	NN6700	56°10·7′	4°8·1′W	X	57
Hillhead	Stir	NS7193	56°7·0′	4°4·0′W	X	57
Hillhead	Stir	NS7692	56°6·5′	3°59·2′W	X	57
Hillhead	Stir	NS8089	56°5·0′	3°55·3′W	X	57,65
Hillhead	Stir	NS8588	56°4·5′	3°50·4′W	X	65
Hillhead Cross	Devon	SX6756	50°23·6′	3°51·9′W	X	202
Hillhead Cross	Somer	SS8540	51°9·1′	3°38·3′W	X	181
Hillhead Dairy	Aberd	NK0644	57°29·4′	1°53·5′W	X	30
Hillhead Fm	Angus	NO5342	56°34·3′	2°45·4′W	FM	54
Hillhead Fm	Corn	SW7833	50°9·6′	5°6·1′W	FM	204
Hillhead Fm	Derby	SK0769	53°13·3′	1°53·3′W	FM	119
Hillhead Fm	Devon	SX9053	50°22·2′	3°32·4′W	FM	202
Hillhead Fm	D & G	NY2974	55°3·6′	3°6·3′W	FM	85
Hill Head Fm	Ghead	NZ2258	54°55·2′	1°39·0′W	FM	88
Hillhead of Ardlethen	Aberd	NJ9230	57°21·9′	2°7·5′W	X	30
Hillhead of Ardmiddle	Aberd	NJ6946	57°30·4′	2°30·6′W	X	29
Hillhead of Ardo	Aberd	NJ8539	57°26·7′	2°14·5′W	X	30
Hillhead of Ashogle	Aberd	NJ7053	57°34·2′	2°29·6′W	X	29
Hillhead of Auchenten	Aberd	NK0434	57°24·0′	1°55·5′W	X	30
Hillhead of Auchentumb	Aberd	NJ9258	57°37·0′	2°7·6′W	X	30
Hillhead of Auchreddie	Aberd	NJ8646	57°30·5′	2°13·6′W	X	30
Hillhead of Auquharney	Aberd	NK0139	57°26·7′	1°58·5′W	X	30
Hillhead of Auquhirie	Aberd	NO8383	56°56·5′	2°16·3′W	X	45
Hillhead of Avochie	Aberd	NJ5447	57°30·9′	2°45·6′W	X	29
Hillhead of Bogfouton	Aberd	NJ6336	57°25·0′	2°36·5′W	X	29
Hillhead of Braco	Aberd	NK0538	57°26·2′	1°54·5′W	X	30
Hillhead of Burghill	Angus	NO6058	56°43·0′	2°38·8′W	X	54
Hillhead of Carnie	Aberd	NJ8205	57°8·4′	2°17·4′W	X	38
Hillhead of Cocklaw	Aberd	NK0844	57°29·4′	1°51·5′W	X	30
Hillhead of Coldwells	Aberd	NK1040	57°27·3′	1°49·5′W	X	30
Hillhead of Cowie	Aberd	NO8990	57°0·3′	2°10·4′W	X	38,45
Hillhead of Craichmore	D & G	NX0363	54°55·6′	5°4·0′W	X	82
Hillhead of Craigellie	Aberd	NK0159	57°37·5′	1°58·5′W	X	30
Hillhead of Craigie	Aberd	NJ9120	57°16·5′	2°8·5′W	X	38
Hillhead of Denend	Aberd	NJ9953	57°34·3′	2°0·5′W	X	30
Hillhead of Derbeth	C of Aber	NJ8608	57°10·0′	2°13·4′W	X	38
Hillhead of Esslemont	Aberd	NJ9129	57°21·3′	2°8·5′W	X	38
Hillhead of Fechil	Aberd	NJ9529	57°21·3′	2°4·5′W	X	38
Hillhead of Gask	Aberd	NK0840	57°27·3′	1°51·5′W	X	30
Hillhead of Glasslaw	Aberd	NO8483	56°56·5′	2°15·3′W	X	45

Hillhead of Heathcot	Aberd	NJ8900	57°5·7′	2°10·4′W	X	38
Hillhead of Hedderwick	Angus	NO6961	56°44·6′	2°30·0′W	X	45
Hillhead of Kincraig	Aberd	NJ9724	57°18·7′	2°2·5′W	X	38
Hillhead of Kintocher	Aberd	NJ5708	57°9·9′	2°42·2′W	X	37
Hillhead of Lethenty	Aberd	NJ7625	57°19·2′	2°23·5′W	X	38
Hillhead of Litterty	Aberd	NJ7953	57°34·3′	2°20·6′W	X	29,30
Hillhead of Maryfield	Aberd	NO7295	57°3·0′	2°27·2′W	X	38,45
Hillhead of Mintlaw	Aberd	NK0049	57°32·1′	1°59·5′W	X	30
Hillhead of Mosstown	Aberd	NJ9227	57°20·3′	2°7·5′W	X	38
Hillhead of Mountblairy	Aberd	NJ6853	57°34·2′	2°31·6′W	T	29
Hillhead of Muirton	Aberd	NJ9217	57°14·9′	2°7·5′W	X	38
Hillhead of Mundurno	C of Aber	NJ9313	57°12·7′	2°6·5′W	X	38
Hillhead of Pitforthie	Aberd	NO8179	56°54·4′	2°18·3′W	X	45
Hillhead of Pittulie	Aberd	NJ9666	57°41·3′	2°3·6′W	X	30
Hillhead of Rannas	Moray	NJ4663	57°39·5′	2°53·8′W	X	28,29
Hillhead of Tollo	Aberd	NJ6544	57°29·4′	2°34·6′W	X	29
Hillhead of Torryleith	Aberd	NJ8820	57°16·5′	2°11·5′W	X	38
Hillhead of Troup	Aberd	NJ8263	57°39·7′	2°17·6′W	X	29,30
Hillhead Plantation	Northum	NZ0973	55°3·3′	1°51·1′W	F	88
Hillhead Plantn	D & G	NX8596	55°14·9′	3°48·1′W	F	78
Hill Head Wood	Ghead	NZ2259	54°55·8′	1°39·0′W	F	88
Hill Ho	Bucks	SP9001	51°42·3′	0°41·5′W	X	165
Hill Ho	Ches	SJ5563	53°10·0′	2°40·0′W	X	117
Hill Ho	Ches	SJ6481	53°19·7′	2°32·0′W	X	109
Hill Ho	Ches	SJ7981	53°19·8′	2°18·5′W	X	109
Hill Ho	Cumbr	NY0845	54°47·7′	3°25·4′W	X	85
Hill Ho	Cumbr	NY1448	54°49·4′	3°19·9′W	X	85
Hill Ho	Cumbr	NY4765	54°58·9′	2°49·3′W	X	86
Hill Ho	Cumbr	NY5266	54°59·4′	2°44·6′W	X	86
Hill Ho	Cumbr	NY5456	54°54·0′	2°42·6′W	X	86
Hill Ho	Cumbr	NY6459	54°55·7′	2°33·3′W	X	86
Hill Ho	Cumbr	NY7045	54°48·2′	2°27·6′W	X	86,87
Hill Ho	Cumbr	NY7538	54°44·4′	2°22·9′W	X	91
Hill Ho	Darl	NZ3418	54°33·6′	1°28·0′W	X	93
Hill Ho	Durham	NZ0624	54°36·9′	1°54·0′W	X	92
Hill Ho	Durham	NZ1817	54°33·1′	1°42·9′W	X	92
Hill Ho	Durham	NZ2821	54°35·2′	1°33·6′W	X	93
Hill Ho	Durham	NZ3441	54°46·0′	1°27·9′W	X	88
Hill Ho	Essex	TL8532	51°57·6′	0°42·0′E	X	168
Hill Ho	Essex	TL8928	51°55·3′	0°45·3′E	X	168
Hill Ho	Essex	TM0431	51°56·6′	0°58·5′E	X	168
Hill Ho	Essex	TM2029	51°55·2′	1°12·4′E	X	169
Hill Ho	Essex	TM2221	51°50·8′	1°13·8′E	X	169
Hill Ho	E Yorks	SE8934	53°47·9′	0°38·5′W	X	106
Hill Ho	Heref	SO5251	52°9·5′	2°41·7′W	X	149
Hill Ho	Heref	SO6936	52°1·5′	2°26·7′W	X	149
Hill Ho	Kent	TQ4643	51°10·3′	0°5·7′E	X	188
Hill Ho	Lancs	SD5740	53°51·5′	2°38·8′W	X	102
Hill Ho	Lancs	SD7646	53°54·8′	2°21·5′W	X	103
Hill Ho	Leic	SK3509	52°40·9′	1°28·5′W	X	128,140
Hill Ho	Lincs	TF2431	52°52·0′	0°9·1′W	X	131
Hill Ho	Norf	TG0508	52°38·1′	1°2·2′E	X	144
Hill Ho	Norf	TG0536	52°53·2′	1°3·2′E	X	133
Hill Ho	Norf	TG1139	52°54·6′	1°8·7′E	X	133
Hill Ho	Norf	TG2635	52°52·1′	1°21·9′E	X	133
Hill Ho	Norf	TG2802	52°34·3′	1°22·3′E	X	134
Hill Ho	Norf	TL9691	52°29·1′	0°53·6′E	X	144
Hill Ho	Norf	TM0496	52°31·6′	1°0·8′E	X	144
Hill Ho	Norf	TM1887	52°26·5′	1°12·9′E	X	156
Hill Ho	Norf	TM3999	52°32·4′	1°31·9′E	X	134
Hill Ho	Northum	NY8264	54°58·5′	2°16·4′W	X	86,87
Hill Ho	N Yks	NZ3510	54°29·3′	1°27·2′W	X	93
Hill Ho	N Yks	NZ4904	54°26·0′	1°14·3′W	X	93
Hill Ho	N Yks	NZ6404	54°25·9′	1°0·4′W	X	94
Hill Ho	N Yks	SE3195	54°21·2′	1°31·0′W	X	99
Hill Ho	N Yks	SE3996	54°21·7′	1°23·6′W	X	99
Hill Ho	Oxon	SP4725	51°55·5′	1°18·6′W	X	164
Hill Ho	Oxon	SP5029	51°57·7′	1°15·9′W	X	164
Hill Ho	Pemb	SN0538	52°0·6′	4°50·1′W	X	145
Hill Ho	Pth & Kin	NO1030	56°27·5′	3°27·2′W	X	53
Hill Ho	S Glos	ST6883	51°32·9′	2°27·3′W	X	172
Hill Ho	Sheff	SK2893	53°26·2′	1°34·3′W	X	110
Hill Ho	Somer	ST2542	51°10·6′	3°4·0′W	X	182
Hill Ho	Staffs	SK0558	53°7·4′	1°55·1′W	X	119
Hill Ho	Stir	NN7607	56°14·6′	3°59·6′W	X	57
Hill Ho	Suff	TM0336	51°59·3′	0°57·8′E	X	155
Hill Ho	Suff	TM0375	52°20·4′	0°59·2′E	X	144
Hill Ho	Suff	TM0875	52°20·2′	1°3·6′E	X	144
Hill Ho	Suff	TM1167	52°15·9′	1°5·9′E	X	155
Hill Ho	Suff	TM1665	52°14·7′	1°10·2′E	X	156
Hill Ho	Suff	TM2147	52°4·9′	1°13·9′E	X	169
Hill Ho	Suff	TM2161	52°12·4′	1°14·5′E	X	156
Hill Ho	Suff	TM2336	51°58·9′	1°15·2′E	X	169
Hill Ho	Suff	TM2778	52°21·4′	1°20·4′E	X	156
Hill Ho	Suff	TM3357	52°9·9′	1°24·8′E	X	156
Hill Ho	Warw	SP3493	52°32·3′	1°29·5′W	X	140
Hill Ho	Warw	SP4166	52°17·7′	1°23·5′W	X	151
Hill Ho	W Loth	NT1167	55°53·5′	3°24·9′W	X	65
Hill Ho	Worcs	SO8535	52°1·0′	2°12·7′W	X	150
Hill Ho	Worcs	SP1248	52°8·0′	1°49·1′W	X	150
Hill Ho	W Susx	TQ1132	51°4·8′	0°24·5′W	X	187
Hill Ho	W Susx	TQ1622	50°59·4′	0°20·4′W	X	198
Hill Hoath	Kent	TQ4944	51°10·8′	0°8·3′E	T	188
Hill Ho Fm	Shrops	SO4984	52°27·3′	2°44·6′W	FM	137,138
Hillhole Fm	Heref	SO2842	52°4·5′	3°2·6′W	FM	148,161
Hill Holt Fm	Lincs	SK8660	53°8·0′	0°42·5′W	FM	121
Hill Hook	Birm	SK1000	52°36·1′	1°50·7′W	T	139
Hill Hos	Durham	NY9037	54°43·9′	2°8·9′W	X	91,92
Hill Ho, Th	Beds	TL1644	52°5·2′	0°18·0′W	X	153
Hillhouse	D & G	NY1295	55°14·7′	3°22·6′W	X	78
Hillhouse	D & G	NY1565	54°58·6′	3°19·3′W	X	85
Hill House	Durham	NZ2041	54°46·1′	1°40·9′W	X	88
Hillhouse	E Ayr	NS4146	55°41·1′	4°31·3′W	X	64
Hillhouse	E Ayr	NS4333	55°34·2′	4°29·0′W	X	70
Hillhouse	E Ayr	NS4539	55°37·4′	4°27·3′W	X	70
Hillhouse	E Ayr	NS4933	55°34·3′	4°23·3′W	X	70
Hillhouse	E Ayr	NS5334	55°34·9′	4°19·5′W	X	70
Hill House	Essex	TL7015	51°48·7′	0°28·4′E	A	167
Hill House	Fife	NT0985	56°3·2′	3°27·2′W	A	65
Hill House	Lancs	SD3406	53°33·0′	2°59·4′W	A	108

Hill House	Oxon	SU3689	51°36·2'	1°28·4'W	X	174
Hillhouse	S Ayr	NS3629	55°31·9'	4°35·5'W	X	70
Hillhouse	Scot Bord	NT5055	55°47·4'	2°47·4'W	X	66,73
Hillhouse	Scot Bord	NY4986	55°10·2'	2°47·6'W	X	79
Hillhouse	S Lanak	NS8738	55°37·6'	3°47·2'W	X	71,72
Hillhouse	S Lanak	NS9730	55°33·4'	3°37·5'W	X	72
Hill House	Suff	TM0535	51°58·8'	0°59·5'E	X	155
Hill House	Warw	SP2557	52°12·9'	1°37·6'W	X	151
Hillhouse	W Loth	NT0075	55°57·7'	3°35·7'W	X	65
Hillhouse Burn	Scot Bord	NT5056	55°47·9'	2°47·4'W	W	66,73
Hillhouse Close	Northum	NY6859	54°55·7'	2°29·5'W	X	86,87
Hill House Fm	Cambs	TL1574	52°21·3'	0°18·3'W	FM	142
Hill House Fm	Cambs	TL6158	52°12·0'	0°21·8'E	FM	154
Hill House Fm	Devon	ST2408	50°52·2'	3°4·4'W	FM	192,193
Hill House Fm	Durham	NZ0816	54°32·6'	1°52·2'W	FM	92
Hill House Fm	Essex	TL7521	51°51·8'	0°32·9'E	FM	167
Hill House Fm	Essex	TL8821	51°51·6'	0°44·2'E	FM	168
Hillhouse Fm	Essex	TM0328	51°55·0'	0°57·5'E	FM	168
Hill House Fm	E Susx	TQ7511	50°52·5'	0°29·6'E	FM	199
Hillhouse Fm	Glos	SO7504	51°44·3'	2°21·3'W	FM	162
Hill House Fm	Glos	SO7725	51°55·6'	2°19·7'W	FM	162
Hillhouse Fm	Glos	SO9303	51°43·8'	2°5·7'W	FM	163
Hill House Fm	Glos	SP1215	51°50·2'	1°49·2'W	FM	163
Hill House Fm	Heref	SO3370	52°19·7'	2°58·6'W	FM	137,148
Hill House Fm	Heref	SO6756	52°12·3'	2°28·6'W	FM	149
Hill House Fm	Heref	SO7447	52°7·5'	2°22·4'W	FM	150
Hill House Fm	Kent	TQ7550	51°13·6'	0°30·8'E	FM	188
Hill House Fm	Kent	TR2245	51°9·9'	1°10·9'E	FM	179,189
Hill House Fm	Lancs	SD3111	53°35·7'	3°2·1'W	FM	108
Hill House Fm	Lancs	SD3835	53°48·7'	2°56·1'W	FM	102
Hill House Fm	Lancs	SD4653	53°58·5'	2°49·0'W	FM	102
Hill House Fm	Norf	TF6930	52°50·7'	0°31·0'E	FM	132
Hill House Fm	Norf	TF9435	52°52·9'	0°53·4'E	FM	132
Hillhouse Fm	Norf	TM3093	52°29·4'	1°23·7'E	FM	134
Hill House Fm	Notts	SK6256	53°6·1'	1°4·0'W	FM	120
Hill House Fm	Notts	SK7460	53°8·2'	0°53·2'W	FM	120
Hill House Fm	N Yks	NZ3805	54°26·6'	1°24·4'W	FM	93
Hill House Fm	N Yks	NZ7707	54°27·4'	0°48·3'W	FM	94
Hill House Fm	N Yks	SE2868	54°6·7'	1°33·9'W	FM	99
Hill House Fm	N Yks	SE2962	54°3·4'	1°33·0'W	FM	99
Hill House Fm	Powys	SO2968	52°18·6'	3°2·1'W	FM	137,148
Hillhouse Fm	S Glos	ST7186	51°34·6'	2°24·7'W	FM	172
Hillhouse Fm	Shrops	SO6373	52°21·5'	2°32·2'W	FM	138
Hill House Fm	Sol	SP2579	52°24·7'	1°37·5'W	FM	140
Hill House Fm	Somer	ST5543	51°11·3'	2°38·2'W	FM	182,183
Hill House Fm	Somer	ST7450	51°15·1'	2°22·0'W	FM	183
Hill House Fm	Stock on T	NZ3920	54°34·7'	1°23·4'W	FM	93
Hill House Fm	Stock on T	NZ4108	54°28·2'	1°21·6'W	FM	93
Hill House Fm	Stock on T	NZ4109	54°28·7'	1°21·6'W	FM	93
Hillhouse Fm	Suff	TL9349	52°6·6'	0°49·5'E	FM	155
Hill House Fm	Suff	TM0549	52°6·3'	1°0·0'E	FM	155
Hill House Fm	Suff	TM0855	52°9·5'	1°2·9'E	FM	155
Hill House Fm	Suff	TM2034	51°57·9'	1°12·6'E	FM	169
Hill House Fm	Suff	TM2561	52°12·3'	1°18·0'E	FM	156
Hillhouse Fm	Suff	TM2936	51°58·7'	1°20·5'E	FM	169
Hill House Fm	Suff	TM3663	52°13·1'	1°27·7'E	FM	156
Hill House Fm	Suff	TM3673	52°18·5'	1°28·1'E	FM	156
Hillhouse Fm	Surrey	TQ1036	51°7·0'	0°25·3'W	FM	187
Hillhouse Fm	Surrey	TQ1841	51°9·6'	0°18·4'W	FM	187
Hill House Fm	Warw	SP3358	52°13·4'	1°30·6'W	FM	151
Hillhouse Fm	W Berks	SU5470	51°25·8'	1°13·0'W	FM	174
Hill House Fm	Worcs	SO7666	52°17·7'	2°20·7'W	FM	138,150
Hill House Fm	Worcs	SO9740	52°3·7'	2°2·2'W	FM	150
Hillhouse Fm	W Susx	TQ3427	51°1·8'	0°5·0'W	FM	187,198
Hill House Fold	Lancs	SD5212	53°36·4'	2°43·1'W	X	108
Hillhousehill	E Ayr	NS4641	55°38·5'	4°26·4'W	X	70
Hillhouse Nook	Cumbr	NY3950	54°50·7'	2°56·6'W	X	85
Hillhouseridge	N Lanak	NS8661	55°50·0'	3°48·8'W	X	65
Hillhouses	Angus	NO3835	56°30·4'	3°0·0'W	X	54
Hill Houses	Cumbr	NY4540	54°45·4'	2°50·9'W	X	86
Hill Houses	Derby	SK0587	53°23·0'	1°55·1'W	X	110
Hill Houses	Derby	SK3767	53°12·2'	1°26·4'W	X	119
Hill Houses	Hants	SU5728	51°3·1'	1°10·8'W	X	185
Hill Houses	N Yks	SE6599	54°23·2'	0°59·5'W	X	94,100
Hill Houses	Shrops	SO6379	52°24·7'	2°32·2'W	T	138
Hill House Stables	W Berks	SU3179	51°30·8'	1°32·8'W	X	174
Hill House, The	Arg & Bt	NS3083	56°0·8'	4°43·2'W	X	56
Hill House,The,	Arg & Bt	NS3083	56°0·8'	4°43·2'W	X	56
Hilliard's Cross	Staffs	SK1511	52°42·0'	1°46·3'W	T	128
Hilliclay	Highld	ND1664	58°33·6'	3°26·1'W	X	11,12
Hillidin	Shetld	HU6288	60°34·5'	0°51·6'W	X	1,2
Hilliers	W Berks	SU5869	51°25·3'	1°9·6'W	X	174
Hilliers	W Susx	SU9922	50°59·6'	0°35·0'W	X	197
Hillies Wood	Devon	SS5313	50°54·1'	4°5·1'W	F	180
Hillilees	N Yks	NZ4008	54°28·2'	1°22·5'W	X	93
Hillingdon	Durham	NZ0621	54°35·3'	1°54·0'W	X	92
Hillingdon	Hill	TQ0882	51°31·8'	0°26·2'W	T	176
Hillingdon Heath	Hill	TQ0782	51°31·8'	0°27·1'W	T	176
Hillington	C of Glas	NS5164	55°51·0'	4°22·4'W	T	64
Hillington	Norf	TF7125	52°48·0'	0°32·6'E	T	132
Hillington Hall	Norf	TF7226	52°48·5'	0°33·5'E	X	132
Hillington Industrial Estate	Renf	NS5165	55°51·6'	4°22·4'W	X	64
Hillis	Powys	SO1132	51°59·0'	3°17·4'W	H	161
Hillis Corner	I of W	SZ4793	50°44·3'	1°19·7'W	T	196
Hillis Fm	I of W	SZ4693	50°44·3'	1°20·5'W	FM	196
Hillkirk	Angus	NO5447	56°37·0'	2°44·5'W	X	54
Hillkitty	Pth & Kin	NN9605	56°13·8'	3°40·2'W	X	58
Hill Lands Fm	W Susx	SU8115	50°56·0'	0°50·5'W	FM	197
Hill Leys	Pemb	SM9014	51°47·4'	5°2·3'W	X	157,158
Hill Manor	Swin	SU2382	51°32·4'	1°39·7'W	X	174
Hill Marsh Fm	Lincs	TF2627	52°49·8'	0°7·4'W	FM	131
Hillmoor	Devon	ST1013	50°54·8'	3°16·4'W	T	181,193
Hill Moor	Pemb	SM8913	51°46·8'	5°3·1'W	X	157,158
Hillmoor Fm	Ches	SJ8765	53°11·2'	2°11·3'W	FM	118
Hillmorton	Warw	SP5373	52°21·4'	1°12·9'W	T	140
Hillmott's Fm	Bucks	SU9588	51°35·2'	0°37·3'W	FM	175,176
Hill Mountain	Pemb	SM9708	51°44·3'	4°56·0'W	T	157,158
Hill Ness	Shetld	HP6517	60°50·1'	0°47·8'W	X	1
Hill Oak	Heref	SO6751	52°9·6'	2°28·5'W	X	149
Hillock	Aberd	NJ5105	57°8·3'	2°48·1'W	X	37
Hillock	Aberd	NJ5410	57°11·0'	2°45·2'W	X	37
Hillock	Aberd	NJ5704	57°7·8'	2°42·2'W	X	37
Hillock	Angus	NO4734	56°30·0'	2°51·2'W	X	54
Hillock	Angus	NO5578	56°53·7'	2°43·9'W	X	44
Hillock	Fife	NT0888	56°2·7'	3°28·2'W	X	65
Hillock	Moray	NJ3932	57°22·7'	3°0·4'W	X	37
Hillock	Northum	NY8399	55°17·3'	2°15·6'W	X	80
Hillock Fm	Lancs	SD7035	53°48·9'	2°26·9'W	FM	103
Hillockhead	Aberd	NJ3809	57°10·3'	3°1·1'W	X	37
Hillockhead	Aberd	NJ4042	57°28·1'	2°59·6'W	X	28
Hillockhead	Aberd	NJ4912	57°12·0'	2°50·2'W	X	37
Hillockhead	Aberd	NJ5540	57°27·1'	2°44·5'W	X	29
Hillockhead	Angus	NO3052	56°39·5'	3°8·1'W	X	53
Hillockhead	Highld	NH7460	57°37·0'	4°6·1'W	X	21,27
Hillockhead	Moray	NJ0251	57°32·6'	3°37·8'W	X	27
Hillockhead	Moray	NJ4049	57°31·9'	2°59·7'W	X	28
Hillockhead of Muldearie	Moray	NJ3950	57°32·4'	3°0·7'W	X	28
Hillock of Baywest	Orkney	HY6124	59°6·3'	2°40·4'W	X	5
Hillock of Baywest (Brock)	Orkney	HY6124	59°6·3'	2°40·4'W	A	5
Hillock of Breakna	Orkney	HY3505	58°55·9'	3°7·3'W	A	6,7
Hillock of Breakna (Broch)	Orkney	HY3505	58°55·9'	3°7·3'W	A	6,7
Hillock of Keig	Aberd	NJ5821	57°16·9'	2°41·3'W	X	37
Hillock of Terpersie	Aberd	NJ5320	57°16·4'	2°46·3'W	X	37
Hillock O'Leys	Aberd	NJ8556	57°35·9'	2°14·6'W	X	30
Hillocks	Aberd	NJ8324	57°18·6'	2°16·5'W	X	38
Hillocks	Aberd	NO8790	57°0·3'	2°12·4'W	X	38,45
Hillocks	Moray	NJ4263	57°39·5'	2°57·9'W	X	28
Hillocks	Pth & Kin	NO1735	56°30·2'	3°20·5'W	X	53
Hillocks Fm	Shrops	SO6576	52°23·1'	2°30·5'W	FM	138
Hillocks of Garth	Orkney	HY4607	58°57·1'	2°55·8'W	A	6,7
Hillocks of Gourdie	Pth & Kin	NO1143	56°34·5'	3°26·5'W	X	53
Hillock Vale	Lancs	SD7629	53°45·7'	2°21·4'W	T	103
Hillock Wood	Bucks	SP8302	51°42·9'	0°47·5'W	F	165
Hill of Achalone	Highld	ND0363	58°32·9'	3°39·5'W	X	11,12
Hill of Acharole	Highld	ND2249	58°25·6'	3°19·7'W	X	11,12
Hill of Achmore	Moray	NJ2630	57°21·5'	3°13·3'W	H	37
Hill of Adenaich	Angus	NO3065	56°46·5'	3°8·3'W	H	44
Hill of Airlie	Aberd	NJ5920	57°16·4'	2°40·3'W	H	37
Hill of Aitnoch	Highld	NH9739	57°26·0'	3°42·5'W	H	27
Hill of Aldachuie	Aberd	NJ3116	57°14·0'	3°8·1'W	H	37
Hill of Aldie	Aberd	NK0541	57°27·8'	1°54·5'W	H	30
Hill of Allamuc	Aberd	NJ3906	57°8·7'	3°0·0'W	H	37
Hill of Allargue	Aberd	NJ2510	57°10·7'	3°14·0'W	H	37
Hill of Allochie	Aberd	NO8591	57°0·8'	2°14·4'W	X	38,45
Hill of Alvah	Aberd	NJ6759	57°37·4'	2°32·7'W	H	29
Hill of Alyth	Pth & Kin	NO2350	56°38·4'	3°14·9'W	H	53
Hill of Annahar	Aberd	NO6880	56°54·9'	2°31·1'W	X	45
Hill of Ardiffery	Aberd	NK0435	57°24·6'	1°55·5'W	X	30
Hill of Ardo	Aberd	NJ9422	57°17·6'	2°5·5'W	X	38
Hill of Area	Shetld	HU4658	60°18·5'	1°9·6'W	H	2,3
Hill of Arisdale	Shetld	HU4984	60°32·5'	1°5·9'W	H	1,2,3
Hill of Arnmore	Stir	NS6295	56°7·9'	4°12·8'W	X	57
Hill of Ashmore	Pth & Kin	NO1553	56°39·9'	3°22·8'W	H	53
Hill of Auchlee	Aberd	NO8897	57°4·1'	2°11·4'W	H	38,45
Hill of Auchleuchries	Aberd	NK0036	57°25·1'	1°59·5'W	H	30
Hill of Auchmannoch	E Ayr	NS5330	55°32·7'	4°19·4'W	X	70
Hill of Badarclay	Highld	ND2350	58°26·2'	3°18·7'W	X	11,12
Hill of Badymicks	Aberd	NO5885	56°57·5'	2°41·0'W	H	44
Hill of Bainshole	Aberd	NJ6135	57°24·5'	2°38·5'W	H	29
Hill of Bakkanalee	Shetld	HP4903	60°42·7'	1°5·6'W	H	1
Hill of Balbae	Angus	NO3566	56°47·1'	3°3·4'W	H	44
Hill of Baldowrie	Pth & Kin	NO2739	56°32·5'	3°10·8'W	X	53
Hill of Balgair	Stir	NS5988	56°4·1'	4°15·5'W	X	57
Hill of Banchory	Aberd	NO7096	57°3·5'	2°29·2'W	F	38,45
Hill of Bank	Moray	NJ3829	57°21·1'	3°1·4'W	H	37
Hill of Bardister	Shetld	HU3576	60°28·2'	1°21·3'W	X	2,3
Hill of Barnaigh	Renf	NS3661	55°49·1'	4°36·6'W	H	63
Hill of Barnyards	Aberd	NJ7652	57°33·7'	2°23·6'W	H	29
Hill of Barra	Aberd	NJ8025	57°19·2'	2°19·5'W	H	38
Hill of Basta	Shetld	HU5293	60°37·3'	1°2·5'W	H	1,2
Hill of Beath	Fife	NT1390	56°5·9'	3°23·5'W	H	58
Hill of Beath	Fife	NT1490	56°6·0'	3°22·5'W	T	58
Hill of Beith	N Ayr	NS3554	55°45·3'	4°37·3'W	X	63
Hill of Bellaty	Angus	NO2459	56°43·2'	3°14·1'W	H	53
Hill of Bellyhack	Moray	NJ3942	57°28·1'	3°0·6'W	X	28
Hill of Belnagoak	Aberd	NJ8742	57°28·3'	2°12·5'W	H	30
Hill of Beltie	Aberd	NO6399	57°5·1'	2°36·2'W	H	37,45
Hill of Beosetter	Shetld	HU4843	60°10·4'	1°7·6'W	H	4
Hill of Berran	Angus	NO4571	56°49·9'	2°53·6'W	H	44
Hill of Berry	Shetld	HU3940	60°8·8'	1°17·4'W	H	4
Hill of Bixsetter	Shetld	HU5397	60°39·4'	1°1·3'W	H	1
Hill of Blackford	Aberd	NJ7034	57°24·0'	2°29·5'W	H	29
Hill of Blacklodge	Aberd	NO7488	56°59·2'	2°25·2'W	X	45
Hill of Blackroads	Moray	NJ1747	57°30·6'	3°22·7'W	X	28
Hill of Blair	Aberd	NJ8426	57°19·7'	2°15·5'W	X	38
Hill of Blairfowl	Aberd	NJ8037	57°25·6'	2°19·5'W	H	29,30
Hill of Blairs	Aberd	NO8899	57°5·2'	2°11·4'W	X	38,45
Hill of Bogairdy	Aberd	NJ4836	57°24·9'	2°51·5'W	H	28,29
Hill of Boghead	Aberd	NJ7914	57°13·2'	2°20·4'W	X	38
Hill of Bogjurgan	Aberd	NO7585	56°57·6'	2°24·2'W	X	45
Hill of Bolshan	Angus	NO6353	56°40·3'	2°35·8'W	X	54
Hill of Bomo	Orkney	HY5736	59°12·8'	2°44·7'W	X	5
Hill of Borwick	Orkney	HY2216	59°1·7'	3°21·0'W	X	6
Hill of Bousta	Shetld	HU2257	60°18·1'	1°35·6'W	H	3
Hill of Bouster	Shetld	HU4590	60°35·7'	1°10·2'W	H	1,2
Hill of Brackans	Aberd	NJ7653	57°34·2'	2°23·6'W	H	29
Hill of Braewick	Shetld	HU3357	60°18·0'	1°23·7'W	H	2,3
Hill of Braigie	Aberd	NJ7605	57°8·4'	2°23·3'W	X	38
Hill of Breakon	Shetld	HP5104	60°43·2'	1°3·4'W	X	1
Hill of Breibister	Shetld	HU3793	60°37·4'	1°18·9'W	X	1,2
Hill of Bretto	Shetld	HU4253	60°15·8'	1°14·0'W	H	3
Hill of Brimness	Shetld	HP5105	60°43·8'	1°3·4'W	X	1
Hill of Brindister	Shetld	HU4437	60°7·2'	1°12·0'W	X	4
Hill of Brunt Hamarsland	Shetld	HU4351	60°14·7'	1°12·9'W	H	3
Hill of Burnieshag	Aberd	NO6981	56°55·4'	2°30·1'W	X	45
Hill of Burraness	Shetld	HU5495	60°38·3'	1°0·3'W	H	1,2
Hill of Burravoe	Shetld	HU3667	60°23·4'	1°20·3'W	H	2,3
Hill of Burriesness	Shetld	HU2883	60°32·0'	1°28·9'W	H	3
Hill of Burwick	Shetld	HU3941	60°9·4'	1°17·4'W	H	4
Hill of Cairnton	Aberd	NJ9639	57°26·7'	2°3·5'W	H	30
Hill of Cairnton	Aberd	NO6596	57°3·5'	2°34·2'W	H	38,45
Hill of Cairnty	Moray	NJ3353	57°34·0'	3°6·7'W	X	28
Hill of Caldback	Shetld	HP6006	60°44·2'	0°53·5'W	H	1
Hill of Caldback (Chambered Cairn)	Shetld	HP6006	60°44·2'	0°53·5'W	A	1
Hill of Calder	Highld	ND1057	58°29·8'	3°32·2'W	X	11,12
Hill of Calfsound	Orkney	HY5637	59°13·3'	2°45·8'W	X	5
Hill of Cally	Pth & Kin	NO1253	56°39·9'	3°25·7'W	H	53
Hill of Camb	Shetld	HU5092	60°36·8'	1°4·7'W	H	1,2
Hill of Cammie	Angus	NO5285	56°57·5'	2°46·9'W	H	44
Hill of Candacraig	Aberd	NJ3400	57°5·4'	3°4·9'W	H	37
Hill of Canisdale	Shetld	HU5084	60°32·5'	1°4·8'W	X	1,2,3
Hill of Canterland	Aberd	NO7065	56°46·8'	2°29·0'W	X	45
Hill of Carlincraig	Aberd	NJ6744	57°29·4'	2°32·6'W	H	29
Hill of Cat	Angus	NO4887	56°58·5'	2°50·9'W	H	44
Hill of Catfirth	Shetld	HU4454	60°16·3'	1°11·8'W	H	3
Hill of Chattie	Aberd	NJ5962	57°39·0'	2°40·8'W	X	29
Hill of Christ's Kirk	Aberd	NJ6027	57°20·2'	2°39·4'W	H	37
Hill of Clais-na-canaich	Highld	ND2638	58°19·7'	3°15·3'W	H	11
Hill of Clais nan Earb	Moray	NJ3233	57°23·2'	3°7·4'W	H	28
Hill of Clashmadin	Moray	NJ4760	57°37·9'	2°52·8'W	X	28,29
Hill of Clayton	Highld	ND3463	58°33·3'	3°7·6'W	X	12
Hill of Cleftbog	Aberd	NJ6845	57°29·9'	2°31·6'W	H	29
Hill of Clibberswick	Shetld	HP6612	60°47·4'	0°46·8'W	H	1
Hill of Clindrag	Highld	ND1767	58°35·3'	3°25·2'W	H	11,12
Hill of Clindrag (Cairn)	Highld	ND1767	58°35·3'	3°25·2'W	A	11,12
Hill of Clothan	Shetld	HU4681	60°30·9'	1°9·2'W	H	1,2,3
Hill of Cloverycrook	Aberd	NJ7534	57°24·0'	2°24·5'W	H	29
Hill of Clyne	Aberd	NJ8421	57°17·0'	2°15·5'W	X	38
Hill of Collithie	Aberd	NJ5034	57°23·9'	2°49·5'W	H	29
Hill of Colvadale	Shetld	HP6105	60°43·7'	0°52·4'W	H	1
Hill of Colvister	Shetld	HU5095	60°38·4'	1°4·6'W	H	1,2
Hill of Corathro	Angus	NO5572	56°50·5'	2°43·8'W	X	44
Hill of Corfeidly	Aberd	NJ6701	57°6·2'	2°32·2'W	H	38
Hill of Corn	Angus	NO4786	56°58·0'	2°51·8'W	X	44
Hill of Corrachree	Aberd	NJ4504	57°7·7'	2°54·1'W	H	37
Hill of Corsegight	Aberd	NJ8550	57°32·7'	2°14·6'W	H	30
Hill of Corskie	Aberd	NJ5432	57°22·8'	2°45·4'W	H	29,37
Hill of Corskie	Aberd	NJ7509	57°10·5'	2°24·4'W	X	38
Hill of Cotburn	Aberd	NJ7753	57°34·2'	2°22·6'W	H	29,30
Hill of Coull	Aberd	NJ5202	57°6·6'	2°47·1'W	H	37
Hill of Courtstone	Aberd	NJ8333	57°23·5'	2°16·5'W	H	29,30
Hill of Couternach	Angus	NO3565	56°46·6'	3°3·4'W	H	44
Hill of Craighead	Pth & Kin	NO1954	56°40·5'	3°18·9'W	H	53
Hill of Craigmancie	Aberd	NJ5947	57°30·9'	2°40·6'W	H	29
Hill of Creagdearg	Aberd	NJ4525	57°19·0'	2°54·3'W	H	37
Hill of Crimond	Aberd	NJ8223	57°18·1'	2°17·5'W	X	38
Hill of Crogodale	Highld	ND3971	58°37·6'	3°2·5'W	H	7,12
Hill of Crooksetter	Shetld	HU4175	60°27·7'	1°14·8'W	H	2,3
Hill of Cruaday	Orkney	HY2421	59°4·4'	3°19·1'W	X	6
Hill of Cruester	Shetld	HU4842	60°9·8'	1°7·6'W	H	4
Hill of Cuckron	Shetld	HU4151	60°14·7'	1°15·1'W	H	3
Hill of Culbirnie	Aberd	NJ6360	57°38·0'	2°36·7'W	H	29
Hill of Cummerton	Aberd	NJ3513	57°12·4'	3°4·1'W	H	37
Hill of Dale	Orkney	HY3205	58°55·9'	3°10·4'W	H	6,7
Hill of Dale	Shetld	HU4069	60°24·4'	1°15·9'W	H	2,3
Hill of Dale	Shetld	HU4341	60°9·3'	1°13·0'W	H	4
Hill of Dalnapot	Highld	NJ1537	57°25·2'	3°24·5'W	H	28
Hill of Dalsetter	Shetld	HU5098	60°40·0'	1°4·6'W	H	1
Hill of Deepdale	Shetld	HU3926	60°1·3'	1°17·5'W	H	4
Hill of Den	Aberd	NJ7426	57°19·7'	2°25·5'W	H	38
Hill of Denmoss	Aberd	NJ6542	57°28·3'	2°34·6'W	H	29
Hill of Dens	Aberd	NJ9545	57°30·0'	2°4·5'W	H	30
Hill of Dens	Aberd	NK0742	57°28·3'	1°52·5'W	X	30
Hill of Deskie	Moray	NJ2031	57°22·0'	3°19·3'W	H	36
Hill of Doune	Aberd	NJ6963	57°39·6'	2°30·7'W	H	29
Hill of Doune	Angus	NO3885	56°57·4'	3°0·7'W	H	44
Hill of Draidland	Aberd	NJ7762	57°39·1'	2°22·7'W	H	29,30
Hill of Drimmie	Pth & Kin	NO1850	56°38·3'	3°19·8'W	H	53
Hill of Drip	Stir	NS7695	56°8·2'	3°59·3'W	T	57
Hill of Drumfergue	Aberd	NJ4733	57°23·3'	2°52·4'W	H	28,29
Hill of Duchery	Aberd	NO5091	57°0·7'	2°48·9'W	H	44
Hill of Duclash	Aberd	NO6285	56°57·5'	2°37·0'W	H	45
Hill of Dudwick	Aberd	NJ9737	57°25·7'	2°2·5'W	H	30
Hill of Dumeath	Aberd	NJ4137	57°25·4'	2°58·5'W	H	28
Hill of Dun	W Dunb	NS4474	55°56·3'	4°29·4'W	X	64
Hill of Dwarmo	Orkney	HY3925	59°6·7'	3°3·4'W	H	6
Hill of Easter Bleaton	Pth & Kin	NO1457	56°42·1'	3°23·8'W	H	53
Hill of Easterhoull	Shetld	HU4138	60°7·7'	1°15·2'W	H	4
Hill of Easterton	Aberd	NJ7532	57°22·9'	2°24·5'W	H	29
Hill of Easteton	Aberd	NJ7532	57°22·9'	2°24·5'W	H	29
Hill of Eaton	Heref	SO6027	51°56·6'	2°34·5'W	X	162
Hill of Edendocher	Aberd	NO6085	56°57·5'	2°39·0'W	H	45
Hill of Edinvale	Moray	NJ1154	57°34·3'	3°28·8'W	X	28
Hill of Edzell	Angus	NO5770	56°49·4'	2°41·8'W	H	44
Hill of Errol	Pth & Kin	NO2221	56°22·7'	3°15·3'W	X	53,58
Hill of Fare	Aberd	NJ6802	57°6·7'	2°31·2'W	H	38
Hill of Fearn	Highld	NH8377	57°46·3'	3°57·6'W	T	21
Hill of Fechel	Aberd	NJ8625	57°19·2'	2°13·5'W	X	38
Hill of Fernyhirst	Angus	NO2156	56°41·6'	3°16·9'W	H	53
Hill of Fiddes	Aberd	NJ9324	57°18·6'	2°6·5'W	X	38
Hill of Finavon	Angus	NO4954	56°40·8'	2°49·5'W	H	54
Hill of Findon	Aberd	NJ8063	57°39·6'	2°19·7'W	H	29,30
Hill of Findon	Aberd	NO9398	57°4·6'	2°6·5'W	H	38,45
Hill of Fingray	Angus	NO5781	56°55·4'	2°41·9'W	H	44
Hill of Fishrie	Aberd	NJ8258	57°37·0'	2°17·6'W	H	29,30
Hill of Flamister	Shetld	HU4456	60°17·4'	1°11·8'W	H	2,3
Hill of Flinder	Aberd	NJ5927	57°20·2'	2°40·4'W	H	37
Hill of Formal	Angus	NO5370	56°49·4'	2°45·8'W	X	44
Hill of Forrest	Aberd	NK0060	57°38·1'	1°59·5'W	H	30
Hill of Forss	Highld	ND0668	58°35·7'	3°36·6'W	X	11,12
Hill of Fortrose	Highld	NH7157	57°35·3'	4°9·0'W	H	27
Hill of Foudland	Aberd	NJ6033	57°23·4'	2°39·5'W	H	29
Hill of Gairney	Angus	NO4487	56°58·5'	2°54·8'W	H	44
Hill of Garbet	Angus	NO4668	56°48·3'	2°52·6'W	H	44
Hill of Gardin	Shetld	HU4965	60°22·2'	1°6·2'W	H	2,3
Hill of Garmouth	Moray	NJ3262	57°38·8'	3°7·9'W	X	28
Hill of Garth	Shetld	HU4175	60°27·7'	1°14·8'W	H	2,3
Hill of Garvock	Aberd	NO7370	56°49·5'	2°26·1'W	H	45
Hill of Gaschyle	Moray	NJ0448	57°31·0'	3°35·7'W	X	27

Hill of Gask	Aberd	NK0741	57°27·8′	1°52·5′W	X	30
Hill of Gellan	Aberd	NJ5001	57°6·1′	2°49·1′W	X	37
Hill of Girlsta	Shetld	HU4251	60°14·7′	1°14·0′W	H	3
Hill of Glansie	Angus	NO4369	56°48·8′	2°55·6′W	H	44
Hill of Glasserton	D & G	NX4136	54°41·9′	4°27·6′W	H	83
Hill of Glenroads	Moray	NJ3031	57°22·1′	3°9·4′W	H	37
Hill of Goauch	Aberd	NO6694	57°2·4′	2°33·2′W	H	38,45
Hill of Gord	Shetld	HU4021	59°58·6′	1°16·5′W	X	4
Hill of Gothie	Aberd	NO6783	56°56·5′	2°32·1′W	H	45
Hill of Goval	Aberd	NJ8815	57°13·8′	2°11·5′W	X	38
Hill of Graven	Shetld	HU4072	60°26·1′	1°15·9′W	H	2,3
Hill of Greenfold	Aberd	NJ5541	57°27·7′	2°44·5′W	H	29
Hill of Greenhead	Shetld	HU4643	60°10·4′	1°9·8′W	X	4
Hill of Greenstile	Aberd	NJ3813	57°12·5′	3°1·1′W	H	37
Hill of Gremista	Shetld	HU4544	60°10·9′	1°10·8′W	H	4
Hill of Griesta	Shetld	HU4044	60°11·0′	1°16·2′W	H	4
Hill of Gunnista	Shetld	HU4943	60°10·4′	1°6·5′W	H	4
Hill of Gutcher	Shetld	HU5498	60°40·0′	1°0·2′W	X	1
Hill of Gyratesmyre	Aberd	NO7878	56°53·8′	2°21·2′W	H	45
Hill of Haggrister	Shetld	HU3470	60°25·0′	1°22·5′W	H	2,3
Hill of Halsagarth	Shetld	HU4890	60°35·7′	1°6·9′W	X	1,2
Hill of Hamarsland	Shetld	HU4149	60°13·7′	1°15·1′W	H	3
Hill of Hardwall	Shetld	HU3769	60°24·5′	1°19·2′W	H	2,3
Hill of Harland	Highld	ND3253	58°27·9′	3°9·5′W	H	12
Hill of Harley	Highld	ND3765	58°34·4′	3°4·5′W	X	12
Hill of Health	Suff	TL8371	52°18·6′	0°41·5′E	X	144,155
Hill of Health (Tumulus)	Suff	TL8371	52°18·6′	0°41·5′E	A	144,155
Hill of Heddle	Orkney	HY3513	59°0·2′	3°7·4′W	H	6
Hill of Hellister	Shetld	HU3949	60°13·7′	1°17·3′W	H	3
Hill of Heodale	Shetld	HU3071	60°25·6′	1°26·8′W	H	3
Hill of Herrislee	Shetld	HU4344	60°11·0′	1°13·0′W	H	4
Hill of Hobseat	Aberd	NO7587	56°58·7′	2°24·2′W	X	45
Hill of Holligarth	Shetld	HU5184	60°32·4′	1°3·7′W	X	1,2,3
Hill of Houlland	Shetld	HU4040	60°8·8′	1°16·3′W	X	4
Hill of Howness	Orkney	HY6826	59°7·4′	2°33·1′W	X	5
Hill of Huntis	Orkney	HY3623	59°5·6′	3°6·5′W	X	6
Hill of Huxter	Shetld	HU3951	60°14·7′	1°17·2′W	H	3
Hill of Inverkindling	Aberd	NJ5258	57°36·8′	2°47·7′W	H	29
Hill of Itlaw	Aberd	NJ6657	57°36·4′	2°33·7′W	H	29
Hill of Janetstown	Aberd	NJ4143	57°28·7′	2°58·6′W	H	28
Hill of John's Cairn	Aberd	NJ4320	57°16·3′	2°56·3′W	H	37
Hill of Keillor	Angus	NO2840	56°33·0′	3°9·8′W	H	53
Hill of Keir	Aberd	NJ8108	57°10·0′	2°18·4′W	H	38
Hill of Keir	Aberd	NJ9418	57°15·4′	2°5·5′W	X	38
Hill of Kennerty	Aberd	NJ6700	57°5·6′	2°32·2′W	H	38
Hill of Kilncadzow	S Lanak	NS8948	55°43·0′	3°45·6′W	X	72
Hill of Kinglands	Pth & Kin	NO0233	56°29·0′	3°35·0′W	X	52,53
Hill of Kingseat	Pth & Kin	NO1555	56°41·0′	3°22·8′W	H	53
Hill of Kinnaird	Falk	NS8785	56°2·9′	3°48·4′W	X	65
Hill of Kirkabister	Shetld	HU5496	60°38·9′	1°0·2′W	H	1
Hill of Kirkney	Aberd	NJ5031	57°22·3′	2°49·4′W	H	29,37
Hill of Kirny	Angus	NO4483	56°56·4′	2°54·8′W	X	44
Hill of Kirriemuir	Angus	NO3954	56°40·7′	2°59·3′W	H	54
Hill of Knocknashalg	Moray	NJ2234	57°23·6′	3°17·4′W	H	28
Hill of Laithers	Aberd	NJ6748	57°31·5′	2°32·6′W	H	29
Hill of Laxowater	Shetld	HU4464	60°21·7′	1°11·6′W	H	2,3
Hill of Lee	Shetld	HU3762	60°20·7′	1°19·3′W	H	2,3
Hill of Lee	Shetld	HU4474	60°27·1′	1°11·5′W	H	2,3
Hill of Lendrum	Aberd	NJ7745	57°29·9′	2°22·6′W	H	29,30
Hill of Lenshie	Aberd	NJ6741	57°27·7′	2°32·5′W	H	29
Hill of Leodebest	Highld	ND1834	58°17·5′	3°23·4′W	X	11
Hill of Lieurary	Highld	ND0861	58°31·9′	3°34·3′W	H	11,12
Hill of Linkster	Shetld	HU4146	60°12·0′	1°15·1′W	X	4
Hill of Longhaven	Aberd	NK0842	57°28·3′	1°51·5′W	H	30
Hill of Lour	Angus	NO4746	56°36·4′	2°51·4′W	H	54
Hill of Loyal	Pth & Kin	NO2550	56°38·4′	3°12·9′W	H	53
Hill of Lundie	Angus	NO5667	56°47·8′	2°42·8′W	H	44
Hill of Lussetter	Shetld	HU5290	60°35·7′	1°2·5′W	H	1,2
Hill of Lybster	Highld	ND0269	58°36·1′	3°40·7′W	H	12
Hill of Lychrobbie	Highld	ND1732	58°16·4′	3°24·4′W	H	11
Hill of Lynedardy	Orkney	HY2311	58°59·0′	3°19·9′W	X	6
Hill of Lyradale	Orkney	HY3611	58°59·1′	3°6·3′W	H	6
Hill of Mackalea	Moray	NJ3638	57°25·9′	3°3·5′W	H	28
Hill of Marcus	C of Aber	NJ8413	57°12·7′	2°15·4′W	H	38
Hill of Markamouth	Shetld	HP4802	60°42·2′	1°6·7′W	H	1
Hill of Maryfield	Aberd	NO7195	57°3·0′	2°28·2′W	H	38,45
Hill of Maud	Moray	NJ4662	57°38·9′	2°53·8′W	H	28,29
Hill of Maunderlea	Aberd	NJ6356	57°35·8′	2°36·7′W	H	29
Hill of Mayen	Moray	NJ5748	57°31·5′	2°42·6′W	X	29
Hill of Meadaple	Aberd	NJ7234	57°24·0′	2°27·5′W	H	29
Hill of Megray	Aberd	NO8787	56°58·7′	2°12·4′W	X	45
Hill of Melby	Shetld	HU1855	60°17·0′	1°40·0′W	H	3
Hill of Menduff	Moray	NJ4359	57°37·3′	2°56·8′W	X	28
Hill of Menie	Aberd	NJ9620	57°16·5′	2°3·5′W	X	38
Hill of Menmuir	Angus	NO5165	56°46·7′	2°47·7′W	H	44
Hill of Mid Clyth	Highld	ND2838	58°19·7′	3°13·3′W	H	11
Hill of Middleton	Aberd	NJ8519	57°15·9′	2°14·5′W	X	38
Hill of Midland	Orkney	HY3204	58°55·3′	3°10·4′W	H	6,7
Hill of Miffia	Orkney	HY2313	59°0·1′	3°19·9′W	H	6
Hill of Milduan	Aberd	NJ4730	57°21·7′	2°52·4′W	H	29,37
Hill of Millmedden	Aberd	NJ5322	57°17·4′	2°46·3′W	H	37
Hill of Milltimber	C of Aber	NJ8502	57°6·8′	2°14·4′W	X	38
Hill of Minnes	Aberd	NJ9423	57°18·1′	2°5·5′W	X	38
Hill of Mondurran	Angus	NO4670	56°49·4′	2°52·6′W	H	44
Hill of Mongirsdale	Shetld	HU6492	60°36·6′	0°49·4′W	X	1,2
Hill of Montsnaught	Aberd	NO8293	57°1·9′	2°17·3′W	H	38,45
Hill of Morphie	Aberd	NO7264	56°46·3′	2°27·0′W	H	45
Hill of Mossmaud	Aberd	NO7689	56°59·7′	2°23·2′W	H	45
Hill of Mountblairy	Aberd	NJ6753	57°34·2′	2°32·6′W	T	29
Hill of Moustoft	Shetld	HU4052	60°15·3′	1°16·1′W	H	3
Hill of Muchalls	Aberd	NO8791	57°0·9′	2°12·4′W	X	38,45
Hill of Muirden	Aberd	NJ7154	57°34·8′	2°28·6′W	X	29
Hill of Mulderie	Moray	NJ3851	57°33·0′	3°1·7′W	H	28
Hill of Mulundy	Moray	NJ1053	57°33·8′	3°29·8′W	H	28
Hill of Mungo	Aberd	NJ5542	57°28·2′	2°44·6′W	H	29
Hill of Murdostoun	N Lanak	NS8258	55°48·3′	3°52·5′W	X	65,72
Hill of Neap	Shetld	HU5057	60°17·9′	1°5·2′W	H	2,3
Hill of Neegarth	Shetld	HU4271	60°25·5′	1°13·7′W	H	2,3
Hill of Newleslie	Aberd	NJ5825	57°19·1′	2°41·4′W	H	37
Hill of Newton	Moray	NJ3345	57°29·7′	3°6·6′W	X	28
Hill of Norwick	Shetld	HU3681	60°30·9′	1°20·2′W	X	1,2,3
Hill of Noth	Aberd	NJ5030	57°21·7′	2°49·4′W	H	29,37
Hill of Noub	Shetld	HU4685	60°33·0′	1°9·2′W	H	1,2,3
Hill of Oldmerdrum	Aberd	NJ4629	57°21·2′	2°53·4′W	H	37
Hill of Olicelt	Highld	ND2946	58°24·1′	3°12·4′W	H	11,12
Hill of Ollaberry	Shetld	HU3681	60°30·9′	1°20·2′W	H	1,2,3
Hill of Olligarth	Shetld	HU3847	60°12·6′	1°18·4′W	H	3
Hill of Olrig	Highld	ND1765	58°34·2′	3°25·1′W	H	11,12
Hill of Orbister	Shetld	HU3177	60°28·8′	1°25·7′W	H	3
Hill of Ord	Aberd	NJ6157	57°36·3′	2°38·7′W	X	29
Hill of Overbrae	Aberd	NJ8060	57°38·0′	2°19·6′W	H	29,30
Hill of Oxnabool	Shetld	HU4170	60°25·0′	1°14·8′W	H	2,3
Hill of Park	Aberd	NO7799	57°5·1′	2°22·3′W	X	38,45
Hill of Persie	Pth & Kin	NO1256	56°41·5′	3°25·8′W	H	53
Hill of Petty	Aberd	NJ7435	57°24·5′	2°25·5′W	X	29
Hill of Phones	Moray	NJ1940	57°26·8′	3°20·5′W	H	28
Hill of Pitspunkie	Aberd	NO8189	56°59·8′	2°18·3′W	X	45
Hill of Pundsgeo	Shetld	HU5440	60°8·7′	1°1·2′W	H	4
Hill of Queyon	Shetld	HU5386	60°33·5′	1°1·5′W	X	1,2,3
Hill of Quholm	Orkney	HY2411	58°59·0′	3°18·9′W	X	6
Hill of Quintfall	Highld	ND3162	58°32·7′	3°10·6′W	H	11,12
Hill of Quithel	Aberd	NO7785	56°57·6′	2°22·2′W	X	45
Hill of Raga	Shetld	HU4692	60°36·8′	1°9·1′W	X	1,2
Hill of Rangag	Highld	ND1843	58°22·3′	3°23·6′W	H	11,12
Hill of Rattar	Highld	ND2473	58°38·6′	3°18·1′W	H	7,12
Hill of Reafirth	Shetld	HU5088	60°34·6′	1°4·8′W	H	1,2
Hill of Redhall	Angus	NO3958	56°42·8′	2°59·3′W	H	54
Hill of Remora	Aberd	NO6078	56°53·8′	2°38·9′W	H	45
Hill of Rhinstock	Aberd	NJ3217	57°14·6′	3°7·1′W	H	37
Hill of Righorach	Aberd	NJ2915	57°13·5′	3°10·1′W	H	37
Hill of Rigifa'	Highld	ND3072	58°38·1′	3°11·9′W	H	7,12
Hill of Rothin	Aberd	NJ6058	57°36·9′	2°39·7′W	X	29
Hill of Rothmaise	Aberd	NJ6833	57°23·4′	2°31·5′W	H	29
Hill of Roughbank	Aberd	NO7286	56°58·1′	2°27·2′W	X	45
Hill of Rowan	Angus	NO4779	56°54·2′	2°51·8′W	H	44
Hill of Rubislaw	C of Aber	NJ9005	57°8·4′	2°9·5′W	X	38
Hill of Sandvoe	Shetld	HU3589	60°35·2′	1°21·2′W	H	1,2
Hill of Sandwick	Shetld	HU4568	60°23·9′	1°10·5′W	H	2,3
Hill of Sauchenbush	Aberd	NJ7661	57°38·6′	2°23·7′W	X	29
Hill of Saughs	Angus	NO4485	56°57·4′	2°54·8′W	H	44
Hill of Saughs	Angus	NO5583	56°56·4′	2°43·9′W	X	44
Hill of Savock	Aberd	NJ9522	57°17·6′	2°4·5′W	X	38
Hill of Scarvister	Shetld	HU2048	60°13·2′	1°37·8′W	H	3
Hill of Scatsta	Shetld	HU3871	60°25·5′	1°18·1′W	H	2,3
Hill of Scattertie	Aberd	NJ7056	57°35·8′	2°29·7′W	X	29
Hill of Seabeg	Aberd	NO8483	56°56·5′	2°15·3′W	X	45
Hill of Sellafirth	Shetld	HU5199	60°40·5′	1°3·5′W	X	1
Hill of Setter	Shetld	HU4681	60°30·9′	1°9·2′W	H	1,2,3
Hill of Setter	Shetld	HU4990	60°35·7′	1°5·8′W	H	1,2
Hill of Setter	Shetld	HU5042	60°9·8′	1°5·5′W	H	4
Hill of Setter	Shetld	HU5439	60°8·2′	1°1·2′W	H	4
Hill of Shebster	Highld	ND0164	58°33·4′	3°41·6′W	H	11,12
Hill of Shenwall	Aberd	NJ4344	57°29·2′	2°56·6′W	H	28
Hill of Sherin	Shetld	HU4682	60°31·4′	1°9·2′W	X	1,2,3
Hill of Shurton	Shetld	HU4440	60°8·8′	1°12·0′W	H	4
Hill of Skares	Aberd	NJ6334	57°24·0′	2°36·5′W	H	29
Hill of Skea	Shetld	HU3785	60°33·1′	1°19·0′W	H	1,2,3
Hill of Skellister	Shetld	HU4655	60°16·9′	1°9·6′W	H	3
Hill of Skelmonae	Aberd	NJ8839	57°26·7′	2°11·5′W	H	30
Hill of Skeomire	Shetld	HU4128	60°2·3′	1°15·4′W	X	4
Hill of Skilmafilly	Aberd	NJ9040	57°27·3′	2°9·5′W	H	30
Hill of Skurron	Shetld	HU4153	60°15·8′	1°15·0′W	H	3
Hill of Slackmore	Moray	NJ1443	57°28·4′	3°25·6′W	H	28
Hill of Slickly	Highld	ND2967	58°35·4′	3°12·8′W	H	11,12
Hill of Snowy Slack	Aberd	NJ4121	57°16·8′	2°58·3′W	H	37
Hill of Sound	Shetld	HU3751	60°14·8′	1°19·4′W	H	3
Hill of Sour	Highld	ND1161	58°31·9′	3°31·2′W	H	11,12
Hill of Spott	Angus	NO3366	56°47·1′	3°5·3′W	H	44
Hill of Spynie	Moray	NJ2265	57°40·3′	3°18·0′W	X	28
Hill of Stake	N Ayr	NS2763	55°50·0′	4°45·3′W	H	63
Hill of Stanks	Angus	NO2961	56°44·4′	3°9·2′W	X	44
Hill of State	Shetld	HU5173	60°26·5′	1°3·9′W	H	2,3
Hill of St Colm	Aberd	NO4988	56°59·1′	2°49·9′W	X	44
Hill of Steinswall	Shetld	HU4141	60°9·4′	1°15·2′W	H	4
Hill of Stemster	Highld	ND3450	58°26·3′	3°7·4′W	H	12
Hill of St Fink	Pth & Kin	NO2147	56°36·8′	3°16·8′W	X	53
Hill of Stob	Moray	NJ2147	57°30·6′	3°18·7′W	X	28
Hill of Stonyslacks	Moray	NJ4358	57°36·8′	2°56·8′W	X	28
Hill of Strabathie	C of Aber	NJ9513	57°12·7′	2°4·5′W	X	38
Hill of Stracathro	Angus	NO6364	56°46·2′	2°35·9′W	H	45
Hill of Strom	Shetld	HU3948	60°13·1′	1°17·3′W	H	3
Hill of Strone	Angus	NO2867	56°47·6′	3°10·3′W	H	44
Hill of Strone	Angus	NO2872	56°50·3′	3°10·4′W	H	44
Hill of Stroupster	Highld	ND3366	58°34·9′	3°8·7′W	X	12
Hill of Summertown	Moray	NJ5360	57°37·9′	2°46·8′W	H	29
Hill of Susetter	Shetld	HU4165	60°22·3′	1°14·9′W	H	2,3
Hill of Swanley	Aberd	NO8187	56°58·7′	2°18·3′W	H	45
Hill of Swartagill	Shetld	HU3243	60°10·5′	1°24·9′W	H	4
Hill of Swinister	Shetld	HU4372	60°26·0′	1°12·6′W	H	2,3
Hill of Tagdale	Shetld	HU4443	60°10·4′	1°11·9′W	H	4
Hill of Tain	Highld	NH7381	57°48·3′	4°7·8′W	H	21
Hill of Talnamounth	Aberd	NJ4040	57°27·0′	2°59·5′W	H	28
Hill of Tarvit	Fife	NO3811	56°17·5′	2°59·7′W	X	59
Hill of the Taing	Shetld	HU4551	60°14·7′	1°10·7′W	H	3
Hill of the Wangie	Moray	NJ1353	57°33·8′	3°26·8′W	H	28
Hill of the Waters	Shetld	HU4683	60°31·9′	1°9·2′W	H	1,2,3
Hill of Three Cairns	Pth & Kin	NO1955	56°41·0′	3°18·9′W	H	53
Hill of Three Stones	Aberd	NO7788	56°59·2′	2°22·3′W	H	45
Hill of Three Stones	Moray	NJ3422	57°17·3′	3°5·2′W	H	37
Hill of Tillyfair	Aberd	NO6494	57°2·4′	2°35·1′W	H	37,45
Hill of Tillymauld	Aberd	NJ8055	57°35·3′	2°19·6′W	H	29,30
Hill of Tillymorgan	Aberd	NJ6534	57°24·0′	2°34·5′W	H	29
Hill of Tipperty	Aberd	NJ6560	57°38·0′	2°34·7′W	H	29
Hill of Toftcarl	Highld	ND3546	58°24·1′	3°6·3′W	X	12
Hill of Toftgun	Highld	ND2742	58°21·9′	3°14·4′W	H	11,12
Hill of Tomechole	Moray	NJ0649	57°31·5′	3°33·7′W	H	27
Hill of Towanreef	Aberd	NJ4524	57°18·5′	2°54·3′W	H	37
Hill of Towie	Moray	NJ3847	57°30·8′	3°1·6′W	H	28
Hill of Trolliva	Shetld	HU5497	60°39·4′	1°0·2′W	X	1
Hill of Trondavoe	Shetld	HU3870	60°25·0′	1°18·1′W	H	2,3
Hill of Troup	Aberd	NJ8261	57°38·6′	2°17·6′W	H	29,30
Hill of Trusta	Aberd	NO7886	56°58·1′	2°21·3′W	H	45
Hill of Trustach	Aberd	NO6396	57°3·5′	2°36·1′W	H	37,45
Hill of Turlundie	Aberd	NJ8756	57°35·9′	2°12·6′W	H	30
Hill of Turret	Angus	NO5581	56°55·3′	2°43·9′W	X	44
Hill of Ulbster	Highld	ND3342	58°21·9′	3°8·2′W	H	12
Hill of Ulsta	Shetld	HU4780	60°30·3′	1°8·2′W	X	1,2,3
Hill of Urchany	Highld	NH8950	57°31·9′	3°50·8′W	X	27
Hill of Ure	Shetld	HU2180	60°30·5′	1°36·6′W	H	3
Hill of Vatsie	Shetld	HU5188	60°34·6′	1°3·7′W	X	1,2
Hill of Vidlin	Shetld	HU4664	60°21·7′	1°9·5′W	H	2,3
Hill of Vigon	Shetld	HP4803	60°42·7′	1°6·7′W	H	1
Hill of Voe	Shetld	HU3381	60°30·9′	1°23·4′W	H	1,2,3
Hill of Voesgarth	Shetld	HP6007	60°44·8′	0°53·5′W	X	1
Hill of Voxter	Shetld	HU3660	60°19·6′	1°20·4′W	H	2,3
Hill of Wards	Orkney	ND3190	58°47·8′	3°11·2′W	X	7
Hill of Warse	Highld	ND3371	58°37·6′	3°8·7′W	X	7,12
Hill of Wells	Aberd	NJ7136	57°25·1′	2°28·5′W	X	29
Hill of Wester Clova	Aberd	NJ4418	57°15·2′	2°55·2′W	H	37
Hill of Westerhouse	S Lanak	NS8851	55°44·6′	3°46·6′W	X	65,72
Hill of Westersta	Shetld	HU3765	60°22·3′	1°19·2′W	H	2,3
Hill of White Hamars	Orkney	ND3188	58°46·7′	3°11·1′W	X	7
Hill of Windhouse	Shetld	HU4892	60°36·8′	1°6·9′W	X	1,2
Hill of Wirren	Angus	NO5273	56°51·0′	2°46·8′W	H	44
Hill of Yarrows	Highld	ND2942	58°21·9′	3°12·3′W	H	11,12
Hillowton Fm	D & G	NX7664	54°57·6′	3°55·8′W	FM	84
Hill Park	Arg & Bt	NM8206	56°12·1′	5°30·4′W	X	55
Hill Park	Hants	SU5507	50°51·8′	1°12·7′W	T	196
Hill Park	Kent	TQ4355	51°16·8′	0°3·4′E	T	187
Hillpark	Moray	NJ4260	57°37·8′	2°57·8′W	X	28
Hillpark	Moray	NJ4360	57°37·8′	2°56·8′W	X	28
Hill Park	Warw	SP1770	52°19·9′	1°44·6′W	X	139
Hill Park Fm	Cumbr	SD3087	54°16·7′	3°4·1′W	FM	96,97
Hillparks Fm	Leic	SK4320	52°46·8′	1°21·3′W	FM	129
Hillpike	Heref	SO4376	52°23·0′	2°49·9′W	X	137,148
Hill Place	Essex	TL8311	51°46·3′	0°39·5′E	X	168
Hill Place	Hants	SU5816	50°56·7′	1°10·1′W	X	185
Hill Place	Surrey	SU9659	51°19·5′	0°36·9′W	X	175,186
Hill Place Fm	W Susx	TQ3837	51°7·2′	0°1·3′W	FM	187
Hill Plantation	Pth & Kin	NN9425	56°24·6′	3°42·6′W	F	52,53,58
Hill Plantn	N Yks	SE7296	54°21·5′	0°53·1′W	F	94,100
Hillpool	Worcs	SO8976	52°23·2′	2°9·3′W	T	139
Hillpound	Hants	SU5815	50°56·1′	1°10·1′W	T	196
Hillquoy	Orkney	HY2627	59°7·7′	3°17·1′W	X	6
Hill Ridware	Staffs	SK0717	52°45·3′	1°53·4′W	T	128
Hill Rigg	Cumbr	NY4846	54°48·6′	2°48·1′W	X	86
Hill Rigg	S Lanak	NS9049	55°43·6′	3°44·7′W	H	72
Hill Row Doles	Cambs	TL4176	52°22·1′	0°4·7′E	X	142,143
Hills	Moray	NJ3161	57°38·3′	3°8·9′W	X	28
Hills	S Lanak	NS7849	55°43·4′	3°56·1′W	X	64
Hills	Swan	SS4393	51°37·1′	4°15·7′W	X	159
Hills and Holes	Norf	TL9591	52°29·1′	0°52·7′E	F	144
Hills Barn Fm	Leic	SK7820	52°46·6′	0°50·2′W	FM	129
Hillsborough	Corn	SX1091	50°41·5′	4°41·0′W	X	190
Hillsborough	Devon	SS5347	51°12·4′	4°5·9′W	X	180
Hillsborough	Sheff	SK3290	53°24·6′	1°30·7′W	T	110,111
Hills Brough Fm	Lincs	TF1496	53°27·1′	0°16·6′W	FM	113
Hill's Copse	Dorset	SY7596	50°46·0′	2°20·9′W	F	194
Hillsdale	Staffs	SK0855	53°5·8′	1°52·4′W	X	119
Hillsdown Fm	E Susx	TQ4031	51°3·9′	0°0·3′E	FM	187
Hillsea	N Som	ST4366	51°23·6′	2°48·8′W	X	171,172,182
Hillsend	Norf	TM0294	52°30·6′	0°59·0′E	X	144
Hills Flats	S Glos	ST6297	51°40·5′	2°32·6′W	X	162
Hill's Fm	Beds	TL1955	52°11·1′	0°15·2′W	FM	153
Hills Fm	Cambs	TL3090	52°29·8′	0°4·7′W	FM	142
Hills Fm	Derby	SK0384	53°21·4′	1°56·9′W	FM	110
Hills Fm	Devon	SY2797	50°46·3′	3°1·7′W	FM	193
Hills Fm	Essex	TL5844	52°4·5′	0°18·7′E	FM	154
Hills Fm	Heref	SO4827	51°56·6′	2°45·0′W	FM	161
Hill's Fm	Kent	TR0330	51°2·2′	0°54·1′E	FM	189
Hills Fm	Notts	SK5325	52°49·4′	1°12·4′W	FM	129
Hills Fm	Notts	SK7032	52°53·1′	0°57·2′W	FM	129
Hills Fm	Somer	ST4519	50°58·3′	2°46·6′W	FM	193
Hills Fm	Staffs	SJ9950	53°3·1′	2°0·5′W	FM	118
Hills Fm	Suff	TL6846	52°5·4′	0°27·5′E	FM	154
Hills Fm, The	Shrops	SO6990	52°30·7′	2°27·0′W	FM	138
Hill's Folly	Lincs	TF3257	53°5·9′	0°1·3′W	X	122
Hillsford Br	Devon	SS7447	51°12·7′	3°47·9′W	X	180
Hills Green Fm	W Susx	SU9927	51°2·3′	0°34·9′W	FM	186,197
Hillshaw Burn	S Lanak	NT0324	55°30·3′	3°31·7′W	W	72
Hillshaw Head	S Lanak	NT0424	55°30·3′	3°30·8′W	H	72
Hillshaw Sike	S Lanak	NS9923	55°29·7′	3°35·5′W	W	72
Hills Ho	Derby	SK0485	53°22·0′	1°56·0′W	X	110
Hills & Holes	Notts	SK5568	53°12·6′	1°10·2′W	X	120
Hills & Holes	Peterb	TF0704	52°37·6′	0°24·7′W	A	142
Hillside	Aberd	NJ4143	57°28·7′	2°58·6′W	X	28
Hillside	Aberd	NJ4712	57°12·0′	2°52·2′W	X	37
Hillside	Aberd	NJ5607	57°9·4′	2°43·2′W	X	37
Hillside	Aberd	NJ5762	57°39·0′	2°42·8′W	X	29
Hillside	Aberd	NJ6030	57°21·8′	2°39·4′W	X	29,37
Hillside	Aberd	NJ7207	57°9·4′	2°27·3′W	X	38
Hillside	Aberd	NJ7462	57°39·1′	2°25·7′W	X	29
Hillside	Aberd	NJ9856	57°35·9′	2°1·5′W	X	30
Hillside	Aberd	NO9297	57°4·1′	2°7·5′W	T	38,45
Hillside	Angus	NO4064	56°46·1′	2°58·4′W	X	44
Hillside	Angus	NO4549	56°38·0′	2°53·3′W	X	54
Hillside	Angus	NO5550	56°38·6′	2°43·6′W	X	54
Hillside	Angus	NO7061	56°44·6′	2°29·0′W	T	45
Hill Side	Barns	SE2202	53°31·1′	1°39·7′W	T	110
Hillside	Carm	SN3011	51°46·6′	4°27·5′W	X	159
Hillside	C of Aber	NJ8408	57°10·0′	2°15·4′W	X	38
Hillside	Devon	SS5429	51°2·7′	4°4·6′W	X	180
Hillside	Devon	ST1705	50°50·5′	3°10·4′W	T	192,193
Hillside	Devon	SX7060	50°25·8′	3°49·4′W	T	202
Hillside	D & G	NX7573	55°2·4′	3°56·9′W	X	84
Hillside	D & G	NY0279	55°6·0′	3°31·7′W	X	84
Hillside	D & G	NY1385	55°9·4′	3°21·5′W	X	78
Hillside	D & G	NY1965	54°58·6′	3°15·5′W	X	85
Hillside	Durham	NZ3444	54°47·6′	1°27·8′W	X	88
Hillside	Fife	NT0495	56°8·5′	3°32·3′W	X	58

Hillside	Hants	SU7550	51°14·9′	0°55·1′W	T	186
Hill Side	Hants	SU7827	51°2·5′	0°52·9′W	T	186,197
Hillside	Heref	SO2731	51°58·6′	3°3·4′W	X	161
Hillside	Inverc	NS2970	55°53·8′	4°43·7′W	X	63
Hillside	Kent	TQ9759	51°18·0′	0°50·0′E	X	178
Hill Side	Kirk	SE1817	53°39·2′	1°43·2′W	T	110
Hillside	Moray	NJ1560	57°37·6′	3°24·9′W	X	28
Hillside	Northum	NY7462	54°57·4′	2°23·9′W	X	86,87
Hill Side	N Yks	NZ0003	54°25·6′	1°59·6′W	X	92
Hillside	Orkney	HY3124	59°6·1′	3°11·8′W	T	6
Hillside	Orkney	ND3390	58°47·8′	3°9·1′W	X	7
Hillside	Orkney	ND4696	58°51·1′	2°55·7′W	T	6,7
Hillside	Pth & Kin	NO0603	56°12·9′	3°30·5′W	X	58
Hillside	Sefton	SD3214	53°37·3′	3°1·3′W	T	108
Hillside	Shetld	HU3579	60°29·9′	1°21·3′W	X	2,3
Hillside	Shetld	HU4063	60°21·2′	1°16·0′W	T	2,3
Hillside	Shetld	HU5297	60°39·4′	1°2·4′W	X	1
Hillside	Shrops	SO5987	52°29·0′	2°35·8′W	T	137,138
Hillside	S Lanak	NT0847	55°42·7′	3°27·4′W	X	72
Hillside	Warw	SP2489	52°30·1′	1°38·4′W	X	139
Hillside	Wilts	SU0691	51°37·3′	1°54·4′W	X	163,173
Hillside	Wilts	SU0692	51°37·8′	1°54·4′W	T	173
Hill Side	Worcs	SO7561	52°15·0′	2°21·6′W	T	138,150
Hillside Fm	Bucks	SP6412	51°48·4′	1°3·9′W	FM	164,165
Hillside Fm	Cambs	TL2942	52°3·9′	0°6·7′W	FM	153
Hillside Fm	Ches	SJ6569	53°13·3′	2°31·0′W	FM	118
Hillside Fm	Cumbr	NY2946	54°48·5′	3°5·9′W	FM	85
Hillside Fm	Essex	TL6439	52°1·7′	0°23·8′E	FM	154
Hillside Fm	Glos	SP2327	51°56·7′	1°39·5′W	FM	163
Hillside Fm	Lancs	SD4360	54°2·2′	2°51·8′W	FM	97
Hillside Fm	Lincs	SK9263	53°9·6′	0°37·0′W	FM	121
Hillside Fm	Norf	TF6907	52°38·3′	0°30·3′E	FM	143
Hillside Fm	Norf	TG3000	52°33·2′	1°24·0′E	FM	134
Hillside Fm	Norf	TG3000	52°33·2′	1°24·0′E	FM	134
Hillside Fm	Northnts	SP9070	52°19·5′	0°40·4′W	FM	141
Hillside Fm	N Yks	SE4950	53°56·9′	1°14·8′W	FM	105
Hillside Fm	N Yks	SE7264	54°4·3′	0°53·6′W	FM	100
Hillside Fm	Rut	SK8710	52°41·1′	0°42·4′W	FM	130
Hillside Fm	Shrops	SO6087	52°29·0′	2°34·9′W	FM	138
Hillside Fm	Staffs	SJ8041	52°58·2′	2°17·5′W	FM	118
Hillside Fm	Surrey	TQ0850	51°14·6′	0°26·8′W	FM	187
Hillside Fm	Warr	SJ6183	53°20·8′	2°34·7′W	FM	109
Hillside Fm	Wilts	SU0384	51°33·5′	1°57·0′W	FM	173
Hillside Fm	Worcs	SO7364	52°16·6′	2°23·3′W	FM	138,150
Hillside Ho	Notts	SK7385	53°21·6′	0°53·8′W	X	112,120
Hillside of Dendoldrum	Aberd	NO8272	56°50·6′	2°17·3′W	X	45
Hillside of Prieston	Angus	NO3839	56°32·6′	3°0·1′W	X	54
Hillside of Row	Stir	NS7599	56°10·3′	4°0·4′W	X	57
Hillside Woods	Aberd	NJ4422	57°17·4′	2°55·3′W	F	37
Hill Six Acres	Lincs	TF3035	52°54·0′	0°3·6′W	X	131
Hillslap Tower	Scot Bord	NT5139	55°38·8′	2°46·3′W	A	73
Hills of Bendochy	Pth & Kin	NO2041	56°33·5′	3°17·6′W	X	53
Hills of Boyndie	Aberd	NJ6663	57°39·6′	2°33·7′W	H	29
Hills of Cromdale	Moray	NJ1226	57°19·2′	3°27·2′W	H	36
Hills of Dunipace	Falk	NS8381	56°0·7′	3°52·2′W	X	65
Hills of Grobsness	Shetld	HU3763	60°21·2′	1°19·3′W	H	2,3
Hill Somersal	Derby	SK1434	52°54·4′	1°47·1′W	T	128
Hills, The	Beds	TL1335	52°0·3′	0°20·8′W	X	153
Hills, The	Derby	SK3727	52°50·6′	1°26·6′W	X	128
Hills, The	Heref	SO5663	52°16·0′	2°38·3′W	X	137,138,149
Hills, The	Lancs	SD6238	53°50·5′	2°34·2′W	X	102,103
Hills, The	Shrops	SO5378	52°24·1′	2°41·1′W	X	137,138
Hills, The	Staffs	SJ6933	52°53·9′	2°27·2′W	X	127
Hills, The	Suff	TM0438	52°0·4′	0°58·7′E	X	155
Hills, The (Motte & Baileys)	Beds	TL1335	52°0·3′	0°20·8′W	A	153
Hill Stones	N Yks	NZ8215	54°31·7′	0°43·6′W	X	94
Hills Tor	Swan	SS4294	51°37·6′	4°16·6′W	X	159
Hills Town	Derby	SK4869	53°13·2′	1°16·5′W	T	120
Hill Street	Dorset	ST7011	50°54·1′	2°25·2′W	X	194
Hillstreet	Hants	SU3416	50°56·8′	1°30·6′W	T	185
Hill Street	Kent	TR1145	51°10·1′	1°1·5′E	T	179,189
Hillswick	Shetld	HU2877	60°28·8′	1°28·9′W	T	3
Hills Wood	D & G	NX9273	55°2·6′	3°41·0′W	F	84
Hilltarvit Mains	Fife	NO3712	56°18·0′	3°0·6′W	X	59
Hill Teasses	Fife	NO4108	56°15·9′	2°56·7′W	X	59
Hill, The	Bath & NE Somer	ST7768	51°24·9′	2°19·5′W	X	172
Hill, The	Ches	SJ7660	53°8·4′	2°21·1′W	X	118
Hill, The	Cumbr	NY1424	54°36·5′	3°19·5′W	X	89
Hill, The	Cumbr	NY3961	54°56·6′	2°56·7′W	X	85
Hill, The	Cumbr	NY4629	54°39·4′	2°49·8′W	X	90
Hill, The	Cumbr	NY4738	54°44·3′	2°49·0′W	X	90
Hill, The	Cumbr	NY5356	54°54·0′	2°43·6′W	X	86
Hill, The	Cumbr	NY6266	54°59·5′	2°35·2′W	X	86
Hill, The	Cumbr	SD2389	54°17·7′	3°10·6′W	X	96
Hill, The	Cumbr	SD6290	54°18·5′	2°34·6′W	X	97
Hill, The	Devon	SS4622	50°58·8′	4°11·3′W	X	180,190
Hill, The	Devon	SY2698	50°46·8′	3°2·6′W	X	192,193
Hill, The	D & G	NY4080	55°6·9′	2°56·0′W	X	79
Hill, The	Donc	SE6002	53°30·9′	1°5·3′W	X	111
Hill, The	E Ayr	NS4148	55°42·2′	4°31·4′W	X	64
Hill, The	Essex	TL6112	51°47·2′	0°20·5′E	X	167
Hill, The	Glos	SO7132	51°59·4′	2°24·9′W	X	149
Hill, The	Glos	SO7830	51°58·3′	2°18·8′W	X	150
Hill, The	Heref	SO4351	52°9·5′	2°49·6′W	X	148,149
Hill, The	Heref	SO6745	52°6·4′	2°28·5′W	X	149
Hill,The	Lancs	SD6467	54°6·1′	2°32·6′W	X	97
Hill, The	Monm	SO3807	51°45·7′	2°53·5′W	X	161
Hill, The	Northnts	SP5144	52°5·8′	1°14·9′W	X	151
Hill, The	Northum	NY6653	54°52·5′	2°31·4′W	X	86
Hill, The	Powys	SN9390	52°30·1′	3°34·2′W	H	136
Hill, The	Powys	SO2964	52°16·4′	3°2·0′W	X	137,148
Hill, The	Staffs	SJ8040	52°57·7′	2°17·5′W	X	118
Hill, The	Staffs	SK0657	53°6·8′	1°54·2′W	X	119
Hill, The	Warw	SP3767	52°18·2′	1°27·0′W	X	151
Hill, The	Worcs	SO8035	52°1·0′	2°17·1′W	X	150
Hill, The	Worcs	SO8279	52°24·8′	2°15·5′W	X	138
Hill, The	Worcs	SO8439	52°3·2′	2°13·6′W	X	150
Hilltoft	Orkney	HY4704	58°55·5′	2°54·7′W	X	6,7

Hilton	Highld	NH5391	57°53·3′	4°28·3′W	X	20
Hilton	Highld	NH5693	57°54·5′	4°25·3′W	X	21
Hilton	Highld	NH6735	57°23·4′	4°12·3′W	X	26
Hilton of Dunlugas	Aberd	NJ7055	57°35·3′	2°29·6′W	X	29
Hilton of Knapp	Pth & Kin	NO2831	56°28·2′	3°9·7′W	X	53
Hill Top	Barns	SE2705	53°32·7′	1°35·1′W	T	110
Hill Top	Black w Dar	SD7317	53°39·2′	2°24·1′W	X	109
Hilltop	Blae Gw	SO1609	51°46·6′	3°12·7′W	T	161
Hill Top	Brad	SD9937	53°50·0′	2°0·5′W	X	103
Hill Top	Brad	SE0933	53°47·8′	1°51·4′W	T	104
Hill Top	Brad	SE1041	53°52·1′	1°50·5′W	X	104
Hilltop	Bucks	SP9602	51°42·7′	0°36·2′W	T	165
Hill Top	Ches	SJ8777	53°17·6′	2°11·3′W	X	118
Hilltop	Cumbr	NY2042	54°46·2′	3°14·2′W	X	85
Hilltop	Cumbr	NY2942	54°46·3′	3°5·8′W	X	85
Hilltop	Cumbr	NY4275	55°4·2′	2°54·1′W	X	85
Hilltop	Cumbr	NY4343	54°47·0′	2°52·8′W	X	85
Hilltop	Cumbr	NY4673	55°3·2′	2°50·3′W	X	86
Hill Top	Cumbr	NY6905	54°26·6′	2°28·3′W	X	91
Hill Top	Cumbr	NY7513	54°30·9′	2°22·7′W	X	91
Hilltop	Cumbr	NY7843	54°47·1′	2°20·1′W	X	86,87
Hill Top	Cumbr	SD3183	54°14·5′	3°3·1′W	X	96,97
Hill Top	Cumbr	SD3486	54°16·2′	3°0·4′W	X	96,97
Hill Top	Cumbr	SD3695	54°21·0′	2°58·7′W	X	96,97
Hill Top	Cumbr	SD4083	54°14·6′	2°54·8′W	X	96,97
Hill Top	Cumbr	SD5491	54°19·0′	2°42·0′W	X	97
Hill Top	Cumbr	SD6294	54°20·7′	2°34·7′W	X	97
Hill Top	Cumbr	SD7284	54°15·3′	2°25·4′W	X	98
Hilltop	Derby	SK0295	53°27·3′	1°57·8′W	X	110
Hilltop	Derby	SK1845	53°0·4′	1°43·5′W	X	119,128
Hilltop	Derby	SK2950	53°3·0′	1°33·6′W	X	119
Hilltop	Derby	SK3463	53°10·0′	1°29·1′W	T	119
Hill Top	Derby	SK3577	53°17·6′	1°28·1′W	T	119
Hilltop	Derby	SK3655	53°5·7′	1°27·3′W	X	119
Hill Top	Derby	SK4965	53°11·0′	1°15·6′W	X	120
Hilltop	Devon	SS9310	50°53·0′	3°30·9′W	X	192
Hilltop	D & G	NX6052	54°50·8′	4°10·4′W	X	83
Hill Top	Donc	SK4997	53°28·3′	1°15·3′W	T	111
Hill Top	Durham	NY8233	54°41·7′	2°16·3′W	X	91,92
Hill Top	Durham	NY8837	54°43·9′	2°10·8′W	X	91,92
Hill Top	Durham	NY9924	54°36·9′	2°0·5′W	T	92
Hill Top	Durham	NZ1416	54°32·6′	1°46·6′W	X	92
Hill Top	Durham	NZ1654	54°53·1′	1°44·6′W	T	88
Hill Top	Durham	NZ2124	54°36·9′	1°40·1′W	X	93
Hill Top	Durham	NZ2144	54°47·7′	1°40·0′W	T	88
Hill Top	Hants	SU4003	50°49·7′	1°25·5′W	T	196
Hill Top	Hants	SU5717	50°57·2′	1°10·9′W	X	185
Hill Top	Heref	SO4154	52°11·1′	2°51·4′W	X	148,149
Hill Top	Kirk	SE0713	53°37·1′	1°53·2′W	T	110
Hill Top	Kirk	SE0714	53°37·6′	1°53·2′W	X	110
Hill Top	Lancs	SD5067	54°6·0′	2°45·5′W	X	97
Hill Top	Lancs	SD5574	54°9·8′	2°40·9′W	X	97
Hill Top	Lancs	SD6138	53°50·5′	2°35·1′W	X	102,103
Hill Top	Lancs	SD9046	53°54·8′	2°8·7′W	X	103
Hill Top	Leeds	SE2442	53°52·7′	1°37·7′W	X	104
Hill Top	Leeds	SE2534	53°48·3′	1°36·8′W	T	104
Hilltop	Leic	SK6416	52°44·5′	1°2·7′W	X	129
Hill Top	Norf	TG1641	52°55·6′	1°13·2′E	X	133
Hill Top	Northnts	SP8871	52°20·0′	0°42·1′W	X	141
Hill Top	Northum	NY7365	54°59·0′	2°24·9′W	X	86,87
Hill Top	Northum	NY9957	54°54·7′	2°0·5′W	X	87
Hill Top	Northum	NZ0689	55°12·0′	1°53·9′W	X	81
Hill Top	Notts	SK4746	53°0·8′	1°17·6′W	T	129
Hill Top	N Tyne	NZ3269	55°1·1′	1°29·5′W	X	88
Hill Top	N Yks	NY8501	54°24·5′	2°13·4′W	X	91,92
Hill Top	N Yks	SD6568	54°6·6′	2°31·7′W	X	97
Hill Top	N Yks	SD7956	54°0·2′	2°18·8′W	X	103
Hill Top	N Yks	SD9396	54°21·8′	2°6·0′W	X	98
Hill Top	N Yks	SE0042	53°52·7′	1°59·6′W	X	104
Hill Top	N Yks	SE0053	53°58·6′	1°59·6′W	X	104
Hill Top	N Yks	SE0082	54°14·3′	1°59·6′W	X	98
Hill Top	N Yks	SE1762	54°3·5′	1°44·0′W	X	99
Hill Top	N Yks	SE1961	54°2·9′	1°42·2′W	T	99
Hill Top	N Yks	SE2277	54°11·5′	1°39·4′W	X	99
Hill Top	N Yks	SE2662	54°3·4′	1°35·8′W	T	99
Hill Top	Oldham	SD9707	53°33·8′	2°2·3′W	X	109
Hill Top	Roth	SK3992	53°25·6′	1°24·4′W	T	110,111
Hill Top	Salf	SD7303	53°31·6′	2°24·0′W	T	109
Hill Top	Sand	SO9993	52°32·3′	2°0·5′W	T	139
Hill Top	Sheff	SK2889	53°24·1′	1°34·3′W	T	110
Hill Top	Shrops	SJ4337	52°55·9′	2°50·5′W	X	126
Hilltop	Shrops	SO5796	52°33·8′	2°37·7′W	X	137,138
Hilltop	Staffs	SJ8736	52°55·5′	2°11·2′W	X	127
Hill Top	Staffs	SJ8808	52°40·4′	2°10·2′W	T	127
Hill Top	Staffs	SK0243	52°59·3′	1°57·8′W	X	119,128
Hilltop	Staffs	SK0268	53°12·8′	1°57·8′W	X	119
Hill Top	Staffs	SK0914	52°43·7′	1°51·6′W	X	128
Hill Top	Stock	SJ9687	53°23·0′	2°3·2′W	X	109
Hill Top	Wakf	SE3315	53°38·1′	1°29·6′W	X	110,111
Hill Top	Warw	SP2990	52°30·7′	1°34·0′W	T	140
Hill Top	Warw	SP3690	52°30·6′	1°27·8′W	T	140
Hill Top	Worcs	SO6466	52°17·7′	2°31·3′W	X	138,149
Hill Top	W Susx	SU8820	50°58·6′	0°44·4′W	T	197
Hilltop Cott	S Ayr	NX1085	55°7·6′	4°58·4′W	X	76
Hill Top East	N Yks	SE2288	54°17·5′	1°39·3′W	X	99
Hill Top Fm	Cambs	TL1680	52°24·6′	0°17·3′W	FM	142
Hilltop Fm	Ches	SJ6562	53°9·5′	2°31·0′W	FM	118
Hill Top Fm	Ches	SJ7061	53°9·0′	2°26·5′W	FM	118
Hilltop Fm	Ches	SJ9483	53°20·9′	2°5·0′W	FM	109
Hill Top Fm	Cumbr	NY3123	54°36·1′	3°3·7′W	FM	90
Hill Top Fm	Darl	NZ2910	54°29·3′	1°32·7′W	FM	93
Hilltop Fm	Derby	SK1855	53°5·8′	1°43·5′W	FM	119
Hill Top Fm	Derby	SK2236	52°55·5′	1°40·0′W	FM	128
Hilltop Fm	Derby	SK2740	52°57·6′	1°35·5′W	FM	119,128
Hill Top Fm	Derby	SK2743	52°59·3′	1°35·5′W	FM	119,128
Hilltop Fm	Derby	SK3477	53°17·6′	1°29·0′W	FM	119
Hilltop Fm	Derby	SK4141	52°58·1′	1°23·0′W	FM	129
Hill Top Fm	E Yorks	SE8737	53°49·6′	0°40·3′W	FM	106
Hill Top Fm	E Yorks	TA2828	53°44·2′	0°3·2′W	FM	107

Hilltop Fm	Hants	SU3903	50°49·7′	1°26·4′W	FM	196
Hill Top Fm	Heref	SO4148	52°7·9′	2°51·3′W	FM	148,149
Hill Top Fm	Heref	SO7039	52°3·2′	2°25·9′W	FM	149
Hilltop Fm	Leic	SK3820	52°46·8′	1°25·8′W	FM	128
Hill Top fm	Leic	SK4326	52°50·0′	1°21·3′W	FM	129
Hill Top Fm	Leic	SK6623	52°48·3′	1°0·9′W	FM	129
Hill Top Fm	Leic	SP5882	52°26·2′	1°8·4′W	FM	140
Hill Top Fm	Lincs	SK8530	52°51·9′	0°43·8′W	FM	130
Hill Top Fm	Lincs	SK9548	53°1·5′	0°34·6′W	FM	130
Hill Top Fm	Lincs	TF2762	53°8·6′	0°5·7′W	FM	122
Hill Top Fm	Lincs	TF3494	53°25·8′	0°1·4′E	FM	113
Hilltop Fm	Monm	ST4396	51°39·8′	2°49·1′W	FM	171
Hill Top Fm	Notts	SK5627	52°50·5′	1°9·7′W	FM	129
Hill Top Fm	Notts	SK6727	52°50·4′	0°59·9′W	FM	129
Hill Top Fm	N Yks	SE1249	53°56·5′	1°48·6′W	FM	104
Hill Top Fm	N Yks	SE1598	54°22·9′	1°45·7′W	FM	99
Hilltop Fm	N Yks	SE2347	53°55·4′	1°38·6′W	FM	104
Hill Top Fm	N Yks	SE3059	54°1·8′	1°32·1′W	FM	104
Hill Top Fm	N Yks	SE3261	54°2·9′	1°30·3′W	FM	99
Hill Top Fm	N Yks	SE7381	54°13·4′	0°52·4′W	FM	100
Hilltop Fm	Staffs	SK0908	52°40·4′	1°51·6′W	FM	128
Hilltop Fm	Stock	SJ8882	53°20·3′	2°10·4′W	FM	109
Hilltop Fm	Stock	SJ9988	53°23·6′	2°0·5′W	FM	109
Hill Top Fm	Suff	TM1050	52°6·7′	1°4·4′E	FM	155
Hill Top Fm	Suff	TM3266	52°14·8′	1°24·3′E	FM	156
Hilltop Fm	Warw	SP1353	52°10·7′	1°48·2′W	FM	151
Hilltop Fm	Worcs	SO6066	52°17·7′	2°34·8′W	FM	138,149
Hilltop Fm	Worcs	SO6269	52°19·3′	2°33·1′W	FM	138
Hilltop Fm	Worcs	SO7755	52°11·8′	2°19·8′W	FM	150
Hill Top Fm	Worcs	SO9758	52°13·4′	2°2·2′W	FM	150
Hilltop Fm	W Susx	TQ1834	51°5·8′	0°18·5′W	FM	187
Hill Top Fms	Lincs	SK9551	53°3·1′	0°34·6′W	FM	121
Hill Top Hall	N Yks	SE2951	53°57·5′	1°33·1′W	X	104
Hilltop Ho	Hants	SU3903	50°49·7′	1°26·4′W	X	196
Hilltop Ho	Notts	SK5472	53°14·8′	1°11·0′W	X	120
Hill Top Ho	St Hel	SJ4898	53°28·8′	2°46·6′W	X	108
Hill Top House	Glos	SP1732	51°59·4′	1°44·8′W	X	151
Hilltop House Fm	N Yks	SE1978	54°12·1′	1°42·1′W	FM	99
Hill-Top Lodge	Leic	SP6185	52°27·8′	1°5·7′W	X	140
Hill Top West	N Yks	SE2188	54°17·5′	1°40·2′W	X	99
Hill Top Wood	S Lanak	NS8341	55°39·2′	3°51·1′W	F	71,72
Hill Tor	Corn	SX2273	50°32·0′	4°30·3′W	X	201
Hilltown	Aberd	NJ6355	57°35·3′	2°36·7′W	X	29
Hilltown	C of Dun	NO4031	56°28·3′	2°58·0′W	X	54
Hilltown	Devon	SS6523	50°59·7′	3°55·0′W	X	180
Hilltown	Devon	SS7522	50°59·3′	3°46·5′W	X	180
Hilltown	Devon	SS7826	51°1·5′	3°44·0′W	X	180
Hilltown	Devon	SS8516	50°56·2′	3°37·8′W	X	181
Hilltown	Devon	SX5381	50°36·8′	4°4·3′W	X	191,201
Hilltown	Midlo	NT3170	55°55·3′	3°5·8′W	X	66
Hilltown Fm	Devon	SX5595	50°44·4′	4°2·9′W	FM	191
Hilltown of Ballindean	Pth & Kin	NO2529	56°27·1′	3°12·6′W	X	53,59
Hilltown of Balmuir	Angus	NO4034	56°29·9′	2°58·0′W	X	54
Hilltown of Mause	Pth & Kin	NO1647	56°36·7′	3°21·7′W	X	53
Hilluppencott	Shrops	SO5776	52°23·1′	2°37·5′W	X	137,138
Hill View	Dorset	SY9895	50°45·5′	2°1·3′W	T	195
Hillview	Northum	NZ1394	55°14·6′	1°47·3′W	X	81
Hillview	Sund	NZ3954	54°53·0′	1°23·1′W	T	88
Hill View	Wilts	SU1559	51°20·0′	1°46·7′W	X	173
Hill View Fm	Bucks	SP6325	51°55·4′	1°4·6′W	FM	164,165
Hill View Fm	Ches	SJ4876	53°16·9′	2°46·4′W	FM	117
Hill View Fm	Hants	SU6214	50°55·6′	1°6·7′W	FM	196
Hillview Fm	Somer	ST6638	51°8·6′	2°28·8′W	FM	183
Hillwatering Fm	Suff	TL9770	52°17·8′	0°53·7′E	FM	144,155
Hillway	I of W	SZ6386	50°40·4′	1°6·1′W	T	196
Hillway	Somer	SS8236	51°6·9′	3°40·8′W	X	181
Hillwell	Shetld	HU3714	59°54·8′	1°19·8′W	T	4
Hillwicket	Wrekin	SJ6824	52°49·0′	2°28·1′W	X	127
Hill Wood	Aberd	NO6777	56°53·2′	2°32·0′W	F	45
Hill Wood	Birm	SK1200	52°36·1′	1°49·0′W	T	139
Hill Wood	Cambs	TL2078	52°23·4′	0°13·8′W	F	142
Hillwood	C of Edin	NT2073	55°56·9′	3°16·4′W	X	66
Hill Wood	Derby	SK2562	53°9·5′	1°37·2′W	F	119
Hill Wood	Dorset	ST7403	50°49·8′	2°21·8′W	F	194
Hill Wood	E Yorks	SE8346	53°54·4′	0°43·8′W	F	106
Hill Wood	Herts	TL0112	51°48·1′	0°31·7′W	F	166
Hill Wood	Oxon	SP4121	51°53·4′	1°23·9′W	F	164
Hill Wood	Scot Bord	NT6760	55°50·2′	2°31·2′W	F	67
Hill Wood	Scot Bord	NT7862	55°51·3′	2°20·6′W	F	67
Hill Wood	Wilts	ST9652	51°16·3′	2°3·1′W	F	184
Hillwood	Wilts	SU2474	51°28·1′	1°38·9′W	X	174
Hillwood Fm	Worcs	SO6667	52°18·2′	2°29·5′W	FM	138,149
Hill Wootton	Warw	SP3068	52°18·8′	1°33·2′W	T	151
Hillworth	Worcs	SO8337	52°2·1′	2°14·5′W	X	150
Hillyfield	Kent	TQ7271	51°24·9′	0°28·8′E	X	178
Hillyfields	Hants	SU3715	50°56·2′	1°28·0′W	T	196
Hilly Fm	Suff	TL9443	52°3·3′	0°50·2′E	FM	155
Hillyland	Pth & Kin	NO0924	56°24·2′	3°28·0′W	T	52,53,58
Hillylees	Staffs	SJ9764	53°10·6′	2°2·3′W	X	118
Hilly Pool Point	Essex	TL8807	51°44·0′	0°43·8′E	X	168
Hilly Wood	Peterb	TF1104	52°37·6′	0°21·2′W	F	142
Hilmarton	Wilts	SU0275	51°28·7′	1°57·9′W	T	173
Hilmarton Manor	Wilts	SU0174	51°28·1′	1°58·7′W	X	173
Hilperton	Wilts	ST8759	51°20·0′	2°10·8′W	T	173
Hilperton Marsh	Wilts	ST8659	51°20·0′	2°11·7′W	T	173
Hilpsford Scar	Cumbr	SD2161	54°2·6′	3°12·0′W	X	96
Hilsea	C of Port	SU6503	50°49·6′	1°4·2′W	T	196
Hilsea Point	Devon	SX5445	50°17·4′	4°2·6′W	X	201
Hilston	E Yorks	TA2833	53°46·9′	0°3·0′W	T	107
Hilston Park	Monm	SO4418	51°51·7′	2°48·4′W	X	161
Hilter Fm	Glos	SO7027	51°56·7′	2°25·8′W	FM	162
Hiltingbury	Hants	SU4322	51°0·0′	1°22·8′W	T	185
Hiltly	W Loth	NT0075	55°57·7′	3°35·7′W	X	65
Hiltmead	Glos	SO7910	51°47·5′	2°17·9′W	X	162
Hilton	Aberd	NJ5803	57°7·2′	2°41·2′W	X	37
Hilton	Aberd	NJ6461	57°38·5′	2°35·7′W	X	29
Hilton	Aberd	NJ8352	57°33·7′	2°16·6′W	X	29,30
Hilton	Aberd	NO8692	57°1·4′	2°13·4′W	X	38,45
Hilton	Angus	NO2957	56°42·2′	3°9·1′W	X	53
Hilton	Angus	NO6650	56°38·7′	2°32·8′W	X	54

Hilton	Arg & Bt	NS0668	55°52·2′	5°5·6′W	X	63
Hilton	Cambs	TL2866	52°16·9′	0°7·0′W	T	153
Hilton	Clackm	NS9092	56°6·7′	3°45·7′W	X	58
Hilton	C of Aber	NJ8603	57°7·3′	2°13·4′W	X	38
Hilton	C of Aber	NJ9108	57°10·0′	2°8·5′W	T	38
Hilton	Corn	SS2303	50°48·2′	4°30·3′W	X	190
Hilton	Cumbr	NY7320	54°34·7′	2°24·6′W	T	91
Hilton	Derby	SK2430	52°52·3′	1°38·2′W	T	128
Hilton	Dorset	ST7803	50°49·8′	2°18·4′W	T	194
Hilton	Durham	NZ1621	54°35·3′	1°44·7′W	T	92
Hilton	Fife	NO3616	56°20·2′	3°1·7′W	X	59
Hilton	Fife	NT0587	56°4·2′	3°31·1′W	X	65
Hilton	Fife	NT0983	56°2·1′	3°27·2′W	X	65
Hilton	Highld	NH5449	57°30·7′	4°25·8′W	X	26
Hilton	Highld	NH6743	57°27·7′	4°12·6′W	T	26
Hilton	Highld	NH7980	57°47·9′	4°1·7′W	T	21
Hilton	Highld	NH9285	57°50·8′	3°48·7′W	T	21
Hilton	Moray	NJ4363	57°39·5′	2°56·9′W	X	28
Hilton	Orkney	HY4916	59°1·9′	2°52·8′W	X	6
Hilton	Pth & Kin	NO1004	56°13·5′	3°26·6′W	X	58
Hilton	Scot Bord	NT8850	55°44·8′	2°11·0′W	T	67,74
Hilton	Shrops	SO7795	52°33·4′	2°20·0′W	T	138
Hilton	Staffs	SK0805	52°38·8′	1°52·5′W	T	139
Hilton	Stir	NS5997	56°8·9′	4°15·7′W	X	57
Hilton	Stock on T	NZ4611	54°29·8′	1°17·0′W	T	93
Hilton Bay	Scot Bord	NT9659	55°49·7′	2°3·4′W	W	74,75
Hilton Beck	Cumbr	NY7220	54°34·7′	2°25·6′W	W	91
Hilton Bottom	Dorset	ST7704	50°50·3′	2°19·2′W	X	194
Hilton Brook	Derby	SK2528	52°51·2′	1°37·3′W	W	128
Hilton Farm	Stir	NS8489	56°5·0′	3°51·4′W	FM	65
Hilton Fell	Cumbr	NY7722	54°35·8′	2°20·9′W	X	91
Hilton Fields	Derby	SK2432	52°53·3′	1°38·2′W	X	128
Hilton Fm	Aberd	NJ9434	57°24·0′	2°5·5′W	FM	30
Hilton Fm	Aberd	NO8095	57°3·0′	2°19·3′W	FM	38,45
Hilton Fm	C of Aber	NO8299	57°5·2′	2°17·4′W	FM	38,45
Hilton Fm	Fife	NT1594	56°8·1′	3°21·6′W	FM	58
Hilton Fm	Pth & Kin	NO1119	56°21·6′	3°26·0′W	FM	58
Hilton Fm	Shrops	SJ7613	52°43·1′	2°20·9′W	FM	127
Hilton Fm	V of Glam	SS9574	51°27·6′	3°30·3′W	FM	170
Hilton Grange	N Yks	SE3696	54°21·7′	1°26·3′W	X	99
Hilton Hill Fm	Fife	NO3106	56°14·7′	3°6·4′W	FM	59
Hilton Home Fm	Pemb	SM8719	51°50·0′	5°5·1′W	FM	157
Hilton House	Bolton	SD6308	53°34·3′	2°33·1′W	T	109
Hilton House Fm	Stock on T	NZ4611	54°29·8′	1°17·0′W	FM	93
Hilton Lodge	Derby	SK2531	52°52·8′	1°37·3′W	X	128
Hilton Lodge	Highld	NH2824	57°16·7′	4°50·7′W	X	25
Hilton Moor	Durham	NZ1622	54°35·8′	1°44·7′W	X	92
Hilton of Aldie	Pth & Kin	NO0599	56°10·7′	3°31·4′W	X	58
Hilton of Cadboll	Highld	NH8776	57°45·8′	3°53·5′W	T	21
Hilton of Carslogie	Fife	NO3314	56°19·1′	3°4·5′W	X	59
Hilton of Culsh	Aberd	NJ8748	57°31·6′	2°12·6′W	X	30
Hilton of Delnies	Highld	NH8456	57°35·0′	3°55·9′W	X	27
Hilton of Duncrievie	Pth & Kin	NO1309	56°16·2′	3°23·8′W	X	58
Hilton of Fern	Angus	NO5060	56°44·0′	2°48·6′W	X	44
Hilton of Forthar	Fife	NO3005	56°14·2′	3°7·3′W	X	59
Hilton of Gask	Pth & Kin	NN9918	56°20·9′	3°37·6′W	X	58
Hilton of Guthrie	Angus	NO5551	56°39·2′	2°43·6′W	X	54
Hilton of Kirkforthar	Fife	NO3005	56°14·2′	3°7·3′W	X	59
Hiltonpark	Aberd	NJ6460	57°38·0′	2°35·7′W	X	29
Hilton Park	Bury	SD8102	53°31·1′	2°16·8′W	T	109
Hilton Park	Staffs	SJ9505	52°38·8′	2°4·0′W	X	127,139
Hilton Park, Service Area	Staffs	SJ9605	52°38·8′	2°3·1′W	X	127,139
Hiltonshill	Scot Bord	NT5929	55°33·4′	2°38·6′W	X	73,74
Hilton Wood	Moray	NJ4663	57°39·5′	2°53·8′W	F	28,29
Hilts Quarry	Derby	SK3553	53°4·6′	1°28·2′W	X	119
Himbleton	Worcs	SO9458	52°13·4′	2°4·9′W	T	150
Himley	Staffs	SO8791	52°31·2′	2°11·1′W	T	139
Himley Fm	Oxon	SP5623	51°54·4′	1°10·8′W	FM	164
Himmon Hill	Orkney	HY3227	59°7·7′	3°10·8′W	X	6
Hinam Fm	Somer	SS8829	51°3·2′	3°35·5′W	FM	181
Hincaster	Cumbr	SD5084	54°15·2′	2°45·6′W	T	97
Hinchcliffe Mill	Kirk	SE1207	53°33·8′	1°48·7′W	T	110
Hincheslea Moor	Hants	SU2601	50°48·7′	1°37·5′W	X	195
Hincheslea Wood	Hants	SU2700	50°48·2′	1°36·7′W	X	195
Hinchingbrooke House	Cambs	TL2271	52°19·6′	0°12·2′W	A	153
Hinchley Fm	Worcs	SO8768	52°18·8′	2°11·0′W	FM	139
Hinchley Wood	Surrey	TQ1565	51°22·6′	0°20·5′W	T	176
Hinchwick	Glos	SP1430	51°58·3′	1°47·4′W	T	151
Hinchwick Hill Barn	Glos	SP1330	51°58·3′	1°48·3′W	X	151
Hinchwick Manor Fm	Glos	SP1429	51°57·8′	1°47·4′W	FM	163
Hinckley	Leic	SP4294	52°32·8′	1°22·4′W	T	140
Hinckley Fields Fm	Leic	SP4195	52°33·3′	1°23·3′W	FM	140
Hinckley Fields Fm	Leic	SP4196	52°33·9′	1°23·3′W	FM	140
Hincknowle	Dorset	SY4997	50°46·5′	2°43·0′W	T	193,194
Hincks	Wrekin	SJ7016	52°44·7′	2°26·3′W	X	127
Hincks' Hall	N Yks	SE2864	54°4·5′	1°33·9′W	X	99
Hincks Plantation	Wrekin	SJ6916	52°44·7′	2°27·2′W	F	127
Hincks' Wood	N Yks	SE2863	54°4·0′	1°33·9′W	F	99
Hinda Stack	Shetld	HP6612	60°47·4′	0°46·8′W	X	1
Hindatown	Orkney	HY3214	59°0·7′	3°10·6′W	X	6
Hindberries	Durham	NZ1822	54°35·8′	1°42·9′W	X	92
Hind Crag	Cumbr	NY2311	54°29·6′	3°10·9′W	X	89,90
Hindera Field	Orkney	HY3419	59°3·4′	3°8·6′W	X	6
Hinderclay	Suff	TM0276	52°20·9′	0°58·4′E	T	144
Hinderclay Fen	Suff	TM0278	52°22·0′	0°58·4′E	X	144
Hinderton	Ches	SJ3078	53°17·9′	3°2·6′W	T	117
Hinderwell	N Yks	NZ7916	54°32·2′	0°46·3′W	T	94
Hindford	Shrops	SJ3332	52°53·1′	2°59·3′W	T	126
Hind Gill	D & G	NT0807	55°21·2′	3°26·6′W	W	78
Hindhaugh	Northum	NY8784	55°9·3′	2°11·8′W	X	80
Hindhay Fm	Win & Maid	SU8682	51°32·0′	0°45·2′W	FM	175
Hindhead	Surrey	SU8836	51°7·2′	0°44·2′W	T	186
Hindhead Common	Surrey	SU8936	51°7·2′	0°43·3′W	F	186
Hind Hill	D & G	NT0807	55°21·2′	3°26·6′W	H	78
Hindhillock	Aberd	NJ8552	57°33·7′	2°14·6′W	X	30
Hindhillock	Aberd	NJ8655	57°35·3′	2°13·6′W	X	30
Hind Ho	N Yks	SE2568	54°6·7′	1°36·6′W	X	99
Hind Hole Beck	N Yks	NY9102	54°25·0′	2°7·9′W	W	91,92
Hindhope Burn	Northum	NY7799	55°17·3′	2°21·3′W	W	80
Hindhope Burn	Scot Bord	NT7710	55°23·3′	2°21·4′W	W	80
Hindhope Hill	Scot Bord	NT7611	55°23·8′	2°22·3′W	H	80
Hindhope Law	Northum	NY7697	55°16·2′	2°22·2′W	H	80
Hindhope Law	Scot Bord	NT7709	55°22·7′	2°21·3′W	H	80
Hinding Dean	Northum	NU1717	55°27·0′	1°43·4′W	F	81
Hind Keld	Cumbr	SD7191	54°19·1′	2°26·3′W	X	98
Hindleap Fm	E Susx	TQ4032	51°4·4′	0°0·3′E	FM	187
Hindleap Warren	E Susx	TQ4132	51°4·4′	0°1·2′E	F	187
Hindle Fold	Lancs	SD7332	53°47·3′	2°24·2′W	T	103
Hindlethwaite Hall	N Yks	SE0581	54°13·7′	1°55·0′W	X	98
Hindlethwaite Moor	N Yks	SE0580	54°13·2′	1°55·0′W	X	98
Hindley	Northum	NZ0459	54°55·8′	1°55·8′W	T	87
Hindley	Wigan	SD6204	53°32·1′	2°34·0′W	T	109
Hindley Green	Wigan	SD6303	53°31·6′	2°33·1′W	T	109
Hindley Hall	Wigan	SD6105	53°32·7′	2°34·9′W	X	109
Hindley Head	Lancs	SD7458	54°1·3′	2°23·4′W	X	103
Hindley Hill	Northum	NY8057	54°54·7′	2°18·3′W	X	86,87
Hindleysteel	Northum	NY7472	55°2·8′	2°24·0′W	X	86,87
Hindley Wrae	Northum	NY7958	54°55·2′	2°19·2′W	X	86,87
Hindlip	Worcs	SO8758	52°13·4′	2°11·0′W	T	150
Hindlip Pk	Worcs	SO8758	52°13·4′	2°11·0′W	X	150
Hind Low	Derby	SK0868	53°12·8′	1°52·4′W	X	119
Hindog	N Ayr	NS2851	55°43·6′	4°43·9′W	X	63
Hindolveston	Norf	TG0329	52°49·4′	1°1·2′E	T	133
Hindolveston Wood	Norf	TG0428	52°48·9′	1°2·0′E	F	133
Hindon	Durham	NZ0525	54°37·5′	1°54·9′W	X	92
Hindon	Wilts	ST9132	51°5·5′	2°7·3′W	T	184
Hindon Beck	Durham	NZ0625	54°37·5′	1°54·0′W	W	92
Hindon Edge	Durham	NZ0524	54°36·9′	1°54·9′W	X	92
Hindon Fm.	Somer	SS9346	51°12·4′	3°31·5′W	FM	181
Hindpool	Cumbr	SD1969	54°6·9′	3°13·9′W	T	96
Hindrigg	Cumbr	NY1542	54°46·2′	3°18·9′W	X	85
Hindrigg	Northum	NY8180	55°7·1′	2°17·4′W	X	80
Hindringham	Norf	TF9836	52°53·3′	0°57·0′E	T	132
Hindrum	Aberd	NJ6001	57°6·2′	2°39·2′W	X	37
Hindscarth	Cumbr	NY2116	54°32·2′	3°12·8′W	H	89,90
Hindsclough Fm	Ches	SJ9873	53°15·5′	2°1·4′W	FM	118
Hindsford	Wigan	SD6802	53°31·1′	2°28·5′W	T	109
Hindshield	Northum	NY8367	55°0·1′	2°15·5′W	X	86,87
Hindside Knowe	Northum	NT8412	55°24·3′	2°14·7′W	H	80
Hindsike Hill	Northum	NT8404	55°20·0′	2°14·7′W	H	80
Hindstones	Aberd	NJ8860	57°38·0′	2°11·6′W	X	30
Hindsward	E Ayr	NS5216	55°25·2′	4°19·9′W	X	70
Hindwell Brook	Powys	SO3363	52°15·9′	2°58·5′W	W	137,148,149
Hindwell Fm	Powys	SO2560	52°14·2′	3°5·5′W	FM	137,148
Hine Greenie	Orkney	HY7645	59°17·7′	2°24·8′W	X	5
Hine Heath	Shrops	SJ5825	52°49·5′	2°37·0′W	X	126
Hines Fm	Suff	TM1061	52°12·7′	1°4·8′E	FM	155
Hines House Fm	Warw	SP2252	52°10·2′	1°40·3′W	FM	151
Hingcliff Hill	Sheff	SK1999	53°29·5′	1°42·4′W	H	110
Hinger Stone	Orkney	HY6000	58°53·4′	2°41·2′W	X	6
Hingey Fm	Corn	SW6621	50°2·8′	5°15·7′W	FM	203
Hing Geo	Highld	ND0169	58°36·1′	3°41·7′W	X	12
Hingham	Norf	TG0202	52°34·9′	0°59·3′E	T	144
Hingham Mill	Corn	SX0272	50°31·1′	4°47·2′W	X	200
Hingsdon Fm	Dorset	SY4698	50°47·0′	2°45·6′W	FM	193
Hingston Borough	Devon	SX6848	50°19·3′	3°50·9′W	X	202
Hingston Down	Corn	SX3871	50°31·2′	4°16·7′W	X	201
Hingston Down	Devon	SX7685	50°39·3′	3°44·9′W	H	191
Hingston Rocks	Devon	SX7685	50°39·3′	3°44·9′W	X	191
Hining Hall	Cumbr	SD6988	54°17·4′	2°28·2′W	X	98
Hinkle Wood	N Yks	NZ2307	54°27·7′	1°38·3′W	F	93
Hinkley Point Power Stations	Somer	ST2146	51°12·7′	3°7·5′W	X	182
Hinkley Wood	Staffs	SK1250	53°3·1′	1°48·9′W	F	119
Hinksey Hill Fm	Oxon	SP5004	51°44·2′	1°16·2′W	FM	164
Hinksey Stream	Oxon	SP5005	51°44·7′	1°16·2′W	W	164
Hinksford	Staffs	SO8689	52°30·2′	2°12·0′W	X	139
Hinnegar	S Glos	ST8086	51°34·6′	2°16·9′W	X	173
Hinning Ho	Cumbr	SD1188	54°17·0′	3°21·6′W	X	96
Hinning Ho	Cumbr	SD1297	54°21·9′	3°20·8′W	X	96
Hinning Ho	Cumbr	SD2499	54°23·1′	3°9·8′W	X	96
Hinning Ho Close	Cumbr	SD2399	54°23·1′	3°10·7′W	X	96
Hinning House Fell	Cumbr	NY2500	54°23·6′	3°8·9′W	X	89,90
Hinnington Grange	Shrops	SJ7404	52°38·2′	2°22·7′W	X	127
Hinnisdal Bridge	Highld	NG3957	57°31·9′	6°21·2′W	X	23
Hinstock	Shrops	SJ6926	52°50·1′	2°27·2′W	T	127
Hinstock Grange	Shrops	SJ6927	52°50·6′	2°27·2′W	X	127
Hinterland Ho	Surrey	TQ1154	51°16·7′	0°24·1′W	X	187
Hintish Bay	N Eil	NF7603	57°0·5′	7°19·8′W	W	31
Hintlesham	Suff	TM0843	52°3·0′	1°2·4′E	T	155,169
Hintlesham Great Wood	Suff	TM0742	52°2·5′	1°1·5′E	F	155,169
Hintlesham Park	Suff	TM0843	52°3·0′	1°2·4′E	X	155,169
Hintlesham Priory	Suff	TM0745	52°4·1′	1°1·6′E	X	155,169
Hinton	Glos	SO6803	51°43·7′	2°27·4′W	T	162
Hinton	Hants	SZ2095	50°45·5′	1°42·6′W	T	195
Hinton	Heref	SO3338	52°2·4′	2°58·2′W	T	149,161
Hinton	Northnts	SP5352	52°10·1′	1°13·1′W	T	152
Hinton	S Glos	ST7376	51°29·2′	2°22·9′W	T	172
Hinton	Shrops	SJ4008	52°40·2′	2°52·8′W	T	126
Hinton	Shrops	SO6582	52°26·3′	2°30·5′W	X	138
Hinton	Somer	ST5720	50°58·9′	2°36·4′W	T	183
Hinton Admiral	Hants	SZ2096	50°46·0′	1°42·6′W	A	195
Hinton Admiral Sta	Dorset	SZ2094	50°44·9′	1°42·6′W	X	195
Hinton Ampner	Hants	SU5927	51°2·6′	1°9·1′W	T	185
Hinton Ampner Ho	Hants	SU5927	51°2·6′	1°9·1′W	X	185
Hinton Blewett	Bath & NE Somer	ST5956	51°18·3′	2°34·9′W	T	172,182
Hinton Bushes	Dorset	ST9111	50°54·1′	2°7·3′W	F	195
Hinton Charterhouse	Bath & NE Somer	ST7758	51°19·5′	2°19·4′W	T	172
Hinton Cross	Worcs	SP0340	52°3·7′	1°57·0′W	T	150
Hinton Daubnay	Hants	SU6814	50°55·5′	1°1·6′W	X	196
Hinton Downs	Swin	SU2580	51°31·3′	1°38·0′W	X	174
Hinton Field	Bath & NE Somer	ST7656	51°18·4′	2°20·3′W	X	172
Hinton Field Fm	Bath & NE Somer	ST5955	51°17·8′	2°34·9′W	FM	172,182
Hinton Fm	Heref	SO3845	52°6·2′	2°53·9′W	FM	148,149
Hinton Fm	Heref	SO5747	52°7·4′	2°37·3′W	FM	149
Hinton Grounds Fm	Northnts	SP5437	52°2·0′	1°12·4′W	FM	152
Hinton Hall	Shrops	SJ5344	52°59·7′	2°41·6′W	X	117
Hinton Hall	Suff	TM4372	52°17·8′	1°34·2′E	X	156
Hinton Hall Fm	Cambs	TL4675	52°21·4′	0°9·0′E	FM	143
Hinton Hill	Northnts	SP5354	52°11·1′	1°13·1′W	H	152
Hinton Hill	S Glos	ST7476	51°29·2′	2°22·1′W	X	172
Hinton Ho	Bath & NE Somer	ST7758	51°19·5′	2°19·4′W	X	172
Hinton Ho	Hants	SU4933	51°5·9′	1°17·6′W	X	185
Hinton Ho	Hants	SZ2195	50°45·5′	1°41·8′W	X	195
Hinton Ho	Northnts	SP5353	52°10·6′	1°13·1′W	X	152
Hinton Ho	Somer	ST4112	50°54·5′	2°50·0′W	X	193
Hinton-in-the-Hedges	Northnts	SP5536	52°1·4′	1°11·5′W	T	152
Hinton Lodge	Suff	TM4473	52°18·3′	1°35·2′E	X	156
Hinton Lodge	Wok	SU8074	51°27·8′	0°50·5′W	X	175
Hinton Manor	Hants	SU6815	50°56·1′	1°1·5′W	X	196
Hinton Manor	Oxon	SU3799	51°41·5′	1°27·5′W	X	164
Hinton Manor	Shrops	SJ5343	52°59·2′	2°41·6′W	X	117
Hinton Manor Fm	Heref	SO4159	52°13·8′	2°51·4′W	FM	148,149
Hinton Marsh Fm	Swin	SU2285	51°34·0′	1°40·6′W	FM	174
Hinton Martell	Dorset	SU0106	50°51·4′	1°58·8′W	T	195
Hinton Mill Fm	Dorset	ST9904	50°50·4′	2°0·5′W	FM	195
Hinton Old Hall	Shrops	SJ5443	52°59·2′	2°40·7′W	X	117
Hinton on the Green	Worcs	SP0240	52°3·7′	1°57·9′W	T	150
Hinton Park	Hants	SZ2096	50°46·0′	1°42·6′W	X	195
Hinton Park Fm	Somer	ST4110	50°53·4′	2°49·9′W	FM	193
Hinton Parva	Dorset	ST9904	50°50·4′	2°0·5′W	T	195
Hinton Parva	Swin	SU2283	51°33·0′	1°40·6′W	T	174
Hinton Priory	Bath & NE Somer	ST7759	51°20·0′	2°19·4′W	A	172
Hinton Springs	Suff	TM4372	52°17·8′	1°34·2′E	X	156
Hinton St George	Somer	ST4212	50°54·5′	2°49·1′W	T	193
Hinton St Mary	Dorset	ST7816	50°56·8′	2°18·4′W	T	183
Hinton Waldrist	Oxon	SU3798	51°41·0′	1°27·5′W	T	164
Hinton Woodlands Fm	Hants	SU6327	51°2·6′	1°5·7′W	FM	185
Hints	Shrops	SO6175	52°22·5′	2°34·0′W	T	138
Hints	Staffs	SK1502	52°37·2′	1°46·3′W	T	139
Hints Fm	Staffs	SK1501	52°36·6′	1°46·3′W	FM	139
Hinwick	Beds	SP9361	52°14·6′	0°37·9′W	T	153
Hinwick Dungee	Beds	SP9360	52°14·1′	0°37·9′W	X	153
Hinwick Hall School	Beds	SP9362	52°15·1′	0°37·9′W	X	153
Hinwick Ho	Beds	SP9361	52°14·6′	0°37·9′W	X	153
Hinwick Lodge Fm	Beds	SP9561	52°14·6′	0°36·1′W	FM	153
Hinwood	Shrops	SJ3608	52°40·2′	2°56·4′W	T	126
Hinxhill	Kent	TR0442	51°8·7′	0°55·4′E	T	179,189
Hinxton	Cambs	TL4945	52°5·2′	0°10·9′E	T	154
Hinxton Grange	Cambs	TL5046	52°5·7′	0°11·8′E	X	154
Hinxworth	Herts	TL2340	52°2·9′	0°12·0′W	T	153
Hinxworth Place	Herts	TL2339	52°2·4′	0°12·0′W	A	153
Hiora Wick	Shetld	HT9641	60°9·5′	2°3·8′W	W	4
Hipkin's Fm	Norf	TL9498	52°32·9′	0°52·1′E	FM	144
Hipley	Hants	SU6211	50°53·9′	1°6·7′W	X	196
Hipley Copse	Hants	SU6210	50°53·4′	1°6·7′W	F	196
Hipley Hill	Derby	SK2054	53°5·2′	1°41·7′W	X	119
Hiplin	Shetld	HU6187	60°34·0′	0°52·7′W	X	1,2
Hippa Rock	Corn	SS1913	50°53·5′	4°34·0′W	X	190
Hippenscombe	Wilts	SU3156	51°18·4′	1°32·9′W	X	174
Hipperholme	Cald	SE1225	53°43·5′	1°48·7′W	T	104
Hipperley Beck	N Yks	SE9293	54°19·7′	0°34·7′W	W	94,101
Hipper Sick	Derby	SK3068	53°12·7′	1°32·6′W	W	119
Hipping Hall (Hotel)	Lancs	SD6475	54°10·4′	2°32·7′W	X	97
Hipplecote	Worcs	SO7457	52°12·9′	2°22·4′W	T	150
Hipsburn	Northum	NU2310	55°23·3′	1°37·8′W	T	81
Hips Heugh	Northum	NU2518	55°27·6′	1°35·8′W	X	81
Hipshow Fm	Cumbr	SD5496	54°21·7′	2°42·1′W	FM	97
Hipswell	N Yks	SE1897	54°22·3′	1°43·0′W	T	99
Hipswell Moor	N Yks	SE1497	54°22·3′	1°46·6′W	X	99
Hiptoft Fm	Cambs	TF3906	52°38·3′	0°3·7′E	FM	142,143
Hipton Hill	Worcs	SP0348	52°8·1′	1°57·0′W	X	150
Hirael	Gwyn	SH5872	53°13·8′	4°7·2′W	T	114,115
Hiraeth	Carm	SN1721	51°51·7′	4°39·1′W	T	145,158
Hirddu Fach	Powys	SH9420	52°46·3′	3°33·9′W	W	125
Hirddu Fawr	Powys	SH9421	52°46·8′	3°33·9′W	W	125
Hirddywel	Powys	SO0280	52°24·8′	3°26·1′W	X	136
Hirdie Geo	Shetld	HU1560	60°19·7′	1°43·2′W	X	3
Hirdir	Gwyn	SH6165	53°10·1′	4°4·4′W	X	115
Hirdir	Powys	SO0542	52°4·3′	3°22·8′W	X	147,160
Hirdling Ho	Norf	TF5413	52°41·8′	0°17·1′E	X	131,143
Hirdre	Gwyn	SH2538	52°54·9′	4°35·8′W	X	123
Hirdre-faig	I of Angl	SH4874	53°14·7′	4°16·3′W	X	114,115
Hirdre Isaf	Gwyn	SH2538	52°54·9′	4°35·8′W	X	123
Hirdre Uchaf	Gwyn	SH2538	52°54·9′	4°35·8′W	X	123
Hird's Fm	Lincs	TF3292	53°24·7′	0°0·4′W	FM	113
Hird Wood	Cumbr	NY4106	54°27·0′	2°54·2′W	F	90
Hirendean Castle	Midlo	NT2951	55°45·1′	3°7·4′W	A	66,73
Hirfron	I of Angl	SH2675	53°14·9′	4°36·1′W	X	114
Hirfron	Powys	SO0566	52°17·3′	3°23·2′W	X	136,147
Hirfynydd	Nth Pt Talb	SN8205	51°44·1′	3°42·1′W	X	160
Hirgoed-ddu	Cered	SN8083	52°26·2′	3°45·5′W	X	135,136
Hirgwm	Gwyn	SH6620	52°45·9′	3°58·8′W	X	124
Hirgwm	Gwyn	SH8110	52°40·7′	3°45·2′W	X	124,125
Hirllwyn	Powys	SO1055	52°11·4′	3°18·6′W	X	148
Hirllwyn Bank	Powys	SO1055	52°11·4′	3°18·6′W	X	148
Hirlwyn-isaf	Carm	SN7321	51°52·6′	3°50·3′W	X	160
Hirn	Aberd	NJ7300	57°5·7′	2°26·3′W	T	38
Hirnant	Cered	SN7583	52°26·1′	3°49·9′W	X	135
Hirnant	Cered	SN7859	52°13·2′	3°46·8′W	W	146,147
Hirnant	Powys	SJ0522	52°47·5′	3°24·1′W	T	125
Hirnant	Powys	SN8793	52°31·6′	3°39·5′W	X	135,136
Hirnant	Powys	SN8869	52°18·7′	3°38·2′W	X	135,136,147
Hirnant	Powys	SN9857	52°12·3′	3°29·2′W	W	147
Hirnant Claerwen	Powys	SN8466	52°17·0′	3°41·6′W	W	135,136,147
Hirnley	Aberd	NJ5501	57°6·1′	2°44·1′W	X	37
Hirons Hill Fm	Oxon	SP2829	51°57·8′	1°35·2′W	FM	163
Hirrhos Uchaf	Powys	SJ0407	52°39·4′	3°24·8′W	X	125
Hir-rhyd	Powys	SJ1402	52°36·8′	3°15·8′W	X	136
Hirros Hall	Powys	SJ0408	52°39·9′	3°24·8′W	X	125
Hirsel Country Park, The	Scot Bord	NT8240	55°39·4′	2°16·7′W	X	74
Hirsel Lake	Scot Bord	NT8240	55°39·4′	2°16·7′W	W	74
Hirsley Knowe	Scot Bord	NT7015	55°25·9′	2°28·0′W	X	80
Hirst	N Lanak	NS8663	55°51·1′	3°48·8′W	T	65

Hirst	Northum	NY7849	54°50·4′	2°20·1′W	X	86,87
Hirst	Northum	NZ2887	55°10·8′	1°33·2′W	T	81
Hirst	S Ayr	NS4432	55°33·7′	4°28·0′W	X	70
Hirstane Rig	S Lanak	NS9306	55°20·4′	3°40·8′W	X	71,78
Hirst Courtney	N Yks	SE6124	53°42·8′	1°4·1′W	T	105
Hirst Craig	Scot Bord	NY5793	55°14·0′	2°40·1′W	X	80
Hirst Fm	Derby	SK4045	53°0·3′	1°23·8′W	FM	129
Hirst Grove	N Yks	SE2458	54°1·3′	1°37·6′W	X	104
Hirsthead	Cumbr	NY4679	55°6·4′	2°50·4′W	X	86
Hirst Hill	Northum	NY9658	54°55·2′	2°3·3′W	X	87
Hirst Priory	N Lincs	SE7710	53°35·1′	0°49·8′W	X	112
Hirst Rocks	Scot Bord	NT8370	55°55·6′	2°15·9′W	X	67
Hirst Top	Northum	NY7162	54°57·4′	2°26·7′W	X	86,87
Hirta or St Kilda	N Eil	NF0999	57°48·8′	8°34·7′W	X	18
Hirwaen	Denb	SJ1361	53°8·6′	3°17·6′W	T	116
Hirwaun	Gwyn	SH2029	52°50·0′	4°39·9′W	X	123
Hirwaun	Rho Cyn Taf	SN9505	51°44·3′	3°30·8′W	T	160
Hirwaun Common	Brig	SS9383	51°32·4′	3°32·2′W	T	170
Hirwaun Common	Rho Cyn Taf	SN9303	51°43·2′	3°32·6′W	X	170
Hir Ynys	Gwyn	SH6040	52°56·6′	4°4·6′W	X	124
Hisbeer's Fm	Somer	ST2815	50°56·0′	3°1·1′W	FM	193
Hiscocks Hill	Hants	SU2213	50°55·2′	1°40·8′W	X	195
Hiscott	Devon	SS5426	51°1·1′	4°4·5′W	T	180
Hise Hope	Durham	NZ0145	54°48·2′	1°58·6′W	X	87
Hisehope Burn	Durham	NZ0346	54°48·8′	1°56·8′W	W	87
Hisehope Head	Durham	NZ0045	54°48·2′	1°59·6′W	X	87
Hisehope Reservoir	Durham	NZ0246	54°48·8′	1°57·7′W	W	87
Hisland	Shrops	SJ3127	52°50·4′	3°1·1′W	X	126
Hisley	Devon	SX7880	50°36·7′	3°43·1′W	X	191
Hislop	Scot Bord	NT3704	55°19·8′	2°59·2′W	T	79
Hisomley	Wilts	ST8549	51°14·6′	2°12·5′W	T	183
Hissar House Fm	Leic	SP4595	52°33·3′	1°19·8′W	FM	140
Hiss Fm	Suff	TL7286	52°26·9′	0°32·3′E	FM	143
Histon	Cambs	TL4363	52°15·0′	0°6·1′E	T	154
Hitcham	Suff	TL9851	52°7·5′	0°54·0′E	T	155
Hitchambury	Bucks	SU9183	51°32·5′	0°40·9′W	X	175
Hitcham Ho	Bucks	SU9282	51°32·0′	0°40·0′W	X	175
Hitcham Ho	Suff	TL9750	52°7·0′	0°53·0′E	X	155
Hitcham Park	Bucks	SU9282	51°32·0′	0°40·0′W	X	175
Hitchcock's Fm	Devon	ST0412	50°54·2′	3°21·5′W	FM	181
Hitchcombe	Devon	SX5956	50°23·5′	3°58·6′W	X	202
Hitchcombe Wood	Devon	SX7789	50°41·5′	3°44·1′W	F	191
Hitchcopse Fm	Oxon	SU4599	51°41·5′	1°20·5′W	FM	164
Hitchcroft	Northum	NU1707	55°21·7′	1°43·5′W	X	81
Hitchen's Fm	Ches	SJ4448	53°1·8′	2°49·7′W	FM	117
Hitchill	D & G	NY1467	54°59·7′	3°20·2′W	T	85
Hitchin	Herts	TL1930	51°57·6′	0°15·7′W	T	166
Hitchings	Somer	ST3229	51°3·6′	2°57·8′W	X	193
Hitching Stone	N Yks	SD9841	53°52·2′	2°1·4′W	X	103
Hitchin Hill	Herts	TL1828	51°56·5′	0°16·6′W	T	166
Hitch Wood	Herts	TL1923	51°53·8′	0°15·8′W	F	166
Hitcombe Bottom	Wilts	ST8241	51°10·3′	2°15·1′W	T	183
Hithercroft Fm	Oxon	SU5888	51°35·5′	1°9·4′W	FM	174
Hither Fm	Wilts	ST9472	51°27·1′	2°4·8′W	FM	173
Hither Green	Lew	TQ3974	51°27·1′	0°0·4′E	T	177
Hither Hold Fm	Lincs	TF3422	52°47·0′	0°0·4′W	FM	131
Hitter Hill	Derby	SK0866	53°11·7′	1°52·4′W	H	119
Hitterhill Coppice	Worcs	SO7675	52°22·6′	2°20·8′W	F	138
Hitteril	S Lanak	NS9472	55°22·1′	3°38·0′W	X	78
Hitteril Hill	S Lanak	NS9608	55°21·6′	3°38·0′W	H	78
Hittisleigh	Devon	SX7395	50°44·7′	3°47·6′W	X	191
Hittisleigh Barton	Devon	SX7395	50°44·7′	3°47·6′W	T	191
Hittisleigh Mill	Devon	SX7494	50°44·2′	3°46·8′W	X	191
Hitt's Fm	Devon	SY0398	50°46·6′	3°22·2′W	FM	192
Hive	E Yorks	SE8231	53°46·4′	0°44·9′W	T	106
Hives Fm	Leic	SK6615	52°44·0′	1°1·0′W	FM	129
Hivron	Powys	SO2268	52°18·5′	3°8·2′W	X	137,148
Hixham Hall	Essex	TL4526	51°55·0′	0°6·9′E	X	167
Hixon	Staffs	SK0025	52°49·6′	1°59·6′W	T	128
Hjaltasteyn	Shetld	HU3947	60°12·6′	1°17·3′W	X	3
Hjogaland	Shetld	HU3936	60°6·7′	1°17·4′W	X	4
H.M.S. Cambridge	Devon	SX5048	50°19·0′	4°6·0′W	X	201
HMS Collingwood	Hants	SU5604	50°50·2′	1°11·9′W	X	196
HMS Daedalus	Hants	SU5601	50°48·6′	1°11·9′W	X	196
HMS Dolphin	Hants	SZ6298	50°46·9′	1°6·8′W	X	196
HMS Dryad	Hants	SU6308	50°52·3′	1°5·9′W	X	196
H M S Raleigh	Corn	SX4254	50°22·1′	4°12·9′W	X	201
HMS Royal Arthur	Wilts	ST8568	51°24·9′	2°12·6′W	X	173
HMS Sultan	Hants	SU5900	50°48·0′	1°9·4′W	X	196
HMS Victory	C of Port	SU6200	50°48·0′	1°6·8′W	X	196
HMS Warrier	C of Port	SU6200	50°48·0′	1°6·8′W	X	196
HM Young Offenders Institution Werrington House	Staffs	SJ9447	53°1·5′	2°5·0′W	X	118
Hoad Common	Kent	TQ5951	51°14·4′	0°17·1′E	X	188
Hoaden	Kent	TR2659	51°17·3′	1°14·9′E	T	179
Hoaden Ho	Kent	TR2760	51°17·8′	1°15·8′E	X	179
Hoades Court	Kent	TR1862	51°19·1′	1°8·1′E	X	179
Hoad Fm	Kent	TR2143	51°8·8′	1°10·0′E	FM	179,189
Hoads Common	W Susx	SU9625	51°1·2′	0°37·5′W	F	186,197
Hoad's Fm	Kent	TQ8128	51°1·6′	0°35·3′E	FM	188,199
Hoadsherf Fm	W Susx	TQ2823	50°59·8′	0°10·2′W	FM	198
Hoad's Wood	E Susx	TQ6418	50°56·5′	0°20·5′E	F	199
Hoad's Wood	Kent	TQ9542	51°8·9′	0°47·7′E	F	189
Hoaldalbert	Monm	SO3923	51°54·4′	2°52·8′W	X	161
Hoar Cross	Staffs	SK1223	52°48·5′	1°48·9′W	T	128
Hoardland	Devon	SS3720	50°57·6′	4°18·9′W	X	190
Hoardsall	Lancs	SD6338	53°50·5′	2°33·3′W	X	102,103
Hoards Park	Shrops	SO7194	52°32·8′	2°25·3′W	X	138
Hoardweel	Scot Bord	NT7859	55°49·7′	2°20·6′W	X	67,74
Hoar Edge	Shrops	SO5097	52°34·4′	2°43·9′W	X	137,138
Hoar Edge	Shrops	SO5976	52°23·1′	2°35·7′W	X	137,138
Hoar Hall	Warw	SP2591	52°31·2′	1°37·5′W	X	140
Hoar Hill	W Berks	SU4371	51°26·4′	1°22·5′W	H	174
Hoarlake	Shrops	SJ7027	52°50·6′	2°26·3′W	X	127
Hoarlaw	D & G	NT0003	55°18·9′	3°34·1′W	H	78
Hoar Moor	Somer	SS8640	51°9·1′	3°37·4′W	X	181
Hoaroak	Devon	SS7443	51°10·6′	3°47·8′W	X	180
Hoaroak Hill	Somer	SS7342	51°10·0′	3°48·6′W	H	180
Hoar Oak Tree	Somer	SS7443	51°10·6′	3°47·8′W	X	180
Hoaroak Water	Devon	SS7345	51°11·6′	3°48·7′W	W	180
Hoar Park	Warw	SP2693	52°32·3′	1°36·6′W	F	140
Hoar Park Fm	Warw	SP2792	52°31·7′	1°35·7′W	FM	140
Hoar Side Moor	Cald	SD9229	53°45·7′	2°6·9′W	X	103
Hoarston	Glos	SP1940	52°3·7′	1°43·0′W	X	151
Hoar Stone	Glos	SO9606	51°45·4′	2°3·1′W	X	163
Hoar Stone	Oxon	SP3723	51°54·5′	1°27·3′W	X	164
Hoar Stone	Oxon	SP4524	51°55·0′	1°20·3′W	A	164
Hoarstone	Shrops	SJ6033	52°53·8′	2°35·3′W	X	127
Hoar Stone (Burial Chamber)	Oxon	SP3723	51°54·5′	1°27·3′W	A	164
Hoarstone Edge	Tames	SE0101	53°30·6′	1°58·7′W	X	110
Hoarstone Fm	Worcs	SO7976	52°23·1′	2°18·1′W	FM	138
Hoar Stone (Long Barrow)	Glos	SO9606	51°45·4′	2°3·1′W	A	163
Hoarstones	Lancs	SD8237	53°50·0′	2°16·0′W	X	103
Hoarthorns Fm	Glos	SO5913	51°49·1′	2°35·3′W	FM	162
Hoar Tor	Somer	SS7642	51°10·1′	3°46·0′W	X	180
Hoarwithy	Heref	SO5429	51°57·7′	2°39·8′W	T	149
Hoaten	Pemb	SM8209	51°44·5′	5°9·1′W	X	157
Hoath	Kent	TR2064	51°20·2′	1°9·9′E	T	179
Hoath Corner	Kent	TQ4943	51°10·2′	0°8·3′E	T	188
Hoath Fm, The	Kent	TR1757	51°16·5′	1°7·1′E	FM	179
Hoath Ho	Kent	TQ4942	51°9·7′	0°8·2′E	X	188
Hoathly Fm	Kent	TQ6536	51°6·2′	0°21·8′E	FM	188
Hoathwaite Fm	Cumbr	SD2994	54°20·4′	3°5·1′W	FM	96,97
Hoath Wood	Kent	TQ6954	51°15·8′	0°25·7′E	F	188
Hoback Fm	Cambs	TL3449	52°7·6′	0°2·1′W	FM	154
Hoback Fm	Cambs	TL3546	52°6·0′	0°1·3′W	FM	154
Hobajons Cross	Devon	SX6560	50°25·7′	3°53·7′W	A	202
Hobarris	Shrops	SO3178	52°24·0′	3°0·5′W	T	137,148
Hobarrow Bay	Dorset	SY8978	50°36·3′	2°8·9′W	W	195
Hobart's Hall	Essex	TL8042	52°3·1′	0°37·9′E	X	155
Hobbacott	Corn	SS2404	50°48·8′	4°29·5′W	X	190
Hobban's Fm	Essex	TL5205	51°43·6′	0°12·4′E	FM	167
Hobbard's Hill	Oxon	SP4220	51°52·9′	1°23·0′W	X	164
Hobbergate	Staffs	SJ9137	52°56·1′	2°7·6′W	X	127
Hobberill Fm	Northnts	SP5966	52°17·6′	1°9·5′W	FM	152
Hobberlaw	Northum	NU1711	55°23·8′	1°43·5′W	X	81
Hobberley Ho	Leeds	SE3438	53°50·5′	1°28·6′W	X	104
Hobb Hill	Oxon	SP4236	52°1·5′	1°22·9′W	H	151
Hobbie Geo	Highld	ND3662	58°32·7′	3°5·5′W	X	12
Hobbin's Hill	Pemb	SN0417	51°49·3′	4°50·3′W	X	157,158
Hobbins, The	Shrops	SO7393	52°32·3′	2°23·5′W	T	138
Hobbister	Orkney	HY3212	58°59·7′	3°10·5′W	X	6
Hobbister	Orkney	HY3907	58°57·0′	3°3·1′W	X	6,7
Hobbister Hill	Orkney	HY3806	58°56·5′	3°4·2′W	X	6,7
Hobbister House	Orkney	HY3807	58°57·0′	3°4·2′W	X	6,7
Hobble End	Staffs	SK0005	52°38·8′	1°59·6′W	T	139
Hobbles Green	Suff	TL7053	52°9·2′	0°29·5′E	T	154
Hobb's Bottom Fm	Wilts	ST8466	51°23·8′	2°13·4′W	FM	173
Hobbs Cross	Essex	TL4910	51°46·4′	0°10·0′E	T	167
Hobbs Cross	Essex	TQ4799	51°40·5′	0°8·0′E	T	167,177
Hobb's Flow	Scot Bord	NY5690	55°12·4′	2°41·1′W	W	80
Hobbs Fm	Surrey	TQ3747	51°12·6′	0°1·9′W	FM	187
Hobbs Green Fm	Beds	SP9658	52°12·9′	0°35·3′W	FM	153
Hobbs Hayes	Leic	SP4694	52°32·7′	1°18·9′W	X	140
Hobbs Hill	Ches	SJ6882	53°20·3′	2°28·4′W	X	109
Hobb's Hill	Corn	SX1869	50°29·8′	4°33·6′W	X	201
Hobbs Hill Fm	Kent	TQ5040	51°8·6′	0°9·1′E	FM	188
Hobbs Hole	Hav	TQ5885	51°32·7′	0°17·1′E	W	177
Hobbshole Fm	Oxon	SP4129	51°57·7′	1°23·8′W	FM	164
Hobbs Lots Br	Cambs	TF3901	52°35·6′	0°3·5′E	X	142,143
Hobbs Point	Pemb	SM9604	51°42·1′	4°56·7′W	X	157,158
Hobbs Wall	Bath & NE	ST6560	51°20·5′	2°29·8′W	T	172
Hobby Lodge	Devon	SS3323	50°59·2′	4°22·4′W	X	190
Hobby, The	Devon	SS3224	50°59·7′	4°23·3′W	X	190
Hobcarton	Cumbr	NY1923	54°36·0′	3°14·8′W	H	89,90
Hobcarton Crag	Cumbr	NY1922	54°35·5′	3°14·8′W	X	89,90
Hobcarton End	Cumbr	NY1923	54°36·0′	3°14·8′W	X	89,90
Hobcarton Gill	Cumbr	NY1823	54°36·0′	3°15·7′W	W	89,90
Hobclerk's Fm	Essex	TL7900	51°40·4′	0°35·7′E	FM	167
Hobdale Beck	Cumbr	SD6794	54°20·7′	2°30·0′W	W	98
Hobditch	Warw	SP1368	52°18·8′	1°48·2′W	A	139,151
Hob Green	N Yks	SE2764	54°4·5′	1°34·8′W	X	99
Hobground	N Yks	SE7480	54°12·9′	0°51·5′W	X	100
Hobgrumble Gill	Cumbr	NY4911	54°29·8′	2°46·8′W	W	90
Hob Hay	Staffs	SK0559	53°7·9′	1°55·1′W	X	119
Hob Hill	Ches	SJ4651	53°3·5′	2°47·9′W	T	117
Hob Hill	Staffs	SJ8024	52°49·0′	2°17·4′W	X	127
Hob Hill	Worcs	SP0672	52°21·0′	1°54·3′W	H	139
Hob Hole	N Yks	NZ6507	54°27·5′	0°59·4′W	W	94
Hobhole Drain	Lincs	TF3647	53°0·4′	0°2·0′E	W	131
Hobhole Drain	Lincs	TF3857	53°5·8′	0°4·1′E	W	122
Hob Holes	N Yks	NZ8115	54°31·7′	0°44·5′W	X	94
Hob Hurst's Ho	Derby	SK2869	53°13·3′	1°34·4′W	X	119
Hob Hurst's Ho (Tumulus)	Derby	SK2869	53°13·3′	1°34·4′W	A	119
Hobkin Ground	Cumbr	SD2290	54°18·2′	3°11·5′W	X	96
Hobkirk	Scot Bord	NT5810	55°23·2′	2°39·3′W	T	80
Hob Knowe	Scot Bord	NY5997	55°16·2′	2°38·3′W	X	80
Hobland Hall	Norf	TG5101	52°33·2′	1°42·6′E	X	134
Hobletts	Thurr	TQ6282	51°31·0′	0°20·5′E	X	177
Hobley Furze	Warw	SP4685	52°27·9′	1°19·0′W	F	140
Hoblyn's Cove	Corn	SW7658	50°23·0′	5°8·7′W	W	200
Hobmeadows	Staffs	SK0354	53°5·2′	1°56·9′W	X	119
Hob Moor	York	SE5850	53°56·8′	1°6·6′W	X	105
Hob on the Hill	Red & Cl	NZ6412	54°30·2′	1°0·3′W	X	94
Hoborough Hill	Northnts	SP6266	52°17·6′	1°5·1′W	X	152
Hobroyd	Derby	SK0293	53°26·3′	1°57·8′W	T	110
Hobs Aerie	Essex	TL4835	51°59·8′	0°9·7′E	X	154
Hobsburn	Scot Bord	NT5811	55°23·7′	2°39·4′W	X	80
Hobshill	Aberd	NK0437	57°25·7′	1°55·5′W	X	30
Hobshort's Fm	W Susx	TQ1619	50°57·7′	0°20·5′W	FM	198
Hobsic	Notts	SK4553	53°4·6′	1°19·3′W	X	120
Hob's Knowe	Scot Bord	NT3412	55°24·1′	3°2·1′W	H	79
Hobsland	S Ayr	NS3529	55°31·9′	4°36·4′W	X	70
Hobsley Coppice	Shrops	SJ5200	52°36·0′	2°42·1′W	F	126
Hob's Moat	Sol	SP1482	52°26·4′	1°47·2′W	A	139
Hobson	Durham	NZ1755	54°53·6′	1°43·7′W	T	88
Hobson Moss	Sheff	SK2194	53°26·8′	1°40·6′W	X	110
Hobson Moss Dike	Sheff	SK2293	53°26·2′	1°39·7′W	W	110
Hobson's Brook	Cambs	TL4555	52°10·7′	0°7·6′E	W	154
Hobstone Hill	Staffs	SK0810	52°41·5′	1°52·5′W	X	128
Hobstones	Lancs	SD8841	53°52·1′	2°10·5′W	A	103
Hob Tor	Derby	SK0677	53°17·6′	1°54·2′W	X	119
Hoby	Leic	SK6617	52°45·0′	1°0·9′W	T	129
Hocberry	Glos	ST9498	51°41·1′	2°4·8′W	X	163
Hoccombe	Somer	ST1129	51°3·4′	3°15·8′W	T	181,193
Hoccombe Combe	Devon	SS7844	51°11·2′	3°44·4′W	X	180
Hoccombe Hill	Devon	SS7843	51°10·6′	3°44·3′W	H	180
Hoccombe Water	Somer	SS7843	51°10·6′	3°44·3′W	W	180
Hoccum	Shrops	SO7493	52°32·3′	2°22·6′W	X	138
Hock Cliff	Glos	SO7209	51°47·0′	2°24·0′W	X	162
Hockenden	Brom	TQ4968	51°23·7′	0°8·9′E	T	177
Hockenhull Hall	Ches	SJ4866	53°11·6′	2°46·3′W	A	117
Hockenhull Platts	Ches	SJ4765	53°11·0′	2°47·2′W	X	117
Hockerhill Fm	Staffs	SJ8708	52°40·4′	2°11·1′W	FM	127
Hockeridge Bottom	Bucks	SP9706	51°44·9′	0°35·3′W	X	165
Hockerill	Herts	TL4920	51°51·7′	0°10·2′E	T	167
Hockerill's Fm	Worcs	SO6567	52°18·2′	2°30·4′W	FM	138,149
Hockerill's Fm	Worcs	SO6668	52°18·8′	2°29·5′W	FM	138
Hockering	Norf	TG0713	52°40·7′	1°4·1′E	T	133
Hockering Heath	Norf	TG0814	52°41·2′	1°5·1′E	T	133
Hockering Wood	Norf	TG0714	52°41·3′	1°4·2′E	F	133
Hockerley	Derby	SK0082	53°20·3′	1°59·6′W	X	110
Hockerton	Notts	SK7156	53°6·0′	0°56·0′W	T	120
Hockerton Moor Fm	Notts	SK6957	53°6·6′	0°57·7′W	FM	120
Hockerton Moor Wood	Notts	SK6957	53°6·6′	0°57·7′W	F	120
Hockerwood	Notts	SK7155	53°5·5′	0°56·0′W	X	120
Hockett, The	Win & Maid	SU8584	51°33·1′	0°46·0′W	X	175
Hocketwell	Northum	NU2117	55°27·0′	1°39·6′W	X	81
Hockford Waters	Devon	ST0120	50°58·5′	3°24·2′W	X	181
Hockham Belt	Norf	TL8985	52°26·0′	0°47·2′E	F	144
Hockham Heath	Norf	TL9292	52°29·8′	0°50·1′E	F	144
Hockham Lodge	Norf	TL9792	52°29·6′	0°54·5′E	X	144
Hockham's Fm	Worcs	SO7662	52°15·6′	2°20·7′W	FM	138,150
Hockholler	Somer	ST1621	50°59·2′	3°11·4′W	T	181,193
Hockholler Green	Somer	ST1721	50°59·2′	3°10·6′W	T	181,193
Hockinston Tor	Devon	SX6971	50°31·7′	3°50·5′W	X	202
Hocklake Fm	Devon	SX4669	50°30·3′	4°9·9′W	FM	201
Hockland	Shetld	HU3051	60°14·8′	1°27·0′W	X	3
Hockleton	Shrops	SJ2700	52°35·8′	3°4·3′W	X	126
Hockleton Br	Shrops	SJ2700	52°35·8′	3°4·3′W	X	126
Hockley	Ches	SJ9283	53°20·9′	2°6·8′W	T	109
Hockley	Cov	SP2779	52°24·7′	1°35·8′W	T	140
Hockley	Derby	SK3866	53°11·6′	1°25·5′W	X	119
Hockley	Essex	TM0106	51°43·2′	0°55·0′E	X	168
Hockley	Essex	TM0721	51°51·2′	1°0·7′E	X	168,169
Hockley	Essex	TQ8492	51°36·0′	0°39·8′E	T	178
Hockley	Kent	TQ9733	51°4·0′	0°49·1′E	X	189
Hockley	Kent	TQ9855	51°15·8′	0°50·7′E	T	178
Hockley	Staffs	SK2200	52°36·1′	1°40·1′W	T	139
Hockley Brook	Worcs	SO9274	52°22·1′	2°6·7′W	W	139
Hockley Fm	Bucks	TL0000	51°41·6′	0°32·8′W	FM	166
Hockley Heath	Sol	SP1572	52°21·0′	1°46·4′W	T	139
Hockley Hill	Glos	SO7813	51°49·1′	2°18·8′W	X	162
Hockley Ho	Hants	SU5627	51°2·6′	1°11·7′W	X	185
Hockley House Fm	Warw	SP4069	52°19·3′	1°24·4′W	FM	151
Hockley Lands	Surrey	SU9854	51°16·8′	0°35·3′W	X	186
Hockley Lodge	Northnts	SP8270	52°19·5′	0°47·4′W	X	141
Hockley Lodge	Northnts	SP8274	52°21·7′	0°47·3′W	X	141
Hockley Pl	Essex	TM0821	51°51·2′	1°1·6′E	X	168,169
Hockley Sole	Kent	TR2440	51°7·1′	1°12·4′E	X	179,189
Hockley Woods	Essex	TQ8391	51°35·5′	0°38·9′E	F	178
Hockliffe	Beds	SP9726	51°55·7′	0°35·0′W	T	165
Hockliffe Grange	Beds	SP9627	51°56·2′	0°35·8′W	X	165
Hockliffe Ho	Beds	SP9726	51°55·7′	0°35·0′W	X	165
Hockwill	Devon	SS4112	50°53·4′	4°15·3′W	X	180,190
Hockwold cum Wilton	Norf	TL7388	52°28·0′	0°33·2′E	T	143
Hockwold Fens	Norf	TL7087	52°27·5′	0°30·5′E	X	143
Hockworthy	Devon	ST0319	50°58·0′	3°22·5′W	T	181
Hocombe	Hants	SU4322	51°0·0′	1°22·8′W	T	185
Hodbarrow Point	Cumbr	SD1878	54°11·7′	3°15·0′W	X	96
Hodber Hill Plantn	N Yks	SE2798	54°22·8′	1°34·6′W	F	99
Hodcombe Fm	E Susx	TV5795	50°44·2′	0°13·9′E	FM	199
Hodcott Buildings	W Berks	SU4680	51°31·3′	1°19·8′W	X	174
Hodcott Down	W Berks	SU4882	51°32·3′	1°18·1′W	X	174
Hodcott Ho	W Berks	SU4781	51°31·8′	1°19·0′W	X	174
Hoddell Fm	Powys	SO2564	52°16·4′	3°5·6′W	FM	137,148
Hodder Bank	Lancs	SD6548	53°55·9′	2°31·6′W	X	102,103
Hodder Bank Fell	Lancs	SD6749	53°56·4′	2°29·7′W	H	103
Hoddern Fm	E Susx	TQ4202	50°48·2′	0°1·3′E	FM	198
Hodder's Combe	Somer	ST1540	51°9·4′	3°12·5′W	X	181
Hoddesdon	Herts	TL3608	51°45·5′	0°1·4′W	T	166
Hoddesdonpark Wood	Herts	TL3508	51°45·5′	0°2·2′W	F	166
Hoddington Ho	Hants	SU7047	51°13·3′	0°59·5′W	A	186
Hoddins, The	Shetld	HU3761	60°20·1′	1°19·3′W	X	2,3
Hoddlesden	Black w Dar	SD7122	53°41·9′	2°25·9′W	T	103
Hoddlesden Moss	Black w Dar	SD7221	53°41·3′	2°25·0′W	X	103
Hoddnant	V of Glam	SS9768	51°24·3′	3°28·5′W	W	170
Hoddom Castle	D & G	NY1573	55°2·9′	3°19·4′W	A	85
Hoddomcross	D & G	NY1773	55°2·9′	3°17·5′W	X	85
Hoddom Mains	D & G	NY1572	55°2·4′	3°19·4′W	X	85
Hoddom Mill	D & G	NY1473	55°2·9′	3°20·3′W	X	85
Hoddomtown	D & G	NY1774	55°3·5′	3°17·5′W	X	85
Hodd's Fm	Hants	SU6752	51°16·0′	1°2·0′W	FM	185,186
Hodd's Hill	Wilts	SU2875	51°28·6′	1°35·4′W	X	174
Hode Fm	Kent	TR1755	51°15·4′	1°7·0′E	FM	179
Hoden	Worcs	SP0947	52°7·5′	1°51·7′W	T	150
Hodenhoe Manor	Herts	TL3433	51°59·0′	0°2·5′W	X	166
Hod Fen	Cambs	TL1890	52°29·9′	0°15·3′W	X	142
Hodge Beck	N Yks	NZ6000	54°23·8′	1°1·1′W	W	94
Hodge Beck	N Yks	SE6393	54°20·0′	1°1·4′W	W	94,100
Hodge Beck	N Yks	SE6883	54°14·5′	0°57·0′W	W	100
Hodge Close	Cumbr	NY3101	54°24·3′	3°3·4′W	X	90
Hodgecombe Fm	Glos	ST7899	51°41·6′	2°18·7′W	FM	162
Hodgefield	Staffs	SJ9054	53°5·2′	2°8·6′W	T	118

Hodgefold	Tames	SJ9893	53°26·3′	2°1·4′W	X	109
Hodge Hall	Durham	NY8630	54°40·1′	2°12·6′W	X	91,92
Hodgehill	Birm	SP1288	52°29·6′	1°49·0′W	T	139
Hodgehill	Ches	SJ8369	53°13·3′	2°14·9′W	T	118
Hodge Hill	Cumbr	SD4188	54°17·3′	2°54·0′W	X	96,97
Hodge Hill	Dudley	SO9382	52°26·4′	2°5·8′W	X	139
Hodge Hole	N Yks	SD7378	54°12·1′	2°24·4′W	X	98
Hodgemoor Woods	Bucks	SU9693	51°37·9′	0°36·4′W	F	175,176
Hodges	Devon	SS5745	51°11·4′	4°2·4′W	X	180
Hodges	E Loth	NT4571	55°56·0′	2°52·4′W	X	66
Hodges	E Susx	TQ5524	50°59·8′	0°12·9′E	X	199
Hodgeston	Pemb	SS0399	51°39·6′	4°50·5′W	T	158
Hodgeston Hill	Pemb	SN0300	51°40·1′	4°50·5′W	X	158
Hodgeton	Angus	NO6449	56°38·1′	2°34·8′W	T	54
Hodgewood Fm	Wakf	SE4921	53°41·2′	1°15·1′W	FM	105
Hodghurst	Shrops	SO4597	52°34·3′	2°48·3′W	X	137,138
Hodgson Moor	Lancs	SD7045	53°54·3′	2°27·0′W	X	103
Hod Hill	Dorset	ST8510	50°53·6′	2°12·4′W	H	194
Hodhill Fm	Derby	SK5266	53°11·5′	1°12·9′W	FM	120
Hod Hill (Fort)	Dorset	ST8510	50°53·6′	2°12·4′W	A	194
Hodley	Powys	SO1691	52°30·9′	3°13·9′W	T	136
Hodmore Fm	Oxon	SU6878	51°30·0′	1°0·8′W	FM	175
Hodnell Manor	Warw	SP4257	52°12·8′	1°22·7′W	X	151
Hodnet	Shrops	SJ6128	52°51·1′	2°34·3′W	T	127
Hodnet Heath	Shrops	SJ6126	52°50·0′	2°34·3′W	X	127
Hodnetheath	Shrops	SJ6127	52°50·6′	2°34·3′W	T	127
Hodre Hill	Shrops	SO3177	52°23·4′	3°0·4′W	H	137,148
Hodrid	Powys	SN9862	52°15·0′	3°29·3′W	X	147
Hodshill	Bath & NE Somer	ST7460	51°20·5′	2°22·0′W	X	172
Hods Hill	S Lanak	NT0009	55°22·1′	3°34·2′W	H	78
Hodsock	Notts	SK6185	53°21·7′	1°4·6′W	T	111,120
Hodsock Grange	Notts	SK5886	53°22·3′	1°7·3′W	X	111,120
Hodsock Lodge Fm	Notts	SK6086	53°22·3′	1°5·5′W	FM	111,120
Hodsock Manor Fm	Notts	SK6284	53°21·2′	1°3·7′W	FM	111,120
Hodsock Park	Notts	SK5987	53°22·8′	1°6·4′W	X	111,120
Hodsock Plantation	Notts	SK6285	53°21·7′	1°3·7′W	F	120
Hodsock Red Br	Notts	SK6285	53°21·7′	1°3·7′W	X	111,120
Hodsock Woodhouse	Notts	SK5986	53°22·3′	1°6·4′W	X	111,120
Hodsoll Street	Kent	TQ6263	51°20·8′	0°20·0′E	T	177,188
Hodson	Swin	SU1780	51°31·4′	1°44·9′W	T	173
Hodson's Fm	Brad	SE0647	53°55·4′	1°54·1′W	FM	104
Hodthorpe	Derby	SK5476	53°16·9′	1°11·0′W	T	120
Hodyoad	Cumbr	NY0822	54°35·3′	3°25·0′W	X	89
Hoe	Devon	SS6124	51°0·2′	3°58·5′W	X	180
Hoe	Hants	SU5617	50°57·2′	1°11·8′W	T	185
Hoe	Norf	TF9916	52°42·5′	0°57·6′E	T	132
Hoe	Surrey	TQ0945	51°11·9′	0°26·0′W	T	187
Hoe Beg	N Eil	NF9574	57°39·4′	7°6·4′W	X	18
Hoe Benham	W Berks	SU4169	51°25·3′	1°24·2′W	T	174
Hoe Bridge	W Susx	SU9827	51°2·3′	0°35·7′W	X	186,197
Hoe Copse	W Susx	SU8818	50°57·5′	0°44·4′W	F	197
Hoe Court	Heref	SO7543	52°5·3′	2°21·5′W	X	150
Hoe Cross Fm	Hants	SU6314	50°55·5′	1°5·8′W	FM	196
Hoefields Fm	Leic	SK5100	52°36·0′	1°14·4′W	FM	140
Hoe Fm	Essex	TL9025	51°53·7′	0°46·1′E	FM	168
Hoe Fm	Hants	SU3819	50°58·4′	1°27·1′W	FM	185
Hoe Fm	Norf	TF5819	52°45·0′	0°20·9′E	FM	131
Hoe Fm	Somer	SS9137	51°7·6′	3°33·1′W	FM	181
Hoe Fm	W Susx	SU8102	50°48·9′	0°50·6′W	FM	197
Hoe Fm	W Susx	SU9501	50°48·3′	0°38·7′W	FM	197
Hoe Gate	Hants	SU6213	50°55·0′	1°6·7′W	T	196
Hoe Grange	Derby	SK2155	53°5·7′	1°40·8′W	X	119
Hoe Hill	Lincs	TF2195	53°26·5′	0°10·3′W	X	113
Hoe Hill	Lincs	TF3072	53°14·0′	0°2·7′W	X	122
Hoe Hill	Northnts	SP7267	52°18·0′	0°56·2′W	X	152
Hoe Hill	Notts	SK6233	52°53·7′	1°4·3′W	X	129
Hoe Hill	Notts	SK6836	52°55·3′	0°58·9′W	X	129
Hoe Hill Fm	Lincs	TF2195	53°26·5′	0°10·3′W	FM	113
Hoehill Fm	Notts	SK6234	52°54·2′	1°4·3′W	FM	129
Hoe Hill (Long Barrow)	Lincs	TF2195	53°26·5′	0°10·3′W	A	113
Hoe Hills	Lincs	TF1130	52°51·6′	0°20·7′W	X	130
Hoe Lodge	Norf	TF9915	52°42·0′	0°57·1′E	X	132
Hoe Mill Barns	Essex	TL8108	51°44·7′	0°37·7′E	X	168
Hoemoor Fm	Devon	ST2110	50°53·3′	3°7·0′W	FM	192,193
Hoe Moor Fm	Hants	SU6212	50°54·5′	1°6·7′W	FM	196
Hoe Moor Ho	Hants	SU4810	50°53·5′	1°18·7′W	X	196
Hoe Point	Corn	SW5727	50°5·8′	5°23·5′W	X	203
Hoe Point	Highld	NG1641	57°22·5′	6°43·0′W	X	23
Hoe Point	I Scilly	SV8907	49°53·2′	6°19·4′W	X	203
Hoe Rape	Highld	NG1543	57°23·6′	6°44·2′W	X	23
Hoes Fm	W Susx	SU9719	50°58·0′	0°36·7′W	FM	197
Hoe's Fm	W Susx	TQ1223	51°0·0′	0°23·8′W	FM	198
Hoe Skerries	Orkney	HY7555	59°23·1′	2°25·9′W	X	5
Hoe Skerry	Shetld	HU3442	60°9·9′	1°22·7′W	X	4
Hoe Skerry	Shetld	HU3539	60°8·3′	1°21·7′W	X	4
Hoestreet	Essex	TL6507	51°44·5′	0°23·8′E	X	167
Hoe, The	C of Plym	SX4753	50°21·7′	4°8·7′W	X	201
Hoe, The	Highld	NG1641	57°22·5′	6°43·0′W	H	23
Hoe, The	N Eil	NL5987	56°51·2′	7°35·2′W	H	31
Hoewyck Fm	W Susx	SU9126	51°1·8′	0°41·7′W	FM	186,197
Hoff	Cumbr	NY6717	54°33·1′	2°30·2′W	T	91
Hoff Beck	Cumbr	NY6718	54°33·6′	2°30·2′W	W	91
Hoffleet Stow	Lincs	TF2437	52°55·2′	0°8·9′W	T	131
Hoff Lodge	Cumbr	NY6617	54°33·1′	2°31·1′W	X	91
Hoff Lunn	Cumbr	NY6616	54°32·5′	2°31·1′W	F	91
Hoffnant	Cered	SN3152	52°8·7′	4°27·8′W	W	145
Hoga	Shetld	HU4063	60°21·2′	1°16·0′W	X	2,3
Hoga	Shetld	HU4423	59°59·6′	1°12·2′W	X	4
Hoga	Shetld	HU4678	60°29·2′	1°9·3′W	X	2,3
Hogahellias	Shetld	HU6287	60°34·0′	0°51·6′W	X	1,2
Hogaland	Shetld	HU3479	60°29·9′	1°22·4′W	T	2,3
Hogaland	Shetld	HU3946	60°12·1′	1°17·3′W	X	4
Hoga Lee	Shetld	HU5287	60°34·1′	1°2·6′W	X	1,2
Hogalee Burn	Shetld	HU5387	60°34·0′	1°1·5′W	W	1,2
Hogan	Shetld	HU2049	60°13·8′	1°37·8′W	H	3
Hogan	Shetld	HU2647	60°12·7′	1°31·4′W	X	3
Hogan	Shetld	HU3844	60°11·0′	1°18·4′W	X	4
Hoga Ness	Shetld	HP5500	60°41·0′	0°59·1′W	X	1
Hoga Ness	Shetld	HU2747	60°12·7′	1°30·3′W	X	3
Hogarth	Orkney	HY3919	59°3·5′	3°3·3′W	X	6
Hogarth	Orkney	HY4019	59°3·5′	3°2·3′W	X	6
Hogarth Hall	N Yks	NZ9301	54°24·0′	0°33·6′W	X	94
Hogarth Hill Fm	N Yks	NZ9301	54°24·0′	0°33·6′W	FM	94
Hogbarn	Kent	TQ8855	51°16·0′	0°42·1′E	X	178
Hog Bay	Pemb	SM7404	51°41·6′	5°15·8′W	W	157
Hogben Fm	Kent	TR0737	51°5·9′	0°57·8′E	FM	179,189
Hogben's Hill	Kent	TR0356	51°16·2′	0°55·0′E	T	178,179
Hogbrook Fm	Warw	SP3258	52°13·4′	1°31·5′W	FM	151
Hogchester	Dorset	SY3594	50°44·8′	2°54·9′W	X	193
Hog Cliff Bottom	Dorset	SY6196	50°46·0′	2°32·8′W	X	194
Hog Cliff Hill	Dorset	SY6196	50°46·0′	2°32·8′W	X	194
Hogdigging Copse	Hants	SU4450	51°15·1′	1°21·8′W	F	185
Hogdon Law	Northum	NT9412	55°24·4′	2°5·3′W	H	80
Hog Down	Wilts	SU2056	51°18·4′	1°42·4′W	X	174
Hogerston Hill	N Yks	SE2172	54°8·8′	1°40·3′W	X	99
Hog Fell	D & G	NY3989	55°11·7′	2°57·1′W	H	79
Hogganfield	C of Glas	NS6466	55°52·3′	4°10·0′W	T	64
Hogganfield Loch	C of Glas	NS6467	55°52·9′	4°10·0′W	W	64
Hoggard House Fm	E Yorks	TA0539	53°50·4′	0°23·8′W	FM	107
Hoggard's Green	Suff	TL8856	52°10·4′	0°45·4′E	T	155
Hoggarths	N Yks	NY8601	54°24·5′	2°12·5′W	X	91,92
Hoggatts	Hants	SU7839	51°8·9′	0°52·7′W	X	186
Hogg End	Herts	TL1109	51°46·3′	0°23·1′W	X	166
Hoggen Down	Dorset	ST8101	50°48·7′	2°15·8′W	X	194
Hoggeston	Bucks	SP8025	51°55·3′	0°49·8′W	T	165
Hoggfield Hill	Scot Bord	NT5310	55°23·2′	2°44·1′W	H	79
Hogg Hill	D & G	NY1787	55°10·5′	3°17·8′W	H	79
Hoggie	Moray	NJ5160	57°37·9′	2°48·8′W	X	29
Hog Gill	Scot Bord	NY4590	55°12·3′	2°51·4′W	W	79
Hog Gill Bog	Scot Bord	NY4589	55°11·8′	2°51·4′W	X	79
Hoggington	Wilts	ST8255	51°17·9′	2°15·1′W	T	173
Hogg of Linga	Shetld	HU3539	60°8·3′	1°21·7′W	X	4
Hogg of Papa	Shetld	HU3737	60°7·2′	1°19·6′W	X	4
Hoggrill's End	Warw	SP2291	52°31·2′	1°40·1′W	T	139
Hoggs Hills	Cumbr	SD6581	54°13·7′	2°31·8′W	H	97
Hoggs Lodge	Hants	SU6137	51°8·0′	1°7·3′W	X	185
Hoggs of Hoy	Shetld	HU3745	60°11·5′	1°19·5′W	X	4
Hoggs of Oxna	Shetld	HU3437	60°7·2′	1°22·8′W	X	4
Hogg Sound	Shetld	HU3437	60°7·2′	1°22·8′W	W	4
Hogg, The	Shetld	HU6771	60°25·3′	0°46·5′W	X	2
Hogg, The	Shetld	HU6971	60°25·3′	0°44·3′W	X	2
Hog Hall	Bucks	SP9715	51°49·7′	0°35·1′W	X	165
Hog Hatch	Surrey	SU8348	51°13·7′	0°48·2′W	T	186
Hogh Bay	Arg & Bt	NM1657	56°37·4′	6°37·4′W	W	46
Hog Hill	Brad	SE1243	53°53·2′	1°48·6′W	X	104
Hog Hill	D & G	NS6100	55°16·7′	4°10·9′W	X	77
Hog Hill	D & G	NS7008	55°21·2′	4°2·6′W	X	71,77
Hog Hill	D & G	NX6072	55°1·6′	4°11·0′W	X	77
Hog Hill	D & G	NX6686	55°9·3′	4°5·8′W	H	77
Hog Hill	D & G	NY2895	55°14·9′	3°7·5′W	H	79
Hoghill	D & G	NY3789	55°11·7′	2°59·0′W	X	79
Hog Hill	D & G	NY3889	55°11·7′	2°58·0′W	H	79
Hog Hill	Dorset	ST6400	50°48·1′	2°30·3′W	X	194
Hog Hill	Dorset	ST7401	50°48·7′	2°21·8′W	X	194
Hog Hill	Dorset	SY6494	50°44·9′	2°30·2′W	X	194
Hog Hill	Dorset	SY6688	50°41·7′	2°28·5′W	H	194
Hog Hill	E Dunb	NS5982	56°0·9′	4°15·3′W	X	57,64
Hog Hill	Enf	TQ3097	51°39·6′	0°6·8′W	X	166,176,177
Hog Hill	Midlo	NT2851	55°45·1′	3°8·4′W	X	66,73
Hog Hill	N Yks	NY8503	54°25·6′	2°13·5′W	X	91,92
Hog Hill	Redbr	TQ4791	51°36·1′	0°7·8′E	X	177
Hog Hill	Scot Bord	NT1125	55°30·9′	3°24·1′W	H	72
Hog Hill	Scot Bord	NT1642	55°40·1′	3°19·7′W	H	72
Hog Hill	Scot Bord	NT2546	55°42·4′	3°11·2′W	H	73
Hog Hill	Scot Bord	NT4633	55°35·5′	2°51·0′W	H	73
Hog Hill	Scot Bord	NT5159	55°49·6′	2°46·5′W	H	66,73
Hoghill	W Loth	NT0866	55°53·0′	3°27·8′W	X	65
Hoghill Burn	D & G	NY3889	55°11·7′	2°58·0′W	W	79
Hog Holes	Brad	SE0739	53°51·1′	1°53·2′W	X	104
Hogholm	Aberd	NJ8018	57°15·4′	2°19·4′W	X	38
Hoghouse Hill	Cumbr	NY4828	54°39·0′	2°47·9′W	X	90
Hoghton	Lancs	SD6126	53°44·0′	2°35·1′W	T	102,103
Hoghton Bottoms	Lancs	SD6227	53°44·5′	2°34·2′W	T	102,103
Hoghton Tower	Lancs	SD6226	53°44·0′	2°34·1′W	A	102,103
Hog Island	Shetld	HU5158	60°18·4′	1°4·1′W	X	2,3
Hog Knowe	Northum	NT8308	55°22·2′	2°15·7′W	X	80
Hog Knowe	Scot Bord	NT1438	55°37·9′	3°21·5′W	H	72
Hog Knowes	D & G	NY2196	55°15·4′	3°14·1′W	X	79
Hog Knowes	Scot Bord	NT2747	55°42·9′	3°9·3′W	H	73
Hog Knowes	Scot Bord	NT3310	55°23·0′	3°3·0′W	X	79
Hog Lairs	Northum	NT9113	55°24·9′	2°8·1′W	X	80
Hoglan Bay	N Eil	NF7072	57°37·3′	7°31·2′W	W	18
Hog Lane Fm	Bucks	SP9606	51°44·9′	0°36·2′W	FM	165
Hoglayers	Fife	NO1906	56°14·6′	3°18·0′W	X	58
Hog Leaze	Dorset	SY7399	50°47·6′	2°22·6′W	X	194
Hogleaze Fm	Dorset	SY6192	50°43·8′	2°32·8′W	FM	194
Hogley Green	Kirk	SE1207	53°33·8′	1°48·7′W	T	110
Hoglinns Water	Orkney	ND2491	58°48·3′	3°18·4′W	W	7
Hogmoor Inclosure	Hants	SU7935	51°6·8′	0°51·9′W	F	186
Hognaston	Derby	SK2350	53°3·0′	1°39·0′W	T	119
Hognaston Winn	Derby	SK2250	53°3·0′	1°39·9′W	X	119
Hognore Fm	Kent	TQ6259	51°18·6′	0°19·9′E	FM	188
Hog of Breigeo	Shetld	HU3808	59°51·6′	1°18·8′W	X	4
Hog of the Holm	Shetld	HU3807	59°51·1′	1°18·8′W	X	4
Hog of the Ness	Shetld	HU3808	59°51·6′	1°18·8′W	X	4
Hog Park Strand	D & G	NX5480	55°5·8′	4°16·9′W	W	77
Hog Pit Hill	NE Lincs	TA1905	53°31·9′	0°11·8′W	X	113
Hogpits Bottom	Herts	TL0101	51°42·1′	0°31·9′W	T	166
Hog Rig	Scot Bord	NT5854	55°46·9′	2°39·7′W	X	67,73,74
Hog Rigg	Pth & Kin	NO0305	56°13·9′	3°33·4′W	X	58
Hog's Back	Surrey	SU9348	51°13·6′	0°39·7′W	X	186
Hogs Beck	Lincs	TF4770	53°12·6′	0°12·5′E	W	122
Hogsbeck Ho	Lincs	TF4870	53°12·6′	0°13·4′E	X	122
Hogsbrook Fm	Devon	SY0289	50°41·8′	3°22·9′W	FM	192
Hog's Bush	Kent	TR3645	51°9·6′	1°22·9′E	X	179
Hog's Corner	Suff	TM4580	52°22·0′	1°36·3′E	X	156
Hogsdown Fm	Glos	ST7097	51°40·5′	2°25·6′W	FM	162
Hogs Earth	Cumbr	NY2618	54°33·4′	3°8·2′W	X	89,90
Hogshaw Fm	Bucks	SP7322	51°53·7′	0°56·0′W	FM	165
Hogshaw Hill Fm	Bucks	SP7422	51°53·7′	0°55·1′W	FM	165
Hogshead Wood	Ches	SJ5868	53°12·7′	2°37·3′W	F	117
Hogs Hill	Staffs	SK2209	52°40·9′	1°40·1′W	X	128
Hogs Hole	W Berks	SU3759	51°20·0′	1°27·7′W	X	174
Hog's Kailyard	Shetld	HU5143	60°10·4′	1°4·4′W	X	4
Hogs Law	Scot Bord	NT5555	55°47·4′	2°42·6′W	H	66,73
Hogsmill River	King	TQ2067	51°23·6′	0°16·1′W	W	176
Hogstaff Spinney	Northnts	SP5655	52°11·7′	1°10·4′W	F	152
Hogsthorpe	Lincs	TF5372	53°13·6′	0°17·9′E	T	122
Hogstock	Dorset	ST9506	50°51·4′	2°3·9′W	T	195
Hogston	Angus	NO5140	56°33·2′	2°47·4′W	X	54
Hogstow	Shrops	SJ3600	52°35·9′	2°56·3′W	X	126
Hogstow Hall	Shrops	SJ3601	52°36·4′	2°56·3′W	X	126
Hogswood Moor	Northum	NY6795	55°15·1′	2°30·7′W	X	80
Hog, The	Orkney	HY3220	59°4·0′	3°10·7′W	X	6
Hog, The	Shetld	HU2885	60°33·1′	1°28·9′W	X	3
Hog, The	Shetld	HU6197	60°39·4′	0°52·5′W	X	1
Hogtrough Hill	Kent	TQ4556	51°17·3′	0°5·2′E	X	188
Hogtrough Wood	Bucks	TQ0090	51°36·2′	0°33·0′W	F	176
Hogue Hall	Leic	SP4590	52°30·6′	1°19·8′W	X	140
Hogus Point	D & G	NX9958	54°54·6′	3°34·1′W	X	84
Hog Walk	E Yorks	SE9165	54°4·6′	0°36·1′W	X	101
Hogwell Fm	Essex	TQ8297	51°38·8′	0°38·2′E	FM	168
Hogwells	Essex	TL7610	51°45·9′	0°33·4′E	X	167
Hog Wood	Kent	TQ5563	51°20·9′	0°13·9′E	F	177,188
Hog Wood	W Susx	TQ0132	51°4·9′	0°33·1′W	F	186
Hogwood Fm	Wok	SU7764	51°22·4′	0°53·2′W	FM	175,186
Hoiliff	Shetld	HZ2072	59°32·3′	1°38·3′W	X	4
Hoini	Shetld	HZ2071	59°31·7′	1°38·3′W	X	4
Hoish	Stir	NS5392	56°6·1′	4°21·4′W	X	57
Hoist Covert	Suff	TM4874	52°18·7′	1°38·7′E	F	156
Hoist Point	Devon	SX6345	50°17·6′	3°55·0′W	X	202
Holasmul	N Eil	NG0691	57°49·0′	6°56·6′W	X	14,18
Holbach Coppice	Heref	SO5548	52°7·9′	2°39·1′W	F	149
Holban's Fm	E Susx	TQ6223	50°59·2′	0°18·9′E	FM	199
Holbeach	Lincs	TF3625	52°48·6′	0°1·5′E	T	131
Holbeach Bank	Lincs	TF3527	52°49·6′	0°0·6′E	T	131
Holbeach Clough	Lincs	TF3427	52°49·7′	0°0·3′W	T	131
Holbeach Drove	Lincs	TF3212	52°41·6′	0°2·4′W	T	131,142
Holbeach Drove Common	Lincs	TF3111	52°41·1′	0°3·3′W	X	131,142
Holbeache	Worcs	SO7879	52°24·8′	2°19·0′W	T	138
Holbeach Fen	Lincs	TF3420	52°45·9′	0°0·4′W	X	131
Holbeach Hurn	Lincs	TF3927	52°49·6′	0°4·2′E	T	131
Holbeach Marsh	Lincs	TF3829	52°50·7′	0°3·4′E	X	131
Holbeach St Johns	Lincs	TF3418	52°44·8′	0°0·5′W	T	131
Holbeach St Marks	Lincs	TF3731	52°51·8′	0°2·5′E	T	131
Holbeach St Matthew	Lincs	TF4132	52°52·2′	0°6·1′E	T	131
Holbeam	Devon	SX8271	50°31·8′	3°39·5′W	X	202
Holbeam	Kent	TQ9754	51°15·3′	0°49·8′E	X	189
Holbeam Wood	E Susx	TQ6630	51°2·9′	0°22·5′E	X	188
Holbeche Ho	Dudley	SO8890	52°30·7′	2°10·2′W	A	139
Holbeck	Cumbr	SD2270	54°7·4′	3°11·2′W	X	96
Holbeck	Leeds	SE2932	53°47·3′	1°33·2′W	T	104
Holbeck	Notts	SK5473	53°15·3′	1°11·0′W	T	120
Holbeck	N Yks	SE6377	54°11·3′	1°1·7′W	W	100
Holbeck Fm	Notts	SK6552	53°3·9′	1°1·4′W	FM	120
Holbeck Fm	Rut	SK8212	52°42·2′	0°46·8′W	FM	130
Holbeck Ghyll	Cumbr	NY3902	54°24·8′	2°56·0′W	X	90
Holbeck Manor	Lincs	TF3172	53°14·0′	0°1·8′W	X	122
Holbecks	Suff	TM0141	52°2·1′	0°56·2′E	X	155
Holbeck Woodhouse	Notts	SK5473	53°15·3′	1°11·0′W	T	120
Holbein's Fm	Cambs	TL2950	52°8·2′	0°6·5′W	FM	153
Holberrow Green	Worcs	SP0259	52°14·0′	1°57·8′W	T	150
Holbeton	Devon	SX6150	50°20·2′	3°56·8′W	T	202
Holborn	Camden	TQ3081	51°31·0′	0°7·2′W	T	176,177
Holborn	Conwy	SJ0066	53°11·1′	3°29·4′W	X	116
Holborn Fm	Cambs	TL2978	52°23·3′	0°5·9′W	FM	142
Holbornhead	Highld	ND1070	58°36·8′	3°32·5′W	X	12
Holborn Head	Highld	ND1071	58°37·3′	3°32·5′W	X	12
Holborn Hill	Highld	ND0971	58°37·3′	3°33·5′W	H	12
Holbornhill Fm	Bucks	SP7820	51°52·6′	0°51·6′W	FM	165
Holborn Hill Plantn	Notts	SK6069	53°13·1′	1°5·7′W	F	120
Holborough	Kent	TQ7062	51°20·1′	0°26·8′E	T	178,188
Holbrook	Derby	SK3644	52°59·8′	1°27·4′W	T	119,128
Holbrook	Kent	TQ7847	51°11·9′	0°33·3′E	X	188
Holbrook	Sheff	SK4481	53°19·7′	1°20·0′W	T	111,120
Holbrook	Suff	TM1636	51°59·0′	1°9·1′E	T	169
Holbrook Bay	Suff	TM1733	51°57·4′	1°9·9′E	W	168,169
Holbrook Common	S Glos	ST6973	51°27·5′	2°26·4′W	T	172
Holbrook Coppice	Wrekin	SJ6505	52°38·7′	2°30·6′W	F	127
Holbrook Creek	Suff	TM1733	51°57·4′	1°9·9′E	W	168,169
Holbrooke Fm	Devon	ST0414	50°55·3′	3°21·6′W	FM	181
Holbrook Fm	Devon	SX9991	50°42·8′	3°25·5′W	FM	192
Holbrook Fm	Herts	TL2822	51°53·1′	0°8·0′W	FM	166
Holbrook Fm	Staffs	SK0641	52°58·2′	1°52·4′W	FM	119,128
Holbrook Fm	Surrey	TQ1638	51°8·0′	0°20·1′W	FM	187
Holbrook Fm	Wilts	ST8862	51°21·6′	2°10·0′W	FM	173
Holbrook Gardens	Suff	TM1736	51°59·0′	1°10·0′E	X	169
Holbrook Grange	Warw	SP4776	52°23·0′	1°18·2′W	X	140
Holbrook Hall	Shrops	SJ5025	52°49·5′	2°44·1′W	X	126
Holbrook Hall	Suff	TL9145	52°4·4′	0°47·6′E	X	155
Holbrook Hill	Norf	TM2886	52°25·7′	1°21·6′E	X	156
Holbrook Ho	E Susx	TQ5720	50°57·7′	0°14·5′E	X	199
Holbrook House Hotel	Somer	ST6928	51°3·3′	2°26·2′W	X	183
Holbrook Lodge	Suff	TM1735	51°58·5′	1°10·0′E	X	169
Holbrook Moor	Derby	SK3645	53°0·3′	1°27·4′W	T	119,128
Holbrook Park	Suff	TM1438	52°0·2′	1°7·5′E	F	169
Holbrook Park	W Susx	TQ1833	51°5·3′	0°18·5′W	X	187
Holbrooks	Cov	SP3383	52°26·9′	1°30·5′W	T	140
Holburn	Northum	NU0436	55°37·3′	1°55·8′W	T	75
Holburn Grange	Northum	NU0434	55°36·2′	1°55·8′W	X	75
Holburn Hill	Oxon	SU3685	51°34·0′	1°28·4′W	X	174
Holburn Mill	Northum	NU0335	55°36·8′	1°56·7′W	X	75
Holburn Moss	Northum	NU0536	55°37·3′	1°54·8′W	X	75
Holburn Wood	Durham	NZ1941	54°46·1′	1°41·9′W	F	88
Holbury	Hants	SU4303	50°49·7′	1°23·0′W	T	196
Holbury Fm	Hants	SU2827	51°2·7′	1°35·6′W	FM	184
Holbury Manor	Hants	SU4203	50°49·7′	1°23·8′W	A	196
Holbury Mill	Hants	SU2927	51°2·7′	1°34·8′W	X	185
Holbury Purlieu	Hants	SU4204	50°50·3′	1°23·8′W	X	196

Holcombe	Bury	SD7816	53°38·6'	2°19·6'W	T	109
Holcombe	Devon	SX7586	50°39·9'	3°45·7'W	X	191
Holcombe	Devon	SX9574	50°33·6'	3°28·6'W	T	192
Holcombe	Devon	SY3193	50°44·2'	2°58·3'W	T	193
Holcombe	Somer	ST6749	51°14·6'	2°28·0'W	T	183
Holcombe Barton	Devon	SY1196	50°45·6'	3°15·3'W	X	192,193
Holcombe Bottom	Dorset	SY6996	50°46·0'	2°26·0'W	X	194
Holcombe Bottom	Dorset	SY7185	50°40·1'	2°24·2'W	X	194
Holcombe Brook	Bury	SD7714	53°37·6'	2°20·5'W	T	109
Holcombe Burnell Barton	Devon	SX8591	50°42·7'	3°37·4'W	X	191
Holcombe Burrows	Devon	SS7544	51°11·1'	3°46·9'W	X	180
Holcombe Court	Devon	ST0519	50°58·0'	3°20·8'W	A	181
Holcombe Dairy	Dorset	ST6803	50°49·8'	2°26·9'W	X	194
Holcombe Down	Devon	SX9375	50°34·1'	3°30·3'W	H	192
Holcombe Fm	Bath & NE Somer	ST7865	51°23·3'	2°18·6'W	FM	172
Holcombe Fm	Glos	SO8511	51°48·1'	2°12·7'W	FM	162
Holcombe Fm	Somer	ST1228	51°2·9'	3°14·9'W	FM	181,193
Holcombe Fm	Somer	ST6541	51°10·3'	2°29·7'W	FM	183
Holcombe Hey Fold Fm	Bury	SD7616	53°38·6'	2°21·4'W	FM	109
Holcombe Ho	Glos	SO8511	51°48·1'	2°12·7'W	X	162
Holcombe Moor	Lancs	SD7618	53°39·7'	2°21·4'W	X	109
Holcombe Rogus	Devon	ST0518	50°57·5'	3°20·8'W	T	181
Holcombe Water Fm	Somer	ST0533	51°5·5'	3°21·0'W	FM	181
Holcomb Nap	Worcs	SO9938	52°2·7'	2°0·5'W	X	150
Holcot	Northnts	SP7969	52°19·0'	0°50·1'W	T	152
Holcotmoors Fm	Beds	SP9440	52°3·3'	0°37·3'W	FM	153
Holcot Wood	Beds	SP9540	52°3·2'	0°36·5'W	F	153
Holcroft Hall	Warr	SJ6795	53°27·3'	2°29·4'W	A	109
Holcroft Moss	Warr	SJ6893	53°26·2'	2°28·5'W	X	109
Holdbrook	Enf	TQ3699	51°40·6'	0°1·6'W	T	166,177
Hold Cauldron	N Yks	SE6686	54°16·2'	0°58·8'W	X	94,100
Holden	Lancs	SD7749	53°56·4'	2°20·6'W	T	103
Holdenby	Northnts	SP6967	52°18·0'	0°58·9'W	T	152
Holdenby Ho Gdns & Falconry Centre	Northnts	SP6967	52°18·0'	0°58·9'W	X	152
Holdenby Mill	Northnts	SP7068	52°18·6'	0°58·0'W	X	152
Holdenby North Lodge	Northnts	SP6968	52°18·6'	0°58·9'W	X	152
Holdenby South Lodge	Northnts	SP7066	52°17·5'	0°58·0'W	X	152
Holden Clough	Derby	SK0792	53°25·7'	1°53·3'W	X	110
Holden Clough	Lancs	SD7749	53°56·4'	2°20·6'W	X	103
Holden Cross	Devon	SX8683	50°38·4'	3°36·4'W	X	191
Holdenfields	Stock on T	NZ4311	54°29·8'	1°19·7'W	X	93
Holden Fm	Hants	SU5626	51°2·1'	1°11·7'W	FM	185
Holden Fm	I of W	SZ5180	50°37·3'	1°16·4'W	FM	196
Holden Fm	Wilts	ST8832	51°5·5'	2°9·9'W	FM	183
Holden Fold	Oldham	SD9106	53°33·6'	2°7·7'W	T	109
Holden Gate	Brad	SE0644	53°53·8'	1°54·1'W	X	104
Holden Gate	Cald	SD8924	53°43·0'	2°9·6'W	X	103
Holdenhurst	Dorset	SZ1295	50°45·5'	1°49·4'W	T	195
Holden Moor	Lancs	SD7658	54°1·3'	2°21·6'W	X	103
Holden Park	Brad	SE0543	53°53·2'	1°55·0'W	X	104
Holdens Fm	Bolton	SD6613	53°37·0'	2°30·4'W	FM	109
Holdens Fm	E Susx	TQ5415	50°55·1'	0°11·8'E	FM	199
Holden's Fm	W Susx	SZ8197	50°46·2'	0°50·7'W	FM	197
Holden's Wood	Essex	TQ5991	51°35·9'	0°18·1'E	F	177
Holden Wood Resr	Lancs	SD7722	53°41·9'	2°20·5'W	W	103
Holderness Drain	E Yorks	TA0741	53°51·5'	0°22·0'W	W	107
Holderness Drain	K upon H	TA1234	53°47·7'	0°17·6'W	W	107
Holder's Fm	Glos	SO7027	51°56·7'	2°25·8'W	FM	162
Holder's Green	Essex	TL6328	51°55·8'	0°22·6'E	T	167
Holders Hill	Barnet	TQ2390	51°36·0'	0°13·1'W	T	176
Holdfast	Surrey	SU9233	51°5·6'	0°40·8'W	X	186
Holdfast	Worcs	SO8537	52°2·1'	2°12·7'W	T	150
Hold Fm	Suff	TL9233	51°58·0'	0°48·1'E	FM	168
Holdforth Fm	Durham	NZ3431	54°40·6'	1°27·9'W	FM	93
Holdgate	Shrops	SO5689	52°30·1'	2°38·5'W	T	137,138
Hold House Fm	Northum	NZ1770	55°1·7'	1°43·6'W	FM	88
Holdhurst Fm	Surrey	TQ0437	51°7·6'	0°30·4'W	FM	186
Holdingham	Lincs	TF0547	53°0·8'	0°25·7'W	T	130
Holdings	Lancs	SD5051	53°57·4'	2°45·3'W	X	102
Holdings, The	Fife	NS9487	56°4·1'	3°41·7'W	X	65
Holditch	Dorset	ST3402	50°49·1'	2°55·8'W	T	193
Holditch Court	Dorset	ST3402	50°49·1'	2°55·8'W	A	193
Holdridge	Devon	SS7329	51°3·0'	3°48·3'W	X	180
Holdron Castle	Lancs	SD6150	53°56·9'	2°35·2'W	X	102,103
Holdron Moss	Lancs	SD6051	53°57·5'	2°36·2'W	X	102,103
Holdrops Hill	Hants	SU5261	51°21·0'	1°14·8'W	X	174
Holdshott Fm	Hants	SU7460	51°20·3'	0°55·9'W	FM	175,186
Holdstone Down	Devon	SS6147	51°12·6'	3°59·0'W	H	180
Holdstone Fm	Devon	SS6147	51°12·6'	3°59·0'W	FM	180
Holdstrong	Devon	SX4885	50°38·9'	4°8·6'W	X	191,201
Holdsworth	Cald	SE0829	53°45·7'	1°52·3'W	T	104
Holdsworth Fm	Durham	NZ0223	54°36·4'	1°57·7'W	FM	92
Holdworth	Sheff	SK2891	53°25·1'	1°34·3'W	T	110
Hole	Angus	NO2664	56°46·0'	3°12·2'W	X	44
Hole	Brad	SE0336	53°49·5'	1°56·9'W	T	104
Hole	Devon	SS3317	50°55·9'	4°22·2'W	T	190
Hole	Devon	SS7309	50°52·2'	3°47·9'W	X	191
Hole	Devon	SX7764	50°28·0'	3°43·6'W	X	202
Hole	Devon	SX8185	50°39·4'	3°40·6'W	X	191
Hole	Devon	SX8653	50°22·2'	3°35·8'W	X	202
Hole	E Dunb	NS6178	55°58·7'	4°13·2'W	X	64
Hole	Northum	NY8684	55°9·3'	2°12·8'W	X	80
Hole	Renf	NS3457	55°46·9'	4°38·4'W	X	63
Hole	S Ayr	NS4019	55°26·6'	4°31·3'W	X	70
Hole	S Lanak	NS5853	55°45·2'	4°15·3'W	X	64
Hole	S Lanak	NS8948	55°43·0'	3°45·6'W	X	72
Hole	Staffs	SK0657	53°6·8'	1°54·2'W	X	119
Hole and Alchorne Fm	E Susx	TQ4327	51°1·7'	0°2·7'E	FM	187,198
Hole Bars		TA3315	53°37·1'	0°1·1'E	W	113
Hole Beach	Corn	SX0487	50°39·2'	4°46·0'W	X	200
Holebeck	Cumbr	NY0315	54°31·5'	3°29·5'W	X	89
Hole Beck	Cumbr	SD2591	54°18·8'	3°8·8'W	X	96
Hole Beck	N Yks	SE7292	54°19·3'	0°53·2'W	W	94,100
Holebeck Ho	Durham	NZ0536	54°43·4'	1°54·9'W	X	92
Holebiggerah	Cumbr	SD2577	54°11·2'	3°8·5'W	X	96
Holebogs	S Ayr	NS4118	55°26·1'	4°30·4'W	X	70
Hole Bottom	Cald	SD9424	53°43·0'	2°5·0'W	T	103
Holebrae	D & G	NS8606	55°20·3'	3°47·4'W	X	71,78

Hole Brook	Devon	SS5804	50°49·3'	4°0·6'W	W	191
Holebrook Fm	Dorset	ST7411	50°54·1'	2°21·8'W	FM	194
Holebrook Fm	Wrex	SJ4638	52°56·4'	2°47·8'W	FM	126
Hole Burn	Angus	NO2663	56°45·4'	3°12·2'W	W	44
Hole Carr	Staffs	SK0565	53°11·2'	1°55·1'W	X	119
Hole Common	Dorset	SY3494	50°44·7'	2°55·7'W	X	193
Holecroft	D & G	NX5252	54°50·7'	4°17·9'W	X	83
Holedean Fm	W Susx	TQ2215	50°55·5'	0°15·5'W	FM	198
Hole End	Staffs	SK1059	53°7·9'	1°50·6'W	X	119
Holefield	Scot Bord	NT8034	55°36·2'	2°18·6'W	T	74
Hole Fm	Brad	SE0247	53°55·4'	1°57·8'W	FM	104
Hole Fm	Ches	SJ8679	53°18·7'	2°12·2'W	FM	118
Hole Fm	Devon	SS3310	50°52·2'	4°22·0'W	FM	190
Hole Fm	Devon	SS4205	50°49·6'	4°14·2'W	FM	190
Hole Fm	Devon	SS5447	51°12·5'	4°5·0'W	FM	180
Hole Fm	Devon	SS6903	50°48·9'	3°51·2'W	FM	191
Hole Fm	Devon	SS7116	50°56·0'	3°49·8'W	FM	180
Hole Fm	Devon	SS8115	50°55·6'	3°41·2'W	FM	181
Hole Fm	Devon	ST0420	50°58·5'	3°21·7'W	FM	181
Hole Fm	Devon	ST1611	50°53·8'	3°11·3'W	FM	192,193
Hole Fm	Devon	SX3994	50°43·6'	4°16·5'W	FM	190
Hole Fm	Devon	SX4564	50°27·6'	4°10·6'W	FM	201
Hole Fm	Devon	SX6151	50°20·8'	3°56·8'W	FM	202
Hole Fm	Devon	SX6886	50°39·8'	3°51·7'W	FM	191
Hole Fm	Devon	SX7393	50°43·6'	3°47·6'W	FM	191
Hole Fm	Essex	TL5025	51°54·4'	0°11·2'E	FM	167
Hole Fm	Essex	TL6334	51°59·1'	0°22·8'E	FM	154
Hole Fm	Essex	TL6936	52°0·0'	0°28·1'E	FM	154
Hole Fm	Essex	TL8017	51°49·6'	0°37·1'E	FM	168
Hole Fm	Essex	TL8338	52°0·8'	0°40·4'E	FM	155
Hole Fm	Essex	TL8417	51°49·5'	0°40·6'E	FM	168
Hole Fm	Essex	TQ5889	51°34·9'	0°17·2'E	FM	177
Hole Fm	E Susx	TQ3719	50°57·5'	0°2·6'W	FM	198
Hole Fm	E Susx	TQ5222	50°58·9'	0°10·3'E	FM	199
Hole Fm	E Susx	TQ6415	50°54·9'	0°20·4'E	FM	199
Hole Fm	E Susx	TQ8113	50°53·5'	0°34·8'E	FM	199
Hole Fm	Hants	SU6314	50°55·5'	1°5·8'W	FM	196
Hole Fm	Herts	TL3722	51°53·0'	0°0·2'W	FM	166
Hole Fm	Herts	TL4226	51°55·1'	0°4·3'E	FM	167
Hole Fm	Norf	TG1135	52°52·5'	1°8·5'E	FM	133
Hole Fm	Shrops	SJ3412	52°42·3'	2°58·2'W	FM	126
Hole Fm	Suff	TL9144	52°3·9'	0°47·6'E	FM	155
Hole Fm	Wilts	SU1827	51°2·8'	1°44·2'W	FM	184
Hole Fm	Worcs	SO7952	52°10·2'	2°18·0'W	FM	150
Holegill	Cumbr	SD1186	54°16·0'	3°21·6'W	X	96
Holego Fm	Warw	SP2646	52°6·9'	1°36·8'W	FM	151
Hole Haven	Thurr	TQ7682	51°30·8'	0°32·6'E	W	178
Holehaven Creek	Thurr	TQ7483	51°31·4'	0°30·9'E	W	178
Holehead	E Dunb	NS6182	56°0·9'	4°13·3'W	H	57,64
Holehills	N Lanak	NS7666	55°52·5'	3°58·5'W	T	64
Holehird	Cumbr	NY4100	54°23·8'	2°54·1'W	X	90
Hole Ho	Ches	SJ6960	53°8·4'	2°27·4'W	X	118
Hole Ho	Ches	SJ7471	53°14·4'	2°23·0'W	X	118
Hole Ho	Cumbr	NY2431	54°40·3'	3°10·3'W	X	89,90
Hole Ho	Cumbr	NY3735	54°42·6'	2°58·2'W	X	90
Hole Ho	Cumbr	NY7538	54°44·4'	2°22·9'W	X	91
Hole Ho	Cumbr	SD1893	54°19·8'	3°15·2'W	X	96
Hole Ho	Cumbr	SD3699	54°23·2'	2°58·7'W	X	96,97
Hole Ho	Cumbr	SD6294	54°20·7'	2°34·7'W	X	97
Hole Ho	Cumbr	SD6893	54°20·1'	2°29·1'W	X	98
Hole Ho	Cumbr	SD6988	54°17·4'	2°28·2'W	X	98
Hole Ho	Cumbr	SD7091	54°19·1'	2°27·3'W	X	98
Hole Ho	Devon	SY1989	50°41·9'	3°8·4'W	X	192
Hole Ho	Durham	NY9539	54°45·0'	2°4·2'W	X	91,92
Hole Ho	Lancs	SD5565	54°5·0'	2°40·9'W	X	97
Hole Ho	Northum	NY6763	54°57·9'	2°30·5'W	X	86,87
Hole Ho	Northum	NY9361	54°56·9'	2°6·1'W	X	87
Hole Ho	N Yks	SE0558	54°1·3'	1°55·0'W	X	104
Holehouse	Derby	SK0092	53°25·7'	1°59·6'W	T	110
Holehouse	D & G	NS8200	55°17·1'	3°51·0'W	X	78
Holehouse	D & G	NX7747	54°48·4'	3°54·4'W	X	84
Holehouse	D & G	NX7969	55°0·3'	3°53·1'W	X	84
Holehouse	D & G	NX9762	54°56·8'	3°36·1'W	X	84
Holehouse	D & G	NX9982	55°7·6'	3°34·6'W	X	78
Holehouse	D & G	NX9994	55°14·0'	3°34·9'W	X	78
Holehouse	E Ayr	NS4047	55°41·7'	4°32·3'W	X	64
Holehouse	E Ayr	NS4113	55°23·4'	4°30·2'W	X	70
Holehouse	E Ayr	NS4113	55°23·4'	4°30·2'W	X	70
Holehouse	E Ayr	NS4919	55°26·8'	4°22·8'W	X	70
Holehouse	E Renf	NS4656	55°46·6'	4°26·9'W	X	64
Holehouse	E Renf	NS5753	55°45·2'	4°16·3'W	X	64
Holehouse	Falk	NS8971	55°55·4'	3°46·1'W	X	65
Holehouse	N Ayr	NS2159	55°47·7'	4°50·9'W	X	63
Holehouse	N Ayr	NS3056	55°46·3'	4°42·2'W	X	63
Holehouse	N Ayr	NS3541	55°38·3'	4°36·9'W	X	70
Hole House Beck	N Yks	SE1449	53°56·5'	1°46·8'W	X	104
Holehouseburn	W Loth	NS9561	55°50·1'	3°40·2'W	X	65
Holehouse Fm	Ches	SJ7462	53°9·5'	2°22·9'W	FM	118
Holehouse Fm	C of Stoke	SJ9149	53°2·5'	2°7·6'W	FM	118
Hole House Fm	Cumbr	NY4725	54°37·3'	2°48·8'W	FM	90
Holehouse Fm	Derby	SK2952	53°4·1'	1°33·6'W	FM	119
Hole House Fm	Durham	NZ1445	54°48·2'	1°46·5'W	FM	88
Holehouse Gill	Cumbr	SD1793	54°19·8'	3°16·2'W	W	96
Holehouse Hill	D & G	NY0194	55°14·1'	3°33·0'W	H	78
Holehouse Junction	E Ayr	NS4013	55°23·3'	4°31·1'W	X	70
Holehousemuir	Falk	NS8670	55°54·8'	3°49·0'W	X	65
Holehouses	Ches	SJ7179	53°18·7'	2°25·7'W	X	118
Hole in the Wall	Derby	SK2145	53°0·4'	1°40·8'W	X	119,128
Hole-in-the Wall	Heref	SO6128	51°57·2'	2°33·7'W	T	149
Hole in the Wall Fm	Cambs	TL4994	52°31·6'	0°12·2'E	FM	143
Holemill	Angus	NO3645	56°35·8'	3°2·1'W	X	54
Holemill	Angus	NO4843	56°34·8'	2°50·3'W	T	54
Holemill	Angus	NO6755	56°41·4'	2°31·9'W	X	54
Holemill	C of Aber	NJ8202	57°6·8'	2°17·4'W	X	38
Hole Mill	Northum	NY8989	55°12·0'	2°9·9'W	X	80
Holemoor	Devon	SS4205	50°49·6'	4°14·2'W	T	190
Holemouth	Northum	NU1341	55°40·0'	1°47·2'W	W	75
Holen Ho	N Yks	SE2454	53°59·1'	1°37·6'W	X	104
Hole o' Clean	Pth & Kin	NO2023	56°23·8'	3°17·3'W	X	53,58
Hole of Bugars	Shetld	HU5136	60°6·6'	1°4·5'W	X	4

Hole of Ellel	Cumbr	SD3677	54°11·3'	2°58·4'W	X	96,97
Hole of Geuda	Shetld	HU2483	60°32·1'	1°33·3'W	X	3
Hole of Hellier	Shetld	HU3062	60°20·7'	1°26·9'W	X	3
Hole of Horcum	N Yks	SE8493	54°19·8'	0°42·1'W	X	94,100
Hole of Lyne	Cumbr	NY5478	55°5·9'	2°42·8'W	X	86
Hole of Oddsta	Shetld	HU5894	60°37·8'	0°55·9'W	X	1,2
Hole of Roe	Orkney	HY5410	58°58·7'	2°47·5'W	W	6
Hole of Row	Orkney	ND3792	58°48·9'	3°5·0'W	W	7
Hole of Ruthven	Angus	NO3049	56°37·9'	3°8·0'W	X	53
Hole o'Row	Orkney	HY2219	59°3·3'	3°21·1'W	X	6
Hole Park	Kent	TQ8332	51°3·7'	0°37·1'E	X	188
Holes Bay	Poole	SZ0091	50°43·3'	1°59·6'W	W	195
Holes Beck Ho	N Yks	SE0462	54°3·5'	1°55·9'W	X	98
Holesfoot	Cumbr	NY6417	54°33·1'	2°33·0'W	X	91
Holeshields	Cumbr	NY4766	54°59·4'	2°49·3'W	X	86
Hole's Hole	Devon	SX4365	50°28·1'	4°12·4'W	T	201
Hole Sike	Cald	SD9435	53°48·9'	2°5·1'W	W	103
Hole Sike	Cumbr	NY6034	54°42·2'	2°36·8'W	W	91
Holeslack Fm	Cumbr	SD4988	54°17·4'	2°46·6'W	FM	97
Holes of Burro	Shetld	HU4624	60°0·2'	1°10·0'W	X	4
Holes of Scraada	Shetld	HU2179	60°29·9'	1°36·6'W	W	3
Holestane	D & G	NX8799	55°16·6'	3°46·3'W	X	78
Hole Stock Bridge	Devon	SS4800	50°47·0'	4°9·0'W	X	191
Holestone	Derby	SK3361	53°8·9'	1°30·0'W	T	119
Hole Stone	D & G	NX3655	54°52·0'	4°32·9'W	A	83
Hole Stone	D & G	NX7286	55°9·4'	4°0·1'W	A	77
Hole Stone Bay	D & G	NX0646	54°46·5'	5°0·6'W	W	82
Hole Street	W Susx	TQ1414	50°55·1'	0°22·3'W	T	198
Holestrow	Corn	SW6912	49°58·0'	5°12·9'W	X	203
Hole, The	I of M	SC2666	54°3·9'	4°39·1'W	W	95
Hole Trough	N Yks	SE2272	54°8·8'	1°39·4'W	X	99
Holewater	Devon	SS7035	51°6·2'	3°51·0'W	T	180
Holewell Fm	Devon	SX5471	50°31·5'	4°3·2'W	FM	201
Hole Wood	E Susx	TQ5223	50°59·4'	0°10·3'E	F	199
Holey Kame	Shetld	HP6215	60°49·0'	0°51·1'W	X	1
Holey Moor	N Yks	NZ5101	54°24·4'	1°12·4'W	X	93
Holeyn Hall	Northum	NZ1066	54°59·6'	1°50·2'W	X	88
Holfield Grange	Essex	TL8323	51°52·8'	0°39·9'E	X	168
Holford	Somer	ST1541	51°10·0'	3°12·6'W	T	181
Holford Combe	Somer	ST1540	51°9·4'	3°12·5'W	X	181
Holford Fm	Ches	SJ8261	53°9·0'	2°15·7'W	FM	118
Holford Hall	Ches	SJ7075	53°16·5'	2°26·6'W	A	118
Holford Manor	E Susx	TQ3621	50°58·6'	0°3·4'W	X	198
Holford Moss	Ches	SJ7174	53°16·0'	2°25·7'W	F	118
Holgan	Pemb	SN0717	51°49·3'	4°47·6'W	X	158
Holgate	N Yks	NZ0603	54°25·6'	1°54·0'W	X	92
Holgate	York	SE5851	53°57·4'	1°6·6'W	T	105
Holgate Fm	Heref	SO4561	52°14·9'	2°47·9'W	FM	137,138,148
Holgate Head	N Yks	SD8960	54°2·4'	2°9·7'W	X	98
Holgate Moor	N Yks	NZ0605	54°26·7'	1°54·0'W	X	92
Holgate Pasture	N Yks	NZ0704	54°26·1'	1°53·1'W	X	92
Holgates Kilnsey Moor	N Yks	SD9566	54°5·6'	2°4·2'W	X	98
Holiday Fm	Suff	TM0278	52°22·0'	0°58·4'E	FM	144
Holiday House Fm	N Yks	SE5199	54°23·3'	1°12·5'W	FM	100
Holiday Moss	St Hel	SD4901	53°30·4'	2°45·7'W	X	108
Holidays Hill Inclosure	Hants	SU2607	50°51·9'	1°37·4'W	F	195
Holin	Orkney	HY6625	59°6·9'	2°35·1'W	X	5
Holiskeir	N Eil	NF6969	57°35·6'	7°32·0'W	X	18
Holker	Cumbr	SD3677	54°11·3'	2°58·4'W	T	96,97
Holker Hall	Cumbr	SD3577	54°11·3'	2°59·4'W	X	96,97
Holker Park	Cumbr	SD3577	54°11·3'	2°59·4'W	X	96,97
Holkham	Norf	TF8943	52°57·3'	0°49·2'E	T	132
Holkham Bay		TF8746	52°58·9'	0°47·5'E	W	132
Holkham Gap	Norf	TF8945	52°58·4'	0°49·3'E	X	132
Holkham Hall	Norf	TF8842	52°56·8'	0°48·3'E	X	132
Holkham Meals	Norf	TF8945	52°58·4'	0°49·3'E	X	132
Holkham Park	Norf	TF8842	52°56·8'	0°48·3'E	X	132
Holl	Moray	NJ3450	57°32·4'	3°5·7'W	X	28
Hollacombe	Devon	SS3703	50°48·5'	4°18·4'W	T	190
Hollacombe	Devon	SS6443	51°10·4'	3°56·3'W	X	180
Hollacombe	Devon	SS8000	50°47·5'	3°41·8'W	T	191
Hollacombe Cross	Devon	SS7900	50°47·5'	3°42·6'W	X	191
Hollacombe Hill	Devon	SX5250	50°20·1'	4°4·4'W	T	201
Holladon Fm	Devon	SS3003	50°48·3'	4°24·4'W	FM	190
Holladyke	Moray	NJ4652	57°33·6'	2°53·7'W	X	28,29
Hollafrench	Corn	SX3199	50°46·2'	4°23·4'W	X	190
Hollam	Devon	SS5016	50°55·7'	4°7·4'W	X	180
Hollam	Somer	SS9128	51°2·7'	3°32·9'W	X	181
Hollam Fm	Somer	SS9132	51°4·9'	3°33·0'W	FM	181
Hollamoor	Corn	SS2412	50°53·1'	4°29·8'W	X	190
Hollamoor	Devon	SS4316	50°55·6'	4°13·7'W	X	180,190
Hollamoor Clump	Devon	SS5430	51°3·3'	4°4·6'W	F	180
Hollamore Fm	Devon	SS5429	51°2·7'	4°4·6'W	FM	180
Holland	Devon	SX3980	50°36·1'	4°16·1'W	X	201
Holland	Orkney	HY3615	59°1·3'	3°6·4'W	X	6
Holland	Orkney	HY4811	58°59·2'	2°53·8'W	X	6
Holland	Orkney	HY4851	59°20·8'	2°54·4'W	T	5
Holland	Orkney	HY5236	59°12·7'	2°50·0'W	X	5
Holland	Orkney	HY5310	58°58·7'	2°48·6'W	X	6
Holland	Orkney	HY5504	58°55·5'	2°46·4'W	X	6
Holland	Orkney	HY6136	59°12·8'	2°40·5'W	X	5
Holland	Orkney	HY6622	59°5·3'	2°35·1'W	X	5
Holland	Orkney	HY7553	59°22·0'	2°25·9'W	X	5
Holland	Surrey	TQ4050	51°14·1'	0°0·7'E	T	187
Holland Brook	Essex	TM1226	51°53·8'	1°5·3'E	W	168,169
Hollanden Ho	Kent	TQ5649	51°13·4'	0°14·4'E	X	188
Hollanders Graves	Shetld	HU2980	60°30·4'	1°27·8'W	X	1,3
Hollanders Knowe	Shetld	HU4339	60°8·3'	1°13·1'W	X	4
Holland Fen	Lincs	TF2349	53°1·7'	0°9·5'W	T	131
Holland Fen	Lincs	TF2447	53°0·6'	0°8·7'W	X	131
Holland Fm	Devon	SS7215	50°55·5'	3°48·9'W	FM	180
Holland Fm	Somer	ST7335	51°7·1'	2°22·8'W	FM	183
Holland Gap	Essex	TM2318	51°49·2'	1°14·5'E	X	169
Holland Hall	Cambs	TL3642	52°3·8'	0°0·6'W	X	154
Holland Hall	Durham	NZ2036	54°43·4'	1°40·9'W	X	93
Holland Haven	Essex	TM2117	51°48·7'	1°12·8'E	X	169
Holland Ho	E Yorks	SE7425	53°43·2'	0°52·3'W	X	105,106
Holland Ho	Lincs	TF3015	52°43·3'	0°4·1'W	X	131
Holland Ho	Lincs	TF4019	52°45·3'	0°4·9'E	X	131
Hollandhurst	N Lanak	NS7266	55°52·5'	4°2·3'W	X	64

Holland Isle	D & G	NX6669	55°0·1′	4°5·3′W	X	83,84
Holland Lees	Lancs	SD5108	53°34·2′	2°44·0′W	T	108
Hollandmake	Highld	ND2669	58°36·4′	3°15·9′W	X	12
Hollandmey	Highld	ND2970	58°37·0′	3°12·9′W	X	7,12
Hollandmey Moss	Highld	ND2870	58°37·0′	3°13·9′W	X	7,12
Holland Moss	Lancs	SD4803	53°31·5′	2°46·7′W	X	108
Holland-on-Sea	Essex	TM2016	51°48·2′	1°11·9′E	T	169
Holland Park	King	TQ2479	51°30·0′	0°12·4′W	X	176
Holland Park	Wals	SK0406	52°39·3′	1°56·1′W	X	139
Hollandridge Fm	Oxon	SU7291	51°37·0′	0°57·2′W	FM	175
Holland Road Fms	Lincs	TF1036	52°54·8′	0°21·4′W	FM	130
Hollands	Cumbr	NY4575	55°4·2′	2°51·3′W	X	86
Hollands	D & G	NY0465	54°58·5′	3°29·6′W	X	84
Hollands	Somer	ST5517	50°57·3′	2°38·1′W	T	183
Hollands Fm	Sefton	SD3505	53°32·5′	2°58·4′W	FM	108
Holland's Green	Norf	TM2991	52°28·4′	1°22·7′E	X	134
Holland's Hall	Norf	TG0209	52°38·7′	0°59·6′E	X	144
Holland's Heath Fm	W Susx	TQ0228	51°2·8′	0°32·3′W	FM	186,197
Hollands Hill	Norf	TG0908	52°38·0′	1°5·7′E	X	144
Hollandstide Ho	Oxon	SU6395	51°39·2′	1°5·0′W	X	164,165
Hollandstoun	Orkney	HY7553	59°22·0′	2°25·9′W	T	5
Hollands Wood	Hants	SU3004	50°50·3′	1°34·1′W	F	196
Holland's Wood	Norf	TM0582	52°24·1′	1°1·2′E	F	144
Hollandtide Bottom	Oxon	SU6394	51°38·7′	1°5·0′W	X	164,175
Holland Wood	Cambs	TL2378	52°23·4′	0°11·1′W	F	142
Holland Wood	W Susx	SU9825	51°1·2′	0°35·8′W	F	186,197
Holland's Fm	Lincs	TF3510	52°40·5′	0°0·2′E	FM	131,142
Hollee	D & G	NY2769	55°0·9′	3°8·1′W	T	85
Hollens Fm	Cumbr	NY3407	54°27·5′	3°0·7′W	FM	90
Hollerday Hill	Devon	SS7149	51°13·8′	3°50·5′W	H	180
Hollesley	Suff	TM3544	52°2·9′	1°26·0′E	T	169
Hollesley Bay	Suff	TM3944	52°2·8′	1°29·5′E	W	169
Hollesley Bay Colony (HM Young Offender Institution)	Suff	TM3644	52°2·9′	1°26·9′E	X	169
Hollesley Fm	Surrey	TQ3244	51°11·0′	0°6·3′W	FM	187
Hollesley Heath	Suff	TM3546	52°4·0′	1°26·1′E	X	169
Holley Ho	Norf	TF5909	52°39·6′	0°21·5′E	X	143
Hollicarrs Wood	N Yks	SE6339	53°50·8′	1°2·1′W	F	105,106
Hollick Fm	Devon	SS5625	51°0·6′	4°2·8′W	FM	180
Hollicombe	Torbay	SX8962	50°27·1′	3°33·4′W	T	202
Hollies Common	Staffs	SJ8221	52°47·4′	2°15·6′W	T	127
Hollies Fm	Ches	SJ6680	53°19·2′	2°30·2′W	FM	109
Hollies Fm	Lincs	TF2610	52°40·6′	0°7·8′W	FM	131,142
Hollies Fm	Norf	TM2193	52°29·6′	1°15·7′E	FM	134
Hollies Fm	Shrops	SO4891	52°31·1′	2°45·6′W	FM	137,138
Hollies Fm	Worcs	SO8078	52°24·2′	2°17·2′W	FM	138
Hollies Fm	Worcs	SO9680	52°25·3′	2°3·1′W	FM	139
Hollies Hill	Worcs	SO9277	52°23·7′	2°6·7′W	X	139
Hollies Ho	Northum	NY9960	54°56·3′	2°0·5′W	X	87
Hollies, The	Cered	SN6664	52°15·7′	3°57·4′W	X	146
Hollies, The	Derby	SK1744	52°59·8′	1°44·4′W	X	119,128
Hollies, The	Lincs	TF2623	52°47·6′	0°7·5′W	X	131
Hollies, The	Lincs	TF4963	53°8·8′	0°14·1′E	X	122
Hollies, The	Notts	SK8252	53°3·8′	0°46·2′W	T	121
Hollies, The	N Yks	SE3759	54°1·8′	1°25·7′W	X	104
Hollies, The	Powys	SJ2514	52°43·3′	3°6·2′W	X	126
Hollies, The	Shrops	SJ3801	52°36·4′	2°54·5′W	X	126
Hollies, The	Shrops	SJ4728	52°51·1′	2°46·8′W	X	126
Hollies, The	Shrops	SJ4902	52°37·0′	2°44·8′W	X	126
Hollies, The	Shrops	SO3293	52°32·1′	2°59·8′W	X	137
Hollies, The	Shrops	SO3799	52°35·3′	2°55·4′W	X	137
Hollies, The	Shrops	SO3880	52°25·1′	2°54·3′W	X	137
Hollies, The	Staffs	SJ9752	53°4·2′	2°2·3′W	X	118
Hollies, The	Staffs	SO8085	52°28·0′	2°17·3′W	X	138
Hollies, The	Staffs	SO8399	52°35·6′	2°14·7′W	X	138
Holligarth	Shetld	HU4269	60°24·4′	1°13·8′W	X	2,3
Holligarth	Shetld	HU5283	60°31·9′	1°2·6′W	X	1,2,3
Hollin Bank Fm	Cumbr	SD3298	54°22·6′	3°2·4′W	FM	96,97
Hollin Bower	N Yks	SE5793	54°20·0′	1°7·0′W	X	100
Hollin Brown Knoll	Oldham	SE0306	53°33·3′	1°56·9′W	X	110
Hollin Bush Fm	N Yks	SE6999	54°23·1′	0°55·8′W	FM	94,100
Hollin Clough	Cumbr	NY5380	55°7·0′	2°43·8′W	X	79
Hollin Close	Northum	NY8252	54°52·0′	2°16·4′W	X	86,87
Hollin Crag	Cumbr	NY2903	54°25·3′	3°5·2′W	X	89,90
Hollin Crags	Northum	NY7164	54°58·4′	2°26·8′W	X	86,87
Hollin Edge Height	Sheff	SK2896	53°27·8′	1°34·3′W	X	110
Hollinfare	Warr	SJ6990	53°24·6′	2°27·6′W	T	109
Hollin Fm	N Yks	SE2195	54°21·2′	1°40·2′W	FM	99
Hollin Fms	Worcs	SO7270	52°19·9′	2°24·3′W	FM	138
Hollin Garth	N Yks	NZ8202	54°24·6′	0°43·8′W	X	94
Hollingbourne	Kent	TQ8455	51°16·1′	0°38·7′E	T	178,188
Hollingbourne Ho	Kent	TQ8555	51°16·1′	0°39·5′E	X	178
Hollingbury	Bri & Hov	TQ3108	50°51·6′	0°7·9′W	T	198
Hollingbury Castle	Bri & Hov	TQ3207	50°51·1′	0°7·1′W	X	198
Hollingbury Castle (Fort)	Bri & Hov	TQ3207	50°51·1′	0°7·1′W	A	198
Hollingbury Court	W Susx	TQ2526	51°1·4′	0°12·7′W	X	187,198
Holling Dale	Sheff	SK2192	53°25·7′	1°40·6′W	X	110
Holling Dale Plantation	Sheff	SK2191	53°25·2′	1°40·6′W	F	110
Hollingdean	Bri & Hov	TQ3106	50°50·5′	0°8·0′W	T	198
Hollingdon	Bucks	SP8727	51°56·3′	0°43·7′W	T	165
Hollingee	Ches	SJ8180	53°19·2′	2°16·7′W	X	109
Holling Fms	Worcs	SO7558	52°13·4′	2°21·6′W	FM	150
Holling Grange Dingle	Heref	SO3631	51°58·7′	2°55·5′W	X	149,161
Holling Hill	Northum	NZ0696	55°15·7′	1°53·9′W	X	81
Hollinghurst	Derby	SK2845	53°0·3′	1°34·6′W	X	119,128
Hollin Gill	N Yks	NZ9100	54°23·5′	0°35·5′W	W	94
Hollingley Fm	N Yks	SE1250	53°57·0′	1°48·6′W	FM	104
Hollingley Intake	N Yks	SE1351	53°57·5′	1°47·7′W	X	104
Hollingreave Fm	Warr	SJ6891	53°25·1′	2°28·5′W	FM	109
Hollin Green	Ches	SJ5952	53°4·1′	2°36·3′W	X	117
Hollin Green	Ches	SJ6345	53°0·3′	2°32·7′W	X	118
Hollingreen	Northum	NY8055	54°53·6′	2°18·3′W	X	86,87
Hollingrove	E Susx	TQ6920	50°57·5′	0°24·8′E	T	199
Hollings	Brad	SE0237	53°50·0′	1°57·8′W	X	104
Hollings	Northum	NZ0857	54°54·7′	1°52·1′W	X	88
Hollings Hall	Brad	SE1740	53°51·6′	1°44·1′W	X	104
Hollingshead Fm	Worcs	SO8063	52°16·1′	2°17·2′W	FM	138,150
Hollings Hill	Northum	NZ0957	54°54·7′	1°51·2′W	X	88
Hollingthorpe	Wakf	SE3115	53°38·1′	1°31·5′W	T	110,111

Hollington	Beds	TL0636	52°1·0′	0°26·9′W	X	153
Hollington	Derby	SK2239	52°57·1′	1°39·9′W	T	128
Hollington	E Susx	TQ7911	50°52·5′	0°33·0′E	T	199
Hollington	Hants	SU4259	51°19·9′	1°23·4′W	T	174
Hollington	Staffs	SK0539	52°57·1′	1°55·1′W	T	128
Hollington Cross	Hants	SU4358	51°19·4′	1°22·6′W	T	174
Hollington Fm	Heref	SO5633	51°59·9′	2°38·1′W	FM	149
Hollington Grove	Derby	SK2238	52°56·6′	1°40·0′W	T	128
Hollington Ho	Hants	SU4260	51°20·5′	1°23·4′W	X	174
Hollington Wood	Mil Key	SP8948	52°7·6′	0°41·6′W	F	152
Hollingwood	Derby	SK4174	53°15·9′	1°22·7′W	T	120
Hollingwood Fm	Heref	SO3731	51°58·7′	2°54·6′W	FM	149,161
Hollingworth	Tames	SK0096	53°27·9′	1°59·6′W	T	110
Hollingworth Clough	Derby	SK0489	53°24·1′	1°56·0′W	X	110
Hollingworthhall Moor	Tames	SJ9998	53°29·0′	2°0·5′W	X	109
Hollingworth Lake Country Park	Roch	SD9314	53°37·6′	2°5·9′W	X	109
Hollin Hall	Cumbr	SD3081	54°13·4′	3°4·0′W	X	96,97
Hollin Hall	Cumbr	SD4696	54°21·6′	2°49·4′W	X	97
Hollin Hall	Cumbr	SD5879	54°12·5′	2°38·2′W	X	97
Hollin Hall	Durham	NZ1718	54°33·7′	1°43·8′W	X	92
Hollin Hall	Lancs	SD7134	53°48·3′	2°26·0′W	X	103
Hollin Hall	Lancs	SD9138	53°50·5′	2°7·8′W	T	103
Hollin Hall	Leeds	SE3343	53°53·2′	1°29·5′W	X	104
Hollin Hall	N Yks	NZ7405	54°26·3′	0°51·1′W	X	94
Hollin Hall	N Yks	SD7960	54°2·4′	2°18·8′W	X	98
Hollin Hall	N Yks	SE3167	54°6·1′	1°31·1′W	X	99
Hollinhall	Staffs	SJ9563	53°10·1′	2°4·1′W	X	118
Hollin Head Wood	N Yks	SE2773	54°9·4′	1°34·8′W	F	99
Hollin Hill	Cald	SE0331	53°46·8′	1°56·9′W	X	104
Hollin Hill	Cumbr	SD6792	54°19·6′	2°30·0′W	X	98
Hollin Hill	Derby	SK5175	53°16·4′	1°13·7′W	X	120
Hollin Hill	Durham	NZ0623	54°36·4′	1°54·0′W	X	92
Hollin Hill	N Yks	NZ4900	54°23·8′	1°14·3′W	X	93
Hollin Hill	N Yks	SE1271	54°8·3′	1°48·6′W	X	99
Hollin Hill Fm	Ghead	NZ1759	54°55·8′	1°43·7′W	FM	88
Hollin Hill Fm	N Yks	SE2368	54°6·7′	1°38·5′W	FM	99
Hollin Hill Fm	N Yks	SE5664	54°4·4′	1°8·2′W	FM	100
Hollin Hill Wood	Red & Cl	NZ6419	54°34·0′	1°0·2′W	F	94
Hollin Ho	Staffs	SJ9154	53°5·2′	2°7·7′W	X	118
Hollin House Fm	Lancs	SD3805	53°32·5′	2°55·7′W	FM	108
Hollin House Fm	N Yks	NZ8000	54°23·6′	0°45·7′W	FM	94
Hollin House Tongue	Cumbr	SD2296	54°21·5′	3°11·6′W	H	96
Hollinhurst	D & G	NY3975	55°4·2′	2°56·9′W	X	85
Hollinhurst	Staffs	SJ9453	53°4·7′	2°5·0′W	X	118
Hollinhurst	Wakf	SE2816	53°38·6′	1°34·2′W	X	110
Hollinknoll	Derby	SK0679	53°18·7′	1°54·2′W	X	119
Hollinlane Fm	Ches	SJ6145	53°0·3′	2°34·5′W	FM	118
Hollinlea	D & G	NY2166	54°59·2′	3°13·6′W	X	85
Hollin Park	Brad	SE0734	53°48·4′	1°53·2′W	X	104
Hollin Park	Leeds	SE3336	53°49·4′	1°29·5′W	T	104
Hollin Root	Cumbr	NY2949	54°50·1′	3°5·9′W	X	85
Hollin Root	Cumbr	NY3023	54°36·1′	3°4·6′W	X	90
Hollins	Bolton	SD7005	53°32·7′	2°26·8′W	T	109
Hollins	Bury	SD8108	53°34·3′	2°16·8′W	T	109
Hollins	Cumbr	NY0716	54°32·1′	3°25·8′W	X	89
Hollins	Cumbr	NY0719	54°33·7′	3°25·9′W	X	89
Hollins	Cumbr	NY0927	54°38·0′	3°24·2′W	X	89
Hollins	Cumbr	NY1003	54°25·1′	3°22·8′W	X	89
Hollins	Cumbr	NY1522	54°35·4′	3°18·5′W	X	89
Hollins	Cumbr	NY1701	54°24·1′	3°16·3′W	X	89,90
Hollins	Cumbr	SD4189	54°17·8′	2°54·0′W	X	96,97
Hollins	Cumbr	SD5095	54°21·1′	2°45·7′W	X	97
Hollins	Cumbr	SD5482	54°14·1′	2°41·9′W	X	97
Hollins	Cumbr	SD5795	54°21·2′	2°39·3′W	X	97
Hollins	Cumbr	SD6388	54°17·4′	2°33·7′W	X	97
Hollins	Cumbr	SD6791	54°19·1′	2°30·0′W	T	98
Hollins	Derby	SK1384	53°21·4′	1°47·9′W	X	110
Hollins	Derby	SK3271	53°14·3′	1°30·8′W	T	119
Hollins	Lancs	SD8632	53°47·3′	2°12·3′W	X	103
Hollins	N Yks	NZ8004	54°25·7′	0°45·6′W	X	94
Hollins	Roch	SD8707	53°33·8′	2°11·4′W	T	109
Hollins	Staffs	SJ8253	53°4·7′	2°15·7′W	T	118
Hollins	Staffs	SJ9257	53°6·8′	2°6·8′W	T	118
Hollins	Staffs	SJ9947	53°1·5′	2°0·5′W	T	118
Hollins Clough	Derby	SK0598	53°29·0′	1°55·1′W	X	110
Hollinsclough	Staffs	SK0666	53°11·7′	1°54·2′W	T	119
Hollinsclough Moor	Staffs	SK0566	53°11·7′	1°55·1′W	X	119
Hollins Cross	Derby	SK1384	53°21·4′	1°47·9′W	X	110
Hollins End	Sheff	SK3984	53°21·3′	1°24·4′W	T	110,111
Hollins Fm	Ches	SJ7668	53°12·8′	2°21·2′W	FM	118
Hollins Fm	Derby	SK0088	53°23·6′	1°59·6′W	FM	110
Hollins Fm	Derby	SK0667	53°12·2′	1°54·2′W	FM	119
Hollins Fm	Derby	SK3556	53°6·2′	1°28·2′W	FM	119
Hollins Fm	Donc	SE5012	53°36·4′	1°14·2′W	FM	111
Hollins Fm	Lancs	SD7536	53°49·4′	2°22·4′W	FM	103
Hollins Fm	Lancs	SD8035	53°48·9′	2°17·8′W	FM	103
Hollins Fm	Lancs	SD8145	53°54·3′	2°16·9′W	FM	103
Hollins Fm	N Yks	NZ4303	54°25·5′	1°19·8′W	FM	93
Hollins Fm	N Yks	NZ6705	54°26·4′	0°57·6′W	FM	94
Hollins Fm	N Yks	NZ7408	54°28·0′	0°51·1′W	FM	94
Hollins Fm	N Yks	SE0999	54°23·4′	1°51·3′W	FM	99
Hollins Fm	N Yks	SE1587	54°16·9′	1°45·8′W	FM	99
Hollins Fm	N Yks	SE2785	54°15·8′	1°34·7′W	FM	99
Hollins Fm	N Yks	SE4061	54°2·8′	1°22·9′W	FM	99
Hollins Fm	N Yks	SE4393	54°20·1′	1°19·9′W	FM	99
Hollins Fm	N Yks	SE5721	53°41·2′	1°7·8′W	FM	105
Hollins Fm	N Yks	SE6698	54°22·6′	0°58·6′W	FM	94,100
Hollins Fm	N Yks	SE7394	54°20·4′	0°52·2′W	FM	94,100
Hollins Fm	Staffs	SJ7949	53°2·5′	2°18·4′W	FM	118
Hollinsgreen	Ches	SJ7363	53°10·0′	2°23·8′W	T	118
Hollins Green	Derby	SK3763	53°10·0′	1°26·4′W	X	119
Hollins Green	Warr	SJ6990	53°24·6′	2°27·6′W	T	109
Hollins Grove	N Yks	SE5468	54°6·5′	1°10·0′W	X	100
Hollin's Hall	Herts	TL0100	51°41·6′	0°31·9′W	X	166
Hollins Hill	Derby	SK0667	53°12·2′	1°54·2′W	X	119
Hollins Ho	Lancs	SD7155	53°59·7′	2°26·1′W	X	103
Hollins Ho	Lancs	SD8646	53°54·8′	2°12·4′W	X	103
Hollins Ho	N Yks	SE0289	54°18·0′	1°57·7′W	X	98
Hollinside	Durham	NZ1546	54°48·8′	1°45·6′W	X	88

Hollin Side Wood	Durham	NZ0322	54°35·8′	1°56·8′W	F	92
Hollins Lane	Lancs	SD4951	53°57·4′	2°46·2′W	T	102
Hollins Lane	Shrops	SJ5337	52°55·9′	2°41·6′W	T	126
Hollins, The	Brad	SE0443	53°53·2′	1°55·9′W	X	104
Hollins, The	Ches	SJ9167	53°12·2′	2°7·7′W	X	118
Hollins, The	Ches	SJ9272	53°14·9′	2°6·8′W	X	118
Hollins, The	Shrops	SJ4621	52°47·3′	2°47·6′W	X	126
Hollins, The	Shrops	SO5873	52°21·4′	2°36·6′W	X	137,138
Hollinstone	Cumbr	NY4960	54°56·2′	2°47·3′W	X	86
Hollins View	Cumbr	NY8013	54°31·0′	2°18·1′W	X	91,92
Hollins Wood	Cumbr	NY0625	54°36·9′	3°26·9′W	F	89
Hollins Wood	N Yks	SE5783	54°14·6′	1°7·1′W	F	100
Hollinswood	Wrekin	SJ7009	52°40·9′	2°26·2′W	T	127
Hollinswood Fm	Ches	SJ7363	53°10·0′	2°23·8′W	FM	118
Hollinthorpe	Leeds	SE3831	53°46·7′	1°25·0′W	T	104
Hollin Top	Lancs	SD8341	53°52·1′	2°15·1′W	X	103
Hollin Wood	N Yks	SD9755	53°59·7′	2°2·3′W	F	103
Hollinwood	Oldham	SD9002	53°31·1′	2°8·6′W	T	109
Hollinwood	Shrops	SJ5236	52°55·4′	2°42·4′W	T	126
Hollinwood Fm	Derby	SK4677	53°17·5′	1°18·2′W	FM	120
Hollinwood Ho	Notts	SK5949	53°2·3′	1°6·8′W	X	129
Hollinworth Head Fm	Derby	SK0390	53°24·6′	1°56·9′W	FM	110
Hollis Green	Devon	ST0808	50°52·1′	3°18·1′W	T	192
Hollis Head	Devon	SS9900	50°47·7′	3°25·6′W	T	192
Hollis Hill	Dorset	ST4402	50°49·1′	2°47·3′W	H	193
Hollis Street Fm	E Susx	TQ7111	50°52·6′	0°26·2′E	FM	199
Hollist Common	W Susx	SU8724	51°0·8′	0°45·2′W	F	197
Hollister Fm	Surrey	TQ0749	51°14·0′	0°27·7′W	FM	187
Holliwell Fm	Essex	TR0096	51°37·9′	0°53·8′E	FM	168
Holliwell Point	Essex	TR0296	51°37·8′	0°55·5′E	X	168
Hollocombe	Devon	SS6311	50°53·2′	3°56·5′W	T	191
Hollocombe Moor	Devon	SS6012	50°53·7′	3°59·1′W	X	180
Hollocombe Town	Devon	SS6211	50°53·2′	3°57·3′W	T	191
Holloford Fm	Devon	SS2823	50°59·1′	4°26·7′W	FM	190
Hollom Down Fm	Hants	SU2635	51°7·1′	1°37·3′W	FM	184
Hollonds, The	Kent	TQ5438	51°7·5′	0°12·4′E	X	188
Hollorin	Shetld	HU2756	60°17·5′	1°30·2′W	X	3
Holloway	Derby	SK3256	53°6·3′	1°30·9′W	T	119
Holloway	Pemb	SN0822	51°52·1′	4°46·9′W	X	145,158
Holloway	Shrops	SJ5528	52°51·1′	2°39·7′W	X	126
Holloway	Wilts	ST8730	51°4·4′	2°10·7′W	T	183
Holloway	Win & Maid	SU8480	51°31·0′	0°47·0′W	T	175
Holloway Barton	Devon	SX8985	50°39·5′	3°33·8′W	X	192
Holloway Fm	Oxon	SP6204	51°44·1′	1°5·7′W	FM	164,165
Holloway Fm	Shrops	SO5389	52°30·1′	2°41·1′W	FM	137,138
Holloway Fm	Staffs	SJ7640	52°57·6′	2°21·0′W	FM	118
Holloway Fm	Warw	SP2759	52°13·9′	1°35·9′W	FM	151
Holloway Hill	Surrey	SU9742	51°10·4′	0°36·4′W	T	186
Holloway Rocks	Shrops	SO3174	52°21·8′	3°0·4′W	X	137,148
Holloway's Fm	Cambs	TL3598	52°34·0′	0°0·1′W	FM	142
Holloway Spinney	Leic	SP6790	52°30·5′	1°0·4′W	F	141
Hollow Brook	Bath & NE Somer	ST5860	51°20·5′	2°35·8′W	T	172,182
Hollow Brook	Devon	SS6649	51°13·7′	3°54·8′W	W	180
Hollowcombe	Devon	SS5333	51°4·9′	4°5·5′W	X	180
Hollowcombe	Somer	SS8530	51°3·7′	3°38·1′W	X	181
Hollowcombe Fm	Devon	SX6252	50°21·3′	3°56·0′W	FM	202
Hollowcombe Head	Devon	SX8138	50°14·0′	3°39·7′W	X	202
Hollow Court	Worcs	SO9758	52°13·4′	2°2·2′W	X	150
Hollowcowhey Fm	Ches	SJ9877	53°17·6′	2°1·4′W	FM	118
Hollowdub	Pth & Kin	NO1623	56°23·8′	3°21·2′W	X	53,58
Hollowdyke	Aberd	NJ4745	57°29·8′	2°52·6′W	X	28,29
Hollowell	Northnts	SP6871	52°20·2′	0°59·7′W	T	141
Hollowell Grange	Northnts	SP6972	52°20·7′	0°58·8′W	X	141
Hollowell Resr	Northnts	SP6873	52°21·3′	0°59·7′W	W	141
Hollowells	Somer	ST3707	50°51·8′	2°53·3′W	X	193
Hollowfields Fms	Worcs	SO9761	52°15·1′	2°2·2′W	FM	150
Hollow Fm	Cambs	TL2262	52°14·8′	0°12·4′W	FM	153
Hollow Fm	Derby	SK2163	53°10·1′	1°40·7′W	FM	119
Hollow Fm	Glos	SO7814	51°49·7′	2°18·8′W	FM	162
Hollow Fm	Leic	SK4007	52°39·8′	1°24·1′W	FM	140
Hollow Fm	Warw	SP3894	52°32·8′	1°26·0′W	FM	140
Hollow Fm, The	Heref	SO5336	52°1·5′	2°40·7′W	FM	149
Hollowforth	Lancs	SD5036	53°49·3′	2°45·2′W	X	102
Hollow Fosse Fm	Glos	SP0507	51°45·9′	1°55·3′W	FM	163
Hollowgate	Cumbr	NY5403	54°25·5′	2°42·1′W	X	90
Hollow Gill Wood	N Yks	SD8058	54°1·3′	2°17·9′W	F	103
Hollow Heap Fm	Cambs	TL3185	52°27·1′	0°3·9′W	FM	142
Hollow Heath	Norf	TL8198	52°33·2′	0°40·6′E	X	144
Hollow Hedge	Herts	TL0201	51°42·1′	0°31·0′W	X	166
Hollow Marsh	Bath & NE Somer	ST6156	51°18·3′	2°33·2′W	X	172
Hollow Meadow	Warw	SP2158	52°13·4′	1°41·2′W	X	151
Hollow Meadows	Sheff	SK2488	53°23·5′	1°37·9′W	T	110
Hollowmire	Cumbr	SD2781	54°13·4′	3°6·8′W	X	96,97
Hollow Moor	Cumbr	NY1006	54°26·7′	3°22·9′W	X	89
Hollow Moor	Devon	SS4601	50°47·5′	4°10·7′W	X	190
Hollow Moor	Devon	SS4701	50°47·5′	4°9·9′W	X	191
Hollowmoor Heath	Ches	SJ4868	53°12·6′	2°46·3′W	T	117
Hollow Oak	Cumbr	SD3484	54°15·1′	3°0·4′W	X	96,97
Hollow Oak	Dorset	SY8493	50°44·4′	2°13·2′W	T	194
Hollowood Fm	Ches	SJ7080	53°19·2′	2°26·6′W	FM	109
Hollow Panson	Devon	SX3692	50°42·5′	4°19·0′W	X	190
Hollowpark	Corn	SX1860	50°24·9′	4°33·3′W	X	201
Hollow Road Fm	Suff	TL8666	52°15·9′	0°43·9′E	FM	155
Hollows	Cumbr	NY3922	54°35·6′	2°56·2′W	X	90
Hollows	Cumbr	NY6165	54°58·9′	2°36·1′W	X	86
Hollows	D & G	NY3878	55°5·8′	2°57·9′W	T	85
Hollows Burn	Scot Bord	NT1137	55°37·4′	3°24·4′W	W	72
Hollow Scar	Cumbr	SD1767	54°5·8′	3°15·7′W	X	96
Hollows Fm	Cumbr	NY2417	54°32·8′	3°10·1′W	FM	89,90
Hollows Fm	Derby	SK2613	52°43·1′	1°36·5′W	FM	128
Hollows Fm	Heref	SO4375	52°22·4′	2°49·8′W	FM	137,148
Hollows, The	Bucks	SP7829	51°57·5′	0°51·5′W	X	165
Hollows, The	N Yks	SE4194	54°20·6′	1°21·7′W	X	99
Hollows, The	Warw	SP2831	51°58·8′	1°35·1′W	X	151
Hollow Stones	Cumbr	NY2007	54°27·4′	3°13·6′W	X	89,90
Hollowstones	Cumbr	SD1399	54°23·0′	3°20·0′W	X	96
Hollow Street	Kent	TR2264	51°20·1′	1°11·6′E	T	179
Hollows Wood	Kent	TQ4962	51°20·5′	0°8·7′E	F	177,188

Hollow Tor	Devon	SX5774	50°33·1'	4°0·7'W	X	191
Hollow Tor	Devon	SX7376	50°34·4'	3°47·2'W	X	191
Hollow Tree Cross	Devon	SS7012	50°53·8'	3°50·5'W	X	180
Hollow Wall Fm	E Susx	TQ7823	50°59·0'	0°32·5'E	FM	199
Hollow Wood	Ches	SJ4948	53°1·9'	2°45·2'W	X	117
Hollow Wood	Northnts	SP9294	52°32·4'	0°38·2'W	F	141
Hollow Yard	Lincs	TF2470	53°13·0'	0°8·2'W	X	122
Holl Resr	Fife	NO2203	56°13·0'	3°15·0'W	W	58
Hollybank	Arg & Bt	NN3202	56°11·1'	4°42·0'W	X	56
Hollybank	Derby	SK3855	53°5·7'	1°25·5'W	X	119
Hollybank	Hants	SU7408	50°52·2'	0°56·5'W	X	197
Holly Bank	Oldham	SD9603	53°31·7'	2°3·2'W	X	109
Holly Bank	Oxon	SP4420	51°52·8'	1°21·3'W	X	164
Hollybank	Shrops	SJ4210	52°41·3'	2°51·1'W	X	126
Hollybank	Staffs	SJ7539	52°57·1'	2°21·9'W	X	127
Holly Bank	Staffs	SJ9704	52°38·3'	2°2·3'W	X	127,139
Holly Bank	Wals	SK0503	52°37·7'	1°55·2'W	T	139
Holly Bank Fm	Ches	SJ8569	53°13·3'	2°13·1'W	FM	118
Holly Bank Fm	Staffs	SJ9933	52°53·9'	2°0·5'W	FM	127
Holly Bank Ho	Staffs	SJ9602	52°37·2'	2°3·1'W	X	127,139
Hollybank Wood	N Yks	SE2759	54°1·8'	1°34·9'W	F	104
Holly Barn	Glos	SO5615	51°50·1'	2°37·9'W	X	162
Hollybed Common	Worcs	SO7737	52°2·1'	2°19·7'W	X	150
Hollybeds Fm	Worcs	SO8542	52°4·8'	2°12·7'W	FM	150
Hollyberry End	Sol	SP2683	52°26·9'	1°36·6'W	T	140
Hollyberry Hall Fm	Cov	SP2783	52°26·9'	1°35·8'W	FM	140
Holly Brook	Heref	SO5556	52°12·3'	2°39·1'W	W	149
Holly Brook	Somer	ST5048	51°14·0'	2°42·6'W	T	182,183
Hollybush	Caer	SO1603	51°43·4'	3°12·6'W	T	171
Hollybush	C of Stoke	SJ8943	52°59·3'	2°9·4'W	T	118
Holly Bush	Cumbr	NY2955	54°53·3'	3°6·0'W	X	85
Holly Bush	Cumbr	SD7184	54°15·3'	2°26·3'W	X	98
Hollybush	D & G	NY1368	55°0·2'	3°21·2'W	X	85
Hollybush	Durham	NZ1645	54°48·2'	1°44·6'W	X	88
Hollybush	E Ayr	NS3914	55°23·9'	4°32·1'W	T	70
Hollybush	E Ayr	NS4929	55°32·1'	4°23·1'W	X	70
Hollybush	Northum	NY8056	54°54·1'	2°18·3'W	X	86,87
Hollybush	Pemb	SM8629	51°55·3'	5°6·3'W	X	157
Hollybush	Powys	SO0690	52°30·2'	3°22·7'W	X	136
Hollybush	Powys	SO0793	52°31·9'	3°21·9'W	X	136
Hollybush	Scot Bord	NT4833	55°35·5'	2°49·1'W	X	73
Hollybush	Staffs	SK0339	52°57·1'	1°56·9'W	X	128
Holly Bush	Staffs	SK1326	52°50·1'	1°48·0'W	X	128
Hollybush	Torf	ST2893	51°38·1'	3°2·0'W	T	171
Hollybush	Worcs	SO7636	52°1·6'	2°20·6'W	T	150
Holly Bush	Wrex	SJ4044	52°59·6'	2°53·2'W	T	117
Hollybush Corner	Bucks	SU9686	51°34·1'	0°36·5'W	T	175,176
Hollybush Corner	Suff	TL9159	52°12·0'	0°48·1'E	T	155
Holly Bush Corner	Surrey	TQ3849	51°13·6'	0°1·0'W	X	187
Hollybushes	Kent	TQ9157	51°17·0'	0°44·7'E	T	178
Hollybush Fm	Bucks	TQ0286	51°34·0'	0°31·3'W	FM	176
Holly Bush Fm	Ches	SJ5773	53°15·4'	2°38·3'W	FM	117
Hollybush Fm	Kent	TR0135	51°5·0'	0°52·6'E	FM	189
Holly Bush Fm	Lancs	SD8742	53°52·7'	2°11·5'W	FM	103
Hollybush Fm	Norf	TM3492	52°28·8'	1°27·2'E	FM	134
Holly Bush Fm	N Yks	SE6794	54°20·5'	0°57·7'W	FM	94,100
Holly Bush Fm	Shrops	SO5483	52°26·8'	2°40·2'W	FM	137,138
Hollybush Fm	Suff	TL9657	52°10·8'	0°52·4'E	FM	155
Hollybush Fm	Suff	TL9957	52°10·7'	0°55·0'E	FM	155
Holly Bush Fm	Suff	TM4282	52°23·2'	1°33·8'E	FM	156
Hollybush Fm	V of Glam	ST0174	51°27·6'	3°25·1'W	FM	170
Hollybush Green Stud	Suff	TL8059	52°12·2'	0°38·5'E	X	155
Hollybush Hill	Bucks	SU9884	51°33·0'	0°34·8'W	T	175,176
Hollybush Hill	Essex	TM1118	51°49·5'	1°4·1'E	T	168,169
Hollybush Hill	Herts	TL1226	51°55·5'	0°21·9'W	X	166
Hollybush House	N Yks	SE3786	54°16·3'	1°25·5'W	X	99
Hollybush Mains	E Ayr	NS3914	55°23·9'	4°32·1'W	X	70
Holly Bush Wood	D & G	NY1368	55°0·2'	3°21·2'W	F	85
Hollycombe	W Susx	SU8529	51°3·5'	0°46·8'W	X	186,197
Hollycombe Fm	Devon	SX6993	50°43·5'	3°51·0'W	FM	191
Hollycombe Moor	Devon	SX6894	50°44·1'	3°51·9'W	X	191
Hollycoombe	Corn	SX1364	50°27·0'	4°37·7'W	X	200
Holly Coppice	Shrops	SJ5414	52°43·5'	2°40·5'W	F	126
Holly Copse	Oxon	SU6678	51°30·1'	1°2·6'W	X	175
Holly Cott	N Yks	SE4257	54°0·7'	1°21·1'W	X	105
Holly Cottage	Pth & Kin	NN7039	56°31·8'	4°6·4'W	X	51,52
Holly Court Fm	Oxon	SP3814	51°49·6'	1°26·5'W	FM	164
Hollycroft	Leic	SP4194	52°32·8'	1°23·3'W	T	140
Holly Cross	Hants	SU6560	51°20·4'	1°3·6'W	X	175,186
Holly Cross	Wok	SU8080	51°31·0'	0°50·4'W	T	175
Holly Dale	Staffs	SK0155	53°5·8'	1°58·7'W	X	119
Holly Ditch Fm	Wilts	ST9968	51°24·9'	2°0·5'W	FM	173
Holly End	Norf	TF4906	52°38·1'	0°12·5'E	T	143
Hollyfast Fm	Cov	SP3083	52°26·9'	1°33·1'W	FM	140
Holly Fm	Ches	SJ6841	52°58·2'	2°28·2'W	FM	118
Holly Fm	Ches	SJ7466	53°11·7'	2°22·9'W	FM	118
Holly Fm	Ches	SJ8265	53°11·1'	2°15·8'W	FM	118
Holly Fm	E Yorks	SE7349	53°56·2'	0°52·9'W	FM	105,106
Holly Fm	Heref	SO2931	51°58·6'	3°1·6'W	FM	161
Holly Fm	Kent	TQ8052	51°14·5'	0°35·1'E	FM	188
Holly Fm	Norf	TF9313	52°41·0'	0°51·7'E	FM	132
Holly Fm	Norf	TF9315	52°42·1'	0°51·8'E	FM	132
Holly Fm	Norf	TG0931	52°50·4'	1°6·6'E	FM	133
Holly Fm	Norf	TM4893	52°28·9'	1°39·6'E	FM	134
Holly Fm	Notts	SK6265	53°10·9'	1°3·9'W	FM	120
Holly Fm	Notts	SK7642	52°58·4'	0°51·7'W	FM	129
Holly Fm	Notts	SK8068	53°12·4'	0°47·7'W	FM	121
Holly Fm	N Yks	NZ5608	54°28·1'	1°7·7'W	FM	93
Holly Fm	Suff	TM4988	52°26·2'	1°40·2'E	FM	156
Holly Fm	Suff	TM5194	52°29·4'	1°42·2'E	FM	134
Holly Fm	Warw	SP2373	52°21·5'	1°39·3'W	FM	139
Holly Fold Fm	Lancs	SD4603	53°31·5'	2°48·5'W	FM	108
Hollyford Fm	Devon	SS8407	50°51·3'	3°38·5'W	FM	191
Hollygate Fm	Notts	SK6636	52°55·3'	1°0·7'W	FM	129
Holly Grange	Sol	SP2375	52°22·6'	1°39·3'W	X	139
Holly Green	Bucks	SP7703	51°43·5'	0°52·7'W	T	165
Holly Green	Worcs	SO8641	52°4·3'	2°11·9'W	T	150
Holly Grove	Norf	TG3420	52°43·8'	1°28·4'E	X	133,134
Holly Grove	Oxon	SP3614	51°49·6'	1°28·3'W	F	164
Holly Grove	Oxon	SU7084	51°33·3'	0°59·0'W	F	175

Hollygrove	Shrops	SJ6533	52°53·8'	2°30·8'W	X	127
Holly Grove	Suff	TM5182	52°22·9'	1°41·7'E	F	156
Holly Grove Fm	E Susx	TQ5427	51°1·5'	0°12·1'E	FM	188,199
Holly Grove Ho	Norf	TG3026	52°47·2'	1°25·1'E	X	133,134
Holly Hall	Northum	NY9766	54°59·6'	2°2·4'W	X	87
Holly Hang	Suff	TM5183	52°23·5'	1°41·7'E	F	156
Holly Hatch Cottage	Hants	SU2111	50°54·1'	1°41·7'W	X	195
Holly Hatch Inclosure	Hants	SU2111	50°54·1'	1°41·7'W	F	195
Hollyhead Fm	Lancs	SD5254	53°59·0'	2°43·5'W	FM	102
Holly Heath Fm	Norf	TG0930	52°49·8'	1°6·6'E	FM	133
Hollyhedge Fm	Ches	SJ7575	53°16·5'	2°22·1'W	FM	118
Hollyhedge Fm	Warr	SJ5984	53°21·3'	2°36·6'W	FM	108
Holly Hill	Cumbr	NY4137	54°43·7'	2°54·5'W	X	90
Hollyhill	E Susx	TQ4533	51°4·9'	0°4·6'E	X	188
Holly Hill	Kent	TQ6662	51°20·2'	0°23·4'E	H	177,178,188
Holly Hill	Kent	TQ6763	51°20·7'	0°24·3'E	X	177,178,188
Holly Hill	Kent	TR0760	51°18·3'	0°58·6'E	H	179
Holly Hill	Norf	TG0028	52°49·0'	0°58·5'E	X	133
Holly Hill	Norf	TM3391	52°28·3'	1°26·2'E	X	134
Holly Hill	Northum	NY9556	54°54·2'	2°4·3'W	X	87
Holly Hill	N Yks	NZ1600	54°24·0'	1°44·8'W	T	92
Holly Hill	N Yks	SE2681	54°13·7'	1°35·7'W	X	99
Holly Hill	N Yks	SE2748	53°55·9'	1°34·9'W	X	104
Holly Hill	N Yks	SE5773	54°9·2'	1°7·2'W	X	100
Holly Hill Fm	Enf	TL2900	51°41·3'	0°7·6'W	FM	166
Holly Hills	Hants	SU8231	51°4·6'	0°49·4'W	X	186
Holly Hills	Suff	TM4373	52°18·3'	1°34·3'E	F	156
Holly Ho	Ches	SJ7369	53°13·3'	2°23·9'W	X	118
Holly Ho	Derby	SK3348	53°1·9'	1°30·1'W	X	119
Holly Ho	Lancs	SD3907	53°33·6'	2°54·8'W	X	108
Holly Ho	Lancs	SD4852	53°57·9'	2°47·1'W	X	102
Holly Ho	Newp	ST2585	51°33·8'	3°4·5'W	X	171
Holly Ho	N Yks	SD9288	54°17·5'	2°7·0'W	X	98
Holly Ho	N Yks	SE1699	54°23·4'	1°44·8'W	X	99
Holly Ho	Staffs	SK0056	53°6·3'	1°59·6'W	X	119
Hollyhock Fm	Lincs	TF3718	52°44·8'	0°2·2'E	FM	131
Hollyhouse Fm	Cambs	TL4287	52°28·0'	0°5·8'E	FM	142,143
Holly House Fm	Notts	SK6692	53°25·5'	1°0·0'W	FM	111
Holly House Fm	Notts	SK8464	53°10·2'	0°44·2'W	FM	121
Holly House Fm	N Yks	SE5053	53°58·5'	1°13·8'W	FM	105
Holly House Fm, The	Lincs	SK8265	53°10·8'	0°46·0'W	FM	121
Holly Hurst	Birm	SP1096	52°33·9'	1°50·7'W	F	139
Hollyhurst	Shrops	SJ5744	52°59·7'	2°38·0'W	X	117
Hollyhurst	Shrops	SO4797	52°34·3'	2°46·5'W	T	137,138
Hollyhurst	Warw	SP3785	52°27·9'	1°26·9'W	T	140
Hollyhurst Fm	Derby	SK1437	52°56·1'	1°47·1'W	FM	128
Hollyhurst Fm	Shrops	SJ7443	52°59·3'	2°22·8'W	FM	118
Hollyhurst Ho	Staffs	SK1619	52°46·3'	1°45·4'W	X	128
Holly Island	Highld	NH6372	57°43·3'	4°17·5'W	X	21
Hollylane	Staffs	SJ8758	53°7·4'	2°11·2'W	X	118
Holly Lane Fm	Birm	SP1595	52°33·4'	1°46·3'W	FM	139
Holly Lodge	Cambs	TL1578	52°23·5'	0°18·2'W	X	142
Holly Lodge	Kent	TR3046	51°10·2'	1°17·8'E	X	179
Holly Lodge	Norf	TM3199	52°32·6'	1°24·8'E	X	134
Holly Lodge	Northnts	SP7665	52°16·9'	0°52·8'W	X	152
Holly Lodge	Notts	SK5555	53°5·6'	1°10·3'W	X	120
Holly Lodge	Suff	TL8938	52°0·7'	0°45·6'E	X	155
Holly Lodge Fm	Essex	TL9831	51°56·8'	0°53·3'E	FM	168
Hollylodge Fm	Essex	TM0929	51°55·4'	1°2·8'E	FM	168,169
Holly Lodge Fm	Leic	SK6321	52°47·2'	1°3·5'W	FM	129
Hollym	E Yorks	TA3425	53°42·5'	0°2·2'E	T	107,113
Holly Moor	Somer	ST3627	51°2·6'	2°54·4'W	X	193
Hollymoor Fm	Durham	NZ1124	54°36·9'	1°49·4'W	FM	92
Holly Mount	Bury	SD7614	53°37·6'	2°21·4'W	X	109
Hollymount	Heref	SO5622	51°53·9'	2°38·0'W	X	162
Holly Mount Fm	Derby	SK4145	53°0·3'	1°22·9'W	FM	129
Hollyn Bower	N Yks	SE5981	54°13·5'	1°5·3'W	X	100
Hollyovenbeck Ho	Lancs	SD4439	53°50·9'	2°50·7'W	X	102
Holly Park	N Yks	SE6586	54°16·2'	0°59·7'W	X	94,100
Holly Rose Lodge	Cambs	TL0971	52°19·8'	0°23·6'W	X	153
Hollyseat	Derby	SK3248	53°1·9'	1°31·0'W	X	119
Holly Spring	Brackn	SU8769	51°25·0'	0°44·5'W	X	175
Holly Tree	N Yks	SD6767	54°6·1'	2°29·9'W	X	98
Holly Tree Fm	Lincs	TF3512	52°41·6'	0°0·3'E	FM	131,142
Holly Tree Fm	Suff	TM2473	52°18·8'	1°17·6'E	FM	156
Holly Tree Fm	Suff	TM3773	52°18·5'	1°29·0'E	FM	156
Hollytree Fm	Suff	TM3870	52°16·8'	1°29·8'E	FM	156
Holly Tree Fm	Suff	TM4074	52°18·9'	1°31·7'E	FM	156
Hollyvag	Corn	SX2879	50°35·4'	4°25·4'W	X	201
Hollywaste	Shrops	SO6475	52°22·5'	2°31·3'W	T	138
Holly Water	Devon	SS8506	50°50·8'	3°37·6'W	W	191
Hollywater	Hants	SU8034	51°6·2'	0°51·1'W	T	186
Hollywater Barton	Devon	SS8605	50°50·2'	3°36·8'W	X	191
Holly Wood	Oxon	SP5810	51°47·4'	1°9·2'W	F	164
Hollywood	Staffs	SJ9333	52°53·9'	2°5·8'W	X	127
Hollywood	Worcs	SP0877	52°23·7'	1°52·5'W	T	139
Hollywood Fm	Lancs	SD3919	53°40·1'	2°55·0'W	FM	108
Hollywood Fm	N Lincs	SE8504	53°31·8'	0°42·6'W	FM	112
Hollywood Fm	Staffs	SK0637	52°56·1'	1°54·2'W	FM	128
Hollywood Manor	Kent	TQ5761	51°19·8'	0°15·6'E	X	177,188
Hollywood Tower	S Glos	ST5781	51°31·8'	2°36·8'W	X	172
Holm	Aberd	NJ7057	57°36·4'	2°29·7'W	X	29
Holm	Devon	SS6807	50°51·1'	3°52·1'W	X	191
Holm	D & G	NX3777	55°3·9'	4°32·7'W	X	77
Holm	D & G	NX9680	55°6·5'	3°37·4'W	X	78
Holm	D & G	NY2498	55°16·5'	3°11·3'W	X	79
Holm	Highld	NG5151	57°29·1'	6°8·8'W	X	23,24
Holm	N Eil	NB0333	58°11·4'	7°2·8'W	X	13
Holm	Orkney	HY4903	58°54·9'	2°52·7'W	X	6,7
Holm	S Lanak	NS7447	55°42·3'	3°59·9'W	X	64
Holmacott	Devon	SS5028	51°2·1'	4°8·0'W	T	180
Holmains	D & G	NY0876	55°4·4'	3°26·0'W	X	85
Holmains Moor	D & G	NY0776	55°4·4'	3°27·0'W	X	85
Holman Clavel	Somer	ST2216	50°56·5'	3°6·2'W	T	193
Holm and Ivy Fm	Dorset	ST8521	50°59·5'	2°12·4'W	FM	183
Holmans Bridge	E Susx	TQ4116	50°55·8'	0°0·8'E	X	198
Holman's Fm	Kent	TQ9227	51°0·8'	0°44·6'E	FM	189
Holman's Fm	Somer	ST3118	50°57·7'	2°58·6'W	FM	193
Holmbank	D & G	NX8397	55°15·5'	3°50·0'W	X	78
Holm Beag	N Eil	NG0897	57°52·3'	6°55·0'W	X	14,18

Holmbridge	Kirk	SE1106	53°33·3'	1°49·6'W	T	110
Holm Burn	D & G	NS6300	55°16·8'	4°9·0'W	W	77
Holm Burn	E Ayr	NS5819	55°26·9'	4°14·3'W	W	71
Holmbury Fm	Surrey	TQ1042	51°10·2'	0°25·2'W	FM	187
Holmbury Hill	Surrey	TQ1043	51°10·8'	0°25·2'W	X	187
Holmbury Hill (Fort)	Surrey	TQ1043	51°10·8'	0°25·2'W	A	187
Holmbury Ho	Surrey	TQ1042	51°10·2'	0°25·2'W	X	187
Holmbury St Mary	Surrey	TQ1144	51°11·3'	0°24·3'W	T	187
Holmbush	Corn	SX0352	50°20·3'	4°45·7'W	T	200,204
Holmbush	Dorset	ST3602	50°49·1'	2°54·1'W	T	193
Holmbush	E Susx	TQ5813	50°53·9'	0°15·2'E	X	199
Holmbush	W Susx	TQ2233	51°5·2'	0°15·1'W	X	187
Holm Bushes, The	Dorset	ST6310	50°53·5'	2°31·2'W	F	194
Holmbush Fm	W Susx	TQ2414	50°55·0'	0°13·8'W	FM	198
Holmbush Fm	W Susx	TQ3121	50°58·6'	0°7·6'W	FM	198
Holmbush Ho	W Susx	TQ1316	50°56·2'	0°23·1'W	X	198
Holmbush Manor Fm	W Susx	TQ1130	51°3·7'	0°24·6'W	FM	187
Holmbyre	N Ayr	NS2648	55°41·9'	4°45·7'W	X	63
Holmcroft	Staffs	SJ9025	52°49·6'	2°8·5'W	T	127
Holmdale Fm	E Yorks	SE8858	54°0·9'	0°39·0'W	FM	106
Holme	Beds	TL1842	52°4·1'	0°16·3'W	T	153
Holme	Brad	SE1931	53°46·7'	1°42·3'W	T	104
Holme	Cambs	TL1987	52°28·3'	0°14·5'W	T	142
Holme	Cumbr	SD1987	54°16·6'	3°14·2'W	X	96
Holme	Cumbr	SD3775	54°10·3'	2°57·5'W	X	96,97
Holme	Cumbr	SD4183	54°14·6'	2°53·9'W	X	96,97
Holme	Cumbr	SD5278	54°12·0'	2°43·7'W	T	97
Holme	Cumbr	SD6390	54°18·5'	2°33·7'W	X	97
Holme	Donc	SE5610	53°35·3'	1°8·8'W	X	111
Holme	Highld	NH5744	57°28·1'	4°22·6'W	X	26
Holme	Kirk	SE1005	53°32·7'	1°50·5'W	T	110
Holme	N Lincs	SE9206	53°32·8'	0°36·3'W	T	112
Holme	Notts	SK8059	53°7·6'	0°47·9'W	T	121
Holme	N Yks	SE3582	54°14·2'	1°27·4'W	T	99
Holmead Fm	Devon	SS8815	50°55·7'	3°35·2'W	FM	181
Holme Bank	Ches	SJ4767	53°12·1'	2°47·2'W	X	117
Holme Bank	Cumbr	SD2773	54°9·1'	3°6·6'W	X	96,97
Holme Barn Fm	Lincs	SK8450	53°2·7'	0°44·4'W	FM	121
Holme Beck	N Yks	NZ1507	54°27·7'	1°45·7'W	W	92
Holme Bottom	N Yks	SE3058	54°1·3'	1°32·1'W	X	104
Holme Br	N Yks	SD8458	54°1·3'	2°14·2'W	X	103
Holmebridge	Dorset	SY8986	50°40·6'	2°9·0'W	T	195
Holme Brook	Derby	SK3472	53°14·9'	1°29·0'W	W	119
Holme Carr	Notts	SK5579	53°18·5'	1°10·1'W	X	120
Holme Chapel	Lancs	SD8728	53°45·1'	2°11·4'W	T	103
Holme Chase	E Susx	TQ6023	50°59·3'	0°17·2'E	X	199
Holme Clough	Oldham	SE0405	53°32·7'	1°56·0'W	X	110
Holme Common	E Yorks	SE8036	53°49·1'	0°46·7'W	X	106
Holmedale Fm	E Yorks	SE9346	53°54·3'	0°34·6'W	FM	106
Holme Down	Devon	SS5804	50°49·3'	4°0·6'W	X	191
Holme Dub	Cumbr	NY1547	54°48·9'	3°18·9'W	W	85
Holme Dyke	Notts	SK7149	53°2·2'	0°56·1'W	W	129
Holme Eden Abbey	Cumbr	NY4657	54°54·5'	2°50·1'W	X	86
Holme Ends	Cumbr	NY4658	54°55·1'	2°50·1'W	X	86
Holme Fell	Cumbr	NY3100	54°23·7'	3°3·3'W	X	90
Holme Fell	Cumbr	SD6490	54°18·5'	2°32·8'W	X	97
Holme Fen	Cambs	TL2288	52°28·8'	0°11·8'W	X	142
Holme Fen	Cambs	TL4572	52°19·8'	0°8·1'E	X	154
Holme Fm	Ches	SJ4569	53°13·2'	2°49·0'W	FM	117
Holme Fm	Ches	SJ4577	53°17·5'	2°49·1'W	FM	117
Holme Fm	Ches	SJ6161	53°8·9'	2°34·6'W	FM	118
Holme Fm	Cumbr	SD4279	54°12·5'	2°52·9'W	FM	96,97
Holme Fm	D & G	NX6479	55°5·5'	4°7·4'W	FM	77
Holme Fm	Durham	NZ1528	54°39·1'	1°45·6'W	FM	92
Holme Fm	E Yorks	SE9744	53°53·2'	0°31·0'W	FM	106
Holme Fm	Leeds	SE3842	53°52·6'	1°24·9'W	FM	104
Holme Fm	Lincs	SK8294	53°26·4'	0°45·5'W	FM	112
Holme Fm	Lincs	TF3099	53°28·5'	0°2·1'W	FM	113
Holme Fm	Notts	SK6089	53°23·9'	1°5·4'W	FM	111,120
Holme Fm	Notts	SK7140	52°57·4'	0°56·2'W	FM	129
Holme Fm	N Yks	NZ3810	54°29·3'	1°24·4'W	FM	93
Holme Fm	N Yks	NZ5702	54°24·9'	1°6·9'W	FM	93
Holme Fm	N Yks	SE8377	54°11·2'	0°43·3'W	FM	100
Holme Fm	W Susx	SU7509	50°52·8'	0°55·6'W	FM	197
Holme Gate	Cumbr	NY4557	54°54·5'	2°51·0'W	X	86
Holmegate	Cumbr	SD1086	54°16·0'	3°22·5'W	X	96
Holmegate	Dorset	SY8986	50°40·6'	2°9·0'W	X	195
Holme Green	Beds	TL1943	52°4·6'	0°15·4'W	T	153
Holme Green	N Yks	SE5541	53°52·0'	1°9·4'W	T	105
Holme Green	Wok	SU8267	51°24·0'	0°48·9'W	T	175
Holme Ground	Cumbr	NY3101	54°24·2'	3°3·4'W	X	90
Holme Hale	Norf	TF8807	52°37·9'	0°47·1'E	T	144
Holme Hale Hall	Norf	TF9008	52°38·4'	0°48·9'E	X	144
Holme Hall	Derby	SK2169	53°13·3'	1°40·7'W	A	119
Holme Hall	E Yorks	SE8138	53°50·2'	0°45·7'W	X	106
Holme Hall	N Lincs	SE9006	53°32·8'	0°38·1'W	X	112
Holme Hall Fm	Donc	SK5594	53°26·6'	1°9·9'W	FM	111
Holme Head	Cumbr	NY4934	54°42·2'	2°47·1'W	X	90
Holmehead	Cumbr	NY5478	55°5·9'	2°42·8'W	X	86
Holmehead Br	Lancs	SD7153	53°58·6'	2°26·1'W	X	103
Holme Heath	Dorset	SY9084	50°39·6'	2°8·1'W	X	195
Holme Hill	Lincs	TF1376	53°16·4'	0°17·9'W	X	121
Holme Hill	NE Lincs	TA2709	53°34·0'	0°4·5'W	T	113
Holme Hill	N Yks	SD7880	54°13·2'	2°19·8'W	X	98
Holme Hill Fm	Durham	NZ4244	54°47·6'	1°20·4'W	FM	88
Holme Hill Fm	Lincs	TF0298	53°28·4'	0°27·4'W	FM	112
Holme Hill Fm	Lincs	TF0390	53°24·0'	0°26·6'W	FM	112
Holme Ho	Brad	SE0240	53°51·6'	1°57·8'W	X	104
Holme Ho	Cumbr	NY6506	54°27·1'	2°32·0'W	X	91
Holme Ho	Cumbr	SD5297	54°22·2'	2°43·9'W	X	97
Holme Ho	Cumbr	SD6183	54°14·7'	2°35·5'W	X	97
Holme Ho	Donc	SE6505	53°32·5'	1°0·7'W	X	111
Holme Ho	E Yorks	SE7837	53°49·6'	0°48·5'W	X	105,106
Holme Ho	Lancs	SD5746	53°54·7'	2°38·9'W	X	102
Holme Ho	Lancs	SD6077	54°11·5'	2°36·4'W	X	97
Holme Ho	Lincs	TF1745	52°59·6'	0°15·0'W	X	130
Holme Ho	Notts	SK6338	52°56·4'	1°3·3'W	X	129
Holme Ho	N Yks	NZ2214	54°31·5'	1°39·2'W	X	93
Holme Ho	N Yks	SD9454	53°59·2'	2°5·1'W	X	103
Holme Ho	N Yks	SE0557	54°0·8'	1°55·0'W	X	104

Holme House Fell	Lancs	SD5848	53°55·8′	2°38·0′W	X	102
Holme House Fm	Lancs	SD4821	53°41·2′	2°46·8′W	FM	102
Holme House Fm	Notts	SK5783	53°20·7′	1°8·2′W	FM	111,120
Holme Island	Cumbr	SD4278	54°11·9′	2°52·9′W	X	96,97
Holme Knott	Cumbr	SD6489	54°18·0′	2°32·8′W	X	97
Holme Lacy	Heref	SO5535	52°0·9′	2°38·9′W	T	149
Holme Lane	Notts	SK6237	52°55·8′	1°4·3′W	T	129
Holme Lode	Cambs	TL2089	52°29·4′	0°13·6′W	W	142
Holme Lode Covert	Cambs	TL2088	52°28·8′	0°13·6′W	F	142
Holme Lode Fm	Cambs	TL2089	52°29·4′	0°13·6′W	FM	142
Holme Lodge	N Yks	SE3482	54°14·2′	1°28·3′W	X	99
Holme Mains	Highld	NH6542	57°27·2′	4°14·5′W	X	26
Holme Marsh	Heref	SO3454	52°11·1′	2°57·5′W	T	148,149
Holme Mill	D & G	NX6480	55°6·0′	4°7·5′W	X	77
Holme Mills	Cumbr	SD5278	54°12·0′	2°43·7′W	T	97
Holme Moor	Somer	ST0926	51°1·8′	3°17·5′W	X	181
Holme Moss	Derby	SE0804	53°32·2′	1°52·3′W	X	110
Holme next the Sea	Norf	TF7043	52°57·7′	0°32·3′E	T	132
Holme Nook	C of Derb	SK3539	52°57·1′	1°28·3′W	X	128
Holme Nook	Lancs	SD3841	53°51·9′	2°56·2′W	X	102
Holmen's Grove	Surrey	SU9236	51°7·2′	0°40·7′W	F	186
Holme of Setter	Shetld	HU4142	60°9·9′	1°15·2′W	X	4
Holme-on-Spalding-Moor	E Yorks	SE8038	53°50·2′	0°46·6′W	T	106
Holme on the Wolds	E Yorks	SE9646	53°54·3′	0°31·9′W	T	106
Holme Park	E Susx	TQ5628	51°2·0′	0°13·9′E	X	188,199
Holmepark Fell	Cumbr	SD5479	54°12·5′	2°41·9′W	X	97
Holme Park Fm	Cumbr	SD5379	54°12·5′	2°42·8′W	FM	97
Holme Park Fm	Cumbr	SD5995	54°21·2′	2°37·4′W	FM	97
Holme Pierrepont	Notts	SK6239	52°56·9′	1°4·2′W	T	129
Holme Place	Devon	SS9021	50°58·9′	3°33·6′W	X	181
Holme Plantn	N Lincs	SE9105	53°32·3′	0°37·2′W	F	112
Holme Priory	Dorset	SY8986	50°40·6′	2°9·0′W	X	195
Holmer	Heref	SO5042	52°4·7′	2°43·4′W	T	149
Holmer Green	Bucks	SU9097	51°40·1′	0°41·5′W	T	165
Holme Rose	Highld	NH8048	57°30·6′	3°59·7′W	X	27
Holmes	Devon	SS8513	50°54·5′	3°37·8′W	X	181
Holmes	E Ayr	NS4736	55°35·9′	4°25·3′W	X	70
Holmes	Lancs	SD4318	53°39·6′	2°51·3′W	T	108
Holmes	Northum	NY8452	54°52·0′	2°14·5′W	X	86,87
Holmes	N Yks	SD6369	54°7·2′	2°33·5′W	X	97
Holmes	S Ayr	NS3112	55°22·6′	4°39·6′W	X	70
Holmescales	Cumbr	SD5587	54°16·8′	2°41·1′W	X	97
Holmes Carr Great Wood	Donc	SK6098	53°28·8′	1°5·3′W	F	111
Holmes Chapel	Ches	SJ7667	53°12·2′	2°21·2′W	T	118
Holmesdale	Derby	SK3678	53°18·1′	1°27·2′W	T	119
Holmesdale Fm	E Susx	TQ4225	51°0·6′	0°1·8′E	FM	187,198
Holmesfield	Derby	SK3277	53°17·6′	1°30·8′W	T	119
Holmesfield Common	Derby	SK3177	53°17·6′	1°31·7′W	X	119
Holmes Fm	E Susx	TQ7009	50°51·6′	0°25·3′E	FM	199
Holmes Fm	Herts	TL3124	51°54·2′	0°5·4′W	FM	166
Holmes Fm	Lancs	SD6431	53°46·7′	2°32·4′W	FM	102,103
Holme's Fm	Leic	SP8298	52°34·9′	0°58·6′W	FM	141
Holmes Fm	Lincs	SK8248	53°1·6′	0°46·2′W	FM	130
Holmes Fm	Lincs	SK9053	53°4·2′	0°39·0′W	FM	121
Holmes Fm	Lincs	TF1565	53°10·4′	0°16·4′W	FM	121
Holmes Fm	Lincs	TF2841	52°57·3′	0°5·3′W	FM	131
Holmes Fm	Lincs	TF4098	53°27·8′	0°6·9′E	FM	113
Holmes Fm	N Lincs	SE7503	53°31·3′	0°51·7′W	FM	112
Holmes Fm	N Yks	SE2175	54°10·5′	1°40·3′W	FM	99
Holmes Fm	Somer	ST2336	51°7·3′	3°5·6′W	FM	182
Holmes Fm	W Susx	SZ7998	50°46·8′	0°52·4′W	FM	197
Holmeshead Fm	Cumbr	NY3502	54°24·8′	2°59·7′W	FM	90
Holmes Ho	N Yks	SE6932	53°47·0′	0°56·8′W	A	105,106
Holmes Ho	Warw	SP4056	52°12·3′	1°24·5′W	X	151
Holmes Slack	Lancs	SD5531	53°46·6′	2°40·6′W	T	102
Holmesland	Hants	SU5013	50°55·1′	1°16·9′W	X	196
Holmesmill	Cumbr	NY3361	54°56·6′	3°2·3′W	X	85
Holmes Moss	Cumbr	SD7495	54°21·2′	2°23·6′W	X	98
Holmes Moss	Lancs	SD4120	53°40·6′	2°53·2′W	X	102
Holmes Moss Hill	Cumbr	SD7594	54°20·7′	2°22·7′W	X	98
Holmes's Hill	E Susx	TQ5312	50°53·5′	0°10·9′E	T	199
Holmes's Wood	Norf	TG0430	52°50·0′	1°2·1′E	F	133
Holme St Cuthbert	Cumbr	NY1047	54°48·8′	3°23·6′W	T	85
Holmes, The	Derby	SK1479	53°18·7′	1°47·0′W	X	119
Holmes, The	Notts	SK6543	52°59·1′	1°1·5′W	X	129
Holmes, The	N Yks	NZ2513	54°30·9′	1°36·4′W	X	93
Holmes, The	N Yks	NZ3209	54°28·8′	1°29·9′W	X	93
Holmes, The	N Yks	SE6133	53°47·6′	1°4·0′W	X	105
Holmes,The	Pemb	SN0421	51°51·4′	4°50·4′W	X	145,157,158
Holmes, The	Staffs	SK0862	53°9·5′	1°52·4′W	X	119
Holmes, The	Stock on T	NZ4416	54°32·5′	1°18·8′W	X	93
Holme Street Ho	W Susx	TQ0618	50°57·3′	0°29·1′W	X	197
Holmeswood	Lancs	SD4316	53°38·5′	2°51·3′W	T	108
Holme, The	Cambs	TL4266	52°16·7′	0°5·3′E	X	154
Holme, The	D & G	NX6479	55°5·5′	4°7·4′W	X	77
Holme, The	Lancs	SD8828	53°45·1′	2°10·5′W	A	103
Holme, The	Northum	NY7165	54°59·0′	2°26·8′W	X	86,87
Holme, The	N Yks	SE2159	54°1·8′	1°40·3′W	X	104
Holmethorpe	Surrey	TQ2851	51°14·9′	0°9·6′W	T	187
Holme Well	Cumbr	SD3892	54°19·4′	2°56·8′W	X	96,97
Holme Wold Ho	E Yorks	SE9546	53°54·3′	0°32·8′W	X	106
Holme Wood	Brad	SE1931	53°46·7′	1°42·3′W	T	104
Holme Wood	Bucks	SU8188	51°35·3′	0°49·5′W	F	175
Holme Wood	Cumbr	NY1221	54°34·8′	3°21·3′W	F	89
Holmewood	Derby	SK4365	53°11·1′	1°21·0′W	T	120
Holme Wood	Donc	SE6505	53°32·5′	1°0·7′W	X	111
Holme Wood	Lincs	TF2865	53°10·2′	0°4·7′W	F	122
Holmewood Ho	Kent	TQ5538	51°7·4′	0°13·3′E	X	188
Holme Woods	Kirk	SE1004	53°32·2′	1°50·5′W	F	110
Holmfield	Cald	SE0828	53°45·1′	1°52·3′W	T	104
Holm Field	E Yorks	SE8858	54°0·9′	0°39·0′W	X	106
Holm Field	Shetld	HU3930	60°3·4′	1°17·5′W	H	4
Holmfield Fm	E Yorks	SE8958	54°0·9′	0°38·1′W	FM	106
Holmfield Fm	Wakf	SE4624	53°42·9′	1°17·8′W	FM	105
Holmfirth	Kirk	SE1408	53°34·3′	1°46·9′W	T	110
Holm Fm	N Eil	NB4430	58°11·3′	6°20·9′W	FM	8
Holm Fm	S Glos	ST5786	51°34·5′	2°36·8′W	FM	172
Holm Fm	Somer	ST3354	51°17·1′	2°57·3′W	FM	182
Holm Fm	W Susx	TQ2234	51°5·8′	0°15·1′W	FM	187
Holmfoot	Cumbr	NY4166	54°59·4′	2°54·9′W	X	85
Holmgate	Derby	SK3763	53°10·0′	1°26·4′W	X	119
Holmhead	Aberd	NJ5108	57°9·9′	2°48·2′W	X	37
Holmhead	Angus	NO5677	56°53·2′	2°42·9′W	X	44
Holmhead	C of Aber	NJ8709	57°10·6′	2°12·4′W	X	38
Holmhead	D & G	NX7085	55°8·8′	4°2·0′W	X	77
Holmhead	D & G	NX7676	55°4·0′	3°56·1′W	X	84
Holmhead	D & G	NY0571	55°1·7′	3°28·7′W	X	85
Holmhead	D & G	NY3585	55°9·6′	3°0·8′W	X	79
Holmhead	E Ayr	NS5620	55°27·4′	4°16·2′W	T	71
Holmhead	S Ayr	NX2089	55°10·0′	4°49·1′W	X	76
Holmhead	S Lanak	NS6539	55°37·8′	4°8·2′W	X	71
Holmhead	S Lanak	NS8721	55°28·4′	3°46·8′W	X	71,72
Holmhead Hill	D & G	NX7593	55°13·2′	3°57·5′W	H	78
Holmhead Moss	D & G	NY0570	55°1·2′	3°28·7′W	F	85
Holm Hill	D & G	NX5595	55°13·9′	4°16·4′W	H	77
Holmhill	D & G	NX8795	55°14·4′	3°46·2′W	T	78
Holm Hill	Hants	SU2602	50°49·2′	1°37·5′W	X	195
Holmhill Fm	Suff	TM3237	51°59·2′	1°23·1′E	FM	169
Holmhill Inclosure	Hants	SU2508	50°52·5′	1°38·3′W	F	195
Holm Hills	Hants	SU8232	51°5·1′	0°49·4′W	X	186
Holm Ho	Cumbr	NY3644	54°47·5′	2°59·3′W	X	85
Holm House	Pemb	SN0338	52°0·6′	4°51·8′W	X	145,157
Holmhurst St Mary	E Susx	TQ8012	50°53·0′	0°33·9′E	X	199
Holmie	Moray	NJ4161	57°38·4′	2°58·8′W	X	28
Holming Beam	Devon	SX5976	50°34·2′	3°59·1′W	X	191
Holmingham Fm	Devon	SS9520	50°58·4′	3°29·4′W	FM	181
Holmisdale	Highld	NG1848	57°26·3′	6°41·5′W	T	23
Holm Island	Highld	NG5251	57°29·1′	6°7·8′W	X	23,24
Holmlea Fm	Derby	SK1235	52°55·0′	1°48·9′W	FM	128
Holm Leigh Fm	Salf	SJ6895	53°27·3′	2°28·5′W	FM	109
Holmley Common	Derby	SK3579	53°18·6′	1°28·1′W	T	119
Holm Moor	D & G	NX8677	55°4·7′	3°46·7′W	X	84
Holm Nick	S Lanak	NT0526	55°31·4′	3°29·9′W	H	72
Holm of Aikerness	Orkney	HY4652	59°21·3′	2°56·5′W	X	5
Holm of Beosetter	Shetld	HU4945	60°11·5′	1°6·5′W	X	4
Holm of Boray	Orkney	HY4520	59°4·1′	2°57·1′W	X	5,6
Holm of Breibister	Shetld	HU2247	60°12·7′	1°35·7′W	X	3
Holm of Brough	Shetld	HP5404	60°43·5′	0°56·1′W	X	1
Holm of Califf	Shetld	HU4545	60°11·5′	1°10·8′W	X	4
Holm of Copister	Shetld	HU4678	60°29·2′	1°9·3′W	X	2,3
Holm of Cruester	Shetld	HU4742	60°9·8′	1°8·7′W	X	4
Holm of Dalry	D & G	NX6180	55°6·0′	4°10·3′W	X	77
Holm of Daltallochan	D & G	NX5594	55°13·4′	4°16·3′W	X	77
Holm of Drumlanrig	D & G	NX8398	55°16·0′	3°50·1′W	H	78
Holm of Elsness	Orkney	HY6637	59°13·1′	2°35·3′W	X	5
Holm of Faray	Orkney	HY5238	59°13·8′	2°50·0′W	X	5
Holm of Grimbister	Orkney	HY3713	59°0·2′	3°5·3′W	X	6
Holm of Gruting	Shetld	HU2747	60°12·7′	1°30·3′W	X	3
Holm of Gunnista	Shetld	HU4944	60°10·9′	1°6·5′W	X	4
Holm of Helliness	Shetld	HU4628	60°2·3′	1°10·0′W	X	4
Holm of Heogland	Shetld	HU5799	60°40·5′	0°56·9′W	X	1
Holm of Houton	Orkney	HY3103	58°54·8′	3°11·4′W	X	6,7
Holm of Huip	Orkney	HY6231	59°10·1′	2°39·4′W	X	5
Holm of Kirkness	Orkney	HY2918	59°2·9′	3°13·8′W	X	6
Holm of Maywick	Shetld	HU3726	60°1·3′	1°19·7′W	X	4
Holm of Melby	Shetld	HU1958	60°18·6′	1°38·9′W	X	3
Holm of Noss	Shetld	HU5539	60°8·2′	1°0·1′W	X	4
Holm of Odness	Orkney	HY6926	59°7·4′	2°32·0′W	X	5
Holm of Papa	Orkney	HY5051	59°20·8′	2°52·3′W	X	5
Holm of Rendall	Orkney	HY4220	59°4·0′	3°0·2′W	X	5,6
Holm of Sandwick	Shetld	HU5360	60°19·5′	1°1·9′W	X	2,3
Holm of Scockness	Orkney	HY4531	59°10·0′	2°57·2′W	X	5,6
Holm of Skaw	Shetld	HP6617	60°50·1′	0°46·7′W	X	1
Holm of Skellister	Shetld	HU4755	60°16·9′	1°8·5′W	X	3
Holm of Tressaness	Shetld	HU6294	60°37·7′	0°51·5′W	X	1,2
Holm of West Sandwick	Shetld	HU4389	60°35·2′	1°12·4′W	X	1,2
Holm Place	Kent	TQ9273	51°25·6′	0°46·1′E	X	178
Holm Point	Orkney	HY3713	59°0·2′	3°5·3′W	X	6
Holmpton	E Yorks	TA3623	53°41·4′	0°4·0′E	T	107,113
Holmrook	Cumbr	SD0799	54°22·9′	3°25·5′W	T	96
Holmrook Hall	Cumbr	NY0800	54°23·5′	3°24·6′W	X	89
Holms	D & G	NT0902	55°18·5′	3°25·6′W	X	78
Holms	E Ayr	NS3514	55°23·8′	4°35·9′W	X	70
Holms	N Ayr	NS3537	55°36·2′	4°36·7′W	X	70
Holms	N Lanak	NS6969	55°54·0′	4°5·3′W	X	64
Holms	S Lanak	NS6437	55°36·7′	4°9·1′W	X	71
Holmsfoot	Cumbr	NY7743	54°47·1′	2°21·0′W	X	86,87
Holmsgarth	Shetld	HU4642	60°9·9′	1°9·8′W	T	4
Holmshaw	D & G	NT0404	55°19·5′	3°30·4′W	X	78
Holms Hill	Aberd	NJ5622	57°17·4′	2°43·3′W	H	37
Holms Hill Fm	E Susx	TQ5619	50°57·2′	0°13·7′E	FM	199
Holmshill Ho	Herts	TQ2198	51°40·3′	0°14·6′W	X	166,176
Holmshurst	E Susx	TQ6425	51°0·3′	0°20·6′E	X	188,199
Holmside	Durham	NZ2149	54°50·4′	1°40·0′W	T	88
Holmside Hall	Durham	NZ2049	54°50·4′	1°40·9′W	X	88
Holm Sikes	Scot Bord	NY5693	55°14·0′	2°41·1′W	W	80
Holmsleigh Fm	Devon	ST1802	50°48·9′	3°9·5′W	FM	192,193
Holmsleigh Green	Devon	ST2002	50°49·0′	3°7·8′W	T	192,193
Holmsley Inclosure	Hants	SU2200	50°48·2′	1°40·9′W	F	195
Holmsley Lodge	Hants	SU2201	50°48·7′	1°40·9′W	X	195
Holmsley Ridge	Hants	SU2100	50°48·2′	1°41·7′W	X	195
Holmsmill	Scot Bord	NT1033	55°35·2′	3°25·2′W	X	72
Holms of Blossom	Orkney	HY5140	59°14·9′	2°51·1′W	X	5
Holms of Caaf	N Ayr	NS2748	55°41·9′	4°44·7′W	X	63
Holms of Ire	Orkney	HY6546	59°18·2′	2°36·4′W	X	5
Holms of Spurness	Orkney	HY6032	59°10·6′	2°41·5′W	X	5,6
Holms of Uyea-sound	Shetld	HU3161	60°20·2′	1°25·8′W	X	3
Holms of Vatsland	Shetld	HU4745	60°11·5′	1°8·7′W	X	4
Holm Sound	Orkney	HY4816	59°1·9′	2°53·9′W	W	6
Holm Sound	Orkney	HY6637	59°13·4′	2°35·3′W	W	5
Holm Sound	Orkney	ND5099	58°52·8′	2°51·6′W	W	6,7
Holmstall	E Susx	TQ5626	51°1·0′	0°13·8′E	X	188,199
Holmsted Manor	W Susx	TQ2826	51°1·4′	0°10·1′W	X	187,198
Holms, The	N Yks	SE8371	54°7·9′	0°43·4′W	X	100
Holmston	S Ayr	NS3521	55°27·6′	4°36·1′W	T	70
Holmstone	Kent	TR0218	50°55·8′	0°52·9′E	X	189
Holmston Hall	Ches	SJ6062	53°9·5′	2°35·5′W	X	118
Holms Water	Scot Bord	NT0932	55°34·6′	3°26·3′W	W	72
Holms Waterhead	Scot Bord	NT0728	55°32·5′	3°28·0′W	X	72
Holm Taing	Orkney	HY5121	59°4·7′	2°50·8′W	X	5,6
Holm, The	D & G	NX3460	54°54·7′	4°35·0′W	X	82
Holm, The	D & G	NX8254	54°52·3′	3°49·9′W	X	84
Holm, The	Heref	SO3146	52°6·7′	3°0·1′W	X	148
Holm, The	Shetld	HU6771	60°25·3′	0°46·5′W	X	2
Holmwath	Durham	NY8329	54°39·6′	2°15·4′W	X	91,92
Holmwood	Dorset	SZ0698	50°47·1′	1°54·5′W	X	195
Holmwood Common	Surrey	TQ1745	51°11·8′	0°19·1′W	F	187
Holmwood Corner	Surrey	TQ1744	51°11·2′	0°19·2′W	T	187
Holmwood Fm	Devon	ST1508	50°52·2′	3°12·1′W	FM	192,193
Holmwood Fm	Devon	ST1508	50°52·2′	3°12·1′W	FM	192,193
Holmwood Fm	Essex	TL8627	51°54·9′	0°42·7′E	FM	168
Holmwood Fm	Essex	TM0320	51°50·7′	0°57·2′E	FM	168
Holmwood Fm	Lincs	TF2864	53°9·7′	0°4·7′W	FM	122
Holmwood Fm	Surrey	TQ1647	51°12·9′	0°20·0′W	FM	187
Holmwood Park	Surrey	TQ1744	51°11·2′	0°19·2′W	X	187
Holmwood Place	Kent	TQ4748	51°13·0′	0°6·7′E	X	188
Holm Woods	N Yks	SE8589	54°17·6′	0°41·2′W	F	94,100
Holmwood Sta	Surrey	TQ1743	51°10·7′	0°19·2′W	X	187
Holmwrangle	Cumbr	NY5148	54°49·7′	2°45·3′W	T	86
Holne	Devon	SX7069	50°30·6′	3°49·6′W	T	202
Holne Br	Devon	SX7370	50°31·2′	3°47·1′W	A	202
Holne Chase	Devon	SX7271	50°31·7′	3°48·0′W	F	202
Holne Moor	Devon	SX6770	50°31·1′	3°52·2′W	X	202
Holne Park Residential Centre	Devon	SX7370	50°31·2′	3°47·1′W	X	202
Holne Ridge	Devon	SX6669	50°30·6′	3°53·0′W	X	202
Holnest	Dorset	ST6509	50°53·0′	2°29·5′W	T	194
Holnest Fm	Devon	SY1994	50°44·6′	3°8·5′W	FM	192,193
Holnest Park	Dorset	ST6509	50°53·0′	2°29·5′W	X	194
Holne Woods	Devon	SX7070	50°31·2′	3°49·7′W	F	202
Holnicote	Somer	SS9146	51°12·4′	3°33·2′W	T	181
Holodyke	Orkney	HY3020	59°3·9′	3°12·8′W	X	6
Holo-gwyn	I of Angl	SH5071	53°13·1′	4°14·4′W	X	114,115
Holoman Bay	Highld	NG5539	57°22·8′	6°4·1′W	W	24,32
Holoman Island	Highld	NG5440	57°23·3′	6°5·2′W	X	24
Holpur	Shetld	HU4421	59°58·6′	1°12·2′W	X	4
Holride Fm	Surrey	TQ0554	51°16·8′	0°29·3′W	FM	187
Holroyd Ho	Devon	SS4507	50°50·7′	4°11·7′W	X	190
Holsas	Shetld	HU4232	60°4·5′	1°14·2′W	H	4
Holset	Devon	SX7537	50°13·4′	3°44·8′W	X	202
Hols Hellier	Shetld	HP6317	60°50·1′	0°50·0′W	X	1
Holsome	Devon	SX7355	50°23·1′	3°46·8′W	X	202
Holsty Fm	Heref	SO3836	52°1·4′	2°53·8′W	FM	149,161
Holsworthy	Devon	SS3403	50°48·4′	4°21·0′W	T	190
Holsworthy Beacon	Devon	SS3508	50°51·1′	4°20·3′W	T	190
Holsworthy Woods	Devon	SS3501	50°47·3′	4°20·1′W	F	190
Holt	Ches	SK0069	53°13·3′	1°59·6′W	X	119
Holt	Dorset	SU0203	50°49·8′	1°57·9′W	T	195
Holt	Hants	SU7354	51°17·1′	0°56·8′W	T	186
Holt	Norf	TG0838	52°54·2′	1°6·0′E	T	133
Holt	Shrops	SO5396	52°33·8′	2°41·2′W	X	137,138
Holt	St Hel	SJ4891	53°25·0′	2°46·5′W	T	108
Holt	Suff	TL9442	52°2·8′	0°50·1′E	X	155
Holt	Wilts	ST8661	51°21·1′	2°11·7′W	T	173
Holt	Worcs	SO8262	52°15·6′	2°15·4′W	T	138,150
Holt	Wrex	SJ4053	53°4·5′	2°53·3′W	T	117
Holt Ball	Somer	SS9143	51°10·8′	3°33·2′W	X	181
Holtby	York	SE6754	53°58·9′	0°58·3′W	T	105,106
Holtby Grange	N Yks	SE2693	54°20·2′	1°35·6′W	X	99
Holtby Grange	York	SE6653	53°58·4′	0°59·2′W	X	105,106
Holtby Hall	N Yks	SE2692	54°19·6′	1°35·6′W	X	99
Holtby Manor	York	SE6652	53°57·8′	0°59·2′W	X	105,106
Holt Copse	W Berks	SU3374	51°28·1′	1°31·1′W	F	174
Holt Down Plantation	Hants	SU7218	50°57·6′	0°58·1′W	F	197
Holt End	Hants	SU6639	51°9·0′	1°3·0′W	T	185,186
Holt End	Worcs	SP0769	52°19·4′	1°53·4′W	T	139
Holt Fleet	Worcs	SO8263	52°16·1′	2°15·4′W	T	138,150
Holt Fm	Essex	TM1927	51°54·1′	1°11·4′E	FM	168,169
Holt Fm	Glos	SP0324	51°55·1′	1°57·0′W	FM	163
Holt Fm	Glos	SP1435	52°1·0′	1°47·4′W	FM	151
Holt Fm	Glos	ST9295	51°39·5′	2°6·5′W	FM	163
Holt Fm	Herts	TL1203	51°43·1′	0°22·3′W	FM	166
Holt Fm	Leeds	SE2744	53°53·7′	1°34·9′W	FM	104
Holt Fm	Leic	SP5587	52°28·9′	1°11·0′W	FM	140
Holt Fm	Leic	SP6086	52°28·4′	1°6·6′W	FM	140
Holt Fm	Leic	SP6188	52°29·4′	1°5·7′W	FM	140
Holt Fm	N Som	ST5159	51°19·9′	2°41·8′W	FM	172,182
Holt Fm	Somer	ST5739	51°9·2′	2°36·5′W	FM	182,183
Holt Fm	Somer	ST7439	51°9·2′	2°21·9′W	FM	183
Holt Fm	Warw	SP0762	52°15·6′	1°53·4′W	FM	150
Holt Fm	Warw	SP2298	52°35·0′	1°40·1′W	FM	139
Holt Fm	Warw	SP2340	52°3·7′	1°39·5′W	FM	151
Holt Fm	Warw	SP4360	52°14·4′	1°21·8′W	FM	151
Holt Fm	Warw	SP4559	52°13·9′	1°20·1′W	FM	151
Holt Fm	W Susx	TQ1005	50°50·3′	0°25·9′W	FM	198
Holt Fms	Dorset	ST5608	50°52·4′	2°37·1′W	FM	194
Holt Fms	Kent	TR1146	51°10·7′	1°1·5′E	FM	179,189
Holt Fm, The	Herts	TL1619	51°51·7′	0°18·5′W	FM	166
Holt Forest	Dorset	SU0305	50°50·9′	1°57·1′W	F	195
Holt Green	Lancs	SD3904	53°32·0′	2°54·8′W	T	108
Holt Hall (Coll)	Norf	TG0739	52°54·7′	1°5·1′E	X	133
Holt Hall Fm	Warw	SP2692	52°31·8′	1°36·6′W	FM	140
Holtham Garrs	Lincs	TF1586	53°21·7′	0°15·9′W	X	113,121
Holtham Plantn	Dorset	ST7215	50°56·3′	2°23·5′W	F	183
Holt Head	Kirk	SE0712	53°36·5′	1°53·2′W	T	110
Holt Heath	Dorset	SU0504	50°50·4′	1°55·4′W	X	195
Holt Heath	Dorset	SU0604	50°50·4′	1°54·5′W	T	195
Holt Heath	Worcs	SO8163	52°16·1′	2°16·3′W	T	138,150
Holt Hill	Dorset	ST6814	50°55·7′	2°26·9′W	X	194
Holt Hill	Kent	TQ7157	51°17·4′	0°27·5′E	T	178,188
Holt Hill	Staffs	SK1226	52°50·1′	1°48·9′W	T	128
Holt Ho	Ches	SJ8080	53°19·2′	2°17·6′W	X	109
Holt Ho	Lincs	TF2436	52°54·7′	0°9·0′W	X	131
Holt Ho	Norf	TF6718	52°44·3′	0°28·8′E	X	132
Holt Lodge	Norf	TG0737	52°53·7′	1°5·0′E	X	133
Holt Lodge	W Berks	SU3864	51°22·7′	1°26·9′W	X	174
Holt Lodge Fm	Dorset	SU0506	50°51·4′	1°55·4′W	FM	195
Holt Lodge Fm	Wrex	SJ3751	53°3·4′	2°56·0′W	FM	117
Holt Lowes	Norf	TG0837	52°53·6′	1°5·9′E	X	133
Holt Manor	Wilts	ST8562	51°21·6′	2°12·5′W	X	173

Holt Manor Fm	W Berks	SU4064	51°22·6′	1°25·1′W	FM	174
Holton	Corn	SX0869	50°29·6′	4°42·0′W	X	200
Holton	Oxon	SP6006	51°45·2′	1°7·5′W	T	164,165
Holton	Pth & Kin	NO1106	56°14·5′	3°25·7′W	X	58
Holton	Somer	ST6826	51°2·2′	2°27·0′W	T	183
Holton	Suff	TM4077	52°20·5′	1°31·8′E	T	156
Holton Brook	Oxon	SP6107	51°45·7′	1°6·6′W	W	164,165
Holtonburn	Pth & Kin	NO1206	56°14·6′	3°24·8′W	X	58
Holton cum Beckering	Lincs	TF1181	53°19·1′	0°19·6′W	T	121
Holton Fm	Leic	SP6186	52°28·3′	1°5·7′W	FM	140
Holton Grange	Lincs	TA2901	53°29·6′	0°2·9′W	X	113
Holton Grange	Lincs	TF1282	53°19·6′	0°18·7′W	X	121
Holton Hall	Suff	TM0536	51°59·3′	0°59·5′E	X	155
Holton Heath	Dorset	SY9591	50°43·3′	2°3·9′W	X	195
Holton Heath Station	Dorset	SY9490	50°42·8′	2°4·7′W	X	195
Holton Hill	E Susx	TQ6625	51°0·2′	0°22·4′E	X	188,199
Holton Hill	Lancs	SD6142	53°52·6′	2°35·2′W	X	102,103
Holton le Clay	Lincs	TA2802	53°30·2′	0°3·8′W	T	113
Holton le Moor	Lincs	TF0897	53°27·8′	0°22·0′W	T	112
Holton Lodge	Lincs	TA2801	53°29·6′	0°3·8′W	X	113
Holton Mill	Oxon	SP6105	51°44·7′	1°6·6′W	X	164,165
Holton Point	Dorset	SY9791	50°43·3′	2°2·2′W	X	195
Holton St Mary	Suff	TM0536	51°59·3′	0°59·5′E	T	155
Holton Wood	Oxon	SP6008	51°46·3′	1°7·4′W	F	164,165
Holt Park	Leeds	SE2640	53°51·6′	1°35·9′W	T	104
Holt Place	W Susx	SZ8199	50°47·3′	0°50·7′W	X	197
Holt Pound	Hants	SU8143	51°11·1′	0°50·1′W	T	186
Holt Pound Inclosure	Hants	SU8043	51°11·1′	0°50·9′W	F	186
Holtridge	Ches	SJ5648	53°1·9′	2°39·0′W	X	117
Holtroad Downs	Corn	SX1565	50°27·6′	4°36·0′W	X	201
Holts	Essex	TL9431	51°56·8′	0°49·8′E	X	168
Holts	Oldham	SD9503	53°31·7′	2°4·1′W	T	109
Holts Down	Bath & NE Somer	ST7769	51°25·4′	2°19·5′W	X	172
Holt's Fm	Essex	TL6626	51°54·7′	0°25·2′E	FM	167
Holts Fm	Essex	TL7512	51°47·0′	0°32·6′E	FM	167
Holts Fm	Oxon	SP5517	51°51·2′	1°11·7′W	FM	164
Holts Fm	Staffs	SJ8031	52°52·8′	2°17·4′W	FM	127
Holtsmere End	Herts	TL0711	51°47·5′	0°26·5′W	X	166
Holtspur	Bucks	SU9290	51°36·3′	0°39·9′W	T	175
Holt, The	Hants	SU5523	51°0·5′	1°12·6′W	X	185
Holt, The	Hants	SU5561	51°21·0′	1°12·2′W	X	174
Holt, The	Hants	SU5743	51°11·2′	1°10·7′W	F	185
Holt, The	Hants	SU7111	50°53·9′	0°59·0′W	F	197
Holt, The	Notts	SK6390	53°24·4′	1°2·7′W	F	111
Holt, The	Shrops	SJ8208	52°40·4′	2°15·6′W	X	127
Holt, The	Shrops	SO7588	52°29·6′	2°21·7′W	X	138
Holt, The	W Berks	SU3473	51°27·5′	1°30·2′W	X	174
Holtwood	Derby	SK1332	52°53·4′	1°48·0′W	X	128
Holt Wood	Derby	SK3256	53°6·3′	1°30·9′W	F	119
Holtwood	Dorset	ST6914	50°55·7′	2°26·1′W	X	194
Holt Wood	Dorset	SU0305	50°50·9′	1°57·1′W	T	195
Holt Wood	Surrey	TQ3759	51°19·0′	0°1·7′W	F	187
Holtwood	W Berks	SU4164	51°22·6′	1°24·3′W	X	174
Holtwood Fm	Beds	TL0528	51°56·7′	0°27·9′W	FM	166
Holtye	E Susx	TQ4539	51°8·1′	0°4·7′E	T	188
Holtye Common	E Susx	TQ4539	51°8·1′	0°4·7′E	X	188
Holtye Ho	E Susx	TQ4639	51°8·1′	0°5·6′E	X	188
Holverston Hall	Norf	TG3003	52°34·8′	1°24·1′E	X	134
Holway	Dorset	ST3803	50°49·6′	2°52·4′W	T	193
Holway	Dorset	ST6320	50°58·9′	2°31·2′W	T	183
Holway	Flint	SJ1776	53°16·7′	3°14·3′W	T	116
Holway	Somer	ST2423	51°0·3′	3°4·6′W	T	193
Holway Farm	Dorset	ST5801	50°48·7′	2°35·4′W	A	194
Holway Hill	Dorset	ST6320	50°58·9′	2°31·2′W	H	183
Holways Fm	Devon	SY0497	50°46·1′	3°21·3′W	FM	192
Holwell	Corn	SX3775	50°33·4′	4°17·7′W	X	201
Holwell	Devon	SS3723	50°59·2′	4°19·0′W	X	190
Holwell	Devon	SS5742	51°9·8′	4°2·3′W	X	180
Holwell	Devon	SS9510	50°53·0′	3°29·2′W	X	192
Holwell	Devon	SX5073	50°32·5′	4°6·6′W	X	191,201
Holwell	Devon	SX6941	50°15·5′	3°49·9′W	X	202
Holwell	Devon	SX7477	50°35·0′	3°46·4′W	X	191
Holwell	Dorset	ST7011	50°54·1′	2°25·2′W	T	194
Holwell	Herts	TL1633	51°59·2′	0°18·2′W	T	166
Holwell	Leic	SK7323	52°48·2′	0°54·6′W	T	129
Holwell	Oxon	SP2309	51°47·0′	1°39·6′W	T	163
Holwell	Somer	ST7245	51°12·4′	2°23·7′W	T	183
Holwell Barrow	Devon	SS6743	51°10·5′	3°53·8′W	A	180
Holwellbury	Beds	TL1634	51°59·8′	0°18·2′W	T	153
Holwellbury Fm	Beds	TL1634	51°59·8′	0°18·2′W	FM	153
Holwell Castle	Devon	SS6644	51°11·0′	3°54·7′W	A	180
Holwell Combe	Somer	ST2134	51°6·2′	3°7·3′W	X	182
Holwell Court	Herts	TL2710	51°46·7′	0°9·1′W	X	166
Holwell Downs Fm	Oxon	SP2108	51°46·4′	1°41·3′W	FM	163
Holwell Fm	Devon	SS4215	50°55·0′	4°14·5′W	FM	180,190
Holwell Fm	Devon	SS9623	51°0·1′	3°28·5′W	FM	181
Holwell Fm	Dorset	SU0613	50°55·2′	1°54·5′W	FM	195
Holwell Fm	Dorset	SY6583	50°39·0′	2°29·3′W	FM	194
Holwell Fm	Glos	ST7992	51°37·8′	2°17·8′W	FM	162,172
Holwell Fm	Somer	ST7149	51°14·6′	2°24·5′W	FM	183
Holwell Lawn	Devon	SX7478	50°35·5′	3°46·4′W	X	191
Holwell Mouth	Leic	SK7224	52°48·8′	0°55·5′W	X	129
Holwell Tor	Devon	SX7577	50°35·0′	3°45·6′W	X	191
Holwick	Durham	NY9026	54°38·0′	2°8·9′W	T	91,92
Holwick Fell	Durham	NY8826	54°38·0′	2°10·7′W	X	91,92
Holwick Head Ho	Durham	NY8828	54°39·1′	2°10·7′W	X	91,92
Holwick Lodge	Durham	NY9027	54°38·5′	2°8·9′W	X	91,92
Holwick Scars	Durham	NY9026	54°38·0′	2°8·9′W	X	91,92
Holwill	Devon	SS4211	50°52·9′	4°14·4′W	X	190
Holwood	Brom	TQ4263	51°21·1′	0°2·7′E	X	177,187
Holwood	Corn	SX3463	50°26·8′	4°19·9′W	X	201
Holwood	Lancs	SD5839	53°51·0′	2°37·9′W	X	102
Holwood Fm	Brom	TQ4262	51°20·6′	0°2·7′E	FM	177,187
Holwood Fm	Cambs	TL3878	52°23·2′	0°2·1′E	FM	142,143
Holwoods House Fm	Cambs	TL3880	52°24·3′	0°2·1′E	FM	142,143
Holworth	Dorset	SY7683	50°39·0′	2°20·0′W	X	194
Holworth Ho	Dorset	SY7681	50°37·9′	2°20·0′W	X	194
Holworth Village	Dorset	SY7783	50°39·0′	2°19·1′W	A	194
Holworthy	Devon	SS6844	51°11·0′	3°52·9′W	X	180
Holworthy	Somer	SS9730	51°3·8′	3°27·8′W	X	181
Holy Austin Rock	Staffs	SO8383	52°26·9′	2°14·6′W	X	138
Holybourne	Hants	SU7340	51°9·5′	0°57·0′W	T	186
Holybourne Down	Hants	SU7342	51°10·6′	0°57·0′W	X	186
Holybreds Fm	Essex	TL7707	51°44·2′	0°34·2′E	FM	167
Holy Brook	Devon	SX7168	50°30·1′	3°48·8′W	W	202
Holy Brook	W Berks	SU6771	51°26·3′	1°1·8′W	W	175
Holy City	Devon	ST2904	50°50·1′	3°0·1′W	T	193
Holy Cross	Durham	NZ3843	54°47·1′	1°24·1′W	X	88
Holy Cross	N Tyne	NZ3167	55°0·0′	1°30·5′W	T	88
Holy Cross	Worcs	SO9278	52°24·2′	2°6·7′W	T	139
Holydean	Scot Bord	NT5330	55°33·9′	2°44·3′W	X	73
Holy Den	Scot Bord	NY4696	55°15·6′	2°50·5′W	X	79
Holyeat	Devon	SX4779	50°35·7′	4°9·3′W	X	191,201
Holyfield	Essex	TL3803	51°42·8′	0°0·2′E	T	166
Holyfield Hall Fm	Essex	TL3803	51°42·8′	0°0·2′E	FM	166
Holyford	Devon	SY2392	50°43·6′	3°5·1′W	T	192,193
Holygate Fm	Leic	SK8216	52°44·4′	0°46·7′W	FM	130
Holyhead Bay	I of Angl	SH2687	53°21·3′	4°36·5′W	W	114
Holyhead Mountain	I of Angl	SH2182	53°18·5′	4°40·8′W	H	114
Holyhead or Caergybi	I of Angl	SH2482	53°18·6′	4°38·1′W	T	114
Holy Island	N Ayr	NS0629	55°31·2′	5°4·0′W	X	69
Holy Island	Northum	NU1241	55°40·0′	1°48·1′W	T	75
Holy Island	Northum	NU1243	55°41·1′	1°48·1′W	X	75
Holy Island or Ynys Gybi	I of Angl	SH2579	53°17·0′	4°37·1′W	X	114
Holy Island Sands	Northum	NU0942	55°40·5′	1°51·0′W	X	75
Holy Kirk	Orkney	HY2521	59°4·4′	3°18·0′W	X	6
Holy Kirk (Stones)	Orkney	HY2521	59°4·4′	3°18·0′W	A	6
Holylee	Scot Bord	NT3937	55°37·6′	2°57·7′W	T	73
Holylee Burn	Scot Bord	NT3938	55°38·2′	2°57·7′W	W	73
Holy Linn	D & G	NX6580	55°6·0′	4°6·5′W	W	77
Holy Loch	Arg & Bt	NS1682	56°0·0′	4°56·6′W	W	56
Holy Loch	Arg & Bt	NS1780	55°58·9′	4°55·6′W	W	63
Holy Mill	Shrops	SO5595	52°33·3′	2°39·4′W	X	137,138
Holy Moor	Derby	SK3268	53°12·7′	1°30·8′W	X	119
Holymoorside	Derby	SK3369	53°13·3′	1°29·9′W	T	119
Holyoak Fm	Suff	TM0556	52°10·1′	1°0·3′E	FM	155
Holyoaks Lodge	Leic	SP8495	52°33·0′	0°45·3′W	X	141
Holyport	Win & Maid	SU8977	51°29·3′	0°42·7′W	T	175
Holyrood Ho	Devon	SS3016	50°55·3′	4°24·7′W	X	190
Holyrood Ho	E Yorks	TA1438	53°49·8′	0°15·7′W	X	107
Holyroodhouse (Abbey & Palace)	C of Edin	NT2673	55°56·9′	3°10·7′W	A	66
Holyrood Park	C of Edin	NT2773	55°56·9′	3°9·7′W	X	66
Holystone	Northum	NT9502	55°19·0′	2°4·3′W	T	81
Holystone Burn	Northum	NT9401	55°18·4′	2°5·2′W	W	80
Holystone Common	Northum	NT9401	55°18·4′	2°5·2′W	X	80
Holystone Fm	N Tyne	NZ2970	55°1·7′	1°32·4′W	FM	88
Holystone Grange	Northum	NT9600	55°17·9′	2°3·3′W	X	81
Holy Stream	Dorset	SY8488	50°41·7′	2°13·2′W	W	194
Holystreet Manor	Devon	SX6887	50°40·3′	3°51·7′W	X	191
Holy's Wash	Swan	SS4985	51°32·9′	4°10·3′W	X	159
Holytown	N Lanak	NS7660	55°49·3′	3°58·3′W	T	64
Holytown Sta	N Lanak	NS7659	55°48·8′	3°58·3′W	X	64
Holy Vale	I Scilly	SV9211	49°55·4′	6°17·1′W	T	203
Holyway Cross	Corn	SX2782	50°37·0′	4°26·4′W	X	201
Holywell	Aberd	NJ5527	57°20·1′	2°44·4′W	X	37
Holywell	Beds	TL0116	51°50·2′	0°31·6′W	T	166
Holywell	Cambs	TL3370	52°18·9′	0°2·5′W	T	154
Holywell	Ches	SJ4755	53°5·6′	2°47·1′W	X	117
Holy Well	Corn	SW6728	50°6·6′	5°15·2′W	A	203
Holywell	Corn	SW7658	50°23·0′	5°8·7′W	T	200
Holy Well	Corn	SX0976	50°33·4′	4°41·4′W	A	200
Holywell	Cumbr	NY4675	55°4·2′	2°50·3′W	X	86
Holy Well	Cumbr	NY5968	55°0·5′	2°38·0′W	X	86
Holy Well	Cumbr	SD3873	54°9·2′	2°56·5′W	W	96,97
Holy Well	Devon	SS7631	51°4·1′	3°45·8′W	A	180
Holy Well	Devon	SX6647	50°18·7′	3°52·5′W	A	202
Holywell	Dorset	ST5904	50°50·3′	2°34·6′W	T	194
Holy Well	Durham	NY8243	54°47·1′	2°16·4′W	X	86,87
Holywell	Durham	NZ2537	54°43·9′	1°36·3′W	X	93
Holywell	E Susx	TV6096	50°44·7′	0°16·5′E	X	199
Holywell	Glos	ST7693	51°38·4′	2°20·4′W	T	162,172
Holy Well	Gwyn	SH2429	52°50·0′	4°36·4′W	A	123
Holy Well	Hants	SU5914	50°55·6′	1°9·2′W	A	196
Holywell	Heref	SO3741	52°4·1′	2°54·8′W	T	148,149,161
Holywell	Herts	TQ0995	51°38·8′	0°25·1′W	T	166,176
Holywell	Kent	TQ8567	51°22·5′	0°39·9′E	X	178
Holy Well	Lincs	SK9792	53°25·2′	0°32·0′W	A	112
Holy Well	Monm	SO2905	51°44·6′	3°1·3′W	A	161
Holywell	Northum	NU1817	55°27·0′	1°42·5′W	X	81
Holywell	Northum	NZ3174	55°3·8′	1°30·4′W	T	88
Holy Well	Pemb	SN1111	51°46·2′	4°44·0′W	A	158
Holy Well	Peterb	TL1698	52°34·3′	0°16·9′W	A	142
Holy Well	Shrops	SJ6821	52°47·4′	2°28·1′W	W	127
Holy Well	Shrops	SO5175	52°22·5′	2°42·8′W	A	137,138
Holy Well	Somer	ST3740	51°9·6′	2°53·7′W	W	182
Holy Well	Somer	ST3839	51°9·0′	2°52·8′W	A	182
Holywell	Somer	ST5213	50°55·1′	2°40·6′W	T	194
Holywell	Warw	SP1966	52°17·7′	1°42·9′W	T	151
Holywell Bank	Flint	SJ2178	53°17·8′	3°10·7′W	X	117
Holywell Bay	Corn	SW7659	50°23·5′	5°8·7′W	W	200
Holywell Beach	Corn	SW7659	50°23·5′	5°8·7′W	X	200
Holywell Beck	Durham	NZ2438	54°44·4′	1°37·2′W	W	93
Holywell Brook	Oxon	SU3292	51°37·8′	1°31·9′W	W	164,174
Holywell Brook	Powys	SJ2316	52°44·4′	3°8·0′W	W	126
Holy Well Burn	Durham	NZ1834	54°42·3′	1°42·8′W	W	92
Holywell Burn	Northum	NY8879	55°6·6′	2°10·9′W	W	87
Holywell Common	Flint	SJ1873	53°15·1′	3°13·3′W	X	116
Holywell Cross	Devon	SS7631	51°4·1′	3°45·8′W	X	180
Holywell Dingle	Heref	SO3151	52°9·4′	3°0·1′W	X	148
Holywell Fm	Bucks	SP7734	52°0·2′	0°52·3′W	FM	152,165
Holywell Fm	Notts	SK6959	53°7·7′	0°57·7′W	FM	120
Holywell Fm	Oxon	SP3832	51°59·3′	1°26·4′W	FM	151
Holywell Fm	Red & Cl	NZ7216	54°32·3′	0°52·8′W	FM	94
Holywell Grange Fm	N Tyne	NZ3173	55°3·3′	1°30·5′W	FM	88
Holywell Green	Cald	SE0819	53°40·3′	1°52·3′W	T	110
Holywell Hall	Leic	SK5018	52°45·7′	1°15·1′W	X	129
Holywell Hall	Lincs	SK9916	52°44·2′	0°31·6′W	X	130
Holywell Halt	N Yks	SE0253	53°58·6′	1°57·8′W	X	104
Holywell Ho	Ches	SJ5753	53°4·6′	2°38·1′W	X	117
Holywell Ho	Durham	NZ1721	54°35·3′	1°43·8′W	X	92
Holywell Ho	Hants	SU5915	50°56·1′	1°9·2′W	X	196
Holy Well Ho	N Yks	NZ8011	54°29·5′	0°45·5′W	X	94
Holywell Lake	Somer	ST1020	50°58·6′	3°16·5′W	T	181,193
Holywellmoor	Shrops	SJ4630	52°52·1′	2°47·7′W	X	126
Holywell or Treffynnon	Flint	SJ1875	53°16·2′	3°13·4′W	T	116
Holywell Park fm	Kent	TQ6263	51°20·8′	0°20·0′E	FM	177,188
Holywell Resr	Devon	SS7630	51°3·6′	3°45·8′W	W	180
Holywell Rig	Scot Bord	NT4503	55°19·3′	2°51·6′W	H	79
Holywell Row	Suff	TL7077	52°22·1′	0°30·2′E	T	143
Holywells Park	Suff	TM1743	52°2·8′	1°10·3′E	X	169
Holywell Wood	Lincs	SK9815	52°43·7′	0°32·5′W	F	130
Holywick	Bucks	SU8087	51°34·8′	0°50·3′W	X	175
Holywood	D & G	NX9480	55°6·4′	3°39·3′W	T	78
Holywych Fm	E Susx	TQ4840	51°8·6′	0°7·3′E	FM	188
Holywych Ho	E Susx	TQ4840	51°8·6′	0°7·3′E	X	188
Hombush Forest	W Susx	TQ2233	51°5·2′	0°15·1′W	F	187
Homebank	Scot Bord	NT8039	55°38·9′	2°18·6′W	X	74
Homebarns	Shrops	SJ5517	52°45·2′	2°39·6′W	X	126
Home Barton	Devon	SS5647	51°12·5′	4°3·3′W	X	180
Home Bush	Devon	SY2197	50°46·3′	3°6·8′W	F	192,193
Homebush Wood	Somer	SS8645	51°11·8′	3°37·5′W	F	181
Homebyres	Scot Bord	NT7040	55°39·4′	2°28·2′W	X	74
Home Copse	Bucks	SU8285	51°33·7′	0°48·6′W	F	175
Home Cottage Fm	Norf	TM0095	52°31·2′	0°57·3′E	FM	144
Home Covert	Norf	TF7400	52°34·4′	0°34·5′E	F	143
Home Covert	Norf	TL9383	52°24·9′	0°50·7′E	F	144
Home Covert	Norf	TL9981	52°23·7′	0°55·9′E	F	144
Home Covert	Somer	ST7355	51°17·8′	2°22·8′W	F	172
Home Covert	Suff	TM4676	52°19·8′	1°37·0′E	F	156
Home Covert	Suff	TM5084	52°24·0′	1°40·9′E	F	156
Home Dams Fen	Cambs	TL4881	52°24·6′	0°11·0′E	X	143
Home Dams Fen	Cambs	TL4983	52°25·7′	0°11·9′E	X	143
Home Down	Hants	SU6316	50°56·6′	1°5·8′W	X	185
Homedowns	Glos	SO9232	51°59·4′	2°6·6′W	T	150
Home Eweleaze	Dorset	SY7496	50°46·0′	2°21·7′W	X	194
Home Farm	Aberd	NJ5743	57°28·8′	2°42·6′W	FM	29
Home Farm	Aberd	NJ7059	57°37·5′	2°29·7′W	FM	29
Home Farm	Aberd	NK0064	57°40·2′	1°59·5′W	FM	30
Home Farm	Orkney	HY4227	59°7·8′	3°0·3′W	FM	5,6
Home Farm	Scot Bord	NT1737	55°37·4′	3°18·6′W	FM	72
Home Farm Auchry	Aberd	NJ8051	57°33·2′	2°19·6′W	X	29,30
Home Farm Colony	Essex	TQ8086	51°32·9′	0°36·2′E	X	178
Home Farm Ho	Essex	TL7526	51°54·5′	0°33·0′E	X	167
Home Farm Ho	Kent	TQ7746	51°11·4′	0°32·4′E	X	188
Home Farm Kininmonth	Aberd	NK0353	57°34·3′	1°56·5′W	X	30
Home Farm Kinmundy	Aberd	NK0043	57°28·9′	1°59·5′W	X	30
Home Farm of Netherdale	Aberd	NJ6448	57°31·5′	2°35·6′W	X	29
Home Farm of Pitlurg	Aberd	NK0233	57°23·5′	1°57·5′W	X	30
Homefield	Devon	SX7744	50°17·2′	3°43·2′W	X	202
Homefield Fm	Kent	TQ5469	51°24·2′	0°13·2′E	FM	177
Homefield Wood	Bucks	SU8187	51°34·8′	0°49·5′W	F	175
Home Fm	Aberd	NJ5416	57°14·2′	2°45·3′W	FM	37
Home Fm	Aberd	NJ5430	57°21·7′	2°45·4′W	FM	29,37
Home Fm	Aberd	NJ5630	57°21·8′	2°43·4′W	FM	29,37
Home Fm	Aberd	NJ5741	57°27·7′	2°42·5′W	FM	29
Home Fm	Aberd	NJ6811	57°11·6′	2°31·3′W	FM	38
Home Fm	Aberd	NJ6915	57°13·7′	2°30·4′W	FM	38
Home Fm	Aberd	NJ7026	57°19·7′	2°29·4′W	FM	38
Home Fm	Aberd	NJ7032	57°22·9′	2°29·5′W	FM	29
Home Fm	Aberd	NJ7035	57°24·5′	2°29·5′W	FM	29
Home Fm	Aberd	NJ7420	57°16·5′	2°25·4′W	FM	38
Home Fm	Aberd	NJ7546	57°30·5′	2°24·6′W	FM	29
Home Fm	Aberd	NJ7550	57°32·6′	2°24·6′W	FM	29
Home Fm	Aberd	NJ7640	57°27·2′	2°23·5′W	FM	29
Home Fm	Aberd	NJ7921	57°17·0′	2°20·4′W	FM	38
Home Fm	Aberd	NJ8516	57°14·3′	2°14·5′W	FM	38
Home Fm	Aberd	NJ8525	57°19·2′	2°14·5′W	FM	38
Home Fm	Aberd	NJ8621	57°17·0′	2°13·5′W	FM	38
Home Fm	Aberd	NJ8914	57°13·3′	2°10·5′W	FM	38
Home Fm	Aberd	NJ8926	57°19·7′	2°10·5′W	FM	38
Home Fm	Aberd	NJ9337	57°25·7′	2°6·5′W	FM	30
Home Fm	Aberd	NJ9416	57°14·3′	2°5·5′W	FM	38
Home Fm	Aberd	NJ9931	57°22·4′	2°0·5′W	FM	30
Home Fm	Aberd	NJ9959	57°37·5′	2°0·5′W	FM	30
Home Fm	Aberd	NO4795	57°2·8′	2°52·0′W	FM	37,44
Home Fm	Aberd	NO6475	56°52·2′	2°35·0′W	FM	45
Home Fm	Aberd	NO6697	57°4·0′	2°33·2′W	FM	38,45
Home Fm	Aberd	NO7975	56°52·2′	2°20·2′W	FM	45
Home Fm	Aberd	NO8096	57°3·5′	2°19·3′W	FM	38,45
Home Fm	Aberd	NO8486	56°58·2′	2°15·3′W	FM	45
Home Fm	Angus	NO3451	56°39·0′	3°4·1′W	FM	54
Home Fm	Angus	NO4059	56°43·4′	2°58·4′W	FM	54
Home Fm	Angus	NO5642	56°34·3′	2°42·5′W	FM	54
Home Fm	Angus	NO5650	56°38·6′	2°42·6′W	FM	54
Home Fm	Angus	NO6246	56°36·5′	2°36·7′W	FM	54
Home Fm	Angus	NO6862	56°45·2′	2°30·9′W	FM	45
Home Fm	Arg & Bt	NM4153	56°36·1′	6°12·8′W	FM	47
Home Fm	Arg & Bt	NM5439	56°29·0′	5°59·3′W	FM	47,48
Home Fm	Beds	SP9421	51°53·0′	0°37·7′W	FM	165
Home Fm	Beds	SP9541	52°3·8′	0°36·5′W	FM	153
Home Fm	Beds	TL0033	51°59·4′	0°32·2′W	FM	166
Home Fm	Beds	TL0753	52°10·1′	0°25·7′W	FM	153
Home Fm	Beds	TL0836	52°0·9′	0°25·2′W	FM	153
Home Fm	Beds	TL1017	51°50·7′	0°23·8′W	FM	166
Home Fm	Beds	TL2549	52°7·7′	0°10·0′W	FM	153
Home Fm	Brackn	SU9470	51°25·5′	0°38·5′W	FM	175
Home Fm	Bucks	SP6737	52°1·9′	1°1·0′W	FM	152
Home Fm	Bucks	SP6828	51°57·0′	1°0·2′W	FM	164,165
Home Fm	Bucks	SP7135	52°0·8′	0°57·5′W	FM	152
Home Fm	Bucks	SP7142	52°4·5′	0°57·4′W	FM	152
Home Fm	Bucks	SP7225	51°55·4′	0°56·8′W	FM	165
Home Fm	Bucks	SP7237	52°1·8′	0°56·6′W	FM	152
Home Fm	Bucks	SP8825	51°55·2′	0°42·8′W	FM	165
Home Fm	Cambs	TL1886	52°27·8′	0°15·4′W	FM	142
Home Fm	Cambs	TL3056	52°11·4′	0°5·5′W	FM	153
Home Fm	Cambs	TL5456	52°11·1′	0°15·6′E	FM	154
Home Fm	Carm	SN7541	52°3·4′	3°49·0′W	FM	146,147,160
Home Fm	Cered	SN6278	52°23·2′	4°1·3′W	FM	135

Home Fm	Ches	SJ3372	53°14·7′	2°59·8′W	FM	117
Home Fm	Ches	SJ6976	53°17·0′	2°27·5′W	FM	118
Home Fm	Ches	SJ7482	53°20·3′	2°23·0′W	FM	109
Home Fm	Ches	SJ7954	53°5·2′	2°18·4′W	FM	118
Home Fm	Ches	SJ8070	53°13·8′	2°17·6′W	FM	118
Home Fm	Ches	SJ8459	53°7·9′	2°13·9′W	FM	118
Home Fm	Ches	SJ8473	53°15·5′	2°14·0′W	FM	118
Home Fm	Ches	SJ8773	53°15·5′	2°11·3′W	FM	118
Home Fm	C of Edin	NT1777	55°59·0′	3°19·4′W	FM	65,66
Home Fm	Corn	SX1090	50°41·0′	4°41·0′W	FM	190
Home Fm	Cumbr	NY5531	54°40·6′	2°41·4′W	FM	90
Home Fm	Cumbr	NY7709	54°28·8′	2°20·9′W	FM	91
Home Fm	Cumbr	SD5376	54°10·9′	2°42·8′W	FM	97
Home Fm	Derby	SK2513	52°43·1′	1°37·4′W	FM	128
Home Fm	Derby	SK4033	52°53·8′	1°23·9′W	FM	129
Home Fm	Derby	SK4344	52°59·7′	1°21·2′W	FM	129
Home Fm	Devon	ST0509	50°52·6′	3°20·6′W	FM	192
Home Fm	Devon	SX9696	50°45·5′	3°28·1′W	FM	192
Home Fm	Devon	SY1392	50°43·5′	3°13·6′W	FM	192,193
Home Fm	D & G	NW9862	54°55·0′	5°8·7′W	FM	82
Home Fm	D & G	NX4137	54°42·4′	4°27·7′W	FM	83
Home Fm	D & G	NX4745	54°46·8′	4°22·3′W	FM	83
Home Fm	D & G	NX6769	55°0·1′	4°4·3′W	FM	83,84
Home Fm	D & G	NX9356	54°53·5′	3°39·7′W	FM	84
Home Fm	D & G	NY1576	55°4·5′	3°19·5′W	FM	85
Home Fm	Donc	SK5695	53°27·2′	1°9·0′W	FM	111
Home Fm	Dorset	ST3901	50°48·6′	2°51·6′W	FM	193
Home Fm	Dorset	ST6415	50°56·2′	2°30·4′W	FM	183
Home Fm	Dorset	ST9112	50°54·7′	2°7·3′W	FM	195
Home Fm	Dorset	SU1213	50°55·2′	1°49·4′W	FM	195
Home Fm	Dorset	SY7193	50°44·4′	2°24·3′W	FM	194
Home Fm	Dorset	SY7794	50°44·9′	2°19·2′W	FM	194
Home Fm	Dorset	SY8683	50°39·0′	2°11·5′W	FM	194
Home Fm	Durham	NZ2727	54°38·5′	1°34·5′W	FM	93
Home Fm	E Loth	NT3469	55°54·8′	3°2·9′W	FM	66
Home Fm	E Loth	NT4983	56°2·5′	2°48·7′W	FM	66
Home Fm	E Loth	NT5477	55°59·3′	2°43·8′W	FM	66
Home Fm	Essex	TL4101	51°41·6′	0°2·8′E	FM	167
Home Fm	Essex	TL5525	51°54·3′	0°15·6′E	FM	167
Home Fm	Essex	TL7730	51°56·6′	0°34·9′E	FM	167
Home Fm	Essex	TL7916	51°49·1′	0°36·2′E	FM	167
Home Fm	Essex	TL8630	51°56·5′	0°42·8′E	FM	168
Home Fm	Essex	TL9012	51°46·7′	0°45·7′E	FM	168
Home Fm	Essex	TM0629	51°55·5′	1°0·2′E	FM	168
Home Fm	Essex	TM1330	51°55·9′	1°6·3′E	FM	168,169
Home Fm	Essex	TM2031	51°56·3′	1°12·4′E	FM	169
Home Fm	Essex	TQ4495	51°38·3′	0°5·3′E	FM	167,177
Home Fm	Essex	TQ8292	51°36·1′	0°38·1′E	FM	178
Home Fm	E Susx	TQ4930	51°3·2′	0°7·9′E	FM	188
Home Fm	E Yorks	SE7857	54°0·4′	0°48·2′W	FM	105,106
Home Fm	E Yorks	SE8250	53°56·6′	0°44·6′W	FM	106
Home Fm	E Yorks	TA2169	54°6·4′	0°8·5′W	FM	101
Home Fm	Fife	NO3322	56°23·4′	3°4·7′W	FM	53,59
Home Fm	Fife	NO3421	56°22·9′	3°3·7′W	FM	54,59
Home Fm	Glos	SO7823	51°54·5′	2°18·8′W	FM	162
Home Fm	Glos	SO8732	51°59·4′	2°11·0′W	FM	150
Home Fm	Glos	SO9326	51°56·2′	2°5·7′W	FM	163
Home Fm	Glos	SP1714	51°49·7′	1°44·8′W	FM	163
Home Fm	Glos	SP2112	51°48·6′	1°41·3′W	FM	163
Home Fm	Glos	ST8096	51°40·0′	2°17·0′W	FM	162
Home Fm	Glos	ST8690	51°36·8′	2°11·7′W	FM	162,173
Home Fm	Hants	SU1208	50°52·5′	1°49·4′W	FM	195
Home Fm	Hants	SU2342	51°10·8′	1°39·9′W	FM	184
Home Fm	Hants	SU2629	51°3·8′	1°37·4′W	FM	184
Home Fm	Hants	SU3342	51°10·8′	1°31·3′W	FM	185
Home Fm	Hants	SU4125	51°1·6′	1°24·5′W	FM	185
Home Fm	Hants	SU4323	51°0·5′	1°22·8′W	FM	185
Home Fm	Hants	SU4849	51°14·5′	1°18·4′W	FM	185
Home Fm	Hants	SU5756	51°18·2′	1°10·5′W	FM	174
Home Fm	Hants	SU6550	51°15·0′	1°3·7′W	FM	185,186
Home Fm	Hants	SU6962	51°21·4′	1°0·2′W	FM	175,186
Home Fm	Hants	SU7023	51°0·4′	0°59·7′W	FM	197
Home Fm	Hants	SU7159	51°19·8′	0°58·5′W	FM	175,186
Home Fm	Hants	SU8257	51°18·6′	0°49·0′W	FM	175,186
Home Fm	Hav	TQ5293	51°37·1′	0°12·1′E	FM	177
Home Fm	Hav	TQ6185	51°32·7′	0°19·7′E	FM	177
Home Fm	Heref	SO4043	52°5·2′	2°52·1′W	FM	148,149,161
Home Fm	Heref	SO4635	52°0·9′	2°46·8′W	FM	149,161
Home Fm	Heref	SO4830	51°58·2′	2°45·0′W	FM	149,161
Home Fm	Heref	SO5560	52°14·4′	2°39·1′W	FM	137,138,149
Home Fm	Heref	SO6018	51°51·8′	2°34·5′W	FM	162
Home Fm	Herts	TL0012	51°48·1′	0°32·6′W	FM	166
Home Fm	Herts	TL0315	51°49·7′	0°29·9′W	FM	166
Home Fm	Herts	TL0411	51°47·5′	0°29·1′W	FM	166
Home Fm	Herts	TL3118	51°50·9′	0°5·5′W	FM	166
Home Fm	Herts	TL4321	51°52·4′	0°5·0′E	FM	167
Home Fm	Herts	TQ1796	51°39·3′	0°18·1′W	FM	166,176
Home Fm	Highld	NH3962	57°37·4′	4°41·3′W	FM	20
Home Fm	Highld	NH4316	57°12·7′	4°35·5′W	FM	34
Home Fm	Highld	NH4942	57°26·9′	4°30·5′W	FM	26
Home Fm	Highld	NH7273	57°44·0′	4°8·5′W	FM	21
Home Fm	Highld	NJ0330	57°21·3′	3°36·3′W	FM	27,36
Home Fm	Kent	TQ5365	51°22·0′	0°12·3′E	FM	177
Home Fm	Kent	TQ5547	51°12·3′	0°13·5′E	FM	188
Home Fm	Kent	TQ6041	51°9·0′	0°17·7′E	FM	188
Home Fm	Kent	TQ9744	51°9·9′	0°49·5′E	FM	189
Home Fm	Kent	TR0047	51°11·5′	0°52·1′E	FM	189
Home Fm	Kent	TR0639	51°7·0′	0°57·0′E	FM	179,189
Home Fm	Leeds	SE4136	53°49·4′	1°22·2′W	FM	105
Home Fm	Leeds	SE4228	53°45·0′	1°21·4′W	FM	105
Home Fm	Leic	SK3302	52°37·1′	1°30·4′W	FM	140
Home Fm	Leic	SK4227	52°50·6′	1°22·2′W	FM	129
Home Fm	Leic	SK4824	52°48·9′	1°16·9′W	FM	129
Home Fm	Leic	SK5720	52°46·7′	1°8·9′W	FM	129
Home Fm	Leic	SK6113	52°42·9′	1°5·4′W	FM	129
Home Fm	Leic	SK7200	52°35·8′	0°55·8′W	FM	141
Home Fm	Leic	SK7612	52°42·3′	0°52·1′W	FM	129
Home Fm	Leic	SP5481	52°25·7′	1°11·9′W	FM	140
Home Fm	Leic	SP8093	52°32·0′	0°48·8′W	FM	141
Home Fm	Lincs	SK9882	53°19·8′	0°31·3′W	FM	121
Home Fm	Lincs	TF0188	53°23·0′	0°28·5′W	FM	112,121
Home Fm	Lincs	TF1354	53°4·5′	0°18·4′W	FM	121
Home Fm	Lincs	TF1672	53°14·2′	0°15·3′W	FM	121
Home Fm	Lincs	TF1884	53°20·6′	0°13·2′W	FM	122
Home Fm	Lincs	TF1923	52°47·7′	0°13·7′W	FM	130
Home Fm	Lincs	TF1953	53°3·9′	0°13·0′W	FM	122
Home Fm	Lincs	TF2625	52°48·7′	0°7·4′W	FM	131
Home Fm	Lincs	TF2883	53°19·9′	0°4·3′W	FM	122
Home Fm	Lincs	TF3061	53°8·0′	0°3·0′W	FM	122
Home Fm	Lincs	TF3084	53°20·4′	0°2·4′W	FM	122
Home Fm	Lincs	TF3085	53°21·0′	0°2·4′W	FM	122
Home Fm	Lincs	TF3251	53°2·6′	0°1·5′W	FM	122
Home Fm	Lincs	TF3483	53°19·8′	0°1·1′E	FM	122
Home Fm	Lincs	TF3929	52°50·7′	0°4·2′E	FM	131
Home Fm	Lincs	TF4070	53°12·7′	0°6·2′E	FM	122
Home Fm	Lincs	TF4420	52°45·7′	0°8·5′E	FM	131
Home Fm	Lincs	TF4754	53°4·0′	0°12·0′E	FM	122
Home Fm	Lincs	TF5065	53°9·9′	0°15·0′E	FM	122
Home Fm	Mil Key	SP9447	52°7·0′	0°37·2′W	FM	153
Home Fm	Monm	SO4514	51°49·6′	2°47·5′W	FM	161
Home Fm	Moray	NJ3038	57°25·9′	3°9·5′W	FM	28
Home Fm	Moray	NJ3744	57°29·2′	3°2·6′W	FM	28
Home Fm	Moray	NJ4966	57°41·1′	2°50·9′W	FM	28,29
Home Fm	N Ayr	NS1963	55°49·8′	4°53·0′W	FM	63
Home Fm	N Lincs	SE9501	53°30·1′	0°33·7′W	FM	112
Home Fm	Norf	TF6212	52°41·1′	0°24·2′E	FM	132,143
Home Fm	Norf	TF6300	52°34·6′	0°24·7′E	FM	143
Home Fm	Norf	TF6404	52°36·8′	0°25·7′E	FM	143
Home Fm	Norf	TF7029	52°50·1′	0°31·8′E	FM	132
Home Fm	Norf	TF7117	52°43·6′	0°32·3′E	FM	132
Home Fm	Norf	TF7918	52°44·0′	0°39·5′E	FM	132
Home Fm	Norf	TF8004	52°36·5′	0°39·9′E	FM	144
Home Fm	Norf	TF8504	52°36·4′	0°44·3′E	FM	144
Home Fm	Norf	TF9318	52°43·7′	0°51·9′E	FM	132
Home Fm	Norf	TG1804	52°35·6′	1°13·5′E	FM	134
Home Fm	Norf	TG2816	52°41·8′	1°22·9′E	FM	133,134
Home Fm	Norf	TG2837	52°53·1′	1°23·7′E	FM	133
Home Fm	Norf	TL5592	52°30·5′	0°17·4′E	FM	143
Home Fm	Norf	TL7789	52°28·4′	0°36·8′E	FM	144
Home Fm	Norf	TL7896	52°32·2′	0°37·9′E	FM	144
Home Fm	Norf	TL8292	52°30·0′	0°41·3′E	FM	144
Home Fm	Norf	TL9098	52°33·0′	0°48·5′E	FM	144
Home Fm	Norf	TL9581	52°23·8′	0°52·4′E	FM	144
Home Fm	Norf	TL9596	52°31·8′	0°52·9′E	FM	144
Home Fm	Norf	TM2084	52°24·8′	1°14·5′E	FM	156
Home Fm	Norf	TM2384	52°24·7′	1°17·1′E	FM	156
Home Fm	Norf	TM2886	52°25·7′	1°21·6′E	FM	156
Home Fm	Northnts	SP6785	52°27·8′	1°0·4′W	FM	141
Home Fm	Northnts	SP7766	52°17·4′	0°51·9′W	FM	152
Home Fm	Northnts	SP8958	52°13·0′	0°41·4′W	FM	152
Home Fm	Northnts	SP9579	52°24·3′	0°35·8′W	FM	141
Home Fm	Northnts	SP9696	52°33·4′	0°34·6′W	FM	141
Home Fm	Northum	NZ2097	55°16·3′	1°40·7′W	FM	81
Home Fm	Northum	NZ2177	55°5·5′	1°39·8′W	FM	88
Home Fm	Notts	SK4652	53°4·0′	1°18·4′W	FM	120
Home Fm	Notts	SK5052	53°4·0′	1°14·8′W	FM	120
Home Fm	Notts	SK6934	52°54·2′	0°58·0′W	FM	129
Home Fm	Notts	SK7031	52°52·5′	0°57·2′W	FM	129
Home Fm	Notts	SK7189	53°23·8′	0°55·5′W	FM	112,120
Home Fm	N Som	ST5168	51°24·8′	2°41·9′W	FM	172,182
Home Fm	N Yks	NZ3505	54°26·6′	1°27·2′W	FM	93
Home Fm	N Yks	SE2193	54°20·2′	1°40·2′W	FM	99
Home Fm	N Yks	SE2298	54°22·9′	1°39·3′W	FM	99
Home Fm	N Yks	SE3060	54°2·3′	1°32·1′W	FM	99
Home Fm	N Yks	SE3252	53°58·0′	1°30·3′W	FM	104
Home Fm	N Yks	SE3276	54°11·0′	1°30·2′W	FM	99
Home Fm	N Yks	SE3568	54°6·6′	1°27·5′W	FM	99
Home Fm	N Yks	SE3586	54°16·3′	1°27·3′W	FM	99
Home Fm	N Yks	SE3749	53°56·4′	1°25·8′W	FM	104
Home Fm	N Yks	SE4388	54°17·4′	1°19·9′W	FM	99
Home Fm	N Yks	SE4440	53°51·5′	1°19·4′W	FM	105
Home Fm	N Yks	SE4595	54°21·2′	1°18·0′W	FM	99
Home Fm	N Yks	SE5367	54°6·0′	1°11·0′W	FM	100
Home Fm	N Yks	SE5640	53°51·4′	1°8·5′W	FM	105
Home Fm	N Yks	SE5670	54°7·6′	1°8·2′W	FM	100
Home Fm	N Yks	SE5863	54°3·8′	1°6·4′W	FM	100
Home Fm	N Yks	SE5934	53°48·2′	1°5·8′W	FM	105
Home Fm	N Yks	SE5942	53°52·5′	1°5·7′W	FM	105
Home Fm	N Yks	SE6572	54°8·6′	0°59·9′W	FM	100
Home Fm	N Yks	SE6943	53°53·0′	0°56·6′W	FM	105,106
Home Fm	N Yks	SE7077	54°11·3′	0°55·2′W	FM	100
Home Fm	N Yks	SE7571	54°8·0′	0°50·7′W	FM	100
Home Fm	Oxon	SP2307	51°45·9′	1°39·6′W	FM	163
Home Fm	Oxon	SP3606	51°45·3′	1°28·3′W	FM	164
Home Fm	Oxon	SP4222	51°53·9′	1°23·0′W	FM	164
Home Fm	Oxon	SP4723	51°54·4′	1°18·6′W	FM	164
Home Fm	Oxon	SP5312	51°48·5′	1°13·5′W	FM	164
Home Fm	Oxon	SP5410	51°47·4′	1°12·6′W	FM	164
Home Fm	Oxon	SP5918	51°51·7′	1°8·2′W	FM	164
Home Fm	Oxon	SP6130	51°58·1′	1°6·3′W	FM	152,165
Home Fm	Oxon	SP7602	51°42·9′	0°53·6′W	FM	165
Home Fm	Oxon	SU2386	51°34·6′	1°39·7′W	FM	174
Home Fm	Oxon	SU2589	51°36·2′	1°37·9′W	FM	174
Home Fm	Oxon	SU3396	51°39·9′	1°31·0′W	FM	164
Home Fm	Oxon	SU5297	51°40·4′	1°14·5′W	FM	164
Home Fm	Oxon	SU7478	51°30·0′	0°55·6′W	FM	175
Home Fm	Pemb	SM9319	51°50·1′	4°59·9′W	FM	157,158
Home Fm	Peterb	TF0400	52°35·5′	0°27·5′W	FM	141
Home Fm	Peterb	TF2004	52°37·5′	0°13·2′W	FM	142
Home Fm	Powys	SO2966	52°17·5′	3°2·1′W	FM	137,148
Home Fm	Pth & Kin	NN7159	56°42·6′	4°6·0′W	FM	42,51,52
Home Fm	Pth & Kin	NN9116	56°19·7′	3°45·3′W	FM	58
Home Fm	Pth & Kin	NO0515	56°19·3′	3°31·7′W	FM	58
Home Fm	Pth & Kin	NO1203	56°12·9′	3°24·7′W	FM	58
Home Fm	Pth & Kin	NO1218	56°21·0′	3°25·0′W	FM	58
Home Fm	Roth	SK5585	53°21·8′	1°10·0′W	FM	111,120
Home Fm	S Ayr	NS4731	55°33·2′	4°25·1′W	FM	70
Home Fm	Scot Bord	NT7029	55°33·5′	2°28·1′W	FM	74
Home Fm	Shrops	SJ4905	52°38·7′	2°44·8′W	FM	126
Home Fm	Shrops	SJ5410	52°41·4′	2°40·4′W	FM	126
Home Fm	Shrops	SJ6339	52°57·1′	2°32·6′W	FM	127
Home Fm	Shrops	SJ7415	52°44·2′	2°22·7′W	FM	127
Home Fm	Shrops	SO6799	52°35·5′	2°28·8′W	FM	138
Home Fm	Sol	SP2479	52°24·7′	1°38·4′W	FM	139
Home Fm	Somer	ST0243	51°10·9′	3°23·7′W	FM	181
Home Fm	Somer	ST5256	51°18·3′	2°40·9′W	FM	172,182
Home Fm	Somer	ST6642	51°10·8′	2°28·8′W	FM	183
Home Fm	Somer	ST7052	51°16·2′	2°25·4′W	FM	183
Home Fm	Staffs	SJ8245	53°0·4′	2°15·7′W	FM	118
Home Fm	Staffs	SJ9216	52°44·7′	2°6·7′W	FM	127
Home Fm	Staffs	SJ9234	52°54·4′	2°6·7′W	FM	127
Home Fm	Staffs	SK1722	52°48·0′	1°44·5′W	FM	128
Home Fm	Staffs	SO8890	52°30·7′	2°10·2′W	FM	139
Home Fm	St Hel	SJ5491	53°25·1′	2°41·1′W	FM	108
Home Fm	Stir	NS5085	56°2·3′	4°24·0′W	FM	57
Home Fm	Stir	NS5387	56°3·5′	4°21·2′W	FM	57
Home Fm	Suff	TL7452	52°8·6′	0°33·0′E	FM	155
Home Fm	Suff	TL8552	52°8·3′	0°42·6′E	FM	155
Home Fm	Suff	TL8961	52°13·1′	0°46·4′E	FM	155
Home Fm	Suff	TL8978	52°22·3′	0°47·0′E	FM	144
Home Fm	Suff	TL9163	52°14·1′	0°48·2′E	FM	155
Home Fm	Suff	TL9354	52°9·3′	0°49·7′E	FM	155
Home Fm	Suff	TL9576	52°21·1′	0°52·2′E	FM	144
Home Fm	Suff	TL9841	52°2·1′	0°53·6′E	FM	155
Home Fm	Suff	TM1257	52°10·5′	1°6·4′E	FM	155
Home Fm	Suff	TM1738	52°0·1′	1°10·1′E	FM	169
Home Fm	Suff	TM1776	52°20·6′	1°11·5′E	FM	156
Home Fm	Suff	TM2259	52°11·3′	1°15·3′E	FM	156
Home Fm	Suff	TM2457	52°10·2′	1°16·9′E	FM	156
Home Fm	Suff	TM2550	52°6·4′	1°17·5′E	FM	156
Home Fm	Suff	TM2954	52°8·4′	1°21·2′E	FM	156
Home Fm	Suff	TM2978	52°21·4′	1°22·2′E	FM	156
Home Fm	Suff	TM3085	52°25·1′	1°23·3′E	FM	156
Home Fm	Suff	TM3472	52°18·0′	1°26·3′E	FM	156
Home Fm	Suff	TM3483	52°23·9′	1°26·8′E	FM	156
Home Fm	Suff	TM3761	52°12·0′	1°28·5′E	FM	156
Home Fm	Suff	TM4996	52°30·5′	1°40·6′E	FM	134
Home Fm	Suff	TM5199	52°32·1′	1°42·5′E	FM	
Home Fm	Suff	TM5299	52°32·1′	1°43·4′E	FM	134
Home Fm	Surrey	TQ1548	51°13·4′	0°20·8′W	FM	187
Home Fm	Surrey	TQ2040	51°9·0′	0°16·7′W	FM	187
Home Fm	Swan	SS4988	51°34·5′	4°10·4′W	FM	159
Home Fm	Thurr	TQ6582	51°31·0′	0°23·1′E	FM	177,178
Home Fm	Traf	SJ7486	53°22·5′	2°23·0′W	FM	109
Home Fm	V of Glam	ST0467	51°23·9′	3°22·4′W	FM	170
Home Fm	V of Glam	ST0478	51°29·8′	3°22·6′W	FM	170
Home Fm	Warw	SK2801	52°36·6′	1°34·8′W	FM	140
Home Fm	Warw	SP1472	52°21·0′	1°47·3′W	FM	139
Home Fm	Warw	SP2467	52°18·3′	1°38·5′W	FM	151
Home Fm	Warw	SP4372	52°20·9′	1°21·7′W	FM	140
Home Fm	Warw	SP4876	52°23·0′	1°17·3′W	FM	140
Home Fm	Warw	SP5178	52°24·1′	1°14·6′W	FM	140
Home Fm	Warw	SP5375	52°22·5′	1°12·9′W	FM	140
Home Fm	W Berks	SU3667	51°24·3′	1°28·6′W	FM	174
Home Fm	W Berks	SU4179	51°30·7′	1°24·2′W	FM	174
Home Fm	W Berks	SU4671	51°26·4′	1°19·9′W	FM	174
Home Fm	W Berks	SU5574	51°28·0′	1°12·1′W	FM	174
Home Fm	W Berks	SU6176	51°29·0′	1°6·9′W	FM	175
Home Fm	W Berks	SU6469	51°25·2′	1°4·4′W	FM	175
Home Fm	W Berks	SU6676	51°29·0′	1°2·6′W	FM	175
Home Fm	Wilts	ST7734	51°6·5′	2°19·3′W	FM	183
Home Fm	Wilts	ST9460	51°20·6′	2°4·8′W	FM	173
Home Fm	Wilts	ST9568	51°24·9′	2°3·9′W	FM	173
Home Fm	Wilts	ST9669	51°25·4′	2°3·1′W	FM	173
Home Fm	Wilts	SU0062	51°21·7′	1°59·6′W	FM	173
Home Fm	Wilts	SU0929	51°3·8′	1°51·9′W	FM	184
Home Fm	Wilts	SU2246	51°13·0′	1°40·7′W	FM	184
Home Fm	Wilts	SU2319	50°58·4′	1°40·0′W	FM	184
Home Fm	Win & Maid	SU9274	51°27·7′	0°40·1′W	FM	175
Home Fm	Win & Maid	SU9875	51°28·2′	0°35·0′W	FM	175,176
Home Fm	W Loth	NT1368	55°54·1′	3°23·0′W	FM	65
Home Fm	Worcs	SO7565	52°17·2′	2°21·6′W	FM	138,150
Home Fm	Worcs	SO8043	52°5·3′	2°17·1′W	FM	150
Home Fm	Worcs	SO8047	52°7·5′	2°17·1′W	FM	150
Home Fm	Wrex	SJ2942	52°58·5′	3°3·0′W	FM	117
Home Fm	Wrex	SJ3642	52°58·5′	2°56·8′W	FM	117
Home Fm	Wrex	SJ4439	52°57·0′	2°49·6′W	FM	126
Home Fm	W Susx	SU8428	51°2·9′	0°47·7′W	FM	186,197
Home Fm	W Susx	SU9008	50°52·1′	0°42·9′W	FM	197
Home Fm	W Susx	SZ8695	50°45·1′	0°46·5′W	FM	197
Home Fm	W Susx	TQ2025	51°0·9′	0°17·0′W	FM	187,198
Home Fm	W Susx	TQ3237	51°7·2′	0°6·4′W	FM	187
Home Fm	York	SE5448	53°55·8′	1°10·2′W	FM	105
Home Fm	York	SE5858	54°1·1′	1°6·5′W	FM	105
Home Fm Auchintoul	Aberd	NJ6152	57°33·6′	2°38·6′W	FM	29
Home Fm of Clunie	Aberd	NJ6350	57°32·6′	2°36·6′W	FM	29
Home Fm, The	Ches	SJ5359	53°7·8′	2°41·7′W	FM	117
Home Fm, The	Ches	SJ5872	53°14·8′	2°37·4′W	FM	117
Home Fm, The	Ches	SJ7563	53°10·1′	2°22·0′W	FM	118
Home Fm, The	Northnts	SP6844	52°5·6′	1°0·0′W	FM	152
Home Fm, The	Pemb	SR9795	51°37·3′	4°55·6′W	FM	158
Home Fm The	Somer	ST1042	51°10·4′	3°16·9′W	FM	181
Home Fm, The	Staffs	SJ8318	52°45·8′	2°14·7′W	FM	127
Home Fm, The	Staffs	SK1144	52°59·8′	1°49·8′W	FM	119,128
Home Fm, The	W Susx	TQ2627	51°1·9′	0°11·8′W	FM	187,198
Homehead	Aberd	NJ4304	57°7·7′	2°56·0′W	X	37
Home Heath	Suff	TL7870	52°18·2′	0°37·0′E	X	144,155
Home Heath	Suff	TL8273	52°19·7′	0°40·7′E	F	144,155
Home Hill	Norf	TF9643	52°57·1′	0°55·5′E	X	132
Home Ho	Heref	SO6956	52°12·3′	2°26·8′W	X	149
Homehouse Fm	Heref	SO7046	52°6·9′	2°25·9′W	FM	149
Homelands	Devon	SX8346	50°18·4′	3°38·2′W	X	202
Homelands Fm	Glos	SO9628	51°57·3′	2°3·1′W	FM	150,163
Homelands Fm	W Susx	TQ1918	50°57·2′	0°18·0′W	FM	198
Home Law	Scot Bord	NT3215	55°25·7′	3°4·0′W	H	79
Homelea Fm	Somer	ST1330	51°4·0′	3°14·1′W	FM	181
Homeleaze Fm	Glos	SP1704	51°44·3′	1°44·8′W	FM	163
Home Loch	Highld	NH2079	57°46·1′	5°1·1′W	W	20
Homelye Fm	Essex	TL6422	51°52·6′	0°23·3′E	FM	167
Home Manor Fm	Northnts	SP6145	52°6·2′	1°6·2′W	FM	152

Homemead Fm	Somer	ST7440	51°9·8′	2°21·9′W	FM	183
Homend	Heref	SO6444	52°5·8′	2°31·1′W	X	149
Home Park	Herts	TL2409	51°46·2′	0°11·8′W	F	166
Home Park	W Susx	SU8129	51°3·5′	0°50·3′W	X	186,197
Home Park, The	Win & Maid	SU9776	51°28·7′	0°35·8′W	X	175,176
Home Pastures	Warw	SP4186	52°28·5′	1°23·4′W	X	140
Homer	Devon	SS5116	50°55·7′	4°6·8′W	X	180
Homer	Shrops	SJ6101	52°36·6′	2°34·2′W	T	127
Home Reach	Suff	TM4655	52°8·5′	1°36·1′E	W	156
Homerell Hole	N Yks	NZ9507	54°27·2′	0°31·7′W	W	94
Homer Fm	Oxon	SU6685	51°33·8′	1°2·5′W	FM	175
Homer Green	Sefton	SD3402	53°30·9′	2°59·3′W	T	108
Homersfield	Suff	TM2885	52°25·1′	1°21·6′E	T	156
Homerton	Hack	TQ3585	51°33·1′	0°2·8′W	T	177
Homerton Hill	Devon	SX5690	50°41·7′	4°2·0′W	X	191
Homestall	Kent	TQ9559	51°18·0′	0°48·2′E	X	178
Homestall	Kent	TR0360	51°18·4′	0°55·1′E	X	178,179
Homestalls	Herts	TL4519	51°51·3′	0°6·7′E	X	167
Homestalls	Wilts	ST7737	51°8·1′	2°19·3′W	X	183
Homestall Stud	E Susx	TQ4238	51°7·6′	0°2·1′E	X	187
Homestall Wood	Derby	SK2214	52°43·6′	1°40·1′W	F	128
Homestall Wood	Kent	TR1158	51°17·1′	1°1·9′E	F	179
Homestead	Wilts	SU2572	51°27·0′	1°38·0′W	A	174
Homestead Fm	E Susx	TQ7018	50°56·4′	0°25·6′E	FM	199
Homestead Fm	Hants	SU3434	51°6·5′	1°30·5′W	FM	185
Homestead Fm	Notts	SK6135	52°54·8′	1°5·2′W	FM	129
Homestead Moat	Highld	NH5353	57°32·9′	4°26·9′W	X	26
Homesteads, The	Stir	NS7793	56°7·1′	3°58·3′W	X	57
Homestead, The	Cambs	TF3905	52°37·7′	0°3·6′E	X	142,143
Homestead, The	E Susx	TQ4925	51°0·5′	0°7·8′E	X	188,199
Homestead, The	Leic	SK5612	52°42·4′	1°9·9′W	X	129
Homestead, The	Leic	SK7617	52°44·9′	0°52·0′W	X	129
Homestead, The	Leic	SP4991	52°31·1′	1°16·3′W	X	140
Homestead, The	York	SE5745	53°54·1′	1°7·5′W	X	105
Homeston	Arg & Bt	NR6715	55°22·7′	5°40·2′W	X	68
Home, The	Shrops	SO3790	52°30·5′	2°55·3′W	X	137
Home Whin Fm	Suff	TM3245	52°3·5′	1°23·5′E	FM	169
Home Wood	Beds	SP9529	51°57·3′	0°36·7′W	F	165
Home Wood	Beds	TL1446	52°6·3′	0°19·7′W	F	153
Home Wood	Bucks	SP6440	52°3·5′	1°3·6′W	F	152
Home Wood	Bucks	SP6840	52°3·5′	1°0·1′W	F	152
Home Wood	Bucks	SP7124	51°54·8′	0°57·7′W	F	165
Home Wood	Herts	TL2903	51°42·9′	0°7·6′W	F	166
Home Wood	N Yks	SE8675	54°10·1′	0°40·5′W	F	101
Home Wood	Oxon	SP3605	51°44·8′	1°28·3′W	F	164
Home Wood	Oxon	SP5223	51°54·4′	1°14·3′W	F	164
Home Wood	Suff	TL9751	52°7·6′	0°53·1′E	F	155
Home Wood	Surrey	SU9131	51°4·5′	0°41·7′W	F	186
Homewoodgate Fm	E Susx	TQ3717	50°56·4′	0°2·6′W	FM	198
Hom Green	Heref	SO5822	51°53·9′	2°36·2′W	T	162
Hom Grove Fm	Heref	SO6318	51°51·8′	2°31·8′W	FM	162
Homilton	Northum	NY9778	55°6·0′	2°2·4′W	X	87
Homilton Hill	Northum	NT8932	55°35·1′	2°10·0′W	H	74
Homing Down	Devon	SX5298	50°46·0′	4°5·5′W	X	191
Homington	Wilts	SU1226	51°2·2′	1°49·3′W	T	184
Homington Down	Wilts	SU1124	51°1·1′	1°50·2′W	X	184
Homington Down	Wilts	SU1226	51°2·2′	1°49·3′W	X	184
Homington Ho	Wilts	SU1126	51°2·2′	1°50·2′W	X	184
Homme Castle	Worcs	SO7361	52°15·0′	2°23·3′W	X	138,150
Homme House	Heref	SO6531	51°58·8′	2°30·2′W	A	149
Homme, The	Heref	SO4152	52°10·0′	2°51·4′W	X	148,149
Homme, The	Heref	SO5722	51°53·9′	2°37·1′W	X	162
Homri	V of Glam	ST0875	51°28·2′	3°19·1′W	X	170
Hom,The	Powys	SO1944	52°5·5′	3°10·5′W	X	148,161
Honddu	Powys	SN9942	52°4·3′	3°28·0′W	W	147,160
Honddu	Powys	SO0335	52°0·5′	3°24·4′W	W	160
Hondon	Powys	SO1549	52°8·2′	3°14·1′W	X	148
Hondslough Fm	Ches	SJ5472	53°14·8′	2°41·0′W	FM	117
Hone	Devon	SS9616	50°56·8′	3°28·4′W	X	181
Hone	Somer	SS9232	51°4·9′	3°32·1′W	X	181
Hone Hill	Devon	SS9617	50°56·8′	3°28·4′W	H	181
Honer Fm	W Susx	SZ8798	50°46·7′	0°45·6′W	FM	197
Honeybag Tor	Devon	SX7278	50°35·5′	3°48·1′W	H	191
Honeybank	Aberd	NO7080	56°54·9′	2°29·1′W	X	45
Honeybarrel	Aberd	NJ4617	57°14·7′	2°53·2′W	X	37
Honeybed Wood	Wilts	ST9874	51°28·1′	2°1·3′W	F	173
Honey Bee Nest	N Yks	NZ6803	54°25·3′	0°56·7′W	X	94
Honeybottom	W Berks	SU4570	51°25·9′	1°20·8′W	X	174
Honey Bottom	Wilts	SU2953	51°16·8′	1°34·7′W	X	185
Honeybourne	Worcs	SP1144	52°5·9′	1°50·0′W	T	150
Honeybourne Sta	Worcs	SP1144	52°5·9′	1°50·0′W	X	150
Honey Br	Cambs	TL4389	52°29·0′	0°6·8′E	X	142,143
Honeybrae	Midlo	NT1656	55°47·7′	3°19·9′W	X	65
Honeybrae	Midlo	NT1656	55°47·7′	3°19·9′W	X	66
Honeybridge Fm	W Susx	TQ1616	50°56·1′	0°20·6′W	FM	198
Honeybrook Fm	Dorset	SU0002	50°49·3′	1°59·6′W	FM	195
Honeybrook Fm	Wilts	ST8473	51°27·6′	2°13·4′W	FM	173
Honeyburge	Bucks	SP6213	51°49·0′	1°5·6′W	X	164,165
Honey Burn	Scot Bord	NT5517	55°26·9′	2°42·3′W	W	80
Honeyburn	Scot Bord	NT5618	55°27·5′	2°41·3′W	X	80
Honeychild Manor	Kent	TR0527	51°0·6′	0°55·7′E	X	189
Honeychurch	Devon	SS6202	50°48·3′	3°57·1′W	T	191
Honeychurch Moor	Devon	SS6303	50°48·9′	3°56·3′W	X	191
Honeycombe Fm	Dorset	ST6214	50°55·7′	2°32·1′W	FM	194
Honeycombe Fm	Glos	SO9208	51°46·5′	2°6·6′W	FM	163
Honeycombe Fm	Worcs	SO6164	52°16·6′	2°33·9′W	FM	138,149
Honeycombe Wood	Dorset	ST6314	50°55·7′	2°31·2′W	F	194
Honeycomb Leaze Fm	Glos	SP1202	51°43·2′	1°49·2′W	FM	163
Honey Corse	Carm	SN2809	51°45·4′	4°29·1′W	X	158
Honeycott	N Yks	SD8689	54°18·0′	2°12·5′W	X	98
Honeycrock	E Susx	TQ6007	50°50·6′	0°16·8′E	X	199
Honeycroft	Devon	SS3308	50°51·1′	4°22·0′W	X	190
Honeycrook Burn	Northum	NY8266	54°59·5′	2°16·5′W	W	86,87
Honeydale Fm	Oxon	SP2818	51°51·8′	1°35·2′W	FM	163
Honeydon	Beds	TL1358	52°12·7′	0°20·4′W	T	153
Honeydown Fm	Dorset	ST4307	50°51·8′	2°48·2′W	FM	193
Honeyend Fm	Ches	SJ5157	53°6·7′	2°43·5′W	FM	117
Honeyfield Wood	Kent	TQ9039	51°7·3′	0°43·3′E	F	189
Honey Fm	Cambs	TL3683	52°25·9′	0°0·4′E	FM	142
Honeyford Fm	Devon	SX7593	50°43·6′	3°45·9′W	FM	191

Honeygar Fm	Somer	ST4242	51°10·7′	2°49·4′W	FM	182
Honey Hall	N Som	ST4361	51°20·9′	2°48·7′W	T	172,182
Honey Hill	Cambs	TL4388	52°28·5′	0°6·7′E	X	142,143
Honey Hill	Cambs	TL5060	52°13·3′	0°12·2′E	X	154
Honey Hill	Devon	ST3103	50°49·6′	2°58·4′W	X	193
Honey Hill	Durham	NZ0546	54°48·8′	1°54·9′W	X	87
Honey Hill	E Yorks	SE9966	54°5·1′	0°28·8′W	X	101
Honeyhill	I of M	SC4081	54°12·2′	4°26·8′W	X	95
Honey Hill	Kent	TR1161	51°18·8′	1°2·1′E	T	179
Honey Hill	Leic	SK2809	52°40·9′	1°34·7′W	X	128,140
Honey Hill	Northnts	SP6376	52°22·9′	1°4·1′W	H	140
Honey Hill	Wok	SU8266	51°23·5′	0°48·9′W	T	175
Honey Hill Fm	Cambs	TL4488	52°28·5′	0°7·6′E	FM	142,143
Honey Hill Fm	Northnts	SP6376	52°22·9′	1°4·1′W	FM	140
Honeyhill Fm	Suff	TL8064	52°14·9′	0°38·6′E	FM	155
Honey Hills	Norf	TF7634	52°52·7′	0°37·3′E	X	132
Honeyhills Wood	Kent	TQ7957	51°17·3′	0°34·4′E	F	178,188
Honeyhill Wood	Cambs	TL0767	52°17·7′	0°25·5′W	F	153
Honeyhive	Aberd	NO7272	56°50·6′	2°27·1′W	X	45
Honey Ho	Cumbr	NY4732	54°41·1′	2°48·9′W	X	90
Honeyhole	D & G	NX8297	55°15·4′	3°51·0′W	X	78
Honeyhole	Pth & Kin	NO1236	56°30·7′	3°25·4′W	X	53
Honey Hook	Pemb	SM8917	51°49·0′	5°3·3′W	X	157,158
Honeyhurst Fm	Somer	ST4750	51°15·0′	2°45·2′W	FM	182
Honeykiln Fm	N Yks	SE4692	54°19·5′	1°17·1′W	FM	100
Honeylake Brook	Heref	SO4654	52°11·1′	2°47·0′W	W	148,149
Honeyland	Devon	SS9212	50°54·1′	3°31·8′W	X	181
Honeylands	Essex	TQ3999	51°40·6′	0°1·0′E	X	166,177
Honey Lane Fm	Notts	SK7750	53°2·7′	0°50·7′W	FM	120
Honeyman Fm	Hants	SU5425	51°1·5′	1°13·4′W	FM	185
Honeymeade Fm	Somer	ST3455	51°17·7′	2°56·4′W	FM	182
Honeymead Fm	Somer	SS7939	51°8·5′	3°43·4′W	FM	180
Honey Moor	Cumbr	SD5898	54°22·8′	2°38·4′W	X	97
Honeymoor Common	Heref	SO4338	52°2·5′	2°49·5′W	X	149,161
Honeyneuk	Aberd	NJ9148	57°31·6′	2°8·6′W	X	30
Honey Pig	D & G	NX2059	54°53·9′	4°48·0′W	X	82
Honeypot	Cumbr	NY5530	54°40·0′	2°41·4′W	X	90
Honeypot	Kent	TR0835	51°4·8′	0°58·6′E	X	179,189
Honeypot Fm	Essex	TM1519	51°49·9′	1°7·6′E	FM	168,169
Honeypots	E Yorks	TA0361	54°2·3′	0°25·2′W	X	101
Honey Pots	N Yks	SE1084	54°15·3′	1°50·4′W	X	99
Honey Pots	Staffs	SJ9215	52°44·2′	2°6·7′W	F	127
Honeypots Fm	Essex	TQ8490	51°35·0′	0°39·7′E	FM	178
Honeypots Fm	Suff	TM2270	52°17·2′	1°15·7′E	FM	156
Honeypots Plantation	Norf	TL9894	52°30·7′	0°55·5′E	F	144
Honeys	Win & Maid	SU8274	51°27·8′	0°48·8′W	X	175
Honeys Croft	Pemb	SN0805	51°42·9′	4°46·4′W	X	158
Honeysgeo	Orkney	ND4893	58°49·5′	2°53·6′W	X	7
Honey's Green	E Susx	TQ5017	50°56·2′	0°8·5′E	X	199
Honeystreet	Wilts	SU1061	51°21·1′	1°51·0′W	T	173
Honey Street Fm	Wilts	SU1061	51°21·1′	1°51·0′W	FM	173
Honeysuckle Fm	E Yorks	TA1848	53°55·1′	0°11·8′W	FM	107
Honeysyke	Roth	SK5179	53°18·6′	1°13·7′W	X	120
Honeytor	Devon	SX4473	50°32·4′	4°11·7′W	X	201
Honey Tye	Suff	TL9535	51°59·0′	0°50·8′E	T	155
Honey Tye Fms	Suff	TL9636	51°59·5′	0°51·7′E	FM	155
Honeywall Fm	Staffs	SJ7945	53°0·4′	2°18·4′W	FM	118
Honeywell Fm	Devon	SS5740	51°8·7′	4°2·3′W	FM	180
Honeywell Ho	Somer	SS9137	51°7·6′	3°33·1′W	X	181
Honeywick	Beds	SP9721	51°53·0′	0°35·0′W	T	165
Honeywick Hill	Somer	ST6532	51°5·4′	2°29·6′W	X	183
Honey Wood	Kent	TR1461	51°18·7′	1°4·6′E	F	179
Honeywood Fm	Kent	TR0532	51°3·3′	0°55·9′E	FM	189
Honeywood Ho	W Susx	TQ1235	51°6·4′	0°23·6′W	X	187
Honga Ness	Shetld	HU6591	60°36·1′	0°48·3′W	X	1,2
Hongar Ho	Heref	SO4922	51°53·9′	2°44·1′W	X	162
Hongrass	Shrops	SO2481	52°25·5′	3°6·7′W	X	137
Honibere Fm	Somer	ST1843	51°11·1′	3°10·0′W	FM	181
Honicknowle	C of Plym	SX4658	50°24·3′	4°9·7′W	T	201
Honicombe	Corn	SX4170	50°30·7′	4°14·2′W	X	201
Honies Fm	Notts	SK7748	53°1·7′	0°50·7′W	FM	129
Honiley	Warw	SP2472	52°21·0′	1°38·5′W	T	139
Honing	Norf	TG3227	52°47·7′	1°26·9′E	T	133,134
Honing Common	Norf	TG3427	52°47·6′	1°28·7′E	X	133,134
Honing Hall	Norf	TG3229	52°48·7′	1°27·0′E	X	133,134
Honingham	Norf	TG1011	52°39·6′	1°6·7′E	T	133
Honington	Lincs	SK9443	52°58·8′	0°35·6′W	T	130
Honington	Suff	TL9174	52°20·1′	0°48·6′E	T	144
Honington	Warw	SP2642	52°4·8′	1°36·8′W	T	151
Honington Beck	Lincs	SK9444	52°59·3′	0°35·6′W	W	130
Honington House Fm	Norf	TF4714	52°42·5′	0°11·0′E	FM	131
Honnington Grange	Lincs	SK9343	52°58·8′	0°36·5′W	X	130
Honister Crag	Cumbr	NY2114	54°31·2′	3°12·8′W	X	89,90
Honister Pass	Cumbr	NY2213	54°30·6′	3°11·9′W	X	89,90
Honiton	Corn	SX2980	50°35·9′	4°24·6′W	X	201
Honiton	Devon	ST1600	50°47·8′	3°11·1′W	T	192,193
Honiton Barton	Devon	SS6824	51°0·3′	3°52·5′W	A	180
Honkley	Wrex	SJ3459	53°7·7′	2°58·8′W	T	117
Honkley Hall	Wrex	SJ3459	53°7·7′	2°58·8′W	X	117
Honley	Kirk	SE1311	53°36·0′	1°47·8′W	T	110
Honley Moor	Kirk	SE1311	53°36·0′	1°47·8′W	T	110
Honley Sta	Kirk	SE1412	53°36·5′	1°46·9′W	X	110
Honley Wood	Kirk	SE1111	53°36·0′	1°49·6′W	F	110
Honley Wood Bottom	Kirk	SE1111	53°36·0′	1°49·6′W	X	110
Honnington	Wrekin	SJ7215	52°44·2′	2°24·5′W	T	127
Honnington Fm	Kent	TQ5843	51°10·1′	0°16·0′E	FM	188
Hononton Fm	Kent	TQ6841	51°8·8′	0°24·5′E	FM	188
Honor End Fm	Bucks	SP8601	51°42·3′	0°44·9′W	FM	165
Honor Oak	Lew	TQ3574	51°27·2′	0°3·0′W	T	177
Honor Oak Park	Lew	TQ3674	51°27·1′	0°2·2′W	T	177
Honresfeld	Roch	SD9416	53°38·7′	2°5·0′W	T	109
Hoo	Kent	TR2964	51°20·0′	1°17·6′E	T	179
Hoo	Suff	TM2558	52°10·7′	1°17·9′E	X	156
Hoo Ash Fm	Leic	SK4014	52°43·6′	1°24·1′W	FM	129
Hoo Back	Orkney	HY6035	59°12·3′	2°41·5′W	X	5,6
Hoober	Lancs	SD8551	53°57·5′	2°13·3′W	X	103
Hoober	Roth	SK4198	53°28·9′	1°22·5′W	T	111
Hoober Hall	Roth	SK4199	53°29·4′	1°22·5′W	X	111
Hoober Stand	Roth	SK4098	53°28·9′	1°23·4′W	X	111
Hooborough Brook	Leic	SK3013	52°43·1′	1°32·9′W	W	128

Hoo Brook	Staffs	SK0855	53°5·8′	1°52·4′W	W	119
Hoobrook	Worcs	SO8374	52°22·1′	2°14·6′W	T	138
Hooby Lodge	Rut	SK9217	52°44·8′	0°37·8′W	X	130
Hoo Coppice	Wrekin	SJ5817	52°45·2′	2°36·9′W	F	126
Hood Ball	Devon	SX7663	50°27·5′	3°44·4′W	H	202
Hood Beck	N Yks	SE4981	54°13·6′	1°14·5′W	W	100
Hoodcroft	Derby	SK4775	53°16·4′	1°17·3′W	X	120
Hoodens Hill	E Ayr	NX4588	55°10·0′	4°25·6′W	H	77
Hood Grange	N Yks	SE5082	54°14·1′	1°13·6′W	X	100
Hood Green	Barns	SE3102	53°31·1′	1°31·5′W	T	110,111
Hood Hill	N Yks	SE5081	54°13·6′	1°13·6′W	H	100
Hood Hill	Roth	SK3697	53°28·3′	1°27·0′W	T	110,111
Hood Hill Plantn	Barns	SK3698	53°28·9′	1°27·0′W	F	110,111
Hood Hole	N Yks	SE3067	54°6·1′	1°32·1′W	X	99
Hood Lane Fm	Warw	SP2891	52°31·2′	1°34·8′W	FM	140
Hood Manor	Warr	SJ5888	53°23·5′	2°37·5′W	T	108
Hood Manor (Sch)	Devon	SX7763	50°27·5′	3°43·6′W	X	202
Hoodown Fm	Devon	SX8852	50°21·7′	3°34·1′W	FM	202
Hood Ridding Fm	Cumbr	SD5787	54°16·9′	2°39·2′W	FM	97
Hood Rigg	N Yks	SD8796	54°21·8′	2°11·6′W	X	98
Hoodshill	Pth & Kin	NO0401	56°11·8′	3°32·4′W	H	58
Hoodston	Angus	NO5562	56°45·1′	2°43·7′W	X	44
Hoodston	E Ayr	NS4521	55°27·8′	4°26·7′W	X	70
Hoodston Br	E Ayr	NS4736	55°35·9′	4°25·3′W	X	70
Hoodstorth Allotment	N Yks	SE1360	54°2·4′	1°47·7′W	X	99
Hoodstorth Allotment	N Yks	SE1359	54°1·9′	1°47·7′W	X	104
Hoodsyard	N Ayr	NS3754	55°45·4′	4°35·4′W	X	63
Hood Tarn	Cumbr	SD5787	54°16·9′	2°39·2′W	W	97
Hood, The	Norf	TG0146	52°58·6′	1°0·0′E	X	133
Hooe	C of Plym	SX5052	50°21·2′	4°6·1′W	T	201
Hooe	Devon	SX4265	50°28·0′	4°13·2′W	X	201
Hooe	E Susx	TQ6809	50°51·6′	0°23·6′E	T	199
Hooe Common	E Susx	TQ6910	50°52·1′	0°24·5′E	T	199
Hooe Level	E Susx	TQ6806	50°50·0′	0°23·5′E	X	199
Hoo End	Herts	TL1819	51°51·7′	0°16·8′W	T	166
Hoofield	Ches	SJ5162	53°9·4′	2°43·6′W	X	117
Hoo Field	Shetld	HU3682	60°31·5′	1°20·1′W	H	1,2,3
Hoo Field	Shetld	HU3965	60°22·3′	1°17·1′W	X	2,3
Hoo Field	Shetld	HU4127	60°1·8′	1°15·4′W	H	4
Hoo Field	Shetld	HU4964	60°21·7′	1°6·2′W	H	2,3
Hoofield Covert	Ches	SJ5262	53°9·4′	2°42·7′W	F	117
Hoo Fields	Shetld	HU4542	60°9·9′	1°10·9′W	X	4
Hoo Flats	Medway	TQ7971	51°24·8′	0°34·8′E	X	178
Hoo Fm	Beds	TL0965	52°16·6′	0°23·7′W	FM	153
Hoo Fm	Beds	TL1147	52°6·8′	0°22·3′W	FM	153
Hoo Fm	Beds	TL1537	52°1·4′	0°19·0′W	FM	153
Hoo Fm	Staffs	SO8387	52°29·1′	2°14·6′W	FM	138
Hoo Fm	Wrekin	SJ6914	52°43·6′	2°27·1′W	FM	127
Hoo Fort	Medway	TQ7970	51°24·3′	0°34·8′E	A	178
Hoo Green	Ches	SJ7182	53°20·3′	2°25·7′W	T	109
Hoo Hall	Essex	TL8317	51°49·5′	0°39·7′E	X	168
Hoohill	Blackp	SD3237	53°49·7′	3°1·6′W	T	102
Hoo Hills Fm	Leic	SK3703	52°37·6′	1°26·8′W	FM	140
Hoohivda	Shetld	HU2379	60°29·9′	1°34·4′W	X	3
Hoo Ho	Suff	TM2557	52°10·1′	1°17·8′E	X	156
Hoo Hole	Cald	SE0025	53°43·5′	1°59·6′W	T	104
Hook	Cambs	TL4293	52°31·2′	0°6·0′E	T	142,143
Hook	Devon	ST3005	50°50·7′	2°59·3′W	T	193
Hook	Devon	SX5896	50°45·0′	4°0·4′W	X	191
Hook	E Yorks	SE7625	53°43·2′	0°50·5′W	T	105,106
Hook	Hants	SU5005	50°50·8′	1°17·0′W	T	196
Hook	Hants	SU7254	51°17·1′	0°57·7′W	T	186
Hook	King	TQ1864	51°22·0′	0°17·9′W	T	176,187
Hook	Pemb	SM9520	51°50·8′	4°58·2′W	X	157,158
Hook	Pemb	SM9711	51°45·9′	4°56·1′W	T	157,158
Hook	Wilts	SU0784	51°33·5′	1°53·6′W	T	173
Hook-a-gate	Shrops	SJ4609	52°40·8′	2°47·5′W	T	126
Hoo Kame	Shetld	HU4258	60°18·5′	1°13·9′W	H	2,3
Hook Bank	Worcs	SO8140	52°3·7′	2°16·2′W	T	150
Hook Br	Somer	ST3327	51°2·5′	2°57·0′W	X	193
Hookcar Hill	N Yks	SE2795	54°21·2′	1°34·7′W	X	99
Hookcliffe	Lancs	SD7842	53°52·7′	2°19·7′W	X	103
Hook Common	Hants	SU7153	51°16·6′	0°58·5′W	X	186
Hook Copse	Hants	SU4355	51°17·8′	1°22·6′W	F	174,185
Hook Copse	Wilts	ST9126	51°2·2′	2°7·3′W	F	184
Hook Drain	Norf	TF5708	52°39·0′	0°19·7′E	W	143
Hooke	Dorset	ST5300	50°48·1′	2°39·6′W	T	194
Hook Ebb	Devon	SY1587	50°40·8′	3°11·8′W	X	192
Hooke Court (School)	Dorset	ST5300	50°48·1′	2°39·6′W	A	194
Hooke Hill	Herts	TL2800	51°41·3′	0°8·5′W	X	166
Hook End	Essex	TQ5899	51°40·3′	0°17·5′E	T	167,177
Hook End	Oxon	SU6681	51°31·7′	1°2·5′W	T	175
Hook End	Sol	SP2080	52°25·3′	1°42·0′W	T	139
Hook End Fm	W Berks	SU5977	51°29·6′	1°8·6′W	FM	174
Hooke Park	Dorset	SY5299	50°47·8′	2°40·5′W	F	194
Hooker Crag	Cumbr	SD1198	54°22·4′	3°21·8′W	H	96
Hooker Edge	Kent	TQ7738	51°7·1′	0°32·1′E	X	188
Hooker Gate	Ghead	NZ1459	54°55·8′	1°46·5′W	T	88
Hooker Mill Scar	N Yks	SD8999	54°23·4′	2°9·7′W	X	98
Hooker's Fm	W Susx	TQ2520	50°58·2′	0°12·8′W	FM	198
Hooker's Gate Fm	Wilts	SU0483	51°33·0′	1°56·1′W	FM	173
Hookerswell Fm	Oxon	SP3827	51°56·6′	1°26·4′W	FM	164
Hooke, The	E Susx	TQ3818	50°56·9′	0°1·7′W	X	198
Hookey's Fm	Worcs	SP0459	52°14·0′	1°56·1′W	FM	150
Hook Fm	Devon	SS4809	50°51·9′	4°9·2′W	FM	191
Hook Fm	Devon	SS6414	50°54·8′	3°55·7′W	FM	180
Hook Fm	Devon	SX7695	50°44·7′	3°45·1′W	FM	191
Hook Fm	Devon	SY3293	50°44·2′	2°57·4′W	FM	193
Hook Fm	E Susx	TQ6733	51°4·5′	0°23·4′E	FM	188
Hook Fm	Pemb	SM9824	51°52·9′	4°55·7′W	FM	157,158
Hook Fm	Shrops	SO7184	52°27·4′	2°25·2′W	FM	138
Hook Fm	Wilts	ST9126	51°2·2′	2°7·3′W	FM	184
Hook Fm	W Susx	SU8302	50°48·9′	0°48·9′W	FM	197
Hook Fm	W Susx	TQ3531	51°4·0′	0°4·0′W	FM	187
Hook Fms	Pemb	SM7708	51°43·8′	5°13·4′W	FM	157
Hookgate	Staffs	SJ7435	52°54·9′	2°22·8′W	T	127
Hookgate Coppice	Hants	SU5205	50°50·8′	1°15·3′W	F	196
Hookgate Fm	Somer	ST7235	51°7·0′	2°23·6′W	FM	183
Hook Green	Kent	TQ5271	51°25·3′	0°11·6′E	X	177
Hook Green	Kent	TQ6170	51°24·6′	0°19·3′E	T	177

Hook Green	Kent	TQ6467	51°22·9′	0°21·8′E	T	177
Hook Green	Kent	TQ6535	51°5·7′	0°21·8′E	T	188
Hook Hall	E Yorks	SE7526	53°43·7′	0°51·4′W	X	105,106
Hookhams Fm	W Susx	SU9328	51°2·9′	0°40·0′W	FM	186,197
Hookhays Fm	Devon	ST0124	51°0·6′	3°24·3′W	FM	181
Hookhead	S Lanak	NS6541	55°38·9′	4°8·3′W	X	71
Hook Heath	Surrey	SU9857	51°18·4′	0°35·3′W	T	175,186
Hookheath Fm	Hants	SU6408	50°52·3′	1°5·0′W	FM	196
Hook Hill Fm	Somer	ST0335	51°6·6′	3°22·8′W	FM	181
Hook Ho	Hants	SU7354	51°17·1′	0°56·8′W	X	186
Hook Ho	Kent	TQ9824	50°59·1′	0°49·7′E	X	189
Hook House Fm	N Yks	SE2695	54°21·2′	1°35·6′W	FM	99
Hookhouse Fm	W Susx	TQ3121	50°58·6′	0°7·6′W	FM	198
Hooking Loch	Orkney	HY7653	59°22·0′	2°24·8′W	W	5
Hook Kennels, The	Herts	TL2801	51°41·8′	0°8·5′W	X	166
Hooklands	W Susx	TQ1417	50°56·7′	0°22·2′W	X	198
Hooklands Fm	W Susx	TQ3622	50°59·1′	0°3·4′W	FM	198
Hooklaw	S Lanak	NS6745	55°41·1′	4°6·5′W	X	64
Hook Moor	Leeds	SE4335	53°48·8′	1°20·4′W	F	105
Hookmoor Fm	E Yorks	SE7119	53°40·0′	0°55·1′W	FM	112
Hooknell	Warw	SP2463	52°16·1′	1°38·5′W	X	151
Hookney	Falk	NS7783	56°1·7′	3°58·0′W	X	57,64
Hookney Tor	Devon	SX6981	50°37·1′	3°50·7′W	H	191
Hook Norton	Oxon	SP3533	51°59·9′	1°29·0′W	T	151
Hook Park	Hants	SU4904	50°50·2′	1°17·9′W	T	196
Hook Reach	Pemb	SM9812	51°46·5′	4°55·3′W	W	157,158
Hooks	Pemb	SM8911	51°45·7′	5°3·1′W	X	157,158
Hooks Beech	E Susx	TQ7620	50°57·4′	0°30·8′E	X	199
Hook's Brook	Ches	SJ4652	53°4·0′	2°47·9′W	W	117
Hook's Car	Derby	SK2483	53°20·8′	1°38·0′W	X	110
Hook's Cross	Herts	TL2720	51°52·1′	0°8·9′W	T	166
Hookses, The	Pemb	SM7906	51°42·8′	5°11·6′W	X	157
Hooksey	Cumbr	NY6802	54°25·0′	2°29·2′W	X	91
Hook's Fm	Bucks	SU8286	51°34·2′	0°48·6′W	FM	175
Hooks Fm	Glos	SO7416	51°50·8′	2°22·3′W	FM	162
Hook's Fm	Lincs	TF0394	53°26·2′	0°26·6′W	FM	112
Hooks Green	Staffs	SJ9037	52°56·1′	2°8·5′W	X	127
Hooks Hall	Suff	TL8050	52°7·4′	0°38·2′E	X	155
Hooks Hill	Pemb	SN0319	51°50·3′	4°51·2′W	X	157,158
Hook's Hill	Somer	ST5854	51°17·2′	2°35·7′W	H	182,183
Hookshouse	Glos	ST8692	51°37·8′	2°11·7′W	X	162,173
Hook's Mill	Cambs	TL2745	52°5·6′	0°8·4′W	X	153
Hooks, The	Shrops	SJ6825	52°49·5′	2°28·1′W	X	127
Hookstile Ho	Surrey	TQ3546	51°12·1′	0°3·7′W	X	187
Hook Street	Glos	ST6799	51°41·6′	2°28·3′W	T	162
Hook Street	Wilts	SU0884	51°33·5′	1°52·7′W	T	173
Hooksway	W Susx	SU8116	50°56·5′	0°50·4′W	T	197
Hookswood Ho	Dorset	ST9415	50°56·3′	2°4·7′W	X	184
Hook Valley Fm	Somer	ST6927	51°2·7′	2°26·1′W	FM	183
Hookway	Devon	SS8910	50°53·0′	3°34·3′W	X	192
Hookway	Devon	SX8598	50°46·4′	3°37·5′W	T	191
Hook Wood	Herts	TL2701	51°41·8′	0°9·3′W	F	166
Hook Wood	Kent	TQ8637	51°6·3′	0°39·8′E	F	189
Hook Wood	Surrey	TQ0750	51°14·6′	0°27·6′W	F	187
Hookwood	Surrey	TQ2642	51°10·0′	0°11·5′W	T	187
Hookwood	Surrey	TQ4153	51°15·7′	0°1·6′E	X	187
Hook Wood Fm	Norf	TM0598	52°32·7′	1°1·8′E	FM	144
Hookwood Ho	Kent	TQ6051	51°14·4′	0°17·9′E	X	188
Hoole	Ches	SJ4267	53°12·1′	2°51·7′W	T	117
Hoole	Pth & Kin	NO2130	56°27·6′	3°16·5′W	X	53
Hoole Bank	Ches	SJ4369	53°13·1′	2°50·8′W	T	117
Hoole Fm	Lancs	SD4645	53°54·1′	2°48·9′W	FM	102
Hoole Fold	Lancs	SD5138	53°50·4′	2°44·3′W	X	102
Hoole Ho	Norf	TG3330	52°49·3′	1°27·9′E	X	133
Hooles Fm	Lancs	SD3948	53°55·7′	2°55·3′W	FM	102
Hooley	Surrey	TQ2856	51°17·5′	0°9·5′W	T	187
Hooley Bridge	Roch	SD8512	53°36·5′	2°13·2′W	T	109
Hooley Brow	Roch	SD8511	53°36·0′	2°13·2′W	T	109
Hooley Hill	Tames	SJ9297	53°28·4′	2°6·8′W	T	109
Hoolgrave Manor	Ches	SJ6758	53°7·3′	2°29·2′W	X	118
Hoo Lodge	Medway	TQ7771	51°24·8′	0°33·1′E	X	178
Hoolster Hill	Lancs	SD6229	53°45·6′	2°34·2′W	H	102,103
Hoo Meavy	Devon	SX5365	50°28·2′	4°3·9′W	T	201
Hoo Mill	Warw	SP1057	52°12·9′	1°50·8′W	X	150
Hoo Moor	Derby	SK0076	53°17·1′	1°59·6′W	X	119
Hoo Nager	Orkney	HY4243	59°16·4′	3°0·6′W	X	5
Hoo Ness	Medway	TQ7870	51°24·3′	0°33·9′E	X	178
Hoon Hay Manor	Derby	SK2229	52°51·7′	1°40·0′W	X	128
Hoon Mount	Derby	SK2331	52°52·8′	1°39·1′W	X	128
Hoon Mount (Tumulus)	Derby	SK2331	52°52·8′	1°39·1′W	A	128
Hoon Ridge	Derby	SK2331	52°52·8′	1°39·1′W	X	128
Hoop	Monm	SO5107	51°45·8′	2°42·2′W	T	162
Hooper Green	Bolton	SD6605	53°32·7′	2°30·4′W	X	109
Hooperhayne	Devon	SY2294	50°44·7′	3°6·0′W	X	192,193
Hoopers Elm Fm	Somer	ST3432	51°5·2′	2°56·2′W	FM	182
Hoopers Fm	Hants	SU3532	51°5·4′	1°29·6′W	FM	185
Hoopers Fm	Surrey	TQ4242	51°9·8′	0°2·2′E	FM	187
Hooper's Hill	Hants	SZ2694	50°44·9′	1°37·5′W	X	195
Hooper's Point	Pemb	SM7806	51°42·8′	5°12·4′W	X	157
Hoopers Pool	Wilts	ST8354	51°17·3′	2°14·2′W	T	183
Hooper's Water Fm	Devon	SS4223	50°59·3′	4°14·7′W	FM	180,190
Hooperton	Devon	SX7492	50°43·1′	3°46·7′W	X	191
Hoop Fm	Devon	ST0201	50°48·3′	3°23·1′W	FM	192
Hoopits, The	Shrops	SO5671	52°20·4′	2°38·4′W	X	137,138
Hoops	Devon	SS3723	50°59·2′	4°19·0′W	T	190
Hoop Side	Wilts	SU0529	51°3·9′	1°55·3′W	X	184
Hooro Nev	Orkney	HY4244	59°17·0′	3°0·6′W	X	5
Hoo Salt Marsh	Medway	TQ7870	51°24·3′	0°33·9′E	W	178
Hoosiefield	Shetld	HU3650	60°14·2′	1°20·5′W	X	3
Hoo Stack	Shetld	HU5052	60°15·2′	1°5·3′W	X	3
Hoo St Werburgh	Medway	TQ7872	51°25·4′	0°34·0′E	T	178
Hootens Fm	Northnts	SP6349	52°8·4′	1°4·4′W	FM	152
Hooterhall	Ches	SJ7358	53°7·4′	2°23·8′W	X	118
Hoo, The	Glos	SP1439	52°3·2′	1°47·4′W	X	151
Hoo, The	Herts	TL0312	51°48·1′	0°30·0′W	X	166
Hoo, The	Herts	TL1819	51°51·7′	0°16·8′W	X	166
Hooton	Ches	SJ3678	53°17·9′	2°57·2′W	T	117
Hooton Common	Roth	SK4797	53°28·3′	1°17·1′W	X	111
Hooton Levitt	Roth	SK5291	53°25·0′	1°12·6′W	T	111
Hooton Pagnell	Donc	SE4808	53°34·2′	1°16·1′W	T	111

Hooton Pagnell Wood	Donc	SE4708	53°34·2′	1°17·0′W	F	111
Hooton Roberts	Roth	SK4897	53°28·3′	1°16·2′W	T	111
Hooton's Fm	Lancs	SD3613	53°36·8′	2°57·6′W	FM	108
Hooton Sta	Ches	SJ3478	53°17·9′	2°59·0′W	X	117
Hoove	N Yks	NZ0006	54°27·2′	1°59·6′W	H	92
Hoove	Shetld	HU3945	60°11·5′	1°17·3′W	X	4
Hoove	Shetld	HU3953	60°15·8′	1°17·2′W	X	3
Hooveth	Orkney	HY2321	59°4·4′	3°20·1′W	X	6
Hoo Wood	Herts	SP9914	51°49·2′	0°33·4′W	F	165
Hoo Wood	Mil Key	SP8445	52°6·0′	0°46·0′W	F	152
Hooze Fm	Worcs	SO8133	51°59·9′	2°16·2′W	FM	150
Hopbrook	Powys	SO0087	52°28·5′	3°27·9′W	X	136
Hop Castle	W Berks	SU4473	51°27·5′	1°21·6′W	X	174
Hopcott Common	Somer	SS9544	51°11·4′	3°29·8′W	F	181
Hopcroft's Holt	Oxon	SP4625	51°55·5′	1°19·5′W	T	164
Hope	Derby	SK1683	53°20·9′	1°45·2′W	T	110
Hope	D & G	NY3897	55°16·0′	2°58·1′W	X	79
Hope	Highld	NC4760	58°30·3′	4°37·1′W	X	9
Hope	Midlo	NT4062	55°51·1′	2°57·1′W	X	66
Hope	Northum	NU0901	55°18·4′	1°51·1′W	X	81
Hope	Powys	SJ2507	52°39·6′	3°6·1′W	X	126
Hope	Scot Bord	NT3040	55°39·2′	3°6·3′W	X	73
Hope	Shrops	SJ3401	52°36·4′	2°58·1′W	T	126
Hope	Shrops	SO3779	52°24·6′	2°55·2′W	X	137,148
Hope	Staffs	SK1255	53°5·8′	1°48·8′W	T	119
Hopealone	Northum	NY7371	55°2·2′	2°24·9′W	X	86,87
Hope Bagot	Shrops	SO5874	52°22·0′	2°36·6′W	T	137,138
Hope Barton	Devon	SX6839	50°14·4′	3°50·7′W	X	202
Hope Beck	Cumbr	NY1623	54°36·0′	3°17·6′W	W	89
Hopebeck	Cumbr	NY1624	54°36·5′	3°17·6′W	T	89
Hope Bowdler	Shrops	SO4792	52°31·6′	2°46·5′W	T	137,138
Hope Bowdler Hill	Shrops	SO4893	52°32·2′	2°45·6′W	X	137,138
Hope Brink	Derby	SK1785	53°21·9′	1°44·3′W	X	110
Hope Burn	D & G	NX9295	55°14·5′	3°41·5′W	W	78
Hope Burn	D & G	NY1785	55°9·4′	3°17·7′W	W	79
Hope Burn	Scot Bord	NT0629	55°33·0′	3°29·0′W	W	72
Hope Burn	Scot Bord	NT3348	55°43·5′	3°3·6′W	W	73
Hope Burn	Scot Bord	NT3350	55°44·6′	3°3·6′W	W	66,73
Hope Burn	Scot Bord	NT3442	55°40·3′	3°2·5′W	W	73
Hope Burn	Scot Bord	NT4342	55°40·3′	2°53·9′W	W	73
Hopecarton	Scot Bord	NT1230	55°33·6′	3°23·3′W	X	72
Hopecarton Burn	Scot Bord	NT1330	55°33·6′	3°22·3′W	W	72
Hope Cleugh	Northum	NY7453	54°52·5′	2°23·9′W	X	86,87
Hope Cottage	Wilts	SU2216	50°56·8′	1°40·8′W	X	184
Hope Court	Shrops	SO5873	52°21·4′	2°36·6′W	X	137,138
Hope Cove	Aberd	NO8881	56°55·5′	2°11·4′W	W	45
Hope Cove	Devon	SX6739	50°14·4′	3°51·5′W	W	202
Hope Cross	Derby	SK1687	53°23·0′	1°45·2′W	X	110
Hope Dale	Shrops	SO4686	52°28·4′	2°47·3′W	X	137,138
Hope Dale	Shrops	SO5190	52°30·6′	2°42·9′W	X	137,138
Hopedale	Staffs	SK1255	53°5·8′	1°48·8′W	T	119
Hope Edge	Durham	NZ0307	54°27·7′	1°56·8′W	X	92
Hope End Green	Essex	TL5720	51°51·6′	0°17·2′E	T	167
Hope End Ho	Heref	SO7241	52°4·2′	2°24·1′W	X	149
Hope Farm Cotts	Somer	ST3254	51°17·1′	2°58·1′W	X	182
Hope Fell	Northum	NY9251	54°51·5′	2°7·1′W	X	87
Hopefield	E Loth	NT4672	55°56·5′	2°51·4′W	X	66
Hopefield	Highld	ND0767	58°35·1′	3°35·5′W	X	11,12
Hopefield	Highld	NH7359	57°36·5′	4°7·1′W	X	27
Hopefield	Midlo	NT3064	55°52·1′	3°6·7′W	X	66
Hope Fleet	Medway	TQ7678	51°28·6′	0°32·5′E	W	178
Hope Fm	Brad	SE1439	53°51·1′	1°46·8′W	FM	104
Hope Fm	Essex	TL4537	52°1·0′	0°7·2′E	FM	154
Hope Fm	E Susx	TQ5217	50°56·2′	0°10·2′E	FM	199
Hope Fm	Glos	SO9123	51°54·6′	2°7·5′W	FM	163
Hope Fm	Heref	SO6658	52°13·4′	2°29·5′W	FM	149
Hope Fm	Kent	TQ6250	51°13·8′	0°19·6′E	FM	188
Hope Fm	Kent	TQ9928	51°1·2′	0°50·6′E	FM	189
Hope Fm	Kent	TR0525	50°59·5′	0°55·7′E	FM	189
Hope Fm	Kent	TR1138	51°6·4′	1°1·2′E	FM	179,189
Hope Fm	Kent	TR2338	51°6·1′	1°11·5′E	FM	179,189
Hope Fm	Lincs	TF5470	53°12·5′	0°18·8′E	FM	122
Hope Fm	Powys	SJ2407	52°39·6′	3°7·0′W	FM	126
Hope Fm	S Glos	ST6789	51°36·2′	2°28·2′W	FM	162,172
Hope Fm	Shrops	SJ3502	52°37·0′	2°57·2′W	FM	126
Hope Fm	Staffs	SJ9116	52°44·7′	2°7·6′W	FM	127
Hope Fm	Worcs	SO6960	52°14·5′	2°26·8′W	FM	138,149
Hope Fm	W Susx	TQ0629	51°3·3′	0°28·9′W	FM	187,197
Hopefoot	Northum	NY8895	55°15·2′	2°10·9′W	X	80
Hope Forest	Derby	SK1291	53°25·2′	1°48·8′W	X	110
Hope Gill	Cumbr	NY1723	54°36·0′	3°16·7′W	W	89,90
Hopegill Head	Cumbr	NY1822	54°35·4′	3°15·7′W	H	89,90
Hope Green	Ches	SJ9182	53°20·3′	2°7·7′W	T	109
Hope Hall	Flint	SJ3158	53°7·8′	3°1·5′W	X	117
Hope Hall	Leeds	SE4043	53°53·1′	1°23·1′W	X	105
Hope Hall	Shrops	SJ3401	52°36·4′	2°58·1′W	X	126
Hope Head	Northum	NY8347	54°49·3′	2°15·5′W	X	86,87
Hopehead	Northum	NY8996	55°15·7′	2°10·0′W	X	80
Hopehead	Scot Bord	NT0725	55°30·8′	3°27·9′W	X	72
Hope Head	Scot Bord	NT2412	55°24·0′	3°11·6′W	H	79
Hopehead Burn	Scot Bord	NT1439	55°38·5′	3°21·5′W	W	72
Hope Hill	D & G	NX5675	55°3·2′	4°14·8′W	X	77
Hope Hill	Highld	NC7718	58°8·3′	4°4·9′W	H	17
Hope Hills	E Loth	NT5561	55°50·7′	2°42·7′W	X	66
Hope Hills	E Loth	NT5661	55°50·7′	2°41·7′W	H	67
Hope Ho	Darl	NZ2422	54°35·6′	1°37·3′W	X	93
Hope Ho	Durham	NY9827	54°38·5′	2°1·4′W	X	92
Hope Ho	Durham	NZ3231	54°40·6′	1°29·8′W	X	93
Hope Ho	Durham	NZ3632	54°41·1′	1°26·1′W	X	93
Hope Ho	Kent	TQ8129	51°2·1′	0°35·3′E	X	188,199
Hope Ho	Northum	NU2503	55°19·5′	1°35·9′W	X	81
Hopehouse	Northum	NY6780	55°7·0′	2°30·6′W	X	80
Hopehouse	Scot Bord	NT2916	55°26·2′	3°6·9′W	X	79
Hopehouse Burn	Scot Bord	NT2816	55°26·2′	3°7·8′W	W	79
Hope House Fm	Durham	NZ3325	54°37·4′	1°28·9′W	FM	93
Hope House Fm	Glos	SO7404	51°44·3′	2°22·2′W	FM	162
Hope House Fm	Heref	SO7051	52°9·6′	2°25·9′W	FM	149
Hopehouse Fm	Worcs	SO7559	52°14·0′	2°21·6′W	FM	150
Hopekist Rig	Scot Bord	NT1330	55°33·6′	3°22·3′W	H	72
Hopeman	Moray	NJ1469	57°42·4′	3°26·1′W	T	28

Hope Mansell	Heref	SO6219	51°52·3′	2°32·7′W	T	162
Hope Marsh	Staffs	SK1255	53°5·8′	1°48·8′W	X	119
Hope Moor	Durham	NZ0207	54°27·7′	1°57·7′W	X	92
Hope Mountain	Flint	SJ2956	53°6·0′	3°3·2′W	H	117
Hope or Yr Hôb	Flint	SJ3058	53°7·1′	3°2·4′W	T	117
Hope Park	Shrops	SJ3201	52°36·4′	2°59·8′W	T	126
Hope Point	Kent	TR3746	51°10·1′	1°23·8′E	X	179
Hopes	E Loth	NT5663	55°51·7′	2°41·7′W	X	67
Hope's Ash Fm	Heref	SO6221	51°53·4′	2°32·7′W	FM	162
Hopesay	Shrops	SO3983	52°26·7′	2°53·5′W	T	137
Hopesay Common	Shrops	SO3983	52°26·7′	2°53·5′W	X	137
Hopesay Hill	Shrops	SO4083	52°26·7′	2°52·6′W	H	137
Hope Scar	Durham	NZ0307	54°27·7′	1°56·8′W	X	92
Hope's Castle Fm	Powys	SO1381	52°25·4′	3°16·4′W	FM	136
Hopesgate	Shrops	SJ3301	52°36·4′	2°59·0′W	T	126
Hope's Green	Essex	TQ7786	51°32·9′	0°33·6′E	T	178
Hopeshield Burn	Northum	NY8373	55°3·3′	2°15·5′W	W	86,87
Hope's Ho	Cumbr	NY4673	55°3·2′	2°50·3′W	X	86
Hope Sike	Northum	NY7371	55°2·2′	2°24·9′W	W	86,87
Hopesike Woods	Cumbr	NY3866	54°59·3′	2°57·7′W	F	85
Hope's Nose	Torbay	SX9463	50°27·7′	3°29·2′W	X	202
Hope's Place	Flint	SJ3664	53°10·4′	2°57·0′W	X	117
Hope Springs	Heref	SO5736	52°1·5′	2°37·2′W	X	149
Hopes Resr	E Loth	NT5462	55°51·2′	2°43·6′W	W	66
Hope's Rough	Heref	SO6347	52°7·4′	2°32·0′W	T	149
Hope Sta	Derby	SK1883	53°20·9′	1°43·4′W	X	110
Hopestead	Scot Bord	NT8566	55°53·5′	2°14·0′W	X	67
Hopes Water	E Loth	NT5562	55°51·2′	2°42·7′W	W	66
Hopes Water	E Loth	NT5665	55°52·8′	2°41·8′W	W	67
Hope, The	Northum	NY7654	54°53·1′	2°22·0′W	X	86,87
Hope, The	Northum	NY8356	54°54·2′	2°15·5′W	X	86,87
Hope, The	Orkney	ND4396	58°51·1′	2°58·8′W	X	6,7
Hope, The	Shrops	SO5178	52°24·1′	2°42·8′W	T	137,138
Hopetoun Craig	Scot Bord	NT1806	55°20·7′	3°17·2′W	H	79
Hopetoun Ho	W Loth	NT0879	56°0·0′	3°28·1′W	X	65
Hopetoun Monument	Fife	NO3316	56°20·2′	3°4·6′W	X	59
Hopetoun Wood	W Loth	NT0877	55°58·9′	3°28·0′W	F	65
Hope Town	N Yks	SE3284	54°15·3′	1°30·1′W	X	99
Hopetown	Wakf	SE3923	53°42·4′	1°24·1′W	T	104
Hopetown Monument	E Loth	NT5076	55°58·7′	2°47·6′W	X	66
Hope under Dinmore	Heref	SO5052	52°10·1′	2°43·5′W	T	149
Hope Valley	Derby	SK1783	53°20·9′	1°44·3′W	X	110
Hope Valley	Shrops	SJ3300	52°35·9′	2°59·0′W	X	126
Hopewell	Darl	NZ2017	54°33·1′	1°41·0′W	X	93
Hopewell Ho	N Yks	SE3758	54°1·2′	1°25·7′W	X	104
Hopewell Lodge	Aberd	NJ4505	57°8·2′	2°54·1′W	X	37
Hope Wood	Glos	SO6817	51°51·3′	2°27·5′W	F	162
Hop Farm	Kent	TQ6747	51°12·1′	0°23·8′E	FM	188
Hop Farm	Kent	TR1955	51°15·3′	1°8·7′E	FM	179
Hopgoods Green	W Berks	SU5369	51°25·3′	1°13·9′W	T	174
Hopgrass Fm	W Berks	SU3268	51°24·8′	1°32·0′W	FM	174
Hopgreen Fm	Essex	TL8525	51°53·8′	0°41·7′E	FM	168
Hophills Nob	Scot Bord	NT7009	55°22·7′	2°28·0′W	H	80
Hophouse Fm	Essex	TL6438	52°1·2′	0°23·8′E	FM	154
Hophurst Fm	W Susx	TQ3538	51°7·7′	0°3·8′W	FM	187
Hopkiln Fm	Wok	SU6968	51°24·6′	1°0·1′W	FM	175
Hopkins	Essex	TL6115	51°48·9′	0°20·5′E	X	167
Hopkin's Fm	Essex	TL7939	52°1·5′	0°36·9′E	FM	155
Hopkins' Fm	Somer	ST1528	51°2·9′	3°12·4′W	FM	181,193
Hopkins Fm	Tames	SD9600	53°30·0′	2°3·2′W	FM	109
Hopkinstown	Carm	SN6412	51°47·6′	3°57·9′W	X	159
Hopkinstown	Rho Cyn Taf	ST0690	51°36·3′	3°21·1′W	T	170
Hoplands	Hants	SU3729	51°3·8′	1°27·9′W	X	185
Hoplands Fm	Kent	TR2061	51°18·6′	1°9·8′E	FM	179
Hoplands Fm	Lincs	TF2357	53°6·0′	0°9·4′W	FM	122
Hoplands Wood	Lincs	TF4571	53°13·2′	0°10·7′E	F	122
Hoplass	Pemb	SM9101	51°40·4′	5°1·0′W	X	157,158
Hopley Coppice	Shrops	SJ5927	52°50·6′	2°36·1′W	F	126
Hopley Fm	Shrops	SJ5927	52°50·6′	2°36·1′W	FM	126
Hopley Ho	Ches	SJ6962	53°9·5′	2°27·4′W	X	118
Hopley's Green	Heref	SO3452	52°10·0′	2°57·5′W	T	148,149
Hopleys, The	Suff	TL8361	52°13·2′	0°41·1′E	X	155
Hoppatown	Devon	SS3102	50°47·8′	4°23·5′W	X	190
Hoppen Hall	Northum	NU1630	55°34·1′	1°44·3′W	X	75
Hopper Ho	Durham	NZ3426	54°37·9′	1°28·0′W	X	93
Hoppersford Fm	Northnts	SP6140	52°3·5′	1°6·2′W	FM	152
Hopperton	N Yks	SE4256	54°0·1′	1°21·1′W	T	105
Hopping Fm	Derby	SK2063	53°10·1′	1°41·6′W	FM	119
Hopping Hill	Northnts	SP7262	52°15·3′	0°56·3′W	X	152
Hoppin Hill	Northnts	SP7475	52°22·3′	0°54·4′W	H	141
Hop Pole	Lincs	TF1813	52°42·3′	0°14·8′W	T	130,142
Hoppringle	Scot Bord	NT4351	55°45·2′	2°54·1′W	X	66,73
Hoppyland Fm	Durham	NZ0932	54°41·2′	1°51·2′W	FM	92
Hoprig	E Loth	NT4574	55°57·6′	2°52·4′W	X	66
Hoprig	Scot Bord	NT7569	55°55·1′	2°23·6′W	X	67
Hoprig Mains	E Loth	NT4473	55°57·1′	2°53·4′W	X	66
Hoprigshiels	Scot Bord	NT7469	55°55·1′	2°24·5′W	X	67
Hops Copse	Northnts	SP8455	52°11·4′	0°45·9′W	F	152
Hopsford	Warw	SP4284	52°27·4′	1°22·5′W	T	140
Hopsford Hall	Warw	SP4183	52°26·8′	1°23·4′W	X	140
Hopsford Ho	Warw	SP4184	52°27·4′	1°23·4′W	X	140
Hopsford Lodge Fm	Warw	SP4185	52°27·9′	1°23·4′W	FM	140
Hopsford Old Hall Fm	Warw	SP4283	52°26·8′	1°22·5′W	FM	140
Hopsford Village	Warw	SP4283	52°26·8′	1°22·5′W	A	140
Hopshort	Shrops	SJ7228	52°51·2′	2°24·5′W	X	127
Hopsnort	Shrops	SJ7228	52°51·2′	2°24·5′W	X	127
Hopsrig	D & G	NY3288	55°11·1′	3°3·6′W	X	79
Hopstone	Shrops	SO7894	52°32·8′	2°19·1′W	T	138
Hopton	Aberd	NJ7803	57°7·3′	2°21·3′W	X	38
Hopton	Derby	SK2553	53°4·7′	1°37·2′W	T	119
Hopton	Powys	SO2391	52°30·9′	3°7·7′W	X	137
Hopton	Scot Bord	NT6024	55°30·7′	2°37·6′W	X	74
Hopton	Shrops	SJ3820	52°46·7′	2°54·7′W	T	126
Hopton	Shrops	SJ5926	52°50·0′	2°36·1′W	X	126
Hopton	Staffs	SJ9426	52°50·1′	2°4·9′W	T	127
Hopton	Suff	TL9979	52°22·6′	0°55·8′E	T	144
Hopton Bank	Powys	SO2389	52°29·8′	3°7·7′W	X	137
Hoptonbank	Shrops	SO6277	52°23·6′	2°33·1′W	T	138
Hopton Brook	Shrops	SO5479	52°24·7′	2°40·2′W	W	137,138
Hopton Cangeford	Shrops	SO5480	52°25·2′	2°40·2′W	T	137,138

Hopton Castle	Shrops	SO3678	52°24·0'	2°56·0'W	T	137,148
Hopton Court	Worcs	SO7552	52°10·2'	2°21·5'W	X	150
Hopton Ct	Shrops	SO6476	52°23·1'	2°31·3'W	X	138
Hopton Dingle	Heref	SO6349	52°8·5'	2°32·0'W	X	149
Hopton Fen	Suff	TL9980	52°23·1'	0°55·9'E	W	144
Hopton Fm	Norf	TL8698	52°33·1'	0°45·0'E	FM	144
Hopton Fm	Shrops	SJ6027	52°50·6'	2°35·2'W	FM	127
Hopton Fm	Staffs	SJ9226	52°50·1'	2°6·7'W	FM	127
Hoptongate	Shrops	SO5380	52°25·2'	2°41·1'W	T	137,138
Hopton Hall	Kirk	SE1918	53°39·7'	1°42·3'W	A	110
Hopton Hall Fm	Shrops	SO5480	52°25·2'	2°40·2'W	FM	137,138
Hoptonheath	Shrops	SO3877	52°23·5'	2°54·3'W	X	137,148
Hopton Heath	Staffs	SJ9526	52°50·1'	2°4·1'W	T	127
Hopton Isaf	Powys	SO2390	52°30·4'	3°7·7'W	X	137
Hopton on Sea	Norf	TG5400	52°32·5'	1°45·2'E	T	134
Hopton Park	Shrops	SO3677	52°23·5'	2°56·0'W	F	137,148
Hopton Point	Norf	TL8697	52°32·6'	0°45·0'E	X	144
Hopton Sollers	Heref	SO6349	52°8·5'	2°32·0'W	X	149
Hopton Titterhill	Shrops	SO3577	52°23·5'	2°56·9'W	H	137,148
Hopton Uchaf	Powys	SO2290	52°30·4'	3°8·6'W	X	137
Hopton Wafers	Shrops	SO6376	52°23·1'	2°32·2'W	T	138
Hopton Wood	Derby	SK2556	53°6·3'	1°37·2'W	F	119
Hopwas	Staffs	SK1705	52°38·8'	1°44·5'W	T	139
Hopwas Hays Wood	Staffs	SK1705	52°38·8'	1°44·5'W	F	139
Hopwas House Fm	Staffs	SK1704	52°38·2'	1°44·5'W	FM	139
Hopwell Hall School	Derby	SK4436	52°55·4'	1°20·3'W	X	129
Hopwell's Fm	Essex	TL7934	51°58·8'	0°36·8'E	FM	155
Hopwood	Roch	SD8609	53°34·9'	2°12·3'W	T	109
Hopwood	Worcs	SP0274	52°22·1'	1°57·8'W	T	139
Hopwood Hall	Roch	SD8708	53°34·3'	2°11·4'W	X	109
Hopwood Ho	Sheff	SK2888	53°23·5'	1°34·3'W	X	110
Hopworthy	Devon	SS3002	50°47·8'	4°24·4'W	T	190
Hopyard Fm	Notts	SK7255	53°5·5'	0°55·1'W	FM	120
Horam	E Susx	TQ5717	50°56·1'	0°14·5'E	T	199
Horbling	Lincs	TF1135	52°54·3'	0°20·6'W	T	130
Horbling Fen	Lincs	TF1535	52°54·2'	0°17·0'W	X	130
Horbury	Wakf	SE2918	53°39·7'	1°33·3'W	T	110
Horbury Bridge	Wakf	SE2817	53°39·2'	1°34·2'W	T	110
Horbury Junction	Wakf	SE3017	53°39·2'	1°32·4'W	T	110,111
Horchester	Dorset	ST5903	50°49·7'	2°34·5'W	X	194
Horcombe	Somer	SS7438	51°7·9'	3°47·7'W	X	180
Horcott	Glos	SP1500	51°42·1'	1°46·6'W	T	163
Horcott Hill	Glos	SU1599	51°41·6'	1°46·6'W	X	163
Horden	Durham	NZ4441	54°46·0'	1°18·5'W	T	88
Horden Fm	Black w Dar	SD6525	53°43·5'	2°31·4'W	FM	102,103
Horden Hall	Durham	NZ4342	54°46·5'	1°19·5'W	A	88
Horden Point	Durham	NZ4443	54°47·0'	1°18·5'W	X	88
Horderley	Shrops	SO4086	52°28·4'	2°52·6'W	X	137
Hordern Fm	Ches	SJ9574	53°16·0'	2°4·1'W	FM	118
Hordern Stoops	Lancs	SD6515	53°38·1'	2°31·3'W	X	109
Hordle	Hants	SZ2795	50°45·5'	1°36·6'W	T	195
Hordle Cliff	Hants	SZ2791	50°43·3'	1°36·7'W	X	195
Hordle Grange	Hants	SZ2696	50°46·0'	1°37·5'W	X	195
Hordle House (Sch)	Hants	SZ2692	50°43·9'	1°37·5'W	X	195
Hordley	Shrops	SJ3830	52°52·1'	2°54·9'W	T	126
Hordley Fm	Oxon	SP4419	51°52·3'	1°21·3'W	FM	164
Hordron	Barns	SK1899	53°29·5'	1°43·3'W	X	110
Hordron Edge	Derby	SK2186	53°22·5'	1°40·7'W	X	110
Hords Covert	E Yorks	TA1062	54°2·8'	0°18·8'W	X	101
Horeb	Carm	SN4905	51°43·6'	4°10·8'W	T	159
Horeb	Carm	SN5128	51°56·1'	4°9·7'W	T	146
Horeb	Cered	SN3942	52°3·4'	4°20·5'W	T	145
Horeb	Flint	SJ2857	53°6·6'	3°4·1'W	T	117
Hore Down Fm	Devon	SS5343	51°10·3'	4°5·8'W	FM	180
Horeham Flat Fm	E Susx	TQ5716	50°55·5'	0°14·4'E	FM	199
Hore Stone	Corn	SX2451	50°20·2'	4°28·0'W	X	201
Horestone	Devon	SS8716	50°56·2'	3°36·1'W	X	181
Horestone Cotts	Devon	SS5925	51°0·7'	4°0·2'W	X	180
Horestone Point	I of W	SZ6390	50°42·6'	1°6·1'W	X	196
Hore Wood	Devon	SX7489	50°41·5'	3°46·7'W	F	191
Horfield	C of Bris	ST5976	51°29·1'	2°35·0'W	T	172
Horgabost	N Eil	NG0496	57°51·6'	6°59·0'W	T	18
Horham	Suff	TM2172	52°18·3'	1°14·9'E	T	156
Horham Hall	Essex	TL5829	51°56·4'	0°18·3'E	A	167
Horisary	N Eil	NF7667	57°34·9'	7°24·8'W	X	18
Horisary River	N Eil	NF7668	57°35·4'	7°24·9'W	W	18
Horish Wood	Kent	TQ7857	51°17·3'	0°33·6'E	F	178,188
Horkstow	N Lincs	SE9818	53°39·2'	0°30·6'W	T	112
Horkstow Br	N Lincs	SE9719	53°39·7'	0°31·5'W	X	112
Horkstow Carrs	N Lincs	SE9718	53°39·2'	0°31·5'W	X	112
Horkstow Grange	N Lincs	SE9817	53°38·7'	0°30·6'W	X	112
Horkstow Wolds	N Lincs	SE9919	53°39·7'	0°29·7'W	T	112
Horlake Moor	Somer	ST3431	51°4·7'	2°56·1'W	X	182
Horleigh Green	E Susx	TQ5626	51°1·0'	0°13·8'E	X	188,199
Horley	Oxon	SP4143	52°5·3'	1°23·7'W	T	151
Horley	Surrey	TQ2843	51°10·5'	0°9·7'W	T	187
Horley Fields Fm	Oxon	SP4045	52°6·3'	1°24·6'W	FM	151
Horley Fm	W Susx	SU8617	50°57·0'	0°46·2'W	FM	197
Horley Lodge	Surrey	TQ2746	51°12·2'	0°10·5'W	X	187
Horn	Somer	ST3407	50°51·8'	2°55·9'W	X	193
Hornacott	Corn	SX3294	50°43·5'	4°22·4'W	X	190
Hornacott Barton	Corn	SX3194	50°43·5'	4°23·3'W	X	190
Hornage Fm	Bucks	SP6710	51°47·3'	1°1·3'W	FM	164,165
Horn Ash	Dorset	ST3904	50°50·2'	2°51·6'W	T	193
Horn Bank Fm	N Yks	SE2950	53°57·0'	1°33·1'W	FM	104
Hornblotton	Somer	ST5934	51°6·5'	2°34·8'W	T	182,183
Hornblotton Green	Somer	ST5833	51°5·9'	2°35·6'W	T	182,183
Hornbriggs	N Yks	NZ0906	54°27·2'	1°51·3'W	X	92
Hornbrook	Kent	TQ9433	51°4·0'	0°46·5'E	X	189
Hornbrook Fm	Sol	SP2281	52°25·8'	1°40·2'W	FM	139
Hornbuckle Fm	Win & Maid	SU8874	51°27·7'	0°43·6'W	FM	175
Horn Burn	Scot Bord	NT8959	55°49·7'	2°10·1'W	W	67,74
Horn Burn	Scot Bord	NT9160	55°50·2'	2°8·2'W	X	67
Hornby	Lancs	SD5868	54°6·6'	2°38·1'W	T	97
Hornby	N Yks	NZ3605	54°26·6'	1°26·3'W	T	93
Hornby	N Yks	SE2293	54°20·2'	1°39·3'W	T	99
Hornby	Powys	SO0089	52°29·6'	3°28·0'W	X	136
Hornby Cave	Conwy	SH7584	53°20·5'	3°52·2'W	X	115
Hornby Grange	N Yks	NZ3604	54°26·1'	1°26·3'W	X	93
Hornby Green Fm	N Yks	NZ3704	54°26·0'	1°25·4'W	FM	93
Hornby Hall	Cumbr	NY5629	54°39·5'	2°40·5'W	X	90
Hornby Hall Fm	N Yks	NZ3605	54°26·6'	1°26·3'W	FM	93
Hornby Park	N Yks	SE2293	54°20·2'	1°39·3'W	X	99
Hornby Park Wood	Lancs	SD5969	54°7·2'	2°37·2'W	F	97
Hornby's Lane	Lancs	SD4044	53°53·6'	2°54·4'W	X	102
Horncastle	Lincs	TF2669	53°12·4'	0°6·4'W	T	122
Horncastle	Northum	NY9884	55°9·3'	2°1·5'W	X	81
Horncastle	Read	SU6772	51°26·8'	1°1·8'W	T	175
Horncastle Canal (disused)	Lincs	TF2464	53°9·8'	0°8·3'W	W	122
Horncastle Hill	Lincs	TF3465	53°10·1'	0°0·7'E	X	122
Horncastle Wood	E Susx	TQ3931	51°3·9'	0°0·6'W	F	187
Hornchurch	Hav	TQ5386	51°33·4'	0°12·8'E	T	177
Hornchurch Country Park	Hav	TQ5384	51°32·3'	0°12·8'E	X	177
Hornchurch Marshes	Hav	TQ5082	51°31·2'	0°10·1'E	X	177
Horncliffe	Northum	NT9249	55°44·3'	2°7·2'W	T	74,75
Horncliffe	Northum	NT9249	55°44·3'	2°7·2'W	X	67
Horncliffe Ho	Northum	NT9350	55°44·8'	2°6·3'W	X	67,74,75
Horncliffe Mains	Northum	NT9349	55°44·3'	2°6·3'W	X	74,75
Horncliffe Mill Fm	Northum	NT9349	55°44·3'	2°6·3'W	FM	74,75
Horncliffe Well	Brad	SE1343	53°53·2'	1°47·7'W	W	104
Horncombe	W Susx	TQ3430	51°3·4'	0°4·9'W	X	187
Horncroft Fm	W Susx	TQ0017	50°56·9'	0°34·2'W	FM	197
Horndean	Hants	SU7013	50°55·0'	0°59·9'W	T	197
Horndean	Scot Bord	NT8949	55°44·3'	2°10·1'W	T	74
Horndean Burn	Scot Bord	NT8848	55°43·8'	2°11·0'W	W	74
Horndean Down	Hants	SU7115	50°56·0'	0°59·0'W	X	197
Horndon	Devon	SX5280	50°36·3'	4°5·1'W	T	191,201
Horndon Ho	Thurr	TQ6782	51°31·0'	0°24·8'E	X	177,178
Horndon on the Hill	Thurr	TQ6683	51°31·5'	0°24·0'E	T	177,178
Horn Down	Oxon	SU4788	51°35·6'	1°18·9'W	X	174
Horndoyne	Aberd	NJ6724	57°18·6'	2°32·4'W	X	38
Horne	Surrey	TQ3344	51°11·0'	0°5·4'W	T	187
Hornecourt Manor Fm	Surrey	TQ3345	51°11·5'	0°5·4'W	FM	187
Horne Ho	Brad	SE0348	53°55·9'	1°56·8'W	X	104
Horne House Fm	Surrey	TQ3344	51°11·0'	0°5·4'W	FM	187
Horn End	N Yks	SE6695	54°21·0'	0°58·7'W	X	94,100
Horne Park Fm	Surrey	TQ3542	51°9·9'	0°3·8'W	FM	187
Horner	Devon	SX7654	50°22·6'	3°44·3'W	X	202
Horner	Somer	SS8945	51°11·8'	3°34·9'W	T	181
Horner Hill	Devon	ST2501	50°48·5'	3°3·5'W	H	192,193
Horner Hill	Somer	SS9044	51°11·3'	3°34·1'W	X	181
Horne Row	Essex	TL7704	51°42·6'	0°34·1'E	T	167
Horner's Green	Suff	TL9641	52°2·2'	0°51·9'E	T	155
Horner, The	Aberd	NJ7415	57°13·8'	2°25·4'W	X	38
Horner Water	Somer	SS8945	51°11·8'	3°34·9'W	W	181
Horner Wood	Somer	SS8944	51°11·3'	3°34·9'W	F	181
Horne's Green	Essex	TL8833	51°58·0'	0°44·6'E	X	168
Hornes Place	Kent	TQ9530	51°2·4'	0°47·3'E	X	189
Hornestreet	Essex	TM0232	51°57·2'	0°56·8'E	T	168
Hornets Fm	Essex	TL5809	51°45·7'	0°17·8'E	FM	167
Horneval	Highld	NG2747	57°26·1'	6°32·5'W	T	23
Horney Common	E Susx	TQ4525	51°0·6'	0°4·4'E	T	188,198
Horneystead	Northum	NY8177	55°5·5'	2°17·4'W	X	86,87
Hornfield Ho	Cambs	TF4116	52°43·6'	0°5·7'E	X	131
Horn Fm	Glos	SP2328	51°57·2'	1°39·5'W	FM	163
Horn Fm	N Yks	SE6741	53°51·9'	0°58·5'W	FM	105,106
Horn Fm	Pth & Kin	NO2526	56°25·5'	3°12·5'W	FM	53,59
Horngrove	Worcs	SO8473	52°21·5'	2°13·7'W	X	138
Horn Heath	Suff	TL7877	52°22·0'	0°37·3'E	X	144
Horn Hill	Bucks	TQ0192	51°37·3'	0°32·1'W	X	176
Horn Hill	Derby	SK3320	52°46·8'	1°30·2'W	X	128
Hornhill	Devon	SS9611	50°53·6'	3°28·3'W	X	192
Horn Hill	Dorset	ST4603	50°49·7'	2°45·6'W	X	193
Horn Hill	Somer	ST2340	51°9·5'	3°5·7'W	T	182
Hornhill	W Berks	SU3366	51°23·8'	1°31·1'W	X	174
Horn Hill Court	Bucks	TQ0192	51°37·3'	0°32·1'W	X	176
Hornhillock	Aberd	NJ9532	57°23·0'	2°4·5'W	X	30
Hornhill Top	E Yorks	SE9749	53°55·9'	0°30·9'W	X	106
Horn Ho	Rut	SK9511	52°41·5'	0°35·3'W	X	130
Hornick	Corn	SW9753	50°20·8'	4°50·8'W	T	200,204
Hornickhill	Cumbr	NY3765	54°58·8'	2°58·6'W	X	85
Horniehaugh	Angus	NO4161	56°44·5'	2°57·4'W	X	44
Hornigals	Essex	TL8822	51°52·1'	0°44·2'E	X	168
Horning	Norf	TG3417	52°42·2'	1°28·2'E	T	133,134
Horning Hall	Norf	TG3716	52°41·6'	1°30·8'E	X	133,134
Horninghold	Leic	SP8097	52°34·1'	0°48·8'W	T	141
Horninglow	Staffs	SK2425	52°49·6'	1°38·2'W	T	128
Horningsea	Cambs	TL4962	52°14·4'	0°11·3'E	T	154
Horningsham	Wilts	ST8141	51°10·3'	2°15·9'W	T	183
Horningtoft	Norf	TF9323	52°46·4'	0°52·1'E	T	132
Hornington Br	N Yks	SE5241	53°52·0'	1°12·1'W	X	105
Hornington Manor	N Yks	SE5141	53°52·0'	1°13·1'W	X	105
Horningtops	Corn	SX2760	50°25·1'	4°25·7'W	T	201
Hornish	N Eil	NF7309	57°3·6'	7°23·2'W	X	31
Hornish	N Eil	NF8776	57°40·2'	7°14·5'W	X	18
Hornish Strand	N Eil	NF8676	57°40·1'	7°15·5'W	X	18
Hornley Common	Hants	SU8258	51°19·1'	0°49·0'W	X	175,186
Horn Mill	Rut	SK9510	52°41·0'	0°35·3'W	X	130
Horn Moor	Somer	ST3406	50°51·2'	2°55·9'W	X	193
Horn of Ramsness	Shetld	HU6187	60°34·0'	0°52·7'W	X	1,2
Horn Park	Dorset	ST4602	50°49·1'	2°45·6'W	X	193
Horn Park Fm	Dorset	ST4602	50°49·1'	2°45·6'W	FM	193
Horn Ridge	N Yks	SE6596	54°21·6'	0°59·6'W	H	94,100
Hornsbarrow	Cumbr	SD5780	54°13·1'	2°39·1'W	X	97
Hornsbury	Somer	ST3310	50°53·4'	2°56·8'W	T	193
Hornsby	Cumbr	NY5150	54°50·8'	2°45·4'W	T	86
Hornsby Gate	Cumbr	NY5250	54°50·8'	2°44·4'W	X	86
Horns Corner	Kent	TQ7429	51°2·3'	0°29·3'E	X	188,199
Hornscroft	Aberd	NJ8035	57°24·6'	2°19·5'W	X	29,30
Horns Cross	Devon	SS3823	50°59·3'	4°18·1'W	T	190
Horn's Cross	Devon	SX6671	50°31·6'	3°53·1'W	A	202
Horns Cross	E Susx	TQ8222	50°58·3'	0°35·9'E	T	199
Horns Cross	Kent	TQ5774	51°26·8'	0°16·0'E	X	177
Hornsea	E Yorks	TA2047	53°54·6'	0°10·0'W	T	107
Hornsea Burton	E Yorks	TA2046	53°54·0'	0°10·0'W	T	107
Hornsea Mere	E Yorks	TA1947	53°54·6'	0°10·9'W	W	107
Hornsea Rail Trail (Cycle Route)	E Yorks	TA1638	53°49·8'	0°13·8'W	X	107
Hornsey	Hargy	TQ3089	51°35·3'	0°7·0'W	T	176,177
Hornsey Brook	Somer	ST5623	51°0·5'	2°37·2'W	W	183
Hornsey Vale	Hargy	TQ3088	51°34·8'	0°7·0'W	T	176,177
Horns Green	Brom	TQ4558	51°18·4'	0°5·2'E	T	188
Hornshayes Br	Devon	ST2304	50°50·1'	3°5·2'W	X	192,193
Hornshay Fm	Somer	ST1422	50°59·7'	3°13·1'W	FM	181,193
Hornshayne Fm	Devon	SY1994	50°44·6'	3°8·5'W	FM	192,193
Hornshill	E Loth	NT5767	55°53·9'	2°40·8'W	X	67
Horns Hill	Glos	SO7301	51°42·7'	2°23·1'W	X	162
Horns Hill	Kent	TQ4552	51°15·1'	0°5·1'E	X	188
Hornshill	N Lanak	NS6669	55°54·0'	4°8·2'W	X	64
Hornshill Fm	W Susx	TQ0733	51°5·4'	0°27·9'W	FM	187
Horn's Ho	Durham	NZ2246	54°48·7'	1°39·0'W	X	88
Hornshurst Wood	E Susx	TQ5531	51°3·7'	0°13·1'E	F	188
Horn Skerry	Shetld	HU7071	60°25·3'	0°43·2'W	X	2
Hornsleasow Fm	Glos	SP1232	51°59·4'	1°49·1'W	FM	150
Horns Lodge	Kent	TQ5949	51°13·3'	0°17·0'E	X	188
Horns Lodge	Kent	TQ6162	51°20·3'	0°19·1'E	X	177,188
Hornsmill Brook	Ches	SJ4775	53°16·4'	2°47·3'W	W	117
Horns of Hagmark	Shetld	HP6612	60°47·4'	0°46·8'W	X	1
Horns of the Roe	Shetld	HU4492	60°36·8'	1°11·3'W	X	1,2
Hornspike	Shrops	SJ4734	52°54·3'	2°46·9'W	X	126
Horns Reservoir	Lancs	SD5738	53°50·4'	2°38·8'W	W	102
Horns, The	E Susx	TQ6106	50°50·1'	0°17·6'E	X	199
Horns, The	Glos	SO8704	51°44·3'	2°10·9'W	X	162
Horn Street	Kent	TQ6860	51°19·1'	0°25·0'E	T	177,178,188
Horn Street	Kent	TQ6960	51°19·1'	0°25·9'E	T	177,178,188
Horn Street	Kent	TR1835	51°4·6'	1°7·1'E	T	179,189
Horn, The	Shetld	HU1461	60°20·2'	1°44·3'W	X	3
Hornton	Oxon	SP3945	52°6·4'	1°25·4'W	T	151
Hornton Grounds	Oxon	SP3844	52°5·8'	1°26·3'W	X	151
Hornton Hall	Oxon	SP3845	52°6·4'	1°26·3'W	X	151
Hornton Hill Fm	Oxon	SP3846	52°6·9'	1°26·3'W	FM	151
Horntowie	Aberd	NJ4847	57°30·9'	2°51·6'W	X	28,29
Horn Wood	Northnts	SP8957	52°12·5'	0°41·5'W	F	152
Horpit	Swin	SU2184	51°33·5'	1°41·4'W	T	174
Hor Point	Corn	SW4941	50°13·2'	5°30·8'W	X	203
Horrabank Fm	N Yks	SD9591	54°19·1'	2°4·2'W	FM	98
Horrabridge	Devon	SX5169	50°30·3'	4°5·7'W	T	201
Horrace	Corn	SW3921	50°2·2'	5°38·3'W	X	203
Horrace	Cumbr	SD2679	54°12·3'	3°7·7'W	X	96,97
Horraldshay	Orkney	HY3614	59°0·8'	3°6·4'W	X	6
Horraquoy	Orkney	HY5805	58°56·1'	2°43·3'W	X	6
Horrathorne	Devon	SX5297	50°45·5'	4°5·5'W	X	191
Horrell	Corn	SX3088	50°40·2'	4°24·0'W	X	190
Horrex Fm	Norf	TL7799	52°33·8'	0°37·1'E	FM	144
Horridge	Devon	SS5335	51°6·0'	4°5·6'W	X	180
Horridge	Devon	SS6235	51°6·1'	3°57·9'W	X	180
Horridge	Devon	SS6413	50°54·3'	3°55·7'W	X	180
Horridge	Devon	SS7219	50°57·6'	3°49·0'W	X	180
Horridge	Devon	SS7910	50°52·8'	3°42·8'W	X	191
Horridge	Devon	SX7674	50°33·4'	3°44·7'W	X	191
Horridge Moor	Devon	SS7015	50°55·4'	3°50·6'W	X	180
Horrid Hill	Medway	TQ8168	51°23·2'	0°36·5'E	X	178
Horrie	Orkney	HY5104	58°55·5'	2°50·6'W	X	6,7
Horries	Orkney	HY5607	58°57·1'	2°45·4'W	X	6
Horringer	Suff	TL8261	52°13·3'	0°40·3'E	T	155
Horringer Court	Suff	TL8362	52°13·8'	0°41·2'E	X	155
Horringer Ho	Suff	TL8260	52°12·7'	0°40·2'E	X	155
Horringford	I of W	SZ5485	50°40·0'	1°13·8'W	X	196
Horris Hill School	Hants	SU4663	51°22·1'	1°20·0'W	X	174
Horrocks Fold	Bolton	SD7013	53°37·0'	2°26·8'W	T	109
Horrocksford	Lancs	SD7443	53°53·2'	2°23·3'W	T	103
Horrocks Hill Fm	Bolton	SD6912	53°36·5'	2°27·7'W	FM	109
Horrockwood	Cumbr	NY4421	54°35·1'	2°51·6'W	X	90
Horroquoy	Orkney	HY3214	59°0·7'	3°10·6'W	X	6
Horrowmore	Devon	SX8489	50°41·6'	3°38·2'W	X	191
Horsacleit	N Eil	NG1496	57°52·0'	6°48·9'W	X	14
Horsacott	Devon	SS5131	51°3·8'	4°7·2'W	X	180
Horsalls	Kent	TQ8754	51°15·5'	0°41·2'E	X	189
Horsanish	N Eil	NA9908	57°57·8'	7°4·9'W	X	13
Horsbere Brook	Glos	SO8420	51°52·9'	2°13·6'W	W	162
Horsbrugh Castle	Scot Bord	NT2939	55°38·6'	3°7·2'W	X	73
Horsbrugh Ford	Scot Bord	NT2939	55°38·6'	3°7·2'W	X	73
Horsburgh Hope	Scot Bord	NT2942	55°40·2'	3°7·3'W	X	73
Horsdon	Northum	NT9827	55°32·5'	2°1·5'W	X	75
Horsea Island	C of Port	SU6304	50°50·2'	1°5·9'W	X	196
Horse Bank	Sefton	SD3220	53°40·6'	3°1·4'W	X	102
Horsebog	Moray	NJ4655	57°35·2'	2°53·7'W	X	28,29
Horse Bog	Scot Bord	NT7940	55°39·4'	2°19·6'W	X	74
Horsebog Loch	D & G	NX8979	55°5·8'	3°43·9'W	X	84
Horse Bones Fm	Kent	TR0322	50°57·9'	0°53·9'E	FM	189
Horse Br	Shrops	SJ3705	52°38·6'	2°55·5'W	X	126
Horsebridge	Devon	SX4074	50°32·9'	4°15·1'W	T	201
Horse Bridge	E Susx	TQ6609	50°51·6'	0°21·9'E	X	199
Horsebridge	Hants	SU3430	51°4·3'	1°30·5'W	T	185
Horsebridge	Shrops	SJ3606	52°39·1'	2°56·4'W	T	126
Horse Bridge	Staffs	SJ9653	53°4·7'	2°3·2'W	T	118
Horsebridge Common	W Susx	TQ1815	50°55·6'	0°18·9'W	X	198
Horsebrook	Devon	SX7158	50°24·7'	3°48·6'W	T	202
Horsebrook	Staffs	SJ8810	52°41·5'	2°10·3'W	T	127
Horsebush Hill	Hants	SU8032	51°5·1'	0°51·1'W	X	186
Horse Carr Wood	Barns	SE3806	53°33·2'	1°25·2'W	F	110,111
Horsecastle	N Som	ST4266	51°23·6'	2°49·6'W	T	171,172,182
Horsecastle Bay	Scot Bord	NT9168	55°54·6'	2°8·2'W	W	67
Horsecleugh Fm	E Ayr	NS5618	55°26·3'	4°16·1'W	FM	71
Horseclose	D & G	NY1167	54°59·6'	3°23·0'W	X	85
Horse Close	Northum	NY6661	54°56·8'	2°31·4'W	X	86
Horse Close	Northum	NY7464	54°58·4'	2°23·9'W	X	86,87
Horseclose Copse	Glos	SP1914	51°49·7'	1°43·1'W	F	163
Horse Close Fm	N Yks	SD9950	53°57·0'	2°0·5'W	FM	103
Horse Close Fm	Red & Cl	NZ6320	54°34·5'	1°1·1'W	FM	94
Horsecombe Fm	Somer	SS8838	51°8·1'	3°35·7'W	FM	181
Horsecombe Vale	Bath & NE Somer	ST7561	51°21·1'	2°21·2'W	X	172
Horse Copse	Wilts	ST9470	51°26·0'	2°4·8'W	F	173
Horse Cove	Devon	SX9675	50°34·2'	3°27·7'W	W	192
Horse Crags	Cumbr	NY2803	54°25·3'	3°6·2'W	X	89,90
Horse Craig	Fife	NT0384	56°2·6'	3°33·0'W	X	65
Horsecraig	Inverc	NS3170	55°53·9'	4°41·7'W	X	63
Horsecroft Fm	Suff	TL8461	52°13·2'	0°42·0'E	FM	155

Horse Croft Fm	Wilts	ST8953	51°16·8′	2°9·1′W	FM	184
Horsecroft Hall	Suff	TL8461	52°13·2′	0°42·0′E	X	155
Horse Crook Bay	Aberd	NO8371	56°50·1′	2°16·3′W	W	45
Horse Cross	Herts	TL4123	51°53·5′	0°3·3′E	X	167
Horsedale Fm	Derby	SK2758	53°7·3′	1°35·4′W	FM	119
Horsedale Plantn	E Yorks	SE8757	54°0·3′	0°39·9′W	F	106
Horse Down	Dorset	ST9609	50°53·1′	2°3·0′W	X	195
Horsedown	Wilts	ST8379	51°30·8′	2°14·3′W	T	173
Horse Down	Wilts	SU0247	51°13·6′	1°57·9′W	X	184
Horse Down	Wilts	SU0840	51°9·8′	1°52·7′W	X	184
Horsedown Common	Hants	SU7648	51°13·8′	0°54·3′W	X	186
Horsedowns	Corn	SW6134	50°9·7′	5°20·4′W	T	203
Horse Edge	Cumbr	NY6845	54°48·2′	2°29·4′W	X	86,87
Horse Eye	E Susx	TQ6208	50°51·2′	0°18·5′E	X	199
Horse Eye Level	E Susx	TQ6209	50°51·7′	0°18·5′E	X	199
Horse Fen Fm	Norf	TL6192	52°30·4′	0°22·7′E	FM	143
Horse Flags	Orkney	HY4849	59°19·7′	2°54·3′W	X	5
Horsefoot Hill	Hants	SU7111	50°53·9′	0°59·0′W	X	197
Horseford Fm	Devon	SS7716	50°56·1′	3°44·6′W	FM	180
Horse Gate	Ghead	NZ1259	54°55·8′	1°48·3′W	X	88
Horse Geo	Orkney	HY6543	59°16·6′	2°36·4′W	X	5
Horse Geo	Orkney	HY7137	59°13·4′	2°30·0′W	X	5
Horse Geo	Shetld	HU4755	60°16·9′	1°8·5′W	X	3
Horsegills	Cumbr	NY4665	54°58·9′	2°50·2′W	X	86
Horseham Hall	Essex	TL6643	52°3·9′	0°25·7′E	X	154
Horse Haven	Devon	SS8218	50°57·2′	3°40·4′W	X	181
Horsehay	Wrekin	SJ6707	52°39·8′	2°28·9′W	T	127
Horsehay Common	Wrekin	SJ6707	52°39·8′	2°28·9′W	X	127
Horsehay Fm	Oxon	SP4527	51°56·6′	1°20·3′W	FM	164
Horse Haylands	Staffs	SJ9862	53°9·5′	2°1·4′W	X	118
Horse Head	Cumbr	NY6181	55°7·6′	2°36·3′W	X	80
Horse Head	N Yks	SD8878	54°12·1′	2°10·6′W	H	98
Horse Head	Scot Bord	NT9563	55°51·9′	2°4·4′W	X	67
Horse Head Moor	N Yks	SD8977	54°11·6′	2°9·7′W	X	98
Horseheath	Cambs	TL6147	52°6·1′	0°21·4′E	T	154
Horseheath Lodge	Cambs	TL5947	52°6·1′	0°19·7′E	X	154
Horseheath Park	Cambs	TL6247	52°6·1′	0°22·3′E	X	154
Horse Hey Fm	Lancs	SD6942	53°52·6′	2°27·9′W	FM	103
Horse Hill	D & G	NX8068	54°59·8′	3°52·1′W	X	84
Horsehill	E Ayr	NS4842	55°39·1′	4°24·5′W	X	70
Horse Hill	Kent	TR0662	51°19·4′	0°57·8′E	X	179
Horse Hill	N Ayr	NS1757	55°46·6′	4°54·6′W	X	63
Horse Hill	Norf	TG0539	52°54·8′	1°3·3′E	F	133
Horse Hill	Oxon	SP3930	51°58·3′	1°25·5′W	X	151
Horse Hill	Wilts	ST9422	51°0·1′	2°4·7′W	H	184
Horse Hill	Worcs	SO8349	52°8·6′	2°14·5′W	X	150
Horsehill Fm	Somer	ST6439	51°9·2′	2°30·5′W	FM	183
Horsehill Fm	Worcs	SO7773	52°21·5′	2°19·9′W	FM	138
Horsehill Tor	Derby	SK0984	53°21·4′	1°51·5′W	X	110
Horsehoes, The	Kent	TQ5046	51°11·8′	0°9·2′E	X	188
Horsehold	Cald	SD9826	53°44·1′	2°1·4′W	X	103
Horseholders Wood	Medway	TQ6864	51°21·2′	0°25·2′E	F	177,178,188
Horse Holm	Angus	NO4474	56°51·5′	2°54·7′W	X	44
Horseholm	D & G	NY0270	55°1·1′	3°31·5′W	X	84
Horseholme	Cumbr	NY6671	55°2·2′	2°31·5′W	X	86
Horse Holme Wood	N Yks	SD9359	54°1·9′	2°6·0′W	F	103
Horse Hope Burn	Scot Bord	NT2131	55°34·2′	3°14·7′W	W	73
Horse Hope Hill	Scot Bord	NT2130	55°33·7′	3°14·7′W	H	73
Horsehouse	N Yks	SE0481	54°13·7′	1°55·9′W	T	98
Horse Island	Highld	NC0204	57°59·1′	5°20·5′W	X	15
Horse Island	Shetld	HU3807	59°51·1′	1°18·8′W	X	4
Horse Isle (Nature Reserve)	N Ayr	NS2142	55°38·6′	4°50·2′W	X	63,70
Horse Isles Bay	D & G	NX8352	54°51·2′	3°48·9′W	W	84
Horse Isle Shelves	N Ayr	NS2142	55°38·6′	4°50·2′W	X	63,70
Horse Knowe	D & G	NY2390	55°12·1′	3°12·2′W	H	79
Horselake	Devon	SX7186	50°39·8′	3°49·1′W	X	191
Horselake	Devon	SX7793	50°43·7′	3°44·2′W	X	191
Horselaw	Fife	NO3514	56°19·1′	3°2·6′W	X	59
Horse Law	S Lanak	NT0349	55°43·7′	3°32·2′W	H	72
Horselea	Pth & Kin	NO0917	56°20·5′	3°27·9′W	X	58
Horse Ledge	I of W	SZ5880	50°37·2′	1°10·4′W	X	196
Horselees	Kent	TR0659	51°17·8′	0°57·7′E	X	179
Horseley	Scot Bord	NT8363	55°51·8′	2°15·9′W	X	67
Horseley Fm	Somer	ST7134	51°6·5′	2°24·5′W	FM	183
Horseley Head Moss	Kirk	SE0609	53°34·9′	1°54·2′W	X	110
Horseley Heath	Sand	SO9792	52°31·8′	2°2·2′W	T	139
Horseley Hill	Scot Bord	NT8362	55°51·3′	2°15·9′W	X	67
Horseleyhills Fm	Worcs	SO8080	52°25·3′	2°17·2′W	FM	138
Horse Leys Fm	Leic	SK6021	52°47·2′	1°6·2′W	FM	129
Horseleys Fm	Warw	SP2539	52°3·2′	1°37·7′W	FM	151
Horsell	Surrey	SU9959	51°19·5′	0°34·4′W	T	175,186
Horsell Birch	Surrey	SU9859	51°19·5′	0°35·2′W	T	175,186
Horsell Common	Surrey	TQ0060	51°20·0′	0°33·5′W	X	176,186
Horse Lochs	Shetld	HU2582	60°31·5′	1°32·2′W	W	3
Horselode Fen Fm	Cambs	TL4082	52°25·3′	0°3·9′E	FM	142,143
Horselunges	E Susx	TQ5811	50°52·8′	0°15·2′E	A	199
Horseman's Green	Wrex	SJ4441	52°58·0′	2°49·6′W	T	117
Horseman's Hill	Devon	SY3292	50°43·7′	2°57·4′W	X	193
Horseman Side	Essex	TQ5496	51°38·7′	0°13·9′E	T	167,177
Horsemans Well Fm	N Yks	SE2457	54°0·7′	1°37·6′W	FM	104
Horse Mark	D & G	NX5650	54°49·7′	4°14·1′W	X	83
Horsemarling Fm	Glos	SO8006	51°45·4′	2°17·0′W	FM	162
Horsemere Green	W Susx	SU9902	50°48·8′	0°35·3′W	T	197
Horsemill	Pth & Kin	NO1219	56°21·6′	3°25·0′W	X	58
Horse Moor	Cambs	TL4394	52°31·7′	0°6·9′E	X	142,143
Horse Moor	Devon	SS5422	50°59·0′	4°4·4′W	X	180
Horsemoor	W Berks	SU4773	51°27·5′	1°19·0′W	X	174
Horsemoor Copse	Hants	SZ3798	50°47·1′	1°28·1′W	F	196
Horsemoor Fm	Cambs	TL4494	52°31·7′	0°7·8′E	FM	142,143
Horsemoor Hills	Cumbr	NY2533	54°41·4′	3°9·4′W	X	89,90
Horsemoor Wood	Staffs	SJ9411	52°41·9′	2°5·9′W	F	127
Horsemuir	E Ayr	NS4144	55°40·1′	4°31·2′W	X	70
Horsenden	Bucks	SP7902	51°42·9′	0°51·0′W	T	165
Horsenden Hill	Ealing	TQ1684	51°32·8′	0°19·2′W	H	176
Horsen Fm	Somer	SS7836	51°6·9′	3°44·2′W	FM	180
Horsen Hill	Somer	SS7835	51°6·3′	3°44·2′W	H	180
Horse of Burravoe	Shetld	HU5381	60°30·8′	1°1·6′W	X	1,2,3
Horse of Copinsay	Orkney	HY6202	58°54·5′	2°39·1′W	X	6
Horse of the Knabb	Shetld	HU4740	60°8·8′	1°8·7′W	X	4
Horse Paddock Wood	Staffs	SJ8607	52°39·9′	2°12·0′W	F	127,139
Horse Park Wood	N Yks	SE2197	54°22·3′	1°40·2′W	F	99
Horsepasture Covert	Staffs	SK0413	52°43·1′	1°56·0′W	F	128
Horse Pasture Fm	Lincs	TF1985	53°21·1′	0°12·3′W	FM	122
Horsepasture Fm	W Susx	SU7410	50°53·3′	0°56·5′W	FM	197
Horsepasture Wood	Notts	SK6453	53°4·5′	1°2·3′W	F	120
Horse Pasture Wood	N Yks	SE0097	54°22·4′	1°59·6′W	F	98
Horse Point	I Scilly	SV8807	49°53·2′	6°20·3′W	X	203
Horse Pool	Notts	SK8161	53°8·6′	0°46·9′W	W	121
Horsepool Fm	Suff	TL7961	52°13·3′	0°37·6′E	FM	155
Horsepool Fm	Worcs	SO9680	52°25·3′	2°3·1′W	FM	139
Horsepool Grange	Leic	SK4610	52°41·4′	1°18·8′W	X	129
Horsepools	Glos	SO8410	51°47·5′	2°13·5′W	T	162
Horse Pow Hill	S Lanak	NS9912	55°23·7′	3°35·3′W	H	78
Horse Rigg	Northum	NT8233	55°35·7′	2°16·7′W	X	74
Horse Rock	Corn	SW6545	50°15·7′	5°17·5′W	X	203
Horse Rock	Corn	SW8364	50°26·4′	5°3·0′W	X	200
Horse Rock	S Ayr	NX1796	55°13·7′	4°52·2′W	X	76
Horse Sand Fort	C of Port	SZ6594	50°44·7′	1°4·3′W	A	196
Horse Sands	Kent	TR0365	51°21·1′	0°55·3′E	X	178,179
Horse Seat	Arg & Bt	NS1376	55°56·7′	4°59·2′W	X	63
Horseshoe Bay	I of W	SZ5777	50°35·6′	1°11·3′W	W	196
Horseshoe Br	Lincs	TF2121	52°46·6′	0°12·0′W	X	131
Horseshoe Corner	Essex	TQ9891	51°35·2′	0°51·9′E	X	178
Horseshoe Craig	Highld	NH4112	57°10·5′	4°37·4′W	X	34
Horseshoe Dale	Derby	SK0970	53°13·9′	1°51·5′W	X	119
Horseshoe Fm	S Glos	ST6790	51°36·7′	2°28·2′W	FM	162,172
Horseshoe Fm	Surrey	TQ4036	51°6·6′	0°0·4′E	FM	187
Horseshoe Hill	Durham	NY9844	54°47·7′	2°1·4′W	H	87
Horseshoe Hill	Hants	SU2733	51°6·0′	1°36·5′W	H	184
Horseshoe Hole Fm	Norf	TF5524	52°47·7′	0°18·3′E	FM	131
Horseshoe Lake	Glos	SP2200	51°42·1′	1°40·5′W	W	163
Horseshoe Pass	Denb	SJ1847	53°1·1′	3°12·9′W	X	116
Horseshoe Plantn	Scot Bord	NT6440	55°39·4′	2°33·9′W	F	74
Horse Shoe Point	Lincs	TA3801	53°29·5′	0°5·2′E	X	113
Horseshoes Fm	Essex	TL4606	51°44·2′	0°7·3′E	FM	167
Horse Shoe, The	Arg & Bt	NM8228	56°23·9′	5°31·5′W	W	49
Horseshoe, The	Lincs	TF4750	53°1·9′	0°11·9′E	X	122
Horse Shoe, The	Pemb	SM9204	51°42·0′	5°0·2′W	X	157,158
Horse Sound	Highld	NC0304	57°59·2′	5°19·5′W	W	15
Horse Sound	Orkney	HY6102	58°54·5′	2°40·1′W	W	6
Horse Stead	Derby	SK1471	53°14·4′	1°47·0′W	X	119
Horse Stone	Sheff	SK1597	53°28·4′	1°46·0′W	X	110
Horse, The	Corn	SW6713	49°58·5′	5°14·6′W	X	203
Horseupcleugh	Scot Bord	NT6658	55°49·1′	2°32·1′W	X	67,74
Horseupcleugh Rig	Scot Bord	NT6659	55°49·6′	2°32·1′W	X	67,74
Horse Water	Shetld	HU5281	60°30·8′	1°2·7′W	W	1,2,3
Horseway	Cambs	TL4286	52°27·4′	0°5·8′E	T	142,143
Horseway Head	Heref	SO3460	52°14·3′	2°57·6′W	T	137,148,149
Horsewells	Aberd	NJ7701	57°6·2′	2°22·3′W	X	38
Horsewold Fm	E Yorks	SE9148	53°55·4′	0°36·4′W	FM	106
Horse Wood	Cald	SD9522	53°41·9′	2°4·1′W	X	103
Horse Wood	Ches	SJ8570	53°13·9′	2°13·1′W	F	118
Horse Wood	Norf	TF9218	52°43·8′	0°51·0′E	F	132
Horsey	Norf	TG4522	52°44·6′	1°38·2′E	T	134
Horsey	Somer	ST3239	51°9·0′	2°57·9′W	T	182
Horsey Corner	Norf	TG4523	52°45·2′	1°38·2′E	T	134
Horsey Down	Wilts	SU0993	51°38·4′	1°51·8′W	T	163,173
Horseyeatt	Devon	SX5470	50°30·9′	4°3·2′W	X	201
Horsey Fm	Somer	ST4326	51°2·1′	2°48·4′W	FM	193
Horsey Hill	Peterb	TL2295	52°32·6′	0°11·7′W	X	142
Horsey Hill (Civil War Fort)	Peterb	TL2295	52°32·6′	0°11·7′W	A	142
Horsey Island	Devon	SS4733	51°4·8′	4°10·7′W	X	180
Horsey Island	Essex	TM2324	51°52·4′	1°14·8′E	X	169
Horsey Knap	Dorset	ST5604	50°50·3′	2°37·1′W	H	194
Horseylane Fm	Staffs	SK0613	52°43·1′	1°54·3′W	FM	128
Horsey Level	Somer	ST3239	51°9·0′	2°57·9′W	X	182
Horsey Mere	Norf	TG4422	52°44·7′	1°37·3′E	W	134
Horsey Mill	Norf	TG4522	52°44·6′	1°38·2′E	X	134
Horsey Pill	Somer	ST3039	51°9·0′	2°59·7′W	X	182
Horsey Ridge	Devon	SS4733	51°4·8′	4°10·7′W	X	180
Horsford	Norf	TG1916	52°42·1′	1°14·9′E	T	133,134
Horsford Brook	Shrops	SO6887	52°29·0′	2°27·9′W	W	138
Horsford Manor	Norf	TG2013	52°40·4′	1°15·7′E	X	133,134
Horsford Woods	Norf	TG1918	52°43·1′	1°15·0′E	F	133,134
Horsforth	Leeds	SE2438	53°50·5′	1°37·7′W	T	104
Horsforth Sta	Leeds	SE2439	53°51·0′	1°37·7′W	X	104
Horsforth Woodside	Leeds	SE2437	53°50·0′	1°37·7′W	T	104
Horsfrith Park Fm	Essex	TL6104	51°42·9′	0°20·2′E	FM	167
Horsgate	W Susx	TQ3125	51°0·8′	0°7·6′W	X	187,198
Horsgate Fm	W Susx	TQ3125	51°0·8′	0°7·6′W	FM	187,198
Horsham	Devon	SX4762	50°26·5′	4°8·9′W	X	201
Horsham	Worcs	SO7357	52°12·9′	2°23·3′W	T	150
Horsham	W Susx	TQ1731	51°4·2′	0°19·4′W	T	187
Horsham Marsh	Kent	TQ8367	51°22·6′	0°38·2′E	X	178
Horsham St Faith	Norf	TG2115	52°41·5′	1°16·6′E	T	133,134
Horshoe Green	Kent	TQ4742	51°9·7′	0°6·5′E	T	188
Horsick	Orkney	HY5104	58°55·5′	2°50·6′W	X	6,7
Horsielands	Surrey	TQ2041	51°9·6′	0°16·6′W	X	187
Horsington	Lincs	TF1968	53°12·0′	0°12·7′W	T	122
Horsington	Somer	ST7023	51°0·6′	2°25·3′W	T	183
Horsington Holmes	Lincs	TF1566	53°11·0′	0°16·3′W	X	121
Horsington Marsh	Somer	ST7124	51°1·1′	2°24·4′W	X	183
Horsington Wood	Lincs	TF1867	53°11·5′	0°13·6′W	F	122
Horsley	Derby	SK3844	52°59·8′	1°25·6′W	T	119,128
Horsley	Glos	ST8398	51°41·1′	2°14·4′W	T	162
Horsley	Northum	NY8496	55°15·7′	2°14·7′W	T	80
Horsley	Northum	NZ0966	54°59·6′	1°51·1′W	T	88
Horsley Burn	Durham	NY9637	54°43·9′	2°3·3′W	W	91,92
Horsley Cross	Essex	TM1227	51°54·3′	1°5·3′E	T	168,169
Horsleycross Street	Essex	TM1228	51°54·8′	1°5·4′E	T	168,169
Horsley Fen	Cambs	TL4083	52°25·9′	0°4·0′E	X	142,143
Horsley Fm	Derby	SK1951	53°3·6′	1°42·6′W	FM	119
Horsley Fm	Staffs	SJ8027	52°50·6′	2°17·4′W	FM	127
Horsley Fm	W Susx	SU7613	50°54·9′	0°54·7′W	FM	197
Horsleygate	Derby	SK3177	53°17·6′	1°31·7′W	X	119
Horsleygate Fm	N Yks	SE2569	54°7·2′	1°36·6′W	FM	99
Horsley Hall	Durham	NY9638	54°44·5′	2°3·3′W	X	91,92
Horsley Hall	Staffs	SJ8128	52°51·2′	2°16·5′W	X	127
Horsley Head	Durham	NY9637	54°43·9′	2°3·3′W	X	91,92
Horsleyhead	N Lanak	NS7952	55°45·0′	3°55·2′W	X	64
Horsley High Barns	Northum	NZ1592	55°13·6′	1°45·4′W	X	81
Horsleyhill	Scot Bord	NT5319	55°28·0′	2°44·2′W	T	79
Horsley Hill	S Tyne	NZ3865	54°58·9′	1°23·9′W	T	88
Horsleyhope	Durham	NZ0547	54°49·3′	1°54·9′W	T	87
Horsley Lodge	Derby	SK3843	52°59·2′	1°25·6′W	X	119,128
Horsleys Green	Bucks	SU7895	51°39·1′	0°52·0′W	T	165
Horsley Sta	Surrey	TQ0954	51°16·7′	0°25·8′W	X	187
Horsley Tower	Northum	NZ1494	55°14·6′	1°46·4′W	A	81
Horsley Towers	Surrey	TQ0953	51°16·2′	0°25·9′W	X	187
Horsley Wood	Northum	NZ1065	54°59·0′	1°50·2′W	F	88
Horsley Woodhouse	Derby	SK3944	52°59·8′	1°24·7′W	T	119,128
Horsmanshoad	W Susx	TQ2723	50°59·8′	0°11·0′W	X	198
Horsmonden	Kent	TQ7040	51°8·3′	0°26·2′E	T	188
Horsnett Fm	Heref	SO6055	52°11·7′	2°34·7′W	FM	149
Horson Ho	Corn	SX4155	50°22·6′	4°13·8′W	X	201
Horspath	Oxon	SP5704	51°44·1′	1°10·1′W	T	164
Horspath Common	Oxon	SP5705	51°44·7′	1°10·1′W	X	164
Horstead	Norf	TG2619	52°43·5′	1°21·2′E	T	133,134
Horstead Keynes Sta	W Susx	TQ3729	51°2·9′	0°2·3′W	X	187,198
Horstead Lodge	Norf	TG2618	52°43·0′	1°21·2′E	X	133,134
Horsted Green	E Susx	TQ4619	50°57·3′	0°5·1′E	T	198
Horsted House Fm	W Susx	TQ3730	51°3·4′	0°2·3′W	FM	187
Horsted Keynes	W Susx	TQ3828	51°2·3′	0°1·5′W	T	187,198
Horsted Place	E Susx	TQ4618	50°56·8′	0°5·1′E	X	198
Horstedpond Fm	E Susx	TQ4719	50°57·3′	0°6·0′E	FM	198
Horswell Fm	Devon	SS5829	51°2·8′	4°1·2′W	FM	180
Horswell Ho	Devon	SX6942	50°16·0′	3°49·9′W	X	202
Hortham Fm	S Glos	ST6284	51°33·5′	2°32·5′W	FM	172
Hortham Wood	S Glos	ST6284	51°33·5′	2°32·5′W	F	172
Horticulture Research International	Warw	SP2757	52°12·9′	1°35·9′W	X	151
Horton	Bucks	SP9219	51°51·9′	0°39·4′W	T	165
Horton	Dorset	SU0307	50°52·0′	1°57·1′W	T	195
Horton	Heref	SO6358	52°13·4′	2°32·1′W	X	149
Horton	Kent	TR1155	51°15·5′	1°1·8′E	T	179
Horton	Lancs	SD8550	53°57·0′	2°13·3′W	T	103
Horton	Northnts	SP8154	52°10·9′	0°48·5′W	T	152
Horton	S Glos	ST7684	51°33·5′	2°20·4′W	T	172
Horton	Shrops	SJ4930	52°52·1′	2°45·1′W	T	126
Horton	Somer	ST3214	50°55·5′	2°57·7′W	T	193
Horton	Staffs	SJ9457	53°6·8′	2°5·0′W	T	118
Horton	Swan	SS4785	51°32·8′	4°12·0′W	T	159
Horton	Wilts	SU0563	51°22·2′	1°55·3′W	T	173
Horton	Win & Maid	TQ0175	51°28·1′	0°32·4′W	T	176
Horton	Wrekin	SJ6814	52°43·6′	2°28·0′W	T	127
Horton Br	Wilts	SU0363	51°22·2′	1°57·0′W	X	173
Horton Bridge	Devon	SS2918	50°56·4′	4°25·7′W	X	190
Horton Brook	Staffs	SJ9357	53°6·8′	2°5·9′W	W	118
Horton Bushes	S Glos	ST7484	51°33·5′	2°22·1′W	F	172
Horton Common	Dorset	SU0706	50°51·4′	1°53·6′W	T	195
Horton Country Park	Surrey	TQ1962	51°20·9′	0°17·1′W	X	176,187
Horton Court	Kent	TR1240	51°7·4′	1°2·2′E	T	179,189
Horton Court	S Glos	ST7684	51°33·5′	2°20·4′W	A	172
Horton Cross	Somer	ST3315	50°56·1′	2°56·8′W	T	193
Horton-cum-Studley	Oxon	SP5912	51°48·4′	1°8·3′W	T	164
Horton Down	Wilts	SU0766	51°23·8′	1°53·6′W	X	173
Horton Fm	Devon	SS3017	50°55·9′	4°24·8′W	FM	190
Horton Grange	Northum	NZ1975	55°4·4′	1°41·7′W	X	88
Horton Grange Low Ho	Northum	NZ1876	55°4·9′	1°42·7′W	X	88
Horton Green	Ches	SJ4549	53°2·4′	2°48·8′W	T	117
Horton Green	Lancs	SD8550	53°57·0′	2°13·3′W	X	103
Horton Hall	Ches	SJ4649	53°2·4′	2°47·9′W	X	117
Horton Hall	Ches	SJ4968	53°12·6′	2°45·4′W	X	117
Horton Hall	W Susx	TQ2011	50°53·4′	0°17·2′W	X	198
Horton Heath	Dorset	SU0606	50°51·4′	1°54·5′W	T	195
Horton Heath	Hants	SU4916	50°56·7′	1°17·6′W	T	185
Horton Inn	Dorset	SU0108	50°52·5′	1°58·8′W	X	195
Horton in Ribblesdale	N Yks	SD8072	54°8·9′	2°18·0′W	T	98
Horton Kirby	Kent	TQ5668	51°23·6′	0°14·9′E	T	177
Hortonlane	Shrops	SJ4411	52°41·9′	2°49·3′W	T	126
Horton Lodge	Win & Maid	TQ0176	51°28·7′	0°32·3′W	X	176
Horton Lodge Fm	Northnts	SP8155	52°11·5′	0°48·5′W	FM	152
Horton Lodge (Sch)	Staffs	SJ9458	53°7·4′	2°5·0′W	X	118
Horton Mill Fm	Wilts	SU0463	51°22·2′	1°56·2′W	FM	173
Horton Moor	Northum	NU0232	55°35·1′	1°57·7′W	X	75
Horton Moor	N Yks	SD8274	54°9·9′	2°16·1′W	X	98
Horton Park Fm	Surrey	TQ1861	51°20·4′	0°18·0′W	FM	187
Horton Pasture	Lancs	SD8651	53°57·5′	2°12·4′W	X	103
Horton Priory	Kent	TR1039	51°6·9′	1°0·4′E	T	179,189
Horton Scar	N Yks	SD8173	54°9·4′	2°17·0′W	X	98
Hortons Fm	W Susx	SU9529	51°3·4′	0°38·3′W	FM	186,197
Horton Tower	Dorset	SU0306	50°51·4′	1°57·1′W	X	195
Horton Wharf	Bucks	SP9319	51°51·9′	0°38·6′W	T	165
Horton Wood	Bucks	SU8689	51°35·8′	0°45·1′W	F	175
Horton Wood	Kent	TQ5766	51°22·5′	0°15·7′E	F	177
Hortonwood	Wrekin	SJ6813	52°43·1′	2°28·0′W	T	127
Horton Woods	Northnts	SP8252	52°9·8′	0°47·7′W	F	152
Horwell Barton	Devon	SS7600	50°47·4′	3°45·2′W	X	191
Horwell Fm	Oxon	SP5430	51°58·2′	1°12·4′W	FM	152
Horwich	Bolton	SD6311	53°35·9′	2°33·1′W	T	109
Horwich End	Derby	SK0080	53°19·3′	1°59·6′W	T	110
Horwich Ho	Derby	SK0180	53°19·3′	1°58·7′W	X	110
Horwood	Devon	SS5027	51°1·6′	4°8·0′W	T	180
Horwood Barton	Devon	SS4419	50°57·2′	4°12·9′W	X	180,190
Horwood Fm	Wilts	ST9325	51°1·7′	2°5·6′W	FM	184
Horwood Fms	Somer	ST7227	51°2·7′	2°23·6′W	FM	183
Horwood Ho	Bucks	SP7929	51°57·5′	0°50·6′W	X	165
Horwood Riding	S Glos	ST7485	51°34·0′	2°22·1′W	T	172
Hoscar	Lancs	SD4611	53°35·8′	2°48·5′W	T	108
Hoscote	Scot Bord	NT3911	55°23·6′	2°57·4′W	X	79
Hoscote Burn	Scot Bord	NT3711	55°23·6′	2°59·2′W	W	79
Hoscoteshiel	Scot Bord	NT3712	55°24·1′	2°59·3′W	X	79
Hosden Hope	Northum	NT8811	55°23·8′	2°10·9′W	X	80
Hosden's Fm	Essex	TL7934	51°58·8′	0°36·8′E	FM	155
Hose	Leic	SK7329	52°51·4′	0°54·5′W	T	129
Hosedon Burn	Northum	NT9106	55°21·1′	2°8·1′W	W	80
Hose Grange	Leic	SK7329	52°51·4′	0°54·5′W	X	129
Hose Hill	Leic	SK7916	52°44·4′	0°49·4′W	X	129
Hoselaw	Scot Bord	NT8032	55°35·1′	2°18·6′W	T	74

Hoselaw Loch	Scot Bord	NT8031	55°34·6′	2°18·6′W	W	74
Hoselaw Mains	Scot Bord	NT8133	55°35·7′	2°17·7′W	X	74
Hoseley Bank	Wrex	SJ3653	53°4·5′	2°56·9′W	X	117
Hoseley Ho	Wrex	SJ3654	53°5·0′	2°56·9′W	X	117
Hose Lodge	Leic	SK7229	52°51·5′	0°55·4′W	X	129
Hose lodge Fm	Notts	SK7131	52°52·5′	0°56·3′W	FM	129
Hosenett	S Lanak	NS7343	55°40·1′	4°0·7′W	X	71
Hoses	Cumbr	SD2192	54°19·3′	3°12·5′W	X	96
Hoses	Essex	TL7336	52°0·0′	0°31·6′E	X	155
Hosey Br	Dorset	ST7915	50°56·3′	2°17·5′W	X	183
Hosey Hill	Kent	TQ4553	51°15·7′	0°5·1′E	T	188
Hosh	Pth & Kin	NN8523	56°23·4′	3°51·3′W	T	52,58
Hosket Hill	Cumbr	NY3457	54°54·5′	3°1·3′W	X	85
Hoskins	Herts	TL4515	51°49·1′	0°6·6′E	X	167
Hoskins Barn	Oxon	SP3201	51°42·6′	1°31·8′W	X	164
Hoskinshire	Lancs	SD4241	53°52·0′	2°52·5′W	X	102
Hospice	Cumbr	SD3979	54°12·4′	2°55·7′W	X	96,97
Hospital Barn Fm	Kent	TQ7251	51°14·2′	0°28·2′E	FM	188
Hospital Br	N Yks	SD8357	54°0·8′	2°15·1′W	X	103
Hospital Cottages	Lincs	TF3633	52°52·9′	0°1·7′E	X	131
Hospitalfield	Angus	NO6240	56°33·3′	2°36·6′W	X	54
Hospital Fm	Northnts	SP7981	52°25·5′	0°49·9′W	FM	141
Hospital Mill	Fife	NO3411	56°17·5′	3°3·5′W	X	59
Hospital Plantation	Cumbr	NY2123	54°36·0′	3°13·0′W	F	89,90
Hospital Plantn	N Yks	SE9055	53°59·7′	2°8·7′W	F	103
Hospital Shields	Aberd	NO7167	56°47·9′	2°28·0′W	X	45
Hospital Wood	Aberd	NJ7345	57°29·9′	2°26·6′W	F	29
Hosta	N Eil	NF7272	57°37·4′	7°29·2′W	T	18
Hostaberg	Shetld	HU3749	60°13·7′	1°19·4′W	X	3
Hostage Fm	Essex	TL7733	51°58·3′	0°35·0′E	FM	167
Hostage Wood	Northnts	SP9894	52°32·3′	0°32·9′W	F	141
Hostel Fm	Cambs	TL0896	52°33·3′	0°24·0′W	FM	142
Hoston Bay	Orkney	ND4387	58°46·3′	2°58·7′W	W	7
Hoston Head	Orkney	ND4387	58°46·3′	2°58·7′W	X	7
Hostye Fm	Brom	TQ4460	51°19·5′	0°4·4′E	FM	177,187
Hos Wick	Shetld	HU4123	59°59·7′	1°15·4′W	W	4
Hoswick	Shetld	HU4123	59°59·7′	1°15·4′W	T	4
Hotbank	Northum	NY7768	55°0·6′	2°21·2′W	X	86,87
Hotbank Crags	Northum	NY7768	55°0·6′	2°21·2′W	X	86,87
Hotburn Hill	Northum	NY9751	54°51·5′	2°2·4′W	X	87
Hotchley Hill	Notts	SK5528	52°51·0′	1°10·6′W	X	129
Hotham	E Yorks	SE8934	53°47·9′	0°38·5′W	T	106
Hotham Carrs	E Yorks	SE8533	53°47·4′	0°42·2′W	X	106
Hotham Hall	E Yorks	SE8933	53°47·4′	0°38·5′W	X	106
Hotham Ho	E Yorks	SE8934	53°47·9′	0°38·5′W	X	106
Hothe Court Fm	Kent	TR1360	51°18·2′	1°3·7′E	FM	179
Hothersall Hall	Lancs	SD6334	53°48·3′	2°33·3′W	X	102,103
Hothersall Lodge	Lancs	SD6234	53°48·3′	2°34·2′W	X	102,103
Hothfield	Kent	TQ9744	51°9·9′	0°49·5′E	T	189
Hothfield Bogs	Kent	TQ9645	51°10·5′	0°48·6′E	X	189
Hothfield Common	Kent	TQ9645	51°10·5′	0°48·6′E	X	189
Hot Hollow Fm	Rut	SK9409	52°40·5′	0°36·2′W	FM	141
Hothorpe Hall	Northnts	SP6685	52°27·8′	1°1·3′W	X	141
Hothorpe Hills	Northnts	SP6783	52°26·7′	1°0·5′W	H	141
Hoth Wood	E Susx	TQ5631	51°3·7′	0°14·0′E	F	188
Hotley Bottom	Bucks	SP8701	51°42·3′	0°44·1′W	T	165
Hot Moss	Northum	NY6563	54°57·9′	2°32·4′W	X	86
Hoton	Leic	SK5722	52°47·8′	1°8·9′W	T	129
Hoton Hills	Leic	SK5622	52°47·8′	1°9·8′W	X	129
Hot Point	Corn	SW7112	49°58·1′	5°11·2′W	X	203
Hot Ridding	Cumbr	SD5980	54°13·1′	2°37·3′W	X	97
Hott	Cumbr	NY4859	54°55·6′	2°48·3′W	X	86
Hott	Northum	NY7785	55°9·8′	2°21·2′W	X	80
Hott Hill	Scot Bord	NT4210	55°23·1′	2°54·5′W	H	79
Hottia	Denb	SJ0578	53°17·7′	3°25·1′W	X	116
Hottit	Orkney	ND4793	58°49·5′	2°54·6′W	X	7
Hotts	D & G	NY2678	55°5·7′	3°9·1′W	X	85
Hotwells	C of Bris	ST5772	51°27·0′	2°36·7′W	T	172
Houb	Shetld	HU3730	60°3·4′	1°19·6′W	W	4
Houbans	Shetld	HU3574	60°27·2′	1°21·3′W	X	2,3
Houbansetter	Shetld	HU3561	60°20·2′	1°21·5′W	X	2,3
Houbie	Shetld	HU4548	60°13·1′	1°10·8′W	H	3
Houbie	Shetld	HU6290	60°35·6′	0°51·6′W	T	1,2
Houb of Lunnister	Shetld	HU3571	60°25·5′	1°21·4′W	W	2,3
Houb of Scatsta	Shetld	HU3972	60°26·1′	1°17·0′W	W	2,3
Houbridge Hall	Essex	TM1726	51°53·6′	1°9·6′E	X	168,169
Houbs Ayre	Shetld	HU3772	60°26·1′	1°19·2′W	X	2,3
Houb, The	Shetld	HU2277	60°28·8′	1°35·5′W	W	3
Houb, The	Shetld	HU2448	60°13·2′	1°33·5′W	W	3
Houb, The	Shetld	HU3572	60°26·1′	1°21·3′W	W	2,3
Houb, The	Shetld	HU3674	60°27·2′	1°20·2′W	W	2,3
Houb, The	Shetld	HU4075	60°27·7′	1°15·9′W	W	2,3
Houb, The	Shetld	HU4346	60°12·0′	1°13·0′W	W	4
Houb, The	Shetld	HU4472	60°26·0′	1°11·5′W	W	2,3
Houcham Fm	Notts	SK8467	53°11·8′	0°44·1′W	FM	121
Houchin's Fm	Essex	TL8723	51°52·7′	0°43·4′E	FM	168
Houd's Fm	Essex	TL9329	51°55·8′	0°48·8′E	FM	168
Houdston	S Ayr	NX2097	55°14·3′	4°49·4′W	X	76
Hough	Arg & Bt	NL9545	56°30·2′	6°57·0′W	T	46
Hough	Ches	SJ7150	53°3·0′	2°25·6′W	T	118
Hough	Ches	SJ8578	53°18·2′	2°13·1′W	T	118
Houghall College	Durham	NZ2841	54°46·0′	1°33·5′W	X	88
Houghall Fm	Durham	NZ2740	54°45·5′	1°34·4′W	FM	88
Hougham	Lincs	SK8844	52°59·4′	0°40·9′W	T	130
Hougharry	N Eil	NF7071	57°36·8′	7°31·1′W	T	18
Hough Bay	Arg & Bt	NL9346	56°30·6′	6°59·0′W	W	46
Hough Br	Lincs	TF2454	53°4·4′	0°8·5′W	X	122
Hough Common	Ches	SJ7150	53°3·0′	2°25·6′W	X	118
Houghen Plantn	Norf	TG1717	52°42·7′	1°13·2′E	F	133,134
Hough Fm	Shrops	SJ5531	52°52·7′	2°39·7′W	FM	126
Houghgate Hill	Notts	SK7486	53°22·2′	0°52·9′W	X	112,120
Hough Grange	Lincs	SK9047	53°1·0′	0°39·1′W	X	130
Hough Green	Halton	SJ4886	53°22·3′	2°46·5′W	T	108
Hough Green Fm	Ches	SJ7784	53°21·4′	2°20·3′W	FM	109
Hough Green Fm	Ches	SJ8579	53°18·7′	2°13·1′W	FM	118
Hough Hall Fm	Ches	SJ8680	53°19·2′	2°12·2′W	FM	109
Hough Hill	Lancs	SD5922	53°41·8′	2°36·8′W	X	102
Houghlane Fm	Ches	SJ6376	53°17·0′	2°32·9′W	FM	118
Hough Manor	Ches	SJ7051	53°3·6′	2°26·5′W	X	118
Hough-on-the-Hill	Lincs	SK9246	53°0·4′	0°37·3′W	T	130

Houghpark	Derby	SK2445	53°0·3′	1°38·1′W	X	119,128
Hough Side	Leeds	SE2333	53°47·8′	1°38·6′W	T	104
Hough Skerries	Arg & Bt	NL9147	56°31·1′	7°1·0′W	X	46
Hough, The	Ches	SJ4945	53°0·2′	2°45·2′W	X	117
Hough, The	Shrops	SO4591	52°31·1′	2°48·2′W	X	137,138
Hough, The	Staffs	SJ8129	52°51·7′	2°16·5′W	X	127
Houghton	Cambs	TL2872	52°20·1′	0°6·9′W	T	153
Houghton	Cumbr	NY4059	54°55·6′	2°55·7′W	T	85
Houghton	Devon	SX6546	50°18·1′	3°53·4′W	X	202
Houghton	Hants	SU3432	51°5·4′	1°30·5′W	T	185
Houghton	Northum	NZ1266	54°59·6′	1°48·3′W	T	88
Houghton	Pemb	SM9807	51°43·8′	4°55·1′W	T	157,158
Houghton	Pemb	SN0401	51°40·7′	4°49·7′W	X	157,158
Houghton	W Susx	TQ0111	50°53·6′	0°33·4′W	T	197
Houghton Bank	Darl	NZ2222	54°35·8′	1°39·1′W	T	93
Houghton Conquest	Beds	TL0441	52°3·7′	0°28·6′W	T	153
Houghton Court	Heref	SO5551	52°9·6′	2°39·1′W	X	149
Houghton Down	Hants	SU3335	51°7·0′	1°31·3′W	X	185
Houghton Down Fm	Hants	SU3335	51°7·0′	1°31·3′W	FM	185
Houghton Drayton	Hants	SU3332	51°5·4′	1°31·3′W	X	185
Houghton Fm	Devon	SY0988	50°41·3′	3°16·9′W	FM	192
Houghton Fm	Norf	TF8605	52°36·9′	0°45·3′E	FM	144
Houghton Forest	W Susx	SU9911	50°53·6′	0°35·2′W	F	197
Houghton Gate	Durham	NZ2951	54°51·4′	1°32·5′W	X	88
Houghton Grange	Cambs	TL2972	52°20·1′	0°6·0′W	X	153
Houghton Green	E Susx	TQ9222	50°58·1′	0°44·5′E	T	189
Houghton Green	Warr	SJ6291	53°25·1′	2°33·9′W	T	109
Houghton Hall	Beds	TL0223	51°54·0′	0°30·7′W	X	166
Houghton Hall	Cumbr	NY4159	54°55·6′	2°54·8′W	X	85
Houghton Hall	E Yorks	SE8839	53°50·6′	0°39·3′W	X	106
Houghton Hall	Suff	TL7846	52°5·2′	0°36·3′E	X	155
Houghton Hill Fm	Cambs	TL2972	52°20·1′	0°6·0′W	FM	153
Houghton Ho	Cumbr	NY4060	54°56·1′	2°55·8′W	X	85
Houghton Ho	Durham	NZ1528	54°39·1′	1°45·6′W	X	92
Houghton House Fm	Lancs	SD5133	53°47·7′	2°44·2′W	FM	102
Houghton-le-Side	Darl	NZ2221	54°35·3′	1°39·2′W	T	93
Houghton-Le-Spring	Sund	NZ3449	54°50·3′	1°27·8′W	T	88
Houghton Lodge	Barns	SE4308	53°34·2′	1°20·6′W	X	111
Houghton Lodge	Hants	SU3433	51°5·9′	1°30·5′W	X	185
Houghton Lodge	Leic	SK6602	52°36·9′	1°1·1′W	X	141
Houghton Moor	E Yorks	SE8837	53°49·5′	0°39·4′W	F	106
Houghton North Down	Dorset	ST8005	50°50·9′	2°16·7′W	X	194
Houghton on the Hill	Leic	SK6703	52°37·5′	1°0·2′W	T	141
Houghton Park	Norf	TF7928	52°49·4′	0°39·8′E	X	132
Houghton Plantn	Darl	NZ2120	54°34·7′	1°40·1′W	F	93
Houghton Regis	Beds	TL0124	51°54·6′	0°31·5′W	T	166
Houghton St Giles	Norf	TF9235	52°52·9′	0°51·6′E	T	132
Houghwood	St Hel	SD5100	53°29·9′	2°43·9′W	T	108
Hougoumont Fm	Wilts	SU2352	51°16·2′	1°39·8′W	FM	184
Hougton House	Beds	TL0339	52°2·6′	0°29·5′W	A	153
Hougton Park Fm	Beds	TL0439	52°2·6′	0°28·6′W	FM	153
Hou Hatch	Essex	TQ5694	51°37·6′	0°15·6′E	X	167,177
Houkler Hall	Cumbr	SD2888	54°17·2′	3°5·9′W	X	96,97
Houll	Shetld	HU3791	60°36·3′	1°19·0′W	X	1,2
Houll	Shetld	HU3850	60°14·2′	1°18·3′W	X	3
Houll	Shetld	HU6589	60°35·0′	0°48·3′W	X	1,2
Houlland	Shetld	HP5910	60°46·9′	0°54·5′W	X	1
Houlland	Shetld	HU3453	60°15·9′	1°22·6′W	T	3
Houlland	Shetld	HU4040	60°8·8′	1°16·3′W	T	4
Houlland	Shetld	HU4223	59°59·6′	1°14·3′W	T	4
Houlland	Shetld	HU4654	60°16·3′	1°9·6′W	X	3
Houlland	Shetld	HU5080	60°30·3′	1°4·9′W	T	1,2,3
Houlland Hill	Shetld	HP5203	60°42·7′	1°2·3′W	X	1
Houllna Gruna	Shetld	HP5911	60°46·9′	0°54·5′W	H	1
Houllnan	Shetld	HP5705	60°43·7′	0°56·8′W	X	1
Houllnan Ness	Shetld	HP5605	60°43·7′	0°57·9′W	X	1
Houllscarpa	Shetld	HU4052	60°15·3′	1°16·1′W	X	3
Houlls Geo	Shetld	HU6689	60°35·0′	0°47·2′W	X	1,2
Houlls-nef	Shetld	HP6617	60°50·1′	0°46·7′W	X	1
Houlls Water	Shetld	HU3367	60°23·4′	1°23·6′W	W	2,3
Houlls Water	Shetld	HU4595	60°38·4′	1°10·1′W	W	1,2
Houll, The	Shetld	HU4423	59°59·6′	1°12·2′W	X	4
Houll, The	Shetld	HU5664	60°21·6′	0°58·6′W	X	2
Houlma Sound	Shetld	HU2675	60°27·7′	1°31·1′W	W	3
Houlma Water	Shetld	HU2657	60°18·0′	1°31·3′W	W	3
Houlston	Shrops	SJ4725	52°49·4′	2°46·8′W	X	126
Houlston Manor	Shrops	SJ4724	52°48·9′	2°46·8′W	X	126
Houlsyke	N Yks	NZ7307	54°27·4′	0°52·0′W	T	94
Houlton Fm	N Lincs	TA1515	53°37·4′	0°15·3′W	FM	113
Houlton's Covert	N Lincs	TA1716	53°37·9′	0°13·4′W	F	113
Houm Field	Shetld	HU3578	60°29·3′	1°21·3′W	H	2,3
Hound	Hants	SU4708	50°52·4′	1°19·5′W	T	196
Houndalee	Northum	NZ2594	55°14·6′	1°36·0′W	X	81
Houndaller Fm	Devon	ST0513	50°54·8′	3°20·7′W	FM	181
Houndapit Fm	Corn	SS2110	50°51·9′	4°32·2′W	FM	190
Houndean Bottom	E Susx	TQ3909	50°52·1′	0°1·1′W	X	198
Houndean Mill	Northum	NU2306	55°21·1′	1°37·8′W	X	81
Hound Green	Hants	SU7259	51°19·8′	0°57·6′W	T	175,186
Hound Hill	Barns	SE3304	53°32·1′	1°29·7′W	X	110,111
Hound Hill	Cumbr	NY7039	54°45·0′	2°27·5′W	X	91
Hound Hill	Dorset	ST9901	50°48·7′	2°0·5′W	T	195
Hound Hill	Northum	NY7468	55°0·6′	2°24·0′W	H	86,87
Hound Hill	Staffs	SK1330	52°52·3′	1°48·0′W	H	128
Hound Hillock	Aberd	NO6279	56°54·3′	2°37·9′W	H	45
Hound Ho	Surrey	TQ0744	51°11·3′	0°27·7′W	X	187
Houndkirk Moor	Sheff	SK2881	53°19·7′	1°34·4′W	X	110
Houndmills	Hants	SU6252	51°16·1′	1°6·3′W	T	185
Houndown	Surrey	SU8940	51°9·4′	0°43·3′W	F	186
Hound Point	C of Edin	NT1579	56°0·0′	3°21·3′W	X	65
Houndridge	Scot Bord	NT7438	55°38·3′	2°24·3′W	X	74
Hound Rig	D & G	NY0097	55°15·7′	3°34·0′W	X	78
Houndscroft	Glos	SO8502	51°43·2′	2°12·6′W	T	162
Houndsell Place	E Susx	TQ5931	51°3·6′	0°16·5′E	X	188
Houndshall	Scot Bord	NT5127	55°32·3′	2°46·2′W	X	73
Houndslow	Scot Bord	NT6347	55°43·2′	2°34·9′W	T	74
Houndsmoor	Somer	ST1225	51°1·3′	3°14·9′W	T	181,193
Houndstone	Somer	ST5217	50°57·3′	2°40·6′W	T	183
Houndswood	Herts	TL1601	51°42·0′	0°18·9′W	F	166
Hound Tor	Devon	SX6288	50°40·8′	3°56·8′W	H	191
Hound Tor	Devon	SX7478	50°35·5′	3°46·4′W	H	191

Houndtor Wood	Devon	SX7780	50°36·6′	3°43·9′W	F	191
Houndwood	Scot Bord	NT8463	55°51·8′	2°14·9′W	T	67
Hound Wood	Wilts	SU2330	51°4·4′	1°39·9′W	F	184
Houndwood Ho	Scot Bord	NT8562	55°51·3′	2°13·9′W	X	67
Hounsdale	E Yorks	TA0459	54°1·2′	0°24·3′W	X	107
Hounsdown	Hants	SU3512	50°54·6′	1°29·7′W	T	196
Hounsell Wood	E Susx	TQ7226	51°0·7′	0°27·5′E	F	188,199
Hounsley Batch	N Som	ST5463	51°22·1′	2°39·3′W	T	172,182
Hounslow	Houns	TQ1475	51°28·0′	0°21·1′W	T	176
Hounslow Heath	Houns	TQ1274	51°27·5′	0°22·9′W	X	176
Hounslow West	Houns	TQ1276	51°28·5′	0°22·8′W	T	176
Houns-tout Cliff	Dorset	SY9577	50°35·8′	2°3·9′W	X	195
Hourne Fm	E Susx	TQ5231	51°3·7′	0°10·5′E	FM	188
Hourston	Orkney	HY2919	59°3·4′	3°13·8′W	T	6
Housabister	Shetld	HU4958	60°18·5′	1°6·3′W	T	2,3
Housa Voe	Shetld	HU1860	60°19·7′	1°39·9′W	W	3
Housa Water	Shetld	HU2844	60°11·0′	1°29·2′W	W	4
Housa Water	Shetld	HU4047	60°12·6′	1°16·2′W	W	3
Housa Wick	Shetld	HU5491	60°36·2′	1°0·3′W	W	1,2
Housay	Shetld	HU6771	60°25·3′	0°46·5′W	T	2
Housebay	Orkney	HY5016	59°2·0′	2°51·8′W	X	6
Housebay	Orkney	HY6721	59°4·7′	2°34·1′W	X	5
Housebrough	N Yks	SE4885	54°15·7′	1°15·4′W	X	100
Houseby	Orkney	HY2922	59°5·0′	3°13·8′W	X	6
Houseclose Plantn	E Yorks	SE8853	53°58·2′	0°39·1′W	F	106
House Close Wood	N Yks	SE2882	54°14·2′	1°33·8′W	F	99
Housecroft Fm	Wilts	ST9154	51°17·3′	2°7·4′W	FM	184
Housedale	Aberd	NJ7508	57°10·0′	2°24·3′W	X	38
Housedale Rigg	N Yks	SE8687	54°16·5′	0°40·3′W	H	94,101
Housedean Fm	E Susx	TQ3609	50°52·1′	0°3·6′W	FM	198
Housedon Hill	Northum	NT9032	55°35·1′	2°9·1′W	H	74,75
House Fm	N Yks	NZ5702	54°24·9′	1°6·9′W	FM	93
House Fm	Suff	TL7049	52°7·0′	0°29·4′E	FM	154
House Fm	Wilts	SU2470	51°25·9′	1°38·9′W	FM	174
Housegarth	Orkney	HY2520	59°3·9′	3°18·0′W	X	6
House Geo	Orkney	ND3792	58°48·9′	3°5·0′W	X	7
House Gill	N Yks	SE1181	54°13·7′	1°49·5′W	W	99
Househill	Falk	NS8482	56°1·3′	3°51·2′W	X	65
Househill	Highld	NH8855	57°34·5′	3°51·9′W	X	27
Households Fm	Cambs	TL3589	52°29·2′	0°0·3′W	FM	142
House in the Wood, The	Hants	SU3804	50°50·3′	1°27·2′W	X	196
Housel Bay	Corn	SW7011	49°57·5′	5°12·0′W	W	203
Houselop Beck	Durham	NZ0939	54°45·0′	1°51·2′W	W	92
Housenea	Orkney	HY2519	59°3·4′	3°18·0′W	X	6
Housenrigg	Cumbr	NY1644	54°47·3′	3°18·0′W	X	85
Housensellar	Shetld	HU3827	60°1·8′	1°18·6′W	X	4
House of Auchiries	Aberd	NJ9760	57°38·1′	2°2·6′W	X	30
House of Cockburn	C of Edin	NT1465	55°52·5′	3°22·0′W	X	65
House of Corse, The	Aberd	NJ5407	57°9·4′	2°45·2′W	X	37
House of Daviot	Highld	NH7240	57°26·2′	4°7·5′W	X	27
House of Dun	Angus	NO6759	56°43·5′	2°31·9′W	X	54
House of Falkland Sch	Fife	NO2407	56°15·2′	3°13·2′W	X	59
House of Glenmuick	Aberd	NO3794	57°2·2′	3°1·8′W	X	37,44
House of Joseph	D & G	NX8087	55°10·0′	3°52·6′W	X	78
House of Knock	D & G	NW9857	54°52·3′	5°8·5′W	X	82
House of Lynturk	Aberd	NJ6113	57°12·6′	2°38·3′W	X	37
House of Monymusk	Aberd	NJ6815	57°13·7′	2°31·3′W	X	38
House of Rosskeen, The	Highld	NH6969	57°41·8′	4°11·4′W	X	21
House of Schivas	Aberd	NJ8936	57°25·1′	2°10·5′W	A	30
House of Water	E Ayr	NS5512	55°23·1′	4°16·9′W	X	71
House o' Hill	Aberd	NJ9758	57°37·0′	2°2·6′W	X	30
House o' Hill Hotel	D & G	NX3576	55°3·3′	4°34·6′W	X	77
House-o-Muir	C of Edin	NT1264	55°51·9′	3°23·9′W	X	65
House o' Muir	E Loth	NT4166	55°53·3′	2°56·2′W	X	66
House O'Muir Fm	Midlo	NT2362	55°51·0′	3°13·4′W	FM	66
Houses Hill	Kirk	SE1916	53°38·7′	1°42·3′W	T	110
Houses of Parliament	C of West	TQ3079	51°29·9′	0°7·2′W	X	176,177
Housesteads	Northum	NY7869	55°1·2′	2°20·2′W	X	86,87
Housetter	Shetld	HU3684	60°32·5′	1°20·1′W	T	1,2,3
Housey Crags	Northum	NT9521	55°29·2′	2°4·3′W	X	74,75
Housham	Lincs	SK8964	53°10·2′	0°39·7′W	X	121
Housham Hall	Essex	TL5011	51°46·9′	0°10·9′E	X	167
Housham Tye	Essex	TL5010	51°46·3′	0°10·8′E	T	167
Housi Field	Shetld	HP6318	60°48·0′	0°50·0′W	H	1
Housley	Derby	SK1975	53°16·5′	1°42·5′W	X	119
Houss	Shetld	HU3731	60°4·0′	1°19·6′W	T	4
Houss Ness	Shetld	HU3729	60°2·9′	1°19·6′W	X	4
Houstard	D & G	NX8858	54°54·5′	3°44·4′W	X	84
Houster	Shetld	HU3354	60°16·4′	1°23·7′W	X	3
Houster	Shetld	HU4446	60°12·0′	1°11·9′W	X	4
Houston	Renf	NS4066	55°51·9′	4°33·0′W	T	64
Houston Ho	Renf	NS4167	55°52·4′	4°32·0′W	X	64
Houston Ind Est	W Loth	NT0569	55°54·5′	3°30·7′W	X	65
Houstoun Mains Holdings	W Loth	NT0570	55°55·1′	3°30·8′W	X	65
Houstry	Highld	ND1357	58°29·8′	3°29·1′W	X	11,12
Houstry	Highld	ND1535	58°18·0′	3°26·5′W	T	11,17
Houstry	Highld	ND2154	58°28·3′	3°20·8′W	X	11,12
Houstry of Dunn	Highld	ND2054	58°28·3′	3°21·8′W	X	11,12
Housty	Northum	NY8357	54°54·7′	2°15·5′W	X	86,87
Houth	Orkney	HY3104	58°55·3′	3°11·4′W	X	6,7
Houtley	Northum	NY9461	54°56·9′	2°5·2′W	X	87
Houton	Orkney	HY3104	58°55·3′	3°11·4′W	T	6,7
Houton Head	Orkney	HY3003	58°54·8′	3°12·4′W	X	6,7
Houtsay Park	Cumbr	NY6227	54°38·4′	2°34·9′W	X	91
Houx Hill	Northum	NT7704	55°20·0′	2°21·3′W	H	80
Houxty	Northum	NY8578	55°6·0′	2°13·7′W	X	87
Houxty Burn	Northum	NY8379	55°6·6′	2°15·6′W	W	86,87
Hove	Bri & Hov	TQ2805	50°50·0′	0°10·5′W	T	198
Hove Burn	Shetld	HP6014	60°48·5′	0°53·3′W	W	1
Hove Edge	Cald	SE1324	53°43·0′	1°47·8′W	T	104
Hovel Hill	Leic	SP5980	52°25·1′	1°7·5′W	X	140
Hovells Fm	Essex	TL8223	51°52·8′	0°39·1′E	FM	168
Hovels Fm	Thurr	TQ7086	51°33·1′	0°27·5′E	FM	178
Hovenden Ho	Lincs	TF3926	52°49·0′	0°4·2′E	X	131
Hoveringham	Notts	SK6946	53°0·6′	0°57·9′W	T	129
Hoversta	Shetld	HU4941	60°9·3′	1°6·5′W	X	4
Hoveton	Norf	TG3018	52°42·9′	1°24·7′E	T	133,134
Hoveton Great Broad	Norf	TG3116	52°41·8′	1°25·5′E	W	133,134
Hoveton Hall	Norf	TG3120	52°43·9′	1°25·7′E	X	133,134
Hoveton Ho	Norf	TG3117	52°42·3′	1°25·6′E	X	133,134

Hoveton Little Broad	Norf	TG3317	52°42·3′	1°27·3′E	W	133,134
Hoveton Marshes	Norf	TG3217	52°42·3′	1°26·5′E	W	133,134
Hoveton Old Hall	Norf	TG3020	52°43·9′	1°24·8′E	X	133,134
Hovingham	N Yks	SE6675	54°10·2′	0°58·9′W	T	100
Hovingham Carrs	N Yks	SE6676	54°10·8′	0°58·9′W	X	100
Hovingham High Wood	N Yks	SE6475	54°10·2′	1°0·8′W	F	100
Hovingham Lodge	N Yks	SE6574	54°9·7′	0°59·9′W	X	100
Hovingham Park	N Yks	SE6575	54°10·2′	0°59·8′W	X	100
Hovingham Spa	N Yks	SE6576	54°10·8′	0°59·8′W	W	100
How	Cumbr	NY2424	54°36·6′	3°10·2′W	X	89,90
How	Cumbr	NY5056	54°54·0′	2°46·4′W	T	86
How	Durham	NY9221	54°35·3′	2°7·0′W	X	91,92
How	Orkney	HY6639	59°14·4′	2°35·3′W	X	5
How	Orkney	HY7445	59°17·7′	2°26·9′W	X	5
Howaback	Orkney	HY2919	59°3·4′	3°13·8′W	X	6
Howahill	Scot Bord	NT5609	55°22·6′	2°41·2′W	X	80
Howally	Orkney	HY3024	59°6·1′	3°12·8′W	X	6
Howan	Orkney	HY2821	59°4·5′	3°14·9′W	X	6
Howan	Orkney	HY4729	59°8·9′	2°55·1′W	X	5,6
Howana Gruna	Orkney	HY3326	59°7·2′	3°9·7′W	X	6
Howana Gruna (Cairn)	Orkney	HY3326	59°7·2′	3°9·7′W	A	6
Howan Lickan	Orkney	HY5909	58°58·2′	2°42·3′W	X	6
Howar	Orkney	HY6137	59°13·3′	2°40·5′W	X	5
Howar	Orkney	HY7651	59°20·9′	2°24·8′W	X	5
Howard	Corn	SS2305	50°49·3′	4°30·4′W	X	190
Howard Barton	Devon	SX7396	50°45·2′	3°47·6′W	X	191
Howardian Hills	N Yks	SE6472	54°8·6′	1°0·8′W	H	100
Howards	Herts	TL2426	51°55·4′	0°11·4′W	A	166
Howard's Common	Norf	TG4702	52°33·8′	1°39·1′E	X	134
Howard's Hill	Norf	TG3228	52°48·2′	1°26·9′E	X	133,134
Howards Ho	Beds	TL0848	52°7·4′	0°24·9′W	X	153
Howath	D & G	NY2476	55°4·6′	3°11·0′W	X	85
Howatoft	Orkney	ND4691	58°48·5′	2°55·6′W	X	7
Howat's Hill	D & G	NY2279	55°6·2′	3°12·9′W	H	85
Howbalk	Northum	NU0513	55°24·9′	1°54·8′W	X	81
Howbank	Cumbr	SD1196	54°21·4′	3°21·8′W	X	96
Howbarrow	Cumbr	SD3679	54°12·4′	2°58·5′W	X	96,97
Howbeck Bank	Ches	SJ6849	53°2·5′	2°28·2′W	T	118
Howbeck Fm	Ches	SJ6849	53°2·5′	2°28·2′W	FM	118
Howber Hill Fm	N Yks	SE0852	53°58·1′	1°52·3′W	FM	104
Howber Hill or Beamsley Beacon	N Yks	SE0952	53°58·1′	1°51·4′W	H	104
Howberry	Cumbr	NY4264	54°58·3′	2°53·9′W	X	85
Howberry Barn	Heref	SO5845	52°6·3′	2°36·4′W	X	149
Howberrywood	Oxon	SU6885	51°33·8′	1°0·7′W	X	175
Howbourne Fm	E Susx	TQ5125	51°0·5′	0°9·5′E	FM	188,199
Howbrook	Barns	SK3298	53°28·9′	1°30·7′W	T	110,111
Howburn	Cumbr	NY2836	54°43·1′	3°6·6′W	X	89,90
Howburn	Cumbr	NY7143	54°47·1′	2°26·6′W	X	86,87
Howburn	Midlo	NT3055	55°47·2′	3°6·5′W	X	66,73
Howburn	Northum	NT8235	55°36·7′	2°16·7′W	X	74
How Burn	Northum	NZ1080	55°7·1′	1°50·2′W	W	81
How Burn	Northum	NZ2088	55°11·4′	1°40·7′W	W	81
How Burn	Scot Bord	NT7312	55°24·3′	2°25·2′W	W	80
Howburn	Scot Bord	NT8562	55°51·3′	2°13·9′W	X	67
How Burn	S Lanak	NS9940	55°38·8′	3°35·9′W	W	72
Howburn	S Lanak	NT0743	55°40·5′	3°28·3′W	X	72
How Burn	W Loth	NS9265	55°52·2′	3°43·1′W	W	65
Howburn Br	Northum	NZ1380	55°7·1′	1°47·3′W	X	81
Howbury Hall	Beds	TL0951	52°9·0′	0°24·0′W	X	153
How Caple	Heref	SO6030	51°58·3′	2°34·5′W	T	149
Howcleuchshiel	Scot Bord	NT4214	55°25·2′	2°54·5′W	X	79
Howcommon	E Ayr	NS4233	55°34·2′	4°29·9′W	X	70
Howcore	Moray	NJ3962	57°38·9′	3°0·9′W	X	28
Howcraig	N Ayr	NS2458	55°47·3′	4°48·0′W	X	63
Howcraigs Hill	E Renf	NS4555	55°46·1′	4°27·8′W	H	64
Howcroft Barn	Lancs	SD7739	53°51·0′	2°20·6′W	X	103
Howdale	Cumbr	NY5269	55°1·0′	2°44·6′W	X	86
How Dale	N Yks	NZ9502	54°24·5′	0°31·8′W	X	94
Howdale Fm	N Yks	NZ9501	54°24·0′	0°31·8′W	FM	94
Howdale Moor	N Yks	NZ9501	54°24·0′	0°31·8′W	X	94
Howdales	D & G	NY2076	55°4·6′	3°14·8′W	X	85
Howdales	Lincs	TF4291	53°24·0′	0°8·6′E	X	113
Howden	E Loth	NT4967	55°53·9′	2°48·5′W	X	66
Howden	E Loth	NT5780	56°0·9′	2°40·9′W	X	67
Howden	E Yorks	SE7428	53°44·8′	0°52·3′W	T	105,106
Howden	Scot Bord	NT4527	55°32·3′	2°51·9′W	X	73
Howden	Scot Bord	NT6425	55°31·3′	2°33·8′W	X	74
Howden	Scot Bord	NT6519	55°28·1′	2°32·8′W	X	80
Howden	W Loth	NT0567	55°53·5′	3°30·7′W	T	65
Howden 20	E Yorks	SE7129	53°45·4′	0°55·0′W	X	105,106
Howden 20	E Yorks	SE7135	53°48·6′	0°54·9′W	X	105,106
Howden 20	E Yorks	SE7534	53°48·1′	0°51·3′W	X	105,106
Howden 20	E Yorks	SE7534	53°48·1′	0°51·3′W	X	105,106
Howden Burn	C of Edin	NT2267	55°53·6′	3°14·4′W	W	66
Howden Burn	Durham	NZ0034	54°42·3′	1°59·6′W	W	92
Howden Burn	Durham	NZ1648	54°49·8′	1°44·6′W	W	88
Howden Burn	Northum	NY7462	54°57·4′	2°23·9′W	W	86,87
Howden Clough	Kirk	SE2326	53°44·0′	1°38·7′W	T	104
Howden Clough	Sheff	SK1893	53°26·2′	1°43·3′W	X	110
Howden Dean	Sheff	SK1892	53°25·7′	1°43·3′W	X	110
Howden Dene	Northum	NZ0064	54°58·5′	1°59·6′W	X	87
Howdendyke	E Yorks	SE7526	53°43·7′	0°51·4′W	X	105,106
Howden Edge	Sheff	SK1598	53°29·0′	1°46·0′W	X	110
Howden Hall	Stock on T	NZ4122	54°35·7′	1°21·5′W	X	93
Howden Hill	Northum	NY8369	55°1·2′	2°15·5′W	X	86,87
Howden Hill	N Yks	NZ2413	54°30·9′	1°37·3′W	X	93
Howden Hill	N Yks	SE9391	54°18·6′	0°33·8′W	X	94,101
Howden Hill	Scot Bord	NT4527	55°32·3′	2°51·9′W	H	73
Howden Ho	Brad	SE0444	53°53·8′	1°55·9′W	X	104
Howden-le-Wear	Durham	NZ1533	54°41·8′	1°45·6′W	T	92
Howden Lodge	N Yks	SE0484	54°15·3′	1°55·9′W	X	98
Howden Moors	Sheff	SK1697	53°28·4′	1°45·1′W	X	110
Howden Moors	Sheff	SK1893	53°26·2′	1°43·3′W	X	110
Howden Moss	Durham	NY8626	54°38·0′	2°12·6′W	X	91,92
Howden Park	Brad	SE0545	53°54·3′	1°55·0′W	X	104
Howden Parks	E Yorks	SE7429	53°45·4′	0°52·2′W	X	105,106
Howden Reservoir	Sheff	SK1793	53°26·2′	1°44·2′W	W	110
Howden Sta	E Yorks	SE7530	53°45·9′	0°51·3′W	X	105,106
Howden Well	Northum	NY9694	55°14·7′	2°3·3′W	W	81
Howdiemont Sands	Northum	NU2615	55°25·9′	1°34·9′W	X	81
Howdon	N Tyne	NZ3267	55°0·0′	1°29·6′W	T	88
Howdon Pans	N Tyne	NZ3366	54°59·5′	1°28·6′W	T	88
Howdub Knowe	Scot Bord	NT2909	55°22·4′	3°6·8′W	X	79
Howe	Aberd	NJ9841	57°27·8′	2°1·5′W	X	30
Howe	Aberd	NK0754	57°34·8′	1°52·5′W	X	30
Howe	Cumbr	NY4919	54°34·1′	2°46·9′W	X	90
Howe	Highld	ND0963	58°33·0′	3°33·3′W	X	11,12
Howe	Highld	ND3062	58°32·7′	3°11·7′W	X	11,12
Howe	Norf	TM2799	52°32·7′	1°21·3′E	T	134
Howe	N Yks	SE3580	54°13·1′	1°27·4′W	T	99
Howe	Orkney	HY2323	59°5·5′	3°20·1′W	X	6
Howe	Orkney	HY2710	58°58·5′	3°15·7′W	X	6
Howe	Orkney	HY3526	59°7·2′	3°7·6′W	X	6
Howe	Orkney	HY4630	59°9·5′	2°56·2′W	X	5,6
Howe	Orkney	HY5116	59°2·0′	2°50·7′W	X	6
Howe Bottom	Scot Bord	NT4127	55°32·2′	2°55·7′W	X	73
Howe Bridge	Wigan	SD6602	53°31·1′	2°30·4′W	T	109
Howe Bridge Fm	N Yks	SE8176	54°10·6′	0°45·1′W	FM	100
Howe Brook Ho	Lancs	SD5215	53°38·0′	2°43·1′W	A	108
Howe Burn	Scot Bord	NT7850	55°44·8′	2°20·6′W	W	67,74
Howe Cleuch	S Lanak	NT0124	55°30·2′	3°33·6′W	X	72
Howe Copse East	Wilts	SU2528	51°3·3′	1°38·2′W	F	184
Howe Downs	Corn	SW6235	50°10·3′	5°19·6′W	X	203
Howe End	N Yks	NZ6907	54°27·5′	0°55·7′W	X	94
Howe Farm	Cumbr	SD3597	54°22·1′	2°59·6′W	FM	96,97
Howefield Ho	N Yks	SE3676	54°11·0′	1°26·5′W	X	99
Howe Fm	Bucks	SU7788	51°35·4′	0°52·9′W	FM	175
Howe Fm	Cumbr	SD4193	54°20·0′	2°54·0′W	FM	96,97
Howe Fm	Essex	TL6734	51°59·0′	0°26·3′E	FM	154
Howe Fm	Essex	TM0102	51°41·1′	0°54·9′E	FM	168
Howe Fm	N Yks	SE1881	54°13·7′	1°43·0′W	FM	99
Howe Fm	N Yks	SE8075	54°10·1′	0°46·1′W	FM	100
Howe Fm	N Yks	TA0875	54°9·8′	0°20·3′W	FM	101
Howe Fm	Orkney	HY3316	59°1·8′	3°9·6′W	FM	6
Howe Fm	Suff	TM1159	52°11·6′	1°5·6′E	FM	155
Howegill Head	Cumbr	SD6484	54°15·3′	2°32·7′W	X	97
Howegill Rig	S Lanak	NT0131	55°34·0′	3°33·8′W	H	72
Howe Grain	Cumbr	NY4318	54°33·5′	2°52·5′W	X	90
Howe Green	Derby	SK0468	53°12·8′	1°56·0′W	X	119
Howe Green	Essex	TL5118	51°50·6′	0°11·9′E	T	167
Howe Green	Essex	TL7403	51°42·1′	0°31·5′E	T	167
Howegreen	Essex	TL8301	51°40·9′	0°39·2′E	T	168
Howe Green	Herts	TL2809	51°46·1′	0°8·3′W	X	166
Howe Green	Warw	SP3188	52°29·6′	1°32·2′W	T	140
Howe Hall	Essex	TL4938	52°1·5′	0°10·7′E	X	154
Howe Hall	Essex	TL6933	51°58·4′	0°28·0′E	X	167
Howe Harper	Orkney	HY3414	59°0·7′	3°8·5′W	X	6
Howe Harper (Cairn)	Orkney	HY3414	59°0·7′	3°8·5′W	A	6
Howe Hill	N Lincs	TA0715	53°37·5′	0°22·5′W	A	112
Howe Hill	Norf	TF8743	52°57·3′	0°47·4′E	X	132
Howe Hill	N Yks	NZ5111	54°29·7′	1°12·3′W	X	93
Howe Hill	N Yks	SE3495	54°21·2′	1°28·2′W	X	99
Howe Hill	N Yks	SE3951	53°57·5′	1°23·9′W	X	104
Howe Hill	Orkney	HY5116	59°2·0′	2°50·7′W	A	6
Howe Hill Cottages	N Yks	NZ3510	54°29·3′	1°27·2′W	X	93
Howe Hill (Motte)	N Yks	SE3495	54°21·2′	1°28·2′W	A	99
Howe Hill (Motte)	N Yks	SE3951	53°57·5′	1°23·9′W	A	104
Howe Hill of Haggagmalag	D & G	NX4535	54°41·4′	4°23·9′W	X	83
Howe Hills	Durham	NZ3224	54°36·9′	1°29·8′W	X	93
Howe Hills	N Yks	SE1189	54°18·0′	1°49·4′W	X	99
Howe Ho	N Yks	NZ7907	54°27·4′	0°46·5′W	X	94
Howe Hole of Shaddock	D & G	NX4739	54°43·6′	4°22·1′W	X	83
Howell	Lincs	TF1346	53°0·2′	0°18·6′W	T	130
Howell Fen	Lincs	TF1546	53°0·2′	0°16·8′W	X	130
Howell Hill	Surrey	TQ2362	51°20·9′	0°13·6′W	X	176,187
Howell Ho	Barns	SE4408	53°34·2′	1°19·7′W	X	111
Howell's Fm	Essex	TL8509	51°45·2′	0°41·2′E	FM	168
Howells Fm	Herts	TL2728	51°56·4′	0°8·7′W	FM	166
Howell's School	Denb	SJ0565	53°10·7′	3°24·9′W	X	116
Howell Wood	Donc	SE4309	53°34·8′	1°20·6′W	F	111
Howels Head	Oldham	SE0503	53°31·7′	1°55·1′W	X	110
Howelston	Pemb	SM8511	51°45·6′	5°6·5′W	X	157
Howe Mill Fm	V of Glam	ST0072	51°26·5′	3°25·9′W	FM	170
Howemoss	Aberd	NJ7908	57°10·0′	2°20·4′W	X	38
Howemoss	C of Aber	NJ8612	57°12·2′	2°13·4′W	X	38
How End	Beds	TL0340	52°3·2′	0°29·5′W	T	153
Howend	Cumbr	NY3149	54°50·1′	3°4·0′W	X	85
Howend	Cumbr	NY3867	54°59·9′	2°57·7′W	X	85
Howe Nook	Cumbr	NY6009	54°28·7′	2°36·6′W	X	91
Howe o'Buchan	Aberd	NK1046	57°30·5′	1°49·5′W	X	30
Howe of Alford	Aberd	NJ5816	57°14·2′	2°41·3′W	X	37
Howe of Ashalloch	Aberd	NJ6140	57°27·2′	2°38·5′W	X	29
Howe of Auchterless	Aberd	NJ7242	57°28·3′	2°27·6′W	X	29
Howe of Blair	Aberd	NJ8426	57°19·7′	2°15·5′W	X	38
Howe of Bruxie	Aberd	NJ9348	57°31·6′	2°6·6′W	X	30
Howe of Cushnie	Aberd	NJ5211	57°11·5′	2°47·2′W	X	37
Howe of Fife	Fife	NO2810	56°16·9′	3°9·3′W	X	59
Howe of Forgue	Aberd	NJ6044	57°29·3′	2°39·6′W	X	29
Howe of Kinmuck	Aberd	NJ9935	57°24·6′	2°0·5′W	X	30
Howe of Laggan	S Ayr	NX3192	55°11·9′	4°38·9′W	X	76
Howe of Rora	Aberd	NK0549	57°32·1′	1°54·5′W	X	30
Howe of Teuchar	Aberd	NJ7946	57°30·5′	2°20·6′W	T	29,30
Howe of the Mearns	Aberd	NO6974	56°51·6′	2°30·1′W	X	45
Howe Park Wood	Mil Key	SP8334	52°0·1′	0°47·1′W	F	152,165
Howequoy	Orkney	HY4601	58°53·8′	2°55·7′W	X	6,7
Howequoy Head	Orkney	HY4600	58°53·3′	2°55·7′W	X	6,7
Howerigg	Cumbr	SD6281	54°13·6′	2°34·6′W	X	97
Howe Rock	Somer	ST2759	51°19·8′	3°2·5′W	X	182
Howes	Cumbr	NY4240	54°45·3′	2°53·7′W	X	85
Howes	Cumbr	NY4910	54°29·2′	2°46·8′W	H	90
Howes	D & G	NY1866	54°59·2′	3°16·5′W	X	85
Howes Beck	Cumbr	NY5017	54°33·0′	2°46·0′W	W	90
Howes Fm	E Yorks	TA0852	53°57·4′	0°20·8′W	FM	107
Howe's Fm	Suff	TL7452	52°8·6′	0°33·0′E	FM	155
Howe's Fm	Suff	TM2645	52°3·7′	1°18·2′E	FM	169
Howe's Hill	Norf	TG1341	52°55·7′	1°10·5′E	X	133
Howe's Hill (Tumulus)	Norf	TG1341	52°55·7′	1°10·5′E	A	133
Howe Slacks	Cumbr	NY6714	54°31·5′	2°30·2′W	X	91
Howes of Quoyawa	Orkney	HY2302	58°54·2′	3°19·7′W	X	6,7
Howes, The	Cumbr	NY5017	54°33·0′	2°46·0′W	X	90
Howestone	Cumbr	SD5598	54°22·8′	2°41·1′W	X	97
Howe Street	Essex	TL6914	51°48·2′	0°27·5′E	T	167
Howe Street	Essex	TL6934	51°58·9′	0°28·1′E	T	154
Howes Well	Cumbr	NY6808	54°28·2′	2°29·2′W	W	91
Howes Wick	Orkney	HY5100	58°53·3′	2°50·5′W	W	6,7
Howe Taing	Orkney	ND4294	58°50·0′	2°59·8′W	X	7
Howe, The	Cumbr	NX9828	54°38·5′	3°33·3′W	X	89
Howe, The	Cumbr	NY4102	54°24·8′	2°54·1′W	X	90
Howe,The	Cumbr	SD4395	54°21·1′	2°52·2′W	X	97
Howe, The	Essex	TL8131	51°57·1′	0°38·4′E	X	168
Howe, The	I of M	SC1967	54°4·3′	4°45·6′W	X	95
Howe, The	Midlo	NT1962	55°50·9′	3°17·2′W	X	65,66
Howe, The	N Yks	NZ6907	54°27·5′	0°55·7′W	X	94
Howe, The	Oxon	SU6992	51°37·6′	0°59·8′W	X	175
Howe, The	Scot Bord	NT5357	55°48·5′	2°44·6′W	X	66,73
Howetown Fm	Somer	SS9332	51°4·9′	3°31·3′W	FM	181
Howe Wood	Essex	TL4939	52°2·0′	0°10·7′E	F	154
Howe Wood	Essex	TL5434	51°59·2′	0°15·0′E	F	154
Howe Wood	Oxon	SU6991	51°37·0′	0°59·8′W	F	175
Howe Wood	Suff	TL6447	52°6·0′	0°24·1′E	F	154
Howe Wood	Suff	TL9844	52°3·8′	0°53·7′E	F	155
Howey	Powys	SO0558	52°13·0′	3°23·0′W	T	147
How Fen	Cambs	TL4186	52°27·5′	0°4·9′E	X	142,143
Howfield	Cumbr	NY4347	54°49·1′	2°52·8′W	X	85
Howfield Fm	Kent	TR1156	51°16·1′	1°1·9′E	FM	179
Howfields	Essex	TQ5099	51°40·4′	0°10·6′E	X	167,177
Howfield Wood	Kent	TR1157	51°16·6′	1°1·9′E	F	179
How Fm	Cumbr	NY0302	54°24·5′	3°29·3′W	FM	89
Howfold Fm	Pth & Kin	NT0095	56°8·5′	3°36·1′W	FM	58
Howford	Aberd	NJ9554	57°34·8′	2°4·6′W	X	30
Howford	Highld	NH8753	57°33·4′	3°52·9′W	X	27
Howford	Scot Bord	NT3136	55°37·0′	3°5·3′W	T	73
Howford	Scot Bord	NT3924	55°30·6′	2°57·5′W	T	73
Howford	S Lanak	NS9140	55°38·7′	3°43·5′W	X	71,72
Howford Bridge	Cumbr	NY4765	54°58·9′	2°49·3′W	X	86
Howford Hill	Scot Bord	NT3923	55°30·1′	2°57·5′W	H	73
Howgarth Scar	D & G	NY1364	54°58·0′	3°21·1′W	X	85
Howgate	Cumbr	NX9921	54°34·7′	3°33·3′W	T	89
Howgate	Midlo	NT2458	55°48·8′	3°12·3′W	T	66,73
Howgate	Scot Bord	NT7820	55°28·6′	2°20·5′W	X	74
Howgate	S Lanak	NS9135	55°36·0′	3°43·4′W	X	71,72
Howgate Foot	Cumbr	NY5119	54°34·1′	2°45·1′W	X	90
Howgate Hill	S Lanak	NS9134	55°35·5′	3°43·3′W	H	71,72
Howgate Ho	Cumbr	NY5924	54°36·8′	2°37·7′W	X	91
Howgate Mouth	S Lanak	NS9234	55°35·5′	3°42·4′W	X	71,72
Howgate Nick	Scot Bord	NT2746	55°42·4′	3°9·3′W	X	73
How-Gill	Cumbr	NY3640	54°45·3′	2°59·2′W	X	85
Howgill	Cumbr	NY5364	54°58·4′	2°43·6′W	X	86
How Gill	Cumbr	NY5755	54°53·5′	2°39·8′W	W	86
Howgill	Cumbr	NY5820	54°34·7′	2°38·6′W	X	91
Howgill	Cumbr	NY5957	54°54·6′	2°37·9′W	X	86
Howgill	Cumbr	SD6396	54°21·7′	2°33·7′W	T	97
Howgill	Lancs	SD8246	53°54·8′	2°16·0′W	T	103
Howgill	N Yks	SD9667	54°6·2′	2°3·3′W	X	98
Howgill	N Yks	SE0659	54°1·9′	1°54·1′W	T	104
How Gill	N Yks	SE0975	54°10·5′	1°51·3′W	W	99
Howgill Beck	Cumbr	NY5957	54°54·6′	2°37·9′W	W	86
Howgill Burn	D & G	NY2065	54°58·6′	3°14·6′W	W	85
Howgill Castle	Cumbr	NY6629	54°39·5′	2°31·2′W	A	91
Howgillcleuch	D & G	NY3981	55°7·4′	2°57·0′W	X	79
Howgill Fell	D & G	NY1496	55°15·3′	3°20·8′W	H	78
Howgill Fells	Cumbr	SD6798	54°22·8′	2°30·1′W	H	98
Howgill Fm	N Yks	SE0953	53°58·6′	1°51·4′W	FM	104
Howgill Foot	Cumbr	NY8209	54°28·8′	2°16·2′W	X	91,92
Howgill Grange	Durham	NY9520	54°34·8′	2°4·2′W	X	91,92
Howgill Hill	D & G	NY4392	55°13·4′	2°53·3′W	H	79
Howgill Ho	Durham	NY9028	54°39·1′	2°8·9′W	X	91,92
How Gill Ho	N Yks	SE0975	54°10·5′	1°51·3′W	X	99
How Gill Moss	Cumbr	SD7485	54°15·8′	2°23·5′W	X	98
Howgill Rigg	Cumbr	NY7048	54°49·8′	2°27·6′W	X	86,87
Howgillside	D & G	NY2873	55°3·0′	3°7·2′W	X	85
Howgill Side	N Yks	SE0953	53°58·6′	1°51·4′W	X	104
Howgillsike	Cumbr	NY7540	54°45·5′	2°22·9′W	X	86,87
Howgill Sike	Cumbr	NY8209	54°28·8′	2°16·2′W	W	91,92
Howgill Tongue	Cumbr	NY2726	54°37·7′	3°7·4′W	X	89,90
Howgill Wood	Cumbr	NY1933	54°41·4′	3°15·0′W	F	89,90
Howgrave Hall	N Yks	SE3179	54°12·6′	1°31·1′W	X	99
Howgrave Village	N Yks	SE3179	54°12·6′	1°31·1′W	A	99
How Green	Kent	TQ4746	51°11·9′	0°6·6′E	T	188
Howgrove Fm	Bath & NE Somer	ST5262	51°21·5′	2°41·0′W	FM	172,182
How Hall Fm	Cumbr	NY0916	54°32·1′	3°24·0′W	FM	89
How Ham Fm	N Som	ST4674	51°28·0′	2°46·3′W	FM	171,172
How Head	Cumbr	SD3197	54°22·1′	3°3·3′W	X	96,97
How Hill	Cumbr	NY3935	54°42·6′	2°56·4′W	H	90
How Hill	Norf	TG3719	52°43·2′	1°31·0′E	X	133,134
How Hill	N Yks	SE0098	54°22·9′	1°59·6′W	A	98
How Hill	N Yks	SE1098	54°22·9′	1°50·3′W	H	99
How Hill	N Yks	SE2767	54°6·1′	1°34·8′W	X	99
How Hill	Suff	TL7576	52°21·5′	0°34·6′E	X	143
Howhill Clump	Suff	TL7577	52°22·0′	0°34·6′E	F	143
How Hills	Cumbr	NY0409	54°28·3′	3°28·5′W	H	89
How Hill (Tumulus)	Suff	TL7576	52°21·5′	0°34·6′E	A	143
Howick	Monm	ST5095	51°39·3′	2°43·0′W	T	162
Howick	Northum	NU2517	55°27·0′	1°35·9′W	T	81
Howick	W Susx	SU9928	51°2·8′	0°34·9′W	X	186,197
Howick Cross	Lancs	SD5027	53°44·5′	2°45·1′W	T	102
Howick Fm	W Susx	TQ0831	51°4·3′	0°27·1′W	FM	187
Howick Grange	Northum	NU2416	55°26·5′	1°36·8′W	X	81
Howick Hall	Northum	NU2416	55°26·5′	1°36·8′W	X	81
Howick Haven	Northum	NU2616	55°26·5′	1°34·9′W	W	81
Howicks	Surrey	TQ0034	51°6·0′	0°33·9′W	X	186
Howick Scar	Northum	NU2519	55°28·1′	1°35·8′W	X	81
Howierig	Falk	NS8478	55°59·1′	3°51·1′W	X	65
Howie Sound	Orkney	HY4631	59°10·0′	2°56·2′W	W	5,6
Howietoun Fishery	Stir	NS7888	56°4·4′	3°57·2′W	X	57
Howith	N Yks	SD7663	54°4·0′	2°21·6′W	X	98
Howitt Ho (School)	Staffs	SK1627	52°50·7′	1°45·3′W	X	128
Howk	Cumbr	NY3139	54°44·7′	3°3·9′W	X	90

Howkeld Mill	N Yks	SE6885	54°15·6'	0°56·9'W	X	94,100
Howkerse	Falk	NS9083	56°1·9'	3°45·5'W	X	65
Howkwood	S Lanak	NS9116	55°25·8'	3°42·9'W	X	71,78
Howla Hay Fm	Red & Cl	NZ6317	54°32·9'	1°1·1'W	FM	94
Howland	Orkney	HY6643	59°16·6'	2°35·3'W	X	5
Howlands	Aberd	NJ5855	57°35·2'	2°41·7'W	X	29
Howlands	Aberd	NJ9419	57°16·0'	2°5·5'W	X	38
Howlands	Stir	NS7889	56°5·0'	3°57·2'W	X	57
Howlanehead	Ches	SJ9078	53°18·2'	2°8·6'W	X	118
Howl Beck	N Yks	NZ2603	54°25·5'	1°35·5'W	W	93
Howl Beck	N Yks	SE4396	54°21·7'	1°19·9'W	W	99
Howl Beck	N Yks	SE7458	54°1·0'	0°51·8'W	W	105,106
Howl Beck	N Yks	SE7666	54°5·3'	0°49·9'W	W	100
Howlbeck Fm	Red & Cl	NZ6117	54°32·9'	1°3·0'W	FM	94
Howl Dale Wood	N Yks	SE8184	54°15·0'	0°45·0'W	X	100
Howle	Wrekin	SJ6923	52°48·5'	2°27·2'W	T	127
Howlea Br	Durham	NZ1132	54°41·2'	1°49·3'W	X	92
Howle Beck	Durham	NZ0825	54°37·4'	1°52·1'W	W	92
Howle Hill	Heref	SO6020	51°52·9'	2°34·5'W	X	162
Howle Hope Fm	Durham	NZ3630	54°40·1'	1°26·1'W	FM	93
Howleigh	Somer	ST2018	50°57·6'	3°8·0'W	T	193
Howle Manor	Wrekin	SJ6923	52°48·5'	2°27·2'W	X	127
Howler's Heath	Glos	SO7435	52°1·0'	2°22·3'W	F	150
Howletburn	E Ayr	NS5038	55°37·0'	4°22·5'W	X	70
Howlet Hall	Northum	NU2305	55°20·6'	1°37·8'W	X	81
Howlet Hall	N Yks	NZ8807	54°27·3'	0°38·1'W	X	94
Howlet Ho	Lincs	TF5370	53°12·5'	0°17·9'E	X	122
Howlets Fm	Kent	TQ4543	51°10·3'	0°4·8'E	FM	188
Howlet's Ha'	Scot Bord	NT6149	55°44·2'	2°36·8'W	X	74
Howlet's House	Midlo	NT1962	55°50·9'	3°17·2'W	A	65,66
Howlett End	Essex	TL5834	51°59·1'	0°18·5'E	T	154
Howlett Hall	Northum	NZ1084	55°9·3'	1°50·2'W	X	81
Howletts	Essex	TL7119	51°50·8'	0°29·4'E	X	167
Howletts	Kent	TQ9964	51°20·6'	0°51·8'E	X	178
Howlett's Fm	Kent	TR0152	51°14·1'	0°53·2'E	FM	189
Howlett's Hall	Essex	TL6102	51°41·8'	0°20·2'E	X	167
Howletts Hall	Essex	TL6610	51°46·1'	0°24·7'E	X	167
Howletts Hall	Essex	TQ5297	51°39·3'	0°12·2'E	X	167,177
Howletts Zoo Park	Kent	TR1956	51°15·9'	1°8·7'E	X	179
Howley	Devon	SS4022	50°58·7'	4°16·4'W	X	180,190
Howley	Glos	ST7494	51°38·9'	2°22·2'W	T	162,172
Howley	Somer	ST2609	50°52·8'	3°2·7'W	T	192,193
Howley	Warr	SJ6188	53°23·5'	2°34·8'W	T	109
Howley Hall	Leeds	SE2525	53°43·5'	1°36·9'W	X	104
Howlgate Head Wood	N Yks	SE7487	54°16·6'	0°51·4'W	F	94,100
Howlgate Nab	N Yks	SE8289	54°17·6'	0°44·0'W	X	94,100
Howliggat	D & G	NX9473	55°2·7'	3°39·1'W	X	84
Howlish Hall	Durham	NZ2428	54°39·0'	1°37·3'W	X	93
Howliston	Scot Bord	NT4148	55°43·6'	2°55·9'W	X	73
Howliston Burn	Scot Bord	NT4049	55°44·1'	2°56·9'W	W	73
Howl John	Durham	NY9638	54°44·5'	2°3·3'W	X	91,92
Howl Moor	N Yks	SE8297	54°22·0'	0°43·9'W	X	94,100
Howl Wood Fm	N Yks	SE6189	54°17·8'	1°3·3'W	FM	94,100
Howmae Brae	Orkney	HY7552	59°21·5'	2°25·9'W	X	5
Howmae Brae (Settlement)	Orkney	HY7552	59°21·5'	2°25·9'W	A	5
Howmains	D & G	NX9969	55°0·6'	3°34·3'W	X	84
Howmains	S Lanak	NS7347	55°42·2'	4°0·8'W	X	64
How Man	Cumbr	NX9810	54°28·8'	3°34·0'W	X	89
How Mea	N Yks	SD8196	54°21·8'	2°17·1'W	X	98
Howmill	Aberd	NJ4819	57°15·8'	2°51·3'W	X	37
How Moor	Cambs	TL3889	52°29·1'	0°2·3'E	X	142,143
How Moor	Cumbr	NY5842	54°46·5'	2°38·8'W	X	86
How Moor	Northum	NU0710	55°23·3'	1°52·9'W	X	81
Howmoor Cott	S Ayr	NS2712	55°22·5'	4°43·4'W	X	70
Howmuir	Angus	NO4954	56°40·8'	2°49·5'W	X	54
Howmuir	D & G	NX7576	55°4·0'	3°57·0'W	X	84
Howmuir	E Loth	NT6176	55°58·8'	2°37·1'W	X	67
Hownam	Scot Bord	NT7719	55°28·1'	2°21·4'W	T	80
Hownam Burn	Scot Bord	NT7820	55°28·6'	2°20·5'W	W	74
Hownam Grange	Scot Bord	NT7822	55°29·7'	2°20·5'W	X	74
Hownam Law	Scot Bord	NT7921	55°29·2'	2°19·5'W	H	74
Hownam Mains	Scot Bord	NT7820	55°28·6'	2°20·5'W	X	74
Hownam Rings	Scot Bord	NT7919	55°28·1'	2°19·5'W	X	80
Hownam Rings (Fort & Settlement)	Scot Bord	NT7919	55°28·1'	2°19·5'W	A	80
Hownam Steeple	Scot Bord	NT7819	55°28·1'	2°20·4'W	H	80
Howney Stone	Pemb	SM7709	51°44·4'	5°13·4'W	X	157
Howney Stone	Pemb	SM8212	51°46·1'	5°9·2'W	X	157
Howning's Fm	Worcs	SO9462	52°15·6'	2°4·9'W	FM	150
Hown's Fm	Durham	NZ0949	54°50·4'	1°51·2'W	FM	88
Howpark	Scot Bord	NT8266	55°53·5'	2°16·8'W	X	67
Howpark Burn	Scot Bord	NT8266	55°53·5'	2°16·8'W	W	67
Howpasley	Scot Bord	NT3407	55°21·4'	3°2·0'W	T	79
Howpasley Burn	Scot Bord	NT3405	55°20·3'	3°2·0'W	W	79
Howpasley Hope	Scot Bord	NT3405	55°20·3'	3°2·0'W	X	79
Howrigg	Cumbr	NY1444	54°47·3'	3°19·8'W	X	85
Howrigg	Cumbr	NY3247	54°49·0'	3°3·1'W	X	85
Howrigg	Cumbr	NY6330	54°40·1'	2°34·0'W	X	91
Howroyd Beck	Kirk	SE2318	53°39·7'	1°38·7'W	W	110
Howroyde	Cald	SE0519	53°40·3'	1°55·0'W	A	110
Hows	Cumbr	NY1701	54°24·1'	3°16·3'W	X	89,90
Howscales	Cumbr	NY5841	54°46·0'	2°38·7'W	X	86
Howsen	Worcs	SO7954	52°11·3'	2°18·0'W	T	150
Howses	Essex	TL6336	52°0·1'	0°22·9'E	X	154
Howsham	N Lincs	TA0404	53°31·6'	0°25·5'W	T	112
Howsham	N Yks	SE7362	54°3·2'	0°52·7'W	T	100
Howsham Barff	N Lincs	TA0305	53°32·1'	0°26·3'W	X	112
Howsham Br	N Yks	SE7362	54°3·2'	0°52·7'W	X	100
Howsham Grange	N Lincs	TA0305	53°32·1'	0°26·3'W	X	112
Howsham Wood	N Yks	SE7464	54°4·2'	0°51·7'W	F	100
Howshaw Tor	Sheff	SK1991	53°25·2'	1°42·4'W	X	110
Howshoots	Warr	SJ6585	53°21·9'	2°31·1'W	X	109
Howslack	D & G	NT0708	55°21·7'	3°27·6'W	X	78
Howslack Fm	Scot Bord	NT0635	55°36·2'	3°29·1'W	FM	72
Howson Ridge	N Yks	SE1568	54°6·7'	1°45·8'W	X	99
Howson's Lodge	Cambs	TL1078	52°23·6'	0°23·7'W	X	142
How Stean Beck	N Yks	SE0673	54°9·4'	1°54·1'W	W	99
How Stean Gorge	N Yks	SE0973	54°9·4'	1°51·3'W	X	99
Howstrake	I of M	SC4178	54°10·6'	4°25·8'W	X	95
Howsyke	N Yks	SD9784	54°15·3'	2°2·3'W	X	98
How Tallon	Durham	NZ0507	54°27·7'	1°55·0'W	A	92
Howtel	Northum	NT8934	55°36·2'	2°10·0'W	T	74
Howt Green	Kent	TQ8965	51°21·4'	0°43·3'E	T	178
Howthat	D & G	NY0870	55°1·2'	3°25·9'W	X	85
Howthat Burn	D & G	NY1491	55°12·6'	3°20·7'W	W	78
Howthorpe Fm	N Yks	SE6772	54°8·6'	0°58·0'W	FM	100
Howton	Aberd	NJ4828	57°20·6'	2°51·4'W	X	37
Howton	Corn	SX3763	50°26·9'	4°17·4'W	X	201
Howton	Heref	SO4129	51°57·6'	2°51·1'W	T	149,161
Howton Fm	Devon	SX7487	50°40·4'	3°46·6'W	FM	191
Howton Grove Fm	Heref	SO4230	51°58·2'	2°50·3'W	FM	149,161
Howtown	Cumbr	NY4419	54°34·0'	2°51·5'W	T	90
Howwell	D & G	NX6944	54°46·7'	4°1·8'W	X	83,84
Howwell Bay	D & G	NX6943	54°46·1'	4°1·8'W	W	83,84
How Wood	Herts	TL1303	51°43·1'	0°21·5'W	T	166
How Wood	Herts	TL2429	51°57·0'	0°11·3'W	F	166
Howwood	Renf	NS3960	55°48·6'	4°33·7'W	T	63
Hoxa	Orkney	ND4293	58°49·5'	2°59·8'W	X	7
Hoxa Head	Orkney	ND4092	58°48·9'	3°1·8'W	X	7
Hoxa Hill	Orkney	ND4393	58°49·5'	2°58·7'W	X	7
Hoxall Cottage	I of W	SZ4083	50°38·9'	1°25·7'W	X	196
Hoxne	Suff	TM1877	52°21·1'	1°12·5'E	T	156
Hoxne Wood	Suff	TM1975	52°20·0'	1°13·3'E	F	156
Hoxton	Hack	TQ3383	51°32·0'	0°4·6'W	T	176,177
Hoy	Highld	ND1460	58°31·4'	3°28·1'W	X	11,12
Hoy	Highld	ND2163	58°33·1'	3°21·0'W	X	11,12
Hoy	Orkney	HY2203	58°54·7'	3°20·8'W	T	6,7
Hoy	Orkney	ND2499	58°52·6'	3°18·6'W	X	6,7
Hoy	Shetld	HU3744	60°11·0'	1°19·5'W	X	4
Hoy Ho	Durham	NZ0816	54°32·6'	1°52·2'W	X	92
Hoylake	Wirral	SJ2188	53°23·2'	3°10·9'W	T	108
Hoyland	Barns	SE3700	53°30·0'	1°26·1'W	T	110,111
Hoyland Common	Barns	SE3500	53°30·0'	1°27·9'W	T	110,111
Hoylandswaine	Barns	SE2604	53°32·2'	1°36·1'W	T	110
Hoyle	W Susx	SU9018	50°57·5'	0°42·7'W	T	197
Hoyle Bottom	Lancs	SD7426	53°44·0'	2°23·2'W	X	103
Hoyle Fm	Surrey	TQ1742	51°10·1'	0°19·2'W	FM	187
Hoyle Fm	W Susx	SU9118	50°57·5'	0°41·9'W	FM	197
Hoyle Green	Cald	SE0524	53°43·0'	1°55·0'W	X	104
Hoyle Mill	Barns	SE3606	53°33·2'	1°27·0'W	T	110,111
Hoyle Mill Dam	Wakf	SE4314	53°37·5'	1°20·6'W	W	111
Hoyles Moss Fm	Warr	SJ6792	53°25·7'	2°29·4'W	FM	109
Hoy Lodge	Orkney	HY2203	58°54·7'	3°20·8'W	X	6,7
Hoy Outdoor Centre	Orkney	HY2303	58°54·7'	3°19·7'W	X	6,7
Hoys Fm	Essex	TL5837	52°0·8'	0°18·5'E	FM	154
Hoy Sound	Orkney	HY2307	58°56·9'	3°19·8'W	W	6,7
Hoys Wood	N upon Ty	NZ2275	55°4·4'	1°38·9'W	F	88
Hozen	Orkney	HY3021	59°4·5'	3°12·8'W	X	6
Huan	Orkney	HY2320	59°3·9'	3°20·1'W	X	6
Huan	Pemb	SN1337	52°0·2'	4°43·1'W	X	145
Huanaraigh	N Eil	NF9057	57°30·1'	7°10·1'W	X	22
Hubbage	Heref	SO6359	52°13·9'	2°32·1'W	X	149
Hubbard's Fm	Essex	TL7127	51°55·1'	0°29·6'E	FM	167
Hubbard's Fm	Kent	TQ9049	51°12·7'	0°43·6'E	FM	189
Hubbards Fm	Norf	TF8534	52°52·5'	0°45·3'E	FM	132
Hubbard's Hall	Essex	TL4810	51°46·4'	0°9·1'E	X	167
Hubbard's Hall Fm	Suff	TM1339	52°0·7'	1°6·6'E	FM	169
Hubbard's Hill	Kent	TQ5352	51°15·0'	0°11·9'E	T	188
Hubbards Hills	Lincs	TF3186	53°21·5'	0°1·5'W	F	113,122
Hubbards Lodge	Rut	SK8511	52°41·6'	0°44·1'W	X	130
Hubber Dale	Derby	SK1469	53°13·3'	1°47·0'W	X	119
Hubberholme	N Yks	SD9278	54°12·1'	2°6·9'W	T	98
Hubberston	Pemb	SM8906	51°43·0'	5°2·9'W	T	157,158
Hubbersty Head	Cumbr	SD4291	54°18·9'	2°53·1'W	T	96,97
Hubberton Green	Cald	SE0322	53°41·9'	1°56·9'W	T	104
Hubbert's Bridge	Lincs	TF2643	52°58·4'	0°7·0'W	T	131
Hubbet, The	Orkney	HY4628	59°8·4'	2°56·1'W	X	5,6
Huby	N Yks	SE2747	53°55·3'	1°34·9'W	T	104
Huby	N Yks	SE5665	54°4·9'	1°8·2'W	T	100
Huby Burn	N Yks	SE5465	54°4·9'	1°10·1'W	X	100
Huccaby	Devon	SX6672	50°32·2'	3°53·1'W	X	191
Huccaby Ring	Devon	SX6573	50°32·7'	3°53·9'W	A	191
Huccaby Tor	Devon	SX6574	50°33·2'	3°54·0'W	X	191
Hucclecote	Glos	SO8617	51°51·3'	2°11·8'W	T	162
Huck Barrow	Dorset	SY7488	50°41·7'	2°21·7'W	A	194
Huckerby	Lincs	SK9093	53°25·8'	0°38·3'W	X	112
Huckham	Devon	SX8040	50°15·1'	3°40·6'W	X	202
Huckham Fm	Devon	SS6340	51°8·8'	3°57·1'W	FM	180
Huckham Fm	Somer	ST4435	51°6·9'	2°47·6'W	FM	182
Huck Hill	Kirk	SE0412	53°36·5'	1°56·0'W	X	110
Huckhoe	Northum	NZ0782	55°8·2'	1°53·0'W	H	81
Hucking	Kent	TQ8458	51°17·7'	0°38·7'E	T	178,188
Hucking Hill Ho	Kent	TQ8357	51°17·2'	0°37·9'E	X	178,188
Huckles Brook	Hants	SU1711	50°54·1'	1°45·1'W	W	195
Hucklesbrook Fm	Hants	SU1510	50°53·6'	1°46·8'W	FM	195
Hucklinsower	Orkney	HY6846	59°18·2'	2°33·2'W	X	5
Hucklow Edge	Derby	SK1878	53°18·2'	1°43·4'W	X	119
Hucklow Lees Barn	Derby	SK1490	53°24·6'	1°47·0'W	X	110
Hucklow Moor	Derby	SK1578	53°18·2'	1°46·1'W	X	119
Hucknall	Notts	SK5349	53°2·4'	1°12·2'W	T	129
Hucknall Fm	Ches	SJ7475	53°16·5'	2°23·0'W	FM	118
Hucknall Wood	Derby	SK4665	53°11·0'	1°18·3'W	F	120
Hucksbarn	Shrops	SO5073	52°21·4'	2°43·7'W	X	137,138
Hucks Fm	Worcs	SO7657	52°12·9'	2°20·7'W	FM	150
Huckshott Fm	W Susx	SU7716	50°56·5'	0°53·9'W	FM	197
Huckworthy Br	Devon	SX5370	50°30·9'	4°4·0'W	A	201
Hudbeck	Cumbr	NY3743	54°46·9'	2°58·3'W	X	85
Huddale	Staffs	SK0949	53°2·5'	1°51·5'W	X	119
Hudder Down	Corn	SW6042	50°14·0'	5°21·6'W	X	203
Huddersfield	Kirk	SE1416	53°38·7'	1°46·9'W	T	110
Hudderstone	S Lanak	NT0227	55°31·9'	3°32·7'W	H	72
Huddington	Worcs	SO9457	52°12·9'	2°4·9'W	T	150
Huddington Court	Worcs	SO9457	52°12·9'	2°4·9'W	A	150
Huddington Hill Fm	Worcs	SO9456	52°12·4'	2°4·9'W	FM	150
Huddinknoll Hill	Glos	SO8410	51°47·5'	2°13·5'W	X	162
Huddisford	Devon	SS3019	50°57·0'	4°24·8'W	T	190
Huddispitt	Devon	SX4688	50°40·5'	4°10·4'W	X	190
Huddlecross Plantn	E Yorks	TA1444	53°53·0'	0°15·5'W	F	107
Huddlesceugh Hall	Cumbr	NY5942	54°46·5'	2°37·8'W	X	86
Huddlesford	Staffs	SK1509	52°40·9'	1°46·3'W	T	128
Huddlestone Fm	W Susx	TQ1813	50°54·5'	0°18·9'W	FM	198
Huddleston Hall	N Yks	SE4633	53°47·7'	1°17·7'W	A	105
Huddleston Old Wood	N Yks	SE4633	53°47·7'	1°17·7'W	F	105
Hudeshope Beck	Durham	NY9428	54°39·1'	2°5·2'W	W	91,92
Hudeshope Grains	Durham	NY9332	54°41·2'	2°6·1'W	W	91,92
Hudford Fm	Somer	ST0631	51°4·5'	3°20·1'W	FM	181
Hudgery	Devon	SS8209	50°52·3'	3°40·2'W	X	191
Hudgillrigg	Cumbr	NY7445	54°48·2'	2°23·8'W	X	86,87
Hud Hey	Lancs	SD7824	53°43·0'	2°19·6'W	T	103
Hud Holes	Lincs	TF3881	53°18·7'	0°4·7'E	X	122
Hud Lee	Lancs	SD6638	53°50·5'	2°30·6'W	X	103
Hudley Mill	Devon	SS6732	51°4·6'	3°53·5'W	X	180
Hudnall	Herts	TL0013	51°48·6'	0°32·6'W	T	166
Hudnall Corner	Beds	TL0113	51°48·6'	0°31·7'W	X	166
Hudnalls	Glos	SO5403	51°43·7'	2°39·6'W	T	162
Huds Brook Fm	Lancs	SD5444	53°53·7'	2°41·6'W	FM	102
Hudscales	Cumbr	NY3337	54°43·7'	3°2·0'W	X	90
Hudscott	Devon	SS6424	51°0·2'	3°55·9'W	X	180
Huds Head	Northum	NU0150	55°44·9'	1°58·6'W	X	75
Hudshouse Rig	Scot Bord	NY5798	55°16·7'	2°40·2'W	X	80
Hudson	Devon	SS2909	50°51·6'	4°25·4'W	X	190
Hudson Place	Cumbr	NY1122	54°35·4'	3°22·2'W	X	89
Hudsons Fm	Lancs	SD4441	53°52·0'	2°50·7'W	FM	102
Hudson Way	E Yorks	SE9542	53°52·5'	0°32·9'W	X	106
Hudson Way	E Yorks	TA0141	53°51·6'	0°27·4'W	X	106,107
Hudswell	N Yks	NZ1400	54°24·0'	1°46·6'W	T	92
Hudswell	Wilts	ST8569	51°25·4'	2°12·6'W	T	173
Hudswell Grange	N Yks	SE1398	54°22·9'	1°47·6'W	X	99
Huel Crag	Northum	NY8399	55°17·3'	2°15·6'W	X	80
Huffley	Shrops	SJ4917	52°45·1'	2°44·9'W	X	126
Hu Field	Shetld	HU2775	60°27·7'	1°30·0'W	X	3
Hugbridge	Ches	SJ9363	53°10·1'	2°5·9'W	X	118
Huggan Ing	Lancs	SD7947	53°55·4'	2°18·8'W	X	103
Huggate	E Yorks	SE8855	53°59·3'	0°39·1'W	T	106
Huggate Heads	E Yorks	SE8854	53°58·7'	0°39·1'W	X	106
Huggate Lodge	E Yorks	SE9257	54°0·3'	0°35·4'W	X	106
Huggate Wold	E Yorks	SE8657	54°0·3'	0°40·9'W	X	106
Huggester Fm	Derby	SK4476	53°17·0'	1°20·0'W	FM	120
Huggett's Furnace	E Susx	TQ5326	51°1·0'	0°11·3'E	X	188,199
Hug Gill	Durham	NY9712	54°30·4'	2°2·4'W	X	92
Huggill Force	Durham	NY9712	54°30·4'	2°2·4'W	W	92
Huggin Carr or Low Grounds	Donc	SE6705	53°32·5'	0°58·9'W	X	111
Huggin's Hall	Kent	TQ7535	51°5·5'	0°30·3'E	X	188
Hugginshayes	Devon	ST2005	50°50·6'	3°7·8'W	X	192,193
Hugglepit	Devon	SS3024	50°59·7'	4°25·0'W	T	190
Hugglescote	Leic	SK4212	52°42·5'	1°22·3'W	T	129
Huggon Ho	N Yks	SD7960	54°2·4'	2°18·8'W	X	98
Hughenden Manor	Bucks	SU8695	51°39·1'	0°45·0'W	X	165
Hughenden Valley	Bucks	SU8696	51°39·6'	0°45·0'W	T	165
Hughes's Hill	W Susx	TQ0626	51°1·6'	0°28·9'W	X	187,197
Hughley	Shrops	SO5697	52°34·4'	2°38·6'W	T	137,138
Hughley Brook	Shrops	SO5798	52°34·9'	2°37·7'W	W	137,138
Hugh Mill	Lancs	SD8321	53°41·4'	2°15·0'W	T	103
Hugh Seat	Cumbr	SD8099	54°23·4'	2°18·1'W	X	98
Hugh's Hill	Northum	NY7071	55°2·2'	2°27·7'W	X	86,87
Hughslade Fm	Devon	SX5593	50°43·3'	4°2·9'W	FM	191
Hugh's Laithes Pike	Cumbr	NY5015	54°31·9'	2°45·9'W	H	90
Hughsrigg	D & G	NY3776	55°4·7'	2°58·8'W	X	85
Hughston	Highld	NH5549	57°30·7'	4°24·8'W	X	26
Hughton	Highld	NH4741	57°26·3'	4°32·5'W	T	26
Hugh Town	I Scilly	SV9010	49°54·8'	6°18·7'W	T	203
Hugill Fell	Cumbr	SD4599	54°23·3'	2°50·4'W	H	97
Hugill Hall	Cumbr	SD4599	54°23·3'	2°50·4'W	X	97
Huglets Fm	E Susx	TQ6121	50°58·2'	0°18·0'E	FM	199
Huglets Stream	E Susx	TQ6614	50°54·3'	0°22·1'E	W	199
Huglith Fm	Shrops	SJ4002	52°37·0'	2°52·8'W	FM	126
Huglith Hill	Shrops	SJ4102	52°37·0'	2°51·9'W	X	126
Hugmore Ho	Wrex	SJ3751	53°3·4'	2°56·0'W	X	117
Hugset Wood	Barns	SE3006	53°33·2'	1°32·4'W	F	110,111
Hugus	Corn	SW7743	50°14·9'	5°7·3'W	T	204
Hugus Fm	Corn	SW7843	50°15·0'	5°6·5'W	FM	204
Huilish Point	N Eil	NF8278	57°41·0'	7°19·7'W	X	18
Huilish Point	N Eil	NL6194	56°55·1'	7°33·8'W	X	31
Huip	Orkney	HY6330	59°9·6'	2°38·3'W	X	5
Huip Ness	Orkney	HY6430	59°9·6'	2°37·3'W	X	5
Huip Sound	Orkney	HY6330	59°9·6'	2°38·3'W	W	5
Huisgill	Highld	NG3231	57°17·7'	6°26·5'W	X	32
Huisgill Burn	Highld	NG3232	57°18·3'	6°26·5'W	W	32
Huish	Devon	SS4829	51°2·7'	4°9·7'W	T	180
Huish	Devon	SS5311	50°53·0'	4°5·0'W	T	191
Huish	Dorset	SY9097	50°46·6'	2°8·1'W	X	195
Huish	Wilts	SU1463	51°22·2'	1°47·5'W	T	173
Huish Barton	Somer	ST0538	51°8·2'	3°21·1'W	X	181
Huish Champflower	Somer	ST0429	51°3·4'	3°21·8'W	T	181
Huish Champflower Barrow	Somer	ST0234	51°6·1'	3°23·6'W	A	181
Huish Cross	Devon	SX8479	50°36·2'	3°38·0'W	X	191
Huish Episcopi	Somer	ST4326	51°2·1'	2°48·4'W	T	193
Huish Fm	Dorset	SY6398	50°47·1'	2°31·1'W	FM	194
Huish Hill	Wilts	SU1564	51°22·7'	1°46·7'W	H	173
Huish Ho	Hants	SU6751	51°15·5'	1°2·0'W	X	185,186
Huish Ho	Somer	ST6953	51°16·8'	2°26·3'W	X	183
Huish Moor	Devon	SS5029	51°2·7'	4°8·0'W	X	180
Huish Moor	Somer	ST0428	51°2·8'	3°21·8'W	X	181
Huit Fm	Leic	SP4796	52°33·8'	1°18·0'W	FM	140
Hukeley Fm	Devon	SS9723	51°0·1'	3°27·7'W	FM	181
Hula-geo	N Eil	NF7376	57°39·6'	7°28·6'W	X	18
Hulam	Durham	NZ1520	54°34·7'	1°45·7'W	X	92
Hulam	Durham	NZ4436	54°43·3'	1°18·6'W	X	93
Hulands Fm	Durham	NZ0114	54°31·5'	1°58·7'W	FM	92
Hulberry	Kent	TQ5265	51°22·0'	0°11·4'E	X	177
Hulcote	Beds	SP9438	52°2·2'	0°37·4'W	T	153
Hulcote	Northnts	SP7049	52°8·3'	0°58·2'W	T	152
Hulcote Fm	Beds	SP9538	52°2·2'	0°36·5'W	FM	153
Hulcott	Bucks	SP8516	51°50·4'	0°45·6'W	T	165
Huldies Park	Scot Bord	NT9261	55°50·8'	2°7·2'W	X	67
Hule Moss	Scot Bord	NT7149	55°44·3'	2°27·3'W	W	74
Hulford's Copse	Hants	SU7658	51°19·2'	0°54·2'W	F	175,186
Hulgrave Hall	Ches	SJ5360	53°8·3'	2°41·8'W	X	117

Hulham	Devon	SY0183	50°38·5′	3°23·6′W	T	192
Hulk	Shetld	HU4494	60°37·9′	1°11·2′W	X	1,2
Hulke's Fm	Essex	TL6005	51°43·5′	0°19·4′E	FM	167
Hulk Waters	Shetld	HU4494	60°37·9′	1°11·2′W	W	1,2
Hulland	Derby	SK2446	53°0·9′	1°38·1′W	T	119,128
Hulland Grange	Derby	SK2547	53°1·4′	1°37·2′W	X	119,128
Hulland Moss	Derby	SK2546	53°0·9′	1°37·2′W	X	119,128
Hulland Ward	Derby	SK2547	53°1·4′	1°37·2′W	T	119,128
Hullasey Ho	Glos	ST9699	51°41·6′	2°3·1′W	X	163
Hullasey Village	Glos	ST9799	51°41·6′	2°2·2′W	A	163
Hullavington	Wilts	ST8982	51°32·4′	2°9·1′W	T	173
Hullavington Airfield	Wilts	ST9081	51°31·9′	2°8·3′W	X	173
Hullback's Fm	Suff	TL9335	51°59·0′	0°49·0′E	FM	155
Hull Bank	Cumbr	NY7312	54°30·4′	2°24·6′W	X	91
Hullbridge	Essex	TQ8194	51°37·2′	0°37·3′E	T	168,178
Hull Bridge	E Yorks	TA0541	53°51·5′	0°23·8′W	X	107
Hullbrook Ho	Surrey	TQ0243	51°10·9′	0°32·0′W	X	186
Hullderow	Orkney	ND3792	58°48·9′	3°5·0′W	X	7
Hull End	Derby	SK0582	53°20·3′	1°55·1′W	T	110
Huller Bush	Durham	NZ0422	54°35·8′	1°55·9′W	X	92
Hulleter	Cumbr	SD3387	54°16·7′	3°1·3′W	X	96,97
Hullet Hall	Lancs	SD8843	53°53·2′	2°10·5′W	X	103
Hulleys, The	N Yks	TA0096	54°21·2′	0°27·3′W	X	101
Hull Fm	Essex	TM0427	51°54·5′	0°58·3′E	FM	168
Hull Fm	Oxon	SP3229	51°57·7′	1°31·7′W	FM	164
Hull Fm	Somer	ST6723	51°0·6′	2°27·8′W	FM	183
Hull Green	Essex	TL5410	51°46·3′	0°14·3′E	X	167
Hull Ho	N Yks	SD8656	54°0·2′	2°12·4′W	X	103
Hullion	Orkney	HY3927	59°7·8′	3°3·5′W	X	6
Hullockhowe	Cumbr	NY5018	54°33·5′	2°46·0′W	X	90
Hullockpit Hill	Herts	TL2436	52°0·7′	0°11·2′W	X	153
Hullock's Pool	Staffs	SJ8051	53°3·6′	2°17·5′W	X	118
Hull Pot	N Yks	SD8274	54°9·9′	2°16·1′W	X	98
Hull Pot Beck	N Yks	SD8275	54°10·5′	2°16·1′W	W	98
Hull Roads	K upon H	TA1027	53°43·9′	0°19·5′W	W	107
Hull Roads	K upon H	TA1027	53°43·9′	0°19·5′W	W	107
Hulls	Cumbr	NY6314	54°31·4′	2°33·9′W	X	91
Hull Sand	Norf	TF5429	52°50·4′	0°17·6′E	X	131
Hull's Mill Fm	Essex	TL7933	51°58·2′	0°36·8′E	FM	167
Hulls, The	Oxon	SP5832	51°59·2′	1°8·9′W	X	152
Hully, The	Wrex	SJ4741	52°58·1′	2°46·9′W	X	117
Hulmalees	Shetld	HU2952	60°15·3′	1°28·1′W	X	3
Hulma Water	Shetld	HU2952	60°15·3′	1°28·1′W	W	3
Hulme	Man	SJ8396	53°27·9′	2°15·0′W	T	109
Hulme	Staffs	SJ9345	53°0·4′	2°5·9′W	T	118
Hulme	Warr	SJ6091	53°25·1′	2°35·7′W	T	109
Hulme Barns Fm	Ches	SJ7282	53°20·3′	2°24·8′W	FM	109
Hulme End	Staffs	SK1059	53°7·9′	1°50·6′W	T	119
Hulme Hall	Ches	SJ7272	53°14·9′	2°24·8′W	A	118
Hulme Ho	Staffs	SK0961	53°9·0′	1°51·5′W	X	119
Hulmetray	N Eil	NF9875	57°40·1′	7°3·4′W	X	18
Hulme Walfield	Ches	SJ8465	53°11·2′	2°14·0′W	T	118
Hulme Walfield Fm	Ches	SJ8564	53°10·6′	2°13·1′W	FM	118
Hulne Park	Northum	NU1514	55°25·4′	1°45·3′W	F	81
Hulne Priory	Northum	NU1615	55°26·0′	1°44·4′W	A	81
Hulse Fm	Ches	SJ7073	53°15·4′	2°26·6′W	FM	118
Hulse Grounds Fm	Oxon	SP2302	51°43·2′	1°39·6′W	FM	163
Hulseheath	Ches	SJ7283	53°20·8′	2°24·8′W	T	109
Hulse House Fm	Ches	SJ7172	53°14·9′	2°25·7′W	FM	118
Hulse, The	Shetld	HU3715	59°55·4′	1°19·8′W	H	4
Hultness	Shetld	HU3765	60°22·3′	1°19·2′W	X	2,3
Hulton Park	Bolton	SD6805	53°32·7′	2°28·6′W	X	109
Hulver Hill	Norf	TF9117	52°43·2′	0°50·1′E	X	132
Hulverhill Covert	Suff	TM0952	52°7·8′	1°3·6′E	F	155
Hulverstone	I of W	SZ3984	50°39·5′	1°26·5′W	T	196
Hulver Street	Suff	TM4786	52°25·2′	1°38·4′E	T	156
Hulverton Hill	Somer	SS9225	51°1·1′	3°32·0′W	H	181
Humabery	Shetld	HU1857	60°18·1′	1°40·0′W	X	3
Humasun Point	Orkney	HY2815	59°1·2′	3°14·8′W	X	6
Humber	Devon	SX8974	50°33·5′	3°33·6′W	T	192
Humber	Heref	SO5356	52°12·3′	2°40·9′W	T	149
Humber Bridge	E Yorks	TA0224	53°42·4′	0°26·9′W	X	106,107,112
Humber Brook	Heref	SO5354	52°11·2′	2°40·9′W	W	149
Humber Brook	Warw	SP2148	52°8·0′	1°41·2′W	W	151
Humber Dale	E Yorks	TA0027	53°44·0′	0°28·6′W	X	106,107
Humber Field Fm	E Yorks	TA0026	53°43·5′	0°28·6′W	FM	106,107
Humber Fm	E Yorks	TA3419	53°39·3′	0°2·1′E	FM	113
Humber House Fm	Durham	NZ1346	54°48·8′	1°47·4′W	FM	88
Humber Pilot Station	E Yorks	TA3910	53°34·3′	0°6·4′E	X	113
Humber's Ball	Somer	SS8232	51°4·7′	3°40·7′W	X	181
Humberside International Airport	N Lincs	TA0910	53°34·8′	0°20·8′W	X	112
Humberston	Highld	NH5457	57°35·0′	4°26·1′W	X	26
Humberston	NE Lincs	TA3105	53°31·8′	0°1·0′W	T	113
Humberstone	C of Leic	SK6205	52°38·6′	1°4·6′W	T	140
Humberstone Bank	N Yks	SE1360	54°2·4′	1°47·7′W	X	99
Humberston Fitties	NE Lincs	TA3305	53°31·7′	0°0·8′E	T	113
Humbers Wood	Hants	SU3529	51°3·8′	1°29·6′W	F	185
Humberton	N Yks	SE4268	54°6·6′	1°21·0′W	X	99
Humber Wildfowl Refuge	N Lincs	SE8824	53°42·5′	0°39·6′W	X	106,112
Humber Wood	Dorset	ST7304	50°50·3′	2°22·6′W	F	194
Humbie	E Loth	NT4562	55°51·1′	2°52·3′W	T	66
Humbie	Fife	NT1986	56°3·9′	3°17·6′W	X	65,66
Humbie	W Loth	NT1167	55°53·5′	3°24·9′W	X	65
Humbie Fm	C of Edin	NT1175	55°57·8′	3°25·1′W	FM	65
Humbie Ho	E Loth	NT4764	55°52·2′	2°50·4′W	X	66
Humbie Mains	E Loth	NT4762	55°51·2′	2°50·4′W	X	66
Humbie Mill	E Loth	NT4663	55°51·7′	2°51·3′W	X	66
Humbie Water	E Loth	NT4664	55°52·2′	2°51·3′W	W	66
Humbie Wood	E Loth	NT4665	55°52·8′	2°51·4′W	F	66
Humbie Wood	Fife	NT1986	56°3·9′	3°17·6′W	F	65,66
Humblebee	Glos	SP0225	51°55·6′	1°57·9′W	F	163
Humblebee Fm	N Yks	TA0378	54°11·5′	0°24·9′W	FM	101
Humblebee Hall	Worcs	SO9555	52°11·8′	2°4·0′W	X	150
Humble Burn	Durham	NZ2349	54°50·4′	1°38·1′W	W	88
Humble Burn	Northum	NY6483	55°8·7′	2°33·5′W	W	80
Humblecairn	Aberd	NJ9939	57°26·7′	2°0·5′W	X	30
Humble Dodd	Northum	NY7256	54°54·1′	2°25·8′W	X	86,87
Humbledon	Sund	NZ3755	54°53·5′	1°25·0′W	T	88
Humble Green	Suff	TL9345	52°4·4′	0°49·4′E	T	155
Humbleheugh	Northum	NU1718	55°27·6′	1°43·4′W	X	81
Humble Hill	Northum	NY6481	55°7·6′	2°33·4′W	H	80
Humble Knowle Fm	Durham	NZ3832	54°41·1′	1°24·2′W	FM	93
Humblemoor Hill	Scot Bord	NT7714	55°25·4′	2°21·4′W	H	80
Humble Point	Devon	SY3089	50°42·0′	2°59·1′W	X	193
Humblescough Fm	Lancs	SD4644	53°53·6′	2°48·9′W	FM	102
Humbles Knowe	Scot Bord	NT7859	55°49·7′	2°20·6′W	X	67,74
Humbletoft	Norf	TF9814	52°41·5′	0°56·2′E	X	132
Humbleton	Durham	NZ0917	54°33·1′	1°51·2′W	X	92
Humbleton	E Yorks	TA2234	53°47·5′	0°8·5′W	T	107
Humbleton	Northum	NT9728	55°33·0′	2°2·4′W	X	75
Humbleton	Northum	NY8361	54°56·8′	2°15·5′W	X	86,87
Humbleton Beck	E Yorks	TA2333	53°47·0′	0°7·6′W	W	107
Humbleton Buildings	Northum	NT9729	55°33·5′	2°2·4′W	X	75
Humbleton Burn	Northum	NT9731	55°34·6′	2°2·4′W	W	75
Humbleton Fm	Darl	NZ2519	54°34·2′	1°36·4′W	FM	93
Humbleton Grange	E Yorks	TA2133	53°47·0′	0°9·4′W	X	107
Humbleton Hill	Northum	NT9628	55°33·0′	2°3·4′W	H	74,75
Humbleton Hill	Northum	NU0610	55°23·3′	1°53·9′W	H	81
Humbleton Hill	Northum	NU1632	55°35·1′	1°44·3′W	X	75
Humbleton Ho	E Yorks	TA2234	53°47·5′	0°8·5′W	X	107
Humbleton Manor	E Yorks	TA2234	53°47·5′	0°8·5′W	X	107
Humbly Grove	Hants	SU7045	51°12·2′	0°59·5′W	X	186
Humbly Grove Copse	Hants	SU7045	51°12·2′	0°59·5′W	F	186
Humbrack	Moray	NJ2556	57°35·5′	3°14·8′W	X	28
Humby	Lincs	TF0032	52°52·8′	0°30·4′W	T	130
Hume	Scot Bord	NT7041	55°39·9′	2°28·2′W	T	74
Hume Craigs	Scot Bord	NT7041	55°39·9′	2°28·2′W	X	74
Humehall	Scot Bord	NT7141	55°40·0′	2°27·2′W	X	74
Hume Mill	Scot Bord	NT7040	55°39·4′	2°28·2′W	X	74
Hume Orchard	Scot Bord	NT6941	55°39·9′	2°29·1′W	X	74
Hume Platn	Scot Bord	NT6942	55°40·5′	2°29·1′W	F	74
Humesett	N Yks	SD8493	54°20·2′	2°14·3′W	X	98
Humeston	S Ayr	NS2611	55°22·0′	4°44·3′W	X	70
Humford Mill	Northum	NZ2680	55°7·1′	1°35·1′W	X	81
Humla	Highld	NG1900	57°0·6′	6°37·3′W	X	39
Humla Stack	Shetld	HP5917	60°50·2′	0°54·4′W	X	1
Humla Stack	Shetld	HU2445	60°11·6′	1°33·5′W	X	4
Humlataes	Shetld	HP6017	60°50·1′	0°53·3′W	X	1
Hummacott	Devon	SS7019	50°57·6′	3°50·7′W	X	180
Hummel Craig	Aberd	NJ6523	57°18·0′	2°34·4′W	H	38
Hummelknows	Scot Bord	NT5012	55°24·2′	2°46·9′W	X	79
Hummell Knowe	Northum	NY7071	55°2·2′	2°27·7′W	X	86,87
Hummell Rocks	E Loth	NT4683	56°2·5′	2°51·6′W	X	66
Hummel Ridges	E Loth	NT5485	56°3·6′	2°43·9′W	X	66
Hummel Rocks	Fife	NT2786	56°3·9′	3°9·9′W	X	66
Hummel Side	Scot Bord	NT4116	55°26·3′	2°55·5′W	H	79
Hummer	Dorset	ST5919	50°58·4′	2°34·7′W	X	183
Hummer Beck	Durham	NZ1825	54°37·4′	1°42·9′W	W	92
Hummerbeck Fm	Durham	NZ1825	54°37·4′	1°42·9′W	FM	92
Hummersea Fm	Red & Cl	NZ7219	54°33·9′	0°52·8′W	FM	94
Hummersea Scar	Red & Cl	NZ7220	54°34·4′	0°52·8′W	X	94
Hummersknott	Darl	NZ2614	54°31·5′	1°35·5′W	T	93
Humphreston Hall	Shrops	SJ8105	52°38·8′	2°16·4′W	X	127
Humphrey Head	Cumbr	SD3974	54°9·7′	2°55·6′W	X	96,97
Humphrey Head Point	Cumbr	SD3973	54°9·2′	2°55·6′W	X	96,97
Humphreys	Essex	TL5007	51°44·7′	0°10·8′E	X	167
Humphrey's Fm	Essex	TL6812	51°47·1′	0°26·5′E	FM	167
Humphrey's Fm	E Susx	TQ8512	50°52·9′	0°38·2′E	FM	199
Humphrey's Well	Aberd	NJ4709	57°10·4′	2°52·1′W	W	37
Humshaugh	Northum	NY9171	55°2·3′	2°8·0′W	T	87
Humster	Highld	ND3548	58°25·2′	3°6·3′W	X	12
Huna	Highld	ND3673	58°38·7′	3°5·7′W	X	7,12
Huna	N Eil	NF7172	57°37·3′	7°30·2′W	X	18
Huna Ho	Highld	ND3673	58°38·7′	3°5·7′W	X	7,12
Hunchaquoy	Orkney	HY2827	59°7·7′	3°15·0′W	X	6
Hunchar	Angus	NO4362	56°45·0′	2°55·5′W	X	44
Huncieoroft	Notts	SK5473	53°15·3′	1°11·0′W	X	120
Hunclett	Orkney	HY4127	59°7·8′	3°1·5′W	X	5,6
Huncoat	Lancs	SD7730	53°46·2′	2°20·5′W	T	103
Huncote	Leic	SP5197	52°34·3′	1°14·4′W	T	140
Huncote Grange	Leic	SK5100	52°36·0′	1°14·4′W	X	140
Hunda	Orkney	ND4396	58°51·2′	2°58·8′W	X	6,7
Hundah	Durham	NZ0212	54°30·4′	1°57·7′W	X	92
Hundalee	Scot Bord	NT6418	55°27·5′	2°33·7′W	T	80
Hundale Point	N Yks	TA0294	54°20·1′	0°25·5′W	X	101
Hundall	Derby	SK3877	53°17·6′	1°25·4′W	T	119
Hunda Reef	Orkney	ND4496	58°51·1′	2°57·8′W	X	6,7
Hunda Sound	Orkney	ND4496	58°51·1′	2°57·8′W	W	6,7
Hundatora Village	Devon	SX7478	50°35·5′	3°46·4′W	A	191
Hundavaig	N Eil	NF9785	57°45·4′	7°5·2′W	X	18
Hunday	Cumbr	NY0226	54°37·4′	3°30·7′W	X	89
Hundayfield	N Yks	SE4363	54°3·9′	1°20·2′W	X	99
Hunder Beck	Durham	NY9016	54°32·6′	2°8·9′W	W	91,92
Hunder Hill	Durham	NY9016	54°32·6′	2°8·9′W	X	91,92
Hunder Holm	Shetld	HU5163	60°21·1′	1°4·1′W	X	2,3
Hunder Rigg	Durham	NY9216	54°32·6′	2°7·0′W	X	91,92
Hunderthwaite	Durham	NY9821	54°35·3′	2°1·4′W	T	92
Hunderthwaite Moor	Durham	NY9219	54°34·2′	2°7·0′W	X	91,92
Hunderton	Heref	SO4938	52°2·5′	2°44·2′W	T	149
Hund Geo	Shetld	HU1461	60°20·2′	1°44·3′W	X	3
Hundhowe	Cumbr	SD4998	54°22·7′	2°46·7′W	X	97
Hundi Stack	Shetld	HZ1971	59°31·7′	1°39·4′W	X	4
Hundith Hill	Cumbr	NY1428	54°38·6′	3°19·5′W	X	89
Hundland	Orkney	HY2423	59°5·5′	3°19·1′W	X	6
Hundland	Orkney	HY3026	59°7·2′	3°12·9′W	X	6
Hundland	Orkney	HY5053	59°21·9′	2°52·3′W	X	5
Hundland Hill	Orkney	HY3027	59°7·7′	3°12·9′W	H	6
Hundleby	Lincs	TF3866	53°10·6′	0°4·3′E	T	122
Hundle Houses	Lincs	TF2453	53°3·8′	0°8·6′W	T	122
Hundleshope	Scot Bord	NT2336	55°36·9′	3°12·9′W	T	73
Hundleshope Burn	Scot Bord	NT2336	55°36·9′	3°12·9′W	W	73
Hundleshope Heights	Scot Bord	NT2533	55°35·3′	3°11·0′W	H	73
Hundleton	Pemb	SM9600	51°39·9′	4°56·6′W	T	157,158
Hundon	Suff	TL7348	52°6·4′	0°32·0′E	T	155
Hundon Great Lodge	Suff	TL7351	52°8·0′	0°32·1′E	X	155
Hundon Hall	Suff	TL7449	52°6·9′	0°32·9′E	X	155
Hundon Manor	Lincs	TA1102	53°30·4′	0°19·2′W	X	113
Hundred Acre Fm	Cambs	TF3810	52°40·4′	0°2·9′E	FM	131,142,143
Hundred Acre Fm	Cambs	TL5869	52°18·0′	0°19·4′E	FM	154
Hundred Acre Fm	Lincs	TF3335	52°54·0′	0°1·0′W	FM	131
Hundred Acre Fm	N Yks	SE6162	54°3·3′	1°3·7′W	FM	100
Hundred Acre Fm	Suff	TM7070	52°18·3′	0°30·0′E	FM	154
Hundred Acre Plantation	Norf	TG1624	52°46·4′	1°12·5′E	F	133
Hundred Acre Plantn	Durham	NZ2037	54°43·9′	1°40·9′W	F	93
Hundred Acres	Cambs	TL5877	52°22·3′	0°19·7′E	X	143
Hundred Acres	Hants	SU5911	50°54·0′	1°9·3′W	X	196
Hundred-acres	Staffs	SJ8929	52°51·7′	2°9·4′W	X	127
Hundred Acres	W Susx	TQ3336	51°6·7′	0°5·6′W	F	187
Hundred Acres Fm	Notts	SK5648	53°1·8′	1°9·5′W	FM	129
Hundred Acre Wood	Norf	TG1140	52°55·2′	1°8·7′E	F	133
Hundred Acre Wood	Notts	SK6182	53°20·1′	1°4·6′W	F	111,120
Hundred Barrow	Dorset	SY8493	50°44·4′	2°13·2′W	A	194
Hundred Dike	Norf	TG3816	52°41·6′	1°31·7′E	W	133,134
Hundred End	Lancs	SD4122	53°41·7′	2°53·2′W	T	102
Hundred Fen	Lincs	TF1731	52°52·1′	0°15·3′W	X	130
Hundred Fm	Cambs	TL4486	52°27·4′	0°7·6′E	FM	142,143
Hundred Foot Drain or New Bedford River	Cambs	TL4178	52°23·1′	0°4·7′E	W	142,143
Hundred Foot Drain or New Bedford River	Cambs	TL5088	52°28·4′	0°12·9′E	W	143
Hundred Foot Washes, The	Cambs	TL4178	52°23·1′	0°4·7′E	X	142,143
Hundred Foot Washes, The	Cambs	TL5292	52°30·5′	0°14·8′E	X	143
Hundred Ho Hotel	Worcs	SO7566	52°17·7′	2°21·6′W	X	138,150
Hundred Ho, The	E Susx	TQ5121	50°58·3′	0°9·4′E	X	199
Hundred House	Powys	SO1154	52°10·9′	3°17·7′W	T	148
Hundred House Fm	Shrops	SO6992	52°31·7′	2°27·0′W	FM	138
Hundred River	Suff	TM4460	52°11·3′	1°34·6′E	W	156
Hundred River	Suff	TM4887	52°25·7′	1°39·3′E	W	156
Hundreds Fm	Beds	SP9233	51°59·5′	0°39·2′W	FM	152,165
Hundreds Fm	Peterb	TF2407	52°39·0′	0°9·6′W	FM	142
Hundreds, The	Cumbr	NY4004	54°25·9′	2°55·1′W	X	90
Hundreds, The	Lincs	TF4962	53°8·3′	0°14·1′E	X	122
Hundred Stone	Somer	ST5517	50°57·3′	2°38·1′W	A	183
Hundred Stream	Norf	TG4621	52°44·1′	1°39·0′E	W	134
Hundred, The	Heref	SO5264	52°16·6′	2°41·8′W	T	137,138,149
Hundsetts	Shetld	HU1561	60°20·2′	1°43·2′W	X	3
Hunds Heelor	Shetld	HZ2071	59°31·7′	1°38·3′W	X	4
Hundwith Beck	N Yks	SE1549	53°56·5′	1°45·9′W	W	104
Hundy Mundy	Scot Bord	NT6637	55°37·8′	2°32·0′W	X	74
Hune Bay	Orkney	ND4388	58°46·8′	2°58·7′W	W	7
Huney	Shetld	HP6506	60°44·2′	0°48·0′W	X	1
Hungarian Hall	Suff	TM2853	52°7·9′	1°20·3′E	X	156
Hungarton	Leic	SK6907	52°39·6′	0°58·4′W	T	141
Hungary Hall	Cambs	TL2775	52°21·7′	0°7·7′W	X	142
Hungary Hall	Essex	TL8527	51°54·9′	0°41·8′E	X	168
Hungary Hall	Mil Key	SP8652	52°9·8′	0°44·2′W	X	152
Hungary Hill	Essex	TL8632	51°57·5′	0°42·8′E	X	168
Hungary Hill Fm	Staffs	SJ8507	52°39·9′	2°12·9′W	FM	127,139
Hungate	Leeds	SE3726	53°44·0′	1°25·9′W	T	104
Hungate	N Yks	SE2368	54°6·7′	1°38·5′W	X	99
Hungate End	Mil Key	SP7846	52°6·6′	0°51·3′W	X	152
Hunger Barn	Notts	SK7659	53°7·6′	0°51·4′W	X	120
Hungercut Hall	Suff	TM1054	52°8·9′	1°4·6′E	X	155
Hungerdowns	Essex	TM0729	51°55·5′	1°1·0′E	X	168,169
Hungerford	Hants	SU1612	50°54·7′	1°46·0′W	X	195
Hungerford	Shrops	SO5389	52°30·1′	2°41·1′W	T	137,138
Hungerford	Somer	ST0440	51°9·3′	3°22·0′W	T	181
Hungerford	W Berks	SU3368	51°24·8′	1°31·1′W	T	174
Hungerford	Win & Maid	SU8274	51°27·8′	0°48·8′W	T	175
Hungerford Common	W Berks	SU3467	51°24·3′	1°30·3′W	X	174
Hungerford Green	W Berks	SU5579	51°30·7′	1°12·1′W	T	174
Hungerford Ho	Shrops	SO5489	52°30·1′	2°40·3′W	X	137,138
Hungerford House Fm	Staffs	SJ7844	52°59·8′	2°19·3′W	FM	118
Hungerford Newtown	W Berks	SU3571	51°26·4′	1°29·4′W	T	174
Hunger Hatch	Kent	TQ9347	51°11·6′	0°46·1′E	X	189
Hunger Hill	Bolton	SD6706	53°33·2′	2°29·5′W	T	109
Hunger Hill	Cald	SE0115	53°38·1′	1°58·7′W	X	110
Hunger Hill	Ches	SJ5471	53°14·3′	2°40·9′W	X	117
Hungerhill	Cumbr	NY5117	54°33·0′	2°45·0′W	X	90
Hunger Hill	Darl	NZ3312	54°30·4′	1°29·0′W	X	93
Hunger Hill	Derby	SK1752	53°4·1′	1°44·4′W	X	119
Hunger Hill	Derby	SK3267	53°12·2′	1°30·8′W	X	119
Hunger Hill	Dorset	ST8023	51°0·6′	2°16·7′W	H	183
Hunger Hill	Lancs	SD5311	53°35·9′	2°42·2′W	T	108
Hunger Hill	Lincs	TF4565	53°10·0′	0°10·6′E	X	122
Hunger Hill	Notts	SK6246	53°0·7′	1°4·1′W	X	129
Hunger Hill	Shrops	SJ4706	52°39·2′	2°46·6′W	X	126
Hunger Hill	Somer	ST6827	51°2·7′	2°27·0′W	X	183
Hunger Hill	Staffs	SK0918	52°45·8′	1°51·6′W	X	128
Hunger Hill	Warw	SP1465	52°17·2′	1°47·3′W	X	151
Hunger Hill Fm	Dorset	ST8024	51°1·1′	2°16·7′W	FM	183
Hungerhill Fm	W Susx	TQ1120	50°58·3′	0°24·8′W	FM	198
Hunger Hills	Cumbr	SD5781	54°13·6′	2°39·2′W	X	97
Hungerhills	E Yorks	TA1633	53°47·1′	0°13·9′W	X	107
Hunger Hills	Leeds	SE2338	53°50·5′	1°38·6′W	X	104
Hungerhill Wood	Beds	SP9629	51°57·3′	0°35·8′W	F	165
Hunger Pill	Monm	ST5490	51°36·7′	2°39·5′W	W	162,172
Hungers Green	Suff	TM2165	52°14·5′	1°14·6′E	X	156
Hungershall Park	Kent	TQ5738	51°7·4′	0°15·0′E	T	188
Hungerstone	Heref	SO4435	52°0·9′	2°48·6′W	T	149,161
Hungerton	Lincs	SK8730	52°51·9′	0°42·1′W	T	130
Hungladder	Highld	NG3871	57°39·4′	6°23·1′W	T	23
Hungram Gorse	Lincs	TF1974	53°15·2′	0°12·6′W	X	122
Hungram Ho	Lincs	TF1974	53°15·2′	0°12·6′W	X	122
Hungreyhatton	Shrops	SJ6726	52°50·1′	2°29·0′W	T	127
Hungriff Hall	Suff	TL7951	52°7·9′	0°37·3′E	X	155
Hungriggs	Cumbr	NY6921	54°35·2′	2°28·4′W	X	91
Hungrill	Lancs	SD7750	53°57·0′	2°20·6′W	X	103
Hungry Bentley Village	Derby	SK1738	52°56·6′	1°44·4′W	A	128
Hungry Green	Powys	SO1153	52°10·3′	3°17·7′W	X	148
Hungry Hall	Essex	TL8018	51°50·1′	0°37·2′E	X	168
Hungry Hill	Cambs	TL0866	52°17·1′	0°24·6′W	X	153
Hungry Hill	Cambs	TL5957	52°11·5′	0°20·0′E	X	154
Hungry Hill	Dorset	SY5397	50°46·5′	2°39·6′W	X	194
Hungryhill	E Ayr	NS4938	55°37·0′	4°23·4′W	X	70
Hungry Hill	E Ayr	NS5812	55°23·1′	4°14·1′W	X	71

Hungry Hill	Norf	TF8213	52°41·3'	0°42·0'E	X	132
Hungry Hill	Norf	TF9518	52°43·7'	0°53·7'E	X	132
Hungry Hill	Norf	TG2539	52°54·3'	1°21·2'E	X	133
Hungry Hill	Norf	TM0490	52°28·4'	1°0·6'E	X	144
Hungry Hill	Norf	TM3693	52°29·3'	1°29·0'E	X	134
Hungry Hill	Scot Bord	NT4023	55°30·1'	2°56·6'W	X	73
Hungry Hill	Shrops	SO7075	52°22·6'	2°26·0'W	X	138
Hungry Hill	Surrey	SU8449	51°14·3'	0°47·4'W	X	186
Hungry Hill	Surrey	TQ0555	51°17·3'	0°29·3'W	X	187
Hungryhills	Aberd	NJ6858	57°36·9'	2°31·7'W	X	29
Hungryhills	Aberd	NJ7461	57°38·6'	2°25·7'W	X	29
Hungryhill Wood	Oxon	SU7393	51°38·1'	0°56·3'W	F	175
Hungry Law	Northum	NT7406	55°21·1'	2°24·2'W	H	80
Hungry Lodge	Hants	SU6950	51°14·9'	1°0·3'W	X	186
Hungry Snout	E Loth	NT6663	55°51·8'	2°32·2'W	X	67
Hunish	Highld	NG4076	57°42·2'	6°21·4'W	X	23
Hunkington	Shrops	SJ5613	52°43·0'	2°38·7'W	X	126
Hunley	Cumbr	NY4564	54°58·3'	2°51·1'W	X	86
Hunmanby	N Yks	TA0977	54°10·9'	0°19·4'W	T	101
Hunmanby Gap	N Yks	TA1277	54°10·8'	0°16·6'W	X	101
Hunmanby Grange	N Yks	TA0775	54°9·8'	0°21·3'W	X	101
Hunmanby Moor	N Yks	TA1177	54°10·8'	0°17·5'W	T	101
Hunmanby Sands	N Yks	TA1278	54°11·4'	0°16·6'W	X	101
Hunnacott	Devon	SS6030	51°3·4'	3°59·5'W	X	180
Hunnacott	Devon	SS6440	51°8·8'	3°56·3'W	X	180
Hunndagro	N Eil	NB4042	58°17·6'	6°25·7'W	W	8
Hunningham	Warw	SP3768	52°18·8'	1°27·0'W	T	151
Hunningham Hill	Warw	SP3867	52°18·2'	1°26·2'W	T	151
Hunnington	Worcs	SO9681	52°25·9'	2°3·1'W	T	139
Hunnington Ho	Warw	SP3967	52°18·2'	1°25·3'W	X	151
Hunniwins Fm	Devon	SS7132	51°4·6'	3°50·1'W	FM	180
Hunny Hill	I of W	SZ4989	50°42·1'	1°18·0'W	T	196
Hunridge Manor	Bucks	SP9301	51°42·2'	0°38·9'W	X	165
Hunsbury Hill	Northnts	SP7358	52°13·2'	0°55·5'W	X	152
Hunscote	Warw	SP2454	52°11·3'	1°38·5'W	X	151
Hunscott Fm	Devon	SX3999	50°46·3'	4°16·6'W	FM	190
Hunsdale Fm	E Yorks	SE9230	53°45·7'	0°35·8'W	FM	106
Hunsdon	Herts	TL4114	51°48·6'	0°3·1'E	T	167
Hunsdonbury	Herts	TL4113	51°48·1'	0°3·1'E	T	167
Hunsdon Fm	Devon	SX6155	50°22·9'	3°56·9'W	FM	202
Hunsdon Ho	Herts	TL4112	51°47·6'	0°3·1'E	X	167
Hunsdon Lodge Fm	Herts	TL4214	51°48·6'	0°4·0'E	FM	167
Hunshaw Fm	Devon	SS4915	50°55·1'	4°8·5'W	FM	180
Hunshelf Bank	Sheff	SK2898	53°28·9'	1°34·3'W	X	110
Hunshelf Hall	Barns	SK2799	53°29·5'	1°35·2'W	X	110
Hunsingore	N Yks	SE4253	53°58·5'	1°21·2'W	T	105
Hunslet	Leeds	SE3031	53°46·7'	1°32·3'W	T	104
Hunslet Carr	Leeds	SE3030	53°46·2'	1°32·3'W	T	104
Hunsley Ho	E Yorks	SE9535	53°48·4'	0°33·0'W	X	106
Hunsonby	Cumbr	NY5835	54°42·7'	2°38·7'W	T	91
Hunspow	Highld	ND2172	58°38·0'	3°21·2'W	X	7,12
Hunsta	Shetld	HP5802	60°42·1'	0°55·8'W	X	1
Hunstanton	Norf	TF6740	52°56·1'	0°29·5'E	T	132
Hunstanton Park	Norf	TF6941	52°56·6'	0°31·3'E	X	132
Hunstanworth	Durham	NY9449	54°50·4'	2°5·2'W	T	87
Hunstanworth Moor	Durham	NY9246	54°48·8'	2°7·0'W	X	87
Hunster Grange Fm	Donc	SK6296	53°27·7'	1°3·6'W	FM	111
Hunsterson	Ches	SJ6946	53°0·9'	2°27·3'W	T	118
Hunston	Suff	TL9768	52°16·7'	0°53·7'E	T	155
Hunston	W Susx	SU8601	50°48·4'	0°46·4'W	T	197
Hunstone	Devon	SS7031	51°4·1'	3°50·9'W	X	180
Hunston Green	Suff	TL9866	52°15·6'	0°54·5'E	T	155
Hunston House Fm	Lincs	TF3853	53°3·6'	0°4·0'E	FM	122
Hunston Lodge	Suff	TL9867	52°16·2'	0°54·5'E	X	155
Hunstrete	Bath & NE Somer	ST6462	51°21·6'	2°30·6'W	T	172
Hunstrete Ho(Hotel)	Bath & NE Somer	ST6461	51°21·1'	2°30·6'W	X	172
Hunsworth	Kirk	SE1827	53°44·6'	1°43·2'W	T	104
Hunsworth Lodge Fm	Kirk	SE1927	53°44·6'	1°42·3'W	FM	104
Huntacott	Devon	SS7014	50°54·9'	3°50·6'W	X	180
Huntacott Water	Devon	SS7216	50°56·0'	3°48·9'W	W	180
Huntbourn	Hants	SU6213	50°55·0'	1°6·7'W	X	196
Huntbourne Fm	Kent	TQ9035	51°5·2'	0°43·2'E	FM	189
Hunt Cliff	Red & Cl	NZ6921	54°35·0'	0°55·5'W	X	94
Hunt Court Fm	Glos	SO9017	51°51·3'	2°8·3'W	FM	163
Hunt End	Worcs	SP0364	52°16·7'	1°57·0'W	T	150
Huntenhull Green	Wilts	ST8247	51°13·5'	2°15·1'W	T	183
Hunter Banks	N Yks	NZ4508	54°28·2'	1°17·9'W	X	93
Hunter Bark	N Yks	SD8361	54°2·9'	2°15·2'W	X	98
Huntercombe End	Oxon	SU6887	51°34·9'	1°0·7'W	T	175
Huntercombe Manor	Bucks	SU9380	51°30·9'	0°39·2'W	X	175
Huntercrook	Northum	NY7665	54°59·0'	2°22·1'W	X	86,87
Hunterhall	Pth & Kin	NO1920	56°22·2'	3°18·2'W	X	53,58
Hunterheck	D & G	NT1004	55°19·6'	3°24·7'W	X	78
Hunterheck Hill	D & G	NT1105	55°20·1'	3°23·8'W	H	78
Hunterheugh Crags	Northum	NU1116	55°26·5'	1°49·1'W	H	81
Hunter Hill	Cald	SE0529	53°45·7'	1°55·0'W	X	104
Hunter Hill	N Yks	NZ5110	54°29·2'	1°12·3'W	X	93
Hunter Hill	Scot Bord	NT2023	55°29·9'	3°15·6'W	H	73
Hunter Hill Fm	Brad	SE0737	53°50·0'	1°53·2'W	FM	104
Hunter Hill Fm	Red & Cl	NZ6114	54°31·3'	1°3·0'W	FM	94
Hunter Ho	D & G	NY0581	55°7·1'	3°28·9'W	X	78
Hunter Ho	Durham	NY9220	54°34·8'	2°7·0'W	X	91,92
Hunter Ho	Durham	NZ0052	54°52·0'	1°59·6'W	X	87
Hunter Howe	N Yks	SE9897	54°21·8'	0°29·1'W	A	94,101
Hunterlee Hill	Northum	NY9290	55°12·5'	2°7·1'W	H	80
Hunterlees	S Lanak	NS7347	55°42·2'	4°0·8'W	X	64
Hunter Oak	Northum	NY7957	54°54·7'	2°19·2'W	X	86,87
Hunters Br	Dorset	ST6611	50°54·1'	2°28·6'W	X	194
Hunter's Burgh	E Susx	TQ5403	50°48·6'	0°11·5'E	X	199
Hunter's Burgh (Long Barrow)	E Susx	TQ5403	50°48·6'	0°11·5'E	A	199
Hunter's Burn	Northum	NY7293	55°14·1'	2°26·0'W	W	80
Hunter's Clough	Lancs	SD5749	53°56·4'	2°38·9'W	X	102
Hunter's Cott	Cumbr	NY1849	54°50·0'	3°16·2'W	X	85
Hunters Fm	E Susx	TQ4426	51°1·1'	0°3·6'E	FM	187,198
Hunter's Fm	E Susx	TQ7021	50°58·0'	0°25·7'E	FM	199
Hunters Forstal	Kent	TR1866	51°21·3'	1°8·3'E	T	179
Hunter's Gate	D & G	NY1574	55°3·4'	3°19·4'W	X	85
Hunters Geo	Orkney	HY6715	59°1·5'	2°34·0'W	X	5
Hunters Hall	N Som	ST5164	51°22·6'	2°41·9'W	X	172,182
Huntershall	Scot Bord	NT4758	55°49·0'	2°50·3'W	X	66,73
Huntershall	Scot Bord	NT7332	55°35·1'	2°25·3'W	X	74
Hunters Hall	S Glos	ST7970	51°26·0'	2°17·7'W	X	172
Hunter's Hall Fm	Essex	TL4304	51°43·2'	0°4·6'E	FM	167
Hunter's Hall Fm	E Susx	TQ6534	51°5·1'	0°21·7'E	FM	188
Huntershield	Northum	NY7860	54°56·3'	2°20·2'W	X	86,87
Hunter's Hill	Aberd	NO6676	56°52·7'	2°33·0'W	H	45
Hunters Hill	Angus	NO3946	56°36·4'	2°59·2'W	H	54
Hunter's Hill	N Yks	SE4693	54°20·1'	1°17·1'W	X	100
Hunters Hill Fm	Notts	SK6446	53°0·7'	1°2·4'W	FM	129
Hunter's Hill Fm	N Yks	SE2391	54°19·1'	1°38·4'W	FM	99
Hunters Hill Fm	N Yks	SE3299	54°23·4'	1°30·0'W	FM	99
Hunters Hole	N Yks	SD9181	54°13·7'	2°7·9'W	W	98
Hunter's Holme	Cumbr	NY4267	54°59·9'	2°54·0'W	X	85
Hunter's Inn	Devon	SS6548	51°13·2'	3°55·6'W	X	180
Hunters Inn Hill	Hants	SU3511	50°54·1'	1°29·8'W	X	196
Hunter's Lodge	Aberd	NO6097	57°4·0'	2°39·1'W	X	37,45
Hunters Lodge	N Yks	SE4760	54°2·3'	1°16·5'W	X	100
Hunter's Lodge	Somer	ST2114	50°55·4'	3°7·1'W	X	193
Hunter's Lodge	Somer	ST4030	51°4·2'	2°51·0'W	X	182
Hunter's Lodge Fm	Dorset	ST4905	50°50·8'	2°43·1'W	FM	193,194
Hunter's Meadow	E Ayr	NS5045	55°40·8'	4°22·7'W	X	64
Hunters Moon	Hants	SU8634	51°6·2'	0°45·9'W	X	186
Hunters Oak	Lancs	SD8134	53°48·4'	2°16·9'W	X	103
Hunter's Path	Angus	NO5741	56°33·8'	2°41·5'W	X	54
Hunter's Pool Fm	Ches	SJ8877	53°17·6'	2°10·4'W	FM	118
Hunter's Quay	Arg & Bt	NS1879	55°58·4'	4°54·6'W	T	63
Huntersrace Fm	W Susx	SU8407	50°51·6'	0°48·0'W	FM	197
Hunter's Scar	N Yks	NZ5810	54°29·2'	1°5·9'W	X	93
Hunters Stone	Devon	SX6863	50°27·4'	3°51·2'W	X	202
Hunters Stone	N Yks	SD9976	54°11·0'	2°0·5'W	X	98
Hunter's Stones	N Yks	SE2151	53°57·5'	1°40·4'W	X	104
Hunterston	E Ayr	NS4621	55°27·8'	4°25·7'W	X	70
Hunterston Ho	N Ayr	NS1951	55°43·4'	4°52·5'W	X	63
Hunterston Sands	N Ayr	NS1852	55°43·9'	4°53·5'W	X	63
Hunter's Tor	Devon	SX7289	50°41·4'	3°48·4'W	X	191
Hunter's Tor	Devon	SX7682	50°37·7'	3°44·8'W	H	191
Hunters' Well	Essex	TL5436	52°0·3'	0°15·0'E	W	154
Huntfield	D & G	NX8686	55°9·6'	3°46·9'W	X	78
Huntfield	S Lanak	NT0140	55°38·9'	3°34·0'W	X	72
Huntford	Scot Bord	NT6808	55°22·1'	2°29·9'W	X	80
Hunt Green Fm	Worcs	SO8561	52°15·1'	2°12·8'W	FM	150
Hunt Hall	Durham	NY8530	54°40·1'	2°13·5'W	X	91,92
Hunthall	Pth & Kin	NN9605	56°13·8'	3°40·2'W	X	58
Hunthall	Scot Bord	NT7847	55°43·2'	2°20·6'W	X	74
Hunt Hall Fm	Warw	SP1450	52°9·1'	1°47·3'W	FM	151
Hunthall Hill	Scot Bord	NT7711	55°23·8'	2°21·4'W	H	80
Huntham	Somer	ST3325	51°1·5'	2°56·9'W	T	193
Hunthayes Fm	Devon	ST1202	50°48·9'	3°14·6'W	FM	192,193
Hunthay Fm	Devon	SY2898	50°46·9'	3°0·9'W	FM	193
Hunt Hill	Aberd	NO3386	56°57·9'	3°5·7'W	X	44
Hunt Hill	Angus	NO2671	56°49·7'	3°12·3'W	H	44
Hunt Hill	Angus	NO3780	56°54·7'	3°1·6'W	H	44
Hunt Hill	Glos	SO7314	51°49·7'	2°23·1'W	X	162
Hunt Hill	Moray	NJ2346	57°30·1'	3°12·6'W	H	28
Hunt Hill	Moray	NJ2754	57°34·5'	3°12·8'W	X	28
Hunthill	Scot Bord	NT6619	55°28·1'	2°31·8'W	X	80
Hunt Hill Fm	E Yorks	TA0850	53°56·3'	0°20·9'W	FM	107
Hunthill Lodge	Angus	NO4771	56°49·9'	2°51·7'W	X	44
Hunthills	D & G	NX9987	55°10·3'	3°34·7'W	X	78
Hunthill Wood	Corn	SS2408	50°50·9'	4°29·6'W	F	190
Hunt Ho	N Yks	SD9896	54°21·8'	2°1·4'W	X	98
Hunt Ho	N Yks	SE5576	54°10·9'	1°9·0'W	X	100
Hunt Ho	N Yks	SE8198	54°22·5'	0°44·8'W	X	94,100
Hunt Ho	Staffs	SJ9559	53°7·9'	2°4·1'W	X	118
Hunt House Fm	Worcs	SO6970	52°19·9'	2°26·9'W	FM	138
Hunthouse Fms	Heref	SO3326	51°55·9'	2°58·1'W	FM	161
Hunting Butts	Glos	SO9424	51°55·1'	2°4·8'W	X	163
Huntingdon	Cambs	TL2472	52°20·2'	0°10·4'W	T	153
Huntingdon Cross	Devon	SX6666	50°28·9'	3°53·0'W	A	202
Huntingdon Hall	Lancs	SD6638	53°50·5'	2°30·6'W	A	103
Huntingdon Warren	Devon	SX6567	50°29·5'	3°53·8'W	X	202
Huntingdrop Fm	Worcs	SO9262	52°15·6'	2°6·6'W	FM	150
Huntingfaulds	Angus	NO4039	56°32·6'	2°58·1'W	X	54
Huntingfield	Kent	TQ9755	51°15·8'	0°49·8'E	X	178
Huntingfield	Suff	TM3374	52°19·1'	1°25·5'E	T	156
Huntingfield Hall	Norf	TF9309	52°38·9'	0°51·6'E	X	144
Huntingford	Dorset	ST8029	51°3·8'	2°16·7'W	T	183
Huntingford	Glos	ST7193	51°38·3'	2°24·8'W	T	162,172
Hunting Hall	Northum	NU0241	55°40·0'	1°57·7'W	X	75
Hunting Hill	Highld	NH8180	57°47·9'	3°59·7'W	X	21
Hunting Hill	Lancs	SD4970	54°7·6'	2°46·4'W	H	97
Hunting Stile	Cumbr	NY3306	54°26·9'	3°1·6'W	X	90
Huntington	Ches	SJ4164	53°10·4'	2°52·6'W	T	117
Huntington	Ches	SJ4264	53°10·4'	2°51·7'W	T	117
Huntington	E Loth	NT4874	55°57·6'	2°49·5'W	T	66
Huntington	Heref	SO2553	52°10·4'	3°5·4'W	T	148
Huntington	Heref	SO4841	52°4·1'	2°45·1'W	T	148,149,161
Huntington	Scot Bord	NT5349	55°44·2'	2°44·5'W	X	73
Huntington	Shrops	SO5371	52°20·3'	2°41·0'W	X	137,138
Huntington	Staffs	SJ9712	52°42·6'	2°2·3'W	T	127
Huntington	Wrekin	SJ6507	52°39·8'	2°30·6'W	T	127
Huntington	York	SE6155	53°59·5'	1°3·8'W	T	105
Huntington	York	SE6356	54°0·0'	1°1·9'W	X	105,106
Huntington Castle	Heref	SO2453	52°10·4'	3°6·3'W	A	148
Huntington Hall	Ches	SJ4262	53°9·4'	2°51·6'W	X	117
Huntington Park	Heref	SO2653	52°10·5'	3°4·5'W	X	148
Huntingtower	Pth & Kin	NO0724	56°24·2'	3°30·0'W	T	52,53,58
Huntingtower Castle	Pth & Kin	NO0825	56°24·8'	3°29·0'W	A	52,53,58
Huntingtower Haugh	Pth & Kin	NO0725	56°24·7'	3°30·0'W	T	52,53,58
Huntland	Devon	SS9210	50°53·0'	3°31·7'W	X	192
Huntlands	Heref	SO7155	52°11·8'	2°25·1'W	X	149
Huntlaw	E Loth	NT4367	55°53·8'	2°54·3'W	X	66
Huntlaw	Northum	NZ0975	55°4·4'	1°51·1'W	X	88
Hunt Law	Scot Bord	NT1426	55°31·5'	3°21·3'W	H	72
Hunt Law	Scot Bord	NT1834	55°35·8'	3°17·6'W	H	72
Hunt Law	Scot Bord	NT3654	55°46·8'	3°0·8'W	X	66,73
Hunt Law	Scot Bord	NT4107	55°21·5'	2°55·4'W	H	79
Huntlaw	Scot Bord	NT5321	55°29·1'	2°44·2'W	X	73
Hunt Law	Scot Bord	NT5758	55°49·1'	2°40·7'W	X	67,73,74
Hunt Law	S Lanak	NS8716	55°25·7'	3°46·7'W	H	71,78
Huntlaw Burn	Scot Bord	NT5322	55°29·6'	2°44·2'W	W	73
Huntley	Glos	SO7219	51°52·4'	2°24·0'W	T	162
Huntley	Staffs	SK0041	52°58·2'	1°59·6'W	T	119,128
Huntley Hill	Glos	SO7019	51°52·4'	2°25·8'W	H	162
Huntley Manor	Glos	SO7120	51°52·9'	2°24·9'W	X	162
Huntley's Cave	Highld	NJ0435	57°24·0'	3°35·4'W	X	27
Huntley's Fm	Heref	SO6534	52°0·4'	2°30·2'W	FM	149
Huntly	Aberd	NJ5240	57°27·1'	2°47·5'W	T	29
Huntlybank	S Lanak	NS9144	55°40·9'	3°43·6'W	X	71,72
Huntly Burn	Pth & Kin	NO2928	56°26·6'	3°8·7'W	W	53,59
Huntlyburn Ho	Scot Bord	NT5233	55°35·5'	2°45·3'W	X	73
Huntly Cot	Midlo	NT3052	55°45·6'	3°6·5'W	X	66,73
Huntly Cot Hills	Midlo	NT3151	55°45·1'	3°5·5'W	X	66,73
Huntly Covert	Scot Bord	NT4223	55°30·1'	2°54·7'W	F	73
Huntly Fm	Pth & Kin	NO3231	56°28·2'	3°5·8'W	FM	53
Huntly Hall	Pth & Kin	NO0905	56°14·0'	3°27·6'W	X	58
Huntlyhill	Angus	NO6263	56°45·7'	2°36·8'W	X	45
Huntly Hill	Scot Bord	NT4224	55°30·6'	2°54·7'W	H	73
Huntlyhill	S Lanak	NS9144	55°40·9'	3°43·6'W	X	71,72
Huntly Lodge Farm	Aberd	NJ5341	57°27·7'	2°46·5'W	FM	29
Huntly Rig	Scot Bord	NT4223	55°30·1'	2°54·7'W	H	73
Huntly's Cave	Highld	NJ0232	57°22·3'	3°37·3'W	X	27,36
Huntlywood	Scot Bord	NT6143	55°41·0'	2°36·8'W	X	74
Hunton	Hants	SU4839	51°9·1'	1°18·4'W	T	185
Hunton	Kent	TQ7149	51°13·1'	0°27·3'E	T	188
Hunton	N Yks	SE1892	54°19·6'	1°43·0'W	T	99
Hunton	Orkney	HY6527	59°8·0'	2°36·2'W	X	5
Hunton Br	Heref	SO3358	52°13·2'	2°58·5'W	X	148,149
Hunton Bridge	Herts	TL0800	51°41·5'	0°25·9'W	T	166
Hunton Clump	N Yks	SE1994	54°20·7'	1°42·0'W	X	99
Hunton Court	Kent	TQ7249	51°13·1'	0°28·2'E	X	188
Hunton Down Fm	Hants	SU4941	51°10·2'	1°17·6'W	FM	185
Hunton Fm	Heref	SO3358	52°13·2'	2°58·5'W	FM	148,149
Hunton Grange Fm	Hants	SU4840	51°9·7'	1°18·4'W	FM	185
Hunton Mill	N Yks	SE2092	54°19·6'	1°41·1'W	X	99
Hunt Pot	N Yks	SD8274	54°9·9'	2°16·1'W	X	98
Huntrods	Northum	NY8452	54°52·0'	2°14·5'W	X	86,87
Huntroyde	Lancs	SD7835	53°48·9'	2°19·6'W	X	103
Huntroyde Demesne	Lancs	SD7834	53°48·4'	2°19·6'W	X	103
Huntsbank Fm	Ches	SJ6853	53°4·6'	2°28·3'W	FM	118
Hunt's Bridge	Lincs	SK8466	53°11·3'	0°44·2'W	X	121
Huntscarth	Orkney	HY3317	59°2·4'	3°9·6'W	X	6
Hunt's Corner	Norf	TM0588	52°27·3'	1°1·4'E	T	144
Huntscott	Somer	SS9243	51°10·8'	3°32·3'W	T	181
Hunt's Cross	Liv	SJ4284	53°21·2'	2°51·9'W	T	108
Huntsdown	Devon	SX3789	50°40·9'	4°18·1'W	X	190
Hunt's Down	Wilts	SU0729	51°3·8'	1°53·6'W	X	184
Hunt's Fm	Essex	TL7028	51°55·7'	0°28·8'E	FM	167
Hunts Fm	Essex	TQ7095	51°37·9'	0°27·8'E	FM	167
Hunts Fm	E Susx	TQ5136	51°6·4'	0°9·8'E	FM	188
Hunts Fm	Hants	SU3525	51°1·6'	1°29·7'W	FM	185
Hunt's Fm	Oxon	SU7480	51°31·1'	0°55·6'W	FM	175
Hunts Fm	Swan	SS5687	51°34·0'	4°4·3'W	FM	159
Hunt's Green	Bucks	SP8903	51°43·3'	0°42·3'W	T	165
Hunts Green	Warw	SP1897	52°34·5'	1°43·7'W	T	139
Hunt's Green	W Berks	SU4370	51°25·9'	1°22·5'W	T	174
Huntsgreen Fm	W Berks	SU4369	51°25·3'	1°22·5'W	FM	174
Hunt's Hall	Essex	TL8432	51°57·6'	0°41·1'E	X	168
Hunt's Hall Fm	Wilts	ST8561	51°21·1'	2°12·5'W	FM	173
Huntsham	Devon	ST0020	50°58·5'	3°25·1'W	T	181
Huntsham Barton	Devon	ST0021	50°59·0'	3°25·1'W	X	181
Huntsham Castle	Devon	SS9917	50°56·9'	3°25·9'W	X	181
Huntsham Castle (Settlement)	Devon	SS9917	50°56·9'	3°25·9'W	A	181
Huntsham Court	Heref	SO5617	51°51·2'	2°37·9'W	X	162
Huntsham Fm	York	SE5452	53°57·9'	1°10·2'W	FM	105
Huntsham Hill	Heref	SO5616	51°50·7'	2°37·9'W	H	162
Huntsham Wood	Devon	ST0018	50°57·4'	3°25·0'W	F	181
Huntshaw	Devon	SS5022	50°58·9'	4°7·8'W	T	180
Huntshaw	Scot Bord	NT5739	55°38·8'	2°40·6'W	X	73,74
Huntshaw Cross	Devon	SS5322	50°59·0'	4°5·3'W	X	180
Huntshaw Hill	Scot Bord	NT5640	55°39·3'	2°41·5'W	X	73
Huntshaw Mill Bridge	Devon	SS4922	50°58·9'	4°8·7'W	X	180
Huntshaw Water	Devon	SS5023	50°59·4'	4°7·9'W	T	180
Huntshield Ford	Durham	NY8838	54°44·5'	2°10·8'W	X	91,92
Hunt's Hill	Bucks	SU8496	51°39·6'	0°46·7'W	T	165
Hunts Holm	Shetld	HP6300	60°41·0'	0°50·3'W	X	1
Huntsland	W Susx	TQ3337	51°7·2'	0°5·6'W	X	187
Huntsland Fm	Devon	SX9595	50°44·9'	3°28·9'W	FM	192
Hunt's Lane	Leic	SK4503	52°37·6'	1°19·7'W	T	140
Huntsman's Fm	Essex	TL8244	52°4·1'	0°39·7'E	FM	155
Huntsman's Inn	Cumbr	NY4778	55°5·9'	2°49·4'W	X	86
Huntsman's Leap	Pemb	SM7911	51°45·5'	5°11·8'W	X	157
Huntsman's Leap	Pemb	SR9593	51°36·2'	4°57·2'W	X	158
Huntsmill Fm	Bucks	SP6335	52°0·8'	1°4·5'W	FM	152
Hunt's Moat	Suff	TL8851	52°7·7'	0°45·2'E	A	155
Huntsmoor Hill	Hants	SU5362	51°21·5'	1°13·9'W	H	174
Huntsmoor Park	Bucks	TQ0481	51°31·3'	0°29·7'W	X	176
Hunts Park Fm	Suff	TL6649	52°7·1'	0°25·9'E	FM	154
Huntspill	Somer	ST3145	51°12·2'	2°58·9'W	T	182
Huntspill Level	Somer	ST3245	51°12·2'	2°58·0'W	X	182
Huntspill Moor	Somer	ST3544	51°11·7'	2°55·4'W	X	182
Huntspill River	Somer	ST3443	51°11·2'	2°56·3'W	W	182
Huntstile	Somer	ST2633	51°5·7'	3°3·0'W	T	182
Huntstreet	Kent	TR0948	51°11·8'	0°59·9'E	X	179,189
Hunt's Wood	Bucks	SU9183	51°32·5'	0°40·9'W	F	175
Hunt's Wood	Essex	TL7838	52°0·9'	0°36·0'E	F	155
Hunt's Wood	Kent	TQ9634	51°4·5'	0°48·3'E	F	189
Hunts Wood Fm	Bucks	SU9484	51°33·1'	0°38·3'W	FM	175
Huntwell	Northum	NY8447	54°49·3'	2°14·5'W	X	86,87
Huntwick Grange Fm	Wakf	SE4019	53°40·2'	1°23·3'W	FM	111
Huntworth	N Yks	SD8065	54°5·1'	2°17·9'W	X	98
Huntworth	Somer	ST3134	51°6·3'	2°58·7'W	T	182
Hunwellspring Plantn	Suff	TL8478	52°22·4'	0°42·6'E	F	144
Hunwick	Durham	NZ1932	54°41·2'	1°41·9'W	T	92
Hunworth	Norf	TG0635	52°52·6'	1°4·1'E	T	133
Hùpridh	N Eil	NB4637	58°15·2'	6°19·3'W	X	8

Hurbuck Cottages	Durham	NZ1348	54°49·8'	1°47·4'W	X	88
Hurcot Hill	Somer	ST5030	51°4·3'	2°42·4'W	H	182,183
Hurcott	Somer	ST3916	50°56·6'	2°51·7'W	T	193
Hurcott	Somer	ST5029	51°3·7'	2°42·4'W	T	183
Hurcott	Worcs	SO8577	52°23·7'	2°12·8'W	T	139
Hurcott Wood	Worcs	SO8578	52°24·2'	2°12·8'W	F	139
Hurda Field	Shetld	HU3469	60°24·5'	1°22·5'W	H	2,3
Hurdcott	Wilts	SU1733	51°6·0'	1°45·0'W	T	184
Hurdcott Fm	Wilts	SU1534	51°6·5'	1°46·8'W	FM	184
Hurdcott Ho	Wilts	SU0431	51°4·9'	1°56·2'W	X	184
Hurden Hall	Staffs	SJ9039	52°57·1'	2°8·5'W	X	127
Hurdiback	Shetld	HU1760	60°19·7'	1°41·0'W	X	3
Hurdi Field	Shetld	HU2656	60°17·5'	1°31·3'W	H	3
Hurdiss Fm	Warw	SP3758	52°13·4'	1°27·1'W	FM	151
Hurdlaw	Scot Bord	NT6650	55°44·8'	2°32·1'W	X	67,74
Hurd Law	Scot Bord	NT6651	55°45·3'	2°32·1'W	X	67,74
Hurdlesgrove	Bucks	SP8022	51°53·7'	0°49·8'W	X	165
Hurdletree Ho	Lincs	TF3622	52°46·9'	0°1·4'E	X	131
Hurdley	Powys	SO2994	52°32·6'	3°2·4'W	T	137
Hurd Low	Derby	SK1381	53°19·8'	1°47·9'W	X	110
Hurdlow	Staffs	SK0260	53°8·5'	1°57·8'W	X	119
Hurdlow Town	Derby	SK1166	53°11·7'	1°49·7'W	X	119
Hurdon Down	Corn	SX3482	50°37·1'	4°20·4'W	X	201
Hurdon Fm	Corn	SX3382	50°37·1'	4°21·3'W	FM	201
Hurds	Shetld	HU2857	60°18·0'	1°29·1'W	X	3
Hurdsfield	Ches	SJ9274	53°16·0'	2°6·8'W	T	118
Hurd, The	Shetld	HU4452	60°15·3'	1°11·8'W	X	3
Hurdwick Farm	Devon	SX4775	50°33·5'	4°9·2'W	FM	191,201
Hurgill	N Yks	NZ1601	54°24·5'	1°44·8'W	T	92
Hurgin	Shrops	SO2379	52°24·5'	3°7·5'W	H	137,148
Hurker	Scot Bord	NT8770	55°55·6'	2°12·0'W	X	67
Hurkisgarth	Orkney	HY2517	59°2·3'	3°17·9'W	X	6
Hurkledale	D & G	NY1366	54°59·1'	3°21·1'W	X	85
Hurkledown Hill	D & G	NX7372	55°1·8'	3°58·8'W	X	77,84
Hurkle Rig	Scot Bord	NT3616	55°26·3'	3°0·3'W	H	79
Hurklewinter Knowe	Scot Bord	NY5590	55°12·4'	2°42·0'W	X	80
Hurkling Stones	Derby	SK2087	53°23·0'	1°41·5'W	X	110
Hurlands	Surrey	SU9447	51°13·1'	0°38·9'W	X	186
Hurlands	Surrey	TQ0034	51°6·0'	0°33·9'W	X	186
Hurlawcrook Fm	S Lanak	NS6451	55°44·3'	4°9·5'W	FM	64
Hurlbarrow	Cumbr	NY0705	54°26·2'	3°25·6'W	X	89
Hurlbridge	Devon	SS5403	50°48·7'	4°4·0'W	X	191
Hurlditch Court	Devon	SX4477	50°34·6'	4°11·8'W	X	201
Hurlditch Horn	Devon	SX4572	50°31·9'	4°10·8'W	X	201
Hurlers, The	Corn	SX2571	50°31·0'	4°27·7'W	A	201
Hurleston Junction	Ches	SJ6255	53°5·7'	2°33·6'W	X	118
Hurlet	C of Glas	NS5161	55°49·4'	4°22·3'W	T	64
Hurley	Warw	SP2496	52°33·9'	1°38·4'W	T	139
Hurley	Win & Maid	SU8283	51°32·6'	0°48·7'W	T	175
Hurley Beacon	Somer	ST1438	51°8·3'	3°13·4'W	X	181
Hurley Beacon (Tumulus)	Somer	ST1438	51°8·3'	3°13·4'W	A	181
Hurley Bottom	Win & Maid	SU8283	51°32·6'	0°48·7'W	T	175
Hurley Common	Warw	SP2496	52°33·9'	1°38·4'W	T	139
Hurley Fm	Somer	ST1337	51°7·8'	3°14·2'W	FM	181
Hurley Fm	Somer	ST2317	50°57·1'	3°5·4'W	FM	193
Hurley Fm	W Susx	TQ3636	51°6·7'	0°3·0'W	FM	187
Hurley Hall Fm	Warw	SP2595	52°33·4'	1°37·5'W	FM	140
Hurlford	E Ayr	NS4536	55°35·8'	4°27·2'W	T	70
Hurlie Bog	Aberd	NO7986	56°58·1'	2°20·3'W	X	45
Hurliness	Orkney	ND2889	58°47·2'	3°14·3'W	T	7
Hurlingbarrow	Corn	SW7249	50°18·1'	5°11·7'W	X	204
Hurlingham Ho	Wan	TQ2475	51°27·8'	0°12·5'W	X	176
Hurlingpot Fm	Somer	ST6444	51°11·9'	2°30·5'W	FM	183
Hurlmakin	Fife	NO5308	56°16·0'	2°45·1'W	X	59
Hurlston	Lancs	SD4010	53°35·2'	2°54·0'W	T	108
Hurl Stone	Northum	NU0324	55°30·8'	1°56·7'W	A	75
Hurlstone Point	Somer	SS8949	51°14·0'	3°35·0'W	X	181
Hurlston Green	Lancs	SD3911	53°35·8'	2°54·9'W	T	108
Hurly Hawkin (Broch)	C of Dun	NO3332	56°28·8'	3°4·8'W	A	53
Hurn	Dorset	SZ1296	50°46·0'	1°49·4'W	T	195
Hurn	E Yorks	TA0240	53°51·0'	0°26·6'W	T	106,107
Hurn Br	Lincs	TF2154	53°4·4'	0°11·2'W	X	122
Hurn Court	Bourne	SZ1295	50°45·5'	1°49·4'W	X	195
Hurnel Moss	N Yks	SD7472	54°8·8'	2°23·5'W	X	98
Hurn Fm	Hants	SU1804	50°50·3'	1°44·3'W	FM	195
Hurn Fm	Peterb	TF2305	52°38·0'	0°10·5'W	FM	142
Hurn Fm	Somer	ST2953	51°16·5'	3°0·7'W	FM	182
Hurn Fm	Somer	ST4944	51°11·8'	2°43·4'W	FM	182,183
Hurn Forest	Dorset	SZ1199	50°47·7'	1°50·3'W	F	195
Hurn Hall	Lincs	TF3926	52°49·0'	0°4·2'E	X	131
Hurnip's Point	Orkney	HY5406	58°56·6'	2°47·5'W	X	6,7
Hurns Br	York	SE5657	54°0·6'	1°8·3'W	X	105
Hurn's End	Lincs	TF4249	53°1·4'	0°7·4'E	T	131
Hurn Wood	Lincs	SK8868	53°12·3'	0°40·5'W	F	121
Hurn Wood	Lincs	SK9833	52°53·4'	0°32·2'W	F	130
Hurrell's Fm	Suff	TL9340	52°1·7'	0°49·2'E	FM	155
Hurr Gill	N Yks	NZ0007	54°27·7'	1°59·6'W	W	92
Hurries Fm	N Yks	SD8858	54°1·3'	2°10·6'W	FM	103
Hurscott	Devon	SS6131	51°3·9'	3°58·6'W	X	180
Hursdon	Devon	SX5392	50°42·8'	4°4·6'W	X	191
Hursey	Dorset	ST4302	50°49·1'	2°48·2'W	T	193
Hursley	Hants	SU4225	51°1·6'	1°23·7'W	T	185
Hursley Bottom	Wilts	SU1566	51°23·8'	1°46·7'W	X	173
Hursley Fm	Worcs	SO6463	52°16·1'	2°31·3'W	FM	138,149
Hursley Hill	Bath & NE Somer	ST6165	51°23·2'	2°33·2'W	X	172
Hursley Park	Hants	SU4225	51°1·6'	1°23·7'W	X	185
Hurst	Cald	SD9927	53°44·6'	2°0·5'W	X	103
Hurst	Cumbr	NY4140	54°45·3'	2°54·6'W	T	85
Hurst	Dorset	SY7990	50°42·8'	2°17·5'W	T	194
Hurst	N Yks	NZ0402	54°25·0'	1°55·9'W	X	92
Hurst	Sheff	SK3292	53°25·7'	1°30·7'W	X	110,111
Hurst	Shrops	SO3180	52°25·1'	3°0·5'W	X	137
Hurst	Somer	ST4518	50°57·8'	2°46·6'W	T	193
Hurst	Tames	SD9400	53°30·0'	2°5·0'W	T	109
Hurst	Wok	SU7973	51°27·3'	0°51·4'W	T	175
Hurstage, The	Staffs	SJ9435	52°55·0'	2°4·9'W	X	127
Hurst Barn Fm	Glos	SP2111	51°48·1'	1°41·3'W	FM	163
Hurst Barns	E Susx	TQ3816	50°55·8'	0°1·8'W	X	198
Hurst Beach	Hants	SZ3090	50°42·8'	1°34·1'W	X	196

Hurstbourne Hill	Hants	SU3752	51°16·2'	1°27·8'W	X	185
Hurstbourne Park	Hants	SU4447	51°13·5'	1°21·8'W	X	185
Hurstbourne Priors	Hants	SU4346	51°12·9'	1°22·7'W	T	185
Hurstbourne Tarrant	Hants	SU3853	51°16·7'	1°26·9'W	T	185
Hurst Brook	Derby	SK0693	53°26·3'	1°54·2'W	W	110
Hurst Castle	Hants	SZ3189	50°42·2'	1°33·3'W	A	196
Hurst Copse	Hants	SU2941	51°10·3'	1°34·7'W	F	185
Hurstead	Roch	SD9115	53°38·1'	2°7·8'W	T	109
Hurst End	Mil Key	SP9243	52°4·9'	0°39·0'W	X	152
Hurstend Fm	Mil Key	SP9243	52°4·9'	0°39·0'W	FM	152
Hurst Farm Ho	W Susx	TQ0429	51°3·3'	0°30·6'W	X	186,197
Hurst Fm	Bury	SD7804	53°32·2'	2°19·5'W	FM	109
Hurst Fm	Glos	SO6403	51°43·7'	2°30·9'W	FM	162
Hurst Fm	Glos	SO7102	51°43·2'	2°24·8'W	FM	162
Hurst Fm	Hants	SU5121	50°59·4'	1°16·0'W	FM	185
Hurst Fm	Hants	SU6544	51°11·7'	1°3·8'W	FM	185,186
Hurst Fm	Hants	SU6927	51°2·5'	1°0·6'W	FM	186,197
Hurst Fm	Hants	SU7620	50°58·7'	0°54·7'W	FM	197
Hurst Fm	Hants	SU7754	51°17·0'	0°53·4'W	FM	186
Hurst Fm	Kent	TQ4350	51°14·1'	0°3·3'E	FM	187
Hurst Fm	Kent	TQ9353	51°14·8'	0°46·3'E	FM	189
Hurst Fm	Kent	TR0651	51°13·5'	0°57·4'E	FM	179,189
Hurst Fm	Kent	TR0733	51°3·8'	0°57·6'E	FM	179,189
Hurst Fm	Leic	SK4918	52°45·7'	1°16·0'W	FM	129
Hurst Fm	Northnts	SP7440	52°3·4'	0°54·8'W	FM	152
Hurst Fm	Shrops	SJ6627	52°50·6'	2°29·9'W	FM	127
Hurst Fm	Somer	ST3843	51°11·2'	2°52·8'W	FM	182
Hurst Fm	Staffs	SK1610	52°41·5'	1°45·4'W	FM	128
Hurst Fm	Surrey	TQ2055	51°17·1'	0°16·4'W	FM	187
Hurst Fm	Warr	SJ6083	53°20·8'	2°35·6'W	FM	109
Hurst Fm	Warw	SP2875	52°22·6'	1°34·9'W	FM	140
Hurst Fm	Wilts	ST9856	51°18·4'	2°1·3'W	FM	173
Hurst Fm	Worcs	SO7939	52°3·2'	2°18·0'W	FM	150
Hurst Fm	Worcs	SO7963	52°16·1'	2°18·1'W	FM	138,150
Hurst Fm	Worcs	SO9275	52°22·6'	2°6·7'W	FM	139
Hurst Fm	W Susx	SU8426	51°1·9'	0°47·7'W	FM	186,197
Hurst Fms	Wilts	ST9356	51°18·4'	2°5·6'W	FM	173
Hurst Fm, The	Shrops	SJ3507	52°39·7'	2°57·3'W	FM	126
Hurstfold Fm	W Susx	SU9027	51°2·3'	0°42·6'W	FM	186,197
Hurst Green	Ches	SJ5546	53°0·8'	2°39·8'W	X	117
Hurst Green	Dudley	SO9885	52°28·0'	2°1·4'W	T	139
Hurst Green	Essex	TM0916	51°48·4'	1°2·3'E	T	168,169
Hurst Green	E Susx	TQ7327	51°1·2'	0°28·4'E	T	188,199
Hurst Green	Kent	TQ7647	51°11·9'	0°31·5'E	X	188
Hurst Green	Lancs	SD6838	53°50·5'	2°28·8'W	T	103
Hurst Green	Surrey	TQ3951	51°14·7'	0°0·1'W	T	187
Hurst Green Fm	Birm	SP1592	52°31·8'	1°46·3'W	FM	139
Hurst Grove	Wok	SU7872	51°26·7'	0°52·3'W	X	175
Hurst Hall	Ches	SJ5746	53°0·8'	2°38·1'W	X	117
Hurst Hall	Warr	SJ6696	53°27·8'	2°30·3'W	X	109
Hurst Haven	E Susx	TQ6308	50°51·1'	0°19·3'E	W	199
Hursthead Cote	Derby	SK1887	53°23·0'	1°43·3'W	X	110
Hurst Heath	Dorset	SY7889	50°42·2'	2°18·3'W	F	194
Hurst Hill	Dudley	SO9394	52°32·9'	2°5·8'W	T	139
Hurst Hill	Kent	TQ9443	51°9·4'	0°46·9'E	X	189
Hurst Hill	Lancs	SD6217	53°39·1'	2°34·1'W	X	109
Hurst Hill	Oxon	SP4704	51°44·2'	1°18·8'W	H	164
Hursthill Inclosure	Hants	SU2805	50°50·9'	1°35·8'W	F	195
Hurst Ho	Carm	SN2908	51°44·9'	4°28·2'W	X	159
Hurst Ho	E Susx	TQ7819	50°56·8'	0°32·4'E	X	199
Hurst Ho	Warw	SP1465	52°17·2'	1°47·3'W	X	151
Hurst Ho	Wok	SU7973	51°27·3'	0°51·4'W	X	175
Hursthole Point	Cumbr	NY2127	54°38·2'	3°13·0'W	X	89,90
Hurstley	Heref	SO3548	52°7·8'	2°56·6'W	T	148,149
Hurst Lodge	Wok	SU8073	51°27·2'	0°50·5'W	X	175
Hurst Mill	Dorset	SY8883	50°39·0'	2°9·8'W	X	194
Hurst Moor	Derby	SK0692	53°25·7'	1°54·2'W	X	110
Hurst Moor	N Yks	NZ0403	54°25·6'	1°55·9'W	X	92
Hurstnook Fm	Derby	SK0493	53°26·3'	1°56·0'W	FM	110
Hurston	Devon	SX6884	50°38·7'	3°51·6'W	X	191
Hurstone	Devon	SS6422	50°59·1'	3°55·9'W	X	180
Hurstone Fm	Somer	ST0525	51°1·2'	3°20·9'W	FM	181
Hurston Ho	Dorset	SX8792	50°43·2'	3°35·7'W	X	192
Hurston Place	W Susx	TQ0716	50°56·2'	0°28·2'W	X	197
Hurston Ridge	Devon	SX6782	50°37·6'	3°52·4'W	X	191
Hurston Warren	W Susx	TQ0716	50°56·2'	0°28·2'W	X	197
Hurst Park	Surrey	TQ1368	51°24·2'	0°22·1'W	T	176
Hurst Peat Moss	N Yks	NZ0303	54°25·6'	1°56·8'W	X	92
Hurstpierpoint	W Susx	TQ2816	50°56·0'	0°10·3'W	T	198
Hurstpierpoint College	W Susx	TQ2917	50°56·5'	0°9·4'W	X	198
Hurst Resr	Derby	SK0593	53°26·3'	1°55·1'W	W	110
Hurst's Fm	Wilts	SU1060	51°20·6'	1°51·0'W	FM	173
Hurst, The	Cumbr	NY5868	55°0·5'	2°39·0'W	X	86
Hurst, The	Derby	SK4561	53°8·9'	1°19·2'W	X	120
Hurst, The	Heref	SO3952	52°10·0'	2°53·1'W	X	148,149
Hurst, The	Shrops	SO6796	52°33·9'	2°28·8'W	X	138
Hurst, The	Staffs	SJ8311	52°42·0'	2°14·7'W	X	127
Hurst Wickham	W Susx	TQ2916	50°56·0'	0°9·5'W	T	198
Hurst Wood	E Susx	TQ7112	50°53·2'	0°26·3'E	F	199
Hurst Wood	E Susx	TQ7819	50°56·8'	0°32·4'E	F	199
Hurst Wood	Kent	TQ6354	51°15·9'	0°20·6'E	F	188
Hurst Wood	Kent	TQ9348	51°12·1'	0°46·2'E	F	189
Hurstwood	Lancs	SD8831	53°46·8'	2°10·5'W	T	103
Hurstwood Hall	Lancs	SD8831	53°46·8'	2°10·5'W	R	103
Hurstwood Ho	W Susx	TQ3322	50°59·1'	0°5·9'W	X	198
Hurstwood Resr	Lancs	SD8831	53°46·8'	2°10·5'W	W	103
Hurthill Copse	Surrey	SU9035	51°6·7'	0°42·5'W	F	186
Hurtiso	Orkney	HY4431	59°10·0'	2°58·3'W	X	5,6
Hurtiso	Orkney	HY5001	58°53·9'	2°51·9'W	X	6,7
Hurtle Hill	Worcs	SO7770	52°19·9'	2°19·9'W	X	138
Hurtle Pot	N Yks	SD7377	54°11·5'	2°24·4'W	X	98
Hurtleton	Cumbr	NY4961	54°56·7'	2°47·3'W	X	86
Hurtmore	Surrey	SU9545	51°12·0'	0°38·0'W	T	186
Hurts Hall	Suff	TM3862	52°12·5'	1°29·4'E	X	156
Hurtstocks Wood	Corn	SX1067	50°28·6'	4°40·3'W	F	200
Hurt's Wood	Staffs	SK1453	53°4·7'	1°47·1'W	F	119
Hurt Wood	Surrey	TQ0943	51°10·8'	0°26·0'W	F	187
Hurtwood Ho	Surrey	TQ1042	51°10·2'	0°25·2'W	X	187
Hurtwood, The	Surrey	SU9938	51°8·2'	0°34·7'W	F	186
Hur Wood	Somer	SS9842	51°10·3'	3°27·2'W	F	181

Hurworth Bryan Fm	Durham	NZ3935	54°42·8'	1°23·3'W	FM	93
Hurworth Burn	Durham	NZ4133	54°41·7'	1°21·4'W	X	93
Hurworth Burn Reservoir	Durham	NZ4033	54°41·7'	1°22·3'W	W	93
Hurworth Moor	Darl	NZ3112	54°30·4'	1°30·9'W	X	93
Hurworth Moor Ho	Darl	NZ3112	54°30·4'	1°30·9'W	X	93
Hurworth-on-Tees	Darl	NZ3010	54°29·3'	1°31·8'W	T	93
Hurworth Place	Darl	NZ2910	54°29·3'	1°32·7'W	T	93
Hury	Durham	NY9519	54°34·2'	2°4·2'W	T	91,92
Hury Reservoir	Durham	NY9619	54°34·2'	2°3·3'W	W	91,92
Husabost	Highld	NG2051	57°28·0'	6°39·7'W	X	23
Husbandry Fm	Cambs	TL4282	52°25·3'	0°5·7'E	FM	142,143
Husbands Bosworth	Leic	SP6484	52°27·2'	1°3·1'W	T	140
Husbandtown	Angus	NO4839	56°32·7'	2°50·3'W	X	54
Husborne Crawley	Beds	SP9535	52°0·5'	0°36·6'W	T	153
Huscote Fm	Oxon	SP4742	52°4·7'	1°18·5'W	FM	151
Husheath Manor	Kent	TQ7540	51°8·2'	0°30·5'E	X	188
Hushinish	N Eil	NA9812	57°59·9'	7°6·2'W	T	13
Hushinish Bay	N Eil	NA9911	57°59·4'	7°5·2'W	W	13
Hushinish Glorigs	N Eil	NA9809	57°58·3'	7°6·0'W	X	13
Hushinish Point	N Eil	NA9811	57°59·4'	7°6·2'W	X	13
Husival Beag	N Eil	NB0012	58°0·0'	7°4·2'W	H	13
Husival Mór	N Eil	NB0211	57°59·6'	7°2·1'W	H	13
Huskisson's Lodge	Northnts	TL0197	52°33·9'	0°30·2'W	X	141
Huslan	I of Angl	SH5283	53°19·6'	4°12·9'W	X	114,115
Huspeth	Northum	NY9494	55°14·7'	2°5·2'W	X	80
Husphins Fm	Staffs	SJ8404	52°38·2'	2°13·8'W	FM	127
Husseys Fm	Hants	SU7644	51°11·6'	0°54·4'W	FM	186
Huster Roo	Shetld	HU5239	60°8·2'	1°3·3'W	X	4
Hus, The	Shetld	HU1655	60°17·0'	1°42·1'W	X	3
Husthwaite	N Yks	SE5175	54°10·3'	1°12·7'W	T	100
Hustyn	Corn	SX0068	50°28·9'	4°48·8'W	X	200
Hustyn Downs	Corn	SX0068	50°28·9'	4°48·8'W	H	200
Hustyn Downs (Tumuli)	Corn	SX0065	50°27·3'	4°48·7'W	A	200
Hustyn Gate	Corn	SW9867	50°28·3'	4°50·4'W	X	200
Hustyn Wood	Corn	SX0069	50°29·4'	4°48·8'W	F	200
Hut Bottom	Wilts	SU0427	51°2·8'	1°56·2'W	X	184
Hut Burn	Northum	NY6551	54°51·4'	2°32·3'W	W	86
Hutchen Gill Head	N Yks	SE0256	54°0·2'	1°57·8'W	X	104
Hutcherleigh	Devon	SX7850	50°20·5'	3°42·5'W	T	202
Hutcherton	Devon	SS6332	51°4·5'	3°57·0'W	X	180
Hutcherton Down	Devon	SS6333	51°5·0'	3°57·0'W	H	180
Hutchesontown	C of Glas	NS5963	55°50·6'	4°14·7'W	T	64
Hutches, The	Corn	SW7928	50°6·9'	5°5·1'W	X	204
Hutchinghayes	Devon	ST1403	50°49·4'	3°12·9'W	X	192,193
Hutchinson's Ho	N Yks	NZ7911	54°29·5'	0°46·4'W	X	94
Hutchins's Copse	Oxon	SU4391	51°37·2'	1°22·3'W	F	174
Hutchison	Stir	NN7804	56°13·0'	3°57·6'W	X	57
Hutchison Memorial Hut	Aberd	NO0299	57°4·6'	3°36·5'W	X	36,43
Hutchwns Point	Brig	SS8076	51°28·5'	3°43·3'W	X	170
Hut Covert	Norf	TL9682	52°24·3'	0°53·3'E	F	144
Hut Crag	N Yks	SE0156	54°0·2'	1°58·7'W	X	104
Hut Green	N Yks	SE5623	53°42·3'	1°8·7'W	T	105
Huthead Cott	Renf	NS3962	55°49·7'	4°33·8'W	X	63
Hut Hill	Suff	TL9580	52°23·2'	0°52·3'E	X	144
Hut Hill (Tumulus)	Suff	TL9580	52°23·2'	0°52·3'E	A	144
Huthwaite	Notts	SK4659	53°7·8'	1°18·3'W	T	120
Huthwaite Green	N Yks	NZ4900	54°23·8'	1°14·3'W	X	93
Huthwaite Hall	Barns	SE2800	53°30·0'	1°34·3'W	X	110
Hut Knowe	Scot Bord	NT7915	55°26·0'	2°19·5'W	H	80
Hutlerburn	Scot Bord	NT4024	55°30·6'	2°56·6'W	T	73
Hutler Burn	Scot Bord	NT4322	55°29·6'	2°53·7'W	W	73
Hutlerburn Hill	Scot Bord	NT4123	55°30·1'	2°55·6'W	H	73
Hutlerburn Loch	Scot Bord	NT4123	55°30·1'	2°55·6'W	W	73
Hutshayes Fm	Devon	ST1408	50°52·1'	3°12·9'W	FM	192,193
Hutswell	Devon	SS9017	50°56·8'	3°33·6'W	X	181
Hutswell	Devon	SS9022	50°59·4'	3°33·7'W	X	181
Hutter	Orkney	HY2514	59°0·7'	3°17·9'W	X	6
Hut, The	Ches	SJ7177	53°17·6'	2°25·7'W	X	118
Hut, The	Wilts	SU0422	51°0·1'	1°56·2'W	X	184
Huttock Top	Lancs	SD8622	53°41·9'	2°12·3'W	T	103
Huttoft	Lincs	TF5176	53°15·8'	0°16·2'E	T	122
Huttoft Bank	Lincs	TF5477	53°16·3'	0°19·0'E	X	122
Hutton	Cumbr	NY4326	54°37·8'	2°52·6'W	T	90
Hutton	Cumbr	SD2090	54°18·2'	3°13·3'W	X	96
Hutton	Essex	TQ6395	51°38·0'	0°21·7'E	T	167,177
Hutton	E Yorks	TA0253	53°58·0'	0°26·3'W	T	106,107
Hutton	Lancs	SD4926	53°43·9'	2°46·0'W	T	102
Hutton	N Som	ST3558	51°19·3'	2°55·6'W	T	182
Hutton	Scot Bord	NT9053	55°46·5'	2°9·1'W	T	67,74,75
Hutton Beck	Cumbr	NY4439	54°44·8'	2°51·8'W	W	90
Hutton Beck	Durham	NZ1212	54°30·4'	1°48·5'W	W	92
Hutton Beck	N Yks	SE7091	54°18·8'	0°55·0'W	W	94,100
Hutton Bonville	N Yks	NZ3400	54°23·9'	1°28·2'W	T	93
Hutton Buscel	N Yks	SE9784	54°14·8'	0°30·3'W	T	101
Hutton Castle	Scot Bord	NT8854	55°47·0'	2°11·0'W	A	67,74
Hutton Common	N Yks	SE7088	54°17·2'	0°55·1'W	X	94,100
Hutton Conyers	N Yks	SE3273	54°9·4'	1°30·2'W	T	99
Hutton Court	N Som	ST3558	51°19·3'	2°55·6'W	A	182
Hutton Cranswick	E Yorks	TA0252	53°57·5'	0°26·3'W	T	106,107
Hutton End	Cumbr	NY4438	54°44·3'	2°51·8'W	T	90
Hutton Fields	Durham	NZ1311	54°29·9'	1°47·5'W	X	92
Hutton Fields Fm	N Yks	NZ4403	54°25·5'	1°18·9'W	FM	93
Hutton Gate	Red & Cl	NZ5915	54°31·9'	1°4·9'W	T	93
Hutton Grange	Cumbr	NY4637	54°43·8'	2°49·9'W	X	90
Hutton Grange	N Yks	NZ4506	54°27·1'	1°17·9'W	X	93
Hutton Grange	N Yks	SE3575	54°10·4'	1°27·4'W	X	99
Hutton Grange	N Yks	SE5148	53°55·8'	1°13·0'W	X	105
Hutton Grange Fm	N Yks	NZ3500	54°23·9'	1°27·2'W	FM	93
Hutton Grange Fm	Oxon	SP3232	51°59·4'	1°31·6'W	FM	151
Hutton Hall	N Yks	SE3374	54°9·9'	1°29·3'W	X	99
Hutton Hall	Red & Cl	NZ5914	54°31·3'	1°4·9'W	X	93
Hutton Hall Barns	Scot Bord	NT8954	55°47·0'	2°10·1'W	X	67,74
Hutton Hang	N Yks	SE1788	54°17·5'	1°43·9'W	T	99
Hutton Henry	Durham	NZ4236	54°43·3'	1°20·5'W	T	93
Hutton Hill	N Som	ST3558	51°19·3'	2°55·6'W	H	182
Hutton Hill	N Yks	SE1689	54°18·0'	1°44·8'W	X	99
Hutton Hill	N Yks	SE7368	54°6·4'	0°52·6'W	X	100
Hutton Ho	Durham	NZ4236	54°43·3'	1°20·5'W	X	93
Hutton-in-the-Forest	Cumbr	NY4635	54°42·7'	2°49·9'W	A	90
Hutton John	Cumbr	NY4326	54°37·8'	2°52·6'W	X	90

Hutton-le-Hole	N Yks	SE7089	54°17·7′	0°55·0′W	T	94,100
Hutton Lowcross Woods	Red & Cl	NZ5913	54°30·8′	1°4·9′W	F	93
Hutton Magna	Durham	NZ1212	54°30·4′	1°48·5′W	T	92
Hutton Mains	Scot Bord	NT9152	55°45·9′	2°8·2′W	X	67,74,75
Hutton Marsh	Lancs	SD4527	53°44·4′	2°49·6′W	W	102
Hutton Moor	N Yks	SE3574	54°9·9′	1°27·4′W	X	99
Hutton Moor Closes	N Yks	SE3672	54°8·8′	1°26·5′W	X	99
Hutton Moor End	Cumbr	NY3627	54°38·3′	2°59·1′W	X	90
Hutton Moor Ho	N Yks	SE3474	54°9·9′	1°28·3′W	X	99
Hutton Mote	D & G	NY1689	55°11·5′	3°18·7′W	A	79
Hutton Mount	Essex	TQ6194	51°37·5′	0°20·0′E	T	167,177
Hutton Mulgrave	N Yks	NZ8310	54°29·0′	0°42·7′W	X	94
Hutton Mulgrave Wood	N Yks	NZ8309	54°28·4′	0°42·7′W	F	94
Hutton Park	Cumbr	SD5792	54°19·6′	2°39·3′W	X	97
Hutton Ridge	N Yks	SE7092	54°19·4′	0°55·0′W	X	94,100
Hutton Roof	Cumbr	NY3734	54°42·1′	2°58·2′W	T	90
Hutton Roof	Cumbr	SD5778	54°12·0′	2°39·1′W	T	97
Hutton Roof Crags	Cumbr	SD5577	54°11·5′	2°41·0′W	H	97
Hutton Roof Park	Cumbr	SD5677	54°11·5′	2°40·0′W	X	97
Hutton Row	Cumbr	NY4538	54°44·3′	2°50·8′W	X	90
Hutton Rudby	N Yks	NZ4606	54°27·1′	1°17·0′W	T	93
Huttons Ambo	N Yks	SE7667	54°5·8′	0°49·9′W	T	100
Hutton Sands	Lancs	SD4427	53°44·4′	2°50·5′W	X	102
Huttons Bank Wood	N Yks	SE7467	54°5·9′	0°51·7′W	F	100
Hutton Sceugh	Cumbr	NY3537	54°43·7′	3°0·1′W	X	90
Hutton Sessay	N Yks	SE4776	54°10·9′	1°16·4′W	T	100
Hutton's Fm	Bucks	SU7987	51°34·8′	0°51·2′W	FM	175
Hutton's Mon	N Yks	SE0999	54°23·4′	1°51·3′W	X	99
Hutton Thorn	N Yks	SE5151	53°57·4′	1°13·0′W	F	105
Hutton Village	Red & Cl	NZ6013	54°30·8′	1°4·0′W	T	94
Hutton Wandesley	N Yks	SE5050	53°56·9′	1°13·9′W	T	105
Hutts Fm, The	N Yks	SE2177	54°11·5′	1°40·3′W	FM	99
Hutts Fm, The	Staffs	SK1244	52°59·8′	1°48·9′W	FM	119,128
Hutts Gill	N Yks	SE2277	54°11·5′	1°39·4′W	W	99
Hutts Wood	N Yks	SE2177	54°11·5′	1°40·3′W	F	99
Hut Wood	Hants	SU4218	50°57·8′	1°23·7′W	F	185
Huxbear Ho	Devon	SX8580	50°36·7′	3°37·1′W	X	191
Huxford Fm	Devon	SS6920	50°58·1′	3°51·6′W	FM	180
Huxham	Devon	SX9497	50°46·0′	3°29·8′W	T	192
Huxham Brake	Devon	SX9496	50°45·5′	3°29·8′W	F	192
Huxham Green	Somer	ST5936	51°7·5′	2°34·8′W	T	182,183
Huxham's Cross	Devon	SX7863	50°27·5′	3°42·7′W	X	202
Huxhill	Devon	SS4923	50°59·4′	4°8·7′W	X	180
Huxley	Ches	SJ5061	53°8·9′	2°44·5′W	T	117
Huxley Gorse	Ches	SJ5261	53°8·9′	2°42·7′W	F	117
Huxloe Lo	Northnts	SP9678	52°23·7′	0°34·9′W	X	141
Huxtable Fm	Devon	SS6630	51°3·5′	3°54·3′W	FM	180
Huxter	Shetld	HU1757	60°18·1′	1°41·0′W	T	3
Huxter	Shetld	HU3950	60°14·2′	1°17·2′W	X	3
Huxter	Shetld	HU5662	60°20·6′	0°58·6′W	X	2
Huxton	Scot Bord	NT8666	55°53·5′	2°13·0′W	X	67
Huxton Cross	Devon	SX7044	50°17·1′	3°49·1′W	X	202
Huyton	Know	SJ4491	53°25·0′	2°50·1′W	T	108
Huyton Hill	Cumbr	NY3701	54°24·3′	2°57·8′W	X	90
Huyton Park	Know	SJ4490	53°24·5′	2°50·1′W	T	108
Huyton Quarry	Know	SJ4590	53°24·5′	2°49·2′W	T	108
Huyton-With-Roby	Know	SJ4491	53°25·0′	2°50·1′W	T	108
Hwlffordd	Conwy	SH9565	53°10·5′	3°33·9′W	X	116
Hwylfa	Conwy	SH8151	53°2·8′	3°46·1′W	H	116
Hwylfa-ddu	Conwy	SH8358	53°6·6′	3°44·5′W	X	116
Hyam Fm	Wilts	ST9187	51°35·1′	2°7·4′W	FM	173
Hyam Wood	Wilts	ST9087	51°35·1′	2°8·3′W	F	173
Hyatt Sarnesfield	Heref	SO3749	52°8·4′	2°54·8′W	X	148,149
Hyatt's Hill	Somer	ST6547	51°13·5′	2°29·7′W	X	183
Hyattswood Fm	N Som	ST5067	51°24·2′	2°42·7′W	FM	172,182
Hybreck	Orkney	HY3114	59°0·7′	3°11·6′W	X	6
Hybrid Fm	Devon	SS5041	51°9·2′	4°8·3′W	FM	180
Hycemoor	Cumbr	SD0989	54°17·6′	3°23·5′W	T	96
Hycemoor Side	Cumbr	SD0888	54°17·0′	3°24·4′W	X	96
Hycemoor Side Fm	Cumbr	SD0890	54°18·1′	3°24·4′W	FM	96
Hyddgen	Powys	SN7790	52°29·9′	3°48·3′W	X	135
Hyde	Dorset	SY4792	50°43·7′	2°44·7′W	T	193
Hyde	Dorset	SY8790	50°42·8′	2°10·7′W	X	194
Hyde	Glos	SO8801	51°42·7′	2°10·0′W	T	162
Hyde	Glos	SP0828	51°57·3′	1°52·6′W	T	150,163
Hyde	Hants	SU1612	50°54·7′	1°46·0′W	T	195
Hyde	Hants	SU4830	51°4·3′	1°18·5′W	T	185
Hyde	Heref	SO4555	52°11·7′	2°47·9′W	T	148,149
Hyde	Swin	SU1589	51°36·2′	1°46·6′W	X	173
Hyde	Tames	SJ9494	53°26·8′	2°5·0′W	T	109
Hyde Ash	Heref	SO4455	52°11·7′	2°48·8′W	X	148,149
Hyde Brook	Glos	SO9625	51°55·6′	2°3·1′W	W	163
Hyde Chase	Essex	TL8003	51°42·0′	0°36·7′E	T	168
Hyde Common	Hants	SU1712	50°54·7′	1°45·1′W	X	195
Hyde Cotts	Suff	TL8166	52°16·0′	0°39·6′E	X	155
Hyde End	W Berks	SU5563	51°22·0′	1°12·2′W	T	174
Hyde End	Wok	SU7366	51°23·5′	0°56·7′W	X	175
Hyde Field	Heref	SO4451	52°9·5′	2°48·7′W	X	148,149
Hyde Fm	Bucks	SP9100	51°41·7′	0°40·6′W	FM	165
Hyde Fm	Bucks	SU9589	51°35·7′	0°37·3′W	FM	175,176
Hyde Fm	Essex	TL6227	51°55·3′	0°21·7′E	FM	167
Hyde Fm	Essex	TL7330	51°56·7′	0°31·4′E	FM	167
Hyde Fm	Essex	TL9210	51°45·6′	0°47·3′E	FM	168
Hyde Fm	Essex	TL9615	51°48·2′	0°51·0′E	FM	168
Hyde Fm	Glos	SO6812	51°48·6′	2°27·5′W	FM	162
Hyde Fm	Glos	SO8901	51°42·7′	2°9·2′W	FM	163
Hyde Fm	Glos	SO9425	51°55·6′	2°4·8′W	FM	163
Hyde Fm	Hants	SU0814	50°55·8′	1°52·8′W	FM	195
Hyde Fm	Hants	SU3224	51°1·1′	1°32·2′W	FM	185
Hyde Fm	Hants	SU5061	51°21·0′	1°16·5′W	FM	174
Hyde Fm	Hants	SU7446	51°12·7′	0°56·0′W	FM	186
Hyde Fm	Heref	SO6234	52°0·4′	2°32·8′W	FM	149
Hyde Fm	Heref	SO6652	52°10·2′	2°29·4′W	FM	149
Hyde Fm	Herts	TL0804	51°43·7′	0°25·8′W	FM	166
Hyde Fm	Northnts	SP7451	52°9·4′	0°54·7′W	FM	152
Hyde Fm	Oxon	SU3191	51°37·2′	1°32·7′W	FM	164,174
Hyde Fm	Oxon	SU3892	51°37·8′	1°26·7′W	FM	164,174
Hyde Fm	Somer	ST2625	51°1·4′	3°2·9′W	FM	193
Hyde Fm	Somer	ST5411	50°54·0′	2°38·9′W	FM	194
Hyde Fm	Staffs	SJ8707	52°39·9′	2°11·1′W	FM	127,139

Hyde Fm	Surrey	SU8838	51°8·3′	0°44·1′W	FM	186
Hyde Fm	Win & Maid	SU8583	51°32·6′	0°46·1′W	FM	175
Hyde Fm	Worcs	SO6261	52°15·0′	2°33·0′W	FM	138,149
Hyde Fm, The	Essex	TL7739	52°1·5′	0°35·2′E	FM	155
Hydegate	Glos	ST7798	51°41·1′	2°19·6′W	X	162
Hydegreen	Tames	SJ9899	53°29·5′	2°1·4′W	X	109
Hyde Hall	Essex	TL7015	51°48·7′	0°28·4′E	A	167
Hyde Hall	Essex	TQ7899	51°39·9′	0°34·8′E	X	167
Hyde Hall	Norf	TF9112	52°40·5′	0°49·9′E	X	132
Hyde Hall	Tames	SJ9194	53°26·8′	2°7·7′W	A	109
Hyde Hall Fm	Herts	TL3432	51°58·4′	0°2·5′W	FM	166
Hyde Heath	Bucks	SP9300	51°41·7′	0°38·9′W	T	165
Hydeheath Common	Bucks	SP9200	51°41·7′	0°39·7′W	X	165
Hyde Hill	W Susx	TQ2336	51°6·8′	0°14·2′W	X	187
Hyde Hill Fm	Cambs	TL3741	52°3·3′	0°0·3′E	FM	154
Hyde Hill Plantation	Dorset	ST9410	50°53·6′	2°4·7′W	F	195
Hyde Ho	Bucks	SP9201	51°42·2′	0°39·7′W	X	165
Hyde Home Fm	Beds	TL1317	51°50·6′	0°21·2′W	FM	166
Hydelane Fm	Bucks	SP7235	52°0·8′	0°56·7′W	FM	152
Hyde Lea	Staffs	SJ9120	52°46·9′	2°7·6′W	T	127
Hyde Marsh	Heref	SO4554	52°11·1′	2°47·9′W	X	148,149
Hyde Mill	Glos	SP1724	51°55·1′	1°44·8′W	X	163
Hyden Fm	Hants	SU6717	50°57·1′	1°2·4′W	FM	185
Hyden Hill	Hants	SU6819	50°58·2′	1°1·5′W	H	185
Hyde North Sta	Tames	SJ9496	53°27·9′	2°5·0′W	X	109
Hyden Wood	Hants	SU6818	50°57·7′	1°1·5′W	F	185
Hyden Wood	Hants	SU6918	50°57·7′	1°0·7′W	F	197
Hyde Park	C of West	TQ2780	51°30·5′	0°9·8′W	X	176
Hydepark	Cumbr	NY5431	54°40·6′	2°42·4′W	X	90
Hyde Park	Donc	SE5702	53°30·9′	1°8·0′W	T	111
Hyde Park	Norf	TF8034	52°52·6′	0°40·9′E	X	132
Hyde Park	W Susx	SU9119	50°58·0′	0°41·9′W	X	197
Hydes Fm	Dorset	ST7312	50°54·6′	2°22·7′W	FM	194
Hydes Fm	Essex	TQ4698	51°39·9′	0°7·1′E	FM	167,177
Hyde's Fm	Stock	SJ9691	53°25·2′	2°3·2′W	FM	109
Hydes Pastures	Warw	SP3992	52°31·7′	1°25·1′W	X	140
Hydes, The	Essex	TL6431	51°57·4′	0°23·6′E	X	167
Hydestile	Surrey	SU9640	51°9·3′	0°37·2′W	T	186
Hyde, The	Beds	TL1317	51°50·6′	0°21·2′W	X	166
Hyde, The	Bucks	SU7888	51°35·4′	0°52·1′W	X	175
Hyde, The	Essex	TL6100	51°40·8′	0°20·1′E	X	167
Hyde, The	Staffs	SO8484	52°27·5′	2°13·7′W	X	138
Hyde, The	W Susx	TQ2430	51°3·6′	0°13·4′W	X	187
Hyde Wood	Suff	TL8166	52°16·0′	0°39·6′E	F	155
Hyde Woods	Essex	TL8004	51°42·6′	0°36·7′E	F	168
Hydon Heath	Surrey	SU9739	51°8·7′	0°36·4′W	F	186
Hydon Hill	Wilts	SU0427	51°2·8′	1°56·2′W	X	184
Hydon's Ball	Surrey	SU9739	51°8·7′	0°36·4′W	H	186
Hydro Ho	Highld	NM6768	56°45·0′	5°48·2′W	X	40
Hyes	W Susx	TQ1033	51°5·4′	0°25·4′W	X	187
Hyfield	Ches	SJ3176	53°16·8′	3°1·7′W	X	117
Hygga	Monm	SO4803	51°43·6′	2°44·8′W	X	171
Hygrove Ho	Glos	SO7818	51°51·8′	2°18·8′W	X	162
Hyham Hill	Kent	TR1139	51°6·9′	1°1·3′E	X	179,189
Hykeham Grange	Lincs	SK9264	53°10·1′	0°37·0′W	X	121
Hykeham Sta	Lincs	SK9367	53°11·8′	0°36·1′W	X	121
Hylands Park	Essex	TL6804	51°42·8′	0°26·3′E	X	167
Hyles Moor	Lancs	SD8052	53°58·1′	2°17·9′W	X	103
Hyles Moor Fm	Lancs	SD8053	53°58·6′	2°17·9′W	FM	103
Hylters	W Susx	SU8413	50°54·8′	0°47·9′W	X	197
Hylton Castle	Sund	NZ3558	54°55·2′	1°26·8′W	A	88
Hylton Castle	Sund	NZ3558	54°55·2′	1°26·8′W	T	88
Hylton Grove Fm	S Tyne	NZ3359	54°55·7′	1°28·7′W	FM	88
Hylton Red House	Sund	NZ3659	54°55·7′	1°25·9′W	T	88
Hyltons Crossways	Norf	TG2328	52°48·4′	1°18·9′E	T	133,134
Hymns Fm	Powys	SO2461	52°14·8′	3°6·4′W	FM	137,148
Hynam	Cumbr	NY5655	54°53·5′	2°40·7′W	X	86
Hyndal Hill	Inverc	NS2866	55°51·6′	4°44·5′W	X	63
Hyndberry	Scot Bord	NT6448	55°43·7′	2°34·0′W	X	74
Hyndburn Bridge	Lancs	SD7432	53°47·3′	2°23·3′W	T	103
Hyndburn Brook	Lancs	SD7330	53°46·2′	2°24·2′W	W	103
Hynd Castle	Angus	NO5041	56°33·8′	2°48·4′W	A	54
Hyndford	S Lanak	NS9041	55°39·3′	3°44·5′W	X	71,72
Hyndford Bridge	S Lanak	NS9141	55°39·3′	3°43·5′W	T	71,72
Hyndfordwell	Scot Bord	NT1448	55°43·3′	3°21·7′W	X	72
Hyndgreenie	Orkney	HY4954	59°22·4′	2°53·4′W	X	5
Hyndhope	Scot Bord	NT3621	55°29·0′	3°0·3′W	T	73
Hyndhope Burn	Scot Bord	NT3519	55°27·9′	3°1·3′W	W	79
Hyndhope Burn	Scot Bord	NT3620	55°28·4′	3°0·3′W	W	73
Hyndlee	Scot Bord	NT5906	55°21·0′	2°38·4′W	X	80
Hyndlee Burn	Scot Bord	NT6003	55°19·4′	2°37·4′W	W	80
Hyndshaw	S Lanak	NS8453	55°45·6′	3°50·5′W	X	65,72
Hyndshawland	S Lanak	NT0442	55°40·0′	3°31·1′W	H	72
Hyndsidehill	Scot Bord	NT6047	55°43·1′	2°37·8′W	X	74
Hyne	Arg & Bt	NM2054	56°35·9′	6°33·3′W	X	46,47
Hyner Fm	Devon	SX8382	50°37·8′	3°38·9′W	FM	191
Hynett Fm	Heref	SO5542	52°4·7′	2°39·0′W	FM	149
Hyning	Cumbr	SD4986	54°16·3′	2°46·6′W	X	97
Hyning	Cumbr	SD5598	54°22·8′	2°41·1′W	X	97
Hyning	Cumbr	SD5896	54°21·7′	2°38·4′W	X	97
Hyning Home Fm	Lancs	SD5173	54°9·3′	2°44·6′W	FM	97
Hynish	Arg & Bt	NL9839	56°27·0′	6°53·7′W	T	46
Hynish Bay	Arg & Bt	NM0041	56°28·2′	6°51·9′W	W	46
Hyrlas Rock	Corn	SW7716	50°0·4′	5°6·4′W	X	204
Hysbackie	Highld	NC5955	58°27·9′	4°24·5′W	T	10
Hyssington	Powys	SO3194	52°32·6′	3°0·6′W	T	137
Hyssington Marsh	Powys	SO3196	52°33·7′	3°0·7′W	X	137
Hystfield	Glos	ST6696	51°39·9′	2°29·1′W	T	162
Hythe	Durham	NZ1244	54°47·7′	1°48·4′W	X	88
Hythe	Hants	SU4207	50°51·9′	1°23·8′W	T	196
Hythe	Kent	TR1634	51°4·1′	1°5·4′E	T	179,189
Hythe	Somer	ST4452	51°16·1′	2°47·8′W	T	182
Hythe	Surrey	TQ0270	51°25·4′	0°31·6′W	T	176
Hythe End	Win & Maid	TQ0172	51°26·5′	0°32·4′W	T	176
Hythe Ranges	Kent	TR1433	51°3·6′	1°3·6′E	X	179,189
Hythie	Aberd	NK0051	57°33·2′	1°59·5′W	T	30
Hyton	Cumbr	SD0987	54°16·5′	3°23·4′W	T	96
Hyton	Cumbr	SD1087	54°16·5′	3°22·5′W	X	96
Hyval	Orkney	HY2320	59°3·9′	3°20·1′W	X	6
Hyver Hall	Barnet	TQ2194	51°38·1′	0°14·7′W	X	166,176

I

Iagro	N Eil	NB5257	58°26·1′	6°14·5′W	X	8
Ianstown	Moray	NJ4366	57°41·1′	2°56·9′W	T	28
Iasg Loch	Arg & Bt	NM8715	56°17·0′	5°26·0′W	W	55
Ibberton	Dorset	ST7807	50°52·0′	2°18·4′W	T	194
Ibberton Hill	Dorset	ST7907	50°52·0′	2°17·5′W	X	194
Ibberton Long Down	Dorset	ST8007	50°52·0′	2°16·7′W	X	194
Ibert	Stir	NS5286	56°2·9′	4°22·1′W	X	57
Ibert, The	Pth & Kin	NN8825	56°24·5′	3°48·5′W	X	52,58
Ible	Derby	SK2457	53°6·8′	1°38·1′W	T	119
Ibornden Fm	Kent	TQ8440	51°8·0′	0°38·2′E	FM	188
Ibornden Park	Kent	TQ8439	51°7·5′	0°38·2′E	X	188
Ibrox	C of Glas	NS5564	55°51·1′	4°18·5′W	T	64
Ibsley	Hants	SU1509	50°53·0′	1°46·8′W	T	195
Ibsley Common	Hants	SU1710	50°53·6′	1°45·1′W	X	195
Ibstock	Leic	SK4010	52°41·4′	1°24·1′W	T	129
Ibstock Grange	Leic	SK4109	52°40·9′	1°23·2′W	X	140
Ibstone	Bucks	SU7593	51°38·1′	0°54·6′W	T	175
Ibstone Common	Bucks	SU7493	51°38·1′	0°55·5′W	X	175
Ibstone Ho	Bucks	SU7592	51°37·5′	0°54·6′W	X	175
Ibthorpe	Hants	SU3753	51°16·7′	1°27·8′W	T	185
Iburndale	N Yks	NZ8707	54°27·3′	0°39·1′W	X	94
Ibworth	Hants	SU5654	51°17·2′	1°11·4′W	T	185
Icaron Lodge	Durham	NY9723	54°36·4′	2°2·4′W	X	92
Iceland Skerry	Orkney	HY4513	59°0·3′	2°57·0′W	X	6
Icelton	N Som	ST3765	51°23·1′	2°53·9′W	T	171,182
Icen Barrow	Dorset	SY9283	50°39·0′	2°6·4′W	A	195
Icen Fm	Dorset	SY6783	50°39·0′	2°27·6′W	FM	194
Iceni Village	Norf	TF7904	52°36·5′	0°39·0′E	X	144
Ichrachan	Arg & Bt	NN0130	56°25·5′	5°13·2′W	T	50
Ichrachan Ho	Arg & Bt	NN0129	56°24·9′	5°13·1′W	X	50
Ickburgh	Norf	TL8194	52°31·1′	0°40·5′E	T	144
Ickburgh Fields	Norf	TL8296	52°32·1′	0°41·4′E	F	144
Ickenham	Hill	TQ0785	51°33·5′	0°27·0′W	T	176
Ickenham Manor	Hill	TQ0885	51°33·4′	0°26·1′W	X	176
Ickenthwaite	Cumbr	SD3289	54°17·8′	3°2·3′W	T	96,97
Ickford	Bucks	SP6407	51°45·7′	1°4·0′W	T	164,165
Ickham	Kent	TR2258	51°16·9′	1°11·4′E	T	179
Ickleford	Herts	TL1831	51°58·1′	0°16·5′W	T	166
Icklesham	E Susx	TQ8716	50°55·0′	0°40·0′E	T	189,199
Ickleton	Cambs	TL4943	52°4·1′	0°10·8′E	T	154
Ickleton Granges	Cambs	TL4642	52°3·7′	0°8·2′E	X	154
Icklingham	Suff	TL7772	52°19·3′	0°36·2′E	T	144,155
Icklingham Belt	Suff	TL7972	52°19·2′	0°38·0′E	X	144,155
Icklingham Plains	Suff	TL7573	52°19·9′	0°34·5′E	X	155
Icknield Fm	Oxon	SU6283	51°32·8′	1°6·0′W	FM	175
Icknield Ho	Bucks	SP9011	51°47·7′	0°41·3′W	X	165
Icknield Ho	Oxon	SU6993	51°38·1′	0°59·8′W	X	175
Icknield Way	Beds	TL0322	51°53·5′	0°29·8′W	A	166
Icknield Way	Cambs	TL4041	52°3·2′	0°2·9′E	A	154
Icknield Way	Herts	TL1530	51°57·6′	0°19·2′W	A	166
Icknield Way	Oxon	SU6285	51°33·9′	1°5·9′W	A	175
Icknield Way	Oxon	SU6892	51°37·6′	1°0·7′W	A	164,175
Icknield Way	Suff	TL7770	52°18·2′	0°36·2′E	A	144,155
Icknield Way	Suff	TL8176	52°21·4′	0°39·9′E	A	144
Icknield Way Fm	Beds	SP9919	51°51·9′	0°33·3′W	FM	165
Icknield Way Path	Beds	TL0925	51°55·0′	0°24·5′W	X	166
Icknield Way Path	Bucks	SP9618	51°51·4′	0°36·0′W	X	165
Icknield Way Path	Cambs	TL5849	52°7·2′	0°18·9′E	X	154
Icknield Way Path	Herts	TL2638	52°1·8′	0°9·4′W	X	153
Icknield Way Path	Herts	TL3438	52°1·7′	0°2·4′W	X	154
Icknield Way Path	Suff	TL8171	52°18·7′	0°39·7′E	X	144,155
Icknield Way Path	Suff	TL8877	52°21·8′	0°46·1′E	X	144
Ickornshaw	N Yks	SD9642	53°52·7′	2°3·2′W	T	103
Ickornshaw Moor	N Yks	SD9640	53°51·6′	2°3·2′W	X	103
Ickwell	Beds	TL1545	52°5·7′	0°18·9′W	T	153
Ickwell Bury	Beds	TL1445	52°5·7′	0°19·8′W	X	153
Ickwell Green	Beds	TL1545	52°5·7′	0°18·9′W	T	153
Ickworth Ho	Suff	TL8161	52°13·3′	0°39·4′E	X	155
Ickworth Lodge	Suff	TL8162	52°13·8′	0°39·4′E	X	155
Ickworth Park	Suff	TL8161	52°13·3′	0°39·4′E	X	155
Icomb	Glos	SP2122	51°54·0′	1°41·3′W	T	163
Icomb Hill	Glos	SP2023	51°54·5′	1°42·2′W	X	163
Icomb Place	Glos	SP2122	51°54·0′	1°41·3′W	A	163
Icy Park	Devon	SX6947	50°18·7′	3°50·0′W	T	202
Idbury	Oxon	SP2219	51°52·4′	1°40·4′W	A	163
Idbury	Oxon	SP2319	51°52·4′	1°39·6′W	T	163
Iddenshall Grange	Ches	SJ5363	53°10·0′	2°41·8′W	X	117
Iddesleigh	Devon	SS5608	50°51·5′	4°2·4′W	T	191
Iddlecott	Devon	SS5612	50°53·6′	4°2·5′W	X	180
Ide	Devon	SX8990	50°42·2′	3°33·9′W	T	192
Ideal Fm	Herts	TL4224	51°54·0′	0°4·2′E	FM	167
Ideford	Devon	SX8977	50°35·2′	3°33·7′W	T	192
Ideford Arch	Devon	SX8877	50°35·2′	3°34·5′W	X	192
Ideford Common	Devon	SX9078	50°35·7′	3°32·9′W	X	192
Ide Hill	Kent	TQ4851	51°14·6′	0°7·6′E	T	188
Idehurst Copse	W Susx	TQ0325	51°1·1′	0°31·5′W	F	186,197
Idehurst Fm	W Susx	TQ0325	51°1·1′	0°31·5′W	FM	186,197
Iden	E Susx	TQ9123	50°58·7′	0°43·6′E	T	189
Iden	Kent	TQ9147	51°11·6′	0°44·4′E	X	189
Iden Grange	Kent	TQ7841	51°8·7′	0°33·1′E	X	188
Iden Green	Kent	TQ7437	51°6·6′	0°29·5′E	T	188
Iden Green	Kent	TQ8031	51°3·2′	0°34·5′E	T	188
Iden Park	E Susx	TQ9123	50°58·7′	0°43·6′E	X	189
Iden Wood	E Susx	TQ8923	50°58·7′	0°41·9′E	F	189
Ide's Barn	W Susx	SU9112	50°54·2′	0°42·0′W	X	197
Idestone	Devon	SX7048	50°19·3′	3°49·2′W	X	202
Idestone	Devon	SX8788	50°41·1′	3°35·6′W	X	192
Idle	Brad	SE1737	53°50·0′	1°44·1′W	T	104
Idlebush Barrow	Oxon	SU3084	51°33·5′	1°33·6′W	A	174
Idlecombe Down	I of W	SZ4585	50°40·0′	1°21·4′W	X	196

Idlecombe Fm	I of W	SZ4686	50°40·5′	1°20·6′W	FM	196
Idle Hill	Cumbr	NY4005	54°26·5′	2°55·1′W	X	90
Idle Hill	Herts	TL3021	51°52·6′	0°6·3′W	X	166
Idle Hill	Tames	SJ9793	53°26·3′	2°2·3′W	X	109
Idleigh Court	Kent	TQ6265	51°21·9′	0°20·0′E	X	177
Idle Moor	Brad	SE1637	53°50·0′	1°45·0′W	T	104
Idlerocks	Staffs	SJ9337	52°56·1′	2°5·8′W	X	127
Idless	Corn	SW8247	50°17·2′	5°3·2′W	T	204
Idlestone	Aberd	NO6493	57°1·9′	2°35·1′W	X	37,45
Idlicote	Warw	SP2844	52°5·9′	1°35·1′W	T	151
Idlicote Hill	Warw	SP2843	52°5·3′	1°35·1′W	X	151
Idlicote Ho	Warw	SP2844	52°5·9′	1°35·1′W	X	151
Idmiston	Wilts	SU1937	51°8·1′	1°43·3′W	T	184
Idmiston Down	Wilts	SU2236	51°7·6′	1°40·7′W	X	184
Idoch Water	Aberd	NJ7548	57°31·5′	2°24·6′W	W	29
Idole	Carm	SN4215	51°48·9′	4°17·1′W	T	159
Idover Demesne Fm	Wilts	ST9883	51°33·0′	2°1·3′W	FM	173
Idover Ho	Wilts	ST9882	51°32·4′	2°1·3′W	X	173
Idridgehay	Derby	SK2849	53°2·5′	1°34·5′W	T	119
Idridgehay Green	Derby	SK2849	53°2·5′	1°34·5′W	T	119
Idridge Scar	Cumbr	SD3071	54°8·1′	3°3·9′W	X	96,97
Idrigill	Highld	NG2537	57°20·7′	6°33·8′W	X	23
Idrigill	Highld	NG3863	57°35·1′	6°22·6′W	T	23
Idrigill Point	Highld	NG2436	57°20·1′	6°34·7′W	X	23
Idson Fm	Somer	ST2244	51°11·6′	3°6·6′W	FM	182
Idstone	Oxon	SU2584	51°33·5′	1°38·0′W	T	174
Idstone Down	Swin	SU2780	51°31·3′	1°36·3′W	X	174
Idsworth Down	Hants	SU7314	50°55·5′	0°57·3′W	X	197
Idsworth Ho	Hants	SU7213	50°54·9′	0°58·2′W	X	197
Idvies	Angus	NO5347	56°37·0′	2°45·5′W	X	54
Idvies Hill	Angus	NO5347	56°37·0′	2°45·5′W	X	54
Idvies Mill	Angus	NO5448	56°37·6′	2°44·5′W	X	54
Iet-y-bwlch	Carm	SN1628	51°55·4′	4°40·2′W	T	145,158
Iffcomb Wood	Glos	SP0112	51°48·6′	1°58·7′W	F	163
Iffen Meadows Fm	Kent	TR1454	51°14·9′	1°4·4′E	FM	179,189
Ifferdale	Arg & Bt	NR7733	55°32·6′	5°31·7′W	X	68,69
Ifferdale Burn	Arg & Bt	NR7533	55°32·6′	5°33·6′W	W	68,69
Ifferdale Cottage	Arg & Bt	NR7633	55°32·6′	5°32·6′W	X	68,69
Iffin Fm	Kent	TR1454	51°14·9′	1°4·4′E	FM	179,189
Iffin Wood	Kent	TR1353	51°14·4′	1°3·5′E	F	179,189
Iffley	Oxon	SP5203	51°43·6′	1°14·4′W	T	164
Ifield	W Susx	TQ2537	51°7·3′	0°12·4′W	T	187
Ifield Court	Kent	TQ6469	51°24·0′	0°21·9′E	A	177
Ifield Court	W Susx	TQ2438	51°7·9′	0°13·3′W	X	187
Ifield Green	W Susx	TQ2538	51°7·9′	0°12·4′W	T	187
Ifieldwood	W Susx	TQ2338	51°7·9′	0°14·1′W	T	187
Ifold	W Susx	TQ0231	51°4·4′	0°32·3′W	T	186
Iford	Bourne	SZ1393	50°44·4′	1°48·6′W	T	195
Iford	E Susx	TQ4007	50°51·0′	0°0·3′W	T	198
Iford Br	Bourne	SZ1393	50°44·4′	1°48·6′W	X	195
Iford Hill	E Susx	TQ3906	50°50·4′	0°1·2′W	X	198
Iford Manor	Wilts	ST8058	51°19·5′	2°16·8′W	A	173
Ifton Fm	Shrops	SJ3237	52°55·8′	3°0·3′W	FM	126
Ifton Great Wood	Monm	ST4588	51°35·5′	2°47·2′W	F	171,172
Ifton Hall	Shrops	SJ3238	52°56·3′	3°0·3′W	X	126
Ifton Heath	Shrops	SJ3337	52°55·8′	2°59·4′W	T	126
Ifton Manor	Monm	ST4687	51°35·0′	2°46·4′W	X	171,172
Ightfield	Shrops	SJ5938	52°56·5′	2°36·2′W	T	126
Ightfield Hall	Shrops	SJ6039	52°57·1′	2°35·3′W	X	127
Ightfield Heath	Shrops	SJ5937	52°56·0′	2°36·2′W	T	126
Ightham	Kent	TQ5956	51°17·1′	0°17·2′E	T	188
Ightham Court	Kent	TQ5957	51°17·6′	0°17·2′E	X	188
Ightham Mote	Kent	TQ5853	51°15·5′	0°16·3′E	A	188
Ightham Warren	Kent	TQ5955	51°16·5′	0°17·2′E	T	188
Igtham Common	Kent	TQ5855	51°16·6′	0°16·3′E	T	188
Iken	Suff	TM4155	52°8·7′	1°31·7′E	T	156
Iken Boot	Suff	TM4154	52°8·1′	1°31·7′E	X	156
Ikencliff	Suff	TM4056	52°9·2′	1°30·9′E	X	156
Iken Common	Suff	TM4155	52°8·7′	1°31·7′E	X	156
Iken Heath	Suff	TM4055	52°8·7′	1°30·9′E	X	156
Iken Marshes	Suff	TM4256	52°9·2′	1°32·7′E	X	156
Iken Wood	Suff	TM3956	52°9·3′	1°30·0′E	F	156
Ilam	Staffs	SK1350	53°3·1′	1°48·0′W	T	119
Ilam Country Park	Staffs	SK1351	53°3·6′	1°48·0′W	X	119
Ilam Estate Country Park	Staffs	SK1350	53°3·1′	1°48·0′W	X	119
Ilam Rock	Staffs	SK1453	53°4·7′	1°47·1′W	X	119
Ilam Tops	Staffs	SK1352	53°4·1′	1°48·0′W	X	119
Ilbury Fm	Oxon	SP4331	51°58·8′	1°22·0′W	FM	151
Ilchester	Somer	ST5222	51°0·0′	2°40·7′W	T	183
Ilchester Mead	Somer	ST5122	51°0·0′	2°41·5′W	T	183
Ilderton	Northum	NU0121	55°29·2′	1°58·6′W	T	75
Ildertonmoor	Northum	NU0120	55°28·7′	1°58·6′W	X	75
Ileach Bhàn	Highld	NH6410	57°9·9′	4°14·5′W	H	35
Ileden	Kent	TR2052	51°13·7′	1°9·5′E	T	179,189
Ileden Wood	Kent	TR2151	51°13·1′	1°10·3′E	F	179,189
Ilford	Redbr	TQ4486	51°33·5′	0°5·0′E	T	177
Ilford	Somer	ST3617	50°57·2′	2°54·3′W	T	193
Ilford Bridges	Somer	ST3717	50°57·2′	2°53·4′W	X	193
Ilfracombe	Devon	SS5147	51°12·4′	4°7·6′W	T	180
Ilgar's Manor	Essex	TQ7998	51°39·4′	0°35·7′E	X	167
Il Holm	Shetld	HU6394	60°37·7′	0°50·4′W	X	1,2
Ilkerton Ridge	Devon	SS7145	51°11·6′	3°50·4′W	H	180
Ilkeston	Derby	SK4642	52°58·6′	1°18·5′W	T	129
Ilketshall Hall	Suff	TM3785	52°24·9′	1°29·5′E	X	156
Ilketshall St Andrew	Suff	TM3887	52°26·0′	1°30·5′E	T	156
Ilketshall St Lawrence	Suff	TM3883	52°23·8′	1°30·3′E	T	156
Ilketshall St Margaret	Suff	TM3585	52°25·0′	1°27·8′E	T	156
Ilkley	Brad	SE1147	53°55·4′	1°49·5′W	T	104
Ilkley Crags	Brad	SE1246	53°54·8′	1°48·6′W	X	104
Ilkley Moor	Brad	SE1046	53°54·8′	1°50·5′W	X	104
Illa	Monm	SO3706	51°45·2′	2°54·4′W	X	161
Illand	Corn	SX2878	50°34·8′	4°25·4′W	T	201
Illawalla	Lancs	SD3541	53°51·9′	2°58·9′W	X	102
Illbeare	Somer	ST1928	51°3·0′	3°9·0′W	X	181,193
Ill Bell	Cumbr	NY4307	54°27·6′	2°52·3′W	H	90
Ill Crag	Cumbr	NY2207	54°27·4′	3°11·8′W	X	89,90
Illeray	N Eil	NF7863	57°32·8′	7°22·5′W	T	18
Illers Leary	Devon	SS6530	51°3·4′	3°55·2′W	X	180
Illey	Dudley	SO9881	52°25·9′	2°1·4′W	T	139
Illgill Head	Cumbr	NY1604	54°25·7′	3°17·3′W	H	89

Illidge Green	Ches	SJ7963	53°10·1′	2°18·4′W	T	118
Illieston	W Loth	NT1069	55°54·6′	3°25·9′W	A	65
Illington	Norf	TL9489	52°28·1′	0°51·8′E	T	144
Illingworth	Cald	SE0728	53°45·1′	1°53·2′W	T	104
Illiswilgig	I Scilly	SV8513	49°56·3′	6°23·1′W	X	203
Illogan	Corn	SW6744	50°15·2′	5°15·8′W	T	203
Illogan Highway	Corn	SW6741	50°13·6′	5°15·6′W	T	203
Illshaw Heath	Sol	SP1374	52°22·1′	1°48·1′W	T	139
Illston Grange	Leic	SP6998	52°34·8′	0°58·5′W	X	141
Illston on the Hill	Leic	SP7099	52°35·3′	0°57·6′W	T	141
Illwills Border	W Berks	SU4066	51°23·7′	1°25·1′W	F	174
Ilmer	Bucks	SP7605	51°44·5′	0°53·6′W	T	165
Ilmington	Warw	SP2143	52°5·3′	1°41·2′W	T	151
Ilminster	Somer	ST3614	50°55·5′	2°54·3′W	T	193
Ilsington	Devon	SX7876	50°34·5′	3°43·0′W	T	191
Ilsington	Dorset	SY7591	50°43·3′	2°20·9′W	X	194
Ilsington Ho	Dorset	SY7594	50°44·9′	2°20·9′W	A	194
Ilsington Wood	Dorset	SY7592	50°43·9′	2°20·9′W	F	194
Ilsley Barn Fm	W Berks	SU5081	51°31·8′	1°16·4′W	FM	174
Ilsom	Glos	ST9094	51°38·9′	2°8·3′W	X	163,173
Ilston	Swan	SS5590	51°35·7′	4°5·2′W	T	159
Ilston Cwm	Swan	SS5589	51°35·1′	4°5·2′W	X	159
Iltney Fm	Essex	TL8804	51°42·4′	0°43·7′E	FM	168
Ilton	Devon	SX7240	50°15·0′	3°47·4′W	X	202
Ilton	N Yks	SE1878	54°12·1′	1°43·0′W	T	99
Ilton	Somer	ST3517	50°57·2′	2°55·1′W	T	193
Ilton Castle Fm	Devon	SX7240	50°15·0′	3°47·4′W	FM	202
Ilton Grange Fm	N Yks	SE2078	54°12·1′	1°41·2′W	FM	99
Ilton Moor	N Yks	SE1676	54°11·0′	1°44·9′W	X	99
Imachar	N Ayr	NR8640	55°36·7′	5°23·4′W	T	62,69
Imachar Point	N Ayr	NR8640	55°36·7′	5°23·4′W	X	62,69
Imber	Wilts	ST9648	51°14·1′	2°3·1′W	T	184
Imberhorne Fm	W Susx	TQ3738	51°7·7′	0°2·1′W	FM	187
Imberley	W Susx	TQ3836	51°6·6′	0°1·3′W	X	187
Imbhams Fm	Surrey	SU9233	51°5·6′	0°40·8′W	FM	186
Imeraval	Arg & Bt	NR3545	55°37·8′	6°12·2′W	T	60
Imirfada	Highld	NC0631	58°13·8′	5°17·8′W	X	15
Immeroin	Stir	NN5317	56°19·6′	4°22·2′W	X	57
Immervoulin	Stir	NN5616	56°19·1′	4°19·3′W	X	57
Immingham	NE Lincs	TA1814	53°36·8′	0°12·6′W	T	113
Immingham Dock	NE Lincs	TA1916	53°37·9′	0°11·6′W	X	113
Immingham Grange	NE Lincs	TA1813	53°36·3′	0°14·4′W	X	113
Impaugh Fm	Suff	TM1460	52°12·0′	1°8·3′E	FM	156
Impen's Fm	Somer	ST2931	51°4·7′	3°0·4′W	FM	182
Imperial War Museum	Cambs	TL4546	52°5·8′	0°7·4′E	X	154
Impington	Cambs	TL4463	52°15·0′	0°7·0′E	T	154
Inadown Fm	Hants	SU7133	51°5·7′	0°58·8′W	FM	186
Inaltry	Moray	NJ5162	57°39·0′	2°48·8′W	X	29
Inbhir a' Gharraidh	Highld	NG2436	57°20·1′	6°34·7′W	W	23
Inbhir Beag	Highld	NM7392	56°58·1′	5°43·6′W	W	33,40
Inbhir Dhorrcail	Highld	NG8505	57°5·4′	5°32·5′W	W	33
Inbhir-fhaolain	Highld	NN1650	56°36·6′	4°59·4′W	X	41
Inbhir Ghil	Highld	NM3592	56°56·9′	6°21·0′W	X	39
Inbhir Ghualann	Highld	NG7924	57°15·5′	5°39·4′W	X	33
Inbhir nan-giubhas	Arg & Bt	NN1832	56°27·0′	4°56·7′W	W	50
Inbhir Scaddail	Highld	NN0168	56°45·9′	5°19·4′W	W	41
Ince	Ches	SJ4576	53°16·9′	2°49·1′W	T	117
Ince Banks	Ches	SJ4478	53°18·0′	2°50·0′W	X	117
Ince Blundell	Sefton	SD3203	53°31·4′	3°1·1′W	T	108
Ince Castle	Corn	SX4056	50°23·2′	4°14·7′W	A	201
Ince in Makerfield	Wigan	SD5804	53°32·1′	2°37·6′W	T	108
Ince Marshes	Ches	SJ4676	53°16·9′	2°48·2′W	X	117
Inces	W Susx	TQ3622	50°59·1′	0°3·4′W	X	198
Inch	Clackm	NS8791	56°6·2′	3°48·6′W	X	58
Inch	Cumbr	NY4175	55°4·2′	2°55·0′W	X	85
Inch	D & G	NX4447	54°47·9′	4°25·2′W	X	83
Inch	Fife	NO5303	56°13·3′	2°45·0′W	X	59
Inch	Highld	NH6756	57°40·1′	4°13·3′W	X	21
Inchaffray Abbey	Pth & Kin	NN9522	56°23·0′	3°41·6′W	A	52,53,58
Inchallon	Moray	NJ1557	57°36·0′	3°24·9′W	X	28
Incharnock	Moray	NJ1657	57°36·0′	3°23·9′W	X	28
Incharvie	Fife	NO4802	56°12·7′	2°49·9′W	X	59
Inchbae Forest	Highld	NH3776	57°44·9′	4°43·9′W	X	20
Inchbae Lodge	Highld	NH3969	57°41·2′	4°41·6′W	X	20
Inchbare	Angus	NO6065	56°46·7′	2°38·8′W	T	45
Inchbean	E Ayr	NS4334	55°34·7′	4°29·0′W	X	70
Inchbelle Fm	E Dunb	NS6675	55°57·2′	4°8·3′W	FM	64
Inchberry	Highld	NH5845	57°28·6′	4°21·6′W	X	26
Inchberry	Moray	NJ3155	57°35·0′	3°8·8′W	T	28
Inchberry Hill	Highld	NH5944	57°28·1′	4°20·6′W	H	26
Inchbrakie Fm	Pth & Kin	NN8922	56°22·9′	3°47·4′W	FM	52,58
Inchbraoch or Rossie Island	Angus	NO7056	56°41·9′	2°28·9′W	T	54
Inchbrayock	Angus	NO7156	56°41·9′	2°28·0′W	X	54
Inchbroke	Highld	NJ0525	57°18·6′	3°34·2′W	X	36
Inchbrook	Glos	SO8400	51°42·1′	2°13·5′W	T	162
Inchbroom	Moray	NJ2566	57°40·9′	3°15·0′W	X	28
Inch Burn	Scot Bord	NT2222	55°29·4′	3°13·6′W	W	73
Inch Burn	Scot Bord	NT3422	55°29·5′	3°2·3′W	W	73
Inchcailloch	Stir	NS4090	56°4·8′	4°33·8′W	X	56
Inchcape	Highld	NC6903	58°0·1′	4°12·5′W	X	16
Inchcolm	Fife	NT1882	56°1·7′	3°18·5′W	X	65,66
Inchconnachan	Arg & Bt	NS3791	56°5·3′	4°36·7′W	X	56
Inchcoonans	Pth & Kin	NO2323	56°23·8′	3°14·4′W	X	53,58
Inchcorsie	Moray	NJ5548	57°31·5′	2°44·6′W	X	29
Inchcross	W Loth	NS9666	55°52·8′	3°39·3′W	X	65
Inchcruin	Stir	NS3891	56°5·3′	4°35·8′W	X	56
Inchdairniemuir Plantation	Fife	NT2497	56°9·8′	3°13·0′W	F	59
Inchdowrie Ho	Angus	NO3472	56°50·3′	3°4·5′W	X	44
Inchdrewer	Aberd	NJ6560	57°38·0′	2°34·7′W	X	29
Inchdryne	Highld	NH9716	57°13·7′	3°41·9′W	X	36
Inchechart	Highld	NH4030	57°20·2′	4°39·0′W	X	26
Incheoch	Pth & Kin	NO2452	56°39·5′	3°13·9′W	X	53
Incheril	Highld	NH0362	57°36·6′	5°17·4′W	T	19
Inches	Aberd	NK0025	57°19·2′	1°59·5′W	X	38
Inches	Aberd	NO7682	56°56·0′	2°23·2′W	X	45
Inchewan Burn	Pth & Kin	NO0140	56°32·8′	3°36·2′W	W	52,53
Inchfad	Stir	NS3990	56°4·8′	4°34·8′W	X	56
Inchfield Moor	Cald	SD9122	53°41·9′	2°7·8′W	X	103
Inch Fm	Fife	NS9486	56°3·6′	3°41·7′W	FM	65

Inchford	Aberd	NJ5657	57°36·3′	2°43·7′W	X	29
Inchford Brook	Warw	SP2671	52°20·4′	1°36·7′W	W	140
Inchfuir	Highld	NH7272	57°43·4′	4°8·5′W	X	21
Inchgalbraith	Arg & Bt	NS3690	56°4·7′	4°37·7′W	X	56
Inchgarth	Angus	NO4450	56°38·6′	2°54·3′W	X	54
Inchgarth	Pth & Kin	NN7650	56°37·8′	4°0·8′W	X	42,51,52
Inch Garvie	C of Edin	NT1379	56°0·0′	3°23·3′W	X	65
Inch Geck	Aberd	NJ9927	57°20·3′	2°0·5′W	X	38
Inchgll Fm	Fife	NT1895	56°8·7′	3°18·7′W	FM	58
Inchgotrick	E Ayr	NS4133	55°34·1′	4°30·9′W	X	70
Inchgray Fm	Aberd	NO6674	56°51·6′	2°33·0′W	FM	45
Inchgreen	Aberd	NJ8346	57°30·5′	2°16·6′W	X	29,30
Inchgrundle	Angus	NO4179	56°54·2′	2°57·7′W	X	44
Inch Ho	Fife	NS9386	56°3·6′	3°42·7′W	X	65
Inch House	C of Edin	NT2770	55°55·3′	3°9·6′W	A	66
Inchie	Stir	NN5900	56°10·6′	4°15·8′W	X	57
Inchina	Highld	NG9691	57°52·0′	5°25·9′W	X	19
Inchindown	Highld	NH6974	57°44·5′	4°11·6′W	X	21
Inchinnan	Renf	NS4769	55°53·6′	4°26·4′W	T	64
Inchintaury	Highld	NH6983	57°49·3′	4°11·9′W	X	21
Inchkeil	Moray	NJ1465	57°40·3′	3°26·0′W	X	28
Inchkeith	Fife	NT2982	56°1·8′	3°7·9′W	X	66
Inchkeith Hill	Scot Bord	NT4848	55°43·6′	2°49·2′W	H	73
Inch Kenneth	Arg & Bt	NM4335	56°26·5′	6°9·7′W	X	47,48
Inchkinloch	Highld	NC5944	58°22·0′	4°24·1′W	X	10
Inchlaggan	Highld	NH1701	57°4·1′	5°0·7′W	X	34
Inchloan	Aberd	NO7692	57°1·4′	2°23·3′W	X	38,45
Inchlonaig	Arg & Bt	NS3893	56°6·4′	4°35·9′W	X	56
Inchlumpie	Highld	NH5875	57°44·8′	4°22·7′W	X	21
Inchmagrannachan	Pth & Kin	NO0044	56°34·9′	3°37·2′W	X	52,53
Inchmahome	Stir	NN5700	56°10·5′	4°17·8′W	X	57
Inchmarlo	Aberd	NO6796	57°3·5′	2°32·2′W	X	38,45
Inchmarnoch	Aberd	NO4296	57°3·3′	2°56·9′W	T	37,44
Inchmarnock	Arg & Bt	NS0259	55°47·3′	5°9·0′W	X	63
Inchmartine Ho	Pth & Kin	NO2628	56°26·6′	3°11·6′W	X	53,59
Inchmery Ho	Hants	SZ4398	50°47·0′	1°23·0′W	X	196
Inchmichael	Pth & Kin	NO2425	56°24·9′	3°13·5′W	X	53,59
Inchmickery	C of Edin	NT2080	56°0·6′	3°16·5′W	X	66
Inchmoan	Arg & Bt	NS3790	56°4·8′	4°36·7′W	X	56
Inchmoor	Heref	SO4965	52°17·1′	2°44·5′W	X	137,138,148
Inch Moor	Scot Bord	NT7053	55°46·4′	2°28·3′W	X	67,74
Inchmore	Aberd	NJ2108	57°9·6′	3°17·9′W	X	36
Inchmore	Highld	NH3940	57°25·6′	4°40·4′W	X	26
Inchmore	Highld	NH5745	57°28·6′	4°22·6′W	T	26
Inchmore Hotel	Highld	NH5644	57°28·1′	4°23·6′W	X	26
Inchmulloch Hill	D & G	NX1039	54°42·9′	4°56·6′W	H	82
Inchmurrin	W Dunb	NS3887	56°3·2′	4°35·6′W	X	56
Inchnabobart	Aberd	NO3087	56°58·4′	3°8·6′W	X	44
Inchnacape	Moray	NJ2020	57°16·1′	3°19·1′W	X	36
Inchnacardoch Forest	Highld	NH3309	57°8·8′	4°45·2′W	X	34
Inchnacardoch Lodge Hotel	Highld	NH3710	57°9·4′	4°41·2′W	X	34
Inchnadamph	Highld	NC2521	58°8·9′	4°57·9′W	T	15
Inchnadamph Forest	Highld	NC2721	58°8·9′	4°55·9′W	X	15
Inchnadamph National Nature Reserve	Highld	NC2619	58°7·8′	4°56·8′W	X	15
Inchneuk Fm	N Lanak	NS7169	55°54·1′	4°3·4′W	FM	64
Inchnye	Fife	NO2716	56°20·1′	3°10·4′W	X	59
Inchock	Angus	NO6848	56°37·6′	2°30·8′W	X	54
Inch of Arnhall	Aberd	NO6270	56°49·5′	2°36·9′W	X	45
Inch of Culter	Aberd	NJ8500	57°5·7′	2°14·4′W	X	38
Inch of Ferryton	Clackm	NS9089	56°5·1′	3°45·6′W	X	65
Inch-of-Leckie	Stir	NS6795	56°8·0′	4°8·0′W	X	57
Inch Parks	D & G	NX0962	54°55·2′	4°58·4′W	X	82
Inchree	Highld	NN0263	56°43·3′	5°13·7′W	T	41
Inchreed Fm	E Susx	TQ5226	51°1·0′	0°10·4′E	FM	188,199
Inchrory	Highld	NH5046	57°29·0′	4°29·7′W	X	26
Inchrory	Moray	NJ1708	57°9·6′	3°21·9′W	X	36
Inchs	Corn	SW9963	50°26·2′	4°49·5′W	T	200
Inchstelly	Moray	NJ1463	57°39·2′	3°26·0′W	X	28
Inchtavannach	Arg & Bt	NS3691	56°5·3′	4°37·7′W	X	56
Inch, The	Pth & Kin	NO1039	56°32·3′	3°27·4′W	X	53
Inch, The	Pth & Kin	NO1340	56°32·9′	3°24·5′W	X	53
Inch, The	Scot Bord	NT3421	55°29·0′	3°2·2′W	X	73
Inchture	Pth & Kin	NO2828	56°26·6′	3°9·6′W	T	53,59
Inchtuthill Cott	Pth & Kin	NO1139	56°32·3′	3°26·4′W	X	53
Inchully	Highld	NH3936	57°23·4′	4°40·3′W	X	26
Inchvannie	Highld	NH4959	57°36·0′	4°31·1′W	X	26
Inchvuilt	Highld	NH2238	57°24·1′	4°57·3′W	X	25
Inchvuilt Wood	Highld	NH2337	57°23·6′	4°56·3′W	F	25
Inchyettle	Highld	NH8348	57°30·7′	3°56·7′W	X	27
Inchyra	Pth & Kin	NO1820	56°22·2′	3°19·2′W	T	53,58
Inchyra Grange Hotel	Falk	NS9379	55°59·8′	3°42·5′W	X	65
Inchyra Ho	Pth & Kin	NO1921	56°22·7′	3°18·3′W	X	53,58
Incledon Fm	Devon	SS4640	51°8·6′	4°11·7′W	FM	180
Incledon Fm	Devon	SS4738	51°7·5′	4°10·8′W	FM	180
Incline, The	Somer	ST0234	51°6·1′	3°23·6′W	X	181
Incline Top	N Yks	NZ6102	54°24·8′	1°3·2′W	X	94
Incott Fm	Devon	SX6298	50°46·1′	3°57·0′W	FM	191
Indian Fm	N Yks	NZ4708	54°28·2′	1°16·1′W	FM	93
Indian Queens	Corn	SW9159	50°23·9′	4°56·1′W	T	200
Indicknowle	Devon	SS5944	51°10·9′	4°0·7′W	X	180
Indicombe	Devon	SS6630	51°3·5′	3°54·3′W	X	180
Indicott	Devon	SS5741	51°9·3′	4°2·3′W	X	180
Indio	Devon	SX8177	50°35·1′	3°40·5′W	X	191
Ineraval	Arg & Bt	NR3241	55°35·6′	6°14·8′W	X	60
Inett	Shrops	SJ6900	52°36·1′	2°27·1′W	X	127
In Fell	N Yks	SD9959	54°1·9′	2°0·5′W	X	103
In Field	E Yorks	SE8352	53°57·7′	0°43·7′W	X	106
Infield Ho	Lancs	SD5344	53°53·6′	2°42·5′W	X	102
Infield's Fm	Cambs	TL3599	52°34·6′	0°0·1′W	FM	142
Ingale Skerry	Orkney	HY6719	59°3·7′	2°34·0′W	X	5
Ingale Sound	Orkney	HY6620	59°4·2′	2°35·1′W	W	5
Inga Ness	Orkney	HY2115	59°1·2′	3°22·1′W	X	6
Inga Ness	Orkney	HY4143	59°16·4′	3°1·6′W	X	5
Inganess	Orkney	HY4609	58°58·2′	2°55·9′W	X	6,7
Inganess Bay	Orkney	HY4810	58°58·7′	2°53·8′W	W	6
Inganoust	Orkney	HY6522	59°5·3′	2°36·2′W	X	5
Ingardine	Shrops	SO6281	52°25·8′	2°33·1′W	X	138
Ingardine Brook	Shrops	SO6281	52°25·8′	2°33·1′W	W	138

Ingarsby Old Hall	Leic	SK6805	52°38·5′	0°59·3′W	A	141
Ingarsby Village	Leic	SK6805	52°38·5′	0°59·3′W	X	141
Ingashowe	Orkney	HY3812	58°59·7′	3°4·3′W	X	6
Ingatestone	Essex	TQ6499	51°40·2′	0°22·7′E	T	167,177
Ingatestone Hall	Essex	TQ6598	51°39·6′	0°23·5′E	A	167,177
Ingatus, The	Orkney	HY6222	59°5·3′	2°39·3′W	X	5
Ing Barn	Lancs	SD6848	53°55·9′	2°28·8′W	X	103
Ingbarrow Fm	N Yks	SE3849	53°56·4′	1°24·9′W	FM	104
Ingber Ho	N Yks	SD9054	53°59·2′	2°8·7′W	X	103
Ingber Plantn	N Yks	SD9054	53°59·2′	2°8·7′W	F	103
Ingbirchworth	Barns	SE2206	53°33·2′	1°39·7′W	T	110
Ingbirchworth Resr	Barns	SE2105	53°32·7′	1°40·6′W	W	110
Ing Bridge	Cumbr	NY4104	54°25·9′	2°54·2′W	X	90
Ing Close	N Yks	SD7262	54°3·4′	2°25·2′W	X	98
Ingebeck	I of M	SC3584	54°13·8′	4°31·5′W	X	95
Ing Ends	Lancs	SD8140	53°51·6′	2°16·9′W	X	103
Ingerthorpe	N Yks	SE2966	54°5·6′	1°33·0′W	T	99
Ingestone	Heref	SO6029	51°57·7′	2°34·5′W	X	149
Ingestre	Staffs	SJ9824	52°49·1′	2°1·4′W	T	127
Ingfield Manor (Sch)	W Susx	TQ0928	51°2·7′	0°26·3′W	X	187,198
Ingham	Lincs	SK9483	53°20·4′	0°34·9′W	T	121
Ingham	Norf	TG3926	52°46·9′	1°33·1′E	T	133,134
Ingham	Suff	TL8570	52°18·0′	0°43·2′E	T	144,155
Ingham Cliff	Lincs	SK9683	53°20·3′	0°33·1′W	X	121
Ingham Cliff Fm	Lincs	SK9584	53°20·9′	0°34·0′W	FM	121
Ingham Corner	Norf	TG3927	52°47·5′	1°33·1′E	T	133,134
Inghams	Suff	TM1049	52°6·2′	1°4·4′E	X	155,169
Ing Head Fm	Lancs	SD8140	53°51·6′	2°16·9′W	FM	103
Ingheads	Cumbr	SD7790	54°18·6′	2°20·8′W	X	98
Ing Heads	Cumbr	SD7898	54°22·9′	2°19·9′W	X	98
Ing Hey	Lancs	SD8833	53°47·8′	2°10·5′W	X	103
Inghey Br	N Yks	SD9651	53°57·5′	2°3·2′W	X	103
Ing Heys	Lancs	SD9140	53°51·6′	2°7·8′W	X	103
Ing Hill	Cumbr	NY7802	54°25·0′	2°19·9′W	X	91
Ingimster	Highld	ND2953	58°27·8′	3°12·5′W	X	11,12
Ing Lands	Lincs	TF4094	53°25·7′	0°6·8′E	X	113
Ingleberry Lodge	Leic	SK4817	52°45·1′	1°16·9′W	X	129
Ingleborough	Norf	TF4715	52°43·0′	0°11·0′E	T	131
Ingleborough	N Yks	SD7474	54°9·9′	2°23·5′W	X	98
Ingleborough Cave	N Yks	SD7571	54°8·3′	2°22·5′W	X	98
Ingleborough Common	N Yks	SD7373	54°9·4′	2°24·4′W	X	98
Ingleborough Fm	Norf	TF4715	52°43·0′	0°11·0′E	FM	131
Ingleborough (Fort)	N Yks	SD7474	54°9·9′	2°23·5′W	A	98
Ingleborough Hall	N Yks	SD7469	54°7·2′	2°23·5′W	X	98
Ingle Br	N Yks	SD8859	54°1·9′	2°10·6′W	X	103
Ingleby	Derby	SK3427	52°50·6′	1°29·3′W	T	128
Ingleby	Lincs	SK8977	53°17·2′	0°39·5′W	X	121
Ingleby Arncliffe	N Yks	NZ4400	54°23·9′	1°18·9′W	T	93
Ingleby Barwick	Stock on T	NZ4414	54°31·4′	1°18·8′W	X	93
Ingleby Beck	N Yks	NZ5707	54°27·6′	1°6·8′W	W	93
Ingleby Beck	N Yks	NZ5904	54°25·9′	1°5·0′W	W	93
Ingleby Chase	Lincs	SK8978	53°17·7′	0°39·5′W	X	121
Ingleby Cross	N Yks	NZ4500	54°23·9′	1°18·0′W	T	93
Ingleby Grange	Lincs	SK8977	53°17·2′	0°39·5′W	X	121
Ingleby Greenhow	N Yks	NZ5806	54°27·0′	1°5·9′W	T	93
Ingleby Hill	Stock on T	NZ4412	54°30·3′	1°18·8′W	X	93
Ingleby Lodge	N Yks	SD9290	54°18·6′	2°7·0′W	X	98
Ingleby Manor	N Yks	NZ5805	54°26·5′	1°5·9′W	A	93
Ingleby Mill	N Yks	NZ5706	54°27·0′	1°6·8′W	X	93
Ingleby Moor	N Yks	NZ6004	54°25·9′	1°4·1′W	X	94
Ingleby Plantn	N Yks	NZ5805	54°26·5′	1°5·9′W	F	93
Ingleby Toft	Derby	SK3526	52°50·1′	1°28·4′W	X	128
Ingleby Village	Lincs	SK8977	53°17·2′	0°39·5′W	A	121
Ingleden	Kent	TQ8934	51°4·7′	0°42·3′E	X	189
Ingleigh Green	Devon	SS6007	50°51·0′	3°58·9′W	T	191
Inglemire	K upon H	TA0731	53°46·1′	0°22·2′W	T	107
Inglenook Fm	St Hel	SD4700	53°29·9′	2°47·5′W	FM	108
Inglesbatch	Bath & NE Somer	ST7061	51°21·1′	2°25·5′W	T	172
Inglesham	Swin	SU2098	51°41·1′	1°42·2′W	T	163
Inglesham Village	Swin	SU2098	51°41·1′	1°42·2′W	A	163
Ingleside	Card	ST2183	51°32·7′	3°8·0′W	X	171
Ingleston	D & G	NX6048	54°48·7′	4°10·3′W	X	83
Ingleston	D & G	NX6653	54°51·5′	4°4·8′W	X	83,84
Ingleston	D & G	NX7757	54°53·8′	3°54·7′W	X	84
Ingleston	D & G	NX9178	55°5·3′	3°42·0′W	X	84
Ingleston	D & G	NX9865	54°58·4′	3°35·2′W	X	84
Ingleston	D & G	NY0597	55°15·7′	3°29·3′W	X	78
Ingleston	Renf	NS4271	55°54·6′	4°31·2′W	X	64
Inglestone	D & G	NS8604	55°19·3′	3°47·4′W	X	78
Ingle Stone	D & G	NX6553	54°51·5′	4°5·8′W	X	83,84
Inglestone Common	S Glos	ST7588	51°35·7′	2°21·3′W	X	162,172
Inglestone Fm	S Glos	ST7488	51°35·6′	2°22·1′W	FM	162,172
Inglestonford	D & G	NX9764	54°57·9′	3°36·1′W	X	84
Ingleston Hill Cotts	D & G	NX9864	54°57·9′	3°35·2′W	X	84
Ingleston Mains	D & G	NX7989	55°11·1′	3°53·6′W	X	78
Ingleston Moor	D & G	NX7755	54°52·7′	3°54·6′W	X	84
Inglethorpe Manor	Norf	TF4807	52°38·7′	0°11·7′E	X	143
Ingleton	Durham	NZ1720	54°34·7′	1°43·8′W	T	92
Ingleton	N Yks	SD6973	54°9·4′	2°28·1′W	T	98
Ingleton Grange	Durham	NZ1620	54°34·7′	1°44·7′W	X	92
Inglewhite	Lancs	SD5439	53°51·0′	2°41·5′W	T	102
Inglewhite Lodge Fm	Lancs	SD5539	53°51·0′	2°40·6′W	FM	102
Inglewood	Clackm	NS8794	56°7·8′	3°48·6′W	X	58
Inglewood	W Berks	SU3666	51°23·7′	1°28·6′W	X	174
Inglewood Bank	Cumbr	NY5334	54°42·2′	2°43·3′W	X	90
Inglewoodbank Cottages	Cumbr	NY5233	54°41·6′	2°44·3′W	X	90
Inglewood Cottage	Cumbr	NY4843	54°47·0′	2°48·1′W	X	86
Inglewood Edge	Cumbr	NY3937	54°43·7′	2°56·4′W	X	90
Inglewood Fm	W Berks	SU3666	51°23·7′	1°28·6′W	FM	174
Inglewood Forest	Cumbr	NY4141	54°45·9′	2°54·6′W	X	85
Inglewood Forest	Cumbr	NY4539	54°44·8′	2°50·8′W	F	90
Inglewood Forest	Cumbr	NY4741	54°45·9′	2°49·0′W	X	86
Inglewood Ho	Cumbr	NY4742	54°46·5′	2°49·0′W	X	86
Inglewood Inn Fm	Cumbr	NY5033	54°41·6′	2°46·1′W	FM	90
Ingli Geo	Shetld	HU3779	60°29·8′	1°19·1′W	X	2,3
Inglisfield	E Loth	NT5168	55°54·4′	2°46·6′W	X	66
Inglismaldie	Aberd	NO6466	56°47·3′	2°34·9′W	A	45
Ingliston	Angus	NO3345	56°35·8′	3°5·0′W	X	53
Ingliston	Angus	NO4148	56°37·5′	2°57·2′W	T	54
Ingliston	C of Edin	NT1372	55°56·2′	3°23·1′W	X	65
Ingliston Hill	Angus	NO3444	56°35·3′	3°4·0′W	X	54
Inglistown	Aberd	NJ7922	57°17·5′	2°20·4′W	X	38
Ingmanthorpe	Derby	SK3373	53°15·4′	1°29·9′W	X	119
Ingmanthorpe	N Yks	SE4150	53°56·9′	1°22·1′W	T	105
Ingmanthorpe Park	Leeds	SE4249	53°56·4′	1°21·2′W	X	105
Ingmire Hall	Cumbr	SD6391	54°19·0′	2°33·7′W	X	97
Ingmote Hill	Norf	TG0637	52°53·7′	1°4·2′E	X	133
Ingo Brake	Devon	SX5184	50°38·4′	4°6·1′W	X	191,201
Ingoe	Northum	NZ0374	55°3·9′	1°56·8′W	T	87
Ingoe Moor	Northum	NZ0476	55°5·0′	1°55·8′W	X	87
Ingol	Lancs	SD5131	53°46·6′	2°44·3′W	T	102
Ingoldisthorpe	Norf	TF6832	52°51·8′	0°30·1′E	T	132
Ingoldmells	Lincs	TF5668	53°11·4′	0°20·5′E	T	122
Ingoldmells Point	Lincs	TF5768	53°11·4′	0°21·4′E	X	122
Ingoldsby	Lincs	TF0130	52°51·7′	0°29·6′W	T	130
Ingoldsby Wood	Lincs	SK9930	52°51·7′	0°31·4′W	F	130
Ingol, The	Norf	TF6532	52°51·8′	0°27·5′E	W	132
Ingon	Warw	SP2157	52°12·9′	1°41·2′W	T	151
Ingon Manor Hotel	Warw	SP2157	52°12·9′	1°41·2′W	X	151
Ingram	Northum	NU0116	55°26·5′	1°58·6′W	T	81
Ingram Grange	N Yks	NZ3804	54°26·0′	1°24·4′W	X	93
Ingram Mill	Northum	NU0216	55°26·5′	1°57·7′W	X	81
Ingram's Fm	E Susx	TQ7112	50°53·2′	0°26·3′E	FM	199
Ingrams Fm	W Susx	TQ0324	51°0·6′	0°31·5′W	FM	197
Ingrams Green	W Susx	SU8420	50°58·6′	0°47·8′W	T	197
Ingraston	Scot Bord	NT1148	55°43·3′	3°24·6′W	X	72
Ingra Tor	Devon	SX5572	50°32·0′	4°2·4′W	H	191
Ingrave	Essex	TQ6292	51°36·4′	0°20·8′E	T	177
Ingrave Hall	Essex	TQ6293	51°37·0′	0°20·8′E	X	177
Ingrebourne River	Hav	TQ5485	51°32·8′	0°13·7′E	W	177
Ingrebourne Valley	Hav	TQ5485	51°32·8′	0°13·7′E	X	177
Ingrie	Fife	NO2302	56°12·5′	3°14·0′W	X	58
Ingrow	Brad	SE0539	53°51·1′	1°55·0′W	T	104
Ings	Cumbr	SD4498	54°22·7′	2°51·3′W	T	97
Ingsay	Orkney	HY2828	59°8·2′	3°15·0′W	X	6
Ings Beck	Lancs	SD8044	53°53·8′	2°17·8′W	W	103
Ings Br	N Yks	SE9880	54°12·6′	0°29·4′W	X	101
Ingsdon	Devon	SX8172	50°32·4′	3°40·4′W	X	191
Ingsdon Hill	Devon	SX8173	50°32·9′	3°40·4′W	H	191
Ingsdons Hill	Somer	ST6343	51°11·3′	2°31·4′W	X	183
Ings End	Lancs	SD8144	53°53·8′	2°16·9′W	X	103
Ings Fm	K upon H	TA0735	53°48·3′	0°22·1′W	FM	107
Ings Fm	Lincs	SE8200	53°29·7′	0°45·4′W	FM	112
Ings Fm	Lincs	TA0200	53°29·4′	0°27·3′W	FM	112
Ings Fm	Lincs	TF0389	53°23·5′	0°26·7′W	FM	112,121
Ings Fm	Lincs	TF0570	53°13·2′	0°25·2′W	FM	121
Ings Fm	Lincs	TF1482	53°19·6′	0°16·9′W	FM	121
Ings Fm	Lincs	TF1882	53°19·5′	0°13·3′W	FM	122
Ings Fm	Lincs	TF2977	53°16·7′	0°3·5′W	FM	122
Ings Fm	Lincs	TF3948	53°0·9′	0°4·7′E	FM	131
Ings Fm	N Lincs	SE8304	53°31·8′	0°44·5′W	FM	112
Ings Fm	N Lincs	SK9298	53°28·5′	0°36·4′W	FM	112
Ings Fm	N Yks	NZ5407	54°27·6′	1°9·6′W	FM	93
Ings Fm	N Yks	SE1760	54°2·4′	1°44·0′W	FM	99
Ings Fm	N Yks	SE2646	53°54·8′	1°35·8′W	FM	104
Ings Fm	N Yks	SE8878	54°11·7′	0°38·7′W	FM	101
Ings Fm	N Yks	SE9880	54°12·6′	0°29·4′W	FM	101
Ings Fm	Red & Cl	NZ7518	54°33·3′	0°50·0′W	FM	94
Ings Ho	N Yks	SD9961	54°2·9′	2°0·5′W	X	98
Ings Ho	N Yks	SE4188	54°17·4′	1°21·8′W	X	99
Ings Laithe	N Yks	SD9158	54°1·3′	2°7·8′W	X	103
Ings Plantn	K upon H	TA0834	53°47·7′	0°21·2′W	F	107
Ings Plantn	N Yks	SE8559	54°1·4′	0°41·7′W	W	106
Ings Plantn	N Yks	SE9882	54°13·7′	0°29·4′W	F	101
Ings Point	Lancs	SD4772	54°8·7′	2°48·3′W	X	97
Ingsque Woods	N Yks	SE1098	54°22·9′	1°50·3′W	F	99
Ingst	S Glos	ST5887	51°35·1′	2°36·0′W	T	172
Ings, The	Lincs	SK9549	53°2·0′	0°34·6′W	X	130
Ings, The	Lincs	TF2157	53°6·0′	0°11·2′W	X	122
Ings, The	Lincs	TF3669	53°12·3′	0°2·6′E	X	122
Ings, The	Lincs	TF4462	53°8·4′	0°9·6′E	X	122
Ings, The	N Yks	SE7575	54°10·2′	0°50·7′W	X	100
Ingst Rhine	S Glos	ST5887	51°35·1′	2°36·0′W	W	172
Ings Wood	E Yorks	SE8130	53°45·8′	0°45·9′W	F	106
Ingthorpe	Rut	SK9908	52°39·9′	0°31·8′W	T	141
Ingthorpe Grange	N Yks	SD8952	53°58·1′	2°9·6′W	X	103
Ingulfs	Essex	TQ9192	51°35·9′	0°45·9′E	X	178
Ing Wood	Lancs	SD6545	53°54·2′	2°31·5′W	F	102,103
Ingworth	Norf	TG1929	52°49·1′	1°15·4′E	T	133,134
Inham Down	Wilts	SU2256	51°18·4′	1°40·7′W	X	174
Inham Hall	Cambs	TF4107	52°38·8′	0°5·5′E	X	142,143
Inhams	Hants	SU6412	50°54·5′	1°5·0′W	X	196
Inham's End	Cambs	TL2796	52°33·1′	0°7·2′W	X	142
Inholmes	N Yks	SE4743	53°53·1′	1°16·7′W	X	105
Inholmes	W Berks	SU3373	51°27·5′	1°31·1′W	X	174
Inholmes Court	Hants	SU7557	51°18·7′	0°55·0′W	X	175,186
Inholmes Wood	W Susx	SU8012	50°54·3′	0°51·3′W	F	197
Inholms Copse	W Susx	SU8526	51°1·9′	0°46·9′W	F	186,197
Inholms Fm	E Susx	TQ3617	50°56·4′	0°3·5′W	FM	198
Inholms Fm	E Yorks	TA1153	53°57·9′	0°18·1′W	FM	107
Inholms Fm	Surrey	TQ1747	51°12·8′	0°19·1′W	FM	187
Inhurst	Hants	SU5761	51°20·9′	1°10·5′W	T	174
Inhurst Fm	Hants	SU5761	51°20·9′	1°10·5′W	FM	174
Inhurst Ho (Sch)	Hants	SU5762	51°21·5′	1°10·5′W	X	174
Inion	Arg & Bt	NM9635	56°28·0′	5°18·3′W	X	49
Inions Fm	Beds	TL0720	51°52·3′	0°26·3′W	FM	166
Inishail	Arg & Bt	NN1024	56°22·5′	5°4·2′W	X	50
Inistrynich	Arg & Bt	NN1023	56°21·9′	5°4·1′W	X	50
Inivea	Arg & Bt	NM3651	56°34·9′	6°17·5′W	X	47
Injebreck Hill	I of M	SC3585	54°14·3′	4°31·5′W	H	95
Injebreck Plantation	I of M	SC3684	54°13·8′	4°30·5′W	F	95
Inkberrow	Worcs	SP0157	52°12·9′	1°58·7′W	T	150
Inkerman	Durham	NZ1139	54°45·0′	1°49·3′W	T	92
Inkerman	Orkney	HY5219	59°3·6′	2°49·7′W	X	6
Inkerman Fm	Bucks	SP9096	51°39·6′	0°41·5′W	FM	165
Inkerman Fm	Oxon	SP5230	51°58·2′	1°14·2′W	FM	151
Inkerman Br	Gwyn	SH2832	52°51·7′	4°32·9′W	X	123
Inkersall	Derby	SK4272	53°14·8′	1°21·8′W	T	120
Inkersall Fm	Notts	SK6260	53°8·2′	1°4·0′W	FM	120
Inkersall Grange Fm	Notts	SK6159	53°7·7′	1°4·9′W	FM	120
Inkersall Green	Derby	SK4272	53°14·8′	1°21·8′W	T	120
Inkerson Fen	Cambs	TF3406	52°38·3′	0°0·8′W	X	142
Inkford	Worcs	SP0774	52°22·1′	1°53·4′W	T	139
Inkley's Fm	Lincs	TF3509	52°39·9′	0°0·2′E	FM	142
Ink Moss	D & G	NX2766	54°57·8′	4°41·7′W	X	82
Inkpen	W Berks	SU3764	51°22·7′	1°27·7′W	T	174
Inkpen Common	W Berks	SU3863	51°22·1′	1°26·9′W	T	174
Inkpen Hill	W Berks	SU3562	51°21·6′	1°29·4′W	H	174
Inkstack	Highld	ND2570	58°37·0′	3°17·0′W	X	7,12
Inkster	Orkney	HY4119	59°3·5′	3°1·2′W	X	6
Inlandpasture	Northum	NU0149	55°44·3′	1°58·6′W	X	75
Inlands	W Susx	SU7706	50°51·1′	0°54·0′W	T	197
Inlands Fm	Wilts	SU1661	51°21·1′	1°45·8′W	FM	173
Inlay's Fm	Cambs	TF4005	52°37·7′	0°4·5′E	FM	142,143
Inmans	Cumbr	SD0988	54°17·0′	3°23·5′W	X	96
Inmarsh	Wilts	ST9460	51°20·6′	2°4·8′W	T	173
In Meadow Gate	Warw	SP4860	52°14·4′	1°17·4′W	X	151
Inmere Fm	Norf	TF7034	52°52·8′	0°32·0′E	FM	132
In Moor	N Yks	SE0875	54°10·5′	1°52·2′W	X	99
Innage	Monm	ST5291	51°37·2′	2°41·2′W	X	162,172
Innan Neb	Orkney	ND3592	58°48·9′	3°7·0′W	X	7
Innbanks	Shetld	HU3369	60°24·5′	1°23·6′W	X	2,3
Innean Glen	Arg & Bt	NR6016	55°23·0′	5°46·9′W	X	68
Innellan	Arg & Bt	NS1469	55°53·0′	4°58·0′W	T	63
Innellan Fm	Arg & Bt	NS1470	55°53·5′	4°58·0′W	FM	63
Innellan Hill	Arg & Bt	NS1370	55°53·5′	4°59·0′W	X	63
Inneraer	Orkney	HY3309	58°58·0′	3°9·4′W	X	6,7
Inner Anchorage	Devon	SS1444	51°10·1′	4°39·3′W	W	180
Inner Bay	Fife	NT1282	56°1·6′	3°24·3′W	W	65
Inner Black Hill	E Dunb	NS6181	56°0·4′	4°13·3′W	X	64
Inner Blair	D & G	NX0854	54°50·9′	4°59·0′W	X	82
Inner Booth	Shetld	HU3795	60°38·5′	1°18·9′W	X	1,2
Inner Br	Fife	NO4519	56°21·9′	2°53·0′W	X	59
Inner Brigurd Point	N Ayr	NS1852	55°43·9′	4°53·5′W	X	63
Inner Brough	Shetld	HU6693	60°37·2′	0°47·1′W	X	1,2
Innercochill	Pth & Kin	NN9138	56°31·5′	3°45·9′W	X	52
Innercraigie	Pth & Kin	NN9220	56°21·9′	3°44·4′W	X	52,58
Inner Dodd	Northum	NY6868	55°0·6′	2°29·6′W	X	86,87
Innerdouny Hill	Pth & Kin	NO0307	56°15·0′	3°33·5′W	H	58
Innerdownie	Pth & Kin	NN9603	56°12·8′	3°40·2′W	H	58
Innerdunning	Pth & Kin	NO0217	56°20·4′	3°34·7′W	X	58
Innerdunning Ho	Pth & Kin	NO0216	56°19·8′	3°34·7′W	X	58
Inner Farne	Northum	NU2135	55°36·7′	1°39·6′W	X	75
Inner Flaess	Shetld	HP6617	60°50·1′	0°46·7′W	X	1
Inner Froward Point	Devon	SX9049	50°20·1′	3°32·4′W	X	202
Innergask	Pth & Kin	NO0021	56°22·5′	3°36·7′W	X	52,53,58
Inner Gat	Lincs	TF4738	52°55·4′	0°11·6′E	X	131
Innergellie	Fife	NO5705	56°14·4′	2°41·2′W	X	59
Innerhadden	Pth & Kin	NN6757	56°41·4′	4°9·8′W	X	42,51
Innerhadden Burn	Pth & Kin	NN6655	56°40·3′	4°10·8′W	W	42,51
Inner Head	I Scilly	SV9009	49°54·3′	6°18·7′W	X	203
Inner Head	Swan	SS3987	51°33·8′	4°19·0′W	X	159
Inner Hebrides	Arg & Bt	NM1353	56°35·1′	6°40·0′W	X	46
Inner Hebrides	Arg & Bt	NM3929	56°23·1′	6°13·3′W	X	48
Inner Hebrides	Highld	NG3549	57°27·5′	6°24·6′W	X	23
Inner Hebrides	Highld	NG5020	57°12·4′	6°7·9′W	X	32
Inner Hebrides	Highld	NM3797	56°59·6′	6°19·4′W	X	39
Inner Heisker	N Eil	NL5886	56°50·6′	7°36·1′W	X	31
Inner Hill	Northum	NT8707	55°21·7′	2°11·9′W	H	80
Inner Hill	Northum	NT8708	55°22·2′	2°11·9′W	H	80
Inner Hill	Northum	NT9111	55°23·8′	2°8·1′W	H	80
Inner Hill	Northum	NT9210	55°23·3′	2°7·1′W	H	80
Inner Hill	Scot Bord	NT4407	55°21·5′	2°52·6′W	H	79
Inner Hill	Scot Bord	NT7264	55°52·4′	2°26·4′W	X	67
Inner Holm	Orkney	HY2508	58°57·4′	3°17·7′W	X	6,7
Inner Holm of Skaw	Shetld	HU5967	60°23·2′	0°55·3′W	X	2
Inner Hope	Devon	SX6739	50°14·4′	3°51·5′W	T	202
Inner Huntly	Scot Bord	NT4124	55°30·6′	2°55·6′W	X	73
Inner Knock	Lincs	TF5756	53°4·9′	0°21·1′E	X	122
Innerleith	Fife	NO2811	56°17·4′	3°9·3′W	X	59
Innerleithen	Scot Bord	NT3336	55°37·0′	3°3·4′W	T	73
Innerleven	Fife	NO3700	56°11·6′	3°0·5′W	T	59
Innermessan	D & G	NX0863	54°55·7′	4°59·4′W	X	82
Inner Mid Hill	D & G	NY1998	55°16·4′	3°16·1′W	X	79
Inner Nebbock	N Ayr	NS2440	55°37·6′	4°47·3′W	X	70
Innernyte Fm	Pth & Kin	NO1235	56°30·2′	3°25·3′W	FM	53
Inner Owers	W Susx	SZ8794	50°44·6′	0°45·6′W	X	197
Inner Park Wall	Glos	SP0426	51°56·2′	1°56·1′W	A	163
Innerpeffray	Pth & Kin	NN9018	56°20·8′	3°46·3′W	X	58
Innerpeffray Wood	Pth & Kin	NN9119	56°21·3′	3°45·4′W	F	58
Innersand	Shetld	HU3547	60°12·6′	1°21·6′W	X	3
Inner Score	Shetld	HU5145	60°11·4′	1°4·3′W	X	4
Inner Skaw	Shetld	HP6615	60°49·0′	0°46·7′W	X	1
Inner Skerry	Shetld	HU3633	60°5·1′	1°20·7′W	X	4
Inner Sound	Highld	ND3575	58°39·7′	3°6·7′W	W	7,12
Inner Sound	Highld	NG6441	57°24·2′	5°55·3′W	W	24
Inner Sound	Northum	NU2035	55°36·7′	1°40·5′W	W	75
Inner Sound	Orkney	HY6445	59°17·7′	2°37·4′W	W	5
Inner Tod Hill	S Lanak	NS6733	55°34·6′	4°6·1′W	X	71
Innertown	Orkney	HY2408	58°57·4′	3°18·8′W	T	6,7
Inner Voder	Shetld	HU5054	60°16·3′	1°5·3′W	X	3
Innerwell Fishery	D & G	NX4749	54°49·0′	4°22·4′W	X	83
Innerwell Port	D & G	NX4749	54°49·0′	4°22·4′W	W	83
Inner Westmark Knock	Lincs	TF5130	52°51·0′	0°15·0′E	X	131
Innerwick	E Loth	NT7274	55°57·7′	2°26·5′W	T	67
Innerwick	Pth & Kin	NN5847	56°35·9′	4°18·3′W	T	51
Innerwick Castle	E Loth	NT7373	55°57·2′	2°25·5′W	A	67
Innes Canal	Moray	NJ2666	57°39·9′	3°14·0′W	W	28
Innes House	Moray	NJ2764	57°39·9′	3°13·0′W	A	28
Innes Links	Moray	NJ2867	57°41·5′	3°12·0′W	X	28
Innesmill	Moray	NJ2863	57°39·3′	3°11·9′W	X	28
Inn Fm	Beds	TL0265	52°16·7′	0°29·9′W	FM	153
Innie	Arg & Bt	NM8716	56°17·6′	5°26·1′W	X	55
Inniemore Lodge	Arg & Bt	NM5421	56°19·3′	5°58·3′W	X	48
Inniens Bay	Orkney	HY5238	59°13·8′	2°50·0′W	W	5
Inninbeg	Highld	NM6943	56°31·6′	5°44·9′W	X	49
Inninmore Bay	Highld	NM7241	56°30·6′	5°41·9′W	W	49
Innins, The	Shetld	HU3681	60°30·9′	1°20·2′W	X	1,2,3
Innis	Corn	SX0262	50°25·7′	4°46·9′W	X	200

Innis a' Chròtha	Highld	NG9721	57°14·3'	5°21·4'W	X	25,33
Innis Ard	Stir	NN4600	56°10·3'	4°28·4'W	H	57
Innischoarach	Stir	NN4936	56°29·8'	4°26·7'W	X	51
Innis Chonain	Arg & Bt	NN1025	56°23·0'	5°4·2'W	T	50
Innis Chonnell	Arg & Bt	NM9711	56°15·1'	5°16·2'W	X	55
Inniscord Lochs	Shetld	HU3289	60°35·3'	1°24·5'W	W	1
Innis Downs	Corn	SX0262	50°25·7'	4°46·9'W	X	200
Innis Dubh	N Ayr	NR9825	55°28·9'	5°11·4'W	X	69
Innishewan	Stir	NN4828	56°25·4'	4°27·4'W	X	51
Innisidgen	I Scilly	SV9212	49°56·0'	6°17·2'W	X	203
Inn Island	Arg & Bt	NM8946	56°33·8'	5°25·6'W	X	49
Innis Loch	Shetld	HU3390	60°35·8'	1°23·3'W	W	1,2
Innis Mhòr	Highld	NH8485	57°50·6'	3°56·8'W	X	21
Innis nan Damh	Highld	NC4500	57°58·0'	4°36·7'W	X	16
Innisraineach Burn	Stir	NN4537	56°30·2'	4°30·7'W	W	51
Innis Sea-ràmhach	Arg & Bt	NM9710	56°14·6'	5°16·1'W	X	55
Innis Stiùre	Arg & Bt	NM9408	56°13·5'	5°18·9'W	X	55
Innister	Orkney	HY3833	59°11·0'	3°4·6'W	X	6
Innox Hill	Somer	ST7749	51°14·6'	2°19·4'W	T	183
Innri Geo	Shetld	HU3088	60°34·7'	1°26·7'W	X	1
Innsacre	Dorset	SY4992	50°43·8'	2°43·0'W	X	193,194
Innseag na h-Iuraiche	Arg & Bt	NN1840	56°31·3'	4°57·1'W	X	50
Inns Holm	Shetld	HU3620	59°58·1'	1°20·8'W	X	4
Innsker	Orkney	HY5221	59°4·7'	2°49·8'W	W	5,6
Innsworth	Glos	SO8621	51°53·5'	2°11·8'W	T	162
Inny Foot	Corn	SX3877	50°34·5'	4°16·9'W	W	201
Inny Ham	Corn	SX3777	50°34·4'	4°17·7'W	X	201
Inon	D & G	NX6748	54°48·8'	4°3·8'W	X	83,84
Inpark Fm	Dorset	ST5701	50°48·6'	2°36·2'W	FM	194
Insabysetter	Orkney	HY2826	59°7·2'	3°15·0'W	X	6
In Scar	Cumbr	NY5419	54°34·1'	2°42·3'W	X	90
Insch	Aberd	NJ6328	57°20·7'	2°36·4'W	T	37
Insch	Highld	NH7156	57°34·8'	4°9·0'W	X	27
Inschfield	Aberd	NJ6229	57°21·3'	2°37·4'W	X	37
Insch of Ury	Aberd	NO8492	57°1·4'	2°15·4'W	X	38,45
Inschtammack	Aberd	NJ4942	57°28·2'	2°50·6'W	X	28,29
Insetton Ho	Worcs	SO9274	52°22·1'	2°6·7'W	X	139
Insh	Highld	NH8101	57°5·3'	3°57·4'W	T	35
Insh	Highld	NN2680	56°53·0'	4°50·9'W	X	34,41
Inshanks	D & G	NX1034	54°40·2'	4°56·4'W	X	82
Inshanks Fell	D & G	NX1135	54°40·7'	4°55·5'W	H	82
Insharn	Highld	NH8422	57°16·7'	3°55·0'W	X	35
Inshegra	Highld	NC2455	58°27·1'	5°0·5'W	T	9
Inshewan	Angus	NO4456	56°41·8'	2°54·4'W	X	54
Insh Ho	Highld	NH8303	57°6·4'	3°55·4'W	X	35
Insh Island	Arg & Bt	NM7319	56°18·8'	5°39·8'W	X	55
Inshlampie	Highld	NC7146	58°23·3'	4°11·9'W	X	10
Inshlampie Burn	Highld	NC7145	58°22·7'	4°11·9'W	W	10
Inshoch Fm	Highld	NH9356	57°35·1'	3°46·9'W	FM	27
Inshoch Wood	Highld	NH9558	57°36·3'	3°45·0'W	F	27
Inshore	Highld	NC3269	58°34·9'	4°52·9'W	X	9
Inshriach	Highld	NH8907	57°8·7'	3°49·6'W	X	35,36
Inshriach Forest	Highld	NH8302	57°5·9'	3°55·4'W	F	35
Inshriach Ho	Highld	NH8707	57°8·7'	3°51·6'W	X	35,36
Inskip	Lancs	SD4637	53°49·8'	2°48·8'W	T	102
Inskip Moss Side	Lancs	SD4539	53°50·9'	2°49·7'W	T	102
In Sleets	N Yks	SD8672	54°8·9'	2°12·4'W	X	98
Instaple Fm	Devon	SS3211	50°52·7'	4°22·9'W	FM	190
Instead Manor Ho	Suff	TM2380	52°22·6'	1°17·0'E	X	156
Instone	Heref	SO6555	52°11·8'	2°30·3'W	X	149
Instone Court	Heref	SO6550	52°9·1'	2°30·3'W	X	149
Instoneville	Donc	SE5512	53°36·3'	1°9·7'W	T	111
Instow	Devon	SS4730	51°3·2'	4°10·6'W	T	180
Instow Sands	Devon	SS4731	51°3·7'	4°10·6'W	X	180
Insworke	Corn	SX4252	50°21·0'	4°12·9'W	T	201
Intack	Black w Dar	SD7028	53°45·1'	2°26·9'W	T	103
Intack	Cumbr	NY4347	54°49·1'	2°52·8'W	X	85
Intack	Cumbr	NY7043	54°47·1'	2°27·6'W	X	86,87
Intack	Lancs	SD5362	54°3·4'	2°42·7'W	X	97
Intack	Lancs	SD6639	53°51·0'	2°30·6'W	X	103
Intack	N Yks	SD7880	54°13·2'	2°19·8'W	X	98
Intack Fm	Cumbr	NY2644	54°47·4'	3°8·6'W	FM	85
Intack Fm	E Yorks	TA3525	53°42·5'	0°3·1'E	FM	107,113
Intack Fm	Lancs	SD5168	54°6·6'	2°44·6'W	FM	97
Intack Head	Cumbr	NY3144	54°47·4'	3°4·0'W	X	85
Intake	Cumbr	NY6304	54°26·1'	2°33·8'W	X	91
Intake	Cumbr	SD7797	54°22·3'	2°20·8'W	X	98
Intake	Donc	SE5903	53°31·5'	1°6·2'W	T	111
Intake	Leeds	SE2235	53°48·9'	1°39·5'W	T	104
Intake	Northum	NU1711	55°23·8'	1°43·5'W	X	81
Intake	N Yks	SD9642	53°52·1'	2°3·2'W	X	103
Intake	N Yks	SE0955	53°59·7'	1°51·3'W	X	104
Intake	Sheff	SK3884	53°21·3'	1°25·3'W	T	110,111
Intake Beck	N Yks	NZ9107	54°27·3'	0°35·4'W	W	94
Intake Fm	Brad	SE0136	53°49·5'	1°58·7'W	FM	104
Intake Fm	Derby	SK1679	53°18·7'	1°45·2'W	FM	119
Intake Fm	Durham	NZ0238	54°44·5'	1°57·7'W	FM	92
Intake Fm	E Yorks	SE7232	53°47·0'	0°54·0'W	FM	105,106
Intake Fm	Leeds	SE1843	53°53·2'	1°43·2'W	FM	104
Intake Fm	Leeds	SE3639	53°51·0'	1°26·8'W	FM	104
Intake Fm	N Yks	NZ8704	54°25·7'	0°39·1'W	FM	94
Intake Fm	N Yks	SD9954	53°59·2'	2°0·5'W	FM	103
Intake Fm	N Yks	SE0874	54°9·9'	1°52·2'W	FM	99
Intake Fm	Staffs	SJ9461	53°9·0'	2°5·0'W	FM	118
Intake Fm	Staffs	SK0355	53°5·8'	1°56·9'W	FM	119
Intake Gate	Leeds	SE1442	53°52·7'	1°46·8'W	X	104
Intake Gill	N Yks	SE0974	54°9·9'	1°51·3'W	W	99
Intake Ho	N Yks	SE1491	54°19·1'	1°46·7'W	X	99
Intake Lodge	N Yks	SE5973	54°9·2'	1°5·4'W	X	100
Intake Plantation	N Yks	SE0459	54°1·9'	1°55·9'W	F	104
Intakes	Staffs	SJ9461	53°9·0'	2°5·0'W	X	118
Intakes Fm	Derby	SJ9991	53°25·2'	2°0·5'W	FM	109
Intake Side	Cumbr	NY8015	54°32·0'	2°18·1'W	X	91,92
Intake Side Fm	Leeds	SE1541	53°52·1'	1°45·9'W	FM	104
Intakes, The	Derby	SK0389	53°24·1'	1°56·9'W	X	110
Intakes, The	N Yks	SE1267	54°6·2'	1°48·6'W	X	99
Intake, The	Cumbr	SD1394	54°20·3'	3°19·9'W	X	96
Intake Wood	Notts	SK5964	53°10·4'	1°6·6'W	F	120
Intake Wood	N Yks	SE9889	54°17·5'	0°29·2'W	F	94,101

Interfield	Worcs	SO7749	52°8·6'	2°19·8'W	T	150
International Centre	Bourne	SZ0890	50°42·8'	1°52·8'W	X	195
Intockhouse	S Lanak	NS8641	55°39·2'	3°48·3'W	X	71,72
Intwood	Norf	TG1904	52°35·6'	1°14·4'E	T	134
Inver	Aberd	NO2393	57°1·6'	3°15·7'W	T	36,44
Inver	Arg & Bt	NM9945	56°33·5'	5°15·8'W	X	49
Inver	Highld	ND1629	58°14·8'	3°25·4'W	X	11,17
Inver	Highld	NG5542	57°24·4'	6°4·3'W	X	24
Inver	Highld	NH1455	57°33·1'	5°6·0'W	X	25
Inver	Highld	NH8682	57°49·0'	3°54·7'W	T	21
Inver	Pth & Kin	NO0142	56°33·8'	3°36·2'W	T	52,53
Inverae	Arg & Bt	NR9796	56°7·1'	5°15·5'W	X	55
Inverailort	Highld	NM7681	56°52·2'	5°40·1'W	T	40
Inveraldie	Angus	NO4136	56°31·0'	2°57·1'W	X	54
Inveralivaig	Highld	NG4842	57°24·2'	6°11·3'W	T	23
Inverallan Ho	Highld	NJ0226	57°19·1'	3°37·2'W	X	36
Inveralligin	Highld	NG8457	57°33·4'	5°36·2'W	T	24
Inverallochy	Aberd	NK0465	57°40·7'	1°55·5'W	T	30
Inverallochy Castle	Aberd	NK0462	57°39·1'	1°55·5'W	A	30
Inveramsay	Aberd	NJ7423	57°18·1'	2°25·4'W	X	38
Inveran	Highld	NG8778	57°44·7'	5°34·3'W	X	19
Inveran	Highld	NH5797	57°56·6'	4°24·5'W	X	21
Inveraray	Arg & Bt	NN0908	56°13·8'	5°4·4'W	T	56
Inverar Burn	Pth & Kin	NN6549	56°37·1'	4°11·6'W	W	51
Inverardoch Mains	Stir	NN7300	56°10·8'	4°2·3'W	X	57
Inverardran	Stir	NN3924	56°23·1'	4°36·0'W	X	50
Inverarish	Highld	NG5535	57°20·6'	6°3·9'W	T	24,32
Inverarish Burn	Highld	NG5737	57°21·8'	6°2·0'W	W	24,32
Inverarity	Angus	NO4544	56°35·3'	2°53·3'W	T	54
Inverarnan	Arg & Bt	NN3118	56°19·7'	4°43·6'W	T	50,56
Inverarnie	Highld	NH6833	57°22·4'	4°11·2'W	X	26
Inverarnie Lodge	Highld	NH6934	57°22·9'	4°10·3'W	X	26
Inverasdale	Highld	NG8186	57°48·9'	5°40·8'W	H	19
Inver Aulavaig	Highld	NG6012	57°8·4'	5°57·6'W	W	32
Inveravon	Falk	NS9579	55°59·8'	3°40·6'W	X	65
Inverawe Ho	Arg & Bt	NN0231	56°26·0'	5°12·2'W	X	50
Inverbain	Highld	NG7854	57°31·6'	5°42·0'W	X	24
Inver Bay	Highld	NH8683	57°49·6'	3°54·7'W	W	21
Inverbeg	Arg & Bt	NS3497	56°8·5'	4°39·9'W	T	56
Inverbervie	Aberd	NO8272	56°50·6'	2°17·3'W	T	45
Inverblye	Moray	NJ2423	57°17·7'	3°15·2'W	X	36
Inverboyndie	Aberd	NJ6664	57°40·1'	2°33·7'W	T	29
Inverbreakie	Highld	NH7169	57°41·8'	4°9·4'W	X	21,27
Inverbroom Lodge	Highld	NH1883	57°48·2'	5°3·3'W	X	20
Inverbrora	Highld	NC8903	58°0·4'	3°52·2'W	X	17
Inverbrough Lodge	Highld	NH8130	57°21·0'	3°58·2'W	X	27
Invercarney	Aberd	NJ7837	57°25·6'	2°21·5'W	X	29,30
Invercannich	Highld	NH3432	57°21·2'	4°45·1'W	X	26
Invercassley	Highld	NC4701	57°58·6'	4°34·8'W	T	16
Invercauld Bridge	Aberd	NO1891	57°0·4'	3°20·6'W	X	43
Invercauld House	Aberd	NO1792	57°1·0'	3°21·6'W	X	43
Inverchaolain	Arg & Bt	NS0975	55°56·1'	5°3·0'W	T	63
Inverchaolain Fm	Arg & Bt	NS0975	55°56·1'	5°3·0'W	FM	63
Inverchaolain Glen	Arg & Bt	NS1076	55°56·6'	5°2·1'W	X	63
Inverchapel	Arg & Bt	NS1486	56°2·1'	4°58·7'W	X	56
Inverchapel Burn	Arg & Bt	NS1586	56°2·1'	4°57·7'W	W	56
Invercharnan	Highld	NN1448	56°35·5'	5°1·3'W	X	50
Invercharron Hill	Highld	NH5791	57°53·4'	4°24·3'W	X	21
Invercharron Ho	Highld	NH5991	57°53·4'	4°22·2'W	X	21
Invercharron Mains	Highld	NH5992	57°54·0'	4°22·3'W	X	21
Inverchor	Moray	NJ1723	57°17·7'	3°22·2'W	X	36
Inverchorachan	Arg & Bt	NN2217	56°19·0'	4°52·2'W	X	50,56
Inverchoran	Highld	NH2650	57°30·7'	4°53·8'W	T	25
Inverchroskie	Pth & Kin	NO0662	56°44·7'	3°31·8'W	X	43
Invercoe Ho	Highld	NN1059	56°41·3'	5°5·7'W	X	41
Invercomrie	Pth & Kin	NN4956	56°40·5'	4°27·4'W	X	42,51
Inver Cott	Arg & Bt	NR4471	55°52·1'	6°5·1'W	X	60,61
Invercreran	Arg & Bt	NN0147	56°34·6'	5°13·9'W	X	50
Invercrynoch	Aberd	NO8697	57°4·1'	2°13·4'W	X	38,45
Inver Dalavil	Highld	NG5706	57°4·6'	6°0·1'W	W	32,39
Inverden	Aberd	NJ4414	57°13·1'	2°55·2'W	X	37
Inverdovat	Fife	NO4327	56°26·2'	2°55·0'W	X	54,59
Inverdruie	Highld	NH9011	57°10·9'	3°48·7'W	T	36
Inverebrie	Aberd	NJ9233	57°23·5'	2°7·5'W	X	30
Invereck	Arg & Bt	NS1482	56°0·0'	4°58·5'W	X	56
Invereddrie	Pth & Kin	NO1368	56°48·0'	3°25·0'W	T	43
Invereen	Highld	NH7931	57°21·5'	4°0·2'W	X	27
Invereigh	Arg & Bt	NN2938	56°30·4'	4°46·3'W	X	50
Invereighty Ho	Angus	NO4345	56°35·9'	2°55·3'W	X	54
Invereighty Mill	Angus	NO4345	56°35·9'	2°55·3'W	X	54
Invereil Ho	E Loth	NT5285	56°3·6'	2°45·8'W	X	66
Inverernan Ho	Aberd	NJ3211	57°11·3'	3°7·1'W	X	37
Inverernie	Moray	NJ0360	57°37·4'	3°37·0'W	X	27
Invereshie Ho	Highld	NH8405	57°7·5'	3°54·5'W	X	35
Inveresk	E Loth	NT3572	55°56·5'	3°2·0'W	T	66
Inveresragan	Arg & Bt	NM9835	56°28·1'	5°16·3'W	T	49
Inverewe Garden	Highld	NG8582	57°46·8'	5°36·5'W	X	19
Inverey	Aberd	NO0889	56°59·2'	3°30·4'W	T	43
Inverey	Aberd	NO6295	57°2·9'	2°37·1'W	X	37,45
Inverfarigaig	Highld	NH5223	57°16·7'	4°26·8'W	T	26,35
Inverfolla	Arg & Bt	NM9544	56°32·9'	5°19·6'W	X	49
Invergarry	Highld	NH3001	57°4·4'	4°47·8'W	T	34
Invergarry Castle	Highld	NH3100	57°3·9'	4°46·8'W	A	34
Invergaunan	Arg & Bt	NN2736	56°29·3'	4°48·1'W	X	50
Invergelder	Aberd	NO2393	57°1·6'	3°15·7'W	T	36,44
Invergeldie	Pth & Kin	NN7427	56°25·4'	4°2·1'W	X	51,52
Invergeldie Burn	Pth & Kin	NN7529	56°26·5'	4°1·2'W	W	51,52
Inverghiusachan Point	Arg & Bt	NN0940	56°31·1'	5°5·8'W	X	50
Invergighty Cottage	Angus	NO6149	56°38·3'	2°38·2'W	X	54
Inverglen	Arg & Bt	NN0901	56°10·1'	5°4·1'W	X	56
Invergloy Ho	Highld	NN2288	56°57·2'	4°55·2'W	X	34,41
Invergordon	Highld	NH7168	57°41·3'	4°9·4'W	T	21,27
Invergordon Mains	Highld	NH7069	57°41·8'	4°10·4'W	X	21,27
Invergowrie	Pth & Kin	NO3430	56°27·7'	3°3·8'W	T	54
Invergroin	Arg & Bt	NS3099	56°9·5'	4°43·8'W	X	56
Inverguseran	Highld	NG7407	57°6·2'	5°43·4'W	T	33
Inverhaggernie	Stir	NN3726	56°24·1'	4°38·0'W	X	50
Inverhaggernie Burn	Stir	NN3827	56°24·7'	4°37·1'W	W	50
Inverharity	Angus	NO1963	56°45·4'	3°19·0'W	X	43
Inverharroch Fm	Moray	NJ3831	57°22·2'	3°1·4'W	FM	37

Inverherive	Stir	NN3626	56°24·1'	4°39·0'W	X	50
Inver Hill	Highld	ND1121	58°10·4'	3°30·3'W	X	17
Inver Ho	Aberd	NJ6914	57°13·2'	2°30·3'W	X	38
Inverhope	Highld	NC4761	58°30·9'	4°37·1'W	X	9
Inverhoulin	Arg & Bt	NN3206	56°13·3'	4°42·1'W	X	56
Inverhouse	Highld	NH5696	57°56·1'	4°25·5'W	X	21
Inverianvie River	Highld	NG9688	57°50·4'	5°25·7'W	W	19
Inverichnie Ho	Aberd	NJ6960	57°38·0'	2°30·7'W	X	29
Inverie	Highld	NG7600	57°2·5'	5°41·1'W	T	33
Inverie Bay	Highld	NM7599	57°1·9'	5°42·0'W	W	33,40
Inverie House	Highld	NM7799	57°2·0'	5°40·1'W	X	33,40
Inverie River	Highld	NM8099	57°2·0'	5°37·1'W	W	33,40
Inverinain	Pth & Kin	NN6547	56°36·0'	4°11·5'W	X	51
Inverinain Burn	Pth & Kin	NN6546	56°35·4'	4°11·5'W	W	51
Inverinan	Arg & Bt	NM9917	56°18·4'	5°14·5'W	T	55
Inverinan Mór	Arg & Bt	NM9917	56°18·4'	5°14·5'W	X	55
Inverinate	Highld	NG9221	57°14·2'	5°26·3'W	T	25,33
Inverinate Forest	Highld	NG9925	57°16·6'	5°19·6'W	X	25,33
Inverinate Ho	Highld	NG9221	57°14·2'	5°26·3'W	X	25,33
Inveriscandye	Angus	NO6267	56°47·8'	2°36·9'W	X	45
Inverkeilor	Angus	NO6649	56°38·2'	2°32·8'W	T	54
Inverkeithing Bay	Fife	NT1381	56°1·1'	3°23·3'W	W	65
Inverkeithing	Fife	NT1382	56°1·6'	3°23·3'W	T	65
Inverkeithny	Aberd	NJ6247	57°31·0'	2°37·6'W	T	29
Inverkindling	Aberd	NJ5357	57°36·3'	2°46·7'W	X	29
Inverkip	Inverc	NS2072	55°54·7'	4°52·4'W	T	63
Inverkip Bay	Inverc	NS1971	55°54·1'	4°53·3'W	W	63
Inverkirkaig	Highld	NC0719	58°7·3'	5°16·2'W	T	15
Inverlael	Highld	NH1885	57°49·3'	5°3·4'W	X	20
Inverlael Fm	Highld	NH1885	57°49·3'	5°3·4'W	FM	20
Inverlael Forest	Highld	NH2286	57°50·0'	4°59·4'W	X	20
Inverlaidnan	Highld	NH8621	57°16·2'	3°53·0'W	X	35,36
Inverlaidnan Hill	Highld	NH8522	57°16·7'	3°54·0'W	H	35,36
Inverlair	Highld	NN3379	56°52·6'	4°44·0'W	T	41
Inverlair Falls	Highld	NN3380	56°53·1'	4°44·0'W	W	34,41
Inverlauren	Arg & Bt	NS3185	56°1·9'	4°42·3'W	X	56
Inverleith	C of Edin	NT2475	55°58·0'	3°12·6'W	T	66
Inverliever Forest	Arg & Bt	NM9310	56°14·5'	5°20·0'W	F	55
Inverliever Lodge	Arg & Bt	NM8905	56°11·7'	5°23·6'W	X	55
Inverliver	Arg & Bt	NN0635	56°28·3'	5°8·5'W	X	50
Inverliver Bay	Arg & Bt	NN0636	56°28·8'	5°8·6'W	W	50
Inverlochlarig	Stir	NN4318	56°20·0'	4°31·9'W	X	56
Inverlochlarig Burn	Stir	NN4319	56°20·5'	4°32·0'W	W	56
Inverlochlarig Glen	Stir	NN4319	56°20·5'	4°32·0'W	X	56
Inverlochty	Moray	NJ1861	57°38·2'	3°21·9'W	X	28
Inverlochy	Angus	NO6044	56°35·4'	2°38·6'W	X	54
Inverlochy	Arg & Bt	NN1927	56°24·3'	4°55·6'W	X	50
Inverlochy	Highld	NN1174	56°49·4'	5°5·4'W	T	41
Inverlochy	Moray	NJ1324	57°18·2'	3°26·2'W	X	36
Inverlochy Castle (Hotel)	Highld	NN1376	56°50·5'	5°3·5'W	X	41
Inverlounin	Arg & Bt	NS2099	56°9·2'	4°53·4'W	X	56
Inverlussa	Arg & Bt	NR6486	56°0·8'	5°46·7'W	T	55,61
Inver Mallie (Bothy)	Highld	NN1388	56°57·0'	5°4·0'W	X	34,41
Invermarkie	Aberd	NJ4239	57°26·5'	2°57·5'W	X	28
Invermark Lodge	Angus	NO4380	56°54·7'	2°55·7'W	X	44
Invermay	Pth & Kin	NO0616	56°19·9'	3°30·8'W	X	58
Inver Meadale	Highld	NG3834	57°19·5'	6°20·7'W	X	32
Invermoidart	Highld	NM6673	56°47·6'	5°49·5'W	T	40
Invermoriston	Highld	NH4116	57°12·7'	4°37·5'W	T	34
Invernahyle	Arg & Bt	NM9544	56°32·9'	5°19·6'W	X	49
Invernauld Ho	Highld	NC4900	57°58·1'	4°32·7'W	X	16
Invernaver	Highld	NC7060	58°30·8'	4°13·4'W	T	10
Inverneil Burn	Arg & Bt	NR8281	55°58·6'	5°29·2'W	W	55
Inverneil Burn	Arg & Bt	NS0573	55°54·9'	5°6·8'W	W	63
Inverneill	Arg & Bt	NR8481	55°58·7'	5°27·3'W	T	55
Inverneill Fm	Arg & Bt	NR8480	55°58·1'	5°27·2'W	FM	55
Invernenty Burn	Stir	NN4616	56°18·9'	4°28·9'W	W	57
Inverness	Highld	NH6645	57°28·8'	4°13·6'W	T	26
Inverness Airport	Highld	NH7752	57°32·7'	4°2·8'W	X	27
Invernettie	Aberd	NJ3415	57°13·5'	3°5·1'W	X	37
Invernettie	Aberd	NK1244	57°29·4'	1°47·5'W	T	30
Invernoaden	Arg & Bt	NS1297	56°8·0'	5°1·1'W	T	56
Invernorth	Aberd	NK0162	57°39·1'	1°58·5'W	X	30
Inverockle	Highld	NM5571	56°46·2'	6°0·1'W	X	39,47
Inveroe	W Loth	NT1265	55°52·5'	3°24·0'W	X	65
Inveronich	Arg & Bt	NN2002	56°10·9'	4°53·6'W	X	56
Inveroran Hotel	Arg & Bt	NN2741	56°32·0'	4°48·3'W	X	50
Inverord	Aberd	NJ8103	57°7·3'	2°18·4'W	X	38
Inveroykel	Highld	NC4600	57°58·0'	4°35·7'W	X	16
Inverpattack Lodge	Highld	NN5590	56°59·0'	4°22·7'W	X	35
Inverpolly Forest	Highld	NC1111	58°3·1'	5°11·7'W	X	15
Inverpolly Lodge	Highld	NC0614	58°4·6'	5°16·9'W	X	15
Inverpolly National Nature Reserve	Highld	NC1412	58°3·8'	5°8·7'W	X	15
Inverquharity	Angus	NO4057	56°42·3'	2°58·3'W	X	54
Inverquharity Mill	Angus	NO4157	56°42·3'	2°57·4'W	X	54
Inverquhomery	Aberd	NK0246	57°30·5'	1°57·5'W	X	30
Inverquiech	Pth & Kin	NO2749	56°37·9'	3°11·0'W	X	53
Inverquinzie Cotts	Aberd	NK1051	57°33·2'	1°49·5'W	X	30
Inverroy	Highld	NN2581	56°53·5'	4°51·9'W	T	34,41
Inversanda	Highld	NM9359	56°40·9'	5°22·3'W	T	49
Inversanda Bay	Highld	NM9459	56°40·9'	5°21·3'W	W	49
Inverscaddle Bay	Highld	NN0268	56°46·0'	5°13·9'W	W	41
Invershiel	Highld	NG9319	57°13·2'	5°25·3'W	T	33
Invershin	Highld	NH5796	57°56·1'	4°24·4'W	T	21
Invershin Castle	Highld	NH5796	57°56·1'	4°24·4'W	A	21
Invershin Sta	Highld	NH5796	57°55·6'	4°24·4'W	X	21
Invershore	Highld	ND2434	58°17·5'	3°17·3'W	T	11
Inverskilavulin	Highld	NN1283	56°54·3'	5°4·8'W	X	34,41
Inversnaid	Stir	NN3308	56°14·4'	4°41·2'W	X	56
Invertiel	Fife	NT2689	56°5·5'	3°10·9'W	X	66
Inverton	Highld	NN7499	57°4·2'	4°4·2'W	X	35
Inver Tote	Highld	NG5260	57°34·0'	6°8·4'W	W	23,24
Invertromie	Highld	NH7800	57°4·8'	4°0·3'W	X	35
Invertrossachs	Stir	NN5605	56°13·2'	4°18·9'W	X	57
Invertruim	Highld	NN6895	57°1·9'	4°10·0'W	X	35
Inverugie	Aberd	NK1048	57°31·6'	1°49·5'W	T	30
Inverugie	Moray	NJ1568	57°41·9'	3°25·1'W	X	28
Inveruglas	Arg & Bt	NN3109	56°14·9'	4°43·2'W	T	56
Inveruglas Isle	Arg & Bt	NN3209	56°14·9'	4°42·2'W	X	56

Inveruglass	Highld	NH8000	57°4·8′	3°58·3′W	T	35
Inveruglas Water	Arg & Bt	NN2910	56°15·4′	4°45·2′W	W	50,56
Inveruglas Water	Arg & Bt	NN3009	56°14·8′	4°44·2′W	W	56
Inveruplan	Highld	NC1223	58°9·6′	5°11·3′W	X	15
Inverurie	Aberd	NJ7721	57°17·0′	2°22·4′W	T	38
Invervack	Pth & Kin	NN8365	56°46·0′	3°54·4′W	X	43
Invervar	Pth & Kin	NN6648	56°36·5′	4°10·5′W	T	51
Inverveddie	Aberd	NK0545	57°30·0′	1°54·5′W	X	30
Invervegain	Arg & Bt	NS0778	55°57·6′	5°5·1′W	X	63
Invervegain Burn	Arg & Bt	NS0879	55°58·2′	5°4·2′W	W	63
Invervegain Glen	Arg & Bt	NS0879	55°58·2′	5°4·2′W	X	63
Invervigar Burn	Highld	NH3205	57°6·6′	4°46·0′W	W	34
Inverwick	Highld	NH3213	57°10·9′	4°46·3′W	X	34
Inverwick Forest	Highld	NH3413	57°10·9′	4°44·3′W	X	34
Invery Ho	Aberd	NO6993	57°1·9′	2°30·2′W	X	38,45
Inveryne Fm	Arg & Bt	NR9175	55°55·6′	5°20·3′W	FM	62
Inverythan	Aberd	NJ7541	57°27·8′	2°24·5′W	T	29
Inwardleigh	Devon	SX5699	50°46·6′	4°2·2′W	T	191
Inwood	Glos	SO5608	51°46·4′	2°37·9′W	X	162
Inwood	Shrops	SO4696	52°33·8′	2°47·4′W	T	137,138
Inwood	Somer	ST7120	50°59·0′	2°24·4′W	F	183
Inwood	Wilts	ST8063	51°22·2′	2°16·9′W	F	173
Inwood Copse	Hants	SU6046	51°12·8′	1°8·1′W	F	185
Inwood Fm	Somer	ST2039	51°8·9′	3°8·2′W	FM	182
Inwood Fm	Surrey	SU9148	51°13·7′	0°41·4′W	FM	186
Inwoods	Wilts	ST8063	51°22·2′	2°16·9′W	X	173
Inwoods Fm	Warw	SP5072	52°20·9′	1°15·6′W	FM	140
Inworth	Essex	TL8717	51°49·4′	0°43·2′E	T	168
Inworth Grange	Essex	TL8715	51°48·4′	0°43·1′E	X	168
Inzie Head	Aberd	NK0662	57°39·1′	1°53·5′W	X	30
Inzievar	Fife	NT0287	56°4·2′	3°34·0′W	X	65
Inzievar Wood	Fife	NT0288	56°4·7′	3°34·0′W	F	65
Inzion Burn	Angus	NO2856	56°41·7′	3°10·1′W	W	53
Iochdar	N Eil	NF7746	57°23·6′	7°22·2′W	T	22
Iodhlann Dubh	Highld	NG4054	57°30·4′	6°20·0′W	X	23
Ioidse Mhorsgail	N Eil	NB1322	58°5·9′	6°51·8′W	X	13,14
Iolairig	Highld	NN5195	57°1·6′	4°26·8′W	X	35
Iolarig	Arg & Bt	NR7467	55°50·9′	5°36·2′W	X	62
Iola-Sgorr	Highld	NG2104	57°2·8′	6°35·6′W	X	39
Iolla Bheag	Highld	NC0303	57°58·6′	5°19·4′W	X	15
Iolla Mhór	Highld	NC0203	57°58·6′	5°20·4′W	X	15
Iolyn Park	Conwy	SH7775	53°15·7′	3°50·2′W	X	115
Iomairaghradain	Highld	NG8420	57°13·5′	5°34·2′W	X	33
Iomallach	Arg & Bt	NR4344	55°37·6′	6°4·5′W	X	60
Iona	Arg & Bt	NM2724	56°20·0′	6°24·6′W	X	48
Ionadal Burn	Highld	NG1942	57°23·2′	6°40·1′W	W	23
Ion Bridge Fm	Beds	TL1033	51°59·3′	0°23·5′W	FM	166
Ion Fm	Beds	TL1034	51°59·8′	0°23·5′W	FM	153
Iorcail	Highld	NG2606	57°4·1′	6°30·8′W	X	39
Iorsa Water	N Ayr	NR9239	55°36·3′	5°17·7′W	W	68,69
Iosaigh	N Eil	NB1002	57°55·0′	6°53·4′W	X	14
Iphs	Orkney	HY4249	59°19·7′	3°0·7′W	X	5
Iping	W Susx	SU8523	51°0·2′	0°46·9′W	T	197
Iping Common	W Susx	SU8421	50°59·2′	0°47·8′W	X	197
Ipley Inclosure	Hants	SU3607	50°51·9′	1°28·9′W	F	196
Ipley Manor	Hants	SU3706	50°51·4′	1°28·1′W	X	196
Ipplepen	Devon	SX8366	50°29·2′	3°38·6′W	T	202
Ipsden	Oxon	SU6385	51°33·9′	1°5·1′W	T	175
Ipsden Heath	Oxon	SU6685	51°33·8′	1°2·5′W	F	175
Ipsden Ho	Oxon	SU6385	51°33·9′	1°5·1′W	X	175
Ipsden Wood	Oxon	SU6783	51°32·7′	1°1·6′W	F	175
Ipsley	Worcs	SP0666	52°17·8′	1°54·3′W	T	150
Ipstones	Staffs	SK0249	53°2·5′	1°57·8′W	T	119
Ipstones Edge	Staffs	SK0251	53°3·6′	1°57·8′W	X	119
Ipstones Park	Staffs	SK0349	53°2·5′	1°56·9′W	X	119
Ipswich	Suff	TM1644	52°4·3′	1°9·4′E	T	169
Ipswich Airport	Suff	TM1941	52°1·7′	1°11·9′E	X	169
Irams, The	Cambs	TL4369	52°18·3′	0°6·2′E	X	154
Irby	Wirral	SJ2584	53°21·1′	3°7·2′W	T	108
Irby Dales Fm	NE Lincs	TA1904	53°31·4′	0°11·9′W	FM	113
Irby Dales Wood	Lincs	TA1805	53°31·9′	0°12·8′W	F	113
Irby Hill	Wirral	SJ2585	53°21·6′	3°7·2′W	X	108
Irby Holmes Wood	NE Lincs	TA2003	53°30·8′	0°11·0′W	F	113
Irby in the Marsh	Lincs	TF4763	53°8·9′	0°12·3′E	T	122
Irby Manor Fm	N Yks	NZ4003	54°25·5′	1°22·6′W	FM	93
Irby upon Humber	NE Lincs	TA1904	53°31·4′	0°11·9′W	T	113
Irchester	Northnts	SP9265	52°16·8′	0°38·7′W	T	152
Irchester Grange	Northnts	SP9264	52°16·2′	0°38·7′W	X	152
Ireby	Cumbr	NY2338	54°44·1′	3°11·3′W	T	89,90
Ireby	Lancs	SD6575	54°10·4′	2°31·8′W	T	97
Ireby Beck	N Yks	SD6676	54°11·0′	2°30·8′W	W	98
Ireby Fell	Lancs	SD6676	54°11·0′	2°30·8′W	X	98
Ireby Fell Cavern	Lancs	SD6777	54°11·5′	2°29·9′W	X	98
Ireby Hall Fm	Lancs	SD6475	54°10·4′	2°32·7′W	FM	97
Iredale Place	Cumbr	NY1122	54°35·4′	3°22·2′W	X	89
Ireland	Angus	NO5166	56°47·2′	2°47·7′W	X	44
Ireland	Beds	TL1341	52°3·6′	0°20·7′W	T	153
Ireland	Orkney	HY3009	58°58·0′	3°12·6′W	T	6,7
Ireland	Powys	SO1448	52°7·7′	3°15·0′W	X	148
Ireland	Shetld	HU3722	59°59·1′	1°19·7′W	T	4
Ireland	Shrops	SO4687	52°28·9′	2°47·3′W	X	137,138
Ireland	Wilts	ST8454	51°17·3′	2°13·4′W	T	183
Irelandbrae	Aberd	NJ7029	57°21·3′	2°29·5′W	X	38
Ireland Cott	Shrops	SO4483	52°26·8′	2°49·0′W	X	137
Ireland Fm	Lincs	TF3749	53°1·5′	0°3·0′E	FM	131
Ireland Fm	Warw	SP3652	52°10·1′	1°28·0′W	FM	151
Ireland Moss	Cumbr	SD3384	54°15·1′	3°1·3′W	F	96,97
Ireland's Cross	Shrops	SJ7341	52°58·2′	2°23·7′W	T	118
Ireland's Fm	E Susx	TQ7915	50°54·6′	0°33·2′E	FM	199
Ireland's Fm	Lincs	TF2932	52°52·4′	0°4·6′W	FM	131
Irelands Fm	Warw	SP1667	52°18·3′	1°45·5′W	FM	151
Irelandton	D & G	NX6456	54°53·1′	4°6·8′W	X	83
Irelandton Moor	D & G	NX6457	54°53·6′	4°6·8′W	X	83
Ireland Wick	Shetld	HU3721	59°58·6′	1°19·7′W	W	4
Ireland Wood	Leeds	SE2638	53°50·5′	1°35·9′W	T	104
Ireleth	Cumbr	SD2277	54°11·2′	3°11·3′W	T	96
Ireley Fm	Glos	SP0330	51°58·3′	1°57·0′W	FM	150
Ires Geo	Highld	ND3545	58°23·6′	3°6·2′W	X	12
Ireshope Burn	Durham	NY8537	54°43·9′	2°13·6′W	W	91,92
Ireshopeburn	Durham	NY8638	54°44·5′	2°12·6′W	T	91,92
Ireshope Moor	Durham	NY8436	54°43·4′	2°14·5′W	X	91,92
Ireshope Plains	Durham	NY8637	54°43·9′	2°12·6′W	X	91,92
Ireton Fm	Derby	SK3141	52°58·2′	1°31·9′W	FM	119,128
Ireton Houses	Derby	SK3747	53°1·4′	1°26·5′W	X	119,128
Ireton Wood	Derby	SK2847	53°1·4′	1°34·5′W	T	119,128
Irfon	Powys	SN9749	52°8·0′	3°29·9′W	W	147
Irfon Forest	Powys	SN8650	52°8·4′	3°39·6′W	F	147
Iridge Place	E Susx	TQ7326	51°0·7′	0°28·4′E	X	188,199
Iriewells	Aberd	NJ9028	57°20·8′	2°9·5′W	X	38
Irine Burn	Highld	NM7277	56°50·0′	5°43·8′W	W	40
Irish	Corn	SX1177	50°34·0′	4°39·8′W	X	200
Irishcombe Fm	Devon	SS7817	50°56·6′	3°43·8′W	FM	180
Irish Fm	Leic	SK4613	52°43·0′	1°18·7′W	FM	129
Irish Hill	W Berks	SU4066	51°23·7′	1°25·1′W	H	174
Irish Lady	Corn	SW3426	50°4·7′	5°42·7′W	X	203
Irish Law	N Ayr	NS2559	55°47·8′	4°47·1′W	H	63
Irishman's Ledge	I Scilly	SV9414	49°57·1′	6°15·6′W	X	203
Irishman's Wall	Devon	SX6191	50°42·4′	3°57·7′W	X	191
Irish Sea		NX1530	54°38·1′	4°51·6′W	W	82
Irish Sea		SH2797	53°26·7′	4°35·9′W	W	114
Irish Sea	I of M	SC3265	54°3·5′	4°33·6′W	W	95
Irlam	Salf	SJ7294	53°26·8′	2°24·9′W	T	109
Irlams o' th' Height	Salf	SD7900	53°30·0′	2°18·6′W	T	109
Irlam Sta	Salf	SJ7193	53°26·2′	2°25·8′W	X	109
Irlick Chaoile	Highld	NN3072	56°48·8′	4°46·6′W	X	41
Irmingland Hall	Norf	TG1229	52°49·2′	1°9·2′E	A	133
Irnham	Lincs	TF0226	52°49·5′	0°28·8′W	T	130
Irnham Hall	Lincs	TF0226	52°49·5′	0°28·8′W	A	130
Irnham Pasture	Lincs	TF0225	52°49·0′	0°28·8′W	X	130
Iron Acton	S Glos	ST6783	51°32·9′	2°28·2′W	T	172
Iron Band	Cumbr	NY8318	54°33·7′	2°15·4′W	H	91,92
Iron Banks	N Yks	SE1899	54°23·4′	1°42·9′W	X	99
Ironbower Moss	Derby	SK1199	53°29·5′	1°49·6′W	X	110
Iron Bridge	Cambs	TL4898	52°33·8′	0°11·4′E	T	143
Iron Bridge	Ches	SJ4160	53°8·3′	2°52·5′W	X	117
Ironbridge	Wrekin	SJ6703	52°37·7′	2°28·9′W	T	127
Ironbridge Cycle Way	Shrops	SJ7600	52°36·1′	2°20·9′W	X	127
Iron Bridge Fm	Essex	TL7328	51°55·6′	0°31·4′E	FM	167
Iron Buildings	Oxon	SP3023	51°54·5′	1°33·4′W	X	164
Iron Crag	Cumbr	NY1212	54°30·0′	3°21·1′W	X	89
Iron Crag	Cumbr	NY2919	54°33·9′	3°5·5′W	X	89,90
Iron Crag	Cumbr	NY3034	54°42·0′	3°4·8′W	X	90
Iron Craig	Fife	NT2982	56°1·8′	3°7·9′W	X	66
Iron Cross	Northnts	SP5054	52°11·2′	1°15·7′W	X	151
Iron Cross	Warw	SP0552	52°10·2′	1°55·2′W	T	150
Iron Down	Oxon	SP4131	51°58·8′	1°23·8′W	X	151
Irondown Fm	Oxon	SP4231	51°58·8′	1°22·9′W	FM	151
Irongate Fm	Glos	ST9497	51°40·5′	2°4·8′W	FM	163
Irongate Fm	Monm	ST3196	51°39·7′	2°59·5′W	FM	171
Irongate Fm	Suff	TM3371	52°17·5′	1°25·4′E	FM	156
Iron Geo	Orkney	HY2403	58°54·7′	3°18·7′W	X	6,7
Iron Geo	Shetld	HP6117	60°50·1′	0°52·2′W	X	1
Iron Gill	Cumbr	NY3445	54°48·0′	3°1·2′W	W	85
Irongray	D & G	NX9179	55°5·9′	3°42·1′W	T	84
Ironharrow Well (spring)	Angus	NO4143	56°34·8′	2°57·2′W	W	54
Ironhash Hill	D & G	NX8656	54°53·4′	3°46·2′W	H	84
Iron Hellia	Orkney	HY5407	58°57·1′	2°47·5′W	X	6,7
Ironhill	Aberd	NJ9165	57°40·7′	2°8·6′W	X	30
Iron Hill	Kent	TR0658	51°17·3′	0°57·7′E	X	179
Iron Hill	W Susx	SU8529	51°3·5′	0°46·8′W	X	186,197
Iron Hill Fm	Northnts	SP5054	52°11·2′	1°15·7′W	FM	151
Ironhirst	D & G	NY0572	55°2·3′	3°28·8′W	X	85
Ironhirst Moss	D & G	NY0471	55°1·7′	3°29·7′W	X	84
Iron Ho	Staffs	SO8283	52°26·9′	2°15·5′W	X	138
Iron Howe	Cumbr	NY6931	54°40·6′	2°28·4′W	X	91
Iron Keld	Cumbr	NY3301	54°24·3′	3°1·5′W	X	90
Iron Lodge	Highld	NH0429	57°18·8′	5°14·8′W	X	25,33
Ironlosh	D & G	NX6779	55°5·5′	4°4·6′W	X	77,84
Ironmacannie	D & G	NX6675	55°3·3′	4°5·4′W	X	77,84
Ironmill Bay	Fife	NT0584	56°2·6′	3°31·1′W	W	65
Iron Mill Fm	Somer	ST7642	51°10·8′	2°20·2′W	FM	183
Iron Mills	Shrops	SJ3133	52°53·6′	3°1·1′W	X	126
Iron Mill Stream	Devon	SS9120	50°58·4′	3°32·8′W	W	181
Iron Pear Tree Fm	Essex	TL7727	51°55·0′	0°34·8′E	FM	167
Iron Pear Tree Fm	Wilts	ST9962	51°21·7′	2°0·5′W	FM	173
Iron Pits Fm	Staffs	SK0651	53°3·6′	1°54·2′W	FM	119
Iron Point	Pemb	SM7905	51°42·3′	5°11·5′W	X	157
Ironrieves	Aberd	NJ9221	57°17·0′	2°7·5′W	X	38
Iron River	E Susx	TQ4415	50°55·2′	0°3·3′E	W	198
Irons Bottom	Surrey	TQ2546	51°12·2′	0°12·3′W	T	187
Ironshill	Angus	NO6750	56°38·7′	2°31·8′W	X	54
Ironshill Inclosure	Hants	SU3109	50°53·0′	1°33·2′W	F	196
Ironshill Lodge	Hants	SU3110	50°53·5′	1°33·2′W	X	196
Ironside Hill	Angus	NO4041	56°33·7′	2°58·1′W	H	54
Irons Well	Hants	SU2314	50°55·7′	1°40·0′W	X	195
Iron Tongue	Tames	SE0001	53°30·6′	1°59·6′W	W	110
Irontongue Hill	Tames	SE0100	53°30·0′	1°58·7′W	X	110
Iron Tors	Derby	SK1456	53°6·3′	1°47·0′W	X	119
Ironville	Derby	SK4351	53°3·5′	1°21·1′W	T	120
Iron Works Fm	Derby	SK3849	53°2·5′	1°25·6′W	FM	119
Iroshill	Carm	SN4904	51°43·1′	4°10·8′W	X	159
Irrigation Fm	Northnts	SP8362	52°15·2′	0°46·6′W	FM	152
Irstead	Norf	TG3620	52°43·8′	1°30·1′E	X	133,134
Irstead Street	Norf	TG3519	52°43·3′	1°29·2′E	T	133,134
Irthing Head	Northum	NY6378	55°6·0′	2°34·4′W	X	86
Irthing Ho	Northum	NY6367	55°0·0′	2°34·3′W	X	86
Irthington	Cumbr	NY4961	54°56·7′	2°47·3′W	T	86
Irthlingborough	Northnts	SP9470	52°19·4′	0°36·8′W	T	141,153
Irthlingborough Grange	Northnts	SP9168	52°18·4′	0°39·5′W	X	152
Irton	N Yks	TA0184	54°14·7′	0°26·6′W	T	101
Irton Fell	Cumbr	NY1302	54°24·6′	3°20·0′W	X	89
Irton Hall	Cumbr	NY1000	54°23·5′	3°22·7′W	X	89
Irton Ho	Cumbr	NY2034	54°41·9′	3°14·1′W	X	89,90
Irton Manor	N Yks	TA0185	54°15·3′	0°26·6′W	X	101
Irton Moor	N Yks	SE9987	54°16·4′	0°28·4′W	X	94,101
Irton Park	Cumbr	NY1100	54°23·5′	3°21·8′W	X	89
Irton Pike	Cumbr	NY1201	54°24·1′	3°20·9′W	H	89
Irton Road Sta	Cumbr	SD1399	54°23·0′	3°20·0′W	X	96
Irvine	N Ayr	NS3239	55°37·2′	4°39·6′W	T	70
Irvine Bar	N Ayr	NS2937	55°36·1′	4°42·4′W	X	70
Irvine Bay	N Ayr	NS2937	55°36·1′	4°42·4′W	W	70
Irvine Burn	D & G	NY3680	55°6·9′	2°59·8′W	W	79
Irvinehill	E Ayr	NS3845	55°40·5′	4°34·1′W	X	63
Irvine Ho	D & G	NY3780	55°6·9′	2°58·8′W	X	79
Irving House Fm	N Yks	NZ4004	54°26·0′	1°22·6′W	FM	93
Irvington	D & G	NY2566	54°59·2′	3°9·9′W	X	85
Irvington	D & G	NY2670	55°1·4′	3°9·0′W	X	85
Irwell Spring	Lancs	SD8626	53°44·1′	2°12·3′W	W	103
Irwell Vale	Lancs	SD7920	53°40·8′	2°18·7′W	T	103
Irwell Valley Way	Lancs	SD8724	53°43·0′	2°11·4′W	X	103
Isaacstown	Aberd	NJ8021	57°17·0′	2°19·4′W	X	38
Isabella Pit	Northum	NZ3080	55°7·1′	1°31·4′W	T	81
Isabella Plantation	Rich	TQ1971	51°25·8′	0°16·9′W	F	176
Is-afon	Gwyn	SH9131	52°52·2′	3°36·8′W	X	125
Isaford	Devon	SX7279	50°36·0′	3°48·1′W	X	191
Isallt	Gwyn	SH5344	52°58·6′	4°11·0′W	X	124
Isallt Bach	I of Angl	SH2579	53°17·0′	4°37·1′W	T	114
Isauld	Highld	NC9765	58°33·9′	3°45·8′W	T	11
Isauld Ho	Highld	NC9765	58°33·9′	3°45·8′W	X	11
Isay	Highld	NG2157	57°31·3′	6°39·1′W	X	23
Isbister	Orkney	HY2623	59°5·5′	3°17·0′W	T	6
Isbister	Orkney	HY3918	59°2·9′	3°3·3′W	T	6
Isbister	Orkney	ND4684	58°44·7′	2°55·5′W	X	7
Isbister	Shetld	HU3790	60°35·8′	1°19·0′W	T	1,2
Isbister	Shetld	HU5763	60°21·1′	0°57·5′W	T	2
Isbister Holm	Shetld	HU6064	60°21·6′	0°54·2′W	X	2
Isca (Caerleon or Caerllion)	Newp	ST3390	51°36·5′	2°57·7′W	R	171
Isca (Exeter)	Devon	SX9292	50°43·3′	3°31·4′W	R	192
Iscoed Home Fm	Carm	SN3811	51°46·7′	4°20·5′W	FM	159
Iscoed-uchaf	Carm	SN3812	51°47·2′	4°20·5′W	X	159
Iscoyd Park	Wrex	SJ5042	52°58·6′	2°44·3′W	A	117
Iseanach Mór	Arg & Bt	NR4245	55°38·1′	6°5·5′W	X	60
Isel	Cumbr	NY1533	54°41·3′	3°18·7′W	T	89
Iselgate	Cumbr	NY1633	54°41·4′	3°17·8′W	X	89
Isel Hall	Cumbr	NY1533	54°41·3′	3°18·7′W	A	89
Isel Old Park	Cumbr	NY1934	54°41·9′	3°15·0′W	X	89,90
Isenhurst	E Susx	TQ5623	50°59·3′	0°13·8′E	X	199
Isfield	E Susx	TQ4517	50°56·3′	0°4·2′E	T	198
Isfield Place	E Susx	TQ4418	50°56·8′	0°3·4′E	A	198
Isgaer-wen	Conwy	SH9954	53°4·7′	3°30·1′W	X	116
Ishag Burn	Stir	NN4018	56°19·9′	4°34·8′W	W	56
Ishag Glen	Stir	NN4018	56°19·9′	4°34·8′W	X	56
Isham	Northnts	SP8873	52°21·1′	0°42·1′W	T	141
Is-Helen	Gwyn	SH4662	53°8·2′	4°17·7′W	X	114,115
Ishriff	Arg & Bt	NM6331	56°25·0′	5°50·1′W	X	49
Isington	Hants	SU7742	51°10·6′	0°53·5′W	T	186
Isington Close	Hants	SU7842	51°10·5′	0°52·7′W	X	186
Isinvrank	I Scilly	SV8607	49°53·1′	6°21·9′W	X	203
Islabank	Pth & Kin	NO1941	56°33·5′	3°18·6′W	X	53
Island	Arg & Bt	NS1494	56°6·4′	4°59·0′W	X	56
Island	Hants	SU7325	51°1·4′	0°57·2′W	X	186,197
Islandadd Bridge	Arg & Bt	NR8092	56°4·5′	5°31·7′W	X	55
Island Barn Reservoir	Surrey	TQ1367	51°23·7′	0°22·2′W	W	176
Island Carr	N Lincs	SE9906	53°32·7′	0°29·9′W	T	112
Island Davaar	Arg & Bt	NR7520	55°25·6′	5°32·9′W	X	68,69
Island Fm	Ches	SJ5877	53°17·5′	2°37·4′W	FM	117
Island Fm	Devon	SY0995	50°45·1′	3°17·0′W	FM	192
Island Fm	Durham	NZ3331	54°40·6′	1°28·9′W	FM	93
Island Fm	Lancs	SD4545	53°54·1′	2°49·8′W	FM	102
Island Fm	Lancs	SD4546	53°54·7′	2°49·8′W	FM	102
Island Fm	N Lincs	SE8620	53°40·4′	0°41·5′W	FM	106,112
Island Fm	Pemb	SN0140	52°1·6′	4°53·7′W	FM	145,157
Island Fm	Warw	SP3662	52°15·5′	1°28·0′W	FM	151
Island Ho	Arg & Bt	NL9843	56°29·2′	6°53·9′W	X	46
Island Ho	Arg & Bt	NR3056	55°43·6′	6°17·6′W	X	60
Island Ho	Norf	TM2292	52°29·1′	1°16·6′E	X	134
Island Ho	Swan	SS5797	51°39·5′	4°3·7′W	X	159
Island I Vow	Arg & Bt	NN3312	56°16·5′	4°41·4′W	X	50,56
Island Macaskin	Arg & Bt	NR7899	56°8·2′	5°33·9′W	X	55
Island of Bute	Arg & Bt	NS0664	55°50·1′	5°5·4′W	X	63
Island of Danna	Arg & Bt	NR6978	55°56·6′	5°41·5′W	X	61,62
Island of Mull	Arg & Bt	NM5435	56°26·8′	5°59·1′W	X	47,48
Island of Mull	Arg & Bt	NM6531	56°25·0′	5°48·2′W	X	49
Island of Raasay	Highld	NG5644	57°25·5′	6°3·4′W	X	24
Island of Skye	Highld	NG3349	57°27·4′	6°26·6′W	X	23
Island of Skye	Highld	NG3549	57°27·5′	6°24·6′W	X	23
Island of Skye	Highld	NG5325	57°15·2′	6°5·3′W	X	32
Island of Skye	Highld	NG5804	57°4·1′	5°59·1′W	X	32,39
Island of Skye	Highld	NG7017	57°11·4′	5°47·9′W	X	33
Island of Stroma	Highld	ND3577	58°40·8′	3°6·8′W	X	7,12
Island Ross	Arg & Bt	NR7827	55°29·4′	5°30·4′W	X	68,69
Islands Common	Cambs	TL1861	52°14·3′	0°15·9′W	T	153
Islands Fm	Pemb	SN0903	51°41·8′	4°45·4′W	FM	158
Islands of Fleet	D & G	NX5748	54°48·6′	4°13·1′W	X	83
Islands Thorns Inclosure	Hants	SU2114	50°55·7′	1°41·7′W	F	195
Islands Thorns Inclosure	Hants	SU2115	50°56·3′	1°41·7′W	F	184
Island, The	Corn	SX0489	50°40·3′	4°46·1′W	X	200
Island, The	Norf	TG4502	52°33·9′	1°37·3′E	X	134
Island, The	N Yks	SE9898	54°22·3′	0°29·1′W	X	94,101
Island, The	Somer	ST2945	51°12·2′	3°0·6′W	X	182
Island, The or St Ives Head	Corn	SW5241	50°13·3′	5°28·2′W	X	203
Isla Park	Pth & Kin	NO2341	56°33·5′	3°14·7′W	X	53
Islawr-dref	Gwyn	SH6815	52°43·2′	3°56·9′W	X	124
Islay	Arg & Bt	NR3960	55°46·0′	6°9·2′W	X	60
Islay Ho	Arg & Bt	NR3362	55°46·9′	6°15·3′W	X	60,61
Isle	D & G	NX8156	54°53·3′	3°50·9′W	X	84
Isle	D & G	NX9383	55°8·0′	3°40·3′W	X	78
Isle	E Ayr	NX4999	55°16·0′	4°22·2′W	X	77
Isle	Pth & Kin	NN9523	56°23·5′	3°41·6′W	X	52,53,58
Isle	Staffs	SJ9662	53°9·5′	2°3·2′W	X	118
Isle Abbotts	Somer	ST3520	50°58·8′	2°55·2′W	T	193
Isle Beck	N Yks	SE4577	54°11·4′	1°18·2′W	W	99
Islebeck Grange	N Yks	SE4577	54°11·4′	1°18·2′W	X	99
Isle Brewers	Somer	ST3621	50°59·3′	2°54·3′W	T	193
Isle Croft	D & G	NX4736	54°42·0′	4°22·0′W	X	83
Isle Fm	Ches	SJ4551	53°3·4′	2°48·8′W	FM	117
Isle Fm	D & G	NX4737	54°42·5′	4°22·1′W	FM	83
Isle Grange	Shrops	SJ4515	52°44·0′	2°48·5′W	X	126

Isleham	Cambs	TL6474	52°20·6′	0°24·9′E	T	143
Isleham Fen	Cambs	TL6276	52°21·7′	0°23·2′E	X	143
Isleham Marina	Suff	TL6575	52°21·1′	0°25·8′E	X	143
Isleham Plantn	Cambs	TL6571	52°19·0′	0°25·6′E	F	154
Isle Hill	Hants	SU5058	51°19·4′	1°16·6′W	H	174
Islekirk Hall	Cumbr	NY2544	54°47·4′	3°9·6′W	X	85
Isle Maree	Highld	NG9372	57°41·7′	5°27·9′W	X	19
Isle Martin	Highld	NC0900	57°57·2′	5°13·2′W	X	15,19
Isle Martin	Highld	NH0999	57°56·6′	5°13·1′W	X	19
Isle Of Arran	N Ayr	NR9536	55°34·7′	5°14·7′W	X	68,69
Isle of Axholme	N Lincs	SE7806	53°32·9′	0°49·0′W	T	112
Isle of Canty	Fife	NT0688	56°4·8′	3°30·2′W	X	65
Isle of Dalton	D & G	NY1173	55°2·9′	3°23·2′W	X	85
Isle of Dogs	T Ham	TQ3778	51°29·3′	0°1·2′W	T	177
Isle of Ewe	Highld	NG8588	57°50·1′	5°36·8′W	X	19
Isle of Fethaland	Shetld	HU3794	60°37·9′	1°18·9′W	X	1,2
Isle of Flosh	D & G	NY1173	55°2·9′	3°23·2′W	X	85
Isle of Gigha	Arg & Bt	NR6449	55°40·9′	5°44·8′W	X	62
Isle of Grain	Medway	TQ8776	51°27·3′	0°41·9′E	X	178
Isle of Gunnister	Shetld	HU3073	60°26·6′	1°26·8′W	X	3
Isle of Harty	Kent	TR0267	51°22·2′	0°54·5′E	X	178
Isle of Lewis (Eilean Leodhais)	N Eil	NB3741	58°17·0′	6°28·7′W	X	8
Isle of Lewis or Eilean Leòdhais	N Eil	NB2022	58°6·2′	6°44·7′W	X	13,14
Isle of Man	D & G	NY0075	55°3·8′	3°33·5′W	T	84
Isle of Man	I of M	SC3585	54°14·3′	4°31·5′W	X	95
Isle of Man (Ronaldsway) Airport	I of M	SC2868	54°5·0′	4°37·4′W	X	95
Isle of Man Steam Railway	I of M	SC2469	54°5·5′	4°41·1′W	X	95
Isle of May	Fife	NT6599	56°11·2′	2°33·4′W	X	59
Isle of Mull Railway	Arg & Bt	NM7236	56°27·9′	5°41·6′W	X	49
Isle of Nibon	Shetld	HU3073	60°26·6′	1°26·8′W	X	3
Isle of Niddister	Shetld	HU2675	60°27·7′	1°31·1′W	X	3
Isle of Noss	Shetld	HU5440	60°8·7′	1°1·2′W	X	4
Isle of Oxney	Kent	TQ9127	51°0·9′	0°43·8′E	X	189
Isle of Portland	Dorset	SY6972	50°33·0′	2°25·9′W	X	194
Isle of Purbeck	Dorset	SY9681	50°38·0′	2°3·0′W	X	195
Isle of Rhé	Glos	ST7396	51°40·0′	2°23·0′W	X	162
Isle of Sheppey	Kent	TQ9669	51°23·4′	0°49·4′E	X	178
Isle of Skye Fm	Lancs	SD5451	53°57·4′	2°41·6′W	FM	102
Isle of Stenness	Shetld	HU2076	60°28·3′	1°37·7′W	X	3
Isle of Thanet	Kent	TR3167	51°21·5′	1°19·5′E	X	179
Isle of Thorns	E Susx	TQ4130	51°3·3′	0°1·1′E	X	187
Isle of West Burrafirth	Shetld	HU2458	60°18·6′	1°33·4′W	X	3
Isle of Westerhouse	Shetld	HU2675	60°27·7′	1°31·1′W	X	3
Isle of Whithorn	D & G	NX4736	54°42·0′	4°22·0′W	T	83
Isle of Wight	I of W	SZ4986	50°40·5′	1°18·0′W	X	196
Isle of Wight Airport	I of W	SZ5884	50°39·4′	1°10·4′W	X	196
Isle of Wight Fm	Beds	TL0118	51°51·3′	0°31·6′W	FM	166
Isle of Wight Fm	Bucks	TQ0188	51°35·1′	0°32·1′W	FM	176
Isle of Wight Hill	Hants	SU2437	51°8·1′	1°39·0′W	H	184
Isle of Wight Steam Rly	I of W	SZ5589	50°42·1′	1°12·9′W	X	196
Isleornsay or Eilean Iarmain	Highld	NG6912	57°8·7′	5°48·7′W	T	32
Isleornsay or Eilean Iarmain	Highld	NG7012	57°8·7′	5°47·7′W	X	32,33
Isle Park Fm	Shrops	SJ4617	52°45·1′	2°47·6′W	FM	126
Isle Pool	Shrops	SJ4617	52°45·1′	2°47·6′W	W	126
Isle Port	S Ayr	NS2412	55°22·5′	4°46·2′W	W	70
Isleport Fm	Somer	ST3347	51°13·3′	2°57·2′W	FM	182
Isle Ristol	Highld	NB9711	58°2·8′	5°25·9′W	X	15
Isle Rough	Orkney	HY6001	58°53·9′	2°41·2′W	X	6
Isles	D & G	NX8662	54°56·6′	3°46·4′W	X	84
Islesburgh	Shetld	HU3369	60°24·5′	1°23·6′W	X	2,3
Isles Field Fm	Lancs	SD5639	53°51·0′	2°39·7′W	FM	102
Isles Fm	Somer	ST5311	50°54·0′	2°39·7′W	FM	194
Isles of Scilly	I Scilly	SV9111	49°55·4′	6°18·0′W	X	203
Islesteps	D & G	NX9672	55°2·2′	3°37·2′W	T	84
Islestone	Northum	NU1934	55°36·2′	1°41·5′W	X	75
Isle, The	Shrops	SJ4516	52°44·6′	2°48·5′W	X	126
Isleworth	Houns	TQ1575	51°28·0′	0°20·3′W	T	176
Isley Walton	Leic	SK4225	52°49·5′	1°22·2′W	T	129
Islington	Isling	TQ3184	51°32·6′	0°6·3′W	T	176,177
Islington	Wrekin	SJ7420	52°46·9′	2°22·7′W	T	127
Islington Hall Fm	Norf	TF5716	52°43·4′	0°19·9′E	FM	131
Islington Hill	Durham	NZ0029	54°39·6′	1°59·6′W	H	92
Islington Lodge	Norf	TF5717	52°43·9′	0°19·9′E	X	131
Islip	Northnts	SP9879	52°24·2′	0°33·2′W	T	141
Islip	Oxon	SP5214	51°49·6′	1°14·3′W	T	164
Islip Lo	Northnts	SP9678	52°23·7′	0°34·9′W	X	141
Islivig	N Eil	NA9927	58°8·0′	7°6·4′W	T	13
Ismere Ho	Worcs	SO8679	52°24·8′	2°12·0′W	X	139
Is Mynydd	Gwyn	SH6019	52°45·3′	4°4·1′W	X	124
Is-mynydd	Gwyn	SH8838	52°55·9′	3°39·6′W	X	124,125
Isnage Fm	Hants	SU7745	51°12·2′	0°53·5′W	FM	186
Isombridge	Wrekin	SJ6113	52°43·0′	2°34·2′W	T	127
Israel Fm	N Yks	SD7463	54°4·0′	2°23·4′W	FM	98
Israel's Fm	Bolton	SD6905	53°32·7′	2°27·7′W	FM	109
Israel's Fm	Essex	TL6713	51°47·7′	0°25·7′E	FM	167
Issue Edge	Kirk	SE0805	53°32·7′	1°52·3′W	X	110
Istead Rise	Kent	TQ6370	51°24·6′	0°21·0′E	T	177
Isurium (Roman Town)	N Yks	SE4066	54°5·5′	1°22·9′W	R	99
Isworth Fm	Northnts	SP7844	52°5·6′	0°51·3′W	FM	152
Is-y-coed	Powys	SH7700	52°35·3′	3°48·5′W	X	135
Isycoed	V of Glam	SS9878	51°29·7′	3°27·8′W	X	170
Isycoed	Wrex	SJ4050	53°2·9′	2°53·3′W	T	117
Is-y-llan	Carm	SN4916	51°49·6′	4°11·1′W	X	159
Italian Chapel	Orkney	HY4800	58°53·3′	2°53·7′W	X	6,7
Itchel Home Fm	Hants	SU7849	51°14·3′	0°52·6′W	FM	186
Itchen	C of Soton	SU4411	50°54·0′	1°22·1′W	T	196
Itchen Abbas	Hants	SU5332	51°5·3′	1°14·2′W	T	185
Itchen Down Fm	Hants	SU5434	51°6·4′	1°13·3′W	FM	185
Itchen Navigation, The	Hants	SU4622	51°0·0′	1°20·3′W	W	185
Itchenor Ho	W Susx	SU7900	50°47·9′	0°52·4′W	X	197
Itchen Stoke	Hants	SU5532	51°5·3′	1°12·5′W	T	185
Itchen Stoke Down	Hants	SU5534	51°6·4′	1°12·5′W	X	185
Itchen Valley Country Park	Hants	SU4515	50°56·2′	1°21·2′W	X	196
Itchen Valley Country Park	Hants	SU4516	50°56·7′	1°21·2′W	X	185
Itchen Way	Hants	SU5432	51°5·3′	1°13·3′W	X	185

Itchen Wood	Hants	SU5235	51°6·9′	1°15·0′W	F	185
Itchill	I of W	SZ5279	50°36·7′	1°15·5′W	X	196
Itchingfield	W Susx	TQ1328	51°2·6′	0°22·9′W	T	187,198
Itchington	S Glos	ST6586	51°34·5′	2°29·9′W	T	172
Itchington Holt	Warw	SP3755	52°11·8′	1°27·1′W	F	151
Itchingwood Common	Surrey	TQ4150	51°14·1′	0°1·6′E	X	187
Itford Fm	E Susx	TQ4305	50°49·8′	0°2·2′E	FM	198
Itford Hill	E Susx	TQ4305	50°49·8′	0°2·2′E	X	198
Ithells Bridge Fm	Wrex	SJ3956	53°6·1′	2°54·3′W	FM	117
Itherie Geo	Orkney	HY3733	59°11·0′	3°5·7′W	X	6
Itlaw	Aberd	NJ6757	57°36·4′	2°32·7′W	X	29
Itlay	Glos	SO9905	51°44·9′	2°0·5′W	X	163
Itteringham	Norf	TG1430	52°49·7′	1°11·0′E	T	133
Itteringham Common	Norf	TG1529	52°49·2′	1°11·9′E	T	133
Ittinge Fm	Kent	TR1146	51°10·7′	1°1·5′E	FM	179,189
Ittingstone	Aberd	NJ5039	57°26·6′	2°49·5′W	X	29
Itton	Devon	SX6898	50°46·2′	3°51·9′W	X	191
Itton	Monm	ST4995	51°39·3′	2°43·8′W	T	162
Itton Common	Monm	ST4896	51°39·9′	2°44·7′W	T	171
Itton Court	Monm	ST4995	51°39·3′	2°43·8′W	X	162
Itton Hill	Monm	ST4895	51°39·3′	2°44·7′W	X	171
Itton Moor	Devon	SX6899	50°46·8′	3°52·0′W	X	191
Iuchair	N Eil	NB2649	58°20·9′	6°40·5′W	X	8
Ivah	Lancs	SD6564	54°4·5′	2°31·7′W	X	97
Ivar's Knowe	Orkney	HY7143	59°16·6′	2°30·0′W	X	5
Ivar's Knowe (Burnt Mound)	Orkney	HY7143	59°16·6′	2°30·0′W	A	5
Ivegill	Cumbr	NY4143	54°47·0′	2°54·6′W	T	85
Ivelet	N Yks	SD9397	54°22·4′	2°6·0′W	T	98
Ivelet Moor	N Yks	NY9100	54°24·0′	2°7·9′W	X	91,92
Ivelet Wood	N Yks	SD9198	54°22·9′	2°7·9′W	F	98
Ivelle Fm	Surrey	TQ0635	51°6·5′	0°28·8′W	FM	187
Iver	Bucks	TQ0381	51°31·3′	0°30·5′W	T	176
Iver Heath	Bucks	TQ0283	51°32·4′	0°31·4′W	T	176
Iverley	Staffs	SO8781	52°25·8′	2°11·1′W	T	139
Iverley House Fm	Staffs	SO8781	52°25·8′	2°11·1′W	FM	139
Iver Sta	Bucks	TQ0379	51°30·3′	0°30·6′W	X	176
Ivescar	N Yks	SD7479	54°12·6′	2°23·5′W	X	98
Ives Fm	Hants	SU6860	51°20·3′	1°1·0′W	FM	175,186
Ives Fm	N Yks	SE4161	54°2·8′	1°22·0′W	FM	99
Ives Head	Leic	SK4717	52°45·1′	1°17·8′W	H	129
Iveson Ho	Leeds	SE2638	53°50·5′	1°35·9′W	X	104
Iveston	Durham	NZ1350	54°50·9′	1°47·4′W	T	88
Ivetsey Bank	Staffs	SJ8310	52°41·5′	2°14·7′W	X	127
Ivetsey Bank Fm	Staffs	SJ8310	52°41·5′	2°14·7′W	FM	127
Ivey	Corn	SX1276	50°33·4′	4°38·9′W	X	200
Ivinghoe	Bucks	SP9416	51°50·3′	0°37·7′W	T	165
Ivinghoe Aston	Bucks	SP9518	51°51·4′	0°36·8′W	T	165
Ivinghoe Br	Bucks	SP9317	51°50·9′	0°38·6′W	X	165
Ivinghoe Common	Bucks	SP9714	51°49·2′	0°35·2′W	F	165
Ivinghoe Hills	Bucks	SP9615	51°49·8′	0°36·0′W	H	165
Iving Howe	Cumbr	NY3203	54°25·3′	3°2·5′W	X	90
Ivington	Heref	SO4756	52°12·2′	2°46·1′W	T	148,149
Ivington Camp	Heref	SO4854	52°11·1′	2°45·2′W	A	148,149
Ivington Common	Heref	SO4657	52°12·8′	2°47·0′W	X	148,149
Ivington Court	Heref	SO4656	52°12·2′	2°47·0′W	X	148,149
Ivington Green	Heref	SO4656	52°12·2′	2°47·0′W	T	148,149
Ivington Park	Heref	SO4755	52°11·7′	2°46·1′W	X	148,149
Ivin Waite	N Yks	SE1365	54°5·1′	1°47·7′W	X	99
Ivol Barn	Oxon	SU6183	51°32·8′	1°6·8′W	X	175
Ivory Fm	Hants	SU4557	51°18·8′	1°20·9′W	FM	174
Ivorys	W Susx	TQ1923	50°59·9′	0°17·9′W	X	198
Ivrigar	Orkney	HY3524	59°6·1′	3°7·6′W	X	6
Ivy Bank Fm	Staffs	SK1424	52°49·0′	1°47·1′W	FM	128
Ivy Barn	Norf	TM3394	52°29·9′	0°26·4′E	X	134
Ivy Br	Gwyn	SH6539	52°56·1′	4°0·1′W	X	124
Ivybridge	Devon	SX6356	50°23·5′	3°55·3′W	T	202
Ivybridge	Monm	ST3592	51°37·6′	2°56·0′W	X	171
Ivy Chimneys	Essex	TL4500	51°41·0′	0°6·2′E	T	167
Ivychurch	Kent	TR0227	51°0·6′	0°53·2′E	T	189
Ivycott	Devon	SS4742	51°9·6′	4°10·9′W	X	180
Ivy Cott	Durham	NZ1323	54°36·4′	1°47·5′W	X	92
Ivy Cott	Kent	TQ7265	51°21·7′	0°28·6′E	X	178
Ivy Cottage	Cumbr	NY4547	54°49·1′	2°50·9′W	X	86
Ivy Cove	Devon	SX9150	50°20·6′	3°31·5′W	W	202
Ivy Crag	Cumbr	NY3100	54°23·7′	3°3·3′W	H	90
Ivy Crag	Cumbr	NY3504	54°25·9′	2°59·7′W	H	90
Ivy Cross	Dorset	ST8623	51°0·6′	2°11·6′W	T	183
Ivyend Fm	Shrops	SJ3612	52°42·4′	2°56·4′W	FM	126
Ivy Farm Ho	Staffs	SJ8421	52°47·4′	2°13·8′W	X	127
Ivy Fm	Cambs	TL1985	52°27·2′	0°14·5′W	FM	142
Ivy Fm	Ches	SJ5158	53°7·3′	2°43·5′W	FM	117
Ivy Fm	Hants	SU3838	51°8·6′	1°27·0′W	FM	185
Ivy Fm	Hants	SU7034	51°6·3′	0°59·6′W	FM	186
Ivy Fm	Herts	TL3440	52°2·8′	0°2·4′W	FM	154
Ivy Fm	Lancs	SD3730	53°46·0′	2°56·9′W	FM	102
Ivy Fm	Lancs	SD4045	53°54·1′	2°54·4′W	FM	102
Ivy Fm	Norf	TF5912	52°41·2′	0°21·5′E	FM	131,143
Ivy Fm	Norf	TF6112	52°41·1′	0°23·3′E	FM	132,143
Ivy Fm	Norf	TF9323	52°46·4′	0°52·1′E	FM	132
Ivy Fm	Norf	TG0500	52°33·8′	1°1·9′E	FM	144
Ivy Fm	Norf	TG2121	52°44·7′	1°16·9′E	FM	133,134
Ivy Fm	Suff	TM5192	52°28·3′	1°42·2′E	FM	134
Ivy Fm	Wilts	ST8574	51°28·1′	2°12·6′W	FM	173
Ivy Grange	N Yks	SE6035	53°48·7′	1°4·9′W	X	105
Ivy Hall	Essex	TL7225	51°54·0′	0°30·4′E	X	167
Ivy Hall	N Yks	NZ6707	54°27·5′	0°57·6′W	X	94
Ivy Hatch	Kent	TQ5854	51°16·0′	0°16·3′E	T	188
Ivy Ho	Ches	SJ5254	53°5·2′	2°44·3′W	X	117
Ivy Ho	Ches	SJ5748	53°1·9′	2°38·1′W	X	117
Ivy Ho	Derby	SK1078	53°18·2′	1°50·6′W	X	119
Ivy Ho	Derby	SK1659	53°7·9′	1°45·2′W	X	119
Ivy Ho	Essex	TM0615	51°48·0′	0°59·7′E	X	168
Ivy Ho	E Susx	TQ8212	50°52·9′	0°35·6′E	X	199
Ivy Ho	E Yorks	SE7832	53°46·9′	0°48·6′W	X	105,106
Ivy Ho	E Yorks	TA2820	53°39·9′	0°3·3′W	X	107,113
Ivy Ho	Lincs	TF1483	53°20·1′	0°16·9′W	X	121
Ivy Ho	Lincs	TF2356	53°5·5′	0°9·4′W	X	122
Ivy Ho	Lincs	TF3261	53°8·0′	0°1·2′W	X	122
Ivy Ho	Lincs	TF3367	53°11·2′	0°0·2′W	X	122

Ivy Ho	Lincs	TF3898	53°27·9′	0°5·1′E	X	113
Ivy Ho	Lincs	TF4856	53°5·1′	0°13·0′E	X	122
Ivy Ho	Northum	NU0736	55°37·3′	1°52·9′W	X	75
Ivy Ho	N Yks	SE0298	54°22·9′	1°57·7′W	X	98
Ivy Ho	Powys	SJ2403	52°37·4′	3°7·0′W	X	126
Ivy Ho	Staffs	SK0857	53°6·8′	1°52·4′W	X	119
Ivy Ho	York	SE6951	53°57·3′	0°56·5′W	X	105,106
Ivyhole Hill	Hants	SU7857	51°18·6′	0°52·5′W	X	175,186
Ivy Holme Fm	Norf	TM1399	52°33·1′	1°8·9′E	FM	144
Ivy House	Flint	SJ1472	53°14·5′	3°16·9′W	X	116
Ivyhouse Cross	Devon	SX4093	50°43·1′	4°15·6′W	X	190
Ivy House Fm	Bucks	TQ0485	51°33·5′	0°29·6′W	FM	176
Ivy House Fm	Cambs	TL4899	52°34·3′	0°11·4′E	FM	143
Ivy House Fm	Ches	SJ8179	53°18·7′	2°16·7′W	FM	118
Ivyhouse Fm	Derby	SK3043	52°59·2′	1°32·8′W	FM	119,128
Ivyhouse Fm	Hants	SU7127	51°2·5′	0°58·9′W	FM	186,197
Ivy House Fm	Kent	TQ8749	51°12·8′	0°41·0′E	FM	189
Ivy House Fm	Leic	SK3501	52°36·6′	1°28·6′W	FM	140
Ivy House Fm	Lincs	SK9457	53°6·3′	0°35·3′W	FM	121
Ivy House Fm	Lincs	TF3748	53°0·9′	0°2·9′E	FM	131
Ivy House Fm	Norf	TF5607	52°38·5′	0°18·7′E	FM	143
Ivyhouse Fm	Norf	TM4093	52°29·1′	1°32·5′E	FM	134
Ivy House Fm	Northnts	SP6162	52°15·4′	1°6·0′W	FM	152
Ivy House Fm	N Yks	SE1466	54°5·6′	1°46·7′W	FM	99
Ivy House Fm	Sol	SP1673	52°21·5′	1°45·5′W	FM	139
Ivy House Fm	Sol	SP2684	52°27·4′	1°36·6′W	FM	140
Ivy House Fm	Staffs	SK2300	52°36·1′	1°39·2′W	FM	139
Ivy House Fm	Suff	TM2773	52°18·7′	1°20·2′E	FM	156
Ivyhouse Fm	Surrey	TQ2139	51°8·5′	0°15·8′W	FM	187
Ivy House Fm	Wilts	SU0382	51°32·4′	1°57·0′W	FM	173
Ivy Island	Devon	SX5746	50°18·0′	4°0·1′W	X	202
Ivyland Fm	E Susx	TQ7118	50°56·4′	0°26·4′E	FM	199
Ivy Lane Fm	Bucks	SP9029	51°57·4′	0°41·0′W	FM	165
Ivyleaf Fm	Corn	SS2308	50°50·9′	4°30·5′W	FM	190
Ivy Lea Fm	N Yks	SE8475	54°10·1′	0°42·4′W	FM	100
Ivy Lodge	Essex	TM0922	51°51·7′	1°2·5′E	X	168,169
Ivy Lodge	Glos	SO9902	51°43·2′	2°0·5′W	X	163
Ivy Lodge Fm	Leic	SP6687	52°28·8′	1°1·3′W	FM	141
Ivy Lodge Fm	Suff	TM0670	52°17·6′	1°1·7′E	FM	144,155
Ivy Lodge Fm	Suff	TM2357	52°10·2′	1°16·1′E	FM	156
Ivy Mill Fm	Wilts	ST9254	51°17·3′	2°6·5′W	FM	184
Ivy Nook Fm	Suff	TL9875	52°20·5′	0°54·8′E	FM	144
Ivy Scar	N Yks	SD9890	54°18·6′	2°1·4′W	X	98
Ivy Stone	Somer	SS8348	51°13·4′	3°40·1′W	X	181
Ivy Thorn Manor	Somer	ST4834	51°6·4′	2°44·2′W	X	182
Ivytodd	Essex	TL5840	52°2·4′	0°18·6′E	X	154
Ivy Todd	Norf	TF8909	52°39·0′	0°48·0′E	T	144
Ivyton Fm	Somer	ST2031	51°4·6′	3°8·1′W	FM	182
Ivy Tower	Nth Pt Talb	SS7798	51°40·3′	3°46·3′W	X	170
Ivy Tree	Cumbr	SD2887	54°16·7′	3°5·9′W	X	96,97
Ivytree Fm	Suff	TM0139	52°1·0′	0°56·2′E	FM	155
Ivytree Fm	Suff	TM0144	52°3·7′	0°56·3′E	FM	155
Ivy Villa	Staffs	SJ8412	52°42·6′	2°13·8′W	X	127
Ivywell Fm	Suff	TM1143	52°2·9′	1°5·0′E	FM	155,169
Ivy Wood	Essex	TL7716	51°49·1′	0°34·5′E	F	167
Iwade	Kent	TQ8967	51°22·5′	0°43·3′E	T	178
Iwerddon	Conwy	SH7852	53°3·3′	3°48·8′W	H	115
Iwerne Courtney or Shroton	Dorset	ST8512	50°54·7′	2°12·4′W	T	194
Iwerne Hill	Dorset	ST8814	50°55·8′	2°9·9′W	X	194
Iwerne Minster	Dorset	ST8614	50°55·7′	2°11·6′W	T	194
Iwood	N Som	ST4563	51°22·0′	2°47·0′W	T	172,182
Iwood Place Fm	E Susx	TQ6316	50°55·4′	0°19·5′E	FM	199
Ixhill	Bucks	SP6510	51°47·3′	1°3·1′W	X	164,165
Ixworth	Suff	TL9270	52°17·9′	0°49·4′E	T	144,155
Ixworth Thorpe	Suff	TL9172	52°19·0′	0°48·5′E	T	144,155
Izaak Walton Hotel	Staffs	SK1450	53°3·1′	1°47·1′W	X	119
Izaak Walton's Cottage and Museum	Staffs	SJ8729	52°51·7′	2°11·2′W	X	127

J

Jaapston	E Renf	NS4655	55°46·1′	4°26·9′W	X	64
Jackaments Bottom	Glos	ST9697	51°40·5′	2°3·1′W	X	163
Jack Anderton Br	Lancs	SD5645	53°54·2′	2°39·8′W	X	102
Jacka Point	Corn	SW9339	50°13·1′	4°53·7′W	X	204
Jacka, The	Corn	SW9339	50°13·1′	4°53·7′W	X	204
Jackbarrow Fm	Glos	SO9507	51°45·9′	2°4·0′W	FM	163
Jack Bridge	Cald	SD9628	53°45·1′	2°3·2′W	X	103
Jack (Clayton Windmills)	W Susx	TQ3013	50°54·3′	0°8·7′W	X	198
Jackdaw Hill	Beds	SP9938	52°2·1′	0°33·0′W	X	153
Jackdaw Hole	N Yks	SD8075	54°10·5′	2°18·0′W	X	98
Jackdaw Point	V of Glam	ST2264	51°22·4′	3°6·9′W	X	182
Jacket's Point	Corn	SX0383	50°37·0′	4°46·7′W	X	200
Jack Field	N Yks	SD9943	53°53·2′	2°0·5′W	X	103
Jackfield	Wrekin	SJ6902	52°37·1′	2°27·1′W	T	127
Jack Field's Fm	Ches	SJ8666	53°11·7′	2°12·2′W	FM	118
Jack Gap Plantn	Cumbr	SD3395	54°21·0′	3°1·4′W	F	96,97
Jack Green	Lancs	SD5925	53°43·4′	2°36·9′W	T	102
Jack Hayes	Staffs	SJ9349	53°2·5′	2°5·9′W	T	118
Jack Hey Gate Fm	Traf	SJ7089	53°24·1′	2°26·7′W	FM	109
Jack Hill	N Yks	SE2051	53°57·5′	1°41·3′W	X	104
Jack Ho	Cumbr	NY3843	54°46·9′	2°57·4′W	X	85
Jack Ho	Lancs	SD8546	53°54·8′	2°13·3′W	X	103
Jack Hole Flat	N Yks	SE0864	54°4·6′	1°52·2′W	X	99
Jack Hole Moss	N Yks	SE0864	54°4·6′	1°52·2′W	X	99
Jack in the Basket	Hants	SZ3493	50°44·4′	1°30·7′W	X	196
Jack-in-the-Green	Devon	SY0195	50°45·0′	3°23·8′W	T	192
Jacklett's Fm	Essex	TL8002	51°41·5′	0°36·7′E	FM	168
Jackmoor	Devon	SX9098	50°46·5′	3°33·2′W	X	192
Jack Mytton Way	Shrops	SO2576	52°22·9′	3°5·7′W	X	148
Jack Nook Fm	Lancs	SD5238	53°50·4′	2°43·4′W	FM	102

Jack O'Sherwood	Notts	SK5452	53°4·0′	1°11·2′W	F	120
Jacksbank	Aberd	NO7683	56°56·5′	2°23·2′W	X	45
Jacksbridge Fm	Surrey	TQ3843	51°10·4′	0°1·2′W	FM	187
Jack's Bush Fm	Hants	SU2636	51°7·6′	1°37·3′W	FM	184
Jack's Castle	Somer	ST7435	51°7·1′	2°21·9′W	X	183
Jack's Corse	Aberd	NO7872	56°50·6′	2°21·2′W	X	45
Jack's Court	Kent	TR0521	50°57·3′	0°55·5′E	X	189
Jack Scout	Lancs	SD4573	54°9·2′	2°50·1′W	X	97
Jacksdale	Notts	SK4451	53°3·5′	1°20·2′W	T	120
Jack's Furze	Lincs	TF2986	53°21·5′	0°3·3′W	F	113,122
Jack's Green	Essex	TL5721	51°52·2′	0°17·2′E	T	167
Jack's Green	Glos	SO8809	51°47·0′	2°10·0′W	T	162
Jack's Hatch	Essex	TL4306	51°44·3′	0°4·7′E	T	167
Jack's Hill	Dorset	SY4998	50°47·0′	2°43·0′W	H	193,194
Jack's Hill	Essex	TQ4399	51°40·5′	0°4·5′E	X	167,177
Jack's Hill	Herts	TL2329	51°57·0′	0°12·2′W	X	166
Jacks Law	Northum	NT9542	55°40·5′	2°4·3′W	H	74,75
Jacks Law	Northum	NT9542	55°40·5′	2°4·3′W	X	74,75
Jack's Law	S Lanak	NS8828	55°32·2′	3°46·1′W	H	71,72
Jacksom's Fm	Wilts	ST9175	51°28·7′	2°7·4′W	FM	173
Jackson Bridge	Kirk	SE1607	53°33·8′	1°45·1′W	T	110
Jackson Ground	Cumbr	SD2392	54°19·3′	3°10·6′W	X	96
Jackson Rigg	Cumbr	NY4269	55°1·0′	2°54·0′W	X	85
Jackson's Banks	Lancs	SD6232	53°47·2′	2°34·2′W	X	102,103
Jackson's Br	Traf	SJ8092	53°25·7′	2°17·7′W	X,	109
Jacksons Fm	Hants	SU4915	50°56·2′	1°17·8′W	FM	196
Jackson's Fm	Northnts	SP5944	52°5·7′	1°7·9′W	FM	152
Jackson's Fm	Suff	TM2867	52°15·5′	1°20·9′E	FM	156
Jackson's Hill	Notts	SK5854	53°5·0′	1°7·6′W	X	120
Jackson's Hill	Wakf	SE4917	53°39·1′	1°15·1′W	X	111
Jackson's Ho	Lancs	SD8443	53°53·2′	2°14·2′W	X	103
Jackson's Plantn	E Yorks	SE9446	53°54·3′	0°33·7′W	F	106
Jackson's Ridge	Lancs	SD9536	53°49·5′	2°4·1′W	X	103
Jackson's Wood	Notts	SK6454	53°5·0′	1°2·3′W	F	120
Jack Sound	Pemb	SM7508	51°43·8′	5°15·1′W	W	157
Jacks Reef	Orkney	HY6529	59°9·0′	2°36·2′W	X	5
Jackston	Aberd	NJ8744	57°29·4′	2°12·6′W	X	30
Jackston	Aberd	NO7767	56°47·9′	2°22·1′W	X	45
Jackstone	Pth & Kin	NO0633	56°29·0′	3°31·1′W	X	52,53
Jackstown	Aberd	NJ7531	57°22·4′	2°24·5′W	X	29
Jack the Treacle Eater	Somer	ST5614	50°55·7′	2°37·2′W	X	194
Jackton	S Lanak	NS5952	55°44·7′	4°14·3′W	X	64
Jackville	Shetld	HU3743	60°10·5′	1°19·5′W	X	4
Jack White's Gibbet	Somer	ST6729	51°3·8′	2°27·9′W	X	183
Jackwood	Gren	TQ4376	51°28·1′	0°3·9′E	F	177
Jacky's Rock	I Scilly	SV8306	49°52·5′	6°24·4′W	X	203
Jacob's Bank	Kent	TQ9275	51°26·7′	0°46·2′E	X	178
Jacob's Fm	E Susx	TQ7919	50°56·8′	0°33·3′E	FM	199
Jacob's Gill	Cumbr	NY3147	54°49·0′	3°4·0′W	X	85
Jacobshall	Aberd	NJ8265	57°40·7′	2°17·6′W	X	29,30
Jacob's Ladder	Derby	SK0886	53°22·5′	1°52·4′W	X	110
Jacob's Ladder	Staffs	SK1452	53°4·1′	1°47·1′W	X	119
Jacob's Ladder	Worcs	SO7978	52°24·2′	2°18·1′W	X	138
Jacobstow	Corn	SX1995	50°43·8′	4°33·5′W	T	190
Jacobstowe	Devon	SS5801	50°47·7′	4°0·5′W	T	191
Jacobs Well	Surrey	SU9952	51°15·7′	0°34·5′W	T	186
Jacob's Wood	Mil Key	SP9545	52°5·9′	0°36·4′W	F	153
Jacotts Hill	Herts	TQ0897	51°39·9′	0°25·9′W	X	166,176
Jacques Bay	Essex	TM1531	51°56·4′	1°8·1′E	W	168,169
Jacques Court	Kent	TR1746	51°10·5′	1°6·7′E	X	179,189
Jacque's Fm	N Lincs	SE7410	53°35·1′	0°52·5′W	FM	112
Jacques Hall	Essex	TM1531	51°56·4′	1°8·1′E	X	168,169
Jaggard's Fm	Cambs	TL3958	52°12·4′	0°2·5′E	FM	154
Jagger Green	Cald	SE0919	53°40·3′	1°51·4′W	T	110
Jaggers	Essex	TM0319	51°50·2′	0°57·2′E	X	168
Jaggers Clough	Derby	SK1487	53°23·0′	1°47·0′W	X	110
Jakeman's Hill Fm	Worcs	SO8864	52°16·7′	2°10·2′W	FM	150
Jam	Aberd	NJ4945	57°29·8′	2°50·6′W	X	28,29
Jamaica Fm	Hants	SU4350	51°15·1′	1°22·6′W	FM	185
Jamaica Inn	Corn	SX1876	50°33·6′	4°33·8′W	X	201
Jamesfield	Pth & Kin	NO1918	56°21·1′	3°18·2′W	X	58
Jamesford	Powys	SO2197	52°34·1′	3°9·5′W	X	137
Jame's Hill	E Renf	NS4852	55°44·5′	4°24·8′W	H	64
Jameson's Fm	Wigan	SJ5999	53°29·4′	2°36·7′W	FM	108
James's Fm	Wrex	SJ3043	52°59·0′	3°2·2′W	FM	117
James Steel Park, The	Sund	NZ3255	54°53·6′	1°29·6′W	X	88
James's Thorn	Derby	SK0894	53°26·8′	1°52·4′W	X	110
James's Thorns	Glos	ST5498	51°41·0′	2°39·5′W	F	162
Jameston	Aberd	NO9099	57°5·2′	2°9·4′W	X	38,45
Jameston	N Ayr	NS3146	55°40·9′	4°40·8′W	X	63
Jameston	Pemb	SS0598	51°39·1′	4°48·7′W	T	158
Jameston	S Ayr	NS2207	55°19·7′	4°47·9′W	X	70,76
Jamestown	Aberd	NJ5335	57°24·4′	2°46·5′W	X	29
Jamestown	D & G	NY2996	55°15·4′	3°6·6′W	X	79
Jamestown	Fife	NT1281	56°1·1′	3°24·3′W	X	65
Jamestown	Highld	NH4756	57°34·4′	4°33·0′W	T	26
Jamestown	W Dunb	NS3981	56°0·0′	4°34·5′W	T	63
Jamie Cheyne's Loch	Shetld	HU3942	60°9·9′	1°17·3′W	W	4
Jamie's Hill Sike	Cumbr	NY6169	55°1·1′	2°36·2′W	W	86
Jamieson's Point	D & G	NX0371	54°59·9′	5°4·4′W	X	76,82
Jamie Wright's Well	E Dunb	NS6180	55°59·8′	4°13·3′W	W	64
Jamphlars	Fife	NT2095	56°8·7′	3°16·8′W	T	58
Jane Austen's Ho	Hants	SU7037	51°7·9′	0°59·6′W	X	186
Janecroft	Cumbr	NY0226	54°37·4′	3°30·7′W	X	89
Janefield	Aberd	NJ6151	57°33·1′	2°38·6′W	X	29
Janefield	Highld	NH7259	57°36·4′	4°8·1′W	X	27
Janesmoor Plain	Hants	SU2413	50°55·2′	1°39·1′W	X	195
Janeston	Angus	NO5947	56°37·0′	2°39·6′W	X	54
Janet's Foss	N Yks	SD9163	54°4·0′	2°7·8′W	W	98
Janetstown	Highld	ND0866	58°34·6′	3°34·4′W	T	11,12
Janetstown	Highld	ND3550	58°26·3′	3°6·3′W	T	12
Jangye-ryn	Corn	SW6520	50°2·3′	5°16·5′W	X	203
Janke's Green	Essex	TL9029	51°55·8′	0°46·2′E	T	168
Jankinsfield Fm	Norf	TF5317	52°44·0′	0°16·4′E	FM	131
Jan's Hill	Dorset	SY4295	50°45·3′	2°49·0′W	H	193
Jarbruck	D & G	NX8089	55°11·1′	3°52·7′W	X	78
Jarbruck Burn	D & G	NX7988	55°10·5′	3°53·6′W	W	78
Jardinefield	Scot Bord	NT8749	55°44·3′	2°12·0′W	X	74
Jardinefield	Scot Bord	NT8750	55°44·8′	2°12·0′W	X	67,74
Jardine Hall Mains	D & G	NY1087	55°10·4′	3°24·4′W	X	78

Jardine's Fm	Cumbr	NY6135	54°42·8′	2°35·9′W	FM	91
Jarlshof	Shetld	HU3909	59°52·1′	1°17·7′W	A	4
Jarman Centre	Cambs	TL6662	52°14·1′	0°26·3′E	X	154
Jarmons Fm	Kent	TQ7047	51°12·0′	0°26·4′E	FM	188
Jarnett, The	Derby	SK1469	53°13·3′	1°47·0′W	X	119
Jarney Burn	D & G	NX7599	55°16·4′	3°57·6′W	W	78
Jarney Knowes	D & G	NS7803	55°18·6′	3°54·9′W	H	78
Jarn Mound	Oxon	SP4802	51°43·1′	1°17·9′W	X	164
Jarratt Hills	E Yorks	SE8830	53°45·8′	0°39·5′W	X	106
Jarrow	S Tyne	NZ3465	54°59·0′	1°27·7′W	T	88
Jarrow Slake	S Tyne	NZ3465	54°59·0′	1°27·7′W	X	88
Jarves Fm	Surrey	TQ3445	51°11·5′	0°4·5′W	FM	187
Jarvis Brook	E Susx	TQ5329	51°2·6′	0°11·3′E	T	188,199
Jarvis Carr	Lancs	SD4247	53°55·2′	2°52·6′W	X	102
Jarvis Clough	Derby	SK2186	53°22·5′	1°40·7′W	X	110
Jarvis Fm	Kent	TQ9236	51°5·7′	0°44·9′E	FM	189
Jarvishayes	Devon	SX9796	50°45·5′	3°27·2′W	X	192
Jarvis Hill	Lincs	SK8093	53°25·9′	0°47·3′W	X	112
Jarvis Hill	Suff	TL6748	52°6·5′	0°26·7′E	X	154
Jarvis's Wood	E Susx	TQ6013	50°53·9′	0°16·9′E	F	199
Jason Hall	Pemb	SS0298	51°39·0′	4°51·3′W	X	158
Jasonshill Fm	Bucks	SP9802	51°42·7′	0°34·5′W	FM	165
Jaspers Fm	Worcs	SO9757	52°12·9′	2°2·2′W	FM	150
Jasper's Green	Essex	TL7226	51°54·6′	0°30·4′E	T	167
Java	Arg & Bt	NM7137	56°28·4′	5°42·7′W	T	49
Java Point	Arg & Bt	NM7137	56°28·4′	5°42·7′W	X	49
Jaw	Stir	NS6285	56°2·5′	4°12·5′W	X	57
Jawcraig	Falk	NS8475	55°57·5′	3°51·0′W	X	65
Jaw Hill	Leeds	SE2923	53°42·4′	1°33·2′W	T	104
Jawhills	Falk	NS8173	55°56·4′	3°53·9′W	X	65
Jaw Resr	W Dunb	NS4975	55°56·9′	4°24·7′W	W	64
Jay	Heref	SO3974	52°21·9′	2°53·4′W	X	137,148
Jayes Park	Surrey	TQ1440	51°9·1′	0°21·8′W	X	187
Jay Fm	Glos	SP2223	51°54·5′	1°40·4′W	FM	163
Jays	Devon	SX3687	50°39·8′	4°18·9′W	X	190
Jay's Copse	W Susx	SU9330	51°3·9′	0°40·0′W	F	186
Jay's Fm	Suff	TM5079	52°21·3′	1°40·7′E	FM	156
Jay's Fm	Wilts	ST9372	51°27·0′	2°5·7′W	FM	173
Jay's Grave	Devon	SX7379	50°36·0′	3°47·3′W	X	191
Jay's Hatch	Herts	TL0001	51°42·2′	0°32·8′W	X	166
Jay's Hill	Suff	TM4686	52°25·2′	1°37·5′E	X	156
Jaywick	Essex	TM1513	51°46·7′	1°7·4′E	T	168,169
Jealott's Hill	Brackn	SU8673	51°27·2′	0°45·3′W	T	175
Jeancroft	S Ayr	NS2003	55°17·5′	4°49·7′W	X	76
Jeanfield	Angus	NO3636	56°31·0′	3°2·0′W	X	54
Jeanfield	Pth & Kin	NN9814	56°18·7′	3°38·5′W	X	58
Jeanfield	S Ayr	NS3830	55°32·5′	4°33·6′W	X	70
Jeanfield	S Lanak	NS9851	55°44·8′	3°37·1′W	X	65,72
Jeaniefield	Scot Bord	NT5342	55°40·4′	2°44·4′W	T	73
Jeanie's Wood	Scot Bord	NT7555	55°47·5′	2°23·5′W	F	67,74
Jeater Houses	N Yks	SE4394	54°20·6′	1°19·9′W	X	99
Jedbank	Scot Bord	NT6521	55°29·1′	2°32·8′W	X	74
Jedburgh	Scot Bord	NT6520	55°28·6′	2°32·8′W	T	74
Jedburgh Knees	D & G	NS6102	55°17·8′	4°10·9′W	H	77
Jedderfield	Scot Bord	NT2340	55°39·1′	3°13·0′W	X	73
Jedderfield Plantn	Scot Bord	NT2340	55°39·1′	3°13·0′W	F	73
Jedforest Hotel	Scot Bord	NT6615	55°25·9′	2°31·8′W	X	80
Jedhead	Scot Bord	NT6205	55°20·5′	2°35·5′W	X	80
Jedurgh	Scot Bord	NT6519	55°28·1′	2°32·8′W	T	80
Jed Water	Scot Bord	NT6206	55°21·0′	2°35·5′W	W	80
Jed Water	Scot Bord	NT6614	55°25·4′	2°31·8′W	W	80
Jeffery Pot	N Yks	SD8783	54°14·8′	2°11·6′W	X	98
Jeffrey Hill	Lancs	SD6440	53°51·5′	2°32·4′W	X	102,103
Jeffreymeadow	Staffs	SK0740	52°57·7′	1°53·3′W	X	119,128
Jeffrey Rig	Scot Bord	NT2428	55°32·6′	3°11·8′W	H	73
Jeffrey's Fm	Essex	TL7720	51°51·3′	0°34·6′E	FM	167
Jeffrey's Mount	Cumbr	NY6002	54°25·0′	2°36·6′W	H	91
Jeffreystock Fm	Renf	NS3357	55°46·9′	4°39·3′W	FM	63
Jeffreyston	Pemb	SN0806	51°43·4′	4°46·4′W	T	158
Jeffrie's Corse	Midlo	NT2849	55°44·0′	3°8·4′W	H	73
Jeffrons Heys	Staffs	SJ7749	53°2·5′	2°20·2′W	X	118
Jeffry Bog Plantn	N Yks	SE7566	54°5·3′	0°50·8′W	F	100
Jeffs	Herts	TL4514	51°48·6′	0°6·6′E	X	167
Jekelow Grange	N Yks	SE3594	54°20·7′	1°27·3′W	X	99
Jekyll's Fm	Essex	TL6935	51°59·5′	0°28·1′E	FM	154
Jelliston	S Ayr	NS3917	55°25·5′	4°32·2′W	X	70
Jellyhill	E Dunb	NS6171	55°55·0′	4°13·0′W	X	64
Jellyholm	Clackm	NS9093	56°7·3′	3°45·7′W	X	58
Jemimaville	Highld	NH7165	57°39·6′	4°9·3′W	T	21,27
Jenden's Fm	W Susx	TQ1221	50°58·9′	0°23·9′W	FM	198
Jenet, The	Oxon	SP6000	51°42·0′	1°7·5′W	X	164,165
Jenkin	Brad	SE0249	53°56·5′	1°57·8′W	X	104
Jenkin	Cumbr	NY1528	54°38·6′	3°18·6′W	X	89
Jenkin Beck	N Yks	SD7072	54°8·8′	2°27·1′W	W	98
Jenkin Chapel	Ches	SJ9876	53°17·1′	2°1·4′W	X	118
Jenkin Crag	Cumbr	NY3802	54°24·8′	2°56·9′W	X	90
Jenkin Cross	Cumbr	NY2847	54°49·0′	3°6·8′W	X	85
Jenkin Hill	Cumbr	NY2727	54°38·2′	3°7·4′W	X	89,90
Jenkinhogs Fm	Essex	TL6036	52°0·2′	0°20·3′E	FM	154
Jenkins Burn	Northum	NY7869	55°1·2′	2°20·2′W	W	86,87
Jenkin's Fm	Essex	TL7823	51°52·9′	0°35·6′E	FM	167
Jenkin's Fm	Essex	TL8010	51°45·8′	0°36·9′E	FM	168
Jenkins Fm	Essex	TL9330	51°56·3′	0°48·9′E	FM	168
Jenkins Fm	Essex	TQ5295	51°38·2′	0°12·2′E	FM	167,177
Jenkins Park	Highld	NH3709	57°8·8′	4°41·2′W	X	34
Jenkins Point	Pemb	SN0005	51°42·7′	4°53·3′W	X	157,158
Jenkins's Fm	Glos	SO8509	51°47·0′	2°12·7′W	FM	162
Jenkinstown	Cumbr	NY4671	55°2·1′	2°50·3′W	X	86
Jenkyn Place	Hants	SU7844	51°11·6′	0°52·6′W	X	186
Jennetts Hill	W Berks	SU5771	51°26·3′	1°10·4′W	T	174
Jennetts Resr	Devon	SS4424	50°59·9′	4°13·0′W	W	180,190
Jenningsbury Fm	Herts	TL3411	51°47·1′	0°3·0′W	FM	166
Jennings Fm	Bucks	SU9487	51°34·7′	0°38·2′W	FM	175
Jenningtree Point	Bexley	TQ5080	51°30·2′	0°10·1′E	X	177
Jennison's Plantn	Suff	TL7960	52°12·8′	0°37·6′E	F	155
Jenny Bells Carr	Northum	NU2423	55°30·3′	1°36·8′W	X	75
Jenny Binks Moss	N Yks	SE1083	54°14·8′	1°50·4′W	H	99
Jenny Brown's Point	Lancs	SD4573	54°9·2′	2°50·1′W	X	97
Jennycliff Bay	C of Plym	SX4852	50°21·1′	4°7·8′W	W	201
Jennyfield	N Yks	SE2856	54°0·2′	1°34·0′W	T	104

Jenny Firkin Wood	E Yorks	SE8250	53°56·6′	0°44·6′W	F	106
Jennygill	D & G	NY0073	55°2·7′	3°33·5′W	X	84
Jenny Gray's Fm	Cambs	TL4592	52°30·6′	0°8·6′E	FM	143
Jenny Hurn	Lincs	SK8198	53°28·6′	0°46·4′W	X	112
Jenny Mill	Wilts	ST9859	51°20·0′	2°1·3′W	X	173
Jenny's Burn	D & G	NX3978	55°4·5′	4°30·9′W	W	77
Jenny's Cove	Devon	SS1345	51°10·7′	4°40·1′W	W	180
Jenny's Hill	D & G	NX3978	55°4·5′	4°30·9′W	X	77
Jenny's Lantern	Northum	NU1115	55°26·0′	1°49·1′W	X	81
Jenny's Portion	Devon	SS9403	50°49·2′	3°29·9′W	X	192
Jennystown	Fife	NO3211	56°17·5′	3°5·5′W	X	59
Jenny Twigg and her Daughter Tib	N Yks	SE1274	54°9·9′	1°48·6′W	X	99
Jennyval	Orkney	HY3510	58°58·6′	3°7·4′W	X	6
Jenny Wood	Lincs	TF3483	53°19·8′	0°1·1′E	F	122
Jennywoodston	Stir	NS6193	56°6·8′	4°13·7′W	X	57
Jepcrack's Fm	Essex	TL8711	51°46·2′	0°43·0′E	FM	168
Jeppe Knave Grave	Lancs	SD7537	53°50·0′	2°22·4′W	A	103
Jepson's Pond	Merth Tyd	SO0809	51°46·6′	3°19·6′W	W	160
Jerah	Stir	NS8399	56°10·4′	3°52·6′W	X	57
Jerby East	I of M	SC3899	54°21·9′	4°29·2′W	T	95
Jerdonfield	Scot Bord	NT6523	55°30·2′	2°32·8′W	X	74
Jeremiah's Tree	Beds	TL0829	51°57·2′	0°25·3′W	X	166
Jericho	Aberd	NJ6333	57°23·4′	2°36·5′W	X	29
Jericho	Angus	NO4047	56°36·9′	2°58·2′W	X	54
Jericho	Bury	SD8311	53°36·0′	2°15·0′W	T	109
Jericho	Cumbr	NY1146	54°48·3′	3°22·7′W	X	85
Jericho Barns	Oxon	SP4511	51°48·0′	1°20·5′W	FM	164
Jericho Fm	Bucks	SP6311	51°47·9′	1°4·8′W	FM	164,165
Jericho Fm	Corn	SW3931	50°7·5′	5°38·7′W	FM	203
Jericho Fm	Derby	SK0867	53°12·2′	1°52·4′W	FM	119
Jericho Fm	Lincs	SK9041	52°57·8′	0°39·2′W	FM	130
Jericho Fm	Notts	SK6246	53°0·7′	1°4·1′W	FM	129
Jericho Hill	Powys	SJ1620	52°46·5′	3°14·3′W	H	125
Jericho Lodge	Leic	SK7635	52°54·7′	0°51·8′W	X	129
Jericho Lodge	Leic	SK7915	52°43·8′	0°49·4′W	X	129
Jericho Priory	Essex	TL6001	51°41·3′	0°19·3′E	X	167
Jericho Wood	Lincs	SK9141	52°57·8′	0°38·3′W	F	130
Jermyns Fm	Suff	TM0839	52°0·8′	1°2·3′E	FM	155,169
Jermyns Ho	Hants	SU3823	51°0·5′	1°27·1′W	X	185
Jerome Coutts' Head	Shetld	HU1762	60°20·8′	1°41·0′W	X	3
Jerriestown	Cumbr	NY3963	54°57·7′	2°56·7′W	X	85
Jerrings Hall Fm	Sol	SP1276	52°23·1′	1°49·0′W	FM	139
Jerrycalf Rigg	Cumbr	NY6372	55°2·7′	2°34·3′W	X	86
Jerry's Bog	Lincs	SK8498	53°28·6′	0°43·6′W	X	112
Jerry's Linn	Northum	NY7481	55°7·6′	2°24·0′W	W	80
Jerry's New Plantn	Suff	TL8373	52°19·7′	0°41·5′E	F	144,155
Jerry's Point	Dorset	SZ0286	50°40·6′	1°57·9′W	X	195
Jerry's Pond	E Susx	TQ4904	50°49·2′	0°7·3′E	W	199
Jersay	N Lanak	NS8361	55°49·9′	3°51·6′W	X	65
Jersey Fm	Devon	ST0513	50°54·8′	3°20·7′W	FM	181
Jersey Marine	Nth Pt Talb	SS7194	51°38·0′	3°51·5′W	T	170
Jerusalem	Cumbr	NY6519	54°34·1′	2°32·1′W	X	91
Jerusalem Fm	E Loth	NT4770	55°55·5′	2°50·5′W	FM	66
Jervaulx Abbey	N Yks	SE1785	54°15·9′	1°43·9′W	A	99
Jervaulx Hall	N Yks	SE1685	54°15·9′	1°44·8′W	X	99
Jervaulx Park	N Yks	SE1785	54°15·9′	1°43·9′W	X	99
Jerviswood	S Lanak	NS8845	55°41·4′	3°46·5′W	T	72
Jerviswood Mains	S Lanak	NS8945	55°41·4′	3°45·5′W	X	72
Jervoise Fm	Wilts	SU0923	51°0·6′	1°51·9′W	FM	184
Jeskyns Fm	Kent	TQ6669	51°24·0′	0°23·6′E	FM	177,178
Jesmond	N upon Ty	NZ2566	54°59·5′	1°36·1′W	T	88
Jesmond Fm	Lincs	TF0492	53°25·1′	0°25·7′W	FM	112
Jesmor Fm	Surrey	TQ4144	51°10·9′	0°1·4′E	FM	187
Jessamine	Cered	SN5157	52°11·7′	4°10·4′W	X	146
Jessamine House Fm	Lincs	TF2653	53°3·8′	0°6·8′W	FM	122
Jesse Fm	Derby	SK4040	52°57·6′	1°23·9′W	FM	129
Jessiefield	C of Aber	NJ8805	57°8·4′	2°11·4′W	X	38
Jessop's Hill	E Susx	TQ4327	51°1·7′	0°2·7′E	X	187,198
Jester's Hill	Oxon	SP3839	52°3·1′	1°26·4′W	X	151
Jesus Hospl	Win & Maid	SU9079	51°30·4′	0°41·8′W	A	175
Jesus Well	Corn	SW9376	50°33·1′	4°55·0′W	A	200
Jett Hall	Donc	SE5914	53°37·4′	1°6·1′W	X	111
Jevington	E Susx	TQ5601	50°47·5′	0°13·2′E	T	199
Jevington Place	E Susx	TQ5601	50°47·5′	0°13·2′E	A	199
Jewell's Cross	Devon	SS2603	50°48·3′	4°27·8′W	T	190
Jewell's Fm	Devon	ST1512	50°54·3′	3°12·2′W	FM	181,193
Jewel Seat Well	N Yks	SD8699	54°23·4′	2°12·5′W	W	98
Jew House Fm	Cambs	TF4405	52°37·6′	0°8·1′E	FM	142,143
Jews Fm	Somer	ST0529	51°3·4′	3°20·9′W	FM	181
Jews Wood	E Susx	TQ6236	51°6·2′	0°19·2′E	F	188
Jill (Clayton Windmills)	W Susx	TQ3013	50°54·3′	0°8·7′W	X	198
Jilling's Fm	Suff	TL7461	52°13·4′	0°33·2′E	FM	155
Jill's Hole	Suff	TM2437	51°59·4′	1°16·2′E	W	169
Jimpies	Aberd	NJ6732	57°22·9′	2°32·5′W	X	29
Jingleby Ho	N Yks	SE8989	54°17·6′	0°37·5′W	X	94,101
Jingle Pot	N Yks	NZ0401	54°24·5′	1°55·9′W	X	92
Jingle Pot	N Yks	NZ1001	54°24·5′	1°50·3′W	X	92
Jingle Pot	N Yks	SD7377	54°11·5′	2°24·4′W	X	98
Jingle Pot Edge	N Yks	SD9399	54°23·4′	2°6·0′W	X	98
Jinglepot Hole	Durham	NZ0008	54°28·3′	1°59·6′W	X	92
Jingle Street	Monm	SO4710	51°47·4′	2°45·7′W	T	161
Jingling Pot	N Yks	SD6978	54°12·1′	2°28·1′W	X	98
Jinkinson's Fm	Lancs	SD6134	53°48·3′	2°35·1′W	FM	102,103
Joan Beech Wood	Kent	TR0756	51°16·2′	0°58·4′E	F	179
Joan Eaton's Cross	Staffs	SJ8417	52°45·3′	2°13·8′W	X	127
Joaney How	Somer	SS9042	51°10·2′	3°34·0′W	A	181
Joanland Fm	W Susx	TQ1535	51°6·4′	0°21·0′W	FM	187
Joan's Acre	Hants	SU6126	51°2·0′	1°7·4′W	X	185
Joan's Acre Wood	Hants	SU6126	51°2·0′	1°7·4′W	F	185
Joan's Hole	Worcs	SO7670	52°19·9′	2°20·7′W	X	138
Job Cross	Red & Cl	NZ6811	54°29·6′	0°56·6′W	A	94
Job's Copse	Oxon	SP3613	51°49·1′	1°28·3′W	F	164
Job's Ferry	Wirral	SJ3682	53°20·1′	2°57·3′W	X	108
Job's Fm	Beds	SP9332	51°59·0′	0°38·4′W	FM	165
Jobsgreen Fm	S Glos	ST6194	51°38·8′	2°33·4′W	FM	162,172
Jobs Hill	Northnts	SP5149	52°8·4′	1°14·9′W	X	151
Job's Hill Ho	Durham	NZ1734	54°42·3′	1°43·7′W	X	92
Job's Lodge	Durham	NZ0526	54°38·0′	1°54·9′W	X	92
Jobsons Fm	I of W	SZ5077	50°35·7′	1°17·2′W	FM	196

Job's Tenement	Corn	SX0075	50°32·7'	4°49·0'W	X	200
Job's Water	Corn	SW7431	50°8·4'	5°9·4'W	X	204
Jockasey	Orkney	HY3108	58°57·5'	3°11·5'W	X	6,7
Jockey Cap Clump	N Yks	NZ1403	54°25·6'	1°46·6'W	F	92
Jockey End	Herts	TL0413	51°48·6'	0°29·1'W	T	166
Jockey Ho	Notts	SK6876	53°16·8'	0°58·4'W	X	120
Jockey's Hall	Suff	TM0256	52°10·1'	0°57·6'E	X	155
Jockey Shield	Cumbr	NY5555	54°53·5'	2°41·7'W	X	86
Jockhedge	Lincs	TF5064	53°9·4'	0°15·0'E	X	122
Jock Ho	Durham	NZ0213	54°31·0'	1°57·7'W	X	92
Jock's Burn	Scot Bord	NT5656	55°48·0'	2°41·7'W	W	67,73
Jock's Burn	S Lanak	NS8250	55°44·0'	3°52·3'W	W	65,72
Jock's Castle	N Ayr	NS2557	55°46·7'	4°47·0'W	X	63
Jock's Crag	Northum	NT7502	55°18·9'	2°23·2'W	X	80
Jock's Craig	Inverc	NS3269	55°53·3'	4°40·7'W	X	63
Jock's Hill	Aberd	NJ9544	57°29·4'	2°4·5'W	F	30
Jock's Hill	Cumbr	NY6074	55°3·8'	2°37·1'W	X	86
Jock's Hill	Moray	NJ3136	57°24·8'	3°8·5'W	H	28
Jock's Hole	Fife	NO3725	56°25·0'	3°0·8'W	W	54,59
Jock's Hope	D & G	NY3594	55°14·4'	3°0·9'W	X	79
Jocksleys	Moray	NJ3949	57°31·9'	3°0·7'W	X	28
Jock's Pike	Northum	NY6784	55°9·2'	2°30·6'W	H	80
Jock's Road	Aberd	NO1982	56°55·6'	3°19·4'W	X	43
Jock's Road	Angus	NO2477	56°52·9'	3°14·4'W	X	44
Jock's Ruck	D & G	NS8205	55°19·7'	3°51·2'W	X	71,78
Jock's Shoulder	D & G	NY1702	55°18·6'	3°18·0'W	H	79
Jocksthorn	E Ayr	NS4141	55°38·5'	4°31·1'W	X	70
Jockston	Aberd	NJ8900	57°5·7'	2°10·4'W	X	38
Jockstown	D & G	NY2171	55°1·9'	3°13·7'W	X	85
Jodrell Bank	Ches	SJ7970	53°13·8'	2°18·5'W	T	118
Joe's Hill	Norf	TG0243	52°57·0'	1°0·8'E	X	133
John Ball Hill	Leic	SP6390	52°30·5'	1°3·9'W	X	140
John Bell's Banner	Cumbr	NY4109	54°28·6'	2°54·2'W	X	90
John Boyne's Burn	Shetld	HU4341	60°9·3'	1°13·0'W	W	4
Johnby	Cumbr	NY4333	54°41·6'	2°52·6'W	T	90
John Fell	N Yks	SD7062	54°3·4'	2°27·1'W	X	98
Johnfield	D & G	NY0085	55°9·2'	3°33·7'W	X	78
John Field Howden	Derby	SK1990	53°24·6'	1°42·4'W	X	110
Johnfield Moss	D & G	NY0085	55°9·2'	3°33·7'W	X	78
Johnmans Barn	Glos	SP1507	51°45·9'	1°46·6'W	X	163
John Muir Country Park	E Loth	NT6479	56°0·4'	2°34·2'W	X	67
Johnnie Mann's Loch	Shetld	HU3372	60°26·1'	1°23·5'W	W	2,3
Johnnygate	Derby	SK3175	53°16·5'	1°31·7'W	X	119
Johnny Pye's Clough Top	Lancs	SD5751	53°57·4'	2°38·9'W	X	102
Johnny's Crags	Northum	NY6677	55°5·4'	2°31·5'W	X	86
Johnny Sinclair's Nose	Shetld	HU3243	60°10·5'	1°24·9'W	X	4
John of Gaunt's Castle	N Yks	SE2154	53°59·1'	1°40·4'W	A	104
John of Gaunt's Deer Park	Hants	SU3531	51°4·9'	1°29·6'W	A	185
John of Gaunts House	Norf	TG2735	52°52·1'	1°22·8'E	A	133
John O'Gaunt	Leic	SK7309	52°40·7'	0°54·8'W	T	141
John O' Gaunt (Fox Covert)	Leic	SK7407	52°39·6'	0°54·0'W	F	141
John O' Gaunts	Leeds	SE3529	53°45·6'	1°27·7'W	T	104
John O' Gaunt's Hill	Beds	TL2247	52°6·7'	0°12·7'W	A	153
John o' Groats	Highld	ND3872	58°38·2'	3°3·6'W	T	7,12
John's Boat	Orkney	HY4955	59°23·0'	2°53·4'W	X	5
John's Burn	Cumbr	NY7735	54°42·8'	2°21·0'W	W	91
Johnscales	Cumbr	SD4686	54°16·3'	2°49·3'W	X	97
Johnscleugh	E Loth	NT6366	55°53·4'	2°35·1'W	X	67
John's Cross	E Susx	TQ7421	50°57·9'	0°29·1'E	T	199
Johnsfield	Scot Bord	NT7955	55°47·5'	2°19·7'W	X	67,74
John's Forest	Aberd	NJ7617	57°14·8'	2°23·4'W	F	38
Johnshaven	Aberd	NO7967	56°47·9'	2°20·2'W	T	45
John's Head	Shetld	HU2861	60°20·2'	1°29·1'W	X	3
Johnshill	Aberd	NJ7154	57°34·8'	2°28·6'W	X	29
John's Hill	Orkney	HY6328	59°8·5'	2°38·3'W	H	5
Johns Hill	Pth & Kin	NO0008	56°15·5'	3°36·4'W	H	58
Johnshill	Pth & Kin	NO2248	56°37·3'	3°15·8'W	X	53
Johnshill	S Lanak	NS8137	55°37·0'	3°52·9'W	X	71,72
John Side	Northum	NY8088	55°11·4'	2°18·4'W	X	80
Johns Lane Fm	Bucks	SP9706	51°44·9'	0°35·3'W	FM	165
John's Lee Wood	Leic	SK5010	52°41·4'	1°15·2'W	F	129
Johnson Fold	Bolton	SD6811	53°35·9'	2°28·6'W	T	109
Johnson Hall	Staffs	SJ8228	52°51·2'	2°15·6'W	X	127
Johnson Ho	Cumbr	SD5776	54°10·9'	2°39·1'W	X	97
Johnson House Fm	Lancs	SD5020	53°40·7'	2°45·0'W	FM	102
Johnson's Fm	E Yorks	SE7734	53°48·0'	0°49·4'W	FM	105
Johnson's Fm	E Yorks	SE7734	53°48·0'	0°49·4'W	FM	105,106
Johnson's Fm	Oxon	SU4584	51°33·6'	1°20·7'W	FM	174
Johnson's Hillock	Lancs	SD5921	53°41·3'	2°36·8'W	T	102
Johnson's Knoll	Derby	SK1557	53°6·8'	1°46·1'W	H	119
Johnson Street	Norf	TG3717	52°42·1'	1°30·9'E	T	133,134
Johnston	Aberd	NJ5824	57°18·5'	2°41·4'W	X	37
Johnston	Fife	NO2917	56°20·7'	3°8·5'W	X	59
Johnston	Pemb	SM9310	51°45·3'	4°59·6'W	T	157,158
Johnstone	Devon	SS7325	51°0·9'	3°48·2'W	X	180
Johnstone	Renf	NS4362	55°49·8'	4°30·0'W	T	64
Johnstonebank	D & G	NY1875	55°4·0'	3°16·6'W	X	85
Johnstonebridge	D & G	NY0992	55°13·1'	3°25·4'W	T	78
Johnstone Cas, The	Renf	NS4262	55°49·8'	4°30·9'W	A	64
Johnstonecleugh	D & G	NY0890	55°12·0'	3°26·3'W	X	78
Johnstone Hall	D & G	NY2275	55°4·1'	3°12·9'W	X	85
Johnstone Moors	Devon	SS7326	51°1·4'	3°48·3'W	X	180
Johnstonlee	D & G	NY2170	55°1·3'	3°13·7'W	X	85
Johnston Loch	N Lanak	NS6968	55°53·5'	4°5·2'W	W	64
Johnston Lodge	Aberd	NO7170	56°49·5'	2°28·1'W	X	45
Johnston Mains	Aberd	NO7270	56°49·5'	2°27·1'W	X	45
Johnston's Point	Arg & Bt	NR7612	55°21·3'	5°31·6'W	X	68
Johnstown	Carm	SN3919	51°51·0'	4°19·9'W	T	159
Johnstown	Wrex	SJ3046	53°0·6'	3°2·2'W	T	117
Johnstripe	Moray	NJ0447	57°30·4'	3°35·7'W	X	27
Joiner Stones	Cald	SE0016	53°38·7'	1°59·6'W	X	110
Jointer's Fm	Oxon	SP6601	51°42·5'	1°2·3'W	FM	164,165
Jointure	Moray	NJ2664	57°39·9'	3°14·0'W	X	28
Joist Fen	Cambs	TL5269	52°18·1'	0°14·2'E	X	154
Joist Fen	Suff	TL6985	52°26·4'	0°29·6'E	X	143
Joist Fm	Cambs	TL5269	52°18·1'	0°14·2'E	FM	154
Jolby Fm	N Yks	NZ2509	54°28·8'	1°36·4'W	FM	93
Jolby Grange	N Yks	NZ2510	54°29·3'	1°36·4'W	X	93
Jolby Manor	N Yks	NZ2510	54°29·3'	1°36·4'W	X	93
Joldwynds	Surrey	TQ1042	51°10·2'	0°25·2'W	X	187
Jolesfield Ho	W Susx	TQ1819	50°57·7'	0°18·8'W	X	198
Joles Fm	W Susx	TQ1823	50°59·9'	0°18·7'W	FM	198
Jolliffes Fm	Dorset	ST8119	50°58·4'	2°15·9'W	FM	183
Jolliffe's Fm	Dorset	ST8321	50°59·5'	2°14·1'W	FM	183
Jollyboys	Essex	TL6819	51°50·9'	0°26·7'E	X	167
Jolly Rock	I Scilly	SV8306	49°52·5'	6°24·4'W	X	203
Jolly's Bottom	Corn	SW7545	50°15·8'	5°9·1'W	T	204
Jolly's Fm	Suff	TM3356	52°9·4'	1°24·8'E	FM	156
Jolly's Fm	Wilts	SU3052	51°16·2'	1°33·8'W	FM	185
Jol Pool	Staffs	SJ9431	52°52·8'	2°4·9'W	W	127
Jones' Fm	Hants	SU4160	51°20·5'	1°24·3'W	FM	174
Jones's Covert	Cambs	TL1693	52°31·6'	0°17·0'W	F	142
Jones's Wood	S Glos	ST6889	51°36·2'	2°27·3'W	F	162,172
Joppa	Cered	SN5666	52°16·6'	4°6·3'W	X	135
Joppa	C of Edin	NT3173	55°57·0'	3°5·9'W	T	66
Joppa	Corn	SW3829	50°6·4'	5°39·5'W	X	203
Joppa	Corn	SW5636	50°10·7'	5°24·7'W	T	203
Joppa	S Ayr	NS4019	55°26·6'	4°31·3'W	T	70
Jordan	Devon	SX5291	50°42·2'	4°5·4'W	X	191
Jordan	Devon	SX7075	50°33·9'	3°49·8'W	X	191
Jordan Castle	Notts	SK6766	53°11·4'	0°59·4'W	A	120
Jordan Crags	N Yks	SE1470	54°7·8'	1°46·7'W	X	99
Jordan Fm	E Susx	TQ8916	50°55·0'	0°41·7'E	FM	189
Jordan Green	Norf	TG0721	52°45·0'	1°4·4'E	T	133
Jordan Hill	Surrey	SU9754	51°16·8'	0°36·2'W	X	186
Jordan Moss	N Yks	SE1175	54°10·5'	1°49·5'W	W	99
Jordans	Bucks	SU9791	51°36·8'	0°35·5'W	T	175,176
Jordans	Somer	ST3316	50°56·6'	2°56·8'W	X	193
Jordans	Surrey	TQ2138	51°7·9'	0°15·8'W	X	187
Jordan's Fm	Essex	TL6504	51°42·9'	0°23·7'E	FM	167
Jordanston	Pemb	SM9132	51°57·1'	5°2·1'W	T	157
Jordanstone	Pth & Kin	NO2747	56°36·8'	3°10·9'W	X	53
Jordanston Fm	Pemb	SM9407	51°43·7'	4°58·6'W	FM	157,158
Jordanthorpe	Sheff	SK3581	53°19·7'	1°28·1'W	T	110,111
Jordieland	D & G	NX7153	54°51·6'	4°0·2'W	X	83,84
Jordieland Loch	D & G	NX7153	54°51·6'	4°0·2'W	W	83,84
Jordon	Roth	SK4092	53°25·6'	1°23·5'W	T	111
Jordon Castle Fm	Notts	SK6766	53°11·4'	0°59·4'W	FM	120
Jordonhill	C of Glas	NS5366	55°53·2'	4°20·6'W	T	64
Jordonlaw	Scot Bord	NT6249	55°44·2'	2°35·9'W	X	74
Jordonlaw Moss	Scot Bord	NT6149	55°44·2'	2°36·8'W	X	74
Joros Fm	Lincs	SK8688	53°23·1'	0°42·0'W	FM	112,121
Joseph's Cairn	Northum	NU0902	55°19·0'	1°51·1'W	X	81
Jose's Cross	Devon	SS6921	50°58·6'	3°51·6'W	X	180
Joshua Fm	Bucks	SP6209	51°46·8'	1°5·7'W	FM	164,165
Joshua Plantn	Scot Bord	NT8451	55°45·4'	2°14·9'W	F	67,74
Joss Bay	Kent	TR4070	51°22·9'	1°27·3'E	W	179
Josselyns	Essex	TL9131	51°56·9'	0°47·2'E	X	168
Josselyns	Essex	TL9632	51°57·3'	0°51·5'E	A	168
Jotmans Hall Fm	Essex	TQ7687	51°33·5'	0°32·7'E	FM	178
Jowett Ho	Barns	SE2607	53°33·8'	1°36·0'W	X	110
Joyce Green Hospital	Kent	TQ5476	51°27·9'	0°13·4'E	X	177
Joyce Grove	Oxon	SU7086	51°34·3'	0°59·0'W	X	175
Joyce's Fm	Essex	TL9108	51°44·5'	0°46·4'E	FM	168
Joyce's Fm	Essex	TQ9299	51°39·6'	0°47·0'E	FM	168
Joyce's Head	Essex	TL9712	51°46·5'	0°51·7'E	X	168
Joyden's Wood	Bexley	TQ4971	51°25·3'	0°9·0'E	F	177
Joyford	Glos	SO5713	51°49·1'	2°37·0'W	T	162
Joy Hill	Lincs	TF4250	53°1·9'	0°7·5'E	X	122
Joy Lane Fm	Warr	SJ5591	53°25·1'	2°40·2'W	FM	108
Joylers Fm	Somer	ST4417	50°57·2'	2°47·5'W	FM	193
Joy's Green	Glos	SO6016	51°50·7'	2°34·4'W	T	162
Joytail Fm	Brad	SE0644	53°53·8'	1°54·1'W	FM	104
Juanhill	S Lanak	NS7441	55°39·0'	3°59·7'W	X	71
Juanjorge	Angus	NO2679	56°54·0'	3°12·4'W	X	44
Jubilee	Oldham	SD9410	53°35·4'	2°5·0'W	T	109
Jubilee Br	Worcs	SP0045	52°6·4'	1°59·6'W	X	150
Jubilee Cave	N Yks	SD8365	54°5·1'	2°15·2'W	A	98
Jubilee Corner	Kent	TQ8447	51°11·8'	0°38·4'E	X	188
Jubilee Fm	Bucks	SP6729	51°57·6'	1°1·1'W	FM	164,165
Jubilee Fm	Lincs	TF2263	53°9·2'	0°10·1'W	FM	122
Jubilee Fm	Lincs	TF2740	52°56·8'	0°6·2'W	FM	131
Jubilee Fm	Norf	TL6791	52°29·7'	0°28·0'E	FM	143
Jubilee Fm	Notts	SK6485	53°21·7'	1°1·9'W	FM	111,120
Jubilee Hill	Hants	SU8350	51°14·8'	0°48·3'W	X	186
Jubilee Lodge	Essex	TQ4394	51°37·8'	0°4·4'E	X	167,177
Jubilee Lodge	Rut	SK8404	52°37·9'	0°45·1'W	X	141
Jubilee Mills	N Yks	SE3563	54°3·9'	1°27·5'W	X	99
Jubilee Park	Enf	TQ3494	51°38·0'	0°3·4'W	X	166,176,177
Jubilee Rock	Corn	SX1074	50°32·3'	4°40·5'W	X	200
Jubilee Tower	Denb	SJ1662	53°9·2'	3°15·0'W	X	116
Jubilee Way	Cered	SN6588	52°28·6'	3°58·9'W	X	162,172
Jubilee Way	Leic	SK7623	52°48·2'	0°52·0'W	X	129
Jubilee Way	Leic	SK8234	52°54·1'	0°46·4'W	X	130
Juby's Fm	Norf	TG2817	52°42·4'	1°22·9'E	FM	133,134
Juddmonte Fm North	Win & Maid	SU8081	51°31·6'	0°50·4'W	FM	175
Juddmonte Ho	Win & Maid	SU8081	51°31·6'	0°50·4'W	X	175
Judd's Hill	Kent	TQ9960	51°18·5'	0°51·7'E	X	178
Judegate Fm	Lincs	TF4451	53°2·4'	0°9·3'E	FM	122
Judge House Fm	Kent	TQ8748	51°12·3'	0°41·0'E	FM	189
Judge's Cairn, The	Stir	NN7305	56°13·5'	4°2·5'W	A	57
Judge's Plantn	Cumbr	NY5434	54°42·2'	2°42·4'W	F	90
Judy Cross	Lincs	TF2333	52°53·1'	0°9·9'W	X	131
Jugbank	Staffs	SJ7535	52°55·0'	2°21·9'W	T	127
Jugger Howe Beck	N Yks	SE9398	54°22·4'	0°33·7'W	W	94,101
Jugger Howes	N Yks	NZ9400	54°23·4'	0°32·7'W	A	94
Jugger How Moor	N Yks	SE9499	54°22·9'	0°32·7'W	X	94,101
Jugg's Wood	Wilts	SU3066	51°23·8'	1°33·7'W	F	174
Jughole Wood	Derby	SK2759	53°7·9'	1°35·4'W	F	119
Jugsholme Fm	Northnts	SP7084	52°27·2'	0°57·8'W	FM	141
Julian Bower	Cumbr	NY6026	54°37·9'	2°36·8'W	X	91
Julian Ho	Norf	TM1886	52°25·9'	1°12·8'E	X	156
Julian Holme	Cumbr	NY0903	54°25·1'	3°23·7'W	X	89
Julian Park	N Yks	NZ8100	54°23·6'	0°44·7'W	X	94
Julian's	Devon	SS3614	50°54·4'	4°19·6'W	X	190
Julians	Herts	TL3032	51°58·5'	0°6·0'W	X	166
Julian's Barn	Lincs	TF2591	53°24·3'	0°6·8'W	X	113
Julian's Bower (Maze)	N Lincs	SE8721	53°40·9'	0°40·6'W	A	106,112
Julian's Bridge	Dorset	SZ0099	50°47·7'	1°59·6'W	A	195
Julian's Brimstone	Brom	TQ4763	51°21·0'	0°7·1'E	X	177,188
Julliberrie Downs	Kent	TR0753	51°14·5'	0°58·3'E	X	179,189
Jultock Point	D & G	NX4849	54°49·0'	4°21·5'W	X	83
July Course	Cambs	TL6062	52°14·2'	0°21·0'E	X	154
Jumble	Derby	SK0493	53°26·3'	1°56·0'W	X	110
Jumbles	Lancs	SD7037	53°49·9'	2°26·9'W	X	103
Jumbles Country Park	Bolton	SD7314	53°37·6'	2°24·1'W	X	109
Jumbles Resr	Black w Dar	SD7314	53°37·6'	2°24·1'W	W	109
Jump	Barns	SE3801	53°30·5'	1°25·2'W	T	110,111
Jumpers Common	Dorset	SZ1494	50°45·0'	1°47·7'W	T	195
Jumper's Town	E Susx	TQ4632	51°4·3'	0°5·4'E	T	188
Jumps, The	Hants	SU6628	51°3·1'	1°3·1'W	X	185,186
Jumps, The (Tumulli)	Hants	SU6628	51°3·1'	1°3·1'W	A	185,186
Junction	N Yks	SE0145	53°54·3'	1°58·7'W	T	104
Junction Pool	Devon	SS6617	50°56·4'	3°54·1'W	W	180
Jungle, The	Lincs	SK8868	53°12·3'	0°40·5'W	X	121
Juniper	Northum	NY9358	54°55·2'	2°6·1'W	X	87
Juniper Banks	Durham	NY9934	54°42·3'	2°0·5'W	X	92
Juniper Craigs	Scot Bord	NT2435	55°36·4'	3°11·9'W	X	73
Juniper Green	C of Edin	NT2068	55°54·2'	3°16·3'W	T	66
Juniper Gulf	N Yks	SD7673	54°9·4'	2°21·6'W	X	98
Juniper Hall	Surrey	TQ1752	51°15·5'	0°19·0'W	X	187
Juniper Hill	Bucks	SU8588	51°35·3'	0°46·0'W	X	175
Juniper Hill	Hants	SU6038	51°8·5'	1°8·1'W	X	185
Juniper Hill	Oxon	SP5832	51°59·2'	1°8·9'W	X	152
Juniperhill	Surrey	TQ1752	51°15·5'	0°19·0'W	X	187
Juniper Hill	Surrey	TQ2352	51°15·5'	0°13·8'W	X	187
Juniper Rock	D & G	NW9564	54°56·0'	5°11·6'W	X	82
Juniper Top	Surrey	TQ1852	51°15·5'	0°18·1'W	X	187
Juniper Valley	Surrey	SU9840	51°9·3'	0°35·5'W	X	186
Junk	Shetld	HU3645	60°11·5'	1°20·6'W	X	4
Jupiter Point	Corn	SX4156	50°23·2'	4°13·8'W	X	201
Jura	Arg & Bt	NR4970	55°51·7'	6°0·2'W	X	60,61
Jura	Arg & Bt	NR5683	55°58·9'	5°54·3'W	X	61
Jura	Arg & Bt	NR6079	55°56·9'	5°50·2'W	X	61,62
Jura	Arg & Bt	NR6694	56°5·2'	5°45·2'W	X	55,61
Jura Forest	Arg & Bt	NR4975	55°54·4'	6°0·5'W	X	60,61
Jura Forest	Arg & Bt	NR5075	55°54·4'	5°59·6'W	X	61
Jura Forest	Arg & Bt	NR5370	55°51·9'	5°56·4'W	F	61
Jura Ho	Arg & Bt	NR4863	55°47·9'	6°0·8'W	X	60,61
Jurassic Way	Oxon	SP3948	52°8·0'	1°25·4'W	X	151
Jurby Head	I of M	SC3498	54°21·3'	4°32·8'W	X	95
Jurby West	I of M	SC3598	54°21·3'	4°31·9'W	T	95
Jurishayes	Devon	SS9112	50°54·1'	3°32·6'W	X	181
Jurston	Devon	SX6984	50°38·7'	3°50·8'W	T	191
Jurston Fm	Somer	ST1420	50°58·6'	3°13·1'W	FM	181,193
Jury Fm	Surrey	TQ0754	51°16·7'	0°27·6'W	FM	187
Jury Fm	W Susx	SU8400	50°47·8'	0°48·1'W	FM	197
Jury Fms	Heref	SO4032	51°59·2'	2°52·0'W	FM	149,161
Jury Hill	Essex	TQ6189	51°34·8'	0°19·8'E	X	177
Jury's Gap	E Susx	TQ9818	50°55·9'	0°49·5'E	T	189
Jury's Gut Sewer	E Susx	TR0019	50°56·4'	0°51·2'E	W	189
Justenlees	D & G	NY1667	54°59·7'	3°18·4'W	X	85
Justicehall	Scot Bord	NT4953	55°46·3'	2°48·3'W	X	66,73
Justice Hill	Herts	TL2804	51°43·4'	0°8·4'W	X	166
Justice's Hill	Essex	TL6932	51°57·9'	0°28·0'E	X	167
Justicetown	Cumbr	NY3764	54°58·2'	2°58·6'W	X	85
Justinhaugh	Angus	NO4657	56°42·4'	2°52·5'W	X	54

K

Kaber	Cumbr	NY7911	54°29·9'	2°19·0'W	T	91
Kaber Fell	Cumbr	NY8608	54°28·3'	2°12·5'W	X	91,92
Kadelands Ho	N Yks	NZ7008	54°28·0'	0°54·8'W	X	94
Kaellan Hellier	Orkney	HY2114	59°0·6'	3°22·0'W	X	6
Kaemuir Fm	Falk	NS9372	55°56·0'	3°42·4'W	FM	65
Kaeside	Scot Bord	NT5134	55°36·1'	2°46·2'W	X	73
Kaila	Shetld	HU1958	60°18·6'	1°38·9'W	W	3
Kaila Ness	Shetld	HU2447	60°12·7'	1°33·5'W	X	3
Kail Hill	N Yks	SE0161	54°2·9'	1°58·7'W	H	98
Kail Hill	N Yks	SE0460	54°2·4'	1°55·9'W	H	98
Kaills Burn	Scot Bord	NT7467	55°54·0'	2°24·5'W	W	67
Kail Pot	N Yks	SD6876	54°11·0'	2°29·0'W	X	98
Kailzie	Scot Bord	NT2738	55°38·1'	3°9·1'W	X	73
Kailzie Hill	Scot Bord	NT2736	55°37·0'	3°9·1'W	X	73
Kailzie Mains	Scot Bord	NT2737	55°37·5'	3°9·1'W	X	73
Kaim	Renf	NS3561	55°49·1'	4°37·6'W	X	63
Kaim Brae	Scot Bord	NY5486	55°10·2'	2°42·9'W	X	79
Kaim Burn	Scot Bord	NT8520	55°28·7'	2°13·8'W	W	74
Kaim Dam	Renf	NS3462	55°49·6'	4°38·6'W	W	63
Kaimend	Scot Bord	NT5113	55°24·8'	2°46·0'W	X	79
Kaimend	S Lanak	NS9945	55°41·5'	3°36·0'W	T	72
Kaimes	C of Edin	NT1266	55°53·0'	3°24·0'W	X	65
Kaimes	C of Edin	NT2668	55°54·2'	3°10·6'W	T	66
Kaimes	Scot Bord	NT1650	55°44·4'	3°19·8'W	X	65,66,72
Kaimes	Stir	NS7694	56°7·6'	3°59·3'W	X	57
Kaimes Hill	C of Edin	NT1266	55°53·0'	3°24·0'W	X	65
Kaimflat	Scot Bord	NT7338	55°38·3'	2°25·3'W	X	74
Kaimhill	C of Aber	NJ9203	57°7·3'	2°7·5'W	T	38
Kaim Hill	N Ayr	NS2253	55°44·5'	4°49·7'W	H	63
Kaimhill Fm	Renf	NS4065	55°51·4'	4°32·9'W	FM	64
Kaimhouse	Scot Bord	NT1649	55°43·9'	3°19·8'W	X	72
Kaimknowe	Scot Bord	NT7135	55°36·7'	2°27·2'W	X	74
Kaimknowe Fm	Pth & Kin	NN9505	56°13·8'	3°41·2'W	FM	58
Kaim Rig	Scot Bord	NT8224	55°30·8'	2°16·7'W	H	74
Kaimrig End	Scot Bord	NT0941	55°39·5'	3°26·3'W	T	72
Kaims Castle (Roman Fortlet)	Pth & Kin	NN8612	56°17·5'	3°50·1'W	R	58
Kaimshill	E Ayr	NS4436	55°35·8'	4°28·1'W	X	70
Kaims of Airlie	Angus	NO3252	56°39·5'	3°6·1'W	X	53
Kaims, The	Scot Bord	NT6950	55°44·8'	2°29·2'W	X	67,74

Kair Ho	Aberd	NO7676	56°52·7'	2°23·2'W	X	45
Kaker Mill	Cumbr	SD5484	54°15·2'	2°41·9'W	X	97
Kale Croft	N Yks	NZ9302	54°24·5'	0°33·6'W	X	94
Kaledna	Corn	SW6923	50°4·0'	5°13·3'W	X	203
Kalemouth	Scot Bord	NT7027	55°32·4'	2°28·1'W	X	74
Kale Water	Scot Bord	NT7326	55°31·9'	2°25·2'W	W	74
Kale Water	Scot Bord	NT7614	55°25·4'	2°22·3'W	W	80
Kallee Ness	Shetld	HU3835	60°6·1'	1°18·5'W	X	4
Kallow Point	I of M	SC2167	54°4·3'	4°43·7'W	X	95
Kalnakill	Highld	NG6954	57°31·3'	5°51·0'W	T	24
Kamarad Fm	Lincs	TF5124	52°47·8'	0°14·8'E	FM	131
Kame	Fife	NO3807	56°15·3'	2°59·6'W	X	59
Kame	Shetld	HU3344	60°11·0'	1°23·8'W	X	4
Kame Bridge	Fife	NO3807	56°15·3'	2°59·6'W	X	59
Kamehill	E Loth	NT5779	56°0·4'	2°40·9'W	X	67
Kame of Camy	Orkney	HY5608	58°57·7'	2°45·4'W	X	6
Kame of Corrigall	Orkney	HY3320	59°4·0'	3°9·6'W	H	6
Kame of Flouravoug	Shetld	HP5916	60°49·6'	0°54·4'W	X	1
Kame of Hoy	Orkney	HY1904	58°55·2'	3°23·9'W	X	7
Kame of Isbister	Shetld	HU3891	60°36·3'	1°17·9'W	X	1,2
Kame of Isbister (Settlement)	Shetld	HU3891	60°36·3'	1°17·9'W	A	1,2
Kame of Riven Noup	Shetld	HU3631	60°4·0'	1°20·7'W	X	4
Kame of Sandwick	Shetld	HU4787	60°34·1'	1°8·1'W	H	1,2
Kame of Stews	Orkney	ND4688	58°46·8'	2°55·6'W	X	7
Kames	Arg & Bt	NR9771	55°53·6'	5°14·4'W	T	62
Kames	E Ayr	NS6926	55°30·9'	4°4·0'W	T	71
Kames	Scot Bord	NT7845	55°42·1'	2°20·6'W	X	74
Kames	S Lanak	NS8424	55°30·0'	3°49·8'W	X	71,72
Kames Bay	Arg & Bt	NM8211	56°14·8'	5°30·7'W	W	55
Kames Bay	Arg & Bt	NM9814	56°16·8'	5°15·3'W	W	55
Kames Bay	Arg & Bt	NS0767	55°51·7'	5°4·6'W	W	63
Kames Castle	Arg & Bt	NS0667	55°51·7'	5°5·6'W	A	63
Kames East Mains	Scot Bord	NT7845	55°42·1'	2°20·6'W	X	74
Kames Fm	Arg & Bt	NM8111	56°14·7'	5°31·6'W	FM	55
Kames Fm	Arg & Bt	NR9771	55°53·6'	5°14·4'W	FM	62
Kames Geo	Orkney	HY6101	58°53·9'	2°40·1'W	X	6
Kames Hill	Arg & Bt	NS0569	55°52·7'	5°6·6'W	H	63
Kames, River	Arg & Bt	NM9910	56°14·7'	5°14·2'W	W	55
Kames, The	Shetld	HU3876	60°28·2'	1°18·0'W	X	2,3
Kames, The	S Lanak	NT0152	55°45·3'	3°34·2'W	X	65,72
Kames West Mains	Scot Bord	NT7844	55°41·6'	2°20·6'W	X	74
Kame, The	Shetld	HT9340	60°8·9'	2°7·1'W	X	4
Kame, The	Shetld	HU3414	59°54·8'	1°23·0'W	X	4
Kandahar Cott	Arg & Bt	NS0082	55°59·6'	5°12·0'W	X	55
Kandy	Pth & Kin	NO1109	56°16·2'	3°25·8'W	X	58
Kapleston Hill	D & G	NY4492	55°13·4'	2°52·4'W	X	79
Kapleston Sike	D & G	NY4392	55°13·4'	2°53·3'W	W	79
Kate Brook	Devon	SX8779	50°36·2'	3°35·4'W	W	192
Kate Mc Nieven's Craig	Pth & Kin	NN8723	56°23·4'	3°49·4'W	X	52,58
Kateridden	Red & Cl	NZ6714	54°31·3'	0°57·5'W	X	94
Kate's Bench Fm	Wilts	ST7939	51°9·2'	2°17·6'W	FM	183
Kate's Br	Lincs	TF1014	52°43·0'	0°21·9'W	X	130
Kate's Cott	I of M	SC3882	54°12·7'	4°28·6'W	X	95
Kateshaw Hill	Northum	NY6586	55°10·3'	2°32·5'W	H	80
Kates Hill	Dudley	SO9590	52°30·7'	2°4·0'W	T	139
Kates Hill	Leic	SK7202	52°36·9'	0°55·8'W	X	141
Kate's Hill Fm	Suff	TM0541	52°2·0'	0°59·7'E	FM	155
Kat Fell	Shetld	HU3268	60°23·9'	1°24·7'W	H	3
Katherines	Essex	TL4308	51°45·4'	0°4·7'E	X	167
Katherine's Cross	Beds	TL0238	52°2·1'	0°30·4'W	X	153
Katherine's Fm	Glos	ST7294	51°38·9'	2°23·9'W	FM	162,172
Kathlea	Monm	SO3621	51°53·3'	2°55·4'W	X	161
Katty or Catherine White's Allotment	N Yks	SE1162	54°3·5'	1°49·5'W	X	99
Kaye Edge	Kirk	SE0904	53°32·2'	1°51·4'W	X	110
Kaye Wood	Notts	SK7032	52°53·1'	0°57·2'W	F	129
Kay Field	Lancs	SD8946	53°54·8'	2°9·6'W	X	103
Kay Head Allotment	N Yks	SE0575	54°10·5'	1°55·0'W	X	98
Kay Hill	Northum	NU0727	55°32·4'	1°52·9'W	H	75
Kay Holm	Shetld	HU5291	60°36·2'	1°2·5'W	X	1,2
Kaylane Brook	Warr	SJ6985	53°21·9'	2°27·5'W	W	109
Kays Bank	Cumbr	NY5172	55°2·7'	2°45·6'W	X	86
Kays Fm	Ches	SJ6878	53°18·1'	2°28·4'W	FM	118
Kays Fm	Lancs	SD5351	53°57·4'	2°42·6'W	FM	102
Kays Fm	Lancs	SD6016	53°38·6'	2°35·9'W	FM	109
Kay's Hill	Durham	NZ2929	54°39·6'	1°32·6'W	X	93
Kayshill	E Ayr	NS4517	55°25·6'	4°26·5'W	X	70
Kay's Wood	N Yks	SE6168	54°6·5'	1°3·6'W	F	100
Kayte Fm	Glos	SO9525	51°55·6'	2°4·0'W	FM	163
Kaywick	Shetld	HU5291	60°36·2'	1°2·5'W	X	1,2
KCC Centenary Walk	Kent	TR1156	51°16·1'	1°1·9'E	X	179
Kea	Corn	SW8042	50°14·5'	5°4·8'W	T	204
Keabog	Aberd	NO8082	56°56·0'	2°19·3'W	X	45
Keadby	N Lincs	SE8311	53°35·6'	0°44·3'W	T	112
Keadby Grange	N Lincs	SE8110	53°35·1'	0°46·2'W	X	112
Kealasay	N Eil	NB1441	58°16·1'	6°52·2'W	X	13
Keal Cotes	Lincs	TF3661	53°8·0'	0°2·4'E	T	122
Kealcup Hill	N Yks	SD9365	54°5·1'	2°6·0'W	X	98
Keal Fm	Lincs	TF3775	53°15·5'	0°3·6'E	FM	122
Keallasay Beg	N Eil	NF9171	57°37·6'	7°10·1'W	X	18
Keallasay More	N Eil	NF9172	57°38·2'	7°10·2'W	X	18
Keam Farm	Moray	NJ1567	57°41·4'	3°25·1'W	FM	28
Keanchulish House	Highld	NH1299	57°56·7'	5°10·1'W	X	19
Keanloch	Highld	NH9626	57°19·0'	3°43·1'W	X	36
Kearby Town End	N Yks	SE3447	53°55·3'	1°28·5'W	T	104
Kearnsey	Kent	TR2843	51°8·7'	1°16·0'E	T	179
Kearra	Highld	NG3528	57°16·2'	6°23·3'W	X	32
Kearsinish	N Eil	NF7917	57°8·2'	7°17·9'W	H	31
Kearsley	Bolton	SD7505	53°32·7'	2°22·2'W	T	109
Kearsley	Northum	NZ0275	55°4·4'	1°57·7'W	X	87
Kearsley Fell	Northum	NZ0276	55°5·0'	1°57·7'W	X	87
Kearsney Abbey	Kent	TR2943	51°8·6'	1°16·8'E	X	179
Kearstay	N Eil	NA9617	58°2·5'	7°8·7'W	X	13
Kearstwick	Cumbr	SD6079	54°12·6'	2°36·4'W	T	97
Kearton	N Yks	SD9999	54°23·4'	2°0·5'W	T	98
Kearton's Wood	N Yks	SD9396	54°21·8'	2°6·0'W	F	98
Kearvaig	Highld	NC2972	58°36·4'	4°56·1'W	X	9
Kearvaig River	Highld	NC2970	58°35·3'	4°56·0'W	W	9
Keasbeck Fm	N Yks	SE9695	54°20·7'	0°31·0'W	FM	94,101
Keasbeck Hill Fm	N Yks	SE9695	54°20·7'	0°31·0'W	FM	94,101
Keasden	N Yks	SD7266	54°5·6'	2°25·3'W	T	98
Keasden Beck	N Yks	SD7163	54°4·0'	2°26·2'W	W	98
Keasden Head	N Yks	SD7163	54°4·0'	2°26·2'W	X	98
Keasey Fm	E Yorks	SE8753	53°58·2'	0°40·0'W	FM	106
Keason	Corn	SX3167	50°28·9'	4°22·6'W	X	201
Keason	Corn	SX3665	50°27·9'	4°18·3'W	X	201
Keaton	Devon	SX5947	50°18·6'	3°58·4'W	X	202
Keaton	Devon	SX6454	50°22·4'	3°54·4'W	X	202
Kebb	Lancs	SD7232	53°47·3'	2°25·1'W	X	103
Kebbaty	Aberd	NJ6708	57°10·0'	2°32·3'W	X	38
Kebbuck Knowe	Aberd	NJ4122	57°17·3'	2°58·3'W	H	37
Kebbuck Stone	Highld	NH8255	57°34·4'	3°57·9'W	A	27
Keb Fm	N Lincs	SE9515	53°37·6'	0°33·4'W	FM	112
Keb Hill	D & G	NX7599	55°16·4'	3°57·6'W	H	78
Kebholes	Aberd	NJ6455	57°35·3'	2°35·7'W	X	29
Kebister Ness	Shetld	HU4746	60°12·0'	1°8·6'W	X	4
Kebro	Orkney	HY3510	58°58·6'	3°7·4'W	X	6
Kebroyd	Cald	SE0421	53°41·4'	1°56·0'W	T	104
Keb Wood	N Lincs	SE9512	53°36·0'	0°33·5'W	F	112
Kebwood Fm	N Lincs	SE9612	53°36·0'	0°32·5'W	FM	112
Keckwick	Halton	SJ5783	53°20·8'	2°38·3'W	T	108
Keckwick Brook	Halton	SJ5683	53°20·8'	2°39·2'W	W	108
Keddington	Lincs	TF3488	53°22·5'	0°1·3'E	T	113,122
Keddington Corner	Lincs	TF3589	53°23·1'	0°2·2'E	T	113,122
Keddington Grange	Lincs	TF3489	53°23·1'	0°1·3'E	X	113,122
Kedills Mires	Shetld	HP5100	60°41·1'	1°3·5'W	W	1
Kedington	Suff	TL7046	52°5·4'	0°29·3'E	T	154
Kedington Hill	Suff	TL8938	52°0·7'	0°45·6'E	X	155
Kedleston	Derby	SK3041	52°58·2'	1°32·8'W	T	119,128
Kedleston Park	Derby	SK3040	52°57·6'	1°32·8'W	X	119,128
Kedlock	Fife	NO3819	56°21·8'	2°59·8'W	T	59
Kedlock Feus	Fife	NO3719	56°21·8'	3°0·7'W	T	59
Kedslie	Scot Bord	NT5540	55°39·3'	2°42·5'W	T	73
Kedslie Hill	Scot Bord	NT5340	55°39·3'	2°44·4'W	X	73
Kedworthy	Devon	SS7037	51°7·3'	3°51·1'W	X	180
Keekham Beck	Durham	NY8222	54°35·8'	2°16·3'W	W	91,92
Keekham Beck Head	Durham	NY8123	54°36·4'	2°17·2'W	X	91,92
Keekle	Cumbr	NY0016	54°32·0'	3°32·3'W	T	89
Keekle Grove	Cumbr	NY0015	54°31·5'	3°32·3'W	X	89
Keekle Head Fm	Cumbr	NY0421	54°34·8'	3°28·7'W	FM	89
Keelam	Cald	SE0028	53°45·1'	1°59·6'W	X	104
Keelam Heights	Cald	SD9426	53°44·1'	2°5·0'W	X	103
Keelars Tye	Essex	TM0523	51°52·3'	0°59·1'E	T	168
Keelby	Lincs	TA1610	53°34·7'	0°14·5'W	T	113
Keelby Grange	Lincs	TA1410	53°34·7'	0°16·3'W	X	113
Keele	Staffs	SJ8045	53°0·4'	2°17·5'W	T	118
Keele Service Area	Staffs	SJ8044	52°59·8'	2°17·5'W	X	118
Keeley Green	Beds	TL0046	52°6·4'	0°32·0'W	T	153
Keel Fm	Kent	TR2266	51°21·2'	1°11·7'E	FM	179
Keelham	Brad	SE0732	53°47·3'	1°53·2'W	T	104
Keel Head	Northum	NU1343	55°41·1'	1°47·2'W	X	75
Keeling Hall Fm	Norf	TG0425	52°47·3'	1°1·9'E	FM	133
Keelings	Essex	TL9901	51°40·6'	0°53·1'E	X	168
Keelings	Essex	TQ7099	51°40·1'	0°27·9'E	X	167
Keels, The	Shetld	HZ2069	59°30·7'	1°38·3'W	X	4
Keelylang Hill	Orkney	HY3710	58°58·6'	3°5·3'W	H	6
Keen	Shetld	HU3682	60°31·5'	1°20·1'W	X	1,2,3
Keen	Shetld	HU5965	60°22·1'	0°55·3'W	X	2
Keenabonus	Shetld	HU3827	60°1·8'	1°18·6'W	X	4
Keen Ground	Cumbr	SD3498	54°22·6'	3°0·5'W	X	96,97
Keen Hall Fm	Somer	ST5242	51°10·7'	2°40·8'W	FM	182,183
Keenie	Angus	NO5277	56°53·2'	2°46·8'W	X	44
Keenley	Northum	NY7956	54°54·1'	2°19·2'W	T	86,87
Keenley Fell	Northum	NY7956	54°54·1'	2°19·2'W	X	86,87
Keenleyside Hill	Northum	NY7855	54°53·6'	2°20·2'W	X	86,87
Keen of Hamar	Shetld	HP6409	60°45·8'	0°49·0'W	H	1
Keen Point	Shetld	HU3359	60°19·1'	1°23·7'W	I	2,3
Keens	Devon	SS9607	50°51·4'	3°28·3'W	X	192
Keens	Devon	SS9624	51°0·6'	3°28·6'W	X	181
Keen's Fm	Suff	TM2454	52°8·6'	1°16·8'E	FM	156
Keenshaw Burn	Northum	NY9599	55°17·4'	2°4·3'W	W	81
Keen, The	Shetld	HP5504	60°43·2'	0°59·0'W	X	1
Keen, The	Shetld	HP6215	60°49·0'	0°51·1'W	X	1
Keen, The	Shetld	HU4968	60°23·8'	1°6·2'W	X	2,3
Keen, The	Shetld	HU5057	60°17·9'	1°5·2'W	X	2,3
Keenthorne	Somer	ST2139	51°8·9'	3°7·4'W	T	182
Keeper's Cott	D & G	NX8259	54°55·0'	3°50·0'W	X	84
Keepers Cott	Wilts	SU2428	51°3·3'	1°39·1'W	X	184
Keepers Cottage	Cumbr	NY2840	54°45·2'	3°6·7'W	X	85
Keepers Cottage	N Yks	SE4578	54°12·0'	1°18·2'W	X	99
Keepers Cottage	Staffs	SJ8115	52°44·2'	2°16·5'W	X	127
Keepers Fm	Leic	SP5796	52°33·8'	1°9·1'W	FM	140
Keepers Fm	Surrey	TQ3341	51°9·4'	0°5·5'W	FM	187
Keepershield	Northum	NY8766	54°59·6'	2°11·8'W	X	87
Keepershield	Northum	NY9072	55°2·8'	2°9·0'W	X	87
Keeper's Lo	Brad	SE0133	53°47·8'	1°58·7'W	X	104
Keepers Lodge	Staffs	SJ9514	52°43·7'	2°4·0'W	X	127
Keeper's Lodge	Wilts	ST7636	51°7·6'	2°20·2'W	X	183
Keepers Lodge Fm	V of Glam	ST0379	51°30·3'	3°23·5'W	FM	170
Keeper's Old Ho	N Yks	SE8891	54°18·7'	0°38·4'W	X	94,101
Keeper's Pool	Birm	SP1096	52°33·9'	1°50·7'W	W	139
Keepers' Warren	Beds	TL1241	52°3·6'	0°21·6'W	F	153
Keepers Wood	N Yks	SE2588	54°17·5'	1°36·5'W	F	99
Keep Hatch	Wok	SU8269	51°25·1'	0°48·9'W	X	175
Keephill	Devon	SS3402	50°47·9'	4°21·0'W	X	190
Keep Hill	Heref	SO6354	52°11·2'	2°32·1'W	X	149
Keeping	Hants	SU4000	50°48·1'	1°25·6'W	X	196
Keeping Copse	Hants	SU3900	50°48·1'	1°26·4'W	F	196
Keep, The	Cumbr	NY5461	54°56·7'	2°42·7'W	X	86
Keepwick Fell	Northum	NY9569	55°1·2'	2°4·3'W	X	87
Keepwick Fm	Northum	NY9571	55°2·3'	2°4·3'W	FM	87
Keer Channel	Lancs	SD4569	54°7·1'	2°50·1'W	W	97
Keeres Green	Essex	TL5914	51°48·3'	0°18·8'E	T	167
Keer Holme	Lancs	SD5573	54°9·3'	2°40·9'W	X	97
Keer Side	Lancs	SD5675	54°10·4'	2°40·0'W	X	97
Keeston	Pemb	SM9019	51°50·1'	5°2·5'W	T	157,158
Keeston Br	Pemb	SM9018	51°49·5'	5°2·5'W	X	157,158
Keeston Moor	Pemb	SM8918	51°49·5'	5°3·3'W	X	157,158
Keetham Beck Head	Durham	NY8023	54°36·4'	2°18·2'W	H	92
Keevil	Wilts	ST9258	51°19·5'	2°6·5'W	T	173
Kegga	Shetld	HU6692	60°36·6'	0°47·2'W	X	1,2
Kegworth	Leic	SK4826	52°50·0'	1°16·8'W	T	129
Kehelland	Corn	SW6241	50°13·5'	5°19·8'W	T	203
Keig	Aberd	NJ6119	57°15·9'	2°38·3'W	T	37
Keigar	Orkney	HY5506	58°56·6'	2°46·4'W	X	6
Keighley	Brad	SE0641	53°52·2'	1°54·1'W	T	104
Keighley Moor	Brad	SD9939	53°51·1'	2°0·5'W	X	103
Keighley Moor	Brad	SE0039	53°51·1'	1°59·6'W	X	104
Keighley Moor Resr	Brad	SD9839	53°51·1'	2°1·4'W	W	103
Keighley & Worth Valley Rly	Brad	SE0438	53°50·5'	1°55·9'W	X	104
Keightley House Fm	Lincs	TF3529	52°50·7'	0°0·7'E	FM	131
Keigwin	Corn	SW3934	50°9·2'	5°38·9'W	X	203
Keil	Highld	NM9753	56°37·8'	5°18·1'W	X	49
Keilarsbrae	Clackm	NS8993	56°7·3'	3°46·7'W	T	58
Keilator	Stir	NN3724	56°23·1'	4°38·0'W	X	50
Keilburn	Aberd	NO7372	56°50·6'	2°26·1'W	X	45
Keilhill	Aberd	NJ7159	57°37·5'	2°28·7'W	T	29
Keil Ho	Highld	NN0064	56°43·8'	5°15·7'W	X	41
Keillbeg	Arg & Bt	NR6980	55°57·7'	5°41·6'W	T	55,61
Keillmore	Arg & Bt	NR6880	55°57·7'	5°42·6'W	T	55,61
Keillor	Pth & Kin	NO2640	56°33·0'	3°11·8'W	X	53
Keillor Hill	Angus	NO2838	56°32·0'	3°9·8'W	H	53
Keillour Castle	Pth & Kin	NN9725	56°24·6'	3°39·7'W	X	52,53,58
Keillour Forest	Pth & Kin	NN9523	56°23·5'	3°41·6'W	X	52,53,58
Keills	Arg & Bt	NR4168	55°50·4'	6°7·8'W	X	60,61
Keills Ho	Arg & Bt	NR6980	55°57·7'	5°41·6'W	X	55,61
Keillyford	Aberd	NJ8133	57°23·5'	2°18·5'W	X	29,30
Keiloch	Aberd	NO1891	57°0·4'	3°20·6'W	X	43
Keil Point	Arg & Bt	NR6707	55°18·4'	5°39·8'W	X	68
Keils	Arg & Bt	NR5268	55°50·7'	5°57·3'W	T	61
Keilthusthag	I of M	NX4201	54°23·1'	4°25·6'W	X	95
Keinton Mandeville	Somer	ST5430	51°4·3'	2°39·0'W	T	182,183
Keir	Fife	NS9588	56°4·7'	3°40·8'W	X	65
Keir Hills	D & G	NX8490	55°11·7'	3°48·9'W	H	78
Keir Ho	Stir	NS7698	56°9·8'	3°59·4'W	X	57
Keir Mill	D & G	NX8593	55°13·3'	3°48·0'W	T	78
Keirn	Moray	NJ3623	57°17·8'	3°3·3'W	H	37
Keirn Burn	Moray	NJ3624	57°18·4'	3°3·3'W	W	37
Keirs	E Ayr	NS4308	55°20·7'	4°28·1'W	X	70,77
Keirs Hill	E Ayr	NS4207	55°20·2'	4°29·0'W	H	70,77
Keirsleywell Row	Northum	NY7751	54°51·4'	2°21·1'W	X	86,87
Keirsmill	E Ayr	NS3911	55°22·3'	4°32·0'W	X	70
Keirton	Angus	NO4343	56°34·8'	2°55·2'W	X	54
Keirwoodhead	Pth & Kin	NO0118	56°20·9'	3°35·7'W	X	58
Keisby	Lincs	TF0328	52°50·6'	0°27·8'W	T	130
Keisby Ho	Lincs	TF0329	52°51·2'	0°27·8'W	X	130
Keisgaig River	Highld	NC2568	58°34·2'	5°0·1'W	W	9
Keisley	Cumbr	NY7123	54°36·3'	2°26·5'W	X	91
Keiss	Highld	ND3461	58°32·2'	3°7·5'W	T	12
Keiss Castle	Highld	ND3561	58°32·2'	3°6·5'W	X	12
Keiss Links	Highld	ND3359	58°31·1'	3°8·5'W	X	12
Keistle	Highld	NG4351	57°28·8'	6°16·8'W	T	23
Keith	Moray	NJ4250	57°32·4'	2°57·7'W	T	28
Keithen	Aberd	NJ7945	57°29·9'	2°20·6'W	X	29,30
Keith Hall	Aberd	NJ7821	57°17·0'	2°21·4'W	A	38
Keithhall	Angus	NO3235	56°30·4'	3°5·8'W	X	53
Keith Hill	E Loth	NT4761	55°50·6'	2°50·3'W	X	66
Keith Hills	Pth & Kin	NO0398	56°10·1'	3°33·3'W	X	58
Keithick	Pth & Kin	NO2038	56°31·9'	3°17·6'W	X	53
Keith Inch	Aberd	NK1345	57°30·0'	1°46·5'W	T	30
Keith Mains	E Loth	NT4465	55°52·7'	2°53·3'W	X	66
Keith Marischal	E Loth	NT4464	55°52·2'	2°53·3'W	A	66
Keithmore	Moray	NJ3539	57°26·5'	3°4·5'W	X	28
Keithney	Aberd	NJ7219	57°15·9'	2°27·4'W	X	38
Keithock	Angus	NO6063	56°45·7'	2°38·8'W	X	45
Keiths' Muir	Aberd	NO7998	57°4·6'	2°20·3'W	X	38,45
Keiths' Tower	Aberd	NO8098	57°4·6'	2°19·3'W	X	38,45
Keith Water	E Loth	NT4563	55°51·7'	2°52·3'W	W	66
Kelbarrow	Cumbr	NY3307	54°27·5'	3°1·6'W	X	90
Kelbarrow Fm	Cumbr	NY4634	54°42·1'	2°49·9'W	FM	90
Kelber	N Yks	SD8854	53°59·2'	2°10·6'W	X	103
Kelber	N Yks	SE0068	54°6·7'	1°59·6'W	X	98
Kelbrick Fm	Lancs	SD5346	53°54·7'	2°42·5'W	FM	102
Kelbrook	Lancs	SD9044	53°53·8'	2°8·7'W	T	103
Kelbrook Moor	Lancs	SD9143	53°53·2'	2°7·8'W	H	103
Kelburn	N Ayr	NS2156	55°46·1'	4°50·8'W	A	63
Kelburn Country Centre	N Ayr	NS2156	55°46·1'	4°50·8'W	X	63
Kelby	Lincs	TF0041	52°57·7'	0°30·3'W	T	130
Kelby Fm	Lincs	TF0242	52°58·2'	0°28·5'W	FM	130
Kelcar Fish Pond	N Yks	SE4450	53°56·9'	1°19·4'W	X	105
Kelcliffe	Leeds	SE1842	53°52·7'	1°43·2'W	T	104
Keld	Cumbr	NY5514	54°31·4'	2°41·3'W	T	90
Keld	Cumbr	NY6222	54°35·8'	2°34·9'W	X	91
Keld	Cumbr	NY6722	54°35·8'	2°30·2'W	X	91
Keld	N Yks	NY8901	54°24·5'	2°9·7'W	T	91,92
Kelda Ber	Orkney	HY3949	59°19·6'	3°3·8'W	X	5
Keldas	Cumbr	NY3816	54°32·4'	2°57·1'W	X	90
Keldcarrs Drain	N Yks	SE6642	53°52·4'	0°59·4'W	W	105,106
Keld Fm	Cumbr	NY5337	54°43·8'	2°43·4'W	FM	90
Keldgate	E Yorks	TA0233	53°47·2'	0°26·7'W	X	106,107
Keld Gill	Cumbr	NY5413	54°30·9'	2°42·2'W	W	90
Keld Gill	N Yks	SD7994	54°20·7'	2°19·0'W	X	98
Keldhead	Cumbr	NY4819	54°34·1'	2°47·8'W	X	90
Keld Head	N Yks	SD6976	54°11·0'	2°28·1'W	X	98
Keld Head Scar	N Yks	SD6977	54°11·5'	2°28·1'W	X	98
Keldholme	N Yks	SE7086	54°16·1'	0°55·1'W	T	94,100
Keld Houses	N Yks	SE1063	54°4·0'	1°50·4'W	T	99
Keld Knowle	N Yks	SE7685	54°15·5'	0°49·6'W	X	94,100
Keldlands	N Yks	SE8189	54°17·7'	0°44·9'W	X	94,100
Keldray	Cumbr	SD2784	54°15·0'	3°6·8'W	X	96,97
Keld Runnels Fm	N Yks	SE9989	54°17·5'	0°28·3'W	FM	94,101
Keld Side	N Yks	NY8700	54°24·0'	2°11·6'W	X	91,92
Keldside Plantn	E Yorks	SE7756	53°59·9'	0°49·1'W	F	105,106
Keld, The	E Yorks	TA0157	54°0·2'	0°27·1'W	W	106,107
Keld,The	Orkney	HY6033	59°11·2'	2°41·5'W	W	5,6
Keld View	Cumbr	NY1448	54°49·4'	3°19·9'W	X	85
Keldy Br	N Yks	SE7790	54°18·2'	0°48·6'W	X	94,100
Keldy Castle Forest Cabins	N Yks	SE7791	54°18·8'	0°48·6'W	X	94,100

Kelfield	N Lincs	SE8201	53°30·2'	0°45·4'W	T	112
Kelfield	N Yks	SE5938	53°50·3'	1°5·8'W	T	105
Kelfield Catchwater	N Lincs	SE7904	53°31·8'	0°48·1'W	W	112
Kelfield Grange	Leeds	SE3940	53°51·5'	1°24·0'W	X	104
Kelfield Grange	Lincs	SE8200	53°29·7'	0°45·4'W	X	112
Kelfield Grange	N Lincs	SE8102	53°30·7'	0°46·3'W	X	112
Kelfield Grange	N Yks	SE5839	53°50·9'	1°6·7'W	X	105
Kelfield Ings	N Yks	SE5738	53°50·3'	1°7·6'W	X	105
Kelfield Lodge	N Yks	SE6038	53°50·3'	1°4·9'W	X	105
Kelfield Ridge Fm	N Yks	SE6039	53°50·9'	1°4·9'W	FM	105
Kelham	Notts	SK7755	53°5·4'	0°50·6'W	T	120
Kelham Bridge Fm	Leic	SK4012	52°42·5'	1°24·1'W	FM	129
Kelham Fm	Lincs	TF2656	53°5·4'	0°6·7'W	FM	122
Kelham Hills	Notts	SK7656	53°6·0'	0°51·5'W	F	120
Kelham Hills Fm	Notts	SK7656	53°6·0'	0°51·5'W	FM	120
Kelhead	D & G	NY1469	55°0·7'	3°20·3'W	X	85
Kelhead Flow	D & G	NY1469	55°0·7'	3°20·3'W	X	85
Kelhead Moss Plantation	D & G	NY1369	55°0·7'	3°21·2'W	F	85
Kelhead Quarry	D & G	NY1469	55°0·7'	3°20·3'W	X	85
Kelhope Hill	Scot Bord	NT4959	55°49·5'	2°48·4'W	H	66,73
Kelhurn	Arg & Bt	NS3377	55°57·7'	4°40·1'W	T	63
Kelig	N Eil	NF8476	57°40·0'	7°17·5'W	X	18
Kelk Beck	E Yorks	TA0957	54°0·1'	0°19·8'W	W	107
Kelker Well	Cumbr	SD5578	54°12·0'	2°41·0'W	X	97
Kelk Hill	Kent	TR2752	51°13·5'	1°15·5'E	X	179
Kelky Fell	Cumbr	NY5756	54°54·1'	2°39·8'W	X	86
Kella	I of M	SC3995	54°19·8'	4°28·1'W	T	95
Kellacott	Devon	SX4088	50°40·4'	4°15·5'W	T	190
Kellah	Northum	NY6561	54°56·8'	2°32·4'W	X	86
Kellah Burn	Northum	NY6460	54°56·3'	2°33·3'W	W	86
Kellalees	S Lanak	NS7642	55°39·6'	3°57·8'W	X	71
Kellamergh	Lancs	SD4029	53°45·5'	2°54·2'W	T	102
Kellam's Fm	Leic	SK4613	52°43·0'	1°18·7'W	FM	129
Kellan	Arg & Bt	NM5240	56°29·5'	6°1·3'W	X	47,48
Kelland Barton	Devon	SS7206	50°50·6'	3°48·7'W	X	191
Kelland Cross	Devon	SS7207	50°51·1'	3°48·7'W	X	191
Kellan Head	Corn	SW9681	50°35·8'	4°52·6'W	X	200
Kellan Mill	Arg & Bt	NM5040	56°29·4'	6°3·2'W	X	47,48
Kellas	Angus	NO4535	56°30·5'	2°53·2'W	T	54
Kellas	Moray	NJ1754	57°34·4'	3°22·8'W	T	28
Kellas Ho	Moray	NJ1654	57°34·4'	3°23·8'W	X	28
Kellas Plantation	Northum	NZ0056	54°54·2'	1°59·6'W	F	87
Kellaton	Devon	SX7748	50°19·4'	3°43·3'W	X	202
Kellaton	Devon	SX8039	50°14·6'	3°40·6'W	T	202
Kellaways	Wilts	ST9575	51°28·7'	2°3·9'W	T	173
Kell Burn	E Loth	NT6364	55°52·3'	2°35·0'W	W	67
Kellerstain	C of Edin	NT1671	55°55·7'	3°20·2'W	X	65,66
Kelleth	Cumbr	NY6605	54°26·6'	2°31·0'W	T	91
Kelleth Rigg	Cumbr	NY6606	54°27·1'	2°31·0'W	H	91
Kellet Lane Br	Lancs	SD5171	54°8·2'	2°44·6'W	X	97
Kellet Park Wood	Lancs	SD5371	54°8·2'	2°42·7'W	F	97
Kellet's Br	Lancs	SD4634	53°48·2'	2°48·8'W	X	102
Kellets Fm	Lancs	SD6337	53°49·9'	2°33·3'W	FM	102,103
Kelleybank	Clackm	NS9698	56°10·1'	3°40·0'W	X	58
Kelleythorpe	E Yorks	TA0156	53°59·6'	0°27·1'W	X	106,107
Kell House Fm	Ches	SJ7782	53°20·3'	2°20·3'W	FM	109
Kellie Castle	Angus	NO6040	56°33·2'	2°38·6'W	A	54
Kellie Castle	Fife	NO5205	56°14·4'	2°46·0'W	A	59
Kellie Law	Fife	NO5106	56°14·9'	2°47·0'W	H	59
Kellinch	Devon	SX8070	50°31·3'	3°41·2'W	X	202
Kelling	Norf	TG0942	52°56·3'	1°7·0'E	T	133
Kelling Hard	Norf	TG0943	52°56·8'	1°7·1'E	X	133
Kelling Heath	Norf	TG1041	52°55·7'	1°7·9'E	X	133
Kellingley	N Yks	SE5224	53°42·8'	1°12·3'W	T	105
Kellington	N Yks	SE5524	53°42·8'	1°9·6'W	T	105
Kellington Common	N Yks	SE5422	53°41·7'	1°10·5'W	X	105
Kellister	Shetld	HP5402	60°42·1'	1°0·1'W	T	1
Kellister	Shetld	HU2455	60°17·0'	1°33·5'W	X	3
Kellock, The	Aberd	NJ6430	57°21·8'	2°35·4'W	W	29,37
Kelloe	Durham	NZ3436	54°43·3'	1°27·9'W	T	93
Kelloe	Scot Bord	NT8453	55°46·5'	2°14·9'W	X	67,74
Kelloe Law	Durham	NZ3637	54°43·8'	1°26·0'W	X	93
Kelloe Mains	Scot Bord	NT8353	55°46·5'	2°15·8'W	X	67,74
Kelloholm	D & G	NS7411	55°22·9'	3°58·9'W	T	71
Kelloside	D & G	NS7211	55°22·8'	4°0·8'W	X	71
Kello Water	D & G	NS6808	55°21·2'	4°4·5'W	W	71,77
Kells	Cumbr	NX9616	54°32·0'	3°36·0'W	T	89
Kells	D & G	NX9457	54°54·0'	3°38·8'W	X	84
Kells Burn	D & G	NX9457	54°54·0'	3°38·8'W	W	84
Kell, The	Pemb	SM9522	51°51·8'	4°58·3'W	X	157,158
Kellwood	Cumbr	NY5263	54°57·8'	2°44·6'W	X	86
Kelly	Corn	SX0173	50°31·6'	4°48·1'W	T	200
Kelly	Devon	SX3981	50°36·6'	4°16·2'W	T	201
Kelly	Devon	SX7981	50°37·2'	3°42·3'W	X	191
Kellybeare	Devon	SX3983	50°37·7'	4°16·2'W	X	201
Kelly Br	Clackm	NS9698	56°10·1'	3°40·0'W	X	58
Kelly Bray	Corn	SX3571	50°31·2'	4°19·3'W	T	201
Kelly Burn	N Ayr	NS2168	55°52·6'	4°51·2'W	W	63
Kelly Burn	Scot Bord	NT6029	55°33·4'	2°37·6'W	W	74
Kellyburn Hill	Northum	NY8395	55°15·2'	2°15·6'W	H	80
Kelly Castle	Angus	NO6040	56°33·3'	2°38·6'W	X	54
Kelly College	Devon	SX4875	50°33·5'	4°8·4'W	X	191,201
Kellyfield	Angus	NO5840	56°33·3'	2°40·5'W	X	54
Kelly Fm	Devon	SS8613	50°54·5'	3°36·9'W	FM	181
Kellygreen	Corn	SX0475	50°32·8'	4°45·6'W	X	200
Kelly Heads	Scot Bord	NT1849	55°43·9'	3°17·9'W	H	72
Kelly Ho	Devon	SX3981	50°36·6'	4°16·2'W	X	201
Kelly Lake	Aberd	NJ8835	57°24·6'	2°11·5'W	W	30
Kelly Mains	N Ayr	NS1968	55°52·5'	4°53·2'W	X	63
Kelly Port	D & G	NX4461	54°55·4'	4°25·6'W	X	83
Kelly Resr	Inverc	NS2268	55°52·6'	4°50·3'W	W	63
Kelly's Cove	Devon	SX9049	50°20·1'	3°32·4'W	W	202
Kelly's Pike	Northum	NY8195	55°15·2'	2°17·5'W	H	80
Kelman Hill	Moray	NJ3832	57°22·7'	3°1·4'W	H	37
Kelmarsh	Northnts	SP7379	52°24·5'	0°55·2'W	T	141
Kelmarsh Field Fm	Northnts	SP7281	52°25·6'	0°56·1'W	FM	141
Kelmire Grange	N Yks	SE4783	54°14·7'	1°16·3'W	X	100
Kelmore Hill Fm	Cumbr	NY0223	54°35·8'	3°30·6'W	FM	89
Kelmscot	Oxon	SU2599	51°41·6'	1°37·9'W	T	163
Kelmscott	Scot Bord	NT6349	55°44·2'	2°34·9'W	X	74
Kelphope	Scot Bord	NT5158	55°49·0'	2°46·5'W	X	66,73
Kelphope Burn	Scot Bord	NT5156	55°47·9'	2°46·5'W	W	66,73
Kelpie Strand	Northum	NT9520	55°28·7'	2°4·3'W	X	74,75
Kelsale	Suff	TM3865	52°14·1'	1°29·5'E	T	156
Kelsale Hall	Suff	TM3766	52°14·7'	1°28·7'E	X	156
Kelsale Lodge	Suff	TM3867	52°15·2'	1°29·6'E	X	156
Kelsall	Ches	SJ5268	53°12·7'	2°42·7'W	T	117
Kelsall Hill	Ches	SJ5368	53°12·7'	2°41·8'W	X	117
Kelsay	Arg & Bt	NR1956	55°43·2'	6°28·1'W	X	60
Kelsborrow Castle	Ches	SJ5367	53°12·1'	2°41·8'W	X	117
Kelsborrow Castle (Fort)	Ches	SJ5367	53°12·1'	2°41·8'W	A	117
Kelsey Br	Lincs	TF3446	52°59·9'	0°0·2'E	X	131
Kelsey Hall	Lincs	TF4464	53°9·4'	0°9·6'E	X	122
Kelsey Head	Corn	SW7660	50°24·1'	5°8·8'W	X	200
Kelsey Ho	E Yorks	TA2326	53°43·2'	0°7·7'W	X	107
Kelsey Ho	W Susx	TQ3031	51°4·0'	0°8·3'W	X	187
Kelseys, The	Corn	SW7759	50°23·6'	5°7·9'W	X	200
Kelshall	Herts	TL3236	52°0·6'	0°4·2'W	T	153
Kelsham Fm	Kent	TQ8144	51°10·2'	0°35·7'E	FM	188
Kelsick	Cumbr	NY1950	54°50·5'	3°15·3'W	T	85
Kelsickhouse Fm	Cumbr	NY1849	54°50·0'	3°16·2'W	FM	85
Kelsit Grange	N Yks	SE5463	54°3·8'	1°10·1'W	X	100
Kelso	Scot Bord	NT7234	55°36·2'	2°26·2'W	T	74
Kelso Abbey	Scot Bord	NT7233	55°35·6'	2°26·2'W	A	74
Kelsocleuch	Scot Bord	NT8517	55°27·0'	2°13·8'W	X	80
Kelsocleuch Burn	Scot Bord	NT8517	55°27·0'	2°13·8'W	W	80
Kelsocleuch Rig	Scot Bord	NT8416	55°26·5'	2°14·7'W	X	80
Kelso Hill	Scot Bord	NT7216	55°26·5'	2°26·1'W	H	80
Kelstedge	Derby	SK3363	53°10·0'	1°30·0'W	T	119
Kelstern	Lincs	TF2590	53°23·8'	0°6·8'W	T	113
Kelstern Grange	Lincs	TF2489	53°23·2'	0°7·7'W	X	113,122
Kelsterton	Flint	SJ2770	53°13·6'	3°5·2'W	T	117
Kelston	Bath & NE Somer	ST7067	51°24·3'	2°25·5'W	T	172
Kelston Fm	Flint	SJ1082	53°19·9'	3°20·7'W	FM	116
Kelston Park	Bath & NE Somer	ST7066	51°23·8'	2°25·5'W	X	172
Kelston Round Hill	Bath & NE Somer	ST7167	51°24·3'	2°24·6'W	H	172
Kelswick	Cumbr	NY1929	54°39·2'	3°14·9'W	X	89,90
Kels Wick	Shetld	HU4969	60°24·4'	1°6·1'W	W	2,3
Keltie Burn	Pth & Kin	NN8527	56°25·5'	3°51·4'W	W	52,58
Keltie Water	Stir	NN6309	56°15·5'	4°12·3'W	W	57
Keltney Burn	Pth & Kin	NN7650	56°37·8'	4°0·8'W	W	42,51,52
Keltney Burn	Pth & Kin	NN7749	56°37·3'	3°59·8'W	W	51,52
Keltneyburn	Pth & Kin	NN7749	56°37·3'	3°59·8'W	T	51,52
Kelton	D & G	NX9870	55°1·1'	3°35·3'W	T	84
Kelton	Durham	NY9220	54°34·8'	2°7·0'W	T	91,92
Kelton	Orkney	HY4210	58°58·7'	3°0·1'W	X	6
Keltonbank	D & G	NX9871	55°1·6'	3°35·3'W	X	84
Kelton Fell	Cumbr	NY0918	54°33·2'	3°24·0'W	H	89
Kelton Fell	Durham	NY8919	54°34·2'	2°9·8'W	X	91,92
Keltonfell Top	Cumbr	NY0818	54°33·2'	3°24·9'W	H	89
Kelton Head	Cumbr	NY0618	54°33·2'	3°26·8'W	X	89
Kelton Hill	D & G	NX7560	54°55·4'	3°56·6'W	H	84
Kelton Hill	Durham	NY9219	54°34·2'	2°7·0'W	H	91,92
Keltonhill Farm	D & G	NX7460	54°55·4'	3°57·5'W	FM	83,84
Kelton Hill or Rhonehouse	D & G	NX7459	54°54·8'	3°57·5'W	T	83,84
Kelton Ho	D & G	NX9871	55°1·6'	3°35·3'W	X	84
Kelton Mains	D & G	NX7461	54°55·9'	3°57·6'W	X	83,84
Keltswells	Aberd	NJ6834	57°24·0'	2°31·5'W	X	29
Kelty	Fife	NT1494	56°8·1'	3°22·6'W	T	58
Keltybridge	Pth & Kin	NT1495	56°8·7'	3°22·6'W	T	58
Kelty Burn	Pth & Kin	NO0813	56°18·3'	3°28·8'W	W	58
Kelty Water	Stir	NS5396	56°8·3'	4°21·5'W	W	57
Kelvedon	Essex	TL8618	51°50·0'	0°42·4'E	T	168
Kelvedon Grange	Essex	TL5600	51°40·8'	0°15·8'E	X	167
Kelvedon Hall	Essex	TL5500	51°40·9'	0°14·9'E	X	167
Kelvedon Hall Fm	Essex	TL8616	51°48·9'	0°42·3'E	FM	168
Kelvedon Hatch	Essex	TQ5698	51°39·8'	0°15·7'E	T	167,177
Kelvin	Pth & Kin	NO2749	56°37·9'	3°11·0'W	X	53
Kelvin	S Lanak	NS6352	55°44·8'	4°10·5'W	T	64
Kelvindale	C of Glas	NS5568	55°53·3'	4°18·7'W	T	64
Kelvinhead	N Lanak	NS7578	55°59·0'	3°59·8'W	X	64
Kelvinside	C of Glas	NS5667	55°52·7'	4°17·7'W	T	64
Kelwell Fm	E Yorks	TA1436	53°48·7'	0°15·7'W	FM	107
Kelwood	D & G	NY0171	55°1·7'	3°33·5'W	X	84
Kelwood Burn	D & G	NY0071	55°1·7'	3°33·4'W	W	84
Kelynack	Corn	SW3729	50°6·4'	5°40·3'W	T	203
Kemacott	Devon	SS6647	51°12·6'	3°54·7'W	T	180
Kemback	Fife	NO4115	56°19·7'	2°56·8'W	T	59
Kemback Ho	Fife	NO4115	56°19·7'	2°56·8'W	X	59
Kemback Wood	Fife	NO4215	56°19·7'	2°55·8'W	F	59
Kemberton	Shrops	SJ7304	52°38·2'	2°23·5'W	T	127
Kemble	Glos	ST9897	51°40·5'	2°1·3'W	T	163
Kemble Airfield	Wilts	ST9696	51°40·0'	2°3·1'W	X	163
Kemble Ho	Glos	ST9896	51°40·0'	2°1·3'W	X	163
Kemble Wick	Glos	ST9895	51°39·5'	2°1·3'W	T	163
Kemble Wood	Glos	ST9796	51°40·0'	2°2·2'W	F	163
Kembroke Hall	Suff	TM2641	52°1·5'	1°18·1'E	X	169
Kemerton	Worcs	SO9437	52°2·1'	2°4·9'W	T	150
Kemeys Commander	Monm	SO3404	51°44·1'	2°57·0'W	X	171
Kemeys Folly	Newp	ST3892	51°37·6'	2°53·4'W	X	171
Kemeys Folly (Earthwork)	Newp	ST3892	51°37·6'	2°53·4'W	A	171
Kemeys Graig	Newp	ST3892	51°37·6'	2°53·4'W	X	171
Kemeys Ho	Newp	ST3892	51°37·6'	2°53·4'W	A	171
Kemeys Inferior	Monm	ST3792	51°37·6'	2°54·2'W	X	171
Kemhill	Aberd	NJ7214	57°13·2'	2°27·4'W	X	38
Kemincham	Ches	SJ8068	53°12·8'	2°17·6'W	T	118
Kemland	E Susx	TQ6722	50°58·6'	0°23·1'E	X	199
Kemnal Manor	Brom	TQ4471	51°25·4'	0°4·7'E	X	177
Kemnay	Aberd	NJ7316	57°14·3'	2°26·4'W	T	38
Kemnay Ho	Aberd	NJ7315	57°13·8'	2°26·4'W	X	38
Kemnay Quarries	Aberd	NJ7316	57°14·3'	2°26·4'W	X	38
Kempe's Corner	Kent	TR0346	51°10·9'	0°54·7'E	T	179,189
Kempfield	Aberd	NJ5553	57°34·2'	2°44·7'W	X	29
Kemphill	Pth & Kin	NO2039	56°32·4'	3°17·6'W	X	53
Kemphills	Angus	NO5042	56°34·3'	2°48·4'W	X	54
Kemp Howe	Cumbr	NY5612	54°30·3'	2°40·3'W	X	90
Kempie	Highld	NC4457	58°28·7'	4°40·0'W	X	9
Kemping Moss	Northum	NT9937	55°37·8'	2°0·5'W	X	75
Kemping Moss Ho	Northum	NU0037	55°37·8'	1°59·6'W	X	75
Kempland Fm	Devon	SS7115	50°55·4'	3°49·7'W	FM	180
Kemplee	Cumbr	NY6121	54°35·2'	2°35·8'W	X	91
Kemple End	Lancs	SD6940	53°51·6'	2°27·9'W	X	103
Kemplerigg	Cumbr	NY0802	54°24·6'	3°24·6'W	X	89
Kempleton	D & G	NX6854	54°52·1'	4°3·0'W	X	83,84
Kempleton Mill	D & G	NX6855	54°52·6'	4°3·0'W	X	83,84
Kemple View	Lancs	SD6933	53°47·8'	2°27·8'W	X	103
Kempley	Glos	SO6729	51°57·7'	2°28·4'W	T	149
Kempley Brook	Glos	SO6731	51°58·8'	2°28·4'W	W	149
Kempley Court	Glos	SO6731	51°58·8'	2°28·4'W	X	149
Kempley Green	Glos	SO6729	51°57·7'	2°28·4'W	T	149
Kempley, The	Shrops	SJ5936	52°55·4'	2°36·2'W	X	126
Kempock Point	Inverc	NS2478	55°58·0'	4°48·8'W	X	63
Kemps	Somer	SS8936	51°7·0'	3°34·8'W	X	181
Kemp's Castle	Angus	NO5153	56°40·2'	2°47·5'W	X	54
Kemp's Castle (forts)	Angus	NO5153	56°40·2'	2°47·5'W	A	54
Kemp's Corner	Norf	TM2186	52°25·9'	1°15·5'E	X	156
Kempsey	Worcs	SO8549	52°8·6'	2°12·8'W	T	150
Kempsey Common	Worcs	SO8648	52°8·0'	2°11·9'W	X	150
Kemp's Fm	Essex	TL9224	51°53·1'	0°47·8'E	FM	168
Kemps Fm	Essex	TL9916	51°48·7'	0°53·6'E	FM	168
Kemp's Fm	Surrey	TQ2251	51°14·9'	0°14·7'W	FM	187
Kemps Fm	Thurr	TQ5883	51°31·7'	0°17·1'E	FM	177
Kempsford	Glos	SU1696	51°40·0'	1°45·7'W	T	163
Kemps Green	Warw	SP1470	52°19·9'	1°47·3'W	T	139
Kemp's Hill	Aberd	NJ4933	57°23·3'	2°50·4'W	H	28,29
Kemp's Hill	Kent	TR0523	50°58·4'	0°55·6'E	X	189
Kempshill Fm	Derby	SK1177	53°17·6'	1°49·7'W	FM	119
Kemps Ho	W Susx	TQ3029	51°3·0'	0°8·3'W	A	187,198
Kempshott	Hants	SU6050	51°15·0'	1°8·0'W	T	185
Kempson's Spinney	Notts	SK6729	52°51·5'	0°59·9'W	F	129
Kempster's Hill	Powys	SJ3114	52°43·4'	3°0·9'W	H	126
Kempston	Beds	TL0348	52°7·5'	0°29·3'W	T	153
Kempston Church End	Beds	TL0147	52°7·0'	0°31·1'W	T	153
Kempstone Hill	Aberd	NO8789	56°59·8'	2°12·4'W	H	45
Kempstone Lodge	Norf	TF8816	52°42·8'	0°47·4'E	X	132
Kempstone Manor Fm	Norf	TF8815	52°42·2'	0°47·4'E	FM	132
Kempston Hardwick	Beds	TL0344	52°5·3'	0°29·4'W	T	153
Kempston Hill	Aberd	NO8789	56°59·8'	2°12·4'W	X	45
Kempston Ho	Beds	TL0047	52°7·0'	0°32·0'W	X	153
Kempston West End	Beds	SP9947	52°7·0'	0°32·8'W	T	153
Kempston Wood	Beds	SP9947	52°7·0'	0°32·8'W	F	153
Kempswithen	N Yks	NZ6508	54°28·0'	0°59·4'W	H	94
Kemp's Wood	E Susx	TQ6219	50°57·1'	0°18·8'E	F	199
Kempthorne	Devon	SX3497	50°45·2'	4°20·8'W	X	190
Kempton	Shrops	SO3582	52°26·2'	2°57·0'W	T	137
Kempton Park Fm	Norf	TG1822	52°45·3'	1°14·2'E	FM	133,134
Kempton Park Race Course	Surrey	TQ1170	51°25·3'	0°23·8'W	X	176
Kemp Town	Bri & Hov	TQ3203	50°48·9'	0°7·2'W	T	198
Kempwood	Oxon	SU6779	51°30·6'	1°1·7'W	X	175
Kemsdale	Kent	TQ8331	51°3·2'	0°37·1'E	X	188
Kemsdale Ho	Kent	TR0560	51°18·4'	0°56·9'E	X	179
Kemsey Manor	Staffs	SJ7524	52°49·0'	2°21·9'W	X	127
Kemsing	Kent	TQ5558	51°18·2'	0°13·8'E	T	188
Kemsing Sta	Kent	TQ5657	51°17·7'	0°14·6'E	X	188
Kemsley	Kent	TQ9066	51°21·9'	0°44·2'E	T	178
Kemsley Down Sta	Kent	TQ9266	51°21·9'	0°45·9'E	X	178
Kemsley Street	Kent	TQ8062	51°19·9'	0°35·4'E	T	178,188
Kemvel Point	Corn	SW4524	50°3·9'	5°33·4'W	X	203
Kemyel	Corn	SW4524	50°3·9'	5°33·4'W	X	203
Kemyel Wartha	Corn	SW4524	50°3·9'	5°33·4'W	X	203
Kemys Hall	D & G	NX9782	55°7·6'	3°36·5'W	X	78
Kenardington	Kent	TQ9732	51°3·4'	0°49·1'E	T	189
Kenbank	D & G	NX6281	55°6·5'	4°9·4'W	X	77
Ken Br	D & G	NX6478	55°4·9'	4°7·4'W	X	77
Kenchester	Heref	SO4343	52°5·2'	2°49·5'W	T	148,149,161
Kench Hill	Kent	TQ9032	51°3·6'	0°43·1'E	X	189
Kencot	Oxon	SP2504	51°44·3'	1°37·9'W	T	163
Kencot Hill Fm	Oxon	SP2406	51°45·4'	1°38·7'W	FM	163
Kendal	Cumbr	SD5192	54°19·5'	2°44·8'W	T	97
Kendal End	Worcs	SP0074	52°22·1'	1°59·6'W	T	139
Kendal Fell	Cumbr	SD5093	54°20·1'	2°45·7'W	X	97
Kendal Hill	Lancs	SD4454	53°59·0'	2°50·8'W	X	102
Kendal Hill	N Yks	SD8957	54°0·8'	2°9·7'W	X	103
Kendall Ground	Cumbr	SD2786	54°16·1'	3°6·8'W	X	96,97
Kendall Lodge	Norf	TM1092	52°29·4'	1°6·0'E	X	144
Kendalls, The	Dorset	ST8028	51°3·3'	2°16·7'W	X	183
Kendal's Wood	Staffs	SK1703	52°37·7'	1°44·5'W	F	139
Kendal Park	Cumbr	SD5391	54°19·0'	2°42·9'W	X	97
Kendell Beck	N Yks	SE0189	54°18·0'	1°58·7'W	W	98
Kendell Bottom	N Yks	SD9996	54°21·8'	2°0·5'W	X	98
Kendieshill	Falk	NS9475	55°57·6'	3°41·4'W	X	65
Kendle Fm	Somer	SS9433	51°5·4'	3°30·4'W	FM	181
Kendleshire	S Glos	ST6679	51°30·8'	2°29·0'W	T	172
Kendon	Caer	ST1998	51°40·7'	3°9·9'W	T	171
Kendon	Devon	SX7181	50°37·1'	3°49·0'W	X	191
Kendoon	D & G	NX6087	55°9·7'	4°11·4'W	T	77
Kendoon Loch	D & G	NX6090	55°11·3'	4°11·5'W	W	77
Kendown Wood	D & G	NX5952	54°50·8'	4°11·3'W	F	83
Kendram	Highld	NG4374	57°41·2'	6°18·3'W	T	23
Kendray	Barns	SE3605	53°32·7'	1°27·0'W	T	110,111
Kendrum Burn	Stir	NN5623	56°22·9'	4°19·5'W	W	51
Kenegie	Corn	SW4832	50°8·3'	5°31·2'W	X	203
Ken Ervie	D & G	NX6674	55°2·8'	4°5·4'W	X	77,84
Kenfield Hall	Kent	TR1252	51°13·9'	1°2·6'E	A	179,189
Kenfig	Brig	SS8081	51°31·1'	3°43·4'W	T	170
Kenfig Burrows	Brig	SS7881	51°31·1'	3°45·1'W	X	170
Kenfig Castle	Brig	SS8082	51°31·7'	3°43·4'W	A	170
Kenfig Hill	Brig	SS8383	51°32·3'	3°40·8'W	T	170
Kenfig House Fm	Nth Pt Talb	SS8084	51°32·8'	3°43·4'W	FM	170
Kenfig Pool	Brig	SS7981	51°31·1'	3°44·3'W	W	170
Kenfig Sands	Brig	SS7881	51°31·1'	3°45·1'W	X	170
Kengharair Fm	Arg & Bt	NM4348	56°33·5'	6°10·5'W	FM	47,48
Ken Hill	Norf	TF6734	52°52·9'	0°29·3'E	X	132
Ken Hill Wood	Norf	TF6735	52°53·4'	0°29·3'E	F	132
Kenibus	Lancs	SD7057	54°0·7'	2°27·1'W	X	103

Kenick Burn	D & G	NX6565	54°57·9′	4°6·1′W	W	83,84
Kenick Hill	D & G	NX6566	54°58·5′	4°6·1′W	H	83,84
Kenick Wood	D & G	NX6566	54°57·9′	4°6·1′W	F	83,84
Kenidjack Castle	Corn	SW3532	50°8·0′	5°42·1′W	A	203
Kenidjack Fm	Corn	SW3632	50°8·0′	5°41·3′W	FM	203
Kenilworth	Warw	SP2971	52°20·4′	1°34·1′W	T	140
Kenilworth Castle	Warw	SP2772	52°21·0′	1°35·8′W	A	140
Kenknock	Pth & Kin	NN5243	56°33·6′	4°24·0′W	X	51
Kenknock	Stir	NN4636	56°29·7′	4°29·6′W	X	51
Kenley	Croy	TQ3259	51°19·1′	0°6·0′W	T	187
Kenley	Shrops	SJ5600	52°36·0′	2°38·6′W	T	126
Kenley Bottom	Somer	ST1833	51°5·7′	3°9·9′W	X	181
Kenley Common	Croy	TQ3358	51°18·6′	0°5·1′W	X	187
Kenley Common	Shrops	SO5698	52°34·9′	2°38·6′W	X	137,138
Kenley Gorse	Shrops	SJ5700	52°36·0′	2°37·7′W	F	126
Kenley Ho	Croy	TQ3258	51°18·6′	0°6·0′W	X	187
Kenley House Fm	E Yorks	TA0737	53°49·3′	0°22·1′W	FM	107
Kenley Reach Fm	E Yorks	TA0737	53°49·3′	0°22·1′W	FM	107
Kenlum Hill	D & G	NX5658	54°54·0′	4°14·3′W	H	83
Kenlygreen	Fife	NO5613	56°18·7′	2°42·2′W	X	59
Kenly Water	Fife	NO5612	56°18·2′	2°42·2′W	W	59
Kenmoor Coppice	Heref	SO4045	52°6·2′	2°52·2′W	F	148,149
Kenmore	Arg & Bt	NN0601	56°10·0′	5°7·0′W	X	56
Kenmore	Highld	NG7557	57°33·1′	5°45·2′W	T	24
Kenmore	Pth & Kin	NN7745	56°35·1′	3°59·7′W	T	51,52
Kenmore Wood	Arg & Bt	NN3207	56°13·8′	4°42·2′W	F	56
Kenmuir	C of Glas	NS6562	55°50·2′	4°8·9′W	X	64
Kenmuir	D & G	NX0746	54°46·6′	4°59·6′W	X	82
Kenmure	D & G	NX3059	54°54·1′	4°38·7′W	X	82
Kenmure	D & G	NX6376	55°3·8′	4°8·3′W	X	77
Kenmure	D & G	NX8384	55°8·4′	3°49·7′W	X	78
Kenmure Castle	D & G	NX6376	55°3·8′	4°8·3′W	A	77
Kenmure Holms	D & G	NX6376	55°3·8′	4°8·3′W	X	77
Kenn	Devon	SX9285	50°39·5′	3°31·3′W	T	192
Kenn	N Som	ST4169	51°25·3′	2°50·5′W	T	171,172,182
Kennaa	I of M	SC2880	54°11·5′	4°37·8′W	X	95
Kennachy	Highld	ND0268	58°35·6′	3°40·7′W	X	11,12
Kennack Sands	Corn	SW7316	50°0·3′	5°9·7′W	X	204
Kennacoil	Pth & Kin	NN9941	56°33·3′	3°38·1′W	X	52,53
Kennacott	Corn	SS2101	50°47·1′	4°32·0′W	X	190
Kennacott	Corn	SX2989	50°40·8′	4°24·8′W	X	190
Kennacott	Devon	SS5226	51°1·1′	4°6·2′W	X	180
Kennacott Fm	Devon	SS5637	51°7·1′	4°3·1′W	FM	180
Kennacraig	Arg & Bt	NR8262	55°48·4′	5°28·3′W	X	62
Kennall Vale	Corn	SW7437	50°11·6′	5°9·6′W	X	204
Kennan's Isle	D & G	NX7055	54°52·6′	4°1·1′W	X	83,84
Kennard Moor	Somer	ST5236	51°7·5′	2°40·8′W	X	182,183
Kennards House	Corn	SX2883	50°37·5′	4°25·5′W	T	201
Kennaways	Kent	TQ9958	51°17·4′	0°51·6′E	X	178
Kennedies	S Lanak	NS6953	55°45·4′	4°4·8′W	X	64
Kennedy's Cairn	D & G	NX1430	54°38·1′	4°52·5′W	X	82
Kennedy's Corner	D & G	NY2776	55°4·6′	3°8·2′W	X	85
Kennedy's Pass	S Ayr	NX1593	55°12·1′	4°54·0′W	X	76
Kenneggy	Corn	SW5628	50°6·4′	5°24·4′W	T	203
Kenneggy Downs	Corn	SW5629	50°6·9′	5°24·4′W	X	203
Kenneggy Sands	Corn	SW5628	50°6·4′	5°24·4′W	X	203
Kennel Burn	Angus	NO3871	56°49·8′	3°0·5′W	W	44
Kennel Fm	Beds	TL2144	52°5·1′	0°13·6′W	FM	153
Kennel Fm	Dorset	SY8583	50°39·0′	2°12·3′W	FM	194
Kennel Fm	Hants	SU6047	51°13·4′	1°8·1′W	FM	185
Kennel Fm	N Yks	SE4689	54°17·9′	1°17·2′W	FM	100
Kennel Fm	Surrey	SU8442	51°10·5′	0°47·5′W	FM	186
Kennel Fm	Wilts	SU1728	51°3·3′	1°45·1′W	FM	184
Kennel Hall Fm	Herts	TL2809	51°46·1′	0°8·3′W	FM	166
Kennel Ho	Durham	NZ1222	54°35·8′	1°48·4′W	X	92
Kennel Holt Hotel	Kent	TQ7637	51°6·5′	0°31·2′E	X	188
Kennels	Heref	SO3258	52°13·2′	2°59·3′W	X	148
Kennels	Lancs	SD8149	53°56·4′	2°17·0′W	X	103
Kennels	Wilts	SU0929	51°3·8′	1°51·9′W	X	184
Kennels	Worcs	SO8578	52°24·2′	2°12·8′W	X	139
Kennels Dairy	Devon	ST0417	50°56·9′	3°21·6′W	X	181
Kennels Fm	Notts	SK6874	53°15·8′	0°58·4′W	FM	120
Kennels Fm	N Yks	SE7766	54°5·3′	0°49·0′W	FM	100
Kennels Fm	Surrey	TQ3248	51°13·2′	0°6·2′W	FM	187
Kennels, The	Cumbr	NY4070	55°1·5′	2°55·9′W	X	85
Kennels, The	Dorset	ST6415	50°56·2′	2°30·4′W	X	183
Kennels The	Dorset	SY7493	50°44·4′	2°21·7′W	X	194
Kennels, The	E Yorks	SE9843	53°52·7′	0°30·1′W	X	106
Kennels, The	Hants	SU2910	50°53·6′	1°34·9′W	X	196
Kennels, The	N Yks	NZ2013	54°31·0′	1°41·0′W	X	93
Kennels, The	Scot Bord	NT5830	55°34·0′	2°39·5′W	X	73,74
Kennel Whin	N Yks	SE2194	54°20·7′	1°40·2′W	X	99
Kennel Wood	Heref	SO3059	52°13·7′	3°1·1′W	F	148
Kennel Wood	N Yks	SE5641	53°52·0′	1°8·5′W	F	105
Kennerland Cross	Devon	SS3221	50°58·1′	4°23·2′W	X	190
Kennerland Fm	Devon	SS3321	50°58·1′	4°22·3′W	FM	190
Kennerleigh	Devon	SS8107	50°51·3′	3°41·1′W	T	191
Kennerley Fm	I of W	SZ5283	50°38·9′	1°15·5′W	FM	196
Kennerty	Aberd	NO6799	57°5·1′	2°32·2′W	X	38,45
Kennerty	C of Aber	NJ8300	57°5·7′	2°16·4′W	X	38
Kennet	Clackm	NS9291	56°6·2′	3°43·7′W	T	58
Kennet and Avon Canal	W Berks	SU6470	51°25·8′	1°4·4′W	W	175
Kennet & Avon Canal	Bath & NE Somer	ST7864	51°22·7′	2°18·6′W	W	172
Kennet & Avon Canal	W Berks	SU3967	51°24·3′	1°26·0′W	W	174
Kennet & Avon Canal	Wilts	SU0363	51°22·2′	1°57·0′W	W	173
Kennet End	Cambs	TL7066	52°16·2′	0°29·9′E	T	154
Kennet Gardens	Clackm	NS9290	56°5·7′	3°43·7′W	X	58
Kennethmont	Aberd	NJ5328	57°20·7′	2°46·4′W	T	37
Kennetholme	W Berks	SU5466	51°23·7′	1°13·0′W	X	174
Kennetpans	Clackm	NS9189	56°5·1′	3°44·7′W	X	65
Kennetsideheads	Scot Bord	NT7241	55°40·0′	2°26·3′W	X	74
Kennett	Cambs	TL6968	52°17·3′	0°29·1′E	T	154
Kennett Sta	Cambs	TL6967	52°16·7′	0°29·0′E	X	154
Kennexstone	Swan	SS4591	51°36·0′	4°13·9′W	X	159
Kennford	Devon	SX9186	50°40·0′	3°32·2′W	T	192
Kennick	Devon	SX7983	50°38·3′	3°42·3′W	X	191
Kennick Reservoir	Devon	SX8084	50°38·8′	3°41·5′W	W	191
Kennicott	Devon	SX3598	50°45·7′	4°20·0′W	X	190
Kennieshillock	Moray	NJ3060	57°37·7′	3°9·9′W	X	28
Kenniford Fm	Devon	SX9889	50°41·7′	3°26·3′W	FM	192
Kenninghall	Norf	TM0386	52°26·3′	0°59·6′E	T	144
Kenninghall Fen	Norf	TM0487	52°26·8′	1°0·5′E	X	144
Kenninghall Heath	Norf	TM0384	52°25·2′	0°59·5′E	X	144
Kenninghall Lodge	Norf	TM0785	52°25·7′	1°3·1′E	X	144
Kenninghall Place	Norf	TM0685	52°25·7′	1°2·2′E	X	144
Kenningham Hall	Norf	TG2000	52°33·4′	1°15·1′E	X	134
Kennington	Kent	TR0144	51°9·8′	0°52·9′E	T	189
Kennington	Lam	TQ3077	51°28·8′	0°7·3′W	T	176,177
Kennington	Oxon	SP5202	51°43·1′	1°14·4′W	T	164
Kennington Cliff	Lincs	SK9492	53°25·2′	0°34·7′W	X	112
Kennington Hall	Kent	TR0245	51°10·3′	0°53·8′E	X	189
Kenningtons	Thurr	TQ5681	51°30·6′	0°15·3′E	X	177
Kennisham Hill	Somer	SS9636	51°7·1′	3°28·8′W	X	181
Kennishead	C of Glas	NS5460	55°48·9′	4°19·4′W	T	64
Kenn Moor	N Som	ST4368	51°24·7′	2°48·8′W	X	171,172,182
Kenn Moor Gate	N Som	ST4467	51°24·2′	2°47·9′W	T	171,172,182
Kennon Hill	Devon	SX6489	50°41·3′	3°55·1′W	H	191
Kennoway	Fife	NO3502	56°12·6′	3°2·4′W	T	59
Kennox	E Ayr	NS3844	55°40·0′	4°34·1′W	A	63,70
Kennox	S Lanak	NS7926	55°31·0′	3°54·5′W	X	71
Kennoxhead	S Lanak	NS7724	55°29·9′	3°56·4′W	X	71
Kennox Hill	S Lanak	NS7824	55°29·9′	3°55·4′W	X	71
Kennox Moss	E Ayr	NS3745	55°40·5′	4°35·1′W	X	63
Kennox Water	S Lanak	NS7825	55°30·5′	3°55·5′W	W	71
Kenn's Fm	Oxon	SP2706	51°45·4′	1°36·1′W	FM	163
Kennulph's Fm	Lincs	TF2208	52°39·6′	0°11·4′W	FM	142
Kenny	Somer	ST3117	50°57·1′	2°58·6′W	T	193
Kennydown Fm	Devon	SS6512	50°53·7′	3°54·8′W	FM	180
Kenny Hill	Suff	TL6679	52°23·3′	0°26·8′E	T	143
Kennythorpe	N Yks	SE7865	54°4·7′	0°48·0′W	T	100
Kenovay	Arg & Bt	NL9946	56°30·8′	6°53·2′W	T	46
Kenriva Burn	D & G	NX9599	55°16·7′	3°38·7′W	W	78
Kensaleyre	Highld	NG4251	57°28·8′	6°17·8′W	T	23
Kensal Green	Brent	TQ2382	51°31·6′	0°13·2′W	T	176
Kensal Rise	Brent	TQ2483	51°32·2′	0°12·3′W	T	176
Kensal Town	Wan	TQ2482	51°31·6′	0°12·4′W	T	176
Kensary	Highld	ND2248	58°25·1′	3°19·6′W	X	11,12
Kensey	Corn	SX2187	50°39·5′	4°31·6′W	X	190
Kensgriff	Cumbr	SD6899	54°23·4′	2°29·1′W	X	98
Kensham Fm	Bucks	SU7992	51°37·5′	0°51·1′W	FM	175
Kensham Fm	Kent	TQ8229	51°2·1′	0°36·1′E	FM	188,199
Kensham Ho	Devon	ST0003	50°49·3′	3°24·8′W	X	192
Kenshot Hill	Aberd	NO7871	56°50·1′	2°21·2′W	H	45
Kensington	Ken & Ch	TQ2579	51°30·0′	0°11·6′W	T	176
Kensington	Liv	SJ3691	53°25·0′	2°57·4′W	T	108
Kensington Gardens	C of West	TQ2680	51°30·5′	0°10·7′W	X	176
Kenslow Fm	Derby	SK1862	53°9·5′	1°43·4′W	FM	119
Kenslow Knoll	Derby	SK1861	53°9·0′	1°43·4′W	H	119
Kenson	V of Glam	ST0568	51°24·4′	3°21·6′W	X	170
Kenson River	V of Glam	ST0368	51°24·4′	3°23·3′W	W	170
Kenstey	E Ayr	NS5224	55°29·5′	4°20·1′W	X	70
Kenstone	Shrops	SJ5928	52°51·1′	2°36·1′W	X	126
Kenswick Manor	Worcs	SO7958	52°13·4′	2°18·0′W	X	150
Kensworth	Beds	TL0218	51°51·3′	0°30·7′W	T	166
Kensworth Ho	Beds	TL0418	51°51·3′	0°29·0′W	X	166
Kensworth Lynch	Beds	TL0418	51°51·3′	0°29·0′W	X	166
Kent	Gwyn	SH5063	53°8·8′	4°14·2′W	X	114,115
Kentallen	Arg & Bt	NM5547	56°33·3′	5°58·8′W	X	47,48
Kentallen	Highld	NN0057	56°40·0′	5°15·4′W	T	41
Kentallen Bay	Highld	NN0057	56°40·0′	5°15·4′W	W	41
Kent and East Sussex Steam Railway	Kent	TQ8631	51°3·1′	0°39·6′E	X	189
Kent and Sussex Steam Railway	E Susx	TQ8226	51°0·5′	0°36·1′E	X	188,199
Kentangaval	N Eil	NL6598	56°57·4′	7°30·2′W	T	31
Kent Brook	Surrey	TQ4246	51°12·0′	0°2·3′E	W	187
Kent Channel	Lancs	SD4269	54°7·1′	2°52·8′W	W	96,97
Kentchurch	Heref	SO4125	51°55·5′	2°51·1′W	T	161
Kentchurch Court	Heref	SO4225	51°55·5′	2°50·2′W	A	161
Kent College	Kent	TQ6243	51°10·0′	0°19·4′E	X	188
Kent Ditch	E Susx	TQ9621	50°57·6′	0°47·8′E	W	189
Kent Ditch	Kent	TQ7926	51°0·6′	0°33·5′E	W	188,199
Kent & East Sussex Rly	Kent	TQ8628	51°1·5′	0°39·5′E	X	199
Kent End	Wilts	SU0594	51°38·9′	1°55·3′W	X	163,173
Kent Fm	Somer	ST4139	51°9·1′	2°50·2′W	FM	182
Kentford	Suff	TL7066	52°16·2′	0°29·9′E	T	154
Kentford Heath	Suff	TL7168	52°17·2′	0°30·8′E	X	154
Kentford Lake	Hants	SU3219	50°58·4′	1°32·3′W	W	185
Kent Hatch	Kent	TQ4351	51°14·6′	0°3·3′E	X	187
Kent Hill	Essex	TQ7094	51°37·4′	0°27·7′E	X	167,178
Kent Hill	Hants	SU1310	50°53·6′	1°48·5′W	X	195
Kent House Fm	Kent	TQ6549	51°13·2′	0°22·2′E	FM	188
Kent House Fm	N Yks	SE2848	53°55·9′	1°34·0′W	FM	104
Kentie Burn	D & G	NX3781	55°6·1′	4°32·9′W	W	77
Kentie Hill	D & G	NX3385	55°8·1′	4°36·8′W	X	76
Kent International Airport	Kent	TR3365	51°20·4′	1°21·1′E	X	179
Kentisbeare	Devon	ST0608	50°52·1′	3°19·8′W	T	192
Kentisbeare Ho	Devon	ST0607	50°51·5′	3°19·8′W	X	192
Kentisbury	Devon	SS6243	51°10·4′	3°58·1′W	T	180
Kentisbury Down	Devon	SS6343	51°10·4′	3°57·2′W	H	180
Kentisbury Ford	Devon	SS6142	51°9·9′	3°58·9′W	T	180
Kentisbury Grange	Devon	SS6242	51°9·9′	3°58·0′W	X	180
Kentishes Fm	Essex	TL7926	51°54·4′	0°36·5′E	FM	167
Kentish Fm	Essex	TL7535	51°59·4′	0°33·3′E	FM	155
Kentish Lane Fm	Herts	TL2605	51°44·0′	0°10·1′W	FM	166
Kentish Town	Camden	TQ2884	51°32·6′	0°8·9′W	T	176
Kentis Moor	Devon	ST0506	50°51·0′	3°20·6′W	X	192
Kentmere	Cumbr	NY4504	54°26·0′	2°50·5′W	T	90
Kentmere Common	Cumbr	NY4408	54°28·1′	2°51·4′W	X	90
Kentmere Park	Cumbr	NY4303	54°25·4′	2°52·3′W	X	90
Kentmere Pike	Cumbr	NY4607	54°27·6′	2°49·6′W	H	90
Kentmere Reservoir	Cumbr	NY4408	54°28·1′	2°51·4′W	W	90
Kenton	Brent	TQ1788	51°34·9′	0°18·3′W	T	176
Kenton	Devon	SX9583	50°38·5′	3°28·7′W	T	192
Kenton	N upon Ty	NZ2267	55°0·1′	1°38·9′W	T	88
Kenton	Suff	TM1965	52°14·6′	1°12·9′E	T	156
Kenton Bankfoot	N upon Ty	NZ2068	55°0·6′	1°40·8′W	T	88
Kenton Bar	N upon Ty	NZ2167	55°0·1′	1°39·9′W	T	88
Kenton Corner	Suff	TM2065	52°14·6′	1°13·8′E	T	156
Kenton Green	Glos	SO7714	51°49·7′	2°19·6′W	T	162
Kenton Hall	Suff	TM1865	52°14·6′	1°12·0′E	X	156
Kenton Hills	Suff	TM4664	52°13·4′	1°36·5′E	X	156
Kenton Lodge	Suff	TM2064	52°14·0′	1°13·7′E	X	156
Kentor	D & G	NX6673	55°2·3′	4°5·4′W	X	77,84
Kentra	Highld	NM6569	56°45·5′	5°50·2′W	T	40
Kentra Bay	Highld	NM6468	56°44·9′	5°51·1′W	W	40
Kentra Moss	Highld	NM6569	56°45·5′	5°50·2′W	X	40
Kentraugh	I of M	SC2269	54°5·4′	4°42·9′W	X	95
Kentraw	Arg & Bt	NR2662	55°46·7′	6°21·8′W	X	60
Kentrigg	Cumbr	SD5194	54°20·6′	2°44·8′W	T	97
Kents	Corn	SX1995	50°43·8′	4°33·5′W	T	190
Kents	Devon	SS8621	50°58·9′	3°37·1′W	X	181
Kents Bank	Cumbr	SD3976	54°10·8′	2°55·7′W	T	96,97
Kents Bank	Shrops	SO1883	52°26·6′	3°12·0′W	X	136
Kentsboro	Hants	SU3040	51°9·7′	1°33·9′W	X	185
Kent's Br	Lincs	TF4060	53°7·4′	0°5·9′E	X	122
Kents Cavern	Torbay	SX9364	50°28·2′	3°30·1′W	A	202
Kents Fm	Somer	SS9231	51°4·3′	3°32·1′W	FM	181
Kent's Fm	Warw	SP3349	52°8·5′	1°30·7′W	FM	151
Kent's Fm	W Susx	TQ2918	50°57·0′	0°9·4′W	FM	198
Kentsford Fm	Somer	ST0542	51°10·4′	3°21·2′W	FM	181
Kent's Green	Glos	SO7423	51°54·5′	2°22·3′W	T	162
Kent's Green Fm	Ches	SJ7456	53°6·3′	2°22·9′W	FM	118
Kent's Hill	Hants	SU8634	51°6·2′	0°45·9′W	X	186
Kents Hill	Mil Key	SP8937	52°1·7′	0°41·8′W	T	152
Kent's Hill	Oxon	SU7280	51°31·1′	0°57·3′W	X	175
Kents Hill	Somer	SS9125	51°1·1′	3°32·9′W	X	181
Kentshill Fm	Essex	TM1923	51°52·0′	1°11·3′E	FM	168,169
Kents Oak	Hants	SU3224	51°1·1′	1°32·2′W	T	185
Kentstone	Northum	NU0341	55°40·0′	1°56·7′W	X	75
Kent Street	E Susx	TQ7815	50°54·6′	0°32·3′E	X	199
Kent Street	Kent	TQ6654	51°15·9′	0°23·2′E	T	188
Kent Street	W Susx	TQ2221	50°58·8′	0°15·3′W	T	198
Kentucky Fm	Lancs	SD4446	53°54·7′	2°50·7′W	FM	102
Kentucky Ho	N Yks	SD9880	54°13·2′	2°1·4′W	X	98
Kent Viaduct	Cumbr	SD4579	54°12·5′	2°50·2′W	X	97
Kent Water	E Susx	TQ4940	51°8·6′	0°8·2′E	W	188
Kentwell Downs	Suff	TL8548	52°6·2′	0°42·5′E	X	155
Kentwell Hall	Suff	TL8647	52°5·6′	0°43·2′E	A	155
Kenward	Kent	TQ6243	51°10·0′	0°19·4′E	X	188
Kenward	Kent	TQ6951	51°14·2′	0°25·6′E	X	188
Kenwards Fm	W Susx	TQ3426	51°1·3′	0°5·0′W	FM	187,198
Kenwater	Heref	SO4859	52°13·8′	2°45·3′W	W	148,149
Kenwick	Shrops	SJ4230	52°52·1′	2°51·3′W	T	126
Kenwick Bar	Lincs	TF3384	53°20·4′	0°0·3′E	X	122
Kenwick Fm	Norf	TF5618	52°44·5′	0°19·1′E	FM	131
Kenwick Hall	Lincs	TF3485	53°20·9′	0°1·2′E	X	122
Kenwick Hall	Norf	TF5719	52°45·0′	0°20·0′E	X	131
Kenwick Lodge	Shrops	SJ4228	52°51·0′	2°51·3′W	X	126
Kenwick Park	Shrops	SJ4129	52°51·6′	2°52·2′W	T	126
Kenwith	Devon	SS4327	51°1·5′	4°13·9′W	X	180
Kenwood	Camden	TQ2787	51°34·3′	0°9·7′W	X	176
Kenwyn	Corn	SW8245	50°16·1′	5°3·2′W	T	204
Kenylon Fm	Kent	TQ9551	51°13·7′	0°48·0′E	FM	189
Kenyon	Warr	SJ6295	53°27·3′	2°33·9′W	T	109
Kenyon Hall	Warr	SJ6294	53°26·7′	2°33·9′W	X	109
Kenziels	D & G	NY1965	54°58·6′	3°15·5′W	X	85
Keoch Lane	D & G	NX6299	55°16·2′	4°9·9′W	W	77
Keoch Rig	D & G	NX6199	55°16·2′	4°10·8′W	X	77
Keoldale	Highld	NC3866	58°33·4′	4°46·6′W	X	9
Keolki Field	Shetld	HU2545	60°11·6′	1°32·5′W	X	4
Keostinse	Shetld	HP5708	60°45·3′	0°56·7′W	X	1
Kepculloch	Stir	NS5491	56°5·6′	4°20·4′W	X	57
Kepdarroch	Stir	NS7095	56°8·1′	4°5·1′W	X	57
Kepdowrie	Stir	NS5594	56°7·3′	4°19·5′W	T	57
Kepier Fm	Durham	NZ2843	54°47·1′	1°33·5′W	A	88
Kepplahill	Aberd	NK0148	57°31·6′	1°58·5′W	X	30
Kepnal	Wilts	SU1760	51°20·6′	1°45·0′W	T	173
Kepollsmore	Arg & Bt	NR3866	55°49·2′	6°10·5′W	X	60,61
Keppanach	Highld	NN0262	56°42·7′	5°13·7′W	X	41
Keppel Cove	Cumbr	NY3416	54°32·3′	3°0·8′W	X	90
Keppel Gate	I of M	SC3882	54°12·7′	4°28·6′W	X	95
Keppel Pier	N Ayr	NS1754	55°44·9′	4°54·5′W	X	63
Keppel's Column	Roth	SK3894	53°26·7′	1°25·3′W	X	110,111
Keppernach	Highld	NH9148	57°30·8′	3°48·7′W	X	27
Kepp Ho	N Yks	SD6672	54°8·8′	2°30·8′W	X	98
Kepple Crag	Cumbr	SD1999	54°23·1′	3°14·4′W	X	96
Kepple Crag	Cumbr	SD2198	54°22·5′	3°12·6′W	X	96
Kepplehill Fm	N Lanak	NS8758	55°48·4′	3°47·7′W	FM	65,72
Kepplestone	C of Aber	NJ8609	57°10·6′	2°13·4′W	X	38
Keppoch	Arg & Bt	NR7163	55°48·6′	5°38·8′W	X	62
Keppoch	Highld	NG9024	57°15·8′	5°28·5′W	X	25,33
Keppoch	Highld	NM6486	56°54·6′	5°52·1′W	X	40
Keppoch	Highld	NN2680	56°53·0′	4°50·9′W	X	34,41
Keppochan	Arg & Bt	NN0821	56°20·8′	5°6·0′W	X	50,56
Keppochan River	Arg & Bt	NN0619	56°19·7′	5°7·8′W	W	50,56
Keppoch Ho	Arg & Bt	NS3279	55°58·7′	4°41·1′W	X	63
Keppoch Ho	Highld	NH5059	57°36·0′	4°30·1′W	X	26
Keppoch Ho	Highld	NM6586	56°54·6′	5°51·2′W	X	40
Keppoch Ho	Pth & Kin	NT0398	56°10·1′	3°33·3′W	X	58
Keppoch Point	Arg & Bt	NR7063	55°48·6′	5°39·8′W	X	61,62
Kepranich	Pth & Kin	NN7141	56°32·9′	4°5·5′W	X	51,52
Keprigan	Arg & Bt	NR6910	55°20·0′	5°38·1′W	X	68
Kepscaith	W Loth	NS9463	55°51·2′	3°41·2′W	X	65
Kepwick	N Yks	SE4690	54°18·5′	1°17·2′W	T	100
Kepwick Moor	N Yks	SE4892	54°19·5′	1°15·3′W	X	100
Keramenach	Arg & Bt	NR6309	55°19·3′	5°43·7′W	X	68
Kerchesters	Scot Bord	NT7735	55°36·7′	2°21·5′W	T	74
Kercock	Pth & Kin	NO1238	56°31·8′	3°25·4′W	X	53
Kerdiston	Norf	TG0824	52°46·6′	1°5·4′E	T	133
Kerelaw	N Ayr	NS2642	55°38·7′	4°45·5′W	X	63,70
Keresforth Hill	Barns	SE3205	53°32·7′	1°30·6′W	T	110,111
Keresley	Cov	SP3184	52°27·4′	1°32·2′W	T	140
Keresley Ho	Cov	SP3084	52°27·4′	1°33·1′W	X	140
Keresley Newlands	Warw	SP3284	52°27·4′	1°31·3′W	T	140
Kerewhip Bank	Fife	NO2219	56°21·7′	3°15·3′W	X	58
Kerfield	Scot Bord	NT2540	55°39·1′	3°11·1′W	T	73
Kerfield Ho	Ches	SJ7777	53°17·6′	2°20·3′W	X	118
Kergilliack	Corn	SW7733	50°9·5′	5°7·0′W	X	204

Kergord	Shetld	HU3954	60°16·4′	1°17·2′W	X	3
Keristal	I of M	SC3573	54°7·8′	4°31·1′W	T	95
Kerketh Fm	Corn	SW8773	50°31·3′	4°59·9′W	FM	200
Kerley	Corn	SX2097	50°44·9′	4°32·7′W	X	190
Kerley Downs	Corn	SW7644	50°15·4′	5°8·2′W	T	204
Kerloch	Aberd	NO6987	56°58·6′	2°30·1′W	H	45
Kermincham Hall	Ches	SJ7967	53°12·2′	2°18·5′W	X	118
Kermincham Ho	Ches	SJ8068	53°12·8′	2°17·6′W	X	118
Ker Moor	Somer	ST0143	51°10·9′	3°24·6′W	X	181
Kernalhill	Cumbr	NY4870	55°1·6′	2°48·4′W	X	86
Kernborough	Devon	SX7941	50°15·6′	3°41·5′W	T	202
Kerne Bridge	Heref	SO5818	51°51·8′	2°36·2′W	T	162
Kernewas	Corn	SW7420	50°2·5′	5°9·0′W	X	204
Kern Fm	I of W	SZ5786	50°40·5′	1°11·2′W	FM	196
Kernick	Corn	SW9663	50°26·1′	4°52·0′W	X	200
Kernick	Corn	SX0871	50°30·7′	4°42·1′W	X	200
Kernick Fm	Corn	SX1791	50°41·6′	4°35·1′W	FM	190
Kernick Ho	Corn	SW7733	50°9·5′	5°7·0′W	X	204
Kernock	Corn	SX3763	50°26·9′	4°17·4′W	X	201
Kernoon	Aberd	NO8682	56°56·0′	2°13·4′W	X	45
Kernow Mill	Corn	SX3359	50°24·7′	4°20·7′W	X	201
Kernsary	Highld	NG8979	57°45·3′	5°32·3′W	X	19
Kernstone Fm	Devon	SS2323	50°59·0′	4°30·9′W	FM	190
Kerr	D & G	NY3479	55°6·3′	3°1·6′W	X	85
Kerrachar	Highld	NC1734	58°15·7′	5°6·7′W	X	15
Kerrachar Bay	Highld	NC1834	58°15·7′	5°5·7′W	W	15
Kerranbeg	Arg & Bt	NR7112	55°21·2′	5°36·3′W	X	68
Kerran Hill	Arg & Bt	NR7313	55°21·8′	5°34·5′W	H	68
Kerrcleuch	Scot Bord	NT2016	55°26·1′	3°15·4′W	X	79
Kerrcleuch Burn	Scot Bord	NT1917	55°26·7′	3°16·4′W	W	79
Kerrera	Arg & Bt	NM8128	56°23·9′	5°32·5′W	X	49
Kerr Height	D & G	NY3380	55°6·8′	3°2·6′W	X	79
Kerricks	D & G	NX9583	55°8·1′	3°38·4′W	X	78
Kerridge	Ches	SJ9376	53°17·1′	2°5·9′W	T	118
Kerridge-end	Ches	SJ9475	53°16·6′	2°5·0′W	T	118
Kerridge Hill	Ches	SJ9475	53°16·6′	2°5·0′W	H	118
Kerriemore Hill	D & G	NX3986	55°8·8′	4°31·2′W	H	77
Kerriers	Corn	SW9964	50°26·7′	4°49·5′W	X	200
Kerris	Corn	SW4427	50°5·5′	5°34·4′W	T	203
Kerrison Sch	Suff	TM1370	52°17·4′	1°7·8′E	X	144,156
Kerroodhoo	I of M	SC2678	54°10·3′	4°39·5′W	X	95
Kerroodhoo Plantation	I of M	SC2276	54°9·2′	4°43·1′W	F	95
Kerroogarroo	I of M	SC3997	54°20·8′	4°28·2′W	T	95
Kerrow	Corn	SX1174	50°32·4′	4°39·7′W	X	200
Kerrow	Highld	NH3330	57°20·1′	4°46·0′W	T	26
Kerrow	Highld	NH7601	57°5·3′	4°2·3′W	X	35
Kerrow	Moray	NH9941	57°27·1′	3°40·5′W	X	27
Kerrowaird	Highld	NH7649	57°31·1′	4°3·8′W	X	27
Kerrowdhoo	I of M	SC4080	54°11·7′	4°26·7′W	X	95
Kerrowdown Fm	Highld	NH5230	57°20·5′	4°27·1′W	FM	26
Kerrow Downs	Corn	SX1175	50°32·9′	4°39·7′W	X	200
Kerrowe Fm	Corn	SW4537	50°10·9′	5°34·0′W	FM	203
Kerrow Glass	I of M	SC3082	54°12·6′	4°36·0′W	X	95
Kerrowglass	I of M	SC3088	54°15·8′	4°36·2′W	X	95
Kerrowkeil	I of M	SC2673	54°7·7′	4°39·4′W	X	95
Kerrowkneale	I of M	SC3898	54°21·4′	4°29·2′W	X	95
Kerrowmoar	I of M	SC2673	54°7·7′	4°39·4′W	X	95
Kerrowmoar	I of M	SC3994	54°19·2′	4°28·1′W	X	95
Kerrowmoar	I of M	SC3999	54°21·9′	4°28·3′W	X	95
Kerrowmore	Pth & Kin	NN5846	56°35·3′	4°18·3′W	X	51
Kerrow Wood	Highld	NH3531	57°20·6′	4°44·1′W	F	26
Kerr's Port	N Ayr	NS0532	55°32·8′	5°5·0′W	W	69
Kerry	Powys	SO1489	52°29·8′	3°15·6′W	T	136
Kerrycroy	Arg & Bt	NS1061	55°48·6′	5°1·5′W	T	63
Kerrycroy Bay	Arg & Bt	NS1061	55°48·6′	5°1·5′W	W	63
Kerrycrusach	Arg & Bt	NS0861	55°48·5′	5°3·4′W	X	63
Kerryfearn	Arg & Bt	NS0561	55°48·4′	5°6·3′W	X	63
Kerry Geo	Highld	ND2373	58°38·5′	3°19·1′W	X	7,12
Kerry Hill	Powys	SO1385	52°27·6′	3°16·4′W	H	136
Kerry Hill	Staffs	SJ9249	53°2·5′	2°6·8′W	T	118
Kerrylamont	Arg & Bt	NS1158	55°47·0′	5°0·4′W	X	63
Kerrylamont Bay	Arg & Bt	NS1157	55°46·4′	5°0·4′W	W	63
Kerrymenoch	Arg & Bt	NS0757	55°46·3′	5°4·2′W	X	63
Kerry Pole	Powys	SO1686	52°28·2′	3°13·8′W	X	136
Kerry Ridgeway (Cefnffordd Ceri)	Shrops	SO2789	52°29·9′	3°4·1′W	X	137
Kerrysdale	Highld	NG8273	57°41·9′	5°39·0′W	X	19
Kerry's Gate	Heref	SO3933	51°59·8′	2°52·9′W	T	149,161
Kerrytonlia	Arg & Bt	NS1156	55°45·9′	5°0·3′W	X	63
Kerrytonlia Point	Arg & Bt	NS1156	55°45·9′	5°0·3′W	X	63
Kerry Wood	Highld	NG8174	57°42·4′	5°40·1′W	F	19
Kersal	Salf	SD8101	53°30·6′	2°16·8′W	T	109
Kersall	Notts	SK7162	53°9·3′	0°55·9′W	T	120
Kersall Lodge	Notts	SK7162	53°9·3′	0°55·9′W	X	120
Kersbrook	Devon	SY0683	50°38·6′	3°19·4′W	T	192
Kersbrook Cross	Corn	SX3175	50°33·3′	4°22·8′W	T	201
Kerscott	Devon	SS6329	51°2·9′	3°56·9′W	T	180
Kerscott	Devon	SS7925	51°0·9′	3°43·1′W	X	180
Kerse	D & G	NY0690	55°12·0′	3°28·2′W	X	78
Kerse	Renf	NS3355	55°45·8′	4°39·3′W	X	63
Kerse	S Lanak	NS8141	55°39·1′	3°53·0′W	X	71,72
Kersebrock	Falk	NS8685	56°2·9′	3°49·4′W	X	65
Kerse Fm	Devon	SX6843	50°16·6′	3°50·8′W	FM	202
Kerse Loch	E Ayr	NS4214	55°23·9′	4°29·3′W	W	70
Kerse Moor	D & G	NY0690	55°12·0′	3°28·2′W	X	78
Kersepark	E Ayr	NS4214	55°23·9′	4°29·3′W	X	70
Kersewell Mains	S Lanak	NT0148	55°43·2′	3°34·1′W	X	72
Kersey	Suff	TM0044	52°3·7′	0°55·5′E	T	155
Kerseycleugh	Scot Bord	NY6195	55°15·1′	2°36·4′W	X	80
Kersey Green Scar	N Yks	NZ0804	54°26·1′	1°52·2′W	X	92
Kerseys	Essex	TL9832	51°57·3′	0°53·3′E	X	168
Kersey's Fm	Suff	TM0964	52°14·4′	1°4·1′E	FM	155
Kersey Tye	Suff	TL9843	52°3·2′	0°53·7′E	T	155
Kersey Upland	Suff	TL9942	52°2·7′	0°54·5′E	T	155
Kersey Vale	Suff	TM0043	52°3·2′	0°55·4′E	X	155
Kersford Barton	Devon	SX4986	50°39·5′	4°7·8′W	X	191,201
Kersham	Somer	SS9438	51°8·1′	3°30·5′W	X	181
Kersham Br	Devon	SS6613	50°54·3′	3°54·0′W	X	180
Kersham Hill	Somer	SS9438	51°8·1′	3°30·5′W	H	181
Kershay Fms	Dorset	SY4597	50°46·4′	2°46·4′W	FM	193
Kersheugh	Scot Bord	NT6517	55°27·0′	2°32·8′W	X	80
Kershope Bridge	Cumbr	NY5083	55°8·6′	2°46·6′W	X	79
Kershope Burn	Cumbr	NY5184	55°9·1′	2°45·7′W	W	79
Kershope Burn	Cumbr	NY5586	55°10·2′	2°42·0′W	W	80
Kershopefoot	Cumbr	NY4782	55°8·0′	2°49·4′W	T	79
Kershope Forest	Cumbr	NY5181	55°7·5′	2°45·7′W	F	79
Kershope Forest	Cumbr	NY5582	55°8·1′	2°41·9′W	F	80
Kershopehead	Cumbr	NY5486	55°10·2′	2°42·9′W	H	79
Kershope Ho	Cumbr	NY4782	55°8·0′	2°49·4′W	X	79
Kersie Mains	Falk	NS8791	56°6·2′	3°48·6′W	X	58
Kersiepow	Clackm	NS8996	56°8·9′	3°46·8′W	X	58
Kersknowe	Scot Bord	NT7528	55°33·0′	2°23·3′W	X	74
Kersland	N Ayr	NS3050	55°43·1′	4°41·9′W	X	63
Kersley Hall	Suff	TM2272	52°18·3′	1°15·8′E	X	156
Kerslochmuir	N Ayr	NS3149	55°42·6′	4°41·0′W	X	63
Kersmains	Scot Bord	NT7031	55°34·6′	2°28·1′W	X	74
Kersmoor Head	Scot Bord	NT8021	55°29·2′	2°18·6′W	H	74
Kersoe	Worcs	SO9939	52°3·2′	2°0·5′W	T	150
Kersons Cleugh	Scot Bord	NT6059	55°49·6′	2°37·9′W	X	67,74
Kersquarter	Scot Bord	NT7634	55°36·2′	2°22·4′W	X	74
Kerswell	Devon	SS5203	50°48·7′	4°5·7′W	X	191
Kerswell	Devon	ST0806	50°51·0′	3°18·0′W	T	192
Kerswell Barton	Devon	ST0120	50°58·5′	3°24·2′W	X	181
Kerswell Fm	Devon	SS7829	51°3·1′	3°44·1′W	FM	180
Kerswell Fm	Devon	SX9286	50°40·1′	3°31·3′W	FM	192
Kerswell Gardens	Torbay	SX8866	50°29·2′	3°34·4′W	X	202
Kerswell Green	Worcs	SO8646	52°7·0′	2°11·9′W	T	150
Kerswell Ho	Devon	SX9895	50°45·0′	3°26·4′W	X	192
Kerswell Priory	Devon	ST0706	50°51·0′	3°18·9′W	A	192,193
Kerswill	Devon	SX7358	50°24·7′	3°46·9′W	X	202
Kersworthy	Corn	SX2593	50°42·9′	4°28·4′W	X	190
Kerthen Wood	Corn	SW5833	50°9·1′	5°22·9′W	T	203
Kesgrave	Suff	TM2145	52°3·8′	1°13·8′E	T	169
Kesgrave Hall	Suff	TM2346	52°4·3′	1°15·6′E	X	169
Keskadale Beck	Cumbr	NY2018	54°33·3′	3°13·8′W	W	89,90
Keskadale Fm	Cumbr	NY2119	54°33·9′	3°12·9′W	FM	89,90
Keskeys	Corn	SW5734	50°9·6′	5°23·8′W	X	203
Kessingland	Suff	TM5286	52°25·1′	1°42·8′E	T	156
Kessingland Beach	Suff	TM5385	52°24·5′	1°43·6′E	T	156
Kessingland Cliffs	Suff	TM5387	52°25·6′	1°43·7′E	X	156
Kessingland Level	Suff	TM5285	52°24·5′	1°42·7′E	X	156
Kessington	E Dunb	NS5571	55°54·9′	4°18·8′W	X	64
Kessockbank	Aberd	NJ9865	57°40·7′	2°1·6′W	X	30
Kessock Bridge	Highld	NH6647	57°29·9′	4°13·7′W	X	26
Kestal	Corn	SW5531	50°7·9′	5°25·3′W	X	203
Kester	Kent	TQ5659	51°18·7′	0°14·7′E	X	188
Kester Brook	Devon	SX8171	50°31·8′	3°40·4′W	W	202
Kesters	E Yorks	TA0563	54°3·4′	0°23·3′W	X	101
Kestle	Corn	SW7525	50°5·2′	5°8·4′W	X	204
Kestle	Corn	SW8559	50°23·7′	5°1·1′W	X	200
Kestle	Corn	SW9945	50°16·5′	4°48·9′W	T	204
Kestle	Corn	SX2984	50°38·1′	4°24·7′W	X	201
Kestle Fm	Corn	SW8749	50°18·4′	4°59·1′W	FM	204
Kestlemerris Fm	Corn	SW7619	50°2·0′	5°7·3′W	FM	204
Kestle Mill	Corn	SW8559	50°23·7′	5°1·1′W	T	200
Keston	Brom	TQ4164	51°21·7′	0°1·9′E	T	177,187
Keston Court	Brom	TQ4163	51°21·1′	0°1·9′E	X	177,187
Keston Mark	Brom	TQ4265	51°22·2′	0°2·8′E	T	177
Kestor Rock	Devon	SX6686	50°39·7′	3°53·4′W	X	191
Kestrel Lodge	Cumbr	NY2432	54°40·9′	3°10·3′W	X	89,90
Keswick	Cumbr	NY2623	54°36·1′	3°8·3′W	T	89,90
Keswick	Norf	TG2004	52°35·6′	1°15·3′E	T	134
Keswick	Norf	TG3533	52°50·8′	1°29·8′E	T	133
Keswick Beck	Leeds	SE3644	53°53·7′	1°26·7′W	W	104
Keswick Beck	N Yks	SE3147	53°55·3′	1°31·3′W	W	104
Keswick Hall (Coll)	Norf	TG2004	52°35·6′	1°15·3′E	X	134
Ket Brae	S Lanak	NS9527	55°31·8′	3°39·4′W	X	72
Ketches	E Susx	TQ4120	50°58·0′	0°0·9′E	X	198
Ketche's Fm	E Susx	TQ4024	51°0·1′	0°0·1′E	FM	198
Kete	Pemb	SM8004	51°41·7′	5°10·6′W	T	157
Ketford	Glos	SO7230	51°58·3′	2°24·1′W	T	149
Kethole Reach	Kent	TQ8472	51°25·2′	0°39·2′E	W	178
Ketill Holm	Shetld	HU5264	60°21·7′	1°2·9′W	X	2,3
Ketley	Wrekin	SJ6710	52°41·4′	2°28·9′W	T	127
Ketley Bank	Wrekin	SJ6910	52°41·4′	2°27·1′W	T	127
Ketley Fm	E Susx	TQ7031	51°3·4′	0°25·9′E	FM	188
Ketligill Head	Shetld	HU2784	60°32·6′	1°30·0′W	X	3
Ketsby	Lincs	TF3676	53°16·0′	0°2·8′E	T	122
Ketsby House Fm	Lincs	TF3676	53°16·0′	0°2·8′E	FM	122
Kettelshiel	Scot Bord	NT7051	55°45·3′	2°28·2′W	X	67,74
Kettering	Northnts	SP8778	52°23·8′	0°42·9′W	T	141
Ketteringham	Norf	TG1602	52°34·6′	1°11·7′E	T	144
Ket, The	D & G	NX4239	54°43·5′	4°26·8′W	W	83
Kettins	Pth & Kin	NO2338	56°31·9′	3°14·7′W	T	53
Kettla Ness	Shetld	HU3428	60°2·4′	1°22·9′W	X	4
Kettle	I Scilly	SV8816	49°58·0′	6°20·7′W	X	203
Kettlebaston	Suff	TL9650	52°7·0′	0°52·2′E	T	155
Kettlebridge	Fife	NO3007	56°15·3′	3°7·3′W	T	59
Kettlebrook	Staffs	SK2103	52°37·7′	1°41·0′W	T	139
Kettleburgh	Suff	TM2660	52°11·7′	1°18·8′E	T	156
Kettleburgh Lodge	Suff	TM2562	52°12·8′	1°18·0′E	X	156
Kettleburn	Northum	NU0836	55°37·3′	1°51·9′W	X	75
Kettlebury Hill	Surrey	SU8840	51°9·4′	0°44·1′W	X	186
Kettleby Beck	N Lincs	TA0206	53°32·7′	0°27·2′W	W	112
Kettleby Carrs Fm	Lincs	TA0207	53°33·2′	0°27·2′W	FM	112
Kettleby Ho	Lincs	TA0307	53°33·2′	0°26·3′W	X	112
Kettleby Thorpe Fm	Lincs	TA0407	53°33·2′	0°25·4′W	FM	112
Kettle Corner	Kent	TQ7253	51°15·2′	0°28·3′E	T	188
Kettle Crag	Cumbr	NY2704	54°25·8′	3°7·1′W	X	89,90
Kettledean Fm	Beds	TL1231	51°58·2′	0°21·8′W	FM	166
Kettle Green	Herts	TL4118	51°50·8′	0°3·2′E	T	167
Kettle Hall	Cumbr	NY5581	55°7·5′	2°41·9′W	X	80
Kettlehill	Fife	NO3207	56°15·3′	3°5·4′W	T	59
Kettle Hill	Norf	TG0143	52°57·0′	0°59·9′E	X	133
Kettle Ho	Derby	SK3280	53°19·2′	1°30·9′W	X	110
Kettle Holes	Moray	NJ0143	57°28·3′	3°38·6′W	W	27
Kettleholm	D & G	NY1476	55°4·5′	3°20·5′W	T	85
Kettle Howe	N Yks	SE6897	54°22·1′	0°56·8′W	A	94,100
Kettleman Br	N Yks	SE4842	53°52·6′	1°15·8′W	X	105
Kettleness	N Yks	NZ8315	54°31·6′	0°42·6′W	X	94
Kettle Ness	N Yks	NZ8316	54°32·2′	0°42·6′W	X	94
Kettlesbeck	N Yks	SD7463	54°4·0′	2°23·4′W	X	98
Kettles Beck	N Yks	SD7464	54°4·5′	2°23·4′W	W	98
Kettle's Bottom	Corn	SW3225	50°4·1′	5°44·4′W	X	203
Kettleshill Fm	Kent	TQ5552	51°15·0′	0°13·7′E	FM	188
Kettleshulme	Ches	SJ9879	53°18·7′	2°1·4′W	T	118
Kettle Sike	Cumbr	NY5581	55°7·5′	2°41·9′W	W	80
Kettlesing	N Yks	SE2256	54°0·2′	1°39·4′W	T	104
Kettlesing Bottom	N Yks	SE2257	54°0·8′	1°39·4′W	T	104
Kettlesing Head	N Yks	SE2255	53°59·7′	1°39·4′W	X	104
Kettle Spring	N Yks	SE2662	54°3·4′	1°35·8′W	X	99
Kettlestang Hill	N Yks	SE1571	54°8·3′	1°45·8′W	H	99
Kettlestang Shooting Ho	N Yks	SE1671	54°8·3′	1°44·9′W	X	99
Kettlester	Shetld	HU5179	60°29·8′	1°3·8′W	T	2,3
Kettles, The	Moray	NJ2350	57°32·3′	3°16·7′W	X	28
Kettlestone	Norf	TF9631	52°50·7′	0°55·0′E	T	132
Kettlestounhills	W Loth	NS9875	55°57·7′	3°37·6′W	X	65
Kettles Wood	Worcs	SO9880	52°25·3′	2°1·4′W	F	139
Kettle, The	Northum	NU2136	55°37·3′	1°39·6′W	W	75
Kettle, The	Orkney	ND4677	58°40·9′	2°55·4′W	X	7
Kettlethorpe	Lincs	SK8475	53°16·2′	0°44·0′W	T	121
Kettlethorpe	Wakef	SE3216	53°38·6′	1°30·5′W	T	110,111
Kettlethorpe Fm	E Yorks	SE9133	53°47·4′	0°36·7′W	FM	106
Kettletoft	Orkney	HY6538	59°13·9′	2°36·3′W	T	5
Kettletoft Bay	Orkney	HY6638	59°13·9′	2°35·3′W	W	5
Kettleton Burn	D & G	NS9001	55°17·7′	3°43·5′W	W	78
Kettlewell	N Yks	SD9772	54°8·9′	2°2·3′W	T	98
Kettlewell Fm	N Yks	SE3898	54°22·8′	1°24·5′W	FM	99
Kettlewells Fm	Herts	TL1008	51°45·8′	0°24·0′W	FM	166
Kettock Burn	Aberd	NO5981	56°55·4′	2°40·0′W	W	44
Kettock Burn	Aberd	NO6081	56°55·4′	2°39·0′W	W	45
Ketton	Rut	SK9704	52°37·7′	0°33·6′W	T	141
Ketton Hall	Darl	NZ3019	54°34·2′	1°31·7′W	X	93
Ketton House	Suff	TL7046	52°5·4′	0°29·3′E	A	154
Kett's Fm	Suff	TM2881	52°23·0′	1°21·4′E	FM	156
Kett's Oak	Norf	TF6200	52°34·6′	0°23·9′E	A	143
Kett's Oak	Norf	TG1303	52°35·2′	1°9·1′E	A	144
Kevans	D & G	NX4642	54°45·2′	4°23·2′W	X	83
Kevelin Moor	Northum	NY8050	54°50·9′	2°18·3′W	H	86,87
Keveral	Corn	SX2955	50°22·4′	4°23·9′W	X	201
Keveral Beach	Corn	SX2954	50°21·9′	4°23·9′W	X	201
Keveral Wood	Corn	SX2955	50°22·4′	4°23·9′W	F	201
Keverstone Grange	Durham	NZ1322	54°35·8′	1°47·5′W	X	92
Kevingtown	Brom	TQ4867	51°23·2′	0°8·0′E	T	177
Kew	Rich	TQ1977	51°29·0′	0°16·8′W	T	176
Kewaigue	I of M	SC3574	54°8·4′	4°31·1′W	X	95
Keward	Somer	ST5444	51°11·8′	2°39·1′W	T	182,183
Kew Br	Rich	TQ1977	51°29·0′	0°16·8′W	X	176
Kewing	Orkney	HY4022	59°5·1′	3°2·3′W	X	5,6
Kewland Hall	Suff	TM1651	52°7·1′	1°9·7′E	X	156
Kewnston	S Ayr	NS3213	55°23·2′	4°38·7′W	X	70
Kew's Holt	Lincs	SK9474	53°15·5′	0°35·0′W	F	121
Kewsland	Devon	SS6026	51°1·2′	3°59·4′W	X	180
Kewstoke	N Som	ST3363	51°22·0′	2°57·4′W	T	182
Kew, The	I of M	SC2783	54°13·1′	4°38·8′W	X	95
Kex Beck	N Yks	SE1054	53°59·2′	1°50·4′W	W	104
Kex Beck	N Yks	SE2274	54°9·9′	1°39·4′W	W	99
Kexbrough	Barns	SE3009	53°34·8′	1°32·4′W	T	110,111
Kexby	Lincs	SK8785	53°21·5′	0°41·2′W	T	112,121
Kexby	York	SE7051	53°57·3′	0°55·6′W	T	105,106
Kexby Grange	Lincs	SK8685	53°21·5′	0°42·1′W	X	112,121
Kexby Ho	E Yorks	SE7051	53°57·3′	0°55·6′W	X	105,106
Kexby Stray Fm	York	SE6749	53°56·2′	0°58·3′W	FM	105,106
Kexgill Fm	N Yks	SE1255	53°59·7′	1°48·6′W	FM	104
Kex Gill Moor	N Yks	SE1355	53°59·7′	1°47·7′W	X	104
Kex Moor	N Yks	SE2074	54°9·9′	1°41·2′W	X	99
Kexwith	N Yks	NZ0505	54°26·7′	1°55·0′W	X	92
Kexwith Moor	N Yks	NZ0305	54°26·7′	1°56·8′W	X	92
Keybridge	Corn	SX0873	50°31·8′	4°42·2′W	T	200
Key Brook	Dorset	ST8217	50°57·4′	2°15·0′W	W	183
Keycol	Kent	TQ8764	51°20·9′	0°41·5′E	T	178
Keycol Hill	Kent	TQ8665	51°21·4′	0°40·7′E	X	178
Keyes Fm	Bucks	SP7040	52°3·5′	0°58·3′W	FM	152
Keyethern Fm	Devon	SS5105	50°49·8′	4°6·6′W	FM	191
Key Fm	Norf	TL5994	52°31·5′	0°21·0′E	FM	143
Keyford	Somer	ST5514	50°55·7′	2°38·0′W	X	194
Keyford	Somer	ST7747	51°13·5′	2°19·4′W	T	183
Keyfox Fm	W Susx	SU9724	51°0·7′	0°36·6′W	FM	197
Key Green	Ches	SJ9164	53°10·6′	2°7·7′W	X	118
Key Green	N Yks	NZ8004	54°25·7′	0°45·6′W	T	94
Keyham	Leic	SK6706	52°39·1′	1°0·2′W	T	141
Keyham Fm	Hants	SU7330	51°4·1′	0°57·1′W	FM	186
Keyhaven	Hants	SZ3091	50°43·3′	1°34·1′W	T	196
Keyhaven Marshes	Hants	SZ3191	50°43·3′	1°33·3′W	X	196
Keyhead	Aberd	NK0755	57°35·4′	1°52·5′W	T	30
Keyholme Fm	Lincs	TF3799	53°28·4′	0°4·3′E	FM	113
Keyhow	Cumbr	NY1300	54°23·5′	3°20·0′W	X	89
Keyingham	E Yorks	TA2425	53°42·6′	0°6·9′W	T	107,113
Keyingham Drain	E Yorks	TA2224	53°42·1′	0°8·7′W	W	107,113
Keyingham Grange	E Yorks	TA2323	53°41·6′	0°7·8′W	X	107,113
Keyingham Marsh	E Yorks	TA2223	53°41·6′	0°8·7′W	X	107,113
Keylands	Kent	TQ6746	51°11·6′	0°23·8′E	X	188
Keymelford	Devon	SX7799	50°46·9′	3°44·3′W	X	191
Keymer	W Susx	TQ3115	50°55·4′	0°7·8′W	T	198
Key Moss	Cumbr	SD4284	54°15·2′	2°53·0′W	X	96,97
Keynedon Barton	Devon	SX7743	50°16·7′	3°43·2′W	X	202
Keynes Park Country Park	Glos	SU0295	51°39·5′	1°57·9′W	X	163
Keynor Ho	W Susx	SZ8497	50°46·2′	0°48·1′W	X	197
Keynsham	Bath & NE Somer	ST6568	51°24·8′	2°29·8′W	T	172
Keynsham	Glos	ST5899	51°41·5′	2°36·1′W	X	162
Keynsham Hams	Bath & NE Somer	ST6569	51°25·4′	2°29·8′W	X	172
Keynsham Manor	Bath & NE Somer	ST6767	51°24·3′	2°28·1′W	X	172
Keynston Down	Dorset	ST9205	50°50·9′	2°6·4′W	H	195
Keypitts Fm	Devon	SS5445	51°11·4′	4°5·0′W	FM	180
Keysbeck	N Yks	SE6694	54°20·5′	0°58·7′W	X	94,100
Key's Englebourne	Devon	SX7757	50°24·2′	3°43·5′W	X	202
Keysers Estate	Essex	TL3706	51°44·4′	0°0·6′W	T	166

Keyses Fm	Worcs	SO8038	52°2·6'	2°17·1'W	FM	150
Keys Fm	Derby	SK4436	52°55·4'	1°20·3'W	FM	129
Keys Fm	Worcs	SO9865	52°17·2'	2°1·4'W	FM	150
Key's Green	Kent	TQ6539	51°7·8'	0°21·9'E	T	188
Keyshill	E Ayr	NS4422	55°28·3'	4°27·6'W	X	70
Keysley Down	Wilts	ST8634	51°6·5'	2°11·6'W	X	183
Keysley Fm	Wilts	ST8635	51°7·1'	2°11·6'W	FM	183
Keysmount	Cumbr	NY4062	54°57·2'	2°55·8'W	X	85
Keysoe	Beds	TL0762	52°15·0'	0°25·6'W	T	153
Keysoe Row	Beds	TL0861	52°14·4'	0°24·7'W	T	153
Keys, The	Orkney	ND4992	58°49·0'	2°52·5'W	X	7
Keys Toft Ho	Lincs	TF4958	53°6·1'	0°13·9'E	X	122
Keyston	Cambs	TL0475	52°22·0'	0°28·0'W	T	141
Key Street	Kent	TQ8864	51°20·9'	0°42·4'E	T	178
Keysworth Fm	Dorset	SY9389	50°42·3'	2°5·6'W	FM	195
Keysworth Point	Dorset	SY9589	50°42·3'	2°3·9'W	X	195
Keythorpe Grange	Leic	SK7700	52°35·8'	0°51·4'W	X	141
Keythorpe Hall	Leic	SK7600	52°35·8'	0°52·3'W	X	141
Keythorpe Hall Fm	Leic	SP7699	52°35·2'	0°52·3'W	FM	141
Keythorpe Lodge Fm	Leic	SP7698	52°34·7'	0°52·3'W	FM	141
Keythorpe Wood	Leic	SP7698	52°34·7'	0°52·3'W	F	141
Key West	Durham	NZ0449	54°50·4'	1°55·8'W	X	87
Keywood	Corn	SX2599	50°46·1'	4°28·5'W	X	190
Keyworth	Notts	SK6130	52°52·1'	1°5·2'W	T	129
Keyworth House Fm	Cambs	TL3392	52°30·8'	0°2·0'W	FM	142
Keyworth Wolds	Notts	SK6129	52°51·5'	1°5·2'W	X	129
Khantore	Aberd	NO2893	57°1·6'	3°10·7'W	X	37,44
Kibanes Burn	N Ayr	NS3159	55°47·9'	4°41·3'W	W	63
Kibbear	Somer	ST2221	50°59·2'	3°6·3'W	T	193
Kibbens Geo	Orkney	HY5430	59°9·5'	2°47·8'W	X	5,6
Kibber Hill	N Yks	SE3976	54°10·9'	1°23·7'W	X	99
Kibble Ditch	Oxon	SU5689	51°36·1'	1°11·1'W	W	174
Kibbleston	Renf	NS3961	55°49·2'	4°33·8'W	X	63
Kibblestone Camp	Staffs	SJ9136	52°55·5'	2°7·6'W	X	127
Kibblesworth	Ghead	NZ2456	54°54·1'	1°37·1'W	T	88
Kibblesworth Common	Ghead	NZ2355	54°53·6'	1°38·1'W	X	88
Kibblesworth Grange	Ghead	NZ2356	54°54·1'	1°38·1'W	X	88
Kiberick Cove	Corn	SW9237	50°12·0'	4°54·5'W	W	204
Kibworth Beauchamp	Leic	SP6893	52°32·1'	0°59·4'W	T	141
Kibworth Br	Leic	SP6694	52°32·6'	1°1·2'W	X	141
Kibworth Hall	Leic	SP6895	52°33·1'	0°59·4'W	X	141
Kibworth Harcourt	Leic	SP6894	52°32·6'	0°59·4'W	T	141
Kickle's Fm	Mil Key	SP8644	52°5·5'	0°44·3'W	FM	152
Kidbeck Fm	Cumbr	NY1104	54°25·7'	3°21·9'W	FM	89
Kidbrooke	Gren	TQ4176	51°28·1'	0°2·2'E	T	177
Kidbrooke Park	E Susx	TQ4234	51°5·5'	0°2·1'E	X	187
Kidbrooke Wood	E Susx	TQ4133	51°5·0'	0°1·2'E	F	187
Kidburngill	Cumbr	NY0621	54°34·8'	3°26·8'W	T	89
Kiddal Hall	Leeds	SE3939	53°51·0'	1°24·0'W	X	104
Kiddal Lane End	Leeds	SE4039	53°51·0'	1°23·1'W	T	105
Kiddamhill	D & G	NT2002	55°18·6'	3°15·2'W	X	79
Kiddemore Green	Staffs	SJ8508	52°40·4'	2°12·9'W	T	127
Kiddens Plantation	Devon	SX8784	50°38·9'	3°35·5'W	F	192
Kidderminster	Worcs	SO8376	52°23·1'	2°15·5'W	T	138
Kiddington	Oxon	SP4122	51°53·9'	1°23·9'W	T	164
Kiddington Cottage	W Berks	SU5780	51°31·2'	1°10·3'W	X	174
Kiddle's Bottom	Dorset	ST6800	50°48·2'	2°26·9'W	X	194
Kiddshill	Aberd	NJ9343	57°28·9'	2°6·5'W	T	30
Kidd's Moor	Norf	TG1103	52°35·3'	1°7·3'E	T	144
Kidds Scar	Scot Bord	NT3306	55°20·9'	3°3·0'W	X	79
Kiddygreen	Northum	NY8157	54°54·7'	2°17·4'W	X	86,87
Kidfield Ho	Barns	SE2505	53°32·7'	1°37·0'W	X	110
Kidhow	N Yks	SD8383	54°14·8'	2°15·2'W	X	98
Kid Islands	D & G	NX2952	54°50·3'	4°39·3'W	X	82
Kidland	Devon	SS8022	50°59·3'	3°42·2'W	X	181
Kidland Forest	Northum	NT9112	55°24·4'	2°8·1'W	X	80
Kidlandlee	Northum	NT9109	55°22·7'	2°8·1'W	X	80
Kidlandlee Dean	Northum	NT9109	55°22·7'	2°8·1'W	X	80
Kidlaw	E Loth	NT5064	55°52·2'	2°47·5'W	X	66
Kidlaw	Northum	NZ0181	55°7·6'	1°58·6'W	X	81
Kidlaw Burn	E Loth	NT5165	55°52·8'	2°46·6'W	W	66
Kidley Hill	Heref	SO5632	51°59·3'	2°38·1'W	H	149
Kidlington	Oxon	SP4913	51°49·0'	1°17·0'W	T	164
Kid Moor	Cumbr	NY4819	54°34·1'	2°47·8'W	X	90
Kidmore End	Oxon	SU6979	51°30·6'	1°0·0'W	T	175
Kidnal	Ches	SJ4749	53°2·4'	2°47·0'W	T	117
Kidnal Hall	Ches	SJ4748	53°1·8'	2°47·0'W	X	117
Kidnalls	Glos	SO6205	51°44·8'	2°32·6'W	X	162
Kidney Wood	Beds	TL0919	51°51·8'	0°24·6'W	F	166
Kidsdale	D & G	NX4336	54°41·9'	4°25·8'W	X	83
Kidsgrove	Staffs	SJ8354	53°5·2'	2°14·8'W	T	118
Kidshiel	Scot Bord	NT7456	55°48·0'	2°24·4'W	X	67,74
Kidshielhaugh	Scot Bord	NT7457	55°48·6'	2°24·5'W	X	67,74
Kidside	Cumbr	SD5282	54°14·1'	2°43·8'W	X	97
Kidsnape	Lancs	SD5738	53°50·4'	2°38·8'W	X	102
Kid Stone	N Yks	SD9941	53°52·2'	2°0·5'W	X	103
Kid Stones	Cald	SD9730	53°46·2'	2°2·3'W	X	103
Kidstones	N Yks	SD9581	54°13·7'	2°4·2'W	X	98
Kidstones Fell	N Yks	SD9481	54°13·7'	2°5·1'W	X	98
Kidstones Gill	N Yks	SD9581	54°13·7'	2°4·2'W	W	98
Kidstones Scar	N Yks	SD9481	54°13·7'	2°5·1'W	X	98
Kidston Mill	Scot Bord	NT2443	55°40·7'	3°12·1'W	X	73
Kidsty Howes	Cumbr	NY4612	54°30·3'	2°49·6'W	X	90
Kidsty Pike	Cumbr	NY4412	54°30·3'	2°51·5'W	H	90
Kidwelly (Cydweli)	Carm	SN4006	51°44·0'	4°18·6'W	T	159
Kiel Crofts	Arg & Bt	NM9039	56°30·0'	5°24·3'W	T	49
Kielder	Northum	NY6293	55°14·0'	2°35·4'W	T	80
Kielder Burn	Northum	NY6595	55°15·1'	2°32·6'W	W	80
Kielder Castle	Northum	NY6393	55°14·0'	2°34·5'W	X	80
Kielder Forest	Northum	NY6690	55°12·4'	2°31·6'W	F	80
Kielder Head	Northum	NY6698	55°16·7'	2°31·7'W	X	80
Kielderhead Moor	Northum	NT6700	55°17·8'	2°30·8'W	X	80
Kielder Stone	Northum	NT6300	55°17·8'	2°34·5'W	X	80
Kielderstone Cleugh	Northum	NT6400	55°17·8'	2°33·6'W	X	80
Kielder Water	Northum	NY6787	55°10·8'	2°30·7'W	W	80
Kielhope Law	Scot Bord	NT7814	55°25·4'	2°20·4'W	H	80
Kierallan	Pth & Kin	NN8308	56°15·3'	3°52·9'W	X	57
Kierfea Hill	Orkney	HY4232	59°10·5'	3°0·4'W	H	5,6
Kier Fiold	Orkney	HY2418	59°2·8'	3°19·0'W	X	6
Kierfiold House	Orkney	HY2518	59°2·8'	3°18·0'W	X	6

Kiessimul Castle	N Eil	NL6697	56°56·9'	7°29·2'W	A	31
Kiff Green	W Berks	SU5768	51°24·7'	1°10·4'W	T	174
Kiftsgate Court	Glos	SP1743	52°5·3'	1°44·7'W	X	151
Kiftsgate Stone	Glos	SP1338	52°2·6'	1°48·2'W	A	151
Kigbeare	Devon	SX5396	50°44·9'	4°4·6'W	X	191
Kighill Fm	Notts	SK5653	53°4·5'	1°9·4'W	FM	120
Kiladam	D & G	NX3556	54°52·5'	4°33·9'W	X	83
Kilail Burn	Arg & Bt	NR9483	56°0·0'	5°17·8'W	W	55
Kilandan Burn	Stir	NS4593	56°6·5'	4°29·1'W	W	57
Kilanow	Pemb	SN1508	51°44·7'	4°40·4'W	X	158
Kilantringan Loch	S Ayr	NX0879	55°4·4'	5°0·0'W	W	76
Kilbagie	Clackm	NS9290	56°5·7'	3°43·7'W	X	58
Kilbanes Burn	N Ayr	NS3159	55°47·9'	4°41·3'W	W	63
Kilbank	S Lanak	NS8543	55°40·3'	3°49·3'W	X	71,72
Kilbarchan	Renf	NS4063	55°50·3'	4°32·9'W	T	64
Kilbarth	Pemb	SM9520	51°50·7'	4°58·2'W	X	157,158
Kilbeg	Highld	NG6406	57°5·3'	5°53·3'W	X	32
Kilberry	Arg & Bt	NR7164	55°49·2'	5°38·9'W	T	62
Kilberry Bay	Arg & Bt	NR7063	55°48·6'	5°39·8'W	W	61,62
Kilberry Castle	Arg & Bt	NR7064	55°49·1'	5°39·9'W	X	61,62
Kilberry Head	Arg & Bt	NR7064	55°49·1'	5°39·9'W	X	61,62
Kilberry Point	Arg & Bt	NR7063	55°48·6'	5°39·8'W	X	61,62
Kilbert How	Cumbr	NY4018	54°33·5'	2°55·2'W	X	90
Kilbirnie	N Ayr	NS3154	55°45·2'	4°41·1'W	T	63
Kilbirnie Loch	N Ayr	NS3354	55°45·3'	4°39·2'W	W	63
Kilblaan	Arg & Bt	NN1213	56°16·6'	5°1·8'W	X	50,56
Kilblaan	Arg & Bt	NR7009	55°19·5'	5°37·1'W	X	68
Kilblaan Burn	Arg & Bt	NN1513	56°16·7'	4°58·8'W	W	50,56
Kilblane	D & G	NX9881	55°7·0'	3°35·5'W	X	78
Kilblean	Aberd	NJ8328	57°20·8'	2°16·5'W	X	38
Kilbo	Angus	NO2470	56°49·2'	3°14·3'W	X	44
Kilbo Path	Angus	NO2472	56°50·3'	3°14·3'W	X	44
Kilbowie	Arg & Bt	NM8429	56°24·5'	5°29·6'W	X	49
Kilbowie	W Dunb	NS5071	55°54·8'	4°23·6'W	T	64
Kilbrackmont	Fife	NO4706	56°14·9'	2°50·9'W	X	59
Kilbrackmont Place	Fife	NO4705	56°14·3'	2°50·9'W	X	59
Kilbrannan Sound		NR8340	55°36·6'	5°26·3'W	W	62,69
Kilbraur	Highld	NC8210	58°4·1'	3°59·5'W	X	17
Kilbraur Hill	Highld	NC8208	58°3·0'	3°59·5'W	H	17
Kilbreece	Heref	SO5223	51°54·4'	2°41·5'W	X	162
Kilbreen	D & G	NX0654	54°50·8'	5°0·9'W	X	82
Kilbrennan	Arg & Bt	NM4342	56°30·3'	6°10·1'W	X	47,48
Kilbride	Arg & Bt	NM1954	56°35·9'	6°34·2'W	X	46
Kilbride	Arg & Bt	NM7516	56°17·2'	5°37·7'W	T	55
Kilbride	Arg & Bt	NM8308	56°13·2'	5°29·6'W	X	55
Kilbride	Arg & Bt	NM8525	56°22·4'	5°28·5'W	T	49
Kilbride	Arg & Bt	NM9124	56°22·0'	5°22·6'W	X	49
Kilbride	Arg & Bt	NR3846	55°38·5'	6°9·4'W	X	60
Kilbride	Arg & Bt	NR7108	55°19·0'	5°36·1'W	X	68
Kilbride	Arg & Bt	NR7280	55°57·8'	5°38·7'W	X	55
Kilbride	Arg & Bt	NR8596	56°6·8'	5°27·0'W	X	55
Kilbride	Arg & Bt	NS0367	55°51·6'	5°8·4'W	X	63
Kilbride	Highld	NG5920	57°12·7'	5°59·0'W	X	32
Kilbride	N Ayr	NR9721	55°26·7'	5°12·1'W	X	69
Kilbride Bay or Bàgh Osde	Arg & Bt	NR9566	55°50·9'	5°16·0'W	W	62
Kilbride Fm	Arg & Bt	NR9668	55°52·0'	5°15·2'W	FM	62
Kilbride Hill	Arg & Bt	NS0369	55°52·7'	5°8·5'W	H	63
Kilbride Hill	Arg & Bt	NS1475	55°56·2'	4°58·2'W	H	63
Kilbride Hill	N Ayr	NR9821	55°26·7'	5°11·2'W	X	69
Kilbride Island	Arg & Bt	NS0096	56°7·2'	5°12·6'W	X	55
Kilbridemore	Arg & Bt	NS0390	56°4·0'	5°9·4'W	T	55
Kilbridemore Burn	Arg & Bt	NS0392	56°5·1'	5°9·5'W	W	55
Kilbride Point	Highld	NG3766	57°36·7'	6°23·8'W	X	23
Kilbride River	Arg & Bt	NR3945	55°38·0'	6°8·4'W	W	60
Kilbrook	D & G	NY1197	55°15·8'	3°23·6'W	X	78
Kilbryd	Arg & Bt	NR7381	55°58·4'	5°37·8'W	X	55
Kilbryde Castle	Stir	NN7503	56°12·4'	4°0·5'W	X	57
Kilbucho Burn	Scot Bord	NT0834	55°35·7'	3°27·2'W	W	72
Kilbucho Church	Scot Bord	NT0633	55°35·1'	3°29·0'W	A	72
Kilbucho Ho	Scot Bord	NT0834	55°35·7'	3°27·2'W	X	72
Kilbucho Mains	Scot Bord	NT0935	55°36·3'	3°26·2'W	X	72
Kilbucho Place	Scot Bord	NT0935	55°36·3'	3°26·2'W	X	72
Kilburn	Angus	NO3568	56°48·2'	3°3·4'W	X	44
Kilburn	Brent	TQ2483	51°32·2'	0°12·3'W	T	176
Kilburn	Derby	SK3845	53°0·3'	1°25·6'W	T	119,128
Kilburn	D & G	NY2095	55°14·8'	3°15·1'W	X	79
Kil Burn	D & G	NY2196	55°15·4'	3°14·1'W	W	79
Kilburn	E Renf	NS4756	55°46·6'	4°25·9'W	X	64
Kilburn	N Yks	SE5179	54°12·5'	1°12·7'W	T	100
Kilburn Fm	N Ayr	NS2160	55°48·3'	4°50·9'W	FM	63
Kilburn Granges	N Yks	SE5178	54°12·0'	1°12·7'W	X	100
Kilburn Hill	D & G	NY2196	55°15·4'	3°14·1'W	H	79
Kilburnie House	N Ayr	NS3054	55°45·2'	4°42·1'W	A	63
Kilburns	Fife	NO3725	56°25·0'	3°0·8'W	X	54,59
Kilburn Thicket	N Yks	SE5278	54°11·9'	1°11·8'W	F	100
Kilbury Camp	Heref	SO7238	52°2·6'	2°24·1'W	A	149
Kilby	Leic	SP6295	52°33·2'	1°4·7'W	T	140
Kilby Bridge	Leic	SP6197	52°34·3'	1°5·6'W	T	140
Kilby Bridge Fm	Leic	SP6097	52°34·3'	1°6·5'W	FM	140
Kilby Grange Fms	Leic	SP6294	52°32·7'	1°4·7'W	FM	140
Kilby Lodge	Leic	SP6395	52°33·2'	1°3·8'W	X	140
Kilchamaig	Arg & Bt	NR8061	55°47·8'	5°30·2'W	X	62
Kilchamaig Bay	Arg & Bt	NR8061	55°47·8'	5°30·2'W	W	62
Kilchattan Bay	Arg & Bt	NS1055	55°45·3'	5°1·2'W	T	63
Kilchattan Bay	Arg & Bt	NS1055	55°45·3'	5°1·2'W	W	63
Kilchattan Hill	Arg & Bt	NR7111	55°20·6'	5°36·3'W	X	68
Kilchatton	Arg & Bt	NM7408	56°12·9'	5°38·2'W	X	55
Kilchenzie	Arg & Bt	NR6724	55°27·5'	5°40·7'W	T	68
Kilcheran	Arg & Bt	NM8238	56°29·3'	5°32·0'W	X	49
Kilcheran Loch	Arg & Bt	NM8239	56°29·8'	5°32·1'W	W	49
Kilchiaran	Arg & Bt	NR2060	55°45·4'	6°27·3'W	T	60
Kilchiaran Bay	Arg & Bt	NR1959	55°44·8'	6°28·2'W	W	60
Kilchoan	Highld	NM4863	56°41·7'	6°6·5'W	T	47
Kilchoan	Highld	NM7799	57°2·0'	5°40·1'W	X	33,40
Kilchoan Bay	Arg & Bt	NM7912	56°15·2'	5°33·6'W	W	55
Kilchoan Bay	Highld	NM4863	56°41·7'	6°6·5'W	W	47
Kilchoan Ho	Arg & Bt	NM7913	56°15·7'	5°33·7'W	X	55
Kilchoan Lochs	Arg & Bt	NM7914	56°16·3'	5°33·7'W	W	55
Kilchoman	Arg & Bt	NR2163	55°47·0'	6°26·6'W	T	60
Kilchrenan	Arg & Bt	NN0322	56°21·2'	5°10·9'W	T	50

Kilchrenan Burn	Arg & Bt	NN0323	56°21·8'	5°10·9'W	W	50
Kilchrist Cas	Arg & Bt	NR6917	55°23·8'	5°38·5'W	X	68
Kilchurn Castle	Arg & Bt	NN1327	56°24·2'	5°1·4'W	A	50
Kilcluan	Moray	NJ2562	57°38·8'	3°14·9'W	X	28
Kilconquhar	Fife	NO4802	56°12·7'	2°49·9'W	T	59
Kilconquhar Castle	Fife	NO4902	56°12·7'	2°48·9'W	X	59
Kilconquhar Loch	Fife	NO4801	56°12·2'	2°49·8'W	W	59
Kilconquhar Mains	Fife	NO4802	56°12·7'	2°49·9'W	X	59
Kilcot	Glos	SO6925	51°55·6'	2°26·7'W	T	162
Kilcot Wood	Glos	SO6924	51°55·1'	2°26·7'W	F	162
Kilcoy	Highld	NH5751	57°31·9'	4°22·8'W	T	26
Kilcoy Castle	Highld	NH5751	57°31·9'	4°22·8'W	X	26
Kilcoy Mill	Highld	NH5851	57°31·9'	4°21·8'W	X	26
Kilcreggan	Arg & Bt	NS2380	55°59·1'	4°49·8'W	T	63
Kildale	N Yks	NZ6009	54°28·6'	1°4·0'W	T	94
Kildale Moor	N Yks	NZ6208	54°28·1'	1°2·2'W	X	94
Kildale Moor	N Yks	NZ6211	54°29·7'	1°2·1'W	X	94
Kildalloig	Arg & Bt	NR7518	55°24·5'	5°32·8'W	X	68,69
Kildalloig Bay	Arg & Bt	NR7519	55°25·1'	5°32·9'W	W	68,69
Kildalton Church	Arg & Bt	NR4550	55°40·8'	6°3·0'W	A	60
Kildalton Ho	Arg & Bt	NR4347	55°39·2'	6°4·7'W	X	60
Kildanes Bottom	Glos	SP1432	51°59·4'	1°47·4'W	X	151
Kildarroch	D & G	NX3162	54°55·7'	4°37·8'W	X	82
Kildarroch	D & G	NX3849	54°48·8'	4°30·8'W	X	83
Kildary	Highld	NH7675	57°45·1'	4°4·6'W	T	21
Kildary Ho	Highld	NH7674	57°44·6'	4°5·5'W	X	21
Kildavaig	Arg & Bt	NR9866	55°51·0'	5°13·2'W	X	62
Kildavanan	Arg & Bt	NS0266	55°51·1'	5°9·3'W	X	63
Kildavanan Point	Arg & Bt	NS0266	55°51·1'	5°9·3'W	X	63
Kildavie	Arg & Bt	NR7210	55°20·1'	5°35·3'W	X	68
Kildean	Stir	NS7894	56°7·6'	3°57·3'W	X	57
Kilderhayes Fm	Devon	ST2402	50°49·0'	3°4·3'W	FM	192,193
Kildermorie Forest	Highld	NH4678	57°46·2'	4°34·9'W	X	20
Kildermorie Lodge	Highld	NH5178	57°46·3'	4°29·8'W	X	20
Kildhu	Aberd	NO4897	57°3·9'	2°51·0'W	X	37,44
Kildinny	Pth & Kin	NO0617	56°20·4'	3°30·8'W	X	58
Kildoach Hill	S Ayr	NS3903	55°17·9'	4°31·7'W	H	77
Kildonald Bay	Arg & Bt	NR7827	55°29·4'	5°30·4'W	W	68,69
Kildonald Point	Arg & Bt	NR7827	55°29·4'	5°30·4'W	X	68,69
Kildonan	Arg & Bt	NR7728	55°30·0'	5°31·4'W	X	68,69
Kildonan	D & G	NX0551	54°49·2'	5°1·7'W	X	82
Kildonan	Highld	NG3554	57°30·2'	6°25·0'W	T	23
Kildonan	Highld	NH0790	57°51·7'	5°14·7'W	X	19
Kildonan	N Ayr	NS0221	55°26·8'	5°7·4'W	T	69
Kildonan	S Ayr	NX2283	55°6·8'	4°47·0'W	X	76
Kildonan Burn	Highld	NC9224	58°11·8'	3°49·8'W	W	17
Kildonan Fm	Highld	NC9120	58°9·6'	3°50·7'W	FM	17
Kildonan Lodge	Highld	NC9022	58°10·7'	3°51·7'W	X	17
Kildonnan	Highld	NM4885	56°53·5'	6°7·8'W	T	39
Kildonnan Burn	D & G	NX0550	54°48·7'	5°1·7'W	W	82
Kildoon Hill	S Ayr	NS2907	55°19·9'	4°41·3'W	X	70,76
Kildown Point	Corn	SW7214	49°59·2'	5°10·5'W	X	204
Kildrochet Ho	D & G	NX0856	54°52·0'	4°59·1'W	X	82
Kildrum	N Lanak	NS7675	55°57·4'	3°58·7'W	T	64
Kildrummy	Aberd	NJ4617	57°14·7'	2°53·2'W	T	37
Kildrummy Castle	Aberd	NJ4516	57°14·1'	2°54·2'W	A	37
Kilduff	E Loth	NT5277	55°59·3'	2°45·7'W	X	66
Kilduff Hill	E Loth	NT5177	55°59·3'	2°46·7'W	X	66
Kilduff Ho	E Loth	NT5177	55°59·3'	2°46·7'W	X	66
Kildun	Highld	NH5457	57°35·0'	4°26·1'W	X	26
Kilduncan	Fife	NO5712	56°18·2'	2°41·3'W	T	59
Kilduncan Burn	Fife	NO5711	56°17·6'	2°41·2'W	W	59
Kilduskland	Arg & Bt	NR8485	56°0·8'	5°27·5'W	X	55
Kilduskland Burn	Arg & Bt	NR8386	56°1·3'	5°28·5'W	W	55
Kilduskland Resr	Arg & Bt	NR8386	56°1·3'	5°28·5'W	W	55
Kildutie	Aberd	NJ7200	57°5·7'	2°27·3'W	X	38
Kildwick	N Yks	SE0145	53°54·3'	1°58·7'W	T	104
Kildwick Grange	N Yks	SE0246	53°54·9'	1°57·8'W	X	104
Kildwick Hall (Hotel)	N Yks	SE0146	53°54·9'	1°58·7'W	A	104
Kildwick Moor	N Yks	SE0147	53°55·4'	1°58·7'W	X	104
Kilearnan	Highld	NC9218	58°8·5'	3°49·6'W	X	17
Kilearnan Hill	Highld	NC9317	58°8·0'	3°48·6'W	X	17
Kileekie	S Ayr	NS3206	55°19·4'	4°38·4'W	X	70,76
Kilennan	Arg & Bt	NR3757	55°44·4'	6°11·0'W	X	60
Kilennan River	Arg & Bt	NR3757	55°44·4'	6°11·0'W	W	60
Kilewnan Burn	Stir	NS6085	56°2·5'	4°14·4'W	W	57
Kilfasset	Stir	NS5588	56°4·0'	4°19·3'W	X	57
Kilfeddar	D & G	NX1568	54°58·6'	4°53·0'W	X	82
Kilfillan	D & G	NX2054	54°51·2'	4°47·8'W	X	82
Kilfinan	Arg & Bt	NR9378	55°57·3'	5°18·5'W	T	62
Kilfinan Bay	Arg & Bt	NR9178	55°57·2'	5°20·4'W	W	62
Kilfinan Burn	Arg & Bt	NR9479	55°57·8'	5°17·6'W	W	62
Kilfinichen Bay	Arg & Bt	NM4828	56°22·9'	6°4·5'W	W	48
Kilfinnan	Highld	NN2795	57°1·1'	4°50·5'W	X	34
Kilfinnan Burn	Highld	NN2796	57°1·6'	4°50·6'W	W	34
Kilfinnan Fall	Highld	NN2796	57°1·6'	4°50·6'W	W	34
Kilford Fm	Denb	SJ0766	53°11·2'	3°23·1'W	FM	116
Kilforge Ho	Heref	SO5632	51°59·3'	2°38·1'W	X	149
Kilgarie	Angus	NO5666	56°47·3'	2°42·8'W	X	44
Kilgetty	Pemb	SN1207	51°44·1'	4°43·0'W	T	158
Kilgetty Fm	Pemb	SN1308	51°44·6'	4°42·1'W	FM	158
Kilgogue Fm	Corn	SX0954	50°21·5'	4°40·7'W	FM	200
Kilgour	Fife	NO2208	56°15·7'	3°15·1'W	X	58
Kilgourieknowe	Fife	NO2606	56°14·7'	3°11·2'W	X	59
Kilgram Grange	N Yks	SE1985	54°15·9'	1°42·1'W	X	99
Kilgrammie	S Ayr	NS2501	55°16·6'	4°44·9'W	T	76
Kilgwrrwg Common	Monm	ST4798	51°40·9'	2°45·6'W	T	171
Kilgwrrwg Ho	Monm	ST4698	51°40·9'	2°46·5'W	X	171
Kilhallon	Corn	SX0754	50°21·5'	4°42·4'W	T	200
Kilham	E Yorks	TA0664	54°3·9'	0°22·4'W	T	101
Kilham	Northum	NT8832	55°35·1'	2°11·0'W	T	74
Kilham Fm	Donc	SE6502	53°30·9'	1°0·8'W	FM	111
Kilham Grange Fm	E Yorks	TA0766	54°5·0'	0°21·4'W	FM	101
Kilham Hill	Northum	NT8831	55°34·6'	2°11·0'W	H	74
Kilham West Field	E Yorks	TA0064	54°4·0'	0°27·9'W	X	101
Kilhendre Hall Fm	Shrops	SJ3538	52°56·4'	2°57·6'W	FM	126
Kilhenzie Castle	S Ayr	NS3008	55°20·5'	4°40·4'W	A	70,76
Kilhern	D & G	NX2064	54°56·0'	4°48·2'W	X	82
Kilhern Loch	D & G	NX2064	54°56·5'	4°48·2'W	W	82
Kilhern Moss	D & G	NX1962	54°55·4'	4°49·0'W	X	82

Kilhey Court (Hotel)	Wigan	SD5810	53°35·3'	2°37·7'W	X	108
Kilhill	Fife	NO4012	56°18·1'	2°57·7'W	X	59
Kilhilt	D & G	NX0656	54°51·9'	5°1·0'W	X	82
Kili Holm	Orkney	HY4732	59°10·6'	2°55·1'W	X	5,6
Kilirvan Cottage	Arg & Bt	NR6912	55°21·1'	5°38·2'W	X	68
Kilivington Hall	N Yks	SE4486	54°16·3'	1°19·0'W	X	99
Kilka Water	Shetld	HU3365	60°22·3'	1°23·6'W	W	2,3
Kilkeddan	Arg & Bt	NR7526	55°28·8'	5°33·2'W	X	68,69
Kilkenneth	Arg & Bt	NL9444	56°29·6'	6°57·9'W	T	46
Kilkenny	Glos	SP0018	51°51·9'	1°59·6'W	T	163
Kilkenny	I of M	SC3375	54°8·9'	4°33·0'W	X	95
Kilkenny	Somer	ST6035	51°7·0'	2°33·9'W	X	183
Kilkenny Bay	N Som	ST4577	51°29·6'	2°47·1'W	W	171,172
Kilkenny Cotts	Glos	SP1308	51°46·5'	1°48·3'W	X	163
Kilkenny Fm	Glos	SP1309	51°47·0'	1°48·3'W	FM	163
Kilkenny Fm	Oxon	SP2808	51°46·4'	1°35·3'W	FM	163
Kilkerran	Arg & Bt	NR7219	55°25·0'	5°35·7'W	T	68
Kilkerran	S Ayr	NS3003	55°17·8'	4°40·2'W	A	76
Kilkhampton	Corn	SS2511	50°52·6'	4°28·9'W	T	190
Kilkiehill	Aberd	NK0754	57°34·8'	1°52·5'W	X	30
Kilkiffeth	Pemb	SN0133	51°57·8'	4°53·4'W	X	145,157
Kilkington Manor	Heref	SO3745	52°6·2'	2°54·8'W	X	148,149
Kilkivan	Arg & Bt	NR6520	55°25·3'	5°42·4'W	X	68
Kilknockiebank	Pth & Kin	NO1515	56°19·4'	3°22·0'W	X	58
Killabrega	I of M	SC3790	54°17·0'	4°29·8'W	X	95
Killabury	Corn	SX3078	50°34·9'	4°23·7'W	A	201
Killadam Burn	D & G	NX3356	54°52·5'	4°35·7'W	W	82
Killagorden	Corn	SW8246	50°16·7'	5°3·2'W	X	204
Killail	Arg & Bt	NR9384	56°0·5'	5°18·8'W	X	55
Killallan	Renf	NS3868	55°52·9'	4°35·0'W	X	63
Killamarsh	Derby	SK4580	53°19·1'	1°19·1'W	T	111,120
Killandrist	Arg & Bt	NM8542	56°31·5'	5°29·3'W	X	49
Killane River	I of M	SC3596	54°20·2'	4°31·9'W	W	95
Killantrae	D & G	NX3246	54°47·1'	4°36·3'W	X	82
Killantrae Burn	D & G	NX3444	54°46·1'	4°34·4'W	W	82
Killantrae Burn	D & G	NX3548	54°48·2'	4°33·6'W	W	83
Killantringan	D & G	NW9957	54°52·3'	5°7·5'W	X	82
Killantringan	S Ayr	NX2681	55°5·8'	4°43·2'W	X	76
Killantringan Bay	D & G	NW9856	54°51·7'	5°8·4'W	W	82
Killarow	Arg & Bt	NR6628	55°29·6'	5°41·8'W	X	68
Killaser Burn	D & G	NX0846	54°46·6'	4°58·7'W	W	82
Killaser Castle	D & G	NX0945	54°46·1'	4°57·7'W	A	82
Killatown	Corn	SX1966	50°28·2'	4°32·7'W	X	201
Killatree	Devon	SS3203	50°48·4'	4°22·7'W	X	190
Killaworgey	Corn	SW9060	50°24·4'	4°57·0'W	T	200
Killay	Swan	SS6093	51°37·3'	4°1·0'W	T	159
Kill Barrow	Wilts	ST9948	51°14·1'	2°0·5'W	X	184
Kill Barrow (Long Barrow)	Wilts	ST9948	51°14·1'	2°0·5'W	A	184
Killbeg	Arg & Bt	NM6041	56°30·3'	5°53·6'W	X	49
Kill Brae	Scot Bord	NT3738	55°38·1'	2°59·6'W	X	73
Kill Burn	Scot Bord	NT2832	55°34·8'	3°8·1'W	W	73
Killchianaig	Arg & Bt	NR6486	56°0·8'	5°46·7'W	X	55,61
Killcrash	Lancs	SD4851	53°57·4'	2°47·1'W	X	102
Killcrow Hill	Monm	ST4990	51°36·6'	2°43·8'W	X	162,172
Killeal	D & G	NX3561	54°55·2'	4°34·0'W	X	83
Killean	Arg & Bt	NM7129	56°24·1'	5°42·2'W	X	49
Killean	Arg & Bt	NM8441	56°30·9'	5°30·2'W	X	49
Killean	Arg & Bt	NN0404	56°11·6'	5°9·1'W	X	56
Killean	Arg & Bt	NR6944	55°38·3'	5°39·8'W	T	62
Killean Burn	Arg & Bt	NR7044	55°38·4'	5°38·8'W	W	62
Killean Ho	Arg & Bt	NR6944	55°38·3'	5°39·8'W	X	62
Killearn	Stir	NS5285	56°2·4'	4°22·1'W	T	57
Killearn Br	Stir	NS5087	56°3·4'	4°24·1'W	X	57
Killearn Ho	Stir	NS5084	56°1·8'	4°24·0'W	X	57,64
Killeganogue Fm	Corn	SW9465	50°27·2'	4°53·7'W	FM	200
Killegray	N Eil	NF9783	57°44·3'	7°5·0'W	X	18
Killegray House	N Eil	NF9784	57°44·9'	7°5·1'W	X	18
Killegrews	Essex	TL6802	51°41·7'	0°26·2'E	A	167
Killegruer	Arg & Bt	NR6635	55°33·4'	5°42·2'W	X	68
Killellan	Arg & Bt	NS1069	55°52·9'	5°1·8'W	X	63
Killellan Lodge	Arg & Bt	NR6814	55°22·2'	5°39·2'W	X	68
Killellan Park	Arg & Bt	NR6815	55°22·7'	5°39·3'W	X	68
Killen	Highld	NH6758	57°35·8'	4°13·1'W	T	26
Killen Burn	Highld	NH6756	57°34·7'	4°13·0'W	W	26
Killeonan	Arg & Bt	NR6818	55°24·3'	5°39·4'W	X	68
Killeonan Burn	Arg & Bt	NR7017	55°23·8'	5°37·5'W	W	68
Killerby	Darl	NZ1919	54°34·2'	1°41·9'W	T	92
Killerby Beck	Durham	NZ1820	54°34·7'	1°42·9'W	W	92
Killerby Fm	N Yks	SE2595	54°21·2'	1°36·5'W	FM	99
Killerby Grange	N Yks	TA0682	54°13·6'	0°22·0'W	X	101
Killerby Hall	N Yks	SE2596	54°21·8'	1°36·5'W	X	99
Killerby Halls	N Yks	TA0682	54°13·6'	0°22·0'W	X	101
Killern	D & G	NX5858	54°54·0'	4°12·4'W	X	83
Killernie	Fife	NT0392	56°6·9'	3°33·2'W	X	58
Killerton Ho	Devon	SS9700	50°47·7'	3°27·3'W	X	192
Killerton Park	Devon	SS9700	50°47·7'	3°27·3'W	X	192
Killervan	Arg & Bt	NR6812	55°21·1'	5°39·1'W	X	68
Killgallioch	D & G	NX2271	55°0·4'	4°46·6'W	X	76
Killhogs Fm	Essex	TL7227	51°55·1'	0°30·5'E	FM	167
Killhope Burn	Durham	NY8143	54°47·1'	2°17·3'W	W	86,87
Killhope Cross	Durham	NY8043	54°47·1'	2°18·2'W	X	86,87
Killhope Law	Northum	NY8144	54°47·7'	2°17·3'W	H	86,87
Killhope Lead Mining Centre	Cumbr	NY8243	54°47·1'	2°16·4'W	X	86
Killhope Moor	Durham	NY8043	54°47·1'	2°18·2'W	X	86,87
Killhope Wheel (Mus)	Durham	NY8242	54°46·6'	2°16·4'W	X	86,87
Killichonan	Pth & Kin	NN5458	56°41·7'	4°22·6'W	T	42,51
Killichoran Burn	Pth & Kin	NN5660	56°42·8'	4°20·7'W	W	42
Killick's Bank	Kent	TQ5444	51°10·7'	0°12·6'E	X	188
Killiechassie	Pth & Kin	NN8650	56°37·9'	3°51·1'W	X	52
Killiechoilum	Highld	NH4713	57°11·2'	4°31·4'W	X	34
Killiechoinich	Arg & Bt	NM8827	56°23·5'	5°25·6'W	X	49
Killiechonate	Highld	NN2481	56°53·5'	4°52·9'W	X	34,41
Killiechonate Forest	Highld	NN2273	56°49·1'	4°54·5'W	X	41
Killiechronan	Arg & Bt	NM5441	56°30·1'	5°59·4'W	X	47,48
Killiecrankie	Pth & Kin	NN9162	56°44·5'	3°46·5'W	T	43
Killiecrankie Battle	Pth & Kin	NN9063	56°45·0'	3°47·5'W	A	43
Killiegowan	D & G	NX5857	54°53·5'	4°12·4'W	X	83
Killiegowan Wood	D & G	NX5857	54°53·5'	4°12·4'W	F	83
Killiehuntly	Highld	NN7998	57°3·7'	3°59·3'W	X	35
Killiemor	Arg & Bt	NM4839	56°28·8'	6°5·1'W	X	47,48
Killiemor Cott	Arg & Bt	NM5040	56°29·4'	6°3·2'W	X	47,48
Killiemore	Arg & Bt	NM5029	56°23·5'	6°2·6'W	X	48
Killiemore Ho	Arg & Bt	NM4928	56°22·9'	6°3·5'W	X	48
Killiemore Ho	D & G	NX3559	54°54·2'	4°34·0'W	X	83
Killievair Stone	Angus	NO5660	56°44·0'	2°42·7'W	A	44
Killiewarren	D & G	NX7993	55°13·2'	3°53·7'W	X	78
Killifreth Fm	Corn	SW7243	50°14·8'	5°11·5'W	FM	204
Killiganoon	Corn	SW8040	50°13·4'	5°4·7'W	X	204
Killigerran Head	Corn	SW8732	50°9·2'	4°58·5'W	X	204
Killigorrick	Corn	SX2261	50°25·5'	4°30·0'W	X	201
Killigrew Fm	Corn	SW8452	50°19·9'	5°1·7'W	FM	200,204
Killilan	Highld	NG9430	57°19·1'	5°24·8'W	T	25
Killilan Forest	Highld	NH0231	57°19·9'	5°16·9'W	X	25
Killimster	Highld	ND3156	58°29·5'	3°10·5'W	T	11,12
Killimster Mains	Highld	ND3254	58°28·4'	3°9·5'W	X	12
Killin	Highld	NC8507	58°2·5'	3°56·4'W	X	17
Killin	Stir	NN5732	56°27·8'	4°18·8'W	T	51
Killinallan	Arg & Bt	NR3171	55°51·7'	6°17·5'W	X	60,61
Killinallan Point	Arg & Bt	NR3072	55°52·2'	6°18·5'W	X	60
Killin Fm	Highld	NH3960	57°36·3'	4°41·2'W	FM	20
Killingbeck	Leeds	SE3334	53°48·3'	1°29·5'W	T	104
Killinghall	N Yks	SE2858	54°1·3'	1°33·9'W	T	104
Killinghall Moor	N Yks	SE2756	54°0·2'	1°34·9'W	X	104
Killingholme Marshes	N Lincs	TA1718	53°39·0'	0°13·4'W	X	113
Killinghurst	Surrey	SU9333	51°5·6'	0°39·9'W	X	186
Killings Knap Fm	Somer	ST6551	51°15·7'	2°29·7'W	FM	183
Killington	Cumbr	SD6188	54°17·4'	2°35·5'W	T	97
Killington	Devon	SS6646	51°12·1'	3°54·7'W	T	180
Killington Reservoir	Cumbr	SD5991	54°19·0'	2°37·4'W	W	97
Killington Service Area	Cumbr	SD5891	54°19·0'	2°38·3'W	X	97
Killingwoldgraves	E Yorks	TA0039	53°50·5'	0°28·4'W	X	106,107
Killingworth	N Tyne	NZ2771	55°2·2'	1°34·2'W	T	88
Killingworth Moor	N Tyne	NZ2870	55°1·7'	1°33·3'W	T	88
Killingworth Village	N Tyne	NZ2870	55°1·7'	1°33·3'W	T	88
Killin Lodge	Highld	NH5209	57°9·1'	4°26·3'W	X	35
Killinochonoch	Arg & Bt	NR8395	56°6·2'	5°28·9'W	T	55
Killin Rock	Highld	NC8605	58°1·4'	3°55·3'W	H	17
Killiow	Corn	SW8042	50°14·5'	5°4·8'W	X	204
Killiow Fm	Corn	SW9045	50°16·3'	4°56·5'W	FM	204
Killiserth	Corn	SW8551	50°19·4'	5°0·9'W	X	200,204
Killivose	Corn	SW6438	50°11·9'	5°18·0'W	T	203
Killivose	Corn	SW8049	50°18·2'	5°5·0'W	X	204
Killmade Burn	E Loth	NT6662	55°51·3'	2°32·1'W	W	67
Killmade Burn	E Loth	NT6662	55°51·3'	2°32·1'W	W	67
Killoch	E Ayr	NS4720	55°27·3'	4°24·7'W	X	70
Killoch	E Ayr	NS5131	55°33·3'	4°21·3'W	X	70
Killoch	E Renf	NS4858	55°47·7'	4°25·0'W	X	64
Killochan Castle	S Ayr	NS2200	55°16·0'	4°47·7'W	A	76
Killoch Burn	E Ayr	NS5031	55°33·2'	4°22·2'W	W	70
Killoch Burn	Pth & Kin	NO0602	56°12·3'	3°30·5'W	W	58
Killoch Colliery	E Ayr	NS4720	55°27·3'	4°24·7'W	X	70
Killochend	Inverc	NS2672	55°54·8'	4°46·6'W	X	63
Killochhead	E Ayr	NS5132	55°33·8'	4°21·3'W	X	70
Killochries	Inverc	NS3467	55°52·3'	4°38·8'W	X	63
Killochy	D & G	NX6476	55°3·8'	4°7·3'W	X	77
Killochyett	Scot Bord	NT4545	55°42·0'	2°52·1'W	T	73
Killock Fm	Corn	SS2309	50°51·4'	4°30·5'W	FM	190
Killocraw	Arg & Bt	NR6530	55°30·7'	5°42·9'W	X	68
Killoeter	Arg & Bt	NS3481	55°59·9'	4°39·3'W	H	63
Killowent	Powys	SO1580	52°24·9'	3°14·6'W	X	136
Killpallet	E Loth	NT6260	55°50·2'	2°36·0'W	X	67
Killpallet Heights	E Loth	NT6060	55°50·1'	2°37·9'W	H	67
Killumpha	D & G	NX1140	54°43·4'	4°55·7'W	X	82
Killunaig	Arg & Bt	NM4925	56°21·3'	6°3·3'W	X	48
Killundine	Highld	NM5849	56°34·5'	5°56·0'W	X	47,48
Killundine River	Highld	NM5850	56°35·0'	5°56·0'W	W	47
Killyleoch	D & G	NX8682	55°7·4'	3°46·8'W	X	78
Killyleoch Hill	D & G	NX8782	55°7·4'	3°45·9'W	H	78
Killylung	D & G	NX9581	55°7·0'	3°38·3'W	X	78
Killymingan	D & G	NX8567	54°59·3'	3°47·4'W	X	84
Killymingan Hill	D & G	NX8466	54°58·8'	3°48·3'W	H	84
Killyminshaw Hill	D & G	NX9896	55°15·1'	3°35·8'W	H	78
Killypole	Arg & Bt	NR6417	55°23·7'	5°43·2'W	X	68
Killypole Loch	Arg & Bt	NR6417	55°23·7'	5°43·2'W	W	68
Killyquharn	Aberd	NJ8962	57°39·1'	2°10·6'W	X	30
Killyvarder Rock	Corn	SX0852	50°20·4'	4°41·5'W	X	200,204
Killywhan	D & G	NX8869	55°0·4'	3°44·6'W	X	84
Kilmacfadzean	D & G	NX2067	54°58·2'	4°48·3'W	X	82
Kilmachalmack	Highld	NH5098	57°57·0'	4°31·6'W	X	20
Kilmachalmack Burn	Highld	NH4696	57°55·9'	4°35·6'W	W	20
Kilmacolm	Inverc	NS3669	55°53·4'	4°36·9'W	T	63
Kilmacolm High Dam	Inverc	NS3167	55°52·3'	4°41·6'W	W	63
Kilmaha	Arg & Bt	NM9408	56°13·5'	5°18·9'W	X	55
Kilmahew Fm	Arg & Bt	NS3578	55°58·3'	4°38·2'W	FM	63
Kilmahew Ho	Arg & Bt	NS3578	55°58·3'	4°38·2'W	X	63
Kilmaho	Arg & Bt	NR6824	55°27·5'	5°39·7'W	X	68
Kilmahog	Stir	NN6108	56°14·9'	4°14·2'W	T	57
Kilmahumaig	Arg & Bt	NR7893	56°5·0'	5°33·6'W	T	55
Kilmalieu	Highld	NM8955	56°38·6'	5°26·0'W	X	49
Kilmaluag	Arg & Bt	NR6937	55°34·6'	5°39·4'W	X	68
Kilmaluag	Highld	NG4273	57°40·6'	6°19·2'W	T	23
Kilmaluag Bay	Highld	NG4475	57°41·8'	6°17·3'W	W	23
Kilmaluag River	Highld	NG4372	57°40·1'	6°18·1'W	W	23
Kilmannan Reservoir	W Dunb	NS4978	55°58·5'	4°24·8'W	W	64
Kilmany	Fife	NO3821	56°22·9'	2°59·8'W	T	54,59
Kilmarie	Highld	NG5417	57°10·9'	6°3·8'W	T	32
Kilmarnock	E Ayr	NS4237	55°36·3'	4°30·1'W	T	70
Kilmarnock Hill	Arg & Bt	NS1073	55°55·0'	5°2·0'W	X	63
Kilmaron	Fife	NO3516	56°20·2'	3°2·6'W	X	59
Kilmaronaig	Arg & Bt	NM9334	56°27·4'	5°21·1'W	X	49
Kilmaron Castle	Fife	NO3516	56°20·2'	3°2·6'W	X	59
Kilmaron Den	Fife	NO3516	56°20·2'	3°2·6'W	X	59
Kilmaron Fm	Fife	NO3516	56°20·2'	3°2·6'W	FM	59
Kilmaron Hill	Fife	NO3516	56°20·2'	3°2·6'W	H	59
Kilmaronock Ho	W Dunb	NS4587	56°3·3'	4°28·9'W	X	57
Kilmarth	Corn	SX0952	50°20·5'	4°40·7'W	X	200,204
Kilmartin	Arg & Bt	NR8398	56°7·8'	5°29·1'W	T	55
Kilmartin Burn	Arg & Bt	NR8297	56°7·2'	5°30·0'W	W	55
Kilmartin Fm	Highld	NH4230	57°20·3'	4°37·0'W	FM	26
Kilmartin Ho	Highld	NH4330	57°20·3'	4°36·0'W	X	26
Kilmartin River	Highld	NG4865	57°36·5'	6°12·7'W	W	23
Kilmar Tor	Corn	SX2574	50°32·6'	4°27·8'W	H	201
Kilmashenachan	Arg & Bt	NR7107	55°18·5'	5°36·1'W	X	68
Kilmaurs	E Ayr	NS4041	55°38·4'	4°32·1'W	T	70
Kilmaurs Mains	N Ayr	NS3841	55°38·4'	4°34·0'W	X	70
Kilmaurs Place	E Ayr	NS4141	55°38·5'	4°31·1'W	A	70
Kilmein Hill	E Ayr	NS4511	55°22·4'	4°26·3'W	H	70
Kilmelford	Arg & Bt	NM8413	56°15·9'	5°28·8'W	T	55
Kilmeny	Arg & Bt	NR3965	55°48·7'	6°9·5'W	T	60,61
Kilmersdon	Somer	ST6952	51°16·2'	2°26·3'W	T	183
Kilmester's Fm	Oxon	SU2497	51°40·5'	1°38·8'W	FM	163
Kilmeston	Hants	SU5926	51°2·0'	1°9·1'W	T	185
Kilmichael	Arg & Bt	NR6922	55°26·5'	5°38·7'W	X	68
Kilmichael	Arg & Bt	NR9970	55°53·1'	5°12·4'W	X	62
Kilmichael	D & G	NX7562	54°56·5'	3°56·7'W	X	84
Kilmichael Beg	Arg & Bt	NR9593	56°5·4'	5°17·3'W	T	55
Kilmichael Glassary	Arg & Bt	NR8593	56°5·1'	5°26·9'W	T	55
Kilmichael Hill	Arg & Bt	NR7885	56°0·7'	5°33·2'W	H	55
Kilmichael Ho	N Ayr	NS0035	55°34·3'	5°9·9'W	X	69
Kilmichael of Inverlussa	Arg & Bt	NR7785	56°0·6'	5°34·2'W	T	55
Kilmington	Devon	SY2797	50°46·3'	3°1·7'W	T	193
Kilmington	Wilts	ST7736	51°7·6'	2°19·3'W	T	183
Kilmington Common	Wilts	ST7735	51°7·1'	2°19·3'W	T	183
Kilminning Castle	Fife	NO6308	56°16·0'	2°35·4'W	X	59
Kilminorth	Corn	SX2353	50°21·3'	4°28·9'W	X	201
Kilmluaig House	Arg & Bt	NR7269	55°51·9'	5°38·2'W	X	62
Kilmoluaig	Arg & Bt	NL9646	56°30·7'	6°56·1'W	T	46
Kilmond Wood	Durham	NZ0313	54°31·0'	1°56·8'W	F	92
Kilmonivaig	Highld	NN1783	56°54·4'	4°59·9'W	T	34,41
Kilmorack	Highld	NH4944	57°27·9'	4°30·6'W	T	26
Kilmoray	S Ayr	NX1478	55°4·0'	4°54·3'W	H	76
Kilmore	Arg & Bt	NM8825	56°22·4'	5°25·5'W	T	49
Kilmore	Highld	NG6507	57°5·9'	5°52·3'W	T	32
Kilmore	S Ayr	NS3813	55°23·3'	4°33·0'W	X	70
Kilmorich	Pth & Kin	NO0050	56°38·1'	3°37·4'W	X	52,53
Kilmorie	Stir	NS5385	56°2·4'	4°21·1'W	X	57
Kilmorie	Torbay	SX9363	50°27·7'	3°30·1'W	X	202
Kilmory	Arg & Bt	NR7044	55°38·4'	5°38·8'W	X	62
Kilmory	Arg & Bt	NR7075	55°55·0'	5°40·4'W	T	61,62
Kilmory	Arg & Bt	NR7183	55°59·4'	5°39·9'W	X	55
Kilmory	Highld	NG3603	57°2·8'	6°20·7'W	X	32,39
Kilmory	Highld	NM5270	56°45·6'	6°3·0'W	T	39,47
Kilmory	N Ayr	NR9621	55°26·7'	5°13·1'W	T	68,69
Kilmory Bay	Arg & Bt	NR6974	55°54·5'	5°41·3'W	W	61,62
Kilmory Burn	Arg & Bt	NR7075	55°55·0'	5°40·4'W	W	61,62
Kilmory Castle	Arg & Bt	NR8686	56°1·4'	5°25·6'W	X	55
Kilmory Glen	Highld	NG3602	57°2·3'	6°20·7'W	X	32,39
Kilmory Hill	Arg & Bt	NS0560	55°47·9'	5°6·2'W	H	63
Kilmory Lodge	Arg & Bt	NM7105	56°11·2'	5°41·0'W	X	55
Kilmory River	Highld	NG3602	57°2·3'	6°20·7'W	W	32,39
Kilmory Water	N Ayr	NR9723	55°27·8'	5°12·2'W	W	69
Kilmote	Highld	NC9711	58°4·8'	3°44·3'W	X	17
Kilmuir	Highld	NG2547	57°26·1'	6°34·5'W	T	23
Kilmuir	Highld	NG3870	57°38·9'	6°23·0'W	T	23
Kilmuir	Highld	NH6749	57°31·0'	4°12·8'W	T	26
Kilmuir	Highld	NH7573	57°44·0'	4°5·5'W	T	21
Kilmun	Arg & Bt	NM9214	56°16·6'	5°21·1'W	X	55
Kilmun	Arg & Bt	NM9714	56°16·8'	5°16·3'W	X	55
Kilmun	Arg & Bt	NN0712	56°15·9'	5°6·5'W	X	50,56
Kilmun	Arg & Bt	NS1781	55°59·5'	4°55·6'W	T	63
Kilmun Hill	Arg & Bt	NS1782	56°0·0'	4°55·6'W	H	56
Kilmux Fm	Fife	NO3605	56°14·2'	3°1·5'W	FM	59
Kilnair	D & G	NX6686	55°9·3'	4°5·8'W	X	77
Kilnair Hill	D & G	NX6687	55°9·8'	4°5·8'W	H	77
Kilnaish	Arg & Bt	NR7761	55°47·7'	5°33·0'W	X	62
Kilnaughton Bay	Arg & Bt	NR3445	55°37·8'	6°13·1'W	W	60
Kilnave	Arg & Bt	NR2871	55°51·6'	6°20·4'W	T	60
Kiln Bank	Cumbr	SD2787	54°16·7'	3°6·9'W	X	96,97
Kiln Burn	D & G	NS7708	55°21·3'	3°56·0'W	W	71,78
Kiln Burn	D & G	NS7713	55°24·0'	3°56·1'W	W	71,78
Kiln Burn	Scot Bord	NY5694	55°14·5'	2°41·1'W	W	80
Kilncadzow	S Lanak	NS8848	55°43·0'	3°46·5'W	T	72
Kilncroft	D & G	NX8575	55°3·6'	3°47·6'W	X	84
Kiln Down	Devon	SX8284	50°38·9'	3°39·8'W	X	191
Kilndown	Kent	TQ7035	51°5·6'	0°26·1'E	T	188
Kilndown Wood	Kent	TQ6935	51°5·6'	0°25·2'E	F	188
Kilnerfoot	Cumbr	SD5778	54°12·0'	2°39·1'W	X	97
Kilness	D & G	NX9479	55°5·9'	3°39·2'W	X	84
Kilneuair	Arg & Bt	NM8803	56°10·6'	5°24·5'W	X	55
Kiln Farm	Mil Key	SP8039	52°2·8'	0°49·6'W	FM	152
Kiln Fm	Herts	SP9208	51°46·0'	0°39·6'W	FM	165
Kiln Fm	Oldham	SD9603	53°31·7'	2°3·2'W	FM	109
Kiln Fm	Oxon	SP5702	51°43·1'	1°10·1'W	FM	164
Kiln Fm	Suff	TL8649	52°6·7'	0°43·4'E	FM	155
Kiln Fm	Suff	TL9669	52°17·3'	0°52·8'E	FM	155
Kiln Fm	Suff	TM0066	52°15·6'	0°56·2'E	FM	155
Kiln Fm	Suff	TM1075	52°20·2'	1°5·4'E	FM	144
Kiln Fm	Suff	TM1771	52°17·9'	1°11·4'E	FM	156
Kiln Fm	W Berks	SU5073	51°27·5'	1°16·4'W	FM	174
Kilnford	D & G	NX9375	55°3·7'	3°40·1'W	X	84
Kilnford	S Ayr	NS3535	55°35·1'	4°36·6'W	X	70
Kiln Gate	Cumbr	NY3442	54°46·4'	3°1·1'W	X	85
Kiln Green	Hants	SU6056	51°18·2'	1°8·0'W	X	175
Kiln Green	Heref	SO6019	51°52·3'	2°34·5'W	T	162
Kiln Green	Oldham	SE0007	53°33·8'	1°59·6'W	X	110
Kiln Green	Wok	SU8178	51°29·9'	0°49·6'W	T	175
Kiln Green	Wrex	SJ4942	52°58·6'	2°45·2'W	X	117
Kiln Grove	Suff	TL8962	52°13·6'	0°46·4'E	F	155
Kiln Head	Cumbr	SD5795	54°21·2'	2°39·3'W	X	97
Kilnhill	Aberd	NO7073	56°51·1'	2°29·1'W	X	45
Kilnhill	Angus	NO4154	56°40·7'	2°57·3'W	X	54
Kilnhill	Cumbr	NY2132	54°40·9'	3°13·1'W	T	89,90
Kiln Hill	Cumbr	NY6166	54°59·5'	2°36·1'W	X	86
Kiln Hill	D & G	NX4161	54°55·4'	4°28·4'W	X	83
Kilnhill	Highld	NH9257	57°35·7'	3°47·9'W	X	27
Kiln Hill	Lancs	SD8938	53°50·5'	2°9·6'W	X	103
Kilnhill	S Lanak	NS8539	55°38·1'	3°49·2'W	X	71,72
Kilnhillock	Aberd	NJ5365	57°40·6'	2°46·8'W	X	57
Kiln Ho	E Yorks	TA3031	53°45·8'	0°1·3'W	X	107

Kilnholme	Cumbr	NY4377	55°5·3'	2°53·2'W	X	85
Kilnhouse Fm	Kent	TQ5048	51°12·9'	0°9·3'E	FM	188
Kilnhurst	Roth	SK4697	53°28·3'	1°18·0'W	T	111
Kilninian	Arg & Bt	NM3945	56°31·7'	6°14·2'W	T	47,48
Kilninver	Arg & Bt	NM8221	56°20·1'	5°31·2'W	T	49
Kilnknowe	D & G	NY2371	55°1·9'	3°11·9'W	X	85
Kilnmaichlie	Moray	NJ1832	57°22·5'	3°21·4'W	X	36
Kilnmark	D & G	NX7696	55°14·8'	3°56·6'W	X	78
Kilnmire	Cumbr	NY7103	54°25·5'	2°26·4'W	X	91
Kilnotrie	D & G	NX7567	54°59·2'	3°56·8'W	X	84
Kiln Pit Hill	Northum	NZ0355	54°53·6'	1°56·8'W	H	87
Kilnpothall	S Lanak	NS9651	55°44·7'	3°39·0'W	X	65,72
Kilnpotlees	S Lanak	NS9329	55°32·8'	3°41·3'W	X	71,72
Kiln Rig	Scot Bord	NY4790	55°12·3'	2°49·5'W	X	79
Kilnsea	E Yorks	TA4115	53°37·0'	0°8·3'E	T	113
Kilnsea Clays	E Yorks	TA4014	53°36·5'	0°7·4'E	X	113
Kilnsea Grange	E Yorks	TA4016	53°37·5'	0°7·4'E	X	113
Kilnsea Warren	E Yorks	TA4115	53°37·0'	0°8·3'E	X	113
Kilnsey	N Yks	SD9767	54°6·2'	2°2·3'W	T	98
Kilnsey Crag	N Yks	SD9767	54°6·2'	2°2·3'W	X	98
Kilnsey Ho	N Yks	NZ2403	54°25·6'	1°37·4'W	X	93
Kilnsey Moor	N Yks	SD9566	54°5·6'	2°4·2'W	X	98
Kilnsey Park	N Yks	SD9767	54°6·2'	2°2·3'W	X	98
Kilnsey Wood	N Yks	SD9766	54°5·6'	2°2·3'W	F	98
Kilns of Brin-Novan	Orkney	HY3834	59°11·6'	3°4·6'W	X	6
Kilns, The	Scot Bord	NT6916	55°26·5'	2°29·0'W	X	80
Kilnstones	Cumbr	NY5002	54°24·9'	2°45·8'W	X	90
Kilnstown	Cumbr	NY5374	55°3·7'	2°43·7'W	X	86
Kiln, The	D & G	NS7708	55°21·3'	3°56·0'W	X	71,78
Kiln, The	Harrow	TQ1492	51°37·1'	0°20·8'W	X	176
Kiln, The	Orkney	HY5239	59°14·4'	2°50·0'W	X	5
Kiln, The	Orkney	ND3690	58°47·8'	3°6·0'W	X	7
Kiln, The	Shetld	HU3679	60°29·9'	1°20·2'W	X	2,3
Kiln Trees Fm	Lancs	SD4848	53°55·8'	2°47·1'W	FM	102
Kilnwick	E Yorks	SE9949	53°55·9'	0°29·1'W	T	106
Kilnwick New Cut	E Yorks	TA0149	53°55·9'	0°27·3'W	W	106,107
Kilnwick New Fm	E Yorks	SE9850	53°56·4'	0°30·0'W	FM	106
Kilnwick Percy	E Yorks	SE8250	53°56·6'	0°44·6'W	T	106
Kilnwick Percy Wood	E Yorks	SE8248	53°55·5'	0°44·7'W	F	106
Kiln Wood	Corn	SX2254	50°21·8'	4°29·8'W	F	201
Kiln Wood	Suff	TL9572	52°18·9'	0°52·1'E	F	144,155
Kilnwood	W Susx	TQ2235	51°6·3'	0°15·1'W	X	187
Kilnwood End	W Susx	TQ2335	51°6·3'	0°14·2'W	X	187
Kiloran	Arg & Bt	NR3996	56°5·4'	6°11·3'W	T	61
Kiloran	E Loth	NT4268	55°54·4'	2°55·2'W	X	66
Kiloran Bay	Arg & Bt	NR3998	56°6·5'	6°11·4'W	W	61
Kilpaison Burrows	Pemb	SM8900	51°39·8'	5°2·7'W	X	157,158
Kilpale	Monm	ST4692	51°37·7'	2°46·4'W	X	171,172
Kilpatrick	Arg & Bt	NM7334	56°26·9'	5°40·6'W	X	49
Kilpatrick	N Ayr	NR9027	55°29·8'	5°19·0'W	T	68,69
Kilpatrick	S Ayr	NX2190	55°10·6'	4°48·2'W	X	76
Kilpatrick Braes	W Dunb	NS4574	55°56·3'	4°28·5'W	X	64
Kilpatrick Hills	W Dunb	NS4776	55°57·4'	4°26·6'W	H	64
Kilpatrick Point	N Ayr	NR8926	55°29·2'	5°19·9'W	X	68,69
Kilpeck	Heref	SO4430	51°58·2'	2°48·5'W	T	149,161
Kilpeck Castle	Heref	SO4430	51°58·2'	2°48·5'W	A	149,161
Kilphedder	N Eil	NF7274	57°38·5'	7°29·4'W	X	18
Kilpheder	N Eil	NF7419	57°9·0'	7°23·0'W	T	31
Kilphedir	Highld	NC9818	58°8·6'	3°43·5'W	T	17
Kilpin	E Yorks	SE7726	53°43·7'	0°49·6'W	T	105,106
Kilpin Pike	E Yorks	SE7626	53°43·7'	0°50·5'W	T	105,106
Kilpunt	W Loth	NT0971	55°55·7'	3°26·9'W	X	65
Kilquhanity	D & G	NX7670	55°0·8'	3°55·9'W	X	84
Kilquhockadale	D & G	NX2967	54°58·4'	4°39·9'W	X	82
Kilquhockadale Flow	D & G	NX2769	54°59·4'	4°41·8'W	X	82
Kilranny	S Ayr	NX1593	55°12·1'	4°54·0'W	X	76
Kilravock Castle	Highld	NH8149	57°31·2'	3°58·7'W	A	27
Kilreague Fm	Heref	SO5121	51°53·4'	2°42·3'W	FM	162
Kilrenny	Fife	NO5704	56°13·9'	2°41·2'W	T	59
Kilrenny Common	Fife	NO5705	56°14·4'	2°41·2'W	X	59
Kilrenny Mill	Fife	NO5804	56°13·9'	2°40·2'W	X	59
Kilrenzie	S Ayr	NX1783	55°6·7'	4°51·7'W	X	76
Kilrie	Fife	NT2489	56°5·5'	3°12·8'W	X	66
Kilrie Fm	Fife	NT2489	56°5·5'	3°12·8'W	FM	66
Kilroom	Pemb	SM8605	51°42·4'	5°5·5'W	X	157
Kilroy	D & G	NX9183	55°8·0'	3°42·2'W	X	78
Kilrubie Hill	Scot Bord	NT2146	55°42·3'	3°15·0'W	H	73
Kilry Lodge	Angus	NO2355	56°41·1'	3°15·0'W	X	53
Kilsall Hall	Shrops	SJ7906	52°39·3'	2°18·2'W	X	127
Kilsby	Northnts	SP5671	52°20·3'	1°10·3'W	T	140
Kilsby	Powys	SN8648	52°7·4'	3°39·5'W	X	147
Kilsby Grange	Northnts	SP5770	52°19·8'	1°9·4'W	X	140
Kilsham Fm	W Susx	SU9619	50°58·0'	0°37·6'W	FM	197
Kilslevan	Arg & Bt	NR4167	55°49·5'	6°7·7'W	X	60,61
Kilspindie	E Loth	NT4580	56°0·8'	2°52·5'W	X	66
Kilspindie	Pth & Kin	NO2125	56°24·9'	3°16·4'W	T	53,58
Kilstay	D & G	NX1238	54°42·4'	4°54·7'W	W	82
Kilsture Forest	D & G	NX4360	54°54·9'	4°26·5'W	F	83
Kilsyth	N Lanak	NS7178	55°58·9'	4°3·6'W	T	64
Kilsyth Hills	N Lanak	NS6980	56°0·0'	4°5·6'W	H	64
Kiltarie Fm	N Lanak	NS7964	55°51·5'	3°55·6'W	FM	64
Kiltarlity	Highld	NH5041	57°26·3'	4°29·5'W	T	26
Kiltarlity Cotts	Highld	NH4943	57°27·4'	4°30·6'W	X	26
Kilter	Corn	SW7819	50°2·0'	5°5·6'W	X	204
Kiltersan	D & G	NX2961	54°55·1'	4°39·7'W	X	82
Kilt Fm	Falk	NS7976	55°58·0'	3°55·9'W	FM	64
Kilthorpe Grange	Rut	SK9803	52°37·2'	0°32·7'W	X	141
Kilton	Notts	SK5979	53°18·5'	1°6·5'W	T	120
Kilton	Red & Cl	NZ7018	54°33·4'	0°54·6'W	T	94
Kilton	Somer	ST1643	51°11·0'	3°11·7'W	T	181
Kilton Beck	Red & Cl	NZ7017	54°32·8'	0°54·6'W	X	94
Kilton Ho	N Yks	NZ4501	54°24·4'	1°18·0'W	X	93
Kilton Thorpe	Red & Cl	NZ6917	54°32·9'	0°55·6'W	T	94
Kilt Rock	Highld	NG5066	57°37·1'	6°10·7'W	X	23,24
Kiltryknock	Aberd	NJ6656	57°35·8'	2°33·7'W	X	29
Kiltyrie	Pth & Kin	NN6236	56°30·0'	4°14·1'W	X	51
Kilvaree	Arg & Bt	NM9231	56°25·8'	5°22·0'W	X	49
Kilvaxter	Highld	NG3869	57°38·4'	6°22·9'W	T	23
Kilve	Somer	ST1443	51°11·0'	3°13·4'W	T	181
Kilve Court	Somer	ST1442	51°10·5'	3°13·4'W	X	181

Kilverstone Belt	Norf	TL9185	52°26·0'	0°49·0'E	F	144
Kilverstone Hall	Norf	TL8984	52°25·5'	0°47·2'E	X	144
Kilverstone Heath	Norf	TL9087	52°27·1'	0°48·2'E	X	144
Kilvey Hill	Swan	SS6794	51°38·0'	3°54·9'W	H	159
Kilvington	Notts	SK8042	52°58·4'	0°48·1'W	T	130
Kilvrough Fm	Swan	SS5689	51°35·1'	4°4·3'W	FM	159
Kilvrough Manor	Swan	SS5689	51°35·1'	4°4·3'W	X	159
Kilwhannel	S Ayr	NX1181	55°5·5'	4°57·3'W	X	76
Kilwhinleck	Arg & Bt	NS0562	55°49·0'	5°6·3'W	X	63
Kilwhipnach	Arg & Bt	NR6716	55°23·2'	5°40·3'W	X	68
Kilwick Wood	Mil Key	SP8653	52°10·3'	0°44·1'W	F	152
Kilwinning	N Ayr	NS3043	55°39·3'	4°41·7'W	T	63,70
Kilworth Sticks Fm	Leic	SP6084	52°27·3'	1°6·6'W	FM	140
Kilworthy	Devon	SX4876	50°34·1'	4°8·4'W	X	191,201
Kimber Court Fm	Derby	SK2382	53°20·3'	1°38·9'W	FM	110
Kimberley	Norf	TG0704	52°35·9'	1°3·8'E	T	144
Kimberley	Notts	SK4944	52°59·7'	1°15·8'W	T	129
Kimberley Hall Fm	Warw	SP2695	52°33·4'	1°36·6'W	FM	140
Kimberley Ho	Norf	TG0904	52°35·8'	1°5·6'E	X	144
Kimberley Home Fm	Norf	TG0904	52°35·8'	1°5·6'E	FM	144
Kimberley Park	Norf	TG0804	52°35·9'	1°4·7'E	X	144
Kimberworth	Roth	SK4093	53°26·2'	1°23·5'W	T	111
Kimberworth Park	Roth	SK4094	53°26·7'	1°23·5'W	T	111
Kimbland Cross	Devon	SS6634	51°5·6'	3°54·4'W	X	180
Kimbland Fm	Devon	SS6634	51°5·6'	3°54·4'W	FM	180
Kimble Fm	Bucks	SU7589	51°35·9'	0°54·6'W	FM	175
Kimblesworth	Durham	NZ2547	54°49·3'	1°36·2'W	T	88
Kimblesworth Grange	Durham	NZ2546	54°48·7'	1°36·2'W	X	88
Kimble Wick	Bucks	SP8007	51°45·6'	0°50·1'W	T	165
Kimblewick Fm	Bucks	SP8107	51°45·6'	0°49·2'W	FM	165
Kimbolton	Cambs	TL0967	52°17·6'	0°23·7'W	T	153
Kimbolton	Heref	SO5261	52°14·9'	2°41·8'W	T	137,138,149
Kimbolton Court Fm	Heref	SO5362	52°15·5'	2°40·9'W	FM	137,138,149
Kimbolton Park	Cambs	TL0967	52°17·6'	0°23·7'W	X	153
Kimbridge	Hants	SU3325	51°1·6'	1°31·4'W	T	185
Kimcote	Leic	SP5886	52°28·4'	1°8·4'W	T	140
Kimkerrick	D & G	NX9858	54°54·6'	3°35·0'W	X	84
Kimleymoor	Swan	SS4387	51°33·8'	4°15·5'W	X	159
Kimmeragh Fm	I of M	NX4400	54°22·5'	4°23·7'W	FM	95
Kimmer Crags	Northum	NU1117	55°27·1'	1°49·1'W	X	81
Kimmer Fm	Hants	SU3956	51°18·3'	1°26·0'W	FM	174
Kimmerghame Heugh	Scot Bord	NT8251	55°45·4'	2°16·8'W	X	67,74
Kimmerghame House	Scot Bord	NT8151	55°45·4'	2°17·7'W	X	67,74
Kimmerghame Mains	Scot Bord	NT8150	55°44·8'	2°17·7'W	X	67,74
Kimmeridge	Dorset	SY9179	50°36·9'	2°7·3'W	T	195
Kimmeridge Bay	Dorset	SY9078	50°36·3'	2°8·1'W	W	195
Kimmeridge Ledges	Dorset	SY9177	50°35·8'	2°7·2'W	X	195
Kimmer Lough	Northum	NU1217	55°27·1'	1°48·2'W	W	81
Kimmerston	Northum	NT9535	55°36·8'	2°4·3'W	T	74,75
Kimpton	Hants	SU2846	51°13·0'	1°35·6'W	T	184
Kimpton	Herts	TL1718	51°51·1'	0°17·7'W	T	166
Kimpton Down Fm	Hants	SU2647	51°13·5'	1°37·3'W	FM	184
Kimpton Grange	Herts	TL1618	51°51·1'	0°18·5'W	X	166
Kimpton Hall Fm	Herts	TL1717	51°50·6'	0°17·7'W	FM	166
Kimpton Mill	Herts	TL1918	51°51·1'	0°15·9'W	X	166
Kimpton Wood	Hants	SU2647	51°13·5'	1°37·3'W	F	184
Kimsbury Ho	Glos	SO8612	51°48·6'	2°11·8'W	X	162
Kimworthy	Devon	SS3112	50°53·2'	4°23·8'W	T	190
Kinakyle	Highld	NH8811	57°10·8'	3°50·7'W	X	35,36
Kinaldie	Aberd	NJ4205	57°8·2'	2°57·0'W	X	37
Kinaldie	Aberd	NJ8315	57°13·8'	2°16·4'W	X	38
Kinaldie	Angus	NO6646	56°36·5'	2°32·8'W	X	54
Kinaldy	Fife	NO5110	56°17·1'	2°47·0'W	X	59
Kinaldy	Pth & Kin	NN7764	56°45·3'	4°0·3'W	X	42
Kinaldy Burn	Fife	NO5110	56°17·1'	2°47·0'W	W	59
Kinalty	Angus	NO3551	56°39·0'	3°3·2'W	X	54
Kinalty	Angus	NO3960	56°43·9'	2°59·4'W	X	44
Kinalty Haughs	Angus	NO3649	56°38·0'	3°2·1'W	X	54
Kinardochy	Moray	NJ1426	57°19·2'	3°25·2'W	X	36
Kinbate	Aberd	NJ7353	57°34·2'	2°26·6'W	X	29
Kinbattoch	Aberd	NJ4212	57°12·0'	2°57·1'W	X	37
Kinbeachie	Highld	NH6362	57°37·9'	4°17·2'W	T	21
Kinbeam Hill	Aberd	NJ8260	57°38·0'	2°17·6'W	H	29,30
Kinblethmont	Angus	NO6347	56°37·1'	2°35·7'W	X	54
Kinblethmont	Angus	NO6446	56°36·5'	2°34·7'W	A	54
Kinbog	Aberd	NJ9962	57°39·1'	2°0·5'W	X	30
Kinbrace	Highld	NC8631	58°15·4'	3°56·1'W	T	17
Kinbrace Burn	Highld	NC8929	58°14·4'	3°53·0'W	W	17
Kinbrace Fm	Highld	NC8728	58°13·8'	3°55·0'W	FM	17
Kinbrace Hill	Highld	NC8829	58°14·4'	3°54·0'W	H	17
Kinbreack	Highld	NN0096	57°1·0'	5°17·2'W	X	33
Kinbroon	Aberd	NJ7135	57°24·5'	2°28·5'W	X	29
Kinbuck	Stir	NN7904	56°13·0'	3°56·6'W	T	57
Kinburn	Pth & Kin	NN8407	56°14·7'	3°51·9'W	X	58
Kincaidston	S Ayr	NS3519	55°26·5'	4°36·1'W	T	70
Kincairney Ho	Pth & Kin	NO0844	56°35·0'	3°29·4'W	X	52,53
Kincaldrum Hill	Angus	NO4244	56°35·3'	2°56·2'W	X	54
Kincaldrum Ho	Angus	NO4344	56°35·3'	2°55·2'W	X	54
Kincaple	Fife	NO4618	56°21·3'	2°52·0'W	T	59
Kincardine	Aberd	NJ6000	57°5·6'	2°39·2'W	X	37
Kincardine	Fife	NS9387	56°4·1'	3°42·7'W	T	65
Kincardine	Highld	NH6089	57°52·4'	4°21·2'W	T	21
Kincardine	Pth & Kin	NN9411	56°17·0'	3°42·3'W	X	58
Kincardine Castle	Aberd	NO6775	56°52·2'	2°32·0'W	A	45
Kincardine Castle	Pth & Kin	NN9411	56°17·0'	3°42·3'W	X	58
Kincardine Fm	Pth & Kin	NN8721	56°22·3'	3°49·3'W	FM	52,58
Kincardine O'Neil	Aberd	NO5899	57°5·1'	2°41·1'W	T	37,44
Kincham Wood	Scot Bord	NT8341	55°40·0'	2°15·8'W	F	74
Kinchie Burn	E Loth	NT4366	55°53·3'	2°54·2'W	W	66
Kinchley Hill	Leic	SK5613	52°42·9'	1°9·9'W	X	129
Kinchurdy	Highld	NH9315	57°13·1'	3°45·9'W	X	36
Kinchyle	Highld	NH6237	57°24·4'	4°17·4'W	X	26
Kinchyle	Highld	NH8552	57°32·9'	3°54·8'W	X	27
Kinclaven	Pth & Kin	NO1538	56°31·8'	3°22·5'W	X	53
Kinclaven Fm	Pth & Kin	NO1537	56°31·3'	3°22·4'W	FM	53
Kinclune	Aberd	NJ4513	57°12·5'	2°54·2'W	X	37
Kinclune	Angus	NO3155	56°41·2'	3°7·1'W	X	53
Kinclune Hill	Angus	NO3156	56°41·7'	3°7·2'W	H	53
Kincluny	Aberd	NO8097	57°4·1'	2°19·3'W	T	38,45
Kincorth	C of Aber	NJ9303	57°7·3'	2°6·5'W	T	38

Kincorth Ho	Moray	NJ0161	57°37·9'	3°39·0'W	X	27
Kincraig	Aberd	NJ9624	57°18·7'	2°3·5'W	X	38
Kincraig	Angus	NO6258	56°43·0'	2°36·8'W	X	54
Kincraig	Fife	NO4600	56°11·6'	2°51·8'W	X	59
Kincraig	Highld	NH8305	57°7·5'	3°55·5'W	T	35
Kincraig	Scot Bord	NT6941	55°39·9'	2°29·1'W	X	74
Kincraig Ho	Highld	NH6970	57°42·3'	4°11·4'W	X	21
Kincraig Ho	Highld	NH8206	57°8·0'	3°56·5'W	X	35
Kincraigie	Aberd	NJ5604	57°7·7'	2°43·2'W	X	37
Kincraigie	Aberd	NJ6013	57°12·6'	2°39·3'W	X	37
Kincraigie	Fife	NO1910	56°16·8'	3°18·1'W	X	58
Kincraigie	Pth & Kin	NN8867	56°47·1'	3°49·5'W	X	43
Kincraigie	Pth & Kin	NN9849	56°37·6'	3°39·3'W	X	52,53
Kincraigie Law	Fife	NO1911	56°17·3'	3°18·1'W	X	58
Kincraig Point	Fife	NT4699	56°11·1'	2°51·8'W	X	59
Kincreich	Angus	NO4344	56°35·3'	2°55·2'W	X	54
Kincreich Mill	Angus	NO4444	56°35·3'	2°54·3'W	X	54
Kincurdy Ho	Highld	NH7358	57°35·9'	4°7·0'W	X	27
Kindallachan	Pth & Kin	NN9949	56°37·6'	3°38·3'W	T	52,53
Kindar Ho	D & G	NX9665	54°58·4'	3°37·1'W	X	84
Kindeace Ho	Highld	NH7273	57°44·0'	4°8·5'W	X	21
Kinder Bank	Derby	SK0487	53°23·0'	1°56·0'W	X	110
Kinder Downfall	Derby	SK0888	53°23·6'	1°52·4'W	X	110
Kinder Intake	Oldham	SE0103	53°31·7'	1°58·7'W	X	110
Kinder Low	Derby	SK0787	53°23·0'	1°53·3'W	X	110
Kinderlow End	Derby	SK0686	53°22·5'	1°54·2'W	X	110
Kinder Resr	Derby	SK0588	53°23·6'	1°55·1'W	W	110
Kinder Scout	Derby	SK0888	53°23·6'	1°52·4'W	H	110
Kinderton Hall	Ches	SJ7067	53°12·2'	2°26·5'W	X	118
Kinderton Lodge	Ches	SJ7266	53°11·7'	2°24·7'W	X	118
Kindie Burn	Aberd	NJ4116	57°14·1'	2°58·2'W	W	37
Kindle	Northum	NY6856	54°54·1'	2°29·5'W	X	86,87
Kindrochet	Pth & Kin	NN7223	56°23·2'	4°3·9'W	X	51,52
Kindrochet Lodge	Pth & Kin	NN8065	56°45·9'	3°57·3'W	X	43
Kindrochid	Arg & Bt	NR2368	55°49·8'	6°25·0'W	X	60
Kindrogan	Pth & Kin	NO0562	56°44·7'	3°32·7'W	X	43
Kindrogan Hill	Pth & Kin	NO0462	56°44·6'	3°33·7'W	H	43
Kindrogan Wood	Pth & Kin	NO0461	56°44·1'	3°33·7'W	F	43
Kindrought	Aberd	NJ6064	57°40·1'	2°39·8'W	X	29
Kindrought	Aberd	NJ9753	57°34·3'	2°2·5'W	X	30
Kindrummond	Highld	NH5932	57°21·7'	4°20·2'W	X	26
Kindrumpark	Pth & Kin	NN9730	56°27·3'	3°39·8'W	X	52,53
Kindy Burn	Moray	NJ3923	57°17·9'	3°0·3'W	W	37
Kinellan Fm	Highld	NH4757	57°34·9'	4°33·1'W	FM	26
Kinellan Lodge	Highld	NH4757	57°34·9'	4°33·1'W	X	26
Kinellar	Aberd	NJ8112	57°12·2'	2°18·4'W	X	38
Kinellar Ho	Aberd	NJ8112	57°12·2'	2°18·4'W	X	38
Kine Moor	Barns	SE2704	53°32·2'	1°35·1'W	X	110
Kinerarach	Arg & Bt	NR6653	55°43·1'	5°43·1'W	X	62
Kinermony	Moray	NJ2541	57°27·4'	3°14·5'W	X	28
Kinerras	Highld	NH4740	57°25·7'	4°32·4'W	X	26
Kineton	Glos	SP0926	51°56·2'	1°51·8'W	T	163
Kineton	Warw	SP3351	52°9·6'	1°30·7'W	T	151
Kineton Grange Fm	Warw	SP3351	52°9·6'	1°30·7'W	FM	151
Kineton Green	Sol	SP1281	52°25·8'	1°49·0'W	T	139
Kineton Hill	Glos	SP1226	51°56·2'	1°49·1'W	X	163
Kinetonhill Fm	Glos	SP1227	51°56·7'	1°49·1'W	FM	163
Kinfauns	Pth & Kin	NO1622	56°23·2'	3°21·2'W	T	53,58
Kinfauns Castle	Pth & Kin	NO1522	56°23·2'	3°22·2'W	X	53,58
Kingairloch	Highld	NM8452	56°36·9'	5°30·8'W	T	49
Kingairloch	Highld	NM8452	56°36·9'	5°30·8'W	X	49
Kingairloch Ho	Highld	NM8353	56°37·4'	5°31·8'W	X	49
Kingarth	Arg & Bt	NS0956	55°45·8'	5°2·2'W	T	63
Kingarth	Pth & Kin	NN7624	56°23·8'	4°0·1'W	X	51,52
King Arthur's Bed	Corn	SX2475	50°33·1'	4°28·7'W	X	201
King Arthur's Cave	Heref	SO5415	51°50·1'	2°39·7'W	A	162
King Arthur's Downs	Corn	SX1378	50°34·5'	4°38·1'W	X	200
King Arthur's Hall	Corn	SX1277	50°34·0'	4°38·9'W	A	200
Kingask	Fife	NO3816	56°20·2'	2°59·7'W	X	59
Kingask	Fife	NO5414	56°19·2'	2°44·2'W	X	59
Kingask Ho	Fife	NO3716	56°20·2'	3°0·7'W	X	59
Kingates	I of W	SZ5177	50°35·7'	1°16·4'W	T	196
King Bank Head	S Lanak	NT0530	55°33·5'	3°29·9'W	H	72
King Barrow	Dorset	SU0912	50°54·7'	1°51·9'W	X	195
King Barrow	Dorset	SZ0481	50°38·0'	1°56·2'W	A	195
King Barrow	Wilts	ST8944	51°11·9'	2°9·1'W	A	184
King Barrow (Tumulus)	Dorset	SU0912	50°54·7'	1°51·9'W	A	195
Kingbeare	Corn	SX2774	50°32·6'	4°26·1'W	T	201
Kingbridge Ford Br	Cumbr	NY5767	55°0·0'	2°39·9'W	X	86
Kingcausie	Aberd	NJ8600	57°5·7'	2°13·4'W	X	38
Kingcoed	Monm	SO4305	51°44·7'	2°49·1'W	T	161
Kingcomb	Glos	SP1440	52°3·7'	1°47·4'W	X	151
Kingcombe	Dorset	ST7400	50°48·2'	2°21·8'W	X	194
Kingcombe Cross Roads	Dorset	ST5500	50°48·1'	2°37·9'W	X	194
King Dick's Hole	Leic	SP3199	52°35·5'	1°32·1'W	X	140
Kingdom	Pth & Kin	NO2425	56°24·9'	3°13·5'W	X	53,59
Kingdon Gardens	Devon	SS5834	51°5·5'	4°1·3'W	X	180
King Donier's Stone	Corn	SX2368	50°29·3'	4°29·3'W	A	201
Kingdown	Bath & NE Somer	ST5264	51°22·6'	2°41·0'W	T	172,182
King Down	Dorset	ST9703	50°49·8'	2°2·2'W	X	195
King Down Fm	Dorset	ST9703	50°49·8'	2°2·2'W	FM	195
King Down Fm	Somer	ST5054	51°17·2'	2°42·6'W	FM	182,183
King Edward	Aberd	NJ7157	57°36·4'	2°28·7'W	T	29
King Edward 1 Mon	Cumbr	NY3260	54°56·1'	3°3·3'W	X	85
King Edwards Fm	Lincs	TF3811	52°41·0'	0°2·9'E	FM	131,142,143
King Edward's Place	Swin	SU2281	51°31·9'	1°40·6'W	X	174
King Edward V11 Hospital	W Susx	SU8724	51°0·8'	0°45·2'W	X	197
Kingencleugh Ho	E Ayr	NS5025	55°30·0'	4°22·1'W	X	70
Kingennie House	Angus	NO4735	56°30·5'	2°51·2'W	X	54
Kingerby	Lincs	TF0592	53°25·1'	0°24·8'W	T	112
Kingerby Beck	Lincs	TF0593	53°25·6'	0°24·8'W	W	112
Kingerby Wood	Lincs	TF0491	53°24·6'	0°25·7'W	F	112
Kingfield	Surrey	TQ0057	51°18·4'	0°33·5'W	T	186
Kingfield Ho	Cumbr	NY4577	55°5·3'	2°51·3'W	X	86
King Fm	Kent	TQ9336	51°5·7'	0°45·8'E	FM	189
Kingford	Devon	SS2806	50°49·9'	4°26·2'W	T	190
Kingford	Devon	SS6219	50°57·5'	3°57·5'W	T	180
Kingford Fm	Devon	SX5075	50°33·6'	4°6·7'W	FM	191,201
King George Dock	K upon H	TA1428	53°44·4'	0°15·9'W	X	107

King George's Reservoir	Enf	TQ3796	51°39.0'	0°0.8'W	W	166,177
King George V1 Reservoir	Surrey	TQ0473	51°27.0'	0°29.8'W	W	176
King George V Dock	Newham	TQ4280	51°30.3'	0°3.2'E	X	177
Kingham	Oxon	SP2523	51°54.5'	1°37.8'W	T	163
Kingham Hill Fm	Oxon	SP2726	51°56.1'	1°36.0'W	FM	163
Kingham Hill School	Oxon	SP2626	51°56.1'	1°36.9'W	X	163
Kinghams Fm	Hants	SU4259	51°19.9'	1°23.4'W	FM	174
Kingham Sta	Oxon	SP2522	51°54.0'	1°37.8'W	X	163
King Harry	Cumbr	NY5447	54°49.2'	2°42.5'W	X	86
King Harry Ferry V	Corn	SW8439	50°12.9'	5°1.3'W	X	204
King Harry's Plantn	Cumbr	NY5349	54°50.3'	2°43.5'W	F	86
Kinghay	Wilts	ST8929	51°3.8'	2°9.0'W	T	184
Kingheriot	Pemb	SM8126	51°53.6'	5°10.6'W	X	157
King Hill	Cumbr	NY5465	54°58.9'	2°42.7'W	X	86
Kingholm Quay	D & G	NX9773	55°2.7'	3°36.3'W	T	84
Kinghorn	Aberd	NJ8721	57°17.0'	2°12.5'W	X	38
Kinghorn	Fife	NT2686	56°3.9'	3°10.9'W	T	66
Kinghornie	Aberd	NO8372	56°50.6'	2°16.3'W	X	45
Kinghorn Loch	Fife	NT2587	56°4.5'	3°11.9'W	W	66
Kinghorn Ness	Fife	NT2786	56°3.9'	3°9.9'W	X	66
Kingie	Highld	NH0901	57°3.9'	5°8.6'W	X	33
Kingie	Highld	NH1001	57°3.9'	5°7.6'W	X	34
Kingie Lang	Orkney	HY2600	58°53.1'	3°16.5'W	H	6,7
Kingie Pool	Highld	NH1000	57°3.4'	5°7.5'W	W	34
Kingillie Ho	Highld	NH5545	57°28.6'	4°24.6'W	X	26
King John Fm	Lincs	TF4724	52°47.8'	0°11.2'E	FM	131
King John's Castle	Warw	SP3350	52°9.1'	1°30.7'W	A	151
King John's Hill	Hants	SU7537	51°7.9'	0°55.3'W	H	186
King John's Ho	Wilts	ST9417	50°57.4'	2°4.7'W	A	184
King John's Palace	Notts	SK6064	53°10.4'	1°5.7'W	A	120
Kingland	Shetld	HU3580	60°30.4'	1°21.3'W	X	1,2,3
Kinglass	Falk	NT0080	56°0.4'	3°35.8'W	X	65
Kinglasser	Aberd	NJ9963	57°39.7'	2°0.5'W	X	30
Kinglassie	Fife	NO5513	56°18.7'	2°43.2'W	X	59
Kinglassie	Fife	NT2398	56°10.4'	3°14.0'W	T	58
Kinglas Water	Arg & Bt	NN2309	56°14.7'	4°50.9'W	W	56
Kinglas Water	Arg & Bt	NN2511	56°15.8'	4°49.1'W	W	50,56
Kingledoors Burn	Scot Bord	NT0725	55°30.8'	3°27.9'W	W	72
Kingledores	Scot Bord	NT1028	55°32.5'	3°25.1'W	T	72
Kingle Rig	Scot Bord	NT0827	55°31.9'	3°27.0'W	X	72
Kingley	Warw	SP0854	52°11.3'	1°52.6'W	X	150
Kingley Vale (Nature Reserve)	W Susx	SU8210	50°53.2'	0°49.7'W	X	197
Kinglia	Shetld	HT9739	60°8.4'	2°2.7'W	X	4
King Lud's Entrenchments	Leic	SK8627	52°50.3'	0°43.0'W	A	130
King Manor Hill	Wilts	SU1829	51°3.8'	1°44.2'W	X	184
Kingman's Fm	Somer	ST7253	51°16.8'	2°23.7'W	FM	183
Kingmoor	Cumbr	NY1649	54°50.0'	3°18.0'W	X	85
Kingmoor Ho	Cumbr	NY3858	54°55.0'	2°57.6'W	X	85
King Oak	Wilts	SU2265	51°23.2'	1°40.6'W	X	174
Kingole	Corn	SX1556	50°22.7'	4°35.7'W	X	201
King o' Muirs	Clackm	NS8795	56°8.3'	3°48.7'W	X	58
Kingoodie	Pth & Kin	NO3329	56°27.2'	3°4.8'W	T	53,59
King Orry's Grave	I of M	SC4384	54°13.9'	4°24.1'W	X	95
King Orry's Grave (Chambered Cairn)	I of M	SC4384	54°13.9'	4°24.1'W	X	95
King & Queen Rocks	N Yks	TA1675	54°9.7'	0°13.0'W	X	101
Kingrigg	Cumbr	NY3753	54°52.3'	2°58.5'W	X	85
King Road	C of Bris	ST4878	51°30.1'	2°44.6'W	W	171,172
Kingrove Bottom	Dorset	SY6999	50°47.6'	2°26.0'W	X	194
Kingrove Common	S Glos	ST7381	51°31.9'	2°23.0'W	X	172
Kingrow Fm	Norf	TF9404	52°36.2'	0°52.3'E	FM	144
Kings	Gwyn	SH6816	52°43.8'	3°56.9'W	X	124
King's Acre	Heref	SO4741	52°4.1'	2°46.0'W	T	148,149,161
Kingsand	Corn	SX4350	50°20.0'	4°12.0'W	T	201
Kingsash	Bucks	SP8805	51°44.4'	0°43.1'W	T	165
King's Ash Cross	Torbay	SX8760	50°26.0'	3°35.1'W	X	202
Kings Bank	E Susx	TQ8523	50°58.8'	0°38.5'E	X	189,199
Kings Barn	W Susx	TQ2321	50°58.7'	0°14.5'W	X	198
Kings Barn Fm	Bucks	SU8185	51°33.7'	0°49.5'W	FM	175
King's Barn Fm	W Susx	TQ1615	50°55.6'	0°20.6'W	FM	198
Kings Barn Fm	W Susx	TQ1811	50°53.4'	0°18.9'W	FM	198
Kingsbarns	Fife	NO5912	56°18.2'	2°39.3'W	T	59
King's Barrow	Devon	SX7081	50°37.1'	3°49.9'W	A	191
Kings Barrow	Dorset	SY9285	50°40.4'	2°6.4'W	A	195
Kings Barrow, The	Dorset	SY9185	50°40.1'	2°7.3'W	X	195
Kings Beck	S Lanak	NT0330	55°33.5'	3°31.8'W	W	72
King's Beeches	Win & Maid	SU9366	51°23.4'	0°39.4'W	X	175
Kingsborough Fm	Kent	TQ9772	51°25.0'	0°50.4'E	FM	178
King's Bottom	Wilts	ST8343	51°11.4'	2°14.2'W	X	183
King's Br	Swan	SS5997	51°39.5'	4°1.9'W	X	159
Kings Brake Fm	Warw	SP2733	51°59.9'	1°36.0'W	FM	151
Kingsbridge	Angus	NO4355	56°41.3'	2°55.4'W	X	54
Kingsbridge	Devon	SX7344	50°17.2'	3°46.6'W	T	202
Kingsbridge	Somer	SS9837	51°7.6'	3°27.1'W	T	181
Kingsbridge Estuary	Devon	SX7441	50°15.6'	3°45.7'W	W	202
Kingsbridge Fm	Bucks	SP7028	51°57.0'	0°58.5'W	FM	165
Kingsbridge Fm	Bucks	SP8427	51°54.7'	0°46.3'W	FM	165
Kingsbridgefork Cross	Devon	SX7746	50°18.3'	3°43.3'W	X	202
King's Bromley	Staffs	SK1216	52°44.7'	1°48.9'W	T	128
King's Brompton Fm	Somer	SS9533	51°5.4'	3°29.6'W	FM	181
Kings Brompton Forest	Somer	SS9632	51°4.9'	3°28.7'W	F	181
King's Brook	Leic	SK5623	52°48.3'	1°9.8'W	W	129
Kingsburgh	Highld	NG3955	57°30.9'	6°21.0'W	T	23
King's Burn	Aberd	NJ7530	57°21.8'	2°24.5'W	W	29
Kings Burn	N Ayr	NS2859	55°47.9'	4°44.2'W	W	63
Kingsbury	Brent	TQ1988	51°34.9'	0°16.6'W	T	176
Kingsbury	Warw	SP2196	52°33.9'	1°41.0'W	T	139
Kingsbury Episcopi	Somer	ST4321	50°59.4'	2°48.3'W	T	193
Kingsbury Regis	Somer	ST6719	50°58.4'	2°27.8'W	T	183
Kingsbury Water Park	Warw	SP2096	52°33.9'	1°41.9'W	X	139
Kingsbury Wood	Warw	SP2397	52°34.5'	1°39.2'W	F	139
Kings Cairn	D & G	NX3785	55°8.2'	4°33.0'W	A	77
King's Caple	Heref	SO5628	51°57.2'	2°38.0'W	T	149
King Scar	Lancs	SD3050	53°56.7'	3°3.6'W	X	102
King's Castle	Somer	ST5645	51°12.4'	2°37.4'W	A	182,183
King's Cave	Highld	NH8371	57°43.1'	3°57.4'W	X	21
King's Cave	N Ayr	NR8830	55°31.3'	5°21.1'W	A	68,69
Kingscavil	W Loth	NT0376	55°58.3'	3°32.8'W	T	65
King's Chair	Ches	SJ5368	53°12.7'	2°41.8'W	X	117
King's Chair	Derby	SK2553	53°4.7'	1°37.2'W	X	119
Kings Chair	D & G	NX7973	55°2.5'	3°53.2'W	X	84
King Schaw's Grave	D & G	NY2593	55°13.8'	3°10.3'W	A	79
Kingsclere	Hants	SU5258	51°19.4'	1°14.8'W	T	174
Kingsclere Woodlands	Hants	SU5361	51°21.0'	1°13.9'W	T	174
King's Cleuch	Scot Bord	NT7008	55°22.2'	2°28.0'W	X	80
King's Cliffe	Northnts	TL0097	52°33.9'	0°31.1'W	T	141
King's Cliff Wood	Somer	ST2531	51°4.6'	3°3.9'W	F	182
King's Copse	Northnts	SP7344	52°5.6'	0°55.7'W	F	152
Kings Copse Inclosure	Hants	SU4201	50°48.6'	1°23.8'W	F	196
King's Corner	Derby	SK4039	52°57.0'	1°23.9'W	X	129
Kingscote	Glos	ST8196	51°40.0'	2°16.1'W	T	162
Kingscote	Wok	SU8370	51°25.6'	0°48.0'W	X	175
Kingscote Station	W Susx	TQ3635	51°6.1'	0°3.1'W	X	187
Kingscote Wood	Glos	ST8297	51°40.5'	2°15.2'W	F	162
Kingscott	Devon	SS5318	50°56.8'	4°5.2'W	T	180
King's Cott	Devon	SS5728	51°2.3'	4°2.0'W	X	180
King's Coughton	Warw	SP0858	52°13.4'	1°52.6'W	T	150
Kingscourt	Glos	SO8403	51°43.8'	2°13.5'W	T	162
King's Court Palace	Dorset	ST8126	51°2.2'	2°15.9'W	A	183
King's Court Wood	Dorset	ST8226	51°2.2'	2°15.0'W	F	183
King's Cr0ss Sta	Isling	TQ3083	51°32.1'	0°7.1'W	X	176,177
King's Crags	Northum	NY7971	55°2.2'	2°19.3'W	X	86,87
Kingscross	N Ayr	NS0428	55°30.6'	5°5.8'W	T	69
Kingscross Point	N Ayr	NS0528	55°30.7'	5°4.9'W	X	69
King's Cross Sta	Isling	TQ3083	51°32.1'	0°7.1'W	X	176,177
King's Crown	Aberd	NJ9645	57°30.0'	2°3.5'W	X	30
Kingsdale	Fife	NO3401	56°12.1'	3°3.4'W	X	59
Kingsdale	N Yks	SD6976	54°11.0'	2°28.1'W	X	98
King's Dale	Orkney	HY3711	58°59.2'	3°5.3'W	X	6
Kingsdale	Orkney	HY3711	58°59.2'	3°5.3'W	X	6
Kingsdale Beck	N Yks	SD6977	54°11.5'	2°28.1'W	W	98
Kingsdale Head	N Yks	SD7079	54°12.6'	2°27.2'W	X	98
King's Deer Park	Aberd	NO6477	56°53.2'	2°35.0'W	A	45
King's Delph	Cambs	TL2495	52°32.6'	0°9.9'W	X	142
King's Delph Gate Fm	Cambs	TL2294	52°32.0'	0°11.7'W	FM	142
Kingsden Fm	Kent	TQ8845	51°10.6'	0°41.8'E	FM	189
King's Dike	Cambs	TL2596	52°33.1'	0°9.0'W	W	142
Kingsditch	Glos	SO9324	51°55.1'	2°5.7'W	T	163
King's Dod	Northum	NY9694	55°14.7'	2°3.3'W	H	81
Kingsdon	Devon	SY2594	50°44.7'	3°3.4'W	T	192,193
Kingsdon	Somer	ST5126	51°2.1'	2°41.5'W	T	183
Kingsdon Hill	Somer	ST5126	51°2.1'	2°41.5'W	H	183
Kingsdon Manor School	Somer	ST5125	51°1.6'	2°41.5'W	X	183
Kingsdon Wood	Somer	ST5127	51°2.6'	2°41.6'W	F	183
Kingsdown	Kent	TQ9359	51°18.1'	0°46.5'E	T	178
Kingsdown	Kent	TR3748	51°11.1'	1°23.9'E	T	179
Kingsdown	Swin	SU1688	51°35.7'	1°45.7'W	T	173
Kingsdown	W Berks	SU3180	51°31.3'	1°32.8'W	X	174
Kingsdown	Wilts	ST8167	51°24.3'	2°16.0'W	T	173
Kingsdown Fm	E Susx	TQ6322	50°58.7'	0°19.7'E	FM	199
Kingsdown Fm	Kent	TQ5664	51°21.4'	0°14.8'E	FM	177,188
Kingsdown Ho	Kent	TQ5863	51°20.9'	0°16.5'E	X	177,188
Kingsdown Wood	Kent	TQ9158	51°17.6'	0°44.8'E	F	178
King's Dyke	Cambs	TL2496	52°33.1'	0°9.9'W	T	142
Kingseat	Fife	NT1290	56°5.9'	3°24.4'W	T	58
Kingseat	Pth & Kin	NO1454	56°40.4'	3°23.8'W	X	53
King Seat	Scot Bord	NT1153	55°46.0'	3°24.7'W	H	65,72
Kingseat Fm	Aberd	NJ9019	57°15.9'	2°9.5'W	FM	38
Kingseathill	Fife	NT1088	56°4.8'	3°26.3'W	T	65
King's End	Oxon	SP5822	51°53.8'	1°9.0'W	T	164
King's End	Worcs	SO8251	52°9.7'	2°15.4'W	T	150
Kingsett	Devon	SX5180	50°36.3'	4°6.0'W	T	191,201
Kingsett Down	Devon	SX5181	50°36.8'	4°6.0'W	X	191,201
Kingsey	Bucks	SP7406	51°45.1'	0°55.3'W	T	165
Kings Farm	Kent	TQ6572	51°25.6'	0°22.8'E	FM	177,178
King's Fene	Suff	TM3783	52°23.8'	1°29.4'E	X	156
Kingsferry Br	Kent	TQ9169	51°23.5'	0°45.1'E	X	178
Kingsfield	Heref	SO5249	52°8.5'	2°41.7'W	T	149
Kingsfield	Monm	SO4025	51°55.5'	2°52.0'W	X	161
Kingsfield	W Loth	NT0277	55°58.8'	3°33.8'W	X	65
King's Fleet	Suff	TM3037	51°59.4'	1°21.4'E	W	169
Kings Fm	Beds	TL0538	52°2.1'	0°27.8'W	FM	153
King's Fm	Cambs	TL6180	52°23.9'	0°22.4'E	FM	143
King's Fm	Dorset	SY5395	50°45.4'	2°39.6'W	FM	194
King's Fm	Essex	TL6617	51°49.8'	0°24.9'E	FM	167
Kings Fm	Essex	TL8634	51°58.6'	0°42.9'E	FM	155
Kings Fm	Essex	TL9328	51°55.2'	0°48.8'E	FM	168
Kings Fm	Essex	TL9503	51°41.7'	0°49.7'E	FM	168
King's Fm	Essex	TM2021	51°50.9'	1°12.1'E	FM	169
King's Fm	Glos	SO9304	51°44.3'	2°5.7'W	FM	163
King's Fm	Hants	SU2920	50°59.0'	1°34.8'W	FM	185
Kings Fm	Hants	SU6862	51°21.4'	1°1.0'W	FM	175,186
King's Fm	Hants	SZ2897	50°46.5'	1°35.8'W	FM	195
King's Fm	Kent	TQ7073	51°26.1'	0°27.1'E	FM	178
King's Fm	Norf	TM2697	52°31.7'	1°20.3'E	FM	134
King's Fm	Somer	SS8435	51°6.4'	3°39.0'W	FM	181
King's Fm	Somer	ST3439	51°9.0'	2°56.2'W	FM	182
King's Fm	Suff	TM1671	52°17.9'	1°10.5'E	FM	144,156
Kings Fm	Suff	TM1771	52°17.9'	1°11.4'E	FM	156
King's Fm	Suff	TM4468	52°15.6'	1°34.9'E	FM	156
King's Fm	W Berks	SU5467	51°24.2'	1°13.0'W	FM	174
King's Fm	W Susx	TQ3032	51°4.6'	0°8.3'W	FM	187
Kingsfold	Lancs	SD5326	53°43.9'	2°42.3'W	T	102
Kingsfold	Pemb	SR9799	51°39.4'	4°55.7'W	A	158
Kingsfold	W Susx	TQ1636	51°6.9'	0°20.2'W	T	187
Kingsfold	W Susx	TQ2416	50°56.0'	0°13.7'W	X	198
Kingsford	Aberd	NJ5614	57°13.1'	2°43.3'W	X	37
Kingsford	Aberd	NJ7244	57°29.4'	2°27.6'W	X	29
Kingsford	C of Aber	NJ8506	57°8.9'	2°14.4'W	X	38
Kingsford	Devon	ST0408	50°52.0'	3°21.5'W	X	192
Kingsford	Devon	SX8391	50°42.6'	3°39.0'W	X	191
Kingsford	E Ayr	NS4448	55°42.3'	4°28.5'W	T	64
Kingsford	Worcs	SO8181	52°25.8'	2°16.4'W	T	138
Kingsford Country Park	Worcs	SO8281	52°25.8'	2°15.5'W	X	138
King's Forest of Geltsdale	Cumbr	NY6053	54°52.5'	2°37.0'W	X	86
King's Forest or Greeba Plantation	I of M	SC3181	54°12.1'	4°35.0'W	F	95
King's Forest, The	Suff	TL8173	52°19.7'	0°39.8'E	F	144,155
Kingsforth	N Lincs	TA0219	53°39.7'	0°27.0'W	X	112
King's Furlong	Hants	SU6251	51°15.5'	1°6.3'W	T	185
King's Garden	Hants	SU2009	50°53.0'	1°42.6'W	X	195
King's Garn Gutter	Hants	SU2613	50°55.2'	1°37.4'W	W	195
King's Garn Gutter Inclosure	Hants	SU2513	50°55.2'	1°38.3'W	F	195
King's Gate	Ches	SJ5367	53°12.1'	2°41.8'W	X	117
Kingsgate	Kent	TQ8530	51°2.6'	0°38.7'E	X	189
Kingsgate	Kent	TR3970	51°22.9'	1°26.5'E	T	179
Kingsgate Bay	Kent	TR3970	51°22.9'	1°26.5'E	W	179
Kingsgate Ho	Kent	TQ8928	51°1.4'	0°42.1'E	X	189
Kings Grain	Scot Bord	NT2817	55°26.7'	3°7.9'W	W	79
King's Grange	D & G	NX7867	54°59.2'	3°54.0'W	X	84
King's Green	Glos	SO7633	51°59.9'	2°20.6'W	T	150
King's Green	Worcs	SO7760	52°14.5'	2°19.8'W	T	138,150
King's Grove	Derby	SK2542	52°58.7'	1°37.3'W	X	119,128
Kingshall	Swan	SS4389	51°34.9'	4°15.6'W	X	159
Kingshall Green	Suff	TL9160	52°12.5'	0°48.1'E	T	155
King's Hall Hill	Heref	SO5064	52°16.6'	2°43.6'W	X	137,138,149
Kingshall Street	Suff	TL9161	52°13.1'	0°48.2'E	T	155
Kingsham Wood	W Susx	SU8425	51°1.3'	0°47.8'W	F	186,197
King's Hat Inclosure	Hants	SU3805	50°50.8'	1°27.2'W	F	196
Kingshaugh Fm	Notts	SK7673	53°15.1'	0°51.2'W	FM	120
Kingshead	Devon	SX7177	50°34.9'	3°49.0'W	X	191
Kingsheanton	Devon	SS5537	51°7.1'	4°3.9'W	T	180
King's Heath	Birm	SP0781	52°25.9'	1°53.4'W	T	139
Kings Heath	Northnts	SP7362	52°15.3'	0°55.4'W	T	152
Kings Hedges	Cambs	TL4561	52°13.9'	0°7.8'E	T	154
Kingshill	C of Aber	NJ8605	57°8.4'	2°13.4'W	X	38
Kings Hill	Devon	SS6516	50°55.9'	3°54.9'W	X	180
Kings Hill	Glos	SP0301	51°42.7'	1°57.0'W	T	163
Kingshill	Glos	ST7598	51°41.0'	2°21.3'W	T	162
King's Hill	Lincs	TF1270	53°13.1'	0°18.9'W	A	121
King's Hill	Lincs	TF4153	53°3.6'	0°6.6'E	X	122
King's Hill	Rut	SP8498	52°34.6'	0°45.2'W	X	141
King's Hill	S Ayr	NS3606	55°19.5'	4°34.7'W	X	70,77
King's Hill	Somer	ST5938	51°8.6'	2°34.8'W	X	182,183
King's Hill	Suff	TM2362	52°12.9'	1°16.3'E	X	156
King's Hill	Surrey	SU9465	51°22.8'	0°38.6'W	X	175
Kingshill	Swin	SU1484	51°33.5'	1°47.5'W	T	173
King's Hill	Wals	SO9896	52°33.9'	2°1.4'W	T	139
King's Hill	Warw	SP3274	52°22.0'	1°31.4'W	X	140
King's Hill	Wilts	ST8436	51°7.6'	2°13.3'W	X	183
Kings Hill Fm	Beds	TL1644	52°5.2'	0°18.0'W	FM	153
Kingshill Fm	Glos	SO6803	51°43.7'	2°27.4'W	FM	162
Kings Hill Fm	Kent	TQ9367	51°22.4'	0°46.8'E	FM	178
Kingshill Fm	Northnts	SP6341	52°4.1'	1°4.5'W	FM	152
Kingshill Fm	Wilts	SU1192	51°37.8'	1°50.1'W	FM	163,173
Kingshill Fm	Worcs	SO7550	52°9.1'	2°21.5'W	FM	150
King's Hill Lodge	Rut	SP8498	52°34.6'	0°45.2'W	X	141
King's Hill (Motte and Bailey)	Lincs	TF4153	53°3.6'	0°6.6'E	A	122
Kingshill Plantation	S Lanak	NS8753	55°45.7'	3°47.6'W	F	65,72
King's Hills	Norf	TG0736	52°53.1'	1°5.0'E	X	133
King's Hills	Surrey	TQ0950	51°14.6'	0°25.9'W	X	187
Kingshill Wood	C of Aber	NJ8505	57°8.4'	2°14.4'W	F	38
Kingsholm	Glos	SO8319	51°52.4'	2°14.4'W	T	162
Kings Horses	Leic	SK6700	52°35.9'	1°0.2'W	X	141
Kingshouse	Stir	NN5620	56°21.3'	4°19.4'W	T	51,57
Kings House Hotel	Highld	NN2554	56°39.0'	4°50.8'W	X	41
King's How	Cumbr	NY2516	54°32.3'	3°9.1'W	H	89,90
Kingshurst	Sol	SP1688	52°29.6'	1°45.5'W	T	139
Kingside	Scot Bord	NT2455	55°47.2'	3°12.3'W	X	66,73
Kingside Burn	E Loth	NT6265	55°52.9'	2°36.0'W	W	67
Kingside Hill	Cumbr	NY1551	54°51.0'	3°19.0'W	T	85
Kingside Hill	E Loth	NT6365	55°52.9'	2°35.0'W	H	67
Kingside Loch	Scot Bord	NT3413	55°24.6'	3°2.1'W	W	79
Kings Inch	Scot Bord	NT4557	55°48.4'	2°52.2'W	X	66,73
King's Inn	S Lanak	NS9952	55°45.3'	3°36.1'W	X	65,72
Kingsisland	Pth & Kin	NN8864	56°45.5'	3°49.5'W	X	43
Kingskerswell	Devon	SX8867	50°29.8'	3°34.4'W	T	202
Kingskettle	Fife	NO3008	56°15.8'	3°7.4'W	T	59
King's Knot	Stir	NS7893	56°7.1'	3°57.3'W	A	57
Kingsknowe	C of Edin	NT2170	55°55.3'	3°15.4'W	T	66
Kings Laggan	D & G	NX5657	54°53.5'	4°14.3'W	X	83
Kingslake	Devon	SS4403	50°48.6'	4°12.5'W	X	190
Kingsland	Cambs	TL3398	52°34.0'	0°1.9'W	X	142
Kingsland	Dorset	SY4597	50°46.4'	2°46.4'W	T	193
Kingsland	Glos	SO6708	51°46.4'	2°28.3'W	X	162
Kingsland	Hack	TQ3384	51°32.6'	0°4.5'W	T	176,177
Kingsland	Heref	SO4461	52°14.9'	2°48.8'W	T	137,148,149
Kingsland	I of Angl	SH2481	53°18.1'	4°38.1'W	T	114
Kingsland	Kent	TQ9945	51°10.4'	0°51.2'E	X	189
Kingsland	Shrops	SJ4811	52°41.9'	2°45.8'W	T	126
Kingsland	V of Glam	ST0271	51°26.0'	3°24.2'W	X	170
Kingsland	V of Glam	ST0875	51°28.2'	3°19.1'W	X	170
Kingsland Barton	Devon	SS6925	51°0.8'	3°51.7'W	X	180
Kingsland Fm	Cambs	TL2782	52°25.5'	0°7.5'W	FM	142
Kingsland Fm	Cambs	TL3499	52°34.6'	0°0.9'W	FM	142
Kings Langley	Herts	TL0702	51°42.6'	0°26.7'W	T	166
Kingslaw	E Loth	NT4172	55°56.5'	2°56.2'W	X	66
King's Law	Northum	NY8954	54°53.1'	2°9.9'W	X	87
King's Law	S Lanak	NS8753	55°45.7'	3°47.6'W	X	65,72
Kingslea	W Susx	TQ0824	51°0.5'	0°27.2'W	X	197
Kingslee	Ches	SJ4253	53°4.5'	2°51.5'W	X	117
Kingsley	Ches	SJ5574	53°15.9'	2°40.1'W	T	117
Kingsley	Hants	SU7838	51°8.4'	0°52.7'W	T	186
Kingsley	Staffs	SK0046	53°0.9'	1°59.6'W	T	119,128
Kingsley Common	Hants	SU7937	51°7.8'	0°51.9'W	F	186
Kingsley Fm	Shrops	SO6995	52°33.4'	2°27.0'W	FM	138
Kingsley Green	W Susx	SU8930	51°4.0'	0°43.4'W	T	186
Kingsley Hill Fm	E Susx	TQ6117	50°56.0'	0°17.9'E	FM	199
Kingsley Holt	Staffs	SK0246	53°0.9'	1°57.8'W	T	119,128
Kingsley Moor	Staffs	SJ9946	53°0.9'	2°0.5'W	T	118
Kingsley Park	Northnts	SP7662	52°15.3'	0°52.8'W	T	152
King's Links or Old Town	C of Aber	NJ9508	57°10.0'	2°4.5'W	X	38
Kings Lodge	Warw	SP1548	52°8.0'	1°46.5'W	X	151
King's Loop	D & G	NX3343	54°45.5'	4°35.3'W	W	82
Kingslow	Shrops	SO7998	52°35.0'	2°18.2'W	T	138
King's Low	Staffs	SJ9523	52°48.5'	2°4.0'W	A	127

King's Lynn	Norf	TF6120	52°45·4′	0°23·6′E	T	132
Kings Manor	I of W	SZ3488	50°41·7′	1°30·7′W	X	196
King's Marshes	Suff	TM4449	52°5·4′	1°34·1′E	X	169
King's Marshes	Suff	TM4450	52°5·9′	1°34·2′E	X	156
King's Meaburn	Cumbr	NY6221	54°35·2′	2°34·9′W	T	91
Kingsmead	Hants	SU5813	50°55·0′	1°10·1′W	T	196
Kingsmead	Kent	TQ6440	51°8·4′	0°21·1′E	X	188
Kingsmead	Win & Maid	SU9372	51°26·6′	0°39·3′W	X	175
Kingsmead Fm	Warw	SP2655	52°11·8′	1°36·8′W	FM	151
King's Meadow	Read	SU7274	51°27·9′	0°57·4′W	X	175
Kingsmeadow	Scot Bord	NT2639	55°38·6′	3°10·1′W	X	73
King's Meads	Herts	TL3413	51°48·2′	0°3·0′W	X	166
Kings Men	Oxon	SP2930	51°58·3′	1°34·3′W	X	151
Kings Men (Stone Circle)	Oxon	SP2930	51°58·3′	1°34·3′W	A	151
King's Mere	Wok	SU8164	51°22·4′	0°49·8′W	W	175,186
King's Mill Br	Dorset	ST7617	50°57·3′	2°20·1′W	X	183
Kingsmill Down	Kent	TR1043	51°9·1′	1°0·6′E	X	179,189
Kingsmill Lake	Corn	SX4360	50°25·4′	4°12·2′W	W	201
Kings Mills	Fife	NO3401	56°12·1′	3°3·4′W	X	59
King's Mills	Leic	SK4127	52°50·6′	1°23·1′W	T	129
King's Mills	Wrex	SJ3449	53°2·3′	2°58·7′W	T	117
Kingsmoor	Devon	SS4404	50°49·1′	4°12·5′W	X	190
Kingsmoor	Essex	TL4407	51°44·8′	0°5·6′E	T	167
King's Moor	Pemb	SN1106	51°43·5′	4°43·8′W	X	158
King's Moor	Somer	ST1527	51°2·4′	3°12·4′W	X	181,193
King's Moor	Somer	ST4823	51°0·5′	2°44·1′W	X	193
King's Moors Plantn	York	SE6658	54°1·1′	0°59·1′W	F	105,106
King's Moss	Aberd	NJ6415	57°13·7′	2°35·3′W	X	37
King's Moss	E Ayr	NS6035	55°35·6′	4°12·9′W	X	71
Kings Moss	St Hel	SD5001	53°30·4′	2°44·8′W	T	108
Kingsmuir	Angus	NO4749	56°38·0′	2°51·4′W	T	54
Kings Muir	Scot Bord	NT2539	55°38·6′	3°11·1′W	T	73
Kingsmuir Ho	Fife	NO5308	56°16·0′	2°45·1′W	X	59
King's Myre	Pth & Kin	NO1136	56°30·7′	3°26·3′W	W	53
King's Newnham	Warw	SP4577	52°23·6′	1°19·9′W	T	140
King's Newton	Derby	SK3926	52°50·0′	1°24·9′W	T	128
Kingsnoad	Kent	TQ8547	51°11·8′	0°39·3′E	X	189
Kingsnordley	Shrops	SO7787	52°29·1′	2°19·9′W	T	138
Kingsnorth	Kent	TR0039	51°7·1′	0°51·9′E	T	189
Kingsnorth	Medway	TQ8072	51°25·3′	0°35·7′E	X	178
King's Norton	Birm	SP0579	52°24·8′	1°55·2′W	T	139
King's Norton	Leic	SK6800	52°35·8′	0°59·4′W	T	141
King's Nympton	Devon	SS6819	50°57·6′	3°52·4′W	T	180
Kingsnympton Park	Devon	SS6719	50°57·5′	3°53·2′W	X	180
King's Nympton Sta	Devon	SS6616	50°55·9′	3°54·0′W	X	180
King's Park	Bourne	SZ1192	50°43·9′	1°50·3′W	X	195
Kings Park	Carm	SN5945	52°5·4′	4°3·1′W	X	146
Kings Park	C of Glas	NS5961	55°49·6′	4°14·6′W	T	64
King's Park	Stir	NS7893	56°7·1′	3°57·3′W	X	57
Kingspark Wood	W Susx	SU9931	51°4·4′	0°34·8′W	F	186
King's Pier	Dorset	SY7073	50°33·6′	2°25·0′W	X	194
King's Pitts	Heref	SO5033	51°59·8′	2°43·3′W	X	149
King's Play Hill	Wilts	SU0065	51°23·3′	1°59·6′W	H	173
King's Pyon	Heref	SO4350	52°9·0′	2°49·6′W	T	148,149
King's Pyon Ho	Heref	SO4350	52°9·0′	2°49·6′W	X	148,149
King's Quay	I of W	SZ5394	50°44·8′	1°14·5′W	X	196
King's Quoit	Pemb	SS0697	51°38·5′	4°47·8′W	X	158
King's Quoit (Burial Chamber)	Pemb	SS0697	51°38·5′	4°47·8′W	A	158
Kings Ride	Herts	TL3239	52°2·2′	0°4·1′W	X	153
Kings Ride Ho	Brackn	SU9168	51°24·5′	0°41·1′W	X	175
Kingsrig	Scot Bord	NT7639	55°38·9′	2°22·4′W	X	74
Kings Ripton	Cambs	TL2676	52°22·3′	0°8·5′W	T	142
Kings-seat	Fife	NT0895	56°8·6′	3°28·4′W	X	58
King's Seat	Pth & Kin	NO0042	56°33·8′	3°37·2′W	X	52,53
King's Seat	Pth & Kin	NO0340	56°32·8′	3°34·2′W	H	52,53
King's Seat	Pth & Kin	NO2333	56°29·2′	3°14·6′W	H	53
King's Seat	Scot Bord	NT8717	55°27·1′	2°11·9′W	X	80
Kingsseat Burn	Scot Bord	NT8618	55°27·6′	2°12·9′W	W	80
King's Seat Hill	Clackm	NS9399	56°10·6′	3°43·0′W	H	58
King's Sedge Moor	Somer	ST4233	51°5·8′	2°49·3′W	X	182
King's Sedgemoor Drain	Somer	ST3835	51°6·9′	2°52·8′W	W	182
King's Somborne	Hants	SU3631	51°4·9′	1°28·8′W	T	185
King's Stag	Dorset	ST7210	50°53·6′	2°23·5′W	T	194
King's Standing	Birm	SP0895	52°33·4′	1°52·5′W	A	139
King's Standing	E Susx	TQ4730	51°3·3′	0°6·2′E	X	188
King's Stanley	Glos	SO8103	51°43·8′	2°16·1′W	T	162
King's Step	Aberd	NO8472	56°50·6′	2°15·3′W	X	45
King's Stone	Derby	SK2463	53°10·1′	1°38·1′W	A	119
King's Stone	Pth & Kin	NO0928	56°26·4′	3°28·1′W	A	52,53,58
King's Stone,The	Northum	NT8838	55°38·4′	2°11·0′W	A	74
Kings Sutton	Northnts	SP5036	52°1·4′	1°15·9′W	T	151
Kingstall Wood	Suff	TM3873	52°18·4′	1°29·9′E	F	156
King's Tamerton	C of Plym	SX4558	50°24·3′	4°10·5′W	T	201
Kingstand Fm	Leic	SK5102	52°37·0′	1°14·4′W	FM	140
King Stand Fm	Notts	SK6465	53°10·9′	1°2·1′W	FM	120
Kingstanding	Birm	SP0894	52°32·9′	1°52·5′W	T	139
Kingstanding Fm	Oxon	SP3117	51°51·3′	1°32·6′W	FM	164
Kingstanding Fm	Warw	SP2568	52°18·8′	1°37·6′W	FM	151
Kingstanding Hill	Oxon	SU5783	51°32·8′	1°10·3′W	X	174
Kingsteignton	Devon	SX8773	50°33·0′	3°35·3′W	T	192
Kingsteps	Highld	NH9057	57°35·6′	3°50·0′W	T	27
King Sterndale	Derby	SK0972	53°14·9′	1°51·5′W	T	119
King's, The or Bruce's Stone	D & G	NX5576	55°3·7′	4°15·8′W	A	77
King's Thorn	Heref	SO5031	51°58·8′	2°43·3′W	T	149
Kingsthorpe	Northnts	SP7563	52°15·8′	0°53·7′W	T	152
Kingsthorpe Hollow	Northnts	SP7562	52°15·3′	0°53·7′W	T	152
Kingsthorpe Lodge	Northnts	TL0885	52°27·4′	0°24·2′W	X	142
Kingston	Angus	NO4749	56°38·0′	2°51·4′W	X	54
Kingston	Cambs	TL3455	52°10·8′	0°2·0′W	T	154
Kingston	C of Port	SU6501	50°48·5′	1°4·3′W	T	196
Kingston	Corn	SX1458	50°23·8′	4°36·7′W	X	200
Kingston	Corn	SX3675	50°33·3′	4°18·5′W	X	201
Kingston	Devon	SX6347	50°18·7′	3°55·1′W	T	202
Kingston	Devon	SX8454	50°22·7′	3°37·5′W	X	202
Kingston	Devon	SX9051	50°21·2′	3°32·4′W	T	202
Kingston	Devon	SY0687	50°40·7′	3°19·4′W	T	192
Kingston	Dorset	ST7509	50°53·0′	2°20·9′W	T	194
Kingston	Dorset	SY9579	50°36·9′	2°3·9′W	T	195

Kingston	E Loth	NT5482	56°2·0′	2°43·9′W	T	66
Kingston	Essex	TL6113	51°47·8′	0°20·5′E	X	167
Kingston	Hants	SU1402	50°49·3′	1°47·7′W	T	195
Kingston	I of W	SZ4781	50°37·8′	1°19·7′W	T	196
Kingston	Kent	TR1951	51°13·2′	1°8·6′E	T	179,189
Kingston	Mil Key	SP9038	52°2·2′	0°40·9′W	T	152
Kingston	Moray	NJ3365	57°40·5′	3°6·9′W	T	28
Kingston	Pemb	SR9999	51°39·5′	4°54·0′W	X	158
Kingston	Suff	TM2647	52°4·7′	1°18·3′E	T	169
Kingston	Tames	SJ9495	53°27·3′	2°5·0′W	T	109
Kingston Bagpuize	Oxon	SU4098	51°41·0′	1°24·9′W	T	164
Kingston Bagpuize Ho	Oxon	SU4097	51°40·5′	1°24·9′W	X	164
Kingston Barn	Warw	SP3757	52°12·8′	1°27·1′W	X	151
Kingston Beacon	Somer	ST2230	51°4·1′	3°6·4′W	X	182
Kingston Blount	Oxon	SU7399	51°41·3′	0°56·2′W	T	165
Kingston Br	Mil Key	SP9038	52°2·2′	0°40·9′W	X	152
Kingston Brook	Notts	SK5326	52°50·0′	1°12·4′W	W	129
Kingston by Sea	W Susx	TQ2305	50°50·1′	0°14·8′W	T	198
Kingston Common Fm	Oxon	SU3388	51°35·6′	1°31·0′W	FM	174
Kingston Deverill	Wilts	ST8437	51°8·2′	2°13·3′W	T	183
Kingstone	Barns	SE3305	53°32·7′	1°29·7′W	T	110,111
Kingstone	Heref	SO4235	52°0·9′	2°50·3′W	T	149,161
Kingstone	Heref	SO6324	51°55·0′	2°31·9′W	T	162
King Stone	Oxon	SP2930	51°58·3′	1°34·3′W	A	151
Kingstone	Somer	ST3713	50°55·0′	2°53·4′W	T	193
Kingstone	Staffs	SK0629	52°51·7′	1°54·2′W	T	128
Kingstone Coombes	Oxon	SU2785	51°34·0′	1°36·2′W	X	174
Kingstone Down	Oxon	SU2882	51°32·4′	1°35·4′W	X	174
Kingstone Fm	N Yks	SE1866	54°5·6′	1°43·1′W	FM	99
Kingstone Grange	Heref	SO4234	52°0·3′	2°50·3′W	X	149,161
Kingstones Fm	Wilts	SU2065	51°23·3′	1°42·4′W	FM	174
Kingstone Warren	Oxon	SU3185	51°34·0′	1°32·8′W	X	174
Kingstone Winslow	Oxon	SU2685	51°34·0′	1°37·1′W	T	174
Kingstone Wood	Staffs	SK0628	52°51·2′	1°54·3′W	F	128
Kingston Fields Fm	Notts	SK5128	52°51·1′	1°14·2′W	FM	129
Kingston Fm	E Loth	NT5382	56°2·0′	2°44·8′W	FM	66
Kingston Fm	Pth & Kin	NO2927	56°26·0′	3°8·6′W	FM	53,59
Kingston Fm	Warw	SP3656	52°12·3′	1°28·0′W	FM	151
Kingston Gorse	W Susx	TQ0801	50°48·1′	0°27·7′W	T	197
Kingston Grange	Warw	SP3556	52°12·3′	1°28·9′W	X	151
Kingston Great Common	Hants	SU1802	50°49·3′	1°44·3′W	X	195
Kingston Grove	Oxon	SU7397	51°40·3′	0°56·3′W	X	165
Kingston Hill	Oxon	SU4099	51°41·5′	1°24·9′W	X	164
Kingston Hill Fm	Oxon	SU4099	51°41·5′	1°24·9′W	FM	164
Kingston Ho	Devon	SX7965	50°28·6′	3°41·9′W	X	202
Kingston Ho	E Loth	NT5382	56°2·0′	2°44·8′W	X	66
Kingston Ho	Oxon	SU7399	51°41·3′	0°56·2′W	X	165
Kingston Hollow	E Susx	TQ3908	50°51·5′	0°1·1′W	X	198
Kingston Holt	Warw	SP3656	52°12·3′	1°28·0′W	X	151
Kingston Island	Notts	SK6270	53°13·6′	1°3·9′W	X	120
Kingston Lacy Ho	Dorset	ST9701	50°48·7′	2°2·2′W	A	195
Kingston Lisle	Oxon	SU3287	51°35·1′	1°31·9′W	T	174
Kingston Maurward	Dorset	SY7191	50°43·3′	2°24·3′W	T	194
Kingston Mood Fm	Cambs	TL3253	52°9·8′	0°3·8′W	FM	153
Kingston near Lewes	E Susx	TQ3908	50°51·5′	0°1·1′W	T	198
Kingston on Soar	Notts	SK5027	52°50·5′	1°15·1′W	T	129
Kingston Park	N upon Ty	NZ2168	55°0·6′	1°39·9′W	T	88
Kingston Pastures Fm	Cambs	TL3252	52°9·3′	0°3·8′W	FM	153
Kingston Pastures Fm	Cambs	TL3352	52°9·2′	0°3·0′W	FM	154
Kingston Russell	Dorset	SY5891	50°43·3′	2°35·3′W	T	194
Kingston Russell Ho	Dorset	SY5789	50°42·2′	2°36·2′W	A	194
Kingstons	Essex	TL5612	51°47·3′	0°16·1′E	X	167
Kingston Seymour	N Som	ST4066	51°23·6′	2°51·4′W	T	171,172,182
Kingstons Fm	Essex	TL5312	51°47·4′	0°13·5′E	FM	167
Kingston Stert	Oxon	SP7201	51°42·4′	0°57·1′W	T	165
Kingston St Mary	Somer	ST2229	51°3·5′	3°6·4′W	T	193
Kingston upon Hull	K upon H	TA0929	53°45·0′	0°20·4′W	T	107
Kingston Upon Thames	King	TQ1870	51°25·2′	0°17·8′W	T	176
Kingston Vale	King	TQ2171	51°25·7′	0°15·2′W	T	176
Kingston Warren Down	Oxon	SU3084	51°33·5′	1°33·6′W	X	174
Kingstonwell Fm	Somer	ST3507	50°51·8′	2°55·0′W	FM	193
Kingston Wood	Cambs	TL3254	52°10·3′	0°3·8′W	F	153
Kingston Wood	Oxon	SU7497	51°40·2′	0°55·4′W	F	165
King's Tor	Devon	SX5573	50°32·6′	4°2·4′W	H	191
Kingstown	Cumbr	NY3959	54°55·6′	2°56·7′W	T	85
Kingstree	Devon	SS7119	50°57·6′	3°49·8′W	X	180
King Street	Essex	TL5803	51°42·4′	0°17·6′E	T	167
Kingstreet	Stock	SJ8782	53°20·3′	2°11·3′W	X	109
Kingstreet Grange	Shrops	SJ7712	52°42·5′	2°20·0′W	X	127
Kingstreet Hall	Ches	SJ6969	53°13·3′	2°27·5′W	X	118
King Street (Roman Road)	Ches	SJ6970	53°13·8′	2°27·5′W	R	118
King Street (Roman Road)	Lincs	TF1012	52°41·9′	0°21·9′W	R	130,142
King Street (Roman Road)	Peterb	TF1106	52°38·7′	0°21·2′W	R	142
King's Walden	Herts	TL1623	51°53·8′	0°18·4′W	T	166
Kingsway	Bath & NE Somer	ST7363	51°22·2′	2°22·9′W	T	172
Kingsway	Halton	SJ5185	53°21·8′	2°43·8′W	T	108
Kingsway Fm	Beds	SP9428	51°56·8′	0°37·5′W	FM	165
Kingswear	Devon	SX8851	50°21·1′	3°34·1′W	T	202
King's Weir	Essex	TL3705	51°43·8′	0°0·6′W	X	166
King's Weir	Oxon	SP4710	51°47·4′	1°18·7′W	X	164
King's Weir	Devon	SX8592	50°43·2′	3°37·4′W	X	191
King's Well	D & G	NX5091	55°11·7′	4°21·0′W	W	77
Kingswell	E Ayr	NS5047	55°41·9′	4°22·8′W	X	64
Kingswell	Pth & Kin	NO1631	56°28·1′	3°21·4′W	X	53
Kingswell Burn	E Ayr	NS4947	55°41·8′	4°23·7′W	W	64
Kingswell End	Herts	TL1524	51°54·4′	0°19·3′W	X	166
Kingswells Fm	E Susx	TQ7317	50°55·8′	0°28·1′E	FM	199
Kingswells	C of Aber	NJ8606	57°8·9′	2°12·9′W	X	38
Kings Weston Hill	C of Bris	ST5477	51°29·6′	2°39·4′W	H	172
Kingswinford	Dudley	SO8888	52°29·6′	2°10·2′W	T	139
King's Wood	Beds	SP9229	51°57·3′	0°39·3′W	F	165
King's Wood	Beds	TL0440	52°3·1′	0°28·6′W	F	153
Kingswood	Bucks	SP9005	51°44·4′	0°41·4′W	X	165
King's Wood	Bucks	SU8993	51°38·0′	0°42·4′W	F	175
King's Wood	Corn	SX0048	50°18·1′	4°48·1′W	F	204
Kings Wood	Croy	TQ3560	51°19·6′	0°3·3′W	F	177,187
King's Wood	Devon	SX7166	50°29·0′	3°48·7′W	F	202
Kingswood	Essex	TQ7087	51°33·6′	0°27·5′E	T	178
Kingswood	Glos	ST7491	51°37·3′	2°22·1′W	T	162,172

Kingswood	Heref	SO2954	52°11·0′	3°1·9′W	T	148
Kingswood	Herts	TL1000	51°41·5′	0°24·1′W	T	166
King's Wood	Herts	TL3723	51°53·5′	0°0·1′W	F	166
Kingswood	Kent	TQ8450	51°13·4′	0°38·5′E	T	188
Kings Wood	Kent	TQ8451	51°13·9′	0°38·5′E	F	188
King's Wood	Kent	TR0350	51°13·0′	0°54·8′E	F	179,189
King's Wood	Monm	SO4712	51°48·5′	2°45·7′W	F	161
King's Wood	Northnts	SP8687	52°28·7′	0°43·6′W	F	141
Kingswood	Northum	NY7861	54°56·8′	2°20·2′W	X	86,87
King's Wood	N Som	ST4564	51°22·6′	2°47·0′W	F	172,182
King's Wood	Oxon	SP4018	51°51·8′	1°24·8′W	F	164
Kingswood	Powys	SJ2402	52°36·9′	3°7·0′W	T	126
Kingswood	Pth & Kin	NO0638	56°31·7′	3°31·2′W	X	52,53
King's Wood	Roth	SK3899	53°29·4′	1°25·2′W	F	110,111
King's Wood	Roth	SK5489	53°23·9′	1°10·9′W	F	111,120
Kingswood	S Glos	ST6473	51°27·5′	2°30·7′W	T	172
Kingswood	Shrops	SO2796	52°33·7′	3°4·2′W	X	137
Kingswood	Shrops	SO7377	52°23·7′	2°23·4′W	X	138
Kingswood	Somer	ST1037	51°7·7′	3°16·8′W	T	181
King's Wood	Somer	ST4155	51°17·7′	2°50·4′W	F	172,182
King's Wood	Staffs	SJ8639	52°57·1′	2°12·1′W	F	127
King's Wood	Suff	TL7849	52°6·9′	0°36·4′E	F	155
Kingswood	Surrey	TQ2456	51°17·6′	0°12·9′W	T	187
Kingswood	Warr	SJ5790	53°24·5′	2°38·4′W	T	108
Kingswood	Warw	SP1871	52°20·4′	1°43·7′W	T	139
Kingswood	W Susx	TQ1209	50°52·4′	0°24·1′W	X	198
Kingswood Bank	Staffs	SJ8540	52°57·7′	2°13·0′W	X	118
Kingswood Bank Fm	Staffs	SJ8302	52°37·2′	2°14·7′W	FM	127
Kingswood Brook	Warw	SP1970	52°19·9′	1°42·9′W	T	139
Kingswood Burn	Northum	NY7760	54°56·3′	2°21·1′W	W	86,87
Kingswoodbury Fm	Herts	TL2931	51°58·0′	0°6·9′W	FM	166
Kingswood Common	Northum	NY7560	54°56·3′	2°23·0′W	X	86,87
Kingswood Common	Staffs	SJ8402	52°37·2′	2°13·8′W	T	127
Kingswood Common	Worcs	SO7365	52°17·2′	2°23·4′W	T	138,150
Kingswood Common	Worcs	SO7460	52°14·5′	2°22·5′W	X	138,150
Kingswood Downs	Corn	SX1166	50°28·0′	4°39·4′W	X	200
Kingswood Fm	Dorset	SZ0081	50°38·0′	1°59·6′W	FM	195
Kingswood Fm	Oxon	SP4019	51°52·3′	1°24·7′W	FM	164
Kingswood Fm	Somer	ST4909	50°52·9′	2°43·1′W	FM	193,194
Kingswood Fm	Surrey	TQ3542	51°9·9′	0°3·8′W	FM	187
Kingswood Fm	Warw	SP3173	52°21·5′	1°32·3′W	FM	140
Kingswoodgreen Fm	Ches	SJ6144	52°59·8′	2°34·5′W	FM	118
Kingswood Ho	Bucks	SP8300	51°41·8′	0°47·5′W	X	165
Kingswood Ho	Suff	TL9139	52°1·2′	0°47·4′E	X	155
Kingswood Ho	Wok	SU8078	51°29·9′	0°50·5′W	X	175
Kingswoodlane Fm	Bucks	SP6818	51°51·6′	1°0·4′W	FM	164,165
Kingswood Lodge	Croy	TQ3560	51°19·6′	0°3·3′W	X	177,187
Kingswood Manor	Surrey	TQ2553	51°16·0′	0°12·1′W	X	187
Kingswood Rigg	Northum	NY7660	54°56·3′	2°22·1′W	X	86,87
King's Wood Warren	Somer	ST7436	51°7·6′	2°21·9′W	F	183
Kingswood Warren	Surrey	TQ2455	51°17·1′	0°12·9′W	X	187
Kings Worthy	Hants	SU4933	51°5·9′	1°17·6′W	T	185
King Syke	Lancs	SD7151	53°57·5′	2°26·1′W	W	103
Kingthorn Mill	Northnts	SP6549	52°8·4′	1°2·6′W	X	152
Kingthorn Wood	Northnts	SP6648	52°7·8′	1°1·8′W	F	152
Kingthorpe	Lincs	TF1275	53°15·8′	0°18·8′W	X	121
Kingthorpe Ho	N Yks	SE8385	54°15·5′	0°43·1′W	X	94,100
Kington	Heref	SO2956	52°12·1′	3°1·9′W	T	148
Kington	S Glos	ST6290	51°36·7′	2°32·5′W	T	162,172
Kington	Worcs	SO9955	52°11·8′	2°0·5′W	T	150
Kington Down Fm	Wilts	ST7977	51°29·7′	2°17·8′W	FM	172
Kington Grange	Warw	SP1864	52°16·7′	1°43·8′W	X	151
Kington Ho	S Glos	ST6291	51°37·2′	2°32·5′W	X	162,172
Kington Langley	Wilts	ST9277	51°29·7′	2°6·5′W	T	173
Kington Magna	Dorset	ST7623	51°0·6′	2°20·1′W	T	183
Kington St Michael	Wilts	ST9077	51°29·7′	2°8·3′W	T	173
King Tor	Devon	SX7081	50°37·1′	3°49·9′W	H	191
Kingturn Rigg	Cumbr	NY6370	55°1·6′	2°34·3′W	X	86
Kingussie	Highld	NH7500	57°4·7′	4°3·3′W	T	35
King Water	Cumbr	NY5868	55°0·5′	2°39·0′W	W	86
King Water	Cumbr	NY6371	55°2·2′	2°34·3′W	W	86
Kingway Barn	Wilts	ST9182	51°32·4′	2°7·4′W	X	173
Kingweston	Somer	ST5230	51°4·3′	2°40·7′W	T	182,183
Kingweston Ho	Somer	ST5231	51°4·8′	2°40·7′W	X	182,183
King William's Coll	I of M	SC2768	54°5·0′	4°38·3′W	X	95
King Wood	Essex	TL6603	51°42·3′	0°24·5′E	F	167
King Wood	Lancs	SD6134	53°48·3′	2°35·1′W	F	102,103
Kingwood Common	Oxon	SU6982	51°32·2′	0°59·9′W	X	175
Kingwood Ho	W Berks	SU3077	51°29·7′	1°33·7′W	X	174
Kinharrachie Cottage	Aberd	NJ9231	57°22·4′	2°7·5′W	X	30
Kinharvie	D & G	NX9266	54°58·9′	3°40·8′W	X	84
Kinharvie Burn	D & G	NX9265	54°58·3′	3°40·8′W	W	84
Kinharvie Hill	D & G	NX9364	54°57·8′	3°39·8′W	H	84
Kinharvie Plantation	D & G	NX9366	54°58·9′	3°39·9′W	F	84
Kinhrive	Highld	NH7075	57°45·0′	4°10·6′W	X	21
Kinigallin	Pth & Kin	NN7546	56°35·6′	4°1·7′W	X	51,52
Kininvie Ho	Moray	NJ3144	57°29·1′	3°8·6′W	A	28
Kinkeadly	Pth & Kin	NO2151	56°38·9′	3°16·9′W	X	53
Kinkell	Aberd	NO7479	56°54·4′	2°25·2′W	T	45
Kinkell	E Dunb	NS6375	55°57·2′	4°11·2′W	X	64
Kinkell Br	Pth & Kin	NN9316	56°19·7′	3°43·4′W	X	58
Kinkell Castle	Highld	NH5554	57°33·4′	4°24·9′W	A	26
Kinkell Church	Aberd	NJ7819	57°15·9′	2°21·4′W	A	38
Kinkell Fm	Fife	NO5016	56°19·2′	2°44·2′W	FM	59
Kinkell Ness	Fife	NO5315	56°19·8′	2°45·2′W	X	59
Kinknockie	Aberd	NJ9425	57°19·2′	2°5·5′W	X	38
Kinknockie	Aberd	NK0041	57°27·8′	1°59·5′W	T	30
Kinknockie Hill	Aberd	NK0040	57°27·3′	1°59·5′W	H	30
Kinkry Hill	Cumbr	NY5175	55°4·3′	2°45·6′W	T	86
Kinkwall	Shetld	HU2150	60°14·3′	1°36·7′W	X	3
Kinkwell Braes	Fife	NO5215	56°19·8′	2°46·1′W	X	59
Kinlea Wood	Highld	NH6145	57°28·7′	4°18·6′W	F	26
Kinlet	Shrops	SO7180	52°25·3′	2°25·2′W	T	138
Kinlet Hall	Shrops	SO7081	52°25·8′	2°26·1′W	A	138
Kinlet Park	Shrops	SO7180	52°25·3′	2°25·2′W	X	138
Kinley	Heref	SO3247	52°7·3′	2°59·2′W	X	148
Kinley Fm	Heref	SO3642	52°4·6′	2°55·6′W	FM	148,149,161
Kinley Fm	Wrekin	SJ6614	52°43·6′	2°29·8′W	FM	127
Kinley Hill	Durham	NZ4346	54°48·7′	1°19·4′W	X	88
Kinloch	Aberd	NK0950	57°32·7′	1°50·5′W	X	30

Kinloch	Arg & Bt	NM8940	56°30·5′	5°25·3′W	X	49
Kinloch	Fife	NO2812	56°18·0′	3°9·4′W	T	59
Kinloch	Highld	NC3434	58°16·1′	4°49·3′W	T	15
Kinloch	Highld	NG6917	57°11·4′	5°48·9′W	X	32
Kinloch	Highld	NH4757	57°34·9′	4°33·1′W	X	26
Kinloch	Highld	NM4099	57°0·8′	6°16·5′W	T	39
Kinloch	Highld	NM6554	56°37·4′	5°49·4′W	X	49
Kinloch	Highld	NN5388	56°57·9′	4°24·6′W	X	42
Kinloch	N Eil	NL6599	56°57·9′	7°30·3′W	T	31
Kinloch	Pth & Kin	NO1444	56°35·1′	3°23·6′W	X	53
Kinloch	Pth & Kin	NO2644	56°35·2′	3°11·8′W	X	53
Kinlochaline	Highld	NM6947	56°33·8′	5°45·1′W	X	49
Kinlochan	Highld	NM8167	56°44·9′	5°34·5′W	X	40
Kinlochard	Stir	NN4502	56°11·4′	4°29·4′W	T	57
Kinlocharkaig	Highld	NM9890	56°57·7′	5°18·9′W	X	33,40
Kinlochbeoraid	Highld	NM8585	56°54·7′	5°31·4′W	X	40
Kinlochbervie	Highld	NC2156	58°27·6′	5°3·6′W	T	9
Kinloch Burn	Pth & Kin	NN8837	56°31·0′	3°48·8′W	W	52
Kinloch Castle	Highld	NM4099	57°0·8′	6°16·5′W	X	39
Kinloch Cottage	Highld	NC5552	58°26·2′	4°28·5′W	X	10
Kinloch Damph	Highld	NG8647	57°28·0′	5°33·6′W	X	24
Kinlocheil	Highld	NM9779	56°51·7′	5°19·4′W	T	40
Kinlochetive	Highld	NN1245	56°33·8′	5°3·1′W	X	50
Kinlochewe	Highld	NH0261	57°36·0′	5°18·4′W	T	19
Kinlochewe Forest	Highld	NH0666	57°38·8′	5°14·6′W	X	19
Kinlochewe River	Highld	NH0263	57°37·1′	5°18·5′W	W	19
Kinlochfollart	Highld	NG2546	57°25·5′	6°34·4′W	X	23
Kinloch Glen	Highld	NG3800	57°1·3′	6°18·6′W	X	32,39
Kinloch Ho	Fife	NO2712	56°17·9′	3°10·3′W	X	59
Kinloch Ho	Pth & Kin	NN9138	56°31·5′	3°45·9′W	X	52
Kinloch Hourn	Highld	NG9507	57°6·8′	5°22·7′W	X	33
Kinlochhourn Forest	Highld	NG9409	57°7·8′	5°23·8′W	X	33
Kinloch House Hotel	Pth & Kin	NO1345	56°35·6′	3°24·6′W	X	53
Kinlochlaich	Arg & Bt	NM9346	56°33·9′	5°21·7′W	X	49
Kinlochlaich Farm	Arg & Bt	NM9346	56°33·9′	5°21·7′W	FM	49
Kinlochleven	Highld	NN1861	56°42·6′	4°58·0′W	T	41
Kinloch Lodge	Highld	NC5552	58°26·2′	4°28·5′W	X	10
Kinloch Lodge Hotel	Highld	NG7015	57°10·4′	5°47·8′W	X	32,33
Kinloch Loggan	Highld	NN5489	56°58·4′	4°23·7′W	T	42
Kinlochluichart Forest	Highld	NH2769	57°40·9′	4°53·6′W	X	20
Kinlochmoidart	Highld	NM7072	56°47·2′	5°45·5′W	T	40
Kinlochmorar	Highld	NM8690	56°57·4′	5°30·7′W	X	33,40
Kinlochmore	Highld	NN1862	56°43·1′	4°58·0′W	T	41
Kinloch Rannoch	Pth & Kin	NN6658	56°41·9′	4°10·9′W	T	42,51
Kinloch River	Highld	NC5551	58°25·7′	4°28·5′W	W	10
Kinloch River	Highld	NG3800	57°1·3′	6°18·6′W	W	32,39
Kinloch River	Highld	NN6554	56°38·0′	5°48·5′W	W	49
Kinlochruel	Arg & Bt	NS0177	55°56·9′	5°10·8′W	X	63
Kinlochspelve	Arg & Bt	NM6526	56°22·3′	5°47·9′W	X	49
Kinlochy	Highld	ND3347	58°24·6′	3°8·3′W	X	12
Kinloid	Highld	NM6587	56°55·1′	5°51·2′W	T	40
Kinloss	Moray	NJ0661	57°38·0′	3°34·0′W	T	27
Kinloss Burn	Moray	NJ0862	57°38·6′	3°32·0′W	W	27
Kinloss Ho	Fife	NO3615	56°19·6′	3°1·7′W	X	59
Kinloss Sch	Worcs	SO7659	52°14·0′	2°20·7′W	X	150
Kinmel Bay (Bae Cinmel)	Conwy	SH9880	53°18·7′	3°31·5′W	T	116
Kinmel Hall	Conwy	SH9874	53°15·4′	3°31·3′W	X	116
Kinmel Park	Conwy	SH9875	53°16·0′	3°31·4′W	X	116
Kinminity Fm	Aberd	NO5696	57°3·4′	2°43·1′W	FM	37,44
Kinminty	Aberd	NJ7553	57°34·2′	2°24·6′W	X	29
Kinmohr	Aberd	NJ8213	57°12·7′	2°17·4′W	X	38
Kinmont Beck	Cumbr	SD1390	54°18·1′	3°19·8′W	W	96
Kinmont Buck Barrow	Cumbr	SD1491	54°18·7′	3°18·9′W	X	96
Kinmonth	Pth & Kin	NO1619	56°21·6′	3°21·1′W	X	58
Kinmount Ho	D & G	NY1468	55°0·2′	3°20·2′W	X	85
Kinmuck	Aberd	NJ8119	57°15·9′	2°18·4′W	T	38
Kinmundy	Aberd	NJ8307	57°9·5′	2°16·4′W	X	38
Kinmundy	Aberd	NJ8917	57°14·9′	2°10·5′W	X	38
Kinmylies	Highld	NH6444	57°28·2′	4°15·6′W	T	26
Kinn	Cumbr	NY2223	54°36·0′	3°12·0′W	X	89,90
Kinnaber	Angus	NO7261	56°44·6′	2°27·0′W	X	45
Kinnabus	Arg & Bt	NR2942	55°36·0′	6°17·7′W	X	60
Kinnadie	Aberd	NJ9643	57°28·9′	2°3·5′W	T	30
Kinnahaird	Highld	NH4655	57°33·8′	4°34·0′W	X	26
Kinnaird	Angus	NO2954	56°40·6′	3°9·1′W	X	53
Kinnaird	Fife	NO2717	56°20·6′	3°10·4′W	X	59
Kinnaird	Pth & Kin	NN9559	56°42·9′	3°42·5′W	T	52,53
Kinnaird	Pth & Kin	NO0817	56°20·4′	3°28·9′W	X	58
Kinnaird	Pth & Kin	NO2328	56°26·5′	3°14·5′W	T	53,58
Kinnaird	Pth & Kin	NO2428	56°26·5′	3°13·5′W	T	53,59
Kinnaird	Pth & Kin	NT1396	56°9·2′	3°23·6′W	X	58
Kinnaird Burn	Pth & Kin	NN9559	56°42·9′	3°42·5′W	W	52,53
Kinnaird Castle	Angus	NO6357	56°42·5′	2°35·8′W	X	54
Kinnaird Fm	Fife	NO4216	56°20·2′	2°55·8′W	FM	59
Kinnaird Head	Aberd	NJ9967	57°41·8′	2°0·5′W	X	30
Kinnaird Ho	Falk	NS8884	56°2·4′	3°47·4′W	X	65
Kinnaird Ho	Pth & Kin	NN9849	56°37·6′	3°39·3′W	X	52,53
Kinnaird Park	Angus	NO6257	56°42·4′	2°36·8′W	X	54
Kinnaird Park Farm	Angus	NO6257	56°42·4′	2°36·8′W	FM	54
Kinnairds Mill	Angus	NO6258	56°43·0′	2°36·8′W	X	54
Kinnairdy Castle	Moray	NJ6049	57°32·0′	2°39·6′W	A	29
Kinnaker, The	Pth & Kin	NN9208	56°15·4′	3°44·2′W	X	58
Kinnaniel	Angus	NO3153	56°40·1′	3°7·1′W	X	53
Kinnauld	Highld	NC7301	57°59·1′	4°8·4′W	T	16
Kinneddar	Moray	NJ2269	57°42·5′	3°18·1′W	X	28
Kinneddar Mains	Fife	NT0291	56°6·4′	3°34·1′W	X	58
Kinneff	Aberd	NO8574	56°51·7′	2°14·3′W	T	45
Kinneil	Falk	NS9880	56°0·4′	3°37·7′W	X	65
Kinneil House	Falk	NS9880	56°0·4′	3°37·7′W	A	65
Kinneil Kerse	Falk	NS9680	56°0·4′	3°39·6′W	X	65
Kinnelbanks	D & G	NY0884	55°8·8′	3°26·2′W	X	78
Kinnel Br	D & G	NY0885	55°9·3′	3°26·2′W	X	78
Kinnelhead	D & G	NT0301	55°17·9′	3°31·2′W	X	78
Kinnell	Angus	NO6050	56°38·7′	2°38·7′W	T	54
Kinnell	Stir	NN5732	56°27·8′	4°18·8′W	X	51
Kinnelside	D & G	NY0885	55°9·3′	3°26·2′W	X	78
Kinnel Water	D & G	NY0693	55°13·6′	3°28·2′W	W	78
Kinneries	Angus	NO5245	56°35·9′	2°46·5′W	X	54
Kinnerley	Shrops	SJ3320	52°46·6′	2°59·2′W	T	126
Kinnernie	Aberd	NJ7210	57°11·1′	2°27·3′W	X	38

Kinnernie Burn	Aberd	NJ7409	57°10·5′	2°25·3′W	W	38
Kinnersley	Heref	SO3449	52°8·4′	2°57·5′W	T	148,149
Kinnersley	Worcs	SO8743	52°5·3′	2°11·0′W	T	150
Kinnersley Manor	Surrey	TQ2646	51°12·2′	0°11·4′W	X	187
Kinnerton	Powys	SO2463	52°15·8′	3°6·4′W	T	137,148
Kinnerton	Shrops	SO3796	52°33·7′	2°55·4′W	X	137
Kinnerton Green	Flint	SJ3361	53°8·8′	2°59·7′W	T	117
Kinnerton Lodge	Flint	SJ3261	53°8·8′	3°0·6′W	X	117
Kinness Burn	Fife	NO4715	56°19·7′	2°51·0′W	W	59
Kinnesswood	Pth & Kin	NO1702	56°12·5′	3°19·8′W	T	58
Kinneston	Pth & Kin	NO1901	56°11·9′	3°17·9′W	X	58
Kinneston Craigs	Pth & Kin	NO1902	56°12·5′	3°17·9′W	X	58
Kinnettles Ho	Angus	NO4246	56°36·4′	2°56·2′W	X	54
Kinniegar	S Ayr	NX0881	55°5·4′	5°0·1′W	X	76
Kinninghall	Scot Bord	NT5315	55°25·8′	2°44·1′W	X	79
Kinnings	Devon	SS6220	50°58·0′	3°57·5′W	X	180
Kinninmonth	Fife	NO4212	56°18·1′	2°55·8′W	X	59
Kinninmonth	Fife	NT2199	56°10·9′	3°15·9′W	X	58
Kinninmonth Hill	Fife	NO4312	56°18·1′	2°54·8′W	X	59
Kinninvie	Durham	NZ0521	54°35·3′	1°54·9′W	T	92
Kinniside Common	Cumbr	NY0711	54°29·4′	3°25·7′W	X	89
Kinnoir	Aberd	NJ5543	57°28·8′	2°44·6′W	X	29
Kinnon Park	Pth & Kin	NO0324	56°24·2′	3°33·9′W	X	52,53,58
Kinnordy	Angus	NO3655	56°41·2′	3°2·2′W	X	54
Kinnoull Hill	Pth & Kin	NO1322	56°23·2′	3°24·1′W	H	53,58
Kinnudie	Highld	NH9055	57°34·6′	3°49·9′W	X	27
Kinoulton	Notts	SK6730	52°52·0′	0°59·9′W	T	129
Kinoulton Grange	Notts	SK7030	52°52·0′	0°57·2′W	X	129
Kinoulton Wolds	Notts	SK6530	52°52·0′	1°1·7′W	X	129
Kinpauch	Pth & Kin	NN8907	56°14·8′	3°47·0′W	X	58
Kinpauch Hill	Pth & Kin	NN8906	56°14·3′	3°47·0′W	X	58
Kinpurney	Angus	NO3142	56°34·2′	3°6·9′W	X	53
Kinpurney Hill	Angus	NO3241	56°33·6′	3°6·0′W	H	53
Kinpurnie Castle	Angus	NO2840	56°33·0′	3°9·8′W	X	53
Kinrara	Highld	NH8708	57°9·2′	3°51·6′W	X	35,36
Kinrea Cornmill	Highld	NH7846	57°29·5′	4°1·7′W	X	27
Kinrive	Angus	NO3862	56°45·0′	3°0·4′W	X	44
Kinrive Hill	Highld	NH6875	57°45·0′	4°12·6′W	H	21
Kinrive Plantation	Angus	NO3864	56°46·1′	3°0·4′W	F	44
Kinrive Wood	Highld	NH6975	57°45·0′	4°11·6′W	F	21
Kinross	Pth & Kin	NO1102	56°12·4′	3°25·6′W	T	58
Kinross Ho	Pth & Kin	NO1202	56°12·4′	3°24·7′W	X	58
Kinrossie	Pth & Kin	NO1832	56°28·6′	3°19·4′W	T	53
Kinsadel	Highld	NM6791	56°57·4′	5°49·5′W	X	40
Kinsaile	Highld	NC2154	58°26·5′	5°3·5′W	X	9
Kinsale Tower	D & G	NW9962	54°55·0′	5°7·7′W	X	82
Kinsall	Shrops	SJ3432	52°53·1′	2°58·4′W	X	126
Kinsbourne Green	Herts	TL1016	51°50·1′	0°23·8′W	T	166
Kinsey Cave	N Yks	SD8065	54°5·1′	2°17·9′W	A	98
Kinsey Heath	Ches	SJ6742	52°58·7′	2°29·1′W	T	118
Kinsford Gate	Somer	SS7436	51°6·8′	3°47·6′W	X	180
Kinsford Water	Somer	SS7536	51°6·8′	3°46·8′W	W	180
Kinshaldy	Fife	NO4823	56°24·0′	2°50·1′W	X	54,59
Kinsham	Worcs	SO9335	52°1·0′	2°5·7′W	T	150
Kinsley	Wakf	SE4114	53°37·5′	1°22·4′W	T	111
Kinsley Common	Wakf	SE4214	53°37·5′	1°21·5′W	X	111
Kinsley Wood	Shrops	SO2972	52°20·7′	3°2·1′W	F	137,148
Kinson	Bourne	SZ0696	50°46·0′	1°54·5′W	T	195
Kinson	Shrops	SO5782	52°26·3′	2°37·6′W	X	137,138
Kinstair	Aberd	NJ5714	57°13·1′	2°42·3′W	X	37
Kinsteary Ho	Highld	NH9254	57°34·1′	3°47·9′W	X	27
Kintail Forest	Highld	NG9917	57°12·2′	5°19·2′W	X	33
Kintail Lodge (Hotel)	Highld	NG9319	57°13·2′	5°25·3′W	X	33
Kintaline Mill	Arg & Bt	NM8939	56°30·0′	5°25·3′W	X	49
Kintallan	Arg & Bt	NR7487	56°1·6′	5°37·2′W	T	55
Kintbury	W Berks	SU3866	51°23·7′	1°26·8′W	T	174
Kintbury Cross Ways	W Berks	SU3865	51°23·2′	1°26·8′W	X	174
Kintbury Fm	W Berks	SU3766	51°23·7′	1°27·7′W	FM	174
Kintbury Holt Fm	W Berks	SU3965	51°23·2′	1°26·0′W	FM	174
Kintessack	Moray	NJ0060	57°37·4′	3°40·0′W	T	27
Kintewline	Aberd	NJ8600	57°5·7′	2°13·4′W	X	38
Kinthall Fm	Heref	SO6664	52°16·6′	2°29·5′W	FM	138,149
Kintillo	Pth & Kin	NO1317	56°20·5′	3°24·0′W	T	58
Kintley Fm	Heref	SO2749	52°8·3′	3°3·6′W	FM	148
Kintocher	Aberd	NJ5709	57°10·4′	2°42·2′W	X	37
Kintocher	Pth & Kin	NN9222	56°22·9′	3°44·5′W	X	52,58
Kinton	Heref	SO4074	52°21·9′	2°52·5′W	T	137,148
Kinton	Shrops	SJ3719	52°46·1′	2°55·6′W	T	126
Kinton	Shrops	SO2899	52°35·3′	3°3·4′W	X	137
Kintore	Aberd	NJ7816	57°14·3′	2°21·4′W	T	38
Kintour	Arg & Bt	NR4551	55°41·4′	6°3·0′W	X	60
Kintour River	Arg & Bt	NR4452	55°41·9′	6°4·0′W	W	60
Kintra	Arg & Bt	NM3125	56°20·7′	6°20·8′W	T	48
Kintra	Arg & Bt	NR3248	55°39·4′	6°15·2′W	X	60
Kintradwell	Highld	NC9107	58°2·6′	3°50·3′W	X	17
Kintrae	Moray	NJ1765	57°40·3′	3°23·0′W	X	28
Kintra River	Arg & Bt	NR3349	55°39·9′	6°14·3′W	W	60
Kintraw	Arg & Bt	NM8205	56°11·5′	5°30·4′W	X	55
Kintrockat Ho	Angus	NO5659	56°43·5′	2°42·7′W	X	54
Kintyre	Arg & Bt	NR7023	55°27·1′	5°37·8′W	X	68
Kintyre	Arg & Bt	NR7240	55°36·3′	5°36·7′W	X	62
Kintyrie	Angus	NO3857	56°42·3′	3°0·3′W	X	54
Kinuachdrachd	Arg & Bt	NR7098	56°7·4′	5°41·6′W	T	55,61
Kinuachdrachd Harbour	Arg & Bt	NR7098	56°7·4′	5°41·6′W	W	55,61
Kinvaid	Pth & Kin	NO0630	56°27·4′	3°31·1′W	X	52,53
Kinvaston Hall Fm	Staffs	SJ9012	52°42·6′	2°8·5′W	FM	127
Kinveachy	Highld	NH9118	57°14·6′	3°47·9′W	T	36
Kinveachy Forest	Highld	NH8517	57°14·0′	3°53·9′W	X	35,36
Kinveachy Lodge	Highld	NH9018	57°14·6′	3°48·9′W	X	36
Kinver	Staffs	SO8483	52°26·9′	2°13·7′W	T	138
Kinver Edge	Staffs	SO8382	52°26·4′	2°14·6′W	X	138
Kinwalsey	Warw	SP2585	52°28·0′	1°37·5′W	T	140
Kinwardstone Fm	Wilts	SU2360	51°20·5′	1°39·8′W	FM	174
Kinwarton	Warw	SP1058	52°13·4′	1°50·8′W	X	150
Kinwarton Ho	Warw	SP0958	52°13·4′	1°51·7′W	X	150
Kiondroughad	I of M	NX3900	54°22·5′	4°28·3′W	X	95
Kione Beg	I of M	SC1666	54°3·7′	4°48·3′W	X	95
Kionedroghad	I of M	SC3292	54°18·0′	4°34·5′W	X	95
Kionehenin	I of M	SC4686	54°15·0′	4°21·4′W	X	95
Kione ny Garee	I of M	SC1868	54°4·8′	4°46·5′W	X	95

Kione ny Halby	I of M	SC1665	54°3·1′	4°48·2′W	X	95
Kione y Ghoggan	I of M	SC1966	54°3·7′	4°45·5′W	X	95
Kionlough	I of M	SC4598	54°21·5′	4°22·7′W	X	95
Kionslieu	I of M	SC2878	54°10·4′	4°37·7′W	X	95
Kip Burn	S Lanak	NS7334	55°35·2′	4°0·5′W	W	71
Kip Hill	Durham	NZ2053	54°52·5′	1°40·9′W	T	88
Kip Hill	Northum	NZ0267	55°0·1′	1°57·7′W	H	87
Kip Knowe	Scot Bord	NT8324	55°30·8′	2°15·7′W	X	74
Kiplaw	Aberd	NK0534	57°24·0′	1°54·6′W	X	30
Kip Law	Northum	NY7150	54°50·9′	2°26·7′W	X	86,87
Kiplaw	Northum	NZ1181	55°7·6′	1°49·2′W	X	81
Kiplaw Croft	Aberd	NK0533	57°23·5′	1°54·6′W	X	30
Kiplin	N Yks	SE2797	54°22·3′	1°34·6′W	T	99
Kiplingcotes	E Yorks	SE9245	53°53·8′	0°35·6′W	X	106
Kiplingcotes Fm	E Yorks	SE9345	53°53·8′	0°34·7′W	FM	106
Kipling Cotes Race Course	E Yorks	SE9046	53°54·4′	0°37·4′W	X	106
Kipling Ho	E Yorks	SE9047	53°54·9′	0°37·4′W	X	106
Kiplin Hall	N Yks	SE2797	54°22·3′	1°34·6′W	A	99
Kipney	Pth & Kin	NN9630	56°27·3′	3°40·8′W	X	52,53
Kipp	D & G	NX8455	54°52·8′	3°48·1′W	X	84
Kipp	Stir	NN5516	56°19·1′	4°20·2′W	X	57
Kippax	Leeds	SE4130	53°46·1′	1°22·3′W	T	105
Kippen	Kent	TQ8957	51°17·1′	0°43·0′E	X	178
Kippen	Stir	NS6594	56°7·4′	4°9·9′W	T	57
Kippen Ho	Pth & Kin	NO0112	56°17·7′	3°35·5′W	X	58
Kippen Muir	Stir	NS6192	56°6·3′	4°13·7′W	X	57
Kippenrait	Stir	NN7900	56°10·9′	3°56·5′W	X	57
Kippenrait Glen	Stir	NS7999	56°10·4′	3°56·5′W	X	57
Kippenross House	Stir	NS7899	56°10·3′	3°57·5′W	X	57
Kipperknoll	Heref	SO4951	52°9·5′	2°44·3′W	X	148,149
Kipperlynn	Northum	NZ0657	54°54·7′	1°54·0′W	X	87
Kipperoch Fm	W Dunb	NS3777	55°57·8′	4°36·2′W	FM	63
Kippetlaw	Scot Bord	NT6854	55°46·9′	2°30·2′W	X	67,74
Kippetlaw Burn	Scot Bord	NT6955	55°47·5′	2°29·2′W	W	67,74
Kippford or Scaur	D & G	NX8354	54°52·3′	3°49·0′W	T	84
Kippielaw	E Loth	NT5875	55°58·2′	2°39·9′W	X	67
Kippilaw	Midlo	NT3466	55°53·2′	3°2·9′W	X	66
Kippilaw	Scot Bord	NT5428	55°32·9′	2°43·3′W	T	73
Kippilaw Mains	Scot Bord	NT5429	55°33·4′	2°43·3′W	T	73
Kipping's Cross	Kent	TQ6439	51°7·8′	0°21·0′E	T	188
Kippington	Kent	TQ5254	51°16·1′	0°11·1′E	T	188
Kippit Fm	Scot Bord	NT1147	55°42·8′	3°24·6′W	FM	72
Kippo Fm	Fife	NO5710	56°17·1′	2°41·2′W	FM	59
Kippo Plantn	Fife	NO5610	56°17·1′	2°42·2′W	F	59
Kippsbyre	N Lanak	NS7466	55°52·5′	4°0·4′W	X	64
Kipps Fm	N Lanak	NS7366	55°52·5′	4°1·4′W	FM	64
Kipps, The	Midlo	NT3049	55°44·0′	3°6·4′W	H	73
Kipps, The	Midlo	NT3049	55°44·0′	3°6·4′W	X	73
Kipscombe	Devon	SS6739	51°8·3′	3°53·7′W	X	180
Kipscombe Hill	Devon	SS7649	51°13·8′	3°46·2′W	H	180
Kipscott Barton	Devon	SS8026	51°1·5′	3°42·3′W	X	181
Kipson Ho	W Susx	SU8500	50°47·8′	0°47·2′W	X	197
Kip, The	Scot Bord	NT3119	55°27·9′	3°5·0′W	H	79
Kip,The	Scot Bord	NT7831	55°34·6′	2°20·5′W	X	74
Kip, The	Scot Bord	NT8019	55°28·1′	2°18·5′W	H	80
Kipton Ash Fm	Norf	TF8423	52°46·6′	0°44·1′E	FM	132
Kipton Heath	Norf	TF8324	52°47·2′	0°43·2′E	F	132
Kirbist	Orkney	HY4243	59°16·4′	3°0·6′W	X	5
Kirbist	Orkney	HY4729	59°8·9′	2°55·1′W	X	5,6
Kirbist	Orkney	HY7552	59°21·5′	2°25·9′W	X	5
Kirbister	Orkney	HY2414	59°0·6′	3°18·9′W	T	6
Kirbister	Orkney	HY3607	58°57·0′	3°6·3′W	T	6,7
Kirbuster	Orkney	HY2825	59°6·6′	3°15·0′W	T	6
Kirbuster	Orkney	HY6823	59°5·8′	2°33·0′W	X	5
Kirbuster Hill	Orkney	HY2826	59°7·2′	3°15·0′W	H	6
Kirbuster Ho	Orkney	ND3290	58°47·8′	3°10·1′W	X	7
Kirby	I of M	SC3676	54°9·5′	4°30·3′W	T	95
Kirby Bedon	Norf	TG2805	52°35·9′	1°22·4′E	T	134
Kirby Bellars	Leic	SK7117	52°45·0′	0°56·5′W	T	129
Kirby Br	N Yks	NZ5307	54°27·6′	1°10·5′W	X	93
Kirby Cane	Norf	TM3793	52°29·2′	1°29·9′E	T	134
Kirby Corner	Cov	SP2976	52°23·1′	1°34·0′W	T	140
Kirby Creek	Essex	TM2224	51°52·4′	1°13·9′E	W	169
Kirby Cross	Essex	TM2220	51°50·3′	1°13·8′E	T	169
Kirby Fields	Leic	SK5203	52°37·6′	1°13·5′W	T	140
Kirby Fm	Warw	SP3044	52°5·8′	1°33·3′W	FM	151
Kirby Gate	Leic	SK7117	52°45·0′	0°56·5′W	X	129
Kirby Grange	Leic	SK4805	52°38·7′	1°17·0′W	X	140
Kirby Grange	N Yks	NZ5404	54°26·0′	1°9·6′W	X	93
Kirby Grange	N Yks	SE3685	54°15·8′	1°26·4′W	X	99
Kirby Grange	N Yks	SE9064	54°4·1′	0°37·1′W	X	101
Kirby Green	Norf	TM3794	52°29·8′	1°29·9′E	T	134
Kirby Grindalythe	N Yks	SE9067	54°5·7′	0°37·0′W	T	101
Kirby Grounds	Northnts	SP6449	52°8·4′	1°3·5′W	X	152
Kirby Grove	N Yks	SE3585	54°15·8′	1°27·3′W	X	99
Kirby Hall	Essex	TL7737	52°0·4′	0°35·1′E	X	155
Kirby Hall	Northnts	SP9292	52°31·3′	0°38·2′W	A	141
Kirby Hall	N Yks	SE4561	54°2·8′	1°18·3′W	X	99
Kirby Hall Fm	Northnts	SP9193	52°31·9′	0°39·1′W	FM	141
Kirby Hall Fm	N Yks	SE4560	54°2·3′	1°18·4′W	FM	99
Kirby Hall Park	N Yks	SE4561	54°2·8′	1°18·3′W	X	99
Kirby Hall Park	N Yks	SE4661	54°2·8′	1°17·4′W	X	100
Kirby Hill	Norf	TM3793	52°29·2′	1°29·9′E	X	134
Kirby Hill	N Yks	NZ1306	54°27·2′	1°47·5′W	T	92
Kirby Ho	W Berks	SU3763	51°22·1′	1°27·7′W	X	174
Kirby Knowle	N Yks	SE4687	54°16·8′	1°17·2′W	T	100
Kirby Knowle Moor	N Yks	SE4788	54°17·4′	1°16·3′W	X	100
Kirby Lane Fm	N Yks	NZ5306	54°27·0′	1°10·5′W	FM	93
Kirby-le-Soken	Essex	TM2221	51°50·8′	1°13·8′E	T	169
Kirby Lodge	Northnts	SP9192	52°31·3′	0°39·1′W	X	141
Kirby Lodge Fm	Leic	SK7214	52°43·4′	0°55·6′W	FM	129
Kirby Lodge Fm	Leic	SK7216	52°44·4′	0°55·6′W	FM	129
Kirby Misperton	N Yks	SE7779	54°12·3′	0°48·8′W	T	100
Kirby Moor	Cumbr	NY5261	54°56·7′	2°44·5′W	X	86
Kirby Mount	Lincs	TF0944	52°59·2′	0°22·2′W	X	130
Kirby Muxloe	Leic	SK5104	52°38·1′	1°14·4′W	T	140
Kirby-O-Carr	N Yks	SE7778	54°11·8′	0°48·8′W	FM	100
Kirby Plantn	N Yks	SE9167	54°5·7′	0°36·1′W	F	101
Kirby Row	Norf	TM3792	52°28·7′	1°29·8′E	T	134
Kirby Sigston	N Yks	SE4194	54°20·6′	1°21·7′W	T	99

Kirby's Manor Fm	Herts	TL2642	52°4·0'	0°9·3'W	FM	153
Kirby Underdale	E Yorks	SE8058	54°0·9'	0°46·3'W	T	106
Kirby Wiske	N Yks	SE3784	54°15·3'	1°25·5'W	T	99
Kirby Wold Fm	N Yks	SE9069	54°6·8'	0°37·0'W	FM	101
Kirclachie Burn	D & G	NX1064	54°56·3'	4°57·5'W	W	82
Kircram	Aberd	NO6482	56°55·9'	2°35·0'W	H	45
Kirdellbeg	Moray	NJ1741	57°27·4'	3°22·5'W	X	28
Kirdford	W Susx	TQ0126	51°1·7'	0°33·2'W	T	186,197
Kirerroch	D & G	NX4878	55°4·6'	4°22·4'W	X	77
Kirk	Highld	ND2859	58°31·1'	3°13·7'W	X	11,12
Kirkabister	Shetld	HU4866	60°22·8'	1°7·3'W	T	2,3
Kirkabister	Shetld	HU4938	60°7·7'	1°6·6'W	X	4
Kirkabister	Shetld	HU4958	60°18·5'	1°6·3'W	T	2,3
Kirkabister	Shetld	HU5395	60°38·4'	1°1·4'W	X	1,2
Kirkabister Ness	Shetld	HU4837	60°7·1'	1°7·7'W	X	4
Kirkaby	Shetld	HP5606	60°44·3'	0°57·9'W	X	1
Kirka Dale	Shetld	HU5093	60°37·3'	1°4·7'W	X	1,2
Kirkaig Point	Highld	NC0521	58°8·4'	5°18·3'W	X	15
Kirkandrews	D & G	NX5948	54°48·7'	4°11·2'W	X	83
Kirkandrews Bay	D & G	NX5947	54°48·1'	4°11·2'W	W	83
Kirkandrews-on-Eden	Cumbr	NY3558	54°55·0'	3°0·4'W	T	85
Kirkandrews Tower	Cumbr	NY3871	55°2·0'	2°57·8'W	A	85
Kirka Ness	Shetld	HU3043	60°10·5'	1°27·1'W	X	4
Kirka Ness	Shetld	HU3346	60°12·1'	1°23·8'W	X	4
Kirkapol	Arg & Bt	NM0447	56°31·6'	6°48·4'W	T	46
Kirka Taing	Orkney	ND3396	58°51·0'	3°9·2'W	X	6,7
Kirkaton	Shetld	HP6514	60°48·5'	0°47·8'W	T	1
Kirka Ward	Shetld	HU3648	60°13·2'	1°20·5'W	X	3
Kirkbampton	Cumbr	NY3056	54°53·9'	3°5·1'W	T	85
Kirkbank	Cumbr	SD1382	54°13·8'	3°19·7'W	X	96
Kirk Bank	Cumbr	SD7287	54°16·9'	2°25·4'W	X	98
Kirkbank	D & G	NY0990	55°12·0'	3°25·4'W	X	78
Kirkbank	D & G	NY1275	55°4·0'	3°22·3'W	X	85
Kirk Bank	N Yks	NZ2405	54°26·6'	1°37·4'W	X	93
Kirkbarrow	Cumbr	NY4428	54°38·9'	2°51·6'W	X	90
Kirkbarrow	Cumbr	NY4926	54°37·8'	2°47·0'W	X	90
Kirk Bay	Orkney	ND3692	58°48·9'	3°6·0'W	W	7
Kirkbean	D & G	NX9759	54°55·2'	3°36·0'W	T	84
Kirkbean Burn	D & G	NX9560	54°55·7'	3°37·9'W	W	84
Kirkbean Glen	D & G	NX9659	54°55·1'	3°36·9'W	X	84
Kirk Beck	Cumbr	NY0311	54°29·4'	3°29·4'W	W	89
Kirk Beck	Cumbr	NY5774	55°3·8'	2°40·0'W	W	86
Kirk Beck	N Yks	NZ2304	54°26·1'	1°38·3'W	W	93
Kirkbeck	N Yks	SD6568	54°6·6'	2°31·7'W	X	97
Kirkbeckstown	Cumbr	NY5474	55°3·8'	2°42·8'W	X	86
Kirkber	Cumbr	NY7020	54°34·7'	2°27·4'W	X	91
Kirkblane Fm	D & G	NY0269	55°0·6'	3°31·5'W	FM	84
Kirkbog	D & G	NX8793	55°13·4'	3°46·2'W	X	78
Kirkborough	Cumbr	NY0536	54°42·9'	3°28·1'W	T	89
Kirkbrae	Orkney	HY4546	59°18·1'	2°57·5'W	X	5
Kirk Bramwith	Donc	SE6111	53°35·8'	1°4·3'W	T	111
Kirkbreck	Orkney	HY4603	58°54·9'	2°55·8'W	X	6,7
Kirkbride	Cumbr	NY2256	54°53·8'	3°12·5'W	T	85
Kirkbride	D & G	NS8505	55°19·8'	3°48·3'W	X	71,78
Kirkbride	D & G	NX1140	54°43·4'	4°55·7'W	X	82
Kirkbride	D & G	NX4855	54°52·3'	4°21·7'W	X	83
Kirkbride	D & G	NX5655	54°52·4'	4°14·2'W	X	83
Kirkbride	D & G	NX7454	54°52·1'	3°57·4'W	X	83,84
Kirkbride	D & G	NX8887	55°10·1'	3°45·1'W	X	78
Kirkbride	S Ayr	NS3303	55°17·8'	4°37·4'W	X	76
Kirkbride Burn	D & G	NX4956	54°52·8'	4°20·8'W	W	83
Kirkbride Ho	S Ayr	NS3304	55°18·4'	4°37·4'W	X	76
Kirkbridge	N Yks	SE2590	54°18·5'	1°36·5'W	T	99
Kirkbryde	D & G	NX0070	54°59·3'	5°7·1'W	X	76,82
Kirkbuddo Ho	Angus	NO5043	56°34·8'	2°48·4'W	X	54
Kirk Burn	D & G	NS7805	55°19·7'	3°55·0'W	W	71,78
Kirk Burn	D & G	NS9005	55°19·9'	3°43·6'W	W	71,78
Kirk Burn	D & G	NY1383	55°8·3'	3°21·5'W	W	78
Kirkburn	D & G	NY1383	55°8·3'	3°21·5'W	X	78
Kirk Burn	D & G	NY2679	55°6·2'	3°9·2'W	W	85
Kirk Burn	D & G	NY3191	55°12·8'	3°4·6'W	W	79
Kirkburn	E Yorks	SE9855	53°59·1'	0°29·9'W	T	106
Kirk Burn	Highld	ND3164	58°33·8'	3°10·7'W	W	11,12
Kirk Burn	Northum	NU0722	55°29·8'	1°52·9'W	W	75
Kirk Burn	Northum	NY8378	55°6·0'	2°15·6'W	W	86,87
Kirk Burn	Scot Bord	NT2515	55°25·6'	3°10·7'W	W	79
Kirk Burn	Scot Bord	NT2937	55°37·5'	3°7·2'W	W	73
Kirkburn	Scot Bord	NT2938	55°38·1'	3°7·2'W	T	73
Kirk Burn	Scot Bord	NT3111	55°23·5'	3°4·9'W	W	79
Kirk Burn	Scot Bord	NT7650	55°44·8'	2°22·5'W	W	67,74
Kirk Burn	S Lanak	NS9635	55°36·1'	3°38·6'W	W	72
Kirkburn Grange	E Yorks	SE9657	54°0·2'	0°31·7'W	X	106
Kirkburn Manor	E Yorks	SE9855	53°59·1'	0°29·9'W	X	106
Kirkburton	Kirk	SE1912	53°36·5'	1°42·4'W	T	110
Kirkby	Know	SJ4198	53°28·8'	2°52·9'W	T	108
Kirkby	Lincs	TF0692	53°25·1'	0°23·9'W	T	112
Kirkby	N Yks	NZ5306	54°27·0'	1°10·5'W	T	93
Kirkby Beck	N Yks	SD8860	54°2·4'	2°10·6'W	W	98
Kirkby Fell	N Yks	SD8763	54°4·0'	2°11·5'W	X	98
Kirkby Fenside	Lincs	TF3261	53°8·0'	0°1·2'W	T	122
Kirkby Fleetham	N Yks	SE2894	54°20·7'	1°33·7'W	T	99
Kirkby Fleetham Hall	N Yks	SE2895	54°21·2'	1°33·7'W	X	99
Kirkby Forest	Notts	SK5254	53°5·1'	1°13·0'W	F	120
Kirkby Grange Fm	Kirk	SE2414	53°37·6'	1°37·8'W	FM	110
Kirkby Green	Lincs	TF0857	53°6·2'	0°22·8'W	T	121
Kirkby Hall	Cumbr	SD2383	54°14·5'	3°10·5'W	A	96
Kirkby Hill	Lincs	TF3364	53°9·6'	0°0·2'W	X	122
Kirkby Hill	N Yks	SE3868	54°6·6'	1°24·7'W	T	99
Kirkby Ho	Cumbr	SD4692	54°19·5'	2°49·4'W	X	97
Kirkby - In - Ashfield	Notts	SK5056	53°6·2'	1°14·8'W	T	120
Kirkby-in-Furness	Cumbr	SD2282	54°13·9'	3°11·4'W	T	96
Kirkby la Thorpe	Lincs	TF0945	52°59·7'	0°22·1'W	T	130
Kirkby Lodge	Leic	SK4401	52°36·5'	1°20·6'W	X	140
Kirkby Lonsdale	Cumbr	SD6178	54°12·0'	2°35·5'W	T	97
Kirkby Malham	N Yks	SD8961	54°2·9'	2°9·6'W	T	98
Kirkby Mallory	Leic	SK4500	52°36·0'	1°19·7'W	T	140
Kirkby Malzeard	N Yks	SE2374	54°9·9'	1°38·4'W	T	99
Kirkby Malzeard Moor	N Yks	SE1674	54°9·9'	1°44·9'W	X	99
Kirkby Mills	N Yks	SE7085	54°15·6'	0°55·1'W	T	94,100
Kirkby Moats	Leic	SK4501	52°36·5'	1°19·7'W	A	140
Kirkby Moor	Cumbr	SD2584	54°15·0'	3°8·6'W	X	96
Kirkby Moor	Lincs	TF2163	53°9·3'	0°11·0'W	X	122
Kirkbymoorside	N Yks	SE6986	54°16·1'	0°56·0'W	T	94,100
Kirkby Moss	Know	SJ4498	53°28·8'	2°50·2'W	X	108
Kirkby Old Parks	Leic	SK4502	52°37·1'	1°19·7'W	X	140
Kirkby on Bain	Lincs	TF2462	53°8·7'	0°8·4'W	T	122
Kirkby Overblow	N Yks	SE3249	53°56·4'	1°30·3'W	T	104
Kirkby Park's Fm	Notts	SK4654	53°5·1'	1°18·4'W	FM	120
Kirkby Park Wood	Cumbr	SD2386	54°16·1'	3°10·5'W	F	96
Kirkby Pool	Cumbr	SD2386	54°16·1'	3°10·5'W	W	96
Kirkby Stephen	Cumbr	NY7708	54°28·3'	2°20·9'W	T	91
Kirkby Stephen Common	Cumbr	NY7501	54°24·5'	2°22·7'W	X	91
Kirkby Stephen Sta	Cumbr	NY7606	54°27·2'	2°21·8'W	X	91
Kirkby Thore	Cumbr	NY6325	54°37·4'	2°34·0'W	T	91
Kirkby Top	N Yks	SD8962	54°3·5'	2°9·7'W	X	98
Kirkby Underwood	Lincs	TF0727	52°50·0'	0°24·3'W	T	130
Kirkby Wharfe	N Yks	SE5040	53°51·5'	1°14·0'W	T	105
Kirkby Woodhouse	Notts	SK4954	53°5·1'	1°15·7'W	T	120
Kirkcaldy	Fife	NT2791	56°6·6'	3°10·0'W	T	59
Kirkcaldy Sands	Fife	NT2891	56°6·6'	3°9·0'W	X	59
Kirkcalla	D & G	NX3074	55°2·1'	4°39·2'W	X	76
Kirkcambeck	Cumbr	NY5368	55°0·5'	2°43·7'W	T	86
Kirkcarrion	Durham	NY9423	54°36·4'	2°5·2'W	X	91,92
Kirkchrist	D & G	NX3659	54°54·2'	4°33·0'W	X	83
Kirkchrist	D & G	NX6651	54°50·4'	4°4·8'W	X	83,84
Kirkclaugh	D & G	NX5352	54°50·7'	4°16·9'W	X	83
Kirk Cleuch Rig	D & G	NY2998	55°16·5'	3°6·6'W	H	79
Kirkcolm	D & G	NX0268	54°58·3'	5°5·2'W	T	82
Kirkconnel	D & G	NS7312	55°23·4'	3°59·9'W	T	71
Kirkconnel Church	D & G	NY2575	55°4·1'	3°10·0'W	A	85
Kirkconnell	D & G	NX6760	54°55·3'	4°4·1'W	X	83,84
Kirkconnell	D & G	NX7694	55°13·7'	3°56·6'W	X	78
Kirkconnell	D & G	NX9768	55°0·0'	3°36·2'W	X	84
Kirkconnell Burn	D & G	NX7694	55°13·7'	3°56·6'W	W	78
Kirkconnell Flow	D & G	NX9769	55°0·5'	3°36·2'W	X	84
Kirkconnell Linn	D & G	NX6761	54°55·8'	4°4·1'W	W	83,84
Kirkconnell Merse	D & G	NX9868	55°0·0'	3°35·2'W	X	84
Kirkcowan	D & G	NX3261	54°55·2'	4°36·9'W	T	82
Kirk Craig	Stir	NN3625	56°23·6'	4°39·0'W	X	50
Kirk Craigs	Clackm	NS9298	56°10·0'	3°43·9'W	X	58
Kirkcudbright	D & G	NX6850	54°49·9'	4°2·9'W	T	83,84
Kirkcudbright Bay	D & G	NX6645	54°47·2'	4°4·6'W	W	83,84
Kirkcudbright Fm	D & G	NX7789	55°11·1'	3°55·5'W	FM	78
Kirkdale	Cumbr	NY6634	54°42·2'	2°31·2'W	X	91
Kirk Dale	Derby	SK1868	53°12·8'	1°43·4'W	X	119
Kirkdale	Liv	SJ3493	53°26·0'	2°59·2'W	T	108
Kirk Dale	N Yks	SE6686	54°16·2'	0°58·8'W	X	94,100
Kirk Dale	N Yks	SE8984	54°14·9'	0°37·6'W	X	101
Kirkdale Burn	D & G	NX5153	54°51·2'	4°18·8'W	W	83
Kirkdale Church	D & G	NX5154	54°51·8'	4°18·9'W	A	83
Kirkdale Fm	N Yks	SE6585	54°15·6'	0°59·7'W	FM	94,100
Kirkdale Ho	D & G	NX5153	54°51·2'	4°18·8'W	X	83
Kirkdale Manor (School)	N Yks	SE6585	54°15·6'	0°59·7'W	X	94,100
Kirkdale Port	D & G	NX5053	54°51·2'	4°19·8'W	X	83
Kirkdale Slack	N Yks	SE8484	54°14·9'	0°42·2'W	X	100
Kirkdale Woods	N Yks	SE6786	54°16·2'	0°57·9'W	F	94,100
Kirk Dam	Arg & Bt	NS0863	55°49·6'	5°3·5'W	W	63
Kirkdean	Scot Bord	NT1244	55°41·1'	3°23·5'W	X	72
Kirk Deighton	N Yks	SE3950	53°56·9'	1°23·9'W	T	104
Kirk Ella	E Yorks	TA0229	53°45·1'	0°26·8'W	T	106,107
Kirk Ella Grange	E Yorks	TA0030	53°45·6'	0°28·6'W	X	106,107
Kirkennan	D & G	NX8258	54°54·4'	3°50·0'W	X	84
Kirkennan Burn	D & G	NX3984	55°7·7'	4°31·1'W	W	77
Kirkeoch	D & G	NX6649	54°49·3'	4°4·7'W	X	83,84
Kirkeoch Hill	D & G	NX6649	54°49·3'	4°4·7'W	H	83,84
Kirke's Plantn	Notts	SK7674	53°15·7'	0°51·2'W	F	120
Kirkettle	Midlo	NT2661	55°50·4'	3°10·5'W	X	66
Kirk Fell	Cumbr	NY1726	54°37·6'	3°16·7'W	H	89,90
Kirk Fell	Cumbr	NY1910	54°29·0'	3°14·6'W	H	89,90
Kirkfell Crags	Cumbr	NY1911	54°29·5'	3°14·6'W	X	89,90
Kirkfield	Highld	ND1865	58°34·2'	3°24·1'W	X	11,12
Kirkfield	Highld	NH3127	57°18·4'	4°47·9'W	X	26
Kirkfield	Northum	NY8578	55°6·0'	2°13·7'W	X	87
Kirkfieldbank	S Lanak	NS8643	55°40·3'	3°48·3'W	T	71,72
Kirkfield Ho	S Lanak	NS8643	55°40·3'	3°48·3'W	X	71,72
Kirkforthar	Fife	NO3004	56°13·7'	3°7·3'W	X	59
Kirkforthar Feus	Fife	NO2804	56°13·6'	3°9·2'W	T	59
Kirkforthar Ho	Fife	NO2904	56°13·7'	3°8·3'W	A	59
Kirkgate Bridge	Cambs	TF4316	52°43·6'	0°7·5'E	X	131
Kirkgate Lodge	N Yks	SE9484	54°14·8'	0°33·0'W	X	101
Kirk Gates	N Yks	SE7460	54°2·1'	0°51·8'W	X	100
Kirk Geo	Orkney	HY2504	58°55·3'	3°17·7'W	X	6,7
Kirk Geo	Orkney	ND4893	58°49·5'	2°53·6'W	X	7
Kirk Gill	S Lanak	NS9120	55°28·0'	3°43·0'W	W	71,72
Kirk Gill Moor	N Yks	SD9177	54°11·6'	2°7·9'W	X	98
Kirkgunzeon	D & G	NX8666	54°58·8'	3°46·5'W	T	84
Kirkgunzeon Lane	D & G	NX8463	54°57·1'	3°48·3'W	W	84
Kirkhall	N Lanak	NS8655	55°46·7'	3°48·6'W	X	65,72
Kirk Hallam	Derby	SK4540	52°57·6'	1°19·4'W	T	129
Kirkham	Lancs	SD4232	53°47·1'	2°52·4'W	T	102
Kirkham	N Yks	SE7365	54°4·8'	0°52·6'W	T	100
Kirkham Fm	Glos	SP1623	51°54·6'	1°45·6'W	FM	163
Kirkhamgate	Wakf	SE2922	53°41·9'	1°33·2'W	T	104
Kirkham Ho	Torbay	SX8860	50°26·0'	3°34·2'W	X	202
Kirkham i'th'Fields	Lancs	SD3939	53°50·9'	2°55·2'W	X	102
Kirk Hammerton	N Yks	SE4655	53°59·6'	1°17·5'W	T	105
Kirkhams	Bury	SD8105	53°32·7'	2°16·8'W	T	109
Kirkharle	Northum	NZ0182	55°8·2'	1°58·6'W	T	81
Kirkhaugh	Northum	NY6949	54°50·3'	2°28·5'W	X	86,87
Kirkhead	Cumbr	NY1320	54°34·3'	3°20·3'W	X	89
Kirkheaton	Kirk	SE1818	53°39·7'	1°43·2'W	T	110
Kirkheaton	Northum	NZ0177	55°5·5'	1°58·6'W	T	87
Kirkhill	Aberd	NJ4718	57°15·2'	2°52·3'W	X	37
Kirkhill	Aberd	NJ5335	57°24·4'	2°46·5'W	X	29
Kirk Hill	Aberd	NJ6539	57°26·7'	2°34·5'W	H	29
Kirkhill	Aberd	NJ9334	57°24·0'	2°6·5'W	X	30
Kirkhill	Aberd	NJ9622	57°17·6'	2°3·5'W	X	38
Kirkhill	Aberd	NJ9834	57°24·0'	2°1·5'W	X	30
Kirkhill	Angus	NO6860	56°44·1'	2°30·9'W	T	45
Kirkhill	C of Aber	NJ8709	57°10·6'	2°12·4'W	X	38
Kirk Hill	D & G	NS7705	55°19·7'	3°55·9'W	X	71,78
Kirkhill	D & G	NY0874	55°3·4'	3°26·0'W	X	85
Kirkhill	D & G	NY1092	55°13·1'	3°24·5'W	X	78
Kirkhill	D & G	NY1396	55°15·3'	3°21·7'W	X	78
Kirk Hill	D & G	NY1499	55°16·9'	3°20·8'W	H	78
Kirkhill	E Renf	NS5555	55°46·3'	4°18·3'W	T	64
Kirkhill	Highld	NH5545	57°28·6'	4°24·6'W	T	26
Kirkhill	Midlo	NT2360	55°49·9'	3°13·3'W	T	66
Kirkhill	Moray	NJ1263	57°39·2'	3°28·0'W	X	28
Kirkhill	Moray	NJ2462	57°38·8'	3°15·9'W	X	28
Kirkhill	Moray	NJ2733	57°23·2'	3°12·4'W	X	28
Kirkhill	Moray	NJ3051	57°32·9'	3°9·7'W	X	28
Kirkhill	Northum	NZ0287	55°10·9'	1°57·7'W	X	81
Kirk Hill	N Yks	SE8469	54°6·8'	0°42·5'W	X	100
Kirkhill	Pth & Kin	NN9618	56°20·8'	3°40·5'W	X	58
Kirk Hill	S Ayr	NS2604	55°18·2'	4°44·0'W	H	76
Kirkhill	S Ayr	NS4029	55°32·0'	4°31·7'W	X	70
Kirk Hill	Scot Bord	NT3212	55°24·1'	3°4·0'W	H	79
Kirkhill	Scot Bord	NT5943	55°41·0'	2°38·7'W	X	73,74
Kirk Hill	Scot Bord	NT9168	55°54·6'	2°8·2'W	H	67
Kirk Hill	Scot Bord	NY4686	55°10·2'	2°50·4'W	H	79
Kirkhill	W Loth	NT0772	55°56·2'	3°28·9'W	T	65
Kirkhill Fm	Lincs	TF2030	52°51·5'	0°12·7'W	FM	131
Kirkhill Forest	C of Aber	NJ8413	57°12·7'	2°15·4'W	F	38
Kirkhill Ho	N Lanak	NS7754	55°46·1'	3°57·2'W	X	64
Kirkhill Ho	S Ayr	NX1485	55°7·7'	4°54·6'W	X	76
Kirkhill Hotel	Midlo	NT3262	55°51·0'	3°4·7'W	X	66
Kirkhill Pendicle	Aberd	NJ9345	57°30·0'	2°6·5'W	X	30
Kirk Ho	Cumbr	NY6528	54°39·0'	2°32·1'W	X	91
Kirk Ho	Lancs	SD5269	54°7·1'	2°43·6'W	X	97
Kirk Holm	Shetld	HU3346	60°12·1'	1°23·8'W	X	4
Kirkholt	Roch	SD8911	53°36·0'	2°9·6'W	T	109
Kirk Hope	Orkney	ND3389	58°47·3'	3°9·1'W	W	7
Kirkhope	Scot Bord	NT3823	55°30·1'	2°58·5'W	T	73
Kirkhope	S Lanak	NS9605	55°19·9'	3°37·9'W	X	78
Kirkhope Burn	Scot Bord	NT2012	55°24·0'	3°15·4'W	W	79
Kirkhope Cleuch	S Lanak	NS9506	55°20·5'	3°38·9'W	W	78
Kirkhope Hill	Scot Bord	NT3825	55°31·1'	2°58·5'W	H	73
Kirkhope Law	Scot Bord	NT2735	55°36·4'	3°9·1'W	H	73
Kirkhouse	Cumbr	NY5659	54°55·7'	2°40·8'W	T	86
Kirkhouse	D & G	NX9859	54°55·2'	3°35·1'W	X	84
Kirkhouse	Orkney	HY4952	59°21·3'	2°53·3'W	X	5
Kirkhouse	Orkney	ND4391	58°48·4'	2°58·7'W	X	7
Kirkhouse	Orkney	ND4690	58°47·9'	2°55·6'W	X	7
Kirkhouse	Scot Bord	NT3233	55°35·4'	3°4·3'W	X	73
Kirkhouse	Shetld	HU4062	60°20·7'	1°16·0'W	X	2,3
Kirkhouse	Shetld	HU4583	60°32·0'	1°10·3'W	X	1,2,3
Kirkhouse	S Lanak	NT0946	55°42·2'	3°26·4'W	X	72
Kirkhouse Green	Donc	SE6213	53°36·8'	1°3·4'W	X	111
Kirkhouse Loch	Shetld	HU4765	60°22·2'	1°8·4'W	W	2,3
Kirkhouse Point	Orkney	ND4790	58°47·9'	2°54·6'W	X	7
Kirkhouse Water	Shetld	HU3153	60°15·9'	1°25·9'W	W	3
Kirkiboll	Highld	NC5956	58°28·4'	4°24·6'W	X	10
Kirkibost	Highld	NG5417	57°10·9'	6°3·8'W	T	32
Kirkibost Island	N Eil	NF7565	57°33·8'	7°25·7'W	X	18
Kirkie Hill	Orkney	ND4390	58°47·9'	2°58·7'W	H	7
Kirkie Loch	S Ayr	NX1982	55°6·2'	4°49·8'W	W	76
Kirkill	I of M	SC2172	54°7·0'	4°43·9'W	X	95
Kirkinch	Angus	NO3144	56°35·2'	3°7·0'W	X	53
Kirkinner	D & G	NX4251	54°50·0'	4°27·2'W	T	83
Kirkintilloch	E Dunb	NS6573	55°56·1'	4°9·2'W	T	64
Kirk Ireton	Derby	SK2650	53°3·0'	1°36·3'W	T	119
Kirk Knowe	Shetld	HU5893	60°37·2'	0°55·9'W	X	1,2
Kirk Lakes	Aberd	NK0563	57°39·7'	1°54·5'W	X	30
Kirkland	Aberd	NJ6045	57°29·9'	2°39·6'W	X	29
Kirkland	Cumbr	NY0717	54°32·6'	3°25·8'W	T	89
Kirkland	Cumbr	NY2648	54°49·5'	3°8·7'W	T	85
Kirkland	Cumbr	NY6432	54°41·2'	2°33·1'W	T	91
Kirkland	D & G	NS7214	55°24·4'	4°0·9'W	X	71
Kirkland	D & G	NX0164	54°56·1'	5°6·0'W	X	82
Kirkland	D & G	NX4166	54°58·1'	4°28·6'W	X	83
Kirkland	D & G	NX6280	55°6·0'	4°9·3'W	X	77
Kirkland	D & G	NX6950	54°49·9'	4°1·9'W	X	83,84
Kirkland	D & G	NX7560	54°55·4'	3°56·6'W	X	84
Kirkland	D & G	NX7869	55°0·3'	3°54·0'W	X	84
Kirkland	D & G	NX8090	55°11·6'	3°52·7'W	T	78
Kirkland	D & G	NX8093	55°13·3'	3°52·8'W	X	78
Kirkland	D & G	NX8792	55°12·8'	3°46·1'W	X	78
Kirkland	D & G	NX8997	55°15·5'	3°44·4'W	X	78
Kirkland	D & G	NX9376	55°4·3'	3°40·1'W	X	84
Kirkland	D & G	NY0389	55°11·4'	3°31·0'W	X	78
Kirkland	E Renf	NS5852	55°44·7'	4°15·3'W	X	64
Kirkland	Falk	NS8282	56°1·2'	3°53·1'W	X	57,65
Kirkland	Fife	NO3600	56°11·6'	3°1·4'W	T	59
Kirkland	Fife	NT1897	56°9·8'	3°18·8'W	X	58
Kirkland	Moray	NJ3961	57°38·3'	3°0·8'W	X	28
Kirkland	S Ayr	NX2492	55°11·7'	4°45·5'W	X	76
Kirkland	S Lanak	NT0648	55°43·2'	3°29·4'W	X	72
Kirklandbank	Pth & Kin	NO2349	56°37·8'	3°14·9'W	X	53
Kirkland Beck	Cumbr	NY6533	54°41·7'	2°32·2'W	W	91
Kirkland Burn	D & G	NY0388	55°10·9'	3°31·0'W	W	78
Kirkland Dam	Fife	NO3500	56°11·5'	3°2·4'W	T	59
Kirkland Fell	Cumbr	NY6733	54°41·7'	2°30·3'W	X	91
Kirkland Glen	N Ayr	NS2146	55°40·7'	4°50·4'W	X	63
Kirkland Guards	Cumbr	NY1840	54°45·1'	3°16·0'W	T	85
Kirkland Hall	Lancs	SD4843	53°53·1'	2°47·1'W	X	102
Kirkland Hill	D & G	NS7216	55°25·5'	4°0·9'W	H	71
Kirkland Hill	D & G	NX7869	55°0·3'	3°54·0'W	H	84
Kirkland Hill	D & G	NY0191	55°12·5'	3°32·9'W	X	78
Kirklandhill	E Loth	NT6177	55°59·3'	2°37·1'W	X	67
Kirklandhill	S Ayr	NS2910	55°21·5'	4°41·4'W	X	70
Kirkland Hill	S Ayr	NX2493	55°12·3'	4°45·5'W	H	76
Kirklandhill	Scot Bord	NT4053	55°46·3'	2°56·9'W	X	66,73
Kirkland Ho	Cumbr	NY2461	54°56·5'	3°10·8'W	X	85
Kirklandholm Fm	S Ayr	NS3824	55°29·2'	4°33·4'W	FM	70
Kirkland Howe	Cumbr	NY0419	54°33·7'	3°28·7'W	X	89
Kirkland of Gelston	D & G	NX7757	54°53·8'	3°54·7'W	X	84
Kirkland of Longcastle	D & G	NX3747	54°47·7'	4°32·1'W	X	83
Kirkland Plantn	D & G	NX7213	55°23·9'	4°0·8'W	F	71
Kirklandrigg	D & G	NY1272	55°2·3'	3°22·2'W	X	85

Kirklands	E Loth	NT4969	55°54·9′	2°48·5′W	X	66
Kirklands	Fife	NO6108	56°16·0′	2°37·3′W	X	59
Kirklands	Scot Bord	NT3337	55°37·6′	3°3·4′W	X	73
Kirklands	Scot Bord	NT5735	55°36·7′	2°40·5′W	X	73,74
Kirklands	Scot Bord	NT6125	55°31·3′	2°36·6′W	X	74
Kirklands	W Loth	NT0774	55°57·3′	3°28·9′W	X	65
Kirkland Scar	Cumbr	NY2462	54°57·1′	3°10·8′W	X	85
Kirklands Fm	Cumbr	NY0800	54°23·5′	3°24·6′W	FM	89
Kirklands Fm	N Yks	NZ1906	54°27·2′	1°42·0′W	FM	92
Kirklands of Damside	Pth & Kin	NN9614	56°18·7′	3°40·4′W	X	58
Kirk Langley	Derby	SK2838	52°56·6′	1°34·6′W	T	128
Kirklauchline	D & G	NX0450	54°48·6′	5°2·6′W	X	82
Kirklawhill	Scot Bord	NT0837	55°37·3′	3°27·2′W	X	72
Kirklawhill Burn	Scot Bord	NT0938	55°37·9′	3°26·3′W	W	72
Kirklea	D & G	NS7718	55°26·7′	3°56·2′W	H	71,78
Kirklea Fm	Somer	ST3952	51°16·1′	2°52·1′W	FM	182
Kirkleatham	Red & Cl	NZ5921	54°35·1′	1°4·8′W	T	93
Kirklebride	D & G	NX7674	55°3·0′	3°56·0′W	X	84
Kirkleegreen Rest	N Ayr	NS3855	55°45·9′	4°34·5′W	W	63
Kirklees	Bury	SD7812	53°36·5′	2°19·5′W	T	109
Kirklees Hall	Cald	SE1722	53°41·9′	1°44·1′W	X	104
Kirklees Light Rly	Kirk	SE2411	53°35·9′	1°37·8′W	X	110
Kirklees Way	Kirk	SE1320	53°40·8′	1°47·8′W	X	104
Kirklees Way	Kirk	SE2426	53°44·0′	1°37·8′W	X	104
Kirkless Fm	N Yks	SE9893	54°19·6′	0°29·2′W	FM	94,101
Kirklevington	Stock on T	NZ4209	54°28·7′	1°20·7′W	T	93
Kirklevington Hall	Stock on T	NZ4210	54°29·3′	1°20·7′W	X	93
Kirkley	Suff	TM5391	52°27·7′	1°43·9′E	T	134
Kirkley Hall College	Northum	NZ1577	55°5·5′	1°45·5′W	X	88
Kirkley March	Northum	NZ1477	55°5·5′	1°46·4′W	X	88
Kirkley Mill	Northum	NZ1676	55°4·9′	1°44·5′W	X	88
Kirkley West Fm	Northum	NZ1276	55°4·9′	1°48·3′W	FM	88
Kirklington	Notts	SK6757	53°6·6′	0°59·5′W	T	120
Kirklington	N Yks	SE3181	54°13·7′	1°31·1′W	T	99
Kirklington Grange	N Yks	SE3279	54°12·6′	1°30·1′W	X	99
Kirklington Low Wood	N Yks	SE3081	54°13·7′	1°32·0′W	F	99
Kirklinton	Cumbr	NY4367	54°59·9′	2°53·0′W	T	85
Kirklinton Hall	Cumbr	NY4367	54°59·9′	2°53·0′W	X	85
Kirklinton Park	Cumbr	NY4566	54°59·4′	2°51·1′W	X	86
Kirkliston	C of Edin	NT1274	55°57·3′	3°24·1′W	T	65
Kirk Loch	Angus	NO7048	56°37·6′	2°28·9′W	W	54
Kirkloch	D & G	NX4874	55°2·5′	4°23·4′W	H	77
Kirk Loch	D & G	NY0782	55°7·7′	3°27·1′W	W	78
Kirk Loch	Shetld	HP5304	60°43·2′	1°1·2′W	W	1
Kirkmabreck	D & G	NX0948	54°47·7′	4°57·8′W	X	82
Kirkmabreck	D & G	NX4856	54°52·8′	4°21·7′W	X	83
Kirkmadrine	D & G	NX4748	54°48·5′	4°22·4′W	A	83
Kirkmadrine Church	D & G	NX0848	54°47·7′	4°58·8′W	A	82
Kirkmaiden	D & G	NX1236	54°41·3′	4°54·6′W	T	82
Kirkmaiden	D & G	NX3639	54°43·4′	4°32·4′W	A	83
Kirkmaiden Church	D & G	NX1332	54°39·2′	4°53·5′W	A	82
Kirkmains	Scot Bord	NT6825	55°31·3′	2°30·0′W	X	74
Kirkmay	Fife	NO6007	56°15·5′	2°38·3′W	X	59
Kirk Merrington	Durham	NZ2631	54°40·6′	1°35·4′W	T	93
Kirk Michael	I of M	SC3190	54°16·9′	4°35·3′W	T	95
Kirkmichael	Pth & Kin	NO0860	56°43·6′	3°29·8′W	T	43
Kirkmichael	S Ayr	NS3408	55°20·5′	4°36·6′W	T	70,76
Kirkmichael Fell	D & G	NY0189	55°11·4′	3°32·9′W	H	78
Kirkmichael Ho	D & G	NY0187	55°10·3′	3°32·8′W	X	78
Kirkmichael Ho (Sch)	S Ayr	NS3408	55°20·5′	4°36·6′W	X	70,76
Kirkmichael Mains	D & G	NY0187	55°10·3′	3°32·8′W	T	78
Kirkmirran	D & G	NX7954	54°52·2′	3°52·7′W	X	84
Kirk Moor	N Yks	NZ9202	54°24·5′	0°34·5′W	X	94
Kirkmuir	D & G	NX5154	54°51·8′	4°18·9′W	X	83
Kirkmuir Fm	E Ayr	NS4045	55°40·6′	4°32·2′W	FM	64
Kirkmuirhill	S Lanak	NS7943	55°40·2′	3°55·0′W	T	71
Kirkmyres	Aberd	NJ9262	57°39·1′	2°7·6′W	X	30
Kirk Ness	Orkney	HY2818	59°2·8′	3°14·8′W	X	6
Kirkness	Orkney	HY2818	59°2·8′	3°14·8′W	X	6
Kirk Ness	Orkney	ND4791	58°48·5′	2°54·6′W	X	7
Kirkness	Pth & Kin	NT1898	56°10·3′	3°18·8′W	X	58
Kirk Ness	Shetld	HU5565	60°22·2′	0°59·7′W	X	2
Kirknewton	Northum	NT9130	55°34·1′	2°8·1′W	T	74,75
Kirknewton	W Loth	NT1167	55°53·5′	3°24·9′W	T	65
Kirknewton Ho	W Loth	NT1166	55°53·0′	3°24·9′W	X	65
Kirknewton Mains	W Loth	NT1067	55°53·5′	3°25·9′W	X	65
Kirkney	Aberd	NJ5132	57°22·8′	2°48·4′W	T	29,37
Kirkney Water	Aberd	NJ4328	57°20·6′	2°56·4′W	W	37
Kirkney Water	Aberd	NJ4831	57°22·2′	2°51·4′W	W	29,37
Kirk Noust	Orkney	HY4429	59°8·9′	2°58·3′W	X	5,6
Kirk of Shotts	N Lanak	NS8462	55°50·5′	3°50·7′W	T	65
Kirk o' Muir Cemy	Stir	NS7084	56°2·1′	4°4·7′W	X	57,64
Kirkoswald	Cumbr	NY5541	54°46·0′	2°41·5′W	T	86
Kirkoswald	S Ayr	NS2407	55°19·8′	4°46·0′W	T	70,76
Kirk o' Tang	Highld	ND2574	58°39·1′	3°17·1′W	X	7,12
Kirk o'the Muir	Pth & Kin	NO1136	56°30·7′	3°26·3′W	X	53
Kirkpatrick	D & G	NX9090	55°11·8′	3°43·3′W	T	78
Kirkpatrick Durham	D & G	NX7870	55°0·8′	3°54·1′W	T	84
Kirkpatrick-Fleming	D & G	NY2770	55°1·4′	3°8·1′W	T	85
Kirkpatrick Hill	D & G	NX8990	55°11·8′	3°44·2′W	H	78
Kirk Plantation	D & G	NX8896	55°15·0′	3°45·3′W	F	78
Kirk Quoy	Orkney	HY2917	59°2·3′	3°13·7′W	X	6
Kirk Rigg	Cumbr	NY4435	54°42·7′	2°51·7′W	X	90
Kirk Road	D & G	NX7065	54°58·0′	4°1·4′W	X	83,84
Kirk Rocks	Orkney	HY2307	58°56·9′	3°19·8′W	X	6,7
Kirks	Shetld	HP5004	60°43·2′	1°4·5′W	X	1
Kirk Sand	Shetld	HU1759	60°19·2′	1°41·0′W	X	3
Kirk Sandall	Donc	SE6107	53°33·6′	1°4·3′W	T	111
Kirksanton	Cumbr	SD1380	54°12·7′	3°19·6′W	T	96
Kirksanton Haws	Cumbr	SD1379	54°12·2′	3°19·6′W	X	96
Kirkshaw	N Lanak	NS7263	55°50·9′	4°2·2′W	T	64
Kirksheaf	Highld	NH7882	57°48·9′	4°2·7′W	X	21
Kirkside	Aberd	NJ6862	57°39·1′	2°31·7′W	X	29
Kirkside	Aberd	NO7363	56°45·7′	2°26·0′W	X	45
Kirkside Wood	Northum	NY7049	54°50·3′	2°27·6′W	F	86,87
Kirk Sink	N Yks	SD9453	53°58·6′	2°5·1′W	X	103
Kirk Skerry	Shetld	HU3944	60°11·0′	1°17·3′W	X	4
Kirkslight Hill	D & G	NY2289	55°11·6′	3°13·1′W	H	79
Kirk Smeaton	N Yks	SE5116	53°38·5′	1°13·3′W	T	111
Kirkstall	Leeds	SE2635	53°48·9′	1°35·9′W	T	104
Kirkstane Grain	S Lanak	NS9206	55°20·4′	3°41·7′W	W	71,78
Kirkstead	Cumbr	NY3346	54°48·5′	3°2·1′W	X	85
Kirkstead	Scot Bord	NT2624	55°30·5′	3°9·9′W	T	73
Kirkstead Br	Lincs	TF1762	53°8·8′	0°14·6′W	X	121
Kirkstead Burn	Scot Bord	NT2425	55°31·0′	3°11·8′W	W	73
Kirkstead Hall	Lincs	TF1962	53°8·7′	0°12·8′W	X	122
Kirkstead Hill	Scot Bord	NT2524	55°30·5′	3°10·8′W	H	73
Kirksteads	N Yks	SD6674	54°9·9′	2°30·8′W	X	98
Kirksteads	Staffs	SK0856	53°6·3′	1°52·4′W	X	119
Kirkstile	Aberd	NJ5235	57°24·4′	2°47·5′W	X	29
Kirkstile	D & G	NY3690	55°12·3′	2°59·9′W	X	79
Kirk Stone	Cumbr	NY4008	54°28·1′	2°55·1′W	X	90
Kirkstone Pass	Cumbr	NY4009	54°28·6′	2°55·1′W	X	90
Kirkstyle	D & G	NY1069	55°0·7′	3°24·0′W	X	85
Kirkstyle	Highld	ND3472	58°38·1′	3°7·7′W	T	7,12
Kirk Styles	Kirk	SE2109	53°34·9′	1°40·6′W	X	110
Kirk Syke	N Yks	SD8958	54°1·3′	2°9·7′W	X	103
Kirk Sykes Fm	N Yks	SD9547	53°55·4′	2°4·2′W	FM	103
Kirk Taing	Orkney	HY4542	59°15·9′	2°57·4′W	X	5
Kirk Taing	Orkney	HY5633	59°11·2′	2°45·7′W	X	5,6
Kirk Taing	Orkney	HY7043	59°16·6′	2°31·1′W	X	5
Kirk Taing	Orkney	ND4996	58°51·2′	2°52·6′W	X	6,7
Kirk, The	Orkney	HY5428	59°8·4′	2°47·8′W	X	5,6
Kirk, The	Shetld	HU2883	60°32·0′	1°28·9′W	X	3
Kirkthorpe	Wakf	SE3620	53°40·8′	1°26·9′W	T	104
Kirkthwaite Cottage	Cumbr	SD3287	54°16·7′	3°2·2′W	X	96,97
Kirkton	Aberd	NJ5409	57°10·4′	2°45·2′W	X	37
Kirkton	Aberd	NJ5840	57°27·2′	2°41·5′W	X	29
Kirkton	Aberd	NJ6425	57°19·1′	2°35·4′W	T	37
Kirkton	Aberd	NJ6950	57°32·6′	2°30·6′W	X	29
Kirkton	Aberd	NJ8214	57°13·2′	2°17·4′W	X	38
Kirkton	Aberd	NK0152	57°33·7′	1°58·5′W	X	30
Kirkton	Aberd	NO8074	56°51·7′	2°19·2′W	X	45
Kirkton	Aberd	NO8793	57°1·9′	2°12·4′W	X	38,45
Kirkton	Angus	NO2941	56°33·6′	3°8·9′W	X	53
Kirkton	Angus	NO3437	56°31·5′	3°3·9′W	X	54
Kirkton	Angus	NO4037	56°31·5′	2°58·1′W	T	54
Kirkton	Angus	NO4246	56°36·4′	2°56·2′W	T	54
Kirkton	Angus	NO4380	56°54·7′	2°55·7′W	X	44
Kirkton	Angus	NO6342	56°34·4′	2°35·7′W	T	54
Kirkton	Arg & Bt	NM7701	56°9·2′	5°35·0′W	X	55
Kirkton	Arg & Bt	NS3478	55°58·2′	4°39·2′W	X	63
Kirkton	C of Aber	NJ8714	57°13·3′	2°12·5′W	X	38
Kirkton	D & G	NX9781	55°7·0′	3°36·5′W	T	78
Kirkton	Fife	NO3625	56°25·0′	3°1·8′W	T	54,59
Kirkton	Fife	NS9787	56°4·1′	3°38·8′W	X	65
Kirkton	Fife	NT2190	56°6·0′	3°15·8′W	X	58
Kirkton	Fife	NT2386	56°3·9′	3°13·8′W	T	66
Kirkton	Highld	NC8862	58°32·2′	3°54·9′W	X	10
Kirkton	Highld	NG8327	57°17·2′	5°35·6′W	T	33
Kirkton	Highld	NG9141	57°24·9′	5°28·3′W	T	25
Kirkton	Highld	NH6038	57°24·9′	4°19·4′W	X	26
Kirkton	Highld	NH6045	57°28·7′	4°19·6′W	X	26
Kirkton	Highld	NH7066	57°40·2′	4°10·3′W	X	21,27
Kirkton	Highld	NH7856	57°34·9′	4°2·0′W	X	27
Kirkton	Highld	NH7998	57°57·6′	4°2·2′W	T	21
Kirkton	Highld	NJ0226	57°19·1′	3°37·2′W	X	36
Kirkton	Midlo	NT2163	55°51·5′	3°15·3′W	X	66
Kirkton	Moray	NJ1363	57°39·2′	3°27·0′W	X	28
Kirkton	N Ayr	NS1555	55°45·4′	4°56·5′W	X	63
Kirkton	Orkney	HY5318	59°3·1′	2°48·7′W	X	6
Kirkton	Pth & Kin	NN7858	56°42·1′	3°59·1′W	X	42,51,52
Kirkton	Pth & Kin	NN8910	56°16·4′	3°47·1′W	X	58
Kirkton	Pth & Kin	NN9618	56°20·8′	3°40·5′W	X	58
Kirkton	Pth & Kin	NO2631	56°28·2′	3°11·6′W	X	53
Kirkton	Renf	NS4471	55°54·7′	4°29·3′W	X	64
Kirkton	Scot Bord	NT5413	55°24·8′	2°43·2′W	T	79
Kirkton	S Lanak	NS9321	55°28·5′	3°41·1′W	X	71,72
Kirkton	Stir	NN5100	56°10·4′	4°23·6′W	T	57
Kirkton	Stir	NN7003	56°12·4′	4°5·3′W	X	57
Kirkton	W Loth	NT0366	55°52·9′	3°32·6′W	T	65
Kirkton Barns	Fife	NO4426	56°25·6′	2°54·0′W	X	54,59
Kirktonbridge Cotts	Aberd	NJ7907	57°9·5′	2°20·4′W	X	38
Kirkton Dam	E Renf	NS4856	55°46·7′	4°25·0′W	W	64
Kirkton Fm	Aberd	NK0634	57°24·0′	1°53·6′W	FM	30
Kirkton Fm	Fife	NT1592	56°7·0′	3°21·6′W	FM	58
Kirkton Fm	Renf	NS3868	55°52·9′	4°35·0′W	FM	63
Kirkton Fm	Stir	NN3628	56°25·2′	4°39·1′W	FM	50
Kirkton Glen	Stir	NN5322	56°22·3′	4°22·4′W	X	51
Kirkton Head	Aberd	NK1250	57°32·7′	1°47·5′W	X	30
Kirkton Hill	Angus	NO3355	56°41·2′	3°5·2′W	H	53
Kirktonhill	D & G	NY3190	55°12·2′	3°4·6′W	X	79
Kirkton Hill	Pth & Kin	NO1020	56°22·1′	3°27·0′W	H	53,58
Kirktonhill	Scot Bord	NT4754	55°46·8′	2°50·3′W	X	66,73
Kirkton Hill	Scot Bord	NT5312	55°24·2′	2°44·1′W	X	79
Kirktonhill	W Dunb	NS3874	55°56·2′	4°35·2′W	T	63
Kirktonhill Ho	Aberd	NO6965	56°46·8′	2°30·0′W	X	45
Kirktonhill Tower	Angus	NO7067	56°47·9′	2°29·0′W	X	45
Kirkton Ho	Aberd	NJ8007	57°9·5′	2°19·4′W	X	38
Kirktonlees	Pth & Kin	NN9313	56°18·1′	3°43·3′W	X	58
Kirkton Manor	Scot Bord	NT2237	55°37·5′	3°13·9′W	X	73
Kirkton Muir	Aberd	NO6795	57°3·0′	2°32·2′W	X	38,45
Kirkton Muir	Highld	NH6044	57°28·1′	4°19·6′W	X	26
Kirkton of Airlie	Angus	NO3151	56°39·0′	3°7·1′W	X	53
Kirkton of Auchterhouse	Angus	NO3438	56°32·0′	3°3·9′W	T	54
Kirkton of Auchterless	Aberd	NJ7141	57°27·8′	2°28·5′W	T	29
Kirkton of Balfour	Aberd	NO6073	56°51·1′	2°38·9′W	X	45
Kirkton of Bourtie	Aberd	NJ8024	57°18·6′	2°19·5′W	X	38
Kirkton of Collace	Pth & Kin	NO1932	56°28·6′	3°18·5′W	X	53
Kirkton of Coull	Aberd	NJ5102	57°6·6′	2°48·1′W	X	37
Kirkton of Craig	Angus	NO7055	56°41·4′	2°28·9′W	T	54
Kirkton of Culsalmond	Aberd	NJ6432	57°22·9′	2°35·5′W	T	29,37
Kirkton of Cults	Fife	NO3409	56°16·4′	3°3·5′W	T	59
Kirkton of Durris	Aberd	NO7796	57°3·5′	2°22·3′W	T	38,45
Kirkton of Forbes	Aberd	NJ5116	57°14·2′	2°48·3′W	X	37
Kirkton of Glenbuchat	Aberd	NJ3715	57°13·5′	3°2·1′W	T	37
Kirkton of Glenisla	Angus	NO2160	56°43·8′	3°17·0′W	T	44
Kirkton of Kingoldrum	Angus	NO3354	56°40·6′	3°5·2′W	T	53
Kirkton of Largo or Upper Largo	Fife	NO4203	56°13·2′	2°55·7′W	T	59
Kirkton of Lethendy	Pth & Kin	NO1342	56°34·0′	3°24·5′W	T	53
Kirkton of Logie Buchan	Aberd	NJ9829	57°21·3′	2°1·5′W	X	38
Kirkton of Lude	Pth & Kin	NN9068	56°47·7′	3°47·6′W	T	43
Kirkton of Lundie	Angus	NO2936	56°30·9′	3°8·8′W	X	53
Kirkton of Mailer	Pth & Kin	NO1020	56°22·1′	3°27·0′W	X	53,58
Kirkton of Maryculter	Aberd	NO8599	57°5·2′	2°14·4′W	T	38,45
Kirkton of Menmuir	Angus	NO5364	56°46·2′	2°45·7′W	T	44
Kirkton of Monikie	Angus	NO5138	56°32·1′	2°47·4′W	T	54
Kirkton of Nevay	Angus	NO3243	56°34·7′	3°6·0′W	X	53
Kirkton of Oyne	Aberd	NJ6825	57°19·1′	2°31·4′W	T	38
Kirkton of Rayne	Aberd	NJ6930	57°21·8′	2°30·5′W	T	29
Kirkton of Skene	Aberd	NJ8007	57°9·5′	2°19·4′W	T	38
Kirkton of Tough	Aberd	NJ6113	57°12·6′	2°38·3′W	T	37
Kirkton Park	Pth & Kin	NN9313	56°18·1′	3°43·3′W	X	58
Kirkton Rig	S Lanak	NS9320	55°28·0′	3°41·1′W	X	71,72
Kirktoun	E Ayr	NS4140	55°37·9′	4°31·1′W	T	70
Kirktown	Aberd	NJ9262	57°39·1′	2°7·6′W	X	30
Kirktown	Aberd	NK0951	57°33·2′	1°50·5′W	T	30
Kirktown	Aberd	NK1246	57°30·5′	1°47·5′W	T	30
Kirktown	Moray	NJ3826	57°19·5′	3°1·3′W	X	37
Kirktown of Alvah	Aberd	NJ6760	57°38·0′	2°32·7′W	T	29
Kirktown of Deskford	Moray	NJ5061	57°38·4′	2°49·8′W	T	29
Kirktown of Fetteresso	Aberd	NO8585	56°57·6′	2°14·3′W	T	45
Kirktown of Mortlach	Moray	NJ3239	57°26·4′	3°7·5′W	T	28
Kirktown of Slains	Aberd	NK0329	57°21·3′	1°56·6′W	X	38
Kirktown Wood	Aberd	NJ6814	57°13·2′	2°31·3′W	F	38
Kirkurd	Scot Bord	NT1244	55°41·1′	3°23·5′W	T	72
Kirkwall	Orkney	HY4510	58°58·7′	2°56·9′W	T	6
Kirkwall Airport	Orkney	HY4808	58°57·6′	2°53·8′W	X	6,7
Kirk Ward	Shetld	HU4758	60°18·5′	1°8·5′W	X	2,3
Kirkwhelpington	Northum	NY9984	55°9·3′	2°0·5′W	T	81
Kirkwhelpington Common	Northum	NY9786	55°10·3′	2°2·4′W	X	81
Kirkwood	D & G	NY1275	55°4·0′	3°22·3′W	T	85
Kirkwood	E Ayr	NS3947	55°41·6′	4°33·3′W	X	63
Kirkwood	N Lanak	NS7163	55°50·8′	4°3·2′W	T	64
Kirkwood Ho	S Lanak	NS6840	55°38·4′	4°5·4′W	X	71
Kirkwood Ho	S Lanak	NT0235	55°36·2′	3°32·9′W	X	72
Kirkwood Mains	D & G	NY1274	55°3·4′	3°22·2′W	X	85
Kirk Yetholm	Scot Bord	NT8228	55°33·0′	2°16·7′W	T	74
Kirland	Corn	SX0665	50°27·4′	4°43·6′W	X	200
Kirmington	N Lincs	TA1011	53°35·3′	0°19·9′W	T	113
Kirminnoch	D & G	NX0067	54°57·7′	5°7·0′W	X	82
Kirminnoch	D & G	NX1258	54°53·1′	4°55·4′W	X	82
Kirmond le Mire	Lincs	TF1892	53°24·9′	0°13·1′W	T	113
Kirmond Top	Lincs	TF1890	53°23·9′	0°13·1′W	X	113
Kirn	Arg & Bt	NS1877	55°57·4′	4°54·5′W	T	63
Kirn	Orkney	ND4092	58°48·9′	3°1·8′W	X	7
Kirnan	Arg & Bt	NR8795	56°6·3′	5°25·1′W	X	55
Kirnashie Hill	Arg & Bt	NR8041	55°37·0′	5°29·2′W	H	62,69
Kirna, The	Scot Bord	NT3437	55°37·6′	3°2·5′W	X	73
Kirn Brae	D & G	NX4084	55°7·7′	4°30·1′W	X	77
Kirncleuch	D & G	NY1494	55°14·2′	3°20·7′W	X	78
Kirn Cleuch	Scot Bord	NT5906	55°21·0′	2°38·4′W	X	80
Kirndean	Scot Bord	NY5291	55°12·9′	2°44·8′W	X	79
Kirnie Law	Scot Bord	NT3438	55°38·1′	3°2·5′W	H	73
Kirn Law	Scot Bord	NT2940	55°39·2′	3°7·3′W	H	73
Kirn of Gula	Shetld	HU6493	60°37·2′	0°49·3′W	X	1,2
Kirn, The	Shetld	HU4222	59°59·1′	1°14·3′W	X	4
Kirranrae	D & G	NX0268	54°58·3′	5°5·2′W	X	82
Kirreoch Burn	D & G	NX4889	55°10·6′	4°22·8′W	W	77
Kirriemore	D & G	NX3785	55°8·2′	4°33·0′W	X	77
Kirriemore Burn	D & G	NX3786	55°8·7′	4°33·0′W	W	77
Kirriemore Loch	D & G	NX3785	55°8·2′	4°33·0′W	W	77
Kirriemuir	Angus	NO3853	56°40·1′	3°0·3′W	T	54
Kirriereoch	D & G	NX3687	55°9·3′	4°34·0′W	X	77
Kirriereoch Hill	D & G	NX4187	55°9·4′	4°29·3′W	H	77
Kirriereoch Loch	D & G	NX3686	55°8·7′	4°34·0′W	W	77
Kirsgill How	Cumbr	NY0217	54°32·6′	3°30·5′W	X	89
Kirshinnoch Burn	D & G	NX4086	55°8·8′	4°30·2′W	W	77
Kirstead Green	Norf	TM2997	52°31·6′	1°23·0′E	T	134
Kirstead Hall	Norf	TM2998	52°32·1′	1°23·0′E	A	134
Kirstead House Fm	Norf	TM2998	52°32·1′	1°23·0′E	FM	134
Kirtlebridge	D & G	NY2372	55°2·4′	3°11·9′W	T	85
Kirtlehead	D & G	NY2682	55°7·9′	3°9·2′W	X	79
Kirtlehead Hill	D & G	NY2683	55°8·4′	3°9·2′W	H	79
Kirtleside	D & G	NY2967	54°59·8′	3°6·2′W	X	85
Kirtleton	D & G	NY2680	55°6·8′	3°9·2′W	T	79
Kirtle Water	D & G	NY2869	55°0·9′	3°7·1′W	W	85
Kirtling	Cambs	TL6856	52°10·8′	0°27·8′E	T	154
Kirtling Green	Cambs	TL6855	52°10·3′	0°27·8′E	T	154
Kirtlington	Oxon	SP4919	51°52·3′	1°16·9′W	T	164
Kirtlington Park	Oxon	SP5019	51°52·3′	1°16·0′W	X	164
Kirtling Towers	Cambs	TL6857	52°11·4′	0°27·9′E	X	154
Kirtomy	Highld	NC7463	58°32·5′	4°9·4′W	T	10
Kirtomy Bay	Highld	NC7464	58°33·0′	4°9·4′W	W	10
Kirtomy Burn	Highld	NC7462	58°31·9′	4°9·4′W	W	10
Kirtomy Point	Highld	NC7465	58°33·6′	4°9·5′W	X	10
Kirton	Falk	NS8983	56°1·9′	3°46·4′W	X	65
Kirton	Lincs	TF3038	52°55·7′	0°3·6′W	T	131
Kirton	Notts	SK6969	53°13·1′	0°57·6′W	T	120
Kirton	Suff	TM2739	52°0·4′	1°18·9′E	T	169
Kirton Campus	W Loth	NT0366	55°52·9′	3°32·6′W	T	65
Kirton Cliff	N Lincs	SK9598	53°28·4′	0°33·7′W	X	112
Kirton Creek	Suff	TM2941	52°1·4′	1°20·7′E	W	169
Kirton End	Lincs	TF2840	52°56·8′	0°5·3′W	T	131
Kirton Fen Fm	Lincs	TF2448	53°1·1′	0°8·7′W	FM	131
Kirton Fm	Hants	SU4233	51°5·9′	1°23·6′W	FM	185
Kirton Holme	Lincs	TF2641	52°57·3′	0°7·1′W	T	131
Kirton in Lindsey	N Lincs	SK9398	53°28·5′	0°35·5′W	T	112
Kirton Lindsey Sta	N Lincs	SK9399	53°29·0′	0°35·5′W	X	112
Kirton Lodge	Suff	TM2840	52°0·9′	1°19·8′E	X	169
Kirton Marsh	Lincs	TF3436	52°54·5′	0°0·0′W	X	131
Kirton Meeres	Lincs	TF2739	52°56·2′	0°6·2′W	X	131
Kirton of Barevan	Highld	NH8347	57°30·1′	3°56·7′W	X	27
Kirton of Mailer	Pth & Kin	NO1020	56°22·1′	3°27·0′W	X	53,58
Kirton's Fm	W Berks	SU6969	51°25·2′	1°0·1′W	FM	175
Kirton Tunnel	N Lincs	SE9400	53°29·5′	0°34·6′W	X	112
Kirton Wood	Lincs	SK9832	52°52·8′	0°32·2′W	F	130
Kirton Wood	Notts	SK7068	53°12·5′	0°56·7′W	F	120
Kirt Shun	Shetld	HU3473	60°26·6′	1°22·4′W	W	2,3

Kirvennie	D & G	NX4155	54°52·1'	4°28·2'W	X	83
Kirwar Plantation	D & G	NX2850	54°49·2'	4°40·2'W	F	82
Kirwaugh	D & G	NX4054	54°51·6'	4°29·1'W	X	83
Kirwaugh Moor	D & G	NX3954	54°51·5'	4°30·1'W	X	83
Kisby's Fm	Hants	SU5060	51°20·4'	1°16·5'W	FM	174
Kisdon	N Yks	SD8999	54°23·4'	2°9·7'W	H	98
Kisdon	N Yks	SD9098	54°22·9'	2°8·8'W	X	98
Kisdon Force	N Yks	NY8900	54°24·0'	2°9·7'W	W	91,92
Kishinish	N Eil	NF8788	57°46·6'	7°15·5'W	X	18
Kishorn	Highld	NG8340	57°24·2'	5°36·3'W	X	24
Kishorn Island	Highld	NG8037	57°22·5'	5°39·1'W	X	24
Kisima Fm	N Yks	SE6633	53°47·6'	0°59·5'W	FM	105,106
Kiskin	Cumbr	SD0986	54°15·9'	3°23·4'W	T	96
Kislingbury	Northnts	SP6959	52°13·7'	0°59·0'W	T	152
Kislingbury Grange	Northnts	SP7057	52°12·6'	0°58·1'W	X	152
Kismeldon Bridge	Devon	SS3516	50°55·4'	4°20·5'W	X	190
Kismeldon Fm	Devon	SS3416	50°55·4'	4°21·3'W	FM	190
Kissock	D & G	NX9068	54°59·9'	3°42·8'W	X	84
Kissthorn Fm	N Yks	SE7059	54°1·6'	0°55·5'W	FM	105,106
Kista	Shetld	HZ2071	59°31·7'	1°38·3'W	X	4
Kist, The	Orkney	ND4387	58°46·3'	2°58·7'W	X	7
Kitbridge	Devon	ST3003	50°49·6'	2°59·3'W	T	193
Kitbridge Fm	I of W	SZ4889	50°42·1'	1°18·8'W	FM	196
Kit Brow	Lancs	SD4956	54°0·1'	2°46·3'W	X	102
Kitchadon	Devon	SS6808	50°51·6'	3°52·2'W	X	191
Kitcham	Devon	SX3788	50°40·4'	4°18·0'W	X	190
Kitchen Barrow	Wilts	SU0664	51°22·7'	1°54·4'W	A	173
Kitchen Copse	Surrey	TQ3252	51°15·3'	0°6·1'W	F	187
Kitchen Corner	Swan	SS4087	51°33·8'	4°18·1'W	X	159
Kitchenend Fm	Beds	TL0733	51°59·3'	0°26·1'W	FM	166
Kitchener Memorial	Orkney	HY2225	59°6·6'	3°21·2'W	X	6
Kitchen Fm	Powys	SO2158	52°13·1'	3°9·0'W	FM	148
Kitchen Gill	Cumbr	NY7805	54°26·6'	2°19·9'W	W	91
Kitchen Green	Fife	NS9992	56°6·9'	3°37·0'W	X	58
Kitchen Ground	Cumbr	SD1099	54°23·0'	3°22·7'W	X	96
Kitchenham	E Susx	TQ8825	50°59·8'	0°41·1'E	X	189,199
Kitchenham Fm	E Susx	TQ6813	50°53·7'	0°23·7'E	FM	199
Kitchenhill	Cumbr	NY4934	54°42·2'	2°47·1'W	X	90
Kitchen Linn	N Lanak	NS9157	55°47·9'	3°43·9'W	W	65,72
Kitchen Moss	C of Edin	NT1560	55°49·8'	3°21·0'W	X	65
Kitchenour	E Susx	TQ8624	50°59·3'	0°39·4'E	X	189,199
Kitchen Rig	N Lanak	NS9157	55°47·9'	3°43·9'W	X	65,72
Kitchenroyd	Kirk	SE2309	53°34·9'	1°38·7'W	T	110
Kitchens	Lancs	SD6944	53°53·7'	2°27·9'W	X	103
Kitchen's Yard	Lincs	TF5360	53°7·1'	0°17·6'E	X	122
Kitchers	Herts	TL4225	51°54·6'	0°4·3'E	X	167
Kitchingham Fm	E Susx	TQ7027	51°1·3'	0°25·8'E	FM	188,199
Kitchlow Fm	Lancs	SD5672	54°8·8'	2°40·0'W	FM	97
Kitcombe Ho	Hants	SU7034	51°6·3'	0°59·6'W	X	186
Kit Crag	Cumbr	NY4814	54°31·4'	2°47·8'W	X	90
Kitcrag	Cumbr	SD5599	54°23·3'	2°41·2'W	X	97
Kitebrook	Warw	SP2431	51°58·9'	1°38·6'W	T	151
Kite Green	Warw	SP1666	52°17·7'	1°45·5'W	T	151
Kite Hill	I of W	SZ5592	50°43·7'	1°12·9'W	T	196
Kite Hill	W Berks	SU3878	51°30·2'	1°26·8'W	X	174
Kitelands	Hants	SU5042	51°10·7'	1°16·7'W	X	185
Kitemoor Fm	Oxon	SU3094	51°38·9'	1°33·6'W	FM	164,174
Kitemore Ho	Oxon	SU3194	51°38·9'	1°32·7'W	X	164,174
Kitesbridge Fm	Oxon	SP2911	51°48·0'	1°34·4'W	FM	164
Kites Fm	Glos	ST7389	51°36·2'	2°23·0'W	FM	162,172
Kites Hall Fm	Northnts	SP7975	52°22·3'	0°50·0'W	FM	141
Kites Hardwick	Warw	SP4768	52°18·7'	1°18·2'W	T	151
Kites Hill	Glos	SO8712	51°48·6'	2°10·9'W	X	162
Kites Hill	S Glos	ST6584	51°33·5'	2°29·9'W	X	172
Kite's Hill	Worcs	SP1344	52°5·9'	1°48·2'W	X	151
Kites Nest	Shrops	SO5678	52°24·1'	2°38·4'W	X	137,138
Kitesnest	Shrops	SO6094	52°32·8'	2°35·0'W	X	138
Kite's Nest	Worcs	SP1035	52°1·0'	1°50·9'W	X	150
Kites Nest Fm	Glos	ST7294	51°38·9'	2°23·9'W	FM	162,172
Kites Nest Fm	Hants	SU0617	50°57·4'	1°54·5'W	FM	184
Kitfield Fm	Hants	SU6633	51°5·8'	1°3·1'W	FM	185,186
Kitford	Dorset	ST7708	50°52·5'	2°19·2'W	X	194
Kitford	Oxon	SU4286	51°34·5'	1°23·2'W	X	174
Kitford Br	Dorset	ST6612	50°54·6'	2°28·6'W	X	194
Kit Hill	Corn	SX3771	50°31·2'	4°17·6'W	H	201
Kithill	Devon	SS4206	50°50·2'	4°14·3'W	X	190
Kit Hill	Dorset	ST8419	50°58·4'	2°13·3'W	T	183
Kit Hill	Somer	ST5210	50°53·5'	2°40·6'W	H	194
Kithurst Fm	W Susx	TQ0713	50°54·6'	0°28·3'W	FM	197
Kithurst Hill	W Susx	TQ0812	50°54·1'	0°27·5'W	H	197
Kitlake	Devon	SS8903	50°49·2'	3°34·2'W	X	192
Kitlands	Surrey	TQ1543	51°10·7'	0°20·9'W	X	187
Kitleigh	Corn	SX2499	50°46·1'	4°29·4'W	X	190
Kitley Caves	Devon	SX5751	50°20·7'	4°0·2'W	X	202
Kitley Hill	Bath & NE Somer	ST6755	51°17·8'	2°28·0'W	X	172,183
Kitley Hill Ho	N Yks	NY9805	54°26·7'	2°1·4'W	X	92
Kitley (Hotel)	Devon	SX5651	50°20·7'	4°1·1'W	X	202
Kitleyknowe	Scot Bord	NT1755	55°47·1'	3°19·0'W	X	65,66,72
Kit Loch	Orkney	ND2794	58°49·9'	3°15·4'W	W	7
Kitlye	Glos	SO8904	51°44·3'	2°9·2'W	T	163
Kitmere	Cumbr	SD6085	54°15·8'	2°36·4'W	W	97
Kitnocks	Hants	SU5213	50°55·1'	1°15·2'W	X	196
Kitnor Heath	Somer	SS8739	51°8·6'	3°36·5'W	X	181
Kitridding	Cumbr	SD5883	54°14·7'	2°38·3'W	X	97
Kitridding Hill	Cumbr	SD5884	54°15·2'	2°38·3'W	X	97
Kit's Coty	Kent	TQ7461	51°19·5'	0°30·2'E	T	178,188
Kit's Coty Ho	Kent	TQ7460	51°19·0'	0°30·2'E	A	178,188
Kitscrew Wood	N Yks	SE6674	54°9·7'	0°58·9'W	F	100
Kits Croft	Hants	SU7960	51°20·2'	0°51·6'W	X	175,186
Kitsham	Corn	SS2300	50°46·6'	4°30·3'W	X	190
Kit's Hill	Essex	TQ8599	51°39·8'	0°40·9'E	X	168
Kitstone Hill	Devon	SS5446	51°11·9'	4°5·0'W	H	180
Kitta Taing	Orkney	ND3291	58°48·3'	3°10·1'W	X	7
Kitten Tom	Northum	NY6952	54°52·0'	2°28·6'W	X	86,87
Kitterford Cross	Devon	SX6956	50°23·6'	3°50·2'W	X	202
Kitter Green Fm	N Yks	NZ8209	54°28·4'	0°43·7'W	FM	94
Kitterland	I of M	SC1766	54°3·7'	4°47·4'W	X	95
Kittern Hill	I Scilly	SV8808	49°53·7'	6°20·3'W	H	203
Kittern Rock	I Scilly	SV8808	49°53·7'	6°20·3'W	X	203

Kitt Green	Wigan	SD5505	53°32·6'	2°40·3'W	T	108
Kittington Fm	Kent	TR2751	51°13·0'	1°15·4'E	FM	179
Kittisford	Somer	ST0722	50°59·6'	3°19·1'W	T	181
Kittisford Barton	Somer	ST0723	51°0·2'	3°19·1'W	X	181
Kittisford Fm	Somer	ST0623	51°0·2'	3°20·0'W	FM	181
Kittitoe	Devon	SS6646	51°12·1'	3°54·7'W	X	180
Kittle	Swan	SS5789	51°35·1'	4°3·5'W	T	159
Kittlegairy Hill	Scot Bord	NT2741	55°39·7'	3°9·2'W	X	73
Kittlehill	Swan	SS4692	51°36·6'	4°13·1'W	X	159
Kittlemanoch	Aberd	NJ4936	57°25·0'	2°50·5'W	X	28,29
Kittlenaked Wood	Fife	NO5305	56°14·4'	2°45·1'W	F	59
Kittle's Corner	Suff	TM2259	52°11·3'	1°15·3'E	X	156
Kittle Top	Swan	SS4988	51°34·5'	4°10·4'W	X	159
Kittochside	S Lanak	NS6156	55°46·9'	4°12·5'W	X	64
Kittow's Moor	Corn	SX2086	50°39·0'	4°32·4'W	X	201
Kitts End	Herts	TQ2498	51°40·3'	0°12·0'W	T	166,176
Kitt's Green	Birm	SP1587	52°29·1'	1°46·3'W	T	139
Kitts Green Fm	Glos	ST7098	51°41·0'	2°25·6'W	FM	162
Kitt's Moss	Stock	SJ8884	53°21·4'	2°10·4'W	T	109
Kittuck	Somer	SS8143	51°10·7'	3°41·8'W	X	181
Kittwhistle	Dorset	ST3903	50°49·6'	2°51·6'W	T	193
Kittybrewster	C of Aber	NJ9207	57°9·5'	2°7·5'W	T	38
Kitty Brewster Fm	Northum	NZ2882	55°8·1'	1°33·2'W	FM	81
Kittycarter Burn	Northum	NU1922	55°29·7'	1°41·5'W	W	75
Kittyfield	Scot Bord	NT5635	55°36·6'	2°41·5'W	X	73
Kittyflat	Scot Bord	NT4549	55°44·1'	2°52·1'W	X	73
Kitty Hill	E Yorks	SE7856	53°59·9'	0°48·2'W	X	105,106
Kitty Hill (Tumulus)	E Yorks	SE7856	53°59·9'	0°48·2'W	A	105,106
Kittymuir	S Lanak	NS7548	55°42·8'	3°58·9'W	X	64
Kitty's Cairn	D & G	NY2883	55°8·4'	3°7·3'W	X	79
Kitty's Fm	Suff	TM4998	52°31·6'	1°40·7'E	FM	134
Kittythirst	Northum	NY6096	55°15·6'	2°37·3'W	X	80
Kitty Tor	Devon	SX5687	50°40·1'	4°1·9'W	H	191
Kitwell	Birm	SO9981	52°25·9'	2°0·5'W	T	139
Kitwhistle Fm	Dorset	ST5003	50°49·7'	2°42·2'W	FM	194
Kitwood	Hants	SU6633	51°5·8'	1°3·1'W	T	185,186
Kiverley	Devon	SS5415	50°55·2'	4°4·3'W	X	180
Kivernoll	Heref	SO4632	51°59·3'	2°46·8'W	T	149,161
Kiveton Bridge Sta	Roth	SK4882	53°20·2'	1°16·3'W	X	111,120
Kiveton Park	Roth	SK4983	53°20·7'	1°15·4'W	T	111,120
Kiveton Park	Roth	SK5083	53°20·7'	1°14·5'W	X	111,120
Kiveton Park Sta	Roth	SK5082	53°20·2'	1°14·5'W	X	111,120
Kiwi, The	Wilts	SU1943	51°11·4'	1°43·3'W	X	184
Kixley Fm	Sol	SP1877	52°23·7'	1°43·7'W	FM	139
Klettar	Orkney	HY4852	59°21·3'	2°54·4'W	X	5
Klevar	Shetld	HU3370	60°25·0'	1°23·5'W	X	2,3
Klibreck Burn	Highld	NC5832	58°15·5'	4°24·7'W	W	16
Klifts	Shetld	HU6089	60°35·1'	0°53·8'W	X	1,2
Klondyke	Orkney	ND4696	58°51·1'	2°55·7'W	X	6,7
Klyptir of Garth	Shetld	HU5398	60°40·0'	1°1·3'W	X	1
Knabbe's Hall Fm	Barns	SE2803	53°31·6'	1°34·2'W	FM	110
Knabbs Farmhouse	E Susx	TQ4324	51°0·1'	0°2·7'E	X	198
Knabbygates	Moray	NJ5552	57°33·6'	2°44·7'W	X	29
Knabs Grove	N Yks	SE2356	54°0·2'	1°38·5'W	X	104
Knabs Ridge	N Yks	SE2355	53°59·7'	1°38·5'W	X	104
Knab, The	Swan	SS6287	51°34·1'	3°59·1'W	T	159
Knachly	Angus	NO3366	56°47·1'	3°5·3'W	H	44
Knackers Hole	Dorset	ST7811	50°54·1'	2°18·4'W	X	194
Knaggy House Fm	N Yks	NZ8905	54°26·2'	0°37·2'W	FM	94
Knagshill	E Ayr	NS5322	55°28·4'	4°19·1'W	X	70
Knaith	Lincs	SK8284	53°21·0'	0°45·7'W	T	121
Knaith Park	Lincs	SK8485	53°21·5'	0°43·9'W	T	112,121
Knap	Arg & Bt	NS2090	56°4·4'	4°53·1'W	X	56
Knap Barrow	Hants	SU0819	50°58·5'	1°52·8'W	X	184
Knap Barrow (Long Barrow)	Hants	SU0819	50°58·5'	1°52·8'W	A	184
Knap Burn	Arg & Bt	NS2091	56°4·9'	4°53·1'W	W	56
Knapdale	Arg & Bt	NR7879	55°57·4'	5°32·9'W	X	62
Knapdale	Arg & Bt	NR7880	55°58·0'	5°33·0'W	X	55
Knap Down	Devon	SS5946	51°12·0'	4°0·7'W	H	180
Knapeney Fm	Notts	SK7365	53°10·9'	0°54·1'W	FM	120
Knap Fm	Dorset	SY7686	50°40·6'	2°20·0'W	FM	194
Knap Head	Devon	SS2118	50°56·3'	4°32·5'W	X	190
Knap Hill	Somer	ST6946	51°13·0'	2°26·2'W	X	183
Knaphill	Surrey	SU9658	51°19·0'	0°37·0'W	T	175,186
Knap Hill	Wilts	SU1263	51°22·2'	1°49·3'W	H	173
Knap Hill (Causewayed Enclosure)	Wilts	SU1263	51°22·2'	1°49·3'W	A	173
Knaphill Manor	Surrey	SU9760	51°20·1'	0°36·1'W	X	175,176,186
Knaplock	Somer	SS8633	51°5·3'	3°37·3'W	X	181
Knaplock	Somer	ST2342	51°10·6'	3°5·7'W	X	182
Knap Mill	Devon	SX7047	50°18·8'	3°49·2'W	X	202
Knap of Howar	Orkney	HY4851	59°20·8'	2°54·4'W	A	5
Knap of Lawhardie	Aberd	NO7877	56°53·3'	2°21·2'W	X	45
Knap of Trowieglen	Orkney	ND2398	58°52·0'	3°19·6'W	H	6,7
Knapp	Hants	SU4023	51°0·5'	1°25·4'W	T	185
Knapp	Pth & Kin	NO2831	56°28·2'	3°9·7'W	T	53
Knapp	Somer	ST3025	51°1·4'	2°59·5'W	T	193
Knapp	Wilts	SU0225	51°1·7'	1°57·9'W	T	184
Knappach	Aberd	NO7395	57°3·0'	2°26·2'W	X	38,45
Knappach	Highld	NN7599	57°4·2'	4°3·2'W	X	35
Knapp Br	Somer	ST3026	51°2·0'	2°59·5'W	X	193
Knapp Down	Wilts	ST9049	51°14·6'	2°8·2'W	X	184
Knapp Down	Wilts	SU0227	51°2·8'	1°57·9'W	X	184
Knapperfield	Highld	ND2656	58°29·4'	3°15·7'W	X	11,12
Knapperna	Aberd	NK0431	57°22·4'	1°55·6'W	X	30
Knapperthaw	Cumbr	SD2783	54°14·5'	3°6·8'W	X	96,97
Knapp Fm	Devon	ST2209	50°52·7'	3°6·1'W	FM	192,193
Knapp Fm	Dorset	ST4102	50°49·1'	2°49·9'W	FM	193
Knapp Fm	Dorset	ST5403	50°49·7'	2°38·8'W	FM	194
Knapp Fm	Dorset	SY3695	50°45·3'	2°54·1'W	FM	193
Knapp Fm	Heref	SO6638	52°2·6'	2°29·3'W	FM	149
Knapp Fm	Pemb	SM9909	51°44·9'	4°54·3'W	FM	157,158
Knapp Fm	Powys	SO2459	52°13·7'	3°6·4'W	FM	148
Knapp Fm	Somer	ST2610	50°53·3'	3°2·7'W	FM	192,193
Knapp Hill	Dorset	ST8527	51°2·8'	2°12·5'W	T	183
Knapp Hill	Somer	ST5646	51°12·9'	2°37·4'W	H	182,183
Knappieround	Aberd	NJ4805	57°8·2'	2°51·1'W	X	37
Knapps	Aberd	NJ3014	57°12·9'	3°9·1'W	H	37
Knapps	Pemb	SN0610	51°45·5'	4°48·3'W	X	158

Knapps	S Ayr	NX3387	55°9·2'	4°36·8'W	H	76
Knapps Hill Fm	Dorset	ST6805	50°50·9'	2°26·9'W	FM	194
Knapps Loch	Inverc	NS3668	55°52·9'	4°36·9'W	W	63
Knapps, The	Shrops	SJ3307	52°39·6'	2°59·0'W	X	126
Knapp, The	Heref	SO3244	52°5·6'	2°59·2'W	X	148,161
Knapp, The	Oxon	SU7196	51°39·7'	0°58·0'W	X	165
Knapp, The	Shrops	SO6471	52°20·4'	2°31·3'W	X	138
Knappy Park	Aberd	NO5397	57°4·0'	2°46·1'W	F	37,44
Knaps	Aberd	NJ8522	57°17·6'	2°14·5'W	X	38
Knaps	Angus	NO3562	56°45·0'	3°3·3'W	X	44
Knapside Hill	Cumbr	NY6438	54°44·4'	2°33·1'W	H	91
Knapsleask	Aberd	NK0332	57°23·0'	1°56·5'W	X	30
Knaps Longpeak	Devon	SS2018	50°56·2'	4°33·3'W	X	190
Knaps of Auchlee	Aberd	NK0349	57°32·1'	1°56·5'W	X	30
Knaps of Bedlam	Aberd	NJ8744	57°29·4'	2°12·6'W	X	30
Knaps of Birness	Aberd	NJ9833	57°23·5'	2°1·5'W	X	30
Knaps of Fafernie	Aberd	NO2180	56°54·5'	3°17·4'W	X	44
Knap, The	Arg & Bt	NM9247	56°34·4'	5°22·7'W	X	49
Knap, The	Swan	SS5787	51°34·1'	4°3·4'W	X	159
Knapthorpe	Notts	SK7458	53°7·1'	0°53·3'W	T	120
Knaptoft	Leic	SP6289	52°30·0'	1°4·8'W	T	140
Knaptoft Grange	Leic	SP6288	52°29·4'	1°4·8'W	X	140
Knaptoft House Fm	Leic	SP6189	52°30·0'	1°5·7'W	FM	140
Knaptoft Lodge	Leic	SP6387	52°28·9'	1°3·9'W	X	140
Knapton	Norf	TG3034	52°51·5'	1°25·4'E	T	133
Knapton	York	SE5652	53°57·9'	1°8·4'W	T	105
Knapton Grange	N Yks	SE8975	54°10·0'	0°37·8'W	X	101
Knapton Green	Heref	SO4452	52°10·0'	2°48·7'W	T	148,149
Knapton Hall	N Yks	SE8875	54°10·0'	0°38·7'W	X	101
Knapton Ho	Norf	TG2933	52°51·0'	1°24·5'E	X	133
Knapton Lodge	N Yks	SE8777	54°11·1'	0°39·6'W	X	101
Knapton Plantn	N Yks	SE8974	54°9·5'	0°37·8'W	F	101
Knapwell	Cambs	TL3362	52°14·6'	0°2·7'W	T	154
Knar	Ches	SK0067	53°12·2'	1°59·6'W	X	119
Knar	Northum	NY6651	54°51·4'	2°31·4'W	X	86
Knar Burn	Northum	NY6549	54°50·3'	2°32·3'W	W	86
Knaresborough	N Yks	SE3557	54°0·7'	1°27·5'W	T	104
Knares, The	Northum	NY6480	55°7·0'	2°33·4'W	X	80
Knarie Burn	D & G	NX7877	55°4·6'	3°54·2'W	W	84
Knarr Cross Fm	Peterb	TF3301	52°35·7'	0°1·8'W	FM	142
Knarr End Fm	Lancs	SD9442	53°52·7'	2°5·1'W	FM	103
Knarr Fm	Peterb	TF3304	52°37·3'	0°1·7'W	FM	142
Knarrs	Lancs	SD9341	53°52·2'	2°6·0'W	X	103
Knarrs Hill	Lancs	SD9342	53°52·7'	2°6·0'W	X	103
Knarrs Nook	Derby	SK0290	53°24·6'	1°57·8'W	X	110
Knarsdale	Northum	NY6753	54°52·5'	2°30·4'W	T	86,87
Knarsdale Common	Northum	NY6550	54°50·9'	2°32·3'W	X	86
Knarsdale Forest	Northum	NY6452	54°51·9'	2°33·2'W	X	86
Knarsdale Hall	Northum	NY6754	54°53·0'	2°30·4'W	A	86,87
Knarston	Orkney	HY3020	59°3·9'	3°12·8'W	T	6
Knarston	Orkney	HY4429	59°8·9'	2°58·3'W	X	5,6
Knathorne	Devon	SS7604	50°49·6'	3°45·3'W	X	191
Knathorne Brook	Devon	SS7604	50°49·6'	3°45·3'W	W	191
Knatta Barrow	Devon	SX6564	50°27·9'	3°53·8'W	A	202
Knatts Valley	Kent	TQ5661	51°19·8'	0°14·7'E	T	177,188
Knauchland	Moray	NJ5651	57°33·1'	2°43·7'W	X	29
Knave Holes Hill	Cald	SD9819	53°40·3'	2°1·4'W	X	109
Knaven	Aberd	NJ8943	57°28·9'	2°10·5'W	T	30
Knavenhill Fm	Warw	SP2449	52°8·6'	1°38·6'W	FM	151
Knavenhill Wood	Warw	SP2449	52°8·6'	1°38·6'W	F	151
Knaves Ash	Hants	SU1804	50°50·3'	1°44·3'W	X	195
Knave's Ash	Kent	TR1964	51°20·2'	1°9·0'E	X	179
Knaves Ash Cross	Devon	SX8264	50°28·1'	3°39·4'W	X	202
Knaves Green	Suff	TM1265	52°14·8'	1°6·7'E	T	155
Knavesmire	Durham	NZ1128	54°39·1'	1°49·3'W	X	92
Knavesmire	York	SE5849	53°56·3'	1°6·6'W	X	105
Knaveston	Pemb	SM8724	51°52·7'	5°5·3'W	X	157
Knave, The	Swan	SS4386	51°33·3'	4°15·5'W	X	159
Knavocks, The	Corn	SW5943	50°14·5'	5°22·4'W	X	203
Knaworthy	Devon	SS4317	50°56·1'	4°13·7'W	X	180,190
Knayton	N Yks	SE4387	54°16·9'	1°20·0'W	T	99
Knayton Grange	N Yks	SE4287	54°16·9'	1°20·9'W	X	99
Knebworth	Herts	TL2520	51°52·1'	0°10·7'W	T	166
Knebworth Ho	Herts	TL2220	51°52·1'	0°13·3'W	X	166
Knedlington	E Yorks	SE7328	53°44·8'	0°53·2'W	T	105,106
Knee Brook	Glos	SP2136	52°1·6'	1°41·2'W	W	151
Kneedeep	Moray	NJ3024	57°18·3'	3°9·3'W	X	37
Kneefill Ness	Shetld	HU2965	60°22·3'	1°27·9'W	X	3
Knee of Cairnsmore	D & G	NX5165	54°57·7'	4°19·2'W	X	83
Kneep	N Eil	NB0936	58°13·3'	6°56·9'W	T	13
Kneesall	Notts	SK7064	53°10·3'	0°56·8'W	T	120
Kneesall Green Fm	Notts	SK7164	53°10·3'	0°55·9'W	FM	120
Kneesall Lodge	Notts	SK7263	53°9·8'	0°55·0'W	X	120
Kneesall Wood	Notts	SK7164	53°10·3'	0°55·9'W	F	120
Kneesend	S Lanak	NS9213	55°24·2'	3°41·9'W	X	71,78
Kneesend Wood	S Lanak	NT0122	55°29·2'	3°33·6'W	F	72
Kneeset Nose	Devon	SX5886	50°39·6'	4°0·2'W	X	191
Knees Hill	S Lanak	NS8121	55°28·4'	3°52·5'W	X	71,72
Knees, The	Orkney	HY5740	59°14·9'	2°44·7'W	X	5
Kneesworth	Cambs	TL3444	52°4·9'	0°2·3'W	T	154
Kneesworth Ho (Hospl)	Cambs	TL3544	52°4·9'	0°1·4'W	X	154
Knee, The	Highld	ND4072	58°38·2'	3°1·5'W	X	7,12
Knee, The	Orkney	HY4433	59°11·1'	2°58·3'W	X	5,6
Kneeton	Notts	SK7146	53°0·6'	0°56·1'W	T	129
Kneeton Hall	N Yks	NZ2106	54°27·2'	1°40·1'W	X	93
Kneller Court	Hants	SU5608	50°52·4'	1°11·9'W	X	196
Kneller Hall	Rich	TQ1474	51°27·4'	0°21·2'W	X	176
Knelle Wood	E Susx	TQ8525	50°59·9'	0°38·6'E	F	189,199
Knell Fm	Kent	TR2859	51°17·3'	1°16·6'E	FM	179
Knellock	Angus	NO4842	56°34·3'	2°50·3'W	X	54
Knells Ho	Cumbr	NY4160	54°56·1'	2°54·8'W	X	85
Knellstone	E Susx	TQ8718	50°56·1'	0°40·1'E	X	189,199
Knelston	Swan	SS4688	51°34·4'	4°13·0'W	T	159
Knenhall	Staffs	SJ9237	52°56·1'	2°6·7'W	T	127
Knepp Castle	W Susx	TQ1521	50°58·8'	0°21·3'W	X	198
Knepp Castle	W Susx	TQ1620	50°58·3'	0°20·5'W	A	198
Kneppmill Pond	W Susx	TQ1521	50°58·8'	0°21·3'W	W	198
Knettishall	Suff	TL9780	52°23·2'	0°54·1'E	T	144
Knettishall Heath Country Park	Suff	TL9480	52°23·2'	0°51·5'E	X	144

Knevocklaw	E Ayr	NS5638	55°37·1'	4°16·8'W	X	71
Kneysbeck	N Yks	SE6694	54°20·5'	0°58·7'W	X	94,100
Knightacott	Devon	SS5030	51°3·2'	4°8·0'W	X	180
Knightacott	Devon	SS6439	51°8·3'	3°56·3'W	T	180
Knight Close or Bella	N Yks	SD8986	54°16·4'	2°9·7'W	X	98
Knightcote	Warw	SP3954	52°11·2'	1°25·4'W	T	151
Knightcott	N Som	ST3859	51°19·8'	2°53·0'W	T	182
Knightland Burn	Aberd	NJ5640	57°27·1'	2°43·5'W	W	29
Knightley	Staffs	SJ8125	52°49·6'	2°16·5'W	T	127
Knightley Dale	Staffs	SJ8123	52°48·5'	2°16·5'W	T	127
Knightley Eaves	Staffs	SJ8026	52°50·1'	2°17·4'W	X	127
Knightley Gorse	Staffs	SJ8125	52°49·6'	2°16·5'W	X	127
Knightley Grange	Staffs	SJ8024	52°49·0'	2°17·4'W	X	127
Knightley Hall	Staffs	SJ8123	52°48·5'	2°16·5'W	X	127
Knightley Park	Staffs	SK1923	52°48·5'	1°42·7'W	F	128
Knightley Way	Northnts	SP6353	52°10·5'	1°4·3'W	X	152
Knightley Wood	Northnts	SP6054	52°11·1'	1°6·9'W	F	152
Knightlow Hill	Warw	SP4073	52°21·5'	1°24·4'W	X	140
Knighton	C of Leic	SK5901	52°36·4'	1°7·3'W	T	140
Knighton	Corn	SX2579	50°35·3'	4°28·0'W	X	201
Knighton	Devon	SX5249	50°19·6'	4°4·4'W	T	201
Knighton	Devon	SX7547	50°18·8'	3°45·0'W	X	202
Knighton	Dorset	ST6111	50°54·1'	2°32·9'W	T	194
Knighton	Hants	SU4924	51°1·0'	1°17·7'W	X	185
Knighton	Oxon	SU2887	51°35·1'	1°35·4'W	T	174
Knighton	Poole	SZ0497	50°46·6'	1°56·2'W	T	195
Knighton	Somer	SS8335	51°6·4'	3°39·9'W	X	181
Knighton	Somer	ST1944	51°11·6'	3°9·2'W	T	181
Knighton	Somer	ST3920	50°58·8'	2°51·8'W	X	193
Knighton	Staffs	SJ7240	52°57·6'	2°24·6'W	T	118
Knighton	Staffs	SJ7426	52°50·1'	2°22·8'W	X	127
Knighton	Wilts	SU2971	51°26·5'	1°34·6'W	T	174
Knighton	Worcs	SP0356	52°12·4'	1°57·0'W	T	150
Knighton Barn	Oxon	SU2885	51°34·0'	1°35·4'W	X	174
Knighton Combe	Somer	SS8234	51°5·8'	3°40·7'W	X	181
Knighton Common	Worcs	SO6270	52°19·8'	2°33·1'W	X	138
Knighton Down	Oxon	SU2983	51°32·9'	1°34·5'W	X	174
Knighton Down	Wilts	SU1244	51°11·9'	1°49·3'W	X	184
Knighton Fields	C of Leic	SK5901	52°36·4'	1°7·3'W	T	140
Knighton Fm	I of W	SZ5686	50°40·5'	1°12·1'W	FM	196
Knighton Fm	Wilts	SU1545	51°12·5'	1°46·7'W	FM	184
Knighton Grange Fm	Staffs	SJ7427	52°50·6'	2°22·8'W	FM	127
Knighton Heath	Devon	SX8477	50°35·1'	3°37·9'W	X	191
Knighton Heath	Dorset	SY8186	50°40·6'	2°15·8'W	X	194
Knighton Heath Wood	Dorset	SY7488	50°41·7'	2°21·7'W	F	194
Knighton Hill	Dorset	ST6112	50°54·6'	2°32·9'W	H	194
Knighton Hill	Wilts	SU0524	51°1·2'	1°55·3'W	H	184
Knighton Hill Fm	Wilts	SU0524	51°1·2'	1°55·3'W	FM	184
Knighton Ho (Sch)	Dorset	ST8508	50°52·5'	2°12·4'W	X	194
Knighton Manor	Wilts	SU0525	51°1·7'	1°55·3'W	X	184
Knighton on Teme	Worcs	SO6370	52°19·8'	2°32·2'W	T	138
Knighton or Tref-y-Clawdd	Powys	SO2872	52°20·7'	3°3·0'W	T	137,148
Knighton Park	C of Leic	SK6000	52°35·9'	1°6·4'W	X	140
Knighton Reservoir	Shrops	SJ7328	52°51·2'	2°23·7'W	W	127
Knightons	Surrey	TQ0134	51°6·0'	0°33·1'W	X	186
Knighton Sutton Fm	Bath & NE Somer	ST5960	51°20·5'	2°34·9'W	FM	172,182
Knighton Wood	Wilts	SU0522	51°0·1'	1°55·3'W	F	184
Knighton Wood Fm	Wilts	SU0622	51°0·1'	1°55·4'W	FM	184
Knightor	Corn	SX0356	50°22·5'	4°45·9'W	T	200
Knight Resr	Surrey	TQ1167	51°23·7'	0°23·9'W	W	176
Knight's	Somer	ST0834	51°6·1'	3°18·5'W	X	181
Knights Bottom	Kent	TR3648	51°11·2'	1°23·0'E	X	179
Knightsbridge	Glos	SO8926	51°56·2'	2°9·2'W	T	163
Knightsbridge	Ken & Ch	TQ2779	51°30·0'	0°9·8'W	T	176
Knightsbridge Fm	E Susx	TQ6015	50°55·0'	0°17·0'E	FM	199
Knightsbridge Fm	Oxon	SU6897	51°40·3'	1°0·6'W	FM	164,165
Knightsbridge Ho	Hants	SU5163	51°22·1'	1°15·7'W	X	174
Knights Copse	Hants	SU3700	50°48·1'	1°28·1'W	F	196
Knightscote Fm	Hill	TQ0590	51°36·2'	0°28·6'W	FM	176
Knight's End	Cambs	TL4094	52°31·8'	0°4·2'E	T	142,143
Knights Enham	Hants	SU3648	51°14·0'	1°28·7'W	T	185
Knightsfield Fm	Staffs	SK0831	52°52·8'	1°52·5'W	FM	128
Knight's Fm	Essex	TL9630	51°56·3'	0°51·5'E	FM	168
Knight's Fm	E Susx	TQ5611	50°52·9'	0°13·4'E	FM	199
Knight's Fm	I of W	SZ5389	50°42·1'	1°14·6'W	FM	196
Knight's Fm	Lancs	SD6028	53°45·1'	2°36·0'W	FM	102,103
Knight's Fm	Leic	SP7898	52°34·7'	0°50·5'W	FM	141
Knight's Fm	S Glos	ST6194	51°38·8'	2°33·4'W	FM	162,172
Knight's Fm	Somer	ST1128	51°2·9'	3°15·8'W	FM	181,193
Knights Fm	Suff	TM2034	51°57·9'	1°12·6'E	FM	169
Knight's Fm	Suff	TM2678	52°21·4'	1°19·5'E	FM	156
Knight's Fm	W Berks	SU6869	51°25·2'	1°0·9'W	FM	175
Knight's Fm	W Susx	TQ1322	50°59·4'	0°23·0'W	FM	198
Knightsford Fm	Carm	SN3824	51°53·7'	4°20·9'W	FM	145,159
Knight's Grange	Ches	SJ6367	53°12·2'	2°32·8'W	X	118
Knight's Green	Glos	SO7131	51°58·8'	2°24·9'W	X	149
Knightshayes Court	Devon	SS9615	50°55·7'	3°28·4'W	X	181
Knightshayne Fm	Devon	ST2310	50°53·3'	3°5·3'W	FM	192,193
Knight's Hill	Dorset	SY4996	50°45·9'	2°43·0'W	H	193,194
Knightshill	Heref	SO6621	51°53·4'	2°29·3'W	X	162
Knight's Hill	Lam	TQ3273	51°26·7'	0°5·6'W	T	176,177
Knights Hill	Worcs	SO8644	52°5·9'	2°11·9'W	X	150
Knights Hill Fm	Herts	TL3725	51°54·6'	0°0·1'W	FM	166
Knights Hill Fm	Suff	TL9152	52°8·2'	0°47·9'E	FM	155
Knightsland Fm	Staffs	SK0830	52°52·3'	1°52·5'W	FM	128
Knightsland Wood	Essex	TL5101	51°41·5'	0°11·5'E	F	167
Knight's Lodge	Cumbr	NY4044	54°47·5'	2°55·6'W	X	85
Knightsmill	Aberd	NJ5942	57°28·2'	2°40·6'W	X	29
Knightsmill	Corn	SX0780	50°35·5'	4°43·2'W	T	200
Knights Place	Kent	TQ7068	51°23·4'	0°27·0'E	X	178
Knightsridge	W Loth	NT0469	55°54·5'	3°31·7'W	T	65
Knightstone	Devon	SS7806	50°50·7'	3°43·6'W	X	191
Knightstone	Devon	SY1094	50°44·6'	3°16·2'W	A	192,193
Knightstone	N Som	ST3161	51°20·9'	2°59·1'W	X	182
Knightstone Down	Devon	SS7807	50°51·2'	3°43·6'W	X	191
Knightston Fm	Pemb	SN1202	51°41·4'	4°42·8'W	FM	158
Knights Ward	Fife	NO5007	56°15·4'	2°48·0'W	X	59
Knights Ward Wood	Fife	NO5007	56°15·4'	2°48·0'W	F	59
Knightswood	C of Glas	NS5269	55°53·7'	4°21·6'W	T	64
Knightswood Common	Glos	SO9505	51°44·9'	2°4·0'W	F	163
Knight Templar Rock	Devon	SS1346	51°11·2'	4°40·2'W	X	180
Knight, The	Cumbr	NY4017	54°32·9'	2°55·2'W	X	90
Knightwick	Worcs	SO7255	52°11·8'	2°24·2'W	T	149
Knightwick	Worcs	SO7355	52°11·8'	2°23·3'W	X	150
Knightwick Manor	Worcs	SO7255	52°11·8'	2°24·2'W	X	149
Knightwood Fm	Hants	SU4121	50°59·4'	1°24·6'W	FM	185
Knightwood Inclosure	Hants	SU2506	50°51·4'	1°38·3'W	F	195
Knightwood Oak	Hants	SU2606	50°51·4'	1°37·5'W	X	195
Knill	Heref	SO2960	52°14·3'	3°2·0'W	T	137,148
Knill Court	Heref	SO2960	52°14·3'	3°2·0'W	X	137,148
Knill Garraway	Heref	SO2959	52°13·7'	3°2·0'W	X	148
Knill Wood	Heref	SO2962	52°15·3'	3°2·0'W	F	137,148
Knipe Fold	Cumbr	SD3499	54°23·2'	3°0·6'W	T	96,97
Knipe Moor	Cumbr	NY5219	54°34·1'	2°44·1'W	X	90
Knipe Scar	N Yks	SD9770	54°7·8'	2°2·3'W	X	98
Knipe Tarn	Cumbr	SD4294	54°20·5'	2°53·1'W	W	96,97
Knipe, The	E Ayr	NS6511	55°22·7'	4°7·4'W	X	71
Knipoch	Arg & Bt	NM8523	56°21·3'	5°28·4'W	T	49
Knipton	Leic	SK8231	52°52·4'	0°46·5'W	T	130
Knipton Pasture	Leic	SK8232	52°53·0'	0°46·5'W	X	130
Knipton Resr	Leic	SK8130	52°51·9'	0°47·4'W	W	130
Knitchen Hill	Orkney	HY4228	59°8·4'	3°0·3'W	H	5,6
Knitsley	Durham	NZ1148	54°49·8'	1°49·3'W	T	88
Knitsley Fell	Durham	NZ0934	54°42·3'	1°51·2'W	X	92
Knitsley Mill	Durham	NZ1148	54°49·8'	1°49·3'W	X	88
Knitson Fm	Dorset	SZ0080	50°37·4'	1°59·6'W	FM	195
Knittleton	Cumbr	SD2586	54°16·1'	3°8·7'W	X	96
Kniveden	Staffs	SK0056	53°6·3'	1°59·6'W	X	119
Knivestone	Northum	NU2539	55°38·9'	1°35·7'W	X	75
Kniveton	Derby	SK2050	53°3·1'	1°41·7'W	T	119
Kniveton Brook	Derby	SK2148	53°2·0'	1°40·8'W	W	119
Knivetonwood	Derby	SK2050	53°3·1'	1°41·7'W	X	119
Knoake's Court	Heref	SO4555	52°11·7'	2°47·9'W	X	148,149
Knobbs Fm	Warw	SP1649	52°8·6'	1°45·6'W	FM	151
Knob Fm	Derby	SK3153	53°4·6'	1°31·8'W	FM	119
Knob Fm	Derby	SK3748	53°1·9'	1°26·5'W	FM	119
Knob Fm	Derby	SK4029	52°51·7'	1°23·9'W	FM	129
Knob Hill	Leic	SP8298	52°34·7'	0°47·0'W	H	141
Knob Hill	W Susx	TQ1534	51°5·9'	0°21·1'W	X	187
Knob's Crook	Dorset	SU0507	50°52·0'	1°55·4'W	X	195
Knob, The	Derby	SK2345	53°0·4'	1°39·0'W	X	119,128
Knock	Aberd	NJ9746	57°30·5'	2°2·5'W	X	30
Knock	Aberd	NO3595	57°2·7'	3°3·8'W	X	37,44
Knock	Arg & Bt	NM5438	56°28·5'	5°59·2'W	X	47,48
Knock	Arg & Bt	NR9190	56°3·7'	5°21·0'W	X	55
Knock	Cumbr	NY6727	54°38·5'	2°30·3'W	T	91
Knock	D & G	NW9857	54°52·3'	5°8·5'W	X	82
Knock	D & G	NX3739	54°43·4'	4°31·4'W	X	83
Knock	Moray	NJ1527	57°19·8'	3°24·2'W	X	36
Knock	Moray	NJ5452	57°33·6'	2°45·7'W	T	29
Knock	Moray	NJ5453	57°34·1'	2°45·7'W	X	29
Knock	Scot Bord	NT7557	55°48·6'	2°23·5'W	X	67,74
Knock	W Loth	NS9971	55°55·5'	3°36·5'W	X	65
Knockailan	Highld	NJ0417	57°14·3'	3°35·0'W	X	36
Knockalava	Arg & Bt	NR9196	56°6·9'	5°21·3'W	X	55
Knockaldie	D & G	NW9859	54°53·4'	5°8·6'W	X	82
Knockali	Pth & Kin	NO1458	56°42·6'	3°23·8'W	H	53
Knockallan	D & G	NX7465	54°58·1'	3°57·7'W	X	83,84
Knockalls Inclosure	Glos	SO5411	51°48·0'	2°39·6'W	F	162
Knockally	Highld	ND1429	58°14·7'	3°27·4'W	X	11,17
Knockaloe Moar	I of M	SC2382	54°12·4'	4°42·4'W	X	95
Knockan	Aberd	NO2293	57°1·6'	3°16·6'W	T	36,44
Knockan	Arg & Bt	NM4023	56°19·9'	6°11·9'W	T	48
Knockan	Highld	NC2110	58°2·8'	5°1·5'W	T	15
Knockan	Moray	NJ3346	57°30·2'	3°6·6'W	X	28
Knockan	Moray	NJ3546	57°30·2'	3°4·6'W	H	28
Knockanbearach	Arg & Bt	NR3363	55°47·5'	6°15·1'W	X	60,61
Knockanbeg	Moray	NJ2632	57°22·6'	3°13·4'W	X	37
Knockanbuie	Highld	NH8452	57°32·9'	3°55·8'W	X	27
Knockanbuie	Highld	NJ1135	57°24·1'	3°28·4'W	X	28
Knockan Crag	Highld	NC1909	58°2·3'	5°3·5'W	X	15
Knockancurin	Highld	NH5865	57°39·4'	4°22·3'W	X	21
Knockandhu	Moray	NJ2123	57°17·7'	3°18·2'W	T	36
Knockandhu	Moray	NJ3246	57°30·2'	3°7·6'W	X	28
Knock and Maize	D & G	NW9958	54°52·8'	5°7·6'W	X	82
Knock and Maize	D & G	NX0059	54°53·4'	5°6·7'W	X	82
Knockando	Moray	NJ1941	57°27·4'	3°20·5'W	T	28
Knockando Burn	Moray	NJ1744	57°29·0'	3°22·6'W	W	28
Knockandoch	Aberd	NJ5711	57°11·5'	2°42·2'W	X	37
Knockando Ho	Moray	NJ2042	57°27·9'	3°19·6'W	X	28
Knockandoo	Highld	NH7825	57°18·2'	4°1·0'W	X	35
Knockandy Hill	Aberd	NJ5431	57°22·3'	2°45·4'W	H	29,37
Knockangle	Highld	NH8945	57°29·1'	3°50·6'W	X	27
Knockangle Point	Arg & Bt	NR3151	55°40·9'	6°16·3'W	X	60
Knockanicken	D & G	NX2671	55°0·4'	4°42·8'W	X	76
Knockann	D & G	NX4151	54°50·0'	4°28·1'W	X	83
Knockanrioch	Moray	NJ1844	57°29·0'	3°21·6'W	X	28
Knockanrock	Highld	NC1808	58°1·7'	5°4·5'W	X	15
Knockantivore	Arg & Bt	NM5736	56°27·5'	5°56·2'W	X	47,48
Knockarthur	Highld	NC7506	58°1·8'	4°6·5'W	T	16
Knockatoul	D & G	NX2572	55°1·0'	4°43·8'W	X	76
Knockaughley	D & G	NX7291	55°12·1'	4°0·2'W	X	77
Knockbain	Highld	NH5358	57°35·6'	4°27·1'W	X	26
Knockbain	Highld	NH5543	57°27·5'	4°24·6'W	X	26
Knockbain	Highld	NH6255	57°34·1'	4°18·0'W	X	26
Knockbain	S Ayr	NX1690	55°10·5'	4°52·9'W	X	76
Knockbain Mains	Highld	NH6155	57°34·1'	4°19·0'W	X	26
Knockban	Highld	NH2161	57°36·5'	4°59·3'W	X	20
Knockbank Fm	Aberd	NO7479	56°54·4'	2°25·2'W	FM	45
Knockbarrie	Pth & Kin	NN9658	56°42·4'	3°41·5'W	X	52,53
Knock Barrie	Pth & Kin	NN9659	56°42·9'	3°41·5'W	X	52,53
Knockbartnock	Renf	NS3560	55°48·6'	4°37·5'W	X	63
Knock Bay	D & G	NW9757	54°52·2'	5°9·4'W	W	82
Knock Bay	Highld	NG6608	57°6·5'	5°48·3'W	W	32
Knockbennan Hill	D & G	NW9866	54°57·1'	5°8·8'W	H	82
Knockbog	Moray	NJ5354	57°34·7'	2°46·7'W	T	29
Knockbrack	D & G	NX9395	55°14·5'	3°40·5'W	H	78
Knockbrake	S Ayr	NS2907	55°19·9'	4°41·3'W	H	70,76
Knockbreck	E Ayr	NS6422	55°28·6'	4°8·7'W	X	71
Knockbreck	Highld	NG2660	57°33·1'	6°34·4'W	T	23
Knockbreck	Highld	NH7881	57°48·4'	4°2·7'W	X	21
Knockbrex	D & G	NX5849	54°49·2'	4°12·2'W	T	83
Knockbridge Fm	E Susx	TQ8715	50°54·5'	0°40·0'E	FM	189,199
Knock Brook	Pemb	SM9118	51°49·5'	5°1·6'W	W	157,158
Knockbuckle	S Ayr	NX3899	55°15·8'	4°32·5'W	X	77
Knock Burn	D & G	NX4667	54°58·7'	4°24·0'W	W	83
Knock Burn	D & G	NX8563	54°57·2'	3°47·3'W	W	84
Knock Burn	Moray	NJ1427	57°19·8'	3°25·2'W	W	36
Knockburn	Northum	NY8350	54°50·9'	2°15·5'W	X	86,87
Knock Burn	S Lanak	NT0328	55°32·4'	3°31·8'W	W	72
Knockburnie	E Ayr	NS5610	55°22·0'	4°15·9'W	X	71
Knockburnie Burn	E Ayr	NS5509	55°21·5'	4°16·8'W	W	71,77
Knockcarrach	Highld	NH4613	57°11·2'	4°32·4'W	X	34
Knock Castle	Highld	NG6708	57°6·5'	5°50·4'W	A	32
Knock Castle	N Ayr	NS1962	55°49·3'	4°52·9'W	X	63
Knockclune	D & G	NX5886	55°9·1'	4°13·3'W	X	77
Knockcoid	D & G	NX0169	54°58·8'	5°6·2'W	X	82
Knockconey Dod	D & G	NS8507	55°20·9'	3°48·4'W	H	71,78
Knock Craggie	Highld	NC3205	58°0·4'	4°50·1'W	H	15
Knockcravie Burn	D & G	NX3783	55°7·1'	4°32·9'W	W	77
Knockcroon	S Ayr	NX2680	55°5·3'	4°43·2'W	X	76
Knock Cross	Cumbr	NY6726	54°37·9'	2°30·3'W	X	91
Knockdal Ring	Inverc	NS2867	55°52·2'	4°44·5'W	X	63
Knockdamph	Highld	NH2895	57°54·9'	4°53·7'W	X	20
Knockdavie Castle	Fife	NT2188	56°5·0'	3°15·7'W	A	66
Knockdaw	S Ayr	NX1589	55°9·9'	4°53·8'W	X	76
Knockdaw Hill	S Ayr	NX1688	55°9·4'	4°52·9'W	H	76
Knockdawn	D & G	NX6158	54°54·1'	4°9·6'W	H	83
Knockdee	Highld	ND1661	58°32·0'	3°26·1'W	X	11,12
Knockderry Cas	Arg & Bt	NS2183	56°0·7'	4°51·8'W	X	56
Knockderry Fm	Arg & Bt	NS2283	56°0·7'	4°50·9'W	FM	56
Knock Dhu	Highld	NH8380	57°47·9'	3°57·6'W	X	21
Knockdhu	Highld	NH9135	57°23·8'	3°48·4'W	X	27
Knockdhu	S Ayr	NX1483	55°6·6'	4°54·5'W	H	76
Knockdhu Burn	Arg & Bt	NS0974	55°55·5'	5°3·0'W	W	63
Knockdolian	S Ayr	NX1184	55°7·1'	4°57·4'W	H	76
Knockdolian	S Ayr	NX1285	55°7·7'	4°56·5'W	X	76
Knockdollochan	D & G	NX6685	55°8·7'	4°5·7'W	X	77
Knockdon	Arg & Bt	NR3364	55°48·0'	6°15·2'W	X	60,61
Knockdon	E Ayr	NS5631	55°33·3'	4°16·5'W	X	71
Knockdon	S Ayr	NS3014	55°23·7'	4°40·6'W	X	70
Knockdon	S Ayr	NS4300	55°16·4'	4°27·9'W	X	77
Knockdon Burn	S Ayr	NS4301	55°16·9'	4°27·9'W	W	77
Knockdow	Arg & Bt	NS1070	55°53·4'	5°1·9'W	X	63
Knockdown	Wilts	ST8388	51°35·7'	2°14·3'W	T	162,173
Knockdunder	E Ayr	NS5316	55°25·2'	4°18·9'W	X	70
Knockdurn	Aberd	NJ5863	57°39·6'	2°41·8'W	X	29
Knockeans	D & G	NX4958	54°53·9'	4°20·9'W	X	83
Knockeans Hill	D & G	NX4957	54°53·3'	4°20·8'W	H	83
Knock-e-Dooney	I of M	NX4002	54°23·6'	4°27·4'W	X	95
Knockeen	S Ayr	NX3095	55°13·5'	4°39·9'W	X	76
Knockeffrick	D & G	NX4149	54°48·9'	4°28·0'W	X	83
Knockelly	D & G	NX8097	55°15·4'	3°52·9'W	X	78
Knockenae Plantn	E Renf	NS4554	55°45·5'	4°27·8'W	F	64
Knockenbaird	Aberd	NJ6329	57°21·3'	2°36·4'W	T	37
Knockencorsan	N Ayr	NS2467	55°52·1'	4°48·3'W	H	63
Knockencule	D & G	NX0935	54°40·7'	4°57·3'W	X	82
Knockencurr	D & G	NX4249	54°48·9'	4°27·1'W	X	83
Knockendale	S Ayr	NS3832	55°33·5'	4°33·7'W	X	70
Knockendoch	D & G	NX9563	54°57·3'	3°38·0'W	H	84
Knockendon	N Ayr	NS2451	55°43·5'	4°47·7'W	X	63
Knockendon Resr	N Ayr	NS2452	55°44·0'	4°47·8'W	W	63
Knockendurrick	D & G	NX6357	54°53·6'	4°7·7'W	H	83
Knock-e-nean	I of M	NX4101	54°23·0'	4°26·5'W	X	95
Knockengalie Burn	D & G	NS8306	55°20·3'	3°50·2'W	W	71,78
Knockengorroch	D & G	NX5597	55°15·0'	4°16·4'W	X	77
Knockenhair	D & G	NS7912	55°23·5'	3°54·2'W	X	71,78
Knockenhair	D & G	NS7913	55°24·0'	3°54·2'W	H	71,78
Knockenjig	D & G	NS7511	55°22·9'	3°57·9'W	X	71,78
Knockenkelly	N Ayr	NS0427	55°30·1'	5°5·8'W	T	69
Knockenlee Burn	E Ayr	NS5208	55°20·9'	4°19·6'W	W	70,77
Knockenny	Angus	NO3845	56°35·8'	3°0·1'W	X	54
Knockenshag	D & G	NS7518	55°26·7'	3°58·1'W	H	71,78
Knockenshang	D & G	NX9793	55°13·5'	3°36·7'W	X	78
Knockenstob	D & G	NS7811	55°22·9'	3°55·1'W	X	71,78
Knockentiber	E Ayr	NS3939	55°37·3'	4°33·0'W	T	70
Knockenzie	Aberd	NJ4700	57°5·5'	2°52·0'W	X	37
Knockerdown	Derby	SK2351	53°3·6'	1°39·0'W	T	119
Knockerhill Fm	Heref	SO4935	52°0·9'	2°44·2'W	FM	149
Knockespen	D & G	NX9890	55°11·9'	3°35·7'W	H	78
Knockespock Ho	Aberd	NJ5424	57°18·5'	2°45·4'W	X	37
Knocketie Moss	D & G	NX2858	54°53·5'	4°40·5'W	X	82
Knock-e-vriew	I of M	SC2972	54°7·2'	4°36·6'W	X	95
Knockewart	N Ayr	NS2447	55°41·3'	4°47·6'W	X	63
Knockewart Hills	N Ayr	NS2347	55°41·3'	4°48·5'W	H	63
Knockeycaw	S Ayr	NX2675	55°2·6'	4°43·0'W	X	76
Knockfarrel	Highld	NH5058	57°35·5'	4°30·1'W	T	26
Knock Farril	Highld	NH4958	57°35·5'	4°31·1'W	X	26
Knock Fell	Cumbr	NY7230	54°40·1'	2°25·6'W	X	91
Knock Fell	D & G	NX2555	54°51·8'	4°43·2'W	H	82
Knockfin	Highld	NC8935	58°17·6'	3°53·1'W	X	17
Knockfin	Highld	NH2926	57°17·8'	4°49·8'W	X	25
Knockfin Heights	Highld	NC9134	58°17·1'	3°51·1'W	H	17
Knock Fm	Pemb	SM9318	51°49·6'	4°59·9'W	FM	157,158
Knock Fm	Pemb	SN0321	51°51·4'	4°51·3'W	FM	145,157,158
Knockfullertree Fm	Aberd	NJ6609	57°10·5'	2°33·3'W	FM	38
Knockgardner	S Ayr	NS3503	55°17·9'	4°35·5'W	X	77
Knockgarty	Highld	NH7474	57°44·5'	4°6·5'W	T	21
Knockgerran	S Ayr	NX2497	55°14·4'	4°45·7'W	X	76
Knockglass	D & G	NX0458	54°53·0'	5°2·9'W	T	82
Knockglass	E Renf	NS4454	55°45·5'	4°28·7'W	X	64
Knockglass	Highld	ND0563	58°32·9'	3°37·5'W	T	11,12
Knockglass	Highld	ND1753	58°27·7'	3°24·9'W	X	11,12
Knockglass	Highld	NH7994	57°55·4'	4°2·1'W	X	21
Knockgour	D & G	NW9859	54°53·4'	5°8·6'W	H	82
Knockgranish	Highld	NH9014	57°12·5'	3°48·8'W	X	36
Knockgray	D & G	NX5793	55°12·9'	4°14·4'W	X	77
Knockgray Burn	D & G	NX5793	55°12·9'	4°14·4'W	W	77
Knockguldron	E Ayr	NS4813	55°23·5'	4°23·6'W	X	70

Knock Gune	N Eil	NF9282	57°43·6'	7°10·0'W	X	18
Knockhall	Kent	TQ5974	51°26·8'	0°17·7'E	T	177
Knockhall	Orkney	ND4593	58°49·5'	2°56·7'W	X	7
Knockhall Castle	Aberd	NJ9926	57°19·7'	2°0·5'W	A	38
Knockhall Point	Orkney	ND4594	58°50·1'	2°56·7'W	X	7
Knockhanty	Arg & Bt	NR6420	55°25·3'	5°43·3'W	X	68
Knock Head	Aberd	NJ6566	57°41·2'	2°34·8'W	X	29
Knock Hill	Aberd	NJ5710	57°11·0'	2°42·2'W	H	37
Knockhill	Aberd	NJ5722	57°17·5'	2°42·3'W	X	37
Knockhill	Aberd	NO7091	57°0·8'	2°29·2'W	X	38,45
Knock Hill	Aberd	NO7579	56°54·4'	2°24·2'W	H	45
Knockhill	Angus	NO5847	56°37·0'	2°40·6'W	X	54
Knockhill	D & G	NY1674	55°3·5'	3°18·5'W	X	85
Knock Hill	E Loth	NT5563	55°51·7'	2°42·7'W	X	66
Knock Hill	Fife	NO4416	56°20·2'	2°53·9'W	X	59
Knock Hill	Fife	NT0593	56°7·5'	3°31·3'W	H	58
Knock Hill	Moray	NJ5355	57°35·2'	2°46·7'W	H	29
Knock Hill	Northum	NT9916	55°26·5'	2°0·5'W	H	81
Knock Hill	Scot Bord	NT6144	55°41·5'	2°36·8'W	H	74
Knock Hill	Scot Bord	NT7455	55°47·5'	2°24·4'W	X	67,74
Knock Hill	S Lanak	NT0428	55°32·4'	3°30·8'W	H	72
Knockhill Ho	Fife	NO4225	56°25·1'	2°56·0'W	X	54,59
Knock Hills	Scot Bord	NT6909	55°22·7'	2°28·9'W	H	80
Knockhill Wood	Moray	NJ5356	57°35·8'	2°46·7'W	F	29
Knockhoe	Highld	NG3770	57°38·9'	6°24·0'W	X	23
Knockholt	Kent	TQ4859	51°18·9'	0°7·8'E	T	188
Knockholt Pound	Kent	TQ4859	51°18·9'	0°7·8'E	X	188
Knockholt Sta	Brom	TQ4862	51°20·5'	0°7·9'E	X	177,188
Knockhourn	Moray	NJ1742	57°27·9'	3°22·6'W	X	28
Knockhouse	Fife	NT0786	56°3·7'	3°29·2'W	X	65
Knockie	Aberd	NO5289	56°59·6'	2°46·9'W	X	44
Knockiebae	D & G	NX1765	54°57·0'	4°51·0'W	X	82
Knockie Branar	Aberd	NO4092	57°1·2'	2°58·8'W	H	44
Knockie Lodge (Hotel)	Highld	NH4413	57°11·1'	4°34·4'W	X	34
Knockiemill	Aberd	NJ7151	57°33·1'	2°28·6'W	X	29
Knockiemore	Aberd	NJ9957	57°36·4'	2°0·5'W	X	30
Knockienausk Head	D & G	NX0251	54°49·1'	5°4·5'W	X	82
Knockieside	Aberd	NJ4605	57°8·4'	2°53·1'W	X	37
Knockieston	Pth & Kin	NN8320	56°21·7'	3°53·2'W	X	52,57
Knockilsine Hill	D & G	NY0498	55°16·3'	3°30·2'W	H	78
Knockin	Shrops	SJ3322	52°47·7'	2°59·2'W	T	126
Knockinaam Lodge	D & G	NX0252	54°49·7'	5°4·5'W	X	82
Knockinculloch	S Ayr	NS3300	55°16·2'	4°37·3'W	H	76
Knockingalloch	Stir	NS5890	56°5·2'	4°16·5'W	X	57
Knocking Tofts	Cumbr	NY7813	54°31·0'	2°20·0'W	X	91
Knockin Hall	Shrops	SJ3422	52°47·7'	2°58·3'W	X	126
Knockin Heath	Shrops	SJ3521	52°47·2'	2°57·4'W	T	126
Knockinheath Fm	Shrops	SJ3522	52°47·7'	2°57·4'W	FM	126
Knockinlaw	E Ayr	NS4239	55°37·4'	4°30·1'W	T	70
Knockinlochie	S Ayr	NX3188	55°9·7'	4°38·7'W	X	76
Knockinnon	Highld	ND1731	58°15·9'	3°24·4'W	X	11
Knockintorran	N Eil	NF7367	57°34·7'	7°27·8'W	T	18
Knockishee	D & G	NX2559	54°54·0'	4°43·3'W	X	82
Knockjarder	S Ayr	NS3515	55°24·3'	4°35·9'W	X	70
Knocklach Burn	S Ayr	NX3889	55°10·4'	4°32·2'W	W	77
Knocklae	D & G	NX6478	55°4·9'	4°7·4'W	X	77
Knocklandside	E Ayr	NS3941	55°38·4'	4°33·0'W	X	70
Knocklaugh	S Ayr	NX1791	55°11·0'	4°52·0'W	X	76
Knocklaugh Lodge	S Ayr	NX1892	55°11·6'	4°51·1'W	X	76
Knocklaw	Northum	NU0601	55°18·4'	1°53·9'W	T	81
Knocklea	Aberd	NJ3310	57°10·8'	3°6·0'W	X	37
Knocklea	Highld	NH4640	57°25·7'	4°33·4'W	X	26
Knocklearn	D & G	NX7579	55°5·6'	3°57·1'W	X	84
Knocklearn Moor	D & G	NX7479	55°5·6'	3°58·0'W	X	77,84
Knocklearn Moor	D & G	NX7579	55°5·6'	3°57·1'W	X	84
Knocklearoch	Arg & Bt	NR3964	55°48·2'	6°9·5'W	X	60,61
Knock Leaven	S Lanak	NS9026	55°31·2'	3°44·1'W	H	71,72
Knockleith	Aberd	NK0544	57°29·4'	1°54·5'W	X	30
Knockleith Ho	Aberd	NJ7040	57°27·2'	2°29·5'W	X	29
Knockline	N Eil	NF7467	57°34·8'	7°26·8'W	T	18
Knocklin Ends	Northum	NU2236	55°37·3'	1°38·6'W	X	75
Knockloam	Highld	NH8751	57°32·4'	3°52·8'W	X	27
Knocklom	Aberd	NJ6510	57°11·0'	2°34·3'W	X	38
Knockmade Hill	Renf	NS3561	55°49·1'	4°37·6'W	X	63
Knockmade Plantn	E Ayr	NS4353	55°45·0'	4°29·6'W	F	64
Knock & Maize	D & G	NW9957	54°52·3'	5°7·5'W	X	82
Knockmalloch	S Ayr	NX2384	55°7·4'	4°46·1'W	X	76
Knockman	D & G	NX6782	55°7·1'	4°4·7'W	X	77
Knockman Hill	D & G	NX6783	55°7·7'	4°4·7'W	H	77
Knockman Loch	D & G	NX6683	55°7·6'	4°5·7'W	W	77
Knockman Wood	D & G	NX4168	54°59·1'	4°28·7'W	F	83
Knockmill	Kent	TQ5761	51°19·8'	0°15·6'E	T	177,188
Knockminwood Hill	Inverc	NS2868	55°52·7'	4°44·5'W	X	63
Knock Moor	Cumbr	NY6727	54°38·5'	2°30·3'W	X	91
Knockmore	D & G	NX3857	54°53·1'	4°31·1'W	X	83
Knockmore	Fife	NO2202	56°12·5'	3°15·0'W	X	58
Knock More	Inverc	NS2968	55°52·7'	4°43·6'W	X	63
Knock More	Moray	NJ3149	57°31·8'	3°8·7'W	H	28
Knock Moss	D & G	NX2657	54°52·9'	4°42·3'W	X	82
Knockmountain	Renf	NS3671	55°54·5'	4°37·0'W	X	63
Knock Mugary	N Eil	NF8172	57°37·8'	7°20·2'W	X	18
Knockmuir	Highld	NH7055	57°34·2'	4°10·0'W	X	27
Knockmullock	D & G	NX6148	54°48·7'	4°9·4'W	X	83
Knockmult	D & G	NX7947	54°48·4'	3°52·5'W	H	84
Knockmurran Fm	S Ayr	NS4416	55°25·0'	4°27·4'W	FM	70
Knock Murton	Cumbr	NY0919	54°33·7'	3°24·0'W	H	89
Knocknafenaig	Arg & Bt	NM3619	56°17·7'	6°15·6'W	X	48
Knocknagael	Highld	NH6540	57°26·1'	4°14·5'W	X	26
Knocknagillan	Highld	NH8954	57°34·0'	3°50·9'W	X	27
Knocknagore	Moray	NJ1844	57°29·0'	3°21·6'W	X	28
Knocknaha	Arg & Bt	NR6817	55°23·8'	5°39·4'W	X	68
Knocknahar	Highld	NH8681	57°48·5'	3°54·6'W	X	21
Knocknahighle	Highld	NJ0828	57°20·3'	3°31·2'W	X	36
Knocknaib	E Ayr	NS5921	55°28·0'	4°13·4'W	X	71
Knocknain	D & G	NW9764	54°56·0'	5°9·7'W	X	82
Knocknair	E Dunb	NS5980	55°59·8'	4°15·2'W	X	64
Knocknairling	D & G	NX6276	55°3·8'	4°9·2'W	X	77
Knocknairling Burn	D & G	NX5977	55°4·3'	4°12·1'W	W	77
Knocknalling	D & G	NX5984	55°8·1'	4°12·3'W	X	77
Knocknashalavaig	Highld	NH4340	57°25·7'	4°36·4'W	X	26
Knocknashalg	Moray	NJ2035	57°24·2'	3°19·4'W	X	28
Knock na Snaird	Moray	NJ1048	57°31·1'	3°29·7'W	X	28
Knocknassie	D & G	NW9768	54°58·2'	5°9·9'W	X	82
Knockneen	D & G	NW9970	54°59·3'	5°8·1'W	X	76,82
Knocknevis	D & G	NX5573	55°2·1'	4°15·7'W	X	77
Knocknide Hill	E Ayr	NS5909	55°21·5'	4°13·0'W	X	71,77
Knock Noddimull	N Eil	NL6391	56°53·5'	7°31·6'W	H	31
Knockodhar	S Ayr	NX2589	55°10·1'	4°44·4'W	X	76
Knock of Auchnahannet	Highld	NJ0633	57°22·9'	3°33·4'W	X	27
Knock of Balmyle	Pth & Kin	NO1156	56°41·5'	3°26·7'W	H	53
Knock of Braemoray	Moray	NJ0141	57°27·2'	3°38·5'W	H	27
Knock of Buchromb	Moray	NJ3042	57°28·0'	3°9·6'W	H	28
Knock of Crieff	Pth & Kin	NN8623	56°23·4'	3°50·4'W	H	52,58
Knock of Findowie	Pth & Kin	NO0447	56°36·6'	3°33·4'W	H	52,53
Knock of Formal	Angus	NO2554	56°40·6'	3°13·0'W	H	53
Knock of Gownie	Moray	NJ2942	57°28·0'	3°10·6'W	X	28
Knock of Luce	D & G	NX2555	54°51·8'	4°43·2'W	X	82
Knock Old Man	Cumbr	NY7230	54°40·1'	2°25·6'W	X	91
Knockollochie	Aberd	NJ7025	57°19·1'	2°29·4'W	X	38
Knockomie	Moray	NJ0257	57°35·8'	3°37·9'W	X	27
Knockoner	S Ayr	NX3699	55°15·7'	4°34·4'W	H	77
Knock Ore Gill	Cumbr	NY7030	54°40·1'	2°27·5'W	W	91
Knockormal	S Ayr	NX1388	55°9·3'	4°55·7'W	X	76
Knockormal Hill	S Ayr	NX1388	55°9·3'	4°55·7'W	H	76
Knock-o-Ronald	Stir	NS6893	56°6·9'	4°6·9'W	X	57
Knockothie	Aberd	NJ9531	57°22·4'	2°4·5'W	X	30
Knockoure	D & G	NX7985	55°8·9'	3°53·5'W	H	78
Knockower	D & G	NX5194	55°13·3'	4°20·1'W	H	77
Knock Pike	Cumbr	NY6828	54°39·0'	2°29·3'W	H	91
Knockpin	S Ayr	NS3402	55°17·3'	4°36·4'W	X	76
Knockquharn	Aberd	NJ7607	57°9·5'	2°23·4'W	X	38
Knockquhassen	D & G	NX0259	54°53·4'	5°4·8'W	X	82
Knockraich	Stir	NS6187	56°3·6'	4°13·5'W	X	57
Knockreoch Fm	D & G	NX5785	55°8·6'	4°14·2'W	FM	77
Knockrivoch	N Ayr	NS2544	55°39·7'	4°46·5'W	X	63,70
Knockrochar	S Ayr	NS2900	55°16·1'	4°41·1'W	X	76
Knockrome	Arg & Bt	NR5571	55°52·5'	5°54·6'W	T	61
Knockroon	E Ayr	NS5521	55°27·9'	4°17·2'W	X	71
Knockroon	S Ayr	NS3105	55°18·9'	4°39·4'W	X	70,76
Knockroy	Arg & Bt	NM4729	56°23·4'	6°5·5'W	X	48
Knockruan Loch	Arg & Bt	NR7322	55°26·6'	5°34·9'W	W	68
Knocksallie	D & G	NX5378	55°4·7'	4°17·7'W	X	77
Knock Saul	Aberd	NJ5723	57°18·0'	2°42·4'W	H	37
Knock Scalbart	Arg & Bt	NR7322	55°26·6'	5°34·9'W	H	68
Knockshannoch	Angus	NO2359	56°43·2'	3°15·0'W	X	53
Knockshanoch	W Dunb	NS4379	55°59·0'	4°30·5'W	X	64
Knocksharry	I of M	SC2785	54°14·1'	4°38·9'W	T	95
Knocksheen	D & G	NX5782	55°7·0'	4°14·1'W	X	77
Knock Shield	Northum	NY8350	54°50·9'	2°15·5'W	X	86,87
Knockshield Burn	Northum	NY8350	54°50·9'	2°15·5'W	W	86,87
Knockshield Moor	Northum	NY8248	54°49·8'	2°16·4'W	X	86,87
Knockshiffnock	E Ayr	NS5118	55°26·2'	4°20·9'W	X	70
Knockshin	S Ayr	NX2279	55°4·7'	4°46·9'W	X	76
Knockshinnan	Pth & Kin	NO1235	56°30·2'	3°25·3'W	X	53
Knockshinnoch	D & G	NX8876	55°4·2'	3°44·8'W	X	84
Knockshinnoch	E Ayr	NS4314	55°23·8'	4°28·3'W	X	70
Knockshoggle	S Ayr	NS4223	55°28·8'	4°29·6'W	X	70
Knockside Hills	N Ayr	NS2558	55°47·3'	4°47·0'W	X	63
Knockskae	S Ayr	NS3601	55°16·8'	4°34·5'W	X	77
Knockskae	S Ayr	NS3701	55°16·8'	4°33·5'W	X	77
Knockskelly Hill	D & G	NX7254	54°52·1'	3°59·3'W	X	83,84
Knockskeog Fm	D & G	NX3958	54°53·7'	4°30·2'W	FM	83
Knock Smerclett	N Eil	NF8875	57°39·7'	7°13·5'W	X	18
Knocksoul	Aberd	NJ4206	57°8·7'	2°57·1'W	X	37
Knockstapple	Arg & Bt	NR6912	55°21·1'	5°38·2'W	H	68
Knockstapplebeg	Arg & Bt	NR6912	55°21·1'	5°38·2'W	X	68
Knockstapplemore	Arg & Bt	NR6911	55°20·6'	5°38·2'W	X	68
Knocksting	D & G	NX6988	55°10·4'	4°3·0'W	X	77
Knocksting Loch	D & G	NX6988	55°10·4'	4°3·0'W	W	77
Knockstocks	D & G	NX3966	54°58·0'	4°30·5'W	X	83
Knockterra	E Ayr	NS5418	55°26·3'	4°18·0'W	X	70
Knock, The	Aberd	NO3495	57°2·7'	3°4·8'W	H	37,44
Knock, The	D & G	NY2291	55°12·7'	3°13·1'W	H	79
Knock, The	Pth & Kin	NO2001	56°11·9'	3°16·9'W	H	58
Knock, The	Pth & Kin	NO2001	56°11·9'	3°16·9'W	X	58
Knock, The	S Lanak	NT0337	55°37·3'	3°32·0'W	X	72
Knocktim	D & G	NW9869	54°58·7'	5°9·0'W	X	82
Knocktim	D & G	NX4963	54°56·6'	4°21·0'W	X	83
Knocktimpen	D & G	NX9494	55°14·0'	3°39·6'W	H	78
Knockton	Angus	NO1958	56°42·7'	3°18·9'W	H	53
Knocktulchan Fm	Highld	NJ1135	57°24·1'	3°28·4'W	FM	28
Knock Ullinish	Highld	NG3338	57°21·4'	6°25·9'W	X	23,32
Knockupple	W Dunb	NS4579	55°59·0'	4°28·6'W	X	64
Knockupple Burn	W Dunb	NS4579	55°59·0'	4°28·6'W	W	64
Knockupworth	Cumbr	NY3656	54°53·9'	2°59·5'W	X	85
Knockvennie	D & G	NX7571	55°1·3'	3°56·9'W	X	84
Knockville	D & G	NX3672	55°1·2'	4°33·5'W	X	77
Knockvologan	Arg & Bt	NM3119	56°17·5'	6°20·4'W	X	48
Knockvuy	Highld	NH4538	57°24·6'	4°34·4'W	X	26
Knockwalloch	D & G	NX7970	55°0·8'	3°53·1'W	X	84
Knockwhirn	D & G	NX6095	55°14·0'	4°11·7'W	H	77
Knockwhirr	D & G	NX6457	54°53·6'	4°6·8'W	X	83
Knock Wood	Aberd	NO7191	57°0·8'	2°28·2'W	F	38,45
Knock Wood	Kent	TQ8935	51°5·2'	0°42·3'E	F	189
Knock Wood	Moray	NJ5454	57°34·7'	2°45·7'W	F	29
Knockworthy	Devon	SS5122	50°58·9'	4°7·0'W	X	180
Knockycoid	S Ayr	NX2679	55°4·8'	4°43·1'W	X	76
Knockylaight	S Ayr	NX2677	55°3·7'	4°43·0'W	X	76
Knockytinnal	S Ayr	NX2284	55°7·4'	4°47·1'W	X	76
Knockytoul	S Ayr	NX2780	55°5·3'	4°42·2'W	X	76
Knoc-lochy Well	Moray	NJ1620	57°16·0'	3°23·1'W	W	36
Knodishall	Suff	TM4261	52°11·9'	1°32·9'E	T	156
Knodishall Common	Suff	TM4360	52°11·3'	1°33·7'E	X	156
Knodishall Green	Suff	TM4163	52°13·0'	1°32·1'E	X	156
Knodishall Whin	Suff	TM4159	52°10·8'	1°31·9'E	X	156
Knole	Kent	TQ5354	51°16·1'	0°12·0'E	A	188
Knole	Somer	ST4825	51°1·6'	2°44·1'W	T	193
Knole Hill	Kent	TQ8649	51°12·8'	0°40·2'E	X	189
Knole Knapp	Somer	ST5025	51°1·6'	2°42·4'W	X	183
Knole Park	Kent	TQ5453	51°15·5'	0°12·8'E	X	188
Knoles Fm	I of W	SZ4975	50°34·6'	1°18·1'W	FM	196
Knole, The	Devon	SX5087	50°40·0'	4°7·0'W	X	191
Knole, The	Suff	TM1449	52°6·1'	1°7·9'E	X	169
Knoll	Dorset	ST7004	50°50·3'	2°25·2'W	H	194
Knolland's Fm	Warw	SP2840	52°3·7'	1°35·1'W	FM	151
Knoll Barn	Glos	SP1306	51°45·4'	1°48·3'W	X	163
Knollbuck	Highld	NH3605	57°6·7'	4°42·0'W	X	34
Knollbury	Monm	ST4388	51°35·5'	2°49·0'W	T	171,172
Knollbury	Oxon	SP3123	51°54·5'	1°32·6'W	A	164
Knoll Down	Hants	SU0818	50°57·9'	1°52·8'W	X	184
Knoll Down	Wilts	SU0769	51°25·4'	1°53·6'W	X	173
Knollend Down	Oxon	SU4583	51°32·9'	1°20·7'W	X	174
Knoll Fm	Dorset	SY9797	50°46·6'	2°2·2'W	FM	195
Knoll Fm	Glos	SO5203	51°43·7'	2°41·3'W	FM	162
Knoll Fm	Hants	SU0917	50°57·4'	1°51·9'W	FM	184
Knoll Fm	Leic	SK4900	52°36·0'	1°16·2'W	FM	140
Knoll Fm	Surrey	TQ1638	51°8·0'	0°20·1'W	FM	187
Knoll Fm	Wilts	ST7937	51°8·1'	2°17·6'W	FM	183
Knoll Fm, The	Kent	TR0734	51°4·3'	0°57·7'E	FM	179,189
Knoll Fm, The	Worcs	SO8760	52°14·5'	2°11·0'W	FM	150
Knoll Green	Somer	ST2339	51°8·9'	3°5·7'W	T	182
Knollhead	N Ayr	NS3349	55°42·6'	4°39·1'W	X	63
Knollhead	Pth & Kin	NO2439	56°32·5'	3°13·7'W	X	53
Knoll Hill	Devon	SY3294	50°44·7'	2°57·4'W	X	193
Knoll Hill	Somer	ST4037	51°8·0'	2°51·1'W	H	182
Knoll Hill	Somer	ST6526	51°2·2'	2°29·6'W	X	183
Knoll Hill	Worcs	SO8878	52°24·2'	2°10·2'W	X	139
Knoll Ho	Shrops	SJ7908	52°40·4'	2°18·2'W	X	127
Knoll House Hotel	Dorset	SZ0383	50°39·0'	1°57·1'W	X	195
Knoll Pins	Devon	SS1446	51°11·2'	4°39·3'W	X	180
Knolls	Dorset	SY5685	50°40·0'	2°37·0'W	X	194
Knolls	Shrops	SO4190	52°30·5'	2°51·8'W	X	137
Knolls Green	Ches	SJ8079	53°18·7'	2°17·6'W	T	118
Knolls Hill Fm	Essex	TQ4994	51°37·7'	0°9·6'E	FM	167,177
Knolls, The	Glos	SO9731	51°58·9'	2°2·2'W	H	150
Knolls, The	Shrops	SO3697	52°34·3'	2°56·3'W	X	137
Knolls, The	Suff	TM3556	52°9·4'	1°26·5'E	F	156
Knoll, The	Bucks	SU9193	51°37·9'	0°40·7'W	A	175
Knoll, The	C of Edin	NT1978	55°59·5'	3°17·5'W	X	65,66
Knoll, The	Dorset	SY5387	50°41·1'	2°39·5'W	H	194
Knoll, The	Dorset	SY6784	50°39·5'	2°27·6'W	X	194
Knoll, The	Herts	TL2637	52°1·3'	0°9·4'W	X	153
Knoll, The	Newp	ST4290	51°36·6'	2°49·9'W	H	171,172
Knoll, The	N Som	ST5461	51°21·0'	2°39·2'W	X	172,182
Knoll, The	Shrops	SO2898	52°34·7'	3°3·4'W	X	137
Knoll, The	Wilts	ST9141	51°10·3'	2°7·3'W	X	184
Knoll, The	Wilts	SU0662	51°21·7'	1°54·4'W	H	173
Knoll, The	Worcs	SO8156	52°12·4'	2°16·3'W	X	150
Knoll Top	N Yks	SE1965	54°5·1'	1°42·2'W	T	99
Knoll Top Fm	Sheff	SK2785	53°21·9'	1°35·2'W	FM	110
Knoltlairs	S Lanak	NS6847	55°42·2'	4°5·6'W	X	64
Knoltlairs	Somer	ST6848	51°14·1'	2°27·1'W	X	162
Knolton	Shrops	SJ3738	52°56·4'	2°55·8'W	T	126
Knolton Bryn	Wrex	SJ3739	52°56·9'	2°55·9'W	T	126
Knolton Fm	Wrex	SJ3640	52°57·5'	2°56·8'W	FM	117
Knolton Hall	Wrex	SJ3540	52°57·4'	2°57·7'W	A	117
Knook	Wilts	ST9341	51°10·3'	2°5·6'W	T	184
Knook Barrow	Wilts	ST9544	51°11·9'	2°3·9'W	X	184
Knook Barrow (Long Barrow)	Wilts	ST9544	51°11·9'	2°3·9'W	A	184
Knook Camp	Wilts	ST9442	51°10·9'	2°4·8'W	X	184
Knook Castle	Wilts	ST9643	51°11·4'	2°3·0'W	A	184
Knook Down	Wilts	ST9543	51°11·4'	2°3·9'W	X	184
Knook Horse Hill	Wilts	ST9441	51°10·3'	2°4·8'W	X	184
Knook Manor	Wilts	ST9341	51°10·3'	2°5·6'W	A	184
Knorren Beck	Cumbr	NY5467	55°0·0'	2°42·7'W	W	86
Knorren Lodge	Cumbr	NY5367	55°0·0'	2°43·7'W	X	86
Knossington	Leic	SK8008	52°40·1'	0°49·7'W	T	141
Knossington Grange	Leic	SK7908	52°40·1'	0°49·5'W	X	141
Knotbury	Staffs	SK0168	53°12·8'	1°58·7'W	T	119
Knot Hill	Lancs	SD6444	53°53·7'	2°32·5'W	H	102,103
Knotlow	Derby	SK1467	53°12·2'	1°47·0'W	X	119
Knot Moor	Shrops	SJ3302	52°36·9'	2°59·0'W	X	126
Knot or Sugar Loaf	Lancs	SD6750	53°56·9'	2°29·8'W	X	103
Knots	Derby	SK1190	53°24·6'	1°47·9'W	X	110
Knots Flat	N Yks	SE0465	54°5·1'	1°55·9'W	X	98
Knots Wood	Lancs	SD5162	54°3·3'	2°44·5'W	F	97
Knott	Cumbr	NY2933	54°41·5'	3°5·7'W	H	89,90
Knott	Cumbr	NY6302	54°25·0'	2°33·8'W	X	91
Knott	Cumbr	NY6408	54°28·2'	2°32·9'W	X	91
Knott	Cumbr	NY7101	54°24·5'	2°26·4'W	H	91
Knott	Cumbr	SD4792	54°19·5'	2°48·5'W	X	97
Knott	Cumbr	SD6794	54°20·7'	2°30·0'W	X	98
Knott	Highld	NG3853	57°29·8'	6°21·9'W	T	23
Knottallow Tarn	Cumbr	SD2780	54°12·9'	3°6·7'W	W	96,97
Knott End	Cumbr	SD1397	54°21·9'	3°19·9'W	X	96
Knott End	Cumbr	SD2291	54°18·8'	3°11·5'W	X	96
Knott End	Cumbr	SD2586	54°16·1'	3°8·7'W	X	96
Knott End-on-Sea	Lancs	SD3548	53°55·7'	2°59·0'W	T	102
Knott Ends	Cumbr	NY1608	54°27·9'	3°17·3'W	X	89
Knotteranum	Lancs	SD7360	54°2·4'	2°24·3'W	X	98
Knotteranum	N Yks	SD7360	54°2·4'	2°24·3'W	X	98
Knott Fm	Lancs	SD6140	53°51·5'	2°35·2'W	FM	102,103
Knott Fm	N Yks	SD9546	53°54·9'	2°4·2'W	FM	103
Knott Fm	N Yks	SE1972	54°8·9'	1°42·1'W	FM	99
Knott Fm, The	Brad	SE0144	53°53·8'	1°58·7'W	FM	104
Knott Hall Fm	Cumbr	SD6298	54°22·8'	2°34·7'W	FM	97
Knott Hill	Cumbr	NY4850	54°50·8'	2°48·2'W	X	86
Knott Hill	Cumbr	SD1787	54°16·6'	3°16·1'W	H	96
Knott Hill	Cumbr	SD5180	54°13·0'	2°44·7'W	X	97
Knott Hill	Durham	NY8529	54°39·6'	2°13·5'W	X	91,92
Knotting	Beds	TL0063	52°15·6'	0°31·7'W	T	153
Knotting Green	Beds	TL0062	52°15·1'	0°31·7'W	T	153
Knottingley	Wakf	SE4923	53°42·3'	1°15·0'W	T	105
Knott Lanes	Oldham	SD9201	53°30·6'	2°6·8'W	T	109
Knott Oak	Somer	ST3714	50°55·6'	2°53·4'W	T	193
Knott Rigg	Cumbr	NY1918	54°33·3'	3°14·7'W	H	89,90
Knotts	Cumbr	NY2614	54°31·2'	3°8·2'W	H	89,90
Knotts	Cumbr	NY4321	54°35·1'	2°52·5'W	X	90
Knotts	Cumbr	SD5387	54°16·8'	2°42·9'W	X	97

Knotts	Cumbr	SD6293	54°20·1'	2°34·6'W	H	97
Knotts	Lancs	SD7653	53°58·6'	2°21·5'W	T	103
Knotts	N Yks	SD9469	54°7·3'	2°5·1'W	X	98
Knotts Fm	Lancs	SD5161	54°2·8'	2°44·5'W	FM	97
Knotts Fm	N Yks	SE1759	54°1·8'	1°44·0'W	FM	104
Knott's Gill	N Yks	SE1170	54°7·8'	1°49·5'W	W	99
Knott Side	N Yks	SE1765	54°5·1'	1°44·0'W	X	99
Knotts Plantn	Durham	NY9926	54°38·0'	2°0·5'W	F	92
Knott's Plantn	N Yks	SE1270	54°7·8'	1°48·6'W	F	99
Knotts Wood	Cumbr	NY5754	54°53·0'	2°39·8'W	F	86
Knott, The	Cumbr	NY4312	54°30·3'	2°52·4'W	H	90
Knott, The	Cumbr	NY5012	54°30·3'	2°45·9'W	X	90
Knott, The	Cumbr	NY5347	54°49·2'	2°43·5'W	X	86
Knott, The	Cumbr	SD1495	54°20·8'	3°19·0'W	X	96
Knott, The	Cumbr	SD2493	54°19·9'	3°9·7'W	H	96
Knott, The	Derby	SK0489	53°24·1'	1°56·0'W	X	110
Knott, The	Liv	SJ4091	53°25·0'	2°53·8'W	T	108
Knotty Ash	Devon	SS4125	51°0·4'	4°15·6'W	T	180,190
Knotty Corner	Bucks	SU9392	51°37·4'	0°39·0'W	T	175
Knotty Green	Durham	NZ3430	54°40·1'	1°27·9'W	X	93
Knotty Hill	S Lanak	NS9918	55°27·0'	3°35·4'W	X	78
Knotty Hill	Northnts	SP7742	52°4·5'	0°52·2'W	FM	152
Knotwood Fields Fm	Derby	SK2375	53°16·5'	1°38·9'W	FM	119
Knouchley Fm	Cumbr	NY7001	54°24·5'	2°27·3'W	X	91
Knoutberry	N Yks	SD7817	54°13·7'	2°20·8'W	X	98
Knoutberry Bank	N Yks	SD8298	54°22·9'	2°16·2'W	X	98
Knoutberry Currack	Cumbr	SD7391	54°19·1'	2°24·5'W	H	98
Knoutberry Haw	Durham	NY8041	54°46·1'	2°18·2'W	X	86,87
Knoutberry Hill	N Yks	SD9462	54°3·5'	2°5·1'W	X	98
Know Bank	Cumbr	NY4638	54°44·3'	2°49·9'W	X	90
Knowbrow						
Knowbury	Shrops	SO5774	52°22·0'	2°37·5'W	T	137,138
Knowe	Cumbr	NY5377	55°5·4'	2°43·8'W	X	86
Knowe	D & G	NX3171	55°0·5'	4°38·1'W	T	76
Knowe	D & G	NX3172	55°1·1'	4°38·2'W	X	76
Knowe	E Ayr	NS5122	55°28·4'	4°21·0'W	X	70
Knowe	E Ayr	NS5636	55°36·0'	4°16·7'W	X	71
Knowe	Moray	NJ2835	57°24·2'	3°11·4'W	X	28
Knowe	N Ayr	NS0328	55°34·3'	5°9·9'W	X	69
Knowe	Orkney	HY3108	58°57·5'	3°11·5'W	X	6,7
Knowe	Shetld	HU3363	60°21·2'	1°23·6'W	X	2,3
Knowe	Shetld	HU5383	60°31·9'	1°1·6'W	X	1,2,3
Knowebog Hill	Scot Bord	NT3308	55°21·9'	3°3·0'W	H	79
Knowe Crags	Cumbr	NY3127	54°38·3'	3°3·7'W	X	90
Knowe Dod	S Lanak	NT0231	55°34·0'	3°32·8'W	H	72
Knowe Fell	N Yks	SD8768	54°6·7'	2°11·5'W	X	98
Knowefield	Cumbr	NY4057	54°54·5'	2°55·7'W	T	85
Knowe Fm	Cumbr	NY4939	54°44·9'	2°47·1'W	FM	90
Knowe Fm, The	N Ayr	NS0328	55°30·6'	5°6·8'W	FM	69
Knowehead	Aberd	NJ4713	57°12·5'	2°52·2'W	X	37
Knowehead	Aberd	NJ4715	57°13·6'	2°52·2'W	X	37
Knowehead	Aberd	NJ5604	57°7·7'	2°43·2'W	X	37
Knowehead	Aberd	NJ5715	57°13·7'	2°42·3'W	X	37
Knowehead	Aberd	NJ5853	57°34·2'	2°41·7'W	X	29
Knowehead	Aberd	NJ6613	57°12·6'	2°33·3'W	X	38
Knowehead	Aberd	NJ6627	57°20·2'	2°33·4'W	X	38
Knowehead	Aberd	NJ9466	57°41·3'	2°5·6'W	X	30
Knowehead	Angus	NO2354	56°40·5'	3°15·0'W	X	53
Knowehead	Angus	NO4436	56°31·0'	2°54·2'W	X	54
Knowehead	Angus	NO4659	56°43·4'	2°52·5'W	X	54
Knowehead	Angus	NO5263	56°45·6'	2°46·7'W	X	44
Knowehead	Clackm	NS9794	56°7·9'	3°39·0'W	X	58
Knowehead	D & G	NS6713	55°23·8'	4°5·6'W	X	71
Knowehead	D & G	NX6090	55°11·3'	4°11·5'W	X	77
Knowehead	D & G	NX8695	55°14·4'	3°47·1'W	X	78
Knowe Head	D & G	NY4481	55°7·5'	2°52·3'W	X	79
Knowehead	E Ayr	NS4736	55°35·9'	4°25·3'W	X	70
Knowehead	E Ayr	NS4929	55°32·1'	4°23·1'W	X	70
Knowehead	E Dunb	NS6079	55°59·3'	4°14·2'W	X	64
Knowehead	N Ayr	NS3543	55°39·4'	4°36·9'W	X	63,70
Knowehead	N Lanak	NS8865	55°52·2'	3°47·0'W	X	65
Knowe Head	Northum	NY6855	54°53·6'	2°29·5'W	X	86,87
Knowehead	Pth & Kin	NN8807	56°14·8'	3°48·0'W	X	58
Knowehead	Pth & Kin	NO0309	56°16·1'	3°33·5'W	X	58
Knowehead	Pth & Kin	NO0546	56°36·0'	3°32·4'W	X	52,53
Knowehead	Pth & Kin	NO1434	56°29·7'	3°23·4'W	X	53
Knowehead	S Ayr	NS4330	55°32·6'	4°28·9'W	X	70
Knowehead	Scot Bord	NT0435	55°36·2'	3°31·0'W	X	72
Knowehead	S Lanak	NS6646	55°41·6'	4°7·5'W	X	64
Knowehead	S Lanak	NS8851	55°44·6'	3°46·6'W	X	65,72
Knowehead	Stir	NS6492	56°6·3'	4°10·8'W	X	57
Knowehead Caircake	Aberd	NJ8248	57°31·6'	2°17·6'W	X	29,30
Knowehead of Auldallan	Angus	NO2958	56°42·8'	3°9·1'W	X	53
Knowehill	Cumbr	NY1851	54°51·1'	3°16·2'W	X	85
Knowe Hill	Lancs	SD5056	54°0·1'	2°45·4'W	X	102
Knowe Kniffling	Scot Bord	NT0833	55°35·2'	3°27·1'W	X	72
Knowe o'Burristae	Orkney	HY4342	59°15·9'	2°59·5'W	X	5
Knowe o'Burristae (Broch)	Orkney	HY4342	59°15·9'	2°59·5'W	A	5
Knowe of Bracklach	Moray	NJ3824	57°18·4'	3°1·3'W	H	37
Knowe of Bugarth	Shetld	HU4492	60°36·8'	1°11·3'W	X	1,2
Knowe of Burgarth	Shetld	HU3724	60°0·2'	1°19·7'W	X	4
Knowe of Craie	Orkney	HY4131	59°10·0'	3°1·4'W	X	5,6
Knowe of Craie (Chambered Cairn)	Orkney	HY4131	59°10·0'	3°1·4'W	A	5,6
Knowe of Crippley	Angus	NO4084	56°56·9'	2°58·7'W	X	44
Knowe of Finistry	Shetld	HU4556	60°17·4'	1°10·7'W	X	2,3
Knowe of Holland	Orkney	HY2423	59°5·5'	3°19·1'W	A	6
Knowe of Lee	Angus	NO3480	56°54·7'	3°4·6'W	X	44
Knowe of Midgarth	Orkney	HY3923	59°5·6'	3°3·4'W	X	6
Knowe of Midgarth (Chambered Cairn)	Orkney	HY3923	59°5·6'	3°3·4'W	A	6
Knowe of Rowiegar	Orkney	HY3729	59°8·9'	3°5·6'W	X	6
Knowe of Rowiegar (Chambered Cairn)	Orkney	HY3729	59°8·9'	3°5·6'W	A	6
Knowe of Sandywater	Shetld	HU3086	60°33·7'	1°26·7'W	X	1,3
Knowe of Scorn	Orkney	HY2423	59°5·5'	3°19·1'W	A	6
Knowe of Setter	Shetld	HP5906	60°44·2'	0°54·6'W	X	1
Knowe of Stenso	Orkney	HY3626	59°7·2'	3°6·6'W	X	6
Knowe of Stenso (Brock)	Orkney	HY3626	59°7·2'	3°6·6'W	A	6
Knowe of Tronamires	Shetld	HP5809	60°45·9'	0°55·6'W	X	1
Knowe of Verron	Orkney	HY2219	59°3·3'	3°21·1'W	X	6
Knowe of Verron (Brock)	Orkney	HY2219	59°3·3'	3°21·1'W	A	6
Knowe of Yarrow	Orkney	HY6544	59°17·1'	2°36·4'W	X	5
Knowe of Yarso	Orkney	HY4028	59°8·3'	3°2·4'W	X	5,6
Knowe of Yarso (Chambered Cairn)	Orkney	HY4028	59°8·3'	3°2·4'W	A	5,6
Knowe o'Samilands	Orkney	HY7653	59°22·0'	2°24·8'W	X	5
Knowe o'Samilands (Burnt Mound)	Orkney	HY7653	59°22·0'	2°24·8'W	A	5
Knowes	Aberd	NO6192	57°1·3'	2°38·1'W	X	45
Knowes	D & G	NX1132	54°39·1'	4°55·4'W	X	82
Knowes	E Loth	NT6177	55°59·3'	2°37·1'W	T	67
Knowes	Moray	NJ5161	57°38·4'	2°48·8'W	X	29
Knowes	Orkney	HY6338	59°13·9'	2°38·4'W	X	5
Knowes	Pth & Kin	NO0211	56°17·1'	3°34·5'W	X	58
Knowes	Renf	NS3656	55°46·4'	4°36·4'W	X	63
Knowes	Renf	NS4366	55°52·0'	4°30·1'W	X	64
Knowes Fm	N Ayr	NS3455	55°45·9'	4°38·3'W	FM	63
Knowesgate	Northum	NY9885	55°9·8'	2°1·5'W	T	81
Knowes Head	Scot Bord	NT4203	55°19·3'	2°54·4'W	H	79
Knowes Hill	Scot Bord	NT4338	55°38·2'	2°53·9'W	H	73
Knoweside	S Ayr	NS2512	55°22·5'	4°45·3'W	X	70
Knoweside Hill	S Ayr	NS2613	55°23·1'	4°44·4'W	H	70
Knowes of Bratta	Shetld	HU4898	60°40·0'	1°6·8'W	H	1
Knowes of Cunnister	Shetld	HU5297	60°39·4'	1°2·4'W	X	1
Knowes of Elrick	Aberd	NJ6053	57°34·2'	2°39·7'W	T	29
Knowes of Euro	Orkney	HY4118	59°3·0'	3°1·2'W	X	6
Knowes of Euro (Tumuli)	Orkney	HY4118	59°3·0'	3°1·2'W	A	6
Knowes of Lingro	Orkney	HY2829	59°8·8'	3°15·0'W	X	6
Knowes of Lingro (Tumuli)	Orkney	HY2829	59°8·8'	3°15·0'W	A	6
Knowes of Swinister	Shetld	HU3481	60°30·9'	1°22·3'W	X	1,2,3
Knowes of Trinnawin	Orkney	HY3318	59°2·9'	3°9·6'W	X	6
Knowes of Trinnawin (Tumuli)	Orkney	HY3318	59°2·9'	3°9·6'W	A	6
Knowes of Trotty	Orkney	HY3417	59°2·4'	3°8·5'W	X	6
Knowes of Trotty (Tumuli)	Orkney	HY3417	59°2·4'	3°8·5'W	A	6
Knowes of Westerskeld	Shetld	HU2944	60°11·0'	1°28·1'W	H	4
Knowes of Yonbell	Orkney	HY2422	59°5·0'	3°19·1'W	X	6
Knowes of Yonbell (Tumuli)	Orkney	HY2422	59°5·0'	3°19·1'W	A	6
Knowes O' the Rue	D & G	NX2665	54°57·2'	4°42·6'W	X	82
Knowesouth	Scot Bord	NT6021	55°29·1'	2°37·5'W	X	74
Knowe, The	Angus	NO3960	56°43·9'	2°59·4'W	X	44
Knowe, The	Cumbr	NY4508	54°28·1'	2°50·5'W	H	90
Knowe, The	D & G	NS7112	55°23·4'	4°1·8'W	X	71
Knowe, The	D & G	NY0074	55°3·3'	3°33·5'W	X	84
Knowe, The	N Ayr	NS0328	55°30·6'	5°6·8'W	X	69
Knowetop	D & G	NX7178	55°5·0'	4°0·8'W	X	77,84
Knowetop	N Lanak	NS7555	55°46·6'	3°59·1'W	T	64
Knowetop	S Lanak	NS7351	55°44·4'	4°0·9'W	X	64
Knowetop Fm	S Lanak	NS7344	55°40·6'	4°0·7'W	FM	71
Knowetownhead	Scot Bord	NT5318	55°27·5'	2°44·2'W	X	79
Knowfaulds	Clackm	NS8595	56°8·3'	3°50·6'W	X	58
Knowhead	Aberd	NJ7431	57°22·4'	2°25·5'W	X	29
Knowhead	Aberd	NJ9255	57°35·4'	2°7·6'W	X	30
Knowhead	E Ayr	NS5429	55°32·2'	4°18·4'W	X	70
Knowhead	Moray	NJ2331	57°22·0'	3°16·4'W	X	36
Knowhead	Moray	NJ3652	57°33·5'	3°3·7'W	X	28
Knowhead	Pth & Kin	NO1623	56°23·8'	3°21·2'W	X	53,58
Know Hill	Lancs	SD4674	54°9·8'	2°49·2'W	X	97
Knowiemoor	Aberd	NJ5559	57°37·4'	2°44·7'W	X	29
Knowl	Wilts	ST8430	51°4·4'	2°13·3'W	X	183
Knowlands Fm	E Susx	TQ4216	50°55·8'	0°1·6'E	FM	198
Knowlands Wood	E Susx	TQ4117	50°56·3'	0°0·8'E	F	198
Knowlbank	Shrops	SJ7208	52°40·4'	2°24·4'W	X	127
Knowl Bank	Staffs	SJ7749	53°2·5'	2°20·2'W	T	118
Knowle	C of Bris	ST6070	51°25·9'	2°34·1'W	T	172
Knowle	Corn	SX2299	50°46·0'	4°31·1'W	X	190
Knowle	Devon	SS2502	50°47·7'	4°28·6'W	X	190
Knowle	Devon	SS4938	51°7·5'	4°9·1'W	T	180
Knowle	Devon	SS5821	50°58·5'	4°1·0'W	X	180
Knowle	Devon	SS7801	50°48·0'	3°43·5'W	T	191
Knowle	Devon	ST0007	50°51·5'	3°24·9'W	T	192
Knowle	Devon	SX5191	50°42·2'	4°6·2'W	X	191
Knowle	Devon	SX7469	50°30·7'	3°46·2'W	X	202
Knowle	Devon	SX7880	50°36·7'	3°43·1'W	X	191
Knowle	Devon	SX7967	50°29·7'	3°42·0'W	X	202
Knowle	Devon	SY0582	50°38·0'	3°20·2'W	T	192
Knowle	E Susx	TQ5725	51°0·4'	0°14·7'E	X	188,199
Knowle	E Susx	TQ6034	51°5·2'	0°17·5'E	X	188
Knowle	Powys	SO2457	52°12·6'	3°6·3'W	X	148
Knowle	Shrops	SO5973	52°21·5'	2°35·7'W	T	137,138
Knowle	Sol	SP1876	52°23·1'	1°43·7'W	T	139
Knowle	Somer	SS9643	51°10·8'	3°28·9'W	X	181
Knowle	Somer	ST3339	51°9·0'	2°57·1'W	T	182
Knowle	Surrey	TQ1942	51°10·1'	0°17·5'W	X	187
Knowle	Wilts	SU1660	51°20·6'	1°45·8'W	T	173
Knowle Cross	Devon	SY0497	50°46·1'	3°21·3'W	X	192
Knowle Cross	Dorset	ST4103	50°49·6'	2°49·9'W	X	193
Knowle End	Warw	SP3848	52°8·0'	1°26·3'W	X	151
Knowle Fields	Worcs	SP0457	52°12·9'	1°56·1'W	T	150
Knowle Fm	Corn	SX2772	50°31·6'	4°26·1'W	FM	201
Knowle Fm	Devon	SS5028	51°2·1'	4°8·0'W	FM	180
Knowle Fm	Devon	SX4584	50°38·3'	4°11·1'W	FM	201
Knowle Fm	Devon	SX5996	50°45·0'	3°59·5'W	FM	191
Knowle Fm	Dorset	ST4600	50°48·1'	2°45·6'W	FM	193
Knowle Fm	Hants	SU5509	50°53·1'	1°12·7'W	FM	196
Knowle Fm	Heref	SO2752	52°9·9'	3°3·6'W	FM	148
Knowle Fm	Powys	SO2261	52°14·7'	3°8·2'W	FM	137,148
Knowle Fm	Somer	SS8926	51°1·6'	3°34·6'W	FM	181
Knowle Fm	Somer	ST4507	50°51·8'	2°46·5'W	FM	193
Knowle Fm	Somer	ST4947	51°13·4'	2°43·4'W	FM	182,183
Knowle Fm	Somer	ST5842	51°10·8'	2°35·7'W	FM	182,183
Knowle Fm	Staffs	SK0125	52°49·6'	1°58·7'W	FM	128
Knowle Fm	Staffs	SK1107	52°39·9'	1°49·8'W	FM	139
Knowle Fm	Surrey	SU8347	51°13·2'	0°48·3'W	FM	186
Knowle Fm	Wilts	SU2567	51°24·3'	1°38·0'W	FM	174
Knowlegate	Shrops	SO5973	52°21·5'	2°35·7'W	T	137,138
Knowle Green	Lancs	SD6338	53°50·5'	2°33·3'W	T	102,103
Knowle Green	Surrey	TQ0470	51°25·4'	0°29·9'W	T	176
Knowle Grove	Sol	SP1775	52°22·6'	1°44·6'W	T	139
Knowle Hall	Sol	SP1976	52°23·1'	1°42·9'W	X	139
Knowle Hall	Somer	ST3340	51°9·6'	2°57·1'W	X	182
Knowle Hassock	Hants	SU4846	51°12·9'	1°18·4'W	X	185
Knowle Hill	Bath & NE Somer	ST5861	51°21·0'	2°35·8'W	H	172,182
Knowle Hill	Devon	SX9289	50°41·7'	3°31·4'W	X	192
Knowle Hill	Devon	SY2094	50°44·6'	3°7·7'W	H	192,193
Knowle Hill	Dorset	SU0309	50°53·1'	1°57·1'W	X	195
Knowle Hill	Dorset	SY5294	50°44·8'	2°40·4'W	H	194
Knowle Hill	Dorset	SY6391	50°43·3'	2°31·1'W	X	194
Knowle Hill	Dorset	SY9382	50°38·5'	2°5·6'W	H	195
Knowle Hill	Hants	SU5018	50°57·8'	1°16·9'W	X	185
Knowle Hill	Powys	SO2161	52°14·7'	3°9·0'W	H	137,148
Knowle Hill	Shrops	SO6981	52°25·8'	2°27·0'W	H	138
Knowle Hill	Somer	SS9643	51°10·8'	3°28·9'W	X	181
Knowle Hill	Somer	ST1827	51°2·4'	3°9·8'W	X	181,193
Knowle Hill	Somer	ST4407	50°51·8'	2°47·4'W	X	193
Knowle Hill	Somer	ST4808	50°52·4'	2°44·0'W	H	193
Knowle Hill	Somer	ST4946	51°12·9'	2°43·4'W	H	182,183
Knowle Hill	Somer	ST5942	51°10·8'	2°34·8'W	H	182,183
Knowle Hill	Surrey	SU9866	51°23·3'	0°35·1'W	T	175,176
Knowle Hill	Surrey	TQ1259	51°19·4'	0°23·2'W	X	187
Knowle Hill	Wilts	SU0323	51°0·6'	1°57·0'W	H	184
Knowle Hill Fm	Derby	SK3425	52°49·5'	1°29·3'W	FM	128
Knowle Ho	Devon	SX9788	50°41·2'	3°27·1'W	X	192
Knowle Ho	Devon	SY0482	50°38·0'	3°21·1'W	X	192
Knowle Ho	Devon	SY1590	50°42·4'	3°11·8'W	X	192,193
Knowle Hospital	Hants	SU5609	50°52·9'	1°11·9'W	X	196
Knowle Moor	Somer	ST4846	51°12·9'	2°44·3'W	X	182
Knowl End	Staffs	SJ7751	53°3·6'	2°20·2'W	X	118
Knowle Park	Brad	SE0540	53°51·6'	1°55·0'W	T	104
Knowle Park	Surrey	TQ0538	51°8·1'	0°29·6'W	X	187
Knowle Park Fm	Somer	ST6931	51°4·9'	2°26·2'W	FM	183
Knowle Rock Fm	Somer	ST7031	51°4·9'	2°25·3'W	FM	183
Knowles	Barns	SE1704	53°32·2'	1°44·2'W	X	110
Knowles	Cumbr	SD6398	54°22·8'	2°33·8'W	X	97
Knowles	Staffs	SK0161	53°9·0'	1°58·7'W	X	119
Knowlesands	Shrops	SO7291	52°31·2'	2°24·4'W	T	138
Knowles Bank	Kent	TQ6244	51°10·6'	0°19·4'E	X	188
Knowles Fm	Derby	SK2343	52°59·3'	1°39·0'W	FM	119,128
Knowles Fm	Derby	SK3076	53°17·0'	1°32·6'W	FM	119
Knowles Fm	N Yks	NZ9110	54°28·9'	0°35·3'W	FM	94
Knowles Fm	Pemb	SN0208	51°44·4'	4°51·7'W	FM	157,158
Knowles Fm	Staffs	SJ9254	53°5·2'	2°6·8'W	FM	118
Knowles Fm	Stock on T	NZ4209	54°28·7'	1°20·7'W	FM	93
Knowles Hill	Devon	SX8571	50°31·9'	3°37·0'W	T	202
Knowles Pit Fm	Ches	SJ7281	53°19·8'	2°24·8'W	FM	109
Knowles's Fm	Essex	TL9630	51°56·3'	0°51·5'E	FM	168
Knowles St Giles	Somer	ST3411	50°53·9'	2°55·9'W	T	193
Knowles Wood	Devon	ST0907	50°51·6'	3°17·2'W	F	192
Knowle's Wood	Warw	SP1863	52°16·1'	1°43·8'W	F	151
Knowle, The	Derby	SK3245	53°0·3'	1°31·0'W	X	119,128
Knowle, The	Devon	ST1710	50°53·2'	3°10·4'W	X	192,193
Knowle, The	Kent	TQ6842	51°9·4'	0°24·5'E	X	188
Knowle, The	Kent	TQ7171	51°25·0'	0°27·9'E	X	178
Knowle Top	Somer	SS9144	51°11·3'	3°33·2'W	H	181
Knowley	Aberd	NJ6933	57°23·4'	2°30·5'W	X	29
Knowl Green	Essex	TL7841	52°2·6'	0°36·1'E	T	155
Knowl Hill	Bucks	SP7024	51°54·8'	0°58·5'W	H	165
Knowl Hill	Flint	SJ2864	53°10·3'	3°4·2'W	X	117
Knowl Hill	Win & Maid	SU8279	51°30·5'	0°48·7'W	T	175
Knowlhill Fm	Bucks	SP7023	51°54·3'	0°58·6'W	FM	165
Knowlmere Manor	Lancs	SD6749	53°56·4'	2°29·7'W	X	103
Knowl Moor	Lancs	SD8146	53°54·8'	2°16·9'W	X	103
Knowl's Tooth	W Susx	TQ2717	50°56·5'	0°11·1'W	X	198
Knowlton	Dorset	SU0210	50°53·6'	1°57·9'W	T	195
Knowlton	Kent	TR2853	51°14·1'	1°16·4'E	T	179
Knowlton Court	Kent	TR2853	51°14·1'	1°16·4'E	A	179
Knowlton Park	Kent	TR2753	51°14·1'	1°15·5'E	X	179
Knowl Top	Lancs	SD7740	53°51·6'	2°20·6'W	X	103
Knowl Wall	Staffs	SJ8539	52°57·1'	2°13·0'W	T	127
Knowl Water	Devon	SS5236	51°6·5'	4°6·5'W	W	180
Knowl Wood	Cald	SD9322	53°41·9'	2°5·9'W	T	103
Knowl Wood	Shrops	SJ7308	52°40·4'	2°23·6'W	F	127
Knownoble	N Lanak	NS7958	55°48·3'	3°55·4'W	X	64
Knowslade	Devon	SS6728	51°2·4'	3°53·4'W	X	180
Knowsley	Know	SJ4395	53°27·2'	2°51·1'W	T	108
Knowsley	Lancs	SD9020	53°40·8'	2°8·7'W	X	103
Knowsley Cott	Know	SJ4394	53°26·6'	2°51·1'W	X	108
Knowsley Cross	Staffs	SK1064	53°10·6'	1°50·6'W	X	119
Knowsley Hall	Know	SJ4493	53°26·1'	2°50·2'W	X	108
Knowsley Industrial Park	Know	SJ4398	53°28·8'	2°51·1'W	X	108
Knowsley Park	Know	SJ4595	53°27·2'	2°49·3'W	X	108
Knowsthorpe	Leeds	SE3132	53°47·2'	1°31·4'W	T	104
Knowstone	Devon	SS8223	50°59·9'	3°40·5'W	T	181
Knowstone Inner Moor	Devon	SS8321	50°58·8'	3°39·6'W	X	181
Knowstone Outer Moor	Devon	SS8421	50°58·8'	3°38·8'W	X	181
Knowton Fm	N Lanak	NS8958	55°48·4'	3°45·8'W	FM	65,72
Knowts Hall Fm	Derby	SK4150	53°3·0'	1°22·9'W	FM	120
Knox	N Yks	SE2957	54°0·7'	1°33·0'W	X	104
Knox Bridge	Kent	TQ7840	51°8·1'	0°33·0'E	T	188
Knoxes Reef	Northum	NU2236	55°37·3'	1°38·6'W	X	75
Knoxfauld	Pth & Kin	NN8007	56°14·7'	3°55·7'W	X	57
Knox Hall	N Yks	SE1963	54°4·0'	1°42·2'W	X	99
Knoxhill	Aberd	NJ9238	57°26·2'	2°7·5'W	X	30
Knox Hill	Aberd	NO8171	56°50·1'	2°18·2'W	H	45
Knox Knowe	Scot Bord	NT6502	55°18·9'	2°32·7'W	H	80
Knoyle Down Fm	Wilts	ST8934	51°6·5'	2°9·0'W	FM	184
Knuck Bank	Shrops	SO2586	52°28·2'	3°5·8'W	X	137
Knucker Hill	Orkney	HY4247	59°18·6'	3°0·6'W	H	5
Knucklas	Powys	SO2574	52°21·8'	3°5·7'W	T	137,148
Knuckle Bone Pasture	N Yks	SD9576	54°11·0'	2°4·2'W	X	98
Knudmaning	Cumbr	SD7791	54°19·1'	2°20·8'W	X	98
Knugdale	Orkney	HY4347	59°18·6'	2°59·6'W	X	5
Knuston	Northnts	SP9366	52°17·3'	0°37·8'W	T	153
Knuston High Fm	Northnts	SP9465	52°16·7'	0°36·9'W	FM	153
Knuston Lodge Fm	Northnts	SP9266	52°17·3'	0°38·7'W	FM	152
Knutsford	Ches	SJ7578	53°18·1'	2°22·1'W	T	118
Knutsford Service Area	Ches	SJ7378	53°18·1'	2°23·9'W	X	118
Knutton	Staffs	SJ8347	53°1·4'	2°14·8'W	T	118

Knuzden Brook	Lancs	SD7127	53°44·6′	2°26·0′W	T	103
Knuzden Hall	Lancs	SD7227	53°44·6′	2°25·1′W	X	103
Knypersley	Staffs	SJ8856	53°6·3′	2°10·3′W	T	118
Knypersley End	Staffs	SJ8955	53°5·8′	2°9·5′W	X	118
Knypersley Park	Staffs	SJ8956	53°6·3′	2°9·5′W	X	118
Knypersley Reservoir	Staffs	SJ8955	53°5·8′	2°9·5′W	W	118
Koda Skerry	Shetld	HU1862	60°20·8′	1°39·9′W	X	3
Koffs Fm	Wilts	SU0685	51°34·1′	1°54·4′W	FM	173
Kokoarrah	Cumbr	SD0496	54°21·3′	3°28·2′W	X	96
Kongie Geo	Orkney	HY4034	59°11·6′	3°2·5′W	X	5,6
Koogrew	Orkney	HY4030	59°9·4′	3°2·5′W	X	5,6
Kraiknish	Highld	NG3723	57°13·6′	6°21·0′W	X	32
Kroklahellia	Shetld	HU6190	60°35·6′	0°52·7′W	X	1,2
Kronyhillock	Highld	NH9349	57°31·4′	3°46·7′W	X	27
Krumlin	Cald	SE0518	53°39·7′	1°55·0′W	T	110
Kuggar	Corn	SW7216	50°0·3′	5°10·5′W	T	204
Kurkigarth	Shetld	HU3851	60°14·8′	1°18·3′W	X	3
Kurkigarth	Shetld	HU3963	60°21·2′	1°17·1′W	X	2,3
Kussa Waters	Shetld	HP5102	60°42·1′	1°3·4′W	W	1
Kweevnie Geos	Orkney	HY4954	59°22·4′	2°53·4′W	X	5
Kye Hill	Aberd	NJ4837	57°25·5′	2°51·5′W	X	28,29
Kyle	E Ayr	NS6519	55°27·0′	4°7·6′W	X	71
Kyle Akin	Highld	NG7526	57°16·4′	5°43·5′W	W	33
Kyleakin	Highld	NG7526	57°16·4′	5°43·5′W	T	33
Kyle Forest	E Ayr	NS4911	55°22·4′	4°22·5′W	F	70
Kyle Ho	Highld	NG7426	57°16·4′	5°44·5′W	X	33
Kyle of Durness	Highld	NC3765	58°32·8′	4°47·6′W	W	9
Kyle of Lochalsh	Highld	NG7627	57°17·0′	5°42·5′W	T	33
Kyle of Lochalsh	Highld	NH4059	57°35·8′	4°40·2′W	X	26
Kyle of Sutherland	Highld	NH5198	57°57·0′	4°30·6′W	W	20
Kyle of Sutherland	Highld	NH5795	57°55·6′	4°24·4′W	W	21
Kyle of Tongue	Highld	NC5858	58°29·5′	4°25·7′W	W	10
Kylepark	S Lanak	NS6961	55°49·7′	4°5·0′W	T	64
Kylerhea	Highld	NG7820	57°13·3′	5°40·2′W	T	33
Kyle Rhea	Highld	NG7922	57°14·4′	5°39·3′W	W	33
Kylerhea Glen	Highld	NG7720	57°13·3′	5°41·2′W	W	33
Kylerhea River	Highld	NG7620	57°13·2′	5°42·2′W	W	33
Kylesbeg	Highld	NM6773	56°47·7′	5°48·5′W	X	40
Kyles Campay	N Eil	NB1442	58°16·7′	6°52·3′W	W	13
Kyles Flodday	N Eil	NB1340	58°15·6′	6°53·1′W	W	13
Kyles Hill	Scot Bord	NT7250	55°44·8′	2°26·3′W	H	67,74
Kylesknoydart	Highld	NM8093	56°58·8′	5°36·8′W	X	33,40
Kylesku	Highld	NC2233	58°15·3′	5°1·5′W	T	15
Kyles Lodge	N Eil	NF9987	57°46·6′	7°3·3′W	X	18
Kylesmorar	Highld	NM8093	56°58·8′	5°36·8′W	X	33,40
Kyles of Bute	Arg & Bt	NR9968	55°52·1′	5°12·3′W	W	62
Kyles of Bute	Arg & Bt	NS0473	55°54·9′	5°7·7′W	W	63
Kyles Pabay	N Eil	NB1036	58°13·3′	6°55·9′W	W	13
Kyles-paible	N Eil	NF7567	57°34·8′	7°25·8′W	X	18
Kyleston	S Ayr	NS2918	55°25·8′	4°41·7′W	X	70
Kylestrome	Highld	NC2134	58°15·8′	5°2·6′W	T	15
Kyles Valasay	N Eil	NB1336	58°13·4′	6°52·8′W	W	13
Kyles Vuia	N Eil	NB1335	58°12·9′	6°52·8′W	W	13
Kylesyke Hill	Cumbr	NY5049	54°57·8′	2°44·8′W	X	86
Kyle, The	N Yks	SE5271	54°8·2′	1°11·8′W	W	100
Kylie	N Eil	NF9781	57°43·3′	7°4·9′W	X	18
Kylieford	Aberd	NJ5627	57°20·1′	2°43·4′W	X	37
Kyllachy House	Highld	NH7825	57°18·2′	4°1·0′W	X	35
Kylnadrochit Lodge	Moray	NJ1419	57°15·5′	3°25·1′W	X	36
Kyloag	Highld	NH6691	57°53·6′	4°15·2′W	X	21
Kyloe Cott	Northum	NU0440	55°39·5′	1°55·8′W	X	75
Kyloe Crags	Northum	NY6983	55°8·7′	2°28·8′W	X	80
Kyloe Hills	Northum	NU0439	55°38·9′	1°55·8′W	H	75
Kyloe Ho	Northum	NZ1070	55°1·7′	1°50·2′W	X	88
Kyloe Wood	Northum	NU0438	55°38·4′	1°55·8′W	F	75
Kymah Burn	Moray	NJ2922	57°17·2′	3°10·2′W	W	37
Kyme Eau	Lincs	TF1649	53°1·8′	0°15·8′W	W	130
Kyme Eau	Lincs	TF1952	53°3·4′	0°13·1′W	W	122
Kymin	Heref	SO5845	52°6·3′	2°36·4′W	T	149
Kymin	Monm	SO5212	51°48·5′	2°41·4′W	T	162
Kynachan	Pth & Kin	NN7759	56°42·7′	4°0·1′W	X	42,51,52
Kynagarry	Arg & Bt	NR3758	55°44·9′	6°11·0′W	X	60
Kynance Cliff	Corn	SW6713	49°58·5′	5°14·6′W	X	203
Kynance Cove	Corn	SW6813	49°58·6′	5°13·8′W	W	203
Kynance Fm	Corn	SW6814	49°59·1′	5°13·8′W	FM	203
Kynaston	Heref	SO5427	51°56·6′	2°39·8′W	T	162
Kynaston	Heref	SO6435	52°1·0′	2°31·1′W	X	149
Kynaston	Shrops	SJ3520	52°46·7′	2°57·4′W	T	126
Kynballoch	Pth & Kin	NO1848	56°37·3′	3°19·7′W	X	53
Kynnersley	Wrekin	SJ6716	52°44·7′	2°28·9′W	T	127
Kynnersley Moor	Wrekin	SJ6816	52°44·7′	2°28·0′W	X	127
Kynoch Plantn	Aberd	NO6599	57°5·1′	2°34·2′W	F	38,45
Kynsal Fm	Ches	SJ6641	52°58·2′	2°30·0′W	FM	118
Kynsal Lodge Fm	Ches	SJ6742	52°58·7′	2°29·1′W	FM	118
Kyo Burn	Durham	NZ1853	54°52·5′	1°42·7′W	W	88
Kyo Hall	Ghead	NZ1261	54°56·9′	1°48·3′W	X	88
Kype Lodge	S Lanak	NS7338	55°37·4′	4°0·6′W	X	71
Kype Muir	S Lanak	NS7139	55°37·9′	4°2·5′W	X	71
Kype Reservoir	S Lanak	NS7338	55°37·4′	4°0·6′W	W	71
Kypes Rig	S Lanak	NS7140	55°38·4′	4°2·5′W	X	71
Kype Water	S Lanak	NS7242	55°39·5′	4°1·6′W	W	71
Kype Water	S Lanak	NS7438	55°37·4′	3°59·6′W	W	71
Kypewaterhead	S Lanak	NS7439	55°38·0′	3°59·7′W	X	71
Kypie	Northum	NT9134	55°36·2′	2°8·1′W	X	74,75
Kypie Hill	Northum	NT9033	55°35·7′	2°9·1′W	H	74,75
Kyre	Worcs	SO6263	52°16·1′	2°33·0′W	T	138,149
Kyrebatch	Heref	SO6261	52°15·0′	2°33·0′W	X	138,149
Kyre Brook	Worcs	SO6167	52°18·2′	2°33·9′W	W	138,149
Kyre Green	Worcs	SO6062	52°15·5′	2°34·8′W	T	138,149
Kyre Green Fm	Worcs	SO6162	52°15·5′	2°33·9′W	FM	138,149
Kyre Park	Worcs	SO6263	52°16·1′	2°33·0′W	T	138,149
Kyrewood	Worcs	SO6067	52°18·2′	2°34·8′W	T	138,149
Kyrewood Ho	Worcs	SO6068	52°18·8′	2°34·8′W	X	138
Kyrse	Corn	SX2186	50°39·0′	4°31·6′W	X	201
Kytra Lock	Highld	NH3506	57°7·2′	4°43·1′W	X	34
Kytton Barton	Devon	ST0620	50°58·5′	3°20·0′W	X	181

L

Laalt Mór	Arg & Bt	NM2922	56°19·0′	6°22·5′W	W	48
Labbett's Cross	Devon	SS7211	50°53·3′	3°48·8′W	X	191
Labdens Fm	Herts	TL3620	51°51·9′	0°1·1′W	FM	166
Labdon	Devon	SS6611	50°53·2′	3°53·9′W	X	191
Labost	N Eil	NB2749	58°20·9′	6°39·5′W	T	8
Labothie	Angus	NO4642	56°34·3′	2°52·3′W	X	54
Labothie Hill	Angus	NO4742	56°34·3′	2°51·3′W	X	54
Labour in Vain Fm	Dorset	SY5486	50°40·5′	2°38·7′W	FM	194
Labourn's Fell	Northum	NZ0958	54°55·2′	1°51·1′W	X	88
Labrador Bay	Devon	SX9370	50°31·4′	3°30·2′W	W	202
Labrador Fm	Warw	SP1260	52°14·5′	1°49·1′W	FM	150
Laburnum Ho	Lincs	TF2649	53°1·6′	0°6·9′W	X	131
Lacasaidh	N Eil	NB3321	58°6·1′	6°31·4′W	T	13,14
Lacasdal	N Eil	NB4234	58°13·4′	6°23·2′W	T	8
Lacastal	N Eil	NB4240	58°16·6′	6°23·6′W	W	8
Laceby	NE Lincs	TA2106	53°32·4′	0°10·0′W	T	113
Laceby Acres	NE Lincs	TA2307	53°32·9′	0°8·2′W	T	113
Laceby Beck	NE Lincs	TA2207	53°33·0′	0°9·1′W	W	113
Laceby Manor Fm	NE Lincs	TA2306	53°32·4′	0°8·2′W	FM	113
Lacesston	Fife	NO1708	56°15·7′	3°20·0′W	X	58
Lacesston Muir	Fife	NO1806	56°14·6′	3°18·9′W	X	58
Lacey Green	Bucks	SP8200	51°41·8′	0°48·4′W	T	165
Lacey Green	Ches	SJ8482	53°20·3′	2°14·0′W	T	109
Lacey's Fm	Essex	TQ7598	51°39·4′	0°32·2′E	FM	167
Lacey's FM	Norf	TG2231	52°50·1′	1°18·2′E	X	133
Lachasay	Highld	NG4071	57°39·5′	6°21·1′W	X	23
Lach Dennis	Ches	SJ7071	53°14·4′	2°26·6′W	T	118
Lache	Ches	SJ3864	53°10·4′	2°55·2′W	T	117
Lache Eyes, The	Ches	SJ3763	53°9·9′	2°56·1′W	X	117
Laches, The	Ches	SJ9673	53°15·5′	2°3·2′W	X	118
Lachlan Bay	Arg & Bt	NS0095	56°6·6′	5°12·6′W	W	55
Lachlanstrype	Aberd	NJ8660	57°38·0′	2°13·6′W	X	30
Lachlanwells	Moray	NJ1360	57°37·6′	3°26·9′W	X	28
Lackenby	Red & Cl	NZ5619	54°34·0′	1°7·6′W	T	93
Lackford	Suff	TL7870	52°18·2′	0°37·0′E	T	144,155
Lackgie	Highld	NH9621	57°16·3′	3°43·0′W	X	36
Lackham College of Agriculture	Wilts	ST9270	51°26·0′	2°6·5′W	X	173
Lackmore Wood	Oxon	SU6681	51°31·7′	1°2·5′W	F	175
Lackstone	Shrops	SO5780	52°25·2′	2°37·5′W	X	137,138
Lacock	Wilts	ST9168	51°24·9′	2°7·4′W	T	173
Lacock Abbey	Wilts	ST9168	51°24·9′	2°7·4′W	A	173
Laconby	Cumbr	NY0902	54°24·6′	3°23·7′W	X	89
Lacon Fm	Shrops	SJ5332	52°53·2′	2°41·5′W	FM	126
Lacon Hall	N Yks	SE2466	54°5·6′	1°37·6′W	X	99
Lacon Hall	Shrops	SJ5330	52°52·2′	2°41·5′W	X	126
Lacques, The	Carm	SN2910	51°46·0′	4°28·3′W	X	159
Lactodorvm (Towcester)	Northnts	SP6948	52°7·8′	0°59·1′W	R	152
Lacton Manor	Kent	TQ9748	51°12·1′	0°49·6′E	X	189
Lacys	E Susx	TQ4509	50°52·0′	0°4·0′E	X	198
Lacy's Caves	Cumbr	NY5638	54°44·4′	2°40·6′W	X	90
Lada Sgeir	N Eil	NB5040	58°16·9′	6°15·4′W	X	8
Lad Barrow	Glos	SP1609	51°47·0′	1°45·7′W	A	163
Ladbarrow Fm	Glos	SP1709	51°47·0′	1°44·8′W	FM	163
Ladbroke	Warw	SP4158	52°13·4′	1°23·6′W	T	151
Ladbroke Grove Fm	Warw	SP4358	52°13·3′	1°21·8′W	FM	151
Ladbroke Hill Fm	Warw	SP4359	52°13·9′	1°21·8′W	FM	151
Ladbrook Hall	Warw	SP0971	52°20·5′	1°51·7′W	X	139
Lad Crags	Cumbr	NY4715	54°31·9′	2°48·7′W	X	90
Ladden Brook	S Glos	ST6785	51°34·0′	2°28·2′W	W	172
Laddenside Fm	S Glos	ST6683	51°32·9′	2°29·0′W	FM	172
Laddenvean	Corn	SW7821	50°3·1′	5°5·7′W	T	204
Ladder Burn	Angus	NO4184	56°56·9′	2°57·7′W	W	44
Ladder Burn	Moray	NJ2719	57°15·6′	3°12·2′W	W	37
Ladderfoot	Moray	NJ2620	57°16·1′	3°13·2′W	X	37
Ladder Hill	Derby	SK0279	53°18·7′	1°57·8′W	X	119
Ladder Hills	Moray	NJ2719	57°15·6′	3°12·2′W	H	37
Ladder Law	Scot Bord	NT3204	55°19·8′	3°3·9′W	H	79
Ladder Stile	Ches	SJ9065	53°11·2′	2°8·6′W	X	118
Laddie Wood	Highld	NH2201	57°4·2′	4°55·7′W	F	34
Laddin Fm	Heref	SO6635	52°1·0′	2°29·3′W	FM	149
Laddingford	Kent	TQ6948	51°12·6′	0°25·6′E	T	188
Laddow Rocks	Derby	SE0501	53°30·6′	1°55·1′W	X	110
Laddus Fens	Cambs	TF4701	52°35·4′	0°10·6′E	X	143
Laddus Fm	Cambs	TF4702	52°36·0′	0°10·6′E	FM	143
Laddy Green	N Yks	SD7957	54°0·8′	2°18·8′W	X	103
Lade	Kent	TR0820	50°56·7′	0°58·1′E	T	189
Lade Bank	Lincs	TF3954	53°4·1′	0°4·9′E	T	122
Lade Bank Br	Lincs	TF3754	53°4·2′	0°3·1′E	X	122
Ladeddie	Fife	NO4412	56°18·1′	2°53·9′W	X	59
Ladeddie Hill	Fife	NO4413	56°18·6′	2°53·9′W	H	59
Ladehead	S Lanak	NS7941	55°39·1′	3°54·9′W	X	71
Ladenford	Angus	NO4747	56°37·0′	2°51·4′W	X	54
Ladenford Fm	Angus	NO4747	56°37·0′	2°51·4′W	FM	54
Ladenhar	Aberd	NJ7434	57°24·0′	2°25·5′W	X	29
Lade of Basta	Shetld	HU5295	60°38·4′	1°2·5′W	X	1,2
Ladeside	E Ayr	NS4746	55°41·3′	4°25·6′W	X	64
Ladford	Devon	SS4311	50°52·9′	4°13·5′W	X	190
Lad Gill	N Yks	NY8904	54°26·1′	2°9·8′W	W	91,92
Ladham Ho	Kent	TQ7338	51°7·1′	0°28·7′E	X	188
Ladhar Bheinn	Highld	NG8203	57°4·3′	5°35·3′W	H	33
Ladhill Beck	N Yks	SE5492	54°19·5′	1°9·8′W	W	100
Lad Hope	Scot Bord	NT3425	55°31·1′	3°2·3′W	X	73
Ladhope	Scot Bord	NT3426	55°31·6′	3°2·3′W	X	73
Ladhope Middle	Scot Bord	NT3524	55°30·6′	3°1·3′W	H	73
Ladhope Moor	Scot Bord	NT4938	55°38·2′	2°48·2′W	X	73
Lad Hows	Cumbr	NY1719	54°33·8′	3°16·6′W	X	89,90
Ladie	Shetld	HU3561	60°20·2′	1°21·5′W	X	2,3
Ladie Hill	Shetld	HU3668	60°23·9′	1°20·3′W	H	2,3
Ladie Loch	Shetld	HU4590	60°35·7′	1°10·2′W	W	1,2
Ladies' Cross	Pemb	SN0114	51°47·6′	4°52·8′W	X	157,158
Ladies Hill	Lancs	SD4048	53°55·7′	2°54·4′W	X	102
Ladies Hole	Shetld	HU5380	60°30·3′	1°1·6′W	W	1,2,3
Ladies Mount	Powys	SJ2106	52°39·0′	3°9·7′W	X	126
Ladies Mount (Motte & Bailey)	Powys	SJ2106	52°39·0′	3°9·7′W	A	126
Ladies Parlour	E Yorks	SE8336	53°49·1′	0°43·9′W	X	106
Ladies Riggs	N Yks	SE1465	54°5·1′	1°46·7′W	T	99
Ladies Skerrs	Northum	NU0053	55°46·5′	1°59·6′W	X	75
Ladies Table	Cumbr	NY2028	54°38·7′	3°14·0′W	H	89,90
Ladies Window	Corn	SX0790	50°40·9′	4°43·5′W	X	190
Lad Law	Lancs	SD9235	53°48·9′	2°6·9′W	H	103
Ladle Hill	Hants	SU4756	51°18·3′	1°19·2′W	H	174
Ladle Hill (Fort)	Hants	SU4756	51°18·3′	1°19·2′W	A	174
Ladle Well	Northum	NY8752	54°52·0′	2°11·7′W	X	87
Ladmanlow	Derby	SK0471	53°14·4′	1°56·0′W	T	119
Ladock	Corn	SW8950	50°19·0′	4°57·5′W	T	200,204
Ladock Wood	Corn	SW8851	50°19·5′	4°58·3′W	F	200,204
Ladram Bay	Devon	SY0984	50°39·1′	3°16·9′W	W	192
Lad's Cleugh	Northum	NT7600	55°17·9′	2°22·2′W	X	80
Lad's Fm	Kent	TQ6863	51°20·7′	0°25·1′E	FM	177,178,188
Lads Grave	Derby	SK2315	52°44·2′	1°39·2′W	X	128
Ladshaw Fell	D & G	NT3104	55°19·8′	3°4·8′W	H	79
Lad's Leap	Derby	SK0599	53°29·5′	1°55·1′W	X	110
Lads Lodge	Cumbr	NY4778	55°5·9′	2°49·4′W	X	86
Lad Stones	Cumbr	NY2900	54°23·7′	3°5·2′W	X	89,90
Ladswood Fm	Kent	TR0035	51°5·0′	0°51·7′E	FM	189
Ladthwaite	Cumbr	NY7906	54°27·2′	2°19·0′W	X	91
Ladwell	Hants	SU4223	51°0·5′	1°23·7′W	T	185
Ladwood	Kent	TR2043	51°8·9′	1°9·1′E	X	179,189
Lady	Orkney	HY6840	59°15·0′	2°33·2′W	T	5
Lady Arbour Fm	Heref	SO3048	52°7·8′	3°1·0′W	FM	148
Ladybank	Aberd	NJ6445	57°29·9′	2°35·6′W	X	29
Lady Bank	C of Dun	NO4930	56°27·8′	2°49·2′W	X	54
Ladybank	Fife	NO3009	56°16·4′	3°7·4′W	T	59
Ladybank	Orkney	HY6740	59°15·0′	2°34·2′W	X	5
Ladybank	S Ayr	NS2102	55°17·0′	4°48·7′W	X	76
Lady Bay	D & G	NX0271	54°59·9′	5°5·3′W	W	76,82
Lady Bell's Moss	N Lanak	NS8065	55°52·1′	3°54·6′W	X	65
Lady Bench	Monm	ST5187	51°35·0′	2°42·0′W	X	172
Lady Blantyre's Rock	Brad	SE0839	53°51·1′	1°52·3′W	X	104
Ladybog	Aberd	NJ6536	57°25·0′	2°34·5′W	X	29
Lady Booth Brook	Derby	SK1486	53°22·5′	1°47·0′W	W	110
Ladybower Ho	Derby	SK2086	53°22·5′	1°41·6′W	X	110
Ladybower Reservoir	Derby	SK1888	53°23·6′	1°43·4′W	W	110
Ladybower Tor	Derby	SK2086	53°22·5′	1°41·6′W	X	110
Lady Br	Staffs	SK2003	52°37·7′	1°41·9′W	X	139
Lady Bray Fm	Herts	TL0916	51°50·1′	0°24·7′W	FM	166
Ladybridge	N Yks	SE2980	54°13·1′	1°32·9′W	X	99
Ladybrook	Notts	SK5261	53°8·9′	1°12·9′W	T	120
Lady Brook	Stock	SJ9085	53°21·9′	2°8·6′W	W	109
Ladybrow	E Ayr	NS5837	55°36·6′	4°14·8′W	X	71
Lady Burn	D & G	NX2259	54°53·9′	4°46·1′W	W	82
Ladyburn	Inverc	NS3075	55°56·5′	4°42·9′W	T	63
Lady Burn	S Ayr	NS2102	55°17·0′	4°48·7′W	W	76
Ladyburn	S Ayr	NS3103	55°17·8′	4°39·3′W	X	76
Lady Burn	S Ayr	NS3202	55°17·3′	4°38·3′W	W	76
Ladyburn Lake	Northum	NU2600	55°17·9′	1°35·0′W	W	81
Lady Bute's Lodge	Beds	TL1016	51°50·1′	0°23·8′W	X	166
Ladycairn	Highld	NH5538	57°24·8′	4°24·4′W	X	26
Lady Cairn	S Lanak	NS9717	55°26·4′	3°37·3′W	H	78
Lady Canning's Plantation	Sheff	SK2883	53°20·8′	1°34·4′W	F	110
Ladyclose Wood	Durham	NZ1021	54°35·3′	1°50·3′W	F	92
Lady Clough	Derby	SK1091	53°25·2′	1°50·6′W	X	110
Lady Clough Moor	Derby	SK1092	53°25·7′	1°50·6′W	X	110
Lady Copse	Northnts	SP7344	52°5·6′	0°55·7′W	F	152
Ladycroft	Moray	NJ2444	57°29·1′	3°15·6′W	X	28
Lady Croft Fm	N Lincs	SK8098	53°28·6′	0°47·3′W	FM	112
Lady Cross	Barns	SK1499	53°29·5′	1°46·9′W	A	110
Ladycross	Corn	SX3288	50°40·3′	4°22·3′W	T	190
Lady Cross	N Yks	NZ4805	54°26·5′	1°15·2′W	X	93
Ladycross Fm	Surrey	TQ4141	51°9·3′	0°1·4′E	FM	187
Ladycross Lodge	Hants	SU3302	50°49·2′	1°31·5′W	X	196
Lady Dane Fm	Kent	TR0260	51°18·4′	0°54·3′E	FM	178
Lady Down	Corn	SX1076	50°33·4′	4°40·6′W	X	200
Ladydown	Devon	SX6956	50°23·6′	3°50·2′W	X	202
Lady Down	Wilts	ST9530	51°4·4′	2°3·9′W	X	184
Lady Down Fm	Wilts	ST8559	51°20·0′	2°12·5′W	FM	173
Lady Downs	Corn	SW4736	50°10·4′	5°32·2′W	H	203
Ladye Bay	N Som	ST4072	51°26·9′	2°51·4′W	W	171,172
Lady Edge	Staffs	SK0562	53°9·5′	1°55·1′W	X	119
Ladye Grove	Heref	SO4552	52°10·1′	2°47·9′W	X	148,149
Lady Elizabeth's Hill	Warw	SP3442	52°4·8′	1°29·8′W	X	151
Ladye Park	Corn	SX2364	50°27·2′	4°29·4′W	X	201
Ladye Point	C of Bris	ST4073	51°27·4′	2°51·4′W	X	171,172
Ladyes Hill	Warw	SP2972	52°21·0′	1°34·1′W	T	140
Lady Fen	Norf	TL5595	52°32·1′	0°17·5′E	X	143
Lady Ferrers Wood	Norf	TF8926	52°48·1′	0°48·6′E	F	132
Ladyfield	Arg & Bt	NN0815	56°17·6′	5°5·7′W	X	50,56
Ladyfield	D & G	NY1568	55°0·2′	3°19·3′W	X	85
Ladyfield Fm	N Yks	SE3393	54°20·1′	1°29·1′W	FM	99
Ladyfield Fm	N Yks	SE3593	54°20·1′	1°27·3′W	FM	99
Ladyfield Fm	Shrops	SO5372	52°20·9′	2°41·0′W	FM	137,138
Ladyfields	Staffs	SJ9549	53°2·5′	2°4·1′W	X	118
Ladyflat	Scot Bord	NT7750	55°44·8′	2°21·5′W	X	67,74
Lady Fm	Bath & NE Somer	ST6362	51°21·6′	2°31·5′W	FM	172
Ladyford	Cumbr	SD5195	54°21·1′	2°44·8′W	X	97
Ladygill	S Lanak	NS9428	55°32·3′	3°40·4′W	X	71,72
Ladygill Burn	S Lanak	NS9227	55°31·7′	3°42·2′W	W	71,72
Lady Green	N.Yks	SE6598	54°22·6′	0°59·5′W	X	94,100
Lady Green	Sefton	SD3103	53°31·4′	3°2·0′W	T	108
Lady Grove	Herts	TL1823	51°53·8′	0°16·7′W	F	166
Ladygrove Fm	Oxon	SU5391	51°37·2′	1°13·7′W	FM	164,174
Ladygrove Fm	Surrey	TQ0053	51°16·3′	0°33·6′W	FM	186
Lady Hall	Cumbr	SD1985	54°15·5′	3°14·2′W	T	96
Ladyhall	D & G	NY0966	54°59·1′	3°24·9′W	X	85
Lady Halton	Shrops	SO4775	52°22·5′	2°46·3′W	T	137,138,148
Lady Hay Wood	Leic	SK5108	52°40·3′	1°14·3′W	F	140
Lady Heyes Fm	Ches	SJ5375	53°16·4′	2°41·9′W	FM	117

Ladyhill	Aberd	NJ9127	57°20·3'	2°8·5'W	X	38
Ladyhill	Northum	NY8075	55°4·4'	2°18·4'W	X	86,87
Lady Hill	N Yks	SE1972	54°8·9'	1°42·1'W	X	99
Lady Hill	Staffs	SK0217	52°45·3'	1°57·8'W	X	128
Lady Hill	Warw	SP4359	52°13·9'	1°21·8'W	X	151
Ladyhill Fm	Shrops	SJ3325	52°49·3'	2°59·3'W	FM	126
Ladyhills	N Yks	SE9072	54°8·4'	0°36·9'W	X	101
Lady Hole	Derby	SK2045	53°0·4'	1°41·7'W	X	119,128
Lady Holme	Cumbr	SD3997	54°22·1'	2°55·9'W	X	96,97
Ladyholt	W Susx	SU7516	50°56·5'	0°55·6'W	X	197
Lady House	Roch	SD9211	53°36·0'	2°6·8'W	T	109
Lady House Fm	Shrops	SJ3402	52°36·9'	2°58·1'W	FM	126
Ladyhousesteads	D & G	NY3576	55°4·7'	3°0·7'W	X	85
Lady I	E Yorks	TA1846	53°54·0'	0°11·8'W	X	107
Lady Ing Fm	Cumbr	NY7711	54°29·9'	2°20·9'W	FM	91
Lady Isle	S Ayr	NS2729	55°31·7'	4°44·0'W	X	70
Lady Jane's Plantation	Aberd	NO6671	56°50·0'	2°33·0'W	F	45
Lady Katherine's Wood	Suff	TL8160	52°12·7'	0°39·4'E	F	155
Ladykirk	S Ayr	NS3826	55°30·3'	4°33·5'W	X	70
Ladykirk	Scot Bord	NT8847	55°43·2'	2°11·0'W	T	74
Ladykirk Home Farm	Scot Bord	NT8846	55°42·7'	2°11·0'W	FM	74
Ladykirk House	Scot Bord	NT8845	55°42·1'	2°11·0'W	X	74
Ladykirk Shiels	Scot Bord	NT8645	55°42·1'	2°12·9'W	X	74
Ladyland	D & G	NX9657	54°54·1'	3°36·9'W	X	84
Ladyland	Essex	TL6211	51°46·7'	0°21·3'E	X	167
Ladyland	N Ayr	NS3257	55°46·9'	4°40·3'W	X	63
Ladyland Fm	Surrey	TQ2745	51°11·6'	0°10·6'W	FM	187
Ladyland Moor	N Ayr	NS2959	55°47·9'	4°43·2'W	X	63
Ladylands	Essex	TL6004	51°42·9'	0°19·4'E	X	167
Lady Lane Fm	Sol	SP1175	52°22·6'	1°49·9'W	FM	139
Ladylea Hill	Aberd	NJ3416	57°14·1'	3°5·1'W	H	37
Lady Lee	Notts	SK5679	53°18·5'	1°9·2'W	X	120
Ladyleys	Aberd	NJ8229	57°21·3'	2°17·5'W	X	38
Lady Leys	Derby	SK2313	52°43·1'	1°39·2'W	X	128
Ladylift Clump	Heref	SO3947	52°7·3'	2°53·1'W	F	148,149
Lady Low	Derby	SK0678	53°18·2'	1°54·2'W	A	119
Lady Margaret Manor	Kent	TQ9255	51°15·9'	0°45·5'E	X	178
Lady Masham Fox Covert	Notts	SK7750	53°2·7'	0°50·7'W	F	120
Ladymeade Fm	N Som	ST4460	51°20·4'	2°47·9'W	FM	172,182
Ladymead Fm	Bucks	SP7520	51°52·6'	0°54·2'W	FM	165
Lady Meadow	Heref	SO4864	52°16·5'	2°45·3'W	X	137,138,148
Ladymeads Fm	E Susx	TQ6633	51°4·6'	0°22·6'E	FM	188
Ladymill	Aberd	NJ5611	57°11·5'	2°43·2'W	X	37
Ladymire	Aberd	NJ9729	57°21·3'	2°2·5'W	X	38
Lady Mires	Durham	NY9812	54°30·4'	2°1·4'W	X	92
Ladymoor Gate	Staffs	SJ9055	53°5·8'	2°8·6'W	X	118
Ladymuir	Inverc	NS3464	55°50·7'	4°38·6'W	X	63
Ladymuir Resr	Renf	NS3463	55°50·2'	4°38·6'W	W	63
Lady Nance	Corn	SW8660	50°24·3'	5°0·3'W	X	200
Lady Nunn's Old Eau	Lincs	TF3812	52°41·5'	0°2·9'E	W	131,142,143
Ladyoak	Shrops	SJ3603	52°37·5'	2°56·3'W	T	126
Lady Park	Ghead	NZ2458	54°55·2'	1°37·1'W	T	88
Ladypark	Orkney	ND4587	58°46·3'	2°56·6'W	X	7
Lady Park Wood	Monm	SO5414	51°49·6'	2°39·7'W	F	162
Ladypit Drain	N Yks	SE6836	53°49·2'	0°57·6'W	W	105,106
Lady Port	I of M	SC2887	54°15·2'	4°38·0'W	W	95
Ladyridge	Heref	SO5931	51°58·8'	2°35·4'W	T	149
Ladyrig	Scot Bord	NT7230	55°34·0'	2°26·2'W	X	74
Lady Royd	Cald	SD9730	53°46·2'	2°2·3'W	X	103
Lady's Chapel	N Yks	SE4598	54°22·8'	1°18·0'W	X	99
Lady's Cross	Derby	SK2778	53°18·1'	1°35·3'W	A	119
Ladyseat Fm	Cambs	TL2189	52°29·4'	0°12·7'W	FM	142
Lady's Edge	Somer	ST1440	51°9·4'	3°13·4'W	X	181
Ladysford	Aberd	NJ8960	57°38·0'	2°10·6'W	X	30
Lady's Green	Suff	TL7559	52°12·3'	0°34·1'E	T	155
Ladysheets	Aberd	NJ6357	57°36·3'	2°36·7'W	X	29
Lady's Hole	Northum	NU2328	55°33·0'	1°37·7'W	X	75
Lady's Holm	Shetld	HU3709	59°52·1'	1°19·9'W	X	4
Ladyside	Scot Bord	NT3650	55°44·6'	3°0·7'W	X	66,73
Ladyside	Staffs	SK0954	53°5·2'	1°51·5'W	X	119
Ladyside Burn	Scot Bord	NT3648	55°43·5'	3°0·7'W	W	73
Ladyside Height	Scot Bord	NT3647	55°43·0'	3°0·7'W	H	73
Ladyside Hill	N Ayr	NS2549	55°42·4'	4°46·7'W	X	63
Ladyside Pike	Cumbr	NY1822	54°35·4'	3°15·7'W	X	89,90
Lady's Knowe	Scot Bord	NY4896	55°15·6'	2°48·7'W	H	79
Ladysmith Fm	Staffs	SK1122	52°48·0'	1°49·8'W	FM	128
Lady's Rake	Cumbr	NY2721	54°35·0'	3°7·3'W	X	89,90
Lady's Rock	Arg & Bt	NM7734	56°27·0'	5°36·7'W	X	49
Lady's Seat	Arg & Bt	NM8200	56°8·8'	5°30·1'W	X	55
Ladyston	Pth & Kin	NN9016	56°19·7'	3°46·3'W	X	58
Ladystone	Highld	NH6143	57°27·6'	4°18·6'W	X	26
Ladyswell	Aberd	NJ8144	57°29·4'	2°18·6'W	X	29,30
Lady's Well	Aberd	NO6185	56°57·5'	2°38·0'W	W	45
Lady's Well	Dorset	ST6506	50°51·4'	2°29·5'W	A	194
Lady's Well	Glos	SO8117	51°51·3'	2°16·2'W	A	162
Lady's Well	Northum	NT9503	55°19·5'	2°4·3'W	A	81
Lady's Well	Northum	NU1715	55°26·0'	1°43·4'W	A	81
Lady's Well	Suff	TL9762	52°13·5'	0°53·5'E	A	155
Lady's Wood	Cambs	TL2482	52°25·5'	0°10·2'W	F	142
Lady's Wood	S Glos	ST7385	51°34·0'	2°23·0'W	F	172
Ladyswood	Wilts	ST8784	51°33·5'	2°10·9'W	X	173
Lady Syke	Cumbr	SD3283	54°14·5'	3°2·2'W	X	96,97
Ladythorne Ho	Northum	NU0346	55°42·7'	1°56·7'W	X	75
Ladythorpe Fm	Donc	SE5814	53°37·4'	1°7·0'W	FM	111
Ladyton	E Ayr	NS4837	55°36·4'	4°24·3'W	X	70
Ladyurd	Scot Bord	NT1442	55°40·1'	3°21·6'W	X	72
Ladyurd Hill	Scot Bord	NT1540	55°39·0'	3°20·6'W	H	72
Ladyward	D & G	NY1181	55°7·2'	3°23·3'W	X	78
Ladywash Fm	Derby	SK2177	53°17·6'	1°40·7'W	FM	119
Lady Wasset Well	N Yks	SD9983	54°14·8'	2°0·5'W	W	98
Lady Wath's Beck	Lincs	TF4364	53°9·5'	0°8·7'E	W	122
Ladywell	Aberd	NJ6327	57°20·2'	2°36·4'W	X	37
Ladywell	Angus	NO3851	56°39·1'	3°0·5'W	X	54
Ladywell	D & G	NX9858	54°54·6'	3°35·0'W	X	84
Lady Well	Durham	NZ1230	54°40·1'	1°48·4'W	A	92
Ladywell	Essex	TL5118	51°50·6'	0°11·9'E	X	167
Ladywell	Lew	TQ3774	51°27·1'	0°1·3'W	T	177
Ladywell	Northum	NY9981	55°7·6'	2°0·1'W	X	87
Lady Well	N Yks	SE1867	54°6·2'	1°43·1'W	A	99
Ladywell	Pth & Kin	NO0241	56°33·7'	3°35·2'W	X	52,53
Ladywell	Pth & Kin	NO2127	56°26·0'	3°16·4'W	X	53,58
Ladywell	S Ayr	NS2000	55°15·9'	4°49·6'W	X	76
Ladywell	Scot Bord	NT7955	55°47·5'	2°19·7'W	X	67,74
Ladywell	Shrops	SJ4934	52°54·3'	2°45·1'W	T	126
Lady Well	Suff	TM0655	52°9·5'	1°1·1'E	A	155
Ladywell	W Loth	NT0468	55°54·0'	3°31·7'W	T	65
Ladywells	D & G	NY2276	55°4·6'	3°12·9'W	X	85
Ladywood	Birm	SP0586	52°28·6'	1°55·2'W	T	139
Lady Wood	Leeds	SE3337	53°49·9'	1°29·5'W	T	104
Lady Wood	Leeds	SE3943	53°53·1'	1°24·0'W	F	104
Lady Wood	Leic	SK8107	52°39·5'	0°47·7'W	F	141
Lady Wood	Northnts	SP9784	52°27·0'	0°34·0'W	F	141
Lady Wood	Notts	SK7258	53°7·1'	0°55·0'W	F	120
Lady Wood	Notts	SK7568	53°12·5'	0°52·2'W	F	120
Lady Wood	Peterb	TF0902	52°36·5'	0°23·0'W	F	142
Ladywood	Shrops	SJ6703	52°37·7'	2°28·9'W	T	127
Ladywood	Worcs	SO8761	52°15·1'	2°11·0'W	T	150
Ladywood Fm	Derby	SK4439	52°57·0'	1°20·3'W	FM	129
Ladywood Fm	Notts	SK7568	53°12·5'	0°52·2'W	FM	120
Ladywood Fm	N Yks	SE6484	54°15·1'	1°0·6'W	FM	100
Lady Wood Fm	Warw	SP2994	52°32·8'	1°33·9'W	FM	140
Ladyyard	S Ayr	NS4729	55°32·1'	4°25·0'W	X	70
Laeca Burn	Aberd	NK0639	57°26·7'	1°53·5'W	W	30
Lael Forest	Highld	NH1982	57°47·7'	5°2·3'W	F	20
Laffak	St Hel	SJ5298	53°28·8'	2°43·0'W	T	108
Laffitt's Hall	Suff	TM1759	52°11·4'	1°10·9'E	X	156
Lag	Arg & Bt	NM3653	56°35·9'	6°17·6'W	X	47
Lag	D & G	NX8878	55°5·3'	3°44·9'W	X	84
Laga	Highld	NM6361	56°41·1'	5°51·7'W	T	40
Laga Bay	Highld	NM6361	56°41·1'	5°51·7'W	W	40
Lag a' Bhainne	Arg & Bt	NM9806	56°12·5'	5°15·0'W	X	55
Lag a' Bhàsdair	Arg & Bt	NM5233	56°25·7'	6°0·9'W	X	47,48
Lag a'Choire	Arg & Bt	NR6492	56°4·0'	5°47·1'W	X	55,61
Lag a' Choire	Highld	NM4664	56°42·2'	6°8·5'W	X	47
Lag a' Chomhaich	Arg & Bt	NM6924	56°21·4'	5°43·9'W	X	49
Lagachro	Moray	NJ3243	57°28·6'	3°7·6'W	X	28
Laga-'horie	Moray	NJ2940	57°26·9'	3°10·5'W	X	28
Lagalochan	Arg & Bt	NM8711	56°14·9'	5°25·8'W	X	55
Lag a' Mhàim	Arg & Bt	NM8150	56°35·7'	5°33·6'W	X	49
Lag a' Mhuilinn-luaidh	Arg & Bt	NM6321	56°19·6'	5°49·6'W	X	49
Lagan	N Eil	NB4212	58°1·6'	6°21·7'W	W	14
Laganabeastie Burn	D & G	NX1273	55°1·2'	4°56·0'W	W	76
Lagan a' Bhuic	Highld	NM7643	56°31·8'	5°38·1'W	X	49
Lagan Arnal	N Eil	NF7266	57°34·2'	7°28·7'W	X	18
Laganbuidhe	Arg & Bt	NN1627	56°24·2'	4°58·5'W	T	50
Laganbuidhe Fm	Arg & Bt	NN1628	56°24·8'	4°58·5'W	FM	50
Lagan an Daer	N Ayr	NS0228	55°30·6'	5°7·7'W	X	69
Lagan an Daimh	Arg & Bt	NR9478	55°57·3'	5°17·5'W	X	62
Lagan-Dhu	Pth & Kin	NO1152	56°39·3'	3°26·7'W	X	53
Lagan Domhain	N Eil	NG1492	57°49·8'	6°48·6'W	X	14
Lagandorain	Arg & Bt	NM2825	56°20·6'	6°23·7'W	X	48
Lagangarbh	Highld	NN2255	56°39·4'	4°53·8'W	X	41
Lagan Loisgte	Highld	NM7797	57°0·9'	5°39·9'W	X	33,40
Lagan Maskeir	N Eil	NF7266	57°34·2'	7°28·7'W	X	18
Lag an Taigh-cloiche	N Eil	NB1110	57°59·4'	6°52·9'W	X	13,14
Lag an t-Seilich	Arg & Bt	NM4923	56°20·2'	6°3·2'W	X	48
Lag a' Phuill	Stir	NN5014	56°17·9'	4°25·0'W	X	57
Lagars Geo	Shetld	HU4422	59°59·1'	1°12·2'W	X	4
Lagavaich	Moray	NJ2230	57°21·5'	3°17·3'W	X	36
Lagavulin	Arg & Bt	NR4045	55°38·0'	6°7·4'W	T	60
Lagavulin Bay	Arg & Bt	NR4045	55°38·0'	6°7·4'W	W	60
Lag Bank	Cumbr	SD2594	54°20·4'	3°8·8'W	X	96
Lag Birragh	I of M	SC4177	54°10·1'	4°25·7'W	X	95
Lag Buidhe	Moray	NJ2336	57°24·7'	3°16·4'W	X	28
Lag Burn	Aberd	NJ4733	57°23·3'	2°52·4'W	W	28,29
Lag Choan	Arg & Bt	NN0234	56°27·7'	5°12·4'W	X	50
Lag Dearg	Arg & Bt	NR2570	55°50·9'	6°23·2'W	X	60
Lagentivm (Castleford)	Wakf	SE4225	53°43·4'	1°21·4'W	R	105
Lagg	Arg & Bt	NR5978	55°56·3'	5°51·1'W	T	61
Lagg	D & G	NX5959	54°54·6'	4°11·5'W	X	83
Lagg	Highld	NG8826	57°16·8'	5°30·6'W	X	33
Lagg	Highld	NJ0332	57°22·3'	3°36·3'W	X	27,36
Lagg	Highld	NN6293	57°0·7'	4°15·9'W	X	35
Lagg	N Ayr	NR9521	55°26·7'	5°14·0'W	T	68,69
Lagg	S Ayr	NS2717	55°25·2'	4°43·6'W	X	70
Laggan	Arg & Bt	NM8427	56°23·4'	5°29·5'W	X	49
Laggan	Arg & Bt	NR2855	55°43·0'	6°19·4'W	X	60
Laggan	D & G	NX5453	54°51·3'	4°16·0'W	X	83
Laggan	D & G	NX7083	55°7·7'	4°1·9'W	X	77
Laggan	D & G	NX8855	54°52·9'	3°44·3'W	X	84
Laggan	D & G	NX8884	55°8·5'	3°45·0'W	X	78
Laggan	Highld	NH6340	57°26·0'	4°16·5'W	X	26
Laggan	Highld	NH7422	57°16·5'	4°4·9'W	X	35
Laggan	Highld	NM7180	56°51·6'	5°44·9'W	X	40
Laggan	Highld	NN2996	57°1·7'	4°48·6'W	T	34
Laggan	Highld	NN6194	57°1·2'	4°16·9'W	T	35
Laggan	Moray	NJ2026	57°19·3'	3°19·2'W	X	36
Laggan	Moray	NJ3436	57°24·8'	3°5·5'W	X	28
Laggan	N Ayr	NR9750	55°42·3'	5°13·4'W	X	62,69
Laggan	Pth & Kin	NN8422	56°22·8'	3°52·3'W	X	52,58
Laggan	S Ayr	NX0982	55°6·0'	4°59·2'W	X	76
Laggan	S Ayr	NX2582	55°6·3'	4°44·2'W	X	76
Laggan	Stir	NN5614	56°18·1'	4°19·2'W	X	57
Lagganallachie	Pth & Kin	NN9840	56°32·7'	3°39·1'W	X	52,53
Lagganauld	Moray	NJ1807	57°9·1'	3°20·9'W	X	36
Laggan Bay	Arg & Bt	NM4540	56°29·2'	6°8·1'W	W	47,48
Laggan Bay	Arg & Bt	NR2951	55°40·9'	6°18·2'W	W	60
Lagganbeg	Arg & Bt	NM8520	56°19·7'	5°28·2'W	X	49
Laggan Br	Arg & Bt	NR3457	55°44·3'	6°13·8'W	X	60
Laggan Br	Highld	NN6194	57°1·2'	4°16·9'W	X	35
Laggan Burn	Arg & Bt	NM9825	56°22·7'	5°15·8'W	W	49
Laggan Burn	Arg & Bt	NS0072	55°54·2'	5°11·5'W	W	63
Laggan Burn	D & G	NX9084	55°8·5'	3°43·1'W	W	78
Laggan Burn	S Ayr	NX3092	55°11·8'	4°39·8'W	W	76
Laggan Camp	D & G	NX3937	54°42·4'	4°29·5'W	A	83
Laggan Cott	Aberd	NJ3200	57°5·4'	3°6·9'W	X	37
Laggan Dam	Highld	NN3780	56°53·2'	4°40·1'W	X	34,41
Laggan Deer Forest	Arg & Bt	NM6221	56°19·6'	5°50·5'W	X	49
Laggandhu	Highld	NJ0519	57°15·4'	3°34·0'W	X	36
Lagganesgair Cotts	Pth & Kin	NN6259	56°42·4'	4°14·8'W	X	42,51
Laggangairn	D & G	NX2271	55°0·4'	4°46·6'W	X	76
Lagganhill	D & G	NX8983	55°8·0'	3°44·0'W	X	78
Laggan Hill	D & G	NX9056	54°53·5'	3°42·5'W	H	84
Laggan Hill	Highld	NJ0026	57°19·1'	3°39·2'W	H	36
Laggan Hill	S Ayr	NX2094	55°12·7'	4°49·3'W	H	76
Laggan Ho	Moray	NJ2341	57°27·4'	3°16·5'W	X	28
Laggan Ho	S Ayr	NX1183	55°6·6'	4°57·4'W	X	76
Lagganlees	D & G	NX8784	55°8·5'	3°45·9'W	X	78
Lagganlia	Highld	NH8503	57°6·5'	3°53·5'W	T	35,36
Laggan Loch	S Ayr	NX2095	55°13·2'	4°49·4'W	W	76
Laggan Loch	S Ayr	NX2582	55°6·3'	4°44·2'W	W	76
Laggan Locks	Highld	NN2896	57°1·6'	4°49·6'W	X	34
Laggan Lodge	Arg & Bt	NM6223	56°20·6'	5°50·6'W	X	49
Lagganmore	Arg & Bt	NM8420	56°19·6'	5°29·2'W	X	49
Lagganmore	D & G	NX0154	54°50·7'	5°5·5'W	X	82
Lagganmullan	D & G	NX5655	54°52·4'	4°14·2'W	X	83
Laggan o' Dee	D & G	NX5774	55°2·7'	4°13·9'W	X	77
Laggan Park	D & G	NX8390	55°11·7'	3°49·9'W	X	78
Laggan Point	Arg & Bt	NR2755	55°42·9'	6°20·4'W	X	60
Lagganroaig	Arg & Bt	NR9064	55°49·7'	5°20·7'W	X	62
Laggansarroch	S Ayr	NX2088	55°9·5'	4°49·1'W	X	76
Laggan Swing Bridge	Highld	NN2998	57°2·7'	4°48·7'W	X	34
Laggantalluch Head	D & G	NX0836	54°41·2'	4°58·3'W	X	82
Laggantygown	Highld	NH9017	57°14·1'	3°48·9'W	X	36
Lagganulva	Arg & Bt	NM4541	56°29·8'	6°8·1'W	X	47,48
Lagganvoulin	Moray	NJ1817	57°14·4'	3°21·1'W	X	36
Laggan Wood	Pth & Kin	NN7723	56°23·3'	3°59·1'W	F	51,52
Lag Garbh	N Eil	NB0709	57°58·7'	6°56·9'W	X	13,14
Lagg Bay	Arg & Bt	NR5978	55°56·3'	5°51·1'W	W	61
Laggen Gill	S Lanak	NS9019	55°27·4'	3°43·9'W	W	71,78
Laggeran Burn	D & G	NX5698	55°15·6'	4°15·5'W	W	77
Laggeran Hill	D & G	NX5798	55°15·6'	4°14·6'W	X	77
Lagget	Cumbr	NY0512	54°29·9'	3°27·6'W	X	89
Lagg Fm	D & G	NX8786	55°9·6'	3°46·0'W	FM	78
Laggie Burn	D & G	NX1376	55°2·9'	4°55·2'W	W	76
Laggish	S Ayr	NX2378	55°4·2'	4°45·9'W	X	76
Laggish Burn	S Ayr	NX2278	55°4·1'	4°46·8'W	W	76
Lag Glas	N Eil	NB0611	57°59·7'	6°58·1'W	X	13,14
Lag Glas	N Eil	NB1208	57°58·3'	6°51·8'W	X	13,14
lag Glas Oireabhal	N Eil	NB0611	57°59·7'	6°58·1'W	X	13,14
Laggon Agneash	I of M	SC4186	54°15·0'	4°26·0'W	X	95
Lag Gorm	N Eil	NF7762	57°32·2'	7°23·4'W	X	22
Laghall	D & G	NX9773	55°2·7'	3°36·3'W	X	84
Lagham Lodge Fm	Surrey	TQ3747	51°12·6'	0°1·9'W	FM	187
Laghead	D & G	NX6060	54°55·2'	4°10·6'W	X	83
Laght Hill	S Lanak	NS9108	55°21·5'	3°42·7'W	H	71,78
Lag Iain	Highld	NM8592	56°58·4'	5°31·8'W	H	33,40
Lag Kilmichael	Arg & Bt	NR7840	55°36·4'	5°31·0'W	X	62,69
Laglaff	E Ayr	NS6010	55°22·1'	4°12·1'W	X	71
Laglanny	S Ayr	NX3590	55°10·9'	4°35·1'W	X	77
Laglass Hill	E Ayr	NS6408	55°21·1'	4°8·3'W	X	71,77
Laglingarten	Arg & Bt	NN1407	56°13·4'	4°59·6'W	X	56
Lagloskine	Arg & Bt	NR7246	55°39·5'	5°37·1'W	X	62
Lag MacCodruim	N Eil	NB0609	57°58·6'	6°57·9'W	X	13,14
Lag ma Leatha	N Eil	NB0030	58°9·7'	7°5·6'W	X	13
Lag Mór	Highld	NM6747	56°33·7'	5°47·1'W	X	49
Lag Mór	N Eil	NB0214	58°1·2'	7°2·3'W	H	13
Lagmore	Moray	NJ1735	57°24·1'	3°22·4'W	X	28
Lag na Ballaig	Arg & Bt	NM5049	56°34·2'	6°3·7'W	X	47,48
Lagnabenae Moss	D & G	NX1767	54°58·1'	4°51·1'W	X	82
Lag na Bò Maoile	Highld	NM5364	56°42·4'	6°1·7'W	X	47
Lag na Cnàpaiche	Highld	NN7699	57°4·2'	4°2·3'W	X	35
Lag na Criche	Arg & Bt	NR2765	55°48·3'	6°21·0'W	X	60
Lag na Croise	N Ayr	NR9731	55°32·1'	5°12·6'W	X	69
Lag na Driseige	Arg & Bt	NS1886	56°2·2'	4°54·8'W	X	56
Lag-na-Keil	Arg & Bt	NM8525	56°22·4'	5°28·5'W	X	49
Lag na Làire	N Eil	NG2394	57°51·2'	6°39·7'W	X	14
Lagnalean	Highld	NH6241	57°26·6'	4°17·5'W	X	26
Lag na Linne	N Eil	NB2925	58°8·1'	6°35·8'W	X	13,14
Lag na Luinge	Arg & Bt	NN1225	56°23·1'	5°2·3'W	W	50
Lag nam Buinneag	N Eil	NB2639	58°15·5'	6°39·8'W	X	8,13
Lag nan Capull	Arg & Bt	NR2670	55°51·0'	6°22·4'W	X	60
Lag na Saille	Highld	NC0513	58°4·1'	5°17·9'W	W	15
Lag na Sliseig	Arg & Bt	NM6524	56°21·3'	5°47·8'W	X	49
Lagness	W Susx	SU8900	50°47·8'	0°43·8'W	T	197
Lag Odhar	Arg & Bt	NR3270	55°51·2'	6°16·5'W	X	60,61
Lagoes	Warw	SP2293	52°32·3'	1°40·1'W	X	139
Lagos Fm	Leic	SK3305	52°38·7'	1°30·3'W	FM	140
Lagrae	D & G	NS7014	55°24·4'	4°2·8'W	X	71
Lagrae Burn	D & G	NS7015	55°25·0'	4°2·8'W	W	71
Lag Sleitir	Highld	NM3497	56°59·5'	6°22·3'W	X	39
Lags Strand	D & G	NX6588	55°10·3'	4°6·7'W	W	77
Lagstoban	Arg & Bt	NR3064	55°47·9'	6°18·1'W	X	60
Lag Uaine	Arg & Bt	NN2609	56°14·8'	4°48·0'W	X	56
Lagual	Moray	NJ2423	57°17·7'	3°15·2'W	X	36
Laguna House	Pth & Kin	NO1036	56°30·7'	3°27·3'W	X	53
Lagvag	D & G	NX1530	54°38·1'	4°51·6'W	X	82
Lagwholt Moor	D & G	NX3983	55°7·2'	4°31·0'W	X	77
Lagwyne	D & G	NX5593	55°12·9'	4°16·3'W	X	77
Lahill Craig	Fife	NO4304	56°13·8'	2°54·7'W	X	59
Lahill Ho	Fife	NO4403	56°13·2'	2°53·7'W	X	59
Lahill Mains	Fife	NO4404	56°13·8'	2°53·8'W	X	59
La Hogue Fm	Cambs	TL6767	52°16·8'	0°27·3'E	FM	154
Laiaval	N Eil	NF8875	57°39·7'	7°13·5'W	H	18
Laid	Highld	NC4159	58°29·7'	4°42·3'W	X	9
Laid	Highld	ND2155	58°28·8'	3°20·8'W	X	11,12
Laid	Highld	ND2538	58°19·7'	3°16·4'W	X	11
Laide	Highld	NG8992	57°52·3'	5°33·0'W	T	19
Laidie Hill	Shetld	HU2949	60°13·7'	1°28·1'W	H	3
Laidlawsteil	Scot Bord	NT4236	55°37·1'	2°54·8'W	X	73
Laidlawsteil Fm	Scot Bord	NT4237	55°37·6'	2°54·8'W	FM	73
Laidlehope Burn	Scot Bord	NY5399	55°17·2'	2°44·0'W	W	79
Laidlehope Head	Scot Bord	NT5401	55°18·3'	2°43·0'W	X	79
Laidneskea	Pth & Kin	NN8951	56°38·5'	3°48·2'W	X	52
Laidwinley	Angus	NO4768	56°48·3'	2°51·6'W	H	44
Laig	Highld	NM4687	56°54·5'	6°9·9'W	X	39
Laig Drumlamford	S Ayr	NX2778	55°4·2'	4°42·1'W	X	76
Laigh Alderstocks	S Lanak	NS6144	55°40·4'	4°12·2'W	X	71
Laigh Auchenharvie	E Ayr	NS3644	55°40·0'	4°36·0'W	X	63,70
Laigh Auchenharvie	E Ayr	NS3644	55°40·0'	4°36·0'W	X	70

Laigh Baidland	N Ayr	NS2749	55°42·5′	4°44·8′W	X	63
Laigh Balernock	Arg & Bt	NS2588	56°3·4′	4°48·2′W	X	56
Laigh Balsarroch Fm	S Ayr	NS3615	55°24·3′	4°35·0′W	FM	70
Laigh Borland	S Ayr	NS4332	55°33·6′	4°28·9′W	X	70
Laigh Braidley	E Ayr	NS5740	55°38·2′	4°15·9′W	X	71
Laigh Cairn	D & G	NS6812	55°23·3′	4°4·6′W	X	71
Laigh Carnduff	S Lanak	NS6646	55°41·6′	4°7·5′W	T	64
Laigh Cleughearn	S Lanak	NS6249	55°43·1′	4°11·4′W	X	64
Laigh Crewburn	S Lanak	NS6642	55°39·4′	4°7·4′W	X	71
Laigh Fenwick	E Ayr	NS4642	55°39·1′	4°26·4′W	T	70
Laigh Glencroe	Arg & Bt	NN2405	56°12·6′	4°49·8′W	X	56
Laigh Glengall	S Ayr	NS3418	55°25·9′	4°37·0′W	T	70
Laigh Glenmuir	E Ayr	NS6120	55°27·5′	4°11·5′W	X	71
Laigh Gooseloan	N Ayr	NS3245	55°40·4′	4°39·9′W	X	63
Laigh Grange	S Ayr	NS3112	55°22·6′	4°39·6′W	X	70
Laigh Hall	E Ayr	NS6728	55°31·9′	4°6·0′W	X	71
Laigh Hapton	E Ayr	NS5541	55°38·7′	4°17·8′W	X	71
Laigh Hazliebank	S Lanak	NS6940	55°38·4′	4°4·4′W	X	71
Laighhill	Moray	NJ3362	57°38·8′	3°6·9′W	X	28
Laigh Hill	Scot Bord	NT1228	55°32·5′	3°23·2′W	H	72
Laigh Hillhouse	S Ayr	NS3433	55°34·0′	4°37·5′W	X	70
Laigh Hillhouse	S Ayr	NS3433	55°34·0′	4°37·5′W	X	70
Laigh Hook	S Lanak	NS6745	55°41·1′	4°6·5′W	X	64
Laigh Huntlawrig	S Lanak	NS6048	55°42·6′	4°13·3′W	X	64
Laigh Kilphin	S Ayr	NX1080	55°4·9′	4°58·2′W	X	76
Laigh Knoweglass	S Lanak	NS6450	55°43·7′	4°9·5′W	X	64
Laigh Langmuir	E Ayr	NS3941	55°38·4′	4°33·0′W	X	70
Laigh Langside	S Ayr	NS4131	55°33·1′	4°30·8′W	X	70
Laigh Letterpin	S Ayr	NX2092	55°11·6′	4°49·2′W	X	76
Laigh Mains	S Lanak	NS6356	55°46·9′	4°10·6′W	X	64
Laigh McGownston	S Ayr	NS2203	55°17·6′	4°47·8′W	X	76
Laighmilldown	D & G	NX1275	55°2·3′	4°56·1′W	X	76
Laighmuir	Aberd	NJ5529	57°21·2′	2°44·4′W	X	37
Laighmuir	E Ayr	NS4745	55°40·7′	4°25·6′W	X	64
Laigh Netherfield	S Lanak	NS7245	55°41·2′	4°1·7′W	X	64
Laigh Netherfielddyke	S Lanak	NS7246	55°41·7′	4°1·8′W	X	64
Laigh Newton	E Ayr	NS5937	55°36·6′	4°13·9′W	X	71
Laigh of Rossie	Pth & Kin	NN9815	56°19·2′	3°38·5′W	X	58
Laigh Overmuir	E Ayr	NS5843	55°39·8′	4°15·0′W	X	71
Laighpark	E Dunb	NS5376	55°57·5′	4°20·8′W	X	64
Laighpark	S Ayr	NS4019	55°26·6′	4°31·3′W	X	70
Laighparks	Stir	NS5184	56°1·8′	4°23·0′W	X	57,64
Laigh Patterton	N Ayr	NS3443	55°39·4′	4°37·9′W	X	63,70
Laigh Plewland	S Lanak	NS6535	55°35·7′	4°8·1′W	X	71
Laigh Sinniness	D & G	NX2152	54°50·1′	4°46·8′W	X	82
Laigh Smithston	S Ayr	NS3212	55°22·7′	4°38·7′W	X	70
Laigh Smithstone	N Ayr	NS2846	55°40·9′	4°43·7′W	X	63
Laighs of Cannahars	Aberd	NJ9120	57°16·5′	2°8·5′W	X	38
Laighstonehall	S Lanak	NS7054	55°46·0′	4°3·9′W	T	64
Laight	D & G	NX8195•	55°14·3′	3°51·9′W	X	78
Laight	E Ayr	NS4507	55°20·2′	4°26·2′W	X	70,77
Laigh Tarbeg	E Ayr	NS4820	55°27·3′	4°23·8′W	X	70
Laight Castle	E Ayr	NS4508	55°20·8′	4°26·2′W	A	70,77
Laight Fm	E Ayr	NS6111	55°22·7′	4°11·2′W	FM	71
Laight Hill	D & G	NX8095	55°14·3′	3°52·8′W	X	78
Laight Moor	D & G	NX0671	55°0·0′	5°1·6′W	X	76
Laigh Unthank	S Lanak	NS6743	55°40·0′	4°6·4′W	X	71
Laighwood	Pth & Kin	NO0745	56°35·5′	3°30·4′W	X	52,53
Laigh Woodston	S Ayr	NS3211	55°22·1′	4°38·6′W	X	70
Laigland Auchincruive Holdings	S Ayr	NS3822	55°28·2′	4°33·3′W	X	70
Laiken Forest	Highld	NH9052	57°32·9′	3°49·8′W	F	27
Lailt	Arg & Bt	NR6509	55°19·4′	5°41·8′W	X	68
Laimhrig	Highld	NM4196	56°59·2′	6°15·4′W	X	39
Laimhrig	N Eil	NB5558	58°26·8′	6°11·4′W	X	8
Laimhrig Mhurchaidh	N Eil	NB3609	57°59·8′	6°27·6′W	X	14
Laimhrig na Mòine	Highld	NG3523	57°13·5′	6°23·0′W	X	32
Laimhrig na Seoraid	N Eil	NA9822	58°5·3′	7°7·0′W	X	13
Lainchoil	Highld	NJ0618	57°14·8′	3°33·0′W	X	36
Lain Copse	Hants	SU3028	51°3·3′	1°33·9′W	F	185
Laindon	Essex	TQ6789	51°34·7′	0°25·0′E	T	177,178
Laindon Common	Essex	TQ6692	51°36·4′	0°24·2′E	X	177,178
Laines	Wilts	SU2374	51°28·1′	1°39·7′W	X	174
Lainger Beck	N Yks	SD9563	54°4·0′	2°4·2′W	W	98
Lainger Ho	N Yks	SD9562	54°3·5′	2°4·2′W	X	98
Laingseat	Aberd	NJ9415	57°13·8′	2°5·5′W	X	38
Laingshill	Northum	NY9396	55°15·7′	2°6·2′W	X	80
Lainish	N Eil	NB0000	57°53·6′	7°3·3′W	X	18
Lainish	N Eil	NF8568	57°35·8′	7°15·9′W	X	18
Lainne Sgeir	Arg & Bt	NM3650	56°34·3′	6°17·4′W	X	47
Lains Barn	Oxon	SU4289	51°36·1′	1°23·2′W	X	174
Lains Fm	Hants	SU2744	51°11·9′	1°36·4′W	FM	184
Lainshaw Ho	E Ayr	NS4045	55°40·6′	4°32·2′W	X	64
Lainshaw Mains	E Ayr	NS4045	55°40·6′	4°32·2′W	X	64
Lainston Ho	Hants	SU4431	51°4·8′	1°21·9′W	X	185
Laintachan	Highld	NJ0518	57°14·8′	3°34·0′W	X	36
Lair	Highld	NH0148	57°29·0′	5°18·7′W	T	25
Lair	Pth & Kin	NO1463	56°45·3′	3°23·9′W	X	43
Laira	C of Plym	SX5055	50°22·8′	4°6·2′W	T	201
Laira Br	C of Plym	SX5054	50°22·2′	4°6·2′W	X	201
Làir Bhàn	Arg & Bt	NM7606	56°11·9′	5°36·2′W	X	55
Laird Knowe	S Lanak	NS5932	55°33·9′	4°13·7′W	X	71
Lairdlaugh	D & G	NX8071	55°1·4′	3°52·2′W	X	84
Lairdmannoch Lodge	D & G	NX6559	54°54·7′	4°5·9′W	X	83,84
Laird's Burn	Aberd	NO5790	57°0·2′	2°42·0′W	W	44
Laird's Burn	S Lanak	NS7421	55°28·3′	3°59·2′W	W	71
Lairds Cleuch Rig	Scot Bord	NT1219	55°27·7′	3°23·1′W	X	78
Laird's Hill	D & G	NX0669	54°58·9′	5°1·5′W	X	82
Laird's Hill	N Lanak	NS6980	56°0·0′	4°5·6′W	H	64
Laird's Hill	Scot Bord	NT3507	55°21·4′	3°1·1′W	H	79
Lairdside Hill	N Ayr	NS2254	55°45·1′	4°49·7′W	X	63
Lairdside Hill	N Ayr	NS2756	55°46·2′	4°45·0′W	X	63
Lairdside Hill	Renf	NS3160	55°48·5′	4°41·4′W	X	63
Lairdside Knowe	Scot Bord	NT1527	55°32·0′	3°20·4′W	H	72
Laird's Loch	Pth & Kin	NO2535	56°30·3′	3°12·7′W	W	53
Lairds Loch	Shetld	HU3065	60°22·3′	1°26·9′W	W	3
Lairds Seat	Inverc	NS2967	55°52·2′	4°43·5′W	X	63
Laird's Seat	Moray	NJ3134	57°23·7′	3°8·4′W	X	28
Laird's Seat	S Lanak	NS6045	55°41·0′	4°13·2′W	H	64

Lairg	Highld	NC5806	58°1·5′	4°23·8′W	T	16
Lairgandour	Highld	NH7237	57°24·6′	4°7·4′W	X	27
Lair Geos	Orkney	HY4032	59°10·5′	3°2·5′W	X	5,6
Lairg Lodge	Highld	NC5707	58°2·0′	4°24·8′W	X	16
Lairgmore	Highld	NH5937	57°24·4′	4°20·4′W	X	26
Lairg Muir	Highld	NC5807	58°2·0′	4°23·8′W	T	16
Lairgs of Tain	Highld	NH7279	57°47·2′	4°8·7′W	X	21
Lairg Station	Highld	NC5803	57°59·9′	4°23·7′W	X	16
Lairhill	Stir	NN8302	56°12·0′	3°52·7′W	X	57
Lairhill Fm	E Yorks	SE9347	53°54·9′	0°34·6′W	FM	106
Lairhope	Scot Bord	NT3806	55°20·9′	2°58·2′W	X	79
Lairhope Burn	Scot Bord	NT3705	55°20·4′	2°59·2′W	W	79
Lairig a' Mhuic	Pth & Kin	NN5749	56°36·9′	4°19·4′W	X	51
Lairig an Laoigh	Aberd	NJ0300	57°5·1′	3°35·6′W	X	36
Lairig Arnan	Arg & Bt	NN2918	56°19·7′	4°45·5′W	X	50,56
Lairig Breisleich	Stir	NN5541	56°32·6′	4°21·1′W	X	51
Lairig Charnach	Pth & Kin	NO0670	56°49·0′	3°31·9′W	X	43
Lairig Dhoireann	Arg & Bt	NN1534	56°28·0′	4°59·7′W	X	50
Lairig Duirinnis	Arg & Bt	NN0235	56°28·2′	5°12·4′W	X	50
Lairig Eilde	Highld	NN1753	56°38·2′	4°58·6′W	X	41
Lairig Gartain	Highld	NN1953	56°38·3′	4°56·6′W	X	41
Lairig Ghallabhaich	Pth & Kin	NN5951	56°38·0′	4°17·5′W	X	42,51
Lairig Ghru	Highld	NH9602	57°6·1′	3°42·6′W	X	36
Lairig Hill	Arg & Bt	NN2433	56°27·6′	4°50·9′W	H	50
Lairig Leacach	Highld	NN2872	56°48·7′	4°48·6′W	X	41
Lairig Liaran	Stir	NN4738	56°30·8′	4°28·7′W	X	51
Lairigmór	Highld	NN1264	56°44·0′	5°4·0′W	X	41
Lairig Noe	Arg & Bt	NN1031	56°26·2′	5°4·5′W	X	50
Lairig, The	Highld	NN2578	56°51·9′	4°51·8′W	X	41
Lair of Aldararie	Angus	NO3178	56°53·6′	3°7·5′W	H	44
Lair of Whitestone	Angus	NO3176	56°52·5′	3°7·5′W	H	44
Lairo Water	Orkney	HY5019	59°3·6′	2°51·8′W	W	6
Lairs	E Dunb	NS6379	55°59·3′	4°11·3′W	X	64
Lairs	E Yorks	SE8649	53°56·0′	0°41·0′W	X	106
Lairs	S Lanak	NS7844	55°40·7′	3°56·0′W	X	71
Lairshill	Aberd	NJ8618	57°15·4′	2°13·5′W	X	38
Lais	Brig	SS9381	51°31·3′	3°32·1′W	X	170
Laisterdyke	Brad	SE1833	53°47·8′	1°43·2′W	T	104
Laith	Orkney	HY2716	59°1·8′	3°15·8′W	X	6
Laitha	Cumbr	NY6223	54°36·3′	2°34·9′W	X	91
Laithbuts Laithe	Lancs	SD8748	53°55·9′	2°11·5′W	X	103
Laithbutts	Lancs	SD6374	54°9·9′	2°33·6′W	X	97
Laithbutts	N Yks	SD7369	54°7·2′	2°24·4′W	X	98
Laithe	Cald	SD9830	53°46·2′	2°1·4′W	X	103
Laithes	Cumbr	NY4633	54°41·6′	2°49·8′W	T	90
Laithes, The	Cumbr	NY4533	54°41·6′	2°50·8′W	X	90
Laithkirk	Durham	NY9524	54°36·9′	2°4·2′W	T	91,92
Laithwaite Fm	Cumbr	SD5097	54°22·2′	2°45·8′W	FM	97
Laity	Corn	SW6930	50°7·7′	5°13·6′W	X	203
Laity Moor	Corn	SW6945	50°15·8′	5°14·1′W	T	203
Laity Moor	Corn	SW7536	50°11·1′	5°8·7′W	X	204
Laival a Deas	N Eil	NB0223	58°6·0′	7°3·0′W	H	13
Laival a Tuath	N Eil	NB0224	58°6·5′	7°3·1′W	H	13
Lake	Devon	SS4402	50°48·0′	4°12·4′W	X	190
Lake	Devon	SS4409	50°51·8′	4°12·6′W	T	190
Lake	Devon	SS5405	50°49·8′	4°4·0′W	X	191
Lake	Devon	SS5531	51°3·8′	4°3·8′W	T	180
Lake	Devon	SS5806	50°50·4′	4°0·6′W	X	191
Lake	Devon	SS6403	50°48·9′	3°55·5′W	X	191
Lake	Devon	SX5288	50°40·6′	4°5·3′W	T	191
Lake	Devon	SX5368	50°29·8′	4°4·0′W	X	201
Lake	Devon	SX7968	50°30·2′	3°42·0′W	X	202
Lake	I of W	SZ5883	50°38·9′	1°10·4′W	T	196
Lake	Pemb	SS0298	51°39·0′	4°51·3′W	X	158
Lake	Poole	SY9890	50°42·8′	2°1·3′W	T	195
Lake	Wilts	SU1339	51°9·2′	1°48·5′W	T	184
Lake Bank	Cumbr	SD2889	54°17·7′	3°6·0′W	X	96,97
Lake Bank	Cumbr	SD3696	54°21·6′	2°58·7′W	X	96,97
Lake Cottage	D & G	NX0948	54°47·7′	4°57·8′W	X	82
Lake Covert	Norf	TM3292	52°28·8′	1°25·4′E	F	134
Lake Dike	E Yorks	TA2038	53°49·7′	0°10·2′W	W	107
Lake Down	Devon	SX5388	50°40·6′	4°4·5′W	H	191
Lake Down	Wilts	SU1139	51°9·2′	1°50·2′W	X	184
Lake Drain	N Yks	SE5617	53°39·0′	1°8·8′W	W	111
Lake End	Bucks	SU9279	51°30·4′	0°40·1′W	T	175
Lake Farm Ho	Ches	SJ6280	53°19·2′	2°33·8′W	X	109
Lakefield Fm	Arg & Bt	NM9831	56°25·9′	5°16·1′W	FM	49
Lake Fm	Devon	SS4808	50°51·3′	4°9·2′W	FM	191
Lake Fm	Devon	ST0112	50°54·2′	3°24·1′W	FM	181
Lake Fm	Devon	ST2304	50°50·1′	3°5·2′W	FM	192,193
Lake Fm	Devon	ST2504	50°50·1′	3°3·5′W	FM	192,193
Lake Fm	Devon	SX4083	50°37·7′	4°15·4′W	FM	201
Lake Fm	Devon	SX8799	50°47·0′	3°35·8′W	FM	192
Lake Fm	Dorset	ST6113	50°55·1′	2°32·9′W	FM	194
Lake Fm	Hants	SU4817	50°57·3′	1°18·6′W	FM	185
Lake Fm	Kent	TQ7947	51°11·9′	0°34·1′E	FM	188
Lake Fm	Kent	TQ8147	51°11·8′	0°35·8′E	FM	188
Lake Fm	Lincs	TF1999	53°28·7′	0°12·0′W	FM	113
Lake Fm	Poole	SY9998	50°47·1′	2°0·5′W	FM	195
Lake Fm	Powys	SO2491	52°30·9′	3°6·8′W	FM	137
Lake Fm	Somer	ST4019	50°58·3′	2°50·9′W	FM	193
Lake Fm	Swan	SS4689	51°35·0′	4°13·0′W	FM	159
Lake Fm	Wilts	ST9377	51°29·7′	2°5·7′W	FM	173
Lake Group	Wilts	SU1140	51°9·8′	1°50·2′W	X	184
Lake Group (Tumuli)	Wilts	SU1140	51°9·8′	1°50·2′W	A	184
Lakehead Fm	Devon	SS6716	50°55·9′	3°53·2′W	FM	180
Lakehead Fm	D & G	NX9988	55°10·8′	3°34·7′W	FM	78
Lake Ho	Lincs	TF4577	53°16·4′	0°10·9′E	X	122
Lake Ho	Shrops	SO7685	52°28·0′	2°20·8′W	X	138
Lake Ho	Somer	ST3551	51°15·5′	2°55·5′W	X	182
Lake Ho	Suff	TG5000	52°32·6′	1°41·6′E	X	134
Lake Ho	Wilts	SU1338	51°8·7′	1°48·5′W	A	184
Lake Ho Fm	Shrops	SO5293	52°32·2′	2°42·1′W	FM	137,138
Lake House	Northum	NY9482	55°8·2′	2°5·2′W	X	80
Lakehouse Brook	Shrops	SO5292	52°31·7′	2°42·1′W	W	137,138
Lakehouse Fm	Essex	TL6638	52°1·2′	0°25·6′E	FM	154
Lakeland	Devon	SX6883	50°38·1′	3°51·6′W	X	191
Lakelands	Devon	SS8014	50°55·0′	3°42·0′W	X	181
Lake Lothing	Suff	TM5392	52°28·3′	1°43·9′E	W	134
Lake Louise	Highld	NH7387	57°51·5′	4°8·0′W	W	21

Lake Meadows	Essex	TQ6795	51°38·0′	0°25·2′E	X	167,177
Lake Mochdre	Powys	SO0787	52°28·6′	3°21·8′W	W	136
Lakemoor	Devon	SX6967	50°29·5′	3°50·4′W	X	202
Lakemoor Brook	Wrekin	SJ6119	52°46·3′	2°34·3′W	W	127
Lakenham	Norf	TG2307	52°37·1′	1°18·1′E	T	134
Lakenheath	Suff	TL7182	52°24·8′	0°31·3′E	T	143
Lakenheath Airfield	Suff	TL7481	52°24·2′	0°33·9′E	X	143
Lakenheath Sta	Suff	TL7286	52°26·9′	0°32·3′E	X	143
Lakenheath Warren	Suff	TL7580	52°23·6′	0°34·7′E	X	143
Lakenheath Warren	Suff	TL7780	52°23·6′	0°36·5′E	X	144
Lake of Menteith	Stir	NN5700	56°10·5′	4°17·8′W	W	57
Lake of Moy	Moray	NJ0162	57°38·5′	3°39·0′W	X	27
Laker Hall	Northum	NZ0467	55°0·1′	1°55·8′W	X	87
Laker's Green	Surrey	TQ0335	51°6·5′	0°31·3′W	T	186
Lakers Lodge	W Susx	TQ0430	51°3·8′	0°30·6′W	X	186
Lakes	Devon	SS3604	50°49·0′	4°19·3′W	X	190
Lakes End	Norf	TL5196	52°32·7′	0°14·0′E	X	143
Lake Settlement	Peterb	TL2298	52°34·2′	0°11·6′W	A	142
Lakes Fm	Hants	SU1602	50°49·3′	1°46·0′W	FM	195
Lakeside	Cumbr	SD3787	54°16·7′	2°57·6′W	T	96,97
Lakeside	Thurr	TQ5879	51°29·5′	0°17·0′E	T	177
Lakeside	Worcs	SP0567	52°18·3′	1°55·2′W	T	150
Lakeside Fm	Devon	SX5648	50°19·1′	4°1·0′W	FM	202
Lakeside Fm	Lincs	SK9347	53°1·0′	0°36·4′W	FM	130
Lakeside & Haverthwaite Rly	Cumbr	SD3585	54°15·6′	2°59·5′W	X	96,97
Lakes Sta, The	Warw	SP1073	52°21·5′	1°50·8′W	X	139
Lakestreet Manor	E Susx	TQ5929	51°2·5′	0°16·5′E	X	188,199
Lake Superior	D & G	NX0870	54°59·5′	4°59·7′W	W	76
Lake's Wood	E Yorks	TA0045	53°53·7′	0°28·3′W	F	106,107
Lake, The	Bucks	SP6716	51°50·5′	1°1·3′W	W	164,165
Lake, The	Bucks	SP6736	52°1·3′	1°1·0′W	W	152
Lake, The	Card	ST1879	51°30·5′	3°10·5′W	W	171
Lake, The	Derby	SK4038	52°56·5′	1°23·9′W	W	129
Lake, The	D & G	NX6847	54°48·3′	4°2·8′W	X	83,84
Lake, The	D & G	NX8792	55°12·8′	3°46·1′W	W	78
Lake, The	Norf	TG0330	52°50·0′	1°1·2′E	W	133
Lake, The	N Yks	SD7469	54°7·2′	2°23·5′W	W	98
Lake, The	Oxon	SP4316	51°50·7′	1°22·2′W	W	164
Lake, The	Oxon	SP5630	51°58·2′	1°10·7′W	W	152
Lake, The	Surrey	TQ2752	51°15·4′	0°10·4′W	W	187
Lake, The	W Susx	SU9630	51°3·9′	0°37·4′W	W	186
Lakethwaite	Cumbr	SD6095	54°21·2′	2°36·5′W	X	97
Lake Village (site of)	Somer	ST4941	51°10·2′	2°43·4′W	A	182,183
Lake Villages (sites of)	Somer	ST4442	51°10·7′	2°47·7′W	A	182
Lake Vyrnwy or Llyn Efyrnwy (Nature Reserve)	Powys	SH9821	52°46·9′	3°30·3′W	W	125
Lakin Fm	N Ayr	NR9030	55°31·4′	5°19·2′W	FM	68,69
Lalathan Fm	Fife	NO3404	56°13·7′	3°3·4′W	FM	59
Lalbuss Plantation	Cumbr	NY4045	54°48·0′	2°55·6′W	F	85
La Lee Fm	Dorset	ST8301	50°48·7′	2°14·1′W	FM	194
Laleham	Surrey	TQ0568	51°24·3′	0°29·0′W	T	176
Laleham Abbey	Surrey	TQ0568	51°24·3′	0°29·0′W	X	176
Laleham Burway	Surrey	TQ0467	51°23·8′	0°29·9′W	X	176
Laleston	Brig	SS8779	51°30·2′	3°37·3′W	T	170
Lalu Fm	Worcs	SO9639	52°3·2′	2°3·1′W	FM	150
Lamachan	D & G	NX4374	55°2·4′	4°27·0′W	X	77
Lamachan Hill	D & G	NX4377	55°4·0′	4°27·1′W	H	77
Lamagowan	D & G	NX5761	54°55·6′	4°13·5′W	X	83
Lamahip	Aberd	NO5592	57°1·3′	2°44·0′W	H	44
Lamaload Reservoir	Ches	SJ9775	53°16·6′	2°2·3′W	W	118
Lamalum	N Eil	NF7303	57°0·4′	7°22·8′W	X	31
La Mancha	Lancs	SD3612	53°36·3′	2°57·6′W	X	108
Lamancha	Scot Bord	NT1952	55°45·5′	3°17·0′W	X	65,66,72
Lama Ness	Orkney	HY6843	59°16·6′	2°33·2′W	X	5
Lamaness Firth	Orkney	HY6842	59°16·1′	2°33·2′W	W	5
Lamanva	Corn	SW7631	50°8·4′	5°7·7′W	T	204
Lamarsh	Essex	TL8935	51°59·1′	0°45·5′E	T	155
Lamarth Fm	Corn	SW6724	50°4·5′	5°15·0′W	FM	203
Lamas	Norf	TG2423	52°45·7′	1°19·6′E	T	133,134
Lamawhillis	Aberd	NO5393	57°1·8′	2°46·0′W	X	37,44
Lamb	E Loth	NT5386	56°4·1′	2°44·9′W	X	66
Lamba	Shetld	HU3981	60°30·9′	1°16·9′W	X	1,2,3
Lamba Dale	Shetld	HP5808	60°45·3′	0°55·6′W	X	1
Lamba Ness	Orkney	HY6138	59°13·9′	2°40·5′W	X	5
Lamba Ness	Shetld	HP6715	60°49·0′	0°45·6′W	X	1
Lamba Ness	Shetld	HU1662	60°20·8′	1°42·1′W	X	3
Lamba Scord	Shetld	HU4055	60°16·9′	1°16·1′W	X	3
Lamba Stack	Shetld	HP5503	60°42·6′	0°59·0′W	X	1
Lamba Stack	Shetld	HU6972	60°25·8′	0°44·3′W	X	2
Lamba Taing	Shetld	HU4326	60°1·3′	1°13·2′W	X	4
Lamba Water	Shetld	HU3856	60°17·4′	1°18·3′W	W	2,3
Lamba Wick	Shetld	HU3060	60°19·6′	1°26·9′W	W	3
Lamb Bay	Orkney	HY6921	59°4·8′	2°32·0′W	W	5
Lamb Beck Ing	Cumbr	NY4334	54°42·1′	2°52·6′W	X	90
Lamb Burn	E Loth	NT5962	55°51·2′	2°38·9′W	W	67
Lamb Close	Notts	SK4748	53°1·9′	1°17·5′W	X	129
Lamb Close	N Yks	SE1368	54°6·7′	1°47·7′W	X	99
Lamb Corner	Essex	TM0431	51°56·6′	0°58·5′E	T	168
Lambcote Fm	Warw	SP2647	52°7·5′	1°36·8′W	FM	151
Lambcote Grange	Donc	SK5393	53°26·1′	1°11·7′W	X	111
Lamb Crags	Northum	NU1003	55°19·5′	1°50·1′W	X	81
Lamb Craig	Arg & Bt	NR9971	55°53·7′	5°12·4′W	X	62
Lamb Craig	D & G	NT2104	55°19·7′	3°14·3′W	X	79
Lamb Craigs	D & G	NX7797	55°15·4′	3°55·7′W	H	78
Lambcroft Fm	Lincs	TF2593	53°25·4′	0°6·7′W	FM	113
Lambden	Scot Bord	NT7443	55°41·0′	2°24·4′W	T	74
Lambden Burn	Northum	NT9123	55°30·3′	2°8·1′W	W	74,75
Lambden Burn	Scot Bord	NT7543	55°41·0′	2°23·4′W	W	74
Lambden Ho	Scot Bord	NT7443	55°41·0′	2°24·4′W	X	74
Lambdens, The	W Berks	SU6170	51°25·8′	1°7·0′W	X	175
Lambdoughty	S Ayr	NX2591	55°11·2′	4°44·5′W	X	76
Lambdoughty Burn	S Ayr	NS4106	55°19·6′	4°29·9′W	W	70,77
Lambdoughty Hill	S Ayr	NS4006	55°19·6′	4°30·9′W	X	70,77
Lamb Down	Wilts	ST9839	51°9·2′	2°1·3′W	X	184
Lamb Down	Wilts	SU2548	51°14·1′	1°38·1′W	X	184
Lambdown Hill	W Susx	SU8112	50°54·3′	0°50·5′W	H	197
Lambeeth Fm	Pemb	SM9301	51°40·4′	4°59·2′W	FM	157,158
Lamberal Water	Corn	SS2712	50°53·1′	4°27·2′W	W	190

Lamberden	Kent	TQ8228	51°1·6'	0°36·1'E	T	188,199
Lamberhead Green	Wigan	SD5404	53°32·1'	2°41·2'W	T	108
Lamberhurst	Kent	TQ6736	51°6·2'	0°23·5'E	T	188
Lamberhurst Fm	Kent	TR0862	51°19·4'	0°59·5'E	FM	179
Lamberhurst Quarter	Kent	TQ6538	51°7·3'	0°21·9'E	T	188
Lamberkine	Pth & Kin	NO0622	56°23·1'	3°30·9'W	X	52,53,58
Lamber Low	Staffs	SK0850	53°3·1'	1°52·4'W	X	119
Lambert	Devon	SS5200	50°47·1'	4°5·6'W	X	191
Lambert	Devon	SX7592	50°43·1'	3°45·9'W	X	191
Lambert Fm	Devon	SS4714	50°54·5'	4°10·2'W	FM	180
Lambert Hill Fm	N Yks	NZ8808	54°27·8'	0°38·1'W	FM	94
Lamberton	Scot Bord	NT9656	55°48·1'	2°3·4'W	X	74,75
Lamberton Beach	Scot Bord	NT9758	55°49·2'	2°2·4'W	X	75
Lamberton Moor	Scot Bord	NT9558	55°49·2'	2°4·4'W	X	67,74,75
Lamberton Shiels	Scot Bord	NT9658	55°49·2'	2°3·4'W	X	74,75
Lambert's Castle	Dorset	SY3799	50°47·5'	2°53·2'W	X	193
Lambert's Castle (Fort)	Dorset	SY3799	50°47·5'	2°53·2'W	A	193
Lambert's Castle Hill	Dorset	SY3698	50°46·9'	2°54·1'W	H	193
Lambert's Coppice	Staffs	SJ9625	52°49·6'	2°3·2'W	F	127
Lambert's End	Sand	SO9991	52°31·2'	2°0·5'W	T	139
Lambert's Fm	Essex	TL8727	51°54·8'	0°43·5'E	FM	168
Lambert's Hill	Dorset	SY6390	50°42·7'	2°31·1'W	X	194
Lambert's Hill	Suff	TM0258	52°11·2'	0°57·7'E	X	155
Lambert's Hill Fm	Somer	ST6042	51°10·8'	2°33·9'W	FM	183
Lambert's Marsh	Wilts	ST8354	51°17·3'	2°14·2'W	X	183
Lambert's Mill	Fife	NT2390	56°6·1'	3°13·8'W	X	58
Lambert's Spinney	Beds	SP9747	52°7·0'	0°34·6'W	F	153
Lambesso	Corn	SW8444	50°15·6'	5°1·5'W	X	204
Lambest	Corn	SX3063	50°26·8'	4°23·3'W	X	201
Lambeth	C of West	TQ3078	51°29·4'	0°7·3'W	T	176,177
Lambeth Br	C of West	TQ3078	51°29·4'	0°7·3'W	X	176,177
Lambfair Green	Suff	TL7153	52°9·2'	0°30·4'E	T	154
Lambfell Beg	I of M	SC2985	54°14·2'	4°37·0'W	X	95
Lambfell Moar	I of M	SC2984	54°13·6'	4°37·0'W	X	95
Lambfield Fm	Cumbr	NY3843	54°46·9'	2°57·4'W	FM	85
Lamb Fm	Essex	TM1216	51°48·4'	1°4·9'E	FM	168,169
Lamb Fm	E Susx	TQ9522	50°58·1'	0°47·0'E	FM	189
Lambfoot	Cumbr	NY1630	54°39·7'	3°17·7'W	T	89
Lambgang Plantn	D & G	NX8396	55°14·9'	3°50·0'W	F	78
Lambgarth Head	Shetld	HU4550	60°14·2'	1°10·7'W	X	3
Lambgreen Hills	Cumbr	NY7136	54°43·3'	2°26·6'W	X	91
Lamb Head	Orkney	HY6921	59°4·8'	2°32·0'W	X	5
Lambhellia-cuddies	Shetld	HU6087	60°34·0'	0°53·8'W	X	1,2
Lamb Hill	Aberd	NJ4410	57°10·9'	2°55·1'W	H	37
Lambhill	Aberd	NJ6235	57°24·5'	2°37·5'W	X	29
Lambhill	Aberd	NJ7733	57°23·5'	2°22·5'W	X	29,30
Lambhill	Aberd	NJ9055	57°35·4'	2°9·6'W	X	30
Lambhill	C of Glas	NS5769	55°53·8'	4°16·8'W	T	64
Lamb Hill	Cumbr	NY0627	54°38·0'	3°27·0'W	X	89
Lamb Hill	D & G	NT2905	55°20·3'	3°6·7'W	H	79
Lamb Hill	D & G	NX1069	54°59·0'	4°57·7'W	H	82
Lamb Hill	D & G	NX9492	55°12·9'	3°39·5'W	H	78
Lamb Hill	D & G	NY0099	55°16·8'	3°34·0'W	X	78
Lamb Hill	D & G	NY2798	55°16·5'	3°8·5'W	H	79
Lamb Hill	Durham	NZ0213	54°31·0'	1°57·7'W	X	92
Lamb Hill	E Ayr	NS5841	55°38·8'	4°15·0'W	X	71
Lamb Hill	E Ayr	NS6203	55°18·4'	4°10·0'W	X	77
Lamb Hill	N Ayr	NS3158	55°47·4'	4°41·3'W	X	63
Lamb Hill	Northum	NT8113	55°24·9'	2°17·6'W	H	80
Lamb Hill	N Yks	SE1464	54°4·5'	1°46·7'W	X	99
Lamb Hill	N Yks	SE2479	54°12·6'	1°37·5'W	X	99
Lamb Hill	Pth & Kin	NO0007	56°15·0'	3°36·4'W	H	58
Lamb Hill	Scot Bord	NT6358	55°49·1'	2°35·0'W	X	67,74
Lambhill	S Lanak	NS6939	55°37·9'	4°4·4'W	X	71
Lamb Hill	S Lanak	NS9702	55°18·3'	3°36·9'W	H	78
Lamb Hill Fell	Lancs	SD6859	54°1·8'	2°28·9'W	X	103
Lamb Hill Fm	Lancs	SD7057	54°0·7'	2°27·1'W	FM	103
Lamb Hoga	Shetld	HU6088	60°34·5'	0°53·8'W	X	1,2
Lambhoga Head	Shetld	HU4014	59°54·8'	1°16·6'W	X	4
Lambholm	D & G	NY0286	55°9·8'	3°31·9'W	X	78
Lamb Holm	Orkney	HY4800	58°53·3'	2°53·7'W	X	6,7
Lamb Howe	Cumbr	SD4291	54°18·9'	2°53·1'W	X	96,97
Lambhowe Plantn	Cumbr	SD4191	54°18·9'	2°54·0'W	F	96,97
Lambigart	Shetld	HU2841	60°9·4'	1°29·2'W	X	4
Lambi Loch	Shetld	HU2742	60°10·0'	1°30·3'W	W	4
Lambing Clough	Lancs	SD6837	53°49·9'	2°28·8'W	X	103
Lamb Knowe	D & G	NS7917	55°26·2'	3°54·3'W	H	71,78
Lamb Knowe	Northum	NT8337	55°37·8'	2°15·8'W	X	74
Lamb Knowe	Scot Bord	NT1622	55°29·3'	3°19·3'W	H	72
Lamb Knowe	Scot Bord	NT4017	55°26·8'	2°56·5'W	H	79
Lamblair Edge	Scot Bord	NT3303	55°19·2'	3°2·9'W	X	79
Lamblair Edge	Scot Bord	NT7208	55°22·2'	2°26·1'W	X	80
Lamblair Hill	Scot Bord	NT5701	55°18·3'	2°40·2'W	H	80
Lamblair Knowe	D & G	NT2903	55°19·2'	3°6·7'W	H	79
Lamblairknowe	Scot Bord	NT7010	55°23·2'	2°28·0'W	X	80
Lamblair Wood	E Loth	NT4772	55°56·5'	2°50·5'W	F	66
Lamb Law	Scot Bord	NT2845	55°41·8'	3°8·3'W	H	73
Lamb Law	Scot Bord	NT3544	55°41·4'	3°1·6'W	H	73
Lamb Lea	W Susx	SU9215	50°55·9'	0°41·1'W	X	197
Lamb Leer Cavern	Somer	ST5455	51°17·8'	2°39·2'W	X	172,182
Lambley	Northum	NY6758	54°55·2'	2°30·5'W	T	86,87
Lambley	Notts	SK6345	53°0·2'	1°3·3'W	T	129
Lambley Common	Northum	NY6757	54°54·6'	2°30·5'W	X	86,87
Lambley Dumble	Notts	SK6245	53°0·2'	1°4·2'W	W	129
Lambley Fm	Northum	NY6759	54°55·7'	2°30·5'W	FM	86,87
Lambley Ho	Notts	SK6146	53°0·7'	1°5·0'W	X	129
Lambley Lodge	Rut	SK8102	52°36·8'	0°47·8'W	X	141
Lambleys Barn	W Susx	TQ1506	50°50·7'	0°21·6'W	X	198
Lamb Ness	Orkney	HY6921	59°4·8'	2°32·0'W	X	5
Lamborough	Pemb	SN0220	51°50·9'	4°52·1'W	X	145,157,158
Lamborough Camp	Pemb	SN0219	51°50·3'	4°52·1'W	A	157,158
Lamborough Hill	Oxon	SP4700	51°42·0'	1°18·8'W	T	164
Lambourn	W Berks	SU3278	51°30·2'	1°31·9'W	T	174
Lambourn Downs	W Berks	SU3481	51°31·8'	1°30·2'W	X	174
Lambourne	Corn	SW7651	50°19·2'	5°8·4'W	T	200,204
Lambourne	Essex	TQ4796	51°38·8'	0°7·9'E	T	167,177
Lambourne End	Essex	TQ4794	51°37·8'	0°7·8'E	T	167,177
Lambourne Hall	Essex	TQ9194	51°37·0'	0°45·9'E	X	168,178
Lambourne Place	Essex	TQ4897	51°39·4'	0°8·8'E	A	167,177
Lambourne's Hill	Hants	SU2950	51°15·1'	1°34·7'W	X	185
Lambourn Woodlands	W Berks	SU3275	51°28·6'	1°32·0'W	T	174
Lamb Pasture	Cumbr	NY5302	54°24·9'	2°43·0'W	H	90
Lambpit Hill	Norf	TL8382	52°24·5'	0°41·8'E	X	144
Lambpits, The	Suff	TM4470	52°16·7'	1°35·0'E	X	156
Lambrenny	Corn	SX1786	50°38·9'	4°34·9'W	X	201
Lambridden Fm	N Ayr	NS3148	55°42·0'	4°40·9'W	FM	63
Lambridge	Bath & NE Somer	ST7666	51°23·8'	2°20·3'W	T	172
Lambridge Wood	Oxon	SU7384	51°33·2'	0°56·4'W	F	175
Lamb Rig	D & G	NY0397	55°15·7'	3°31·2'W	X	78
Lamb Rig	Scot Bord	NT1154	55°46·5'	3°24·7'W	X	65,72
Lamb Rig	Scot Bord	NT5459	55°49·6'	2°43·6'W	X	66,73
Lamb Rig	Scot Bord	NT6404	55°20·2'	2°33·6'W	X	80
Lambriggan	Corn	SW7651	50°19·2'	5°8·4'W	X	200,204
Lambrigg Fell	Cumbr	SD5894	54°20·6'	2°38·3'W	H	97
Lambrigg Foot	Cumbr	SD5696	54°21·7'	2°40·2'W	X	97
Lambrigg Head	Cumbr	SD5995	54°21·2'	2°37·4'W	X	97
Lambrigg Mill	Norf	TG4325	52°46·3'	1°36·6'E	X	134
Lambrigg Park	Cumbr	SD5994	54°20·6'	2°37·4'W	X	97
Lambrigg Park Fm	Cumbr	SD5994	54°20·6'	2°37·4'W	FM	97
Lambrig Wood	D & G	NX9387	55°10·2'	3°40·4'W	F	78
Lamb Roe	Lancs	SD7337	53°50·0'	2°24·2'W	X	103
Lambrook	Dorset	SY4796	50°45·9'	2°44·7'W	T	193
Lambrook	Monm	SO2903	51°43·5'	3°1·3'W	X	
Lambrook Brook	Somer	ST4218	50°57·7'	2°49·2'W	W	193
Lambrook Fm	Somer	ST5923	51°0·5'	2°34·7'W	FM	183
Lambsceugh	Cumbr	NY4638	54°44·3'	2°49·9'W	X	90
Lambscombe	Devon	SS7629	51°3·1'	3°45·8'W	X	180
Lamb's Common	Norf	TF7317	52°43·6'	0°34·1'E	X	132
Lambs' Cross	Cambs	TL4265	52°16·1'	0°5·3'E	X	154
Lamb's Cross	Kent	TQ7948	51°12·4'	0°34·1'E	T	188
Lambsdale Leans	Highld	ND0454	58°28·1'	3°38·3'W	X	11,12
Lambs Down	Devon	SX6965	50°28·4'	3°50·4'W	X	202
Lambsgate Fm	Somer	ST8048	51°14·1'	2°16·8'W	FM	183
Lambs Green	Dorset	SY9998	50°47·1'	2°0·5'W	T	195
Lambs Green	W Susx	TQ2136	51°6·9'	0°15·9'W	T	187
Lamb's Head	Durham	NY8040	54°45·5'	2°18·2'W	H	86,87
Lamb Shield	Durham	NZ0248	54°49·9'	1°57·7'W	X	87
Lamb Shield	Northum	NY9461	54°56·9'	2°5·2'W	X	87
Lambshillock	Aberd	NJ9444	57°29·4'	2°5·5'W	X	30
Lamb's Holes	Norf	TG2118	52°43·1'	1°16·7'E	X	133,134
Lambs House Fm	Hartpl	NZ4632	54°41·1'	1°16·8'W	FM	93
Lambside	Devon	SX5747	50°18·6'	4°0·1'W	X	202
Lambskin Dale	Staffs	SK0343	52°59·3'	1°56·9'W	X	119,128
Lambslack	Aberd	NJ6739	57°26·7'	2°32·5'W	X	29
Lambslair Plantn	Scot Bord	NT5721	55°29·1'	2°40·4'W	F	73,74
Lambsland Fm	Kent	TQ8529	51°2·1'	0°38·7'E	FM	189,199
Lambsleaze	I of W	SZ4491	50°43·2'	1°22·2'W	X	196
Lambs Rigg	Northum	NY8756	54°54·2'	2°11·7'W	X	87
Lambston	Pemb	SM9016	51°48·4'	5°2·4'W	T	157,158
Lambswick Fms	Worcs	SO6869	52°19·3'	2°27·8'W	FM	138
Lambtech	Aberd	NJ7750	57°32·6'	2°22·6'W	X	29,30
Lambton	Highld	NH7159	57°36·4'	4°9·1'W	X	27
Lambton	Sund	NZ2955	54°53·6'	1°32·4'W	T	88
Lambton Castle	Durham	NZ2952	54°52·0'	1°32·5'W	X	88
Lambton Park	Durham	NZ2951	54°51·4'	1°32·5'W	X	88
Lambwath Stream	E Yorks	TA1840	53°50·8'	0°12·0'W	W	107
Lamby	Card	ST2277	51°29·4'	3°7·0'W	X	171
Lamcote Field	Notts	SK6338	52°56·4'	1°3·3'W	X	129
Lamehead	Ches	SJ9566	53°11·7'	2°4·1'W	X	118
Lame Hill	Somer	ST4624	51°1·0'	2°45·8'W	X	193
Lamelgate	Corn	SX2170	50°30·4'	4°31·1'W	X	201
Lamellen	Corn	SX0577	50°33·9'	4°44·8'W	X	200
Lamellion	Corn	SX2463	50°26·7'	4°28·4'W	T	201
Lamellyn	Corn	SW8948	50°17·9'	4°57·4'W	X	204
Lamellyon	Corn	SX1352	50°20·5'	4°37·3'W	X	200
Lamer Fm	Herts	TL1815	51°49·5'	0°16·9'W	FM	166
Lamer Ho	Herts	TL1816	51°50·0'	0°16·8'W	X	166
Lamerhooe	Devon	SX3973	50°32·3'	4°15·9'W	X	201
Lamerton	Devon	SS3504	50°49·0'	4°20·2'W	X	190
Lamerton	Devon	SX4476	50°34·0'	4°11·8'W	T	201
Lamerton Cross	Devon	SX5799	50°46·6'	4°1·3'W	X	191
Lamesley	Ghead	NZ2558	54°55·2'	1°36·2'W	T	88
Lametton Mill	Corn	SX2561	50°25·6'	4°27·5'W	X	201
Lamford	D & G	NX5299	55°16·0'	4°19·3'W	X	77
Lamford Burn	D & G	NX5387	55°9·6'	4°18·0'W	W	77
Lamford Hill	D & G	NX5398	55°15·5'	4°18·3'W	H	77
Lamgarroch	D & G	NX7198	55°15·8'	4°1·4'W	H	77
Làmh a' Sgeir Bheag	N Eil	NA7246	58°17·1'	7°35·4'W	X	13
Làmh a' Sgeir Mhòr	N Eil	NA7246	58°17·1'	7°35·4'W	X	13
Lamh-bheinn	Arg & Bt	NR3064	55°47·9'	6°18·1'W	X	60
Lamh Dearg	Pth & Kin	NO1263	56°45·3'	3°25·9'W	H	43
Lamigo Bay	Highld	NC6563	58°32·3'	4°18·7'W	W	10
Laminess	Orkney	HY6137	59°13·3'	2°40·5'W	T	5
Lamington	Aberd	NJ6526	57°19·7'	2°34·4'W	X	38
Lamington	Highld	NH7476	57°45·6'	4°6·6'W	T	21
Lamington	S Lanak	NS9731	55°34·0'	3°37·6'W	T	72
Lamington Burn	S Lanak	NS9828	55°32·4'	3°36·5'W	W	72
Lamington Hill	S Lanak	NT0030	55°33·5'	3°34·7'W	H	72
Lamington Park	Highld	NH7477	57°46·2'	4°6·6'W	F	21
Lamlash	N Ayr	NS0230	55°31·7'	5°7·8'W	T	69
Lamlash Bay	N Ayr	NS0330	55°31·7'	5°6·8'W	W	69
Lamledra	Corn	SX0141	50°14·4'	4°47·1'W	T	204
Lamloch	D & G	NX5296	55°14·4'	4°19·2'W	X	77
Lamloch Burn	D & G	NX5195	55°13·9'	4°20·1'W	W	77
Lammack	Black w Dar	SD6629	53°45·6'	2°30·5'W	T	103
Lammacott Fm	Devon	SS7403	50°49·0'	3°46·9'W	FM	191
Lammas Field	Warw	SP2764	52°16·6'	1°35·9'W	X	151
Lammas Hill	Warw	SP4175	52°22·5'	1°23·5'W	X	140
Lammas Muir	Aberd	NO6577	56°53·2'	2°34·0'W	X	45
Lammaston Fm	Pemb	SS0099	51°39·5'	4°53·1'W	FM	158
Lammerbogs	Aberd	NJ9940	57°27·3'	2°0·5'W	X	30
Lammer Geo	Orkney	ND4193	58°49·5'	3°1·8'W	X	7
Lammer Law	E Loth	NT5261	55°50·6'	2°45·6'W	H	66
Lammerlaw	S Lanak	NT0544	55°41·1'	3°30·2'W	X	72
Lammerloch Resr	E Loth	NT5163	55°51·7'	2°46·5'W	W	66
Lammermuir	Aberd	NJ9437	57°25·7'	2°5·5'W	X	30
Lammermuir	Scot Bord	NT7458	55°49·1'	2°24·5'W	X	67,74
Lammermuir Hills	E Loth	NT5460	55°50·1'	2°43·6'W	H	66
Lammermuir Hills	E Loth	NT6165	55°52·8'	2°37·0'W	H	67
Lammerside Castle	Cumbr	NY7704	54°26·1'	2°20·9'W	A	91
Lammerton	C of Dun	NO4533	56°29·4'	2°53·1'W	X	54
Lammerview	E Loth	NT5377	55°59·3'	2°44·8'W	X	66
Lamming's Marsh Fm	Lincs	TF3334	52°53·5'	0°1·0'W	FM	131
Lammy Down	Swin	SU2481	51°31·9'	1°38·8'W	X	174
Lamode	I of M	SC2272	54°7·0'	4°43·0'W	X	95
Lamonby	Cumbr	NY4035	54°42·6'	2°55·5'W	T	90
Lamonby Hall	Cumbr	NY4134	54°42·1'	2°54·5'W	X	90
Lamorbey Park	Bexley	TQ4673	51°26·5'	0°6·4'E	X	177
Lamorick	Corn	SX0364	50°26·8'	4°46·1'W	T	200
Lamorna	Corn	SW4424	50°3·9'	5°34·3'W	T	203
Lamorna Cove	Corn	SW4523	50°3·4'	5°33·4'W	W	203
Lamorna Valley	Corn	SW4424	50°3·9'	5°34·3'W	X	203
Lamorran	Corn	SW8741	50°14·1'	4°58·8'W	T	204
Lamorran Wood	Corn	SW8842	50°14·6'	4°58·0'W	F	204
Lampardbrook	Suff	TM2761	52°12·2'	1°19·7'E	X	156
Lampardbrook Fm	Suff	TM2762	52°12·8'	1°19·8'E	FM	156
Lampay	Highld	NG2155	57°30·2'	6°39·0'W	X	23
Lampen	Corn	SX1867	50°28·7'	4°33·5'W	X	201
Lampern Ho	Glos	ST7997	51°40·5'	2°17·8'W	X	162
Lampert	Northum	NY6874	55°3·8'	2°29·6'W	X	86,87
Lampeter	Cered	SN5748	52°7·0'	4°4·9'W	T	146
Lampeter Vale	Pemb	SN1615	51°48·4'	4°39·8'W	X	158
Lampeter Velfrey	Pemb	SN1514	51°47·9'	4°40·6'W	T	158
Lampetts	Essex	TL5607	51°44·6'	0°16·0'E	X	167
Lamphey	Pemb	SN0100	51°40·1'	4°52·3'W	T	158
Lamphill Woods	Corn	SX0877	50°33·9'	4°42·3'W	F	200
Lamphitt	D & G	NX9989	55°11·4'	3°34·8'W	X	78
Lampinsdub	W Loth	NT0775	55°57·8'	3°28·9'W	X	65
Lampits	S Lanak	NS9645	55°41·5'	3°38·8'W	X	72
Lampits Fm	Suff	TM1467	52°15·8'	1°8·6'E	FM	156
Lamplands	N Yks	NZ8206	54°26·8'	0°43·7'W	X	94
Lamplugh	Cumbr	NY0820	54°34·3'	3°25·1'W	T	89
Lamplugh Fell	Cumbr	NY1019	54°33·7'	3°23·1'W	H	89
Lampool	Aberd	NO8482	56°56·0'	2°15·3'W	X	45
Lamport	Bucks	SP6837	52°1·9'	1°0·1'W	X	152
Lamport	Northnts	SP7574	52°21·8'	0°53·5'W	T	141
Lampretten	Corn	SX2367	50°28·8'	4°29·3'W	X	201
Lamps Moss	N Yks	NY8104	54°26·1'	2°17·2'W	X	91,92
Lampton	Houns	TQ1376	51°28·5'	0°22·0'W	T	176
Lamsey Fm	Herts	SP9914	51°49·2'	0°33·4'W	FM	165
Lamyatt	Somer	ST6535	51°7·0'	2°29·6'W	T	183
Lamyatt Lodge	Somer	ST6636	51°7·6'	2°28·8'W	X	183
Lan	Brig	SS9184	51°32·9'	3°33·9'W	X	170
Lan	Carm	SN1620	51°51·1'	4°39·9'W	X	145,158
Lan	Carm	SN1925	51°53·9'	4°37·5'W	X	145,158
Lan	Carm	SN2024	51°53·4'	4°36·6'W	X	145,158
Lan	Carm	SN3323	51°53·1'	4°25·2'W	X	145,159
Lan	Carm	SN3729	51°56·4'	4°21·9'W	X	145
Lan	Carm	SN4713	51°47·9'	4°12·7'W	X	159
Lan	Carm	SN4725	51°54·4'	4°13·1'W	X	146
Lan	Carm	SN5825	51°54·6'	4°3·5'W	X	146
Lan	Carm	SN6125	51°54·6'	4°0·9'W	X	146
Lan	Carm	SN6132	51°58·4'	4°1·0'W	X	146
Lan	Carm	SN7522	51°53·2'	3°48·6'W	X	160
Lan	Cered	SN2547	52°5·9'	4°32·9'W	X	145
Lan	Powys	SN8689	52°29·5'	3°40·3'W	X	135,136
Lana	Devon	SS3007	50°50·5'	4°24·5'W	T	190
Lana	Devon	SS4405	50°49·6'	4°12·5'W	X	190
Lana	Devon	SX3496	50°44·6'	4°20·8'W	T	190
Lanacombe	Somer	SS7742	51°10·1'	3°45·2'W	X	180
Lanacre	Somer	SS8236	51°6·9'	3°40·8'W	X	181
Lana Cross	Devon	SS4206	50°50·2'	4°14·3'W	X	190
Lanagan	Corn	SX0681	50°36·0'	4°44·1'W	X	200
Lana Lake	Devon	SX3497	50°45·2'	4°20·8'W	W	190
Lanamoor Plantn	Devon	SX3495	50°44·1'	4°20·8'W	F	190
Lanark	S Lanak	NS8843	55°40·3'	3°46·4'W	T	71,72
Lanarkland	D & G	NY0267	54°59·5'	3°31·5'W	X	84
Lanark Moor	S Lanak	NS9043	55°40·3'	3°44·5'W	X	71,72
Lanarth	Corn	SW7621	50°3·1'	5°7·4'W	X	204
Lanaways Fm	W Susx	TQ1528	51°2·6'	0°21·2'W	FM	187,198
Lancare Fm	Corn	SX1955	50°22·3'	4°32·3'W	FM	201
Lancarffe	Corn	SX0869	50°29·6'	4°42·0'W	X	200
Lancarrow	Corn	SW6937	50°11·5'	5°13·8'W	X	203
Lancashire Coastal Way	Lancs	SD4463	54°3·8'	2°50·9'W	X	97
Lancashire College of Agriculture	Lancs	SD4940	53°51·5'	2°46·1'W	X	102
Lancashire Cycle Way	Black w Dar	SD6916	53°38·6'	2°27·7'W	X	109
Lancashire Cycle Way	Lancs	SD5339	53°51·0'	2°42·5'W	X	102
Lancashire Cycle Way	Lancs	SD6932	53°47·2'	2°27·8'W	X	103
Lanca Skerry	Shetld	HP6405	60°43·6'	0°49·1'W	X	1
Lancaster	Lancs	SD4761	54°2·8'	2°48·2'W	T	97
Lancaster Canal	Lancs	SD5040	53°51·5'	2°45·2'W	W	102
Lancaster Canal	Lancs	SD5176	54°10·9'	2°44·6'W	W	97
Lancaster Hole	Cumbr	SD6680	54°13·1'	2°30·9'W	X	98
Lancasters	Essex	TL5414	51°48·4'	0°14·4'E	X	167
Lancaster Sound	Cumbr	SD3366	54°5·4'	3°1·0'W	W	96,97
Lancaut	Glos	ST5396	51°39·9'	2°40·4'W	X	162
Lance Beck	Durham	NZ0119	54°34·2'	1°58·6'W	W	92
Lance Butts	N Yks	SE7382	54°13·9'	0°52·4'W	X	100
Lance Coppice	S Glos	ST7588	51°35·7'	2°21·3'W	F	162,172
Lance Levy Fm	Hants	SU6957	51°18·7'	1°0·2'W	FM	175,186
Lancen Cotts	Hants	SU5524	51°1·0'	1°12·6'W	X	185
Lanchester	Durham	NZ1647	54°49·3'	1°44·6'W	T	88
Lanchester Valley Walk	Durham	NZ1946	54°48·8'	1°41·9'W	X	88
Lanchestoo	Shetld	HU3791	60°36·3'	1°19·0'W	H	1,2
Lancin Fm	Somer	ST2807	50°51·7'	3°1·0'W	FM	193
Lancing	W Susx	TQ1804	50°49·6'	0°19·1'W	T	198
Lancing Hill	W Susx	TQ1806	50°50·7'	0°19·0'W	X	198
Lan-clyn-Adda	Carm	SN4531	51°57·6'	4°15·0'W	X	146
Lancombe Fm	Dorset	SY5699	50°47·6'	2°37·1'W	FM	194
Lancorla Fm	Corn	SW9664	50°26·7'	4°52·0'W	FM	200
Lancrigg	Cumbr	NY3308	54°28·0'	3°1·6'W	X	90
Lancwm	Cered	SN4046	52°5·6'	4°19·7'W	X	146
Lancwmbrawd	Carm	SN5029	51°56·6'	4°10·5'W	X	146
Lancych	Pemb	SN2538	52°1·0'	4°32·6'W	X	145
Landacre Bridge	Somer	SS8136	51°6·9'	3°41·5'W	X	181
Landare Fm	Corn	SX2058	50°23·9'	4°31·6'W	FM	201

Landaviddy	Corn	SX1951	50°20·1′	4°32·2′W	X	201
Landbarn Fm	Surrey	TQ1349	51°14·0′	0°22·5′W	FM	187
Landbeach	Cambs	TL4765	52°16·0′	0°9·7′E	T	154
Landberrick	D & G	NX3645	54°46·6′	4°32·6′W	X	83
Land Brook	Oxon	SU3692	51°37·8′	1°28·4′W	W	164,174
Landcombe Ho	Devon	SX8447	50°18·9′	3°37·4′W	X	202
Landcross	Devon	SS4623	50°59·4′	4°11·3′W	T	180,190
Land Drain	N Lincs	SE9914	53°37·0′	0°29·8′W	W	112
Lan Ddu	Powys	SN8756	52°11·7′	3°38·8′W	X	147
Lan Ddu Cilwenau	Carm	SN5837	52°1·0′	4°3·8′W	X	146
Land Ends	Cumbr	NY4324	54°36·7′	2°52·5′W	X	90
Landerberry	Aberd	NJ7404	57°7·8′	2°25·3′W	T	38
Landermere Hall	Essex	TM1923	51°52·0′	1°11·3′E	X	168,169
Landews Meadow Fm	Kent	TQ9950	51°13·1′	0°51·4′E	FM	189
Land Fm	Devon	SS9604	50°49·8′	3°28·2′W	FM	192
Land Fm	Devon	ST2605	50°50·6′	3°2·7′W	FM	192,193
Land Fm	D & G	NY2175	55°4·0′	3°13·8′W	FM	85
Landford	Wilts	SU2519	50°58·4′	1°38·2′W	T	184
Landford Common	Wilts	SU2618	50°57·9′	1°37·4′W	X	184
Landford lodge	Wilts	SU2420	50°59·0′	1°39·1′W	X	184
Landford Manor	Wilts	SU2620	50°59·0′	1°37·4′W	X	184
Landfordwood	Wilts	SU2521	50°59·5′	1°38·2′W	T	184
Land Gate	Wigan	SD5701	53°30·5′	2°38·5′W	T	108
Landgreek	Corn	SX1951	50°20·1′	4°32·2′W	X	201
Landguard Fort	Suff	TM2831	51°56·1′	1°19·4′E	A	169
Landguard Manor	I of W	SZ5782	50°38·3′	1°11·3′W	T	196
Landguard Point	Suff	TM2831	51°56·1′	1°19·4′E	X	169
Landhallow	Highld	ND1833	58°16·9′	3°23·4′W	X	11
Landheads	D & G	NY2069	55°0·8′	3°14·6′W	X	85
Landhill	Devon	SX4297	50°45·3′	4°14·0′W	T	190
Land Hill	D & G	NX8660	54°55·6′	3°46·3′W	H	84
Landhillick	Corn	SX2295	50°43·9′	4°31·0′W	X	190
Land Ho	Durham	NZ1244	54°47·7′	1°48·4′W	X	88
Land Ho	Lancs	SD4742	53°52·5′	2°48·0′W	X	102
Landican	Wirral	SJ2885	53°21·7′	3°4·5′W	T	108
Landieu	Durham	NZ0436	54°43·4′	1°55·9′W	X	92
Landigwynnet	Pemb	SN0604	51°42·3′	4°48·1′W	X	158
Landimore	Swan	SS4693	51°37·1′	4°13·1′W	T	159
Landimore Marsh	Swan	SS4594	51°37·6′	4°14·0′W	W	159
Landing Beach, The	Devon	SS1443	51°9·6′	4°39·2′W	X	180
Landing How	Cumbr	SD3787	54°16·7′	2°57·6′W	X	96,97
Landinner	Corn	SX2383	50°37·4′	4°29·8′W	X	201
Landkey	Devon	SS5931	51°3·9′	4°0·4′W	T	180
Landkey Newland	Devon	SS5931	51°3·9′	4°0·4′W	T	180
Landlake	Corn	SX3281	50°36·5′	4°22·1′W	X	201
Landlooe Br	Corn	SX2459	50°24·5′	4°28·2′W	X	201
Landmead Fm	Oxon	SU4494	51°38·8′	1°21·5′W	FM	164,174
Landmoor Fm	N Lincs	SE8903	53°31·2′	0°39·0′W	FM	112
Landmoth Hall	N Yks	SE4292	54°19·6′	1°20·8′W	X	99
Landmoth Wood	N Yks	SE4292	54°19·6′	1°20·8′W	F	99
Land of Canaan	Ches	SJ5244	52°59·7′	2°42·5′W	X	117
Land of Nod	E Yorks	SE8436	53°49·0′	0°43·0′W	X	106
Land of Nod	Hants	SU8437	51°7·8′	0°47·6′W	X	186
Land o' Nod Fm	N Yks	NZ7812	54°30·1′	0°47·3′W	FM	94
Landore	Swan	SS6595	51°38·5′	3°56·7′W	T	159
Landport	C of Port	SU6401	50°48·5′	1°5·1′W	T	196
Landport	E Susx	TQ4010	50°52·6′	0°0·2′W	T	198
Landrake	Corn	SX3760	50°25·3′	4°17·3′W	T	201
Landrake	Devon	SS9718	50°57·4′	3°27·6′W	X	181
Landrends	Corn	SX3284	50°38·1′	4°22·2′W	X	201
Landreyne	Corn	SX2876	50°33·7′	4°25·3′W	X	201
Landrick	Stir	NN7902	56°12·0′	3°56·6′W	X	57
Landrine	Corn	SW8652	50°20·0′	5°0·1′W	X	200,204
Landrion Point	Corn	SX0451	50°19·8′	4°44·9′W	X	200,204
Landrivick	Corn	SW7424	50°4·6′	5°9·2′W	X	204
Lands	Devon	SS8425	51°1·0′	3°38·8′W	X	181
Lands	D & G	NY0365	54°58·5′	3°30·5′W	X	84
Landsceugh	Cumbr	NY3546	54°48·5′	3°0·3′W	X	85
Landscove	Devon	SX7766	50°29·1′	3°43·7′W	T	202
Landsdale Ho	Lincs	SK9562	53°9·0′	0°34·4′W	X	121
Land's End	Corn	SW3425	50°4·2′	5°42·7′W	X	203
Lands End	W Berks	SU4483	51°32·9′	1°21·5′W	X	174
Landsend Barton	Devon	SS7400	50°47·4′	3°46·9′W	X	191
Landsend Fm	Devon	SS4901	50°47·6′	4°8·2′W	FM	191
Lands End Fm	Somer	ST4146	51°12·8′	2°50·3′W	FM	182
Land's End or St Just Aerodrome	Corn	SW3729	50°6·4′	5°40·3′W	X	203
Landsend Point	Essex	TQ8896	51°38·1′	0°43·4′E	X	168
Landsend Wood	Scot Bord	NT7864	55°52·4′	2°20·7′W	F	67
Lands Fm	Norf	TM2087	52°26·4′	1°14·6′E	FM	156
Landsfoot	Cumbr	NY4538	54°44·3′	2°50·8′W	X	90
Landshipping	Pemb	SN0111	51°46·0′	4°52·7′W	T	157,158
Landshipping Quay	Pemb	SN0010	51°45·4′	4°53·5′W	T	157,158
Landshire Br	Somer	ST7319	50°58·4′	2°22·7′W	X	183
Landshot Hill	Northum	NY9593	55°14·1′	2°4·3′W	H	81
Landshott	Northum	NY9493	55°14·1′	2°5·2′W	X	80
Land Side	Wigan	SJ6598	53°28·9′	2°31·2′W	X	109
Landsker Borderlands Trail	Carm	SN1723	51°52·8′	4°39·1′W	X	145,145
Landskill	Lancs	SD5345	53°54·2′	2°42·5′W	X	102
Landslip, The	I of W	SZ5878	50°36·2′	1°10·4′W	X	196
Landslip, The	Surrey	TQ1443	51°10·7′	0°21·8′W	X	187
Landslow Green	Tames	SJ9997	53°28·4′	2°0·5′W	T	109
Lands Point	Cumbr	SD3096	54°21·5′	3°4·2′W	X	96,97
Landspring Beck	Norf	TM4596	52°30·6′	1°37·0′E	W	134
Land Taing	Shetld	HU5274	60°27·1′	1°2·8′W	X	2,3
Landue	Corn	SX3479	50°35·5′	4°20·3′W	X	201
Landulph	Corn	SX4361	50°25·9′	4°12·3′W	T	201
Landulph Cross	Corn	SX4262	50°26·4′	4°13·1′W	X	201
Landvillas	Shetld	HU3515	59°55·4′	1°21·9′W	X	4
Landwade	Suff	TL6268	52°17·4′	0°22·9′E	T	154
Landward Geo	Orkney	HY6546	59°18·2′	2°36·4′W	X	5
Landward Taing	Shetld	HU6398	60°39·9′	0°50·3′W	X	1
Landwick Fm	Essex	TL9901	51°40·6′	0°53·1′E	FM	168
Land Yeo	N Som	ST4771	51°26·4′	2°45·4′W	W	171,172
Landyke Lane Fm	Leic	SK7424	52°48·7′	0°53·7′W	FM	129
Landymoors Fm	Northnts	SP7070	52°19·6′	0°58·0′W	FM	141
Landynod	Heref	SO6556	52°12·3′	2°30·3′W	X	149
Landywood	Staffs	SJ9906	52°39·3′	2°0·5′W	T	127,139
Lane	Corn	SW8260	50°24·2′	5°3·7′W	T	200
Lane	Devon	SS6735	51°6·2′	3°53·6′W	X	180

Lane	Kirk	SE1005	53°32·7′	1°50·5′W	X	110
Lane Acres Fm	Ches	SJ5649	53°2·4′	2°39·0′W	FM	117
Laneast	Corn	SX2283	50°37·4′	4°30·6′W	T	201
Laneast Downs	Corn	SX2384	50°38·0′	4°29·8′W	X	201
Lane Bottom	Brad	SE0535	53°48·9′	1°55·0′W	T	104
Lane Bottom	Lancs	SD8735	53°48·9′	2°11·4′W	T	103
Lane Bottom	N Yks	SE1358	54°1·3′	1°47·7′W	X	104
Lane Burn	E Ayr	NS5711	55°22·6′	4°15·0′W	W	71
Lanecroft	D & G	NX9070	55°1·0′	3°42·8′W	X	84
Lane End	Brad	SE0238	53°50·5′	1°57·8′W	T	104
Lane End	Bucks	SU8092	51°37·5′	0°50·3′W	T	175
Lane End	Ches	SJ4249	53°2·3′	2°51·5′W	X	117
Lane End	Corn	SW9761	50°25·1′	4°51·1′W	X	200
Lane-end	Corn	SX0369	50°29·5′	4°46·3′W	T	200
Lane End	Corn	SX2288	50°40·1′	4°30·8′W	X	190
Lane End	Cumbr	NY5368	55°0·5′	2°43·7′W	X	86
Lane End	Cumbr	NY6123	54°36·3′	2°35·8′W	X	91
Lane End	Cumbr	SD1093	54°19·7′	3°22·6′W	T	96
Lane End	Cumbr	SD2189	54°17·7′	3°12·4′W	X	96
Lane End	Derby	SK2951	53°3·6′	1°33·6′W	X	119
Lane End	Derby	SK4461	53°8·9′	1°20·1′W	T	120
Lane End	Devon	SS4300	50°46·9′	4°13·2′W	T	190
Lane End	Devon	SS6510	50°52·7′	3°54·8′W	X	191
Lane End	Devon	SX5382	50°37·4′	4°4·3′W	X	191,201
Lane End	Dorset	SY8492	50°43·9′	2°13·2′W	T	194
Lane End	Flint	SJ2863	53°9·8′	3°4·2′W	T	117
Lane End	Hants	SU5525	51°1·5′	1°12·6′W	T	185
Lane End	Hants	SU6729	51°3·6′	1°2·2′W	T	185,186
Lane End	Heref	SO6419	51°52·3′	2°31·0′W	T	162
Lane End	Heref	SO7445	52°6·4′	2°22·4′W	X	150
Lane End	I of W	SZ6587	50°41·0′	1°4·4′W	T	196
Lane End	Kent	TQ5671	51°25·2′	0°15·0′E	T	177
Lane End	Lancs	SD5165	54°5·0′	2°44·5′W	X	97
Lane End	Lancs	SD8747	53°55·4′	2°11·5′W	T	103
Lane End	Northum	NZ1887	55°10·9′	1°42·6′W	X	81
Lane End	N Yks	SE0452	53°58·1′	1°55·9′W	X	104
Lane End	N Yks	SE4397	54°22·2′	1°19·9′W	X	99
Lane End	Roch	SD8609	53°34·9′	2°12·3′W	X	109
Lane End	Sheff	SK3596	53°27·8′	1°28·0′W	T	110,111
Lane End	Shrops	SJ3624	52°48·8′	2°56·6′W	X	126
Lane-end	Staffs	SJ9261	53°9·0′	2°6·8′W	X	118
Lane End	Surrey	SU8441	51°10·0′	0°47·5′W	T	186
Lane End	Wilts	ST8145	51°12·5′	2°15·9′W	T	183
Lane End	Wrekin	SJ7222	52°47·9′	2°24·5′W	X	127
Lane End Common	E Susx	TQ4022	50°59·0′	0°0·1′E	X	198
Lane End Down	Hants	SU5526	51°2·1′	1°12·5′W	X	185
Lane End Fm	Beds	SP9527	51°56·2′	0°36·7′W	FM	165
Lane End Fm	Ches	SJ6265	53°11·1′	2°33·7′W	FM	118
Lane End Fm	Cumbr	SD4887	54°16·8′	2°47·5′W	FM	97
Lane End Fm	Devon	SS6328	51°2·3′	3°56·9′W	FM	180
Lane End Fm	Devon	ST1005	50°50·5′	3°16·3′W	FM	192,193
Lane End Fm	E Yorks	TA1535	53°48·1′	0°14·8′W	FM	107
Lane End Fm	Hants	SU5525	51°1·5′	1°12·6′W	FM	185
Lane End Fm	Leeds	SE2541	53°52·1′	1°36·8′W	FM	104
Lane End Fm	Monm	ST4597	51°40·4′	2°47·3′W	FM	171
Lane End Fm	N Yks	SE3048	53°55·9′	1°32·2′W	FM	104
Lane End Fm	Oxon	SU6195	51°39·3′	1°6·7′W	FM	164,165
Lane End Fm	Surrey	TQ0845	51°11·9′	0°26·9′W	FM	187
Lane End Fm	Worcs	SO7572	52°21·0′	2°21·6′W	FM	138
Lane End Ho	N Yks	SE7865	54°5·1′	2°19·8′W	X	98
Lane Ends	Ches	SJ7059	53°7·9′	2°26·5′W	T	118
Lane Ends	Ches	SJ9883	53°20·9′	2°1·4′W	T	109
Lane Ends	C of Stoke	SJ8754	53°5·2′	2°11·2′W	T	118
Lane Ends	Cumbr	SD3484	54°15·1′	3°0·4′W	T	96,97
Lane Ends	Cumbr	SD6691	54°19·1′	2°30·9′W	X	98
Lane Ends	Derby	SK2334	52°54·4′	1°39·1′W	T	128
Lane Ends	Derby	SK2448	53°2·0′	1°38·1′W	X	119
Lane Ends	Derby	SK3554	53°5·2′	1°28·2′W	T	119
Lane Ends	Lancs	SD6115	53°38·0′	2°35·0′W	T	109
Lane Ends	Lancs	SD6232	53°47·2′	2°34·2′W	X	102,103
Lane Ends	Lancs	SD6538	53°50·5′	2°31·5′W	X	102,103
Lane Ends	Lancs	SD7550	53°57·0′	2°22·4′W	T	103
Lane Ends	Lancs	SD7930	53°46·2′	2°18·7′W	T	103
Lane Ends	Leeds	SE2239	53°51·0′	1°39·5′W	T	104
Lane Ends	N Yks	SD9843	53°53·2′	2°1·4′W	T	103
Lane Ends	Stock	SJ9790	53°24·6′	2°2·3′W	T	109
Lane Ends Amenity Area	Lancs	SD4149	53°56·3′	2°53·5′W	X	102
Lanefield	Lancs	SD8441	53°52·1′	2°14·2′W	X	103
Lane Fm	Cumbr	SD5283	54°14·7′	2°43·8′W	FM	97
Lane Fm	Essex	TL8929	51°55·9′	0°45·3′E	FM	168
Lane Fm	Heref	SO2749	52°8·3′	3°3·6′W	FM	148
Lane Fm	Powys	SJ2417	52°45·2′	3°7·2′W	FM	126
Lane Fm	Powys	SJ3015	52°43·9′	3°1·8′W	FM	126
Lane Fm	Powys	SO1747	52°7·1′	3°12·3′W	FM	148
Lane Fm	Red & Cl	NZ7416	54°32·3′	0°51·0′W	FM	94
Lane Fm	Shrops	SJ3211	52°41·8′	3°0·0′W	FM	126
Lane Fm	Shrops	SJ6541	52°58·2′	2°30·9′W	FM	118
Lane Fm	Staffs	SJ9530	52°52·3′	2°4·1′W	FM	127
Lane Fm	Suff	TM1039	52°0·8′	1°4·0′E	FM	155,169
Lane Fm	Worcs	SO7780	52°25·3′	2°19·9′W	FM	138
Lane Fm	Wrex	SJ4637	52°55·9′	2°47·8′W	FM	126
Lane Fm, The	Powys	SO1244	52°5·5′	3°16·7′W	FM	148,161
Lanefoot	Cumbr	NY0615	54°31·5′	3°26·7′W	X	89
Lanefoot	Cumbr	NY0620	54°34·2′	3°26·8′W	X	89
Lane Foot	Cumbr	SD5094	54°20·6′	2°45·7′W	X	97
Lanefoot Fm	Cumbr	NY1326	54°37·5′	3°20·4′W	FM	89
Lanefoot Fm	Cumbr	NY2224	54°36·6′	3°12·0′W	FM	89,90
Lane Foot Fm	Lancs	SD5974	54°9·9′	2°37·3′W	FM	97
Lane Green	Staffs	SJ8803	52°37·7′	2°10·2′W	T	127,139
Laneham	Notts	SK8076	53°16·7′	0°47·6′W	T	121
Laneham Field Fm	Notts	SK7975	53°16·2′	0°48·5′W	FM	120,121
Lane Head	Cald	SD9932	53°47·3′	2°0·5′W	X	103
Lane Head	Ches	SJ9378	53°18·2′	2°5·9′W	X	118
Lanehead	Cumbr	NX9614	54°30·9′	3°36·0′W	X	89
Lane Head	Cumbr	NY2241	54°45·7′	3°12·3′W	X	85
Lanehead	Cumbr	NY3643	54°46·9′	2°59·3′W	X	85
Lane Head	Cumbr	NY3727	54°38·3′	2°58·1′W	X	90
Lane Head	Cumbr	NY3914	54°31·3′	2°56·1′W	X	90
Lanehead	Cumbr	NY5964	54°58·4′	2°38·0′W	X	86
Lane Head	Cumbr	NY6013	54°30·9′	2°36·7′W	X	91

Lane Head	Cumbr	SD3184	54°15·1′	3°3·1′W	X	96,97
Lane Head	Cumbr	SD5090	54°18·4′	2°45·7′W	X	97
Lane Head	Derby	SK1676	53°17·1′	1°45·2′W	T	119
Lanehead	Derby	SK3053	53°4·6′	1°32·7′W	X	119
Lanehead	Durham	NY8441	54°46·1′	2°14·5′W	T	86,87
Lane Head	Durham	NY9220	54°34·8′	2°7·0′W	X	91,92
Lane Head	Durham	NZ0449	54°50·4′	1°55·8′W	X	87
Lane Head	Durham	NZ0825	54°37·4′	1°52·1′W	X	92
Lane Head	Durham	NZ1211	54°29·9′	1°48·5′W	X	92
Lanehead	E Ayr	NS5510	55°22·0′	4°16·8′W	X	71
Lane Head	Kirk	SE1908	53°34·3′	1°42·4′W	T	110
Lane Head	Kirk	SE2012	53°36·5′	1°41·5′W	T	110
Lane Head	Lancs	SD5442	53°52·6′	2°41·6′W	X	102
Lane Head	Lancs	SD9141	53°52·2′	2°7·8′W	X	103
Lanehead	Northum	NY6859	54°55·7′	2°29·5′W	X	86,87
Lanehead	Northum	NY7957	54°54·7′	2°19·2′W	X	86,87
Lanehead	Northum	NY7985	55°9·8′	2°19·3′W	T	80
Lane Head	N Yks	SD9446	53°54·8′	2°5·1′W	X	103
Lane Head	N Yks	SD9563	54°4·0′	2°4·2′W	X	98
Lane Head	Pemb	SN0004	51°42·2′	4°53·3′W	T	157,158
Lanehead	Staffs	SJ9155	53°5·8′	2°7·7′W	X	118
Lanehead	Staffs	SK0548	53°2·0′	1°55·1′W	X	119
Lane Head	Wals	SJ9700	52°36·1′	2°2·3′W	T	127,139
Lane Head	Wigan	SJ6296	53°27·8′	2°33·9′W	T	109
Lane Head Fm	Durham	NY8520	54°34·7′	2°13·5′W	FM	91,92
Lane Head Fm	Heref	SO4439	52°3·0′	2°48·6′W	FM	149,161
Lane Head Fm	Northum	NU1702	55°19·0′	1°43·5′W	FM	81
Lane Head Fm	N Yks	SE1848	53°55·9′	1°43·1′W	FM	104
Lane Head Fm	Red & Cl	NZ7113	54°30·7′	0°53·8′W	FM	94
Lane Heads	Lancs	SD4339	53°50·9′	2°51·6′W	T	102
Lane Ho	Durham	NZ1330	54°40·1′	1°47·5′W	X	92
Lane Ho	E Yorks	TA1148	53°55·2′	0°18·2′W	X	107
Lane Ho	Lancs	SD5976	54°10·9′	2°37·3′W	X	97
Lane Ho	Northum	NY8769	55°1·2′	2°11·8′W	X	87
Lane Ho	Northum	NZ0871	55°2·3′	1°52·1′W	X	88
Lane Ho	N Yks	SD6968	54°6·7′	2°28·0′W	X	98
Lane Ho	N Yks	SD6971	54°8·3′	2°28·1′W	X	98
Lane Ho	N Yks	SE0246	53°54·9′	1°57·8′W	X	104
Lane Ho	N Yks	SE0884	54°15·3′	1°52·2′W	X	99
Lane Ho	N Yks	SE1885	54°15·9′	1°43·0′W	X	99
Lane Ho	N Yks	SE5293	54°20·0′	1°11·6′W	X	100
Lane Ho	Stock on T	NZ4413	54°30·9′	1°18·8′W	X	93
Lanehouse	Dorset	SY6578	50°36·3′	2°29·3′W	T	194
Lane House Fm	Powys	SO2156	52°12·0′	3°9·0′W	FM	148
Lanehurst	W Susx	TQ2518	50°57·0′	0°12·8′W	X	198
Lanelands	W Susx	TQ0129	51°3·3′	0°33·1′W	X	186,197
Lanemark	E Ayr	NS5811	55°22·6′	4°14·0′W	X	71
Lanercost	Cumbr	NY5563	54°57·8′	2°41·7′W	T	86
Lanercost Br	Cumbr	NY5563	54°57·8′	2°41·7′W	A	86
Lane Royds Park	Barns	SE3100	53°30·0′	1°31·5′W	X	110,111
Lanerton	Cumbr	NY5964	54°58·4′	2°38·0′W	X	86
Lanes	S Ayr	NX2695	55°13·4′	4°43·7′W	X	76
Lanescot	Corn	SX0855	50°22·1′	4°41·6′W	T	200
Lanes End	Bucks	SP9007	51°45·5′	0°41·4′W	T	165
Lanesend	Pemb	SN0706	51°43·4′	4°47·3′W	T	158
Lane's End	Shrops	SO6380	52°25·2′	2°32·2′W	T	138
Lanes End Fm	Warw	SP3036	52°1·5′	1°33·4′W	FM	151
Lanesfield	Wolv	SO9295	52°33·4′	2°6·7′W	T	139
Lanes Fm	Ches	SJ5160	53°8·3′	2°43·5′W	FM	117
Lanes Fm	Derby	SK4866	53°11·6′	1°16·5′W	FM	120
Lane's Fm	Essex	TL8011	51°46·3′	0°36·9′E	FM	168
Lane's Fm	Somer	ST2413	50°54·9′	3°4·5′W	FM	193
Lanes Fm	Wakf	SE4415	53°38·0′	1°19·7′W	FM	111
Lanes Foot	N Yks	SE1861	54°2·9′	1°43·1′W	X	99
Laneshaw Bridge	Lancs	SD9240	53°51·6′	2°6·9′W	T	103
Laneshaw Resr	N Yks	SD9441	53°52·2′	2°5·1′W	W	103
Laneside	D & G	NX9671	55°1·6′	3°37·2′W	X	84
Lane Side	Lancs	SD7546	53°54·8′	2°22·4′W	X	103
Lane Side	Lancs	SD7641	53°52·1′	2°21·5′W	X	103
Lane Side	Lancs	SD7822	53°41·9′	2°19·6′W	T	103
Lane Side	Lancs	SD7953	53°58·6′	2°18·8′W	X	103
Lane Side	Lancs	SD8445	53°54·3′	2°14·2′W	X	103
Lane Side	N Yks	SD7466	54°5·6′	2°23·4′W	X	98
Lane Side	N Yks	SD8055	53°59·7′	2°17·9′W	X	103
Laneside Fm	Derby	SK0188	53°23·6′	1°58·7′W	FM	110
Laneside Fm	Derby	SK1178	53°18·2′	1°49·7′W	FM	119
Laneside Fm	Lancs	SD7746	53°54·8′	2°20·6′W	FM	103
Laneskin Wood	Corn	SX1265	50°27·5′	4°38·5′W	F	200
Lane, The	Cumbr	NY6904	54°26·1′	2°28·3′W	X	91
Lane, The	D & G	NX4364	54°57·0′	4°26·7′W	W	83
Lane, The	Powys	SJ2012	52°42·2′	3°10·6′W	X	126
Lane, The	Staffs	SK0663	53°10·1′	1°54·2′W	X	119
Lane Top Fm	Lancs	SD7926	53°44·0′	2°18·7′W	FM	103
Lane Wood	Bucks	SU9898	51°40·6′	0°34·6′W	F	165,176
Laney Green	Staffs	SJ9606	52°39·3′	2°3·1′W	T	127,139
Lan-Farm	V of Glam	SS9269	51°24·8′	3°32·8′W	X	170
Lanfawr	Carm	SN5216	51°49·6′	4°8·5′W	X	159
Lan Fawr	Cered	SN6950	52°8·2′	3°54·5′W	H	146
Lan Fawr	Cered	SN8376	52°22·4′	3°42·7′W	X	135,136,147
Lan Fawr	Powys	SN9457	52°12·3′	3°32·7′W	X	147
Lan Fawr	Powys	SO2996	52°33·7′	3°2·4′W	H	137
Lanfine	E Ayr	NS5536	55°36·0′	4°17·7′W	X	71
Lanfine Home Fm	E Ayr	NS5436	55°36·0′	4°18·6′W	FM	70
Lan Fm	Brig	SS9389	51°34·0′	3°32·2′W	FM	170
Lan Fm	Carm	SN2920	51°51·4′	4°28·6′W	FM	145,159
Lan Fm	Carm	SN3512	51°47·2′	4°23·1′W	FM	159
Lan Fm	Carm	SN4634	51°59·2′	4°14·2′W	FM	146
Lan Fm	Rho Cyn Taf	ST1184	51°33·1′	3°16·6′W	FM	171
Lan Fraith	Powys	SN8772	52°20·3′	3°39·1′W	H	135,136,147
Lan-fraith	Powys	SO0374	52°21·6′	3°25·1′W	X	136,147
Lanfro	Carm	SN2914	51°48·2′	4°28·4′W	X	159
Langa	Arg & Bt	NR6724	55°27·5′	5°40·7′W	X	68
Langa	Shetld	HU3739	60°8·3′	1°19·5′W	X	4
Langabeare Barton	Devon	SS5501	50°47·7′	4°3·1′W	X	191
Langabeer	Devon	SX6496	50°45·1′	3°55·3′W	X	191
Langabeer Moor	Devon	SS5600	50°47·1′	4°2·2′W	X	191
Langacre Rhyne	Somer	ST3932	51°5·3′	2°51·9′W	W	182
Langadon Fm	Devon	SS3509	50°51·7′	4°20·3′W	FM	190
Langafater Lodge	D & G	NX1376	55°2·9′	4°55·2′W	X	76
Langaford	Devon	SX4199	50°46·4′	4°14·9′W	T	190

Langaford Moor	Devon	SS4100	50°46·9'	4°15·0'W	X	190
Langage	Devon	SX5654	50°22·3'	4°1·1'W	T	202
Langage	Devon	SX5756	50°23·4'	4°0·3'W	X	202
Langal	Highld	NM7069	56°45·6'	5°45·3'W	T	40
Langalbuinoch	Arg & Bt	NS0856	55°45·8'	5°3·2'W	X	63
Langal Burn	Highld	NM7070	56°46·2'	5°45·4'W	W	40
Langaller	Devon	SX8076	50°34·5'	3°41·3'W	X	191
Langaller	Somer	ST2626	51°2·0'	3°2·9'W	T	193
Langaller Fm	Somer	SS9125	51°1·1'	3°32·9'W	FM	181
Langa Mae	Orkney	HY6720	59°4·2'	2°34·1'W	X	5
Langamay	Orkney	HY7544	59°17·2'	2°25·8'W	X	5
Langamull	Arg & Bt	NM3853	56°36·0'	6°15·7'W	X	47
Langa Ness	Orkney	HY2626	59°7·1'	3°17·1'W	X	6
Lang Aoineadh	Arg & Bt	NR4879	55°56·5'	6°1·7'W	X	60,61
Langar	Notts	SK7234	52°54·2'	0°55·4'W	T	129
Langar Grange	Notts	SK7232	52°53·1'	0°55·4'W	X	129
Langar Lodge	Notts	SK7332	52°53·1'	0°54·5'W	X	129
Langarth	Corn	SW7745	50°16·0'	5°7·4'W	X	204
Langary Gate Fm	Lincs	TF3414	52°42·7'	0°0·6'W	FM	131
Langa Sgeir	N Eil	NG0084	57°45·0'	7°2·1'W	X	18
Langa Sgeir Mhòr	N Eil	NB4732	58°12·5'	6°17·9'W	X	8
Langass	N Eil	NF8365	57°34·1'	7°17·7'W	X	18
Langa Taing	Orkney	ND4695	58°50·6'	2°55·7'W	X	7
Langaton	Corn	SS2700	50°46·7'	4°26·9'W	X	190
Langaton	Devon	SS6525	51°0·7'	3°55·1'W	X	180
Langaton Point	Highld	ND3479	58°41·9'	3°7·9'W	X	7,12
Langay	N Eil	NG0181	57°43·4'	7°0·9'W	X	18
Lang Ayre	Shetld	HU2885	60°33·1'	1°28·9'W	X	3
Langbank	E Dunb	NS5673	55°56·0'	4°17·9'W	X	64
Langbank	Renf	NS3873	55°55·6'	4°35·1'W	T	63
Langbank	Stir	NN8205	56°13·6'	3°53·8'W	X	57
Langbar	N Yks	SE0951	53°57·5'	1°51·4'W	T	104
Langbar Moor	N Yks	SE1152	53°58·1'	1°49·5'W	X	104
Langbaurgh	N Yks	NZ5511	54°29·7'	1°8·6'W	T	93
Langbaurgh Ridge	N Yks	NZ5512	54°30·3'	1°8·6'W	X	93
Langber	N Yks	SD6870	54°7·7'	2°29·0'W	X	98
Langber	N Yks	SD9049	53°56·5'	2°8·7'W	X	103
Langbigging	Orkney	HY7644	59°17·2'	2°24·8'W	X	5
Langbourne	Dorset	ST9008	50°52·5'	2°8·1'W	X	195
Langbridge	I of W	SZ5585	50°40·0'	1°12·9'W	X	196
Langbridge Fm	Bucks	SP7634	52°0·2'	0°53·2'W	FM	152,165
Langbrook	Devon	SX6252	50°21·3'	3°56·0'W	X	202
Lang Burn	Scot Bord	NT5205	55°20·5'	2°45·0'W	W	79
Langburnshiels	Scot Bord	NT5304	55°19·9'	2°44·0'W	X	79
Lang Cleuch	D & G	NS8708	55°21·4'	3°46·5'W	X	71,78
Lang Cleuch	S Lanak	NS9110	55°22·6'	3°42·8'W	X	71,78
Langcliffe	N Yks	SD8265	54°5·1'	2°16·1'W	T	98
Langcliffe	N Yks	SD9871	54°8·3'	2°1·4'W	X	98
Langcliffe Place	N Yks	SD8165	54°5·1'	2°17·0'W	X	98
Lang Clodie Loch	Shetld	HU3187	60°34·2'	1°25·6'W	W	1
Lang Clodie Wick	Shetld	HU3088	60°34·7'	1°26·7'W	W	1
Lang Combe	Somer	SS8742	51°10·2'	3°36·6'W	X	181
Langcombe Head	Devon	SX6166	50°28·9'	3°57·2'W	W	202
Langcombe Hill	Devon	SX6165	50°28·3'	3°57·2'W	H	202
Lang Craig	Angus	NO7048	56°37·6'	2°28·9'W	X	54
Langcraig	S Ayr	NS4132	55°33·6'	4°30·8'W	X	70
Lang Craigs	W Dunb	NS4375	55°57·3'	4°30·4'W	X	64
Langdale	Cumbr	NY6502	54°25·0'	2°31·9'W	X	91
Langdale	Devon	SX8390	50°42·1'	3°39·0'W	X	191
Lang Dale	E Yorks	TA0476	54°10·4'	0°24·0'W	X	101
Langdale	Highld	NC6944	58°22·2'	4°13·9'W	X	10
Langdale	N Yks	NZ1909	54°28·8'	1°42·0'W	X	92
Langdale Burn	Highld	NC6744	58°22·1'	4°15·9'W	W	10
Langdale Combe	Cumbr	NY2608	54°28·0'	3°8·1'W	X	89,90
Langdale End	N Yks	SE9391	54°18·6'	0°33·8'W	X	94,101
Langdale Fell	Cumbr	NY2706	54°26·9'	3°7·1'W	X	89,90
Langdale Fell	Cumbr	NY6500	54°23·9'	2°31·9'W	H	91
Langdale Forest	N Yks	SE9095	54°20·8'	0°36·5'W	F	94,101
Langdale Knott	Cumbr	NY6602	54°25·0'	2°31·0'W	H	91
Langdale Pikes	Cumbr	NY2707	54°27·4'	3°7·1'W	H	89,90
Langdale Rigg End	N Yks	SE9294	54°20·2'	0°34·7'W	X	94,101
Langdales	N Lanak	NS7971	55°55·3'	3°55·7'W	X	64
Langdales	Scot Bord	NT7022	55°29·7'	2°28·1'W	X	74
Langden Br	Lancs	SD6549	53°56·4'	2°31·6'W	X	102,103
Langden Brook	Lancs	SD6250	53°56·9'	2°34·3'W	W	102,103
Langden Castle	Lancs	SD6050	53°56·9'	2°36·2'W	X	102,103
Langden Head	Lancs	SD5851	53°57·4'	2°38·0'W	X	102
Langdike Moss	N Ayr	NS2757	55°46·8'	4°45·1'W	X	63
Langdon	Corn	SX2092	50°42·2'	4°32·6'W	X	190
Langdon	Devon	SS3600	50°46·8'	4°19·2'W	X	190
Langdon	Devon	SX7282	50°37·7'	3°48·2'W	X	191
Langdon	Kent	TR0331	51°2·8'	0°54·2'E	X	189
Langdon	Pemb	SN0907	51°44·0'	4°45·6'W	X	158
Langdon Abbey	Kent	TR3246	51°10·2'	1°19·5'E	X	179
Langdon Barton	Devon	SX9379	50°36·3'	3°30·3'W	X	192
Langdon Bay	Kent	TR3442	51°8·0'	1°21·1'E	W	179
Langdon Beck	Durham	NY8531	54°40·7'	2°13·5'W	T	91,92
Langdon Beck	Durham	NY8532	54°41·2'	2°13·5'W	W	91,92
Langdon Common	Durham	NY8433	54°41·8'	2°14·5'W	X	91,92
Langdon Court	Kent	TR0461	51°18·9'	0°56·0'E	X	178,179
Langdon Cross	Corn	SX3089	50°40·8'	4°24·0'W	X	190
Langdon Fell	Durham	NY8633	54°41·8'	2°12·6'W	X	91,92
Langdon Fm	Corn	SX3091	50°41·9'	4°24·1'W	FM	190
Langdon Fm	Dorset	ST5001	50°48·6'	2°42·2'W	FM	194
Langdon Hall Fm	Thurr	TQ6786	51°33·1'	0°24·9'E	FM	177,178
Langdon Head	Durham	NY8534	54°42·3'	2°13·5'W	X	91,92
Langdon Hill	Dorset	SY4192	50°43·7'	2°49·8'W	H	193
Langdon Hill	Oxon	SU5483	51°32·8'	1°12·9'W	X	174
Langdon Hills	Essex	TQ6787	51°33·7'	0°25·0'E	T	177,178
Langdon Ho	Devon	SX9478	50°35·8'	3°29·5'W	X	192
Langdon's Way	Somer	SS8839	51°8·6'	3°35·7'W	X	181
Langdown	Devon	SX6796	50°45·1'	3°52·7'W	X	191
Langdown	Hants	SU4206	50°51·3'	1°23·8'W	T	196
Lang Down	Oxon	SU3782	51°32·4'	1°27·6'W	X	174
Langdyke	D & G	NY0971	55°1·8'	3°25·0'W	X	85
Langdyke	D & G	NY1976	55°4·6'	3°15·7'W	X	85
Langdyke	E Ayr	NS4942	55°39·1'	4°23·6'W	X	70
Langdyke	Fife	NO3304	56°13·7'	3°4·4'W	X	59
Langdyke	Northum	NT9945	55°42·2'	2°0·5'W	X	75
Langenhoe	Essex	TM0018	51°49·7'	0°54·5'E	T	168
Langenhoe Hall	Essex	TM0117	51°49·1'	0°55·4'E	X	168
Langenhoe Marsh	Essex	TM0417	51°49·1'	0°58·0'E	X	168
Langergill	Highld	ND1855	58°28·8'	3°23·9'W	X	11,12
Langerstone Point	Devon	SX7835	50°12·4'	3°42·2'W	X	202
Langerth	Corn	SW9752	50°20·2'	4°50·8'W	FM	200,204
Langerton Fm	N Yks	SD9960	54°2·4'	2°0·5'W	FM	98
Langerton Hill	N Yks	SE0462	54°3·5'	1°55·9'W	H	98
Langfaulds Fm	Fife	NT0093	56°7·4'	3°36·1'W	FM	58
Langfauld Wood	D & G	NY3586	55°10·1'	3°0·8'W	F	79
Langfield Common	Cald	SD9521	53°41·4'	2°4·1'W	X	103
Langfield Copse	Wilts	SU2563	51°22·2'	1°38·1'W	F	174
Langford	Beds	TL1840	52°3·0'	0°16·4'W	T	153
Langford	Corn	SS2709	50°51·5'	4°27·1'W	X	190
Langford	Cumbr	NY7315	54°32·0'	2°24·6'W	X	91
Langford	Devon	SS7201	50°47·9'	3°48·6'W	X	191
Langford	Devon	ST0202	50°48·8'	3°23·1'W	T	192
Langford	Devon	SX9097	50°46·0'	3°33·2'W	T	192
Langford	Essex	TL8309	51°45·2'	0°39·5'E	T	168
Langford	Norf	TL8396	52°32·1'	0°42·3'E	X	144
Langford	Notts	SK8258	53°7·0'	0°46·1'W	T	121
Langford	Oxon	SP2402	51°43·2'	1°38·8'W	T	163
Langford	Somer	ST2026	51°1·9'	3°8·1'W	T	193
Langford Barton	Corn	SS2301	50°47·1'	4°30·3'W	X	190
Langford Barton	Devon	SX6956	50°23·6'	3°50·2'W	X	202
Langford Br	Devon	ST1702	50°48·9'	3°10·3'W	X	192,193
Langford Br	Devon	SX8769	50°30·8'	3°35·3'W	X	202
Langford Br	Essex	TL5501	51°41·4'	0°14·9'E	X	167
Langford Bridge Fm	Essex	TL5500	51°40·9'	0°14·9'E	FM	167
Langford Brook	Oxon	SP2301	51°42·7'	1°39·6'W	W	163
Langford Budville	Somer	ST1122	50°59·7'	3°15·7'W	T	181,193
Langford Court	Devon	ST0302	50°48·8'	3°22·2'W	X	192
Langford Court	N Som	ST4560	51°20·4'	2°47·0'W	X	172,182
Langford Downs Fm	Oxon	SP2203	51°43·7'	1°40·5'W	FM	163
Langford Fm	Ches	SJ7074	53°16·0'	2°26·6'W	FM	118
Langford Fm	Devon	SX4675	50°33·5'	4°10·1'W	FM	201
Langford Fm	Devon	SX7558	50°24·7'	3°45·2'W	FM	202
Langford Fm	Northnts	SP6549	52°8·4'	1°2·6'W	FM	152
Langford Fm	W Susx	SU8410	50°53·2'	0°48·0'W	FM	197
Langford Green	Devon	ST0302	50°48·8'	3°22·2'W	T	192
Langford Green	N Som	ST4759	51°19·9'	2°45·3'W	T	172,182
Langford Grounds	N Som	ST3567	51°24·1'	2°55·7'W	X	171,182
Langford Grove	Essex	TL8410	51°45·7'	0°40·4'E	X	168
Langford Hall	Essex	TM0232	51°57·2'	0°56·8'E	X	168
Langford Hall	Notts	SK8257	53°6·5'	0°46·1'W	X	121
Langford Heathfield	Somer	ST1023	51°0·2'	3°16·6'W	X	181,193
Langford Hele	Corn	SS2201	50°47·1'	4°31·1'W	X	190
Langford Ho	N Som	ST4560	51°20·4'	2°47·0'W	X	172,182
Langford Ho	Oxon	SP2201	51°42·7'	1°40·5'W	X	163
Langford Lane	Oxon	SP5720	51°52·8'	1°9·9'W	X	164
Langford Manor	Somer	ST3522	50°59·9'	2°55·2'W	X	193
Langford Moor Fm	Notts	SK8456	53°5·9'	0°44·3'W	FM	121
Langford Park	Essex	TL8409	51°45·2'	0°40·3'E	X	168
Langford Park Fm	Oxon	SP5821	51°53·3'	1°9·0'W	FM	164
Langgadlie Hill	Aberd	NJ5113	57°12·6'	2°48·2'W	H	37
Lang Geo	Orkney	ND1899	58°52·5'	3°24·8'W	X	7
Lang Geo	Orkney	ND2392	58°48·8'	3°19·5'W	X	7
Lang Gill	S Lanak	NT0428	55°32·4'	3°30·8'W	W	72
Langhale Ho	Norf	TM3096	52°31·0'	1°23·8'E	X	134
Langham	Devon	SS5511	50°53·1'	4°3·3'W	X	191
Langham	Dorset	ST7725	51°1·7'	2°19·3'W	T	183
Langham	Essex	TM0231	51°56·7'	0°56·7'E	T	168
Langham	Norf	TG0041	52°56·0'	0°59·0'E	T	133
Langham	Rut	SK8411	52°41·6'	0°45·0'W	T	130
Langham	Somer	SS9040	51°9·2'	3°34·0'W	X	181
Langham	Somer	ST3210	50°53·4'	2°57·6'W	T	193
Langham	Suff	TL9769	52°17·3'	0°53·7'E	T	155
Langham Br	Suff	TM3758	52°10·4'	1°28·4'E	X	156
Langham Fm	Lincs	TF1093	53°25·6'	0°20·3'W	FM	113
Langham Fm	Lincs	TF5374	53°14·7'	0°18·0'E	FM	122
Langham Fm	Somer	SS9836	51°7·1'	3°27·1'W	FM	181
Langham Glass	Norf	TG0041	52°56·0'	0°59·0'E	X	133
Langham Hall	Essex	TM0333	51°57·7'	0°57·7'E	X	168
Langham Hill	Somer	SS9735	51°6·5'	3°27·9'W	X	181
Langham Hills	Suff	TL9669	52°17·3'	0°52·8'E	X	155
Langham Lake	Devon	SS5725	51°0·6'	4°1·9'W	W	180
Langham Lodge	Essex	TM0129	51°55·6'	0°55·8'E	X	168
Langham Lodge	Norf	TG0041	52°56·0'	0°59·0'E	X	133
Langham Lodge	Rut	SK8511	52°41·6'	0°44·1'W	X	130
Langham Park Fm	Kent	TR1751	51°13·2'	1°6·8'E	FM	179,189
Langhat Ditch	Oxon	SP2603	51°43·7'	1°37·0'W	W	163
Langhaugh	Angus	NO5662	56°45·1'	2°42·7'W	X	44
Langhaugh	Scot Bord	NT2031	55°34·2'	3°15·7'W	T	73
Langhaugh Hill	Scot Bord	NT2030	55°33·7'	3°15·7'W	H	73
Lang Head	Shetld	HU3070	60°25·0'	1°26·8'W	X	3
Langhill	D & G	NY1480	55°6·7'	3°20·5'W	X	78
Langhill	Falk	NS7684	56°2·2'	3°59·0'W	X	57,64
Langhill	Inverc	NS2172	55°54·7'	4°51·4'W	X	63
Lang Hill	N Ayr	NS2561	55°48·9'	4°47·1'W	H	63
Lang Hill	Orkney	HY4806	58°56·6'	2°53·7'W	X	6,7
Lang Hill	Shetld	HU2757	60°18·0'	1°30·2'W	H	3
Langhill Fm	Midlo	NT2664	55°52·1'	3°10·5'W	FM	66
Lang Hillock	Moray	NJ3823	57°17·9'	3°1·3'W	H	37
Langhill Plantn	N Yks	SE8064	54°4·2'	0°46·2'W	F	100
Langhill Wood	N Yks	SE8165	54°4·7'	0°45·3'W	F	100
Langho	Lancs	SD7034	53°48·3'	2°26·9'W	T	103
Lang Hoevdi	Shetld	HT9737	60°7·3'	2°2·7'W	X	4
Langholm	Arg & Bt	NR7110	55°20·1'	5°36·2'W	X	68
Langholm	D & G	NY3684	55°9·0'	2°59·8'W	T	79
Langholm	E Ayr	NS5021	55°27·8'	4°21·9'W	X	70
Langholm	S Ayr	NS3632	55°33·5'	4°35·6'W	X	70
Lang Holm	Shetld	HP5606	60°44·3'	0°57·9'W	X	1
Langholm	S Lanak	NS9832	55°34·5'	3°36·6'W	X	72
Langholme	Lancs	SD7034	53°48·3'	2°26·9'W	X	103
Langholme	N Lincs	SK7597	53°28·1'	0°51·8'W	T	112
Langholme Fm	N Lincs	SK7598	53°28·6'	0°51·8'W	FM	112
Langhope	Northum	NY8864	54°58·5'	2°10·8'W	X	87
Langhope	Scot Bord	NT4220	55°28·5'	2°54·6'W	T	73
Langhope Burn	Scot Bord	NT4119	55°28·0'	2°55·6'W	W	79
Langhope Height	Scot Bord	NT3800	55°17·7'	2°58·2'W	H	79
Langhope Rig	Scot Bord	NT4019	55°27·9'	2°56·5'W	X	79
Langhouse (Hotel)	Inverc	NS2171	55°54·2'	4°51·4'W	X	63
Lang How	Cumbr	NY3106	54°26·9'	3°3·4'W	X	90
Langhowe Pike	Cumbr	NY5213	54°30·8'	2°44·1'W	H	90
Lang Hurst	Durham	NY8326	54°38·0'	2°15·4'W	X	91,92
Langhurst	Surrey	TQ4249	51°13·6'	0°2·4'E	X	187
Langhurst	W Susx	TQ1735	51°6·4'	0°19·3'W	X	187
Langhurst	W Susx	TQ2238	51°7·9'	0°15·0'W	X	187
Langhurst Fm	W Susx	SU9825	51°1·2'	0°35·8'W	FM	186,197
Langhurst Ho	Surrey	SU9435	51°6·6'	0°39·0'W	X	186
Langhurst Manor	Surrey	SU9435	51°6·6'	0°39·0'W	X	186
Langie Geos	Orkney	HY5236	59°12·7'	2°50·0'W	X	5
Langi Fea	Orkney	HY2501	58°53·7'	3°17·6'W	X	6,7
Langi Geo	Orkney	ND2489	58°47·2'	3°18·4'W	X	7
Langknowe	D & G	NS8702	55°18·2'	3°46·4'W	X	78
Langlanburn	Moray	NJ4958	57°36·8'	2°50·8'W	X	28,29
Langland	Devon	SS7709	50°52·3'	3°44·5'W	X	191
Langland	Swan	SS6087	51°34·1'	4°0·8'W	T	159
Langland Bay	Swan	SS6087	51°34·1'	4°0·8'W	W	159
Langlands	Angus	NO5651	56°39·2'	2°42·6'W	X	54
Langlands	D & G	NX6552	54°50·9'	4°5·7'W	X	83,84
Langlands	Essex	TL5814	51°48·4'	0°17·9'E	X	167
Langlands	Falk	NS8285	56°2·9'	3°53·2'W	X	57,65
Langlands	N Ayr	NS3155	55°45·8'	4°41·2'W	X	63
Langlands	N Yks	SE3290	54°18·5'	1°30·1'W	X	99
Langlands	S Ayr	NS3829	55°31·9'	4°33·6'W	X	70
Langlands	S Ayr	NS4226	55°30·4'	4°29·7'W	X	70
Langlands	S Lanak	NS6350	55°43·7'	4°10·5'W	X	64
Langlands Fm	Devon	ST0511	50°53·7'	3°20·7'W	FM	192
Langlands Fm	N Ayr	NS3842	55°38·9'	4°34·0'W	FM	63,70
Langlands Fm	Somer	ST3939	51°9·1'	2°51·9'W	FM	182
Langlawhill	Scot Bord	NT0938	55°37·9'	3°26·3'W	X	72
Langleas	Fife	NT0187	56°4·2'	3°35·0'W	X	65
Langlee	E Renf	NS5151	55°44·0'	4°21·9'W	X	64
Langlee	Northum	NT9623	55°30·3'	2°3·4'W	X	74,75
Langlee	Scot Bord	NT5135	55°36·6'	2°46·2'W	T	73
Langlee	Scot Bord	NT6417	55°27·0'	2°33·7'W	X	80
Langlee Crags	Northum	NT9621	55°29·2'	2°3·4'W	H	74,75
Langleeford	Northum	NT9421	55°29·2'	2°5·3'W	X	74,75
Langleeford Hope	Northum	NT9320	55°28·7'	2°6·2'W	X	74,75
Langlee Mains	Scot Bord	NT5136	55°37·2'	2°46·2'W	T	73
Langlees	Falk	NS8982	56°1·3'	3°46·4'W	T	65
Langlees	Fife	NT0688	56°4·8'	3°30·2'W	X	65
Langlees Fm	S Lanak	NT0237	55°37·3'	3°32·9'W	FM	72
Langlees Ho	S Lanak	NT0237	55°37·3'	3°32·9'W	X	72
Langleigh	Devon	SS5146	51°11·9'	4°7·6'W	X	180
Langley	Ches	SJ9471	53°14·4'	2°5·0'W	T	118
Langley	Cumbr	SD0991	54°18·6'	3°23·5'W	X	96
Langley	Derby	SK4446	53°0·8'	1°20·2'W	T	129
Langley	Devon	SS7319	50°57·6'	3°48·1'W	X	180
Langley	Devon	SS9109	50°52·4'	3°32·6'W	X	192
Langley	Devon	SX7991	50°42·6'	3°42·4'W	X	191
Langley	Durham	NZ2046	54°48·8'	1°40·9'W	X	88
Langley	Essex	TL4434	51°59·4'	0°6·2'E	T	154
Langley	Glos	SP0028	51°57·3'	1°59·6'W	T	150,163
Langley	Hants	SU4400	50°48·1'	1°22·2'W	T	196
Langley	Herts	TL2122	51°53·2'	0°14·1'W	T	166
Langley	Kent	TQ8151	51°14·0'	0°36·0'E	T	188
Langley	Kent	TQ8940	51°7·9'	0°42·5'E	X	189
Langley	Moray	NJ5156	57°35·7'	2°48·7'W	X	29
Langley	Northum	NY8261	54°56·8'	2°16·4'W	T	86,87
Langley	Oxon	SP3015	51°50·2'	1°33·5'W	T	164
Langley	Roch	SD8606	53°33·3'	2°12·3'W	T	109
Langley	Sand	SO9988	52°29·6'	2°0·5'W	T	139
Langley	Shrops	SO4880	52°25·2'	2°45·5'W	X	137,138
Langley	Shrops	SO5879	52°24·7'	2°36·7'W	X	137,138
Langley	Slough	TQ0079	51°30·3'	0°33·2'W	T	176
Langley	Somer	ST0828	51°2·9'	3°18·4'W	T	181
Langley	Surrey	SU8029	51°3·5'	0°51·1'W	T	186,197
Langley	Warw	SP1962	52°15·6'	1°42·9'W	T	151
Langley Barton	Devon	SS5624	51°0·1'	4°2·8'W	X	180
Langley Beck	Durham	NZ0822	54°35·8'	1°52·1'W	W	92
Langley Beck	Durham	NZ1419	54°34·2'	1°46·6'W	W	92
Langley Brook	Warw	SP1697	52°34·5'	1°45·4'W	W	139
Langley Burn	Cumbr	NY5180	55°7·0'	2°45·7'W	W	79
Langley Burrell	Wilts	ST9375	51°28·7'	2°5·7'W	T	173
Langleybury	Herts	TL0700	51°41·5'	0°26·7'W	T	166
Langley Castle (Hotel)	Northum	NY8362	54°57·4'	2°15·5'W	A	86,87
Langley Chapel	Shrops	SJ5300	52°36·0'	2°41·2'W	A	126
Langley Common	Derby	SK2937	52°56·0'	1°33·7'W	T	128
Langley Common	Wok	SU7666	51°23·5'	0°54·1'W	T	175
Langley Corner	Bucks	TQ0184	51°33·0'	0°32·2'W	T	176
Langley Court	W Susx	SU8128	51°3·0'	0°50·3'W	X	186,197
Langley Cross	Devon	SS5724	51°0·1'	4°1·9'W	X	180
Langleydale Common	Durham	NZ0424	54°36·9'	1°55·9'W	X	92
Langley Fm	Bucks	SU9097	51°40·1'	0°41·5'W	FM	165
Langley Fm	Oxon	SP2915	51°50·2'	1°34·4'W	FM	164
Langley Fm	Warw	SP1857	52°12·9'	1°43·8'W	FM	151
Langley Fm	W Berks	SU4976	51°29·1'	1°17·3'W	FM	174
Langley Gate Fm	Wilts	ST9377	51°29·7'	2°5·7'W	FM	173
Langley Gorse	Birm	SP1494	52°32·9'	1°47·2'W	X	139
Langley Green	Derby	SK2738	52°56·6'	1°35·5'W	T	128
Langley Green	Essex	TL8721	51°51·6'	0°43·3'E	T	168
Langley Green	Norf	TG3503	52°34·7'	1°28·5'E	X	134
Langley Green	Sand	SO9987	52°29·1'	2°0·5'W	T	139
Langley Green	Warw	SP1962	52°15·6'	1°42·9'W	T	151
Langley Green	W Susx	TQ2638	51°7·9'	0°11·6'W	T	187
Langley Hall	Birm	SP1595	52°33·4'	1°46·3'W	X	139
Langley Hall	Derby	SK2839	52°57·1'	1°34·6'W	X	128
Langley Hall	Durham	NZ2146	54°48·8'	1°40·0'W	A	88
Langley Hall	Oxon	SU6396	51°39·8'	1°5·0'W	X	164,165
Langley Hall	Shrops	SJ5300	52°36·0'	2°41·2'W	X	126
Langley Hall Fm	Durham	NZ2440	54°45·5'	1°37·2'W	FM	88
Langley Hall Fm	Staffs	SO8696	52°33·9'	2°12·0'W	FM	139
Langley Heath	Kent	TQ8151	51°14·0'	0°36·0'E	T	188
Langley Hill	Glos	SP0029	51°57·8'	1°59·6'W	H	150,163
Langley Hill Fm	Glos	SP0028	51°57·3'	1°59·6'W	FM	150,163
Langleyhill Fm	Herts	TL2122	51°53·2'	0°14·1'W	FM	166
Langley Ho	Wilts	ST9275	51°28·7'	2°6·5'W	X	173
Langley Lawn	Essex	TL4234	51°59·4'	0°4·5'E	X	154
Langley Lawn Fm	Staffs	SJ8406	52°39·3'	2°13·8'W	FM	127

Langley Lodge	Hants	SU3610	50°53·5′	1°28·9′W	X	196
Langley Lodge	Kent	TQ8150	51°13·5′	0°35·9′E	X	188
Langley Lodge Fm	Herts	TL0601	51°42·1′	0°27·6′W	FM	166
Langley Marsh	Somer	ST0729	51°3·4′	3°19·2′W	T	181
Langley Marshes	Norf	TG3702	52°34·1′	1°30·2′E	X	134
Langley Marshes	Norf	TG4604	52°34·9′	1°38·3′E	X	134
Langley Mill	Derby	SK4447	53°1·3′	1°20·2′W	T	129
Langley Mill Fm	Birm	SP1597	52°34·5′	1°46·3′W	FM	139
Langley Moor	Durham	NZ1850	54°50·9′	1°42·8′W	X	88
Langley Moor	Durham	NZ2540	54°45·5′	1°36·3′W	T	88
Langley Park	Angus	NO6860	56°44·1′	2°30·9′W	X	45
Langley Park	Bucks	TQ0181	51°31·4′	0°32·3′W	X	176
Langley Park	Cumbr	SD0992	54°19·2′	3°23·5′W	X	96
Langley Park	Durham	NZ2144	54°47·7′	1°40·0′W	T	88
Langley Park Fm	Kent	TQ7951	51°14·0′	0°34·2′E	FM	188
Langley Priory	Leic	SK4323	52°48·4′	1°21·3′W	A	129
Langleys	Aberd	NJ8657	57°36·4′	2°13·6′W	X	30
Langleys	Aberd	NJ9443	57°28·9′	2°5·5′W	X	30
Langleys	Essex	TL6320	51°51·5′	0°22·4′E	X	167
Langleys	Essex	TL6913	51°47·6′	0°27·4′E	A	167
Langley School	Norf	TG3500	52°33·0′	1°28·4′E	X	134
Langley's Fm	Essex	TL6611	51°46·6′	0°24·8′E	FM	167
Langleys Fm	Wilts	ST9788	51°35·7′	2°2·2′W	FM	173
Langley Street	Norf	TG3601	52°33·6′	1°29·3′E	T	134
Langley Vale	Surrey	TQ2157	51°18·2′	0°15·5′W	T	187
Langley West Ho	Durham	NZ1946	54°48·8′	1°41·8′W	X	88
Langley Wood	Cambs	TL6042	52°3·4′	0°20·4′E	F	154
Langley Wood	Hants	SU3509	50°53·0′	1°29·8′W	F	196
Langley Wood	Suff	TL9448	52°6·0′	0°50·4′E	F	155
Langley Wood	W Berks	SU4876	51°29·1′	1°18·1′W	F	174
Langley Wood	Wilts	SU2220	50°59·0′	1°40·8′W	F	184
Langloan	N Lanak	NS7264	55°51·4′	4°2·3′W	T	64
Lang Loch	Shetld	HU2658	60°18·6′	1°31·3′W	W	3
Langloch	S Lanak	NS9042	55°39·8′	3°44·5′W	X	71,72
Lang Lochs	Shetld	HU4238	60°7·7′	1°14·1′W	W	4
Langlogie	Pth & Kin	NO3145	56°35·8′	3°7·0′W	X	53
Langmead	Devon	SS6302	50°48·3′	3°56·3′W	X	191
Langmead	Somer	ST3633	51°5·8′	2°54·5′W	X	182
Langmere	Norf	TM1881	52°23·2′	1°12·6′E	X	156
Langmere Boxes	Norf	TL9183	52°24·9′	0°48·9′E	X	144
Langmere Fm	Norf	TG2419	52°43·6′	1°19·4′E	FM	133,134
Langmere Hill	Norf	TL9183	52°24·9′	0°48·9′E	X	144
Lang Moor	Somer	ST3535	51°6·9′	2°55·3′W	X	182
Langmuirhead Fm	N Lanak	NS6569	55°54·0′	4°9·1′W	FM	64
Langmyre Mains	D & G	NX8796	55°15·0′	3°46·2′W	X	78
Langness	I of M	SC2866	54°3·9′	4°37·3′W	X	95
Langness Point	I of M	SC2765	54°3·4′	4°38·2′W	X	95
Langney	E Susx	TQ6202	50°47·9′	0°18·3′E	T	199
Langney Point	E Susx	TQ6401	50°47·3′	0°20·0′E	X	199
Lan Goch	Powys	SN9156	52°11·7′	3°35·3′W	X	147
Langold	Notts	SK5887	53°22·8′	1°7·3′W	T	111,120
Langold Country Park	Notts	SK5786	53°22·3′	1°8·2′W	X	111,120
Langold Fm	Roth	SK5786	53°22·3′	1°8·2′W	FM	111,120
Langold Lake	Notts	SK5786	53°22·3′	1°8·2′W	W	111,120
Langore	Corn	SX2986	50°39·2′	4°24·8′W	T	201
Langot Lane	Staffs	SJ7631	52°52·8′	2°21·0′W	X	127
Langport	Somer	ST4226	51°2·1′	2°49·2′W	T	193
Langracleit	N Eil	NG1498	57°53·1′	6°49·0′W	H	14
Langraw	Fife	NO4913	56°18·7′	2°49·0′W	X	59
Langraw	Scot Bord	NT5811	55°23·7′	2°39·4′W	X	80
Langrick	Lincs	TF2648	53°1·1′	0°6·9′W	T	131
Langrick Bridge	Lincs	TF2647	53°0·6′	0°6·9′W	T	131
Langrick Grange	Lincs	TF2648	53°1·1′	0°6·9′W	X	131
Langridge	Bath & NE Somer	ST7469	51°25·4′	2°22·0′W	T	172
Langridge	Devon	SS5722	50°59·0′	4°1·9′W	X	180
Langridge	Devon	SX7896	50°45·3′	3°43·4′W	X	191
Langridge	Essex	TL3804	51°43·3′	0°0·3′E	X	166
Langridge	Somer	SS9024	51°0·5′	3°33·7′W	X	181
Langridgeford	Devon	SS5722	50°59·0′	4°1·9′W	T	180
Langridge Ho	Bath & NE Somer	ST7369	51°25·4′	2°22·9′W	X	172
Langridge Wood	Somer	ST0137	51°7·7′	3°24·5′W	F	181
Langrig	Scot Bord	NT8045	55°42·1′	2°18·7′W	X	74
Lang Rig	Scot Bord	NY3399	55°17·1′	3°2·9′W	X	79
Langrigg	Cumbr	NY1645	54°47·8′	3°18·0′W	T	85
Langrigg	Cumbr	NY7614	54°31·5′	2°21·8′W	T	91
Langrigg	N Yks	SD7763	54°4·0′	2°20·7′W	X	98
Langrigg	N Yks	SD9683	54°14·8′	2°3·3′W	X	98
Langrigg	Scot Bord	NT8550	55°44·8′	2°13·9′W	X	67,74
Langrigg Beck	Cumbr	NY1646	54°48·4′	3°18·0′W	W	85
Langrish	Hants	SU7023	51°0·4′	0°59·7′W	T	197
Langrish Ho	Hants	SU7023	51°0·4′	0°59·7′W	X	197
Lang Scar	N Yks	SE0792	54°19·7′	1°53·1′W	X	99
Langsett	Barns	SE2100	53°30·0′	1°40·6′W	T	110
Langsett Moors	Barns	SK1699	53°29·5′	1°45·1′W	X	110
Langsett Resr	Sheff	SE2000	53°30·0′	1°41·5′W	W	110
Langshaw	Scot Bord	NT5139	55°38·8′	2°46·3′W	T	73
Langshaw	S Lanak	NS8549	55°43·5′	3°49·4′W	X	72
Langshawburn	D & G	NT2804	55°19·7′	3°7·7′W	X	79
Langshaw Burn	D & G	NT2805	55°20·3′	3°7·7′W	W	79
Langshawburn Rig	D & G	NT2704	55°19·7′	3°8·6′W	H	79
Langshawbush	D & G	NT0804	55°19·5′	3°26·6′W	X	78
Langshaw Ho	D & G	NY2472	55°2·5′	3°10·9′W	X	85
Langshawmuir	D & G	NY2573	55°3·0′	3°10·0′W	X	85
Langshot Fm	E Dunb	NS6175	55°57·1′	4°13·1′W	FM	64
Langside	C of Glas	NS5761	55°49·5′	4°16·5′W	T	64
Langside	D & G	NY1293	55°13·7′	3°22·6′W	X	78
Langside	E Ayr	NS4233	55°34·2′	4°29·9′W	X	70
Langside	E Ayr	NS5233	55°34·3′	4°20·4′W	X	70
Langside	Fife	NO3403	56°13·2′	3°3·4′W	X	59
Langside	Midlo	NT3568	55°54·3′	3°1·9′W	X	66
Langside	N Ayr	NS2952	55°44·1′	4°43·0′W	X	63
Langside	N Ayr	NS3840	55°37·9′	4°34·0′W	X	70
Langside	N Lanak	NS8163	55°51·0′	3°53·6′W	X	65
Langside	Pth & Kin	NN7913	56°17·9′	3°56·9′W	X	57
Langside	Pth & Kin	NO1208	56°15·6′	3°24·8′W	X	58
Langside	Renf	NS3571	55°54·5′	4°37·9′W	X	63
Langside	Scot Bord	NT5528	55°32·9′	2°42·4′W	X	73
Langsidebrae	Scot Bord	NT5005	55°20·4′	2°46·9′W	X	79
Langside Burn	Scot Bord	NT4903	55°19·4′	2°47·8′W	W	79
Langside Fm	Scot Bord	NT2442	55°40·2′	3°12·1′W	FM	73
Langside Fm	S Lanak	NS8641	55°39·2′	3°48·3′W	FM	71,72
Langside Head	Midlo	NT3567	55°53·8′	3°1·9′W	X	66
Langside Hill	Fife	NO3403	56°13·2′	3°3·4′W	H	59
Langside Hill	N Ayr	NS2453	55°44·6′	4°47·8′W	X	63
Langskaill	Orkney	HY2414	59°0·6′	3°18·9′W	X	6
Langskaill	Orkney	HY4032	59°10·5′	3°2·5′W	X	5,6
Langskaill	Orkney	HY4321	59°4·6′	2°59·2′W	A	5,6
Langskaill	Orkney	HY4342	59°15·9′	2°59·5′W	X	5
Langskaill	Orkney	HY4845	59°17·6′	2°54·3′W	X	5
Langskaill	Orkney	HY5005	58°56·0′	2°51·6′W	X	6,7
Lang Sound	Shetld	HU3834	60°5·6′	1°18·5′W	W	4
Lang Stack	Shetld	HU1753	60°15·9′	1°41·1′W	X	3
Lang Stack	Shetld	HU2357	60°18·1′	1°34·5′W	X	3
Lang Stane	Aberd	NJ4813	57°12·5′	2°51·2′W	A	37
Lang Stane	Aberd	NO8290	57°0·3′	2°17·3′W	A	38,45
Lang Stane o'Craigearn	Aberd	NJ7214	57°13·2′	2°27·4′W	A	38
Langston	Devon	SX6448	50°19·2′	3°54·3′W	X	202
Langston	Devon	SX6790	50°41·9′	3°52·6′W	X	191
Langstone	Corn	SX2977	50°34·3′	4°24·5′W	X	201
Langstone	Devon	SX7482	50°37·7′	3°46·5′W	T	191
Langstone	Hants	SU7105	50°50·6′	0°59·1′W	T	197
Langstone	Newp	ST3790	51°36·6′	2°54·2′W	T	171
Langstone Bridge	Hants	SU7204	50°50·1′	0°58·3′W	X	197
Langstone Channel	Hants	SU6901	50°48·5′	1°0·9′W	W	197
Langstone Court	Heref	SO5322	51°53·9′	2°40·6′W	A	162
Langstone Court	Newp	ST3789	51°36·0′	2°54·2′W	X	171
Langstone Downs	Corn	SX2573	50°32·1′	4°27·8′W	X	201
Langstone Harbour	C of Port	SU6802	50°49·0′	1°1·7′W	W	196
Langstone Harbour	C of Port	SU6902	50°49·0′	1°0·8′W	W	197
Langstone Manor	Devon	SX4882	50°37·3′	4°8·6′W	X	191,201
Langstone Moor	Devon	SX5578	50°35·3′	4°2·5′W	X	191
Langstone Rock	Devon	SX9777	50°35·3′	3°26·9′W	X	192
Langstrath	Cumbr	NY2610	54°29·0′	3°8·1′W	X	89,90
Langstrath Beck	Cumbr	NY2611	54°29·6′	3°8·1′W	W	89,90
Langstrothdale	N Yks	SD9078	54°12·1′	2°8·8′W	X	98
Langstrothdale Chase	N Yks	SD8879	54°12·6′	2°10·6′W	X	98
Langtae Burn	Durham	NY8237	54°43·9′	2°16·3′W	W	91,92
Langtae Hill	Scot Bord	NT4400	55°17·7′	2°52·5′W	H	79
Langtae Moss	Durham	NY8138	54°44·4′	2°17·3′W	X	91,92
Langtae Sike	Scot Bord	NT4400	55°17·7′	2°52·5′W	W	79
Lang Taing	Orkney	HY6938	59°13·9′	2°32·1′W	X	5
Langthorne	N Yks	SE2591	54°19·1′	1°36·5′W	T	99
Langthorns	Essex	TL5920	51°51·6′	0°18·9′E	X	167
Langthorn Wood	N Yks	SE2589	54°18·0′	1°36·5′W	F	99
Langthorpe	N Yks	SE3867	54°6·1′	1°24·7′W	T	99
Langthorpe Hall	E Yorks	TA1639	53°50·3′	0°13·8′W	X	107
Langthwaite	Cumbr	SD6380	54°13·1′	2°33·6′W	X	97
Langthwaite	Lancs	SD4959	54°1·7′	2°46·3′W	X	102
Langthwaite	N Yks	NZ0002	54°25·1′	1°59·6′W	T	92
Langthwaite Fm	Cumbr	SD1580	54°12·8′	3°17·8′W	FM	96
Langtoft	E Yorks	TA0166	54°5·0′	0°26·9′W	T	101
Langtoft	Lincs	TF1212	52°41·9′	0°20·2′W	T	130,142
Langtoft Fen	Lincs	TF1413	52°42·4′	0°18·4′W	X	130,142
Langtoft Grange	E Yorks	SE9965	54°4·5′	0°28·8′W	X	101
Langton	Cumbr	NY7020	54°34·7′	2°27·4′W	X	91
Langton	Durham	NZ1619	54°34·2′	1°44·7′W	T	92
Langton	Lincs	TF2368	53°11·9′	0°9·1′W	T	122
Langton	Lincs	TF3970	53°12·8′	0°5·3′E	T	122
Langton	N Yks	SE7967	54°5·8′	0°47·1′W	T	100
Langton	Pemb	SM9433	51°57·7′	4°59·5′W	X	157
Langton Bank Wood	Durham	NZ1619	54°34·2′	1°44·7′W	F	92
Langton Beck	Durham	NZ1619	54°34·2′	1°44·7′W	W	92
Langton Br	Lincs	TF1477	53°16·9′	0°17·0′W	X	121
Langton Burn	Scot Bord	NT7851	55°45·4′	2°20·6′W	W	67,74
Langton Burn	Scot Bord	NT7852	55°45·9′	2°20·6′W	W	67,74
Langton by Wragby	Lincs	TF1476	53°16·4′	0°17·0′W	T	121
Langton Caudle	Leic	SP7493	52°32·0′	0°54·1′W	X	141
Langton Court Fm	Rho Cyn Taf	ST0488	51°35·2′	3°22·8′W	FM	170
Langton Cross	Dorset	SY6282	50°38·4′	2°31·9′W	A	194
Langton Edge	Scot Bord	NT7454	55°47·0′	2°24·4′W	X	67,74
Langton Field	Cumbr	NY7020	54°34·7′	2°27·4′W	X	91
Langton Fm	E Renf	NS5054	55°45·6′	4°23·0′W	FM	64
Langton Fm	Leic	SP4795	52°33·3′	1°18·0′W	FM	140
Langton Fm	W Loth	NT0866	55°53·0′	3°27·8′W	FM	65
Langton Grange	N Yks	SE3097	54°22·3′	1°31·9′W	X	99
Langton Grange	W Susx	TQ2717	50°56·5′	0°11·1′W	X	198
Langton Grange Fm	Lincs	TF3972	53°13·8′	0°5·4′E	FM	122
Langton Green	Kent	TQ5439	51°8·0′	0°12·5′E	T	188
Langton Green	Suff	TM1474	52°19·6′	1°8·8′E	T	144,156
Langton Hall	Leic	SP7193	52°32·0′	0°56·8′W	X	141
Langton Hall	Notts	SK4755	53°5·6′	1°17·5′W	X	120
Langton Hall	N Yks	SE3095	54°21·2′	1°31·9′W	X	99
Langton Herring	Dorset	SY6182	50°38·4′	2°32·7′W	T	194
Langton Hill	Lincs	TF1575	53°15·8′	0°16·1′W	X	121
Langton Hill	Lincs	TF2469	53°12·4′	0°8·2′W	X	122
Langton Hill	Lincs	TF3971	53°13·3′	0°5·3′E	X	122
Langtonlees	Scot Bord	NT7353	55°46·4′	2°25·4′W	X	67,74
Langton Lodge	Kent	TR1561	51°18·7′	1°5·5′E	X	179
Langton Long Blandford	Dorset	ST8905	50°50·9′	2°9·0′W	T	195
Langton Matravers	Dorset	SY9978	50°36·3′	2°0·5′W	T	195
Langton Mill	Scot Bord	NT7752	55°45·9′	2°21·6′W	X	67,74
Langtons	Essex	TQ5794	51°37·6′	0°16·5′E	X	167,177
Langton Wold	N Yks	SE8068	54°6·3′	0°46·2′W	X	100
Langton Wood	N Yks	SE2996	54°21·8′	1°32·8′W	F	99
Langtree	Devon	SS4515	50°55·1′	4°11·9′W	T	180,190
Langtree Common	Devon	SS4616	50°55·6′	4°11·1′W	X	180,190
Langtree Hall	Wigan	SD5611	53°35·9′	2°39·5′W	X	108
Langtree Old Hall	Wigan	SD5512	53°36·4′	2°40·4′W	X	108
Langtree Week	Devon	SS4715	50°55·1′	4°10·2′W	T	180
Langtye Fm	E Susx	TQ5109	50°51·9′	0°9·1′E	FM	199
Langunnett	Corn	SX1557	50°23·3′	4°35·8′W	X	201
Lang Ware Taing	Orkney	HY7843	59°16·6′	2°22·7′W	X	5
Langwathby	Cumbr	NY5633	54°41·7′	2°40·5′W	T	90
Langwathby Moor	Cumbr	NY5832	54°41·1′	2°38·7′W	X	91
Langwell	Highld	NC4101	57°58·5′	4°40·8′W	X	16
Langwell	Orkney	HY3106	58°56·4′	3°11·5′W	X	6,7
Langwell Forest	Highld	ND0325	58°12·5′	3°38·6′W	X	17
Langwell Hill	Highld	NC4112	58°4·4′	4°41·3′W	H	16
Langwell Ho	Highld	ND1122	58°10·9′	3°30·3′W	X	17
Langwell Lodge	Highld	NC1702	57°58·4′	5°5·2′W	X	15
Langwell Water	Highld	ND0224	58°11·9′	3°39·6′W	W	17
Langwith	Derby	SK5269	53°13·2′	1°12·9′W	T	120
Langwith	N Yks	SE2882	54°14·2′	1°33·8′W	X	99
Langwith Ho	N Yks	SE2881	54°13·7′	1°33·8′W	X	99
Langwith Ho	York	SE6547	53°55·1′	1°0·2′W	X	105,106
Langwith Junction	Derby	SK5268	53°12·6′	1°12·9′W	T	120
Langwith Lodge	Notts	SK5370	53°13·7′	1°12·0′W	X	120
Langwith Lodge	York	SE6548	53°55·7′	1°0·2′W	X	105,106
Langwith Mill Ho	Notts	SK5470	53°13·7′	1°11·1′W	X	120
Langwith Wood	Derby	SK5068	53°12·6′	1°14·7′W	F	120
Langwood Fen	Cambs	TL4385	52°26·9′	0°6·7′E	X	142,143
Langwood Fm	Cambs	TL4285	52°26·9′	0°5·8′E	FM	142,143
Langwood Hill	Cambs	TL4185	52°26·9′	0°4·9′E	X	142,143
Langworth	Lincs	TF0576	53°16·5′	0°25·1′W	T	121
Langworth Grange	Lincs	TF2456	53°5·4′	0°8·5′W	X	122
Langworthy	Devon	SX4794	50°43·8′	4°9·7′W	X	191
Lanhadron Fm	Corn	SW9947	50°17·6′	4°48·9′W	FM	204
Lanham Green	Essex	TL7921	51°51·8′	0°36·4′E	T	167
Lanhargy	Corn	SX3275	50°33·3′	4°21·9′W	X	201
Lanhay	Corn	SW8635	50°10·8′	4°59·5′W	X	204
Lanherne	Corn	SW8765	50°27·0′	4°59·7′W	A	200
Lan Hill	Wilts	ST8774	51°28·1′	2°10·8′W	H	173
Lanhill Fm	Wilts	ST8875	51°28·7′	2°10·0′W	FM	173
Lan Ho	Carm	SN4215	51°48·9′	4°17·1′W	X	159
Lanhoose	Corn	SW8537	50°11·9′	5°0·4′W	X	204
Lanhydrock House	Corn	SX0863	50°26·4′	4°41·9′W	A	200
Laniewee Burn	D & G	NX3182	55°6·5′	4°38·5′W	W	76
Laniley	Corn	SW8448	50°17·8′	5°1·6′W	X	204
Lanimer Burn	S Lanak	NS9633	55°35·0′	3°38·6′W	W	72
Laninval Ho	Corn	SX0465	50°27·4′	4°45·3′W	X	200
Lan Isaf	Powys	SN8954	52°10·6′	3°37·0′W	X	147
Lanivet	Corn	SX0364	50°26·8′	4°46·1′W	T	200
Lanjaghan	I of M	SC3881	54°12·2′	4°28·6′W	X	95
Lanjeth	Corn	SW9752	50°20·2′	4°50·8′W	T	200,204
Lanjew	Corn	SW9864	50°26·7′	4°50·3′W	T	200
Lanjore	Corn	SX3458	50°24·1′	4°19·8′W	X	201
Lank	Corn	SX0875	50°32·8′	4°42·2′W	T	200
Lankaber	Cumbr	NY6218	54°33·6′	2°34·8′W	X	91
Lank Combe	Devon	SS7745	51°11·7′	3°45·2′W	X	180
Lankelly Fm	Corn	SX1151	50°20·0′	4°39·0′W	FM	200,204
Lanket's Grove	Suff	TL9375	52°20·6′	0°50·4′E	X	144
Lankey Burn	Northum	NY8285	55°9·8′	2°16·5′W	W	80
Lankham Bottom	Dorset	SY6099	50°47·6′	2°33·7′W	X	194
Lankhurst Fm	E Susx	TQ8114	50°54·0′	0°34·8′E	FM	199
Lank Rigg	Cumbr	NY0911	54°29·4′	3°23·9′W	H	89
Lankrigg Moss	Cumbr	NY0712	54°29·9′	3°25·7′W	X	89
Lanky Hill	Norf	TF7421	52°45·7′	0°35·1′E	X	132
Lanlas	Cered	SN4860	52°13·3′	4°13·1′W	X	146
Lan-las	Cered	SN6047	52°6·5′	4°2·3′W	X	146
Lanlash	Carm	SN5722	51°52·9′	4°4·3′W	X	159
Lanlavery Rock	Corn	SX1582	50°36·7′	4°36·5′W	X	201
Lanlawren	Corn	SX1653	50°21·1′	4°34·8′W	X	201
Lanlivery	Corn	SX0759	50°24·2′	4°42·6′W	T	200
Lanlliwe	Carm	SN1817	51°49·6′	4°38·1′W	X	158
Lanlluest	Powys	SO1874	52°21·7′	3°11·9′W	X	136,148
Lanlwyd	Cered	SN6175	52°21·6′	4°2·1′W	X	135
Lanmartin	Carm	SN3313	51°47·7′	4°24·9′W	X	159
Lannacombe Bay	Devon	SX8036	50°12·9′	3°40·5′W	W	202
Lannacombe Beach	Devon	SX8037	50°13·5′	3°40·6′W	X	202
Lannarth	Corn	SW7624	50°4·7′	5°7·5′W	X	204
Lanner	Corn	SW7139	50°12·6′	5°12·2′W	T	203
Lanner	Corn	SW8341	50°14·0′	5°2·2′W	X	204
Lanner Barton	Corn	SW8249	50°18·3′	5°3·3′W	X	204
Lanner Vean	Corn	SW6427	50°6·0′	5°17·6′W	X	203
Lannhall	D & G	NX8092	55°12·7′	3°52·7′W	X	78
Lannock Hill	Herts	TL2430	51°57·5′	0°11·3′W	X	166
Lannock Manor Fm	Herts	TL2430	51°57·5′	0°11·3′W	FM	166
Lannygore Burn	D & G	NX2758	54°53·5′	4°41·4′W	W	82
Lanolway Fm	Monm	SO4002	51°43·0′	2°51·7′W	FM	171
Lanow Fm	Corn	SX0277	50°33·8′	4°47·4′W	FM	200
Lanoy	Corn	SX2977	50°34·3′	4°24·5′W	X	201
Lanpill	Monm	SO4600	51°42·0′	2°46·5′W	X	171
Lanreath	Corn	SX1856	50°22·8′	4°33·2′W	T	201
Lanrest	Corn	SX2560	50°25·1′	4°27·4′W	X	201
Lanrick	Stir	NN6803	56°12·3′	4°7·2′W	X	57
Lanrick Hall	D & G	NX9886	55°9·7′	3°35·6′W	X	78
Lansallos	Corn	SX1751	50°20·1′	4°33·9′W	T	201
Lansbury Fm	Cambs	TL2057	52°12·1′	0°14·2′W	FM	153
Lansbury Park	Caer	ST1687	51°34·8′	3°12·3′W	T	171
Lansdown	Bath & NE Somer	ST7268	51°24·9′	2°23·8′W	T	172
Lansdown	Bath & NE Somer	ST7466	51°23·8′	2°22·0′W	T	172
Lansdown	Glos	SO9321	51°53·5′	2°5·7′W	T	163
Lansdowne	Sol	SP1875	52°22·6′	1°43·7′W	X	139
Lansdowne Ho (Hotel)	N Lincs	SE8309	53°34·5′	0°44·4′W	X	112
Lansdown Hill	Bath & NE Somer	ST7268	51°24·9′	2°23·8′W	X	172
Lanshaw	Brad	SE1245	53°54·3′	1°48·6′W	X	104
Lanshaw	Lancs	SD6765	54°5·0′	2°29·9′W	X	98
Lanshaw Fm	N Yks	SD7566	54°5·6′	2°22·5′W	FM	98
Lanshaw Fm	N Yks	SE2451	53°57·5′	1°37·6′W	FM	104
Lanshaw Ho	Cumbr	NY2754	54°52·8′	3°7·8′W	X	85
Lansic Ho	Notts	SK6946	53°0·6′	0°57·9′W	X	129
Lansmere Fm	Cumbr	NY5821	54°35·2′	2°38·6′W	FM	91
Lan Sor	Monm	ST3494	51°38·7′	2°56·8′W	A	171
Lantallack Cross	Corn	SX3560	50°25·2′	4°19·0′W	X	201
Lanteague	Corn	SW8053	50°20·4′	5°5·1′W	X	200,204
Lanteglos	Corn	SX0882	50°36·6′	4°42·4′W	T	200
Lanteglos Highway	Corn	SX1453	50°21·1′	4°36·5′W	T	200
Lantern Marshes	Suff	TM4551	52°6·4′	1°35·1′E	X	156
Lantern Pike	Derby	SK0288	53°23·6′	1°57·8′W	H	110
Lantern Rock	Devon	SX6937	50°13·3′	3°49·8′W	X	202
Lanterrick	Corn	SX0576	50°33·3′	4°44·8′W	X	200
Lante Shop Cave	N Yks	SD8377	54°11·6′	2°15·2′W	X	98
Lantewey	Corn	SX1668	50°29·2′	4°35·3′W	X	201
Lanthwaite	Cumbr	NY1520	54°34·3′	3°18·5′W	X	89
Lantic Bay	Corn	SX1450	50°19·5′	4°36·4′W	W	200

Lantivet Bay	Corn	SX1650	50°19·5′	4°34·7′W	W	201
Lant Lodge Fm	Derby	SK3261	53°8·9′	1°30·9′W	FM	119
Lanton	Northum	NT9231	55°34·6′	2°7·2′W	X	74,75
Lanton	Scot Bord	NT6221	55°29·1′	2°35·6′W	T	74
Lantonhall	Scot Bord	NT6222	55°29·7′	2°35·7′W	X	74
Lanton Hill	Scot Bord	NT6220	55°28·6′	2°35·6′W	H	74
Lanton Mill	Northum	NT9130	55°34·1′	2°8·1′W	X	74,75
Lanton Moor	Scot Bord	NT6321	55°29·1′	2°34·7′W	F	74
Lantonside	D & G	NY0166	54°59·0′	3°32·4′W	X	84
Lantuel	Corn	SW9767	50°28·3′	4°51·3′W	T	200
Lantundle Fm	Corn	SX2158	50°23·9′	4°30·7′W	FM	201
Lantyan	Corn	SX1057	50°23·2′	4°40·0′W	T	200
Lantyan Wood	Corn	SX1156	50°22·6′	4°39·1′W	F	200
Lan Uchaf	Powys	SN8953	52°10·1′	3°37·0′W	X	147
Lanwades Park	Suff	TL6966	52°16·2′	0°29·0′E	X	154
Lan Wen	Powys	SN9057	52°12·3′	3°36·2′W	X	147
Lan Wen	Powys	SN9070	52°19·3′	3°36·4′W	X	136,147
Lan Wen	Powys	SN9172	52°20·4′	3°35·6′W	X	136,147
Lan-wen	Powys	SO0669	52°18·9′	3°22·3′W	X	136,147
Lanwithan	Corn	SX1059	50°24·2′	4°40·1′W	X	200
Lanyar Taing	Shetld	HU3893	60°37·4′	1°17·8′W	X	1,2
Lanyew	Corn	SW8141	50°13·9′	5°3·9′W	X	204
Lanygors	Carm	SN3018	51°50·3′	4°27·7′W	X	159
Lanyon	Corn	SW6037	50°11·3′	5°21·4′W	X	203
Lanyon Fm	Corn	SW4234	50°9·2′	5°36·3′W	FM	203
Lanyon Fm	Corn	SW6838	50°12·0′	5°14·7′W	FM	203
Lanyon Quoit	Corn	SW4333	50°8·7′	5°35·5′W	A	203
Lan Ystenu	Powys	SN9653	52°10·2′	3°30·8′W	X	147
Lanzion	Corn	SX2487	50°39·6′	4°29·0′W	X	190
Laorin Bay	Arg & Bt	NM4257	56°38·3′	6°12·0′W	W	47
Lapal	Dudley	SO9883	52°26·9′	2°1·4′W	T	139
Lapford	Devon	SS7308	50°51·7′	3°47·9′W	T	191
Lapford Cross	Devon	SS7207	50°51·1′	3°48·7′W	T	191
Lapfordwood Ho	Devon	SS7108	50°51·7′	3°49·6′W	X	191
Laphroaig	Arg & Bt	NR3845	55°37·9′	6°9·3′W	T	60
Lapley	Staffs	SJ8712	52°42·6′	2°11·1′W	T	127
Lapley Fm	Glos	SO7602	51°43·2′	2°20·5′W	FM	162
Lapley Wood Fm	Staffs	SJ8612	52°42·6′	2°12·0′W	FM	127
Laplow Bank	Shrops	SO3884	52°27·3′	2°54·3′W	X	137
Laployd Barton	Devon	SX8085	50°39·4′	3°41·5′W	X	191
Laployd Plantation	Devon	SX8084	50°38·8′	3°41·5′W	F	191
Lappa Valley Steam Rly	Corn	SW8356	50°22·1′	5°2·7′W	X	200
Lappel, The	Kent	TQ9073	51°25·7′	0°44·4′E	X	178
Lappie	Fife	NO1707	56°15·2′	3°19·9′W	X	58
Lappiemoss	Fife	NO1707	56°15·2′	3°19·9′W	X	58
Lappingwell Wood	Glos	SP1707	51°45·9′	1°44·8′W	F	163
Lappock Rock		NS3034	55°34·5′	4°41·4′W	X	70
Lapstone Fm	Glos	SP1436	52°1·6′	1°47·4′W	FM	151
Lapthorne	Devon	SX8553	50°22·2′	3°36·7′W	X	202
Lapwater Fm	Lincs	TF3159	53°7·0′	0°2·2′W	FM	122
Lapwinghall	Ches	SJ8173	53°15·5′	2°16·7′W	X	118
Lapwing Lodge	E Renf	NS4359	55°48·2′	4°29·9′W	X	64
Lapwings	Suff	TM0862	52°13·2′	1°3·1′E	X	155
Lapworth	Warw	SP1671	52°20·4′	1°45·5′W	T	139
Lapworth Grange	Warw	SP1570	52°19·9′	1°46·4′W	X	139
Lapworth Park	Warw	SP1669	52°19·4′	1°45·5′W	X	139,151
Lapworth Sta	Warw	SP1871	52°20·4′	1°43·7′W	X	139
Laques	Carm	SN3310	51°46·1′	4°24·8′W	X	159
Laques-fawr	Carm	SN3209	51°45·5′	4°25·7′W	X	159
Laraben	Stir	NS6295	56°7·9′	4°12·8′W	X	57
Larabridge Fm	N Yks	SE6634	53°48·1′	0°59·5′W	FM	105,106
Larachantivore	Highld	NH0580	57°46·3′	5°16·3′W	X	19
Larachbeg	Highld	NM6948	56°34·3′	5°45·2′W	X	49
Larach Bhan	Arg & Bt	NN0723	56°21·9′	5°7·0′W	X	50
Larach Hill	Arg & Bt	NS1591	56°4·8′	4°57·9′W	H	56
Larachmòr Burn	Arg & Bt	NR8457	55°45·7′	5°26·1′W	W	62
Larachpark	Arg & Bt	NN2603	56°11·5′	4°47·8′W	X	56
Làrach Tigh Mhic Dhomhnuill	Highld	NG8525	57°16·2′	5°33·5′W	X	33
Laramie	Lincs	TF4299	53°28·3′	0°8·8′E	X	113
Larberry Pastures	Stock on T	NZ3717	54°33·1′	1°25·3′W	X	93
Larbert	Falk	NS8682	56°1·3′	3°49·3′W	T	65
Larbert Ho	Falk	NS8482	56°1·3′	3°51·2′W	X	65
Larbrax	D & G	NW9760	54°53·9′	5°9·5′W	X	82
Larbrax Moor	D & G	NW9761	54°54·4′	5°9·6′W	X	82
Larbreck	D & G	NX8878	55°5·3′	3°44·9′W	X	84
Larbreck	Lancs	SD4040	53°51·4′	2°54·3′W	T	102
Larbreck Hall	Lancs	SD3940	53°51·4′	2°55·2′W	X	102
Larch Covert	Warw	SP2768	52°18·8′	1°35·8′W	F	151
Larchery, The	Staffs	SJ9419	52°46·4′	2°4·9′W	X	127
Larches	Lancs	SD5030	53°46·1′	2°45·1′W	T	102
Larches Fm, The	Worcs	SO9949	52°8·6′	2°0·5′W	FM	150
Larches, The	Brom	TQ4363	51°21·1′	0°3·6′E	F	177,187
Larches, The	W Susx	TQ4039	51°8·2′	0°0·5′E	X	187
Larchet Hill	E Ayr	NS5244	55°40·3′	4°20·8′W	H	70
Larchet Hill	Northum	NY6555	54°53·6′	2°32·3′W	X	86
Larchfield	D & G	NX8975	55°3·8′	3°35·4′W	X	84
Larchfield Community	Midd	NZ5013	54°30·8′	1°13·2′W	X	93
Larch Fm, The	Notts	SK5555	53°5·6′	1°10·3′W	FM	120
Larch Grove	C of Edin	NT1566	55°53·0′	3°21·1′W	X	65
Larch Grove	Powys	SO1461	52°14·7′	3°15·2′W	X	148
Larch-hillock	Aberd	NJ8620	57°16·5′	2°13·5′W	X	38
Larch Tree Hole	N Yks	SD8271	54°8·3′	2°16·1′W	X	98
Larch Wood	Norf	TF7606	52°37·6′	0°36·4′E	F	143
Larch Wood	Scot Bord	NT2932	55°34·8′	3°7·1′W	F	73
Larchwood Fm	Shrops	SO5395	52°33·3′	2°41·2′W	FM	137,138
Larchwood Fm	Wok	SU7864	51°22·4′	0°52·4′W	FM	175,186
Larcombe	Devon	SX7457	50°24·2′	3°46·0′W	X	202
Larcombe Brook	Somer	SS8937	51°7·5′	3°34·8′W	W	181
Larcombe Fm	Devon	SX7949	50°19·9′	3°41·6′W	FM	202
Larcombe Fm	Somer	SS8738	51°8·0′	3°36·5′W	FM	181
Larden Cott	Shrops	SO5794	52°32·8′	2°37·6′W	X	137,138
Larden Grange	Shrops	SO5693	52°32·2′	2°38·5′W	X	137,138
Larden Green	Ches	SJ5851	53°3·5′	2°37·2′W	T	117
Larden Hall	Shrops	SO5693	52°32·2′	2°38·5′W	X	137,138
Larennie	Fife	NO4409	56°16·5′	2°53·8′W	X	59
Larford Fm	Worcs	SO8169	52°19·4′	2°16·3′W	FM	138
Larg	D & G	NX3674	55°2·3′	4°33·6′W	X	77
Larg	D & G	NX4365	54°57·5′	4°26·7′W	X	83
Larg	D & G	NX4858	54°53·9′	4°21·8′W	X	83

Largate	Norf	TG2520	52°44·1′	1°20·4′E	X	133,134
Largbrae Head	D & G	NS7815	55°25·1′	3°55·2′W	X	71,78
Large Fm	Lincs	SK8668	53°12·4′	0°42·3′W	FM	121
Largess Fm	Essex	TL8139	52°1·4′	0°38·7′E	FM	155
Larg Fell	D & G	NX3874	55°2·3′	4°31·7′W	X	77
Larghan	Pth & Kin	NO2240	56°33·0′	3°15·7′W	X	53
Larg Hill	D & G	NX4275	55°2·9′	4°28·0′W	H	77
Larg Hill	D & G	NX4365	54°57·5′	4°26·7′W	H	83
Larg Hill	D & G	NX4857	54°53·3′	4°21·8′W	H	83
Larghill	D & G	NX8274	55°3·0′	3°50·4′W	X	84
Larg Hill	S Ayr	NX3193	55°12·4′	4°38·9′W	H	76
Largh Kenmure	E Dunb	NS5970	55°54·4′	4°14·9′W	X	64
Largie	Aberd	NJ6131	57°22·3′	2°38·5′W	T	29,37
Largie	Aberd	NO8375	56°52·2′	2°16·3′W	X	45
Largiebaan	Arg & Bt	NR6114	55°22·0′	5°45·9′W	X	68
Largiebeg	Arg & Bt	NR6725	55°28·1′	5°40·7′W	X	68
Largie Fm	Arg & Bt	NR7046	55°39·4′	5°38·9′W	FM	62
Largiemore	Arg & Bt	NR6725	55°28·1′	5°40·7′W	X	68
Largiemore	Arg & Bt	NR9486	56°1·6′	5°17·9′W	T	55
Largiemore Burn	Arg & Bt	NR9686	56°1·7′	5°16·0′W	W	55
Largievrechtan	Arg & Bt	NS0464	55°50·0′	5°7·3′W	X	63
Largin	Corn	SX1663	50°26·5′	4°35·1′W	X	201
Largin Castle	Corn	SX1664	50°27·1′	4°35·1′W	A	201
Largin Wood	Corn	SX1664	50°27·1′	4°35·1′W	F	201
Largizean	Arg & Bt	NS0854	55°44·7′	5°3·1′W	X	63
Larglanglee	D & G	NX8374	55°3·1′	3°49·5′W	X	84
Larglanglee Hill	D & G	NX8274	55°3·0′	3°50·4′W	H	84
Larglea	D & G	NX8373	55°2·5′	3°49·4′W	X	84
Larglea Moss	D & G	NX8474	55°3·1′	3°48·5′W	X	84
Larglear Hill	D & G	NX7176	55°4·0′	4°0·8′W	H	77,84
Largmore	D & G	NX5682	55°6·9′	4°15·0′W	X	77
Largo Bay	Fife	NO4201	56°12·1′	2°55·6′W	W	59
Largo Ho	Fife	NO4203	56°13·2′	2°55·7′W	X	59
Largo Law	Fife	NO4205	56°14·3′	2°55·7′W	H	59
Largoward	Fife	NO4607	56°15·4′	2°51·9′W	T	59
Largs	D & G	NX6755	54°52·6′	4°3·9′W	X	83,84
Largs	N Ayr	NS2059	55°47·7′	4°51·8′W	T	63
Largs	S Ayr	NS2917	55°25·3′	4°41·7′W	X	70
Largs	S Ayr	NS3805	55°19·0′	4°32·7′W	X	70,77
Largs Bay	N Ayr	NS2059	55°47·7′	4°51·8′W	W	63
Largs Hill	S Ayr	NS3904	55°18·5′	4°31·8′W	X	77
Largue	Aberd	NJ4018	57°15·2′	2°59·2′W	X	37
Largue	Aberd	NJ6341	57°27·7′	2°36·5′W	T	29
Largue Fm	Aberd	NJ6441	57°27·7′	2°35·5′W	FM	29
Largvey Hill	D & G	NX5684	55°8·0′	4°15·1′W	X	77
Largybeg	N Ayr	NS0523	55°28·0′	5°4·7′W	T	69
Largybeg Point	N Ayr	NS0523	55°28·0′	5°4·7′W	X	69
Largymeanoch	N Ayr	NS0424	55°28·5′	5°5·6′W	T	69
Largymore	N Ayr	NS0424	55°28·5′	5°5·6′W	T	69
Larichfraskhan	Pth & Kin	NN8133	56°28·7′	3°55·5′W	X	52
Larick Scalp	Fife	NO4628	56°26·7′	2°52·1′W	X	54,59
Larig Fell	D & G	NX2063	54°56·0′	4°48·2′W	H	82
Larig Hill	Highld	NJ0840	57°26·7′	3°31·5′W	H	27
Larkbarrow	Somer	SS8242	51°10·1′	3°40·9′W	X	181
Larkbeare	Devon	SY0697	50°46·1′	3°19·6′W	T	192
Larkbeare Court	Devon	SY0697	50°46·1′	3°19·6′W	X	192
Larkborough	Worcs	SP1042	52°4·8′	1°50·8′W	X	150
Lark Cott	Durham	NZ1342	54°46·6′	1°47·4′W	X	88
Larkenshaw	Surrey	SU9962	51°21·1′	0°34·3′W	X	175,176,186
Larker's Fm	Lincs	SK9260	53°8·0′	0°37·1′W	FM	121
Larkethill Wood	Glos	SP1411	51°47·9′	1°47·4′W	F	163
Larkeyvalley Wood	Kent	TR1255	51°15·5′	1°2·7′E	F	179
Larkfield	Inverc	NS2375	55°56·4′	4°49·6′W	T	63
Larkfield	Kent	TQ7058	51°18·0′	0°26·7′E	T	178,188
Larkfield	Leeds	SE2139	53°51·0′	1°40·4′W	T	104
Larkfield Hall	Kent	TQ6140	51°8·4′	0°18·5′E	X	188
Larkfield Ho	Warw	SP4260	52°14·4′	1°22·7′W	X	151
Lark Grange	Suff	TL6181	52°24·4′	0°22·4′E	X	143
Larkhall	Bath & NE Somer	ST7566	51°23·8′	2°21·2′W	T	172
Lark Hall	Cambs	TL5854	52°9·9′	0°19·0′E	X	154
Larkhall	Northum	NY9684	55°9·3′	2°3·3′W	X	81
Lark Hall	N Yks	SE3492	54°19·6′	1°28·2′W	X	99
Larkhall	Scot Bord	NT6319	55°28·1′	2°34·7′W	X	80
Larkhall	S Lanak	NS7650	55°43·9′	3°58·0′W	T	64
Lark Hall	Staffs	SJ9349	53°2·5′	2°5·9′W	X	118
Lark Hall	Staffs	SK0156	53°6·3′	1°58·7′W	X	119
Lark Hall Fm	Cambs	TL6170	52°18·5′	0°22·1′E	FM	154
Lark Hall Fm	Suff	TL7568	52°17·2′	0°34·3′E	FM	155
Lark Hall Heath Fm	Cambs	TL5755	52°10·5′	0°18·2′E	FM	154
Lark Hill	Beds	TL0641	52°3·7′	0°26·8′W	X	153
Lark Hill	Kent	TQ9047	51°11·7′	0°43·6′E	X	189
Lark Hill	Lancs	SD6223	53°42·4′	2°34·1′W	X	102,103
Lark Hill	Oldham	SD9907	53°33·8′	2°0·5′W	X	109
Lark Hill	Oxon	SU4187	51°35·1′	1°24·1′W	X	174
Larkhill	Salf	SJ7095	53°27·3′	2°26·7′W	X	109
Lark Hill	Wigan	SD6900	53°30·0′	2°27·6′W	T	109
Larkhill	Wilts	SU1244	51°11·9′	1°49·3′W	T	184
Larkhill Artillery Range	Wilts	SU0949	51°14·6′	1°51·9′W	X	184
Lark Hill Fm	Oxon	SU4187	51°35·1′	1°24·1′W	FM	174
Lark Ho	Darl	NZ2315	54°32·0′	1°38·3′W	X	93
Larkins Fm	Essex	TL5802	51°41·9′	0°17·6′E	FM	167
Larklands	Derby	SK4741	52°58·1′	1°17·6′W	T	129
Lark Law	N Lanak	NS8956	55°47·3′	3°45·8′W	X	65,72
Lark Park	Staffs	SK0353	53°4·7′	1°56·9′W	X	119
Larkrigg	Cumbr	SD5188	54°17·4′	2°44·7′W	X	97
Larkrigg Spring	Cumbr	SD5187	54°16·8′	2°44·7′W	F	97
Larks Fm	Somer	ST7437	51°8·1′	2°21·9′W	FM	183
Larkshall	Norf	TL9188	52°27·6′	0°49·1′E	X	144
Larks' Hill	Suff	TM1949	52°6·0′	1°12·3′E	T	169
Larks in the Wood	Essex	TL8044	52°4·1′	0°38·0′E	X	155
Lark Spit	Somer	ST2750	51°14·9′	3°2·4′W	X	182
Lark Stoke	Warw	SP1943	52°5·3′	1°43·0′W	X	151
Larkstoke Stud	Oxon	SU6285	51°33·9′	1°5·9′W	X	175
Larkton Hill	Ches	SJ4952	53°4·0′	2°45·3′W	H	117
Larkwhistle Fm	Hants	SU4444	51°11·8′	1°21·8′W	FM	185
Larkwhistle Fm	Hants	SU4536	51°7·5′	1°21·0′W	FM	185
Larkwhistle Fm	Hants	SU5130	51°4·2′	1°15·9′W	FM	185
Larkworthy	Devon	SX3795	50°44·1′	4°18·2′W	X	190
Larling	Norf	TL9889	52°28·0′	0°55·3′E	T	144

Larling Heath	Suff	TL7978	52°22·5′	0°38·2′E	X	144
Larmer Tree Grounds	Wilts	ST9416	50°56·8′	2°4·7′W	X	184
Larpool Hall	N Yks	NZ8909	54°28·4′	0°37·2′W	X	94
Larport	Heref	SO5738	52°2·6′	2°37·2′W	T	149
Larrick	Corn	SX1950	50°19·6′	4°32·2′W	X	201
Larrick	Corn	SX3078	50°34·9′	4°23·7′W	T	201
Larrick	Corn	SX3280	50°36·0′	4°22·1′W	X	201
Larriston	Scot Bord	NY5494	55°14·5′	2°43·0′W	T	79
Larriston Burn	Scot Bord	NY5694	55°14·5′	2°41·1′W	W	80
Larriston Fells	Scot Bord	NY5792	55°13·5′	2°40·1′W	H	80
Larriston Rig	Scot Bord	NY5794	55°14·5′	2°40·1′W	X	80
Larriston Rigg	Scot Bord	NY5594	55°14·5′	2°42·0′W	X	80
Larroch	D & G	NX3740	54°44·0′	4°31·5′W	X	83
Larryvarry	Moray	NJ2320	57°16·1′	3°16·1′W	X	36
Larter Fm	Norf	TG1619	52°43·8′	1°12·3′E	FM	133
Lartington	Durham	NZ0117	54°33·1′	1°58·7′W	T	92
Lartington High Moor	Durham	NY9215	54°32·1′	2°7·0′W	X	91,92
Larton	Wirral	SJ2487	53°22·7′	3°8·1′W	X	108
Lary	Aberd	NJ3300	57°5·4′	3°5·9′W	X	37
Lary Burn	Aberd	NJ3401	57°6·0′	3°4·9′W	W	37
Lary Hill	Aberd	NJ3301	57°6·0′	3°5·9′W	H	37
Lary Syke	Lancs	SD6259	54°1·8′	2°34·4′W	W	102,103
Lasborough	Glos	ST8294	51°38·9′	2°15·2′W	T	162,173
Lasborough Park	Glos	ST8293	51°38·4′	2°15·2′W	X	162,173
Lascelles Hall	Kirk	SE1816	53°38·7′	1°43·3′W	X	110
Lascombe	Surrey	SU9147	51°13·1′	0°41·4′W	X	186
Lascot Hill	Somer	ST4348	51°13·9′	2°48·6′W	H	182
Lasgair	N Eil	NF7820	57°9·7′	7°19·2′W	X	31
Lasgarn	Torf	SO2803	51°43·5′	3°2·2′W	X	171
Lasgarn Wood	Torf	SO2704	51°44·0′	3°3·0′W	F	171
Lasham	Hants	SU6742	51°10·6′	1°2·1′W	T	185,186
Lasham Hill	Hants	SU6642	51°10·6′	1°3·0′W	X	185,186
Lasham Wood	Hants	SU6842	51°10·6′	1°1·2′W	F	185,186
Lashbrook	Devon	SS4007	50°50·7′	4°16·0′W	X	190
Lashbrook Fm	Devon	SS4305	50°49·6′	4°13·4′W	FM	190
Lashbrook Fm	Devon	SY0799	50°47·2′	3°18·8′W	FM	192
Lashbrook Moor Plantation	Devon	SS4102	50°48·0′	4°15·0′W	F	190
Lashenden	Kent	TQ8440	51°8·0′	0°38·2′E	T	188
Lashingcott Moor	Devon	SS5323	50°59·5′	4°5·3′W	X	180
Lashley Hall	Essex	TL6426	51°54·7′	0°23·5′E	X	167
Lashmars Hall	W Susx	TQ1916	50°56·1′	0°18·0′W	X	198
Lash,The	Orkney	HY2506	58°56·3′	3°17·7′W	X	6,7
Lash, The	Orkney	HY3704	58°55·4′	3°5·2′W	X	6,7
Lashy Skerries	Orkney	HY5938	59°13·9′	2°42·6′W	X	5
Lashy Sound	Orkney	HY5937	59°13·3′	2°42·6′W	W	5
Lashy Taing	Orkney	HY5938	59°13·9′	2°42·6′W	X	5
Lask Edge	Staffs	SJ9156	53°6·3′	2°7·7′W	T	118
Laskey Ho	Warr	SJ6587	53°23·0′	2°31·2′W	X	109
Laskill Ho	N Yks	SE5690	54°18·4′	1°7·9′W	X	100
Laskill Pasture Moor	N Yks	SE5891	54°18·9′	1°6·1′W	X	100
Lason Field	Durham	NZ0637	54°43·9′	1°54·0′W	X	92
Lassington	Glos	SO7921	51°53·5′	2°17·9′W	X	162
Lassintullich	Pth & Kin	NN6957	56°41·4′	4°7·9′W	X	42,51
Lassodie	Fife	NT1292	56°7·0′	3°24·5′W	T	58
Last Drop Village, The	Bolton	SD7214	53°37·6′	2°25·0′W	X	109
Lastingham	N Yks	SE7290	54°18·3′	0°53·2′W	T	94,100
Lasynys	Gwyn	SH5932	52°52·3′	4°5·3′W	X	124
Latan	Orkney	HY6322	59°5·3′	2°38·3′W	X	5
Latch	Aberd	NJ9624	57°18·7′	2°3·5′W	X	38
Latch	E Loth	NT5264	55°52·3′	2°45·6′W	X	66
Latcham	Somer	ST4447	51°13·4′	2°47·7′W	T	182
Latchbrook	Corn	SX4059	50°24·8′	4°14·7′W	T	201
Latch Burn	Midlo	NT3354	55°46·7′	3°3·7′W	W	66,73
Latch Burn	W Loth	NS9765	55°52·3′	3°38·3′W	W	65
Latchensfen Fm	Cambs	TL4291	52°30·1′	0°5·9′E	FM	142,143
Latches Fen	Cambs	TL4392	52°30·7′	0°6·8′E	X	142,143
Latchetts	E Susx	TQ3826	51°1·2′	0°1·6′W	X	187,198
Latch Fm	W Loth	NT0965	55°52·4′	3°26·8′W	FM	65
Latchford	Herts	TL3920	51°51·9′	0°1·5′E	T	166
Latchford	Oxon	SP6501	51°42·5′	1°3·2′W	T	164,165
Latchford	Warr	SJ6187	53°22·9′	2°34·8′W	T	109
Latchingdon	Essex	TL8800	51°40·3′	0°43·5′E	T	168
Latchley	Corn	SX4073	50°32·3′	4°15·1′W	T	201
Latchley's Fm	Essex	TL6739	52°1·7′	0°26·5′E	A	154
Latchly Hill	Scot Bord	NT8424	55°30·8′	2°14·8′W	H	74
Latchmere Green	Hants	SU6360	51°20·4′	1°5·3′W	T	175
Latchmore Bank	Essex	TL4918	51°50·7′	0°10·2′E	T	167
Latchmore Bottom	Hants	SU1812	50°54·7′	1°44·3′W	X	195
Latchmore Brook	Hants	SU2013	50°55·2′	1°42·5′W	W	195
Lategillan Rig	Scot Bord	NT1123	55°29·8′	3°24·1′W	H	72
Lately Common	Warr	SJ6698	53°28·9′	2°30·3′W	T	109
Lat Gill	N Yks	SD8082	54°14·2′	2°18·0′W	W	98
Lathallan	Falk	NS9577	55°58·7′	3°40·5′W	X	65
Lathallan Home Fm	Fife	NO4506	56°14·9′	2°52·8′W	FM	59
Lathallan Mill	Fife	NO4605	56°14·3′	2°51·8′W	X	59
Lathallen School	Aberd	NO8067	56°47·9′	2°19·2′W	X	45
Lathalmond	Fife	NT0992	56°7·0′	3°27·4′W	X	58
Latham Hall	Staffs	SK1149	53°2·5′	1°49·8′W	X	119
Latha Skerry	Orkney	HY2326	59°7·1′	3°20·2′W	X	6
Lathbury	Durham	NZ0119	54°34·2′	1°58·6′W	X	92
Lathbury	Mil Key	SP8745	52°6·0′	0°43·4′W	T	152
Lathbury Park	Mil Key	SP8744	52°5·5′	0°43·4′W	X	152
Latherford	Staffs	SJ9307	52°39·9′	2°5·8′W	X	127,139
Latheron	Highld	ND1933	58°17·0′	3°22·4′W	T	11
Latheronwheel	Highld	ND1932	58°16·4′	3°22·4′W	T	11
Latheronwheel Ho	Highld	ND1832	58°16·4′	3°23·4′W	X	11
Lathgreen Fm	Norf	TM2596	52°31·1′	1°19·4′E	FM	134
Lathkill Dale	Derby	SK1865	53°11·1′	1°43·4′W	X	119
Lathochar Mains	Fife	NO4809	56°16·5′	2°49·9′W	X	59
Lathockar	Fife	NO4911	56°17·6′	2°49·0′W	X	59
Lathockar Burn	Fife	NO4909	56°16·5′	2°49·0′W	W	59
Lathockar Ho	Fife	NO4910	56°17·0′	2°49·0′W	X	59
Lathockar Mill	Fife	NO4909	56°16·5′	2°49·0′W	X	59
Lathom	Lancs	SD4510	53°35·3′	2°49·4′W	T	108
Lathom Ho	Lancs	SD4609	53°34·7′	2°48·5′W	X	108
Lathones	Fife	NO4708	56°15·9′	2°50·9′W	T	59
Lathries	Aberd	NJ6830	57°21·8′	2°31·5′W	X	29
Lathrisk Ho	Fife	NO2708	56°15·8′	3°10·3′W	X	59
Lathro	Pth & Kin	NO1103	56°12·9′	3°25·7′W	X	58
Lathwaite	Lancs	SD4649	53°56·3′	2°48·9′W	X	102

Lathwells Fm	Bucks	SP7724	51°54·8′	0°52·4′W	FM	165
Latimer	Bucks	TQ0099	51°41·1′	0°32·8′W	T	166,176
Latimer House	Bucks	SU9998	51°40·6′	0°33·7′W	X	165,176
Latimer Park Fm	Bucks	SU9998	51°40·6′	0°33·7′W	FM	165,176
Latneys	Essex	TL8012	51°46·9′	0°37·0′E	X	168
Latrigg	Cumbr	NY2724	54°36·6′	3°7·4′W	H	89,90
Latrigg	Cumbr	NY4101	54°24·3′	2°54·1′W	X	90
Lattenbury Fm	Cambs	TL2766	52°16·9′	0°7·9′W	FM	153
Lattenden Fm	E Susx	TQ6616	50°55·4′	0°22·1′E	FM	199
Latter Barrow	Cumbr	NY0711	54°29·4′	3°25·7′W	H	89
Latterbarrow	Cumbr	SD3699	54°23·2′	2°58·7′W	H	96,97
Latterbarrow Beck	Cumbr	NY0711	54°29·4′	3°25·7′W	W	89
Latterbarrow Fm	Cumbr	SD4383	54°14·6′	2°52·1′W	FM	97
Latterbarrow Moss	Cumbr	NY0711	54°29·4′	3°25·7′W	X	89
Latterford	Northum	NY8676	55°4·9′	2°12·7′W	X	87
Latter Gate Hills	N Yks	NZ9204	54°25·6′	0°34·5′W	X	94
Latterhaw Crag	Cumbr	NY3813	54°30·8′	2°57·0′W	X	90
Latterhead	Cumbr	NY1422	54°35·4′	3°19·4′W	X	89
Latteridge	S Glos	ST6684	51°33·5′	2°29·0′W	T	172
Latteridge Hill	S Glos	ST6685	51°34·0′	2°29·0′W	X	172
Lattersey Hill	Cambs	TL2896	52°33·0′	0°6·3′W	X	142
Lattiford	Somer	ST6926	51°2·2′	2°26·1′W	T	183
Lattiford Fm	Somer	ST6826	51°2·2′	2°27·0′W	FM	183
Lattin Down	Oxon	SU4183	51°32·9′	1°24·1′W	X	174
Lattin Down Kiln	Oxon	SU4183	51°32·9′	1°24·1′W	X	174
Lattinford Hill	Suff	TM0736	51°59·3′	1°1·3′E	T	155,169
Latton	Wilts	SU0995	51°39·5′	1°51·8′W	T	163
Latton Bush	Essex	TL4608	51°45·3′	0°7·3′E	T	167
Latton Park	Essex	TL4707	51°44·8′	0°8·2′E	F	167
Latton Priory	Essex	TL4606	51°44·2′	0°7·3′E	A	167
Latus Hall Fm	Lancs	SD5439	53°51·0′	2°41·5′W	FM	102
Latymer Courtenays	Devon	SX7696	50°45·3′	3°45·1′W	X	191
Latymere Dam	Suff	TM5086	52°25·1′	1°41·0′E	W	156
Lauchentyre	D & G	NX5557	54°53·5′	4°15·2′W	X	83
Lauchintilly	Aberd	NJ7412	57°12·1′	2°25·4′W	X	38
Lauchintilly Moss	Aberd	NJ7313	57°12·7′	2°26·4′W	X	38
Lauchintilly Wood	Aberd	NJ7312	57°12·1′	2°26·4′W	F	38
Lauchlansbrae	Aberd	NJ8650	57°32·7′	2°13·6′W	X	30
Laudale Ho	Highld	NM7459	56°40·4′	5°40·9′W	X	49
Laudale River	Highld	NM7258	56°39·8′	5°42·8′W	W	49
Lauder	Scot Bord	NT5247	55°43·1′	2°45·4′W	T	73
Lauder Barns	Scot Bord	NT5446	55°42·6′	2°43·5′W	T	73
Lauder Common	Scot Bord	NT5046	55°42·5′	2°47·3′W	X	73
Lauderdale	Scot Bord	NT5743	55°41·0′	2°40·6′W	X	73,74
Lauderhaugh	Scot Bord	NT5250	55°44·7′	2°45·4′W	X	66,73
Lauderhill	Scot Bord	NT5147	55°43·1′	2°46·4′W	X	73
Laugharne	Carm	SN3010	51°46·0′	4°27·4′W	T	159
Laugharne Burrows	Carm	SN2807	51°44·4′	4°29·1′W	X	158
Laugharne Burrows	Carm	SN2907	51°44·4′	4°28·2′W	X	159
Laugharne Sands	Carm	SN3106	51°43·9′	4°26·4′W	X	159
Laughenghie Hill	D & G	NX6165	54°57·9′	4°9·8′W	H	83
Laughern Brook	Worcs	SO7661	52°15·0′	2°20·7′W	W	138,150
Laughern Brook	Worcs	SO8058	52°13·4′	2°17·2′W	W	150
Laughern Hill	Worcs	SO7758	52°13·4′	2°19·8′W	T	150
Laughing Law	Scot Bord	NT7364	55°52·4′	2°25·5′W	H	67
Laughman Tor	Derby	SK1078	53°18·2′	1°50·6′W	H	119
Laughter Hole	Devon	SX6575	50°33·8′	3°54·0′W	X	191
Laughterton	Lincs	SK8375	53°16·2′	0°44·9′W	T	121
Laughterton Marsh	Lincs	SK8276	53°16·7′	0°45·8′W	X	121
Laughter Tor	Devon	SX6575	50°33·8′	3°54·0′W	H	191
Laught Mains	D & G	NX8994	55°13·9′	3°44·3′W	X	78
Laughton	E Susx	TQ5013	50°54·0′	0°8·4′E	T	199
Laughton	Leic	SP6589	52°29·9′	1°2·1′W	T	141
Laughton	Lincs	SK8497	53°28·0′	0°43·7′W	T	112
Laughton	Lincs	TF0731	52°52·2′	0°24·2′W	T	130
Laughton Common	E Susx	TQ4914	50°54·6′	0°7·6′E	T	199
Laughton Common	Lincs	SK8296	53°27·5′	0°45·5′W	F	112
Laughton Common	Roth	SK5187	53°22·9′	1°13·6′W	T	111,120
Laughton en le Morthen	Roth	SK5288	53°23·4′	1°12·7′W	T	111,120
Laughton Hills	Leic	SP6687	52°28·8′	1°1·3′W	X	141
Laughton Lodge	Lincs	SK8498	53°28·6′	0°43·6′W	X	112
Laughton Lodge	Lincs	TF0631	52°52·2′	0°25·1′W	X	130
Laughton Manor	Lincs	TF0832	52°52·7′	0°23·3′W	X	130
Laughton Park Fm	E Susx	TQ5014	50°54·6′	0°8·4′E	FM	199
Laughton Place	E Susx	TQ4811	50°53·0′	0°6·6′E	A	198
Laughton's Fm	Glos	SO7922	51°54·0′	2°17·9′W	FM	162
Laughton's Fm	Lincs	SK8945	52°59·9′	0°40·0′W	FM	130
Laughton Wood	Lincs	SK8698	53°28·5′	0°41·8′W	F	112
Laughton Woods	Lincs	SK8499	53°29·1′	0°43·6′W	F	112
Launcells Barton	Corn	SS2405	50°49·3′	4°29·5′W	A	190
Launcells Cross	Corn	SS2606	50°49·9′	4°27·9′W	T	190
Launceston	Corn	SX3384	50°38·1′	4°21·3′W	T	201
Launceston Down	Dorset	ST9510	50°53·6′	2°3·9′W	X	195
Launceston Steam Rly	Corn	SX3185	50°38·6′	4°23·0′W	X	201
Launcherley	Somer	ST5443	51°11·3′	2°39·1′W	T	182,183
Launcherley Hill	Somer	ST5542	51°10·8′	2°38·2′W	H	182,183
Launchy Gill	Cumbr	NY2915	54°31·8′	3°5·4′W	W	89,90
Launchy Gill	Cumbr	NY3015	54°31·8′	3°4·5′W	W	90
Laund	Lancs	SD8023	53°42·4′	2°17·8′W	T	103
Laund	Lancs	SD8438	53°50·5′	2°14·2′W	X	103
Laund Clough	Barns	SK1699	53°29·5′	1°45·1′W	X	110
Launde Abbey	Leic	SK7904	52°37·9′	0°49·6′W	A	141
Launde Big Wood	Leic	SK7803	52°37·4′	0°50·5′W	F	141
Launde Fm	Rut	SK8700	52°35·7′	0°42·5′W	FM	141
Launde Park	Leic	SK7904	52°37·9′	0°49·6′W	X	141
Launde Park Wood	Leic	SK8003	52°37·4′	0°48·7′W	F	141
Launder's Fm	Oxon	SU7292	51°37·6′	0°57·2′W	FM	175
Launde Wood Fm	Leic	SK7803	52°37·4′	0°50·5′W	FM	141
Laund Ho	N Yks	NZ8906	54°26·7′	0°37·2′W	X	94
Laund Ho	N Yks	SE0756	54°0·2′	1°53·2′W	X	104
Laund Ho	N Yks	SE5157	54°0·6′	1°12·9′W	X	105
Laund Ho	N Yks	SE5560	54°2·2′	1°9·2′W	X	100
Laund House Fm	Brad	SE1745	53°54·3′	1°44·1′W	FM	104
Laund House Fm	N Yks	SE5661	54°2·8′	1°8·3′W	FM	100
Laundimer Woods	Northnts	SP9387	52°28·6′	0°37·4′W	F	141
Launditch	Norf	TF9217	52°43·2′	0°51·0′E	A	132
Laund Pasture Plantation	N Yks	SE0757	54°0·8′	1°53·2′W	F	104
Laundry Fm	Cambs	TL4257	52°11·8′	0°5·1′E	FM	154
Laund's Fm	Essex	TL7342	52°3·2′	0°31·8′E	FM	155
Launds Fm	N Yks	SE5770	54°7·6′	1°7·2′W	FM	100
Launds, The	Lancs	SD4653	53°58·5′	2°49·0′W	X	102
Launton	Oxon	SP6022	51°53·8′	1°7·3′W	T	164,165
Laurel Bank	I of M	SC2883	54°13·1′	4°37·9′W	X	95
Laurel Fm	Barnet	TQ2593	51°37·5′	0°11·3′W	FM	176
Laurel Fm	Bucks	SP7632	51°59·1′	0°53·2′W	FM	152,165
Laurel Fm	Ches	SJ6582	53°20·3′	2°31·1′W	FM	109
Laurel Fm	N Som	ST4366	51°23·6′	2°48·8′W	FM	171,172,182
Laurel Fm	Suff	TL9258	52°11·4′	0°48·9′E	FM	155
Laurel Fm	Suff	TM2051	52°7·0′	1°13·2′E	FM	156
Laurel Fm	Suff	TM2580	52°22·5′	1°18·7′E	FM	156
Laurel Fm	Suff	TM2883	52°24·1′	1°21·5′E	FM	156
Laurel Ho	Bucks	SP7031	51°58·6′	0°58·5′W	X	152,165
Laurel Lodge Fm	Lincs	TF3725	52°48·5′	0°2·4′E	FM	131
Laurels Fm	Suff	TM0053	52°8·6′	0°55·8′E	FM	155
Laurels Fm	Suff	TM3889	52°27·0′	1°30·6′E	FM	156
Laurels Fm, The	Norf	TF5623	52°47·1′	0°19·2′E	FM	131
Laurels, The	Ches	SJ6445	53°0·3′	2°31·8′W	X	118
Laurels, The	Flint	SJ2465	53°10·8′	3°7·8′W	X	117
Laurels, The	Lincs	TA1708	53°33·6′	0°13·6′W	X	113
Laurels, The	Lincs	TF3764	53°9·6′	0°3·4′E	X	122
Laurels, The	Norf	TM3397	52°31·5′	1°26·5′E	X	134
Laurels, The	S Glos	ST6296	51°39·9′	2°32·6′W	X	162
Laurencekirk	Aberd	NO7171	56°50·0′	2°28·1′W	T	45
Laurence Loch	Shetld	HU3685	60°33·1′	1°20·1′W	W	1,2,3
Laurieclose	D & G	NY2679	55°6·2′	3°9·2′W	X	85
Laurieston	D & G	NX6864	54°57·4′	4°3·3′W	T	83,84
Laurieston	E Ayr	NS4114	55°23·9′	4°30·2′W	X	70
Laurieston	Falk	NS9079	55°59·7′	3°45·4′W	T	65
Laurieston	S Ayr	NS3734	55°34·6′	4°34·7′W	X	70
Laurieston Forest	D & G	NX6464	54°57·4′	4°7·0′W	F	83
Laurieston Forest	D & G	NX6564	54°57·4′	4°6·1′W	F	83,84
Laurieston Hall	D & G	NX6765	54°58·0′	4°4·2′W	X	83,84
Lauriston Castle	Aberd	NO7666	56°47·4′	2°23·1′W	A	45
Lauriston Castle	C of Edin	NT2076	55°58·5′	3°16·5′W	A	66
Lauriston Fm	Essex	TL9208	51°44·5′	0°47·3′E	FM	168
Laurland	E Ayr	NS4827	55°31·0′	4°24·0′W	X	70
Lavan Sands or Traeth Lafan	Gwyn	SH6376	53°16·0′	4°2·8′W	X	114,115
Lavant Down	W Susx	SU8710	50°53·2′	0°45·4′W	X	197
Lavant Ho (Sch)	W Susx	SU8508	50°52·1′	0°47·1′W	X	197
Lavatris (Roman Fort)	Durham	NY9813	54°31·0′	2°1·4′W	R	92
Laveddon	Corn	SX0566	50°27·9′	4°44·5′W	X	200
Lavell's Fm	Hants	SU6661	51°20·9′	1°2·7′W	FM	175,186
Lavender Line	E Susx	TQ4517	50°56·3′	0°4·2′E	X	198
Lavendon	Mil Key	SP9153	52°10·3′	0°39·8′W	T	152
Lavendon Grange	Mil Key	SP9053	52°10·3′	0°40·6′W	A	152
Lavendon Mill	Mil Key	SP9052	52°9·8′	0°40·7′W	X	152
Lavendon Wood	Mil Key	SP9255	52°11·4′	0°38·9′W	F	152
Lavenham	Suff	TL9149	52°6·6′	0°47·8′E	T	155
Lavenham Hill Fm	Suff	TL9151	52°7·7′	0°47·8′E	FM	155
Lavenham Lodge	Suff	TL9051	52°7·7′	0°47·0′E	X	155
Lavenham Park Fm	Suff	TL9051	52°7·7′	0°47·0′E	FM	155
Lavenie	Aberd	NJ6819	57°15·9′	2°31·4′W	X	38
Laver Banks	N Yks	SE2671	54°8·3′	1°35·7′W	X	99
Laverhay	D & G	NY1498	55°16·4′	3°20·8′W	X	78
Laverhay Height	D & G	NY1598	55°16·4′	3°19·8′W	H	79
Laver Ho	N Yks	SE2372	54°8·8′	1°38·5′W	X	99
Laverick Hall	Lancs	SD5166	54°5·5′	2°44·5′W	X	97
Laverick Hall Fm	S Tyne	NZ3161	54°56·8′	1°30·5′W	FM	88
Laverickstone	Cumbr	NY2855	54°53·3′	3°6·9′W	X	85
Laverlaw	Scot Bord	NT2937	55°37·5′	3°7·2′W	T	73
Laverley	Somer	ST5639	51°9·1′	2°37·4′W	T	182,183
Laverlock Law	Scot Bord	NT8568	55°54·5′	2°14·0′W	X	67
Lavern Burn	D & G	NS9007	55°20·9′	3°43·7′W	W	71,78
Lavernock	V of Glam	ST1868	51°24·5′	3°10·4′W	T	171
Lavernock Point	V of Glam	ST1867	51°24·0′	3°10·3′W	X	171
Laveroc Hall Fm	Brad	SE0436	53°49·5′	1°55·9′W	FM	104
Laverockbank	Pth & Kin	NN9829	56°26·8′	3°38·8′W	X	52,53,58
Laverockbrae	Aberd	NJ8332	57°22·9′	2°16·5′W	X	29,30
Laverock Braes	C of Aber	NJ9211	57°11·6′	2°7·5′W	X	38
Laverock Braes	Scot Bord	NT8567	55°54·0′	2°14·0′W	X	67
Laverock Bridge Ho	Cumbr	SD5395	54°21·1′	2°43·0′W	X	97
Laverockcairn	Aberd	NJ9840	57°27·3′	2°1·5′W	X	30
Laverockhall	Angus	NO5644	56°35·4′	2°42·5′W	X	54
Laverock Hall	Brad	SE0138	53°50·5′	1°58·7′W	X	104
Laverock Hall	Durham	NY9925	54°37·5′	2°0·5′W	X	92
Laverock Hall	Northum	NZ2878	55°6·0′	1°33·2′W	X	88
Laverock Hall	N Yks	SE1666	54°5·6′	1°44·9′W	X	99
Laverock Hall	S Lanak	NS8814	55°24·7′	3°45·7′W	X	71,78
Laverock Hall Fm	N Yks	SE5792	54°19·5′	1°7·0′W	FM	100
Laverock How	Cumbr	NY0606	54°26·7′	3°26·6′W	X	89
Laverockclaw	E Loth	NT4775	55°58·2′	2°50·5′W	X	66
Laverock Law	Northum	NU0336	55°37·3′	1°56·7′W	X	75
Laverockloch	Moray	NJ1963	57°39·2′	3°21·0′W	X	28
Laverock Stone	Inverc	NS2969	55°53·3′	4°43·6′W	X	63
Laversdale	Cumbr	NY4762	54°57·2′	2°49·2′W	T	86
Lavers Geos	Shetld	HU5999	60°40·5′	0°54·7′W	X	1
Laverstock	Wilts	SU1530	51°4·4′	1°46·8′W	T	184
Laverstock Fm	Dorset	ST4200	50°48·0′	2°49·0′W	FM	193
Laverstoke	Hants	SU4948	51°14·0′	1°17·5′W	T	185
Laverstoke Grange Fm	Hants	SU4946	51°12·9′	1°17·5′W	FM	185
Laverstoke Ho	Hants	SU4949	51°14·5′	1°17·5′W	X	185
Laverstoke Wood	Hants	SU5045	51°12·4′	1°16·7′W	F	185
Laverton	Glos	SP0735	52°1·0′	1°53·5′W	T	150
Laverton	N Yks	SE2273	54°9·4′	1°39·4′W	T	99
Laverton	Somer	ST7753	51°16·8′	2°19·4′W	T	183
Lavery Burn	S Ayr	NX2678	55°4·2′	4°43·1′W	W	76
Lavethan	Corn	SX0973	50°31·8′	4°41·3′W	A	200
Lavey Sound	Orkney	HY5238	59°13·8′	2°50·0′W	W	5
Lavington Common	W Susx	SU9418	50°57·5′	0°39·3′W	F	197
Lavington Down	Wilts	SU0049	51°14·6′	1°59·6′W	X	184
Lavington Folly	Wilts	SU1249	51°14·6′	1°49·3′W	X	184
Lavington Sands	Wilts	SU0055	51°17·9′	1°59·6′W	T	173
Lavington Stud Fm	W Susx	SU9316	50°56·4′	0°40·2′W	FM	197
Lavister	Wrex	SJ3758	53°7·2′	2°56·1′W	T	117
Lavrean	Corn	SX0358	50°23·6′	4°45·9′W	T	200
Lavrean Fm	Corn	SX0359	50°24·1′	4°46·0′W	FM	200
Law	Aberd	NJ5727	57°20·1′	2°42·4′W	X	37
Law	E Ayr	NS3746	55°41·1′	4°35·1′W	X	63
Law	E Dunb	NS5173	55°55·9′	4°22·7′W	X	64
Law	Kirk	SE1605	53°32·7′	1°45·1′W	X	110
Law	Renf	NS3863	55°50·2′	4°34·8′W	X	63
Law	S Lanak	NS7733	55°34·8′	3°56·6′W	X	71
Law	S Lanak	NS8252	55°45·1′	3°52·4′W	T	65,72
Law	W Loth	NT0372	55°56·1′	3°32·7′W	X	65
Lawbrook	Surrey	TQ0846	51°12·4′	0°26·8′W	X	187
Law Cairn	Aberd	NJ8859	57°37·5′	2°11·6′W	A	30
Law Castle	N Ayr	NS2148	55°41·8′	4°50·5′W	A	63
Law Drum	Fife	NO5511	56°17·6′	2°43·2′W	H	59
Lawdyke	E Ayr	NS5333	55°34·4′	4°19·5′W	X	70
Lawell Ho	Devon	SX8678	50°35·7′	3°36·3′W	X	191
Lawers	Pth & Kin	NN6739	56°31·7′	4°9·3′W	T	51
Lawers	Pth & Kin	NN7922	56°22·7′	3°57·1′W	T	51,52
Lawersbridge	E Ayr	NS4931	55°33·2′	4°23·2′W	X	70
Lawers Burn	Pth & Kin	NN6742	56°33·3′	4°9·4′W	W	51
Lawesknowe	D & G	NT0603	55°19·0′	3°28·4′W	X	78
Lawfield	E Loth	NT7572	55°56·7′	2°23·6′W	X	67
Lawfield	Fife	NO3210	56°16·9′	3°5·5′W	X	59
Lawfield	Midlo	NT3565	55°52·7′	3°1·9′W	X	66
Lawfield Dam	Renf	NS3769	55°53·5′	4°36·0′W	W	63
Lawfield Fm	Renf	NS3769	55°53·5′	4°36·0′W	FM	63
Lawflat	W Loth	NT1077	55°58·9′	3°26·1′W	X	65
Law Fm	Brad	SE0833	53°47·8′	1°52·3′W	FM	104
Law Fm	Lancs	SD7735	53°48·9′	2°20·5′W	FM	103
Law Fm	S Ayr	NS4128	55°31·4′	4°30·7′W	FM	70
Lawfolds	Aberd	NJ6679	57°20·7′	2°30·4′W	X	38
Lawford	Essex	TM0931	51°56·5′	1°2·8′E	T	168,169
Lawford	Somer	ST1336	51°7·2′	3°14·2′W	T	181
Lawford Hall	Essex	TM0831	51°56·5′	1°2·0′E	A	168,169
Lawford Heath	Warw	SP4573	52°21·4′	1°20·0′W	T	140
Lawford Hill Fm	Warw	SP4674	52°22·0′	1°19·1′W	FM	140
Lawford Ho	Essex	TM0930	51°56·0′	1°2·8′E	X	168,169
Lawfordhouse Fm	Essex	TM0930	51°56·0′	1°2·8′E	FM	168,169
Lawford Lodge Fm	Warw	SP4474	52°22·0′	1°20·8′W	FM	140
Lawglass	D & G	NX6987	55°9·9′	4°3·0′W	H	77
Law Hall Fm	Herts	TL1622	51°53·3′	0°18·5′W	FM	166
Lawhead	E Loth	NT6079	56°0·4′	2°38·0′W	X	67
Lawhead	Fife	NO4609	56°16·5′	2°51·9′W	X	59
Lawhead	S Lanak	NS9653	55°45·8′	3°39·0′W	X	65,72
Lawhead Fm	Midlo	NT2161	55°50·4′	3°15·3′W	FM	66
Lawhead Fm	S Lanak	NT0254	55°46·4′	3°33·3′W	FM	65,72
Lawhead Ho	S Lanak	NT0253	55°45·9′	3°33·3′W	X	65,72
Lawhead Plantn	E Loth	NT5872	55°56·6′	2°39·9′W	F	67
Lawheads	W Loth	NT0966	55°53·0′	3°26·8′W	X	65
Lawhibbet Fm	Corn	SX1055	50°22·1′	4°39·9′W	FM	200
Law Hill	Clackm	NS9799	56°10·6′	3°39·1′W	H	58
Lawhill	E Ayr	NS4622	55°28·3′	4°25·7′W	X	70
Law Hill	Lancs	SD9041	53°52·1′	2°8·7′W	X	103
Lawhill	N Ayr	NS2147	55°41·3′	4°50·4′W	X	63
Law Hill	N Ayr	NS2148	55°41·8′	4°50·5′W	H	63
Law Hill	N Ayr	NS3448	55°42·1′	4°38·1′W	X	63
Lawhill	Pth & Kin	NN9617	56°20·3′	3°40·5′W	X	58
Lawhill	S Ayr	NS3429	55°31·8′	4°37·4′W	X	70
Law Hill	S Lanak	NS8251	55°44·5′	3°52·3′W	T	65,72
Lawhill Ho	Clackm	NS9798	56°10·1′	3°39·1′W	X	58
Law Hillock	Moray	NJ4567	57°41·6′	2°54·9′W	X	28,29
Lawhitton	Corn	SX3582	50°37·1′	4°19·6′W	T	201
Lawhitton Barton	Corn	SX3682	50°37·1′	4°18·7′W	X	201
Law Ho	S Lanak	NS7243	55°40·1′	4°1·7′W	X	71
Lawhouses	Fife	NO4526	56°25·6′	2°53·1′W	X	54,59
Lawkland	N Yks	SD7766	54°5·6′	2°20·7′W	T	98
Lawkland Green	N Yks	SD7865	54°5·1′	2°19·8′W	T	98
Lawkland Hall Wood	N Yks	SD7765	54°5·1′	2°20·7′W	F	98
Law Kneis	Scot Bord	NT2913	55°24·6′	3°6·9′W	H	79
Lawless Fm	Somer	ST3113	50°55·0′	2°58·5′W	FM	193
Lawley	Shrops	SO5098	52°34·9′	2°43·9′W	X	137,138
Lawley	Wrekin	SJ6708	52°40·4′	2°28·9′W	T	127
Lawley Common	Wrekin	SJ6708	52°40·4′	2°28·9′W	X	127
Lawley Fm	Shrops	SO4998	52°34·9′	2°44·8′W	FM	137,138
Lawley, The	Shrops	SO4997	52°34·3′	2°44·8′W	H	137,138
Lawling Creek	Essex	TL9004	51°42·4′	0°45·4′E	W	168
Lawling Hall	Essex	TL9001	51°40·8′	0°45·3′E	X	168
Lawmarnock	Renf	NS3763	55°50·2′	4°35·7′W	X	63
Lawmuir	E Dunb	NS5172	55°55·3′	4°22·6′W	X	64
Lawmuir	Pth & Kin	NO0226	56°25·2′	3°34·9′W	X	52,53,58
Lawmuir	S Lanak	NS5953	55°45·2′	4°14·4′W	X	64
Lawmuir Fm	Clackm	NS9496	56°9·0′	3°41·9′W	FM	58
Lawn	Swin	SU1683	51°33·0′	1°45·8′W	T	173
Lawn Barn Fm	Dorset	SY7998	50°47·1′	2°17·5′W	FM	194
Lawn Brook	Powys	SO1875	52°22·3′	3°11·9′W	W	136,148
Lawn Coppice	Wilts	SU2869	51°25·4′	1°35·4′W	F	174
Lawn Cottage	Shrops	SJ6035	52°54·9′	2°35·3′W	X	127
Lawndowns	Corn	SW9151	50°19·5′	4°55·8′W	X	200,204
Lawness	Essex	TQ6596	51°38·5′	0°23·5′E	X	167,177
Lawney's Fm	Suff	TL9261	52°13·0′	0°49·0′E	FM	155
Lawn Fm	Bucks	SP6715	51°50·0′	1°1·3′W	FM	164,165
Lawn Fm	Cambs	TL3160	52°13·6′	0°4·5′W	FM	153
Lawn Fm	Derby	SK3050	53°3·0′	1°32·7′W	FM	119
Lawn Fm	Derby	SK3450	53°3·0′	1°29·2′W	FM	119
Lawn Fm	Dorset	ST8228	51°3·3′	2°15·0′W	FM	183
Lawn Fm	Glos	SO7927	51°56·7′	2°17·9′W	FM	162
Lawn Fm	Glos	SO8431	51°58·9′	2°13·6′W	FM	150
Lawn Fm	Hants	SU7060	51°20·3′	0°59·3′W	FM	175,186
Lawn Fm	Leic	SK5201	52°36·5′	1°13·5′W	FM	140
Lawn Fm	Norf	TG0740	52°55·3′	1°5·2′E	FM	133
Lawn Fm	Powys	SO2076	52°22·8′	3°10·1′W	FM	137,148
Lawn Fm	Staffs	SJ9350	53°3·1′	2°5·9′W	FM	118
Lawn Fm	Staffs	SJ9353	53°4·7′	2°5·9′W	FM	118
Lawn Fm	Suff	TL9962	52°13·4′	0°55·2′E	FM	155
Lawn Fm	Suff	TM2878	52°21·4′	1°21·3′E	FM	156
Lawn Fm	Wilts	ST9229	51°3·8′	2°6·5′W	FM	184
Lawn Fm	Wilts	ST9385	51°34·1′	2°5·7′W	FM	173
Lawn Hall	Essex	TL6517	51°49·9′	0°24·1′E	X	167
Lawnhead	Staffs	SJ8324	52°49·0′	2°14·7′W	T	127
Lawn Hill	Oxon	SP4649	52°8·5′	1°19·3′W	X	151
Lawn Hill	Shrops	SJ4102	52°37·0′	2°51·9′W	H	126
Lawn Hill Fm	Lincs	TF1750	53°2·3′	0°14·9′W	FM	121
Lawnhill Fm	Northnts	SP5449	52°8·4′	1°12·3′W	FM	152
Lawn Hollow Plantation	Leic	SK8127	52°50·3′	0°47·4′W	X	130
Lawns	Cumbr	SD4385	54°15·7′	2°52·1′W	X	97

Lawns	Essex	TQ5298	51°39·8′	0°12·3′E	X	167,177
Lawns	Wakf	SE3124	53°42·9′	1°31·4′W	T	104
Lawns Fm	Essex	TL7413	51°47·5′	0°31·8′E	FM	167
Lawns Fm	Heref	SO6222	51°54·0′	2°32·7′W	FM	162
Lawns Fm	N Lincs	SE7805	53°32·4′	0°49·0′W	FM	112
Lawns Fm	N Yks	NZ7407	54°27·4′	0°51·1′W	FM	94
Lawn's Fm	N Yks	SE1858	54°1·3′	1°43·1′W	FM	104
Lawns Fm	Shrops	SJ6035	52°54·9′	2°35·3′W	FM	127
Lawns Fm	Somer	ST2418	50°57·6′	3°4·5′W	FM	193
Lawns Fm	Staffs	SK2122	52°47·9′	1°40·9′W	FM	128
Lawns Fm	Warw	SP3786	52°28·5′	1°26·9′W	FM	140
Lawns Fm,The	Monm	SO4024	51°54·9′	2°51·9′W	FM	161
Lawns Gate	N Yks	NZ7506	54°26·9′	0°50·2′W	X	94
Lawns House Fm	N Yks	SE6839	53°50·8′	0°57·6′W	FM	105,106
Lawns, The	Cambs	TL4478	52°23·1′	0°7·4′E	X	142,143
Lawns, The	Heref	SO4832	51°59·3′	2°45·0′W	X	149,161
Lawns, The	Shrops	SJ5505	52°38·7′	2°39·5′W	X	126
Lawns, The	Somer	SS9943	51°10·9′	3°26·3′W	X	181
Lawns, The	Warw	SP3489	52°30·1′	1°29·5′W	X	140
Lawnswood	Leeds	SE2638	53°50·5′	1°35·9′W	T	104
Lawns Wood	Staffs	SO8786	52°28·5′	2°11·1′W	X	139
Lawnt	Denb	SJ0465	53°10·7′	3°25·8′W	T	116
Lawnt	Powys	SJ0412	52°42·1′	3°24·8′W	X	125
Lawnt	Powys	SJ0703	52°37·3′	3°22·0′W	X	136
Lawn, The	Essex	TQ8590	51°34·9′	0°40·6′E	X	178
Lawn, The	Leic	SK4201	52°36·5′	1°22·4′W	X	140
Lawn, The	Norf	TG0633	52°51·5′	1°4·0′E	X	133
Lawn, The	Shrops	SJ4833	52°53·8′	2°46·0′W	X	126
Lawn, The	Shrops	SO3881	52°25·6′	2°54·3′W	X	137
Lawn, The	Suff	TL9971	52°18·3′	0°55·5′E	X	144,155
Lawn Top	Northum	NY6365	54°58·9′	2°34·3′W	X	86
Lawnt, The	Powys	SJ1730	52°51·9′	3°13·6′W	X	125
Lawnt, The	Powys	SO1757	52°12·5′	3°12·5′W	X	148
Lawnwith	N Yks	SE2474	54°9·9′	1°37·5′W	X	99
Lawn Wood	Leic	SK5009	52°40·8′	1°15·2′W	F	140
Lawn Wood	Suff	TL6348	52°6·6′	0°23·2′E	F	154
Law of Brigton	Angus	NO2848	56°37·4′	3°10·0′W	X	53
Law of Lumgair	Aberd	NO8581	56°55·5′	2°14·3′W	X	45
Lawoodhead	N Ayr	NS2149	55°42·3′	4°50·5′W	X	63
Lawpark	Inverc	NS3468	55°52·9′	4°38·8′W	X	63
Law Plantn	Scot Bord	NT6309	55°22·7′	2°34·6′W	F	80
Lawrence Bridge Fm	Cambs	TL4590	52°29·5′	0°8·5′E	FM	143
Lawrence Burn	Cumbr	NY6776	55°4·9′	2°30·6′W	W	86,87
Lawrence Castle	Devon	SX8786	50°40·0′	3°35·6′W	X	192
Lawrence Edge	Derby	SK0898	53°29·0′	1°52·4′W	X	110
Lawrence End	Herts	TL1419	51°51·7′	0°20·3′W	X	166
Lawrence Field	Derby	SK2579	53°18·7′	1°37·1′W	X	119
Lawrencefield	Pth & Kin	NO0018	56°20·9′	3°36·6′W	X	58
Lawrence Fm	Norf	TF9610	52°39·4′	0°54·3′E	FM	132
Lawrence Hill	Newp	ST3488	51°35·5′	2°56·8′W	T	171
Lawrenceholme	Cumbr	NY2352	54°51·7′	3°11·6′W	X	85
Lawrence House Fm	Cumbr	SD4985	54°15·7′	2°46·6′W	FM	97
Lawrence of Arabia's Cottage	Dorset	SY8290	50°42·8′	2°14·9′W	X	194
Lawrence's Cottage	Dorset	SY5585	50°40·0′	2°37·8′W	X	194
Lawrence's Fm	Oxon	SU7284	51°33·2′	0°57·3′W	FM	175
Lawrence's Hill	Wrekin	SJ6409	52°40·9′	2°31·6′W	X	127
Lawrence's Lodge	Cambs	TL1192	52°31·1′	0°21·4′W	X	142
Lawrence's Piece	Orkney	HY3949	59°19·6′	3°3·8′W	X	5
Lawrence Weston	C of Bris	ST5478	51°30·2′	2°39·4′W	T	172
Lawrenny	Pemb	SN0107	51°43·8′	4°52·5′W	T	157,158
Lawrenny Quay	Pemb	SN0106	51°43·3′	4°52·5′W	T	157,158
Lawridding	D & G	NX9983	55°8·1′	3°34·6′W	X	78
Lawrie's Den	E Loth	NT7078	55°59·9′	2°28·4′W	X	67
Lawriesmuir	S Lanak	NS7839	55°38·0′	3°55·8′W	X	71
Law Rocks	E Loth	NT5486	56°4·1′	2°43·9′W	X	66
Lawr-y-pant	Shrops	SJ2632	52°53·1′	3°5·6′W	X	126
Laws	Angus	NO4935	56°30·5′	2°49·3′W	X	54
Law's Castle	N Lanak	NS8261	55°49·9′	3°52·6′W	X	65
Laws Fell	Northum	NY7457	54°54·7′	2°23·9′W	X	86,87
Law's Fm	Lincs	TF2113	52°42·3′	0°12·1′W	FM	131,142
Laws Hall	Cumbr	NY4271	55°2·1′	2°54·0′W	X	85
Lawshall	Suff	TL8654	52°9·4′	0°43·5′E	T	155
Lawshall Green	Suff	TL8753	52°8·8′	0°44·4′E	T	155
Lawside	S Lanak	NS5952	55°44·7′	4°14·3′W	X	64
Lawsie	Aberd	NO2696	57°3·2′	3°12·7′W	X	37,44
Lawsings	N Yks	SD7366	54°5·6′	2°24·4′W	X	98
Law's Lawn	Northnts	TL0298	52°34·4′	0°29·3′W	X	141
Laws Moor Plantn	Scot Bord	NT8349	55°44·3′	2°15·8′W	F	74
Lawsonhall	Angus	NO5041	56°33·8′	2°48·4′W	X	54
Lawson Hill	Cumbr	NY5348	54°49·7′	2°43·5′W	H	86
Lawson Ho	Lancs	SD7747	53°55·4′	2°20·6′W	X	103
Lawson Park	Cumbr	SD3195	54°21·0′	3°3·3′W	X	96,97
Lawson's Barn Fm	Notts	SK6740	52°57·4′	0°59·8′W	FM	129
Laws, The	Northum	NY7757	54°54·7′	2°21·1′W	X	86,87
Laws, The	Scot Bord	NT8350	55°44·8′	2°15·8′W	X	67,74
Lawston	D & G	NX8770	55°1·0′	3°45·6′W	X	84
Lawston	Scot Bord	NY4681	55°7·5′	2°50·4′W	X	79
Lawsuit Law	Scot Bord	NT7113	55°24·9′	2°27·1′W	H	80
Law,The	Aberd	NJ8166	57°41·3′	2°18·7′W	A	29,30
Law, The	Angus	NO5137	56°31·6′	2°47·3′W	X	54
Law, The	Clackm	NS9199	56°10·5′	3°44·9′W	H	58
Law, The	Clackm	NS9199	56°10·5′	3°44·9′W	X	58
Law, The	D & G	NX9797	55°15·6′	3°36·8′W	H	78
Law,The	Scot Bord	NT6731	55°34·5′	2°31·0′W	X	74
Lawthorn	N Ayr	NS3440	55°37·8′	4°37·8′W	X	70
Law Ting Holm	Shetld	HU4143	60°10·4′	1°15·2′W	A	4
Lawton	Angus	NO6348	56°37·6′	2°35·7′W	X	54
Lawton	Heref	SO4459	52°13·8′	2°48·8′W	T	148,149
Lawton	Shrops	SO5183	52°26·8′	2°42·9′W	T	137,138
Lawton-gate	Ches	SJ8056	53°6·3′	2°17·5′W	T	118
Lawton Grange	Staffs	SK1005	52°38·7′	1°50·7′W	X	139
Lawton Hall	Ches	SJ8255	53°5·8′	2°15·7′W	X	118
Lawton Heath	Ches	SJ8056	53°6·3′	2°17·5′W	X	118
Lawton Heath End	Ches	SJ7956	53°6·3′	2°18·4′W	T	118
Lawton Ho	Pth & Kin	NO2034	56°29·7′	3°17·5′W	X	53
Lawton's Hope	Heref	SO4750	52°9·0′	2°46·1′W	X	148,149
Lawyer's Cross	Cumbr	NY6248	54°49·8′	2°35·1′W	X	86
Lawyers' Fm	Lincs	TF4233	52°52·8′	0°7·0′E	FM	131
Laxa Burn	Shetld	HU5089	60°35·1′	1°4·7′W	W	1,2

Lax Dale	Shetld	HU4031	60°4·0′	1°16·4′W	X	4
Laxe's Fm	Warw	SP2691	52°31·2′	1°36·6′W	FM	140
Laxey	I of M	SC4384	54°13·9′	4°24·1′W	T	95
Laxey Bay	I of M	SC4382	54°12·8′	4°24·0′W	W	95
Laxey Glen	I of M	SC4285	54°14·4′	4°25·1′W	X	95
Laxey Glen Gdns	I of M	SC4284	54°13·9′	4°25·0′W	X	95
Laxey Head	I of M	SC4483	54°13·4′	4°23·2′W	H	95
Laxey River	I of M	SC4285	54°14·4′	4°25·1′W	W	95
Laxfield	Suff	TM2972	52°18·1′	1°21·9′E	T	156
Laxfield Ho	Suff	TM2870	52°17·1′	1°21·0′E	X	156
Laxfield Wood	Suff	TM2969	52°16·5′	1°21·8′E	F	156
Laxfirth	Shetld	HU4346	60°12·0′	1°13·0′W	X	4
Lax Firth	Shetld	HU4447	60°12·6′	1°11·9′W	W	3
Laxfirth	Shetld	HU4759	60°19·0′	1°8·5′W	T	2,3
Laxford Bay	Highld	NC2248	58°23·3′	5°2·2′W	W	9
Laxford Bridge	Highld	NC2346	58°22·3′	5°1·1′W	X	9
Lax-Hill	Rut	SK8806	52°38·9′	0°41·6′W	H	141
Laxigar	Orkney	ND4396	58°51·1′	2°58·8′W	X	6,7
Laxo	Shetld	HU4463	60°21·2′	1°11·7′W	T	2,3
Laxobigging	Shetld	HU4173	60°26·6′	1°14·8′W	T	2,3
Laxo Burn	Shetld	HU4362	60°20·7′	1°12·8′W	W	2,3
Laxo Knowe	Shetld	HU4264	60°21·7′	1°13·8′W	H	2,3
Laxo Voe	Shetld	HU4563	60°21·2′	1°10·6′W	W	2,3
Laxo Water	Shetld	HU4465	60°22·3′	1°11·6′W	W	2,3
Laxton	E Yorks	SE7925	53°43·2′	0°47·8′W	T	105,106
Laxton	Northnts	SP9496	52°33·5′	0°36·4′W	T	141
Laxton	Notts	SK7267	53°11·9′	0°54·9′W	T	120
Laxton Common	Notts	SK6967	53°12·0′	0°57·6′W	X	120
Laxton Grange	E Yorks	SE8828	53°44·7′	0°39·5′W	X	106
Laxton Hall	Northnts	SP9597	52°34·0′	0°35·5′W	X	141
Laxton Lodge	Notts	SK7263	53°9·8′	0°55·0′W	X	120
Laxton's Covert	Leic	SK8016	52°44·4′	0°48·5′W	F	130
Laxy Wheel	I of M	SC4385	54°14·4′	4°24·1′W	X	95
Laybrook Fm	W Susx	TQ1118	50°57·3′	0°24·8′W	FM	198
Layburn Moor	N Yks	SE0892	54°19·7′	1°52·2′W	X	99
Laycock	Brad	SE0340	53°51·6′	1°56·8′W	T	104
Laycock Fm	Dorset	SY7194	50°44·9′	2°24·3′W	FM	194
Layer Breton	Essex	TL9418	51°49·8′	0°49·3′E	T	168
Layer Breton Hall	Essex	TL9417	51°49·3′	0°49·3′E	X	168
Layer Breton Heath	Essex	TL9418	51°49·8′	0°49·3′E	X	168
Layer Brook	Essex	TL9115	51°48·3′	0°46·6′E	W	168
Layer de la Haye	Essex	TL9720	51°50·9′	0°52·0′E	T	168
Layer Hall	Essex	TL9619	51°50·3′	0°51·1′E	X	168
Layer Knowe	Scot Bord	NT2227	55°32·1′	3°13·7′W	H	73
Layer Marney	Essex	TL9217	51°49·3′	0°47·6′E	T	168
Layer Marney Tower	Essex	TL9217	51°49·3′	0°47·6′E	A	168
Layerthorpe	York	SE6151	53°57·3′	1°3·8′W	T	105
Layer Wood	Essex	TL9118	51°49·9′	0°46·7′E	F	168
Layhams Fm	Brom	TQ3962	51°20·6′	0°0·1′E	FM	177,187
Laylands Fm	N Yks	SE2698	54°22·9′	1°35·6′W	FM	99
Laylands Fm	Surrey	TQ3541	51°9·4′	0°3·8′W	FM	187
Laymore	Dorset	ST3804	50°50·2′	2°52·4′W	T	193
Laynes Fm	Glos	SO7812	51°48·6′	2°18·8′W	FM	162
Laynes Fm	Wilts	ST9794	51°38·9′	2°2·2′W	FM	163,173
Layriggs	Cumbr	SD1380	54°12·7′	3°19·6′W	X	96
Lays Fm	Bath & NE Somer	ST6467	51°24·3′	2°30·7′W	FM	172
Lay's Fm	Norf	TL9898	52°32·9′	0°55·6′E	FM	144
Layside	Northum	NY7565	54°59·0′	2°23·0′W	X	86,87
Laystone	Pth & Kin	NO1838	56°31·9′	3°19·5′W	X	53
Lay Taing	Orkney	ND4686	58°45·8′	2°55·5′W	X	7
Layters Green	Bucks	SU9890	51°36·2′	0°34·7′W	T	175,176
Laytham	E Yorks	SE7439	53°50·8′	0°52·1′W	T	105,106
Laytham Grange	E Yorks	SE7540	53°51·3′	0°51·2′W	X	105,106
Laytham Green Fm	E Yorks	SE7441	53°51·8′	0°52·1′W	FM	105,106
Laythams	Lancs	SD6952	53°58·0′	2°27·9′W	X	103
Lay, The	Corn	TQ4406	50°50·4′	0°3·1′E	X	198
Lay, The	Norf	TM3088	52°26·7′	1°23·5′E	W	156
Laythes, The	Cumbr	NY2455	54°53·3′	3°10·7′W	X	85
Laythorpe Fm	Brad	SE1040	53°51·6′	1°50·5′W	FM	104
Laythorpe House Fm	Lincs	TF3562	53°8·5′	0°1·5′E	FM	122
Laythwaite Crags	Cumbr	NY4714	54°31·4′	2°48·7′W	X	90
Layton	Blackp	SD3236	53°49·2′	3°1·6′W	T	102
Layton Fields	N Yks	NZ1512	54°30·4′	1°45·7′W	X	92
Layton Ho	Durham	NZ3727	54°38·4′	1°25·2′W	X	93
Layton Lings	Durham	NZ3926	54°37·9′	1°23·3′W	X	93
Layton Sta	Blackp	SD3238	53°50·3′	3°1·6′W	X	102
Layton Village	Durham	NZ3726	54°37·9′	1°25·2′W	A	93
Lazaretto Point	Arg & Bt	NS1780	55°58·9′	4°55·6′W	X	63
Lazenby	Red & Cl	NZ5719	54°34·0′	1°6·7′W	T	93
Lazenby Bank	Red & Cl	NZ5719	54°34·0′	1°6·7′W	X	93
Lazenby Grange	N Yks	SE3499	54°23·4′	1°28·2′W	X	99
Lazenby Hall	N Yks	SE3398	54°22·8′	1°29·1′W	A	99
Lazencroft Fm	Leeds	SE3834	53°48·3′	1°25·0′W	FM	104
Lazonby	Cumbr	NY5439	54°44·9′	2°42·5′W	T	90
Lazonby Fell	Cumbr	NY5139	54°44·9′	2°45·3′W	H	90
Lazonby Hall	Cumbr	NY5440	54°45·4′	2°42·5′W	X	86
Lazybeds Plantn	Scot Bord	NT8956	55°48·1′	2°10·1′W	F	67,74
Lazyfold	Aberd	NJ5726	57°19·7′	2°42·4′W	X	37
Lazy Knowe	Cumbr	NY5687	55°10·8′	2°41·0′W	H	80
Lazy Well	Aberd	NJ4408	57°9·8′	2°55·1′W	X	37
L Dubh	Highld	NH6075	57°44·8′	4°20·7′W	W	21
Lea	Derby	SK3257	53°6·8′	1°30·9′W	T	119
Lea	Devon	SY2499	50°47·4′	3°4·3′W	T	192,193
Lea	Heref	SO6521	51°53·4′	2°30·1′W	T	162
Lea	Lancs	SD4930	53°46·1′	2°46·0′W	T	102
Lea	Lincs	SK8286	53°22·1′	0°45·6′W	T	112,121
Lea	Orkney	HY2426	59°7·1′	3°19·2′W	X	6
Lea	Shetld	HU3051	60°14·8′	1°27·0′W	X	3
Lea	Shrops	SJ4108	52°40·2′	2°52·0′W	T	126
Lea	Shrops	SO3589	52°29·9′	2°57·1′W	T	137
Lea	Wilts	ST9586	51°34·6′	2°3·9′W	T	173
Leaba Bhaltair	Highld	NH4582	57°48·3′	4°36·0′W	X	20
Leaba Bhruic	Highld	NH4384	57°49·3′	4°38·1′W	X	20
Leabaidh a' Mhinisteir	N Eil	NB4929	58°11·0′	6°15·7′W	X	8
Leabaidh an Daimh Bhuidhe	Aberd	NJ1301	57°5·8′	3°25·7′W	H	36
Leabaidh Fhéidh	Highld	NC3002	57°58·8′	4°52·0′W	H	15
Lea Bailey Inclosures	Heref	SO6419	51°52·3′	2°31·0′W	F	162
Leaba Mhór	Arg & Bt	NR3688	56°1·0′	6°13·7′W	X	61

Leabank	Aberd	NJ6600	57°5·6′	2°33·2′W	X	38
Lea Bank Fm	Sheff	SK3090	53°24·6′	1°32·5′W	FM	110,111
Lea Barton	Devon	ST0420	50°58·5′	3°21·7′W	X	181
Lea Bridge	Derby	SK3156	53°6·3′	1°31·8′W	X	119
Lea Bridge	Hack	TQ3586	51°33·6′	0°2·8′W	T	177
Lea Brook	Roth	SK4098	53°28·9′	1°23·4′W	X	111
Leabrooks	Derby	SK4153	53°4·6′	1°22·9′W	T	120
Leaburn	S Lanak	NS6449	55°43·2′	4°9·5′W	X	64
Lea by Backford	Ches	SJ3971	53°14·2′	2°54·4′W	T	117
Leac a' Bhaid-bheithe	Highld	NH0390	57°51·6′	5°18·8′W	X	19
Leac a' Bheithe	Highld	NM6473	56°47·6′	5°51·4′W	H	40
Leac a' Chaisteil	Highld	NM3693	56°57·4′	6°20·1′W	X	39
Leac a'Chaoruinn	Arg & Bt	NM9605	56°11·9′	5°16·9′W	X	55
Leac a' Chlobha	Highld	NG4047	57°26·6′	6°19·5′W	H	23
Leacach Stùlabhal	N Eil	NF7923	57°11·4′	7°18·4′W	X	22
Leac a' Ghille	N Ayr	NR9736	55°34·8′	5°12·8′W	X	69
Leac a' Ghobhainn	Highld	NC3437	58°17·7′	4°49·5′W	H	15
Leac a' Ghuidhal	Highld	NM4985	56°53·6′	6°6·8′W	X	39
Leacainn	Highld	NN6584	56°55·9′	4°12·7′W	H	42
Leacainn	N Eil	NB1301	57°54·6′	6°50·3′W	T	14
Leac Airigh Choinnich	Arg & Bt	NM6623	56°20·8′	5°46·8′W	X	49
Leac a' Langich	N Eil	NL5680	56°47·3′	7°37·6′W	X	31
Leac a Li	N Eil	NG1292	57°49·8′	6°50·6′W	T	14
Leaca Mór	N Ayr	NR9523	55°27·7′	5°14·1′W	X	68,69
Leac an Aiseig	Highld	NG8906	57°6·1′	5°28·6′W	X	33
Leacanashie	Highld	NG8535	57°21·5′	5°34·0′W	T	24
Leac an t-Sidhein	Highld	NH6117	57°13·6′	4°17·7′W	X	35
Leac an Daimh	Highld	NH8931	57°21·6′	3°50·3′W	X	27,36
Leacan Donna	Highld	NG8392	57°52·2′	5°39·1′W	X	19
Leacan Dubha	Arg & Bt	NM6829	56°24·0′	5°45·1′W	X	49
Leacan Dubha	Highld	NH1942	57°26·2′	5°0·5′W	X	25
Leacan Dubha	Highld	NH2602	57°4·8′	4°51·8′W	X	34
Leac an Fhaobhair	Highld	NG8997	57°55·0′	5°33·3′W	X	19
Leac an Fhidleir	Highld	NM6363	56°42·2′	5°51·9′W	H	40
Leac an Fhuarain	Highld	NM8774	56°48·8′	5°28·9′W	X	40
Leac an Ime	Highld	NG9895	57°54·2′	5°24·1′W	X	19
Leac an Leathaid	Arg & Bt	NM5936	56°27·5′	5°54·3′W	X	47,48
Leacan Mhór	Arg & Bt	NM0709	56°14·3′	5°6·4′W	X	56
Leacann	Arg & Bt	NS1798	56°8·6′	4°56·3′W	X	56
Leacann a' Chnoic	Arg & Bt	NR4150	55°40·7′	6°6·8′W	X	60
Leacann an Daimh	Moray	NJ1106	57°8·4′	3°27·8′W	X	36
Leacann an Dòthaidh	Arg & Bt	NN3041	56°32·1′	4°45·4′W	X	50
Leacann an Sgàilean	Pth & Kin	NN5570	56°48·2′	4°22·0′W	X	42
Leacann Beinn Dòrain	Arg & Bt	NN3138	56°30·5′	4°44·3′W	X	50
Leacann Bhreac	Highld	NN4869	57°41·4′	4°32·5′W	X	20
Leacann Bhuidhe	Pth & Kin	NN6813	56°17·7′	4°7·5′W	X	57
Leacann Doire Bainneir	Highld	NN2994	57°0·6′	4°48·5′W	H	34
Leacann Fiadhach	Highld	NH4708	57°8·5′	4°31·3′W	X	34
Leacann Ghlasa	Pth & Kin	NN6138	56°31·1′	4°15·1′W	X	51
Leacann Ghorm	Highld	NH3588	57°51·3′	4°46·4′W	X	20
Leacann Gortain	Arg & Bt	NN3748	56°36·0′	4°38·9′W	X	50
Leacann Nighean an t-Siosalaich	Highld	NG3941	57°23·3′	6°20·1′W	X	23
Leacann nam Braonan	Highld	NN2650	56°36·8′	4°49·7′W	X	41
Leacann nam Fuaran	Highld	NM7296	57°0·2′	5°44·8′W	X	33,40
Leacann nam Fuaran	Highld	NN3658	56°41·4′	4°40·2′W	X	41
Leacann nan Gall	Arg & Bt	NS1079	55°58·2′	5°2·2′W	H	63
Leacann nan Giomach	Pth & Kin	NN4461	56°43·1′	4°32·5′W	X	42
Leacann na Sguabaich	Highld	NN5783	56°55·2′	4°20·5′W	X	42
Leacann na Sguaibe	Arg & Bt	NN0744	56°33·2′	5°8·0′W	X	50
Leacann Riabhach	Stir	NN4624	56°23·3′	4°29·2′W	X	51
Leacann Water	Arg & Bt	NN0202	56°10·4′	5°10·9′W	W	55
Leacan Riabhach	Highld	NH1732	57°20·8′	5°2·2′W	X	25
Leacan Ruadha	N Ayr	NR8832	55°32·4′	5°21·2′W	X	68,69
Leac an Staoin	Arg & Bt	NM5524	56°21·0′	5°57·5′W	X	48
Leac an Tobair	N Ayr	NR9643	55°38·5′	5°14·1′W	X	62,69
Leac an Tuadh	Highld	NH2778	57°45·8′	4°54·0′W	X	20
Leac an Tuairneir	Highld	NM6261	56°41·1′	5°52·7′W	X	40
Leacantuim	Highld	NN1157	56°40·3′	5°4·6′W	X	41
Leac a' Phris	Highld	NM7850	56°35·6′	5°36·5′W	X	49
Lea Castle Fm	Worcs	SO8479	52°24·8′	2°13·7′W	FM	138
Leac Bhàn	N Eil	NF9079	57°41·9′	7°11·8′W	X	18
Leac Bharainn	Arg & Bt	NN0649	56°35·8′	5°9·2′W	H	50
Leac Bhuidhe	Arg & Bt	NM4200	56°7·6′	6°8·7′W	H	61
Leac Bhuidhe	Arg & Bt	NR2874	55°53·2′	6°20·6′W	X	60
Leac Bhuidhe	Arg & Bt	NR3489	56°1·5′	6°15·7′W	X	61
Leac Bhuidhe	Arg & Bt	NR3788	56°1·0′	6°12·8′W	X	61
Leac Bhuidhe	Arg & Bt	NR6119	55°24·7′	5°46·1′W	X	68
Leac Bhuidhe	Highld	NM8692	56°58·4′	5°30·8′W	X	33,40
Leac Buidhe	Highld	NC3372	58°36·5′	4°52·0′W	X	9
Leac Chlann Dòmhnuill Mhic Dhùghail	Highld	NM7765	56°43·7′	5°38·3′W	X	40
Leac Chogaidh	Arg & Bt	NM1455	56°36·2′	6°39·2′W	X	46
Leac Choinnich	Highld	NG4336	57°20·8′	6°15·9′W	X	23,32
Leac Chorrach	Highld	NN2090	56°58·2′	4°57·2′W	H	34
Leac Dhonn	Highld	NH0199	57°56·4′	5°21·2′W	X	19
Leac Dhubh Earrainn	Arg & Bt	NR7458	55°46·0′	5°35·7′W	X	62
Leac Dhubh Poll Ula	N Eil	NB1336	58°13·4′	6°52·8′W	X	13
Leac Doire Lochaidh	Highld	NH0602	57°4·4′	5°11·6′W	X	33
Leac Dubh Gob Thais	N Eil	NB5349	58°21·9′	6°12·9′W	X	8
Leac Eascadail	N Eil	NG2399	57°53·9′	6°40·0′W	X	14
Leac Eidhne	Arg & Bt	NR4351	55°41·3′	6°4·9′W	X	60
Leacet Hill	Cumbr	NY5626	54°37·9′	2°40·5′W	X	90
Leac Fhola	Arg & Bt	NR5577	55°55·7′	5°54·9′W	H	61
Leac Gallain	Highld	ND2434	58°17·5′	3°17·3′W	X	11
Leac Gharbh	N Ayr	NS0047	55°40·8′	5°10·4′W	X	63,69
Leac Ghorm	Aberd	NO2295	57°2·6′	3°16·7′W	H	36,44
Leac Ghorm	Highld	NH4285	57°49·8′	4°39·2′W	X	20
Leac Ghorm	Highld	NN9493	57°1·2′	3°44·3′W	X	36,43
Leachachan	Highld	NG8922	57°14·7′	5°29·4′W	X	33
Leach Castle Fm	V of Glam	ST0573	51°27·1′	3°21·6′W	FM	170
Leachd	Arg & Bt	NS0498	56°8·3′	5°8·8′W	X	56
Leachd	Highld	NG4445	57°25·7′	6°15·4′W	X	23
Leachdann Féith Seasgachain	Pth & Kin	NN9181	56°54·7′	3°47·0′W	H	43
Leachd an Nostarie	Highld	NM6896	57°0·1′	5°48·8′W	X	40
Leachd Dhubh	Highld	NM7495	56°59·7′	5°42·8′W	X	33,40
Leachd Fheadanach	Highld	NM7273	56°47·8′	5°43·6′W	X	40
Leachd Mhór	Highld	NH3410	57°9·3′	4°44·2′W	X	34
Leachd na Ruadhaig	Highld	NH3109	57°8·7′	4°47·1′W	X	34

Leachd ri Grèin	Highld	NN5488	56°57·9'	4°23·6'W	H	42
Leachd Thuilm	Highld	NG4224	57°14·3'	6°16·1'W	X	32
Leaches	Roch	SD8313	53°37·0'	2°15·0'W	X	109
Leache's Br	Brad	SE0742	53°52·7'	1°53·2'W	X	104
Leachfield Grange	N Yks	SE3986	54°16·3'	1°23·6'W	X	99
Leach Ho	Lancs	SD4856	54°0·1'	2°47·2'W	X	102
Leach Ho	Lancs	SD6241	53°52·1'	2°34·3'W	X	102,103
Leachie Hill	Aberd	NO7385	56°57·6'	2°26·2'W	H	45
Leachive Fm	Arg & Bt	NR7487	56°1·6'	5°37·2'W	FM	55
Leachkin	Highld	NH6344	57°28·2'	4°16·6'W	T	26
Leachonich	Highld	NH6885	57°50·4'	4°12·9'W	X	21
Leachpool	Pemb	SM9719	51°50·2'	4°56·4'W	X	157,158
Leac Iain	N Eil	NB0538	58°14·2'	7°1·1'W	X	13
Leac Iain Tailleir	N Eil	HW8132	59°7·4'	5°49·1'W	X	8
Leac Innis nan Gobhar	Highld	NG9390	57°51·4'	5°28·9'W	X	19
Leack	Arg & Bt	NS0498	56°8·3'	5°8·8'W	X	56
Leac Ladaidh	Highld	NN2399	57°3·1'	4°54·6'W	X	34
Leac Liath	Pth & Kin	NN8073	56°50·2'	3°57·6'W	H	43
Leac Liutha	Arg & Bt	NR6080	55°57·4'	5°50·3'W	X	61
Lea Close	Darl	NZ3422	54°35·8'	1°28·0'W	X	93
Leac Mhòr	Highld	NG8897	57°55·0'	5°34·3'W	X	19
Leac Mhòr	Highld	NN0661	56°42·3'	5°9·7'W	X	41
Leac Mhòr Fianuis	N Eil	HW8133	59°7·9'	5°49·2'W	X	8
Leac na Ban	Arg & Bt	NR7891	56°3·9'	5°33·5'W	X	55
Leac na Banaraich	N Eil	NF7908	57°3·3'	7°17·2'W	X	31
Leac na Bò Riabhaich	Arg & Bt	NM4558	56°38·9'	6°9·1'W	X	47
Leac na Carnaich	Highld	NM9889	56°58·2'	5°18·8'W	H	40
Leac na' Fealla	N Eil	NL5580	56°47·3'	7°38·6'W	X	31
Leac na Fearna	Highld	NG9701	57°3·6'	5°20·4'W	X	33
Leac na Fidhle	Highld	NM8049	56°35·1'	5°34·5'W	X	49
Leac na Hoe	N Eil	NF9772	57°38·4'	7°4·2'W	X	18
Leac na h-Uaigh	Highld	NH6509	57°9·4'	4°13·5'W	X	35
Leac nam Bà	Arg & Bt	NM4044	56°31·2'	6°13·2'W	X	47,48
Leac nam Buidheag	Highld	NH3322	57°15·8'	4°45·7'W	X	26
Leac nam Faoileann	Highld	NG4214	57°8·9'	6°15·5'W	X	32
Leac nam Fionn	Arg & Bt	NN1040	56°31·1'	5°4·9'W	X	50
Leac nam Frith-allt	Highld	NM8171	56°47·0'	5°34·7'W	X	40
Leac nam Fuaran	Highld	NM7376	56°49·5'	5°42·8'W	X	40
Leac nam Leum	Arg & Bt	NM4918	56°17·5'	6°2·9'W	X	48
Leac nan Caiseachan	Highld	NG7701	57°3·0'	5°40·2'W	X	33
Leac nan Carn	Highld	NN3062	56°43·4'	4°46·2'W	X	41
Leac nan Cisteachan	Highld	NH5114	57°11·8'	4°27·5'W	H	35
Leac nan Cliabhan	Pth & Kin	NN7075	56°51·2'	4°7·5'W	X	42
Leac nan Craobh	Highld	NG5720	57°12·6'	6°1·0'W	H	32
Leac nan Cudaigean	N Eil	NB1434	58°12·4'	6°51·7'W	X	13
Leac nan Fionn	Highld	NG4570	57°39·1'	6°16·0'W	H	23
Leac nan Gaidhseich	Highld	NG9804	57°5·2'	5°19·6'W	X	33
Leac nan Geadh	Arg & Bt	NR3688	56°1·0'	6°13·7'W	X	61
Leac na Nighinn	Highld	NH0231	57°19·9'	5°16·9'W	X	25
Leac nan Uan	Highld	NH3796	57°55·7'	4°44·7'W	H	34
Leacnasaide	Highld	NG7972	57°41·3'	5°42·0'W	X	19
Leac na Saighde	Highld	NM7155	56°38·1'	5°43·6'W	X	49
Leac Nighe	N Eil	NG4196	57°53·0'	6°21·7'W	X	14
Leacon Fm	Kent	TQ9547	51°11·6'	0°47·8'E	FM	189
Lea Court Fm	Glos	SO7510	51°47·5'	2°21·4'W	FM	162
Leacraithnaich	Highld	NM7447	56°33·9'	5°40·3'W	X	49
Leac Reidh	N Eil	NB3909	57°59·9'	6°24·6'W	X	14
Leac Ribhach	Highld	NM8573	56°48·2'	5°30·8'W	X	40
Leacroft Hall	Staffs	SJ9639	52°57·1'	2°3·2'W	X	127
Lea Cross	Shrops	SJ4208	52°40·2'	2°51·1'W	X	126
Leac Shleamhuinn	N Eil	NF7714	57°6·5'	7°19·7'W	X	31
Leac Shoilleir	Highld	NM6065	56°43·2'	5°54·9'W	H	40
Leac-stearnan	Highld	NG4513	57°8·5'	6°12·5'W	X	32
Leac Suenish	N Eil	NF8878	57°41·3'	7°13·7'W	X	18
Leac Tressirnish	Highld	NG5257	57°32·4'	6°8·2'W	X	23,24
Leadbeater's Fm	Bolton	SD6904	53°32·1'	2°27·7'W	FM	109
Lead Brook	Flint	SJ2670	53°13·6'	3°6·1'W	W	117
Leadbrook Hall	Flint	SJ2571	53°14·1'	3°7·0'W	X	117
Lead Burn	Scot Bord	NT2254	55°46·6'	3°14·2'W	W	66,73
Leadburn	Scot Bord	NT2355	55°47·2'	3°13·2'W	T	66,73
Lead Burn	S Lanak	NS9216	55°25·8'	3°42·0'W	W	71,78
Leadburn Rig	S Lanak	NS9216	55°25·8'	3°42·0'W	H	71,78
Leadclune	Highld	NH5625	57°17·8'	4°22·9'W	X	26,35
Leadendale	Staffs	SJ9239	52°57·1'	2°6·7'W	T	127
Leaden Hall	Lincs	TF3531	52°51·8'	0°0·7'E	X	131
Leaden Hall	Suff	TL9537	52°0·1'	0°50·8'E	X	155
Leadenhall Fm	Lincs	TF3633	52°52·9'	0°1·7'E	FM	131
Leadenham	Lincs	SK9552	53°3·6'	0°34·5'W	T	121
Leadenham Heath	Lincs	SK9751	53°3·1'	0°32·8'W	X	121
Leadenham Ho	Lincs	SK9451	53°3·1'	0°35·4'W	X	121
Leadenham Low Fields	Lincs	SK9352	53°3·7'	0°36·3'W	X	121
Leadenporch Fm	Oxon	SP4730	51°58·2'	1°18·6'W	FM	151
Leaden Roding	Essex	TL5913	51°48·8'	0°18·7'E	T	167
Leadensider Burn	Aberd	NJ3419	57°15·7'	3°5·2'W	W	37
Leaderfoot	Scot Bord	NT5734	55°36·1'	2°40·5'W	X	73,74
Leadervale Ho	Scot Bord	NT5639	55°38·8'	2°41·5'W	X	73
Leader Water	Scot Bord	NT5151	55°45·2'	2°46·4'W	W	66,73
Leader Water	Scot Bord	NT5542	55°40·4'	2°42·5'W	W	73
Leadgate	Cumbr	NY7043	54°47·1'	2°27·6'W	T	86,87
Leadgate	Durham	NZ1251	54°51·5'	1°48·4'W	T	88
Leadgate	Ghead	NZ1159	54°55·8'	1°49·3'W	T	88
Leadgate	Northum	NY7854	54°53·1'	2°20·2'W	X	86,87
Leadgate	Northum	NY8177	55°5·5'	2°17·4'W	X	86,87
Leadgate Fm	Ches	SJ5062	53°9·4'	2°44·5'W	FM	117
Lead Hall Fm	N Yks	SE4636	53°49·3'	1°17·7'W	FM	105
Leadhills	S Lanak	NS8815	55°25·2'	3°45·7'W	T	71,78
Leadie	Shetld	HU2875	60°27·7'	1°29·0'W	X	3
Leadingcross Green	Kent	TQ8951	51°13·8'	0°42·8'E	T	189
Leading Stead	N Yks	NY9406	54°27·2'	2°5·1'W	X	91,92
Leading Stead Bottom	N Yks	NY9507	54°27·7'	2°4·2'W	X	91,92
Leadketty	Pth & Kin	NO0115	56°19·3'	3°35·6'W	X	58
Leadlich	Aberd	NJ5205	57°8·3'	2°47·1'W	H	37
Leadloch Fm	N Lanak	NS9160	55°49·5'	3°44·0'W	FM	65
Leadmachany	Pth & Kin	NN8715	56°19·1'	3°49·2'W	X	58
Leadmill	Derby	SK2380	53°19·2'	1°38·9'W	T	110
Leadmill	Flint	SJ2464	53°10·3'	3°7·8'W	T	117
Lead Mill Fm	N Yks	SE4737	53°49·9'	1°16·7'W	FM	105
Lead Mine Burn	S Ayr	NX3091	55°11·3'	4°39·8'W	W	76
Lead Mine Moss	N Yks	SD7274	54°9·9'	2°25·3'W	X	98
Lead Mines Clough	Lancs	SD6316	53°38·6'	2°33·2'W	X	109
Leadmines Fm	Derby	SK2260	53°8·4'	1°39·9'W	FM	119
Leadmore Fm	Pth & Kin	NO0532	56°28·5'	3°32·1'W	FM	52,53
Leadon Court	Heref	SO6846	52°6·9'	2°27·6'W	X	149
Leadpipe Hill	Northum	NY9456	54°54·2'	2°5·2'W	X	87
Lead Stone or Flat Rock	Torbay	SX9563	50°27·7'	3°28·4'W	X	202
Lead Up Gill	N Yks	SE0681	54°13·7'	1°54·1'W	W	99
Lea End	Worcs	SP0475	52°22·6'	1°56·1'W	T	139
Leafea	Orkney	HY2309	58°57·9'	3°19·9'W	X	6,7
Leaf Howe	N Yks	SE7894	54°20·4'	0°47·6'W	A	94,100
Leaf Howe Hill	N Yks	SE7795	54°20·9'	0°48·5'W	X	94,100
Leafield	D & G	NY1074	55°3·4'	3°24·1'W	X	85
Leafield	Oxon	SP3115	51°50·2'	1°32·6'W	T	164
Leafield	Wilts	ST8669	51°25·4'	2°11·7'W	T	173
Leafield Edge	Northum	NT9813	55°24·9'	2°1·5'W	H	81
Leafield Fm	Glos	SP1503	51°43·8'	1°46·6'W	FM	163
Lea Fields	Shrops	SO6472	52°20·9'	2°31·3'W	X	138
Lea Fm	Arg & Bt	NS3676	55°57·2'	4°37·2'W	FM	63
Lea Fm	Ches	SJ3870	53°13·6'	2°55·3'W	FM	117
Lea Fm	C of Derb	SK3530	52°52·2'	1°28·4'W	FM	128
Lea Fm	E Susx	TQ9022	50°58·2'	0°42·8'E	FM	189
Lea Fm	Hants	SU8049	51°14·3'	0°50·9'W	FM	186
Lea Fm	Heref	SO5362	52°15·5'	2°40·9'W	FM	137,138,149
Lea Fm	Kent	TQ8953	51°14·9'	0°42·9'E	FM	189
Lea Fm	Midlo	NT2762	55°51·0'	3°9·5'W	FM	66
Lea Fm	Powys	SO2361	52°14·7'	3°7·3'W	FM	137,148
Lea Fm	Shrops	SJ4327	52°50·5'	2°50·4'W	FM	126
Lea Fm	Shrops	SO6676	52°23·1'	2°29·6'W	FM	138
Lea Fm	Shrops	SO7794	52°32·8'	2°20·0'W	FM	138
Lea Fm	Suff	TL6783	52°25·4'	0°27·8'E	FM	143
Lea Fm	Suff	TL9966	52°15·6'	0°55·4'E	FM	155
Lea Fm	Surrey	TQ0142	51°10·3'	0°32·9'W	FM	186
Lea Fm	Wok	SU7663	51°21·9'	0°54·1'W	FM	175,186
Lea Forge	Ches	SJ7048	53°1·9'	2°26·4'W	T	118
Leaf Sails Fm	E Yorks	TA1928	53°44·3'	0°11·3'W	FM	107
Leafy Rigg	Cumbr	NY6075	55°4·3'	2°37·2'W	X	86
Leagag	Pth & Kin	NN5153	56°39·0'	4°25·4'W	H	42,51
Leagate	Cumbr	NY5400	54°23·9'	2°42·1'W	X	90
Lea Gate Fm	Lincs	TF2458	53°6·5'	0°8·4'W	FM	122
Leager Ho	Northum	NZ1069	55°1·2'	1°50·2'W	X	88
Lea Gill	S Lanak	NT0228	55°32·4'	3°32·7'W	W	72
Leagram Hall Fm	Lancs	SD6244	53°53·7'	2°34·3'W	FM	102,103
Lea Grange	Lincs	SK8386	53°22·1'	0°44·7'W	X	112,121
Lea Grange	Staffs	SK1011	52°42·0'	1°50·7'W	X	128
Lea Grange Fm	Leic	SK3205	52°38·7'	1°31·2'W	FM	140
Leagrave	Luton	TL0523	51°54·0'	0°28·0'W	T	166
Leagreen	Hants	SZ2793	50°44·4'	1°36·7'W	T	195
Lea Green	Heref	SO6764	52°16·6'	2°28·6'W	X	138,149
Lea Green	Lancs	SD5150	53°56·9'	2°44·4'W	X	102
Lea Green	St Hel	SJ5092	53°25·6'	2°44·7'W	T	108
Lea Green Hall	Ches	SJ6662	53°9·5'	2°30·1'W	X	118
Lea Green Villa Fm	Ches	SJ6662	53°9·5'	2°30·1'W	FM	118
League Hill	D & G	NY0598	55°16·3'	3°29·3'W	X	78
League Hole	Norf	TM5399	52°32·0'	1°44·2'E	W	134
Lea Hall	Birm	SP0591	52°31·2'	1°55·2'W	X	139
Lea Hall	Birm	SP1486	52°28·5'	1°47·2'W	T	139
Lea Hall	Ches	SJ4358	53°7·2'	2°50·7'W	X	117
Lea Hall	Ches	SJ6864	53°10·6'	2°28·3'W	X	118
Lea Hall	Ches	SJ7148	53°2·0'	2°25·5'W	X	118
Lea Hall	Derby	SK1951	53°3·6'	1°42·6'W	X	119
Lea Hall	Derby	SK3357	53°6·8'	1°30·0'W	X	119
Lea Hall	Durham	NZ3122	54°35·8'	1°30·8'W	X	93
Lea Hall	Essex	TL5215	51°49·0'	0°12·7'E	X	167
Lea Hall	Northum	NY8258	54°55·2'	2°16·4'W	X	86,87
Lea Hall	Shrops	SJ4921	52°47·3'	2°45·0'W	A	126
Lea Hall	Shrops	SJ5838	52°56·5'	2°37·1'W	X	126
Lea Hall	Shrops	SJ8002	52°37·2'	2°17·3'W	X	127
Lea Hall Fm	Derby	SK3457	53°6·8'	1°29·1'W	FM	119
Lea Hall Fm	Staffs	SK0421	52°48·0'	1°56·0'W	FM	128
Leahaugh	Scot Bord	NY5092	55°13·4'	2°46·7'W	X	79
Leahaugh Cottage	Scot Bord	NY4991	55°12·9'	2°47·7'W	X	79
Lea Head Manor	Staffs	SJ7542	52°58·7'	2°21·9'W	A	118
Leaheads Hill	D & G	NY3179	55°6·3'	3°4·5'W	X	85
Lea Heath	Staffs	SK0226	52°50·1'	1°57·8'W	T	128
Lea Hill Fm	Shrops	SO5196	52°33·8'	2°43·0'W	FM	137,138
Leahouse Fm	Ches	SJ6864	53°10·6'	2°28·3'W	FM	118
Leahurst	Ches	SJ3177	53°17·4'	3°1·7'W	X	117
Lea Hurst	Derby	SK3255	53°5·7'	1°30·9'W	X	119
Leake	Lincs	TF4249	53°1·4'	0°7·4'E	T	131
Leake	N Yks	SE4390	54°18·5'	1°19·9'W	T	99
Leake Commonside	Lincs	TF3952	53°3·1'	0°4·8'E	T	122
Leake Fold Hill	Lincs	TF4051	53°2·5'	0°5·7'E	T	122
Leake Gride	Lincs	TF3850	53°2·0'	0°3·9'E	X	122
Leake Ho	N Yks	SE4290	54°18·5'	1°20·8'W	X	99
Leake Ings	Lincs	TF3851	53°2·5'	0°3·9'E	X	122
Leake Lane Ho	N Yks	SE4391	54°19·0'	1°19·9'W	X	99
Leake Stell	N Yks	SE4392	54°19·5'	1°19·9'W	W	99
Leakin	Moray	NJ1642	57°27·9'	3°23·6'W	X	28
Lea Knowl	Staffs	SJ7828	52°51·2'	2°19·2'W	X	127
Leak Wood	E Yorks	SE8344	53°53·4'	0°43·8'W	F	106
Lealands	E Susx	TQ5337	51°6·9'	0°11·5'E	X	188
Lealands	E Susx	TQ5713	50°53·9'	0°14·4'E	X	199
Lealholm	N Yks	NZ7607	54°27·4'	0°49·2'W	T	94
Lealholm Hall	N Yks	NZ7707	54°27·4'	0°48·3'W	X	94
Lealholm Moor	N Yks	NZ7509	54°28·5'	0°50·1'W	X	94
Lealholm Rigg	N Yks	NZ7608	54°27·9'	0°49·2'W	X	94
Lealholm Side	N Yks	NZ7608	54°27·9'	0°49·2'W	T	94
Lea Line	Heref	SO6621	51°53·4'	2°29·3'W	T	162
Lealt	Arg & Bt	NR6690	56°3·0'	5°45·0'W	X	55,61
Lealt	Highld	NG5060	57°33·9'	6°9·7'W	T	23,24
Lealt Burn	Arg & Bt	NR6693	56°4·6'	5°45·2'W	W	55,61
Lealt River	Highld	NG4960	57°33·9'	6°11·4'W	W	23
Lealty Ho	Highld	NH6073	57°43·8'	4°20·6'W	X	21
Leam	Derby	SK2379	53°18·7'	1°38·9'W	T	119
Lea Manor Fm	Ches	SJ3872	53°14·7'	2°55·3'W	FM	117
Lea Manor Fm	Ches	SJ4357	53°6·7'	2°50·7'W	FM	117
Lea Marsh	Lancs	SD4829	53°45·5'	2°46·9'W	W	102
Lea Marsh	Lincs	SK8187	53°22·7'	0°46·5'W	X	112,121
Lea Marston	Warw	SP2093	52°32·3'	1°41·9'W	T	139
Leam Fm	N Lincs	SE8014	53°37·2'	0°47·0'W	FM	112
Leam Hall	Derby	SK2379	53°18·7'	1°38·9'W	X	119
Leamington Hall Fm	Warw	SP3461	52°15·0'	1°29·7'W	FM	151
Leamington Hastings	Warw	SP4467	52°18·2'	1°20·9'W	T	151
Leamlands	Lincs	TF4726	52°48·9'	0°11·3'E	X	131
Leam Lane	Ghead	NZ2960	54°56·3'	1°32·4'W	X	88
Leamnamuic	Arg & Bt	NR7959	55°46·7'	5°31·0'W	X	62
Leamonsley	Staffs	SK1009	52°41·0'	1°50·7'W	T	128
Leamoor Common	Shrops	SO4286	52°28·4'	2°50·8'W	T	137
Leamore	Wals	SJ9900	52°36·1'	2°0·5'W	T	127,139
Leamside	Durham	NZ3146	54°48·7'	1°30·6'W	T	88
Leam, The	Ghead	NZ2959	54°55·7'	1°32·4'W	X	88
Leana an Fheòir	N Eil	NG0689	57°47·9'	6°56·5'W	X	14,18
Leana Burn	S Ayr	NX1278	55°3·9'	4°56·2'W	W	76
Leanach	Arg & Bt	NS0498	56°8·3'	5°8·8'W	X	56
Leanach	Highld	NH1457	57°34·2'	5°6·1'W	X	25
Leanach	Highld	NH7544	57°28·4'	4°4·6'W	T	27
Leanachan	Highld	NN2178	56°51·8'	4°55·7'W	X	41
Leanachan Forest	Highld	NN1978	56°51·8'	4°57·7'W	F	41
Lean a' Chneamh	N Ayr	NR9326	55°29·3'	5°16·2'W	X	68,69
Leana Hill	S Ayr	NX1278	55°3·9'	4°56·2'W	X	76
Leanaidh	Highld	NH2054	57°32·7'	5°0·0'W	H	25
Leanaig	Highld	NH5554	57°33·4'	4°24·9'W	X	26
Lèana Mhòr	Highld	NN2887	56°56·8'	4°49·2'W	H	34,41
Lèana Mhòr	Highld	NN3187	56°56·9'	4°46·3'W	H	34,41
Lèana na Feannaige	Arg & Bt	NR3046	55°38·2'	6°17·0'W	X	60
Lean an Tubhaidh	N Ayr	NR8940	55°36·7'	5°20·6'W	X	62,69
Lea Newbold Fm	Ches	SJ4459	53°7·8'	2°49·8'W	FM	117
Leanish	N Eil	NL6998	56°57·5'	7°26·3'W	X	31
Lean Low	Derby	SK1462	53°9·5'	1°47·0'W	H	119
Leanlow Fm	Derby	SK1562	53°9·5'	1°46·1'W	FM	119
Leàn Mhór	Arg & Bt	NR4266	55°49·4'	6°6·7'W	X	60,61
Lèan Mór	Arg & Bt	NR7464	55°49·2'	5°36·0'W	X	62
Lean nan Coileach	Arg & Bt	NS0887	56°2·5'	5°4·5'W	X	56
Leanoch	Moray	NJ1954	57°34·4'	3°20·8'W	X	28
Leanoch Burn	Moray	NJ1951	57°32·8'	3°20·7'W	W	28
Lean Park Fm	Corn	SX2660	50°25·1'	4°26·6'W	FM	201
Leantack	Highld	NH9725	57°18·5'	3°42·1'W	X	36
Leap Burn	Scot Bord	NT5203	55°19·4'	2°45·0'W	W	79
Leap Edge	Derby	SK0469	53°13·3'	1°56·0'W	X	119
Leap Gate	Dorset	SY6893	50°44·4'	2°26·8'W	X	194
Leapgate	Worcs	SO8372	52°21·0'	2°14·6'W	T	138
Leap Hill	Northum	NT7207	55°21·6'	2°26·1'W	H	80
Leap Hill	Scot Bord	NT4419	55°27·9'	2°52·7'W	H	79
Leap Hill	Scot Bord	NT5101	55°18·3'	2°45·9'W	H	79
Leapingwells	Essex	TL8419	51°50·6'	0°40·7'E	X	168
Leaplish	Northum	NY6587	55°10·6'	2°32·5'W	X	80
Leap Moor	Inverc	NS2370	55°53·7'	4°49·4'W	X	63
Leapmoor Forest	Inverc	NS2270	55°53·7'	4°50·4'W	F	63
Leapool	Notts	SK5847	53°1·3'	1°7·7'W	X	129
Leaps Beck	Cumbr	NY0918	54°33·2'	3°24·0'W	W	89
Leaps Rigg	Cumbr	NY5067	55°0·0'	2°46·5'W	X	86
Leaquoy	Orkney	HY2424	59°6·0'	3°19·1'W	X	6
Learable	Highld	NC8923	58°11·2'	3°52·8'W	X	17
Learable Hill	Highld	NC8924	58°11·7'	3°52·8'W	X	17
Learân Fm	Pth & Kin	NN5757	56°41·2'	4°19·6'W	FM	42,51
Leargan	Pth & Kin	NN6459	56°42·4'	4°12·8'W	X	42,51
Leargybreck	Arg & Bt	NR5471	55°52·4'	5°55·5'W	T	61
Learielaw	W Loth	NT0871	55°55·7'	3°27·9'W	X	65
Learney Hill	Aberd	NJ6204	57°7·8'	2°37·2'W	H	37
Learney Ho	Aberd	NJ6304	57°7·8'	2°36·2'W	X	37
Learnie	Highld	NH7560	57°37·0'	4°5·1'W	X	21,27
Lear's Fm	Somer	ST1714	50°55·4'	3°10·5'W	FM	181,193
Leary	Orkney	HY2424	59°6·0'	3°19·1'W	X	6
Leary Moors	Devon	SS6529	51°2·9'	3°55·2'W	X	180
Leary Rock	S Glos	ST5690	51°36·7'	2°37·7'W	X	162,172
Leasam Ho	E Susx	TQ9021	50°57·6'	0°42·7'E	X	189
Leascar	N Yks	SE3698	54°22·8'	1°26·3'W	X	99
Leascole	Shetld	HU2279	60°29·9'	1°35·5'W	X	3
Leasefield Fm	Devon	SS4201	50°47·5'	4°9·9'W	FM	191
Leaselands, The	Norf	TG1526	52°47·5'	1°11·7'E	F	133
Lease Rigg	N Yks	NZ8204	54°25·7'	0°43·7'W	T	94
Leasers Barn	Surrey	TQ1148	51°13·4'	0°24·2'W	X	187
Leases	Cumbr	NY7409	54°28·8'	2°23·7'W	X	91
Leases Fm	N Yks	SE2495	54°21·2'	1°37·4'W	FM	99
Leases Grange	N Yks	SE2791	54°19·1'	1°34·7'W	X	99
Leases Hall	N Yks	SE2891	54°19·1'	1°33·9'W	X	99
Leasey Bridge	Herts	TL1614	51°49·0'	0°18·6'W	T	166
Leas Fm	N Yks	SE7982	54°13·9'	0°46·9'W	FM	100
Leasgill	Cumbr	SD4984	54°15·2'	2°46·5'W	T	97
Leashaw Fm	Derby	SK3355	53°5·7'	1°30·0'W	FM	119
Leas Head Fm	N Yks	NZ8703	54°25·1'	0°39·1'W	FM	94
Leash Fen	Derby	SK2973	53°15·4'	1°33·5'W	X	119
Leas Ho	N Yks	SD9391	54°19·1'	2°6·0'W	X	98
Lea Shun	Orkney	HY6621	59°4·7'	2°35·1'W	W	5
Leaside	Durham	NZ1722	54°35·8'	1°43·8'W	X	92
Leasingham	Lincs	TF0548	53°1·4'	0°25·7'W	T	130
Leasingham Moor	Lincs	TF0748	53°1·3'	0°23·9'W	X	130
Leasingthorne	Durham	NZ2529	54°39·6'	1°36·3'W	T	93
Leaskie Knowe	Shetld	HU3749	60°13·7'	1°19·4'W	X	3
Leason	Swan	SS4892	51°36·6'	4°11·3'W	T	159
Leasow	Derby	SK2944	52°59·8'	1°33·7'W	X	119,128
Leasowe	Wirral	SJ2791	53°24·9'	3°5·5'W	T	108
Leasowe Fm	Warw	SP3564	52°16·6'	1°28·8'W	FM	151
Leasowes	Shrops	SJ5704	52°38·2'	2°37·7'W	X	126
Leasowes	Shrops	SO2881	52°25·6'	3°3·1'W	X	137
Leasowes	Shrops	SO4899	52°35·4'	2°45·7'W	X	137,138
Leasowes Bank Fm	Shrops	SO3999	52°35·4'	2°53·7'W	FM	137
Leasowes Fm	Warw	SP3147	52°7·5'	1°32·4'W	FM	151
Leasowes Fm	Worcs	SO9964	52°16·7'	2°0·5'W	FM	150
Leasowes Fm	Wrekin	SJ6318	52°45·7'	2°32·5'W	FM	127
Leasowe Sta	Wirral	SJ2690	53°24·3'	3°6·4'W	X	108
Leasowes, The	Glos	SO9503	51°43·8'	2°4·0'W	X	163
Leasowes The	Shrops	SJ3328	52°51·0'	2°59·3'W	X	126
Leasowes, The	Shrops	SO5698	52°34·9'	2°38·6'W	X	137,138
Leasowes, The	Shrops	SO6993	52°32·3'	2°27·0'W	X	138
Leasowes, The	Warw	SP1270	52°19·9'	1°49·0'W	X	139
Leasowes, The	Warw	SP3275	52°22·6'	1°31·4'W	X	140
Leasow Ho	Glos	SP0536	52°1·6'	1°55·2'W	X	150
Leasows Fm	Shrops	SJ6505	52°38·7'	2°30·6'W	FM	127
Leasows Fm	Staffs	SJ8610	52°41·5'	2°12·0'W	FM	127
Leasows, The	Heref	SO5357	52°12·8'	2°40·9'W	X	149

Leasows, The	Shrops	SJ4521	52°47·3'	2°48·5'W	X	126
Leasows, The	Shrops	SO6574	52°22·0'	2°30·4'W	X	138
Leasows, The	Staffs	SJ9536	52°55·5'	2°4·1'W	X	127
Leas, The	D & G	NT3000	55°17·6'	3°5·7'W	X	79
Leas, The	S Tyne	NZ3866	54°59·5'	1°23·9'W	X	88
Leas, The	Wok	SU7663	51°21·9'	0°54·1'W	X	175,186
Leaston	E Loth	NT4863	55°51·7'	2°49·4'W	X	66
Leaswood Fm	Ches	SJ3376	53°16·8'	2°59·9'W	FM	117
Leat	Corn	SX3087	50°39·7'	4°23·9'W	X	190
Lea Taing	Orkney	HY5240	59°14·9'	2°50·0'W	X	5
Lea Taing	Orkney	HY5410	58°58·7'	2°47·5'W	X	6
Leat Fm	Devon	SS8216	50°56·1'	3°40·4'W	FM	181
Leathabhal	N Eil	NF7723	57°11·3'	7°20·4'W	H	22
Leathad a' Chaorainn	Highld	NH6998	57°57·4'	4°12·4'W	X	21
Leathad a' Charra	Highld	NH0939	57°24·3'	5°10·3'W	X	25
Leathad a' Mhuidhe	Highld	NH3383	57°48·6'	4°48·2'W	X	20
Leathad an Dubh-alltain	Highld	NC6610	58°3·8'	4°15·8'W	X	16
Leathad an Locha	Highld	NC6913	58°5·5'	4°12·9'W	X	16
Leathad an Lochain	Arg & Bt	NM6338	56°28·7'	5°50·5'W	X	49
Leathad an Taobhain	Highld	NN8185	56°56·7'	3°56·9'W	H	43
Leathad Beag	Highld	NG7506	57°5·7'	5°42·4'W	X	33
Leathad Beag	Highld	NN3550	56°37·0'	4°40·9'W	X	41
Leathad Beithe	Highld	NG3229	57°16·6'	6°26·3'W	X	32
Leathad Buan	Highld	NC2443	58°20·7'	4°59·9'W	X	9
Leathad Buidhe	Highld	NC1922	58°9·3'	5°4·1'W	X	15
Leathad Buidhe	Highld	NG9961	57°35·9'	5°21·4'W	X	19
Leathad Cas	Highld	NC6416	58°7·0'	4°18·0'W	X	16
Leathad Chrithinn	Highld	NG5529	57°17·4'	6°3·5'W	H	32
Leathad Creagach	Highld	NC6103	57°59·9'	4°20·6'W	X	16
Leathad Dail nan Cliabh	Highld	NC3715	58°5·9'	4°45·5'W	H	16
Leathad Doire Beithe	Highld	NH0352	57°31·2'	5°16·9'W	X	25
Leathad Dubh	Highld	NC5665	58°33·2'	4°28·0'W	X	10
Leathad Dubh	Highld	NG5130	57°17·8'	6°7·5'W	X	24,32
Leathad Dubh	Highld	NH0745	57°27·5'	5°12·6'W	X	25
Leathad Fearna	Arg & Bt	NM6039	56°29·2'	5°53·5'W	X	49
Leathad Fiag	Highld	NC4421	58°9·3'	4°38·6'W	X	16
Leathad Gaothach	Highld	NN5298	57°3·2'	4°26·0'W	X	35
Leathad Ghaicarain	Highld	NC6404	58°0·5'	4°17·6'W	X	16
Leathad Leamhach	Highld	NH5193	57°54·4'	4°30·4'W	X	20
Leathad Lianach	Highld	NC2320	58°8·3'	4°59·9'W	X	15
Leathad Liath	Highld	NC6814	58°6·0'	4°13·9'W	X	16
Leathad Màiri Sheog	Highld	NC6618	58°8·1'	4°16·1'W	X	16
Leathad Mór	Highld	NG7605	57°5·2'	5°41·4'W	X	33
Leathad Mor	Highld	NG8786	57°49·0'	5°34·7'W	X	19
Leathad Mór	Highld	NH0055	57°32·7'	5°20·1'W	X	25
Leathad Mòr	Highld	NN3751	56°37·6'	4°39·0'W	X	41
Leathad na Cloiche	Highld	NH7496	57°56·4'	4°7·2'W	X	21
Leathad na Cloiche Mòire	Highld	NC5617	58°7·4'	4°26·2'W	X	16
Leathad nan Con Dearga	Highld	NH3891	57°53·0'	4°43·5'W	X	20
Leathad nan Craobh Fearna	Pth & Kin	NN5761	56°43·4'	4°19·8'W	H	42
Leathad nan Uan	Highld	NH7193	57°54·7'	4°10·2'W	X	21
Leathad na Seamraig	Highld	NC6515	58°6·5'	4°17·0'W	X	16
Leathad na Steiseig	Highld	NG4629	57°17·1'	6°12·4'W	H	32
Leathad na Stioma	Highld	NC2841	58°19·7'	4°55·8'W	X	9
Leathad na Surraig	Highld	NC3849	58°24·2'	4°45·9'W	X	9
Leathad Riabhach	Highld	NH5377	57°45·8'	4°27·8'W	X	20
Leathad Sùileach	Highld	NH6893	57°54·7'	4°13·2'W	X	21
Leathaid Choinneach	Highld	NH1030	57°19·5'	5°8·9'W	X	25
Leathan Dhail	Stir	NN6510	56°16·1'	4°10·3'W	X	57
Lea, The	Bucks	TQ0586	51°34·0'	0°28·7'W	X	176
Lea, The	Staffs	SJ7728	52°51·2'	2°20·1'W	X	127
Leathead Beag	Highld	NN3549	56°36·5'	4°40·9'W	X	50
Leather Barrow	Somer	SS9835	51°6·5'	3°27·0'W	A	181
Leatherfield Common	Herts	TL2921	51°52·6'	0°7·2'W	X	166
Leatherhead	Surrey	TQ1656	51°17·7'	0°19·8'W	T	187
Leatherhead Common	Surrey	TQ1658	51°18·8'	0°19·7'W	T	187
Leatherhead Downs	Surrey	TQ1754	51°16·6'	0°19·0'W	X	187
Leather Mill Fms	Warw	SP3495	52°33·3'	1°29·5'W	FM	140
Leathern Bottle	Glos	SO7200	51°42·1'	2°23·9'W	T	162
Leatherslade Fm	Bucks	SP6512	51°48·4'	1°3·0'W	FM	164,165
Leathersley Fm	Derby	SK1731	52°52·8'	1°44·4'W	FM	128
Leathers, The	Heref	SO4266	52°17·6'	2°50·6'W	X	137,148,149
Leather Tor	Devon	SX5670	50°31·0'	4°1·5'W	X	202
Leathgill Bridge	Cumbr	NY6800	54°23·9'	2°29·2'W	X	91
Leath Ho	Norf	TF8542	52°56·8'	0°45·6'E	X	132
Leathley	N Yks	SE2347	53°55·4'	1°38·6'W	T	104
Leathley Br	N Yks	SE2346	53°54·8'	1°38·6'W	X	104
Leathley Grange	N Yks	SE2347	53°55·4'	1°38·6'W	X	104
Leathley Hall	N Yks	SE2346	53°54·8'	1°38·6'W	X	104
Leat Ho	N Yks	SE7970	54°7·4'	0°47·1'W	X	100
Leaths	D & G	NX7862	54°56·5'	3°53·8'W	X	84
Leath, The	Shrops	SO5889	52°30·1'	2°36·7'W	T	137,138
Leaton	Shrops	SJ4618	52°45·7'	2°47·6'W	T	126
Leaton	Wrekin	SJ6111	52°42·0'	2°34·2'W	T	127
Leaton Hall	Staffs	SO8190	52°30·7'	2°16·4'W	X	138
Leaton Heath	Shrops	SJ4518	52°45·6'	2°48·5'W	T	126
Leaton Knolls	Shrops	SJ4716	52°44·6'	2°46·7'W	X	126
Leaton Lodge	Shrops	SJ4618	52°45·7'	2°47·6'W	X	126
Leaton Shelf	Shrops	SJ4617	52°45·1'	2°47·6'W	F	126
Lea Town	Lancs	SD4731	53°46·6'	2°47·8'W	T	102
Leault	Highld	NH8205	57°7·5'	3°56·5'W	X	35
Lea Valley	Herts	TL1515	51°49·5'	0°19·5'W	T	166
Lea Valley Walk	Enf	TQ3693	51°37·4'	0°1·7'W	X	167,177
Leavanin	Arg & Bt	NN1201	56°10·1'	5°1·2'W	W	56
Leaveland	Kent	TR0053	51°14·7'	0°52·3'E	T	189
Leaveland Court	Kent	TR0054	51°15·2'	0°52·4'E	X	189
Leavenhalls, The	Shrops	SO7299	52°35·5'	2°24·4'W	X	138
Leavenheath	Suff	TL9536	51°59·5'	0°50·8'E	T	155
Leavening	N Yks	SE7863	54°3·7'	0°48·1'W	T	100
Leavening Brow	N Yks	SE7962	54°3·1'	0°47·2'W	X	100
Leavesden Airport	Herts	TL0900	51°41·5'	0°25·0'W	X	166
Leavesden Green	Herts	TL0900	51°41·5'	0°25·0'W	T	166
Leaves Green	Brom	TQ4161	51°20·1'	0°1·8'E	T	177,187
Leavisgarth	Orkney	HY6941	59°15·5'	2°32·1'W	X	5
Lea Wood	Glos	SP1503	51°43·8'	1°46·6'W	F	163
Lea Wood	Leic	SK5011	52°41·9'	1°15·2'W	F	129
Lea Wood	Lincs	SK8387	53°22·6'	0°44·7'W	F	112,121
Leawood	Staffs	SJ7624	52°49·0'	2°21·0'W	X	127
Lea Wood	Wilts	ST9685	51°34·1'	2°3·1'W	F	173
Leawood Fm	Derby	SK2760	53°8·4'	1°35·4'W	FM	119
Leawood Ho	Devon	SX5188	50°40·6'	4°6·2'W	X	191
Leawood Pumphouse	Derby	SK3155	53°5·7'	1°31·8'W	X	119
Lea Yeat	Cumbr	SD7686	54°16·4'	2°21·7'W	T	98
Leaze	Corn	SX1376	50°33·5'	4°38·0'W	X	200
Leaze Burn	E Ayr	NS7132	55°34·1'	4°2·3'W	W	71
Leaze Fm	Glos	SO8002	51°43·2'	2°17·0'W	FM	162
Leaze Fm	N Som	ST5057	51°18·8'	2°42·7'W	FM	172,182
Leaze Fm	Wilts	ST9179	51°30·8'	2°7·4'W	FM	173
Leazers Wood	W Susx	SU9128	51°2·9'	0°41·7'W	F	186,197
Leazes	Northum	NY9164	54°58·5'	2°8·0'W	X	87
Leazes Fm	Durham	NZ0637	54°43·9'	1°54·0'W	FM	92
Leazes Hall	Durham	NZ1657	54°54·7'	1°44·6'W	X	88
Leazes Head	Northum	NY9071	55°2·3'	2°9·0'W	X	87
Leball Wood	Corn	SX1265	50°27·5'	4°38·5'W	F	200
Lebberston	N Yks	TA0782	54°13·6'	0°21·1'W	T	101
Lebberston Carr Fm	N Yks	TA0681	54°13·1'	0°22·0'W	FM	101
Lebberston Cliff	N Yks	TA0883	54°14·1'	0°20·2'W	X	101
Leburnick	Corn	SX3581	50°36·6'	4°19·5'W	T	201
Lecha Fm	Pemb	SM8127	51°54·2'	5°10·6'W	FM	157
Lechlade	Glos	SU2199	51°41·6'	1°41·4'W	T	163
Lechlade Mill	Glos	SU2299	51°41·6'	1°40·5'W	X	163
Lechrea	Pth & Kin	NN7733	56°28·6'	3°59·4'W	X	51,52
Lechrea Hill	Pth & Kin	NN7634	56°29·2'	4°0·4'W	H	51,52
Lecht Mine	Moray	NJ2315	57°13·4'	3°16·1'W	X	36
Lecht Road	Moray	NJ2413	57°12·3'	3°15·0'W	X	36
Leck	Lancs	SD6476	54°11·0'	2°32·7'W	T	97
Leck Beck	Lancs	SD6477	54°11·5'	2°32·7'W	W	97
Leckby Fm	N Yks	SE6761	54°2·7'	0°58·2'W	FM	100
Leckby Grange	N Yks	SE4174	54°9·9'	1°21·9'W	X	99
Leckby Palace Fm	N Yks	SE4174	54°9·9'	1°21·9'W	FM	99
Leckby Villa Fm	N Yks	SE4173	54°9·3'	1°21·9'W	FM	99
Leckerston	Fife	NT0292	56°6·9'	3°34·1'W	X	58
Leckerstone	Fife	NT0884	56°2·7'	3°28·2'W	X	65
Lecket Hill	E Dunb	NS6481	56°0·4'	4°10·4'W	H	64
Leckethill	N Lanak	NS5770	55°54·6'	4°3·4'W	X	64
Leck Fell	Lancs	SD6678	54°12·0'	2°30·9'W	X	98
Leck Fell Ho	Lancs	SD6779	54°12·6'	2°29·9'W	X	98
Leckford	Hants	SU3737	51°8·1'	1°27·9'W	T	185
Leckford Abbas	Hants	SU3737	51°8·1'	1°27·9'W	X	185
Leckfurin	Highld	NC7059	58°30·3'	4°13·4'W	T	10
Leckgruinart Cott	Arg & Bt	NR2769	55°50·5'	6°20·2'W	X	60
Leckhampstead	Bucks	SP7237	52°1·8'	0°56·6'W	T	152
Leckhampstead	W Berks	SU4376	51°29·1'	1°22·5'W	T	174
Leckhampstead Thicket	W Berks	SU4276	51°29·1'	1°23·3'W	T	174
Leckhampstead Wood	Bucks	SP7240	52°3·5'	0°56·6'W	F	152
Leckhampton	Glos	SO9419	51°52·4'	2°4·8'W	T	163
Leckhampton Hill	Glos	SO9418	51°51·9'	2°4·8'W	H	163
Leckie	Highld	NH0964	57°37·8'	5°11·5'W	X	19
Leckiebank	Fife	NO2212	56°17·9'	3°15·2'W	X	58
Leckie Burn	Stir	NS6893	56°6·9'	4°6·9'W	W	57
Leckmelm	Highld	NH1690	57°52·0'	5°5·6'W	T	20
Leckmelm Fm	Highld	NH1690	57°52·0'	5°5·6'W	FM	20
Leckmelm Wood	Highld	NH1691	57°52·5'	5°5·7'W	F	20
Leckmoram Ness	E Loth	NT5785	56°3·6'	2°41·0'W	X	67
Lecknacreive Burn	Arg & Bt	NR6514	55°22·1'	5°42·1'W	W	68
Leckroy	Highld	NN3592	56°59·6'	4°42·5'W	X	34
Leckuary	Arg & Bt	NR8795	56°6·3'	5°25·1'W	X	55
Leck Villa Fm	Lancs	SD6576	54°11·0'	2°31·8'W	FM	97
Leckwith	Card	ST1574	51°27·8'	3°13·0'W	T	171
Leckwith Moors	V of Glam	ST1674	51°27·8'	3°12·2'W	X	171
Leckwith Woods	V of Glam	ST1575	51°28·3'	3°13·0'W	F	171
Leconfield	E Yorks	TA0143	53°52·6'	0°27·4'W	T	106,107
Leconfield Grange	E Yorks	TA0244	53°53·2'	0°26·5'W	X	106,107
Leconfield Low Parks	E Yorks	TA0342	53°52·1'	0°25·6'W	X	107
Leconfield Parks Ho	E Yorks	TA0242	53°52·1'	0°26·5'W	X	106,107
Le Court	Hants	SU7631	51°4·6'	0°54·5'W	X	186
Ledaig	Arg & Bt	NM3920	56°18·3'	6°12·7'W	X	48
Ledaig	Arg & Bt	NM5055	56°37·5'	6°4·1'W	T	47
Ledaig	Arg & Bt	NM9037	56°29·0'	5°24·2'W	T	49
Ledaig	N Eil	NL6697	56°56·9'	7°29·2'W	T	31
Ledaig Point	Arg & Bt	NM8935	56°27·9'	5°25·1'W	X	49
Ledard	Stir	NN4602	56°11·4'	4°28·5'W	X	57
Ledard Burn	Stir	NN4504	56°12·5'	4°29·5'W	W	57
Ledbeg	Highld	NC2413	58°4·5'	4°58·6'W	X	15
Ledbeg River	Highld	NC2412	58°4·0'	4°58·5'W	W	15
Ledburn	Bucks	SP9021	51°53·0'	0°41·1'W	T	165
Ledburn Fm	Bucks	SP9021	51°53·0'	0°41·1'W	FM	165
Ledbury	Heref	SO7037	52°2·1'	2°25·8'W	T	149
Ledbury Park	Heref	SO7137	52°2·1'	2°25·0'W	X	149
Ledcameroch	Stir	NN7801	56°11·4'	3°57·5'W	X	57
Ledcharrie	Stir	NN5028	56°25·5'	4°25·5'W	X	51
Ledcharrie Burn	Stir	NN5026	56°24·4'	4°25·4'W	W	51
Ledcrieff	Angus	NO2637	56°31·4'	3°11·7'W	X	53
Ledcrieff Loch	Angus	NO2737	56°31·4'	3°10·7'W	W	53
Leddach	Aberd	NJ8106	57°8·9'	2°18·4'W	X	38
Ledderhowe	Cumbr	NY8415	54°32·0'	2°14·4'W	X	91,92
Leddington	Glos	SO6934	52°0·5'	2°26·7'W	T	149
Leddriegreen Ho	Stir	NS5679	55°59·2'	4°18·1'W	X	64
Leden Urquhart	Fife	NO1711	56°17·3'	3°20·0'W	X	58
Ledge Beck	N Yks	SE5796	54°21·6'	1°6·9'W	W	100
Ledgemoor	Heref	SO4150	52°8·9'	2°51·3'W	X	148,149
Ledgemore Bottom	Glos	ST8696	51°40·0'	2°11·8'W	X	162
Ledgemore Fm	Herts	TL0412	51°48·0'	0°29·1'W	FM	166
Ledger Fm	Win & Maid	SU9076	51°28·8'	0°41·8'W	FM	175
Ledgerland	Pemb	SN1808	51°44·7'	4°37·8'W	X	158
Ledgers Fm	Surrey	TQ3858	51°18·5'	0°0·8'W	FM	187
Ledgertlaw	Pth & Kin	NO2133	56°29·2'	3°16·5'W	X	53
Ledges, The	S Glos	ST6196	51°39·9'	2°33·4'W	X	162
Ledgowan	Highld	NH1355	57°33·1'	5°7·1'W	X	25
Ledgowan Forest	Highld	NH1155	57°33·0'	5°9·1'W	X	25
Ledgowan Lodge	Highld	NH1558	57°34·7'	5°5·2'W	X	25
Ledgrianach	Arg & Bt	NM9243	56°32·2'	5°22·5'W	X	49
Ledicot	Heref	SO4162	52°15·4'	2°51·5'W	T	137,148,149
Ledlanet	Pth & Kin	NO0806	56°14·0'	3°29·6'W	X	58
Ledlation	Pth & Kin	NO0605	56°14·0'	3°30·5'W	X	58
Ledlewan	Stir	NS5182	56°0·7'	4°23·0'W	X	57,64
Ledmacay	Aberd	NJ3413	57°12·4'	3°5·1'W	X	37
Ledmore	Angus	NO5364	56°46·2'	2°45·7'W	X	44
Ledmore	Arg & Bt	NM5146	56°32·7'	6°2·6'W	X	47,48
Ledmore	Highld	NC2412	58°4·0'	4°58·5'W	X	15
Ledmore River	Arg & Bt	NM5146	56°32·7'	6°2·6'W	W	47,48
Ledmore River	Highld	NC2511	58°3·5'	4°57·5'W	W	15
Lednabirichen	Highld	NH7592	57°54·3'	4°6·1'W	T	21
Lednabra	Stir	NS5089	56°4·5'	4°24·2'W	X	57
Lednagullin	Highld	NC8064	58°33·1'	4°3·3'W	T	10
Ledrishbeg	W Dunb	NS3982	56°0·5'	4°34·5'W	X	56
Ledrishmore	W Dunb	NS4083	56°1·1'	4°33·6'W	X	56,64
Ledsham	Ches	SJ3574	53°15·8'	2°58·1'W	T	117
Ledsham	Leeds	SE4529	53°45·6'	1°18·6'W	T	105
Ledston	Leeds	SE4328	53°45·0'	1°20·5'W	T	105
Ledstone	Devon	SX7446	50°18·3'	3°45·8'W	T	202
Ledston Hall	Leeds	SE4328	53°45·0'	1°20·5'W	A	105
Ledston Luck	Leeds	SE4230	53°46·1'	1°21·4'W	T	105
Ledston Park	Leeds	SE4430	53°46·1'	1°19·5'W	X	105
Leduckie	Pth & Kin	NO0646	56°36·0'	3°31·4'W	X	52,53
Ledwell	Oxon	SP4228	51°57·2'	1°22·9'W	T	164
Ledwich Br	Shrops	SO5768	52°18·7'	2°37·4'W	X	137,138
Ledwyche Brook	Heref	SO5471	52°20·3'	2°40·1'W	W	137,138
Ledwyche Brook	Shrops	SO5579	52°24·7'	2°39·3'W	W	137,138
Ledyatt	Angus	NO2935	56°30·4'	3°8·8'W	X	53
Lee	Arg & Bt	NM4021	56°18·9'	6°11·8'W	X	48
Lee	Ches	SJ9270	53°13·9'	2°6·8'W	X	118
Lee	Devon	SS4846	51°11·8'	4°10·1'W	T	180
Lee	Devon	SS5546	51°11·9'	4°4·1'W	T	180
Lee	Devon	SS8226	51°1·5'	3°40·6'W	X	181
Lee	Devon	SX7966	50°29·1'	3°42·0'W	X	202
Lee	Hants	SU3617	50°57·3'	1°28·9'W	T	185
Lee	Lancs	SD5655	53°59·6'	2°39·9'W	X	102
Lee	Lew	TQ3974	51°27·1'	0°0·4'E	T	177
Lee	Northum	NY9459	54°55·8'	2°5·2'W	T	87
Lee	Orkney	HY2513	59°0·1'	3°17·8'W	X	6
Lee	Scot Bord	NT3239	55°38·6'	3°4·4'W	X	73
Lee	Shetld	HU2877	60°28·8'	1°28·9'W	X	3
Lee	Shetld	HU3465	60°22·3'	1°22·5'W	X	2,3
Lee	Shetld	HU4268	60°23·9'	1°13·8'W	X	2,3
Lee	Shrops	SJ4032	52°53·2'	2°53·1'W	T	126
Lee Abbey	Devon	SS6949	51°13·7'	3°52·2'W	X	180
Leea Geo	Shetld	HU4333	60°5·0'	1°13·1'W	X	4
Leeans	Shetld	HU2049	60°13·8'	1°37·8'W	X	3
Leeans	Shetld	HU2256	60°17·5'	1°35·6'W	H	3
Leeans	Shetld	HU3347	60°12·6'	1°23·8'W	T	3
Leeans	Shetld	HU3790	60°35·8'	1°19·0'W	X	1,2
Leeans	Shetld	HU6187	60°34·0'	0°52·7'W	X	1,2
Leeans, The	Shetld	HU5764	60°21·6'	0°57·5'W	X	2
Lee Ball	Devon	SS6839	51°8·3'	3°52·8'W	X	180
Lee Bank	Birm	SP0686	52°28·6'	1°54·3'W	T	139
Lee Barton	Corn	SS2212	50°53·0'	4°31·5'W	X	190
Lee Barton	Devon	SS5720	50°57·9'	4°1·8'W	X	180
Lee Bay	Devon	SS4746	51°11·8'	4°11·0'W	W	180
Lee Bay	Devon	SS6949	51°13·7'	3°52·2'W	W	180
Lee Beck	Notts	SK7779	53°18·4'	0°50·3'W	W	120
Leebotten	Shetld	HU4224	60°0·2'	1°14·3'W	T	4
Leebotwood	Shrops	SO4798	52°34·9'	2°46·5'W	T	137,138
Lee Br	Lancs	SD5655	53°59·6'	2°39·9'W	X	102
Lee Bridges	Shrops	SJ4031	52°52·6'	2°53·1'W	X	126
Lee Brockhurst	Shrops	SJ5427	52°50·6'	2°40·6'W	T	126
Lee Brook	Cambs	TL6674	52°20·6'	0°26·6'E	W	143
Lee Brook	Suff	TL6672	52°19·5'	0°26·6'E	W	154
Lee Burn	Pth & Kin	NO0305	56°13·9'	3°33·4'W	W	58
Lee Burn	S Lanak	NS8648	55°43·0'	3°48·4'W	W	72
Lee Burn Head	Scot Bord	NT3139	55°38·6'	3°5·3'W	H	73
Lee Castle	S Lanak	NS8546	55°41·9'	3°49·3'W	X	72
Leece	Cumbr	SD2469	54°6·9'	3°9·3'W	T	96
Leece's Wood	Lancs	SD6234	53°48·3'	2°34·2'W	F	102,103
Lee Chapel	Essex	TQ6988	51°34·2'	0°26·7'E	T	177,178
Leeches	Corn	SX0274	50°32·2'	4°47·3'W	X	200
Leeches	Devon	SX4565	50°28·1'	4°10·7'W	X	201
Leeches	W Susx	TQ1915	50°55·6'	0°18·0'W	X	198
Leech-hope Crag	Northum	NY9595	55°15·2'	2°4·3'W	H	81
Leechmeadow Cott	Shrops	SJ6104	52°38·2'	2°34·2'W	X	127
Leechmere Fm	Cambs	TL6471	52°19·0'	0°24·8'E	FM	154
Leechmire	Durham	NZ4235	54°42·7'	1°20·5'W	X	93
Leechmore Fm	I of W	SZ5080	50°37·3'	1°17·2'W	FM	196
Leech Pool	Corn	SW7120	50°2·4'	5°11·5'W	W	203
Leechpool	Monm	ST5089	51°36·1'	2°42·9'W	T	162,172
Lee Clump	Bucks	SP9004	51°43·9'	0°41·4'W	T	165
Lee Common	Bucks	SP9004	51°43·9'	0°41·4'W	T	165
Lee Copse	I of W	SZ3889	50°42·2'	1°27·3'W	F	196
Lee Craig	Orkney	ND3793	58°49·5'	3°5·0'W	X	7
Lee Cross	Devon	SS9305	50°50·3'	3°30·8'W	X	192
Leedale Fm	Brad	SE1442	53°52·7'	1°46·8'W	FM	104
Leeden Tor	Devon	SX5671	50°31·5'	4°1·5'W	H	202
Leedes Fm	Suff	TM1453	52°8·3'	1°8·0'E	FM	156
Leedon	Beds	SP9425	51°55·2'	0°37·6'W	X	165
Lee Downs	Devon	SX4483	50°37·8'	4°12·0'W	X	201
Leeds	Kent	TQ8252	51°14·5'	0°36·8'E	T	188
Leeds	Leeds	SE3034	53°48·3'	1°32·3'W	T	104
Leeds and Liverpool Canal	Lancs	SD6124	53°42·9'	2°35·0'W	W	102,103
Leeds and Liverpool Canal	Lancs	SD8436	53°49·4'	2°14·2'W	W	103
Leeds and Liverpool Canal	Leeds	SE2137	53°50·0'	1°40·4'W	W	104
Leeds and Liverpool Canal	Wigan	SJ6299	53°29·4'	2°34·0'W	W	109
Leeds, Bradford International Airport	Leeds	SE2241	53°52·1'	1°39·5'W	X	104
Leeds Country Way	Leeds	SE2231	53°46·7'	1°39·6'W	X	104
Leeds Country Way	Leeds	SE4031	53°46·7'	1°23·2'W	X	105
Leedsgate Br	Lincs	TF3617	52°44·2'	0°1·3'E	X	131
Leeds & Liverpool Canal	Lancs	SD4112	53°36·3'	2°53·7'W	W	108
Leeds & Liverpool Canal	Wigan	SD5809	53°34·8'	2°37·7'W	W	108
Leedstown	Corn	SW6034	50°9·7'	5°21·3'W	T	203
Lee End	Lancs	SD5059	54°1·7'	2°45·4'W	X	102
Lee End	Lancs	SD6455	53°59·6'	2°32·5'W	X	102,103
Lee Fell	Lancs	SD5758	54°1·2'	2°39·0'W	X	102
Lee Field	Shetld	HU4689	60°35·2'	1°9·1'W	H	1,2
Lee Fm	Beds	SP9760	52°14·0'	0°34·4'W	FM	153
Lee Fm	Derby	SK1378	53°18·2'	1°47·9'W	FM	119
Lee Fm	Devon	SX4483	50°37·8'	4°12·0'W	FM	201
Lee Fm	Devon	SX7973	50°32·9'	3°42·1'W	FM	191
Lee Fm	Essex	TL5508	51°45·2'	0°15·1'E	FM	167

Lee Fm	Essex	TL6604	51°42·8'	0°24·6'E	FM	167
Lee Fm	Hants	SU6745	51°12·2'	1°2·1'W	FM	185,186
Lee Fm	I of W	SZ3888	50°41·7'	1°27·3'W	FM	196
Lee Fm	Lancs	SD4939	53°50·9'	2°46·1'W	FM	102
Lee Fm	Suff	TL6673	52°20·0'	0°26·6'E	FM	154
Lee Fm	Win & Maid	SU8582	51°32·1'	0°46·1'W	FM	175
Lee Fm	W Susx	TQ0118	50°57·4'	0°33·3'W	FM	197
Lee Fm	W Susx	TQ0710	50°53·0'	0°28·3'W	FM	197
Lee Fm, The	Shrops	SJ6626	52°50·1'	2°29·9'W	FM	127
Leeford	Devon	SS7748	51°13·3'	3°45·3'W	T	180
Leeford	Devon	SY0482	50°38·0'	3°21·1'W	X	192
Lee Gate	Bucks	SP8905	51°44·4'	0°42·3'W	T	165
Leegate	Cumbr	NY0925	54°37·0'	3°24·1'W	X	89
Lee Gate	N Yks	SD9264	54°4·6'	2°6·9'W	X	98
Leegate Ho	Cumbr	NY1946	54°48·4'	3°15·2'W	X	85
Leegomery	Wrekin	SJ6612	52°42·5'	2°29·8'W	T	127
Lee Green	Medway	TQ7372	51°25·5'	0°29·7'E	X	178
Lee Ground	Hants	SU5408	50°52·4'	1°13·6'W	T	196
Lee Ground Coppice	Hants	SU5309	50°52·9'	1°14·4'W	F	196
Lee Hall	Northum	NY8679	55°6·6'	2°12·7'W	X	87
Lee Hall Fm	Northum	NY8680	55°7·1'	2°12·7'W	FM	80
Lee Hall Fm	Powys	SO1971	52°20·1'	3°10·9'W	FM	136,148
Leeham Ford Bridge	Devon	SS6739	51°8·3'	3°53·7'W	X	180
Lee Head	Derby	SK0092	53°25·7'	1°59·6'W	T	110
Lee Hills	Devon	SS5546	51°11·9'	4°4·1'W	H	180
Leehinish	N Eil	NL6590	56°53·1'	7°29·6'W	X	31
Lee Ho	Bucks	SP7221	51°53·2'	0°56·8'W	X	165
Lee Ho	Derby	SK0985	53°21·9'	1°51·5'W	X	110
Lee Ho	Devon	SS5337	51°7·0'	4°5·6'W	X	180
Lee Ho	Hants	SU3519	50°58·4'	1°29·7'W	X	185
Lee Ho	Lancs	SD6140	53°51·5'	2°35·2'W	X	102,103
Lee Ho	Staffs	SJ8859	53°7·9'	2°10·4'W	X	118
Lee Ho	Staffs	SJ9361	53°9·0'	2°5·9'W	X	118
Lee Ho	Staffs	SJ9552	53°4·2'	2°4·1'W	X	118
Leeholme	Durham	NZ2430	54°40·1'	1°37·2'W	T	93
Lee Hos	Cumbr	NY7539	54°45·0'	2°22·9'W	X	91
Leehouses	E Loth	NT4965	55°52·8'	2°48·5'W	X	66
Leek	Arg & Bt	NR2367	55°49·3'	6°24·9'W	X	60
Leek	Highld	NH3304	57°6·1'	4°45·0'W	X	34
Leek	Staffs	SJ9856	53°6·3'	2°1·4'W	T	118
Leekbrook	Staffs	SJ9853	53°4·7'	2°1·4'W	T	118
Leekscriadan	Pth & Kin	NN9265	56°46·1'	3°45·6'W	X	43
Leekshedge Fm	Wilts	SU0075	51°28·7'	1°59·6'W	FM	173
Leek Wootton	Warw	SP2969	52°19·3'	1°34·1'W	T	151
Lee Lane Fm	Barns	SE3411	53°35·9'	1°28·8'W	FM	110,111
Lee Lane Fm	Leeds	SE2338	53°50·5'	1°38·6'W	FM	104
Leelaw	S Lanak	NS8540	55°38·7'	3°49·2'W	X	71,72
Leelawmuir	S Lanak	NS8540	55°38·7'	3°49·2'W	X	71,72
Lee Meadow	S Lanak	NS8548	55°43·0'	3°49·4'W	X	72
Lee Mill	Devon	SX5955	50°22·9'	3°58·6'W	T	202
Leeming	Brad	SE0434	53°48·4'	1°55·9'W	T	104
Leeming	N Yks	SE2989	54°18·0'	1°32·8'W	T	99
Leeming Bar	N Yks	SE2890	54°18·5'	1°33·8'W	T	99
Leeming Beck	N Yks	SE1890	54°18·5'	1°43·0'W	W	99
Leeming Ho (Hotel)	Cumbr	NY4421	54°35·1'	2°51·6'W	X	90
Leeming Lodge	N Yks	SE2988	54°17·5'	1°32·8'W	X	99
Leemings	Lancs	SD7245	53°54·2'	2°25·2'W	T	103
Lee Moor	Devon	SX5661	50°26·1'	4°1·3'W	T	202
Lee Moor	Devon	SX5964	50°27·8'	3°58·8'W	X	202
Lee Moor	Northum	NU2118	55°27·6'	1°39·6'W	X	81
Lee Moor	Wakf	SE3425	53°43·5'	1°28·7'W	T	104
Leemuir	S Lanak	NS8648	55°43·0'	3°48·4'W	X	72
Lee Navigation	Herts	TL3704	51°43·3'	0°0·6'W	W	166
Leeniesdale Hill	Orkney	HY5531	59°10·3'	2°46·7'W	X	5,6
Leen, The	Heref	SO3859	52°13·8'	2°54·1'W	X	148,149
Lee of Burrafirth	Shetld	HU3559	60°19·1'	1°21·5'W	X	2,3
Lee of Gonfirth	Shetld	HU3762	60°20·7'	1°19·3'W	X	2,3
Lee of Saxavord	Shetld	HP6216	60°49·6'	0°51·1'W	X	1
Lee of Vollister	Shetld	HU4695	60°38·4'	1°9·0'W	X	1,2
Lee Old Hall	Shrops	SJ4032	52°53·2'	2°53·1'W	A	126
Leeon	Orkney	HY3513	59°0·2'	3°7·4'W	X	6
Lee-on-the-Solent	Hants	SU5600	50°48·0'	1°11·9'W	T	196
Lee-over-Sands	Essex	TM1012	51°46·3'	1°3·0'E	T	168,169
Lee Park Fm	Hants	SU3518	50°57·9'	1°29·7'W	FM	185
Lee Pen	Scot Bord	NT3238	55°38·1'	3°4·4'W	H	73
Lee Place	W Susx	TQ0523	51°0·0'	0°29·8'W	X	197
Lee Priory	Kent	TR2156	51°15·8'	1°10·5'E	X	179
Leera Stack	Shetld	HP6217	60°50·1'	0°51·1'W	X	1
Lees	Brad	SE0437	53°50·0'	1°55·9'W	X	104
Lees	Derby	SK2637	52°56·0'	1°36·4'W	T	128
Lees	Lancs	SD6644	53°53·7'	2°30·6'W	X	103
Lees	Oldham	SD9504	53°32·2'	2°4·1'W	T	109
Lees	Scot Bord	NT8439	55°38·9'	2°14·8'W	X	74
Lees Barn	Notts	SK6438	52°56·4'	1°2·5'W	X	129
Lees Burn	Aberd	NJ6940	57°27·2'	2°30·5'W	W	29
Lees Coppice	Shrops	SJ3904	52°38·1'	2°53·7'W	F	126
Lees Court	Kent	TR0156	51°16·3'	0°53·3'E	A	178
Leese Hill	Staffs	SK0430	52°52·3'	1°56·0'W	X	128
Leese House Fm	Staffs	SJ9738	52°56·6'	2°2·3'W	FM	127
Lee's Fm	Devon	ST0225	51°1·2'	3°23·5'W	FM	181
Lees Fm	Kent	TR1438	51°6·3'	1°3·8'E	FM	179,189
Lees Fm	Northum	NY8263	54°57·9'	2°16·4'W	FM	86,87
Lees Fm, The	Shrops	SJ3728	52°51·0'	2°55·7'W	FM	126
Lees Hall	Derby	SK0392	53°25·7'	1°56·9'W	X	110
Lees Hall	Northum	NY7065	54°59·0'	2°27·7'W	X	86,87
Lees Hall Fm	Derby	SK1734	52°54·4'	1°44·4'W	FM	128
Lees Heugh	Northum	NY8163	54°57·9'	2°17·4'W	X	86,87
Lees Hill	Cumbr	NY5567	55°0·0'	2°41·8'W	X	86
Lees Hill	Scot Bord	NT7252	55°45·9'	2°26·3'W	X	67,74
Lees Hill	S Lanak	NS8026	55°31·0'	3°53·6'W	X	71,72
Lees Hill	Stir	NS6590	56°5·3'	4°9·7'W	H	57
Lees Hill	Tames	SK0099	53°29·5'	1°59·6'W	H	110
Lees Ho	Kent	TQ6949	51°13·1'	0°25·6'E	X	188
Lees House Fm	Ches	SJ9570	53°13·9'	2°4·1'W	FM	118
Lees House Fm	Lancs	SD6643	53°53·2'	2°30·6'W	FM	103
Lees House Fm	Staffs	SK1448	53°2·0'	1°47·1'W	FM	119
Leeside	Staffs	SJ9360	53°8·5'	2°5·9'W	X	118
Lees Marshes	Medway	TQ8778	51°28·4'	0°42·0'E	X	178
Lees Moor	Brad	SE0538	53°50·5'	1°55·0'W	X	104
Lees Moor Wood	Derby	SK2467	53°12·2'	1°38·0'W	F	119
Leeson Ho	Dorset	SZ0078	50°36·3'	1°59·6'W	X	195
Lee's Rest	Oxon	SP3719	51°52·3'	1°27·4'W	X	164
Leesrig Fm	Cumbr	NY1942	54°46·2'	3°15·1'W	FM	85
Lees Scar Lighthouse	Cumbr	NY0952	54°51·5'	3°24·6'W	X	85
Lees, The	Kent	TQ6949	51°13·1'	0°25·6'E	X	188
Lees, The	Oxon	SU5786	51°34·4'	1°10·3'W	F	174
Lees, The	Shrops	SJ5912	52°42·5'	2°36·0'W	X	126
Lees, The	Shrops	SJ6638	52°56·5'	2°30·0'W	X	127
Leesthorpe	Leic	SK7813	52°42·8'	0°50·3'W	T	129
Leesthorpe Hill	Leic	SK7814	52°43·3'	0°50·3'W	X	129
Lees Wood	Herts	TQ0798	51°40·5'	0°26·8'W	F	166,176
Leeswood Hall	Flint	SJ2561	53°8·7'	3°6·9'W	X	117
Leeswood Old Hall	Flint	SJ2561	53°8·7'	3°6·9'W	X	117
Leeswood or Coed-Llai	Flint	SJ2759	53°7·6'	3°5·1'W	T	117
Lee Taing	Shetld	HU4118	59°57·0'	1°15·5'W	X	4
Lee, The	Northum	NZ0897	55°16·3'	1°52·0'W	X	81
Lee, The	Shetld	HU2878	60°29·4'	1°28·9'W	X	3
Lee, The	Shetld	HU3291	60°36·3'	1°24·4'W	X	1
Lee, The	Shrops	SO3072	52°20·7'	3°1·3'W	X	137,148
Lee, The	Staffs	SK0957	53°6·8'	1°51·5'W	X	119
Leet Hill	Norf	TM3892	52°28·7'	1°30·7'E	X	134
Leet Moss	Aberd	NJ8035	57°24·6'	2°19·5'W	X	29,30
Leetown	Highld	NH5437	57°24·3'	4°25·3'W	X	26
Leetown	Pth & Kin	NO2121	56°22·7'	3°16·3'W	T	53,58
Leetside	Scot Bord	NT8651	55°45·4'	2°12·9'W	X	67,74
Leet Water	Scot Bord	NT8044	55°41·6'	2°18·7'W	W	74
Lee View	Devon	SS7130	51°3·5'	3°50·1'W	X	180
Lee Wick Fm	Essex	TM1014	51°47·3'	1°3·1'E	FM	168,169
Lee Wood	Corn	SS2111	50°52·5'	4°32·3'W	F	190
Lee Wood	Hants	SU7847	51°13·2'	0°52·6'W	F	186
Lee Wood	Shrops	SJ4132	52°53·2'	2°52·2'W	F	126
Leez Lodge Lakes	Essex	TL7018	51°50·3'	0°28·5'E	W	167
Lefesant	Corn	SW9949	50°18·6'	4°49·0'W	X	204
Leffey Hall	Suff	TL9957	52°10·7'	0°55·0'E	X	155
Leffin Donald	S Ayr	NX1482	55°6·1'	4°54·5'W	X	76
Leffin Donald Hill	S Ayr	NX1481	55°5·6'	4°54·5'W	X	76
Leffinwyne	S Ayr	NS2607	55°19·8'	4°44·2'W	X	70,76
Leffnoll	D & G	NX0765	54°56·8'	5°0·4'W	X	82
Leffnoll Point	D & G	NX0765	54°56·8'	5°0·4'W	X	82
Left Law	S Lanak	NT0550	55°44·3'	3°30·3'W	X	65,72
Leftshaw Hill	S Lanak	NS7620	55°27·7'	3°57·2'W	H	71
Leftwich	Ches	SJ6672	53°14·9'	2°30·2'W	T	118
Leftwich Grange Fm	Ches	SJ6571	53°14·3'	2°31·1'W	FM	118
Legar	Powys	SO2117	51°51·0'	3°8·4'W	T	161
Legars	Scot Bord	NT7140	55°39·4'	2°27·2'W	X	74
Legaston	Angus	NO5848	56°37·6'	2°40·6'W	X	54
Legatesden House	Aberd	NJ7425	57°19·1'	2°25·4'W	X	38
Legbarrow Point	Cumbr	SD3182	54°14·0'	3°3·1'W	X	96,97
Legbourne	Lincs	TF3684	53°20·4'	0°3·0'E	T	122
Legbourne Furze	Lincs	TF3786	53°21·4'	0°3·9'E	X	113,122
Legbourne Grange	Lincs	TF3885	53°20·9'	0°4·8'E	X	122
Legbourne Wood	Lincs	TF3683	53°19·8'	0°2·9'E	F	122
Legbranock	N Lanak	NS7860	55°49·3'	3°56·4'W	X	64
Legbranock Burn	N Lanak	NS7759	55°48·8'	3°57·3'W	W	64
Legburthwaite	Cumbr	NY3119	54°33·9'	3°3·6'W	T	90
Legerwood	Scot Bord	NT5843	55°41·0'	2°39·6'W	T	73,74
Legerwood Hill	Scot Bord	NT5841	55°39·9'	2°39·6'W	H	73,74
Leggat	Aberd	NJ7920	57°16·5'	2°20·4'W	X	38
Leggatt Hill	W Susx	SU9223	51°0·2'	0°40·9'W	T	197
Leggatts	Essex	TM0003	51°41·6'	0°54·0'E	X	168
Leggatts Fm	Essex	TL5730	51°57·0'	0°17·5'E	FM	167
Leggatts Fm	Wilts	ST9025	51°1·7'	2°8·2'W	FM	184
Leggatts Park	Herts	TL2602	51°42·4'	0°10·2'W	X	166
Leggerdale	Aberd	NJ7110	57°11·1'	2°28·3'W	X	38
Leggetts Fm	Suff	TM3479	52°21·8'	1°26·6'E	FM	156
Legg Fm	Kent	TQ9632	51°3·5'	0°48·2'E	FM	189
Legglands	Somer	ST1418	50°57·5'	3°13·1'W	X	181,193
Legg's Cross Fm	Durham	NZ2022	54°35·8'	1°41·0'W	FM	93
Leggsmill	Aberd	NJ5859	57°37·4'	2°41·7'W	X	29
Legh Hall	Ches	SJ8878	53°18·2'	2°10·4'W	X	118
Legh Manor	W Susx	TQ2822	50°59·2'	0°10·2'W	X	198
Legholmshiels	S Lanak	NT0335	55°36·2'	3°31·9'W	X	72
Legis Tor	Devon	SX5765	50°28·3'	4°0·5'W	X	202
Legonna	Corn	SW8359	50°23·7'	5°2·8'W	X	200
Legsby	Lincs	TF1385	53°21·2'	0°17·7'W	T	121
Legsby Wood	Lincs	TF1286	53°21·8'	0°18·6'W	F	113,121
Legs Cross	Durham	NZ2022	54°35·8'	1°41·0'W	A	93
Legsheath Fm	E Susx	TQ3933	51°5·0'	0°0·5'W	FM	187
Le Hurst	Essex	TL7136	52°0·0'	0°29·9'E	X	154
Leicester	C of Leic	SK5804	52°38·1'	1°8·2'W	T	140
Leicester Airport	Leic	SK6501	52°36·4'	1°2·0'W	X	141
Leicester Fm	Norf	TF8022	52°46·2'	0°40·5'E	FM	132
Leicester Forest East	Leic	SK5303	52°37·6'	1°12·6'W	T	140
Leicester Forest East Service Area	Leic	SK5302	52°37·0'	1°12·6'W	X	140
Leicester Grange	Warw	SP4390	52°30·6'	1°21·6'W	T	140
Leicester House Fm	Warw	SP3559	52°13·9'	1°28·9'W	FM	151
Leicestershire Round, The	Leic	SP4789	52°30·0'	1°18·1'W	X	140
Leicestershire Round, The	Leic	SP7796	52°33·6'	0°51·4'W	X	141
Leicester Square Fm	Norf	TF8633	52°52·0'	0°46·2'E	FM	132
Leicester Tower	Worcs	SP0345	52°6·4'	1°57·0'W	X	150
Leicestshire Round, The	Leic	SK6114	52°43·4'	1°5·4'W	X	129
Leidchruich	Highld	NH5361	57°37·2'	4°27·2'W	X	20
Leidle River	Arg & Bt	NM5323	56°20·4'	5°59·4'W	W	48
Leids Hill	Moray	NJ4126	57°19·5'	2°58·3'W	H	37
Leigasdail	N Eil	NB5249	58°21·8'	6°13·9'W	X	8
Leigh	Corn	SS2407	50°50·4'	4°29·6'W	X	190
Leigh	Corn	SX2498	50°45·5'	4°29·3'W	X	190
Leigh	Devon	SS7212	50°53·8'	3°48·8'W	T	180
Leigh	Devon	SS7609	50°52·3'	3°45·4'W	X	191
Leigh	Devon	SS9114	50°55·1'	3°32·7'W	X	181
Leigh	Devon	SX4488	50°40·5'	4°12·1'W	X	190
Leigh	Devon	SX4667	50°29·2'	4°9·9'W	X	201
Leigh	Devon	SX5063	50°27·1'	4°6·4'W	X	201
Leigh	Devon	SX7246	50°18·2'	3°47·5'W	A	202
Leigh	Dorset	ST6108	50°52·4'	2°32·9'W	T	194
Leigh	Dorset	ST7808	50°52·5'	2°18·4'W	T	194
Leigh	Dorset	SZ0299	50°47·7'	1°57·9'W	T	195
Leigh	Kent	TQ5546	51°11·8'	0°13·5'E	T	188
Leigh	Shrops	SJ3303	52°37·5'	2°59·0'W	T	126
Leigh	Somer	SS9032	51°4·8'	3°33·8'W	X	181
Leigh	Surrey	TQ2246	51°12·2'	0°14·8'W	T	187
Leigh	Wigan	SD6500	53°30·0'	2°31·2'W	T	109
Leigh	Wilts	SU0692	51°37·8'	1°54·4'W	T	163,173
Leigh	Worcs	SO7853	52°10·7'	2°18·9'W	T	150
Leigham	C of Plym	SX5158	50°24·4'	4°5·4'W	T	201
Leigham's Fm	Essex	TL7801	51°41·0'	0°34·9'E	FM	167
Leighbank Fm	Staffs	SK0137	52°56·1'	1°58·7'W	FM	128
Leigh Barton	Devon	SS9114	50°55·1'	3°32·7'W	X	181
Leigh Barton	Devon	SS9505	50°50·3'	3°29·1'W	X	192
Leigh Barton	Somer	SS9727	51°2·2'	3°27·8'W	X	181
Leigh Barton	Somer	ST0235	51°6·6'	3°23·6'W	X	181
Leigh Barton Fm	Devon	SX3977	50°34·5'	4°16·1'W	FM	201
Leigh Beck	Essex	TQ8182	51°30·7'	0°36·9'E	T	178
Leigh Br	Devon	SX6887	50°40·3'	3°51·7'W	X	191
Leighbridge Fm	Kent	TQ8145	51°10·8'	0°35·8'E	FM	188
Leigh Brook	Glos	SO8826	51°56·2'	2°10·1'W	W	162
Leigh Brook	Worcs	SO7752	52°10·2'	2°19·8'W	W	150
Leigh Common	Somer	ST7429	51°3·8'	2°21·9'W	T	183
Leigh Cott	Somer	ST1136	51°7·2'	3°15·9'W	X	181
Leigh Court	Devon	ST1111	50°53·7'	3°15·6'W	X	192,193
Leigh Court	N Som	ST5474	51°28·0'	2°39·3'W	X	172
Leigh Court	Somer	ST1918	50°57·6'	3°8·8'W	X	181,193
Leigh Creek	Sou-on-Sea	TQ8385	51°32·3'	0°38·7'E	W	178
Leigh Cross	Devon	SS6904	50°49·5'	3°51·2'W	X	191
Leigh Cross	Devon	SX8387	50°40·5'	3°39·0'W	X	191
Leigh Delamere	Wilts	ST8879	51°30·8'	2°10·0'W	T	173
Leigh End	Glos	SO8625	51°55·6'	2°11·8'W	X	162
Leighfield Lodge Fm	Wilts	SU0690	51°36·8'	1°54·4'W	FM	163,173
Leigh Fm	Bath & NE Somer	ST6263	51°22·1'	2°32·4'W	FM	172
Leigh Fm	Corn	SX3364	50°27·4'	4°20·8'W	FM	201
Leigh Fm	Corn	SX3862	50°26·4'	4°16·5'W	FM	201
Leigh Fm	Devon	SS2523	50°59·0'	4°29·2'W	FM	190
Leigh Fm	Lancs	SD6124	53°42·9'	2°35·0'W	FM	102,103
Leigh Fm	S Glos	ST6978	51°30·2'	2°26·4'W	FM	172
Leigh Fm	Somer	SS9633	51°5·4'	3°28·7'W	FM	181
Leigh Fm	Somer	ST0924	51°0·7'	3°17·4'W	FM	181
Leigh Fm	Somer	ST1919	50°58·1'	3°8·8'W	FM	181,193
Leigh Fm	Somer	ST7429	51°3·8'	2°21·9'W	FM	183
Leigh Fm	W Berks	SU3174	51°28·1'	1°32·8'W	FM	174
Leigh Gate	Dorset	SY5096	50°45·9'	2°42·2'W	X	194
Leigh Grange	Devon	SX7061	50°26·3'	3°49·5'W	X	202
Leigh Green	Kent	TQ9032	51°3·6'	0°43·1'E	T	189
Leigh Hall	Shrops	SJ3303	52°37·5'	2°59·0'W	X	126
Leigh Hill	Somer	ST1917	50°57·0'	3°8·8'W	H	181,193
Leigh Hill	Wilts	SU2164	51°22·7'	1°41·5'W	X	174
Leigh Hill Copse	Wilts	SU2263	51°22·2'	1°40·6'W	F	174
Leigh Hill Fm	Devon	ST1010	50°53·2'	3°16·4'W	FM	192,193
Leigh Ho	Devon	SS6714	50°54·8'	3°53·1'W	X	180
Leigh Ho	Glos	SO8725	51°55·6'	2°10·9'W	X	162
Leigh Ho	Hants	SU4321	50°59·4'	1°22·9'W	X	185
Leigh Ho	Somer	ST3506	50°51·3'	2°55·0'W	A	193
Leigh Holt	Somer	ST4835	51°7·0'	2°44·2'W	X	182
Leigh House Fm	Staffs	SO8186	52°28·5'	2°16·4'W	FM	138
Leighland Chapel	Somer	ST0336	51°7·1'	3°22·8'W	T	181
Leigh Lees	Rut	SK8203	52°37·3'	0°46·9'W	X	141
Leigh Lodge	Rut	SK8204	52°37·9'	0°46·9'W	X	141
Leigh Manor	Shrops	SJ3302	52°36·9'	2°59·0'W	X	126
Leigh Middle	Essex	TQ8382	51°30·7'	0°38·6'E	W	178
Leighon	Devon	SX7579	50°36·1'	3°45·6'W	X	191
Leigh-on-Sea	Sou-on-Sea	TQ8486	51°32·8'	0°39·6'E	T	178
Leigh Park	Hants	SU7108	50°52·3'	0°59·1'W	T	197
Leigh Park Fm	Kent	TQ5347	51°12·3'	0°11·8'E	FM	188
Leigh Place	Surrey	TQ2247	51°12·8'	0°14·8'W	X	187
Leigh Place	Surrey	TQ3651	51°14·7'	0°2·7'W	X	187
Leigh Resr	Somer	ST1917	50°57·0'	3°8·8'W	W	181,193
Leigh Sand	Sou-on-Sea	TQ8484	51°31·7'	0°39·6'E	X	178
Leigh Sinton	Worcs	SO7750	52°9·1'	2°19·8'W	T	150
Leighs Lodge	Essex	TL7019	51°50·8'	0°28·5'E	X	167
Leighswood	Wals	SK0501	52°36·6'	1°55·2'W	T	139
Leighterton	Glos	ST8291	51°37·3'	2°15·2'W	T	162,173
Leigh, The	Orkney	HY2909	58°58·0'	3°13·6'W	X	6,7
Leightnie	Angus	NO5267	56°47·8'	2°46·7'W	X	44
Leighton	N Yks	SE1679	54°12·6'	1°44·9'W	T	99
Leighton	Powys	SJ2405	52°38·5'	3°7·0'W	T	126
Leighton	Shrops	SJ6105	52°38·7'	2°34·2'W	T	127
Leighton	Somer	ST7043	51°11·4'	2°25·4'W	T	183
Leighton Beck	Lancs	SD4977	54°11·4'	2°46·5'W	W	97
Leighton Bromswold	Cambs	TL1175	52°21·9'	0°21·8'W	T	142
Leighton Buzzard	Beds	SP9225	51°55·2'	0°39·3'W	T	165
Leighton Buzzard Railway	Beds	SP9326	51°55·7'	0°38·4'W	X	165
Leighton Court	Heref	SO6446	52°6·9'	2°31·1'W	X	149
Leighton Gorse	Cambs	TL0975	52°22·0'	0°23·5'W	F	142
Leighton Grange	Ches	SJ6757	53°6·8'	2°29·2'W	X	118
Leighton Hall	Ches	SJ6757	53°6·8'	2°29·2'W	X	118
Leighton Hall	Lancs	SD4974	54°9·8'	2°46·4'W	X	97
Leighton Hall	Powys	SJ2404	52°37·9'	3°7·0'W	X	126
Leighton Hall Fm	Ches	SJ2879	53°18·4'	3°4·4'W	FM	117
Leightonhill	Angus	NO6361	56°44·6'	2°35·8'W	T	45
Leighton Hill	Northum	NY9095	55°15·2'	2°9·0'W	H	80
Leighton Ho	Cumbr	SD4877	54°11·4'	2°47·4'W	X	97
Leighton Lodge	Ches	SJ6858	53°7·3'	2°28·3'W	X	118
Leighton Lodge	Northnts	SP6469	52°19·2'	1°3·3'W	X	152
Leighton Manor Fm	Kent	TQ4541	51°9·2'	0°4·8'E	FM	188
Leighton Moss (Nature Reserve)	Lancs	SD4875	54°10·3'	2°47·4'W	X	97
Leighton Resr	N Yks	SE1578	54°12·1'	1°45·8'W	W	99
Leigh Tor	Devon	SX7071	50°31·7'	3°49·7'W	X	202
Leigh upon Mendip	Somer	ST6947	51°13·5'	2°26·2'W	T	183
Leigh Wood	Corn	SS2506	50°49·9'	4°28·7'W	F	190
Leigh Wood	Devon	SX3977	50°34·5'	4°16·1'W	F	201
Leigh Wood	Glos	SP1027	51°56·7'	1°50·9'W	F	163
Leigh Woods	N Som	ST5572	51°26·9'	2°38·5'W	T	172
Leigh Woods	N Som	ST5574	51°28·0'	2°38·5'W	F	172
Lèig Mhùthoir	N Eil	NB2338	58°14·9'	6°42·8'W	W	8,13
Leign Fm	Devon	SX7887	50°40·4'	3°43·2'W	FM	191
Leim Fm	Arg & Bt	NR6346	55°39·2'	5°45·6'W	FM	62
Leiniscal	N Eil	NB3729	58°10·6'	6°27·9'W	X	8

Leinish	Highld	NG2050	57°27·5′	6°39·7′W	X	23
Leinish Bay	Highld	NG2050	57°27·5′	6°39·7′W	W	23
Leinster Park	Highld	NH7776	57°45·7′	4°3·6′W	F	21
Leinthall Common	Heref	SO4467	52°18·1′	2°48·9′W	X	137,148,149
Leinthall Earls	Heref	SO4467	52°18·1′	2°48·9′W	T	137,148,149
Leinthall Moor	Heref	SO4270	52°19·7′	2°50·7′W	X	137,148
Leinthall Starkes	Heref	SO4369	52°19·2′	2°49·8′W	T	137,148
Leintwardine	Heref	SO4074	52°21·9′	2°52·5′W	T	137,148
Leintwardine Fishery	Heref	SO4172	52°20·8′	2°51·6′W	W	137,148
Leintwardine Manor	Heref	SO4074	52°21·9′	2°52·5′W	X	137,148
Leipsic Wood	Suff	TL7361	52°13·4′	0°32·4′E	F	155
Leira Ness	Shetld	HU4841	60°9·3′	1°7·6′W	X	4
Leiravay Bay	N Eil	NF9167	57°35·5′	7°9·8′W	W	18
Leire	Leic	SP5290	52°30·6′	1°13·6′W	T	140
Leiregeo	N Eil	NB0031	58°10·2′	7°5·7′W	W	13
Leirinbeg	Highld	NC4167	58°34·0′	4°43·5′W	X	9
Leirinmore	Highld	NC4266	58°33·5′	4°42·5′W	T	9
Leir Mhaodail	Highld	NM5799	57°1·4′	5°59·8′W	X	32,39
Leishfoot Hill	Scot Bord	NT0628	55°32·5′	3°28·9′W	H	72
Leishmore	Highld	NH4040	57°25·6′	4°39·4′W	X	26
Leiston	Suff	TM4462	52°12·4′	1°34·7′E	T	156
Leiston Abbey	Suff	TM4464	52°13·4′	1°34·8′E	A	156
Leiston Common	Suff	TM4563	52°12·9′	1°35·6′E	X	156
Leisure Lakes	Lancs	SD4017	53°39·0′	2°54·1′W	W	108
Leisure World	Essex	TM0025	51°53·5′	0°54·8′E	X	168
Leitcheston	Moray	NJ4062	57°38·9′	2°59·9′W	X	28
Leitchestown	Moray	NJ5263	57°39·5′	2°47·8′W	X	29
Leitchill	Pth & Kin	NO1321	56°22·7′	3°24·1′W	X	53,58
Leitchland	Inverc	NS2274	55°55·8′	4°50·5′W	X	63
Leitchland Fm	Renf	NS4461	55°49·3′	4°29·0′W	FM	64
Leitch's Wood	Moray	NJ3557	57°36·2′	3°4·8′W	F	28
Leiterchullin	Highld	NH6331	57°21·2′	4°16·2′W	X	26
Leitfié	Pth & Kin	NO2545	56°35·7′	3°12·8′W	T	53
Leith	C of Edin	NT2776	55°58·5′	3°9·7′W	T	66
Leith	Orkney	ND4996	58°51·2′	2°52·6′W	X	6,7
Leith Bank	Cumbr	NY5924	54°36·8′	2°37·7′W	X	91
Leith Copse	W Susx	SU7619	50°58·2′	0°54·7′W	F	197
Leithenhall	D & G	NY1296	55°15·3′	3°22·6′W	X	78
Leithenhall Burn	D & G	NY1397	55°15·8′	3°21·7′W	W	78
Leithen Hopes	Scot Bord	NT3344	55°41·3′	3°3·5′W	H	73
Leithen Lodge	Scot Bord	NT3242	55°40·3′	3°4·4′W	X	73
Leithen Water	Scot Bord	NT3341	55°39·7′	3°3·5′W	W	73
Leithenwater Forest	Scot Bord	NT2945	55°41·8′	3°7·3′W	F	73
Leithfield	Aberd	NO7576	56°52·7′	2°24·2′W	X	45
Leith Hall	Aberd	NJ5429	57°21·2′	2°45·4′W	A	37
Leithhead Fm	W Loth	NT1163	55°51·4′	3°24·9′W	FM	65
Leith Hill	Surrey	TQ1343	51°10·7′	0°22·6′W	H	187
Leith Hill Place	Surrey	TQ1342	51°10·2′	0°22·6′W	X	187
Leith Hill Wood	Surrey	TQ1242	51°10·2′	0°23·5′W	F	187
Leithies, The	E Loth	NT5785	56°3·6′	2°41·0′W	X	67
Leith Links	C of Edin	NT2775	55°58·0′	3°9·7′W	X	66
Leitholm	Scot Bord	NT7944	55°41·6′	2°19·6′W	T	74
Leithope Forest	Scot Bord	NT7408	55°22·2′	2°24·2′W	F	80
Leith Vale	Surrey	TQ1338	51°8·0′	0°22·7′W	X	187
Leitir a' Chuilinn	Arg & Bt	NN0903	56°11·1′	5°4·2′W	X	56
Leitir an Stacca	Highld	NC2742	58°20·2′	4°56·8′W	X	9
Leitir Beithe	Highld	NH2521	57°15·0′	4°53·6′W	F	25
Leitir Bheag	Highld	NC6249	58°24·7′	4°21·3′W	X	10
Leitir Bo Fionn	Highld	NN2161	56°42·6′	4°55·0′W	X	41
Leitir Dhubh	Highld	NC2728	58°12·7′	4°56·2′W	X	15
Leitir Dhubh	Highld	NM8367	56°44·9′	5°32·5′W	X	40
Leitir Dhubh	Highld	NM9662	56°42·6′	5°19·5′W	F	40
Leitir Dhubh	Highld	NN4068	56°46·8′	4°36·7′W	X	42
Leitirfearn	Highld	NH3201	57°4·4′	4°45·8′W	X	34
Leitir Fhearna	Highld	NH1574	57°43·3′	5°5·9′W	X	20
Leitir Fhearna	Highld	NN3299	57°3·3′	4°45·7′W	H	34
Leitir Fhoinnlaigh	Highld	NN2792	56°59·5′	4°50·4′W	H	34
Leitir Mhuiseil	Highld	NC4646	58°22·8′	4°37·5′W	X	9
Leitir Riabhach	Highld	NH4291	57°53·1′	4°39·4′W	X	20
Leitir Ruadh	Highld	NH1267	57°39·5′	5°8·6′W	X	19
Leitters	Stir	NN5720	56°21·3′	4°18·4′W	X	51,57
Leland Trail	Somer	ST7133	51°6·0′	2°24·5′W	X	183
Lelant	Corn	SW5437	50°11·2′	5°26·4′W	T	203
Lelant Downs	Corn	SW5236	50°10·6′	5°28·0′W	T	203
Lelant Saltings Sta	Corn	SW5436	50°10·6′	5°26·4′W	X	203
Lelley	E Yorks	TA2032	53°46·5′	0°10·3′W	T	107
Lelley Dyke Fm	E Yorks	TA2133	53°47·0′	0°9·4′W	FM	107
Lelleyfield Ho	E Yorks	TA2231	53°45·9′	0°8·5′W	X	107
Lelley Grange	E Yorks	TA2231	53°45·9′	0°8·5′W	X	107
Lellizzick	Corn	SW9077	50°33·5′	4°57·5′W	X	200
Lelum Hall	N Yks	NZ8005	54°26·3′	0°45·6′W	X	94
Lemail	Corn	SX0272	50°31·1′	4°47·2′W	X	200
Lemanis (Stutfall Castle) (Roman Fort)	Kent	TR1134	51°4·2′	1°1·1′E	R	179,189
Leman Wood	E Yorks	SE9844	53°53·2′	0°30·1′W	F	106
Lemar	Corn	SX0969	50°29·6′	4°41·2′W	X	200
Lem Brook	Shrops	SO7175	52°22·6′	2°25·2′W	W	138
Lem Hill	Worcs	SO7274	52°22·0′	2°24·3′W	T	138
Lemington	Ghead	NZ1764	54°58·5′	1°43·6′W	T	88
Lemington	Scot Bord	NT8663	55°51·8′	2°13·0′W	X	67
Lemington Grange	Glos	SP2133	51°59·9′	1°41·3′W	X	151
Lemington Manor	Glos	SP2234	52°0·5′	1°40·4′W	X	151
Lemlair	Highld	NH5762	57°37·8′	4°23·2′W	X	21
Lemmington Branch	Northum	NU1311	55°23·8′	1°47·3′W	X	81
Lemmington Hall	Northum	NU1211	55°23·8′	1°48·2′W	X	81
Lemmington Mill	Northum	NU1111	55°23·8′	1°49·1′W	X	81
Lemnas	Aberd	NJ8462	57°39·1′	2°15·6′W	X	29,30
Lemno Burn	Angus	NO4755	56°41·3′	2°51·5′W	W	54
Lemon's Hill	Devon	ST1511	50°53·8′	3°12·1′W	X	192,193
Lemon's Hill Fm	Devon	ST1511	50°53·8′	3°12·1′W	FM	192,193
Lemore	Heref	SO3151	52°9·4′	3°0·1′W	X	148
Lemoria Rock	Corn	SW9237	50°12·0′	4°54·5′W	X	204
Le Mote Hall	Essex	TL8634	51°58·6′	0°42·9′E	X	155
Lempitlaw	Scot Bord	NT7832	55°35·1′	2°20·5′W	T	74
Lempock Wells	E Loth	NT4467	55°53·8′	2°53·3′W	X	66
Lemsford	Herts	TL2111	51°47·3′	0°14·3′W	T	166
Lenacre	Cumbr	SD6689	54°18·0′	2°30·9′W	T	98
Lenacre Hall Fm	Kent	TR0145	51°10·4′	0°52·9′E	FM	189
Lenady	Orkney	HY5004	58°55·5′	2°51·6′W	X	6,7
Lenahowe	Orkney	HY2320	59°3·9′	3°20·1′W	X	6
Lenahowe	Orkney	HY2815	59°1·2′	3°14·8′W	X	6
Lenaig	Arg & Bt	NR7048	55°40·5′	5°39·0′W	X	62
Lenamhor Fm	N Ayr	NR9620	55°26·1′	5°13·0′W	FM	68,69
Lenaston Fm	Heref	SO5027	51°56·6′	2°43·3′W	FM	162
Lenavore	Arg & Bt	NR3043	55°36·6′	6°16·8′W	X	60
Lenborough	Bucks	SP6931	51°58·6′	0°59·3′W	T	152,165
Lenborough Fm	Bucks	SP7030	51°58·1′	0°58·5′W	FM	152,165
Lenborough Wood	Bucks	SP6631	51°58·6′	1°1·9′W	F	152,165
Lench Ditch	Worcs	SO9746	52°7·0′	2°2·2′W	W	150
Lenchie	Aberd	NJ5931	57°22·3′	2°40·4′W	X	29,37
Lenchwick	Worcs	SP0347	52°7·5′	1°57·0′W	T	150
Lenda	Devon	SX7975	50°34·0′	3°42·1′W	X	191
Lendales	N Yks	SE7879	54°12·3′	0°47·8′W	X	100
Lendalfoot	S Ayr	NX1389	55°9·9′	4°55·7′W	T	76
Lendal Lodge	S Ayr	NX1590	55°10·4′	4°53·9′W	X	76
Lenders Dale	Orkney	HY2104	58°55·2′	3°21·8′W	X	6,7
Lendersfield Ho	N Yks	SE6599	54°23·2′	0°59·5′W	X	94,100
Lendrick Hill	Pth & Kin	NO0103	56°12·8′	3°35·3′W	H	58
Lendrick Lodge	Angus	NO3550	56°38·5′	3°3·1′W	X	54
Lendrick Lodge	Stir	NN5406	56°13·7′	4°20·9′W	X	57
Lendrick Muir School	Pth & Kin	NO0200	56°11·2′	3°34·3′W	X	58
Lendrum	Aberd	NJ7644	57°29·4′	2°23·6′W	X	29
Lendrum Terrace	Aberd	NK1241	57°27·8′	1°47·5′W	X	30
Lengemire	Orkney	HY4345	59°17·5′	2°59·6′W	X	5
Lenhall Fm	Kent	TR1752	51°13·8′	1°6·9′E	FM	179,189
Lenham	Kent	TQ8952	51°14·4′	0°42·9′E	T	189
Lenham Forstal	Kent	TQ9150	51°13·3′	0°44·5′E	T	189
Lenham Heath	Kent	TQ9149	51°12·7′	0°44·5′E	T	189
Lenibrick Point	Cumbr	SD3475	54°10·2′	3°0·2′W	X	96,97
Lenihall	Arg & Bt	NS0168	55°52·1′	5°10·4′W	X	63
Lenimore	N Ayr	NR8847	55°40·5′	5°21·9′W	X	62,69
Lennel	Scot Bord	NT8540	55°39·4′	2°13·9′W	T	74
Lennelhill	Scot Bord	NT8542	55°40·5′	2°13·9′W	X	74
Lennerton Fm	N Yks	SE5232	53°47·1′	1°12·2′W	FM	105
Lennie	S Ayr	NX3597	55°14·6′	4°35·3′W	H	77
Lennie Mains	C of Edin	NT1674	55°57·4′	3°20·3′W	X	65,66
Lennie Park	C of Edin	NT1773	55°56·8′	3°19·3′W	X	65,66
Lennies	D & G	NX4759	54°54·4′	4°22·8′W	X	83
Lennieston Muir	Stir	NN6203	56°12·2′	4°13·0′W	X	57
Lennoch	Pth & Kin	NN8021	56°22·2′	3°56·1′W	X	52,57
Lennox Fm	Lancs	SD6539	53°51·0′	2°31·5′W	FM	102,103
Lennoxlove	E Loth	NT5172	55°56·6′	2°46·6′W	A	66
Lennoxlove Acredales	E Loth	NT5173	55°57·1′	2°46·6′W	X	66
Lennoxlove Mains	E Loth	NT5172	55°56·6′	2°46·6′W	X	66
Lennox Plunton	D & G	NX6051	54°50·3′	4°10·4′W	X	83
Lennox Tower	C of Edin	NT1767	55°53·6′	3°19·2′W	A	65,66
Lennoxtown	E Dunb	NS6277	55°58·2′	4°12·2′W	T	64
Lenny Hill	Cumbr	SD1870	54°7·4′	3°14·9′W	X	96
Lenshaw	Aberd	NJ6641	57°27·7′	2°33·5′W	X	29
Lensty	Orkney	ND3793	58°49·5′	3°5·0′W	X	7
Lens Wick	Orkney	HY7655	59°23·1′	2°24·9′W	W	5
Lent	Bucks	SU9282	51°32·0′	0°40·0′W	T	175
Lenten Pool	Denb	SJ0466	53°11·2′	3°25·8′W	T	116
Lent Fm	Norf	TM1090	52°28·3′	1°5·9′E	FM	144
Lenthay Common	Dorset	ST6115	50°56·2′	2°32·9′W	X	183
Lenthay Dairy Ho	Dorset	ST6215	50°56·2′	2°32·1′W	X	183
Lentney Fm	Somer	ST6953	51°16·8′	2°26·3′W	FM	183
Lenton	C of Nott	SK5539	52°57·0′	1°10·5′W	T	129
Lenton	Devon	SS6620	50°58·1′	3°54·1′W	X	180
Lenton	Lincs	TF0230	52°51·7′	0°28·7′W	T	130
Lenton Abbey	C of Nott	SK5338	52°56·4′	1°12·3′W	T	129
Lenton Fm	Wilts	ST8663	51°22·2′	2°11·7′W	FM	173
Lentran	Highld	NH5845	57°28·6′	4°21·6′W	T	26
Lentran Ho	Highld	NH5745	57°28·6′	4°22·6′W	X	26
Lentran Point	Highld	NH5846	57°29·2′	4°21·7′W	X	26
Lent Rise	Bucks	SU9281	51°31·5′	0°40·0′W	T	175
Lentworth Hall	Lancs	SD5454	53°59·0′	2°41·7′W	X	102
Lenwade	Norf	TG1018	52°43·4′	1°7·0′E	T	133
Leny Ho	Stir	NN6108	56°14·9′	4°14·2′W	X	57
Lenzie	E Dunb	NS6572	55°55·6′	4°9·2′W	T	64
Lenziemill	N Lanak	NS7673	55°56·3′	3°58·7′W	T	64
Leob	Arg & Bt	NM4023	56°19·9′	6°11·9′W	X	48
Leoch	Angus	NO3536	56°31·0′	3°2·9′W	T	54
Leochel Burn	Aberd	NJ5710	57°11·0′	2°42·2′W	W	37
Leochel-Cushnie	Aberd	NJ5210	57°11·0′	2°47·2′W	T	37
Leochrie	Aberd	NJ3917	57°14·6′	3°0·2′W	X	37
Leodebest	Highld	ND1834	58°17·5′	3°23·4′W	X	11
Leodest Fm	I of M	NX4000	54°22·5′	4°27·4′W	FM	95
Leogh	Shetld	HZ2070	59°31·2′	1°38·3′W	X	4
Leomadal	N Eil	NF9793	57°49·7′	7°5·8′W	X	18
Leominster	Heref	SO4959	52°13·8′	2°44·4′W	T	148,149
Leon	Shetld	HU3581	60°30·9′	1°21·3′W	X	1,2,3
Leonach	Moray	NJ1150	57°32·1′	3°28·7′W	X	28
Leonach Burn	Highld	NH9136	57°24·3′	3°48·4′W	W	27
Leonard Childs Br	Cambs	TL3888	52°28·6′	0°2·3′E	X	142,143
Leonard Fm	Devon	ST0009	50°52·5′	3°24·9′W	FM	192
Leonard Moor	Devon	ST0513	50°54·8′	3°20·7′W	X	181
Leonard Scar	Cumbr	SD2668	54°6·4′	3°7·5′W	X	96,97
Leonard's Cove	Devon	SX8648	50°19·5′	3°35·7′W	W	202
Leonards Cragg	Cumbr	NY8214	54°31·5′	2°16·3′W	X	91,92
Leonard's Hill	Northum	NY8088	55°11·4′	2°18·4′W	H	80
Leonard Stanley	Glos	SO8003	51°43·8′	2°17·0′W	T	162
Leonardston	Pemb	SM9405	51°42·6′	4°58·5′W	T	157,158
Leorin	Arg & Bt	NR3548	55°39·5′	6°12·4′W	T	60
Leorin Lochs	Arg & Bt	NR3748	55°39·5′	6°10·5′W	W	60
Leosaval	N Eil	NB0309	57°58·5′	7°1·0′W	H	13
Lepe	Hants	SZ4598	50°47·0′	1°21·3′W	T	196
Lepe Country Park	Hants	SZ4598	50°47·0′	1°21·3′W	X	196
Lepe Fm	Hants	SZ4499	50°47·6′	1°22·2′W	FM	196
Leper Ho	Staffs	SJ8605	52°38·8′	2°12·0′W	X	127,139
Leperstone Resr	Inverc	NS3571	55°54·5′	4°37·9′W	W	63
Lephams Bridge Ho	E Susx	TQ4823	50°59·5′	0°6·9′E	X	198
Lephenstrath	Arg & Bt	NR6608	55°18·9′	5°40·8′W	X	68
Lephenstrath Br	Arg & Bt	NR6609	55°19·4′	5°40·9′W	X	68
Lephin	Highld	NG1749	57°26·8′	6°42·6′W	T	23
Lephinchapel	Arg & Bt	NR9690	56°3·8′	5°16·2′W	T	55
Lephincorrach	Arg & Bt	NR7835	55°33·7′	5°30·8′W	X	68,69
Lephincorrach Burn	Arg & Bt	NR7735	55°33·7′	5°31·8′W	W	68,69
Lephinkill	Arg & Bt	NR9983	56°0·1′	5°13·0′W	X	55
Lephinmore	Arg & Bt	NR7832	55°32·1′	5°30·7′W	X	68,69
Lephinmore	Arg & Bt	NR9892	56°4·9′	5°14·3′W	T	55
Lephinmore Point	Arg & Bt	NR9892	56°4·9′	5°14·3′W	X	55
Leppington	N Yks	SE7661	54°2·6′	0°49·9′W	T	100
Leppington Beck	N Yks	SE7560	54°2·1′	0°50·9′W	W	100
Leppington Grange	N Yks	SE7561	54°2·6′	0°50·9′W	X	100
Leppington Lodge Fm	N Yks	SE7662	54°3·1′	0°49·9′W	FM	100
Leppington Wood	N Yks	SE7661	54°2·6′	0°49·9′W	F	100
Lepton	Kirk	SE2015	53°38·1′	1°41·4′W	T	110
Lepton Edge	Kirk	SE2115	53°38·1′	1°40·5′W	T	110
Lerabeck	Shetld	HT9738	60°7·9′	2°2·7′W	X	4
Lerags Fm	Arg & Bt	NM8324	56°21·8′	5°30·3′W	FM	49
Lerags House	Arg & Bt	NM8424	56°21·8′	5°29·4′W	X	49
Lera Voe	Shetld	HU2248	60°13·2′	1°35·7′W	W	3
Le Rette Fm	E Susx	TQ7417	50°55·8′	0°29·0′E	FM	199
Ler Geo	Shetld	HU2585	60°33·1′	1°32·1′W	X	3
Lergeo Water	Shetld	HU2584	60°32·6′	1°32·2′W	W	3
Lergychoniemore	Arg & Bt	NM8108	56°13·1′	5°31·5′W	X	55
Lerigoligan	Arg & Bt	NM8105	56°11·5′	5°31·3′W	X	55
Ler Ness	Shetld	HZ2073	59°32·8′	1°38·3′W	X	4
Leroch	Pth & Kin	NO2545	56°35·7′	3°12·8′W	X	53
Lerquoy	Shetld	HP5901	60°41·5′	0°54·7′W	X	1
Lerrocks	Stir	NN7303	56°12·4′	4°2·4′W	X	57
Lerryn	Corn	SX1456	50°22·7′	4°36·6′W	T	200
Lertwell	Oxon	SU2684	51°33·5′	1°37·1′W	X	174
Ler Wick	Shetld	HU4492	60°36·8′	1°11·3′W	W	1,2
Lerwick	Shetld	HU4741	60°9·3′	1°8·7′W	T	4
Lerwill Fm	Devon	SS6426	51°1·3′	3°56·0′W	FM	180
Lesbury	Northum	NU2311	55°23·8′	1°37·8′W	T	81
Lesceave Fm	Corn	SW5827	50°5·9′	5°22·7′W	FM	203
Leschangie	Aberd	NJ7314	57°13·2′	2°26·4′W	X	38
Leschangie Hill	Aberd	NJ7414	57°13·2′	2°25·4′W	H	38
Lescraigie	Aberd	NJ7545	57°29·9′	2°24·6′W	X	29
Lescrow	Corn	SX1152	50°20·5′	4°39·0′W	X	200,204
Les Graham Memorial Shelter	I of M	SC3987	54°15·5′	4°27·9′W	X	95
Lesingey Round	Corn	SW4530	50°7·2′	5°33·7′W	A	203
Leskernick	Corn	SX1879	50°35·2′	4°33·9′W	X	201
Leskernick Hill	Corn	SX1880	50°35·7′	4°33·9′W	H	201
Leskine	Stir	NN5329	56°26·1′	4°22·6′W	X	51
Leslie	Aberd	NJ5924	57°18·5′	2°40·4′W	T	37
Leslie	Fife	NO2401	56°12·0′	3°13·1′W	T	59
Lesliedale	Orkney	HY4010	58°58·6′	3°2·1′W	X	6
Leslie Ho	Fife	NO2601	56°12·0′	3°11·1′W	X	59
Leslie Mains	Fife	NO2601	56°12·0′	3°11·1′W	X	59
Lesmahagow	S Lanak	NS8139	55°38·1′	3°53·0′W	T	71,72
Lesmurdie Ho	Moray	NJ2263	57°39·3′	3°18·0′W	X	28
Lesneague	Corn	SW7722	50°3·6′	5°6·6′W	X	204
Lesnes Abbey Woods	Bexley	TQ4778	51°29·1′	0°7·4′E	F	177
Lesnewth	Corn	SX1390	50°41·0′	4°38·5′W	T	190
Lesquite Fm	Corn	SX0662	50°25·8′	4°43·5′W	FM	200
Lessendrum	Aberd	NJ5741	57°27·7′	2°42·5′W	X	29
Lesser Linn	S Lanak	NS8442	55°39·7′	3°50·2′W	X	71,72
Lesser Poston	Shrops	SO5382	52°26·3′	2°41·1′W	X	137,138
Lesshamar	Orkney	HY5537	59°13·3′	2°46·8′W	X	5
Lessingham	Norf	TG3928	52°48·0′	1°33·1′E	T	133,134
Lessland Fm	I of W	SZ5482	50°38·3′	1°13·8′W	FM	196
Lessness Heath	Bexley	TQ4978	51°29·1′	0°9·2′E	T	177
Lessnessock	E Ayr	NS4819	55°26·7′	4°23·8′W	X	70
Lessonhall	Cumbr	NY2250	54°50·6′	3°12·5′W	T	85
Lessor Fm	Oxon	SP3934	52°0·4′	1°25·5′W	FM	151
Lessudden Bank	Scot Bord	NT6031	55°34·5′	2°37·6′W	X	74
Lester Cliff	Devon	SS5847	51°12·5′	4°1·6′W	X	180
Lester Point	Devon	SS5747	51°12·5′	4°2·4′W	X	180
Lestoon	Corn	SX0358	50°23·6′	4°45·9′W	X	200
Lestowder	Corn	SW7924	50°4·7′	5°5·0′W	X	204
Lestow Fm	Corn	SX1667	50°28·7′	4°35·2′W	FM	201
Lestraynes	Corn	SW7332	50°8·9′	5°10·3′W	X	204
Leswalt	D & G	NX0163	54°55·6′	5°5·9′W	T	82
Leswidden	Corn	SW3930	50°7·0′	5°38·7′W	X	203
Letall Fm	Cambs	TL2591	52°30·4′	0°9·1′W	FM	142
Letche's Fm	Essex	TL8028	51°55·5′	0°37·5′E	FM	168
Letchmoor Fm	Heref	SO3464	52°16·5′	2°57·6′W	FM	137,148,149
Letchmore Heath	Herts	TQ1597	51°39·8′	0°19·8′W	T	166,176
Letchworth	Herts	TL2132	51°58·6′	0°13·9′W	T	166
Letcombe Bassett	Oxon	SU3785	51°34·0′	1°27·6′W	T	174
Letcombe Bassett Field	Oxon	SU3686	51°34·5′	1°28·4′W	X	174
Letcombe Bowers Fm	Oxon	SU3882	51°32·4′	1°26·7′W	FM	174
Letcombe Brook	Oxon	SU4193	51°38·3′	1°24·1′W	W	164,174
Letcombe Regis	Oxon	SU3886	51°34·5′	1°26·7′W	T	174
Leth Allt	Arg & Bt	NS0488	56°2·9′	5°8·4′W	W	56
Leth Allt	Highld	NH2299	57°57·0′	5°0·0′W	W	20
Leth Allt	Highld	NN0182	56°53·5′	5°15·6′W	W	41
Leth-allt Beag	Highld	NJ0823	57°17·6′	3°31·1′W	W	36
Leth-allt Mór	Highld	NJ0722	57°17·0′	3°32·1′W	W	36
Letham	Angus	NO5248	56°37·5′	2°46·5′W	T	54
Letham	E Renf	NS5655	55°46·3′	4°17·3′W	X	64
Letham	Falk	NS8985	56°3·0′	3°46·5′W	T	65
Letham	Fife	NO3014	56°19·1′	3°7·5′W	T	59
Letham	Fife	NO3704	56°13·7′	3°0·5′W	X	59
Letham	Fife	NT1483	56°2·2′	3°22·4′W	X	65
Letham	Pth & Kin	NO0632	56°28·5′	3°31·1′W	X	52,53
Letham	Pth & Kin	NO0924	56°24·2′	3°28·0′W	T	52,53,58
Letham	Pth & Kin	NO1511	56°17·3′	3°21·9′W	X	58
Letham	S Lanak	NS8038	55°37·5′	3°53·9′W	X	71,72
Lethame Ho	S Lanak	NS6844	55°40·5′	4°5·5′W	X	71
Letham Feus	Fife	NO3704	56°13·7′	3°0·5′W	X	59
Letham Grange (Hotel)	Angus	NO6245	56°36·0′	2°36·7′W	X	54
Lethamhill	Northum	NT9339	55°38·9′	2°6·2′W	X	74,75
Letham Hill Haugh	Northum	NT9238	55°38·4′	2°7·2′W	X	74,75
Letham Hill Wood	Fife	NT1483	56°2·2′	3°22·4′W	F	65
Letham Ho	E Loth	NT4973	55°57·1′	2°48·6′W	X	66
Letham Mains	E Loth	NT4872	55°56·5′	2°49·5′W	X	66
Letham Moss	Falk	NS8886	56°3·5′	3°47·5′W	X	65
Letham Shank	Northum	NT9753	55°46·5′	2°2·4′W	X	75
Lethangie	Pth & Kin	NO1203	56°12·9′	3°24·7′W	X	58
Lethanhill	E Ayr	NS4310	55°21·8′	4°28·2′W	X	70
Lethans	E Ayr	NS6916	55°25·5′	4°3·8′W	X	71
Lethans Hill	D & G	NS6915	55°24·9′	4°3·7′W	X	71
Lethans Muir	Fife	NT0794	56°8·0′	3°29·3′W	X	58
Leth Bheinn	Highld	NN0678	56°51·4′	5°10·5′W	X	41

Leth Chreag	Highld	NG9771	57°41·2'	5°23·9'W	X	19
Leth Chreag	Highld	NG9848	57°28·9'	5°21·7'W	X	25
Leth-chreag	Highld	NN9293	57°1·2'	3°46·3'W	X	36,43
Leth Dhearc-ola	Arg & Bt	NM6538	56°28·7'	5°48·5'W	X	49
Lethegus Rocks	I Scilly	SV8707	49°53·1'	6°21·1'W	X	203
Lethem	Scot Bord	NT6708	55°22·1'	2°30·8'W	T	80
Lethen	Aberd	NJ7533	57°23·5'	2°24·5'W	X	29
Lethen Bar	Highld	NH9549	57°31·4'	3°44·7'W	H	27
Lethendry	Highld	NJ0727	57°19·7'	3°32·2'W	X	36
Lethendrychule	Highld	NH8921	57°16·2'	3°50·0'W	X	35,36
Lethendryveole	Highld	NH8919	57°15·2'	3°49·9'W	X	35,36
Lethendybank	Pth & Kin	NO1342	56°34·0'	3°24·5'W	X	53
Lethenhill	Moray	NJ1058	57°36·4'	3°29·9'W	X	28
Lethen Ho	Highld	NH9351	57°32·5'	3°46·8'W	X	27
Lethenty	Aberd	NJ5820	57°16·4'	2°41·3'W	X	37
Lethenty	Aberd	NJ7624	57°18·6'	2°23·4'W	X	38
Lethenty	Aberd	NJ8041	57°27·8'	2°19·5'W	T	29,30
Lethenty Hill	Aberd	NJ5821	57°16·9'	2°41·3'W	H	37
Letheringham	Suff	TM2757	52°10·1'	1°19·6'E	T	156
Letheringham Lodge	Suff	TM2757	52°10·1'	1°19·6'E	X	156
Letheringsett	Norf	TG0638	52°54·2'	1°4·2'E	T	133
Leth-fhonn	Arg & Bt	NM7232	56°25·8'	5°41·4'W	X	49
Leth-ghleann	Highld	NC9540	58°20·4'	3°47·1'W	X	11
Leth Sgeir	Arg & Bt	NR7085	56°0·4'	5°40·9'W	X	55,61
Leth Sgeir	Arg & Bt	NR7389	56°2·7'	5°38·2'W	X	55
Leth Uillt	Arg & Bt	NR7250	55°41·7'	5°37·2'W	W	62
Letocetum (Roman Town)	Staffs	SK1006	52°39·3'	1°50·7'W	R	139
Letrualt	Arg & Bt	NS2684	56°1·3'	4°47·1'W	X	56
Lettach	Aberd	NJ4039	57°26·5'	2°59·5'W	X	28
Lettaford	Devon	SX7084	50°38·7'	3°49·9'W	T	191
Lettaly	Orkney	HY3618	59°2·9'	3°6·4'W	X	6
Lettan	Orkney	HY7545	59°17·7'	2°25·8'W	T	5
Lettar of Ballied	Pth & Kin	NO1246	56°36·1'	3°25·6'W	X	53
Letter	Aberd	NJ7511	57°11·6'	2°24·4'W	T	38
Letter	Arg & Bt	NS2186	56°2·3'	4°52·0'W	X	56
Letter	Highld	NH5640	57°25·9'	4°23·5'W	X	26
Letter	Pth & Kin	NO0543	56°34·4'	3°32·3'W	X	52,53
Letter	Stir	NN4610	56°15·7'	4°28·7'W	X	57
Letter	Stir	NN6003	56°12·2'	4°15·0'W	X	57
Letterach	Moray	NJ2720	57°16·2'	3°12·2'W	H	37
Letterage Copse	Wilts	SU0984	51°33·5'	1°51·8'W	F	173
Letteraitten	Highld	NJ0917	57°14·3'	3°30·0'W	X	36
Letterbeg	Aberd	NO6692	57°1·3'	2°33·1'W	X	38,45
Letterbox Meml	Devon	SX6267	50°29·4'	3°56·4'W	X	202
Letter Burn	Stir	NN4612	56°16·8'	4°28·8'W	W	57
Letterewe	Highld	NG9571	57°41·2'	5°25·9'W	T	19
Letterewe Forest	Highld	NG9872	57°41·8'	5°22·9'W	X	19
Letterfearn	Highld	NG8823	57°15·2'	5°30·4'W	T	33
Letter F Fm	Cambs	TL6185	52°26·6'	0°22·5'E	FM	143
Letterfinlay Lodge Hotel	Highld	NN2491	56°58·9'	4°53·3'W	X	34
Letterfourie	Moray	NJ4462	57°38·9'	2°55·8'W	X	28
Letter Hill	Highld	NG8331	57°19·3'	5°35·8'W	H	24
Lettermay	Arg & Bt	NN1800	56°9·7'	4°55·4'W	X	56
Lettermay Burn	Arg & Bt	NS1799	56°9·2'	4°56·3'W	W	56
Letter Moor	Corn	SX1770	50°30·3'	4°34·5'W	X	201
Lettermorar	Highld	NM7389	56°56·5'	5°43·5'W	T	40
Lettermore	Arg & Bt	NM4948	56°33·7'	6°4·7'W	X	47,48
Lettermore	Highld	NC6147	58°23·6'	4°22·2'W	X	10
Letter Muir	Stir	NN6103	56°12·2'	4°14·0'W	X	57
Letters	Highld	NH1687	57°50·3'	5°5·5'W	T	20
Lettershaws	S Lanak	NS9020	55°27·9'	3°44·0'W	X	71,72
Letterston	Pemb	SM9329	51°55·5'	5°0·2'W	T	157,158
Letterston Moorland	Pemb	SM9328	51°55·0'	5°0·2'W	F	157,158
Letterwalton House	Arg & Bt	NM9139	56°30·1'	5°23·3'W	X	49
Lettie River or Abhainn Deataidh	Highld	NC6805	58°1·1'	4°13·6'W	W	16
Lettoch	Highld	NH6248	57°30·3'	4°17·7'W	X	26
Lettoch	Highld	NJ0219	57°15·3'	3°37·0'W	X	36
Lettoch	Highld	NJ0932	57°22·4'	3°30·3'W	X	27,36
Lettoch	Moray	NJ2221	57°16·6'	3°17·2'W	X	36
Lettoch	Moray	NJ3037	57°25·3'	3°9·5'W	X	28
Lettoch	Pth & Kin	NN9064	56°45·5'	3°47·5'W	X	43
Lettoch	Pth & Kin	NN9359	56°42·9'	3°44·4'W	X	52
Letton	Heref	SO3346	52°6·7'	2°58·3'W	T	148,149
Letton	Heref	SO3770	52°19·7'	2°55·1'W	T	137,148
Letton Court Fm	Heref	SO3445	52°6·2'	2°57·4'W	FM	148,149
Letton Green	Norf	TF9806	52°37·2'	0°55·9'E	T	144
Letton Hall	Norf	TF9705	52°36·6'	0°55·0'E	X	144
Letton Lake	Heref	SO3547	52°7·3'	2°56·6'W	W	148,149
Letton Park	Dorset	ST9007	50°52·0'	2°8·1'W	X	195
Lettravane Fm	Monm	SO4218	51°51·7'	2°50·1'W	FM	161
Lettre Cottage	Stir	NS5284	56°1·8'	4°22·1'W	X	57,64
Lettrick	D & G	NX7882	55°7·3'	3°54·4'W	X	78
Lettrick Hill	D & G	NX7882	55°7·3'	3°54·4'W	H	78
Lettrickhills	S Lanak	NS6556	55°47·0'	4°8·7'W	X	64
Lett's Green	Kent	TQ4559	51°18·9'	0°5·2'E	T	188
Letty Brongu	Brig	SS8888	51°35·0'	3°36·6'W	T	170
Letty Green	Herts	TL2810	51°46·7'	0°8·3'W	T	166
Lettymoel	Cered	SN6472	52°20·0'	3°59·4'W	X	135
Letwell	Roth	SK5687	53°22·8'	1°9·1'W	T	111,120
Leuan	Orkney	HY4018	59°3·0'	3°2·3'W	X	6
Leuchar	C of Aber	NJ7904	57°7·8'	2°20·4'W	X	38
Leuchar Burn	C of Aber	NJ7904	57°7·8'	2°20·4'W	W	38
Leuchar Moss	C of Aber	NJ7904	57°7·8'	2°20·4'W	X	38
Leuchars	Fife	NO4521	56°22·9'	2°53·0'W	T	54,59
Leuchars Airfield	Fife	NO4620	56°22·4'	2°52·0'W	X	54,59
Leuchars Castle	Fife	NO4522	56°23·5'	2°53·0'W	X	54,59
Leuchars Ho	Moray	NJ2564	57°39·8'	3°15·0'W	X	28
Leuchars Lodge	Fife	NO4422	56°23·5'	2°54·0'W	X	54,59
Leuchatsbeath	Fife	NT1592	56°7·0'	3°21·6'W	X	58
Leuchland	Angus	NO6259	56°43·5'	2°36·8'W	X	54
Leuchland Plantation	Angus	NO6360	56°44·1'	2°35·8'W	F	45
Leuchlands	C of Aber	NJ9313	57°12·7'	2°6·5'W	X	38
Leuchold	C of Edin	NT1578	55°59·5'	3°21·3'W	X	65
Leud-lainn	Highld	NH5625	57°17·8'	4°22·9'W	X	26,35
Leumadair Mór	N Eil	NA9822	58°5·3'	7°7·0'W	X	13
Leum an Fhéidh	Highld	NC0801	57°57·7'	5°14·3'W	X	15
Leum Beathaig	Arg & Bt	NR5264	55°48·6'	5°57·0'W	X	61
Leum Langa	N Eil	NB5654	58°24·6'	6°10·2'W	X	8
Leum Langa	N Eil	NB5657	58°26·3'	6°10·4'W	X	8

Leum na Muice Duibhe	Arg & Bt	NM6923	56°20·8'	5°43·9'W	X	49
Leumrabhagh	N Eil	NB3711	58°0·9'	6°26·7'W	T	14
Leum Uilleim	Highld	NN3364	56°44·5'	4°43·4'W	H	41
Leur Thòb	N Eil	NB1934	58°12·6'	6°46·6'W	W	8,13
Leusdon	Devon	SX7073	50°32·8'	3°49·7'W	X	191
Leva Green	N Yks	SD7562	54°3·4'	2°22·5'W	X	98
Levalsa	Corn	SW9948	50°18·1'	4°49·0'W	X	204
Levalsa Meor	Corn	SX0049	50°18·7'	4°48·2'W	T	204
Levan	Inverc	NS2176	55°56·9'	4°51·6'W	T	63
Levaneap	Shetld	HU4863	60°21·2'	1°7·3'W	T	2,3
Levant Zawn	Corn	SW3634	50°9·1'	5°41·4'W	W	203
Levardro	Corn	SW8749	50°18·4'	4°59·1'W	X	204
Levaton	Devon	SX8067	50°29·7'	3°41·1'W	X	202
Levedale	Staffs	SJ8916	52°44·7'	2°9·4'W	T	127
Level	I of M	SC2269	54°5·4'	4°42·9'W	X	95
Level Court Fm	Newp	ST3582	51°32·2'	2°55·8'W	FM	171
Level Ho	N Yks	NY9601	54°24·5'	2°3·3'W	X	91,92
L Evelix	Highld	NH7387	57°51·5'	4°8·0'W	W	21
Level of Mendalgief	Newp	ST3086	51°34·3'	3°0·2'W	T	171
Levels Fm	Notts	SK7098	53°28·7'	0°56·3'W	FM	112
Level's Green	Essex	TL4724	51°53·9'	0°8·6'E	T	167
Level, The	Moray	NJ2258	57°36·6'	3°17·9'W	X	28
Leven	E Yorks	TA1045	53°53·6'	0°19·1'W	T	107
Leven	Fife	NO3800	56°11·6'	2°59·5'W	T	59
Leven Br	Stock on T	NZ4412	54°30·3'	1°18·8'W	X	93
Leven Canal	E Yorks	TA0744	53°53·1'	0°21·9'W	W	107
Leven Carrs	E Yorks	TA0745	53°53·6'	0°21·9'W	X	107
Leven Close Fm	Stock on T	NZ4511	54°29·8'	1°17·9'W	FM	93
Levencorroch	N Ayr	NS0021	55°26·8'	5°9·3'W	T	69
Levencorroch Hill	N Ayr	NS0021	55°26·8'	5°9·3'W	X	69
Leven Grange	E Yorks	TA1144	53°53·1'	0°18·3'W	X	107
Levenhall	E Loth	NT3673	55°57·0'	3°1·1'W	T	66
Levenish	N Eil	NF1396	57°47·4'	8°30·4'W	X	18
Leven Links	Fife	NO3800	56°11·6'	2°59·5'W	T	59
Leven Mouth	N Yks	NZ5107	54°27·6'	1°12·4'W	W	93
Levenmouth	Pth & Kin	NO1700	56°11·4'	3°19·8'W	X	58
Levenmouth Plantn	Pth & Kin	NO1700	56°11·4'	3°19·8'W	F	58
Levens	Cumbr	SD4886	54°16·3'	2°47·5'W	T	97
Levens Br	Cumbr	SD4985	54°15·7'	2°46·6'W	A	97
Leven Seat	W Loth	NS9457	55°47·9'	3°41·0'W	H	65,72
Leven Seat	W Loth	NS9459	55°49·0'	3°41·1'W	T	65,72
Levens Green	Herts	TL3522	51°53·0'	0°1·9'W	T	166
Levens Hall	Cumbr	SD4985	54°15·7'	2°46·6'W	A	97
Levens Hall	N Yks	SE2757	54°0·7'	1°34·9'W	X	104
Levenshulme	Man	SJ8794	53°26·8'	2°11·3'W	T	109
Levens Moss	Cumbr	SD4787	54°16·8'	2°48·4'W	X	97
Levens Park	Cumbr	SD5085	54°15·7'	2°45·6'W	X	97
Leventhorpe	Brad	SE1233	53°47·8'	1°48·7'W	T	104
Leventhorpe Hall	Leeds	SE3630	53°46·1'	1°26·8'W	X	104
Leven Viaduct	Cumbr	SD3278	54°11·8'	3°2·1'W	X	96,97
Levenwick	Shetld	HU4021	59°58·6'	1°16·5'W	T	4
Leven Wick	Shetld	HU4121	59°58·6'	1°15·4'W	W	4
Levenwick Ness	Shetld	HU4121	59°58·6'	1°15·4'W	X	4
Leverburgh	N Eil	NG0186	57°46·1'	7°1·3'W	T	18
Lever-Edge	Bolton	SD7006	53°33·2'	2°26·8'W	T	109
Lever Hill	Heref	SO5361	52°14·9'	2°40·9'W	X	137,138,149
Leverington	Cambs	TF4411	52°40·9'	0°8·2'E	T	131,142,143
Leverington Common	Cambs	TF4109	52°39·9'	0°5·5'E	X	142,143
Leverington Common	Cambs	TF4210	52°40·4'	0°6·4'E	T	131,142,143
Levern Water	E Renf	NS4958	55°47·8'	4°24·1'W	W	64
Lever Park	Lancs	SD6313	53°37·0'	2°33·1'W	X	109
Levers Hawse	Cumbr	SD2699	54°23·1'	3°7·9'W	X	96,97
Leverstock Green	Herts	TL0806	51°44·8'	0°25·7'W	T	166
Levers Water	Cumbr	SD2799	54°23·1'	3°7·0'W	W	96,97
Leverton	Lincs	TF3947	53°0·4'	0°4·7'E	T	131
Leverton	W Berks	SU3370	51°25·9'	1°31·1'W	T	174
Leverton Highgate	Lincs	TF4047	53°0·4'	0°5·6'E	T	131
Leverton Ings	Lincs	TF3849	53°1·5'	0°3·9'E	X	131
Leverton Lucasgate	Lincs	TF4147	53°0·3'	0°6·5'E	T	131
Leverton Outgate	Lincs	TF4248	53°0·9'	0°7·4'E	T	131
Levin Down	W Susx	SU8813	50°54·8'	0°44·5'W	H	197
Levington	Suff	TM2339	52°0·5'	1°15·4'E	T	169
Levington Heath	Suff	TM2440	52°1·0'	1°16·3'E	X	169
Levisham	N Yks	SE8390	54°18·2'	0°43·0'W	T	94,100
Levisham Beck	N Yks	SE8391	54°18·7'	0°43·0'W	W	94,100
Levisham Mill Fm	N Yks	SE8390	54°18·2'	0°43·0'W	FM	94,100
Levisham Moor	N Yks	SE8392	54°19·2'	0°43·0'W	X	94,100
Levisham Sta	N Yks	SE8190	54°18·2'	0°44·9'W	X	94,100
Levishie	Highld	NH4017	57°13·2'	4°38·5'W	X	34
Levishie Forest	Highld	NH3818	57°13·7'	4°40·6'W	X	34
Levitt's Fm	Essex	TL7037	52°0·5'	0°29·0'E	FM	154
Levrattich	Highld	NH9445	57°29·2'	3°45·6'W	X	27
Levy Beck	Cumbr	SD2877	54°11·3'	3°5·8'W	W	96,97
Levy Pool	Durham	NY9615	54°32·1'	2°3·3'W	X	91,92
Lew	Oxon	SP3206	51°45·3'	1°31·8'W	T	164
Lewaigue	I of M	SC4692	54°18·3'	4°21·6'W	X	95
Lewaigue Cott	I of M	SC4692	54°18·3'	4°21·6'W	X	95
Lewannick	Corn	SW7759	50°23·6'	5°7·9'W	X	200
Lewannick	Corn	SX2780	50°35·9'	4°26·3'W	T	201
Lewcombe	Dorset	ST5507	50°51·9'	2°38·0'W	T	194
Lewcoombe	Corn	SX3683	50°37·7'	4°18·8'W	X	201
Lew Cross Fm	Kent	TQ5043	51°10·2'	0°9·1'E	FM	188
Lewdon	Devon	SS7710	50°52·8'	3°44·5'W	X	191
Lewdon Fm	Devon	SX7794	50°44·2'	3°44·2'W	FM	191
Lewdons Fm	Devon	SX7883	50°38·3'	3°43·1'W	FM	191
Lewdown	Devon	SX4486	50°39·4'	4°12·0'W	T	201
Lewell Lodge	Dorset	SY7388	50°41·7'	2°22·6'W	X	194
Lewenshope	Scot Bord	NT3929	55°33·3'	2°57·6'W	X	73
Lewenshope Burn	Scot Bord	NT3730	55°33·8'	2°59·5'W	W	73
Lewenshope Hope	Scot Bord	NT3631	55°34·4'	3°0·5'W	X	73
Lewenshope Rig	Scot Bord	NT3830	55°33·8'	2°58·6'W	H	73
Lewer	Devon	SS5205	50°49·8'	4°5·7'W	X	191
Lewersland Fm	Devon	SS6204	50°49·4'	3°57·2'W	FM	191
Lewes	E Susx	TQ4110	50°52·6'	0°0·6'E	T	198
Lewesdon Hill	Dorset	ST4301	50°48·6'	2°48·2'W	X	193
Lewes Heath	Kent	TQ7039	51°7·7'	0°26·2'E	X	188
Lewesk	Aberd	NJ6928	57°20·7'	2°30·4'W	X	38
Leweston	Pemb	SM9422	51°51·8'	4°59·1'W	T	157,158
Leweston Fm	Dorset	ST6413	50°55·2'	2°30·3'W	FM	194
Leweston Mountain	Pemb	SM9223	51°52·3'	5°0·9'W	X	157,158

Lewes Wood	Fife	NO3422	56°23·4'	3°3·7'W	F	54,59
Lew Gorse	Oxon	SP3106	51°45·3'	1°32·7'W	F	164
Lew Heath Ho	Oxon	SP3105	51°44·8'	1°32·7'W	X	164
Lewhurst Fm	E Susx	TQ5915	50°55·0'	0°16·1'E	FM	199
Lewidden	Corn	SW8771	50°30·2'	4°59·9'W	X	200
Lewin Br	Leic	SK6213	52°42·9'	1°4·5'W	X	129
Lewinside	S Lanak	NS9350	55°44·2'	3°41·8'W	X	65,72
Lewis Burn	Northum	NY5986	55°10·2'	2°38·2'W	W	80
Lewis Burn	Northum	NY6389	55°11·9'	2°34·4'W	W	80
Lewis Fm	Suff	TM1559	52°11·5'	1°9·1'E	FM	156
Lewisham	Lew	TQ3875	51°27·7'	0°0·4'W	T	177
Lewisham Castle	Wilts	SU2473	51°27·6'	1°38·9'W	A	174
Lewis Hill	Stir	NS7688	56°4·4'	3°59·1'W	H	57
Lewishillock	Aberd	NJ4619	57°15·8'	2°53·3'W	X	37
Lewiston	Highld	NH5028	57°19·3'	4°29·0'W	T	26,35
Lewistown	Brig	SS9388	51°35·1'	3°32·3'W	T	170
Lewis Wych	Heref	SO3357	52°12·7'	2°58·4'W	X	148,149
Lewknor	Oxon	SU7197	51°40·3'	0°58·0'W	T	165
Lew Mill	Devon	SX4686	50°39·4'	4°10·3'W	X	201
Lewmoor	Devon	SX5102	50°48·1'	4°6·5'W	X	191
Leworthy	Devon	SS3201	50°47·3'	4°22·6'W	X	190
Leworthy	Devon	SS3519	50°57·0'	4°20·6'W	X	190
Leworthy	Devon	SS6738	51°7·8'	3°53·7'W	X	180
Leworthy Cross	Devon	SS6638	51°7·8'	3°54·5'W	X	180
Lewsey Farm	Luton	TL0323	51°54·0'	0°29·8'W	FM	166
Lewsome Fm	Kent	TQ8850	51°13·3'	0°41·9'E	FM	189
Lewson Street	Kent	TQ9661	51°19·1'	0°49·2'E	T	178
Lewstone	Heref	SO5317	51°51·2'	2°40·6'W	X	162
Lewth	Lancs	SD4836	53°49·3'	2°47·0'W	T	102
Lewthorn Cross	Devon	SX7776	50°34·5'	3°43·8'W	T	191
Lewtrenchard	Devon	SX4586	50°39·4'	4°11·2'W	T	201
Lew Wood	Devon	SX4685	50°38·9'	4°10·3'W	F	201
Lexden	Essex	TL9725	51°53·5'	0°52·2'E	T	168
Lexden Lodge	Essex	TL9726	51°54·1'	0°52·2'E	X	168
Lex Fm	Surrey	SU9143	51°11·0'	0°41·5'W	FM	186
Lexham Hall	Norf	TF8617	52°43·3'	0°45·7'E	X	132
Lexhayne Fm	Devon	SY2496	50°45·8'	3°4·3'W	FM	192,193
Lexworthy Fm	Somer	ST2535	51°6·8'	3°3·9'W	FM	182
Ley	Aberd	NJ4614	57°13·1'	2°53·2'W	X	37
Ley	Aberd	NJ5312	57°12·0'	2°46·2'W	X	37
Ley	Aberd	NJ5363	57°39·5'	2°46·8'W	X	29
Ley	Aberd	NO7297	57°4·0'	2°27·3'W	X	38,45
Ley	Angus	NO2660	56°43·8'	3°12·1'W	X	44
Ley	Corn	SX1766	50°28·2'	4°34·4'W	X	201
Ley	Corn	SX2871	50°31·0'	4°25·2'W	X	201
Ley	Devon	SS7123	50°59·8'	3°49·9'W	X	180
Ley	Devon	SX5755	50°22·9'	4°0·3'W	X	202
Ley	Devon	SX6749	50°19·8'	3°51·7'W	X	202
Ley	Devon	SX7154	50°22·5'	3°48·5'W	X	202
Ley	Devon	SX9098	50°46·5'	3°33·2'W	X	192
Ley	Shrops	SJ3023	52°48·2'	3°1·9'W	X	126
Ley	Somer	SS8438	51°8·0'	3°39·1'W	T	181
Leybourne	Kent	TQ6858	51°18·0'	0°25·0'E	T	178,188
Leybrook Common	Dorset	SU1302	50°49·3'	1°48·5'W	F	195
Leyburn	N Yks	SE1190	54°18·6'	1°49·4'W	T	99
Leyburn Shawl	N Yks	SE0990	54°18·6'	1°51·3'W	X	99
Leycett	Staffs	SJ7946	53°0·9'	2°18·4'W	T	118
Leycote	Derby	SK0567	53°12·2'	1°55·1'W	X	119
Ley Court	Glos	SO7416	51°50·8'	2°22·3'W	X	162
Leycourt Fm	Cambs	TL2757	52°12·0'	0°8·1'W	FM	153
Leycroft	Herts	TL3225	51°54·7'	0°4·5'W	X	166
Leyden	W Loth	NT0964	55°51·9'	3°26·8'W	X	65
Leyes Fm	Glos	SP2011	51°48·1'	1°42·2'W	FM	163
Leyfield Fm	Glos	SP0135	52°1·0'	1°58·7'W	FM	150
Leyfield Fm	Leeds	SE4137	53°49·9'	1°22·2'W	FM	105
Leyfield Fm	Notts	SK7188	53°23·3'	0°55·5'W	FM	112,120
Leyfield Fm	N Yks	SE0950	53°57·0'	1°51·4'W	FM	104
Leyfield Fm	N Yks	SE2749	53°56·4'	1°34·9'W	FM	104
Leyfield Fm	N Yks	SE7271	54°8·0'	0°53·5'W	FM	100
Leyfields	Notts	SK6863	53°9·8'	0°58·6'W	X	120
Ley Fields	Staffs	SK0158	53°7·4'	1°58·7'W	X	119
Leyfields	Staffs	SK1905	52°38·8'	1°42·7'W	T	139
Ley Fields Fm	Staffs	SJ9945	53°0·4'	2°0·5'W	FM	118
Ley Fm	Devon	SS3716	50°55·5'	4°18·8'W	FM	190
Ley Fm	Devon	SS4521	50°58·3'	4°12·1'W	FM	180,190
Ley Fm	Devon	SS5218	50°56·8'	4°6·0'W	FM	180
Ley Fm	Devon	SS5624	51°0·1'	4°2·8'W	FM	180
Ley Fm	Devon	ST2406	50°51·1'	3°4·4'W	FM	192,193
Ley Fm	Devon	SX4564	50°27·6'	4°10·6'W	FM	201
Ley Fm	Wilts	ST9830	51°4·4'	2°1·3'W	FM	184
Ley Fm	Wirral	SJ2983	53°20·6'	3°3·6'W	FM	108
Ley Fm	Worcs	SO8839	52°3·2'	2°10·1'W	FM	150
Ley Fm	Wrex	SJ2939	52°56·9'	3°3·0'W	FM	126
Leygatehead Moor	Derby	SK0589	53°24·1'	1°55·1'W	X	110
Leygore Manor	Glos	SP1116	51°50·8'	1°50·0'W	X	163
Ley Grange	Shrops	SJ4511	52°41·9'	2°48·4'W	X	126
Leygreen	Devon	SX8474	50°33·5'	3°37·9'W	X	191
Ley Green	Herts	TL1524	51°54·4'	0°19·3'W	T	166
Leygreen Fm	Hants	SU3703	50°49·7'	1°28·1'W	FM	196
Ley Ground Fm	Ches	SJ7146	53°0·9'	2°25·5'W	FM	118
Leygrove's Wood	Bucks	SU7893	51°38·1'	0°52·0'W	F	175
Ley Hey Park	Stock	SJ9589	53°24·1'	2°4·1'W	T	109
Ley Hill	Birm	SP1198	52°35·0'	1°49·9'W	T	139
Ley Hill	Bucks	SP9802	51°42·7'	0°34·5'W	T	165
Ley Hill	D & G	NY2781	55°7·3'	3°8·3'W	H	79
Leyhill	S Glos	ST6992	51°37·8'	2°26·5'W	T	162,172
Ley Hill	Somer	SS8844	51°11·3'	3°35·8'W	H	181
Leyhill Fm	Shrops	SO5196	52°33·8'	2°43·0'W	FM	137,138
Ley House	W Susx	TQ3137	51°7·3'	0°7·3'W	X	187
Leyhurst Fm	E Susx	TQ5814	50°54·5'	0°15·2'E	FM	199
Leyland	Lancs	SD5422	53°41·8'	2°41·4'W	T	102
Leyland Fm	Lancs	SD6265	54°5·0'	2°34·4'W	FM	97
Leylands	Kent	TQ6364	51°21·3'	0°20·9'E	X	177,188
Leylands	Lancs	SD3941	53°51·9'	2°55·2'W	X	102
Leylands Fm	Bucks	SP9008	51°46·0'	0°41·3'W	FM	165
Leyland's Fm	Essex	TL7514	51°48·1'	0°32·7'E	FM	167
Leylands Fm	E Susx	TQ3821	50°58·5'	0°1·7'W	FM	198
Leylands Fm	Norf	TL7587	52°27·4'	0°34·9'E	FM	143
Leyland's Fm	Somer	ST1318	50°57·5'	3°13·9'W	FM	181,193
Leylands Fm	Worcs	SO8971	52°20·5'	2°9·3'W	FM	139

Leylodge	Aberd	NJ7613	57°12·7'	2°23·4'W	T	38
Ley Mill	Corn	SX2871	50°31·0'	4°25·2'W	X	201
Leymoor	Kirk	SE1016	53°38·7'	1°50·5'W	T	110
Leyni Geo	Orkney	ND4093	58°49·5'	3°1·9'W	X	7
Leyonne	Corn	SX1054	50°21·6'	4°39·9'W	X	200
Ley Park	Glos	SO7117	51°51·3'	2°24·9'W	F	162
Leys	Aberd	NJ4602	57°6·6'	2°53·0'W	X	37
Leys	Aberd	NJ5742	57°28·2'	2°42·6'W	X	29
Leys	Aberd	NJ9932	57°23·0'	2°0·5'W	X	30
Leys	Aberd	NK0052	57°33·7'	1°59·5'W	X	30
Leys	Cumbr	NY0618	54°33·2'	3°26·8'W	T	89
Leys	Derby	SK2557	53°6·8'	1°37·2'W	X	119
Leys	Falk	NS7681	56°0·6'	3°58·9'W	X	64
Leys	N Yks	SE3879	54°12·6'	1°24·6'W	X	99
Leys	Pth & Kin	NO2524	56°24·4'	3°12·5'W	X	53,59
Leys	Pth & Kin	NO2537	56°31·4'	3°12·7'W	X	53
Leys	Staffs	SK0347	53°1·5'	1°56·9'W	T	119,128
Leys	Wakf	SE4921	53°41·2'	1°15·1'W	X	105
Leys Barn	N Yks	SE4870	54°7·7'	1°15·5'W	X	100
Leys Beach	V of Glam	ST0265	51°22·8'	3°24·1'W	X	170
Leysbent	Falk	NS7781	56°0·6'	3°57·9'W	X	64
Leysburnfoot	Scot Bord	NY5397	55°16·1'	2°44·0'W	X	79
Leys Castle	Highld	NH6840	57°26·1'	4°11·5'W	X	26
Leys Cross	Devon	SS8607	50°51·3'	3°36·8'W	X	191
Leysdown Marshes	Kent	TR0369	51°23·2'	0°55·5'E	X	178,179
Leysdown-on-Sea	Kent	TR0370	51°23·8'	0°55·5'E	T	178,179
Ley Seat	Cumbr	NY8220	54°34·7'	2°16·3'W	X	91,92
Leys Fm	Beds	SP9341	52°3·8'	0°38·9'W	FM	153
Leys Fm	Fife	NO5808	56°16·0'	2°40·2'W	FM	59
Leys Fm	Glos	ST7592	51°37·8'	2°21·3'W	FM	162,172
Leys Fm	N Lincs	TA0922	53°41·2'	0°20·6'W	FM	107,112
Leys Fm	Norf	TF9409	52°38·9'	0°52·5'E	FM	144
Ley's Fm	Norf	TG0914	52°41·2'	1°5·9'E	FM	133
Leys Fm	Norf	TM0493	52°30·0'	1°0·7'E	FM	144
Leys Fm	Notts	SK7492	53°25·4'	0°52·8'W	FM	112
Leys Fm	Oxon	SP3336	52°1·5'	1°30·7'W	FM	151
Leys Fm	Oxon	SP3725	51°55·6'	1°27·3'W	FM	164
Leys Fm	Oxon	SP4623	51°54·5'	1°19·5'W	FM	164
Leys Fm	Suff	TL7148	52°6·5'	0°30·2'E	FM	154
Leys Fm	Suff	TL7545	52°4·8'	0°33·6'E	FM	155
Leys Fm	Warw	SP1751	52°9·7'	1°44·7'W	FM	151
Leyshade	Angus	NO4237	56°31·5'	2°56·1'W	X	54
Leys Hill	Aberd	NO8278	56°53·8'	2°17·3'W	X	45
Leys Hill	Heref	SO5819	51°52·3'	2°36·2'W	T	162
Leys Ho	N Yks	SD9745	53°54·3'	2°2·3'W	X	103
Leysmill	Angus	NO6047	56°37·0'	2°38·7'W	T	54
Leys of Barras	Aberd	NO8277	56°53·3'	2°17·3'W	X	45
Leys of Boysack	Angus	NO6147	56°37·1'	2°37·7'W	X	54
Leys of Cossans	Angus	NO3749	56°38·0'	3°1·2'W	X	54
Leys of Dummuies	Aberd	NJ5537	57°25·5'	2°44·5'W	X	29
Leys of Dun	Angus	NO6560	56°44·1'	2°33·9'W	X	45
Leys of Lindertis	Angus	NO3349	56°37·9'	3°5·1'W	X	53
Leys of Marlee	Pth & Kin	NO1544	56°35·1'	3°22·6'W	X	53
Leys Plantn	Norf	TM0392	52°29·5'	0°59·8'E	F	144
Leysters	Heref	SO5663	52°16·0'	2°38·3'W	T	137,138,149
Leysters Pole	Heref	SO5563	52°16·0'	2°39·2'W	X	137,138,149
Leys, The	Bucks	SP8332	51°59·0'	0°47·1'W	X	152,165
Leys, The	Clackm	NS9999	56°10·6'	3°37·2'W	X	58
Leys, The	Suff	TM1175	52°20·2'	1°6·2'E	X	144
Leys, The	Suff	TM1870	52°17·3'	1°12·2'E	A	156
Leys, The	Worcs	SP0273	52°21·5'	1°57·8'W	X	139
Leysthorpe	N Yks	SE6378	54°11·9'	1°1·6'W	F	100
Leyswood	E Susx	TQ5235	51°5·9'	0°10·6'E	X	188
Leys Wood	N Yks	SE8266	54°5·2'	0°44·4'W	F	100
Leytack	Angus	NO4664	56°46·1'	2°52·6'W	X	44
Ley, The	Heref	SO3951	52°9·5'	2°53·1'W	A	148,149
Ley, The	Scot Bord	NT3239	55°38·6'	3°4·4'W	X	73
Leythe Ho	Hants	SU7021	50°59·3'	0°59·8'W	X	197
Leyton	Aberd	NJ6000	57°5·6'	2°39·2'W	X	37
Leyton	Aberd	NJ9820	57°16·5'	2°1·5'W	X	38
Leyton	Wal F	TQ3786	51°33·6'	0°1·0'W	T	177
Leyton Cross	Kent	TQ5272	51°25·8'	0°11·6'E	X	177
Leyton Lees	N Yks	SE3164	54°4·5'	1°31·2'W	X	99
Leytonstone	Wal F	TQ3987	51°34·1'	0°0·7'E	T	177
Leywell Spinney	Northnts	SP7576	52°22·8'	0°53·5'W	F	141
Lezant	Corn	SX3379	50°35·4'	4°21·2'W	T	201
Lezerea	Corn	SW6833	50°9·3'	5°14·5'W	T	203
Leziate	Norf	TF6719	52°44·8'	0°28·9'E	T	132
Leziate Fen	Norf	TF7020	52°45·3'	0°31·6'E	X	132
L Ghille - caluim	Arg & Bt	NM2560	56°39·3'	6°28·8'W	W	46,47
Lhanbryde	Moray	NJ2761	57°38·2'	3°12·9'W	T	28
Lhargee Ruy	I of M	SC3383	54°13·2'	4°33·3'W	H	95
Lheakerrow	I of M	SC2878	54°10·4'	4°37·7'W	X	95
Lheeah-rio	I of M	SC2666	54°3·9'	4°39·1'W	X	95
Lhen, The	I of M	NX3801	54°23·0'	4°29·3'W	T	95
Lhen Trench, The	I of M	SC3999	54°21·9'	4°28·3'W	W	95
Lhergycholvine	I of M	SC2785	54°14·1'	4°38·9'W	X	95
Lhergyrhenny	I of M	SC3888	54°16·0'	4°28·8'W	X	95
Lhergy Vreck	I of M	SC3290	54°16·9'	4°34·4'W	X	95
Lhiattee ny Beinnee	I of M	SC2172	54°7·0'	4°43·9'W	H	95
Lhoob Doo	I of M	SC2178	54°10·2'	4°44·1'W	X	95
Li	Highld	NG8307	57°6·4'	5°34·5'W	X	33
Liacam	N Eil	NB1137	58°13·9'	6°54·9'W	X	13
Liade Ho	Highld	NG8990	57°51·2'	5°32·9'W	X	19
Lianach	Stir	NN5215	56°18·5'	4°23·1'W	X	57
Liana Horgabost	N Eil	NG0596	57°51·6'	6°58·0'W	X	14,18
Lian Airigh nan Geadh	Highld	NG2750	57°27·8'	6°32·7'W	X	23
Lianamul	N Eil	NL5483	56°48·8'	7°39·8'W	X	31
Lian Mór	Arg & Bt	NM6725	56°21·9'	5°45·9'W	X	49
Liathach	Highld	NG9257	57°33·6'	5°28·2'W	H	25
Liath Bhad	Highld	NC2530	58°13·7'	4°58·3'W	X	15
Liath Bheinn	Moray	NJ1712	57°11·7'	3°22·0'W	H	36
Liath-choire Mhór	Aberd	NO1698	57°4·2'	3°22·7'W	X	36,43
Liath Dhoire	Arg & Bt	NM6136	56°27·6'	5°52·3'W	X	49
Liath Dhoire	Arg & Bt	NR5981	55°58·0'	5°51·3'W	X	61
Liath Dhoire	Highld	NH1602	57°4·6'	5°1·7'W	X	34
Liath Dhoire	Highld	NH2657	57°34·4'	4°54·1'W	X	25
Liath Dhoire	Highld	NH3704	57°6·1'	4°41·0'W	X	34
Liath Dhoire	Highld	NM5970	56°45·8'	5°56·2'W	X	39,47
Liath Eilean	Arg & Bt	NR6878	55°56·6'	5°42·5'W	X	61,62

Liath Eilean	Arg & Bt	NR8883	55°59·8'	5°23·5'W	X	55
Liath Eilean	Arg & Bt	NR7172	55°53·5'	5°39·3'W	X	62
Liath Sgeir	Arg & Bt	NM6909	56°13·3'	5°43·1'W	X	55
Liath Sgeir	Arg & Bt	NM7806	56°12·0'	5°34·3'W	X	55
Liath Sgeir	Arg & Bt	NM7837	56°28·6'	5°35·8'W	X	49
Liath Sgeir	Arg & Bt	NR5264	55°48·6'	5°57·0'W	X	61
Liath-sgeir Bheag	Arg & Bt	NR7798	56°7·6'	5°34·8'W	X	55
Liath-sgeir Mhór	Arg & Bt	NR7797	56°7·1'	5°34·8'W	X	55
Liatrie	Highld	NH2432	57°20·9'	4°55·0'W	X	25
Liatrie Burn	Highld	NH2534	57°22·0'	4°54·1'W	W	25
Libanus	Powys	SN9925	51°55·1'	3°27·7'W	T	160
Libbaton	Devon	SS6019	50°57·4'	3°59·2'W	X	180
Libbear Barton	Devon	SS4506	50°50·2'	4°11·7'W	X	190
Libbers Hill	Shetld	HP5813	60°48·0'	0°55·6'W	H	1
Libberton	S Lanak	NS9843	55°40·4'	3°36·9'W	T	72
Libbery	Worcs	SO9555	52°11·8'	2°4·0'W	T	150
Li Ber	Orkney	HY4333	59°11·1'	2°59·4'W	X	5,6
Liberton	C of Edin	NT2769	55°54·8'	3°9·6'W	T	66
Liberton Ho	C of Edin	NT2669	55°54·8'	3°10·6'W	A	66
Liberton Tower	C of Edin	NT2669	55°54·8'	3°10·6'W	A	66
Liberty Fm	Dorset	ST5508	50°52·4'	2°38·0'W	FM	194
Liberty Fm	Somer	ST3744	51°11·7'	2°53·7'W	FM	182
Liberty Hall	Denb	SJ0840	52°57·2'	3°21·8'W	X	125
Liberty Hall	E Loth	NT4672	55°56·5'	2°51·4'W	X	66
Liberty Hall	Essex	TL7115	51°48·7'	0°29·2'E	X	167
Liberty Lodge	Darl	NZ3409	54°28·8'	1°28·1'W	X	93
Librig Bheag	Arg & Bt	NM0947	56°31·8'	6°43·5'W	X	46
Librig Mhór	Arg & Bt	NM0947	56°31·8'	6°43·5'W	X	46
Libry Moor	D & G	NS7110	55°22·3'	4°1·7'W	X	71
Libury Hall	Herts	TL3423	51°53·6'	0°2·8'W	X	166
Liceasto	N Eil	NG1292	57°49·8'	6°50·6'W	T	14
Lichett Plain	Hants	SU8056	51°18·1'	0°50·8'W	F	175,186
Lichfield	Staffs	SK1109	52°41·0'	1°49·8'W	T	128
Lichfield or Trent Valley Sta	Staffs	SK1309	52°40·9'	1°48·1'W	X	128
Lichnet	Aberd	NJ8064	57°40·2'	2°19·7'W	X	29,30
Lich Way	Devon	SX5779	50°35·8'	4°0·9'W	A	191
Lick	Angus	NO2771	56°49·7'	3°11·3'W	X	44
Lick	Pth & Kin	NN8258	56°42·2'	3°55·2'W	X	52
Lickar Dean	Northum	NU0142	55°40·5'	1°58·6'W	X	75
Lickar Lea	Northum	NU0141	55°40·0'	1°58·6'W	X	75
Lickar Moor	Northum	NT9642	55°40·5'	2°3·4'W	X	74,75
Lickey	Worcs	SO9975	52°22·6'	2°0·5'W	T	139
Lickey End	Worcs	SO9772	52°21·0'	2°2·2'W	T	139
Lickey Hills	Worcs	SO9975	52°22·6'	2°0·5'W	H	139
Lickey Hills Country Park	Worcs	SO9975	52°22·6'	2°0·5'W	X	139
Lickey Incline	Worcs	SO9870	52°19·9'	2°1·4'W	X	139
Lickfold	W Susx	SU9225	51°1·2'	0°40·9'W	T	186,197
Lickfold	W Susx	TQ0617	50°56·8'	0°29·1'W	X	197
Lickham Bottom	Devon	ST1212	50°54·3'	3°14·7'W	X	181,193
Lickham Hall	E Yorks	TA0246	53°54·2'	0°26·4'W	X	106,107
Lickhill	Worcs	SO8072	52°21·0'	2°17·2'W	T	138
Lickhill Fm	Wilts	ST9972	51°27·1'	2°0·5'W	FM	173
Lickhurst	Lancs	SD5543	53°53·1'	2°40·7'W	X	102
Lickhurst Fm	Lancs	SD6345	53°54·2'	2°33·4'W	FM	102,103
Lickleyhead Castle	Aberd	NJ6223	57°18·0'	2°37·4'W	A	37
Lickshead	Staffs	SK0745	53°0·4'	1°53·3'W	X	119,128
Lidale Lodge	N Yks	SE2188	54°17·5'	1°40·2'W	X	99
Lid Brook	Wilts	ST8270	51°26·0'	2°15·1'W	W	173
Lidbury Camp	Wilts	SU1653	51°16·8'	1°45·8'W	A	184
Lidcombe Hill	Glos	SP0732	51°59·4'	1°53·5'W	H	150
Lidcombe Wood	Glos	SP0732	51°59·4'	1°53·5'W	F	150
Lidcote Village	Bucks	SP8324	51°54·7'	0°47·2'W	A	165
Lidcott	Corn	SX1068	50°29·1'	4°40·3'W	X	200
Lidcutt Fm	Corn	SX0665	50°27·4'	4°43·6'W	FM	200
Lidcutt Wood	Corn	SX1068	50°29·1'	4°40·3'W	F	200
Lidda	Orkney	HY5309	58°58·2'	2°48·6'W	X	6,7
Liddaton	Devon	SX4582	50°37·3'	4°11·1'W	T	201
Lidde Hill Fm	W Susx	TQ2117	50°56·6'	0°16·3'W	FM	198
Liddel	Orkney	ND4583	58°44·1'	2°56·5'W	X	7
Liddell Hall	Northum	NY9675	55°4·4'	2°3·3'W	X	87
Liddel Loch	Orkney	ND4583	58°44·1'	2°56·5'W	W	7
Liddel Lodge	Cumbr	NY4679	55°6·4'	2°50·4'W	X	86
Liddell's Monument	C of Aber	NJ8615	57°13·8'	2°13·5'W	A	38
Liddel Park	Cumbr	NY4677	55°5·3'	2°50·3'W	X	86
Liddel Strength	Cumbr	NY4074	55°3·7'	2°55·9'W	X	85
Liddel Strength (Motte & Baileys)	Cumbr	NY4074	55°3·7'	2°55·9'W	A	85
Liddel Water	Cumbr	NY4276	55°4·8'	2°54·1'W	W	85
Liddel Water	Cumbr	NY4579	55°6·4'	2°51·3'W	W	86
Liddel Water	Scot Bord	NY5292	55°13·4'	2°44·8'W	W	79
Liddel Water	Scot Bord	NY5797	55°16·2'	2°40·2'W	W	80
Liddesdale	D & G	NX0461	54°54·6'	5°3·0'W	X	82
Liddesdale	Highld	NM7759	56°40·4'	5°38·0'W	X	49
Liddesdale Burn	Highld	NM7759	56°40·4'	5°38·0'W	W	49
Liddeston	Pemb	SM8906	51°43·0'	5°2·9'W	T	157,158
Liddimore Fm	Somer	ST0742	51°10·4'	3°19·4'W	FM	181
Liddington	Swin	SU2081	51°31·9'	1°42·3'W	T	174
Liddington Castle	Swin	SU2079	51°30·8'	1°42·3'W	X	174
Liddington Castle (Fort)	Swin	SU2079	51°30·8'	1°42·3'W	A	174
Liddington Hill	Swin	SU2179	51°30·8'	1°41·5'W	H	174
Liddington Warren Fm	Swin	SU2279	51°30·8'	1°40·6'W	FM	174
Liddle Stack	Durham	NZ4348	54°49·7'	1°19·4'W	X	88
Liden	Swin	SU1883	51°33·0'	1°44·0'W	T	173
Lidgate	Derby	SK0481	53°19·8'	1°56·0'W	X	110
Lidgate	Derby	SK3077	53°17·6'	1°32·6'W	T	119
Lidgate	Suff	TL7257	52°11·3'	0°31·4'E	T	154
Lidget	Donc	SE6500	53°29·8'	1°0·8'W	T	111
Lidget Green	Brad	SE1432	53°47·3'	1°46·8'W	T	104
Lidgett	Notts	SK6265	53°10·9'	1°3·9'W	T	120
Lidgett Flatt Fm	Lancs	SD8647	53°55·4'	2°12·4'W	FM	103
Lidgett Park	Leeds	SE3238	53°50·5'	1°30·4'W	T	104
Lidham Hill	E Susx	TQ8416	50°55·1'	0°37·5'E	T	199
Lidistrom	N Eil	NF8350	57°26·0'	7°16·5'W	X	22
Lidlington	Beds	SP9839	52°2·7'	0°33·9'W	T	153
Lidmoor Fms	N Yks	SE6295	54°21·0'	1°2·3'W	FM	94,100
Lidmore	V of Glam	ST0970	51°25·5'	3°18·1'W	X	171
Lidsey	W Susx	SU9303	50°49·4'	0°40·3'W	T	197
Lidsey Lodge	W Susx	SU9402	50°48·8'	0°39·6'W	X	197
Lidsing	Kent	TQ7862	51°20·0'	0°33·7'E	T	178,188

Lidstone	Oxon	SP3524	51°55·0'	1°29·1'W	T	164
Lidwell	Corn	SX3774	50°32·8'	4°17·7'W	X	201
Lidwell Fm	Devon	SX9275	50°34·1'	3°31·1'W	FM	192
Lidwells Ho	Kent	TQ7238	51°7·1'	0°27·9'E	X	188
Lienassie	Highld	NG9621	57°14·3'	5°24·7'W	X	25,33
Liernis	N Eil	NF8758	57°30·5'	7°13·1'W	X	22
Lieurary	Highld	ND0762	58°32·4'	3°35·4'W	X	11,12
Liever Island	Arg & Bt	NM8904	56°11·2'	5°23·6'W	X	55
Life Hill	E Yorks	SE9361	54°2·4'	0°34·4'W	X	101
Life Hill	Leic	SK7204	52°38·0'	0°55·8'W	X	141
Life Ho	N Yks	SE7893	54°19·8'	0°47·6'W	X	94,100
Life Wood	Norf	TF6831	52°51·2'	0°30·1'E	F	132
Liff	Angus	NO3333	56°29·3'	3°4·8'W	T	53
Lifford	Birm	SP0579	52°24·8'	1°55·2'W	T	139
Liffs, The	Derby	SK1557	53°6·8'	1°46·1'W	H	119
Liftingstane	D & G	NX8990	55°11·8'	3°44·2'W	X	78
Lifton	Devon	SX3885	50°38·8'	4°17·1'W	T	201
Liftondown	Devon	SX3685	50°38·7'	4°18·8'W	T	201
Lifton Park	Devon	SX3884	50°38·2'	4°17·1'W	X	201
Liggars	Corn	SX2262	50°26·1'	4°30·0'W	X	201
Liggat	D & G	NX5693	55°12·9'	4°15·4'W	X	77
Liggat Hill	D & G	NX1573	55°1·3'	4°53·2'W	X	76
Ligger or Perran Bay	Corn	SW7556	50°21·9'	5°9·5'W	W	200
Ligger Point	Corn	SW7558	50°23·0'	5°9·5'W	X	200
Liggetcheek	S Ayr	NX1185	55°7·7'	4°57·4'W	X	76
Lighe nan Leac	N Eil	NB5452	58°23·5'	6°12·1'W	X	8
Lightbeck	Cumbr	SD4792	54°19·5'	2°48·5'W	X	97
Light Birks	Northum	NY8463	54°57·9'	2°14·6'W	X	86,87
Light Burn	S Lanak	NS6660	55°49·1'	4°7·9'W	W	64
Lightcliffe	Cald	SE1425	53°43·5'	1°46·9'W	T	104
Lighteach	Shrops	SJ5434	52°54·3'	2°40·6'W	T	126
Lighteach Coppice	Shrops	SJ5435	52°54·9'	2°40·6'W	F	126
Lightfield	Scot Bord	NT6441	55°39·9'	2°33·9'W	X	74
Lightfoot Green	Lancs	SD5133	53°47·7'	2°44·2'W	T	102
Lightfoot Green Fm	Ches	SJ7863	53°10·1'	2°19·3'W	FM	118
Lightfoots	Essex	TL4009	51°46·0'	0°2·1'E	X	167
Lightfoots	Essex	TL6408	51°45·0'	0°22·9'E	X	167
Lightgreen Coppice	Shrops	SJ5003	52°37·6'	2°43·9'W	F	126
Light Hall Fm	Sol	SP1277	52°23·7'	1°49·0'W	FM	139
Lighthazles	Cald	SE0220	53°40·8'	1°57·8'W	X	104
Light Hazzles Resr	Roch	SD9620	53°40·8'	2°3·2'W	W	103
Lightney	Ches	SJ8865	53°11·2'	2°10·4'W	X	118
Light Hill	N Yks	SE1470	54°7·8'	1°46·7'W	X	99
Light Ho	Lincs	TF2152	53°3·3'	0°11·3'W	X	122
Lighthorne	Warw	SP3355	52°11·8'	1°30·6'W	T	151
Lighthorne Heath	Warw	SP3555	52°11·8'	1°28·9'W	T	151
Lighthorne Rough	Warw	SP3154	52°11·2'	1°32·4'W	F	151
Lighthorne Rough	Warw	SP3255	52°11·8'	1°31·5'W	T	151
Lighthouse Fm	Lincs	TF4924	52°47·8'	0°13·0'E	FM	131
Lighthouse Hill	N Ayr	NS1451	55°43·3'	4°57·3'W	H	63,69
Lighthouse Hill	N Ayr	NS1451	55°43·3'	4°57·3'W	X	63,69
Lighthouse Point	V of Glam	ST2264	51°22·4'	3°6·9'W	X	171,182
Lightlands	E Susx	TQ5933	51°4·7'	0°16·6'E	A	188
Lightmire Field	N Yks	SE4562	54°3·4'	1°18·3'W	X	99
Lightmoor	Wrekin	SJ6705	52°38·7'	2°28·9'W	T	127
Lightning Hill	Scot Bord	NT4101	55°18·2'	2°55·3'W	H	79
Lightnot	Aberd	NJ7930	57°21·9'	2°20·5'W	X	29,30
Light Oaks	Staffs	SJ9250	53°3·1'	2°6·8'W	T	118
Lightoaks	Staffs	SK0444	52°59·8'	1°56·0'W	X	119,128
Lightoaks Fm	Staffs	SK0441	52°58·2'	1°56·0'W	FM	119,128
Light Oaks Moss Fm	Salf	SJ6896	53°27·8'	2°28·5'W	FM	109
Lightpill	Glos	SO8403	51°43·8'	2°13·5'W	T	162
Lightshaw	E Ayr	NS7128	55°32·0'	4°2·2'W	X	71
Lightshaw Hall	Wigan	SJ6199	53°29·4'	2°34·9'W	A	109
Lights, The	Staffs	SJ8511	52°42·0'	2°12·9'W	X	127
Light Trees	Cumbr	NY8414	54°31·5'	2°14·4'W	X	91,92
Light Water	D & G	NX7079	55°5·6'	4°1·8'W	W	77,84
Lightwater	Surrey	SU9262	51°21·2'	0°40·3'W	T	175,186
Lightwater Ho	Northum	NZ1585	55°9·8'	1°45·4'W	X	81
Lightwaters Fm	Essex	TL7224	51°53·5'	0°30·4'E	FM	167
Lightwater Valley	N Yks	SE2875	54°10·4'	1°33·8'W	X	99
Lightwood	Aberd	NO7299	57°5·1'	2°27·3'W	X	38,45
Lightwood	C of Stoke	SJ9241	52°58·2'	2°6·7'W	T	118
Lightwood	Cumbr	SD4089	54°17·8'	2°54·9'W	X	96,97
Lightwood	Derby	SK3782	53°20·3'	1°26·3'W	T	110,111
Lightwood	Shrops	SJ6929	52°51·7'	2°27·2'W	T	127
Lightwood	Shrops	SO6491	52°31·2'	2°31·2'W	X	138
Lightwood	Staffs	SK0142	52°58·8'	1°58·7'W	T	119,128
Lightwood Fm	Ches	SJ5979	53°18·6'	2°36·5'W	FM	117
Lightwood Fm	Ches	SJ8065	53°11·1'	2°17·6'W	FM	118
Light Wood Fm	Shrops	SJ6829	52°51·7'	2°28·1'W	FM	127
Light Wood Fms	Worcs	SO7955	52°11·8'	2°18·0'W	FM	150
Lightwood Green	Ches	SJ6342	52°58·7'	2°32·7'W	T	118
Lightwood Green	Wrex	SJ3840	52°57·5'	2°55·0'W	T	117
Lightwood Hall	Wrex	SJ3840	52°57·5'	2°55·0'W	X	117
Lightwood Resrs	Derby	SK0575	53°16·6'	1°55·1'W	W	119
Liglartrie	S Ayr	NX2186	55°8·4'	4°48·1'W	X	76
Likely Burn	Scot Bord	NT3232	55°34·9'	3°4·3'W	W	73
Likely Hill	Suff	TL9151	52°7·7'	0°47·8'E	X	155
Likely Wood	Suff	TM4485	52°24·7'	1°35·7'E	F	156
Likilk	Shetld	HU6588	60°34·5'	0°48·3'W	X	1,2
Lilac Fm	N Yks	SE9078	54°11·6'	0°36·8'W	FM	101
Lilac Lodge	Notts	SK5985	53°21·8'	1°6·4'W	X	111,120
Lilbourne	Northnts	SP5676	52°23·0'	1°10·2'W	T	140
Lilburn Burn	Northum	NU0022	55°29·8'	1°59·6'W	W	75
Lilburn Glebe	Northum	NU0322	55°29·8'	1°56·7'W	X	75
Lilburn Grange	Northum	NU0324	55°30·8'	1°56·7'W	X	75
Lilburn Hill	Northum	NU0125	55°31·4'	1°58·6'W	X	75
Lilburn Pond	Northum	NU0422	55°29·8'	1°55·8'W	W	75
Lilburn South Steads	Northum	NU0323	55°30·3'	1°56·7'W	X	75
Lilburn Tower	Northum	NU0224	55°30·8'	1°57·7'W	X	75
Lilburntower Fm	Northum	NU0224	55°30·8'	1°57·7'W	FM	75
Liley Wood	Kirk	SE2117	53°39·2'	1°40·5'W	F	110
Lilford	Wigan	SD6600	53°30·0'	2°30·3'W	T	109
Lilford Lodge Fm	Northnts	TL0384	52°26·9'	0°27·9'W	FM	141
Lilford Park	Northnts	TL0283	52°26·4'	0°29·6'W	X	141
Lilford Park	Wigan	SD6701	53°30·5'	2°29·4'W	F	109
Lilford Wood	Northnts	SP9884	52°26·9'	0°33·1'W	F	141
Lilies	Bucks	SP8118	51°51·5'	0°49·0'W	X	165
Lilie's Loch	D & G	NX5174	55°2·5'	4°19·5'W	W	77

Lilies, The	Derby	SK2945	53°0·3′	1°33·7′W	X	119,128
Lilies, The	Kent	TQ9266	51°21·9′	0°45·9′E	W	178
Lilla Howe	N Yks	SE8898	54°22·4′	0°38·3′W	A	94,101
Lilla Rigg	N Yks	SE8798	54°22·4′	0°39·2′W	X	94,101
Lillechurch Fm	Kent	TQ7273	51°26·0′	0°28·9′E	FM	178
Lillends	Heref	SO6636	52°1·5′	2°29·3′W	X	149
Lillery's Cove	Corn	SX4248	50°18·9′	4°12·8′W	W	201
Lillesden	Kent	TQ7528	51°1·7′	0°30·1′E	X	188,199
Lillesdon	Somer	ST3023	51°0·4′	2°59·5′W	T	193
Lillesdon Court	Somer	ST2923	51°0·4′	3°0·3′W	X	193
Lilleshall	Wrekin	SJ7315	52°44·2′	2°23·6′W	T	127
Lilleshall Grange	Wrekin	SJ7214	52°43·6′	2°24·5′W	X	127
Lilleshall Grove	Wrekin	SJ7213	52°43·1′	2°24·5′W	X	127
Lilleshall Hall	Shrops	SJ7414	52°43·6′	2°22·7′W	X	127
Lilley	Herts	TL1126	51°55·5′	0°22·7′W	T	166
Lilley	W Berks	SU4479	51°30·7′	1°21·6′W	T	174
Lilley Bottom	Herts	TL1324	51°54·4′	0°21·0′W	X	166
Lilley Copse	W Berks	SU4379	51°30·7′	1°22·4′W	F	174
Lilley Fm	Kent	TQ6245	51°11·1′	0°19·5′E	FM	188
Lilley Fm	Oxon	SU6777	51°29·5′	1°1·7′W	FM	175
Lilley Green Hall Fm	Worcs	SP0672	52°21·0′	1°54·3′W	FM	139
Lilley Hoo	Herts	TL1227	51°56·0′	0°21·9′W	X	166
Lilley Hoo Fm	Herts	TL1227	51°56·0′	0°21·9′W	FM	166
Lilley Manor Fm	Herts	TL1127	51°56·1′	0°22·7′W	FM	166
Lilley's Br	Lincs	TF2841	52°57·3′	0°5·3′W	X	131
Lilley Wood	Herts	TL1126	51°55·5′	0°22·7′W	F	166
Lilliardsedge	Scot Bord	NT6127	55°32·4′	2°36·6′W	X	74
Lilliardsedge Park	Scot Bord	NT6226	55°31·8′	2°35·7′W	X	74
Lillibrooke Manor	Win & Maid	SU8678	51°29·9′	0°45·3′W	X	175
Lillicrapp	Devon	SX5291	50°42·2′	4°5·4′W	X	191
Lilliesleaf	Scot Bord	NT5325	55°31·2′	2°44·2′W	T	73
Lilliestead	Northum	NT9652	55°45·9′	2°3·4′W	X	74,75
Lilling Green	N Yks	SE6463	54°3·8′	1°0·9′W	X	100
Lilling Hall	N Yks	SE6664	54°4·3′	0°59·1′W	X	100
Lilling Hall Fm	N Yks	SE6764	54°4·3′	0°58·1′W	FM	100
Lillingstone Dayrell	Bucks	SP7039	52°2·9′	0°58·4′W	T	152
Lillingstone Ho	Bucks	SP7039	52°2·9′	0°58·4′W	X	152
Lillingstone Lovell	Bucks	SP7140	52°3·5′	0°57·5′W	T	152
Lillington	Dorset	ST6212	50°54·6′	2°32·0′W	T	194
Lillington	Warw	SP3267	52°18·2′	1°31·4′W	T	151
Lillington Hill	Dorset	ST6213	50°55·1′	2°32·1′W	H	194
Lilling Wood	N Yks	SE6464	54°4·3′	1°0·9′W	F	100
Lilliput	Poole	SZ0489	50°42·3′	1°56·2′W	T	195
Lillisford Fm	Devon	SX8264	50°28·1′	3°39·4′W	FM	202
Lill Rig	Scot Bord	NT6747	55°43·2′	2°31·1′W	X	74
Lilly	Devon	SS5833	51°5·0′	4°1·3′W	X	180
Lilly Brook	Devon	SX8293	50°43·7′	3°39·9′W	W	191
Lillycombe Ho	Somer	SS8247	51°12·8′	3°41·0′W	X	181
Lillyfee Fm	Bucks	SU9288	51°35·2′	0°39·9′W	FM	175
Lilly Hall Fm	Roth	SK5192	53°25·6′	1°13·5′W	FM	111
Lillyhall Industrial Estate	Cumbr	NY0225	54°36·9′	3°30·6′W	X	89
Lilly Holt	Cambs	TL3490	52°29·7′	0°1·2′W	X	142
Lilly Loch	N Lanak	NS8266	55°52·6′	3°52·7′W	W	65
Lillymill Fm	Hants	SU6759	51°19·8′	1°1·9′W	FM	175,186
Lillypool Fm	Somer	ST4456	51°18·3′	2°47·8′W	FM	172,182
Lillyput	V of Glam	ST0574	51°27·7′	3°21·7′W	X	170
Lillyputts	Hav	TQ5588	51°34·4′	0°14·6′E	X	177
Lilstock	Somer	ST1644	51°11·6′	3°11·7′W	T	181
Lilswood Fm	Northum	NY9153	54°52·5′	2°8·0′W	FM	87
Lilswood Grange	Northum	NY9153	54°52·5′	2°8·0′W	X	87
Lilswood Moor	Northum	NY8952	54°52·0′	2°9·9′W	H	87
Lilybank	Aberd	NJ6339	57°26·6′	2°36·5′W	X	29
Lilybank	Inverc	NS3074	55°56·0′	4°42·8′W	T	63
Lily Beds	W Susx	TQ2130	51°3·6′	0°16·0′W	X	187
Lily Broad	Norf	TG4514	52°40·3′	1°37·8′E	W	134
Lilyburn	Midlo	NT2658	55°48·8′	3°10·4′W	X	66,73
Lily Fm	Bucks	SP8301	51°42·3′	0°47·5′W	FM	165
Lily Fm	Dorset	SY3593	50°44·2′	2°54·9′W	FM	193
Lily Green	N Yks	SE1064	54°4·6′	1°50·4′W	X	99
Lily Hall	Shrops	SJ5433	52°53·8′	2°40·6′W	X	126
Lily Hill	Cambs	TL2355	52°11·0′	0°11·7′W	X	153
Lily Hill	Durham	NZ0612	54°30·4′	1°54·0′W	X	92
Lily Hoo	Kent	TQ6747	51°12·1′	0°23·8′E	X	188
Lilyhurst	Shrops	SJ7413	52°43·1′	2°22·7′W	T	127
Lilylaw	S Ayr	NS4229	55°32·0′	4°29·8′W	X	70
Lily Loch	Aberd	NJ9214	57°13·3′	2°7·5′W	W	38
Lily Loch	W Dunb	NS4777	55°58·0′	4°26·6′W	W	64
Lily Mere	Cumbr	SD6091	54°19·0′	2°36·5′W	W	97
Lily Mere Ho	Cumbr	SD6091	54°19·0′	2°36·5′W	X	97
Lilystone Hall	Essex	TQ6898	51°39·6′	0°26·1′E	X	167,177
Lily's Wood	Gwyn	SH9637	52°55·5′	3°32·4′W	F	125
Lilyvale	Kent	TR0839	51°7·0′	0°58·7′E	T	179,189
Lilyvale	S Lanak	NS9939	55°38·3′	3°35·8′W	X	72
Lilywood	Shrops	SO5190	52°30·6′	2°42·9′W	X	137,138
Limb Brook	Oxon	SP4107	51°45·8′	1°24·0′W	W	164
Limb Brook	Sheff	SK3082	53°20·3′	1°32·6′W	W	110,111
Limbeck Fm	Oxon	SP4118	51°51·8′	1°23·9′W	FM	164
Limber Hill	Lincs	TA1507	53°33·1′	0°15·4′W	X	113
Limber Hill	Lincs	TF2293	53°25·4′	0°9·4′W	X	113
Limber Hill Wood	N Yks	NZ7905	54°26·3′	0°46·5′W	F	94
Limbo Fm	W Susx	SU9624	51°0·7′	0°37·5′W	FM	197
Limbourne Creek	Essex	TL8705	51°43·0′	0°42·8′E	W	168
Limbourne Park Fm	Essex	TL8701	51°40·8′	0°42·7′E	FM	168
Limbrick	Lancs	SD6016	53°38·6′	2°35·9′W	T	109
Limbrick Hall	Herts	TL1412	51°47·9′	0°20·4′W	X	166
Limbury	Dorset	SY4595	50°45·4′	2°46·4′W	X	193
Limbury	Glos	SO7724	51°55·1′	2°19·7′W	X	162
Limbury	Luton	TL0624	51°54·5′	0°27·1′W	T	166
Limbury Hill	Glos	SO7725	51°55·6′	2°19·7′W	H	162
Limby Hall	Leic	SK4116	52°44·6′	1°23·2′W	X	129
Lime Banks	Orkney	ND4892	58°49·0′	2°53·5′W	X	7
Lime Breach Wood	N Som	ST4672	51°26·9′	2°46·2′W	F	171,172
Limebrook	Heref	SO3766	52°17·6′	2°55·0′W	T	137,148,149
Limebrook Fm	Essex	TL8305	51°43·1′	0°39·4′E	FM	168
Limeburn	Moray	NJ5154	57°34·7′	2°48·7′W	X	29
Limebury	Devon	SS3622	50°58·7′	4°19·8′W	X	190
Lime Cleuch	D & G	NS8406	55°20·3′	3°49·3′W	X	71,78
Lime Combe	Somer	SS7640	51°9·0′	3°46·0′W	X	180
Limecrofts	Staffs	SK0837	52°56·1′	1°52·5′W	X	128
Limefield	Bury	SD8012	53°36·5′	2°17·7′W	T	109
Limefield	S Lanak	NS9231	55°33·9′	3°42·3′W	X	71,72
Limefield	W Loth	NS9869	55°54·5′	3°37·5′W	X	65
Lime Field Fm	York	SE6953	53°58·3′	0°56·5′W	FM	105,106
Limefield Ho	W Loth	NT0364	55°51·8′	3°32·6′W	X	65
Limefitt Park	Cumbr	NY4103	54°25·4′	2°54·1′W	X	90
Lime Fm	Bucks	SU9299	51°41·2′	0°39·8′W	FM	165
Lime Fm	Cambs	TL4764	52°15·5′	0°9·6′E	FM	154
Lime Fm	Derby	SK3940	52°57·6′	1°24·8′W	FM	119,128
Lime Fm	Heref	SO4259	52°13·8′	2°50·6′W	FM	148,149
Lime Hill	Stir	NS4796	56°8·2′	4°27·3′W	H	57
Limehillock	Moray	NJ5152	57°33·6′	2°48·7′W	T	29
Limehouse	T Ham	TQ3681	51°30·9′	0°2·0′W	T	177
Limehouse Fm	Lancs	SD7439	53°51·0′	2°23·3′W	FM	103
Limehouse Reach	Medway	TQ7468	51°23·3′	0°30·4′E	W	178
Limehouse Reach	T Ham	TQ3679	51°29·8′	0°2·1′W	W	177
Lime House School	Cumbr	NY3747	54°49·1′	2°58·4′W	X	85
Limehurst	Tames	SD9300	53°30·0′	2°5·9′W	T	109
Limekiln Bank	N Yks	NZ4800	54°23·8′	1°15·2′W	X	93
Limekilnburn	S Lanak	NS7050	55°43·8′	4°3·8′W	T	64
Lime Kiln Dairy	Dorset	SY8483	50°39·0′	2°13·2′W	X	194
Lime Kiln Edge	Scot Bord	NT5401	55°18·3′	2°43·0′W	H	79
Limekiln Field	Derby	SK4771	53°14·3′	1°17·3′W	T	120
Limekiln Fm	Ches	SJ8559	53°7·9′	2°13·0′W	FM	118
Limekiln Fm	Dorset	ST6315	50°56·2′	2°31·2′W	FM	183
Limekiln Fm	E Susx	TQ5311	50°52·9′	0°10·9′E	FM	199
Lime Kiln Fm	Kent	TQ7744	51°10·3′	0°32·3′E	FM	188
Limekiln Fm	Kent	TQ8641	51°8·5′	0°39·9′E	FM	189
Limekiln Fm	Norf	TG2224	52°46·3′	1°17·9′E	FM	133,134
Lime Kiln Fm	N Yks	SE2396	54°21·8′	1°38·3′W	FM	99
Limekiln Fm	Suff	TL7586	52°26·9′	0°34·9′E	FM	143
Lime Kiln Fm	Suff	TM4777	52°20·3′	1°38·0′E	FM	156
Limekiln Hill	Dorset	SY5387	50°41·1′	2°39·5′W	H	194
Lime Kiln Hovel	Oxon	SP5629	51°57·6′	1°10·7′W	X	164
Lime Kiln Nook	Cumbr	NY3640	54°45·3′	2°59·2′W	X	85
Lime Kiln Oast	E Susx	TQ5330	51°3·2′	0°11·5′E	X	188
Limekiln Plantn	Norf	TF7007	52°38·3′	0°31·1′E	F	143
Limekiln Plantn	Suff	TL8371	52°18·6′	0°41·5′E	F	144,155
Limekiln Platation	Norf	TF8101	52°34·8′	0°40·7′E	F	144
Limekilns	D & G	NY1769	55°0·8′	3°17·5′W	X	85
Limekilns	Fife	NT0783	56°2·1′	3°29·1′W	T	65
Lime Kilns Fm	N Yks	SE3262	54°3·4′	1°30·3′W	FM	99
Limekilns, The	Cambs	TL6665	52°15·7′	0°26·3′E	X	154
Limekiln Wood	E Susx	TQ5331	51°3·7′	0°11·4′E	F	188
Limekiln Wood	N Yks	SE4841	53°52·0′	1°15·8′W	F	105
Limekiln Wood	Wrekin	SJ6509	52°40·9′	2°30·7′W	F	127
Lime Knowe	D & G	NT2806	55°20·8′	3°7·7′W	H	79
Limelands	Fife	NO5310	56°17·1′	2°45·1′W	X	59
Lime Park	E Susx	TQ6312	50°53·3′	0°19·4′E	X	199
Limepit Hill	Cambs	TL5055	52°10·6′	0°12·0′E	X	154
Lime Ridge Wood	Somer	ST2419	50°58·2′	3°4·6′W	F	193
Limerigg	Falk	NS8570	55°54·8′	3°50·0′W	T	65
Limers Cross	Devon	ST1404	50°50·0′	3°12·9′W	X	192,193
Limer Shank	Aberd	NJ5121	57°16·9′	2°48·3′W	X	37
Limerstone	I of W	SZ4482	50°38·4′	1°22·3′W	T	196
Limerstone Down	I of W	SZ4483	50°38·9′	1°22·3′W	X	196
Limesbrook	Essex	TL9112	51°46·7′	0°46·5′E	X	168
Limes Fm	Lincs	TF2834	52°53·5′	0°5·4′W	FM	131
Limes Fm	Lincs	TF3561	53°8·0′	0°1·5′E	FM	122
Limes Fm, The	Ches	SJ7651	53°3·6′	2°21·1′W	FM	118
Lime Side	Oldham	SD9102	53°31·1′	2°7·7′W	T	109
Limeslade Bay	Swan	SS6286	51°33·6′	3°59·1′W	W	159
Limeslake Fm	Devon	SS7428	51°2·5′	3°47·5′W	FM	180
Limes, The	Bucks	SP7413	51°48·9′	0°55·2′W	X	165
Limes, The	Cambs	TL4896	52°32·7′	0°11·4′E	X	143
Limes, The	Ches	SJ4767	53°12·1′	2°47·2′W	X	117
Limes, The	Ches	SJ7366	53°11·7′	2°23·8′W	X	118
Limes, The	E Yorks	TA1629	53°44·9′	0°14·0′W	X	107
Limes, The	Lincs	TF2173	53°14·6′	0°10·8′W	X	122
Limes, The	Lincs	TF3310	52°40·5′	0°1·6′W	X	131,142
Limes, The	Norf	TF4810	52°40·3′	0°11·7′E	X	131,143
Limes, The	Norf	TF5616	52°43·4′	0°19·0′E	X	131
Limes, The	Notts	SK6737	52°55·8′	0°59·8′W	X	129
Limes, The	Staffs	SJ9637	52°56·1′	2°3·2′W	X	127
Limestone Brae	Northum	NY7949	54°50·4′	2°19·2′W	T	86,87
Limestone Hall	Warw	SP4475	52°22·5′	1°20·8′W	X	140
Limestone Hill	Donc	SK5792	53°25·5′	1°8·1′W	X	111
Limestone Hill	Staffs	SK1346	53°0·9′	1°47·9′W	X	119,128
Limestone Hill Fm	Carm	SN4612	51°47·4′	4°13·6′W	FM	159
Limestone Knowe	Northum	NT6701	55°18·4′	2°30·8′W	H	80
Limestone Link	Bath & NE Somer	ST6657	51°18·9′	2°28·9′W	X	172,182
Limestone Link	Cumbr	SD5179	54°12·5′	2°44·7′W	X	97
Limestone Link	N Som	ST4558	51°19·3′	2°47·0′W	X	
Limestones	Aberd	NJ5458	57°36·8′	2°45·7′W	X	29
Limestone Trail	Lancs	SD8928	53°45·1′	2°9·6′W	X	103
Limestone Way	Derby	SK1381	53°19·8′	1°47·9′W	X	110
Limestone Way	Derby	SK1665	53°11·1′	1°45·2′W	X	119
Lime Street	Worcs	SO8130	51°58·3′	2°16·2′W	T	150
Lime St Sta	Liv	SJ3590	53°24·4′	2°58·3′W	X	108
Limetree Fm	Ches	SJ5664	53°10·5′	2°39·1′W	FM	117
Limetree Fm	Ches	SJ7084	53°21·4′	2°26·6′W	FM	109
Lime Tree Fm	Kent	TQ7337	51°6·6′	0°28·7′E	FM	188
Lime Tree Fm	Lincs	TF3339	52°56·1′	0°0·9′W	FM	131
Lime Tree Fm	Norf	TM1493	52°29·8′	1°9·6′E	FM	144
Lime Tree Fm	Norf	TM1990	52°28·1′	1°13·9′E	FM	134
Lime Tree Fm	Norf	TM2195	52°30·7′	1°15·8′E	FM	134
Lime Tree Fm	Suff	TM1169	52°16·9′	1°6·0′E	FM	155
Lime Tree Fm	Suff	TM2774	52°19·2′	1°20·3′E	FM	156
Limetree Fm	Suff	TM3656	52°9·3′	1°27·4′E	FM	156
Lime Tree Park	Cov	SP2978	52°24·2′	1°34·0′W	T	140
Limetree Walk	E Loth	NT6180	56°0·9′	2°37·1′W	X	67
Limetree Wood	Derby	SK2767	53°12·2′	1°35·3′W	F	119
Lime Wharf	Wirral	SJ2085	53°21·6′	3°11·7′W	X	108
Limiecleuch Burn	Scot Bord	NT3802	55°18·7′	2°58·2′W	W	79
Limie Hill	Scot Bord	NT3902	55°18·7′	2°57·2′W	H	79
Limington	Somer	ST5422	51°0·0′	2°38·9′W	T	183
Limley Fm	N Yks	SE1075	54°10·5′	1°50·4′W	FM	99
Limlow Hill	Cambs	TL3241	52°3·3′	0°4·1′W	X	153
Limmer Copse	Wilts	SU2954	51°17·3′	1°34·7′W	F	185
Limmerhaugh Muir	E Ayr	NS6127	55°31·3′	4°11·7′W	X	71
Limmer Hill	S Lanak	NS8731	55°33·8′	3°47·1′W	H	71,72
Limmerhill	Wok	SU7968	51°24·6′	0°51·5′W	X	175
Limmer Pond	Wilts	SU2955	51°17·8′	1°34·7′W	W	174,185
Limmicks	Corn	SX2653	50°21·3′	4°26·4′W	X	201
Limney Fm	E Susx	TQ5427	51°1·5′	0°12·1′E	FM	188,199
Limpenhoe	Norf	TG3903	52°34·6′	1°32·1′E	T	134
Limpenhoe Hill	Norf	TG4002	52°34·0′	1°32·9′E	T	134
Limpenhoe Marshes	Norf	TG3902	52°34·0′	1°32·0′E	X	134
Limpers Hill	Wilts	ST8231	51°4·9′	2°15·0′W	T	183
Limpert	V of Glam	ST0266	51°23·3′	3°24·1′W	X	170
Limpert Bay	V of Glam	ST0166	51°23·3′	3°25·0′W	W	170
Limpet Craig	N Ayr	NS1946	55°40·7′	4°52·3′W	X	63
Limpet Rocks	Devon	SX8241	50°15·7′	3°39·0′W	X	202
Limpin Lake	Pemb	SN0208	51°44·4′	4°51·7′W	W	157,158
Limpit Hill	Shrops	SJ4024	52°48·9′	2°53·0′W	X	126
Limpley Stoke	Bath & NE Somer	ST7860	51°20·6′	2°18·6′W	T	172
Limpool Fm	Donc	SK6194	53°26·6′	1°4·5′W	FM	111
Limpsfield	Surrey	TQ3953	51°15·8′	0°0·1′W	T	187
Limpsfield Chart	Surrey	TQ4251	51°14·7′	0°2·5′E	T	187
Limpsfield Common	Surrey	TQ4152	51°15·2′	0°1·6′E	T	187
Limpsfield Grange	Surrey	TQ4053	51°15·8′	0°0·8′E	X	187
Limsboro'	Devon	SX5680	50°36·4′	4°1·7′W	X	191
Limy Water	Lancs	SD8127	53°44·6′	2°16·9′W	W	103
Linacre Ho	Halton	SJ5087	53°22·9′	2°44·7′W	X	108
Linacre Resrs	Derby	SK3372	53°14·9′	1°29·9′W	W	119
Linacres	Northum	NY8178	55°6·0′	2°17·4′W	X	86,87
Linacre Wood	Derby	SK3372	53°14·9′	1°29·9′W	F	119
Linbeck	Cumbr	SD1498	54°22·5′	3°19·0′W	X	96
Linbeck Gill	Cumbr	SD1497	54°21·9′	3°19·0′W	W	96
Linbriggs	Northum	NT8906	55°21·1′	2°10·0′W	T	80
Lin Brook	Staffs	SK1622	52°48·0′	1°45·4′W	W	128
Linburn	E Ayr	NS6929	55°32·5′	4°4·1′W	X	71
Linburn	Renf	NS4570	55°54·1′	4°28·3′W	X	64
Linburn	W Loth	NT1268	55°54·1′	3°24·0′W	T	65
Linburn Beck	Durham	NZ1129	54°39·6′	1°49·3′W	W	92
Linburn Hall	Durham	NZ0729	54°39·6′	1°53·1′W	X	92
Linburn Head	Durham	NZ0627	54°38·5′	1°54·0′W	X	92
Linby	Notts	SK5351	53°3·5′	1°12·1′W	T	120
Linces Fm	Herts	TL2216	51°50·0′	0°13·4′W	FM	166
Linceter Fm	Heref	SO6957	52°12·9′	2°26·8′W	FM	149
Lince, The	Oxon	SP4414	51°49·6′	1°21·3′W	X	164
Linchball Wood	W Susx	SU8416	50°56·5′	0°47·9′W	F	197
Linchborough Park	Hants	SU8133	51°5·7′	0°50·2′W	X	186
Linch Clough	Derby	SK1694	53°26·8′	1°45·1′W	X	110
Linch Down	W Susx	SU8417	50°57·0′	0°47·9′W	H	197
Linches, The	Northnts	TL0283	52°26·4′	0°29·6′W	F	141
Linch Fm	W Susx	SU8418	50°57·5′	0°47·8′W	FM	197
Linch Hill	Oxon	SP4103	51°43·7′	1°24·0′W	X	164
Linchmere	W Susx	SU8631	51°4·5′	0°46·0′W	T	186
Linchmere Common	W Susx	SU8631	51°4·5′	0°46·0′W	F	186
Lincluden	D & G	NX9677	55°4·8′	3°37·3′W	T	84
Lincoln	Lincs	SK9771	53°13·9′	0°32·4′W	T	121
Lincoln Flats	E Yorks	SE7737	53°49·7′	0°49·4′W	X	105,106
Lincoln Fm	N Yks	NZ4906	54°27·1′	1°14·2′W	FM	93
Lincoln Hall	Norf	TG3907	52°36·7′	1°32·2′E	X	134
Lincoln Hill	Herts	TL3932	51°58·4′	0°1·8′E	X	166
Lincoln Hill	Lincs	SK8445	53°0·0′	0°44·5′W	X	130
Lincoln Hill	N Lincs	SE9705	53°32·2′	0°31·8′W	X	112
Lincoln Hill	Northum	NY9071	55°2·3′	2°9·0′W	X	87
Lincoln Island	Redbr	TQ4187	51°34·1′	0°2·5′E	X	177
Lincoln Lane Fm	Lincs	SK9563	53°9·6′	0°34·3′W	FM	121
Lincoln Lodge	Mil Key	SP7845	52°6·1′	0°51·3′W	X	152
Lincoln Lodge	Notts	SK6728	52°51·0′	0°59·9′W	X	129
Lincolns	Essex	TL4625	51°54·5′	0°7·7′E	X	167
Lincolns	Essex	TQ5695	51°38·2′	0°15·7′E	X	167,177
Lincoln's Fir	Suff	TM5083	52°23·5′	1°40·9′E	F	156
Lincolnshire Gate	Lincs	SK9914	52°43·1′	0°31·7′W	X	130
Lincomb	Worcs	SO8268	52°18·8′	2°15·4′W	T	138
Lincombe	Devon	SS4946	51°11·8′	4°9·3′W	T	180
Lincombe	Devon	SX7340	50°15·0′	3°46·5′W	X	202
Lincombe	Devon	SX7458	50°24·7′	3°46·0′W	X	202
Lincombe Fm	Devon	SY1393	50°44·0′	3°13·6′W	FM	192,193
Lincott	Dorset	SY7885	50°40·1′	2°18·3′W	X	194
Lincowell	Cumbr	NY5844	54°47·6′	2°38·8′W	X	86
Lin Crag Fm	Cumbr	SD2787	54°16·7′	3°6·9′W	FM	96,97
Lindal Cote Cottage	Cumbr	SD2475	54°10·2′	3°9·4′W	X	96
Lindale	Cumbr	SD4180	54°13·0′	2°53·9′W	T	96,97
Lin Dale	Derby	SK1551	53°3·6′	1°46·2′W	X	119
Lindal in Furness	Cumbr	SD2575	54°10·2′	3°8·5′W	T	96
Lindal Moor	Cumbr	SD2476	54°10·7′	3°9·4′W	X	96
Linday Geo	Orkney	HY6338	59°13·9′	2°38·4′W	X	5
Lindean	Scot Bord	NT4931	55°34·5′	2°48·1′W	T	73
Lindean Moor	Scot Bord	NT5029	55°33·4′	2°47·1′W	X	73
Linden	Glos	SO8216	51°50·8′	2°15·3′W	T	162
Linden	Heref	SO7642	52°4·8′	2°20·6′W	X	150
Lind End	Cumbr	SD2391	54°18·8′	3°10·6′W	X	96
Linden End Field	Cambs	TL4674	52°20·9′	0°9·0′E	X	143
Linden Fm	Cumbr	NY5833	54°41·7′	2°38·7′W	FM	91
Linden Fm	Somer	ST3233	51°5·8′	2°57·9′W	FM	182
Linden Grange	N Yks	NZ4605	54°26·5′	1°17·0′W	X	93
Linden Hall	Northum	NZ1596	55°15·7′	1°45·4′W	X	81
Linden Hill	Wok	SU8178	51°29·9′	0°49·6′W	X	175
Linden Hill Head	Northum	NZ1496	55°15·7′	1°46·4′W	X	81
Lindenlane	Northum	NZ1495	55°15·2′	1°46·4′W	X	81
Lindens Fm, The	Lincs	TA1808	53°33·6′	0°12·7′W	FM	113
Lindens, The	Lincs	TA1908	53°33·5′	0°11·8′W	X	113
Lindertis	Angus	NO3351	56°39·0′	3°5·1′W	X	53
Lindeth	Cumbr	SD4195	54°21·1′	2°54·0′W	X	96,97
Lindeth Twr	Lancs	SD4674	54°9·8′	2°49·2′W	X	97
Lindfield	W Susx	TQ3425	51°0·7′	0°5·0′W	T	187,198
Lindfield Fm	W Susx	TQ3822	50°59·1′	0°1·6′W	FM	198
Lindford	Hants	SU8036	51°7·3′	0°51·0′W	T	186
Lindhead Beck	N Yks	SE9993	54°19·6′	0°28·2′W	W	94,101
Lindhead Beck	N Yks	TA0093	54°19·6′	0°27·3′W	W	101
Lindhead Gorse	N Yks	SE9993	54°19·6′	0°28·2′W	X	94,101
Lindholme Grange	Donc	SE7207	53°33·5′	0°54·4′W	X	112
Lindholme Hall	Donc	SE7006	53°33·0′	0°56·2′W	X	112
Lindhope Burn	Northum	NT9112	55°24·4′	2°8·1′W	W	80

Lindhope Linn	Northum	NT9113	55°24·9'	2°8·1'W	W	80
Lindhurst Fm	Notts	SK5657	53°6·7'	1°9·4'W	FM	120
Lindifferon	Fife	NO3116	56°20·1'	3°6·5'W	X	59
Lindifferon Hill	Fife	NO3216	56°20·1'	3°5·5'W	X	59
Lindisfarne	Durham	NZ0746	54°48·8'	1°53·0'W	X	88
Lindisfarne	Northum	NU1243	55°41·1'	1°48·1'W	A	75
Lindley	Kirk	SE1118	53°39·7'	1°49·6'W	T	110
Lindley	N Yks	SE2249	53°56·4'	1°39·5'W	T	104
Lindley Br	N Yks	SE2248	53°55·9'	1°39·5'W	X	104
Lindley Grange	Leic	SP3695	52°33·3'	1°27·7'W	X	140
Lindley Hall Fm	Leic	SP3696	52°33·9'	1°27·7'W	FM	140
Lindley Lodge	Leic	SP3794	52°32·8'	1°26·9'W	X	140
Lindley Moor	N Yks	SE2351	53°57·5'	1°38·6'W	X	104
Lindley Wood	N Yks	SE2149	53°56·4'	1°40·4'W	F	104
Lindley Wood Resr	N Yks	SE2149	53°56·4'	1°40·4'W	W	104
Lindop Wood	Derby	SK2567	53°12·2'	1°37·1'W	F	119
Lindores	Fife	NO2616	56°20·1'	3°11·4'W	T	59
Lindores Hill	Fife	NO2518	56°21·2'	3°12·4'W	H	59
Lindores Ho	Fife	NO2616	56°20·1'	3°11·4'W	X	59
Lindores Loch	Fife	NO2616	56°20·1'	3°11·4'W	W	59
Lindors Fm	Glos	SO5404	51°44·2'	2°39·6'W	FM	162
Lindowan Resr	Arg & Bt	NS2481	55°59·6'	4°48·9'W	W	63
Lindow Common	Ches	SJ8381	53°19·8'	2°14·9'W	X	109
Lindow End	Ches	SJ8178	53°18·2'	2°16·7'W	T	118
Lindow Fm	Ches	SJ8180	53°19·2'	2°16·7'W	FM	109
Lindow Lea Fm	Kent	TQ6646	51°11·6'	0°22·9'E	FM	188
Lindow Moss	Ches	SJ8281	53°19·8'	2°15·8'W	X	109
Lindreth Brow	Cumbr	SD4693	54°20·0'	2°49·4'W	X	97
Lindrick Common	Roth	SK5482	53°20·2'	1°10·9'W	X	111,120
Lindrick Dale	Roth	SK5482	53°20·2'	1°10·9'W	T	111,120
Lindridge	Kent	TQ7644	51°10·3'	0°31·5'E	X	188
Lindridge	Shrops	SO7986	52°28·5'	2°18·2'W	X	138
Lindridge	Worcs	SO6769	52°19·3'	2°28·7'W	T	138
Lindridge Fm	Leic	SK4605	52°38·7'	1°18·8'W	FM	140
Lindridge Hall Fm	Leic	SK4604	52°38·1'	1°18·8'W	FM	140
Lindridge Hill	Devon	SX8774	50°33·5'	3°35·3'W	X	192
Lindridge Lodge Fm	Kent	TQ6638	51°7·3'	0°22·7'E	FM	188
Lindridge Park	Devon	SX8975	50°34·1'	3°33·7'W	X	192
Lindridge, The	Birm	SP1596	52°33·9'	1°46·3'W	X	139
Lindsaig	Arg & Bt	NR9379	55°57·8'	5°18·6'W	X	62
Lindsayfield	Aberd	NO8284	56°57·1'	2°17·3'W	X	45
Lindsaylands	S Lanak	NT0237	55°37·3'	3°32·9'W	X	72
Lindsayston	S Ayr	NS2800	55°16·1'	4°42·0'W	X	76
Lindsayston Fm	S Ayr	NS3413	55°23·2'	4°36·8'W	FM	70
Lindsell	Essex	TL6427	51°55·3'	0°23·5'E	T	167
Lindsey	Suff	TL9744	52°3·8'	0°52·8'E	T	155
Lindsey Fm	Oxon	SP3708	51°46·4'	1°27·4'W	FM	164
Lindsey Tye	Suff	TL9845	52°4·3'	0°53·7'E	T	155
Lindston	S Ayr	NS3716	55°24·9'	4°34·1'W	X	70
Lindston Loch	S Ayr	NS3716	55°24·9'	4°34·1'W	W	70
Lindsway Bay	Pemb	SM8406	51°42·9'	5°7·2'W	W	157
Lindum Ho	Lincs	TF2223	52°47·7'	0°11·0'W	X	131
Lindvm (Lincoln)	Lincs	SK9771	53°13·9'	0°32·4'W	R	121
Lindwaylane Fm	Derby	SK3558	53°7·3'	1°28·2'W	FM	119
Lindway Springs	Derby	SK3557	53°6·8'	1°28·2'W	F	119
Lindwell	Cald	SE0921	53°41·4'	1°51·4'W	T	104
Lineage Fm	Leic	SK3804	52°38·2'	1°25·9'W	FM	140
Lineage Wood	Suff	TL8848	52°6·1'	0°45·1'E	F	155
Line Croft Fm	Notts	SK7793	53°25·9'	0°50·1'W	FM	112
Linefoot	Cumbr	NY0734	54°41·8'	3°26·2'W	X	89
Linegar	Orkney	ND4193	58°49·5'	3°0·8'W	X	7
Lineham Fm	Leeds	SE2842	53°52·6'	1°34·0'W	FM	104
Linehams	Cumbr	NY7611	54°29·9'	2°21·8'W	X	91
Lineholme Burn	Cumbr	NY5658	54°55·1'	2°40·8'W	W	86
Lineholt	Worcs	SO8266	52°17·7'	2°15·4'W	T	138,150
Lineholt Common	Worcs	SO8267	52°18·3'	2°15·4'W	T	138,150
Linekiln Wood	N Yks	SE2396	54°21·8'	1°38·3'W	F	99
Linen Sike	Northum	NY6974	55°3·8'	2°28·7'W	W	86,87
Linen Well	Monm	ST5398	51°41·0'	2°40·4'W	W	162
Lineover Wood	Glos	SO9818	51°51·9'	2°1·3'W	F	163
Line Riggs	Cumbr	SD3886	54°16·2'	2°56·7'W	X	96,97
Linethwaite	Cumbr	NX9813	54°30·4'	3°34·1'W	X	89
Linewath	Cumbr	NY3534	54°42·1'	3°0·1'W	X	90
Liney	Somer	ST3535	51°6·9'	2°55·3'W	T	182
Linfairn	S Ayr	NS3801	55°16·8'	4°32·6'W	X	77
Linfern Loch	S Ayr	NX3697	55°14·7'	4°34·4'W	W	77
Linfield	Pth & Kin	NN9925	56°24·6'	3°37·8'W	X	52,53,58
Linfit	Kirk	SE2013	53°37·0'	1°41·4'W	X	110
Linfitts	Oldham	SD9708	53°34·4'	2°2·3'W	T	109
Linfold Fm	W Susx	TQ0225	51°1·1'	0°32·4'W	FM	186,197
Linford	Hants	SU1806	50°51·4'	1°44·3'W	T	195
Linford	Thurr	TQ6779	51°29·3'	0°24·7'E	T	177,178
Linford Brook	Hants	SU1908	50°52·5'	1°43·4'W	W	195
Linford Fm	Shrops	SJ5630	52°52·2'	2°38·8'W	FM	126
Linford Wood	Mil Key	SP8345	52°6·1'	0°46·9'W	F	152
Linford Wood	Mil Key	SP8440	52°3·4'	0°46·1'W	F	152
Linga	Shetld	HU2348	60°13·2'	1°34·6'W	X	3
Linga	Shetld	HU2859	60°19·1'	1°29·1'W	X	3
Linga	Shetld	HU3563	60°21·2'	1°21·4'W	X	2,3
Linga	Shetld	HU3639	60°8·3'	1°20·6'W	X	4
Linga	Shetld	HU4673	60°26·6'	1°9·3'W	X	2,3
Linga	Shetld	HU5598	60°40·0'	0°59·1'W	X	1
Linga Fiold	Orkney	HY2615	59°1·2'	3°16·8'W	H	6
Lingague	I of M	SC2172	54°7·0'	4°43·9'W	X	95
Linga Holm	Orkney	HY6127	59°7·9'	2°40·4'W	X	5
Lingamend	Aberd	NJ5608	57°9·9'	2°43·2'W	X	37
Linganbo	Aberd	NJ7059	57°37·5'	2°29·7'W	X	29
Lingara Bay	N Eil	NG0684	57°45·2'	6°56·1'W	W	18
Lingarabay	N Eil	NG0687	57°45·8'	6°56·2'W	T	18
Lingarabay Island	N Eil	NG0684	57°45·2'	6°56·1'W	X	18
Lingards Fm	Ches	SJ8672	53°14·9'	2°12·2'W	FM	118
Lingards Wood	Kirk	SE0612	53°36·5'	1°54·1'W	T	110
Lingart	Lancs	SD5046	53°54·7'	2°45·3'W	X	102
Lingarth	Shetld	HU4018	59°57·0'	1°16·5'W	X	4
Linga Skerries	Shetld	HU4955	60°16·8'	1°6·3'W	X	3
Linga Sound	Orkney	HY6228	59°8·5'	2°39·4'W	W	5
Linga Sound	Shetld	HU5364	60°21·7'	1°1·9'W	W	2,3
Lingavi Geo	Orkney	HY5316	59°2·0'	2°48·6'W	X	6
Lingay	N Eil	NF7511	57°4·8'	7°21·4'W	X	31
Lingay	N Eil	NF8778	57°41·2'	7°14·7'W	X	18
Lingay	N Eil	NG0178	57°41·8'	7°0·7'W	X	18
Lingay	N Eil	NL6089	56°52·3'	7°34·4'W	X	31
Lingay-fhada	N Eil	NF7303	57°0·4'	7°22·8'W	X	31
Lingay Hill	Cambs	TL6160	52°13·1'	0°21·8'E	X	154
Lingay Strand	N Eil	NF8777	57°40·7'	7°14·6'W	X	18
Lingbank	Cumbr	NY0504	54°25·6'	3°27·4'W	X	89
Lingber Hill	N Yks	SD8757	54°0·8'	2°11·5'W	H	103
Lingbob	Brad	SE0935	53°48·9'	1°51·4'W	T	104
Ling Bob	Leeds	SE2439	53°51·0'	1°37·7'W	X	104
Ling Chapel Fm	N Yks	SE0952	53°58·1'	1°51·4'W	FM	104
Ling Comb	Cumbr	NY1515	54°31·6'	3°18·4'W	X	89
Ling Common	Norf	TF6523	52°47·0'	0°27·2'E	X	132
Ling Common	Norf	TG2720	52°44·0'	1°22·1'E	X	133,134
Ling Cottages	Cumbr	NY4644	54°47·5'	2°50·0'W	X	86
Lingcove Beck	Cumbr	NY2304	54°25·8'	3°10·8'W	W	89,90
Ling Covert	Suff	TL8574	52°20·2'	0°43·3'E	F	144
Ling Crags	Cumbr	NY1518	54°33·3'	3°18·4'W	X	89
Lingcroft	Cumbr	NY0722	54°35·3'	3°25·9'W	X	89
Lingcroft	N Yks	SE4451	53°57·4'	1°19·4'W	X	105
Lingcroft Fm	York	SE6147	53°55·2'	1°3·9'W	FM	105
Lingdale	Red & Cl	NZ6616	54°32·3'	0°58·4'W	T	94
Lingdowey Burn	D & G	NX1466	54°57·5'	4°53·9'W	W	82
Lingeigh	N Eil	NF8544	57°22·9'	7°14·1'W	X	22
Lingen	Heref	SO3667	52°18·1'	2°55·9'W	T	137,148,149
Lingen	Powys	SN9873	52°21·0'	3°29·5'W	X	136,147
Lingen Br	Shrops	SO3572	52°20·8'	2°56·9'W	X	137,148
Lingen Fm	Worcs	SO7660	52°14·5'	2°20·7'W	FM	138,150
Lingens Fm, The	Worcs	SO7856	52°12·3'	2°18·9'W	FM	150
Lingen Vallet Wood	Heref	SO3566	52°17·5'	2°56·8'W	F	137,148,149
Lingerfield	N Yks	SE3359	54°1·8'	1°29·4'W	X	104
Linger Hill	Norf	TL9791	52°29·1'	0°54·5'E	X	144
Lingermans	Oxon	SP2809	51°47·0'	1°35·3'W	X	163
Lingerwood	Midlo	NT3363	55°51·6'	3°3·8'W	X	66
Lingeybank	Cumbr	NY2033	54°41·4'	3°14·0'W	X	89,90
Lingey Close	Durham	NZ2136	54°43·4'	1°40·0'W	X	93
Lingey Field	Northum	NZ0258	54°55·2'	1°57·7'W	X	87
Ling Fell	Cumbr	NY1728	54°38·7'	3°16·7'W	H	89,90
Lingfield	Darl	NZ3114	54°31·5'	1°30·8'W	T	93
Lingfield	Surrey	TQ3843	51°10·4'	0°1·2'W	T	187
Lingfield Common	Surrey	TQ3844	51°10·9'	0°1·1'W	T	187
Lingfield Cottage	N Yks	SE4455	53°59·6'	1°19·3'W	X	105
Lingfield Fm	Darl	NZ3114	54°31·5'	1°30·8'W	FM	93
Lingfield Fm	Midd	NZ5113	54°30·8'	1°12·3'W	FM	93
Lingfield Fm	N Yks	NZ3901	54°24·4'	1°23·5'W	FM	93
Lingfield Hospital School	Surrey	TQ4043	51°10·4'	0°0·6'E	X	187
Ling Fm	Cumbr	NY5725	54°37·3'	2°39·5'W	FM	91
Ling Fm	E Yorks	SE8862	54°3·0'	0°38·9'W	FM	101
Ling Fm	Norf	TM0182	52°24·2'	0°57·7'E	FM	144
Ling Fm	Notts	SK5656	53°6·1'	1°9·4'W	FM	120
Ling Fm	N Yks	SE9968	54°6·1'	0°28·7'W	FM	101
Ling Gill	N Yks	SD8078	54°12·1'	2°18·0'W	X	98
Ling Hall	N Yks	SE1074	54°9·9'	1°50·4'W	X	99
Ling Hall Fm	N Yks	SE9273	54°8·9'	0°35·1'W	FM	101
Lingham Fm	Wirral	SJ2591	53°24·9'	3°7·3'W	FM	108
Lingham Lane Fm	N Yks	SE3972	54°8·8'	1°23·8'W	FM	99
Linghaw	Cumbr	SD6398	54°22·8'	2°33·8'W	X	97
Linghaw Fm	N Yks	SD6868	54°6·7'	2°29·0'W	FM	98
Ling Haw Hill	N Yks	SE0045	53°54·3'	1°59·6'W	X	104
Ling Heath	Norf	TL8993	52°30·4'	0°47·5'E	X	144
Lingheath Fm	Suff	TL7985	52°26·2'	0°38·4'E	FM	144
Ling Hill	Lancs	SD7553	53°58·6'	2°22·5'W	X	103
Ling Hill	Leic	SK5212	52°42·4'	1°13·4'W	X	129
Ling Hill	Stir	NS6789	56°4·8'	4°7·8'W	H	57
Ling Hills	Norf	TF6610	52°40·0'	0°27·7'E	X	132,143
Linghills Fm	Norf	TF8300	52°34·2'	0°42·4'E	FM	144
Ling Ho	Donc	SE6310	53°35·3'	1°2·5'W	X	111
Ling Ho	Norf	TF7330	52°50·6'	0°34·5'E	X	132
Lingholm	Cumbr	NY2522	54°35·5'	3°9·2'W	X	89,90
Ling Holm	Orkney	HY3005	59°0·7'	3°12·6'W	X	6
Ling Holm	Orkney	HY5019	59°3·6'	2°51·8'W	X	6
Ling Holme	Cumbr	SD3893	54°20·0'	2°56·8'W	X	96,97
Lingholm Fm	N Yks	TA0781	54°13·1'	0°21·1'W	FM	101
Ling Holms	Orkney	HY2815	59°1·2'	3°14·8'W	X	6
Ling Hope	E Loth	NT7069	55°55·0'	2°28·4'W	X	67
Linghope Burn	Scot Bord	NT1722	55°29·3'	3°18·4'W	W	72
Linghope Burn	Scot Bord	NT2128	55°32·6'	3°14·7'W	W	73
Ling Hurst	Notts	SK6986	53°22·2'	0°57·4'W	F	111,120
Ling Hut	Highld	NG9556	57°33·1'	5°25·1'W	X	25
Lingie Hill	E Ayr	NS5111	55°22·5'	4°20·7'W	X	70
Lingieston	Moray	NJ0360	57°37·4'	3°37·0'W	X	27
Linginis	N Eil	NB2101	57°54·9'	6°42·2'W	X	14
Lingla Beck	Cumbr	NY0316	54°32·0'	3°29·5'W	W	89
Linglands Fm	N Yks	SE9896	54°21·2'	0°29·1'W	FM	94,101
Lingley Green	Warr	SJ5589	53°24·0'	2°40·2'W	T	108
Lingley Knoll	Oxon	SU5782	51°32·3'	1°10·3'W	X	174
Lingley Mere	Warr	SJ5589	53°24·0'	2°40·2'W	T	108
Linglie	Scot Bord	NT4629	55°33·4'	2°51·9'W	X	73
Linglie Hill	Scot Bord	NT4530	55°33·9'	2°51·9'W	H	73
Linglow	Cumbr	NY6811	54°29·8'	2°29·2'W	X	91
Lingmell	Cumbr	NY1413	54°30·6'	3°19·3'W	X	89
Lingmell	Cumbr	NY2008	54°27·9'	3°13·6'W	X	89,90
Lingmell Beck	Cumbr	NY1909	54°28·4'	3°14·6'W	W	89,90
Lingmell Crag	Cumbr	NY2008	54°27·9'	3°13·6'W	X	89,90
Lingmell End	Cumbr	NY4409	54°28·6'	2°51·4'W	H	90
Lingmell Gill	Cumbr	NY1907	54°27·4'	3°14·5'W	W	89,90
Lingmoor Fell	Cumbr	NY3004	54°25·8'	3°4·3'W	H	90
Lingmoor Fm	N Yks	SE7188	54°17·2'	0°54·1'W	FM	94,100
Lingmoor Tarn	Cumbr	NY3005	54°26·4'	3°4·3'W	W	90
Ling Ness	Orkney	HY3930	59°9·4'	3°3·5'W	X	6
Ling Ness	Shetld	HU4954	60°16·3'	1°6·4'W	X	3
Lingodell Fm	Roth	SK5488	53°23·4'	1°10·9'W	FM	111,120
Lingoe	Orkney	HY3005	58°55·9'	3°12·5'W	X	6,7
Lingo House	Fife	NO5008	56°16·0'	2°48·0'W	X	59
Lingore Linn	N Lanak	NS9058	55°48·4'	3°44·9'W	W	65,72
Ling Park	N Yks	SE1050	53°57·0'	1°50·4'W	X	104
Ling Plantation	Norf	TF9722	52°45·8'	0°55·6'E	F	132
Ling Rig	E Loth	NT6466	55°53·4'	2°34·1'W	X	67
Lingro	Orkney	HY4308	58°57·6'	2°59·0'W	X	6,7
Lingro	Orkney	HY5220	59°4·1'	2°49·7'W	X	5,6
Lingrove Howe	N Yks	NZ7917	54°32·8'	0°46·3'W	X	94
Lingrow Knock	N Yks	NZ8017	54°32·8'	0°45·4'W	X	94
Lings Covert	Leic	SK8027	52°50·3'	0°48·3'W	F	130
Ling's End	Norf	TF8911	52°40·1'	0°48·1'E	X	132
Lings Fm	Derby	SK4166	53°11·6'	1°22·8'W	FM	120
Lings Fm	Donc	SE6507	53°33·6'	1°0·7'W	FM	111
Lings Fm	E Yorks	SE9540	53°51·1'	0°32·9'W	FM	106
Lings Fm	Leic	SK8127	52°50·3'	0°47·4'W	FM	130
Lings Fm	Lincs	TF0416	52°44·1'	0°27·2'W	FM	130
L'Ings Fm	Lincs	TF1798	53°28·2'	0°13·8'W	FM	113
Lings Fm	Notts	SK5624	52°48·9'	1°9·7'W	FM	129
Lings Fm, The	Notts	SK5625	52°49·4'	1°9·7'W	FM	129
Lings Hill	Leic	SK8128	52°50·8'	0°47·4'W	X	130
Ling Side	Cumbr	NY3445	54°48·0'	3°1·2'W	X	85
Lings Plantn	E Yorks	SE8552	53°57·7'	0°41·9'W	F	106
Lingspot Fm	Notts	SK8356	53°5·9'	0°45·2'W	FM	121
Lings, The	Donc	SE6508	53°34·1'	1°0·7'W	T	111
Lings, The	Norf	TF9733	52°51·7'	0°56·0'E	F	132
Lings, The	Norf	TG0306	52°37·1'	1°0·3'E	X	144
Lings, The	Notts	SK5967	53°12·0'	1°6·6'W	F	120
Lingstubbs	Cumbr	NY4930	54°40·0'	2°47·0'W	X	90
Lings Windmill	Donc	SE6508	53°34·1'	1°0·7'W	X	111
Ling's Wood	Notts	SK6691	53°24·9'	1°0·0'W	F	111
Lingthwaite	N Yks	SD7564	54°4·5'	2°22·5'W	X	98
Ling Walk	E Yorks	SE9462	54°3·0'	0°33·4'W	X	101
Lingwhite	Norf	TG0000	52°33·9'	0°57·5'E	X	144
Lingwood	Norf	TG3608	52°37·3'	1°29·6'E	T	134
Lingwood Common	Essex	TL7705	51°43·2'	0°34·1'E	X	167
Lingwood Fm	Cambs	TL4571	52°19·3'	0°8·1'E	FM	154
Lingwood Lodge	Norf	TG3709	52°37·8'	1°30·5'E	X	134
Lingyclose Head	Cumbr	NY3752	54°51·8'	2°58·5'W	X	85
Lingy Crag	Cumbr	NY4113	54°30·8'	2°54·3'W	X	90
Lingy Hill	Durham	NY8233	54°41·7'	2°16·3'W	X	91,92
Lingy Knowe	S Lanak	NT0251	55°44·8'	3°33·2'W	X	65,72
Lingy Moor	N Yks	NZ2503	54°25·6'	1°36·5'W	X	93
Lingy Pits Moss	Lancs	SD5950	53°56·9'	2°37·1'W	X	102
Linhay Meads	Hants	SU3325	51°1·6'	1°31·4'W	X	185
Linhead	Aberd	NJ6755	57°35·3'	2°32·7'W	X	29
Linhead	Fife	NT2088	56°4·9'	3°16·7'W	X	66
Linhead	Scot Bord	NT7871	55°56·1'	2°20·7'W	X	67
Linhope	Northum	NT9616	55°26·5'	2°3·4'W	T	81
Linhope	Scot Bord	NT4001	55°18·2'	2°56·3'W	T	79
Linhope Burn	Northum	NT9517	55°27·1'	2°4·3'W	W	81
Linhope Burn	Scot Bord	NT4100	55°17·7'	2°55·3'W	W	79
Linhope Spout	Northum	NT9517	55°27·1'	2°4·3'W	W	81
Linhouse Fm	Falk	NS9071	55°55·4'	3°45·2'W	FM	65
Linhouse Water	W Loth	NT0764	55°51·9'	3°28·7'W	W	65
Linicro	Highld	NG3967	57°37·3'	6°21·8'W	T	23
Lining Crag	Cumbr	NY2508	54°28·0'	3°9·0'W	X	89,90
Lining Crag	Cumbr	NY2811	54°29·6'	3°6·3'W	X	89,90
Link	N Som	ST4759	51°19·9'	2°45·3'W	T	172,182
Linkataing	Orkney	HY5539	59°14·4'	2°46·8'W	X	5
Link Burn	Highld	ND2969	58°36·5'	3°12·8'W	W	12
Link Cove	Cumbr	NY3711	54°29·7'	2°57·9'W	X	90
Linkend	Worcs	SO8331	51°58·9'	2°14·5'W	T	150
Linkenholt	Hants	SU3658	51°19·4'	1°28·6'W	T	174
Linkeylaw	Northum	NU0829	55°33·5'	1°52·0'W	X	75
Linkfield	Falk	NS8886	56°3·5'	3°47·5'W	X	65
Link Hall	York	SE6546	53°54·6'	1°0·2'W	X	105,106
Linkhall Moor	Northum	NU1521	55°29·2'	1°45·3'W	X	75
Linkhill	Kent	TQ8128	51°1·6'	0°35·3'E	T	188,199
Link Ho	Northum	NZ3179	55°6·5'	1°30·4'W	X	88
Linkholms	Pth & Kin	NO1946	56°36·2'	3°18·7'W	X	53
Link House	Kent	TQ8947	51°11·7'	0°42·7'E	X	189
Linkhouse	Northum	NU2230	55°34·0'	1°38·6'W	X	75
Link House Fm	Essex	TL7300	51°40·6'	0°30·5'E	FM	167
Link House Pier	Shetld	HU5190	60°35·7'	1°3·6'W	X	1,2
Linkim Shore	Scot Bord	NT9265	55°52·9'	2°7·2'W	X	67
Linkinhorne	Corn	SX3173	50°32·2'	4°22·7'W	T	201
Linkins Glen	D & G	NX7655	54°52·7'	3°55·5'W	X	84
Linklater	Orkney	ND4587	58°46·3'	2°56·6'W	T	7
Linklet	Orkney	HY7654	59°22·6'	2°24·9'W	T	5
Linklet Bay	Orkney	HY7754	59°22·6'	2°23·8'W	W	5
Links	Pth & Kin	NO1738	56°31·9'	3°20·5'W	X	53
Link Sands	Fife	NT2890	56°6·1'	3°9·0'W	X	59
Links Bay	Aberd	NJ5966	57°41·2'	2°40·8'W	W	29
Linksfield	Moray	NJ2264	57°39·8'	3°18·0'W	X	28
Link's Fm	Essex	TL8021	51°51·7'	0°37·2'E	FM	168
Linkshill	Aberd	NJ9022	57°17·6'	2°9·5'W	X	38
Links Ho	Cambs	TL6361	52°13·6'	0°23·6'E	X	154
Linksness	Orkney	HY2403	58°54·7'	3°18·7'W	X	6,7
Linksness	Orkney	HY5310	58°58·7'	2°48·6'W	T	6
Links Ness	Orkney	HY6129	59°9·0'	2°40·4'W	X	5
Links of Dunnet	Highld	ND2270	58°36·9'	3°20·1'W	X	7,12
Links of Greenland	Highld	ND2268	58°35·8'	3°20·0'W	X	11,12
Links of Machrihanish	Arg & Bt	NR6523	55°26·9'	5°42·5'W	X	68
Links of Montrose	Angus	NO7258	56°43·0'	2°27·0'W	X	54
Links of Old Tain	Highld	ND2168	58°35·8'	3°21·1'W	X	11,12
Links of Quendale	Shetld	HU3813	59°54·3'	1°18·7'W	X	4
Linkster	Shetld	HU4246	60°12·0'	1°14·0'W	X	4
Links, The	Aberd	NK0065	57°40·7'	1°59·5'W	X	30
Links, The	Fife	NO4918	56°21·4'	2°49·1'W	X	59
Links, The	Moray	NJ3664	57°39·9'	3°3·9'W	X	28
Links, The	Orkney	HY4349	59°19·7'	2°59·6'W	X	5
Links, The	Shrops	SJ7026	52°50·1'	2°26·3'W	X	127
Links Wood	Fife	NO4124	56°24·5'	2°56·9'W	F	54,59
Linktown	Fife	NT2790	56°6·1'	3°10·0'W	T	59
Linkumtoy Burn	S Ayr	NX2187	55°9·0'	4°48·1'W	W	76
Linkwood	Moray	NJ2361	57°38·2'	3°16·9'W	X	28
Link Wood	Suff	TL8960	52°12·6'	0°46·4'E	F	155
Linkylea	E Loth	NT5470	55°55·5'	2°43·7'W	X	66
Linlathen	C of Dun	NO4633	56°29·4'	2°52·2'W	X	54
Linley	Shrops	SO3592	52°31·6'	2°57·1'W	T	137
Linley	Shrops	SO6898	52°35·0'	2°27·9'W	X	138
Linley Big Wood	Shrops	SO3494	52°32·6'	2°58·0'W	F	137
Linley Brook	Shrops	SO6897	52°34·4'	2°27·9'W	T	138
Linley Fm	Wilts	ST8929	51°3·8'	2°9·0'W	FM	184
Linley Green	Heref	SO6953	52°10·7'	2°26·8'W	T	149
Linleygreen	Shrops	SO6898	52°35·0'	2°27·9'W	T	138
Linley Hall	Staffs	SJ8154	53°5·2'	2°16·6'W	X	118
Linley Hill	E Yorks	TA0646	53°54·2'	0°22·8'W	X	107

Linley Hill	Shrops	SO3594	52°32·6'	2°57·1'W	X	137
Linlithgow	W Loth	NT0076	55°58·3'	3°35·7'W	T	65
Linlithgow Bridge	W Loth	NS9877	55°58·8'	3°37·6'W	T	65
Linlithgow Loch	W Loth	NT0077	55°58·8'	3°35·7'W	W	65
Linmere Moss	Ches	SJ5470	53°13·7'	2°40·9'W	X	117
Linna Brake	Orkney	HY6328	59°8·5'	2°38·3'W	X	5
Linnabreck	Orkney	HY3022	59°5·0'	3°12·8'W	X	6
Linnacombe	Devon	SX5392	50°42·8'	4°4·6'W	X	191
Linna Dale	Orkney	HY3206	58°56·4'	3°10·4'W	X	6,7
Linn Burn	D & G	NS8002	55°18·1'	3°53·0'W	W	78
Linn Burn	Northum	NY8853	54°52·5'	2°10·8'W	W	87
Linn Burn	S Lanak	NT0225	55°30·8'	3°32·7'W	W	72
Linnburn Fm	Scot Bord	NT2740	55°39·1'	3°9·2'W	FM	73
Linnburn Hill	D & G	NX9295	55°14·5'	3°41·5'W	H	78
Linn Dean Water	Midlo	NT4659	55°49·5'	2°51·3'W	W	66,73
Linn Dhu	S Ayr	NX2281	55°5·7'	4°46·9'W	W	76
Linndhu Ho	Arg & Bt	NM5153	56°36·4'	6°3·0'W	X	47
Linne a' Dhuais	Arg & Bt	NM3921	56°18·8'	6°12·8'W	X	48
Linne Ghorm	Highld	NM7569	56°45·8'	5°40·4'W	W	40
Linnel Hill	Northum	NY9559	54°55·8'	2°4·3'W	X	87
Linnels	Northum	NY9561	54°56·9'	2°4·3'W	X	87
Linnel Wood	Northum	NY9559	54°55·8'	2°4·3'W	F	87
Linne Mhuirich	Arg & Bt	NR7284	55°59·9'	5°39·0'W	W	55
Linne na Craige	Arg & Bt	NM9533	56°26·9'	5°19·1'W	W	49
Linne nan Ribheid	Arg & Bt	NM3219	56°17·5'	6°19·4'W	W	48
Linneraineach	Highld	NC1209	58°2·1'	5°10·6'W	X	15
Linney	Pemb	SR8996	51°37·6'	5°2·5'W	X	158
Linney Burrows	Pemb	SR8997	51°38·2'	5°2·6'W	X	158
Linney Head	Pemb	SR8895	51°37·1'	5°3·4'W	X	158
Linngeam	N Eil	NB1433	58°11·8'	6°51·6'W	X	13
Linnhall	D & G	NY2282	55°7·8'	3°13·0'W	X	79
Linnhead	Aberd	NJ9824	57°18·7'	2°1·5'W	X	38
Linnhead	E Ayr	NS4353	55°45·0'	4°29·6'W	X	64
Linnhead Fm	S Lanak	NS8840	55°38·7'	3°46·3'W	FM	71,72
Linnheads	Northum	NY9386	55°10·3'	2°6·2'W	X	80
Linn Hill	D & G	NX6660	54°55·3'	4°5·0'W	H	83,84
Linn Hill	Pth & Kin	NO0308	56°15·5'	3°33·5'W	X	58
Linn Ho	D & G	NX3779	55°5·0'	4°32·8'W	X	77
Linnhous	W Loth	NT0662	55°50·8'	3°29·6'W	A	65
Linnhouse	D & G	NX8192	55°12·7'	3°51·8'W	X	78
Linnick	Corn	SX3280	50°36·0'	4°22·1'W	X	201
Linnie	Highld	NH5951	57°31·9'	4°20·8'W	T	26
Linnington	Somer	ST2907	50°51·7'	3°0·1'W	X	193
Linn Kern	Northum	NZ0596	55°15·7'	1°54·8'W	X	81
Linn Mill	Clackm	NS9292	56°6·8'	3°43·8'W	X	58
Linn Mill	D & G	NY1176	55°4·5'	3°23·2'W	X	85
Linnmill	S Lanak	NS8443	55°40·3'	3°50·2'W	X	71,72
Linn Moor Home	C of Aber	NJ8202	57°6·8'	2°17·4'W	X	38
Linn of Avon	Moray	NJ1707	57°9·0'	3°21·9'W	W	36
Linn of Barnoise	D & G	NX3462	54°55·8'	4°35·0'W	X	82
Linn of Corriemulzie	Aberd	NO1189	56°59·3'	3°27·4'W	W	43
Linn of Dee	Aberd	NO0689	56°59·2'	3°32·4'W	W	43
Linn of Muick Cottage	Aberd	NO3389	56°59·5'	3°5·7'W	X	44
Linn of Muick (Waterfall)	Aberd	NO3389	56°59·5'	3°5·7'W	W	44
Linn of Pattack	Highld	NN5587	56°57·4'	4°22·6'W	X	42
Linn of Quoich	Aberd	NO1191	57°0·4'	3°27·5'W	W	43
Linn of Tummel	Pth & Kin	NN9159	56°42·9'	3°46·4'W	W	52
Linnorie	Aberd	NJ5239	57°26·6'	2°47·5'W	X	29
Linn Park	C of Glas	NS5859	55°48·5'	4°15·5'W	X	64
Linns	Angus	NO1970	56°49·1'	3°19·2'W	T	43
Linns	D & G	NY0476	55°4·4'	3°29·8'W	X	84
Linns	Falk	NS7581	56°0·6'	3°59·9'W	X	64
Linns Burn	D & G	NY0475	55°3·9'	3°29·8'W	W	84
Linn's Grave	D & G	NX2472	55°0·9'	4°44·7'W	A	76
Linnshalloch	S Ayr	NX4097	55°14·7'	4°30·6'W	H	77
Linnshaw Burn	N Ayr	NS2359	55°47·8'	4°49·0'W	W	63
Linnside	S Lanak	NS8347	55°42·4'	3°51·3'W	X	72
Linns Knowe	D & G	NY4093	55°13·9'	2°56·2'W	X	79
Linn Slack	D & G	NT2702	55°18·7'	3°8·6'W	X	79
Linns, The	D & G	NY1681	55°7·2'	3°18·6'W	X	79
Linn, The	Moray	NJ2548	57°31·2'	3°14·7'W	W	28
Linn, The	Northum	NY7273	55°3·3'	2°25·9'W	X	86,87
Linn Water	E Ayr	NS5207	55°20·3'	4°19·6'W	W	70,77
Linnyshaw	Salf	SD7403	53°31·6'	2°23·1'W	T	109
Linplum Ho	E Loth	NT5570	55°55·5'	2°42·8'W	X	66
Linross	Angus	NO3549	56°38·0'	3°3·1'W	X	54
Linscott	Devon	SS5427	51°1·7'	4°4·5'W	X	180
Linscott	Devon	SX7387	50°40·3'	3°47·5'W	X	191
Linsgreave	Cald	SD9914	53°37·6'	2°0·5'W	X	109
Linshart	Aberd	NK0346	57°30·5'	1°56·5'W	X	30
Linshiels	Northum	NT8906	55°21·1'	2°10·0'W	X	80
Linshiels Lake	Northum	NT8904	55°20·0'	2°10·0'W	W	80
Linshire Copse	Northnts	SP7042	52°4·5'	0°58·3'W	F	152
Linsiadar	N Eil	NB2131	58°11·0'	6°44·3'W	T	8,13
Linsidecroy	Highld	NH5598	57°57·1'	4°26·5'W	X	21
Linsidemore	Highld	NH5499	57°57·6'	4°27·6'W	T	21
Linskeldfield	Cumbr	NY1734	54°41·9'	3°16·9'W	X	89,90
Linslade	Beds	SP9125	51°55·2'	0°40·2'W	T	165
Linstead Fm	Suff	TM3176	52°20·2'	1°23·9'E	FM	156
Linstead Hall	Suff	TM3276	52°20·2'	1°24·7'E	X	156
Linstead Parva	Suff	TM3377	52°20·7'	1°25·7'E	X	156
Linsteads	Essex	TL6413	51°47·7'	0°23·1'E	X	167
Linstock	Cumbr	NY4258	54°55·0'	2°53·9'W	T	85
Linstock Ho	Cumbr	NY4258	54°55·0'	2°53·9'W	X	85
Lint	Northum	NT9336	55°37·3'	2°6·2'W	X	74,75
Lintalee	Scot Bord	NT6418	55°27·5'	2°33·7'W	X	80
Lint Brae	Orkney	HY4006	58°56·5'	3°2·1'W	X	6,7
Lintfield Bank	S Lanak	NS8335	55°35·9'	3°51·0'W	X	71,72
Linthaugh	Aberd	NJ4720	57°16·3'	2°52·3'W	X	37
Linthaugh	S Lanak	NS7547	55°42·3'	3°58·9'W	X	64
Linthill	Scot Bord	NT5426	55°31·8'	2°43·3'W	X	73
Linthill	Scot Bord	NT9263	55°51·9'	2°7·2'W	X	67
Linthills	Renf	NS3459	55°48·0'	4°38·5'W	X	63
Linthorpe	Midd	NZ4818	54°33·5'	1°15·0'W	T	93
Linthouse	C of Glas	NS5466	55°52·2'	4°19·6'W	X	64
Linthurst	Worcs	SO9972	52°21·0'	2°0·5'W	T	139
Linthwaite	Kirk	SE1014	53°37·6'	1°50·5'W	T	110
Lint Lands	Northum	NT9016	55°26·5'	2°9·1'W	H	80
Lintlaw	Scot Bord	NT8257	55°48·6'	2°16·8'W	X	67,74
Lintlaw Burn	Scot Bord	NT8358	55°49·1'	2°15·8'W	W	67,74

Lintley	Northum	NY6851	54°51·4'	2°29·5'W	X	86,87
Lint Lochs	Highld	ND3769	58°36·5'	3°4·6'W	W	12
Lintmill	Aberd	NK0250	57°32·7'	1°57·5'W	X	30
Lintmill	Moray	NJ5165	57°40·6'	2°48·8'W	T	29
Lintmill of Boyne	Aberd	NJ6064	57°40·1'	2°39·8'W	X	29
Lintmiln	Stir	NS6192	56°6·3'	4°13·7'W	X	57
Linton	Cambs	TL5646	52°5·6'	0°17·0'E	T	154
Linton	Derby	SK2716	52°44·7'	1°35·6'W	T	128
Linton	Devon	SS2318	50°56·3'	4°30·8'W	X	190
Linton	Heref	SO6625	51°55·6'	2°29·3'W	T	162
Linton	Kent	TQ7549	51°13·0'	0°30·7'E	T	188
Linton	Leeds	SE3846	53°54·8'	1°24·9'W	T	104
Linton	Northum	NZ2691	55°13·0'	1°35·1'W	T	81
Linton	N Yks	SD9962	54°3·5'	2°0·5'W	T	98
Linton	Orkney	HY5218	59°3·0'	2°49·7'W	X	6
Linton	Scot Bord	NT7726	55°31·9'	2°21·4'W	X	74
Linton	Somer	ST0341	51°9·8'	3°22·9'W	X	181
Linton Burn	Northum	NZ2692	55°13·5'	1°35·0'W	W	81
Linton Burnfoot	Scot Bord	NT7825	55°31·3'	2°20·5'W	X	74
Linton Court	Fife	NT2787	56°4·5'	3°9·9'W	X	66
Linton Covert	Scot Bord	NT7727	55°32·4'	2°21·4'W	F	74
Linton Fm	Glos	SO7919	51°52·4'	2°17·9'W	FM	162
Linton Fm	Scot Bord	NT7726	55°31·9'	2°21·4'W	FM	74
Linton Heath	Derby	SK2816	52°44·7'	1°34·7'W	T	128
Linton Hill	Dorset	SY5884	50°39·5'	2°35·3'W	H	194
Linton Hill	Heref	SO6624	51°55·0'	2°29·3'W	T	162
Linton Hill	Scot Bord	NT7827	55°32·4'	2°20·5'W	H	74
Linton Hills	Leeds	SE3847	53°55·3'	1°24·9'W	X	104
Linton Ho	Aberd	NJ7010	57°11·0'	2°29·3'W	X	38
Linton Ings	Leeds	SE3947	53°55·3'	1°24·0'W	X	104
Linton Lock	N Yks	SE4960	54°2·3'	1°14·7'W	X	100
Linton Moor	N Yks	SD9761	54°2·9'	2°2·3'W	X	98
Linton Muir	Scot Bord	NT1554	55°46·6'	3°20·9'W	X	65,72
Linton-on-Ouse	N Yks	SE4960	54°2·3'	1°14·7'W	T	100
Linton-on-Ouse Airfield	N Yks	SE4861	54°2·8'	1°15·6'W	X	100
Linton Park	Kent	TQ7549	51°13·0'	0°30·7'E	X	188
Linton Springs (Hotel)	Leeds	SE3748	53°55·8'	1°25·8'W	X	104
Linton Wold	N Yks	SE9071	54°7·9'	0°36·9'W	X	101
Linton Wold Fm	N Yks	SE9070	54°7·3'	0°37·0'W	FM	101
Linton Wood	Heref	SO6626	51°56·1'	2°29·3'W	F	162
Linton Woods	N Yks	SE5062	54°3·3'	1°13·8'W	X	100
Lintpots	Moray	NJ3052	57°33·4'	3°9·7'W	X	28
Lintrathen Lodge	Angus	NO2853	56°40·1'	3°10·0'W	X	53
Lintridge	Glos	SO7432	51°59·4'	2°22·3'W	T	150
Lintrigs	Aberd	NJ9338	57°26·2'	2°6·5'W	X	30
Lintrose Ho	Pth & Kin	NO2237	56°31·4'	3°15·6'W	X	53
Lintseedridge Fm	N Ayr	NS2951	55°43·6'	4°42·9'W	FM	63
Lints Tor	Devon	SX5887	50°40·2'	4°0·2'W	H	191
Lintz	Durham	NZ1656	54°54·2'	1°44·6'W	T	88
Lintzford	Ghead	NZ1457	54°54·7'	1°46·5'W	T	88
Lintzford Wood	Ghead	NZ1457	54°54·7'	1°46·5'W	F	88
Lintzgarth	Durham	NY9242	54°46·6'	2°7·0'W	T	87
Lintzgarth Common	Durham	NY9142	54°46·6'	2°8·0'W	X	87
Lintz Green	Durham	NZ1556	54°54·2'	1°45·5'W	X	88
Lintz Hall Fm	Durham	NZ1555	54°53·6'	1°45·5'W	FM	88
Linwood	Hants	SU1809	50°53·0'	1°44·3'W	T	195
Linwood	Lincs	TF1086	53°21·8'	0°20·4'W	T	113,121
Linwood	Renf	NS4464	55°50·9'	4°29·1'W	T	64
Linwood Fm	Hants	SU1809	50°53·0'	1°44·3'W	FM	195
Linwood Hall Fm	Lincs	TF1260	53°7·8'	0°19·2'W	FM	121
Linwood Ho	Cambs	TL4093	52°31·2'	0°4·2'E	X	142,143
Linwood Moor	Lincs	TF1160	53°7·8'	0°20·1'W	X	121
Linwood Moss	Renf	NS4365	55°51·4'	4°30·1'W	X	64
Linwood Warren	Lincs	TF1387	53°22·3'	0°17·7'W	F	113,121
Lioag	Shetld	HT9639	60°8·4'	2°3·8'W	X	4
Lionacleit	N Eil	NF7849	57°25·3'	7°21·4'W	T	22
Lionacuidhe	N Eil	NF7546	57°23·6'	7°24·2'W	T	22
Lional	N Eil	NB5363	58°29·4'	6°13·8'W	T	8
Lion Fm	Suff	TM1574	52°19·5'	1°9·7'E	FM	144,156
Liongam	N Eil	NA9919	58°3·7'	7°5·8'W	X	13
Lion Hill	S Lanak	NS9710	55°22·6'	3°37·1'W	H	78
Lion Ho	E Susx	TQ6008	50°51·2'	0°16·8'E	X	199
Lion Inn, The	N Yks	SE6799	54°23·2'	0°57·7'W	X	94,100
Lionlane Wood	Shrops	SJ4038	52°56·4'	2°53·2'W	F	126
Lion Lodge	Dorset	SY9398	50°47·1'	2°5·6'W	X	195
Lion Lodges	Staffs	SJ9623	52°48·5'	2°1·4'W	X	127
Lion Rock	Corn	SW6812	49°58·0'	5°13·7'W	X	203
Lion Rock	Gwyn	SH5750	53°1·9'	4°7·5'W	X	115
Lion Rock	I Scilly	SV9118	49°59·2'	6°18·3'W	X	203
Lion's Den	Corn	SW7011	49°57·5'	5°12·0'W	X	203
Lion's Den	E Yorks	SE9635	53°48·4'	0°32·1'W	X	106
Lion's Den	Staffs	SK0118	52°45·8'	1°58·7'W	X	128
Lion's Den	Suff	TM3049	52°5·7'	1°21·9'E	X	169
Lion's Face	Aberd	NO1691	57°0·4'	3°22·5'W	X	43
Lions Green	E Susx	TQ5518	50°56·7'	0°12·8'E	T	199
Lion's Head	Aberd	NJ8366	57°41·3'	2°16·6'W	X	29,30
Lions Hill	Dorset	SU1004	50°50·4'	1°51·1'W	X	195
Lion's Mouth	Norf	TG1840	52°55·0'	1°15·0'E	X	133
Lion, The	N Ayr	NS1754	55°44·9'	4°54·5'W	X	63
Lion Wharf	Essex	TQ9294	51°36·9'	0°46·8'E	X	168,178
Lipe Hill	Somer	ST1821	50°59·2'	3°9·7'W	X	181,193
Lipgate Fm	Somer	ST7237	51°8·1'	2°23·6'W	FM	183
Liphook	Hants	SU8431	51°4·6'	0°47·7'W	T	186
Lipley	Shrops	SJ7331	52°52·8'	2°23·7'W	T	127
Lipley Fm	Shrops	SJ7431	52°52·8'	2°22·8'W	FM	127
Lipley Hall Fm	Shrops	SJ7330	52°52·2'	2°23·7'W	FM	127
Lippen Cotts	Hants	SU6324	51°0·9'	1°5·7'W	X	185
Lippering Fm	W Susx	SZ8199	50°47·3'	0°50·7'W	FM	197
Lippetts Fm	Worcs	SO7464	52°16·6'	2°22·5'W	FM	138,150
Lippitts Hill	Essex	TQ3996	51°39·0'	0°0·9'E	T	166,177
Lipton Fm	Devon	SX7947	50°18·9'	3°41·6'W	FM	202
Lipwood Hall	Northum	NY8164	54°58·5'	2°17·4'W	X	86,87
Lipwood Well	Northum	NY8264	54°58·5'	2°16·4'W	X	86,87
Lipyeate	Somer	ST6750	51°15·1'	2°28·0'W	T	183
Lipyeate Ho	Somer	ST6850	51°15·1'	2°27·1'W	X	183
Liquo or Bowhousebog	N Lanak	NS8558	55°48·4'	3°49·7'W	T	65,72
Lisburne Fm	Devon	SX7359	50°25·3'	3°46·9'W	FM	202
Liscard	Wirral	SJ3092	53°25·5'	3°2·8'W	T	108
Liscleugh	S Lanak	NS8621	55°28·4'	3°47·8'W	X	71,72
Liscoe Fm	Lancs	SD3840	53°51·4'	2°56·1'W	FM	102

Lisco Fm	Cumbr	NY3627	54°38·3'	2°59·1'W	FM	90
Liscombe	Devon	SS8727	51°2·1'	3°36·3'W	X	181
Liscombe	Somer	SS8732	51°4·8'	3°36·4'W	X	181
Liscombe Ho	Bucks	SP8825	51°55·2'	0°42·8'W	A	165
Liscombe Park	Bucks	SP8825	51°55·2'	0°42·8'W	X	165
Lisgear Mhòr	N Eil	HW8133	59°7·9'	5°49·2'W	X	8
Lishaw Burn	Northum	NY5984	55°9·2'	2°38·2'W	W	80
Lishaw Rigg	Northum	NY6086	55°10·3'	2°37·2'W	H	80
Lisieux Hall	Lancs	SD5721	53°41·3'	2°38·7'W	X	102
Liskeard	Corn	SX2564	50°27·2'	4°27·5'W	T	201
Lisle Court	Hants	SZ3495	50°45·4'	1°30·7'W	X	196
Lisles Burn	Northum	NY9186	55°10·3'	2°8·0'W	W	80
Lismore	Arg & Bt	NM8441	56°30·9'	5°30·2'W	X	49
Lismore	Arg & Bt	NM8845	56°33·2'	5°26·5'W	X	49
Liss	Hants	SU7827	51°2·5'	0°52·9'W	T	186,197
Lissens Moss	N Ayr	NS3346	55°41·0'	4°38·9'W	X	63
Lisset Br	E Yorks	TA1356	53°59·5'	0°16·2'W	X	107
Lissett	E Yorks	TA1458	54°0·6'	0°15·2'W	T	107
Liss Forest	Hants	SU7828	51°3·0'	0°52·8'W	T	186,197
Lissington	Lincs	TF1083	53°20·2'	0°20·5'W	T	121
Lisson Grove	C of West	TQ2782	51°31·6'	0°9·8'W	T	176
Listean	N Eil	NB5164	58°29·9'	6°15·9'W	X	8
Listercombe Bottom	Glos	SP0612	51°48·6'	1°54·4'W	F	163
Listerdale	Roth	SK4691	53°25·1'	1°18·1'W	T	111
Lister Ho	N Yks	SE3372	54°8·8'	1°29·3'W	X	99
Lister Institute	Herts	TQ1695	51°38·7'	0°19·0'W	X	166,176
Listock	Somer	ST3223	51°0·4'	2°57·8'W	T	193
Listoft	Lincs	TF5172	53°13·6'	0°16·1'E	T	122
Liston	Essex	TL8544	52°4·0'	0°42·3'E	T	155
Liston Garden	Essex	TL8445	52°4·6'	0°41·5'E	T	155
Liston Hall Fm	Essex	TL7631	51°57·2'	0°34·1'E	FM	167
Listonshiels	C of Edin	NT1361	55°50·3'	3°22·9'W	X	65
Lists Ho	N Yks	SE5274	54°9·8'	1°11·8'W	X	100
Lisvane	Card	ST1883	51°32·6'	3°10·6'W	T	171
Liswerry	Newp	ST3487	51°34·9'	2°56·8'W	T	171
Litchadon Fm	Devon	SS6930	51°3·5'	3°51·8'W	FM	180
Litcham	Norf	TF8817	52°43·3'	0°47·4'E	T	132
Litcham Common (Nature Reserve)	Norf	TF8817	52°43·3'	0°47·4'E	X	132
Litcham Heath	Norf	TF8619	52°44·4'	0°45·7'E	X	132
Litchard	Brig	SS9081	51°31·3'	3°34·7'W	T	170
Litchardon	Devon	SS5229	51°2·7'	4°6·3'W	X	180
Litchborough	Northnts	SP6354	52°11·1'	1°4·3'W	T	152
Litchborough Ho	Northnts	SP6254	52°11·1'	1°5·2'W	X	152
Litchfield	Hants	SU4653	51°16·7'	1°20·0'W	T	185
Litchfield Fm	Oxon	SP3624	51°55·0'	1°28·2'W	FM	164
Litchfield Grange	Hants	SU5345	51°12·3'	1°14·1'W	X	185
Litchmere Fm	Norf	TM3694	52°29·8'	1°29·0'E	FM	134
Litchurch	C of Derb	SK3635	52°54·9'	1°27·5'W	T	128
Litfield Fm	Derby	SK3980	53°19·2'	1°24·5'W	FM	110,111
Litharge	Northum	NY9154	54°53·1'	2°8·0'W	X	87
Litherland	Sefton	SJ3398	53°28·7'	3°0·2'W	T	108
Litherskew	N Yks	SD8991	54°19·1'	2°9·7'W	X	98
Lithiack	Corn	SX3558	50°24·2'	4°18·9'W	X	201
Lith Sgeir	N Eil	NB5166	58°30·9'	6°16·1'W	X	8
Litigan	Pth & Kin	NN7649	56°37·2'	4°0·8'W	X	51,52
Litla Billan	Shetld	HU5355	60°16·8'	1°2·0'W	X	3
Litlagill	Shetld	HU4866	60°22·8'	1°7·3'W	X	2,3
Litlapund	Shetld	HU2053	60°15·9'	1°37·8'W	X	3
Litla Stack	Shetld	HU1754	60°16·5'	1°41·1'W	X	3
Litla Water	Shetld	HU4585	60°33·0'	1°10·3'W	W	1,2,3
Litley	Staffs	SJ9942	52°58·8'	2°0·5'W	X	118
Litley Court	Heref	SO5339	52°3·1'	2°40·7'W	X	149
Litley Fm	Ches	SJ6980	53°19·2'	2°27·5'W	FM	109
Litlington	Cambs	TL3142	52°3·9'	0°4·9'W	T	153
Litlington	E Susx	TQ5201	50°47·5'	0°9·8'E	T	199
Litmarsh	Heref	SO5249	52°8·5'	2°41·7'W	T	149
Littaford Tors	Devon	SX6176	50°34·3'	3°57·4'W	X	191
Litterty	Aberd	NJ7854	57°34·8'	2°21·6'W	X	29,30
Little Abbot's Fm	Surrey	TQ2147	51°12·8'	0°15·7'W	FM	187
Little Abington	Cambs	TL5349	52°7·3'	0°14·5'E	T	154
Little Acre Fm	Wilts	SU2574	51°28·1'	1°38·0'W	FM	174
Little Acton Fm	Worcs	SO8568	52°18·8'	2°12·8'W	FM	139
Little Addington	Northnts	SP9573	52°21·0'	0°35·9'W	T	141,153
Little Aiden	Arg & Bt	NS2380	55°59·1'	4°49·8'W	X	63
Little Ailsa	S Ayr	NX0199	55°15·0'	5°7·4'W	X	76
Little Airies	D & G	NW9867	54°57·7'	5°8·9'W	X	82
Little Airies	D & G	NX4248	54°48·4'	4°27·1'W	X	83
Little Airmyn	E Yorks	SE7225	53°43·2'	0°54·1'W	T	105,106
Little Aitnoch	Highld	NH9640	57°26·6'	3°43·5'W	X	27
Little Allamoor	Notts	SK6057	53°6·6'	1°5·8'W	X	120
Little Allt Bheithachan	Moray	NJ1511	57°11·2'	3°23·9'W	W	36
Little Alms Cliff or Almias Cliff	N Yks	SE2352	53°58·1'	1°38·5'W	X	104
Little Almshoe	Herts	TL1925	51°54·9'	0°15·8'W	T	166
Little Alne	Warw	SP1361	52°15·1'	1°48·2'W	T	151
Little Altcar	Sefton	SD3006	53°33·0'	3°3·0'W	T	108
Little Ambrook	Devon	SX8165	50°28·6'	3°40·3'W	A	202
Little Ann	Hants	SU3343	51°11·3'	1°31·3'W	T	185
Little Ansty or Pleck	Dorset	ST7604	50°50·3'	2°20·1'W	X	194
Little Antron	Corn	SW6327	50°6·0'	5°18·5'W	X	203
Little Appledore	Kent	TR0429	51°1·7'	0°54·9'E	X	189
Little Ardinn	Aberd	NJ7548	57°31·5'	2°24·6'W	X	29
Little Ardo	Aberd	NJ8538	57°26·2'	2°14·5'W	X	30
Little Ardrone	Moray	NJ4551	57°33·0'	2°54·7'W	X	28,29
Little Ardyne	Arg & Bt	NS1069	55°52·9'	5°1·8'W	X	63
Little Argham	E Yorks	TA1070	54°7·1'	0°18·6'W	X	101
Little Arnage	Aberd	NJ9333	57°23·5'	2°6·5'W	X	30
Little Arnewood Ho	Hants	SZ2796	50°46·0'	1°36·6'W	X	195
Little Arnot	Pth & Kin	NO2101	56°12·0'	3°16·0'W	X	58
Little Arowry	Wrex	SJ4540	52°57·5'	2°48·7'W	T	117
Little Arram	E Yorks	TA1749	53°55·7'	0°12·7'W	X	107
Little Arrow	Cumbr	SD2895	54°21·0'	3°6·0'W	X	96,97
Little Arrow	Heref	SO4856	52°12·2'	2°45·3'W	W	148,149
Little Arrow Moor	Cumbr	SD2796	54°21·5'	3°7·0'W	X	96,97
Little Asby	Cumbr	NY6909	54°28·8'	2°28·3'W	T	91
Little Ashcombe	Somer	SS7840	51°9·0'	3°44·3'W	X	180
Little Ashfold	W Susx	TQ2727	51°1·9'	0°10·9'W	X	187,198
Little Ashley	Wilts	ST8162	51°21·6'	2°16·0'W	T	173
Little Assynt	Highld	NC1524	58°10·2'	5°8·3'W	X	15

Little Aston	Staffs	SK0900	52°36·1′	1°51·6′W	T	139
Little Atherfield	I of W	SZ4680	50°37·3′	1°20·6′W	T	196
Little Atwick	E Yorks	TA1849	53°55·7′	0°11·8′W	X	107
Little Auchenfad Hill	D & G	NX9568	55°0·0′	3°38·1′W	H	84
Little Auchengibbert	E Ayr	NS5819	55°26·9′	4°14·3′W	X	71
Little Auchinstilloch	E Ayr	NS7531	55°33·7′	3°58·5′W	X	71
Little Auchmillie	Aberd	NJ5864	57°40·1′	2°41·8′W	X	29
Little Auchnarie	Aberd	NJ9054	57°34·8′	2°9·6′W	X	30
Little Avon River	Glos	ST7094	51°38·9′	2°25·6′W	W	162,172
Little Ayre	Orkney	ND3092	58°48·9′	3°12·2′W	X	7
Little-ayre	Shetld	HU3262	60°20·7′	1°24·7′W	X	3
Little Ayton	N Yks	NZ5710	54°29·2′	1°6·8′W	T	93
Little Bache Ho	Ches	SJ6155	53°5·7′	2°34·5′W	X	118
Little Baddow	Essex	TL7707	51°44·2′	0°34·2′E	T	167
Little Baddow Hall	Essex	TL7608	51°44·8′	0°33·4′E	A	167
Little Badminton	S Glos	ST8084	51°33·5′	2°16·9′W	T	173
Little Bainden Fm	E Susx	TQ6026	51°0·9′	0°17·3′E	FM	188,199
Little Baldon Fm	Oxon	SU5698	51°40·9′	1°11·0′W	FM	164
Little Ballia Clett	Shetld	HU3282	60°31·5′	1°24·5′W	X	1,3
Little Ballinluig	Pth & Kin	NN9152	56°39·1′	3°46·2′W	T	52
Little Ballo	Fife	NO2205	56°14·1′	3°15·1′W	X	58
Little Ballo	Pth & Kin	NO2634	56°29·8′	3°11·7′W	X	53
Little Balloch Hill	Aberd	NJ4949	57°32·0′	2°50·6′W	H	28,29
Little Balloch Hill	Moray	NJ3433	57°23·2′	3°5·4′W	H	28
Little Balmae	D & G	NX6944	54°46·7′	4°1·8′W	X	83,84
Little Balquhomrie	Fife	NO2303	56°13·1′	3°14·1′W	X	58
Little Balvie	E Dunb	NS5275	55°57·0′	4°21·8′W	X	64
Little Bamff	Pth & Kin	NO2252	56°39·5′	3°15·9′W	X	53
Little Bampton	Cumbr	NY2655	54°53·3′	3°8·8′W	T	85
Little Bank	Fife	NO2419	56°21·7′	3°13·4′W	X	59
Littlebank	N Yks	SD7962	54°3·5′	2°18·8′W	X	98
Little Bardfield	Essex	TL6530	51°56·9′	0°24·4′E	T	167
Little Barford	Beds	TL1856	52°11·6′	0°16·0′W	T	153
Little Barn	W Susx	SU8121	50°59·2′	0°50·4′W	X	197
Little Barningham	Norf	TG1333	52°51·4′	1°10·2′E	T	133
Little Barnsley Fm	Shrops	SO7592	52°31·8′	2°21·7′W	FM	138
Little Barone	Arg & Bt	NS0764	55°50·1′	5°4·5′W	X	63
Little Barras	Aberd	NO8178	56°53·8′	2°18·3′W	X	45
Little Barrington	Glos	SP2012	51°48·6′	1°42·2′W	T	163
Little Barrington Hall Fm	Essex	TL5419	51°51·1′	0°14·6′E	FM	167
Little Barrow	Ches	SJ4670	53°13·7′	2°48·1′W	T	117
Little Barrow	Glos	SP2029	51°57·8′	1°42·1′W	X	163
Little Barton	Devon	SS2423	50°59·0′	4°30·1′W	X	190
Little Barton Fm	Devon	SY0298	50°46·6′	3°23·0′W	FM	192
Little Barton Fm	Kent	TR1657	51°16·5′	1°6·2′E	FM	179
Little Barugh	N Yks	SE7679	54°12·3′	0°49·7′W	T	100
Little Bavington	Northum	NY9878	55°6·0′	2°1·5′W	T	87
Little Bayhall	Kent	TQ6139	51°7·9′	0°18·5′E	X	188
Little Bayham	E Susx	TQ6336	51°6·2′	0°20·1′E	T	188
Little Bay Point	Pemb	SM7305	51°42·1′	5°16·7′W	X	157
Little Bealings	Suff	TM2347	52°4·8′	1°15·7′E	T	169
Littlebeck	Cumbr	NY6219	54°34·1′	2°34·8′W	X	91
Little Beck	NE Lincs	TA2107	53°33·0′	0°10·0′W	X	113
Little Beck	N Yks	NZ8401	54°24·1′	0°41·9′W	W	94
Little Beck	N Yks	NZ8706	54°26·8′	0°39·1′W	W	94
Littlebeck	N Yks	NZ8804	54°25·7′	0°38·2′W	X	94
Little Beck	N Yks	SE7591	54°18·8′	0°50·4′W	W	94,100
Littlebeck Fm	Norf	TM2897	52°31·6′	1°22·1′E	FM	134
Little Beckford	Worcs	SO9734	52°0·5′	2°2·2′W	T	150
Little Beck Wood	N Yks	NZ8804	54°25·7′	0°38·2′W	F	94
Little Bedwyn	Wilts	SU2965	51°23·2′	1°34·6′W	T	174
Little Beeby	Leic	SK6607	52°39·6′	1°1·0′W	X	141
Little Beech Hill	N Yks	SE4297	54°22·2′	1°20·8′W	X	99
Little Bendauch	C of Aber	NJ8314	57°13·2′	2°16·4′W	X	38
Little Bendysh Wood	Essex	TL6139	52°1·8′	0°21·2′E	F	154
Little Bennane	S Ayr	NX1086	55°8·2′	4°58·4′W	X	76
Little Bentley	Essex	TM1125	51°53·2′	1°4·4′E	T	168,169
Little Bentley Hall	Essex	TM1224	51°52·7′	1°5·2′E	X	168,169
Little Benton Fm	N upon Ty	NZ2867	55°0·1′	1°33·3′W	FM	88
Little Berkamstead	Herts	TL2908	51°45·6′	0°7·5′W	T	166
Little Bernera	N Eil	NB1440	58°15·6′	6°52·1′W	X	13
Little Berry Burn	Moray	NJ0643	57°28·3′	3°33·6′W	W	27
Little Biggin Common	Cambs	TL6241	52°2·8′	0°22·1′E	X	154
Little Billia Fiold	Orkney	HY3421	59°4·5′	3°8·6′W	X	6
Little Billing	Northnts	SP8062	52°15·3′	0°49·3′W	T	152
Little Billington	Beds	SP9322	51°53·6′	0°38·5′W	T	165
Little Bin	Moray	NJ4864	57°40·0′	2°51·8′W	H	28,29
Little Bin	Stir	NS6782	56°1·0′	4°7·6′W	H	57,64
Little Birch	Heref	SO5131	51°58·8′	2°42·4′W	T	149
Little Birch Holt Fm	Essex	TL9121	51°51·5′	0°46·8′E	FM	168
Little Bispham	Blackp	SD3141	53°51·9′	3°2·5′W	T	102
Little Bittering Village	Norf	TF9417	52°43·2′	0°52·8′E	A	132
Little Bixbottom Fm	Oxon	SU7386	51°34·3′	0°56·4′W	FM	175
Little Black Hill	Angus	NO4574	56°51·5′	2°53·7′W	H	44
Little Black Hill	Devon	SS7845	51°11·7′	3°44·4′W	H	180
Little Black Hill	Heref	SO2832	51°59·1′	3°2·5′W	H	161
Little Blackton	Aberd	NJ6558	57°36·9′	2°34·7′W	X	29
Little Blairlusk	W Dunb	NS4184	56°1·6′	4°32·6′W	X	56,64
Little Blakenham	Suff	TM1048	52°5·7′	1°4·3′E	T	155,169
Little Blakesware	Herts	TL4017	51°50·3′	0°2·3′E	X	167
Little Blakey Howe	N Yks	SE6899	54°23·2′	0°56·8′W	A	94,100
Little Bleak Law	Scot Bord	NT3314	55°25·2′	3°3·1′W	H	79
Little Blencow	Cumbr	NY4532	54°41·1′	2°50·8′W	T	90
Little Blithe	Staffs	SK0921	52°47·4′	1°51·6′W	W	128
Little Bloxwich	Wals	SK0003	52°37·7′	1°59·6′W	T	139
Little Blunts	Essex	TQ6797	51°39·0′	0°25·2′E	X	167,177
Little Boarzell	E Susx	TQ7128	51°1·8′	0°26·7′E	X	188,199
Little Bogburn	Aberd	NO7882	56°56·0′	2°21·2′W	X	45
Little Bog Hill	S Lanak	NT0415	55°25·4′	3°30·6′W	H	78
Little Bognor	W Susx	TQ0020	50°58·5′	0°34·1′W	T	197
Little Bolas	Shrops	SJ6321	52°47·4′	2°32·5′W	X	127
Little Bolehill	Derby	SK2954	53°5·2′	1°33·6′W	T	119
Little Bollington	Ches	SJ7286	53°22·4′	2°24·8′W	T	109
Little Bolton	Salf	SJ7898	53°28·9′	2°19·5′W	T	109
Little Bonnet of Lorn or Sidhean an Aoinidh Bhig	Highld	NM6750	56°35·3′	5°47·2′W	X	49
Little Bonny Cliff	N Yks	NZ5001	54°24·4′	1°13·4′W	X	93
Little Bookham	Surrey	TQ1254	51°16·7′	0°23·3′W	T	187
Little Bookham Common	Surrey	TQ1256	51°17·8′	0°23·2′W	X	187
Littleborough	Devon	SS8210	50°52·9′	3°40·3′W	T	191
Littleborough	Notts	SK8282	53°19·9′	0°45·7′W	T	121
Littleborough	Roch	SD9316	53°38·7′	2°5·9′W	T	109
Little Bosullow	Corn	SW4133	50°8·7′	5°37·1′W	T	203
Littlebourne	Kent	TR2057	51°16·4′	1°9·6′E	T	179
Little Bourton	Oxon	SP4544	52°5·8′	1°20·2′W	T	151
Little Bouts Fm	Worcs	SP0258	52°13·4′	1°57·8′W	FM	150
Little Bovey	Devon	SX8376	50°34·6′	3°38·8′W	X	191
Little Bowden	Leic	SP7487	52°28·8′	0°54·2′W	T	141
Little Bowden Lodge Fm	Leic	SP7587	52°28·8′	0°53·3′W	FM	141
Little Box	Glos	SO6807	51°45·9′	2°27·4′W	X	162
Little Boys Heath	Bucks	SU9098	51°40·6′	0°41·5′W	T	165
Little Boyton Hall	Essex	TL6410	51°46·1′	0°23·0′E	X	167
Little Bradley	Suff	TL6852	52°8·7′	0°27·7′E	T	154
Little Bradley Wood	Wilts	ST7941	51°10·3′	2°17·6′W	F	183
Little Braiswick	Essex	TL9827	51°54·6′	0°53·1′E	X	168
Little Braithwaite	Cumbr	NY2323	54°36·0′	3°11·1′W	T	89,90
Little Brampton	Heref	SO3061	52°14·8′	3°1·1′W	A	137,148
Little Brampton	Shrops	SO3681	52°25·6′	2°56·1′W	T	137
Little Bratt-houll	Shetld	HP5100	60°41·1′	1°3·5′W	X	1
Little Braxted	Essex	TL8314	51°47·9′	0°39·6′E	T	168
Little Bray	Devon	SS6835	51°6·2′	3°52·7′W	T	180
Little Bray Cross	Devon	SS6637	51°7·2′	3°54·5′W	X	180
Little Brechin	Angus	NO5862	56°45·1′	2°40·8′W	T	44
Littlebredy	Dorset	SY5889	50°42·2′	2°35·3′W	T	194
Littlebredy Fm	Dorset	SY5988	50°41·6′	2°34·4′W	FM	194
Little Brickhill	Mil Key	SP9032	51°59·0′	0°41·0′W	T	152,165
Little Brickhill Copse	Mil Key	SP9233	51°59·5′	0°39·2′W	F	152,165
Little Bridge	Cambs	TL2798	52°34·1′	0°7·2′W	X	142
Littlebridge	Heref	SO6757	52°12·9′	2°28·6′W	X	149
Little Bridgeford	Staffs	SJ8727	52°50·7′	2°11·2′W	T	127
Little Briggens	Herts	TL3912	51°47·6′	0°1·3′E	X	166
Little Brigham	E Yorks	TA0853	53°57·9′	0°20·8′W	X	107
Little Brigurd	N Ayr	NS1751	55°43·3′	4°54·4′W	X	63
Little Brington	Northnts	SP6663	52°15·9′	1°1·6′W	T	152
Little Bristol	S Glos	ST7291	51°37·3′	2°23·9′W	T	162,172
Little Britain	Warw	SP1154	52°11·3′	1°49·9′W	T	150
Little Broach Dale	E Yorks	TA0467	54°5·5′	0°24·2′W	X	101
Little Broadreed Fm	E Susx	TQ5425	51°0·4′	0°12·1′E	FM	188,199
Little Bromley	Essex	TM0928	51°54·9′	1°2·7′E	T	168,169
Little Bromley Hall	Essex	TM0927	51°54·4′	1°2·7′E	X	168,169
Little Bromwich	Birm	SP1086	52°28·5′	1°50·8′W	T	139
Littlebrook	E Susx	TQ5033	51°4·8′	0°8·9′E	X	188
Little Brook	Kent	TR0059	51°17·9′	0°52·5′E	X	178
Littlebrook Fm	Surrey	SU9236	51°7·2′	0°40·7′W	FM	186
Little Brooks Ho	Lancs	SD5440	53°51·5′	2°41·5′W	X	102
Little Brookwood	Kent	TQ8242	51°9·1′	0°36·5′E	X	188
Little Broughton	Cumbr	NY0731	54°40·2′	3°26·1′W	T	89
Little Brownhill	Aberd	NJ9837	57°25·7′	2°1·5′W	X	30
Little Brown Hill	Moray	NJ5751	57°33·1′	2°42·6′W	H	29
Little Browns Fm	Kent	TQ4247	51°12·5′	0°2·4′E	FM	187
Little Bryngwyn	Swan	SS5190	51°35·6′	4°8·7′W	X	159
Little Brynn	Corn	SW9762	50°25·6′	4°51·1′W	X	200
Little Buckham Fm	E Susx	TQ4419	50°57·4′	0°3·4′E	FM	198
Little Buckland	Glos	SP0736	52°1·6′	1°53·5′W	X	150
Little Bucksteep Fm	E Susx	TQ6417	50°56·0′	0°20·4′E	FM	199
Little Budbridge Fm	I of W	SZ5383	50°38·9′	1°14·6′W	FM	196
Little Budds Fm	Kent	TQ8258	51°17·7′	0°37·0′E	FM	178,188
Little Budgate	Highld	NH8350	57°31·8′	3°56·8′W	X	27
Little Budworth	Ches	SJ5965	53°11·1′	2°36·4′W	T	117
Little Budworth Country Park	Ches	SJ5865	53°11·1′	2°37·3′W	X	117
Little Bull Stones	Lancs	SD6757	54°0·7′	2°29·8′W	X	103
Little Burcombe	Devon	SY0993	50°44·0′	3°17·0′W	X	192
Little Burdon	Darl	NZ3216	54°32·5′	1°29·9′W	X	93
Little Burgate Fm	Surrey	SU9839	51°8·7′	0°35·5′W	FM	186
Little Burn	Aberd	NJ3602	57°6·5′	3°2·9′W	W	37
Littleburn	Highld	NH6353	57°33·0′	4°16·9′W	X	26
Little Burn	Northum	NY6090	55°12·4′	2°37·3′W	W	80
Littleburn	N Yks	SD9986	54°16·4′	2°0·5′W	X	98
Little Burn	Scot Bord	NT3113	55°24·6′	3°5·0′W	W	79
Littleburn Fm	Durham	NZ2539	54°45·0′	1°36·3′W	FM	93
Little Burntshields	Renf	NS3861	55°49·2′	4°34·7′W	X	63
Little Burrows	Carm	SN2708	51°44·9′	4°30·0′W	X	158
Little Burstead	Essex	TQ6692	51°36·4′	0°24·2′E	T	177,178
Little Bursteads	Essex	TL4916	51°49·6′	0°10·1′E	X	167
Little Burton	E Yorks	TA1147	53°54·7′	0°18·2′W	X	107
Littlebury	Essex	TL5139	52°2·0′	0°12·5′E	T	154
Littlebury Fm	Cambs	TL2768	52°18·0′	0°7·9′W	FM	153
Littlebury Fm	Essex	TL7618	51°50·2′	0°33·7′E	FM	167
Littlebury Green	Essex	TL4838	52°1·5′	0°9·8′E	T	154
Littlebury Hall	Essex	TL5501	51°41·4′	0°14·9′E	X	167
Little Bustard Fm	E Yorks	TA0052	53°57·5′	0°28·1′W	FM	106,107
Little Butts Fm	E Susx	TQ6532	51°4·0′	0°21·7′E	FM	188
Little Byth	Aberd	NJ8257	57°36·4′	2°17·6′W	X	29,30
Little Bytham	Lincs	TF0117	52°44·7′	0°29·8′W	T	130
Little Bytham Lodge	Lincs	TF0217	52°44·7′	0°28·9′W	X	130
Little Cairnandrew	Aberd	NJ7560	57°38·0′	2°24·7′W	X	29
Little Cairnbrock	D & G	NW9766	54°57·1′	5°9·8′W	X	82
Little Cairn Table	S Lanak	NS7325	55°30·4′	4°0·2′W	H	71
Little Calder	S Lanak	NS6444	55°40·5′	4°9·3′W	W	71
Little Caldon	Stir	NS4982	56°0·7′	4°24·9′W	X	57,64
Little Calf Hill	Aberd	NO6182	56°55·9′	2°38·0′W	X	45
Little Callestock	Corn	SW7951	50°19·3′	5°5·9′W	X	200,204
Little Calva	Cumbr	NY2831	54°40·4′	3°6·6′W	H	89,90
Little Cambridge	Essex	TL6127	51°55·3′	0°20·9′E	T	167
Little Camdore	Heref	SO4527	51°56·6′	2°47·6′W	X	161
Little Canfield Hall	Essex	TL5821	51°52·1′	0°18·1′E	X	167
Little Canford	Dorset	SZ0499	50°47·7′	1°56·2′W	T	195
Little Canon	Kent	TQ6854	51°15·8′	0°24·9′E	X	188
Little Canons Fm	Essex	TL4306	51°44·3′	0°4·7′E	FM	167
Little Cansiron Fm	E Susx	TQ4538	51°7·6′	0°4·7′E	FM	188
Little Carcary	Angus	NO6355	56°41·4′	2°35·8′W	X	54
Little Carleith	E Ayr	NS5332	55°33·8′	4°19·4′W	X	70
Little Carleton	Blackp	SD3338	53°50·3′	3°0·7′W	T	102
Little Carleton	S Ayr	NX1389	55°9·9′	4°55·7′W	X	76
Little Carlton	Lincs	TF3985	53°20·8′	0°5·7′E	T	122
Little Carlton	Notts	SK7757	53°6·5′	0°50·6′W	T	120
Little Carne Fm	Corn	SX0455	50°22·0′	4°45·0′W	FM	200
Little Carr	Northum	NU2620	55°28·6′	1°34·9′W	X	75
Little Carrs	Cumbr	NY2701	54°24·2′	3°7·1′W	X	89,90
Little Carr Side Fm	Lancs	SD3929	53°45·5′	2°55·1′W	FM	102
Little Casterton	Rut	TF0109	52°40·4′	0°30·0′W	T	141
Little Castle Head	Pemb	SM8506	51°42·9′	5°6·4′W	X	157
Little Castle Point	Pemb	SM7903	51°41·2′	5°11·5′W	X	157
Little Cathpair	Scot Bord	NT4546	55°42·5′	2°52·1′W	X	73
Little Cattie	Aberd	NJ8429	57°21·3′	2°15·5′W	X	38
Little Catwick	E Yorks	TA1244	53°53·0′	0°17·3′W	T	107
Little Catworth	Cambs	TL1072	52°20·3′	0°22·7′W	T	153
Little Cawthorpe	Lincs	TF3583	53°19·8′	0°2·0′E	T	122
Littlecell Bottom	Cumbr	SD1491	54°18·7′	3°18·9′W	X	96
Little Chalfield	Wilts	ST8563	51°22·2′	2°12·5′W	T	173
Little Chalfont	Bucks	SU9997	51°40·0′	0°33·7′W	T	165,176
Little Chalvedon Hall	Essex	TQ7589	51°34·6′	0°31·9′E	X	178
Little Chapel	Aberd	NJ8134	57°24·0′	2°18·5′W	X	29,30
Little Chart	Kent	TQ9446	51°11·0′	0°46·9′E	T	189
Little Chart Forstal	Kent	TQ9545	51°10·5′	0°47·8′E	T	189
Little Chase Fm	Warw	SP2673	52°21·5′	1°36·7′W	FM	140
Little Chell	C of Stoke	SJ8752	53°4·1′	2°11·2′W	T	118
Little Chessell	I of W	SZ4086	50°40·6′	1°25·6′W	X	196
Little Chester	C of Derb	SK3537	52°56·0′	1°28·4′W	T	128
Little Chesterford	Essex	TL5141	52°3·0′	0°12·5′E	T	154
Little Chesterton	Oxon	SP5520	51°52·8′	1°11·7′W	T	164
Little Cheveney Fm	Kent	TQ7244	51°10·4′	0°28·0′E	FM	188
Little Cheverell	Wilts	ST9953	51°16·8′	2°0·5′W	T	184
Little Cheyne Court	Kent	TQ9821	50°57·5′	0°49·6′E	X	189
Little Chilfords	Cambs	TL5547	52°6·2′	0°16·2′E	X	154
Little Chilton	Durham	NZ2931	54°40·6′	1°32·6′W	X	93
Little Chishill	Cambs	TL4137	52°1·0′	0°3·7′E	T	154
Little Clachdubh	Aberd	NJ4018	57°15·2′	2°59·2′W	X	37
Little Clacton	Essex	TM1619	51°49·9′	1°8·5′E	T	168,169
Little Clacton Lodge	Essex	TM1819	51°49·8′	1°10·2′E	X	168,169
Little Clanfield	Oxon	SP2701	51°42·7′	1°36·2′W	T	163
Little Clark's	Essex	TL6333	51°58·5′	0°22·8′E	X	167
Little Claw Moor	Devon	SS3902	50°47·9′	4°16·7′W	X	190
Little Claydons Fm	Essex	TL7401	51°41·1′	0°31·4′E	FM	167
Little Clegg	Roch	SD9214	53°37·6′	2°6·8′W	T	109
Little Clett	Highld	ND2274	58°39·1′	3°20·2′W	X	7,12
Little Cliffsend	Kent	TR3564	51°19·8′	1°22·8′E	X	179
Little Clifton	Cumbr	NY0528	54°38·5′	3°27·9′W	T	89
Little Clinterty	C of Aber	NJ8312	57°12·2′	2°16·4′W	X	38
Little Cloak	D & G	NX8659	54°55·0′	3°46·3′W	X	84
Little Cloverley	Shrops	SJ6036	52°55·4′	2°35·3′W	X	127
Little Clyde	S Lanak	NS9916	55°25·9′	3°35·3′W	X	78
Little Coates	NE Lincs	TA2408	53°33·5′	0°7·3′W	T	113
Little Cockcairn	Aberd	NO4689	56°59·6′	2°52·9′W	H	44
Little Cocklick	D & G	NX8467	54°59·3′	3°48·4′W	X	84
Little Cockup	Cumbr	NY2633	54°41·4′	3°8·5′W	X	89,90
Little Cogill	N Yks	NY8403	54°25·6′	2°14·4′W	W	91,92
Little Colesbourne	Glos	SP0013	51°49·2′	1°59·6′W	X	163
Little Colonsay	Arg & Bt	NM3736	56°26·8′	6°15·6′W	X	47,48
Little Colp	Aberd	NJ7448	57°31·5′	2°25·6′W	X	29
Littlecombe	Devon	SX7068	50°30·1′	3°49·6′W	X	202
Littlecombe Bottom	Dorset	ST8816	50°56·8′	2°9·9′W	X	183
Littlecombe Bottom	Wilts	ST9039	51°9·2′	2°8·2′W	X	184
Littlecombe Hill	Wilts	ST8939	51°9·2′	2°9·1′W	X	184
Little Comberton	Worcs	SO9643	52°5·4′	2°3·1′W	T	150
Littlecombe Shoot	Devon	SY1887	50°40·8′	3°9·3′W	W	192
Little Comfort	Corn	SX3480	50°36·0′	4°20·4′W	T	201
Little Comfort	Devon	SS5140	51°8·6′	4°7·4′W	X	180
Little Common	Cambs	TL1884	52°26·7′	0°15·4′W	X	142
Little Common	E Susx	TQ7107	50°50·5′	0°26·1′E	T	199
Little Common	Lincs	TF3427	52°49·7′	0°0·3′W	T	131
Little Common	Shrops	SO3977	52°23·5′	2°53·4′W	T	137,148
Little Common	W Berks	SU3565	51°23·2′	1°29·4′W	X	174
Little Common	W Susx	SU9421	50°59·1′	0°39·3′W	T	197
Little Compton	Warw	SP2630	51°58·3′	1°36·9′W	T	151
Little Conachcraig	Aberd	NO2789	56°59·4′	3°11·6′W	H	44
Little Conghurst	Kent	TQ7729	51°2·2′	0°31·9′E	X	188,199
Little Conval	Moray	NJ2939	57°26·4′	3°10·5′W	H	28
Little Cooks	Essex	TQ8598	51°39·2′	0°40·9′E	X	168
Little Coombe Fm	W Berks	SU4182	51°32·4′	1°24·1′W	FM	174
Little Cooperhill	Aberd	NJ6654	57°34·7′	2°33·7′W	X	29
Little Coop House Fm	Durham	NZ4045	54°48·1′	1°22·2′W	FM	88
Little Corby	Cumbr	NY4757	54°54·5′	2°49·2′W	T	86
Little Corkhill Fm	Notts	SK7056	53°6·0′	0°56·9′W	FM	120
Little Cornard	Suff	TL9039	52°1·2′	0°46·5′E	T	155
Little Corr Riabhach	Aberd	NJ2512	57°11·8′	3°14·0′W	X	37
Little Corum	Stir	NN8503	56°12·6′	3°50·8′W	H	58
Littlecote	Bucks	SP8324	51°54·7′	0°47·2′W	T	165
Littlecote	Wilts	SU3070	51°25·9′	1°33·7′W	A	174
Littlecote Park Fm	Wilts	SU2969	51°25·4′	1°34·6′W	FM	174
Littlecott	Wilts	SU0376	51°29·2′	1°57·0′W	X	173
Littlecott	Wilts	SU1451	51°15·7′	1°47·6′W	T	184
Littlecott Down	Wilts	SU1653	51°16·8′	1°45·8′W	X	184
Little Coum	Cumbr	SD6099	54°23·3′	2°36·5′W	X	97
Little Coursehorne	Kent	TQ7934	51°4·9′	0°33·7′E	X	188
Little Court	Northnts	SP6154	52°11·1′	1°6·1′W	X	152,152
Little Cove	Cumbr	SD2598	54°22·6′	3°8·9′W	X	96
Little Cowarne	Heref	SO6051	52°9·6′	2°34·7′W	T	149
Little Cowbridge Grange	Essex	TQ6595	51°38·0′	0°23·4′E	X	167,177
Little Cowden	E Yorks	TA2340	53°50·7′	0°7·4′W	X	107
Little Coxwell	Oxon	SU2893	51°38·3′	1°35·3′W	T	163,174
Little Crag	N Yks	SE1053	53°58·6′	1°50·4′W	X	104
Little Craig	Scot Bord	NT1724	55°30·4′	3°18·4′W	H	72
Little Craigherbs	Aberd	NJ6564	57°40·1′	2°34·7′W	X	29
Little Craig Minnan	Inverc	NS3164	55°50·6′	4°41·5′W	X	63
Little Craigs	S Ayr	NS3229	55°31·8′	4°39·3′W	X	70
Little Craigtarson	D & G	NX4786	55°8·9′	4°23·6′W	X	77
Little Crakehall	N Yks	SE2490	54°18·5′	1°37·4′W	T	99
Little Cranecleugh Burn	Northum	NY6586	55°10·3′	2°32·5′W	W	80
Little Cransley	Northnts	SP8376	52°22·8′	0°46·4′W	T	141
Little Crawley	Mil Key	SP9245	52°6·0′	0°39·0′W	T	152
Little Creaton	Northnts	SP7071	52°20·2′	0°58·0′W	T	141
Little Crebawethan	I Scilly	SV8206	49°52·4′	6°25·2′W	X	203
Little Creich	Highld	NH6389	57°52·4′	4°18·1′W	X	21
Little Creigiau	Powys	SO1963	52°15·8′	3°10·8′W	X	148
Little Creoch	E Ayr	NS5914	55°24·2′	4°13·2′W	X	71
Little Cressingham	Norf	TF8700	52°34·2′	0°46·0′E	T	144
Little Creuch Hill	Inverc	NS2769	55°53·2′	4°45·5′W	H	63

Little Crimbles	Lancs	SD4650	53°56·8'	2°49·0'W	X	102
Little Croft West	Corn	SW7746	50°16·5'	5°7·4'W	X	204
Little Crosby	Sefton	SD3101	53°30·3'	3°2·0'W	T	108
Little Crosthwaite	Cumbr	NY2327	54°38·2'	3°11·2'W	X	89,90
Little Cubley	Derby	SK1637	52°56·0'	1°45·3'W	T	128
Little Culand	Kent	TQ7361	51°19·5'	0°29·4'E	X	178,188
Little Cullendoch Moss	D & G	NX5565	54°57·8'	4°15·5'W	X	83
Little Culloch	D & G	NX8465	54°58·2'	3°48·3'W	X	84
Little Culmain	D & G	NX8468	54°59·8'	3°48·4'W	X	84
Little Cultain	Moray	NJ5362	57°39·0'	2°46·8'W	X	29
Little Cumbrae Island	N Ayr	NS1451	55°43·3'	4°57·3'W	X	63,69
Little Cushnie	Aberd	NJ7860	57°38·0'	2°21·6'W	X	29,30
Little Cutmadoc Fm	Corn	SX0964	50°26·9'	4°41·0'W	FM	200
Little Cutstraw	E Ayr	NS4245	55°40·6'	4°30·3'W	X	64
Little Cwm	Powys	SJ1605	52°38·4'	3°14·1'W	X	125
Little Daan	Highld	NH6783	57°49·3'	4°13·9'W	X	21
Little Dalby	Leic	SK7714	52°43·3'	0°51·2'W	T	129
Little Dalby Hall	Leic	SK7713	52°42·8'	0°51·2'W	X	129
Little Dale	Cumbr	NY2016	54°32·2'	3°13·8'W	X	89,90
Littledale	Lancs	SD5461	54°2·8'	2°41·7'W	X	97
Littledale	Notts	SK6755	53°5·5'	0°59·6'W	X	120
Little Dale	N Yks	SD7681	54°13·7'	2°21·7'W	X	98
Little Dale Beck	N Yks	SD7581	54°13·7'	2°22·6'W	W	98
Littledale Edge	Cumbr	NY2016	54°32·2'	3°13·8'W	X	89,90
Littledale Hall	Lancs	SD5661	54°2·8'	2°39·9'W	X	97
Little Dallas	Highld	NH6985	57°50·4'	4°11·9'W	X	21
Little Dalrachie	Moray	NJ1729	57°20·9'	3°22·3'W	X	36
Little Danby Hall	N Yks	SE3496	54°21·7'	1°28·2'W	X	99
Little Dane Fm	Kent	TR2038	51°6·2'	1°8·9'E	FM	179,189
Little Dartmouth	Devon	SX8749	50°20·0'	3°34·9'W	X	202
Little Dart River	Devon	SS7013	50°54·3'	3°50·6'W	W	180
Little Dart River	Devon	SS7413	50°54·4'	3°47·1'W	W	180
Little Dart River	Devon	SS8316	50°56·1'	3°39·5'W	W	181
Little Daugh	Aberd	NJ5047	57°30·9'	2°49·6'W	X	29
Little Dawley	Wrekin	SJ6806	52°39·3'	2°28·0'W	T	127
Littledean	Glos	SO6713	51°49·1'	2°28·3'W	T	162
Littledean	Scot Bord	NT6231	55°34·5'	2°35·7'W	X	74
Little Deane Wood	Hants	SU5151	51°15·6'	1°12·3'W	F	185
Little Dean Fm	Hants	SU7148	51°13·8'	0°58·6'W	FM	186
Littledean Fm	Scot Bord	NT9262	55°51·3'	2°7·2'W	FM	67
Littledean Hill	Glos	SO6614	51°49·7'	2°29·2'W	T	162
Littledeanlees	Scot Bord	NT6823	55°30·2'	2°30·0'W	X	74
Little Deerholme Grange	N Yks	SE8178	54°11·7'	0°45·1'W	X	100
Little Dene	E Susx	TQ4507	50°50·9'	0°4·0'E	X	198
Little Dennis	Corn	SW7825	50°5·3'	5°5·8'W	A	204
Little Denny Resr	Falk	NS7981	56°0·7'	3°56·0'W	W	64
Little Dens	Aberd	NK0743	57°28·9'	1°52·5'W	X	30
Little Deuchries	Aberd	NJ6455	57°35·3'	2°35·7'W	X	29
Little Dewchurch	Heref	SO5331	51°58·8'	2°40·7'W	T	149
Little Dibbin Hill	D & G	NX6896	55°14·7'	4°4·1'W	X	77
Little Dilwyn	Heref	SO4353	52°10·6'	2°49·6'W	X	148,149
Little Dingle	Suff	TM4771	52°17·1'	1°37·7'E	X	156
Little Ditch	Essex	TL9813	51°47·1'	0°52·6'E	W	168
Little Ditton	Cambs	TL6658	52°11·9'	0°26·1'E	X	154
Little Dod	Northum	NT9514	55°25·4'	2°4·3'W	H	81
Little Dod	Scot Bord	NT7366	55°53·4'	2°25·5'W	X	67
Little Dodd	Cumbr	NY1319	54°33·8'	3°20·3'W	H	89
Little Dodd	Cumbr	NY1415	54°31·6'	3°19·3'W	X	89
Little Dodd Hill	Northum	NY7078	55°5·3'	2°27·8'W	X	86,87
Little Doggetts	Essex	TQ8793	51°36·5'	0°42·4'E	X	178
Little Don River or The Porter	Sheff	SK1899	53°29·5'	1°43·3'W	W	110
Little Dornell	D & G	NX7066	54°58·6'	4°1·4'W	H	83,84
Little Doward	Heref	SO5416	51°50·7'	2°39·7'W	T	162
Little Dowden's Fm	Somer	ST2245	51°12·2'	3°6·6'W	FM	182
Little Down	Bath & NE Somer	ST7068	51°24·8'	2°25·5'W	X	172
Littledown	Bourne	SZ1293	50°44·4'	1°49·4'W	T	195
Little Down	Dorset	ST8503	50°49·8'	2°12·4'W	X	194
Little Down	Dorset	ST9508	50°52·5'	2°3·9'W	X	195
Littledown	Hants	SU3457	51°18·9'	1°30·3'W	T	174
Little Down	I of W	SZ4386	50°40·6'	1°23·1'W	X	196
Little Down	Shrops	SO6274	52°22·0'	2°33·1'W	X	138
Little Down	Wilts	ST8738	51°8·7'	2°10·8'W	X	183
Little Down	Wilts	SU0138	51°8·7'	1°58·8'W	X	184
Little Down	Wilts	SU0527	51°2·8'	1°55·3'W	X	184
Little Down	Wilts	SU3055	51°17·8'	1°33·8'W	X	174,185
Little Down	W Susx	SU9609	50°52·6'	0°37·7'W	X	197
Little Down (Fort)	Bath & NE Somer	ST7068	51°24·8'	2°25·5'W	A	172
Little Downham	Cambs	TL5283	52°25·7'	0°14·5'E	T	143
Little Drayton	Shrops	SJ6633	52°53·8'	2°29·9'W	T	127
Little Driesh	Angus	NO2673	56°50·8'	3°12·3'W	X	44
Little Driffield	E Yorks	TA0057	54°0·2'	0°28·0'W	T	106,107
Little Drum Loin	Moray	NJ1108	57°9·5'	3°27·8'W	X	36
Little Drumquharn	Stir	NS5187	56°3·4'	4°23·1'W	X	57
Little Drumrash	D & G	NX6772	55°1·7'	4°4·4'W	X	77,84
Little Drumtie	Stir	NS5790	56°5·1'	4°17·4'W	X	57
Little Drybrook	Glos	SO5907	51°45·8'	2°35·3'W	T	162
Little Dully	Kent	TQ9362	51°19·7'	0°46·6'E	X	178
Little Dunchrae	D & G	NX6669	55°0·1'	4°5·3'W	X	83,84
Little Dunclent Fm	Worcs	SO8676	52°23·1'	2°11·9'W	FM	139
Little Dun Fell	Cumbr	NY7033	54°41·7'	2°27·5'W	H	91
Little Dunham	Norf	TF8612	52°40·7'	0°45·5'E	T	132
Little Dunkeld	Pth & Kin	NO0242	56°33·8'	3°35·2'W	T	52,53
Little Dunks Fm	Kent	TQ6638	51°7·3'	0°22·7'E	FM	188
Little Dunmow	Essex	TL6521	51°52·0'	0°24·2'E	T	167
Little Dunster Fm	Dorset	SY4397	50°46·4'	2°48·1'W	FM	193
Little Durnford	Wilts	SU1234	51°6·5'	1°49·3'W	T	184
Little Duxmore	I of W	SZ5587	50°41·0'	1°12·9'W	X	196
Little Dytach	Aberd	NJ5464	57°40·1'	2°45·8'W	X	29
Little Eachaig River	Arg & Bt	NS1281	55°59·4'	5°0·4'W	W	63
Little Earl	Stir	NS5682	56°0·8'	4°18·2'W	X	57,64
Little Eastbury	Worcs	SO8257	52°12·9'	2°15·4'W	T	150
Little Easton	Essex	TL6023	51°53·2'	0°19·9'E	T	167
Little East Standen Fm	I of W	SZ5287	50°41·0'	1°15·5'W	FM	196
Little Eaton	Derby	SK3641	52°58·1'	1°27·4'W	T	119,128
Little Eccleston	Lancs	SD4140	53°51·4'	2°53·4'W	T	102
Little Eddieston	C of Aber	NJ7802	57°6·8'	2°21·3'W	X	38
Little Ednie	Aberd	NK0850	57°32·7'	1°51·5'W	X	30
Little Edstone	N Yks	SE7184	54°15·0'	0°54·2'W	X	100
Little Eela Water	Shetld	HU3278	60°29·3'	1°24·6'W	W	3
Little Eggleston Beck	Durham	NY9929	54°39·6'	2°0·5'W	W	92
Little Eldrig	D & G	NX3466	54°57·9'	4°35·2'W	X	82
Little Eller Beck	N Yks	SE8798	54°22·4'	0°39·2'W	W	94,101
Little Ellingham	Norf	TM0099	52°33·3'	0°57·4'E	T	144
Little Elmridge	Lancs	SD5941	53°52·1'	2°37·0'W	X	102
Little Elrick	Aberd	NJ9244	57°29·4'	2°7·5'W	X	30
Little Elrick	Aberd	NO1694	57°2·0'	3°22·6'W	H	36,43
Little End	Cambs	TL1758	52°12·7'	0°16·9'W	T	153
Little End	Essex	TL5400	51°40·9'	0°14·1'E	T	167
Little End	E Yorks	SE8038	53°50·2'	0°46·6'W	T	106
Little End	Mil Key	SP8945	52°6·0'	0°41·6'W	X	152
Little Endovie	Aberd	NJ5814	57°13·1'	2°41·3'W	X	37
Little England Fm	E Susx	TQ5423	50°59·4'	0°12·0'E	FM	199
Little England Hill	E Yorks	TA3227	53°43·6'	0°0·5'E	X	107
Little Ennochie	Aberd	NO6391	57°0·8'	2°36·1'W	X	45
Little Ensdon	Shrops	SJ4117	52°45·1'	2°52·0'W	X	126
Little Eriff Hill	E Ayr	NS5000	55°16·5'	4°21·2'W	H	77
Little Everdon	Northnts	SP5958	52°13·3'	1°7·8'W	T	152
Little Eversden	Cambs	TL3753	52°9·7'	0°0·6'E	T	154
Little Eye	Wirral	SJ1986	53°22·1'	3°12·6'W	X	108
Little Eye	Wirral	SJ2086	53°22·1'	3°11·7'W	X	108
Little Fardle	Pth & Kin	NO1440	56°32·9'	3°23·5'W	X	53
Little Faringdon	Oxon	SP2201	51°42·7'	1°40·5'W	T	163
Little Farmcote	Glos	SP0528	51°57·3'	1°55·2'W	X	150,163
Little Fell	Cumbr	NY3202	54°24·8'	3°2·4'W	H	90
Little Fell	Cumbr	NY7601	54°24·5'	2°21·8'W	H	91
Little Fell	Cumbr	NY7822	54°35·8'	2°20·0'W	H	91
Little Fell	Cumbr	SD1286	54°16·0'	3°20·7'W	X	96
Little Fell	D & G	NS9100	55°17·2'	3°42·5'W	H	78
Little Fell	N Yks	SD8097	54°22·3'	2°18·1'W	X	98
Little Fell	N Yks	SD8878	54°12·1'	2°10·6'W	X	98
Little Fell	S Ayr	NX1381	55°5·5'	4°55·4'W	X	76
Little Fen	Cambs	TL5868	52°17·5'	0°19·4'E	X	154
Little Fen	Norf	TM0479	52°22·5'	1°0·2'E	W	144
Little Fencote	N Yks	SE2893	54°20·2'	1°33·7'W	T	99
Little Fenton	N Yks	SE5235	53°48·8'	1°12·2'W	T	105
Little Fenton Lodge	N Yks	SE5235	53°48·8'	1°12·2'W	X	105
Little Fenwick	E Ayr	NS4543	55°39·6'	4°27·4'W	X	70
Little Fernhill	Shrops	SJ3133	52°53·6'	3°1·1'W	X	126
Littleferry	Highld	NH8095	57°56·0'	4°1·1'W	T	21
Little Ffordd-fawr	Powys	SO2040	52°3·4'	3°9·6'W	X	148,161
Littlefield	Aberd	NJ6054	57°34·7'	2°39·7'W	X	29
Littlefield	Cumbr	NY4770	55°1·6'	2°49·3'W	X	86
Littlefield	NE Lincs	TA2608	53°33·4'	0°5·5'W	T	113
Littlefield Common	Surrey	SU9552	51°15·8'	0°37·9'W	T	186
Littlefield Green	Win & Maid	SU8576	51°28·8'	0°46·2'W	T	175
Littlefield Manor	Surrey	SU9552	51°15·8'	0°37·9'W	X	186
Littlefields	Somer	ST4116	50°56·7'	2°50·0'W	X	193
Littlefields Fm	Notts	SK5046	53°0·8'	1°14·9'W	FM	129
Little Finborough	Suff	TM0254	52°9·1'	0°57·6'E	T	155
Little Findowie	Pth & Kin	NN9438	56°31·6'	3°42·9'W	X	52,53
Little Finnart	Pth & Kin	NN5056	56°40·6'	4°26·4'W	X	42,51
Little Finnery	W Dunb	NS4485	56°2·2'	4°29·8'W	X	57
Little Firbriggs Hill	Aberd	NJ3917	57°14·6'	3°0·2'W	H	37
Little Fir Covert	Suff	TL8167	52°16·5'	0°39·6'E	F	155
Little Fithie	Angus	NO6254	56°40·8'	2°36·8'W	X	54
Little Flanchford	Surrey	TQ2348	51°13·3'	0°13·9'W	X	187
Little Flinder	Aberd	NJ5827	57°20·2'	2°41·4'W	X	37
Little Float	D & G	NX0647	54°47·1'	5°0·6'W	X	82
Little Fm	Devon	SY1892	50°43·5'	3°9·3'W	FM	192,193
Littlefold	Pth & Kin	NN9320	56°21·9'	3°43·5'W	X	52,58
Littleford	Devon	SS3213	50°53·8'	4°23·0'W	X	190
Littleford	Glos	SO7326	51°56·1'	2°23·2'W	X	162
Little Forest	Hants	SU6011	50°53·9'	1°8·4'W	X	196
Little Forest Hall	Essex	TL5705	51°43·5'	0°16·8'E	X	167
Little Forgie	Moray	NJ4052	57°33·5'	2°59·7'W	X	28
Little Forgue	Aberd	NJ6144	57°29·3'	2°38·6'W	X	29
Little Forter	Angus	NO1864	56°45·9'	3°20·0'W	X	43
Little France	C of Edin	NT2870	55°55·3'	3°8·7'W	X	66
Little Fransham	Norf	TF9012	52°40·6'	0°49·0'E	T	132
Little Freuchie	Fife	NO2706	56°14·7'	3°10·2'W	X	59
Little Friars' Thornes	Norf	TF7909	52°39·2'	0°39·2'E	X	144
Little Frith	Kent	TQ9455	51°15·9'	0°47·2'E	T	178
Little Frith	Wilts	SU2467	51°24·3'	1°38·9'W	F	174
Little Froome	Heref	SO6553	52°10·7'	2°30·3'W	X	149
Little Fryup Beck	N Yks	NZ7105	54°26·4'	0°53·9'W	W	94
Little Furzenip	Pemb	SR8899	51°39·2'	5°3·5'W	X	158
Little Gaddesden	Herts	SP9913	51°48·6'	0°33·4'W	T	165
Littlegain	Shrops	SO7896	52°33·9'	2°19·1'W	T	138
Little Gala	S Lanak	NS9132	55°34·4'	3°43·3'W	X	71,72
Little Galt Skerry	Orkney	HY4821	59°4·6'	2°53·9'W	X	5,6
Little Galver	Corn	SW4335	50°9·8'	5°35·5'W	X	203
Little Ganilly	I Scilly	SV9314	49°57·1'	6°16·4'W	X	203
Little Ganinick	I Scilly	SV9313	49°56·5'	6°16·4'W	X	203
Littlegarth	Shetld	HP6100	60°41·0'	0°52·5'W	X	1
Little Garve	Highld	NH3962	57°37·4'	4°41·3'W	X	20
Little Garvoun	Moray	NJ1309	57°10·1'	3°25·9'W	H	36
Little Garway Fm	Heref	SO4424	51°54·9'	2°48·5'W	FM	161
Littlegates Fm	Lincs	SK8747	53°1·0'	0°41·8'W	FM	130
Little Geal Charn	Aberd	NJ2919	57°15·6'	3°10·2'W	H	37
Little Geal Charn	Moray	NJ1905	57°8·0'	3°19·8'W	H	36
Little Genoch	D & G	NX1357	54°52·6'	4°54·5'W	X	82
Little Gibcracks	Essex	TL7703	51°42·1'	0°34·1'E	X	167
Little Gidding	Cambs	TL1281	52°25·2'	0°20·8'W	T	142
Little Gight	Aberd	NJ8339	57°26·7'	2°16·5'W	X	29,30
Littlegill	Cumbr	NY7142	54°46·6'	2°26·6'W	X	86,87
Little Gill	Cumbr	NY7739	54°45·0'	2°21·0'W	W	91
Little Gill	Cumbr	NY7740	54°45·5'	2°21·0'W	W	86,87
Littlegill	S Lanak	NS9326	55°31·2'	3°41·3'W	X	71,72
Littlegill Fm	S Lanak	NS8143	55°40·2'	3°53·1'W	FM	71,72
Little Givendale	N Yks	SE3469	54°7·2'	1°28·4'W	X	99
Little Givendale Fm	E Yorks	SE8253	53°58·2'	0°44·6'W	FM	106
Little Glas Maol	Angus	NO1775	56°51·8'	3°21·2'W	H	43
Little Glemham	Suff	TM3458	52°10·5'	1°25·7'E	T	156
Little Glen	E Ayr	NS5739	55°37·7'	4°15·8'W	X	71
Littleglen Burn	Aberd	NJ3017	57°14·6'	3°9·1'W	W	37
Little Glengyre	D & G	NX0066	54°57·2'	5°7·0'W	X	82
Little Glenshee	Pth & Kin	NN9834	56°29·5'	3°39·0'W	X	52,53
Little Gornhay	Devon	SS9713	50°54·7'	3°27·5'W	X	181
Little Gorsley	Heref	SO6825	51°55·6'	2°27·5'W	T	162
Little Gourdas	Aberd	NJ7641	57°27·8'	2°23·5'W	X	29
Little Goval	Aberd	NJ8914	57°13·3'	2°10·5'W	X	38
Little Gowder Crag	Cumbr	NY1411	54°29·5'	3°19·2'W	X	89
Little Goytre	Monm	SO3523	51°54·3'	2°56·3'W	X	161
Little Grain Noddle	N Yks	SE8994	54°20·3'	0°37·4'W	X	94,101
Little Grange	Essex	TL8103	51°42·0'	0°37·6'E	X	168
Little Gransden	Cambs	TL2755	52°10·9'	0°8·1'W	T	153
Little Grassoms	Cumbr	SD1488	54°17·1'	3°18·8'W	X	96
Little Gravenhurst	W Susx	TQ2722	50°59·2'	0°11·0'W	X	198
Little Grays	Kent	TR2267	51°21·7'	1°11·7'E	X	179
Little Green	Cambs	TL2845	52°5·5'	0°7·5'W	T	153
Little Green	Notts	SK7243	52°59·0'	0°55·2'W	T	129
Little Green	Somer	ST7248	51°14·1'	2°23·7'W	T	183
Little Green	Suff	TM0671	52°18·1'	1°1·7'E	T	144,155
Little Green	Suff	TM0774	52°19·7'	1°2·7'E	T	144
Little Green	Wrex	SJ4140	52°57·5'	2°52·3'W	X	117
Little Green	Wrex	SJ4840	52°57·5'	2°46·0'W	T	117
Little Greencroft Fm	Durham	NZ1248	54°49·8'	1°48·4'W	FM	88
Little Green Fm	Oxon	SP4011	51°48·0'	1°24·8'W	FM	164
Little Green Holm	Orkney	HY5226	59°7·4'	2°49·8'W	X	5,6
Littlegreen (Sch)	W Susx	SU7715	50°56·0'	0°53·9'W	X	197
Little Gregories	Essex	TL4500	51°41·0'	0°6·2'E	X	167
Little Grenach	Arg & Bt	NS0861	55°48·5'	5°3·4'W	X	63
Little Gribbin	Corn	SX0850	50°19·4'	4°41·5'W	X	200,204
Little Grimsby	Lincs	TF3291	53°24·2'	0°0·5'W	T	113
Little Gringley	Notts	SK7380	53°18·9'	0°53·8'W	T	120
Little Gruinard	Highld	NG9489	57°50·9'	5°27·8'W	X	19
Little Gruinard River	Highld	NG9486	57°49·2'	5°27·6'W	W	19
Little Gruna Stacks	Shetld	HU2886	60°33·7'	1°28·9'W	X	1,3
Little Habton	N Yks	SE7477	54°11·2'	0°51·5'W	T	100
Little Haddo	Aberd	NJ9925	57°19·2'	2°0·5'W	X	38
Little Hadham	Herts	TL4422	51°52·9'	0°5·9'E	T	167
Little Hadham Place	Herts	TL4322	51°52·9'	0°5·1'E	X	167
Little Halden	Kent	TQ8532	51°3·7'	0°38·8'E	X	189
Little Halden Place	Kent	TQ8633	51°4·2'	0°39·7'E	X	189
Little Haldon	Devon	SX9176	50°34·6'	3°32·0'W	X	192
Little Hale	Lincs	TF1441	52°57·5'	0°17·8'W	T	130
Little Hale	Norf	TF9406	52°37·3'	0°52·4'E	T	144
Little Hale Fen	Lincs	TF1740	52°56·9'	0°15·1'W	X	130
Little Hales Manor Fm	Wrekin	SJ7416	52°44·7'	2°22·7'W	FM	127
Little Hales Wood	Essex	TL5740	52°2·4'	0°17·7'E	F	154
Little Hall	Carm	SN7937	52°1·3'	3°45·4'W	X	146,160
Little Hall	Cumbr	NY4757	54°54·5'	2°49·2'W	X	86
Little Hall	Devon	SS6023	50°59·6'	3°59·3'W	X	180
Little Hall	Shrops	SO2782	52°26·1'	3°4·0'W	X	137
Little Hall	Wrex	SJ4536	52°55·4'	2°48·7'W	X	126
Little Hallam	Derby	SK4640	52°57·6'	1°18·5'W	T	129
Little Hall Fm	Kent	TR1460	51°18·2'	1°4·6'E	FM	179
Little Hallingbury	Essex	TL5017	51°50·1'	0°11·0'E	T	167
Little Hallingbury Hall	Essex	TL5016	51°49·6'	0°11·0'E	X	167
Little Hallingbury Park	Essex	TL5116	51°49·6'	0°11·9'E	X	167
Little Halstead Fm	Kent	TQ7761	51°19·5'	0°32·8'E	FM	178,188
Little Halveor	Corn	SW8964	50°26·5'	4°57·9'W	X	200
Littleham	Devon	SS4323	50°59·3'	4°13·8'W	T	180,190
Littleham	Devon	SY0281	50°37·5'	3°22·7'W	T	192
Littlehamar	Shetld	HP6409	60°45·8'	0°49·0'W	X	1
Littleham Court	Devon	SS4324	50°59·9'	4°13·9'W	X	180,190
Littleham Cove	Devon	SY0480	50°36·9'	3°21·0'W	W	192
Little Ham Fm	Hants	SU5660	51°20·4'	1°11·4'W	FM	174
Little Hampden	Bucks	SP8603	51°43·4'	0°44·9'W	T	165
Little Hampden Common	Bucks	SP8504	51°43·9'	0°45·8'W	F	165
Littlehampton	W Susx	TQ0202	50°48·7'	0°32·7'W	T	197
Little Hanford	Dorset	ST8411	50°54·1'	2°13·3'W	X	194
Little Hangman	Devon	SS5848	51°13·1'	4°1·6'W	H	180
Little Harcar	Northum	ND2438	55°38·3'	1°36·7'W	X	75
Little Hard Hill	D & G	NX9263	54°57·2'	3°40·8'W	X	84
Little Haresfield	Glos	SO8009	51°47·0'	2°17·0'W	T	162
Littleharle Tower	Northum	NZ0183	55°8·7'	1°58·6'W	X	81
Little Harmers Fm	E Susx	TQ8522	50°58·3'	0°38·5'E	FM	189,199
Little Harrowden	Northnts	SP8671	52°20·1'	0°43·9'W	T	141
Little Hart Crag	Cumbr	NY3810	54°29·1'	2°57·0'W	H	90
Little Hartfell	D & G	NY2288	55°11·1'	3°13·1'W	X	79
Little Hartmidden	S Lanak	NS6032	55°34·0'	4°12·8'W	H	71
Little Harwood	Black w Dar	SD6929	53°45·6'	2°27·8'W	T	103
Little Harwood	W Loth	NT0161	55°50·2'	3°34·4'W	X	65
Little Haseley	Oxon	SP6400	51°41·9'	1°4·0'W	T	164,165
Little Hasguard	Pemb	SM8410	51°45·1'	5°7·4'W	X	157
Little Hatfield	E Yorks	TA1743	53°52·4'	0°12·8'W	T	107
Little Haugh Hall	Suff	TL9566	52°15·7'	0°51·8'E	X	155
Little Hautbois	Norf	TG2521	52°44·6'	1°20·4'E	T	133,134
Little Haven	Pemb	SM8512	51°46·2'	5°6·6'W	T	157
Little Haven	W Susx	TQ1832	51°4·7'	0°18·5'W	T	187
Little Havra	Shetld	HU3526	60°1·3'	1°21·8'W	X	4
Little Haw	N Yks	SE0780	54°13·2'	1°53·1'W	X	99
Little Haw Wood	Lincs	SK9617	52°44·8'	0°34·3'W	F	130
Little Hay	Staffs	SK1202	52°37·2'	1°49·0'W	T	139
Little Hayfield	Derby	SK0388	53°23·6'	1°56·9'W	T	110
Little Haywood	Staffs	SK0021	52°47·4'	1°59·6'W	T	128
Little Heateth	E Ayr	NS5323	55°29·0'	4°19·1'W	X	70
Little Heath	Ches	SJ4465	53°11·0'	2°49·9'W	T	117
Little Heath	Ches	SJ6644	52°59·8'	2°30·0'W	T	118
Little Heath	Cov	SP3482	52°26·3'	1°29·6'W	T	140
Little Heath	Devon	SS8811	50°53·5'	3°35·2'W	X	192
Little Heath	Herts	TL0108	51°45·9'	0°31·8'W	T	166
Little Heath	Herts	TL2502	51°42·4'	0°11·1'W	T	166
Little Heath	Redbr	TQ4788	51°34·5'	0°7·7'E	T	177
Little Heath	Shrops	SJ3722	52°47·8'	2°55·7'W	X	126
Little Heath	Staffs	SJ9017	52°45·3'	2°8·5'W	T	127
Little Heath	Suff	TL8577	52°21·8'	0°43·4'E	X	144
Little Heath	Surrey	TQ1360	51°19·9'	0°22·3'W	T	176,187
Little Heath	W Berks	SU6063	51°22·0'	1°7·9'W	X	175
Little Heath	W Berks	SU6573	51°27·4'	1°3·5'W	T	175
Little Heath Fm	Cambs	TL2351	52°8·8'	0°11·7'W	FM	153
Little Heath Fm	Shrops	SJ3522	52°47·7'	2°57·4'W	FM	126
Little Heatley	Warr	SJ7187	53°23·0'	2°25·8'W	X	109
Little Heaven	E Susx	TQ4411	50°53·1'	0°3·2'E	X	198
Little Heck	N Yks	SE5922	53°41·7'	1°6·0'W	T	105

Little Hele	Devon	SS7224	51°0·3′	3°49·1′W	X	180
Little Hell	Corn	SX0852	50°20·4′	4°41·5′W	X	200,204
Little Hemingfold Fm	E Susx	TQ7714	50°54·1′	0°31·4′E	FM	199
Littlehempston	Devon	SX8162	50°27·0′	3°40·2′W	T	202
Little Hendra	Corn	SW3629	50°6·4′	5°41·2′W	X	203
Little Henham	Essex	TL5330	51°57·1′	0°14·0′E	T	167
Little Hen Hill	Cumbr	NY6275	55°4·3′	2°35·3′W	H	86
Little Herbert's	Glos	SO9619	51°52·4′	2°3·1′W	T	163
Little Hereford	Heref	SO5568	52°18·7′	2°39·2′W	T	137,138
Little Hermitage	Kent	TQ7270	51°24·4′	0°28·8′E	X	178
Little Heydon	Somer	ST0228	51°2·8′	3°23·5′W	X	181
Little Hey Ho	Essex	TL8924	51°53·2′	0°45·2′E	X	168
Little Hidden Fm	W Berks	SU3571	51°26·4′	1°29·4′W	FM	174
Little Higham	Kent	TQ9257	51°17·0′	0°45·6′E	X	178
Little Hilbre Island	Wirral	SJ1887	53°22·7′	3°13·6′W	X	108
Little Hill	Aberd	NJ5401	57°6·1′	2°45·1′W	H	37
Littlehill	Aberd	NJ9247	57°31·0′	2°7·6′W	X	30
Littlehill	Aberd	NK0054	57°34·8′	1°59·5′W	X	30
Little Hill	Angus	NO3886	56°57·9′	3°0·7′W	X	44
Little Hill	Cambs	TL4980	52°24·1′	0°11·8′E	X	143
Little Hill	Devon	SS5926	51°1·2′	4°0·2′W	H	180
Little Hill	Devon	SS7824	51°0·4′	3°44·0′W	X	180
Littlehill	Fife	NT1089	56°5·4′	3°26·3′W	X	65
Little Hill	Heref	SO4727	51°56·6′	2°45·9′W	T	161
Little Hill	Heref	SO6038	52°2·6′	2°34·6′W	X	149
Little Hill	Oxon	SP3322	51°54·0′	1°30·8′W	X	164
Little Hill	Powys	SO0745	52°6·0′	3°21·1′W	H	147
Little Hill	Powys	SO0760	52°14·1′	3°21·3′W	X	147
Little Hill	Powys	SO1267	52°17·9′	3°17·0′W	X	136,148
Little Hill	Powys	SO1453	52°10·4′	3°15·1′W	H	148
Little Hill	Powys	SO1653	52°10·4′	3°13·3′W	H	148
Little Hill	Pth & Kin	NN7717	56°20·0′	3°58·9′W	H	57
Littlehill	S Ayr	NS4630	55°32·6′	4°26·0′W	X	70
Little Hill	Shrops	SJ6107	52°39·8′	2°34·2′W	H	127
Little Hill	S Lanak	NS9603	55°18·9′	3°37·9′W	X	78
Little Hill	Somer	ST2613	50°54·9′	3°2·8′W	T	193
Little Hill	Warw	SP2756	52°12·3′	1°35·9′W	X	151
Little Hill	Wilts	SU0553	51°16·8′	1°55·3′W	X	184
Little Hilla Green	N Yks	SE9489	54°17·5′	0°32·9′W	X	94,101
Little Hillbrae	Aberd	NJ7923	57°18·1′	2°20·5′W	X	38
Littlehill Common	Powys	SO1473	52°21·1′	3°15·4′W	X	136,148
Little Hillend	Staffs	SK0165	53°11·2′	1°58·7′W	X	119
Little Hill Fm	Northnts	SP7537	52°1·8′	0°54·0′W	FM	152
Littlehillie	Aberd	NJ7635	57°24·5′	2°23·5′W	X	29
Littlehill of Knaven	Aberd	NJ8743	57°28·9′	2°12·5′W	X	30
Littlehill Platn	Scot Bord	NT6440	55°39·4′	2°33·9′W	F	74
Little Hills	Arg & Bt	NN3012	56°16·5′	4°44·3′W	H	50,56
Little Hills	D & G	NX4250	54°49·4′	4°27·1′W	X	83
Littlehills	Swan	SS4586	51°33·3′	4°13·8′W	X	159
Little Hills	Swan	SS5492	51°36·7′	4°6·1′W	X	159
Little Hilton	Aberd	NJ7351	57°33·2′	2°26·6′W	X	29
Little Hilton	Pemb	SM8819	51°50·0′	5°4·2′W	X	157
Little Hockham	Norf	TL9490	52°28·6′	0°51·8′E	X	144
Little Hograh Moor	N Yks	NZ6506	54°27·0′	0°59·4′W	X	94
Little Hogus	Corn	SW5130	50°7·3′	5°28·6′W	X	203
Little Holbury	Hants	SU4204	50°50·3′	1°23·8′W	T	196
Little Holcombe Covert	Oxon	SU6296	51°39·8′	1°5·8′W	F	164,165
Little Holm	Shetld	HU3709	59°52·1′	1°19·9′W	X	4
Little Holm	Shetld	HU4086	60°33·6′	1°15·7′W	X	1,2,3
Little Holm	Shetld	HU4452	60°15·3′	1°11·8′W	X	3
Little Holmhill Inclosure	Hants	SU3206	50°51·4′	1°32·3′W	F	196
Little Holmside Fm	Durham	NZ1949	54°50·4′	1°41·8′W	FM	88
Little Holtby	N Yks	SE2791	54°19·1′	1°34·7′W	X	99
Little Honeyborough	Pemb	SM9506	51°43·2′	4°57·7′W	T	157,158
Little Hook Fm	Kent	TQ9449	51°12·7′	0°47·0′E	FM	189
Little Hookstead Fm	Kent	TQ8837	51°6·3′	0°41·5′E	FM	189
Little Hoole Moss Houses	Lancs	SD4823	53°42·3′	2°46·9′W	T	102
Little Horkesley	Essex	TL9632	51°57·3′	0°52·0′E	T	168
Little Hormead	Herts	TL4029	51°56·7′	0°2·6′E	T	167
Little Hormead Bury	Herts	TL3929	51°56·8′	0°1·7′E	X	166
Little Horringer Hall	Suff	TL8162	52°13·8′	0°39·4′E	X	155
Little Horse Shoe, The	Arg & Bt	NM8127	56°23·3′	5°32·4′W	W	49
Little Horsted	E Susx	TQ4718	50°56·8′	0°5·9′E	T	198
Little Horton	Brad	SE1531	53°46·7′	1°45·9′W	T	104
Little Horton	Wilts	SU0462	51°21·7′	1°56·2′W	T	173
Little Horton Wood	Northnts	SP8152	52°9·9′	0°48·5′W	F	152
Little Horwood	Bucks	SP7930	51°58·0′	0°50·6′W	T	152,165
Little Houghton	Barns	SE4205	53°32·6′	1°21·6′W	T	111
Little Houghton	Northnts	SP8059	52°13·6′	0°49·3′W	T	152
Littlehoughton	Northum	NU2316	55°26·5′	1°37·8′W	T	81
Little Houghton Lodge	Northnts	SP8058	52°13·1′	0°49·3′W	X	152
Little Houndbeare Fm	Devon	SY0593	50°44·0′	3°20·4′W	FM	192
Little Hound Tor	Devon	SX6389	50°41·3′	3°56·0′W	X	191
Little House Fm	Powys	SO1481	52°25·5′	3°15·5′W	FM	136
Little Houses	Kent	TQ9046	51°11·1′	0°43·5′E	X	189
Little How Crags	Cumbr	SD2799	54°23·1′	3°7·0′W	X	96,97
Little Howden Moor	Sheff	SK1891	53°25·2′	1°43·3′W	X	110
Little Huckham Fm	Somer	ST4535	51°6·9′	2°46·8′W	FM	182
Little Hucklow	Derby	SK1678	53°18·2′	1°45·2′W	T	119
Little Hudwick	Shrops	SO6292	52°31·7′	2°33·2′W	X	138
Little Hulton	Salf	SD7203	53°31·6′	2°24·9′W	T	109
Little Humber	E Yorks	TA1923	53°41·6′	0°11·4′W	X	107,113
Little Hunclett	Orkney	HY4705	58°56·0′	2°54·8′W	X	6,7
Little Hundridge Fm	Bucks	SP9202	51°42·8′	0°39·7′W	FM	165
Little Hungerford	W Berks	SU5173	51°27·5′	1°15·6′W	T	174
Little Hunsley	E Yorks	SE9635	53°48·4′	0°32·1′W	X	106
Little Hutton	Durham	NZ1412	54°30·4′	1°46·6′W	X	92
Little Hutton	N Yks	SE4576	54°10·9′	1°18·2′W	X	99
Little Hyde	Glos	SO6812	51°48·6′	2°27·5′W	X	162
Little Hyde Fm	Essex	TL6500	51°40·7′	0°23·6′E	FM	167
Little Hyde Hall	Essex	TL5015	51°49·0′	0°11·0′E	X	167
Little Ickford	Bucks	SP6507	51°45·7′	1°3·1′W	X	164,165
Little Idoch	Aberd	NJ7648	57°31·6′	2°23·6′W	X	29
Little Ilford	Newham	TQ4385	51°33·0′	0°4·1′E	T	177
Little Inch	Fife	NO3824	56°24·5′	2°59·8′W	X	54,59
Little Ingestre	Staffs	SJ9924	52°49·1′	2°0·5′W	T	127
Little Ing Fm	Cumbr	SD7899	54°23·4′	2°19·9′W	FM	98
Little Ing Gill	N Yks	SD8485	54°15·9′	2°14·3′W	W	98
Little Inkberrow	Worcs	SP0057	52°12·9′	1°59·6′W	T	150
Little Intake	Derby	SE1001	53°30·6′	1°50·5′W	X	110
Little Ion	Beds	TL1034	51°59·8′	0°23·5′W	X	153
Little Irchester	Northnts	SP9066	52°17·3′	0°40·4′W	T	152
Little Iridge Fm	E Susx	TQ7426	51°0·6′	0°29·2′E	FM	188,199
Little Isegarth	Orkney	HY6639	59°14·4′	2°35·3′W	X	5
Little Island	V of Glam	ST1066	51°23·4′	3°17·2′W	X	171
Little Isle	Durham	NZ3027	54°38·5′	1°31·7′W	X	93
Little Isle	Shrops	SO6074	52°22·0′	2°34·9′W	X	138
Little John	Leic	SK5008	52°40·3′	1°15·2′W	X	140
Little John	Peterb	TL1398	52°34·3′	0°19·6′W	A	142
Little John's Fm	Read	SU6974	51°27·9′	1°0·0′W	FM	175
Little John's Haven	Aberd	NO8574	56°51·7′	2°14·3′W	W	45
Little John's Well	Derby	SK2679	53°18·7′	1°36·2′W	W	119
Littlejoy	Devon	SX8371	50°31·9′	3°38·7′W	X	202
Little Keithick	Pth & Kin	NO1938	56°31·9′	3°18·6′W	X	53
Little Keithock	Angus	NO6062	56°45·1′	2°38·8′W	X	45
Little Kelk	E Yorks	TA1060	54°1·7′	0°18·8′W	X	101
Little Kelk Fm	E Yorks	TA1060	54°1·7′	0°18·8′W	FM	101
Little Kendale	E Yorks	TA0259	54°1·3′	0°26·2′W	X	106,107
Little Kendals Fm	Herts	TQ1698	51°40·4′	0°19·0′W	FM	166,176
Little Kenny	Angus	NO3053	56°40·1′	3°8·1′W	X	53
Little Kerloch	Aberd	NO6887	56°58·6′	2°31·1′W	H	45
Little Kerse	Falk	NS9379	55°59·8′	3°42·5′W	X	65
Little Kerse	Stir	NS6596	56°8·5′	4°9·9′W	X	57
Little Ketton	Darl	NZ3119	54°34·2′	1°30·8′W	X	93
Little Keyford	Somer	ST7746	51°13·0′	2°19·4′W	T	183
Little Kilchattan	Arg & Bt	NS1056	55°45·9′	5°1·3′W	X	63
Little Kildale	N Yks	NZ6109	54°28·6′	1°3·1′W	X	94
Little Kildrummie	Highld	NH8653	57°33·4′	3°53·9′W	X	27
Little Kilham Fm	E Yorks	TA0465	54°4·5′	0°24·2′W	FM	101
Little Kilmory	Arg & Bt	NS0459	55°47·3′	5°7·1′W	X	63
Little Kilmundie	Angus	NO3844	56°35·3′	3°0·1′W	X	54
Little Kilrannoch	Angus	NO2177	56°52·9′	3°17·3′W	X	44
Little Kilry	Angus	NO2255	56°41·1′	3°15·9′W	X	53
Little Kilsture	D & G	NX4348	54°48·4′	4°26·1′W	X	83
Little Kimble	Bucks	SP8207	51°45·6′	0°48·3′W	T	165
Little Kineton	Warw	SP3350	52°9·1′	1°30·7′W	T	151
Little King Seat	Scot Bord	NT1252	55°45·5′	3°23·7′W	X	65,72
Little Kingshill	Bucks	SU8999	51°41·2′	0°42·4′W	T	165
Little Kington Fm	Dorset	ST7723	51°0·6′	2°19·3′W	FM	183
Little Kirkhill	Aberd	NJ9445	57°30·0′	2°5·5′W	X	30
Little Kit's Coty Ho	Kent	TQ7460	51°19·0′	0°30·2′E	A	178,188
Little Knapside Hill	Cumbr	NY6439	54°44·9′	2°33·1′W	H	91
Little Kneeset	Devon	SX5984	50°38·6′	3°59·3′W	H	191
Little Knighton Fm	Worcs	SP0457	52°12·9′	1°56·1′W	FM	150
Little Knight's Oast	E Susx	TQ8217	50°55·6′	0°35·8′E	X	199
Little Knockoure	D & G	NX8084	55°8·4′	3°52·5′W	X	78
Little Knoll	Wilts	ST8037	51°8·1′	2°16·8′W	H	183
Little Knowle	Devon	SY0682	50°38·0′	3°19·4′W	T	192
Little Knowle Fm	Devon	SS3202	50°47·8′	4°22·7′W	FM	190
Little Knowles Green	Suff	TL7758	52°11·7′	0°35·8′E	T	155
Little Knox	D & G	NX8060	54°55·5′	3°51·9′W	X	84
Little Kype East	S Lanak	NS7440	55°38·5′	3°59·7′W	X	71
Little Kype West	S Lanak	NS7440	55°38·5′	3°59·7′W	X	71
Little Laight	D & G	NX0670	54°59·5′	5°1·5′W	X	76
Little Laith	Lancs	SD9238	53°50·5′	2°6·9′W	X	103
Littlelake Fm	Surrey	TQ2944	51°11·1′	0°8·9′W	FM	187
Little Lakes	Worcs	SO7672	52°21·0′	2°20·7′W	X	138
Little Landside	Devon	ST0315	50°55·8′	3°22·4′W	X	181
Little Langdale	Cumbr	NY3103	54°25·3′	3°3·4′W	T	90
Little Langdale Tarn	Cumbr	NY3003	54°25·3′	3°4·3′W	W	90
Little Langford	Devon	SS7100	50°47·3′	3°49·4′W	X	191
Little Langford	Wilts	SU0436	51°7·6′	1°56·2′W	T	184
Little Langford Fm	Norf	TL8197	52°32·7′	0°40·6′E	FM	144
Little Langley Fm	Kent	TQ8939	51°7·4′	0°42·4′E	FM	189
Little Langton Grange	N Yks	SE3094	54°20·7′	1°31·9′W	X	99
Little Larg	D & G	NX1666	54°57·5′	4°52·0′W	X	82
Little Laught	N Ayr	NS2645	55°40·3′	4°45·6′W	X	63
Little Laver	Essex	TL5409	51°45·7′	0°14·3′E	T	167
Little Laver Hall	Essex	TL5410	51°46·3′	0°14·3′E	X	167
Little Law	Pth & Kin	NN9908	56°15·5′	3°37·4′W	X	58
Little Law	Scot Bord	NT5959	55°49·6′	2°38·8′W	H	67,73,74
Little Law	S Lanak	NS9228	55°32·3′	3°42·2′W	H	71,72
Little Lawford	Warw	SP4677	52°23·6′	1°19·0′W	T	140
Little Lawsley	Northum	NY8757	54°54·7′	2°11·7′W	X	87
Little Layton	Blackp	SD3237	53°49·7′	3°1·6′W	T	102
Little Leake	N Yks	SE4391	54°19·0′	1°19·9′W	X	99
Little Lediken	Aberd	NJ6529	57°21·3′	2°34·4′W	X	38
Little Leigh	Ches	SJ6175	53°16·5′	2°34·7′W	T	118
Little Leigh	Devon	SX7996	50°45·3′	3°42·5′W	X	191
Little Leighs	Essex	TL7116	51°49·2′	0°29·3′E	T	167
Little Lemhill Fm	Glos	SP2001	51°42·7′	1°42·2′W	FM	163
Little Lepton	Kirk	SE2014	53°37·6′	1°41·4′W	T	110
Little Leven	E Yorks	TA1045	53°53·6′	0°19·1′W	T	107
Little Lever	Bolton	SD7507	53°33·8′	2°22·2′W	T	109
Little Ley	Aberd	NJ6511	57°11·6′	2°34·3′W	X	38
Little Ley	Angus	NO2661	56°44·3′	3°12·1′W	H	44
Little Leyfields	Notts	SK6764	53°10·4′	0°59·4′W	X	120
Little Leys	Essex	TL6416	51°49·3′	0°23·2′E	X	167
Little Limber	Lincs	TA1210	53°34·7′	0°18·1′W	T	113
Little Limber Grange	Lincs	TA1009	53°34·2′	0°19·9′W	X	113
Little Linford	Mil Key	SP8444	52°5·5′	0°46·0′W	T	152
Little Linford Inclosure	Hants	SU1807	50°52·0′	1°44·3′W	F	195
Little Linga	Orkney	HY6030	59°9·6′	2°41·5′W	X	5,6
Little Linga	Shetld	HU5265	60°22·2′	1°2·9′W	X	2,3
Little Links Tor	Devon	SX5486	50°39·6′	4°3·6′W	X	191,201
Little Linton	Cambs	TL5547	52°6·2′	0°16·2′E	X	154
Little Liverpool	Derby	SK2414	52°43·6′	1°38·3′W	X	128
Little Llwygy	Monm	SO3122	51°53·8′	2°59·8′W	X	161
Little Load	Somer	ST4624	51°1·0′	2°45·8′W	T	193
Little Loch	Aberd	NK0231	57°22·4′	1°57·5′W	W	30
Little Loch	E Renf	NS5052	55°44·5′	4°22·9′W	W	64
Little Loch	Orkney	ND2198	58°52·0′	3°21·7′W	W	6,7
Little Lochans	D & G	NX0757	54°52·5′	5°0·1′W	X	82
Little Loch Borve	N Eil	NF9181	57°43·0′	7°10·9′W	W	18
Little Loch Broom	Highld	NH0392	57°52·7′	5°18·9′W	W	19
Little Lochlair	Angus	NO5143	56°34·8′	2°47·4′W	X	54
Little Loch Roag	N Eil	NB1227	58°8·6′	6°53·2′W	W	13
Little Loch Scye	Highld	ND0155	58°28·6′	3°41·4′W	W	11,12
Little Loch Skiach	Pth & Kin	NN9546	56°35·9′	3°42·2′W	W	52,53
Little Lodge	Essex	TL6828	51°55·7′	0°27·0′E	X	167
Little Lodge	Powys	SO1838	52°2·3′	3°11·3′W	X	161
Little Lodge	Suff	TM2864	52°13·8′	1°20·7′E	X	156
Little Lodge Fm	Lincs	TF2412	52°41·7′	0°9·5′W	FM	131,142
Little Lodge Fm	Suff	TL8387	52°27·2′	0°42·0′E	FM	144
Little Lodge Fm	Worcs	SO9561	52°15·1′	2°4·0′W	FM	150
Little London	Brad	SE2039	53°51·1′	1°41·3′W	T	104
Little London	Bucks	SP6412	51°48·4′	1°3·9′W	T	164,165
Little London	Bucks	SP8605	51°44·5′	0°44·9′W	T	165
Little London	Cambs	TL4196	52°32·8′	0°5·2′E	T	142,143
Little London	Corn	SW5230	50°7·3′	5°27·8′W	X	203
Little London	Essex	TL4729	51°56·6′	0°8·7′E	T	167
Little London	Essex	TL6835	51°59·5′	0°27·2′E	T	154
Little London	E Susx	TQ5719	50°57·2′	0°14·5′E	T	199
Little London	Glos	SO7018	51°51·8′	2°25·7′W	T	162
Little London	Hants	SU3749	51°14·6′	1°27·8′W	T	185
Little London	Hants	SU6259	51°19·8′	1°6·2′W	T	175
Little London	Heref	SO3546	52°6·7′	2°56·6′W	X	148,149
Little London	I of M	SC3286	54°14·8′	4°34·3′W	X	95
Little London	Kent	TR1148	51°11·8′	1°1·6′E	X	179,189
Little London	Kent	TR2544	51°9·3′	1°13·4′E	X	179
Little London	Lincs	TF1486	53°21·7′	0°16·8′W	T	113,121
Little London	Lincs	TF2320	52°46·0′	0°10·2′W	T	131
Little London	Lincs	TF3375	53°15·6′	0°0·0′E	T	122
Little London	Lincs	TF4323	52°47·4′	0°7·6′E	T	131
Little London	NE Lincs	TA1811	53°35·2′	0°12·6′W	X	113
Little London	Norf	TG1030	52°49·8′	1°7·4′E	T	133
Little London	Norf	TG1823	52°45·9′	1°14·3′E	T	133,134
Little London	Norf	TG2931	52°49·9′	1°24·4′E	T	133
Little London	Norf	TL7696	52°32·2′	0°36·1′E	T	143
Little London	Oxon	SP5201	51°42·6′	1°14·5′W	T	164
Little London	Powys	SO0489	52°29·7′	3°24·4′W	T	136
Little London	Shrops	SO5088	52°29·5′	2°43·8′W	T	137,138
Little London	Somer	ST6247	51°13·5′	2°32·3′W	T	183
Little London	Suff	TM0063	52°14·0′	0°56·1′E	X	155
Little London	Suff	TM0455	52°9·6′	0°59·4′E	T	155
Little London	Wilts	SU0671	51°26·5′	1°54·4′W	X	173
Little London	Worcs	SO6371	52°20·4′	2°32·2′W	T	138
Little London	W Susx	SU9119	50°58·0′	0°41·9′W	X	197
Little london Fm	Essex	TL8809	51°45·1′	0°43·8′E	FM	168
Little Longstone	Derby	SK1871	53°14·4′	1°43·4′W	T	119
Little Lough	Northum	NY9795	55°15·2′	2°2·4′W	W	81
Little Lour	Angus	NO4744	56°35·4′	2°51·3′W	X	54
Little Loveny Hall	Essex	TL8831	51°57·0′	0°44·5′E	X	168
Little Luddington Fm	Warw	SP1753	52°10·7′	1°44·7′W	FM	151
Little Lude	Pth & Kin	NN9068	56°47·7′	3°47·6′W	X	43
Little Lun	Fife	NT3399	56°11·0′	3°4·3′W	X	59
Little Lunga Water	Shetld	HU3288	60°34·7′	1°24·5′W	W	1
Little Lyne	Highld	NH9745	57°29·3′	3°42·6′W	X	27
Little Lynturk	Aberd	NJ5712	57°12·1′	2°42·2′W	X	37
Little Lyth	Shrops	SJ4706	52°39·2′	2°46·6′W	T	126
Little Madeley	Staffs	SJ7745	53°0·3′	2°20·2′W	T	118
Little Mains of Hatton	Aberd	NJ6842	57°28·3′	2°31·6′W	X	29
Little Maldron	Aberd	NJ6303	57°7·2′	2°36·2′W	X	37
Little Malgraves	Thurr	TQ6686	51°33·1′	0°24·1′E	X	177,178
Little Malvern	Worcs	SO7640	52°3·7′	2°20·6′W	T	150
Little Man	Cumbr	NY2627	54°38·2′	3°8·4′W	H	89,90
Little Mancot	Flint	SJ3266	53°11·4′	3°0·7′W	T	117
Little Manor Fm	Halton	SJ5781	53°19·7′	2°38·3′W	FM	108
Little Manor Fm	N Yks	SE6486	54°16·2′	1°0·6′W	FM	94,100
Little Maplestead	Essex	TL8234	51°58·7′	0°39·4′E	T	155
Little Marcle	Heref	SO6736	52°1·5′	2°28·5′W	T	149
Little Mark	D & G	NX0359	54°53·5′	5°3·9′W	X	82
Littlemark	E Ayr	NS5710	55°22·0′	4°14·9′W	X	71
Little Marland	Devon	SS4911	50°53·0′	4°8·4′W	X	191
Little Marland	Devon	SS4912	50°53·5′	4°8·4′W	X	180
Little Marles Fm	Essex	TL4406	51°44·3′	0°5·5′E	FM	167
Little Marloes Fm	Pemb	SM7907	51°43·3′	5°11·6′W	FM	157
Little Marlow	Bucks	SU8788	51°35·3′	0°44·3′W	T	175
Little Marl Point	Norf	TG2938	52°53·7′	1°24·7′E	X	133
Little Marsden	Lancs	SD8537	53°50·0′	2°13·3′W	T	103
Little Marsh	Bucks	SP6523	51°54·3′	1°2·9′W	T	164,165
Little Marsh	Hants	SZ4096	50°46·0′	1°25·6′W	X	196
Little Marsh	Norf	TG0038	52°54·4′	0°58·9′E	T	133
Little Marsh	Wilts	ST8959	51°20·0′	2°9·1′W	T	173
Little Marston Fm	Somer	ST5722	51°0·0′	2°36·4′W	FM	183
Little Marton	Blackp	SD3434	53°48·1′	2°59·7′W	T	102
Little Mascalls	Essex	TL7302	51°41·6′	0°30·6′E	T	167
Little Massingham	Norf	TF7924	52°47·3′	0°39·7′E	T	132
Littlemayne	Dorset	SY7287	50°41·2′	2°23·4′W	X	194
Little Mearley Hall	Lancs	SD7741	53°52·1′	2°20·6′W	A	103
Little Meaton	Shrops	SO7078	52°24·2′	2°26·1′W	X	138
Little Meend	Glos	SO5600	51°42·1′	2°37·8′W	X	162
Little Meg	Cumbr	NY5737	54°43·8′	2°39·6′W	A	91
Little Meldrum	Aberd	NJ8833	57°23·5′	2°11·5′W	X	38
Little Mell Fell	Cumbr	NY4224	54°36·7′	2°53·5′W	H	90
Little Melton	Norf	TG1606	52°36·8′	1°11·8′E	T	144
Little Mere River	Devon	SS5210	50°52·5′	4°5·8′W	W	191
Littlemerk Hill	D & G	NS8106	55°20·3′	3°52·1′W	H	71,78
Little Merthyr	Heref	SO2648	52°7·8′	3°4·5′W	T	148
Little Methlick	Aberd	NJ8537	57°25·6′	2°14·5′W	X	30
Little Mew Stone	Devon	SX7235	50°12·3′	3°47·2′W	X	202
Little Middop	Lancs	SD8445	53°54·3′	2°14·2′W	X	103
Little Milford	Pemb	SM9611	51°45·9′	4°57·0′W	T	157,158
Littlemill	Aberd	NJ4521	57°16·8′	2°54·3′W	X	37
Littlemill	Aberd	NJ5147	57°30·9′	2°48·6′W	X	29
Littlemill	Aberd	NJ5824	57°18·5′	2°41·4′W	X	37
Littlemill	Aberd	NJ6737	57°25·6′	2°32·5′W	X	29
Littlemill	Aberd	NJ9644	57°29·4′	2°3·5′W	X	30
Littlemill	Aberd	NO3295	57°2·7′	3°6·8′W	X	37,44
Little Mill	Angus	NO4349	56°38·0′	2°55·3′W	X	54
Littlemill	E Ayr	NS4515	55°24·5′	4°26·5′W	T	70
Littlemill	Highld	NH7037	57°24·6′	4°9·4′W	X	27
Littlemill	Highld	NH9150	57°31·9′	3°48·8′W	T	27
Little Mill	Kent	TQ6548	51°12·7′	0°22·1′E	T	188
Little Mill	Monm	SO3202	51°43·0′	2°58·7′W	T	171
Littlemill	Northum	NU2218	55°27·6′	1°38·7′W	X	81
Little Millbrex	Aberd	NJ8144	57°29·4′	2°18·6′W	X	29,30
Little Mill of Clinterty	C of Aber	NJ8310	57°11·1′	2°16·4′W	X	38
Littlemill of Esslemont	Aberd	NJ9228	57°20·8′	2°7·5′W	X	38
Little Millriggs	D & G	NY1690	55°12·1′	3°18·8′W	X	79

Little Millyea	D & G	NX5181	55°6·3′	4°19·7′W	H	77
Little Milton	D & G	NX8471	55°1·5′	3°48·4′W	X	84
Little Milton	Oxon	SP6100	51°42·0′	1°6·6′W	T	164,165
Little Minalto	I Scilly	SV8611	49°55·2′	6°22·1′W	X	203
Little Minch, The		NG0273	57°39·2′	6°59·3′W	W	18
Little Minch, The		NG1768	57°37·1′	6°43·9′W	W	23
Little Minch, The	N Eil	NG1986	57°46·8′	6°43·2′W	W	14
Little Minster	Oxon	SP3111	51°48·0′	1°32·6′W	T	164
Little Minterne Hill	Dorset	ST6604	50°50·3′	2°28·6′W	H	194
Little Missnden	Bucks	SU9298	51°40·6′	0°39·8′W	T	165
Little Mis Tor	Devon	SX5676	50°34·2′	4°1·6′W	H	191
Little Moat Fm	Kent	TQ9741	51°8·3′	0°49·4′E	FM	189
Little Mochrum	D & G	NX7375	55°3·4′	3°58·9′W	X	77,84
Little Modbury	Devon	SX6550	50°20·3′	3°53·5′W	X	202
Little Mongeham	Kent	TR3350	51°12·3′	1°20·5′E	T	179
Little Monkside	Northum	NY7094	55°14·6′	2°27·9′W	X	80
Littlemoor	Derby	SK3663	53°10·0′	1°27·3′W	T	119
Littlemoor	Dorset	SY6882	50°38·4′	2°26·8′W	T	194
Little Moor	Lancs	SD7440	53°51·6′	2°23·3′W	T	103
Little Moor	N Yks	SE4991	54°19·0′	1°14·4′W	X	100
Little Moor	N Yks	SE5085	54°15·7′	1°13·5′W	X	100
Little Moor	N Yks	TA0095	54°20·7′	0°27·3′W	X	101
Little Moor	Somer	ST3232	51°5·2′	2°57·9′W	X	182
Little Moor	Somer	ST3946	51°12·8′	2°52·0′W	X	182
Little Moor	Staffs	SO8398	52°35·0′	2°14·7′W	X	138
Little Moor	Stock	SJ9189	53°24·1′	2°7·7′W	T	109
Little Moor End	Lancs	SD7327	53°44·6′	2°24·2′W	T	103
Little Moor Fm	Durham	NZ1427	54°38·5′	1°46·6′W	FM	92
Littlemoor Fm	Leeds	SE3839	53°51·0′	1°24·9′W	FM	104
Littlemoor Fm	Norf	TG0125	52°47·3′	0°59·3′E	FM	133
Little Moor Hall Fm	Lancs	SD4005	53°32·5′	2°53·9′W	FM	108
Little Moorsholm Fm	Red & Cl	NZ6816	54°32·3′	0°56·5′W	FM	94
Littlemoor Wood	Derby	SK3158	53°7·3′	1°31·8′W	F	119
Littlemore	Oxon	SP5302	51°43·1′	1°13·6′W	T	164
Little Moreton Hall	Ches	SJ8358	53°7·4′	2°14·8′W	A	118
Little Morrell	Warw	SP3156	52°12·3′	1°32·4′W	T	151
Little Morton Fm	Notts	SK6778	53°17·9′	0°59·3′W	FM	120
Little Morven	Highld	ND0027	58°13·5′	3°41·7′W	X	17
Little Mosedale Beck	Cumbr	NY5009	54°28·7′	2°45·9′W	W	90
Little-moss	Ches	SJ8356	53°6·3′	2°14·8′W	X	118
Littlemoss	Tames	SJ9199	53°29·5′	2°7·7′W	T	109
Little Moss Fm	Ches	SJ8277	53°17·6′	2°15·8′W	FM	118
Little Mountain	Flint	SJ2963	53°9·8′	3°3·3′W	T	117
Little Mountain	Heref	SO2842	52°4·5′	3°2·6′W	X	148,161
Little Mountain	Powys	SO1442	52°4·4′	3°14·9′W	X	148,161
Little Mountain	Powys	SO2149	52°8·3′	3°8·9′W	H	148
Little Mountain	Torf	SO2802	51°43·0′	3°2·1′W	H	171
Little Mount Meddin	Moray	NJ3922	57°17·3′	3°0·3′W	H	37
Little Mulltaggart	D & G	NX5267	54°58·8′	4°18·3′W	X	83
Little Munden Fm	Herts	TL1300	51°41·5′	0°21·5′W	FM	166
Little Murston	Kent	TQ9365	51°21·3′	0°46·7′E	X	178
Little Musgrave	Cumbr	NY7513	54°30·9′	2°22·7′W	T	91
Little Myles	Essex	TL5601	51°41·4′	0°15·8′E	X	167
Little Narrowcove	Cumbr	NY2206	54°26·9′	3°11·8′W	X	89,90
Little Ness	I of M	SC3672	54°7·3′	4°30·2′W	X	95
Little Ness	Shetld	HU3067	60°23·4′	1°26·8′W	X	3
Littleness	Shetld	HU3616	59°55·9′	1°20·9′W	X	4
Little Ness	Shetld	HU4761	60°20·1′	1°8·4′W	X	2,3
Little Ness	Shrops	SJ4019	52°46·2′	2°53·0′W	T	126
Little Neston	Ches	SJ2976	53°16·8′	3°3·5′W	T	117
Little Newarks	Essex	TL6411	51°46·6′	0°23·0′E	X	167
Little Newbury Fm	Oxon	SU3092	51°37·8′	1°33·6′W	FM	164,174
Little Newcastle	Pemb	SM9728	51°55·1′	4°56·7′W	T	157,158
Little Newcombes	Devon	SX8899	50°47·0′	3°34·9′W	X	192
Little Newsham	Durham	NZ1217	54°33·1′	1°48·4′W	T	92
Little Newsome	E Yorks	TA3026	53°43·1′	0°1·4′W	X	107
Little Newton	Aberd	NJ5525	57°19·1′	2°44·4′W	X	37
Little Newton	N Yks	SD8557	54°0·8′	2°13·3′W	X	103
Little Nineveh	Kent	TQ7832	51°3·8′	0°32·8′E	X	188
Little Nobury	Worcs	SP0256	52°12·4′	1°57·8′W	X	150
Little Norlington	E Susx	TQ4514	50°54·7′	0°4·1′E	T	198
Little North Fen	Cambs	TL4367	52°17·2′	0°6·2′E	X	154
Little Norton	Somer	ST4715	50°56·2′	2°44·9′W	T	193
Little Norwood	Kent	TQ8765	51°21·4′	0°41·5′E	X	178
Little Noup Head	Orkney	HY5539	59°14·4′	2°46·8′W	X	5
Little Oak	Newp	ST4193	51°38·2′	2°50·8′W	X	171,172
Little Oakleigh	Kent	TQ7273	51°26·0′	0°28·9′E	X	178
Little Oakley	Essex	TM2229	51°55·1′	1°14·1′E	T	169
Little Oakley	Northnts	SP8985	52°27·6′	0°41·0′W	T	141
Little Oakley Hall	Essex	TM2128	51°54·6′	1°13·2′E	X	169
Little Oaks	Rut	SK9511	52°41·5′	0°35·3′W	F	130
Little Oak Square	Notts	SK6373	53°15·3′	1°2·9′W	F	120
Little Ochiltree	W Loth	NT0474	55°57·2′	3°31·8′W	X	65
Little Odell	Beds	SP9657	52°12·4′	0°35·3′W	T	153
Little Offley	Herts	TL1328	51°56·6′	0°21·0′W	T	166
Little Olantigh Fm	Kent	TR0648	51°11·9′	0°57·3′E	FM	179,189
Little Omenden Fm	Kent	TQ8739	51°7·4′	0°40·7′E	FM	189
Little Onn	Staffs	SJ8316	52°44·7′	2°14·7′W	T	127
Little Orcheton	Devon	SX6350	50°20·3′	3°55·1′W	X	202
Little Ormes Head	Conwy	SH8182	53°19·5′	3°46·8′W	X	116
Little Ormside	Cumbr	NY7016	54°32·5′	2°27·4′W	T	91
Little or North Port of Spittal	D & G	NX0253	54°50·2′	5°4·6′W	X	82
Little or South Haw	N Yks	SE0878	54°12·1′	1°52·2′W	X	99
Little Orton	Cumbr	NY3555	54°53·4′	3°0·4′W	T	85
Little Orton	Leic	SK3105	52°38·7′	1°32·1′W	T	140
Little Ossa	Shetld	HU2184	60°32·6′	1°36·5′W	X	3
Littleour	Pth & Kin	NO1740	56°32·9′	3°20·6′W	X	53
Little Ouse	Cambs	TL6289	52°28·7′	0°23·5′E	T	143
Little Ouseburn	N Yks	SE4460	54°2·3′	1°19·3′W	T	99
Little Ouse River	Cambs	TL6487	52°27·6′	0°25·2′E	W	143
Little Ouse River	Norf	TL8585	52°26·1′	0°43·7′E	W	144
Little Ouse River	Norf	TL9080	52°23·3′	0°47·9′E	W	144
Littleover	C of Derb	SK3233	52°53·8′	1°31·1′W	T	128
Little Overton	Wrex	SJ3741	52°58·0′	2°55·9′W	T	117
Little Owens Ct	Kent	TR0358	51°17·3′	0°55·1′E	X	178,179
Little Ox	E Loth	NT3673	55°57·0′	3°1·1′W	X	66
Little Oxenbold	Shrops	SO5891	52°31·2′	2°36·7′W	X	137,138
Little Oxendon	Northnts	SP7284	52°27·2′	0°56·0′W	X	141
Little Oxendon Village	Northnts	SP7384	52°27·2′	0°55·1′W	A	141
Little Oxney Green	Essex	TL6605	51°43·4′	0°24·6′E	T	167
Little Packington	Warw	SP2184	52°27·4′	1°41·1′W	T	139
Little Pale	Carm	SN2315	51°48·6′	4°33·7′W	X	158
Little Palgrave Hall	Norf	TF8313	52°41·3′	0°42·9′E	X	132
Little Pap	Aberd	NO2684	56°56·7′	3°12·5′W	X	44
Little Park	Barns	SE4206	53°33·2′	1°21·6′W	F	111
Little Park	D & G	NX4565	54°57·6′	4°24·8′W	X	83
Little-Park	D & G	NX7672	55°1·9′	3°56·0′W	X	84
Little Park	Powys	SO0571	52°20·0′	3°23·3′W	X	136,147
Littlepark	Staffs	SK1549	53°2·5′	1°46·2′W	X	119
Little Park Copse	Hants	SU6946	51°12·8′	1°0·3′W	F	186
Littlepark Farm	Beds	TL0237	52°1·6′	0°30·4′W	FM	153
Little Park Fm	E Susx	TQ5414	50°54·5′	0°11·8′E	FM	199
Little Park Fm	E Susx	TQ7516	50°55·2′	0°29·8′E	FM	199
Little Park Fm	Hants	SU3344	51°11·9′	1°31·3′W	FM	185
Little Park Fm	Suff	TM0847	52°5·2′	1°2·6′E	FM	155,169
Little Park Fm	W Berks	SU6763	51°22·0′	1°1·9′W	FM	175,186
Little Park Fm	Wilts	SU0580	51°31·4′	1°55·3′W	FM	173
Little Park Ho	W Berks	SU5464	51°22·6′	1°13·1′W	X	174
Little Park Wood	D & G	NX4565	54°57·6′	4°24·8′W	F	83
Little Park Wood	E Susx	TQ8518	50°56·1′	0°38·4′E	F	189,199
Little Park Wood	N Yks	SE8285	54°15·5′	0°44·1′W	F	94,100
Little Parndon	Essex	TL4310	51°46·4′	0°4·8′E	T	167
Little Parrock	E Susx	TQ4434	51°5·5′	0°3·8′E	X	187
Little Pasture	N Yks	SE9667	54°5·6′	0°31·5′W	X	101
Little Pattenden	Kent	TQ7445	51°10·9′	0°29·8′E	X	188
Little Paxton	Cambs	TL1862	52°14·8′	0°15·9′W	T	153
Little Paxton Wood	Cambs	TL1663	52°15·4′	0°17·6′W	F	153
Little Pednor Fm	Bucks	SP9202	51°42·8′	0°39·7′W	FM	165
Little Pell Fm	E Susx	TQ6432	51°4·1′	0°20·8′E	FM	188
Little Penlan	Heref	SO2751	52°9·4′	3°3·6′W	X	148
Little Pennard Fm	Somer	ST6037	51°8·1′	2°33·9′W	FM	183
Little Pennatillies	Corn	SW9167	50°28·2′	4°56·3′W	X	200
Little Pen-y-lan Fm	Heref	SO4027	51°56·5′	2°52·0′W	FM	161
Little Petherick	Corn	SW9172	50°30·9′	4°56·5′W	T	200
Little Petherick Creek	Corn	SW9173	50°31·4′	4°56·5′W	W	200
Little Pett Fm	Kent	TQ8560	51°18·8′	0°39·7′E	FM	178
Little Peverels	Essex	TL7101	51°41·1′	0°28·8′E	X	167
Little Piece, The	Kent	TR1132	51°3·1′	1°1·0′E	X	189
Little Pillhead	Devon	SS4926	51°1·1′	4°8·8′W	X	180
Little Pilmuir	Fife	NO4003	56°13·2′	2°57·6′W	X	59
Little Pinkerton	E Loth	NT6976	55°58·8′	2°29·4′W	X	67
Little Pinmore	S Ayr	NX1988	55°9·4′	4°50·0′W	X	76
Little Pipe Fm	Staffs	SK0710	52°41·5′	1°53·4′W	FM	128
Little Pitinnan	Aberd	NJ7530	57°21·8′	2°24·5′W	X	29
Little Pitlurg	Moray	NJ4245	57°29·8′	2°57·6′W	X	28
Little Pix Hall Fm	Kent	TQ7331	51°3·4′	0°28·5′E	FM	188
Little Plantn	York	SE6759	54°1·6′	0°58·2′W	F	105,106
Little Plowland	E Yorks	TA3422	53°40·9′	0°2·1′E	X	107,113
Little Plumpton	Lancs	SD3732	53°47·1′	2°57·0′W	T	102
Little Plumstead	Norf	TG3112	52°39·6′	1°25·4′E	T	133,134
Little Ponton	Lincs	SK9232	52°52·9′	0°37·6′W	T	130
Littleport	Cambs	TL5686	52°27·2′	0°18·2′E	T	143
Littleport	Norf	TF7236	52°53·9′	0°33·8′E	X	132
Little Port Hill	Pth & Kin	NN7024	56°23·7′	4°5·9′W	X	51,52
Little Posbrook	Hants	SU5304	50°50·2′	1°14·5′W	T	196
Little Postland	Lincs	TF3113	52°42·2′	0°3·3′W	X	131,142
Little Potheridge	Devon	SS5213	50°54·1′	4°5·9′W	X	180
Little Poulton	Lancs	SD3539	53°50·8′	2°58·9′W	T	102
Little Powgavie Fm	Pth & Kin	NO2826	56°25·5′	3°9·6′W	FM	53,59
Little Preston	Kent	TQ7358	51°17·9′	0°29·3′E	T	178,188
Little Preston	Leeds	SE3830	53°46·1′	1°25·0′W	T	104
Little Preston	Northnts	SP5854	52°11·1′	1°8·7′W	X	152
Little Prideaux	Corn	SX0656	50°22·6′	4°43·3′W	X	200
Little Puddle Bottom	Dorset	SY7196	50°46·0′	2°24·3′W	X	194
Little Puddle Hill	Dorset	SY7095	50°45·5′	2°25·1′W	X	194
Little Punchard Gill	N Yks	NY9603	54°25·6′	2°3·3′W	W	91,92
Little Punchard Head	N Yks	NY9503	54°25·6′	2°4·2′W	X	91,92
Little Purnel	Hants	SZ3999	50°47·6′	1°26·4′W	X	196
Little Purston	Northnts	SP5139	52°3·1′	1°15·0′W	X	151
Little Quantock Fm	Somer	ST1436	51°7·2′	3°13·3′W	FM	181
Little Quay Bay	Cered	SN4160	52°13·2′	4°19·3′W	W	146
Littlequoy	Orkney	ND4496	58°51·1′	2°57·8′W	X	6,7
Littler	Ches	SJ6366	53°11·6′	2°32·8′W	T	118
Little Rackenford Fm	Devon	SS8618	50°57·2′	3°37·0′W	FM	181
Little Rack Wick	Orkney	ND2392	58°48·8′	3°19·5′W	W	7
Little Rahane	Arg & Bt	NS2386	56°2·3′	4°50·0′W	X	56
Little Raith	Fife	NT2091	56°6·6′	3°16·7′W	X	58
Little Rakefairs	Essex	TL6225	51°54·2′	0°21·7′E	X	167
Little Ranch	Somer	ST4740	51°9·6′	2°45·1′W	X	182
Little Range Cleuch	Scot Bord	NT3220	55°28·4′	3°4·1′W	X	73
Little Raveley	Cambs	TL2579	52°23·9′	0°9·4′W	T	142
Little Raws	E Ayr	NS4739	55°37·5′	4°25·4′W	X	70
Little Reedness	E Yorks	SE8022	53°41·5′	0°46·9′W	T	106,112
Little Renters Fm	Essex	TL8910	51°45·6′	0°44·7′E	FM	168
Little Revel End	Herts	TL0810	51°46·9′	0°25·7′W	X	166
Little Reynoldston	Swan	SS4889	51°35·0′	4°11·2′W	T	159
Little Rhyndaston	Pemb	SM8923	51°52·2′	5°3·5′W	X	157,158
Little Ribston	N Yks	SE3853	53°58·5′	1°24·8′W	T	104
Little Richorn	D & G	NX8359	54°55·0′	3°49·1′W	X	84
Little Ridsdale	Northum	NY8986	55°10·3′	2°9·9′W	X	80
Littlerig	Pth & Kin	NO0107	56°15·0′	3°35·4′W	X	58
Little Rigend Hill	E Ayr	NS5311	55°22·5′	4°18·8′W	X	70
Little Rissington	Glos	SP1919	51°52·4′	1°43·0′W	T	163
Little River	Highld	ND1647	58°24·5′	3°25·8′W	W	11,12
Little River	N Som	ST4066	51°23·6′	2°51·4′W	W	171,172,182
Little River	Somer	SS8732	51°4·8′	3°36·4′W	W	181
Little Rock	Northum	NU2428	55°33·0′	1°36·7′W	X	75
Little Rodmore Fm	Dorset	ST7111	50°54·1′	2°24·4′W	FM	194
Little Roe	Shetld	HU4079	60°29·8′	1°15·8′W	X	2,3
Little Rogart	Highld	NC7203	58°0·1′	4°9·5′W	T	16
Little Rollright	Oxon	SP2930	51°58·3′	1°34·3′W	T	151
Little Rooks, The	Scot Bord	NT8571	55°56·2′	2°14·0′W	X	67
Little Rookwood Fm	Suff	TL8756	52°10·5′	0°44·5′E	FM	155
Little Ross	D & G	NX6543	54°46·1′	4°5·5′W	X	83,84
Little Rough Tor	Corn	SX1481	50°36·2′	4°37·3′W	X	200
Little Rowley	Devon	SS6542	51°9·9′	3°55·5′W	X	180
Little Rundale Beck	Cumbr	NY7126	54°37·9′	2°26·5′W	W	91
Little Rundale Tarn	Cumbr	NY7327	54°38·5′	2°24·7′W	W	91
Little Ryburgh	Norf	TF9628	52°49·1′	0°54·9′E	T	132
Little Ryle	Northum	NU0211	55°23·8′	1°57·7′W	X	81
Little Ryton	Shrops	SJ4803	52°37·6′	2°45·7′W	T	126
Little Salisbury	Wilts	SU1860	51°20·6′	1°44·1′W	T	173
Little Salkeld	Cumbr	NY5636	54°43·3′	2°40·6′W	T	90
Little Sampford	Essex	TL6533	51°58·5′	0°24·5′E	T	167
Little Sand Fm	Highld	NG7578	57°44·4′	5°46·3′W	FM	19
Little Sandhurst	Brackn	SU8362	51°21·3′	0°48·1′W	T	175,186
Little Saredon	Staffs	SJ9407	52°39·9′	2°4·9′W	T	127,139
Little Sarnesfield	Heref	SO3852	52°10·0′	2°54·0′W	X	148,149
Little Sauchen	Aberd	NJ6809	57°10·5′	2°31·3′W	X	38
Little Saxham	Suff	TL7963	52°14·4′	0°37·7′E	T	155
Little Says Law	E Loth	NT5961	55°50·7′	2°38·8′W	H	67
Little Scar	Hartpl	NZ5230	54°40·0′	1°11·2′W	X	93
Little Scar	N Yks	SD8088	54°17·5′	2°18·0′W	X	98
Little Scarcar	Northum	NU2236	55°37·3′	1°38·6′W	X	75
Little Scares	D & G	NX2634	54°40·5′	4°41·5′W	X	82
Little Scatwell	Highld	NH3856	57°34·2′	4°42·1′W	X	26
Little Scaw'd Law	D & G	NS9104	55°19·3′	3°42·6′W	X	78
Little Scotland	Wigan	SD6010	53°35·3′	2°35·8′W	T	109
Little Scotney	Kent	TR0121	50°57·4′	0°52·1′E	X	189
Little Scotney Fm	Kent	TQ6936	51°6·1′	0°25·2′E	FM	188
Little Scotston	Angus	NO3339	56°32·6′	3°4·9′W	X	53
Little Scraulac	Aberd	NJ3107	57°9·2′	3°8·0′W	X	37
Little Sea	Dorset	SZ0384	50°39·6′	1°57·1′W	W	195
Little Sea	Orkney	HY6739	59°14·4′	2°34·2′W	W	5
Little Seabrook	Bucks	SP9317	51°50·9′	0°38·6′W	X	165
Little Sessay	N Yks	SE4674	54°9·8′	1°17·3′W	X	100
Littles Fm	Kent	TR0058	51°17·4′	0°52·5′E	FM	178
Little Shalloch	E Ayr	NS4502	55°17·5′	4°26·0′W	X	77
Little Shalloch	S Ayr	NX2688	55°9·6′	4°43·4′W	X	76
Little Shank	Moray	NJ2434	57°23·7′	3°15·4′W	X	28
Little Sharpshaw Fm	Somer	ST7545	51°12·5′	2°21·1′W	FM	183
Little Sharsted Fm	Kent	TQ9458	51°17·5′	0°47·3′E	FM	178
Little Sheil Hill	Aberd	NO7991	57°0·8′	2°20·3′W	H	38,45
Little Shelfin Fm	Devon	SS5044	51°10·8′	4°8·4′W	FM	180
Little Shelford	Cambs	TL4551	52°8·5′	0°7·5′E	T	154
Little Shellwood	Surrey	TQ2145	51°11·7′	0°15·7′W	X	187
Little Shillay	N Eil	NF8790	57°47·7′	7°15·6′W	X	18
Little Shoddesden	Hants	SU2848	51°14·1′	1°35·5′W	T	184
Little Shrawardine	Shrops	SJ3915	52°44·0′	2°53·8′W	X	126
Little Shrewley	Warw	SP2267	52°18·3′	1°40·2′W	T	151
Little Shurdington	Glos	SO9117	51°51·3′	2°7·4′W	T	163
Little Sidcup	Kent	TQ5148	51°12·9′	0°10·1′E	X	188
Little Silver	Devon	SS5119	50°57·3′	4°6·9′W	X	180
Little Silver	Devon	SS5440	51°8·7′	4°4·9′W	T	180
Little Silver	Devon	SS6220	50°58·0′	3°57·5′W	X	180
Little Silver	Devon	SS9109	50°52·4′	3°32·6′W	T	192
Little Simon's Seat	N Yks	SE0860	54°2·4′	1°52·3′W	X	99
Little Singleton	Lancs	SD3739	53°50·9′	2°57·0′W	T	102
Little Sir Hughes	Essex	TL7402	51°41·6′	0°31·5′E	X	167
Little Skerries	Moray	NJ2271	57°43·6′	3°18·1′W	X	28
Little Skerry	Orkney	HY5111	58°59·3′	2°50·7′W	X	6
Little Skerry	Orkney	ND4776	58°40·4′	2°54·4′W	X	7
Little Skerry	Shetld	HU6371	60°25·3′	0°50·9′W	X	2
Little Skillymarno	Aberd	NJ9553	57°34·3′	2°4·6′W	X	30
Little Skipwith	N Yks	SE6538	53°50·3′	1°0·3′W	T	105,106
Little Sled Dale	N Yks	NY8200	54°24·0′	2°16·2′W	X	91,92
Little Sleddale Beck	N Yks	NY8201	54°24·5′	2°16·2′W	W	91,92
Little Smeaton	N Yks	NZ3403	54°25·5′	1°28·1′W	T	93
Little Smeaton	N Yks	SE5216	53°38·5′	1°12·4′W	T	111
Little Smithcott Fm	Wilts	ST9982	51°32·4′	2°0·5′W	FM	173
Little Snoring	Norf	TF9532	52°51·2′	0°54·2′E	T	132
Little Sodbury	S Glos	ST7583	51°33·0′	2°21·2′W	T	172
Little Sodbury End	S Glos	ST7483	51°33·0′	2°22·1′W	T	172
Little Solsbury Hill	Bath & NE Somer	ST7668	51°24·9′	2°20·3′W	H	172
Little Solsbury Hill (Fort)	Bath & NE Somer	ST7668	51°24·9′	2°20·3′W	A	172
Little Somborne	Hants	SU3832	51°5·4′	1°27·1′W	T	185
Little Somborne Ho	Hants	SU3832	51°5·4′	1°27·1′W	X	185
Little Somerford	Wilts	ST9684	51°33·5′	2°3·1′W	T	173
Little Sorn	E Ayr	NS4933	55°34·3′	4°23·3′W	X	70
Little Soudley	Shrops	SJ7128	52°51·2′	2°25·4′W	T	127
Little Sound	Pemb	SM7409	51°44·3′	5°16·0′W	W	157
Little Spear	D & G	NX4285	55°8·3′	4°28·3′W	X	77
Little Spierston	E Ayr	NS4722	55°28·3′	4°24·8′W	X	70
Little Spott	E Loth	NT6574	55°57·7′	2°33·2′W	X	67
Little Stainforth	N Yks	SD8167	54°6·2′	2°17·0′W	T	98
Little Stainton	Darl	NZ3420	54°34·7′	1°28·0′W	T	93
Little Stainton	N Yks	SD8953	53°58·6′	2°9·6′W	X	103
Little Stairs Point	I of W	SZ5882	50°38·3′	1°10·4′W	X	196
Little Stambridge Hall	Essex	TQ8892	51°35·9′	0°43·3′E	X	178
Little Stand	Cumbr	NY2403	54°25·3′	3°9·9′W	X	89,90
Little Stanmore	Harrow	TQ1890	51°36·0′	0°17·4′W	T	176
Little Stanney	Ches	SJ4174	53°15·8′	2°52·7′W	T	117
Little Staughton	Beds	TL1062	52°14·9′	0°22·9′W	T	153
Littlestead Green	Oxon	SU7376	51°28·9′	0°56·5′W	T	175
Little Steeping	Lincs	TF4362	53°8·4′	0°8·7′E	T	122
Little Stepple	Shrops	SO6577	52°23·6′	2°30·5′W	X	138
Littlester	Shetld	HU5080	60°30·3′	1°4·9′W	T	1,2,3
Little Stirk	Highld	NM5357	56°38·6′	6°1·3′W	X	47
Little Stock Fm	Kent	TR0638	51°6·5′	0°57·0′E	FM	179,189
Little Stoke	S Glos	ST6181	51°31·8′	2°33·3′W	T	172
Little Stoke	Staffs	SJ9132	52°53·4′	2°7·6′W	T	127
Littlestoke Manor	Oxon	SU6085	51°33·9′	1°7·7′W	X	175
Littlestone-on-Sea	Kent	TR0724	50°58·9′	0°57·3′E	T	189
Little Stonham	Suff	TM1159	52°11·6′	1°5·6′E	T	155
Little Stour	Kent	TR2462	51°19·0′	1°13·3′E	W	179
Little Strand	Corn	SX1295	50°43·7′	4°39·5′W	X	190
Little Strath	Aberd	NO6371	56°50·0′	2°35·9′W	X	45
Little Streele	E Susx	TQ5021	50°58·4′	0°8·6′E	X	199
Little Stretton	Leic	SK6600	52°35·9′	1°1·1′W	T	141
Little Stretton	Shrops	SO4491	52°31·1′	2°49·1′W	T	137
Little Strickland	Cumbr	NY5619	54°34·1′	2°40·4′W	T	90
Little Strudgate Fm	W Susx	TQ3232	51°4·6′	0°6·6′W	FM	187
Little Studdridge	Bucks	SU7595	51°39·2′	0°54·6′W	X	165
Little Studley	N Yks	SE3172	54°8·8′	1°31·1′W	T	99
Little Stukeley	Cambs	TL2075	52°21·8′	0°13·9′W	T	142
Little Sugnall	Staffs	SJ8031	52°52·8′	2°17·4′W	T	127
Little Sutton	Ches	SJ3777	53°17·4′	2°56·3′W	T	117

Little Sutton	Lincs	TF4522	52°46·8′	0°9·4′E	T	131
Little Sutton	Shrops	SO5182	52°26·3′	2°42·9′W	T	137,138
Little Sutton Hoo	Suff	TM2848	52°5·2′	1°20·1′E	X	169
Little Swart Houll	Shetld	HU4993	60°37·3′	1°5·8′W	X	1,2
Little Swattesfield Hall	Suff	TM0871	52°18·1′	1°3·4′E	X	144,155
Little Swinburne	Northum	NY9477	55°5·5′	2°5·2′W	T	87
Little Swinburne Reservoir	Northum	NY9477	55°5·5′	2°5·2′W	W	87
Little Swinton	Scot Bord	NT8245	55°42·1′	2°16·7′W	X	74
Little Sypland	D & G	NX7253	54°51·6′	3°59·2′W	X	83,84
Little Tahall	D & G	NX4052	54°50·5′	4°29·1′W	X	83
Little Tangley	Surrey	TQ0246	51°12·5′	0°32·0′W	X	186
Little Tarn	Cumbr	NY2433	54°41·4′	3°10·3′W	W	89,90
Little Tarras Water	D & G	NY3985	55°9·6′	2°57·0′W	W	79
Little Tarrington	Heref	SO6241	52°4·2′	2°32·9′W	T	149
Little Tawney Hall	Essex	TQ5099	51°40·4′	0°10·6′E	X	167,177
Little Tearie	Moray	NH9856	57°35·2′	3°41·9′W	X	27
Little Tearle	Moray	NH9856	57°35·2′	3°41·9′W	X	27
Little Testwood Fm	Hants	SU3415	50°56·2′	1°30·6′W	FM	196
Little Tew	Oxon	SP3828	51°57·2′	1°26·4′W	T	164
Little Tew Grounds Fm	Oxon	SP3727	51°56·6′	1°27·3′W	FM	164
Little Tey	Essex	TL8923	51°52·6′	0°45·1′E	T	168
Little Thakeham	W Susx	TQ1015	50°55·7′	0°25·7′W	X	198
Little Thetford	Cambs	TL5376	52°21·9′	0°15·2′E	T	143
Little Thickthorn Fm	Beds	TL0443	52°4·8′	0°28·5′W	FM	153
Little Thirkleby	N Yks	SE4778	54°12·0′	1°16·4′W	X	100
Little Thornage	Norf	TG0538	52°54·2′	1°3·3′E	T	133
Little Thorness	I of W	SZ4593	50°44·3′	1°21·4′W	X	196
Little Thornton	Aberd	NO6771	56°50·0′	2°32·0′W	X	45
Little Thornton	Lancs	SD3541	53°51·9′	2°58·9′W	T	102
Little Thorpe	Durham	NZ4242	54°46·5′	1°20·4′W	T	88
Littlethorpe	E Yorks	TA1069	54°6·5′	0°18·6′W	X	101
Little Thorpe	Kirk	SE1822	53°41·9′	1°43·2′W	T	104
Littlethorpe	Leic	SP5496	52°33·8′	1°11·8′W	T	140
Littlethorpe	N Yks	SE3269	54°7·2′	1°30·2′W	T	99
Little Thurlow	Suff	TL6751	52°8·1′	0°26·8′E	T	154
Little Thurlow Green	Suff	TL6851	52°8·1′	0°27·7′E	T	154
Little Thurrock	Thurr	TQ6279	51°29·4′	0°20·4′E	T	177
Littlethwaite	Cumbr	NY1424	54°36·5′	3°19·5′W	X	89
Little Tiffenden Fm	Kent	TQ9236	51°5·7′	0°44·9′E	FM	189
Little Tilden Fm	Kent	TQ7547	51°11·9′	0°30·7′E	FM	188
Little Tind	Shetld	HU4007	59°51·0′	1°16·7′W	X	4
Littleton	Aberd	NJ8143	57°28·9′	2°18·6′W	X	29,30
Littleton	Bath & NE Somer	ST5563	51°22·1′	2°38·4′W	T	172,182
Littleton	Ches	SJ4466	53°11·5′	2°49·9′W	T	117
Littleton	D & G	NX6255	54°52·5′	4°8·6′W	X	83
Littleton	Dorset	ST8904	50°50·4′	2°9·0′W	T	195
Littleton	Hants	SU4532	51°5·4′	1°21·1′W	T	185
Littleton	Pth & Kin	NN8725	56°24·5′	3°49·4′W	X	52,58
Littleton	Pth & Kin	NN9944	56°34·9′	3°38·2′W	X	52,53
Littleton	Pth & Kin	NO2633	56°29·3′	3°11·7′W	X	53
Littleton	S Ayr	NS3108	55°20·5′	4°39·5′W	X	70,76
Littleton	Somer	ST4930	51°4·3′	2°43·3′W	T	182,183
Littleton	Surrey	SU9847	51°13·1′	0°35·4′W	T	186
Littleton	Surrey	TQ0768	51°24·3′	0°27·3′W	T	176
Littleton	Wilts	ST9160	51°20·6′	2°7·4′W	T	173
Littleton Common	Surrey	TQ0870	51°25·3′	0°26·4′W	T	176
Littleton Copse	Hants	SU2848	51°14·1′	1°35·5′W	F	184
Littleton Down	Wilts	ST9750	51°15·2′	2°2·2′W	X	184
Littleton Down	W Susx	SU9415	50°55·8′	0°39·4′W	H	197
Littleton Drew	Wilts	ST8380	51°31·4′	2°14·3′W	T	173
Littleton Fm	S Ayr	NS2104	55°18·1′	4°48·8′W	FM	76
Littleton Fm	W Susx	SU9514	50°55·3′	0°38·5′W	FM	197
Little Tongue	D & G	NX1263	54°55·8′	4°55·6′W	X	82
Little Tongues	Lancs	SD3748	53°55·7′	2°57·2′W	X	102
Littleton Hill	S Ayr	NX1286	55°8·2′	4°56·5′W	H	76
Littleton Ho	Hants	SU4433	51°5·9′	1°21·9′W	X	185
Littleton Manor Fm	Bucks	SP7317	51°51·0′	0°56·0′W	FM	165
Littleton Manor Fm	Surrey	TQ2349	51°13·8′	0°13·9′W	FM	187
Littleton of Airlie	Angus	NO3350	56°38·5′	3°5·1′W	X	53
Littleton Panell	Wilts	ST9954	51°17·3′	2°0·5′W	T	184
Littleton Pastures	Worcs	SP1045	52°6·4′	1°50·8′W	X	150
Littleton-upon-severn	S Glos	ST5990	51°36·7′	2°35·1′W	T	162,172
Littleton Warth	S Glos	ST5890	51°36·7′	2°36·0′W	X	162,172
Little Torboll	Highld	NH7598	57°57·5′	4°6·3′W	T	21
Little Tor Hill	Glos	ST7692	51°37·8′	2°20·4′W	X	162,172
Little Torhouse	D & G	NX3856	54°52·6′	4°31·1′W	X	83
Little Torrington	Devon	SS4916	50°55·7′	4°8·5′W	T	180
Little Tosson	Northum	NU0101	55°18·4′	1°58·6′W	X	81
Little Totham	Essex	TL8811	51°46·2′	0°43·9′E	T	168
Little Totham Hall	Essex	TL8810	51°45·6′	0°43·9′E	X	168
Little Tottingworth Fm	E Susx	TQ6021	50°58·2′	0°17·1′E	FM	199
Little Toux	Aberd	NJ5459	57°37·4′	2°45·7′W	X	29
Littletown	Aberd	NJ6909	57°10·5′	2°30·3′W	X	38
Little Town	Cumbr	NY2319	54°33·9′	3°11·0′W	T	89,90
Littletown	Devon	SY1699	50°47·3′	3°11·1′W	T	192,193
Littletown	Durham	NZ3443	54°47·1′	1°27·9′W	T	88
Little Town	Highld	NH8089	57°52·7′	4°0·9′W	T	21
Littletown	I of W	SZ5390	50°42·7′	1°14·6′W	T	196
Littletown	Kirk	SE2024	53°43·0′	1°41·4′W	T	104
Little Town	Lancs	SD6039	53°51·0′	2°36·1′W	X	102,103
Little Town	Lancs	SD6535	53°48·9′	2°31·5′W	T	102,103
Little Town	Warr	SJ6494	53°26·7′	2°32·1′W	T	109
Littletown Farmhouse	Wilts	SU0978	51°30·3′	1°51·8′W	X	173
Littletown Fm	Suff	TM3077	52°20·8′	1°23·0′E	FM	156
Littletown Ho	Durham	NZ3343	54°47·1′	1°28·8′W	X	88
Little Tows	Lincs	TF2188	53°22·7′	0°10·4′W	X	113,122
Little Toyd Down	Wilts	SU0921	50°59·5′	1°51·9′W	X	184
Little Treffgarne	Pemb	SM9624	51°52·4′	4°57·5′W	T	157,158
Little Treffgarne Mountain	Pemb	SM9625	51°53·4′	4°57·5′W	H	157,158
Little Treleaver	Corn	SW7618	50°1·4′	5°7·3′W	X	204
Little Tring	Herts	SP9112	51°48·2′	0°40·4′W	T	165
Little Trochry	Pth & Kin	NN9840	56°32·7′	3°39·1′W	X	52,53
Little Trochry Hill	Pth & Kin	NN9938	56°31·6′	3°38·1′W	H	52,53
Little Trodgers Fm	E Susx	TQ5830	51°3·1′	0°15·6′E	FM	188
Little Tullo	Angus	NO5771	56°50·0′	2°41·8′W	X	44
Little Tulloch	Aberd	NO4496	57°3·4′	2°54·9′W	X	37,44
Little Tulloch	Aberd	NO7795	57°3·0′	2°22·3′W	X	38,45
Little Tullybelton	Pth & Kin	NO0334	56°29·5′	3°34·1′W	X	52,53
Little Turnberry	S Ayr	NS2106	55°19·2′	4°48·8′W	X	70,76
Little Twinness	Orkney	HY5206	58°56·6′	2°49·6′W	X	6,7
Little Twycross	Leic	SK3305	52°38·7′	1°30·3′W	T	140
Little Tyes	Suff	TM3252	52°7·3′	1°23·7′E	X	156
Little Urchany	Highld	NH8748	57°30·7′	3°52·7′W	X	27
Little Urswick	Cumbr	SD2673	54°9·1′	3°7·6′W	T	96,97
Little Vandra Water	Shetld	HU4989	60°35·2′	1°5·8′W	W	1,2
Little Vantage	W Loth	NT1063	55°51·4′	3°25·8′W	T	65
Little Varracombe	Devon	SX6283	50°38·1′	3°56·7′W	X	191
Little Virda Field	Shetld	HU1561	60°20·2′	1°43·2′W	X	3
Little Wadden Hall	Kent	TR1348	51°11·7′	1°3·3′E	X	179,189
Little Wadd Fm	Kent	TQ7940	51°8·1′	0°33·9′E	FM	188
Little Wairds	Aberd	NO7978	56°53·8′	2°20·2′W	X	45
Little Wakering	Essex	TQ9388	51°33·7′	0°47·5′E	T	178
Little Wakering Hall	Essex	TQ9488	51°33·7′	0°48·3′E	X	178
Little Wakering Wick	Essex	TQ9388	51°33·7′	0°47·5′E	X	178
Little Walden	Essex	TL5441	52°3·0′	0°15·2′E	T	154
Little Waldingfield	Suff	TL9245	52°4·4′	0°48·5′E	T	155
Little Walsingham	Norf	TF9336	52°53·4′	0°52·5′E	T	132
Little Waltham	Essex	TL7012	51°47·1′	0°28·3′E	T	167
Little Walton	Warw	SP4983	52°26·8′	1°16·3′W	T	140
Little Ward	Shetld	HU3246	60°12·1′	1°24·9′W	X	4
Littleward	Stir	NS6597	56°9·1′	4°10·0′W	X	57
Little Ward Law	Northum	NT8614	55°25·4′	2°12·8′W	H	80
Littleward Wester	Stir	NS6597	56°9·1′	4°10·0′W	X	57
Little Warley	Essex	TQ6090	51°35·4′	0°19·0′E	T	177
Little Warley Hall	Essex	TQ6088	51°34·3′	0°18·9′E	A	177
Little Warley Lodge	Essex	TQ6090	51°35·4′	0°19·0′E	X	177
Little Warrington Sike	Scot Bord	NY5592	55°13·5′	2°42·0′W	W	80
Little Warton	Warw	SK2803	52°37·7′	1°34·8′W	T	140
Little Washbourne	Glos	SO9933	52°0·0′	2°0·5′W	T	150
Little Water	Aberd	NJ8441	57°27·8′	2°15·5′W	W	29,30
Littlewater	Cumbr	NY5017	54°33·0′	2°46·0′W	X	90
Little Waterfall Fm	Red & Cl	NZ6315	54°31·8′	1°1·2′W	FM	94
Little Water of Fleet	D & G	NX5865	54°57·8′	4°12·7′W	W	83
Little Watersend	Kent	TR2744	51°9·2′	1°15·2′E	X	179
Little Wauldby Fm	E Yorks	SE9829	53°45·1′	0°30·4′W	FM	106
Little Waver	Cumbr	NY2343	54°46·8′	3°11·4′W	W	85
Little Weald Hall	Essex	TL4905	51°43·7′	0°9·8′E	X	167
Little Weare Barton	Devon	SS4823	50°59·4′	4°9·6′W	X	180
Little Weghill	E Yorks	TA2029	53°44·8′	0°10·4′W	X	107
Little Weighton	E Yorks	SE9833	53°47·3′	0°30·3′W	T	106
Little Weir	Devon	SS6024	51°0·1′	3°59·3′W	X	180
Little Welland	Worcs	SO8038	52°2·6′	2°17·1′W	T	150
Little Welnetham	Suff	TL8960	52°12·6′	0°46·4′E	T	155
Little Welton	Lincs	TF3087	53°22·1′	0°2·4′W	T	113,122
Little Wenderton Fm	Kent	TR2458	51°16·8′	1°13·1′E	FM	179
Little Wenham	Suff	TM0839	52°0·8′	1°2·3′E	T	155,169
Little Wenlock	Wrekin	SJ6406	52°39·3′	2°31·5′W	T	127
Little West End Fm	Hants	SU6519	50°58·2′	1°4·1′W	FM	185
Little Westfield	Lancs	SD5437	53°49·9′	2°41·5′W	X	102
Little Weston	Somer	ST6225	51°1·6′	2°32·1′W	T	183
Little Whatmans	Kent	TQ8536	51°5·8′	0°38·9′E	X	189
Little Whernside	N Yks	SE0277	54°11·6′	1°57·7′W	H	98
Little Whickhope Burn	Northum	NY6984	55°9·2′	2°28·8′W	W	80
Little White	Durham	NZ2238	54°44·4′	1°39·1′W	X	93
Little Whitefield	Aberd	NJ6653	57°34·2′	2°33·6′W	X	29
Little Whitefield	Pth & Kin	NO1733	56°29·2′	3°20·4′W	X	53
Little Whitehill	Aberd	NJ8951	57°33·2′	2°10·6′W	X	30
Little Whitehouse	I of W	SZ4591	50°43·2′	1°21·4′W	T	196
Little Whitriggs	D & G	NY1987	55°10·5′	3°15·9′W	X	79
Little Whittingham Green	Suff	TM2876	52°20·3′	1°21·2′E	T	156
Little Whittington	Northum	NY9969	55°1·2′	2°0·5′W	X	87
Littlewick	Surrey	SU9759	51°19·5′	0°36·1′W	X	175,186
Littlewick Green	Win & Maid	SU8380	51°31·0′	0°47·8′W	T	175
Little Wigborough	Essex	TL9715	51°48·2′	0°51·8′E	T	168
Little Wigston	Leic	SK3009	52°40·9′	1°33·0′W	X	128,140
Little Wilbraham	Cambs	TL5458	52°12·1′	0°15·6′E	T	154
Little Wilbraham River	Cambs	TL5258	52°12·2′	0°13·9′E	W	154
Little Wildage	Kent	TR1646	51°10·6′	1°5·8′E	X	179,189
Little Wildwood Fm	Surrey	TQ0535	51°6·5′	0°29·6′W	FM	187
Little Willicote	Warw	SP1848	52°8·0′	1°43·8′W	X	151
Little Wilscombe	Somer	ST0327	51°2·3′	3°22·6′W	X	181
Little Winceys Fm	Essex	TL6732	51°57·9′	0°26·3′E	FM	167
Littlewindsor	Dorset	ST4404	50°50·2′	2°47·3′W	T	193
Little Wisbeach	Lincs	TF1231	52°52·1′	0°19·8′W	T	130
Little Wishford	Wilts	SU0736	51°7·6′	1°53·6′W	X	184
Little Witchingham Hall	Norf	TG1220	52°44·4′	1°8·8′E	X	133
Little Witcombe	Glos	SO9115	51°50·2′	2°7·4′W	T	163
Little Witley	Worcs	SO7863	52°16·1′	2°18·9′W	T	138,150
Little Wittenham	Oxon	SU5693	51°38·2′	1°11·1′W	T	164,174
Little Wittenham Wood	Oxon	SU5792	51°37·7′	1°10·2′W	F	164,174
Little Wold Plantn	E Yorks	SE9332	53°46·8′	0°34·9′W	F	106
Little Wolford	Warw	SP2635	52°1·0′	1°36·9′W	T	151
Little Wolford Heath	Warw	SP2734	52°0·5′	1°36·0′W	F	151
Little Wollascott	Shrops	SJ4717	52°45·1′	2°46·7′W	X	126
Littlewood	Derby	SK5365	53°11·0′	1°12·0′W	X	120
Littlewood	Devon	SS5304	50°49·3′	4°4·8′W	X	191
Littlewood	Dorset	SY6294	50°44·9′	2°31·9′W	X	194
Little Wood	E Yorks	SE9537	53°49·5′	0°33·0′W	F	106
Little Wood	Hants	SU6845	51°12·2′	1°1·2′W	F	185,186
Little Wood	Norf	TG0031	52°50·6′	0°58·6′E	F	133
Little Wood	Norf	TG1034	52°52·0′	1°7·6′E	F	133
Little Wood	Norf	TM2594	52°30·1′	1°19·3′E	F	134
Little Wood	Norf	TM2597	52°31·7′	1°19·4′E	F	134
Little Wood	Shrops	SO5881	52°25·8′	2°36·7′W	X	137,138
Littlewood	Staffs	SJ9807	52°39·9′	2°1·4′W	T	127,139
Little Wood	Suff	TM1970	52°17·3′	1°13·1′E	F	156
Little Wood	Wilts	SU2872	51°27·0′	1°35·4′W	F	174
Little Woodbarns	Essex	TL6200	51°40·7′	0°21·0′E	X	167
Little Woodbury	Wilts	SU1427	51°2·8′	1°47·6′W	A	184
Little Wood Corner	Bucks	SP9101	51°42·3′	0°40·6′W	T	165
Little Woodcote	Sutton	TQ2861	51°20·2′	0°9·4′W	T	176,187
Little Woodend Fm	Glos	SO7129	51°57·8′	2°24·9′W	FM	149
Littlewood Fm	Cumbr	SD4899	54°23·3′	2°47·6′W	FM	97
Littlewood Fm	Devon	SS7021	50°58·7′	3°50·7′W	FM	180
Littlewood Fm	Durham	NY9237	54°43·9′	2°7·0′W	FM	91,92
Littlewood Fm	E Yorks	SE9536	53°48·9′	0°33·0′W	FM	106
Littlewood Fm	W Susx	SU8715	50°55·9′	0°45·3′W	FM	197
Littlewood Green	Warw	SP0762	52°15·6′	1°53·4′W	T	150
Little Woodhill	Oxon	SU3890	51°36·7′	1°26·7′W	X	164,174
Little Woodlands	Shrops	SO7385	52°28·0′	2°23·4′W	X	138
Littlewood Lodge	E Yorks	SE9537	53°49·5′	0°33·0′W	X	106
Littlewood Park	Aberd	NJ5118	57°15·3′	2°48·3′W	X	37
Little Woolden Hall	Salf	SJ6894	53°26·8′	2°28·5′W	X	109
Little Woolden Moss	Salf	SJ6995	53°27·3′	2°27·6′W	X	109
Little Woolgarston	Dorset	SY9781	50°38·0′	2°2·2′W	T	195
Little Worge Fm	E Susx	TQ6521	50°58·1′	0°21·4′E	FM	199
Littleworth	Beds	TL0744	52°5·3′	0°25·9′W	T	153
Littleworth	Donc	SK6298	53°28·7′	1°3·5′W	T	111
Littleworth	Glos	SO8501	51°42·7′	2°12·6′W	T	162
Littleworth	Glos	SP1439	52°3·2′	1°47·4′W	T	151
Littleworth	Northnts	SP6750	52°8·9′	1°0·9′W	X	152
Littleworth	Oxon	SP5805	51°44·7′	1°9·2′W	T	164
Littleworth	Oxon	SU3197	51°40·5′	1°32·7′W	T	164
Littleworth	Oxon	SU6191	51°37·1′	1°6·7′W	T	164,175
Littleworth	Rut	SK8100	52°35·7′	0°47·8′W	X	141
Littleworth	Staffs	SJ7925	52°49·6′	2°18·3′W	X	127
Littleworth	Staffs	SJ9323	52°48·5′	2°5·8′W	T	127
Littleworth	Staffs	SK0112	52°42·6′	1°58·7′W	T	128
Littleworth	Warw	SP2363	52°16·1′	1°39·4′W	T	151
Littleworth	Wilts	SU1861	51°21·1′	1°44·1′W	T	173
Littleworth	Worcs	SO8849	52°8·6′	2°10·1′W	T	150
Littleworth	Worcs	SO9962	52°15·6′	2°0·5′W	T	150
Little Worth	Wrekin	SJ6506	52°39·3′	2°30·6′W	X	127
Littleworth	W Susx	TQ1920	50°58·3′	0°17·9′W	T	198
Littleworth Common	Bucks	SU9386	51°34·1′	0°39·1′W	T	175
Littleworth Common	Surrey	TQ1465	51°22·6′	0°21·3′W	X	176
Littleworth Cross	Surrey	SU8945	51°12·1′	0°43·2′W	X	186
Little Worthen	Shrops	SJ3305	52°38·6′	2°59·0′W	T	126
Littleworth End	Staffs	SP1597	52°34·5′	1°46·3′W	T	139
Littleworth Fm	Bucks	SP7327	51°56·4′	0°55·9′W	FM	165
Littleworth Fm	Oxon	SP4117	51°51·2′	1°23·9′W	FM	164
Littleworth Fm	Warw	SP2942	52°4·8′	1°34·2′W	FM	151
Little Wratting	Suff	TL6847	52°6·0′	0°27·6′E	T	154
Little Wretchwick Fm	Oxon	SP6021	51°53·3′	1°7·3′W	FM	164,165
Little Wymington	Beds	SP9565	52°16·7′	0°36·0′W	T	153
Little Wymondley	Herts	TL2127	51°55·9′	0°14·0′W	T	166
Little Wyrley	Staffs	SK0105	52°38·8′	1°58·7′W	T	139
Little Wytheford	Shrops	SJ5619	52°46·2′	2°38·7′W	T	126
Little Wyvis	Highld	NH4364	57°38·6′	4°37·4′W	H	20
Little Yarlside	Cumbr	NY5307	54°27·6′	2°43·1′W	H	90
Little Yarrow	Scot Bord	NT2217	55°26·7′	3°13·6′W	W	79
Little Yeldham	Essex	TL7739	52°1·5′	0°35·2′E	T	155
Little Yews	Wilts	SU1324	51°1·1′	1°48·5′W	F	184
Littley Green	Essex	TL6917	51°49·8′	0°27·6′E	T	167
Littleypark	Essex	TL6917	51°49·8′	0°27·6′E	X	167
Little Ythsie	Aberd	NJ8931	57°22·4′	2°10·5′W	X	30
Littley Wood	S Glos	ST7487	51°35·1′	2°22·1′W	F	172
Littley Wood	Suff	TL6448	52°6·6′	0°24·1′E	F	154
Littly Wood	Suff	TL7459	52°12·3′	0°33·2′E	F	155
Litton	Derby	SK1675	53°16·5′	1°45·2′W	T	119
Litton	Devon	SS8032	51°4·7′	3°42·4′W	X	181
Litton	N Yks	SD9074	54°9·9′	2°8·8′W	T	98
Litton	Somer	SS8033	51°5·3′	3°42·4′W	X	181
Litton	Somer	ST5954	51°17·3′	2°34·9′W	T	182,183
Litton Cheney	Dorset	SY5590	50°42·7′	2°37·9′W	T	194
Litton Dale	Derby	SK1574	53°16·0′	1°46·1′W	X	119
Littondale	N Yks	SD9172	54°8·9′	2°7·9′W	X	98
Littonfields	Derby	SK1775	53°16·5′	1°44·3′W	X	119
Litton Hill	Powys	SO2666	52°17·5′	3°4·7′W	X	137,148
Litton Mill	Derby	SK1572	53°14·9′	1°46·1′W	T	119
Littonslack	Derby	SK1673	53°15·5′	1°45·2′W	X	119
Litton Water	Devon	SS8032	51°4·7′	3°42·4′W	W	181
Littywood	Staffs	SJ8918	52°45·8′	2°9·4′W	X	127
Liundale	Arg & Bt	NR5479	55°56·7′	5°56·0′W	X	61
Liurbost	N Eil	NB3526	58°8·9′	6°29·8′W	T	8
Liurbost	N Eil	NB3725	58°8·4′	6°27·7′W	T	14
Liuri	N Eil	NF9693	57°49·7′	7°6·8′W	X	18
Liursaigh Dubh	N Eil	NF8640	57°20·8′	7°12·8′W	X	22
Liursaigh Glas	N Eil	NF8640	57°20·8′	7°12·8′W	X	22
Liuthaid	N Eil	NB1713	58°1·2′	6°47·1′W	H	13,14
Livaton	Devon	SX6793	50°43·5′	3°52·7′W	X	191
Live Moor	N Yks	NZ5001	54°24·4′	1°13·4′W	X	93
Livenhayes Fm	Devon	ST2307	50°51·7′	3°5·3′W	FM	192,193
Liver Hill	Lancs	SD8226	53°44·0′	2°16·0′W	X	103
Liveridge Fm	Worcs	SO7772	52°21·0′	2°19·9′W	FM	138
Liveridge Hill	Warw	SP1568	52°18·8′	1°46·4′W	X	139,151
Livermead	Torbay	SX9062	50°27·1′	3°32·6′W	T	202
Livermere Heath	Suff	TL8773	52°19·6′	0°45·1′E	X	144,155
Livermere Park	Suff	TL8771	52°18·5′	0°45·0′E	X	144,155
Liverpool	Liv	SJ3791	53°25·0′	2°56·5′W	T	108
Liverpool Airport	Liv	SJ4283	53°20·7′	2°51·9′W	X	108
Liverpool Bay	Liv	SJ2395	53°27·0′	3°9·2′W	W	108
Liverpool St Sta	C of Lon	TQ3381	51°31·0′	0°4·6′W	X	176,177
Liversedge	Kirk	SE2023	53°42·4′	1°41·4′W	T	104
Liverton	Devon	SX8075	50°34·0′	3°41·3′W	T	191
Liverton	Devon	SY0382	50°38·0′	3°21·9′W	X	192
Liverton	Red & Cl	NZ7115	54°31·8′	0°53·8′W	T	94
Liverton Lodge	Red & Cl	NZ7117	54°32·8′	0°53·7′W	X	94
Liverton Mill	Red & Cl	NZ7015	54°31·8′	0°54·7′W	X	94
Liverton Mines	Red & Cl	NZ7117	54°32·8′	0°53·7′W	T	94
Liverton Moor	Red & Cl	NZ7112	54°30·1′	0°53·8′W	X	94
Liverton Street	Kent	TQ8750	51°13·3′	0°41·1′E	T	189
Livery, The	Wilts	SU2329	51°3·8′	1°39·9′W	X	184
Livesey Street	Kent	TQ7054	51°15·8′	0°26·6′E	T	188
Liviness	Orkney	HY4916	59°1·9′	2°52·8′W	X	6
Livingshayes	Devon	SS9603	50°49·3′	3°28·2′W	T	192
Livingston	W Loth	NT0668	55°54·0′	3°29·8′W	T	65
Livingstone	D & G	NX7167	54°59·1′	4°0·5′W	X	83,84
Livingstone Hill	D & G	NX7067	54°59·1′	4°1·5′W	H	83,84
Livingstone Ho	Cumbr	NY4073	55°3·1′	2°55·9′W	X	85
Livingston's Rocks	Arg & Bt	NM3117	56°16·4′	6°20·3′W	X	48
Livingston Village	W Loth	NT0366	55°52·9′	3°32·6′W	T	65
Living World	Essex	TQ5199	51°40·4′	0°11·4′E	X	199
Livox Fm	Monm	ST5397	51°40·4′	2°40·4′W	FM	162
Livthorpe Kennels	N Lincs	SE8415	53°37·7′	0°43·4′W	X	112
Lixton	Devon	SX6950	50°20·4′	3°50·1′W	X	202
Lixwm	Flint	SJ1671	53°14·0′	3°15·1′W	T	116
Liza Beck	Cumbr	NY1521	54°34·9′	3°18·5′W	W	89
Lizard	Corn	SW7012	49°58·1′	5°12·1′W	T	203

Lizard Downs	Corn	SW6913	49°58·6′	5°12·9′W	X	203
Lizard Fm	Norf	TG0423	52°46·2′	1°1·9′E	FM	133
Lizard Fm	Shrops	SJ7708	52°40·4′	2°20·0′W	FM	127
Lizard Grange	Shrops	SJ7810	52°41·5′	2°19·1′W	X	127
Lizard Hill	Shrops	SJ7709	52°40·9′	2°20·0′W	H	127
Lizardmill Fm	Shrops	SJ7809	52°40·9′	2°19·1′W	FM	127
Lizard Point	Corn	SW6911	49°57·5′	5°12·9′W	X	203
Lizard Point	I Scilly	SV9014	49°57·0′	6°18·9′W	X	203
Lizard Point	S Tyne	NZ4164	54°58·4′	1°21·1′W	X	88
Lizard Pool	Corn	SW9939	50°13·2′	4°48·7′W	W	204
Lizards	Durham	NZ1548	54°49·8′	1°45·6′W	X	88
Lizards Fm	Durham	NZ3531	54°40·6′	1°27·0′W	FM	93
Lizards Fm	S Tyne	NZ4063	54°57·8′	1°22·1′W	FM	88
Lizwell	Devon	SX7074	50°33·3′	3°49·7′W	X	191
Lizwell Meet	Devon	SX7173	50°32·8′	3°48·9′W	W	191
Lizzen	Corn	SX1851	50°20·1′	4°33·1′W	X	201
Lizziewells	Fife	NO2712	56°17·9′	3°10·3′W	X	59
Llabwst Fm	Gwyn	SH5706	52°38·2′	4°6·4′W	FM	124
Llachdolt	Powys	SO1441	52°3·9′	3°14·9′W	X	148,161
Llaethbwlch	Powys	SJ1116	52°44·3′	3°18·7′W	X	125
Llaethdy	Carm	SN3616	51°49·4′	4°22·4′W	X	159
Llaethdy	Pemb	SM7327	51°54·0′	5°17·6′W	X	157
Llaethdy	Powys	SO0680	52°24·8′	3°22·5′W	T	136
Llaethliw	Cered	SN4759	52°12·7′	4°14·0′W	X	146
Llaethnant	Gwyn	SH8821	52°46·7′	3°39·2′W	W	124,125
Llaethwryd	Conwy	SH9347	53°0·8′	3°35·3′W	A	116
Llain	Carm	SN5232	51°58·2′	4°8·9′W	X	146
Llain	Cered	SN3348	52°6·5′	4°25·9′W	X	145
Llain	Cered	SN3442	52°3·3′	4°24·9′W	X	145
Llain	Cered	SN4259	52°12·6′	4°18·4′W	X	146
Llain	Pemb	SM8930	51°56·0′	5°3·8′W	X	157
Llain	Pemb	SN1329	51°55·9′	4°42·8′W	X	145,158
Llainbanal	Pemb	SN1633	51°58·1′	4°40·3′W	X	145
Llain-dderwen-lŵyd	Carm	SN5127	51°55·5′	4°9·6′W	X	146
Llainfachwen	Gwyn	SH5649	53°1·4′	4°8·4′W	X	115
Llaingarreglwyd	Cered	SN4158	52°12·1′	4°19·2′W	X	146
Llaingoch	I of Angl	SH2382	53°18·6′	4°39·0′W	T	114
Llainlas	Carm	SN5240	52°2·6′	4°9·1′W	X	146
Llain-lwyd	Carm	SN2818	51°50·3′	4°29·4′W	X	158
Llain-lwyd	Carm	SN2829	51°56·2′	4°29·7′W	X	145,158
Llainoleu	Carm	SN5332	51°58·3′	4°8·0′W	X	146
Llain-wen	Carm	SN3930	51°57·0′	4°20·2′W	X	145
Llain-wen	Cered	SN3253	52°9·2′	4°27·0′W	X	145
Llainwen	Denb	SJ1552	53°3·8′	3°15·7′W	X	116
Llain Wen Fm	Gwyn	SH7036	52°54·6′	3°55·6′W	FM	124
Llain Wen Fm	I of Angl	SH3574	53°14·5′	4°28·0′W	FM	114
Llaithgwm	Gwyn	SH9240	52°57·0′	3°36·0′W	X	125
L Lake	Notts	SK5858	53°7·2′	1°7·6′W	W	120
Llambed	Pemb	SM8832	51°57·0′	5°4·7′W	X	157
Llambed Hill	Pemb	SM8932	51°57·0′	5°3·8′W	H	157
Llam Carw	I of Angl	SH4593	53°24·9′	4°19·5′W	X	114
Llam-march	Monm	SO2111	51°47·8′	3°8·3′W	X	161
Llampha	V of Glam	SS9275	51°28·1′	3°32·9′W	T	170
Llampha Court	V of Glam	SS9275	51°28·1′	3°32·9′W	X	170
Llam-y-trwsgl	Gwyn	SH5750	53°1·9′	4°7·5′W	X	115
Llan	Monm	SO3304	51°44·1′	2°57·8′W	X	171
Llan	Powys	SH8800	52°35·4′	3°38·8′W	X	135,136
Llan	Powys	SO1325	51°55·2′	3°15·5′W	X	161
Llan	Rho Cyn Taf	ST0487	51°34·7′	3°22·7′W	X	170
Llanaber	Gwyn	SH6017	52°44·2′	4°4·0′W	T	124
Llanadevy	Shrops	SO3378	52°24·0′	2°58·7′W	X	137,148
Llanaelhaearn	Gwyn	SH3844	52°58·4′	4°24·4′W	T	123
Llanaeron	Cered	SN4760	52°13·3′	4°14·0′W	X	146
Llanafan	Cered	SN6872	52°20·1′	3°55·8′W	T	135
Llanafan-fawr	Powys	SN9655	52°11·2′	3°30·9′W	T	147
Llanallgo	I of Angl	SH4985	53°20·7′	4°15·7′W	T	114
Llananno	Powys	SO0974	52°21·6′	3°19·8′W	T	136,147
Llan-a'r-Ithon	Powys	SO0459	52°13·5′	3°23·9′W	X	147
Llanarmon	Gwyn	SH4239	52°55·8′	4°20·6′W	T	123
Llanarmon Dyffryn Ceiriog	Wrex	SJ1532	52°53·0′	3°15·4′W	T	125
Llanarmon Mynydd-mawr	Powys	SJ1327	52°50·3′	3°17·1′W	T	125
Llanarmon-yn-Ial	Denb	SJ1956	53°5·9′	3°12·2′W	T	116
Llanarrow Cott	Heref	SO2552	52°9·9′	3°5·4′W	X	148
Llanarth	Cered	SN4257	52°11·6′	4°18·3′W	T	146
Llanarth	Monm	SO3710	51°47·3′	2°54·4′W	T	161
Llanarth Court	Monm	SO3810	51°47·4′	2°53·5′W	X	161
Llanarthne	Carm	SN5320	51°51·8′	4°7·7′W	T	159
Llanasa	Flint	SJ1081	53°19·3′	3°20·7′W	T	116
Llanbabo	I of Angl	SH3786	53°21·0′	4°26·5′W	T	114
Llanbachowey	Powys	SO1345	52°6·0′	3°15·8′W	X	148
Llanbad	Rho Cyn Taf	SS9884	51°33·0′	3°27·9′W	T	170
Llanbadarn Fawr	Cered	SN6080	52°24·2′	4°3·1′W	T	135
Llanbadarn Fynydd	Powys	SO0978	52°23·8′	3°19·8′W	T	136,147
Llanbadarn-y-garreg	Powys	SO1148	52°7·6′	3°17·6′W	T	148
Llanbadoc	Monm	SO3700	51°41·9′	2°54·3′W	T	171
Llanbadrig	I of Angl	SH3794	53°25·3′	4°26·8′W	T	114
Llanbeder	Newp	ST3890	51°36·6′	2°53·3′W	T	171
Llanbedr	Gwyn	SH5826	52°49·0′	4°6·0′W	T	124
Llanbedr	Powys	SO1446	52°6·6′	3°15·0′W	T	148
Llanbedr	Powys	SO2320	51°52·6′	3°6·7′W	T	161
Llanbedr-Dyffryn-Clwyd	Denb	SJ1459	53°7·5′	3°16·7′W	T	116
Llanbedrgoch	I of Angl	SH5180	53°18·0′	4°13·7′W	T	114,115
Llanbedr Hall	Denb	SJ1459	53°7·5′	3°16·7′W	X	116
Llanbedr Hill	Powys	SO1448	52°7·7′	3°15·0′W	H	148
Llanbedrog	Gwyn	SH3231	52°51·3′	4°29·3′W	T	123
Llanbedr-y-cennin	Conwy	SH7569	53°12·4′	3°51·9′W	T	115
Llanbella	Powys	SO2353	52°10·4′	3°7·2′W	X	148
Llanberis	Gwyn	SH5760	53°7·3′	4°7·8′W	T	114,115
Llanberis Lake Railway	Gwyn	SH5761	53°7·9′	4°7·8′W	X	114,115
Llanberis Path	Gwyn	SH6056	53°5·2′	4°5·0′W	X	115
Llanbethêry	V of Glam	ST0369	51°24·9′	3°23·3′W	T	170
Llanbister	Powys	SO1073	52°21·1′	3°18·9′W	T	136,148
Llanbister Br	Powys	SO1072	52°20·6′	3°18·9′W	X	136,148
Llanbister Road Sta	Powys	SO1771	52°20·1′	3°12·7′W	X	136,148
Llanblethian	V of Glam	SS9974	51°27·6′	3°26·8′W	T	170
Llanboidy	Carm	SN2123	51°52·9′	4°35·7′W	T	145,158
Llanbradach	Caer	ST1490	51°36·4′	3°14·1′W	T	171
Llanbradach Fawr	Caer	ST1392	51°37·4′	3°15·0′W	X	171
Llanbradach Isaf	Caer	ST1491	51°36·9′	3°14·1′W	X	171
Llanbrook	Shrops	SO3578	52°24·0′	2°56·9′W	X	137,148
Llanbrynmair	Powys	SH8902	52°36·5′	3°38·0′W	T	135,136
Llanbwchllyn	Powys	SO1146	52°6·5′	3°17·6′W	X	148
Llan Bwch-llyn Lake	Powys	SO1146	52°6·5′	3°17·6′W	W	148
Llancadle	V of Glam	ST0368	51°24·4′	3°23·3′W	T	170
Llancaeo Hill	Monm	SO3702	51°43·0′	2°54·3′W	H	171
Llancaiach	Caer	ST1196	51°39·6′	3°16·8′W	T	171
Llancaiach Fawr	Caer	ST1196	51°39·6′	3°16·8′W	A	171
Llancarfan	V of Glam	ST0570	51°25·5′	3°21·6′W	T	170
Llancayo	Monm	SO3603	51°43·6′	2°55·2′W	T	171
Llancillo Court	Heref	SO3625	51°55·4′	2°55·4′W	X	161
Llancillo Hall	Heref	SO3625	51°55·4′	2°55·4′W	X	161
Llancloudy	Heref	SO4920	51°52·8′	2°44·1′W	T	162
Llancoch	Powys	SO2073	52°21·2′	3°10·1′W	X	137,148
Llancowrid	Powys	SO1990	52°30·4′	3°11·2′W	T	136
Llancwm Fm	Carm	SN4411	51°46·8′	4°15·3′W	FM	159
Llancyfelyn	Cered	SN6492	52°30·8′	3°59·9′W	T	135
Llan-dafal	Caer	SO1803	51°43·4′	3°10·8′W	T	171
Llandaff	Card	ST1577	51°29·4′	3°13·1′W	T	171
Llandaff North	Card	ST1578	51°29·9′	3°13·1′W	T	171
Llandanwg	Gwyn	SH5628	52°50·1′	4°7·9′W	T	124
Llandarcy	Nth Pt Talb	SS7195	51°38·6′	3°51·5′W	T	170
Llandawke	Carm	SN2811	51°46·5′	4°29·2′W	T	158
Llanddaniel Fab	I of Angl	SH4970	53°12·6′	4°15·3′W	T	114,115
Llanddarog	Carm	SN5016	51°49·6′	4°10·2′W	T	159
Llanddeiniol	Cered	SN5672	52°19·9′	4°6·4′W	T	135
Llanddeiniolen	Gwyn	SH5466	53°10·5′	4°10·7′W	T	114,115
Llandderfel	Gwyn	SH9837	52°55·5′	3°30·6′W	T	125
Llanddetty Hall	Powys	SO1220	51°52·5′	3°16·3′W	X	161
Llanddeusant	Carm	SN7724	51°54·3′	3°46·9′W	X	160
Llanddeusant	I of Angl	SH3485	53°20·4′	4°29·2′W	T	114
Llanddew	Powys	SO0530	51°57·9′	3°22·6′W	T	160
Llanddewi	Powys	SO1344	52°5·5′	3°15·8′W	X	148,161
Llanddewi	Swan	SS4689	51°35·0′	4°13·0′W	T	159
Llanddewi-Brefi	Cered	SN6655	52°10·9′	3°57·2′W	T	146
Llanddewi Court	Monm	SO3417	51°51·1′	2°57·1′W	X	161
Llanddewi Court	Monm	ST3197	51°40·3′	2°59·5′W	A	171
Llanddewi Fach	Monm	ST3395	51°39·2′	2°57·7′W	T	171
Llanddewi Gaer	Pemb	SN1416	51°48·9′	4°41·5′W	A	158
Llanddewi'r Cwm	Powys	SO0348	52°7·5′	3°24·6′W	T	147
Llanddewi Rhydderch	Monm	SO3413	51°48·9′	2°57·1′W	T	161
Llanddewi Skirrid	Monm	SO3416	51°50·6′	2°57·1′W	T	161
Llanddewi Velfrey	Pemb	SN1416	51°48·9′	4°41·5′W	T	158
Llanddewi Ystradenni	Powys	SO1068	52°18·4′	3°18·8′W	T	136,148
Llanddinog	Pemb	SM8327	51°54·2′	5°8·9′W	X	157
Llanddoged	Conwy	SH8063	53°9·3′	3°47·3′W	T	116
Llanddona	I of Angl	SH5779	53°17·6′	4°8·3′W	T	114,115
Llanddowror	Carm	SN2514	51°48·1′	4°31·9′W	T	158
Llanddulas	Conwy	SH9078	53°17·5′	3°38·6′W	T	116
Llanddwyn Bay	I of Angl	SH4062	53°8·1′	4°23·1′W	W	114,115
Llanddwyn Island (Ynys Llanddwyn)	I of Angl	SH3862	53°8·1′	4°24·9′W	X	114
Llanddwywe	Gwyn	SH5822	52°46·9′	4°5·9′W	T	124
Llanddyfnan	I of Angl	SH5078	53°16·9′	4°14·6′W	X	114,115
Llanddygfael Hir	I of Angl	SH3590	53°23·1′	4°28·5′W	X	114
Llandecwyn	Gwyn	SH6337	52°55·0′	4°1·9′W	T	124
Llandecwyn Sta	Gwyn	SH6137	52°55·0′	4°3·6′W	X	124
Llandefaelog	Powys	SO0332	51°58·9′	3°24·4′W	T	160
Llandefaelog-tre'r-graig	Powys	SO1229	51°57·4′	3°16·4′W	T	161
Llandefalle	Powys	SO1035	52°0·6′	3°18·3′W	T	161
Llandefalle Hill	Powys	SO0737	52°1·7′	3°20·9′W	X	160
Llandegai	Gwyn	SH5970	53°12·7′	4°6·3′W	T	114,115
Llandegfan	I of Angl	SH5673	53°14·3′	4°9·1′W	T	114,115
Llandegfedd Reservoir	Torf	ST3299	51°41·4′	2°58·6′W	W	171
Llandegla	Denb	SJ1952	53°3·8′	3°12·1′W	T	116
Llandegla Forest	Denb	SJ2251	53°3·3′	3°9·4′W	F	117
Llandegley	Powys	SO1362	52°15·2′	3°16·1′W	T	148
Llandegley Rhos	Powys	SO1360	52°14·1′	3°16·0′W	X	148
Llandegley Rocks	Powys	SO1361	52°14·7′	3°16·1′W	H	148
Llandegveth	Monm	ST3395	51°39·2′	2°57·7′W	T	171
Llandegwning	Gwyn	SH2630	52°50·6′	4°34·6′W	X	123
Llandeilo	Carm	SN6222	51°53·0′	3°59·9′W	T	159
Llandeilo Graban	Powys	SO0944	52°5·5′	3°19·3′W	T	147,161
Llandeilo Hill	Powys	SO0946	52°6·5′	3°19·3′W	H	147
Llandeilo Hill	Powys	SO1047	52°7·1′	3°18·5′W	H	148
Llandeilo'r-Fan	Powys	SN8934	51°59·8′	3°36·6′W	T	160
Llandeloy	Pemb	SM8526	51°53·7′	5°7·1′W	T	157
Llandenny	Monm	SO4103	51°43·6′	2°50·9′W	T	171
Llandenny Court	Monm	SO4203	51°43·6′	2°50·0′W	X	171
Llandenny Walks	Monm	SO3904	51°44·1′	2°52·6′W	T	171
Llandevaud	Newp	ST4090	51°36·6′	2°51·6′W	T	171,172
Llandevenny	Monm	ST4186	51°34·4′	2°50·7′W	T	171,172
Llandigige	Pemb	SM7929	51°55·2′	5°12·4′W	X	157
Llandilo	Pemb	SN1027	51°54·8′	4°45·4′W	T	145,158
Llandilo-abercowin	Carm	SN3113	51°47·6′	4°26·7′W	X	159
Llandilo-yr-ynys	Carm	SN4920	51°51·7′	4°11·2′W	T	159
Llandinabo Fm	Heref	SO5128	51°57·1′	2°42·4′W	FM	149
Llandinam	Powys	SO0288	52°29·1′	3°26·2′W	T	136
Llandinam Hall	Powys	SO0290	52°30·2′	3°26·2′W	X	136
Llandinier	Powys	SO1798	52°34·7′	3°13·1′W	X	136
Llandinshop	Shrops	SO2577	52°23·4′	3°5·7′W	X	137,148
Llandishty	Monm	SO4415	51°50·1′	2°48·4′W	X	161
Llandissilio	Pemb	SN1221	51°51·6′	4°43·4′W	T	145,158
Llandochau or Llandough	V of Glam	ST1673	51°27·2′	3°12·1′W	T	171
Llandogo	Monm	SO5204	51°44·2′	2°41·3′W	T	162
Llandough	V of Glam	SS9972	51°26·5′	3°26·8′W	T	170
Llandough or Llandochau	V of Glam	ST1673	51°27·2′	3°12·1′W	T	171
Llandovery (Llanymddyfri)	Carm	SN7634	51°59·7′	3°48·0′W	T	146,160
Llandow	V of Glam	SS9473	51°27·0′	3°31·1′W	T	170
Llandow Industrial Estate	V of Glam	SS9572	51°26·5′	3°30·3′W	X	170
Llandowlais	Monm	ST3798	51°40·9′	2°54·3′W	X	171
Llandre	Carm	SN1523	51°52·7′	4°40·9′W	X	145,158
Llandre	Carm	SN6742	52°3·9′	3°56·0′W	X	146
Llandre	Cered	SN6286	52°27·5′	4°1·5′W	T	135
Llandre	Pemb	SN1328	51°55·4′	4°42·8′W	X	145,158
Llandre Br	Carm	SN0920	51°51·0′	4°46·0′W	X	145,158
Llandre Egremont	Carm	SN0920	51°51·0′	4°46·0′W	X	145,158
Llandremor	Swan	SN6105	51°43·8′	4°0·4′W	X	159
Llandrillo	Denb	SJ0337	52°55·5′	3°26·2′W	T	125
Llandrillo-yn-Rhôs	Conwy	SH8380	53°18·5′	3°45·0′W	T	116
Llandrindod or (Llandrindod Wells)	Powys	SO0561	52°14·6′	3°23·1′W	T	147
Llandrindod Wells or (Llandrindod)	Powys	SO0561	52°14·6′	3°23·1′W	T	147
Llandrinio	Powys	SJ2817	52°45·0′	3°3·6′W	T	126
Llandruidion	Pemb	SM7824	51°52·5′	5°13·1′W	T	157
Llandruidion	Pemb	SM9037	51°59·7′	5°3·2′W	X	157
Llandudno	Conwy	SH7881	53°19·0′	3°49·5′W	T	115
Llandudno Bay or Ormes Bay	Conwy	SH7983	53°20·1′	3°48·6′W	W	115
Llandudno Bay or Ormes Bay	Conwy	SH8082	53°19·5′	3°47·7′W	W	116
Llandudno Junction	Conwy	SH7978	53°17·4′	3°48·5′W	T	115
Llandudno Junction	Conwy	SH8078	53°17·4′	3°47·6′W	T	116
Llandudwen	Gwyn	SH2736	52°53·9′	4°33·9′W	X	123
Llandwrog	Gwyn	SH4556	53°5·0′	4°18·5′W	T	115,123
Llandybie	Carm	SN6115	51°49·2′	4°0·6′W	T	159
Llandyfan	Carm	SN6417	51°50·3′	3°58·1′W	T	159
Llandyfriog	Cered	SN3341	52°2·8′	4°25·7′W	T	145
Llandyfrydog	I of Angl	SH4485	53°20·6′	4°20·2′W	T	114
Llandygwydd	Cered	SN2443	52°3·7′	4°33·7′W	T	145
Llandynan	Denb	SJ1944	52°59·5′	3°12·0′W	T	125
Llandyn Hall	Denb	SJ2242	52°58·4′	3°9·3′W	X	117
Llandyrnog	Denb	SJ1065	53°10·7′	3°20·4′W	T	116
Llandyry	Carm	SN4304	51°43·0′	4°16·0′W	X	159
Llandysilio	Powys	SJ2619	52°46·1′	3°5·4′W	T	126
Llandyssil	Powys	SO1995	52°33·1′	3°11·3′W	T	136
Llandysul	Cered	SN4140	52°2·4′	4°18·7′W	T	146
Llaneast	Pemb	SM9635	51°58·8′	4°57·8′W	X	157
Llaneast Fm	Powys	SO1447	52°7·1′	3°15·0′W	FM	148
Llanedeyrn	Card	ST2080	51°31·0′	3°8·8′W	T	171
Llanedeyrn	Card	ST2181	51°31·6′	3°7·9′W	T	171
Llanedi	Carm	SN5807	51°44·9′	4°3·0′W	X	159
Llanedw	Powys	SO1153	52°10·3′	3°17·7′W	X	148
Llanedw	Powys	SO1250	52°8·7′	3°16·8′W	X	148
Llaneglwys	Powys	SO0638	52°2·2′	3°21·8′W	T	160
Llaneglwys Wood	Powys	SO0439	52°2·7′	3°23·6′W	F	160
Llanegryn	Gwyn	SH6005	52°37·7′	4°3·7′W	T	124
Llanegwad	Carm	SN5121	51°52·3′	4°9·5′W	T	159
Llaneilian	I of Angl	SH4792	53°24·4′	4°17·7′W	T	114
Llaneithyr	Cered	SN7677	52°22·9′	3°48·9′W	X	135,147
Llanelian yn-Rhôs	Conwy	SH8676	53°16·4′	3°42·2′W	T	116
Llanelidan	Denb	SJ1050	53°2·6′	3°20·1′W	T	116
Llanelieu	Powys	SO1834	52°0·1′	3°11·3′W	T	161
Llanellan	Swan	SS5193	51°37·2′	4°8·8′W	X	159
Llanellen	Monm	SO3010	51°47·3′	3°0·5′W	T	161
Llanelli	Carm	SN5000	51°41·0′	4°9·8′W	T	159
Llanelltyd	Gwyn	SH7119	52°45·4′	3°54·3′W	T	124
Llanelly	Monm	SO2314	51°49·4′	3°6·6′W	T	161
Llanelly Hill	Monm	SO2211	51°47·8′	3°7·5′W	T	161
Llanelwedd	Powys	SO0451	52°9·2′	3°23·8′W	T	147
Llanelwedd Rocks	Powys	SO0552	52°9·7′	3°22·9′W	X	147
Llanelwy or St Asaph	Denb	SJ0374	53°15·5′	3°26·8′W	T	116
Llanenddwyn	Gwyn	SH5723	52°47·4′	4°6·8′W	T	124
Llanengan	Gwyn	SH2926	52°48·5′	4°31·8′W	T	123
Llaneon	Powys	SO1255	52°11·4′	3°16·8′W	X	148
Llanerch	Carm	SN5605	51°43·8′	4°4·7′W	X	159
Llanerch	Gwyn	SH8816	52°44·0′	3°39·1′W	X	124,125
Llanerch	Pemb	SN0535	51°59·0′	4°50·0′W	X	145
Llanerch	Powys	SO1531	51°58·5′	3°13·9′W	X	161
Llanerch	Powys	SO1680	52°24·9′	3°13·7′W	X	136
Llanerch	Powys	SO3093	52°32·1′	3°1·5′W	T	137
Llanerchbrochwel	Powys	SJ1910	52°41·1′	3°11·5′W	X	125
Llanerch Brook	Heref	SO5120	51°52·8′	2°42·3′W	W	162
Llanerch Cawr	Powys	SN9061	52°14·4′	3°36·3′W	X	147
Llanerchclwydau	Cered	SN6885	52°27·1′	3°56·2′W	X	135
Llanerch Elsi	Conwy	SH7854	53°4·4′	3°48·9′W	X	115
Llanerchemrys	Powys	SJ2023	52°48·2′	3°10·8′W	T	126
Llanerch-fraith	Powys	SO0871	52°20·0′	3°20·6′W	X	136,147
Llanerch-goch	Carm	SN8131	51°58·1′	3°43·5′W	X	160
Llanerchigwynion	Conwy	SH8049	53°1·7′	3°47·0′W	X	116
Llanerchindda	Carm	SN8042	52°4·0′	3°44·6′W	X	147,160
Llanerchir	Powys	SO1749	52°8·2′	3°12·4′W	X	148
Llanerch Lâs	Gwyn	SH8837	52°55·4′	3°39·6′W	X	124,125
Llanerchllwyd	Powys	SN9755	52°11·3′	3°30·0′W	X	147
Llanerchllyn	Gwyn	SN6198	52°34·0′	4°2·7′W	X	135
Llanerch-Panna	Wrex	SJ4139	52°57·0′	2°52·3′W	X	126
Llanerch Pentir	Cered	SN6975	52°21·7′	3°55·0′W	X	135
Llanerchpesgi	Powys	SN9653	52°10·2′	3°30·8′W	X	147
Llanerchrugog Hall	Wrex	SJ2847	53°1·2′	3°4·0′W	X	117
Llanerch-y-coed	Heref	SO2742	52°4·5′	3°3·5′W	X	148,161
Llanerchydol Hall	Powys	SJ2007	52°39·5′	3°10·6′W	X	126
Llanerchymedd	I of Angl	SH4184	53°20·0′	4°22·9′W	T	114,115
Llanerch-yr-aur	Powys	SJ1422	52°47·6′	3°16·1′W	X	125
Llanerfyl	Powys	SJ0309	52°40·4′	3°25·7′W	T	125
Llanerthill	Monm	SO4304	51°44·1′	2°49·1′W	X	171
Llaneuddog	I of Angl	SH4688	53°22·2′	4°18·5′W	T	114
Llan-eurgain or Northop	Flint	SJ2468	53°12·5′	3°7·9′W	T	117
Llanevan	Powys	SO1561	52°14·7′	3°14·3′W	X	148
Llan-Evan Hill	Powys	SO1661	52°14·7′	3°13·4′W	X	148
Llanfabon	Caer	ST1093	51°38·0′	3°17·6′W	T	171
Llanfach	Caer	ST2295	51°39·1′	3°7·3′W	T	171
Llanfachraeth	I of Angl	SH3182	53°18·7′	4°31·8′W	T	114
Llanfachreth	Gwyn	SH7522	52°47·1′	3°50·8′W	T	124
Llan-faelog	Cered	SN5961	52°14·0′	4°3·5′W	X	146
Llanfaelog	I of Angl	SH3373	53°13·9′	4°29·7′W	T	114
Llanfaelrhys	Gwyn	SH2126	52°48·4′	4°38·9′W	X	123
Llanfaenor	Monm	SO4316	51°50·6′	2°49·3′W	X	161
Llanfaes	I of Angl	SH6077	53°16·5′	4°5·6′W	T	114,115
Llanfaes	Powys	SO0328	51°56·8′	3°24·3′W	T	160
Llanfaethlu	I of Angl	SH3186	53°20·9′	4°31·9′W	T	114
Llanfaglan	Gwyn	SH4760	53°7·2′	4°16·8′W	T	114,115
Llanfair	Cered	SN4341	52°3·0′	4°17·0′W	X	146
Llanfair	Gwyn	SH5729	52°50·6′	4°7·0′W	T	124
Llanfair Caereinion	Powys	SJ1006	52°38·9′	3°19·4′W	T	125
Llanfair Clydogau	Cered	SN6251	52°8·6′	4°0·6′W	T	146
Llanfair Dyffryn Clwyd	Denb	SJ1355	53°5·4′	3°17·5′W	T	116
Llanfair-fach	Cered	SN6050	52°8·1′	4°2·3′W	X	146
Llanfairfechan	Conwy	SH6874	53°15·0′	3°58·3′W	T	115
Llanfair Fm	Heref	SO2545	52°6·1′	3°5·3′W	FM	148

Llanfair Grange	Monm	SO3919	51°52·2′	2°52·8′W	X	161
Llanfair Hall	Gwyn	SH5066	53°10·4′	4°14·3′W	X	114,115
Llanfair Hill	Shrops	SO2579	52°24·5′	3°5·8′W	H	137,148
Llanfair Kilgeddin	Monm	SO3407	51°45·7′	2°57·0′W	T	161
Llanfair-Nant-Gwyn	Pemb	SN1637	52°0·3′	4°40·5′W	T	145
Llanfair Pwllgwyngyll	I of Angl	SH5371	53°13·2′	4°11·7′W	T	114,115
Llanfair Talhaiarn	Conwy	SH9270	53°13·2′	3°36·6′W	T	116
Llanfair Waterdine	Shrops	SO2476	52°22·8′	3°6·6′W	T	137,148
Llanfair-Ym-Muallt or (Builth Wells)	Powys	SO0350	52°8·6′	3°24·7′W	T	147
Llanfairyneubwll	I of Angl	SH3076	53°15·5′	4°32·5′W	T	114
Llanfairynghornwy	I of Angl	SH3290	53°23·1′	4°31·2′W	T	114
Llanfallteg	Carm	SN1519	51°50·6′	4°40·7′W	T	158
Llanfallteg	Carm	SN1520	51°51·1′	4°40·8′W	T	145
Llanfallteg West	Carm	SN1419	51°50·6′	4°41·6′W	T	158
Llanfarach	V of Glam	ST0679	51°30·4′	3°20·9′W	X	170
Llanfaredd	Powys	SO0650	52°8·7′	3°22·0′W	T	147
Llanfarian	Cered	SN5877	52°22·6′	4°4·8′W	T	135
Llanfawr	Carm	SN3926	51°54·8′	4°20·1′W	X	145
Llanfawr	I of Angl	SH4473	53°14·1′	4°19·8′W	X	114,115
Llanfawr	Powys	SO1040	52°3·3′	3°18·4′W	X	148,161
Llan-fawr	Powys	SO2566	52°17·5′	3°5·6′W	H	137,148
Llanfechain	Powys	SJ1820	52°46·5′	3°12·5′W	T	125
Llanfechan	Cered	SN5145	52°5·2′	4°10·1′W	X	146
Llanfechan	Powys	SH7705	52°38·0′	3°48·7′W	H	124
Llanfechan	Powys	SN9750	52°8·6′	3°29·9′W	X	147
Llanfechan Ho	Powys	SN9750	52°8·6′	3°29·9′W	X	147
Llanfechell	I of Angl	SH3691	53°23·7′	4°27·6′W	T	114
Llanfellte	Powys	SO1421	51°53·1′	3°14·6′W	X	161
Llanfendigaid	Gwyn	SH5605	52°37·7′	4°7·3′W	X	124
Llanferran	Pemb	SM7528	51°54·5′	5°15·9′W	X	157
Llanferran	Pemb	SM8837	51°59·7′	5°4·9′W	X	157
Llanferres	Denb	SJ1860	53°8·1′	3°13·1′W	T	116
Llanfflewyn	I of Angl	SH3589	53°22·6′	4°28·4′W	T	114
Llanfigael	I of Angl	SH3282	53°18·7′	4°30·9′W	T	114
Llanfihangel	Gwyn	SH3034	52°52·8′	4°31·2′W	X	123
Llanfihangel-ar-arth	Carm	SN4539	52°1·9′	4°15·2′W	T	146
Llanfihangel Glyn Myfyr	Conwy	SH9949	53°2·0′	3°30·0′W	T	116
Llanfihangel-helygen	Powys	SO0464	52°16·2′	3°24·0′W	T	147
Llanfihangel Hill	Powys	SO1955	52°11·5′	3°10·7′W	H	148
Llanfihangel Nant Bran	Powys	SN9434	51°59·9′	3°32·2′W	T	160
Llanfihangel-nant-Melan	Powys	SO1858	52°13·1′	3°11·6′W	T	148
Llanfihangel Rhydithon	Powys	SO1566	52°17·4′	3°14·4′W	T	136,148
Llanfihangel Rogiet	Monm	ST4587	51°35·0′	2°47·2′W	T	171,172
Llanfihangel Tal-y-llyn	Powys	SO1128	51°56·8′	3°17·3′W	T	161
Llanfihangel Tor y Mynydd	Monm	SO4502	51°43·1′	2°47·4′W	T	171
Llanfihangel-uwch-Gwili	Carm	SN4822	51°52·8′	4°12·1′W	T	159
Llanfihangel-y-Creuddyn	Cered	SN6676	52°22·2′	3°57·7′W	T	135
Llanfihangel-yng-Ngwynfa	Powys	SJ0816	52°44·3′	3°21·4′W	T	125
Llanfihangel yn Nhowyn	I of Angl	SH3277	53°16·1′	4°30·7′W	T	114
Llanfihangel-y-pennant	Gwyn	SH5244	52°58·6′	4°11·9′W	X	124
Llanfihangel-y-pennant	Gwyn	SH6708	52°39·4′	3°57·6′W	T	124
Llanfihangel-y-traethau	Gwyn	SH5935	52°53·9′	4°5·4′W	T	124
Llanfilo	Powys	SO1133	51°59·5′	3°17·4′W	T	161
Llan Fm	Heref	SO3142	52°4·6′	3°0·0′W	FM	148,161
Llan Fm	Shrops	SO3579	52°24·5′	2°56·9′W	FM	137,148
Llanfoist	Monm	SO2813	51°48·9′	3°2·3′W	T	161
Llanfor	Gwyn	SH9336	52°54·9′	3°35·1′W	T	125
Llan-fraith Hill	Powys	SO1150	52°8·7′	3°17·6′W	H	148
Llanfrechfa	Torf	ST3193	51°38·1′	2°59·4′W	T	171
Llanfrothen	Gwyn	SH6241	52°57·2′	4°2·8′W	T	124
Llanfrother	Heref	SO5428	51°57·2′	2°39·8′W	X	149
Llanfrynach	Powys	SO0725	51°55·2′	3°20·7′W	T	160
Llanfwrog	Denb	SJ1157	53°6·4′	3°19·4′W	T	116
Llanfwrog	I of Angl	SH3084	53°19·8′	4°32·8′W	T	114
Llanfyllin	Powys	SJ1419	52°45·9′	3°16·1′W	T	125
Llanfynydd	Carm	SN5527	51°55·6′	4°6·1′W	T	146
Llanfynydd	Flint	SJ2756	53°6·0′	3°5·0′W	T	117
Llanfyrnach	Pemb	SN2231	51°57·2′	4°35·0′W	T	145
Llangadfan	Powys	SJ0110	52°41·0′	3°27·5′W	T	125
Llangadog	Carm	SN4207	51°44·6′	4°16·9′W	T	159
Llangadog	Carm	SN7028	51°56·4′	3°53·1′W	T	146,160
Llangadwaladr	I of Angl	SH3869	53°11·9′	4°25·1′W	T	114
Llangadwaladr	Powys	SJ1830	52°51·9′	3°12·7′W	T	125
Llangaffo	I of Angl	SH4468	53°11·4′	4°19·7′W	T	114,115
Llangain	Carm	SN3815	51°48·9′	4°20·6′W	T	159
Llangammarch Wells	Powys	SN9347	52°6·9′	3°33·4′W	T	147
Llangan	V of Glam	SS9577	51°29·2′	3°30·3′W	T	170
Llangarron	Heref	SO5221	51°53·4′	2°41·5′W	T	162
Llangarron Court	Heref	SO5221	51°53·4′	2°41·5′W	X	162
Llangarthginning	Carm	SN2721	51°51·9′	4°30·4′W	X	145,158
Llangasty-Talyllyn	Powys	SO1326	51°55·5′	3°15·5′W	T	161
Llangathen	Carm	SN5822	51°52·9′	4°3·4′W	T	159
Llangattock	Powys	SO2117	51°51·0′	3°8·4′W	T	161
Llangattock Ho	Monm	SO3310	51°47·3′	2°57·9′W	X	161
Llangattock Lingoed	Monm	SO3620	51°52·7′	2°55·4′W	T	161
Llangattock Park Ho	Powys	SO2017	51°51·0′	3°9·3′W	X	161
Llangattock-Vibon-Avel	Monm	SO4515	51°50·1′	2°47·5′W	T	161
Llangedwyn	Powys	SJ1824	52°48·7′	3°12·6′W	T	125
Llangefni	I of Angl	SH4675	53°15·2′	4°18·1′W	T	114,115
Llangeinor	Brig	SS9187	51°34·5′	3°34·0′W	T	170
Llangeitho	Cered	SN6159	52°12·9′	4°1·7′W	T	146
Llangeler	Carm	SN3739	52°1·8′	4°22·2′W	T	145
Llangelynnin	Gwyn	SH5707	52°38·8′	4°6·4′W	T	124
Llangennech	Carm	SN5501	51°41·6′	4°5·5′W	T	159
Llangennith	Swan	SS4291	51°36·0′	4°16·5′W	T	159
Llangennith Burrows	Swan	SS4192	51°36·5′	4°17·4′W	X	159
Llangennith Moors	Swan	SS4191	51°36·0′	4°17·4′W	X	159
Llangenny	Powys	SO2417	51°51·0′	3°5·8′W	T	161
Llangernyw	Conwy	SH8767	53°11·5′	3°41·1′W	T	116
Llangeview	Monm	SO3900	51°42·0′	2°52·6′W	T	171
Llangewydd	Brig	SS8681	51°31·2′	3°38·2′W	X	170
Llangewydd Court Fm	Brig	SS8781	51°31·2′	3°37·3′W	FM	170
Llangian	Gwyn	SH2928	52°49·6′	4°31·9′W	T	123
Llangibby Castle Fm	Monm	ST3697	51°40·3′	2°55·1′W	FM	171
Llangiwg	Nth Pt Talb	SN7205	51°44·0′	3°50·8′W	X	160
Llangloffan	Pemb	SM9032	51°57·1′	5°3·0′W	T	157
Llangloffan Cross	Pemb	SM9032	51°57·1′	5°3·0′W	X	157
Llanglydwen	Carm	SN1826	51°54·4′	4°38·4′W	T	145,158
Llangoed	I of Angl	SH6079	53°17·6′	4°5·6′W	T	114,115
Llangoed	Powys	SO1240	52°3·3′	3°16·6′W	X	148,161
Llangoedmor	Cered	SN2045	52°4·7′	4°37·2′W	T	145
Llangollan	Corn	SW9477	50°33·6′	4°54·1′W	X	200
Llangollen	Denb	SJ2141	52°57·9′	3°10·2′W	T	117
Llangollen Steam Railway	Denb	SJ1642	52°58·4′	3°14·7′W	X	125
Llangolman	Pemb	SN1126	51°54·3′	4°44·5′W	T	145,158
Llangolman Common	Pemb	SN1127	51°54·8′	4°44·5′W	X	145,158
Llangorse	Powys	SO1327	51°56·3′	3°15·5′W	T	161
Llangorse Lake	Powys	SO1326	51°55·8′	3°15·5′W	W	161
Llangorwen	Cered	SN6083	52°25·9′	4°3·2′W	T	135
Llangovan	Monm	SO4505	51°44·7′	2°47·4′W	T	161
Llangower	Gwyn	SH9032	52°52·7′	3°37·7′W	T	125
Llangower Point	Gwyn	SH9032	52°52·7′	3°37·7′W	X	125
Llangranog	Cered	SN3154	52°9·7′	4°27·9′W	T	145
Llangristiolus	I of Angl	SH4373	53°14·1′	4°20·7′W	T	114,115
Llangrove	Heref	SO5219	51°52·3′	2°41·4′W	T	162
Llangua	Monm	SO3925	51°55·4′	2°52·8′W	T	161
Llangunllo	Powys	SO2171	52°20·1′	3°9·2′W	T	137,148
Llangunllo Sta	Powys	SO2073	52°21·2′	3°10·1′W	X	137,148
Llangunnock	Heref	SO5123	51°54·4′	2°42·3′W	X	162
Llangunnock Br	Heref	SO5022	51°53·9′	2°43·2′W	X	162
Llangunnog	Monm	SO4501	51°42·5′	2°47·4′W	X	171
Llangunnor	Carm	SN4320	51°51·6′	4°16·4′W	T	159
Llangunville Fm	Heref	SO4916	51°50·7′	2°44·0′W	FM	162
Llangurig	Powys	SN9079	52°24·1′	3°36·6′W	T	136,147
Llangwarren	Pemb	SM9231	51°56·6′	5°1·2′W	X	157
Llangwathan	Powys	SO2440	52°3·4′	3°6·1′W	X	148,161
Llangwm	Conwy	SH9644	52°59·2′	3°32·6′W	T	125
Llangwm	Monm	SO4200	51°42·0′	2°50·0′W	T	171
Llangwm	Pemb	SM9909	51°44·9′	4°54·3′W	T	157,158
Llangwm	Pemb	SN1022	51°52·1′	4°45·2′W	X	145,158
Llangwm-isaf Fm	Monm	SO4201	51°42·5′	2°50·0′W	FM	171
Llangwnnadl	Gwyn	SH2032	52°51·6′	4°40·0′W	T	123
Llangwryd-isaf	Wrex	SJ2337	52°55·7′	3°8·3′W	X	126
Llangwstenin Hall	Conwy	SH8279	53°17·9′	3°46·2′W	X	116
Llangwyfan	Denb	SJ1166	53°11·3′	3°19·5′W	T	116
Llangwyfan-isaf	I of Angl	SH3369	53°11·8′	4°29·6′W	X	114
Llangwyllog	I of Angl	SH4379	53°17·3′	4°20·9′W	T	114,115
Llan-gwyn	Powys	SO2373	52°21·2′	3°7·4′W	X	137,148
Llangwyryfon	Cered	SN5970	52°18·8′	4°3·7′W	T	135
Llangybi	Cered	SN6053	52°9·7′	4°2·4′W	T	146
Llangybi	Gwyn	SH4241	52°56·8′	4°20·7′W	T	123
Llangybi	Monm	ST3796	51°39·8′	2°54·3′W	T	171
Llangybi Common	Cered	SN5954	52°10·2′	4°3·3′W	X	146
Llangyfelach	Swan	SS6498	51°40·1′	3°57·6′W	T	159
Llangyfrwys	Powys	SO1356	52°12·0′	3°16·0′W	X	148
Llangyndeyrn	Carm	SN4514	51°48·4′	4°14·5′W	T	159
Llangynhafal	Denb	SJ1263	53°9·7′	3°18·6′W	T	116
Llangynidr	Powys	SO1519	51°52·0′	3°13·7′W	T	161
Llangynidr Bridge	Powys	SO1520	51°52·6′	3°13·7′W	X	161
Llangynidr Reservoir	Powys	SO1514	51°49·3′	3°13·6′W	W	161
Llangyniew	Powys	SJ1208	52°40·0′	3°17·7′W	T	125
Llangynin	Carm	SN2519	51°50·8′	4°32·0′W	T	158
Llangynllo	Cered	SN3543	52°3·9′	4°24·0′W	X	145
Llangynog	Carm	SN3316	51°49·3′	4°25·0′W	T	159
Llangynog	Powys	SJ0526	52°49·6′	3°24·2′W	T	125
Llangynwyd	Brig	SS8688	51°35·0′	3°38·3′W	T	170
Llanhailo	Powys	SO1255	52°11·4′	3°16·8′W	X	148
Llanhamlach	Powys	SO0926	51°55·7′	3°19·0′W	T	161
Llanharan	Rho Cyn Taf	ST0083	51°32·5′	3°26·1′W	T	170
Llanharry	Rho Cyn Taf	ST0080	51°30·8′	3°26·1′W	T	170
Llanhaylow	Powys	SO2053	52°10·4′	3°9·8′W	X	148
Llanhedrick	Shrops	SO2884	52°27·1′	3°3·2′W	X	137
Llanhedry Fm	Heref	SO2750	52°8·8′	3°3·6′W	FM	148
Llanhennock	Monm	ST3592	51°37·6′	2°56·0′W	T	171
Llanhilleth	Blae Gw	SO2100	51°41·8′	3°8·2′W	T	171
Llanhowel	Pemb	SM8127	51°54·2′	5°10·6′W	T	157
Llanhowell	Powys	SO1355	52°11·4′	3°16·0′W	X	148
Llan-Howell	Powys	SO2356	52°12·1′	3°7·2′W	X	148
Llanhowell Fm	Shrops	SO3479	52°24·5′	2°57·8′W	FM	137,148
Llanidan Ho	I of Angl	SH4966	53°10·4′	4°15·2′W	A	114,115
Llanidloes	Powys	SN9584	52°26·9′	3°32·3′W	T	136
Llaniestyn	Gwyn	SH2633	52°52·2′	4°34·7′W	T	123
Llanifyny	Powys	SN8681	52°25·1′	3°40·2′W	T	135,136
Llanigon	Powys	SO2140	52°3·4′	3°8·7′W	T	148,161
Llanilar	Cered	SN6275	52°21·6′	4°1·2′W	T	135
Llanilid	Rho Cyn Taf	SS9781	51°31·3′	3°28·7′W	X	170
Llanilid	Rho Cyn Taf	ST0086	51°34·1′	3°26·2′W	X	170
Llanio-fawr	Cered	SN6457	52°11·9′	3°59·0′W	X	146
Llanio-isaf	Cered	SN6456	52°11·4′	3°59·0′W	X	146
Llanion	Pemb	SM9703	51°41·6′	4°55·8′W	T	157,158
Llanishen	Card	ST1781	51°31·5′	3°11·4′W	T	171
Llanishen	Monm	SO4703	51°43·6′	2°45·7′W	T	171
Llanishen Court	Monm	SO4304	51°44·1′	2°49·1′W	X	171
Llanishen Cross	Monm	SO4703	51°43·6′	2°45·7′W	X	171
Llanishen Resr	Card	ST1881	51°31·6′	3°10·5′W	W	171
Llanithog Fm	Heref	SO4326	51°56·0′	2°49·4′W	FM	161
Llaniwared	Powys	SN8877	52°23·0′	3°38·3′W	X	135,136,147
Llanllawddog	Carm	SN4529	51°56·5′	4°14·9′W	X	146
Llanllawen	Gwyn	SH1426	52°48·2′	4°45·2′W	X	123
Llanllechid	Gwyn	SH6268	53°11·7′	4°3·5′W	T	115
Llanlleiana	I of Angl	SH3894	53°25·3′	4°25·9′W	X	114
Llanllibio Fawr	I of Angl	SH3282	53°18·7′	4°30·9′W	X	114
Llanllibio Groes	I of Angl	SH3381	53°18·2′	4°30·0′W	X	114
Llanllowell	Monm	ST3998	51°40·9′	2°52·5′W	T	171
Llanllugan	Powys	SJ0502	52°36·7′	3°23·8′W	T	136
Llanllwch	Carm	SN3818	51°50·5′	4°20·7′W	T	159
Llanllwchaiarn	Powys	SO1192	52°31·4′	3°18·3′W	T	136
Llanllwni	Carm	SN4939	52°2·0′	4°11·7′W	T	146
Llanllwyd	Shrops	SO1981	52°25·5′	3°11·1′W	T	136
Llanllwyda	Gwyn	SH6507	52°38·9′	3°59·3′W	X	124
Llanllwydd	Monm	SO4117	51°51·1′	2°51·0′W	X	161
Llanllyfni	Gwyn	SH4751	53°2·3′	4°16·5′W	T	115,123
Llanllyr	Cered	SN5455	52°10·7′	4°7·7′W	X	146
Llanmadoc	Shrops	SO1781	52°25·5′	3°12·8′W	X	136
Llanmadoc	Swan	SS4493	51°37·1′	4°14·8′W	T	159
Llanmadoc Hill	Swan	SS4392	51°36·5′	4°15·7′W	H	159
Llanmaes	Card	ST1276	51°28·8′	3°15·6′W	T	171
Llanmaes	V of Glam	SS9869	51°24·9′	3°27·6′W	T	170
Llan-Marlais	Pemb	SN1716	51°49·0′	4°38·9′W	X	158
Llanmartin	Newp	ST3989	51°36·0′	2°52·5′W	T	171
Llanmerwig	Powys	SO1592	52°31·4′	3°14·8′W	T	136
Llanmihangel	Nth Pt Talb	SS8182	51°31·7′	3°42·5′W	X	170
Llanmihangel	V of Glam	SS9871	51°26·0′	3°27·7′W	T	170
Llan-mill	Pemb	SN1414	51°47·9′	4°41·5′W	T	158
Llanmiloe	Carm	SN2508	51°44·8′	4°31·7′W	T	158
Llanmorlais	Swan	SS5394	51°37·8′	4°7·0′W	T	159
Llannant	Swan	SN5700	51°41·1′	4°3·7′W	X	159
Llannefydd	Conwy	SH9870	53°13·3′	3°31·3′W	T	116
Llannerch	Gwyn	SH3538	52°55·1′	4°26·9′W	X	123
Llannerch	Gwyn	SH5538	52°55·4′	4°9·0′W	X	124
Llannerch	Powys	SO1558	52°13·1′	3°14·3′W	X	148
Llannerch-celli	Powys	SJ2417	52°45·0′	3°7·2′W	X	126
Llannerchfydaf	Gwyn	SH9017	52°44·6′	3°37·4′W	X	125
Llannerch Hall	Denb	SJ0572	53°14·4′	3°25·0′W	X	116
Llannerchwen	Powys	SO0232	51°58·9′	3°25·2′W	X	160
Llannerch-y-môr	Flint	SJ1779	53°18·3′	3°14·3′W	T	116
Llannerch-yr-aur	Powys	SN8697	52°33·8′	3°40·5′W	X	135,136
Llannerch-yrfa	Powys	SN8355	52°11·1′	3°42·3′W	X	147
Llannon	Carm	SN5308	51°45·3′	4°7·4′W	T	159
Llan-non	Cered	SN5167	52°17·1′	4°10·7′W	T	135
Llannor	Gwyn	SH3537	52°54·6′	4°26·8′W	T	123
Llanoddian Hall	Powys	SJ0907	52°39·4′	3°20·3′W	X	125
Llanol	I of Angl	SH3788	53°22·1′	4°26·6′W	X	114
Llanoley	Powys	SO0860	52°14·1′	3°20·4′W	X	147
Llanoley Fm	Powys	SO1949	52°8·2′	3°10·6′W	FM	148
Llanon	Pemb	SM8331	51°56·4′	5°9·0′W	T	157
Llanover	Heref	SO3132	51°59·2′	2°59·9′W	X	161
Llanover	Monm	SO3108	51°46·2′	2°59·6′W	T	161
Llan-pica	Powys	SO2250	52°8·8′	3°8·0′W	X	148
Llanpumsaint	Carm	SN4129	51°56·4′	4°18·4′W	T	146
Llanreath	Pemb	SM9503	51°41·5′	4°57·6′W	T	157,158
Llanreithan	Pemb	SM8628	51°54·8′	5°6·3′W	X	157
Llanrhaeadr	Denb	SJ0863	53°9·6′	3°22·2′W	T	116
Llanrhaeadr-ym-Mochnant	Powys	SJ1226	52°49·7′	3°18·0′W	T	125
Llanrhian	Pemb	SM8131	51°56·3′	5°10·8′W	T	157
Llanrhidian	Swan	SS4992	51°36·6′	4°10·5′W	T	159
Llanrhidian Marsh	Swan	SS4993	51°37·2′	4°10·5′W	W	159
Llanrhidian Pill	Swan	SS5094	51°37·7′	4°9·6′W	W	159
Llanrhidian Sands	Swan	SS4995	51°38·3′	4°10·5′W	X	159
Llanrhos	Conwy	SH7980	53°18·4′	3°48·6′W	T	115
Llanrhychwyn	Conwy	SH7761	53°8·2′	3°49·9′W	X	115
Llanrhyddlad	I of Angl	SH3389	53°22·5′	4°30·2′W	T	114
Llanrhydd Mill	Denb	SJ1457	53°6·4′	3°16·7′W	X	116
Llanrhys	Powys	SO1578	52°23·8′	3°14·6′W	X	136,148
Llanrhystud	Cered	SN5369	52°18·2′	4°9·0′W	T	135
Llanrosser	Heref	SO2837	52°1·8′	3°2·6′W	X	161
Llanrothal	Heref	SO4718	51°51·7′	2°45·8′W	X	161
Llanrothal	Monm	SO4618	51°51·7′	2°46·7′W	X	161
Llanrug	Gwyn	SH5363	53°8·9′	4°11·5′W	T	114,115
Llanrumney	Card	ST2280	51°31·0′	3°7·1′W	T	171
Llanrwst	Conwy	SH8061	53°8·2′	3°47·2′W	T	116
Llansabbath	Monm	SO3109	51°46·8′	2°59·6′W	X	161
Llansadurnen	Carm	SN2810	51°46·0′	4°29·2′W	T	158
Llansadwrn	Carm	SN6931	51°58·0′	3°54·0′W	T	146,160
Llansadwrn	I of Angl	SH5676	53°15·9′	4°9·1′W	T	114,115
Llansaint	Carm	SN3808	51°45·1′	4°20·4′W	T	159
Llansamlet	Swan	SS6897	51°39·6′	3°54·1′W	T	159
Llansanffraid Glan Conwy	Conwy	SH8075	53°15·8′	3°47·5′W	T	116
Llansannan	Conwy	SH9365	53°10·5′	3°35·7′W	T	116
Llansannor	V of Glam	SS9977	51°29·2′	3°26·9′W	T	170
Llansantffraed	Cered	SN5167	52°17·1′	4°10·7′W	T	135
Llansantffraed	Powys	SO1223	51°54·2′	3°16·4′W	T	161
Llansantffraed Court (Hotel)	Monm	SO3510	51°47·3′	2°56·2′W	X	161
Llansantffraed-Cwmdeuddwr	Powys	SN9667	52°17·7′	3°31·1′W	T	136,147
Llansantffraed-in-Elwel	Powys	SO0954	52°10·8′	3°19·5′W	T	147
Llansantffraid-ym-Mechain	Powys	SJ2120	52°46·6′	3°9·9′W	T	126
Llansawel	Carm	SN6136	52°0·5′	4°1·1′W	T	146
Llanshay	Powys	SO2971	52°20·2′	3°2·1′W	X	137,148
Llanshiver	Powys	SO2047	52°7·2′	3°9·7′W	X	148
Llan-Shon-Dorthy	Powys	SO2052	52°9·9′	3°9·8′W	X	148
Llansilin	Powys	SJ2028	52°50·9′	3°10·9′W	T	126
Llansoar Fawr	Monm	ST3593	51°38·2′	2°56·0′W	X	171
Llansoy	Monm	SO4402	51°43·1′	2°48·2′W	T	171
Llanspyddid	Powys	SO0128	51°56·7′	3°26·0′W	T	160
Llanstadwell	Pemb	SM9405	51°42·6′	4°58·5′W	T	157,158
Llansteffan	Carm	SN3510	51°46·1′	4°23·1′W	T	159
Llanstephan	Powys	SO1242	52°4·4′	3°16·6′W	T	148,161
Llanstephan Ho	Powys	SO1141	52°3·9′	3°17·5′W	X	148,161
Llanstinan Home Fm	Pemb	SM9532	51°57·2′	4°58·6′W	FM	157
Llantarnam	Torf	ST3093	51°38·1′	3°0·3′W	T	171
Llantarnam Abbey	Torf	ST3192	51°37·6′	2°59·4′W	X	171
Llantarnam Hall	Torf	ST3091	51°37·0′	3°0·3′W	X	171
Llanteems	Monm	SO3320	51°52·7′	2°58·0′W	T	161
Llanteg	Pemb	SN1810	51°45·8′	4°37·9′W	T	158
Llanteglos	Pemb	SN1709	51°45·2′	4°38·7′W	X	158
Llantellen	Monm	SO4120	51°52·8′	2°51·0′W	X	161
Llantellen, The	Powys	SO3194	52°32·6′	3°0·6′W	X	137
Llanthomas	Powys	SO2140	52°3·4′	3°8·7′W	X	148,161
Llanthony	Monm	SO2827	51°56·4′	3°2·5′W	T	161
Llanthony Priory	Glos	SO8218	51°51·9′	2°15·3′W	A	162
Llantilio Crossenny	Monm	SO3914	51°49·5′	2°52·7′W	T	161
Llantilio Pertholey	Monm	SO3116	51°50·5′	2°59·7′W	T	161
Llantood	Pemb	SN1541	52°2·4′	4°41·5′W	X	145
Llantrisant	I of Angl	SH3683	53°19·4′	4°27·3′W	T	114
Llantrisant	Monm	ST3996	51°39·8′	2°52·5′W	T	171
Llantrisant	Rho Cyn Taf	ST0483	51°32·5′	3°22·7′W	T	170
Llantrisant Common	Rho Cyn Taf	ST0484	51°33·0′	3°22·7′W	X	170
Llantrisant Forest	Rho Cyn Taf	ST0284	51°33·0′	3°24·4′W	F	170
Llantrithyd	V of Glam	ST0472	51°26·6′	3°22·5′W	T	170
Llantrithyd Place	V of Glam	ST0472	51°26·6′	3°22·5′W	A	170
Llantroft	Shrops	SO2379	52°24·5′	3°7·5′W	X	137,148
Llantrwssa	Powys	SO2157	52°12·6′	3°9·0′W	X	148
Llantwit	Nth Pt Talb	SS7697	51°39·7′	3°47·2′W	T	170
Llantwit Fardre	Rho Cyn Taf	ST0784	51°33·1′	3°20·1′W	T	170
Llantwit Major	V of Glam	SS9768	51°24·3′	3°28·5′W	T	170
Llantysilio Hall	Denb	SJ1943	52°58·9′	3°12·0′W	X	125
Llantysilio Mountain	Denb	SJ1545	53°0·0′	3°15·6′W	H	116

Llantywaun Brook	Heref	SO4921	51°53·4′	2°44·1′W	W	162
Llanungar	Pemb	SM7925	51°53·0′	5°12·3′W	X	157
Llanunwas	Pemb	SM7924	51°52·5′	5°12·3′W	X	157
Llanusk Fm	Monm	ST3799	51°41·4′	2°54·3′W	FM	171
Llanuwchllyn	Gwyn	SH8730	52°51·6′	3°40·3′W	T	124,125
Llanvaches	Newp	ST4391	51°37·1′	2°49·0′W	T	171,172
Llanvair	Monm	SO4604	51°44·2′	2°46·5′W	X	171
Llanvair-Discoed	Monm	ST4492	51°37·7′	2°48·2′W	T	171,172
Llanvair Grange	Monm	SO3307	51°45·7′	2°57·9′W	X	161
Llanvapley	Monm	SO3614	51°49·5′	2°55·3′W	T	161
Llanvetherine	Monm	SO3617	51°51·1′	2°55·4′W	T	161
Llanveynoe	Heref	SO3031	51°58·6′	3°0·8′W	T	161
Llanvihangel Court	Monm	SO3220	51°52·7′	2°58·9′W	A	161
Llanvihangel Court	Monm	SO4601	51°42·5′	2°46·5′W	X	171
Llanvihangel Crucorney	Monm	SO3220	51°52·7′	2°58·9′W	T	161
Llanvihangel Gobion	Monm	SO3409	51°46·8′	2°57·0′W	T	161
Llanvihangel Pontymoel	Torf	SO3001	51°42·4′	3°0·4′W	X	171
Llanvihangel-Ystern-Llewern	Monm	SO4313	51°49·0′	2°49·2′W	T	161
Llanvithyn	V of Glam	ST0571	51°26·0′	3°21·6′W	X	170
Llanwarne	Heref	SO5028	51°57·1′	2°43·3′W	T	149
Llanwarne Court	Heref	SO5027	51°56·6′	2°43·3′W	X	162
Llanwddyn	Powys	SJ0219	52°45·8′	3°26·7′W	T	125
Llanwefr Pool	Powys	SO1359	52°13·6′	3°16·0′W	W	148
Llanwenarth	Monm	SO2714	51°49·4′	3°3·2′W	T	161
Llanwenarth Breast	Monm	SO2616	51°50·5′	3°4·1′W	X	161
Llanwenarth Ho	Monm	SO2513	51°48·9′	3°4·9′W	X	161
Llan-wen Hill	Powys	SO2969	52°19·1′	3°2·1′W	X	137,148
Llanwenog	Cered	SN4945	52°5·2′	4°11·8′W	T	146
Llanwensan	V of Glam	ST0779	51°30·4′	3°20·0′W	X	170
Llanwern	Newp	ST3688	51°35·5′	2°55·0′W	T	171
Llanwilcae	Monm	SO3806	51°45·2′	2°53·5′W	X	161
Llanwinio	Carm	SN2626	51°54·6′	4°31·4′W	T	145,158
Llanwinio Common	Carm	SN2429	51°56·1′	4°33·2′W	X	145,158
Llanwinney	Monm	SO4604	51°44·2′	2°46·5′W	X	171
Llanwnda	Gwyn	SH4758	53°6·1′	4°16·7′W	T	115,123
Llanwnda	Pemb	SM9339	52°0·9′	5°0·6′W	T	157
Llanwnnen	Cered	SN5347	52°6·4′	4°8·4′W	T	146
Llanwnog	Powys	SO0293	52°31·8′	3°26·3′W	T	136
Llanwnwr	Pemb	SM8940	52°1·3′	5°4·1′W	X	157
Llanwolley	Shrops	SO2177	52°23·4′	3°9·3′W	H	137,148
Llanwonno	Rho Cyn Taf	ST0395	51°39·0′	3°23·7′W	X	170
Llanwonog Fm	Heref	SO3229	51°57·6′	2°59·0′W	FM	161
Llanwrda	Carm	SN7131	51°58·0′	3°52·3′W	T	146,160
Llanwrin	Powys	SH7803	52°36·9′	3°47·7′W	T	135
Llanwrthwl	Powys	SN9763	52°15·6′	3°30·2′W	T	147
Llanwrtyd	Powys	SN8647	52°6·8′	3°39·5′W	T	147
Llanwrtyd Wells	Powys	SN8746	52°6·3′	3°38·6′W	T	147
Llanwyddelan	Powys	SJ0701	52°36·2′	3°22·0′W	T	136
Llanyblodwel	Shrops	SJ2422	52°47·7′	3°7·2′W	T	126
Llanybri	Carm	SN3312	51°47·1′	4°24·9′W	T	159
Llanybydder	Carm	SN5244	52°4·7′	4°9·2′W	T	146
Llanycefn	Pemb	SN0923	51°52·6′	4°46·1′W	T	145,158
Llan-y-cefn	Wrex	SJ3541	52°58·0′	2°57·7′W	X	117
Llanychaer	Pemb	SM9835	51°58·8′	4°56·1′W	T	157
Llanycil	Gwyn	SH9134	52°53·8′	3°36·8′W	T	125
Llanycrwys	Carm	SN6445	52°5·4′	3°58·7′W	X	146
Llanyfaelog	Carm	SN4111	51°46·7′	4°17·9′W	T	159
Llan-y-Felin	Powys	SO2454	52°11·0′	3°6·3′W	X	148
Llanymawddwy	Gwyn	SH9019	52°45·7′	3°37·4′W	T	125
Llanymddyfri (Llandovery)	Carm	SN7634	51°59·7′	3°48·0′W	T	146,160
Llanymynech	Powys	SJ2620	52°46·6′	3°5·4′W	T	126
Llanymynech Hill	Powys	SJ2622	52°47·7′	3°5·4′W	H	126
Llan-y-nant	Monm	SO4902	51°43·1′	2°43·9′W	X	162
Llanynghenedl	I of Angl	SH3181	53°18·2′	4°31·8′W	T	114
Llanynys	Denb	SJ1062	53°9·1′	3°20·3′W	T	116
Llanyoyne	Powys	SO2051	52°9·3′	3°9·8′W	X	148
Llan-y-pwll	Wrex	SJ3751	53°3·4′	2°56·0′W	T	117
Llanyrafon	Torf	ST3094	51°38·7′	3°0·3′W	T	171
Llanyre	Powys	SO0462	52°15·1′	3°24·0′W	T	147
Llanystumdwy	Gwyn	SH4738	52°55·3′	4°16·2′W	T	123
Llanywern	Powys	SO1028	51°56·8′	3°18·2′W	T	161
Llathige	Carm	SN6636	52°0·6′	3°56·8′W	X	146
Llatho	Powys	SO1151	52°9·2′	3°17·7′W	X	148
Llawcoed-du	Powys	SO1449	52°8·2′	3°15·0′W	X	148
Llawes-heli	Powys	SN9049	52°7·9′	3°36·0′W	X	147
Llawhaden	Pemb	SN0617	51°49·3′	4°48·5′W	T	158
Llawlech	Gwyn	SH6321	52°46·4′	4°1·5′W	H	124
Llawndy	Flint	SJ1183	53°20·4′	3°19·8′W	X	116
Llawnt	Shrops	SJ2430	52°52·0′	3°7·3′W	T	126
Llawog	Denb	SJ1063	53°9·6′	3°20·4′W	X	116
Llawr Cilan	Denb	SJ0237	52°55·5′	3°27·1′W	X	125
Llawr-cwrt	Cered	SN4150	52°7·8′	4°19·0′W	X	146
Llawr Dref	Gwyn	SH2728	52°49·6′	4°33·7′W	X	123
Llawr-dre-fawr	Powys	SN8545	52°5·7′	3°40·3′W	X	147
Llawr-tyddyn	I of Angl	SH3581	53°18·3′	4°28·2′W	X	114
Llawr-y-cwm-bach	Cered	SN7185	52°27·1′	3°53·5′W	X	135
Llawryglyn	Powys	SN9391	52°30·6′	3°34·2′W	T	136
Llay	Wrex	SJ3355	53°5·5′	2°59·6′W	T	117
Llechan Ucha	Conwy	SH7575	53°15·7′	3°52·0′W	X	115
Llechart	Swan	SN6904	51°43·4′	3°53·4′W	X	170
Llechau	Rho Cyn Taf	ST0180	51°30·9′	3°25·2′W	X	170
Llechaucochion	Pemb	SM7831	51°56·2′	5°13·4′W	W	157
Llechau-isaf	Pemb	SM6823	51°51·7′	5°21·8′W	X	157
Llechau-uchaf	Pemb	SM6824	51°52·2′	5°21·8′W	X	157
Llech Ciste	Carm	SN5128	51°56·1′	4°9·7′W	A	146
Llechclawdd	Carm	SN2423	51°52·9′	4°33·0′W	X	145,158
Llechcynfarwy	I of Angl	SH3881	53°18·3′	4°25·5′W	T	114
Llech Dafad	Pemb	SM8835	51°58·3′	5°4·8′W	X	157
Llech Daniel	Denb	SH9956	53°5·7′	3°30·1′W	X	116
Llechdwnni	Carm	SN4210	51°46·2′	4°17·0′W	X	159
Llecheiddior	Gwyn	SH4743	52°58·0′	4°16·3′W	T	123
Llecheiddior	Gwyn	SH6022	52°46·9′	4°4·1′W	X	124
Llecheigon	Carm	SN3822	51°52·6′	4°20·8′W	X	145,159
Llechenhinen	Pemb	SM7228	51°54·5′	5°18·5′W	X	157
Llechfaen	Powys	SO0828	51°56·8′	3°19·9′W	T	160
Llechfraith	Gwyn	SH6619	52°45·4′	3°58·7′W	T	124
Llech Ganol	Pemb	SM7731	51°56·2′	5°14·3′W	X	157
Llech Idris	Gwyn	SH7331	52°51·9′	3°52·8′W	A	124
Llech Isaf	Pemb	SM7631	51°56·2′	5°15·1′W	X	157

Llechlwyd	Carm	SN3622	51°52·6′	4°22·6′W	X	145,159
Llech Lydan	Gwyn	SH3343	52°57·7′	4°28·8′W	X	123
Llechog	Gwyn	SH5953	53°3·6′	4°5·8′W	X	115
Llechog	Gwyn	SH6056	53°5·2′	4°5·0′W	X	115
Llechog isaf	I of Angl	SH4293	53°24·9′	4°22·2′W	X	114
Llechollwyn	Gwyn	SH5932	52°52·3′	4°5·3′W	X	124
Llechryd	Caer	SO1009	51°46·6′	3°17·9′W	T	161
Llechryd	Cered	SN2143	52°3·6′	4°36·3′W	T	145
Llechryd	Conwy	SJ0068	53°12·2′	3°29·4′W	X	116
Llechrydau	Wrex	SJ2234	52°54·1′	3°9·2′W	X	126
Llechryd-isaf	Cered	SN2143	52°3·6′	4°36·3′W	X	145
Llech Uchaf	Pemb	SM7832	51°56·8′	5°13·4′W	X	157
Llechwedd	Cered	SN4944	52°4·7′	4°11·8′W	X	146
Llechwedd	Conwy	SH7676	53°16·2′	3°51·2′W	T	115
Llechwedd	Conwy	SH9650	53°2·5′	3°32·7′W	X	116
Llechwedd	Denb	SJ0336	52°55·0′	3°26·2′W	X	125
Llechwedd	Powys	SH9512	52°42·0′	3°32·8′W	X	125
Llechwedd Bryniau Defaid	Conwy	SH7845	52°59·6′	3°48·7′W	X	115
Llechwedd Cilan	Denb	SJ0236	52°55·0′	3°27·0′W	X	125
Llechwedd Crin	Powys	SN8192	52°31·0′	3°44·8′W	X	135,136
Llechwedd-dderi	Cered	SN5050	52°7·9′	4°11·1′W	X	146
Llechwedd Diffwys	Gwyn	SH8915	52°43·5′	3°38·2′W	X	124,125
Llechwedd Diflas	Powys	SN7893	52°31·5′	3°47·5′W	H	135
Llechwedd Du	Powys	SH9205	52°38·2′	3°35·4′W	X	125
Llechwedd Du	Powys	SH9616	52°44·1′	3°32·0′W	X	125
Llechwedd-du	Powys	SH9701	52°36·1′	3°30·9′W	X	136
Llechwedd-du	Powys	SJ0006	52°38·8′	3°28·3′W	X	125
Llechwedd-du	Powys	SJ0020	52°46·3′	3°28·5′W	X	125
Llechwedd Du	Powys	SN8793	52°31·6′	3°39·5′W	X	135,136
Llechwedd du-bach	Gwyn	SH5932	52°52·3′	4°5·3′W	X	124
Llechwedd-du-mawr	Gwyn	SH6032	52°52·3′	4°4·4′W	X	124
Llechwedd Erwent	Gwyn	SH8234	52°53·7′	3°44·8′W	X	124,125
Llechwedd Figyn	Gwyn	SH9144	52°59·2′	3°37·0′W	X	125
Llechwedd-fwyalchen	Gwyn	SH8627	52°50·0′	3°41·1′W	X	124,125
Llechwedd-gwyn	Wrex	SJ2034	52°54·1′	3°11·0′W	X	126
Llechweddhafod	Conwy	SH7648	53°1·1′	3°50·5′W	X	115
Llechwedd Hirgoed	Powys	SN8183	52°26·2′	3°44·6′W	X	135,136
Llechwedd Llwyd	Powys	SH9317	52°44·6′	3°34·7′W	H	125
Llechwedd Llwyd	Powys	SJ1123	52°48·1′	3°18·8′W	H	125
Llechwedd Llwyd	Powys	SN8381	52°25·1′	3°42·8′W	X	135,136
Llechwedd llyfn	Conwy	SH9450	53°2·5′	3°34·5′W	X	116
Llechwedd-llyfn	Gwyn	SH8644	52°59·1′	3°41·5′W	H	124,125
Llechwedd Mawr	Conwy	SH7743	52°58·5′	3°49·5′W	X	124
Llechwedd Mawr	Powys	SH8609	52°40·2′	3°40·8′W	H	124,125
Llechwedd Melyn	Gwyn	SN6198	52°34·0′	4°2·7′W	H	135
Llechwedd Oernant	Conwy	SH7847	53°0·6′	3°48·7′W	X	115
Llechwedd Rudd	Gwyn	SH8035	52°54·2′	3°46·6′W	X	124,125
Llechwedd Slate Caverns	Gwyn	SH6946	53°0·0′	3°56·7′W	X	115
Llechwedd-y-gaer	Conwy	SH9748	53°1·4′	3°31·7′W	H	116
Llechwedd-y-garth	Powys	SJ0326	52°49·6′	3°26·0′W	X	125
Llechwedd y Glyn	Powys	SN8687	52°28·4′	3°40·3′W	X	135,136
Llechweddystrad	Gwyn	SH8930	52°51·7′	3°38·5′W	X	124,125
Lledfron	Powys	SJ1120	52°46·5′	3°18·8′W	X	125
Llednant	Powys	SN9054	52°10·6′	3°36·1′W	X	147
Lledrod	Cered	SN6470	52°18·9′	3°59·3′W	T	135
Lledrod	Powys	SJ1918	52°45·5′	3°11·6′W	X	125
Lledrod	Powys	SJ2130	52°51·9′	3°10·0′W	X	126
Lledrod	Powys	SJ2229	52°51·4′	3°9·1′W	X	126
Lledwigan	Conwy	SH7562	53°8·7′	3°51·7′W	X	115
Lledwigan	I of Angl	SH4574	53°14·7′	4°19·0′W	X	114,115
Lledwyn Mawr	Gwyn	SH9028	52°50·5′	3°37·6′W	H	125
Llefn	Gwyn	SH6368	53°11·7′	4°2·6′W	X	115
Llegodig	Powys	SO1896	52°33·6′	3°12·2′W	X	136
Lleina	Cered	SN2150	52°7·4′	4°36·5′W	X	145
Lleinau	Carm	SN2323	51°52·9′	4°33·9′W	X	145,158
Lleinau	Pemb	SN1734	51°58·7′	4°39·5′W	X	145
Lleine	Carm	SN3422	51°52·6′	4°24·3′W	X	145,159
Lleine	Carm	SN4126	51°54·8′	4°18·3′W	X	146
Lleine	Pemb	SN0943	52°3·4′	4°46·8′W	X	145
Lleiniau	Gwyn	SH1931	52°51·0′	4°40·9′W	X	123
Lleiniog	I of Angl	SH6179	53°17·6′	4°4·7′W	X	114,115
Lleiriog	Powys	SJ1527	52°50·3′	3°15·3′W	W	125
Lleithyr	Pemb	SM7427	51°54·0′	5°16·7′W	X	157
Lle'r Gaer	Rho Cyn Taf	ST0587	51°34·7′	3°21·9′W	A	170
Lle'r-neuaddau	Cered	SN7584	52°26·6′	3°50·0′W	X	135
Llether	Cered	SN7253	52°9·9′	3°51·9′W	X	146,147
Llethercynon	Powys	SO0536	52°1·1′	3°22·7′W	X	160
Lletherddu	Powys	SN9654	52°10·7′	3°30·9′W	X	147
Llethergynuen	Powys	SO0333	51°59·5′	3°24·4′W	X	160
Lletherhir	Carm	SN8240	52°3·0′	3°42·9′W	X	147,160
Llethermadin	Pemb	SN1023	51°52·6′	4°45·2′W	X	145,158
Llethr	Carm	SN4128	51°55·9′	4°18·4′W	X	146
Llethr	Cered	SN7470	52°19·1′	3°50·5′W	X	135,147
Llethr	Conwy	SH8962	53°8·9′	3°39·2′W	X	116
Llethr	Pemb	SM8523	51°52·1′	5°7·0′W	X	157
Llethr	Pemb	SN1632	51°57·6′	4°40·3′W	X	145
Llethr	Powys	SN9119	51°51·8′	3°34·6′W	X	160
Llethr	Powys	SN9761	52°14·5′	3°30·1′W	X	147
Llethr	Powys	SO0058	52°12·9′	3°27·4′W	X	147
Llethr	Powys	SO0776	52°22·7′	3°21·6′W	X	136,147
Llethr	Powys	SO1282	52°26·0′	3°17·3′W	X	136
Llethrach	Carm	SN3419	51°50·9′	4°24·2′W	X	159
Llethrau	Powys	SO1483	52°26·5′	3°15·5′W	X	136
Llethr Brith	Cered	SN7662	52°14·8′	3°48·6′W	X	146,147
Llethr Brith	Cered	SN7768	52°18·0′	3°47·8′W	X	135,147
Llethr-ddu	Gwyn	SH4045	52°59·0′	4°22·6′W	X	115,123
Llethr Ddu	Powys	SN9345	52°5·8′	3°33·3′W	X	147
Llethr Du	Cered	SN7050	52°8·2′	3°53·6′W	X	146,147
Llethr Du	Powys	SO1965	52°16·9′	3°10·8′W	X	148
Llethr Erwast	Cered	SN7150	52°8·2′	3°52·7′W	X	146,147
Llethr Garw	Powys	SN8556	52°11·7′	3°40·6′W	X	147
Llethr Gwinau	Carm	SN7246	52°6·1′	3°51·7′W	X	146,147
Llethr Gwngu	Powys	SN8572	52°20·3′	3°40·9′W	X	135,136,147
Llethr Gwyn	Cered	SN7151	52°8·8′	3°52·7′W	X	146,147
Llethr Hafodydd	Cered	SN7355	52°11·0′	3°51·1′W	X	146,147
Llethr Hir	Powys	SN8366	52°17·0′	3°42·5′W	H	135,136,147
Llethr-hir	Powys	SO1479	52°24·4′	3°15·5′W	X	136,148
Llethrid Br	Swan	SS5391	51°36·2′	4°7·0′W	X	159
Llethr Las	Rho Cyn Taf	SN9304	51°43·7′	3°32·6′W	X	170
Llethr-llwyd	Carm	SN6134	51°59·5′	4°1·1′W	X	146

Llethr Llwyd	Cered	SN7353	52°9·9′	3°51·0′W	H	146,147
Llethrllymwynt	Powys	SO1077	52°23·3′	3°19·0′W	X	136,148
Llethr Lwyd	Cered	SN7869	52°18·6′	3°47·0′W	X	135,147
Llethr Mawr	Cered	SN7054	52°10·4′	3°53·7′W	X	146,147
Llethr Melyn	Powys	SN8753	52°10·1′	3°38·7′W	X	147
Llethr-moel	Carm	SN3627	51°55·3′	4°22·7′W	X	145
Llethr Tirion	Cered	SN7970	52°19·1′	3°46·1′W	X	135,147
Llethyr Melyn	Powys	SN9658	52°12·9′	3°30·9′W	X	147
Lletty	Carm	SN1619	51°50·6′	4°39·9′W	X	158
Lletty	Carm	SN5306	51°44·2′	4°7·3′W	X	159
Lletty	Carm	SN6219	51°51·4′	3°59·8′W	X	159
Lletty	Carm	SN7123	51°53·7′	3°52·1′W	X	160
Lletty	Conwy	SH7861	53°8·2′	3°49·0′W	X	115
Lletty	Denb	SJ0846	53°0·4′	3°21·9′W	X	116
Lletty	Gwyn	SH5060	53°7·2′	4°14·1′W	X	114,115
Lletty	Powys	SJ0916	52°44·3′	3°20·5′W	X	125
Lletty	Powys	SO0359	52°13·5′	3°24·8′W	X	147
Llettybella Fm	Nth Pt Talb	SN7800	51°41·4′	3°45·5′W	FM	170
Llettybowen	Cered	SN5155	52°10·6′	4°10·4′W	X	146
Lletty-clyd	Carm	SN2737	52°0·5′	4°30·8′W	X	145
Lletty Fm	Denb	SJ1264	53°10·2′	3°18·6′W	FM	116
Llettyglyd	Carm	SN6120	51°51·9′	4°0·7′W	X	159
Lletty Gwilym Isaf	Powys	SJ0503	52°37·2′	3°23·8′W	X	136
Lletty-Ifan-Ddu	Carm	SN7430	51°57·5′	3°49·6′W	X	146,160
Llettyllwyd	Cered	SN6588	52°28·6′	3°58·9′W	X	135
Llettyllwynde	Carm	SN5535	51°59·9′	4°6·3′W	X	146
Lletty-Mawr	Powys	SH9810	52°40·9′	3°30·1′W	X	125
Llettypeod	Powys	SO1648	52°7·7′	3°13·2′W	X	148
Lletty'r-afel-fawr	Nth Pt Talb	SN7801	51°41·9′	3°45·5′W	X	170
Llettyrcadwgan	Carm	SN6535	52°0·1′	3°57·6′W	X	146
Llety'r Cymro	Cered	SN3554	52°9·8′	4°24·4′W	X	145
Llety'r-dryw	Carm	SN5303	51°42·6′	4°7·3′W	X	159
Lletyrhaflaeth	Carm	SN7839	52°2·4′	3°46·3′W	X	146,160
Lletty-Rhŷs	Nth Pt Talb	SN7101	51°41·8′	3°51·6′W	X	170
Llettyrychen	Carm	SN4501	51°41·4′	4°14·2′W	T	159
Lletty Shon	Cered	SN4761	52°13·8′	4°14·0′W	X	146
Llettytwppa Fm	Cered	SN5848	52°7·0′	4°4·0′W	FM	146
Lletty Watkin	Conwy	SH8569	53°12·6′	3°42·9′W	X	116
Lletty-wyn	Gwyn	SH8121	52°46·7′	3°45·5′W	X	124,125
Llety	Powys	SJ1427	52°50·3′	3°16·2′W	X	125
Llety Cadwgan	Carm	SN6535	52°0·1′	3°57·6′W	X	146
Llety-dau-filwr	Carm	SN4717	51°50·1′	4°12·8′W	X	159
Llety-du	Conwy	SH8875	53°15·9′	3°40·3′W	X	116
Lletygynfach	Powys	SJ2502	52°36·9′	3°6·1′W	X	126
Llety Ifan	Wrex	SJ2239	52°56·8′	3°9·2′W	X	126
Llety-Ifan-Hên	Cered	SN6885	52°27·1′	3°56·2′W	X	135
Llety-Morfil	Swan	SN6401	51°41·7′	3°57·7′W	X	159
Llety'r Adar	Conwy	SH8675	53°15·8′	3°42·1′W	X	116
Llety'r Eos	Flint	SJ1968	53°12·4′	3°12·4′W	X	116
Lletyrhyddod	Carm	SN7428	51°56·4′	3°49·6′W	X	146,160
Lletyrhys	Gwyn	SH7619	52°45·5′	3°49·9′W	X	124
Lletyr-neuadd	Carm	SN4728	51°56·0′	4°13·1′W	X	146
Llety'r Wyn	Gwyn	SH1930	52°50·5′	4°40·8′W	X	123
Lleuar Bach	Gwyn	SH4451	53°2·3′	4°19·2′W	X	115,123
Lleuar Fawr	Gwyn	SH4552	53°2·8′	4°18·3′W	X	115,123
Lleust-mawr	Cered	SN5063	52°14·9′	4°11·4′W	X	146
Lleustuchaf	Powys	SO0098	52°34·5′	3°28·1′W	X	136
Llewelyn	Flint	SJ2359	53°7·6′	3°8·6′W	X	117
Llewelyn Park	Swan	SS6696	51°39·0′	3°55·8′W	X	159
Llewelyn's Cave	Powys	SO0846	52°6·5′	3°20·2′W	X	147
Llewelyn's Dingle	Monm	ST4099	51°41·4′	2°51·7′W	W	171
Llewenau	Powys	SO1823	51°54·2′	3°11·1′W	X	161
Llewenau Draw	Powys	SO1923	51°54·2′	3°10·3′W	X	161
Lleweni Hall	Denb	SJ0868	53°12·3′	3°22·2′W	X	116
Llewerllyd	Denb	SJ0479	53°18·2′	3°26·0′W	X	116
Llewesog Hall	Denb	SJ0561	53°8·5′	3°24·8′W	X	116
Llewetrog	Powys	SJ1246	52°6·6′	3°16·7′W	X	148
Llewitha Br	Swan	SS6196	51°39·0′	4°0·2′W	X	159
Lleyn Peninsula (Penrhyn Llŷn)	Gwyn	SH3437	52°54·5′	4°27·7′W	X	123
Llidiad-Nenog	Carm	SN5437	52°1·0′	4°7·3′W	X	146
Llidiardau	Cered	SN6374	52°21·1′	4°0·3′W	X	135
Llidiardau	Gwyn	SH8738	52°55·9′	3°40·5′W	T	124,125
Llidiarddau	Powys	SN9778	52°23·7′	3°30·4′W	X	136,147
Llidiardu	Powys	SJ1201	52°36·2′	3°17·6′W	X	136
Llidiart-cae-hir	Wrex	SJ1430	52°51·9′	3°16·2′W	X	125
Llidiart-fawr	Denb	SJ1652	53°3·8′	3°14·8′W	X	116
Llidiart y Barwn	Gwyn	SH9012	52°41·9′	3°37·3′W	X	125
Llidiart-y-gwinedd	Denb	SJ0546	53°0·4′	3°24·5′W	X	116
Llidiart-y-Parc	Denb	SJ1143	52°58·9′	3°19·1′W	T	125
Llifior Brook	Powys	SO1698	52°34·6′	3°14·0′W	W	136
Llig-fynydd	Denb	SJ0754	53°4·8′	3°22·9′W	X	116
Lligwy Bay	I of Angl	SH4987	53°21·7′	4°15·7′W	W	114
Llithfaen	Gwyn	SH3543	52°57·8′	4°27·0′W	T	123
Lloc	Flint	SJ1476	53°16·7′	3°17·0′W	T	116
Lloegr	Powys	SO0434	52°0·0′	3°23·5′W	X	160
Lloegr-fâch	Cered	SN4962	52°14·4′	4°12·3′W	X	146
Llofft-y-bardd	Powys	SN8953	52°10·1′	3°37·0′W	X	147
Llofftyddgleision	Powys	SN9371	52°19·8′	3°33·8′W	X	136,147
Llolans	Scot Bord	NT1037	55°37·3′	3°25·3′W	X	72
Llong	Flint	SJ2662	53°9·2′	3°6·0′W	T	117
Llongley	Flint	SJ2073	53°15·1′	3°11·5′W	X	117
Lloran Isaf	Powys	SJ1827	52°50·3′	3°12·6′W	X	125
Lloran Uchaf	Powys	SJ1627	52°50·3′	3°14·4′W	X	125
Llorfa	Powys	SN7815	51°49·5′	3°45·8′W	X	160
Llowes	Powys	SO1941	52°3·9′	3°10·5′W	T	148,161
Llowes Hall	Powys	SO1743	52°5·0′	3°12·3′W	X	148,161
Lloyd Ho	Staffs	SO8894	52°32·9′	2°10·2′W	X	139
Lloyd Jack	Cered	SN5256	52°11·2′	4°9·5′W	X	146
Lloyd's Fm	Lincs	TF5163	53°8·8′	0°15·9′E	FM	122
Lloyds, The	Wrekin	SJ6903	52°37·7′	2°27·1′W	X	127
Lloyd, The	Staffs	SJ7133	52°53·9′	2°25·5′W	X	127
Lloyney	Powys	SO1341	52°3·9′	3°15·8′W	X	148,161
Lloyney	Powys	SO2044	52°5·6′	3°9·7′W	X	148,161
Lloyney	Powys	SO2151	52°9·3′	3°8·9′W	X	148
Lloyney	Powys	SO2475	52°22·3′	3°6·6′W	T	137,148
Lloysey Fm	Monm	SO4906	51°45·3′	2°43·9′W	FM	162
Lloyts Fm	W Susx	TQ1818	50°57·2′	0°18·8′W	FM	198
Lluast	Powys	SJ0104	52°37·7′	3°27·4′W	X	125
Lluest	Brig	SS9089	51°35·6′	3°34·9′W	X	170

Lluest	Cered	SN4659	52°12·7'	4°14·8'W	X	146
Lluest	Cered	SN5767	52°17·2'	4°5·4'W	X	135
Lluest	Cered	SN5954	52°10·2'	4°3·3'W	X	146
Lluest	Cered	SN7974	52°21·3'	3°46·2'W	X	135,147
Lluest	Powys	SH9708	52°39·8'	3°31·0'W	X	125
Lluest	Powys	SJ0212	52°42·1'	3°26·6'W	X	125
Lluest	Powys	SJ1417	52°44·9'	3°16·0'W	X	125
Lluest Abercaethon	Powys	SN8768	52°18·2'	3°39·0'W	X	135,136,147
Lluest-dolgwiail	Powys	SN8476	52°22·4'	3°41·8'W	X	135,136,147
Lluestfach	Cered	SN6682	52°25·4'	3°57·8'W	X	135
Lluest-newydd	Cered	SN5966	52°16·7'	4°3·6'W	X	135
Lluestnewydd	Powys	SN9759	52°13·4'	3°30·1'W	X	147
Lluest Ty-mawr	Powys	SN8595	52°32·7'	3°41·4'W	X	135,136
Lluest-wen	Brig	SS8489	51°35·5'	3°40·1'W	X	170
Lluest-wen	Powys	SN9488	52°29·0'	3°33·3'W	X	136
Lluest-wen Resr	Rho Cyn Taf	SN9401	51°42·1'	3°31·6'W	W	170
Lluestycerrig	Powys	SO0299	52°35·0'	3°26·4'W	X	136
Lluest y Graig	Powys	SN8088	52°28·8'	3°45·6'W	X	135,136
Llugwy	Gwyn	SN7199	52°34·7'	3°53·8'W	T	135
Llundain-fach	Cered	SN5556	52°11·2'	4°6·9'W	T	146
Llwch-is-awel	Carm	SN6511	51°47·1'	3°57·0'W	X	159
Llwch-yr-hâl	Cered	SN3342	52°3·3'	4°25·8'W	X	145
Llwybr Heulen	Powys	SJ0621	52°46·9'	3°23·2'W	X	125
Llwybr-hir	Flint	SJ1275	53°16·1'	3°18·8'W	X	116
Llwych-iwrch	Brig	SS9485	51°33·5'	3°31·4'W	X	170
Llwydarth	Brig	SS8590	51°36·1'	3°39·2'W	T	170
Llwydcoed	Carm	SN5409	51°45·9'	4°6·6'W	X	159
Llwydcoed	Carm	SN5509	51°45·9'	4°5·7'W	X	159
Llwydcoed	Carm	SN6224	51°54·1'	4°0·0'W	X	159
Llwydcoed	Powys	SO0596	52°33·5'	3°23·7'W	X	136
Llwydcoed	Rho Cyn Taf	SN9904	51°43·8'	3°27·4'W	T	170
Llwydcoed-fawr	Powys	SH9911	52°41·5'	3°29·3'W	X	125
Llwydfaen	Conwy	SH7872	53°14·1'	3°49·3'W	X	115
Llwydgoed Isa	Conwy	SH8376	53°16·3'	3°44·9'W	X	116
Llwydiarth	Powys	SN9880	52°24·8'	3°29·6'W	X	136
Llwydiarth	Wrex	SJ2237	52°55·7'	3°9·2'W	X	126
Llwydiarth Esgob Fm	I of Angl	SH4384	53°20·0'	4°21·1'W	FM	114,115
Llwydiarth Fawr	I of Angl	SH4285	53°20·5'	4°22·0'W	X	114
Llwydiarth Hall	Powys	SH7710	52°40·7'	3°48·8'W	X	124
Llwydiarth Hall	Powys	SJ0616	52°44·3'	3°23·1'W	X	125
Llwyd Mawr	Gwyn	SH5046	52°59·7'	4°13·7'W	X	115
Llwyfen	Powys	SO1521	51°53·1'	3°13·7'W	X	161
Llwyn	Carm	SN5116	51°49·6'	4°9·3'W	X	159
Llwyn	Carm	SN6443	52°4·4'	3°58·7'W	X	146
Llwyn	Cered	SN6555	52°10·8'	3°58·2'W	X	146
Llwyn	Denb	SJ0864	53°10·2'	3°22·2'W	T	116
Llwyn	Denb	SJ0951	53°3·2'	3°21·1'W	X	116
Llwyn	Gwyn	SH6839	52°56·2'	3°57·4'W	X	124
Llwyn	Powys	SO0267	52°17·8'	3°25·8'W	X	136,147
Llwyn	Powys	SO0963	52°15·7'	3°19·6'W	X	147
Llwyn	Powys	SO1272	52°20·6'	3°17·1'W	X	136,148
Llwyn	Shrops	SO2880	52°25·0'	3°3·1'W	T	137
Llwynadam	Swan	SN5801	51°41·6'	4°2·9'W	X	159
Llwyna Fm	Monm	SO4704	51°44·2'	2°45·7'W	FM	171
Llwyna Fm	Monm	ST3995	51°39·3'	2°52·5'W	FM	171
Llwynarddisgyn	Carm	SN4436	52°0·3'	4°16·0'W	X	146
Llwyn Arfon Fm	Caer	SO1603	51°43·4'	3°12·6'W	FM	171
Llwynaumawr Fm	Powys	SO1723	51°54·2'	3°12·0'W	FM	161
Llwyn-barried Hall	Powys	SO0265	52°16·7'	3°25·8'W	X	136,147
Llwynbedw	Carm	SN2736	52°0·0'	4°30·8'W	X	145
Llwyn-bedw	Carm	SN6521	51°52·5'	3°57·3'W	X	159
Llwynbedw	Cered	SN6069	52°18·3'	4°2·8'W	X	135
Llwyn-bedw	Gwyn	SH5358	53°6·2'	4°11·3'W	A	115
Llwynbedw	Powys	SO0024	51°54·6'	3°26·8'W	X	160
Llwyn Bedw	Powys	SO1429	51°57·4'	3°14·7'W	X	161
Llwyn Bedw Uchaf	Gwyn	SH4550	53°1·7'	4°18·3'W	X	115,123
Llwynberried	Powys	SO2038	52°2·3'	3°9·6'W	X	161
Llwynbeudy	Cered	SN6765	52°16·3'	3°56·6'W	X	135
Llwyn Braich Ddu	Gwyn	SJ0040	52°57·1'	3°28·9'W	X	125
Llwynbrain	Cered	SN6576	52°22·2'	3°58·6'W	X	135
Llwynbrain	Powys	SN9248	52°7·4'	3°34·3'W	X	147
Llwynbrain	Powys	SO0557	52°12·4'	3°23·0'W	X	147
Llwynbrain	Powys	SO2039	52°2·9'	3°9·6'W	X	161
Llwyn Bryn-dinas	Powys	SJ1724	52°48·7'	3°13·5'W	A	125
Llwyn-bŵch	Cered	SN6363	52°15·1'	4°0·0'W	X	146
Llwynbychan	Carm	SN2618	51°50·3'	4°31·1'W	X	158
Llwyncadfor	Cered	SN3342	52°3·3'	4°25·8'W	X	145
Llwyncadwgan	Powys	SN9149	52°8·0'	3°35·2'W	X	147
Llwyncalenig	Carm	SN4329	51°56·5'	4°16·7'W	X	146
Llwyn-cecil Fm	Monm	SO3211	51°47·8'	2°58·8'W	FM	161
Llwyncelyn	Carm	SN4113	51°47·8'	4°18·0'W	X	159
Llwyn-celyn	Carm	SN4628	51°56·0'	4°14·0'W	X	146
Llwyn celyn	Carm	SN5130	51°57·2'	4°9·7'W	X	146
Llwyn-celyn	Carm	SN5931	51°57·8'	4°2·7'W	X	146
Llwyncelyn	Carm	SN7232	51°58·5'	3°51·4'W	X	146,160
Llwyncelyn	Cered	SN4459	52°12·7'	4°16·6'W	T	146
Llwyncelyn	Gwyn	SH6798	52°34·1'	3°57·3'W	X	135
Llwyncelyn	Monm	SO3021	51°53·2'	3°0·6'W	X	161
Llwyncelyn	Monm	ST3594	51°38·7'	2°56·0'W	X	171
Llwyncelyn	Pemb	SN2042	52°3·1'	4°37·1'W	X	145
Llwyncelyn	Powys	SO0132	51°58·9'	3°26·1'W	X	160
Llwyncelyn Fm	Carm	SN6023	51°53·5'	4°1·7'W	FM	159
Llwyncelyn Fm	Powys	SO1618	51°51·5'	3°12·8'W	FM	161
Llwyncelyn-lan	Pemb	SN2330	51°56·7'	4°34·1'W	X	145
Llwyncelyn Uchaf	Carm	SN2419	51°50·8'	4°32·9'W	X	158
Llwynceubren	Powys	SO0659	52°13·5'	3°22·2'W	X	147
Llwyn Coch	Powys	SO1396	52°33·5'	3°16·6'W	X	136
Llwyncoch	Rho Cyn Taf	SN9706	51°44·8'	3°29·1'W	X	160
Llwyn-coed	Carm	SN2549	52°6·9'	4°33·0'W	X	145
Llwyn-coedwr	Nth Pt Talb	SN8301	51°42·0'	3°41·2'W	X	170
Llwyn-cor	Powys	SN8728	51°56·6'	3°38·2'W	X	160
Llwyn-croes	Carm	SN4126	51°54·8'	4°18·3'W	X	146
Llwyncrwn	Carm	SN2318	51°50·2'	4°33·8'W	X	158
Llwyn-crwn	Carm	SN3126	51°54·7'	4°27·0'W	X	145
Llwyn-crwn	Gwyn	SH7137	52°55·1'	3°54·7'W	X	124
Llwyncrwn Isaf	Rho Cyn Taf	ST0584	51°33·1'	3°21·8'W	X	170
Llwyn-cus	Powys	SN9250	52°8·5'	3°34·3'W	X	147
Llwyncwtta Fm	Powys	SN9869	52°18·8'	3°29·4'W	FM	136,147
Llwyncynhyrys	Carm	SN7436	52°0·7'	3°49·8'W	X	146,160
Llwyncynog	Powys	SO0833	51°59·5'	3°20·0'W	X	160
Llwyncytrych	Powys	SO2316	51°50·5'	3°6·7'W	X	161
Llwyndafydd	Cered	SN3755	52°10·4'	4°22·6'W	T	145
Llwynddewi	Carm	SN4719	51°51·2'	4°12·9'W	X	159
Llwynddu	V of Glam	ST0277	51°29·2'	3°24·3'W	X	170
Llwyn-Dedwydd	Conwy	SH9843	52°58·7'	3°30·7'W	X	125
Llwynderi Fm	Monm	SO3812	51°48·4'	2°53·6'W	FM	161
Llwynderw	Cered	SN4358	52°12·1'	4°17·5'W	X	146
Llwynderw	Powys	SJ2003	52°37·4'	3°10·5'W	X	126
Llwyn-derw	Powys	SN9184	52°26·8'	3°35·8'W	T	136
Llwyndewi	Carm	SN2317	51°49·7'	4°33·7'W	X	158
Llwyndewi	Carm	SN6517	51°50·4'	3°57·2'W	X	159
Llwyndinawed	Carm	SN7542	52°4·0'	3°49·0'W	X	146,147,160
Llwyn-diried	Carm	SN6845	52°5·5'	3°55·2'W	X	146
Llwyndrain	Pemb	SN2634	51°58·9'	4°31·6'W	X	145
Llwyndrissi	Carm	SN2917	51°49·8'	4°28·5'W	X	159
Llwyndrissi	Carm	SN5641	52°3·2'	4°5·6'W	F	146
Llwyn-du	Carm	SN3715	51°48·8'	4°21·5'W	X	159
Llwyn-du	Carm	SN5418	51°50·7'	4°6·8'W	X	159
Llwyndu	Carm	SN6724	51°54·2'	3°55·6'W	X	159
Llwyn-du	Conwy	SH8169	53°12·5'	3°46·5'W	X	116
Llwyn Du	Gwyn	SH5910	52°40·4'	4°4·7'W	X	124
Llwyn-du	Monm	SO2816	51°50·5'	3°2·3'W	T	161
Llwyn-du	Swan	SN7101	51°41·8'	3°51·6'W	X	170
Llwyndu Court	Monm	SO2815	51°50·0'	3°2·3'W	X	161
Llwyndu Fm	Gwyn	SH5918	52°44·7'	4°4·9'W	FM	124
Llwyn Du Isa	Conwy	SH8665	53°10·4'	3°41·9'W	X	116
Llwynduris	Cered	SN2343	52°3·7'	4°34·5'W	T	145
Llwyn-dwfr	Carm	SN1023	51°52·6'	4°45·2'W	X	145,158
Llwyn-dwyfog	Gwyn	SH4439	52°55·4'	4°18·9'W	X	123
Llwyndyrys	Gwyn	SH3741	52°56·7'	4°25·2'W	T	123
Llwyndyrys	Pemb	SN1018	51°49·9'	4°45·1'W	X	158
Llwyn Ednyfed	I of Angl	SH4674	53°14·7'	4°18·1'W	X	114,115
Llwynegrin	Flint	SJ2465	53°10·8'	3°7·8'W	X	117
Llwyneinion	Wrex	SJ2847	53°1·2'	3°4·0'W	X	117
Llwyn-Einon	Powys	SN9448	52°7·4'	3°32·5'W	X	147
Llwyneôs	Cered	SN3347	52°6·0'	4°25·9'W	X	145
Llwyn-erwyn	Conwy	SH9267	53°11·6'	3°36·6'W	X	116
Llwyneuadd	Powys	SN8645	52°5·7'	3°39·5'W	X	147
Llwyneuadd	Powys	SN8824	51°54·4'	3°37·3'W	X	160
Llwynfedw	Carm	SN5342	52°3·7'	4°8·3'W	X	146
Llwynfedw	Cered	SN4753	52°9·5'	4°13·8'W	X	146
Llwynfedwen	Carm	SN5625	51°54·5'	4°5·2'W	X	146
Llwynffynnon	Carm	SN4038	52°1·3'	4°19·5'W	X	146
Llwynfilltir	Carm	SN4316	51°49·5'	4°16·3'W	X	159
Llwynfilly	Powys	SO1938	52°2·3'	3°10·5'W	X	161
Llwynfilwr	Carm	SN4611	51°46·8'	4°13·6'W	X	159
Llwyn Fm	Powys	SO1149	52°8·2'	3°17·6'W	FM	148
Llwynfortune	Carm	SN5221	51°52·3'	4°8·6'W	X	159
Llwyn Franc	Monm	SO3219	51°52·2'	2°58·9'W	X	161
Llwynfron	Carm	SN7523	51°53·7'	3°48·6'W	X	160
Llwynfynwent	Powys	SN8942	52°4·2'	3°36·8'W	X	147,160
Llwyngaru	Cered	SN7058	52°12·5'	3°53·8'W	X	146,147
Llwyngibbon	V of Glam	ST0779	51°30·4'	3°20·0'W	X	170
Llwyn-glas	Cered	SN6490	52°29·7'	3°59·8'W	X	135
Llwyn-glas	Powys	SJ1021	52°47·0'	3°19·7'W	X	125
Llwyn Gogau	Cered	SN6972	52°20·1'	3°55·0'W	X	135
Llwyngoras	Pemb	SN0939	52°1·2'	4°46·6'W	X	145
Llwyn-Goronwy	Conwy	SH8261	53°8·2'	3°45·4'W	X	116
Llwyn-grawys	Cered	SN2146	52°5·2'	4°36·4'W	X	145
Llwyngriffith Fm	Nth Pt Talb	SN7802	51°42·4'	3°45·6'W	FM	170
Llwyngronw	Cered	SN6483	52°25·9'	3°59·6'W	X	135
Llwyngronw	Powys	SN8631	51°58·2'	3°39·2'W	X	160
Llwyngwair	Pemb	SN0739	52°1·2'	4°48·4'W	X	145
Llwyngwcw	Carm	SN4113	51°47·8'	4°18·0'W	X	159
Llwyngwenno	Swan	SN6303	51°42·8'	3°58·6'W	X	159
Llwyn-gwern	Gwyn	SH8528	52°50·5'	3°42·0'W	X	124,125
Llwyn-Gwgan	Gwyn	SH9244	52°59·2'	3°36·1'W	X	125
Llwyngwilliam	Powys	SO2247	52°7·2'	3°8·0'W	X	148
Llwyngwilym	Powys	SN9150	52°8·5'	3°35·2'W	X	147
Llwyngwilym	Powys	SN9869	52°18·8'	3°29·4'W	X	136,147
Llwyngwin	Nth Pt Talb	SN9006	51°44·8'	3°35·2'W	X	160
Llwyn-gwinau	Cered	SN6763	52°15·2'	3°56·5'W	X	146
Llwyngwinau	Cered	SN7292	52°30·9'	3°52·8'W	X	135
Llwyngwnadl	Gwyn	SH4548	53°0·7'	4°18·2'W	X	115,123
Llwyngwnadl Uchaf	Gwyn	SH4548	53°0·7'	4°18·2'W	X	123
Llwyn-Gwrgan	Powys	SN9353	52°10·1'	3°33·5'W	X	147
Llwyngwril	Gwyn	SH5909	52°39·9'	4°4·7'W	T	124
Llwyngwydd	Carm	SN2120	51°51·2'	4°35·6'W	X	145,158
Llwyngwydd	Pemb	SN1143	52°3·4'	4°45·0'W	X	145
Llwyn-gwyddel	Cered	SN7468	52°18·0'	3°50·5'W	X	135,147
Llwyngwyddil	Pemb	SN1615	51°48·4'	4°39·8'W	X	158
Llwyn Gwyn	Caer	ST1886	51°34·3'	3°10·6'W	X	171
Llwyn-gwyn	Carm	SN3614	51°48·3'	4°22·3'W	X	159
Llwyn-gwyn	Carm	SN4825	51°54·4'	4°12·2'W	X	146
Llwyn-gwyn	Cered	SN6894	52°31·9'	3°56·4'W	X	135
Llwyn-gwyn	Monm	SO3018	51°51·6'	3°0·6'W	X	161
Llwyn-gwyn	Powys	SN9079	52°24·1'	3°36·6'W	X	136,147
Llwyngwyn	Powys	SN9751	52°9·1'	3°29·9'W	X	147
Llwyn-gwyn	Powys	SO0295	52°32·9'	3°26·3'W	X	136
Llwyn-gwyn	Powys	SO0841	52°3·8'	3°20·1'W	X	147,160
Llwynhelig	Carm	SN4115	51°48·9'	4°18·0'W	X	159
Llwynhelig	Carm	SN6123	51°53·5'	4°0·8'W	X	159
Llwyn-helyg	Rho Cyn Taf	SN9802	51°42·7'	3°28·2'W	X	170
Llwynhelyg Ho	V of Glam	SS9875	51°28·1'	3°27·7'W	X	170
Llwyn-hên	Nth Pt Talb	SN7010	51°46·7'	3°52·7'W	X	160
Llwynhendy	Carm	SS5499	51°40·5'	4°6·3'W	T	159
Llwyn Howel	Powys	SN9350	52°8·5'	3°33·4'W	X	147
Llwyn Howel	Wrex	SJ3143	52°59·0'	3°1·3'W	X	117
Llwynhowell	Carm	SN7635	52°0·2'	3°48·0'W	X	146,160
Llwynhugh	Carm	SN1626	51°54·4'	4°40·1'W	X	145,158
Llwynieir	Cered	SN5948	52°7·0'	4°3·2'W	X	146
Llwyn-Ifan	Swan	SN6707	51°45·0'	3°55·2'W	X	159
Llwyn-Ifan-ddu	Swan	SN6107	51°44·9'	4°0·4'W	X	159
Llwyn Ifor	Flint	SJ1678	53°17·8'	3°15·2'W	X	116
Llwynihirion	Pemb	SN1036	51°59·6'	4°45·7'W	X	145
Llwynioli	Card	ST0880	51°30·9'	3°19·2'W	X	170
Llwyniolyn	Gwyn	SH9539	52°56·5'	3°33·4'W	X	125
Llwynion-fechan	Gwyn	SH5925	52°48·5'	4°5·1'W	X	124
Llwyniorwerth	Cered	SN6481	52°24·8'	3°59·6'W	X	135
Llwyn Knottia	Wrex	SJ3550	53°2·8'	2°57·8'W	X	117
Llwyn-llwyd	Carm	SN1925	51°53·9'	4°37·5'W	X	145,158
Llwynllwyd	Powys	SN9938	52°2·1'	3°28·0'W	X	160
Llwynllwydyn	Gwyn	SH8528	52°50·5'	3°42·0'W	X	124,125
Llwyn Llydan	Conwy	SH8564	53°9·9'	3°42·8'W	X	116
Llwyn Madoc	Powys	SN9052	52°9·6'	3°36·1'W	X	147
Llwynmadoc	Powys	SO0855	52°11·4'	3°20·4'W	X	147
Llwynmadoc Fm	Powys	SO1794	52°32·5'	3°13·0'W	FM	136
Llwyn Mafon	Gwyn	SH5141	52°57·0'	4°12·7'W	X	124
Llwyn Mali	Conwy	SH9544	52°59·2'	3°33·4'W	X	125
Llwynmalus	Cered	SN6968	52°17·9'	3°54·9'W	X	135
Llwyn-mawr	Gwyn	SH8833	52°53·2'	3°39·5'W	X	124,125
Llwynmawr	Wrex	SJ2237	52°55·7'	3°9·2'W	T	126
Llwynmelyn	Carm	SN4617	51°50·1'	4°13·7'W	X	159
Llwynmilwas	Rho Cyn Taf	ST0682	51°32·0'	3°20·9'W	X	170
Llwynmwyn	Cered	SN7469	52°18·5'	3°50·5'W	X	135,147
Llwyn-neuadd	Powys	SO0738	52°2·2'	3°21·0'W	X	160
Llwynneuadd	Powys	SO0769	52°18·9'	3°21·5'W	X	136,147
Llwynobin	Powys	SO2295	52°33·1'	3°8·6'W	X	137
Llwyn Offa	Flint	SJ2565	53°10·9'	3°6·9'W	X	117
Llwynon	Carm	SN5305	51°43·7'	4°7·3'W	X	159
Llwynon	Gwyn	SH6217	52°44·2'	4°2·2'W	X	124
Llwyn-on	Monm	SO2728	51°57·0'	3°3·3'W	X	161
Llwyn-on	Powys	SO2620	51°52·7'	3°4·1'W	X	161
Llwyn-onn	Conwy	SH7572	53°14·1'	3°52·0'W	X	115
Llwyn-onn	Conwy	SH8950	53°2·4'	3°38·9'W	X	116
Llwyn Onn	Gwyn	SH6127	52°49·6'	4°3·4'W	X	124
Llwyn-onn	Gwyn	SH9741	52°57·6'	3°31·6'W	X	125
Llwyn-onn	I of Angl	SH5170	53°12·6'	4°13·5'W	X	114,115
Llwyn-onn	Powys	SJ0327	52°50·2'	3°26·0'W	X	125
Llwyn-onn	Powys	SJ0425	52°49·1'	3°25·1'W	X	125
Llwyn Onn	Powys	SJ0726	52°49·7'	3°22·4'W	X	125
Llwyn Onn Hall	Wrex	SJ3549	53°2·3'	2°57·8'W	A	117
Llwyn-on Reservoir	Rho Cyn Taf	SO0011	51°47·6'	3°26·6'W	W	160
Llwyn-on Village	Merth Tyd	SO0111	51°47·6'	3°25·7'W	T	160
Llwyn-Owen	Carm	SN7039	52°2·3'	3°53·3'W	X	146,160
Llwynowen	Powys	SN9152	52°9·6'	3°35·2'W	X	147
Llwynpenderi	Powys	SO1642	52°4·4'	3°13·1'W	X	148,161
Llwynpentre Bank	Powys	SO1171	52°20·0'	3°18·0'W	X	136,148
Llwynpinner	Pemb	SN1715	51°48·5'	4°38·9'W	X	158
Llwynpiod	Carm	SN4322	51°52·7'	4°16·5'W	X	159
Llwynpiod	Carm	SN6628	51°56·3'	3°56·6'W	X	146
Llwynpiod	Cered	SN1747	52°5·7'	4°39·9'W	X	145
Llwynpiod	Powys	SN9549	52°8·0'	3°31·7'W	X	147
Llwynpiod Fm	Carm	SN4516	51°49·5'	4°14·6'W	FM	159
Llwyn Prisg	Cered	SN6784	52°26·5'	3°57·0'W	X	135
Llwyn-pur	Carm	SN3736	52°0·2'	4°22·1'W	X	145
Llwynrheol	Cered	SN4456	52°11·1'	4°16·5'W	X	146
Llwynrhida	Powys	SO0829	51°57·4'	3°19·9'W	X	160
Llwyn-rhidyll	Powys	SO0042	52°4·3'	3°27·1'W	X	147,160
Llwyn-rhyddid	V of Glam	ST0477	51°29·3'	3°22·6'W	X	170
Llwyn-rhyd-Owen	Cered	SN4444	52°4·6'	4°16·2'W	X	146
Llwynrhyn	Powys	SO1518	51°51·5'	3°13·7'W	X	161
Llwyn-Richard	Conwy	SH8262	53°8·8'	3°45·5'W	X	116
Llwyn Saint	Conwy	SH8760	53°7·8'	3°40·9'W	X	116
Llwyn-têg	Cered	SN5508	51°45·4'	4°5·7'W	T	159
Llwyn-teg-isaf	Powys	SN9135	52°0·4'	3°34·9'W	X	160
Llwyntew	Powys	SN9428	51°56·7'	3°32·1'W	X	160
Llwyntidmon Hall	Shrops	SJ2820	52°46·6'	3°3·6'W	X	126
Llwyntudor	Powys	SO1251	52°9·3'	3°16·8'W	X	148
Llwyn-uchaf	Denb	SJ0664	53°10·1'	3°24·0'W	X	116
Llwyn-Walter	Carm	SN5128	51°56·1'	4°9·7'W	X	146
Llwynwccws Fm	Gwyn	SH5919	52°45·3'	4°5·0'W	FM	124
Llwynwennol	Carm	SN7521	51°52·7'	3°48·6'W	X	160
Llwynwermod	Cered	SN3758	52°12·0'	4°22·7'W	X	145
Llwynwernau	Cered	SN4155	52°10·5'	4°19·1'W	X	146
Llwyn-nwydog	V of Glam	ST0178	51°29·8'	3°25·2'W	X	170
Llwyn-y-barcud	Carm	SN4109	51°45·7'	4°17·8'W	X	159
Llwyn-y-berllan	Carm	SN7538	52°1·8'	3°48·9'W	X	146,160
Llwyn-y-berth	I of Angl	SH2180	53°17·5'	4°40·7'W	X	114
Llwyn-y-brain	Card	ST0782	51°32·0'	3°20·1'W	X	170
Llwyn-y-brain	Carm	SN1915	51°48·5'	4°37·1'W	T	158
Llwyn-y-brain	Carm	SN7332	51°58·6'	3°50·6'W	X	146,160
Llwyn y Brain	Gwyn	SH5263	53°8·9'	4°12·4'W	X	114,115
Llwyn-y-brain	Gwyn	SH9141	52°57·6'	3°37·0'W	X	125
Llwynybrain	Powys	SO0492	52°31·3'	3°24·5'W	X	136
Llwyn-y-brain	Powys	SO2723	51°54·3'	3°3·3'W	X	161
Llwyn-y-bwch	Swan	SS4891	51°36·1'	4°11·3'W	X	159
Llwynycaedu	Powys	SO1770	52°19·5'	3°12·7'W	X	136,148
Llwynycelyn	Monm	SO3911	51°47·9'	2°52·7'W	X	161
Llwyn-y-celyn	Monm	SO4706	51°45·2'	2°45·7'W	X	161
Llwyn-y-celyn	Monm	ST4794	51°38·8'	2°45·6'W	X	171,172
Llwyn-y-celyn	Powys	SN9638	52°2·1'	3°30·6'W	X	160
Llwyn-y-celyn	Powys	SN9722	51°53·5'	3°29·4'W	X	160
Llwyn Ych	Powys	SO1172	52°20·6'	3°18·0'W	X	136,148
Llwyn-y-ci	Gwyn	SH9238	52°56·0'	3°36·0'W	X	125
Llwyn-y-cil	Wrex	SJ2738	52°56·3'	3°4·8'W	X	126
Llwyn-y-cosyn Fm	Flint	SJ1772	53°14·6'	3°14·2'W	FM	116
Llwyn-y-crwth	Powys	SJ2000	52°35·8'	3°10·5'W	X	126
Llwyn-y-cwn	Carm	SN6410	51°46·6'	3°57·9'W	X	159
Llwyn-y-domen	Swan	SN6702	51°42·3'	3°55·1'W	X	159
Llwyn-y-fedwen	Powys	SN9512	51°48·0'	3°31·0'W	X	160
Llwyn-y-gaer	Monm	SO4011	51°47·9'	2°51·8'W	X	161
Llwyn-y-go	Shrops	SJ3121	52°47·2'	3°1·0'W	T	126
Llwyn-y-gôg	Cered	SN7267	52°17·4'	3°52·2'W	X	135,147
Llwynygog	Powys	SN8792	52°31·1'	3°39·5'W	T	135,136
Llwyn-y-gog	Powys	SO0493	52°31·8'	3°24·5'W	X	136
Llwyn-y-gorras	Pemb	SM8931	51°56·5'	5°3·8'W	X	157
Llwyn-y-groes	Cered	SN5248	52°6·9'	4°9·3'W	X	146
Llwyn-y-groes	Cered	SN5956	52°11·3'	4°3·4'W	T	146
Llwyn-y-groes	Shrops	SJ2820	52°46·6'	3°3·6'W	X	126
Llwynymaen	Shrops	SJ2728	52°50·9'	3°4·6'W	X	126
Llwyn-y-môch	Carm	SN7414	51°48·9'	3°49·3'W	X	160
Llwyn-y-ynn Hall	Denb	SJ1353	53°4·3'	3°17·5'W	X	116
Llwyn-y-pennau	Rho Cyn Taf	ST0680	51°30·9'	3°20·9'W	X	170
Llwynypia	Rho Cyn Taf	SS9993	51°37·8'	3°27·2'W	T	170
Llwyn-y-piod	Carm	SN5103	51°42·6'	4°9·0'W	X	159
Llwynypiod	Carm	SN6316	51°49·8'	3°58·9'W	X	159
Llwynyrebol	Carm	SN1326	51°54·3'	4°42·7'W	X	145,158
Llwyn-yr-êos	Powys	SO1319	51°52·0'	3°15·4'W	X	161
Llwynyrhedydd	Powys	SJ2501	52°36·3'	3°6·1'W	X	126

Llwyn-yr-hwrdd	Pemb	SN2232	51°57·7'	4°35·1'W	T	145
Llwynyrynn	Carm	SN6723	51°53·6'	3°55·6'W	X	159
Llwyn-yr-ynn	Powys	SN8418	51°51·2'	3°40·7'W	X	160
Llwyn-y-saint	Conwy	SH9844	52°59·3'	3°30·8'W	X	125
Llwynysgaw	I of Angl	SH3767	53°10·8'	4°25·9'W	X	114
Llwynywen	Cered	SN5363	52°15·0'	4°8·8'W	X	146
Llwynywormwood	Carm	SN7631	51°58·1'	3°47·9'W	X	146,160
Llwytmor	Gwyn	SH6769	53°12·3'	3°58·2'W	H	115
Llydyadyway	Heref	SO2442	52°4·5'	3°6·1'W	X	148,161
Llyfnant Brook	Powys	SO0689	52°29·7'	3°22·7'W	W	136
Llyfnant Valley	Cered	SN7297	52°33·6'	3°52·9'W	X	135
Llygad-y-cleddau	Pemb	SM9733	51°57·7'	4°56·9'W	X	157
Llygnant	Powys	SN7891	52°30·4'	3°47·5'W	W	135
Llymgwyn	Gwyn	SH4236	52°54·1'	4°20·6'W	X	123
Llymon Brook	Monm	SO4118	51°51·7'	2°51·0'W	W	161
Llymwynt Brook	Powys	SO1178	52°23·8'	3°18·1'W	W	136,148
Llyn	Flint	SJ1969	53°13·0'	3°12·4'W	X	116
Llyn Alaw	I of Angl	SH3986	53°21·0'	4°24·7'W	W	114
Llyn Aled	Conwy	SH9157	53°6·2'	3°37·3'W	W	116
Llyn Alwen	Conwy	SH8956	53°5·6'	3°39·1'W	W	116
Llyn Anafon	Gwyn	SH6969	53°12·4'	3°57·3'W	W	115
Llyn Arenig Fach	Gwyn	SH8241	52°57·4'	3°45·0'W	W	124,125
Llyn Arenig Fawr	Gwyn	SH8438	52°55·9'	3°43·1'W	W	124,125
Llyn Arran	Gwyn	SH7313	52°42·2'	3°52·4'W	W	124
Llynau Diwaunedd	Conwy	SH6853	53°3·7'	3°57·8'W	W	115
Llyn Barfog	Gwyn	SN6598	52°34·0'	3°59·1'W	W	135
Llyn Barfog or Bearded Lake	Gwyn	SN6598	52°34·0'	3°59·1'W	W	135
Llyn Bedydd	Wrex	SJ4739	52°57·0'	2°46·9'W	W	126
Llyn Berwyn	Cered	SN7456	52°11·5'	3°50·2'W	W	146,147
Llyn Blaenmelindwr	Cered	SN7183	52°26·0'	3°53·5'W	W	135
Llyn Bochlwyd	Conwy	SH6559	53°6·9'	4°0·6'W	W	115
Llyn Bodgylched	I of Angl	SH5877	53°16·5'	4°7·4'W	W	114,115
Llyn Bodgynydd	Conwy	SH7659	53°7·1'	3°50·8'W	W	115
Llyn Bodlyn	Gwyn	SH6423	52°47·5'	4°0·6'W	W	124
Llyn Bowydd	Gwyn	SH7246	53°0·0'	3°54·0'W	W	115
Llyn Brân	Denb	SH9659	53°7·3'	3°32·8'W	W	116
Llyn Brenig	Conwy	SH9755	53°5·2'	3°31·9'W	W	116
Llyn Brianne	Carm	SN7948	52°7·3'	3°45·6'W	W	146,147
Llyn Brianne	Cered	SN7951	52°8·9'	3°45·7'W	W	146,147
Llyn Brianne Resr	Cered	SN8049	52°7·8'	3°44·8'W	W	147
Llyn Bychan	Conwy	SH7559	53°7·1'	3°51·7'W	W	115
Llyn Cadarn	I of Angl	SH4981	53°18·5'	4°15·6'W	W	114,115
Llyn Caer-Euni	Gwyn	SH9840	52°57·1'	3°30·7'W	W	125
Llyn Caerwych	Gwyn	SH6435	52°54·0'	4°0·9'W	W	124
Llyn Carw	Powys	SN8561	52°14·4'	3°40·7'W	W	147
Llyn Caseg-fraith	Conwy	SH6758	53°6·4'	3°58·8'W	W	115
Llyn Cau	Gwyn	SH7112	52°41·7'	3°54·1'W	W	124
Llyn Celyn	Gwyn	SH8540	52°56·9'	3°42·3'W	W	124,125
Llyn Cerrigllwydion Isaf	Powys	SN8470	52°19·2'	3°41·7'W	W	135,136,147
Llyn Cerrigllwydion Uchaf	Powys	SN8369	52°18·6'	3°42·6'W	W	135,136,147
Llyn Clogwyn-brith	Gwyn	SH6646	52°59·9'	3°59·4'W	W	115
Llyn Clyd	Gwyn	SH6359	53°6·9'	4°2·4'W	W	115
Llynclys	Shrops	SJ2823	52°48·2'	3°3·7'W	T	126
Llynclys Hill	Shrops	SJ2723	52°48·2'	3°4·6'W	H	126
Llyn Clywedog (Reservoir)	Powys	SN8889	52°29·5'	3°38·6'W	W	135,136
Llyn Coch	Gwyn	SH5954	53°4·1'	4°5·9'W	W	115
Llyn Coch	Gwyn	SH6647	53°0·5'	3°59·4'W	W	115
Llyn Coch-hwyad	Powys	SH9210	52°40·9'	3°35·5'W	W	125
Llyn Coethlyn	Powys	SJ0114	52°43·1'	3°27·5'W	W	125
Llyn Conach	Cered	SN7393	52°31·4'	3°51·9'W	W	135
Llyn Conglog	Gwyn	SH6747	53°0·5'	3°58·5'W	W	115
Llyn Conglog-mawr	Gwyn	SH7538	52°55·7'	3°51·2'W	W	124
Llyn Conwy	Conwy	SH7846	53°0·1'	3°48·7'W	W	115
Llyn Coron	I of Angl	SH3770	53°12·4'	4°26·0'W	W	114
Llyn Cors-y-barcud	Gwyn	SH7639	52°56·3'	3°50·3'W	W	124
Llyn Cowlyd Reservoir	Conwy	SH7262	53°8·6'	3°54·4'W	W	115
Llyn Crafnant Resr	Conwy	SH7461	53°8·1'	3°52·6'W	W	115
Llyn Craigypistyll	Cered	SN7285	52°27·1'	3°52·6'W	W	135
Llyn Croesor	Gwyn	SH6645	52°59·4'	3°59·4'W	W	115
Llyn Crugnant	Cered	SN7561	52°14·2'	3°49·4'W	W	146,147
Llyn Cwellyn	Gwyn	SH5554	53°4·1'	4°9·4'W	W	115
Llyn Cwm Bychan	Gwyn	SH6431	52°51·8'	4°0·8'W	W	124
Llyn Cwm-byr	Powys	SN8192	52°31·0'	3°44·8'W	W	135
Llyn Cwm corsiog	Gwyn	SH6647	53°0·5'	3°59·4'W	W	115
Llyn Cwm Dulyn	Gwyn	SH4949	53°1·3'	4°14·7'W	W	115,123
Llyn Cwmffynnon	Gwyn	SH6456	53°5·3'	4°1·4'W	W	115
Llyn Cwmhosan	Gwyn	SH6627	52°49·7'	3°58·9'W	W	124
Llyn Cwm Llwch	Powys	SO0022	51°53·5'	3°26·8'W	W	160
Llyn Cwm-mynach	Gwyn	SH6723	52°47·5'	3°57·9'W	W	124
Llyn Cwmorthin	Gwyn	SH6746	52°59·9'	3°58·5'W	W	115
Llyn Cwmystradllyn	Gwyn	SH5644	52°58·7'	4°8·3'W	W	124
Llyn Cyfynwy	Denb	SJ2154	53°4·9'	3°10·4'W	W	117
Llyn Cynwch	Gwyn	SH7320	52°46·0'	3°52·5'W	W	124
Llyn Cyri	Gwyn	SH6511	52°41·0'	3°59·4'W	W	124
Llyn Cywion	Gwyn	SH6360	53°7·4'	4°2·4'W	W	115
Llynddu	Cered	SN3851	52°8·3'	4°21·6'W	X	145
Llyn Dinam	I of Angl	SH3177	53°16·0'	4°31·6'W	W	114
Llyn Dinas	Gwyn	SH6149	53°1·5'	4°3·9'W	W	115
Llyn Du	Cered	SN7661	52°14·2'	3°48·6'W	X	146,147
Llyn Du	Cered	SN7969	52°18·6'	3°46·1'W	W	135,147
Llyn Du	Cered	SN8069	52°18·6'	3°45·2'W	W	135,136,147
Llyn Du	Denb	SH9957	53°6·3'	3°30·1'W	W	116
Llyn Du	Gwyn	SH5642	52°57·6'	4°8·2'W	W	124
Llyn Du	Gwyn	SH6529	52°50·7'	3°59·9'W	W	124
Llyn Du	Powys	SJ1712	52°42·2'	3°13·3'W	W	125
Llyn Du	Powys	SO0096	52°33·4'	3°28·1'W	W	136
Llyn Du-bâch	Gwyn	SH7146	53°0·0'	3°54·9'W	W	115
Llyn Dulyn	Gwyn	SH6624	52°48·1'	3°58·9'W	W	124
Llyn Du'r Arddu	Gwyn	SH6055	53°4·7'	4°5·0'W	W	115
Llyn Dwfn	Cered	SN7392	52°30·9'	3°51·9'W	W	135
Llyn Dŵr	Powys	SN9536	52°1·0'	3°31·4'W	W	160
Llyn Dwythwch	Gwyn	SH5757	53°5·7'	4°7·7'W	W	115
Llyndy	Gwyn	SH6249	53°1·5'	4°3·1'W	X	115
Llyn Ebyr	Powys	SN9788	52°29·1'	3°30·6'W	W	136
Llyn Edno	Gwyn	SH6649	53°1·5'	3°59·5'W	W	115
Llyn Efyrnwy or Lake Vyrnwy (Nature Reserve)	Powys	SH9821	52°46·9'	3°30·3'W	W	125
Llyn Egnant	Cered	SN7967	52°17·5'	3°46·1'W	W	135,147
Llyn Eiddew-bach	Gwyn	SH6434	52°53·4'	4°0·9'W	W	124

Llyn Eiddew-mawr	Gwyn	SH6433	52°52·9'	4°0·9'W	W	124
Llyn Eiddwen	Cered	SN6066	52°16·7'	4°2·7'W	W	135
Llyn Eigiau Reservoir	Conwy	SH7265	53°10·2'	3°54·5'W	W	115
Llyn Elsi Resr	Conwy	SH7855	53°4·9'	3°48·9'W	W	115
Llyn Fach	Nth Pt Talb	SN9003	51°43·1'	3°35·2'W	W	170
Llynfaes	I of Angl	SH4078	53°16·7'	4°23·6'W	T	114,115
Llyn Fanod	Cered	SN6064	52°15·6'	4°2·7'W	W	146
Llyn Ffridd-y-bwlch	Gwyn	SH6948	53°1·0'	3°56·8'W	W	115
Llyn Ffynhonnau	Gwyn	SH5255	53°4·5'	4°12·2'W	W	115
Llyn Ffynnon-y-gwas	Gwyn	SH5955	53°4·7'	4°5·9'W	W	115
Llynfi River	Brig	SS8788	51°35·0'	3°37·5'W	W	170
Llynfi Valley	Brig	SS8788	51°35·0'	3°37·5'W	X	170
Llyn Frogwy	I of Angl	SH4277	53°16·2'	4°21·8'W	W	114,115
Llyn Frongoch	Cered	SN7275	52°21·7'	3°52·4'W	W	135,147
Llyn Fyrddon Fach	Cered	SN7970	52°19·1'	3°46·1'W	W	135,147
Llyn Fyrddon Fawr	Cered	SN8070	52°19·1'	3°45·2'W	W	135,136,147
Llyn Gafr	Gwyn	SH7114	52°42·7'	3°54·2'W	W	124
Llyn Garreg-lwyd	I of Angl	SH3188	53°22·0'	4°32·0'W	W	114
Llyn Geirionydd	Conwy	SH7660	53°7·6'	3°50·8'W	W	115
Llyn Gelli Gain	Gwyn	SH7332	52°52·5'	3°52·8'W	W	124
Llyngeren	Merth Tyd	SO0512	51°48·2'	3°22·3'W	X	160
Llyn Glanmerin	Powys	SN7599	52°34·7'	3°50·3'W	W	135
Llyn Glas	Gwyn	SH6155	53°4·7'	4°4·1'W	W	115
Llyn Glasfryn	Gwyn	SH4042	52°57·3'	4°22·5'W	W	123
Llyn Gloyw	Conwy	SH9945	52°59·8'	3°29·9'W	W	116
Llyn Goddionduon	Conwy	SH7558	53°6·5'	3°51·6'W	W	115
Llyn Gorast	Cered	SN7963	52°15·4'	3°46·0'W	W	146,147
Llyn Grych-y-waun	Gwyn	SH8129	52°51·0'	3°45·6'W	W	124,125
Llyn Gwernan	Gwyn	SH7016	52°43·8'	3°55·1'W	W	124
Llyn Gweryd	Denb	SJ1755	53°5·4'	3°14·0'W	W	116
Llyn Gwngu	Cered	SN8372	52°20·3'	3°42·6'W	W	135,136,147
Llyn Gwyddior	Powys	SH9307	52°39·3'	3°34·5'W	W	125
Llyn Gwyn	Powys	SO0164	52°16·2'	3°26·7'W	W	147
Llyn Gwynant	Gwyn	SH6451	53°2·6'	4°1·3'W	W	115
Llyn Gynon	Cered	SN7964	52°15·9'	3°46·0'W	W	146,147
Llyn Hafodol	I of Angl	SH3989	53°22·6'	4°24·8'W	W	114
Llynheilyn	Powys	SO1658	52°13·1'	3°13·4'W	W	148
Llyn Helyg	Flint	SJ1177	53°17·2'	3°19·7'W	W	116
Llyn Hendref	I of Angl	SH3976	53°15·6'	4°24·4'W	W	114
Llyn Hesgyn	Gwyn	SH8844	52°59·1'	3°39·7'W	W	124,125
Llyn Hir	Cered	SN7867	52°17·5'	3°46·9'W	W	135,147
Llyn Hir	Powys	SJ0205	52°38·3'	3°26·5'W	W	125
Llyn Hiraethlyn	Gwyn	SH7437	52°55·2'	3°52·0'W	W	124
Llyn Hywel	Gwyn	SH6626	52°49·1'	3°58·9'W	W	124
Llyn Idwal	Gwyn	SH6459	53°6·9'	4°1·5'W	W	115
Llyn Irddyn	Gwyn	SH6222	52°46·9'	4°2·4'W	W	124
Llyn Isaf	Cered	SN8075	52°21·8'	3°45·3'W	W	135,136,147
Llyn Iwerddon	Gwyn	SH6847	53°0·5'	3°57·6'W	W	115
Llyn Llaethdy	I of Angl	SH4491	53°23·8'	4°20·4'W	W	114
Llyn Llagi	Gwyn	SH6448	53°1·0'	4°1·2'W	W	115
Llyn Llech Owen Country Park	Carm	SN5615	51°49·1'	4°5·0'W	X	159
Llyn Llenyrch	Gwyn	SH6537	52°55·1'	4°0·1'W	W	124
Llyn Lliwbran	Gwyn	SH8725	52°48·9'	3°40·4'W	W	124,125
Llynlloedd	Powys	SH7500	52°35·2'	3°50·3'W	X	135
Llyn Lluncaws	Powys	SJ0731	52°52·3'	3°22·5'W	W	125
Llyn Llydaw	Gwyn	SH6254	53°4·2'	4°3·2'W	W	115
Llyn Llygad Rheidol	Cered	SN7987	52°28·3'	3°46·5'W	W	135
Llyn Llygeirian	I of Angl	SH3489	53°22·6'	4°29·3'W	W	114
Llyn Llywelyn	Gwyn	SH5649	53°1·4'	4°8·4'W	W	115
Llyn Llywenan	I of Angl	SH3481	53°18·2'	4°29·1'W	W	114
Llyn Login	Powys	SO0044	52°5·4'	3°27·2'W	W	147,160
Llyn Lort	Powys	SJ0104	52°37·7'	3°27·4'W	W	136
Llyn Maelog	I of Angl	SH3272	53°13·4'	4°30·6'W	W	114
Llyn Maen Bras	Gwyn	SH9239	52°56·5'	3°36·0'W	W	125
Llyn Mair	Gwyn	SH6541	52°57·2'	4°0·2'W	W	124
Llyn Mawr	Powys	SO0097	52°33·9'	3°28·1'W	W	136
Llyn Moelfre	Powys	SJ1728	52°50·8'	3°13·5'W	W	125
Llyn Morwynion	Gwyn	SH6530	52°51·3'	3°59·9'W	W	124
Llyn Morwynion	Gwyn	SH7342	52°57·9'	3°53·1'W	W	124
Llyn Mynyllod	Gwyn	SJ0140	52°57·1'	3°28·0'W	W	125
Llyn Nadroedd	Gwyn	SH5954	53°4·1'	4°5·9'W	W	115
Llyn Nant-ddeiliog	Powys	SN8695	52°32·7'	3°40·5'W	W	135,136
Llyn Nantlle Uchaf	Gwyn	SH5153	53°3·5'	4°13·0'W	W	115
Llyn Nantycagl	Cered	SN7290	52°29·8'	3°52·7'W	W	135
Llynnau Barlwyd	Gwyn	SH7148	53°1·1'	3°55·0'W	W	115
Llynnau Cerrig-y-myllt	Gwyn	SH6347	53°0·4'	4°2·1'W	W	115
Llynnau Cregennen	Gwyn	SH6614	52°42·7'	3°58·6'W	W	124
Llynnau Cwm Silyn	Gwyn	SH5150	53°1·8'	4°12·9'W	W	115
Llynnau Diffwys	Gwyn	SH6546	52°59·9'	4°0·3'W	W	115
Llynnau Gamallt	Gwyn	SH7444	52°59·0'	3°52·2'W	W	124
Llynnau Mymbyr	Conwy	SH7057	53°5·9'	3°56·0'W	W	115
Llynnau'r Cwn	Gwyn	SH6648	53°1·0'	3°59·5'W	W	115
Llyn Newydd	Gwyn	SH7247	53°0·5'	3°54·1'W	W	115
Llynnoedd Ieuan	Cered	SN7981	52°25·1'	3°46·4'W	X	135
Llynnon Mill	I of Angl	SH3385	53°20·4'	4°30·1'W	X	114
Llynoedd Ieuan	Cered	SN8081	52°25·1'	3°45·5'W	W	135,136
Llyn Ogwen	Gwyn	SH6560	53°7·5'	4°0·6'W	W	115
Llynon Hall	I of Angl	SH3384	53°19·8'	4°30·1'W	X	114
Llyn Oror	Denb	SJ0947	53°1·0'	3°21·0'W	W	116
Llyn Padarn	Gwyn	SH5761	53°7·9'	4°7·8'W	W	114,115
Llyn Padrig	I of Angl	SH3672	53°13·4'	4°27·0'W	W	114
Llyn Pendam	Cered	SN7083	52°26·0'	3°54·3'W	W	135
Llyn Penrhaeadr	Cered	SN7593	52°31·5'	3°50·5'W	W	135
Llyn Penrhyn	I of Angl	SH3176	53°15·5'	4°31·6'W	W	114
Llyn Perfeddau	Gwyn	SH6526	52°49·1'	3°59·8'W	W	124
Llyn Peris	Gwyn	SH5959	53°6·8'	4°6·0'W	W	115
Llyn Pryfed	Gwyn	SH6632	52°52·4'	3°59·1'W	W	124
Llyn Rhos-ddu	I of Angl	SH4264	53°9·3'	4°21·4'W	W	114,115
Llyn Rhosgoch	Cered	SN7183	52°26·0'	3°53·5'W	W	135
Llyn Rhuddwyn	Shrops	SJ2328	52°50·9'	3°8·2'W	W	126
Llyn Serw	Conwy	SH7742	52°57·9'	3°49·5'W	W	124
Llyn Stwlan	Gwyn	SH6644	52°58·8'	3°59·4'W	W	124
Llyn Syberi	Conwy	SH7969	53°12·5'	3°48·3'W	W	115
Llyn Syfydrin	Cered	SN7284	52°26·6'	3°52·6'W	W	135
Llyn Tecwyn Uchaf	Gwyn	SH6438	52°55·6'	4°1·0'W	W	124
Llyn Tegid or Bala Lake	Gwyn	SH9033	52°53·2'	3°37·7'W	W	125
Llyn Teifi	Cered	SN7867	52°17·5'	3°46·9'W	W	135,147
Llyn Terfyn	Gwyn	SH6647	53°0·5'	3°59·4'W	W	115
Llyn Teyrn	Gwyn	SH6454	53°4·2'	4°1·4'W	W	115

Llyn Traffwll	I of Angl	SH3276	53°15·5'	4°30·7'W	W	114
Llyn Trawsfynydd	Gwyn	SH6936	52°54·6'	3°56·5'W	W	124
Llyntro Fm	Wrex	SJ3457	53°6·6'	2°58·8'W	FM	117
Llyn Tryweryn	Gwyn	SH7838	52°55·8'	3°48·5'W	W	124
Llyn Ty'n-y-llyn	Conwy	SH8470	53°13·1'	3°43·8'W	W	116
Llyn Ty'n-y-mynydd Reservoir	Conwy	SH7658	53°6·5'	3°50·7'W	W	115
Llyn Uchaf	Cered	SN8076	52°22·4'	3°45·4'W	W	135,136,147
Llyn y Bi	Gwyn	SH6626	52°49·1'	3°58·9'W	W	124
Llyn y Biswail	Gwyn	SH6447	53°0·4'	4°1·2'W	W	115
Llyn y Cwm	Gwyn	SH6358	53°6·3'	4°2·4'W	W	115
Llyn y Cwrt	Conwy	SH9051	53°2·9'	3°38·1'W	W	116
Llyn-y-dywarchen	Gwyn	SH5653	53°3·5'	4°8·5'W	W	115
Llyn y Dywarchen	Gwyn	SH7642	52°57·9'	3°50·4'W	W	124
Llyn y Fan	Powys	SN9387	52°28·5'	3°34·1'W	W	136
Llyn y Fan Fach	Carm	SN8021	51°52·7'	3°44·2'W	W	160
Llyn y Fan Fawr	Powys	SN8321	51°52·8'	3°41·6'W	W	160
Llyn y Fedw	Gwyn	SH6232	52°52·3'	4°2·6'W	W	124
Llyn y Fign	Gwyn	SH8319	52°45·6'	3°43·6'W	W	124,125
Llyn y Figyn	Cered	SN8170	52°19·2'	3°44·4'W	W	135,136,147
Llyn y Foel	Conwy	SH7154	53°4·3'	3°55·1'W	W	115
Llyn y Foel-frech	Conwy	SH9159	53°7·3'	3°37·3'W	W	116
Llyn y Frithgraig	Conwy	SH7445	52°59·5'	3°52·2'W	W	115
Llyn y Gadair	Gwyn	SH7013	52°42·2'	3°55·0'W	W	124
Llyn y Gader	Gwyn	SH5652	53°3·0'	4°8·5'W	W	115
Llyn y Garn	Gwyn	SH7637	52°55·2'	3°50·3'W	W	124
Llyn y Garnedd-uchaf	Gwyn	SH6542	52°57·7'	4°0·2'W	W	124
Llyn y Garn-fawr	Powys	SO1214	51°49·3'	3°16·2'W	W	161
Llyn y Gorlan	Cered	SN7866	52°17·0'	3°46·9'W	W	135,147
Llyn y Gors	Conwy	SH7545	52°59·5'	3°51·3'W	W	115
Llyn y Gors	I of Angl	SH5774	53°14·9'	4°8·2'W	X	114,115
Llyn y Graig-wen	Gwyn	SH7339	52°56·2'	3°53·0'W	W	124
Llyn y Grinwydden	Powys	SJ0206	52°38·8'	3°26·5'W	W	125
Llyn y Gwaith	Cered	SN6750	52°8·2'	3°56·2'W	W	146
Llyn y Manod	Gwyn	SH7144	52°58·9'	3°54·9'W	W	124
Llyn y Mynydd	Powys	SJ0025	52°49·0'	3°28·6'W	W	125
Llyn-y-pandy	Flint	SJ2065	53°10·8'	3°11·4'W	X	117
Llyn y Parc	Conwy	SH7958	53°6·6'	3°48·1'W	W	115
Llyn y Pennau	Powys	SJ0024	52°48·5'	3°28·6'W	W	125
Llyn yr Adar	Gwyn	SH6548	53°1·0'	4°0·3'W	W	115
Llyn yr Arddu	Gwyn	SH6246	52°59·9'	4°3·0'W	W	115
Llyn-Yr-Oerfa	Cered	SN7279	52°23·9'	3°52·5'W	W	135,147
Llyn yr Oerfel	Gwyn	SH7138	52°55·7'	3°54·7'W	W	124
Llyn yr Wyth-Eidion	I of Angl	SH4781	53°18·5'	4°17·4'W	W	114,115
Llyn y Sarnau	Conwy	SH7759	53°7·1'	3°49·9'W	W	115
Llyn-ysgubor-wen	Cered	SN6389	52°29·1'	4°0·7'W	X	135
Llyn Ystumllyn	Gwyn	SH5238	52°55·4'	4°11·7'W	W	124
Llyn y Tarw	Powys	SO0297	52°34·0'	3°26·4'W	W	136
Llyn y Tomla	Conwy	SH7548	53°1·1'	3°51·4'W	W	115
Llyn-y-waun	Powys	SO1455	52°11·4'	3°15·1'W	W	148
Llys	Denb	SJ0564	53°10·1'	3°24·9'W	X	116
Llys	Denb	SJ0681	53°19·3'	3°24·3'W	X	116
Llys	Denb	SJ0851	53°3·1'	3°22·0'W	X	116
Llys	Flint	SJ2373	53°15·1'	3°8·8'W	X	117
Llys	Powys	SJ1720	52°46·5'	3°13·4'W	X	125
Llys Arthur	Cered	SN7882	52°25·6'	3°47·3'W	A	135
Llys Bradwen	Gwyn	SH6513	52°42·1'	3°59·5'W	A	124
Llys Cwmllorwg	Brig	SS9389	51°35·6'	3°32·3'W	X	170
Llysdinam	Powys	SO0058	52°12·9'	3°27·4'W	X	147
Llysdulas	I of Angl	SH4889	53°22·8'	4°16·7'W	X	114
Llys Dymper	Conwy	SH8959	53°7·2'	3°39·1'W	H	116
Llŷs Edwin	Flint	SJ2369	53°13·0'	3°8·8'W	A	117
Llys Euryn	Conwy	SH8380	53°18·5'	3°45·0'W	A	116
Llysfaen	Cered	SN5249	52°7·4'	4°9·3'W	X	146
Llysfaen	Conwy	SH8877	53°16·9'	3°40·4'W	T	116
Llysfasi (College of Agriculture)	Denb	SJ1452	53°3·7'	3°16·6'W	X	116
Llys-Hendy	Carm	SN3310	51°46·1'	4°24·8'W	X	159
Llys Hill	Powys	SJ1721	52°47·1'	3°13·4'W	H	125
Llysin Hill	Powys	SO1668	52°18·5'	3°13·5'W	H	136,148
Llys Lew	I of Angl	SH4768	53°11·5'	4°17·0'W	X	114,115
Llŷs Meirchion	Conwy	SJ0168	53°12·2'	3°28·5'W	X	116
Llysnant	Rho Cyn Taf	ST0493	51°37·9'	3°22·8'W	X	170
Llys Nant	Rho Cyn Taf	ST0593	51°37·9'	3°22·0'W	W	170
Llysnewydd	Carm	SN3539	52°1·7'	4°23·9'W	X	145
Llys Newydd	Conwy	SH9465	53°10·5'	3°34·8'W	X	116
Llys-nini	Swan	SS6099	51°40·6'	4°1·1'W	X	159
Llys Onnen	Carm	SN3320	51°51·5'	4°25·1'W	X	145,159
Llysty	Shrops	SO3085	52°27·7'	3°1·4'W	X	137
Llystyn	Carm	SN5230	51°57·2'	4°8·8'W	X	146
Llystyn	Pemb	SN0838	52°0·7'	4°47·5'W	X	145
Llystyn-ganol	Gwyn	SH4844	52°58·6'	4°15·4'W	X	123
Llystyn-gwyn	Gwyn	SH4845	52°59·1'	4°15·5'W	X	115,123
Llys Uchaf	Powys	SJ1620	52°46·5'	3°14·3'W	X	125
Llysun	Powys	SJ0310	52°41·0'	3°25·7'W	X	125
Llyswen	Powys	SJ2213	52°42·8'	3°8·9'W	X	126
Llyswen	Powys	SO1337	52°1·7'	3°15·7'W	T	161
Llysworney	V of Glam	SS9674	51°27·6'	3°29·4'W	T	170
Llys-y-defaid	Pemb	SM9731	51°56·7'	4°56·8'W	X	157
Llys-y-frân	Cered	SN0424	51°53·0'	4°50·5'W	T	145,157,158
Llys-y-frân Reservoir	Pemb	SN0325	51°53·6'	4°51·4'W	W	145,157,158
Llys-y-meidw	Cered	SN1745	52°4·6'	4°39·8'W	X	145
Llywel	Powys	SN8730	51°57·7'	3°38·3'W	T	160
Llywernog	Cered	SN7380	52°24·4'	3°51·6'W	T	135
Llywy	Powys	SO0570	52°19·4'	3°23·2'W	H	136,147
Loach Brook	Ches	SJ8164	53°10·6'	2°16·7'W	W	118
Loachbrook Fm	Ches	SJ8363	53°10·1'	2°14·9'W	FM	118
Load Bridge	Somer	ST4623	51°0·5'	2°45·8'W	A	193
Load Brook	Sheff	SK2788	53°23·5'	1°35·2'W	T	110
Loadman	Northum	NY9060	54°56·3'	2°8·9'W	X	87
Loadpit Beck	Brad	SE1239	53°51·1'	1°48·6'W	W	104
Loadpot Hill	Cumbr	NY4518	54°33·5'	2°50·6'W	H	90
Loads Head Fm	Derby	SK3169	53°13·3'	1°31·7'W	FM	119
Loaf Hill	Northum	NY7698	55°16·8'	2°22·2'W	H	80
Loak	Pth & Kin	NO0733	56°29·1'	3°30·2'W	X	52,53
Loam Castle	Devon	SX6642	50°16·0'	3°52·4'W	X	202
Loan	Falk	NS9575	55°57·6'	3°40·5'W	T	65
Loan	Highld	NH0851	57°30·8'	5°11·9'W	X	25
Loanamain	Highld	NH5691	57°53·4'	4°25·3'W	X	21
Loanbaan	Arg & Bt	NR3158	55°44·7'	6°16·7'W	X	60

Loanburn	Aberd	NJ8959	57°37·5'	2°10·6'W	X	30
Loan Burn	D & G	NX3783	55°7·1'	4°32·9'W	W	77
Loan Burn	Midlo	NT2360	55°49·9'	3°13·3'W	W	66
Loand Ho	N Yks	SE7586	54°16·1'	0°50·5'W	X	94,100
Loandhu	Highld	NH8178	57°46·8'	3°59·6'W	T	21
Loan Edge	Northum	NT8008	55°22·2'	2°18·5'W	H	80
Loanend	Aberd	NJ5012	57°12·0'	2°49·2'W	X	37
Loanend	Aberd	NJ5403	57°7·2'	2°45·1'W	X	37
Loanend	Aberd	NJ5543	57°28·8'	2°44·6'W	X	29
Loanend	Aberd	NJ6023	57°18·0'	2°39·4'W	X	37
Loanend	Aberd	NJ9855	57°35·4'	2°1·5'W	X	30
Loanend	Northum	NT9450	55°44·9'	2°5·3'W	T	67,74,75
Loanend	S Lanak	NS6658	55°48·1'	4°7·8'W	X	64
Loanend Plantation	Aberd	NJ5012	57°12·0'	2°49·2'W	F	37
Loanends of Durno	Aberd	NJ7129	57°21·3'	2°28·5'W	X	38
Loan Fm	N Lanak	NS9065	55°52·2'	3°45·0'W	FM	65
Loanfolds	Pth & Kin	NO1231	56°28·0'	3°25·3'W	X	53
Loanfoot	E Ayr	NS5835	55°35·5'	4°14·8'W	X	71
Loanfoot	Falk	NS8477	55°58·6'	3°51·1'W	X	65
Loanhead	Aberd	NJ4205	57°8·2'	2°57·0'W	X	37
Loanhead	Aberd	NJ4746	57°30·3'	2°52·6'W	X	28,29
Loanhead	Aberd	NJ5407	57°9·4'	2°45·2'W	X	37
Loanhead	Aberd	NJ5739	57°26·6'	2°42·5'W	X	29
Loanhead	Aberd	NJ6059	57°37·4'	2°39·7'W	X	29
Loanhead	Aberd	NJ6457	57°36·4'	2°35·7'W	X	29
Loanhead	Aberd	NJ6830	57°21·8'	2°31·5'W	X	29
Loanhead	Aberd	NJ7428	57°20·8'	2°25·5'W	X	38
Loanhead	Aberd	NJ9138	57°26·2'	2°8·5'W	X	30
Loanhead	Aberd	NJ9925	57°19·2'	2°0·5'W	X	38
Loanhead	Angus	NO2255	56°41·1'	3°15·9'W	X	53
Loanhead	Angus	NO4347	56°36·9'	2°55·3'W	X	54
Loanhead	C of Aber	NJ8704	57°7·9'	2°12·4'W	X	38
Loanhead	E Ayr	NS3848	55°42·2'	4°34·2'W	X	63
Loanhead	Falk	NS8472	55°55·9'	3°51·0'W	X	65
Loanhead	Fife	NO5506	56°14·9'	2°43·1'W	X	59
Loanhead	Fife	NT0590	56°5·9'	3°31·2'W	X	58
Loanhead	Midlo	NT2765	55°52·6'	3°9·6'W	T	66
Loanhead	Midlo	NT4064	55°52·2'	2°57·1'W	X	66
Loanhead	Moray	NH9859	57°36·8'	3°42·0'W	X	27
Loanhead	Moray	NJ1864	57°39·8'	3°22·0'W	X	28
Loanhead	Moray	NJ4152	57°33·5'	2°58·7'W	X	28
Loanhead	Moray	NJ4466	57°41·1'	2°55·9'W	X	28
Loanhead	N Lanak	NS7471	55°55·2'	4°0·5'W	X	64
Loanhead	N Lanak	NS7871	55°55·3'	3°56·7'W	X	64
Loanhead	Pth & Kin	NN9715	56°19·2'	3°39·5'W	X	58
Loanhead	Pth & Kin	NO0634	56°29·6'	3°31·2'W	X	52,53
Loanhead	Pth & Kin	NO1432	56°28·6'	3°23·3'W	X	53
Loanhead	Renf	NS3655	55°45·9'	4°36·4'W	X	63
Loanhead	Renf	NS4267	55°52·5'	4°31·1'W	X	64
Loanhead	S Lanak	NS9931	55°34·0'	3°35·7'W	X	72
Loanhead	S Lanak	NS9938	55°37·8'	3°35·8'W	X	72
Loanhead	S Lanak	NT0155	55°46·9'	3°34·3'W	X	65,72
Loanhead	Stir	NS8192	56°6·6'	3°54·4'W	X	57
Loanhead Cott	Fife	NT0892	56°7·0'	3°28·3'W	X	58
Loanhead Fm	Clackm	NS9496	56°9·0'	3°41·9'W	FM	58
Loanhead of Duchally	Pth & Kin	NN9409	56°16·0'	3°42·2'W	X	58
Loanhead of Fedderate	Aberd	NJ8849	57°32·1'	2°11·6'W	X	30
Loanhead of Pitinnan	Aberd	NJ7430	57°21·8'	2°25·5'W	X	29
Loaning	Pth & Kin	NO1045	56°35·6'	3°27·5'W	X	53
Loaningdale	E Yorks	SE8748	53°55·5'	0°40·1'W	X	106
Loaningdale	S Lanak	NT0338	55°37·8'	3°32·0'W	X	72
Loaningfoot	D & G	NX9655	54°53·0'	3°36·8'W	X	84
Loaning Head	Cumbr	NY7441	54°46·0'	2°23·8'W	X	86,87
Loaning Head	Northum	NU1915	55°26·0'	1°41·6'W	X	81
Loaninghead	Stir	NS5189	56°4·5'	4°23·2'W	X	57
Loaning Ho	Cumbr	NY7147	54°49·3'	2°26·7'W	X	86,87
Loaning Ho	Northum	NY9152	54°52·0'	2°8·0'W	X	87
Loaning Side	Northum	NY8353	54°52·5'	2°15·5'W	X	86,87
Loanknowe	Scot Bord	NT7441	55°40·0'	2°24·4'W	X	74
Loanleven	Pth & Kin	NO0525	56°24·7'	3°31·9'W	X	52,53,58
Loan of Durno	Aberd	NJ7128	57°20·8'	2°28·5'W	X	38
Loanreoch	Highld	NH6275	57°44·9'	4°18·7'W	X	21
Loanrigg	Falk	NS8773	55°56·5'	3°48·1'W	X	65
Loanroidge	Highld	NH5974	57°44·3'	4°21·6'W	X	21
Loans	S Ayr	NS3431	55°32·9'	4°37·4'W	T	70
Loansdean	Northum	NZ1984	55°9·2'	1°41·7'W	T	81
Loanside	Clackm	NS9089	56°5·1'	3°45·6'W	X	65
Loanside	Scot Bord	NT8761	55°50·8'	2°12·0'W	X	67
Loans of Tullich	Highld	NH8576	57°45·8'	3°55·5'W	X	21
Loans, The	S Glos	ST6387	51°35·1'	2°31·7'W	X	172
Loanstone	Midlo	NT2460	55°49·9'	3°12·4'W	X	66
Loanthwaite	Cumbr	SD3599	54°23·2'	2°59·6'W	X	96,97
Loath Hill	Notts	SK6353	53°4·5'	1°3·2'W	X	120
Loath Knowe	D & G	NT3101	55°18·1'	3°4·8'W	H	79
Loatland Lodge Fm	Northnts	SP7882	52°26·1'	0°50·8'W	FM	141
Loatmead	Devon	SS2916	50°55·3'	4°25·6'W	X	190
Lòba Sgeir	N Eil	HW8031	59°6·8'	5°50·1'W	X	8
Lobb	Devon	SS4737	51°7·0'	4°10·8'W	T	180
Lobber Point	Corn	SW9981	50°35·9'	4°50·0'W	X	200
Lobbersdown Fm	Oxon	SP6704	51°44·1'	1°1·4'W	FM	164,165
Lobbersdown Hill	Oxon	SP6703	51°43·5'	1°1·4'W	X	164,165
Lobb Fm	Devon	SX5658	50°24·5'	4°1·2'W	FM	202
Lobb Fm	Oxon	SP6602	51°43·0'	1°2·3'W	FM	164,165
Lobbington Hall Fm	Warw	SP3050	52°9·1'	1°33·3'W	FM	151
Lobbs	Cumbr	NY3524	54°36·7'	3°0·0'W	X	90
Lobb's Shop	Corn	SX0249	50°18·7'	4°46·5'W	X	204
Lobb's Valley	Norf	TG0334	52°52·1'	1°1·4'E	X	133
Lober Rock	Orkney	ND4394	58°50·0'	2°58·8'W	X	7
Lobhillcross	Devon	SX4686	50°39·4'	4°10·3'W	T	201
Lobley Hall	N Yks	SE1979	54°12·6'	1°42·1'W	X	99
Lobley Hill	Ghead	NZ2360	54°56·3'	1°38·0'W	T	88
Lobster Ho	N Yks	SE6860	54°2·1'	0°57·3'W	X	100
Lobstone Band	Cumbr	NY2315	54°31·7'	3°11·0'W	X	89,90
Lobthorpe	Lincs	SK9520	52°46·4'	0°35·1'W	T	130
Lobust	Orkney	HY3734	59°11·5'	3°5·7'W	X	6
Lobwood Ho	N Yks	SE0751	53°57·5'	1°53·2'W	X	104
Loch	Aberd	NK0154	57°34·8'	1°58·5'W	X	30
Loch	D & G	NY2663	54°57·6'	3°8·9'W	X	85
Loch	Shetld	HT9639	60°8·4'	2°3·8'W	X	4
Loch A'an or Loch Avon	Moray	NJ0102	57°6·2'	3°37·6'W	W	36

Lochaber	Angus	NO6041	56°33·8'	2°38·6'W	X	54
Lochaber	Highld	NM9994	56°59·9'	5°18·1'W	X	33,40
Lochaber	Highld	NN0594	57°0·0'	5°12·2'W	X	33
Lochaber	Highld	NN1392	56°59·1'	5°4·2'W	X	34
Lochaber	Highld	NN2383	56°54·5'	4°54·0'W	X	34,41
Lochaber	Moray	NJ0759	57°36·9'	3°32·9'W	X	27
Lochaber	Shetld	HU2551	60°14·8'	1°32·4'W	X	3
Lochaber Loch	D & G	NX9270	55°1·0'	3°40·9'W	W	84
Lochaber Rock	Fife	NO6309	56°16·6'	2°35·4'W	X	59
Loch a' Bhac-ghlais	Highld	NG3427	57°15·6'	6°24·2'W	W	32
Loch a' Bhada Dharaich	Highld	NM6994	56°59·0'	5°47·7'W	W	40
Loch a' Bhadaidh Daraich	Highld	NC1644	58°21·0'	5°8·2'W	W	9
Loch a' Bhagh Ghainmhich	Highld	NC1945	58°21·6'	5°5·2'W	W	9
Loch a' Bhaid-bheithe	Highld	NH5090	57°52·7'	4°31·3'W	W	20
Loch a' Bhaid-choille	Highld	NH0091	57°52·1'	5°21·9'W	W	19
Loch a' Bhaid-fhearna	Highld	NG7566	57°37·9'	5°45·7'W	W	19,24
Loch a' Bhaid Ghainmheich	Highld	NG8596	57°54·4'	5°37·3'W	W	19
Loch a' Bhaid-luachraich	Highld	NG8986	57°49·1'	5°32·7'W	W	19
Loch a' Bhaid-rabhain	Highld	NG7682	57°46·6'	5°45·6'W	W	19
Loch a' Bhaid-shambraidh	Highld	NG8184	57°47·8'	5°40·6'W	W	19
Loch a' Bhaile	N Eil	NB1938	58°14·7'	6°46·9'W	W	8,13
Loch a' Bhaile	N Eil	NB2547	58°19·8'	6°41·4'W	W	8
Loch' a Bhaile-Mhargaidh	Arg & Bt	NR4967	55°50·1'	6°0·1'W	W	60,61
Loch a' Bhàillidh	Arg & Bt	NR7563	55°48·7'	5°35·0'W	W	62
Loch a' Bhainne	Highld	NH2704	57°5·9'	4°50·9'W	W	34
Loch a' Bhainne	Highld	NH3616	57°12·6'	4°42·5'W	W	34
Loch a' Bhàird	N Eil	NB3001	57°55·3'	6°33·1'W	W	14
Loch a' Bhalaich	Arg & Bt	NR6085	56°0·1'	5°50·5'W	W	61
Loch a' Bhàna	Highld	NH2231	57°20·4'	4°57·0'W	W	25
Loch a' Bhànain	Highld	NN4292	56°59·8'	4°35·6'W	W	34
Loch a' Bharaille	Highld	NC1225	58°10·7'	5°11·4'W	W	15
Loch a'Bharain	Arg & Bt	NR8291	56°4·0'	5°29·7'W	W	55
Loch a' Bharp	N Eil	NF7821	57°10·3'	7°19·2'W	W	31
Loch a' Bharpa	N Eil	NF8360	57°31·4'	7°17·3'W	W	22
Loch a' Bharpa	N Eil	NF8366	57°34·6'	7°17·8'W	W	18
Loch a'Bharrain	Arg & Bt	NM9624	56°22·1'	5°17·7'W	W	49
Loch a' Bharra Leathain	Arg & Bt	NR7762	55°48·2'	5°33·1'W	W	62
Lochabhat	N Eil	NB2728	58°9·7'	6°38·0'W	W	8,13
Loch a'Bhealaich	Arg & Bt	NR7486	56°1·1'	5°37·1'W	W	55
Loch a' Bhealaich	Highld	NC5926	58°12·3'	4°23·5'W	W	16
Loch a' Bhealaich	Highld	NG7554	57°31·5'	5°45·0'W	W	24
Loch a' Bhealaich	Highld	NG8329	57°18·3'	5°35·7'W	W	33
Loch a' Bhealaich	Highld	NG8664	57°37·2'	5°34·5'W	W	19,24
Loch a' Bhealaich	Highld	NH0221	57°14·5'	5°16·4'W	W	25,33
Loch a' Bhealaich	Highld	NH0693	57°53·3'	5°15·9'W	W	19
Loch a' Bhealaich	Highld	NH3356	57°34·1'	4°47·1'W	W	26
Loch a' Bhealaich	Highld	NH3459	57°35·7'	4°46·2'W	W	26
Loch a' Bhealaich	Highld	NH3560	57°36·3'	4°45·2'W	W	20
Loch a' Bhealaich	Highld	NH3612	57°10·4'	4°42·3'W	W	34
Loch a' Bhealaich	Highld	NH4262	57°37·5'	4°38·3'W	W	20
Loch a' Bhealaich	Highld	NH4420	57°14·9'	4°34·7'W	W	26
Loch a' Bhealaich	N Eil	NG0995	57°51·2'	6°53·9'W	W	14
Loch a' Bhealaich Aird	Arg & Bt	NR3369	55°50·7'	6°15·5'W	W	60,61
Loch a' Bhealaich Bheithe	Highld	NN5171	56°48·7'	4°26·0'W	W	42
Loch a' Bhealaich Dhuibh	Highld	NC5548	58°24·1'	4°28·4'W	W	10
Loch a' Bhealaich Leamhain	Highld	NN4979	56°52·9'	4°28·2'W	W	42
Loch a' Bhealaich Mhóir	Arg & Bt	NM6523	56°20·7'	5°47·7'W	W	49
Loch a Bhealaich Mhóir	Highld	NG8058	57°33·8'	5°40·2'W	W	24
Loch a' Bhealaich Mhóir	Highld	NG9649	57°29·4'	5°23·8'W	W	25
Loch a' Bheannaich	N Eil	NB0437	58°13·6'	7°2·1'W	W	13
Loch a' Bheannaich	N Eil	NB0529	58°9·3'	7°0·4'W	W	13
Loch a' Bheannan Mhòir	N Eil	NB2909	57°59·5'	6°34·7'W	W	13,14
Loch a' Bhìdidh	Highld	NC8108	58°3·0'	4°0·5'W	W	17
Loch á Bhiocair	Highld	NH7899	57°58·1'	4°3·3'W	W	21
Loch a' Bhith	Highld	NC3200	57°57·7'	4°49·9'W	W	15
Loch a' Bhith	Highld	NC3099	57°57·1'	4°51·9'W	W	20
Loch a' Bhlàr Bhuidhe	N Eil	NB3929	58°10·6'	6°25·9'W	W	8
Loch a' Bhodaich	Highld	NH5524	57°17·3'	4°23·9'W	W	26,35
Loch a' Bhogaidh	Arg & Bt	NR2257	55°43·9'	6°25·3'W	W	60
Loch a' Bhoineid	N Eil	NB2316	58°3·1'	6°41·2'W	W	13,14
Loch a' Bhonnaich	Highld	NG8594	57°53·3'	5°37·2'W	W	19
Loch a' Bhraghad	N Eil	NB1731	58°10·9'	6°48·4'W	W	8,13
Loch a' Bhraghad	Highld	NM7792	56°58·2'	5°39·7'W	W	33,40
Loch a Bhràige	Highld	NG6260	57°34·3'	5°58·4'W	W	24
Loch a' Bhraighe	Highld	NC1330	58°13·4'	5°10·6'W	W	15
Loch a' Bhraoin	Highld	NH1374	57°43·3'	5°7·9'W	W	19
Loch a' Bhraoin	Highld	NH1474	57°43·3'	5°6·9'W	W	20
Loch a' Bhric Chàim	Highld	NH1163	57°37·3'	5°9·4'W	W	19
Loch a' Bhrisidh	Highld	NH0575	57°43·6'	5°16·0'W	W	19
Loch a' Bhrochain	Highld	NC3703	57°59·4'	4°45·0'W	W	15
Loch a' Bhroduinn	N Eil	NB3504	57°57·1'	6°28·3'W	W	14
Loch a' Bhuic	Highld	NC8153	58°27·2'	4°1·9'W	W	10
Loch a' Bhualaidh	Highld	NC5356	58°28·3'	4°30·8'W	W	10
Loch a' Bhuic	Highld	NC5141	58°20·2'	4°32·2'W	W	9
Loch a' Bhùic	Highld	NN2678	56°51·9'	4°50·8'W	W	41
Loch a' Bhuird	N Eil	NF8866	57°34·8'	7°12·8'W	W	18
Loch a' Bhuna	N Eil	NB3430	58°11·0'	6°31·0'W	W	8,13
Loch a Bhùrra	Arg & Bt	NR6696	56°6·2'	5°45·3'W	W	55,61
Loch a'Bhursta	N Eil	NF8053	57°27·5'	7°19·7'W	W	22
Loch a' Broma	N Eil	NB2524	58°7·4'	6°39·8'W	W	13,14
Loch a' Chadha-chàrmaich	Highld	NG5839	57°22·9'	6°1·1'W	W	24,32
Loch a' Chadha Dheirg	Highld	NH2885	57°49·6'	4°53·3'W	W	20
Loch a' Chadh- Fi	Highld	NC2151	58°24·9'	5°3·4'W	W	9
Loch a' Chafain	N Eil	NF7424	57°11·7'	7°23·4'W	W	22
Loch Achaidh na h-Inich	Highld	NG8130	57°18·7'	5°37·7'W	W	24
Loch a Chairn	Highld	ND0749	58°25·4'	3°35·1'W	W	11,12
Loch a' Chàirn	N Eil	NB3411	58°0·8'	6°29·8'W	W	13,14
Loch a' Chairn	N Eil	NB4744	58°19·0'	6°18·7'W	W	8
Loch a' Chairn Beag	Highld	NH1586	57°49·8'	5°6·5'W	W	20
Loch a' Chairn Bhàin	Highld	NG9539	57°24·0'	5°24·3'W	W	25
Loch a' Chairn Duibh	Highld	NH3358	57°35·1'	4°47·1'W	W	26
Loch a' Chàirne Bhàin	Highld	NC1933	58°15·2'	5°4·6'W	W	15
Loch a' Chairn Mhoir	Highld	NM6877	56°49·9'	5°47·7'W	W	40
Loch a' Chairn Mór	Highld	NH1486	57°49·8'	5°7·5'W	W	20
Loch a' Chàise	Highld	NC6511	58°4·3'	4°16·9'W	W	16
Loch a' Chaisil	Highld	NM6764	56°42·8'	5°48·0'W	W	40
Loch a' Chaisteil	Highld	NG7241	57°24·4'	5°47·3'W	W	24
Loch Achall	Highld	NH1795	57°54·7'	5°4·9'W	W	20

Loch a' Chama	N Eil	NB0324	58°6·6'	7°2·1'W	W	13
Loch a' Cham Alltain	Highld	NC2844	58°21·3'	4°55·9'W	W	9
Loch Acha Mòr	N Eil	NB3028	58°9·8'	6°35·0'W	W	8,13
Loch Achanalt	Highld	NH2760	57°36·1'	4°53·2'W	W	20
Loch Ach' an Lochaidh	Highld	NC4560	58°30·3'	4°39·1'W	W	9
Loch a' Chaol-thuil	Highld	NG7889	57°50·4'	5°43·9'W	W	19
Loch a' Chaorainn	Arg & Bt	NM8813	56°16·0'	5°25·0'W	W	55
Loch a'Chaorainn	Arg & Bt	NM9300	56°9·1'	5°19·5'W	W	55
Loch a' Chaorainn	Arg & Bt	NR3769	55°50·8'	6°11·7'W	W	60,61
Loch a'Chaorainn	Arg & Bt	NR7774	55°54·7'	5°33·7'W	W	62
Loch a'Chaorainn	Arg & Bt	NR7866	55°50·4'	5°32·3'W	W	62
Loch a'Chaorainn	Arg & Bt	NR8050	55°41·9'	5°29·6'W	W	62,69
Loch a' Chaorainn	Highld	NG7442	57°25·0'	5°45·3'W	W	24
Loch a' Chaorainn	Highld	NG7654	57°31·5'	5°44·0'W	W	24
Loch a' Chaorainn	Highld	NG8146	57°27·4'	5°38·6'W	W	24
Loch a' Chaorainn	Highld	NG9262	57°36·3'	5°28·4'W	W	19
Loch a' Chaorainn	Highld	NH1399	57°56·7'	5°9·1'W	W	19
Loch a' Chaorainn	Highld	NH4679	57°46·7'	4°34·9'W	W	20
Loch a' Chaorainn Beag	Highld	NG8061	57°35·4'	5°40·4'W	W	19,24
Loch a' Chaoruinn	Highld	NB9813	58°3·9'	5°25·0'W	W	15
Loch a' Chaoruinn	Highld	NC2353	58°26·0'	5°1·4'W	W	9
Loch a' Chaoruinn	Highld	NC6660	58°30·7'	4°17·5'W	W	10
Loch à Chaoruinn	Highld	NH7537	57°24·6'	4°4·4'W	W	27
Loch a' Chaphail	N Eil	NB1732	58°11·4'	6°48·5'W	W	8,13
Loch a' Chaplaich	Highld	NH5770	57°42·1'	4°23·5'W	W	21
Loch a' Chapuill	Arg & Bt	NM0245	56°30·4'	6°50·2'W	W	46
Loch a' Chapuill	Highld	NC0917	58°6·3'	5°14·0'W	W	15
Loch a' Chapuill	N Eil	NF8073	57°38·3'	7°21·3'W	W	18
Loch a' Charnain	N Eil	NF8044	57°22·7'	7°19·0'W	T	22
Loch a' Chàrnain Bhàin	Highld	NH1389	57°51·4'	5°8·6'W	W	19
Loch a' Charra	N Eil	NF7768	57°35·4'	7°23·9'W	W	18
Loch a' Charraigein	Arg & Bt	NM4322	56°19·5'	6°9·0'W	W	48
Loch a' Chas Bhràighe Ruaidh	N Eil	NB0417	58°2·9'	7°0·6'W	W	13
Loch Achbuiligan	Highld	NC9865	58°33·9'	3°44·7'W	W	11
Loch Achcheargary	Highld	NC7153	58°27·0'	4°12·2'W	W	10
Loch a' Cheann-dubhain	N Eil	NF7834	57°17·2'	7°20·2'W	W	22
Loch a' Cheibhle	N Eil	NB0915	58°2·0'	6°55·3'W	W	13,14
Loch a'Cheigein	Arg & Bt	NM8713	56°16·0'	5°25·9'W	W	55
Loch a' Cheisteir	N Eil	NB4655	58°24·8'	6°20·5'W	W	8
Loch a' Cheracher	Highld	ND1339	58°20·1'	3°28·7'W	W	11,12,17
Loch a' Cherigal	Highld	ND0948	58°24·9'	3°33·0'W	W	11,12
Loch Achilty	Highld	NH4356	57°34·3'	4°37·0'W	W	26
Loch a' Chinn Ghairbh	Arg & Bt	NR5991	56°3·3'	5°51·8'W	W	61
Loch a' Chinn Ghairbh	Highld	NG7951	57°30·0'	5°40·9'W	W	24
Loch a Chiteadh	Highld	ND0450	58°25·9'	3°38·2'W	W	11,12
Loch a' Chitear	N Eil	NB4847	58°20·6'	6°17·9'W	W	8
Loch a'Chlachain	Arg & Bt	NM8511	56°14·8'	5°27·8'W	W	55
Loch a' Chlachain	Highld	NH6532	57°21·8'	4°14·2'W	W	26
Loch a' Chlachain	N Eil	NB3632	58°12·1'	6°29·1'W	W	8
Loch a' Chlachain	N Eil	NB4652	58°23·2'	6°20·3'W	W	8
Loch a' Chlachain	N Eil	NF7529	57°14·4'	7°22·8'W	W	22
Loch a' Chlachain	N Eil	NF7531	57°15·5'	7°23·0'W	W	22
Loch a' Chlachain	N Eil	NG1089	57°48·1'	6°52·4'W	W	14
Loch a' Chladaich	N Eil	NF8663	57°33·1'	7°14·5'W	W	18
Loch a' Chlaidheimh	Arg & Bt	NR3469	55°50·7'	6°14·5'W	W	60,61
Loch a' Chlaidheimh	Highld	NH1446	57°28·2'	5°5·6'W	W	25
Loch a' Chlaidheimh	Highld	NH2223	57°16·0'	4°56·7'W	W	25
Loch a' Chlaiginn	Highld	NC1203	57°58·9'	5°10·3'W	W	15
Loch a' Chlàir	Arg & Bt	NL9844	56°29·7'	6°54·0'W	W	46
Loch a' Chlarain	Highld	NH4358	57°35·3'	4°37·1'W	W	26
Loch a' Chléirich	Highld	NH0022	57°15·0'	5°18·5'W	W	25,33
Loch Achnacloich	Highld	NH6673	57°43·9'	4°14·6'W	W	21
Loch Achnamoine	Highld	NC8132	58°15·9'	4°1·2'W	W	17
Loch a' Chnoic Bhuidhe	N Eil	NF7635	57°17·7'	7°22·3'W	W	22
Loch a' Chnoic Duibhe	N Eil	NB3628	58°10·0'	6°28·9'W	W	8
Loch a' Chnoic Mhóir	N Eil	NF8762	57°32·6'	7°13·5'W	W	22
Loch a' Chnoic Ruadh	Highld	NC6954	58°27·5'	4°14·2'W	W	10
Loch a' Chnuic	Arg & Bt	NR4348	55°39·7'	6°4·7'W	W	60
Loch a' Chnuic	Highld	NJ0414	57°12·7'	3°34·9'W	W	36
Loch a' Chnuic	N Eil	NB1538	58°14·6'	6°50·9'W	W	13
Loch a' Chnuic Bhric	Arg & Bt	NR3269	55°50·6'	6°16·4'W	W	60,61
Loch a' Chnuic Bhric	Arg & Bt	NR4473	55°53·2'	6°5·2'W	W	60,61
Loch a' Choin	Highld	NC0818	58°6·8'	5°15·1'W	W	15
Loch a' Choin	N Eil	NB0633	58°11·5'	6°59·7'W	W	13
Loch a' Choin	N Eil	NB2228	58°9·5'	6°43·1'W	W	8,13
Loch a' Choin Bhàin	Highld	NG9467	57°39·0'	5°26·7'W	W	19
Loch a' Choin Bhàin	N Eil	NB3514	58°2·4'	6°28·9'W	W	14
Loch a' Choin-bhoirinn	Highld	NC4557	58°28·7'	4°39·0'W	W	9
Loch a' Choin Duibh	Highld	NG8157	57°33·3'	5°39·2'W	W	24
Loch a' Choin Duibh	Highld	NH8111	57°10·7'	3°57·7'W	W	35
Loch a' Chòinich	Highld	NH1416	57°12·1'	5°4·3'W	W	34
Loch a' Choire	Highld	NC4661	58°30·9'	4°38·1'W	W	9
Loch a' Choire	Highld	NG8695	57°53·9'	5°36·2'W	W	19
Loch a' Choire	Highld	NH5395	57°55·5'	4°28·5'W	W	20
Loch a' Choire	Highld	NH6229	57°20·1'	4°17·1'W	W	26,35
Loch a' Choire	Highld	NM8452	56°36·9'	5°30·8'W	W	49
Loch a' Choire	N Eil	NF7614	57°6·4'	7°20·7'W	W	31
Loch a' Choire	N Eil	NF8135	57°17·9'	7°17·3'W	W	22
Loch a' Choire	Pth & Kin	NN9462	56°44·5'	3°43·5'W	W	43
Loch a' Choireachain	Highld	NC1124	58°10·1'	5°12·3'W	W	15
Loch a' Choire Bheithe	Highld	NG9703	57°4·7'	5°20·5'W	W	33
Loch a' Choire Bhig	Highld	NH1633	57°21·3'	5°3·1'W	W	25
Loch a' Choire Bhuidhe	Highld	NG7555	57°32·0'	5°45·1'W	W	24
Loch a' Choire Bhuidhe	Highld	NH4026	57°18·1'	4°38·9'W	W	26
Loch a' Choire Bhuig	Highld	NH1698	57°56·3'	5°6·0'W	W	20
Loch a' Choire Dheirg	Highld	NC2527	58°12·1'	4°58·2'W	W	15
Loch a' Choire Dhomhain	Highld	NH1326	57°17·4'	5°5·7'W	W	25
Loch a' Choire Dhuibh	Highld	NC1618	58°7·0'	5°7·0'W	W	15
Loch a' Choire Dhuibh	Highld	NC2528	58°12·6'	4°58·2'W	W	15
Loch a' Choire Dhuibh	Highld	NH1693	57°53·6'	5°5·8'W	W	20
Loch a'Choire Dhuinn	Arg & Bt	NM9648	56°35·0'	5°18·9'W	W	49
Loch a' Choire Ghlais	Highld	NN2295	57°1·0'	4°55·5'W	W	34
Loch a' Choire Ghrànda	Highld	NC3443	58°20·9'	4°49·7'W	W	9
Loch a' Choire Ghrànda	Highld	NH2780	57°46·8'	4°54·1'W	W	20
Loch a' Choire Leacaich	Highld	NC4434	58°16·3'	4°39·1'W	W	16
Loch a' Choire Leith	Highld	NG8739	57°23·8'	5°32·2'W	W	24
Loch a' Choire Léith	Highld	NH2708	57°8·1'	4°51·1'W	W	34
Loch á Choire Leith	Highld	NH2718	57°13·5'	4°51·5'W	W	34
Loch a' Choire Léith	Highld	NH3257	57°34·6'	4°48·1'W	W	26

Loch a' Choire Mhóir	Highld	NG9060	57°35·1'	5°30·3'W	W	19
Loch a' Choire Mhóir	Highld	NH3088	57°51·2'	4°51·4'W	W	20
Loch a' Choire Mhóir	Highld	NH4769	57°41·4'	4°33·5'W	W	20
Loch a' Choire Riabhaich	Highld	NG4726	57°15·5'	6°11·3'W	W	32
Loch a' Choire Riabhaich	Highld	NG4921	57°12·9'	6°9·0'W	W	32
Loch a' Choire Riabhaich	Highld	NH3450	57°30·9'	4°45·8'W	W	26
Loch a' Choire Riabhaich	Highld	NM7187	56°55·3'	5°45·3'W	W	40
Loch a' Choire Ridbhaich	Highld	NH3152	57°31·9'	4°48·9'W	W	26
Loch Achonachie	Highld	NH4354	57°33·2'	4°37·0'W	W	26
Loch a' Chonnachair	N Eil	NF9066	57°34·9'	7°10·8'W	W	18
Loch a' Chracaich	Highld	NG7657	57°33·1'	5°44·2'W	W	24
Loch a' Chràthaich	Highld	NH3621	57°15·3'	4°42·7'W	W	26
Loch Achray	Stir	NN5106	56°13·7'	4°23·8'W	W	57
Loch a'Chreachain	Arg & Bt	NM8814	56°16·5'	5°25·0'W	W	55
Loch a' Chreadha	Highld	NC1861	58°30·2'	5°6·9'W	W	9
Loch a' Chreagain Daraich	Highld	NC1739	58°18·4'	5°6·9'W	W	15
Loch a' Chreagain Thet	Highld	NC1642	58°19·9'	5°8·1'W	W	9
Loch a' Chrion-doire	Arg & Bt	NN0022	56°21·1'	5°13·8'W	W	50
Loch a' Chrioslaich	Highld	NC7816	58°7·2'	4°3·8'W	W	17
Loch a' Chrochaire	N Eil	NB4010	58°0·5'	6°23·6'W	W	14
Loch a' Chroisg	Highld	NC2102	57°58·5'	5°1·1'W	W	15
Loch a' Chroisg	Highld	NC2115	58°5·5'	5°1·7'W	W	15
Loch a' Chroisg	Highld	NH1258	57°34·6'	5°8·2'W	W	25
Loch a' Chromain	Arg & Bt	NR7545	55°39·0'	5°34·1'W	W	62,69
Loch a' Chrotha	Arg & Bt	NM2359	56°38·7'	6°30·7'W	W	46,47
Loch Achrugan	Highld	NC8262	58°32·1'	4°1·1'W	W	10
Loch Achtriochtan	Highld	NN1456	56°39·8'	5°1·7'W	W	41
Loch a' Chuilinn	Highld	NH2861	57°36·6'	4°52·3'W	W	20
Loch a'Chuirn	Arg & Bt	NR7846	55°39·7'	5°31·3'W	W	62,69
Loch a' Chùirn	Highld	NG8781	57°46·4'	5°34·4'W	W	19
Loch a' Chuirn Deirg	Highld	NH0018	57°12·8'	5°18·3'W	W	33
Loch a' Chumhainn	Arg & Bt	NM4252	56°35·6'	6°11·7'W	W	47
Loch a' Churragan	Arg & Bt	NR3672	55°52·4'	6°12·8'W	W	60,61
Loch a' Coire Uaine	Highld	NG9213	57°9·9'	5°25·9'W	W	33
Locha Dubh	N Eil	NF8272	57°37·8'	7°19·2'W	W	18
Locha Dubha	N Eil	NG0688	57°47·4'	6°56·4'W	W	14,18
Locha Fada Ghasgain	Highld	NG6413	57°9·1'	5°53·7'W	W	32
Loch Affric	Highld	NH1522	57°15·8'	5°3·6'W	W	25
Loch a' Fhraoich	N Eil	NB0818	58°3·6'	6°56·6'W	W	13,14
Lochagan	Aberd	NJ6359	57°37·4'	2°36·7'W	X	29
Loch a' Garbh-bhaid Mór	Highld	NC2748	58°23·4'	4°57·1'W	W	9
Loch a' Ghael	Arg & Bt	NM4147	56°32·9'	6°12·4'W	W	47,48
Loch a' Ghainmhich	N Eil	NB2929	58°10·3'	6°36·1'W	T	8,13
Loch a' Ghainmhich	N Eil	NB4242	58°17·7'	6°23·7'W	W	8
Loch a' Ghàraidh	N Eil	NB0720	58°4·6'	6°57·7'W	W	13,14
Loch a' Ghàraidh	N Eil	NB3002	57°55·8'	6°33·2'W	W	14
Loch a' Ghàraidh	N Eil	NG1090	57°48·6'	6°52·5'W	W	14
Loch a' Gharbh-bhaid	Highld	NC4559	58°29·8'	4°39·1'W	W	9
Loch a' Gharbh-bhaid Beag	Highld	NC2650	58°24·5'	4°58·2'W	W	9
Loch a' Gharbh-choire	Highld	NJ0111	57°11·0'	3°37·8'W	W	36
Loch a' Gharbh-doire	Highld	NG7979	57°45·0'	5°42·4'W	W	19
Loch a' Gharbhrain	Highld	NH2775	57°44·2'	4°53·9'W	W	20
Loch a'Gharbh-uisge	Arg & Bt	NR5483	55°58·9'	5°56·2'W	W	61
Loch a' Gharb-uillt	Highld	NC5537	58°18·1'	4°28·0'W	W	16
Loch a'Ghatha	Arg & Bt	NR7751	55°42·3'	5°32·5'W	W	62,69
Loch a' Gheàdais	N Eil	NF9159	57°31·2'	7°9·2'W	W	22
Loch a' Ghearraidh Dhuibh	N Eil	NF7418	57°8·5'	7°22·9'W	W	31
Loch a' Gheodha Ruaidh	Highld	NC2467	58°33·6'	5°1·1'W	W	9
Loch a' Gheòidh	Arg & Bt	NR2565	55°48·3'	6°22·9'W	W	60
Loch a'Gheoidh	Arg & Bt	NR6695	56°5·7'	5°45·3'W	W	55,61
Loch a' Gheòidh	N Eil	NB0531	58°10·4'	7°0·6'W	W	13
Loch a' Gheòidh	N Eil	NB0734	58°12·1'	6°58·8'W	W	13
Loch a' Gheòidh	N Eil	NB2925	58°8·1'	6°35·8'W	W	13,14
Loch a' Gheòidh	N Eil	NG0687	57°46·8'	6°56·3'W	W	14,18
Loch a'Ghille	Arg & Bt	NM8910	56°14·4'	5°23·9'W	W	55
Loch a' Ghille	Highld	NC1116	58°5·8'	5°11·9'W	W	15
Loch a' Ghille	Highld	NH1986	57°49·9'	5°2·4'W	W	20
Loch a'Ghille Bhain	Arg & Bt	NR8175	55°55·4'	5°29·9'W	W	62
Loch a' Ghille-chnapain	Highld	NG3332	57°18·3'	6°25·5'W	W	32
Loch a' Ghille Ghobaich	Highld	NM6894	56°59·0'	5°48·7'W	W	40
Loch a' Ghille Reamhra	Highld	NM3499	57°0·6'	6°22·4'W	W	39
Loch a' Ghille Ruaidh	Highld	NC2235	58°16·3'	5°1·6'W	W	15
Loch a' Ghiubhais	Highld	NC5523	58°10·6'	4°27·5'W	W	16
Loch a' Ghiubhais	Highld	NC6506	58°1·6'	4°16·7'W	W	16
Loch a' Ghiubhais	Highld	NH7193	57°54·7'	4°10·2'W	W	21
Loch a' Ghiuthais	N Eil	NB3213	58°1·8'	6°31·9'W	W	13,14
Loch a' Ghleannain	Arg & Bt	NM7231	56°25·2'	5°41·4'W	W	49
Loch a' Ghleannain	Highld	NG7915	57°10·6'	5°38·9'W	W	33
Loch a' Ghleannain Shalaich	Highld	NC1427	58°11·8'	5°9·4'W	W	15
Loch a'Ghlinn Bhig	Arg & Bt	NR7445	55°39·0'	5°35·1'W	W	62
Loch a'Ghlinne	Arg & Bt	NM9317	56°18·3'	5°20·3'W	W	55
Loch a' Ghlinne	Highld	NG5905	57°4·6'	5°58·1'W	W	32,39
Loch a' Ghlinne	N Eil	NB0212	58°0·1'	7°2·2'W	W	13
Loch a' Ghlinne Bhig	Highld	NG4144	57°25·0'	6°18·3'W	W	23
Loch a' Ghlinne Dhuirch	Highld	NG8329	57°18·3'	5°35·7'W	W	33
Loch a' Ghlinne-dorcha	N Eil	NF9162	57°32·8'	7°9·5'W	W	22
Loch a' Ghlinnein	Highld	NC1623	58°9·7'	5°7·2'W	W	15
Loch a' Ghlinne or Glen Bay	N Eil	NA0800	57°49·3'	8°35·8'W	W	18
Loch a' Ghlinne Sgoilte	Highld	NC1019	58°7·4'	5°13·1'W	W	15
Loch a' Ghluair	N Eil	NB2431	58°11·2'	6°41·3'W	W	8,13
Loch a' Ghobha- Dhuibh	Highld	NC4949	58°24·5'	4°34·6'W	W	9
Loch a' Ghobhainn	Highld	NG7441	57°24·5'	5°45·3'W	W	24
Loch a' Ghobhainn	N Eil	NB3618	58°4·6'	6°28·2'W	W	14
Loch a' Ghobhair	Highld	NH6593	57°54·6'	4°16·2'W	W	21
Loch a' Ghoghainn	Highld	NG8565	57°37·7'	5°35·6'W	W	19,24
Loch a' Ghoill	N Eil	NF8763	57°33·2'	7°13·5'W	W	18
Loch a' Ghoirtein	N Eil	NB0009	57°58·4'	7°4·0'W	W	13
Loch a' Ghorm-choire	Highld	NC4433	58°15·7'	4°39·1'W	W	16
Loch a' Ghriama	Highld	NC3926	58°11·9'	4°43·9'W	W	16
Loch a' Ghrobain	Highld	NG4430	57°17·6'	6°14·5'W	W	32
Loch a' Ghruagaich	N Eil	NB4117	58°4·3'	6°23·1'W	W	14
Loch a' Ghruibe	Arg & Bt	NM2562	56°40·4'	6°28·9'W	W	46,47
Loch a' Ghuib Aird	Highld	NC1823	58°9·8'	5°5·2'W	W	15
Loch Ahaltair	N Eil	NB1529	58°9·7'	6°50·3'W	W	13
Loch Aighearail	N Eil	NB3104	57°56·9'	6°32·3'W	W	13,14
Loch Ailort	Highld	NM7379	56°51·1'	5°42·9'W	W	40
Lochailort	Highld	NM7682	56°52·8'	5°40·1'W	T	40
Loch Ailsh	Highld	NC3110	58°3·1'	4°51·4'W	W	15
Lochain a' Chaorainn	Highld	NC1942	58°20·0'	5°5·0'W	W	9
Lochain a' Chleirich	Highld	NC9655	58°28·5'	3°46·5'W	W	11
Lochain a' Mhill Dheirg	Highld	NC3033	58°15·4'	4°53·4'W	W	15
Lochain a' Mhullaich	Highld	NG6820	57°13·0'	5°50·1'W	W	32
Lochain an Ais	Highld	NC1809	58°2·2'	5°4·5'W	W	15
Lochain an t- Sochaich	Highld	NC2558	58°28·8'	4°59·6'W	W	9
Lochain Bealach an Eilein	Highld	NC1546	58°22·1'	5°9·3'W	W	9
Lochain Beinne Brice	Highld	NM5868	56°44·7'	5°57·0'W	W	47
Lochain Beinn na Caillich	Highld	NG6124	57°14·9'	5°57·3'W	W	32
Lochain Bheag a' Bhaile-dhoire	Arg & Bt	NR5892	56°3·8'	5°52·8'W	W	61
Lochain Ceann na Mòine	Highld	NH0697	57°55·5'	5°16·1'W	W	19
Lochain Cnapach	Highld	NG9284	57°48·1'	5°29·6'W	W	19
Lochain Coir' an Eich Ghlais	Highld	NH1278	57°45·4'	5°9·1'W	W	19
Lochain Doimhain	Highld	NC2242	58°20·1'	5°1·9'W	W	9
Lochain Doire an Ròin	Highld	NM6766	56°43·9'	5°48·1'W	W	40
Lochain Druim na Luinge	Highld	NM7367	56°44·6'	5°42·3'W	W	40
Lochain Dubh	Highld	NH0981	57°46·9'	5°12·3'W	W	19
Lochain Dubha	Highld	NC2955	58°27·3'	4°55·4'W	W	9
Lochain Dubha	Highld	NG6720	57°13·0'	5°51·1'W	W	32
Lochain Dubha	Highld	NH1704	57°5·7'	5°0·8'W	W	34
Lochain Dubh nan Dubhan	Highld	NM8563	56°42·8'	5°30·3'W	W	40
Lochain Fèith an Leothaid	Highld	NH0459	57°35·0'	5°16·3'W	W	25
Lochain Gleann Locha	Highld	NM4663	56°41·6'	6°8·5'W	W	47
Lochain Meallan a' Chuail	Highld	NC3529	58°13·4'	4°48·1'W	W	15
Lochain Ainm na Gaibhre	Highld	NG8829	57°18·4'	5°30·7'W	W	33
Lochain na Coille	Highld	NG7890	57°50·9'	5°44·0'W	W	19
Lochain na Creige Duibhe	Highld	NC1840	58°18·9'	5°5·9'W	W	9
Lochain na Creige Gile	Highld	NC2745	58°21·8'	4°57·0'W	W	9
Lochain na Cuthaige	Highld	NM7464	56°43·0'	5°41·1'W	W	40
Lochain nan Cnaimh	Arg & Bt	NS1697	56°8·1'	4°57·2'W	W	56
Lochain nan Ealachan	Highld	NC3235	58°16·6'	4°51·4'W	W	15
Lochain nan Gillean	Highld	NM5567	56°44·1'	5°59·9'W	W	47
Lochain nan Sac	Highld	NC1962	58°30·8'	5°6·0'W	W	9
Lochain nan Seasgach	Highld	NG8182	57°46·7'	5°40·5'W	W	19
Lochain Ainort	Highld	NG5528	57°16·9'	6°3·4'W	W	32
Lochain Ruighe a' Bhainne	Highld	NM6966	56°44·0'	5°46·1'W	W	40
Lochain Sidheanan Dubha	Highld	NG7779	57°45·0'	5°44·4'W	W	19
Lochain Stratha Mhóir	Highld	NG5625	57°15·3'	6°2·3'W	W	32
Lochain Teanna	Highld	NG6821	57°13·5'	5°50·1'W	W	32
Lochain Uvie	Highld	NN6795	57°1·9'	4°11·0'W	W	35
Loch Aird	N Eil	NB1732	58°11·4'	6°48·5'W	W	8,13
Loch Aird a' Mhuile	N Eil	NF7129	57°14·3'	7°26·8'W	W	22
Loch Aird an Dùin	N Eil	NF9176	57°40·3'	7°10·5'W	W	18
Loch Aird an Sgairbh	N Eil	NF7326	57°12·7'	7°24·6'W	W	22
Loch Airdeglais	Arg & Bt	NM6228	56°23·3'	5°50·9'W	W	49
Loch Airgh Riabhach	N Eil	NB3730	58°11·1'	6°28·0'W	W	8
Loch Airigh a' Bhaird	Highld	NC2845	58°21·9'	4°55·9'W	W	9
Loch Airigh a' Bhealaich	N Eil	NB1825	58°7·7'	6°46·9'W	W	13,14
Loch Airigh a'Chruidh	Arg & Bt	NM7003	56°10·1'	5°41·8'W	W	55
Loch Airigh a' Ghille Ruaidhe	N Eil	NB2418	58°4·2'	6°40·4'W	W	13,14
Loch Airigh Alasdair	Highld	NG7436	57°21·8'	5°45·0'W	W	24
Loch Airigh a' Mhill	Highld	NG7862	57°35·9'	5°42·5'W	W	19,24
Loch Airigh Amhlaidh	N Eil	NF7935	57°17·8'	7°19·3'W	W	22
Loch Airigh an Eilein	Highld	NG7989	57°50·4'	5°42·9'W	W	19
Loch Airigh an Sgairbh	N Eil	NB4031	58°11·7'	6°25·0'W	W	8
Loch Airigh an t-Sagairt	N Eil	NB3828	58°10·1'	6°26·8'W	W	8
Loch Airigh an Uisge	N Eil	NB1027	58°8·5'	6°55·2'W	W	13
Loch Airigh a' Phuill	Highld	NG8475	57°43·0'	5°37·1'W	W	19
Loch Airigh Ard	N Eil	NF8439	57°20·2'	7°14·7'W	W	22
Loch Airigh Blàir	Highld	NB9816	58°5·5'	5°25·1'W	W	15
Loch Airigh Brocaig	N Eil	NB2733	58°12·3'	6°38·4'W	W	8,13
Loch Airigh Choinnich	N Eil	NB4846	58°20·1'	6°17·8'W	W	8
Loch Airigh Dhaibhaidh	Arg & Bt	NR3155	55°43·1'	6°16·6'W	W	60
Loch Airigh Eachainn	Highld	NG8260	57°34·9'	5°38·3'W	W	19,24
Loch Airighe Bheg	Highld	NC7002	57°59·6'	4°11·5'W	W	16
Loch Airighe Mhór	Highld	NC6902	57°59·5'	4°12·5'W	W	16
Loch Airigh Iain Oig	N Eil	NG1393	57°50·3'	6°49·7'W	W	14
Loch Airigh Lochain	Highld	NH2848	57°29·6'	4°51·7'W	W	25
Loch Airigh Meall Bhreide	Arg & Bt	NM2156	56°37·0'	6°32·4'W	W	46,47
Loch Airigh Mhic Criadh	Highld	NG8276	57°43·5'	5°39·2'W	W	19
Loch Airigh Mhic Fhionnlaidh Dhuibh	N Eil	NB2738	58°15·0'	6°38·7'W	W	8,13
Loch Airigh na Beinne	Highld	NC2041	58°19·5'	5°3·9'W	W	9
Loch Airigh na Beinne	Highld	NC2131	58°14·1'	5°2·5'W	W	15
Loch Airigh na Beinne	Highld	NC3266	58°33·2'	4°52·8'W	W	9
Loch Airigh na Ceardaich	N Eil	NB2722	58°6·4'	6°37·6'W	W	13,14
Loch Airigh na Creige	Arg & Bt	NM9903	56°10·9'	5°13·9'W	W	55
Loch Airigh na h-Achlais	N Eil	NF8038	57°19·5'	7°18·6'W	W	22
Loch Airigh na h-Airde	N Eil	NB2123	58°6·7'	6°43·8'W	W	13,14
Loch Airigh na Lic	N Eil	NB4034	58°13·3'	6°25·2'W	W	8
Loch Airigh nan Caisteal	Arg & Bt	NR3769	55°50·8'	6°11·7'W	W	60,61
Loch Airigh nan Gleann	N Eil	NB3930	58°11·2'	6°26·0'W	W	8
Loch Airigh nan Sloc	N Eil	NB2933	58°12·4'	6°36·3'W	W	8,13
Loch Airigh na Saorach	Highld	NG6820	57°13·0'	5°50·1'W	W	32
Loch Airigh Nualaidh	Arg & Bt	NR5586	56°0·5'	5°55·4'W	W	61
Loch Airigh Seibh	N Eil	NB2538	58°15·0'	6°40·8'W	W	8,13
Loch Airigh Thormoid	N Eil	NB2913	58°1·7'	6°34·9'W	W	13,14
Loch Airigh Uilleim	Highld	NG7571	57°40·6'	5°46·0'W	W	19
Loch Aisavat	N Eil	NF7515	57°6·9'	7°21·7'W	W	31
Loch Aiseabhat	N Eil	NB0711	57°59·8'	6°57·1'W	W	13,14
Loch Aisir	Highld	NC1960	58°29·7'	5°5·9'W	W	9
Loch Aisir Mór	Highld	NC2159	58°29·2'	5°3·8'W	W	9
Loch Akran	Highld	NC9260	58°31·2'	3°50·8'W	W	11
Lochala	Highld	NH6854	57°33·7'	4°11·9'W	X	26
Loch a' Laip	N Eil	NF8647	57°24·6'	7°13·3'W	W	22
Loch Alatair	N Eil	NG0587	57°46·8'	6°57·3'W	W	14,18
Loch a' Leadharain	N Eil	NB3833	58°12·7'	6°27·2'W	W	8
Lochaline	Highld	NM6744	56°32·1'	5°46·5'W	T	49
Loch Aline	Highld	NM6846	56°33·2'	5°46·0'W	W	49
Loch Allabhat	N Eil	NB4348	58°21·0'	6°23·1'W	W	8
Loch Allagro	N Eil	NB1330	58°10·2'	6°52·4'W	W	13
Loch Allallaidh	Arg & Bt	NR4158	55°45·0'	6°7·2'W	W	60
Loch Allan	Arg & Bt	NR4267	55°49·9'	6°6·8'W	W	60,61
Loch Allt an Daraich	Highld	NG9863	57°37·0'	5°22·5'W	W	19
Loch Allt Eigin	Highld	NH1382	57°47·6'	5°8·3'W	W	19
Loch Allt Eoin Thòmais	Highld	NG8089	57°50·5'	5°41·9'W	W	19
Loch Allt na h-Airbe or Loch Yucal	Highld	NC2036	58°16·8'	5°3·7'W	W	15
Loch Allt nam Bearnach	N Eil	NB3608	57°59·2'	6°27·5'W	W	14
Loch Allt nan Ramh	Highld	NC2136	58°16·8'	5°2·7'W	W	15
Loch Almaistean	N Eil	NB2139	58°15·3'	6°44·9'W	W	8,13
Loch Alsh	Highld	NG8025	57°16·0'	5°38·5'W	W	33
Lochalsh Dam	Highld	NG8528	57°17·8'	5°33·7'W	X	33
Loch Altabrug	N Eil	NF7434	57°17·1'	7°24·2'W	W	22
Loch Alty	S Ayr	NX2379	55°4·7'	4°45·9'W	W	76
Loch Alvie	Highld	NH8609	57°9·7'	3°52·6'W	W	35,36
Loch Amar Sine	N Eil	NB2237	58°14·3'	6°43·7'W	W	8,13
Loch a' Meallard	Highld	NC1533	58°15·1'	5°8·7'W	W	15
Loch a' Mhachaire	N Eil	NF9783	57°44·3'	7°5·0'W	W	18
Loch a'Mhadaidh	Arg & Bt	NM8006	56°12·0'	5°32·4'W	W	55
Loch a'Mhadaidh	Arg & Bt	NR7982	55°59·1'	5°32·1'W	W	55
Loch a' Mhadaidh	Highld	NC9841	58°21·0'	3°44·1'W	W	11
Loch a' Mhadaidh	Highld	NG7783	57°47·1'	5°44·6'W	W	19
Loch a' Mhadaidh	Highld	NH1973	57°42·9'	5°1·8'W	W	20
Loch a' Mhadaidh	Highld	NH4148	57°29·9'	4°38·7'W	W	26
Loch a' Mhadaidh Mór	Highld	NG9686	57°49·3'	5°25·6'W	W	19
Loch á Mhadaidh-ruaidh	Highld	NC5546	58°23·0'	4°28·3'W	W	10
Loch a' Mhadail	Highld	NC1514	58°4·9'	5°7·8'W	W	15
Loch a' Mhaide	N Eil	NB2518	58°4·2'	6°39·3'W	W	13,14
Loch a' Mhaim	Arg & Bt	NM6438	56°28·8'	5°49·5'W	W	49
Loch a' Mhairt	N Eil	NB1630	58°10·3'	6°49·3'W	W	13
Loch a' Mhàla	Arg & Bt	NR3371	55°51·8'	6°15·6'W	W	60,61
Loch a' Mhaoil Dhisnich	Highld	NH0709	57°8·1'	5°10·9'W	W	33
Loch Amhastar	N Eil	NB2335	58°13·3'	6°42·6'W	W	8,13
Loch a' Mheallain	Highld	NB9911	58°2·8'	5°23·9'W	W	15
Loch a' Mheallain	Highld	NC2810	58°3·0'	4°54·4'W	W	15
Loch a' Mheallain	Highld	NG8361	57°35·5'	5°37·4'W	W	19,24
Loch a' Mheallain-chaorainn	Highld	NH3367	57°40·0'	4°47·5'W	W	20
Loch a' Mheallain Leith	Highld	NC6517	58°7·5'	4°17·1'W	W	16
Loch a' Mheallain Odhair	Highld	NH0768	57°39·9'	5°13·7'W	W	19
Loch a' Mheig	Highld	NH4119	57°14·3'	4°37·6'W	W	34
Loch a' Mhile	Arg & Bt	NR5184	55°59·5'	5°59·1'W	W	61
Loch a' Mhill	Arg & Bt	NM2560	56°39·3'	6°28·8'W	W	46,47
Loch a' Mhill Aird	Arg & Bt	NM2360	56°39·2'	6°30·7'W	W	46,47
Loch a' Mhill Dheirg	Highld	NC1543	58°20·5'	5°9·2'W	W	9
Loch a' Mhinidh	Highld	NC1837	58°17·3'	5°5·8'W	W	15
Loch a'Mhinn	Arg & Bt	NM8612	56°15·4'	5°26·9'W	W	55
Loch a'Mhinn	Arg & Bt	NM8907	56°12·8'	5°23·7'W	W	55
Loch a' Mhi Runaich	Highld	NC0429	58°12·6'	5°19·7'W	W	15
Loch a' Mhòid	Highld	NC5640	58°19·8'	4°27·1'W	W	10
Loch a' Mhòil	N Eil	NF7334	57°17·0'	7°25·2'W	W	22
Loch a' Mhonaidh	N Eil	NG1695	57°51·5'	6°46·8'W	W	14
Loch a' Mhonaidh-dhroighinn	Highld	NG9388	57°50·3'	5°28·8'W	W	19
Loch a' Mhorghain	N Eil	NB1504	57°56·3'	6°48·5'W	W	13,14
Loch a' Mhuilinn	Arg & Bt	NR5166	55°49·6'	5°58·1'W	W	61
Loch a' Mhuilinn	Arg & Bt	NR6083	55°59·1'	5°50·4'W	W	61
Loch a' Mhuilinn	Arg & Bt	NR7683	55°59·5'	5°35·1'W	W	55
Loch a'Mhuilinn	Arg & Bt	NR7948	55°40·8'	5°30·5'W	W	62,69
Loch a' Mhuilinn	Highld	NC1639	58°18·3'	5°7·9'W	W	15
Loch a' Mhuilinn	Highld	NC1924	58°10·3'	5°4·2'W	W	15
Loch a' Mhuilinn	Highld	NC2063	58°31·3'	5°5·0'W	W	9
Loch a' Mhuilinn	Highld	NC5660	58°30·5'	4°27·8'W	W	10
Loch a' Mhuilinn	Highld	NC8756	58°28·9'	3°55·8'W	W	10
Loch a' Mhuilinn	Highld	ND0142	58°21·6'	3°41·0'W	W	11,12
Loch a' Mhuilinn	Highld	ND0556	58°29·2'	3°37·3'W	W	11,12
Loch a' Mhuilinn	Highld	NG5536	57°21·2'	6°3·9'W	W	24,32
Loch a' Mhuilinn	Highld	NG6229	57°17·6'	5°56·6'W	W	32
Loch a' Mhuilinn	Highld	NG7043	57°25·4'	5°49·4'W	W	24
Loch a' Mhuilinn	Highld	NG7754	57°31·5'	5°43·0'W	W	24
Loch a' Mhuilinn	Highld	NG8275	57°43·0'	5°39·1'W	W	19
Loch a'Mhuilinn	Highld	NG8418	57°12·4'	5°34·1'W	W	33
Loch a' Mhuilinn	Highld	NG9025	57°16·3'	5°28·5'W	W	25,33
Loch a' Mhuilinn	Highld	NG9245	57°27·1'	5°27·6'W	W	25
Loch a' Mhuilinn	Highld	NH3622	57°15·8'	4°42·7'W	W	26
Loch a' Mhuilinn	Highld	NH3824	57°16·9'	4°40·8'W	W	26
Loch a' Mhuilinn	Highld	NH3854	57°33·1'	4°42·0'W	W	26
Loch a' Mhuilinn	Highld	NH4014	57°11·6'	4°38·4'W	W	34
Loch a' Mhuilinn	Highld	NH4138	57°24·5'	4°38·3'W	W	26
Loch a' Mhuilinn	Highld	NM6484	56°53·5'	5°52·0'W	W	40
Loch a' Mhuilinn	N Eil	NB0806	57°57·1'	6°55·7'W	W	13,14
Loch a' Mhuilinn	N Eil	NF7852	57°26·9'	7°21·6'W	W	22
Loch a' Mhuilinn-ghaoithe	Arg & Bt	NR4256	55°44·0'	6°6·1'W	W	60
Loch a' Mhuillidh	Highld	NH2738	57°24·2'	4°52·3'W	W	25
Loch a' Mhuilt Dhuibh	N Eil	NG1392	57°49·8'	6°49·6'W	W	14
Loch a' Mhuim	N Eil	NB2402	57°55·6'	6°39·2'W	W	14
Loch a' Mhuirt	Highld	NC2044	58°21·1'	5°4·1'W	W	9
Loch a' Mhula	N Eil	NB0010	57°58·9'	7°4·1'W	W	13
Loch a' Mhullaich	Highld	NG8060	57°34·9'	5°40·3'W	W	19,24
Lochan	Highld	NN0698	57°2·2'	5°11·4'W	X	33
Lochan	N Eil	NB4010	58°0·5'	6°23·6'W	W	14
Lochan a' Bhàigh	Arg & Bt	NM2563	56°40·9'	6°29·0'W	W	46,47
Lochan a'Bhailis	Arg & Bt	NM9015	56°17·1'	5°23·1'W	W	55
Lochan a' Bhainne	Arg & Bt	NM8018	56°18·5'	5°33·0'W	W	55
Lochan a' Bhainne	Moray	NJ0404	57°7·3'	3°34·7'W	W	36
Lochan a' Bhàthaich	Highld	NH4036	57°23·4'	4°39·3'W	W	26
Lochan a' Bhealaich	Highld	NC3839	58°18·8'	4°45·4'W	W	16
Lochan a' Bhealaich	Highld	NM7187	56°55·3'	5°45·3'W	W	40
Lochan a' Bhealaich	Highld	NM7482	56°52·7'	5°42·1'W	W	40
Lochan a' Bhealaich	Pth & Kin	NN4568	56°46·9'	4°31·8'W	W	42
Lochan a' Bhealaich Bhig	Highld	NG4952	57°29·6'	6°10·9'W	W	23
Lochan a' Bhràghad	Highld	NH0276	57°44·1'	5°19·1'W	W	19
Lochan a' Bhrodainn	Highld	NM8387	56°55·7'	5°33·5'W	W	40
Lochan a' Bhruic	Arg & Bt	NM9210	56°14·5'	5°21·0'W	W	55
Lochan a' Bhuàlt	Highld	NC3303	57°59·4'	4°49·0'W	W	15
Lochan a' Bhuinn-a'-Sè	Highld	NM6647	56°33·7'	5°48·1'W	W	49
Loch an Acha	Highld	NH2091	57°52·6'	5°1·7'W	W	20
Loch an Achaidh	Highld	NC0233	58°14·7'	5°21·9'W	W	15
Loch an Achaidh Mhóir	Highld	NC6142	58°20·9'	4°22·0'W	W	10
Lochan a' Chairn	Highld	NH5184	57°49·5'	4°30·1'W	W	20
Lochan a' Chaisteil	Highld	NM6150	56°35·1'	5°53·1'W	W	49
Lochan a' Chaisteil	Stir	NN3418	56°19·8'	4°40·6'W	W	50,56
Lochan a' Chait	Highld	NN3962	56°43·6'	4°37·4'W	W	41
Lochan a' Chait	Pth & Kin	NN8456	56°41·1'	3°53·2'W	W	52

Lochan a' Chait	Pth & Kin	NO0551	56°38·7'	3°32·5'W	W	52,53
Lochan a' Chaorainn	Highld	NG8934	57°21·1'	5°30·0'W	W	24
Lochan a' Chaorainn	Highld	NG9059	57°34·6'	5°30·3'W	W	25
Lochan a' Chaorainn	Moray	NJ0340	57°26·7'	3°36·5'W	W	27
Lochan a' Chapuill	Arg & Bt	NM6423	56°20·7'	5°48·7'W	W	49
Lochan a' Chàrra Mhóir	Highld	NN4573	56°49·6'	4°32·0'W	W	42
Lochan a' Charr Mhóir	Highld	NN7980	56°54·0'	3°58·7'W	W	42
Lochan a' Chinn Mhonaich	Highld	NH4615	57°12·3'	4°32·5'W	W	34
Lochan a' Chlaidheimh	Highld	NH7377	57°46·1'	4°7·6'W	W	21
Lochan a' Chlaidheimh	Highld	NN4060	56°42·5'	4°36·4'W	W	42
Lochan a'Chlaiginn	Arg & Bt	NM8105	56°11·5'	5°31·3'W	W	55
Lochan Achlarich	Pth & Kin	NN4338	56°30·7'	4°32·6'W	W	51
Lochan a' Chleirich	Highld	NG8770	57°40·4'	5°33·9'W	W	19
Lochan a' Chleirich	Highld	NM6791	56°57·4'	5°49·5'W	W	40
Lochan a' Chleite Tuath	N Eil	NB1118	58°3·7'	6°53·5'W	W	13,14
Lochan a' Chnapaich	Highld	NH2583	57°48·4'	4°56·3'W	W	20
Lochan a' Chneamh	Highld	NM6988	56°55·8'	5°47·3'W	W	40
Lochan a'Choinneachain	Arg & Bt	NM9125	56°22·5'	5°22·6'W	W	49
Lochan a' Choin Uire	Highld	NH4616	57°12·8'	4°32·5'W	W	34
Lochan a' Choire	Highld	NC4613	58°5·0'	4°36·2'W	W	16
Lochan a' Choire	Highld	NC6860	58°30·8'	4°15·5'W	W	10
Lochan a' Choire	Highld	NN4388	56°57·7'	4°34·5'W	W	34,42
Lochan a' Choire	Highld	NN5698	57°3·3'	4°22·0'W	W	35
Lochan a' Choire Bhuidhe	Highld	NC7038	58°18·9'	4°12·7'W	W	16
Lochan a' Choire Bhuidhe	Highld	NH2296	57°55·3'	4°59·9'W	W	20
Lochan a' Choire Dhuibh	Highld	NG7151	57°29·7'	5°48·8'W	W	24
Lochan a' Choire Dhuibh	Highld	NG9259	57°34·7'	5°28·3'W	W	25
Lochan a' Choire Dhuibh	Highld	NM9865	56°44·2'	5°17·7'W	W	40
Lochan a' Choire Ghlais	Highld	NH4405	57°6·8'	4°34·1'W	W	34
Lochan a' Choire Ghuirm	Highld	NC2626	58°11·6'	4°57·1'W	W	15
Lochan a' Chomhlain	Highld	NM9686	56°55·5'	5°20·7'W	W	40
Lochan a' Chothruim	Highld	NM8960	56°41·3'	5°26·3'W	W	40
Lochan a' Chothruim	Highld	NM8965	56°44·0'	5°26·5'W	W	40
Lochan a' Chreachain	Arg & Bt	NN3644	56°33·8'	4°39·7'W	W	50
Lochan a'Chreimh	Arg & Bt	NR8054	55°44·0'	5°29·8'W	W	62
Lochan a' Chreobhair	Highld	NC3239	58°18·7'	4°51·6'W	W	15
Lochan a' Chroin	Stir	NN3818	56°19·9'	4°36·8'W	W	50,56
Lochan a' Chroin	Stir	NN6116	56°19·2'	4°14·4'W	W	57
Lochan a' Chrom-leathaid	Highld	NM6262	56°41·6'	5°52·8'W	W	40
Lochan a Chùirn	Arg & Bt	NM1152	56°34·5'	6°41·9'W	W	46
Lochan a' Chuirn	Arg & Bt	NM3849	56°33·9'	6°15·4'W	W	47,48
Lochan a' Chuirn Dheirg	Highld	NN2766	56°45·5'	4°49·3'W	W	41
Lochan a' Chuirn Duibh	Highld	NM7492	56°58·1'	5°42·6'W	W	33,40
Lochan a' Churra	Highld	NM5568	56°44·6'	6°0·0'W	W	47
Lochan a' Churraichd	Highld	NN1047	56°34·8'	5°5·2'W	W	50
Lochan a' Churraidh	Arg & Bt	NM3441	56°29·4'	6°18·8'W	W	47,48
Lochan a' Craoi	Stir	NN3929	56°25·8'	4°36·2'W	W	50
Loch an Add	Arg & Bt	NR8088	56°2·3'	5°31·5'W	W	55
Lochan Add	Arg & Bt	NR8697	56°7·3'	5°26·1'W	W	55
Lochan a' Garbh Choire	Highld	NN4971	56°48·6'	4°28·0'W	W	42
Lochan a' Ghaorra	Highld	NN7583	56°55·5'	4°2·8'W	W	42
Lochan a'Ghille-bhlain	Arg & Bt	NR8072	55°53·7'	5°30·7'W	W	62
Lochan a' Ghille Ruaidh	N Eil	NB4952	58°23·3'	6°17·2'W	W	8
Lochan a' Ghiubhais	Highld	NC6901	57°59·0'	4°12·5'W	W	16
Lochan a' Ghobhainn	Highld	NM7382	56°52·7'	5°43·1'W	W	40
Lochan a' Ghobhainn	Highld	NM8084	56°54·0'	5°36·3'W	W	40
Lochan a' Ghriasaiche	Highld	NM7688	56°56·0'	5°40·5'W	W	40
Lochan a' Ghurrabain	Arg & Bt	NM5253	56°36·5'	6°2·0'W	W	47
Loch an Aigeil	Highld	NC0428	58°12·1'	5°19·7'W	W	15
Loch an Airceil	Highld	NH1583	57°48·2'	5°6·3'W	W	20
Loch an Aircill	Arg & Bt	NR5077	55°55·5'	5°59·7'W	W	61
Loch an Aircill	Arg & Bt	NR6192	56°3·9'	5°49·9'W	W	61
Loch an Airidh Fhraoich	Highld	NH3338	57°24·4'	4°46·3'W	W	26
Lochan Airigh	Arg & Bt	NN0416	56°18·0'	5°9·6'W	W	50,56
Lochan Airigh Chaluim	Highld	NB9915	58°5·0'	5°24·1'W	W	15
Lochan Airigh Leathaid	Highld	NC9939	58°19·9'	3°43·0'W	W	11,17
Lochan Airigh na Creige	Highld	NC7258	58°29·8'	4°11·3'W	W	10
Lochan Airigh-shamhraidh	Arg & Bt	NM9520	56°19·9'	5°18·5'W	W	49
Loch an Alaskie	Highld	NC4726	58°12·0'	4°35·7'W	W	16
Loch an Alltain-bheithe	Highld	NH3159	57°35·6'	4°49·2'W	W	26
Loch an Alltain Duibh	Highld	NB9712	58°3·3'	5°26·0'W	W	15
Loch an Alltain Duibh	Highld	NC1420	58°8·1'	5°9·1'W	W	15
Loch an Alltan Fheàrna	Highld	NC7433	58°16·3'	4°8·4'W	W	16
Lochan Allt an Sgadain	Arg & Bt	NN0110	56°14·7'	5°12·3'W	W	50,55
Lochan Allt Fearna	Highld	NH6918	57°14·3'	4°9·8'W	H	35
Lochan Allt Leacaich	Highld	NH2897	57°56·0'	4°53·8'W	W	20
Loch an Amair	Highld	NH2626	57°17·8'	4°52·8'W	W	25
Lochan a' Mhadaidh	Arg & Bt	NN1115	56°17·6'	5°2·8'W	W	50,56
Lochan a' Mhadaidh	Stir	NN2621	56°21·2'	4°48·5'W	X	50
Lochan a' Mhadaidh Riabhaich	Highld	NM5565	56°43·0'	5°59·8'W	W	47
Lochan a' Mhàidseir	Pth & Kin	NN4154	56°39·3'	4°35·2'W	W	42,51
Lochan a' Mhaim	Highld	NM9094	56°59·6'	5°27·0'W	W	33,40
Lochan a' Mheadhoin	Highld	NM6994	56°59·0'	5°47·7'W	W	40
Lochan a' Mhill	N Ayr	NR9147	55°40·5'	5°19·0'W	W	62,69
Lochan a' Mhill Bhig	Arg & Bt	NN2213	56°16·8'	4°52·1'W	W	50,56
Lochan a' Mhill Dhuibh	Highld	NH3032	57°21·1'	4°49·1'W	W	26
Lochan a' Mhonaidh	Highld	NM4198	57°0·3'	6°15·5'W	W	39
Lochan a Mhuilinn	Highld	NM6974	56°48·3'	5°46·6'W	W	40
Lochan a' Mhuilinn	Highld	NM7570	56°46·3'	5°40·5'W	W	40
Lochan a' Mhuilinn	Pth & Kin	NN8435	56°29·8'	3°52·6'W	W	52
Lochan a' Mhùinean	Highld	NC1547	58°22·6'	5°9·3'W	W	9
Lochanan a' Ghiubhais	Moray	NJ0844	57°28·9'	3°31·6'W	W	27
Loch an Anama	Arg & Bt	NM9902	56°10·4'	5°13·8'W	W	55
Lochan Anama	Arg & Bt	NR9098	56°8·0'	5°22·3'W	W	55
Lochanan a' Mhuilinn	Highld	NH1991	57°52·6'	5°2·7'W	W	20
Lochanan an Uillt Mhór	Highld	NH1997	57°55·8'	5°2·9'W	W	20
Lochan an Aodainn	Highld	NM4566	56°43·2'	6°9·6'W	W	47
Lochan an Aonaich	Highld	NM7380	56°51·6'	5°43·0'W	W	40
Lochanan Cùl Beinn Dònuill	Highld	NH2098	57°56·4'	5°2·0'W	W	20
Lochan an Dàim	Pth & Kin	NN7157	56°41·5'	4°5·9'W	W	42,51,52
Lochan an Daimh	Arg & Bt	NM6221	56°19·6'	5°50·5'W	W	49
Lochan an Daimh	Highld	NN3861	56°43·0'	4°38·4'W	W	41
Lochanan Deabharan	Highld	NH1987	57°50·4'	5°2·5'W	W	20
Lochan an Diamh	Highld	NG9892	57°52·6'	5°23·9'W	W	19
Lochan an Dobhrain	Highld	NM4770	56°45·4'	6°7·9'W	W	39,47
Lochan an Doire Dharaich	Arg & Bt	NM7133	56°26·3'	5°42·4'W	W	49
Lochanan Dubha	Highld	NC1405	58°0·0'	5°8·4'W	W	15
Lochanan Dubha	Highld	NM7053	56°37·0'	5°44·5'W	W	49
Lochanan Dubha	Highld	NM7745	56°32·9'	5°37·2'W	W	49
Lochan an Duibhe	Highld	NC2125	58°10·9'	5°2·2'W	W	15
Lochan an Eas Bhàin	Highld	NM7786	56°55·0'	5°39·4'W	W	40
Lochan an Eireannaich	Stir	NN5124	56°23·3'	4°24·4'W	W	51
Lochan an Eisg Mhóir	Pth & Kin	NN4254	56°39·3'	4°34·2'W	W	42,51
Lochan an Eoin Ruadha	Highld	NH6132	57°21·7'	4°18·2'W	W	26
Lochan an Fhaing	Highld	NM7648	56°34·5'	5°38·4'W	W	49
Lochan an Fhéidh	Highld	NC2047	58°22·7'	5°4·2'W	W	9
Lochan an Fheòir	Highld	NG7051	57°29·7'	5°49·8'W	W	24
Lochan an Fheòir	Highld	NN4875	56°50·8'	4°29·1'W	W	42
Lochan an Fheòir	N Eil	NB0715	58°1·9'	6°57·4'W	W	13,14
Lochan an Fheòir	N Eil	NB1012	58°0·4'	6°54·1'W	W	13,14
Lochan an Fheòir	N Eil	NB2103	57°56·0'	6°42·3'W	W	13,14
Lochan an Fhithich	Highld	NN1394	57°0·2'	5°4·3'W	W	34
Lochan an Fhleasgaich	N Eil	NB4448	58°21·0'	6°22·1'W	W	8
Lochanan Fiodha	Highld	NH1992	57°53·1'	5°2·7'W	W	20
Lochan an Frigheadair	Highld	NH0600	57°3·3'	5°11·5'W	W	33
Lochan an Iasgaich	Highld	NC1524	58°10·2'	5°8·3'W	W	15
Lochan an Iasgair	Highld	NG9556	57°33·1'	5°25·1'W	W	25
Lochan an Ime	Highld	NM5568	56°44·6'	6°0·0'W	W	47
Lochanan Lacasdail	N Eil	NB1801	57°54·8'	6°45·2'W	W	14
Lochan an Làir	Arg & Bt	NN0743	56°32·6'	5°7·9'W	W	50
Lochan an Laoigh	Highld	NC5020	58°8·9'	4°32·4'W	W	16
Lochan an Laoigh Bhain	Arg & Bt	NR3587	56°0·4'	6°14·6'W	W	61
Lochan an Liath-truisg	Highld	NG8722	57°14·6'	5°31·4'W	W	33
Lochan Anma	Arg & Bt	NR8179	55°57·5'	5°30·1'W	W	62
Lochanan Meall nan Eun	Highld	NG9005	57°5·5'	5°27·5'W	W	33
Lochanan Móra	N Eil	NG1397	57°52·5'	6°50·0'W	W	14
Lochanan na Ceireag	Highld	NC2101	57°58·0'	5°1·1'W	W	15
Lochanan nan Learga	N Eil	NB1523	58°6·5'	6°49·8'W	W	13,14
Lochanan nan Sàilean Beaga	Highld	NC2100	57°57·5'	5°1·0'W	W	15
Lochanan nan Sàilean Móra	Highld	NH2099	57°56·9'	5°2·0'W	W	20
Lochan Annie	Highld	NG9935	57°21·9'	5°20·1'W	W	25
Lochan an Obain Bhig	Highld	NM8789	56°56·9'	5°29·7'W	W	40
Lochanan Sgeireach	N Eil	NB0727	58°8·4'	6°58·3'W	W	13
Lochan an Staic	Highld	NN1199	57°2·9'	5°6·5'W	W	34
Lochan an Tairbh	Highld	NC0824	58°10·1'	5°15·4'W	W	15
Lochan an Tairbh-uisge	Pth & Kin	NN5939	56°31·6'	4°17·1'W	W	51
Lochan an Tairt	Highld	NH4433	57°21·9'	4°35·2'W	W	26
Lochanan Tana	Arg & Bt	NR5275	55°54·5'	5°57·7'W	W	61
Lochanan Tana	Arg & Bt	NR6193	56°4·5'	5°50·0'W	W	61
Lochan an Torra Bhuidhe	Highld	NH4832	57°21·5'	4°31·1'W	W	26
Lochan an Torrnalaich	Arg & Bt	NR8595	56°6·2'	5°27·0'W	W	55
Lochan an t-Sagairt	Highld	NG7437	57°22·3'	5°45·1'W	W	24
Lochan an t-Sluic	Highld	NN8290	56°59·4'	3°56·1'W	W	35,43
Lochan An Tuirc	Highld	NN4280	56°53·3'	4°35·2'W	W	34,42
Loch an Aoinidh Dhuibh	Arg & Bt	NR5185	55°59·9'	5°59·2'W	W	61
Loch an Aonaich Odhair	Highld	NN4499	57°3·6'	4°33·9'W	W	34
Loch an Aon Aite	Highld	NC0828	58°12·2'	5°15·6'W	W	15
Loch an Aon-bhric	Highld	NC5546	58°23·0'	4°28·3'W	W	10
Lochan a' Phuill	Arg & Bt	NM4222	56°19·5'	6°9·9'W	W	48
Loch an Arbhair	Highld	NC0718	58°6·8'	5°16·1'W	W	15
Lochan Arbhair	Highld	NC6757	58°29·1'	4°16·4'W	W	10
Loch an Arbhair	Highld	NG8834	57°21·1'	5°31·0'W	W	24
Lochan Ard na Beinne Baine	Highld	NM9465	56°44·1'	5°21·6'W	W	40
Loch an Armuinn	N Eil	NF9074	57°39·2'	7°11·4'W	W	18
Lochan a' Sgeil	N Eil	NB4343	58°18·3'	6°22·7'W	W	8
Loch an Aslaird	Highld	NC4236	58°17·3'	4°41·2'W	W	16
Lochana' Tana	Arg & Bt	NR5680	55°57·3'	5°54·1'W	W	61
Loch an Athain	Highld	NG5122	57°13·5'	6°7·1'W	W	32
Loch an Athain	N Eil	NF7632	57°16·1'	7°22·1'W	W	22
Loch an Ath Ghairbh	Highld	NG8597	57°54·9'	5°37·3'W	W	19
Loch an Ath Ruaidh	N Eil	NB0518	58°3·4'	6°59·6'W	W	13,14
Loch an Ath Ruaidh	N Eil	NF7526	57°12·8'	7°22·6'W	W	22
Lochan Bac an Lochain	Highld	NM7665	56°43·6'	5°39·2'W	W	40
Lochan Badan Glasliath	Highld	NH2691	57°52·7'	4°55·6'W	W	20
Lochan Bad an Losguinn	Highld	NH1503	57°5·1'	5°2·7'W	W	34
Lochan Ballach	Highld	NC0609	58°1·9'	5°16·7'W	W	15
Lochan Balloch	Stir	NN5904	56°12·7'	4°16·0'W	W	57
Lochan Barr a' Bhealaich	Arg & Bt	NR5788	56°1·7'	5°53·6'W	W	61
Lochan beag	N Eil	NB0507	57°57·5'	6°58·8'W	W	13,14
Lochan Bealach Carra	Arg & Bt	NN0237	56°29·3'	5°12·5'W	W	50
Lochan Bealach Cornaidh	Highld	NC2028	58°12·5'	5°3·3'W	W	15
Lochan Beanaidh	Highld	NH9102	57°6·0'	3°47·5'W	W	36
Lochan Beannach Beag	Highld	NG9477	57°44·4'	5°27·2'W	W	19
Lochan Beannach Mór	Highld	NG9477	57°44·4'	5°27·2'W	W	19
Lochan Beinn Chabhair	Stir	NN3517	56°19·3'	4°39·6'W	W	50,56
Lochan Beinn Chaorach	Highld	NN3151	56°37·5'	4°44·8'W	W	41
Lochan Beinn Damhain	Arg & Bt	NN2917	56°19·1'	4°45·5'W	W	50,56
Lochan Beinn Dònuill	Highld	NH2198	57°56·4'	5°1·0'W	W	20
Lochan Beinne-ri-Oitir	N Eil	NF7722	57°10·8'	7°20·3'W	W	31
Lochan Beinn Iadain	Highld	NM6953	56°37·0'	5°45·4'W	W	49
Lochan Beoil Chathaiche	Pth & Kin	NN7456	56°41·0'	4°3·0'W	W	42,51,52
Lochan Beul na Faireachan	Highld	NC2464	58°32·0'	5°0·9'W	W	9
Lochan Blàr a' Bhainne	Highld	NC6661	58°31·3'	4°17·6'W	W	10
Lochan Blàr nan Lochan	Arg & Bt	NM9749	56°35·6'	5°17·9'W	W	49
Lochan Bràighe	Highld	NC7651	58°26·1'	4°7·0'W	W	10
Lochan Breac	Highld	NM6966	56°44·0'	5°46·1'W	W	40
Lochan Breaclaich	Stir	NN6231	56°27·3'	4°13·9'W	W	51
Lochan Breac-liath	Arg & Bt	NN0316	56°18·0'	5°10·6'W	W	50,55
Lochan Breac-liath	Arg & Bt	NR9198	56°8·0'	5°21·4'W	W	55
Lochan Broach	Arg & Bt	NR3570	55°51·3'	6°13·6'W	W	60,61
Lochan Buic	Arg & Bt	NR7888	56°2·3'	5°33·4'W	W	55
Lochan Buidhe	Highld	NC1620	58°8·1'	5°7·0'W	W	15
Lochan Buidhe	Highld	ND0369	58°36·2'	3°39·7'W	W	12
Lochan Buidhe	Moray	NH9801	57°5·6'	3°40·5'W	W	36
Lochan Buidhe	Stir	NN5515	56°18·6'	4°20·2'W	W	57
Lochan Burn	D & G	NT0200	55°17·3'	3°32·2'W	W	78
Lochan Burn	D & G	NT0811	55°23·3'	3°26·7'W	W	78
Lochan Cairn Dierg	Arg & Bt	NN0749	56°35·9'	5°8·2'W	W	50
Lochan Caitidhriridh	Highld	NH0568	57°39·8'	5°15·7'W	W	19
Lochan Caol Fada	Pth & Kin	NN4156	56°40·4'	4°35·2'W	W	42,51
Lochan Caorainn	Arg & Bt	NN0850	56°36·4'	5°7·2'W	W	41
Lochan Caoruinn	Highld	NC1328	58°12·3'	5°10·5'W	W	15
Lochan Capuill Bhàin	Arg & Bt	NM9910	56°14·7'	5°14·2'W	W	55
Lochan Carn a' Chuilinn	Highld	NH4303	57°5·7'	4°35·0'W	W	34
Lochan Carn na Feòla	Highld	NG9261	57°35·7'	5°28·4'W	W	19
Lochan Ceann Caol Glas Bheinn	Highld	NN1196	57°1·2'	5°6·4'W	W	34
Lochan Chailein	Stir	NN4030	56°26·4'	4°35·3'W	W	51
Lochan Chairn Léith	Highld	ND0544	58°22·7'	3°37·0'W	W	11,12
Lochan Chaorann	Arg & Bt	NR7368	55°51·4'	5°37·2'W	W	62
Lochan Charn nan Caorach	Highld	NG9108	57°7·2'	5°26·7'W	W	33
Lochan Chìpeagal Bheag	N Eil	NB2405	57°57·2'	6°39·5'W	W	13,14
Lochan Chrois Bheinn	Highld	NM5854	56°37·2'	5°56·2'W	W	47
Lochan Chuilceachan	Arg & Bt	NR9888	56°2·8'	5°14·2'W	W	55
Lochan Chuir	Pth & Kin	NN9156	56°41·2'	3°46·3'W	W	52
Lochan Clach a' Chorrach	Highld	NM5065	56°42·8'	6°4·7'W	W	47
Lochan Clach na Boiteig	Highld	NM5867	56°44·2'	5°57·0'W	W	47
Lochan Cleit an Eòin	N Eil	NB0518	58°3·4'	6°59·6'W	W	13,14
Lochan Cnapach	Highld	NH0078	57°45·1'	5°21·2'W	W	19
Lochan Coir' a' Ghobhainn	Highld	NG4118	57°11·0'	6°16·7'W	W	32
Lochan Coire an Iubhair	Highld	NM9063	56°42·9'	5°25·4'W	W	40
Lochan Coire an Lochain	Highld	NN3674	56°50·0'	4°40·8'W	W	41
Lochan Coire Chaolais Bhig	Highld	NG9004	57°5·0'	5°27·5'W	W	33
Lochan Coire Choille-rais	Highld	NN4386	56°56·6'	4°34·4'W	W	34,42
Lochan Coire Cholle-rais	Highld	NN4386	56°56·6'	4°34·4'W	W	34,42
Lochan Coire Ghàidheil	Highld	NH0922	57°15·2'	5°9·5'W	W	25,33
Lochan Coire Laogh	Arg & Bt	NN0749	56°35·9'	5°8·2'W	W	50
Lochan Coire Mhàim	Highld	NM5866	56°43·6'	5°56·9'W	W	47
Lochan Coire na Beinne	Highld	ND1439	58°20·1'	3°27·7'W	W	11,12,17
Lochan Coire na Mèinne	Pth & Kin	NN3952	56°38·2'	4°37·1'W	W	41
Lochan Coire na Mòine	Highld	NM6461	56°41·1'	5°50·8'W	W	40
Lochan Coire na Poite	Highld	NG8145	57°26·8'	5°38·5'W	W	24
Lochan Coire Thoraidh	Arg & Bt	NN2131	56°26·5'	4°53·8'W	W	50
Lochan Coir'Orain	Arg & Bt	NN2537	56°29·8'	4°50·1'W	W	50
Lochan Còrr Chnoic	Arg & Bt	NM9026	56°23·0'	5°23·7'W	W	49
Lochan Coulbackie	Highld	NC8761	58°31·6'	3°55·9'W	W	10
Lochan Cràgach	N Eil	NB0521	58°5·1'	6°59·8'W	W	13,14
Lochan Creag a' Mhadaidh	Pth & Kin	NN7045	56°35·0'	4°6·5'W	W	51,52
Lochan Creag nan Caorann	Stir	NN3021	56°21·3'	4°44·6'W	W	50,56
Lochan Creag nan Con	Highld	NM5667	56°44·1'	5°58·9'W	W	47
Lochan Creige Ruaidhe	Arg & Bt	NM9825	56°22·7'	5°15·8'W	W	49
Lochan Cròc nan Làir	Highld	ND0345	58°23·2'	3°39·1'W	W	11,12
Lochan Cruachan	Stir	NN3507	56°13·9'	4°39·3'W	W	56
Lochan Cruaiche Bige	Arg & Bt	NN0414	56°16·9'	5°9·5'W	W	50,56
Lochan Cruinn	Highld	NG6821	57°13·5'	5°50·1'W	W	32
Lochan Cuilce	Highld	NC1225	58°10·7'	5°11·4'W	W	15
Lochan Cùl a' Mhoil	Highld	NG8424	57°15·6'	5°34·4'W	W	33
Lochan Cùl na Creige	Highld	NC2853	58°26·2'	4°56·3'W	W	9
Loch an Dabhaich	Highld	NN7296	57°2·5'	4°6·1'W	W	35
Lochan da Chean-fhinn	Arg & Bt	NR8570	55°52·8'	5°25·8'W	W	62
Loch an Daimh	Arg & Bt	NM8610	56°14·3'	5°26·8'W	W	55
Loch an Daimh	Highld	NH2794	57°54·4'	4°54·7'W	W	20
Loch an Daimh	N Eil	NB2727	58°9·1'	6°37·9'W	W	8,13
Loch an Daimh	N Eil	NB3918	58°4·7'	6°25·2'W	W	14
Loch an Daimh	N Eil	NF8867	57°35·4'	7°12·8'W	W	18
Loch an Daimh	Pth & Kin	NN4846	56°35·1'	4°28·1'W	W	51
Loch an Daimh Ghlais	Highld	NH3152	57°31·9'	4°48·9'W	W	26
Loch an Daimh Mór	Highld	NC1543	58°20·5'	5°9·2'W	W	9
Lochan Dalach	Arg & Bt	NM9110	56°14·5'	5°21·9'W	W	55
Lochan Daraich	Highld	NC1231	58°13·9'	5°11·6'W	W	15
Lochan Dearg	Arg & Bt	NM4850	56°34·7'	6°5·8'W	W	47
Lochan Dearg	Highld	NB9912	58°3·4'	5°23·9'W	W	15
Lochan Dearg	Highld	NC0907	58°0·9'	5°13·5'W	W	15
Lochan Dearg	Highld	NC1509	58°2·2'	5°7·5'W	W	15
Lochan Dearg	Highld	NG9252	57°30·9'	5°27·9'W	W	25
Lochan Dearg	Highld	NH1496	57°55·1'	5°7·9'W	W	20
Lochan Dearg a' Chùil Mhóir	Highld	NC1510	58°2·7'	5°7·6'W	W	15
Lochan Dearg Beag	Highld	NG9452	57°30·9'	5°25·9'W	W	25
Lochan Dearg Uillt	Highld	NH4103	57°5·7'	4°37·0'W	W	34
Loch an Dherue	Highld	NC5348	58°24·0'	4°30·4'W	W	10
Lochan Dhonnachaidh	Highld	NM7060	56°40·8'	5°44·8'W	W	40
Loch an Dhubhaich	Arg & Bt	NR3972	55°52·5'	6°9·9'W	W	60,61
Lochan Diota	Highld	NN2697	57°2·1'	4°51·6'W	W	34
Lochan Dobhrain	Arg & Bt	NR8079	55°57·5'	5°31·0'W	W	62
Lochan Doilead	Highld	NM6794	56°59·0'	5°49·6'W	W	40
Lochan Doire a'Bhraghaid	Highld	NM9258	56°40·3'	5°23·2'W	W	49
Lochan Doire an Dollain	Arg & Bt	NN3950	56°37·1'	4°37·0'W	W	41
Lochan Doire Cadha	Highld	NH3102	57°4·9'	4°46·9'W	W	34
Loch an Doire Crionaich	Highld	NG9377	57°44·4'	5°28·2'W	W	19
Loch an Doire Dhuibh	Highld	NC1310	58°2·7'	5°9·6'W	W	15
Loch an Doire Ghairbh	Highld	NG8878	57°44·8'	5°33·3'W	W	19
Lochan Doire Meall an Eilein	Highld	NH0100	57°3·1'	5°16·4'W	W	33
Lochan Domhain	Highld	NG9151	57°30·3'	5°28·9'W	W	25
Lochan Domhuill	Highld	NM7076	56°49·4'	5°45·7'W	W	40
Loch an Dornabac	Highld	NM3597	56°59·6'	6°21·3'W	W	39
Loch an Dràic	Highld	NC0513	58°4·1'	5°17·9'W	W	15
Loch an Draing	Highld	NG7790	57°50·9'	5°45·0'W	W	19
Loch an Dreaghain	Arg & Bt	NM3322	56°19·2'	6°18·7'W	W	48
Loch an Droighinn	Arg & Bt	NN0224	56°22·3'	5°11·9'W	W	50
Loch an Droighinn	Highld	NG9536	57°22·4'	5°24·1'W	W	25
Loch an Droma	Highld	NH0528	57°18·3'	5°13·8'W	W	25,33
Loch an Droma	Highld	NH4257	57°34·8'	4°38·1'W	W	26
Loch an Droma	N Eil	NF8261	57°31·9'	7°18·4'W	W	22
Loch an Droma Bhàin	Highld	NG6620	57°12·9'	5°52·1'W	W	32
Lochan Druim an Aionidh	Arg & Bt	NM4128	56°22·7'	6°11·3'W	W	48
Lochan Druim an Dùin	Highld	NC6961	58°31·3'	4°14·5'W	W	10
Lochan Druim an Iubhair	Highld	NM9361	56°42·0'	5°22·4'W	W	40
Lochan Druim an Rathaid	Arg & Bt	NM8203	56°10·4'	5°30·3'W	W	55
Lochan Druim na Claise	Highld	NM4264	56°42·0'	6°12·4'W	W	47
Lochan Druim na Fearna	Highld	NG8270	57°40·3'	5°38·9'W	W	19
Loch an Drunga	N Eil	NB2624	58°7·5'	6°38·8'W	W	13,14
Lochan Dubh	Arg & Bt	NM8622	56°20·8'	5°27·3'W	W	49
Lochan Dubh	Arg & Bt	NM8632	56°26·2'	5°27·8'W	W	49
Lochan Dubh	Arg & Bt	NM9039	56°30·0'	5°24·3'W	W	49
Lochan Dubh	Arg & Bt	NM9112	56°15·5'	5°22·0'W	W	55
Lochan Dubh	Arg & Bt	NM9208	56°13·4'	5°20·9'W	W	55
Lochan Dubh	Arg & Bt	NM9313	56°16·1'	5°20·1'W	W	55

Lochan Dubh	Arg & Bt	NN0008	56°13·6′	5°13·1′W	W	55
Lochan Dubh	Arg & Bt	NN0304	56°11·5′	5°10·1′W	W	55
Lochan Dubh	Arg & Bt	NN0409	56°14·2′	5°9·3′W	W	56
Lochan Dubh	Arg & Bt	NN0616	56°18·1′	5°7·7′W	W	50,56
Lochan Dubh	Arg & Bt	NR4158	55°45·0′	6°7·2′W	W	60
Lochan Dubh	Arg & Bt	NR7366	55°50·3′	5°37·1′W	W	62
Lochan Dubh	Arg & Bt	NR9393	56°5·4′	5°19·2′W	W	55
Lochan Dubh	Highld	NC3538	58°18·2′	4°48·5′W	W	15
Lochan Dubh	Highld	NC6259	58°30·1′	4°21·6′W	W	10
Lochan Dubh	Highld	NC6459	58°30·1′	4°19·6′W	W	10
Lochan Dubh	Highld	NC6659	58°30·2′	4°17·5′W	W	10
Lochan Dubh	Highld	NC7132	58°15·7′	4°11·4′W	W	16
Lochan Dubh	Highld	NC7412	58°5·0′	4°7·7′W	W	16
Lochan Dubh	Highld	NC8064	58°33·1′	4°3·3′W	W	10
Lochan Dubh	Highld	NC8652	58°26·8′	3°56·7′W	W	10
Lochan Dubh	Highld	NC8837	58°18·7′	3°54·2′W	W	17
Lochan Dubh	Highld	NC9552	58°26·9′	3°47·5′W	W	11
Lochan Dubh	Highld	ND0644	58°22·7′	3°36·0′W	W	11,12
Lochan Dubh	Highld	ND0946	58°23·8′	3°32·9′W	W	11,12
Lochan Dubh	Highld	NG6512	57°8·6′	5°52·6′W	W	32
Lochan Dubh	Highld	NG7052	57°30·3′	5°49·9′W	W	24
Lochan Dubh	Highld	NG7763	57°36·4′	5°43·5′W	W	19,24
Lochan Dubh	Highld	NG7861	57°35·3′	5°42·4′W	W	19,24
Lochan Dubh	Highld	NG7958	57°33·7′	5°41·2′W	W	24
Lochan Dubh	Highld	NG8161	57°35·4′	5°39·4′W	W	19,24
Lochan Dubh	Highld	NG9586	57°49·3′	5°26·6′W	W	19
Lochan Dubh	Highld	NH3382	57°48·1′	4°48·1′W	W	20
Lochan Dubh	Highld	NH3632	57°21·2′	4°43·1′W	W	26
Lochan Dubh	Highld	NH4396	57°55·8′	4°38·6′W	W	20
Lochan Dubh	Highld	NH4933	57°22·0′	4°30·2′W	W	26
Lochan Dubh	Highld	NH6730	57°20·7′	4°12·1′W	W	26
Lochan Dubh	Highld	NH7378	57°46·7′	4°7·7′W	W	21
Lochan Dubh	Highld	NH8712	57°11·4′	3°51·7′W	W	35,36
Lochan Dubh	Highld	NH9216	57°13·6′	3°46·9′W	W	36
Lochan Dubh	Highld	NH9532	57°22·2′	3°44·3′W	W	27,36
Lochan Dubh	Highld	NM4195	56°58·7′	6°15·3′W	W	39
Lochan Dubh	Highld	NM4870	56°45·5′	6°6·9′W	W	39,47
Lochan Dubh	Highld	NM6067	56°44·2′	5°55·0′W	W	40
Lochan Dubh	Highld	NM7882	56°52·8′	5°38·2′W	W	40
Lochan Dubh	Highld	NM8057	56°39·4′	5°34·9′W	W	49
Lochan Dubh	Highld	NM8074	56°48·6′	5°35·8′W	W	40
Lochan Dubh	Highld	NM8971	56°47·2′	5°26·8′W	W	40
Lochan Dubh	Highld	NN0695	57°0·6′	5°11·2′W	W	33
Lochan Dubh	Highld	NN7195	57°1·9′	4°7·1′W	W	35
Lochan Dubh	N Eil	NB1523	58°6·5′	6°49·8′W	W	13,14
Lochan Dubh	N Eil	NB3750	58°21·8′	6°29·3′W	W	8
Lochan Dubh	N Eil	NB3813	58°2·0′	6°25·8′W	W	14
Lochan Dubh	Pth & Kin	NN7260	56°43·1′	4°5·0′W	W	42
Lochan Dubh	Stir	NN3414	56°17·6′	4°40·5′W	W	50,56
Lochan Dubha	Arg & Bt	NM9821	56°20·6′	5°15·7′W	W	49
Lochan Dubha	Highld	NB9714	58°4·4′	5°26·1′W	W	15
Lochan Dubha	Highld	NG4924	57°14·5′	6°9·2′W	W	32
Loch an Dubha	Highld	NG7445	57°26·6′	5°45·5′W	W	24
Lochan Dubha	Highld	NG8332	57°19·9′	5°35·9′W	W	24
Lochan Dubha	Highld	NG8337	57°22·6′	5°36·1′W	W	24
Lochan Dubha	Highld	NG9131	57°19·6′	5°27·8′W	W	25
Lochan Dubha	Highld	NG9440	57°24·5′	5°25·3′W	W	25
Lochan Dubha	Highld	NH8139	57°25·8′	3°58·5′W	W	27
Lochan Dubha Airigh Skelpick	Highld	NC7356	58°28·7′	4°10·2′W	W	10
Lochan Dubh a' Chadha	Highld	NH9606	57°8·2′	3°42·6′W	W	36
Lochan Dubh a' Chracairnie	Highld	ND0651	58°26·5′	3°36·1′W	W	11,12
Lochan Dubha Cùl a' Mhill	Highld	NG8953	57°31·3′	5°31·0′W	W	24
Loch an Dubhair	Highld	NH3920	57°14·8′	4°39·6′W	W	26
Lochan Dubh a' Phluic	Highld	NG9370	57°40·6′	5°27·8′W	W	19
Lochan Dubh Cadhafuaraich	Highld	NC6818	58°8·1′	4°14·0′W	W	16
Lochan Dubh Cùl an Lòin	Highld	ND0552	58°27·0′	3°37·2′W	W	11,12
Lochan Dubh Cùl na Beinne	Highld	NC9854	58°28·0′	3°44·4′W	W	11
Lochan Dubh Cùl na h-Amaite	Highld	NC7514	58°6·1′	4°6·8′W	W	16
Lochan Dubh Grundd nan Darachan	Pth & Kin	NN4753	56°38·9′	4°29·3′W	W	42,51
Loch an Dubh-Lochain	Highld	NG8200	57°2·6′	5°35·2′W	W	33
Lochan Dubh Mhuilinn	Arg & Bt	NN0110	56°14·7′	5°12·3′W	W	50,55
Lochan Dubh Mór	Highld	NH3467	57°40·0′	4°46·5′W	W	20
Lochan Dubh na Bèiste	Highld	NH2586	57°50·0′	4°56·4′W	W	20
Lochan Dubh na Caorach	Highld	NG7965	57°37·5′	5°41·6′W	W	19,24
Lochan Dubh na Cruaiche	Arg & Bt	NN0616	56°18·1′	5°7·7′W	W	50,56
Lochan Dubh na Féithe Caoile	Highld	NC9844	58°22·6′	3°44·2′W	W	11
Lochan Dubh nam Biast	Highld	NH2849	57°30·2′	4°51·8′W	W	25
Lochan Dubh nam Breac	Highld	NG6719	57°12·4′	5°51·0′W	W	32
Lochan Dubh nam Breac	Highld	NG9788	57°50·4′	5°24·7′W	W	19
Lochan Dubh nan Cailleach	Highld	NG8173	57°41·9′	5°40·0′W	W	19
Lochan Dubh nan Geodh	Highld	ND0547	58°24·3′	3°37·1′W	W	11,12
Lochan Dubh Torr an Tairbeirt	Highld	NM9378	56°51·1′	5°23·2′W	W	40
Lochan Dughaill	Arg & Bt	NR8080	55°58·0′	5°31·1′W	W	55
Loch an Duibhe	Highld	NH1387	57°50·3′	5°8·5′W	W	19
Loch an Dùin	Arg & Bt	NM2157	56°37·6′	6°32·5′W	W	46,47
Lochan Duin	Arg & Bt	NR8089	56°2·9′	5°31·5′W	W	55
Loch an Duin	N Eil	NB0201	57°54·2′	7°1·4′W	W	18
Loch an Dùin	N Eil	NB1840	58°15·8′	6°48·0′W	W	8,13
Loch an Dùin	N Eil	NB3954	58°24·1′	6°27·6′W	W	8
Loch an Dùin	N Eil	NB5130	58°11·6′	6°13·7′W	W	8
Loch an Dùin	N Eil	NB5535	58°14·4′	6°10·0′W	W	8
Loch an Dùin	N Eil	NF6903	57°0·2′	7°26·7′W	W	31
Loch an Duin	N Eil	NF7415	57°6·9′	7°22·7′W	W	31
Loch an Dùin	N Eil	NF8974	57°39·2′	7°12·4′W	W	18
Loch an Dùin	N Eil	NF9572	57°38·3′	7°6·2′W	W	18
Loch an Dùin	N Eil	NG0394	57°50·5′	6°59·8′W	W	18
Loch an Duin	N Eil	NG2296	57°52·3′	6°40·8′W	W	14
Loch an Dùin	Pth & Kin	NN7279	56°53·3′	4°5·6′W	W	42
Loch an Dùin	Pth & Kin	NN8855	56°40·7′	3°49·2′W	W	52
Lochan Dùin	Stir	NN3121	56°21·3′	4°43·7′W	W	50,56
Loch an Duine	Highld	ND0450	58°25·9′	3°38·2′W	X	11,12
Loch an Dùin Mhòir	N Eil	NF7741	57°21·0′	7°21·8′W	W	22
Lochan Duinte	Highld	NC7158	58°29·7′	4°12·3′W	W	10
Loch an Dùna	N Eil	NB2847	58°19·9′	6°38·3′W	W	8
Loch an Duna	N Eil	NB3926	58°9·0′	6°25·7′W	W	8
Loch an Dùnain	N Eil	NB1939	58°15·3′	6°46·9′W	W	8,13
Lochan Dùnan nan Nighean	Arg & Bt	NM4634	56°26·0′	6°6·8′W	W	47,48
Loch an Dùn-chàirn	Highld	NG8698	57°55·5′	5°36·4′W	W	19
Lochan Dùn Dubhaich	Arg & Bt	NM8118	56°18·5′	5°32·0′W	W	55
Lochan Ealach	Highld	NC8165	58°33·7′	4°2·3′W	W	10
Lochan Ealach	Highld	ND0460	58°31·3′	3°38·4′W	W	11,12
Lochan Ealach Beag	Highld	NC9649	58°25·3′	3°46·4′W	W	11
Lochan Ealach Mór	Highld	NC9648	58°24·7′	3°46·3′W	W	11
Lochan Eanaiche	Highld	NM8992	56°58·5′	5°27·9′W	W	33,40
Loch an Eang	Highld	NH2423	57°16·1′	4°54·7′W	W	25
Loch an Earbaill	N Eil	NB2126	58°8·4′	6°44·0′W	W	8,13
Loch an Easa Ghil	N Eil	NB1925	58°7·7′	6°45·9′W	W	13,14
Loch an Easain	Highld	NC0629	58°12·7′	5°17·7′W	W	15
Loch an Easain	Highld	NN2549	56°36·3′	4°50·6′W	W	50
Loch an Easain Uaine	Highld	NC3246	58°22·5′	4°51·9′W	W	9
Loch an Eas Ghairbh	Highld	NC2652	58°25·6′	4°58·3′W	W	9
Loch an Eich	N Eil	NB2602	57°55·7′	6°37·2′W	W	14
Loch an Eich Bhàin	Highld	NH4258	57°35·3′	4°38·1′W	W	26
Loch an Eich Duibh	Highld	NH0285	57°48·9′	5°19·5′W	W	19
Loch an Eich Uidhir	Highld	NC0829	58°12·7′	5°15·6′W	W	15
Loch an Eich-uisge	Highld	NG8336	57°22·0′	5°36·1′W	W	24
Loch an Eilean	Highld	NG6416	57°10·7′	5°53·8′W	W	32
Loch an Eilean	Highld	NH2495	57°54·8′	4°57·8′W	W	20
Loch an Eilean	N Eil	NF7416	57°7·4′	7°22·8′W	W	31
Loch an Eilean	N Eil	NF7475	57°39·1′	7°27·5′W	W	18
Loch an Eilean Bhig	N Eil	NB3508	57°59·2′	6°28·5′W	W	14
Loch an Eilean Liath	N Eil	NB3323	58°7·2′	6°31·6′W	W	13,14
Loch an Eilein	Arg & Bt	NL9843	56°29·2′	6°53·9′W	W	46
Loch an Eilein	Arg & Bt	NM6229	56°23·9′	5°51·0′W	W	49
Loch an Eilein	Arg & Bt	NR7980	55°58·0′	5°32·0′W	W	55
Loch an Eilein	Highld	NC7550	58°25·5′	4°7·9′W	W	10
Loch an Eilein	Highld	NG6318	57°11·8′	5°54·9′W	W	32
Loch an Eilein	Highld	NG7243	57°25·5′	5°47·4′W	W	24
Loch an Eilein	Highld	NG9083	57°47·5′	5°31·5′W	W	19
Loch an Eilein	Highld	NG9280	57°46·0′	5°29·4′W	W	19
Loch an Eilein	Highld	NH1487	57°50·3′	5°7·5′W	W	20
Loch an Eilein	Highld	NH2370	57°41·4′	4°57·7′W	W	20
Loch an Eilein	Highld	NH3058	57°35·1′	4°50·2′W	W	26
Loch an Eilein	Highld	NH8907	57°8·7′	3°49·6′W	W	35,36
Loch an Eilein	Highld	NH9415	57°13·1′	3°44·9′W	W	36
Loch an Eilein	N Eil	NB1625	58°7·6′	6°49·0′W	W	13,14
Loch an Eilein	N Eil	NB3213	58°1·8′	6°31·9′W	W	13,14
Loch an Eilein	N Eil	NB4443	58°18·3′	6°21·7′W	W	8
Loch an Eilein	N Eil	NF7423	57°11·2′	7°23·3′W	W	22
Loch an Eilein	N Eil	NF7637	57°18·8′	7°22·5′W	W	22
Loch an Eilein	N Eil	NF8237	57°19·0′	7°16·5′W	W	22
Loch an Eilein Beag	Arg & Bt	NR7953	55°43·5′	5°30·7′W	W	62
Loch an Eilein Choinnich	N Eil	NB1127	58°8·5′	6°54·2′W	W	13
Loch an Eilein Duibh	Arg & Bt	NN0212	56°15·8′	5°11·4′W	W	50,55
Loch an Eilein Duibh	N Eil	NB3614	58°2·5′	6°27·9′W	W	14
Loch an Eilein Mór	Arg & Bt	NR8053	55°43·5′	5°29·8′W	W	62
Loch an Eilich	Highld	NG9991	57°52·1′	5°22·9′W	W	19
Loch an Eiligh	Highld	NG9283	57°47·6′	5°29·5′W	W	19
Loch an Eion	Highld	NG9251	57°30·4′	5°27·9′W	W	25
Loch an Eircill	Highld	NC3027	58°12·2′	4°53·1′W	W	15
Loch an Eisg-brachaidh	Highld	NC0717	58°6·3′	5°16·1′W	W	15
Lochan Eisge Mhóir	Arg & Bt	NN0110	56°14·7′	5°12·3′W	W	50,55
Lochan Eligar	N Eil	NF8222	57°11·0′	7°15·4′W	W	31
Loch an Ellen	Arg & Bt	NM6229	56°23·9′	5°51·0′W	W	49
Loch an Eòin	Highld	NC7014	58°6·0′	4°11·9′W	W	16
Lochan Eòin	Pth & Kin	NN4455	56°39·9′	4°32·3′W	W	42,51
Lochan Erallich	Arg & Bt	NN0310	56°14·8′	5°10·3′W	W	50,55
Lochan Eun	Arg & Bt	NR7468	55°51·4′	5°36·2′W	W	62
Lochan Fada	Highld	NC0509	58°1·9′	5°17·7′W	W	15
Lochan Fada	Highld	NC0817	58°6·3′	5°15·0′W	W	15
Lochan Fada	Highld	NC1130	58°13·4′	5°12·6′W	W	15
Lochan Fada	Highld	NC1808	58°1·7′	5°4·5′W	W	15
Lochan Fada	Highld	NC2016	58°6·1′	5°2·8′W	W	15
Lochan Fada	Highld	NG6513	57°9·1′	5°52·7′W	W	32
Lochan Fada	Highld	NG7355	57°32·0′	5°47·1′W	W	24
Lochan Fada	Highld	NG9262	57°36·3′	5°28·4′W	W	19
Lochan Fada	Highld	NH0271	57°41·4′	5°18·8′W	W	19
Lochan Fada	Highld	NH1079	57°45·9′	5°11·2′W	W	19
Lochan Fada	Highld	NH4243	57°27·3′	4°37·5′W	W	26
Lochan Fada	Highld	NM7088	56°55·8′	5°46·4′W	W	40
Lochan Fearna	Highld	NC0830	58°13·3′	5°15·7′W	W	15
Lochan Fearna	Highld	NC1224	58°10·2′	5°11·3′W	W	15
Lochan Fearna	Highld	NC1231	58°13·9′	5°11·6′W	W	15
Lochan Fearphorm	Arg & Bt	NM8303	56°10·5′	5°29·3′W	W	55
Lochan Féith a' Mhadaidh	Highld	NM7487	56°55·4′	5°42·4′W	W	40
Lochan Féith an Leòthaid	Highld	NC2930	58°13·8′	4°54·3′W	W	15
Lochan Feith Easain	Highld	NM8179	56°51·3′	5°35·1′W	W	40
Lochan Féith Mhic'-ilean	Highld	NH0177	57°44·6′	5°20·1′W	W	19
Lochan Féith nan Laogh	Highld	NM8367	56°44·9′	5°32·5′W	W	40
Lochan Fenella	Stir	NN3426	56°24·1′	4°40·9′W	W	50
Lochan Feòir	Highld	NC2225	58°10·9′	5°1·2′W	W	15
Lochan Feoir	Highld	NG9088	57°50·2′	5°31·8′W	W	19
Lochan Feur	Highld	NC4349	58°24·3′	4°40·7′W	W	9
Lochan Feurach	Stir	NN5928	56°25·6′	4°16·7′W	W	51
Loch an Fhada Bhig	N Eil	NB2526	58°8·5′	6°39·9′W	W	8,13
Loch an Fhaing	N Eil	NF8457	57°29·8′	7°16·1′W	W	22
Loch an Fhaing Bhuidhe	N Eil	NF8161	57°31·9′	7°19·4′W	W	22
Loch an Fhamhair	Highld	NG9687	57°49·8′	5°25·7′W	W	19
Loch an Fhearainn Duibh	Highld	NM7182	56°52·6′	5°45·0′W	W	40
Loch an Fheidh	N Eil	NF8548	57°25·1′	7°14·4′W	W	22
Lochan Fhéith Dhùinn	Highld	NM6971	56°46·7′	5°46·4′W	W	40
Loch an Fheòir	Highld	NC4923	58°10·5′	4°33·6′W	W	16
Loch an Fheòir	Highld	NC5025	58°11·6′	4°32·6′W	W	16
Loch an Fheòir	Highld	NC8456	58°28·9′	3°58·9′W	W	10
Loch an Fheòir	Highld	NG7343	57°25·5′	5°46·4′W	W	24
Loch an Fheòir	Highld	NG8693	57°52·8′	5°36·1′W	W	19
Loch an Fheòir	Highld	NG9540	57°24·5′	5°24·3′W	W	25
Loch an Fheòir	Highld	NH3953	57°32·6′	4°40·9′W	W	26
Loch an Fheòir	N Eil	NB3218	58°4·5′	6°32·3′W	W	13,14
Loch an Fheoir	N Eil	NB4127	58°9·6′	6°23·7′W	W	8
Loch an Fheoir	N Eil	NB4446	58°19·9′	6°21·9′W	W	8
Loch an Fheòir	N Eil	NB4652	58°23·2′	6°20·3′W	W	8
Loch an Fheoir Bheag	N Eil	NB4241	58°17·2′	6°23·6′W	W	8
Loch an Fheòir Mhòir	N Eil	NB4142	58°17·7′	6°24·7′W	W	8
Loch an Fhiarlaid	Highld	NH0556	57°33·4′	5°15·1′W	W	25
Loch an Fhidhleir	Highld	NG7258	57°33·5′	5°48·2′W	W	24
Loch an Fhìona	Highld	NH1684	57°48·7′	5°5·4′W	W	20
Lochan Fhionnlaidh	Highld	NC1209	58°2·1′	5°10·6′W	W	15
Lochan Fhionnlaidh	Highld	NC1910	58°2·8′	5°3·5′W	W	15
Loch an Fhir-bhallaich	Highld	NG4220	57°12·2′	6°15·9′W	W	32
Loch an Fhir Mhaoil	Arg & Bt	NR7489	56°2·7′	5°37·3′W	W	55
Loch an Fhir Mhaoil	N Eil	NB1826	58°8·2′	6°47·0′W	W	8,13
Loch an Fhir Mhór	Arg & Bt	NR2669	55°50·4′	6°22·2′W	W	60
Loch an Fhithich	Highld	NG8592	57°52·2′	5°37·0′W	W	19
Loch an Fhorsa	N Eil	NB1123	58°6·4′	6°53·9′W	W	13,14
Loch an Fhraoich	Arg & Bt	NR7447	55°40·1′	5°35·2′W	W	62
Loch an Fhraoich	N Eil	NB2336	58°13·8′	6°42·7′W	W	8,13
Loch an Fhraoich	N Eil	NB2839	58°15·6′	6°37·8′W	W	8,13
Loch an Fhraoich-choire	Highld	NH0525	57°16·7′	5°13·6′W	W	25,33
Loch an Fhreiceadain	Highld	NC5116	58°6·7′	4°31·3′W	W	16
Loch an Fhridein	Highld	NG1939	57°21·6′	6°39·9′W	W	23
Loch an Fhuarain	Highld	NC5827	58°12·8′	4°24·5′W	W	16
Loch an Fhuar-thuill Mhóir	Highld	NH2344	57°27·4′	4°56·6′W	W	25
Loch an Fhuar Thuill Mhór	Highld	NH2170	57°41·3′	4°59·7′W	W	20
Loch an Fhuath	Highld	NC2035	58°16·3′	5°3·7′W	W	15
Lochan Fhùdair	Highld	NN2095	57°0·9′	4°57·4′W	W	34
Lochan Fhurain Mhóir	Highld	NB9812	58°3·3′	5°24·9′W	W	15
Lochan Fiarach	Stir	NN3426	56°24·1′	4°40·9′W	W	50
Lochan Fraoich	Arg & Bt	NR8155	55°44·6′	5°28·9′W	W	62
Lochan Fraoich	Highld	NH1382	57°47·6′	5°8·3′W	W	19
Lochan Fuar	Highld	NG7970	57°40·2′	5°41·9′W	W	19
Lochan Fuar	Highld	NG9435	57°21·8′	5°25·1′W	W	25
Lochan Fuara	Highld	NG9738	57°23·5′	5°22·2′W	W	25
Loch an Gaineamh	Highld	NG9179	57°45·4′	5°30·3′W	W	19
Lochan Gaineamhach	Arg & Bt	NM9904	56°11·4′	5°13·9′W	W	55
Lochan Gaineamhach	Highld	NH0945	57°27·6′	5°10·6′W	W	25
Lochan Gaineamhach	Highld	NN3053	56°38·5′	4°45·9′W	W	41
Lochan Gaineamhaich	Highld	NH0187	57°50·0′	5°20·6′W	W	19
Lochan Gainmheich	Highld	NC1311	58°3·2′	5°9·7′W	W	15
Lochan Geal	Highld	NH8505	57°7·6′	3°53·5′W	W	35,36
Lochan Ghiubhais	Pth & Kin	NN4154	56°39·3′	4°35·2′W	W	42,51
Lochan Ghlas Laoigh	Arg & Bt	NS2189	56°3·9′	4°52·1′W	W	56
Lochan Giubhais	Highld	NG9787	57°49·9′	5°24·7′W	W	19
Lochan Gleann Astaile	Arg & Bt	NR4771	55°52·2′	6°2·2′W	W	60,61
Lochan Gleann Dubh Mhurchaidh	Arg & Bt	NM4920	56°18·6′	6°3·1′W	W	48
Lochan Gobhlach	Highld	NG7216	57°11·0′	5°45·9′W	W	33
Lochan Gobhlach	Highld	NG7638	57°22·9′	5°43·1′W	W	24
Lochan Gobhlach	Highld	NG9853	57°31·6′	5°22·0′W	W	25
Lochan Gobhlach	Highld	NH0837	57°23·2′	5°11·2′W	W	25
Lochan Gobhlach	N Eil	NF7821	57°10·3′	7°19·2′W	W	31
Lochan Gorma	Highld	NM6875	56°48·8′	5°47·6′W	W	40
Lochan gun Ghrunnd	Highld	NG6051	57°29·4′	5°59·8′W	W	24
Lochan Hakel	Highld	NC5652	58°26·2′	4°27·5′W	W	10
Lochan Havurn	Highld	NC3954	58°26·9′	4°45·1′W	W	9
Lochanhead	D & G	NT0200	55°17·3′	3°32·2′W	X	78
Lochanhead	D & G	NX9171	55°1·5′	3°41·9′W	X	84
Lochanhead Ho	D & G	NX9071	55°1·5′	3°42·8′W	X	84
Lochanhully	Highld	NH9123	57°17·3′	3°48·0′W	T	36
Lochan Iain	Highld	NH4800	57°4·2′	4°30·0′W	W	34
Lochan Iain Bhuidhe	Highld	NC5225	58°11·6′	4°30·6′W	W	16
Lochan Iain Bhuidhe	Highld	NC6801	57°59·0′	4°13·5′W	W	16
Lochan Iamhair	Highld	NC2253	58°26·0′	5°2·5′W	W	9
Loch an Iar	N Eil	NB2617	58°3·7′	6°38·3′W	W	13,14
Loch an Iasaich	Highld	NG9535	57°21·8′	5°24·1′W	W	25
Loch an Iasgaich	Highld	NG6714	57°9·7′	5°50·7′W	W	32
Loch an Iasgaich	N Eil	NF8262	57°32·4′	7°18·4′W	W	22
Loch an Iasgair	Highld	NC1935	58°16·3′	5°4·7′W	W	15
Loch an Iasgair	Highld	NG8083	57°47·2′	5°41·6′W	W	19
Loch an Iasgair	Highld	NG9284	57°48·1′	5°29·6′W	W	19
Loch an Iasgair	Highld	NM7784	56°53·9′	5°39·3′W	W	40
Loch an Iasgair	N Eil	NF7430	57°14·9′	7°23·9′W	W	22
Lochan Iliter	Arg & Bt	NM7410	56°14·0′	5°38·3′W	W	55
Loch an Ime	Highld	NG6710	57°7·6′	5°50·5′W	W	32
Loch an Ime	Highld	NG7121	57°13·6′	5°47·2′W	W	33
Lochan Imheir	Highld	NC4502	57°59·1′	4°36·8′W	W	16
Loch an Inneil	Highld	NC2237	58°17·4′	5°1·7′W	W	15
Lochan Innis Eanruig	Highld	NM7393	56°58·6′	5°43·7′W	W	33,40
Loch an Iònaire	N Eil	NF7843	57°22·1′	7°20·9′W	W	22
Lochan Kilmallie	Highld	NN0979	56°52·0′	5°7·6′W	W	41
Loch an Lagain	Highld	NH6595	57°55·7′	4°16·3′W	W	21
Loch an Lagain Aintheach	Highld	NG9202	57°4·0′	5°25·4′W	W	33
Loch Anlaimh	Arg & Bt	NM1855	56°36·4′	6°35·3′W	W	46
Lochan Lairig Cheile	Stir	NN5527	56°25·0′	4°20·6′W	W	51
Lochan Lairig Laoigh	Pth & Kin	NN8254	56°40·0′	3°55·1′W	W	52
Lochan Laoigh	Arg & Bt	NR7764	55°49·3′	5°33·2′W	W	62
Loch an Laoigh	Highld	NC1810	58°2·8′	5°4·5′W	W	15
Loch an Laoigh	Highld	NH0241	57°25·2′	5°17·4′W	W	25
Loch an Laoigh	N Eil	NB2333	58°12·2′	6°42·4′W	W	8,13
Loch an Laoigh	N Eil	NB2635	58°13·4′	6°39·5′W	W	8,13
Lochan Laraiche	Arg & Bt	NR7885	56°0·7′	5°33·2′W	W	55
Lochanlea	D & G	NX8783	55°8·0′	3°45·9′W	X	78
Lochan Leacach	Highld	NC0509	58°1·9′	5°17·7′W	W	15
Lochan Leacach	Highld	NC6857	58°29·1′	4°15·4′W	W	10
Lochan Leac an Iubhair	Highld	NM9972	56°48·0′	5°17·1′W	W	40
Lochan Learg nan Lunn	Stir	NN4438	56°30·8′	4°31·7′W	W	51
Loch an Leathad Rainich	Highld	NC0627	58°11·6′	5°17·6′W	W	15
Loch an Leathaid Bhuain	Highld	NC2736	58°17·0′	4°56·6′W	W	15
Lochan Leathann	Highld	NG7442	57°25·0′	5°45·3′W	W	24
Loch an Leinibh	Arg & Bt	NR3469	55°50·7′	6°14·5′W	W	60,61
Loch an Leòid	Arg & Bt	NN0124	56°22·2′	5°12·9′W	W	50
Loch an Leòid	Highld	NG5916	57°10·6′	5°58·8′W	W	32
Loch an Leòid	Highld	NG6130	57°18·1′	5°57·6′W	W	24,32
Loch an Leòthaid	Highld	NC1422	58°9·1′	5°9·2′W	W	15
Loch an Leothaid	Highld	NC1729	58°13·0′	5°6·5′W	W	15
Loch an Leth-uillt	Highld	NG3621	57°12·5′	6°21·9′W	W	32
Lochan Leum an t-Sagairt	Highld	NM9189	56°57·0′	5°25·7′W	W	40
Lochan Liath	Arg & Bt	NR8165	55°50·0′	5°29·4′W	W	62
Lochan Liath Dhoireachan	Pth & Kin	NN4962	56°43·8′	4°27·6′W	W	42

Lochan Lice	Highld	NH4979	57°46·8′	4°31·9′W	W	20
Loch an Lobain	N Eil	NB4152	58°23·1′	6°25·4′W	W	8
Lochan Lodge	Pth & Kin	NN8936	56°30·4′	3°47·8′W	X	52
Loch an Lòin	Highld	NG8544	57°26·4′	5°34·5′W	W	24
Lochan Lòin nan Donnlaich	Pth & Kin	NN4661	56°43·2′	4°30·5′W	W	42
Lochan Loisgte	Highld	NM6264	56°42·7′	5°52·9′W	W	40
Lochan Lon a' Ghairt	Highld	NM7985	56°54·5′	5°37·3′W	W	40
Lochan Long	Arg & Bt	NN0209	56°14·2′	5°11·2′W	W	55
Loch an Losgainn Mór	Arg & Bt	NM8611	56°14·9′	5°26·8′W	W	55
Lochan Luing	Arg & Bt	NR6948	55°40·5′	5°40·0′W	W	62
Lochan Lunadail	N Eil	NB0623	58°6·2′	6°59·0′W	W	13,14
Lochan Lunn Dà-Bhrà	Highld	NN0865	56°44·5′	5°7·9′W	W	41
Lochan Lus Dubha	Arg & Bt	NM9310	56°14·5′	5°20·0′W	W	55
Lochan Màm a' Chullaich	Highld	NM7343	56°31·7′	5°41·0′W	W	49
Lochan Màm-chuil	Highld	NH4311	57°10·0′	4°35·3′W	W	34
Lochan Màm na Guaille	Highld	NH5515	57°12·4′	4°23·6′W	W	35
Lochan Maoil Dhuinne	Stir	NS3697	56°8·5′	4°37·9′W	W	56
Lochan Maol an t-sornaich	Arg & Bt	NR5480	55°57·3′	5°56·0′W	W	61
Lochan Marbh	Highld	NH3828	57°19·1′	4°40·9′W	W	26
Lochan Mathair Eite	Highld	NN2854	56°39·0′	4°47·9′W	W	41
Lochan Meadhonach	N Eil	NB5353	58°24·0′	6°13·2′W	W	8
Lochan Meall a' Mhadaidh	Highld	NM7175	56°48·9′	5°44·7′W	W	40
Lochan Meallan Mhic Iamhair	Highld	NH0754	57°32·4′	5°13·0′W	W	25
Lochan Meall an Tiompain	Highld	NN2859	56°41·7′	4°48·1′W	W	41
Lochan Meall an t-Suidhe	Highld	NN1472	56°48·4′	5°2·3′W	W	41
Lochan Meall a' Phuill	Highld	NN3156	56°40·2′	4°45·0′W	W	41
Lochan Meall na Caillich	Highld	NG8743	57°25·9′	5°32·4′W	W	24
Lochan Meall na Cloiche	Stir	NN5928	56°25·6′	4°16·7′W	W	51
Lochan Meall na Curra	Highld	NM6960	56°40·7′	5°45·8′W	W	40
Lochan Meoigeach	Pth & Kin	NN4564	56°44·8′	4°31·6′W	W	42
Lochan Mhàim nan Carn	Stir	NN3907	56°14·0′	4°35·4′W	W	56
Lochan Mhàiri	Highld	NH3932	57°21·3′	4°40·1′W	W	26
Lochan Mhaoil na Meidhe	Pth & Kin	NN7029	56°26·4′	4°6·1′W	W	51,52
Lochan Mhic-a-phi	Arg & Bt	NR5380	55°57·2′	5°57·0′W	W	61
Lochan Mhic Chuaraig	Arg & Bt	NM8809	56°13·8′	5°24·8′W	W	55
Lochan Mhic Earoich	Arg & Bt	NM9411	56°15·1′	5°19·1′W	W	55
Lochan Mhic Gille Dhuibh	Highld	NM8567	56°45·0′	5°30·5′W	W	40
Lochan Mhic Leòid	Highld	NC1525	58°10·8′	5°8·3′W	W	15
Lochan Mhic Pheadair Ruaidh	Highld	NN2847	56°35·3′	4°47·6′W	W	50
Lochan Mór	Arg & Bt	NM3923	56°19·9′	6°12·9′W	W	48
Loch Anna	Highld	NG8729	57°18·4′	5°31·7′W	W	33
Lochan na Bà Glaise	Highld	NM7188	56°55·9′	5°45·4′W	W	40
Lochan na Bearta	Highld	NG9980	57°46·1′	5°22·3′W	W	19
Lochan na Beinne	Highld	NH1296	57°55·1′	5°10·0′W	W	19
Lochan na Beinne	Highld	NJ0008	57°9·4′	3°38·7′W	W	36
Lochan na Beinne	Pth & Kin	NO0348	56°37·1′	3°34·4′W	W	52,53
Lochan na Beinne Baine	Highld	NM9366	56°44·6′	5°22·7′W	W	40
Lochan na Beinne Bàine	Highld	NN0894	57°0·1′	5°9·2′W	W	33
Lochan na Beinne Brice	Highld	NH2192	57°53·2′	5°0·7′W	W	20
Lochan na Beinne Brice	Highld	NN2599	57°3·2′	4°52·7′W	W	34
Lochan na Beinne Buidhe	N Eil	NB4012	58°1·5′	6°23·7′W	W	14
Lochan na Beinn Fhadae	Highld	NG8623	57°15·1′	5°32·4′W	W	33
Lochan na Beithe	Arg & Bt	NM9135	56°27·9′	5°23·1′W	W	49
Lochan na Bi	Arg & Bt	NN3031	56°26·7′	4°45·0′W	W	50
Lochan na Bracha	Highld	NM6965	56°43·4′	5°46·1′W	W	40
Lochan na Bradhan	Highld	NH0882	57°47·5′	5°13·3′W	W	19
Lochan na Caillich	Highld	NM7074	56°48·3′	5°45·6′W	W	40
Lochan na Cailliche	Highld	NN4183	56°54·9′	4°36·3′W	W	34,42
Lochan na Cairill	Highld	NG9791	57°52·0′	5°24·9′W	W	19
Lochan na Caisil	Highld	NM6064	56°42·6′	5°54·8′W	W	40
Lochan na Canaich or Lochan nan Lorg	Highld	NM6855	56°38·0′	5°46·5′W	W	49
Lochan na Carnaich	Highld	NM9281	56°52·7′	5°24·4′W	W	40
Lochan na Càrr	Pth & Kin	NN7961	56°43·8′	3°58·2′W	W	42
Lochan na Carraige	Highld	NM5666	56°43·6′	5°58·9′W	W	47
Lochan na Cartach	N Eil	NF6902	56°59·7′	7°26·6′W	W	31
Lochan na Ceàrdaich	Highld	NC8354	58°27·8′	3°59·9′W	W	10
Lochan na Ceardaich	Highld	NM7568	56°45·2′	5°40·4′W	W	40
Lochan na Cille	Highld	NM6647	56°33·7′	5°48·1′W	W	49
Lochan na Circe	Arg & Bt	NM8028	56°23·8′	5°33·5′W	W	49
Lochan na Claise	Highld	NC1313	58°4·3′	5°9·8′W	W	15
Lochan na Claise Domhain	Highld	NC5665	58°33·2′	4°28·0′W	W	10
Lochan na Cloiche	Highld	NC2052	58°25·4′	5°4·5′W	W	9
Lochan na Cloiche Sgoilte	Highld	NM6975	56°48·8′	5°46·6′W	W	40
Lochan na Clòidheig	Arg & Bt	NM6824	56°21·3′	5°44·9′W	W	49
Lochan na Corragain Seilich	Highld	NM8283	56°53·5′	5°34·3′W	W	40
Lochan na Craim	Arg & Bt	NM9907	56°13·0′	5°14·1′W	W	55
Lochan na Cràlaig	Highld	NH0915	57°11·4′	5°9·2′W	W	33
Lochan na Crannaig	Highld	NM4665	56°42·7′	6°8·6′W	W	47
Lochan na Craoibhe	Highld	NH3323	57°16·3′	4°45·7′W	W	26
Lochan na Craoibhe	Highld	NM7087	56°55·3′	5°46·3′W	W	40
Lochan na Craoibhe	Highld	NM7275	56°48·9′	5°43·7′W	W	40
Lochan na Craoibhe	Highld	NM7886	56°55·0′	5°38·4′W	W	40
Lochan na Craoibhe	Highld	NM8795	57°0·1′	5°30·0′W	W	33,40
Lochan na Craoibhe	Highld	NN3359	56°41·8′	4°43·2′W	W	41
Lochan na Craoibhe-beithe	Highld	NH5423	57°16·7′	4°24·8′W	W	26,35
Lochan na Craoibhe-caoruinn	Arg & Bt	NM6322	56°20·1′	5°49·6′W	W	49
Lochan na Craoibhe-fearna	Highld	NH3732	57°21·2′	4°42·1′W	W	26
Lochan na Creige	Arg & Bt	NR7674	55°54·7′	5°34·6′W	W	62
Lochan na Creige	Highld	NM7571	56°46·8′	5°40·5′W	W	40
Lochan na Creige	Highld	NM7572	56°47·4′	5°40·6′W	W	40
Lochan na Creige Duibhe	Highld	NM6466	56°43·8′	5°51·0′W	W	40
Lochan na Creige Duibhe	Highld	NM7584	56°53·8′	5°41·2′W	W	40
Lochan na Creige Riabhaich	Highld	NC4137	58°17·8′	4°42·3′W	W	16
Lochan na Creige Ruaidhe	Pth & Kin	NN6729	56°26·3′	4°9·0′W	W	51
Lochan na Criche	Highld	NM9257	56°39·8′	5°23·2′W	W	49
Lochan na Croraig	Highld	NH2353	57°32·2′	4°57·0′W	W	25
Lochan na Cruadhach	Highld	NM9299	57°2·4′	5°25·2′W	W	33,40
Lochan na Cruaich	Highld	NN0271	56°47·6′	5°14·1′W	W	41
Lochan na Cruaiche	Arg & Bt	NN1421	56°20·9′	5°0·2′W	W	50,56
Lochan na Cruaiche	Highld	NM7176	56°49·4′	5°44·7′W	W	40
Lochan na Cuaig	Arg & Bt	NN0626	56°23·4′	5°8·1′W	W	50
Lochan na Cuidhe	Highld	NH2931	57°20·5′	4°50·0′W	W	25
Lochan na Cuilce	Highld	NC5753	58°26·8′	4°26·5′W	W	10
Lochan na Curaich	Arg & Bt	NR8696	56°6·8′	5°26·1′W	W	55
Lochan na Curr	Highld	NH6580	57°47·6′	4°15·8′W	W	21
Lochan na Curra	Highld	NN1099	57°2·8′	5°7·5′W	W	34
Lochan na Doire-uaine	Highld	NN5886	56°56·9′	4°19·6′W	W	42
Lochan na Dubh Leitir	Highld	NC1734	58°15·7′	5°6·7′W	W	15
Lochan na Dubh Leitir	Highld	NM6765	56°43·4′	5°48·0′W	W	40
Lochan na Faoileige	Highld	NC3244	58°21·4′	4°51·8′W	W	9
Lochan na Faolaig	Highld	NC6400	57°58·4′	4°17·5′W	W	16
Lochan na Feàrna	Highld	NC4550	58°24·9′	4°38·7′W	W	9
Lochan na Féithe	Highld	NN2257	56°40·5′	4°53·9′W	W	41
Lochan na Fola	Arg & Bt	NN0948	56°35·4′	5°6·2′W	W	50
Lochan na Freagairt	Highld	NC1844	58°21·1′	5°6·1′W	W	9
Lochan na Gaoithe	Highld	NC6600	57°58·4′	4°15·5′W	W	16
Lochan na Garbh-bheinne	Arg & Bt	NM8317	56°18·0′	5°30·0′W	W	55
Lochan na Gealaich	Arg & Bt	NN0423	56°21·8′	5°9·9′W	W	50
Lochan na Geàrr Leacainn	Highld	NN1896	57°1·4′	4°59·4′W	W	34
Lochan na Glace	Highld	NM6068	56°44·8′	5°55·1′W	W	40
Lochan na Glaic Gille	Highld	NG7670	57°40·1′	5°44·9′W	W	19
Lochan na Glamhaichd	Highld	NC2866	58°33·2′	4°56·9′W	W	9
Lochan na Glamhaichd	Highld	NC3459	58°29·5′	4°50·4′W	W	9
Lochan na Glas Bheinn	Highld	NN1498	57°2·4′	5°3·5′W	W	34
Lochan na Goirt	Arg & Bt	NM8405	56°11·6′	5°28·4′W	W	55
Lochan na Gruagaich	Highld	NM5565	56°43·0′	5°59·8′W	W	47
Lochan na Guailne Duibhe	Arg & Bt	NM5252	56°35·9′	6°2·0′W	W	47
Lochan na h-Achlaise	Highld	NN3148	56°35·9′	4°44·7′W	W	50
Lochan na h-Airigh	Arg & Bt	NM8218	56°18·5′	5°31·0′W	W	55
Lochan na h-Airigh Bige	Arg & Bt	NM9309	56°14·0′	5°19·9′W	W	55
Lochan na h-Airighe Riabhaich	Highld	NG7451	57°29·8′	5°45·8′W	W	24
Lochan na h-Aon Chraoibh	Pth & Kin	NN4863	56°44·3′	4°28·7′W	W	42
Lochan na h-Earba	Arg & Bt	NM4048	56°33·4′	6°13·4′W	W	47,48
Lochan na Hearba	Highld	NN4883	56°55·1′	4°29·4′W	W	34,42
Lochan na h-Iùraiche	Arg & Bt	NN1941	56°31·8′	4°56·1′W	W	50
Lochan na h-Iubhraich	Highld	NM8268	56°45·4′	5°33·5′W	W	40
Lochan na h-Uimheachd	Highld	NC6054	58°27·4′	4°23·5′W	W	10
Lochan na Lairige	Pth & Kin	NN5940	56°32·1′	4°17·1′W	W	51
Lochan na Leathain	Pth & Kin	NN8461	56°43·8′	3°53·3′W	W	43
Lochan na Leirg	Arg & Bt	NS0478	55°57·6′	5°8·0′W	W	63
Lochan na Leitreach	Arg & Bt	NM6324	56°21·2′	5°49·7′W	W	49
Lochan na Maoile	Highld	NN0149	56°35·7′	5°14·0′W	W	50
Lochan nam Ban Uaine	Arg & Bt	NM6035	56°27·0′	5°53·2′W	W	49
Lochan nam Béistean	Highld	NN1377	56°51·1′	5°3·5′W	W	41
Lochan nam Bò	Highld	NN8691	57°0·0′	3°52·2′W	W	35,43
Lochan nam Bò Riabhach	Highld	ND0332	58°16·2′	3°38·7′W	W	11,17
Lochan nam Breac	Highld	NC1740	58°18·9′	5°7·0′W	W	9
Lochan nam Breac	Highld	ND0047	58°24·3′	3°42·2′W	W	11,12
Lochan nam Breac	Highld	NG8178	57°44·6′	5°40·3′W	W	19
Lochan nam Breac	Highld	NH3866	57°39·6′	4°42·5′W	W	20
Lochan nam Breac	Highld	NM9199	57°2·3′	5°26·2′W	W	33,40
Lochan nam Breac	Pth & Kin	NN4253	56°38·8′	4°34·2′W	W	42,51
Lochan nam Breac Buidhe	Arg & Bt	NM9010	56°14·4′	5°22·9′W	W	55
Lochan nam Breac Buidhe	Highld	NC3368	58°34·3′	4°51·8′W	W	9
Lochan nam Breac Buidhe	Highld	NC5264	58°32·6′	4°32·1′W	W	10
Lochan nam Breac Odhar	Highld	NG7672	57°41·2′	5°45·0′W	W	19
Lochan nam Breac Peatair	N Eil	NF7836	57°18·3′	7°20·4′W	W	22
Lochan nam Breac Reamhar	Highld	NN2458	56°41·1′	4°52·0′W	W	41
Lochan nam Breac Reamhra	Arg & Bt	NM9426	56°23·1′	5°19·8′W	W	49
Lochan nam Burag	Highld	NC6561	58°31·2′	4°18·6′W	W	10
Lochan nam Faoileag	Highld	NH4203	57°5·7′	4°36·0′W	W	34
Lochan nam Faoileann	Highld	NM6365	56°43·3′	5°52·0′W	W	40
Lochan nam Faoileann	N Eil	NF7001	56°59·2′	7°25·6′W	W	31
Lochan nam Fiann	Highld	NM6164	56°42·7′	5°53·9′W	W	40
Lochan nam Meallan	Highld	NC1957	58°28·1′	5°5·7′W	W	9
Lochan nam Meur Liath	Highld	NC5159	58°29·9′	4°32·9′W	W	9
Lochan na Mòine	Pth & Kin	NN6361	56°43·5′	4°13·9′W	W	42
Lochan na Mòinteich	Highld	NN5380	56°53·5′	4°24·3′W	W	42
Lochan nan Allt Ruadh	N Eil	NB0723	58°6·2′	6°58·0′W	W	13,14
Lochan nan Arm	Stir	NN3328	56°25·1′	4°42·0′W	W	50
Lochan nan Atrabhat	N Eil	NB5355	58°25·1′	6°13·3′W	W	8
Lochan nan Caorach	Arg & Bt	NM6324	56°21·2′	5°49·7′W	W	49
Lochan nan Caorach	Arg & Bt	NM9517	56°18·3′	5°18·4′W	W	55
Lochan nan Caorach	Arg & Bt	NR5167	55°50·2′	5°58·2′W	W	61
Lochan nan Caorach	Highld	NM5963	56°42·1′	5°55·8′W	W	47
Lochan nan Caorach	Highld	NN3678	56°52·1′	4°41·0′W	W	41
Lochan nan Carn	Highld	NC6853	58°27·0′	4°15·2′W	W	10
Lochan nan Cat	Pth & Kin	NN4339	56°31·3′	4°32·7′W	W	51
Lochan nan Cat	Pth & Kin	NN4844	56°34·1′	4°28·0′W	W	51
Lochan nan Cat	Pth & Kin	NN6442	56°33·3′	4°12·3′W	W	51
Lochan nan Ceardach	Arg & Bt	NM7915	56°16·8′	5°33·8′W	W	55
Lochan nan Clach Geala	Highld	NC8452	58°26·7′	3°58·8′W	W	10
Lochan nan Clach Geala	Highld	NC9159	58°30·6′	3°51·8′W	W	10
Lochan nan Clach Geala	Highld	NC9349	58°25·2′	3°49·4′W	W	11
Lochan nan Cnamh	N Ayr	NR9141	55°37·3′	5°18·7′W	W	62,69
Lochan nan Cnamh	N Eil	NB4213	58°2·1′	6°21·8′W	W	14
Lochan nan Cnàmh	N Eil	NB4226	58°9·1′	6°22·6′W	W	8
Lochan nan Corp	Stir	NN5511	56°16·4′	4°20·1′W	W	57
Lochan nan Craobh	Highld	NM7748	56°34·5′	5°37·4′W	W	49
Lochan nan Criònach	Highld	NG9110	57°8·3′	5°26·8′W	W	33
Lochan nan Damh	Stir	NN5233	56°28·2′	4°23·7′W	W	51
Lochan nan Daoine	Arg & Bt	NM4443	56°30·8′	6°9·2′W	W	47,48
Lochan nan Dearcag	Highld	NM5567	56°44·1′	5°59·9′W	W	47
Lochan nan Doirb	Highld	NH0457	57°33·9′	5°16·2′W	W	25
Lochan nan Eun	Highld	NC9861	58°31·8′	3°44·6′W	W	11
Lochan nan Gabhar	Moray	NJ1403	57°6·9′	3°24·8′W	W	36
Lochan nan Gad	Highld	NC1833	58°15·2′	5°5·6′W	W	15
Lochan nan Geadas	Highld	NH9508	57°9·3′	3°43·7′W	W	36
Lochan nan Geadas	Stir	NN6029	56°26·2′	4°15·8′W	W	51
Lochan nan Gobhar	Highld	NC6858	58°29·7′	4°15·4′W	W	10
Lochan na Nigheadaireachd	Arg & Bt	NR2855	55°43·0′	6°19·4′W	W	60
Lochan na Nighinn	Highld	NM6766	56°43·9′	5°48·1′W	W	40
Lochan nan Lachan	N Eil	NF8746	57°24·1′	7°12·2′W	W	22
Lochan nan Leac	Highld	NH3686	57°50·3′	4°45·3′W	W	20
Lochan nan Leacann Dearga	Highld	NG8468	57°39·3′	5°36·8′W	W	19,24
Lochan nan Liath Bhreac	Highld	NC1226	58°11·2′	5°11·4′W	W	15
Lochan nan Lorg or Lochan na Canaich	Highld	NM6855	56°38·0′	5°46·5′W	W	49
Lochan nan Ni	Stir	NN5009	56°15·2′	4°24·8′W	W	57
Lochan nan Nighean	Highld	NH4514	57°11·7′	4°33·5′W	W	34
Lochan nan Nighean	Pth & Kin	NN8461	56°43·8′	3°53·3′W	W	43
Lochan nan Ràth	Arg & Bt	NM9235	56°27·9′	5°22·1′W	W	49
Lochan nan Reamh	Highld	NN7998	57°3·7′	3°59·3′W	W	35
Lochan nan Sac	Highld	NC2365	58°32·5′	5°2·0′W	W	9
Lochan nan Sgùd	Highld	NN0698	57°2·2′	5°11·4′W	W	33
Lochan nan Sioman	Highld	NM5766	56°43·6′	5°57·9′W	W	47
Lochan nan Sleubhaich	Highld	NM8779	56°51·5′	5°29·2′W	W	40
Lochan nan Slochd	Highld	NG7339	57°23·4′	5°46·2′W	W	24
Lochan nan Smugaidean	Highld	NC3622	58°9·7′	4°46·8′W	W	16
Lochan nan Stob	Highld	NM9271	56°47·3′	5°23·9′W	W	40
Lochan nan Tri-chriochan	Highld	NM7692	56°58·2′	5°40·7′W	W	33,40
Lochan nan Tri-chriochan	Highld	NM8192	56°58·3′	5°35·7′W	W	33,40
Lochan nan Uan	Highld	NM7593	56°58·7′	5°41·7′W	W	33,40
Lochan nan Uidhean Beaga	N Eil	NB3314	58°2·4′	6°31·0′W	W	13,14
Lochan na Saighe Glaise	Highld	ND0051	58°26·4′	3°42·3′W	W	11,12
Lochan na Sàile	Highld	NC1931	58°14·1′	5°4·5′W	W	15
Lochan na Sàile	Highld	NG7222	57°14·2′	5°46·2′W	W	33
Lochan na Saobhaidhe	Arg & Bt	NN0846	56°34·3′	5°7·1′W	W	50
Lochan na Saobhaidhe	Arg & Bt	NN1941	56°31·8′	4°56·1′W	W	50
Lochan na Seilg	Highld	NC5365	58°33·2′	4°31·1′W	W	10
Lochan na Sgàil	N Eil	NB0314	58°1·2′	7°1·3′W	W	13
Lochan na Sgine	Arg & Bt	NR9673	55°54·7′	5°15·4′W	W	62
Lochan na Stainge	Highld	NN3049	56°36·4′	4°45·7′W	W	50
Lochan na Stairne	Highld	NH4405	57°6·8′	4°34·1′W	W	34
Lochan na Teanga	Highld	NG7342	57°25·0′	5°46·3′W	W	24
Lochan na Teanga Riabhaich	Highld	NG4414	57°9·0′	6°13·5′W	W	32
Lochan na Tuaidh	Highld	NM5567	56°44·1′	5°59·9′W	W	47
Lochan Neimhe	Highld	NG9454	57°32·0′	5°26·0′W	W	25
Loch an Nid	Highld	NH0874	57°43·2′	5°13·0′W	W	19
Lochan Nigheadh	Highld	NC1814	58°4·9′	5°4·7′W	W	15
Lochan Nighean an t-Saoir	Highld	NM6164	56°42·7′	5°53·9′W	W	40
Lochan Nighean Dughaill	Highld	NM4585	56°53·4′	6°10·8′W	W	39
Loch an Nighe Leathaid	Highld	NC2944	58°21·3′	4°54·9′W	W	9
Loch an Nostarie	Highld	NM6995	56°59·6′	5°47·7′W	W	40
Loch an Obain	Highld	NC1640	58°18·9′	5°8·0′W	W	9
Loch an Ochdaimh	Highld	NH4799	57°57·5′	4°34·7′W	W	20
Lochan Odhar	Highld	NH8527	57°19·4′	3°54·1′W	W	35,36
Lochan Odhar	Highld	NH9503	57°6·6′	3°43·6′W	W	36
Lochan Odhar	Highld	NN7397	57°3·1′	4°5·2′W	W	35
Loch an Oir	Arg & Bt	NR4975	55°54·4′	6°0·5′W	W	60,61
Loch an Ois	N Eil	NB3240	58°16·3′	6°33·8′W	W	8,13
Loch an Ois	N Eil	NB3332	58°12·0′	6°32·2′W	W	8,13
Lochan Oisinneach	Pth & Kin	NO0355	56°40·9′	3°34·5′W	W	52,53
Lochan Oisinneach Mór	Pth & Kin	NO0354	56°40·3′	3°34·5′W	W	52,53
Loch an Ordain	Highld	NC0625	58°10·5′	5°17·5′W	W	15
Loch an Ordain	Highld	NC0924	58°10·1′	5°14·4′W	W	15
Loch an Ordain	Highld	NH5523	57°16·7′	4°23·9′W	W	26,35
Loch an Os	N Eil	NF7845	57°23·1′	7°21·1′W	W	22
Lochan Phail	Highld	NH3998	57°56·8′	4°42·7′W	W	20
Lochan Pollaig	Highld	NH3887	57°50·9′	4°43·3′W	W	20
Lochan Pollan Dhughaill	Highld	NC3148	58°23·5′	4°53·0′W	W	9
Lochan Poll an Dubhaidh	Highld	NM5364	56°42·4′	6°1·7′W	W	47
Lochan Prapa	Highld	NG8150	57°29·5′	5°38·8′W	W	24
Loch an Raoin	Arg & Bt	NR2764	55°47·8′	6°20·9′W	W	60
Lochan Raonuill	Arg & Bt	NN0735	56°28·3′	5°7·6′W	W	50
Lochan Rapach	Highld	NC1432	58°14·5′	5°9·7′W	W	15
Loch an Ràsail	Highld	NC4708	58°2·4′	4°35·0′W	W	16
Loch an Rathaid	Highld	NG5541	57°23·9′	6°4·2′W	W	24
Loch an Rathaid	N Eil	NB2215	58°2·5′	6°42·2′W	W	13,14
Loch an Reithe	N Eil	NB2002	57°55·4′	6°43·3′W	W	14
Lochan Reòidhte	Stir	NN5203	56°12·1′	4°22·7′W	W	57
Lochan Riabhach	Highld	NC5066	58°33·6′	4°34·2′W	W	9
Loch an Righ	Highld	NN5087	56°57·3′	4°27·5′W	W	42
Loch an Ròin	Highld	NC1954	58°26·5′	5°5·6′W	W	9
Lochan Ròmach	Arg & Bt	NN0315	56°17·5′	5°10·5′W	W	50,55
Lochan Ròpach	Highld	NM7493	56°58·6′	5°42·7′W	W	33,40
Loch an Rothaid	N Eil	NG1491	57°49·3′	6°48·5′W	W	14
Lochan Ruadh	Arg & Bt	NR8147	55°40·3′	5°28·5′W	W	62,69
Lochan Ruadh	Highld	NC0728	58°12·2′	5°16·6′W	W	15
Lochan Ruadh	Highld	NC6361	58°31·2′	4°20·7′W	W	10
Lochan Ruadh	Highld	NH0485	57°49·0′	5°17·5′W	W	19
Lochan Ruadh	Highld	NN6594	57°1·3′	4°13·0′W	W	35
Loch an Ruadhlaich	Highld	NC2012	58°3·9′	5°2·6′W	W	15
Loch an Ruathair	Highld	NC8636	58°18·1′	3°56·2′W	W	17
Loch an Rubha Dhuibh	Highld	NG4513	57°8·5′	6°12·5′W	W	32
Loch an Ruighein	Highld	NC1526	58°11·3′	5°8·3′W	W	15
Loch an Ruighein	Highld	NC1836	58°16·8′	5°5·8′W	W	15
Lochan Ruighe na Doire Macmhadagain	Pth & Kin	NN4660	56°42·6′	4°30·5′W	W	42
Lochan Ruighe nan Sligean	Pth & Kin	NN4054	56°39·3′	4°36·2′W	W	42,51
Lochan Ruigh Phail	Highld	NN3669	56°47·3′	4°40·6′W	W	41
Loch an Ruisg	N Eil	NB1805	57°57·0′	6°45·5′W	W	13,14
Lochans	Aberd	NJ4618	57°15·2′	2°53·2′W	X	37
Lochans	D & G	NX0656	54°51·9′	5°1·0′W	T	82
Lochan's Airde Beinn	Arg & Bt	NM4753	56°36·3′	6°6·9′W	W	47
Lochan Sàl	Highld	NC0715	58°5·2′	5°16·0′W	W	15
Loch an Salich	Moray	NJ1145	57°29·5′	3°28·6′W	W	28
Lochan Sanndabhat	N Eil	NB4347	58°20·4′	6°23·0′W	W	8
Lochan Scristan	Highld	NH4717	57°13·4′	4°31·6′W	W	34
Lochan Seogh	Highld	NH2818	57°13·5′	4°50·5′W	W	34
Loch an Sgàlain	Arg & Bt	NM3419	56°17·6′	6°17·5′W	W	48
Lochan Sgaothaichean	Highld	NC4844	58°21·8′	4°35·4′W	W	9
Lochan Sgaradh Gobhair	Pth & Kin	NN8857	56°41·7′	3°49·3′W	W	52
Loch an Sgath	N Eil	NB2421	58°5·8′	6°40·6′W	W	13,14
Lochan Sgeirach	Highld	NG7157	57°33·0′	5°49·2′W	W	24
Lochan Sgeirach	Highld	NG7343	57°25·5′	5°46·4′W	W	24
Lochan Sgeireach	Highld	NC0409	58°1·9′	5°18·7′W	W	15
Lochan Sgeireach	Highld	NC0429	58°12·6′	5°19·7′W	W	15
Lochan Sgeireach	Highld	NC0725	58°10·6′	5°16·4′W	W	15
Lochan Sgeireach	Highld	NC1643	58°20·5′	5°8·1′W	W	9
Lochan Sgeireach	Highld	NC2711	58°3·5′	4°55·5′W	W	15
Lochan Sgeireach	Highld	NC3056	58°27·8′	4°54·4′W	W	9

Lochan Sgeireach	Highld	NC3846	58°22·6′	4°45·7′W	W	9
Lochan Sgeireach	Highld	NC5544	58°21·9′	4°28·2′W	W	10
Lochan Sgeireach	Highld	NC6715	58°6·5′	4°15·0′W	W	16
Lochan Sgeireach	Highld	NC7543	58°21·7′	4°7·7′W	W	10
Lochan Sgeireach	Highld	NG7882	57°46·6′	5°43·6′W	W	19
Lochan Sgeireach	Highld	NG8063	57°36·5′	5°40·5′W	W	19,24
Lochan Sgeireach	Highld	NG8170	57°40·3′	5°39·9′W	W	19
Lochan Sgeireach	Highld	NG8281	57°46·2′	5°39·5′W	W	19
Lochan Sgeireach	Highld	NG8697	57°54·9′	5°36·3′W	W	19
Lochan Sgeireach	Highld	NG9034	57°21·2′	5°29·0′W	W	25
Lochan Sgeireach	Highld	NG9181	57°46·5′	5°30·4′W	W	19
Loch an Sgeireach	Highld	NH0569	57°40·4′	5°15·7′W	W	19
Lochan Sgeireach	Highld	NH0955	57°33·0′	5°11·1′W	W	25
Lochan Sgeireach	Highld	NH1397	57°55·7′	5°9·0′W	W	19
Lochan Sgeireach	Highld	NH3984	57°49·3′	4°42·2′W	W	20
Lochan Sgeireach	N Eil	NB1535	58°13·0′	6°50·7′W	W	13
Lochan Sgeireach	N Eil	NB3202	57°55·9′	6°31·2′W	W	14
Loch an Sgeireich Mhóir	N Eil	NB2942	58°17·3′	6°37·0′W	W	8,13
Loch an Sgòir	Highld	NN4874	56°50·2′	4°29·0′W	W	42
Loch an Sgoltaire	Arg & Bt	NR3897	56°5·9′	6°12·3′W	W	61
Lochan Sgrabach	Highld	ND0244	58°22·7′	3°40·1′W	W	11,12
Lochan Sgrathach	Arg & Bt	NR7968	55°51·5′	5°31·4′W	W	62
Lochan Sgreadach	Highld	NC1800	57°57·4′	5°4·1′W	W	15
Lochan Sgreagach	Arg & Bt	NR7867	55°51·0′	5°32·4′W	W	62
Lochan Sguat	Highld	NG7869	57°39·6′	5°42·8′W	W	19,24
Loch an Sgùid	Highld	NH1719	57°13·8′	5°1·4′W	W	34
Loch an Sgùirr Mhóir	Highld	NG3131	57°17·7′	6°27·5′W	W	32
Lochan Sheileach	Pth & Kin	NN4654	56°39·4′	4°30·3′W	W	42,51
Lochan Sheileachan	Arg & Bt	NN1116	56°18·2′	5°2·8′W	W	50,56
Lochan Sheumais	Highld	NH3596	57°55·6′	4°46·7′W	W	20
Lochan Shira	Arg & Bt	NN1720	56°20·5′	4°57·2′W	W	50,56
Lochan Sholum	Arg & Bt	NR4049	55°40·2′	6°7·7′W	W	60
Lochanside	Highld	NH2939	57°24·8′	4°50·4′W	X	25
Lochan Sidhein Bhuidhe	Arg & Bt	NR7274	55°54·6′	5°38·4′W	W	62
Lochan Sidhein Duibh	Highld	NN3348	56°35·9′	4°42·8′W	W	50
Lochan Sìl	Highld	NG9454	57°32·0′	5°26·0′W	W	25
Lochan Sligneach	Highld	NM6465	56°43·3′	5°51·0′W	W	40
Lochans Moor	D & G	NX0757	54°52·5′	5°0·1′W	X	82
Lochan Smùirneach	Highld	NC0508	58°1·4′	5°17·6′W	W	15
Lochan Smurach	Highld	NC1502	57°58·4′	5°7·2′W	W	15
Lochans of Auchniebut	D & G	NX5183	55°7·4′	4°19·8′W	W	77
Lochans of Cairndoon	D & G	NX3738	54°42·9′	4°31·4′W	W	83
Lochan Soireach	N Eil	NB4118	58°4·8′	6°23·1′W	W	14
Loch an Spardain	Highld	NH3249	57°30·3′	4°47·8′W	W	26
Loch an Spioraid	Highld	NJ0316	57°13·7′	3°35·9′W	W	36
Lochan Spling	Stir	NN5000	56°10·4′	4°24·5′W	W	57
Lochan Srath Dubh - Uisge	Arg & Bt	NN2815	56°18·0′	4°46·3′W	W	50,56
Lochan Sròn Mór	Arg & Bt	NN1619	56°19·9′	4°58·1′W	W	50,56
Lochan Sròn nan Sionnach	Highld	NM4865	56°42·8′	6°6·6′W	W	47
Lochan Sròn Smeur	Pth & Kin	NN4460	56°42·6′	4°32·5′W	W	42
Loch an Stacain	Arg & Bt	NN1522	56°21·5′	4°59·2′W	W	50
Loch an Staing	Highld	NC5218	58°7·8′	4°30·3′W	W	16
Loch an Starsaich	Highld	NG6419	57°12·3′	5°54·0′W	W	32
Loch an Sticir	N Eil	NF8977	57°40·8′	7°12·6′W	W	18
Lochan Stob a' Glas-chairn	Highld	NM8383	56°53·5′	5°33·3′W	W	40
Lochan Stole	Highld	NM7493	56°58·6′	5°42·7′W	W	33,40
Loch an Stroim	N Eil	NB1331	58°10·7′	6°52·5′W	W	13
Loch an Strumore	N Eil	NF8969	57°36·5′	7°12·0′W	W	18
Loch an Tachdaich	Highld	NH0938	57°23·8′	5°10·3′W	W	25
Loch an Taigh-sgoile	N Eil	NF7636	57°18·2′	7°22·4′W	W	22
Lochan Tain Mhic Dhughaill	Highld	NM8486	56°55·2′	5°32·5′W	W	40
Loch an Tairbeairt	N Eil	NG1896	57°52·1′	6°44·9′W	W	14
Loch an Tairbeart	N Eil	NB2527	58°9·0′	6°40·0′W	W	8,13
Loch an Tairbeart	N Eil	NB2532	58°11·7′	6°40·3′W	W	8,13
Loch an Tairbeart nan Cleitichean	N Eil	NB2636	58°13·9′	6°39·6′W	W	8,13
Loch an Tairbeirt	N Eil	NB3519	58°5·1′	6°29·3′W	W	14
Loch an Tairbeirt	N Eil	NG0988	57°47·5′	6°53·4′W	W	14
Loch an Tairbh	Highld	NC5631	58°14·9′	4°26·7′W	W	16
Loch an Tairbh	N Eil	NB3814	58°2·5′	6°25·9′W	W	14
Loch an Tairbh Duinn	N Eil	NG1399	57°53·6′	6°50·1′W	W	14
Lochan Tana	Arg & Bt	NM5625	56°21·5′	5°56·6′W	W	48
Lochan Tana	N Eil	NB2315	58°2·5′	6°41·2′W	W	13,14
Lochan Tana	N Eil	NB3716	58°3·6′	6°27·0′W	W	14
Loch an Taobh Sear	N Eil	NB2224	58°7·3′	6°42·8′W	W	13,14
Lochan Taynish	Arg & Bt	NR7385	56°0·5′	5°38·0′W	W	55
Loch an Teas	Highld	NG8791	57°51·7′	5°35·0′W	W	19
Loch an Teas	Highld	NG8891	57°51·8′	5°34·0′W	W	19
Loch an Teine	N Eil	NB1411	58°0·0′	6°50·0′W	W	13,14
Lochan Thulachan	Highld	ND1041	58°21·2′	3°31·8′W	W	11,12
Loch an Tigh-choimhid	Highld	NC6660	58°30·7′	4°17·5′W	W	10
Lochan Tigh Choinnich	Arg & Bt	NM7904	56°10·9′	5°33·2′W	W	55
Loch an Tigh Sheilg	Highld	NC2948	58°23·5′	4°55·1′W	W	9
Loch an Tiompain	Highld	NH1584	57°48·7′	5°6·4′W	W	20
Lochan Tiormachd	Highld	NC7664	58°33·1′	4°7·4′W	W	10
Loch an Tobair	N Eil	NB3034	58°13·0′	6°35·4′W	W	8,13
Loch an Tobair	N Eil	NB4345	58°19·4′	6°22·9′W	W	8
Lochan Tobhta Ruairidh Dhuibh	N Eil	NB3912	58°1·5′	6°24·8′W	W	14
Loch an Toim	N Eil	NF7965	57°33·9′	7°21·7′W	W	18
Loch an Tolla Bhaid	Highld	NC1129	58°12·8′	5°12·6′W	W	15
Lochan Tom Ailein	Highld	NN2764	56°44·4′	4°49·3′W	W	41
Loch an Tomain	N Eil	NB2521	58°5·8′	6°39·6′W	W	13,14
Loch an Tomain	N Eil	NF9160	57°31·7′	7°9·3′W	W	22
Lochan Tom Mhic Iain	Highld	NM5166	56°43·4′	6°3·8′W	W	47
Loch an Torr	Arg & Bt	NM4552	56°35·7′	6°8·8′W	W	47
Lochan Torr a' Choit	Highld	NG9308	57°7·2′	5°24·7′W	W	33
Lochan Torr a' Gharbh-uillt	Highld	NH1601	57°4·1′	5°1·6′W	W	34
Lochan Torr an Fhamhair	Highld	NM9358	56°40·3′	5°22·3′W	W	49
Lochan Torr an Lochain	Highld	NC1834	58°15·7′	5°5·7′W	W	15
Lochan Torr an Tuill	Highld	NH5222	57°16·1′	4°26·8′W	W	26,35
Loch-an-treel	Highld	NH7789	57°52·7′	4°4·0′W	W	21
Lochan Treshtil	Arg & Bt	NM8137	56°28·7′	5°32·9′W	W	49
Lochan Tri-chrioch	Arg & Bt	NM8325	56°22·3′	5°30·4′W	W	49
Loch an Truim	N Eil	NB0917	58°3·1′	6°55·5′W	W	13,14
Loch an t-Sabhail	Highld	NG9525	57°16·4′	5°23·6′W	W	25,33
Loch an t-Sabhail-mhoine	Highld	NG8276	57°43·5′	5°39·2′W	W	19
Loch an t-Sagairt	Arg & Bt	NM2560	56°39·3′	6°28·8′W	W	46,47
Loch an t-Sagairt	N Eil	NF9472	57°38·3′	7°7·2′W	W	18
Loch an t-Sàile	N Eil	NF7546	57°23·6′	7°24·2′W	W	22
Loch an t-Sàilein	Arg & Bt	NR4246	55°38·6′	6°5·6′W	W	60
Loch an t-Seachrain	Highld	NG7724	57°15·4′	5°41·4′W	W	33
Loch an t-Seana-bhaile	Highld	NG7680	57°45·5′	5°45·5′W	W	19
Loch an t-Seana Phuill	Highld	NC2145	58°21·7′	5°3·1′W	W	9
Loch an t-Sean-inbhir	Highld	NG7891	57°51·5′	5°44·1′W	W	19
Loch an t-Searraich	N Eil	NF8470	57°36·8′	7°17·1′W	W	18
Loch an t-Seasgain	N Eil	NF8660	57°31·5′	7°14·3′W	W	22
Lochan t-Seilach	Highld	NH9100	57°4·9′	3°47·4′W	W	36
Loch an t-Seilg	Highld	NC4136	58°17·3′	4°42·3′W	W	16
Loch an t-Seilich	Highld	NG5703	57°3·5′	6°0·0′W	W	32,39
Loch an t-Seilich	Highld	NN7586	56°57·2′	4°2·9′W	W	42
Loch an t-sidhein	Arg & Bt	NM6723	56°20·8′	5°45·8′W	W	49
Loch an t-Sidhein	Highld	NH1580	57°46·6′	5°6·2′W	W	20
Loch an t-Sidhein	Highld	NH9732	57°22·3′	3°42·3′W	W	27,36
Loch an t-Sìdhein	N Eil	NB5432	58°12·8′	6°10·8′W	W	8
Loch an t-Siob	Arg & Bt	NR5173	55°53·4′	5°58·5′W	W	61
Loch an t-Sionnaich	Highld	NH4321	57°15·4′	4°35·7′W	W	26
Loch an t-Sìthein Tarsuinn	Arg & Bt	NR5985	56°0·1′	5°51·5′W	W	61
Loch an t-Siùmpain	N Eil	NB5637	58°15·5′	6°9·1′W	W	8
Loch an t-Slagain	Highld	NG8593	57°52·7′	5°37·1′W	W	19
Loch an t-Slios	N Eil	NB2124	58°7·3′	6°43·8′W	W	13,14
Loch an t-Slugaite	Highld	NC6715	58°6·5′	4°15·0′W	W	16
Loch an t-Sroim	N Eil	NF7927	57°13·5′	7°18·7′W	W	22
Loch an t-Suidhe	Arg & Bt	NM3721	56°18·8′	6°14·7′W	W	48
Lochan Tuath	Highld	NC1005	57°59·9′	5°12·4′W	W	15
Loch an Tubairnaich	Highld	NC8708	58°3·1′	3°54·4′W	W	17
Loch an Tuill Chreagaich	Highld	NH2844	57°27·5′	4°51·6′W	W	25
Loch an Tuill Riabhaich	Highld	NH4092	57°53·6′	4°41·5′W	W	20
Loch an Tuim	Highld	NG6209	57°6·9′	5°55·4′W	W	32
Loch an Tuim	N Eil	NB2535	58°13·3′	6°40·5′W	W	8,13
Loch an Tuim	N Eil	NB4243	58°18·3′	6°23·8′W	W	8
Loch an Tùim Aird	N Eil	NB2529	58°10·1′	6°40·1′W	W	8,13
Loch an Tuim Bhuidhe	Highld	NC4035	58°16·7′	4°43·2′W	W	16
Loch an Tuim Uaine	Arg & Bt	NR5386	56°0·5′	5°57·3′W	W	61
Loch an Tùir	Highld	NC1126	58°11·2′	5°12·4′W	W	15
Loch an Tuirc	Highld	NC1125	58°10·7′	5°12·4′W	W	15
Loch an Tuirc	Highld	NC5439	58°19·2′	4°29·1′W	W	16
Loch an Tuirc	Highld	NH4162	57°37·5′	4°39·3′W	W	20
Loch an Tuirc	N Eil	NF7529	57°14·4′	7°22·8′W	W	22
Loch an Turaraich	Highld	NG8849	57°29·2′	5°31·8′W	W	24
Lochan Tùtach	Moray	NH9840	57°26·6′	3°41·5′W	W	27
Loch an Uachdair	Highld	NG5847	57°27·2′	6°1·6′W	W	24
Lochan Uaine	Aberd	NN9598	57°3·9′	3°43·4′W	W	36,43
Lochan Uaine	Aberd	NO0098	57°4·0′	3°38·5′W	W	36,43
Lochan Uaine	Aberd	NO0298	57°4·0′	3°36·5′W	W	36,43
Lochan Uaine	Arg & Bt	NM9637	56°29·1′	5°18·3′W	W	49
Lochan Uaine	Arg & Bt	NN0009	56°14·1′	5°13·2′W	W	55
Lochan Uaine	Arg & Bt	NN1931	56°26·4′	4°55·7′W	W	50
Lochan Uaine	Arg & Bt	NS3399	56°9·5′	4°40·9′W	W	56
Lochan Uaine	Highld	NG9652	57°31·0′	5°23·9′W	W	25
Lochan Uaine	Highld	NH1314	57°11·0′	5°5·2′W	W	34
Lochan Uaine	Highld	NH6122	57°16·3′	4°17·9′W	W	26,35
Lochan Uaine	Highld	NH7381	57°48·3′	4°7·8′W	W	21
Lochan Uaine	Highld	NN4288	56°57·6′	4°35·5′W	W	34,42
Lochan Uaine	Moray	NJ1415	57°13·3′	3°25·0′W	W	36
Lochan Uaine	Pth & Kin	NN7830	56°27·0′	3°58·3′W	W	51,52
Lochan Uaine	Pth & Kin	NN8335	56°29·8′	3°53·6′W	W	52
Lochan Uaine	Pth & Kin	NO0479	56°53·8′	3°34·1′W	W	43
Lochan Uaine	Stir	NN2922	56°21·8′	4°45·6′W	W	50
Lochan Uamhalt	Highld	NG8707	57°6·5′	5°30·6′W	W	33
Loch an Uidh	Highld	NH1696	57°55·2′	5°5·9′W	W	20
Loch an Uillt-bheithe	Highld	NG9252	57°30·9′	5°27·9′W	W	25
Loch an Uillt-ghiubhais	Highld	NH0565	57°38·2′	5°15·5′W	W	19
Loch an Uillt-ghiubhais	Highld	NH3754	57°33·1′	4°43·0′W	W	26
Lochan Uisge	Highld	NH6303	57°6·1′	4°15·2′W	W	35
Lochan Uisge	Highld	NN5271	56°48·7′	4°25·0′W	W	42
Loch an Uisge-ghil	N Eil	NF7940	57°20·5′	7°19·7′W	W	22
Loch an Uisge Mhaith Mór	N Eil	NB3912	58°1·5′	6°24·8′W	W	14
Lochan Ulbha	Highld	NC3545	58°22·0′	4°48·8′W	W	9
Loch an Ulbhaidh	Highld	NC4922	58°9·9′	4°33·5′W	W	16
Loch an Umhlaich	N Eil	NB4348	58°21·0′	6°23·1′W	W	8
Lochan Vungie	Highld	NH4407	57°7·9′	4°34·2′W	W	34
Loch Aoghnais Mhic Fhionnlaidh	N Eil	NG0687	57°46·8′	6°56·3′W	W	14,18
Loch Aonghais	Highld	NC5547	58°23·5′	4°28·4′W	W	10
Loch Aonghais	N Eil	NF8573	57°38·5′	7°16·3′W	W	18
Loch Aoraidh	N Eil	NB3545	58°19·1′	6°31·0′W	W	8
Loch a' Phealuir Mór	N Eil	NB0930	58°10·0′	6°56·5′W	W	13
Loch a' Phearcail	N Eil	NB0915	58°2·0′	6°55·3′W	W	13,14
Loch a'Phearsain	Arg & Bt	NM8513	56°15·9′	5°27·9′W	W	55
Loch a' Phobuill	N Eil	NF8263	57°33·0′	7°18·5′W	W	18
Loch a' Phollain	Highld	NC0726	58°11·1′	5°16·5′W	W	15
Loch a' Phollain Bheithe	Highld	NC0932	58°14·4′	5°14·8′W	W	15
Loch a' Phollain Drisich	Highld	NC0726	58°11·1′	5°16·5′W	W	15
Loch a' Phollain Riabhaich	Highld	NC1911	58°3·3′	5°3·6′W	W	15
Loch a' Phreasain Challtuinne	Highld	NC1846	58°22·1′	5°6·2′W	W	9
Loch a' Phreasan Chailltean	Highld	NC2153	58°26·0′	5°3·5′W	W	9
Loch a' Phriosain	Highld	NC6345	58°22·6′	4°20·1′W	W	10
Loch a' Phris	Highld	NC2006	58°0·7′	5°2·3′W	W	15
Loch a' Phuill	Arg & Bt	NL9541	56°28·0′	6°56·7′W	W	46
Loch a' Phuill Bhuidhe	Highld	NC2659	58°29·3′	4°58·6′W	W	9
Loch a' Phuill Bhuidhe	Highld	NC2663	58°31·5′	4°58·8′W	W	9
Loch a' Phuill Dhuibh	Highld	NH3056	57°34·0′	4°50·1′W	W	26
Loch a' Phuirt-ruaidh	N Eil	NF7635	57°17·7′	7°22·3′W	W	22
Loch Aradaidh	Highld	NH3751	57°31·5′	4°42·9′W	W	26
Loch Arail	Arg & Bt	NR8079	55°57·5′	5°31·0′W	W	62
Loch a Rathaid	N Eil	NG2295	57°51·7′	6°40·8′W	W	14
Locharbriggs	D & G	NX9979	55°6·0′	3°34·5′W	T	84
Locharbriggs	D & G	NX9980	55°6·5′	3°34·6′W	T	78
Loch Ard	Highld	NG6409	57°6·9′	5°53·4′W	W	32
Loch Ard	Stir	NN4601	56°10·9′	4°28·4′W	W	57
Loch Ard Achadh	Arg & Bt	NR3142	55°36·1′	6°15·8′W	W	60
Loch Ard Airigh a' Ghille Ruaidh	N Eil	NB3728	58°10·0′	6°27·9′W	W	8
Loch Ard a' Phuill	Highld	NM6974	56°48·3′	5°46·6′W	W	40
Loch Ardbhair	Highld	NC1633	58°15·1′	5°7·7′W	W	15
Loch Ard Forest	Stir	NN4107	56°14·0′	4°33·5′W	F	56
Loch Ard Forest	Stir	NS4898	56°9·3′	4°26·4′W	F	57
Lochardil	Highld	NH6642	57°27·2′	4°13·5′W	T	26
Loch Ardinning	Stir	NS5677	55°58·1′	4°18·0′W	W	64
Loch Arichlinie	Highld	NC8435	58°17·6′	3°58·3′W	W	17
Loch Arienas	Highld	NM6851	56°35·9′	5°46·3′W	W	49
Loch Arish	Arg & Bt	NM4628	56°22·8′	6°6·4′W	W	48
Loch Arish	Arg & Bt	NR2670	55°51·0′	6°22·2′W	W	60
Loch Arkaig	Highld	NM9991	56°58·3′	5°18·0′W	W	33,40
Loch Arkaig	Highld	NN0791	56°58·5′	5°10·1′W	W	33
Loch Arkaig	Highld	NN1290	56°58·0′	5°5·1′W	W	34
Loch Arklet	Stir	NN3709	56°15·0′	4°37·4′W	W	56
Loch Arm	Arg & Bt	NM4121	56°18·9′	6°10·9′W	W	48
Lochar Moss	D & G	NY0077	55°4·9′	3°33·6′W	X	84
Lochar Moss	D & G	NY0371	55°1·7′	3°30·6′W	X	84
Loch Arnicle	Arg & Bt	NR7135	55°33·6′	5°37·4′W	W	68
Loch Arnish	Highld	NG5848	57°27·7′	6°1·6′W	W	24
Loch Arnish	N Eil	NB4230	58°11·3′	6°22·9′W	W	8
Loch Arnoil	N Eil	NB3048	58°20·5′	6°36·4′W	W	8
Loch Arroch	D & G	NX3583	55°7·1′	4°34·8′W	W	77
Loch Arron	D & G	NX4483	55°7·3′	4°26·4′W	W	77
Loch Arthur	D & G	NX9068	54°59·9′	3°42·8′W	W	84
Locharthur	D & G	NX9069	55°0·5′	3°42·8′W	X	84
Locharthur Hill	D & G	NX9169	55°0·5′	3°41·8′W	H	84
Loch Aruisg	Highld	NG5700	57°1·9′	5°59·8′W	W	32,39
Lochar Water	D & G	NY0273	55°2·8′	3°31·6′W	W	84
Lochar Water	D & G	NY0566	54°59·0′	3°28·6′W	W	85
Lochar Water	S Lanak	NS6939	55°37·9′	4°4·4′W	W	71
Locharwoods	D & G	NY0467	54°59·6′	3°29·6′W	X	84
Loch as Airde	Highld	NH6990	57°53·1′	4°12·1′W	W	21
Loch Ascaig	Highld	NC8425	58°12·2′	3°58·0′W	W	17
Loch Ascog	Arg & Bt	NS0962	55°49·1′	5°2·5′W	W	63
Loch a' Sgàil	N Eil	NB1307	57°57·8′	6°50·7′W	W	13,14
Loch a' Sgail	N Eil	NB1339	58°15·0′	6°53·1′W	W	13
Loch a' Sgàth	Highld	NG4731	57°18·2′	6°11·6′W	W	32
Loch a' Sguair	N Eil	NB1623	58°6·6′	6°48·8′W	W	13,14
Loch a' Sguirr	Highld	NG6052	57°29·9′	5°59·9′W	W	24
Loch Ashie	Highld	NH6234	57°22·8′	4°17·3′W	W	26
Loch Ashik	Highld	NG6923	57°14·6′	5°49·3′W	W	32
Loch a Siar	N Eil	NB0603	57°55·4′	6°57·5′W	W	13,14
Loch Aslaich	Highld	NH4023	57°16·4′	4°38·8′W	W	26
Loch Assapol	Arg & Bt	NM4020	56°18·3′	6°11·8′W	W	48
Loch Assynt	Highld	NC2024	58°10·4′	5°3·2′W	W	15
Lochassynt Lodge	Highld	NC1726	58°11·4′	5°6·3′W	X	15
Loch Athabhat Beag	N Eil	NB2745	58°18·8′	6°39·2′W	W	8
Loch Athabhat Mòr	N Eil	NB2745	58°18·8′	6°39·2′W	W	8
Loch Atrabhat Iarach	N Eil	NB3751	58°22·4′	6°29·4′W	W	8
Loch Atrabhat Uarach	N Eil	NB3851	58°22·4′	6°28·4′W	W	8
Loch a' Tuath	N Eil	NB1120	58°4·8′	6°53·7′W	W	13,14
Loch Aulasary	N Eil	NF9473	57°38·8′	7°7·3′W	W	18
Loch Avich	Arg & Bt	NM9314	56°16·7′	5°20·2′W	W	55
Lochavich Ho	Arg & Bt	NM9315	56°17·2′	5°20·2′W	X	55
Loch Avon or Loch A'an	Moray	NJ0102	57°6·2′	3°37·6′W	W	36
Loch Awe	Arg & Bt	NM9914	56°16·8′	5°14·4′W	W	55
Loch Awe	Arg & Bt	NN0015	56°17·4′	5°13·5′W	W	50,55
Loch Awe	Arg & Bt	NN0722	56°21·3′	5°7·0′W	W	50
Lochawe	Arg & Bt	NN1227	56°24·1′	5°2·4′W	T	50
Loch Awe	Highld	NC2415	58°5·6′	4°58·7′W	W	15
Loch Bà	Arg & Bt	NM5637	56°28·0′	5°57·2′W	W	47,48
Loch Ba	Highld	NN3149	56°36·4′	4°44·8′W	W	50
Loch Bà Alasdair	N Eil	NF8549	57°25·6′	7°14·4′W	W	22
Loch Bacabhat	N Eil	NB3644	58°18·6′	6°30·0′W	W	8
Loch Bacabhat	N Eil	NB3955	58°24·6′	6°27·6′W	W	8
Loch Bacabhat	N Eil	NB5044	58°19·1′	6°15·7′W	W	8
Loch Bacabhat Ard	N Eil	NB5555	58°25·2′	6°11·3′W	W	8
Loch Bacabhat Chrois	N Eil	NB5356	58°25·6′	6°13·4′W	W	8
Loch Bacabhat Iarach	N Eil	NB5556	58°25·7′	6°11·3′W	W	8
Loch Bachach	Highld	NC4551	58°25·5′	4°38·8′W	W	9
Loch Bad a' Bhàthaich	Highld	NH5378	57°46·3′	4°27·8′W	W	20
Loch Bad a' Bhàthaich	Highld	NH5478	57°46·3′	4°26·8′W	W	21
Loch Bad a' Bhothain	Highld	NC9150	58°25·8′	3°51·5′W	W	10
Loch Bad a' Channain	Highld	NC9340	58°20·4′	3°49·2′W	W	11
Loch Bad a' Chigean	Highld	NC1627	58°11·9′	5°7·4′W	W	15
Loch Bad a' Choille	Highld	NH3399	57°57·2′	4°48·9′W	W	20
Loch Bad a' Chreamh	Highld	NG8180	57°45·6′	5°40·4′W	W	19
Loch Bad a' Chròtha	Highld	NG7872	57°41·2′	5°43·0′W	W	19
Loch Bad a' Ghaill	Highld	NC0710	58°2·5′	5°15·7′W	W	15
Loch Badaidh na Meana	Highld	NC8557	58°29·4′	3°57·9′W	W	10
Loch Badaireach na Gaoithe	Highld	NC8451	58°26·2′	3°58·7′W	W	10
Loch Bad an Fhèidh	Highld	NG7953	57°31·1′	5°41·0′W	W	24
Loch Bad an Fheoir	Highld	NC6441	58°20·5′	4°18·9′W	W	10
Loch Bad an Fheur-loch	Highld	NC3367	58°33·8′	4°51·8′W	W	9
Loch Bad an Loch	Highld	NC5428	58°13·3′	4°28·7′W	W	16
Loch Badanloch	Highld	NC7734	58°16·9′	4°5·4′W	W	17
Loch Badan na Mòine	Highld	NH1678	57°45·5′	5°5·1′W	W	20
Loch Bad an Og	Highld	NC1131	58°13·9′	5°12·7′W	W	15
Loch Bad an Sgalaig	Highld	NG8571	57°40·9′	5°35·9′W	W	19
Loch Bad an t-Seabhaig	Highld	NC2345	58°21·7′	5°1·1′W	W	9
Loch Bad an t-Sean-tighe	Highld	NC7313	58°5·5′	4°8·8′W	W	16
Loch Bad an t-Sluic	Highld	NC1521	58°8·6′	5°8·1′W	W	15
Loch Bad Leabhraidh	Highld	NH3665	57°39·0′	4°44·4′W	W	20
Loch Bad na Gallaig	Highld	NC6342	58°21·0′	4°20·0′W	W	10
Loch Bad na Goibhre	Highld	NC1022	58°9·0′	5°13·2′W	W	15
Loch Bad na h-Achlaise	Highld	NC0808	58°1·4′	5°14·6′W	W	15
Loch Bad na h-Achlaise	Highld	NC3852	58°25·8′	4°46·0′W	W	9
Loch Bad na h-Achlaise	Highld	NG7673	57°41·7′	5°45·1′W	W	19
Loch Bad na h-Achlaise	Highld	NH1599	57°56·8′	5°7·1′W	W	20
Loch Bad na h-Earba	Highld	NC7613	58°5·6′	4°5·7′W	W	17
Loch Bad nam Mult	Highld	NC1741	58°19·4′	5°7·0′W	W	9
Loch Bad na Muirichinn	Highld	NC0919	58°7·4′	5°14·1′W	W	15
Loch Bad nan Aighean	Highld	NC1325	58°10·7′	5°10·3′W	W	15
Loch Bad nan Earb	Highld	NH4534	57°22·5′	4°34·2′W	W	26
Loch Baile a' Ghobhainn	Arg & Bt	NM8542	56°31·5′	5°29·3′W	W	49
Loch Baile Mhic Chailein	Arg & Bt	NN0247	56°34·7′	5°13·0′W	W	50
Loch Bail'-fhionnlaidh	N Eil	NF7753	57°27·4′	7°22·7′W	W	22

Loch Baimilidh	N Eil	NF7425	57°12·2′	7°23·5′W	W	22
Loch Baligill	Highld	NC8562	58°32·1′	3°58·0′W	W	10
Loch Ballach	Highld	NH4447	57°29·4′	4°35·7′W	W	26
Loch Ballygrant	Arg & Bt	NR4066	55°49·3′	6°8·6′W	W	60,61
Lochbank	D & G	NX7561	54°55·9′	3°56·6′W	X	84
Lochbank	D & G	NX9168	54°59·9′	3°41·8′W	X	84
Lochbank	D & G	NX9782	55°7·6′	3°36·5′W	X	78
Lochbank	D & G	NY0783	55°8·2′	3°27·1′W	X	78
Lochbank	Pth & Kin	NO2345	56°35·7′	3°14·8′W	X	53
Lochbank Hill	D & G	NX9169	55°0·5′	3°41·8′W	H	84
Loch Barabhaig	Highld	NG6809	57°7·1′	5°49·5′W	W	32
Loch Baravat	N Eil	NB0334	58°12·0′	7°2·9′W	W	13
Loch Baravat	N Eil	NB1535	58°13·0′	6°50·7′W	W	13
Loch Barnluasgan	Arg & Bt	NR7991	56°3·9′	5°32·6′W	W	55
Loch Barraglom	N Eil	NB1734	58°12·5′	6°48·6′W	W	8,13
Loch Barr-lice	Arg & Bt	NR7943	55°38·1′	5°30·2′W	W	62,69
Loch Battan	Highld	NH5339	57°25·3′	4°26·4′W	W	26
Loch Bà Una	N Eil	NF8152	57°27·0′	7°18·7′W	W	22
Loch Bay	Highld	NG2555	57°30·4′	6°35·0′W	W	23
Loch Beacrabhaig	N Eil	NG1190	57°48·6′	6°51·5′W	W	14
Loch Beag	Arg & Bt	NM7600	56°8·7′	5°35·9′W	W	55
Loch Beag	Arg & Bt	NR7340	55°36·3′	5°35·8′W	W	62
Loch Beag	Highld	NC2729	58°13·2′	4°56·3′W	W	15
Loch Beag	Highld	NC6544	58°22·1′	4°18·0′W	W	10
Loch Beag	Highld	NG3437	57°21·0′	6°24·9′W	W	23,32
Loch Beag	Highld	NG4059	57°33·0′	6°20·3′W	W	23
Loch Beag	Highld	NG5847	57°27·2′	6°1·6′W	W	24
Loch Beag	Highld	NG7756	57°32·6′	5°43·1′W	W	24
Loch Beag	Highld	NG9407	57°6·7′	5°23·7′W	W	33
Loch Beag	Highld	NG9481	57°46·5′	5°27·4′W	W	19
Loch Beag	Highld	NH1435	57°22·3′	5°5·1′W	W	25
Loch Beag	Highld	NH3646	57°28·7′	4°43·7′W	W	26
Loch Beag	Highld	NH6383	57°49·2′	4°17·9′W	W	21
Loch Beag	Highld	NH8609	57°9·7′	3°52·6′W	W	35,36
Loch Beag	Highld	NM7283	56°53·2′	5°44·1′W	W	40
Loch Beag	N Eil	NB2102	57°55·5′	6°42·3′W	W	14
Loch Beag	N Eil	NB2631	58°11·2′	6°39·2′W	W	8,13
Loch Beag	N Eil	NB4026	58°9·1′	6°24·7′W	W	8
Loch Beag	N Eil	NF8265	57°34·1′	7°18·7′W	W	18
Loch Beag	N Eil	NF8480	57°42·2′	7°17·9′W	W	18
Loch Beag a' Chòcair	N Eil	NB3434	58°13·1′	6°31·3′W	W	8,13
Loch Beag Airigh nan Linntean	N Eil	NB2021	58°5·6′	6°44·6′W	W	13,14
Loch Beag an Stàirr	N Eil	NB3839	58°16·0′	6°27·6′W	W	8
Loch Beag Caitiosbhal	N Eil	NB4017	58°4·2′	6°24·1′W	W	14
Loch Beag Eileabhat	N Eil	NB5154	58°24·5′	6°15·3′W	W	8
Loch Beag Gaineamhaich	N Eil	NB5047	58°20·7′	6°15·9′W	W	8
Loch Beag Léig Tàdh	N Eil	NB4951	58°22·8′	6°17·1′W	W	8
Loch Beag na Beiste	N Eil	NB1829	58°9·9′	6°47·2′W	W	8,13
Loch Beag na Craoibhe	N Eil	NB3729	58°10·6′	6°27·9′W	W	8
Loch Beag na Fuaralachd	Highld	NC6015	58°6·4′	4°22·1′W	W	16
Loch Beag nan Ian	N Eil	NF7674	57°38·6′	7°25·4′W	W	18
Loch Beag Ruadh	N Eil	NB1125	58°7·4′	6°54·1′W	W	13,14
Loch Beag Sgeireach	N Eil	NB4947	58°20·6′	6°16·9′W	W	8
Loch Beag Shanndabhat	N Eil	NB4953	58°23·9′	6°17·3′W	W	8
Loch Beag Shèilibridh	N Eil	NB1319	58°4·3′	6°51·6′W	W	13,14
Loch Beag Thoma Dhuibhe	N Eil	NB3331	58°11·5′	6°32·1′W	W	8,13
Loch Bealach a' Bhùirich	Highld	NC2628	58°12·7′	4°57·2′W	W	15
Loch Bealach a' Mhadaidh	Highld	NC3123	58°10·1′	4°51·9′W	W	15
Loch Bealach an Fhiodhain	Arg & Bt	NM9926	56°23·3′	5°14·9′W	W	49
Loch Bealach Coire Sgoireadail	Highld	NG9709	57°7·9′	5°20·8′W	W	33
Loch Bealach Cùlaidh	Highld	NH4472	57°42·9′	4°36·7′W	W	20
Loch Bealach Ghearran	Arg & Bt	NR9494	56°5·9′	5°18·3′W	W	55
Loch Bealach Mhic Neill	Highld	NM3798	57°0·2′	6°19·4′W	W	39
Loch Bealach na Gaoithe	Highld	NM6876	56°49·3′	5°47·7′W	W	40
Loch Bealach na h-Oidhche	Highld	NG8313	57°9·7′	5°34·9′W	W	33
Loch Bealach na h-Uidhe	Highld	NC2625	58°11·0′	4°57·1′W	W	15
Loch Bealach nan Creagan Dubha	Highld	NG8007	57°6·3′	5°37·5′W	W	33
Loch Bealach na Sgeulachd	Highld	NC4253	58°26·5′	4°41·9′W	W	9
Loch Bealach Odhrsgaraidh	Highld	NC4250	58°24·9′	4°41·8′W	W	9
Loch Bealach Stocleit	N Eil	NG1195	57°51·3′	6°51·9′W	W	14
Loch Beanie	Pth & Kin	NO1668	56°48·0′	3°22·1′W	W	43
Loch Beannach	Highld	NC1326	58°11·3′	5°10·4′W	W	15
Loch Beannach	Highld	NC5912	58°4·7′	4°23·0′W	W	16
Loch Beannach	Highld	NC6814	58°6·0′	4°13·9′W	W	16
Loch Beannach	Highld	NC7311	58°4·5′	4°8·7′W	W	16
Loch Beannacharain	Highld	NH2351	57°31·1′	4°56·9′W	W	25
Loch Beannacharan	Highld	NH2938	57°24·3′	4°50·3′W	W	25
Loch Beannacharan	Highld	NH3039	57°24·8′	4°49·4′W	W	26
Loch Bearasta Mòr	N Eil	NG1295	57°51·4′	6°50·8′W	W	14
Loch Bearnach	Arg & Bt	NM6932	56°25·7′	5°44·3′W	W	49
Loch Beg	Arg & Bt	NM5229	56°23·6′	6°0·7′W	W	48
Loch Beg	Highld	ND0846	58°23·8′	3°34·0′W	W	11,12
Loch Bèin	N Eil	NF8437	57°19·1′	7°14·5′W	W	22
Loch Beinn a' Chaoinich	Highld	NG8518	57°12·4′	5°33·1′W	W	33
Loch Beinn a' Charra	N Eil	NF7731	57°15·6′	7°21·0′W	W	22
Loch Beinn a' Mheadhoin	Highld	NG9228	57°18·0′	5°26·7′W	W	25,33
Loch Beinn a' Mheadhoin	Highld	NH2324	57°16·6′	4°55·7′W	W	25
Loch Beinn an Eòin Bheag	Highld	NC3806	58°1·1′	4°44·1′W	W	16
Loch Beinn an t-Sidhein	Highld	NH2315	57°11·8′	4°55·3′W	W	34
Loch Beinn Bhreac	N Eil	NB4027	58°9·6′	6°24·7′W	W	8
Loch Beinn Dearg	Highld	NG8592	57°52·2′	5°37·0′W	W	19
Loch Beinn Dearg	Highld	NH0278	57°45·1′	5°19·2′W	W	19
Loch Beinn Dearg Bheag	Highld	NG9088	57°50·2′	5°31·8′W	W	19
Loch Beinn Deirg	Highld	NC1500	57°57·3′	5°7·1′W	W	15
Loch Beinn Deirg	Highld	NH1599	57°56·8′	5°7·1′W	W	15
Loch Beinn Domhnaill	Highld	NH6795	57°55·7′	4°14·3′W	W	21
Loch Beinn Iobheir	N Eil	NB4943	58°18·5′	6°16·6′W	W	8
Loch Beinn Iosbhal	N Eil	NB0819	58°4·1′	6°56·6′W	W	13,14
Loch Beinn na Gainmhich	N Eil	NB3727	58°9·5′	6°27·8′W	W	8
Loch Beinn nan Carn	Arg & Bt	NM5041	56°29·9′	6°3·3′W	W	47,48
Loch Beinn nan Sgalag	N Eil	NB2236	58°13·8′	6°43·7′W	W	8,13
Loch Beinn nan Sgalag	N Eil	NB2237	58°14·3′	6°43·7′W	W	8,13

Loch Beinn Tighe	Highld	NM4486	56°53·9′	6°11·8′W	W	39
Loch Beinn Uraraidh	Arg & Bt	NR4053	55°42·3′	6°7·9′W	W	60
Loch Belivat	Highld	NH9547	57°30·3′	3°44·7′W	W	27
Loch Benachally	Pth & Kin	NO0750	56°38·2′	3°30·5′W	W	52,53
Loch Ben Harrald	Highld	NC5233	58°15·9′	4°30·9′W	W	16
Loch Ben Tearabert	N Eil	NB5245	58°19·7′	6°13·7′W	W	8
Loch Beoraid	Highld	NM8285	56°54·6′	5°34·4′W	W	40
Loch Beoun Mhòir	N Eil	NF7621	57°10·2′	7°21·2′W	W	31
Loch Bhac	Pth & Kin	NN8262	56°44·3′	3°55·3′W	W	43
Loch Bhacasaraidh	N Eil	NF7532	57°16·0′	7°23·1′W	W	22
Loch Bhad Ghaineamhaich	Highld	NH3259	57°35·7′	4°48·2′W	W	26
Loch Bhalamuis	N Eil	NB2901	57°55·2′	6°34·1′W	W	14
Loch Bhaltois	N Eil	NB3121	58°6·0′	6°33·5′W	W	13,14
Loch Bhanamhòir	Highld	NG9764	57°37·5′	5°23·5′W	W	19
Loch Bharabhat	N Eil	NB2234	58°12·7′	6°43·5′W	W	8,13
Loch Bharabhat	N Eil	NB4659	58°27·0′	6°20·7′W	W	8
Loch Bharcasaig	Highld	NG2542	57°23·4′	6°34·1′W	W	23
Loch Bharradail	Arg & Bt	NR3963	55°47·6′	6°9·4′W	W	60,61
Loch Bharranch	Highld	NG9757	57°33·7′	5°23·2′W	W	25
Loch Bhasapoll	Arg & Bt	NL9747	56°31·3′	6°55·2′W	W	46
Loch Bhata Cuil	N Eil	NB4848	58°21·2′	6°18·0′W	W	8
Loch Bhataleòis	N Eil	NB5253	58°24·0′	6°14·2′W	W	8
Loch Bhatandìob	N Eil	NB3533	58°12·6′	6°30·2′W	W	8
Loch Bhiorain	N Eil	NF7369	57°35·8′	7°28·0′W	W	18
Loch Bhoisimid	N Eil	NB1013	58°1·0′	6°54·2′W	W	13,14
Loch Bhorghastail	N Eil	NB2140	58°15·9′	6°45·0′W	W	8,13
Loch Bhornais	N Eil	NF7329	57°14·4′	7°24·8′W	W	22
Loch Bhraighaig	Highld	NG7556	57°32·6′	5°45·1′W	W	24
Loch Bhraomisaig	Highld	NM7897	57°0·9′	5°39·3′W	W	33,40
Loch Bhreacaich	N Eil	NB3711	58°0·9′	6°26·7′W	W	14
Loch Bhreagleit	N Eil	NB4239	58°16·1′	6°23·5′W	W	8
Loch Bhrodainn	Highld	NN7483	56°55·5′	4°3·8′W	W	42
Loch Bhrolluim	N Eil	NB3102	57°55·8′	6°32·2′W	W	14
Loch Bhrolluim	N Eil	NB3104	57°56·9′	6°32·3′W	W	13,14
Loch Bhruist	N Eil	NF9182	57°43·5′	7°11·0′W	W	18
Loch Bhruthadail	N Eil	NB3146	58°19·5′	6°35·2′W	W	8
Loch Bhuic Mhòir	Highld	NG9226	57°16·9′	5°26·6′W	W	25,33
Loch Bì	N Eil	NF7743	57°22·0′	7°21·9′W	W	22
Loch Bioda Mór	Highld	NG3727	57°15·7′	6°21·2′W	W	32
Loch Blain	Highld	NM6770	56°46·1′	5°48·3′W	W	40
Loch Blàir	Highld	NN0594	57°0·0′	5°12·2′W	W	33
Loch Blashaval	N Eil	NF9071	57°37·6′	7°11·1′W	W	18
Loch Bodabhat	N Eil	NB0619	58°4·0′	6°58·7′W	W	13,14
Loch Bog	Scot Bord	NT4311	55°23·6′	2°53·6′W	X	79
Loch Boidheach	Arg & Bt	NM2056	56°36·4′	6°39·3′W	W	46,47
Lochboisdale	N Eil	NF7919	57°9·2′	7°18·1′W	T	31
Loch Boisdale	N Eil	NF8018	57°8·7′	7°17·0′W	W	31
Loch Boltachan	Pth & Kin	NN6926	56°24·7′	4°7·0′W	W	51
Loch Boor	Highld	NG8379	57°45·2′	5°38·4′W	W	19
Loch Borasdail	N Eil	NF7852	57°26·9′	7°21·6′W	W	22
Loch Bornais Uarach	N Eil	NF7429	57°14·4′	7°23·8′W	W	22
Loch Borralan	Highld	NC2610	58°3·0′	4°56·4′W	W	15
Loch Borralie	Highld	NC3867	58°33·9′	4°46·6′W	W	9
Loch Borve	N Eil	NF9080	57°42·4′	7°11·8′W	W	18
Loch Borve	N Eil	NG0494	57°50·5′	6°58·8′W	W	18
Loch Bowie	W Dunb	NS4275	55°56·8′	4°31·4′W	W	64
Loch Bracadale	Highld	NG2837	57°20·8′	6°30·8′W	W	23
Loch Brack	D & G	NX6882	55°7·1′	4°3·8′W	W	77
Loch Braig	Highld	NG6259	57°33·8′	5°58·3′W	W	24
Loch Braigh a' Bhaile	Highld	NC0623	58°9·5′	5°17·4′W	W	15
Loch Braigh a'Choire	Arg & Bt	NR5980	55°57·4′	5°51·2′W	W	61
Loch Braigh an Achaidh	Highld	NG7440	57°23·9′	5°45·2′W	W	24
Loch Bràigh an t-Sìdhean	N Eil	NA9615	58°1·5′	7°8·5′W	W	13
Loch Bràigh Bheagarais	N Eil	NB0412	58°0·2′	7°0·2′W	W	13
Loch Braigh Bhlàir	Highld	NG6117	57°11·2′	5°56·9′W	W	32
Loch Bràigh Bhruthaich	Highld	NH8829	57°20·5′	3°51·2′W	W	35,36
Loch Bràighe Griomaval	N Eil	NB0122	58°5·4′	7°4·0′W	W	13
Loch Bràigh Horrisdale	Highld	NG7970	57°40·2′	5°41·9′W	W	19
Loch Bràigh na h-Aibhne	Highld	NC9931	58°15·6′	3°42·8′W	W	11,17
Loch Bràigh na h-Aoidhe	N Eil	NB4731	58°12·0′	6°17·9′W	W	8
Loch Braigh na h-Imrich	N Eil	NG1999	57°53·8′	6°44·1′W	W	14
Loch Bràigh nan Ròn	N Eil	NB3408	57°59·2′	6°29·5′W	W	13,14
Loch Bran	Highld	NH5019	57°14·5′	4°28·7′W	W	35
Loch Branahuie	N Eil	NB4732	58°12·5′	6°17·9′W	W	8
Loch Brandy	Angus	NO3375	56°52·0′	3°5·5′W	W	44
Lochbranside	Highld	NH5119	57°14·5′	4°27·7′W	X	35
Loch Breac	Arg & Bt	NR3590	56°2·0′	6°14·8′W	W	61
Loch Breac	Highld	ND0637	58°19·0′	3°35·8′W	W	11,17
Loch Breacam	Arg & Bt	NR8152	55°43·0′	5°28·8′W	W	62,69
Loch Breachacha	Arg & Bt	NM1552	56°34·7′	6°38·0′W	W	46
Loch Breag Cnoc a' Choilich	N Eil	NB3831	58°11·2′	6°27·0′W	W	8
Loch Brecbowie	S Ayr	NX4396	55°14·2′	4°27·7′W	W	77
Loch Breibhat	N Eil	NB3245	58°19·0′	6°34·1′W	W	8
Loch Breugach	N Eil	NB3730	58°11·1′	6°28·0′W	W	8
Loch Brinnaval	N Eil	NB0329	58°9·3′	7°2·5′W	W	13
Loch Briobaig	Highld	NN1189	56°57·5′	5°6·0′W	W	34,41
Loch Briodag	N Eil	NB3831	58°11·7′	6°27·0′W	W	8
Loch Brittle	Highld	NG4019	57°11·5′	6°17·8′W	W	32
Loch Broom	Highld	NH1293	57°53·5′	5°9·8′W	W	19
Loch Broom	Highld	NH1689	57°51·4′	5°5·6′W	W	20
Loch Broom	Pth & Kin	NO0158	56°42·5′	3°36·6′W	W	52,53
Lochbroom Burn	Pth & Kin	NN9956	56°41·3′	3°38·5′W	W	52,53
Loch Brora	Highld	NC8508	58°3·0′	3°56·3′W	W	17
Lochbrow	D & G	NY0988	55°10·9′	3°25·3′W	X	78
Lochbrowan	E Ayr	NS6209	55°21·6′	4°10·2′W	X	71,77
Lochbrowan Hill	E Ayr	NS6210	55°22·1′	4°10·2′W	H	71
Loch Bru	N Eil	NF8973	57°38·6′	7°12·3′W	W	18
Loch Bruaiche Bheibheat	N Eil	NB1821	58°5·6′	6°46·7′W	W	13,14
Loch Bruicheach	Highld	NH4536	57°23·5′	4°34·3′W	W	26
Loch Bruist	N Eil	NF7768	57°35·4′	7°23·9′W	W	18
Loch Brunabhal	N Eil	NB0615	58°1·9′	6°58·4′W	W	13,14
Loch Brùnabhal	N Eil	NB1206	57°57·3′	6°51·6′W	W	13,14
Loch Buaile Bhig	N Eil	NB4229	58°10·7′	6°22·8′W	W	8
Loch Buaile Gramasdail	N Eil	NF8661	57°32·1′	7°14·4′W	W	22
Loch Buaile Miravat	N Eil	NB1537	58°14·0′	6°50·9′W	W	13
Loch Buaile nan Caorach	N Eil	NB0334	58°12·0′	7°2·9′W	W	13
Loch Buidhe	Aberd	NO2582	56°55·7′	3°13·5′W	W	44
Loch Buidhe	Highld	NC5637	58°18·1′	4°27·0′W	W	16
Loch Buidhe	Highld	NC6359	58°30·1′	4°20·6′W	W	10

Loch Buidhe	Highld	NG6319	57°12·3′	5°55·0′W	W	32
Loch Buidhe	Highld	NH6698	57°57·3′	4°15·4′W	W	21
Loch Buidhe	Highld	NN2948	56°35·8′	4°46·7′W	W	50
Loch Buidhe Beag	Highld	NC7759	58°30·4′	4°6·2′W	W	10
Loch Buidhe Mór	Highld	NC7758	58°29·8′	4°6·1′W	W	10
Loch Buie	Arg & Bt	NM5922	56°20·0′	5°53·5′W	W	48
Lochbuie	Arg & Bt	NM6125	56°21·7′	5°51·7′W	T	49
Lochbuie	Moray	NJ2153	57°33·9′	3°18·8′W	X	28
Lochbuie Ho	Arg & Bt	NM6124	56°21·1′	5°51·7′W	X	49
Loch Builg	Moray	NJ1803	57°6·9′	3°20·8′W	W	36
Lochbuilg Lodge	Aberd	NJ1802	57°6·4′	3°20·8′W	X	36
Loch Buine Mòire	Highld	NC0915	58°5·2′	5°13·9′W	W	15
Loch Bun Abhainn Eadarra	N Eil	NB1203	57°55·7′	6°51·4′W	W	13,14
Loch Bunachton	Highld	NH6634	57°22·9′	4°13·3′W	W	26
Loch Burifa'	Highld	ND2076	58°40·1′	3°22·3′W	W	7,12
Lochburn	Aberd	NO8583	56°56·5′	2°14·3′W	X	45
Loch Burn	D & G	NS8009	55°21·9′	3°53·2′W	W	71,78
Loch Burn	E Ayr	NS5841	55°38·8′	4°15·0′W	W	71
Loch Burn	S Ayr	NX3694	55°13·0′	4°34·2′W	W	77
Loch Burn	Scot Bord	NT2653	55°46·1′	3°10·3′W	W	66,73
Loch Burn	S Lanak	NS9010	55°22·6′	3°43·7′W	W	71,78
Lochburnfoot	Scot Bord	NT4609	55°22·6′	2°50·7′W	X	79
Lochbuy	Aberd	NJ9364	57°40·2′	2°6·6′W	X	30
Loch Cadh' a' Ghobhainn	Highld	NH0467	57°39·3′	5°16·6′W	W	19
Loch Cadh'an Eididh	Highld	NG9046	57°27·6′	5°29·6′W	W	25
Loch Caillich	Arg & Bt	NR7951	55°42·4′	5°30·6′W	W	62,69
Loch Caise	Highld	ND0246	58°23·8′	3°40·1′W	W	11,12
Loch Caithlim	Arg & Bt	NM7618	56°18·4′	5°36·8′W	W	55
Loch Caladail	Highld	NC3966	58°33·4′	4°45·6′W	W	9
Loch Calavie	Highld	NH0538	57°23·7′	5°14·2′W	W	25
Loch Calder	Highld	ND0760	58°31·4′	3°35·3′W	W	11,12
Loch Call an Uidhean	Highld	NC0914	58°4·7′	5°13·9′W	W	15
Loch Callater	Aberd	NO1884	56°56·7′	3°20·4′W	W	43
Lochcallater Lodge	Aberd	NO1784	56°56·6′	3°21·4′W	X	43
Loch Caluim	Highld	ND0251	58°26·4′	3°40·2′W	W	11,12
Loch Cam	Arg & Bt	NR3466	55°49·1′	6°14·4′W	W	60,61
Loch Càm a'Phuirt	Arg & Bt	NR7481	55°58·4′	5°36·9′W	W	55
Loch Camasach	Highld	NC4728	58°13·1′	4°35·8′W	W	16
Loch Camas an Fhéidh	Highld	NB9911	58°2·8′	5°23·9′W	W	15
Loch Camas an Lochain	Highld	NH0098	57°55·9′	5°22·2′W	W	19
Loch Camas an Raoigh	Highld	NM7382	56°52·7′	5°43·1′W	W	40
Loch Camas-duibhe	N Eil	NF9177	57°40·9′	7°10·6′W	W	18
Loch Camasord	N Eil	NB0334	58°12·0′	7°2·9′W	W	13
Loch Camasord	N Eil	NB0531	58°10·4′	7°0·6′W	W	13
Loch Cam nan-Eilidean	N Eil	NB2443	58°17·6′	6°42·1′W	W	8
Loch Caoireach	Highld	NH3227	57°18·4′	4°46·9′W	W	26
Loch Caol	Arg & Bt	NM0245	56°30·4′	6°50·2′W	W	46
Loch Caol	Arg & Bt	NM3522	56°19·2′	6°16·7′W	W	48
Loch Caol	Highld	NG4730	57°17·7′	6°11·5′W	W	32
Loch Caol	N Eil	NB3612	58°1·4′	6°27·8′W	W	14
Loch Caol	N Eil	NB4112	58°1·6′	6°22·7′W	W	14
Loch Caoldair	Highld	NN6189	56°58·5′	4°16·8′W	W	42
Loch Caol Duin Othail	N Eil	NB5352	58°23·5′	6°13·1′W	W	8
Loch Caol Eiseal	N Eil	NB3718	58°4·6′	6°27·2′W	W	14
Loch Caolisport	Arg & Bt	NR7374	55°54·6′	5°37·5′W	W	62
Loch Caol na h-Innse-geamhraidh	Highld	NG8792	57°52·3′	5°35·0′W	W	19
Loch Caorach	Highld	NM4365	56°42·6′	6°11·5′W	W	47
Loch Carabhat	N Eil	NF8461	57°32·0′	7°16·4′W	W	22
Loch Carabhat	N Eil	NF8556	57°29·3′	7°15·0′W	W	22
Loch Carn a' Chaochain	Highld	NH2418	57°13·4′	4°54·5′W	W	34
Loch Carn a' Chuilinn	Highld	NH4403	57°5·8′	4°34·0′W	W	34
Loch Carnain an Amais	Arg & Bt	NM4752	56°35·8′	6°6·8′W	W	47
Loch Carn a' Mhaoil	Arg & Bt	NR4350	55°40·8′	6°4·9′W	W	60
Loch Càrnan	N Eil	NF8243	57°22·2′	7°17·0′W	W	22
Loch Carn Bingally	Highld	NH3328	57°19·0′	4°45·9′W	W	26
Loch Carnlia	Highld	ND2644	58°23·0′	3°15·5′W	W	11,12
Loch Càrn Mharasaid	Highld	NC2358	58°28·7′	5°1·7′W	W	9
Loch Carn Mhartuin	Highld	NH1754	57°32·6′	5°3·0′W	W	25
Loch Carn na Cloiche Mòire	Highld	NH3853	57°32·6′	4°41·9′W	W	26
Loch Carn na Glas-leitire	Highld	NH2525	57°17·2′	4°53·8′W	W	25
Loch Carn nam Badan	Highld	NH3934	57°22·3′	4°40·2′W	W	26
Loch Carn nan Conbhairean	Highld	NC3417	58°6·9′	4°48·6′W	W	15
Loch Carn nan Gall	Arg & Bt	NR3770	55°51·3′	6°11·7′W	W	60,61
Loch Càrn nan Gillean	Arg & Bt	NR6593	56°4·6′	5°46·1′W	W	55,61
Loch Carn na Toiteil	Highld	NH3035	57°22·7′	4°49·2′W	W	26
Loch Caroy	Highld	NG3042	57°23·6′	6°29·2′W	W	23
Loch Carran	N Eil	NG0896	57°51·7′	6°55·0′W	W	14,18
Loch Carrie	Highld	NH2633	57°21·5′	4°53·1′W	W	25
Loch Carron	Highld	NG8334	57°21·0′	5°36·0′W	W	24
Lochcarron	Highld	NG8939	57°23·8′	5°30·2′W	T	24
Lochcarron	Highld	NG9039	57°23·8′	5°29·2′W	T	25
Loch Carron	Highld	NG9139	57°23·9′	5°28·2′W	W	25
Loch Cartach	N Eil	NB4010	58°0·5′	6°23·6′W	W	14
Loch Casgro	N Eil	NB3447	58°20·1′	6°32·2′W	W	8
Loch Cathrine	Highld	NH4799	57°57·5′	4°34·7′W	W	20
Loch Catrina	Highld	NH7173	57°44·0′	4°9·5′W	W	21
Loch Caulan	Highld	NH6836	57°24·0′	4°11·3′W	W	26
Loch Ceadraiseal	N Eil	NB3123	58°7·1′	6°33·6′W	W	13,14
Loch Ceann a' Bhaigh	N Eil	NF7630	57°15·0′	7°21·9′W	W	22
Loch Ceann a' Chàrnaich	Highld	NG7789	57°50·4′	5°45·0′W	W	19
Loch Ceann Dibig	N Eil	NG1597	57°52·6′	6°48·0′W	W	14
Loch Ceann Eastail	N Eil	NB3812	58°1·5′	6°25·8′W	W	14
Loch Ceann Hulabhig	N Eil	NB2131	58°11·0′	6°44·3′W	W	8,13
Loch Ceann na Saile	Highld	NC2155	58°27·1′	5°3·6′W	W	9
Loch Ceann Thallabhat	N Eil	NB2739	58°15·6′	6°38·8′W	W	8,13
Loch Cearsabhat	N Eil	NB4555	58°24·8′	6°21·5′W	W	8
Loch Ceartabhat	N Eil	NB3543	58°18·0′	6°30·9′W	W	8
Loch Ceartabhat	N Eil	NB4152	58°23·1′	6°25·4′W	W	8
Loch Ceo Glais	Highld	NH5828	57°19·5′	4°21·0′W	W	26,35
Loch Ceòpach	Highld	NG7653	57°31·0′	5°44·0′W	W	24
Loch Chaitiosbhal	N Eil	NB4018	58°4·8′	6°24·1′W	W	14
Loch Chaolartan	N Eil	NB0624	58°6·7′	6°59·1′W	W	13,14
Loch Chaorainn	Arg & Bt	NR8371	55°53·3′	5°27·8′W	W	62
Loch Chaorainn Beag	Arg & Bt	NR8168	55°51·6′	5°29·5′W	W	62
Loch Chàrlabhaigh	N Eil	NB1842	58°16·8′	6°48·2′W	W	8,13
Loch Charles	Pth & Kin	NO0854	56°40·4′	3°29·6′W	W	52,53

Loch Charn	Arg & Bt	NM8120	56°19·6'	5°32·1'W	W	49
Loch Chealamy	Highld	NC7250	58°25·4'	4°11·0'W	W	10
Loch Cheallair	Arg & Bt	NM8615	56°17·0'	5°27·0'W	W	55
Loch Cheann Chuisil	N Eil	NB0320	58°4·4'	7°1·8'W	W	13
Loch Chearabhaigh	N Eil	NF8648	57°25·1'	7°13·4'W	W	22
Loch Chearasaidh	N Eil	NB4658	58°26·5'	6°20·7'W	W	8
Loch Cheòis	N Eil	NB3622	58°6·8'	6°28·5'W	W	14
Loch Chesney	D & G	NX3354	54°51·4'	4°35·7'W	W	82
Loch Chiarain	Highld	NN2963	56°43·9'	4°47·3'W	W	41
Loch Chill Donnain	N Eil	NF7327	57°13·3'	7°24·6'W	W	22
Loch Chill Eireabhaigh	N Eil	NF8447	57°24·5'	7°15·3'W	W	22
Loch Chipeagal Mòr	N Eil	NB2305	57°57·2'	6°40·5'W	W	13,14
Loch Chlachan Dearga	N Eil	NB3009	57°59·6'	6°33·7'W	W	13,14
Loch Chleistir	N Eil	NB1213	58°1·0'	6°52·2'W	W	13,14
Loch Chliostair	N Eil	NB0610	57°59·2'	6°58·0'W	W	13,14
Loch Chliuthair	N Eil	NG1490	57°48·8'	6°48·5'W	W	14
Loch Chnoc Iain Duibh	N Eil	NB3422	58°6·7'	6°30·5'W	W	13,14
Loch Choilleigar	N Eil	NB0421	58°5·0'	7°0·9'W	W	13
Loch Chòinnich Mór	Highld	NM5967	56°44·2'	5°56·0'W	W	47
Loch Choire	Highld	NC6328	58°13·4'	4°19·5'W	W	16
Loch Choire Forest	Highld	NC6329	58°14·0'	4°19·5'W	X	16
Loch Choire Lodge	Highld	NC6530	58°14·5'	4°17·5'W	X	16
Loch Cholarich	Arg & Bt	NM3418	56°17·1'	6°17·4'W	W	48
Loch Cholla	Arg & Bt	NR3891	56°2·7'	6°12·0'W	W	61
Loch Chollaim	N Eil	NG1590	57°48·8'	6°47·5'W	W	14
Loch Chon	Stir	NN4105	56°12·9'	4°33·4'W	W	56
Loch Chorra-riabhaich	Arg & Bt	NR8055	55°44·6'	5°29·9'W	W	62
Loch Chragoil	N Eil	NB3218	58°4·5'	6°32·3'W	W	13,14
Loch Chriostina	Highld	NG8381	57°46·2'	5°38·5'W	W	19
Loch Chromor	N Eil	NB4020	58°5·8'	6°24·3'W	W	14
Loch Chuibhe	Highld	NC6960	58°30·8'	4°14·4'W	W	10
Loch Chùilean Dubha	Highld	NH0567	57°39·3'	5°15·6'W	W	19
Loch Chuinneag	Highld	NH4984	57°49·5'	4°32·1'W	W	20
Loch Chulain	N Eil	NB1839	58°15·2'	6°48·0'W	W	8,13
Loch Chulapuill	N Eil	NB4843	58°18·5'	6°17·6'W	W	8
Loch Chùmraborgh	N Eil	NB3007	57°58·5'	6°33·5'W	W	13,14
Loch Ciaran	Arg & Bt	NR7754	55°43·9'	5°32·7'W	W	62
Loch Cill an Aonghais	Arg & Bt	NR7761	55°47·7'	5°33·0'W	W	62
Loch Cill Chriosd	Highld	NG6020	57°12·7'	5°58·0'W	W	32
Loch Cille Bhànain	N Eil	NF7641	57°20·9'	7°22·8'W	W	22
Loch Cistavat	N Eil	NG0395	57°51·0'	6°59·9'W	W	18
Loch Clach a' Bhuaile	Arg & Bt	NR2164	55°47·6'	6°26·6'W	W	60
Loch Clach a' Chinn Duibh	Highld	NC2438	58°18·0'	4°59·7'W	W	15
Loch Clachaig	Arg & Bt	NR8187	56°1·8'	5°30·5'W	W	55
Loch Clachaig	Highld	NM7455	56°38·2'	5°40·7'W	W	49
Loch Clach an Duilisg	N Eil	NF7839	57°19·9'	7°20·6'W	W	22
Loch Clacharan	N Eil	NB2436	58°13·8'	6°41·6'W	W	8,13
Loch Clach na h-Iolaire	N Eil	NB3018	58°4·4'	6°34·3'W	W	13,14
Loch Claidh	N Eil	NB2604	57°56·7'	6°37·4'W	W	13,14
Loch Claidh	N Eil	NB2702	57°55·7'	6°36·2'W	W	14
Loch Clàir	Highld	NG7771	57°40·7'	5°43·9'W	W	19
Loch Clàir	Highld	NG8176	57°43·5'	5°40·2'W	W	19
Loch Clair	Highld	NG9957	57°33·8'	5°21·2'W	W	25
Loch Clais a' Chreadha	Highld	NH8681	57°48·5'	3°54·6'W	W	21
Loch Claisein	Highld	NC6559	58°30·2'	4°18·5'W	W	10
Loch Clais nan Coinneal	Highld	NC2163	58°31·4'	5°4·0'W	W	9
Loch Clash	Highld	NC2156	58°27·6'	5°3·6'W	W	9
Loch Cleadaich	N Eil	NB2433	58°12·2'	6°41·4'W	W	8,13
Loch Cleap	Highld	NG4666	57°37·0'	6°14·7'W	W	23
Loch Cleat	Highld	NG4467	57°37·5'	6°16·8'W	W	23
Loch Cleit a' Ghuib Choille	N Eil	NB3109	57°59·6'	6°32·7'W	W	13,14
Loch Cleit an Aiseig	N Eil	NB3002	57°55·8'	6°33·2'W	W	14
Loch Cleit Duastal	N Eil	NB0920	58°4·7'	6°55·7'W	W	13,14
Loch Cleit Eirmis	N Eil	NB2427	58°9·0'	6°41·0'W	W	8,13
Loch Cleit na Stùire	N Eil	NB2114	58°1·9'	6°43·1'W	W	13,14
Loch Cleit Steirmeis	N Eil	NB2326	58°8·4'	6°41·9'W	W	8,13
Loch Cliad	Arg & Bt	NM2058	56°38·1'	6°33·5'W	W	46,47
Loch Cliasam Creag	N Eil	NB2040	58°15·8'	6°46·0'W	W	8,13
Loch Clibh Cracaval	N Eil	NB0225	58°7·1'	7°3·2'W	W	13
Loch Cluaineach	Arg & Bt	NR7449	55°41·2'	5°35·3'W	W	62
Loch Cluanie	Highld	NH0811	57°9·2'	5°10·0'W	W	33
Loch Cluanie	Highld	NH1409	57°8·3'	5°4·0'W	W	34
Loch Cnoc a' Buidhe	N Eil	NF7425	57°12·2'	7°23·5'W	W	22
Loch Cnoc a' Charraich	Arg & Bt	NR4674	55°53·8'	6°3·3'W	W	60,61
Loch Cnoc a' Choilich	N Eil	NB3931	58°11·7'	6°26·0'W	W	8
Loch Cnoc a' Choilich	N Eil	NF9672	57°38·4'	7°5·2'W	W	18
Loch Cnoc a' Chròchaire	Highld	NG3244	57°24·7'	6°27·3'W	W	23
Loch Cnoc an Loch	N Ayr	NR9328	55°30·4'	5°16·2'W	W	68,69
Loch Cnoc Bearuil	N Eil	NB3823	58°7·4'	6°26·5'W	W	14
Loch Cnoc Ibrig	Arg & Bt	NM0245	56°30·4'	6°50·2'W	W	46
Loch Cnoc na h-Iolaire	N Eil	NB3226	58°8·8'	6°32·8'W	W	8,13
Loch Cnoc na Mòinteich	Highld	NH1151	57°30·8'	5°8·9'W	W	25
Loch Cnoc nan Sligean	N Eil	NG1694	57°51·0'	6°46·7'W	W	14
Loch Coill' a' Ghorm Locha	Highld	NC1843	58°20·5'	5°6·1'W	W	9
Loch Coille-Bharr	Arg & Bt	NR7890	56°3·3'	5°33·5'W	W	55
Loch Coille Shuardail	N Eil	NB3723	58°7·3'	6°27·5'W	W	14
Loch Coir' a' Ghrunnda	Highld	NG4520	57°12·3'	6°12·9'W	W	32
Loch Coir' an Eoin	Highld	NC8216	58°7·3'	3°59·7'W	W	17
Loch Coir' a' Phris	Highld	NC2559	58°29·3'	4°59·7'W	W	9
Lochcoire	Highld	NH5394	57°54·9'	4°28·4'W	X	20
Loch Coire a' Bhaic	Highld	NC2429	58°13·1'	4°59·3'W	W	15
Loch Coire a' Bhuic	Highld	NH1652	57°31·5'	5°3·9'W	W	25
Loch Coireag nam Mang	Highld	NH1150	57°30·3'	5°8·8'W	W	25
Loch Coire a' Mhuilinn	Highld	NH2655	57°33·4'	4°54·0'W	W	25
Loch Coire an Daimh	Highld	NG8421	57°14·0'	5°34·3'W	W	33
Loch Coire an Lochain	Highld	NH9400	57°5·0'	3°44·5'W	W	36
Loch Coire an Ruadh-staic	Highld	NG9248	57°28·7'	5°27·7'W	W	25
Loch Coire an Uillt Ghiubhais	Highld	NH3235	57°22·7'	4°47·2'W	W	26
Loch Coire a' Phuill	Highld	NG7203	57°4·0'	5°45·2'W	W	33
Loch Coire Attadale	Highld	NG7846	57°27·3'	5°41·6'W	W	24
Loch Coire Bheachain	Highld	NH4272	57°42·9'	4°38·7'W	W	20
Loch Coire Chaorachain	Highld	NH1082	57°47·5'	5°11·3'W	W	19
Loch Coire Cheap	Highld	NN4775	56°50·7'	4°30·1'W	W	42
Loch Coire Chuir	Highld	NN5084	56°55·6'	4°27·4'W	W	42
Loch Coire Doire na Seilg	Highld	NG4512	57°8·0'	6°12·4'W	W	32
Loch Coire Fionnaraich	Highld	NG9449	57°29·3'	5°25·8'W	W	25
Loch Coire Geurad	N Eil	NB1721	58°5·5'	6°47·7'W	W	13,14
Loch Coire Làir	Highld	NG9750	57°29·9'	5°22·8'W	W	25
Loch Coire Làir	Highld	NH2878	57°45·8'	4°53·0'W	W	20

Loch Coire Mhic Dhughaill	Highld	NC3439	58°18·8'	4°49·5'W	W	15
Loch Coire Mhic Fhearchair	Highld	NG9460	57°35·2'	5°26·3'W	W	19
Loch Coire Mhic Mhathain	Highld	NH3185	57°49·6'	4°50·3'W	W	20
Loch Coire na Bà Buidhe	Highld	NH2091	57°52·6'	5°1·7'W	W	20
Loch Coire na Bruaiche	Highld	NC6316	58°7·0'	4°19·1'W	W	16
Loch Coire na Caime	Highld	NG9258	57°34·1'	5°28·2'W	W	25
Loch Coire na Circe	Highld	NG7608	57°6·8'	5°41·5'W	W	33
Loch Coire na Creiche	Highld	NM8763	56°42·9'	5°28·4'W	W	40
Loch Coire na Creige	Highld	NC1621	58°8·6'	5°7·1'W	W	15
Loch Coire na h-Airigh	Highld	NG8078	57°44·5'	5°41·3'W	W	19
Loch Coire nam Beith	Highld	NN5799	57°3·9'	4°21·0'W	W	35
Loch Coire nam Meidhe	Highld	NC3113	58°4·7'	4°51·5'W	W	15
Loch Coire nam Feuran	Highld	NC6635	58°17·3'	4°16·7'W	W	16
Loch Coire nam Mang	Highld	NC8040	58°20·2'	4°2·5'W	W	10
Loch Coire nan Arr	Highld	NG8042	57°25·2'	5°39·4'W	W	24
Loch Coire nan Cadha	Highld	NG9102	57°4·0'	5°26·4'W	W	33
Loch Coire nan Cnàmh	Highld	NG9703	57°4·7'	5°20·5'W	W	33
Loch Coire nan Crogachan	Highld	NG9116	57°11·5'	5°27·1'W	W	33
Loch Coire nan Dearcag	Highld	NH0722	57°15·1'	5°11·5'W	W	25,33
Loch Coire nan Grunnd	Highld	NM4095	56°58·6'	6°16·3'W	W	39
Loch Coire na Rainich	Highld	NH3921	57°15·3'	4°39·7'W	W	26
Loch Coire na Saidhe Duibhe	Highld	NC4436	58°17·4'	4°39·2'W	W	16
Loch Coire na Sgùile	Highld	NH2543	57°26·9'	4°54·5'W	W	25
Loch Coire Shùbh	Highld	NG9605	57°5·7'	5°21·6'W	W	33
Loch Coirgavat	N Eil	NB1126	58°8·0'	6°54·1'W	W	13
Loch Collas Sgairbhe	N Eil	NB0708	57°58·2'	6°56·8'W	W	13,14
Loch Comhnard	Highld	NH3627	57°18·5'	4°42·9'W	W	26
Loch Con	Pth & Kin	NN6867	56°46·8'	4°9·2'W	W	42
Loch Conagleann	Highld	NH5821	57°15·7'	4°20·8'W	W	26,35
Loch Conailbhe	Arg & Bt	NR2160	55°45·4'	6°26·4'W	W	60
Loch Connan	Highld	NG3843	57°24·4'	6°21·3'W	W	23
Loch Connell	D & G	NX0168	54°58·3'	5°6·1'W	W	82
Loch Coradail	N Eil	NF8333	57°16·9'	7°15·2'W	W	22
Loch Coragrimsaig	N Eil	NF7922	57°10·8'	7°18·3'W	W	31
Loch Corcasgil	Highld	NG4564	57°35·9'	6°15·6'W	W	23
Loch Corlarach	Highld	NG2352	57°28·7'	6°36·8'W	W	23
Loch Cormaic	Highld	NC6258	58°29·6'	4°21·6'W	W	10
Loch Còrr	Arg & Bt	NR2269	55°50·3'	6°26·0'W	W	60
Loch Corsabhat	N Eil	NB4944	58°19·0'	6°16·7'W	W	8
Loch Coruisk	Highld	NG4820	57°12·4'	6°9·9'W	W	32
Lochcote Resr	W Loth	NS9773	55°56·6'	3°38·5'W	W	65
Loch Cottage	Pth & Kin	NO0661	56°44·1'	3°31·7'W	X	43
Loch Coulavie	Highld	NH1321	57°14·8'	5°5·5'W	W	25
Loch Coulin	Highld	NH0155	57°32·7'	5°19·1'W	W	25
Loch Coull Ho	Aberd	NJ5103	57°7·2'	2°48·1'W	X	37
Loch Coulside	Highld	NC5843	58°21·4'	4°25·1'W	W	10
Loch Coulter Burn	Stir	NS7787	56°3·9'	3°58·1'W	W	57
Loch Coulter Reservoir	Stir	NS7686	56°3·3'	3°59·0'W	W	57
Loch Coultrie	Highld	NG8546	57°27·5'	5°34·6'W	W	24
Loch Cracail Beag	Highld	NC6300	57°58·4'	4°18·5'W	W	16
Loch Cracail Mór	Highld	NC6202	57°59·4'	4°19·6'W	W	16
Loch Cragach	N Eil	NB1221	58°5·3'	6°52·7'W	W	13,14
Loch Cragaidh	Highld	NC4560	58°30·3'	4°39·1'W	W	9
Loch Craggie	Highld	NC3205	58°0·4'	4°50·1'W	W	15
Loch Craggie	Highld	NC6152	58°26·3'	4°22·4'W	W	10
Loch Craggie	Highld	NC6207	58°2·1'	4°19·8'W	W	16
Lochcraig Head	Scot Bord	NT1617	55°26·6'	3°19·2'W	H	79
Loch Craignish	Arg & Bt	NM7801	56°9·3'	5°34·0'W	W	55
Lochcraig Resr	E Renf	NS5351	55°44·1'	4°20·0'W	W	64
Lochcraig Rig	Scot Bord	NT1717	55°26·6'	3°18·3'W	X	79
Lochcraigs	N Ayr	NS2743	55°39·2'	4°44·5'W	X	63,70
Loch Craisg	Highld	NC5957	58°29·0'	4°24·6'W	W	10
Loch Crakavaig	N Eil	NF7910	57°4·4'	7°17·4'W	W	31
Loch Crann	Highld	NH0957	57°34·0'	5°11·1'W	W	25
Loch Crannach	Pth & Kin	NO0567	56°47·4'	3°32·9'W	W	43
Loch Crasgach	Highld	NC8354	58°27·8'	3°59·9'W	W	10
Loch Craskie	Highld	NH3033	57°21·6'	4°49·1'W	W	26
Loch Cravadale	N Eil	NB0114	58°1·1'	7°3·4'W	W	13
Loch Creabhat	N Eil	NG1193	57°50·3'	6°51·7'W	W	14
Loch Creagach	N Eil	NB0817	58°3·0'	6°56·5'W	W	13,14
Loch Creag a' Mhadaidh	Highld	NH3199	57°57·2'	4°50·9'W	W	20
Loch Creag Forthill	N Eil	NB3424	58°7·8'	6°30·6'W	W	13,14
Loch Creagh	Pth & Kin	NN9044	56°34·8'	3°47·0'W	W	52
Loch Creran	Arg & Bt	NM9441	56°31·2'	5°20·5'W	W	49
Loch Creran	Arg & Bt	NN0044	56°33·0'	5°14·8'W	W	50
Loch Criadha	N Eil	NB3814	58°2·5'	6°25·9'W	W	14
Loch Crinan	Arg & Bt	NR7995	56°6·1'	5°32·8'W	W	55
Loch Cròcach	Highld	NC1027	58°11·7'	5°13·5'W	W	15
Loch Cròcach	Highld	NC1939	58°18·4'	5°4·9'W	W	15
Loch Cròcach	Highld	NC2252	58°25·5'	5°2·4'W	W	9
Loch Cròcach	Highld	NC4249	58°24·3'	4°41·8'W	W	9
Loch Cròcach	Highld	NC6459	58°30·1'	4°19·6'W	W	10
Loch Cròcach	Highld	NC8043	58°21·8'	4°2·6'W	W	10
Loch Crocach	N Eil	NB1530	58°10·3'	6°50·4'W	W	13
Loch Crò Chriosdaig	N Eil	NB0820	58°4·6'	6°56·7'W	W	13,14
Loch Crogabhat	N Eil	NB3727	58°9·5'	6°27·8'W	W	8
Loch Crogabhat	N Eil	NF9262	57°32·9'	7°8·5'W	W	22
Loch Crogach	N Eil	NB2429	58°10·1'	6°41·1'W	W	8,13
Loch Crogavat	N Eil	NF7522	57°10·7'	7°22·3'W	W	31
Loch Crois Ailein	N Eil	NB3816	58°3·5'	6°26·0'W	W	14
Loch Croispol	Highld	NC3968	58°34·5'	4°45·6'W	W	9
Loch Croistean	N Eil	NB1129	58°9·6'	6°54·3'W	W	13
Loch Cròm	Highld	NC1421	58°8·6'	5°9·1'W	W	15
Loch Cromlach	N Eil	NB0200	57°53·7'	7°1·3'W	W	18
Loch Crongart	S Ayr	NX2882	55°6·4'	4°41·4'W	W	76
Loch Croot	S Ayr	NS3712	55°22·8'	4°33·9'W	W	70
Loch Cruinn	Arg & Bt	NR8357	55°45·8'	5°27·1'W	W	62
Loch Crunachdan	Highld	NN5492	57°0·0'	4°23·8'W	W	35
Loch Cruoshie	Highld	NH0536	57°22·6'	5°14·2'W	W	25
Loch Cuaich	Highld	NN6987	56°57·6'	4°8·8'W	W	42
Loch Cuilc	N Eil	NB5029	58°11·0'	6°14·7'W	W	8
Loch Cuilce	N Eil	NF9470	57°37·2'	7°7·1'W	W	18
Loch Cuilceach	N Eil	NG2396	57°52·3'	6°39·8'W	W	14
Loch Cuileig	Highld	NH2615	57°11·5'	4°52·3'W	W	34
Loch Cùil na Creig	Highld	NG6025	57°15·4'	5°58·3'W	W	32
Loch Cuithir	Highld	NG4759	57°33·3'	6°13·3'W	W	23
Loch Cùl	Highld	NH3058	57°35·1'	4°50·2'W	W	26
Loch Culabhal	N Eil	NB2031	58°11·0'	6°45·3'W	W	8,13

Loch Cùl a' Chleit	N Eil	NB2530	58°10·7'	6°40·2'W	W	8,13
Loch Culag	Highld	NC0921	58°8·5'	5°14·2'W	W	15
Loch Culaidh	Highld	NC8639	58°19·8'	3°56·3'W	W	17
Loch Cul Airigh a' Flod	N Eil	NB2722	58°6·4'	6°37·6'W	W	13,14
Loch Cùl a' Mhill	Highld	NC3530	58°13·9'	4°48·1'W	W	15
Loch Culbokie	Highld	NH6159	57°36·2'	4°19·1'W	W	26
Loch Cùl Duibh	Highld	NG7728	57°17·6'	5°41·6'W	W	33
Loch Cùl Fraioch	Highld	NC0232	58°14·2'	5°21·9'W	W	15
Loch Cul Làimhe Bige	N Eil	NB1722	58°6·1'	6°47·7'W	W	13,14
Loch Cùl na Beinne	N Eil	NG1694	57°51·0'	6°46·7'W	W	14
Loch Cul Uidh an Tuim	Highld	NC2949	58°24·0'	4°55·1'W	W	9
Loch Curran	Pth & Kin	NO0460	56°43·6'	3°33·7'W	W	43
Loch Cuthaig	N Eil	NB2721	58°5·9'	6°37·5'W	W	13,14
Loch Dail Fhearna	Highld	NH2162	57°37·0'	4°59·3'W	W	20
Loch Dallas	Highld	NH9315	57°13·1'	3°45·9'W	W	36
Loch Dallas	Moray	NJ0947	57°30·5'	3°30·7'W	W	27
Loch Damh	Highld	NG8651	57°30·2'	5°33·9'W	W	24
Loch Davan	Aberd	NJ4400	57°5·5'	2°55·0'W	W	37
Loch Dearg	Arg & Bt	NR7874	55°54·7'	5°32·7'W	W	62
Loch Dearg	Highld	NG4535	57°20·3'	6°13·8'W	W	32
Loch Dearg	Highld	NM7374	56°48·4'	5°42·7'W	W	40
Loch Dearg an Sgòrra	Arg & Bt	NR4052	55°41·8'	6°7·8'W	W	60
Loch Dee	D & G	NX4678	55°4·6'	4°24·3'W	W	77
Loch Deibheadh	Highld	NC2260	58°29·8'	5°2·8'W	W	9
Loch Deireadh Bànaig	N Eil	NB0637	58°13·7'	7°0·0'W	W	13
Loch Deoravat	N Eil	NF8966	57°34·9'	7°11·8'W	W	18
Loch Derculich	Pth & Kin	NN8654	56°40·1'	3°51·2'W	W	52
Loch Derry	D & G	NX2573	55°1·5'	4°43·8'W	W	76
Loch Dhailbeag	N Eil	NB2245	58°18·6'	6°44·3'W	W	8
Loch Dhiobadail	N Eil	NB4761	58°28·1'	6°19·8'W	W	8
Loch Dhomhnaill	Arg & Bt	NR3353	55°42·1'	6°14·5'W	W	60
Loch Dhomhnaill Bhig	N Eil	NB2922	58°6·5'	6°35·6'W	W	13,14
Loch Dhonnachaidh	Highld	NC1706	58°0·6'	5°5·4'W	W	15
Loch Dhrinisiadair	N Eil	NG1695	57°51·5'	6°46·8'W	W	14
Loch Dhrombaig	Highld	NC1133	58°15·0'	5°12·8'W	W	15
Loch Dhu	Arg & Bt	NS0661	55°48·5'	5°5·3'W	W	63
Lochdhu	Highld	ND0144	58°22·7'	3°41·1'W	X	11,12
Loch Dhu	Stir	NN4303	56°11·9'	4°31·4'W	W	56
Loch Dhu	Stir	NN6202	56°11·7'	4°13·0'W	W	57
Lochdhu Fm	Highld	NH8655	57°34·5'	3°53·9'W	FM	27
Loch Dhùghaill	Highld	NG6108	57°6·3'	5°56·3'W	W	32
Loch Diabaig	Highld	NG7959	57°34·3'	5°41·3'W	W	24
Loch Diabaigas Airde	Highld	NG8159	57°34·3'	5°39·3'W	W	24
Loch Diobadail	N Eil	NB0523	58°6·1'	7°0·0'W	W	13,14
Loch Dionach-caraidh	Highld	NC5540	58°19·7'	4°28·1'W	W	10
Loch Dionard	Highld	NC3549	58°24·2'	4°48·9'W	W	9
Loch Direcleit	N Eil	NG1598	57°53·1'	6°48·0'W	W	14
Loch Diridean	N Eil	NB5148	58°21·3'	6°14·9'W	W	8
Loch Dirigadale	Arg & Bt	NR7245	55°39·0'	5°37·0'W	W	62
Loch Dithreabn na Cuileige	Highld	NG7741	57°24·5'	5°42·3'W	W	24
Loch Diubaig	Highld	NG3254	57°30·1'	6°28·0'W	W	23
Loch Dòbhrain	N Eil	NF7634	57°17·2'	7°22·2'W	W	22
Loch Dochard	Arg & Bt	NN2141	56°31·9'	4°54·2'W	W	50
Loch Dochart	Stir	NN4025	56°23·7'	4°35·1'W	W	51
Lochdochart Ho	Stir	NN4327	56°24·8'	4°32·2'W	X	51
Loch Dochfour	Highld	NH6038	57°24·9'	4°19·4'W	W	26
Loch Doilet	Highld	NM8067	56°44·8'	5°35·4'W	W	40
Loch Doimhne	N Eil	NB3506	57°58·1'	6°28·4'W	W	14
Loch Doine	Stir	NN4619	56°20·6'	4°29·1'W	W	57
Loch Doir' a' Chatha	Highld	NC4903	57°59·7'	4°32·8'W	W	16
Loch Doir' a' Chreamha	Highld	NG4313	57°8·4'	6°14·4'W	W	32
Loch Doir' a' Ghearrain	Highld	NM7281	56°52·1'	5°44·0'W	W	40
Loch Doire an Lochain	Highld	NG4514	57°9·0'	6°12·5'W	W	32
Loch Doire Ghloghain	Highld	NM6384	56°53·5'	5°53·0'W	W	40
Loch Doire na h-Achlaise	Arg & Bt	NR6595	56°5·7'	5°46·2'W	W	55,61
Loch Doire na h-Airbhe	Highld	NC1012	58°3·7'	5°12·8'W	W	15
Loch Doire na h-Airighe	Highld	NG8774	57°42·6'	5°34·1'W	W	19
Loch Doire nam Mart	Highld	NM6652	56°36·4'	5°48·3'W	W	49
Loch Doire nan Sgiath	Highld	NN5186	56°56·7'	4°26·5'W	W	42
Loch Dola	Highld	NC6008	58°2·6'	4°21·8'W	W	16
Lochdon	Arg & Bt	NM7333	56°26·3'	5°40·5'W	T	49
Loch Don	Arg & Bt	NM7431	56°25·3'	5°39·4'W	W	49
Loch Donnaig	Highld	NC0831	58°13·8'	5°15·7'W	W	15
Loch Doon	D & G	NX1068	54°58·5'	4°57·7'W	W	82
Loch Doon	D & G	NX2851	54°49·7'	4°40·2'W	W	82
Loch Doon	E Ayr	NX4998	55°15·4'	4°22·1'W	W	77
Loch Doon Castle	E Ayr	NX4894	55°13·3'	4°22·9'W	A	77
Loch Dornal	S Ayr	NX2976	55°3·2'	4°40·2'W	W	76
Lochdougan	D & G	NX7356	54°53·2'	3°58·4'W	X	83,84
Lochdougan Dairy	D & G	NX7357	54°53·8'	3°58·4'W	X	83,84
Loch Dow	D & G	NX3584	55°7·6'	4°34·8'W	W	77
Loch Driomoir	N Eil	NF7740	57°20·4'	7°21·7'W	W	22
Loch Droighinn	Highld	NG4571	57°39·7'	6°16·1'W	W	23
Loch Drollabhat	N Eil	NB4760	58°27·6'	6°19·8'W	W	8
Loch Drollabhat	N Eil	NF7925	57°12·5'	7°18·6'W	W	22
Loch Drolsay	Arg & Bt	NR3366	55°49·1'	6°15·3'W	W	60,61
Loch Droma	Highld	NH2675	57°44·1'	4°54·9'W	W	20
Loch Drovinish	N Eil	NB1432	58°11·3'	6°51·5'W	W	13
Loch Druidibeag	N Eil	NF7937	57°18·9'	7°19·5'W	W	22
Loch Druim a' Chliabhain	Highld	NC8039	58°19·7'	4°2·5'W	W	17
Loch Druim a' Chliabhain	Highld	NC8041	58°20·7'	4°2·5'W	W	10
Loch Druim an Iasgair	N Eil	NB2340	58°16·0'	6°42·9'W	W	8,13
Loch Druim an Iasgair	N Eil	NF8043	57°22·2'	7°19·0'W	W	22
Loch Druim na Coille	Highld	NC1849	58°23·8'	5°6·4'W	W	9
Loch Druim nam Bideannan	N Eil	NB4019	58°5·3'	6°24·2'W	W	14
Loch Druim nan Caorach	N Eil	NB2503	57°56·2'	6°38·3'W	W	13,14
Loch Druim nan Goban Rainich	N Eil	NB2504	57°56·7'	6°38·4'W	W	13,14
Loch Druim nan Sgorach	N Eil	NB3530	58°11·0'	6°30·0'W	W	8
Loch Druim Suardalain	Highld	NC1121	58°8·5'	5°12·2'W	W	15
Lochdrum	Falk	NS8177	55°58·5'	3°54·0'W	X	65
Loch Drumbeg	Highld	NC1132	58°14·4'	5°12·7'W	W	15
Loch Drunkie	Stir	NN5404	56°12·6'	4°20·8'W	W	57
Loch Duagrich	Highld	NG4039	57°22·3'	6°18·7'W	W	23,32
Loch Duail	Highld	NC4263	58°31·9'	4°42·3'W	W	9
Loch Duartbeg	Highld	NC1638	58°17·8'	5°7·9'W	W	15

Loch Duartmore	Highld	NC1837	58°17·3'	5°5·8'W	W	15
Loch Duastal	N Eil	NB0920	58°4·7'	6°55·7'W	W	13,14
Loch Dubh	Arg & Bt	NM0348	56°32·1'	6°49·4'W	W	46
Loch Dubh	Arg & Bt	NR3253	55°42·0'	6°15·5'W	W	60
Loch Dubh	Highld	NC0724	58°10·0'	5°16·4'W	W	15
Loch Dubh	Highld	NC1648	58°23·2'	5°8·4'W	W	9
Loch Dubh	Highld	NC3329	58°13·4'	4°50·1'W	W	15
Loch Dubh	Highld	NC4045	58°22·1'	4°43·7'W	W	9
Loch Dubh	Highld	NC8147	58°24·0'	4°1·7'W	W	10
Loch Dubh	Highld	ND0144	58°22·7'	3°41·1'W	W	11,12
Loch Dubh	Highld	ND0536	58°18·4'	3°36·8'W	W	11,17
Loch Dubh	Highld	ND1442	58°21·7'	3°27·7'W	W	11,12
Loch Dubh	Highld	NG3132	57°18·2'	6°27·5'W	W	32
Loch Dubh	Highld	NG4828	57°16·7'	6°10·4'W	W	32
Loch Dubh	Highld	NG6129	57°17·6'	5°57·5'W	W	32
Loch Dubh	Highld	NG7138	57°22·8'	5°48·1'W	W	24
Loch Dubh	Highld	NG8146	57°27·4'	5°38·6'W	W	24
Loch Dubh	Highld	NH1498	57°56·2'	5°8·0'W	W	20
Loch Dubh	Highld	NH4627	57°18·7'	4°33·0'W	W	26
Loch Dubh	Highld	NH4725	57°17·7'	4°31·9'W	W	26
Loch Dubh	Highld	NH6301	57°5·0'	4°15·2'W	W	35
Loch Dubh	Highld	NH9037	57°24·9'	3°49·4'W	W	27
Loch Dubh	Highld	NM6677	56°49·8'	5°49·7'W	W	40
Loch Dubh	Highld	NM6784	56°53·6'	5°49·1'W	W	40
Loch Dubh	Highld	NM7483	56°53·3'	5°42·2'W	W	40
Loch Dubh	N Eil	NB1120	58°4·8'	6°53·7'W	W	13,14
Loch Dubh	N Eil	NB1231	58°10·7'	6°53·5'W	W	13
Loch Dubh	N Eil	NB2136	58°13·7'	6°44·7'W	W	8,13
Loch Dubh	N Eil	NB2919	58°4·9'	6°35·4'W	W	13,14
Loch Dubh	N Eil	NB3317	58°4·0'	6°31·2'W	W	13,14
Loch Dubh	N Eil	NB4038	58°15·5'	6°25·5'W	W	8
Loch Dubh	N Eil	NB5060	58°27·7'	6°16·7'W	W	8
Loch Dubh	N Eil	NF7968	57°35·5'	7°21·9'W	W	18
Loch Dubh	N Eil	NF8533	57°17·0'	7°13·2'W	W	22
Loch Dubh	Stir	NN4003	56°11·8'	4°34·3'W	W	56
Loch Dubhach	Highld	NG9128	57°18·0'	5°27·7'W	W	25,33
Loch Dubh a' Chleite	N Eil	NB2244	58°18·1'	6°44·2'W	W	8
Loch Dubh a' Chnoic Ghairbh	Highld	NC2135	58°16·3'	5°2·6'W	W	15
Loch Dubh a' Chuail	Highld	NC3428	58°12·8'	4°49·1'W	W	15
Loch Dubh a' Ghobha	N Eil	NB5253	58°24·0'	6°14·2'W	W	8
Loch Dubha na Claise Càrnaich	Highld	NG8989	57°50·7'	5°32·8'W	W	19
Loch Dubh an Duine	N Eil	NB3540	58°16·4'	6°30·7'W	W	8
Loch Dubh an Iònaire	N Eil	NF7943	57°22·1'	7°19·9'W	W	22
Loch Dubh an Sgòir	Highld	NM3891	56°56·4'	6°18·0'W	W	39
Loch Dubhar-sgoth	Highld	NG4563	57°35·4'	6°15·6'W	W	23
Loch Dubh Beag	Highld	NH1498	57°56·2'	5°8·0'W	W	20
Loch Dubh Beul na Fàire	Highld	NC6459	58°30·1'	4°19·6'W	W	10
Loch Dubh-bheag	Arg & Bt	NM8913	56°16·0'	5°24·0'W	W	55
Loch Dubh Camas an Lochain	Highld	NG8797	57°55·0'	5°35·3'W	W	19
Loch Dubh Cnoc na File	N Eil	NF8761	57°32·1'	7°13·4'W	W	22
Loch Dubh Cùl na Capulich	Highld	NC5223	58°10·5'	4°30·5'W	W	16
Loch Dubh Deas	Highld	NG7051	57°29·7'	5°49·8'W	W	24
Loch Dubh Geodhachan Tharailt	Highld	NG8996	57°54·5'	5°33·2'W	W	19
Loch Dubh-ghlas	Arg & Bt	NN0005	56°12·0'	5°13·0'W	W	55
Loch Dubh-ghruamach	Highld	NC7108	58°2·8'	4°10·7'W	W	16
Loch Dubh Gormailleabhat	N Eil	NB3643	58°18·0'	6°29·9'W	W	8
Loch Dubh Haca	N Eil	NF8352	57°27·1'	7°16·7'W	W	22
Loch Dubh Màs Holasmul	N Eil	NG0690	57°48·4'	6°56·5'W	W	14,18
Loch Dubh Meallan Mhurchaidh	Highld	NC2119	58°7·7'	5°1·9'W	W	15
Loch Dubh-mór	Arg & Bt	NM8914	56°16·6'	5°24·0'W	W	55
Loch Dubh Mór	N Eil	NF8047	57°24·3'	7°19·3'W	W	22
Loch Dubh na Creige	Highld	NG7846	57°27·3'	5°41·6'W	W	24
Loch Dubh na h-Airde	N Eil	NB3652	58°22·9'	6°30·5'W	W	8
Loch Dubh na Maoil	Highld	NG8996	57°54·5'	5°33·2'W	W	19
Loch Dubh na Mòine	N Eil	NF9076	57°40·3'	7°11·5'W	W	18
Loch Dubh nan Stearnag	N Eil	NB3237	58°14·7'	6°33·6'W	W	8,13
Loch Dubh Sciasgro	N Eil	NB4646	58°20·0'	6°19·9'W	W	8
Loch Dubh Shleiteabhal	N Eil	NG0589	57°47·9'	6°57·5'W	W	14,18
Loch Dubh Sòbhail	N Eil	NB3324	58°7·7'	6°31·6'W	W	13,14
Loch Dubh Thorraidh	N Eil	NB3749	58°21·3'	6°29·3'W	W	8
Loch Dubh Thurtail	N Eil	NB4953	58°23·9'	6°17·3'W	W	8
Loch Dubh Uiseal	N Eil	NB2641	58°16·6'	6°40·0'W	W	8,13
Loch Dùghaill	Highld	NC1952	58°25·4'	5°5·5'W	W	9
Loch Dughaill	Highld	NG8251	57°30·1'	5°37·9'W	W	24
Loch Dùghaill	Highld	NG9947	57°28·4'	5°20·7'W	W	25
Loch Duich	Highld	NG8923	57°15·2'	5°29·4'W	W	33
Loch Duich	Highld	NG9021	57°14·2'	5°28·3'W	W	25,33
Loch Duisk	S Ayr	NX2679	55°4·8'	4°43·1'W	W	76
Loch Dùn an t-Siamain	N Eil	NF8859	57°31·1'	7°12·2'W	W	22
Loch Dungeon	D & G	NX5284	55°8·0'	4°18·9'W	W	77
Loch Dùn Mhurchaidh	N Eil	NF7954	57°28·0'	7°20·8'W	W	22
Loch Dùn na Cille	N Eil	NF7418	57°8·5'	7°22·9'W	W	31
Loch Duntelchaig	Highld	NH6131	57°21·2'	4°18·2'W	W	26
Loch Dunvegan	Highld	NG2153	57°29·1'	6°38·9'W	W	23
Loch Dusary	N Eil	NF7767	57°34·9'	7°23·8'W	W	18
Loch Duvat	N Eil	NF8011	57°5·0'	7°16·5'W	W	31
Loch Eachkavar	N Eil	NG0393	57°49·9'	6°59·8'W	W	18
Lochead	Arg & Bt	NR7778	55°56·9'	5°33·9'W	X	62
Lochead	Arg & Bt	NS0080	55°58·5'	5°11·9'W	X	55,63
Lochead	Renf	NS3456	55°46·4'	4°38·4'W	X	63
Loch Eadaraidh	N Eil	NF7631	57°15·6'	7°22·0'W	W	22
Loch Eadar dà Bhaile	Highld	NG5540	57°23·3'	6°4·2'W	W	24
Loch Eagasgro	N Eil	NB3744	58°18·6'	6°28·9'W	W	8
Loch Ealaidh	N Eil	NB3318	58°4·5'	6°31·2'W	W	13,14
Loch Eanin	Arg & Bt	NR3153	55°42·0'	6°16·5'W	W	60
Loch Earacha	Highld	NC8960	58°31·1'	3°53·9'W	W	10
Loch Earn	Pth & Kin	NN6423	56°23·0'	4°11·7'W	W	51
Lochearnhead	Stir	NN5823	56°22·9'	4°17·5'W	T	51
Loch Earraid	N Eil	NB2239	58°15·4'	6°43·9'W	W	8,13
Loch Eas Domhain	Pth & Kin	NN6629	56°26·3'	4°10·0'W	W	51
Loch Eashader	N Eil	NF8072	57°37·7'	7°21·2'W	W	18
Loch Eas na Maoile	Highld	NC3734	58°16·1'	4°46·3'W	W	16
Loch Eastapair	N Eil	NB3323	58°7·2'	6°31·6'W	W	13,14
Loch Eatharna	Arg & Bt	NM2256	56°37·1'	6°31·5'W	W	46,47

Loch Eaval	N Eil	NF7271	57°36·8'	7°29·1'W	W	18
Loch Eck	Arg & Bt	NS1391	56°4·8'	4°59·9'W	W	56
Loch Eddy	Scot Bord	NT2830	55°33·8'	3°8·1'W	W	73
Loch Ederline	Arg & Bt	NM8602	56°10·0'	5°26·4'W	W	55
Lochee	C of Dun	NO3731	56°28·3'	3°0·9'W	X	54
Loch Eidhbhat	N Eil	NB3643	58°18·0'	6°29·9'W	W	8
Loch Eidhinn	Arg & Bt	NR3349	55°39·9'	6°14·3'W	W	60
Loch Eigheach	Pth & Kin	NN4457	56°41·0'	4°32·4'W	W	42,51
Loch Eighinn	Arg & Bt	NR3350	55°40·5'	6°14·4'W	W	60
Loch Eik	N Eil	NF7674	57°38·6'	7°25·4'W	W	18
Loch Eil	Highld	NN0277	56°50·8'	5°14·3'W	W	41
Loch Eilastar	N Eil	NB2238	58°14·8'	6°43·8'W	W	8,13
Loch Eilde Beag	Highld	NN2565	56°44·9'	4°51·3'W	W	41
Loch Eilde Mór	Highld	NN2364	56°44·3'	4°53·2'W	W	41
Loch Eileabhat	N Eil	NB4154	58°24·1'	6°25·5'W	W	8
Loch Eileag	Highld	NC3006	58°0·9'	4°52·2'W	W	15
Loch Eileanach	Highld	NC0931	58°13·8'	5°14·7'W	W	15
Loch Eileanach	Highld	NC1951	58°24·9'	5°5·4'W	W	9
Loch Eileanach	Highld	NC2053	58°26·0'	5°4·5'W	W	9
Loch Eileanach	Highld	NC2240	58°19·0'	5°1·9'W	W	9
Loch Eileanach	Highld	NC2442	58°20·1'	4°59·9'W	W	9
Loch Eileanach	Highld	NC2747	58°22·9'	4°57·1'W	W	9
Loch Eileanach	Highld	NC4827	58°12·6'	4°34·7'W	W	16
Loch Eileanach	Highld	NC5940	58°19·8'	4°24·0'W	W	10
Loch Eileanach	Highld	NC7960	58°30·9'	4°4·2'W	W	10
Loch Eileanach	Highld	ND0747	58°24·4'	3°35·0'W	W	11,12
Loch Eilean a' Ghille-ruaidh	N Eil	NF7636	57°18·2'	7°22·4'W	W	22
Loch Eilean an Staoir	N Eil	NF7326	57°12·7'	7°24·6'W	W	22
Loch Eilean Iain	N Eil	NF7852	57°26·9'	7°21·6'W	W	22
Loch Eilean Iain	N Eil	NF7853	57°27·4'	7°21·7'W	W	22
Loch Eilean na Craoibhe Mòire	Highld	NC2043	58°20·6'	5°4·0'W	W	9
Locheil Forest	Highld	NN0788	56°56·8'	5°9·9'W	X	41
Loch Eilleagbhal	N Eil	NB5252	58°23·4'	6°14·1'W	W	8
Loch Eil (Outward Bound) Station	Highld	NN0578	56°51·4'	5°11·4'W	X	41
Locheilside Sta	Highld	NM9978	56°51·3'	5°17·3'W	X	40
Loch Eilt	Highld	NM8082	56°52·9'	5°36·2'W	W	40
Loch Einich	Highld	NN9198	57°3·9'	3°47·4'W	W	36,43
Loch Eireachain	Arg & Bt	NM9209	56°13·9'	5°20·9'W	W	55
Loch Eireagoraidh	Highld	NM7295	56°59·7'	5°44·8'W	W	33,40
Loch Eireannaich	Arg & Bt	NR7944	55°38·6'	5°30·3'W	W	62,69
Loch Eirearaigh	N Eil	NB3250	58°21·7'	6°34·5'W	W	8
Loch Eireasort	N Eil	NB3420	58°5·6'	6°30·4'W	W	13,14
Loch Eisg	Pth & Kin	NO0458	56°42·5'	3°33·6'W	W	52,53
Loch Eisgean	N Eil	NB3112	58°1·2'	6°32·9'W	W	13,14
Loch Eishort	Highld	NG1645	57°24·7'	6°43·3'W	W	23
Loch Eishort	Highld	NG6114	57°9·5'	5°56·7'W	W	32
Lochelbank	Pth & Kin	NO1312	56°17·8'	3°23·9'W	X	58
Loch Eldrig	D & G	NX3566	54°57·9'	4°34·2'W	W	83
Loch Ellrig	Falk	NS8874	55°57·0'	3°47·2'W	W	65
Lochenbreck Cott	D & G	NX6465	54°57·9'	4°7·0'W	X	83
Lochenbreck Loch	D & G	NX6465	54°57·9'	4°7·0'W	W	83
Lochend	Aberd	NJ7030	57°21·8'	2°29·5'W	X	29
Lochend	Aberd	NJ9001	57°6·2'	2°9·5'W	X	38
Lochend	Arg & Bt	NS0862	55°49·0'	5°3·4'W	X	63
Lochend	C of Edin	NT1272	55°56·2'	3°24·1'W	X	65
Lochend	C of Edin	NT2774	55°57·5'	3°9·7'W	T	66
Lochend	D & G	NX8968	54°59·9'	3°43·7'W	X	84
Lochend	Falk	NS8774	55°57·0'	3°48·1'W	X	65
Lochend	Fife	NO5113	56°18·7'	2°47·1'W	X	59
Lochend	Fife	NT0990	56°5·9'	3°27·3'W	X	58
Lochend	Fife	NT1391	56°6·5'	3°23·5'W	X	58
Lochend	Fife	NT2092	56°7·1'	3°16·8'W	X	58
Lochend	Highld	ND1841	58°21·3'	3°23·6'W	X	11,12
Lochend	Highld	ND2668	58°35·9'	3°15·9'W	T	11,12
Lochend	Highld	NH5937	57°24·4'	4°20·4'W	T	26
Lochend	N Lanak	NS8569	55°54·3'	3°49·9'W	X	65
Lochend	Orkney	HY6224	59°6·3'	2°39·3'W	X	5
Lochend	Pth & Kin	NO0816	56°19·9'	3°28·8'W	X	58
Lochend	Pth & Kin	NO1800	56°11·4'	3°18·8'W	X	58
Lochend	Renf	NS3764	55°50·8'	4°35·8'W	X	63
Lochend	S Ayr	NS4120	55°27·1'	4°30·4'W	X	70
Lochend	S Ayr	NX2680	55°5·3'	4°43·2'W	X	76
Lochend	Scot Bord	NT5134	55°36·1'	2°46·2'W	X	73
Lochend	Shetld	HU3684	60°32·5'	1°20·1'W	X	1,2,3
Lochend	Shetld	HU4963	60°21·1'	1°6·2'W	X	2,3
Lochend	Stir	NS7585	56°2·8'	4°0·0'W	X	57
Lochend Cott	Pth & Kin	NO0130	56°27·4'	3°35·9'W	X	52,53
Lochend Cott	W Dunb	NS4383	56°1·1'	4°30·7'W	X	56,64
Lochend Fm	Stir	NS5999	56°10·0'	4°15·8'W	FM	57
Lochend Hill	E Renf	NS4753	55°45·0'	4°25·8'W	H	64
Lochend Ho	N Lanak	NS6968	55°53·5'	4°5·2'W	X	64
Lochend Ho	Stir	NS5999	56°10·0'	4°15·8'W	X	57
Lochend Loch	N Lanak	NS7066	55°52·4'	4°4·2'W	W	64
Lochend of Barra	Aberd	NJ7825	57°19·2'	2°21·5'W	X	38
Lochend Wood	Moray	NJ3443	57°28·6'	3°5·6'W	F	28
Lochengower	D & G	NX6966	54°58·5'	4°2·4'W	W	83,84
Lochenkit Bennan	D & G	NX8176	55°4·1'	3°51·4'W	H	84
Lochenkit Burn	D & G	NX8076	55°4·1'	3°52·3'W	W	84
Lochenkit Loch	D & G	NX8075	55°3·6'	3°52·3'W	W	84
Lochen Enoch	D & G	NX4485	55°8·3'	4°26·4'W	W	77
Lochenoun	Moray	NJ0242	57°27·7'	3°37·6'W	X	27
Loch Eoe	Highld	NG7259	57°34·1'	5°48·3'W	W	24
Locheport	N Eil	NF8563	57°33·1'	7°15·5'W	T	18
Loch Eport	N Eil	NF8863	57°33·2'	7°12·5'W	W	18
Locherbain	Moray	NJ2140	57°26·9'	3°18·5'W	X	28
Locherben	D & G	NX9597	55°15·6'	3°38·9'W	X	78
Loch Erbusaig	Highld	NG7730	57°18·6'	5°41·7'W	W	24
Loch Erghallan	Highld	NG2248	57°26·5'	6°37·5'W	W	23
Loch Eriboll	Highld	NC4460	58°30·3'	4°40·2'W	W	9
Loch Ericht	Highld	NN5675	56°50·9'	4°21·2'W	W	42
Loch Ericht Forest	Highld	NN5981	56°54·2'	4°18·5'W	F	42
Locherlour	Pth & Kin	NN8222	56°22·8'	3°54·2'W	X	52
Lochermill	Renf	NS4165	55°50·8'	4°32·9'W	X	64
Loch Errochty	Pth & Kin	NN6865	56°45·7'	4°9·1'W	W	42
Locherside	Renf	NS4165	55°51·4'	4°32·0'W	X	64
Locher Water	Renf	NS3763	55°50·2'	4°35·7'W	W	63
Loch Esk	Angus	NO2379	56°54·0'	3°15·4'W	W	44

Loch Essan	Stir	NN4128	56°25·3'	4°34·2'W	W	51
Loch Etchachan	Aberd	NJ0000	57°5·1'	3°38·5'W	W	36
Loch Etive	Arg & Bt	NM9534	56°27·5'	5°19·2'W	W	49
Loch Etive	Arg & Bt	NN0637	56°29·4'	5°8·6'W	W	50
Lochetive Ho	Highld	NN1246	56°34·4'	5°3·2'W	X	50
Loch Etteridge	Highld	NN6993	57°0·8'	4°9·0'W	W	35
Loch Ettrick	D & G	NX9493	55°13·4'	3°39·6'W	W	78
Loch Eun	Highld	NC9842	58°21·5'	3°44·1'W	W	11
Loch Ewe	Highld	NG8486	57°49·0'	5°37·7'W	W	19
Locheye	Aberd	NJ9114	57°13·3'	2°8·5'W	X	38
Locheye	Highld	NH8279	57°47·4'	3°58·6'W	X	21
Loch Eye	Highld	NH8379	57°47·4'	3°57·6'W	W	21
Loch Eynort	Highld	NG3624	57°14·1'	6°22·0'W	W	32
Loch Eynort or Loch Aineort	N Eil	NF8026	57°13·0'	7°17·6'W	W	22
Loch Eyre	Highld	NG4152	57°29·3'	6°18·9'W	W	23
Loch Fad	Arg & Bt	NS0761	55°48·5'	5°4·4'W	W	63
Loch Fada	Arg & Bt	NM1958	56°38·0'	6°34·5'W	W	46
Loch Fada	Arg & Bt	NM2561	56°39·9'	6°28·8'W	W	46,47
Loch Fada	Arg & Bt	NM7804	56°10·9'	5°34·2'W	W	55
Loch Fada	Arg & Bt	NR3895	56°4·8'	6°12·2'W	W	61
Loch Fada	Arg & Bt	NR4063	55°47·7'	6°8·5'W	W	60,61
Loch Fada	Highld	NC5264	58°32·6'	4°32·1'W	W	10
Loch Fada	Highld	NG3431	57°17·8'	6°24·5'W	W	32
Loch Fada	Highld	NG4569	57°38·6'	6°15·9'W	W	23
Loch Fada	Highld	NG4949	57°28·0'	6°10·7'W	W	23
Loch Fada	Highld	NG5037	57°21·6'	6°9·0'W	W	23,24,32
Loch Fada	Highld	NG6016	57°10·6'	5°57·8'W	W	32
Loch Fada	Highld	NG7159	57°34·0'	5°49·3'W	W	24
Loch Fada	Highld	NG9186	57°49·2'	5°30·7'W	W	19
Loch Fada	N Eil	NB3124	58°7·7'	6°33·7'W	W	13,14
Loch Fada	N Eil	NF7534	57°17·1'	7°23·2'W	W	22
Loch Fada	N Eil	NF7622	57°10·7'	7°21·3'W	W	31
Loch Fada	N Eil	NF7751	57°26·3'	7°22·6'W	W	22
Loch Fada	N Eil	NF7953	57°27·5'	7°20·7'W	W	22
Loch Fada	N Eil	NF7966	57°34·5'	7°21·8'W	W	18
Loch Fada	N Eil	NF8236	57°18·5'	7°16·4'W	W	22
Loch Fada	N Eil	NF8660	57°31·5'	7°14·3'W	W	22
Loch Fada	N Eil	NF8770	57°36·9'	7°14·1'W	W	18
Loch Fada Ben Garrisdale	Arg & Bt	NR6394	56°5·1'	5°48·1'W	W	61
Loch Fada Caol	N Eil	NB4344	58°18·8'	6°22·8'W	W	8
Loch Fad'a Chruib	Arg & Bt	NR5785	56°0·0'	5°53·4'W	W	61
Loch Fada Cùl a Chruib	Arg & Bt	NR5585	56°0·0'	5°55·3'W	W	61
Loch Fada Cul na Beinne	Arg & Bt	NR6092	56°3·9'	5°50·9'W	W	61
Loch Fad a Gobha	N Eil	NB2424	58°7·4'	6°40·8'W	W	13,14
Loch Fada na Gearrachun	N Eil	NF7674	57°38·6'	7°25·4'W	W	18
Loch Fada nam Faoileag	N Eil	NB5051	58°22·8'	6°16·1'W	W	8
Loch Fad Oram	N Eil	NB4849	58°21·7'	6°18·0'W	W	8
Loch Fannich	Highld	NH2165	57°38·6'	4°59·5'W	W	20
Loch Fannie	E Ayr	NX4492	55°12·1'	4°26·6'W	W	77
Loch Faoghail an Tuim	N Eil	NB2027	58°8·9'	6°45·1'W	W	8,13
Loch Faoghail Charrasan	N Eil	NB2026	58°8·3'	6°45·0'W	W	8,13
Loch Faoghail Chiorabhal	N Eil	NB2125	58°7·8'	6°43·9'W	W	13,14
Loch Faoghail nan Caorach	N Eil	NB2122	58°6·2'	6°43·7'W	W	13,14
Loch Faoileag	N Eil	NB3529	58°10·5'	6°30·0'W	W	8
Loch Farlary	Highld	NC7704	58°0·8'	4°4·4'W	W	17
Loch Farleyer	Pth & Kin	NN8152	56°38·9'	3°56·0'W	W	52
Loch Farr	Highld	NH6830	57°20·7'	4°11·2'W	W	26
Loch Farroch	S Ayr	NX2585	55°8·0'	4°44·3'W	W	76
Loch Fasgro	N Eil	NB2041	58°16·4'	6°46·1'W	W	8,13
Loch Faskally	Pth & Kin	NN9158	56°42·3'	3°46·4'W	W	52
Loch Fath	N Eil	NB2812	58°1·1'	6°35·9'W	W	13,14
Lochfauld	C of Glas	NS5870	55°54·4'	4°15·9'W	X	64
Loch Fearna	Highld	NH0503	57°4·9'	5°12·6'W	W	33
Loch Feirma	N Eil	NF7968	57°35·5'	7°21·9'W	W	18
Loch Fèith a' Mhadaidh	Highld	NG9937	57°23·0'	5°20·2'W	W	25
Loch Fèith an Leòthaid	Highld	NC1822	58°9·2'	5°5·1'W	W	15
Loch Fèith a' Phuill	Highld	NH5508	57°8·7'	4°23·3'W	W	35
Loch Fèith nan Cleireach	Highld	NH2379	57°46·2'	4°58·1'W	W	20
Loch Fell	D & G	NT1704	55°19·6'	3°18·1'W	H	79
Loch Fender	Pth & Kin	NN8741	56°33·1'	3°49·8'W	W	52
Loch Feochan	Arg & Bt	NM8423	56°21·3'	5°29·3'W	W	49
Loch Feòir	N Eil	NB4015	58°3·1'	6°23·9'W	W	14
Lochfergus	D & G	NX6951	54°50·5'	4°2·0'W	X	83,84
Lochfergus	S Ayr	NS3918	55°26·0'	4°32·2'W	X	70
Loch Fern	D & G	NX8662	54°56·6'	3°46·4'W	W	84
Loch Feur	Highld	NG8078	57°44·5'	5°41·3'W	W	19
Loch Feurach	Highld	NH3152	57°31·9'	4°48·9'W	W	26
Loch Feusaige	Highld	NC7446	58°23·3'	4°8·8'W	W	10
Loch Fhionnaich	Highld	NC5556	58°28·4'	4°28·7'W	W	10
Loch Fhionnaich	Highld	NC5648	58°24·1'	4°27·4'W	W	10
Loch Fhleoideabhaigh	N Eil	NG1087	57°47·0'	6°52·3'W	W	14
Loch Fhreunadail	N Eil	NB1631	58°10·9'	6°49·4'W	W	13
Loch Fiachanis	Highld	NM3594	56°57·9'	6°21·1'W	W	39
Loch Fiag	Highld	NC4429	58°13·6'	4°38·9'W	W	16
Loch Fiart	Arg & Bt	NM8037	56°28·7'	5°33·9'W	W	49
Loch Fidhle	Arg & Bt	NR8090	56°3·4'	5°31·6'W	W	55
Lochfield	D & G	NY2066	54°59·2'	3°14·6'W	X	85
Lochfield	E Ayr	NS5841	55°38·8'	4°15·0'W	X	71
Lochfield	Stir	NN7000	56°10·8'	4°5·2'W	X	57
Loch Finlaggan	Arg & Bt	NR3867	55°49·8'	6°10·6'W	W	60,61
Loch Finlas	E Ayr	NX4598	55°15·4'	4°25·9'W	W	77
Loch Finnart	Pth & Kin	NN5255	56°40·1'	4°24·5'W	W	42,51
Loch Fionna-choire	Highld	NG5321	57°13·1'	6°5·0'W	W	32
Loch Fionnacleit	N Eil	NB2139	58°15·3'	6°44·9'W	W	8,13
Loch Fionn-Ghleann	Arg & Bt	NR7444	55°38·5'	5°35·0'W	W	62
Loch Fionnsabhagh	N Eil	NG0886	57°46·4'	6°54·2'W	W	14,18
Loch Fir Dhuirinis	Highld	NC3747	58°23·1'	4°46·8'W	W	9
Loch Fir Raoilt	Highld	NH5195	57°55·4'	4°30·5'W	W	20
Loch Fithie	Angus	NO4851	56°39·1'	2°50·4'W	W	54
Loch Fitty	Fife	NT1291	56°6·5'	3°24·5'W	W	58
Lochfitty Burn	Fife	NT1694	56°8·1'	3°20·7'W	W	58
Loch Fleet	D & G	NX5570	55°0·5'	4°15·6'W	W	77
Loch Fleet	D & G	NX5669	54°59·9'	4°14·6'W	W	83
Loch Fleet	Highld	NH7996	57°56·5'	4°2·2'W	W	21
Loch Flemington	Highld	NH8152	57°32·8'	3°58·8'W	W	27
Loch Fleodach Coire	Highld	NC2724	58°10·5'	4°56·0'W	W	15
Loch Fm	E Dunb	NS6471	55°55·0'	4°10·1'W	FM	64
Loch Foid	N Eil	NB3127	58°9·3'	6°33·9'W	W	8,13

Loch Foireabhal Bheag	N Eil	NB2211	58°0·3'	6°41·9'W	W	13,14
Loch Foisneabhat	N Eil	NB4350	58°21·1'	6°23·2'W	W	8
Lochfoot	D & G	NX8973	55°2·6'	3°43·8'W	T	84
Loch Formal	Pth & Kin	NN8645	56°35·2'	3°50·9'W	W	52
Loch Fraing	Arg & Bt	NM5422	56°19·9'	5°58·3'W	W	48
Loch Fraochach	Highld	NH4508	57°8·5'	4°33·2'W	W	34
Loch Freasdail	Arg & Bt	NR8159	55°46·7'	5°29·1'W	W	62
Loch Freuchie	Pth & Kin	NN8637	56°30·9'	3°50·7'W	W	52
Loch Freumhach	Highld	NG8161	57°35·4'	5°39·4'W	W	19,24
Loch Frisa	Arg & Bt	NM4848	56°33·6'	6°5·6'W	W	47,48
Loch Frith Cheannardaidh	Highld	NH4494	57°54·8'	4°37·5'W	W	20
Loch Fuarail	N Eil	NB1224	58°6·9'	6°53·0'W	W	13,14
Loch Fuar-Bheinne	Arg & Bt	NR8178	55°57·0'	5°30·0'W	W	62
Loch Fuaron	Arg & Bt	NM5826	56°22·1'	5°54·7'W	W	48
Loch Fyne	Arg & Bt	NN0804	56°11·7'	5°5·2'W	W	56
Loch Fyne	Arg & Bt	NN1710	56°15·1'	4°56·8'W	W	50,56
Loch Fyne	Arg & Bt	NR8970	55°52·9'	5°22·0'W	W	62
Loch Fyne	Arg & Bt	NR9590	56°3·8'	5°17·1'W	W	55
Loch Gaineamhach	Highld	NC4247	58°23·2'	4°41·7'W	W	9
Loch Gaineamhach	Highld	NC5125	58°11·6'	4°31·6'W	W	16
Loch Gaineamhach	Highld	NC5824	58°11·2'	4°24·4'W	W	16
Loch Gaineamhach	Highld	NC6344	58°22·1'	4°20·0'W	W	10
Loch Gaineamhach	Highld	NG7553	57°30·9'	5°45·0'W	W	24
Loch Gaineamhach	Highld	NG8146	57°27·4'	5°38·6'W	W	24
Loch Gaineamhach	Highld	NG8367	57°38·7'	5°37·7'W	W	19,24
Loch Gaineamhach Beag	Highld	NG8362	57°36·0'	5°37·4'W	W	19,24
Loch Gaineamhaich	N Eil	NB3713	58°2·0'	6°26·8'W	W	14
Loch Gaineamhaich	N Eil	NB5147	58°20·7'	6°14·8'W	W	8
Loch Gaineanhach	Arg & Bt	NM9100	56°9·1'	5°21·5'W	W	55
Loch Gaineimh	Highld	NC7660	58°30·9'	4°7·2'W	W	10
Loch Gaineimh	Highld	NC7943	58°21·8'	4°3·6'W	W	10
Loch Gaineimh	Highld	ND0546	58°23·8'	3°37·0'W	W	11,12
Loch Gaineimh	Highld	ND0748	58°24·9'	3°35·0'W	W	11,12
Loch Gainmheach Eitseal Bheag	N Eil	NB2734	58°12·9'	6°38·4'W	W	8,13
Loch Gainmheach nam Faoileag	N Eil	NB3138	58°15·2'	6°34·6'W	W	8,13
Loch Gainmhich	Highld	NC8165	58°33·7'	4°2·3'W	W	10
Loch Gainmhich	Highld	NM3898	57°0·2'	6°18·4'W	W	39
Loch Gainmhich	N Eil	NB1223	58°6·4'	6°52·9'W	W	13,14
Loch Gair	Arg & Bt	NR9290	56°3·7'	5°20·0'W	W	55
Lochgair	Arg & Bt	NR9290	56°3·7'	5°20·0'W	T	55
Loch Gairloch	Highld	NG7776	57°43·4'	5°44·2'W	W	19
Loch Galabhat	N Eil	NB2840	58°16·1'	6°37·8'W	W	8,13
Loch Galtarsay	N Eil	NF8870	57°37·0'	7°13·1'W	W	18
Loch Gamhna	Highld	NH8906	57°8·2'	3°49·6'W	W	35,36
Loch Gaorsaic	Highld	NH0222	57°15·0'	5°16·5'W	W	25,33
Loch Garasdale	Arg & Bt	NR7651	55°42·3'	5°33·5'W	W	62,69
Loch Garbad	N Ayr	NS0123	55°27·9'	5°8·4'W	W	69
Loch Garbh	Arg & Bt	NM9803	56°10·9'	5°14·8'W	W	55
Loch Garbh	Highld	NC9360	58°31·2'	3°49·7'W	W	11
Loch Garbhaig	Highld	NG8969	57°40·0'	5°31·8'W	W	19,24
Loch Garbhaig	Highld	NH0070	57°40·8'	5°20·8'W	W	19
Loch Garbhaig	N Eil	NB3735	58°13·8'	6°28·3'W	W	8
Loch Garbh Bhreac	Highld	NH4335	57°23·0'	4°36·2'W	W	26
Loch Garbh Iolachan	Highld	NH4235	57°22·9'	4°37·2'W	W	26
Loch Gàrradh nan Capull	Arg & Bt	NL9741	56°28·1'	6°54·8'W	W	46
Loch Garraidh Mhóir	Highld	NH1892	57°53·1'	5°3·7'W	W	20
Loch Garry	Highld	NH2302	57°4·8'	4°54·8'W	W	34
Loch Garry	Pth & Kin	NN6270	56°48·3'	4°15·2'W	W	42
Lochgarry Ho	Pth & Kin	NN7058	56°42·0'	4°6·9'W	X	42,51,52
Loch Garten	Highld	NH9718	57°14·7'	3°42·0'W	W	36
Lochgarthside	Highld	NH5219	57°14·5'	4°26·7'W	X	35
Loch Garve	Highld	NH4060	57°36·4'	4°40·2'W	W	20
Loch Garve	Highld	NH4159	57°35·8'	4°39·2'W	W	26
Lochgate	S Lanak	NS6347	55°36·7'	4°11·0'W	X	71
Loch Gauscavaig	Highld	NG5910	57°7·3'	5°58·4'W	W	32
Loch Geal	N Eil	NB1539	58°15·1'	6°51·0'W	W	13
Loch Geal	N Eil	NB2928	58°9·7'	6°36·0'W	W	8,13
Loch Gearach	Arg & Bt	NR2259	55°44·9'	6°25·4'W	W	60
Lochgelly	Fife	NT1893	56°7·6'	3°18·7'W	T	58
Loch Gelly	Fife	NT2092	56°7·1'	3°16·8'W	W	58
Loch Geòidh	Arg & Bt	NM9503	56°10·8'	5°17·7'W	W	55
Loch Geshader	N Eil	NB1131	58°10·7'	6°54·5'W	W	13
Loch Geumasgairbhe	N Eil	NG1091	57°49·1'	6°52·6'W	W	14
Loch Gheocrab	N Eil	NG1189	57°48·1'	6°51·4'W	W	14
Loch Gheornish	N Eil	NF9167	57°35·5'	7°9·8'W	W	18
Loch Ghiuragarstidh	Highld	NG8881	57°46·4'	5°33·4'W	W	19
Loch Ghiuthsachan	Highld	NN8699	57°4·3'	3°52·4'W	W	35,36,43
Loch Ghreosabhagh	N Eil	NG1492	57°49·8'	6°48·6'W	W	14
Loch Ghreosabhagh	N Eil	NG1591	57°49·3'	6°47·5'W	W	14
Loch Ghriais	N Eil	NB4450	58°22·1'	6°22·2'W	W	8
Loch Ghrinnabhat	N Eil	NB4745	58°19·5'	6°18·8'W	W	8
Loch Ghrinneabhat	N Eil	NB2545	58°18·7'	6°41·3'W	W	8
Loch Ghrinneabhat	N Eil	NB2947	58°19·9'	6°37·3'W	W	8
Loch Ghuibhsachain	Highld	NH0082	57°47·2'	5°21·4'W	W	19
Loch Ghuilbinn	Highld	NN4174	56°50·1'	4°35·9'W	W	42
Loch Gill	D & G	NX2757	54°52·9'	4°41·4'W	W	82
Loch Gill Breinadale	N Eil	NB1532	58°11·4'	6°50·5'W	W	13
Loch Gille-ghoid	N Eil	NF9571	57°37·8'	7°6·1'W	W	18
Loch Gilp	Arg & Bt	NR8684	56°0·3'	5°25·5'W	W	55
Lochgilphead	Arg & Bt	NR8688	56°2·5'	5°25·7'W	T	55
Loch Gil Speireig Mhòr	N Eil	NB3230	58°10·9'	6°33·1'W	W	8,13
Loch Girvan Eye	S Ayr	NX4192	55°12·1'	4°29·5'W	W	77
Loch Giùr-bheinn	Arg & Bt	NR3872	55°52·5'	6°10·9'W	W	60,61
Loch Glac an Ime	Highld	NG5930	57°18·1'	5°59·6'W	W	24,32
Loch Glanaidh	Highld	NH5232	57°21·5'	4°27·2'W	W	26
Loch Glasail	Highld	NC6540	58°19·9'	4°17·9'W	W	10
Loch Glas-bheinn	Arg & Bt	NR6795	56°5·7'	5°44·3'W	W	55,61
Loch Glascarnoch	Highld	NH3172	57°42·6'	4°49·7'W	W	20
Loch Glas-choire	Highld	NN6290	56°59·1'	4°15·8'W	W	35
Loch Glashan	Arg & Bt	NR9193	56°5·3'	5°21·1'W	W	55
Loch Glass	Highld	NH5172	57°43·1'	4°29·6'W	W	20
Loch Glassie	Pth & Kin	NN8452	56°39·0'	3°53·1'W	W	52
Loch Gleann a Bhearraidh	Arg & Bt	NM8426	56°22·9'	5°29·5'W	W	49
Loch Gleannan a' Choit	Highld	NC1627	58°11·9'	5°7·4'W	W	15
Loch Gleannan a' Mhadaidh	Highld	NC1516	58°5·9'	5°7·9'W	W	15
Loch Gleannan na Gaoithe	Highld	NC1019	58°7·4'	5°13·1'W	W	15
Loch Gleann na Moine	N Eil	NG0694	57°50·6'	6°56·8'W	W	14,18
Loch Gleann na Muice	Highld	NH0568	57°39·8'	5°15·7'W	W	19
Loch Glencoul	Highld	NC2531	58°14·2'	4°58·4'W	W	15
Loch Glendhu	Highld	NC2633	58°15·3'	4°57·5'W	W	15
Loch Glen Ionadal	Highld	NG1941	57°22·6'	6°40·0'W	W	23
Loch Glinneabhat	N Eil	NB4154	58°24·1'	6°25·5'W	W	8
Loch Glow	Fife	NT0895	56°8·6'	3°28·4'W	W	58
Loch Glumradh Beag	N Eil	NG1293	57°50·3'	6°50·7'W	W	14
Loch Glumradh Mòr	N Eil	NG1293	57°50·3'	6°50·7'W	W	14
Loch Gobhlach	Highld	NH4274	57°43·9'	4°38·8'W	W	20
Loch Gobhlach	N Eil	NB1736	58°13·6'	6°48·8'W	W	8,13
Loch Gobhlaich	N Eil	NB2527	58°9·0'	6°40·0'W	W	8,13
Loch Gobhloch	Highld	NC1749	58°23·7'	5°7·4'W	W	9
Loch Goil	Arg & Bt	NS2097	56°8·2'	4°53·4'W	W	56
Lochgoilhead	Arg & Bt	NN1901	56°10·3'	4°54·5'W	T	56
Lochgoin Fm	E Ayr	NS5346	55°41·4'	4°19·9'W	FM	64
Lochgoin Resr	E Renf	NS5347	55°41·9'	4°19·9'W	W	64
Loch Goosey	S Ayr	NX2982	55°6·4'	4°40·4'W	W	76
Loch Goosie	S Ayr	NX4494	55°13·2'	4°26·7'W	W	77
Loch Gorm	Arg & Bt	NR2365	55°48·2'	6°24·8'W	W	60
Loch Gorm	Highld	NH2369	57°40·8'	4°57·7'W	W	20
Loch Gorm	Highld	NH4833	57°22·0'	4°31·2'W	W	26
Lochgorm	Highld	NH9225	57°18·4'	3°47·1'W	X	36
Loch Gormag Mòr	N Eil	NB5247	58°20·8'	6°13·8'W	W	8
Loch Gorm Ho	Arg & Bt	NR2661	55°46·1'	6°21·7'W	X	60
Loch Gorm Mór	Highld	NG9125	57°16·3'	5°27·5'W	W	25,33
Loch Gortan	Arg & Bt	NM1752	56°34·7'	6°36·1'W	W	46
Loch Gowan	Highld	NH1556	57°33·6'	5°5·1'W	W	25
Loch Gower	D & G	NX3254	54°51·4'	4°36·6'W	W	82
Loch Gower	D & G	NX5473	55°2·1'	4°16·6'W	W	77
Loch Gower	E Ayr	NX4493	55°12·7'	4°26·7'W	W	77
Loch Gower	S Ayr	NX2877	55°3·7'	4°41·2'W	W	76
Loch Gower Burn	D & G	NX3253	54°50·9'	4°36·6'W	W	82
Loch Grànnda	N Eil	NG1892	57°50·0'	6°44·6'W	W	14
Loch Grannoch	D & G	NX5469	54°59·9'	4°16·5'W	W	83
Loch Grannoch	D & G	NX5470	55°0·4'	4°16·6'W	W	77
Loch Grannoch Lodge	D & G	NX5368	54°59·3'	4°17·4'W	X	83
Loch Grasabhat	N Eil	NB4858	58°26·5'	6°18·6'W	W	8
Lochgreen	Falk	NS8177	55°58·5'	3°54·0'W	X	65
Lochgreen Ho	S Ayr	NS3429	55°31·8'	4°37·4'W	X	70
Lochgreens	Aberd	NJ9115	57°13·8'	2°8·5'W	X	38
Loch Greivat	N Eil	NA9826	58°7·5'	7°7·3'W	W	13
Loch Greshornish	Highld	NG3453	57°29·6'	6°25·9'W	W	23
Loch Gretchen	Orkney	HY7452	59°21·5'	2°27·0'W	W	5
Loch Grigadale	Highld	NM4366	56°43·2'	6°11·6'W	W	47
Loch Grinneabhat	N Eil	NB4036	58°14·4'	6°25·3'W	W	8
Loch Griomsiadair	N Eil	NB4125	58°8·5'	6°23·6'W	W	14
Loch Grobaig	Highld	NG9259	57°34·7'	5°28·3'W	W	25
Lochgrog	E Dunb	NS6371	55°55·0'	4°11·1'W	X	64
Loch Grogary	N Eil	NF7171	57°36·8'	7°30·1'W	W	18
Loch Groigearraidh	N Eil	NF7639	57°19·8'	7°22·6'W	W	22
Loch Grosabhat	N Eil	NB5246	58°20·2'	6°13·8'W	W	8
Loch Grosvenor	Highld	NC2843	58°20·8'	4°55·9'W	W	9
Loch Grota	N Eil	NF9570	57°37·3'	7°6·1'W	W	18
Loch Gruamach	Highld	NH3151	57°31·3'	4°48·9'W	W	26
Loch Gruama Mòr	Highld	NC6139	58°19·3'	4°21·9'W	W	16
Loch Grùdaidh	Highld	NC7410	58°3·9'	4°7·7'W	W	16
Loch Gruinart	Arg & Bt	NR2971	55°51·6'	6°19·4'W	W	60
Loch Gruineabhat	N Eil	NB3726	58°8·9'	6°27·7'W	W	8
Loch Grunavat	N Eil	NB0419	58°3·9'	7°0·7'W	W	13
Loch Grunavat	N Eil	NB0827	58°8·4'	6°57·2'W	W	13
Loch Grunavet	N Eil	NF7371	57°36·9'	7°28·1'W	W	18
Loch Gynack	Highld	NH7402	57°5·8'	4°4·3'W	W	35
Loch Hacklett	N Eil	NF9471	57°37·8'	7°7·1'W	W	18
Loch Halladale	N Eil	NB0208	57°58·0'	7°1·9'W	W	13
Loch Hallan	N Eil	NF7322	57°10·6'	7°24·2'W	W	31
Loch Haluim	Highld	NC5545	58°22·4'	4°28·3'W	W	10
Loch Hamasord	N Eil	NB1632	58°11·4'	6°49·5'W	W	13
Loch Harmasaig	N Eil	NG1593	57°50·4'	6°47·7'W	W	14
Loch Harport	Highld	NG3733	57°19·0'	6°21·6'W	W	32
Loch Harrow	D & G	NX5286	55°9·0'	4°18·9'W	W	77
Loch Hasco	Highld	NG4570	57°39·1'	6°16·0'W	W	23
Lochhead	Aberd	NJ4300	57°5·5'	2°56·0'W	X	37
Lochhead	Aberd	NJ7808	57°10·0'	2°21·4'W	X	38
Lochhead	Aberd	NK0550	57°32·7'	1°54·5'W	X	30
Lochhead	Arg & Bt	NS0583	56°0·3'	5°7·2'W	X	56
Loch Head	D & G	NX3249	54°48·7'	4°36·4'W	X	82
Loch Head	E Ayr	NX4892	55°12·2'	4°22·9'W	X	77
Lochhead	Fife	NT0890	56°5·9'	3°28·3'W	X	58
Lochhead	Fife	NT1891	56°6·5'	3°18·7'W	X	58
Lochhead	S Lanak	NS7746	55°41·8'	3°57·0'W	X	64
Loch Head Burn	D & G	NX4892	55°12·2'	4°22·9'W	W	77
Lochhead Farm	Fife	NT3196	56°9·4'	3°6·2'W	FM	59
Lochhead of Leys	Aberd	NO6997	57°4·0'	2°30·2'W	X	38,45
Loch Heddal More	N Eil	NF8888	57°46·6'	7°14·5'W	W	18
Loch Heileasbhal	N Eil	NG0794	57°50·6'	6°55·8'W	W	14,18
Loch Heilen	Highld	ND2568	58°35·9'	3°17·0'W	W	11,12
Loch Hempriggs	Highld	ND3447	58°24·6'	3°7·3'W	W	12
Loch Hempton	D & G	NX3054	54°51·4'	4°38·5'W	W	82
Loch Heodha Beag	N Eil	NB0109	57°58·5'	7°3·0'W	W	13
Loch Heron	D & G	NX2764	54°56·7'	4°41·6'W	W	82
Loch Hill	Aberd	NO6779	56°54·3'	2°32·1'W	X	45
Loch Hill	D & G	NX6365	54°57·9'	4°8·0'W	H	83
Lochhill	D & G	NX6657	54°53·6'	4°4·9'W	X	83,84
Loch Hill	D & G	NX6684	55°8·2'	4°5·7'W	X	77
Loch-hill	D & G	NX8686	55°9·6'	3°46·9'W	X	78
Lochhill	D & G	NX9665	54°58·4'	3°37·1'W	X	84
Loch Hill	D & G	NY3790	55°12·3'	2°59·0'W	H	79
Lochhill	E Ayr	NS4623	55°28·9'	4°25·8'W	X	70
Lochhill	E Ayr	NS4829	55°32·1'	4°24·1'W	X	70
Lochhill	E Ayr	NS6015	55°24·8'	4°12·3'W	X	71
Lochhill	E Loth	NT4777	55°59·2'	2°50·5'W	X	66
Loch Hill	E Renf	NS5647	55°42·0'	4°17·0'W	H	64
Lochhill	Moray	NJ2964	57°39·9'	3°10·9'W	T	28
Lochhill	N Lanak	NS8165	55°52·1'	3°53·7'W	X	65
Loch Hill	S Ayr	NX1681	55°5·6'	4°52·6'W	X	76
Loch Hill	S Ayr	NX2888	55°9·6'	4°41·6'W	X	76
Loch Hill	Scot Bord	NT1315	55°25·5'	3°22·0'W	X	78
Loch Hill	Scot Bord	NT2650	55°44·5'	3°10·3'W	X	66,73
Lochhills	Aberd	NJ9064	57°40·2'	2°9·6'W	X	30
Loch-Hills	Aberd	NJ9332	57°23·0'	2°6·5'W	X	30
Lochhills	Aberd	NK0154	57°34·8'	1°58·5'W	X	30
Loch-Hills Fm	Aberd	NJ9114	57°13·3'	2°8·5'W	FM	38
Loch Hirta or Village Bay	N Eil	NF1098	57°48·4'	8°33·6'W	W	18
Loch Ho	D & G	NX8456	54°53·4'	3°48·1'W	X	84
Loch Ho	Falk	NS8770	55°54·8'	3°48·0'W	X	65
Loch Ho	W Loth	NS9977	55°58·8'	3°36·7'W	X	65
Loch Hoil	Pth & Kin	NN8643	56°34·2'	3°50·9'W	W	52
Loch Holmasaig	N Eil	NG0887	57°46·9'	6°54·3'W	W	14,18
Loch Hope	Highld	NC4654	58°27·1'	4°37·9'W	W	9
Loch Horaveg	Highld	NG5701	57°2·4'	5°59·9'W	W	32,39
Loch Horisary	N Eil	NF7768	57°35·4'	7°23·9'W	W	18
Loch Horn	Highld	NC7905	58°1·3'	4°2·4'W	W	17
Loch Hosta	N Eil	NF7272	57°37·4'	7°29·2'W	W	18
Loch Houram	N Eil	NF9169	57°36·6'	7°10·0'W	W	18
Loch Hourn	Highld	NG8209	57°7·5'	5°35·6'W	W	33
Lochhouses	E Loth	NT6181	56°1·5'	2°37·1'W	X	67
Loch Howie	D & G	NX6983	55°7·7'	4°2·8'W	W	77
Loch Huamnabhat	N Eil	NG0888	57°47·5'	6°54·4'W	W	14,18
Loch Humphrey	W Dunb	NS4576	55°57·4'	4°28·5'W	W	64
Loch Humphrey Burn	W Dunb	NS4874	55°56·4'	4°25·6'W	W	64
Loch Huna	N Eil	NF8166	57°34·5'	7°19·8'W	W	18
Loch Hunda	N Eil	NF8368	57°35·7'	7°17·9'W	W	18
Loch Hunder	N Eil	NF9065	57°34·4'	7°10·7'W	W	18
Loch Hungavat	N Eil	NF8772	57°38·0'	7°14·2'W	W	18
Loch Hunish	Highld	NG4076	57°42·2'	6°21·4'W	W	23
Loch Hurivag	N Eil	NF9175	57°39·8'	7°10·5'W	W	18
Loch Iain	Highld	NG4000	57°1·3'	6°16·6'W	W	32,39
Loch Iain Mhic Aonghais	Highld	NG8716	57°11·4'	5°31·0'W	W	33
Loch Iain Oig	Highld	NG7929	57°18·2'	5°39·7'W	W	33
Loch Ialaidh	N Eil	NF8970	57°37·0'	7°12·1'W	W	18
Loch Iarnan	Arg & Bt	NR4148	55°39·6'	6°6·6'W	W	60
Loch Iarras	N Eil	NF7830	57°15·1'	7°19·9'W	W	22
Loch Ibheir	N Eil	NB2622	58°6·4'	6°38·6'W	W	13,14
Loch 'ic Colla	N Eil	NF8660	57°31·5'	7°14·3'W	W	22
Loch Ic Iain	Highld	NG6006	57°5·2'	5°57·2'W	W	32
Lochie	Pth & Kin	NN9511	56°17·0'	3°41·3'W	X	58
Lochieheads	Fife	NO2513	56°18·5'	3°12·3'W	X	59
Loch Ille Chiopain	N Eil	NB2013	58°1·3'	6°44·1'W	W	13,14
Loch Ille Mhór	Highld	NH9332	57°22·2'	3°46·3'W	W	27,36
Loch Inbhair	Stir	NN4226	56°24·2'	4°33·2'W	W	51
Lochinch	C of Glas	NS5562	55°50·0'	4°18·5'W	X	64
Loch Inchard	Highld	NC2354	58°26·6'	5°1·5'W	W	9
Lochinch Castle	D & G	NX1061	54°54·7'	4°57·4'W	X	82
Loch Indaal	Arg & Bt	NR2658	55°44·5'	6°21·5'W	W	60
Lochindorb	Highld	NH9736	57°24·4'	3°42·4'W	W	27
Lochindorb Castle	Highld	NH9736	57°24·4'	3°42·4'W	A	27
Lochindorb Lodge	Highld	NH9635	57°23·9'	3°43·4'W	X	27
Lochindores	Angus	NO2635	56°30·3'	3°11·7'W	W	53
Lochingerroch	E Ayr	NS6209	55°21·6'	4°10·2'W	X	71,77
Lochingerroch Burn	E Ayr	NS6108	55°21·0'	4°11·1'W	W	71,77
Loch Innis	N Eil	NB5432	58°12·8'	6°10·8'W	W	8
Loch Innis Gheamhraidh	Highld	NH2926	57°17·8'	4°49·8'W	W	25
Loch Innis na Bà Buidhe	Highld	NC2256	58°27·6'	5°2·6'W	W	9
Loch Innis nan Seangan	Highld	NG9132	57°20·1'	5°27·9'W	W	25
Loch Innis Thorcaill	Highld	NC1528	58°12·4'	5°8·4'W	W	15
Loch Innseag	N Eil	NB4028	58°10·1'	6°24·8'W	W	8
Loch Insh	Highld	NH8304	57°7·0'	3°55·5'W	W	35
Loch Inshore	Highld	NC3269	58°34·9'	4°52·9'W	W	9
Lochinvar	D & G	NX6585	55°8·7'	4°6·7'W	W	77
Lochinvar Burn	D & G	NX6582	55°7·1'	4°6·6'W	W	77
Lochinvar Lodge	D & G	NX6585	55°8·7'	4°6·7'W	X	77
Loch Inver	Highld	NC0721	58°8·4'	5°16·2'W	W	15
Lochinver	Highld	NC0922	58°9·0'	5°14·3'W	T	15
Lochinver	Moray	NJ1861	57°38·2'	3°21·9'W	X	28
Loch Iobhair	N Eil	NB3927	58°9·6'	6°25·8'W	W	8
Loch Iochdarach a' Chruaidh-ghlinn	Arg & Bt	NR5790	56°2·7'	5°53·7'W	W	61
Loch Iochdarach Airigh Nualaidh	Arg & Bt	NR5486	56°0·5'	5°56·3'W	W	61
Loch Iol-ghaoith	Highld	NC3530	58°13·9'	4°48·1'W	W	15
Loch Ionadagro	N Eil	NB5146	58°20·2'	6°14·8'W	W	8
Loch Ionail	N Eil	NB1536	58°13·5'	6°50·8'W	W	13
Loch Iorsa	N Ayr	NR9138	55°35·7'	5°18·6'W	W	68,69
Loch Iosal a' Bhruic	N Eil	NB2827	58°9·2'	6°36·9'W	W	8,13
Loch Iosal an Dùin	N Eil	NF9177	57°40·9'	7°10·6'W	W	18
Loch Isbister	Shetld	HU5764	60°21·6'	0°57·5'W	W	2
Lochivraon	Highld	NH1173	57°42·7'	5°9·9'W	X	19
Loch Kanaird	Highld	NH1099	57°56·7'	5°12·1'W	W	19
Loch Kander	Aberd	NO1980	56°54·5'	3°19·4'W	W	43
Loch Katrine	Stir	NN3912	56°16·6'	4°35·6'W	W	50,56
Loch Katrine	Stir	NN4209	56°15·1'	4°32·6'W	W	56
Loch Katrine	Stir	NN4609	56°15·2'	4°28·7'W	W	57
Loch Kearsinish	N Eil	NF7916	57°7·6'	7°17·9'W	W	31
Loch Keisgaig	Highld	NC2667	58°33·6'	4°59·0'W	W	9
Loch Kemp	Highld	NH4616	57°12·8'	4°32·5'W	W	34
Loch Ken	D & G	NX6672	55°1·7'	4°5·4'W	W	77,84
Loch Kennard	Pth & Kin	NN9046	56°35·8'	3°47·0'W	W	52
Loch Ken or River Dee	D & G	NX7168	54°59·6'	4°0·6'W	W	83,84
Loch Ken Viaduct	D & G	NX6870	55°0·7'	4°3·4'W	X	77,84
Loch Kernsary	Highld	NG8880	57°45·8'	5°33·4'W	W	19
Loch Kerry	Highld	NG8073	57°41·8'	5°41·0'W	W	19
Loch Killin	Highld	NH5210	57°9·7'	4°26·4'W	W	35
Loch Kinardochy	Pth & Kin	NN7755	56°40·5'	4°0·0'W	W	42,51,52
Loch Kindar	D & G	NX9664	54°57·8'	3°37·0'W	W	84
Loch Kinellan	Highld	NH4757	57°34·9'	4°33·1'W	W	26
Loch Kinnabus	Arg & Bt	NR3042	55°36·1'	6°16·8'W	W	60
Loch Kinord	Aberd	NO4499	57°5·0'	2°55·0'W	W	37,44
Loch Kirkaig	Highld	NC0719	58°7·3'	5°16·2'W	W	15
Loch Kirkaldy	Highld	NH9641	57°27·1'	3°43·5'W	W	27
Loch Kishorn	Highld	NG8138	57°23·0'	5°38·2'W	W	24
Loch Knockie	Highld	NH4513	57°11·2'	4°33·4'W	W	34
Loch Knowe	D & G	NY4287	55°10·7'	2°54·2'W	X	79
Loch Knowe	Scot Bord	NY5893	55°14·0'	2°39·2'W	H	80
Loch Labharaig	Highld	NH2892	57°53·3'	4°53·6'W	W	20
Loch Lacasdail	N Eil	NB2706	57°57·8'	6°36·5'W	W	13,14
Loch Lacasdail	N Eil	NG1096	57°51·8'	6°52·9'W	W	14
Loch Lacsabhat Iarach	N Eil	NB2338	58°14·9'	6°42·8'W	W	8,13
Loch Laga	Highld	NM6463	56°42·2'	5°50·9'W	W	40
Loch Lagaidh	Highld	NH1189	57°51·3'	5°10·6'W	W	19
Loch Laggan	Highld	NN4886	56°56·7'	4°29·5'W	W	34,42

Loch Laggan	Stir	NS6292	56°6·3'	4°12·7'W	W	57
Loch Laich	Arg & Bt	NM9246	56°33·9'	5°22·7'W	W	49
Loch Laicheard	Highld	NC1746	58°22·1'	5°7·3'W	W	9
Loch Laide	Highld	NH5435	57°23·2'	4°25·3'W	W	26
Loch Laidon	Pth & Kin	NN3854	56°39·2'	4°38·1'W	W	41
Loch Laidon	Pth & Kin	NN4056	56°40·4'	4°36·2'W	W	42,51
Loch Laingeadail	Arg & Bt	NR2671	55°51·5'	6°22·3'W	W	60
Loch Laingeadail Beag	Arg & Bt	NR2671	55°51·5'	6°22·3'W	W	60
Lochlair	Angus	NO5243	56°34·8'	2°46·4'W	X	54
Lochlait	Highld	NH5435	57°23·2'	4°25·3'W	X	26
Loch Lamadale	N Eil	NB0417	58°2·9'	7°0·6'W	W	13
Loch Lamascaig	Highld	NG5803	57°3·5'	5°59·0'W	W	32,39
Lochlands	Angus	NO4447	56°36·9'	2°54·3'W	X	54
Lochlands	Angus	NO6341	56°33·8'	2°35·7'W	X	54
Lochlands	Pth & Kin	NO2145	56°35·7'	3°16·7'W	X	53
Lochlands	S Ayr	NS3109	55°21·0'	4°39·5'W	X	70,76
Lochlands Hill	N Ayr	NS3755	55°45·9'	4°35·4'W	H	63
Loch Lane	D & G	NX6066	54°58·4'	4°10·8'W	W	83
Lochlane	Pth & Kin	NN8321	56°22·3'	3°53·2'W	X	52,57
Loch Langabhat	N Eil	NB1718	58°3·9'	6°47·5'W	W	13,14
Loch Langabhat	N Eil	NB2143	58°17·5'	6°45·2'W	W	8
Loch Langabhat	N Eil	NB4844	58°19·0'	6°17·7'W	W	8
Loch Langabhat	N Eil	NB5254	58°24·5'	6°14·3'W	W	8
Loch Langabhat	N Eil	NF8348	57°25·0'	7°16·4'W	W	22
Loch Langaig	Highld	NG4670	57°39·2'	6°15·0'W	W	23
Loch Langass	N Eil	NF8464	57°33·6'	7°16·6'W	W	18
Loch Langavat	N Eil	NB0209	57°58·5'	7°2·0'W	W	13
Loch Langavat	N Eil	NG0489	57°47·8'	6°58·5'W	W	18
Loch Langdale	Highld	NC6846	58°23·2'	4°15·0'W	W	10
Loch Langwell	Highld	NC4113	58°4·9'	4°41·3'W	W	16
Loch Lanlish	Highld	NC3868	58°34·5'	4°46·7'W	W	9
Loch Lànnsaidh	Highld	NH7394	57°55·3'	4°8·2'W	W	21
Loch Laoigh	Highld	NH7395	57°55·8'	4°8·2'W	W	21
Loch Laoim	Arg & Bt	NR3748	55°39·5'	6°10·5'W	W	60
Loch Lapagial	Highld	NH7382	57°48·8'	4°7·8'W	W	21
Loch Lapaich	Highld	NH1524	57°16·4'	5°3·7'W	W	25
Loch Laphroaig	Arg & Bt	NR3845	55°37·9'	6°9·3'W	W	60
Loch Laraig	Highld	NG8477	57°44·1'	5°37·2'W	W	19
Loch Laro	Highld	NH6099	57°57·8'	4°21·5'W	W	21
Loch Lathamul	N Eil	NB3930	58°11·2'	6°26·0'W	W	8
Loch Laxavat Ard	N Eil	NB2438	58°14·9'	6°41·8'W	W	8,13
Loch Laxford	Highld	NC1949	58°23·8'	5°5·3'W	W	9
Lochlea	S Ayr	NS4530	55°32·6'	4°27·0'W	X	70
Loch Leacann	Arg & Bt	NM9903	56°10·9'	5°13·9'W	W	55
Loch Leachd	Arg & Bt	NM9504	56°11·3'	5°17·8'W	W	55
Loch Leatha	N Eil	NB1018	58°3·6'	6°54·5'W	W	13,14
Loch Leathad an Lochain	Highld	NC0720	58°7·9'	5°16·2'W	W	15
Loch Leathad nan Aighean	Highld	NC0527	58°11·6'	5°18·6'W	W	15
Loch Leathad nan Cruineachd	Highld	NC1643	58°20·5'	5°8·1'W	W	9
Loch Leathain	N Eil	NB3418	58°4·5'	6°30·2'W	W	13,14
Loch Leathan	Arg & Bt	NR3467	55°49·6'	6°14·4'W	W	60,61
Loch Leathan	Arg & Bt	NR8798	56°7·9'	5°25·2'W	W	55
Loch Leathan	Highld	NG5051	57°29·1'	6°9·8'W	W	23,24
Loch Leathan an Sgòrra	Arg & Bt	NR4052	55°41·8'	6°7·8'W	W	60
Loch Leathann	Arg & Bt	NR4163	55°47·7'	6°7·5'W	W	60,61
Loch Leathann	Highld	NG7441	57°24·5'	5°45·3'W	W	24
Loch Leathed a' Bhaile Fhoghair	Highld	NC0527	58°11·6'	5°18·6'W	W	15
Loch Lednock Reservoir	Pth & Kin	NN7129	56°26·4'	4°5·1'W	W	51,52
Loch Lee	Angus	NO4279	56°54·2'	2°56·7'W	W	44
Lochlee Hill	D & G	NX6789	55°10·9'	4°4·9'W	H	77
Loch Leineabhat	N Eil	NB4860	58°27·6'	6°18·8'W	W	8
Loch Leiniscal	N Eil	NB3629	58°10·5'	6°28·9'W	W	8
Loch Lèir	Highld	NC9545	58°23·1'	3°47·3'W	W	11
Loch Leisabhat	N Eil	NB4357	58°25·8'	6°23·7'W	W	8
Loch Leisgein	Highld	NH6097	57°56·7'	4°21·4'W	W	21
Loch Leitir	N Eil	NB3238	58°15·2'	6°33·6'W	W	8,13
Loch Leitir Easaidh	Highld	NC1626	58°11·3'	5°7·3'W	W	15
Loch Lennous	D & G	NX3353	54°50·9'	4°35·6'W	W	82
Loch Leòdamais	Arg & Bt	NR3645	55°37·9'	6°11·2'W	W	60
Loch Leodasay	N Eil	NF8063	57°32·9'	7°20·5'W	W	18
Loch Leòsaid	N Eil	NB0608	57°58·1'	6°57·9'W	W	13,14
Loch Lesgamaill	Arg & Bt	NR5777	55°55·7'	5°53·0'W	W	61
Lochletter	Highld	NH4429	57°19·8'	4°35·0'W	X	26
Lochletter Wood	Highld	NH4329	57°19·7'	4°36·0'W	F	26
Loch Leum na Luirginn	Highld	NG4467	57°37·5'	6°16·8'W	W	23
Loch Leum nam Bràdh	Highld	NG4670	57°39·2'	6°15·0'W	W	23
Loch Leven	Highld	NN0960	56°41·8'	5°6·7'W	W	41
Loch Leven	Pth & Kin	NO1401	56°11·9'	3°22·7'W	W	58
Lochleven Castle	Pth & Kin	NO1301	56°11·9'	3°23·7'W	A	58
Loch Leven Hotel	Highld	NN0559	56°41·2'	5°10·6'W	X	41
Loch Li	Highld	NH2270	57°41·3'	4°58·7'W	W	20
Loch Lianarich	N Eil	NB0307	57°57·5'	7°0·8'W	W	13
Loch Liath	Highld	NH3319	57°14·1'	4°45·6'W	W	34
Loch Liath	Highld	NH3920	57°14·8'	4°39·6'W	W	26
Loch Liath	Highld	NH4022	57°15·9'	4°38·7'W	W	26
Loch Libo	E Renf	NS4355	55°46·0'	4°29·7'W	W	64
Lochliboside Hills	E Renf	NS4557	55°47·1'	4°27·8'W	X	64
Loch Lic-aird	Highld	NG3332	57°18·3'	6°25·5'W	W	32
Lochliesk	Moray	NJ3245	57°29·7'	3°7·6'W	X	28
Loch Lig	S Ayr	NX2084	55°7·3'	4°48·9'W	W	76
Loch Lighigeag	N Eil	NB4224	58°8·0'	6°22·5'W	W	14
Loch Lingabhat Beag	N Eil	NB5248	58°21·3'	6°13·9'W	W	8
Loch Lingabhat Mòr	N Eil	NB5148	58°21·3'	6°14·9'W	W	8
Loch Linish	N Eil	NB1134	58°12·3'	6°54·7'W	W	13
Loch Linne	Arg & Bt	NR7991	56°3·9'	5°32·6'W	W	55
Loch Linngrabhaigh	N Eil	NB3406	57°58·2'	6°29·4'W	W	13,14
Loch Linnhe	Highld	NM8748	56°34·8'	5°27·6'W	W	49
Lochlip	Aberd	NJ9063	57°39·7'	2°9·6'W	X	30
Lochlip	Aberd	NK0263	57°39·7'	1°57·5'W	X	30
Loch Lite Sithinn	N Eil	NB4115	58°3·2'	6°22·9'W	W	14
Loch Liuravay	Highld	NG4858	57°32·8'	6°12·2'W	W	23
Loch Liurboist	N Eil	NB3724	58°7·9'	6°27·6'W	W	14
Loch Loch	Pth & Kin	NN9874	56°51·0'	3°39·9'W	W	43
Loch Lochton	S Ayr	NX1792	55°11·6'	4°52·1'W	W	76
Loch Lochy	Highld	NN2087	56°56·6'	4°57·1'W	W	34,41
Loch Lochy	Highld	NN2390	56°58·3'	4°54·3'W	W	34
Loch Logan	Stir	NS6893	56°6·9'	4°6·9'W	W	57
Loch Lomhain	N Eil	NB1619	58°4·4'	6°48·5'W	W	13,14
Loch Lomond	Arg & Bt	NN3313	56°17·1'	4°41·4'W	W	50,56
Loch Lomond	Arg & Bt	NS3597	56°8·5'	4°38·9'W	W	56
Loch Lomond National Nature Reserve	W Dunb	NS4189	56°4·3'	4°32·8'W	X	56
Loch Lonachan	Highld	NG6219	57°12·3'	5°56·0'W	W	32
Loch Lonaig	Highld	NG3751	57°28·6'	6°22·8'W	W	23
Loch Long	Arg & Bt	NS2191	56°5·0'	4°52·2'W	W	56
Loch Long	Highld	NG8927	57°17·4'	5°29·6'W	W	33
Loch Long	Highld	NG9029	57°18·5'	5°28·7'W	W	25,33
Loch Lòn Mhurchaidh	Highld	NH0326	57°17·2'	5°15·7'W	W	25,33
Loch Lòn na Gaoithe	Highld	NC7405	58°1·2'	4°7·5'W	W	16
Loch Lòn na h-Uamha	Highld	NC1211	58°3·2'	5°10·7'W	W	15
Loch Loran	Arg & Bt	NR9090	56°3·7'	5°21·9'W	W	55
Loch Losait	Highld	NG2759	57°32·6'	6°33·3'W	W	23
Loch Losgainn	Arg & Bt	NR7443	55°37·9'	5°35·0'W	W	62
Loch Losgainn	Highld	NH6693	57°54·6'	4°15·2'W	W	21
Loch Losgann	Highld	ND0249	58°25·4'	3°40·2'W	W	11,12
Loch Losguinn	Arg & Bt	NR5879	55°56·8'	5°52·1'W	W	61
Loch Losgunn	Arg & Bt	NR7989	56°2·8'	5°32·5'W	W	55
Loch Loskin	Arg & Bt	NS1678	55°57·8'	4°56·4'W	W	63
Loch Lossit	Arg & Bt	NR4065	55°48·8'	6°8·6'W	W	60,61
Lochloy	Highld	NH9257	57°35·7'	3°47·9'W	X	27
Loch Loy	Highld	NH9358	57°36·2'	3°47·0'W	W	27
Loch Loyal	Highld	NC6247	58°23·6'	4°21·2'W	W	10
Loch Loyal Lodge	Highld	NC6146	58°23·1'	4°22·2'W	X	10
Loch Loyne	Highld	NH1604	57°5·7'	5°1·8'W	W	34
Loch Lùbanach	Arg & Bt	NR5483	55°58·9'	5°56·2'W	W	61
Loch Lubnaig	Stir	NN5813	56°17·6'	4°17·2'W	W	57
Loch Lucy	Highld	NC8739	58°19·8'	3°55·3'W	W	17
Lochluichart	Highld	NH3363	57°37·8'	4°47·4'W	T	20
Loch Luichart	Highld	NH3661	57°36·8'	4°44·3'W	W	20
Loch Luichart	Highld	NH3859	57°35·8'	4°42·2'W	W	26
Lochluichart Lodge	Highld	NH3363	57°37·8'	4°47·4'W	X	20
Loch Luireach	Arg & Bt	NR7444	55°38·5'	5°35·0'W	W	62
Loch Lundie	Highld	NG8031	57°19·3'	5°38·8'W	W	24
Loch Lundie	Highld	NG8049	57°28·9'	5°39·7'W	W	24
Loch Lundie	Highld	NH2903	57°5·4'	4°48·9'W	W	34
Loch Lundie	Highld	NH6750	57°31·5'	4°12·8'W	W	26
Lochlundie Moss	Aberd	NK0433	57°23·5'	1°55·6'W	X	30
Loch Lunndaidh	Highld	NC7800	57°58·6'	4°3·3'W	W	17
Loch Lurach	Arg & Bt	NR8157	55°45·7'	5°29·0'W	W	62
Loch Lurgainn	Highld	NC1108	58°1·5'	5°11·6'W	W	15
Loch Lurkie	D & G	NX7270	55°0·7'	3°59·7'W	W	77,84
Lochly	Arg & Bt	NS0862	55°49·0'	5°3·4'W	X	63
Lochlyoch	S Lanak	NS9336	55°36·6'	3°41·5'W	X	71,72
Lochlyoch Reservoir	S Lanak	NS9335	55°36·1'	3°41·5'W	W	71,72
Lochlyock Hill	S Lanak	NS9334	55°35·6'	3°41·4'W	H	71,72
Loch Lyon	Pth & Kin	NN3839	56°31·2'	4°37·5'W	W	50
Loch Lyon	Pth & Kin	NN4240	56°31·8'	4°33·7'W	W	51
Lochmaben	D & G	NY0882	55°7·7'	3°26·1'W	T	78
Lochmaben Castle	D & G	NY0881	55°7·1'	3°26·1'W	A	78
Lochmaben Stone	D & G	NY3165	54°58·7'	3°4·3'W	A	85
Loch Maberry	D & G	NX2875	55°2·6'	4°41·1'W	W	76
Loch Mabrennie	S Ayr	NX2777	55°3·7'	4°42·1'W	W	76
Loch Macanrie	Stir	NS5699	56°10·0'	4°18·7'W	W	57
Loch Macaterick	E Ayr	NX4391	55°11·6'	4°27·6'W	W	77
Loch Mackie	D & G	NX8048	54°49·0'	3°51·6'W	W	84
Lochmaddy	N Eil	NF9168	57°36·0'	7°9·9'W	T	18
Loch Maddy or Loch nam Madadh	N Eil	NF9368	57°36·1'	7°7·9'W	W	18
Loch Magharaidh	Highld	NH4577	57°45·6'	4°35·8'W	W	20
Loch Magillie	D & G	NX0959	54°53·6'	4°58·3'W	W	82
Loch Mahaick	Stir	NN7006	56°14·0'	4°5·4'W	W	57
Lochmailing	D & G	NX9085	55°9·1'	3°43·1'W	X	78
Loch Mall	Highld	NG8935	57°21·7'	5°30·0'W	W	24
Loch Mallachie	Highld	NH9617	57°14·2'	3°42·9'W	W	36
Loch Mallaichte	Highld	NG5949	57°28·3'	6°0·7'W	W	24
Lochmalony Fm	Fife	NO3720	56°22·3'	3°0·8'W	FM	54,59
Lochmalony Ho	Fife	NO3620	56°22·3'	3°1·7'W	X	54,59
Loch Mama	Highld	NM7585	56°54·4'	5°41·3'W	W	40
Loch ma Nàire	Highld	NC7253	58°27·1'	4°11·1'W	W	10
Loch Mannoch	D & G	NX6660	54°55·3'	4°5·0'W	W	83,84
Lochmanse	Aberd	NJ5104	57°7·7'	2°48·1'W	X	37
Loch Maoile	Highld	NC1600	57°57·3'	5°6·1'W	W	15
Loch Maolaig	N Eil	NB0610	57°59·2'	6°58·0'W	W	13,14
Loch Maol Fhraochach	Highld	NG7538	57°22·9'	5°44·1'W	W	24
Loch Maovally	Highld	NC5060	58°30·4'	4°34·0'W	W	9
Loch Marabhat	N Eil	NB4053	58°23·6'	6°26·5'W	W	8
Loch Maragan	Stir	NN4027	56°24·7'	4°35·2'W	W	51
Loch Màraig	N Eil	NB2005	57°57·0'	6°43·5'W	W	13,14
Loch Maree	Highld	NG9570	57°40·7'	5°25·8'W	W	19
Loch Maree Hotel	Highld	NG9170	57°40·5'	5°29·8'W	X	19
Loch Martle	S Ayr	NX2476	55°3·1'	4°44·9'W	W	76
Loch Marulaigh	N Eil	NF8116	57°7·7'	7°15·9'W	W	31
Loch ma Stac	Highld	NH3421	57°15·2'	4°44·6'W	W	26
Loch Màthair Bhorgaidh	Highld	NC5241	58°20·2'	4°31·2'W	W	10
Loch Mckay	Arg & Bt	NR7988	56°2·3'	5°32·4'W	W	55
Loch Meàchdannach	Highld	NG4317	57°10·6'	6°14·7'W	W	32
Loch Meadaidh	Highld	NC4064	58°32·4'	4°44·4'W	W	9
Loch Meadhoin	Arg & Bt	NM4752	56°35·8'	6°6·8'W	W	47
Loch Meadhoin	Highld	ND0651	58°26·5'	3°36·1'W	W	11,12
Loch Meadhonach	Arg & Bt	NR7376	55°55·7'	5°37·6'W	W	62
Loch Meadhonach	Highld	NC2163	58°31·4'	5°4·0'W	W	9
Loch Meadie	Highld	NC4939	58°19·1'	4°34·2'W	W	16
Loch Meadie	Highld	NC4940	58°19·6'	4°34·2'W	W	9
Loch Meadie	Highld	NC7560	58°30·9'	4°8·3'W	W	10
Loch Meadie	Highld	ND0848	58°24·9'	3°34·0'W	W	11,12
Loch Meala	Highld	NC7856	58°28·8'	4°5·1'W	W	10
Loch Meall a' Mhadaidh	Highld	NH2936	57°23·2'	4°50·2'W	W	25
Loch Meall a' Bhainne	Highld	NG7583	57°47·1'	5°46·6'W	W	19
Loch Meall a' Bhuirich	Highld	NC3512	58°4·2'	4°47·4'W	W	15
Loch Meallachain	Highld	NG4941	57°23·7'	6°10·2'W	W	23
Loch Meall a' Chuail	Highld	NG9352	57°30·9'	5°26·9'W	W	25
Loch Meall a' Mhùthaich	Highld	NC1916	58°6·0'	5°3·8'W	W	15
Loch Meallan an Fhùdair	Highld	NH0670	57°40·9'	5°14·8'W	W	19
Loch Meallan Gobhar	Highld	NG8446	57°27·4'	5°35·6'W	W	24
Loch Meallbrodden	Pth & Kin	NN9125	56°24·5'	3°45·5'W	W	52,58
Loch Meall Chuilc	Highld	NC4344	58°21·6'	4°40·5'W	W	9
Loch Meall Daimh	Highld	NG5740	57°23·4'	6°2·2'W	W	24
Loch Meall Dheirgidh	Highld	NH4893	57°54·3'	4°33·4'W	W	20
Loch Meall na Leitreach	Pth & Kin	NN6368	56°47·3'	4°14·1'W	W	42
Loch Meall nam Feadon	Highld	NG7336	57°21·7'	5°46·0'W	W	24
Loch Meall nan Caorach	Highld	NC2922	58°9·5'	4°53·9'W	W	15
Loch Meall nan Dearcag	Highld	NC1906	58°0·6'	5°3·3'W	W	15
Loch Mealt	Highld	NG5065	57°36·6'	6°10·7'W	W	23,24
Loch Meanarbhagh	N Eil	NF8749	57°25·7'	7°12·5'W	W	22
Lochmeharb	E Ayr	NS5604	55°18·8'	4°15·7'W	X	77
Loch Meig	Highld	NH3555	57°33·6'	4°45·0'W	W	26
Loch Meiklie	Highld	NH4330	57°20·3'	4°36·0'W	W	26
Loch Melavat	N Eil	NB0029	58°9·1'	7°5·5'W	W	13
Loch Meleag	Highld	NC6749	58°24·8'	4°16·1'W	W	10
Loch Melemon	S Ayr	NX1185	55°7·7'	4°57·4'W	W	76
Loch Melfort	Arg & Bt	NM8012	56°15·2'	5°32·7'W	W	55
Loch Melldalloch	Arg & Bt	NR9374	55°55·1'	5°18·3'W	W	62
Loch Meodal	Highld	NG6511	57°8·1'	5°52·6'W	W	32
Loch Meraddie	S Ayr	NX1583	55°6·7'	4°53·6'W	W	76
Loch Merkland	Highld	NC3931	58°14·6'	4°44·1'W	W	16
Loch Meurach	N Eil	NG0687	57°46·8'	6°56·3'W	W	14,18
Lochmeyler	Pemb	SM8527	51°54·2'	5°7·1'W	X	157
Loch Mhadadh	Highld	NC9933	58°16·7'	3°42·9'W	W	11,17
Loch Mhairc	Pth & Kin	NN8879	56°53·6'	3°49·9'W	W	43
Loch Mhànais	N Eil	NG0990	57°48·6'	6°53·5'W	W	14
Loch Mhaolach-coire	Highld	NC2719	58°7·8'	4°55·8'W	W	15
Loch Mharabhig	N Eil	NB4119	58°5·3'	6°23·2'W	W	14
Loch Mharaich	Pth & Kin	NO1156	56°41·5'	3°26·7'W	W	53
Loch Mharcoil	N Eil	NB1834	58°12·5'	6°47·6'W	W	8,13
Loch Mheacleit	N Eil	NB0436	58°13·1'	7°2·0'W	W	13
Loch Mheugaidh	Pth & Kin	NN5361	56°43·3'	4°23·7'W	W	42
Loch Mhiabhaig	N Eil	NB0905	57°56·6'	6°54·6'W	W	13,14
Loch Mhic a' Roin	N Eil	NF7568	57°35·4'	7°25·9'W	W	18
Loch Mhic Charmhiceil	Highld	NG6409	57°6·9'	5°53·4'W	W	32
Loch Mhic Dhiarmaid	Arg & Bt	NN0209	56°14·2'	5°11·2'W	W	55
Loch Mhic Eanluig	Arg & Bt	NR7578	55°56·8'	5°35·8'W	W	62
Loch Mhic Ghille-chaoil	Highld	NH9202	57°6·0'	3°46·5'W	W	36
Loch Mhic Gille-bhride	N Eil	NF7769	57°36·0'	7°24·0'W	W	18
Loch Mhic'ille Riabhaich	Highld	NG9084	57°48·0'	5°31·6'W	W	19
Loch Mhic Iomhair	Highld	NH3166	57°39·4'	4°49·5'W	W	20
Loch Mhic Leannain	Highld	NM7194	56°59·1'	5°45·7'W	W	33,40
Loch Mhic Leòid	Highld	NJ0034	57°23·4'	3°39·4'W	W	27
Loch Mhic Leoid	N Eil	NB2731	58°11·3'	6°38·2'W	W	8,13
Loch Mhic Mhàirtein	Arg & Bt	NM7803	56°10·3'	5°34·1'W	W	55
Loch Mhic-Mharsaill	Highld	NH4499	57°57·4'	4°37·7'W	W	20
Loch Mhic Neacail	N Eil	NG1491	57°49·3'	6°48·5'W	W	14
Loch Mhic Phail	N Eil	NF9375	57°39·9'	7°8·5'W	W	18
Loch Mhicreithe	Arg & Bt	NR7851	55°42·4'	5°31·6'W	W	62,69
Loch Mhisteam	N Eil	NB1508	57°58·5'	6°48·8'W	W	13,14
Loch Mhoicean	Highld	NH0731	57°20·0'	5°11·9'W	W	25
Loch Mhor	Highld	NH5420	57°15·1'	4°24·7'W	W	26,35
Loch Mhuilich	Highld	NH1243	57°26·6'	5°7·5'W	W	25
Loch Mhurchaidh	Arg & Bt	NR3975	55°54·1'	6°10·1'W	W	60,61
Loch Mhurchaidh	N Eil	NB2332	58°11·7'	6°42·4'W	W	8,13
Loch Michean	Arg & Bt	NR8098	56°7·7'	5°32·0'W	W	55
Loch Middle	D & G	NX3974	55°2·3'	4°30·7'W	W	77
Loch Migdale	Highld	NH6390	57°53·0'	4°18·2'W	W	21
Lochmill	Angus	NO4249	56°38·0'	2°56·3'W	X	54
Lochmill	Fife	NO2216	56°20·1'	3°15·3'W	X	58
Loch Milleho	N Eil	NB4238	58°15·6'	6°23·4'W	W	8
Lochmill Loch	Fife	NO2216	56°20·1'	3°15·3'W	W	58
Loch Mingary	Arg & Bt	NM4256	56°37·7'	6°12·0'W	W	47
Loch Minish	N Eil	NF9070	57°37·1'	7°11·1'W	W	18
Loch Minnoch	D & G	NX5385	55°8·5'	4°18·0'W	W	77
Loch Mirceabhat	N Eil	NB4016	58°3·7'	6°24·0'W	W	14
Loch Misirich	Highld	NH5068	57°40·9'	4°30·5'W	W	20
Loch Mitchell	Highld	NG3901	57°1·8'	6°17·6'W	W	32,39
Loch Moan	D & G	NX3485	55°8·1'	4°35·8'W	W	76
Loch Modsarie	Highld	NC6461	58°31·2'	4°19·6'W	W	10
Loch Moglabhat	N Eil	NB1918	58°4·0'	6°45·4'W	W	13,14
Loch Moidart	Highld	NM6873	56°47·7'	5°47·5'W	W	40
Loch Moidart	Highld	NM7772	56°47·4'	5°38·6'W	W	40
Loch Moin' a' Chriathair	Highld	NG9347	57°28·2'	5°26·7'W	W	25
Loch Mòine Sheilg	Highld	NG9189	57°50·8'	5°30·8'W	W	19
Loch Molach	Highld	NC6339	58°19·4'	4°19·9'W	W	16
Loch Molach	Highld	NC7241	58°20·6'	4°10·7'W	W	10
Loch Monaghan	Pth & Kin	NN5355	56°40·1'	4°23·5'W	W	42,51
Loch Monaidh	Pth & Kin	NN5668	56°47·1'	4°21·0'W	W	42
Loch Monar	Highld	NH1440	57°25·0'	5°5·4'W	W	25
Loch Monica	Highld	NM3396	56°58·9'	6°23·2'W	W	39
Loch Monzievaird	Pth & Kin	NN8423	56°23·4'	3°52·3'W	W	52,58
Loch Mór	Arg & Bt	NR7340	55°36·3'	5°35·8'W	W	62
Loch Mór	Highld	NC7260	58°30·8'	4°11·4'W	W	10
Loch Mór	Highld	NC8863	58°32·7'	3°55·0'W	W	10
Loch Mór	Highld	NG1448	57°26·2'	6°45·5'W	W	23
Loch Mór	Highld	NG4060	57°33·6'	6°20·4'W	W	23
Loch Mór	Highld	NG4514	57°9·0'	6°12·5'W	W	32
Loch Mór	Highld	NG5851	57°29·3'	6°1·8'W	W	24
Loch Mór	Highld	NH1535	57°22·3'	5°4·1'W	W	25
Loch Mór	Highld	NH9625	57°18·5'	3°43·1'W	W	36
Loch Mór	N Eil	NB0736	58°13·2'	6°58·9'W	W	13
Loch Mór	N Eil	NB2103	57°56·0'	6°42·3'W	W	13,14
Loch Mór	N Eil	NB4954	58°24·4'	6°17·3'W	W	8
Loch Mòr	N Eil	NF7752	57°26·9'	7°22·6'W	W	22
Loch Mòr	N Eil	NF7962	57°32·3'	7°21·4'W	W	22
Loch Mòr	N Eil	NF8481	57°42·7'	7°17·9'W	W	18
Loch Mòr a' Chòcair	N Eil	NB3434	58°13·1'	6°31·3'W	W	8,13
Loch Mòr a' Chraisg	Highld	NC2260	58°29·8'	5°2·8'W	W	9
Loch Mòr a' Chrotaich	N Eil	NB4130	58°11·2'	6°23·9'W	W	8
Loch Mòr a Ghoba	N Eil	NB4847	58°20·6'	6°17·9'W	W	8
Loch Mòr a' Ghrianain	N Eil	NB2637	58°14·5'	6°39·7'W	W	8,13
Loch Mòr a' Ghrianain	N Eil	NB4030	58°11·2'	6°24·9'W	W	8
Loch Moraig	Pth & Kin	NN9066	56°46·6'	3°47·6'W	W	43
Loch Mòr Airigh nan Linntean	N Eil	NB2122	58°6·2'	6°43·7'W	W	13,14
Loch Mòr an Fada Mhòir	N Eil	NB2525	58°8·0'	6°39·8'W	W	13,14
Loch Mòr an Iarainn	N Eil	NB3019	58°4·9'	6°34·3'W	W	13,14
Loch Mòr an Starr	N Eil	NB3938	58°15·5'	6°26·5'W	W	8
Loch Mòr an Tanga	N Eil	NB3719	58°5·2'	6°27·2'W	W	14
Loch Morar	Highld	NM7590	56°57·1'	5°41·5'W	W	33,40
Loch Mòr Ardalanish	Arg & Bt	NM3619	56°17·7'	6°15·6'W	W	48
Loch Mòr Bad an Ducharaich	Highld	NH0086	57°49·4'	5°21·6'W	W	19

Loch Mór Bealach na h-Imriche	Arg & Bt	NR5686	56°0·5′	5°54·4′W	W	61
Loch Mòr Bharabhais	N Eil	NB3450	58°21·7′	6°32·4′W	W	8
Loch Mór Braigh an Tarain	N Eil	NB0426	58°7·7′	7°1·2′W	W	13
Loch Mór Ceann na Sàile	Highld	NC2254	58°26·6′	5°2·5′W	W	9
Loch Mór Connaidh	N Eil	NB2539	58°15·5′	6°40·8′W	W	8,13
Loch Mòr Dùn Tatha	N Eil	NB3916	58°3·6′	6°25·0′W	W	14
Loch More	Highld	NC3237	58°17·6′	4°51·5′W	W	15
Loch More	Highld	ND0745	58°23·3′	3°35·0′W	W	11,12
Lochmore Cott	Highld	ND0846	58°23·8′	3°34·0′W	X	11,12
Loch Moreef	N Eil	NF8314	57°6·7′	7°13·8′W	W	31
Lochmore Lodge	Highld	NC2938	58°18·1′	4°54·6′W	X	15
Lochmore Side	Highld	NC3137	58°17·6′	4°52·5′W	X	15
Loch Morie	Highld	NH5376	57°45·2′	4°27·8′W	W	20
Loch Mòr Lèigh Tàdh	N Eil	NB4951	58°22·8′	6°17·1′W	W	8
Loch Morlich	Highld	NH9609	57°9·9′	3°42·7′W	W	36
Loch Mór na Caiplaich	Highld	NG4731	57°18·2′	6°11·6′W	W	32
Loch Mór na Caorach	Highld	NC7654	58°27·7′	4°7·0′W	W	10
Loch Mór na Clibhe	N Eil	NB0328	58°8·7′	7°2·4′W	W	13
Loch Mòr na Muilne	N Eil	NB3612	58°1·4′	6°27·8′W	W	14
Loch Mòr nan Eileabhat	N Eil	NB5153	58°23·9′	6°15·2′W	W	8
Loch Mòr Sanndabhat	N Eil	NB4346	58°19·9′	6°22·9′W	W	8
Loch Morsgail	N Eil	NB1322	58°5·9′	6°51·8′W	W	13,14
Loch Mòr Sgeireach	N Eil	NB4947	58°20·6′	6°16·9′W	W	8
Loch Mòr Shanndabhat	N Eil	NB4952	58°23·3′	6°17·2′W	W	8
Loch Mòr Sobhal	N Eil	NB4227	58°9·7′	6°22·7′W	W	8
Loch Mòr Stiomrabhaigh	N Eil	NB3313	58°1·8′	6°30·9′W	W	13,14
Lochmoss	Aberd	NJ6338	57°26·1′	2°36·5′W	X	29
Loch Moss	D & G	NX7551	54°50·5′	3°56·4′W	X	84
Loch Mothal Beag	N Eil	NB1725	58°7·7′	6°48·0′W	W	13,14
Loch Mousgrip	N Eil	NF8270	57°36·7′	7°19·1′W	W	18
Loch Moy	Highld	NH7734	57°23·1′	4°2·3′W	W	27
Loch Mùabhat	N Eil	NB3344	58°18·5′	6°33·0′W	W	8
Loch Muchairt	Arg & Bt	NR3247	55°38·8′	6°15·1′W	W	60
Loch Muck	E Ayr	NS5100	55°16·6′	4°20·3′W	W	77
Loch Mudle	Highld	NM5466	56°43·5′	6°0·8′W	W	47
Loch Muick	Aberd	NO2882	56°55·7′	3°10·5′W	W	44
Loch Muidhe	Highld	NC6605	58°1·1′	4°15·6′W	W	16
Loch Muigh-bhlàraidh	Highld	NH6383	57°49·2′	4°17·9′W	W	21
Loch Muileal Ath an Linne	N Eil	NB2113	58°1·4′	6°43·0′W	W	13,14
Lochmuir	Aberd	NO7598	57°4·6′	2°24·3′W	X	38,45
Lochmuir Wood	Fife	NO2903	56°13·1′	3°8·3′W	F	59
Loch Mula	N Eil	NG1390	57°48·7′	6°49·5′W	W	14
Loch Mullardoch	Highld	NH1530	57°19·6′	5°3·9′W	W	25
Loch Mullion	Pth & Kin	NN9833	56°28·9′	3°38·9′W	W	52,53
Loch na Bà	Highld	NG9089	57°50·7′	5°31·8′W	W	19
Loch na Bà	Pth & Kin	NN8855	56°40·7′	3°49·2′W	W	52
Loch na Bà Brice	Highld	NC1731	58°14·1′	5°6·5′W	W	15
Loch na Bà Ceire	N Eil	NF8065	57°34·0′	7°20·7′W	W	18
Loch na Bagh	N Eil	NF7415	57°6·9′	7°22·7′W	W	31
Loch na Ba' Glaise	Highld	NM7194	56°59·1′	5°45·7′W	W	33,40
Loch na Bà Riabhaich	N Eil	NB2434	58°12·8′	6°41·5′W	W	8,13
Loch na Bà Riabhaich	N Eil	NB3917	58°4·2′	6°25·1′W	W	14
Loch na Barrack	Highld	NC1518	58°7·0′	5°8·0′W	W	15
Loch na Bà Ruaidhe	Highld	NG9539	57°24·0′	5°24·3′W	W	25
Loch na Bà Ruaidhe	Highld	NH4933	57°22·0′	4°30·2′W	W	26
Loch na Bà Ruaidhe	N Eil	NB3408	57°59·2′	6°29·5′W	W	13,14
Loch na Beinne Bàine	Highld	NG7946	57°27·3′	5°40·6′W	W	24
Loch na Beinne Baine	Highld	NH2819	57°14·0′	4°50·5′W	W	34
Loch na Beinne Bige	Highld	NH3225	57°17·3′	4°46·8′W	W	26
Loch na Beinne Bige	N Eil	NB2235	58°13·2′	6°43·6′W	W	8,13
Loch na Beinne Brice	Arg & Bt	NR3848	55°39·5′	6°9·5′W	W	60
Loch na Beinne Mòire	Highld	NH3226	57°17·9′	4°46·8′W	W	26
Loch na Beinne Reidhe	Highld	NC2121	58°8·8′	5°2·0′W	W	15
Loch na Bèirè	N Eil	NF8354	57°28·2′	7°16·8′W	W	22
Loch na Beirighe	N Eil	NB2912	58°1·1′	6°34·9′W	W	13,14
Loch na Beiste	Arg & Bt	NM8105	56°11·5′	5°31·3′W	W	55
Loch na Beiste	Arg & Bt	NR7578	55°56·8′	5°35·8′W	W	62
Loch na Bèiste	Arg & Bt	NR7654	55°43·9′	5°33·6′W	W	62
Loch na Bèiste	Highld	NC0012	58°3·4′	5°22·9′W	W	15
Loch na Bèiste	Highld	NC5845	58°22·5′	4°25·2′W	W	10
Loch na Bèiste	Highld	NG7525	57°15·9′	5°43·4′W	W	33
Loch na Bèiste	Highld	NG8894	57°53·4′	5°34·1′W	W	19
Loch na Bèiste	Highld	NH2763	57°37·7′	4°53·4′W	W	20
Loch na Bèiste	Highld	NH3942	57°26·7′	4°40·5′W	W	26
Loch na Bèiste	N Eil	NB0010	57°58·9′	7°4·1′W	W	13
Loch na Bèiste	N Eil	NB1829	58°9·9′	6°47·2′W	W	8,13
Loch na Bèiste	N Eil	NB2537	58°14·4′	6°40·7′W	W	8,13
Loch na Bèiste	N Eil	NB3920	58°5·8′	6°25·3′W	W	14
Loch na Beiste	N Eil	NF7471	57°36·9′	7°27·1′W	W	18
Loch na Beiste	N Eil	NF7870	57°36·6′	7°23·1′W	W	18
Loch na Bèiste	N Eil	NF8645	57°23·5′	7°13·1′W	W	22
Loch na Bèiste	N Eil	NF8649	57°25·6′	7°13·5′W	W	22
Loch na Beiste	N Eil	NF9570	57°37·3′	7°6·1′W	W	18
Loch na Bèiste Brice	Highld	NC1839	58°18·4′	5°5·9′W	W	15
Loch na Beiste Mòire	N Eil	NB3634	58°13·2′	6°29·3′W	W	8
Loch na Bienne	Arg & Bt	NR2941	55°35·5′	6°17·6′W	W	60
Loch na Bioraich	Highld	NM7874	56°48·5′	5°37·8′W	W	40
Loch na Bo	Moray	NJ2860	57°37·7′	3°11·9′W	W	28
Loch na Braan	Moray	NJ0848	57°31·0′	3°31·7′W	W	27
Loch-na-brae	Arg & Bt	NS2388	56°3·4′	4°50·1′W	X	56
Loch na Brae	Pth & Kin	NO0455	56°40·9′	3°33·6′W	W	52,53
Loch na Bràiste	N Eil	NB2536	58°13·9′	6°40·6′W	W	8,13
Loch na Brathan Mòr	N Eil	NB3941	58°17·1′	6°26·7′W	W	8
Loch na Breac Peatair	N Eil	NF7929	57°14·6′	7°18·9′W	W	22
Loch na Bric	Arg & Bt	NR8089	56°2·9′	5°31·5′W	W	55
Loch na Bronn	Highld	NG5746	57°26·6′	6°2·5′W	W	24
Loch na Bruthaich	Highld	NC0731	58°13·8′	5°16·7′W	W	15
Loch na Buaile	N Eil	NF8868	57°35·9′	7°12·9′W	W	18
Loch na Buaile	N Eil	NF9073	57°38·7′	7°11·3′W	W	18
Loch na Buaile Duibhe	N Eil	NB4118	58°4·8′	6°23·1′W	W	14
Loch na Buaile Duibhe	N Eil	NF8762	57°32·6′	7°13·5′W	W	22
Loch na Buaile Gharbha	N Eil	NB3626	58°8·9′	6°28·7′W	W	8
Loch na Buail' Iochdraich	N Eil	NF8066	57°34·5′	7°20·8′W	W	18
Loch na Buidheig	Highld	NC0929	58°12·8′	5°14·6′W	W	15
Loch na Cabhaig	Highld	NG8962	57°36·2′	5°31·4′W	W	19,24
Loch na Cachie	Arg & Bt	NR2264	55°47·6′	6°25·7′W	W	60
Loch na Caiginn	N Eil	NF9571	57°37·8′	7°6·1′W	W	18
Loch na Caillich	Highld	NC2551	58°25·0′	4°59·3′W	W	9
Loch na Caillich	Highld	NC5108	58°2·4′	4°31·0′W	W	16
Loch na Caillich	Highld	NG8641	57°24·8′	5°33·3′W	W	24
Loch na Caillich	Highld	NG9636	57°22·4′	5°23·1′W	W	25
Loch na Caillich	Highld	NH2021	57°14·9′	4°58·6′W	W	25
Loch na Caillich	Highld	NH3351	57°31·4′	4°46·9′W	W	26
Loch na Caillich	N Eil	NB0418	58°3·4′	7°0·6′W	W	13
Loch na Caillich	N Eil	NG0592	57°49·5′	6°57·7′W	W	14,18
Loch na Caillich	Pth & Kin	NN6962	56°44·1′	4°8·0′W	W	42
Loch na Caime	Arg & Bt	NR5383	55°58·8′	5°57·1′W	W	61
Loch na Caiplich	N Eil	NF9055	57°29·0′	7°9·9′W	W	22
Loch na Cairidh	Highld	NG5828	57°17·0′	6°0·5′W	W	32
Loch na Cairteach	N Eil	NB3127	58°9·3′	6°33·9′W	W	8,13
Loch na Cairteach	N Eil	NB3434	58°13·1′	6°31·3′W	W	8,13
Loch na Camaig	Highld	NH1321	57°14·8′	5°5·5′W	W	25
Loch na Caoidhe	Highld	NH2246	57°28·4′	4°57·6′W	W	25
Loch na Caorach	Highld	NC9158	58°30·1′	3°51·7′W	W	10
Loch na Caorach	Highld	NG7256	57°32·5′	5°48·1′W	W	24
Loch na Capulich	Highld	NC5222	58°10·0′	4°30·5′W	W	16
Loch na Carnaich	N Eil	NF9176	57°40·3′	7°10·5′W	W	18
Loch na Carraigeach	Arg & Bt	NN0125	56°22·8′	5°12·9′W	W	50
Loch na Cartach	N Eil	NB1901	57°54·9′	6°44·2′W	W	14
Loch na Cartach	N Eil	NB3217	58°3·9′	6°32·2′W	W	13,14
Loch na Cartach	N Eil	NB3738	58°15·4′	6°28·5′W	W	8
Loch na Cartach	N Eil	NF9272	57°38·2′	7°9·2′W	W	18
Loch na Cartach	N Eil	NG0188	57°47·2′	7°1·4′W	W	13
Loch na Cartach	N Eil	NG0392	57°49·4′	6°59·7′W	W	18
Loch na Cartach	N Eil	NG1191	57°49·2′	6°51·6′W	W	14
Loch na Càthrach Duibhe	Highld	NC4561	58°30·8′	4°39·2′W	W	9
Loch na Cathrach Duibhe	Highld	NG8990	57°51·2′	5°32·9′W	W	19
Loch na Ceannamhóir	N Eil	NB1535	58°13·0′	6°50·7′W	W	13
Loch na Ceàrdaich	N Eil	NF8572	57°37·9′	7°16·2′W	W	18
Loch na Ceithir-Eileana	N Eil	NF8662	57°32·6′	7°14·5′W	W	22
Loch na Ciche	Highld	NC2105	58°0·2′	5°1·3′W	W	15
Loch na Cille	Arg & Bt	NM8312	56°15·3′	5°29·8′W	W	55
Loch na Cille	Arg & Bt	NR6879	55°57·1′	5°42·5′W	W	61,62
Loch na Cille	Arg & Bt	NR6980	55°57·7′	5°41·6′W	W	55,61
Loch na Cille	Arg & Bt	NR7580	55°57·9′	5°35·9′W	W	55
Loch na Cille	N Eil	NF7169	57°35·7′	7°30·0′W	W	18
Loch na Cinneamhuin	Highld	NC6806	58°1·7′	4°13·6′W	W	16
Loch na Circe	Highld	NC1220	58°8·0′	5°11·1′W	W	15
Loch na Ciste	N Eil	NB0926	58°7·9′	6°56·2′W	W	13
Loch na Ciste	N Eil	NB1427	58°8·6′	6°51·2′W	W	13
Loch na Ciste	N Eil	NB1605	57°56·9′	6°47·5′W	W	13,14
Loch na Ciste	N Eil	NB1922	58°6·1′	6°45·7′W	W	13,14
Loch na Ciste	N Eil	NB2425	58°7·9′	6°40·9′W	W	13,14
Loch na Ciste	N Eil	NB3118	58°4·4′	6°33·3′W	W	13,14
Loch na Ciste	N Eil	NB4545	58°19·4′	6°20·8′W	W	8
Loch na Claise	Highld	NC0330	58°13·2′	5°20·8′W	W	15
Loch na Claise	Highld	NC1513	58°4·3′	5°7·7′W	W	15
Loch na Claise Càrnaich	Highld	NC2852	58°25·6′	4°56·3′W	W	9
Loch na Claise Càrnaich	Highld	NG9087	57°49·7′	5°31·7′W	W	19
Loch na Claise Feàrna	Highld	NC2046	58°22·2′	5°4·2′W	W	9
Loch na Claise Luachraich	Highld	NC2249	58°23·9′	5°2·3′W	W	9
Loch na Claise Mòire	Highld	NC3805	58°0·5′	4°44·0′W	W	16
Loch na Cleavag	N Eil	NB0013	58°0·6′	7°4·3′W	W	13
Loch na Clèibh	N Eil	NF8760	57°31·6′	7°13·3′W	W	22
Loch na Clèire	Highld	NH0090	57°51·6′	5°21·8′W	W	19
Loch na Cleith	N Eil	NB2328	58°9·5′	6°42·1′W	W	8,13
Loch na Clibhe	N Eil	NB0124	58°6·5′	7°4·1′W	W	13
Loch na Cloich	N Eil	NB5048	58°21·2′	6°15·9′W	W	8
Loch na Cloich Airde	N Eil	NB0129	58°9·2′	7°4·5′W	W	13
Loch na Cloiche	Arg & Bt	NM2055	56°36·5′	6°33·3′W	W	46,47
Loch na Cloiche	Arg & Bt	NM2461	56°39·8′	6°29·8′W	W	46,47
Loch na Cloiche	Arg & Bt	NR5375	55°54·5′	5°56·7′W	W	61
Loch na Cloiche	Highld	NC9747	58°24·2′	3°45·3′W	W	11
Loch na Cloiche	Highld	NG8281	57°46·2′	5°39·5′W	W	19
Loch na Cloiche Gile	Highld	NG7787	57°49·3′	5°44·8′W	W	19
Loch na Còinnich	N Eil	NF8562	57°32·6′	7°15·5′W	W	22
Loch na Cointich	N Eil	NF9672	57°38·4′	7°5·2′W	W	18
Loch na Coireig	Highld	NH0593	57°53·3′	5°16·9′W	W	19
Loch na Coirnish	N Eil	NB0216	58°2·2′	7°2·5′W	W	13
Loch na Cois	N Eil	NB4026	58°9·1′	6°24·7′W	W	8
Loch na Coit	Highld	NC6661	58°31·3′	4°17·6′W	W	10
Loch na Conaire	Arg & Bt	NR6796	56°6·3′	5°44·4′W	W	55,61
Loch na Corrobha	Arg & Bt	NM4123	56°20·0′	6°11·0′W	W	48
Loch na Craige	Pth & Kin	NN8845	56°35·3′	3°49·0′W	W	52
Loch na Crann	Highld	NH4558	57°35·4′	4°35·1′W	W	26
Loch na Craobhbhaige Mòire	N Eil	NB1028	58°9·0′	6°55·3′W	W	13
Loch na Craobhaig	N Eil	NB0620	58°4·6′	6°58·8′W	W	13,14
Loch na Craobhaig	N Eil	NB1429	58°9·7′	6°51·3′W	W	13
Loch na Craobhaig	N Eil	NB1835	58°13·1′	6°47·7′W	W	8,13
Loch na Craoibhe	N Eil	NB2821	58°5·9′	6°36·5′W	W	13,14
Loch na Craoibhe	N Eil	NB2918	58°4·4′	6°35·3′W	W	13,14
Loch na Craoibhe	N Eil	NB2927	58°9·2′	6°35·9′W	W	8,13
Loch na Craoibhe	N Eil	NB4049	58°21·4′	6°26·2′W	W	8
Loch na Craoibhe	N Eil	NG1590	57°48·8′	6°47·5′W	W	14
Loch na Craoibhe	N Eil	NG2395	57°51·8′	6°39·8′W	W	14
Loch na Craoibhe-caorainn	Highld	NG9250	57°29·8′	5°27·8′W	W	25
Loch na Craoibhe-caoruinn	Highld	NG9025	57°16·3′	5°28·5′W	W	25,33
Loch na Creaganan Gròid	N Eil	NB1119	58°4·2′	6°53·6′W	W	13,14
Loch na Creige	Arg & Bt	NR7341	55°36·8′	5°35·8′W	W	62
Loch na Creige	Highld	NG7457	57°33·1′	5°46·2′W	W	24
Loch na Creige	Highld	NG7655	57°32·0′	5°44·1′W	W	24
Loch na Creige	N Eil	NF8873	57°38·6′	7°13·3′W	W	18
Loch na Creige	N Eil	NF9672	57°38·4′	7°5·2′W	W	18
Loch na Creige Bristè	N Eil	NG0989	57°48·0′	6°53·4′W	W	14
Loch na Creige Cràinde	Arg & Bt	NR7682	55°59·0′	5°35·0′W	W	55
Loch na Creige Duibhe	Highld	NC0011	58°2·8′	5°22·9′W	W	15
Loch na Creige Duibhe	Highld	NC2836	58°17·0′	4°55·5′W	W	15
Loch na Creige Duibhe	Highld	NC4456	58°28·1′	4°40·0′W	W	9
Loch na Creige Duibhe	Highld	NM7685	56°54·4′	5°40·3′W	W	40
Loch na Creige Fraoich	N Eil	NB3424	58°7·8′	6°30·6′W	W	13,14
Loch na Creige Guirme	N Eil	NB2828	58°9·7′	6°37·0′W	W	8,13
Loch na Creige Léithe	Highld	NC0526	58°11·1′	5°18·5′W	W	15
Loch na Creige Riabhaich	Arg & Bt	NM9301	56°9·7′	5°19·6′W	W	55
Loch na Creige Riabhaich	Highld	NC2863	58°31·5′	4°56·8′W	W	9
Loch na Creige Riabhaich	Highld	NC4350	58°24·9′	4°40·8′W	W	9
Loch na Creige Ruaidhe	Highld	NC1736	58°16·7′	5°6·8′W	W	15
Loch na Creige Ruaidhe	N Eil	NB2802	57°55·7′	6°35·2′W	W	14
Loch na Crèitheach	Highld	NG5120	57°12·5′	6°6·9′W	W	32
Loch na Criadha	N Eil	NB3122	58°6·6′	6°33·5′W	W	13,14
Loch na Criadhach	N Eil	NG0686	57°46·3′	6°56·2′W	W	14,18
Loch na Criadhach Mhór	Arg & Bt	NM4754	56°36·8′	6°7·0′W	W	47
Loch na Criathraich	Arg & Bt	NM9519	56°19·4′	5°18·5′W	W	55
Loch na Criche	Highld	NC1603	57°59·0′	5°6·2′W	W	15
Loch na Criche	Highld	NC7343	58°21·7′	4°9·8′W	W	10
Loch na Criche	N Eil	NF9272	57°38·2′	7°9·2′W	W	18
Loch na Crithe	Arg & Bt	NM5151	56°35·4′	6°2·9′W	W	47
Loch na Cròic	Highld	NH4359	57°35·9′	4°37·2′W	W	26
Loch na Cruaich	Arg & Bt	NM8215	56°16·9′	5°30·9′W	W	55
Loch na Cruaiche	Arg & Bt	NM8510	56°14·3′	5°27·7′W	W	55
Loch na Cuilce	Arg & Bt	NM4351	56°35·1′	6°10·7′W	W	47
Loch na Cuilce	Highld	NG4819	57°11·8′	6°9·8′W	W	32
Loch na Cuilce	Highld	NG5747	57°27·2′	6°2·6′W	W	24
Loch na Cuilce	Highld	NH5234	57°22·6′	4°27·2′W	W	26
Loch na Cuilce	N Eil	NL6390	56°53·0′	7°31·6′W	W	31
Loch na Cuithe Mòire	N Eil	NF7323	57°11·1′	7°24·3′W	W	22
Loch na Curach	Highld	NG7356	57°32·5′	5°47·1′W	W	24
Loch na Curra	Highld	NG8280	57°45·7′	5°39·4′W	W	19
Loch na Curra	Highld	NH2363	57°37·6′	4°57·4′W	W	20
Loch na Curra	Highld	NH6032	57°21·7′	4°19·2′W	W	26
Loch na Curraidh	N Eil	NF7532	57°16·0′	7°23·1′W	W	22
Loch na Curraigh	Arg & Bt	NM8613	56°15·9′	5°26·9′W	W	55
Loch na Curs	Moray	NJ1652	57°33·3′	3°23·8′W	W	28
Loch na Dàil	Highld	NC0813	58°4·1′	5°14·8′W	W	15
Loch na Dàiridh	Arg & Bt	NM5740	56°29·6′	5°56·4′W	W	47,48
Loch na Dal	Highld	NG7014	57°9·8′	5°47·8′W	W	32,33
Loch na Davie	N Ayr	NR9545	55°39·6′	5°15·1′W	W	62,69
Loch na Deighe fo Dheas	N Eil	NF8353	57°27·7′	7°16·7′W	W	22
Loch na Deighe fo Thuath	N Eil	NF8353	57°27·7′	7°16·7′W	W	22
Loch na Doireanach	Highld	NG6310	57°7·5′	5°54·5′W	W	32
Loch na Doire Buidhe	Highld	NG4513	57°8·5′	6°12·5′W	W	32
Loch na Doire Duibhe	Highld	NC1739	58°18·4′	5°6·9′W	W	15
Loch na Doire Duinne	Highld	NG8596	57°54·4′	5°37·3′W	W	19
Loch na Doire Mòire	Highld	NG8230	57°18·8′	5°36·7′W	W	24
Loch na Doirlinn	N Eil	NF6400	56°58·4′	7°31·4′W	W	31
Loch na Draipe	Highld	NM6774	56°48·2′	5°48·5′W	W	40
Loch na Droighniche	Highld	NC1534	58°15·6′	5°8·7′W	W	15
Loch na Droma Buidhe	Highld	NM5958	56°39·4′	5°55·5′W	W	47
Loch na Dubh-bhruaich	Highld	NG7256	57°32·5′	5°48·1′W	W	24
Loch na Dubhcha	N Eil	NF9572	57°38·3′	7°6·2′W	W	18
Loch na Duchasaich	N Eil	NF7431	57°15·5′	7°24·0′W	W	22
Loch na Faic	Highld	NC3907	58°1·6′	4°43·1′W	W	16
Loch na Faing	N Eil	NB1021	58°5·3′	6°54·8′W	W	13,14
Loch na Faing	N Eil	NB1732	58°11·4′	6°48·5′W	W	8,13
Loch na Faing	N Eil	NB4248	58°20·9′	6°24·1′W	W	8
Loch na Faoileag	N Eil	NF8656	57°29·4′	7°14·0′W	W	22
Loch na Faoileig	Highld	NC6445	58°22·6′	4°19·1′W	W	10
Loch na Faoileige	Highld	NC2119	58°7·7′	5°1·9′W	W	15
Loch na Faoileige	Highld	NH1387	57°50·3′	5°8·5′W	W	19
Loch na Faoileige	Highld	NH4222	57°15·9′	4°36·7′W	W	26
Loch na Faoileige	Highld	NH4327	57°18·7′	4°35·9′W	W	26
Loch na Faoilinn	Arg & Bt	NR8188	56°2·3′	5°30·5′W	W	55
Loch na Faoilinn	N Eil	NF8051	57°26·5′	7°19·6′W	W	22
Loch na Faoirbh	N Eil	NB0229	58°9·2′	7°3·5′W	W	13
Loch na Faolaig	Highld	NG9025	57°16·3′	5°28·5′W	W	25,33
Loch na Faolinn	Highld	NG2742	57°23·5′	6°32·2′W	W	23
Loch na Feannaig	Highld	NG8061	57°35·4′	5°40·4′W	W	19,24
Loch na Feannaig	Highld	NH3920	57°14·8′	4°39·6′W	W	26
Loch na Fèithe Dirich	Highld	NG7888	57°49·9′	5°43·9′W	W	19
Loch na Fèithe Mùgaig	Highld	NG8574	57°42·5′	5°36·1′W	W	19
Loch na Fèithe Seilich	Highld	NG7020	57°13·0′	5°48·1′W	W	33
Loch na Féithe-seilich	Highld	NG9034	57°21·2′	5°29·0′W	W	25
Loch na Fiacail	Highld	NC2348	58°23·3′	5°1·2′W	W	9
Loch na Fideil	Highld	NG9269	57°40·0′	5°28·8′W	W	19
Loch na Fola	Arg & Bt	NR7579	55°57·3′	5°35·8′W	W	62
Loch na Fola	Highld	NN2056	56°39·9′	4°55·8′W	W	41
Loch na Fola	N Eil	NB4445	58°19·4′	6°21·9′W	W	8
Loch na Frianach	Highld	NG9554	57°32·0′	5°25·0′W	W	25
Loch na Frianich	Highld	NH2646	57°28·5′	4°53·7′W	W	25
Loch na Fuaralachd	Highld	NC6016	58°6·9′	4°22·1′W	W	16
Loch na Fuaralaich	Highld	NC4806	58°1·3′	4°33·9′W	W	16
Loch na Fùdarlaich	Arg & Bt	NR5376	55°55·1′	5°56·7′W	W	61
Loch na Fùdarlaich Beag	Arg & Bt	NR5276	55°55·0′	5°57·7′W	W	61
Loch na Gabhlach	Highld	NH2625	57°17·2′	4°52·8′W	W	25
Loch na Gaghalach Nodha	Highld	NH3685	57°49·7′	4°45·2′W	W	20
Loch na Gaineimh	Highld	NC6912	58°4·9′	4°12·8′W	W	16
Loch na Gaineimh	Highld	NC7630	58°14·7′	4°6·3′W	W	17
Loch na Gainimh	Highld	NC1718	58°7·1′	5°5·9′W	W	15
Loch na Gainimh	Highld	NC2061	58°30·3′	5°4·9′W	W	9
Loch na Gainimh	Highld	NC2756	58°27·7′	4°57·5′W	W	9
Loch na Gainmhich	Highld	NC2428	58°12·6′	4°59·3′W	W	15
Loch na Gainmhich	Highld	NC3065	58°32·7′	4°54·8′W	W	9
Loch na Gainmhich	N Eil	NB2335	58°13·3′	6°42·6′W	W	8,13
Loch na Gainmhich	N Eil	NB3237	58°14·7′	6°33·6′W	W	8,13
Loch na Gaoithe	N Eil	NB0200	57°53·7′	7°1·3′W	W	18
Loch na Gaorach	Highld	NG7456	57°32·5′	5°46·1′W	W	24
Lochnagar	Aberd	NO2585	56°57·3′	3°13·5′W	H	44
Lochnagar	Aberd	NO2585	56°57·3′	3°13·5′W	W	44
Loch na Garbh-abhainn Ard	N Eil	NF8868	57°35·9′	7°12·9′W	W	18
Loch na Garbhe Uidhe	Highld	NC1624	58°10·3′	5°7·2′W	W	15
Loch na Garbh-shròin	Highld	NC6543	58°21·5′	4°18·0′W	W	10
Lochnagar Burn	Aberd	NO2587	56°58·3′	3°13·6′W	W	44
Loch na Geàrra	Highld	NH4262	57°37·5′	4°38·3′W	W	20
Loch na Gearrachun	N Eil	NF7674	57°38·0′	7°25·4′W	W	18
Loch na Géige	Arg & Bt	NM5223	56°20·3′	6°0·3′W	W	48
Loch na Ghreidlein	Highld	NH3126	57°17·9′	4°47·8′W	W	26
Loch na Gile	Arg & Bt	NM0248	56°32·0′	6°50·4′W	W	46
Loch na Gillean	N Eil	NB0616	58°2·8′	6°58·5′W	W	13,14
Loch na Glaic	Highld	NC7513	58°5·6′	4°6·8′W	W	16
Loch na Glaic	Highld	NC7658	58°29·8′	4°7·2′W	W	10
Loch na Glaic Tarsuinn	Highld	NC2966	58°33·2′	4°55·9′W	W	9
Loch na Glasa	Highld	NH4080	57°47·1′	4°41·0′W	W	20
Loch na Glas-choille	Highld	NC5530	58°14·4′	4°27·7′W	W	16
Loch na Gobhlaig	Highld	NH2630	57°19·9′	4°53·0′W	W	25
Loch na Gruagaich	Highld	NC2415	58°5·6′	4°58·7′W	W	15

Loch na Guailne Idhre	Highld	NH0665	57°38·3′	5°14·5′W	W	19
Loch na h-Aibhne Gairbhe	N Eil	NG1195	57°51·3′	6°51·9′W	W	14
Loch na h-Aibhne Ruaidhe	N Eil	NB2115	58°2·5′	6°43·2′W	W	13,14
Loch na h-Airbhe	Highld	NH1092	57°52·9′	5°11·8′W	W	19
Loch na h-Airde	Highld	NG3916	57°9·9′	6°18·6′W	W	32
Loch na h-Airde	N Eil	NB1742	58°16·8′	6°49·2′W	W	8,13
Loch na h-Airde Bige	Highld	NG8879	57°45·3′	5°33·3′W	W	19
Loch na h-Airde Mòire	N Eil	NF9175	57°39·8′	7°10·5′W	W	18
Loch na h-Airgh Uisge	N Eil	NB3126	58°8·7′	6°33·8′W	W	8,13
Loch na h-Airigh	N Eil	NB0617	58°2·9′	6°58·5′W	W	13,14
Loch na h-Airigh	N Eil	NB4016	58°3·7′	6°24·0′W	W	14
Loch na h-Airigh Bige	Highld	NC5554	58°27·3′	4°28·6′W	W	10
Loch na h-Airighe Bige	Highld	NC0526	58°11·1′	5°18·5′W	W	15
Loch na h-Airighe Bige	Highld	NG7254	57°31·4′	5°48·0′W	W	24
Loch na h-Airigh Fraoich	Highld	NC1321	58°8·6′	5°10·1′W	W	15
Loch na h-Airigh Molaich	Highld	NG9280	57°46·0′	5°29·4′W	W	19
Loch na h- Airigh Slèibhe	Highld	NC1843	58°20·5′	5°6·1′W	W	9
Loch na h-Airigh Uir	N Eil	NB3325	58°8·3′	6°31·7′W	W	13,14
Loch na h-Ard Eilig	Highld	NG8891	57°51·8′	5°34·0′W	W	19
Loch na h-Ardlaraich	Arg & Bt	NM8005	56°11·5′	5°32·3′W	W	55
Loch na h-Ath	Highld	NC2341	58°19·6′	5°0·9′W	W	9
Loch na h-Eaglaise Beag	Highld	NC8559	58°30·5′	3°57·9′W	W	10
Loch na h-Eaglaise Mór	Highld	NC8659	58°30·5′	3°56·9′W	W	10
Loch na h-Eangaiche	Highld	NG7454	57°31·5′	5°46·0′W	W	24
Loch na h-Earaig	N Eil	NB4128	58°10·2′	6°23·8′W	W	8
Loch na h-Earrainn	Arg & Bt	NR7378	55°56·7′	5°37·7′W	W	62
Loch na h-Easgainn	N Eil	NF8787	57°46·1′	7°15·4′W	W	18
Loch na h-Eiridh	Highld	NH2422	57°15·6′	4°54·6′W	W	25
Loch na h-Imriche	Highld	NC7664	58°33·1′	4°7·4′W	W	10
Loch na h-Inghinn	Arg & Bt	NR7882	55°59·0′	5°33·1′W	W	55
Loch na h-Inghinn	N Eil	NB3316	58°3·4′	6°31·1′W	W	13,14
Loch na h-Inghinn	N Eil	NB3524	58°7·8′	6°29·6′W	W	14
Loch Nahinie	S Ayr	NX2777	55°3·7′	4°42·1′W	W	76
Loch na h-Innse Fraoich	Highld	NC1626	58°11·3′	5°7·3′W	W	15
Loch na h-Innse Gairbhe	Highld	NG8793	57°52·8′	5°35·1′W	W	19
Loch na h-Iolaire	N Eil	NB2824	58°7·5′	6°36·7′W	W	13,14
Loch na h-Iolaire	N Eil	NF8065	57°34·0′	7°20·7′W	W	18
Loch na h-Iolaire	N Eil	NG1495	57°51·4′	6°48·8′W	W	14
Loch na h-Oidhche	Highld	NG8965	57°37·8′	5°31·6′W	W	19,24
Loch na h-Oidhche	Highld	NH1577	57°44·9′	5°6·1′W	W	20
Loch na h-Ola	N Eil	NB2618	58°4·2′	6°38·3′W	W	13,14
Loch na h-Onaich	Highld	NG9231	57°19·6′	5°26·8′W	W	25
Loch na h-Hostrach	N Eil	NF9166	57°35·0′	7°9·8′W	W	18
Loch na h-Uamha	Highld	NG7766	57°38·0′	5°43·7′W	W	19,24
Loch na h-Uamha	N Eil	NG1791	57°49·4′	6°45·5′W	W	14
Loch na h-Uamhachd	Highld	NC5565	58°33·2′	4°29·0′W	W	10
Loch na h-Uamhaidh	Arg & Bt	NR7683	55°59·5′	5°35·1′W	W	55
Loch na h-Uamhaidh Beag	Highld	NG7991	57°51·5′	5°43·0′W	W	19
Loch na h-Uamhaidh Móire	Highld	NG7991	57°51·5′	5°43·0′W	W	19
Loch na h-Uamhaig	Highld	NG8162	57°36·0′	5°39·4′W	W	19,24
Loch na h-Uidhe	Highld	NG9387	57°49·7′	5°28·7′W	W	19
Loch na h-Uidhe	Highld	NH0493	57°53·3′	5°17·9′W	W	19
Loch na h-Uidhe	N Eil	NB0100	57°53·6′	7°2·3′W	W	18
Loch na h-Uidhe	N Eil	NG0786	57°46·3′	6°55·2′W	W	14,18
Loch na h-Uidhe Doimhne	Highld	NC0628	58°12·2′	5°17·6′W	W	15
Loch Naid	N Eil	NF8044	57°22·7′	7°19·0′W	W	22
Loch na Keal	Arg & Bt	NM4837	56°27·7′	6°5·0′W	W	47,48
Loch na Làimh	Arg & Bt	NR8185	56°0·7′	5°30·4′W	W	55
Loch na Làire Bàine	N Eil	NF8661	57°32·1′	7°14·4′W	W	22
Loch na Làire Duibhe	Highld	NC2352	58°25·5′	5°1·4′W	W	9
Loch na Lairige	Highld	NG7878	57°44·5′	5°43·3′W	W	19
Loch na Lairige	Highld	NH5601	57°4·9′	4°22·1′W	W	35
Loch na Lairige	Highld	NN5591	56°59·5′	4°22·7′W	W	35
Loch na Lap	Highld	NN3971	56°48·4′	4°37·8′W	W	41
Loch na Larach	Highld	NC2158	58°28·7′	5°3·7′W	W	9
Loch na Làrach	Highld	NG7243	57°25·5′	5°47·4′W	W	24
Loch na Làrach	Highld	NG7357	57°33·0′	5°47·2′W	W	24
Loch na Làrach Blàire	Highld	NH3753	57°32·5′	4°42·9′W	W	26
Loch na Larach Lèithe	N Eil	NG1596	57°52·0′	6°47·9′W	W	14
Loch na Làthaich	Arg & Bt	NM3623	56°19·8′	6°15·8′W	W	48
Loch na Làthaich	Arg & Bt	NR2771	55°51·6′	6°21·3′W	W	60
Loch na Leamhain	N Eil	NB2434	58°12·8′	6°41·5′W	W	8,13
Loch na Learg	Highld	NG3155	57°30·6′	6°29·0′W	W	23
Loch na Learga	N Eil	NA9616	58°2·0′	7°8·6′W	W	13
Loch na Leig	N Eil	NF8955	57°29·0′	7°10·9′W	W	22
Loch na Leighe	Arg & Bt	NS1052	55°43·7′	5°1·1′W	W	63,69
Loch na Leirg	Highld	NG8158	57°33·8′	5°39·2′W	W	24
Loch na Leirg	Highld	NG8592	57°52·2′	5°37·0′W	W	19
Loch na Leirg	N Ayr	NS0127	55°30·0′	5°8·6′W	W	69
Loch na Leirisdein	Highld	NH3723	57°16·4′	4°41·7′W	W	26
Loch na Leitir Beithe	Highld	NH2520	57°14·5′	4°53·5′W	W	25
Loch na Leitire	Highld	NG8432	57°19·9′	5°34·9′W	W	24
Loch na Leitreach	Highld	NH0127	57°17·7′	5°17·7′W	W	25,33
Loch na Liana Móire	N Eil	NF7320	57°9·5′	7°24·1′W	W	31
Loch na Liana Móire	N Eil	NF7324	57°11·7′	7°24·4′W	W	22
Loch na Liana Móire	N Eil	NF7653	57°27·4′	7°23·7′W	W	22
Loch na Lice	N Eil	NF7621	57°10·2′	7°21·2′W	W	31
Loch na Lice Bàine	N Eil	NF8142	57°21·7′	7°17·9′W	W	22
Loch na Linne	N Eil	NB3330	58°11·0′	6°32·1′W	W	8,13
Loch na Lochain	Highld	NG8113	57°9·6′	5°36·8′W	W	33
Loch na Loinne	Highld	NC1229	58°12·8′	5°11·5′W	W	15
Loch na Luirg	Highld	NG7787	57°49·3′	5°44·8′W	W	19
Loch na Machrach Bige	Arg & Bt	NR8863	55°49·1′	5°22·6′W	W	62
Loch na Machrach Móire	Arg & Bt	NR8863	55°49·1′	5°22·6′W	W	62
Loch na Maighdein	N Eil	NF8968	57°36·0′	7°11·9′W	W	18
Loch na Main	Highld	NC8154	58°27·8′	4°1·9′W	W	10
Loch na Mang	Highld	NC3939	58°18·9′	4°44·4′W	W	16
Loch na Maoile	Highld	NH1599	57°56·8′	5°7·1′W	W	20
Loch na Maoile Buidhe	Highld	NH0534	57°21·5′	5°14·1′W	W	25
Loch nam Ba	Arg & Bt	NR6293	56°4·5′	5°49·0′W	W	61
Loch nam Badan Boga	Highld	NH0992	57°52·9′	5°12·8′W	W	19
Loch nam Balgan	N Eil	NF7640	57°20·4′	7°22·7′W	W	22
Loch nam Ball	Highld	NG7861	57°35·3′	5°42·4′W	W	19,24
Loch nam Ban	Arg & Bt	NM8712	56°15·4′	5°25·9′W	W	55
Loch nam Ban	Arg & Bt	NR4170	55°51·5′	6°7·9′W	W	60,61
Loch nam Bàn	Arg & Bt	NR7583	55°59·5′	5°36·0′W	W	55
Loch nam Ban	N Eil	NF9078	57°41·4′	7°11·7′W	W	18
Loch nam Ban Móra	Highld	NM4585	56°53·4′	6°10·8′W	W	39
Loch nam Bat	Highld	NH4933	57°22·0′	4°30·2′W	W	26
Loch nam Biast	Highld	NC5066	58°33·6′	4°34·2′W	W	9
Loch nam Bonnach	Highld	NH4848	57°30·1′	4°31·7′W	W	26
Loch nam Bò Uidhre	Highld	NC8457	58°29·4′	3°58·9′W	W	10
Loch nam Brac	Highld	NC1748	58°23·2′	5°7·3′W	W	9
Loch nam Brathain	Highld	NH3921	57°15·3′	4°39·7′W	W	26
Loch nam Breac	Arg & Bt	NR4055	55°43·4′	6°8·0′W	W	60
Loch nam Breac	Arg & Bt	NR5676	55°55·2′	5°53·9′W	W	61
Loch nam Breac	Arg & Bt	NR7948	55°40·8′	5°30·5′W	W	62,69
Loch nam Breac	Highld	NC1031	58°13·9′	5°13·7′W	W	15
Loch nam Breac	Highld	NC6649	58°24·8′	4°17·1′W	W	10
Loch nam Breac	Highld	NC6958	58°29·7′	4°14·4′W	W	10
Loch nam Breac	Highld	NC8247	58°24·0′	4°0·7′W	W	10
Loch nam Breac	N Eil	NB2511	58°0·5′	6°38·9′W	W	13,14
Loch nam Breac	N Eil	NB2837	58°14·5′	6°37·6′W	W	8,13
Loch nam Breac	N Eil	NB3039	58°15·7′	6°35·7′W	W	8,13
Loch nam Breac	N Eil	NB3323	58°7·2′	6°31·6′W	W	13,14
Loch nam Breac	N Eil	NB3623	58°7·3′	6°28·5′W	W	14
Loch nam Breac	N Eil	NB3837	58°14·9′	6°27·4′W	W	8
Loch nam Breac	N Eil	NB4241	58°17·2′	6°23·6′W	W	8
Loch nam Breac	N Eil	NG0692	57°49·5′	6°56·7′W	W	14,18
Loch nam Breac Beag	Highld	NC8160	58°31·0′	4°2·1′W	W	10
Loch nam Breac Beaga	Highld	NC6518	58°8·1′	4°17·1′W	W	16
Loch nam Breac Beaga	Highld	NG7258	57°33·5′	5°48·2′W	W	24
Loch nam Breac Buidge	Highld	NC6456	58°28·5′	4°19·4′W	W	10
Loch nam Breac Buidhe	Arg & Bt	NM9804	56°11·4′	5°14·9′W	W	55
Loch nam Breac Buidhe	Arg & Bt	NR7682	55°59·0′	5°35·0′W	W	55
Loch nam Breac Buidhe	Arg & Bt	NR8185	56°0·7′	5°30·4′W	W	55
Loch nam Breac Buidhe	Highld	NC6143	58°21·5′	4°22·1′W	W	10
Loch nam Breac Buidhe	Highld	NH3884	57°49·2′	4°43·2′W	W	20
Loch nam Breac Dearga	Highld	NH1445	57°27·7′	5°5·6′W	W	25
Loch nam Breac Dearga	Highld	NH4522	57°16·0′	4°33·8′W	W	26
Loch nam Breac Dearga	Highld	NH4734	57°22·5′	4°32·2′W	W	26
Loch nam Breac Dubha	Highld	NG6308	57°6·4′	5°54·4′W	W	32
Loch nam Breac Mèith	Highld	NH0655	57°32·9′	5°14·1′W	W	25
Loch nam Breac Mór	Highld	NC8160	58°31·0′	4°2·1′W	W	10
Loch nam Breac Móra	Highld	NC3227	58°12·3′	4°51·1′W	W	15
Loch nam Breac Móra	Highld	NG8330	57°18·8′	5°35·7′W	W	24
Loch nam Breac Móra	Highld	NG9334	57°21·2′	5°26·0′W	W	25
Loch nam Breac Móra	Highld	NN2761	56°42·8′	4°49·1′W	W	41
Loch nam Breac Mòra	N Eil	NF7844	57°22·6′	7°21·0′W	W	22
Loch nam Breac Ruadh	N Eil	NF7935	57°17·8′	7°19·3′W	W	22
Loch nam Buadh	N Eil	NF6361	57°31·1′	7°37·3′W	W	22
Loch nam Buainichean	Highld	NG8573	57°42·0′	5°36·0′W	W	19
Loch nam Buidheag	Highld	NH4495	57°55·3′	4°37·6′W	W	20
Lochnameal	Arg & Bt	NM5152	56°35·9′	6°2·9′W	W	47
Lochnameal Fm	Arg & Bt	NM5152	56°35·9′	6°2·9′W	FM	47
Loch na Meilich	Highld	NG5739	57°22·9′	6°2·1′W	W	24,32
Loch na Mèine	Highld	NH3737	57°23·9′	4°42·3′W	W	26
Loch nam Falcag	N Eil	NB2926	58°8·7′	6°35·8′W	W	8,13
Loch nam Faoileag	Highld	NC7340	58°20·1′	4°9·7′W	W	10
Loch nam Faoileag	Highld	NH3008	57°8·2′	4°48·1′W	W	34
Loch nam Faoileag	Highld	NH4135	57°22·9′	4°38·2′W	W	26
Loch nam Faoileag	Highld	NH4932	57°21·5′	4°30·1′W	W	26
Loch nam Faoileag	N Ayr	NR9537	55°35·3′	5°14·7′W	W	68,69
Loch nam Faoileag	N Eil	NB2823	58°7·0′	6°36·7′W	W	13,14
Loch nam Faoileag	N Eil	NB3107	57°58·5′	6°32·5′W	W	13,14
Loch nam Faoileag	N Eil	NB3915	58°3·1′	6°25·0′W	W	14
Loch nam Faoileann	N Eil	NF7520	57°9·6′	7°22·1′W	W	31
Loch nam Faoileann	N Eil	NF7928	57°14·1′	7°18·8′W	W	22
Loch nam Faoileann	N Eil	NF7953	57°27·5′	7°20·7′W	W	22
Loch nam Fear	Highld	ND0243	58°22·1′	3°40·0′W	W	11,12
Loch nam Feithean	N Eil	NF7170	57°36·3′	7°30·1′W	W	18
Loch nam Fiadh	Highld	NH3164	57°38·3′	4°49·4′W	W	20
Loch nam Fiasgan	N Eil	NB2128	58°9·4′	6°44·1′W	W	8,13
Loch nam Fiasgan	N Eil	NB2924	58°7·6′	6°35·7′W	W	13,14
Loch nam Fiodhag	Highld	NH3123	57°16·2′	4°47·7′W	W	26
Loch nam Forca	Highld	NG9636	57°22·4′	5°23·1′W	W	25
Loch nam Freumh	Highld	NH3226	57°17·8′	4°46·8′W	W	26
Loch na Mile	Arg & Bt	NR5470	55°51·9′	5°55·5′W	W	61
Loch nam Madadh or Loch Maddy	N Eil	NF9368	57°36·1′	7°7·9′W	W	18
Loch nam Madadh Uisge	Highld	NG5627	57°16·4′	6°2·4′W	W	32
Loch nam Magarlan	N Eil	NF7270	57°36·3′	7°29·1′W	W	18
Loch nam Manaichean	Arg & Bt	NR3955	55°43·3′	6°8·9′W	W	60
Loch nam Meallan Liatha	Highld	NC2220	58°8·3′	5°0·9′W	W	15
Loch nam Meur	Highld	NH3923	57°16·4′	4°39·8′W	W	26
Loch nam Meur	Highld	NH3925	57°17·5′	4°39·8′W	W	26
Loch na Mna	Highld	NG5738	57°22·3′	6°2·1′W	W	24,32
Loch na Mnatha	Highld	NC1944	58°21·1′	5°5·1′W	W	9
Loch na Mòine	Highld	NC6251	58°25·8′	4°21·3′W	W	10
Loch na Mòine	Highld	NC9365	58°33·9′	3°49·9′W	W	11
Loch na Mòine	Highld	NG9278	57°44·9′	5°29·2′W	W	19
Loch na Mòine	N Eil	NB2934	58°13·0′	6°36·4′W	W	8,13
Loch na Mòine	N Eil	NG0590	57°48·4′	6°57·5′W	W	14,18
Loch na Moineach	N Eil	NB2938	58°15·1′	6°36·7′W	W	8,13
Loch na Mòine Beag	Highld	NH1962	57°37·0′	5°1·4′W	W	20
Loch na Mòine Buige	Highld	NG9283	57°47·6′	5°29·5′W	W	19
Loch na Mòine Mòire	Highld	NH0455	57°32·8′	5°16·1′W	W	25
Loch na Mòine Mòr	Highld	NH1863	57°37·5′	5°2·4′W	W	20
Loch na Mola	Highld	NC1735	58°16·2′	5°6·7′W	W	15
Loch na Moracha	N Eil	NF8466	57°34·7′	7°16·8′W	W	18
Loch na Moracha	N Eil	NG0288	57°47·2′	7°0·4′W	W	18
Loch na Morgha	N Eil	NF8674	57°39·0′	7°15·4′W	W	18
Loch nam Paitean	Highld	NM7273	56°47·8′	5°43·6′W	W	40
Loch na Mucnaich	Highld	NC3238	58°18·2′	4°51·5′W	W	15
Loch na Muic	Highld	NH8384	57°50·1′	3°57·8′W	W	21
Loch na Muilne	N Eil	NB0421	58°5·0′	7°0·9′W	W	13
Lochna Muilne	N Eil	NB1224	58°6·9′	6°53·0′W	W	13,14
Loch na Muilne	N Eil	NB1439	58°15·1′	6°52·0′W	W	13
Loch na Muilne	N Eil	NB2038	58°14·8′	6°45·9′W	W	8,13
Loch na Muilne	N Eil	NB2130	58°10·5′	6°44·3′W	W	8,13
Loch na Muilne	N Eil	NB2446	58°19·2′	6°42·2′W	W	8
Loch na Muilne	N Eil	NB2717	58°3·7′	6°37·3′W	W	13,14
Loch na Muilne	N Eil	NB2747	58°19·9′	6°39·4′W	W	8
Loch na Muilne	N Eil	NB3149	58°21·1′	6°35·4′W	W	8
Loch na Muilne	N Eil	NB3622	58°6·8′	6°28·5′W	W	14
Loch na Muilne	N Eil	NB3819	58°5·2′	6°26·2′W	W	14
Loch na Muilne	N Eil	NB5161	58°28·2′	6°15·7′W	W	8
Loch na Muilne	N Eil	NB5247	58°20·8′	6°13·8′W	W	8
Loch na Muilne	N Eil	NF7427	57°13·3′	7°23·7′W	W	22
Loch nan Naich	Arg & Bt	NR7443	55°37·9′	5°35·0′W	W	62
Loch nan Aigheann	Highld	NC5268	58°34·8′	4°32·2′W	W	10
Loch nan Amhaichean	Highld	NH4176	57°45·0′	4°39·8′W	W	20
Loch nan Athan	N Eil	NF7766	57°34·4′	7°23·8′W	W	18
Loch nan Bairness	Highld	NM6575	56°48·7′	5°50·6′W	W	40
Loch nan Cabar	Highld	NG9260	57°35·2′	5°28·3′W	W	19
Loch nan Cabar	Highld	NH0046	57°27·6′	5°19·6′W	W	25
Loch nan Cadhan	Arg & Bt	NR4066	55°49·3′	6°8·6′W	W	60,61
Loch nan Caor	N Eil	NB0607	57°57·6′	6°57·8′W	W	13,14
Loch nan Caor	N Eil	NB3519	58°5·1′	6°29·3′W	W	14
Loch nan Caor	N Eil	NG0987	57°47·0′	6°53·3′W	W	14
Loch nan Caor	N Eil	NG1399	57°53·6′	6°50·1′W	W	14
Loch nan Caorach	Arg & Bt	NR3368	55°50·1′	6°15·4′W	W	60,61
Loch nan Caorach	Arg & Bt	NR6393	56°4·5′	5°48·1′W	W	61
Loch nan Caorach	Highld	NC2923	58°10·0′	4°53·9′W	W	15
Loch nan Caorach	Highld	NC2927	58°12·2′	4°54·1′W	W	15
Loch nan Caorach	Highld	NC8002	57°59·7′	4°1·3′W	W	17
Loch nan Càorach	N Eil	NB2738	58°15·0′	6°38·7′W	W	8,13
Loch nan Caorach	N Eil	NF7625	57°12·3′	7°21·5′W	W	22
Loch nan Càoran	N Eil	NB2931	58°11·3′	6°36·2′W	W	8,13
Loch nan Caorann	N Eil	NB3439	58°15·8′	6°31·7′W	W	8,13
Loch nan Caorann	N Eil	NB3535	58°13·7′	6°30·4′W	W	8
Loch nan Caorann	N Eil	NB4952	58°23·3′	6°17·2′W	W	8
Loch nan Capull	N Eil	NB4126	58°9·1′	6°23·7′W	W	8
Loch nan Capull	N Eil	NF7516	57°7·5′	7°21·8′W	W	31
Loch nan Car	Arg & Bt	NN0312	56°15·8′	5°10·4′W	W	50,55
Loch nan Carn	Highld	NG9379	57°45·4′	5°28·3′W	W	19
Loch nan Carraigean	Highld	NH9015	57°13·0′	3°48·8′W	W	36
Loch nan Ceall	Highld	NM6486	56°54·6′	5°52·1′W	W	40
Loch nan Ceann	Arg & Bt	NM8216	56°17·4′	5°30·9′W	W	55
Loch nan Cèard Beag	Arg & Bt	NM9102	56°10·1′	5°21·5′W	W	55
Loch nan Cèard Mór	Arg & Bt	NM9102	56°10·1′	5°21·5′W	W	55
Loch nan Ceithir Eilean	N Eil	NF8566	57°34·7′	7°15·8′W	W	18
Loch nan Cinneachan	Arg & Bt	NM1856	56°36·9′	6°35·4′W	W	46
Loch nan Ciob	Arg & Bt	NR7540	55°36·4′	5°33·9′W	W	62,69
Loch nan Claban	N Eil	NB5258	58°26·7′	6°14·5′W	W	8
Loch nan Clach	Highld	NC7752	58°26·6′	4°6·0′W	W	10
Loch nan Clach	Highld	NC8659	58°30·5′	3°56·9′W	W	10
Loch nan Clach	Highld	NG6109	57°6·9′	5°56·4′W	W	32
Loch nan Clach	Highld	NM7846	56°33·5′	5°36·3′W	W	49
Loch nan Clach	N Eil	NB3839	58°16·0′	6°27·6′W	W	8
Loch nan Clach	N Eil	NF8261	57°31·9′	7°18·4′W	W	22
Loch nan Clacha-mora	N Eil	NF7521	57°10·1′	7°22·2′W	W	31
Loch nan Clachan	N Eil	NF7673	57°38·1′	7°25·3′W	W	18
Loch nan Clachan	N Eil	NF8152	57°27·0′	7°18·7′W	W	22
Loch nan Clachan Dubha	Highld	NH3551	57°31·4′	4°44·9′W	W	26
Loch nan Clachan Geala	Highld	ND0058	58°30·2′	3°42·5′W	W	11,12
Loch nan Clachan Geala	Highld	NG8595	57°53·8′	5°37·2′W	W	19
Loch nan Clach Corr	N Eil	NF8052	57°27·0′	7°19·7′W	W	22
Loch nan Clach Dubha	Highld	NG9278	57°44·9′	5°29·2′W	W	19
Loch nan Clach Geala	Highld	NC5565	58°33·2′	4°29·0′W	W	10
Loch nan Clach Geala	Highld	NC6053	58°26·8′	4°23·4′W	W	10
Loch nan Clach Geala	Highld	NC9557	58°29·6′	3°47·6′W	W	11
Loch nan Claidhmhnean	Highld	NC1632	58°14·6′	5°7·6′W	W	15
Loch nan Clàr	Highld	NC7535	58°17·4′	4°7·5′W	W	16
Loch-nan Clàr	Highld	NC7635	58°17·4′	4°6·4′W	W	17
Loch nan Cleitichean	N Eil	NB2737	58°14·5′	6°38·7′W	W	8,13
Loch nan Cnaimh	Highld	NH1593	57°53·6′	5°6·8′W	W	20
Loch nan Cnamh	Highld	NC6561	58°31·2′	4°18·6′W	W	10
Loch nan Cnàmh	N Eil	NB2933	58°12·4′	6°36·3′W	W	8,13
Loch nan Cnàmh	N Eil	NB4026	58°9·1′	6°24·7′W	W	8
Loch nan Cnapan	Highld	NN9196	57°2·8′	3°47·3′W	W	36,43
Loch nan Coinean	Highld	NC6746	58°23·2′	4°16·0′W	W	10
Loch nan Con-donna	Highld	NC6751	58°25·9′	4°16·2′W	W	10
Loch nan Craobhag	N Eil	NG1493	57°50·4′	6°48·7′W	W	14
Loch nan Creadha	Highld	NG9640	57°24·5′	5°23·3′W	W	25
Loch nan Cuaran	Highld	NC2923	58°10·0′	4°53·9′W	W	15
Loch nan Cuilcean	Highld	NH4157	57°34·8′	4°39·1′W	W	26
Loch nan Cuile	Highld	NH4343	57°27·3′	4°36·5′W	W	26
Loch nan Culaidhean	N Eil	NB2629	58°10·2′	6°39·1′W	W	8,13
Loch nan Dailthean	Highld	NG8782	57°46·9′	5°34·5′W	W	19
Loch nan Dearcag	Highld	NH3357	57°34·6′	4°47·1′W	W	26
Loch nan Dearcag	Highld	NM8963	56°42·9′	5°26·4′W	W	40
Loch nan Dearcag	N Eil	NB4228	58°10·2′	6°22·8′W	W	8
Loch nan Deas Phoirt	N Eil	NB3021	58°6·0′	6°34·5′W	W	13,14
Loch nan Diol	Arg & Bt	NR4348	55°39·7′	6°4·7′W	W	60
Loch nan Druidean	Highld	NH4671	57°42·4′	4°34·6′W	W	20
Loch nan Druimnean	Arg & Bt	NM8414	56°16·4′	5°28·9′W	W	55
Loch nan Dùbhrachan	Highld	NG6710	57°7·6′	5°50·5′W	W	32
Loch nan Eala	Highld	NM6685	56°54·1′	5°50·1′W	W	40
Loch nan Ealachan	Highld	NC1709	58°2·2′	5°5·5′W	W	15
Loch nan Ealachan	Highld	NC2939	58°18·6′	4°54·7′W	W	15
Loch nan Ealachan	Highld	NC5444	58°21·9′	4°29·3′W	W	10
Loch nan Ealachan	Highld	NC6751	58°25·9′	4°16·2′W	W	10
Loch nan Ealachan	Highld	NG9928	57°18·2′	5°19·7′W	W	25,33
Loch nan Eang	N Eil	NB1408	57°58·4′	6°49·8′W	W	13,14
Loch nan Eang	N Eil	NB1907	57°58·1′	6°44·6′W	W	13,14
Loch nan Eilean	Arg & Bt	NM9403	56°10·8′	5°18·7′W	W	55
Loch nan Eilean	Arg & Bt	NR6696	56°6·2′	5°45·3′W	W	55,61
Loch nan Eilean	Highld	NG4730	57°17·7′	6°11·5′W	W	32
Loch nan Eilean	Highld	NH2779	57°46·3′	4°54·1′W	W	20
Loch nan Eilean	N Eil	NB0633	58°11·5′	6°59·7′W	W	13
Loch nan Eilean	N Eil	NB2022	58°6·2′	6°44·7′W	W	13,14
Loch nan Eilean	N Eil	NB2223	58°6·8′	6°42·7′W	W	13,14
Loch nan Eilean	N Eil	NB3330	58°11·0′	6°32·1′W	W	8,13
Loch nan Eilean	N Eil	NB3505	57°57·6′	6°28·3′W	W	14
Loch nan Eilean	N Eil	NB3617	58°4·1′	6°28·1′W	W	14
Loch nan Eilean	N Eil	NB4112	58°1·6′	6°22·7′W	W	14
Loch nan Eilean	N Eil	NB4127	58°9·6′	6°23·7′W	W	8
Loch nan Eilid	Highld	NH4057	57°34·7′	4°40·1′W	W	26
Loch nan Eilthireach	Arg & Bt	NR7781	55°58·5′	5°34·0′W	W	55
Loch nan Eun	Aberd	NO2385	56°57·2′	3°15·5′W	W	44
Loch nan Eun	Arg & Bt	NR7542	55°37·4′	5°34·0′W	W	62,69
Loch nan Eun	Arg & Bt	NR8052	55°42·9′	5°29·7′W	W	62,69
Loch nan Eun	Highld	NC1023	58°9·6′	5°13·3′W	W	15
Loch nan Eun	Highld	NC2329	58°13·1′	5°0·3′W	W	15
Loch nan Eun	Highld	NG7048	57°28·1′	5°49·7′W	W	24
Loch nan Eun	Highld	NG7050	57°29·2′	5°49·8′W	W	24
Loch nan Eun	Highld	NG7058	57°33·5′	5°50·2′W	W	24

Loch nan Eun	Highld	NG7573	57°41·7′	5°46·1′W	W	19
Loch nan Eun	Highld	NG7791	57°51·4′	5°45·1′W	W	19
Loch nan Eun	Highld	NG8352	57°30·6′	5°36·9′W	W	24
Loch nan Eun	Highld	NG8597	57°54·9′	5°37·3′W	W	19
Loch nan Eun	Highld	NG9385	57°48·7′	5°28·6′W	W	19
Loch nan Eun	Highld	NG9526	57°17·0′	5°23·6′W	W	25,33
Loch nan Eun	Highld	NH1581	57°47·1′	5°6·2′W	W	20
Loch nan Eun	Highld	NH2568	57°40·3′	4°55·6′W	W	20
Loch nan Eun	Highld	NH3120	57°14·6′	4°47·6′W	W	26
Loch nan Eun	Highld	NH4509	57°9·0′	4°33·3′W	W	34
Loch nan Eun	Highld	NH4525	57°17·6′	4°33·9′W	W	26
Loch nan Eun	Highld	NH4648	57°30·0′	4°33·7′W	W	26
Loch nan Eun	N Eil	NF8367	57°35·2′	7°17·8′W	W	18
Loch nan Eun	Pth & Kin	NN8855	56°40·7′	3°49·2′W	W	52
Loch nan Eun	Pth & Kin	NO0678	56°53·3′	3°32·1′W	W	43
Loch nan Faoileag	N Eil	NB1018	58°3·6′	6°54·5′W	W	13,14
Loch nan Gabhar	Arg & Bt	NR3348	55°39·4′	6°14·3′W	W	60
Loch nan Gabhar	Highld	NM9663	56°43·1′	5°19·6′W	W	40
Loch nan Gad	Arg & Bt	NR7857	55°45·6′	5°31·9′W	W	62
Loch nan Gamhna	Highld	NC6458	58°29·6′	4°19·5′W	W	10
Loch nan Gamhna	Highld	NG7961	57°35·4′	5°41·4′W	W	19,24
Loch nan Garbh Chlachan	N Eil	NF8660	57°31·5′	7°14·3′W	W	22
Loch nan Garnach	N Eil	NF7575	57°39·1′	7°26·5′W	W	18
Loch nan Geadas	Highld	NH5930	57°20·6′	4°20·1′W	W	26
Loch nan Gèadh	Arg & Bt	NM2358	56°38·2′	6°30·6′W	W	46,47
Loch nan Geadh	Arg & Bt	NR8153	55°43·5′	5°28·8′W	W	62
Loch nan Geadh	N Eil	NB3036	58°14·1′	6°35·5′W	W	8,13
Loch nan Geadh	N Eil	NB4846	58°20·1′	6°17·8′W	W	8
Loch nan Geadh	N Eil	NF8870	57°37·0′	7°13·1′W	W	18
Loch nan Geadraisean	N Eil	NB1636	58°13·5′	6°49·8′W	W	13
Loch nan Gealag	N Eil	NF8659	57°31·0′	7°14·2′W	W	22
Loch nan Geireann	N Eil	NF8472	57°37·9′	7°17·2′W	W	18
Loch nan Geireann	N Eil	NF8473	57°38·4′	7°17·3′W	W	18
Loch nan Geodhannan	N Eil	NB0318	58°3·4′	7°1·6′W	X	13
Loch nan Gillean	Arg & Bt	NR3043	55°36·6′	6°16·8′W	W	60
Loch nan Gillean	Highld	NG8332	57°19·9′	5°35·9′W	W	24
Loch nan Gillean	Highld	NG9235	57°21·7′	5°27·0′W	W	25
Loch nan Gillean	Highld	NH6892	57°54·1′	4°13·2′W	W	21
Loch nan Gobhar	Highld	NC0623	58°9·5′	5°17·4′W	W	15
Loch nan Gobhar	Highld	NH0145	57°27·4′	5°18·6′W	W	25
Loch nan Gobhar	Highld	NH3019	57°14·1′	4°48·5′W	W	34
Loch nan Gobhar	Highld	NH4137	57°24·0′	4°38·3′W	W	26
Loch nan Gobhar	Highld	NH4444	57°27·8′	4°35·6′W	W	26
Loch nan Gobhar	N Eil	NF8872	57°38·1′	7°13·2′W	W	18
Loch na Nighinn	Highld	ND0041	58°21·0′	3°42·0′W	W	11,12
Loch nan Iolairean	N Eil	NB3616	58°3·5′	6°28·1′W	W	14
Loch nan Lann	Highld	NH4413	57°11·1′	4°34·4′W	W	34
Loch nan Laogh	Highld	NC7555	58°28·2′	4°8·1′W	W	10
Loch nan Laogh	N Eil	NB3728	58°10·0′	6°27·9′W	W	8
Loch nan Leac	Highld	NG6934	57°20·5′	5°49·9′W	X	24,32
Loch nan Leac	N Eil	NB2739	58°15·6′	6°38·8′W	W	8,13
Loch nan Leac	N Eil	NB3140	58°16·2′	6°34·8′W	W	8,13
Loch nan Leac	N Eil	NB4248	58°20·9′	6°24·1′W	W	8
Loch nan Leac	N Eil	NB4445	58°19·4′	6°21·9′W	W	8
Loch nan Leachd	Highld	NG4919	57°11·8′	6°8·9′W	W	32
Loch nan Learg	Arg & Bt	NM4322	56°19·5′	6°9·0′W	W	48
Loch nan Learg	Highld	NG4542	57°24·1′	6°14·2′W	W	23
Loch nan Learg	Highld	NG5919	57°12·2′	5°59·0′W	W	32
Loch nan Learg	N Eil	NB1810	57°59·7′	6°45·9′W	W	13,14
Loch nan Learg	N Eil	NG1394	57°50·9′	6°49·8′W	W	14
Loch nan Learga	N Eil	NB5555	58°25·2′	6°11·3′W	W	8
Loch nan Liagh	Highld	NG8081	57°46·1′	5°41·5′W	W	19
Loch nan Lìon	Highld	NC0927	58°11·7′	5°14·5′W	W	15
Loch nan Lochan	Highld	NM7472	56°47·3′	5°41·6′W	W	40
Loch nan Losganan	Highld	NH5015	57°12·3′	4°28·5′W	W	35
Loch nan Losgann	Arg & Bt	NM9503	56°10·8′	5°17·7′W	W	55
Loch nan Losgann	Arg & Bt	NN0022	56°21·1′	5°13·8′W	W	50
Loch nan Lùb	Highld	NC0630	58°13·2′	5°17·7′W	W	15
Loch nan Lùb	N Eil	NB3414	58°2·4′	6°30·0′W	W	13,14
Loch nan Luch	Highld	NH3225	57°17·3′	4°46·8′W	W	26
Loch nan Luig	N Eil	NB5351	58°22·9′	6°13·0′W	W	8
Loch nan Ràc	Highld	NC1715	58°5·4′	5°5·8′W	W	15
Loch nan Ramh	N Eil	NB0019	58°3·8′	7°4·8′W	W	13
Loch nan Ràmh	N Eil	NB0719	58°4·1′	6°57·7′W	W	13,14
Loch nan Ramh	N Eil	NB3230	58°10·9′	6°33·1′W	W	8,13
Loch nan Rath	Highld	NC4039	58°18·9′	4°43·4′W	W	16
Loch nan Ritheanan	N Eil	NB3523	58°7·3′	6°29·5′W	W	14
Loch nan Ròn	Arg & Bt	NR5578	55°56·2′	5°54·9′W	W	61
Loch nan Ròn	N Eil	NB3509	57°59·7′	6°28·6′W	W	14
Loch nan Sac	Arg & Bt	NM9904	56°11·4′	5°13·9′W	W	55
Loch nan Sean-each	Highld	NH2222	57°15·5′	4°56·6′W	W	25
Loch nan Seileach	Arg & Bt	NN0105	56°12·0′	5°12·0′W	W	55
Loch nan Sgaraig	Highld	NC3424	58°10·7′	4°48·9′W	W	15
Loch nan Sgeireag	N Eil	NF8040	57°20·5′	7°18·7′W	W	22
Loch nan Sgiath	N Eil	NB3630	58°11·1′	6°29·0′W	W	8
Loch nan Sgilleog	Arg & Bt	NM9503	56°10·8′	5°17·7′W	W	55
Loch nan Sìdhean	Highld	NH5001	57°4·8′	4°28·0′W	W	35
Loch nan Sligean	N Eil	NB0208	57°58·0′	7°1·9′W	W	13
Loch nan Smalag	N Eil	NF7920	57°9·8′	7°18·2′W	W	31
Loch nan Smalag	N Eil	NF8264	57°33·5′	7°18·6′W	W	18
Loch nan Smallag	N Eil	NF9572	57°38·3′	7°6·2′W	W	18
Loch nan Spréidh	Highld	NH3893	57°54·1′	4°43·5′W	W	20
Loch nan Starr	N Eil	NB4128	58°10·2′	6°23·8′W	W	8
Loch nan Steall	N Eil	NB3237	58°14·7′	6°33·6′W	W	8,13
Loch nan Stearnag	N Eil	NB3236	58°14·1′	6°33·5′W	W	8,13
Loch nan Stearnag	N Eil	NB4013	58°2·1′	6°23·8′W	W	14
Loch nan Stearnag	N Eil	NB4047	58°20·3′	6°26·1′W	W	8
Loch nan Strùban	N Eil	NF8064	57°33·4′	7°20·6′W	W	18
Loch nan Stuirteag	Aberd	NN9495	57°2·3′	3°44·4′W	W	36,43
Loch nan Stuirteag	Highld	NH7326	57°18·7′	4°6·0′W	W	35
Loch nan Stuirteag	Highld	NH8826	57°18·9′	3°51·1′W	W	35,36
Loch Nant	Arg & Bt	NM9924	56°22·2′	5°14·8′W	W	49
Loch Nant	Arg & Bt	NN0024	56°22·2′	5°13·9′W	W	50
Loch nan Torran	Arg & Bt	NR7568	55°51·4′	5°35·3′W	W	62
Loch nan Tri-eileanan	Highld	NG8259	57°34·4′	5°38·3′W	W	24
Loch nan Trì Tom	N Eil	NB2924	58°7·6′	6°35·7′W	W	13,14
Loch nan Tunnag	Highld	NH4533	57°21·9′	4°34·2′W	W	26
Loch nan Tunnag	Highld	NH8383	57°49·5′	3°57·7′W	W	21
Loch nan Uaighean	Highld	NG7341	57°24·4′	5°46·3′W	W	24
Loch nan Uain	Highld	NG9082	57°47·0′	5°31·5′W	W	19

Loch nan Uamh	Highld	NG6308	57°6·4′	5°54·4′W	W	32
Loch Nan Uamh	Highld	NM7083	56°53·1′	5°46·1′W	W	40
Loch nan Uan	Highld	NC5629	58°13·8′	4°26·7′W	W	16
Loch nan Uan	Highld	NG3332	57°18·3′	6°25·5′W	W	32
Loch nan Uan	Highld	NG8595	57°53·8′	5°37·2′W	W	19
Loch nan Uan	N Eil	NF7325	57°12·2′	7°24·5′W	W	22
Loch nan Ubhlan	Highld	NC6801	57°59·0′	4°13·5′W	W	16
Loch nan Uidh	Highld	NC1941	58°19·5′	5°5·0′W	W	9
Loch nan Uidhean	N Eil	NB0317	58°2·8′	7°1·6′W	W	13
Loch nan Uidhean	N Eil	NB0624	58°6·7′	6°59·1′W	W	13,14
Loch nan Uidhean	N Eil	NB0816	58°2·5′	6°56·4′W	W	13,14
Loch nan Uidhean	N Eil	NB2607	57°58·3′	6°37·6′W	W	13,14
Loch nan Uidhean	N Eil	NG1495	57°51·4′	6°48·8′W	W	14
Loch nan Uidhean	N Eil	NG1692	57°49·9′	6°46·6′W	W	14
Loch nan Uidhean Beaga	Highld	NC0927	58°11·7′	5°14·5′W	W	15
Loch nan Uranan	Highld	NG7916	57°11·2′	5°39·0′W	W	33
Loch na Pearaich	Arg & Bt	NR5883	55°59·0′	5°52·3′W	W	61
Loch na Plaide	N Eil	NB2127	58°8·9′	6°44·0′W	W	8,13
Loch na Plangaid	Highld	NH4242	57°26·7′	4°37·5′W	W	26
Loch na Ploytach	Highld	NB9817	58°6·0′	5°25·2′W	W	15
Loch na Pulaig	Highld	NC6613	58°5·4′	4°15·9′W	W	16
Loch na Ra'fin	Highld	NC5065	58°33·1′	4°34·2′W	W	9
Loch Narroch	D & G	NX4581	55°6·2′	4°25·3′W	W	77
Loch na Ruighe Duibhe	Highld	NH3823	57°16·4′	4°40·8′W	W	26
Loch na Saighe Duibhe	Highld	NC2315	58°5·6′	4°59·7′W	W	15
Loch na Sàil	Highld	NH2399	57°57·0′	4°59·0′W	W	20
Loch na Sailm	Arg & Bt	NM8714	56°16·5′	5°26·0′W	W	55
Loch na Sàlach	Highld	NH3267	57°40·0′	4°48·5′W	W	20
Loch na Salachan	Arg & Bt	NM5523	56°20·4′	5°57·4′W	W	48
Loch na Saobhaidhe	Highld	NC6501	57°58·9′	4°16·5′W	W	16
Loch na Saobhaidhe	Highld	NC8047	58°24·0′	4°2·7′W	W	10
Loch Nasavig	N Eil	NB0436	58°13·1′	7°2·0′W	W	13
Loch na Sealga	Highld	NH0382	57°47·3′	5°18·4′W	W	19
Loch na Seamraig	Highld	NC2872	58°36·4′	4°57·2′W	W	9
Loch na Seilg	Highld	NC3658	58°29·0′	4°48·3′W	W	9
Loch na Seilg	Highld	NC4950	58°25·0′	4°34·6′W	W	9
Loch na Seilge	Highld	NC2543	58°20·7′	4°58·9′W	W	9
Loch na Seilge	Highld	NC3644	58°21·5′	4°47·7′W	W	9
Loch na Seilge	Highld	NC9258	58°30·1′	3°50·7′W	W	11
Loch na Sgàireig Mór	Highld	NG8492	57°52·2′	5°38·1′W	W	19
Loch na' Sgarbh	Highld	NH3656	57°34·1′	4°44·1′W	W	26
Loch na Sgeallaig	Highld	NN3665	56°45·1′	4°40·5′W	W	41
Loch na Sgeireagan Mòr	N Eil	NB1404	57°56·3′	6°49·5′W	W	13,14
Loch na Sgorra	Arg & Bt	NR6797	56°6·8′	5°44·4′W	W	55,61
Loch na Sgorthaich	Highld	NH4414	57°11·7′	4°34·5′W	W	34
Loch na Sgratha	Arg & Bt	NR7682	55°59·0′	5°35·0′W	W	55
Loch na Sgrioba	Arg & Bt	NR4677	55°55·4′	6°3·5′W	W	60,61
Loch na Sguabaidh	Highld	NG5523	57°14·2′	6°3·2′W	W	32
Loch na Smalaig	N Eil	NF8055	57°28·6′	7°19·9′W	W	22
Loch na Smeòraich	Highld	NG8430	57°18·8′	5°34·8′W	W	24
Loch na Speireig	N Eil	NB3224	58°7·7′	6°32·7′W	W	13,14
Loch na Speur	Moray	NJ0948	57°31·0′	3°30·7′W	W	27
Loch na Sreinge	Arg & Bt	NM9217	56°18·2′	5°21·3′W	W	55
Loch na Sròine	Highld	NG9035	57°21·7′	5°29·0′W	W	25
Loch na Sròine	N Eil	NB3204	57°56·9′	6°31·3′W	W	13,14
Loch na Sròine Luime	Highld	NC3421	58°9·1′	4°48·8′W	W	15
Loch na Stàirne	Highld	NC9630	58°15·1′	3°45·8′W	W	11,17
Loch na Staoineig	Highld	NN2965	56°45·0′	4°47·3′W	W	41
Loch na Still	Highld	NH2880	57°46·9′	4°53·1′W	W	20
Loch na Stioma Gile	Highld	NC3049	58°24·1′	4°54·1′W	W	9
Loch na Stròine Móire	N Eil	NB1429	58°9·7′	6°51·3′W	W	13
Loch na Stuirteag	Highld	NJ0032	57°22·3′	3°39·3′W	W	27,36
Loch na Sùiteig	Highld	NG8948	57°28·7′	5°30·7′W	W	24
Loch na Sùla Bige	Highld	NM7746	56°33·4′	5°37·3′W	W	49
Loch na Sùla Móire	Highld	NM7746	56°33·4′	5°37·3′W	W	49
Loch na Tanga	N Eil	NF7323	57°11·1′	7°24·3′W	W	22
Loch na Tarraing	Highld	NC1529	58°12·9′	5°8·5′W	W	15
Loch na Teangaidh Fhiadhaich	Highld	NG9368	57°39·5′	5°27·7′W	W	19
Loch na Thull	Highld	NC2550	58°24·5′	4°59·2′W	W	9
Loch na Totaig	Highld	NB9815	58°4·9′	5°25·1′W	W	15
Loch na Tuadh	Highld	NC3147	58°23·0′	4°53·0′W	W	9
Loch Naver	Highld	NC6136	58°17·7′	4°21·8′W	W	16
Lochnaw Castle	D & G	NW9962	54°55·0′	5°7·7′W	A	82
Lochnawean Hill	Aberd	NO5684	56°57·0′	2°42·9′W	H	44
Loch Neadabhat	N Eil	NB2343	58°17·6′	6°43·2′W	W	8
Loch Neaty	Highld	NH4336	57°23·5′	4°36·3′W	W	26
Loch Nedd	Highld	NC1332	58°14·5′	5°10·7′W	W	15
Loch Neil Bhàin	Highld	NC0430	58°13·2′	5°19·8′W	W	15
Loch Nèill Bhàin	N Eil	NB5255	58°25·1′	6°14·3′W	W	8
Loch Neldricken	D & G	NX4482	55°6·7′	4°26·3′W	W	77
Loch Nell	Arg & Bt	NM8927	56°23·6′	5°24·7′W	W	49
Lochnellan	Highld	NJ0036	57°24·5′	3°39·4′W	X	27
Lochnell Ho	Arg & Bt	NM8838	56°29·4′	5°26·2′W	X	49
Loch Ness	Highld	NH4314	57°11·7′	4°35·4′W	W	34
Loch Ness	Highld	NH4618	57°13·9′	4°32·6′W	W	34
Loch Ness	Highld	NH5023	57°16·6′	4°28·8′W	W	26,35
Loch Nevan	S Ayr	NX2983	55°7·0′	4°40·4′W	W	76
Loch Nevis	Highld	NM7695	56°59·8′	5°40·8′W	W	33,40
Loch Niarsco	Highld	NG3947	57°26·6′	6°20·5′W	W	23
Loch Nic Dhomhnaill	N Eil	NB4949	58°21·7′	6°17·0′W	W	8
Loch nic Ruaidhe	N Eil	NF7001	56°59·2′	7°25·6′W	W	31
Loch Nighe	N Eil	NF8558	57°30·4′	7°15·1′W	W	22
Loch Nighe	N Eil	NF8574	57°39·0′	7°16·4′W	W	18
Loch Nighe	N Eil	NF9166	57°35·0′	7°9·8′W	W	18
Loch Nighe	N Eil	NG1291	57°49·2′	6°50·6′W	W	14
Loch Nighean Aillein	Arg & Bt	NR5986	56°0·6′	5°51·5′W	W	61
Loch Nighean Fhionniadh	Highld	NG5806	57°5·1′	5°59·2′W	W	32,39
Loch Nighean Shomhairle	N Eil	NB2845	58°18·8′	6°38·2′W	W	8
Loch Niosabhat	N Eil	NB3950	58°21·9′	6°27·3′W	W	8
Loch Nishavat	N Eil	NB1635	58°13·0′	6°49·7′W	W	13
Loch Nisreabhal	N Eil	NB3326	58°8·8′	6°31·8′W	W	8,13
Loch Noir	Moray	NJ0945	57°29·4′	3°30·6′W	W	27
Loch Nosinish	N Eil	NF7519	57°9·1′	7°22·0′W	W	31
Loch Nuis	N Ayr	NR9337	55°35·2′	5°16·6′W	W	68,69
Loch Ob an Lochain	Highld	NH1598	57°56·2′	5°7·0′W	W	20
Loch Obasaraigh	N Eil	NF8961	57°32·2′	7°11·4′W	W	22
Loch Obe	N Eil	NF7101	56°59·2′	7°24·6′W	W	31
Loch Ochain	N Eil	NB1430	58°10·2′	6°51·4′W	W	13
Loch Ochiltree	D & G	NX3174	55°2·2′	4°38·2′W	W	76

Loch Odhairn	N Eil	NB4014	58°2·6′	6°23·9′W	W	14
Loch Odhar	Highld	NC1529	58°12·9′	5°8·5′W	W	15
Loch Odhar	Highld	NC2007	58°1·2′	5°2·4′W	W	15
Loch Odhar	Highld	NG7543	57°25·6′	5°44·4′W	W	24
Loch Odhar	Highld	NH2470	57°41·4′	4°56·7′W	W	20
Loch of Aboyne	Aberd	NO5399	57°5·0′	2°46·1′W	W	37,44
Loch of Aesha	Shetld	HU1561	60°20·2′	1°43·2′W	W	3
Loch of Aith	Shetld	HU5042	60°9·8′	1°5·5′W	W	4
Loch of Aithsness	Shetld	HU3258	60°18·6′	1°24·8′W	W	3
Loch of Arg	Shetld	HU3044	60°11·0′	1°27·1′W	W	4
Loch of Assater	Shetld	HU2979	60°29·9′	1°27·8′W	W	3
Loch of Asta	Shetld	HU4141	60°9·4′	1°15·2′W	W	4
Loch of Auckengill	Highld	ND3565	58°34·4′	3°6·6′W	W	12
Loch of Auds	Aberd	NJ6464	57°40·1′	2°35·7′W	X	29
Loch of Balloch	Pth & Kin	NN8319	56°21·2′	3°53·2′W	W	57
Loch of Banks	Orkney	HY2723	59°5·5′	3°16·0′W	X	6
Loch of Basta	Shetld	HU5095	60°38·4′	1°4·6′W	W	1,2
Loch of Bellister	Shetld	HU4658	60°18·5′	1°9·6′W	W	2,3
Loch of Belmont	Shetld	HP5600	60°41·0′	0°58·0′W	W	1
Loch of Benston	Shetld	HU4653	60°15·8′	1°9·6′W	W	3
Loch of Birrier	Shetld	HU5488	60°34·6′	1°0·4′W	W	1,2
Loch of Birriesgirt	Shetld	HU4491	60°36·3′	1°11·3′W	W	1,2
Loch of Blackhill	Shetld	HU3166	60°22·9′	1°25·8′W	W	3
Loch of Blairs	Moray	NJ0255	57°34·7′	3°37·9′W	W	27
Loch of Boardhouse	Orkney	HY2625	59°6·6′	3°17·0′W	W	6
Loch of Boath	Highld	NH8845	57°29·1′	3°51·6′W	W	27
Loch of Bogligarths	Shetld	HP5808	60°45·3′	0°55·6′W	W	1
Loch of Bordigarth	Shetld	HU4273	60°26·6′	1°13·7′W	W	2,3
Loch of Bosquoy	Orkney	HY3018	59°2·9′	3°12·7′W	W	6
Loch of Bottoms	Shetld	HU3264	60°21·8′	1°24·7′W	W	3
Loch of Braehoulland	Shetld	HU2479	60°29·9′	1°33·3′W	W	3
Loch of Breck	Shetld	HU2148	60°13·2′	1°36·8′W	W	3
Loch of Brecksie	Shetld	HP5903	60°42·6′	0°54·6′W	W	1
Loch of Brindister	Shetld	HU4336	60°6·6′	1°13·1′W	W	4
Loch of Brockan	Orkney	HY3919	59°3·5′	3°3·3′W	W	6
Loch of Brough	Shetld	HP5302	60°42·1′	1°1·2′W	W	1
Loch of Brough	Shetld	HU5140	60°8·7′	1°4·4′W	W	4
Loch of Brow	Shetld	HU3815	59°55·4′	1°18·7′W	W	4
Loch of Brue	Orkney	HY7544	59°17·2′	2°25·8′W	W	5
Loch of Brunatwatt	Shetld	HU2551	60°14·8′	1°32·4′W	W	3
Loch of Burness	Orkney	HY4248	59°19·1′	3°0·7′W	W	5
Loch of Burraland	Shetld	HU3474	60°27·2′	1°22·4′W	W	2,3
Loch of Burwick	Shetld	HU3941	60°9·4′	1°17·4′W	W	4
Loch of Bushta	Highld	ND1972	58°38·0′	3°23·2′W	W	7,12
Loch of Butterstone	Pth & Kin	NO0544	56°35·0′	3°32·4′W	W	52,53
Loch of Camster	Highld	ND2644	58°23·0′	3°15·5′W	W	11,12
Loch of Clickimin	Shetld	HU4641	60°9·3′	1°9·8′W	W	4
Loch of Cliff	Shetld	HP5911	60°46·9′	0°54·5′W	W	1
Loch of Clousta	Shetld	HU3158	60°18·6′	1°25·8′W	W	3
Loch of Clumlie	Shetld	HU4017	59°56·4′	1°16·6′W	W	4
Loch of Clumly	Orkney	HY2516	59°1·7′	3°17·9′W	W	6
Loch of Clunie	Pth & Kin	NO1144	56°35·0′	3°26·5′W	W	53
Loch of Collaster	Shetld	HU2057	60°18·1′	1°37·8′W	W	3
Loch of Collaster	Shetld	HU3154	60°16·4′	1°25·9′W	W	3
Loch of Colvister	Shetld	HU4996	60°38·9′	1°5·7′W	W	1
Loch of Couster	Shetld	HU4136	60°6·7′	1°15·3′W	W	4
Loch of Craiglush	Pth & Kin	NO0444	56°34·9′	3°33·3′W	W	52,53
Loch of Cullivoe	Shetld	HP5302	60°42·1′	1°1·2′W	W	1
Loch of Doomy	Orkney	HY5534	59°11·7′	2°46·8′W	W	5,6
Loch of Drumellie or Marlee Loch	Pth & Kin	NO1444	56°35·1′	3°23·6′W	W	53
Loch of Easter Head	Highld	ND2076	58°40·1′	3°22·3′W	W	7,12
Loch of East Yell	Shetld	HU5382	60°31·4′	1°1·6′W	W	1,2,3
Loch of Fladdabister	Shetld	HU4333	60°5·0′	1°13·1′W	W	4
Loch of Flatpunds	Shetld	HU2452	60°15·4′	1°33·5′W	W	3
Loch of Flugarth	Shetld	HU3690	60°35·8′	1°20·1′W	W	1,2
Loch of Forfar	Angus	NO4450	56°38·6′	2°54·3′W	W	54
Loch of Framgord	Shetld	HU2078	60°29·4′	1°37·7′W	W	3
Loch of Freester	Shetld	HU4553	60°15·8′	1°10·7′W	W	3
Loch of Funzie	Shetld	HU6589	60°35·0′	0°48·3′W	W	1,2
Loch of Fyntalloch	D & G	NX3174	55°2·2′	4°38·2′W	W	76
Loch of Fyvie	Aberd	NJ7638	57°26·2′	2°23·5′W	W	29
Loch of Garso	Orkney	HY7755	59°23·1′	2°23·8′W	W	5
Loch of Garth	Shetld	HP5400	60°41·0′	1°0·2′W	W	1
Loch of Garth	Shetld	HU4042	60°9·9′	1°16·3′W	W	4
Loch of Gershon	Shetld	HU3732	60°4·5′	1°19·6′W	W	4
Loch of Girlsta	Shetld	HU4352	60°15·3′	1°12·9′W	W	3
Loch of Gonfirth	Shetld	HU3862	60°20·7′	1°18·2′W	W	2,3
Loch of Goster	Shetld	HU1751	60°14·8′	1°41·1′W	W	3
Loch of Grandtully	Pth & Kin	NN9150	56°38·0′	3°46·2′W	W	52
Loch of Graveland	Shetld	HU4594	60°37·9′	1°10·1′W	W	1,2
Loch of Griesta	Shetld	HU4043	60°10·4′	1°16·2′W	W	4
Loch of Grimsetter	Shetld	HU5139	60°8·2′	1°4·4′W	W	4
Loch of Grunnavoe	Shetld	HU2549	60°13·7′	1°32·4′W	W	3
Loch of Grutfea	Orkney	HY1900	58°53·1′	3°23·8′W	W	7
Loch of Gruting	Shetld	HU2950	60°14·3′	1°28·1′W	W	3
Loch of Grutwick	Shetld	HU5070	60°24·9′	1°5·0′W	W	2,3
Loch of Haggrister	Shetld	HU3370	60°25·0′	1°23·5′W	W	2,3
Loch of Hamarsland	Shetld	HU4148	60°13·1′	1°15·1′W	W	3
Loch of Harray	Orkney	HY2916	59°1·8′	3°13·7′W	W	6
Loch of Hellister	Shetld	HU3950	60°14·2′	1°17·2′W	W	3
Loch of Hillwell	Shetld	HU3713	59°54·3′	1°19·8′W	W	4
Loch of Hollorin	Shetld	HU2755	60°17·0′	1°30·2′W	W	3
Loch of Hookame	Shetld	HU4258	60°18·5′	1°13·9′W	W	2,3
Loch of Houll	Shetld	HU5564	60°21·6′	0°59·7′W	W	2
Loch of Houlland	Shetld	HU2178	60°29·4′	1°36·6′W	W	3
Loch of Houlland	Shetld	HU4041	60°9·4′	1°16·3′W	W	4
Loch of Houlland	Shetld	HU4554	60°16·3′	1°10·7′W	W	3
Loch of Housetter	Shetld	HU3685	60°33·1′	1°20·1′W	W	1,2,3
Loch of Houss	Shetld	HU3732	60°4·5′	1°19·6′W	W	4
Loch of Houster	Shetld	HU3455	60°16·9′	1°22·6′W	W	3
Loch of Hoversta	Shetld	HP6002	60°42·1′	0°53·6′W	W	1
Loch of Huesbreck	Shetld	HU3813	59°54·3′	1°18·7′W	W	4
Loch of Hundland	Orkney	HY2926	59°7·2′	3°13·9′W	W	6
Loch of Huxter	Shetld	HU5562	60°20·6′	0°59·7′W	W	2
Loch of Kebister	Shetld	HU4544	60°10·9′	1°10·8′W	W	4
Loch of Kellister	Shetld	HU2455	60°17·0′	1°33·5′W	W	3
Loch of Kettlester	Shetld	HU5180	60°30·3′	1°3·8′W	W	1,2,3
Loch of Killimster	Highld	ND3055	58°28·9′	3°11·6′W	W	11,12

Loch of Kinnordy	Angus	NO3654	56°40·7'	3°2·2'W	W	54
Loch of Kirbister	Orkney	HY3607	58°57·0'	3°6·3'W	W	6,7
Loch of Kirkabister	Shetld	HU4958	60°18·5'	1°6·3'W	W	2,3
Loch of Kirkigarth	Shetld	HU2349	60°13·7'	1°34·6'W	W	3
Loch of Knitchen	Orkney	HY4228	59°8·4'	3°0·3'W	W	5,6
Loch of Langamay	Orkney	HY7444	59°17·2'	2°26·9'W	W	5
Loch of Liff	Angus	NO3333	56°29·3'	3°4·8'W	X	53
Loch of Lintrathen	Angus	NO2754	56°40·6'	3°11·0'W	W	53
Loch of Littlester	Shetld	HU5179	60°29·8'	1°3·8'W	W	2,3
Loch of Livister	Shetld	HU5563	60°21·1'	0°59·7'W	W	2
Loch of Lomashion	Highld	ND3870	58°37·1'	3°3·6'W	W	7,12
Loch of London	Orkney	HY5634	59°11·7'	2°45·7'W	W	5,6
Loch of Loomachun	Orkney	HY4030	59°9·4'	3°2·5'W	W	5,6
Loch of Lowes	Pth & Kin	NO0443	56°34·4'	3°33·3'W	W	52,53
Loch of Lumgair	Aberd	NO8582	56°56·0'	2°14·4'W	W	45
Loch of Lunklet	Shetld	HU3757	60°18·0'	1°19·3'W	W	2,3
Loch of Lunnister	Shetld	HU3471	60°25·6'	1°22·4'W	W	2,3
Loch of Lythe	Orkney	ND4485	58°45·2'	2°57·6'W	W	7
Loch of Mey	Highld	ND2773	58°38·6'	3°15·0'W	W	7,12
Loch of Mioness	Shetld	HU4278	60°29·3'	1°13·6'W	W	2,3
Loch of Muirs	Highld	ND2073	58°38·5'	3°22·2'W	W	7,12
Loch of Murraster	Shetld	HU2752	60°15·3'	1°30·2'W	W	3
Loch of Norby	Shetld	HU1957	60°18·1'	1°38·9'W	W	3
Loch of North Aywick	Shetld	HU5387	60°34·0'	1°1·5'W	W	1,2
Loch of North-house	Shetld	HU3255	60°16·9'	1°24·8'W	W	3
Loch of Papil	Shetld	HP5404	60°42·0'	1°0·1'W	W	1
Loch of Park	Aberd	NO7698	57°4·6'	2°23·3'W	W	38,45
Loch of Pile	Shetld	HU4752	60°15·2'	1°8·6'W	W	3
Loch of Queyfirth	Shetld	HU3581	60°30·9'	1°21·3'W	W	1,2,3
Loch of Quiensetter	Shetld	HU3660	60°19·6'	1°20·4'W	W	2,3
Loch of Quinnigeo	Shetld	HU2147	60°12·7'	1°36·8'W	W	3
Loch of Raavigeo	Shetld	HU3167	60°23·4'	1°25·8'W	W	3
Loch of Reiff	Highld	NB9614	58°4·4'	5°27·1'W	W	15
Loch of Reva	Shetld	HU2960	60°19·6'	1°28·0'W	W	3
Loch of Rodageo	Shetld	HU3166	60°22·9'	1°25·8'W	W	3
Loch of Roonies	Shetld	HU4652	60°15·2'	1°9·6'W	W	3
Loch of Rummie	Orkney	HY7545	59°17·7'	2°25·8'W	W	5
Loch of Sabiston	Orkney	HY2922	59°5·0'	3°13·8'W	W	6
Loch of Sacquoy	Orkney	HY3835	59°12·1'	3°4·6'W	W	6
Loch of Sandwick	Shetld	HU3632	60°4·5'	1°20·7'W	W	4
Loch of Scadafleck	Shetld	HU3676	60°28·2'	1°20·2'W	W	2,3
Loch of Scattlands	Shetld	HU4588	60°34·6'	1°10·2'W	W	1,2
Loch of Scockness	Orkney	HY4532	59°10·5'	2°57·2'W	W	5,6
Loch of Scrooie	Shetld	HU3247	60°12·6'	1°24·9'W	W	3
Loch of Seligeo	Shetld	HU5139	60°8·2'	1°4·4'W	W	4
Loch of Semblister	Shetld	HU3349	60°13·7'	1°23·8'W	W	3
Loch of Setter	Shetld	HU5141	60°9·3'	1°4·4'W	W	4
Loch of Setterness	Shetld	HU4870	60°24·9'	1°7·2'W	W	2,3
Loch of Skaill	Orkney	HY2418	59°2·8'	3°19·0'W	W	6
Loch of Skellister	Shetld	HU4656	60°17·4'	1°9·6'W	W	2,3
Loch of Skene	Aberd	NJ7807	57°9·5'	2°21·4'W	W	38
Loch of Skiall	Highld	ND0167	58°35·1'	3°41·7'W	W	11,12
Loch of Snabrough	Shetld	HP5602	60°42·1'	0°57·9'W	W	1
Loch of Snarravoe	Shetld	HP5601	60°41·6'	0°58·0'W	W	1
Loch of Sotersta	Shetld	HU2644	60°11·0'	1°31·4'W	W	4
Loch of Spiggie	Shetld	HU3716	59°55·9'	1°19·8'W	W	4
Loch of Stavaness	Shetld	HU4959	60°19·0'	1°6·3'W	W	2,3
Loch of Stenness	Orkney	HY2812	58°59·6'	3°14·7'W	W	6
Loch of Stourdale	Orkney	ND1799	58°52·5'	3°25·9'W	W	7
Loch of Stourhoull	Shetld	HP5702	60°42·1'	0°56·8'W	W	1
Loch of Strathbeg	Aberd	NK0758	57°37·0'	1°52·5'W	W	30
Loch of Strom	Shetld	HU4048	60°13·1'	1°16·2'W	W	3
Loch of St Tredwell	Orkney	HY4950	59°20·3'	2°53·3'W	W	5
Loch of Sung	Shetld	HU1950	60°14·3'	1°38·9'W	W	3
Loch of Swannay	Orkney	HY3128	59°8·3'	3°11·9'W	W	6
Loch of Swartmill	Orkney	HY4745	59°17·6'	2°55·3'W	W	5
Loch of Tankerness	Orkney	HY5109	58°58·2'	2°50·6'W	W	6,7
Loch of the Andris	Shetld	HU4256	60°17·4'	1°13·9'W	W	2,3
Loch of the Clans	Highld	NH8353	57°33·4'	3°56·9'W	W	27
Loch of the Cowlatt	Moray	NJ1244	57°28·9'	3°27·6'W	W	28
Loch of the Graand	Orkney	HY4727	59°7·9'	2°55·1'W	W	5,6
Loch of the Hadd	Shetld	HU3185	60°33·1'	1°25·6'W	W	1,3
Loch of the Lowes	D & G	NX4670	55°0·3'	4°24·1'W	W	77
Loch of the Lowes	Scot Bord	NT2319	55°27·8'	3°12·6'W	W	79
Loch of the Lowes Strand	D & G	NX4569	54°59·8'	4°25·0'W	W	83
Loch of the Lowes Strand	D & G	NX4670	55°0·3'	4°24·1'W	W	77
Loch of the Stack	Orkney	HY3949	59°19·6'	3°3·8'W	W	5
Loch of Tingwall	Shetld	HU4142	60°9·9'	1°15·2'W	W	4
Loch of Toftingall	Highld	ND1952	58°27·2'	3°22·8'W	W	11,12
Loch of Trebister	Shetld	HU4539	60°8·2'	1°10·9'W	W	4
Loch of Trondavoe	Shetld	HU3771	60°25·5'	1°19·2'W	W	2,3
Loch of Ulsta	Shetld	HU4781	60°30·9'	1°8·1'W	W	1,2,3
Loch of Urafirth	Shetld	HU3079	60°29·9'	1°26·7'W	W	3
Loch of Ustaness	Shetld	HU3943	60°10·4'	1°17·3'W	W	4
Loch of Vaara	Shetld	HU3256	60°17·5'	1°24·8'W	W	3
Loch of Vastray	Orkney	HY3925	59°6·7'	3°3·4'W	W	6
Loch of Vatnagarth	Shetld	HP6002	60°42·1'	0°53·6'W	W	1
Loch of Vatsetter	Shetld	HU3723	59°59·7'	1°19·7'W	W	4
Loch of Vatsetter	Shetld	HU5389	60°35·1'	1°1·5'W	W	1,2
Loch of Vatster	Shetld	HU4248	60°13·1'	1°14·0'W	W	3
Loch of Vigga	Shetld	HP5603	60°42·6'	0°57·9'W	W	1
Loch of Voe	Shetld	HU4162	60°20·7'	1°14·9'W	W	2,3
Loch of Vollister	Shetld	HU4794	60°37·9'	1°8·0'W	W	1,2
Loch of Voxterby	Shetld	HU2653	60°15·9'	1°31·3'W	W	3
Loch of Warehouse	Highld	ND2942	58°21·9'	3°12·3'W	W	11,12
Loch of Wasdale	Orkney	HY3414	59°0·7'	3°8·5'W	W	6
Loch of Watlee	Shetld	HP5905	60°43·7'	0°54·6'W	W	1
Loch of Watsness	Shetld	HU1750	60°14·3'	1°41·1'W	W	3
Loch of Wester	Highld	ND3259	58°31·2'	3°9·6'W	W	12
Loch of Westerwick	Shetld	HU2843	60°10·5'	1°29·2'W	W	4
Loch of Whitebrigs	Shetld	HU2453	60°15·9'	1°33·5'W	W	3
Loch of Wick	Shetld	HU4340	60°8·8'	1°13·0'W	W	4
Loch of Windhouse	Shetld	HU4994	60°37·8'	1°5·8'W	W	1,2
Loch of Winless	Highld	ND2954	58°28·4'	3°12·6'W	W	11,12
Loch of Winyadepla	Shetld	HU6392	60°36·7'	0°50·5'W	W	1,2
Loch of Withamo	Orkney	HY4131	59°10·0'	3°1·4'W	W	5,6
Loch of Yaawater	Shetld	HU3723	59°59·7'	1°19·7'W	W	4
Loch of Yarrows	Highld	ND3043	58°22·5'	3°11·3'W	W	11,12
Loch Oich	Highld	NC7945	58°22·9'	4°3·7'W	W	10
Loch Oich	Highld	NH3100	57°3·9'	4°46·8'W	W	34

Loch Oichean	N Eil	NB3827	58°9·5'	6°26·8'W	W	8
Loch Oigheabhat	N Eil	NB2718	58°4·3'	6°37·3'W	W	13,14
Loch Oil	N Eil	NB3003	57°56·3'	6°33·3'W	W	13,14
Loch Oire	Moray	NJ2860	57°37·7'	3°11·9'W	W	28
Loch Olabhat	N Eil	NF7951	57°26·4'	7°20·6'W	W	22
Loch Olabhat	N Eil	NF8050	57°25·9'	7°19·5'W	W	22
Loch Olabhat	N Eil	NF8154	57°28·1'	7°18·8'W	W	22
Loch Olaidh an Ear	N Eil	NF7631	57°15·6'	7°22·0'W	W	22
Loch Olaidh an Iar	N Eil	NF7432	57°16·0'	7°24·0'W	W	22
Loch Olaidh Meadhanach	N Eil	NF7531	57°15·5'	7°23·0'W	W	22
Loch Olavat	N Eil	NF7475	57°39·1'	7°27·5'W	W	18
Loch Olginey	Highld	ND0857	58°29·8'	3°34·2'W	W	11,12
Locholly	Pth & Kin	NO0841	56°33·4'	3°29·4'W	X	52,53
Loch Orasaigh	N Eil	NB3927	58°9·6'	6°25·8'W	W	8
Loch Ordais	N Eil	NB2848	58°20·4'	6°38·4'W	W	8
Loch Ordie	Pth & Kin	NO0350	56°38·2'	3°34·4'W	W	52,53
Lochordie Lodge	Pth & Kin	NO0349	56°37·6'	3°34·4'W	X	52,53
Loch Ore	Fife	NT1695	56°8·7'	3°20·7'W	W	58
Lochore	Fife	NT1796	56°9·2'	3°19·7'W	T	58
Lochore Castle	Fife	NT1795	56°8·7'	3°19·7'W	A	58
Lochore Ho	Fife	NT1797	56°9·8'	3°19·7'W	X	58
Lochore Meadows Coutry Park	Fife	NT1695	56°8·7'	3°20·7'W	X	58
Lochornie	Fife	NT1094	56°8·1'	3°26·4'W	X	58
Lochornie Burn	Fife	NT0994	56°8·1'	3°27·4'W	W	58
Lochorodale	Arg & Bt	NR6615	55°22·6'	5°41·2'W	X	68
Loch Osgaig	Highld	NC0412	58°3·5'	5°18·9'W	W	15
Loch Oss	Stir	NN3025	56°23·5'	4°44·8'W	W	50
Loch Ossian	Highld	NN3867	56°46·2'	4°38·6'W	W	41
Loch Ossian	Highld	NN4068	56°46·8'	4°36·7'W	W	42
Loch o' th' Lowes	E Ayr	NS6014	55°24·3'	4°12·2'W	W	71
Lochouse Tower	D & G	NT0803	55°19·0'	3°26·6'W	A	78
Loch Paible	N Eil	NF7268	57°35·2'	7°28·9'W	W	18
Loch Pàiteag	Highld	NH4715	57°12·3'	4°31·5'W	W	34
Loch Palascaig	Highld	NG7829	57°18·1'	5°40·7'W	W	33
Loch Papadil	Highld	NM3692	56°56·9'	6°20·0'W	W	39
Lochpark	D & G	NX8171	55°1·4'	3°51·3'W	X	84
Loch Park	Moray	NJ3543	57°28·6'	3°4·6'W	W	28
Loch Patrick	D & G	NX7870	55°0·8'	3°54·1'W	W	84
Loch Pattack	Highld	NN5378	56°52·5'	4°24·3'W	W	42
Loch Peallach	Arg & Bt	NM4853	56°36·3'	6°5·9'W	W	47
Loch Peallaig	Highld	NC1020	58°8·0'	5°13·1'W	W	15
Loch Phàdruig	Aberd	NO1786	56°57·7'	3°21·4'W	W	43
Loch Phail	Highld	NG9082	57°47·0'	5°31·5'W	W	19
Loch Pityoulish	Highld	NH9213	57°12·0'	3°46·8'W	W	36
Loch Poit na h-I	Arg & Bt	NM3122	56°19·1'	6°20·6'W	W	48
Loch Poll	Highld	NC1030	58°13·3'	5°13·6'W	W	15
Loch Poll a' Bhacain	Highld	NC1853	58°25·9'	5°6·6'W	W	9
Loch Pollain Buidhe	Highld	NH1822	57°15·4'	5°0·6'W	W	25
Loch Poll an Achaidh Bhuidhe	Highld	NC2538	58°18·0'	4°58·7'W	W	15
Loch Poll an Droighinn	Highld	NC0528	58°12·1'	5°18·6'W	W	15
Loch Poll a' Phac	Highld	NC4628	58°13·1'	4°36·8'W	W	16
Loch Poll Dhaidh	Highld	NC0729	58°12·7'	5°16·6'W	W	15
Loch Pooltiel	Highld	NG1650	57°27·3'	6°43·7'W	W	23
Loch Portain	N Eil	NF9471	57°37·8'	7°7·1'W	W	18
Lochportain	N Eil	NF9471	57°37·8'	7°7·1'W	T	18
Loch Portree	Highld	NG4842	57°24·2'	6°11·3'W	W	23
Loch Poulary	Highld	NH1201	57°4·0'	5°5·6'W	W	34
Loch Preas an Lochan	Highld	NC8453	58°27·3'	3°58·8'W	W	10
Loch Preas an Uisge	Highld	NH8483	57°49·6'	3°56·7'W	W	21
Loch Preas nan Aighean	Highld	NC1127	58°11·7'	5°12·5'W	W	15
Loch Preas nan Sgiathanach	Highld	NC6709	58°3·3'	4°14·8'W	W	16
Loch Prille	Highld	NH2881	57°47·4'	4°53·1'W	W	20
Loch Procrapoil	N Eil	NB1793	57°50·5'	6°45·7'W	W	14
Loch Quie	D & G	NX3472	55°1·1'	4°35·4'W	W	76
Loch Quien	Arg & Bt	NS0659	55°47·4'	5°5·2'W	W	63
Loch Quoich	Highld	NH0102	57°4·2'	5°16·5'W	W	33
Loch Quoich	Highld	NM9499	57°2·4'	5°23·3'W	W	33,40
Lochquoy	Highld	ND1964	58°33·7'	3°23·1'W	X	11,12
Loch Raa	Highld	NC0112	58°3·4'	5°21·9'W	W	15
Loch Racadal	Arg & Bt	NR7665	55°49·8'	5°34·2'W	W	62
Loch Raineachan	Highld	NH4338	57°24·6'	4°36·4'W	W	26
Lochran	Pth & Kin	NT1397	56°9·7'	3°23·6'W	X	58
Loch Rangag	Highld	ND1741	58°21·2'	3°24·6'W	W	11,12
Loch Rangavat	N Eil	NB0431	58°10·4'	7°1·6'W	W	13
Loch Rannoch	Pth & Kin	NN5957	56°41·3'	4°17·7'W	W	42,51
Loch Ranza	N Ayr	NR9350	55°42·2'	5°17·2'W	W	62,69
Lochranza	N Ayr	NR9350	55°42·2'	5°17·2'W	T	62,69
Loch Raoineabhat	N Eil	NB2811	58°0·6'	6°35·8'W	W	13,14
Loch Raoinebhat	N Eil	NB2346	58°19·2'	6°43·4'W	W	8
Loch Rathacleit	N Eil	NB2542	58°17·1'	6°41·0'W	W	8,13
Loch Ravag	Highld	NG3745	57°25·4'	6°22·4'W	W	23
Loch Reabhat	N Eil	NB1943	58°17·4'	6°47·2'W	W	8
Loch Reasort	N Eil	NB0617	58°2·9'	6°58·5'W	W	13,14
Loch Ree	D & G	NX1069	54°59·0'	4°57·7'W	W	82
Loch Reidh Creagain	Highld	NH1887	57°50·4'	5°3·5'W	W	20
Lochrennie	D & G	NX7186	55°9·3'	4°1·0'W	X	77
Loch Reonasgail	N Eil	NB0327	58°8·2'	7°2·3'W	W	13
Loch Reraig	Highld	NG8236	57°22·0'	5°37·1'W	W	24
Loch Restil	Arg & Bt	NN2207	56°13·6'	4°51·8'W	W	56
Loch Riabhachain	Highld	NH3630	57°20·1'	4°43·0'W	W	26
Loch Riaghain	Arg & Bt	NM0347	56°31·5'	6°49·3'W	W	46
Loch Ribavat	N Eil	NB0531	58°10·4'	7°0·6'W	W	13
Loch Riddon or Loch Ruel	Arg & Bt	NS0076	55°56·4'	5°11·7'W	W	62,63
Lochridge	E Ayr	NS4144	55°40·1'	4°31·2'W	X	70
Lochridge	N Ayr	NS3255	55°45·8'	4°40·2'W	X	63
Lochridgehills	E Ayr	NS4151	55°43·8'	4°31·5'W	X	64
Loch Riecawr	S Ayr	NX4393	55°12·6'	4°27·6'W	W	77
Loch Rifa-gil	Highld	NC7448	58°24·4'	4°8·9'W	W	10
Loch Rig	Scot Bord	NT2907	55°21·4'	3°6·8'W	H	79
Lochrig	Scot Bord	NT7945	55°42·1'	2°19·6'W	X	74
Lochrigghead	D & G	NY0587	55°10·3'	3°29·1'W	X	78
Loch Righ Beag	Arg & Bt	NR5283	55°58·8'	5°58·1'W	W	61
Loch Righeachan	Arg & Bt	NN0608	56°13·8'	5°7·3'W	W	56
Loch Righ Guidh	Highld	NH3820	57°14·8'	4°40·6'W	W	26
Loch Righ Meadhonach	Arg & Bt	NR5384	55°59·4'	5°57·2'W	W	61
Loch Righ Mòr	Arg & Bt	NR5485	56°0·0'	5°56·3'W	W	61

Loch Rimsdale	Highld	NC7335	58°17·4'	4°9·5'W	W	16
Loch Rinn na Geodha	N Eil	NB1743	58°17·3'	6°49·3'W	W	8,13
Loch Risay	N Eil	NB1637	58°14·1'	6°49·9'W	W	13
Loch Risord	N Eil	NB2442	58°17·1'	6°42·1'W	W	8,13
Loch Roag	Highld	NG8261	57°35·4'	5°38·4'W	W	19,24
Loch Roag	N Eil	NB1234	58°12·3'	6°53·7'W	W	13
Loch Roan	D & G	NX7469	55°0·2'	3°57·8'W	W	83,84
Loch Rodel	N Eil	NG0482	57°44·1'	6°57·9'W	W	18
Loch Roe	Highld	NC0624	58°10·0'	5°17·4'W	W	15
Loch Ròg	N Eil	NB1932	58°11·5'	6°46·4'W	W	8,13
Loch Ròg	N Eil	NF7535	57°17·7'	7°23·3'W	W	22
Loch Rogabhat	N Eil	NG0689	57°47·9'	6°56·5'W	W	14,18
Loch Ròg an Ear	N Eil	NB1837	58°14·2'	6°47·8'W	W	8,13
Loch Ròinebhal	N Eil	NB2322	58°6·3'	6°41·7'W	W	13,14
Loch Roinich	N Eil	NF7424	57°11·7'	7°23·4'W	W	22
Loch Roinich	N Eil	NF7533	57°16·6'	7°23·1'W	W	22
Loch Roisneabhat	N Eil	NB3939	58°16·0'	6°26·6'W	W	8
Loch Romain	Arg & Bt	NR8253	55°43·5'	5°27·9'W	W	62
Loch Ronald	D & G	NX2664	54°56·7'	4°42·6'W	W	82
Loch Ronard	Arg & Bt	NM2055	56°36·5'	6°33·3'W	W	46,47
Loch Ronard	Arg & Bt	NM2360	56°39·2'	6°30·7'W	W	46,47
Loch Ropàch	N Eil	NF8214	57°6·7'	7°14·7'W	W	31
Loch Rosail	Highld	NC7140	58°20·0'	4°11·7'W	W	10
Lochrosque Forest	Highld	NH2162	57°37·0'	4°59·3'W	X	20
Lochrosque Lodge	Highld	NH1458	57°34·7'	5°6·2'W	X	25
Loch Roy	Highld	NN4189	56°58·2'	4°36·5'W	W	34,42
Loch Ruabhal	N Eil	NF7839	57°19·9'	7°20·6'W	W	22
Loch Ruadh	N Eil	NB1131	58°10·7'	6°54·5'W	W	13
Loch Ruadh	N Eil	NB1326	58°8·1'	6°52·1'W	W	13
Loch Ruadh	N Eil	NB1624	58°7·1'	6°48·9'W	W	13,14
Loch Ruadh	N Eil	NB3107	57°58·5'	6°32·5'W	W	13,14
Loch Ruadh a Deas	N Eil	NB1520	58°4·9'	6°49·6'W	W	13,14
Loch Ruadh Eitseal Bheag	N Eil	NB2732	58°11·8'	6°38·3'W	W	8,13
Loch Ruadh Gheure Dubh Mhòr	N Eil	NB1927	58°8·8'	6°46·1'W	W	8,13
Loch Ruadh Meadhanach	N Eil	NB1521	58°5·4'	6°49·7'W	W	13,14
Loch Ruagaidh	Highld	NH7399	57°58·0'	4°8·3'W	W	21
Loch Ruairidh	Highld	NH5321	57°15·6'	4°25·8'W	W	26,35
Loch Ruairidh	N Eil	NB1221	58°5·3'	6°52·7'W	W	13,14
Loch Ruairidh	N Eil	NB1711	58°0·2'	6°47·0'W	W	13,14
Loch Ruard	Highld	ND1443	58°22·3'	3°27·7'W	W	11,12
Loch Rubha Aird Choinnich	Highld	NG7060	57°34·6'	5°50·4'W	W	24
Loch Rubha na Brèige	Highld	NC0719	58°7·3'	5°16·2'W	W	15
Loch Ruel or Loch Riddon	Arg & Bt	NS0076	55°56·4'	5°11·7'W	W	62,63
Loch Rughean an Aitinn	Highld	NC1232	58°14·5'	5°11·7'W	W	15
Loch Rugh nan Copag	Highld	NC6435	58°17·2'	4°18·7'W	W	16
Loch Ruigleabhat	N Eil	NB4655	58°24·8'	6°20·5'W	W	8
Loch Ruig Sandavat	N Eil	NB1537	58°14·0'	6°50·9'W	W	13
Loch Ruime	Arg & Bt	NR2370	55°50·9'	6°25·1'W	W	60
Loch Ruiseabhat	N Eil	NB4856	58°25·5'	6°18·5'W	W	8
Loch Ruith a' Phuill	Highld	NH4158	57°35·3'	4°39·1'W	W	26
Loch Rumalach	N Eil	NA9714	58°1·0'	7°7·4'W	W	13
Loch Rumsdale	Highld	NC9641	58°21·0'	3°46·1'W	W	11
Loch Runavet	N Eil	NF7369	57°35·8'	7°28·0'W	W	18
Loch Rusky	Stir	NN6103	56°12·2'	4°14·0'W	W	57
Loch Ruthven	Highld	NH6127	57°19·0'	4°18·0'W	W	26,35
Lochrutton Loch	D & G	NX8973	55°2·6'	3°43·8'W	W	84
Loch Ryan	D & G	NX0565	54°56·7'	5°2·3'W	W	82
Lochryan House	D & G	NX0668	54°58·4'	5°1·4'W	X	82
Lochs	Moray	NJ3162	57°38·8'	3°8·9'W	X	28
Lochs	Shetld	HU4463	60°21·2'	1°11·7'W	X	2,3
Loch Sail an Ruathair	Highld	NC3314	58°5·3'	4°49·5'W	W	15
Loch Sail Chalmadale	N Ayr	NR9038	55°35·7'	5°19·5'W	W	68,69
Loch Sàile	N Eil	NG1192	57°49·7'	6°51·6'W	W	14
Loch Saine	Highld	NH6989	57°52·5'	4°12·1'W	W	21
Loch Sàinn	Highld	NC9352	58°26·9'	3°49·5'W	W	11
Loch Saintear	Orkney	HY4347	59°18·6'	2°59·6'W	W	5
Loch Saird	Highld	NC9451	58°26·3'	3°48·5'W	W	11
Loch Salach a' Ghiubhais	Highld	NH1721	57°14·9'	5°1·5'W	W	25
Loch Salachaidh	Highld	NC7503	58°0·2'	4°6·4'W	W	16
Loch Sand	Highld	ND0940	58°20·6'	3°32·8'W	W	11,12
Loch Sandary	N Eil	NF7368	57°35·3'	7°27·9'W	W	18
Loch Sandary	N Eil	NF8074	57°38·8'	7°21·4'W	W	18
Loch Sandavat	N Eil	NB0026	58°7·5'	7°5·3'W	W	13
Loch Sandavat	N Eil	NB0130	58°9·7'	7°4·6'W	W	13
Loch Sandavat	N Eil	NB1129	58°9·6'	6°54·3'W	W	13
Loch Sanndabhat	N Eil	NB5046	58°20·1'	6°15·8'W	W	8
Loch Saorach	Highld	ND0160	58°31·3'	3°41·5'W	W	11,12
Loch Sarclet	Highld	ND3442	58°22·0'	3°7·2'W	W	12
Loch Saugh	Aberd	NO6778	56°53·8'	2°32·1'W	W	45
Loch Scaapar	N Eil	NF9569	57°36·7'	7°6·0'W	W	18
Loch Scadavay	N Eil	NF8568	57°35·8'	7°15·9'W	W	18
Loch Scadavay	N Eil	NF8766	57°34·8'	7°13·8'W	W	18
Loch Scalabsdale	Highld	NC9624	58°11·8'	3°45·7'W	W	17
Loch Scalan	N Eil	NF9670	57°37·3'	7°5·1'W	W	18
Loch Scalloch	S Ayr	NX2889	55°10·2'	4°41·6'W	W	76
Loch Scalpaidh	Highld	NG7828	57°17·6'	5°40·6'W	W	33
Loch Scamadal	Highld	NG5054	57°30·7'	6°10·0'W	W	23,24
Loch Scammadale	Arg & Bt	NM8820	56°19·8'	5°25·3'W	W	49
Loch Scanasdail	N Eil	NB0923	58°6·3'	6°55·9'W	W	13,14
Loch Scàparaid	N Eil	NB2627	58°9·1'	6°39·0'W	W	8,13
Loch Scarabhat Bheag	N Eil	NB3541	58°16·9'	6°30·8'W	W	8
Loch Scarabhat Mhòr	N Eil	NB3540	58°16·4'	6°30·7'W	W	8
Loch Scarasdail	N Eil	NB5049	58°21·8'	6°16·0'W	W	8
Loch Scarie	N Eil	NF7170	57°36·3'	7°30·1'W	W	18
Loch Scarmclate	Highld	ND1859	58°31·0'	3°24·0'W	W	11,12
Loch Scaslavat	N Eil	NB0231	58°10·3'	7°3·6'W	W	13
Loch Scavaig	Highld	NG5015	57°9·7'	6°7·6'W	W	32
Loch Scolpaig	N Eil	NF7375	57°39·0'	7°28·5'W	W	18
Loch Scoly	Pth & Kin	NN9147	56°36·4'	3°46·1'W	W	52
Loch Scourst	N Eil	NB0909	57°58·8'	6°54·9'W	W	13,14
Loch Scresort	Highld	NM4199	57°0·8'	6°15·5'W	W	39
Loch Scriachabhat	N Eil	NB4762	58°28·6'	6°19·9'W	W	8
Loch Scridain	Arg & Bt	NM4625	56°21·2'	6°6·2'W	W	48
Loch Scye	Highld	ND0055	58°28·6'	3°42·4'W	W	11,12
Loch Seaforth or Loch Shiphoirt	N Eil	NB2111	58°0·3'	6°42·9'W	W	13,14
Loch Sealbhanach	Highld	NH2331	57°20·4'	4°56·0'W	W	25
Loch Sealg	N Eil	NB3410	58°0·2'	6°29·7'W	W	13,14

Loch Searrach	Highld	NG9386	57°49·2′	5°28·7′W	W	19
Loch Seil	Arg & Bt	NM8020	56°19·5′	5°33·1′W	W	49
Loch Seogh	Highld	NH3219	57°14·1′	4°46·6′W	W	34
Loch Sgadahagh	N Eil	NG1691	57°49·4′	6°46·5′W	W	14
Loch Sgailler	N Eil	NB0835	58°12·7′	6°57·8′W	W	13
Loch Sgairbheiseal	N Eil	NB2044	58°18·0′	6°46·3′W	W	8
Loch Sgàire	N Eil	NB1928	58°9·4′	6°46·1′W	W	8,13
Loch Sgamhain	Highld	NH1052	57°31·4′	5°9·9′W	W	25
Loch Sgaorishal	Highld	NG3402	57°2·2′	6°22·6′W	W	32,39
Loch Sgeir a' Chadha	Highld	NC2351	58°25·0′	5°1·3′W	W	9
Loch Sgeireach	Highld	NC1201	57°57·8′	5°10·2′W	W	15
Loch Sgeireach	Highld	NC4611	58°3·9′	4°36·2′W	W	16
Loch Sgeireach	Highld	NG8180	57°45·6′	5°40·4′W	W	19
Loch Sgeireach	Highld	NH2373	57°43·0′	4°57·8′W	W	20
Loch Sgeireach	N Eil	NB2433	58°12·2′	6°41·4′W	W	8,13
Loch Sgeireach	N Eil	NB3148	58°20·5′	6°35·3′W	W	8
Loch Sgeireach	N Eil	NB4037	58°15·0′	6°25·4′W	W	8
Loch Sgeireach	N Eil	NB4125	58°8·5′	6°23·6′W	W	14
Loch Sgeireach	N Eil	NB4251	58°22·6′	6°24·3′W	W	8
Loch Sgeireach a' Ghlinn Mhòir	N Eil	NB5150	58°22·3′	6°15·0′W	W	8
Loch Sgeireach Mòr	N Eil	NB4945	58°19·6′	6°16·8′W	W	8
Loch Sgeireach na Creige Brist	N Eil	NB5453	58°24·0′	6°12·2′W	W	8
Loch Sgiathanach	Highld	NC8762	58°32·2′	3°56·0′W	W	10
Loch Sgiobacleit	N Eil	NB3116	58°3·4′	6°33·1′W	W	13,14
Loch Sgiopirt	N Eil	NF8338	57°19·6′	7°15·6′W	W	22
Loch Sgioport	N Eil	NF8238	57°19·6′	7°16·6′W	T	22
Loch Sgitheig	Arg & Bt	NR5779	55°56·8′	5°53·1′W	W	61
Loch Sgolbaidh	Highld	NH3953	57°32·6′	4°40·9′W	W	26
Loch Sgorr Ni Dhonnachaidh	N Eil	NB3817	58°4·1′	6°26·1′W	W	14
Loch Sgriachach	N Eil	NB2729	58°10·2′	6°38·1′W	W	8,13
Loch Sguabain	Arg & Bt	NM6330	56°24·4′	5°50·0′W	W	49
Loch Sguadaig	Highld	NN3687	56°57·0′	4°41·3′W	W	34,41
Loch Sguod	Highld	NG8187	57°49·4′	5°40·8′W	W	19
Loch Sgurr na Caorach	Highld	NG5803	57°3·5′	5°59·0′W	W	32,39
Loch Sgurr na Feartaig	Highld	NH0545	57°27·5′	5°14·6′W	W	25
Loch Sgurr na Gaoithe	Highld	NM6986	56°54·7′	5°47·2′W	W	40
Loch Sgurr na h-Eige	Highld	NH0527	57°17·8′	5°13·7′W	W	25,33
Loch Shaghachain	N Eil	NB3512	58°1·4′	6°28·8′W	W	14
Loch Shamhnan Insir	Highld	NG3702	57°2·3′	6°19·7′W	W	32,39
Loch Shandra	Angus	NO2162	56°44·8′	3°17·1′W	W	44
Loch Shanndabhat	N Eil	NB2437	58°14·4′	6°41·7′W	W	8,13
Loch Shanndabhat	N Eil	NB2440	58°16·0′	6°41·9′W	W	8,13
Loch Shanndabhat	N Eil	NB3413	58°1·9′	6°29·9′W	W	13,14
Loch Shanndabhat	N Eil	NB3627	58°9·4′	6°28·8′W	W	8
Loch Shark	Highld	NC1736	58°16·7′	5°6·8′W	W	15
Loch Sheila	Highld	NC4507	58°1·8′	4°37·0′W	W	16
Loch Sheilah	Highld	NH6778	57°46·6′	4°13·7′W	W	21
Loch Sheileabhaig	N Eil	NF8340	57°20·7′	7°15·7′W	W	22
Loch Sheileasdail	N Eil	NF8230	57°15·3′	7°16·0′W	W	22
Loch Shiabhat	N Eil	NB4759	58°27·0′	6°19·7′W	W	8
Loch Shiaboist	N Eil	NB2548	58°20·3′	6°41·5′W	W	8
Loch Shiadair	N Eil	NB1838	58°14·7′	6°47·9′W	W	8,13
Loch Shiel	Highld	NG9418	57°12·7′	5°24·2′W	W	33
Loch Shiel	Highld	NM8474	56°48·7′	5°31·9′W	W	40
Loch Shieldaig	Highld	NG8055	57°32·2′	5°40·1′W	W	24
Loch Shieldaig	Highld	NG8072	57°41·3′	5°41·0′W	W	19
Loch Shiffin	Arg & Bt	NR6286	56°0·7′	5°48·7′W	W	61
Loch Shin	Highld	NC5015	58°6·2′	4°32·2′W	W	16
Loch Shinnadale	N Eil	NB0201	57°54·2′	7°1·4′W	W	18
Loch Shira	Arg & Bt	NN1009	56°14·4′	5°3·5′W	W	56
Loch Shiùrabhagh	N Eil	NF8250	57°26·0′	7°17·5′W	W	22
Loch Shnathaid	N Eil	NF8242	57°21·7′	7°16·9′W	W	22
Loch Shòbhail	N Eil	NB3425	58°8·3′	6°30·7′W	W	13,14
Loch Shornaraigh	N Eil	NF8657	57°29·9′	7°14·1′W	W	22
Loch Shròmois	N Eil	NB2515	58°2·6′	6°39·1′W	W	13,14
Loch Shuardail	N Eil	NB5031	58°12·1′	6°14·8′W	W	8
Loch Shurabhat	N Eil	NF7824	57°11·9′	7°19·5′W	W	22
Loch Shurrery	Highld	ND0455	58°28·6′	3°38·3′W	W	11,12
Loch Siadar	N Eil	NB4551	58°22·7′	6°21·2′W	W	8
Loch Sian	Highld	NC4463	58°31·9′	4°40·3′W	W	9
Loch Sibhinn	Arg & Bt	NR3265	55°48·5′	6°16·2′W	W	60,61
Lochside	Aberd	NJ7707	57°9·5′	2°22·4′W	X	38
Lochside	Aberd	NK0945	57°30·0′	1°50·5′W	X	30
Lochside	Aberd	NO7364	56°46·3′	2°26·1′W	T	45
Lochside	Aberd	NO7798	57°4·6′	2°22·3′W	X	38,45
Lochside	Angus	NO4350	56°38·6′	2°55·3′W	X	54
Lochside	Angus	NO5333	56°29·5′	2°45·4′W	X	54
Lochside	Angus	NO5969	56°48·9′	2°39·8′W	X	44
Lochside	C of Aber	NJ9401	57°6·3′	2°5·5′W	X	38
Lochside	D & G	NS7910	55°22·4′	3°54·1′W	X	71,78
Lochside	D & G	NX6678	55°5·0′	4°5·5′W	X	77,84
Lochside	D & G	NX8370	55°0·9′	3°49·4′W	X	84
Lochside	D & G	NX9073	55°2·6′	3°42·9′W	X	84
Lochside	D & G	NX9577	55°4·8′	3°38·3′W	T	84
Lochside	D & G	NY1281	55°7·2′	3°22·4′W	X	78
Lochside	E Ayr	NS4143	55°39·5′	4°31·2′W	X	70
Lochside	Highld	NC4758	58°29·3′	4°37·0′W	X	9
Lochside	Highld	NC8735	58°17·6′	3°55·2′W	T	17
Lochside	Highld	ND0858	58°30·3′	3°34·3′W	X	11,12
Lochside	Highld	ND2165	58°34·2′	3°21·0′W	X	11,12
Lochside	Highld	ND2763	58°33·2′	3°14·8′W	X	11,12
Lochside	Highld	ND3443	58°22·5′	3°7·2′W	X	12
Lochside	Highld	NH8152	57°32·8′	3°58·8′W	T	27
Lochside	Moray	NJ2065	57°40·3′	3°20·0′W	X	28
Lochside	Orkney	HY3113	59°0·2′	3°11·6′W	X	6
Lochside	Orkney	HY4745	59°17·6′	2°55·3′W	X	5
Lochside	Pth & Kin	NO1841	56°33·5′	3°19·6′W	X	53
Lochside	S Ayr	NS3422	55°28·1′	4°37·1′W	T	70
Lochside	Scot Bord	NT7928	55°33·0′	2°19·5′W	X	74
Lochside Cottage	D & G	NX3052	54°50·3′	4°38·4′W	X	82
Lochside Ho	Renf	NS3658	55°47·5′	4°36·5′W	X	63
Lochside (Hotel)	E Ayr	NS6014	55°24·3′	4°12·2′W	X	71
Lochside Point	D & G	NX6473	55°2·2′	4°7·3′W	X	77
Loch Sigean	N Eil	NF9466	57°35·1′	7°6·8′W	W	18
Loch Siginish	N Eil	NF9271	57°37·7′	7°9·1′W	W	18
Loch Sike	Scot Bord	NT4523	55°30·1′	2°51·8′W	W	73
Loch Sionascaig	Highld	NC1113	58°4·2′	5°11·8′W	W	15
Loch Sionnaich	Arg & Bt	NN0211	56°15·3′	5°11·3′W	W	50,55
Loch Skabhat	N Eil	NB3627	58°9·4′	6°28·8′W	W	8
Loch Skae	D & G	NX7183	55°7·7′	4°1·0′W	W	77
Loch Skae Burn	D & G	NX7084	55°8·3′	4°1·9′W	W	77
Loch Skealtar	N Eil	NF8968	57°36·0′	7°11·9′W	W	18
Loch Skeen	D & G	NT1716	55°26·1′	3°18·3′W	W	79
Loch Skelloch	S Ayr	NX4096	55°14·2′	4°30·5′W	W	77
Loch Skerray	Highld	NC6660	58°30·7′	4°17·5′W	W	10
Loch Skerrols	Arg & Bt	NR3463	55°47·5′	6°14·2′W	W	60,61
Loch Skerrow	D & G	NX6068	54°59·5′	4°10·9′W	W	83
Loch Skeun	N Eil	NB1427	58°8·6′	6°51·2′W	W	13
Loch Skiach	Pth & Kin	NN9547	56°36·4′	3°42·2′W	W	52,53
Loch Skilivat	N Eil	NF7274	57°38·5′	7°29·4′W	W	18
Loch Slac a' Bhuilg Mór	Highld	NC1001	57°57·7′	5°12·2′W	W	15
Loch Slaim	Highld	NC6253	58°26·9′	4°21·4′W	W	10
Loch Slapin	Highld	NG5717	57°11·0′	6°0·8′W	W	32
Loch Sleadale	Highld	NG3429	57°16·7′	6°24·4′W	W	32
Loch Slèibhe	Arg & Bt	NR7977	55°56·4′	5°31·9′W	W	62
Loch Slèitir	N Eil	NB4049	58°21·4′	6°26·2′W	W	8
Loch Sletill	Highld	NC9547	58°24·2′	3°47·3′W	W	11
Loch Sligachan	Highld	NG5132	57°18·9′	6°7·7′W	W	24,32
Lochslin	Highld	NH8380	57°47·9′	3°57·6′W	T	21
Loch Slochy	S Ayr	NX4292	55°12·1′	4°28·5′W	W	77
Loch Sloy	Arg & Bt	NN2812	56°16·4′	4°46·2′W	W	50,56
Loch Smaddy	D & G	NX7369	55°0·2′	3°58·7′W	W	83,84
Loch Smearal	Highld	NG4465	57°36·4′	6°16·7′W	X	23
Loch Smerclate	N Eil	NF7415	57°6·9′	7°22·7′W	W	31
Loch Smigeadail	Arg & Bt	NR3875	55°54·1′	6°11·1′W	W	60,61
Loch Sminig	N Eil	NB3652	58°22·9′	6°30·5′W	W	8
Loch Smuaisebhal	N Eil	NB2030	58°10·5′	6°45·3′W	W	8,13
Loch Sneabhal	N Eil	NB0518	58°3·4′	6°59·6′W	W	13,14
Loch Sneabhal Beag	N Eil	NB0517	58°2·9′	6°59·5′W	W	13,14
Loch Sneosdal	Highld	NG4169	57°38·5′	6°19·9′W	W	23
Loch Snigiscleit	N Eil	NF8025	57°12·5′	7°17·6′W	W	22
Loch Sniograbhat	N Eil	NF6360	57°30·5′	7°37·2′W	W	22
Loch Snizort	Highld	NG3261	57°33·8′	6°28·4′W	W	23
Loch Snizort Beag	Highld	NG3954	57°30·3′	6°21·0′W	W	23
Lochs o'da Fleck	Shetld	HT9440	60°8·9′	2°6·0′W	W	4
Lochs of Airth	Falk	NS8985	56°3·0′	3°46·5′W	X	65
Lochs of Allt na Craoibhe-caorainn	Moray	NJ2924	57°18·3′	3°10·3′W	W	37
Lochs of Beosetter	Shetld	HU4843	60°10·4′	1°7·6′W	W	4
Lochs of Bogmussach	Moray	NJ1347	57°30·6′	3°26·7′W	W	28
Lochs of Burrafirth	Shetld	HU3658	60°18·5′	1°20·4′W	W	2,3
Lochs of Geniefea	Orkney	ND2495	58°50·4′	3°18·5′W	W	7
Lochs of Heuken	Shetld	HP6306	60°44·2′	0°50·2′W	W	1
Lochs of High Derry	D & G	NX2674	55°2·1′	4°42·9′W	W	76
Lochs of Hostigates	Shetld	HU3159	60°19·1′	1°25·8′W	W	3
Lochs of Little Benshalag	Moray	NJ1043	57°28·4′	3°29·6′W	W	28
Lochs of Littlure	Shetld	HU2048	60°13·2′	1°37·8′W	W	3
Lochs of Lumbister	Shetld	HU4897	60°39·5′	1°6·8′W	W	1
Lochs of Sulma-ness	Shetld	HU2655	60°17·0′	1°31·3′W	W	3
Lochs of the Waters	Shetld	HU4858	60°18·5′	1°7·4′W	W	2,3
Lochs of Withigill	Orkney	ND2497	58°51·5′	3°18·6′W	W	6,7
Loch Sonachan	Arg & Bt	NM9424	56°22·1′	5°19·7′W	W	49
Loch Spallander Reservoir	S Ayr	NS3908	55°20·6′	4°31·9′W	W	70,77
Loch Spealltrabhat	N Eil	NB3145	58°18·9′	6°35·1′W	W	8
Loch Spealtrabhat	N Eil	NB3247	58°20·0′	6°34·2′W	W	8
Loch Speireag	N Eil	NB1929	58°9·9′	6°46·2′W	W	8,13
Loch Speireag	N Eil	NB3631	58°11·6′	6°29·1′W	W	8
Loch Spelve	Arg & Bt	NM6927	56°23·0′	5°44·1′W	W	49
Loch Spey	Highld	NN4293	57°0·3′	4°35·6′W	W	34
Loch Spògach	Highld	NG8692	57°52·2′	5°36·0′W	W	19
Loch Spotail	N Eil	NF8336	57°18·5′	7°15·4′W	W	22
Lochspouts	S Ayr	NS2805	55°18·8′	4°42·2′W	X	70,76
Loch Spynie	Moray	NJ2366	57°40·9′	3°17·0′W	W	28
Loch Srath nan Aisinnin	Highld	NC3232	58°14·9′	4°51·3′W	W	15
Loch Srath Steachran	N Eil	NG1294	57°50·8′	6°50·8′W	W	14
Loch Srùban Beaga	Highld	NH3285	57°49·6′	4°49·3′W	W	20
Loch Srùban Móra	Highld	NH3284	57°49·1′	4°49·2′W	W	20
Loch Stack	Highld	NC2942	58°20·3′	4°54·8′W	W	9
Lochstack Lodge	Highld	NC2643	58°20·7′	4°57·9′W	X	9
Loch Stacsavat	N Eil	NB0631	58°10·5′	6°59·6′W	W	13
Loch Stadhlaigearraidh	N Eil	NF7638	57°19·3′	7°22·5′W	W	22
Loch Staing	Highld	NC5740	58°19·8′	4°26·0′W	W	10
Loch Stànail	Arg & Bt	NL9745	56°30·2′	6°55·0′W	W	46
Loch Staoineig	Arg & Bt	NM2622	56°18·9′	6°25·4′W	W	48
Loch Staoisha	Arg & Bt	NR4071	55°52·0′	6°8·9′W	W	60,61
Loch Staonsaid	Highld	NC3946	58°22·6′	4°44·7′W	W	9
Loch Staosnaig	Arg & Bt	NR3993	56°3·8′	6°11·1′W	W	61
Loch Starabraigh	N Eil	NB0000	57°53·6′	7°3·3′W	W	18
Loch St Clair or Loch Tangusdale	N Eil	NL6499	56°57·9′	7°31·3′W	W	31
Loch Steallaig	Arg & Bt	NM9548	56°35·0′	5°19·8′W	W	49
Loch Steaphain	N Eil	NF7570	57°36·4′	7°26·1′W	W	18
Loch Steinavat	N Eil	NF8774	57°39·1′	7°14·4′W	W	18
Loch Steisevat	N Eil	NG0187	57°46·6′	7°1·3′W	W	18
Loch Steishal	N Eil	NB0435	58°12·5′	7°1·9′W	W	13
Loch Stemster	Highld	ND1842	58°21·8′	3°23·6′W	W	11,12
Loch Stephan	Highld	NC6955	58°28·1′	4°14·3′W	W	10
Loch Stiapabhat	N Eil	NB5264	58°29·9′	6°14·9′W	W	8
Loch Stithcleit	N Eil	NB1200	57°54·1′	6°51·2′W	W	14
Loch Stocinis	N Eil	NG1291	57°49·2′	6°50·6′W	W	14
Loch Storab	Highld	NG5638	57°22·3′	6°3·0′W	W	24,32
Loch Stornoway	Arg & Bt	NR7360	55°47·1′	5°36·8′W	W	62
Loch Strand	D & G	NX2161	54°55·0′	4°47·1′W	W	82
Loch Strand	D & G	NX2468	54°58·8′	4°44·6′W	W	82
Loch Stranndabhat	N Eil	NB2519	58°4·7′	6°39·4′W	W	13,14
Loch Strath Duchally	Highld	NC4226	58°11·9′	4°40·8′W	W	16
Loch Strathy	Highld	NC7747	58°23·9′	4°5·8′W	W	10
Lochstrathy	Highld	NC7948	58°24·5′	4°3·8′W	X	10
Loch Striamabhat	N Eil	NB4455	58°24·8′	6°22·5′W	W	8
Loch Striven	Arg & Bt	NS0582	55°59·7′	5°7·2′W	W	56
Loch Striven	Arg & Bt	NS0872	55°54·4′	5°3·9′W	W	63
Loch Stulabhal	N Eil	NF7923	57°11·4′	7°18·4′W	W	22
Loch Stuladail	N Eil	NB1211	58°0·0′	6°52·0′W	W	13,14
Loch Stulaval	N Eil	NF8022	57°10·9′	7°17·3′W	W	31
Loch Suainagadail	N Eil	NB3241	58°16·8′	6°33·8′W	W	8,13
Loch Suainaval	N Eil	NB0628	58°8·9′	6°59·4′W	W	13
Loch Suardal	Highld	NG2351	57°28·1′	6°36·7′W	W	23
Loch Sunart	Highld	NM5960	56°40·4′	5°55·6′W	W	47
Loch Sunart	Highld	NM6359	56°40·0′	5°51·6′W	W	49
Loch Sunart	Highld	NM7361	56°41·4′	5°42·0′W	W	40
Loch Sunart	Highld	NM7759	56°40·4′	5°38·0′W	W	49
Loch Sùrstabhat	N Eil	NB1425	58°7·6′	6°51·0′W	W	13,14
Loch Swad	D & G	NX3571	55°0·6′	4°34·4′W	W	77
Loch Sween	Arg & Bt	NR7383	55°59·4′	5°37·9′W	W	55
Loch Syre	Highld	NC6644	58°22·1′	4°17·0′W	W	10
Loch Ta	N Eil	NB3726	58°8·9′	6°27·7′W	W	8
Loch Talaheel	Highld	NC9548	58°24·7′	3°47·4′W	W	11
Loch Tallant	Arg & Bt	NR3357	55°44·2′	6°14·8′W	W	60
Loch Tallant	Arg & Bt	NR4450	55°40·8′	6°3·9′W	W	60
Loch Tamanavay	N Eil	NB0220	58°4·4′	7°2·8′W	W	13
Loch Tana	Arg & Bt	NR7947	55°40·2′	5°30·4′W	W	62,69
Loch Tana	N Eil	NB0921	58°5·2′	6°55·8′W	W	13,14
Loch Tana	N Eil	NB1538	58°14·6′	6°50·9′W	W	13
Loch Tana	N Eil	NB1630	58°10·3′	6°49·3′W	W	13
Loch Tana	N Eil	NB2626	58°8·5′	6°38·9′W	W	8,13
Loch Tana	N Eil	NB2728	58°9·7′	6°38·0′W	W	8,13
Loch Tana	N Eil	NB2934	58°13·0′	6°36·4′W	W	8,13
Loch Tana	N Eil	NB3329	58°10·4′	6°32·0′W	W	8,13
Loch Tana	N Eil	NB4954	58°24·4′	6°17·3′W	W	8
Loch Tanabhat	N Eil	NB5246	58°20·2′	6°13·8′W	W	8
Loch Tana na Gile Ruaidhe	N Eil	NB2325	58°7·9′	6°41·9′W	W	13,14
Loch Tana nan Leac	N Eil	NB5151	58°22·9′	6°15·1′W	W	8
Loch Tangusdale or Loch St Clair	N Eil	NL6499	56°57·9′	7°31·3′W	W	31
Loch Tanna	N Ayr	NR9143	55°38·4′	5°18·8′W	W	62,69
Loch Tarbert	Arg & Bt	NR5581	55°57·8′	5°55·1′W	W	61
Loch Tarbhaidh	Highld	NC2955	58°27·3′	4°55·4′W	W	9
Loch Tarbhaidh	Highld	NC6335	58°17·2′	4°19·7′W	W	16
Loch Tarff	Highld	NH4209	57°8·9′	4°36·2′W	W	34
Loch Tarruinn an Eithir	N Eil	NF8764	57°33·7′	7°13·6′W	W	18
Loch Tarsan	Arg & Bt	NS0784	56°0·9′	5°5·3′W	W	56
Loch Tarstabhat	N Eil	NB5045	58°19·6′	6°15·7′W	W	8
Loch Tarsuinn	Highld	NH3411	57°9·9′	4°44·2′W	W	34
Loch Tarsuinn	N Eil	NG2296	57°52·3′	6°40·8′W	W	14
Loch Tarvie	Highld	NH7596	57°56·4′	4°6·2′W	W	21
Loch Tay	Pth & Kin	NN6838	56°31·2′	4°8·3′W	W	51
Loch Teacuis	Highld	NM6356	56°38·4′	5°51·5′W	W	49
Loch Tealasvay	N Eil	NB0218	58°3·3′	7°2·7′W	W	13
Loch Teanga	N Eil	NF8138	57°19·5′	7°17·6′W	W	22
Loch Teàrnait	Highld	NM7446	56°33·4′	5°40·2′W	W	49
Loch Tennet	Angus	NO5385	56°57·5′	2°45·9′W	W	44
Lochter	Aberd	NJ7827	57°20·2′	2°21·5′W	X	38
Loch Tergavat	N Eil	NF9273	57°38·8′	7°9·3′W	W	18
Loch Thamarsiadar	N Eil	NB3925	58°8·5′	6°25·6′W	W	14
Loch Thamascleit	N Eil	NF8038	57°19·5′	7°18·6′W	W	22
Loch Theirmeadail	N Eil	NF8252	57°27·1′	7°17·7′W	W	22
Loch Thobta Bridein	N Eil	NB3327	58°9·3′	6°31·9′W	W	8,13
Loch Tholabhat	N Eil	NB3524	58°7·8′	6°29·6′W	W	14
Loch Thollaidh	Highld	NG8930	57°19·0′	5°29·8′W	W	24
Loch Tholldhoire	Highld	NG8977	57°44·3′	5°32·2′W	W	19
Loch Thom	Inverc	NS2572	55°54·8′	4°47·6′W	W	63
Loch Thonagro	N Eil	NB1840	58°15·8′	6°48·0′W	W	8,13
Loch Thorasdaidh	N Eil	NB3820	58°5·8′	6°26·3′W	W	14
Loch Thormaid	Highld	ND0060	58°31·3′	3°42·5′W	W	11,12
Loch Thormaid	Highld	NH2192	57°53·2′	5°0·7′W	W	20
Loch Thorsagearraidh	N Eil	NG0484	57°45·1′	6°58·1′W	W	18
Loch Thuaimistear	N Eil	NB2645	58°18·8′	6°40·2′W	W	8
Loch Thuill Easaich	Highld	NH0223	57°15·6′	5°16·5′W	W	25,33
Loch Thùlagabhal	N Eil	NB3142	58°17·3′	6°34·9′W	W	8,13
Loch Thùrnaig	Highld	NC3900	57°57·9′	4°42·8′W	W	16
Loch Thùrnaig	Highld	NG8683	57°47·4′	5°35·6′W	W	19
Loch Tigh na Creige	Highld	NC6109	58°3·2′	4°20·8′W	W	16
Loch Tigh-sealga	Arg & Bt	NR5989	56°2·3′	5°51·7′W	W	61
Loch Tilt	Pth & Kin	NN9982	56°55·4′	3°39·1′W	W	43
Loch Tima	Scot Bord	NT2507	55°21·3′	3°10·5′W	W	79
Loch Tinker	Stir	NN4406	56°13·5′	4°30·5′W	W	57
Loch Tiorsdam	N Eil	NB2116	58°3·0′	6°43·3′W	W	13,14
Loch Tobhtaichean Amhlaidh	N Eil	NB3517	58°4·0′	6°29·1′W	W	14
Loch Togul	N Eil	NA9900	57°53·5′	7°4·3′W	W	18
Loch Tollaidh	Highld	NG8478	57°44·7′	5°37·3′W	W	19
Loch Toll a' Mhadaidh	Highld	NG9881	57°46·7′	5°23·4′W	W	19
Loch Toll a' Mhuic	Highld	NH2342	57°26·3′	4°56·5′W	W	25
Loch Toll an Lochain	Highld	NH0280	57°46·2′	5°19·3′W	W	19
Loch Toll an Lochain	Highld	NH0783	57°48·0′	5°14·4′W	W	19
Loch Toll an Lochain	Highld	NH1472	57°42·2′	5°6·8′W	W	20
Loch Toll Lochain	Highld	NH2348	57°29·5′	4°56·7′W	W	25
Loch Toll nam Biast	Highld	NG8661	57°35·6′	5°34·4′W	W	19,24
Loch Toma Dubha	N Eil	NB2534	58°12·8′	6°40·5′W	W	8,13
Loch Tom an Fheidh	N Eil	NB4128	58°10·2′	6°23·8′W	W	8
Loch Tom an Riseal	N Eil	NB4039	58°16·0′	6°25·5′W	W	8
Loch Tom Liabhrat	N Eil	NB2341	58°16·5′	6°43·0′W	W	8,13
Loch Tom nan Aighean	N Eil	NB2928	58°9·7′	6°36·0′W	W	8,13
Lochton	Aberd	NO7592	57°1·4′	2°24·3′W	X	38,45
Lochton	Fife	NO5809	56°16·6′	2°40·3′W	X	59
Lochton	Pth & Kin	NO2533	56°29·2′	3°12·6′W	X	53
Lochton	S Ayr	NX2580	55°5·3′	4°44·1′W	X	76
Lochton	Scot Bord	NT7739	55°38·9′	2°21·5′W	X	74
Lochton Hill	S Ayr	NX1387	55°8·8′	4°55·6′W	X	76
Lochton of Leys	Aberd	NO7097	57°4·0′	2°29·2′W	T	38,45
Loch Torabhat	N Eil	NB4246	58°19·9′	6°24·0′W	W	8
Loch Torascleit	N Eil	NB1701	57°54·8′	6°46·2′W	W	14
Loch Tormasad Beag	N Eil	NF8265	57°34·1′	7°18·7′W	W	18
Loch Toronais	N Eil	NF7330	57°14·9′	7°24·9′W	W	22
Loch Torr a' Bheithe	Highld	NM6484	56°53·5′	5°52·0′W	W	40
Loch Torr an Lochain	Highld	NC1532	58°14·5′	5°8·6′W	W	15
Loch Tòrr an Lochain	Highld	NC1625	58°10·8′	5°7·3′W	W	15
Loch Torridon	Highld	NG7660	57°34·7′	5°44·3′W	W	19,24
Loch Torridon Hotel	Highld	NG8854	57°31·9′	5°32·0′W	X	24
Loch Torr na Ceàrdaich	Highld	NC9751	58°26·4′	3°45·4′W	W	11
Loch Torr na h-Eigin	Highld	NC1230	58°13·4′	5°11·6′W	W	15
Loch Torr nan Uidhean	Highld	NC1231	58°13·9′	5°11·6′W	W	15
Loch Toscaig	Highld	NG7037	57°22·2′	5°49·1′W	W	24
Lochtower	Scot Bord	NT8028	55°33·0′	2°18·6′W	X	74
Loch Tràighidh	N Eil	NB1222	58°5·9′	6°52·8′W	W	13,14
Loch Traighte	N Eil	NB2925	58°8·1′	6°35·8′W	W	13,14

Loch Tralaig	Arg & Bt	NM8816	56°17·6'	5°25·1'W	W	55
Loch Tràth	Arg & Bt	NM4344	56°31·3'	6°10·3'W	W	47,48
Loch Trealabhal	N Eil	NB2723	58°7·0'	6°37·7'W	W	13,14
Loch Treaslane	Highld	NG3952	57°29·2'	6°20·9'W	W	23
Loch Treig	Highld	NN3372	56°48·8'	4°43·7'W	W	41
Loch Treunaidh	Arg & Bt	NR2563	55°47·2'	6°22·8'W	W	60
Loch Trevie	Moray	NJ0944	57°28·9'	3°30·6'W	W	27
Loch Trialavat	N Eil	NB0935	58°12·7'	6°56·8'W	W	13
Loch Trolamaraig	N Eil	NB2201	57°55·0'	6°41·2'W	W	14
Loch Tromlee	Arg & Bt	NN0425	56°22·9'	5°10·0'W	W	50
Loch Trool	D & G	NX4179	55°5·1'	4°29·0'W	W	77
Loch Trosaraidh	N Eil	NF7516	57°7·5'	7°21·8'W	W	31
Loch Trosavat	N Eil	NF7667	57°34·9'	7°24·8'W	W	18
Loch Truderscaig	Highld	NC7132	58°15·7'	4°11·4'W	W	16
Loch Tuamister	N Eil	NB2645	58°18·8'	6°40·2'W	W	8
Loch Tuath	Arg & Bt	NM3943	56°30·7'	6°14·1'W	W	47,48
Loch Tuath	Highld	NH2882	57°47·9'	4°53·2'W	W	20
Loch Tuill Bearnach	Highld	NH1634	57°21·8'	5°3·1'W	W	25
Loch Tuim Ghlais	Highld	NC9752	58°26·9'	3°45·4'W	W	11
Loch Tuirslighe	Highld	NC6559	58°30·2'	4°18·5'W	W	10
Loch Tulla	Arg & Bt	NN2942	56°32·6'	4°46·4'W	W	50
Loch Tullybelton	Pth & Kin	NO0034	56°29·5'	3°37·0'W	W	52,53
Loch Tummel	Pth & Kin	NN7959	56°42·7'	3°58·2'W	W	42,51,52
Loch Tummel	Pth & Kin	NN8159	56°42·7'	3°56·2'W	W	52
Loch Tummel	Pth & Kin	NN8760	56°43·3'	3°50·3'W	W	43
Loch Tungavat	N Eil	NB1628	58°9·2'	6°49·2'W	W	13
Loch Tunnaig	Arg & Bt	NM9101	56°9·6'	5°21·5'W	W	55
Lochturffin	Pemb	SM8529	51°55·3'	5°7·2'W	X	157
Loch Turret Reservoir	Pth & Kin	NN8027	56°25·5'	3°56·3'W	W	52
Loch Twachtan	D & G	NX4286	55°8·8'	4°28·3'W	W	77
Lochty	Angus	NO5362	56°45·1'	2°45·7'W	X	44
Lochty	Fife	NO5208	56°16·0'	2°46·1'W	X	59
Lochty	Pth & Kin	NO0625	56°24·7'	3°31·0'W	T	52,53,58
Lochty Burn	Fife	NT2798	56°10·4'	3°10·1'W	W	59
Lochty Private Railway	Fife	NO5107	56°15·4'	2°47·0'W	X	59
Loch Uacrach nan Caorach	N Eil	NF8349	57°25·5'	7°16·4'W	W	22
Loch Uaille Mhòir	N Eil	NB3718	58°4·6'	6°27·2'W	W	14
Loch Uaine	Highld	NH1225	57°16·9'	5°6·7'W	W	25
Loch Uamasbroc	N Eil	NB0823	58°6·2'	6°56·9'W	W	13,14
Loch Uamasbroc	N Eil	NB1428	58°9·2'	6°51·2'W	W	13
Loch Uamh Dhadhaidh	Highld	NC4564	58°32·5'	4°39·3'W	W	9
Loch Uanadail	N Eil	NG1398	57°53·0'	6°50·1'W	W	14
Loch Uanagan	Highld	NH3607	57°7·7'	4°42·1'W	W	34
Loch Uanalair	N Eil	NB2846	58°19·3'	6°38·3'W	W	8
Loch Ucsabhat	N Eil	NB3206	57°58·0'	6°31·4'W	W	13,14
Loch Udromuil	N Eil	NG1091	57°49·1'	6°52·6'W	W	14
Loch Uidemul	N Eil	NA9714	58°1·0'	7°7·4'W	W	13
Loch Uidh na Ceardaich	Highld	NC1118	58°6·9'	5°12·0'W	W	15
Loch Uidh na Geadaig	Highld	NC1425	58°10·7'	5°9·3'W	W	15
Loch Uidh na h-Iarna	Highld	NC1630	58°13·5'	5°7·5'W	W	15
Loch Uidh Tarraigean	Highld	NC0913	58°4·2'	5°13·8'W	W	15
Loch Uigeadail	Arg & Bt	NR4050	55°40·7'	6°7·7'W	W	60
Loch Uisdein	N Eil	NF8071	57°37·2'	7°21·2'W	W	18
Loch Uiseadair	N Eil	NB0515	58°1·8'	6°59·4'W	W	13,14
Loch Uisg	Arg & Bt	NM6325	56°21·7'	5°49·8'W	W	49
Loch Uisg' an t-Soluis	N Eil	NB3731	58°11·6'	6°28·1'W	W	8
Lochuisge	Highld	NM7955	56°38·3'	5°35·8'W	X	49
Loch Uisge	Highld	NM8055	56°38·4'	5°34·8'W	W	49
Loch Uisgebhagh	N Eil	NF8551	57°26·7'	7°14·6'W	W	22
Loch Uisge Thomais	Highld	NC2005	58°0·1'	5°2·3'W	W	15
Loch Uladale	N Eil	NB0024	58°6·5'	7°5·1'W	W	13
Loch Ulagadale	Arg & Bt	NR7346	55°39·5'	5°36·1'W	W	62
Loch Ulapuil	N Eil	NB3222	58°6·6'	6°32·5'W	W	13,14
Loch Ulbhach Coire	Highld	NC3737	58°17·8'	4°46·4'W	W	16
Loch Ullabhat a' Cli	N Eil	NB4543	58°18·4'	6°20·7'W	W	8
Loch Ullabhat a' Deas	N Eil	NB4543	58°18·4'	6°20·7'W	W	8
Loch Ullachie	Aberd	NO3494	57°2·2'	3°4·8'W	W	37,44
Loch Ulladail	N Eil	NB0714	58°1·4'	6°57·3'W	W	13,14
Loch Ullaveg	N Eil	NF7569	57°35·9'	7°26·0'W	W	18
Loch Unapool	Highld	NC2231	58°14·2'	5°1·4'W	W	15
Loch Urabhal	N Eil	NB3032	58°11·9'	6°35·2'W	W	8,13
Loch Urbhaig	Arg & Bt	NM2357	56°37·6'	6°30·5'W	W	46,47
Lochurd Burn	Scot Bord	NT1142	55°40·1'	3°24·5'W	W	72
Lochurd Fm	Scot Bord	NT1143	55°40·6'	3°24·5'W	FM	72
Lochurd Hills	Scot Bord	NT1242	55°40·1'	3°23·5'W	H	72
Loch Urghag	N Eil	NB3247	58°20·0'	6°34·2'W	W	8
Loch Urigill	Highld	NC2410	58°2·9'	4°58·5'W	W	15
Loch Urr	D & G	NX7684	55°8·3'	3°56·3'W	W	78
Lochurr	D & G	NX7685	55°8·9'	3°56·3'W	X	78
Lochurr Hill	D & G	NX7685	55°8·9'	3°56·3'W	X	78
Lochussie	Highld	NH4956	57°34·4'	4°31·0'W	X	26
Loch Ussie	Highld	NH5058	57°35·5'	4°30·1'W	W	26
Loch Vaa	Highld	NH9117	57°14·1'	3°47·9'W	W	36
Loch Vaich	Highld	NH3477	57°45·4'	4°46·9'W	W	20
Loch Valigan	Pth & Kin	NN9769	56°48·3'	3°40·8'W	W	43
Loch Vallarip	N Eil	NG0583	57°44·6'	6°57·0'W	W	18
Loch Valley	D & G	NX4481	55°6·2'	4°26·3'W	W	77
Lochvane	Pemb	SM8223	51°52·0'	5°9·6'W	X	157
Loch Vasgo	Highld	NC5864	58°32·7'	4°25·9'W	W	10
Loch Vatachan	Highld	NC0110	58°2·3'	5°21·8'W	W	15
Loch Vats-houll	Shetld	HU5765	60°22·2'	0°57·5'W	W	2
Loch Vatten	Highld	NG2843	57°24·0'	6°31·2'W	W	23
Loch Vausary	N Eil	NF7470	57°36·4'	7°27·1'W	W	18
Loch Veiragvat	N Eil	NF8872	57°38·1'	7°13·2'W	W	18
Loch Venachar	Stir	NN5705	56°13·2'	4°17·9'W	W	57
Loch Veyatie	Highld	NC1813	58°4·4'	5°4·7'W	W	15
Loch Vidigill	Highld	NG4037	57°21·2'	6°18·9'W	W	23,32
Lochview	N Lanak	NS8155	55°46·7'	3°53·4'W	X	65,72
Loch Voil	Stir	NN5019	56°20·6'	4°25·2'W	W	57
Loch Vorvin	Highld	NG2854	57°29·9'	6°32·0'W	W	23
Loch Vrotachan	Aberd	NO1278	56°53·4'	3°26·2'W	W	43
Loch Walton	Stir	NS6686	56°3·1'	4°8·7'W	W	57
Loch Warrender	Highld	NC7449	58°24·9'	4°8·9'W	W	10
Loch Watenan	Highld	ND3141	58°21·4'	3°10·3'W	W	11,12
Loch Watersee	N Eil	NF9281	57°43·1'	7°9·9'W	W	18
Loch Watston	Stir	NN7100	56°10·8'	4°4·2'W	W	57
Loch Watten	Highld	ND2256	58°29·4'	3°19·8'W	W	11,12
Loch Wayoch	D & G	NX3056	54°52·4'	4°38·5'W	W	82
Loch Wharral	Angus	NO3574	56°51·4'	3°3·5'W	W	44
Lochwhinnie Hill	D & G	NX6689	55°10·9'	4°5·8'W	X	77
Loch Whinyeon	D & G	NX6260	54°55·2'	4°8·8'W	W	83
Loch Whirr	Pth & Kin	NO1112	56°17·8'	3°25·8'W	W	58
Lochwinnoch	Renf	NS3559	55°48·0'	4°37·5'W	T	63
Loch Winter	Highld	NH8837	57°24·8'	3°51·4'W	W	27
Lochwood	C of Glas	NS6966	55°52·4'	4°5·2'W	T	64
Lochwood	D & G	NY0896	55°15·2'	3°26·4'W	X	78
Lochwood	N Ayr	NS2744	55°39·8'	4°44·6'W	X	63,70
Loch Wood	Scot Bord	NT6352	55°45·8'	2°34·9'W	F	67,74
Lochwood Mains	D & G	NY0996	55°15·2'	3°25·5'W	X	78
Lochwood Moss	D & G	NY0796	55°15·2'	3°27·4'W	X	78
Lochwood Plantn	D & G	NY0997	55°15·8'	3°25·5'W	F	78
Loch Yeor	N Eil	NF9172	57°38·2'	7°10·2'W	W	18
Lochyhill	Moray	NJ0559	57°36·9'	3°35·0'W	X	27
Lochy Law	Scot Bord	NT2211	55°23·5'	3°13·5'W	X	79
Lochymuir Plantn	Fife	NT0884	56°2·7'	3°28·2'W	F	65
Lochyside	Highld	NN1175	56°49·9'	5°5·4'W	T	41
Loch Yucal or Loch Allt na h-Airbe	Highld	NC2036	58°16·8'	5°3·7'W	W	15
Locka Fm	Lancs	SD5771	54°8·2'	2°39·1'W	FM	97
Lockbank Fm	Cumbr	SD6592	54°19·6'	2°31·9'W	FM	97
Lock Br	Lancs	SD7158	54°1·3'	2°26·1'W	X	103
Locke Fm	Dorset	ST5308	50°52·4'	2°39·7'W	FM	194
Locke Fm	Norf	TF6633	52°52·4'	0°28·4'E	FM	132
Lockengate	Corn	SX0361	50°25·2'	4°46·0'W	T	200
Locker Bank	N Yks	SE4993	54°20·1'	1°14·4'W	X	100
Lockerbie	D & G	NY1381	55°7·2'	3°21·4'W	T	78
Lockerbie Ho	D & G	NY1483	55°8·3'	3°20·5'W	X	78
Lockerbrook Fm	Derby	SK1689	53°24·1'	1°45·2'W	FM	110
Lockerbrook Heights	Derby	SK1589	53°24·1'	1°46·1'W	X	110
Lockeridge	Wilts	SU1467	51°24·3'	1°47·5'W	T	173
Lockeridge Dene	Wilts	SU1467	51°24·3'	1°47·5'W	T	173
Lockeridge Ho	Wilts	SU1468	51°24·9'	1°47·5'W	X	173
Lockerley	Hants	SU2926	51°2·2'	1°34·8'W	T	185
Lockerley Hall	Hants	SU2928	51°3·3'	1°34·8'W	X	185
Lockerley Water Fm	Hants	SU2927	51°2·7'	1°34·8'W	FM	185
Locker Low Wood	N Yks	SE5194	54°20·6'	1°12·5'W	F	100
Locker Tarn	N Yks	SE0091	54°19·1'	1°59·6'W	W	98
Locker Wood	N Yks	SE5093	54°20·0'	1°13·4'W	F	100
Lockets	W Susx	TQ1228	51°2·7'	0°23·7'W	X	187,198
Locketts Fm	Dorset	ST7508	50°52·5'	2°20·9'W	FM	194
Lockett's Tenement	Ches	SJ8660	53°8·5'	2°12·2'W	X	118
Lockey Fm	Leic	SK4602	52°37·1'	1°18·8'W	FM	140
Lockey Wood	N Yks	NZ0505	54°26·7'	1°55·0'W	F	92
Lock Fm	E Yorks	SE8439	53°50·7'	0°43·0'W	FM	106
Lock Fm	W Susx	TQ1718	50°57·2'	0°19·7'W	FM	198
Lock Gill	N Yks	SD9978	54°12·1'	2°0·5'W	W	98
Lockham	E Yorks	TA3917	53°38·1'	0°6·6'E	X	113
Lockhartbank	S Lanak	NS8545	55°41·3'	3°49·3'W	X	72
Lockhart Mill	S Lanak	NS8745	55°41·4'	3°47·4'W	X	72
Lock Hill	Norf	TL9192	52°29·8'	0°49·2'E	X	144
Lockhill Hall	Somer	ST4436	51°7·5'	2°47·6'W	X	182
Lockhills	Cumbr	NY5047	54°49·2'	2°46·3'W	T	86
Lock Ho	N Yks	SE3566	54°5·6'	1°27·5'W	X	99
Lock Ho	York	SE6157	54°0·6'	1°3·7'W	X	105
Lockholme	Cumbr	NY7302	54°25·0'	2°24·5'W	X	91
Lockhurst	Kent	TQ4647	51°12·4'	0°5·8'E	X	188
Lockhurst	Lancs	SD5338	53°50·4'	2°42·4'W	X	102
Locking	N Som	ST3659	51°19·8'	2°54·7'W	T	182
Lockinge Down	Oxon	SU4183	51°32·9'	1°24·1'W	X	174
Lockinge Kiln Fm	Oxon	SU4283	51°32·9'	1°23·3'W	FM	174
Locking Head Fm	N Som	ST3660	51°20·4'	2°54·7'W	FM	182
Locking Stumps	Warr	SJ6492	53°25·7'	2°32·1'W	T	109
Lockington	E Yorks	SE9947	53°54·8'	0°29·2'W	T	106
Lockington	Leic	SK4627	52°50·5'	1°18·6'W	T	129
Lockington Carr Ho	E Yorks	TA0347	53°54·8'	0°25·5'W	X	107
Lockington Grange	E Yorks	SE9846	53°54·3'	0°30·1'W	X	106
Lockington Grounds Fm	Leic	SK4730	52°52·2'	1°17·7'W	FM	129
Lockington Wood	E Yorks	SE9845	53°53·8'	0°30·1'W	F	106
Lock Lane Cross	Devon	SS6340	51°8·8'	3°57·1'W	X	180
Lockleaze	C of Bris	ST6076	51°29·1'	2°34·2'W	T	172
Lockley Fm	Herts	TL2416	51°50·0'	0°11·6'W	FM	166
Lockleywood	Shrops	SJ6928	52°51·2'	2°27·2'W	T	127
Lockner Holt	Surrey	TQ0347	51°13·0'	0°31·1'W	X	186
Lock of Isbister	Orkney	HY2523	59°5·5'	3°18·1'W	W	6
Locko Grange Fm	Derby	SK4138	52°56·5'	1°23·0'W	FM	129
Locko Park	Derby	SK4038	52°56·5'	1°23·9'W	X	129
Lockridge Fm	Devon	SX4366	50°28·6'	4°12·4'W	FM	201
Locksash Fm	W Susx	SU7813	50°54·9'	0°53·0'W	FM	197
Locksbottom	Brom	TQ4365	51°22·2'	0°3·7'E	T	177
Locksbrook	Bath & NE Somer	ST7264	51°22·7'	2°23·8'W	T	172
Lock's Common	Brig	SS8077	51°29·0'	3°43·3'W	X	170
Lock's Fm	Hants	SU4008	50°52·4'	1°25·5'W	FM	196
Locks Fm	Hants	SU5516	50°56·7'	1°12·6'W	FM	185
Lock's Fm	W Susx	TQ1312	50°54·0'	0°23·2'W	FM	198
Locksgreen	I of W	SZ4490	50°42·7'	1°22·2'W	T	196
Locks Green Fm	W Susx	TQ2614	50°54·9'	0°12·1'W	FM	198
Lockshaw Moss	Fife	NS9991	56°6·3'	3°37·0'W	X	58
Locks Heath	Hants	SU5107	50°51·8'	1°16·1'W	T	196
Lockshill	Devon	SS5511	50°53·1'	4°3·3'W	X	191
Locks Hill	Heref	SO6646	52°6·9'	2°29·4'W	X	149
Lock's Ho	Wok	SU8367	51°24·0'	0°48·0'W	X	175
Lockskinners Fm	Kent	TQ4944	51°10·8'	0°8·3'E	FM	188
Locksley Farm Ho	Somer	ST5424	51°1·0'	2°39·0'W	X	183
Locks Manor	W Susx	TQ2918	50°57·0'	0°9·4'W	X	198
Locks Park	Devon	SS5102	50°48·1'	4°6·5'W	X	191
Lockthwaite	Cumbr	NY7806	54°27·2'	2°19·9'W	X	91
Lockton	N Yks	SE8489	54°17·6'	0°42·1'W	T	94,100
Lockton High Moor	N Yks	SE8596	54°21·4'	0°41·1'W	X	94,100
Lockton Low Moor	N Yks	SE8592	54°19·2'	0°41·2'W	X	94,100
Lockwell Hill	Notts	SK6358	53°7·2'	1°3·1'W	X	120
Lockwood	Kirk	SE1315	53°38·1'	1°47·8'W	T	110
Lock Wood	Oxon	SU5397	51°40·4'	1°13·6'W	F	164
Lock Wood	Wilts	SU1358	51°19·5'	1°48·4'W	F	173
Lockwood Beck Fm	Red & Cl	NZ6714	54°31·3'	0°57·5'W	FM	94
Lockwood Beck Resr	Red & Cl	NZ6713	54°30·7'	0°57·5'W	W	94
Lockwood Hall	Staffs	SK0245	53°0·4'	1°57·8'W	X	119,128
Lockwood Resr	Wal F	TQ3590	51°35·8'	0°2·7'W	W	177
Lockyers Fm	W Susx	TQ1726	51°1·5'	0°19·5'W	FM	187,198
Lockyer's Hill	Dorset	SY8693	50°44·4'	2°11·5'W	X	194
Locn na Crò	N Eil	NG1692	57°49·9'	6°46·6'W	W	14
Lodan Stiomrabhaigh	N Eil	NB3411	58°0·8'	6°29·8'W	W	13,14
Loddan Hill	Scot Bord	NT7511	55°23·8'	2°23·3'W	H	80
Loddart's Hill	Essex	TL8204	51°42·5'	0°38·5'E	X	168
Loddington	Leic	SK7802	52°36·8'	0°50·5'W	T	141
Loddington	Northnts	SP8178	52°23·9'	0°48·2'W	T	141
Loddington Coppice Fm	Northnts	SP7977	52°23·4'	0°49·9'W	FM	141
Loddington Fm	Kent	TQ7650	51°13·5'	0°31·6'E	FM	188
Loddington Grange	Northnts	SP8277	52°23·3'	0°47·3'W	X	141
Loddington Mill	Leic	SK7701	52°36·3'	0°51·4'W	X	141
Loddington Reddish	Leic	SK7702	52°36·9'	0°51·4'W	F	141
Loddiswell	Devon	SX7148	50°19·3'	3°48·4'W	T	202
Loddon	Norf	TM3698	52°31·9'	1°29·2'E	T	134
Loddon Bridge	Wok	SU7671	51°26·2'	0°54·0'W	X	175
Loddon Court	Wok	SU7164	51°22·5'	0°58·4'W	X	175,186
Loddon Court Fm	Wok	SU7065	51°23·0'	0°59·3'W	FM	175
Loddon Hall	Norf	TM3797	52°31·4'	1°30·0'E	X	134
Loddon Ingloss	Norf	TM3496	52°30·9'	1°27·3'E	T	134
Loddon Park Fm	Wok	SU7876	51°28·9'	0°52·2'W	FM	175
Lode	Cambs	TL5362	52°14·3'	0°14·8'E	T	154
Lode Fm	Cambs	TL5267	52°17·0'	0°14·1'E	FM	154
Lode Fm	Hants	SU7737	51°7·9'	0°53·6'W	FM	186
Lode Heath	Sol	SP1580	52°25·3'	1°46·4'W	T	139
Lode Ho	Staffs	SK1455	53°5·8'	1°47·0'W	X	119
Lodens Moss	D & G	NX2571	55°0·4'	4°43·8'W	X	76
Loder Head	Shetld	HU5243	60°10·4'	1°3·3'W	X	4
Loders	Dorset	SY4994	50°44·8'	2°43·0'W	T	193,194
Loders Hill	Dorset	SY4993	50°44·3'	2°43·0'W	H	193,194
Loder, The	Shetld	HU3710	59°52·7'	1°19·9'W	X	4
Lodesbarn	Derby	SK0978	53°18·2'	1°51·5'W	X	119
Lodes End	Cambs	TL2888	52°28·7'	0°6·5'W	X	142
Lodes Marsh	Derby	SK0978	53°18·2'	1°51·5'W	X	119
Lodfin	Devon	SS9523	51°0·0'	3°29·4'W	X	181
Lodge	Cambs	TL1579	52°24·0'	0°18·2'W	X	142
Lodge	Orkney	HY6424	59°6·3'	2°37·2'W	X	5
Lodge Bank	N Yks	SD7369	54°7·2'	2°24·4'W	X	98
Lodgebank	Shrops	SJ5925	52°49·5'	2°36·1'W	T	126
Lodgebank	Wrekin	SJ7212	52°42·5'	2°24·5'W	X	127
Lodgebarn	Staffs	SJ8336	52°55·5'	2°14·8'W	X	127
Lodge Barn Fm	Kent	TQ4854	51°16·2'	0°7·7'E	FM	188
Lodge Burn	Stir	NN7605	56°13·5'	3°59·6'W	W	57
Lodge Coppice	Northnts	SP9394	52°32·4'	0°37·3'W	F	141
Lodge Copse	Northnts	SP6542	52°4·6'	1°2·7'W	F	152
Lodge Copse	W Berks	SU3877	51°29·7'	1°26·8'W	F	174
Lodge Cott	Shrops	SO5680	52°25·2'	2°38·4'W	X	137,138
Lodge Covert	Lincs	TF1780	53°18·5'	0°14·2'W	F	121
Lodgedale Fm	Staffs	SK0439	52°57·1'	1°56·0'W	FM	128
Lodge Down	W Berks	SU3077	51°29·7'	1°33·7'W	X	174
Lodge Edge	N Yks	NY8101	54°24·5'	2°17·1'W	X	91,92
Lodge Farm	Dudley	SO9387	52°29·1'	2°5·8'W	FM	139
Lodge Farm Ho	Wilts	SU1820	50°59·0'	1°44·2'W	X	184
Lodgefield Fm	E Susx	TQ5038	51°7·5'	0°9·0'E	FM	188
Lodgefield Ho	Notts	SK7046	53°0·6'	0°57·0'W	X	129
Lodge Field Ho	N Yks	SE6177	54°11·3'	1°3·5'W	X	100
Lodge Fm	Beds	SP9449	52°8·1'	0°37·2'W	FM	153
Lodge Fm	Beds	SP9656	52°11·9'	0°35·3'W	FM	153
Lodge Fm	Beds	TL0030	51°57·8'	0°32·3'W	FM	166
Lodge Fm	Beds	TL0269	52°18·8'	0°29·8'W	FM	153
Lodge Fm	Beds	TL0362	52°15·0'	0°29·1'W	FM	153
Lodge Fm	Beds	TL0419	51°51·8'	0°29·0'W	FM	166
Lodge Fm	Bucks	SP7238	52°2·4'	0°56·6'W	FM	152
Lodge Fm	Bucks	SP8911	51°47·7'	0°42·2'W	FM	165
Lodge Fm	Bucks	TQ0096	51°39·5'	0°32·9'W	FM	166,176
Lodge Fm	Cambs	TF4415	52°43·0'	0°8·3'E	FM	131
Lodge Fm	Cambs	TL1369	52°18·7'	0°20·1'W	FM	153
Lodge Fm	Cambs	TL1483	52°26·2'	0°19·0'W	FM	142
Lodge Fm	Cambs	TL1765	52°16·5'	0°16·7'W	FM	153
Lodge Fm	Cambs	TL2068	52°18·0'	0°14·0'W	FM	153
Lodge Fm	Cambs	TL2262	52°14·8'	0°12·4'W	FM	153
Lodge Fm	Cambs	TL2381	52°25·0'	0°11·1'W	FM	142
Lodge Fm	Cambs	TL2574	52°21·2'	0°9·5'W	FM	142
Lodge Fm	Cambs	TL2577	52°22·8'	0°9·4'W	FM	142
Lodge Fm	Cambs	TL2776	52°22·3'	0°7·7'W	FM	142
Lodge Fm	Cambs	TL4669	52°18·2'	0°8·9'E	FM	154
Lodge Fm	Cambs	TL5153	52°9·5'	0°12·8'E	FM	154
Lodge Fm	Cered	SN6593	52°31·3'	3°59·0'W	FM	135
Lodge Fm	Ches	SJ6747	53°1·4'	2°29·1'W	FM	118
Lodge Fm	Ches	SJ8558	53°7·4'	2°13·0'W	FM	118
Lodge Fm	Ches	SJ9278	53°18·2'	2°6·8'W	FM	118
Lodge Fm	C of Stoke	SJ9140	52°57·7'	2°7·6'W	FM	118
Lodge Fm	Cumbr	NY7812	54°30·4'	2°20·0'W	FM	91
Lodge Fm	Denb	SJ0366	53°11·2'	3°26·7'W	FM	116
Lodge Fm	Denb	SJ1072	53°14·5'	3°20·5'W	FM	116
Lodge Fm	Derby	SK1745	53°0·4'	1°44·4'W	FM	119,128
Lodge Fm	Derby	SK2939	52°57·1'	1°33·7'W	FM	128
Lodge Fm	Derby	SK4443	52°59·2'	1°20·3'W	FM	129
Lodge Fm	Derby	SK4771	53°14·3'	1°17·3'W	FM	120
Lodge Fm	Derby	SK5065	53°11·0'	1°14·7'W	FM	120
Lodge Fm	Donc	SK5595	53°27·2'	1°9·9'W	FM	111
Lodge Fm	Dorset	ST5705	50°50·8'	2°36·3'W	FM	194
Lodge Fm	Dorset	ST9702	50°49·3'	2°2·2'W	A	195
Lodge Fm	Durham	NZ2131	54°40·7'	1°40·0'W	FM	93
Lodge Fm	Durham	NZ2344	54°47·7'	1°38·1'W	FM	88
Lodge Fm	Essex	TL4206	51°44·3'	0°3·8'E	FM	167
Lodge Fm	Essex	TL4740	52°2·6'	0°9·4'E	FM	154
Lodge Fm	Essex	TL5218	51°50·6'	0°12·8'E	FM	167
Lodge Fm	Essex	TL5402	51°42·0'	0°14·1'E	FM	167
Lodge Fm	Essex	TL6902	51°41·7'	0°27·1'E	FM	167
Lodge Fm	Essex	TL8013	51°47·4'	0°37·0'E	FM	168
Lodge Fm	Essex	TL8105	51°43·1'	0°37·6'E	FM	168
Lodge Fm	Essex	TL8327	51°54·9'	0°40·1'E	FM	168
Lodge Fm	Essex	TL8436	51°59·7'	0°41·2'E	FM	155
Lodge Fm	Essex	TL9831	51°56·8'	0°53·3'E	FM	168
Lodge Fm	Essex	TM0428	51°55·0'	0°58·4'E	FM	168
Lodge Fm	Essex	TM0725	51°53·3'	1°0·9'E	FM	168,169
Lodge Fm	Essex	TQ6995	51°37·9'	0°26·9'E	FM	167,177
Lodge Fm	Essex	TR0193	51°36·2'	0°54·6'E	FM	178
Lodge Fm	E Yorks	SE6121	53°41·2'	1°4·2'W	FM	105
Lodge Fm	E Yorks	SE8036	53°49·1'	0°46·7'W	FM	106

Lodge Fm	E Yorks	SE8859	54°1·4'	0°39·0'W	FM	106
Lodge Fm	Falk	NS8471	55°55·3'	3°50·9'W	FM	65
Lodge Fm	Glos	SO6003	51°43·7'	2°34·4'W	FM	162
Lodge Fm	Glos	ST8795	51°39·5'	2°10·9'W	FM	162
Lodge Fm	Hants	SU6109	50°52·9'	1°7·6'W	FM	196
Lodge Fm	Hants	SU6654	51°17·1'	1°2·8'W	FM	185,186
Lodge Fm	Hants	SU7352	51°16·0'	0°56·8'W	FM	186
Lodge Fm	Hants	SZ3899	50°47·6'	1°27·3'W	FM	196
Lodge Fm	Heref	SO2653	52°10·5'	3°4·5'W	FM	148
Lodge Fm	Heref	SO3869	52°19·2'	2°54·2'W	FM	137,148
Lodge Fm	Heref	SO4575	52°22·5'	2°48·1'W	FM	137,138,148
Lodge Fm	Heref	SO4667	52°18·1'	2°47·1'W	FM	137,138,148
Lodge Fm	Herts	SP9508	51°46·0'	0°37·0'W	FM	165
Lodge Fm	Herts	TL1424	51°54·4'	0°20·2'W	FM	166
Lodge Fm	Herts	TL2320	51°52·1'	0°12·4'W	FM	166
Lodge Fm	Herts	TL2835	52°0·1'	0°7·7'W	FM	153
Lodge Fm	Herts	TL2934	51°59·6'	0°6·9'W	FM	153
Lodge Fm	Herts	TL3320	51°52·0'	0°3·7'W	FM	166
Lodge Fm	Herts	TL4222	51°52·9'	0°4·2'E	FM	167
Lodge Fm	I of W	SZ4186	50°40·6'	1°24·8'W	FM	196
Lodge Fm	Kent	TQ6868	51°23·4'	0°25·3'E	FM	177,178
Lodge Fm	Lancs	SD7752	53°58·1'	2°20·6'W	FM	103
Lodge Fm	Leic	SK3300	52°36·0'	1°30·4'W	FM	140
Lodge Fm	Leic	SK3409	52°40·9'	1°29·4'W	FM	128,140
Lodge Fm	Leic	SK3921	52°47·3'	1°24·9'W	FM	128
Lodge Fm	Leic	SK4306	52°39·2'	1°21·5'W	FM	140
Lodge Fm	Leic	SK6622	52°47·7'	1°0·9'W	FM	129
Lodge Fm	Leic	SK7430	52°52·0'	0°53·6'W	FM	129
Lodge Fm	Leic	SK7729	52°51·4'	0°51·0'W	FM	129
Lodge Fm	Leic	SK7821	52°47·1'	0°50·2'W	FM	129
Lodge Fm	Leic	SP3596	52°33·9'	1°28·6'W	FM	140
Lodge Fm	Leic	SP3598	52°35·0'	1°28·6'W	FM	140
Lodge Fm	Leic	SP4298	52°34·7'	1°22·4'W	FM	140
Lodge Fm	Leic	SP4986	52°28·4'	1°16·3'W	FM	140
Lodge Fm	Leic	SP5091	52°31·1'	1°15·4'W	FM	140
Lodge Fm	Leic	SP5189	52°30·0'	1°14·5'W	FM	140
Lodge Fm	Leic	SP5192	52°31·6'	1°14·5'W	FM	140
Lodge Fm	Leic	SP5294	52°32·7'	1°13·6'W	FM	140
Lodge Fm	Leic	SP5389	52°30·0'	1°12·8'W	FM	140
Lodge Fm	Leic	SP5692	52°31·6'	1°10·1'W	FM	140
Lodge Fm	Leic	SP5791	52°31·1'	1°9·2'W	FM	140
Lodge Fm	Leic	SP5883	52°26·7'	1°8·4'W	FM	140
Lodge Fm	Leic	SP6385	52°27·8'	1°4·0'W	FM	140
Lodge Fm	Leic	SP6688	52°29·4'	1°1·3'W	FM	141
Lodge Fm	Lincs	SK8759	53°7·5'	0°41·6'W	FM	121
Lodge Fm	Lincs	SK8853	53°4·3'	0°40·8'W	FM	121
Lodge Fm	Lincs	SK8931	52°52·4'	0°40·3'W	FM	130
Lodge Fm	Lincs	SK8948	53°1·5'	0°40·0'W	FM	130
Lodge Fm	Lincs	SK9225	52°49·1'	0°37·7'W	FM	130
Lodge Fm	Lincs	SK9346	53°0·4'	0°36·4'W	FM	130
Lodge Fm	Lincs	SK9444	52°59·3'	0°35·6'W	FM	130
Lodge Fm	Lincs	TF0016	52°44·2'	0°30·7'W	FM	130
Lodge Fm	Lincs	TF0145	52°59·8'	0°29·3'W	FM	130
Lodge Fm	Lincs	TF0174	53°15·4'	0°28·7'W	FM	121
Lodge Fm	Lincs	TF0214	52°43·1'	0°29·0'W	FM	130
Lodge Fm	Lincs	TF0574	53°15·4'	0°25·2'W	FM	121
Lodge Fm	Lincs	TF0713	52°42·5'	0°24·6'W	FM	130,142
Lodge Fm	Lincs	TF0743	52°58·7'	0°24·0'W	FM	130
Lodge Fm	Lincs	TF1143	52°58·6'	0°20·4'W	FM	130
Lodge Fm	Lincs	TF1320	52°46·2'	0°19·1'W	FM	130
Lodge Fm	Lincs	TF1372	53°14·2'	0°18·0'W	FM	121
Lodge Fm	Lincs	TF2058	53°6·6'	0°12·0'W	FM	122
Lodge Fm	Lincs	TF4248	53°0·9'	0°7·4'E	FM	131
Lodge Fm	Lincs	TF4370	53°13·7'	0°8·9'E	FM	122
Lodge Fm	Lincs	TF4589	53°22·9'	0°11·2'E	FM	113,122
Lodge Fm	Lincs	TF4727	52°49·5'	0°11·3'E	FM	131
Lodge Fm	Mil Key	SP8043	52°5·0'	0°49·6'W	FM	152
Lodge Fm	Mil Key	SP9344	52°5·4'	0°38·2'W	FM	153
Lodge Fm	Mil Key	SP9348	52°7·6'	0°38·1'W	FM	153
Lodge Fm	N Lincs	SE9611	53°35·4'	0°32·6'W	FM	112
Lodge Fm	Norf	TF6840	52°56·1'	0°30·4'E	FM	132
Lodge Fm	Norf	TF8000	52°34·3'	0°39·8'E	FM	144
Lodge Fm	Norf	TF8217	52°43·4'	0°42·1'E	FM	132
Lodge Fm	Norf	TF8518	52°43·9'	0°44·8'E	FM	132
Lodge Fm	Norf	TF8803	52°35·8'	0°47·0'E	FM	144
Lodge Fm	Norf	TF9010	52°39·5'	0°49·0'E	FM	132
Lodge Fm	Norf	TF9132	52°51·3'	0°50·6'E	FM	132
Lodge Fm	Norf	TG0107	52°37·6'	0°58·6'E	FM	144
Lodge Fm	Norf	TG1608	52°37·8'	1°11·9'E	FM	144
Lodge Fm	Norf	TG1610	52°38·9'	1°12·0'E	FM	133
Lodge Fm	Norf	TG2000	52°33·4'	1°15·1'E	FM	134
Lodge Fm	Norf	TG2232	52°50·6'	1°18·2'E	FM	133
Lodge Fm	Norf	TG2318	52°43·0'	1°18·5'E	FM	133,134
Lodge Fm	Norf	TG2528	52°48·4'	1°20·7'E	FM	133,134
Lodge Fm	Norf	TG2637	52°53·2'	1°22·0'E	FM	133
Lodge Fm	Norf	TL6197	52°33·0'	0°22·9'E	FM	143
Lodge Fm	Norf	TL8685	52°26·1'	0°44·6'E	FM	144
Lodge Fm	Norf	TL9494	52°30·8'	0°51·9'E	FM	144
Lodge Fm	Norf	TM0482	52°24·1'	1°0·3'E	FM	144
Lodge Fm	Norf	TM0782	52°24·0'	1°3·0'E	FM	144
Lodge Fm	Norf	TM1082	52°24·0'	1°5·6'E	FM	144
Lodge Fm	Norf	TM1087	52°26·7'	1°5·8'E	FM	144
Lodge Fm	Norf	TM1888	52°27·0'	1°12·9'E	FM	156
Lodge Fm	Norf	TM2182	52°23·7'	1°15·3'E	FM	156
Lodge Fm	Norf	TM2484	52°24·7'	1°18·0'E	FM	156
Lodge Fm	Norf	TM2888	52°26·8'	1°21·7'E	FM	156
Lodge Fm	Norf	TM4094	52°29·7'	1°32·5'E	FM	134
Lodge Fm	Northnts	SP5547	52°7·3'	1°11·4'W	FM	152
Lodge Fm	Northnts	SP6381	52°25·6'	1°4·0'W	FM	140
Lodge Fm	Northnts	SP6471	52°20·2'	1°3·2'W	FM	140
Lodge Fm	Northnts	SP6573	52°21·3'	1°2·3'W	FM	141
Lodge Fm	Northnts	SP6749	52°8·3'	1°0·9'W	FM	152
Lodge Fm	Northnts	SP6776	52°22·9'	1°0·5'W	FM	141
Lodge Fm	Northnts	SP7572	52°20·7'	0°53·5'W	FM	141
Lodge Fm	Northnts	SP9161	52°14·6'	0°39·6'W	FM	152
Lodge Fm	Northnts	SP9490	52°30·2'	0°36·5'W	FM	141
Lodge Fm	Northnts	TL0075	52°22·1'	0°31·5'W	FM	141
Lodge Fm	Northnts	TL0194	52°32·3'	0°30·2'W	FM	141
Lodge Fm	Northnts	TL0990	52°30·1'	0°23·3'W	FM	142
Lodge Fm	Northnts	TL1089	52°29·5'	0°22·4'W	FM	142
Lodge Fm	Notts	SK5679	53°18·5'	1°9·2'W	FM	120
Lodge Fm	Notts	SK5928	52°51·0'	1°7·0'W	FM	129
Lodge Fm	Notts	SK6150	53°2·9'	1°5·0'W	FM	120
Lodge Fm	Notts	SK6344	52°59·6'	1°3·3'W	FM	129
Lodge Fm	Notts	SK6629	52°51·5'	1°0·8'W	FM	129
Lodge Fm	Notts	SK7361	53°8·7'	0°54·1'W	FM	120
Lodge Fm	Notts	SK7562	53°9·2'	0°52·3'W	FM	120
Lodge Fm	Notts	SK7570	53°13·5'	0°52·2'W	FM	120
Lodge Fm	Notts	SK7672	53°14·6'	0°51·3'W	FM	120
Lodge Fm	Notts	SK7841	52°57·9'	0°49·9'W	FM	129
Lodge Fm	Notts	SK8259	53°7·5'	0°46·1'W	FM	121
Lodge Fm	Notts	SK8364	53°10·2'	0°45·1'W	FM	121
Lodge Fm	N Yks	NZ2707	54°27·7'	1°34·6'W	FM	93
Lodge Fm	N Yks	NZ9009	54°28·3'	0°36·2'W	FM	94
Lodge Fm	N Yks	SD8261	54°2·9'	2°16·1'W	FM	98
Lodge Fm	N Yks	SE3450	53°56·9'	1°28·5'W	FM	104
Lodge Fm	N Yks	SE4539	53°51·0'	1°18·5'W	FM	105
Lodge Fm	N Yks	SE4764	54°4·4'	1°16·5'W	FM	100
Lodge Fm	N Yks	SE5154	53°59·0'	1°12·9'W	FM	105
Lodge Fm	N Yks	SE5435	53°48·7'	1°10·4'W	FM	105
Lodge Fm	N Yks	SE5826	53°43·9'	1°6·8'W	FM	105
Lodge Fm	N Yks	SE6134	53°48·2'	1°4·0'W	FM	105
Lodge Fm	N Yks	SE6665	54°4·8'	0°59·1'W	FM	100
Lodge Fm	N Yks	SE6735	53°48·7'	0°58·5'W	FM	105,106
Lodge Fm	N Yks	SE6797	54°22·1'	0°57·7'W	FM	94,100
Lodge Fm	Oxon	SP3735	52°1·0'	1°27·3'W	FM	151
Lodge Fm	Oxon	SP3919	51°52·3'	1°25·6'W	FM	164
Lodge Fm	Oxon	SP5228	51°57·1'	1°14·2'W	FM	164
Lodge Fm	Oxon	SP5510	51°47·4'	1°11·8'W	FM	164
Lodge Fm	Oxon	SP5620	51°52·8'	1°10·8'W	FM	164
Lodge Fm	Oxon	SU3486	51°34·5'	1°30·2'W	FM	174
Lodge Fm	Pemb	SM8807	51°43·5'	5°3·8'W	FM	157
Lodge Fm	Peterb	TF2806	52°38·4'	0°6·1'W	FM	142
Lodge Fm	Red & Cl	NZ6914	54°31·2'	0°55·6'W	FM	94
Lodge Fm	Roth	SK5485	53°21·8'	1°10·9'W	FM	111,120
Lodge Fm	S Glos	ST6090	51°36·7'	2°34·3'W	FM	162,172
Lodge Fm	S Glos	ST6486	51°34·5'	2°30·8'W	FM	172
Lodge Fm	S Glos	ST6493	51°38·3'	2°30·8'W	FM	162,172
Lodge Fm	S Glos	ST6775	51°28·6'	2°28·1'W	FM	172
Lodge Fm	Shrops	SJ3823	52°48·3'	2°54·8'W	FM	126
Lodge Fm	Shrops	SJ4730	52°52·1'	2°46·8'W	FM	126
Lodge Fm	Shrops	SJ5925	52°49·5'	2°36·1'W	FM	126
Lodge Fm	Shrops	SJ6600	52°36·0'	2°29·7'W	FM	127
Lodge Fm	Shrops	SO3389	52°29·9'	2°58·8'W	FM	137
Lodge Fm	Shrops	SO6591	52°31·2'	2°30·5'W	FM	138
Lodge Fm	Shrops	SO7388	52°29·6'	2°23·5'W	FM	138
Lodge Fm	Somer	ST0339	51°8·8'	3°22·8'W	FM	181
Lodge Fm	Somer	ST2907	50°51·7'	3°0·1'W	FM	193
Lodge Fm	Somer	ST6445	51°12·4'	2°30·5'W	FM	183
Lodge Fm	Somer	ST6841	51°10·3'	2°27·1'W	FM	183
Lodge Fm	Staffs	SJ7911	52°42·0'	2°18·2'W	FM	127
Lodge Fm	Staffs	SJ9861	53°9·0'	2°1·4'W	FM	118
Lodge Fm	Staffs	SK1801	52°36·6'	1°43·6'W	FM	139
Lodge Fm	Staffs	SK2403	52°37·7'	1°38·3'W	FM	139
Lodge Fm	Staffs	SO8382	52°26·4'	2°14·6'W	FM	138
Lodge Fm	Suff	TL7963	52°14·4'	0°37·7'E	FM	155
Lodge Fm	Suff	TL8056	52°10·6'	0°38·4'E	FM	155
Lodge Fm	Suff	TL8151	52°7·9'	0°39·1'E	FM	155
Lodge Fm	Suff	TL8347	52°5·7'	0°40·7'E	FM	155
Lodge Fm	Suff	TL8575	52°20·7'	0°43·4'E	FM	144
Lodge Fm	Suff	TM0177	52°21·5'	0°57·5'E	FM	144
Lodge Fm	Suff	TM0466	52°15·5'	0°59·7'E	FM	155
Lodge Fm	Suff	TM0865	52°14·9'	1°3·2'E	FM	155
Lodge Fm	Suff	TM0966	52°15·4'	1°4·1'E	FM	155
Lodge Fm	Suff	TM2167	52°15·6'	1°14·7'E	FM	156
Lodge Fm	Suff	TM2242	52°2·1'	1°14·6'E	FM	169
Lodge Fm	Suff	TM2269	52°16·7'	1°15·7'E	FM	156
Lodge Fm	Suff	TM2779	52°21·9'	1°20·5'E	FM	156
Lodge Fm	Suff	TM2973	52°18·7'	1°22·0'E	FM	156
Lodge Fm	Suff	TM2974	52°19·2'	1°22·0'E	FM	156
Lodge Fm	Suff	TM3469	52°16·4'	1°26·2'E	FM	156
Lodge Fm	Suff	TM4089	52°27·0'	1°32·3'E	FM	156
Lodge Fm	Suff	TM4251	52°6·5'	1°32·5'E	FM	156
Lodge Fm	Suff	TM4384	52°24·2'	1°34·8'E	FM	156
Lodge Fm	Suff	TM5188	52°26·2'	1°41·6'E	FM	156
Lodge Fm	Surrey	TQ1845	51°11·7'	0°18·3'W	FM	187
Lodge Fm	Surrey	TQ3346	51°12·1'	0°5·4'W	FM	187
Lodge Fm	Warw	SK2805	52°38·8'	1°34·8'W	FM	140
Lodge Fm	Warw	SP2160	52°14·5'	1°41·1'W	FM	151
Lodge Fm	Warw	SP2776	52°23·1'	1°35·8'W	FM	140
Lodge Fm	Warw	SP3190	52°30·7'	1°32·2'W	FM	140
Lodge Fm	Warw	SP3252	52°10·2'	1°31·5'W	FM	151
Lodge Fm	Warw	SP3558	52°13·4'	1°28·9'W	FM	151
Lodge Fm	Warw	SP4485	52°27·9'	1°20·7'W	FM	140
Lodge Fm	Warw	SP5068	52°18·7'	1°15·6'W	FM	151
Lodge Fm	W Berks	SU2977	51°29·7'	1°34·5'W	FM	174
Lodge Fm	W Berks	SU6166	51°23·6'	1°7·0'W	FM	175
Lodge Fm	Wilts	ST9076	51°29·2'	2°8·3'W	FM	173
Lodge Fm	Wilts	ST9984	51°33·5'	2°0·5'W	FM	173
Lodge Fm	Wilts	SU0422	51°0·1'	1°56·2'W	FM	184
Lodge Fm	Worcs	SO6366	52°17·7'	2°32·2'W	FM	138,149
Lodge Fm	Worcs	SO8341	52°4·3'	2°14·5'W	FM	150
Lodge Fm	Worcs	SO9740	52°3·7'	2°2·2'W	FM	150
Lodge Fm	Worcs	SP0372	52°21·0'	1°57·0'W	FM	139
Lodge Fm	Wrex	SJ2939	52°56·9'	3°3·0'W	FM	126
Lodge Fm	Wrex	SJ3854	53°5·0'	2°55·1'W	FM	117
Lodge Fm	Wrex	SJ4938	52°56·5'	2°45·1'W	FM	126
Lodge Fm	W Susx	SU7612	50°54·4'	0°54·8'W	FM	197
Lodge Fm	W Susx	TQ1622	50°59·4'	0°20·4'W	FM	198
Lodge Fm	W Susx	TQ3023	50°59·7'	0°8·5'W	FM	198
Lodge Fm	W Susx	TQ3114	50°54·9'	0°7·8'W	FM	198
Lodge Fm	York	SE6851	53°57·3'	0°57·4'W	FM	105,106
Lodge Fm, The	Leic	SK6417	52°45·0'	1°2·7'W	FM	129
Lodge Fm, The	Northnts	SP7789	52°29·8'	0°51·5'W	FM	141
Lodgegill	D & G	NY4190	55°12·3'	2°55·2'W	X	79
Lodgegill Sike	Cumbr	NY7830	54°40·1'	2°20·0'W	W	91
Lodge Green	N Yks	SD9598	54°22·9'	2°4·2'W	T	98
Lodge Green	Sol	SP2583	52°26·9'	1°37·5'W	T	140
Lodge Hags	N Yks	NY8002	54°25·0'	2°18·1'W	X	91,92
Lodge Hall	N Yks	SD7877	54°11·5'	2°19·8'W	X	98
Lodge Heath	Suff	TL7678	52°22·5'	0°35·5'E	X	143
Lodge Heath	Suff	TL7778	52°22·5'	0°36·4'E	X	144
Lodge Hill	Birm	SP0282	52°26·4'	1°57·8'W	T	139
Lodge Hill	Bucks	SP7900	51°41·8'	0°51·0'W	H	165
Lodge Hill	Bucks	SP8406	51°45·0'	0°46·6'W	X	165
Lodge Hill	Corn	SX2463	50°26·7'	4°28·4'W	T	201
Lodge Hill	Cumbr	NY4768	55°0·5'	2°49·3'W	X	86
Lodge Hill	E Susx	TQ4202	50°48·2'	0°1·3'E	X	198
Lodge Hill	Herts	TL3129	51°56·9'	0°5·2'W	X	166
Lodge Hill	Lancs	SD9237	53°50·0'	2°6·9'W	X	103
Lodge Hill	Medway	TQ7574	51°26·5'	0°31·5'E	X	178
Lodge Hill	N Yks	NZ7803	54°25·2'	0°47·5'W	X	94
Lodge Hill	N Yks	SE6035	53°48·7'	1°4·9'W	X	105
Lodge Hill	Poole	SZ0295	50°45·5'	1°57·9'W	X	195
Lodge Hill	Scot Bord	NT3808	55°22·0'	2°58·3'W	H	79
Lodge Hill	Shrops	SJ7405	52°38·8'	2°22·7'W	H	127
Lodge Hill	Shrops	SO5199	52°35·4'	2°43·0'W	H	137,138
Lodgehill	S Lanak	NS6653	55°45·4'	4°7·7'W	X	64
Lodge Hill	S Lanak	NS9718	55°27·0'	3°37·3'W	X	78
Lodge Hill	Somer	ST4948	51°14·0'	2°43·4'W	H	182,183
Lodge Hill	Somer	ST6431	51°5·0'	2°30·5'W	H	183
Lodge Hill	Surrey	TQ1852	51°15·5'	0°18·1'W	X	187
Lodge Hill	Wakf	SE2821	53°41·3'	1°34·1'W	T	104
Lodgehill Cottage	Hants	SU3109	50°53·0'	1°33·2'W	X	196
Lodge Hill Fm	Bucks	SU7998	51°40·7'	0°51·0'W	FM	165
Lodge Hill Fm	Derby	SK2134	52°54·4'	1°40·9'W	FM	128
Lodge Hill Fm	Derby	SK3752	53°4·1'	1°26·5'W	FM	119
Lodge Hill Fm	Devon	SS9411	50°53·6'	3°30·0'W	FM	192
Lodge Hill Fm	E Susx	TQ6229	51°2·5'	0°19·0'E	FM	188,199
Lodge Hill Fm	Norf	TF6634	52°52·9'	0°28·4'E	FM	132
Lodgehill Fm	Shrops	SJ7406	52°39·3'	2°22·7'W	FM	127
Lodge Hill Fm	Somer	ST6945	51°12·4'	2°26·2'W	FM	183
Lodge Hill Fm	Somer	ST8148	51°14·1'	2°15·9'W	FM	183
Lodge Hill Fm	Worcs	SO7676	52°23·1'	2°20·8'W	FM	138
Lodge Hill Fm	W Susx	SU8413	50°54·8'	0°47·9'W	FM	197
Lodge Hills	Essex	TL9232	51°57·4'	0°48·1'E	X	168
Lodge Ho	Kent	TR0839	51°7·0'	0°58·7'E	X	179,189
Lodgehouse Fm	Dorset	SY4097	50°46·4'	2°50·7'W	FM	193
Lodge House Fm	Durham	NZ1442	54°46·6'	1°46·5'W	FM	88
Lodge Inclosure	Hants	SU7942	51°10·5'	0°51·8'W	F	186
Lodge Island	D & G	NX7361	54°55·9'	3°58·5'W	X	83,84
Lodgeland Fm	Kent	TR0329	51°1·7'	0°54·1'E	FM	189
Lodgelands	W Susx	TQ3031	51°4·0'	0°8·3'W	X	187
Lodge Lees	Kent	TR2047	51°11·0'	1°9·3'E	T	179,189
Lodge Lower Barn	Wilts	SU2475	51°28·6'	1°38·9'W	X	174
Lodge Marsh	Norf	TF9245	52°58·3'	0°52·0'E	W	132
Lodge Moor	N Yks	SE0174	54°10·0'	1°58·7'W	X	98
Lodge Moor	Sheff	SK2885	53°21·9'	1°34·3'W	T	110
Lodge Mount	Staffs	SJ7812	52°42·6'	2°19·1'W	X	127
Lodge of Kelton	D & G	NX7460	54°55·4'	3°57·5'W	X	83,84
Lodge on the Wolds	Notts	SK6531	52°52·6'	1°1·6'W	X	129
Lodge Park	Cered	SN6693	52°31·3'	3°58·1'W	X	135
Lodge Park	Glos	SP1412	51°48·6'	1°47·4'W	X	163
Lodge Park	Worcs	SP0466	52°17·8'	1°56·1'W	T	150
Lodge Place	Kent	TQ9639	51°7·2'	0°48·4'E	X	189
Lodge Plantn	Norf	TG0634	52°52·1'	1°4·0'E	F	133
Lodge Plantn	Scot Bord	NT4111	55°23·6'	2°55·5'W	F	79
Lodge Pond	Hants	SU8142	51°10·5'	0°50·1'W	W	186
Lodges	Cumbr	NY5963	54°57·8'	2°38·0'W	X	86
Lodges Barn	Glos	SO5507	51°45·8'	2°38·7'W	X	162
Lodges Fm	Glos	SO5407	51°45·8'	2°39·6'W	FM	162
Lodge Side	N Yks	NY8202	54°25·0'	2°16·2'W	X	91,92
Lodge, The	Arg & Bt	NM0447	56°31·6'	6°48·4'W	X	46
Lodge, The	Arg & Bt	NM2157	56°37·6'	6°32·5'W	X	46,47
Lodge, The	Arg & Bt	NS1998	56°8·7'	4°54·4'W	X	56
Lodge, The	Beds	TL1847	52°6·8'	0°16·2'W	X	153
Lodge, The	Ches	SJ4747	53°1·3'	2°47·0'W	X	117
Lodge, The	Cumbr	NY4318	54°33·5'	2°52·5'W	X	90
Lodge, The	Derby	SK0999	53°29·5'	1°51·5'W	X	110
Lodge, The	Devon	SS8519	50°57·8'	3°37·9'W	X	181
Lodge, The	Essex	TL6329	51°56·4'	0°22·7'E	X	167
Lodge, The	Essex	TM1119	51°50·0'	1°4·1'E	X	168,169
Lodge, The	Hants	SU3801	50°48·7'	1°27·3'W	X	196
Lodge, The	Heref	SO4746	52°6·8'	2°46·0'W	X	148,149
Lodge, The	Leic	SK4826	52°50·0'	1°16·8'W	X	129
Lodge, The	Leic	SK6219	52°46·1'	1°4·5'W	X	129
Lodge, The	Leic	SK7627	52°50·3'	0°51·9'W	X	129
Lodge, The	Leic	SP5887	52°28·9'	1°8·4'W	X	140
Lodge, The	Lincs	SK9632	52°52·8'	0°34·0'W	X	130
Lodge, The	N Ayr	NR9350	55°42·2'	5°17·2'W	X	62,69
Lodge, The	Norf	TF7607	52°38·2'	0°36·5'E	X	143
Lodge, The	Norf	TF9002	52°35·2'	0°48·7'E	X	144
Lodge, The	Norf	TG1801	52°34·0'	1°13·4'E	X	134
Lodge, The	Norf	TG2030	52°49·6'	1°16·3'E	X	133
Lodge, The	Norf	TG3310	52°38·5'	1°27·0'E	X	133,134
Lodge, The	Northnts	SP5776	52°23·0'	1°9·4'W	X	140
Lodge, The	Northnts	SP8956	52°11·9'	0°41·5'W	X	152
Lodge, The	N Yks	SE9985	54°15·3'	0°28·4'W	X	94,101
Lodge, The	Oxon	SP3827	51°56·6'	1°26·4'W	X	164
Lodge,The	Peterb	TF1308	52°39·7'	0°19·3'W	X	142
Lodge, The	Scot Bord	NT4343	55°40·9'	2°54·0'W	X	73
Lodge, The	Shrops	SJ5642	52°58·7'	2°38·9'W	X	117
Lodge, The	Shrops	SO6071	52°20·4'	2°34·8'W	X	138
Lodge, The	Suff	TL9057	52°10·9'	0°47·2'E	X	155
Lodge, The	Suff	TL9877	52°21·5'	0°54·9'E	X	144
Lodge, The	Suff	TM1074	52°19·7'	1°5·3'E	X	144
Lodge, The	Suff	TM3344	52°2·9'	1°24·3'E	X	169
Lodge, The	Wrex	SJ4742	52°58·6'	2°47·0'W	X	117
Lodge Wood	Bucks	SP8601	51°42·3'	0°44·9'W	F	165
Lodge Wood	E Susx	TQ4419	50°57·4'	0°3·4'E	F	198
Lodge Wood	Leeds	SE2137	53°50·0'	1°40·4'W	F	104
Lodge Wood	Newp	ST3291	51°37·1'	2°58·5'W	F	171
Lodge Wood	Red & Cl	NZ6916	54°32·3'	0°55·6'W	F	94
Lodge Wood	Scot Bord	NT7358	55°49·1'	2°25·4'W	F	67,74
Lodge Wood	Suff	TM2865	52°14·4'	1°20·8'E	F	156
Lodge Wood	Suff	TM3572	52°18·0'	1°27·2'E	F	156
Lodge Wood	Warw	SP2863	52°16·1'	1°35·0'W	F	151
Lodgeworthy	Devon	SS2702	50°47·7'	4°26·9'W	X	190
Lodgey Cross	Devon	SS6112	50°53·7'	3°58·2'W	X	180
Lodhdrum	Highld	NH2575	57°44·1'	4°55·9'W	X	20

Lodmoor	Dorset	SY6881	50°37·9'	2°26·8'W	X	194
Lodor	Pemb	SN0430	51°56·3'	4°50·7'W	X	145,157
Lodore Falls	Cumbr	NY2618	54°33·4'	3°8·2'W	W	89,90
Lodsworth	W Susx	SU9223	51°0·2'	0°40·9'W	T	197
Lodsworth Common	W Susx	SU9224	51°0·7'	0°40·9'W	T	197
Lodway	N Som	ST5276	51°29·1'	2°41·1'W	T	172
Loe Bar	Corn	SW6424	50°4·4'	5°17·5'W	X	203
Loe Beach	Corn	SW8238	50°12·3'	5°2·9'W	X	204
Loedebest	Highld	ND1332	58°16·3'	3°28·5'W	X	11,17
Loe, The	Corn	SW6424	50°4·4'	5°17·5'W	W	203
Loe Valley	Corn	SW6526	50°5·5'	5°16·8'W	X	203
Lofshaw Hill	Cumbr	NY3827	54°38·3'	2°57·2'W	H	90
Loft Hall	Essex	TQ5396	51°38·7'	0°13·1'E	X	167,177
Lofthall Fm	Thurr	TQ6581	51°30·5'	0°23·1'E	FM	177,178
Loft Hill	Northum	NT8513	55°24·9'	2°13·8'W	H	80
Loft Hill	Northum	NT8725	55°31·4'	2°11·9'W	H	74
Lofthillock	Aberd	NJ7822	57°17·5'	2°21·4'W	X	38
Loft Ho	Durham	NZ1555	54°53·6'	1°45·5'W	X	88
Lofthouse	Leeds	SE3325	53°43·5'	1°29·6'W	T	104
Lofthouse	N Yks	SE1073	54°9·4'	1°50·4'W	T	99
Lofthouse Fm	Leeds	SE3243	53°53·2'	1°30·4'W	FM	104
Lofthouse Gate	Wakf	SE3324	53°42·9'	1°29·6'W	T	104
Lofthouse Grange	Leeds	SE3243	53°53·2'	1°30·4'W	X	104
Lofthouse Hill	Wakf	SE3325	53°43·5'	1°29·6'W	X	104
Lofthouse Moor	N Yks	SE1176	54°11·0'	1°49·5'W	X	99
Loftmans Fm	Essex	TQ9193	51°36·4'	0°45·9'E	FM	178
Loftrans	Lancs	SD8251	53°57·5'	2°16·0'W	X	103
Lofts	Essex	TL8609	51°45·2'	0°42·1'E	X	168
Lofts Hall	Essex	TL4638	52°1·5'	0°8·1'E	X	154
Loftshaw Brook	Barns	SK1599	53°29·5'	1°46·0'W	W	110
Loftshaw Brow	Cumbr	SD6884	54°15·3'	2°29·1'W	X	98
Loftshaw Gill Head	N Yks	SE1152	53°58·1'	1°49·5'W	X	104
Loftshaw Moss	Lancs	SD6766	54°5·6'	2°29·9'W	X	98
Loft Shaws	D & G	NY1694	55°14·2'	3°18·8'W	H	79
Loft Skew	N Yks	SE0793	54°20·2'	1°53·1'W	X	99
Loftsome Br	E Yorks	SE7030	53°45·9'	0°55·9'W	X	105,106
Lofts, The	Lincs	TF2978	53°17·2'	0°3·5'W	A	122
Loft, The	N Yks	SE4748	53°55·8'	1°16·6'W	F	105
Loftus	Red & Cl	NZ7118	54°33·4'	0°53·7'W	T	94
Loftus Hill	N Yks	SE3761	54°2·9'	1°25·7'W	X	99
Logan	D & G	NX0942	54°44·5'	4°57·6'W	X	82
Logan	E Ayr	NS5425	55°30·1'	4°18·3'W	X	70
Logan	E Ayr	NS5920	55°27·5'	4°13·4'W	T	71
Loganbank	Midlo	NT2462	55°51·0'	3°12·4'W	X	66
Logan Beck	Cumbr	SD1790	54°18·2'	3°16·1'W	W	96
Loganbeck	Cumbr	SD1890	54°18·2'	3°15·2'W	X	96
Logan Burn	D & G	NY3073	55°3·0'	3°5·3'W	W	85
Logan Burn	E Ayr	NS5634	55°35·0'	4°16·6'W	W	71
Logan Burn	Midlo	NT1761	55°50·4'	3°19·1'W	W	65,66
Logan Burn	Midlo	NT2063	55°51·5'	3°16·2'W	W	66
Logan Cott	Midlo	NT2063	55°51·5'	3°16·2'W	X	66
Logan Cott	Scot Bord	NT1028	55°32·5'	3°25·1'W	X	72
Logan Craig	Scot Bord	NT1332	55°34·7'	3°22·4'W	H	72
Logan Fm	S Lanak	NS7335	55°35·8'	4°0·5'W	FM	71
Loganhead	D & G	NY2986	55°10·0'	3°6·4'W	X	79
Logan Head	Scot Bord	NT1332	55°34·7'	3°22·4'W	H	72
Loganhill	E Ayr	NS5818	55°26·4'	4°14·2'W	X	71
Logan Ho	Midlo	NT2063	55°51·5'	3°16·2'W	X	66
Loganhouse	D & G	NY3073	55°3·0'	3°5·3'W	X	85
Loganlea	W Loth	NS9862	55°50·7'	3°37·3'W	T	65
Loganlea Resr	Midlo	NT1962	55°50·9'	3°17·2'W	W	65,66
Logan Mains	D & G	NX0943	54°45·0'	4°57·6'W	X	82
Logan Mains	D & G	NY3073	55°3·0'	3°5·3'W	X	85
Logan Mills	D & G	NX1143	54°45·0'	4°55·8'W	X	82
Logan Moss	D & G	NX0943	54°45·0'	4°57·6'W	X	82
Logan Moss	E Ayr	NS5733	55°34·4'	4°15·7'W	X	71
Logan Reservoir	S Lanak	NS7435	55°35·8'	3°59·5'W	W	71
Logan Rock	Corn	SW3922	50°2·7'	5°38·4'W	X	203
Logan Rock	Corn	SX1380	50°35·6'	4°38·2'W	X	200
Logan Rock	Corn	SX1480	50°35·6'	4°37·3'W	X	200
Logan Rock	Devon	SX5687	50°40·1'	4°1·9'W	X	191
Logan Stone	Corn	SW4638	50°11·5'	5°33·2'W	X	203
Logan Stone	Corn	SX0661	50°25·2'	4°43·5'W	X	200
Logan Stone	Devon	SX5587	50°40·1'	4°2·7'W	X	191
Logan Stone	Devon	SX5771	50°31·5'	4°0·7'W	X	202
Logan Stone	Devon	SX7276	50°34·4'	3°48·1'W	X	191
Logan Stone	Devon	SX7475	50°33·9'	3°46·4'W	X	191
Logan Stone	Devon	SX7578	50°35·5'	3°45·6'W	X	191
Loganswell Fm	E Renf	NS5152	55°44·6'	4°22·0'W	FM	64
Logan Water	D & G	NY3184	55°9·0'	3°4·5'W	W	79
Logan Water	S Lanak	NS7437	55°36·9'	3°59·6'W	W	71
Logaston	Heref	SO3451	52°9·4'	2°57·5'W	X	148,149
Log Church	Essex	TL5303	51°42·5'	0°13·3'E	X	167
Loggans Moor	Corn	SW5738	50°11·8'	5°23·9'W	X	203
Loggerheads	Denb	SJ1862	53°9·2'	3°13·2'W	T	116
Loggerheads	Staffs	SJ7336	52°55·5'	2°23·7'W	T	127
Loggerheads Country Park	Denb	SJ1962	53°9·2'	3°12·3'W	X	116
Logg Fm	Oxon	SP5514	51°49·5'	1°11·7'W	FM	164
Loggie	Highld	NH1490	57°51·9'	5°7·7'W	X	20
Logg Wood	Aberd	NJ6447	57°31·0'	2°35·6'W	F	29
Log Ho, The	Hants	SZ4097	50°46·5'	1°25·6'W	X	196
Logie	Aberd	NJ7960	57°38·0'	2°20·6'W	X	29,30
Logie	Aberd	NJ8740	57°27·3'	2°12·5'W	X	30
Logie	Aberd	NO8888	56°59·2'	2°11·4'W	X	45
Logie	Angus	NO3952	56°39·6'	2°59·3'W	X	54
Logie	Angus	NO6963	56°45·7'	2°30·0'W	T	45
Logie	Fife	NO4020	56°22·4'	2°57·8'W	T	54,59
Logie	Highld	NH9646	57°29·8'	3°43·7'W	X	27
Logie	Moray	NJ0150	57°32·0'	3°38·7'W	T	27
Logiealmond	Pth & Kin	NN9930	56°27·3'	3°37·9'W	X	52,53
Logiealmond Lodge	Pth & Kin	NN9631	56°27·8'	3°40·8'W	X	52,53
Logie Aulton	Aberd	NJ6638	57°26·1'	2°33·5'W	X	29
Logiebank	S Lanak	NT0946	55°42·2'	3°26·4'W	X	72
Logiebrae	Pth & Kin	NO1143	56°34·5'	3°26·5'W	X	53
Logiebride	Pth & Kin	NO0434	56°29·6'	3°33·1'W	X	52,53
Logiebuchany	Moray	NH9855	57°34·7'	3°41·9'W	X	27
Logieburn	Moray	NJ2656	57°35·5'	3°13·8'W	X	28
Logie Coldstone	Aberd	NJ4304	57°7·7'	2°56·0'W	T	37
Logie Durno	Aberd	NJ7026	57°19·7'	2°29·4'W	X	38
Logie Durno Church	Aberd	NJ7026	57°19·7'	2°29·4'W	A	38
Logiefair	Aberd	NJ8061	57°38·6'	2°19·6'W	X	29,30
Logie Fm	Aberd	NJ8615	57°13·8'	2°13·5'W	FM	38
Logie Fm	Fife	NO2820	56°22·3'	3°9·5'W	FM	53,59
Logie Head	Aberd	NJ5268	57°42·2'	2°47·9'W	X	29
Logie Hill	Highld	NH7676	57°45·7'	4°4·6'W	T	21
Logie Hill	Shetld	HU4366	60°22·8'	1°12·7'W	H	2,3
Logie Ho	Aberd	NJ5267	57°41·7'	2°47·9'W	X	29
Logie Ho	Fife	NO4020	56°22·4'	2°57·8'W	X	54,59
Logie Ho	Fife	NT0786	56°3·7'	3°29·2'W	X	65
Logie House	Aberd	NJ7025	57°19·1'	2°29·4'W	A	38
Logie House	Moray	NJ0050	57°32·0'	3°39·8'W	X	27
Logie Mill	Angus	NO6963	56°45·7'	2°30·0'W	X	45
Logie Newton	Aberd	NJ6638	57°26·1'	2°33·5'W	X	29
Logie Pert	Angus	NO6664	56°46·2'	2°32·9'W	T	45
Logierait	Pth & Kin	NN9751	56°38·6'	3°40·3'W	T	52,53
Logierait Wood	Pth & Kin	NN9554	56°40·2'	3°42·4'W	F	52,53
Logierieve Ho	Aberd	NJ9226	57°19·7'	2°7·5'W	X	38
Logieside	Highld	NH5252	57°32·3'	4°27·9'W	X	26
Logie Villa	Stir	NS8296	56°8·8'	3°53·5'W	X	57
Login	Carm	SN1623	51°52·8'	4°40·0'W	T	145,158
Login	Cered	SN2050	52°7·4'	4°37·4'W	X	145
Login	Powys	SO0042	52°4·3'	3°27·1'W	X	147,160
Login Fm	Swan	SS6194	51°37·9'	4°0·1'W	FM	159
Logmore Green	Surrey	TQ1447	51°12·9'	0°21·7'W	T	187
Lognaha Fm	Highld	NN0056	56°39·4'	5°15·3'W	FM	41
Logoch	S Lanak	NS6345	55°41·0'	4°10·3'W	X	64
Logshayne Fm	Devon	SY2396	50°45·7'	3°5·1'W	FM	192,193
Loidse Ath Linne	N Eil	NB1912	58°0·8'	6°45·0'W	X	13,14
Loidse Ghriais	N Eil	NB4941	58°17·4'	6°16·5'W	X	8
Loidse Shòbhail	N Eil	NB3424	58°7·8'	6°30·6'W	X	13,14
Loig	Pth & Kin	NN8107	56°14·7'	3°54·8'W	X	57
Loin-a-veaich	Aberd	NO0888	56°58·7'	3°30·4'W	X	43
Loinherry	Aberd	NJ2409	57°10·2'	3°15·0'W	X	36
Loinmarstaig	Pth & Kin	NN9365	56°46·1'	3°44·6'W	X	43
Loinnbuie	Highld	NH8280	57°47·9'	3°58·7'W	X	21
Loinveg	Aberd	NO3193	57°1·6'	3°7·7'W	X	37,44
Loin Water	Arg & Bt	NN3006	56°13·2'	4°44·1'W	W	56
Loirston Country Park	C of Aber	NJ9302	57°6·8'	2°6·5'W	X	38
Loirston Loch	C of Aber	NJ9301	57°6·3'	2°6·5'W	W	38
Lois Weedon Ho	Northnts	SP6047	52°7·3'	1°7·0'W	X	152
Lokati Kame	Shetld	HU3891	60°36·3'	1°17·9'W	X	1,2
Lolham Bridges	Peterb	TF1106	52°38·7'	0°21·2'W	X	142
Lolham Hall	Peterb	TF1107	52°39·2'	0°21·1'W	X	142
Lollesworth Fm	Surrey	TQ0854	51°16·7'	0°26·7'W	FM	187
Lollingdon Fm	Oxon	SU5785	51°33·9'	1°10·3'W	FM	174
Lollingdon Hill	Oxon	SU5685	51°33·9'	1°11·1'W	H	174
Lolworth	Cambs	TL3664	52°15·7'	0°0·0'W	T	154
Lomans Fm	Devon	SX8065	50°28·6'	3°41·1'W	FM	202
Lombard Fm	Corn	SX1353	50°21·1'	4°37·3'W	FM	200
Lomberdale Hall	Derby	SK1963	53°10·1'	1°42·5'W	X	119
Lomber Hey Ho	Stock	SJ9586	53°22·5'	2°4·1'W	X	109
Lomer Fm	Hants	SU5823	51°0·4'	1°10·0'W	FM	185
Lomer Fm	Kent	TQ6465	51°21·8'	0°21·7'E	FM	177
Lomer Village	Hants	SU5923	51°0·4'	1°9·2'W	A	185
Lomeshaye	Lancs	SD8437	53°50·0'	2°14·2'W	T	103
Lomond Hills	Fife	NO2206	56°14·7'	3°15·1'W	H	58
Lomondville	Pth & Kin	NO1505	56°14·1'	3°21·8'W	X	58
Lôn	Denb	SJ0362	53°9·0'	3°26·6'W	X	116
Lôn	Gwyn	SH8831	52°52·1'	3°39·4'W	X	124,125
Lôn	Powys	SO0267	52°17·8'	3°25·8'W	X	136,147
Lonach	Aberd	NJ3210	57°10·8'	3°7·0'W	X	37
Lòn a' Chleirich	Highld	NG2749	57°27·2'	6°32·6'W	X	23
Lòn a' Ghlinne Bhig	Highld	NG4045	57°25·5'	6°19·4'W	W	23
Lòn Airigh an Aonaich	Arg & Bt	NM6629	56°24·0'	5°47·1'W	X	49
Lòn Airigh-uige	Highld	NG4363	57°35·3'	6°17·6'W	W	23
Lòn a' Mhuilinn	Highld	NG4765	57°36·5'	6°13·7'W	W	23
Lòn an Eireannaich	Highld	NG4347	57°26·7'	6°16·5'W	W	23
Lonan Ho	Arg & Bt	NM9929	56°24·9'	5°15·1'W	X	49
Lòn an t-Stratha	Highld	NG4261	57°34·2'	6°18·4'W	W	23
Lòn Bad a' Mhàil	Highld	NC8655	58°28·4'	3°56·8'W	W	10
Lonbain	Highld	NG6853	57°30·7'	5°52·0'W	T	24
Lonban	Arg & Bt	NM1756	56°36·9'	6°36·3'W	X	46
Lòn Bàn	Arg & Bt	NM6037	56°28·1'	5°53·3'W	X	49
Lòn Bàn	Arg & Bt	NR3158	55°44·7'	6°16·7'W	X	60
Lòn Bàn	Arg & Bt	NR3367	55°49·6'	6°15·4'W	X	60,61
Lòn Bàn	Arg & Bt	NR5065	55°49·1'	5°59·0'W	X	61
Lòn Bàn	Highld	NG1643	57°23·6'	6°43·2'W	X	23
Lòn Bàn	Highld	NG3332	57°18·3'	6°25·5'W	X	32
Lòn Bàn	Highld	NG3632	57°18·4'	6°22·6'W	X	32
Lòn Bàn	Highld	NG4318	57°11·1'	6°14·7'W	X	32
Lòn Bàn	Highld	NG4940	57°23·1'	6°10·1'W	W	23
Lon Bàn	N Eil	NB3124	58°7·7'	6°33·7'W	W	13,14
Lonbarn	Essex	TM1530	51°55·8'	1°8·0'E	X	168,169
Lòn Beatha	Highld	NG3351	57°28·5'	6°26·8'W	W	23
Lòn Beinne Thuaith	Highld	NG4252	57°29·4'	6°17·9'W	W	23
Lòn Beinn Iadain	Highld	NM6954	56°37·5'	5°45·5'W	X	49
Lòn Bhearnuis	Arg & Bt	NM3941	56°29·6'	6°14·0'W	W	47,48
Lòn Biolaireach	Arg & Bt	NM5043	56°31·0'	6°3·4'W	X	47,48
Lòn Bota Meanachain	Highld	NG4166	57°36·8'	6°19·7'W	W	23
Lòn Broach	Arg & Bt	NR4164	55°48·2'	6°7·6'W	X	60,61
Lòn Buidhe	Highld	NG6517	57°11·3'	5°52·9'W	X	32
Lòn Buidhe	Highld	NG7832	57°19·7'	5°40·8'W	W	24
Lonbuie	Highld	NH4841	57°26·3'	4°31·5'W	X	26
Lòn Chaorach	Highld	NG4836	57°21·0'	6°10·9'W	W	23,32
Lòn Cleap	Highld	NG4767	57°37·6'	6°13·8'W	W	23
Lonco Brook	Staffs	SJ7522	52°47·9'	2°21·8'W	W	127
Lòn Creadha	Highld	NG6816	57°10·8'	5°49·9'W	W	32
Londesborough	E Yorks	SE8645	53°53·9'	0°41·1'W	T	106
Londesborough Field	E Yorks	SE8646	53°54·4'	0°41·0'W	X	106
Londesborough Lodge	York	SE6952	53°57·8'	0°56·5'W	X	105,106
Londesborough Park	E Yorks	SE8745	53°53·9'	0°40·1'W	X	106
Londesborough Wold	E Yorks	SE8847	53°54·9'	0°39·2'W	X	106
Lòn Doire nan Eala	Highld	NG7771	57°40·7'	5°43·9'W	W	19
London	C of Lon	TQ3181	51°31·0'	0°6·3'W	T	176,177
London Apprentice	Corn	SX0050	50°19·2'	4°48·2'W	T	200,204
London Barn Fm	E Susx	TQ7128	51°1·8'	0°26·7'E	FM	188,199
London Beach	Kent	TQ8836	51°5·8'	0°41·5'E	T	189
London Br	C of Lon	TQ3280	51°30·4'	0°5·5'W	X	176,177
London Bridge	Torbay	SX9262	50°27·1'	3°30·9'W	X	202
London Br Sta	Sthwk	TQ3380	51°30·4'	0°4·6'W	X	176,177
London Colney	Herts	TL1704	51°43·6'	0°18·0'W	T	166
Londonderry	N Yks	SE3087	54°16·9'	1°31·9'W	T	99
Londonderry	Sand	SP0087	52°29·1'	1°59·6'W	T	139
Londonderry Fm	E Susx	TQ4429	51°2·8'	0°3·6'E	FM	187,198
London End	Cambs	TL0968	52°18·2'	0°23·7'W	T	153
London Fields	Dudley	SO9290	52°30·7'	2°6·7'W	T	139
London Fm	I of W	SZ4389	50°42·2'	1°23·1'W	FM	196
London Fm	Somer	ST1533	51°5·6'	3°12·4'W	FM	181
London Hayes	Essex	TQ8799	51°39·7'	0°42·6'E	X	168
London Hill	Hants	SU2945	51°12·4'	1°34·7'W	X	185
London Ho	N Yks	NZ7403	54°25·3'	0°51·2'W	X	94
London Lode Hall	Norf	TL5299	52°34·3'	0°15·0'E	X	143
London Lodge	Leic	SP5782	52°26·2'	1°9·3'W	X	140
London Minstead	Hants	SU2811	50°54·1'	1°35·7'W	T	195
London Ride	Wilts	SU2566	51°23·8'	1°38·0'W	X	174
London Stansted Airport	Essex	TL5322	51°52·8'	0°13·8'E	X	167
London Stone	Medway	TQ8678	51°28·4'	0°41·1'E	X	178
Londonthorpe	Lincs	SK9537	52°55·6'	0°34·8'W	T	130
Lòn Dornaich	Highld	NH7494	57°55·3'	4°7·2'W	X	21
Lòn Druim nan Cliar	Highld	NC5058	58°29·3'	4°33·9'W	W	9
Lòn Dubh	Highld	NG4142	57°23·9'	6°18·2'W	W	23
Lòn Dubh	Highld	NG4547	57°26·8'	6°14·6'W	W	23
Londubh	Highld	NG8681	57°46·3'	5°35·4'W	T	19
Lòn Dubh	N Eil	NF8440	57°20·7'	7°14·8'W	W	22
Lòn Duriseach	Highld	NG4947	57°26·9'	6°10·6'W	W	23
Lone	Highld	NC3042	58°20·3'	4°53·8'W	X	9
Lone Barn	Brom	TQ4866	51°22·6'	0°8·0'E	X	177
Lone Barn	Hants	SU5031	51°4·8'	1°16·8'W	X	185
Lone Barn	Hants	SU5740	51°9·6'	1°10·7'W	X	185
Lone Barn	Oxon	SP5528	51°57·1'	1°11·6'W	X	164
Lone Barn	Surrey	SU9446	51°12·6'	0°38·9'W	X	186
Lone Barn Fm	Kent	TR0037	51°6·1'	0°51·8'E	FM	189
Lone Fm	Hants	SU5334	51°6·4'	1°14·2'W	FM	185
Lone Fm	Hants	SU5641	51°10·2'	1°11·6'W	FM	185
Lone Hill	Highld	NH0849	57°29·7'	5°11·8'W	H	27
Lonely Fm	Suff	TM3665	52°14·2'	1°27·8'E	FM	156
Lonemore	Highld	NG7877	57°43·9'	5°43·3'W	T	19
Lonemore	Highld	NH7688	57°52·1'	4°5·0'W	T	21
Lone Oak Hall	E Susx	TQ4732	51°4·3'	0°6·3'E	X	188
Lone Sheiling	Stir	NN6002	56°11·7'	4°14·9'W	X	57
Lonesome Fm	Oxon	SU6288	51°35·5'	1°5·9'W	FM	175
Lonesome Fm	Surrey	TQ2646	51°12·2'	0°11·4'W	FM	187
Lone Tree (PH), The	Bucks	SP7333	51°59·7'	0°55·8'W	X	152,165
Lonfearn	Highld	NG5162	57°35·0'	6°9·5'W	X	23,24
Lòn Fhiodha	Highld	NH0636	57°22·7'	5°13·2'W	W	25
Longa Berg	Shetld	HU3041	60°9·4'	1°27·1'W	X	4
Longa Berg	Shetld	HU3520	59°58·1'	1°21·9'W	X	4
Long Acre	Denb	SJ0479	53°18·2'	3°26·0'W	X	116
Long Acre Fm	Ghead	NZ2657	54°54·7'	1°35·2'W	FM	88
Long Acres Fm	N Yks	SE5490	54°18·4'	1°9·8'W	FM	100
Longaford Tor	Devon	SX6177	50°34·8'	3°57·4'W	H	191
Longage Fm	Kent	TR1541	51°7·9'	1°4·8'E	FM	179,189
Longa Geo	Shetld	HP5708	60°45·3'	0°56·7'W	X	1
Longa Geo	Shetld	HU4335	60°6·1'	1°13·1'W	X	4
Longa Island	Highld	NG7377	57°43·8'	5°48·3'W	X	19
Longaller	Somer	ST1925	51°1·4'	3°8·9'W	X	181,193
Longa Ness	Shetld	HU2858	60°18·6'	1°29·1'W	X	3
Longannet Point	Fife	NS9485	56°3·0'	3°41·7'W	X	65
Longariva	Shetld	HU6790	60°35·5'	0°46·1'W	X	1,2
Longart Forest	Highld	NH4067	57°40·1'	4°40·5'W	F	20
Long Ashes	Cumbr	NY4932	54°41·1'	2°47·0'W	X	90
Long Ashton	N Som	ST5470	51°25·9'	2°39·3'W	T	172
Longa Skerries	Shetld	HU6261	60°20·0'	0°52·1'W	X	2
Longa Skerry	Shetld	HU3785	60°33·1'	1°19·0'W	X	1,2,3
Longa Skerry	Shetld	HU4327	60°1·8'	1°13·2'W	X	4
Longa Skerry	Shetld	HU4432	60°4·5'	1°12·1'W	X	4
Longa Skerry	Shetld	HU5265	60°22·2'	1°2·9'W	X	2,3
Longa Skerry	Shetld	HU5374	60°27·0'	1°1·7'W	X	2,3
Longa Stacks	Shetld	HP5815	60°49·1'	0°55·5'W	X	1
Longa Taing	Shetld	HP5707	60°44·8'	0°56·8'W	X	1
Longa Tonga	Shetld	HU4978	60°29·2'	1°6·0'W	X	2,3
Longa Voe	Shetld	HU3159	60°19·1'	1°25·8'W	W	3
Longa Water	Shetld	HP6306	60°44·2'	0°50·2'W	W	1
Longa Water	Shetld	HU2656	60°17·5'	1°31·3'W	W	3
Longa Water	Shetld	HU4147	60°12·6'	1°15·1'W	W	3
Longa Water	Shetld	HU4366	60°22·8'	1°12·7'W	W	2,3
Longa Water	Shetld	HU4965	60°22·2'	1°6·2'W	W	2,3
Longay	Highld	NG6531	57°18·8'	5°53·7'W	X	24,32
Long Ayre	Orkney	HY4909	58°58·2'	2°52·7'W	X	6,7
Long Ayre	Shetld	HU3674	60°27·2'	1°20·2'W	X	2,3
Long Band	Cumbr	NY2812	54°30·1'	3°6·3'W	X	89,90
Long Bank	Aberd	NJ4532	57°22·8'	2°54·4'W	H	29,37
Longbank	Angus	NO4055	56°41·2'	2°58·3'W	X	54
Long Bank	Cumbr	SD6687	54°16·9'	2°30·9'W	X	98
Longbank	D & G	NX8783	55°8·0'	3°45·9'W	X	78
Longbank	D & G	NX9684	55°8·6'	3°37·5'W	X	78
Long Bank	Northum	NU2414	55°25·4'	1°36·8'W	X	81
Long Bank	N Yks	SD7365	54°5·1'	2°24·3'W	X	98
Long Bank	N Yks	SD8254	53°59·1'	2°16·1'W	X	103
Longbank	Scot Bord	NT8047	55°43·2'	2°18·7'W	X	74
Long Bank	Sefton	SD3124	53°42·7'	3°2·3'W	X	102
Long Bank	S Lanak	NS6834	55°35·2'	4°5·2'W	X	71
Longbank	Stir	NN7301	56°11·3'	4°2·3'W	X	57
Long Bank	Worcs	SO7674	52°22·0'	2°20·8'W	T	138
Long Bank Br	E Yorks	TA4016	53°37·5'	0°7·4'E	X	113
Long Bank Fm	Red & Cl	NZ5416	54°32·4'	1°9·5'W	FM	93
Long Bar	Cumbr	NY5980	55°7·0'	2°38·1'W	X	80
Long Bar	Devon	SS4441	51°9·1'	4°13·5'W	X	180
Longbar	N Ayr	NS3252	55°44·2'	4°40·1'W	T	63
Longbarn	Cumbr	SD5879	54°12·5'	2°38·2'W	X	97
Long Barn	Devon	SS8401	50°48·1'	3°38·4'W	X	191
Long Barn	Monm	SO3610	51°47·3'	2°55·3'W	X	161
Longbarn	Warr	SJ6390	53°24·6'	2°33·0'W	T	109
Longbarns	Essex	TL5710	51°46·2'	0°16·9'E	X	167
Long Barrow	Cumbr	NY0312	54°29·9'	3°29·4'W	H	89
Long Barrow	Cumbr	SD2464	54°4·2'	3°9·3'W	X	96
Longbarrow Cross Roads	Wilts	SU0941	51°10·3'	1°51·9'W	X	184
Long Batt	Northum	NU1241	55°40·0'	1°48·1'W	X	75
Long Bay	N Ayr	NS1452	55°43·8'	4°57·3'W	W	63,69
Longbeach	D & G	NX8575	55°3·6'	3°47·6'W	X	84

Long Beck	N Yks	SE5477	54°11·4′	1°9·9′W	W	100
Longbeck Station	Red & Cl	NZ6221	54°35·1′	1°2·0′W	X	94
Longbedholm	D & G	NT0506	55°20·6′	3°29·4′W	X	78
Longbedholm Hill	D & G	NT0505	55°20·0′	3°29·4′W	H	78
Long Beech Inclosure	Hants	SU2512	50°54·6′	1°38·3′W	F	195
Longbeech Wood	Kent	TQ9850	51°13·1′	0°50·5′E	F	189
Long Belt	Norf	TL9284	52°25·4′	0°49·8′E	F	144
Long Belt	Notts	SK6562	53°9·3′	1°1·3′W	F	120
Long Belt	Suff	TL7869	52°17·6′	0°37·0′E	F	155
Long Bennington	Lincs	SK8344	52°59·4′	0°45·4′W	T	130
Longbenton	N Tyne	NZ2668	55°0·6′	1°35·2′W	T	88
Longber	N Yks	SD6472	54°8·8′	2°32·7′W	X	97
Longberry Fm	Kent	TQ9441	51°8·3′	0°46·8′E	FM	189
Long Birch Fm	Staffs	SJ8705	52°38·8′	2°11·1′W	FM	127,139
Long Black Belt	Suff	TL7255	52°10·2′	0°31·3′E	F	154
Longbog	Aberd	NJ5920	57°16·4′	2°40·3′W	X	37
Longbog	Aberd	NJ8620	57°16·5′	2°13·5′W	X	38
Longborough	Glos	SP1729	51°57·8′	1°44·8′W	T	163
Long Bottom	Hants	SU1813	50°55·2′	1°44·2′W	X	195
Long Bottom	Surrey	SU8449	51°14·3′	0°47·4′W	X	186
Long Bottom	Wilts	ST8822	51°0·1′	2°9·9′W	X	183
Long Bottom	Wilts	ST9138	51°8·7′	2°7·3′W	X	184
Longbottom Fm	Somer	ST4556	51°18·3′	2°47·0′W	FM	172,182
Longbottom Fm	Wilts	SU3051	51°15·7′	1°33·8′W	FM	185
Long Breach	Devon	SS8131	51°4·2′	3°41·5′W	X	181
Long Bredy	Dorset	SY5690	50°42·7′	2°37·0′W	T	194
Longbridge	Birm	SP0177	52°23·7′	1°58·7′W	T	139
Longbridge	C of Plym	SX5157	50°23·9′	4°5·4′W	T	201
Longbridge	Warw	SP2662	52°15·6′	1°36·7′W	T	151
Longbridge Deverill	Wilts	ST8640	51°9·8′	2°11·6′W	T	183
Longbridge Hayes	Staffs	SJ8550	53°3·1′	2°13·0′W	T	118
Longbridge Muir	D & G	NY0569	55°0·6′	3°28·7′W	X	85
Longbridgemuir	D & G	NY0669	55°0·7′	3°27·8′W	X	85
Long Brook	Devon	SX6152	50°21·3′	3°56·9′W	W	202
Long Brook	Glos	SO7717	51°51·3′	2°19·6′W	W	162
Longbrook Fm	Devon	SX4179	50°35·6′	4°14·4′W	FM	201
Longbrooks Fm	Kent	TQ6843	51°9·9′	0°24·6′E	FM	188
Long Brow	Cumbr	NY3029	54°39·3′	3°4·7′W	X	90
Long Buckby	Northnts	SP6267	52°18·1′	1°5·0′W	T	152
Long Buckby Sta	Northnts	SP6266	52°17·6′	1°5·1′W	X	152
Long Buckby Wharf	Northnts	SP6165	52°17·0′	1°5·9′W	T	152
Longbull Hill	Wakf	SE4722	53°41·8′	1°16·9′W	X	105
Longburgh	Cumbr	NY3158	54°55·0′	3°4·2′W	T	85
Long Burgh	E Susx	TQ5003	50°48·6′	0°8·1′E	X	199
Long Burgh (Long Barrow)	E Susx	TQ5003	50°48·6′	0°8·1′E	A	199
Long Burn	Aberd	NJ4510	57°10·9′	2°54·1′W	W	37
Long Burn	Aberd	NJ4732	57°22·8′	2°52·4′W	W	29,37
Longburn	Cumbr	NY1849	54°50·0′	3°16·2′W	X	85
Long Burn	Scot Bord	NT7309	55°22·7′	2°25·1′W	W	80
Long Burn	S Lanak	NS8629	55°32·7′	3°48·0′W	W	71,72
Longburton	Dorset	ST6412	50°54·6′	2°30·3′W	T	194
Longbury	Dorset	ST7827	51°2·7′	2°18·4′W	X	183
Longbury (Long Barrow)	Dorset	ST7827	51°2·7′	2°18·4′W	A	183
Longbyre	Northum	NY6566	54°59·5′	2°32·4′W	X	86
Longcairn	C of Aber	NJ8407	57°9·5′	2°15·4′W	X	38
Long Cairn	Cumbr	NY5382	55°8·1′	2°43·8′W	A	79
Long Cairn	D & G	NX7279	55°5·6′	3°59·9′W	X	77,84
Long Cairn	D & G	NX8392	55°12·8′	3°49·9′W	A	78
Long Cairn	D & G	NY0498	55°16·3′	3°30·2′W	A	78
Long Cairn	Scot Bord	NY5286	55°10·2′	2°44·8′W	A	79
Long Cairn	Shetld	HU2451	60°14·8′	1°33·5′W	A	3
Long Carn	Corn	SW4136	50°10·3′	5°37·3′W	H	203
Longcarse	Clackm	NS8692	56°6·7′	3°49·6′W	X	58
Longcause	Devon	SX7961	50°26·4′	3°41·9′W	T	202
Long Causeway	N Yks	SE6599	54°23·2′	0°59·5′W	X	94,100
Long Causeway (Roman Road)	Sheff	SK2584	53°21·4′	1°37·1′W	R	110
Long Causeway, The	Lancs	SD8928	53°45·1′	2°9·6′W	A	103
Long Chimney	Devon	SY1791	50°43·0′	3°10·2′W	X	192,193
Long Chimneys	Derby	SK1339	52°57·1′	1°48·0′W	X	128
Long Churn Cave	N Yks	SD7775	54°10·5′	2°20·7′W	X	98
Long Clawson	Leic	SK7227	52°50·4′	0°55·5′W	T	129
Long Cleave	Midlo	NT3048	55°43·5′	3°6·4′W	X	73
Long Cleuch	D & G	NS8507	55°20·9′	3°48·4′W	X	71,78
Longcleughside	Cumbr	NY4468	55°0·5′	2°52·1′W	X	85
Longcleughside	Cumbr	NY4781	55°7·5′	2°49·4′W	X	79
Long Cliff	Corn	SX1699	50°45·9′	4°36·2′W	X	190
Longcliffe	Derby	SK2255	53°5·7′	1°39·9′W	T	119
Longcliffe Fm	Notts	SK6028	52°51·0′	1°6·1′W	FM	129
Longcliffe Lodge Fm	Leic	SK4916	52°44·6′	1°16·0′W	FM	129
Longcliffe Scar	N Yks	SD8565	54°5·1′	2°13·3′W	X	98
Longcliff Hill	Leic	SK6624	52°48·8′	1°0·8′W	X	129
Long Close Fm	Cumbr	NY1733	54°41·4′	3°16·8′W	FM	89,90
Long Close Fm	Cumbr	NY2426	54°37·7′	3°10·2′W	FM	89,90
Long Close Fm	Dorset	ST7900	50°48·2′	2°17·5′W	FM	194
Long Close Plantations	N Lincs	TA0713	53°36·4′	0°22·6′W	F	112
Longclough	Ches	SJ9873	53°15·5′	2°1·4′W	X	118
Long Clough	Derby	SK0391	53°25·2′	1°56·9′W	X	110
Longcoe Fm	Corn	SX2655	50°22·4′	4°26·4′W	FM	201
Longcombe	Devon	SX8359	50°25·4′	3°38·4′W	T	202
Long Combe	Somer	SS8142	51°10·1′	3°41·7′W	X	181
Longcombe Bottom	Dorset	ST8817	50°57·4′	2°9·9′W	X	183
Longcombe Bottom	Wilts	ST9151	51°15·7′	2°7·4′W	X	184
Long Common	Hants	SU5014	50°55·6′	1°16·9′W	T	196
Long Compton	Staffs	SJ8522	52°48·0′	2°12·9′W	T	127
Long Compton	Warw	SP2832	51°59·4′	1°35·1′W	T	151
Long Compton Fm	Staffs	SJ8536	52°55·5′	2°13·0′W	FM	127
Long Compton Woods	Warw	SP2934	52°0·5′	1°34·3′W	F	151
Long Coppice	Heref	SO5046	52°6·8′	2°43·4′W	F	149
Long Copse	Hants	SU4034	51°6·5′	1°25·3′W	F	185
Long Copse	I of W	SZ4884	50°39·4′	1°18·9′W	F	196
Long Copse	Wilts	SU1929	51°3·8′	1°43·3′W	F	184
Longcot	Oxon	SU2790	51°36·7′	1°36·2′W	T	163,174
Longcote	Scot Bord	NT2547	55°42·9′	3°11·2′W	X	73
Longcote Burn	Scot Bord	NT2546	55°42·4′	3°11·2′W	W	73
Longcote Hill	Scot Bord	NT2746	55°42·4′	3°9·3′W	H	73
Longcourse Fm	Derby	SK4470	53°13·8′	1°20·0′W	FM	120
Long Covert	Glos	ST8293	51°38·4′	2°15·2′W	F	162,173
Long Covert	Shrops	SO7487	52°29·1′	2°22·6′W	F	138
Long Covert	Suff	TM1153	52°8·3′	1°5·4′E	F	155
Long Covert	Suff	TM5282	52°22·9′	1°42·6′E	F	156
Long Crag	Cumbr	NY1506	54°26·8′	3°18·2′W	X	89
Long Crag	Cumbr	NY1511	54°29·5′	3°18·3′W	X	89
Long Crag	Cumbr	NY2205	54°26·3′	3°11·7′W	X	89,90
Long Crag	Cumbr	NY2710	54°29·1′	3°7·2′W	X	89,90
Long Crag	Cumbr	NY4019	54°34·0′	2°55·3′W	X	90
Long Crag	Cumbr	NY4621	54°35·1′	2°49·7′W	X	90
Long Crag	Cumbr	NY5105	54°26·5′	2°44·9′W	H	90
Long Crag	Cumbr	NY5878	55°5·9′	2°39·1′W	X	86
Long Crag	Cumbr	NY8415	54°32·0′	2°14·4′W	X	91,92
Long Crag	Cumbr	SD2098	54°22·5′	3°13·5′W	X	96
Long Crag	Cumbr	SD2398	54°22·5′	3°10·7′W	X	96
Long Crag	Cumbr	SD3098	54°22·6′	3°4·2′W	X	96,97
Long Crag	Durham	NY8425	54°37·4′	2°14·4′W	X	91,92
Long Crag	Lancs	SD6256	54°0·2′	2°34·4′W	X	102,103
Long Crag	Northum	NT8904	55°20·0′	2°10·0′W	X	80
Long Crag	Northum	NT9617	55°27·1′	2°3·4′W	X	81
Long Crag	Northum	NU0606	55°21·1′	1°53·9′W	H	81
Long Crag	Northum	NY7296	55°15·7′	2°26·0′W	X	80
Long Crag	Northum	NY7299	55°17·3′	2°26·0′W	X	80
Long Crag	Northum	NY8371	55°2·2′	2°15·5′W	X	86,87
Long Crags	Cumbr	NY6240	54°45·5′	2°35·0′W	X	86
Long Crags	Cumbr	SD3191	54°18·8′	3°3·2′W	X	96,97
Long Crags	Northum	NT9521	55°29·2′	2°4·3′W	X	74,75
Long Crags	Northum	NY6380	55°7·0′	2°34·4′W	X	80
Long Crags	Northum	NY6582	55°8·1′	2°32·5′W	X	80
Long Crags	N Yks	SE0074	54°10·0′	1°59·6′W	X	98
Long Craig	Angus	NO7254	56°40·9′	2°27·0′W	X	54
Long Craig	D & G	NX9066	54°58·8′	3°42·7′W	X	84
Long Craig	E Loth	NT7575	55°58·3′	2°23·6′W	X	67
Long Craig	Fife	NT1280	56°0·5′	3°24·2′W	X	65
Long Craig	Fife	NT1782	56°1·7′	3°19·5′W	X	65,66
Long Craig	Fife	NT2889	56°5·6′	3°9·0′W	X	66
Long Craig	Fife	NT2982	56°1·8′	3°7·9′W	X	66
Long Craig	Pth & Kin	NN9706	56°14·4′	3°39·3′W	X	58
Long Craig Gate	C of Edin	NT1478	55°59·5′	3°22·3′W	X	65
Long Craig Pier	C of Edin	NT1478	55°59·5′	3°22·3′W	X	65
Long Craigs	E Loth	NT4176	55°58·7′	2°56·3′W	X	66
Long Craigs	E Loth	NT6679	56°0·4′	2°32·3′W	X	67
Long Crendon	Bucks	SP6908	51°46·2′	0°59·6′W	T	165
Long Crib Burn	E Loth	NT7067	55°54·0′	2°28·3′W	W	67
Long Crichel	Dorset	ST9710	50°53·6′	2°2·2′W	T	195
Longcroft	Aberd	NJ6627	57°20·2′	2°33·4′W	X	38
Longcroft	Cumbr	NY2158	54°54·9′	3°13·5′W	T	85
Longcroft	Cumbr	SD5382	54°14·1′	2°42·8′W	X	97
Longcroft	Derby	SK3954	53°5·1′	1°24·7′W	X	119
Longcroft	Falk	NS7979	55°59·6′	3°56·0′W	T	64
Longcroft	Herts	SP9108	51°46·0′	0°40·5′W	X	165
Longcroft	Renf	NS3461	55°49·1′	4°38·5′W	X	63
Longcroft	Scot Bord	NT5253	55°46·3′	2°45·5′W	X	66,73
Longcroft	Somer	ST5518	50°57·8′	2°38·1′W	X	183
Longcroft Fm	Glos	SO7115	51°50·2′	2°24·9′W	FM	162
Longcroft Fm	Herts	TL0304	51°43·7′	0°30·1′W	FM	166
Longcroft Fm	Staffs	SK1420	52°46·9′	1°47·1′W	FM	128
Longcroft Spinney	Beds	SP9744	52°5·4′	0°34·7′W	F	153
Longcrook	Moray	NJ2646	57°30·2′	3°13·6′W	X	28
Longcross	Devon	SX4379	50°35·6′	4°12·7′W	T	201
Long Cross	Hants	SU2515	50°56·3′	1°38·3′W	X	184
Long Cross	Northum	NY7450	54°50·9′	2°23·9′W	X	86
Long Cross	Somer	ST6545	51°12·4′	2°29·7′W	X	183
Longcross	Surrey	SU9865	51°22·8′	0°35·1′W	T	175,176
Long Cross	Wilts	ST7832	51°5·4′	2°18·5′W	T	183
Longcross Fm	Card	ST2379	51°30·5′	3°6·2′W	FM	171
Longcross Plain	Hants	SU2415	50°56·3′	1°39·1′W	X	184
Longcross Sta	Surrey	SU9766	51°23·3′	0°36·0′W	X	175,176
Longdale	Cumbr	NY3133	54°41·5′	3°3·8′W	X	90
Longdale	Cumbr	NY6405	54°26·6′	2°32·9′W	T	91
Long Dale	Derby	SK1361	53°9·0′	1°47·9′W	X	119
Long Dale	Derby	SK1860	53°8·4′	1°43·4′W	X	119
Long Dale	Notts	SK5753	53°4·5′	1°8·5′W	X	120
Long Dale	N Yks	SE8360	54°2·0′	0°43·5′W	X	100
Longdale Arts & Craft Centre	Notts	SK5752	53°4·0′	1°8·6′W	X	120
Longdale Cott	N Yks	SD9085	54°15·9′	2°8·8′W	X	98
Longdale Craft Centre & Museum	Notts	SK5752	53°4·0′	1°8·6′W	X	120
Longdales	Cumbr	NY5144	54°47·6′	2°45·3′W	T	86
Long Dam Level	Norf	TM4691	52°27·9′	1°37·7′E	X	134
Long Dean	Wilts	ST8575	51°28·7′	2°12·6′W	T	173
Longdean Bottom	Wilts	ST9336	51°7·6′	2°5·6′W	X	184
Longdell Hills	Norf	TG1411	52°39·5′	1°10·3′E	X	133
Longden	Shrops	SJ4406	52°39·2′	2°49·3′W	T	126
Longden Common	Shrops	SJ4304	52°38·1′	2°50·1′W	T	126
Longdendale	Derby	SK0398	53°29·0′	1°56·9′W	X	110
Longdendale Trail	Derby	SK0798	53°29·0′	1°53·3′W	X	110
Longden End Brook	Roch	SD9613	53°37·1′	2°3·2′W	W	109
Longden Manor	Shrops	SJ4205	52°38·6′	2°51·0′W	X	126
Longden Wood Fm	Shrops	SJ4404	52°38·1′	2°49·2′W	FM	126
Long Dike	Cald	SE0232	53°47·3′	1°57·8′W	W	104
Longdike Burn	Northum	NZ1897	55°16·3′	1°42·6′W	W	81
Long Ditch	Wilts	SU0753	51°16·8′	1°53·6′W	A	184
Long Ditton	Surrey	TQ1666	51°23·1′	0°19·6′W	T	176
Longdole Barn	Glos	SO9212	51°48·6′	2°6·6′W	X	163
Longdon	Staffs	SK0814	52°43·7′	1°52·5′W	T	128
Longdon	Worcs	SO8336	52°1·6′	2°14·5′W	T	150
Longdon Green	Staffs	SK0813	52°43·1′	1°52·5′W	T	128
Longdon Hall	Sol	SP1777	52°23·7′	1°44·6′W	X	139
Longdon Hall	Worcs	SO8434	52°0·5′	2°13·6′W	A	150
Longdon Heath	Worcs	SO8438	52°2·6′	2°13·6′W	T	150
Longdon Hill	Worcs	SP0541	52°4·3′	1°55·2′W	X	150
Longdon Hill End	Worcs	SO8238	52°2·6′	2°15·4′W	T	150
Longdon Ho	Wrekin	SJ6215	52°44·1′	2°33·4′W	X	127
Longdon Manor	Warw	SP2241	52°4·2′	1°40·3′W	X	151
Longdon Marsh	Worcs	SO8235	52°1·0′	2°15·3′W	X	150
Longdon Old Hall	Staffs	SK0612	52°42·6′	1°54·3′W	X	128
Longdon on Tern	Wrekin	SJ6215	52°44·1′	2°33·4′W	T	127
Longdon Orchard	Shrops	SO7477	52°23·7′	2°22·5′W	F	138
Long Down	Devon	SX5358	50°24·4′	4°3·8′W	X	201
Longdown	Devon	SX8691	50°42·7′	3°36·5′W	T	191
Long Down	E Susx	TV5796	50°44·8′	0°13·9′E	X	199
Longdown	I of W	SZ5185	50°40·0′	1°16·3′W	X	196
Long Down	W Susx	SU9309	50°52·6′	0°40·3′W	X	197
Longdown Dairy Fm	Hants	SU3410	50°53·5′	1°30·6′W	FM	196
Longdown Fm	Bucks	SP8304	51°43·9′	0°47·5′W	FM	165
Longdown Inclosure	Hants	SU3508	50°52·5′	1°29·8′W	F	196
Longdowns	Corn	SW7434	50°10·0′	5°9·5′W	T	204
Long Downs	Corn	SX1167	50°28·6′	4°39·5′W	X	200
Long Drax	N Yks	SE6828	53°44·9′	0°57·7′W	T	105,106
Longdrum	Aberd	NJ9217	57°14·9′	2°7·5′W	X	38
Longdrum	Angus	NO2861	56°44·4′	3°10·2′W	X	44
Long Duckmanton	Derby	SK4471	53°14·3′	1°20·0′W	T	120
Long Dyke	Cumbr	NY5354	54°53·0′	2°43·5′W	X	86
Longdyke	Northum	NU2009	55°22·7′	1°40·6′W	X	81
Longdyke	Northum	NZ1796	55°15·7′	1°43·5′W	X	81
Longdyke Fm	Cumbr	NY5353	54°52·4′	2°43·5′W	FM	86
Longdyke Scar	Cumbr	NY1657	54°54·3′	3°18·2′W	X	85
Long Eaton	Derby	SK4933	52°53·8′	1°15·9′W	T	129
Long Eau	Lincs	TF4287	53°21·9′	0°8·5′E	W	113,122
Long Edge	Northum	NY7673	55°3·3′	2°22·1′W	X	86,87
Long Edge Moor	Cald	SE0223	53°42·4′	1°57·8′W	X	104
Longend Fm	Kent	TQ7245	51°10·9′	0°28·1′E	FM	188
Longerend Fm	Surrey	SU9252	51°15·8′	0°40·5′W	FM	186
Longerhallis Hill	D & G	NY1290	55°12·0′	3°22·5′W	H	78
Longfaugh	Midlo	NT4061	55°50·6′	2°57·1′W	X	66
Longfaugh	S Lanak	NS7448	55°42·8′	3°59·9′W	X	64
Longfauld	Pth & Kin	NN8708	56°15·3′	3°49·0′W	X	58
Long Fell	Cumbr	NY1628	54°38·7′	3°17·7′W	X	89
Long Fell	Cumbr	NY5609	54°28·7′	2°40·3′W	X	90
Long Fell	Cumbr	NY7619	54°34·2′	2°21·9′W	X	91
Long Fell	D & G	NX9064	54°57·8′	3°42·7′W	H	84
Longfield	Cald	SD9423	53°42·4′	2°5·0′W	X	103
Longfield	Kent	TQ6069	51°24·1′	0°18·4′E	T	177
Longfield	Shetld	HU3816	59°55·9′	1°18·7′W	T	4
Longfield	Wilts	ST8557	51°18·9′	2°12·5′W	T	173
Longfield Barn	Cumbr	SD5878	54°12·0′	2°38·2′W	X	97
Longfield Fm	Cambs	TL6076	52°21·7′	0°21·4′E	FM	143
Longfield Grange	York	SE5254	53°59·0′	1°12·0′W	X	105
Longfield Hill	Kent	TQ6268	51°23·5′	0°20·1′E	T	177
Longfield Ho	Shrops	SJ6433	52°53·8′	2°31·7′W	X	127
Longfield House Fm	Ghead	NZ1957	54°54·7′	1°41·8′W	FM	88
Longfield Manor	Worcs	SP0473	52°21·5′	1°56·1′W	X	139
Longfield Wood	Cumbr	SD2488	54°17·2′	3°9·6′W	F	96
Longfleet	Poole	SZ0191	50°43·3′	1°58·8′W	T	195
Long Fm	Lincs	TF2766	53°10·8′	0°5·6′W	FM	122
Long Fm	Notts	SK5731	52°52·7′	1°8·8′W	FM	129
Longfold	Aberd	NJ4707	57°9·3′	2°52·1′W	X	37
Longfold	Aberd	NJ6918	57°15·4′	2°30·4′W	X	38
Long Fold	Lancs	SD4721	53°41·2′	2°47·7′W	X	102
Longford	Cov	SP3483	52°26·9′	1°29·6′W	T	140
Longford	Derby	SK2137	52°56·0′	1°40·8′W	T	128
Longford	Devon	SX5174	50°33·0′	4°5·8′W	X	191,201
Longford	Glos	SO8320	51°52·9′	2°14·4′W	T	162
Longford	Hill	TQ0476	51°28·6′	0°29·8′W	T	176
Longford	Kent	TQ5157	51°17·7′	0°10·3′E	T	188
Longford	Shrops	SJ6433	52°53·8′	2°31·7′W	T	127
Longford	Warr	SJ6090	53°24·6′	2°35·7′W	T	109
Longford	W Loth	NS9860	55°49·6′	3°37·3′W	X	65
Longford	Wrekin	SJ7218	52°45·8′	2°24·5′W	T	127
Longford Burn	W Loth	NS9760	55°49·6′	3°38·2′W	W	65
Longford Castle	Wilts	SU1726	51°2·2′	1°45·1′W	A	184
Longford Fm	E Susx	TQ4318	50°56·8′	0°2·5′E	FM	198
Longford Fm	Wilts	SU1526	51°2·2′	1°46·8′W	FM	184
Longford Ho	Shrops	SJ6434	52°54·4′	2°31·7′W	X	127
Longfordlane	Derby	SK2236	52°55·5′	1°40·0′W	T	128
Longford Moors	Wrekin	SJ7118	52°45·8′	2°25·4′W	X	127
Longford Park	Traf	SJ8094	53°26·8′	2°17·7′W	X	109
Longford Park	Wilts	SU1626	51°2·2′	1°45·9′W	X	184
Longford River	Hill	TQ0575	51°28·1′	0°28·9′W	W	176
Longfords	D & G	NY1666	54°59·1′	3°18·3′W	X	85
Longford Stream	E Susx	TQ4218	50°56·9′	0°1·7′E	W	198
Longforgan	Pth & Kin	NO3130	56°27·7′	3°6·7′W	T	53
Longformacus	Scot Bord	NT6957	55°48·6′	2°29·2′W	T	67,74
Longformacus Ho	Scot Bord	NT6957	55°48·6′	2°29·2′W	X	67,74
Long Forth	D & G	NX2352	54°50·1′	4°44·9′W	X	82
Longforth Fm	Somer	ST1321	50°59·1′	3°14·0′W	FM	181,193
Longframlington	Northum	NU1300	55°17·9′	1°47·3′W	T	81
Longframlington Common	Northum	NU1004	55°20·0′	1°50·1′W	X	81
Long Furlong	Devon	SS2526	51°0·6′	4°29·3′W	X	190
Long Furlong	Glos	SP0703	51°43·8′	1°53·5′W	F	163
Long Furlong	Northnts	SP8856	52°11·9′	0°42·3′W	F	152
Longfurlong Barn	W Susx	TQ0907	50°51·4′	0°26·7′W	X	198
Longfurlong Fm	Derby	SK2415	52°44·2′	1°38·3′W	FM	128
Long Furlong Fm	Northnts	SP5357	52°12·8′	1°13·1′W	FM	152
Long Gallop	Norf	TL8095	52°31·6′	0°39·6′E	X	144
Long Gardens	Essex	TL8436	51°59·7′	0°41·2′E	T	155
Long Garth	Cumbr	SD1891	54°18·7′	3°15·2′W	X	96
Long Geo	Orkney	HY4404	58°55·4′	2°57·9′W	X	6,7
Long Geo	Orkney	HY5300	58°53·4′	2°48·4′W	X	6,7
Long Geo	Orkney	HY5409	58°58·2′	2°47·5′W	X	6,7
Long Geo	Shetld	HU3611	59°53·2′	1°20·9′W	X	4
Long Geo	Shetld	HU6692	60°36·6′	0°47·2′W	X	1,2
Longgeo Skerries	Highld	ND2974	58°39·1′	3°12·9′W	X	7,12
Long Gill	Cumbr	NY6704	54°26·1′	2°30·1′W	X	91
Long Gill	Cumbr	NY7500	54°23·9′	2°22·7′W	W	91
Long Gill	Cumbr	SD7692	54°19·6′	2°21·7′W	W	98
Long Gill	N Yks	NY8304	54°26·1′	2°15·3′W	W	91,92
Long Gill	N Yks	SD7180	54°13·1′	2°26·3′W	W	98
Long Gill	N Yks	SD7858	54°1·3′	2°19·7′W	X	103
Long Gill	N Yks	SD7982	54°14·2′	2°18·9′W	W	98
Long Gill	N Yks	SE0980	54°13·2′	1°51·3′W	W	99
Long Gill	Scot Bord	NY4589	55°11·8′	2°51·4′W	W	79
Long Gills	Cumbr	NY6404	54°26·1′	2°32·9′W	X	91
Long Glen	Aberd	NJ8461	57°38·6′	2°15·6′W	X	29,30
Long Goat	Angus	NO3361	56°44·4′	3°5·3′W	H	44
Long Goe Fm	Highld	ND2974	58°39·1′	3°12·9′W	FM	7,12
Long Gore Marsh	Norf	TG4224	52°45·8′	1°35·6′E	W	134
Long Grain	Angus	NO4375	56°52·0′	2°55·6′W	W	44
Long Grain	Cumbr	NY1011	54°29·4′	3°22·9′W	W	89
Long Grain	Cumbr	NY4614	54°31·4′	2°49·6′W	X	90
Long Grain	Cumbr	NY7240	54°45·5′	2°25·7′W	W	86,87

Long Grain	Durham	NY8322	54°35·8'	2°15·4'W	W	91,92
Long Grain	Lancs	SD7519	53°40·3'	2°22·3'W	X	109
Long Grain	N Yks	SE5680	54°13·0'	1°8·1'W	X	100
Long Grain	N Yks	SE8894	54°20·3'	0°38·4'W	W	94,101
Long Grain	Scot Bord	NT1528	55°32·6'	3°20·4'W	W	72
Long Grain	Scot Bord	NT2329	55°33·2'	3°12·8'W	W	73
Long Grain	Scot Bord	NT2922	55°29·5'	3°7·0'W	W	73
Long Grain	Scot Bord	NT3047	55°42·9'	3°6·4'W	W	73
Long Grain	Scot Bord	NT5459	55°49·6'	2°43·6'W	W	66,73
Longgrain Beck	Cumbr	NY4514	54°31·3'	2°50·6'W	W	90
Longgrain Head	D & G	NY3592	55°13·3'	3°0·9'W	H	79
Long Grain Knowe	Scot Bord	NT1629	55°33·1'	3°19·5'W	H	72
Long Grain Moss	Durham	NY8521	54°35·3'	2°13·5'W	X	91,92
Long Grain Rig	Scot Bord	NT2921	55°28·9'	3°7·0'W	H	73
Long Green	Ches	SJ4770	53°13·7'	2°47·2'W	T	117
Long Green	C of Edin	NT1777	55°59·0'	3°19·4'W	X	65,66
Long Green	E Ayr	NS5741	55°38·7'	4°15·9'W	X	71
Long Green	Essex	TL6727	51°55·2'	0°26·1'E	X	167
Long Green	Herts	TL0006	51°44·9'	0°32·7'W	X	166
Long Green	N Yks	NZ0706	54°27·2'	1°53·1'W	X	92
Long Green	Suff	TM0777	52°21·3'	1°2·8'E	T	144
Long Green	Worcs	SO8433	51°59·9'	2°13·6'W	T	150
Long Green Fm	N Yks	NZ6610	54°29·1'	0°58·5'W	FM	94
Long Green Gate	N Yks	NZ0606	54°27·2'	1°54·0'W	X	92
Long Green Head	Cumbr	NY4204	54°25·9'	2°53·2'W	X	90
Long Grove	Essex	TM1517	51°48·8'	1°7·6'E	F	168,169
Long Grove	Suff	TM3455	52°8·8'	1°25·6'E	F	156
Long Guen	Shetld	HU6568	60°23·7'	0°48·7'W	X	2
Longgutter	Ches	SJ9567	53°12·2'	2°4·1'W	X	118
Long Gutter Edge	Derby	SK0797	53°28·4'	1°53·3'W	X	110
Longham	Dorset	SZ0698	50°47·1'	1°54·5'W	T	195
Longham	Norf	TF9415	52°42·1'	0°52·7'E	T	132
Longham Down	Devon	SX4884	50°38·4'	4°8·6'W	H	191,201
Longham Hall	Norf	TF9316	52°42·7'	0°51·8'E	X	132
Longham Wood	Kent	TQ8156	51°16·7'	0°36·1'E	F	178,188
Long Hanborough	Oxon	SP4114	51°49·5'	1°23·9'W	T	164
Longhaugh	Scot Bord	NY5093	55°14·0'	2°46·7'W	X	79
Longhaugh Fm	Aberd	NJ6148	57°31·5'	2°38·6'W	FM	29
Longhaven	Aberd	NK1039	57°26·7'	1°48·5'W	T	30
Long Haven	Aberd	NK1240	57°27·3'	1°47·5'W	W	30
Longhaven Ho	Aberd	NK0938	57°26·2'	1°50·5'W	X	30
Longhaven Mains	Aberd	NK1140	57°27·3'	1°48·5'W	X	30
Longhayne	Devon	SS9717	50°56·8'	3°27·6'W	X	181
Longhead	Cumbr	NY2448	54°49·5'	3°10·6'W	X	85
Long Head	Moray	NJ4668	57°42·2'	2°53·9'W	X	28,29
Longhedge	Wilts	ST8244	51°11·9'	2°15·1'W	T	183
Longhedge Fm	Wilts	SU1434	51°6·5'	1°47·6'W	FM	184
Long Height	Cumbr	SD3798	54°22·7'	2°57·8'W	F	96,97
Longheughshields	Northum	NY8284	55°9·2'	2°16·5'W	X	80
Longhill	Aberd	NJ4637	57°25·5'	2°53·5'W	X	28,29
Long Hill	Aberd	NJ5206	57°8·8'	2°47·1'W	H	37
Longhill	Aberd	NJ8636	57°25·1'	2°13·5'W	X	30
Longhill	Aberd	NJ9954	57°34·8'	2°0·5'W	X	30
Longhill	Aberd	NK0454	57°34·8'	1°55·5'W	X	30
Longhill	Aberd	NK0647	57°31·0'	1°53·5'W	X	30
Long Hill	Cambs	TL6564	52°15·2'	0°25·4'E	X	154
Longhill	Ches	SJ6844	52°59·8'	2°28·2'W	X	118
Long Hill	Darl	NZ2618	54°33·6'	1°35·5'W	X	93
Long Hill	Derby	SK0375	53°16·6'	1°56·9'W	X	119
Longhill	D & G	NX4239	54°43·5'	4°26·8'W	X	83
Long Hill	Durham	NY9542	54°46·6'	2°4·2'W	H	87
Long Hill	E Susx	TQ3709	50°52·1'	0°2·8'W	X	198
Long Hill	Fife	NO3923	56°24·0'	2°58·9'W	H	54,59
Long Hill	Ghead	NZ1959	54°55·8'	1°41·8'W	X	88
Long Hill	Hants	SU8351	51°15·4'	0°48·2'W	X	186
Long Hill	Highld	NC6542	58°21·0'	4°17·9'W	H	10
Longhill	Moray	NJ2662	57°38·8'	3°13·9'W	X	28
Long Hill	N Ayr	NS2661	55°48·9'	4°46·2'W	H	63
Long Hill	Northum	NT8507	55°21·7'	2°13·8'W	H	80
Long Hill	Northum	NY9099	55°17·3'	2°9·0'W	X	80
Long Hill	Notts	SK5149	53°2·4'	1°14·0'W	X	129
Long Hill	N Yks	SE0566	54°5·6'	1°55·0'W	X	98
Long Hill	Oxon	SP3640	52°3·7'	1°28·1'W	H	151
Long Hill	Powys	SJ2019	52°46·0'	3°10·7'W	X	126
Long Hill	Powys	SN9592	52°31·2'	3°32·5'W	X	136
Longhill	S Ayr	NS3118	55°25·5'	4°39·8'W	X	70
Longhill	S Ayr	NS3405	55°18·9'	4°36·5'W	X	70,76
Longhill	Shetld	HU3724	60°0·2'	1°19·7'W	X	4
Long Hill	Shetld	HU4352	60°15·3'	1°12·9'W	H	3
Long Hill	Somer	ST4350	51°15·0'	2°48·6'W	H	182
Long Hill	Warw	SP2551	52°9·6'	1°37·7'W	X	151
Long Hill	Wilts	ST8032	51°5·5'	2°16·7'W	H	183
Long Hill	Worcs	SO6066	52°17·7'	2°34·8'W	X	138,149
Longhill Bottom	Surrey	SU9253	51°16·4'	0°40·5'W	X	186
Longhill Burn	Moray	NJ2663	57°39·3'	3°13·9'W	W	28
Longhill Burn	S Lanak	NS8233	55°34·8'	3°51·9'W	W	71,72
Longhill Burn	W Loth	NS9859	55°49·1'	3°37·2'W	W	65,72
Long Hill End	N Yks	SD9742	53°52·7'	2°2·3'W	X	103
Long Hill Fm	Derby	SK0375	53°16·6'	1°56·9'W	FM	119
Longhill Fm	Glos	SO9705	51°44·9'	2°2·2'W	FM	163
Longhill Fm	Somer	ST6336	51°7·6'	2°31·3'W	FM	183
Longhillock	Moray	NJ1464	57°39·7'	3°26·0'W	X	28
Longhill Point	S Ayr	NS3119	55°26·4'	4°39·9'W	X	70
Longhills	Aberd	NJ8915	57°13·8'	2°10·5'W	X	38
Long Hills	Essex	TQ4096	51°38·9'	0°1·8'E	F	167,177
Long Hills	Norf	TF7422	52°46·3'	0°35·2'E	X	132
Long Hills	Norf	TG0046	52°58·7'	0°59·1'E	X	133
Longhills Hall	Lincs	TF0366	53°11·1'	0°27·1'W	X	121
Long Hill Sike	N Yks	SE0176	54°11·0'	1°58·7'W	W	98
Long Hill Wood	Warw	SP4961	52°14·9'	1°16·5'W	F	151
Longhirst	Cumbr	NY5861	54°56·8'	2°38·9'W	X	86
Longhirst	Northum	NZ2289	55°11·9'	1°38·8'W	T	81
Long Ho	Cumbr	NY3006	54°26·9'	3°4·4'W	X	90
Long Ho	Cumbr	SD2396	54°21·5'	3°10·7'W	X	96
Long Ho	Norf	TM1479	52°22·3'	1°9·0'E	X	144,156
Long Ho	N Yks	SE0142	53°52·7'	1°58·7'W	X	104
Long Ho	Shrops	SO5676	52°23·1'	2°38·4'W	X	137,138
Long Ho	W Susx	TQ2324	51°0·4'	0°14·4'W	X	198
Long Holcombe	Somer	SS7735	51°6·3'	3°45·0'W	H	180
Longhold Lodge	Northnts	SP6881	52°25·6'	0°59·6'W	X	141
Long Hold Spinney	Northnts	SP6980	52°25·1'	0°58·7'W	F	141
Longholes Stud	Cambs	TL6762	52°14·1'	0°27·1'E	X	154
Long Hollow	Lincs	TF0035	52°54·4'	0°30·4'W	X	130
Long Holm	Orkney	HY3014	59°0·7'	3°12·6'W	X	6
Longholme Fm	Notts	SK7182	53°20·0'	0°55·6'W	FM	120
Longhook-fawr	Pemb	SN0028	51°55·1'	4°54·1'W	X	145,157,158
Longhope	Glos	SO6818	51°51·8'	2°27·5'W	T	162
Longhope	Hants	SU7232	51°5·2'	0°57·9'W	X	186
Longhope	Orkney	ND3090	58°47·8'	3°12·2'W	T	7
Longhope	Orkney	ND3191	58°48·3'	3°11·2'W	W	7
Longhope Burn	Scot Bord	NT1809	55°22·3'	3°17·2'W	W	79
Longhope Reach	Monm	ST5395	51°39·3'	2°40·4'W	W	162
Longhorsley	Northum	NZ1494	55°14·6'	1°46·4'W	T	81
Longhorsley Moor	Northum	NZ1592	55°13·6'	1°45·4'W	X	81
Long Ho,The	Wilts	SU2062	51°21·6'	1°42·4'W	X	174
Longhoughton	Northum	NU2415	55°25·9'	1°36·8'W	T	81
Longhoughton Steel	Northum	NU2615	55°25·9'	1°34·9'W	X	81
Longhouse	Bath & NE Somer	ST7060	51°20·5'	2°25·5'W	T	172
Longhouse	E Ayr	NS5820	55°27·5'	4°14·3'W	X	71
Longhouse	Orkney	HY4109	58°58·1'	3°1·1'W	X	6,7
Longhouse	Pemb	SM8433	51°57·5'	5°8·2'W	X	157
Longhouse	S Ayr	NS4631	55°33·2'	4°26·0'W	X	70
Long House Gill	Cumbr	SD2496	54°21·5'	3°9·8'W	W	96
Long Houses	Cumbr	NY4503	54°25·4'	2°50·4'W	X	90
Longhowe End	Cumbr	SD4483	54°14·6'	2°51·1'W	X	97
Longhurst Hill	Surrey	TQ0837	51°7·6'	0°27·0'W	X	187
Longi Geo	Shetld	HU4016	59°55·9'	1°16·6'W	X	4
Longi Geo	Shetld	HU4487	60°34·1'	1°11·3'W	X	1,2
Longi Geo	Shetld	HU5864	60°21·6'	0°56·4'W	X	2
Longiger	Orkney	HY3721	59°4·5'	3°5·5'W	X	6
Long Ing Wood	N Yks	SE0285	54°15·9'	1°57·7'W	F	98
Long Island	Corn	SX0790	50°40·9'	4°43·5'W	X	190
Long Island	D & G	NX3052	54°50·3'	4°38·4'W	X	82
Long Island	Dorset	SY9888	50°41·7'	2°1·3'W	X	195
Long Island	Hants	SU7004	50°50·1'	1°0·0'W	X	197
Long Itchington	Warw	SP4165	52°17·1'	1°23·5'W	T	151
Long Itchington Wood	Warw	SP3862	52°15·5'	1°26·2'W	F	151
Long Ivor Fm	Wilts	ST8841	51°10·3'	2°9·9'W	FM	183
Long John's Hill	Norf	TG2306	52°36·6'	1°18·0'E	T	134
Long Kin West Pot	N Yks	SD7372	54°8·8'	2°24·4'W	X	98
Long Knoll	Wilts	ST7937	51°8·1'	2°17·6'W	H	183
Long Knowe	D & G	NT2100	55°17·5'	3°14·2'W	X	79
Long Knowe	D & G	NY2397	55°15·9'	3°12·3'W	H	79
Longknowe	Northum	NT8630	55°34·1'	2°12·9'W	X	74
Long Knowe	Scot Bord	NT3522	55°29·5'	3°1·3'W	H	73
Long Knowe	Scot Bord	NY5286	55°10·2'	2°44·8'W	X	79
Long Knowe Burn	S Lanak	NS7137	55°36·8'	4°2·5'W	W	71
Longknowe Hill	Northum	NT8730	55°34·1'	2°11·9'W	H	74
Longland	Highld	ND0767	58°35·1'	3°35·5'W	X	11,12
Longland Fm	Notts	SK6255	53°5·6'	1°4·0'W	FM	120
Longland Fm	N Yks	SE6935	53°48·6'	0°56·7'W	FM	105
Longland Fm	N Yks	SE6935	53°48·6'	0°56·7'W	FM	105,106
Longlands	Aberd	NJ4425	57°19·0'	2°55·3'W	X	37
Longlands	Bexley	TQ4472	51°25·9'	0°4·7'E	T	177
Longlands	Corn	SX4058	50°24·2'	4°14·7'W	X	201
Longlands	Cumbr	NY0504	54°25·6'	3°27·4'W	X	89
Longlands	Cumbr	NY2635	54°42·5'	3°8·5'W	T	89,90
Longlands	Cumbr	NY5567	55°0·0'	2°41·8'W	X	86
Longlands	Cumbr	NY5718	54°33·6'	2°39·5'W	X	91
Longlands	Cumbr	SD3879	54°12·4'	2°56·6'W	X	96,97
Longlands	Derby	SK2616	52°44·7'	1°36·5'W	X	128
Longlands	Dorset	SY6089	50°42·2'	2°33·6'W	X	194
Longlands	I of W	SZ6286	50°40·4'	1°7·0'W	X	196
Longlands	Lincs	TF4584	53°20·2'	0°11·1'E	X	122
Longlands	Newp	ST4184	51°33·3'	2°50·7'W	X	171,172
Longlands	N Yks	NZ4301	54°24·4'	1°19·8'W	X	93
Longlands	N Yks	SE3256	54°0·2'	1°30·3'W	X	104
Longlands	N Yks	SE3791	54°19·0'	1°25·5'W	X	99
Longlands	N Yks	SE4492	54°19·5'	1°19·0'W	X	99
Longlands	Pemb	SM8617	51°48·9'	5°5·9'W	X	157
Longlands	Tames	SJ9695	53°27·3'	2°3·2'W	X	109
Longlands Barn	N Yks	SD8862	54°3·5'	2°10·6'W	X	98
Longlands Fell	Cumbr	NY2735	54°42·5'	3°7·6'W	H	89,90
Longlands Fm	Cumbr	SD3980	54°13·0'	2°55·7'W	FM	96,97
Longlands Fm	Devon	SX8355	50°23·2'	3°38·4'W	FM	202
Longlands Fm	Dorset	SY6194	50°44·9'	2°32·8'W	FM	194
Longlands Fm	Glos	SP1641	52°4·3'	1°45·6'W	FM	151
Longlands Fm	Norf	TF8740	52°55·7'	0°47·3'E	FM	132
Longlands Fm	N Yks	NZ3705	54°26·6'	1°25·3'W	FM	93
Longlands Fm	Pemb	SN0318	51°49·8'	4°51·2'W	FM	157,158
Longland's Fm	Somer	ST1827	51°2·4'	3°9·8'W	FM	181,193
Longlands Hall	N Yks	SE7976	54°10·7'	0°47·0'W	X	100
Longlands Head	Cumbr	NY2155	54°53·3'	3°13·5'W	X	85
Longlands Lake	Cumbr	NY0112	54°29·9'	3°31·3'W	W	89
Longlands Moor	Cumbr	NY2554	54°52·8'	3°9·7'W	X	85
Longlane	Derby	SK2538	52°56·6'	1°37·3'W	T	128
Long Lane	N Yks	SE3998	54°22·8'	1°23·6'W	X	99
Longlane	W Berks	SU5071	51°26·4'	1°16·4'W	T	174
Long Lane	Wrekin	SJ6315	52°44·1'	2°32·5'W	T	127
Long Lane Fm	Beds	TL0131	51°58·3'	0°31·4'W	FM	166
Long Lane Fm	Ches	SJ6160	53°8·4'	2°34·6'W	FM	118
Longlane Fm	Ches	SJ7673	53°15·4'	2°21·2'W	FM	118
Long Lane Fm	Dorset	SU0201	50°48·7'	1°57·9'W	FM	195
Long Lane Fm	Kent	TR2548	51°11·4'	1°13·6'E	FM	179
Long Lane Fm	Leic	SK4828	52°51·1'	1°16·8'W	FM	129
Long Lane Fm	Norf	TF9540	52°55·5'	0°54·5'E	FM	132
Long Lane Fm	Win & Maid	SU8775	51°28·3'	0°44·5'W	FM	175
Lòn Glas	Arg & Bt	NM8701	56°9·5'	5°25·4'W	X	55
Lòn Glas	Highld	NG4766	57°37·0'	6°13·7'W	W	23
Lòn Glas	Highld	NG4964	57°36·0'	6°11·6'W	W	23
Long Latch	Scot Bord	NT8468	55°54·5'	2°14·9'W	W	67
Long Lawford	Warw	SP4776	52°23·0'	1°18·2'W	T	140
Long Lea	Cumbr	NY3038	54°44·2'	3°4·8'W	X	90
Longlea	Northum	NZ0989	55°12·0'	1°51·1'W	X	81
Long Lease	N Yks	NZ9208	54°27·8'	0°34·4'W	X	94
Long Leases	N Yks	NZ2111	54°29·9'	1°40·1'W	X	93
Longleat House	Wilts	ST8043	51°11·4'	2°16·8'W	A	183
Longleat Park	Wilts	ST8143	51°11·4'	2°16·0'W	X	183
Longleaze Fm	Swin	SU2087	51°35·1'	1°42·3'W	FM	174
Long Ledge	I of W	SZ6586	50°40·4'	1°4·4'W	X	196
Long Ledge	I Scilly	SV8713	49°56·3'	6°21·4'W	X	203
Long Lee	Brad	SE0740	53°51·6'	1°53·2'W	T	104
Long Lee	Derby	SK0188	53°23·6'	1°58·7'W	X	110
Longlee	Northum	NU2215	55°26·0'	1°38·7'W	X	81
Longlee	Northum	NY8276	55°4·9'	2°16·5'W	X	86,87
Long Lee	Northum	NY9152	54°52·0'	2°8·0'W	X	87
Longleefoot	Scot Bord	NT5431	55°34·5'	2°43·3'W	X	73
Longlee Moor	Northum	NU1519	55°28·1'	1°45·3'W	X	81
Longlevens	Glos	SO8520	51°52·9'	2°12·7'W	T	162
Longley	Aberd	NJ4517	57°14·7'	2°54·2'W	X	37
Longley	Aberd	NJ8531	57°22·4'	2°14·5'W	X	30
Longley	Cald	SE0521	53°41·4'	1°55·0'W	T	104
Longley	Kirk	SE1406	53°33·3'	1°46·9'W	T	110
Longley	Moray	NH9957	57°35·8'	3°40·9'W	X	27
Longley	Shrops	SJ6022	52°47·9'	2°35·2'W	X	127
Longley	Stir	NS7897	56°9·3'	3°57·4'W	X	57
Longley Estate	Sheff	SK3591	53°25·1'	1°28·0'W	T	110,111
Longley Fm	Ches	SJ5269	53°13·2'	2°42·7'W	FM	117
Longley Fm	Glos	SO5706	51°45·3'	2°37·0'W	FM	162
Longley Fm	Moray	NJ0149	57°31·5'	3°38·7'W	FM	27
Longley Green	Worcs	SO7350	52°9·1'	2°23·3'W	T	150
Longley House Fm	Lancs	SD5539	53°51·0'	2°40·6'W	FM	102
Longleys	Aberd	NK0546	57°30·5'	1°54·5'W	X	30
Longleys	Aberd	NO7569	56°49·0'	2°24·1'W	X	45
Longleys	Pth & Kin	NO2643	56°34·6'	3°11·8'W	X	53
Long Leys Fm	Oxon	SP4404	51°44·2'	1°21·4'W	FM	164
Long Liberty Fm	N Yks	SE2354	53°59·1'	1°38·5'W	FM	104
Longlie Common	Somer	ST2611	50°53·9'	3°2·8'W	X	192,193
Long Load	Somer	ST4623	51°0·5'	2°45·8'W	T	193
Long Loch	Angus	NO2838	56°32·0'	3°9·8'W	W	53
Long Loch	E Renf	NS4752	55°44·5'	4°25·8'W	W	64
Longloch	Fife	NT2488	56°5·0'	3°12·8'W	X	66
Long Loch	Highld	ND2075	58°39·6'	3°22·3'W	W	7,12
Long Loch	Highld	NM3698	57°0·1'	6°20·4'W	W	39
Long Loch	S Ayr	NX2376	55°3·1'	4°45·8'W	W	76
Long Loch	Shetld	HU4359	60°19·0'	1°12·8'W	W	2,3
Long Loch of Glenhead	D & G	NX4480	55°5·6'	4°26·3'W	W	77
Long Loch of the Dungeon	D & G	NX4684	55°7·8'	4°24·5'W	W	77
Long Lodge Fm	Northnts	SP8762	52°15·2'	0°43·1'W	FM	152
Long Low	Staffs	SK1253	53°4·7'	1°48·8'W	A	119
Long Lown Wood	Northnts	SP9481	52°25·4'	0°36·7'W	F	141
Longman Cairn	Aberd	NJ7362	57°39·1'	2°26·7'W	A	29
Longmanhill	Aberd	NJ7362	57°39·1'	2°26·7'W	T	29
Long Man Hill	Cumbr	NY7237	54°43·9'	2°25·7'W	X	91
Longman Industrial Estate	Highld	NH6746	57°29·3'	4°12·7'W	X	26
Longman Point	Highld	NH6647	57°29·9'	4°13·7'W	X	26
Longman's Barn Fm	Glos	ST8798	51°41·1'	2°10·9'W	FM	162
Long Man, The	E Susx	TQ5403	50°48·6'	0°11·5'E	A	199
Long Marston	Herts	SP8915	51°49·8'	0°42·1'W	T	165
Long Marston	N Yks	SE5051	53°57·4'	1°13·9'W	T	105
Long Marston	Warw	SP1548	52°8·0'	1°46·5'W	T	151
Long Marton	Cumbr	NY6624	54°36·8'	2°31·2'W	T	91
Long Matthew Point	Pemb	SR9792	51°35·7'	4°55·5'W	X	158
Longmead	Dorset	SY9298	50°47·1'	2°14·9'W	X	194
Long Meadow	Cambs	TL5462	52°14·3'	0°15·7'E	T	154
Long Meadow Barn Fm	Warw	SP2774	52°22·0'	1°35·8'W	FM	140
Long Meadowend	Shrops	SO4182	52°26·2'	2°51·7'W	T	137
Long Meg	Aberd	NO8989	56°59·8'	2°10·4'W	X	45
Longmeg	Cumbr	NY5737	54°43·8'	2°39·6'W	X	91
Long Meg and her Daughters	Cumbr	NY5737	54°43·8'	2°39·6'W	A	91
Long Melford	Suff	TL8645	52°4·6'	0°43·3'E	T	155
Long Mere	Durham	NY8832	54°41·2'	2°10·7'W	X	91,92
Long Mere Fm	Leic	SK4422	52°47·9'	1°20·4'W	FM	129
Longmere Point	W Susx	SU7601	50°48·4'	0°54·9'W	X	197
Longmire	Cumbr	NY4101	54°24·3'	2°54·1'W	X	90
Long Mire	Cumbr	NY5911	54°29·8'	2°37·6'W	W	91
Longmoor	Cumbr	NY0515	54°31·5'	3°27·7'W	X	89
Long Moor	Cumbr	NY5644	54°47·6'	2°40·6'W	X	86
Long Moor	Cumbr	SD6889	54°18·0'	2°29·1'W	X	98
Longmoor	Glos	SP1940	52°3·7'	1°43·0'W	X	151
Longmoor	Lancs	SD5256	54°0·1'	2°43·5'W	X	102
Long Moor	Wok	SU7865	51°22·9'	0°52·4'W	F	175
Longmoor Camp	Hants	SU7930	51°4·1'	0°52·0'W	X	186
Long Moor Clough	Barns	SE1700	53°30·0'	1°44·2'W	X	110
Longmoor Fm	Bucks	SP8420	51°52·6'	0°46·4'W	FM	165
Longmoor Fm	Dorset	ST8229	51°3·8'	2°15·0'W	FM	183
Longmoor Fm	Norf	TG3722	52°44·8'	1°31·1'E	FM	133,134
Long Moor Hill	Donc	SE6501	53°30·3'	1°0·8'W	X	111
Longmoor Hill	S Lanak	NS9034	55°35·5'	3°44·3'W	H	71,72
Longmoor Inclosure	Hants	SU7930	51°4·1'	0°52·0'W	F	186
Longmoor Wood	Aberd	NJ5643	57°28·8'	2°43·6'W	F	29
Longmore	E Ayr	NS5920	55°27·5'	4°13·4'W	X	71
Longmore Fm	Worcs	SO8872	52°21·0'	2°10·9'W	FM	139
Longmore Hill Fm	Worcs	SO8068	52°18·8'	2°17·2'W	FM	138
Longmore Point	W Susx	SU8101	50°48·4'	0°50·6'W	X	197
Longmorn	Moray	NJ2358	57°36·6'	3°16·9'W	X	28
Longmoss	Ches	SJ8874	53°16·0'	2°10·4'W	T	118
Long Moss	Cumbr	NY2914	54°31·2'	3°5·4'W	X	89,90
Long Moss	Cumbr	NY6369	55°1·1'	2°34·3'W	X	86
Long Mountain	Powys	SJ2707	52°39·6'	3°4·4'W	X	126
Longmountain Fm	Powys	SJ2708	52°40·1'	3°4·4'W	FM	126
Longmuir	Aberd	NJ5761	57°38·5'	2°42·8'W	X	29
Longmuir	Aberd	NK0149	57°32·1'	1°58·5'W	X	30
Longmuir	Fife	NO4516	56°20·2'	2°52·9'W	X	59
Longmuir Plantn	W Loth	NT0273	55°56·7'	3°33·7'W	F	65
Longmuir Rig	Scot Bord	NT4651	55°45·2'	2°51·2'W	X	66,73
Long Myers Fm	Durham	NZ3240	54°45·5'	1°29·7'W	FM	88
Long Mynd, The	Shrops	SO4092	52°31·6'	2°52·7'W	X	137
Long Na	N Yks	TA0394	54°20·1'	0°24·5'W	X	101
Long Nanny	Northum	NU2127	55°32·4'	1°39·6'W	W	75
Longnecked Loch	Shetld	HU4251	60°14·7'	1°14·0'W	W	3
Longner Hall	Shrops	SJ5211	52°41·9'	2°42·2'W	X	126
Long Newnton	Glos	ST9092	51°37·8'	2°8·3'W	T	163,173
Longnewton	E Loth	NT5164	55°52·3'	2°46·5'W	X	66
Longnewton	Scot Bord	NT5827	55°32·3'	2°39·5'W	X	73,74
Longnewton	Stock on T	NZ3816	54°32·5'	1°24·3'W	T	93
Longnewton Forest	Scot Bord	NT6027	55°32·4'	2°37·6'W	F	74
Long Newton Grange	Stock on T	NZ3718	54°33·6'	1°25·2'W	X	93

Longnewton Ho	Scot Bord	NT5827	55°32·3′	2°39·5′W	X	73,74
Longnewton Mill Fm	Scot Bord	NT5726	55°31·8′	2°40·4′W	FM	73,74
Longney	Glos	SO7612	51°48·6′	2°20·5′W	T	162
Longney Crib	Glos	SO7611	51°48·1′	2°20·5′W	X	162
Longniddry	E Loth	NT4476	55°58·7′	2°53·4′W	T	66
Longnor	Shrops	SJ4900	52°36·0′	2°44·8′W	T	126
Longnor	Staffs	SJ8614	52°43·6′	2°12·0′W	T	127
Longnor	Staffs	SK0864	53°10·6′	1°52·4′W	T	119
Longnor Gorse Fm	Staffs	SJ8514	52°43·6′	2°12·9′W	FM	127
Longnor Park	Shrops	SJ4600	52°35·9′	2°47·4′W	T	126
Long Nose	Pemb	SM7204	51°41·5′	5°17·6′W	X	157
Long Nose Spit	Kent	TR3871	51°23·5′	1°25·7′E	X	179
Long Oak	Shrops	SJ3523	52°48·3′	2°57·5′W	T	126
Long Oaks	Swan	SS5289	51°35·1′	4°7·8′W	X	159
Lòn Godrum	Highld	NG4159	57°33·1′	6°19·3′W	W	23
Longore Br	Leic	SK8236	52°55·1′	0°46·4′W	X	130
Longovicivm (Roman Fort)	Durham	NZ1546	54°48·8′	1°45·6′W	R	88
Longparish	Hants	SU4344	51°11·8′	1°22·7′W	T	185
Longparish Ho	Hants	SU4344	51°11·8′	1°22·7′W	X	185
Longpark	Cumbr	NY4362	54°57·2′	2°53·0′W	T	85
Long Park	Devon	SY0999	50°47·2′	3°17·1′W	X	192
Longpark	E Ayr	NS4239	55°37·4′	4°30·1′W	T	70
Long Park	Hants	SU4433	51°5·9′	1°21·9′W	T	185
Longpark Plantn	Scot Bord	NT4841	55°39·8′	2°49·2′W	F	73
Longpastures House Fm	Darl	NZ3419	54°34·1′	1°28·0′W	FM	93
Longpeak	Devon	SS2223	50°59·0′	4°31·8′W	X	190
Long Philip Burn	Scot Bord	NT4330	55°33·9′	2°53·8′W	W	73
Long Pike	Cumbr	NY2208	54°27·9′	3°11·8′W	X	89,90
Long Pike Hollow	Shrops	SO2186	52°28·2′	3°9·4′W	X	137
Long Plain Fm	N Yks	SE5186	54°16·3′	1°12·6′W	FM	100
Long Plantation	D & G	NY0382	55°7·6′	3°30·8′W	F	78
Long Plantation	D & G	NY0869	55°0·7′	3°25·9′W	F	85
Long Plantation	Donc	SE6802	53°30·9′	0°58·1′W	F	111
Long Plantation	E Yorks	TA2221	53°40·5′	0°8·8′W	F	107,113
Long Plantation	Norf	TF7509	52°39·3′	0°35·6′E	F	143
Long Plantation	Norf	TG3322	52°44·9′	1°27·6′E	F	133,134
Long Plantation	Northum	NU1007	55°21·7′	1°50·1′W	F	81
Long Plantation	Powys	SO2087	52°28·7′	3°10·3′W	F	137
Long Plantation	Pth & Kin	NN9120	56°21·8′	3°45·4′W	F	52,58
Long Plantation	S Lanak	NS8332	55°34·3′	3°50·9′W	F	71,72
Long Plantation	Suff	TM2986	52°25·7′	1°22·5′E	F	156
Long Plantn	Darl	NZ3714	54°31·4′	1°25·3′W	F	93
Long Plantn	E Yorks	SE9530	53°45·7′	0°33·1′W	F	106
Long Plantn	E Yorks	SE9825	53°43·0′	0°30·5′W	F	106
Long Plantn	Lancs	SD4556	54°0·1′	2°49·9′W	F	102
Long Plantn	Norf	TG3611	52°38·9′	1°29·7′E	F	133,134
Long Plantn	Notts	SK6385	53°21·7′	1°2·8′W	F	111,120
Long Plantn	N Yks	SE3274	54°9·9′	1°30·2′W	F	99
Long Plantn	N Yks	SE5069	54°7·1′	1°13·7′W	F	100
Long Plantn	N Yks	SE5071	54°8·2′	1°13·7′W	F	100
Long Plantn	Suff	TL7769	52°17·7′	0°36·1′E	F	155
Long Plantn	Suff	TM3245	52°3·5′	1°23·5′E	F	169
Long Point	Pemb	SM7405	51°42·1′	5°15·9′W	X	157
Long Point	Pemb	SM7904	51°41·7′	5°11·5′W	X	157
Long Pool	Moray	NJ2041	57°27·4′	3°19·5′W	W	28
Longpools, The	Shrops	SJ7025	52°49·5′	2°26·3′W	X	127
Longport	C of Stoke	SJ8549	53°2·5′	2°13·0′W	T	118
Long Preston	N Yks	SD8358	54°1·3′	2°15·2′W	T	103
Long Preston Beck	N Yks	SD8459	54°1·8′	2°14·2′W	W	103
Long Quarry Point	Torbay	SX9365	50°28·7′	3°30·1′W	X	202
Long Rake	Derby	SK1764	53°10·6′	1°44·3′W	X	119
Long Reach	Essex	TQ7995	51°37·7′	0°35·6′E	W	167
Long Reach	Glos	SO8123	51°54·5′	2°16·2′W	W	162
Long Reach	Kent	TQ5577	51°28·5′	0°14·3′E	W	177
Long Reach	Kent	TQ8971	51°24·6′	0°43·5′E	W	178
Long Reach	Medway	TQ8171	51°24·8′	0°36·6′E	W	178
Long Reach	Suff	TM2237	51°59·4′	1°14·4′E	W	169
Long Reach	Suff	TM4257	52°9·7′	1°32·7′E	W	156
Longreen	Highld	ND3361	58°32·2′	3°8·6′W	X	12
Long Rein Point	Cumbr	SD2065	54°4·7′	3°13·0′W	X	96
Longridge	Carm	SN3007	51°44·4′	4°27·3′W	X	159
Longridge	Corn	SX3171	50°31·1′	4°22·7′W	X	201
Longridge	E Susx	TQ3620	50°58·0′	0°3·4′W	X	198
Longridge	Glos	SO8809	51°47·0′	2°10·0′W	T	162
Longridge	Lancs	SD6037	53°49·9′	2°36·1′W	T	102,103
Long Ridge	Northum	NU1341	55°40·0′	1°47·2′W	X	75
Long Ridge	N Yks	SE0957	54°0·8′	1°51·3′W	X	104
Long Ridge	N Yks	SE1051	53°57·5′	1°50·4′W	X	104
Longridge	Pemb	SN0820	51°51·0′	4°46·9′W	X	145,158
Longridge	Staffs	SJ9115	52°44·2′	2°7·6′W	T	127
Longridge	W Loth	NS9562	55°50·6′	3°40·2′W	T	65
Long Ridge Crags	N Yks	SE1760	54°2·4′	1°44·0′W	X	99
Long Ridge End	Brad	SE0846	53°54·8′	1°52·3′W	X	104
Longridge End	Glos	SO8124	51°55·1′	2°16·2′W	T	162
Longridge Fell	Lancs	SD6540	53°51·5′	2°31·5′W	H	102,103
Long Ridge Moss	Oldham	SE0402	53°31·1′	1°56·0′W	X	110
Longridge Towers	Northum	NT9549	55°44·3′	2°4·3′W	X	74,75
Longrigg	Cumbr	NY2856	54°53·9′	3°6·9′W	X	85
Long Rigg	Cumbr	NY5013	54°30·8′	2°45·9′W	X	90
Longrigg	Cumbr	NY5072	55°2·6′	2°46·5′W	X	86
Long Rigg	Cumbr	NY8009	54°28·8′	2°18·1′W	X	91,92
Long Rigg	Cumbr	SD6497	54°22·3′	2°32·8′W	X	97
Long Rigg	Cumbr	SD6790	54°18·5′	2°30·0′W	X	98
Longrigg	D & G	NY0378	55°5·5′	3°30·8′W	X	84
Longrigg	Highld	NM8062	56°42·1′	5°35·2′W	X	40
Longrigg	N Lanak	NS8370	55°54·8′	3°51·9′W	T	65
Long Rigg	Northum	NY5885	55°9·7′	2°39·1′W	X	80
Long Rigg	Northum	NY6891	55°13·0′	2°29·7′W	H	80
Long Rigg	Northum	NY7176	55°4·9′	2°26·8′W	X	86,87
Long Rigg	Northum	NY8172	55°2·8′	2°17·4′W	X	86,87
Long Rigg	N Yks	NY9103	54°25·6′	2°7·9′W	X	91,92
Long Rigg Beck	Cumbr	SD6496	54°21·7′	2°32·8′W	W	97
Long Rigg Beck	N Yks	NZ9106	54°26·7′	0°35·4′W	W	94
Longrigg Cottage	Cumbr	NY4047	54°49·1′	2°55·6′W	X	85
Longriggend	N Lanak	NS8270	55°54·8′	3°52·8′W	T	65
Longrigging	Orkney	HY6616	59°2·0′	2°35·1′W	X	5
Longrigging Hill	Moray	NJ3722	57°17·3′	3°2·3′W	H	37
Longrigg Moss	Cumbr	NY5071	55°2·1′	2°46·5′W	X	86
Longriggs	Clackm	NS9295	56°8·4′	3°43·8′W	X	58
Long Riston	E Yorks	TA1242	53°52·0′	0°17·4′W	T	107
Long Robin	D & G	NX6745	54°47·2′	4°3·7′W	X	83,84
Long Rock	Corn	SS2009	50°51·4′	4°33·1′W	X	190
Long Rock	Corn	SW4930	50°7·3′	5°30·3′W	X	203
Longrock	Corn	SW4931	50°7·8′	5°30·4′W	T	203
Long Rock	Kent	TR1367	51°21·9′	1°4·0′E	X	179
Longroods Fm	Derby	SK1871	53°14·4′	1°43·4′W	FM	119
Longrope Wood	Kent	TQ9835	51°5·0′	0°50·0′E	F	189
Long Row	Norf	TM3193	52°29·4′	1°24·6′E	F	134
Longrow	Scot Bord	NY4580	55°6·9′	2°51·3′W	X	79
Long Row	Wakf	SE4016	53°38·6′	1°23·3′W	X	111
Long Rue	S Ayr	NS2919	55°26·4′	4°41·8′W	X	70
Long Run	Somer	ST4841	51°10·2′	2°44·2′W	X	182
Long Sand	Lincs	TF5447	53°0·1′	0°18·1′E	X	131
Long Sandall	Donc	SE6006	53°33·1′	1°5·3′W	T	111
Long Sands	Corn	SX3852	50°21·0′	4°16·3′W	X	201
Long Sands	Devon	SX9252	50°21·7′	3°30·7′W	X	202
Long Sands	N Tyne	NZ3770	55°1·6′	1°24·8′W	X	88
Long Saw Croft	Worcs	SO9779	52°24·8′	2°2·2′W	F	139
Longscales	N Yks	SE2257	54°0·8′	1°39·4′W	T	104
Long Scar	Cumbr	NY2703	54°25·3′	3°7·1′W	X	89,90
Long Scar	Hartpl	NZ5331	54°40·5′	1°10·3′W	X	93
Long Scar	N Yks	SD7672	54°8·8′	2°21·6′W	X	98
Long Scar	N Yks	SD7870	54°7·8′	2°19·8′W	X	98
Long Scar	N Yks	SD8795	54°21·3′	2°11·6′W	X	98
Long Scar	N Yks	SE0297	54°22·4′	1°57·7′W	X	98
Longsdon	Staffs	SJ9654	53°5·2′	2°3·2′W	T	118
Longsdon	Staffs	SJ9655	53°5·8′	2°3·2′W	X	118
Longsdon Grange	Staffs	SJ9556	53°6·3′	2°4·1′W	X	118
Long's Fm	Essex	TL7214	51°48·1′	0°30·1′E	FM	167
Long's Fm	Essex	TL8911	51°46·2′	0°44·8′E	FM	168
Long's Fm	Essex	TL9431	51°56·8′	0°49·8′E	FM	168
Longs Fm	Suff	TL8354	52°9·5′	0°40·9′E	FM	155
Long Shank	Angus	NO3577	56°53·0′	3°3·6′W	X	44
Long Shank	Fife	NO5201	56°12·2′	2°46·0′W	X	59
Longshaw	Staffs	SK0154	53°5·2′	1°58·7′W	X	119
Longshaw	Staffs	SK0645	53°0·4′	1°54·2′W	T	119,128
Longshaw	Wigan	SD5202	53°31·0′	2°43·0′W	T	108
Longshaw Estate	Derby	SK2678	53°18·1′	1°36·2′W	X	119
Longshaw Law	Scot Bord	NT3551	55°45·1′	3°1·7′W	H	66,73
Longshaw Lodge	Derby	SK2679	53°18·7′	1°36·2′W	X	119
Longshaws	Northum	NZ1288	55°11·4′	1°48·3′W	X	81
Longshaws Mill	Northum	NZ1189	55°12·0′	1°49·2′W	X	81
Longsheds	D & G	NX7559	54°54·9′	3°56·6′W	X	84
Longships	Corn	SW3225	50°4·1′	5°44·4′W	X	203
Longside	Aberd	NJ6828	57°20·7′	2°31·4′W	X	38
Longside	Aberd	NJ8325	57°19·2′	2°16·5′W	X	38
Longside	Aberd	NK0347	57°31·0′	1°56·5′W	T	30
Longside	C of Aber	NJ8605	57°8·4′	2°13·4′W	X	38
Long Side	Cumbr	NY2428	54°38·7′	3°10·2′W	X	89,90
Long Side	Derby	SK1299	53°29·5′	1°48·7′W	X	110
Longside	Northum	NU0921	55°29·2′	1°51·0′W	X	75
Long Side	N Yks	SE1182	54°14·3′	1°49·5′W	X	99
Longside Edge	Cumbr	NY2428	54°38·7′	3°10·2′W	X	89,90
Longside Fm	Aberd	NK0246	57°30·5′	1°57·5′W	FM	30
Longside Ho	N Yks	SE1172	54°8·9′	1°49·5′W	X	99
Longside Lake	Surrey	TQ0168	51°24·3′	0°32·5′W	W	176
Longside Moor	Derby	SK3168	53°12·7′	1°31·7′W	X	119
Longside Moss	Derby	SE1300	53°30·0′	1°47·8′W	X	110
Longsides	Barns	SE2811	53°35·9′	1°34·2′W	X	110
Longsight	Man	SJ8696	53°27·9′	2°12·2′W	T	109
Long Sight	Oldham	SD9206	53°33·3′	2°6·8′W	T	109
Longsight Fm	E Yorks	TA1630	53°45·4′	0°14·0′W	FM	107
Long Sike	Northum	NY7497	55°16·2′	2°24·1′W	W	80
Longskelly Pt	E Loth	NT5286	56°4·1′	2°45·8′W	X	66
Longskelly Rocks	E Loth	NT5086	56°4·1′	2°47·7′W	X	66
Long Skerry	Shetld	HU2759	60°19·1′	1°30·2′W	X	3
Long Slack Ho	N Yks	SE1956	54°0·2′	1°42·2′W	X	104
Long Slade Bottom	Hants	SU2600	50°48·2′	1°37·5′W	X	195
Longsleddale	Cumbr	NY4903	54°25·4′	2°46·7′W	X	90
Long Slough	C of Aber	NJ9602	57°6·8′	2°3·5′W	W	38
Longslow	Shrops	SJ6535	52°54·9′	2°30·8′W	T	127
Longslow Ho	Shrops	SJ6534	52°54·4′	2°30·8′W	X	127
Longsowerby	Cumbr	NY3954	54°52·9′	2°56·6′W	T	85
Long Spinney	Suff	TL9079	52°22·8′	0°47·9′E	F	144
Long Spinney	Warw	SP4984	52°27·3′	1°16·3′W	F	140
Long Spinneys	Leic	SP4899	52°35·4′	1°17·1′W	F	140
Long Spring	Suff	TM4884	52°24·1′	1°39·2′E	F	156
Longstanton	Cambs	TL3966	52°16·7′	0°2·7′E	T	154
Longster Trail	Ches	SJ4870	53°13·7′	2°46·5′W	X	117
Long Stile	Cumbr	NY4411	54°29·7′	2°51·5′W	X	90
Longstock	Hants	SU3537	51°8·1′	1°29·6′W	T	185
Longstock Ho	Hants	SU3638	51°8·6′	1°28·7′W	X	185
Longstone	C of Edin	NT2170	55°55·3′	3°15·4′W	T	66
Longstone	Corn	SW5338	50°11·7′	5°27·3′W	T	203
Long Stone	Corn	SW7721	50°3·1′	5°6·5′W	A	204
Long Stone	Corn	SW9068	50°28·7′	4°57·2′W	X	200
Longstone	Corn	SW9668	50°28·8′	4°52·2′W	A	200
Longstone	Corn	SX0673	50°31·7′	4°43·9′W	T	200
Long Stone	Devon	SS7715	50°55·5′	3°44·6′W	A	180
Long Stone	Devon	SX6685	50°39·2′	3°53·4′W	A	191
Long Stone	Glos	SO5512	51°48·5′	2°38·8′W	A	162
Longstone	Northum	NU2438	55°38·3′	1°36·7′W	X	75
Long Stone	Northum	NY7766	54°59·5′	2°21·1′W	X	86,87
Long Stone	Pemb	SM8907	51°43·6′	5°2·9′W	A	157,158
Longstone	Pemb	SN1409	51°45·2′	4°41·3′W	X	158
Longstone	Somer	ST3929	51°3·7′	2°51·8′W	T	193
Longstone Barrow	Devon	SS7042	51°10·0′	3°51·2′W	A	180
Longstone Edge	Derby	SK2073	53°15·5′	1°41·6′W	X	119
Longstone Fell	Cumbr	SD6990	54°18·5′	2°28·2′W	X	98
Longstone Fm	Monm	SO5010	51°47·4′	2°43·1′W	FM	162
Longstone Fm	N Yks	NZ7912	54°30·1′	0°46·4′W	FM	94
Longstone Hill	Devon	SX5691	50°42·3′	4°2·0′W	H	191
Longstone Hill	Somer	ST1440	51°9·4′	3°13·4′W	X	181
Longstone Moor	Derby	SK1973	53°15·5′	1°42·5′W	X	119
Long Stone of Convention	E Ayr	NS6827	55°31·4′	4°5·0′W	A	71
Long Stones	Wilts	SU0869	51°25·4′	1°52·7′W	A	173
Long Stone, The	Corn	SX3353	50°21·4′	4°20·5′W	X	201
Longstone, The	Pemb	SN1409	51°45·2′	4°41·3′W	A	158
Longstone Wells	Devon	SS7633	51°5·2′	3°45·8′W	X	180
Longstongs, The	Lincs	TF0370	53°13·3′	0°27·0′W	X	121
Longstowe	Cambs	TL3055	52°10·9′	0°5·5′W	T	153
Longstowe Hall	Cambs	TL3055	52°10·9′	0°5·5′W	X	153
Long Stratton	Norf	TM1992	52°29·1′	1°13·9′E	T	134
Long Stream	Devon	SX8456	50°23·8′	3°37·5′W	W	202
Long Street	Mil Key	SP7947	52°7·2′	0°50·4′W	T	152
Longstreet	Wilts	SU1451	51°15·7′	1°47·6′W	T	184
Longstreet Down	Wilts	SU1852	51°16·2′	1°44·1′W	X	184
Longstreet Ho	Wilts	SU1450	51°15·2′	1°47·6′W	X	184
Longstripes	Lancs	SD6949	53°56·4′	2°27·9′W	X	103
Longstrother	Northum	NY8377	55°5·5′	2°15·6′W	X	86,87
Long Strumble	Cumbr	NY4850	54°50·8′	2°48·2′W	X	86
Long Sutton	Hants	SU7347	51°13·3′	0°56·9′W	T	186
Long Sutton	Lincs	TF4322	52°46·8′	0°7·6′E	T	131
Long Sutton	Somer	ST4625	51°1·5′	2°45·8′W	T	193
Longswood	Wrekin	SJ6216	52°44·7′	2°33·4′W	X	127
Longsyke	Northum	NY7368	55°0·6′	2°24·9′W	X	86,87
Long Syke Edge	N Yks	SD9444	53°53·8′	2°5·1′W	X	103
Long Synalds	Shrops	SO4293	52°32·1′	2°50·9′W	X	137
Long Tae	Scot Bord	NT3007	55°21·4′	3°5·8′W	H	79
Longtae Burn	Northum	NT9001	55°18·4′	2°9·0′W	W	80
Long Taing	Orkney	HY7245	59°17·7′	2°29·0′W	X	5
Long Taing	Shetld	HU3785	60°33·1′	1°19·0′W	X	1,2,3
Long Taing of Newark	Orkney	HY7242	59°16·1′	2°29·0′W	X	5
Long Thong Fm	Northnts	TL0480	52°24·7′	0°27·9′W	FM	141
Longthorn	Midlo	NT3169	55°54·8′	3°5·8′W	X	66
Longthorne Fm	Kent	TR0440	51°7·6′	0°55·3′E	FM	179,189
Longthorn Hill	Cumbr	NY7410	54°29·3′	2°23·7′W	X	91
Longthorns	Dorset	SY8299	50°47·6′	2°14·9′W	X	194
Longthorns	Somer	ST2437	51°7·9′	3°4·8′W	X	182
Longthorns Fm	Dorset	SY8489	50°42·3′	2°13·2′W	FM	194
Longthorpe	Peterb	TL1698	52°34·3′	0°16·9′W	T	142
Long Thurlow	Suff	TM0168	52°16·6′	0°57·2′E	T	155
Longthwaite	Cumbr	NY2514	54°31·2′	3°9·1′W	X	89,90
Longthwaite	Cumbr	NY4322	54°35·6′	2°52·5′W	T	90
Long Tom	D & G	NX0871	55°0·0′	4°59·7′W	X	76
Long Tom (Standing Stone)	D & G	NX0871	55°0·0′	4°59·7′W	A	76
Longton	C of Stoke	SJ9043	52°59·3′	2°8·5′W	T	118
Longton	Lancs	SD4725	53°43·4′	2°47·8′W	T	102
Long Tongue	Cumbr	NY6344	54°47·6′	2°34·1′W	X	86
Long Tongue	Cumbr	SD3790	54°18·4′	2°57·7′W	X	96,97
Longton Marsh	Lancs	SD4526	53°43·9′	2°49·6′W	W	102
Longtons	Lancs	SD7656	54°0·2′	2°21·6′W	X	103
Longton Sands	Lancs	SD4326	53°43·9′	2°51·4′W	X	102
Longton Wood	Kent	TQ8259	51°18·3′	0°37·1′E	F	178,188
Long Top	Cumbr	NY2404	54°25·8′	3°9·9′W	X	89,90
Longtown	Cumbr	NY3868	55°0·4′	2°57·7′W	T	85
Longtown	Heref	SO3228	51°57·0′	2°59·0′W	T	161
Longtown Castle	Heref	SO3229	51°57·6′	2°59·0′W	A	161
Longtownmail	Orkney	HY4907	58°57·1′	2°52·7′W	X	6,7
Longtownmoor	Cumbr	NY3969	55°1·0′	2°56·8′W	X	85
Longtree Barn	Glos	ST8796	51°40·0′	2°10·9′W	A	162
Longtree Bottom	Glos	ST8796	51°40·0′	2°10·9′W	X	162
Long Valley	Hants	SU8352	51°15·9′	0°48·2′W	X	186
Long Valley	Notts	SK5874	53°15·8′	1°7·4′W	X	120
Longview	Know	SJ4492	53°25·6′	2°50·2′W	T	108
Longville Common	Shrops	SO4185	52°27·8′	2°51·7′W	X	137
Longville in the Dale	Shrops	SO5393	52°32·2′	2°41·2′W	T	137,138
Long Walk	Wilts	SU3066	51°23·8′	1°33·7′W	X	174
Long Walk, The	Win & Maid	SU9674	51°27·6′	0°36·7′W	X	175,176
Longwater Lawn	Hants	SU3208	50°52·5′	1°32·3′W	X	196
Longwath	Cumbr	NY3145	54°48·0′	3°4·0′W	X	85
Longway Bank	Derby	SK3154	53°5·2′	1°31·8′W	T	119
Longway Bank	Derby	SK3155	53°5·7′	1°31·8′W	X	119
Long Way Fm	Durham	NY9126	54°38·0′	2°7·9′W	FM	91,92
Longwell	Cumbr	SD5399	54°23·3′	2°43·0′W	X	97
Longwell	Shetld	HU4429	60°2·9′	1°12·1′W	X	4
Longwell	S Lanak	NS9529	55°32·9′	3°39·4′W	X	72
Longwell Green	S Glos	ST6571	51°26·4′	2°29·8′W	T	172
Longwell Moor	Northum	NY8149	54°50·4′	2°17·3′W	X	86,87
Long Whatton	Leic	SK4823	52°48·4′	1°16·9′W	T	129
Long Whatton Brook	Leic	SK4723	52°48·4′	1°17·8′W	W	129
Longwick	Bucks	SP7805	51°44·5′	0°51·8′W	T	165
Long Wittenham	Oxon	SU5493	51°38·2′	1°12·8′W	T	164,174
Longwitton	Northum	NZ0788	55°11·4′	1°53·0′W	T	81
Longwitton Dene	Northum	NZ0787	55°10·9′	1°53·0′W	X	81
Longwitton Village	Northum	NZ0789	55°12·0′	1°53·0′W	A	81
Long Wood	Beds	TL0214	51°49·1′	0°30·8′W	F	166
Longwood	Cambs	TL3761	52°14·0′	0°0·8′E	X	154
Long Wood	Cered	SN6051	52°8·6′	4°2·4′W	F	146
Longwood	Devon	SS4904	50°49·2′	4°8·2′W	X	191
Longwood	Devon	SS5315	50°55·2′	4°5·1′W	F	180
Long Wood	Devon	SS7533	51°5·2′	3°46·7′W	F	180
Longwood	D & G	NX7161	54°55·9′	4°0·4′W	X	83,84
Long Wood	D & G	NX7179	55°5·6′	4°0·9′W	F	77,84
Longwood	D & G	NY3782	55°8·0′	2°58·9′W	X	79
Long Wood	Dorset	ST7707	50°52·0′	2°19·2′W	F	194
Long Wood	Essex	TL9215	51°48·3′	0°47·5′E	F	168
Long Wood	Heref	SO5162	52°15·5′	2°42·7′W	F	137,138,149
Longwood	Kirk	SE1016	53°38·7′	1°50·5′W	T	110
Long Wood	Lincs	SK9724	52°48·5′	0°33·3′W	F	130
Long Wood	Lincs	TF0772	53°14·3′	0°23·4′W	F	121
Long Wood	N Yks	SE4661	54°2·8′	1°17·4′W	F	100
Long Wood	Oxon	SP5310	51°47·4′	1°13·5′W	F	164
Long Wood	Powys	SO3270	52°19·7′	2°59·5′W	F	137,148
Long Wood	Rut	SK8202	52°36·8′	0°46·9′W	F	141
Long Wood	Scot Bord	NT6861	55°50·7′	2°30·2′W	F	67
Long Wood	Somer	ST4855	51°17·7′	2°44·4′W	F	172,182
Long Wood	Suff	TL7849	52°6·9′	0°36·4′E	F	155
Long Wood	Suff	TL8460	52°12·7′	0°42·0′E	F	155
Long Wood	Suff	TL9445	52°4·4′	0°50·2′E	F	155
Long Wood	W Susx	TQ3332	51°4·5′	0°5·7′W	F	187
Longwood Dean Fm	Hants	SU5423	51°0·5′	1°13·4′W	FM	185
Longwood Edge	Kirk	SE1017	53°39·2′	1°50·5′W	T	110
Longwood Hall	Shrops	SJ5941	52°58·1′	2°36·2′W	X	117
Longwood Ho	Hants	SU5424	51°1·0′	1°13·4′W	X	185
Longwood Ho	Norf	TM2791	52°28·4′	1°21·0′E	X	134
Longwood Ho	N Som	ST5271	51°26·4′	2°41·0′W	X	172
Longwood Warren	Hants	SU5326	51°2·1′	1°14·3′W	X	185
Longworth	Heref	SO5639	52°3·1′	2°38·1′W	X	149

Longworth	Oxon	SU3999	51°41·5'	1°25·8'W	T	164
Longworth Manor	Oxon	SU3899	51°41·5'	1°26·6'W	X	164
Longworth Moor	Black w Dar	SD6817	53°39·2'	2°28·6'W	X	109
Longyester	E Loth	NT5465	55°52·8'	2°43·7'W	X	66
Lòn Heastabhal	N Eil	NB2318	58°4·1'	6°41·4'W	W	13,14
Lòn Horro	Highld	NG4371	57°39·6'	6°18·1'W	W	23
Lòn Hulavik	N Eil	NF8379	57°41·6'	7°18·8'W	X	18
Lôn Isaf	Gwyn	SH5969	53°12·2'	4°6·3'W	X	114,115
Lonkhills Fm	Staffs	SK2507	52°39·8'	1°37·4'W	FM	140
Lôn-las	Gwyn	SH4240	52°56·3'	4°20·7'W	X	123
Lon-las	Swan	SS7097	51°39·6'	3°52·4'W	T	170
Lon Leanachain	Highld	NN2078	56°51·8'	4°56·7'W	W	41
Lòn Liath	Arg & Bt	NR7460	55°47·1'	5°35·8'W	X	62
Lòn Liath	Highld	NM6589	56°56·2'	5°51·3'W	W	40
Lòn Loch Mhòir	Highld	NG4159	57°33·1'	6°19·3'W	W	23
Lòn Luachrach	Highld	NG3522	57°13·0'	6°22·9'W	X	32
Lonmay	Aberd	NK0158	57°37·0'	1°58·5'W	T	30
Lòn Mor	Arg & Bt	NM3540	56°28·9'	6°17·8'W	W	47,48
Lòn Mór	Arg & Bt	NR3891	56°2·7'	6°12·0'W	X	61
Lòn Mòr	Highld	NC2362	58°30·9'	5°1·8'W	W	9
Lòn Mór	Highld	NG4552	57°29·5'	6°14·9'W	W	23
Lòn Mór	Highld	NH3206	57°7·1'	4°46·0'W	X	34
Lòn Mòr	N Eil	NF7539	57°19·8'	7°23·6'W	W	22
Lòn Mór	Stir	NN5005	56°13·1'	4°24·7'W	X	57
Lonmore	Highld	NG2646	57°25·6'	6°33·4'W	T	23
Lonnachie Rig	D & G	NY0299	55°16·8'	3°32·1'W	X	78
Lòn na Dubh-sgeir	Arg & Bt	NL9539	56°26·9'	6°56·6'W	X	46
Lòn na Fola	Highld	NH4722	57°16·0'	4°31·8'W	X	26
Lòn na Graidhe	N Eil	NB0313	58°0·7'	7°1·3'W	X	13
Lòn nam Breac	Highld	NG4947	57°26·9'	6°10·6'W	W	23
Lòn na Muice	Highld	NG4733	57°19·3'	6°11·7'W	W	32
Lòn nan Achadhanan	Highld	NG4444	57°25·1'	6°15·4'W	W	23
Lòn nan Airigh	Highld	NG4835	57°20·4'	6°10·8'W	W	32
Lòn nan Earb	Highld	NG4168	57°37·8'	6°19·9'W	W	23
Lon nan Laough	Arg & Bt	NN0009	56°14·1'	5°13·2'W	X	55
Lòn na Saorach	Highld	NG4550	57°28·4'	6°14·7'W	W	23
Lòn na Sunachur	Highld	NH5593	57°54·4'	4°26·4'W	X	21
Lonnie	Highld	NH7349	57°31·1'	4°6·8'W	X	27
Lonning Fm	Cumbr	NY3051	54°51·2'	3°5·0'W	FM	85
Lonning Head	Cumbr	NY3542	54°46·4'	3°0·2'W	X	85
Lonning Park	Cumbr	NY4766	54°59·4'	2°49·3'W	X	86
Lonning, The	Cumbr	NY3850	54°50·7'	2°57·5'W	X	85
Lonning, The	Northum	NZ0797	55°16·3'	1°53·0'W	X	81
Lòn Odhar	Highld	NH3365	57°38·9'	4°47·4'W	X	20
Lòn Reudle	Arg & Bt	NM3645	56°31·6'	6°17·1'W	W	47,48
Lòn Ruadh	Highld	NG4056	57°31·6'	6°20·1'W	W	23
Lonscale	Cumbr	NY2925	54°37·2'	3°5·6'W	X	89,90
Lonscale Fell	Cumbr	NY2826	54°37·7'	3°6·5'W	H	89,90
Lonsdale	S Lanak	NS7444	55°40·6'	3°59·8'W	X	71
Lonsdale Fm	N Yks	NZ6010	54°29·1'	1°4·0'W	FM	94
Lonsdale Plantn	N Yks	NZ6111	54°29·7'	1°3·1'W	F	94
Lòn Tarsuinn	Highld	NC7233	58°16·3'	4°10·5'W	W	16
Lòn Teanga	Highld	NG5058	57°32·8'	6°10·2'W	W	23,24
Lonton	Durham	NY9524	54°36·9'	2°4·2'W	X	91,92
Lòn Tubhaidh	Highld	NN1746	56°34·5'	4°58·3'W	X	50
Loo Cross	Devon	SX7842	50°16·2'	3°42·3'W	X	202
Looe	Corn	SX2553	50°21·3'	4°27·2'W	T	201
Looe Bay	Corn	SX2652	50°20·8'	4°26·4'W	W	201
Looe Mills	Corn	SX2364	50°27·2'	4°29·2'W	T	201
Looe or St George's Island	Corn	SX2551	50°20·2'	4°27·2'W	X	201
Loo Gill	Cumbr	NY6242	54°46·5'	2°35·0'W	W	86
Lookaboutye	Clackm	NS9191	56°6·2'	3°44·7'W	X	58
Lookaboutye	W Loth	NT0970	55°55·1'	3°26·9'W	X	65
Looke Fm	Dorset	SY5488	50°41·6'	2°38·7'W	FM	194
Lookingflatt	Cumbr	NY6817	54°33·1'	2°29·3'W	X	91
Looking Glass	Corn	SX4356	50°23·2'	4°12·1'W	X	201
Looking Stead	Cumbr	NY1811	54°29·5'	3°15·5'W	X	89,90
Lookout	Northum	NT9139	55°38·9'	2°8·1'W	X	74,75
Lookout	Northum	NU2313	55°24·9'	1°37·8'W	X	81
Lookout	Orkney	ND4697	58°51·7'	2°55·7'W	X	6,7
Lookout Fm	Northum	NZ3276	55°4·9'	1°29·5'W	FM	88
Lookout Hill	Surrey	SU9153	51°16·4'	0°41·3'W	X	186
Loom	Durham	NZ4444	54°47·6'	1°18·5'W	X	88
Looma Shun	Orkney	HY3623	59°5·6'	3°6·5'W	W	6
Loomcroft Fm	Somer	ST2708	50°52·2'	3°1·9'W	FM	193
Loomer Shun	Shetld	HP6315	60°49·0'	0°50·0'W	W	1
Loomi Shun	Orkney	HY4805	58°56·0'	2°53·7'W	W	6,7
Loomi Shun	Shetld	HU3965	60°22·3'	1°17·1'W	W	2,3
Loomi Shun	Shetld	HU4569	60°24·4'	1°10·5'W	W	2,3
Loomi Shuns	Orkney	ND2589	58°47·2'	3°17·4'W	W	7
Loomswood Fm	Suff	TM2453	52°8·0'	1°16·8'E	FM	156
Loonan	Orkney	HY3226	59°7·2'	3°10·8'W	X	6
Loons, The	Orkney	HY2410	58°58·5'	3°18·8'W	X	6
Loons, The	Orkney	HY2524	59°6·0'	3°18·1'W	W	6
Loop	Aberd	NJ7543	57°28·9'	2°24·6'W	X	29
Loop Burn	Highld	ND1643	58°22·3'	3°25·7'W	W	11,12
Loop Fm	Durham	NZ1026	54°38·0'	1°50·3'W	FM	92
Loophill	D & G	NY3777	55°5·3'	2°58·8'W	X	85
Loop of Crooie	Orkney	HY2628	59°8·2'	3°17·1'W	X	6
Loop of Geoholdis	Orkney	HY6221	59°4·7'	2°39·3'W	X	5
Loop Wyke	N Yks	NZ8414	54°31·1'	0°41·7'W	W	94
Loose	Kent	TQ7652	51°14·6'	0°31·7'E	T	188
Loosebeare	Devon	SS7105	50°50·0'	3°49·5'W	X	191
Loose Bottom	E Susx	TQ3608	50°51·6'	0°3·7'W	X	198
Loosedon Barton	Devon	SS6008	50°51·5'	3°59·0'W	X	191
Loosedon Cross	Devon	SS5909	50°52·0'	3°59·8'W	X	191
Loose Fm	E Susx	TQ7614	50°54·1'	0°30·6'E	FM	199
Loosegate	Lincs	TF3125	52°48·6'	0°3·0'W	T	131
Loose Hall	Suff	TM0053	52°8·6'	0°55·8'E	X	155
Looseham	Devon	SS4321	50°58·3'	4°13·8'W	X	180,190
Loosehanger Copse	Wilts	SU2119	50°58·4'	1°41·7'W	F	184
Loose Head	Shetld	HU3621	59°58·6'	1°20·8'W	X	4
Loose Hill	Kent	TQ7552	51°14·6'	0°30·8'E	T	188
Loosehill Fm	Derby	SK1178	53°18·2'	1°49·7'W	FM	119
Loose Howe	N Yks	NZ7000	54°23·7'	0°54·9'W	A	94
Loose Howe	N Yks	NZ7811	54°29·5'	0°47·3'W	A	94
Loose Howe Rigg	N Yks	SE6696	54°21·4'	0°40·2'W	H	94,101
Looseland	Devon	SS8613	50°54·5'	3°36·9'W	X	181
Looseland Cross	Devon	SS8514	50°55·1'	3°37·8'W	X	181

Loose Valley	Kent	TQ7553	51°15·2'	0°30·9'E	X	188
Loosley Row	Bucks	SP8100	51°41·8'	0°49·3'W	T	165
Looss Laward	Shetld	HU4110	59°52·6'	1°15·6'W	X	4
Looss Wick	Shetld	HP6018	60°50·7'	0°53·3'W	W	1
Loot	Shetld	HU4473	60°26·6'	1°11·5'W	X	2,3
Lootingstone	Aberd	NK0161	57°38·6'	1°58·5'W	X	30
Lopcombe Corner	Wilts	SU2435	51°7·1'	1°39·0'W	X	184
Lopemede Fm	Bucks	SP6907	51°45·7'	0°59·6'W	FM	165
Lopen	Somer	ST4214	50°55·6'	2°49·1'W	T	193
Lopen Brook	Somer	ST4414	50°55·6'	2°47·4'W	W	193
Lopen Head	Somer	ST4214	50°55·6'	2°49·1'W	T	193
Lopham Grove	Norf	TM0683	52°24·6'	1°2·1'E	F	144
Lopham's Fm	Essex	TL6837	52°0·6'	0°27·3'E	FM	154
Lopham's Hall Fm	Cambs	TL6452	52°8·7'	0°24·2'E	FM	154
Lopham's Wood	Cambs	TL6551	52°8·2'	0°25·1'E	F	154
Lop Ness	Orkney	HY7543	59°16·6'	2°25·8'W	X	5
Lopness	Orkney	HY7543	59°16·6'	2°25·8'W	X	5
Loppergarth	Cumbr	SD2577	54°11·2'	3°8·5'W	T	96
Loppingdale	Essex	TL5525	51°54·3'	0°15·6'E	X	167
Loppinger Fm	Wilts	ST9057	51°19·0'	2°8·2'W	FM	173
Loppington	Shrops	SJ4729	52°51·6'	2°46·8'W	T	126
Loppington Ho	Shrops	SJ4730	52°52·1'	2°46·8'W	X	126
Lopshill	Dorset	SU0813	50°55·2'	1°52·8'W	X	195
Lops Wath	N Yks	NY8401	54°24·5'	2°14·4'W	X	91,92
Lopthorne	Corn	SS2415	50°54·7'	4°29·8'W	X	190
Lopthorne	Devon	SS3907	50°50·6'	4°16·8'W	X	190
Lopthorne Fm	Corn	SS2609	50°51·5'	4°28·0'W	FM	190
Lopwell	Devon	SX4764	50°27·6'	4°9·0'W	T	201
Loquhariot	Midlo	NT3760	55°50·0'	2°59·9'W	X	66
Lorabar	Renf	NS3858	55°47·5'	4°34·6'W	X	63
Lorbottle	Northum	NU0306	55°21·1'	1°56·7'W	X	81
Lorbottle Hall	Northum	NU0408	55°22·2'	1°55·8'W	X	81
Lorbottle Weststeads	Northum	NU0207	55°21·7'	1°57·7'W	X	81
Lord Anson's Wood	Norf	TG2628	52°48·4'	1°21·6'E	F	133,134
Lord Arthur's Hill	Aberd	NJ5119	57°15·8'	2°48·3'W	H	37
Lord Berkeley's Seat	Highld	NH0683	57°47·9'	5°15·4'W	X	19
Lord Crag	Cumbr	NY3507	54°27·5'	2°59·7'W	X	90
Lorden Copse	I of W	SZ4683	50°38·9'	1°20·6'W	F	196
Lordenshaw	Northum	NZ0598	55°16·8'	1°54·8'W	X	81
Lord Hereford's Knob or Twmpa	Powys	SO2234	52°0·2'	3°7·8'W	X	161
Lordine Court	E Susx	TQ8022	50°58·4'	0°34·2'E	X	199
Lordings Fm	W Susx	TQ0724	51°0·6'	0°28·1'W	FM	197
Lordington Ho	W Susx	SU7809	50°52·7'	0°53·1'W	A	197
Lordling Wood	Bucks	SP8905	51°44·4'	0°42·3'W	F	165
Lord Lovat's Bay	Arg & Bt	NM6020	56°19·0'	5°52·4'W	W	49
Lord Macdonald's Table	Highld	NG3679	57°43·7'	6°25·6'W	X	23
Lord Mayor's Whins	E Yorks	TA1349	53°55·7'	0°16·3'W	F	107
Lord Morton's Covert	Leic	SK7205	52°38·5'	0°55·8'W	X	141
Lord of the Manor	Kent	TR3565	51°20·3'	1°22·8'E	X	179
Lords	Lancs	SD8052	53°58·1'	2°17·9'W	X	103
Lord's Barrow	Dorset	SY7784	50°39·5'	2°19·1'W	A	194
Lordsbridge	Norf	TF5712	52°41·2'	0°19·8'E	T	131,143
Lords Buildings Fm	Powys	SJ2707	52°39·6'	3°4·4'W	FM	126
Lord's Burghs	E Susx	TQ4705	50°49·8'	0°5·6'E	X	198
Lord's Burghs (Tumuli)	E Susx	TQ4705	50°49·8'	0°5·6'E	A	198
Lordscairnie	Fife	NO3517	56°20·7'	3°2·7'W	X	59
Lord's Close	Cumbr	NY1143	54°46·7'	3°22·6'W	X	85
Lord's Common	W Susx	SU8725	51°1·3'	0°45·2'W	F	186,197
Lord's Coppice	Shrops	SJ5701	52°36·5'	2°37·7'W	F	126
Lord's Cricket Ground	C of West	TQ2682	51°31·6'	0°10·6'W	X	176
Lords Fields	Ches	SJ3450	53°2·9'	2°50·6'W	X	117
Lordsfields Fm	Northnts	SP6845	52°6·2'	1°0·0'W	FM	152
Lord's Fm	Cambs	TL1991	52°30·5'	0°14·4'W	FM	142
Lord's Fm	Hants	SU7524	51°0·9'	0°55·5'W	FM	197
Lords Fm	Kent	TR0055	51°15·8'	0°52·4'E	FM	178
Lords Fm	Kent	TR0232	51°3·3'	0°53·3'E	FM	189
Lords Fm	Lancs	SD6236	53°49·4'	2°34·2'W	FM	102,103
Lord's Fm	Oxon	SP5724	51°54·9'	1°9·9'W	FM	164
Lordsgate	Cumbr	NY4869	55°1·0'	2°48·4'W	X	86
Lords Gill Shaw	N Yks	SE0277	54°11·6'	1°57·7'W	W	98
Lord's Ground Fm	Cambs	TL5366	52°16·5'	0°15·0'E	FM	154
Lord's Grove	Monm	SO5311	51°48·0'	2°40·5'W	F	162
Lord's Hill	C of Soton	SU3815	50°56·2'	1°27·2'W	T	196
Lord's Hill	Kent	TQ8856	51°16·5'	0°42·1'E	X	178
Lordshill	Shrops	SJ3701	52°36·4'	2°55·4'W	X	126
Lordshill Common	Surrey	TQ0243	51°10·9'	0°32·0'W	T	186
Lord's Hill Fm	Wilts	ST8839	51°9·2'	2°9·9'W	FM	183
Lordship	Herts	TL2923	51°53·7'	0°7·1'W	X	166
Lordship End	Peterb	TF3309	52°40·0'	0°1·6'W	X	142
Lordship Fm	Herts	TL1632	51°58·7'	0°18·3'W	FM	166
Lordship Fm	Herts	TL2923	51°53·7'	0°7·1'W	FM	166
Lordship Fm	Herts	TL4220	51°51·9'	0°4·1'E	FM	167
Lordship Hill	Derby	SK0693	53°26·3'	1°54·2'W	X	110
Lordship's Fm	Herts	TL3322	51°53·1'	0°3·7'W	FM	166
Lordship Stud	Cambs	TL6060	52°13·1'	0°20·9'E	X	154
Lordship, The	Herts	TL3921	51°52·4'	0°1·5'E	A	166
Lordship Wood	E Susx	TQ7622	50°58·5'	0°30·8'E	F	199
Lord's How	Cumbr	NY2813	54°30·7'	3°6·3'W	X	89,90
Lord's Ings	N Yks	SE5740	53°51·4'	1°7·6'W	X	105
Lord's Island	Cumbr	NY2621	54°35·0'	3°8·3'W	X	89,90
Lordsley	Staffs	SJ7437	52°56·0'	2°22·8'W	X	127
Lord's Lot	Cumbr	SD4492	54°19·5'	2°51·2'W	H	97
Lord's Lot	Northum	NY8859	54°55·8'	2°10·8'W	X	87
Lord's Lot Top	N Yks	SD7177	54°11·5'	2°26·3'W	X	98
Lord's Lot Wood	Lancs	SD5470	54°7·7'	2°41·8'W	F	97
Lord's Moor Fm	N Yks	SE2886	54°16·4'	1°33·8'W	FM	99
Lordsmoor Fm	York	SE6460	54°2·2'	1°1·0'W	FM	100
Lord's Park	Carm	SN3309	51°45·5'	4°24·8'W	X	159
Lord's Park Fm	Corn	SX1971	50°30·9'	4°32·8'W	FM	201
Lordspiece	Staffs	SK1446	53°0·9'	1°47·1'W	X	119,128
Lord's Plain	Cumbr	SD4786	54°16·3'	2°48·4'W	X	97
Lord's Rake	Cumbr	NY2006	54°26·8'	3°13·6'W	X	89,90
Lord's Rigg	Northum	NY7454	54°53·1'	2°23·8'W	X	86,87
Lord's Seat	Cumbr	NY2026	54°37·6'	3°13·9'W	H	89,90
Lord's Seat	Cumbr	NY3713	54°30·8'	2°58·0'W	X	90
Lord's Seat	Cumbr	NY5106	54°27·1'	2°44·9'W	X	90
Lord's Seat	Cumbr	SD4487	54°16·8'	2°51·2'W	H	97
Lord's Seat	Derby	SK1183	53°20·9'	1°49·7'W	H	110

Lords Seat	Northum	NT9107	55°21·7'	2°8·1'W	H	80
Lord's Seat	N Yks	SD8276	54°11·0'	2°16·1'W	X	98
Lord's Seat	N Yks	SE0859	54°1·9'	1°52·3'W	X	104
Lord's Seat (Tumulus)	Derby	SK1183	53°20·9'	1°49·7'W	A	110
Lord's Shaw	Northum	NY8291	55°13·0'	2°16·5'W	H	80
Lord's Stone	Shrops	SJ3302	52°36·9'	2°59·0'W	X	126
Lords Stoop Well	N Yks	SE0256	54°0·2'	1°57·8'W	W	104
Lordstown	Cumbr	NY5180	55°7·0'	2°45·7'W	X	79
Lord Stubbins Wood	Notts	SK5368	53°12·6'	1°12·0'W	F	120
Lord's Well	Cumbr	SD6884	54°15·3'	2°29·1'W	W	98
Lord's Well	Staffs	SK2223	52°48·5'	1°40·0'W	W	128
Lord's Well (Chalybeate)	Cumbr	SD6884	54°15·3'	2°29·1'W	W	98
Lord's Wood	Bath & NE Somer	ST6363	51°22·1'	2°31·5'W	F	172
Lordswood	C of Soton	SU4015	50°56·2'	1°25·5'W	T	196
Lord's Wood	Cumbr	SD2692	54°19·3'	3°7·8'W	F	96,97
Lord's Wood	Essex	TL6013	51°47·8'	0°19·6'E	F	167
Lord's Wood	Hants	SU3917	50°57·3'	1°26·3'W	F	185
Lord's Wood	Heref	SO5515	51°50·1'	2°38·8'W	F	162
Lords Wood	Herts	TL4112	51°47·6'	0°3·1'E	F	167
Lords Wood	Kent	TQ5871	51°25·2'	0°16·7'E	F	177
Lord's Wood	Kent	TQ9155	51°15·9'	0°44·7'E	F	178
Lord's Wood	Kent	TR2644	51°9·3'	1°14·3'E	F	179
Lords Wood	Medway	TQ7762	51°20·0'	0°32·8'E	T	178,188
Lord's Wood	N Yks	SD9455	53°59·7'	2°5·1'W	F	103
Lords Wood	Suff	TL7346	52°5·3'	0°31·9'E	F	155
Lord's Wood	Suff	TL9138	52°0·7'	0°47·4'E	F	155
Lord's Wood	W Susx	SU9324	51°0·7'	0°40·1'W	F	197
Lordswood Fm	Wilts	ST8684	51°33·5'	2°11·7'W	FM	173
Lordswood Ho	Wilts	ST8683	51°33·0'	2°11·7'W	X	173
Lord's Yard Coppice	Worcs	SO7575	52°22·6'	2°21·6'W	F	138
Lord Wandsworth College	Hants	SU7446	51°12·7'	0°56·0'W	X	186
Lord Woodstock's Plantn	Notts	SK5871	53°14·2'	1°7·5'W	F	120
Lorenden	Kent	TQ9959	51°17·9'	0°51·7'E	X	178
Lorg	D & G	NS6600	55°16·8'	4°6·1'W	X	77
Lorg Burn	D & G	NS6601	55°17·3'	4°6·2'W	W	77
Lorg Hill	D & G	NS6602	55°17·9'	4°6·2'W	X	77
Lorgie Hill	Arg & Bt	NR7545	55°39·0'	5°34·1'W	X	62,69
Lorgill	Highld	NG1741	57°22·6'	6°42·0'W	X	23
Lorgill Bay	Highld	NG1740	57°22·0'	6°42·0'W	W	23
Lorgill River	Highld	NG1741	57°22·6'	6°42·0'W	W	23
Lorg Rèidh	Arg & Bt	NR4157	55°44·5'	6°7·2'W	X	60
Lorkin's Fm	Essex	TL8635	51°59·2'	0°42·9'E	FM	155
Lorkins Fm	Thurr	TQ6483	51°31·5'	0°22·2'E	FM	177
Lorn	Arg & Bt	NN0835	56°28·3'	5°6·6'W	X	50
Lorn	W Dunb	NS3985	56°2·1'	4°34·6'W	X	56
Lorns Hill	Angus	NO4439	56°32·6'	2°54·2'W	H	54
Lornshill	Clackm	NS8694	56°7·8'	3°49·6'W	X	58
Lornty	Pth & Kin	NO1746	56°36·2'	3°20·7'W	X	53
Lornty Burn	Pth & Kin	NO1447	56°36·7'	3°23·6'W	W	53
Lorridge Fm	Glos	ST7199	51°41·6'	2°24·8'W	FM	162
Lorton Fells	Cumbr	NY1825	54°37·1'	3°15·8'W	X	89,90
Lorton Ho	Dorset	SY6782	50°38·4'	2°27·6'W	X	194
Lorton Vale	Cumbr	NY1525	54°37·0'	3°18·6'W	X	89
Loscar Common	Roth	SK5079	53°18·6'	1°14·6'W	X	120
Loscars	Cumbr	NY6329	54°39·5'	2°34·0'W	H	91
Loscar Wood	Roth	SK5180	53°19·1'	1°13·7'W	F	111,120
Loscoe	Derby	SK4247	53°1·4'	1°22·0'W	T	129
Loscoe	Wakf	SE4023	53°42·4'	1°23·2'W	T	105
Loscoe Fm	Derby	SK3124	52°49·0'	1°32·0'W	FM	128
Loscombe	Dorset	SY5097	50°46·5'	2°42·2'W	T	194
Loscombe Fm	Dorset	SY6189	50°42·2'	2°32·8'W	FM	194
Loseberry Fm	Surrey	TQ1463	51°21·5'	0°21·4'W	FM	176,187
Lose Hill	Derby	SK1585	53°21·9'	1°46·1'W	H	110
Losehill Fm	Derby	SK1584	53°21·4'	1°46·1'W	FM	110
Losehill Hall	Derby	SK1583	53°20·9'	1°46·1'W	X	110
Loseley House	Surrey	SU9747	51°13·1'	0°36·3'W	A	186
Loseley Park	Surrey	SU9747	51°13·1'	0°36·3'W	X	186
Losely	Surrey	TQ1041	51°9·7'	0°25·2'W	X	187
Losgaintir	N Eil	NG0699	57°53·3'	6°57·2'W	T	14,18
Loskay Ho	N Yks	SE6790	54°18·3'	0°57·8'W	X	94,100
Loskey Beck	N Yks	SE7192	54°19·4'	0°54·1'W	W	94,100
Loskeyle Fm	Corn	SX0775	50°32·8'	4°43·1'W	FM	200
L Ospisdale	Highld	NH7388	57°52·1'	4°8·0'W	W	21
Lossat	D & G	NX0171	54°59·9'	5°6·2'W	X	76,82
Lossat	Moray	NJ5448	57°31·4'	2°45·6'W	X	29
Lossburn Resr	Stir	NS8398	56°9·9'	3°52·6'W	W	57
Lossenham	Kent	TQ8427	51°1·0'	0°37·8'E	X	188,199
Loss Gill Bank	N Yks	SE0265	54°5·1'	1°57·7'W	X	98
Loss Hill	Stir	NN8300	56°11·0'	3°52·7'W	H	57
Lossiemouth	Moray	NJ2370	57°43·1'	3°17·1'W	T	28
Lossiemouth Airfield	Moray	NJ2069	57°42·5'	3°20·1'W	X	28
Lossit	Arg & Bt	NR1856	55°43·2'	6°29·0'W	X	60
Lossit	N Lanak	NS6877	55°58·3'	4°6·5'W	X	64
Lossit Bay	Arg & Bt	NR1755	55°42·6'	6°29·9'W	W	60
Lossit Burn	Arg & Bt	NR1955	55°42·7'	6°28·0'W	W	60
Lossit Fm	Arg & Bt	NR4165	55°48·8'	6°7·6'W	FM	60,61
Lossit Ho	Arg & Bt	NR6320	55°25·3'	5°44·3'W	X	68
Lossit Lodge	Arg & Bt	NR4065	55°48·8'	6°8·6'W	X	60,61
Lossit Point	Arg & Bt	NR1756	55°43·1'	6°30·0'W	X	60
Lossley Burn	Pth & Kin	NO1309	56°16·2'	3°23·8'W	W	58
Lost	Aberd	NJ3413	57°12·4'	3°5·1'W	X	37
Lostford	Shrops	SJ6231	52°52·7'	2°33·5'W	T	127
Lostford Hall	Shrops	SJ6232	52°53·3'	2°33·5'W	X	127
Lost John's Cave	Lancs	SD6778	54°12·0'	2°29·9'W	X	98
Lost Lad	Derby	SK1991	53°25·2'	1°42·4'W	X	110
Lostock	Bolton	SD6608	53°34·3'	2°30·4'W	T	109
Lostock Bridge Fm	Lancs	SD5019	53°40·1'	2°45·0'W	FM	108
Lostock Gralam	Ches	SJ6975	53°16·5'	2°27·5'W	T	118
Lostock Green	Ches	SJ6973	53°15·4'	2°27·5'W	T	118
Lostock Hall	Bolton	SD6509	53°34·8'	2°31·3'W	X	109
Lostock Hall	Lancs	SD5425	53°43·4'	2°41·4'W	T	102
Lostockhall Fm	Ches	SJ9083	53°20·9'	2°8·6'W	FM	109
Lostock Junction	Bolton	SD6708	53°34·3'	2°29·5'W	T	109
Lostrigg Beck	Cumbr	NY0425	54°36·9'	3°28·8'W	W	89
Lostwithiel	Corn	SX1059	50°24·2'	4°40·1'W	T	200
Lost Wood	Essex	TL7612	51°47·0'	0°33·5'E	F	167
Lota Corrie	Highld	NG4624	57°14·4'	6°12·1'W	X	32
Lot Fm	Win & Maid	SU8280	51°31·0'	0°48·7'W	FM	175
Loth	Orkney	HY6034	59°11·7'	2°41·5'W	X	5,6

Lothan Ness	Shetld	HU3167	60°23·4'	1°25·8'W	X	3
Lothbeg	Highld	NC9410	58°4·2'	3°47·3'W	T	17
Lothbeg Point	Highld	NC9609	58°3·7'	3°45·3'W	X	17
Lotheran, The	Orkney	HY6446	59°18·2'	2°37·4'W	X	5
Lothersdale	N Yks	SD9645	53°54·3'	2°3·2'W	T	103
Lotherton Br	Devon	SX5953	50°21·8'	3°58·6'W	X	202
Lotherton Hall	Leeds	SE4436	53°49·3'	1°19·5'W	X	105
Lothian	Aberd	NK0455	57°35·4'	1°55·5'W	X	30
Lothian Br	Midlo	NT3964	55°52·2'	2°58·1'W	X	66
Lothianbridge	Midlo	NT3264	55°52·1'	3°4·8'W	T	66
Lothianburn	Midlo	NT2567	55°53·7'	3°11·5'W	X	66
Lothian Edge	E Loth	NT6471	55°56·1'	2°34·1'W	H	67
Lothmore	Highld	NC9611	58°4·8'	3°45·3'W	T	17
Lothrie Burn	Fife	NO2303	56°13·1'	3°14·1'W	W	58
Lothries	Pth & Kin	NO1404	56°13·5'	3°22·8'W	X	58
Lothwaite Side	Cumbr	NY2029	54°39·2'	3°14·0'W	X	89,90
Lotley Fm	Somer	ST0128	51°2·8'	3°24·4'W	FM	181
Lotmans Fm	E Susx	TQ5128	51°2·1'	0°9·6'E	FM	188,199
Lotmead Fm	Swin	SU1985	51°34·0'	1°43·2'W	FM	173
Loton Park	Shrops	SJ3514	52°43·4'	2°57·3'W	X	126
Lotra of Minn	Shetld	HU3530	60°3·5'	1°21·8'W	X	4
Lot's Br	Norf	TL5198	52°33·8'	0°14·1'E	X	143
Lot's Fm	Cambs	TL5782	52°25·0'	0°18·9'E	FM	143
Lots of Callander	Stir	NN6306	56°13·9'	4°12·2'W	X	57
Lots, The	Cumbr	SD2076	54°10·7'	3°13·1'W	X	96
Lot's Wife	D & G	NX8248	54°49·0'	3°49·8'W	X	84
Lot's Wife	D & G	NX9155	54°52·9'	3°41·5'W	X	84
Lotting Fen	Cambs	TL2485	52°27·2'	0°10·1'W	X	142
Lottisham	Somer	ST5734	51°6·5'	2°36·5'W	T	182,183
Lottisham Fm	Somer	ST5735	51°7·0'	2°36·5'W	FM	182,183
Lotus	D & G	NX8968	54°59·9'	3°43·7'W	X	84
Lotus Hill	D & G	NX9067	54°59·4'	3°42·7'W	H	84
Loud Carr	Lancs	SD6342	53°52·6'	2°33·4'W	X	102,103
Loud Carr Side	Lancs	SD6342	53°52·6'	2°33·4'W	X	102,103
Louden Hill	Corn	SX1380	50°35·6'	4°38·2'W	H	200
Loudham Hall	Suff	TM3054	52°8·4'	1°22·1'E	X	156
Loudonston	E Ayr	NS4321	55°27·7'	4°28·6'W	X	70
Loudon Wood	Aberd	NJ9549	57°32·1'	2°4·6'W	F	30
Loudoun Castle	E Ayr	NS5037	55°36·5'	4°22·4'W	A	70
Loudounhill	E Ayr	NS5938	55°37·2'	4°13·9'W	X	71
Loudoun Hill	E Ayr	NS6038	55°37·2'	4°13·0'W	H	71
Loudoun Mains	E Ayr	NS5238	55°37·0'	4°20·6'W	X	70
Loudscales	Lancs	SD5940	53°51·5'	2°37·0'W	X	102
Loudside	Northum	NZ1069	55°1·2'	1°50·2'W	X	88
Loudwater	Bucks	SU9090	51°36·3'	0°41·6'W	T	175
Loudwater	Herts	TQ0596	51°39·4'	0°28·5'W	T	166,176
Loudwell Fm	E Susx	TQ5423	50°59·4'	0°12·0'E	FM	199
Louella Stud	Leic	SK4814	52°43·5'	1°17·0'W	X	129
Loughan	I of M	SC3799	54°21·9'	4°30·1'W	X	95
Loughborough	Leic	SK5319	52°46·2'	1°12·5'W	T	129
Loughborough Moors	Leic	SK5518	52°45·6'	1°10·7'W	X	129
Loughbrow	Northum	NY9362	54°57·4'	2°6·1'W	X	87
Lough Cranstal	I of M	NX4502	54°23·6'	4°22·8'W	W	95
Lough Dhoo	I of M	SC3596	54°20·2'	4°31·9'W	X	95
Lough Down	W Berks	SU5881	51°31·7'	1°9·4'W	X	174
Loughend	Northum	NT9855	55°47·5'	2°1·5'W	X	75
Lough Green	Northum	NY8062	54°57·4'	2°18·3'W	X	86,87
Lough Hill	Northum	NY8557	54°54·7'	2°13·6'W	H	87
Lough Hill	Northum	NY9382	55°8·2'	2°6·2'W	H	80
Lough Hill	Northum	NZ0194	55°14·7'	1°58·6'W	H	81
Lough Ho	Durham	NZ1923	54°36·4'	1°41·9'W	X	92
Lough Ho	Durham	NZ3031	54°40·6'	1°31·7'W	X	93
Lough Ho	Northum	NZ1289	55°11·9'	1°44·5'W	X	81
Lough Ho	Northum	NZ2080	55°7·1'	1°40·8'W	X	81
Lough Ho	N upon Ty	NZ1668	55°0·6'	1°44·6'W	X	88
Loughor	Swan	SS5798	51°40·0'	4°3·7'W	T	159
Loughrigg	Cumbr	NX9812	54°29·8'	3°34·1'W	X	89
Loughrigg Fell	Cumbr	NY3405	54°26·4'	3°0·6'W	H	90
Loughrigg Tarn	Cumbr	NY3404	54°25·9'	3°0·6'W	W	90
Loughrigg Terr	Cumbr	NY3405	54°26·4'	3°0·6'W	X	90
Lough Shaw	Northum	NY8489	55°11·9'	2°14·7'W	H	80
Lough, The	Cumbr	NY4251	54°51·3'	2°53·8'W	X	85
Loughton	Essex	TQ4396	51°38·9'	0°4·4'E	T	167,177
Loughton	Mil Key	SP8337	52°1·7'	0°47·0'W	T	152
Loughton	Shrops	SO6183	52°26·9'	2°34·0'W	T	138
Loughton Camp	Essex	TQ4197	51°39·5'	0°2·7'E	A	167,177
Loughton Camp	Essex	TQ4197	51°39·5'	0°2·7'E	A	167,177
Loughwood Fm	Devon	SY2599	50°47·4'	3°3·5'W	FM	192,193
Louisa Gate	Somer	SS9328	51°2·7'	3°31·2'W	X	181
Louisa Lodge	Kent	TQ7333	51°4·4'	0°28·6'E	X	188
Lound	Lincs	TF0618	52°45·2'	0°25·4'W	X	130
Lound	Notts	SK6986	53°22·2'	0°57·4'W	T	111,120
Lound	Suff	TM5098	52°31·6'	1°41·5'E	T	134
Lounders Fea	Orkney	HY2004	58°55·2'	3°22·9'W	X	7
Loundfield Fm	Notts	SK6886	53°22·2'	0°58·3'W	FM	111,120
Lound Fm	Lincs	SK9173	53°15·0'	0°37·8'W	FM	121
Lound Fm	Norf	TG4125	52°46·3'	1°34·8'E	FM	134
Lound Hall	Notts	SK7073	53°15·2'	0°56·6'W	X	120
Lound Hill	Donc	SE4908	53°34·2'	1°15·2'W	X	111
Loundon Hill	Northum	NT9408	55°22·2'	2°5·2'W	H	80
Lounds Fm	Leic	SK4921	52°47·3'	1°16·0'W	FM	129
Loundsley Green	Derby	SK3572	53°14·9'	1°28·1'W	T	119
Lound Wood	Notts	SK6763	53°9·8'	0°59·5'W	F	120
Lound Wood	Peterb	TF0601	52°36·0'	0°25·7'W	F	142
Lounges Knowe	Northum	NT8710	55°23·3'	2°11·9'W	X	80
Lounston	Devon	SX7875	50°34·0'	3°43·0'W	X	191
Lount	Leic	SK3819	52°46·3'	1°25·8'W	T	128
Lount Fm	Leic	SK4105	52°38·7'	1°23·2'W	FM	140
Lount Fm	Staffs	SK0321	52°47·4'	1°56·9'W	FM	128
Lount Fm	Staffs	SK2126	52°50·1'	1°40·9'W	FM	128
Lounthwaite	Cumbr	NY6430	54°40·1'	2°33·1'W	X	91
Loup	Arg & Bt	NR7758	55°46·1'	5°32·9'W	X	62
Loup Ho	Arg & Bt	NR7658	55°46·1'	5°33·8'W	X	62
Loupin Stanes	D & G	NY2596	55°15·4'	3°10·4'W	A	79
Loup-o-Lees	C of Edin	NT1171	55°55·7'	3°25·0'W	X	65
Loup Scar	N Yks	SE0261	54°2·9'	1°57·8'W	X	98
Loups Fell	Cumbr	NY6004	54°26·0'	2°36·6'W	X	91
Loups of Kenny	Angus	NO3053	56°40·1'	3°8·1'W	X	53
Lour	Angus	NO4746	56°36·4'	2°51·4'W	X	54
Lour	Scot Bord	NT1835	55°36·4'	3°17·7'W	X	72
Louran Burn	D & G	NX4868	54°59·3'	4°22·1'W	W	83
Louran Rig	D & G	NX5068	54°59·3'	4°20·2'W	X	83
Loura Voe	Shetld	HU4452	60°15·3'	1°11·8'W	W	3
Loura Voe	Shetld	HU4761	60°20·1'	1°8·4'W	W	2,3
Lourie's Stane	Shetld	HU4838	60°7·7'	1°7·7'W	X	4
Lousanna	Lancs	SD4144	53°53·6'	2°53·5'W	X	102
Lousey Law	Northum	NY9278	55°6·0'	2°7·1'W	X	87
Lousie Wood Law	S Lanak	NS9315	55°25·3'	3°41·0'W	H	71,78
Louth	Lincs	TF3387	53°22·0'	0°0·3'E	T	113,122
Louth Canal	Lincs	TF3597	53°27·4'	0°2·4'E	W	113
Louther Skerry	Orkney	ND4777	58°40·9'	2°54·4'W	X	7
Louth Park Fm	Lincs	TF3587	53°22·0'	0°2·1'E	FM	113,122
Louven Howe	N Yks	SE8899	54°23·0'	0°38·3'W	A	94,101
Louven Howe Side	N Yks	SE8899	54°23·0'	0°38·3'W	X	94,101
Lovacott	Devon	SS4508	50°51·3'	4°11·8'W	X	190
Lovacott Green	Devon	SS5228	51°2·2'	4°6·3'W	X	180
Lovaig Bay	Highld	NG2355	57°30·3'	6°37·0'W	W	23
Lovat Br	Highld	NH5144	57°28·0'	4°28·6'W	X	26
Lovaton	Devon	SX5466	50°28·8'	4°3·1'W	T	201
Lovaton	Devon	SX6794	50°44·1'	3°52·7'W	X	191
Love Clough	Lancs	SD8127	53°44·6'	2°16·9'W	T	103
Lovecotes Fm	Essex	TL5629	51°56·5'	0°16·6'E	FM	167
Lovedean	Hants	SU6812	50°54·4'	1°1·6'W	T	196
Loveden Hill	Lincs	SK9045	52°59·9'	0°39·1'W	X	130
Lovedere Fm	Somer	ST2535	51°6·8'	3°3·9'W	FM	182
Lovedown	Essex	TQ8494	51°37·1'	0°39·9'E	X	168,178
Love Green	Bucks	TQ0381	51°31·3'	0°30·5'W	T	176
Lovehall	Angus	NO4737	56°31·6'	2°51·2'W	X	54
Lovehayne	Devon	SY1792	50°43·5'	3°10·2'W	X	192,193
Love Hill House Fm	Bucks	TQ0180	51°30·8'	0°32·3'W	FM	176
Lovehurst Manor	Kent	TQ7741	51°8·7'	0°32·2'E	X	188
Lovelace	Kent	TQ9240	51°7·8'	0°45·0'E	X	189
Lovelady Shield (Hotel)	Cumbr	NY7546	54°48·7'	2°22·9'W	X	86,87
Loveland Fm	Devon	SX4898	50°45·9'	4°8·9'W	FM	191
Lovelands Hill	Surrey	SU9158	51°19·1'	0°41·3'W	X	175,186
Love Lane Fm	Ches	SJ7959	53°7·9'	2°18·4'W	FM	118
Lovel Hill	Brackn	SU9271	51°26·1'	0°40·2'W	X	175
Lovell's Court Fm	Oxon	SU3796	51°39·9'	1°27·5'W	FM	164
Lovell's Fm	W Susx	TQ2722	50°59·2'	0°11·0'W	FM	198
Lovell's Hall	Norf	TF5419	52°45·0'	0°17·3'E	A	131
Lovells Lodge	Northnts	SP6575	52°22·4'	1°2·3'W	X	141
Lovelocks	Hants	SU6310	50°53·4'	1°5·9'W	X	196
Lovelocks	W Berks	SU3672	51°27·0'	1°28·5'W	X	174
Love Lodge Fm	Carm	SN6221	51°52·5'	3°59·9'W	FM	159
Lovel Wood	Bucks	SP7041	52°4·0'	0°58·3'W	F	152
Lovely Hall	Lancs	SD6733	53°47·8'	2°29·6'W	X	103
Lovely Seat	N Yks	SD8795	54°21·3'	2°11·6'W	H	98
Loventor Manor	Devon	SX8462	50°27·0'	3°37·7'W	X	202
Lover	Wilts	SU2120	50°59·0'	1°41·7'W	T	184
Lover Gill Head	N Yks	SD8895	54°21·3'	2°10·7'W	X	98
Loversall Carr	Donc	SK5999	53°29·3'	1°6·2'W	X	111
Loversall	Donc	SK5798	53°28·8'	1°8·1'W	T	111
Lover's Bower	D & G	NX7444	54°46·8'	3°57·1'W	X	83,84
Lover's Leap	Derby	SK0772	53°14·9'	1°53·3'W	X	119
Lover's Leap	Derby	SK1451	53°3·6'	1°47·1'W	X	119
Lover's Leap	Devon	SX7272	50°32·3'	3°48·0'W	X	191
Lover's Leap	Monm	ST5296	51°39·9'	2°41·3'W	X	162
Loverstone Fm	I of W	SZ4983	50°38·9'	1°18·0'W	FM	196
Loves	Essex	TL6015	51°48·9'	0°19·7'E	X	167
Love's Copse	Wilts	SU2773	51°27·6'	1°36·3'W	F	174
Love's Fm	Cambs	TL2060	52°13·7'	0°14·2'W	FM	153
Loves Fm	Essex	TL5930	51°57·0'	0°19·2'E	FM	167
Love's Fm	Herts	TL2539	52°2·3'	0°10·3'W	FM	153
Loves Fm	Kent	TQ7341	51°8·7'	0°28·8'E	FM	188
Love's Fm	Wilts	SU2772	51°27·0'	1°36·3'W	FM	174
Loves Fm	W Susx	SU9123	51°0·2'	0°41·8'W	FM	197
Loves Fm	W Susx	TQ0627	51°2·2'	0°28·9'W	FM	187,197
Loves Green	Essex	TL6404	51°42·9'	0°22·8'E	T	167
Lovesgrove	Cered	SN6281	52°24·8'	4°1·3'W	X	135
Love's Hill	Peterb	TL1398	52°34·3'	0°19·6'W	X	142
Lovesome Hill	Darl	NZ3021	54°35·2'	1°31·7'W	X	93
Lovesome Hill	N Yks	SE3599	54°23·4'	1°27·2'W	X	99
Loveston	Pemb	SN0808	51°44·5'	4°46·5'W	T	158
Loveston	Pemb	SR9496	51°37·7'	4°58·2'W	X	158
Lovestone	S Ayr	NX2399	55°15·5'	4°46·7'W	X	76
Lovetts End Fm	Herts	TL0610	51°46·9'	0°27·4'W	FM	166
Lovetts Wood Fm	Glos	ST7688	51°35·7'	2°20·4'W	FM	162,172
Lovington	Somer	ST5930	51°4·3'	2°34·7'W	T	182,183
Lovistone Barton	Devon	SS5410	50°52·5'	4°4·1'W	X	191
Low Abbey	Cumbr	NY6527	54°38·5'	2°32·1'W	X	91
Low Ackworth	Wakf	SE4417	53°39·1'	1°19·6'W	T	111
Low Acton	Northum	NY8352	54°52·0'	2°15·5'W	X	86,87
Low Airies	D & G	NX2666	54°57·8'	4°42·6'W	X	82
Low Airyolland	D & G	NX1662	54°55·4'	4°51·9'W	X	82
Low Alwinton	Northum	NT9205	55°20·6'	2°7·1'W	T	80
Low Ameshaugh	Cumbr	NY7143	54°47·1'	2°26·6'W	X	86,87
Low Angerton	Northum	NZ0984	55°9·3'	1°51·1'W	T	81
Lowan's Hill Fm	Worcs	SP0368	52°18·8'	1°57·0'W	FM	139
Low Ardley	Northum	NY9058	54°55·2'	2°8·9'W	X	87
Low Ardwell	D & G	NX0846	54°46·6'	4°58·7'W	X	82
Low Arkendale	N Yks	SE3861	54°2·9'	1°24·8'W	X	99
Low Arkland	D & G	NX7258	54°54·3'	3°59·4'W	X	83,84
Low Arnsgill Fm	N Yks	SE5295	54°21·1'	1°11·6'W	FM	100
Low Arvie	D & G	NX7477	55°4·5'	3°58·0'W	X	77,84
Low Ash Fm	Sheff	SK3091	53°25·1'	1°32·5'W	FM	110,111
Low Ash Head	N Yks	SE1476	54°11·0'	1°46·7'W	X	99
Low Ash Head Moor	N Yks	SE1475	54°10·5'	1°46·7'W	X	99
Low Ashyard	E Ayr	NS4736	55°35·9'	4°25·3'W	X	70
Low Askew	N Yks	SE7489	54°17·7'	0°51·4'W	X	94,100
Low Auchenlarie	D & G	NX5352	54°50·7'	4°16·9'W	X	83
Low Auchenree	D & G	NX0057	54°52·3'	5°6·6'W	X	82
Low Auchleach	D & G	NX1047	54°47·2'	4°56·9'W	X	82
Low Audlands	Cumbr	SD5786	54°16·3'	2°39·2'W	X	97
Low Auldgirth	D & G	NX9186	55°9·6'	3°42·2'W	X	78
Low Austby	N Yks	SE0949	53°56·5'	1°51·4'W	X	104
Low Balannan	D & G	NX6958	54°54·2'	4°2·2'W	X	83,84
Low Balcray	D & G	NX4538	54°43·0'	4°24·0'W	X	83
Low Ballacottier	I of M	SC3980	54°11·7'	4°27·7'W	X	95
Low Ballevain	Arg & Bt	NR6525	55°28·0'	5°42·6'W	X	68
Low Ballochdowan	S Ayr	NX0878	55°3·8'	5°0·0'W	X	76
Low Balyett	D & G	NX0861	54°54·7'	4°59·3'W	X	82
Lowbands	Glos	SO7731	51°58·9'	2°19·7'W	T	150
Low Bank	Cumbr	NY1717	54°32·7'	3°16·6'W	X	89,90
Low Bank	N Yks	SD7761	54°2·9'	2°20·7'W	X	98
Lowbank	Pth & Kin	NN9417	56°20·3'	3°42·4'W	X	58
Low Bank End	Cumbr	NY7018	54°33·6'	2°27·4'W	X	91
Low Bank Ho	Cumbr	SD6381	54°13·6'	2°33·6'W	X	97
Low Bank Side	Cumbr	SD3677	54°11·3'	2°58·4'W	X	96,97
Low Bank Spring Wood	N Yks	SE4493	54°20·1'	1°19·0'W	F	99
Low Banniscue	N Yks	SE5490	54°18·4'	1°9·8'W	X	100
Low Barford	Durham	NZ1017	54°33·1'	1°50·3'W	X	92
Low Barlay	D & G	NX5958	54°54·1'	4°11·5'W	X	83
Low Barlings	Lincs	TF0873	53°14·8'	0°22·5'W	T	121
Low Barmston Fm	Sund	NZ3356	54°54·1'	1°28·7'W	FM	88
Low Barn	Cumbr	NY1833	54°41·4'	3°15·9'W	X	89,90
Low Barn	Cumbr	NY7021	54°35·2'	2°27·4'W	X	91
Low Barn	Durham	NZ1215	54°32·1'	1°48·5'W	X	92
Low Barn	N Yks	SD8563	54°4·0'	2°13·3'W	X	98
Low Barn	N Yks	SE2385	54°15·9'	1°38·4'W	X	99
Low Barn	Wilts	ST8583	51°33·0'	2°12·6'W	X	173
Low Barness	D & G	NX3954	54°51·5'	4°30·1'W	X	83
Low Barn Farm	N Yks	SE4962	54°3·3'	1°14·7'W	FM	100
Low Barn Fm	Norf	TM0287	52°26·8'	0°58·8'E	FM	144
Low Barn Fm	N Yks	SE3573	54°9·3'	1°27·4'W	FM	99
Low Barns	Northum	NY9267	55°0·1'	2°7·1'W	X	87
Low Barns Fm	Cambs	TL3151	52°8·7'	0°4·7'W	FM	153
Low Barnultoch	D & G	NX0956	54°52·0'	4°58·2'W	X	82
Lowbarrow	Oxon	SP3114	51°49·7'	1°32·6'W	X	164
Low Barrowby	N Yks	SE3247	53°55·3'	1°30·3'W	X	104
Low Barrows Green	Cumbr	SD5287	54°16·8'	2°43·8'W	X	97
Low Barton	Northum	NU0812	55°24·4'	1°52·0'W	X	81
Low Barugh	Barns	SE3108	53°34·3'	1°31·5'W	T	110,111
Low Baswick Fm	E Yorks	TA0746	53°54·2'	0°21·9'W	FM	107
Low Beck	Cumbr	NY1412	54°30·0'	3°19·3'W	W	89
Low Beckfoot	Cumbr	SD6181	54°13·6'	2°35·5'W	X	97
Low Bellafax Grange	N Yks	SE8077	54°11·2'	0°46·0'W	X	100
Low Bell End	N Yks	SE7196	54°21·5'	0°54·0'W	X	94,100
Low Bellmanear	N Yks	SE8569	54°6·8'	0°41·6'W	X	100
Low Belthorpe	E Yorks	SE7852	53°57·7'	0°48·3'W	X	105,106
Low Benbrack	D & G	NX5479	55°5·3'	4°16·8'W	X	77
Low Bentham	N Yks	SD6469	54°7·2'	2°32·6'W	T	97
Low Bergh	N Yks	SD8676	54°11·0'	2°12·5'W	X	98
Low Bethecar	Cumbr	SD3089	54°17·8'	3°4·1'W	X	96,97
Low Biggins	Cumbr	SD6078	54°12·0'	2°36·4'W	T	97
Low Bink Moss	Durham	NY8723	54°36·4'	2°11·7'W	X	91,92
Low Birker	Cumbr	NY1800	54°23·6'	3°15·4'W	X	89,90
Low Birker Pool	Cumbr	SD1899	54°23·0'	3°15·3'W	W	96
Low Birks	N Yks	SD7365	54°5·1'	2°24·3'W	X	98
Low Birkwith	N Yks	SD7976	54°11·0'	2°18·9'W	X	98
Low Bishopside	N Yks	SE1866	54°5·6'	1°43·1'W	X	99
Low Black Hill	Durham	NY9833	54°41·8'	2°1·4'W	H	92
Low Blacklaw	E Ayr	NS4649	55°42·9'	4°26·6'W	X	64
Low Blackwood Yards	S Lanak	NS7642	55°39·6'	3°57·8'W	X	71
Low Blair	D & G	NX4347	54°47·9'	4°26·1'W	X	83
Low Blakey Moor	N Yks	SE6896	54°21·5'	0°56·8'W	X	94,100
Low Blantyre	S Lanak	NS6957	55°47·6'	4°4·9'W	T	64
Low Bleakhope	Northum	NT9315	55°26·0'	2°6·2'W	X	80
Low Blean	N Yks	SD9287	54°17·0'	2°7·0'W	X	98
Low Bleaze	Cumbr	SD5488	54°17·4'	2°42·0'W	X	97
Low Bog Ho	Cumbr	SD1986	54°16·0'	3°14·2'W	X	96
Low Bogside	N Ayr	NS3653	55°44·8'	4°36·3'W	X	63
Low Bohemia Fm	N Yks	SE5761	54°2·7'	1°7·4'W	FM	100
Low Bolton	N Yks	SE0490	54°18·6'	1°55·9'W	X	98
Low Bonwick	E Yorks	TA1653	53°57·8'	0°13·5'W	X	107
Low Boreland	D & G	NX0958	54°53·1'	4°58·2'W	X	82
Low Borland	E Ayr	NS3948	55°42·2'	4°33·3'W	X	63
Low Borrowbridge	Cumbr	NY6101	54°24·4'	2°35·6'W	T	91
Low Borrowby	N Yks	NZ7715	54°31·7'	0°48·2'W	X	94
Low Borrowdale	Cumbr	NY5702	54°24·9'	2°39·3'W	X	91
Low Botaurnie	Stir	NN4936	56°29·8'	4°26·7'W	X	51
Low Bottom	N Yks	SD6568	54°6·6'	2°31·7'W	X	97
Low Bowhill	E Ayr	NS5239	55°37·6'	4°20·6'W	X	70
Low Bowkerstead	Cumbr	SD3391	54°18·9'	3°1·4'W	X	96,97
Low Bracken Hill Fm	Brad	SE0347	53°55·4'	1°56·8'W	FM	104
Low Bradfield	Sheff	SK2691	53°25·1'	1°36·1'W	T	110
Low Bradley	N Yks	SE0048	53°55·9'	1°59·6'W	T	104
Low Bradley Moor	N Yks	SE0047	53°55·4'	1°59·6'W	X	104
Low Bradshaw Hill	Northum	NY7153	54°52·5'	2°26·7'W	X	86,87
Low Bradup	Brad	SE0944	53°53·8'	1°51·4'W	X	104
Low Braithwaite	Cumbr	NY4242	54°46·4'	2°53·7'W	T	85
Low Bramley Grange	N Yks	SE2076	54°11·0'	1°41·2'W	X	99
Low Bride Stones	N Yks	NZ8404	54°25·7'	0°41·9'W	A	94
Low Bridge	Wilts	ST9873	51°27·6'	2°1·3'W	T	173
Lowbridge Fm	Shrops	SO5577	52°23·6'	2°39·3'W	FM	137,138
Lowbridge Ho	Cumbr	NY5301	54°24·4'	2°43·0'W	X	90
Low Bridgend Fm	Cumbr	NY3120	54°34·5'	3°3·6'W	FM	90
Low Brockholme	N Yks	SE3198	54°22·8'	1°30·9'W	X	99
Low Brock Rigg	N Yks	NZ7706	54°26·9'	0°48·3'W	X	94
Lowbrook Fm	Dorset	ST7809	50°53·0'	2°18·4'W	FM	194
Low Brook Fm	Norf	TM1783	52°24·3'	1°11·8'E	FM	156
Low Broomepark	Northum	NU1012	55°24·4'	1°50·1'W	X	81
Low Broomerside	S Lanak	NS7929	55°32·6'	3°54·6'W	X	71
Low Broom Hill	Cumbr	NY5863	54°57·8'	2°38·9'W	X	86
Low Brooms Fm	Durham	NZ1351	54°51·5'	1°47·4'W	FM	88
Low Brown Hill	N Yks	NY8903	54°25·6'	2°9·8'W	X	91,92
Low Brunton	Northum	NU2124	55°30·8'	1°39·6'W	X	75
Low Brunton	Northum	NY9270	55°1·7'	2°7·1'W	X	87
Low Bucker Ho	N Yks	SD9462	54°3·5'	2°5·1'W	X	98
Low Buildings	Cumbr	NY3839	54°44·8'	2°57·4'W	X	90
Low Burnham	N Lincs	SE7802	53°30·8'	0°49·0'W	T	112
Low Burnlea Row	Durham	NZ1032	54°41·2'	1°50·3'W	X	92
Low Burntoft Fm	Hartpl	NZ4528	54°38·9'	1°17·7'W	FM	93
Low Burradon	Northum	NT9705	55°20·6'	2°2·4'W	X	81
Low Burrows	N Yks	NZ8104	54°25·7'	0°44·7'W	X	94
Low Burton	N Yks	SE2381	54°13·7'	1°38·4'W	X	99
Low Burtonfields Fm	E Yorks	SE7355	53°59·4'	0°52·8'W	FM	105,106
Low Burton Wood	N Yks	SE2381	54°13·7'	1°38·4'W	F	99
Lowbury Hill	Oxon	SU5482	51°32·3'	1°12·9'W	H	174
Low Buston	Northum	NU2207	55°21·6'	1°38·7'W	X	81
Low Butterby	Durham	NZ2739	54°45·0'	1°34·4'W	X	93

Low Byer	Northum	NY7159	54°55·7′	2°26·7′W	X	86,87
Low Byrahill	E Ayr	NS4244	55°40·1′	4°30·3′W	X	70
Lowca	Cumbr	NX9821	54°34·7′	3°34·3′W	T	89
Lowca Cott	Cumbr	NX9921	54°34·7′	3°33·3′W	X	89
Low Callis Wold	E Yorks	SE8255	53°59·3′	0°44·5′W	X	106
Low Capple Mere	N Yks	SD7997	54°22·3′	2°19·0′W	X	98
Low Carlingill	Cumbr	SD6299	54°23·4′	2°34·7′W	X	97
Low Carr	N Yks	SE6062	54°3·3′	1°4·6′W	F	100
Low Carr Fm	N Yks	SE6062	54°3·3′	1°4·6′W	FM	100
Low Carriteth	Northum	NY7983	55°8·7′	2°19·3′W	X	80
Low Carry Ho	Northum	NY8578	55°6·0′	2°13·7′W	X	87
Low Carseduchan	D & G	NX3647	54°47·7′	4°32·6′W	X	83
Low Cattadale	Arg & Bt	NR6710	55°20·0′	5°40·0′W	X	68
Low Catton	E Yorks	SE7053	53°58·3′	0°55·6′W	T	105,106
Low Caythorpe	E Yorks	TA1167	54°5·5′	0°17·8′W	X	101
Low Caythorpe Village	E Yorks	TA1167	54°5·5′	0°17·8′W	A	101
Low Chantry	N Yks	NZ2406	54°27·2′	1°37·4′W	X	93
Low Chapel	Cumbr	NY6206	54°27·1′	2°34·7′W	X	91
Low Chapelton	D & G	NX6147	54°48·2′	4°9·3′W	X	83
Low Chibburn	Northum	NZ2696	55°15·7′	1°35·0′W	A	81
Low Chlenry	D & G	NX1359	54°53·7′	4°54·5′W	X	82
Low Clachaig	Arg & Bt	NR6940	55°36·2′	5°39·6′W	X	62
Low Clanyard	D & G	NX1037	54°41·8′	4°56·5′W	X	82
Low Cleaves	N Yks	SE4983	54°14·7′	1°14·5′W	X	100
Lowclose	Cumbr	NY5125	54°37·3′	2°45·1′W	X	90
Low Close Fm	N Yks	SE4265	54°5·0′	1°21·1′W	FM	99
Low Closes Turbary	N Lincs	SE7708	53°34·0′	0°49·8′W	X	112
Low Clunch	E Ayr	NS4647	55°41·8′	4°26·6′W	X	64
Low Coalsgarth	N Yks	NZ1503	54°25·6′	1°45·7′W	X	92
Low Cocken Fm	Durham	NZ2847	54°49·3′	1°33·4′W	FM	88
Low Cock How	Cumbr	NY0514	54°31·0′	3°27·6′W	X	89
Low Cocklaw	Northum	NT9553	55°46·5′	2°4·3′W	X	67,74,75
Lowcocks	Lancs	SD7446	53°54·8′	2°23·3′W	X	103
Low Common	Donc	SK6695	53°27·1′	1°0·0′W	X	111
Low Common	Kirk	SE1806	53°33·3′	1°43·3′W	X	110
Low Common	Norf	TF8702	52°35·2′	0°46·0′E	X	144
Low Common	Norf	TG2133	52°51·2′	1°17·4′E	X	133
Low Common	Norf	TG3203	52°34·7′	1°25·9′E	X	134
Low Common	Norf	TG3301	52°33·6′	1°26·7′E	X	134
Low Common	Norf	TM0580	52°23·0′	1°1·1′E	X	144
Low Common	Norf	TM1491	52°28·7′	1°9·5′E	T	144
Low Common Fm	Norf	TL9297	52°32·0′	0°50·3′E	FM	144
Low Compton	Oldham	SD9208	53°34·4′	2°6·8′W	T	109
Low Coniscliffe	Darl	NZ2413	54°30·9′	1°37·3′W	T	93
Low Coombs Fm	N Yks	NZ7007	54°27·5′	0°54·8′W	FM	94
Low Cop	Heref	SO5623	51°54·5′	2°38·0′W	X	162
Low Copelaw	Durham	NZ2926	54°37·9′	1°32·6′W	X	93
Low Corner Fm	Cambs	TF4600	52°34·9′	0°9·7′E	FM	143
Low Cote Fm	N Yks	SE5194	54°20·6′	1°12·5′W	FM	100
Low Cotehill	Cumbr	NY4750	54°50·8′	2°49·1′W	T	86
Low Cote Moor	N Yks	SD9369	54°7·3′	2°6·0′W	X	98
Low Countam or Fortypenny Hill	D & G	NS6800	55°16·8′	4°4·3′W	X	77
Low Cowden	Northum	NY9178	55°6·0′	2°8·0′W	X	87
Low Cowlam	E Yorks	SE9664	54°4·0′	0°31·6′W	X	101
Low Coylton	S Ayr	NS4219	55°26·6′	4°29·4′W	T	70
Low Crag	Cumbr	SD2296	54°21·5′	3°11·6′W	X	96
Low Crag	Durham	NZ0016	54°32·6′	1°59·6′W	X	92
Low Craghall	Cumbr	SD1891	54°18·7′	3°15·2′W	X	96
Low Crag Wood	Cumbr	SD4485	54°15·7′	2°51·2′W	F	97
Low Craigeazle	D & G	NX5370	55°0·4′	4°17·5′W	X	77
Low Craighead	S Ayr	NS2301	55°16·5′	4°46·8′W	X	76
Low Craighton	E Dunb	NS5376	55°57·5′	4°20·8′W	X	64
Low Craiglemine	D & G	NX3939	54°43·5′	4°29·6′W	X	83
Low Craignell	D & G	NX5275	55°3·1′	4°18·6′W	H	77
Low Cranecleugh	Northum	NY6685	55°9·7′	2°31·6′W	X	80
Lowcray	Cumbr	NY0805	54°26·2′	3°24·7′W	X	89
Low Creoch	D & G	NX5958	54°54·1′	4°11·5′W	X	83
Low Crosby Court Fm	N Yks	SE4092	54°19·6′	1°22·7′W	FM	99
Low Cross	N Yks	SE7388	54°17·2′	0°52·3′W	A	94,100
Low Crossett Fm	N Yks	SE5794	54°20·5′	1°7·0′W	FM	100
Lowcross Fm	Ches	SJ4650	53°2·9′	2°47·9′W	FM	117
Lowcross Fm	Red & Cl	NZ5815	54°31·9′	1°5·9′W	FM	93
Lowcross Hill	Ches	SJ4651	53°3·5′	2°47·9′W	T	117
Low Crow's Ho	Durham	NZ3840	54°45·5′	1°24·1′W	X	88
Low Cuildrynoch	Arg & Bt	NR7661	55°47·7′	5°34·0′W	X	62
Low Culgroat	D & G	NX0952	54°49·8′	4°58·0′W	X	82
Low Cunsey Fm	Cumbr	SD3793	54°20·0′	2°57·7′W	FM	96,97
Low Curghie	D & G	NX1237	54°41·8′	4°54·6′W	X	82
Low Currigg	Cumbr	NY3742	54°46·4′	2°58·3′W	X	85
Low Currochtrie	D & G	NX1237	54°41·8′	4°54·6′W	X	82
Low Dalby	N Yks	SE8587	54°16·5′	0°41·3′W	T	94,100
Low Dalebanks	Cumbr	NY6113	54°30·9′	2°35·7′W	X	91
Low Dale Park	Cumbr	SD3591	54°18·9′	2°59·5′W	X	96,97
Low Dales	N Yks	SE9591	54°18·6′	0°32·0′W	FM	94,101
Lowdales Fm	N Yks	SE9591	54°18·6′	0°32·0′W	FM	94,101
Low Dallars	E Ayr	NS4533	55°34·2′	4°27·1′W	X	70
Low Day Gill	Durham	NZ1226	54°38·0′	1°48·4′W	X	92
Lowden Fm	Kent	TQ8529	51°2·1′	0°38·7′E	FM	189,199
Lowdens Copse	Wilts	SU2322	51°0·0′	1°39·9′W	F	184
Lowdham	Notts	SK6646	53°0·7′	1°0·6′W	T	129
Lowdham Grange	Notts	SK6446	53°0·7′	1°2·4′W	X	129
Lowdham Lodge	Notts	SK6645	53°0·1′	1°0·6′W	X	129
Low Dinsdale	Darl	NZ3411	54°29·8′	1°28·1′W	T	93
Lowdon Ho	N Yks	SE2296	54°21·8′	1°39·3′W	X	99
Low Douk Cave	N Yks	SD6776	54°11·0′	2°29·9′W	X	98
Low Dovengill	Cumbr	SD7299	54°23·4′	2°25·5′W	X	98
Low Dovescar	N Yks	SE0182	54°14·3′	1°58·7′W	X	98
Lowdown Fm	Dorset	ST4002	50°49·1′	2°50·7′W	FM	193
Lowdown Fm	Warw	SP3260	52°14·5′	1°31·5′W	FM	151
Low Drewton	E Yorks	SE9132	53°46·8′	0°36·7′W	X	106
Low Drumclog	S Lanak	NS6340	55°38·3′	4°10·2′W	X	71
Low Drumrae	D & G	NX4042	54°45·1′	4°28·7′W	X	83
Low Drumskeog	D & G	NX3344	54°46·0′	4°35·3′W	X	82
Low Dunashry	Arg & Bt	NR7048	55°40·5′	5°39·0′W	X	62
Lowdy Hall	Heref	SO5850	52°9·0′	2°36·4′W	X	149
Low Dyke	Cumbr	NY4833	54°41·6′	2°48·0′W	X	90
Low Dyke Ho	N Yks	SD7565	54°5·1′	2°22·5′W	X	98
Low Dykes	Cumbr	NY5426	54°37·9′	2°42·3′W	X	90
Lowe	Shrops	SJ4930	52°52·1′	2°45·1′W	T	126
Low Easby	N Yks	NZ5709	54°28·6′	1°6·8′W	X	93
Low East Field Fm	N Yks	TA0383	54°14·2′	0°24·8′W	FM	101
Lowe Bush	Northum	NY6579	55°6·5′	2°32·5′W	X	86
Lowedges	Sheff	SK3480	53°19·2′	1°29·0′W	T	110,111
Lowe Fm	Heref	SO3758	52°13·2′	2°54·9′W	FM	148,149
Lowe Fm	Northnts	SP6982	52°26·1′	0°58·7′W	FM	141
Lowe Fm	Shrops	SO6380	52°25·2′	2°32·2′W	FM	138
Lowe Fm	Shrops	SO7782	52°26·3′	2°19·9′W	FM	138
Lowe Fm	Warw	SP2555	52°11·8′	1°37·7′W	FM	151
Lowe Fm,The	Heref	SO4831	51°58·7′	2°45·0′W	FM	149,161
Lowe Fm, The	Worcs	SO7068	52°18·8′	2°26·0′W	FM	138
Low Ehenside	Cumbr	NY0006	54°26·6′	3°32·1′W	X	89
Lowe Hill	Staffs	SJ9955	53°5·8′	2°0·5′W	T	118
Lowe Hill Ho	Suff	TM0435	51°58·8′	0°58·6′E	X	155
Lowe Hill Villa	Shrops	SJ5030	52°52·2′	2°44·2′W	X	126
Low Eighton	Ghead	NZ2657	54°54·7′	1°35·2′W	T	88
Low Eldrig	D & G	NX1142	54°44·5′	4°55·7′W	X	82
Low Eldrig	D & G	NX2567	54°58·3′	4°43·6′W	X	82
Low Ellington	N Yks	SE2083	54°14·8′	1°41·2′W	T	99
Low End	Durham	NY8232	54°41·2′	2°16·3′W	X	91,92
Low End	N Yks	SE2346	53°54·8′	1°38·6′W	X	104
Lowend	Staffs	SK1060	53°8·5′	1°50·6′W	X	119
Low Entercommon	N Yks	NZ3306	54°27·1′	1°29·0′W	X	93
Lowenva Lodge	Leic	SK7309	52°40·7′	0°54·8′W	X	141
Lower Abbey	Suff	TM4565	52°13·9′	1°35·7′E	X	156
Lower Achachenna	Arg & Bt	NN0221	56°20·7′	5°11·8′W	X	50
Lower Agden	Lancs	SD7953	53°58·6′	2°18·8′W	X	103
Lower Agney	Kent	TQ9921	50°57·5′	0°50·4′E	X	189
Lower Aisholt	Somer	ST2035	51°6·8′	3°8·2′W	T	182
Lower Aldress	Shrops	SO2896	52°33·7′	3°3·3′W	X	137
Lower Alham Fm	Somer	ST6740	51°9·7′	2°27·9′W	FM	183
Lower Allscot	Shrops	SO7396	52°33·9′	2°23·5′W	T	138
Lower Altgaltraig	Arg & Bt	NS0473	55°54·9′	5°7·7′W	X	63
Lower Altofts	Wakf	SE3824	53°42·9′	1°25·0′W	T	104
Lower Amble	Corn	SW9874	50°32·1′	4°50·7′W	T	200
Lower Ansty	Dorset	ST7603	50°49·8′	2°20·1′W	T	194
Lower Apperley	Glos	SO8627	51°56·7′	2°11·8′W	X	162
Lower Arboll	Highld	NH8682	57°49·0′	3°54·7′W	T	21
Lower Ardentallen Ho	Arg & Bt	NM8222	56°20·7′	5°31·2′W	X	49
Lower Ardmannoch	D & G	NX7473	55°2·4′	3°57·9′W	X	77,84
Lower Ardtun	Arg & Bt	NM3822	56°19·3′	6°13·8′W	T	48
Lower Argoed	Monm	ST4694	51°38·8′	2°46·4′W	X	171,172
Lower Arncott	Oxon	SP6018	51°51·7′	1°7·3′W	T	164,165
Lower Ash Fm	Dorset	SY4695	50°45·4′	2°45·6′W	FM	193
Lower Ashtead	Surrey	TQ1757	51°18·2′	0°18·9′W	T	187
Lower Ashton	Devon	SX8484	50°38·9′	3°38·1′W	T	191
Lower Assendon	Oxon	SU7484	51°33·2′	0°55·6′W	T	175
Lower Atchill	Warw	SP3336	52°1·5′	1°30·7′W	X	151
Lower Auchalick	Arg & Bt	NR9174	55°55·1′	5°20·2′W	X	62
Lower Auchenreath	Moray	NJ3763	57°39·4′	3°2·9′W	T	28
Lower Auchinlay	Stir	NN7702	56°11·9′	3°58·5′W	X	57
Lower Auchmill	Aberd	NJ5444	57°29·3′	2°45·3′W	X	29
Lower Auchnamoon	Aberd	NJ8255	57°35·3′	2°17·6′W	X	29,30
Lower Austin Lodge	Kent	TQ5363	51°21·0′	0°12·2′E	X	177,188
Lower Avenue	Staffs	SJ8807	52°39·9′	2°10·2′W	X	127,139
Lower Aylescott	Devon	SS5241	51°9·2′	4°6·6′W	X	180
Lower Aynho Grounds	Northnts	SP5032	51°59·3′	1°15·9′W	X	151
Lower Bach	Heref	SO5461	52°15·0′	2°40·0′W	X	137,138,149
Lower Badcall	Highld	NC1642	58°19·9′	5°8·1′W	T	9
Lower Bagmores Fm	Devon	SX9987	50°40·7′	3°25·4′W	FM	192
Lower Baladdie	Highld	NH8779	57°47·4′	3°53·6′W	X	21
Lower Baldinnie	Fife	NO4211	56°17·5′	2°55·8′W	X	59
Lower Ballaclucas	I of M	SC3479	54°11·0′	4°32·2′W	X	95
Lower Ballaird	Stir	NS5592	56°6·2′	4°19·4′W	X	57
Lower Ballakaighin	I of M	SC2887	54°15·2′	4°38·0′W	X	95
Lower Ballam	Lancs	SD3630	53°46·0′	2°57·8′W	T	102
Lower Ballanorris	I of M	SC2569	54°5·5′	4°40·1′W	X	95
Lower Ballavarkish	I of M	SC2571	54°6·6′	4°40·2′W	X	95
Lower Balmachie	Angus	NO5536	56°31·1′	2°43·4′W	X	54
Lower Bangley	Staffs	SK1601	52°36·6′	1°45·4′W	X	139
Lower Banks Fm	N Yks	SE2647	53°55·4′	1°35·8′W	FM	104
Lower Barden Resr	N Yks	SE0356	54°0·2′	1°56·8′W	W	104
Lower Barker Fm	Lancs	SD5540	53°51·5′	2°40·6′W	FM	102
Lower Barn	Ches	SJ9869	53°13·3′	2°1·4′W	X	118
Lower Barn	Devon	SX7540	50°15·0′	3°44·8′W	X	202
Lower Barn	Kent	TQ5159	51°18·8′	0°10·4′E	X	188
Lower Barn	Lancs	SD6650	53°56·9′	2°30·7′W	X	103
Lower Barn	Lancs	SD7355	53°59·7′	2°24·3′W	X	103
Lower Barn	W Berks	SU4176	51°29·1′	1°24·2′W	X	174
Lower Barn	W Berks	SU4380	51°31·3′	1°22·4′W	X	174
Lower Barn	W Susx	TQ1320	50°58·3′	0°23·0′W	X	198
Lower Barn	W Susx	TQ2120	50°58·2′	0°16·2′W	X	198
Lower Barn Fm	Essex	TM0732	51°57·1′	1°1·1′E	FM	168,169
Lower Barn Fm	Essex	TQ7892	51°36·1′	0°34·6′E	FM	178
Lower Barn Fm	Warw	SP1158	52°13·4′	1°49·9′W	FM	150
Lower Barn Fm	Wilts	ST8340	51°9·8′	2°14·2′W	FM	183
Lower Barn Fm	Worcs	SP0052	52°10·2′	1°59·6′W	FM	150
Lower Barn Fm	W Susx	TQ2221	50°58·8′	0°15·3′W	FM	198
Lower Barns	Worcs	SO8079	52°24·8′	2°17·2′W	X	138
Lower Barnsley Fm	Dorset	ST9903	50°49·8′	2°0·5′W	FM	195
Lower Barpham	W Susx	TQ0709	50°52·5′	0°28·4′W	X	197
Lower Barrihurst Fm	Surrey	TQ0238	51°8·2′	0°32·2′W	FM	186
Lower Bartle	Lancs	SD4933	53°47·7′	2°46·0′W	T	102
Lower Barton Fm	Dorset	SY6699	50°47·6′	2°28·6′W	FM	194
Lower Basildon	W Berks	SU6178	51°30·1′	1°6·9′W	T	175
Lower Basset Down Fm	Swin	SU1180	51°31·4′	1°50·1′W	FM	173
Lower Bassingthorpe	Lincs	SK9629	52°51·2′	0°34·1′W	T	130
Lower Baveney	Shrops	SO6978	52°24·2′	2°26·9′W	X	138
Lower Baynton	Wilts	ST9454	51°17·3′	2°4·8′W	X	184
Lower Bearwood	Heref	SO3957	52°12·7′	2°53·2′W	T	148,149
Lower Beavor	Devon	SY3197	50°46·3′	2°58·3′W	X	193
Lower Bebington	Wirral	SJ3383	53°20·6′	3°0·0′W	T	108
Lower Beeding	W Susx	TQ2227	51°2·0′	0°15·2′W	T	187,198
Lower Beer	Devon	ST0116	50°56·3′	3°24·2′W	X	181
Lower Beesley	Lancs	SD5639	53°51·0′	2°39·7′W	X	102
Lower Beighterton	Staffs	SJ7912	52°42·6′	2°18·2′W	X	127
Lower Benefield	Northnts	SP9888	52°29·1′	0°33·0′W	T	141
Lower Bent	Shrops	SO3392	52°31·5′	2°58·9′W	X	137
Lower Bentley	Worcs	SO9865	52°17·2′	2°1·4′W	T	150
Lower Bents Fm	Brad	SE0837	53°50·0′	1°52·3′W	FM	104
Lower Beobridge	Shrops	SO7891	52°31·2′	2°19·1′W	T	138
Lower Berrick Fm	Oxon	SU6193	51°38·2′	1°6·7′W	FM	164,175
Lower Berrow Fm	Worcs	SP0063	52°16·1′	1°59·6′W	FM	150
Lower Berrycourt	Wilts	ST9123	51°0·6′	2°7·3′W	X	184
Lower Berry Hill	Glos	SO5711	51°48·0′	2°37·0′W	T	162
Lower Berse Fm	Wrex	SJ3150	53°2·8′	3°1·4′W	FM	117
Lower Besley Fm	Devon	ST0418	50°57·4′	3°21·6′W	FM	181
Lower Bettws	Powys	SO2346	52°6·7′	3°7·1′W	X	148
Lower Beversbrook Fm	Wilts	ST9972	51°27·1′	2°0·5′W	FM	173
Lower Bight of Fernham	Devon	SS3324	50°59·7′	4°22·4′W	W	190
Lower Bilfield Fm	Heref	SO5858	52°13·4′	2°36·5′W	FM	149
Lower Bincombe	Dorset	SY6785	50°40·1′	2°27·6′W	X	194
Lower Binton	Warw	SP1453	52°10·7′	1°47·3′W	T	151
Lower Birchwood	Derby	SK4354	53°5·1′	1°21·1′W	T	120
Lower Birtley Fm	Surrey	SU9235	51°6·6′	0°40·8′W	FM	186
Lower Biss Fm	Wilts	ST8756	51°18·4′	2°10·8′W	FM	173
Lower Bisterne Fm	Hants	SU1500	50°48·2′	1°46·8′W	FM	195
Lower Bitchet	Kent	TQ5654	51°16·1′	0°14·6′E	T	188
Lower Bittell Resr	Worcs	SP0174	52°22·1′	1°58·7′W	W	139
Lower Blackgrove Fm	Bucks	SP7617	51°51·0′	0°53·4′W	FM	165
Lower Black Moss	Lancs	SD8241	53°52·1′	2°16·0′W	X	103
Lower Blacon Fm	Warw	SP2162	52°15·6′	1°41·1′W	FM	151
Lower Blairnain	Moray	NJ2738	57°25·8′	3°12·5′W	X	28
Lower Blakemere Fm	Heref	SO3640	52°3·5′	2°55·6′W	FM	148,149,161
Lower Blandford St Mary	Dorset	ST8905	50°50·9′	2°9·0′W	T	195
Lower Bleansley	Cumbr	SD2089	54°17·7′	3°13·3′W	X	96
Lower Blunsdon	Swin	SU1491	51°37·3′	1°47·5′W	T	163,173
Lower Bobbingworth Green	Essex	TL5205	51°43·6′	0°12·4′E	T	167
Lower Bockhampton	Dorset	SY7290	50°42·8′	2°23·4′W	T	194
Lower Boddington	Northnts	SP4852	52°10·1′	1°17·5′W	T	151
Lower Bodham	Norf	TG1139	52°54·6′	1°8·7′E	T	133
Lower Bodinnar	Corn	SW4232	50°8·2′	5°36·3′W	T	203
Lowerbog	Highld	NH5240	57°25·8′	4°27·4′W	X	26
Lower Bogrotten	Moray	NJ4861	57°38·4′	2°51·8′W	X	28,29
Lower Bois	Bucks	SP9600	51°41·7′	0°36·3′W	T	165
Lower Bolney Fm	Oxon	SU7780	51°31·0′	0°53·0′W	FM	175
Lower Bolstone Wood	Heref	SO5533	51°59·9′	2°38·9′W	F	149
Lower Boothlow	Staffs	SK0963	53°10·1′	1°51·5′W	X	119
Lower Bordean	Hants	SU6924	51°0·9′	1°0·6′W	T	197
Lower Borland Park	Pth & Kin	NN9313	56°18·1′	3°43·3′W	X	58
Lower Boscaswell	Corn	SW3734	50°9·1′	5°40·5′W	T	203
Lower Bottom House Fm	Bucks	SU9895	51°38·9′	0°34·6′W	FM	165,176
Lower Bough Fm	E Susx	TQ6523	50°59·2′	0°21·4′E	FM	199
Lower Bourne	Surrey	SU8444	51°11·6′	0°47·5′W	T	186
Lower Bowden	W Berks	SU6176	51°29·0′	1°6·9′W	X	175
Lower Bowden Fm	Somer	ST6820	50°58·9′	2°27·0′W	FM	183
Lower Boxhill Fm	Surrey	TQ1850	51°14·4′	0°18·2′W	FM	187
Lower Boxton	Falk	NS8873	55°56·5′	3°47·2′W	X	65
Lower Brackendale Fm	Notts	SK6937	52°55·8′	0°58·0′W	FM	129
Lower Bradley	Wolv	SO9595	52°33·4′	2°4·0′W	T	139
Lower Brailes	Warw	SP3139	52°3·1′	1°32·5′W	T	151
Lower Bramble Fm	Devon	SX8682	50°37·8′	3°36·3′W	FM	191
Lower Breache Fm	Surrey	TQ1039	51°8·6′	0°25·3′W	FM	187
Lower Breakish	Highld	NG6723	57°14·6′	5°51·3′W	T	32
Lower Bredbury	Stock	SJ9191	53°25·2′	2°7·7′W	T	109
Lower Breinton	Heref	SO4739	52°3·0′	2°46·0′W	T	149,161
Lower Bridmore Fm	Wilts	ST9622	51°0·1′	2°3·0′W	FM	184
Lower Broach	Lancs	SD8942	53°52·7′	2°9·6′W	X	103
Lower Broadfield	Heref	SO5452	52°10·1′	2°40·0′W	X	149
Lower Broadheath	Worcs	SO8057	52°12·9′	2°17·2′W	T	150
Lower Broadmeadow Fm	Heref	SO2642	52°4·5′	3°4·4′W	FM	148,161
Lower Broadrashes	Moray	NJ5159	57°37·4′	2°48·8′W	X	29
Lower Brockhampton	Heref	SO6855	52°11·8′	2°27·7′W	A	149
Lower Brockholes	Lancs	SD5730	53°46·1′	2°38·7′W	X	102
Lower Brockhurst	Staffs	SJ8212	52°42·6′	2°15·6′W	X	127
Lower Brook	Hants	SU3327	51°2·7′	1°31·4′W	T	185
Lower Broomhill	Aberd	NJ6007	57°9·4′	2°39·2′W	X	37
Lower Broughton	Salf	SJ8299	53°29·5′	2°15·9′W	T	109
Lower Broughton	Shrops	SO3190	52°30·5′	3°0·6′W	X	137
Lower Brow Top	Lancs	SD5257	54°0·7′	2°43·5′W	X	102
Lower Bruckland Fm	Devon	SY2793	50°44·2′	3°1·7′W	FM	193
Lower Brynamman	Nth Pt Talb	SN7013	51°48·3′	3°52·7′W	T	160
Lower Brynn	Corn	SW9962	50°25·6′	4°49·4′W	T	200
Lower Bryntalch	Powys	SO1795	52°33·0′	3°13·0′W	X	136
Lower Bryn-y-groes	Powys	SJ1409	52°40·6′	3°15·9′W	X	125
Lower Buckenhill	Heref	SO6033	51°59·9′	2°34·6′W	T	149
Lower Buckland	Hants	SZ3296	50°46·0′	1°32·4′W	T	196
Lower Bullingham	Heref	SO5238	52°2·5′	2°41·6′W	T	149
Lower Bullington	Hants	SU4541	51°10·2′	1°21·0′W	T	185
Lower Bunbury	Ches	SJ5657	53°6·7′	2°39·0′W	T	117
Lower Bunzion	Fife	NO3409	56°16·4′	3°3·5′W	X	59
Lower Burgate	Hants	SU1515	50°56·3′	1°46·8′W	T	184
Lower Burlone	Corn	SX0169	50°29·5′	4°48·0′W	X	200
Lower Burlton Fm	Heref	SO4842	52°4·7′	2°45·1′W	FM	148,149,161
Lower Burncrooks	S Ayr	NS2906	55°19·4′	4°41·3′W	X	70,76
Lower Burnt House Fm	Somer	ST2914	50°55·5′	3°0·2′W	FM	193
Lower Burrow	Lancs	SD4757	54°0·6′	2°48·1′W	X	102
Lower Burrow	Somer	ST4120	50°58·8′	2°50·0′W	T	193
Lower Burrowton	Devon	SY0096	50°45·5′	3°24·7′W	X	192
Lower Burston Fm	Bucks	SP8318	51°51·5′	0°47·3′W	FM	165
Lower Burton	Heref	SO4256	52°12·2′	2°50·5′W	T	148,149
Lower Bush	Medway	TQ6967	51°22·8′	0°26·1′E	T	177,178
Lower Bush	Shrops	SO5882	52°26·3′	2°36·7′W	X	137,138
Lower Bushey Fm	Dorset	SY9783	50°39·0′	2°2·2′W	FM	195
Lower Butterley	Heref	SO6258	52°13·4′	2°33·0′W	X	149
Lower Cadsden	Bucks	SP8204	51°44·0′	0°48·4′W	T	165
Lower Cadshaw	Lancs	SD6634	53°48·3′	2°30·6′W	X	103
Lower Caerfaelog	Powys	SO1073	52°21·1′	3°18·9′W	X	136,148
Lower Caldecote	Beds	TL1746	52°6·2′	0°17·1′W	T	153
Lower Cam	Glos	SO7400	51°42·1′	2°22·2′W	T	162
Lower Camster	Highld	ND2545	58°23·5′	3°16·5′W	X	11,12
Lower Canada	N Som	ST3558	51°19·3′	2°55·6′W	T	182
Lower Canglour	Stir	NS7886	56°3·3′	3°57·1′W	X	57
Lower Carbarns	N Lanak	NS7753	55°45·5′	3°57·2′W	X	64
Lower Carden	Ches	SJ4552	53°4·0′	2°48·8′W	T	117
Lower Carden Hall	Ches	SJ4552	53°4·0′	2°48·8′W	X	117
Lower Carvan	Pemb	SN1714	51°47·9′	4°38·9′W	X	158
Lower Carwood	Shrops	SO4086	52°28·4′	2°52·6′W	X	137
Lower Carwythenack	Corn	SW7127	50°6·2′	5°11·8′W	X	203

Lower Castle Hayes Fm	Staffs	SK1926	52°50·1'	1°42·7'W	FM	128
Lower Catesby	Northnts	SP5159	52°13·8'	1°14·8'W	T	151
Lower Cator	Devon	SX6876	50°34·4'	3°51·5'W	T	191
Lower Caversham	Read	SU7274	51°27·9'	0°57·4'W	T	175
Lower Cefn	Heref	SO3630	51°58·1'	2°55·5'W	X	149,161
Lower Cefn	Powys	SJ1600	52°35·7'	3°14·0'W	X	136
Lower Chadnor	Heref	SO4252	52°10·0'	2°50·5'W	X	148,149
Lower Chalkley Fm	S Glos	ST7586	51°34·6'	2°21·3'W	FM	172
Lower Chancton Fm	W Susx	TQ1313	50°54·5'	0°23·2'W	FM	198
Lower Chapel	Powys	SO0235	52°0·5'	3°25·3'W	T	160
Lower Chapel Ho	N Yks	NZ1814	54°31·5'	1°42·9'W	X	92
Lower Chatwell	Shrops	SO5297	52°34·4'	2°42·1'W	X	137,138
Lower Chedworth	Glos	SP0610	51°47·6'	1°54·4'W	T	163
Lower Chelmscote	Warw	SP3142	52°4·8'	1°32·5'W	X	151
Lower Cheriton	Devon	ST1001	50°48·3'	3°16·3'W	T	192,193
Lower Chicksgrove	Wilts	ST9730	51°4·4'	2°2·2'W	T	184
Lower Chilworth Fm	Oxon	SP6404	51°44·1'	1°4·0'W	FM	164,165
Lower Church Fm	Worcs	SO9854	52°11·3'	2°1·4'W	FM	150
Lower Chute	Wilts	SU3153	51°16·7'	1°32·9'W	T	185
Lower Clapton	Hack	TQ3585	51°33·1'	0°2·8'W	T	177
Lower Claverham Fm	E Susx	TQ5309	50°51·8'	0°10·8'E	FM	199
Lower Claverham Ho	E Susx	TQ5208	50°51·3'	0°10·0'E	X	199
Lower Clent	Worcs	SO9179	52°24·8'	2°7·5'W	T	139
Lower Clicker	Corn	SX2861	50°25·7'	4°24·9'W	T	201
Lower Cliff	Staffs	SK0215	52°44·2'	1°57·8'W	X	128
Lower Cliff	Stock	SJ9792	53°25·7'	2°2·3'W	X	109
Lower Cliffe	Stock	SJ9886	53°22·5'	2°1·4'W	X	109
Lower Clipstone	Norf	TF9729	52°49·6'	0°55·9'E	X	132
Lower Clopton	Warw	SP1645	52°6·4'	1°45·6'W	X	151
Lower Clopton	Warw	SP1957	52°12·9'	1°42·9'W	T	151
Lower Clough	Lancs	SD7258	54°1·3'	2°25·2'W	X	103
Lower Clydach River	Swan	SN6804	51°43·4'	3°54·3'W	W	159
Lower Coed-y-wlad	Powys	SJ2209	52°40·6'	3°8·8'W	X	126
Lower Coignashie	Highld	NH7118	57°14·3'	4°7·8'W	X	35
Lower Coilentowie	Stir	NN6903	56°12·4'	4°6·3'W	X	57
Lower Coillabus	Arg & Bt	NR3143	55°36·6'	6°15·9'W	X	60
Lower Colbiggan	Corn	SX0063	50°26·2'	4°48·6'W	X	200
Lower College Fm	Lancs	SD6136	53°49·4'	2°35·1'W	FM	102,103
Lower Combe	Devon	SX7566	50°29·1'	3°45·3'W	X	202
Lower Comberoy Fm	Devon	SS9900	50°47·7'	3°25·6'W	FM	192
Lower Common	Dorset	SU0906	50°51·4'	1°51·9'W	X	195
Lower Common	Hants	SU6344	51°11·7'	1°5·5'W	T	185
Lower Common	Hants	SU7662	51°21·3'	0°54·1'W	T	175,186
Lower Common	Monm	SO2415	51°49·9'	3°5·8'W	T	161
Lower Common	Monm	SO3300	51°41·9'	2°57·8'W	T	171
Lower Common	Shrops	SJ4505	52°38·6'	2°48·4'W	T	126
Lower Common	W Berks	SU5569	51°25·3'	1°12·1'W	F	174
Lower Cook	Aberd	NJ7956	57°35·9'	2°20·6'W	X	29,30
Lower Cookworthy	Devon	SX3987	50°39·9'	4°16·3'W	X	190
Lower Coombe	Dorset	SY5390	50°42·7'	2°39·6'W	X	194
Lower Coombe Fm	Herts	TL3138	52°1·7'	0°5·0'W	FM	153
Lower Copthurst	Lancs	SD5921	53°41·3'	2°36·8'W	T	102
Lower Core	Lancs	SD5843	53°53·1'	2°37·9'W	X	102
Lower Corry	Devon	ST2401	50°48·4'	3°4·3'W	X	192,193
Lower Corston Fm	S Glos	ST5990	51°36·7'	2°35·1'W	FM	162,172
Lower Coscombe	Glos	SP0730	51°58·3'	1°53·5'W	X	150
Lower Cotburn	Aberd	NJ7654	57°34·8'	2°23·6'W	X	29
Lower Court	Carm	SN3014	51°48·2'	4°27·6'W	X	159
Lower Court	Worcs	SO7251	52°9·6'	2°24·2'W	X	149
Lower Court	Worcs	SO7854	52°11·3'	2°18·9'W	X	150
Lower Court Fm	S Glos	ST6084	51°33·4'	2°34·2'W	FM	172
Lower Court Wood	Hants	SU1114	50°55·8'	1°50·2'W	F	195
Lower Court Wood	Hants	SU1115	50°56·3'	1°50·2'W	F	184
Lower Cousley Wood	E Susx	TQ6633	51°4·6'	0°22·6'E	T	188
Lower Cowley	Staffs	SJ8218	52°45·8'	2°15·6'W	X	127
Lower Cowsden Fm	Worcs	SO9452	52°10·2'	2°4·9'W	FM	150
Lower Cox Street	Kent	TQ8160	51°18·8'	0°36·2'E	T	178,188
Lower Cragabus	Arg & Bt	NR3245	55°37·7'	6°15·0'W	X	60
Lower Craigton	Aberd	NO5999	57°5·1'	2°40·1'W	X	37,44
Lower Crannel Fm	Somer	ST5042	51°10·7'	2°42·5'W	FM	182,183
Lower Creagan Breac	Highld	NN3791	56°59·1'	4°40·5'W	X	34
Lower Creedy	Devon	SS8402	50°48·6'	3°38·4'W	T	191
Lower Croan	Corn	SX0271	50°30·6'	4°47·2'W	T	200
Lower Croft Ho	Lancs	SD8339	53°51·1'	2°15·1'W	X	103
Lower Crossings	Derby	SK0480	53°19·3'	1°56·0'W	T	110
Lower Crundelend Fm	Worcs	SO7266	52°17·7'	2°24·2'W	FM	138,149
Lower Culham Fm	Wok	SU7983	51°32·7'	0°51·3'W	FM	175
Lower Cullamoor	Staffs	SJ9038	52°56·6'	2°8·5'W	X	127
Lower Cullernie	Highld	NH7248	57°30·5'	4°7·7'W	X	27
Lower Cumberworth	Kirk	SE2209	53°34·9'	1°39·7'W	T	110
Lower Cunliffe	Lancs	SD7130	53°46·2'	2°26·0'W	X	103
Lower Cwm	Monm	SO4806	51°45·3'	2°44·8'W	X	161
Lower Cwm	Powys	SO2691	52°31·0'	3°5·0'W	X	137
Lower Cwm Bridge	Powys	SO2419	51°52·1'	3°5·8'W	X	161
Lower Cwmcoched	Heref	SO3225	51°55·4'	2°58·9'W	X	161
Lower Cwmgwannon	Powys	SO1944	52°5·5'	3°10·5'W	X	148,161
Lower Cwmhir	Powys	SO0370	52°19·4'	3°25·0'W	X	136,147
Lower Cwm-twrch	Powys	SO1554	52°10·9'	3°14·2'W	X	148
Lower Cwmtydu	Powys	SO0236	52°1·1'	3°25·3'W	X	160
Lower Daggons	Hants	SU0913	50°55·2'	1°51·9'W	T	195
Lower Dagie	Aberd	NJ6007	57°9·4'	2°39·2'W	X	37
Lower Dairy Ho	Essex	TL9633	51°57·9'	0°51·6'E	X	168
Lower Dairy House Fm	Shrops	SJ8205	52°38·8'	2°15·6'W	FM	127
Lowerdale	Devon	SX7450	50°20·4'	3°45·9'W	X	202
Lower Darwen	Black w Dar	SD6825	53°43·5'	2°28·7'W	T	103
Lower Dean	Beds	TL0569	52°18·8'	0°27·2'W	T	153
Lower Dean	Devon	SX7364	50°28·0'	3°47·0'W	T	202
Lower Dean Fm	Bucks	SP8326	51°55·8'	0°47·2'W	FM	165
Lower Dean Laithe	Brad	SE0140	53°51·6'	1°58·7'W	X	104
Lower Debden Fm	Cambs	TL2468	52°18·0'	0°10·5'W	FM	153
Lower Dell	Highld	NJ0020	57°15·8'	3°39·0'W	X	36
Lower Delphs	Cambs	TL4174	52°21·0'	0°4·6'E	X	142,143
Lower Denby	Kirk	SE2307	53°33·8'	1°38·8'W	T	110
Lower Den Fm	Ches	SJ7348	53°2·0'	2°23·8'W	FM	118
Lower Denham Fm	Bucks	SP7518	51°51·6'	0°54·3'W	FM	165
Lower Derraid	Highld	NJ0332	57°22·3'	3°36·3'W	X	27,36
Lower Deuchries	Aberd	NJ6455	57°35·3'	2°35·7'W	X	29
Lower Diabaig	Highld	NG7960	57°34·8'	5°41·3'W	T	19,24
Lower Dicker	E Susx	TQ5511	50°52·9'	0°12·6'E	T	199

Lower Dinchope	Shrops	SO4584	52°27·3'	2°48·2'W	T	137,138
Lower Ditchford Village	Glos	SP2236	52°1·6'	1°40·4'W	X	151
Lower Dochcarty	Highld	NH5360	57°36·6'	4°27·2'W	X	20
Lower Doiley Fm	Hants	SU4054	51°17·3'	1°25·2'W	FM	185
Lower Dolfawr	Shrops	SO2588	52°29·3'	3°5·9'W	X	137
Lower Dornford Fm	Oxon	SP4420	51°52·8'	1°21·3'W	FM	164
Lower Dorweeke	Devon	SS9406	50°50·9'	3°30·0'W	X	192
Lower Dounreay	Highld	NC9866	58°34·5'	3°44·8'W	T	11
Lower Dowdeswell	Glos	SP0019	51°52·4'	1°59·6'W	X	163
Lower Down	Devon	SX7878	50°35·6'	3°43·0'W	X	191
Lower Down	Shrops	SO3384	52°27·2'	2°58·8'W	T	137
Lower Down	Shrops	SO6374	52°22·0'	2°32·2'W	X	138
Lower Drakemyres	Moray	NJ3954	57°34·6'	3°0·7'W	X	28
Lower Drambuie	Highld	NH5130	57°20·4'	4°28·1'W	X	26
Lower Drayton	Heref	SO5367	52°18·2'	2°41·0'W	X	137,138,149
Lower Drayton	Staffs	SJ9315	52°44·2'	2°5·8'W	X	127
Lower Drum	Highld	NJ0516	57°13·8'	3°34·0'W	X	36
Lower Drumbane	Stir	NN6606	56°13·9'	4°9·3'W	X	57
Lower Drummond	Highld	NH6643	57°27·7'	4°13·6'W	T	26
Lower Duffryn	Powys	SO1037	52°1·7'	3°18·3'W	X	161
Lower Dumball	Glos	SO7311	51°48·1'	2°23·1'W	X	162
Lower Duncliffe Fm	Dorset	ST8223	51°0·6'	2°15·0'W	FM	183
Lower Dunsforth	N Yks	SE4464	54°4·4'	1°19·2'W	T	99
Lower Dunton Hall	Thurr	TQ6587	51°33·7'	0°23·2'E	X	177,178
Lower Durston	Somer	ST2928	51°3·1'	3°0·4'W	T	193
Lower Dutton	Lancs	SD6636	53°49·4'	2°30·6'W	X	103
Lower Dyffryn	Monm	SO4322	51°53·9'	2°49·3'W	X	161
Lower Dyke	Cumbr	NY4638	54°44·3'	2°49·9'W	X	90
Lower Earley	Wok	SU7570	51°25·7'	0°54·9'W	T	175
Lower Earlscourt Fm	Swin	SU2186	51°34·6'	1°41·4'W	FM	174
Lower Earnstrey Park Fm	Shrops	SO5687	52°29·0'	2°38·5'W	FM	137,138
Lower East Carleton	Norf	TG1803	52°35·1'	1°13·5'E	T	134
Lower Eastcombe Fm	Somer	ST7039	51°9·2'	2°25·4'W	FM	183
Lower Eastcott	Devon	SX5199	50°46·5'	4°6·4'W	X	191
Lower Eastern Green	Cov	SP2979	52°24·7'	1°34·0'W	T	140
Lower Easthams Fm	Somer	ST4510	50°53·4'	2°46·5'W	FM	193
Lower Easton Fm	Somer	ST6238	51°8·6'	2°32·2'W	FM	183
Lower Easton Piercy Fm	Wilts	ST8977	51°29·7'	2°9·1'W	FM	173
Lower Eaton Ho	Heref	SO4440	52°3·6'	2°48·4'W	X	148,149,161
Lower Edburton Barn	W Susx	TQ2313	50°54·4'	0°14·6'W	X	198
Lower Edenhope	Shrops	SO2788	52°29·3'	3°4·1'W	X	137
Lower Edge	Lancs	SD7352	53°58·0'	2°24·3'W	X	103
Lower Edgebold	Shrops	SJ4510	52°41·3'	2°48·4'W	X	126
Lower Edmonton	Enf	TQ3493	51°37·4'	0°3·5'W	T	176,177
Lower Eggbeer Fm	Devon	SX7791	50°42·6'	3°44·1'W	FM	191
Lower Egleton	Heref	SO6245	52°6·4'	2°32·9'W	T	149
Lower Eldon Fm	Hants	SU3527	51°2·7'	1°29·7'W	FM	185
Lower Elker	Lancs	SD7135	53°48·9'	2°26·0'W	X	103
Lower Elkstone	Staffs	SK0658	53°7·4'	1°54·2'W	T	119
Lower Ellastone	Staffs	SK1142	52°58·8'	1°49·8'W	T	119,128
Lower Elsford	Devon	SX7982	50°37·7'	3°42·3'W	X	191
Lower Emmetts	Lancs	SD5755	53°59·6'	2°38·9'W	X	102
Lower End	Beds	SP9722	51°53·5'	0°35·0'W	T	165
Lower End	Bucks	SP6809	51°46·8'	1°0·5'W	T	164,165
Lower End	Bucks	SP7333	51°59·7'	0°55·8'W	T	152,165
Lower End	Glos	SO9904	51°44·3'	2°0·5'W	T	163
Lower End	Mil Key	SP9337	52°1·6'	0°38·3'W	T	153
Lower End	Northnts	SP7850	52°8·8'	0°51·2'W	T	152
Lower End	Northnts	SP8159	52°13·6'	0°48·4'W	T	152
Lower End	Northnts	SP8861	52°14·6'	0°42·3'W	T	152
Lower End	Oxon	SP3215	51°50·2'	1°31·7'W	T	164
Lower End Fm	Wilts	SU0375	51°27·6'	1°57·0'W	FM	173
Lower Ensden	Kent	TR0755	51°15·6'	0°58·4'E	X	179
Lower Ettrick	Arg & Bt	NS0367	55°51·6'	5°8·4'W	X	63
Lower Everleigh	Wilts	SU1854	51°17·3'	1°44·1'W	T	184
Lower Exbury	Hants	SZ4298	50°47·0'	1°23·9'W	X	196
Lower Eype	Dorset	SY4491	50°43·2'	2°47·2'W	T	193
Lower Eythorne	Kent	TR2849	51°11·9'	1°16·2'E	T	179
Lower Fachwen	Powys	SO1099	52°35·1'	3°19·3'W	X	136
Lower Failand	N Som	ST5173	51°27·5'	2°41·9'W	T	172
Lower Faintree	Shrops	SO6588	52°29·6'	2°30·5'W	T	138
Lower Fair Snape	Lancs	SD5845	53°54·2'	2°37·9'W	X	102
Lower Falkenham	Suff	TM2938	51°59·8'	1°20·6'E	T	169
Lower Fall	Highld	NH4920	57°15·0'	4°29·7'W	W	26
Lower Farleigh	Devon	SS9413	50°54·6'	3°30·1'W	X	181
Lower Farm	Norf	TG4018	52°42·6'	1°33·6'E	FM	134
Lower Farm Barn	Cambs	TL5956	52°11·0'	0°19·9'E	X	154
Lowerfarm Copse	W Susx	SU7913	50°54·9'	0°52·0'W	F	197
Lower Farringdon	Hants	SU7035	51°6·8'	0°59·6'W	T	186
Lower Feldy Green	Ches	SJ6978	53°18·1'	2°27·5'W	X	118
Lower Fell Plantation	N Yks	SE0658	54°1·3'	1°54·1'W	F	104
Lower Feltham	Houns	TQ0971	51°25·9'	0°25·5'W	T	176
Lower Fence Wood	Lancs	SD6447	53°55·3'	2°32·5'W	X	102,103
Lower Fenemere Fm	Shrops	SJ4522	52°47·8'	2°48·5'W	FM	126
Lower Fernoch	Arg & Bt	NN0119	56°19·6'	5°12·7'W	X	50,55
Lowerfield	Herts	TL3840	52°2·7'	0°1·1'E	X	154
Lower Field Fm	Glos	SP0803	51°43·8'	1°52·7'W	FM	163
Lowerfield Ho	Heref	SO6460	52°14·5'	2°31·2'W	X	138,149
Lower Fields Fm	S Glos	ST7176	51°29·2'	2°24·7'W	FM	172
Lower Fields Fm	Warw	SP4461	52°15·0'	1°20·9'W	FM	151
Lowerfields Fm	Wilts	SU0461	51°21·1'	1°56·2'W	FM	173
Lowerfield Wood	Oxon	SU2288	51°35·7'	1°40·6'W	F	174
Lower Fittleworth	W Susx	TQ0018	50°57·4'	0°34·2'W	T	197
Lower Flass	Lancs	SD7952	53°58·1'	2°18·8'W	X	103
Lower Fleetgreen	Staffs	SK0561	53°9·0'	1°55·1'W	X	119
Lower Fm	Beds	TL0139	52°2·6'	0°31·2'W	FM	153
Lower Fm	Beds	TL0718	51°51·2'	0°26·4'W	FM	166
Lower Fm	Beds	TL2241	52°3·5'	0°12·8'W	FM	153
Lower Fm	Bucks	SP6929	51°57·5'	0°59·4'W	FM	165
Lower Fm	Bucks	SP7523	51°54·3'	0°54·2'W	FM	165
Lower Fm	Bucks	SP7620	51°52·6'	0°53·4'W	FM	165
Lower Fm	Bucks	SP7717	51°51·0'	0°52·5'W	FM	165
Lower Fm	Bucks	SP8710	51°47·1'	0°43·9'W	FM	165
Lower Fm	Cambs	TL6058	52°12·0'	0°20·9'E	FM	154
Lower Fm	Ches	SJ4752	53°4·0'	2°47·1'W	FM	117
Lower Fm	Ches	SJ4872	53°14·8'	2°46·4'W	FM	117
Lower Fm	Ches	SJ5964	53°10·5'	2°36·4'W	FM	117
Lower Fm	Ches	SJ6042	52°58·7'	2°35·3'W	FM	118
Lower Fm	Ches	SJ6065	53°11·1'	2°35·5'W	FM	118
Lower Fm	Devon	ST2502	50°49·0'	3°3·5'W	FM	192,193

Lower Fm	Dorset	ST7522	51°0·0'	2°21·0'W	FM	183
Lower Fm	Dorset	ST7620	50°59·0'	2°20·1'W	FM	183
Lower Fm	Dorset	SU0511	50°54·1'	1°55·3'W	FM	195
Lower Fm	Dorset	SY5689	50°42·2'	2°37·0'W	FM	194
Lower Fm	Dorset	SY7796	50°46·0'	2°19·2'W	FM	194
Lower Fm	Essex	TL9113	51°47·2'	0°46·6'E	FM	168
Lower Fm	Essex	TL9201	51°40·7'	0°47·0'E	FM	168
Lower Fm	Essex	TM0033	51°57·8'	0°55·1'E	FM	168
Lower Fm	Essex	TM0830	51°56·0'	1°1·9'E	FM	168,169
Lower Fm	Essex	TM1017	51°49·0'	1°3·2'E	FM	168,169
Lower Fm	Glos	SO7522	51°54·0'	2°21·4'W	FM	162
Lower Fm	Glos	SO9931	51°58·9'	2°0·5'W	FM	150
Lower Fm	Glos	SP2222	51°54·0'	1°40·4'W	FM	163
Lower Fm	Glos	SP2436	52°1·5'	1°38·6'W	FM	151
Lower Fm	Hants	SU1319	50°58·4'	1°48·5'W	FM	184
Lower Fm	Hants	SU5116	50°56·7'	1°16·1'W	FM	185
Lower Fm	Hants	SU5122	50°59·9'	1°16·0'W	FM	185
Lower Fm	Hants	SU5956	51°18·2'	1°8·8'W	FM	174
Lower Fm	Hants	SU6461	51°20·9'	1°4·5'W	FM	175
Lower Fm	Herts	TL0005	51°44·3'	0°32·7'W	FM	166
Lower Fm	Herts	TL3430	51°57·4'	0°2·6'W	FM	166
Lower Fm	Kent	TQ8046	51°11·3'	0°34·9'E	FM	188
Lower Fm	Lincs	TF0284	53°20·8'	0°27·7'W	FM	121
Lower Fm	Norf	TF6104	52°36·8'	0°23·1'E	FM	143
Lower Fm	Norf	TF6814	52°42·1'	0°29·6'E	FM	132
Lower Fm	Norf	TF7411	52°40·4'	0°34·8'E	FM	132,143
Lower Fm	Norf	TF8505	52°36·9'	0°44·4'E	FM	144
Lower Fm	Norf	TF9211	52°40·0'	0°50·8'E	FM	132
Lower Fm	Northnts	SP5060	52°14·4'	1°15·7'W	FM	151
Lower Fm	Northnts	SP6856	52°12·1'	0°59·9'W	FM	152
Lower Fm	Oxon	SP4108	51°46·4'	1°24·0'W	FM	164
Lower Fm	Oxon	SP4429	51°57·7'	1°21·2'W	FM	164
Lower Fm	Oxon	SP5300	51°42·0'	1°13·6'W	FM	164
Lower Fm	Oxon	SP5512	51°48·5'	1°11·7'W	FM	164
Lower Fm	Oxon	SP5612	51°48·5'	1°10·9'W	FM	164
Lower Fm	Oxon	SP5800	51°42·0'	1°9·3'W	FM	164
Lower Fm	Oxon	SP6703	51°43·5'	1°1·4'W	FM	164,165
Lower Fm	Oxon	SP6800	51°41·9'	1°0·6'W	FM	164,165
Lower Fm	Oxon	SU6681	51°31·7'	1°2·5'W	FM	175
Lower Fm	Oxon	SU6790	51°36·5'	1°1·6'W	FM	164,175
Lower Fm	Powys	SJ2915	52°43·9'	3°2·7'W	FM	126
Lower Fm	S Glos	ST6686	51°34·5'	2°29·0'W	FM	172
Lower Fm	Shrops	SJ3622	52°47·7'	2°56·5'W	FM	126
Lower Fm	Shrops	SO6273	52°21·5'	2°33·1'W	FM	138
Lower Fm	Sol	SP2478	52°24·2'	1°38·4'W	FM	139
Lower Fm	Somer	ST2824	51°0·9'	3°1·2'W	FM	193
Lower Fm	Somer	ST3353	51°16·6'	2°57·2'W	FM	182
Lower Fm	Somer	ST4855	51°17·7'	2°44·4'W	FM	172,182
Lower Fm	Somer	ST5621	50°59·4'	2°37·2'W	FM	183
Lower Fm	Somer	ST6233	51°5·9'	2°32·2'W	FM	183
Lower Fm	Staffs	SK1920	52°46·9'	1°42·7'W	FM	128
Lower Fm	Suff	TL7863	52°14·4'	0°36·8'E	FM	155
Lower Fm	Suff	TL8937	52°0·2'	0°45·6'E	FM	155
Lower Fm	Suff	TL9544	52°3·8'	0°51·1'E	FM	155
Lower Fm	Suff	TL9655	52°9·7'	0°52·3'E	FM	155
Lower Fm	Suff	TM2945	52°3·6'	1°20·8'E	FM	169
Lower Fm	Surrey	TQ1055	51°17·2'	0°25·0'W	FM	187
Lower Fm	Swin	SU1793	51°38·4'	1°44·9'W	FM	163,173
Lower Fm	Warw	SP1996	52°33·9'	1°42·8'W	FM	139
Lower Fm	Warw	SP2698	52°35·0'	1°36·6'W	FM	163
Lower Fm	Warw	SP3694	52°32·8'	1°27·7'W	FM	140
Lower Fm	Warw	SP3775	52°22·5'	1°27·0'W	FM	140
Lower Fm	Warw	SP3955	52°11·7'	1°25·4'W	FM	151
Lower Fm	W Berks	SU3761	51°21·0'	1°27·7'W	FM	174
Lower Fm	W Berks	SU3970	51°25·9'	1°25·9'W	FM	174
Lower Fm	W Berks	SU4472	51°26·9'	1°21·6'W	FM	174
Lower Fm	W Berks	SU4966	51°23·7'	1°17·4'W	FM	174
Lower Fm	Wilts	SU0790	51°36·8'	1°53·5'W	FM	163,173
Lower Fm	Wilts	SU1627	51°2·8'	1°45·9'W	FM	184
Lower Fm	Wilts	SU2759	51°20·0'	1°36·4'W	FM	174
Lower Fm	Wilts	SU2766	51°23·8'	1°36·3'W	FM	174
Lower Fm	Wrex	SJ3341	52°58·0'	2°59·5'W	FM	117
Lower Fm	Wrex	SJ4050	53°2·9'	2°53·3'W	FM	117
Lower Fm	W Susx	SU9804	50°49·9'	0°36·1'W	FM	197
Lower Foel	Powys	SO0983	52°26·5'	3°19·9'W	X	136
Lower Foker Fm	Staffs	SJ9655	53°7·4'	2°2·3'W	FM	118
Lower Fold	Brad	SE0134	53°48·4'	1°58·7'W	X	104
Lower Fold Fm	Lancs	SD6935	53°48·9'	2°27·8'W	FM	103
Lowerford	Lancs	SD8539	53°51·1'	2°13·3'W	T	103
Lower Forest, The	Essex	TL4703	51°42·6'	0°8·1'E	F	167
Lower Forge	Shrops	SO6974	52°22·0'	2°26·9'W	X	138
Lower Forge	Shrops	SO7389	52°30·1'	2°23·5'W	T	138
Lower Fosse Fm	Warw	SP2950	52°9·1'	1°34·2'W	FM	151
Lower Fosse Fm	Warw	SP3562	52°15·5'	1°28·8'W	FM	151
Lower Foxdale	I of M	SC2779	54°10·9'	4°38·6'W	T	95
Lower Foxley	Staffs	SJ7953	53°4·7'	2°18·4'W	X	118
Lower Frankton	Shrops	SJ3631	52°52·6'	2°56·7'W	T	126
Lower Freystrop	Pemb	SM9512	51°46·4'	4°57·9'W	T	157,158
Lower Froyle	Hants	SU7644	51°11·6'	0°54·4'W	T	186
Lower Gabwell	Devon	SX9169	50°30·9'	3°31·9'W	T	202
Lower Gade Fm	Herts	TL0112	51°48·1'	0°31·7'W	FM	166
Lower Gardens	Shrops	SO3585	52°27·8'	2°57·0'W	X	137
Lower Gartally	Highld	NH4930	57°20·4'	4°30·1'W	X	26
Lower Garth	Powys	SJ2110	52°41·2'	3°9·7'W	X	126
Lower Garth	Powys	SO0995	52°33·0'	3°20·1'W	X	136
Lower Gate	Lancs	SD8144	53°53·8'	2°16·9'W	X	103
Lower Gate Fm	E Susx	TQ8621	50°57·7'	0°39·3'E	FM	189,199
Lower Gaufron	Powys	SO0456	52°11·9'	3°23·9'W	X	147
Lower Gentilshurst Fm	W Susx	SU9226	51°1·8'	0°40·9'W	FM	186,197
Lower Gill	Lancs	SD7853	53°58·6'	2°19·7'W	X	103
Lower Gills	Lancs	SD8244	53°53·8'	2°16·0'W	X	103
Lower Glebe Fm	Cambs	TL1586	52°27·8'	0°18·0'W	FM	142
Lower Gledfield	Highld	NH5990	57°52·9'	4°22·2'W	T	21
Lower Gledfield	Highld	NH5991	57°53·4'	4°22·2'W	X	21
Lowerglen	Highld	NG3252	57°29·0'	6°27·8'W	X	23
Lower Glen Astle	Arg & Bt	NR2845	55°37·6'	6°18·8'W	X	60
Lower Glenastle Loch	Arg & Bt	NR2945	55°37·6'	6°17·9'W	W	60
Lower Glendevon Reservoir	Pth & Kin	NN9304	56°13·2'	3°43·1'W	W	58
Lower Glenfintaig Fm	Highld	NN2286	56°56·1'	4°55·1'W	FM	34,41

Lower Glengaber Hill	D & G	NS7417	55°26·1'	3°59·1'W	H	71
Lower Godney	Somer	ST4742	51°10·7'	2°45·1'W	T	182
Lower Godsworthy	Devon	SX5277	50°34·7'	4°5·0'W	X	191,201
Lower Goldstone	Kent	TR2961	51°18·3'	1°17·5'E	T	179
Lower Gordonsburn	Aberd	NJ4738	57°26·0'	2°52·5'W	X	28,29
Lower Gorhuish	Devon	SX5298	50°46·0'	4°5·5'W	X	191
Lower Gornal	Dudley	SO9291	52°31·2'	2°6·7'W	T	139
Lower Gout Fm	N Som	ST3961	51°20·9'	2°52·2'W	FM	182
Lower Goytre	Powys	SO0750	52°8·7'	3°21·2'W	X	147
Lower Grange	Brad	SE1233	53°47·8'	1°48·7'W	T	104
Lower Grange	Monm	ST4285	51°33·9'	2°49·8'W	X	171,172
Lower Grange	Oxon	SU5995	51°39·3'	1°8·4'W	X	164
Lower Grange	Scot Bord	NT1952	55°45·5'	3°17·0'W	X	65,66,72
Lower Grange	Warw	SP3567	52°18·2'	1°28·8'W	X	151
Lower Grange Fm	Heref	SO3632	51°59·2'	2°55·5'W	FM	149,161
Lower Grange Fm	Staffs	SK0243	52°59·3'	1°57·8'W	FM	119,128
Lower Gravenhurst	Beds	TL1135	52°0·4'	0°22·6'W	T	153
Lower Gravenor	Shrops	SO3794	52°32·7'	2°55·3'W	X	137
Lower Green	Essex	TL4334	51°59·4'	0°5·4'E	T	154
Lower Green	Essex	TL7002	51°41·7'	0°28·0'E	T	167
Lower Green	Essex	TL7331	51°57·3'	0°31·5'E	T	167
Lower Green	Essex	TL7404	51°42·7'	0°31·5'E	T	167
Lower Green	Heref	SO3755	52°11·6'	2°54·9'W	X	148,149
Lower Green	Herts	TL1832	51°58·7'	0°16·5'W	T	166
Lower Green	Herts	TL4233	51°58·9'	0°4·5'E	T	167
Lower Green	Kent	TQ5640	51°8·5'	0°14·2'E	T	188
Lower Green	Kent	TQ6241	51°8·9'	0°19·4'E	T	188
Lower Green	Norf	TF9937	52°53·8'	0°57·9'E	T	132
Lower Green	Norf	TG4005	52°35·6'	1°33·0'E	X	134
Lower Green	Powys	SO1378	52°23·8'	3°16·3'W	X	136,148
Lower Green	Staffs	SJ9007	52°39·9'	2°8·5'W	T	127,139
Lower Green	Suff	TL7465	52°15·6'	0°33·4'E	T	155
Lower Green	Suff	TL9457	52°10·9'	0°50·7'E	X	155
Lower Green	Surrey	TQ1366	51°23·1'	0°22·2'W	T	176
Lower Green	Warw	SP5068	52°18·7'	1°15·6'W	T	151
Lower Green	W Berks	SU3564	51°22·7'	1°29·4'W	T	174
Lower Green	Wigan	SJ7099	53°29·5'	2°26·7'W	T	109
Lower Green Bank	Lancs	SD5254	53°59·0'	2°43·5'W	X	102
Lower Green Cross	Devon	SX8145	50°17·8'	3°39·9'W	X	202
Lower Greenfield Fm	Oxon	SU7091	51°37·0'	0°58·9'W	FM	175
Lowergreen Fm	Hants	SU7429	51°3·6'	0°56·3'W	FM	186,197
Lower Green Fm	Norf	TM3089	52°27·3'	1°23·5'E	FM	156
Lower Green Fm	Staffs	SK0458	53°7·4'	1°56·0'W	FM	119
Lower Green Fm	Suff	TM4584	52°24·2'	1°36·5'E	FM	156
Lower Greenland	Highld	ND2367	58°35·3'	3°19·0'W	X	11,12
Lower Green Nook	Lancs	SD5936	53°49·4'	2°37·0'W	X	102
Lower Green Owlers	Kirk	SE0312	53°36·5'	1°56·9'W	X	110
Lower Green Quarries	Cumbr	NY3346	54°48·5'	3°2·1'W	X	85
Lower Greenway	Devon	SX8755	50°23·3'	3°35·0'W	X	202
Lower Greenyards	Stir	NS8290	56°5·6'	3°53·4'W	X	57
Lower Grimmer	Shrops	SJ3403	52°37·5'	2°58·1'W	X	126
Lower Grinacombe	Devon	SX4291	50°42·1'	4°13·9'W	X	190
Lower Grounds	Wrekin	SJ5915	52°44·1'	2°36·0'W	X	126
Lower Grouse Fm	W Susx	TQ2330	51°3·6'	0°14·3'W	FM	187
Lower Grove Common	Heref	SO5525	51°55·5'	2°38·9'W	T	162
Lowergrove Fm	Bucks	SP8029	51°57·5'	0°49·7'W	FM	165
Lower Gull	Suff	TM3946	52°3·9'	1°29·6'E	W	169
Lower Gurney Fm	Bath & NE Somer	ST5657	51°18·9'	2°37·5'W	FM	172,182
Lower Gurrow Point	Devon	SX8655	50°23·3'	3°35·8'W	X	202
Lower Gylen	Arg & Bt	NM8027	56°23·3'	5°33·4'W	X	49
Lower Hacheston	Suff	TM3156	52°9·5'	1°23·0'E	T	156
Lower Haddon Fm	Oxon	SP3005	51°44·8'	1°33·5'W	FM	164
Lower Halistra	Highld	NG2459	57°32·5'	6°36·3'W	T	23
Lower Hall	Ches	SJ5547	53°1·3'	2°39·8'W	X	117
Lower Hall	Essex	TL6223	51°53·1'	0°21·6'E	X	167
Lower Hall	Lancs	SD5931	53°46·7'	2°36·9'W	X	102
Lower Hall	Warr	SJ6281	53°19·7'	2°33·8'W	X	109
Lower Hall	Wrex	SJ4150	53°2·9'	2°52·4'W	X	117
Lowerhall Fm	Ches	SJ4972	53°14·8'	2°45·5'W	FM	117
Lower Hall Fm	Powys	SJ1411	52°41·6'	3°16·0'W	FM	125
Lower Hall Fm	Powys	SO2374	52°21·8'	3°7·5'W	FM	137,148
Lower Hall Fm	Suff	TM3276	52°20·2'	1°24·7'E	FM	156
Lower Halliford	Surrey	TQ0867	51°23·7'	0°26·5'W	T	176
Lower Halstead	Kirk	SE1710	53°35·4'	1°44·2'W	X	110
Lower Halstock	Devon	SX6093	50°43·4'	3°58·6'W	X	191
Lower Halstock Leigh	Dorset	ST5207	50°51·9'	2°40·5'W	T	194
Lower Halstow	Kent	TQ8667	51°22·5'	0°40·7'E	T	178
Lower Ham	Worcs	SO8448	52°8·0'	2°13·6'W	X	150
Lower Hamstead Fm	I of W	SZ4191	50°43·3'	1°24·8'W	FM	196
Lower Hamswell	S Glos	ST7371	51°26·5'	2°22·9'W	T	172
Lower Hamworthy	Poole	SZ0090	50°42·8'	1°59·6'W	T	195
Lower Hanter	Powys	SO2557	52°12·6'	3°5·5'W	X	148
Lower Harcourt	Shrops	SO6982	52°26·3'	2°27·0'W	A	138
Lower Hardacre	N Yks	SD7168	54°6·7'	2°26·2'W	X	98
Lower Hardres	Kent	TR1553	51°14·4'	1°5·2'E	T	179,189
Lower Hardwick	Heref	SO4056	52°12·2'	2°52·3'W	T	148,149
Lower Hare Fm	Devon	SX8593	50°43·7'	3°37·4'W	FM	191
Lower Hare Park Fm	Cambs	TL5959	52°12·6'	0°20·0'E	FM	154
Lower Harford Fm	Glos	SP1322	51°54·0'	1°48·3'W	FM	163
Lower Harford Village	Glos	SP1322	51°54·0'	1°48·3'W	A	163
Lower Harpton	Heref	SO2760	52°14·2'	3°3·7'W	T	137,148
Lower Hartlip	Kent	TQ8464	51°20·9'	0°38·9'E	T	178,188
Lower Hartshay	Derby	SK3851	53°3·5'	1°25·6'W	T	119
Lower Hartwell	Bucks	SP7912	51°48·3'	0°50·9'W	T	165
Lower Hatton	Staffs	SJ8236	52°55·5'	2°15·7'W	T	127
Lower Hawksfold	W Susx	SU8827	51°2·4'	0°44·3'W	X	186,197
Lower Hawthwaite	Cumbr	SD2189	54°17·7'	3°12·4'W	T	96
Lower Hayne	Somer	ST2317	50°57·1'	3°5·4'W	X	193
Lower Haysden	Kent	TQ5645	51°11·2'	0°14·3'E	T	188
Lower Hayston	Pemb	SM9308	51°44·2'	4°59·5'W	X	157,158
Lower Haythog Fm	Pemb	SM9921	51°51·3'	4°54·7'W	FM	157,158
Lower Hayton	Shrops	SO5081	52°25·7'	2°43·7'W	T	137,138
Lower Hazel	S Glos	ST6287	51°35·1'	2°32·5'W	T	172
Lower Hazelcote	Glos	ST8296	51°40·0'	2°15·2'W	X	162
Lower Heath	Ches	SJ8664	53°10·6'	2°12·2'W	T	118
Lower Heathfield	Devon	SX7948	50°19·4'	3°41·6'W	X	202
Lower Heblands	Shrops	SO3290	52°30·5'	2°59·7'W	X	137
Lower Height	N Yks	SD9763	54°4·0'	2°2·3'W	X	98
Lower Heights Fm	Brad	SE0638	53°50·5'	1°54·1'W	FM	104
Lower Hele	Devon	SS3217	50°55·9'	4°23·1'W	X	190
Lower Henwick Fm	W Berks	SU4968	51°24·8'	1°17·3'W	FM	174
Lower Heppington	Kent	TR1453	51°14·4'	1°4·3'E	T	179,189
Lower Hergest	Heref	SO2755	52°11·5'	3°3·7'W	T	148
Lower Herne	Kent	TR1866	51°21·3'	1°8·3'E	T	179
Lower Hernes	Oxon	SU7482	51°32·2'	0°55·6'W	X	175
Lower Hexgreave Fm	Notts	SK6557	53°6·6'	1°1·3'W	FM	120
Lower Heyford	Oxon	SP4824	51°55·0'	1°17·7'W	T	164
Lower Heysham	Lancs	SD4161	54°2·7'	2°53·6'W	T	96,97
Lower Higham	Kent	TQ7173	51°26·0'	0°28·0'E	T	178
Lower Highfield	Lancs	SD5366	54°5·5'	2°42·7'W	X	97
Lower Highfield Fm	Surrey	SU8938	51°8·3'	0°43·3'W	FM	186
Lower Highmoor	Oxon	SU7085	51°33·8'	0°59·0'W	T	175
Lower Hill	Corn	SX1467	50°28·6'	4°36·9'W	X	200
Lower Hill	Devon	SS7927	51°2·0'	3°43·2'W	X	180
Lower Hill	Heref	SO4654	52°11·1'	2°47·0'W	X	148,149
Lower Hill	Pemb	SN0019	51°50·3'	4°53·8'W	X	157,158
Lower Hill	Powys	SO1988	52°29·3'	3°11·2'W	X	136
Lower Hill	Worcs	SO9644	52°5·9'	2°3·1'W	X	150
Lower Hill Fm	Glos	SO9824	51°55·1'	2°1·4'W	FM	163
Lower Hill Fm	Shrops	SO5897	52°34·4'	2°36·8'W	FM	137,138
Lower Hinge Fm	Cambs	TL5166	52°16·5'	0°13·2'E	FM	154
Lower Ho	Ches	SJ5363	53°10·0'	2°41·8'W	X	117
Lower Ho	Ches	SJ8678	53°18·2'	2°12·2'W	X	118
Lower Ho	Essex	TL6114	51°48·3'	0°20·5'E	X	167
Lower Ho	Flint	SJ2765	53°10·9'	3°5·1'W	X	117
Lower Ho	Glos	SO7026	51°56·1'	2°25·8'W	X	162
Lower Ho	Heref	SO3971	52°20·3'	2°53·3'W	X	137,148
Lower Ho	Heref	SO6751	52°9·6'	2°28·5'W	X	149
Lower Ho	Lancs	SD4737	53°49·8'	2°47·9'W	X	102
Lower Ho	Lancs	SD4749	53°56·3'	2°48·0'W	X	102
Lower Ho	Lancs	SD5340	53°51·5'	2°42·5'W	X	102
Lower Ho	Monm	SO4205	51°44·7'	2°50·0'W	X	161
Lower Ho	Powys	SJ2603	52°37·4'	3°5·2'W	X	126
Lower Ho	Powys	SJ3016	52°44·5'	3°1·8'W	X	126
Lower Ho	Powys	SO1249	52°8·2'	3°16·8'W	X	148
Lower Ho	Powys	SO2291	52°30·9'	3°8·6'W	X	137
Lower Ho	Shrops	SJ4029	52°51·6'	2°53·1'W	X	126
Lower Ho	Shrops	SJ5235	52°54·9'	2°42·4'W	X	126
Lower Ho	Surrey	SU9138	51°8·3'	0°41·6'W	X	186
Lower Ho	Worcs	SO6164	52°16·6'	2°33·9'W	X	138,149
Lower Ho	Worcs	SO7152	52°10·2'	2°25·0'W	X	149
Lower Ho	Wrex	SJ4340	52°57·6'	2°50·5'W	X	117
Lower Hockley Hall	Essex	TQ8394	51°37·1'	0°39·0'E	X	168,178
Lower Hodder Br	Lancs	SD7039	53°51·0'	2°26·9'W	X	103
Lower Ho Fm	Monm	ST4599	51°41·5'	2°47·4'W	FM	171
Lower Holbrook	Suff	TM1735	51°58·5'	1°10·0'E	T	169
Lower Holden	Brad	SE0544	53°53·8'	1°55·0'W	X	104
Lower Holditch	Dorset	ST3302	50°49·1'	2°56·7'W	T	193
Lower Hollesley Common	Suff	TM3545	52°3·4'	1°26·1'E	X	169
Lower Holloway	Isling	TQ3085	51°33·2'	0°7·1'W	T	176,177
Lower Hollowfields Fm	Worcs	SO9759	52°14·0'	2°2·2'W	FM	150
Lower Holwell	Dorset	SU0712	50°54·7'	1°53·6'W	T	195
Lower Home Fm	Lincs	TF0508	52°39·8'	0°26·9'W	FM	142
Lowerhone Fm	W Susx	SU8002	50°48·9'	0°51·5'W	FM	197
Lower Hook	Worcs	SO8140	52°3·7'	2°16·2'W	T	150
Lower Hook Fm	Brom	TQ4263	51°21·1'	0°2·7'E	FM	177,187
Lower Hookner	Devon	SX7182	50°37·6'	3°49·1'W	T	191
Lower Hope	Heref	SO5850	52°9·0'	2°36·4'W	X	149
Lower Hope Point	Medway	TQ7178	51°28·7'	0°28·1'E	X	178
Lower Hope, The	Thurr	TQ7077	51°28·2'	0°27·3'E	W	178
Lower Hopton	Kirk	SE1919	53°40·3'	1°42·3'W	T	110
Lower Hopton	Shrops	SJ3720	52°46·7'	2°55·6'W	T	126
Lower Hopton Fm	Heref	SO6349	52°8·5'	2°32·0'W	FM	149
Lower Hordley	Shrops	SJ3929	52°51·5'	2°54·0'W	T	126
Lower Horncroft	W Susx	TQ0017	50°56·9'	0°34·2'W	T	197
Lower Horse	Thurr	TQ7682	51°30·8'	0°32·6'E	X	178
Lower Horsebridge	E Susx	TQ5711	50°52·9'	0°14·3'E	T	199
Lower Horslett	Devon	SX3297	50°45·1'	4°22·5'W	X	190
Lower Ho, The	Worcs	SO8872	52°21·0'	2°10·2'W	X	139
Lower Ho, The	Worcs	SO9970	52°19·9'	2°0·5'W	X	139
Lowerhouse	Ches	SJ9277	53°17·6'	2°6·8'W	T	118
Lowerhouse	Ches	SJ9369	53°13·3'	2°5·9'W	X	118
Lowerhouse	Essex	TL6635	51°59·5'	0°25·5'E	X	154
Lower House	Halton	SJ5085	53°21·8'	2°44·7'W	T	108
Lowerhouse	Lancs	SD8132	53°47·3'	2°16·9'W	T	103
Lower House	Shetld	HU4559	60°19·0'	1°10·6'W	X	2,3
Lower House Bank	Powys	SO1479	52°24·4'	3°15·5'W	H	136,148
Lower House Fm	Ches	SJ5149	53°2·4'	2°43·4'W	FM	117
Lower House Fm	Ches	SJ6344	52°59·8'	2°32·7'W	FM	118
Lower House Fm	Ches	SJ7783	53°20·8'	2°20·3'W	FM	109
Lower House Fm	Dorset	SY4099	50°47·5'	2°50·7'W	FM	193
Lower House Fm	Essex	TL6034	51°59·1'	0°20·2'E	FM	154
Lower House Fm	Essex	TL6038	52°1·3'	0°20·3'E	FM	154
Lowerhouse Fm	Essex	TL6113	51°47·8'	0°20·5'E	FM	167
Lower House Fm	Hants	SU6821	50°59·3'	1°1·5'W	FM	185
Lower House Fm	Heref	SO3036	52°1·3'	3°0·8'W	FM	161
Lower House Fm	Heref	SO3335	52°0·8'	2°58·2'W	FM	149,161
Lower House Fm	Heref	SO6443	52°5·3'	2°31·1'W	FM	149
Lower House Fm	Lancs	SD4329	53°45·5'	2°51·5'W	FM	102
Lower House Fm	Lancs	SD5144	53°53·6'	2°44·3'W	FM	102
Lower House Fm	Lancs	SD6032	53°47·2'	2°36·0'W	FM	102,103
Lower House Fm	Powys	SO1579	52°24·4'	3°14·6'W	FM	136,148
Lower House Fm	Powys	SO2244	52°5·6'	3°7·9'W	FM	148,161
Lower House Fm	Shrops	SJ5443	52°59·2'	2°40·7'W	FM	117
Lower House Fm	Staffs	SJ8130	52°52·3'	2°16·5'W	FM	127
Lower House Fm	Surrey	TQ1139	51°8·6'	0°24·4'W	FM	187
Lowerhouse Fm	Warw	SP2362	52°15·6'	1°39·4'W	FM	151
Lower House Fm	Warw	SP2699	52°35·5'	1°36·6'W	FM	140
Lower House Fm	Wilts	SU2053	51°16·8'	1°42·4'W	FM	184
Lower House Fm	Worcs	SO6368	52°18·8'	2°32·2'W	FM	138
Lowerhouse Fm	Worcs	SO6768	52°18·8'	2°28·6'W	FM	138
Lowerhouse Fm	Worcs	SO7166	52°17·7'	2°25·1'W	FM	138,149
Lower House Fm	Worcs	SO7362	52°15·6'	2°23·3'W	FM	138,150
Lower House Fm	W Susx	SU9028	51°2·9'	0°42·6'W	FM	186,197
Lower Houses	Essex	TL9820	51°50·8'	0°52·9'E	X	168
Lower Houses	Kirk	SE1515	53°38·1'	1°46·0'W	T	110
Lower Houses	Lancs	SD6365	54°5·0'	2°33·5'W	X	97
Lower Houses	Shetld	HU4878	60°29·2'	1°7·1'W	X	2,3
Lower Howsell	Worcs	SO7848	52°8·0'	2°18·9'W	T	150
Lower Hurst Fm	Staffs	SK1159	53°7·9'	1°49·7'W	FM	119
Lower Huxley Hall	Ches	SJ4962	53°9·4'	2°45·4'W	A	117
Lower Hyde Heath	Dorset	SY8891	50°43·3'	2°9·8'W	X	194
Lower Illey	Dudley	SO9781	52°25·9'	2°2·2'W	T	139
Lower Inchdrewer	Aberd	NJ6561	57°38·5'	2°34·7'W	X	29
Lower Ingleston	D & G	NX7989	55°11·1'	3°53·6'W	X	78
Lower Ingley	Devon	SS6007	50°51·0'	3°58·9'W	X	191
Lower Ingon	Warw	SP2057	52°12·9'	1°42·0'W	X	151
Lower Inverbrough	Highld	NH8030	57°20·9'	3°59·2'W	X	27
Lower Island	Kent	TR1066	51°21·5'	1°1·4'E	T	179
Lower Jennies	Essex	TL8932	51°57·5'	0°45·4'E	X	168
Lower Kenly	Fife	NO5612	56°18·2'	2°42·2'W	X	59
Lower Kersal	Salf	SD8101	53°30·6'	2°16·8'W	T	109
Lower Key	Somer	ST5513	50°55·1'	2°38·0'W	X	194
Lower Kidney Wood	Beds	TL1019	51°51·8'	0°23·8'W	F	166
Lower Kilburn	Derby	SK3745	53°0·3'	1°26·5'W	T	119,128
Lower Kilchattan	Arg & Bt	NR3694	56°4·2'	6°14·1'W	T	61
Lower Kilcott	Glos	ST7889	51°36·2'	2°18·7'W	T	162,172
Lower Killeyan	Arg & Bt	NR2743	55°36·5'	6°19·7'W	X	60
Lower Kinachreachan	Arg & Bt	NN1427	56°24·2'	5°0·4'W	X	50
Lower Kincraig	Highld	NH6970	57°42·3'	4°11·4'W	X	21
Lower Kingcombe	Dorset	SY5599	50°47·6'	2°37·9'W	T	194
Lower Kingston Russell	Dorset	SY5788	50°41·6'	2°36·1'W	X	194
Lower Kingswood	Surrey	TQ2453	51°16·0'	0°13·0'W	T	187
Lower Kinnerton	Ches	SJ3462	53°9·3'	2°58·8'W	T	117
Lower Kinsham	Heref	SO3564	52°16·5'	2°56·8'W	T	137,148,149
Lower Knapp	Somer	ST3025	51°1·4'	2°59·5'W	T	193
Lower Knapp Fm	Devon	SY1594	50°44·6'	3°11·9'W	FM	192,193
Lower Knarr Fen	Peterb	TF3202	52°36·2'	0°2·6'W	X	142
Lower Knightley	Staffs	SJ8223	52°48·5'	2°15·6'W	T	127
Lower Knole Fm	S Glos	ST5883	51°32·9'	2°36·0'W	FM	172
Lower Knowle	C of Bris	ST5970	51°25·9'	2°35·0'W	T	172
Lower Lacon	Shrops	SJ5330	52°52·2'	2°41·5'W	X	126
Lower Lady Meadows	Staffs	SK0253	53°4·7'	1°57·8'W	X	119
Lower Laithe Resr	Brad	SE0136	53°49·5'	1°58·7'W	W	104
Lower Lake	Newp	ST3485	51°33·8'	2°56·7'W	X	171
Lower Lake	Notts	SK5453	53°4·5'	1°11·2'W	W	120
Lower Lake	Wakf	SE2812	53°36·5'	1°34·2'W	W	110
Lower Lampetho	Corn	SX0953	50°21·0'	4°40·7'W	X	200,204
Lower Lane	Lancs	SD8038	53°50·5'	2°17·8'W	X	103
Lower Lane	Shrops	SO2597	52°34·2'	3°6·0'W	X	137
Lower Langdon	Corn	SX2172	50°31·5'	4°31·1'W	X	201
Lower Langford	N Som	ST4660	51°20·4'	2°46·1'W	T	172,182
Lower Langley	Shrops	SO6573	52°21·5'	2°30·4'W	X	138
Lower Lanham	Hants	SU6036	51°7·4'	1°8·2'W	X	185
Lower Lanham Copse	Hants	SU6036	51°7·4'	1°8·2'W	F	185
Lower Lanherne	Corn	SW8767	50°28·1'	4°59·7'W	X	200
Lower Lapdown Fm	S Glos	ST7677	51°29·7'	2°20·4'W	FM	172
Lower Larel	Highld	ND1858	58°30·4'	3°24·0'W	X	11,12
Lower Largo	Fife	NO4102	56°12·7'	2°56·6'W	T	59
Lower Lark's Farm	S Glos	ST6785	51°34·0'	2°28·2'W	FM	172
Lower Lark Stoke	Warw	SP1943	52°5·3'	1°43·0'W	X	151
Lower Layham	Suff	TM0340	52°1·5'	0°57·9'E	T	155
Lower Ledge Fm	S Glos	ST7374	51°28·1'	2°22·9'W	FM	172
Lower Ledwyche	Shrops	SO5374	52°22·0'	2°41·0'W	T	137,138
Lower Lee	Shrops	SJ3729	52°51·5'	2°55·7'W	X	126
Lower Lees	Lancs	SD6544	53°53·7'	2°31·5'W	X	102,103
Lower Leesthorpe	Leic	SK7914	52°43·3'	0°49·4'W	X	129
Lower Leigh	Devon	SS6045	51°11·5'	3°59·8'W	X	180
Lower Leigh	Staffs	SK0136	52°55·5'	1°58·7'W	T	128
Lower Leigh Fm	Wilts	ST8828	51°3·3'	2°9·9'W	FM	183
Lower Leighton	Powys	SJ2406	52°39·0'	3°7·0'W	X	126
Lower Lemington	Glos	SP2134	52°0·5'	1°41·2'W	T	151
Lower Lenie	Highld	NH5126	57°18·3'	4°27·9'W	X	26,35
Lower Lewell Fm	Dorset	SY7489	50°42·2'	2°21·7'W	FM	194
Lower Ley	Devon	SX8243	50°16·7'	3°39·0'W	W	202
Lower Ley	Glos	SO7415	51°50·2'	2°22·2'W	X	162
Lower Litton	Powys	SO2666	52°17·5'	3°4·7'W	X	137,148
Lower Llanmellin	Monm	ST4691	51°37·2'	2°46·4'W	X	171,172
Lower Llantrothy	Monm	SO4511	51°47·9'	2°47·5'W	X	161
Lower Llantydwell	Pemb	SN1712	51°46·8'	4°38·8'W	X	158
Lower Lliw Resr	Swan	SN6503	51°42·8'	3°56·9'W	W	159
Lower Lobady	Orkney	HY3124	59°6·1'	3°11·8'W	X	6
Lower Loch of Setter	Shetld	HU3692	60°36·9'	1°20·0'W	W	1,2
Lower Locker Fm	N Yks	SE5093	54°20·0'	1°13·4'W	FM	100
Lower Lode	Glos	SO8731	51°58·9'	2°11·0'W	T	150
Lower Lodge	Leic	SP6887	52°28·8'	0°59·5'W	X	141
Lower Lodge Fm	E Susx	TQ4612	50°53·6'	0°4·9'E	FM	198
Lower Lodge Fm	Northnts	SP8089	52°29·8'	0°48·9'W	FM	141
Lower Lodge Fm	Northnts	SP8585	52°27·6'	0°44·5'W	FM	141
Lower Lodge Fm	Oxon	SU3897	51°40·5'	1°26·6'W	FM	164
Lower Lodge Fm	Warw	SP5078	52°24·1'	1°15·5'W	FM	140
Lower Lodge Fm	Wilts	ST9170	51°26·0'	2°7·4'W	FM	173
Lower Lodge Fm	W Susx	SU8728	51°2·9'	0°45·1'W	FM	186,197
Lower Longbeak	Corn	SS1903	50°48·1'	4°33·7'W	X	190
Lower Longcombe	Devon	SX8359	50°25·4'	3°38·4'W	X	202
Lower Longley Fm	Ches	SJ5269	53°13·2'	2°42·7'W	FM	117
Lower Lovacott	Devon	SS5227	51°1·6'	4°6·2'W	T	180
Lower Lovelynch	Somer	ST1124	51°0·7'	3°15·7'W	X	181,193
Lower Lowery	Devon	SX5569	50°30·4'	4°2·3'W	X	202
Lower Loxhore	Devon	SS6137	51°7·2'	3°58·8'W	T	180
Lower Loxley	Staffs	SK0532	52°53·4'	1°55·1'W	X	128
Lower Luggy	Powys	SJ2002	52°36·8'	3°10·5'W	X	126
Lower Lutheredge Fm	Glos	ST8299	51°41·6'	2°15·2'W	FM	162
Lower Luthrie Fm	Fife	NO3319	56°21·8'	3°4·6'W	FM	59
Lower Lydbrook	Glos	SO5916	51°50·7'	2°35·3'W	T	162
Lower Lyde Court	Heref	SO5143	52°5·2'	2°42·5'W	X	149
Lower Lyde Fm	Heref	SO5144	52°5·8'	2°42·5'W	FM	149
Lower Lye	Devon	ST2405	50°50·6'	3°4·3'W	X	192,193
Lower Lye	Heref	SO4066	52°17·6'	2°52·4'W	T	137,148,149
Lower Machen	Newp	ST2288	51°35·4'	3°7·2'W	T	171
Lower Madeley Fm	Worcs	SO9576	52°23·2'	2°4·0'W	FM	139
Lower Madgell Bank	Lancs	SD6534	53°48·3'	2°31·5'W	X	102,103
Lower Maes-coed	Heref	SO3430	51°58·1'	2°57·3'W	T	149,161
Lower Magiston	Dorset	SY6396	50°46·0'	2°31·1'W	X	194
Lower Main	Powys	SJ1616	52°44·4'	3°12·5'W	X	125
Lower Mains	Clackm	NS9597	56°9·5'	3°41·0'W	T	58
Lower Mains	Moray	NJ1965	57°40·3'	3°21·0'W	X	28
Lower Man	Cumbr	NY3315	54°31·8'	3°1·7'W	H	90
Lower Manaton	Corn	SX3372	50°31·7'	4°21·0'W	X	201

Lower Mannington	Dorset	SU0605	50°50·9′	1°54·5′W	T	195
Lower Manor Fm	Hants	SU4056	51°18·3′	1°25·2′W	FM	174
Lower Marchup Fm	Brad	SE0549	53°56·5′	1°55·0′W	FM	104
Lower Marsh	Somer	ST7420	50°59·0′	2°21·8′W	T	183
Lowermarsh Fm	Essex	TM0918	51°49·5′	1°2·4′E	FM	168,169
Lower Marsh Fm	Somer	ST2227	51°2·5′	3°6·4′W	FM	193
Lower Marston	Somer	ST7644	51°11·9′	2°20·2′W	T	183
Lower Mays Fm	E Susx	TQ5108	50°51·3′	0°9·1′E	FM	199
Lower Medhurst Green Fm	Ches	SJ8163	53°10·1′	2°16·6′W	FM	118
Lower Meend	Glos	SO5504	51°44·2′	2°38·7′W	T	162
Lower Meend Fm	Monm	SO5108	51°46·3′	2°42·2′W	FM	162
Lower Menadue	Corn	SX0359	50°24·1′	4°46·0′W	T	200
Lower Meon	Warw	SP1845	52°6·4′	1°43·8′W	X	151
Lower Merridge	Somer	ST2034	51°6·2′	3°8·2′W	T	182
Lower Micklehurst	Lancs	SD8230	53°46·2′	2°16·0′W	X	103
Lower Mickletown	Leeds	SE4027	53°44·5′	1°23·2′W	T	105
Lower Middleton Cheney	Northnts	SP5041	52°4·1′	1°15·8′W	T	151
Lower Midway	Derby	SK3020	52°46·8′	1°32·9′W	T	128
Lower Mill	Corn	SW9038	50°12·5′	4°56·2′W	T	204
Lower Mill	Hants	SU4344	51°11·8′	1°22·7′W	X	185
Lower Mill Fm	E Yorks	SE9035	53°48·4′	0°37·6′W	FM	106
Lower Mill Fm	Wilts	SU0462	51°21·7′	1°56·2′W	FM	173
Lower Mills	Devon	SX4388	50°40·5′	4°12·9′W	X	190
Lower Milovaig	Highld	NG1450	57°27·3′	6°45·6′W	T	23
Lower Milton	Somer	ST5347	51°13·4′	2°40·0′W	T	182,183
Lower Minchingdown	Devon	SS8209	50°52·3′	3°40·2′W	W	191
Lower Mincombe Fm	Devon	SY1594	50°44·6′	3°11·9′W	FM	192,193
Lower Minnend	Ches	SJ9364	53°10·6′	2°5·9′W	X	118
Lower Moor	Cald	SD9125	53°43·5′	2°7·8′W	X	103
Lower Moor	Corn	SX1482	50°36·7′	4°37·4′W	X	200
Lowermoor	D & G	NY1670	55°1·3′	3°18·4′W	X	85
Lower Moor	Wilts	SU0291	51°37·3′	1°57·9′W	T	163,173
Lower Moor	Worcs	SO9847	52°7·5′	2°1·4′W	T	150
Lower Moorend Fm	Worcs	SO6971	52°20·4′	2°26·9′W	FM	138
Lower Moor Fm	N Yks	SE4579	54°12·5′	1°18·2′W	FM	99
Lower Moor Fm	Wilts	SU0093	51°38·4′	1°59·6′W	FM	163,173
Lower Morton	S Glos	ST6491	51°37·2′	2°30·8′W	T	162,172
Lower Morton	Shrops	SJ3023	52°48·2′	3°1·9′W	X	126
Lower Moulsham's Fm	Essex	TL9515	51°48·2′	0°50·1′E	FM	168
Lower Mountain	Flint	SJ3159	53°7·7′	3°1·5′W	T	117
Lower Mount Fm	Win & Maid	SU8884	51°33·1′	0°43·5′W	FM	175
Lower Muckovie	Highld	NH7043	57°27·8′	4°9·6′W	X	27
Lower Muirden	Aberd	NJ7054	57°34·8′	2°29·6′W	X	29
Lower Munlyn	Powys	SJ2101	52°36·3′	3°9·6′W	X	126
Lower Nabbs Fm	Ches	SJ9668	53°12·8′	2°3·2′W	FM	118
Lower Nash Fm	Pemb	SN0003	51°41·6′	4°53·2′W	FM	157,158
Lower Nash Fm	Shrops	SO5971	52°20·4′	2°35·7′W	FM	137,138
Lower Nazeing	Essex	TL3906	51°44·4′	0°1·2′E	T	166
Lower Netchwood	Shrops	SO6291	52°31·2′	2°33·2′W	T	138
Lower Netley Fm	Shrops	SJ4602	52°37·0′	2°47·5′W	FM	126
Lower New Ho	Lancs	SD7143	53°53·2′	2°26·1′W	X	103
Lower New House Fm	Warw	SP4355	52°11·7′	1°21·9′W	FM	151
Lower New Inn	Torf	ST3098	51°40·8′	3°0·4′W	T	171
Lower Newlands	Kent	TQ9762	51°19·6′	0°50·1′E	X	178
Lower Newmill	Pth & Kin	NO0122	56°23·1′	3°35·8′W	X	52,53,58
Lower Newport	Highld	ND1223	58°11·5′	3°29·3′W	X	17
Lower Newton	Devon	SS6904	50°49·5′	3°51·2′W	X	191
Lower Newton Fm	Shrops	SJ3808	52°40·2′	2°54·6′W	FM	126
Lower Nill Fm	Oxon	SP3635	52°1·0′	1°28·1′W	FM	151
Lower Noar Hill Fm	Hants	SU7332	51°5·2′	0°57·1′W	FM	186
Lower Nobut	Staffs	SK0434	52°54·4′	1°56·0′W	T	128
Lower Norncott	Shrops	SO5686	52°28·4′	2°38·5′W	X	137,138
Lower North Dean	Bucks	SU8598	51°40·7′	0°45·8′W	T	165
Lower Northlands Fm	E Susx	TQ7726	51°0·6′	0°31·8′E	FM	188,199
Lower Norton	Devon	SX8551	50°21·1′	3°36·6′W	X	202
Lower Norton	Warw	SP2363	52°16·1′	1°39·4′W	T	151
Lower Norton Fm	Heref	SO6856	52°12·3′	2°27·7′W	FM	149
Lower Nunton	D & G	NX6548	54°48·8′	4°5·6′W	X	83,84
Lower Nyland	Dorset	ST7421	50°59·5′	2°21·8′W	T	183
Lower Nythe Fm	Somer	ST4134	51°6·4′	2°50·2′W	FM	182
Lower Oakfield	Fife	NT1493	56°7·6′	3°22·6′W	X	58
Lower Ochrwyth	Caer	ST2489	51°35·9′	3°5·4′W	T	171
Lower Odcombe	Somer	ST5115	50°56·2′	2°41·5′W	T	183
Lower Oddington	Glos	SP2325	51°55·6′	1°39·5′W	T	163
Lower Olad	Orkney	ND4488	58°46·8′	2°57·6′W	X	7
Lower Old Park	Surrey	SU8147	51°13·2′	0°50·0′W	X	186
Lower Ollach	Highld	NG5137	57°21·6′	6°8·0′W	T	23,24,32
Lower Padworth	W Berks	SU6067	51°24·2′	1°7·9′W	T	175
Lower Paradise	Lancs	SD8650	53°57·0′	2°12·4′W	X	103
Lower Park	Essex	TM0532	51°57·1′	0°59·4′E	X	168
Lower Park	Oxon	SP4415	51°50·1′	1°21·3′W	X	164
Lower Park Eyton	Wrex	SJ3444	52°59·6′	2°58·6′W	X	117
Lower Park Fm	Dorset	SY3997	50°46·4′	2°51·5′W	FM	193
Lower Park Fm	Kent	TR0836	51°5·4′	0°58·6′E	FM	179,189
Lowerpark Fm	Norf	TM1198	52°32·6′	1°7·1′E	FM	144
Lower Park Fm	Wakf	SE2822	53°41·9′	1°34·1′W	FM	104
Lower Park Fm	Wilts	ST8429	51°3·8′	2°13·3′W	FM	183
Lower Park Fm	Wilts	ST9860	51°20·6′	2°1·3′W	FM	173
Lower Park Fm	Worcs	SP0570	52°19·9′	1°55·2′W	FM	139
Lower Parrock	E Susx	TQ4535	51°6·0′	0°4·6′E	X	188
Lower Part Fm	Wilts	SU1394	51°38·9′	1°48·3′W	FM	163,173
Lower Parting	Glos	SO8118	51°51·9′	2°16·2′W	X	162
Lower Penarth	V of Glam	ST1870	51°25·6′	3°10·4′W	T	171
Lower Pendeford Fm	Staffs	SJ8904	52°38·3′	2°9·4′W	FM	127,139
Lower Pengarth	Powys	SO1245	52°6·0′	3°16·7′W	X	148
Lower Penhale	Corn	SX1784	50°37·9′	4°34·9′W	X	201
Lower Peniarth	Powys	SJ1616	52°44·3′	3°14·3′W	X	125
Lower Penn	Staffs	SO8795	52°33·4′	2°11·1′W	T	139
Lower Penn Fm	Wilts	SU0174	51°28·1′	1°58·7′W	FM	173
Lower Pennington	Hants	SZ3193	50°44·4′	1°33·3′W	T	196
Lower Penrhuddlan	Powys	SO0186	52°28·0′	3°27·0′W	X	136
Lower Penscawn	Corn	SW8754	50°21·1′	4°59·3′W	X	200
Lower Pentre	Powys	SO1569	52°19·0′	3°14·4′W	X	136,148
Lower Pentwyn	Monm	SO3122	51°53·8′	2°59·8′W	X	161
Lower Penwaen	Powys	SO0831	51°58·4′	3°20·0′W	X	160
Lower Penwortham	Lancs	SD5328	53°45·0′	2°42·4′W	T	102
Lower Peover	Ches	SJ7374	53°16·0′	2°23·9′W	T	118
Lower Pertwood	Wilts	ST8836	51°7·6′	2°9·9′W	X	183
Lower Petwick	Oxon	SU3589	51°36·2′	1°29·3′W	X	174
Lower Pexhill	Ches	SJ8771	53°14·4′	2°11·3′W	T	118

Lower Pilehayes Fm	Devon	SY0088	50°41·2′	3°24·6′W	FM	192
Lower Piles	Devon	SX6460	50°25·7′	3°54·5′W	X	202
Lower Pilsley	Derby	SK4163	53°10·0′	1°22·8′W	T	120
Lower Pitham	Hants	SU7060	51°20·3′	0°59·3′W	X	175,186
Lower Pitkerrie	Highld	NH8680	57°48·0′	3°54·6′W	T	21
Lower Pitts Fm	Somer	ST5350	51°15·1′	2°40·0′W	FM	182,183
Lower Place	Brent	TQ2083	51°32·2′	0°15·8′W	T	176
Lower Place	Roch	SD9011	53°36·0′	2°8·7′W	T	109
Lower Pollicot	Bucks	SP7012	51°48·4′	0°58·7′W	T	165
Lower Pool	T Ham	TQ3580	51°30·4′	0°2·9′W	W	177
Lower Porterbelly	D & G	NX8564	54°57·7′	3°47·3′W	X	84
Lower Porthamel	Powys	SO1635	52°0·7′	3°13·0′W	X	161
Lower Porthkerry	V of Glam	ST0766	51°23·4′	3°19·8′W	T	170
Lower Porthpean	Corn	SX0350	50°19·3′	4°45·7′W	T	200,204
Lower Portland Fm	Cambs	TL5964	52°15·3′	0°20·2′E	FM	154
Lower Portman Fm	Somer	ST1828	51°3·0′	3°9·8′W	FM	181,193
Lower Poughley	W Berks	SU3473	51°27·5′	1°30·2′W	X	174
Lower Powburn	Aberd	NO7474	56°51·7′	2°25·1′W	X	45
Lower Prestwood Fm	W Susx	TQ2338	51°7·9′	0°14·1′W	FM	187
Lower Quinton	Warw	SP1847	52°7·5′	1°43·8′W	T	151
Lower Rabber	Powys	SO2554	52°11·0′	3°5·4′W	T	148
Lower Race	Torf	SO2700	51°41·9′	3°3·0′W	T	171
Lower Radley	Oxon	SU5398	51°40·9′	1°13·6′W	T	164
Lower Rainham	Medway	TQ8167	51°22·6′	0°36·4′E	T	178
Lower Rainsbrook Fm	Warw	SP5172	52°20·9′	1°14·7′W	FM	140
Lower Ranachan	Arg & Bt	NR6924	55°27·6′	5°38·8′W	X	68
Lower Rannieshill	Aberd	NJ8919	57°15·9′	2°10·5′W	X	38
Lower Ratley	Hants	SU3223	51°0·6′	1°32·2′W	T	185
Lower Raydon	Suff	TM0338	52°0·4′	0°57·9′E	T	155
Lower Rea	Glos	SO8015	51°50·2′	2°17·0′W	T	162
Lower Reach	Suff	TM2535	51°58·3′	1°16·9′E	W	169
Lower Rectory Fm	Bucks	SP8930	51°57·9′	0°41·9′W	FM	152,165
Lower Rectory Fm	Leic	SK3209	52°40·9′	1°31·2′W	FM	128,140
Lower Reiss	Highld	ND3355	58°28·9′	3°8·5′W	X	12
Lower Relowas	Corn	SW7222	50°3·5′	5°10·8′W	X	204
Lower Reule Fm	Staffs	SJ8419	52°46·3′	2°13·8′W	FM	127
Lower Revels Fm	Dorset	ST6706	50°51·4′	2°27·7′W	FM	194
Lower Rhosgranog	Pemb	SM8627	51°54·3′	5°6·3′W	X	157
Lower Rhynd	Pth & Kin	NN8509	56°15·8′	3°51·0′W	W	58
Lower Ridge	Devon	ST2301	50°48·4′	3°5·2′W	T	192,193
Lower Ridge	Shrops	SJ3432	52°53·1′	2°58·4′W	T	126
Lower Ridge	Shrops	SO2898	52°34·7′	3°3·4′W	X	137
Lower Riess	Highld	ND3355	58°28·9′	3°8·5′W	X	12
Lower Rill	Devon	SS9924	51°0·6′	3°26·0′W	X	181
Lower Rill	I of W	SZ4983	50°38·9′	1°18·0′W	X	196
Low Errington	Northum	NY9672	55°2·8′	2°3·3′W	X	87
Lower Rixdale Fm	Devon	SX9077	50°35·2′	3°32·9′W	FM	192
Lower Roadwater	Somer	ST0338	51°8·2′	3°22·8′W	T	181
Lower-rock Fm	Ches	SJ5359	53°7·8′	2°41·7′W	FM	117
Lower Rocombe Fm	Devon	SX9070	50°31·4′	3°32·7′W	FM	202
Lower Rose	Corn	SW7854	50°20·9′	5°6·9′W	T	200
Lower Rough Head	Cald	SD9825	53°43·5′	2°1·4′W	X	103
Lower Row	Dorset	SU0404	50°50·4′	1°56·2′W	T	195
Lower Row Mires	N Yks	SE7596	54°21·5′	0°50·3′W	X	94,100
Lower Ruthall	Shrops	SO6089	52°30·1′	2°35·0′W	X	138
Lower Rydon Fm	Somer	ST2929	51°3·6′	3°0·4′W	FM	193
Lower Rye Fm	Glos	SP1930	51°58·3′	1°43·0′W	FM	151
Lower Salden Fm	Bucks	SP8131	51°58·5′	0°48·8′W	FM	152,165
Lower Sale Ho	Staffs	SK1127	52°50·7′	1°49·8′W	X	128
Lower Salter	Lancs	SD6063	54°3·9′	2°36·3′W	X	97
Lower Salt Moor	Somer	ST3430	51°4·2′	2°56·1′W	X	182
Lower Sandhill Ho	E Susx	TQ4917	50°56·2′	0°7·6′E	X	199
Lower Sands Fm	Wilts	SU0170	51°26·0′	1°58·7′W	FM	173
Lower Sapey	Worcs	SO6960	52°14·5′	2°26·8′W	T	138,149
Lower Seafield	Highld	NH9083	57°49·6′	3°50·7′W	X	21
Lower Seagry	Wilts	ST9580	51°31·4′	2°3·9′W	T	173
Lower Severalls Fm	Somer	ST4511	50°54·0′	2°46·5′W	FM	193
Lower Shadymoor Fm	Shrops	SJ4603	52°37·6′	2°47·5′W	FM	126
Lower Shampher	Aberd	NO6692	57°1·3′	2°33·1′W	X	38,45
Lower Sharpnose Point	Corn	SS1912	50°53·0′	4°34·0′W	X	190
Lower Sheardale	Clackm	NS9597	56°9·5′	3°41·0′W	X	58
Lower Sheering	Essex	TL4914	51°48·5′	0°10·1′E	T	167
Lower Sheldon Grange	Devon	ST1210	50°53·2′	3°14·7′W	X	192,193
Lower Shelton	Beds	SP9942	52°4·3′	0°32·9′W	T	153
Lower Sherdon	Somer	SS7935	51°6·3′	3°43·3′W	X	180
Lower Shiplake	Oxon	SU7779	51°30·5′	0°53·0′W	T	175
Lower Short Ditch	Shrops	SO2288	52°29·3′	3°8·5′W	A	137
Lower Shuckburgh	Warw	SP4962	52°15·5′	1°16·5′W	T	151
Lower Sketty	Swan	SS6191	51°36·3′	4°0·0′W	T	159
Lower Skilts	Warw	SP0967	52°18·3′	1°51·7′W	X	150
Lower Skippet Fm	Dorset	SY6491	50°43·3′	2°30·2′W	FM	194
Lower Slackbuie	Highld	NH6742	57°27·2′	4°12·5′W	X	26
Lower Slackstead	Hants	SU3925	51°1·6′	1°26·2′W	T	185
Lower Slade	Devon	SS5145	51°11·3′	4°7·5′W	T	180
Lower Slaughter	Glos	SP1622	51°54·0′	1°45·7′W	T	163
Lower Sleights Fm	N Yks	SE7859	54°1·5′	0°48·1′W	FM	105,106
Lower Small Clough	Derby	SK1496	53°27·9′	1°46·9′W	X	110
Lower Smiddyseat	Aberd	NJ7349	57°32·1′	2°26·6′W	X	29
Lower Snailham	E Susx	TQ8517	50°55·6′	0°38·3′E	X	189,199
Lower Snowdon	Staffs	SJ7800	52°36·1′	2°19·1′W	X	127
Low Ersock	D & G	NX4437	54°42·5′	4°24·9′W	X	83
Lower Solva	Pemb	SM8024	51°52·5′	5°11·4′W	T	157
Lower Soothill	Kirk	SE2524	53°42·9′	1°36·9′W	T	104
Lower Soudley	Glos	SO6609	51°47·0′	2°29·2′W	T	162
Lower Sour	Highld	ND1060	58°31·4′	3°32·2′W	X	11,12
Lower Southey Fm	Somer	ST1911	50°53·8′	3°8·7′W	FM	192,193
Lower Southfield	Heref	SO6942	52°4·8′	2°26·7′W	T	149
Lower South Park	Surrey	TQ3447	51°12·6′	0°4·5′W	X	187
Lower Spargo	Corn	SW7532	50°9·0′	5°8·6′W	X	204
Lower Spark's Fm	W Susx	TQ3026	51°1·3′	0°8·4′W	FM	187,198
Lower Spoad	Shrops	SO2582	52°26·1′	3°5·8′W	X	137
Lower Spray Fm	W Berks	SU3463	51°22·1′	1°30·3′W	FM	174
Lower Springs	Shrops	SJ5700	52°36·0′	2°37·7′W	X	126
Lowers Reaps	Lancs	SD8823	53°42·4′	2°10·5′W	X	103
Lower Stanage	Powys	SO3373	52°21·3′	2°58·6′W	X	137,148
Lower Standean	E Susx	TQ3111	50°53·2′	0°7·9′W	X	198
Lower Standen	Lancs	SD7340	53°51·6′	2°24·2′W	X	103
Lower Standen Fm	Kent	TR2340	51°7·2′	1°11·6′E	FM	179,189
Lower Stanton St Quintin	Wilts	ST9181	51°31·9′	2°7·4′W	T	173
Lower Star Post	Brackn	SU8764	51°22·3′	0°44·6′W	X	175,186

Lower St Clere	Kent	TQ5758	51°18·2′	0°15·5′E	X	188
Lower St Cross Fm	I of W	SZ4990	50°42·7′	1°18·0′W	FM	196
Lower Stelling Fm	N Yks	NZ0700	54°24·0′	1°53·1′W	FM	92
Lower Stock Br	Lancs	SD6466	54°5·6′	2°32·6′W	X	97
Lower Stockley Fm	Dorset	SY8591	50°43·3′	2°12·4′W	FM	194
Lower Stoford	Somer	ST1428	51°2·9′	3°13·2′W	X	181,193
Lower Stoke	Cov	SP3578	52°24·2′	1°28·7′W	T	140
Lower Stoke	Medway	TQ8375	51°26·9′	0°38·4′E	T	178
Lower Stondon	Beds	TL1535	52°0·3′	0°19·1′W	T	153
Lower Stone	Glos	ST6794	51°38·9′	2°28·2′W	T	162,172
Lower Stonehouse	Staffs	SJ9054	53°5·2′	2°8·6′W	X	118
Lower Stonehurst Fm	E Susx	TQ4340	51°8·7′	0°3·1′E	FM	187
Lower Stonnall	Staffs	SK0803	52°37·7′	1°52·5′W	T	139
Lower Stony Bank	Lancs	SD7454	53°59·1′	2°23·4′W	X	103
Lower Stow Bedon	Norf	TL9694	52°30·7′	0°53·7′E	T	144
Lower Stratton	Somer	ST4415	50°56·1′	2°47·4′W	T	193
Lower Stratton	Swin	SU1785	51°34·0′	1°44·9′W	T	173
Lower Street	Dorset	SY8499	50°47·7′	2°13·2′W	X	194
Lower Street	E Susx	TQ7012	50°53·2′	0°25·4′E	T	199
Lower Street	Norf	TG1634	52°51·8′	1°12·9′E	T	133
Lower Street	Norf	TG2635	52°52·1′	1°21·9′E	T	133
Lower Street	Suff	TL7852	52°8·5′	0°36·5′E	T	155
Lower Street	Suff	TM1534	51°58·0′	1°8·2′E	T	169
Lower Street Fm	Kent	TQ5448	51°12·8′	0°12·7′E	FM	188
Lower Strensham	Worcs	SO9040	52°3·7′	2°8·4′W	T	150
Lower Stretton	Warr	SJ6281	53°19·7′	2°33·8′W	T	109
Lower Strode	Dorset	SY4599	50°47·5′	2°46·4′W	T	193
Lower Strode Fm	N Som	ST5461	51°21·0′	2°39·2′W	FM	172,182
Lower Studley	Wilts	ST8557	51°18·9′	2°12·5′W	T	173
Lower Sturthill Fm	Dorset	SY5291	50°43·2′	2°40·4′W	FM	194
Lower Sundon	Beds	TL0527	51°56·1′	0°28·0′W	T	166
Lower Swainshead	Lancs	SD5353	53°58·5′	2°42·6′W	X	102
Lower Swainswick	Bath & NE Somer	ST7667	51°24·3′	2°20·3′W	T	172
Lower Swanscoe	Ches	SJ9375	53°16·6′	2°5·9′W	X	118
Lower Swanwick	Hants	SU4909	50°52·9′	1°17·8′W	T	196
Lower Sweeney	Shrops	SJ2825	52°49·3′	3°3·7′W	X	126
Lower Sweetcombe Fm	Devon	SY1592	50°43·5′	3°11·9′W	FM	192,193
Lower Swell	Glos	SP1725	51°55·6′	1°44·8′W	T	163
Lower Sydenham	Brom	TQ3571	51°25·5′	0°3·1′W	T	177
Lower Tadmarton	Oxon	SP4037	52°2·0′	1°24·6′W	T	151
Lower Tale	Devon	ST0601	50°48·3′	3°19·7′W	T	192
Lower Tamar Lake	Devon	SS2911	50°52·6′	4°25·5′W	W	190
Lower Tarr	Stir	NN6200	56°10·6′	4°12·9′W	X	57
Lower Tasburgh	Norf	TM1996	52°31·3′	1°14·1′E	T	134
Lower Taylorton	Stir	NS8294	56°7·7′	3°53·5′W	X	57
Lower Tean	Staffs	SK0138	52°56·6′	1°58·7′W	T	128
Lower Tean Leys Fm	Staffs	SK0037	52°56·1′	1°59·6′W	FM	128
Lower Thornber	N Yks	SD8154	53°59·1′	2°17·0′W	X	103
Lower Thorne	Devon	SS8417	50°56·7′	3°38·7′W	X	181
Lower Thornhill	Staffs	SJ7646	53°0·9′	2°21·1′W	X	118
Lower Thorpe	Northnts	SP5345	52°6·3′	1°13·2′W	T	152
Lower Threapwood	Ches	SJ4444	52°59·7′	2°49·7′W	T	117
Lower Throughburn	S Lanak	NS9352	55°45·2′	3°41·9′W	X	65,72
Lower Thrushgill	Lancs	SD6562	54°3·4′	2°31·7′W	X	97
Lower Thura	Highld	ND2462	58°32·6′	3°17·9′W	X	11,12
Lower Thurlton	Norf	TM4299	52°32·3′	1°34·5′E	T	134
Lower Thurnham	Lancs	SD4554	53°59·0′	2°49·9′W	T	102
Lower Thurvaston	Derby	SK2236	52°55·5′	1°40·0′W	T	128
Lower Tideford	Devon	SX8254	50°22·7′	3°39·2′W	X	202
Lower Tilstock Park	Shrops	SJ5136	52°55·4′	2°43·3′W	X	126
Lower Toch	Pemb	SN0515	51°48·2′	4°49·3′W	X	158
Lower Todding	Heref	SO4075	52°22·4′	2°52·5′W	T	137,148
Lower Tote	Highld	NG5159	57°33·4′	6°9·3′W	X	23,24
Lower Towie	Moray	NJ3945	57°29·7′	3°0·6′W	X	28
Lower Town	Brad	SE0334	53°48·4′	1°56·9′W	T	104
Lowertown	Corn	SW6529	50°7·1′	5°16·9′W	T	203
Lowertown	Corn	SW8661	50°24·8′	5°0·4′W	X	200
Lowertown	Corn	SX0561	50°25·2′	4°44·3′W	T	200
Lower Town	Devon	ST0012	50°54·2′	3°24·9′W	T	181
Lowertown	Devon	SX4684	50°38·4′	4°10·3′W	T	201
Lower Town	Devon	SX7172	50°32·2′	3°48·8′W	X	191
Lower Town	Heref	SO6342	52°4·7′	2°32·0′W	T	149
Lower Town	I Scilly	SV9116	49°58·1′	6°18·2′W	T	203
Lowertown	Orkney	ND4394	58°50·0′	2°58·8′W	X	7
Lower Town	Pemb	SM9637	51°59·9′	4°57·9′W	T	157
Lower Town	Worcs	SO8659	52°14·0′	2°11·9′W	T	150
Lower Towthorpe	N Yks	SE6166	54°5·4′	1°3·6′W	X	100
Lower Trawscoed	Powys	SO0834	52°0·0′	3°20·0′W	X	160
Lower Trebullett	Corn	SX3277	50°34·4′	4°22·0′W	T	201
Lower Tregantle	Corn	SX3953	50°21·5′	4°15·4′W	X	201
Lower Tregarne	Corn	SW7629	50°7·4′	5°7·7′W	X	204
Lower Treludderow Fm	Corn	SW8056	50°22·0′	5°5·2′W	FM	200
Lower Treluswell	Corn	SW7735	50°10·6′	5°7·0′W	X	204
Lower Trenowth	Corn	SW8964	50°26·5′	4°57·9′W	X	200
Lower Tuffley	Glos	SO8214	51°49·7′	2°15·3′W	T	162
Lower Tullochgrue	Highld	NH9109	57°9·8′	3°47·7′W	X	36
Lower Tunbridge Fm	Worcs	SO7351	52°9·6′	2°23·3′W	A	150
Lower Turmer	Hants	SU1309	50°53·1′	1°48·5′W	T	195
Lower Twitchen	Devon	SS3918	50°56·6′	4°17·1′W	T	190
Lower Twydall	Medway	TQ8067	51°22·6′	0°35·6′E	T	178
Lower Tyackesnook	Aberd	NK0359	57°37·5′	1°56·5′W	X	30
Lower Tynes	Corn	SX0581	50°36·0′	4°45·0′W	X	200
Lower Tysoe	Warw	SP3445	52°6·4′	1°29·8′W	T	151
Lower Upcott	Devon	SX8880	50°36·8′	3°34·6′W	X	192
Lower Upham	Hants	SU5219	50°58·3′	1°15·2′W	T	185
Lower Upham Fm	Wilts	SU2077	51°29·7′	1°42·3′W	FM	174
Lower Upnor	Medway	TQ7671	51°24·9′	0°32·3′E	T	178
Lower Upperton	Devon	SX5163	50°27·1′	4°5·6′W	X	201
Lower Upton	Heref	SO5466	52°17·7′	2°40·1′W	X	137,138,149
Lower Valley Fm	Cambs	TL5254	52°10·0′	0°13·8′E	FM	154
Lower Varchoel	Powys	SJ2312	52°42·3′	3°8·0′W	X	126
Lower Venton Fm	Devon	SX5857	50°24·0′	3°59·5′W	FM	202
Lower Vert Wood	E Susx	TQ5113	50°54·0′	0°9·2′E	F	199
Lower Vexford	Somer	ST1135	51°6·7′	3°15·9′W	T	181
Lower Vicar's Fm	Oxon	SU7395	51°39·2′	0°56·3′W	FM	165
Lower Vicarwood	Derby	SK3139	52°57·1′	1°31·9′W	X	128
Lower Vinesend Fm	Heref	SO7447	52°7·5′	2°22·4′W	FM	150
Lower Voaden	Devon	SX4792	50°42·7′	4°9·6′W	X	191
Lower Wadstray	Devon	SX8251	50°21·1′	3°39·1′W	X	202

Lower Wain	Shrops	SO2279	52°24·4′	3°8·4′W	X	137,148
Lower Wainhill	Oxon	SP7601	51°42·4′	0°53·6′W	T	165
Lower Waldridge Fm	Bucks	SP7808	51°46·1′	0°51·8′W	FM	165
Lower Wall	Kent	TR0833	51°3·7′	0°58·5′E	X	179,189
Lower Wallop Fm	Shrops	SJ3207	52°39·6′	2°59·9′W	FM	126
Lower Walton	Warr	SJ6085	53°21·9′	2°35·7′W	T	109
Lower Walton Fm	Heref	SO6547	52°7·4′	2°30·3′W	FM	149
Lower Wanborough	Swin	SU2183	51°33·0′	1°41·4′W	T	174
Lower Warnicombe	Devon	SS9711	50°53·6′	3°27·5′W	X	192
Lower Warren Fm	Bucks	SU8698	51°40·7′	0°45·0′W	FM	165
Lower Washbourne Barton	Devon	SX8055	50°23·2′	3°40·9′W	X	202
Lower Watchbury Fm	Warw	SP2860	52°14·5′	1°35·0′W	FM	151
Lower Watchingwell	I of W	SZ4489	50°42·2′	1°22·2′W	X	196
Lower Waterston	Dorset	SY7395	50°45·5′	2°22·6′W	X	194
Lower Wavensmere	Warw	SP1263	52°16·1′	1°49·1′W	X	150
Lower Way	Devon	SS8914	50°55·1′	3°34·4′W	X	181
Lower Weacombe	Somer	ST1040	51°9·4′	3°16·8′W	T	181
Lower Weald	Mil Key	SP7838	52°2·3′	0°51·4′W	T	152
Lower Wear	Devon	SX9489	50°41·7′	3°29·7′W	T	192
Lower Weare	Somer	ST4053	51°16·6′	2°51·2′W	T	182
Lower Weddington Fm	Kent	TR2959	51°17·3′	1°17·4′E	FM	179
Lower Weedon	Northnts	SP6259	52°13·8′	1°5·1′W	T	152
Lower Week	Devon	SX8849	50°20·1′	3°34·0′W	X	202
Lower Well Fm	Devon	SX8557	50°24·3′	3°36·7′W	FM	202
Lower Welson	Heref	SO2950	52°8·9′	3°1·9′W	T	148
Lower Wern	Pemb	SN0128	51°55·1′	4°53·2′W	X	145,157,158
Lower West Clough	Lancs	SD7544	53°53·7′	2°22·4′W	X	103
Lower Westfield Fm	Oxon	SP4015	51°50·2′	1°24·8′W	FM	164
Lower Westfield Fm	Surrey	TQ0055	51°17·3′	0°33·6′W	FM	186
Lower Westfields Fm	Warw	SP3660	52°14·5′	1°28·0′W	FM	151
Lower Westholme	Somer	ST5640	51°9·7′	2°37·4′W	T	182,183
Lower Westhouse	N Yks	SD6773	54°9·4′	2°29·9′W	T	98
Lower Westmancote	Worcs	SO9337	52°2·1′	2°5·7′W	T	150
Lower Weston	Bath & NE Somer	ST7365	51°23·2′	2°22·9′W	T	172
Lower Weston	Powys	SO2169	52°19·0′	3°9·1′W	X	137,148
Lower Westwater Fm	Devon	SY2898	50°46·9′	3°0·9′W	FM	193
Lower Wetmoor	S Glos	ST7487	51°35·1′	2°22·1′W	F	172
Lower Whatcombe	Dorset	ST8401	50°48·7′	2°13·2′W	T	194
Lower Whatley	Somer	ST7447	51°13·5′	2°22·0′W	T	183
Lower Whitcliffe	Shrops	SO4873	52°21·4′	2°45·4′W	F	137,138,148
Lower Whitcliffe	Shrops	SO4874	52°21·9′	2°45·4′W	X	137,138
Lower Whitehall	Orkney	HY6628	59°8·5′	2°35·2′W	T	5
Lower Whitehill Cotts	Hants	SU5147	51°13·4′	1°15·8′W	X	185
Lower Whitehill Fm	Oxon	SP4718	51°51·7′	1°18·7′W	FM	164
Lower White Lee	Lancs	SD8136	53°49·4′	2°16·9′W	X	103
Lower Whiteston	Stir	NN8004	56°13·1′	3°55·7′W	X	57
Lower White Tor	Devon	SX6179	50°35·9′	3°57·5′W	H	191
Lower Whitley	Ches	SJ6179	53°18·6′	2°34·7′W	T	118
Lower Whitley	Wilts	ST9872	51°27·1′	2°1·3′W	X	173
Lower Whitley Fm	Oxon	SP4405	51°44·7′	1°21·4′W	FM	164
Lower Wick	Glos	ST7196	51°40·0′	2°24·8′W	T	162
Lower Wick	Worcs	SO8352	52°10·2′	2°14·5′W	T	150
Lower Wick Fm	N Som	ST3665	51°23·1′	2°54·8′W	FM	171,182
Lower Widhill Fm	Swin	SU1291	51°37·3′	1°49·2′W	FM	163,173
Lower Wield	Hants	SU6340	51°9·6′	1°5·6′W	T	185
Lower Wilbury Fm	Beds	TL2034	51°59·7′	0°14·7′W	FM	153
Lower Willingdon	E Susx	TQ5803	50°48·5′	0°14·9′E	T	199
Lower Wilting Fm	E Susx	TQ7611	50°52·5′	0°30·5′E	FM	199
Lower Winchendon or Nether Winchendon	Bucks	SP7312	51°48·3′	0°56·1′W	T	165
Lower Wingbury Fm	Bucks	SP8721	51°53·1′	0°43·8′W	FM	165
Lower Winterage Fm	Kent	TR1941	51°7·8′	1°8·2′E	FM	179,189
Lower Wintercott	Heref	SO4755	52°11·7′	2°46·1′W	X	148,149
Lower Wintringham	Cambs	TL2159	52°13·2′	0°13·3′W	X	153
Lower Witheymore Fm	Glos	ST7589	51°36·2′	2°21·3′W	FM	162,172
Lower Withington	Ches	SJ8169	53°13·3′	2°16·7′W	T	118
Lower Wolverton	Worcs	SO9250	52°9·1′	2°6·6′W	T	150
Lower Wood	Cambs	TL6252	52°8·8′	0°22·5′E	F	154
Lower Wood	E Susx	TQ4610	50°52·5′	0°4·9′E	F	198
Lower Wood	Mil Key	SP9241	52°3·8′	0°39·1′W	F	152
Lower Wood	Norf	TM1398	52°32·5′	1°8·9′E	F	144
Lower Wood	Shrops	SJ3002	52°36·9′	3°1·6′W	X	126
Lower Wood	Shrops	SJ3614	52°43·4′	2°56·5′W	X	126
Lower Wood	Shrops	SO4697	52°34·3′	2°47·4′W	X	137,138
Lower Woodbatch Fm	Shrops	SO3188	52°29·4′	3°0·6′W	FM	137
Lower Woodbury Fm	Dorset	SY8693	50°44·4′	2°11·5′W	FM	194
Lower Wood Corner Fm	Staffs	SJ7529	52°51·7′	2°21·9′W	FM	127
Lower Woodcott Down	Hants	SU4555	51°17·8′	1°20·9′W	X	174,185
Lower Woodcott Fm	Hants	SU4454	51°17·2′	1°21·8′W	FM	185
Lower Woodend	Aberd	NJ6718	57°15·3′	2°32·4′W	T	38
Lower Woodend	Bucks	SU8187	51°34·8′	0°49·5′W	T	175
Lower Woodend Fm	Bucks	SU7587	51°34·8′	0°54·7′W	FM	175
Lower Wood Fm	Norf	TG4911	52°38·6′	1°41·2′E	FM	134
Lower Wood Fm	Shrops	SJ8205	52°38·8′	2°15·6′W	FM	127
Lower Woodford	Wilts	SU1235	51°7·1′	1°49·3′W	T	184
Lower Woodhouse	W Susx	TQ1026	51°1·6′	0°25·5′W	X	187,198
Lower Woodhouse Fm	Powys	SO3072	52°20·7′	3°1·3′W	FM	137,148
Lower Woodley	Corn	SX0265	50°27·3′	4°47·0′W	T	200
Lower Woods	Somer	ST7943	51°11·4′	2°17·6′W	F	183
Lower Woods Fm	Oxon	SP5412	51°48·5′	1°12·6′W	FM	164
Lower Woodside	Herts	TL2406	51°44·6′	0°11·8′W	T	166
Lower Woods Lodge	S Glos	ST7488	51°35·6′	2°22·1′W	X	162,172
Lower Woolston	Somer	ST6527	51°2·7′	2°29·6′W	T	183
Lower Woolwich	Kent	TQ8631	51°3·1′	0°39·6′E	X	189
Lower Woon	Corn	SX0363	50°26·3′	4°46·1′W	T	200
Lower Wotton	Devon	SX7698	50°46·3′	3°45·1′W	X	191
Lower Wraxall	Dorset	ST5700	50°48·1′	2°36·2′W	T	194
Lower Wraxall	Somer	ST6035	51°7·0′	2°33·9′W	T	183
Lower Wraxall	Wilts	ST8364	51°22·7′	2°14·3′W	T	173
Lower Wych	Ches	SJ4844	52°59·7′	2°46·1′W	T	117
Lower Wyche	Worcs	SO7744	52°5·9′	2°19·8′W	T	150
Lower Wyke	Brad	SE1525	53°43·5′	1°45·9′W	T	104
Lower Wyke Fm	Hants	SU4048	51°14·0′	1°25·2′W	FM	185
Lower Yard	I of W	SZ5183	50°38·9′	1°16·3′W	X	196
Lower Yelland	Devon	SS4932	51°4·3′	4°8·9′W	T	180
Lower Zeals	Wilts	ST7932	51°5·4′	2°17·6′W	T	183
Lowes	Ches	SJ8970	53°13·9′	2°9·5′W	X	118
Lowes	E Ayr	NS5916	55°25·3′	4°13·2′W	X	71

Lowes	Pth & Kin	NO0544	56°35·0′	3°32·4′W	X	52,53
Lowes Barn	Durham	NZ2641	54°46·0′	1°35·3′W	T	88
Lowesby	Leic	SK7207	52°39·6′	0°55·7′W	T	141
Lowesby Village	Leic	SK7207	52°39·6′	0°55·7′W	A	141
Lowe's Fell	Northum	NY8764	54°58·5′	2°11·8′W	X	87
Lowes Fm	Derby	SK3629	52°51·7′	1°27·5′W	FM	128
Lowes Fm	Norf	TG0735	52°52·6′	1°5·0′E	FM	133
Lowes Fm	Norf	TG0741	52°55·8′	1°5·2′E	FM	133
Lowe's Fm	Norf	TL5995	52°32·0′	0°21·1′E	FM	143
Low Eshells	Northum	NY8957	54°54·7′	2°9·9′W	X	87
Low Esh Fm	Durham	NZ2043	54°47·1′	1°40·9′W	FM	88
Low Eskholme	Cumbr	SD1197	54°21·9′	3°21·8′W	X	96
Low Eskrigg	Cumbr	NY2353	54°52·2′	3°11·6′W	X	85
Lowes Lochs	D & G	NX7078	55°5·0′	4°1·8′W	W	77,84
Lowesmoor Fm	Glos	ST9299	51°41·6′	2°6·6′W	FM	163
Lowesmuir	E Ayr	NS6016	55°25·3′	4°12·3′W	X	71
Low Espley	Northum	NZ1890	55°12·5′	1°42·6′W	X	81
Lowes, The	D & G	NX7079	55°5·6′	4°1·8′W	X	77,84
Lowestoft	Suff	TM5492	52°28·2′	1°44·8′E	T	134
Lowestoft Denes	Suff	TM5594	52°29·3′	1°45·8′E	X	134
Lowestoft Ness	Suff	TM5593	52°28·7′	1°45·7′E	X	134
Lowestoft North Roads	Suff	TM5696	52°30·3′	1°46·7′E	W	134
Lowestoft South Roads	Suff	TM5490	52°27·2′	1°44·7′E	W	134
Loweswater	Cumbr	NY1221	54°34·8′	3°21·3′W	W	89
Loweswater	Cumbr	NY1420	54°34·3′	3°19·4′W	T	89
Loweswater Fell	Cumbr	NY1219	54°33·8′	3°21·2′W	X	89
Lowe's Wood	Beds	SP9232	51°59·0′	0°39·2′W	F	152,165
Lowe, The	Heref	SO4764	52°16·5′	2°46·2′W	X	137,138,148
Low Etherley	Durham	NZ1729	54°39·6′	1°43·8′W	T	92
Low Ewe Cote	N Yks	SE5691	54°18·9′	1°7·9′W	X	100
Low Ewehurst	Durham	NZ1455	54°53·6′	1°46·5′W	X	88
Low Faggergill	N Yks	NY9705	54°26·7′	2°2·4′W	X	92
Low Farm	Notts	SK7278	53°17·9′	0°54·8′W	FM	120
Low Far Moor	N Yks	SD9568	54°6·7′	2°4·2′W	X	98
Low Farnham	Northum	NT9702	55°19·0′	2°2·4′W	X	81
Low Feldom	N Yks	NZ1103	54°25·6′	1°49·4′W	X	92
Low Fell	Cumbr	NY1322	54°35·4′	3°20·4′W	H	89
Low Fell	Cumbr	NY5610	54°29·3′	2°40·3′W	X	90
Low Fell	Cumbr	SD4290	54°18·4′	2°53·1′W	X	96,97
Low Fell	Ghead	NZ2560	54°56·3′	1°36·2′W	T	88
Low Fell	Lancs	SD6855	53°59·6′	2°28·9′W	X	103
Low Fell End	Cumbr	SD4584	54°15·2′	2°50·2′W	X	97
Low Fell Ho	Cumbr	SD5884	54°15·2′	2°38·3′W	X	97
Lowfell Plantns	Northum	NZ1070	55°1·7′	1°50·2′W	F	88
Low Fellside	Cumbr	SD6385	54°15·8′	2°33·7′W	X	97
Low Fen	Cambs	TL4773	52°20·4′	0°9·9′E	X	154
Low Fen	Norf	TF5101	52°35·4′	0°14·1′E	X	143
Lowfewster Gill Fm	Durham	NZ1315	54°32·1′	1°47·5′W	FM	92
Lowfield	Cumbr	NY1832	54°40·8′	3°15·9′W	X	89,90
Lowfield	Cumbr	NY5441	54°46·0′	2°42·5′W	X	86
Lowfield	Cumbr	NY6118	54°33·6′	2°35·8′W	X	91
Lowfield	Cumbr	NY6918	54°33·6′	2°28·3′W	X	91
Low Field	Durham	NZ0013	54°31·0′	1°59·6′W	X	92
Lowfield	Lincs	TF1587	53°22·3′	0°15·9′W	X	113,121
Lowfield	Northum	NU0911	55°23·8′	1°51·0′W	X	81
Low Field	N Yks	NZ1815	54°32·0′	1°42·9′W	X	92
Lowfield	Sheff	SK3585	53°21·9′	1°28·0′W	T	110,111
Lowfield Fm	Beds	TL1850	52°8·4′	0°16·1′W	FM	153
Lowfell Fm	Derby	SK2062	53°9·5′	1°41·6′W	FM	119
Lowfield Fm	Durham	NZ2134	54°42·3′	1°40·0′W	FM	93
Lowfield Fm	Durham	NZ2828	54°39·0′	1°33·5′W	FM	93
Low Field Fm	E Yorks	SE9037	53°49·5′	0°37·5′W	FM	106
Low Field Fm	E Yorks	SE9626	53°43·5′	0°32·3′W	FM	106
Lowfield Fm	Glos	ST8995	51°39·5′	2°9·1′W	FM	163
Lowfield Fm	Lincs	SK8441	52°57·8′	0°44·6′W	FM	130
Lowfield Fm	Lincs	SK8984	53°21·0′	0°39·4′W	FM	121
Lowfield Fm	Lincs	SK9087	53°22·6′	0°38·4′W	FM	112,121
Lowfield Fm	Lincs	TF1470	53°13·1′	0°17·1′W	FM	121
Lowfield Fm	Notts	SK8259	53°7·5′	0°46·1′W	FM	121
Low Field Fm	N Yks	NZ3706	54°27·1′	1°25·3′W	FM	93
Lowfield Fm	N Yks	SE0851	53°57·5′	1°52·3′W	FM	104
Lowfield Fm	N Yks	SE9479	54°12·1′	0°33·1′W	FM	101
Lowfield Fm	N Yks	TA1179	54°11·9′	0°17·5′W	FM	101
Lowfield Fm	Oxon	SU7375	51°28·4′	0°56·5′W	FM	175
Lowfield Fm	Wilts	ST9994	51°38·9′	2°0·5′W	FM	163,173
Lowfield Garden	Durham	NZ0615	54°32·1′	1°54·0′W	X	92
Lowfield Heath	W Susx	TQ2740	51°8·9′	0°10·7′W	T	187
Lowfield Ho	Cumbr	NY2549	54°50·1′	3°9·6′W	X	85
Lowfield Ho	N Yks	SE4187	54°16·9′	1°21·8′W	X	99
Low Fields	Durham	NZ1716	54°32·6′	1°43·8′W	X	92
Low Fields	E Yorks	TA1456	53°59·5′	0°15·3′W	X	107
Low Fields	N Yks	NZ4911	54°29·8′	1°14·2′W	X	93
Lowfields	N Yks	SD6372	54°8·8′	2°33·6′W	X	97
Lowfields	N Yks	SD6672	54°8·8′	2°30·8′W	X	98
Low Fields	N Yks	SE6966	54°5·4′	0°56·3′W	X	100
Low Fields	N Yks	TA1475	54°9·7′	0°14·8′W	X	101
Low Fields Fm	Lincs	SK9660	53°7·9′	0°33·5′W	FM	121
Lowfields Fm	Lincs	SK9663	53°9·6′	0°33·4′W	FM	121
Lowfields Fm	Lincs	TF0381	53°19·2′	0°26·8′W	FM	121
Lowfield's Fm	Lincs	TF2721	52°46·5′	0°6·6′W	FM	131
Low Fiold	Orkney	HY3220	59°4·0′	3°10·7′W	X	6
Low Flask Fm	N Yks	NZ9300	54°23·5′	0°33·6′W	FM	94
Low Flow	Cumbr	NY2459	54°55·4′	3°10·7′W	X	85
Low Floweryhirst	Cumbr	NY5272	55°2·7′	2°44·6′W	X	86
Low Fm	Beds	TL1056	52°11·7′	0°23·0′W	FM	153
Low Fm	Bucks	SU9986	51°34·1′	0°33·9′W	FM	175,176
Low Fm	Cambs	TL2354	52°10·5′	0°11·7′W	FM	153
Low Fm	Cambs	TL3048	52°7·1′	0°5·7′W	FM	153
Low Fm	Cambs	TL3143	52°4·4′	0°4·9′W	FM	153
Low Fm	Cambs	TL5184	52°26·2′	0°13·7′E	FM	143
Low Fm	Derby	SK2858	53°7·3′	1°34·5′W	FM	119
Low Fm	Donc	SE6203	53°31·4′	1°3·5′W	FM	111
Low Fm	E Yorks	SE7846	53°54·5′	0°48·3′W	FM	105,106
Low Fm	E Yorks	SE9658	54°0·8′	0°31·7′W	FM	106
Low Fm	E Yorks	TA0331	53°46·1′	0°25·8′W	FM	107
Low Fm	E Yorks	TA0347	53°54·8′	0°25·5′W	FM	107
Low Fm	E Yorks	TA0535	53°48·3′	0°23·9′W	FM	107
Low Fm	E Yorks	TA1160	54°1·7′	0°17·9′W	FM	101
Low Fm	E Yorks	TA1434	53°47·6′	0°15·7′W	FM	107
Low Fm	E Yorks	TA2637	53°49·1′	0°4·7′W	FM	107

Low Fm	Lincs	SK8986	53°22·0′	0°39·3′W	FM	112,121
Low Fm	Lincs	SK9192	53°25·3′	0°37·4′W	FM	112
Low Fm	Lincs	SK9383	53°20·4′	0°35·8′W	FM	121
Low Fm	Lincs	TA0604	53°31·6′	0°23·6′W	FM	112
Low Fm	Lincs	TA1002	53°30·4′	0°20·1′W	FM	113
Low Fm	Lincs	TA3303	53°30·6′	0°0·8′E	FM	113
Low Fm	Lincs	TA3701	53°29·5′	0°4·3′E	FM	113
Low Fm	Lincs	TF1580	53°18·5′	0°16·0′W	FM	121
Low Fm	Lincs	TF2190	53°23·8′	0°10·4′W	FM	113
Low Fm	Lincs	TF2867	53°11·3′	0°4·6′W	FM	122
Low Fm	Lincs	TF3398	53°27·9′	0°0·6′E	FM	113
Low Fm	Lincs	TF3577	53°16·6′	0°1·9′E	FM	122
Low Fm	Lincs	TF3782	53°19·3′	0°3·8′E	FM	122
Low Fm	Lincs	TF4658	53°6·2′	0°11·3′E	FM	122
Low Fm	NE Lincs	TA2011	53°35·1′	0°10·8′W	FM	113
Low Fm	N Lincs	SE9100	53°29·6′	0°37·3′W	FM	112
Low Fm	N Lincs	TA0008	53°33·8′	0°29·0′W	FM	112
Low Fm	N Lincs	TA0818	53°39·1′	0°21·5′W	FM	112
Low Fm	N Lincs	TA1217	53°38·5′	0°17·9′W	FM	113
Low Fm	Norf	TF9600	52°34·0′	0°53·9′E	FM	144
Low Fm	Norf	TG0800	52°33·7′	1°4·5′E	FM	144
Low Fm	Norf	TG0826	52°47·7′	1°5·5′E	FM	133
Low Fm	Norf	TG3813	52°40·0′	1°31·6′E	FM	133,134
Low Fm	Norf	TM1289	52°27·7′	1°7·6′E	FM	144
Low Fm	Norf	TM1683	52°24·4′	1°10·9′E	FM	144,156
Low Fm	Norf	TM2683	52°24·1′	1°19·7′E	FM	156
Low Fm	Norf	TM2793	52°29·5′	1°21·0′E	FM	134
Low Fm	Norf	TM2986	52°25·7′	1°22·5′E	FM	156
Low Fm	Northum	NY9179	55°6·6′	2°8·0′W	FM	87
Low Fm	N Yks	NZ5005	54°26·5′	1°13·3′W	FM	93
Low Fm	N Yks	NZ6008	54°28·1′	1°4·0′W	FM	94
Low Fm	N Yks	NZ9404	54°25·6′	0°32·6′W	FM	94
Low Fm	N Yks	SE3856	54°0·2′	1°24·8′W	FM	104
Low Fm	N Yks	SE3882	54°14·2′	1°24·6′W	FM	99
Low Fm	N Yks	SE4361	54°2·8′	1°20·2′W	FM	99
Low Fm	N Yks	SE4657	54°0·7′	1°17·5′W	FM	105
Low Fm	N Yks	SE4660	54°2·3′	1°17·4′W	FM	100
Low Fm	N Yks	SE5971	54°8·1′	1°5·4′W	FM	100
Low Fm	N Yks	SE6387	54°16·7′	1°1·5′W	FM	94,100
Low Fm	N Yks	SE7195	54°21·0′	0°54·0′W	FM	94,100
Low Fm	N Yks	SE7659	54°1·5′	0°50·0′W	FM	105,106
Low Fm	N Yks	SE7669	54°6·9′	0°49·8′W	FM	100
Low Fm	N Yks	SE7776	54°10·7′	0°48·8′W	FM	100
Low Fm	Red & Cl	NZ5614	54°31·3′	1°7·7′W	FM	93
Low Fm	Red & Cl	NZ6920	54°34·5′	0°55·5′W	FM	94
Low Fm	Suff	TM0778	52°21·9′	1°2·8′E	FM	144
Low Fm	Suff	TM1749	52°6·0′	1°10·5′E	FM	169
Low Fm	Suff	TM1872	52°18·4′	1°12·3′E	FM	156
Low Fm	Suff	TM2574	52°19·3′	1°18·5′E	FM	156
Low Fm	Suff	TM2759	52°11·2′	1°19·7′E	FM	156
Low Fm	Suff	TM3068	52°15·9′	1°22·6′E	FM	156
Low Fm	Suff	TM3152	52°7·3′	1°22·9′E	FM	156
Low Fm	Suff	TM3274	52°19·1′	1°24·7′E	FM	156
Low Fm	Suff	TM3484	52°24·5′	1°26·8′E	FM	156
Low Fm	Suff	TM3580	52°22·3′	1°27·5′E	FM	156
Low Fm	Suff	TM3850	52°6·0′	1°28·9′E	FM	156
Low Fm	Suff	TM4690	52°27·4′	1°37·7′E	FM	134
Low Fms	Cumbr	SD4588	54°17·3′	2°50·3′W	FM	97
Low Fold	Cumbr	NY4600	54°23·8′	2°49·5′W	X	90
Low Fold	Cumbr	SD4593	54°20·0′	2°50·3′W	X	97
Low Fold	Leeds	SE2337	53°50·0′	1°38·6′W	T	104
Lowfold	W Susx	TQ0424	51°0·6′	0°30·7′W	X	197
Low Folds	Durham	NZ1834	54°42·3′	1°42·8′W	X	92
Low Folds	N Yks	SD7761	54°2·9′	2°20·7′W	X	98
Lowfoot Fm	Derby	SK0873	53°15·5′	1°52·4′W	FM	119
Low Force	Durham	NY9028	54°39·1′	2°8·9′W	W	91,92
Low Force	N Yks	SD9287	54°17·0′	2°7·0′W	X	98
Lowford	Hants	SU4810	50°53·5′	1°18·7′W	T	196
Low Forest Fm	Stock on T	NZ4109	54°28·7′	1°21·6′W	FM	93
Low Fosham	E Yorks	TA2038	53°49·7′	0°10·2′W	X	107
Low Fotherley	Northum	NZ0257	54°54·7′	1°57·7′W	X	87
Low Foulshaw	Cumbr	SD4781	54°13·6′	2°48·4′W	X	97
Low Foxton	N Yks	NZ4609	54°28·7′	1°17·0′W	X	93
Low Friarside	Durham	NZ1557	54°54·7′	1°45·5′W	X	88
Low Frith	Cumbr	SD3379	54°12·4′	3°1·2′W	X	96,97
Low Frith	N Yks	NY8903	54°25·6′	2°9·8′W	X	91,92
Low Fulney	Lincs	TF2621	52°46·5′	0°7·5′W	T	131
Low Gallowberry	E Ayr	NS4349	55°42·8′	4°29·5′W	X	64
Low Gameshill	E Ayr	NS4047	55°41·7′	4°32·3′W	X	64
Low Gartachorrans	Stir	NS4785	56°2·3′	4°26·9′W	X	57
Low Garth	Durham	NZ0021	54°35·3′	1°59·6′W	X	92
Low Garth	N Yks	NZ7305	54°26·4′	0°52·0′W	T	94
Low Gate	Northum	NY9063	54°57·9′	2°8·9′W	T	87
Low Gate	N Yks	SE2567	54°6·1′	1°36·6′W	T	99
Lowgate	N Yks	SE5918	53°39·5′	1°6·0′W	X	111
Lowgate Ho	Lincs	TF4317	52°44·1′	0°7·5′E	X	131
Low Gaterley	N Yks	SE7369	54°6·9′	0°52·6′W	X	100
Low Gatherley	N Yks	NZ2302	54°25·0′	1°38·3′W	X	93
Low Geltbridge	Cumbr	NY5159	54°55·6′	2°45·5′W	X	86
Lowgill	Cumbr	SD6297	54°22·3′	2°34·7′W	T	97
Lowgill	Lancs	SD6564	54°4·5′	2°31·7′W	T	97
Low Gill	N Yks	SD9888	54°17·5′	2°1·4′W	X	98
Low Gill Beck Fm	N Yks	NZ7503	54°25·3′	0°50·2′W	FM	94
Lowgill Fm	Cumbr	NY7714	54°31·5′	2°20·9′W	FM	91
Low Gingerfield Fm	N Yks	NZ1602	54°25·0′	1°44·8′W	FM	92
Low Glasnick	D & G	NX3461	54°55·2′	4°35·0′W	X	82
Low Glenadale	Arg & Bt	NR6411	55°20·4′	5°42·9′W	X	68
Low Glenayes	S Ayr	NS2817	55°25·3′	4°42·6′W	X	70
Low Glenramskill	Arg & Bt	NR7318	55°24·5′	5°34·7′W	X	68
Low Goosepool Fm	Darl	NZ3713	54°30·9′	1°25·3′W	FM	93
Low Grange	Cumbr	NY4341	54°45·9′	2°52·7′W	X	85
Low Grange	Durham	NZ3039	54°44·9′	1°31·6′W	X	93
Low Grange	Durham	NZ3044	54°47·6′	1°31·6′W	X	88
Low Grange	E Yorks	SE8440	53°51·2′	0°43·0′W	X	106
Low Grange	N Yks	NZ1808	54°28·3′	1°42·9′W	X	92
Low Grange	N Yks	SE2986	54°16·4′	1°32·9′W	X	99
Low Grange	N Yks	SE3654	53°59·1′	1°26·6′W	X	104
Low Grange	N Yks	SE4732	53°47·2′	1°16·8′W	X	105
Low Grange Fm	E Yorks	SE7050	53°56·7′	0°55·6′W	FM	105,106
Low Grange Fm	Lincs	TF0989	53°23·4′	0°21·2′W	FM	112,121

Low Grange Fm	Suff	TM3370	52°16·9'	1°25·4'E	FM	156
Low Grantley	N Yks	SE2370	54°7·8'	1°38·5'W	T	99
Low Green	Cumbr	SD4282	54°14·1'	2°53·0'W	X	96,97
Low Green	Leeds	SE2138	53°50·5'	1°40·4'W	T	104
Low Green	N Yks	SE2059	54°1·8'	1°41·3'W	T	104
Low Green	Suff	TL8660	52°12·6'	0°43·7'E	T	155
Low Greenfield	Durham	NZ1728	54°39·1'	1°43·8'W	X	92
Low Green Field	N Yks	SD8480	54°13·2'	2°14·3'W	X	98
Low Green Field Knott	N Yks	SD8479	54°12·6'	2°14·3'W	X	98
Low Green Field Lings	N Yks	SD8380	54°13·2'	2°15·2'W	X	98
Low Green Fm	Leeds	SE3342	53°52·6'	1°29·5'W	FM	104
Low Green Ho	N Yks	SE1467	54°6·2'	1°46·7'W	X	99
Low Greenside	Ghead	NZ1462	54°57·4'	1°46·5'W	T	88
Low Grewburn Fm	Durham	NZ0925	54°37·4'	1°51·2'W	FM	92
Low Ground	Cumbr	SD1798	54°22·5'	3°16·2'W	X	96
Low Ground	N Yks	SD9350	53°57·0'	2°6·0'W	X	103
Low Ground Fm	N Yks	SE6580	54°12·9'	0°59·8'W	FM	100
Low Ground Fm	N Yks	SE7461	54°2·6'	0°51·8'W	FM	100
Low Grounds	Cumbr	NY4838	54°44·3'	2°48·0'W	X	90
Low Grounds	Lincs	TF4758	53°6·2'	0°12·2'E	X	122
Low Grounds Fm	Bucks	SU8384	51°33·2'	0°47·8'W	FM	175
Lowgrounds Fm	Lincs	TF2140	52°56·9'	0°11·5'W	FM	131
Low Grounds Fm	N Yks	SE3972	54°8·8'	1°23·8'W	FM	99
Low Grounds or Huggin Carr	Donc	SE6705	53°32·5'	0°58·9'W	X	111
Low Grove Fm	Cumbr	NY2525	54°37·1'	3°9·3'W	FM	89,90
Lowgroves	Cumbr	SD5295	54°21·1'	2°43·9'W	X	97
Low Grundon Fm	N Yks	SE8280	54°12·8'	0°44·1'W	FM	100
Low Habberley	Worcs	SO8077	52°23·7'	2°17·2'W	T	138
Low Haber	Northum	NY7855	54°53·6'	2°20·2'W	X	86,87
Lowhagstock Scar	Cumbr	NY0749	54°49·9'	3°26·4'W	X	85
Low Hail Fm	Darl	NZ3009	54°28·8'	1°31·8'W	FM	93
Low Haining	Sund	NZ3551	54°51·4'	1°26·9'W	X	88
Low Hall	Cumbr	NX9815	54°31·5'	3°34·1'W	X	89
Low Hall	Cumbr	NY1227	54°38·1'	3°21·4'W	X	89
Low Hall	Cumbr	NY7512	54°30·4'	2°22·7'W	X	91
Low Hall	Cumbr	SD2195	54°20·9'	3°12·5'W	X	96
Low Hall	Cumbr	SD2681	54°13·4'	3°10·4'W	X	96
Low Hall	Lancs	SD6075	54°10·4'	2°36·3'W	X	97
Low Hall	Northum	NU1301	55°18·4'	1°47·3'W	X	81
Low Hall	Northum	NU2701	55°18·4'	1°34·0'W	X	81
Low Hall	Northum	NZ0372	55°2·8'	1°56·8'W	X	87
Low Hall	Northum	NZ0374	55°3·9'	1°56·8'W	X	87
Low Hall	N Yks	SE0460	54°2·4'	1°55·9'W	X	98
Low Hall	N Yks	SE1961	54°2·9'	1°42·2'W	X	99
Low Hall	N Yks	SE1996	54°21·8'	1°42·0'W	X	99
Low Hall	N Yks	SE3249	53°56·4'	1°30·3'W	X	104
Low Hall	N Yks	SE3561	54°2·9'	1°27·5'W	X	99
Low Hall	N Yks	SE9381	54°13·2'	0°34·0'W	X	101
Low Hall	N Yks	SE9884	54°14·8'	0°29·3'W	X	101
Lowhall Building	Cumbr	NY5644	54°47·6'	2°40·6'W	X	86
Low Hallburn	Cumbr	NY4068	55°0·4'	2°55·9'W	X	85
Low Hall Fm	N Lincs	SE7900	53°29·7'	0°48·1'W	FM	112
Low Hall Fm	N Yks	SE5333	53°47·7'	1°11·3'W	FM	105
Low Hall Garth	Cumbr	NY3002	54°24·8'	3°4·3'W	X	90
Low Hall Wood	N Yks	SE1960	54°2·4'	1°42·2'W	F	99
Low Ham	Somer	ST4329	51°3·7'	2°48·4'W	T	193
Low Ham Br	Somer	ST4432	51°5·3'	2°47·6'W	X	182
Low Hamer	N Yks	SE7497	54°22·0'	0°51·2'W	X	94,100
Low Hameringham	Lincs	TF3066	53°10·7'	0°2·9'W	X	122
Low Hangbank	N Yks	NZ2108	54°28·3'	1°40·1'W	X	93
Low Hardwick	Durham	NZ3329	54°39·5'	1°28·9'W	X	93
Low Harker	Cumbr	NY3861	54°56·6'	2°57·6'W	X	85
Low Harperley	Durham	NZ1235	54°42·8'	1°48·4'W	X	92
Low Harthay	Cambs	TL1771	52°19·7'	0°16·6'W	X	153
Low Haswell Fm	Durham	NZ3644	54°47·6'	1°26·0'W	FM	88
Lowhaughs	Northum	NT9652	55°45·9'	2°3·4'W	X	74,75
Low Hauxley	Northum	NU2802	55°18·9'	1°33·1'W	T	81
Low Haw Leas	N Yks	SE2578	54°12·1'	1°36·6'W	X	99
Low Hawsker	N Yks	NZ9207	54°27·2'	0°34·4'W	T	94
Low Hay Bridge	Cumbr	SD3387	54°16·7'	3°1·3'W	X	96,97
Low Haygarth	Cumbr	SD6996	54°21·8'	2°28·2'W	X	98
Low Hazel Heads	N Yks	SE5391	54°19·0'	1°10·7'W	X	100
Low Healey Cote	N Yks	SE1781	54°13·7'	1°43·9'W	X	99
Low Hedgeley Fm	Northum	NU0617	55°27·1'	1°53·9'W	FM	81
Low Hedley	Northum	NZ1498	55°16·8'	1°46·3'W	X	81
Low Hedleyhope Hall	Durham	NZ1440	54°45·5'	1°46·5'W	X	88
Low Heighley	Northum	NZ1788	55°11·4'	1°43·5'W	X	81
Low Hesket	Cumbr	NY4646	54°48·6'	2°50·0'W	T	86
Low Hesleyhurst	Northum	NZ0997	55°16·3'	1°51·1'W	X	81
Low Hill	Brad	SE1540	53°51·6'	1°45·9'W	X	104
Low Hill	E Renf	NS5751	55°44·1'	4°16·2'W	X	64
Low Hill	Wolv	SJ9201	52°36·6'	2°6·7'W	T	127,139
Low Hill	Worcs	SO8473	52°21·5'	2°13·7'W	T	138
Low Hill	Worcs	SO9152	52°10·2'	2°7·5'W	X	150
Low Hill Fm	Hants	SU5020	50°58·9'	1°16·9'W	FM	185
Lowhill Fm	N Lincs	SE8705	53°32·3'	0°40·8'W	FM	112
Low Hill Ho	Lancs	SD6539	53°51·0'	2°31·5'W	X	102,103
Low Hills	Durham	NZ4141	54°46·0'	1°21·3'W	X	88
Lowhillside	Aberd	NJ8023	57°18·1'	2°19·5'W	X	38
Low Ho	Brad	SE1241	53°52·1'	1°48·6'W	X	104
Low Ho	Cumbr	NY0016	54°32·0'	3°32·3'W	X	89
Low Ho	Cumbr	NY0935	54°42·4'	3°24·3'W	X	89
Low Ho	Cumbr	NY1522	54°35·4'	3°18·5'W	X	89
Low Ho	Cumbr	NY2132	54°40·9'	3°13·1'W	X	89,90
Low Ho	Cumbr	NY5101	54°24·4'	2°44·9'W	X	90
Low Ho	Cumbr	NY5148	54°49·7'	2°45·3'W	X	86
Low Ho	Cumbr	NY7604	54°26·1'	2°21·8'W	X	91
Low Ho	Cumbr	SD1681	54°13·3'	3°16·9'W	X	96
Low Ho	Cumbr	SD4389	54°17·9'	2°52·1'W	X	97
Low Ho	Cumbr	SD4599	54°23·3'	2°50·4'W	X	97
Low Ho	Cumbr	SD4989	54°17·9'	2°46·6'W	X	97
Low Ho	Cumbr	SD5693	54°20·1'	2°40·2'W	X	97
Low Ho	Cumbr	SD7389	54°18·0'	2°24·5'W	X	98
Low Ho	Lancs	SD5666	54°5·5'	2°39·9'W	X	97
Low Ho	Lancs	SD5668	54°6·6'	2°40·0'W	X	97
Low Ho	Northum	NT9451	55°45·4'	2°5·3'W	X	67,74,75
Low Ho	Northum	NY9658	54°55·2'	2°3·3'W	X	87
Low Ho	Northum	NZ1174	55°3·9'	1°49·2'W	X	88
Low Ho	N Yks	NZ0707	54°27·7'	1°53·1'W	X	92
Low Ho	N Yks	NZ6706	54°26·9'	0°57·6'W	X	94
Low Ho	N Yks	NZ8015	54°31·7'	0°45·4'W	X	94
Low Ho	N Yks	SE0557	54°0·8'	1°55·0'W	X	104
Low Ho	N Yks	SE4489	54°17·9'	1°19·0'W	X	99
Low Hockett	Northum	NU2117	55°27·0'	1°39·6'W	X	81
Low Holehouse	E Ayr	NS5031	55°33·2'	4°22·2'W	X	70
Low Holm	Cumbr	NY5049	54°50·2'	2°46·3'W	X	86
Low Holme	Cumbr	NY1400	54°23·5'	3°19·1'W	X	89
Low Hood Gap	N Yks	SE1762	54°3·5'	1°44·0'W	X	99
Low Hope	Northum	NY9251	54°51·5'	2°7·1'W	X	87
Low Horcum	N Yks	SE8493	54°19·8'	0°42·1'W	X	94,100
Low Horton Fm	Northum	NZ2879	55°6·5'	1°33·2'W	FM	88
Low Hos	Durham	NY9226	54°38·0'	2°7·0'W	X	91,92
Low Hos	N Yks	SD9897	54°22·4'	2°1·4'W	X	98
Lowhouse	Cumbr	NY4934	54°42·2'	2°47·1'W	X	90
Low House	Durham	NZ2431	54°40·7'	1°37·2'W	X	93
Lowhouse	N Ayr	NS3755	55°45·9'	4°35·4'W	X	63
Lowhouse Beck	Cumbr	SD4092	54°19·5'	2°54·9'W	X	96,97
Low House Fm	Brad	SE1446	53°54·8'	1°46·8'W	FM	104
Low House Fm	Cumbr	NY2219	54°33·9'	3°12·0'W	FM	89,90
Low House Fm	Cumbr	NY2945	54°47·9'	3°5·8'W	FM	85
Lowhouse Fm	Cumbr	NY5048	54°49·7'	2°46·3'W	FM	86
Low House Fm	Cumbr	SD4196	54°21·6'	2°54·1'W	FM	96,97
Low House Fm	Kirk	SE2412	53°36·5'	1°37·8'W	FM	110
Low House Fm	Lancs	SD6475	54°10·4'	2°32·7'W	FM	97
Low House Fm	Northum	NY7264	54°58·4'	2°25·8'W	FM	86,87
Low House Fm	N Yks	NZ4911	54°29·8'	1°14·2'W	FM	93
Low House Fm	N Yks	SE4265	54°5·0'	1°21·1'W	FM	99
Low House Fm	S Tyne	NZ3761	54°56·8'	1°24·9'W	FM	88
Low Houselop	Durham	NZ0940	54°45·5'	1°51·2'W	X	88
Low House Moor	Roch	SD9614	53°37·6'	2°3·2'W	X	109
Low Houses	Cumbr	NY2447	54°49·0'	3°10·5'W	X	85
Low Houses	Cumbr	NY5861	54°56·8'	2°38·9'W	X	86
Low Houses	N Yks	SD8387	54°16·9'	2°15·2'W	X	98
Low Howgill	Cumbr	NY6628	54°39·0'	2°31·2'W	X	91
Low Huddlesceugh	Cumbr	NY5942	54°46·5'	2°37·8'W	X	86
Low Hunsley Fm	E Yorks	SE9533	53°47·3'	0°33·1'W	FM	106
Low Hunsley Plantn	E Yorks	SE9433	53°47·3'	0°34·0'W	F	106
Low Hurst	Cumbr	NY4350	54°50·7'	2°52·8'W	X	85
Low Hutton	N Yks	SE1788	54°17·5'	1°43·9'W	X	99
Low Hutton	N Yks	SE7667	54°5·8'	0°49·9'W	T	100
Lowick	Cumbr	SD2986	54°16·1'	3°5·0'W	T	96,97
Lowick	Northnts	SP9780	52°24·8'	0°34·0'W	T	141
Lowick	Northum	NU0139	55°38·9'	1°58·6'W	T	75
Lowick Bridge	Cumbr	SD2986	54°16·1'	3°5·0'W	T	96,97
Lowick Common	Cumbr	SD2884	54°15·0'	3°5·9'W	X	96,97
Lowick Green	Cumbr	SD2985	54°15·6'	3°5·0'W	T	96,97
Lowick Hall	Cumbr	SD2885	54°15·6'	3°5·9'W	A	96,97
Lowick High Common	Cumbr	SD2683	54°14·5'	3°7·7'W	X	96,97
Lowick High Stead	Northum	NU0038	55°38·4'	1°59·6'W	X	75
Lowick Low Steads	Northum	NU0339	55°38·9'	1°56·7'W	X	75
Lowick Mill	Northum	NU0241	55°40·0'	1°57·7'W	X	75
Lowick Northfield	Northum	NU0039	55°38·9'	1°59·6'W	X	75
Lowicks Ho	Surrey	SU8540	51°9·4'	0°46·7'W	X	186
Lowick Southmoor	Northum	NU0036	55°37·3'	1°59·6'W	X	75
Low Ingleston	D & G	NX8769	55°0·4'	3°45·6'W	X	84
Low Ingram Grange	N Yks	NZ3903	54°25·5'	1°23·5'W	X	93
Low Inhams	N Yks	SE5865	54°4·9'	1°6·4'W	X	100
Low Intake	N Yks	SE2173	54°9·4'	1°40·3'W	X	99
Low Jofless	Durham	NZ0639	54°45·0'	1°54·0'W	X	92
Lowkbers	N Yks	SD7071	54°8·3'	2°27·1'W	X	98
Low Keirs	E Ayr	NS4308	55°20·7'	4°28·1'W	X	70,77
Low Kettlesbeck	N Yks	SD7465	54°5·1'	2°23·4'W	X	98
Low Keverstone	Durham	NZ1422	54°35·8'	1°46·6'W	X	92
Low King Hill	Cumbr	NY6172	55°2·7'	2°36·2'W	X	86
Low Kingthorpe	N Yks	SE8385	54°15·5'	0°43·1'W	X	94,100
Low Kinmont	Cumbr	SD1189	54°17·6'	3°21·6'W	X	96
Low Kiplin	N Yks	SE2896	54°21·8'	1°33·7'W	X	99
Low Kirkbride	D & G	NX8786	55°9·6'	3°46·0'W	X	78
Low Kittymuir	S Lanak	NS7548	55°42·8'	3°58·9'W	X	64
Low Knipe	Cumbr	NY5120	54°34·6'	2°45·1'W	T	90
Low Knockrioch	Arg & Bt	NR6920	55°25·4'	5°38·6'W	X	68
Low Knowle Fm	N Yks	SE1779	54°12·6'	1°43·9'W	FM	99
Low Kop	Cumbr	NY4716	54°32·4'	2°48·7'W	H	90
Low Laithe	Lancs	SD7158	54°1·3'	2°26·1'W	X	103
Low Laithe	N Yks	SE1963	54°4·0'	1°42·2'W	T	99
Low Laithes	Barns	SE3804	53°32·1'	1°25·2'W	T	110,111
Low Laithes	Wakf	SE2921	53°41·3'	1°33·2'W	X	104
Low Laithes Fm	Roth	SK4883	53°20·7'	1°16·3'W	FM	111,120
Low Lambton Fm	Sund	NZ3254	54°53·0'	1°29·6'W	FM	88
Lowland Barn	Oxon	SP3124	51°55·1'	1°32·6'W	X	164
Lowland Fm	Kent	TQ8139	51°7·5'	0°35·6'E	FM	188
Lowland Fm	Wilts	ST9952	51°16·3'	2°0·5'W	FM	184
Lowlandman's Bay	Arg & Bt	NR5672	55°53·0'	5°53·7'W	W	61
Lowland Point	Corn	SW8019	50°2·1'	5°4·0'W	X	204
Lowlands	Devon	SY0795	50°45·1'	3°18·7'W	X	192
Low Lands	Durham	NZ1325	54°37·4'	1°47·5'W	X	92
Lowlands	Torf	ST2996	51°39·7'	3°1·2'W	T	171
Lowlands Fm	Essex	TL7226	51°54·6'	0°30·4'E	FM	167
Lowlands Fm	Essex	TQ8594	51°37·1'	0°40·7'E	FM	168,178
Lowlands Fm	Norf	TG0810	52°39·1'	1°4·9'E	FM	133
Lowlands Fm	Norf	TG3333	52°50·9'	1°28·0'E	FM	133
Lowlands Fm	N Yks	SE4569	54°7·1'	1°18·3'W	FM	99
Lowlands Fm	N Yks	SE5878	54°11·9'	1°6·2'W	FM	100
Lowlands Fm	Peterb	TF1704	52°37·5'	0°15·9'W	FM	142
Lowlands Fm	Stock on T	NZ4111	54°29·8'	1°21·6'W	FM	93
Lowlands Fm	Suff	TM3388	52°26·6'	1°26·1'E	FM	156
Lowlands Fm	W Susx	TQ3120	50°58·1'	0°7·7'W	FM	198
Low Lane Ho	Northum	NY8858	54°55·2'	2°10·8'W	X	87
Low Langshaw Moss	Cumbr	SD7685	54°15·9'	2°21·7'W	X	98
Low Langton	Lincs	TF1576	53°16·3'	0°16·1'W	X	121
Low Langwith	N Yks	SE1876	54°11·0'	1°43·0'W	X	99
Low Lann	D & G	NX8291	55°12·2'	3°50·8'W	X	78
Low Lanrigg	S Lanak	NS7545	55°41·2'	3°58·9'W	X	64
Low Leaf Howe Ho	N Yks	SE7894	54°20·4'	0°47·6'W	X	94,100
Low Leam	Northum	NY8786	55°10·3'	2°11·8'W	X	80
Low Learchild	Northum	NU1011	55°23·8'	1°50·1'W	X	81
Low Leases Fm	N Yks	SE2891	54°19·1'	1°33·8'W	FM	99
Low Leathes	Cumbr	NY1238	54°44·0'	3°21·6'W	X	89
Low Lee Fm	Ches	SJ9468	53°12·8'	2°5·0'W	FM	118
Low Leighton	Derby	SK0085	53°22·0'	1°59·6'W	T	110
Low Levels	Donc	SE7108	53°34·1'	0°55·3'W	X	112
Low Levens Fm	Cumbr	SD4885	54°15·7'	2°47·5'W	FM	97
Lowley	Devon	SX8487	50°40·5'	3°38·1'W	X	191
Lowleybridge	Corn	SX3578	50°34·9'	4°19·5'W	X	201
Lowley Brook	Corn	SX3481	50°36·5'	4°20·4'W	W	201
Low Leys	Cumbr	NY0619	54°33·7'	3°26·8'W	X	89
Lowley's Fm	Essex	TL7215	51°48·7'	0°30·1'E	FM	167
Lowley Wood	Corn	SX3287	50°39·7'	4°22·2'W	F	190
Low Lighthouse	Angus	NO5430	56°27·8'	2°44·3'W	X	54
Low Lindeth	Cumbr	SD4195	54°21·1'	2°54·0'W	X	96,97
Low Lindrick	N Yks	SE2771	54°8·3'	1°34·8'W	X	99
Low Ling	Cumbr	NY3146	54°48·5'	3°4·0'W	X	85
Low Ling Close	Durham	NZ3943	54°47·1'	1°23·2'W	X	88
Low Lion Lodge	N Yks	SE5776	54°10·8'	1°7·2'W	X	100
Low Lochbank	D & G	NX9068	54°59·9'	3°42·8'W	X	84
Low Long Ho	Northum	NY6287	55°10·8'	2°35·4'W	X	80
Low Longmire	Cumbr	SD3287	54°16·7'	3°2·2'W	X	96,97
Low Longrigg	Cumbr	NY1702	54°24·6'	3°16·3'W	X	89,90
Low Longthwaite	Cumbr	NY2447	54°49·0'	3°10·5'W	X	85
Low Lonning Fm	Cumbr	NY5660	54°56·2'	2°40·8'W	FM	86
Low Lorton	Cumbr	NY1525	54°37·0'	3°18·6'W	T	89
Low Lowood	Cumbr	NY5248	54°49·7'	2°44·4'W	X	86
Low Luckens	Cumbr	NY4972	55°2·6'	2°47·5'W	X	86
Low Luddick	N upon Ty	NZ1870	55°1·7'	1°42·7'W	X	88
Low Lynn	Northum	NU0441	55°40·0'	1°55·7'W	X	75
Low Maidendale Fm	Darl	NZ3212	54°30·4'	1°29·9'W	FM	93
Low Mains	D & G	NX4439	54°43·6'	4°24·9'W	X	83
Low Mains Fm	N Yks	SE2282	54°14·2'	1°39·3'W	FM	99
Low Malzie	D & G	NX3753	54°51·0'	4°31·9'W	X	83
Lowman Cross	Devon	ST0115	50°55·8'	3°24·1'W	X	181
Lowmans Fm	Devon	SY1698	50°46·8'	3°11·1'W	FM	192,193
Low Marishes	N Yks	SE8277	54°11·2'	0°44·2'W	T	100
Low Mark	S Ayr	NX0773	55°1·1'	5°0·7'W	X	76
Low Marnham	Notts	SK8069	53°13·0'	0°47·7'W	T	121
Low Marsh	Cumbr	SD3673	54°9·2'	2°58·4'W	W	96,97
Lowmead Fm	Carm	SN1814	51°47·9'	4°38·0'W	FM	158
Low Meadows	Durham	NZ1448	54°49·8'	1°46·5'W	X	88
Low Meadows	Lancs	SD4614	53°37·4'	2°48·6'W	X	108
Low Meathop	Cumbr	SD4379	54°12·5'	2°52·0'W	X	97
Low Meathop Marsh	Cumbr	SD4279	54°12·5'	2°52·9'W	X	96,97
Low Melwood	N Lincs	SE8001	53°30·2'	0°47·2'W	X	112
Low Merrybent	N Yks	NZ2107	54°27·7'	1°40·1'W	X	93
Low Metham Grange	E Yorks	SE8126	53°43·7'	0°45·9'W	X	106
Low Middlefield Fm	Stock on T	NZ4123	54°36·3'	1°21·5'W	FM	93
Low Middle Moor	Northum	NZ2280	55°7·1'	1°38·9'W	X	81
Low Middleton	Darl	NZ3610	54°29·3'	1°26·2'W	X	93
Low Middleton	Northum	NU1036	55°37·3'	1°50·0'W	X	75
Low Mill	Barns	SE2906	53°33·2'	1°33·3'W	X	110
Low Mill	Cumbr	NY0008	54°27·7'	3°32·1'W	X	89
Low Mill	Cumbr	NY2040	54°45·2'	3°14·2'W	X	85
Low Mill	Cumbr	NY3632	54°41·0'	2°59·1'W	X	90
Lowmill	Cumbr	NY3751	54°51·2'	2°58·5'W	X	85
Low Mill	Cumbr	NY5842	54°46·5'	2°38·8'W	X	86
Low Mill	N Yks	SE5795	54°21·1'	1°7·0'W	X	100
Low Mill	N Yks	SE6795	54°21·0'	0°57·7'W	T	94,100
Low Mill Burn	D & G	NX3581	55°6·0'	4°34·7'W	W	77
Lowmill Knowe	D & G	NS8313	55°24·1'	3°50·4'W	H	71,78
Low Milndovan	Arg & Bt	NS3578	55°58·3'	4°38·2'W	X	63
Low Milton	D & G	NX3146	54°47·1'	4°37·3'W	X	82
Low Milton	S Ayr	NS3113	55°23·2'	4°39·6'W	X	70
Lowmoat	Cumbr	NY3973	55°3·1'	2°56·9'W	X	85
Low Moor	Brad	SE1528	53°45·1'	1°45·9'W	T	104
Lowmoor	Cumbr	NY1936	54°43·0'	3°15·0'W	X	89,90
Low Moor	Cumbr	NY4958	54°55·1'	2°47·3'W	X	86
Low Moor	Cumbr	NY5324	54°36·8'	2°43·2'W	X	90
Low Moor	Cumbr	NY6106	54°27·1'	2°35·7'W	X	91
Low Moor	Cumbr	NY6120	54°34·7'	2°35·8'W	X	91
Low Moor	D & G	NX2849	54°48·6'	4°40·2'W	X	82
Low Moor	Lancs	SD7341	53°52·1'	2°24·2'W	T	103
Low Moor	N Yks	NY9904	54°26·1'	2°0·5'W	X	92
Low Moor	N Yks	NZ0103	54°25·6'	1°58·7'W	X	92
Low Moor	N Yks	NZ8501	54°24·1'	0°41·0'W	X	94
Low Moor	N Yks	NZ9103	54°25·1'	0°35·4'W	X	94
Low Moor	N Yks	SD7974	54°9·9'	2°18·9'W	X	98
Low Moor	N Yks	SE1156	54°0·2'	1°49·5'W	X	104
Low Moor	N Yks	SE1463	54°4·0'	1°46·7'W	X	99
Low Moor	N Yks	SE3998	54°22·8'	1°23·6'W	X	99
Low Moor	N Yks	SE8599	54°23·0'	0°41·1'W	X	94,100
Low Moor	Red & Cl	NZ6515	54°31·8'	0°59·3'W	X	94
Low Moor	Sheff	SK2199	53°29·5'	1°40·6'W	X	110
Low Moor	York	SE5352	53°57·9'	1°11·1'W	X	105
Lowmoor Crossing	Northum	NU0938	55°38·4'	1°51·0'W	X	75
Low Moor Dyke	Cumbr	NY3737	54°43·7'	2°58·3'W	X	90
Lowmoor Fm	Derby	SK1956	53°6·3'	1°42·6'W	FM	119
Lowmoor Fm	Devon	ST0812	50°54·2'	3°18·1'W	FM	181
Low Moor Fm	N Yks	NZ3610	54°29·3'	1°26·2'W	FM	93
Low Moor Fm	N Yks	SE2848	53°55·9'	1°34·0'W	FM	104
Lowmoor Fm	N Yks	SE5243	53°53·1'	1°12·1'W	FM	105
Low Moor Fm	N Yks	SE7058	54°1·0'	0°55·5'W	FM	105,106
Low Moor Fm	N Yks	SE7978	54°11·7'	0°46·9'W	FM	100
Low Moor Fm	N Yks	SE8276	54°10·6'	0°44·2'W	FM	100
Low Moor Fm	N Yks	SE9993	54°19·6'	0°28·2'W	FM	94,101
Low Moor Head	Lancs	SD5456	54°0·1'	2°41·7'W	X	102
Low Moor Hill	Durham	NZ1229	54°39·6'	1°48·4'W	X	92
Low Moor Ho	N Yks	SE3569	54°7·2'	1°27·5'W	X	99
Low Moor of Killiemore	D & G	NX3560	54°54·7'	4°34·0'W	X	83
Lowmoor Point	Northum	NU0939	55°38·9'	1°51·0'W	X	75
Lowmoor Row	Cumbr	NY6226	54°37·9'	2°34·9'W	X	91
Low Moors	N Yks	SE7677	54°11·2'	0°49·7'W	X	100
Low Moorside	Cumbr	NY0701	54°24·0'	3°25·5'W	X	89
Low Moorsley	Sund	NZ3446	54°48·7'	1°27·8'W	T	88
Low Moor Wood	Pth & Kin	NN9124	56°24·0'	3°45·5'W	F	52,58
Low Moralee	Northum	NY8476	55°4·9'	2°14·6'W	X	86,87
Low Moresby	Cumbr	NX9920	54°34·2'	3°33·3'W	T	89
Low Moss	Cumbr	NY2820	54°34·5'	3°6·4'W	X	89,90
Low Moss	Cumbr	SD2088	54°17·1'	3°13·3'W	X	96
Low Moss	E Ayr	NS6120	55°27·5'	4°11·5'W	X	71
Low Moss Plantn	E Dunb	NS6271	55°55·0'	4°12·0'W	F	64
Low Mowthorpe	N Yks	SE8965	54°4·6'	0°38·0'W	X	101

Low Mowthorpe	N Yks	SE8966	54°5·2'	0°37·9'W	X	101
Low Muffles	N Yks	SE7694	54°20·4'	0°49·4'W	X	94,100
Low Mye	D & G	NX1053	54°50·4'	4°57·1'W	X	82
Lowna	N Yks	SE6891	54°18·8'	0°56·9'W	T	94,100
Lownde Wood	Suff	TL8060	52°12·8'	0°38·5'E	F	155
Low Neasham Springs	Darl	NZ3210	54°29·3'	1°29·9'W	X	93
Low Neck	Swan	SS3987	51°33·8'	4°19·0'W	X	159
Low Newbiggin	N upon Ty	NZ1968	55°0·6'	1°41·7'W	X	88
Low Newstead Grange	N Yks	SE8478	54°11·7'	0°42·3'W	X	100
Low Newsteads	N Yks	SE1685	54°15·9'	1°44·8'W	X	99
Low Newton	Cumbr	SD4082	54°14·1'	2°54·8'W	T	96,97
Low Newton-by-the-Sea	Northum	NU2424	55°30·8'	1°36·8'W	T	75
Lownie Hill	Angus	NO4948	56°37·5'	2°49·4'W	H	54
Lownie Moor	Angus	NO4848	56°37·5'	2°50·4'W	X	54
Low Nook	Durham	NY9322	54°35·8'	2°6·1'W	X	91,92
Lownorth Beck	N Yks	SE9595	54°20·7'	0°31·9'W	W	94,101
Low North Holme	N Yks	SE6981	54°13·4'	0°56·1'W	X	100
Lownorth Moor	N Yks	SE9397	54°21·8'	0°33·7'W	X	94,101
Low Northsceugh	Cumbr	NY5248	54°49·7'	2°44·4'W	X	86
Low Old Shields	Northum	NY6666	54°59·5'	2°31·5'W	X	86
Lowood	C of Edin	NT1676	55°58·4'	3°20·3'W	X	65,66
Lowood	Scot Bord	NT5135	55°36·6'	2°46·2'W	T	73
Lowood	Suff	TM2451	52°6·9'	1°16·7'E	X	156
Lowerthy	Devon	SX8146	50°18·4'	3°39·9'W	X	202
Low Osgoodby Grange	N Yks	SE4880	54°13·0'	1°15·4'W	X	100
Low Out Wood	Cumbr	NY7908	54°28·3'	2°19·0'W	F	91
Low Over Blow	N Yks	SE8093	54°19·8'	0°45·8'W	X	94,100
Low Oxnop	N Yks	SD9397	54°22·4'	2°6·0'W	X	98
Low Oxque	N Yks	SE1098	54°22·9'	1°50·3'W	X	99
Low Paley Green	N Yks	SD7964	54°4·5'	2°18·8'W	X	98
Low Paradise Fm	N Yks	SE5088	54°17·4'	1°13·5'W	FM	100
Lowpark	Cumbr	NY1420	54°34·3'	3°19·4'W	X	89
Low Park	Cumbr	NY3303	54°25·3'	3°1·5'W	X	90
Low Park	Cumbr	NY5470	55°1·6'	2°42·7'W	X	86
Low Park	Cumbr	NY5672	55°2·7'	2°40·9'W	X	86
Low Park	Cumbr	SD6298	54°22·8'	2°34·7'W	X	97
Low Park	D & G	NX6475	55°3·3'	4°7·3'W	X	77
Low Park	N Yks	SE1950	53°57·0'	1°42·2'W	X	104
Low Park	N Yks	SE2783	54°14·8'	1°34·7'W	X	99
Low Parkamoor	Cumbr	SD3092	54°19·4'	3°4·2'W	X	96,97
Low Parkend	Northum	NY8775	55°4·4'	2°11·8'W	X	87
Low Park Fm	Cumbr	SD5486	54°16·3'	2°42·0'W	FM	97
Low Park Fm	Lincs	TF0729	52°51·1'	0°24·3'W	FM	130
Lowpark Fm	N Yks	SE4639	53°51·0'	1°17·6'W	FM	105
Low Park Fm	N Yks	SE6987	54°16·7'	0°56·0'W	FM	94,100
Low Park Ho	Cumbr	NY8013	54°31·0'	2°18·1'W	X	91,92
Low Parks	N Yks	SE5375	54°10·3'	1°10·9'W	X	100
Low Parks Fm	N Yks	SE6381	54°13·5'	1°2·5'W	FM	100
Low Park Wall	Durham	NZ0418	54°33·7'	1°55·9'W	X	92
Low Pasture	N Yks	NZ1903	54°25·6'	1°42·0'W	X	92
Low Pasture	N Yks	SE2295	54°21·2'	1°39·3'W	X	99
Low Pasture Fm	N Yks	SE8690	54°18·1'	0°40·3'W	FM	94,101
Low Pasture Fm	Suff	TM4886	52°25·2'	1°39·2'E	FM	156
Low Pasture Ho	N Yks	SE5578	54°11·9'	1°9·0'W	X	100
Low Pasture Ho	N Yks	SE6781	54°13·5'	0°57·9'W	X	100
Low Paull	E Yorks	TA1726	53°43·3'	0°13·2'W	X	107
Low Penhowe Fm	N Yks	SE7764	54°4·2'	0°49·0'W	FM	100
Low Pensworth Fm	Wilts	SU2121	50°59·5'	1°41·7'W	FM	184
Low Pike	Cumbr	NY3235	54°42·6'	3°2·9'W	X	90
Low Pike	Cumbr	NY3707	54°27·5'	2°57·9'W	H	90
Low Pinmore	S Ayr	NS3115	55°24·2'	4°39·7'W	X	70
Low Place	Cumbr	NY1501	54°24·1'	3°18·1'W	X	89
Low Place	Lincs	TF0192	53°25·1'	0°28·4'W	X	112
Low Plain	Cumbr	SD4790	54°18·4'	2°48·5'W	X	97
Low Plain Plantn	N Yks	SE3489	54°18·0'	1°28·2'W	F	99
Low Plains	Cumbr	NY4070	55°1·5'	2°55·9'W	X	85
Low Plains	Cumbr	NY4941	54°45·9'	2°47·1'W	X	86
Low Plantation	Suff	TM1766	52°15·2'	1°11·2'E	F	156
Low Plantn	E Yorks	SE8338	53°50·1'	0°43·9'W	F	106
Low Plantn	Norf	TM3795	52°30·3'	1°29·9'E	F	134
Low Pond Ho	N Yks	SE2287	54°16·9'	1°39·3'W	X	99
Low Pow	Cumbr	NY2543	54°46·8'	3°9·5'W	X	85
Low Prudhoe	Northum	NZ1063	54°57·9'	1°50·2'W	T	88
Low Pyke	Northum	NU0514	55°25·4'	1°54·8'W	X	81
Low Quebec	N Yks	NZ8704	54°25·7'	0°39·1'W	X	94
Low Raincliffe Fm	N Yks	TA0182	54°13·7'	0°26·6'W	FM	101
Low Raindale	N Yks	SE8092	54°19·3'	0°45·8'W	X	94,100
Low Raise	Cumbr	NY4513	54°30·8'	2°50·6'W	X	90
Low Rakes	N Yks	SE3262	54°3·4'	1°30·3'W	X	99
Lowran Burn	D & G	NX6473	55°2·2'	4°7·3'W	W	77
Lowrans Law	E Loth	NT5561	55°50·7'	2°42·7'W	X	66
Low Redburn	Durham	NY9243	54°47·2'	2°7·0'W	X	87
Low Rest Park Fm	N Yks	SE5432	53°47·1'	1°10·4'W	FM	105
Lowridding	Cumbr	SD6893	54°20·1'	2°29·1'W	X	98
Lowrie	Aberd	NJ4238	57°26·0'	2°57·5'W	X	28
Lowries Knowes	Scot Bord	NT8569	55°55·1'	2°14·0'W	X	67
Lowrie's Water	Orkney	HY3425	59°6·7'	3°8·7'W	W	6
Low Rigg	Cumbr	NY3022	54°35·5'	3°4·6'W	H	90
Low Rigg	Cumbr	NY5265	54°58·9'	2°44·6'W	X	86
Lowring Burn	D & G	NX5974	55°2·7'	4°12·0'W	W	77
Low Risby	N Lincs	SE9314	53°37·1'	0°35·2'W	T	112
Low Riseborough Fm	N Yks	SE7382	54°13·9'	0°52·4'W	FM	100
Low Road	Suff	TM0679	52°22·4'	1°2·0'E	X	144
Low Roans	N Yks	SE6264	54°4·3'	1°2·7'W	X	100
Low Rockliffe	Darl	NZ3008	54°28·2'	1°31·8'W	X	93
Low Rogerscale Fm	Cumbr	NY1426	54°37·6'	3°19·5'W	FM	89
Low Rookwith	N Yks	SE2086	54°16·4'	1°41·2'W	X	99
Low Row	Cumbr	NY1844	54°47·3'	3°16·1'W	T	85
Low Row	Cumbr	NY5863	54°57·8'	2°38·9'W	T	86
Low Row	Durham	NZ1542	54°46·6'	1°45·6'W	X	88
Low Row	Northum	NY7050	54°50·9'	2°27·6'W	X	86,87
Low Row	N Yks	SD9897	54°22·4'	2°1·4'W	T	98
Low Row Fm	Cumbr	NY1845	54°47·8'	3°16·1'W	FM	85
Low Row Pasture	N Yks	SD9698	54°22·9'	2°3·3'W	X	98
Low Rutter	Cumbr	NY6716	54°32·5'	2°30·2'W	X	91
Low Saddle	Cumbr	NY2813	54°30·7'	3°6·3'W	X	89,90
Low Salchrie	D & G	NX0365	54°56·7'	5°4·1'W	X	82
Low Santon Fm	N Lincs	SE9312	53°36·0'	0°35·3'W	FM	112
Low Saugh Shield	Durham	NY8937	54°43·9'	2°9·8'W	X	91,92
Lowsay Fm	Cumbr	NY1148	54°49·4'	3°22·7'W	FM	85

Low Scale	Cumbr	SD7891	54°19·1'	2°19·9'W	X	98
Low Scales	Cumbr	NY1846	54°48·4'	3°16·1'W	X	85
Low Scales	Cumbr	NY6005	54°26·6'	2°36·6'W	X	91
Low Scales	Cumbr	SD1581	54°13·3'	3°17·8'W	X	96
Low Scales	N Yks	NZ1604	54°26·1'	1°44·8'W	X	92
Low Scar	N Yks	SE0492	54°19·7'	1°55·9'W	X	98
Low Scarth Barn	N Yks	SD8959	54°1·9'	2°9·7'W	X	103
Low Scathaite	Cumbr	SD2982	54°14·0'	3°4·9'W	X	96,97
Low Scawdel	Cumbr	NY2416	54°32·3'	3°10·1'W	X	89,90
Low Scrubs	Bucks	SP8506	51°45·0'	0°45·7'W	X	165
Low Selset	Durham	NY9221	54°35·3'	2°7·0'W	X	91,92
Low Semple	Renf	NS3760	55°48·6'	4°35·6'W	X	63
Low Shaw	Cumbr	SD1984	54°15·0'	3°14·2'W	X	96
Low Shaw	Northum	NY9086	55°10·3'	2°9·0'W	X	80
Lowshield Green	Northum	NY8880	55°7·1'	2°10·9'W	X	80
Low Shilford	Northum	NZ0361	54°56·9'	1°56·8'W	X	87
Low Shipley	Durham	NZ0120	54°34·8'	1°58·6'W	X	92
Low Shipley	Durham	NZ1134	54°42·3'	1°49·3'W	X	92
Low Shires Fm	N Yks	SE5267	54°6·0'	1°11·9'W	FM	100
Low Shotton	Durham	NZ1122	54°35·8'	1°49·4'W	X	92
Lowside	Cumbr	NY3527	54°38·3'	3°0·0'W	X	90
Low Sides	N Yks	SE2677	54°11·5'	1°35·7'W	X	99
Low Sikes	N Yks	SE1172	54°8·9'	1°49·5'W	X	99
Low Sizergh	Cumbr	SD5087	54°16·8'	2°45·7'W	X	97
Low Skelding Fm	N Yks	SE2269	54°7·2'	1°39·4'W	FM	99
Low Skeog	D & G	NX4540	54°44·1'	4°24·0'W	X	83
Low Skibeden	N Yks	SE0152	53°58·1'	1°58·7'W	X	104
Low Skirlington	E Yorks	TA1852	53°57·3'	0°11·7'W	X	107
Low Skydes	Cumbr	NY7242	54°46·6'	2°25·7'W	X	86,87
Low Slakes	Cumbr	NY6628	54°39·0'	2°31·2'W	X	91
Low Sleights	N Yks	SD7579	54°12·6'	2°22·6'W	X	98
Low Smerby	Arg & Bt	NR7522	55°26·7'	5°33·0'W	X	68,69
Low Snab	Cumbr	NY2218	54°33·3'	3°12·0'W	X	89,90
Low Snape Fm	N Yks	SE3049	53°56·4'	1°32·2'W	FM	104
Low Snaygill	N Yks	SD9949	53°56·5'	2°0·5'W	T	103
Low Snowden	N Yks	SE1851	53°57·5'	1°43·1'W	X	104
Low Sober Fm	N Yks	SE3490	54°18·5'	1°28·2'W	FM	99
Lowsonford	Warw	SP1867	52°18·3'	1°43·8'W	T	151
Low Sourmire	N Yks	SE1478	54°12·1'	1°46·7'W	X	99
Low South Ho	N Yks	SE6196	54°21·6'	1°3·3'W	X	94,100
Low Spelder Banks	N Yks	SE2081	54°13·7'	1°41·2'W	X	99
Low Spen Fm	Ghead	NZ1458	54°55·2'	1°46·5'W	FM	88
Low Spinney Fm	Leic	SP5589	52°30·0'	1°11·0'W	FM	140
Low Springs	Brad	SE1541	53°52·1'	1°45·9'W	X	104
Low Staindale	N Yks	SE8690	54°18·1'	0°40·3'W	X	94,101
Low Staindrop Field Ho	Durham	NZ1725	54°37·4'	1°43·8'W	X	92
Low Stead	Northum	NU2515	55°25·9'	1°35·9'W	X	81
Lowstead	Northum	NY8178	55°6·0'	2°17·4'W	X	86,87
Low Stennerley	Cumbr	SD2785	54°15·6'	3°6·8'W	X	96,97
Lowster Hill	Norf	TL9096	52°31·9'	0°48·5'E	X	144
Lowster Hill (Tumulus)	Norf	TL9096	52°31·9'	0°48·5'E	A	144
Low Stillaig	Arg & Bt	NR9267	55°51·3'	5°19·0'W	X	62
Low Stonehills	E Yorks	TA1461	54°2·2'	0°15·1'W	X	101
Low Stony Bank	N Yks	SD9165	54°5·1'	2°7·8'W	X	98
Low Stotfold	Hartpl	NZ4528	54°38·9'	1°17·7'W	X	93
Low Stott Park	Cumbr	SD3788	54°17·3'	2°57·6'W	X	96,97
Low Street	Norf	TG0405	52°36·5'	1°1·2'E	T	144
Low Street	Thurr	TQ6677	51°28·3'	0°23·8'E	T	177,178
Lowstreet Ho	Cumbr	NY4836	54°43·2'	2°48·0'W	X	90
Low Stripe	N Yks	SE2261	54°2·9'	1°39·4'W	X	99
Low Stublick	Northum	NY8660	54°56·3'	2°12·7'W	X	87
Low Swainby Fm	N Yks	SE3385	54°15·8'	1°29·2'W	FM	99
Low Swainston	Durham	NZ4129	54°39·5'	1°21·4'W	X	93
Low Swinston	Durham	NZ0410	54°29·4'	1°55·9'W	X	92
Low Swinton	N Yks	SE2179	54°12·6'	1°40·3'W	X	99
Lowsy Point	Cumbr	SD1874	54°9·6'	3°14·9'W	X	96
Low Tarn	Cumbr	NY1609	54°28·4'	3°17·4'W	W	89
Low Tarn Green	Cumbr	SD4185	54°15·7'	2°53·9'W	X	96,97
Low Tarns	Cumbr	NY1147	54°48·8'	3°22·7'W	X	85
Low Teppermoor	Northum	NY8771	55°2·2'	2°11·8'W	X	87
Low Tharston	Norf	TM1895	52°30·8'	1°13·2'E	T	134
Low, The	Cumbr	SD2094	54°20·4'	3°13·4'W	X	96
Low,The	Northum	NU0240	55°39·5'	1°57·7'W	W	75
Low, The	Staffs	SK0862	53°9·5'	1°52·4'W	X	119
Low, The	Worcs	SP0251	52°9·7'	1°57·8'W	X	150
Lowther	Cumbr	NY5323	54°36·2'	2°43·2'W	T	90
Lowther Brow	Cumbr	NY4205	54°26·5'	2°53·2'W	X	90
Lowther Castle	Cumbr	NY5223	54°36·2'	2°44·2'W	X	90
Lowther Hill	D & G	NS8910	55°22·5'	3°44·7'W	H	71,78
Lowther Hill	N Yks	SD6969	54°7·2'	2°28·0'W	X	98
Lowther Hills	D & G	NS9008	55°21·5'	3°43·7'W	H	71,78
Lowther Hills	D & G	NT0110	55°22·7'	3°33·3'W	H	78
Lowther Leisure Park	Cumbr	NY5322	54°35·7'	2°43·2'W	X	90
Lowther Park	Cumbr	NY0511	54°29·4'	3°27·6'W	F	89
Lowther Park	Cumbr	NY5222	54°35·7'	2°44·2'W	X	90
Lowthers	S Lanak	NS9014	55°24·7'	3°43·8'W	X	71,78
Lowthertown	D & G	NY2466	54°59·2'	3°10·7'W	T	85
Lowtherville	I of W	SZ5578	50°36·2'	1°13·0'W	T	196
Lowthian Gill	Cumbr	NY4648	54°49·7'	2°50·0'W	X	86
Low Thoresby	N Yks	SE0390	54°18·6'	1°56·8'W	X	98
Low Thornhill	N Yks	SE5797	54°22·2'	1°6·9'W	X	100
Low Thornhope	Northum	NY6851	54°51·4'	2°29·5'W	X	86,87
Low Thornley	Ghead	NZ1760	54°56·3'	1°43·7'W	T	88
Lowthorpe	E Yorks	TA0860	54°1·7'	0°20·7'W	T	101
Low Threaber	N Yks	SD6573	54°9·3'	2°31·7'W	X	97
Low Threave	D & G	NX3758	54°53·7'	4°32·1'W	X	83
Low Three Mark	D & G	NX0851	54°49·3'	4°58·9'W	X	82
Lowthwaite	Cumbr	NY2635	54°42·5'	3°8·5'W	X	89,90
Lowthwaite	Cumbr	NY4123	54°36·2'	2°54·4'W	X	90
Lowthwaite Fell	Cumbr	NY2734	54°42·0'	3°7·5'W	X	89,90
Lowthwaite Fm	Cumbr	NY3122	54°35·6'	3°3·7'W	FM	90
Low Thwaites	N Yks	SE5494	54°20·6'	1°9·7'W	X	100
Low Tipalt	Northum	NY6867	55°0·0'	2°29·6'W	X	86,87
Low Tirfergus	Arg & Bt	NR6618	55°24·3'	5°41·3'W	X	68
Low Todhill	E Ayr	NS4343	55°39·6'	4°29·3'W	X	70
Low Todholes	Cumbr	NY5177	55°5·4'	2°45·6'W	X	86
Low Todrigg	Cumbr	NY4126	54°37·8'	2°54·4'W	X	90
Lowton	Devon	SS6604	50°49·4'	3°53·8'W	X	191
Lowton	Devon	SX7485	50°39·2'	3°46·6'W	X	191
Lowton	Devon	SX8087	50°40·5'	3°41·5'W	X	191

Lowton	Somer	ST1918	50°57·6'	3°8·8'W	T	181,193
Lowton	Wigan	SJ6297	53°28·3'	2°33·9'W	T	109
Lowton Common	Wigan	SJ6397	53°28·3'	2°33·0'W	T	109
Lowton Heath	Wigan	SJ6196	53°27·8'	2°34·8'W	T	109
Lowton's Copse	Hants	SU6917	50°57·1'	1°0·7'W	F	197
Lowton St Mary's	Wigan	SJ6397	53°28·3'	2°33·0'W	T	109
Low Tor	Sheff	SK2091	53°25·2'	1°41·5'W	X	110
Low Torry	Fife	NT0186	56°3·7'	3°35·0'W	T	65
Low Town	Northum	NU1300	55°17·9'	1°47·3'W	X	81
Lowtown	Northum	NY6866	54°59·5'	2°29·6'W	X	86,87
Low Town	N Yks	NZ3910	54°29·3'	1°23·5'W	X	93
Low Town	Shrops	SO7293	52°32·3'	2°24·4'W	T	138
Low Townhead	D & G	NX9385	55°9·1'	3°40·3'W	X	78
Lowtown Ho	Cumbr	NY2561	54°56·5'	3°9·8'W	X	85
Low Toynton	Lincs	TF2770	53°12·9'	0°5·5'W	T	122
Low Tranmire	N Yks	NZ7612	54°30·1'	0°49·2'W	X	94
Lowtre	Cered	SN5246	52°5·8'	4°9·2'W	X	146
Low Trenhouse	N Yks	SD8865	54°5·1'	2°10·6'W	X	98
Low Trewhitt	Northum	NU0004	55°20·1'	1°59·6'W	X	81
Lowtrow Cross	Somer	ST0029	51°3·3'	3°25·2'W	X	181
Low Troweir	S Ayr	NX1997	55°14·3'	4°50·4'W	X	76
Low Urpeth	Durham	NZ2555	54°53·6'	1°36·2'W	X	88
Low Valley	Barns	SE4003	53°31·6'	1°23·4'W	T	111
Low Valleyfield	Fife	NT0086	56°3·6'	3°35·9'W	T	65
Low Wall	Cumbr	NY5364	54°58·4'	2°43·6'W	X	86
Low Walton	Cumbr	NX9813	54°30·4'	3°34·1'W	T	89
Low Walworth	Darl	NZ2317	54°33·1'	1°38·2'W	T	93
Low Wardneuk	S Ayr	NS3829	55°31·9'	4°33·6'W	X	70
Low Warren Fm	N Yks	SE6175	54°10·3'	1°3·5'W	FM	100
Low Waskerley	Northum	NZ0853	54°52·5'	1°52·1'W	X	88
Low Water	Cumbr	SD2798	54°22·6'	3°7·0'W	W	96,97
Low Waters	S Lanak	NS7253	55°45·5'	4°1·9'W	T	64
Low Waterside	Cumbr	NY0415	54°31·5'	3°28·6'W	X	89
Low Wathcote	N Yks	NZ1901	54°24·5'	1°42·0'W	X	92
Low Well Fm	York	SE6645	53°54·1'	0°59·3'W	FM	105,106
Low West Ho	Durham	NZ1439	54°45·0'	1°46·5'W	X	92
Low West Thickley	Durham	NZ2125	54°37·4'	1°40·1'W	X	93
Low Westwood	Durham	NZ1156	54°54·2'	1°49·3'W	T	88
Low Wetherhill Fm	Durham	NZ1429	54°39·6'	1°46·6'W	FM	92
Low Wexford	S Ayr	NS3730	55°32·4'	4°34·6'W	X	70
Low Whinholme	N Yks	NZ3100	54°23·9'	1°30·9'W	X	93
Low Whinnow	Cumbr	NY3050	54°50·6'	3°5·0'W	T	85
Low Whita	N Yks	SE0098	54°22·9'	1°59·6'W	T	98
Low Whitsundale Edge	N Yks	NY8504	54°26·1'	2°13·5'W	X	91,92
Low Whittle	Northum	NU1806	55°21·1'	1°42·5'W	X	81
Low Wind Hill	N Yks	SE7595	54°20·9'	0°50·3'W	X	94,100
Low Winsley	N Yks	SE2360	54°2·4'	1°38·5'W	X	99
Low Wiske Moor	N Yks	SE3495	54°21·2'	1°28·2'W	X	99
Low Wood	Cumbr	NY4013	54°30·8'	2°55·2'W	F	90
Low Wood	Cumbr	NY4755	54°53·5'	2°49·2'W	X	86
Low Wood	Cumbr	SD3483	54°14·6'	3°0·3'W	T	96,97
Low Wood	Derby	SK1865	53°11·1'	1°43·4'W	F	119
Low Wood	E Yorks	SE9554	53°58·6'	0°32·7'W	F	106
Low Wood	E Yorks	TA1746	53°54·1'	0°12·7'W	F	107
Low Wood	Kent	TQ9239	51°7·3'	0°45·0'E	X	189
Low Wood	Moray	NH9660	57°37·3'	3°44·0'W	F	27
Low Wood	N Lincs	SE9308	53°33·9'	0°35·4'W	F	112
Low Wood	Northum	NT9641	55°40·0'	2°3·4'W	F	74,75
Low Wood	N Yks	NZ7606	54°26·9'	0°49·3'W	X	94
Low Wood	N Yks	SE0985	54°15·9'	1°51·3'W	F	99
Low Wood	N Yks	SE1366	54°5·6'	1°47·7'W	X	99
Low Wood	N Yks	SE4772	54°8·7'	1°16·4'W	F	100
Low Wood	N Yks	SE5679	54°12·5'	1°8·1'W	F	100
Low Wood	N Yks	SE5791	54°18·9'	1°7·0'W	X	100
Low Wood	Staffs	SK0051	53°3·6'	1°59·6'W	F	119
Low Woodale	N Yks	SE0777	54°11·6'	1°53·1'W	X	99
Low Wood Fm	Cambs	TL3573	52°20·5'	0°0·7'W	FM	154
Low Wood Head	Brad	SE0643	53°53·2'	1°54·1'W	X	104
Low Wood Ho	Durham	NZ0722	54°35·8'	1°53·1'W	X	92
Low Woodnook	Cumbr	NY1940	54°45·2'	3°15·1'W	X	85
Low Woods	Leic	SK4419	52°46·2'	1°20·5'W	X	129
Low Woods	N Yks	SE6580	54°12·9'	0°59·8'W	X	100
Low Woods Fm	N Yks	SE6282	54°14·0'	1°2·5'W	FM	100
Low Woodside	N Yks	NZ7606	54°26·9'	0°49·3'W	X	94
Low Wood Stile	Cumbr	SD2186	54°16·1'	3°12·4'W	X	96
Low Woof Howe	N Yks	SE8996	54°21·3'	0°37·4'W	A	94,101
Low Wool Oaks	Cumbr	NY4641	54°45·9'	2°49·9'W	X	86
Low Worsall	N Yks	NZ3909	54°28·7'	1°23·5'W	T	93
Low Worsall Moor	N Yks	NZ3908	54°28·2'	1°23·5'W	T	93
Low Wray	Cumbr	NY3701	54°24·3'	2°57·8'W	X	90
Low Wray Bay	Cumbr	NY3701	54°24·3'	2°57·8'W	W	90
Low Yarridge	Northum	NY9162	54°57·4'	2°8·0'W	X	87
Low Yedmandale	N Yks	SE9785	54°15·3'	0°30·2'W	X	94,101
Low Yewdale	Cumbr	SD3199	54°23·2'	3°3·3'W	X	96,97
Low Yews	Cumbr	SD4291	54°18·9'	2°53·1'W	X	96,97
Loxbeare	Devon	SS9116	50°56·2'	3°32·7'W	T	181
Loxborough Ho	Bucks	SU8096	51°39·7'	0°50·2'W	X	165
Loxbrook	Devon	SX9997	50°46·1'	3°25·6'W	X	192
Loxford	Redbr	TQ4485	51°33·0'	0°5·0'E	T	177
Loxhill	Surrey	TQ0038	51°8·2'	0°33·9'W	T	186
Loxhole Br	Somer	SS9944	51°11·4'	3°26·3'W	X	181
Loxhore	Devon	SS6138	51°7·7'	3°58·8'W	T	180
Loxhore Cott	Devon	SS6138	51°7·7'	3°58·8'W	T	180
Loxidge Tump	Monm	SO2828	51°57·0'	3°2·5'W	X	161
Lox Lane Fm	Dorset	ST8223	51°0·6'	2°15·0'W	FM	183
Loxley	Sheff	SK3089	53°24·1'	1°32·5'W	T	110,111
Loxley	Warw	SP2552	52°10·2'	1°37·7'W	T	151
Loxley Bank	Staffs	SK0631	52°52·8'	1°54·2'W	X	128
Loxley Chase	Sheff	SK2990	53°24·6'	1°33·4'W	X	110
Loxley Common	Sheff	SK3090	53°24·6'	1°32·5'W	X	110,111
Loxley Fm	Lincs	TF2667	53°11·3'	0°6·4'W	FM	122
Loxley Fm	N Yks	SE3653	53°58·5'	1°26·7'W	FM	104
Loxley Green	Staffs	SK0630	52°52·3'	1°54·2'W	T	128
Loxley Wood	Somer	ST4037	51°8·0'	2°51·1'W	F	182
Loxter	Heref	SO7140	52°3·7'	2°25·0'W	T	149
Loxton	N Som	ST3755	51°17·7'	2°53·8'W	T	182
Loxton Hill	N Som	ST3656	51°18·2'	2°54·7'W	H	182
Loxtree Fm	Dorset	ST5504	50°50·3'	2°38·0'W	FM	194
Loxwell Fm	Wilts	ST9569	51°25·4'	2°3·9'W	FM	173
Loxwood	W Susx	TQ0331	51°4·4'	0°31·4'W	T	186

Loxwood Hall	W Susx	TQ0333	51°5·4'	0°31·4'W	X	186
Lox Yeo River	N Som	ST3857	51°18·8'	2°53·0'W	W	182
Loyalbank	Pth & Kin	NO2549	56°37·9'	3°12·9'W	X	53
Loyn Br	Lancs	SD5869	54°7·2'	2°38·1'W	X	97
Loynton Hall	Staffs	SJ7724	52°49·0'	2°20·1'W	X	127
Loyter's Green	Essex	TL5110	51°46·3'	0°11·7'E	T	167
Loyterton	Kent	TQ9560	51°18·6'	0°48·3'E	T	178
Loyton	Devon	SS9724	51°0·6'	3°27·7'W	X	181
Lozells	Birm	SP0689	52°30·2'	1°54·3'W	T	139
Lr Castle o' Trim	Lancs	SD5255	53°59·6'	2°43·5'W	X	102
Lr Clockhouse Fm	Hants	SZ1696	50°46·0'	1°46·0'W	FM	195
Lr Trotter Hill	Lancs	SD5541	53°52·0'	2°40·6'W	X	102
Lttle Woodcote	Warw	SP2869	52°19·3'	1°35·0'W	X	151
Luachair Mhór	Highld	NH7805	57°7·4'	4°0·5'W	X	35
Luachar Mhór	Highld	NH6879	57°47·1'	4°12·7'W	W	21
Luachrach	Arg & Bt	NM8730	56°25·1'	5°26·8'W	X	49
Luath's Stone	Aberd	NJ6414	57°13·2'	2°35·3'W	A	37
Lubachlaggan	Highld	NH3478	57°45·9'	4°47·0'W	X	20
Lubachoinnich	Highld	NH4195	57°55·2'	4°40·6'W	X	20
Lùb an Arbhair	Highld	NM7246	56°33·3'	5°42·2'W	X	49
Lùban Croma	Highld	NC2812	58°4·1'	4°54·5'W	W	15
Luban Féith a' Mhadaidh	Pth & Kin	NN5153	56°39·0'	4°25·4'W	W	42,51
Lubard's Lodge	Essex	TQ8092	51°36·1'	0°36·3'E	X	178
Lubas	Arg & Bt	NS0854	55°44·7'	5°3·1'W	X	63
Lubas Bay	Arg & Bt	NS0854	55°44·7'	5°3·1'W	W	63
Lub a' Sgiathain	Highld	NG4176	57°42·2'	6°20·4'W	W	23
Lubas Port	Arg & Bt	NS0754	55°44·7'	5°4·1'W	W	63
Lubberland	Shrops	SO6277	52°23·6'	2°33·1'W	T	138
Lùb Chruinn	Highld	NH0336	57°22·6'	5°16·1'W	W	25
Lubchurran	Stir	NN4535	56°29·2'	4°30·6'W	X	51
Lubchurran Burn	Stir	NN4534	56°28·6'	4°30·6'W	W	51
Lubcloud Fm	Leic	SK4716	52°44·6'	1°17·8'W	FM	129
Lubcroy	Highld	NC3501	57°58·3'	4°46·9'W	X	15
Lubenham	Leic	SP7087	52°28·8'	0°57·8'W	T	141
Lubenham Lodge	Leic	SP6888	52°29·4'	0°59·5'W	X	141
Lubfearn	Highld	NH3870	57°41·7'	4°42·6'W	X	20
Lùb Gleann Logain	Arg & Bt	NR4362	55°47·2'	6°5·5'W	X	60,61
Lubinvullin	Highld	NC5764	58°32·7'	4°26·9'W	T	10
Lubmore	Highld	NH0958	57°34·6'	5°11·2'W	X	25
Lubnaclach	Highld	NN3764	56°44·6'	4°39·5'W	X	41
Lùb na Cloiche Duibhe	Arg & Bt	NM5228	56°23·0'	6°0·6'W	X	48
Lùb na Faochaige	Arg & Bt	NR9269	55°52·4'	5°19·1'W	X	62
Lubreoch	Pth & Kin	NN4541	56°32·4'	4°30·8'W	X	51
Lubriach	Highld	NH3573	57°43·3'	4°45·8'W	X	20
Lub Score	Highld	NG3973	57°40·5'	6°22·2'W	W	23
Lùb Stac nam Meann	Highld	NG4376	57°42·3'	6°18·4'W	W	23
Lubstree Park	Wrekin	SJ6915	52°44·1'	2°27·1'W	X	127
Lùbvan	Highld	NN4479	56°52·8'	4°33·2'W	X	42
Lucas End	Herts	TL3203	51°42·8'	0°5·0'W	T	166
Lucas Fm	Essex	TL5713	51°47·8'	0°17·0'E	FM	167
Lucas Fm	Essex	TL6624	51°53·6'	0°25·1'E	FM	167
Lucas Green	Lancs	SD5820	53°40·7'	2°37·7'W	T	102
Lucas Green	Surrey	SU9459	51°19·6'	0°38·7'W	T	175,186
Lucas Hill Wood	Norf	TF8742	52°56·8'	0°47·4'E	F	132
Luccas Fm	Dorset	SY5495	50°45·4'	2°38·7'W	FM	194
Luccombe	Corn	SX3362	50°26·3'	4°20·7'W	X	201
Luccombe	Somer	SS9144	51°11·3'	3°33·2'W	T	181
Luccombe Bay	I of W	SZ5879	50°36·7'	1°10·4'W	W	196
Luccombe Chine	I of W	SZ5879	50°36·7'	1°10·4'W	X	196
Luccombe Down	Dorset	ST8001	50°48·7'	2°16·6'W	X	194
Luccombe Fm	Dorset	SY4599	50°47·5'	2°46·4'W	FM	193
Luccombe Fms	Dorset	ST8101	50°48·7'	2°15·8'W	FM	194
Luccombe Hill	Somer	SS9043	51°10·8'	3°34·0'W	X	181
Luccombe Village	I of W	SZ5879	50°36·7'	1°10·4'W	T	196
Luccombs Fm	Devon	SX9386	50°40·1'	3°30·5'W	FM	192
Luce	D & G	NY1871	55°1·9'	3°16·5'W	X	85
Lucepool	Staffs	SK1519	52°46·3'	1°46·3'W	X	128
Lucern Bank	Worcs	SO8049	52°8·6'	2°17·1'W	F	150
Lucerne Fm	N Yks	SE4544	53°53·7'	1°18·5'W	FM	105
Luce Sands	D & G	NX1754	54°51·1'	4°50·6'W	X	82
Luchruban	N Eil	NB5066	58°30·9'	6°17·1'W	A	8
Lucifer Moss	Highld	ND2670	58°37·0'	3°16·0'W	X	7,12
Luckcroft	Devon	SS4000	50°46·9'	4°15·8'W	X	190
Luckenburn	N Lanak	NS8271	55°55·3'	3°52·9'W	X	65
Lucker	Northum	NU1530	55°34·1'	1°45·3'W	T	75
Lucker South Fm	Northum	NU1529	55°33·6'	1°45·3'W	FM	75
Luckett	Corn	SX3873	50°32·3'	4°16·8'W	T	201
Luckett Fm	Devon	SS8223	50°59·9'	3°40·5'W	FM	181
Luckett Moor	Devon	SS8224	51°0·4'	3°40·5'W	X	181
Lucketts	I of W	SZ3889	50°42·2'	1°27·3'W	X	196
Luckey's Fm	Suff	TL9953	52°8·6'	0°54·9'E	FM	155
Luckford Lake	Dorset	SY8784	50°39·6'	2°10·7'W	W	194
Luckham Fm	Somer	ST1324	51°0·8'	3°14·0'W	FM	181,193
Luckhurst	Kent	TQ9328	51°1·4'	0°45·5'E	X	189
Luckhurst Fm	Kent	TQ8544	51°10·1'	0°39·2'E	FM	189
Luckhurst Fm	Kent	TQ8841	51°8·5'	0°41·6'E	FM	189
Luckie Shiel	Scot Bord	NT7464	55°52·4'	2°24·5'W	X	67
Luckings Fm	Bucks	SU9494	51°38·4'	0°38·1'W	FM	175
Lucking Street	Essex	TL8134	51°58·7'	0°38·5'E	T	155
Luckington	Wilts	ST8383	51°33·0'	2°14·3'W	T	173
Luckington Court	Wilts	ST8384	51°33·5'	2°14·3'W	A	173
Luckington Cross	Somer	ST6950	51°15·1'	2°26·3'W	X	183
Luckington Manor Fm	Somer	ST6950	51°15·1'	2°26·3'W	FM	183
Lucklaw	Fife	NO4120	56°22·4'	2°56·9'W	X	54,59
Lucklaw Hill	Fife	NO4121	56°22·9'	2°56·9'W	H	54,59
Lucklawhill	Fife	NO4221	56°22·9'	2°55·9'W	T	54,59
Luckley Fm	Glos	SP1628	51°57·2'	1°45·6'W	FM	163
Luckley Fm	Wilts	ST8285	51°34·0'	2°15·2'W	FM	173
Luckley Hill	Shrops	SJ3201	52°36·4'	2°59·8'W	H	126
Lucknam Park	Wilts	ST8172	51°27·0'	2°16·0'W	X	173
Lucknow	Angus	NO5133	56°29·4'	2°47·3'W	X	54
Lucknow	E Loth	NT6271	55°56·1'	2°36·1'W	X	67
Lucknow	Orkney	HY5219	59°3·6'	2°49·7'W	X	6
Lucknow Fm	Staffs	SJ8312	52°42·6'	2°14·7'W	FM	127
Luckroft	Devon	SS4700	50°47·0'	4°9·8'W	X	191
Luck's Br	Lincs	TF2319	52°45·5'	0°10·2'W	X	131
Luckwell Bridge	Somer	SS9038	51°8·0'	3°33·9'W	T	181
Luckworthy	Devon	SS8129	51°3·1'	3°41·5'W	X	181
Luckyard Fm	Somer	SS9235	51°6·5'	3°32·2'W	FM	181
Lucky Hole	Corn	SS1915	50°54·6'	4°34·1'W	W	190

Lucky Scalp	Fife	NO4828	56°26·7'	2°50·2'W	X	54,59
Lucott Cross	Somer	SS8443	51°10·7'	3°39·2'W	X	181
Lucott Fm	Somer	SS8645	51°11·8'	3°37·5'W	FM	181
Lucott Moor	Somer	SS8543	51°10·7'	3°38·3'W	X	181
Lucton	Heref	SO4364	52°16·5'	2°49·7'W	T	137,148,149
Lucy Close Fm	Cumbr	NY0425	54°36·9'	3°28·8'W	FM	89
Lucy Cross	N Yks	NZ2112	54°30·4'	1°40·1'W	X	93
Lucy Hill	Hants	SU2204	50°50·3'	1°40·9'W	X	195
Lucy Wood	Cambs	TL6856	52°10·8'	0°27·8'E	F	154
Ludag	N Eil	NF7713	57°5·9'	7°19·6'W	X	31
Ludag Port	N Eil	NF9381	57°43·1'	7°8·9'W	W	18
Ludborough	Lincs	TF2995	53°26·4'	0°3·1'W	T	113
Ludborough Vale	Lincs	TF2894	53°25·9'	0°4·0'W	X	113
Ludbrook	Devon	SX6554	50°22·5'	3°53·5'W	T	202
Lud Brook	Devon	SX6555	50°23·0'	3°53·6'W	W	202
Ludbrook Manor	Devon	SX6553	50°21·9'	3°53·5'W	X	202
Ludburn	Staffs	SK0962	53°9·5'	1°51·5'W	X	119
Lud Castle	Angus	NO6843	56°34·9'	2°30·8'W	X	54
Lud Castle (fort)	Angus	NO6843	56°34·9'	2°30·8'W	A	54
Ludchurch	Pemb	SN1410	51°45·7'	4°41·3'W	T	158
Ludcott Fm	Corn	SX3066	50°28·4'	4°23·4'W	FM	201
Luddenden	Cald	SE0426	53°44·1'	1°55·9'W	T	104
Luddenden Dean	Cald	SE0328	53°45·1'	1°56·9'W	X	104
Luddenden Foot	Cald	SE0424	53°43·0'	1°56·0'W	T	104
Luddenham Court	Kent	TQ9963	51°20·1'	0°51·8'E	X	178
Luddenham Marshes	Kent	TQ9864	51°20·7'	0°51·0'E	X	178
Ludderburn	Cumbr	SD4091	54°18·9'	2°54·9'W	T	96,97
Luddery Hill	Somer	ST1712	50°54·3'	3°10·4'W	H	181,193
Luddesdown	Kent	TQ6766	51°22·3'	0°24·4'E	T	177,178
Luddesdown Court	Kent	TQ6666	51°22·3'	0°23·5'E	A	177,178
Luddington	N Lincs	SE8216	53°38·3'	0°45·2'W	T	112
Luddington	Warw	SP1652	52°10·2'	1°45·6'W	T	151
Luddington in the Brook	Northnts	TL1083	52°26·3'	0°22·5'W	T	142
Luddington Lodge Fm	Northnts	TL0982	52°25·7'	0°23·4'W	FM	142
Luddith Fm	N Yks	SE8366	54°5·2'	0°43·4'W	FM	100
Luddock's Fell	Lancs	SD5749	53°56·4'	2°38·9'W	X	102
Luddon	Devon	SX5093	50°43·3'	4°7·1'W	X	191
Lude Fm	Bucks	SU9191	51°36·9'	0°40·7'W	FM	175
Lude House	Pth & Kin	NN8865	56°46·0'	3°49·5'W	X	43
Ludenhill	Orkney	HY3027	59°7·7'	3°12·9'W	X	6
Ludford	Lincs	TF1989	53°23·3'	0°12·2'W	T	113,122
Ludford	Shrops	SO5173	52°21·4'	2°42·8'W	T	137,138
Ludford Grange	Lincs	TF2089	53°23·3'	0°11·3'W	X	113,122
Lud Gate	Devon	SX6867	50°29·5'	3°51·3'W	X	202
Ludgate	Kent	TQ9360	51°18·6'	0°46·5'E	X	178
Ludgershall	Bucks	SP6617	51°51·1'	1°2·1'W	T	164,165
Ludgershall	Wilts	SU2650	51°15·1'	1°37·3'W	T	184
Ludgershall Castle	Wilts	SU2651	51°15·7'	1°37·3'W	A	184
Ludgrove	Wok	SU8167	51°24·0'	0°49·7'W	X	175
Ludgvan	Corn	SW5033	50°8·9'	5°29·6'W	T	203
Ludham	Norf	TG3818	52°42·7'	1°31·8'E	T	133,134
Ludham Br	Norf	TG3717	52°42·1'	1°30·9'E	X	133,134
Ludham Cottage	I of W	SZ5293	50°44·3'	1°15·4'W	X	196
Ludham Hall	Norf	TG3817	52°42·1'	1°31·8'E	A	133,134
Ludlay	E Susx	TQ5207	50°50·8'	0°9·9'E	X	199
Ludley Fm	E Susx	TQ8520	50°57·2'	0°38·4'E	FM	189,199
Ludlow	Shrops	SO5174	52°22·0'	2°42·8'W	T	137,138
Ludlow's Fm	Wilts	ST8643	51°11·4'	2°11·6'W	FM	183
Ludney	Lincs	TF3995	53°26·2'	0°6·0'E	T	113
Ludney	Somer	ST3812	50°54·5'	2°52·5'W	T	193
Ludowic Stone	Shetld	HU3968	60°23·9'	1°17·0'W	X	2,3
Lud's Church (Cave)	Staffs	SJ9865	53°11·2'	2°1·4'W	X	118
Ludshott Common	Hants	SU8435	51°6·7'	0°47·6'W	F	186
Ludshott Manor	Hants	SU8434	51°6·2'	0°47·6'W	X	186
Ludstock	Heref	SO6835	52°1·0'	2°27·6'W	T	149
Ludstone	Shrops	SO8094	52°32·8'	2°17·3'W	T	138
Ludwell	Durham	NY9438	54°44·5'	2°5·2'W	X	91,92
Ludwell	Wilts	ST9122	51°0·1'	2°7·3'W	T	184
Ludwell	W Susx	TQ3728	51°2·3'	0°2·4'W	X	187,198
Ludwell Fm	Oxon	SP4322	51°53·9'	1°22·1'W	FM	164
Ludwell Fm	W Susx	TQ3530	51°3·4'	0°4·0'W	FM	187
Ludwells Fm	Kent	TQ4541	51°9·2'	0°4·8'E	FM	188
Ludworth	Durham	NZ3641	54°46·0'	1°26·0'W	T	88
Ludworth Intakes	Stock	SJ9991	53°25·2'	2°0·5'W	X	109
Ludworth Moor	Stock	SJ9990	53°24·6'	2°0·5'W	X	109
Lue Fm	Somer	ST3807	50°51·8'	2°52·5'W	FM	193
Luffenhall	Herts	TL2928	51°56·4'	0°7·0'W	T	166
Luffincott	Devon	SX3394	50°43·5'	4°21·6'W	T	190
Luffincott Shop	Devon	SX3494	50°43·5'	4°20·7'W	X	190
Luffincott Wood	Devon	SX3394	50°43·5'	4°21·6'W	F	190
Lufflands	Corn	SX1697	50°44·8'	4°36·1'W	X	190
Lufflands	Devon	SS3209	50°51·6'	4°22·9'W	X	190
Luffness Ho	E Loth	NT4780	56°0·9'	2°50·6'W	A	66
Luffness Links	E Loth	NT4781	56°1·4'	2°50·6'W	X	66
Luffness Mains	E Loth	NT4879	56°0·3'	2°49·6'W	X	66
Luffness Mill Ho	E Loth	NT4880	56°0·9'	2°49·6'W	X	66
Lufkins Fm	Essex	TM0921	51°51·1'	1°2·5'E	FM	168,169
Lufton	Somer	ST5116	50°56·7'	2°41·5'W	T	183
Lugar	E Ayr	NS5821	55°28·0'	4°14·3'W	T	71
Lugar Water	E Ayr	NS5420	55°27·4'	4°18·1'W	W	70
Lugate	Scot Bord	NT4443	55°40·9'	2°53·0'W	T	73
Lugate Water	Scot Bord	NT4145	55°41·9'	2°55·9'W	W	73
Lugbury	Wilts	ST8378	51°30·3'	2°14·3'W	X	173
Lugbury Fm	Wilts	ST8277	51°29·7'	2°15·2'W	FM	173
Lugbury (Long Barrow)	Wilts	ST8378	51°30·3'	2°14·3'W	A	173
Lugden Hill Fm	Norf	TF7739	52°55·4'	0°38·4'E	FM	132
Luge Gill	Cumbr	SD6487	54°16·9'	2°32·8'W	W	97
Lugga Hill	Shetld	HU4988	60°34·6'	1°5·9'W	X	1,2
Luggate	E Loth	NT5974	55°57·7'	2°39·0'W	X	67
Luggate Burn	E Loth	NT5974	55°57·7'	2°39·0'W	T	67
Lugg Br	Heref	SO5341	52°4·2'	2°40·7'W	X	149
Lugg Bridge	Heref	SO3164	52°16·4'	3°0·3'W	X	137,148
Lugg Green	Heref	SO4462	52°15·4'	2°48·8'W	T	137,148,149
Luggiebank	N Lanak	NS7672	55°55·8'	3°58·6'W	T	64
Luggie's Knowe	Shetld	HU4645	60°11·5'	1°9·7'W	X	4
Luggie Water	E Dunb	NS7072	55°55·7'	4°4·4'W	W	64
Lugg's Fm	Devon	ST2506	50°51·2'	3°3·5'W	FM	192,193
Luggy Brook	Powys	SJ1703	52°37·3'	3°13·2'W	W	136
Luggy Brook	Powys	SJ2002	52°36·8'	3°10·5'W	W	126
Lugmarsh Fm	Wilts	ST8530	51°4·4'	2°12·5'W	FM	183

Lugsdale	Halton	SJ5285	53°21·8'	2°42·9'W	T	108
Lugshorn	Somer	ST4831	51°4·8'	2°44·2'W	X	182
Lug, The	Shetld	HP6318	60°50·7'	0°49·9'W	X	1
Lugton	E Ayr	NS4152	55°44·4'	4°31·5'W	T	64
Lugton	Midlo	NT3367	55°53·7'	3°3·8'W	X	66
Lugtonridge	N Ayr	NS3749	55°42·7'	4°35·2'W	X	63
Lugton Water	E Ayr	NS3950	55°43·3'	4°33·4'W	W	63
Lugton Water	E Ayr	NS4052	55°44·4'	4°32·5'W	W	64
Lugton Water	N Ayr	NS3344	55°39·9'	4°38·9'W	W	63,70
Lugwardine	Heref	SO5441	52°4·2'	2°39·9'W	T	149
Lugwardine Br	Heref	SO5440	52°3·6'	2°39·9'W	X	149
Lugwardine Ho	Heref	SO5540	52°3·6'	2°39·0'W	X	149
Lugworthy Cross	Devon	SX4194	50°43·7'	4°14·8'W	X	190
Luham, The	Cumbr	NY5533	54°41·6'	2°41·5'W	X	90
Luib	Highld	NG5627	57°16·4'	6°2·4'W	T	32
Lùib	Highld	NH1354	57°32·5'	5°7·0'W	X	25
Luib	Stir	NN4927	56°24·9'	4°26·4'W	T	51
Luib Bhàn	N Eil	NF7749	57°25·3'	7°22·4'W	X	22
Luib Burn	Stir	NN4926	56°24·4'	4°26·4'W	W	51
Luib-chonnal	Highld	NN3993	57°0·3'	4°38·6'W	X	34
Luibeg	Aberd	NO0393	57°1·3'	3°35·4'W	X	36,43
Luibeg Bridge	Aberd	NO0194	57°1·8'	3°37·4'W	X	36,43
Luibeg Burn	Aberd	NO0194	57°1·8'	3°37·4'W	W	36,43
Lùibeilt	Highld	NN2668	56°46·5'	4°50·4'W	X	41
Lùib Iomaire Mhóir	Arg & Bt	NN0705	56°12·2'	5°6·2'W	W	56
Luiblea	Highld	NN4382	56°54·4'	4°34·2'W	X	34,42
Lùib Luachrach	Arg & Bt	NN2043	56°32·9'	4°55·2'W	X	50
Lùib na Moil	Highld	NG5630	57°18·0'	6°2·6'W	X	24,32
Luib, The	Aberd	NJ2608	57°9·7'	3°13·0'W	X	37
Luidhe nan Ròn	N Eil	NB4631	58°11·9'	6°18·9'W	X	8
Luig an Tairbh	Arg & Bt	NR3143	55°36·6'	6°15·9'W	W	60
Luing	Arg & Bt	NM7409	56°13·5'	5°38·3'W	X	55
Luinga Bheag	Highld	NM6187	56°55·0'	5°55·2'W	X	40
Luinga Mhór	Highld	NM6085	56°53·9'	5°56·0'W	X	40
Lùinleathann	Highld	NN7397	57°3·1'	4°5·2'W	X	35
Luinne Bheinn	Highld	NG8600	57°2·7'	5°31·2'W	H	33
Luipmaldrig	Highld	NH3048	57°29·7'	4°49·7'W	X	26
Lui Water	Aberd	NO0691	57°0·3'	3°32·4'W	W	43
Luke Brook	Heref	SO5521	51°53·4'	2°38·8'W	W	162
Luke Copse	Hants	SU3829	51°3·8'	1°27·1'W	F	185
Lukes Fm	Essex	TL9421	51°51·5'	0°49·4'E	FM	168
Luke's Ho	Cumbr	NY5673	55°3·2'	2°40·9'W	X	86
Lukes Ho	N Yks	SD9291	54°19·1'	2°7·0'W	X	98
Lukesland	Devon	SX6457	50°24·1'	3°54·4'W	X	202
Luke's Shop	Corn	SW8859	50°23·8'	4°58·6'W	X	200
Luke's Stone	D & G	NX6199	55°16·2'	4°10·8'W	X	77
Lukyns	Surrey	TQ1042	51°10·2'	0°25·2'W	X	187
Lulach's Stone	Aberd	NJ4619	57°15·8'	2°53·3'W	A	37
Lul Beck	N Yks	SE1372	54°8·9'	1°47·6'W	W	99
Lulbeck Crags	N Yks	SE1372	54°8·9'	1°47·6'W	X	99
Lulham	Heref	SO4041	52°4·1'	2°52·1'W	T	148,149,161
Lulhams Fm	E Susx	TQ4909	50°51·9'	0°7·4'E	FM	199
Lullenden	Surrey	TQ4240	51°8·7'	0°2·2'E	X	187
Lullings	W Susx	TQ3230	51°3·5'	0°6·6'W	X	187
Lullings Fm	W Susx	TQ3126	51°1·3'	0°7·5'W	FM	187,198
Lullingstone Castle	Kent	TQ5264	51°21·5'	0°11·4'E	A	177,188
Lullingstone Park	Kent	TQ5164	51°21·5'	0°10·5'E	X	177,188
Lullingstone Park Fm	Kent	TQ5264	51°21·5'	0°11·4'E	FM	177,188
Lullington	Derby	SK2513	52°43·1'	1°37·4'W	T	128
Lullington	Somer	ST7851	51°15·7'	2°18·5'W	T	183
Lullington Court	E Susx	TQ5202	50°48·1'	0°9·8'E	X	199
Lullington Heath Nature Reserve	E Susx	TQ5401	50°47·5'	0°11·5'E	X	199
Lulsgate Bottom	N Som	ST5065	51°23·1'	2°42·7'W	T	172,182
Lulsley	Worcs	SO7455	52°11·8'	2°22·4'W	T	150
Lulsley Court	Worcs	SO7455	52°11·8'	2°22·4'W	X	150
Lulworth Camp	Dorset	SY8381	50°37·9'	2°14·0'W	T	194
Lulworth Castle	Dorset	SY8582	50°38·5'	2°12·3'W	A	194
Lulworth Cove	Dorset	SY8279	50°36·9'	2°14·9'W	W	194
Lumb	Kirk	SE1513	53°37·0'	1°46·0'W	T	110
Lumb	Lancs	SD7819	53°40·3'	2°19·6'W	T	109
Lumb	Lancs	SD8324	53°43·0'	2°15·0'W	T	103
Lumb	N Yks	SD9642	53°52·7'	2°3·2'W	X	103
Lumbennie Hill	Fife	NO2115	56°19·5'	3°16·2'W	H	58
Lumber Hill	Cambs	TL1172	52°20·3'	0°21·8'W	X	153
Lumb Fm	Ches	SJ8881	53°19·8'	2°10·4'W	FM	109
Lumb Foot	Brad	SE0137	53°50·0'	1°58·7'W	T	104
Lumb Grange	Derby	SK3346	53°0·9'	1°30·1'W	X	119,128
Lumb Hall	Leeds	SE2229	53°45·7'	1°39·6'W	A	104
Lumbo	Fife	NO4814	56°19·2'	2°50·0'W	X	59
Lumbry Fm	Hants	SU7137	51°7·9'	0°58·7'W	FM	186
Lumbs	Aberd	NK0257	57°36·4'	1°57·5'W	X	30
Lumburn	Devon	SX4573	50°32·4'	4°10·9'W	T	201
Lumbutts	Cald	SD9523	53°42·4'	2°4·1'W	T	103
Lumby	N Yks	SE4830	53°46·1'	1°15·9'W	T	105
Lumby Law	Northum	NU1109	55°22·7'	1°49·2'W	X	81
Lum Edge	Staffs	SK0660	53°8·5'	1°54·2'W	X	119
Lumgair	Aberd	NO8580	56°54·9'	2°14·3'W	X	45
Lumholme	Cumbr	SD2190	54°18·2'	3°12·4'W	X	96
Lumley	W Susx	SU7506	50°51·1'	0°55·7'W	T	197
Lumley Castle	Durham	NZ2851	54°51·4'	1°33·4'W	A	88
Lumley Den	Angus	NO4041	56°33·7'	2°58·1'W	X	54
Lumley Fm	N Yks	SE2270	54°7·8'	1°39·4'W	FM	99
Lumley Grange	Durham	NZ2849	54°50·3'	1°33·4'W	X	88
Lumley Ho	N Yks	NZ6905	54°26·4'	0°55·7'W	X	94
Lumley Ling	Durham	NZ0642	54°46·6'	1°54·0'W	X	87
Lumley Moor	N Yks	SE2271	54°8·3'	1°39·4'W	X	99
Lumley Moor Fm	Durham	NZ3148	54°49·8'	1°30·6'W	FM	88
Lumley Moor Resr	N Yks	SE2270	54°7·8'	1°39·4'W	W	99
Lumley Riding	Durham	NZ2850	54°50·9'	1°33·4'W	X	88
Lumley Seat	W Susx	SU7611	50°53·8'	0°54·8'W	X	197
Lumley Thicks	Durham	NZ3050	54°50·9'	1°31·5'W	T	88
Lumloch	E Dunb	NS6369	55°53·9'	4°11·0'W	X	64
Lummington	Angus	NO5864	56°46·2'	2°40·8'W	X	44
Lumphall Walks	Suff	TM4573	52°18·2'	1°36·0'E	X	156
Lumphanan	Aberd	NJ5804	57°7·8'	2°41·2'W	T	37
Lumphart	Aberd	NJ7627	57°20·2'	2°23·5'W	X	38
Lumphinnans	Fife	NT1792	56°7·1'	3°19·7'W	T	58
Lumphinnans Fm	Fife	NT1793	56°7·6'	3°19·7'W	FM	58
Lumpit Wood	Suff	TL8447	52°5·7'	0°41·6'E	F	155

Lump of the Eglin	E Ayr	NX4488	55°10·0′	4°26·5′W	X	77
Lumps of Garryhorn	D & G	NX5191	55°11·7′	4°20·0′W	X	77
Lumquhat	Fife	NO2413	56°18·5′	3°13·3′W	X	59
Lumquhat Mill	Fife	NO2313	56°18·4′	3°14·2′W	X	58
Lumsdaine	Scot Bord	NT8769	55°55·1′	2°12·0′W	X	67
Lumsdaine Moor	Scot Bord	NT8668	55°54·5′	2°13·0′W	X	67
Lumsdale	Derby	SK3160	53°8·4′	1°31·8′W	X	119
Lumsden	Aberd	NJ4721	57°16·9′	2°52·3′W	T	37
Lumsden Hill	Northum	NU0013	55°24·9′	1°59·6′W	H	81
Lumsdon Burn	Northum	NT7105	55°20·5′	2°27·0′W	W	80
Lumsdon Law	Northum	NT7205	55°20·5′	2°26·1′W	H	80
Luna	Corn	SX1666	50°28·1′	4°35·2′W	X	201
Lunabister	Shetld	HU3716	59°55·9′	1°19·8′W	X	4
Lunan	Angus	NO6851	56°39·2′	2°30·9′W	T	54
Lunan	Orkney	HY3317	59°2·4′	3°9·6′W	X	6
Lunan Bank	Angus	NO6448	56°37·6′	2°34·8′W	X	54
Lunanbank	Pth & Kin	NO0845	56°35·5′	3°29·4′W	X	52,53
Lunan Bay	Angus	NO7051	56°39·2′	2°28·9′W	W	54
Lunan Burn	Pth & Kin	NO0344	56°34·9′	3°34·3′W	W	52,53
Lunan Burn	Pth & Kin	NO0745	56°35·5′	3°30·4′W	W	52,53
Lunan Burn	Pth & Kin	NO1741	56°33·5′	3°20·6′W	W	53
Lunanhead	Angus	NO4752	56°39·7′	2°51·4′W	T	54
Lunan Water	Angus	NO6549	56°38·1′	2°33·8′W	W	54
Luncarty	Aberd	NJ7153	57°34·2′	2°28·6′W	X	29
Luncarty	Pth & Kin	NO0929	56°26·9′	3°28·1′W	T	52,53,58
Lunce's Common	E Susx	TQ3321	50°58·6′	0°5·9′W	X	198
Lunces Hall	E Susx	TQ3320	50°58·1′	0°6·0′W	X	198
Luncheon Huts	Lancs	SD5957	54°0·7′	2°37·1′W	X	102
Lund	Cumbr	NY0719	54°33·7′	3°25·9′W	X	89
Lund	E Yorks	SE9748	53°55·4′	0°31·0′W	T	106
Lund	N Yks	SE6532	53°47·1′	1°0·4′W	T	105,106
Lund	Shetld	HP5703	60°42·6′	0°56·8′W	X	1
Lundale	N Eil	NB1832	58°11·5′	6°47·5′W	X	8,13
Lundavra	Highld	NN0866	56°45·0′	5°8·0′W	X	41
Lunda Wick	Shetld	HP5604	60°43·2′	0°57·9′W	W	1
Lund Court Fm	N Yks	SE6685	54°15·6′	0°58·8′W	FM	94,100
Lunderston	Inverc	NS2174	55°55·8′	4°51·5′W	X	63
Lunderston Bay	Inverc	NS2073	55°55·2′	4°52·4′W	W	63
Lunderton	Aberd	NK1049	57°32·1′	1°49·5′W	X	30
Lund Farms	N Yks	SE5069	54°7·1′	1°13·7′W	FM	100
Lund Fm	N Yks	SD6772	54°8·8′	2°29·9′W	FM	98
Lund Fm	N Yks	SE4968	54°6·6′	1°14·6′W	FM	100
Lund Fm	N Yks	SE5729	53°45·5′	1°7·7′W	FM	105
Lund Fm	N Yks	SE6190	54°18·4′	1°3·3′W	FM	94,100
Lund Garth	E Yorks	TA2031	53°45·9′	0°10·4′W	X	107
Lund Head	N Yks	SE3348	53°55·9′	1°29·4′W	X	104
Lund Head	N Yks	SE6685	54°15·6′	0°58·8′W	X	94,100
Lund Ho	N Yks	SE2853	53°58·6′	1°34·0′W	X	104
Lund Holme	N Yks	SD6872	54°8·8′	2°29·0′W	X	98
Lund House Fm	N Yks	SE4253	53°58·5′	1°21·2′W	FM	105
Lundie	Angus	NO2936	56°30·9′	3°8·8′W	T	53
Lundie	Highld	NH1410	57°8·9′	5°4·0′W	X	34
Lundie Castle	Angus	NO3036	56°30·9′	3°7·8′W	X	53
Lundie Castle	Angus	NO5667	56°47·8′	2°42·8′W	X	44
Lundie Craigs	Angus	NO2737	56°31·4′	3°10·7′W	X	53
Lundie Loch	Angus	NO2837	56°31·4′	3°9·8′W	W	53
Lundie Mains	Angus	NO5767	56°47·8′	2°41·8′W	X	44
Lundin	Pth & Kin	NN8850	56°38·0′	3°49·1′W	X	52
Lundin Br	Fife	NO4627	56°26·2′	2°52·1′W	X	54,59
Lundin Burn	Fife	NO4624	56°24·6′	2°52·1′W	W	54,59
Lundin Fm	Fife	NT0687	56°4·3′	3°30·2′W	FM	65
Lundin Links	Fife	NO4002	56°12·7′	2°57·6′W	X	59
Lundin Wood	Fife	NO3902	56°12·7′	2°58·6′W	F	59
Lund Ridge	N Yks	SE6191	54°18·9′	1°3·3′W	X	94,100
Lunds	N Yks	SD7994	54°20·7′	2°19·0′W	X	98
Lunds Fell	N Yks	SD8096	54°21·8′	2°18·0′W	X	98
Lunds Fm	Brad	SE1640	53°51·6′	1°45·0′W	FM	104
Lundsford Fm	E Susx	TQ7125	51°0·2′	0°26·6′E	FM	188,199
Lunds, The	N Yks	SE4964	54°4·4′	1°14·7′W	X	100
Lund, The	N Yks	SE5068	54°6·6′	1°13·7′W	X	100
Lund, The	N Yks	SE7090	54°18·3′	0°55·0′W	X	94,100
Lund Wold Ho	E Yorks	SE9448	53°55·4′	0°33·7′W	X	106
Lundwood	Barns	SE3707	53°33·7′	1°26·1′W	T	110,111
Lund Wood	N Yks	SE8466	54°5·2′	0°42·5′W	F	100
Lundy	Devon	SS1345	51°10·7′	4°40·1′W	X	180
Lundy	Powys	SO1646	52°6·6′	3°13·2′W	X	148
Lundy Green	Norf	TM2492	52°29·0′	1°18·3′E	T	134
Lundy Roads	Devon	SS1445	51°10·7′	4°39·3′W	W	180
Lundy's Fm	Lincs	TF3834	52°53·4′	0°3·5′E	FM	131
Lunecliffe	Lancs	SD4658	54°1·2′	2°49·0′W	X	102
Lunedale	Durham	NY9221	54°35·3′	2°7·0′W	X	91,92
Lune Forest	Durham	NY8323	54°36·4′	2°15·4′W	X	91,92
Lune Head Beck	Durham	NY8321	54°35·3′	2°15·4′W	W	91,92
Lune Head Moss	Durham	NY8321	54°35·3′	2°15·4′W	X	91,92
Lune Moor	Durham	NY9023	54°36·4′	2°8·9′W	X	91,92
Lunendales	Essex	TL9401	51°40·7′	0°48·8′E	X	168
Luneside	Cumbr	SD6291	54°19·0′	2°34·6′W	X	97
Lu Ness	Shetld	HU3735	60°6·1′	1°19·6′W	X	4
Luney Barton	Corn	SW9648	50°18·0′	4°51·5′W	X	204
Lunga	Arg & Bt	NM2741	56°29·2′	6°25·6′W	X	46,47,48
Lunga	Arg & Bt	NM7008	56°12·8′	5°42·1′W	X	55
Lunga	Arg & Bt	NM7906	56°12·0′	5°33·3′W	X	55
Lunga Crags	Northum	NY9582	55°8·2′	2°4·3′W	X	81
Lunga Skerries	Orkney	HY6616	59°2·0′	2°35·1′W	X	5
Lunga Skerries	Shetld	HU3442	60°9·9′	1°22·7′W	X	4
Lunga Skolla	Shetld	HU4783	60°31·9′	1°8·1′W	X	1,2,3
Lunga Water	Shetld	HU2352	60°15·4′	1°34·6′W	W	3
Lunga Water	Shetld	HU2844	60°11·0′	1°29·2′W	W	4
Lunga Water	Shetld	HU4589	60°35·2′	1°10·2′W	W	1,2
Lunghwa	Corn	SX2263	50°26·6′	4°30·0′W	X	201
Lung Ness	Shetld	HU3550	60°14·2′	1°21·6′W	X	3
Lung Skerry	Shetld	HU6198	60°39·9′	0°52·5′W	X	1
Lunna	Shetld	HU4869	60°24·4′	1°7·2′W	T	2,3
Lunna Holm	Shetld	HU5274	60°27·1′	1°2·8′W	X	2,3
Lunna Kirk	Shetld	HU4869	60°24·4′	1°7·2′W	X	2,3
Lunna Ness	Shetld	HU5071	60°25·5′	1°5·0′W	X	2,3
Lunnasting	Shetld	HU4865	60°22·2′	1°7·3′W	T	2,3
Lunning	Shetld	HU5067	60°23·3′	1°5·1′W	T	2,3
Lunning Head	Shetld	HU5167	60°23·3′	1°4·0′W	X	2,3
Lunning Sound	Shetld	HU5165	60°22·2′	1°4·0′W	W	2,3
Lunnister	Shetld	HU3471	60°25·6′	1°22·4′W	T	2,3
Lunnon	Swan	SS5489	51°35·1′	4°6·1′W	T	159
Lun Rigg	N Yks	SE9295	54°20·8′	0°34·7′W	X	94,101
Lunsford	E Susx	TQ8813	50°53·4′	0°40·8′E	X	199
Lunsford	Kent	TQ6959	51°18·5′	0°25·9′E	T	178,188
Lunsford's Cross	E Susx	TQ7210	50°52·1′	0°27·1′E	T	199
Lunshaw Beck	N Yks	SE4986	54°16·3′	1°14·4′W	W	100
Lunshaw Ho	N Yks	SE4987	54°16·8′	1°14·4′W	X	100
Lunt	Sefton	SD3401	53°30·3′	2°59·3′W	T	108
Lunter Stone	N Yks	SE1871	54°8·3′	1°43·1′W	X	99
Luntley	Heref	SO3955	52°11·6′	2°53·1′W	X	148,149
Lunton Hill	Durham	NZ0527	54°38·5′	1°54·9′W	X	92
Lunts Fm, The	Staffs	SJ7641	52°58·2′	2°21·0′W	FM	118
Lunts Heath	Halton	SJ5188	53°23·4′	2°43·8′W	T	108
Lunways Inn	Hants	SU5136	51°7·5′	1°15·9′W	X	185
Lupin	Staffs	SK1416	52°44·7′	1°47·2′W	T	128
Luppincott	Devon	SS5323	50°59·5′	4°5·3′W	X	180
Luppitt	Devon	ST1606	50°51·1′	3°11·2′W	T	192,193
Luppitt Common	Devon	ST1507	50°51·6′	3°12·1′W	X	192,193
Lupridge	Devon	SX7153	50°22·0′	3°48·5′W	T	202
Lupset	Wakf	SE3119	53°40·2′	1°31·4′W	T	110,111
Lupton	Cumbr	SD5581	54°13·6′	2°41·0′W	T	97
Lupton Beck	Cumbr	SD5780	54°13·1′	2°39·1′W	W	97
Lupton Hall	Cumbr	SD5781	54°13·6′	2°39·2′W	X	97
Lupton High	Cumbr	SD5682	54°14·2′	2°40·1′W	X	97
Lupton Ho (Sch)	Torbay	SX9055	50°23·3′	3°32·5′W	X	202
Lupton Park	Torbay	SX8954	50°22·8′	3°33·3′W	X	202
Lupton Twr	Cumbr	SD5580	54°13·1′	2°41·0′W	X	97
Lupus	S Lanak	NS7838	55°37·5′	3°55·8′W	X	71
Lurchardon	Devon	SX5595	50°44·4′	4°2·9′W	X	191
Lurcher Fm	Notts	SK6156	53°6·1′	1°4·9′W	FM	120
Lurcher's Crag or Creag an Leth-choin	Highld	NH9603	57°6·6′	3°42·6′W	H	36
Lurden	Scot Bord	NT5418	55°27·5′	2°43·2′W	X	79
Lurdenlaw	Scot Bord	NT7631	55°34·6′	2°22·4′W	X	74
Lurg	Aberd	NJ6906	57°8·9′	2°30·3′W	X	38
Lurg	Highld	NJ0317	57°14·3′	3°36·0′W	X	36
Lurg	Moray	NJ0445	57°29·4′	3°35·6′W	X	27
Lurg	Pth & Kin	NN8614	56°18·5′	3°50·1′W	X	58
Lurg	Stir	NS6385	56°2·6′	4°11·5′W	X	57
Lurga	Highld	NM7355	56°38·2′	5°41·7′W	X	49
Lurg á Chuilinn	Highld	NH1502	57°4·6′	5°2·7′W	X	34
Lurg a' Mhula	N Eil	NB1214	58°1·6′	6°52·2′W	X	13,14
Lurgan	Pth & Kin	NN8150	56°37·9′	3°55·9′W	X	52
Lurgan	Pth & Kin	NN8852	56°39·0′	3°49·2′W	X	52
Lurgan Hill	Pth & Kin	NN8118	56°20·6′	3°55·1′W	H	57
Lurg an Tabhail	Highld	NC4042	58°20·5′	4°43·5′W	H	9
Lurgashall	W Susx	SU9327	51°2·3′	0°40·0′W	T	186,197
Lurg Bhàn	Arg & Bt	NN2144	56°33·5′	4°54·3′W	X	50
Lurg Burn	Pth & Kin	NN7627	56°25·4′	4°0·2′W	W	51,52
Lurg Burn	Pth & Kin	NN9032	56°28·3′	3°46·7′W	W	52
Lurg Dhubh	Moray	NJ2214	57°12·9′	3°17·0′W	X	36
Lurg Fm	Fife	NS9586	56°3·6′	3°40·7′W	FM	65
Lurg Hill	Moray	NJ5057	57°36·3′	2°49·7′W	H	29
Lurghill Plantation	Moray	NJ5058	57°36·8′	2°49·8′W	F	29
Lurgie Craigs	Scot Bord	NT6739	55°38·9′	2°31·0′W	X	74
Lurgies Burn	Scot Bord	NT5506	55°21·0′	2°42·1′W	W	80
Lurgiescleuch	Scot Bord	NT5506	55°21·0′	2°42·1′W	X	80
Lurgies, The	Angus	NO6757	56°42·5′	2°31·9′W	X	54
Lurg Loch	Pth & Kin	NT0996	56°9·1′	3°27·5′W	W	58
Lurglomand	Pth & Kin	NN7443	56°34·0′	4°2·6′W	X	51,52
Lurg Mhór	Highld	NH0640	57°24·8′	5°13·3′W	X	25
Lurg Moor	Inverc	NS2973	55°55·4′	4°43·8′W	X	63
Lurignich	Arg & Bt	NM9450	56°36·1′	5°20·9′W	X	49
Lurkeley Hill	Wilts	SU1266	51°23·8′	1°49·3′W	X	173
Lurkenhope	Shrops	SO2874	52°21·8′	3°3·0′W	X	137,148
Lurkeys, The	Shrops	SO5581	52°25·7′	2°39·3′W	X	137,138
Lurley	Devon	SS9214	50°55·2′	3°31·8′W	T	181
Lurneoch	D & G	NX3662	54°55·8′	4°33·1′W	X	83
Lurns of the Sound	Orkney	HY7856	59°23·6′	2°22·8′W	X	5
Lurn, The	Orkney	HY7452	59°21·5′	2°27·0′W	X	5
Lusby	Lincs	TF3367	53°11·2′	0°0·2′W	T	122
Luscar Ho	Fife	NT0589	56°5·3′	3°31·2′W	X	65
Luscombe	Devon	SX7463	50°27·4′	3°46·1′W	X	202
Luscombe	Devon	SX7957	50°24·3′	3°41·8′W	X	202
Luscombe Castle	Devon	SX9476	50°34·7′	3°29·4′W	X	192
Luscombe Cross	Devon	SX7957	50°24·3′	3°41·8′W	A	202
Luscombe Fm	Devon	SX8479	50°36·2′	3°38·0′W	FM	191
Luscombe Fm	Warw	SP2261	52°15·0′	1°40·3′W	FM	151
Luscombe Valley	Poole	SZ0490	50°42·8′	1°56·2′W	X	195
Luscott Barton	Devon	SS5136	51°6·5′	4°7·3′W	X	180
Lushcott	Shrops	SO5595	52°33·3′	2°39·4′W	T	137,138
Lushes Fm	Dorset	ST8117	50°57·4′	2°15·8′W	FM	183
Lus Hill	Swin	SU1693	51°38·4′	1°45·7′W	H	163,173
Luson	Devon	SX6050	50°20·2′	3°57·7′W	T	202
Luson	Devon	SX6153	50°21·9′	3°56·9′W	X	202
Lusragan Burn	Arg & Bt	NM9032	56°26·3′	5°23·9′W	W	49
Luss	Arg & Bt	NS3592	56°6·1′	4°38·7′W	T	56
Lussa Bay	Arg & Bt	NR6486	56°0·8′	5°46·7′W	W	55,61
Lussagiven	Arg & Bt	NR6386	56°0·8′	5°47·7′W	X	61
Lussa Loch	Arg & Bt	NR7130	55°30·9′	5°37·2′W	W	68
Lussa Point	Arg & Bt	NR6486	56°0·8′	5°46·7′W	X	55,61
Lussa River	Arg & Bt	NM6531	56°25·0′	5°48·2′W	W	49
Lussa River	Arg & Bt	NR6391	56°3·4′	5°48·0′W	W	61
Lussa, The	Arg & Bt	NR7784	56°0·1′	5°34·2′W	X	55
Luss Water	Arg & Bt	NS3293	56°6·3′	4°41·6′W	W	56
Lusta	Highld	NG2656	57°30·9′	6°34·1′W	T	23
Lusted Hall Fm	Brom	TQ4157	51°17·9′	0°1·7′E	FM	187
Lusteds	E Susx	TQ6106	50°50·1′	0°17·6′E	X	199
Lustleigh	Devon	SX7881	50°37·2′	3°43·1′W	T	191
Lustleigh Cleave	Devon	SX7681	50°37·2′	3°44·8′W	T	191
Luston	Heref	SO4863	52°16·0′	2°45·3′W	T	137,138,148
Lustruther	Scot Bord	NT6209	55°22·7′	2°35·5′W	X	80
Lusty	Somer	ST6834	51°6·5′	2°27·0′W	T	183
Lusty Glaze	Corn	SW8262	50°25·3′	5°3·8′W	X	200
Lusty Hill Fm	Somer	ST6733	51°6·0′	2°27·9′W	FM	183
Lustylaw	Pth & Kin	NO1313	56°18·3′	3°23·9′W	X	58
Luther Br	Aberd	NO6566	56°47·3′	2°33·9′W	X	45
Luther Moss	Aberd	NO5988	56°59·1′	2°40·0′W	X	44
Luthermuir	Aberd	NO6568	56°48·4′	2°33·9′W	T	45
Luther Water	Aberd	NO6971	56°50·0′	2°30·0′W	W	45
Luthrie	Fife	NO3319	56°21·8′	3°4·6′W	T	59
Lutley	Dudley	SO9483	52°26·9′	2°4·9′W	T	139
Lutley	Staffs	SO8188	52°29·6′	2°16·4′W	X	138
Luton	Devon	ST0802	50°48·8′	3°18·0′W	T	192
Luton	Devon	SX9076	50°34·6′	3°32·8′W	T	192
Luton	Luton	TL0921	51°52·8′	0°24·6′W	T	166
Luton	Medway	TQ7666	51°22·2′	0°32·1′E	T	178
Luton Down	Dorset	ST9107	50°52·0′	2°7·3′W	X	195
Luton Fm	Dorset	ST9407	50°52·0′	2°4·7′W	FM	195
Luton Fm	I of W	SZ4892	50°43·8′	1°18·8′W	FM	196
Luton Hoo	Beds	TL1018	51°51·2′	0°23·8′W	A	166
Luton Hoo Park	Beds	TL1018	51°51·2′	0°23·8′W	X	166
Luton International Airport	Luton	TL1220	51°52·3′	0°22·0′W	X	166
Luton Lye Cotts	Wilts	SU2267	51°24·3′	1°40·6′W	X	174
Lutsey Fm	Wilts	ST9558	51°19·5′	2°3·9′W	FM	173
Lutsford	Devon	SS2519	50°56·9′	4°29·1′W	T	190
Lutson Fm	Devon	SS3010	50°52·1′	4°24·6′W	FM	190
Lutterington Hall	Durham	NZ1824	54°36·9′	1°42·9′W	X	92
Lutterworth	Leic	SP5484	52°27·3′	1°11·9′W	T	140
Lutton	Devon	SX5959	50°25·1′	3°58·7′W	T	202
Lutton	Devon	SX6961	50°26·3′	3°50·3′W	T	202
Lutton	Dorset	SY9080	50°37·4′	2°8·1′W	X	195
Lutton	Lincs	TF4325	52°48·4′	0°7·7′E	T	131
Lutton	Northnts	TL1187	52°28·4′	0°21·5′W	T	142
Lutton Gate Lodge	Lincs	TF3411	52°41·0′	0°0·7′W	X	131,142
Lutton Gowts	Lincs	TF4324	52°47·9′	0°7·7′E	T	131
Lutton Grange	Lincs	TF4426	52°49·0′	0°8·6′E	X	131
Lutton Gwyle	Dorset	SY9081	50°37·9′	2°8·1′W	X	195
Lutton Leam	Lincs	TF4525	52°48·4′	0°9·5′E	W	131
Lutton Lodge Fm	Northnts	TL1287	52°28·4′	0°20·7′W	FM	142
Lutton Marsh	Lincs	TF4526	52°49·0′	0°9·5′E	X	131
Luttrell Fm	Devon	SS9621	50°59·0′	3°28·5′W	FM	181
Lutworthy	Devon	SS7616	50°56·0′	3°45·5′W	X	180
Lutwyche Hall	Shrops	SO5594	52°32·8′	2°39·4′W	X	137,138
Luxborough	Somer	SS9738	51°8·2′	3°27·9′W	T	181
Luxborough Fm	Somer	ST1934	51°6·2′	3°9·0′W	FM	181
Lux Fm	Suff	TM2246	52°4·3′	1°14·8′E	FM	169
Luxhay Resr	Somer	ST2017	50°57·0′	3°8·0′W	W	193
Luxley	Glos	SO6821	51°53·4′	2°27·5′W	T	162
Luxmore Fm	NE Lincs	TA1614	53°36·8′	0°14·4′W	FM	113
Luxted	Brom	TQ4360	51°19·5′	0°3·5′E	T	177,187
Luxters Fm	Bucks	SU7689	51°35·9′	0°53·8′W	FM	175
Luxton	Devon	ST2111	50°53·8′	3°7·0′W	T	192,193
Luxton Barton	Devon	SS6505	50°50·0′	3°54·6′W	X	191
Luxton Moor	Devon	SS6406	50°50·5′	3°55·5′W	X	191
Luxulyan	Corn	SX0558	50°23·6′	4°44·2′W	T	200
Luzley	Tames	SD9601	53°30·6′	2°3·2′W	T	109
Luzley Brook	Oldham	SD9207	53°33·8′	2°6·8′W	T	109
Lwynjack	Carm	SN7533	51°59·1′	3°48·8′W	X	146,160
Lyalls	Devon	SX8886	50°40·0′	3°34·7′W	X	192
Lyatt	Somer	ST5745	51°12·4′	2°36·5′W	X	182,183
Lyatts	Somer	ST5211	50°54·0′	2°40·6′W	T	194
Lybster	Highld	ND0268	58°35·6′	3°40·7′W	X	11,12
Lybster	Highld	ND2435	58°18·1′	3°17·3′W	T	11
Lybster Bay	Highld	ND2434	58°17·5′	3°17·3′W	W	11
Lyburn Fm	Wilts	SU2318	50°57·9′	1°40·0′W	FM	184
Lyburn Ho	Wilts	SU2417	50°57·3′	1°39·1′W	X	184
Lychpole Fm	W Susx	TQ1507	50°51·3′	0°21·6′W	FM	198
Lychpole Hill	W Susx	TQ1507	50°51·3′	0°21·6′W	X	198
Lyckweed Fm	W Berks	SU3174	51°28·1′	1°32·8′W	FM	174
Lycondlich	Pth & Kin	NN9265	56°46·1′	3°45·6′W	X	43
Lydacott	Devon	SS4803	50°48·6′	4°9·1′W	X	191
Lydacott	Devon	SS5130	51°3·2′	4°7·2′W	X	180
Lydall's Wood	Bucks	SU7395	51°39·2′	0°56·3′W	F	165
Lydart Ho	Monm	SO5009	51°46·9′	2°43·1′W	X	162
Lydbridge	Devon	SS5201	50°47·6′	4°5·6′W	X	191
Lydbury North	Shrops	SO3586	52°28·3′	2°57·0′W	T	137
Lydcott	Devon	SS6936	51°6·7′	3°51·9′W	T	180
Lydcott	Devon	SX6297	50°45·6′	3°57·0′W	X	191
Lydcott Hall	Devon	SS6936	51°6·7′	3°51·9′W	X	180
Lydcott Wood	Corn	SX3058	50°24·1′	4°23·2′W	F	201
Lydd	Kent	TR0420	50°56·8′	0°54·6′E	T	189
Lydd Airport	Kent	TR0621	50°57·3′	0°56·4′E	X	189
Lydden	Kent	TR2645	51°9·8′	1°14·3′E	T	179
Lydden	Kent	TR3567	51°21·4′	1°22·9′E	T	179
Lyddendane Fm	Kent	TR0945	51°10·2′	0°59·8′E	FM	179,189
Lydden Hill	Kent	TR2545	51°9·8′	1°13·5′E	X	179
Lydden Spout	Kent	TR2838	51°6·0′	1°15·8′E	W	179
Lydden Valley	Kent	TR3555	51°15·0′	1°22·4′E	X	179
Lyddicombe Bottom	Devon	SS7335	51°6·3′	3°48·5′W	X	180
Lyddington	Rut	SP8797	52°34·1′	0°42·6′W	T	141
Lyddon Ho	Dorset	ST7309	50°53·0′	2°22·6′W	X	194
Lydd-on-Sea	Kent	TR0820	50°56·7′	0°58·1′E	T	189
Lydd Ranges	Kent	TR0118	50°55·8′	0°52·0′E	X	189
Lydds Ho	N Yks	SE8188	54°17·1′	0°44·9′W	X	94,100
Lyde	Orkney	HY3618	59°2·9′	3°6·4′W	X	6
Lyde	Shrops	SJ3101	52°36·4′	3°0·7′W	T	126
Lydeard Cross	Somer	ST2332	51°5·2′	3°5·6′W	X	182
Lydeard Fm	Somer	ST2232	51°5·2′	3°6·4′W	FM	182
Lydeard Hill	Somer	ST1734	51°6·2′	3°10·7′W	H	181
Lydeard St Lawrence	Somer	ST1232	51°5·1′	3°15·0′W	T	181
Lyde Bank	Glos	SO9915	51°50·3′	2°0·5′W	F	163
Lydebrook Dingle	Wrekin	SJ6506	52°39·3′	2°30·6′W	F	127
Lyde Cross	Heref	SO5143	52°5·2′	2°42·5′W	T	149
Lyde Green	Hants	SU7057	51°18·7′	0°59·3′W	T	175,186
Lyde Green	S Glos	ST6778	51°30·2′	2°28·1′W	T	172
Lyde Hill	Heref	SO5243	52°5·2′	2°41·6′W	X	149
Lydehole Fm	Shrops	SO5282	52°26·3′	2°42·0′W	FM	137,138
Lydeland Water	Devon	SS4018	50°56·6′	4°16·3′W	W	180,190
Lydens Fm	Kent	TQ4544	51°10·8′	0°4·9′E	FM	188
Lyde River	Hants	SU6956	51°18·2′	1°0·2′W	W	175,186
Lydes Fm	Glos	SP0433	52°0·0′	1°56·1′W	FM	150
Lydes Fm	S Glos	ST7379	51°30·8′	2°23·0′W	FM	172
Lydes Fm	Somer	ST7451	51°15·7′	2°22·0′W	FM	183
Lydeway	Wilts	SU0458	51°19·5′	1°56·2′W	X	173
Lydford	Devon	SX5184	50°38·4′	4°6·1′W	T	191,201
Lydford Fair Place	Somer	ST5732	51°5·4′	2°36·5′W	T	182,183
Lydford Fm	Devon	SS5547	51°12·5′	4°4·2′W	FM	180
Lydford Gorge	Devon	SX5083	50°37·9′	4°6·9′W	X	191,201

Lydford-on-Fosse	Somer	ST5630	51°4·3'	2°37·3'W	T	182,183
Lydford Tor	Devon	SX5978	50°35·3'	3°59·1'W	H	191
Lydgate	Cald	SD9225	53°43·5'	2°6·9'W	T	103
Lydgate	Oldham	SD9704	53°32·2'	2°2·3'W	T	109
Lydgate	Roch	SD9516	53°38·7'	2°4·1'W	X	109
Lydham	Shrops	SO3390	52°30·5'	2°58·8'W	T	137
Lydham Heath	Shrops	SO3590	52°30·5'	2°57·1'W	X	137
Lydham Manor	Shrops	SO3290	52°30·5'	2°59·7'W	X	137
Lyd Head	Devon	SX5588	50°40·7'	4°2·8'W	W	191
Lydhurst	W Susx	TQ2425	51°0·9'	0°13·5'W	X	187,198
Lydia Br	Devon	SX6960	50°25·7'	3°50·3'W	X	202
Lydiard Country Park	Swin	SU1084	51°33·5'	1°51·0'W	X	173
Lydiard Green	Wilts	SU0885	51°34·1'	1°52·7'W	T	173
Lydiard Millicent	Wilts	SU0985	51°34·1'	1°51·8'W	T	173
Lydiard Plain	Wilts	SU0586	51°34·6'	1°55·3'W	T	173
Lydiard Tregoze	Swin	SU1084	51°33·5'	1°51·0'W	T	173
Lydiate	Sefton	SD3704	53°32·0'	2°56·6'W	T	108
Lydiate Ash	Worcs	SO9775	52°22·6'	2°2·2'W	T	139
Lydiate Fm	Derby	SK0087	53°23·0'	1°59·6'W	FM	110
Lydiates Fm	Staffs	SO8283	52°26·9'	2°15·5'W	FM	138
Lydiate, The	Ches	SJ3178	53°17·9'	3°1·7'W	X	117
Lydiatts	Heref	SO4861	52°14·9'	2°45·3'W	X	137,138,148
Lydlinch	Dorset	ST7413	50°55·2'	2°21·8'W	T	194
Lydlinch Common	Dorset	ST7313	50°55·2'	2°22·7'W	X	194
Lydling Fm	Surrey	SU9346	51°12·6'	0°39·7'W	FM	186
Lydmarsh	Somer	ST3508	50°52·3'	2°55·0'W	T	193
Lydney	Glos	SO6303	51°43·7'	2°31·8'W	T	162
Lydney Harbour	Glos	SO6301	51°42·6'	2°31·7'W	X	162
Lydney Park	Glos	SO6102	51°43·2'	2°33·5'W	X	162
Lydney Park	Glos	SO6202	51°43·2'	2°32·6'W	X	162
Lydney Sand	Glos	ST6399	51°41·5'	2°31·7'W	X	162
Lydox Cotts	Fife	NO4116	56°20·2'	2°56·8'W	X	59
Lydstep	Pemb	SS0898	51°39·1'	4°46·1'W	T	158
Lydstep Haven	Pemb	SS0998	51°39·1'	4°45·3'W	W	158
Lydstep Point	Pemb	SS0997	51°38·6'	4°45·2'W	X	158
Lydsurach	Highld	NH6195	57°55·6'	4°20·4'W	X	21
Lyd Valley Ho	Devon	SX4883	50°37·8'	4°8·6'W	X	191,201
Lydwicke	W Susx	TQ1029	51°3·2'	0°25·4'W	X	187,198
Lye	Dudley	SO9284	52°27·5'	2°6·7'W	T	139
Lye Bridge Fm	Worcs	SP0371	52°20·5'	1°57·0'W	FM	139
Lyeclose Fm	Dudley	SO9882	52°26·4'	2°1·4'W	FM	139
Lye Court	Heref	SO4552	52°10·1'	2°47·9'W	X	148,149
Lye Cross	N Som	ST4962	51°21·5'	2°43·6'W	T	172,182
Lye End Fm	Herts	TL3332	51°58·5'	0°3·4'W	FM	166
Lyefield Fm	Surrey	TQ1140	51°9·1'	0°24·4'W	FM	187
Lye Fm	Hants	SU4154	51°17·2'	1°24·3'W	FM	185
Lye Green	Bucks	SP9703	51°43·3'	0°35·3'W	T	165
Lye Green	E Susx	TQ5134	51°5·3'	0°9·8'E	T	188
Lye Green	Warw	SP1965	52°17·2'	1°42·9'W	T	151
Lye Green	Wilts	ST8159	51°20·0'	2°16·0'W	T	173
Lyegrove Fm	S Glos	ST7781	51°31·9'	2°19·5'W	FM	172
Lyegrove Ho	S Glos	ST7781	51°31·9'	2°19·5'W	X	172
Lye Hall	Shrops	SO7586	52°28·5'	2°21·7'W	X	138
Lye Head	Worcs	SO7573	52°21·5'	2°21·6'W	T	138
Lye Hill	Bath & NE Somer	ST6564	51°22·7'	2°29·8'W	X	172
Lye Hole	N Som	ST5062	51°21·5'	2°42·7'W	T	172,182
Lyeing Hill, The	Arg & Bt	NS0370	55°53·2'	5°8·6'W	H	63
Lyelake Fm	Lancs	SD4505	53°32·6'	2°49·4'W	FM	108
Lyelands Fm	W Susx	TQ2422	50°59·3'	0°13·6'W	FM	198
Lye Rock	Corn	SX0689	50°40·3'	4°44·4'W	X	200
Lye's Fm	W Susx	TQ3021	50°58·6'	0°8·5'W	FM	198
Lye's Green	Wilts	ST8246	51°13·0'	2°15·1'W	X	183
Lye, The	Shrops	SO6793	52°32·3'	2°28·8'W	X	138
Lye Vallets	Heref	SO4652	52°10·1'	2°47·0'W	X	148,149
Lyeway Fm	Hants	SU6632	51°5·2'	1°3·1'W	FM	185,186
Lyewood Common	E Susx	TQ5037	51°7·0'	0°9·0'E	T	188
Lyewood Ho	Hants	SU6531	51°4·7'	1°3·9'W	X	185,186
Lyford	Oxon	SU3994	51°38·8'	1°25·8'W	T	164,174
Lyford Fm	W Susx	SU8426	51°1·9'	0°47·7'W	FM	186,197
Lyford Grange	Oxon	SU3994	51°38·8'	1°25·8'W	X	164,174
Lyford Manor	Oxon	SU3894	51°38·8'	1°26·7'W	X	164,174
Lygan Uchaf	Flint	SJ2068	53°12·4'	3°11·5'W	X	117
Lygan-y-wern	Flint	SJ2072	53°14·6'	3°11·5'W	X	117
Lygos	Swan	SN6708	51°45·5'	3°55·2'W	X	159
Lyham Hill	Northum	NU0731	55°34·6'	1°52·9'W	H	75
Lyham Moor	Northum	NU0731	55°34·6'	1°52·9'W	X	75
Lyke Wake Walk	N Yks	NZ6301	54°24·3'	1°1·3'W	X	94
Lyking	Orkney	HY2715	59°1·2'	3°15·8'W	X	6
Lyking	Orkney	HY4021	59°4·6'	3°2·3'W	X	5,6
Lyking	Orkney	HY5002	58°54·4'	2°51·6'W	X	6,7
Lylands Fm	N Yks	SE4260	54°2·3'	1°21·1'W	FM	99
Lylands Wood	N Yks	SE4160	54°2·3'	1°22·0'W	F	99
Lyle Hill	Inverc	NS2577	55°57·5'	4°47·8'W	H	63
Lylestane	Scot Bord	NT5251	55°45·3'	2°45·5'W	X	66,73
Lyleston	Arg & Bt	NS3379	55°58·8'	4°40·2'W	X	63
Lylestone	N Ayr	NS3245	55°40·4'	4°39·9'W	X	63
Lylestone Hill	Scot Bord	NT5352	55°45·8'	2°44·5'W	H	66,73
Lyleston Fm	Arg & Bt	NS3279	55°58·7'	4°41·1'W	FM	63
Lylowan	Fife	NT0892	56°7·0'	3°28·3'W	X	58
Lymball's Fm	Suff	TM4270	52°16·7'	1°33·3'E	FM	156
Lymbridge Green	Kent	TR1243	51°9·0'	1°2·3'E	T	179,189
Lymburghs Fm	Dorset	ST8119	50°58·4'	2°15·9'W	FM	183
Lymden	E Susx	TQ6729	51°2·4'	0°23·3'E	X	188,199
Lymebridge	Devon	SS2322	50°58·5'	4°30·9'W	X	190
Lyme Brook	Staffs	SJ8543	52°59·3'	2°13·0'W	W	118
Lymecliff	N Yks	SE2679	54°12·6'	1°35·7'W	X	99
Lyme Green	Ches	SJ9170	53°13·9'	2°7·7'W	T	118
Lyme Hall	Ches	SJ9682	53°20·3'	2°3·2'W	A	109
Lyme Ho	Staffs	SJ9456	53°6·3'	2°5·0'W	X	118
Lyme Park Country Park	Ches	SJ9682	53°20·3'	2°3·2'W	X	109
Lyme Regis	Dorset	SY3492	50°43·7'	2°55·7'W	T	193
Lymes, The	Staffs	SJ8243	52°59·3'	2°15·7'W	X	118
Lymiecleuch	Scot Bord	NT3802	55°18·7'	2°58·2'W	T	79
Lyminge	Kent	TR1641	51°7·9'	1°5·6'E	T	179,189
Lymington	Hants	SZ3295	50°45·5'	1°32·4'W	T	196
Lymington River	Hants	SZ3298	50°47·1'	1°32·4'W	W	196
Lymington Spit	Hants	SZ3493	50°44·4'	1°30·7'W	X	196
Lyminster	W Susx	TQ0204	50°49·8'	0°32·7'W	T	197
Lyminster Fm	Somer	ST4107	50°51·8'	2°49·9'W	FM	193

Lymm	Warr	SJ6887	53°23·0'	2°28·5'W	T	109
Lymn Bank Fm	Lincs	TF4861	53°7·8'	0°13·1'E	FM	122
Lymore	Hants	SZ2992	50°43·8'	1°35·0'W	T	196
Lymore	Powys	SO2396	52°33·6'	3°7·8'W	X	137
Lymphoy	C of Edin	NT1767	55°53·6'	3°19·2'W	X	65,66
Lympne	Kent	TR1235	51°4·7'	1°2·0'E	T	179,189
Lympne Castle	Kent	TR1134	51°4·2'	1°1·1'E	A	179,189
Lympscott Fm	Devon	SS2912	50°53·2'	4°25·5'W	FM	190
Lympsham	Somer	ST3354	51°17·1'	2°57·3'W	T	182
Lympstone	Devon	SX9984	50°39·1'	3°25·3'W	T	192
Lympstone Commando Sta	Devon	SX9885	50°39·6'	3°26·2'W	X	192
Lympstone Common	Devon	SY0284	50°39·1'	3°22·8'W	X	192
Lymsworthy Fm	Corn	SS2610	50°52·0'	4°28·0'W	FM	190
Lynaberack Lodge	Highld	NN7694	57°1·5'	4°2·1'W	X	35
Lynachlaggan	Highld	NH8202	57°5·9'	3°56·4'W	X	35
Lynachork	Moray	NJ1518	57°14·9'	3°24·1'W	X	36
Lynague	I of M	SC2886	54°14·7'	4°38·0'W	X	95
Lynamer	Highld	NH9914	57°12·6'	3°39·9'W	X	36
Lynavoir	Moray	NJ2116	57°13·9'	3°18·1'W	X	36
Lynbridge	Devon	SS7248	51°13·2'	3°49·6'W	T	180
Lynbrook	Surrey	SU9659	51°19·5'	0°36·9'W	X	175,186
Lynch	Hants	SU5049	51°14·5'	1°16·6'W	T	185
Lynch	Somer	SS9047	51°12·9'	3°34·1'W	T	181
Lynchat	Highld	NH7801	57°5·3'	4°0·3'W	T	35
Lynch Common	Devon	SX5566	50°28·8'	4°2·2'W	X	202
Lynch Court	Heref	SO4158	52°13·3'	2°51·4'W	X	148,149
Lynches, The	Glos	SP1340	52°3·7'	1°48·2'W	X	151
Lynch Fm	Devon	SS9102	50°48·7'	3°32·4'W	FM	192
Lynch Fm	Dorset	SY5091	50°43·2'	2°42·1'W	FM	194
Lynch Fm	Dorset	SY9580	50°37·4'	2°3·9'W	FM	195
Lynch Fm	Glos	SO7611	51°48·1'	2°20·5'W	FM	162
Lynch Fm	Heref	SO5467	52°18·2'	2°40·1'W	FM	137,138,149
Lynchgate	Shrops	SO3785	52°27·8'	2°55·2'W	T	137
Lynch Hill	Hants	SU4648	51°14·0'	1°20·1'W	T	185
Lynch Hill	Slough	SU9482	51°32·0'	0°38·3'W	T	175
Lynch Knoll	Glos	SO8100	51°42·1'	2°16·1'W	X	162
Lynch, The	Herts	TL3708	51°45·5'	0°0·5'W	X	166
Lynch, The	Kent	TR3154	51°14·5'	1°19·0'E	X	179
Lynch, The	Kent	TR3647	51°10·6'	1°23·0'E	X	179
Lynch, The	Oxon	SU7677	51°29·4'	0°53·9'W	X	175
Lynch Tor	Devon	SX5680	50°36·4'	4°1·7'W	H	191
Lynchurn	Highld	NH9520	57°15·8'	3°44·0'W	X	36
Lynch Wood	W Berks	SU3279	51°30·8'	1°31·9'W	F	174
Lyn Cleave	Devon	SS7249	51°13·8'	3°49·6'W	X	180
Lyncombe	Somer	SS8637	51°7·5'	3°37·4'W	X	181
Lyncombe Fm	Somer	SS9429	51°3·3'	3°30·4'W	FM	181
Lyncombe Hill	N Som	ST4359	51°19·9'	2°48·7'W	X	172,182
Lyncote	Cumbr	NY4639	54°44·8'	2°49·9'W	X	90
Lyndale Ho	Highld	NG3654	57°30·2'	6°24·0'W	X	23
Lyndale Point	Highld	NG3657	57°31·8'	6°24·2'W	X	23
Lynden Down	Wilts	SU2554	51°17·3'	1°38·1'W	X	184
Lyndeor	Highld	NH9225	57°18·4'	3°47·1'W	X	36
Lynders Wood	Heref	SO6426	51°56·1'	2°31·0'W	F	162
Lynderswood Fm	Essex	TL7319	51°50·8'	0°31·1'E	FM	167
Lyndeth	Lancs	SD5841	53°52·1'	2°37·9'W	X	102
Lyndhurst	Hants	SU2908	50°52·5'	1°34·9'W	T	196
Lyndhurst	Herts	TQ1899	51°40·9'	0°17·2'W	X	166,176
Lyndhurst	I of M	SC3292	54°18·0'	4°34·5'W	X	95
Lyndhurst	Northum	NY8675	55°4·4'	2°12·7'W	X	87
Lyndhurst Hill	Hants	SU2808	50°52·5'	1°35·7'W	H	195
Lyndir Hall	Wrex	SJ3658	53°7·2'	2°57·0'W	X	117
Lyndon	Rut	SK9004	52°37·8'	0°39·8'W	T	141
Lyndon Green	Birm	SP1485	52°28·0'	1°47·2'W	T	139
Lyndon Lodge Fm	Leic	SP6393	52°32·1'	1°3·9'W	FM	140
Lyndons, The	Warw	SP0972	52°21·0'	1°51·7'W	X	139
Lyndors Fm	Glos	SO6720	51°52·9'	2°28·4'W	FM	162
Lyn Down	Devon	SS7247	51°12·7'	3°49·6'W	H	180
Lyne	Highld	NC2514	58°5·1'	4°57·6'W	X	15
Lyne	Highld	NH5542	57°27·0'	4°24·5'W	X	26
Lyne	Moray	NJ1628	57°20·3'	3°23·3'W	X	36
Lyne	Scot Bord	NT2041	55°39·6'	3°15·9'W	T	73
Lyne	Surrey	TQ0166	51°23·3'	0°32·5'W	X	176
Lyneal	Shrops	SJ4433	52°53·7'	2°49·5'W	T	126
Lyneal Hall	Shrops	SJ4432	52°53·2'	2°49·5'W	X	126
Lyneal Mill	Shrops	SJ4532	52°53·2'	2°48·6'W	T	126
Lyneal Wood	Shrops	SJ4531	52°52·7'	2°48·6'W	T	126
Lynebeg	Highld	NH8848	57°30·8'	3°51·7'W	X	27
Lynebeg	Highld	NJ0619	57°15·4'	3°33·0'W	X	36
Lynebeg	Moray	NJ1926	57°19·3'	3°20·2'W	X	36
Lynebreck	Highld	NJ0621	57°16·5'	3°33·1'W	X	36
Lyne Burn	Fife	NT0785	56°3·2'	3°29·2'W	W	65
Lyne Burn	Moray	NJ1745	57°29·5'	3°22·6'W	W	28
Lynecrook	Cumbr	NY5073	55°3·2'	2°46·5'W	X	86
Lynedale	Cumbr	NY4771	55°2·1'	2°49·3'W	X	86
Lynedale	Scot Bord	NT1452	55°45·5'	3°21·8'W	X	65,72
Lynedoch Cottage	Pth & Kin	NO0328	56°26·3'	3°33·9'W	X	52,53,58
Lyne Down	Heref	SO6431	51°58·8'	2°31·1'W	T	149
Lynedraw	Cumbr	NY2439	54°44·7'	3°10·4'W	X	89,90
Lynefield Ho	Northum	NZ3089	55°11·9'	1°31·3'W	X	81
Lynefoot	Cumbr	NY3665	54°58·8'	2°59·6'W	X	85
Lynegar	Highld	ND2257	58°29·9'	3°19·8'W	X	11,12
Lyneham	Devon	SX8579	50°36·2'	3°37·1'W	X	191
Lyneham	Oxon	SP2720	51°52·9'	1°36·1'W	T	163
Lyneham	Wilts	SU0278	51°30·3'	1°57·9'W	T	173
Lyneham Airfield	Wilts	SU0078	51°30·3'	1°59·6'W	X	173
Lyneham Barrow	Oxon	SP2921	51°53·4'	1°34·3'W	A	164
Lyneham Ho	Devon	SX5753	50°21·8'	4°0·3'W	A	202
Lyne Hill	Staffs	SJ9212	52°42·6'	2°6·7'W	X	127
Lyne Ho	Surrey	TQ1938	51°8·0'	0°17·6'W	X	187
Lyneholm	D & G	NY2791	55°12·7'	3°8·4'W	X	79
Lyneholme	Cumbr	NY5172	55°2·7'	2°45·6'W	X	86
Lyneholmeford	Cumbr	NY5172	55°2·7'	2°45·6'W	X	86
Lyne House Fm	Notts	SK7893	53°25·9'	0°49·1'W	FM	112
Lynemore	Aberd	NJ3408	57°9·7'	3°5·0'W	X	37
Lynemore	Highld	NH7633	57°22·5'	4°3·3'W	X	27
Lynemore	Highld	NH9239	57°26·0'	3°47·5'W	X	27
Lynemore	Highld	NJ0624	57°18·1'	3°33·1'W	X	36
Lynemore	Moray	NJ1438	57°25·7'	3°25·5'W	X	28
Lynemore	Moray	NJ2935	57°24·3'	3°10·4'W	X	28
Lynemore	Pth & Kin	NN8836	56°30·4'	3°48·7'W	X	52

Lynemouth	Northum	NZ2991	55°13·0'	1°32·2'W	T	81
Lyne of Carron	Moray	NJ2239	57°26·3'	3°17·5'W	X	28
Lyne of Gorthleck	Highld	NH5320	57°15·1'	4°25·7'W	T	26,35
Lyne of Knockando	Moray	NJ1745	57°29·5'	3°22·6'W	X	28
Lyne of Linton	Aberd	NJ7008	57°10·0'	2°29·3'W	X	38
Lyne of Skene	Aberd	NJ7610	57°11·1'	2°23·4'W	T	38
Lyne of Urchany	Highld	NH8748	57°30·7'	3°52·7'W	X	27
Lyne Place Manor	Surrey	TQ0066	51°23·3'	0°33·4'W	X	176
Lynes	Cumbr	NY5473	55°3·2'	2°42·8'W	X	86
Lynes	Moray	NJ2144	57°29·0'	3°18·6'W	X	28
Lynesack	Durham	NZ0926	54°38·0'	1°51·2'W	X	92
Lyne Sands	Northum	NZ3090	55°12·4'	1°31·3'W	X	81
Lynes Barn Fm	Glos	SP0627	51°56·7'	1°54·4'W	FM	163
Lyness	Orkney	ND3094	58°49·9'	3°12·3'W	T	7
Ly Ness	Orkney	ND3194	58°49·9'	3°11·2'W	X	7
Lyne Station	Scot Bord	NT2139	55°38·5'	3°14·9'W	T	73
Lynethobair	Highld	NH8948	57°30·8'	3°50·7'W	X	27
Lyne Water	Scot Bord	NT1257	55°48·2'	3°23·8'W	W	65,72
Lyne Water	Scot Bord	NT1353	55°46·0'	3°22·8'W	W	65,72
Lyn Fawr	Rho Cyn Taf	SN9103	51°43·1'	3°34·3'W	W	170
Lynford	Norf	TL8191	52°29·4'	0°40·4'E	T	144
Lynford Arboretum	Norf	TL8293	52°30·5'	0°41·3'E	X	144
Lynford Hall	Norf	TL8194	52°31·1'	0°40·5'E	X	144
Lynford House Fm	Cambs	TL4892	52°30·6'	0°11·3'E	FM	143
Lynford Point	Norf	TL8389	52°28·3'	0°42·1'E	X	144
Lyng	Norf	TG0617	52°42·9'	1°3·4'E	T	133
Lyng	Somer	ST3228	51°3·1'	2°57·8'W	T	193
Lyngarrie	Highld	NJ0216	57°13·7'	3°36·9'W	X	36
Lyngate	Norf	TG2731	52°49·9'	1°22·6'E	T	133
Lyngate	Norf	TG3026	52°47·2'	1°25·1'E	T	133,134
Lyng Fm	Norf	TF7341	52°56·5'	0°34·9'E	FM	132
Lyng Fm	Norf	TM0295	52°31·1'	0°59·0'E	FM	144
Lyngford	Somer	ST2325	51°1·4'	3°5·5'W	T	193
Lyngham Vallet	Heref	SO4566	52°17·6'	2°48·0'W	X	137,138,148
Lyng Moor	Somer	ST3228	51°3·1'	2°57·8'W	X	193
Lyngrove Fm	Wilts	SO0092	51°37·8'	1°59·6'W	FM	163,173
Lynhales	Heref	SO3255	52°11·6'	2°59·3'W	X	148
Lynhams	E Yorks	TA2070	54°6·9'	0°9·4'W	X	101
Lynher	Corn	SX2775	50°33·2'	4°26·2'W	X	201
Lynher River or St Germans	Corn	SX3955	50°22·6'	4°15·5'W	W	201
Lynmore	Highld	NJ0331	57°21·8'	3°36·3'W	X	27,36
Lynmouth	Devon	SS7249	51°13·8'	3°49·6'W	T	180
Lynmouth Bay	Devon	SS7350	51°14·3'	3°48·8'W	W	180
Lynn	Orkney	HY4509	58°58·1'	2°56·9'W	X	6,7
Lynn	Staffs	SK0804	52°38·3'	1°52·5'W	T	139
Lynn	Wrekin	SJ7815	52°44·2'	2°19·1'W	T	127
Lynn Channel		TF5925	52°48·2'	0°21·9'E	W	131
Lynncot	Pth & Kin	NO0503	56°12·9'	3°31·5'W	X	58
Lynn Deeps		TF5946	52°59·5'	0°22·5'E	W	131
Lynn Deeps		TF6348	53°0·5'	0°26·2'E	W	132
Lynnfield	Orkney	HY4704	58°55·5'	2°54·7'W	X	6,7
Lynn Fm	Fife	NT0792	56°7·0'	3°29·3'W	FM	58
Lynn Fm	I of W	SZ5489	50°42·1'	1°13·7'W	FM	196
Lynn Glen	N Ayr	NS2848	55°42·0'	4°43·8'W	X	63
Lynnholm	Northum	NU0302	55°19·0'	1°56·7'W	X	81
Lynnhouse Fm	Ches	SJ8058	53°7·4'	2°17·5'W	FM	118
Lynn Lane Ho	Staffs	SK0904	52°38·3'	1°51·6'W	X	139
Lynn of Lorn	Arg & Bt	NM8741	56°31·0'	5°27·3'W	W	49
Lynnroad Plantation	Norf	TF6826	52°48·5'	0°30·0'E	F	132
Lynn's Hall	Suff	TL9343	52°3·3'	0°49·3'E	X	155
Lynnshield	Northum	NY6961	54°56·8'	2°28·6'W	X	86,87
Lynnwood	Cumbr	NY0210	54°28·8'	3°30·3'W	X	89
Lynn Wood	Northnts	SP9797	52°34·0'	0°33·7'W	F	141
Lynnwood	Scot Bord	NT4913	55°24·7'	2°47·9'W	T	79
Lynsore Bottom	Kent	TR1649	51°12·2'	1°5·9'E	T	179,189
Lynsore Court	Kent	TR1648	51°11·6'	1°5·9'E	X	179,189
Lynsted	Kent	TQ9460	51°18·6'	0°47·4'E	T	178
Lynsted Court	Kent	TQ9460	51°18·6'	0°47·4'E	A	178
Lynsted Park	Kent	TQ9459	51°18·0'	0°47·4'E	X	178
Lynsters	Herts	TQ0392	51°37·3'	0°30·3'W	X	176
Lynstock	Highld	NJ0120	57°15·9'	3°38·0'W	X	36
Lynstone	Corn	SS2005	50°49·2'	4°33·0'W	T	190
Lynt Br	Oxon	SU2198	51°41·1'	1°41·4'W	X	163
Lyntelloch	Highld	NJ1122	57°17·1'	3°28·1'W	X	36
Lynton	Devon	SS7149	51°13·8'	3°50·5'W	T	180
Lynton Cross	Devon	SS5343	51°10·3'	4°5·8'W	X	180
Lynturk	Aberd	NJ5912	57°12·1'	2°40·3'W	X	37
Lynup Hill	Northum	NZ0375	55°4·4'	1°56·8'W	X	87
Lynwick	W Susx	TQ0733	51°5·4'	0°27·9'W	X	187
Lynwilg	Highld	NH8710	57°10·3'	3°51·7'W	T	35,36
Lynwode Wood	Lincs	TF1285	53°21·2'	0°18·6'W	F	121
Lynworth	Glos	SO9623	51°54·6'	2°3·1'W	T	163
Lynxcross	E Renf	NS5157	55°47·3'	4°22·1'W	X	64
Lyons	Sund	NZ3646	54°48·7'	1°26·0'W	T	88
Lyon's Fm	Sefton	SD4002	53°30·9'	2°53·9'W	FM	108
Lyon's Fm	Suff	TM4376	52°19·9'	1°34·4'E	FM	156
Lyon's Fm	W Susx	TQ0031	51°4·4'	0°34·0'W	FM	186
Lyon's Gate	Dorset	ST6605	50°50·8'	2°28·6'W	T	194
Lyon's Green	Norf	TF9111	52°40·0'	0°49·9'E	T	132
Lyons Hall	Essex	TL7315	51°48·6'	0°31·0'E	T	167
Lyons Hall	Essex	TL7725	51°53·9'	0°34·8'E	X	167
Lyonshall	Heref	SO3355	52°11·6'	2°58·4'W	T	148,149
Lyonshall Park Wood	Heref	SO3256	52°12·1'	2°59·3'W	F	148
Lyonshall Wood	Essex	TL7314	51°48·1'	0°30·9'E	F	167
Lyonshield	N Ayr	NS3753	55°44·8'	4°35·4'W	X	63
Lyon's Hill Fm	Dorset	ST6505	50°50·8'	2°29·4'W	FM	194
Lyons, The	Staffs	SO8186	52°28·0'	2°16·4'W	X	138
Lyonston	S Ayr	NS3010	55°21·5'	4°40·5'W	X	70
Lyons Wood	Shrops	SJ5025	52°49·5'	2°44·1'W	X	126
Lyoth Common	E Susx	TQ3523	50°59·7'	0°4·2'W	X	198
Lype Common	Somer	SS9537	51°7·6'	3°29·6'W	X	181
Lype Fms	Wilts	ST9788	51°35·7'	2°2·2'W	FM	173
Lype Hill	Somer	SS9437	51°7·6'	3°30·5'W	H	181
Lypiatt	Glos	SO9308	51°46·5'	2°5·7'W	T	163
Lypiatt Park	Glos	SO8805	51°44·8'	2°10·0'W	X	162
Lyppard Grange	Worcs	SO8755	52°11·8'	2°11·0'W	X	150
Lyrabus	Arg & Bt	NR2964	55°47·9'	6°19·0'W	X	60
Lyra Skerry	Shetld	HU1461	60°20·2'	1°44·3'W	X	3

Lyrawa Bay	Orkney	ND2998	58°52·1′	3°13·4′W	W	6,7
Lyrawa Burn	Orkney	ND2798	58°52·1′	3°15·5′W	W	6,7
Lyrawa Hill	Orkney	ND2899	58°52·6′	3°14·4′W	X	6,7
Lyrawall	Orkney	ND4392	58°49·0′	2°58·7′W	X	7
Lyre Cliff	Orkney	HY6036	59°12·8′	2°41·5′W	X	5
Lyre Geo	Orkney	HY2114	59°0·6′	3°22·0′W	X	6
Lyre Geo	Orkney	HY2602	58°54·2′	3°16·6′W	X	6,7
Lyrie Geo	Orkney	ND2096	58°50·9′	3°22·7′W	X	7
Lyron	Orkney	HY3819	59°3·5′	3°4·4′W	X	6
Lyscombe Bottom	Dorset	ST7301	50°48·7′	2°22·6′W	X	194
Lyscombe Fm	Dorset	ST7301	50°48·7′	2°22·6′W	FM	194
Lyscombe Hill	Dorset	ST7302	50°49·2′	2°22·6′W	X	194
Lysdon Fm	Northum	NZ3077	55°5·4′	1°31·4′W	FM	88
Lyshwell Fm	Devon	SS8330	51°3·7′	3°39·8′W	FM	181
Lyss Place	Hants	SU7628	51°3·0′	0°54·6′W	X	186,197
Lyston Ho	Heref	SO4928	51°57·1′	2°44·1′W	X	149
Lysways Hall	Staffs	SK0913	52°43·1′	1°51·6′W	X	128
Lytchett Bay	Dorset	SY9791	50°43·3′	2°2·2′W	W	195
Lytchett Heath	Dorset	SY9695	50°45·5′	2°3·0′W	X	195
Lytchett Ho	Dorset	SY9396	50°46·0′	2°5·6′W	X	195
Lytchett Matravers	Dorset	SY9495	50°45·5′	2°4·7′W	T	195
Lytchett Minster	Dorset	SY9592	50°43·9′	2°3·9′W	T	195
Lyte's Cary	Somer	ST5326	51°2·1′	2°39·8′W	A	183
Lyth	Highld	ND2763	58°33·2′	3°14·8′W	X	11,12
Lytham	Lancs	SD3627	53°44·4′	2°58·7′W	T	102
Lytham Hall	Lancs	SD3527	53°44·4′	2°58·7′W	A	102
Lytham Moss	Lancs	SD3430	53°46·0′	2°59·7′W	X	102
Lytham St Anne's	Lancs	SD3327	53°44·4′	3°0·5′W	T	102
Lythanger	Hants	SU7530	51°4·1′	0°55·4′W	X	186
Lythbank	Shrops	SJ4607	52°39·7′	2°47·5′W	T	126
Lythe	Lancs	SD6663	54°4·0′	2°30·8′W	X	98
Lythe	N Yks	NZ8413	54°30·6′	0°41·7′W	X	94
Lythe	Orkney	HY2502	58°54·2′	3°17·6′W	X	6,7
Lythe	Orkney	ND4486	58°45·7′	2°57·6′W	X	7
Lythe Brow	Lancs	SD5262	54°3·3′	2°43·6′W	X	97
Lythecourt	Devon	SS9415	50°55·7′	3°30·1′W	X	181
Lythe Fell	Lancs	SD6762	54°3·4′	2°29·8′W	X	98
Lythe Fm	Hants	SU7224	51°0·9′	0°58·0′W	FM	197
Lythe Hill	Surrey	SU9232	51°5·0′	0°40·8′W	X	186
Lythehill Ho	Surrey	SU9132	51°5·0′	0°41·7′W	X	186
Lythe Ho	N Yks	SE0162	54°3·5′	1°58·7′W	X	98
Lythe-Land	Devon	SS8811	50°53·5′	3°35·2′W	X	192
Lythel's Fm	Cambs	TL5366	52°16·5′	0°15·0′E	FM	154
Lythes	Orkney	ND2990	58°47·8′	3°13·2′W	X	7
Lythes	Orkney	ND4589	58°47·4′	2°56·6′W	T	7
Lytheside Fm	Cumbr	NY7403	54°25·6′	2°23·6′W	FM	91
Lyth Hill Country Park	Shrops	SJ4606	52°39·2′	2°47·5′W	X	126
Lythmore	Highld	ND0566	58°34·6′	3°37·5′W	X	11,12
Lythmore Strath	Highld	ND0465	58°34·0′	3°38·5′W	X	11,12
Lyth, The	Shrops	SJ4133	52°53·7′	2°52·2′W	X	126
Lyth Valley	Cumbr	SD4688	54°17·3′	2°49·4′W	X	97
Lythwell	Shrops	SJ3324	52°48·8′	2°59·2′W	X	126
Lythwood Fm	Shrops	SJ4708	52°40·3′	2°46·6′W	FM	126
Lythwood Hall	Shrops	SJ4708	52°40·3′	2°46·6′W	X	126
Lythwood View	Shrops	SJ4607	52°39·7′	2°47·5′W	X	126
Lyttel Hall	Surrey	TQ3149	51°13·7′	0°7·0′W	X	187
Lyulph's Tower	Cumbr	NY4020	54°34·5′	2°55·3′W	A	90
Lyveden Fm	Northnts	TL0795	52°32·8′	0°24·9′W	FM	142
Lyveden New Bield	Northnts	SP9885	52°27·5′	0°33·1′W	A	141
Lyveden Old Bield	Northnts	SP9885	52°27·5′	0°33·1′W	X	141
Lyvennet Beck	Cumbr	NY6213	54°30·9′	2°34·8′W	W	91
Lyvers Ocle	Heref	SO5746	52°6·9′	2°37·3′W	X	149
Lyzzick Hall (Hotel)	Cumbr	NY2526	54°37·7′	3°9·3′W	X	89,90

M

Maadle Swankie	Shetld	HU3286	60°33·6′	1°24·5′W	W	1,3
Maa Loch	Shetld	HU2960	60°19·6′	1°28·0′W	W	3
Maam	Arg & Bt	NN1212	56°16·1′	5°1·7′W	X	50,56
Maamie of Garth	Shetld	HU2156	60°17·5′	1°36·7′W	W	3
Maa Ness	Shetld	HU3938	60°7·7′	1°17·4′W	X	4
Maari	N Eil	NF8672	57°38·0′	7°15·2′W	H	18
Maatruf	Shetld	HU5036	60°6·6′	1°5·5′W	X	4
Maa Water	Shetld	HU3755	60°16·9′	1°19·4′W	W	3
Mabbin Crag	Cumbr	NY5602	54°24·9′	2°40·3′W	H	90
Mabbin Hall	Cumbr	SD5084	54°15·2′	2°45·6′W	X	97
Mabb's Fm	Essex	TL7016	51°49·2′	0°28·4′E	FM	167
Mabe Burnthouse	Corn	SW7634	50°10·1′	5°7·8′W	T	204
Mabenbank	S Lanak	NT1046	55°42·2′	3°25·5′W	X	72
Mabesgate	Pemb	SM8207	51°43·4′	5°9·0′W	X	157
Mabie Forest	D & G	NX9370	55°1·0′	3°40·0′W	F	84
Mabie Forest	D & G	NY0371	55°1·7′	3°30·6′W	F	84
Mabie Ho	D & G	NX9470	55°1·0′	3°39·0′W	X	84
Mabledon	Kent	TQ5744	51°10·6′	0°15·2′E	T	188
Mabledon Fm	Kent	TQ5844	51°10·6′	0°16·0′E	FM	188
Mablethorpe	Lincs	TF5085	53°20·7′	0°15·6′E	T	122
Mablethorpe Hall	Lincs	TF4984	53°20·1′	0°14·7′E	X	122
Mabonlaw	Scot Bord	NT4515	55°25·8′	2°51·7′W	X	79
Mabws	Pemb	SM8730	51°55·9′	5°5·5′W	X	157
Mabws Hall	Cered	SN5668	52°17·7′	4°6·3′W	X	135
Macaroni Downs Fm	Glos	SP1807	51°45·9′	1°44·0′W	FM	163
Macaroni Fm	Glos	SP1805	51°44·8′	1°44·0′W	FM	163
Macaroni Wood	Glos	SP1804	51°44·3′	1°44·0′W	F	163
Macaterick	E Ayr	NX4390	55°11·0′	4°27·5′W	H	77
Macawston Fm	S Ayr	NS2104	55°18·1′	4°48·8′W	FM	76
Macbeth's Cairn	Aberd	NJ5705	57°8·3′	2°42·2′W	A	37
Macbeth's Castle	Scot Bord	NT2033	55°35·3′	3°15·7′W	H	73
Macbeth's Hillock	Moray	NH9656	57°35·2′	3°43·9′W	X	27
Macbeth's Law	Pth & Kin	NO2034	56°29·7′	3°17·5′W	A	53
Macbeth's Stone	Pth & Kin	NO2843	56°34·7′	3°9·9′W	A	53
Macbiehill	Scot Bord	NT1851	55°45·0′	3°17·9′W	X	65,66,72
Maccallum	E Ayr	NX4392	55°12·1′	4°27·6′W	H	77
Macclesfield	Ches	SJ9173	53°15·5′	2°7·7′W	T	118
Macclesfield Canal	Ches	SJ9168	53°12·8′	2°7·7′W	W	118
Macclesfield Canal	Ches	SJ9483	53°20·9′	2°5·0′W	W	109
Macclesfield Forest	Ches	SJ9772	53°14·9′	2°2·3′W	T	118
Mac Coitir's Cave	Highld	NG4943	57°24·7′	6°10·3′W	X	23
Macduff	Aberd	NJ7064	57°40·2′	2°29·7′W	T	29
Macduff's Castle	Fife	NT3497	56°9·9′	3°3·3′W	A	59
Macduff's Cross	Fife	NO2216	56°20·1′	3°15·3′W	A	58
Macedonia	Fife	NO2501	56°12·0′	3°12·1′W	T	59
Mace Fm	Brom	TQ4560	51°19·5′	0°5·3′E	FM	177,188
Mace Green	Suff	TM1041	52°1·9′	1°4·1′E	T	155,169
Mace Hill	Norf	TG1442	52°56·2′	1°11·5′E	X	133
Maceybank	Cumbr	NY4244	54°47·5′	2°53·7′W	X	85
Macgregor's Leap	Pth & Kin	NN7247	56°36·1′	4°4·7′W	X	51,52
Machair	N Eil	NF8877	57°40·7′	7°13·6′W	X	18
Machair Leathann	N Eil	NF8276	57°40·0′	7°19·5′W	X	18
Machair Mhór	Arg & Bt	NM1756	56°36·9′	6°36·3′W	X	46
Machair Robach	N Eil	NF8676	57°40·1′	7°15·5′W	X	18
Machan	S Lanak	NS7650	55°43·9′	3°58·0′W	T	64
Machany	Pth & Kin	NN9015	56°19·1′	3°46·3′W	X	58
Machany Water	Pth & Kin	NN8815	56°19·1′	3°48·2′W	W	58
Machar Burn	Stir	NS5485	56°2·4′	4°20·2′W	W	57
Macharioch	Arg & Bt	NR7309	55°19·6′	5°34·3′W	X	68
Macharioch Bay	Arg & Bt	NR7308	55°19·1′	5°34·2′W	W	68
Macharmuir	Aberd	NJ9929	57°21·3′	2°0·5′W	X	38
Macharshaugh	Aberd	NJ4818	57°15·2′	2°51·3′W	X	37
Machars, The	D & G	NX3453	54°50·9′	4°34·7′W	X	82
Machars, The	D & G	NX3953	54°51·0′	4°30·0′W	X	83
Machattie's Cairn	Moray	NJ3547	57°30·8′	3°4·6′W	X	28
Machen	Caer	ST2189	51°35·9′	3°8·0′W	T	171
Machermore	D & G	NX2454	54°51·2′	4°44·1′W	X	82
Machermore Castle	D & G	NX4164	54°57·0′	4°28·5′W	X	83
Macherquhat	S Ayr	NX1184	55°7·1′	4°57·4′W	X	76
Macher Stewart	D & G	NX4146	54°47·3′	4°27·9′W	X	83
Machine Fm	Worcs	SO9947	52°7·5′	2°0·5′W	FM	150
Machir Bay	Arg & Bt	NR1962	55°46·4′	6°28·4′W	W	60
Machno Falls	Conwy	SH8053	53°3·9′	3°47·0′W	W	116
Macholws	Carm	SN4423	51°53·3′	4°15·6′W	X	159
Machribeg	Arg & Bt	NR6808	55°18·9′	5°39·0′W	X	68
Machrie	Arg & Bt	NR2063	55°47·0′	6°27·5′W	X	60
Machrie	N Ayr	NR8934	55°33·5′	5°20·3′W	T	68,69
Machrie Bay	N Ayr	NR8834	55°33·5′	5°21·3′W	W	68,69
Machrie Burn	N Ayr	NR9034	55°33·5′	5°19·4′W	W	68,69
Machrie Fm	N Ayr	NR9033	55°33·0′	5°19·3′W	FM	68,69
Machrie Hotel	Arg & Bt	NR3249	55°39·9′	6°15·3′W	X	60
Machrie River	Arg & Bt	NR3250	55°40·4′	6°15·3′W	W	60
Machrie Water	N Ayr	NR9233	55°33·0′	5°17·4′W	W	68,69
Machriewater Foot	N Ayr	NR8933	55°33·0′	5°20·3′W	X	68,69
Machrihanish	Arg & Bt	NR6320	55°25·3′	5°44·3′W	T	68
Machrihanish Bay	Arg & Bt	NR6323	55°26·9′	5°44·4′W	W	68
Machrihanish Water	Arg & Bt	NR6720	55°25·4′	5°40·5′W	W	68
Machrimore	Arg & Bt	NR6908	55°19·0′	5°38·0′W	X	68
Machrins	Arg & Bt	NR3693	56°3·7′	6°14·0′W	X	61
Machroes	Gwyn	SH3126	52°48·5′	4°30·0′W	T	123
Machuim	Pth & Kin	NN6740	56°32·3′	4°9·3′W	X	51
Machynlleth	Powys	SH7400	52°35·2′	3°51·2′W	T	135
Machynys	Carm	SS5198	51°39·9′	4°8·9′W	T	159
Mac is Màthair	Highld	NH0687	57°50·1′	5°15·6′W	H	19
Mackailston	S Ayr	NS3207	55°20·0′	4°38·5′W	X	70,76
Mackay's Court Fm	Medway	TQ8275	51°26·9′	0°37·5′E	FM	178
Mackay's Geo	Orkney	ND2489	58°47·2′	3°18·4′W	X	7
Mackeanston	Stir	NN6800	56°10·7′	4°7·1′W	X	57
Mackenzie's Cairn	Highld	NH2311	57°9·6′	4°55·1′W	X	34
Mackerel Cove	Torbay	SX9269	50°30·9′	3°31·0′W	W	202
Mackerel's Common	W Susx	TQ0128	51°2·8′	0°33·2′W	T	186,197
Mackerel Sike	D & G	NY0788	55°10·9′	3°27·2′W	W	78
Mackerye End	Herts	TL1515	51°49·5′	0°19·5′W	T	166
Mackham	Devon	ST1509	50°52·7′	3°12·1′W	T	192,193
Mackie Rocks	E Loth	NT3874	55°57·6′	2°59·1′W	X	66
Mackie's Mill	Fife	NT3097	56°9·9′	3°7·2′W	X	59
Mackilston	D & G	NX6286	55°9·2′	4°9·5′W	X	77
Mackilston Hill	D & G	NX6287	55°9·7′	4°9·5′W	H	77
Mackinder Fm	Lincs	TF3110	52°40·5′	0°3·3′W	FM	131,142
Mackinnon's Cave	Arg & Bt	NM4332	56°24·9′	6°9·6′W	X	48
Macklands	Medway	TQ8266	51°22·1′	0°37·3′E	X	178
Mackley Fm	Kent	TQ9426	51°0·3′	0°46·3′E	FM	189
Mackley Hill	Oxon	SP4430	51°58·2′	1°21·2′W	X	151
Mackley Ho	Derby	SK1733	52°53·9′	1°44·4′W	X	128
Mackley's Fm	Notts	SK6732	52°53·1′	0°59·9′W	FM	129
Mackney	Oxon	SU5789	51°36·0′	1°10·2′W	T	174
Mackney Court Fm	Oxon	SU5790	51°36·6′	1°10·2′W	FM	164,174
Mackrieston	Stir	NN6700	56°10·7′	4°8·1′W	X	57
Mackside	Scot Bord	NT6010	55°23·2′	2°37·5′W	T	80
Macks Mill	Scot Bord	NT6544	55°41·5′	2°33·0′W	X	74
Mackstead	Aberd	NJ7326	57°19·7′	2°26·4′W	X	38
Mackwhinny Park	D & G	NY1367	54°59·7′	3°21·2′W	X	85
Mackwith	Carm	SN4339	52°1·9′	4°16·9′W	X	146
Mackworth	C of Derb	SK3236	52°55·5′	1°31·0′W	T	128
Mackworth	Derby	SK3137	52°56·0′	1°31·9′W	T	128
Mackworth Brook	Derby	SK3237	52°56·0′	1°31·0′W	W	128
Mackworth Fields	Derby	SK3036	52°55·5′	1°32·8′W	X	128
Maclachrieston	S Ayr	NX2091	55°11·1′	4°49·2′W	X	76
MacLean' Cross	Arg & Bt	NM2824	56°20·1′	6°23·6′W	A	48
Maclean's Nose	Highld	NM5361	56°40·8′	6°1·5′W	X	47
Maclean's Skull Cave	Arg & Bt	NR6497	56°6·7′	5°47·3′W	X	55,61
Maclean's Towel or Tubhailt Mhic'ic Eoghain	Highld	NM9964	56°43·7′	5°16·7′W	W	40
Macleod's Maidens	Highld	NG2436	57°20·1′	6°34·7′W	X	23
Macleod's Table North or Healabhal Mhor	Highld	NG2144	57°24·3′	6°38·3′W	H	23
Macleod's Table South or Halabhal Bheag	Highld	NG2242	57°23·3′	6°37·1′W	H	23
Macmarridge	Pth & Kin	NO0546	56°36·0′	3°32·4′W	X	52,53
Macmaw	D & G	NY1794	55°14·2′	3°17·9′W	X	79
Macmaw Edge	D & G	NY1897	55°15·9′	3°17·0′W	H	79
Macmaw Hill	D & G	NY1795	55°14·8′	3°17·9′W	H	79
Macmerry	E Loth	NT4372	55°56·5′	2°54·3′W	T	66
Macnairston	S Ayr	NS3719	55°26·5′	4°34·2′W	X	70
Macnoshton	E Ayr	NS4319	55°26·6′	4°28·5′W	X	70
Macphee's Hill	N Eil	NL5684	56°49·5′	7°37·9′W	H	31
MacQuarrie's Rock	Arg & Bt	NM4537	56°27·6′	6°7·9′W	X	47,48
Macqueston	D & G	NX7794	55°13·7′	3°55·6′W	X	78
Macquittiston	E Ayr	NS4619	55°26·7′	4°25·6′W	X	70
Macrindlestone	S Ayr	NX2199	55°15·4′	4°48·6′W	X	76
Macringan's Point	Arg & Bt	NR7521	55°26·1′	5°33·0′W	X	68,69
Macritch Hill	Angus	NO2660	56°43·8′	3°12·1′W	H	44
Macrule Hill	Scot Bord	NT0917	55°26·6′	3°25·9′W	H	78
Macterry	Aberd	NJ7842	57°28·3′	2°21·5′W	X	29,30
Macterry	Aberd	NJ8524	57°18·6′	2°14·5′W	X	38
Madacombe	Somer	SS8243	51°10·7′	3°40·9′W	X	181
Madadh Beag	N Eil	NF9568	57°36·2′	7°5·9′W	X	18
Madadh Gruamach	N Eil	NF9566	57°35·1′	7°5·8′W	X	18
Madadh Lounie	N Ayr	NR9248	55°41·1′	5°18·1′W	X	62,69
Madadh Mór	N Eil	NF9567	57°35·7′	7°5·8′W	X	18
Madagan Mòineach	Arg & Bt	NN3948	56°36·0′	4°36·9′W	X	50
Mad Allen's Hole	Ches	SJ5053	53°4·6′	2°44·4′W	X	117
Madame Tussaud's	C of West	TQ2882	51°31·6′	0°8·9′W	X	176
Madam Law	Northum	NT8626	55°31·9′	2°12·9′W	H	74
Madam's Court	Kent	TQ8956	51°16·5′	0°43·0′E	X	178
Madam's End Fm	Glos	SO7713	51°49·1′	2°19·6′W	FM	162
Madamses Fm	E Susx	TQ7823	50°59·0′	0°32·5′E	FM	199
Madam's Fm	Ches	SJ6252	53°4·1′	2°33·6′W	FM	118
Madam's Fm	W Susx	SU8825	51°1·3′	0°44·3′W	FM	186,197
Madam's Hill	Worcs	SO9561	52°15·1′	2°4·0′W	X	150
Mad Bay	Pemb	SM7305	51°42·1′	5°16·7′W	W	157
Mad Bess Wood	Hill	TQ0789	51°35·6′	0°26·9′W	F	176
Madbrain Sands	Somer	SS9846	51°12·5′	3°27·2′W	X	181
Mad Bridge	Cambs	TL1472	52°20·3′	0°19·2′W	X	153
Mad Brook	Shrops	SJ7202	52°37·1′	2°24·4′W	W	127
Mad Brook	Shrops	SO7177	52°23·7′	2°25·2′W	W	138
Madbrook Fm	Wilts	ST8649	51°14·6′	2°11·6′W	FM	183
Mad Burn	W Loth	NS9269	55°54·4′	3°43·2′W	W	65
Maddacleave Wood	Devon	SX4569	50°30·3′	4°10·8′W	F	201
Maddaford	Devon	SX5494	50°43·9′	4°3·8′W	FM	191
Maddasdale	N Eil	NF7309	57°3·6′	7°23·2′W	X	31
Madderly Moor	Corn	SX1059	50°24·2′	4°40·1′W	X	200
Madders Hill	Cambs	TL1670	52°19·2′	0°17·5′W	X	153
Madderty	Pth & Kin	NN9521	56°22·4′	3°41·6′W	T	52,53,58
Maddington	Wilts	SU0644	51°11·9′	1°54·5′W	X	184
Maddington Down	Wilts	SU0343	51°11·4′	1°57·0′W	X	184
Maddington Fm	Wilts	SU0444	51°11·9′	1°56·2′W	FM	184
Maddiston	Falk	NS9476	55°58·2′	3°41·5′W	T	65
Maddle Brook	Heref	SO3844	52°5·7′	2°53·9′W	W	148,149,161
Maddle Brook	Heref	SO3845	52°6·2′	2°53·9′W	W	148,149
Maddle Fm	W Berks	SU3082	51°32·4′	1°33·7′W	FM	174
Maddocks	St Hel	SD5002	53°31·0′	2°44·8′W	X	108
Maddock's Hill	Wrekin	SJ6408	52°40·4′	2°31·5′W	X	127
Maddoms Wood	E Susx	TQ7519	50°56·9′	0°29·9′E	F	199
Maddomswood Fm	E Susx	TQ7619	50°56·8′	0°30·7′E	FM	199
Maddox Fm	Wigan	SD5301	53°30·5′	2°42·1′W	FM	108
Maddoxford Fm	Hants	SU5114	50°55·6′	1°16·1′W	FM	196
Maddox Moor	Pemb	SM9611	51°45·9′	4°57·0′W	T	157,158
Maddox's Coppice	Shrops	SJ3803	52°37·5′	2°54·6′W	F	126
Maddy House Fm	N Yks	NZ6708	54°28·0′	0°57·6′W	FM	94
Maddy Moss	Clackm	NN9201	56°11·6′	3°44·0′W	X	58
Madehurst	W Susx	SU9810	50°53·1′	0°36·0′W	T	197
Madeley	Staffs	SJ7744	52°59·8′	2°20·2′W	T	118
Madeley	Wrekin	SJ6904	52°38·2′	2°27·1′W	T	127
Madeley Court	Wrekin	SJ6905	52°38·8′	2°27·1′W	A	127
Madeley Fm	Staffs	SK0536	52°55·5′	1°55·1′W	FM	128
Madeley Heath	Staffs	SJ7845	53°0·4′	2°19·3′W	T	118
Madeley Heath	Worcs	SO9577	52°23·7′	2°4·0′W	T	139
Madeley Manor	Staffs	SJ7745	53°0·3′	2°20·2′W	X	118
Madeleypark	Staffs	SK0638	52°56·6′	1°54·2′W	X	128
Madeley Park Wood	Staffs	SJ7841	52°58·2′	2°19·3′W	F	118
Madeleywood	Shrops	SJ6703	52°37·7′	2°28·9′W	T	127
Maders	Corn	SX3471	50°31·2′	4°20·1′W	T	201
Madford	Devon	ST1411	50°53·8′	3°13·0′W	T	192,193
Madford River	Devon	ST1411	50°53·8′	3°13·0′W	W	192,193
Madgegill	Cumbr	SD5094	54°20·6′	2°45·7′W	X	97
Madge Hill	Derby	SK2149	53°2·5′	1°40·8′W	H	119
Madge Hill Fm	N Yks	SE1866	54°5·6′	1°43·1′W	FM	99
Madgehole	Surrey	TQ0543	51°10·8′	0°29·5′W	X	187
Mad Geo	Orkney	HY4954	59°22·4′	2°53·4′W	X	5
Madge's Batts	Northum	NU1240	55°39·5′	1°48·1′W	X	75
Madge's Head	Shetld	HU4668	60°23·9′	1°9·4′W	X	2,3
Madgett Hill	Glos	SO5501	51°42·6′	2°38·7′W	X	162
Madgetts Fm	Glos	SO5500	51°42·1′	2°38·7′W	FM	162
Madhouse Plantn	Norf	TL9194	52°30·8′	0°49·3′E	F	144
Madingley	Cambs	TL3960	52°13·5′	0°2·5′E	T	154
Madjeston	Dorset	ST8025	51°1·7′	2°16·7′W	T	183
Madley	Heref	SO4138	52°2·5′	2°51·2′W	T	149,161
Madmarston Hill	Oxon	SP3838	52°2·6′	1°26·4′W	X	151
Madmarston Hill (Fort)	Oxon	SP3838	52°2·6′	1°26·4′W	A	151
Madoc's Haven	Pemb	SM8517	51°48·9′	5°6·8′W	W	157
Madras House	Orkney	HY3118	59°2·9′	3°11·7′W	X	6
Madresfield	Worcs	SO8047	52°7·5′	2°17·1′W	T	150
Madresfield Court	Worcs	SO8047	52°7·5′	2°17·1′W	A	150
Madrigil	Highld	NG4254	57°30·4′	6°18·0′W	X	23
Madrisa Fm	Scot Bord	NT2052	55°45·5′	3°16·1′W	FM	66,73
Madron	Corn	SW4531	50°7·7′	5°33·7′W	T	203
Madron Well	Corn	SW4432	50°8·2′	5°34·6′W	A	203
Madryn	Gwyn	SH6673	53°14·5′	4°0·1′W	X	115
Madryn Castle	Gwyn	SH2836	52°53·9′	4°33·0′W	X	123
Madryn-isaf	Gwyn	SH2837	52°54·4′	4°33·1′W	X	123
Mad Wharf	Sefton	SD2608	53°34·0′	3°6·6′W	X	108
Madwoman's Stones	Derby	SK1388	53°23·6′	1°47·9′W	X	110
Madworthy	Devon	SX4598	50°45·9′	4°11·5′W	X	190
Maea Water	Shetld	HU5298	60°40·0′	1°2·4′W	W	1
Mae Banks	Orkney	HY4830	59°9·5′	2°54·1′W	X	5,6
Maelcombe Ho	Devon	SX7936	50°12·9′	3°41·4′W	X	202
Maelienydd	Powys	SO1371	52°20·1′	3°16·2′W	X	136,148
Maelogen Fawr	Conwy	SH8562	53°8·8′	3°42·8′W	X	116
Maelor Way	Wrex	SJ4039	52°56·9′	2°53·2′W	X	

Maen Achwyfaen	Flint	SJ1278	53°17·7'	3°18·8'W	A	116
Maenaddwyn	I of Angl	SH4584	53°20·1'	4°19·3'W	T	114,115
Maenaidd	Gwyn	SH8718	52°45·1'	3°40·1'W	X	124,125
Maenan	Conwy	SH7966	53°10·9'	3°48·2'W	X	115
Maenan Abbey	Conwy	SH7965	53°10·3'	3°48·2'W	X	115
Maenan Hall	Conwy	SH7965	53°10·3'	3°48·2'W	A	115
Maen ar Dwll	Powys	SN9040	52°3·1'	3°35·9'W	X	147,160
Maen-Arthur	Cered	SN7272	52°20·1'	3°52·3'W	X	135,147
Maen Bâch	Carm	SN7345	52°5·6'	3°50·8'W	A	146,147
Maen Bachau	Pemb	SM7224	51°52·3'	5°18·3'W	X	157
Maen Beuno	Powys	SJ2001	52°36·3'	3°10·5'W	A	126
Maen Bras	Gwyn	SH9239	52°56·5'	3°36·0'W	X	125
Maen Bugail	Gwyn	SH1123	52°46·5'	4°47·7'W	X	123
Maen-cam	Powys	SN9155	52°11·2'	3°35·3'W	A	147
Maen Castle	Corn	SW3425	50°4·2'	5°42·7'W	A	203
Maen Cattwg	Caer	ST1297	51°40·1'	3°16·0'W	X	171
Maen Chynoweth or Morah	Corn	SW8121	50°3·2'	5°3·2'W	X	204
Maenclochog	Pemb	SN0827	51°54·7'	4°47·1'W	T	145,158
Maen-côch	Carm	SN2423	51°52·9'	4°33·0'W	X	145,158
Maen Daufraich	Pemb	SM6623	51°51·6'	5°23·5'W	X	157
Maen Dower	Corn	SW3529	50°6·4'	5°42·0'W	X	203
Maen Du	Gwyn	SH1020	52°44·9'	4°48·5'W	X	123
Maen Du	Gwyn	SH1326	52°48·2'	4°46·0'W	X	123
Maen Du	Gwyn	SH8215	52°43·4'	3°44·4'W	H	124,125
Maen-du-Point	Corn	SW5329	50°6·8'	5°26·9'W	X	203
Maen-du'r Arddu	Gwyn	SH5956	53°5·2'	4°5·9'W	X	115
Maendy	Rho Cyn Taf	SS9885	51°33·5'	3°27·9'W	X	170
Maendy	Rho Cyn Taf	ST0787	51°34·7'	3°20·1'W	X	170
Maendy	V of Glam	ST0176	51°28·7'	3°25·1'W	T	170
Maendy Fm	V of Glam	ST0778	51°29·8'	3°20·0'W	FM	170
Maenease Point or Pen-a-Maen	Corn	SX0141	50°14·4'	4°47·1'W	X	204
Maeneira	Conwy	SH7267	53°11·3'	3°54·5'W	X	115
Maenelin	Cered	SN5771	52°19·4'	4°5·5'W	X	135
Maen Eryr	I of Angl	SH4680	53°17·9'	4°18·2'W	X	114,115
Maeness	Orkney	HY4830	59°9·5'	2°54·1'W	X	5,6
Mae Ness	Orkney	HY4831	59°10·0'	2°54·1'W	X	5,6
Maengowan	Powys	SO0552	52°9·7'	3°22·9'W	X	147
Maen Gwenonwy	Gwyn	SH2025	52°47·8'	4°39·8'W	X	123
Maengwyn	Cered	SN2748	52°6·4'	4°31·2'W	X	145
Maen-gwyn	Cered	SN3843	52°3·9'	4°21·4'W	X	145
Maengwyn	Wrex	SJ1432	52°53·0'	3°16·3'W	H	125
Maengwynedd	Powys	SJ1229	52°51·3'	3°18·0'W	X	125
Maengwyngweddw	Powys	SN9270	52°19·3'	3°34·7'W	A	136,147
Maengwyn Hall	Cered	SN6062	52°14·5'	4°2·6'W	X	146
Maenhinon	Powys	SN9085	52°27·4'	3°36·7'W	X	136
Maen-hir	Carm	SN1525	51°53·8'	4°40·9'W	X	145,158
Maen Hir	I of Angl	SH4566	53°10·4'	4°18·7'W	X	114,115
Maen Iau	Gwyn	SH1122	52°46·0'	4°47·7'W	X	123
Maen Land	Corn	SW8020	50°2·6'	5°4·0'W	X	204
Maen Llia	Powys	SN9219	51°51·8'	3°33·7'W	A	160
Maenllwyd	Carm	SN3215	51°48·7'	4°25·8'W	X	159
Maen Llwyd	Carm	SN3812	51°47·2'	4°20·5'W	A	159
Maen-llwyd	Gwyn	SH4141	52°56·8'	4°21·6'W	X	123
Maen Llwyd	Gwyn	SH7032	52°52·4'	3°55·5'W	A	124
Maen-llwyd	Powys	SN9774	52°21·5'	3°30·4'W	X	136,147
Maenllwyd	Powys	SO1691	52°30·9'	3°13·9'W	X	136
Maen Llwyd	Powys	SO2227	51°56·4'	3°7·7'W	A	161
Maen Madoc	Powys	SN9115	51°49·6'	3°34·5'W	A	160
Maen Mawr	Powys	SN8520	51°52·2'	3°39·8'W	A	160
Maen Mellt	Gwyn	SH1631	52°51·0'	4°43·6'W	X	123
Maen Melyn	Carm	SN3412	51°47·2'	4°24·0'W	A	159
Maen-offeren Quarries	Gwyn	SH7146	53°0·0'	3°54·9'W	X	115
Maenol	Powys	SN9583	52°26·3'	3°32·3'W	X	136
Maen Pebyll	Conwy	SH8456	53°5·6'	3°43·5'W	X	116
Maen Pern	Corn	SW7331	50°8·4'	5°10·2'W	X	204
Maen Piscar	I of Angl	SH2476	53°15·4'	4°37·9'W	X	114
Maenporth	Corn	SW7929	50°7·4'	5°5·1'W	T	204
Maen Rhoson	Pemb	SM6625	51°52·7'	5°23·6'W	X	157
Maen Richard	Powys	SN9634	51°59·9'	3°30·5'W	A	160
Maen-serth	Powys	SN9469	52°18·8'	3°32·9'W	A	136,147
Maentwlch	Heref	SO3634	52°0·3'	2°55·5'W	X	149,161
Maentwrog	Gwyn	SH6640	52°56·7'	3°59·3'W	T	124
Maenuwch	Cered	SN6085	52°26·9'	4°3·2'W	X	135
Maen y Bugael or West Mouse	I of Angl	SH3094	53°25·2'	4°33·1'W	X	114
Maen-y-frân	I of Angl	SH2575	53°14·8'	4°37·0'W	X	114
Maen-y-goron	Denb	SJ1845	53°0·0'	3°12·9'W	X	116
Maen-y-groes	Cered	SN3858	52°12·0'	4°21·8'W	T	145
Maen yr Allor	Nth Pt Talb	SS8898	51°40·4'	3°36·8'W	X	170
Maer	Corn	SS2007	50°50·3'	4°33·0'W	T	190
Maer	Staffs	SJ7938	52°56·6'	2°18·3'W	T	127
Maer Cliff	Corn	SS2008	50°50·8'	4°33·0'W	X	190
Maerdy	Carm	SN6210	51°46·5'	3°59·6'W	X	159
Maerdy	Carm	SN6220	51°51·9'	3°59·9'W	T	159
Maerdy	Carm	SN6527	51°55·7'	3°57·4'W	X	146
Maerdy	Cered	SN3552	52°8·7'	4°24·3'W	X	145
Maerdy	Conwy	SJ0144	52°59·3'	3°28·1'W	T	125
Maerdy	Denb	SJ0748	53°1·5'	3°22·8'W	X	116
Maerdy	Heref	SO3430	51°58·1'	2°57·3'W	X	149,161
Maerdy	Monm	SO3208	51°46·2'	2°58·7'W	X	161
Maerdy	Monm	SO4001	51°42·5'	2°51·7'W	X	171
Maerdy	Monm	SO4314	51°49·5'	2°49·2'W	X	161
Maerdy	Monm	SO4503	51°43·6'	2°47·4'W	X	171
Maerdy	Newp	ST2883	51°32·7'	3°1·9'W	X	171
Maerdy	Pemb	SM8425	51°53·1'	5°7·9'W	X	157
Maerdy	Rho Cyn Taf	SS9798	51°40·5'	3°29·0'W	T	170
Maerdy Brook	Powys	SJ2416	52°44·4'	3°7·1'W	W	126
Maerdy Fm	Card	ST2378	51°30·0'	3°6·2'W	FM	171
Maerdy Fm	Heref	SO3037	52°1·9'	3°0·8'W	FM	161
Maerdy Fm	Monm	SO3724	51°54·9'	2°54·6'W	FM	161
Maerdy Fm	Powys	SJ2516	52°44·4'	3°6·3'W	FM	126
Maerdy-mawr	Denb	SJ0747	53°1·0'	3°22·8'W	X	116
Maerdy-Newydd	V of Glam	ST0474	51°27·6'	3°22·5'W	X	170
Maerfield Gate	Staffs	SJ7939	52°57·1'	2°18·4'W	X	127
Maer Fm	Devon	SY0180	50°36·9'	3°23·6'W	FM	192
Maer Hills	Staffs	SJ7739	52°57·1'	2°20·1'W	H	127
Maer Rocks	Devon	SY0179	50°36·4'	3°23·6'W	X	192
Maer, The	Devon	SY0080	50°36·9'	3°24·4'W	X	192
Maes	Carm	SN4939	52°2·0'	4°11·7'W	X	146
Maes	Powys	SJ1131	52°52·4'	3°18·9'W	X	125
Maesadda	Carm	SN7421	51°52·6'	3°49·4'W	X	160
Maesaeson	V of Glam	ST0778	51°29·8'	3°20·0'W	X	170
Maesafallen	Gwyn	SH9430	52°51·7'	3°34·1'W	X	125
Maes Alyn	Flint	SJ1864	53°10·3'	3°13·2'W	X	116
Maes-Alyn	Flint	SJ2265	53°10·8'	3°9·6'W	X	117
Mae Sand	Orkney	HY4442	59°15·9'	2°58·5'W	X	5
Maes Angharad	Gwyn	SH7017	52°44·3'	3°55·1'W	X	124
Maes-annod	Denb	SJ0859	53°7·5'	3°22·1'W	X	116
Maes Arthur	Newp	ST2786	51°34·3'	3°2·8'W	X	171
Maes Artro	Gwyn	SH5826	52°49·0'	4°6·0'W	X	124
Maesbach	Rho Cyn Taf	ST1085	51°33·6'	3°17·5'W	X	171
Maesbanadlog	Cered	SN7067	52°17·4'	3°54·0'W	X	135,147
Maes-bangor	Cered	SN6680	52°24·3'	3°57·8'W	T	135
Maesbeidog	Cered	SN6069	52°18·3'	4°2·8'W	X	135
Maes Ben-Dinas	Gwyn	SH8615	52°43·5'	3°40·9'W	X	124,125
Maesbrook	Shrops	SJ3021	52°47·2'	3°1·9'W	T	126
Maesbrook Ho	Shrops	SJ2921	52°47·2'	3°2·8'W	X	126
Maesbury	Shrops	SJ3025	52°49·3'	3°1·9'W	T	126
Maesbury Castle	Somer	ST6147	51°13·5'	2°33·1'W	A	183
Maesbury Hall	Shrops	SJ3025	52°49·3'	3°1·9'W	X	126
Maesbury Marsh	Shrops	SJ3125	52°49·3'	3°1·0'W	T	126
Maes Cadarn	Denb	SJ0355	53°5·2'	3°26·5'W	X	116
Maescadlawr	Brig	SS8687	51°34·5'	3°38·3'W	X	170
Maescadog	Carm	SN6839	52°2·3'	3°55·1'W	X	146
Maes-cadw	Denb	SJ0147	53°0·9'	3°28·1'W	X	116
Maescanol	Carm	SN5345	52°5·3'	4°8·3'W	X	146
Maescar	Powys	SN9428	51°56·7'	3°32·1'W	X	160
Maes-Caradoc	Gwyn	SH6362	53°8·5'	4°2·5'W	X	115
Maes-celyn	Powys	SO2019	51°52·1'	3°9·3'W	X	161
Maescelynog	Powys	SJ0411	52°41·5'	3°24·8'W	X	125
Maes-coch	Carm	SN4738	52°1·4'	4°13·4'W	X	146
Maes-côch	Gwyn	SH7415	52°43·3'	3°51·5'W	X	124
Maes-crug	Cered	SN5968	52°17·8'	4°3·7'W	X	135
Maesderwen	Powys	SO0625	51°55·2'	3°21·6'W	X	160
Maes-diofal	Caer	ST1291	51°36·9'	3°15·9'W	X	171
Maes Down	Somer	ST6440	51°9·7'	2°30·5'W	H	183
Maes Down Fm	Somer	ST6440	51°9·7'	2°30·5'W	FM	183
Maes-eglwys	Swan	SN6500	51°41·2'	3°56·8'W	X	159
Maeselwad	Cered	SN7063	52°15·2'	3°53·9'W	X	146,147
Maes Elwy	Denb	SJ0471	53°13·9'	3°25·9'W	X	116
Maes-Evan	Carm	SN6420	51°52·0'	3°58·1'W	X	159
Maesfron	Cered	SN5268	52°17·7'	4°9·8'W	X	135
Maesgarmon	Flint	SJ2164	53°10·3'	3°10·5'W	X	117
Maesgeirchen	Gwyn	SH5871	53°13·3'	4°7·2'W	T	114,115
Maesglas	Carm	SN7227	51°55·8'	3°51·3'W	X	146,160
Maesglas	Cered	SN6662	52°14·6'	3°57·4'W	X	146
Maesglas	Cered	SN7755	52°11·0'	3°47·6'W	X	146,147
Maes-glas	Newp	ST2985	51°33·8'	3°1·1'W	T	171
Maesglase	Gwyn	SH8214	52°42·9'	3°44·4'W	H	124,125
Maesglas Fm	Carm	SN6738	52°1·7'	3°55·9'W	FM	146
Maes-Gwaelod	Wrex	SJ3543	52°59·1'	2°57·7'W	X	117
Maesgwion	Powys	SH8902	52°36·5'	3°38·0'W	X	135,136
Maesgwm	Gwyn	SH7127	52°49·7'	3°54·5'W	X	124
Maesgwrda	Carm	SN2613	51°47·6'	4°31·0'W	X	158
Maesgwyn	Carm	SN5226	51°55·0'	4°8·7'W	X	146
Maes-gwyn	Conwy	SH8259	53°7·2'	3°45·4'W	X	116
Maes Gwyn	Conwy	SH8652	53°3·4'	3°41·7'W	X	116
Maes-gwyn	Conwy	SH9747	53°0·9'	3°31·7'W	X	116
Maes-gwyn	Denb	SJ1647	53°1·1'	3°14·7'W	X	116
Maes-gwyn	Flint	SJ1180	53°18·8'	3°19·7'W	X	116
Maes-gwyn	Gwyn	SH8529	52°51·0'	3°42·1'W	X	124,125
Maes-gwyn	Monm	SO4104	51°44·1'	2°50·9'W	X	171
Maesgwyn	Powys	SO1137	52°1·7'	3°17·4'W	X	161
Maes-gwyn	Powys	SO1577	52°23·3'	3°14·5'W	X	136,148
Maesgwyn	Shrops	SO2388	52°29·3'	3°7·6'W	X	137
Maesgwyn Bungalow	Nth Pt Talb	SN8505	51°44·2'	3°39·5'W	X	160
Maesgwyn Fm	Wrex	SJ4050	53°2·9'	2°53·3'W	FM	117
Maesgwyn Ganol	Powys	SJ1811	52°41·7'	3°12·4'W	X	125
Maesgwyn-Isaf	Powys	SJ1812	52°42·2'	3°12·4'W	X	125
Maes-gwyn-mawr	Flint	SJ2371	53°14·1'	3°8·8'W	X	117
Maesgwynne	Carm	SN2023	51°52·8'	4°36·5'W	T	145,158
Maesgwynne	Carm	SN3513	51°47·7'	4°23·2'W	X	159
Maesgwynne	Powys	SO0656	52°11·9'	3°22·1'W	X	147
Maes Gwyn Uchaf	Gwyn	SH4541	52°56·9'	4°18·0'W	X	123
Maesgwyn Uchaf	Powys	SJ1711	52°41·7'	3°13·3'W	X	125
Maeshafn	Denb	SJ2060	53°8·1'	3°11·3'W	T	117
Maes-hîr	Gwyn	SH9632	52°52·8'	3°32·3'W	X	125
Maes Howe	Orkney	HY3112	58°59·6'	3°11·6'W	A	6
Maes Knoll	Bath & NE Somer	ST5966	51°23·7'	2°35·0'W	X	172,182
Maes Knoll (Fort)	Bath & NE Somer	ST5966	51°23·7'	2°35·0'W	A	172,182
Maesllan	Carm	SN5742	52°3·7'	4°4·8'W	X	146
Maesllanwrthwl	Carm	SN6537	52°1·1'	3°57·7'W	X	146
Maes-llêch	Carm	SN6309	51°46·0'	3°58·7'W	X	159
Maesllech	Powys	SN9349	52°8·0'	3°33·4'W	X	147
Maesllwch Castle	Powys	SO1740	52°3·4'	3°12·2'W	X	148,161
Maesllwyd	Cered	SN5151	52°8·5'	4°10·3'W	X	146
Maesllwydiart Uchaf	Powys	SN9331	51°58·3'	3°33·1'W	X	160
Maes Llwyn	I of Angl	SH5274	53°14·8'	4°12·7'W	X	114,115
Maesllydan Hall	Carm	SN7735	52°0·2'	3°47·1'W	X	146,160
Maes-llymystyn	Powys	SH9711	52°41·5'	3°31·0'W	X	125
Maes llyn	Cered	SN3644	52°4·4'	4°23·2'W	T	145
Maes-llyn	Cered	SN6963	52°15·2'	3°54·8'W	X	146
Maes-Madog	Conwy	SH8264	53°9·8'	3°45·5'W	X	116
Maes Maelor	Denb	SJ2352	53°3·8'	3°8·5'W	X	117
Maes Manor Hotel	Caer	ST1798	51°40·7'	3°11·6'W	X	171
Maesmawr	Carm	SN3810	51°46·2'	4°20·5'W	X	159
Maes-mawr	Flint	SJ1764	53°10·2'	3°14·1'W	X	116
Maes Mawr	Gwyn	SH4353	53°3·3'	4°20·2'W	X	115,123
Maes-mawr	Gwyn	SH7221	52°46·5'	3°53·5'W	X	124
Maes-mawr	Monm	SO3200	51°41·9'	2°58·6'W	X	171
Maes-mawr	Powys	SO0391	52°30·7'	3°25·4'W	X	136
Maesmawr	Powys	SO0690	52°30·2'	3°22·7'W	X	136
Maes-mawr	Powys	SO1122	51°53·6'	3°17·2'W	X	161
Maesmawr Hall	Powys	SJ1609	52°40·6'	3°14·1'W	X	125
Maes-Megan	Powys	SO1337	52°1·7'	3°15·7'W	X	161
Maes-meillion	Gwyn	SH9230	52°51·6'	3°35·8'W	X	125
Maesmelan	Powys	SO1958	52°13·1'	3°10·7'W	X	148
Maes Merddyn	Conwy	SH8654	53°4·5'	3°41·7'W	X	116
Maesmor	Conwy	SJ0144	52°59·3'	3°28·1'W	X	125
Maesmor	Powys	SN9292	52°31·2'	3°35·1'W	X	136
Maesmynach	Cered	SN5250	52°8·0'	4°9·3'W	X	146
Maes-mynan	Flint	SJ1172	53°14·5'	3°19·6'W	X	116
Maesmynis	Powys	SO0147	52°7·0'	3°26·4'W	T	147
Maesnant	Cered	SN7788	52°28·8'	3°48·3'W	X	135
Maesnant	Cered	SN7887	52°28·3'	3°47·4'W	W	135
Maesnant	Powys	SN8486	52°27·8'	3°42·1'W	X	135,136
Maesnewydd	Cered	SN6487	52°28·1'	3°59·7'W	X	135
Maes-newyddion	Conwy	SH9148	53°1·3'	3°37·1'W	X	116
Maes-Nonni	Carm	SN4939	52°2·0'	4°11·7'W	X	146
Maesog	Gwyn	SH4349	53°1·2'	4°20·0'W	X	115,123
Maesoglan	Gwyn	SH2937	52°54·4'	4°32·2'W	X	123
Maesoglan	I of Angl	SH4467	53°10·9'	4°19·7'W	X	114,115
Maesol	Conwy	SH8567	53°11·5'	3°42·9'W	X	116
Maes-pant	Carm	SN5524	51°54·0'	4°6·1'W	X	159
Maes Pennant	Flint	SJ1679	53°18·3'	3°15·2'W	T	116
Maesperthi	Powys	SH7801	52°35·8'	3°47·7'W	X	135
Maespoth	Powys	SN9130	51°57·7'	3°34·8'W	X	160
Maesprydd	Powys	SJ1003	52°37·3'	3°19·4'W	X	136
Maes-pwll	Carm	SN3332	51°57·9'	4°25·5'W	X	145
Maespyllan	Gwyn	SH9241	52°57·6'	3°36·1'W	X	125
Maesquoy	Orkney	HY3116	59°1·8'	3°11·6'W	X	6
Maesrhiw	Carm	SN6833	51°59·0'	3°54·9'W	X	146
Maesrhug	Cered	SN6363	52°15·1'	4°0·0'W	X	146
Maes-siêd	Denb	SJ1068	53°12·3'	3°20·4'W	X	116
Maes Taing	Orkney	HY4421	59°4·6'	2°58·1'W	X	5,6
Maestanyglwyden Fm	Powys	SJ2024	52°48·7'	3°10·8'W	FM	126
Maesteg	Brig	SS8591	51°36·6'	3°39·3'W	T	170
Maesteg	Powys	SH8401	52°35·9'	3°42·4'W	X	135,136
Maesteilo	Carm	SN5826	51°55·1'	4°3·5'W	X	146
Maesterran	Powys	SH7900	52°35·3'	3°46·8'W	X	135
Maestir Fm	Cered	SN5549	52°7·5'	4°6·7'W	FM	146
Maestorglwydd	Powys	SO2137	52°1·8'	3°8·7'W	X	161
Maes-Treylow	Powys	SO2665	52°16·9'	3°4·7'W	X	137,148
Maestron	Gwyn	SH8535	52°54·3'	3°42·2'W	X	124,125
Maes-troyddyn-fawr	Carm	SN6341	52°3·3'	3°59·5'W	X	146
Maes Truan	Denb	SJ1147	53°1·0'	3°19·2'W	X	116
Maestryfer	Gwyn	SH6919	52°45·4'	3°56·1'W	X	124
Maestwynog	Carm	SN6937	52°1·2'	3°54·2'W	X	146,160
Maes Tyddyn	Conwy	SH9749	53°1·9'	3°31·8'W	X	116
Maes-tyddyn	Denb	SJ0553	53°4·2'	3°24·7'W	X	116
Maestyle	Carm	SN5939	52°2·1'	4°2·9'W	X	146
Maeswalter	Powys	SN9323	51°54·0'	3°32·9'W	X	160
Maes-y-Beran	Monm	SO2926	51°55·9'	3°1·6'W	X	161
Maesyblawd	Powys	SN9389	52°29·5'	3°34·2'W	X	136
Maesybont	Carm	SN5616	51°49·7'	4°5·0'W	T	159
Maes-y-bryner	Gwyn	SH7319	52°45·5'	3°52·5'W	X	124
Maesybryn Fm	V of Glam	ST0070	51°25·4'	3°25·9'W	FM	170
Maes-y-bŵch	Powys	SJ0928	52°50·8'	3°20·7'W	X	125
Maesybwlch	Carm	SN8434	51°59·8'	3°41·0'W	X	160
Maes-y-carneddau	Powys	SH9918	52°45·3'	3°29·4'W	X	125
Maes-y-Castell	Carm	SN6327	51°55·7'	3°59·2'W	A	146
Maes-y-castell	Conwy	SH7670	53°13·0'	3°51·0'W	A	115
Maesycelyn	Cered	SN7397	52°33·6'	3°52·0'W	X	135
Maes-y-coed	Powys	SO1036	52°1·1'	3°18·3'W	X	161
Maesycoed	Rho Cyn Taf	ST0689	51°35·8'	3°21·0'W	T	170
Maesycriau	Powys	SH7805	52°38·0'	3°47·8'W	X	124
Maes-y-crochan	Newp	ST2383	51°32·7'	3°6·2'W	X	171
Maesycrugiau	Carm	SN4741	52°3·0'	4°13·5'W	X	146
Maes-y-cwm	Powys	SO0449	52°8·1'	3°23·8'W	X	147
Maesycwmmer	Caer	ST1594	51°38·5'	3°13·3'W	T	171
Maes-y-dderwen	Carm	SN1123	51°52·7'	4°44·4'W	X	145,158
Maesydderwen	Carm	SN6622	51°53·1'	3°56·4'W	X	159
Maesydderwen	Cered	SN4943	52°4·1'	4°11·8'W	X	146
Maesydd, The	Powys	SJ2613	52°42·8'	3°5·3'W	X	126
Maes-y-dre	Flint	SJ2364	53°10·3'	3°8·7'W	T	117
Maes-y-facrell	Conwy	SH7682	53°19·5'	3°51·3'W	X	115
Maes-y-fedw	Gwyn	SH9438	52°56·0'	3°34·2'W	X	125
Maes-y-felin	Carm	SN1626	51°54·4'	4°40·1'W	X	145,158
Maes-y-felin	Pemb	SN1641	52°2·5'	4°40·6'W	X	145
Maes-y-ffin	Monm	SO2530	51°58·0'	3°5·1'W	X	161
Maes-y-ffynnon	Carm	SN7522	51°53·2'	3°48·6'W	X	160
Maes-Y-Ffynnon	Cered	SN3451	52°8·2'	4°25·1'W	X	145
Maes-y-ffynnon	Wrex	SJ2039	52°56·8'	3°11·0'W	X	126
Maesyffynon	Carm	SN1423	51°52·7'	4°41·7'W	X	145,158
Maesyforest	Cered	SN6152	52°9·2'	4°1·5'W	X	146
Maes-y-fron	Powys	SN8113	51°48·4'	3°43·2'W	X	160
Maesygadfa	Gwyn	SH9041	52°57·5'	3°37·9'W	X	125
Maes y Gaer	Gwyn	SH6672	53°13·9'	4°0·1'W	A	115
Maes-y-garn	Cered	SN4749	52°7·3'	4°13·7'W	X	146
Maes-y-garn	Pemb	SN1732	51°57·6'	4°39·4'W	X	145
Maesygarn	Powys	SO0930	51°57·9'	3°19·1'W	X	161
Maes-y-garn	Powys	SO2039	52°2·9'	3°9·6'W	X	161
Maes-y-garnedd	Conwy	SH8254	53°4·5'	3°45·3'W	X	116
Maes-y-garnedd	Gwyn	SH6426	52°49·1'	4°0·7'W	X	124
Maes-y-garnedd	Gwyn	SH7019	52°45·4'	3°55·2'W	X	124
Maes y Gawnen	Powys	SN9013	51°48·5'	3°35·3'W	X	160
Maes-y-glydfa	Powys	SJ0607	52°39·4'	3°23·0'W	X	125
Maesyglyn	Cered	SN3745	52°5·0'	4°22·3'W	X	145
Maes-y-Graig	Shrops	SJ3135	52°54·7'	3°1·2'W	X	126
Maes-y-groes	Flint	SJ1963	53°9·7'	3°12·3'W	X	116
Maes-y-groes Fm	Wrex	SJ4943	52°59·2'	2°45·2'W	FM	117
Maesygroes Isaf	Powys	SN9754	52°10·7'	3°30·0'W	X	147
Maes-y-gwandde	Carm	SN7736	52°0·8'	3°47·1'W	X	146,160
Maesygwartha	Monm	SO2314	51°49·4'	3°6·6'W	T	161
Maes-y-lade	Powys	SO1935	52°0·7'	3°10·4'W	X	161
Maesylan	Carm	SN2325	51°54·0'	4°34·0'W	X	145,158
Maes-y-lan	Carm	SN2614	51°48·1'	4°31·0'W	X	158
Maes-y-llan	Flint	SJ2368	53°12·5'	3°8·8'W	X	117
Maes-y-llan	Powys	SO0834	52°0·0'	3°20·0'W	X	160
Maes-y-llech	Card	ST1279	51°30·4'	3°15·7'W	X	171
Maes-ymdrisiol	Powys	SN8894	52°32·2'	3°38·7'W	X	135,136
Maes-y-meillion	Carm	SN6315	51°49·3'	3°58·9'W	X	159
Maesymeillion	Cered	SN4245	52°5·1'	4°18·0'W	X	146
Maes-y-pandy	Gwyn	SH7008	52°39·5'	3°54·9'W	X	124
Maesypandy	Powys	SN9995	52°32·9'	3°29·0'W	T	136
Maes-y-pant	Carm	SN4928	51°56·0'	4°11·4'W	X	146

Maes-y-porth	I of Angl	SH4565	53°9·8′	4°18·7′W	X	114,115
Maes-y-Prior	Carm	SN3719	51°51·0′	4°21·6′W	X	159
Maesypwll	Cered	SN5647	52°6·4′	4°5·8′W	X	146
Maesyraelfor	Gwyn	SH5930	52°51·2′	4°5·2′W	X	124
Maesyrafon	Pemb	SM9928	51°55·1′	4°55·0′W	X	157,158
Maes yr Esgob	Flint	SJ1469	53°12·9′	3°16·9′W	X	116
Maes-yr-Groes	Conwy	SH7967	53°11·4′	3°48·3′W	X	115
Maes-yr-hâf	Carm	SN2227	51°55·0′	4°34·9′W	X	145,158
Maes-yr-haidd	Carm	SN5630	51°57·2′	4°5·3′W	X	146
Maesyrhaime	Shrops	SO2683	52°26·6′	3°4·9′W	X	137
Maesyrhandir	Powys	SO0990	52°30·3′	3°20·0′W	T	136
Maes'yrhaul	V of Glam	ST0675	51°28·2′	3°20·8′W	X	170
Maes y Rhedyn	Wrex	SJ3356	53°6·1′	2°59·6′W	X	117
Maesyrhelem	Powys	SO0875	52°22·2′	3°20·7′W	X	136,147
Maesyron	Powys	SN9043	52°4·7′	3°35·9′W	X	147,160
Maesyronnen	Powys	SO1740	52°3·4′	3°12·2′W	X	148,161
Maesyrychen Mountain	Denb	SJ1847	53°1·1′	3°12·9′W	H	116
Maes-y-tail	Gwyn	SH8440	52°56·9′	3°43·2′W	X	124,125
Maes y Ward	V of Glam	ST0375	51°28·2′	3°23·4′W	X	170
Maesywerngoch	Gwyn	SH7203	52°36·8′	3°53·0′W	X	135
Mafflat	S Lanak	NS7449	55°43·3′	3°59·9′W	X	64
Magasker	N Eil	NA9800	57°53·5′	7°5·3′W	X	18
Magbiehill	E Ayr	NS4047	55°41·7′	4°32·3′W	X	64
Mag Brook	Warr	SJ6885	53°21·9′	2°28·4′W	W	109
Mag Clough	Derby	SK2377	53°17·6′	1°38·9′W	X	119
Magclough Fm	Derby	SK2277	53°17·6′	1°39·8′W	FM	119
Magdalen Br	Norf	TF5712	52°41·2′	0°19·8′E	X	131,143
Magdalene Hall	Scot Bord	NT6232	55°35·1′	2°35·7′W	X	74
Magdalen Grange Fm	N Yks	TA0880	54°12·5′	0°20·2′W	FM	101
Magdalen Hill Down	Hants	SU5029	51°3·7′	1°16·8′W	X	185
Magdalen Ho	E Yorks	TA2029	53°44·8′	0°10·4′W	X	107
Magdalen Laver	Essex	TL5108	51°45·2′	0°11·7′E	T	167
Magdalen Springs	Kirk	SE0908	53°34·4′	1°51·4′W	W	110
Magdalen Wood	N Yks	SE2377	54°11·5′	1°38·4′W	F	99
Maggie Black's Loch	Shetld	HU3942	60°9·9′	1°17·3′W	W	4
Maggie Kettle's Loch	Shetld	HU3675	60°27·7′	1°20·2′W	W	2,3
Maggieknockater	Moray	NJ3145	57°29·7′	3°8·6′W	T	28
Maggotbox Plantn	Norf	TL8697	52°32·6′	0°45·0′E	F	144
Maggot Hill	D & G	NX5978	55°4·8′	4°12·1′W	H	77
Maggots End	Essex	TL4827	51°55·5′	0°9·5′E	T	167
Maggots Fm	Suff	TM2073	52°18·9′	1°14·1′E	FM	156
Magham Down	E Susx	TQ6011	50°52·8′	0°16·9′E	T	199
Maghannan	N Eil	NB0821	58°5·2′	6°56·8′W	X	13,14
Magher-breck	I of M	SC4690	54°17·2′	4°21·5′W	X	95
Magheuchan Rig	D & G	NS6705	55°19·5′	4°5·3′W	X	71,77
Maghull	Sefton	SD3702	53°30·9′	2°56·6′W	T	108
Maghull Sta	Sefton	SD3801	53°30·4′	2°55·7′W	X	108
Magic Well	Fife	NO4221	56°22·9′	2°55·9′W	X	54,59
Magin Moor Cottages	Lincs	SK8990	53°24·2′	0°39·3′W	X	112
Magiston Fm	Dorset	SY6396	50°46·0′	2°31·1′W	FM	194
Magiston Hill	Dorset	SY6397	50°46·5′	2°31·5′W	X	194
Maglin Burn	Northum	NZ0997	55°16·3′	1°51·1′W	W	81
Mag Low	Derby	SK0781	53°19·8′	1°53·3′W	A	110
Magna Carta Island	Win & Maid	SU9972	51°26·5′	0°34·1′W	X	175,176
Magna Fm	Suff	TM3176	52°20·2′	1°23·9′E	FM	156
Magna Park	Leic	SP5184	52°27·3′	1°14·6′W	X	140
Magnis (Roman Fort)	Northum	NY6665	54°59·0′	2°31·5′W	R	86
Magnis (Roman Town)	Heref	SO4342	52°4·6′	2°49·5′W	R	148,149,161
Magnolia Ho	Essex	TL8435	51°59·2′	0°41·2′E	X	155
Magnolia Ho	Somer	ST3447	51°13·3′	2°56·3′W	X	182
Magnoll's Fm	Lancs	SD7127	53°44·6′	2°26·0′W	FM	103
Magnum	N Ayr	NS3038	55°36·6′	4°41·5′W	X	70
Magog Down	Cambs	TL4853	52°9·6′	0°10·2′E	X	154
Magog Fm	Cambs	TL4952	52°9·0′	0°11·1′E	FM	154
Magor	Monm	ST4287	51°35·0′	2°49·8′W	T	171,172
Magor Fm	Corn	SW6342	50°14·1′	5°19·0′W	FM	203
Magor Pill	Monm	ST4384	51°33·4′	2°48·9′W	W	171,172
Magor Pill Fm	Monm	ST4385	51°33·9′	2°48·9′W	FM	171,172
Magow Rocks	Corn	SW5842	50°13·9′	5°23·2′W	X	203
Magpie Bottom	Kent	TQ5461	51°19·9′	0°13·0′E	X	177,188
Magpie Fm	Norf	TF7314	52°42·0′	0°34·0′E	FM	132
Magpie Fm	Northnts	SP5445	52°6·3′	1°12·3′W	FM	152
Magpie Fm	Oxon	SP3628	51°57·2′	1°28·2′W	FM	164
Magpie Fm	Sol	SP2276	52°23·1′	1°40·2′W	FM	139
Magpie Fm	W Berks	SU5573	51°27·4′	1°12·1′W	FM	174
Magpie Green	Suff	TM0778	52°21·9′	1°2·8′E	T	144
Magpie Hall	Kent	TQ8560	51°18·8′	0°39·7′E	X	178
Magpie Hall Fm	Notts	SK7677	53°17·3′	0°51·2′W	FM	120
Magpie Hill	Shrops	SO6177	52°23·6′	2°34·0′W	X	138
Magpie Inn (PH)	Suff	TM1160	52°12·1′	1°5·7′E	X	155
Magpie Lodge	Bucks	SU9091	51°36·9′	0°41·6′W	X	175
Mag's Hill	Cambs	TL5054	52°10·1′	0°12·0′E	X	154
Magungie House	Angus	NO6345	56°36·0′	2°35·7′W	X	54
Magus Muir	Fife	NO4515	56°19·7′	2°52·9′W	X	59
Mahaar	D & G	NX0170	54°59·3′	5°6·2′W	X	76,82
Mahaar	D & G	NX1057	54°52·6′	4°57·3′W	X	82
Mahago Rig	E Ayr	NS6606	55°20·0′	4°6·3′W	X	71,77
Maharajah's Well	Oxon	SU6784	51°33·3′	1°1·6′W	W	175
Mahollam Br	Heref	SO2754	52°11·0′	3°3·7′W	X	148
Mahon	Aberd	NJ7048	57°31·5′	2°29·6′W	X	29
Mahon Ho	Durham	NZ3333	54°41·7′	1°28·9′W	X	93
Mahorall	Shrops	SO5972	52°20·9′	2°35·7′W	X	137,138
Maich Water	Renf	NS3160	55°48·5′	4°41·4′W	W	63
Maida Vale	C of West	TQ2582	51°31·6′	0°11·5′W	T	176
Maiden Bower	Beds	SP9922	51°53·5′	0°33·3′W	A	165
Maiden Bower	I Scilly	SV8414	49°56·8′	6°23·9′W	X	203
Maiden Bower	N Yks	SE4175	54°10·4′	1°21·9′W	X	99
Maiden Bower	Oxon	SP4623	51°54·5′	1°19·5′W	F	164
Maidenbower	W Susx	TQ2935	51°6·2′	0°9·1′W	T	187
Maiden Bower (Motte & Bailey)	N Yks	SE4175	54°10·4′	1°21·9′W	A	99
Maiden Bradley	Wilts	ST8038	51°8·7′	2°16·8′W	T	183
Maiden Bridge	Lancs	SD6566	54°5·6′	2°31·7′W	X	97
Maidenbrook	Somer	ST2426	51°1·9′	3°4·6′W	X	193
Maidenburn	S Lanak	NS6845	55°41·1′	4°5·5′W	X	64
Maiden Castle	Aberd	NJ6924	57°18·6′	2°30·4′W	X	38
Maiden Castle	Angus	NO6742	56°34·4′	2°31·8′W	X	54
Maiden Castle	Ches	SJ4952	53°4·0′	2°45·3′W	X	117
Maiden Castle	Cumbr	NY1805	54°26·3′	3°15·4′W	X	89,90
Maiden Castle	Cumbr	NY4424	54°36·7′	2°51·6′W	X	90
Maiden Castle	Cumbr	NY4524	54°36·7′	2°50·7′W	A	90
Maiden Castle	Cumbr	NY8713	54°31·0′	2°11·6′W	X	91,92
Maiden Castle	Dorset	SY6688	50°41·7′	2°28·5′W	A	194
Maiden Castle	Durham	NZ2841	54°46·0′	1°33·5′W	A	88
Maiden Castle	E Dunb	NS6478	55°58·8′	4°10·3′W	X	64
Maiden Castle	Fife	NO2206	56°14·7′	3°15·1′W	X	58
Maiden Castle	N Yks	SE0298	54°22·9′	1°57·7′W	A	98
Maiden Castle	Pemb	SM9524	51°52·9′	4°58·3′W	X	157,158
Maiden Castle (Cairn)	Cumbr	NY1805	54°26·3′	3°15·4′W	A	89,90
Maiden Castle Fm	Dorset	SY6789	50°42·2′	2°27·7′W	FM	194
Maiden Castle (Fort)	Aberd	NJ6924	57°18·6′	2°30·4′W	A	38
Maiden Castle (Fort)	Ches	SJ4952	53°4·0′	2°45·3′W	A	117
Maiden Castle (Fort)	Fife	NO2206	56°14·7′	3°15·1′W	A	58
Maiden Castle (Motte & Bailey)	E Dunb	NS6478	55°58·8′	4°10·3′W	A	64
Maiden Castle (Roman Fortlet)	Cumbr	NY8713	54°31·0′	2°11·6′W	R	91,92
Maiden Causeway	Aberd	NJ6822	57°17·5′	2°31·4′W	X	38
Maidencombe	Torbay	SX9268	50°30·3′	3°31·0′W	T	202
Maidencots	S Lanak	NS9226	55°31·2′	3°42·2′W	X	71,72
Maidencourt Fm	W Berks	SU3776	51°29·1′	1°27·6′W	FM	174
Maidencraig	C of Aber	NJ8806	57°8·9′	2°11·4′W	X	38
Maiden Down	Devon	ST0816	50°56·4′	3°18·2′W	X	181
Maidenford	Devon	SS5833	51°5·0′	4°1·3′W	X	180
Maidengill	S Lanak	NS8630	55°33·3′	3°48·0′W	X	71,72
Maiden Hair	Fife	NT6598	56°10·7′	2°33·4′W	X	59
Maidenhall	Scot Bord	NT6133	55°35·6′	2°36·7′W	X	74
Maidenhall	Suff	TM1542	52°2·3′	1°8·5′E	T	169
Maiden Hall Fm	Durham	NZ1749	54°50·4′	1°43·7′W	FM	88
Maidenhall Point	Pemb	SM8520	51°50·5′	5°6·9′W	X	157
Maidenhatch	W Berks	SU6174	51°27·9′	1°6·9′W	X	175
Maidenhatch Fm	W Berks	SU6173	51°27·4′	1°6·9′W	FM	175
Maidenhayne	Devon	SY2795	50°45·2′	3°1·7′W	T	193
Maiden Head	N Som	ST5666	51°23·7′	2°37·6′W	T	172,182
Maidenhead	Win & Maid	SU8781	51°31·5′	0°44·4′W	T	175
Maidenhead Bay	S Ayr	NS2109	55°20·8′	4°49·0′W	W	70,76
Maidenhead Court	Win & Maid	SU9083	51°32·6′	0°41·7′W	T	175
Maidenhead Thicket	Win & Maid	SU8580	51°31·0′	0°46·1′W	F	175
Maidenhill	Cumbr	NY5133	54°41·6′	2°45·2′W	X	90
Maiden Hill	Devon	SX5879	50°35·8′	4°0·0′W	H	191
Maidenhill	E Renf	NS5754	55°45·7′	4°21·1′W	X	64
Maiden Hill	Glos	SO8206	51°45·4′	2°15·3′W	X	162
Maiden Hill	S Lanak	NT0455	55°47·0′	3°31·4′W	X	65,72
Maidenholm	D & G	NX8461	54°56·1′	3°48·2′W	X	84
Maidenhyde Fm	Heref	SO5654	52°11·2′	2°38·2′W	FM	149
Maiden Island	Arg & Bt	NM8431	56°25·6′	5°29·7′W	X	49
Maiden Kaim	Aberd	NO8883	56°56·5′	2°11·4′W	X	45
Maidenkirk	N Yks	SE0954	53°59·2′	1°51·3′W	X	104
Maidenland	Corn	SX0276	50°33·3′	4°47·3′W	X	200
Maiden Law	Durham	NZ1749	54°50·4′	1°43·7′W	T	88
Maiden Law	Scot Bord	NT3941	55°39·8′	2°57·7′W	H	73
Maiden Loch	Highld	NC0426	58°11·0′	5°19·6′W	W	15
Maiden Moor	Cumbr	NY2418	54°33·3′	3°10·1′W	X	89,90
Maiden Newton	Dorset	SY5997	50°46·5′	2°34·5′W	T	194
Maidenpap	D & G	NX8961	54°56·1′	3°43·5′W	H	84
Maiden Pap	Highld	ND0429	58°14·6′	3°37·6′W	H	11,17
Maiden Paps	Scot Bord	NT5002	55°18·8′	2°46·8′W	H	79
Maidenpark	Falk	NS9980	56°0·4′	3°36·7′W	T	65
Maidenplain	Pth & Kin	NN9815	56°19·2′	3°38·5′W	X	58
Maidens	Essex	TL6316	51°49·4′	0°22·3′E	X	167
Maidens	S Ayr	NS2107	55°19·7′	4°48·9′W	T	70,76
Maiden's Bed	S Ayr	NX4090	55°11·0′	4°30·3′W	X	77
Maiden's Bower Fm	Know	SJ4395	53°27·2′	2°51·1′W	FM	108
Maiden's Cottage Fm	E Yorks	TA0168	54°6·1′	0°26·9′W	FM	101
Maiden's Cross	Ches	SJ5173	53°15·3′	2°43·7′W	X	117
Maidensgrave	Suff	TM2648	52°5·3′	1°18·3′E	T	169
Maidensgrave Fm	E Yorks	TA0971	54°7·6′	0°19·5′W	FM	101
Maiden's Green	Brackn	SU8972	51°26·6′	0°42·8′W	T	175
Maidensgrove	Oxon	SU7288	51°35·4′	0°57·2′W	T	175
Maidensgrove Scrubs	Oxon	SU7288	51°35·4′	0°57·2′W	X	175
Maidens Hall	Northum	NZ1488	55°11·4′	1°46·4′W	X	81
Maiden's Hall	Northum	NZ2398	55°16·8′	1°37·8′W	T	81
Maiden's Paps	W Dunb	NS5075	55°56·9′	4°23·7′W	X	64
Maiden Stack	Shetld	HU1860	60°19·7′	1°39·9′W	X	3
Maiden Stane	Angus	NO6844	56°35·5′	2°30·8′W	X	54
Maiden Stone	Aberd	NJ7024	57°18·6′	2°29·4′W	A	38
Maiden's Well	Pth & Kin	NN9601	56°11·7′	3°40·1′W	W	58
Maidensworth Fm	N Yks	SE6173	54°9·2′	1°3·5′W	FM	100
Maiden Tor	Corn	SX1580	50°35·7′	4°36·5′W	X	201
Maiden Way	Cumbr	NY6538	54°44·4′	2°32·2′W	X	91
Maiden Way (Roman Road)	Cumbr	NY6538	54°44·4′	2°32·2′W	R	91
Maiden Way (Roman Road)	Northum	NY6755	54°53·6′	2°30·4′W	R	86,87
Maidenwell	Corn	SX1470	50°30·3′	4°37·0′W	X	200
Maidenwell	Lincs	TF3279	53°17·7′	0°0·8′W	T	122
Maiden Wells	Pemb	SR9799	51°39·4′	4°55·7′W	T	158
Maidford	Northnts	SP6052	52°10·0′	1°7·0′W	T	152
Maidford	Wilts	ST8984	51°33·5′	2°9·1′W	X	173
Maidford Grange	Northnts	SP6053	52°10·6′	1°7·0′W	X	152
Maidford Lodge	Northnts	SP6153	52°10·5′	1°6·1′W	X	152
Maidford Wood	Northnts	SP6152	52°10·0′	1°6·1′W	F	152
Maidland	D & G	NX4354	54°51·6′	4°26·3′W	X	83
Maidscross Hill	Suff	TL7282	52°24·8′	0°32·1′E	X	143
Maid's Moor	Devon	SS3120	50°57·5′	4°24·0′W	X	190
Maids' Moreton	Bucks	SP7035	52°0·8′	0°58·4′W	T	152
Maids Moreton Ho	Bucks	SP7035	52°0·8′	0°58·4′W	X	152
Maids of Bute	Arg & Bt	NS0074	55°55·3′	5°11·6′W	X	63
Maidstone	Kent	TQ7655	51°16·2′	0°31·8′E	T	178,188
Maids Wood	Suff	TM2959	52°11·1′	1°21·4′E	F	156
Maidwell	Northnts	SP7476	52°22·9′	0°54·4′W	T	141
Maikel	Highld	NH5994	57°55·1′	4°22·3′W	X	21
Maikle Wood	Highld	NH6094	57°55·1′	4°21·3′W	F	21
Mail	Shetld	HU4228	60°2·3′	1°14·3′W	T	4
Mailand	Shetld	HP6001	60°41·5′	0°53·6′W	T	1
Maildy	Pemb	SM9034	51°58·1′	5°3·0′W	X	157
Mailer	Pth & Kin	NO0920	56°22·1′	3°27·9′W	X	52,53,58
Mailerbeg	Pth & Kin	NN7217	56°19·9′	4°3·8′W	X	57
Mailermore	Pth & Kin	NN7418	56°20·5′	4°1·9′W	X	57
Mailer's Knowe	Pth & Kin	NN9402	56°12·2′	3°42·1′W	X	58
Mailie's Knowe	Scot Bord	NT1808	55°21·8′	3°17·2′W	X	79
Mailingknowe	Pth & Kin	NN9914	56°18·7′	3°37·5′W	X	58
Mailings	N Lanak	NS7579	55°59·5′	3°59·8′W	X	64
Mailingsland	Scot Bord	NT2443	55°40·7′	3°12·1′W	T	73
Mailscot Wood	Glos	SO5613	51°49·1′	2°37·9′W	F	162
Mail Sike	Cumbr	NY7527	54°38·5′	2°22·8′W	W	91
Maim, The	Aberd	NO2896	57°3·2′	3°10·8′W	X	37,44
Main	Powys	SJ1715	52°43·8′	3°13·3′W	X	125
Main Bench	I of W	SZ3084	50°39·5′	1°34·2′W	X	196
Mainbow	Devon	SX8373	50°32·9′	3°38·7′W	X	191
Main Castle	E Ayr	NS6134	55°35·0′	4°11·9′W	X	71
Main Castle (Earthwork)	E Ayr	NS6134	55°35·0′	4°11·9′W	A	71
Main Channel	Dorset	SZ0389	50°42·3′	1°57·1′W	W	195
Maincombe	Somer	ST4210	50°53·4′	2°49·1′W	X	193
Main Dale	Corn	SW7819	50°2·0′	5°5·6′W	X	204
Maindee	Newp	ST3288	51°35·4′	2°58·5′W	T	171
Main Ditch	Heref	SO5062	52°15·5′	2°43·6′W	W	137,138,149
Main Down	Dorset	ST9314	50°55·8′	2°5·6′W	X	195
Main Down	W Susx	SU7718	50°57·6′	0°53·8′W	H	197
Main Drain	Cambs	TL5085	52°26·8′	0°12·8′E	W	143
Main Drain	Lincs	TF5375	53°15·2′	0°18·0′E	W	122
Maindy	Card	ST1778	51°29·9′	3°11·4′W	T	171
Main Dyke	Lancs	SD3638	53°50·3′	2°57·9′W	W	102
Main End	Lincs	TF4736	52°54·3′	0°11·6′E	X	131
Mainey Wood	Kent	TQ9042	51°9·0′	0°43·4′E	X	189
Mainhead Fm	N Lanak	NS7676	55°57·9′	3°58·8′W	FM	64
Mainhill	D & G	NY1676	55°4·5′	3°18·5′W	X	85
Mainhill	Scot Bord	NT5830	55°34·0′	2°39·5′W	X	73,74
Mainholm	D & G	NY1573	55°2·9′	3°19·4′W	X	85
Mainholm	S Ayr	NS3721	55°27·6′	4°34·2′W	T	70
Mainhouse	Scot Bord	NT7529	55°33·5′	2°23·3′W	X	74
Main Ing	Cumbr	NY6018	54°33·6′	2°36·7′W	X	91
Mainland	Orkney	HY3512	58°59·7′	3°7·4′W	X	6
Mainland	Shetld	HU3863	60°21·2′	1°18·2′W	X	2,3
Mainland	Shetld	HU4028	60°2·4′	1°16·4′W	X	4
Mainnir nam Fiadh	Arg & Bt	NM6735	56°27·2′	5°46·4′W	H	49
Mainoaks	Heref	SO5717	51°51·2′	2°37·1′W	X	162
Main Rig	D & G	NY0393	55°13·6′	3°31·1′W	X	78
Main Road	Lincs	TF3094	53°25·8′	0°2·2′W	X	113
Mains	Aberd	NJ8656	57°35·9′	2°13·6′W	X	30
Mains	Aberd	NK0137	57°25·7′	1°58·5′W	X	30
Mains	Arg & Bt	NR8038	55°35·4′	5°29·0′W	X	68,69
Mains	Cumbr	NY0724	54°36·4′	3°26·0′W	T	89
Mains	D & G	NY0266	54°59·0′	3°31·5′W	X	84
Mains	D & G	NY1372	55°2·3′	3°21·3′W	X	85
Mains	E Ayr	NS4048	55°42·2′	4°32·3′W	X	64
Mains	E Renf	NS5851	55°44·2′	4°15·3′W	X	64
Mains	Fife	NO4528	56°26·7′	2°53·1′W	X	54,59
Mains	Highld	ND2361	58°32·1′	3°18·9′W	X	11,12
Mains	Highld	NH5864	57°38·9′	4°22·3′W	X	21
Mains	Highld	NH6074	57°44·3′	4°20·6′W	X	21
Mains	Highld	NH6463	57°38·4′	4°16·2′W	X	21
Mains	Highld	NH6964	57°39·1′	4°11·2′W	X	21
Mains	Highld	NH8092	57°54·3′	4°1·0′W	X	21
Mains	Highld	NH8149	57°31·2′	3°58·7′W	X	27
Mains	Highld	NH9352	57°33·0′	3°46·8′W	X	27
Mains	Highld	NH9747	57°30·4′	3°42·7′W	X	27
Mains	Moray	NH9949	57°31·5′	3°40·7′W	X	27
Mains	N Ayr	NS3052	55°44·2′	4°42·0′W	X	63
Mains	Pth & Kin	NN9353	56°39·7′	3°44·3′W	X	52
Mains	Scot Bord	NT8955	55°47·5′	2°10·1′W	X	67,74
Mains	Scot Bord	NY5190	55°12·4′	2°45·8′W	X	79
Mains	S Lanak	NS9832	55°34·5′	3°36·6′W	X	72
Mains	W Dunb	NS4078	55°58·4′	4°33·4′W	X	64
Mainsbank	Angus	NO6251	56°39·2′	2°36·7′W	X	54
Mainsbank	Northum	NZ0772	55°2·8′	1°53·0′W	X	88
Mains Burn	W Loth	NT0273	55°56·7′	3°33·7′W	W	65
Mains Castle	S Lanak	NS6256	55°46·9′	4°11·6′W	A	64
Mains Castle	Stir	NN6736	56°30·1′	4°9·2′W	A	51
Mains Cottages	D & G	NY0869	55°0·7′	3°25·9′W	X	85
Mains Croft	Aberd	NK0463	57°39·7′	1°55·5′W	X	30
Mains Fm	Cumbr	NY4724	54°36·8′	2°48·8′W	FM	90
Mains Fm	Highld	NH7966	57°40·3′	4°1·3′W	FM	21,27
Mains Fm	Highld	NM6686	56°54·6′	5°50·2′W	FM	40
Mains Fm	Moray	NJ0048	57°30·9′	3°39·7′W	FM	27
Mains Fm	W Dunb	NS4487	56°3·3′	4°29·9′W	FM	57
Mainsforth	Durham	NZ3131	54°40·6′	1°30·7′W	T	93
Mainsgate	Cumbr	SD0999	54°23·0′	3°23·7′W	X	96
Mainsgill Fm	N Yks	NZ1508	54°28·3′	1°45·7′W	FM	92
Mains Hall (Hotel)	Lancs	SD3740	53°51·4′	2°57·1′W	X	102
Mainshiel Head	Scot Bord	NT4414	55°25·3′	2°52·7′W	H	79
Mainshill	D & G	NY1481	55°7·2′	3°20·5′W	X	78
Mainshill	E Loth	NT5672	55°56·6′	2°41·8′W	X	67
Mains Hill	Scot Bord	NT4538	55°38·2′	2°52·0′W	H	73
Mainshill Fm	Bucks	SP7412	51°48·3′	0°55·2′W	FM	165
Mainshill Wood	S Lanak	NS8531	55°33·8′	3°49·0′W	F	71,72
Mains Ho	Fife	NT3295	56°8·8′	3°5·2′W	X	59
Mains House	Scot Bord	NT8856	55°48·1′	2°11·0′W	X	67,74
Mainslaughter	Scot Bord	NT6660	55°50·2′	2°32·1′W	X	67
Mainsmill	D & G	NX9257	54°54·0′	3°40·6′W	X	84
Mains of Abergeldie	Aberd	NO2895	57°2·7′	3°10·7′W	X	37,44
Mains of Advie	Highld	NJ1334	57°23·5′	3°26·4′W	X	28
Mains of Afforsk	Aberd	NJ6920	57°16·4′	2°30·4′W	X	38
Mains of Airies	D & G	NW9767	54°57·6′	5°9·8′W	X	82
Mains of Airleywight	Pth & Kin	NO0536	56°30·6′	3°32·2′W	X	52,53
Mains of Airlie	Pth & Kin	NO2951	56°39·0′	3°9·0′W	X	53
Mains of Aldbar	Angus	NO5757	56°42·4′	2°41·7′W	X	54
Mains of Allanbuie	Moray	NJ4051	57°33·0′	2°59·7′W	X	28
Mains of Allardice	Aberd	NO8174	56°51·7′	2°18·2′W	X	45
Mains of Altries	Aberd	NO8498	57°4·6′	2°15·4′W	X	38,45
Mains of Annochie	Aberd	NJ9342	57°28·3′	2°6·5′W	X	30
Mains of Arboll	Highld	NH8781	57°48·5′	3°53·6′W	X	21
Mains of Ardestie	Angus	NO5034	56°30·0′	2°48·3′W	T	54
Mains of Ardiffery	Aberd	NK0636	57°25·1′	1°53·5′W	X	30
Mains of Ardlaw	Aberd	NJ9363	57°39·7′	2°6·6′W	X	30
Mains of Ardovie	Angus	NO5856	56°41·9′	2°40·7′W	X	54
Mains of Arnage	Aberd	NJ9335	57°24·6′	2°6·5′W	X	30
Mains of Artamford	Aberd	NJ9048	57°31·6′	2°9·6′W	X	30
Mains of Arthurstone	Pth & Kin	NO2643	56°34·6′	3°11·8′W	X	53

Mains of Artloch	Aberd	NJ4740	57°27·1′	2°52·5′W	X	28,29
Mains of Asleid	Aberd	NJ8344	57°29·4′	2°16·6′W	X	29,30
Mains of Asloun	Aberd	NJ5415	57°13·7′	2°45·3′W	X	37
Mains of Aswanley	Aberd	NJ4439	57°26·5′	2°55·5′W	X	28
Mains of Atherb	Aberd	NJ9249	57°32·1′	2°7·6′W	X	30
Mains of Auchedly	Aberd	NJ8932	57°23·0′	2°10·5′W	X	30
Mains of Auchenfranco	D & G	NX8972	55°2·1′	3°43·8′W	X	84
Mains of Auchinbadie	Aberd	NJ6858	57°36·9′	2°31·7′W	X	29
Mains of Auchindachy	Moray	NJ4048	57°31·4′	2°59·6′W	X	28
Mains of Auchleuchries	Aberd	NK0035	57°24·6′	1°59·5′W	X	30
Mains of Auchmedden	Aberd	NJ8564	57°40·2′	2°14·6′W	X	30
Mains of Auchmithie	Angus	NO6744	56°35·5′	2°31·8′W	X	54
Mains of Auchnagatt	Aberd	NJ9241	57°27·8′	2°7·5′W	X	30
Mains of Auchoynanie	Moray	NJ4549	57°31·9′	2°54·7′W	X	28,29
Mains of Auchreddie	Aberd	NJ9134	57°24·0′	2°8·5′W	X	30
Mains of Auquharney	Aberd	NK0236	57°25·1′	1°57·5′W	X	30
Mains of Badenscoth	Aberd	NJ7039	57°26·7′	2°29·5′W	X	29
Mains of Badenyouchers	Aberd	NJ5458	57°36·8′	2°45·7′W	X	29
Mains of Baldavie	Aberd	NJ6261	57°38·5′	2°37·7′W	X	29
Mains of Baldoon	D & G	NX4352	54°50·5′	4°26·3′W	X	83
Mains of Balfluig	Aberd	NJ5914	57°13·2′	2°40·3′W	X	37
Mains of Balfour	Aberd	NO5596	57°3·4′	2°44·1′W	X	37,44
Mains of Balfour	Aberd	NO6174	56°51·6′	2°37·9′W	X	45
Mains of Balgavies	Angus	NO5351	56°39·2′	2°45·5′W	T	54
Mains of Balgray	E Renf	NS5056	55°46·7′	4°23·1′W	X	64
Mains of Balhaldie	Stir	NN8205	56°13·6′	3°53·8′W	X	57
Mains of Balhall	Angus	NO5163	56°45·6′	2°47·6′W	X	44
Mains of Ballindarg	Angus	NO4051	56°39·1′	2°58·3′W	X	54
Mains of Ballintomb	Moray	NJ2142	57°27·9′	3°18·6′W	X	28
Mains of Balmadies	Angus	NO5449	56°38·1′	2°44·5′W	X	54
Mains of Balmanno	Aberd	NO6966	56°47·3′	2°30·0′W	X	45
Mains of Balmaud	Aberd	NJ7557	57°36·4′	2°24·6′W	X	29
Mains of Balnagowan	Highld	NH8054	57°33·9′	3°59·9′W	X	27
Mains of Balnagown	Highld	NH7674	57°44·6′	4°4·5′W	X	21
Mains of Balnakettle	Aberd	NO6274	56°51·6′	2°36·9′W	X	45
Mains of Balthayock	Pth & Kin	NO1723	56°23·8′	3°20·2′W	X	53,58
Mains of Barrack	Aberd	NJ9142	57°28·3′	2°8·5′W	X	30
Mains of Beldorney	Aberd	NJ4136	57°24·9′	2°58·5′W	X	28
Mains of Bellyhack	Moray	NJ4043	57°28·7′	2°59·6′W	X	28
Mains of Belmont	Pth & Kin	NO2843	56°34·7′	3°9·9′W	X	53
Mains of Benholm	Aberd	NO8070	56°49·5′	2°19·2′W	X	45
Mains of Biffie	Aberd	NJ9647	57°31·0′	2°3·5′W	X	30
Mains of Birkenbog	Aberd	NJ5364	57°40·1′	2°46·8′W	X	29
Mains of Birkenburn	Moray	NJ4548	57°31·4′	2°54·6′W	X	28,29
Mains of Birness	Aberd	NJ9933	57°23·5′	2°0·5′W	X	30
Mains of Blackhall	Aberd	NJ7521	57°17·0′	2°24·4′W	X	38
Mains of Blackton	Aberd	NJ7257	57°36·4′	2°27·7′W	X	29
Mains of Blairingone	Pth & Kin	NS9897	56°9·5′	3°38·1′W	X	58
Mains of Blairmore	Aberd	NJ4143	57°28·7′	2°58·6′W	X	28
Mains of Blairydrine	Aberd	NO7492	57°1·4′	2°25·2′W	X	38,45
Mains of Blervie	Moray	NJ0657	57°35·9′	3°33·9′W	X	27
Mains of Bodinfinnoch	Moray	NJ3748	57°31·3′	3°2·7′W	X	28
Mains of Bogfechel	Aberd	NJ8524	57°18·6′	2°14·5′W	X	38
Mains of Bogfouton	Aberd	NJ6436	57°25·0′	2°35·5′W	X	29
Mains of Bognie	Aberd	NJ5945	57°29·9′	2°40·6′W	X	29
Mains of Bonskeid	Pth & Kin	NN8861	56°43·9′	3°49·4′W	X	43
Mains of Boquhan	Stir	NS6795	56°8·0′	4°8·0′W	X	57
Mains of Bridgeton	Aberd	NO7767	56°47·9′	2°22·1′W	X	45
Mains of Brigton	Angus	NO4248	56°37·5′	2°56·3′W	X	54
Mains of Brotherton	Aberd	NO7967	56°47·9′	2°20·2′W	X	45
Mains of Brux	Aberd	NJ4916	57°14·2′	2°50·2′W	X	37
Mains of Bruxie	Aberd	NJ9448	57°31·6′	2°5·6′W	X	30
Mains of Buckie	Moray	NJ4264	57°40·0′	2°57·9′W	X	28
Mains of Bunachton	Highld	NH6534	57°22·8′	4°14·3′W	X	26
Mains of Bunchrew	Highld	NH6145	57°28·7′	4°18·6′W	X	26
Mains of Burgie	Moray	NJ0959	57°37·0′	3°30·9′W	X	27
Mains of Burnbank	Stir	NS7098	56°9·7′	4°5·2′W	X	57
Mains of Buthlaw	Aberd	NK0648	57°31·6′	1°53·5′W	X	30
Mains of Byth	Aberd	NJ8157	57°36·4′	2°18·6′W	X	29,30
Mains of Cairnborrow	Aberd	NJ4640	57°27·1′	2°53·5′W	X	28,29
Mains of Cairnbrock	D & G	NW9765	54°56·6′	5°9·7′W	X	82
Mains of Cairnbrogie	Aberd	NJ8428	57°20·8′	2°15·5′W	X	38
Mains of Cairnty	Moray	NJ3252	57°33·4′	3°7·7′W	X	28
Mains of Caldons	D & G	NX0853	54°50·4′	4°59·0′W	X	82
Mains of Callander	Pth & Kin	NN8624	56°23·9′	3°50·4′W	X	52,58
Mains of Calrossie	Highld	NH8077	57°46·3′	4°0·6′W	X	21
Mains of Camno	Pth & Kin	NO2742	56°34·1′	3°10·8′W	X	53
Mains of Cardno	Aberd	NJ9764	57°40·2′	2°2·6′W	X	30
Mains of Careston	Angus	NO5359	56°43·5′	2°45·6′W	X	54
Mains of Cargill	Pth & Kin	NO1637	56°31·3′	3°21·5′W	X	53
Mains of Carmyllie	Angus	NO5443	56°34·9′	2°44·5′W	X	54
Mains of Carnousie	Aberd	NJ6750	57°32·6′	2°32·6′W	X	29
Mains of Clackriach	Aberd	NJ9347	57°31·0′	2°6·6′W	X	30
Mains of Clashfarquhar	Aberd	NO9295	57°3·0′	2°7·5′W	X	38,45
Mains of Clunas	Highld	NH8846	57°29·7′	3°51·7′W	X	27
Mains of Clunymore	Moray	NJ3440	57°27·0′	3°5·5′W	X	28
Mains of Coldwells	Aberd	NJ9537	57°25·7′	2°4·5′W	X	30
Mains of Colleonard	Aberd	NJ6763	57°39·6′	2°32·7′W	X	29
Mains of Collieston	Aberd	NK0329	57°21·3′	1°56·6′W	X	38
Mains of Collin	D & G	NX7852	54°51·1′	3°53·6′W	X	84
Mains of Collithie	Aberd	NJ5135	57°24·4′	2°48·5′W	X	29
Mains of Comrie	Fife	NT0089	56°5·3′	3°36·0′W	X	65
Mains of Concraig	Aberd	NJ8309	57°10·5′	2°16·4′W	X	38
Mains of Condie	Pth & Kin	NO0712	56°17·7′	3°29·7′W	X	58
Mains of Corse	Aberd	NJ5407	57°9·4′	2°45·2′W	X	37
Mains of Corse	Aberd	NJ5940	57°27·2′	2°40·5′W	X	29
Mains of Corsindae	Aberd	NJ6809	57°10·5′	2°31·3′W	X	38
Mains of Corskie	Aberd	NJ6253	57°34·2′	2°37·7′W	X	29
Mains of Cotts	Moray	NJ2559	57°37·1′	3°14·9′W	X	28
Mains of Coull	Angus	NO4459	56°43·4′	2°54·5′W	X	54
Mains of Countesswells	C of Aber	NJ8704	57°7·9′	2°12·4′W	X	38
Mains of Craighall	Aberd	NJ5229	57°21·2′	2°47·4′W	X	37
Mains of Craigisla	Angus	NO2553	56°40·0′	3°13·0′W	X	53
Mains of Craigmill	Moray	NJ0954	57°34·3′	3°30·8′W	X	27
Mains of Craigmyle	Aberd	NJ6302	57°6·7′	2°36·2′W	X	37
Mains of Cranna	Aberd	NJ6352	57°33·7′	2°36·6′W	X	29
Mains of Creuchies	Pth & Kin	NO2050	56°38·4′	3°17·8′W	X	53
Mains of Crichie	Aberd	NJ9745	57°30·0′	2°2·5′W	X	30
Mains of Cromdale	Highld	NJ0628	57°20·2′	3°33·2′W	X	36
Mains of Cullen	Aberd	NJ7363	57°39·6′	2°26·7′W	X	29
Mains of Culsh	Aberd	NJ8848	57°31·6′	2°11·6′W	X	30
Mains of Cultmalundie	Pth & Kin	NO0323	56°23·6′	3°33·8′W	X	52,53,58
Mains of Dalbreac	Highld	NH3054	57°32·9′	4°50·0′W	X	26
Mains of Dalhaikie	Aberd	NO6498	57°4·6′	2°35·2′W	X	37,45
Mains of Daltulich	Highld	NH7341	57°26·8′	4°6·5′W	X	27
Mains of Dalvey	Highld	NJ1132	57°22·4′	3°28·3′W	X	36
Mains of Davidston	Aberd	NJ4244	57°29·2′	2°57·6′W	X	28
Mains of Dellavaird	Aberd	NO7481	56°55·4′	2°25·2′W	X	45
Mains of Dhuloch	D & G	NW9966	54°57·1′	5°7·9′W	X	82
Mains of Dounie	Pth & Kin	NO0958	56°42·5′	3°28·7′W	X	52,53
Mains of Drimnin	Highld	NM5455	56°37·6′	6°0·2′W	X	47
Mains of Drum	Aberd	NJ9045	57°30·0′	2°9·6′W	X	30
Mains of Drum	Aberd	NO8099	57°5·2′	2°19·3′W	X	38,45
Mains of Drumduan	Aberd	NJ5600	57°5·6′	2°43·1′W	X	37
Mains of Drumhendry	Aberd	NO6469	56°48·9′	2°34·9′W	X	45
Mains of Druminnor	Aberd	NJ5127	57°20·1′	2°48·4′W	X	37
Mains of Drumlochy	Pth & Kin	NO1646	56°36·2′	3°21·6′W	X	53
Mains of Drummond	Pth & Kin	NN8317	56°20·1′	3°53·1′W	X	57
Mains of Drummuir	Moray	NJ4044	57°29·2′	2°59·6′W	X	28
Mains of Drumtochty	Aberd	NO7180	56°54·9′	2°28·1′W	X	45
Mains of Drumwhindle	Aberd	NJ9235	57°24·6′	2°7·5′W	X	30
Mains of Drynie	Highld	NH6650	57°31·5′	4°13·8′W	X	26
Mains of Duchrae	D & G	NX7068	54°59·6′	4°1·5′W	X	83,84
Mains of Dudwick	Aberd	NJ9737	57°25·7′	2°2·5′W	X	30
Mains of Dumbreck	Aberd	NJ8928	57°20·8′	2°10·5′W	X	38
Mains of Dun	Angus	NO6659	56°43·5′	2°32·9′W	X	54
Mains of Duncrub	Pth & Kin	NO0015	56°19·3′	3°36·6′W	X	58
Mains of Duntanlich	Pth & Kin	NN8559	56°42·8′	3°52·3′W	X	43,52
Mains of Easter Beltie	Aberd	NO6499	57°5·1′	2°35·2′W	X	37,45
Mains of Eden	Aberd	NJ6958	57°36·9′	2°30·7′W	X	29
Mains of Edingight	Moray	NJ5156	57°35·7′	2°48·7′W	X	29
Mains of Edzell	Angus	NO5969	56°48·9′	2°39·8′W	X	44
Mains of Elrick	Aberd	NJ9441	57°27·8′	2°5·5′W	X	30
Mains of Errol	Pth & Kin	NO2421	56°22·8′	3°13·4′W	X	53,59
Mains of Esslemont	Aberd	NJ9329	57°21·3′	2°6·5′W	X	38
Mains of Faillie	Highld	NH7037	57°24·6′	4°9·4′W	X	27
Mains of Fasque	Aberd	NO6574	56°51·6′	2°34·0′W	X	45
Mains of Fedderate	Aberd	NJ8950	57°32·7′	2°10·6′W	X	30
Mains of Fiddie	Aberd	NJ8306	57°8·9′	2°16·4′W	X	38
Mains of Findrack	Aberd	NJ6105	57°8·3′	2°38·2′W	X	37
Mains of Fingask	Highld	NH5545	57°28·6′	4°24·6′W	X	26
Mains of Fisherie	Aberd	NJ7658	57°36·9′	2°23·6′W	X	29
Mains of Flichity	Highld	NH6729	57°20·2′	4°12·1′W	X	26,35
Mains of Fordie	Pth & Kin	NO0941	56°33·4′	3°28·4′W	X	52,53
Mains of Forest	Aberd	NJ9659	57°37·5′	2°3·6′W	X	30
Mains of Fortrie	Aberd	NJ9539	57°26·7′	2°4·5′W	X	30
Mains of Foveran	Aberd	NJ9923	57°18·1′	2°0·5′W	X	38
Mains of Fowlis	Angus	NO3232	56°28·8′	3°5·8′W	X	53
Mains of Frendraught	Aberd	NJ6141	57°27·7′	2°38·5′W	X	29
Mains of Fullarton	Pth & Kin	NO2944	56°35·2′	3°8·9′W	X	53
Mains of Gallachy	Moray	NJ4064	57°40·0′	2°59·9′W	X	28
Mains of Gallery	Angus	NO6765	56°46·8′	2°32·0′W	X	45
Mains of Garten	Highld	NH9620	57°15·8′	3°43·0′W	X	36
Mains of Gartly	Aberd	NJ5333	57°23·4′	2°46·5′W	X	29
Mains of Gask	Highld	NH6836	57°24·0′	4°11·3′W	X	26
Mains of Geanies	Highld	NH8979	57°47·5′	3°51·6′W	X	21
Mains of Gight	Aberd	NJ8239	57°26·7′	2°17·5′W	X	29,30
Mains of Glack	Aberd	NJ7327	57°20·2′	2°26·5′W	X	38
Mains of Glamis	Angus	NO3947	56°36·9′	2°59·2′W	X	54
Mains of Glassaugh	Aberd	NJ5564	57°40·1′	2°44·8′W	X	29
Mains of Glassel	Aberd	NO6699	57°5·1′	2°33·2′W	X	38,45
Mains of Glasswell	Angus	NO4053	56°40·2′	2°58·3′W	X	54
Mains of Glenbrown	Highld	NJ1220	57°16·0′	3°27·1′W	X	36
Mains of Glenbuchat	Aberd	NJ3914	57°13·0′	3°0·1′W	X	37
Mains of Glencarvie	Aberd	NJ3410	57°10·8′	3°5·1′W	X	37
Mains of Glenderby	Pth & Kin	NO0459	56°43·0′	3°33·7′W	X	52,53
Mains of Glenfarquhar	Aberd	NO7180	56°54·9′	2°28·1′W	X	45
Mains of Glenlochy	Highld	NJ1221	57°16·5′	3°27·1′W	X	36
Mains of Glentruim	Highld	NN6894	57°1·4′	4°10·0′W	X	35
Mains of Glinn	Stir	NS6391	56°5·8′	4°11·7′W	X	57
Mains of Gorthy	Pth & Kin	NN9623	56°23·5′	3°40·6′W	X	52,53,58
Mains of Gourdie	Pth & Kin	NO1242	56°34·0′	3°25·5′W	X	53
Mains of Grandhome	C of Aber	NJ8912	57°12·2′	2°10·5′W	T	38
Mains of Gray	C of Dun	NO3332	56°28·8′	3°4·8′W	T	53
Mains of Greenlaw	D & G	NX7464	54°57·5′	3°57·6′W	X	83,84
Mains of Greens	Aberd	NJ8246	57°30·5′	2°17·6′W	X	29,30
Mains of Guynd	Angus	NO5642	56°34·3′	2°42·5′W	X	54
Mains of Haddo	Aberd	NJ8633	57°23·5′	2°13·5′W	X	30
Mains of Hallhead	Aberd	NJ5209	57°10·4′	2°47·2′W	X	37
Mains of Hallyburton	Pth & Kin	NO2438	56°31·9′	3°13·7′W	X	53
Mains of Hatton	Aberd	NJ7042	57°28·3′	2°29·6′W	X	29
Mains of Hatton	Aberd	NJ9658	57°37·0′	2°3·6′W	X	30
Mains of Haulkerton	Aberd	NO7172	56°50·6′	2°28·1′W	X	45
Mains of Hedderwick	Angus	NO7060	56°44·1′	2°29·0′W	X	45
Mains of Hills	D & G	NX9172	55°2·1′	3°41·9′W	X	84
Mains of Hopewell	Aberd	NJ4405	57°8·2′	2°55·1′W	X	37
Mains of Idoch	Aberd	NJ7749	57°32·1′	2°22·6′W	X	29,30
Mains of Inchbreck	Aberd	NO7483	56°56·5′	2°25·2′W	X	45
Mains of Inkhorn	Aberd	NJ9239	57°26·7′	2°7·5′W	X	30
Mains of Innerpeffray	Pth & Kin	NN9018	56°20·8′	3°46·3′W	X	58
Mains of Inveramsay	Aberd	NJ7425	57°19·1′	2°25·4′W	X	38
Mains of Inverebrie	Aberd	NJ9133	57°23·5′	2°8·5′W	X	30
Mains of Inverourie	Moray	NJ1526	57°19·3′	3°24·2′W	X	36
Mains of Inverugie	Aberd	NK1148	57°31·6′	1°48·5′W	X	30
Mains of Kair	Aberd	NO7676	56°52·7′	2°23·2′W	X	45
Mains of Keir	Aberd	NJ8108	57°10·0′	2°18·4′W	X	38
Mains of Keithfield	Aberd	NJ8533	57°23·5′	2°14·5′W	X	30
Mains of Keithick	Pth & Kin	NO2038	56°31·9′	3°17·6′W	X	53
Mains of Kelly	Aberd	NJ8934	57°24·0′	2°10·5′W	X	30
Mains of Kelly	Angus	NO5939	56°32·7′	2°39·6′W	X	54
Mains of Kildrummy	Aberd	NJ4516	57°14·1′	2°54·2′W	X	37
Mains of Killichangie	Pth & Kin	NN9654	56°40·2′	3°41·4′W	X	52,53
Mains of Kinblethmont	Angus	NO6346	56°36·5′	2°35·7′W	X	54
Mains of Kincraigie	Aberd	NJ4904	57°7·7′	2°50·1′W	X	37
Mains of Kindrought	Aberd	NJ9853	57°34·3′	2°1·5′W	X	30
Mains of Kininmonth	Aberd	NK0252	57°33·7′	1°57·5′W	X	30
Mains of Kinmonth	Pth & Kin	NO1618	56°21·1′	3°21·1′W	X	58
Mains of Kinmuck	Aberd	NJ9835	57°24·6′	2°1·5′W	X	30
Mains of Kinmundy	Aberd	NJ8307	57°9·5′	2°16·4′W	X	38
Mains of Kinmundy	Aberd	NK0444	57°29·4′	1°55·5′W	X	30
Mains of Kinnairdy	Aberd	NJ6149	57°32·0′	2°38·6′W	X	29
Mains of Kinnettles	Angus	NO4246	56°36·4′	2°56·2′W	X	54
Mains of Kirdells	Moray	NJ1739	57°26·3′	3°22·5′W	X	28
Mains of Kirkney	Aberd	NJ5133	57°23·3′	2°48·5′W	X	29
Mains of Kirktonhill	Aberd	NO6966	56°47·3′	2°30·0′W	X	45
Mains of Knapperna	Aberd	NJ8823	57°18·1′	2°11·5′W	X	38
Mains of Knockhall	Aberd	NJ9926	57°19·7′	2°0·5′W	X	38
Mains of Knockorth	Aberd	NJ6250	57°32·6′	2°37·6′W	X	29
Mains of Laithers	Aberd	NJ6749	57°32·1′	2°32·6′W	X	29
Mains of Larg	D & G	NX1664	54°56·5′	4°51·9′W	X	82
Mains of Lauriston	Aberd	NO7666	56°47·4′	2°23·1′W	X	45
Mains of Leask	Aberd	NK0333	57°23·5′	1°56·5′W	X	30
Mains of Lesmoir	Aberd	NJ4728	57°20·6′	2°52·4′W	X	37
Mains of Lesmurdie	Moray	NJ3932	57°22·7′	3°0·4′W	X	37
Mains of Letham	Angus	NO6343	56°34·9′	2°35·7′W	X	54
Mains of Linton	Aberd	NJ7010	57°11·0′	2°29·3′W	X	38
Mains of Loanhead	Aberd	NJ6831	57°22·4′	2°31·5′W	X	29
Mains of Logie	Aberd	NJ4402	57°6·6′	2°55·0′W	X	37
Mains of Logie	Aberd	NK0356	57°35·9′	1°56·5′W	X	30
Mains of Logie	Angus	NO7063	56°45·7′	2°29·0′W	X	45
Mains of Luther	Aberd	NO6667	56°47·9′	2°33·0′W	X	45
Mains of Machermore	D & G	NX4264	54°57·0′	4°27·6′W	X	83
Mains of Mause	Pth & Kin	NO1649	56°37·8′	3°21·7′W	X	53
Mains of Mayen	Moray	NJ5747	57°30·9′	2°42·6′W	X	29
Mains of Melginch	Pth & Kin	NO1729	56°27·0′	3°20·3′W	X	53,58
Mains of Melgund	Angus	NO5456	56°41·9′	2°44·6′W	T	54
Mains of Melrose	Aberd	NJ7464	57°40·2′	2°25·7′W	X	29
Mains of Midstrath	Aberd	NO5895	57°2·9′	2°41·1′W	X	37,44
Mains of Minnydow	D & G	NX8070	55°0·9′	3°52·2′W	X	84
Mains of Monaltrie	Aberd	NO2495	57°2·6′	3°14·7′W	X	36,44
Mains of Monduff	Aberd	NO9092	57°1·4′	2°9·4′W	X	38,45
Mains of Mondynes	Aberd	NO7779	56°54·4′	2°22·2′W	X	45
Mains of Montcoffer	Aberd	NJ6861	57°38·5′	2°31·7′W	X	29
Mains of Morinsh	Moray	NJ2130	57°21·5′	3°18·3′W	X	36
Mains of Mosstown	Aberd	NJ9227	57°20·3′	2°7·5′W	X	38
Mains of Moulin	Pth & Kin	NN9932	56°28·4′	3°37·9′W	X	52,53
Mains of Moyness	Highld	NH9553	57°33·6′	3°44·8′W	X	27
Mains of Mulben	Moray	NJ3551	57°32·9′	3°4·7′W	X	28
Mains of Murie	Pth & Kin	NO2322	56°23·3′	3°14·4′W	X	53,58
Mains of Murthly	Pth & Kin	NN8749	56°37·4′	3°50·1′W	X	52
Mains of Newhall	Highld	NH6965	57°39·6′	4°11·3′W	X	21
Mains of New Rayne	Aberd	NJ6729	57°21·3′	2°32·4′W	X	38
Mains of Newton	Aberd	NO7069	56°48·9′	2°29·0′W	X	45
Mains of Newton	Moray	NJ3144	57°29·1′	3°8·6′W	X	28
Mains of Newtongarry	Aberd	NJ5739	57°26·6′	2°42·5′W	X	29
Mains of Novar	Highld	NH6168	57°41·1′	4°19·4′W	X	21
Mains of Ogil	Angus	NO4461	56°44·5′	2°54·5′W	X	44
Mains of Oldmaud	Aberd	NJ9147	57°31·0′	2°8·6′W	X	30
Mains of Olrig	Highld	ND1866	58°34·7′	3°24·1′W	X	11,12
Mains of Orchardtown	Aberd	NJ9126	57°19·7′	2°8·5′W	X	38
Mains of Orchil	Pth & Kin	NN9064	56°45·5′	3°47·5′W	T	43
Mains of Orton	Moray	NJ3154	57°34·5′	3°8·8′W	X	28
Mains of Overhall	Aberd	NJ6326	57°19·6′	2°36·4′W	X	37
Mains of Oxhill	Moray	NJ4059	57°37·3′	2°59·8′W	X	28
Mains of Paithnick	Moray	NJ4752	57°33·6′	2°52·7′W	X	28,29
Mains of Panholes	Pth & Kin	NN8810	56°16·4′	3°48·1′W	X	58
Mains of Panmure	Angus	NO5237	56°31·6′	2°46·4′W	X	54
Mains of Park	Aberd	NK0056	57°35·9′	1°59·5′W	X	30
Mains of Park	D & G	NX1856	54°52·2′	4°49·8′W	X	82
Mains of Parkhill	Angus	NO6445	56°36·0′	2°34·7′W	X	54
Mains of Penninghame	D & G	NX4060	54°54·8′	4°29·3′W	X	83
Mains of Petmathen	Aberd	NJ6627	57°20·2′	2°33·4′W	X	38
Mains of Philorth	Aberd	NK0063	57°39·7′	1°59·5′W	X	30
Mains of Pitforthie	Angus	NO6061	56°44·6′	2°38·8′W	X	45
Mains of Pitfour	Aberd	NJ9849	57°32·1′	2°1·5′W	X	30
Mains of Pitlurg	Moray	NJ4345	57°29·8′	2°56·6′W	X	28
Mains of Pittendreigh	Aberd	NJ6548	57°31·5′	2°34·6′W	X	29
Mains of Pittendriech	Pth & Kin	NO1541	56°33·5′	3°22·5′W	X	53
Mains of Pittrichie	Aberd	NJ8624	57°18·6′	2°13·5′W	X	38
Mains of Powfoulis	Falk	NS9185	56°3·0′	3°44·6′W	X	65
Mains of Pronie	Aberd	NJ4407	57°9·3′	2°55·1′W	X	37
Mains of Quirn	Moray	NJ1924	57°18·2′	3°20·2′W	X	36
Mains of Rannieston	Aberd	NJ9326	57°19·7′	2°6·5′W	X	38
Mains of Ravensby	Angus	NO5335	56°30·5′	2°45·4′W	X	54
Mains of Rhynie	Aberd	NJ4926	57°19·6′	2°50·4′W	X	37
Mains of Rochelhill	Angus	NO3745	56°35·8′	3°1·1′W	X	54
Mains of Rothmaise	Aberd	NJ6732	57°22·9′	2°32·5′W	X	29
Mains of Sauchen	Aberd	NJ6911	57°11·6′	2°30·3′W	X	38
Mains of Seggieden	Aberd	NJ5426	57°19·6′	2°45·4′W	X	37
Mains of Shiels	Aberd	NJ6509	57°10·5′	2°34·3′W	X	38
Mains of Skeith	Moray	NJ5060	57°37·9′	2°49·8′W	X	29
Mains of Skelmanae	Aberd	NJ9158	57°37·0′	2°8·6′W	X	30
Mains of Skene	Aberd	NJ7610	57°11·1′	2°23·4′W	X	38
Mains of Slains	Aberd	NK0430	57°21·9′	1°55·6′W	X	30
Mains of Sluie	Moray	NJ0052	57°33·1′	3°39·8′W	X	27
Mains of Soilzarie	Pth & Kin	NO1259	56°43·1′	3°25·8′W	X	53
Mains of Stobhall	Pth & Kin	NO1335	56°30·2′	3°24·4′W	X	53
Mains of Stroma	Highld	ND3577	58°40·8′	3°6·8′W	X	7,12
Mains of Struie	Pth & Kin	NO0711	56°17·2′	3°29·7′W	X	58
Mains of Struthers	Moray	NJ0760	57°37·5′	3°33·0′W	X	27
Mains of Swailend	Aberd	NJ8817	57°14·9′	2°11·5′W	X	38
Mains of Tannachy	Moray	NJ3863	57°39·4′	3°1·9′W	X	28
Mains of Tarryblake	Moray	NJ5150	57°32·5′	2°48·7′W	X	29
Mains of Tarty	Aberd	NJ9827	57°20·3′	2°1·5′W	X	38
Mains of Taymount	Pth & Kin	NO1234	56°29·6′	3°25·3′W	X	53
Mains of Taymouth	Pth & Kin	NN7745	56°35·1′	3°59·7′W	X	51,52
Mains of Tertowie	Aberd	NJ8110	57°11·1′	2°18·4′W	X	38
Mains of Thornton	Aberd	NJ8224	57°18·6′	2°17·5′W	X	38
Mains of Thornton	Aberd	NO6871	56°50·0′	2°31·0′W	X	45
Mains of Throsk	Stir	NS8590	56°5·6′	3°50·5′W	X	58
Mains of Tig	S Ayr	NX1283	55°6·6′	4°56·4′W	X	76
Mains of Tilliefoure	Aberd	NJ6619	57°15·9′	2°33·4′W	X	38
Mains of Tillyangus	Aberd	NJ5325	57°19·0′	2°46·4′W	X	37
Mains of Tillymorgan	Aberd	NJ6634	57°24·0′	2°33·5′W	X	29
Mains of Tippermallo	Pth & Kin	NO0224	56°24·1′	3°34·8′W	X	52,53,58
Mains of Tollo	Aberd	NJ6645	57°29·9′	2°33·6′W	X	29
Mains of Tonley	Aberd	NJ5913	57°12·6′	2°40·3′W	X	37
Mains of Tore	Highld	NH6153	57°33·0′	4°18·9′W	X	26
Mains of Torryleith	Aberd	NJ8720	57°16·5′	2°12·5′W	X	38
Mains of Towie	Aberd	NJ7444	57°29·4′	2°25·6′W	X	29

Mains of Towiebeg	Moray	NJ3845	57°29·7'	3°1·6'W	X	28
Mains of Tullibardine	Pth & Kin	NN9113	56°18·1'	3°45·2'W	X	58
Mains of Tulloch	Aberd	NJ7832	57°22·9'	2°21·5'W	X	29,30
Mains of Tulloch	Highld	NH9715	57°13·1'	3°41·9'W	X	36
Mains of Tullochgribban	Highld	NH9624	57°17·9'	3°43·1'W	X	36
Mains of Twynholm	D & G	NX6656	54°53·1'	4°4·9'W	X	83,84
Mains of Ulbster	Highld	ND3342	58°21·9'	3°8·2'W	X	12
Mains of Usan	Angus	NO7255	56°41·4'	2°27·0'W	T	54
Mains of Wardhouse	Aberd	NJ5929	57°21·2'	2°40·4'W	X	37
Mains of Waterton	Aberd	NJ9830	57°21·9'	2°1·5'W	X	30
Mains of Watten	Highld	ND2556	58°29·4'	3°16·7'W	X	11,12
Mains of Whitehill	Aberd	NJ7764	57°40·2'	2°22·7'W	X	29,30
Mains of Whitehouse	Aberd	NJ6214	57°13·2'	2°37·3'W	X	37
Mains of Whitewell	Angus	NO4757	56°42·4'	2°51·5'W	X	54
Mains of Williamston	Aberd	NJ6530	57°21·8'	2°34·5'W	X	29
Mains of Woodstone	Aberd	NO7466	56°47·3'	2°25·1'W	X	45
Mains Plantn	D & G	NS7707	55°20·8'	3°55·9'W	F	71,78
Mainsriddle	D & G	NX9456	54°53·5'	3°38·7'W	T	84
Mains Rigg	Cumbr	NY6164	54°58·4'	2°36·1'W	H	86
Mainsrigg	Northum	NY7655	54°53·6'	2°22·0'W	X	86,87
Mainsrigg Fell	Northum	NY7454	54°53·1'	2°23·9'W	X	86,87
Main Stell	Midd	NZ5512	54°30·3'	1°8·6'W	W	93
Mains, The	Cumbr	NY5639	54°44·9'	2°40·6'W	X	90
Mains, The	Highld	NG9055	57°32·4'	5°30·1'W	X	25
Mains, The	Northum	NU0410	55°23·3'	1°55·8'W	X	81
Mainstone	C of Plym	SX5158	50°24·4'	4°5·4'W	X	201
Mainstone	Devon	SS5236	51°6·5'	4°6·5'W	X	180
Mainstone	Shrops	SO2787	52°28·8'	3°4·1'W	T	137
Mainstone Court	Heref	SO6539	52°3·1'	2°30·2'W	X	149
Mainstone Hill	Surrey	SU9157	51°18·5'	0°41·3'W	X	175,186
Mains Wood	Cumbr	NY6116	54°32·5'	2°35·7'W	F	91
Mains Wood	Heref	SO6438	52°2·6'	2°31·1'W	F	149
Mains Wood	Red & Cl	NZ7016	54°32·3'	0°54·7'W	F	94
Maintree	S Ayr	NS4432	55°33·7'	4°28·0'W	X	70
Main Water of Luce	D & G	NX1468	54°58·6'	4°54·0'W	W	82
Main Water of Luce	D & G	NX1474	55°1·8'	4°54·2'W	W	76
Mainwood Fm	Notts	SK7264	53°10·3'	0°55·0'W	FM	120
Maire	Devon	SS8018	50°57·2'	3°42·1'W	X	181
Mairsland	Fife	NO2312	56°17·9'	3°14·2'W	X	58
Maisemore	Glos	SO8121	51°53·5'	2°16·2'W	T	162
Maisemore Ham	Glos	SO8120	51°52·9'	2°16·2'W	X	162
Maisemore Park	Glos	SO8122	51°54·0'	2°16·2'W	X	162
Maisey Fm	Wilts	SU1771	51°26·5'	1°44·9'W	FM	173
Màisgeir	Arg & Bt	NM3439	56°28·3'	6°18·7'W	X	47,48
Maisley	Moray	NJ4049	57°31·9'	2°59·7'W	X	28
Maisondieu	Angus	NO5861	56°44·6'	2°40·8'W	X	44
Maisondieu	Scot Bord	NT7132	55°35·1'	2°27·2'W	X	74
Maisongill	Cumbr	NY6710	54°29·3'	2°30·1'W	X	91
Màithidh Glas	N Eil	NF8849	57°25·7'	7°11·5'W	X	22
Màithidh Riabhach	N Eil	NF8850	57°26·2'	7°11·5'W	X	22
Maitland	S Ayr	NS2902	55°17·2'	4°41·1'W	X	76
Maitland Park	Camden	TQ2884	51°32·6'	0°8·9'W	T	176
Maitlands Fm	Kent	TQ9154	51°15·4'	0°44·6'E	FM	189
Maize Beck	Cumbr	NY7626	54°38·0'	2°21·9'W	W	91
Maize Beck	Cumbr	NY8027	54°38·5'	2°18·2'W	W	91,92
Maizebeck Force	Cumbr	NY8027	54°38·5'	2°18·2'W	W	91,92
Maize Hill	Lincs	TF0421	52°46·8'	0°27·1'W	X	130
Majeston	Inverc	NS2272	55°54·7'	4°50·4'W	X	63
Major Fm	Suff	TM1272	52°18·5'	1°7·0'E	FM	144,155
Major Oak	Notts	SK6267	53°12·0'	1°3·9'W	F	120
Majors Fm	Lincs	TF3430	52°51·3'	0°0·2'W	FM	131
Majors Fm	Notts	SK7832	53°14·6'	0°49·5'W	FM	120,121
Major's Green	Worcs	SP1077	52°23·7'	1°50·8'W	T	139
Major's Leap	Shrops	SO5998	52°34·9'	2°35·9'W	X	137,138
Major Woods	Cumbr	SD4978	54°12·0'	2°46·5'W	F	97
Makants	Wigan	SD7102	53°31·1'	2°25·8'W	X	109
Makemerich	Northum	NZ0379	55°6·6'	1°56·8'W	X	87
Make me Rich	Northum	NZ1977	55°5·5'	1°41·7'W	X	88
Makendon	Northum	NT8009	55°22·7'	2°18·5'W	X	80
Makeness Kipps	Scot Bord	NT2844	55°41·3'	3°8·3'W	H	73
Makeney	Derby	SK3544	52°59·8'	1°28·3'W	T	119,128
Maker Heights	Corn	SX4351	50°20·5'	4°12·0'W	X	201
Makerstoun	Scot Bord	NT6632	55°35·1'	2°31·9'W	X	74
Makerstoun Ho	Scot Bord	NT6731	55°34·5'	2°31·0'W	X	74
Makimrich Wood	Scot Bord	NT4456	55°47·9'	2°53·2'W	F	66,73
Makins Fm	Suff	TL8755	52°9·9'	0°44·5'E	FM	155
Mala Bholsa	Arg & Bt	NR3777	55°55·1'	6°12·1'W	H	60,61
Malach	Aberd	NJ4538	57°26·0'	2°54·5'W	X	28,29
Malaclete	N Eil	NF7974	57°38·8'	7°22·4'W	T	18
Malacombe Bottom	Wilts	ST9419	50°58·5'	2°4·7'W	X	184
Malago, The	C of Bris	ST5769	51°25·3'	2°36·7'W	W	172,182
Malaidh Mora	Arg & Bt	NR7646	55°39·6'	5°33·2'W	X	62,69
Malasgair	N Eil	NB3017	58°3·9'	6°34·2'W	H	13,14
Malborough	Devon	SX7039	50°14·4'	3°49·0'W	T	202
Malborough	Lincs	SK9361	53°8·5'	0°36·2'W	X	121
Malcoff	Derby	SK0782	53°20·3'	1°53·3'W	T	110
Malcolmburn	Moray	NJ3651	57°32·9'	3°3·7'W	X	28
Malcolm's Cross	Northum	NU1914	55°25·4'	1°41·6'W	A	81
Malcolm's Head	Shetld	HZ1970	59°31·2'	1°39·4'W	X	4
Malcolm's Point	Arg & Bt	NM4918	56°17·5'	6°2·9'W	X	48
Malcolmstone	C of Edin	NT1768	55°54·1'	3°19·2'W	X	65,66
Malcomsley	Derby	SK1537	52°56·0'	1°46·2'W	X	128
Malcomston	E Ayr	NS3915	55°24·4'	4°32·1'W	X	70
Malden Rushett	King	TQ1761	51°20·4'	0°18·8'W	T	176,187
Maldie Burn	Highld	NC2534	58°15·9'	4°58·5'W	W	15
Maldon	Essex	TL8407	51°44·1'	0°40·3'E	T	168
Maldon 991	Essex	TL8605	51°43·0'	0°42·0'E	A	168
Maldon Wood	Essex	TM1419	51°49·9'	1°6·8'E	F	168,169
Malecomb	W Susx	SU9214	50°55·3'	0°41·1'W	X	197
Malehurst	Shrops	SJ3806	52°39·1'	2°54·6'W	T	126
Males Burgh	E Susx	TQ4605	50°49·8'	0°4·8'E	X	198
Males Burgh (Tumulus)	E Susx	TQ4605	50°49·8'	0°4·8'E	A	198
Malgwyn	Powys	SN8983	52°26·3'	3°37·6'W	X	135,136
Malham	N Yks	SD9062	54°3·5'	2°8·7'W	T	98
Malham	W Susx	TQ0628	51°2·7'	0°28·9'W	X	187,197
Malham Cove	N Yks	SD8964	54°4·6'	2°9·7'W	X	98
Malham Lings	N Yks	SD8964	54°4·6'	2°9·7'W	X	98
Malham Moor	N Yks	SD9565	54°5·1'	2°4·2'W	X	98
Malham Tarn	N Yks	SD8966	54°5·6'	2°9·7'W	W	98
Malham Tarn Field Centre	N Yks	SD8967	54°6·2'	2°9·7'W	X	98

Malice Fm	Peterb	TF3208	52°39·4'	0°2·5'W	FM	142
Maligar	Highld	NG4864	57°36·0'	6°12·6'W	T	23
Malinbridge	Sheff	SK3289	53°24·0'	1°30·7'W	T	110,111
Malinslee	Wrekin	SJ6908	52°40·4'	2°27·1'W	T	127
Malkin Bower	N Yks	SE5794	54°20·5'	1°7·0'W	X	100
Malkin Hill	Notts	SK6540	52°57·4'	1°1·5'W	X	129
Malkin's Bank	Ches	SJ7659	53°7·9'	2°21·1'W	T	118
Malkins Wood Fm	Salf	SJ7198	53°28·9'	2°25·8'W	FM	109
Mallaig	Highld	NM6796	57°0·0'	5°49·7'W	T	40
Mallaig Bheag	Highld	NM6997	57°0·6'	5°47·8'W	X	33,40
Mallaig Harbour	Highld	NM6797	57°0·6'	5°49·8'W	W	40
Mallaigmore	Highld	NM6997	57°0·6'	5°47·8'W	T	40
Mallands	Devon	SX8272	50°32·4'	3°39·5'W	X	191
Mallard Fm	Lincs	TF1734	52°53·7'	0°15·2'W	FM	130
Mallard Grange	N Yks	SE2670	54°7·8'	1°35·7'W	X	99
Mallard Hurn	Lincs	TF1734	52°53·7'	0°15·2'W	X	130
Mallard's Court	Bucks	SU7696	51°39·7'	0°53·7'W	X	165
Mallards Pike	Glos	SO6309	51°46·9'	2°31·8'W	W	162
Mallard Wood	Hants	SU3209	50°53·0'	1°32·3'W	F	196
Mallart River	Highld	NC6834	58°16·8'	4°14·6'W	W	16
Mallen Dodd	Cumbr	NY2725	54°37·1'	3°7·4'W	X	89,90
Malleny Ho	C of Edin	NT1666	55°53·0'	3°20·1'W	A	65,66
Malleny Mills	C of Edin	NT1665	55°52·5'	3°20·1'W	T	65,66
Mallerstang Common	Cumbr	NY7800	54°23·9'	2°19·9'W	X	91
Mallerstang Common	Cumbr	SD7899	54°23·4'	2°19·9'W	X	98
Mallerstang Edge	Cumbr	NY7901	54°24·5'	2°19·0'W	X	91
Malletsheugh	E Renf	NS5255	55°46·2'	4°21·1'W	X	64
Mallie Side	Scot Bord	NT8619	55°28·1'	2°12·9'W	H	80
Malling	Stir	NN5600	56°10·5'	4°18·7'W	X	57
Mallingdown Fm	E Susx	TQ4423	50°59·5'	0°3·5'E	FM	198
Malling Hill	E Susx	TQ4210	50°52·5'	0°1·5'E	X	198
Mallins Wood	Heref	SO7449	52°8·6'	2°22·4'W	F	150
Mallory Park	Leic	SK4500	52°36·0'	1°19·7'W	X	140
Mallow Burn	Northum	NY8976	55°4·9'	2°9·9'W	X	87
Mallowburn Cottages	Northum	NY8976	55°4·9'	2°9·9'W	X	87
Mallowdale	Lancs	SD6061	54°2·9'	2°36·2'W	X	97
Mallowdale Fell	Lancs	SD6159	54°1·8'	2°35·3'W	X	102,103
Mallowdale Pike	Lancs	SD6160	54°2·3'	2°35·3'W	H	97
Mallows Cotton Village	Northnts	SP9773	52°21·0'	0°34·2'W	A	141,153
Mallow's Fm	Lincs	TF3651	53°2·6'	0°2·1'E	FM	122
Mallows Green	Essex	TL4726	51°55·0'	0°8·6'E	T	167
Mallrenhesken	Pth & Kin	NO1572	56°50·2'	3°23·1'W	H	43
Mallsburn	Cumbr	NY4873	55°3·2'	2°48·4'W	X	86
Mallscastle	D & G	NY1579	55°6·1'	3°19·5'W	X	85
Mallsgate	Cumbr	NY4874	55°3·7'	2°48·4'W	X	86
Malltraeth	I of Angl	SH4068	53°11·3'	4°23·3'W	T	114,115
Malltraeth Bay	I of Angl	SH3764	53°9·1'	4°25·9'W	W	114
Malltraeth Marsh or Cors Ddyga	I of Angl	SH4571	53°13·1'	4°18·9'W	W	114,115
Malltraeth Sands	I of Angl	SH3966	53°10·3'	4°24·1'W	X	114
Mallwyd	Gwyn	SH8612	52°41·9'	3°40·8'W	T	124,125
Mallyan Spout	N Yks	NZ8201	54°24·1'	0°43·8'W	W	94
Mally Brook	Monm	SO5115	51°50·1'	2°42·3'W	W	162
Mallydams Wood	E Susx	TQ8512	50°52·9'	0°38·2'E	F	199
Mallyford	D & G	NX8597	55°15·5'	3°48·1'W	X	78
Mallyrust Fm	Aberd	NJ6659	57°37·4'	2°33·7'W	FM	29
Mally's Crag	Northum	NT7900	55°17·9'	2°19·4'W	X	80
Malmains	Kent	TQ9344	51°10·0'	0°46·0'E	X	189
Malmains Fm	Kent	TR2949	51°11·9'	1°17·1'E	FM	179
Malmaynes Hall Fm	Medway	TQ8175	51°26·9'	0°36·7'E	FM	178
Malmesbury	Wilts	ST9387	51°35·1'	2°5·7'W	T	173
Malmesbury Common	Wilts	ST9085	51°34·1'	2°8·3'W	X	173
Malms Fm	Hants	SU7540	51°9·5'	0°55·3'W	FM	186
Malmsmead	Devon	SS7947	51°12·8'	3°43·6'W	T	180
Malmsmead Hill	Devon	SS7846	51°12·2'	3°44·4'W	H	180
Malo Cross	N Yks	SE8694	54°20·3'	0°40·2'W	A	94,101
Malpas	Ches	SJ4847	53°1·3'	2°46·1'W	T	117
Malpas	Corn	SW8442	50°14·5'	5°1·4'W	T	204
Malpas	Newp	ST3090	51°36·5'	3°0·3'W	T	171
Malpas	W Berks	SU6372	51°26·8'	1°5·2'W	T	175
Malpass Wood	Shrops	SO7076	52°23·1'	2°26·0'W	F	138
Malsach Burn	Aberd	NJ5631	57°22·3'	2°43·4'W	W	29,37
Malshangar Ho	Hants	SU5652	51°16·1'	1°11·4'W	X	185
Malson	Devon	SS8317	50°56·7'	3°39·5'W	X	181
Malston Barton	Devon	SX7745	50°17·8'	3°43·2'W	X	202
Malston Mill	Devon	SX7645	50°17·7'	3°44·1'W	X	202
Malswick	Glos	SO7425	51°55·6'	2°22·3'W	T	162
Maltbeggar's Fm	Essex	TL8624	51°53·2'	0°42·6'E	FM	168
Maltby	Lincs	TF3184	53°20·4'	0°1·5'W	T	122
Maltby	Roth	SK5292	53°25·6'	1°12·6'W	T	111
Maltby	Stock on T	NZ4613	54°30·9'	1°16·9'W	T	93
Maltby Beck	Stock on T	NZ4813	54°30·8'	1°15·1'W	W	93
Maltby Dike	Roth	SK5291	53°25·0'	1°12·6'W	W	111
Maltby Fm	N Lincs	SE9518	53°39·2'	0°33·3'W	FM	112
Maltby Grange	Stock on T	NZ4712	54°30·3'	1°16·0'W	X	93
Maltby le Marsh	Lincs	TF4681	53°18·6'	0°11·9'E	T	122
Maltby Wood	Lincs	TF3483	53°19·8'	0°1·1'E	F	122
Malt Hill Fm	Brackn	SU8872	51°26·6'	0°43·6'W	FM	175
Malt Ho	Dorset	ST9806	50°51·4'	2°1·3'W	X	195
Malt Ho	W Berks	SU3963	51°22·1'	1°26·0'W	X	174
Malthouse	Card	ST2082	51°32·1'	3°8·8'W	X	171
Malthouse	Essex	TM1721	51°50·9'	1°9·4'E	X	168,169
Malthouse	Kent	TQ9461	51°19·1'	0°47·4'E	A	178
Malthouse	W Berks	SU5075	51°28·5'	1°16·4'W	X	174
Malthouse Fm	Hants	SU7938	51°8·4'	0°51·9'W	FM	186
Malthouse Fm	Norf	TF9322	52°45·9'	0°52·0'E	FM	132
Malthouse Fm	Norf	TG2200	52°33·4'	1°16·9'E	FM	134
Malthouse Fm	Norf	TG2723	52°45·6'	1°22·3'E	FM	133,134
Malt House Fm	Shrops	SJ4274	52°25·8'	2°34·0'W	FM	138
Malthouse Fm	Somer	ST3446	51°12·8'	2°56·3'W	FM	182
Malthouse Fm	Staffs	SJ9445	53°0·4'	2°5·0'W	FM	118
Malthouse Fm	Suff	TM1961	52°12·4'	1°12·7'E	FM	156
Malthouse Fm	Surrey	SU9561	51°20·6'	0°37·8'W	FM	175,176,186
Malthouse Fm	W Berks	SU4278	51°30·2'	1°23·3'W	FM	174
Malthouse Fm	W Berks	SU6172	51°26·9'	1°6·9'W	FM	175
Malthouse Fm	Wilts	ST9885	51°34·1'	2°1·3'W	FM	173
Malthouse Point	Devon	SX6147	50°18·6'	3°56·8'W	X	202
Malting End	Suff	TL7454	52°9·6'	0°33·0'E	T	155
Malting Fm	Essex	TL5608	51°45·2'	0°16·0'E	FM	167
Malting Fm	Essex	TL9531	51°56·8'	0°50·6'E	FM	168

Malting Fm	Essex	TM0131	51°56·7'	0°55·9'E	FM	168
Malting Fm	Essex	TM0430	51°56·1'	0°58·5'E	FM	168
Malting Fm	Suff	TL9252	52°8·2'	0°48·7'E	FM	155
Malting Fm	Suff	TL9334	51°58·5'	0°49·0'E	FM	155
Malting Fm	Suff	TM1669	52°16·8'	1°10·4'E	FM	156
Maltings Fm	Essex	TL7817	51°49·6'	0°35·4'E	FM	167
Maltings Fm	Suff	TL8962	52°13·6'	0°46·4'E	FM	155
Maltings Hill	Essex	TL5407	51°44·7'	0°14·2'E	X	167
Maltings, The	Lincs	TF0745	52°59·7'	0°23·9'W	X	130
Maltings, The	Suff	TM3957	52°9·8'	1°30·1'E	X	156
Maltkiln Cotts	Durham	NZ1322	54°35·8'	1°47·5'W	X	92
Maltkiln Fm	Ches	SJ7045	53°0·3'	2°26·4'W	FM	118
Maltkiln Fm	Norf	TG2300	52°33·4'	1°17·8'E	FM	134
Maltkiln Fm	Shrops	SJ5937	52°56·0'	2°36·2'W	FM	126
Maltkiln Hill	N Yks	SE2859	54°1·8'	1°33·9'W	X	104
Maltkiln Hill Fm	Somer	ST7125	51°1·7'	2°24·4'W	FM	183
Malt Land	Arg & Bt	NN0809	56°14·3'	5°5·4'W	X	56
Maltman's Hill	Kent	TQ9043	51°9·5'	0°43·4'E	T	189
Maltmas Fm	Cambs	TF4503	52°36·6'	0°8·9'E	FM	143
Malton	Durham	NZ1746	54°48·8'	1°43·7'W	X	88
Malton	N Yks	SE7871	54°8·0'	0°48·0'W	T	100
Malton Cote	N Yks	SE9085	54°15·4'	0°36·7'W	X	94,101
Malton Fm	Cambs	TL3748	52°7·0'	0°0·5'E	FM	154
Malton Ho	Durham	NZ1744	54°47·7'	1°43·7'W	X	88
Malt Shovel	Leic	SP5982	52°26·2'	1°7·5'W	X	140
Malverleys	Hants	SU4161	51°21·0'	1°24·0'W	X	174
Malvern Common	Worcs	SO7844	52°5·9'	2°18·9'W	T	150
Malvern Hall Fm	Warw	SP4465	52°17·1'	1°20·9'W	FM	151
Malvern Hills	Worcs	SO7641	52°4·2'	2°20·6'W	H	150
Malvern Link	Worcs	SO7847	52°7·5'	2°18·9'W	T	150
Malvern Lodge	Bath & NE Somer	ST5664	51°22·6'	2°37·5'W	X	172,182
Malvern Park Fm	Sol	SP1578	52°24·2'	1°46·4'W	FM	139
Malvern Wells	Worcs	SO7742	52°4·8'	2°19·7'W	T	150
Malwood	Hants	SU2711	50°54·1'	1°36·6'W	X	195
Malyons	Essex	TQ8094	51°37·2'	0°36·4'E	X	168,178
Malzie	D & G	NX3754	54°51·5'	4°31·9'W	X	83
Màm a' Chatha	Highld	NH5741	57°26·5'	4°22·5'W	X	26
Màm a' Choir' Idhir	Arg & Bt	NM5732	56°25·3'	5°56·0'W	X	48
Màm a' Chroisg	Highld	NH2607	57°7·5'	4°52·0'W	H	34
Màm a' Chullaich	Highld	NM7443	56°31·7'	5°40·0'W	H	49
Màm an Doire Dhuinn	Highld	NN0495	57°0·5'	5°13·2'W	H	33
Màman Odhar	Highld	NM7687	56°55·5'	5°40·4'W	X	40
Màman Odhar	Highld	NM7969	56°45·9'	5°36·5'W	X	40
Màm an Staing	Highld	NG7813	57°9·5'	5°39·8'W	X	33
Màm an Tiompain	Arg & Bt	NM6031	56°24·9'	5°53·0'W	X	49
Màm an Trotanaich	Arg & Bt	NM5625	56°21·5'	5°56·6'W	X	48
Màm a' Phobuill	Highld	NG5125	57°15·1'	6°7·2'W	X	32
Màm Bàn	Pth & Kin	NN4366	56°45·8'	4°33·7'W	X	42
Màm Bàn	Pth & Kin	NN5971	56°48·8'	4°18·1'W	H	42
Màm Barrisdale	Highld	NG8501	57°3·3'	5°32·3'W	X	33
Màm Beathaig	Highld	NM8770	56°46·6'	5°28·7'W	X	40
Mambeg	Arg & Bt	NS2389	56°3·9'	4°50·2'W	T	56
Màm Bhradhadail	Arg & Bt	NM6233	56°26·0'	5°51·2'W	X	49
Mamble	Worcs	SO6871	52°20·4'	2°27·8'W	T	138
Mambury	Devon	SS3816	50°55·5'	4°17·9'W	X	190
Màm Carraigh	Arg & Bt	NN2841	56°32·0'	4°47·4'W	X	50
Màm Charaidh	Highld	NH2733	57°21·5'	4°52·1'W	X	25
Màm Choireadail	Arg & Bt	NM5931	56°24·8'	5°54·0'W	X	48
Mameulah	Aberd	NJ8820	57°16·5'	2°11·5'W	X	38
Mam Fm	Derby	SK1383	53°20·9'	1°47·9'W	FM	110
Màm Hael	Arg & Bt	NN0141	56°31·4'	5°13·7'W	H	50
Mamhead Ho	Devon	SX9381	50°37·4'	3°30·4'W	A	192
Mamhilad	Monm	SO3003	51°43·5'	3°0·4'W	T	171
Mamhilad Ho	Monm	SO3004	51°44·1'	3°0·4'W	X	171
Màm Lì	Highld	NG8006	57°5·8'	5°37·5'W	X	33
Màm Lirein	Arg & Bt	NM6734	56°26·7'	5°46·4'W	X	49
Màm Meadail	Highld	NM8497	57°1·1'	5°33·0'W	X	33,40
Mammerton	Derby	SK2136	52°55·5'	1°40·9'W	X	128
Mammie	Aberd	NJ3101	57°5·9'	3°7·9'W	H	37
Màm Mór	Highld	NH5742	57°27·0'	4°22·5'W	X	26
Màm na Céire	Highld	NM7157	56°39·2'	5°43·7'W	X	49
Màm na Cloich Airde	Highld	NM8994	56°59·6'	5°28·0'W	X	33,40
Màm na Gualainn	Highld	NN1162	56°42·9'	5°4·8'W	H	41
Màm na Luirg	Highld	NM8076	56°49·7'	5°35·9'W	X	40
Màm na Luirginn	Highld	NM7173	56°47·8'	5°44·6'W	H	40
Màm nan Carn	Pth & Kin	NO0477	56°52·7'	3°34·1'W	H	43
Màm nan Sac	Arg & Bt	NN2144	56°33·5'	4°54·3'W	X	50
Màm nan Uranan	Highld	NG7916	57°11·2'	5°39·0'W	H	33
Màm na Seilg	Highld	NH1003	57°5·0'	5°7·7'W	X	34
Mamore	Arg & Bt	NS2387	56°2·8'	4°50·1'W	X	56
Mamore Forest	Highld	NN2265	56°44·8'	4°54·2'W	X	41
Mamore Lodge (Hotel)	Highld	NN1862	56°43·1'	4°58·0'W	X	41
Mamores, The	Highld	NN1665	56°44·7'	5°0·1'W	H	41
Màm Ruisgte	Highld	NH0933	57°21·1'	5°10·0'W	X	25
Màm Sodhail	Highld	NH1225	57°16·9'	5°6·7'W	H	25
Màm Suidheig	Highld	NG8101	57°3·1'	5°36·2'W	X	33
Màm Suim	Highld	NJ0109	57°9·9'	3°37·8'W	X	36
Mam Tor	Derby	SK1283	53°20·9'	1°48·8'W	H	110
Màm Tuath	Highld	NM3799	57°0·7'	6°19·5'W	H	39
Màm Uchd	Highld	NM8396	57°0·5'	5°34·0'W	X	33,40
Màm Uidhe	Highld	NG7601	57°3·0'	5°41·1'W	X	33
Màm Unndalain	Highld	NG8900	57°2·8'	5°28·3'W	X	33
Manabattock	Aberd	NJ5319	57°15·8'	2°46·3'W	X	37
Manabattock Hill	Aberd	NJ5319	57°15·8'	2°46·3'W	H	37
Mana Berg	Shetld	HU5137	60°7·1'	1°4·4'W	X	4
Mana Butts	Devon	SX4977	50°35·6'	4°7·6'W	X	191,201
Manaccan	Corn	SW7625	50°5·2'	5°7·5'W	T	204
Manach Hill	Angus	NO5974	56°51·6'	2°39·9'W	H	44
Manachie Fm	Moray	NJ0356	57°35·3'	3°36·9'W	FM	27
Manacle Point	Corn	SW8121	50°3·2'	5°3·2'W	X	204
Manacles, The	Corn	SW8220	50°2·6'	5°2·3'W	X	204
Manadon	C of Plym	SX4758	50°24·4'	4°8·8'W	T	201
Manafon	Powys	SJ1102	52°36·8'	3°18·5'W	T	136
Manais	N Eil	NG1089	57°48·1'	6°52·4'W	T	14
Manannan's Chair (Round House)	I of M	SC2985	54°14·2'	4°37·0'W	A	95
Manare Point	Corn	SW9338	50°12·6'	4°53·7'W	X	204
Man at Edge	Cumbr	NY6535	54°42·8'	2°32·2'W	X	91
Manaton	Devon	SX7581	50°37·2'	3°45·6'W	T	191

Manaton Mill	Corn	SX3372	50°31·7′	4°21·0′W	X	201
Manaton Rocks	Devon	SX7481	50°37·1′	3°46·5′W	X	191
Manaw	I of Angl	SH3579	53°17·2′	4°28·1′W	X	114
Manby	Lincs	TF3986	53°21·4′	0°5·7′E	T	113,122
Mancetter	Warw	SP3196	52°33·9′	1°32·2′W	T	140
Manchester	Man	SJ8398	53°28·9′	2°15·0′W	T	109
Manchester International Airport	Man	SJ8184	53°21·4′	2°16·7′W	X	109
Manchester Lodge	Cambs	TL0473	52°20·9′	0°28·0′W	X	141,153
Manchester Ship Canal	Ches	SJ4577	53°17·5′	2°49·1′W	W	117
Manchester Ship Canal	Halton	SJ5684	53°21·3′	2°39·3′W	W	108
Manchester Ship Canal	Traf	SJ7191	53°25·1′	2°25·8′W	W	109
Mancombe	Somer	ST4210	50°53·4′	2°49·1′W	X	193
Mancot Royal	Flint	SJ3266	53°11·4′	3°0·7′W	T	117
Mancroft	Somer	ST2708	50°52·2′	3°1·9′W	X	193
Mandalay Fm	Essex	TL7029	51°56·2′	0°28·8′E	FM	167
Mandale Rake	Derby	SK1866	53°11·7′	1°43·4′W	X	119
Manderston Ho	Scot Bord	NT8154	55°47·0′	2°17·7′W	X	67,74
Mandeville Stoke Fm	Dorset	SY4096	50°45·9′	2°50·7′W	FM	193
Mandinam	Carm	SN7328	51°56·4′	3°50·5′W	X	146,160
Mandvessedvm	Warw	SP3296	52°33·9′	1°31·3′W	R	140
Manea	Cambs	TL4889	52°29·0′	0°11·2′E	T	143
Manea Fifties	Cambs	TL5092	52°30·5′	0°13·0′E	X	143
Maneight	E Ayr	NS5409	55°21·5′	4°17·8′W	X	70,77
Maneight Hill	E Ayr	NS5408	55°20·9′	4°17·7′W	H	70,77
Manely	Corn	SX1355	50°22·1′	4°37·4′W	X	200
Manest Court	Powys	SO0925	51°55·4′	3°19·0′W	X	161
Manesty	Cumbr	NY2518	54°33·4′	3°9·2′W	X	89,90
Maney	Birm	SP1295	52°33·4′	1°49·0′W	T	139
Manfield	N Yks	NZ2213	54°31·0′	1°39·2′W	T	93
Manfield Fox Covert	N Yks	NZ2212	54°30·4′	1°39·2′W	F	93
Manga Hill	Devon	SX6384	50°38·6′	3°55·9′W	H	191
Mangapps	Essex	TQ9497	51°38·5′	0°48·6′E	X	168
Mangaster	Shetld	HU3270	60°25·0′	1°24·6′W	T	3
Mangaster Voe	Shetld	HU3270	60°25·0′	1°24·6′W	W	3
Mangers	Hants	SU7928	51°3·0′	0°52·0′W	X	186,197
Mangersta	N Eil	NB0031	58°10·2′	7°5·7′W	T	13
Mangersta Sands	N Eil	NB0030	58°9·7′	7°5·6′W	X	13
Manger, The	Oxon	SU2986	51°34·6′	1°34·5′W	X	174
Mangerton	Dorset	SY4895	50°45·4′	2°43·9′W	T	193
Mangerton	Scot Bord	NY4785	55°9·6′	2°49·5′W	X	79
Mangerton Hill	Dorset	SY4896	50°45·9′	2°43·9′W	H	193
Mangerton River	Dorset	SY4895	50°45·4′	2°43·9′W	W	193
Mangland Fm	Bucks	SP7532	51°59·1′	0°54·1′W	FM	152,165
Manglâs	Carm	SN5744	52°4·8′	4°4·8′W	X	146
Mangotsfield	S Glos	ST6576	51°29·1′	2°29·9′W	T	172
Mangreen Fm	Norf	TF9321	52°45·4′	0°52·0′E	FM	132
Mangreen Hall	Norf	TG2103	52°35·0′	1°16·1′E	X	134
Mangrove Green	Herts	TL1223	51°53·9′	0°21·9′W	T	166
Mangthorn Wood	Oxon	SP5122	51°53·9′	1°15·1′W	F	164
Manhay	Corn	SW6930	50°7·7′	5°13·6′W	T	203
Manheirs	Corn	SW9447	50°17·5′	4°53·2′W	X	204
Man & his man or Bawden Rocks	Corn	SW7053	50°20·2′	5°13·6′W	X	203
Manian-fawr	Cered	SN1547	52°5·7′	4°41·7′W	T	145
Manifold Fm	Derby	SK2949	53°2·5′	1°33·6′W	FM	119
Manifold Way	Staffs	SK0952	53°4·1′	1°51·5′W	X	119
Manish	N Eil	NA9513	58°0·4′	7°9·4′W	X	13
Manish Beg	Highld	NG5646	57°26·6′	6°3·5′W	X	24
Manish Island	Highld	NG5648	57°27·7′	6°3·6′W	X	24
Manish Mór	Highld	NG5545	57°26·0′	6°4·5′W	X	24
Manish Point	Highld	NG5648	57°27·7′	6°3·6′W	X	24
Manish Point	N Eil	NF7173	57°37·9′	7°30·3′W	X	18
Manish Strand	N Eil	NF9786	57°45·9′	7°5·3′W	X	18
Maniwan	Carm	SN3130	51°56·8′	4°27·1′W	X	145
Mankinholes	Cald	SD9623	53°42·4′	2°3·2′W	T	103
Manley	Ches	SJ5071	53°14·3′	2°44·5′W	T	117
Manley	Devon	SS9811	50°53·6′	3°26·6′W	T	192
Manley Common	Ches	SJ5272	53°14·8′	2°42·8′W	T	117
Manley Fm	N Yks	SE2686	54°16·4′	1°35·6′W	FM	99
Manley Hall	Wrex	SJ3541	52°58·0′	2°57·7′W	A	117
Manley Ho	Ches	SJ4871	53°14·3′	2°46·3′W	X	117
Manley Old Hall	Ches	SJ5072	53°14·8′	2°44·6′W	X	117
Manley's Fm	Somer	ST1619	50°58·1′	3°11·4′W	FM	181,193
Manmoel	Caer	SO1703	51°43·4′	3°11·7′W	T	171
Mannacott	Devon	SS6648	51°13·2′	3°54·7′W	X	180
Manna Green	E Yorks	SE8255	53°59·3′	0°44·5′W	X	106
Mannal	Arg & Bt	NL9840	56°27·6′	6°53·7′W	T	46
Mannamead	C of Plym	SX4856	50°23·3′	4°7·9′W	T	201
Manners Stone, The	Highld	NG1854	57°29·6′	6°41·9′W	X	23
Mannerston	Falk	NT0478	55°59·4′	3°31·9′W	T	65
Manners Wood	Derby	SK2368	53°12·8′	1°38·9′W	F	119
Manningford Abbots	Wilts	SU1458	51°19·5′	1°47·6′W	T	173
Manningford Bohune	Wilts	SU1357	51°18·9′	1°48·4′W	T	173
Manningford Bohune Common	Wilts	SU1258	51°19·5′	1°49·3′W	X	173
Manningford Bruce	Wilts	SU1358	51°19·5′	1°48·4′W	T	173
Manningham	Brad	SE1534	53°48·4′	1°45·9′W	T	104
Mannings	Essex	TM0923	51°52·2′	1°2·6′E	X	168,169
Manning's Common	Devon	ST2410	50°53·3′	3°4·4′W	X	192,193
Manning's Coppice	Shrops	SJ5823	52°48·4′	2°37·0′W	F	126
Manning's Fm	Suff	TL9742	52°2·7′	0°52·8′E	FM	155
Mannings Heath	W Susx	TQ2028	51°2·6′	0°16·9′W	T	187,198
Mannington	Dorset	SU0605	50°50·9′	1°54·5′W	T	195
Mannington Hall	Norf	TG1432	52°50·8′	1°11·1′E	A	133
Manningtree	Essex	TM1031	51°56·5′	1°3·7′E	T	168,169
Manningtree Sta	Essex	TM0932	51°57·1′	1°2·9′E	X	168,169
Mannoch Cottage	Moray	NJ1944	57°29·0′	3°20·6′W	X	28
Mannoch Hill	Moray	NJ2049	57°31·7′	3°19·7′W	X	28
Mannoch Hill	S Lanak	NS7532	55°34·2′	3°58·5′W	X	71
Mannofield	C of Aber	NJ9104	57°7·9′	2°8·5′W	T	38
Mann's Fm	Essex	TL8326	51°54·4′	0°40·0′E	FM	168
Manns Fm	E Susx	TQ3520	50°58·0′	0°4·3′W	FM	198
Mann's Fm	W Berks	SU6665	51°23·0′	1°2·7′W	FM	175
Manns Fm	W Susx	TQ1936	51°6·9′	0°17·6′W	FM	187
Manns Place	Kent	TQ8760	51°18·7′	0°41·4′E	X	178
Mann Wood	Essex	TL7417	51°49·7′	0°31·9′E	F	167
Manod Bach	Gwyn	SH7144	52°58·9′	3°54·9′W	H	124
Manod Mawr	Gwyn	SH7244	52°58·9′	3°54·0′W	H	124
Manod Mawr	Gwyn	SH7245	52°59·5′	3°54·0′W	X	115

Manod Quarries	Gwyn	SH7345	52°59·5′	3°53·1′W	X	115
Manor	Bucks	SP6436	52°1·4′	1°3·6′W	X	152
Manor	Dorset	ST5900	50°48·1′	2°34·5′W	X	194
Manor	Essex	TL9801	51°40·6′	0°52·2′E	X	168
Manor	Glos	SO8925	51°55·6′	2°9·2′W	X	163
Manor	Glos	SP0333	52°0·0′	1°57·0′W	X	150
Manor	Lincs	TF3361	53°8·0′	0°0·3′W	X	122
Manor	Norf	TG1802	52°34·5′	1°13·4′E	X	134
Manor	Norf	TM3599	52°32·5′	1°28·3′E	X	134
Manor	Northnts	TL0680	52°24·7′	0°26·1′W	X	142
Manor	N Yks	SE5246	53°54·7′	1°12·1′W	X	105
Manor	Oxon	SP2727	51°56·7′	1°36·0′W	X	163
Manor	Oxon	SP5131	51°58·7′	1°15·1′W	X	151
Manor	Shrops	SO6486	52°28·5′	2°31·4′W	X	138
Manor	Somer	ST2126	51°1·9′	3°7·2′W	X	193
Manor	Stir	NS8295	56°8·2′	3°53·5′W	X	57
Manor	Suff	TM4489	52°26·9′	1°35·9′E	X	156
Manor	Warw	SP2367	52°18·3′	1°39·4′W	X	151
Manor	Wilts	ST9065	51°23·3′	2°8·2′W	A	173
Manor	Wilts	SU2053	51°16·8′	1°42·4′W	X	184
Manor	York	SE5555	53°59·5′	1°9·2′W	X	105
Manor	York	SE6048	53°55·7′	1°4·8′W	X	105
Manor Allotment	Somer	SS8043	51°10·7′	3°42·6′W	X	181
Manoravon Fm	Carm	SN6523	51°53·6′	3°57·3′W	FM	159
Manor Barn Fm	Notts	SK6525	52°49·4′	1°1·7′W	FM	129
Manorbier	Pemb	SS0697	51°38·5′	4°47·8′W	T	158
Manorbier Bay	Pemb	SS0597	51°38·5′	4°48·7′W	W	158
Manorbier Newton	Pemb	SS0499	51°39·6′	4°49·6′W	T	158
Manorbier Sta	Pemb	SS0699	51°39·6′	4°47·9′W	X	158
Manor Bourne	Devon	SX4949	50°19·5′	4°6·9′W	T	201
Manor Common	Corn	SX1374	50°32·4′	4°38·0′W	X	200
Manor Cottage Fm	N Yks	NZ4304	54°26·0′	1°19·8′W	FM	93
Manor Cotts	Shrops	SJ3723	52°48·3′	2°55·7′W	X	126
Manor Court	Carm	SN2310	51°45·9′	4°33·5′W	X	158
Manor Dairy Fm	Dorset	ST9104	50°50·4′	2°7·3′W	FM	195
Manordeifi	Pemb	SN2243	52°3·6′	4°35·4′W	X	145
Manordeilo	Carm	SN6626	51°55·2′	3°56·5′W	T	146
Manor Estate	Sheff	SK3885	53°21·9′	1°25·3′W	T	110,111
Manor Farm	Cambs	TL1876	52°22·4′	0°15·6′W	FM	142
Manor Farm	Glos	SP0828	51°57·3′	1°52·6′W	FM	150,163
Manor Farm	Notts	SK5988	53°23·4′	1°6·4′W	FM	111,120
Manor Farm Country Park	Hants	SU4911	50°54·0′	1°17·8′W	X	196
Manorfarm Down	W Susx	SU8816	50°56·4′	0°44·5′W	X	197
Manor Farm Ho	Suff	TM2253	52°8·1′	1°15·0′E	X	156
Manor Fields Fm	Warw	SP3273	52°21·5′	1°31·4′W	FM	140
Manor Fm	Aberd	NJ9761	57°38·6′	2°2·6′W	FM	30
Manor Fm	Barns	SE3102	53°31·1′	1°31·5′W	X	110,111
Manor Fm	Bath & NE Somer	ST6966	51°23·8′	2°26·3′W	FM	172
Manor Fm	Beds	SP9357	52°12·4′	0°37·9′W	FM	153
Manor Fm	Beds	SP9529	51°57·3′	0°36·7′W	FM	165
Manor Fm	Beds	SP9724	51°54·6′	0°35·0′W	FM	165
Manor Fm	Beds	TL0115	51°49·7′	0°31·7′W	FM	166
Manor Fm	Beds	TL0168	52°18·3′	0°30·7′W	FM	153
Manor Fm	Beds	TL0226	51°55·6′	0°30·6′W	FM	166
Manor Fm	Beds	TL0240	52°3·2′	0°30·3′W	FM	153
Manor Fm	Beds	TL0426	51°55·6′	0°28·9′W	FM	166
Manor Fm	Beds	TL0459	52°13·4′	0°28·2′W	FM	153
Manor Fm	Beds	TL0620	51°52·3′	0°27·2′W	FM	166
Manor Fm	Beds	TL0669	52°18·8′	0°26·3′W	FM	153
Manor Fm	Beds	TL0843	52°4·7′	0°25·0′W	FM	153
Manor Fm	Beds	TL0859	52°13·3′	0°24·7′W	FM	153
Manor Fm	Beds	TL1032	51°58·8′	0°23·5′W	FM	166
Manor Fm	Beds	TL1049	52°7·9′	0°23·2′W	FM	153
Manor Fm	Beds	TL1846	52°6·2′	0°16·2′W	FM	153
Manor Fm	Beds	TL2240	52°2·9′	0°12·9′W	FM	153
Manor Fm	Beds	TL2446	52°6·1′	0°11·0′W	FM	153
Manor Fm	Bexley	TQ4871	51°25·3′	0°8·1′E	FM	177
Manor Fm	Brackn	SU8670	51°25·6′	0°45·4′W	FM	175
Manor Fm	Brig	SS8378	51°29·6′	3°40·7′W	FM	170
Manor Fm	Bucks	SP6214	51°49·5′	1°5·6′W	FM	164,165
Manor Fm	Bucks	SP6533	51°59·7′	1°2·8′W	FM	152,165
Manor Fm	Bucks	SP6606	51°45·2′	1°2·2′W	FM	164,165
Manor Fm	Bucks	SP6728	51°57·0′	1°1·1′W	FM	164,165
Manor Fm	Bucks	SP6931	51°58·6′	0°59·3′W	FM	152,165
Manor Fm	Bucks	SP7133	51°59·7′	0°57·6′W	FM	152,165
Manor Fm	Bucks	SP7622	51°53·7′	0°53·3′W	FM	165
Manor Fm	Bucks	SP7806	51°45·1′	0°51·8′W	FM	165
Manor Fm	Bucks	SP8224	51°54·7′	0°48·1′W	FM	165
Manor Fm	Bucks	SP8331	51°58·5′	0°47·1′W	FM	152,165
Manor Fm	Bucks	SP9215	51°49·8′	0°39·5′W	FM	165
Manor Fm	Bucks	SU7592	51°37·5′	0°54·6′W	FM	175
Manor Fm	Bucks	SU7791	51°37·0′	0°52·9′W	FM	175
Manor Fm	Bucks	SU8595	51°39·1′	0°45·9′W	FM	165
Manor Fm	Cambs	TL1164	52°16·0′	0°22·0′W	FM	153
Manor Fm	Cambs	TL1281	52°25·2′	0°20·8′W	FM	142
Manor Fm	Cambs	TL1295	52°32·7′	0°20·5′W	FM	142
Manor Fm	Cambs	TL1388	52°28·9′	0°19·8′W	FM	142
Manor Fm	Cambs	TL1586	52°27·8′	0°18·0′W	FM	142
Manor Fm	Cambs	TL1864	52°15·9′	0°15·9′W	FM	153
Manor Fm	Cambs	TL2182	52°25·6′	0°12·8′W	FM	142
Manor Fm	Cambs	TL2379	52°23·9′	0°11·1′W	FM	142
Manor Fm	Cambs	TL2580	52°24·5′	0°9·3′W	FM	142
Manor Fm	Cambs	TL2795	52°32·5′	0°7·2′W	FM	142
Manor Fm	Cambs	TL2881	52°24·9′	0°6·7′W	FM	142
Manor Fm	Cambs	TL2882	52°25·5′	0°6·7′W	FM	142
Manor Fm	Cambs	TL3044	52°5·0′	0°5·8′W	FM	153
Manor Fm	Cambs	TL3047	52°6·6′	0°5·7′W	FM	153
Manor Fm	Cambs	TL3079	52°23·8′	0°5·0′W	FM	142
Manor Fm	Cambs	TL3149	52°7·7′	0°4·8′W	FM	153
Manor Fm	Cambs	TL3362	52°14·6′	0°2·7′W	FM	154
Manor Fm	Cambs	TL3370	52°18·9′	0°2·5′W	FM	154
Manor Fm	Cambs	TL3378	52°23·3′	0°2·3′W	FM	142
Manor Fm	Cambs	TL3553	52°9·8′	0°1·2′W	FM	154
Manor Fm	Cambs	TL4090	52°29·6′	0°4·1′E	FM	142,143
Manor Fm	Cambs	TL4144	52°4·8′	0°3·9′E	FM	154
Manor Fm	Cambs	TL4149	52°7·5′	0°4·0′E	FM	154
Manor Fm	Cambs	TL4563	52°15·0′	0°7·8′E	FM	154
Manor Fm	Cambs	TL4881	52°24·6′	0°11·0′E	FM	143
Manor Fm	Cambs	TL5057	52°11·7′	0°12·1′E	FM	154

Manor Fm	Cambs	TL6147	52°6·1′	0°21·4′E	FM	154
Manor Fm	Carm	SN2817	51°49·8′	4°29·4′W	FM	158
Manor Fm	Ches	SJ4472	53°14·8′	2°49·9′W	FM	117
Manor Fm	Ches	SJ4845	53°0·2′	2°46·1′W	FM	117
Manor Fm	Ches	SJ5266	53°11·6′	2°42·7′W	FM	117
Manor Fm	Ches	SJ5353	53°4·6′	2°41·7′W	FM	117
Manor Fm	Ches	SJ5876	53°17·0′	2°37·4′W	FM	117
Manor Fm	Ches	SJ6161	53°8·9′	2°34·6′W	FM	118
Manor Fm	Ches	SJ6562	53°9·5′	2°31·0′W	FM	118
Manor Fm	Ches	SJ6743	52°59·2′	2°29·1′W	FM	118
Manor Fm	Ches	SJ6775	53°16·5′	2°29·3′W	FM	118
Manor Fm	Ches	SJ6949	53°2·5′	2°27·3′W	FM	118
Manor Fm	Ches	SJ6963	53°10·0′	2°27·4′W	FM	118
Manor Fm	Ches	SJ7248	53°2·0′	2°24·6′W	FM	118
Manor Fm	Ches	SJ7268	53°12·7′	2°24·8′W	FM	118
Manor Fm	Ches	SJ7568	53°12·7′	2°22·1′W	FM	118
Manor Fm	Ches	SJ7767	53°12·2′	2°20·3′W	FM	118
Manor Fm	Ches	SJ7776	53°17·1′	2°20·3′W	FM	118
Manor Fm	Ches	SJ7856	53°6·3′	2°19·3′W	FM	118
Manor Fm	Ches	SJ8073	53°15·5′	2°17·6′W	FM	118
Manor Fm	Cumbr	SD2188	54°17·1′	3°12·4′W	FM	96
Manor Fm	Derby	SK2255	53°5·7′	1°39·9′W	FM	119
Manor Fm	Derby	SK3257	53°6·8′	1°30·9′W	FM	119
Manor Fm	Derby	SK3543	52°59·2′	1°28·3′W	FM	119,128
Manor Fm	Derby	SK3749	53°2·5′	1°26·5′W	FM	119
Manor Fm	Derby	SK4069	53°13·2′	1°23·6′W	FM	120
Manor Fm	Derby	SK4139	52°57·0′	1°23·0′W	FM	129
Manor Fm	Derby	SK4230	52°52·2′	1°22·2′W	FM	129
Manor Fm	Derby	SK4335	52°54·9′	1°21·2′W	FM	129
Manor Fm	Devon	SS4944	51°10·8′	4°9·2′W	FM	180
Manor Fm	Devon	SS5407	50°50·9′	4°4·1′W	FM	191
Manor Fm	Devon	SS8321	50°58·8′	3°39·6′W	FM	181
Manor Fm	Devon	ST1305	50°50·5′	3°13·8′W	FM	192,193
Manor Fm	Devon	SX7156	50°23·6′	3°48·5′W	FM	202
Manor Fm	Devon	SX7392	50°43·1′	3°47·6′W	FM	191
Manor Fm	Devon	SY0592	50°43·4′	3°20·4′W	FM	192
Manor Fm	Devon	SY2391	50°43·0′	3°5·1′W	FM	192,193
Manor Fm	Donc	SE6100	53°29·8′	1°4·4′W	FM	111
Manor Fm	Dorset	ST4305	50°50·7′	2°48·2′W	FM	193
Manor Fm	Dorset	ST4806	50°51·3′	2°43·9′W	FM	193
Manor Fm	Dorset	ST5305	50°50·8′	2°39·7′W	FM	194
Manor Fm	Dorset	ST5505	50°50·8′	2°38·0′W	FM	194
Manor Fm	Dorset	ST5714	50°55·7′	2°36·3′W	FM	194
Manor Fm	Dorset	ST5807	50°51·9′	2°35·4′W	FM	194
Manor Fm	Dorset	ST6305	50°50·8′	2°31·2′W	FM	194
Manor Fm	Dorset	ST6407	50°51·9′	2°30·3′W	FM	194
Manor Fm	Dorset	ST6607	50°51·9′	2°28·6′W	FM	194
Manor Fm	Dorset	ST6917	50°57·3′	2°26·1′W	FM	183
Manor Fm	Dorset	ST7116	50°56·8′	2°24·4′W	FM	183
Manor Fm	Dorset	ST7615	50°56·3′	2°20·1′W	FM	183
Manor Fm	Dorset	ST7703	50°49·8′	2°19·2′W	FM	194
Manor Fm	Dorset	ST7721	50°59·5′	2°19·3′W	FM	183
Manor Fm	Dorset	ST7829	51°3·8′	2°18·5′W	FM	183
Manor Fm	Dorset	ST8116	50°56·8′	2°15·8′W	FM	183
Manor Fm	Dorset	ST8424	51°1·1′	2°13·3′W	FM	183
Manor Fm	Dorset	ST8617	50°57·4′	2°11·6′W	FM	183
Manor Fm	Dorset	ST9408	50°52·5′	2°4·7′W	FM	195
Manor Fm	Dorset	ST9716	50°56·8′	2°2·2′W	FM	184
Manor Fm	Dorset	ST9811	50°54·1′	2°1·3′W	FM	195
Manor Fm	Dorset	ST9916	50°56·8′	2°0·5′W	FM	184
Manor Fm	Dorset	SU0113	50°55·2′	1°58·8′W	FM	195
Manor Fm	Dorset	SU0413	50°55·2′	1°56·2′W	FM	195
Manor Fm	Dorset	SU0807	50°52·0′	1°52·8′W	FM	195
Manor Fm	Dorset	SY5896	50°46·0′	2°35·4′W	FM	194
Manor Fm	Dorset	SY8097	50°46·6′	2°16·6′W	FM	194
Manor Fm	Durham	NZ2940	54°45·5′	1°32·5′W	FM	88
Manor Fm	Essex	TL8108	51°44·7′	0°37·7′E	FM	168
Manor Fm	Essex	TL9628	51°55·2′	0°51·4′E	FM	168
Manor Fm	Essex	TQ3997	51°39·5′	0°1·0′E	FM	166,177
Manor Fm	E Susx	TQ5717	50°56·1′	0°14·5′E	FM	199
Manor Fm	E Susx	TQ6035	51°5·7′	0°17·5′E	FM	188
Manor Fm	E Susx	TQ6922	50°58·6′	0°24·8′E	FM	199
Manor Fm	E Susx	TQ8816	50°55·0′	0°40·9′E	FM	189,199
Manor Fm	E Yorks	SE6119	53°40·1′	1°4·2′W	FM	111
Manor Fm	E Yorks	SE7635	53°48·6′	0°50·3′W	FM	105,106
Manor Fm	E Yorks	SE7746	53°54·5′	0°49·3′W	FM	105,106
Manor Fm	E Yorks	SE7830	53°45·9′	0°48·6′W	FM	105,106
Manor Fm	E Yorks	SE8030	53°45·8′	0°46·8′W	FM	106
Manor Fm	E Yorks	SE8421	53°41·0′	0°43·3′W	FM	106,112
Manor Fm	E Yorks	SE8443	53°52·8′	0°42·9′W	FM	106
Manor Fm	E Yorks	SE8548	53°55·5′	0°41·9′W	FM	106
Manor Fm	E Yorks	SE8639	53°50·6′	0°41·2′W	FM	106
Manor Fm	E Yorks	SE8838	53°50·1′	0°39·4′W	FM	106
Manor Fm	E Yorks	SE8932	53°46·8′	0°38·5′W	FM	106
Manor Fm	E Yorks	SE8934	53°47·9′	0°38·5′W	FM	106
Manor Fm	E Yorks	SE9631	53°46·2′	0°32·2′W	FM	106
Manor Fm	E Yorks	SE9937	53°49·4′	0°29·3′W	FM	106
Manor Fm	E Yorks	TA0159	54°1·3′	0°27·1′W	FM	106
Manor Fm	E Yorks	TA0753	53°58·0′	0°21·7′W	FM	107
Manor Fm	E Yorks	TA1447	53°54·6′	0°15·5′W	FM	107
Manor Fm	E Yorks	TA1552	53°57·3′	0°14·4′W	FM	107
Manor Fm	E Yorks	TA1646	53°54·1′	0°13·7′W	FM	107
Manor Fm	E Yorks	TA1742	53°51·9′	0°12·8′W	FM	107
Manor Fm	E Yorks	TA1932	53°46·5′	0°11·2′W	FM	107
Manor Fm	E Yorks	TA1944	53°52·9′	0°11·0′W	FM	107
Manor Fm	E Yorks	TA2242	53°51·8′	0°8·3′W	FM	107
Manor Fm	E Yorks	TA3128	53°44·1′	0°0·4′W	FM	107
Manor Fm	E Yorks	TA3520	53°39·8′	0°3·0′E	FM	107,113
Manor Fm	Flint	SJ3365	53°10·9′	2°59·7′W	FM	117
Manor Fm	Glos	SO7612	51°48·6′	2°20·5′W	FM	162
Manor Fm	Glos	SO7808	51°46·4′	2°18·7′W	FM	162
Manor Fm	Glos	SO8113	51°49·2′	2°16·1′W	FM	162
Manor Fm	Glos	SO9609	51°47·0′	2°3·1′W	FM	163
Manor Fm	Glos	SO9729	51°57·8′	2°2·2′W	FM	150,163
Manor Fm	Glos	SP0617	51°51·3′	1°54·4′W	FM	163
Manor Fm	Glos	SP0835	52°1·0′	1°52·6′W	FM	150
Manor Fm	Glos	SP1201	51°42·7′	1°49·2′W	FM	163
Manor Fm	Glos	SP1422	51°54·0′	1°47·4′W	FM	163
Manor Fm	Glos	SP1914	51°49·7′	1°43·1′W	FM	163
Manor Fm	Glos	ST8990	51°36·8′	2°9·1′W	FM	163,173

Manor Fm	Glos	ST9394	51°38·9'	2°5·7'W	FM	163,173
Manor Fm	Glos	ST9395	51°39·5'	2°5·7'W	FM	163
Manor Fm	Glos	SU0798	51°41·1'	1°53·5'W	FM	163
Manor Fm	Halton	SJ4684	53°21·3'	2°48·3'W	FM	108
Manor Fm	Hants	SU1219	50°58·4'	1°49·4'W	FM	184
Manor Fm	Hants	SU2720	50°59·0'	1°36·5'W	FM	184
Manor Fm	Hants	SU2814	50°55·7'	1°35·7'W	FM	195
Manor Fm	Hants	SU2923	51°0·6'	1°34·8'W	FM	185
Manor Fm	Hants	SU2929	51°3·8'	1°34·8'W	FM	185
Manor Fm	Hants	SU3033	51°6·0'	1°33·9'W	FM	185
Manor Fm	Hants	SU3526	51°2·2'	1°29·7'W	FM	185
Manor Fm	Hants	SU3648	51°14·0'	1°28·7'W	FM	185
Manor Fm	Hants	SU3657	51°18·9'	1°28·6'W	FM	174
Manor Fm	Hants	SU4020	50°58·9'	1°25·4'W	FM	185
Manor Fm	Hants	SU4140	51°9·7'	1°24·4'W	FM	185
Manor Fm	Hants	SU4157	51°18·9'	1°24·3'W	FM	174
Manor Fm	Hants	SU4548	51°14·0'	1°20·9'W	FM	185
Manor Fm	Hants	SU5009	50°52·9'	1°17·0'W	FM	196
Manor Fm	Hants	SU5011	50°54·0'	1°17·0'W	FM	196
Manor Fm	Hants	SU5546	51°12·9'	1°12·4'W	FM	185
Manor Fm	Hants	SU6008	50°52·3'	1°8·4'W	FM	196
Manor Fm	Hants	SU6055	51°17·7'	1°8·0'W	FM	175,185
Manor Fm	Hants	SU6146	51°12·8'	1°7·2'W	FM	185
Manor Fm	Hants	SU6348	51°13·9'	1°5·5'W	FM	185
Manor Fm	Hants	SU6645	51°12·3'	1°2·9'W	FM	185,186
Manor Fm	Hants	SU7053	51°16·5'	0°59·4'W	FM	186
Manor Fm	Hants	SZ2398	50°47·1'	1°40·0'W	FM	195
Manor Fm	Hav	TQ5493	51°37·1'	0°13·9'E	FM	177
Manor Fm	Hav	TQ5784	51°32·2'	0°16·2'E	FM	177
Manor Fm	Heref	SO5248	52°7·9'	2°41·7'W	FM	149
Manor Fm	Heref	SO6060	52°14·4'	2°34·8'W	FM	138,149
Manor Fm	Herts	TL1030	51°57·7'	0°23·5'W	FM	166
Manor Fm	Herts	TL2341	52°3·5'	0°12·0'W	FM	153
Manor Fm	Herts	TL2428	51°56·4'	0°11·4'W	FM	166
Manor Fm	Herts	TL2826	51°55·3'	0°7·9'W	FM	166
Manor Fm	Herts	TL2933	51°59·1'	0°6·9'W	FM	166
Manor Fm	Kent	TQ4954	51°16·2'	0°8·5'E	FM	188
Manor Fm	Kent	TQ5745	51°11·2'	0°15·2'E	FM	188
Manor Fm	Kent	TQ5856	51°17·1'	0°16·3'E	FM	188
Manor Fm	Kent	TQ6267	51°23·0'	0°20·1'E	FM	177
Manor Fm	Kent	TQ6948	51°12·6'	0°25·6'E	FM	188
Manor Fm	Kent	TQ9632	51°3·5'	0°48·2'E	FM	189
Manor Fm	Kent	TR0518	50°55·7'	0°55·4'E	FM	189
Manor Fm	Leeds	SE2640	53°51·6'	1°35·9'W	FM	104
Manor Fm	Leeds	SE3342	53°52·6'	1°29·5'W	FM	104
Manor Fm	Leic	SK7824	52°48·7'	0°50·2'W	FM	129
Manor Fm	Leic	SK8009	52°40·6'	0°48·6'W	FM	141
Manor Fm	Leic	SK8024	52°48·7'	0°48·4'W	FM	130
Manor Fm	Leic	SK8524	52°48·6'	0°43·9'W	FM	130
Manor Fm	Leic	SP4398	52°34·9'	1°21·5'W	FM	140
Manor Fm	Leic	SP4888	52°29·5'	1°17·2'W	FM	140
Manor Fm	Lincs	SK8532	52°53·0'	0°43·8'W	FM	130
Manor Fm	Lincs	SK8538	52°56·2'	0°43·7'W	FM	130
Manor Fm	Lincs	SK8676	53°16·7'	0°42·2'W	FM	121
Manor Fm	Lincs	SK8973	53°15·0'	0°39·6'W	FM	121
Manor Fm	Lincs	SK9088	53°23·1'	0°38·4'W	FM	112,121
Manor Fm	Lincs	SK9177	53°17·2'	0°37·7'W	FM	121
Manor Fm	Lincs	SK9219	52°45·9'	0°37·8'W	FM	130
Manor Fm	Lincs	SK9456	53°5·8'	0°35·4'W	FM	121
Manor Fm	Lincs	SK9486	53°22·0'	0°34·8'W	FM	112,121
Manor Fm	Lincs	SK9537	52°55·6'	0°34·8'W	FM	130
Manor Fm	Lincs	SK9582	53°19·8'	0°34·0'W	FM	121
Manor Fm	Lincs	SK9667	53°11·7'	0°33·4'W	FM	121
Manor Fm	Lincs	SK9969	53°12·8'	0°30·6'W	FM	121
Manor Fm	Lincs	TA1000	53°29·3'	0°20·1'W	FM	113
Manor Fm	Lincs	TA1608	53°33·6'	0°14·5'W	FM	113
Manor Fm	Lincs	TF0135	52°54·4'	0°29·5'W	FM	130
Manor Fm	Lincs	TF0274	53°15·4'	0°27·8'W	FM	121
Manor Fm	Lincs	TF0452	53°3·5'	0°26·5'W	FM	121
Manor Fm	Lincs	TF0581	53°19·2'	0°25·0'W	FM	121
Manor Fm	Lincs	TF0596	53°27·3'	0°24·7'W	FM	112
Manor Fm	Lincs	TF0675	53°15·9'	0°24·2'W	FM	121
Manor Fm	Lincs	TF0684	53°20·8'	0°24·1'W	FM	121
Manor Fm	Lincs	TF0813	52°42·5'	0°23·7'W	FM	130,142
Manor Fm	Lincs	TF0885	53°21·3'	0°22·2'W	FM	112,121
Manor Fm	Lincs	TF0889	53°23·4'	0°22·1'W	FM	112,121
Manor Fm	Lincs	TF1183	53°20·2'	0°19·6'W	FM	121
Manor Fm	Lincs	TF1338	52°55·9'	0°18·7'W	FM	130
Manor Fm	Lincs	TF1649	53°1·8'	0°15·8'W	FM	130
Manor Fm	Lincs	TF1794	53°26·0'	0°13·9'W	FM	113
Manor Fm	Lincs	TF2386	53°21·6'	0°8·7'W	FM	113,122
Manor Fm	Lincs	TF2565	53°10·3'	0°7·4'W	FM	122
Manor Fm	Lincs	TF2680	53°18·3'	0°6·1'W	FM	122
Manor Fm	Lincs	TF2770	53°12·9'	0°5·5'W	FM	122
Manor Fm	Lincs	TF2777	53°16·7'	0°5·3'W	FM	122
Manor Fm	Lincs	TF2862	53°8·6'	0°4·8'W	FM	122
Manor Fm	Lincs	TF2875	53°15·6'	0°4·5'W	FM	122
Manor Fm	Lincs	TF2964	53°9·7'	0°3·8'W	FM	122
Manor Fm	Lincs	TF3190	53°23·7'	0°1·4'W	FM	113
Manor Fm	Lincs	TF3264	53°9·6'	0°1·1'W	FM	122
Manor Fm	Lincs	TF3297	53°27·4'	0°0·3'W	FM	113
Manor Fm	Lincs	TF3338	52°55·6'	0°0·9'W	FM	131
Manor Fm	Lincs	TF3395	53°26·3'	0°0·5'E	FM	113
Manor Fm	Lincs	TF3524	52°48·0'	0°0·6'E	FM	131
Manor Fm	Lincs	TF3560	53°7·4'	0°1·5'E	FM	122
Manor Fm	Lincs	TF3610	52°40·5'	0°1·1'E	FM	131,142
Manor Fm	Lincs	TF3775	53°15·5'	0°3·6'E	FM	122
Manor Fm	Lincs	TF3781	53°18·7'	0°3·8'E	FM	122
Manor Fm	Lincs	TF3817	52°44·2'	0°3·0'E	FM	131
Manor Fm	Lincs	TF3864	53°9·5'	0°4·3'E	FM	122
Manor Fm	Lincs	TF4028	52°50·1'	0°5·1'E	FM	131
Manor Fm	Lincs	TF4091	53°24·1'	0°6·8'E	FM	113
Manor Fm	Lincs	TF4152	53°3·0'	0°6·6'E	FM	122
Manor Fm	Lincs	TF4384	53°20·2'	0°9·3'E	FM	122
Manor Fm	Lincs	TF4455	53°4·6'	0°9·4'E	FM	122
Manor Fm	Lincs	TF4581	53°18·6'	0°11·0'E	FM	122
Manor Fm	Lincs	TF4679	53°17·5'	0°11·8'E	FM	122
Manor Fm	Lincs	TF4772	53°13·7'	0°12·5'E	FM	122
Manor Fm	Lincs	TF5374	53°14·7'	0°18·0'E	FM	122
Manor Fm	Lincs	TF5376	53°15·8'	0°18·0'E	FM	122
Manor Fm	Lincs	TF5568	53°11·4'	0°19·6'E	FM	122
Manor Fm	Luton	TL1024	51°54·4'	0°23·7'W	FM	166
Manor Fm	Medway	TQ7376	51°27·6'	0°29·8'E	FM	178
Manor Fm	Mil Key	SP8041	52°3·9'	0°49·6'W	FM	152
Manor Fm	Mil Key	SP8145	52°6·1'	0°48·6'W	FM	152
Manor Fm	Mil Key	SP8748	52°7·6'	0°43·3'W	FM	152
Manor Fm	Mil Key	SP8849	52°8·2'	0°42·5'W	FM	152
Manor Fm	Mil Key	SP9346	52°6·5'	0°38·1'W	FM	153
Manor Fm	Monm	SO3615	51°50·0'	2°55·3'W	FM	161
Manor Fm	NE Lincs	TA2007	53°33·0'	0°10·9'W	FM	113
Manor Fm	NE Lincs	TA2100	53°29·2'	0°10·2'W	FM	113
Manor Fm	N Lincs	SE9302	53°30·6'	0°35·4'W	FM	112
Manor Fm	N Lincs	TA1417	53°38·5'	0°16·1'W	FM	113
Manor Fm	Norf	TF5807	52°38·5'	0°20·5'E	FM	143
Manor Fm	Norf	TF6109	52°39·5'	0°23·2'E	FM	143
Manor Fm	Norf	TF6315	52°42·7'	0°25·2'E	FM	132
Manor Fm	Norf	TF6410	52°40·0'	0°25·9'E	FM	132,143
Manor Fm	Norf	TF6501	52°35·1'	0°26·5'E	FM	143
Manor Fm	Norf	TF6503	52°36·2'	0°26·6'E	FM	143
Manor Fm	Norf	TF6514	52°42·1'	0°26·9'E	FM	132
Manor Fm	Norf	TF6607	52°38·3'	0°27·6'E	FM	143
Manor Fm	Norf	TF6738	52°55·0'	0°29·4'E	FM	132
Manor Fm	Norf	TF6815	52°42·6'	0°29·6'E	FM	132
Manor Fm	Norf	TF7030	52°50·7'	0°31·9'E	FM	132
Manor Fm	Norf	TF7123	52°46·9'	0°32·5'E	FM	132
Manor Fm	Norf	TF7222	52°46·3'	0°33·4'E	FM	132
Manor Fm	Norf	TF7543	52°57·6'	0°36·7'E	FM	132
Manor Fm	Norf	TF8522	52°46·1'	0°44·9'E	FM	132
Manor Fm	Norf	TF8606	52°37·4'	0°45·3'E	FM	144
Manor Fm	Norf	TF8729	52°49·8'	0°47·0'E	FM	132
Manor Fm	Norf	TF8931	52°50·8'	0°48·8'E	FM	132
Manor Fm	Norf	TF9016	52°42·7'	0°49·2'E	FM	132
Manor Fm	Norf	TF9124	52°47·0'	0°50·3'E	FM	132
Manor Fm	Norf	TF9209	52°38·9'	0°50·7'E	FM	144
Manor Fm	Norf	TF9408	52°38·3'	0°52·4'E	FM	144
Manor Fm	Norf	TF9423	52°46·4'	0°53·0'E	FM	132
Manor Fm	Norf	TF9502	52°35·1'	0°53·1'E	FM	144
Manor Fm	Norf	TF9611	52°39·9'	0°54·3'E	FM	132
Manor Fm	Norf	TF9816	52°42·6'	0°56·3'E	FM	132
Manor Fm	Norf	TF9829	52°49·6'	0°56·7'E	FM	132
Manor Fm	Norf	TF9839	52°54·9'	0°57·1'E	FM	132
Manor Fm	Norf	TG0004	52°36·0'	0°57·6'E	FM	144
Manor Fm	Norf	TG0111	52°39·8'	0°58·7'E	FM	133
Manor Fm	Norf	TG0127	52°48·4'	0°59·3'E	FM	133
Manor Fm	Norf	TG0322	52°45·7'	1°0·9'E	FM	133
Manor Fm	Norf	TG0620	52°44·5'	1°3·5'E	FM	133
Manor Fm	Norf	TG0824	52°46·6'	1°5·4'E	FM	133
Manor Fm	Norf	TG1021	52°45·0'	1°7·1'E	FM	133
Manor Fm	Norf	TG1107	52°37·4'	1°7·5'E	FM	144
Manor Fm	Norf	TG1205	52°36·3'	1°8·3'E	FM	144
Manor Fm	Norf	TG1327	52°48·1'	1°10·0'E	FM	133
Manor Fm	Norf	TG1607	52°37·3'	1°11·9'E	FM	144
Manor Fm	Norf	TG1827	52°48·0'	1°14·4'E	FM	133,134
Manor Fm	Norf	TG2034	52°51·7'	1°16·5'E	FM	133
Manor Fm	Norf	TG2535	52°52·1'	1°21·0'E	FM	133
Manor Fm	Norf	TG2804	52°35·4'	1°22·4'E	FM	134
Manor Fm	Norf	TG2815	52°41·3'	1°22·8'E	FM	133,134
Manor Fm	Norf	TG2922	52°45·0'	1°24·0'E	FM	133,134
Manor Fm	Norf	TG3011	52°39·1'	1°24·4'E	FM	133,134
Manor Fm	Norf	TG3224	52°46·0'	1°26·8'E	FM	133,134
Manor Fm	Norf	TG3331	52°49·8'	1°27·9'E	FM	133
Manor Fm	Norf	TG3424	52°46·0'	1°28·5'E	FM	133,134
Manor Fm	Norf	TG3805	52°35·7'	1°31·3'E	FM	134
Manor Fm	Norf	TG4114	52°40·4'	1°34·3'E	FM	134
Manor Fm	Norf	TG4406	52°36·0'	1°36·6'E	FM	134
Manor Fm	Norf	TG4610	52°38·1'	1°38·5'E	FM	134
Manor Fm	Norf	TL7794	52°31·1'	0°36·9'E	FM	144
Manor Fm	Norf	TL9190	52°28·7'	0°49·2'E	FM	144
Manor Fm	Norf	TL9685	52°25·9'	0°53·4'E	FM	144
Manor Fm	Norf	TL9889	52°28·0'	0°55·3'E	FM	144
Manor Fm	Norf	TL9893	52°30·2'	0°55·4'E	FM	144
Manor Fm	Norf	TM0288	52°27·4'	0°58·8'E	FM	144
Manor Fm	Norf	TM0298	52°32·8'	0°59·2'E	FM	144
Manor Fm	Norf	TM1195	52°30·9'	1°7·0'E	FM	144
Manor Fm	Norf	TM1396	52°31·4'	1°8·8'E	FM	144
Manor Fm	Norf	TM2688	52°26·8'	1°19·9'E	FM	156
Manor Fm	Norf	TM2994	52°30·0'	1°22·8'E	FM	134
Manor Fm	Norf	TM3592	52°28·7'	1°28·0'E	FM	134
Manor Fm	Norf	TM3893	52°29·2'	1°30·7'E	FM	134
Manor Fm	Norf	TM4497	52°31·2'	1°36·2'E	FM	134
Manor Fm	Northnts	SP5256	52°12·2'	1°13·9'W	FM	151
Manor Fm	Northnts	SP5438	52°2·5'	1°12·4'W	FM	152
Manor Fm	Northnts	SP5636	52°1·4'	1°10·6'W	FM	152
Manor Fm	Northnts	SP5644	52°5·7'	1°10·6'W	FM	152
Manor Fm	Northnts	SP5951	52°9·5'	1°7·9'W	FM	152
Manor Fm	Northnts	SP6146	52°6·8'	1°6·2'W	FM	152
Manor Fm	Northnts	SP6472	52°20·8'	1°3·2'W	FM	140
Manor Fm	Northnts	SP7050	52°8·9'	0°58·2'W	FM	152
Manor Fm	Northnts	SP7650	52°8·8'	0°53·0'W	FM	152
Manor Fm	Northnts	SP7674	52°21·8'	0°52·6'W	FM	141
Manor Fm	Northnts	SP7743	52°5·0'	0°52·2'W	FM	152
Manor Fm	Northnts	SP7753	52°10·4'	0°52·0'W	FM	152
Manor Fm	Northnts	SP7887	52°28·8'	0°50·7'W	FM	141
Manor Fm	Northnts	SP7982	52°26·0'	0°49·9'W	FM	141
Manor Fm	Northnts	SP8054	52°10·9'	0°49·4'W	FM	152
Manor Fm	Northnts	SP8079	52°24·4'	0°49·0'W	FM	141
Manor Fm	Northnts	SP8353	52°10·4'	0°46·8'W	FM	152
Manor Fm	Northnts	SP9965	52°16·7'	0°32·5'W	FM	153
Manor Fm	Northnts	TL0696	52°33·3'	0°25·8'W	FM	142
Manor Fm	Northnts	TL1187	52°28·4'	0°21·5'W	FM	142
Manor Fm	Northum	NY8378	55°6·0'	2°15·6'W	FM	86,87
Manor Fm	Notts	SK4861	53°8·9'	1°16·5'W	FM	120
Manor Fm	Notts	SK5325	52°49·4'	1°12·4'W	FM	129
Manor Fm	Notts	SK5525	52°49·4'	1°10·6'W	FM	129
Manor Fm	Notts	SK6326	52°49·9'	1°3·5'W	FM	129
Manor Fm	Notts	SK6347	53°1·2'	1°3·2'W	FM	129
Manor Fm	Notts	SK6464	53°10·4'	1°2·1'W	FM	120
Manor Fm	Notts	SK6525	52°49·4'	1°1·7'W	FM	129
Manor Fm	Notts	SK6627	52°50·4'	1°0·8'W	FM	129
Manor Fm	Notts	SK7049	53°2·3'	0°57·0'W	FM	129
Manor Fm	Notts	SK7142	52°58·5'	0°56·2'W	FM	129
Manor Fm	Notts	SK7176	53°16·8'	0°55·7'W	FM	120
Manor Fm	Notts	SK7341	52°57·9'	0°54·4'W	FM	129
Manor Fm	Notts	SK7493	53°26·0'	0°52·8'W	FM	112
Manor Fm	Notts	SK7947	53°1·1'	0°48·9'W	FM	129
Manor Fm	N Som	ST3563	51°22·0'	2°55·6'W	FM	182
Manor Fm	N Som	ST4268	51°24·7'	2°49·7'W	FM	171,172,182
Manor Fm	N Yks	NZ2213	54°31·0'	1°39·2'W	FM	93
Manor Fm	N Yks	NZ5203	54°25·4'	1°11·5'W	FM	93
Manor Fm	N Yks	NZ5405	54°26·5'	1°9·6'W	FM	93
Manor Fm	N Yks	SD9648	53°55·9'	2°3·2'W	FM	103
Manor Fm	N Yks	SE2883	54°14·8'	1°33·8'W	FM	99
Manor Fm	N Yks	SE3451	53°57·5'	1°28·5'W	FM	104
Manor Fm	N Yks	SE4082	54°14·2'	1°22·8'W	FM	99
Manor Fm	N Yks	SE4294	54°20·6'	1°20·8'W	FM	99
Manor Fm	N Yks	SE4357	54°0·7'	1°20·2'W	FM	105
Manor Fm	N Yks	SE4649	53°56·3'	1°17·5'W	FM	105
Manor Fm	N Yks	SE5069	54°7·1'	1°13·7'W	FM	100
Manor Fm	N Yks	SE5938	53°50·3'	1°5·8'W	FM	105
Manor Fm	N Yks	SE6542	53°52·4'	1°0·3'W	FM	105,106
Manor Fm	N Yks	SE6640	53°51·4'	0°59·4'W	FM	105,106
Manor Fm	N Yks	SE6755	53°59·4'	0°58·3'W	FM	105,106
Manor Fm	N Yks	SE6788	54°17·2'	0°57·8'W	FM	94,100
Manor Fm	N Yks	SE7274	54°9·6'	0°53·4'W	FM	100
Manor Fm	N Yks	SE7575	54°10·2'	0°50·7'W	FM	100
Manor Fm	N Yks	SE7766	54°5·3'	0°49·0'W	FM	100
Manor Fm	N Yks	SE7861	54°2·6'	0°48·1'W	FM	100
Manor Fm	N Yks	SE7867	54°5·8'	0°48·0'W	FM	100
Manor Fm	N Yks	SE8185	54°15·5'	0°45·0'W	FM	94,100
Manor Fm	N Yks	SE8375	54°10·1'	0°43·3'W	FM	100
Manor Fm	Oxon	SP2303	51°43·7'	1°39·6'W	FM	163
Manor Fm	Oxon	SP2504	51°44·3'	1°37·9'W	FM	163
Manor Fm	Oxon	SP3007	51°45·9'	1°33·5'W	FM	164
Manor Fm	Oxon	SP3206	51°45·3'	1°31·8'W	FM	164
Manor Fm	Oxon	SP3733	51°59·9'	1°27·3'W	FM	151
Manor Fm	Oxon	SP3805	51°44·8'	1°26·6'W	FM	164
Manor Fm	Oxon	SP4737	52°2·0'	1°18·5'W	FM	151
Manor Fm	Oxon	SP4915	51°50·1'	1°16·9'W	FM	164
Manor Fm	Oxon	SP4921	51°53·4'	1°16·9'W	FM	164
Manor Fm	Oxon	SP4928	51°57·1'	1°16·8'W	FM	164
Manor Fm	Oxon	SP5324	51°55·0'	1°13·4'W	FM	164
Manor Fm	Oxon	SP5807	51°45·8'	1°9·2'W	FM	164
Manor Fm	Oxon	SP6022	51°53·8'	1°7·3'W	FM	164,165
Manor Fm	Oxon	SP6405	51°44·6'	1°4·0'W	FM	164,165
Manor Fm	Oxon	SP6701	51°42·5'	1°1·4'W	FM	164,165
Manor Fm	Oxon	SP6805	51°44·6'	1°0·5'W	FM	164,165
Manor Fm	Oxon	SP7202	51°43·0'	0°57·1'W	FM	165
Manor Fm	Oxon	SU2796	51°40·0'	1°36·2'W	FM	163
Manor Fm	Oxon	SU3895	51°39·4'	1°26·6'W	FM	164
Manor Fm	Oxon	SU3986	51°34·5'	1°25·8'W	FM	174
Manor Fm	Oxon	SU4396	51°39·9'	1°22·3'W	FM	164
Manor Fm	Oxon	SU5887	51°35·0'	1°9·4'W	FM	174
Manor Fm	Oxon	SU7699	51°41·3'	0°53·6'W	FM	165
Manor Fm	Pemb	SN0218	51°49·8'	4°52·0'W	FM	157,158
Manor Fm	Peterb	TF1100	52°35·4'	0°21·3'W	FM	142
Manor Fm	Red & Cl	NZ5822	54°35·6'	1°5·7'W	FM	93
Manor Fm	Roth	SK5081	53°19·7'	1°14·5'W	FM	111,120
Manor Fm	Rut	SK8314	52°43·3'	0°45·9'W	FM	130
Manor Fm	Rut	SK8613	52°42·7'	0°43·2'W	FM	130
Manor Fm	S Glos	ST5789	51°36·1'	2°36·9'W	FM	162,172
Manor Fm	Shrops	SJ6231	52°52·7'	2°33·5'W	FM	127
Manor Fm	Shrops	SO4390	52°30·5'	2°50·0'W	FM	137
Manor Fm	Shrops	SO4587	52°28·9'	2°48·2'W	FM	137,138
Manor Fm	Shrops	SO5192	52°31·7'	2°42·9'W	FM	137,138
Manor Fm	Shrops	SO5293	52°32·2'	2°42·1'W	FM	137,138
Manor Fm	Shrops	SO6384	52°27·4'	2°32·3'W	FM	138
Manor Fm	Somer	ST0831	51°4·5'	3°18·4'W	FM	181
Manor Fm	Somer	ST0927	51°2·3'	3°17·5'W	FM	181
Manor Fm	Somer	ST2730	51°4·1'	3°2·1'W	FM	182
Manor Fm	Somer	ST2829	51°3·6'	3°1·3'W	FM	193
Manor Fm	Somer	ST2839	51°9·0'	3°1·4'W	FM	182
Manor Fm	Somer	ST3239	51°9·0'	2°57·9'W	FM	182
Manor Fm	Somer	ST3306	50°51·2'	2°56·7'W	FM	193
Manor Fm	Somer	ST3311	50°53·9'	2°56·8'W	FM	193
Manor Fm	Somer	ST3337	51°7·9'	2°57·1'W	FM	182
Manor Fm	Somer	ST3431	51°4·7'	2°56·1'W	FM	182
Manor Fm	Somer	ST3553	51°16·6'	2°55·5'W	FM	182
Manor Fm	Somer	ST3607	50°51·8'	2°54·2'W	FM	193
Manor Fm	Somer	ST4138	51°8·5'	2°50·2'W	FM	182
Manor Fm	Somer	ST4307	50°51·8'	2°48·2'W	A	193
Manor Fm	Somer	ST4610	50°53·5'	2°45·7'W	FM	193
Manor Fm	Somer	ST4615	50°56·1'	2°45·7'W	FM	193
Manor Fm	Somer	ST4742	51°10·7'	2°45·1'W	FM	182
Manor Fm	Somer	ST4955	51°17·7'	2°43·5'W	FM	172,182
Manor Fm	Somer	ST5530	51°4·3'	2°38·2'W	FM	182,183
Manor Fm	Somer	ST5610	50°53·5'	2°37·2'W	FM	194
Manor Fm	Somer	ST5718	50°57·8'	2°36·4'W	A	183
Manor Fm	Somer	ST5739	51°9·2'	2°36·5'W	FM	182,183
Manor Fm	Somer	ST6452	51°16·2'	2°30·6'W	FM	183
Manor Fm	Somer	ST6637	51°8·1'	2°28·8'W	FM	183
Manor Fm	Somer	ST6651	51°15·7'	2°28·8'W	FM	183
Manor Fm	Somer	ST6946	51°13·0'	2°26·2'W	FM	183
Manor Fm	Somer	ST7645	51°12·5'	2°20·2'W	FM	183
Manor Fm	Staffs	SJ7742	52°58·7'	2°20·1'W	FM	118
Manor Fm	Staffs	SJ9403	52°37·7'	2°4·9'W	FM	127,139
Manor Fm	Staffs	SK0128	52°51·2'	1°58·7'W	FM	128
Manor Fm	Staffs	SK0458	53°7·4'	1°56·0'W	FM	119
Manor Fm	Staffs	SK0816	52°44·7'	1°52·5'W	FM	128
Manor Fm	St Hel	SJ4990	53°24·5'	2°45·6'W	A	108
Manor Fm	Stock on T	NZ4109	54°28·7'	1°21·6'W	FM	93
Manor Fm	Suff	TL8153	52°9·0'	0°39·1'E	FM	155
Manor Fm	Suff	TL8859	52°12·1'	0°45·5'E	FM	155
Manor Fm	Suff	TL9172	52°19·0'	0°48·5'E	FM	144,155
Manor Fm	Suff	TL9250	52°7·1'	0°48·7'E	FM	155
Manor Fm	Suff	TL9265	52°15·2'	0°49·2'E	FM	155
Manor Fm	Suff	TL9352	52°8·2'	0°49·6'E	FM	155
Manor Fm	Suff	TL9474	52°20·0'	0°51·2'E	FM	144
Manor Fm	Suff	TL9648	52°6·0'	0°52·1'E	FM	155
Manor Fm	Suff	TL9856	52°10·2'	0°54·1'E	FM	155
Manor Fm	Suff	TL9979	52°22·6'	0°55·8'E	FM	144

Manor Fm	Suff	TM0447	52°5·2′	0°59·1′E	FM	155
Manor Fm	Suff	TM0454	52°9·0′	0°59·3′E	FM	155
Manor Fm	Suff	TM1451	52°7·2′	1°8·0′E	FM	156
Manor Fm	Suff	TM1651	52°7·1′	1°9·7′E	FM	156
Manor Fm	Suff	TM1768	52°16·3′	1°11·2′E	FM	156
Manor Fm	Suff	TM2149	52°5·9′	1°14·0′E	FM	169
Manor Fm	Suff	TM2252	52°7·5′	1°15·0′E	FM	156
Manor Fm	Suff	TM2260	52°11·8′	1°15·3′E	FM	156
Manor Fm	Suff	TM2372	52°18·3′	1°16·7′E	FM	156
Manor Fm	Suff	TM2574	52°19·3′	1°18·5′E	FM	156
Manor Fm	Suff	TM2651	52°6·9′	1°18·5′E	FM	156
Manor Fm	Suff	TM3070	52°17·0′	1°22·7′E	FM	156
Manor Fm	Suff	TM3173	52°18·6′	1°23·7′E	FM	156
Manor Fm	Suff	TM3275	52°19·7′	1°24·7′E	FM	156
Manor Fm	Suff	TM3340	52°0·8′	1°24·1′E	FM	169
Manor Fm	Suff	TM3465	52°14·2′	1°26·0′E	FM	156
Manor Fm	Suff	TM3487	52°26·1′	1°27·0′E	FM	156
Manor Fm	Suff	TM3571	52°17·4′	1°27·2′E	FM	156
Manor Fm	Suff	TM3676	52°20·1′	1°28·3′E	FM	156
Manor Fm	Suff	TM3687	52°26·0′	1°28·7′E	FM	156
Manor Fm	Suff	TM3790	52°27·6′	1°29·7′E	FM	134
Manor Fm	Suff	TM3884	52°24·4′	1°30·4′E	FM	156
Manor Fm	Suff	TM3971	52°17·3′	1°30·7′E	FM	156
Manor Fm	Suff	TM4080	52°22·1′	1°31·9′E	FM	156
Manor Fm	Suff	TM4261	52°11·9′	1°32·9′E	FM	156
Manor Fm	Suff	TM4382	52°23·1′	1°34·7′E	FM	156
Manor Fm	Suff	TM4580	52°22·0′	1°36·3′E	FM	156
Manor Fm	Suff	TM5286	52°25·1′	1°42·8′E	FM	156
Manor Fm	Surrey	SU8239	51°8·9′	0°49·3′W	FM	186
Manor Fm	Surrey	SU8848	51°13·7′	0°44·0′W	FM	186
Manor Fm	Surrey	SU9649	51°14·2′	0°37·1′W	FM	186
Manor Fm	Surrey	TQ0147	51°13·0′	0°32·8′W	FM	186
Manor Fm	Surrey	TQ0854	51°16·7′	0°26·7′W	FM	187
Manor Fm	Surrey	TQ1147	51°12·9′	0°24·3′W	FM	187
Manor Fm	Swin	SU1795	51°39·4′	1°44·9′W	FM	163
Manor Fm	Swin	SU1987	51°35·1′	1°43·2′W	FM	173
Manor Fm	Swin	SU2280	51°31·3′	1°40·6′W	FM	174
Manor Fm	Swin	SU2483	51°33·0′	1°38·8′W	FM	174
Manor Fm	Torbay	SX8856	50°23·8′	3°34·2′W	FM	202
Manor Fm	Warw	SP1857	52°12·9′	1°43·8′W	FM	151
Manor Fm	Warw	SP2065	52°17·2′	1°42·0′W	FM	151
Manor Fm	Warw	SP2271	52°20·4′	1°40·2′W	FM	139
Manor Fm	Warw	SP3666	52°17·7′	1°27·9′W	FM	151
Manor Fm	Warw	SP4046	52°6·9′	1°24·6′W	FM	151
Manor Fm	Warw	SP4159	52°13·9′	1°23·6′W	FM	151
Manor Fm	Warw	SP4255	52°11·7′	1°22·7′W	FM	151
Manor Fm	Warw	SP4284	52°27·4′	1°22·5′W	FM	140
Manor Fm	Warw	SP4373	52°21·4′	1°21·7′W	FM	140
Manor Fm	Warw	SP4469	52°19·3′	1°20·9′W	FM	151
Manor Fm	Warw	SP4583	52°26·8′	1°19·9′W	FM	140
Manor Fm	Warw	SP5065	52°17·1′	1°15·6′W	FM	151
Manor Fm	Warw	SP5069	52°19·2′	1°15·6′W	FM	151
Manor Fm	Warw	SP5376	52°23·0′	1°12·9′W	FM	140
Manor Fm	W Berks	SU3477	51°29·7′	1°30·2′W	FM	174
Manor Fm	W Berks	SU3660	51°20·5′	1°28·6′W	FM	174
Manor Fm	W Berks	SU3664	51°22·7′	1°28·6′W	FM	174
Manor Fm	W Berks	SU3775	51°28·6′	1°27·6′W	FM	174
Manor Fm	W Berks	SU4078	51°30·2′	1°25·0′W	FM	174
Manor Fm	W Berks	SU5565	51°23·1′	1°12·2′W	FM	174
Manor Fm	W Berks	SU5570	51°25·8′	1°12·1′W	FM	174
Manor Fm	W Berks	SU5878	51°30·1′	1°9·5′W	FM	174
Manor Fm	W Berks	SU6867	51°24·1′	1°1·0′W	FM	175
Manor Fm	Wilts	ST7838	51°8·7′	2°18·5′W	FM	183
Manor Fm	Wilts	ST8133	51°6·0′	2°15·9′W	FM	183
Manor Fm	Wilts	ST8383	51°33·0′	2°14·3′W	FM	173
Manor Fm	Wilts	ST8740	51°9·8′	2°10·8′W	FM	183
Manor Fm	Wilts	ST9021	50°59·5′	2°8·2′W	FM	184
Manor Fm	Wilts	ST9474	51°28·1′	2°4·8′W	FM	173
Manor Fm	Wilts	ST9576	51°29·2′	2°3·9′W	FM	173
Manor Fm	Wilts	ST9633	51°6·0′	2°3·0′W	FM	184
Manor Fm	Wilts	ST9654	51°17·3′	2°3·1′W	FM	184
Manor Fm	Wilts	ST9666	51°23·8′	2°3·1′W	FM	173
Manor Fm	Wilts	ST9687	51°35·1′	2°3·1′W	FM	173
Manor Fm	Wilts	ST9741	51°10·3′	2°2·2′W	FM	184
Manor Fm	Wilts	ST9828	51°3·3′	2°1·3′W	FM	184
Manor Fm	Wilts	ST9832	51°5·5′	2°1·3′W	FM	184
Manor Fm	Wilts	SU0183	51°33·0′	1°58·7′W	FM	173
Manor Fm	Wilts	SU0229	51°3·9′	1°57·9′W	FM	184
Manor Fm	Wilts	SU0231	51°4·9′	1°57·9′W	FM	184
Manor Fm	Wilts	SU0373	51°27·6′	1°57·0′W	FM	173
Manor Fm	Wilts	SU0671	51°26·5′	1°54·4′W	FM	173
Manor Fm	Wilts	SU0693	51°38·4′	1°54·4′W	FM	163,173
Manor Fm	Wilts	SU0896	51°40·0′	1°52·7′W	FM	163
Manor Fm	Wilts	SU1059	51°20·0′	1°51·0′W	FM	173
Manor Fm	Wilts	SU1077	51°29·7′	1°51·0′W	FM	173
Manor Fm	Wilts	SU1170	51°26·0′	1°50·1′W	FM	173
Manor Fm	Wilts	SU1527	51°2·8′	1°46·8′W	FM	184
Manor Fm	Wilts	SU2132	51°5·4′	1°41·6′W	FM	184
Manor Fm	Wilts	SU2227	51°2·7′	1°40·8′W	FM	184
Manor Fm	Wilts	SU2419	50°58·4′	1°39·1′W	FM	184
Manor Fm	Wilts	SU2459	51°20·0′	1°38·9′W	FM	174
Manor Fm	Wilts	SU2671	51°26·5′	1°37·2′W	FM	174
Manor Fm	Wilts	SU2765	51°23·2′	1°36·3′W	FM	174
Manor Fm	Wilts	SU2859	51°20·0′	1°35·5′W	FM	174
Manor Fm	Wilts	SU3059	51°20·0′	1°33·8′W	FM	174
Manor Fm	Wilts	SU3170	51°25·9′	1°32·9′W	FM	174
Manor Fm	Wilts	SU3360	51°20·5′	1°31·2′W	FM	174
Manor Fm	Wilts	SU3362	51°21·6′	1°31·2′W	FM	174
Manor Fm	Win & Maid	SU9578	51°29·8′	0°37·5′W	FM	175,176
Manor Fm	Win & Maid	SU9875	51°28·2′	0°35·0′W	FM	175,176
Manor Fm	Win & Maid	TQ0175	51°28·1′	0°32·4′W	FM	176
Manor Fm	Worcs	SO8352	52°10·2′	2°14·5′W	FM	150
Manor Fm	Worcs	SO8840	52°3·7′	2°10·1′W	FM	150
Manor Fm	Worcs	SO8968	52°18·8′	2°9·3′W	FM	139
Manor Fm	Worcs	SP0844	52°5·9′	1°52·6′W	FM	150
Manor Fm	Worcs	SP1143	52°5·3′	1°50·0′W	FM	150
Manor Fm	Wrex	SJ3544	52°59·6′	2°57·7′W	FM	117
Manor Fm	W Susx	SU7721	50°59·2′	0°53·8′W	FM	197
Manor Fm	W Susx	SU8218	50°57·6′	0°49·6′W	FM	197
Manor Fm	W Susx	SU9017	50°57·0′	0°42·7′W	FM	197

Manor Fm	W Susx	SU9221	50°59·1′	0°41·0′W	FM	197
Manor Fm	W Susx	SU9516	50°56·4′	0°38·5′W	FM	197
Manor Fm, The	Bucks	SP7931	51°58·5′	0°50·6′W	FM	152,165
Manor France Fm	Dorset	ST8608	50°52·5′	2°11·6′W	FM	194
Manor Hall Fm	Norf	TG4006	52°36·1′	1°33·1′E	FM	134
Manorhead	Scot Bord	NT1927	55°32·1′	3°16·6′W	X	72
Manor Hill	Dorset	ST9215	50°56·3′	2°6·4′W	H	184
Manorhill	Scot Bord	NT6632	55°35·1′	2°31·9′W	T	74
Manor Hill Corner	Lincs	TF4017	52°44·2′	0°4·8′E	T	131
Manor Hill Fm	Lincs	TF4117	52°44·2′	0°5·7′E	FM	131
Manor Hills	Notts	SK5876	53°16·9′	1°7·4′W	X	120
Manor Ho	Aberd	NJ7319	57°15·9′	2°26·4′W	X	38
Manor Ho	Beds	SP9730	51°57·8′	0°34·9′W	X	165
Manor Ho	Beds	TL0232	51°58·9′	0°30·5′W	X	166
Manor Ho	Beds	TL1058	52°12·8′	0°23·0′W	X	153
Manor Ho	Birm	SP0281	52°25·9′	1°57·8′W	X	139
Manor Ho	Bucks	SP6429	51°57·6′	1°3·7′W	X	164,165
Manor Ho	Bucks	SP6430	51°58·1′	1°3·7′W	X	152,165
Manor Ho	Bucks	SP6534	52°0·3′	1°2·8′W	X	152,165
Manor Ho	Bucks	SP7141	52°4·0′	0°57·5′W	X	152
Manor Ho	Bucks	SP8121	51°53·1′	0°49·0′W	A	165
Manor Ho	Bucks	SU7886	51°34·3′	0°52·1′W	X	175
Manor Ho	Bucks	SU8787	51°34·7′	0°44·3′W	X	175
Manor Ho	Bucks	TQ0198	51°40·5′	0°32·0′W	A	166,176
Manor Ho	Cambs	TF4208	52°39·3′	0°6·4′E	X	142,143
Manor Ho	Cambs	TL0869	52°18·7′	0°24·5′W	X	153
Manor Ho	Cambs	TL1876	52°22·4′	0°15·6′W	A	142
Manor Ho	Cambs	TL2883	52°26·0′	0°6·6′W	X	142
Manor Ho	Cambs	TL4551	52°8·5′	0°7·5′E	X	154
Manor Ho	Cambs	TL4874	52°20·9′	0°10·8′E	A	143
Manor Ho	Ches	SJ5050	53°2·9′	2°44·3′W	X	117
Manor Ho	Ches	SJ6751	53°3·6′	2°29·1′W	X	118
Manor Ho	Ches	SJ7356	53°6·3′	2°23·8′W	X	118
Manor Ho	Ches	SJ7759	53°7·9′	2°20·2′W	X	118
Manor Ho	Ches	SJ8967	53°12·2′	2°9·5′W	X	118
Manor Ho	Cumbr	NY7810	54°29·3′	2°20·0′W	A	91
Manor Ho	Derby	SK1640	52°57·7′	1°45·3′W	X	119,128
Manor Ho	Derby	SK1647	53°1·4′	1°45·3′W	X	119,128
Manor Ho	Derby	SK1669	53°13·3′	1°45·2′W	X	119
Manor Ho	Derby	SK2716	52°44·7′	1°35·6′W	X	128
Manor Ho	Devon	SS4440	51°8·5′	4°13·4′W	X	180
Manor Ho	Devon	SS6420	50°58·0′	3°55·8′W	X	180
Manor Ho	Devon	SX5594	50°43·9′	4°2·9′W	X	191
Manor Ho	Devon	SX6454	50°22·4′	3°54·4′W	X	202
Manor Ho	Devon	SY1392	50°43·5′	3°13·6′W	X	192,193
Manor Ho	Donc	SK5796	53°27·7′	1°8·1′W	X	111
Manor Ho	Dorset	ST5602	50°49·2′	2°37·1′W	X	194
Manor Ho	Dorset	ST6502	50°49·2′	2°29·4′W	A	194
Manor Ho	Dorset	ST6808	50°52·5′	2°26·9′W	X	194
Manor Ho	Dorset	ST6810	50°53·5′	2°26·9′W	X	194
Manor Ho	Dorset	ST6902	50°49·2′	2°26·0′W	X	194
Manor Ho	Dorset	ST6917	50°57·3′	2°26·1′W	A	183
Manor Ho	Dorset	ST7000	50°48·2′	2°25·2′W	X	194
Manor Ho	Dorset	ST7500	50°48·2′	2°20·9′W	X	194
Manor Ho	Dorset	ST7706	50°51·4′	2°19·2′W	X	194
Manor Ho	Dorset	ST8303	50°49·8′	2°14·1′W	A	194
Manor Ho	Dorset	ST8312	50°54·7′	2°14·1′W	X	194
Manor Ho	Dorset	ST9906	50°51·4′	2°0·5′W	A	195
Manor Ho	Dorset	SU0212	50°54·7′	1°57·9′W	X	195
Manor Ho	Dorset	SY3694	50°44·8′	2°54·0′W	X	193
Manor Ho	Dorset	SY6182	50°38·4′	2°32·7′W	X	194
Manor Ho	Dorset	SY7099	50°47·6′	2°25·2′W	X	194
Manor Ho	Dorset	SY7282	50°38·5′	2°23·4′W	A	194
Manor Ho	Durham	NZ1747	54°49·3′	1°43·7′W	X	88
Manor Ho	Essex	TL7130	51°56·8′	0°29·7′E	X	167
Manor Ho	Essex	TM1523	51°52·1′	1°7·8′E	X	168,169
Manor Ho	Essex	TQ4097	51°39·5′	0°1·8′E	X	167,177
Manor Ho	E Susx	TQ6916	50°55·3′	0°24·7′E	A	199
Manor Ho	E Yorks	SE7557	54°0·5′	0°50·9′W	X	105,106
Manor Ho	E Yorks	SE7825	53°43·2′	0°48·7′W	X	105,106
Manor Ho	E Yorks	SE8140	53°51·2′	0°45·7′W	X	106
Manor Ho	E Yorks	SE9032	53°46·8′	0°37·6′W	X	106
Manor Ho	E Yorks	SE9352	53°57·6′	0°34·5′W	X	106
Manor Ho	E Yorks	TA0872	54°8·2′	0°20·4′W	X	101
Manor Ho	E Yorks	TA1050	53°56·3′	0°19·0′W	X	107
Manor Ho	E Yorks	TA1242	53°52·0′	0°17·4′W	X	107
Manor Ho	E Yorks	TA1247	53°54·7′	0°17·3′W	X	107
Manor Ho	E Yorks	TA1555	53°58·9′	0°14·4′W	X	107
Manor Ho	E Yorks	TA2234	53°47·5′	0°8·5′W	X	107
Manor Ho	Glos	SO6217	51°51·3′	2°32·7′W	A	162
Manor Ho	Glos	SO9727	51°56·7′	2°2·2′W	X	163
Manor Ho	Glos	SP0700	51°42·2′	1°53·5′W	X	163
Manor Ho	Glos	SP0825	51°55·6′	1°52·6′W	X	163
Manor Ho	Glos	SP1341	52°4·3′	1°48·2′W	X	151
Manor Ho	Glos	SP1927	51°56·7′	1°43·0′W	X	163
Manor Ho	Hants	SU1118	50°57·9′	1°50·2′W	A	184
Manor Ho	Hants	SU1219	50°58·4′	1°49·4′W	X	184
Manor Ho	Hants	SU3658	51°19·4′	1°28·6′W	X	174
Manor Ho	Hants	SU4546	51°12·9′	1°21·0′W	X	185
Manor Ho	Hants	SU7200	50°47·9′	0°58·3′W	X	197
Manor Ho	Hants	SU7229	51°3·6′	0°58·0′W	X	186,197
Manor Ho	Hants	SZ2894	50°44·9′	1°35·8′W	X	195
Manor Ho	Herts	TL0401	51°42·1′	0°29·3′W	A	166
Manor Ho	Herts	TL2630	51°57·5′	0°9·6′W	X	166
Manor Ho	Herts	TL2636	52°0·7′	0°9·4′W	X	153
Manor Ho	Kent	TR0530	51°2·2′	0°55·8′E	X	189
Manor Ho	Kent	TR0539	51°7·0′	0°56·1′E	A	179,189
Manor Ho	Kent	TR2065	51°20·7′	1°9·9′E	A	179
Manor Ho	Lancs	SD5866	54°5·5′	2°38·1′W	X	97
Manor Ho	Lancs	SD6035	53°48·8′	2°36·0′W	X	102,103
Manor Ho	Lancs	SD8143	53°53·2′	2°16·9′W	X	103
Manor Ho	Leeds	SE3141	53°52·1′	1°31·3′W	X	104
Manor Ho	Leic	SK4212	52°42·5′	1°22·3′W	A	129
Manor Ho	Leic	SK4600	52°36·0′	1°18·8′W	X	140
Manor Ho	Leic	SK6800	52°35·8′	0°59·4′W	X	141
Manor Ho	Leic	SK6900	52°35·8′	0°58·5′W	X	141
Manor Ho	Leic	SK7624	52°48·7′	0°51·9′W	X	129
Manor Ho	Leic	SK8008	52°40·1′	0°48·6′W	X	141
Manor Ho	Leic	SP5087	52°29·0′	1°15·4′W	X	140
Manor Ho	Leic	SP5382	52°26·2′	1°12·8′W	X	140

Manor Ho	Leic	SP5385	52°27·9′	1°12·8′W	X	140
Manor Ho	Leic	SP5989	52°30·0′	1°7·5′W	X	140
Manor Ho	Leic	SP6396	52°33·7′	1°3·8′W	X	140
Manor Ho	Leic	SP7089	52°29·9′	0°57·7′W	X	141
Manor Ho	Leic	SP7099	52°35·3′	0°57·6′W	X	141
Manor Ho	Leic	SP7692	52°31·5′	0°52·4′W	X	141
Manor Ho	Leic	SP8095	52°33·1′	0°48·8′W	X	141
Manor Ho	Lincs	SK8898	53°28·5′	0°40·0′W	X	112
Manor Ho	Lincs	SK9154	53°4·8′	0°38·1′W	X	121
Manor Ho	Lincs	SK9396	53°27·4′	0°35·6′W	X	112
Manor Ho	Lincs	SK9983	53°20·3′	0°30·4′W	X	121
Manor Ho	Lincs	TF1892	53°24·9′	0°13·1′W	X	113
Manor Ho	Lincs	TF2368	53°11·9′	0°9·1′W	X	122
Manor Ho	Lincs	TF2374	53°15·2′	0°9·0′W	X	122
Manor Ho	Lincs	TF2787	53°22·1′	0°5·1′W	X	113,122
Manor Ho	Lincs	TF2861	53°8·1′	0°4·8′W	X	122
Manor Ho	Lincs	TF2932	52°52·4′	0°4·6′W	X	131
Manor Ho	Lincs	TF2973	53°14·5′	0°3·6′W	X	122
Manor Ho	Lincs	TF3662	53°8·5′	0°2·4′E	X	122
Manor Ho	Lincs	TF3923	52°47·4′	0°4·1′E	X	131
Manor Ho	Lincs	TF4123	52°47·4′	0°5·9′E	X	131
Manor Ho	Lincs	TF4681	53°18·6′	0°11·9′E	X	122
Manor Ho	Lincs	TF4788	53°22·3′	0°13·0′E	X	113,122
Manor Ho	Lincs	TF5174	53°14·7′	0°16·2′E	X	122
Manor Ho	Mil Key	SP8846	52°6·5′	0°42·5′W	X	152
Manor Ho	NE Lincs	TA2302	53°30·3′	0°8·3′W	X	113
Manor Ho	Norf	TF7042	52°57·1′	0°32·2′E	X	132
Manor Ho	Norf	TF7418	52°44·1′	0°35·0′E	X	132
Manor Ho	Norf	TF7743	52°57·5′	0°38·5′E	X	132
Manor Ho	Norf	TF8015	52°42·4′	0°40·3′E	X	132
Manor Ho	Norf	TF8536	52°53·6′	0°45·4′E	X	132
Manor Ho	Norf	TF8541	52°56·3′	0°45·6′E	X	132
Manor Ho	Norf	TF9028	52°49·2′	0°49·6′E	X	132
Manor Ho	Norf	TF9133	52°51·9′	0°50·7′E	A	132
Manor Ho	Norf	TF9213	52°41·1′	0°50·8′E	X	132
Manor Ho	Norf	TF9317	52°43·2′	0°51·9′E	X	132
Manor Ho	Norf	TF9541	52°56·1′	0°54·5′E	A	132
Manor Ho	Norf	TF9624	52°46·9′	0°54·8′E	X	132
Manor Ho	Norf	TG0123	52°46·3′	0°59·2′E	X	133
Manor Ho	Norf	TG0743	52°56·9′	1°5·3′E	X	133
Manor Ho	Norf	TG1139	52°54·6′	1°8·7′E	X	133
Manor Ho	Norf	TG1236	52°53·0′	1°9·5′E	X	133
Manor Ho	Norf	TG1636	52°52·9′	1°13·0′E	X	133
Manor Ho	Norf	TG2117	52°42·6′	1°16·7′E	X	133,134
Manor Ho	Norf	TG2136	52°52·8′	1°17·5′E	X	133
Manor Ho	Norf	TG2404	52°35·5′	1°18·8′E	X	134
Manor Ho	Norf	TG2719	52°43·5′	1°22·1′E	X	133,134
Manor Ho	Norf	TG3001	52°33·7′	1°24·0′E	X	134
Manor Ho	Norf	TG3625	52°46·5′	1°30·3′E	X	133,134
Manor Ho	Norf	TG3627	52°47·6′	1°30·4′E	X	133,134
Manor Ho	Norf	TG3818	52°42·7′	1°31·8′E	X	133,134
Manor Ho	Norf	TG3928	52°48·0′	1°33·1′E	X	133,134
Manor Ho	Norf	TG4026	52°46·9′	1°33·9′E	X	134
Manor Ho	Norf	TG4104	52°35·0′	1°33·9′E	X	134
Manor Ho	Norf	TG4107	52°36·7′	1°34·0′E	X	134
Manor Ho	Norf	TL9283	52°24·9′	0°49·8′E	X	144
Manor Ho	Norf	TM1286	52°26·1′	1°7·5′E	X	144
Manor Ho	Norf	TM1494	52°30·3′	1°9·6′E	X	144
Manor Ho	Norf	TM2192	52°29·1′	1°15·7′E	X	134
Manor Ho	Norf	TM3496	52°30·9′	1°27·3′E	X	134
Manor Ho	Northnts	SP4950	52°9·0′	1°16·6′W	X	151
Manor Ho	Northnts	SP5158	52°13·3′	1°14·8′W	X	151
Manor Ho	Northnts	SP5361	52°14·9′	1°13·0′W	X	152
Manor Ho	Northnts	SP5539	52°3·0′	1°11·5′W	A	152
Manor Ho	Northnts	SP5754	52°11·1′	1°9·6′W	X	152
Manor Ho	Northnts	SP5768	52°18·7′	1°9·4′W	A	152
Manor Ho	Northnts	SP5946	52°6·8′	1°7·9′W	A	152
Manor Ho	Northnts	SP5948	52°7·9′	1°7·9′W	A	152
Manor Ho	Northnts	SP5957	52°12·7′	1°7·8′W	X	152
Manor Ho	Northnts	SP6273	52°21·3′	1°5·0′W	A	140
Manor Ho	Northnts	SP6354	52°11·1′	1°4·3′W	X	152
Manor Ho	Northnts	SP6757	52°12·7′	1°0·8′W	X	152
Manor Ho	Northnts	SP7054	52°11·0′	0°58·2′W	A	152
Manor Ho	Northnts	SP7581	52°25·5′	0°53·4′W	X	141
Manor Ho	Northnts	SP7991	52°30·9′	0°49·7′W	X	141
Manor Ho	Northnts	SP8253	52°10·4′	0°47·7′W	X	152
Manor Ho	Northnts	SP8569	52°19·0′	0°44·8′W	A	152
Manor Ho	Northnts	SP9197	52°34·0′	0°39·0′W	X	141
Manor Ho	Northnts	TL0588	52°29·0′	0°26·8′W	X	142
Manor Ho	Northum	NZ1381	55°7·6′	1°47·3′W	X	81
Manor Ho	Notts	SK6251	53°3·4′	1°4·1′W	X	120
Manor Ho	Notts	SK6754	53°5·0′	0°59·6′W	X	120
Manor Ho	Notts	SK7288	53°23·3′	0°54·6′W	X	112,120
Manor Ho	Notts	SK7979	53°18·4′	0°48·5′W	X	120,121
Manor Ho	Notts	SK8172	53°14·6′	0°46·8′W	X	121
Manor Ho	Notts	SK8177	53°17·3′	0°46·7′W	X	121
Manor Ho	N Som	ST5473	51°27·5′	2°39·3′W	X	172
Manor Ho	N Yks	NZ2303	54°25·6′	1°38·3′W	A	93
Manor Ho	N Yks	NZ2703	54°25·5′	1°34·6′W	X	93
Manor Ho	N Yks	NZ3002	54°25·0′	1°31·8′W	X	93
Manor Ho	N Yks	NZ3701	54°24·4′	1°25·4′W	X	93
Manor Ho	N Yks	NZ3902	54°25·0′	1°23·5′W	X	93
Manor Ho	N Yks	NZ3906	54°27·1′	1°23·5′W	X	93
Manor Ho	N Yks	NZ4303	54°25·5′	1°19·8′W	X	93
Manor Ho	N Yks	NZ5510	54°29·2′	1°8·6′W	X	93
Manor Ho	N Yks	SD6974	54°9·9′	2°28·1′W	X	98
Manor Ho	N Yks	SD9758	54°1·3′	2°2·3′W	X	103
Manor Ho	N Yks	SE0189	54°18·0′	1°58·7′W	X	98
Manor Ho	N Yks	SE1192	54°19·7′	1°49·4′W	X	99
Manor Ho	N Yks	SE1655	53°59·7′	1°44·9′W	X	104
Manor Ho	N Yks	SE1693	54°20·2′	1°44·8′W	X	99
Manor Ho	N Yks	SE2189	54°18·0′	1°40·2′W	X	99
Manor Ho	N Yks	SE2195	54°21·2′	1°40·2′W	X	99
Manor Ho	N Yks	SE2397	54°22·3′	1°38·3′W	X	99
Manor Ho	N Yks	SE2597	54°22·3′	1°36·5′W	X	99
Manor Ho	N Yks	SE3398	54°22·8′	1°29·1′W	X	99
Manor Ho	N Yks	SE3670	54°7·7′	1°26·5′W	X	99
Manor Ho	N Yks	SE3885	54°15·8′	1°24·6′W	X	99
Manor Ho	N Yks	SE4384	54°15·2′	1°20·0′W	X	99
Manor Ho	N Yks	SE6270	54°7·6′	1°2·7′W	X	100

Manor Ho	N Yks	SE7875	54°10·1'	0°47·9'W	X	100
Manor Ho	N Yks	SE8164	54°4·2'	0°45·3'W	X	100
Manor Ho	N Yks	SE9188	54°17·0'	0°35·7'W	X	94,101
Manor Ho	N Yks	SE9570	54°7·3'	0°32·4'W	X	101
Manor Ho	N Yks	SE9670	54°7·3'	0°31·5'W	X	101
Manor Ho	Oxon	SP3231	51°58·8'	1°31·6'W	X	151
Manor Ho	Oxon	SP3513	51°49·1'	1°29·1'W	X	164
Manor Ho	Oxon	SP3828	51°57·2'	1°26·4'W	A	164
Manor Ho	Oxon	SP4126	51°56·1'	1°23·8'W	X	164
Manor Ho	Oxon	SP4214	51°49·6'	1°23·0'W	X	164
Manor Ho	Oxon	SP4226	51°56·1'	1°23·0'W	X	164
Manor Ho	Oxon	SP4401	51°42·6'	1°21·4'W	X	164
Manor Ho	Oxon	SP4528	51°57·2'	1°20·3'W	X	164
Manor Ho	Oxon	SP4711	51°48·0'	1°18·7'W	A	164
Manor Ho	Oxon	SP5112	51°48·5'	1°15·2'W	A	164
Manor Ho	Oxon	SP5600	51°42·0'	1°11·0'W	X	164
Manor Ho	Oxon	SP5625	51°55·5'	1°10·7'W	X	164
Manor Ho	Oxon	SP5831	51°58·7'	1°8·9'W	A	152
Manor Ho	Oxon	SU2598	51°41·0'	1°37·9'W	A	163
Manor Ho	Oxon	SU5094	51°38·8'	1°16·2'W	X	164,174
Manor Ho	Peterb	TF1005	52°38·1'	0°22·1'W	A	142
Manor Ho	Rut	SP8996	52°33·5'	0°40·8'W	A	141
Manor Ho	Shrops	SJ5634	52°54·3'	2°38·8'W	X	126
Manor Ho	Shrops	SJ7406	52°39·3'	2°22·7'W	X	127
Manor Ho	Shrops	SO4096	52°33·8'	2°52·7'W	X	137
Manor Ho	Shrops	SO5786	52°28·5'	2°37·6'W	X	137,138
Manor Ho	Somer	ST2024	51°0·8'	3°8·0'W	A	193
Manor Ho	Somer	ST2618	50°57·6'	3°2·8'W	X	193
Manor Ho	Somer	ST2730	51°4·1'	3°2·1'W	X	182
Manor Ho	Somer	ST2810	50°53·3'	3°1·0'W	A	193
Manor Ho	Somer	ST6038	51°8·6'	2°33·9'W	A	183
Manor Ho	Staffs	SJ9535	52°55·0'	2°4·1'W	X	127
Manor Ho	Staffs	SK1056	53°6·3'	1°50·6'W	X	119
Manor Ho	Staffs	SO8494	52°32·9'	2°13·8'W	X	138
Manor Ho	Suff	TL7870	52°18·2'	0°37·0'E	X	144,155
Manor Ho	Suff	TL8966	52°15·8'	0°46·6'E	X	155
Manor Ho	Suff	TL9174	52°20·1'	0°48·6'E	X	144
Manor Ho	Suff	TM0837	51°59·8'	1°2·2'E	X	155,169
Manor Ho	Suff	TM1854	52°8·7'	1°11·6'E	X	156
Manor Ho	Suff	TM2460	52°11·8'	1°17·1'E	X	156
Manor Ho	Suff	TM2740	52°0·9'	1°18·9'E	X	169
Manor Ho	Suff	TM4888	52°26·2'	1°39·3'E	X	156
Manor Ho	Suff	TM5294	52°29·4'	1°43·1'E	X	134
Manor Ho	Surrey	TQ0760	51°20·0'	0°27·5'W	X	176,187
Manor Ho	Surrey	TQ1358	51°18·8'	0°22·3'W	X	187
Manor Ho	Surrey	TQ2041	51°9·6'	0°16·6'W	X	187
Manor Ho	Swin	SU2181	51°31·9'	1°41·4'W	X	174,174
Manor Ho	Thurr	TQ6486	51°33·2'	0°22·3'E	X	177
Manor Ho	Warw	SP1359	52°14·0'	1°48·2'W	X	151
Manor Ho	Warw	SP2690	52°30·7'	1°36·6'W	X	140
Manor Ho	Warw	SP2992	52°31·7'	1°34·0'W	X	140
Manor Ho	Warw	SP3196	52°33·9'	1°32·2'W	X	140
Manor Ho	Warw	SP4054	52°11·2'	1°24·5'W	X	151
Manor Ho	Warw	SP4072	52°20·9'	1°24·4'W	X	140
Manor Ho	Warw	SP4453	52°10·6'	1°21·0'W	A	151
Manor Ho	Warw	SP4467	52°18·2'	1°20·9'W	X	151
Manor Ho	W Berks	SU5373	51°27·4'	1°13·8'W	X	174
Manor Ho	Wilts	ST8065	51°23·3'	2°16·9'W	A	173
Manor Ho	Wilts	ST8158	51°19·5'	2°16·0'W	A	173
Manor Ho	Wilts	ST8365	51°23·3'	2°14·3'W	A	173
Manor Ho	Wilts	ST9158	51°19·5'	2°7·4'W	A	173
Manor Ho	Wilts	ST9858	51°19·5'	2°1·3'W	X	173
Manor Ho	Wilts	SU0381	51°31·9'	1°57·0'W	A	173
Manor Ho	Wilts	SU0394	51°38·9'	1°57·0'W	X	163,173
Manor Ho	Wilts	SU0730	51°4·4'	1°53·6'W	X	184
Manor Ho	Wilts	SU0857	51°19·0'	1°52·7'W	X	173
Manor Ho	Wilts	SU0986	51°34·6'	1°51·8'W	X	173
Manor Ho	Wilts	SU1338	51°8·7'	1°48·5'W	X	184
Manor Ho	Wilts	SU3262	51°21·6'	1°32·0'W	X	174
Manor Ho	Wirral	SJ2883	53°20·6'	3°4·5'W	X	108
Manor Ho	Worcs	SO8977	52°23·7'	2°9·3'W	X	139
Manor Ho	Worcs	SO9137	52°2·1'	2°7·5'W	X	150
Manor Ho	Worcs	SO9637	52°2·1'	2°3·1'W	X	150
Manor Ho	Worcs	SO9735	52°1·0'	2°2·2'W	X	150
Manor Ho	Worcs	SP0642	52°4·8'	1°54·4'W	X	150
Manor Ho	Worcs	SP0746	52°7·0'	1°53·5'W	X	150
Manor Ho	W Susx	SU7820	50°58·7'	0°52·9'W	X	197
Manor Ho	W Susx	SU8423	51°0·2'	0°47·8'W	X	197
Manor Ho	York	SE6155	53°59·5'	1°3·8'W	X	105
Manor Ho	York	SE6250	53°56·8'	1°2·9'W	X	105
Manor Ho (Birthplace of Newton)	Lincs	SK9224	52°48·6'	0°37·7'W	A	130
Manor Ho Fm	Hants	SU3515	50°56·2'	1°29·7'W	FM	196
Manor Ho (Hotel)	Wilts	ST8377	51°29·7'	2°14·3'W	X	173
Manor (Hotel)	Glos	SP1939	52°3·2'	1°43·0'W	X	151
Manor Ho, The	Cambs	TL1474	52°21·4'	0°19·2'W	X	142
Manor Ho, The	Devon	ST0004	50°49·8'	3°24·8'W	X	192
Manor Ho, The	Essex	TL6003	51°42·4'	0°19·3'E	X	167
Manor Ho, The	Lincs	SK9031	52°52·4'	0°39·4'W	X	130
Manor Ho, The	Lincs	SK9866	53°11·2'	0°31·6'W	X	121
Manor Ho, The	Wilts	SU1333	51°6·0'	1°48·5'W	X	184
Manor House	Cambs	TL1396	52°33·2'	0°19·6'W	X	142
Manor House	Cambs	TL2664	52°15·8'	0°8·8'W	A	153
Manor House	Cov	SP3682	52°26·3'	1°27·8'W	T	140
Manor House	Darl	NZ3411	54°29·8'	1°28·1'W	X	93
Manor House	Denb	SJ2247	53°1·1'	3°9·4'W	X	117
Manor House	Devon	SS9021	50°58·9'	3°33·6'W	X	181
Manor House	Devon	SY3099	50°47·4'	2°59·2'W	A	193
Manor House	E Susx	TQ7512	50°53·1'	0°29·7'E	A	199
Manor House	E Yorks	TA2530	53°45·3'	0°5·8'W	X	107
Manor House	Glos	SP1522	51°54·0'	1°46·5'W	A	163
Manor House	Glos	SP2003	51°43·8'	1°42·2'W	A	163
Manor House	Glos	ST8891	51°37·3'	2°10·0'W	A	173
Manor House	Hants	SU4622	51°0·0'	1°20·3'W	A	185
Manor House	Lancs	SD4766	54°5·5'	2°48·2'W	A	97
Manor House	Lancs	SD6217	53°39·1'	2°34·1'W	A	109
Manor House	Lincs	TF1108	52°39·7'	0°21·1'W	A	142
Manor House	Norf	TF8829	52°49·8'	0°47·8'E	X	132
Manor House	Norf	TG1125	52°47·1'	1°8·1'E	A	133
Manor House	Northnts	SP9575	52°22·1'	0°35·9'W	A	141
Manor House	Northnts	SP9871	52°19·9'	0°33·3'W	X	141,153
Manor House	Oxon	SU4298	51°41·0'	1°23·2'W	A	164
Manor House	Somer	ST3221	50°59·3'	2°57·7'W	A	193
Manor House	Somer	ST4022	50°59·9'	2°50·9'W	A	193
Manor House	Warw	SP1765	52°17·2'	1°44·6'W	A	151
Manor House	Warw	SP2444	52°5·9'	1°38·6'W	X	151
Manor House	Warw	SP2635	52°1·0'	1°36·9'W	A	151
Manor House Fm	Bucks	SP9214	51°49·3'	0°39·5'W	FM	165
Manor House Fm	Cambs	TL1782	52°25·6'	0°16·4'W	FM	142
Manor House Fm	Cambs	TL3564	52°15·7'	0°0·9'W	FM	154
Manor House Fm	Ches	SJ3374	53°15·8'	2°59·9'W	FM	117
Manor House Fm	Ches	SJ4950	53°2·9'	2°45·2'W	FM	117
Manor House Fm	Derby	SK1184	53°21·4'	1°49·7'W	FM	110
Manor House Fm	E Yorks	SE8637	53°49·6'	0°41·2'W	FM	106
Manor House Fm	E Yorks	SE9859	54°1·3'	0°29·8'W	FM	106
Manor House Fm	E Yorks	TA0942	53°52·0'	0°20·1'W	FM	107
Manor House Fm	E Yorks	TA1561	54°2·2'	0°14·2'W	FM	101
Manor House Fm	Hants	SU6231	51°4·7'	1°6·5'W	FM	185
Manor House Fm	Kirk	SE2415	53°38·1'	1°37·8'W	FM	110
Manor House Fm	Lancs	SD3512	53°36·3'	2°58·5'W	FM	108
Manor House Fm	Lancs	SD4543	53°53·1'	2°49·8'W	FM	102
Manor House Fm	Lancs	SD4740	53°51·5'	2°47·9'W	FM	102
Manor House Fm	Leic	SK3111	52°42·0'	1°32·1'W	FM	128
Manor House Fm	Lincs	SK9364	53°10·1'	0°36·1'W	FM	121
Manor House Fm	Monm	SO3409	51°46·8'	2°57·0'W	FM	161
Manor House Fm	Norf	TF7022	52°46·4'	0°31·6'E	FM	132
Manorhouse Fm	Norf	TF8921	52°45·4'	0°48·5'E	FM	132
Manor House Fm	Norf	TG0039	52°54·9'	0°58·9'E	FM	133
Manor House Fm	Norf	TG0424	52°46·7'	1°1·9'E	FM	133
Manor House Fm	N Yks	NZ3602	54°25·0'	1°26·3'W	FM	93
Manor House Fm	N Yks	NZ4406	54°27·1'	1°18·9'W	FM	93
Manor House Fm	N Yks	NZ5010	54°29·2'	1°13·3'W	FM	93
Manor House Fm	N Yks	NZ9209	54°28·3'	0°34·4'W	FM	94
Manor House Fm	N Yks	SE1287	54°17·0'	1°48·5'W	FM	99
Manor House Fm	N Yks	SE2060	54°2·4'	1°41·3'W	FM	99
Manor House Fm	N Yks	SE4691	54°19·0'	1°17·2'W	FM	100
Manor House Fm	N Yks	SE5683	54°14·6'	1°8·0'W	FM	100
Manor House Fm	N Yks	SE7289	54°17·7'	0°53·2'W	FM	94,100
Manor House Fm	Somer	ST4626	51°2·1'	2°45·8'W	FM	193
Manor House Fm	Somer	ST6747	51°13·5'	2°28·0'W	FM	183
Manor House Fm	Staffs	SJ7537	52°56·0'	2°21·9'W	FM	127
Manor House Fm	Suff	TM3369	52°16·4'	1°25·3'E	FM	156
Manor House Fm	Warw	SK2700	52°36·1'	1°35·7'W	FM	140
Manor House Fm	Warw	SP2197	52°34·5'	1°41·0'W	FM	139
Manor House Fm	Warw	SP2494	52°32·8'	1°38·4'W	FM	139
Manor House Fm	Warw	SP2686	52°28·5'	1°36·6'W	FM	140
Manor House Fm	York	SE6947	53°55·1'	0°56·5'W	FM	105,106
Manor House Hotel	Devon	SX7384	50°38·7'	3°47·4'W	X	191
Manor Houses	Northnts	TL0284	52°26·9'	0°29·5'W	A	141
Manor House, The	Dorset	SY7289	50°42·2'	2°23·4'W	A	194
Manor House, The	Kent	TR1550	51°12·7'	1°5·1'E	X	179
Manor House, The	Oxon	SU2685	51°34·0'	1°37·1'W	A	174
Manor House, The	Worcs	SP0849	52°8·6'	1°52·6'W	A	150
Manorial Earthworks	Derby	SK3418	52°45·7'	1°29·4'W	A	128
Manorial Earthworks	Heref	SO5164	52°16·6'	2°42·7'W	A	137,138,149
Manorial Earthworks	Shrops	SO5194	52°32·7'	2°43·0'W	A	137,138
Manorleys	Fife	NT2588	56°5·0'	3°11·9'W	X	66
Manorleys	Pth & Kin	NT1998	56°10·3'	3°17·8'W	X	58
Manor Lodge	Cambs	TL1476	52°22·4'	0°19·1'W	X	142
Manor Lodge	Northnts	SP9865	52°16·7'	0°33·4'W	X	153
Manor Lodge Fm	Cambs	TL1480	52°24·6'	0°19·0'W	FM	142
Manor Lodge Fm	Leic	SK5720	52°46·7'	1°8·9'W	FM	129
Manor Lodge (Hotel)	Notts	SK5679	53°18·5'	1°9·2'W	A	120
Manor of Dean	W Susx	SU9522	50°59·6'	0°38·4'W	X	197
Manor of Groves, The	Herts	TL4514	51°48·6'	0°6·6'E	X	167
Manorowen	Pemb	SM9336	51°59·3'	5°0·5'W	T	157
Manorowen Hill	Pemb	SM9236	51°59·3'	5°1·4'W	H	157
Manor Park	Brad	SE1547	53°55·4'	1°45·9'W	T	104
Manor Park	Bucks	SP8214	51°49·3'	0°48·2'W	T	165
Manor Park	Ches	SJ6965	53°11·1'	2°27·4'W	T	118
Manor Park	E Susx	TQ4721	50°58·4'	0°6·0'E	T	198
Manor Park	Halton	SJ5583	53°20·8'	2°40·1'W	X	108
Manor Park	Hants	SU2809	50°53·1'	1°35·7'W	X	195
Manor Park	Newham	TQ4285	51°33·0'	0°3·3'E	T	177
Manor Park	Notts	SK5733	52°53·7'	1°8·8'W	T	129
Manor Park	Sheff	SK3786	53°22·4'	1°26·2'W	T	110,111
Manor Park	Slough	SU9681	51°31·4'	0°36·6'W	T	175,176
Manor Park Country Park	Kent	TQ6857	51°17·5'	0°25·0'E	X	178,188
Manor Parsley	Corn	SW7046	50°16·4'	5°13·3'W	T	203
Manor Place	W Susx	SU8214	50°55·4'	0°49·6'W	X	197
Manor Point	D & G	NX6544	54°46·6'	4°5·5'W	X	83,84
Manor Road Sta	Wirral	SJ2289	53°23·8'	3°10·0'W	X	108
Manor Royal	W Susx	TQ2638	51°7·9'	0°11·6'W	T	187
Manor Steps	Stir	NS8395	56°8·3'	3°52·5'W	X	57
Manor Sware	Scot Bord	NT2339	55°38·6'	3°13·0'W	X	73
Manor, The	Bucks	SP7034	52°0·2'	0°58·4'W	X	152,165
Manor, The	Bucks	SP7507	51°45·6'	0°54·4'W	X	165
Manor, The	Ches	SJ3759	53°7·7'	2°56·1'W	X	117
Manor, The	Cov	SP3083	52°26·9'	1°33·1'W	X	140
Manor, The	Dorset	ST6221	50°59·5'	2°32·1'W	A	183
Manor, The	Lancs	SD8941	53°52·1'	2°9·6'W	X	103
Manor, The	Leic	SP7094	52°32·6'	0°57·7'W	X	141
Manor, The	Lincs	TF2752	53°3·2'	0°5·9'W	X	122
Manor, The	Lincs	TF3469	53°12·3'	0°0·8'E	X	122
Manor, The	Lincs	TF3626	52°49·1'	0°1·5'E	X	131
Manor, The	Lincs	TF5175	53°15·3'	0°16·2'E	X	122
Manor, The	NE Lincs	TA2110	53°34·6'	0°9·9'W	X	113
Manor, The	Norf	TM1290	52°28·2'	1°7·7'E	X	144
Manor, The	Northnts	SP6357	52°12·7'	1°4·3'W	X	152
Manor, The	Northnts	SP7546	52°6·7'	0°53·9'W	A	152
Manor, The	N Yks	NZ3304	54°26·1'	1°29·1'W	X	93
Manor, The	N Yks	SE3851	53°57·5'	1°24·8'W	X	104
Manor, The	Oxon	SP2811	51°48·1'	1°35·2'W	A	163
Manor, The	Suff	TM0367	52°16·0'	0°58·9'E	X	155
Manor, The	Wilts	ST8640	51°9·8'	2°11·6'W	X	183
Manor, The	Wilts	ST9057	51°19·0'	2°8·2'W	A	173
Manor, The	Win & Maid	SU8374	51°27·8'	0°47·9'W	X	175
Manor, The	W Susx	SU8404	50°50·0'	0°48·0'W	T	197
Manor, The	York	SE5844	53°53·6'	1°6·6'W	X	105
Manor Top Fm	NE Lincs	TA2205	53°31·9'	0°9·1'W	FM	113
Manor Warren Fm	Lincs	TF2687	53°22·1'	0°6·0'W	FM	113,122
Manor Water	Scot Bord	NT1927	55°32·1'	3°16·6'W	W	72
Manor Water	Scot Bord	NT2034	55°35·8'	3°15·7'W	W	73
Manorway	Glos	SP0634	52°0·5'	1°54·4'W	A	150
Manor Wold Fm	N Lincs	SE9919	53°39·7'	0°29·7'W	FM	112
Manor Wold Fm	N Yks	SE9275	54°10·0'	0°35·0'W	FM	101
Manor Wood	Hants	SU2710	50°53·6'	1°36·6'W	F	195
Manor Wood	Monm	SO5206	51°45·3'	2°41·3'W	F	162
Man o'Scord	Shetld	HU3283	60°32·0'	1°24·5'W	X	1,3
Manquhill	D & G	NX6794	55°13·6'	4°5·0'W	X	77
Manquhill Hill	D & G	NX6694	55°13·6'	4°6·0'W	H	77
Manrahead Fm	N Ayr	NS3452	55°44·2'	4°38·2'W	FM	63
Man Sands	Devon	SX9253	50°22·3'	3°30·7'W	X	202
Mansant	Carm	SN4710	51°46·3'	4°12·7'W	T	159
Mans Br	C of Soton	SU4415	50°56·2'	1°22·0'W	X	196
Man's Cross	Essex	TL7538	52°1·0'	0°33·4'E	T	155
Mansditch Fm	Derby	SK2214	52°43·6'	1°40·1'W	FM	128
Manse	D & G	NS7710	55°22·4'	3°56·0'W	X	71,78
Manse Bay	Orkney	ND4791	58°48·5'	2°54·6'W	W	7
Mansefield	Aberd	NJ7942	57°28·3'	2°20·5'W	X	29,30
Mansefield	D & G	NX8896	55°15·0'	3°45·3'W	X	78
Mansefield	Moray	NJ3246	57°30·2'	3°7·6'W	X	28
Mansefield	Pth & Kin	NO2122	56°23·3'	3°16·3'W	X	53,58
Mansefield	S Lanak	NS9237	55°37·1'	3°42·5'W	X	71,72
Manse Fm	N Yks	SE3656	54°0·2'	1°26·6'W	FM	104
Mansegate	D & G	NX8783	55°8·0'	3°45·9'W	T	78
Manselfield	Swan	SS5988	51°34·6'	4°1·7'W	T	159
Manselfold	Swan	SS4791	51°36·1'	4°12·2'W	X	159
Mansell Gamage	Heref	SO3944	52°5·7'	2°53·0'W	T	148,149,161
Mansell Lacy	Heref	SO4245	52°6·3'	2°50·4'W	T	148,149
Mansellpark	Derby	SK2544	52°59·8'	1°37·2'W	X	119,128
Mansells Fm	Herts	TL2119	51°51·6'	0°14·2'W	FM	166
Manse Loch	Highld	NC0924	58°10·1'	5°14·4'W	W	15
Manse Loch	Orkney	HY4729	59°8·9'	2°55·1'W	W	5,6
Mansel's Barn	Leic	SK8235	52°54·6'	0°46·4'W	X	130
Manselton	Swan	SS6595	51°38·5'	3°56·7'W	T	159
Mansemass	Orkney	HY3731	59°9·9'	3°5·6'W	H	6
Mansergh	Cumbr	SD6082	54°14·2'	2°36·4'W	T	97
Mansergh Hall	Cumbr	SD6081	54°13·6'	2°36·4'W	X	97
Mansergh High	Cumbr	SD6083	54°14·7'	2°36·4'W	X	97
Mansers	Kent	TQ5449	51°13·4'	0°12·7'E	X	188
Manse Taing	Orkney	ND4791	58°48·5'	2°54·6'W	X	7
Manse, The	Powys	SO0274	52°21·6'	3°25·9'W	X	136,147
Manse, The	Shrops	SJ5312	52°42·5'	2°41·3'W	X	126
Mansewood	C of Glas	NS5660	55°49·0'	4°17·5'W	T	64
Mansey Common	Notts	SK6860	53°8·2'	0°58·6'W	X	120
Mansfield	E Ayr	NS6214	55°24·3'	4°10·3'W	T	71
Mansfield	Fife	NO2110	56°16·8'	3°16·1'W	X	58
Mansfield	Inverc	NS2971	55°54·4'	4°43·7'W	X	63
Mansfield	Midlo	NT3563	55°51·6'	3°1·9'W	X	66
Mansfield	Notts	SK5361	53°8·8'	1°12·0'W	T	120
Mansfield	Stir	NN7203	56°12·4'	4°3·4'W	X	57
Mansfield Fm	Bucks	TQ0383	51°32·4'	0°30·5'W	FM	176
Mansfield Fm	Devon	ST2100	50°47·9'	3°6·9'W	FM	192,193
Mansfield Mains	E Ayr	NS6414	55°24·3'	4°8·4'W	X	71
Mansfield Woodhouse	Notts	SK5463	53°9·9'	1°11·1'W	T	120
Mansgrove	Cumbr	NY6223	54°36·3'	2°34·9'W	X	91
Mansgrove Fm	Beds	TL0115	51°49·7'	0°31·7'W	FM	166
Manshay Fm	Dorset	SY3999	50°47·5'	2°51·5'W	FM	193
Man's Head	Wilts	SU1473	51°27·6'	1°47·5'W	X	173
Manshead End	Cald	SD9919	53°40·3'	2°0·5'W	X	109
Manside Cross	Northum	NY9892	55°13·6'	2°1·5'W	A	81
Manside Flow	Northum	NY9791	55°13·0'	2°2·4'W	H	81
Mansie's Berg	Shetld	HU5341	60°9·3'	1°2·2'W	X	4
Mansill Fm	Warw	SP2244	52°5·9'	1°40·3'W	FM	151
Mansion Fm	Kent	TQ8548	51°12·3'	0°39·3'E	FM	189
Mansion House Fm	Kent	TQ8547	51°11·8'	0°39·3'E	FM	189
Mansion House Fm	N Yks	SE2362	54°3·4'	1°38·5'W	FM	99
Mansion, The	Beds	SP9457	52°12·4'	0°37·1'W	X	153
Mansion, The	Glos	SO8001	51°42·7'	2°17·0'W	X	162
Mansion, The	Hants	SU4448	51°14·0'	1°21·8'W	X	185
Mansion, The	Herts	SP9211	51°47·6'	0°39·6'W	A	165
Mansley Cliff	Devon	SS2221	50°57·9'	4°31·7'W	X	190
Mansley Combe	Somer	SS9040	51°9·2'	3°34·0'W	X	181
Man's Newton	Devon	SS6904	50°49·5'	3°51·2'W	X	191
Mansom Plantation	Norf	TG2020	52°44·2'	1°15·9'E	F	133,134
Manson Green	Norf	TG0203	52°35·5'	0°59·3'E	T	144
Mansriggs	Cumbr	SD2980	54°12·9'	3°4·9'W	T	96,97
Mansriggs Hall	Cumbr	SD2881	54°13·4'	3°5·8'W	X	96,97
Manstage	Devon	SX4994	50°43·8'	4°8·0'W	X	191
Manston	Dorset	ST8115	50°56·3'	2°15·8'W	T	183
Manston	Kent	TR3466	51°20·9'	1°22·0'E	T	179
Manston	Leeds	SE3634	53°48·3'	1°26·8'W	T	104
Manston Brook	Dorset	ST8215	50°56·3'	2°15·0'W	W	183
Manstone Fm	W Berks	SU5475	51°28·5'	1°13·0'W	FM	174
Manston Hall	Suff	TL8356	52°10·5'	0°41·0'E	A	155
Manston Ho	Dorset	ST8114	50°55·7'	2°15·8'W	X	194
Manston Ho	Leeds	SE3734	53°48·3'	1°25·9'W	X	104
Mansty Fm	Staffs	SJ9512	52°42·6'	2°4·0'W	FM	127
Mansty Wood	Staffs	SJ9512	52°42·6'	2°4·0'W	F	127
Manswood	Dorset	ST9708	50°52·5'	2°2·2'W	T	195
Mansworn Rig	Angus	NO5064	56°46·2'	2°48·6'W	X	44
Manthorpe	Lincs	SK9137	52°55·6'	0°38·4'W	T	130
Manthorpe	Lincs	TF0715	52°43·6'	0°24·5'W	T	130
Mantle Hill	Northum	NY8184	55°9·2'	2°17·5'W	X	80
Mantle's Fm	Bucks	SU9299	51°41·2'	0°39·8'W	FM	165
Mantles Green	Bucks	SU9597	51°40·1'	0°37·2'W	T	165,176
Mantles Heath	Northnts	SP5955	52°11·6'	1°7·8'W	F	152
Mantles, The	Notts	SK6387	53°22·8'	1°2·8'W	X	111,120
Manton	N Lincs	SE9302	53°30·6'	0°35·4'W	T	112
Manton	Notts	SK5978	53°18·0'	1°6·5'W	T	120
Manton	Rut	SK8804	52°37·8'	0°41·6'W	T	141
Manton	Wilts	SU1768	51°24·9'	1°44·9'W	T	173
Manton Copse	Wilts	SU1767	51°24·3'	1°44·9'W	F	173
Manton Down	Wilts	SU1571	51°26·5'	1°46·7'W	X	173
Manton Forest Fm	Notts	SK6176	53°16·9'	1°4·7'W	FM	120
Manton Ho	Wilts	SU1570	51°26·0'	1°46·7'W	X	173
Manton House Fm	Wilts	SU1770	51°26·0'	1°44·9'W	FM	173
Manton Lodge	Notts	SK6277	53°17·4'	1°3·8'W	X	120
Manton Lodge Fm	Rut	SK8704	52°37·8'	0°42·5'W	FM	141

Manton's Fm	Norf	TL5995	52°32·0′	0°21·1′E	FM	143
Manton Warren	N Lincs	SE9305	53°32·2′	0°35·4′W	T	112
Mantree Cross	Lincs	SK8397	53°28·0′	0°44·6′W	X	112
Manuden	Essex	TL4926	51°55·0′	0°10·4′E	T	167
Manuden Ho	Essex	TL4826	51°55·0′	0°9·5′E	X	167
Manuelhaugh	Falk	NS9776	55°58·2′	3°38·6′W	X	65
Manuel Ho	Falk	NS9676	55°58·2′	3°39·5′W	X	65
Manuels	Corn	SW8360	50°24·2′	5°2·9′W	X	200
Manwar Ings	Lincs	TF2440	52°56·8′	0°8·9′W	A	131
Manwood Copse	Wilts	ST9720	50°59·0′	2°2·2′W	F	184
Manwood Green	Essex	TL5412	51°47·4′	0°14·4′E	T	167
Manworthy Mill	Devon	SS3305	50°49·5′	4°21·9′W	X	190
Manx Electric Railway	I of M	SC4280	54°11·7′	4°24·9′W	X	95
Manxey Level	E Susx	TQ6406	50°50·0′	0°20·1′E	X	199
Manxman's Lake	D & G	NX6748	54°48·8′	4°3·8′W	W	83,84
Manxman's Rock	D & G	NX6144	54°46·6′	4°9·2′W	X	83
Many Crooks	Shetld	HU3186	60°33·6′	1°25·6′W	W	1,3
Manyfold Beck	Durham	NZ0614	54°31·5′	1°54·0′W	W	92
Many Gates Plantn	York	SE6953	53°58·3′	0°56·5′W	F	105,106
Manyleith Head	Scot Bord	NT1224	55°30·4′	3°23·2′W	H	72
Many Lochs	Highld	ND1974	58°39·0′	3°23·3′W	W	7,12
Many Thorns Fm	N Yks	SE8571	54°7·9′	0°41·5′W	FM	100
Manywee	Angus	NO3969	56°48·8′	2°59·5′W	H	44
Manywells Height	Brad	SE0635	53°48·9′	1°54·1′W	T	104
Maodal	N Eil	NF9990	57°48·2′	7°3·6′W	H	18
Maoil an Roll	N Eil	NB2826	58°8·6′	6°36·9′W	H	8,13
Maoil Daimh	N Eil	NF8135	57°17·9′	7°17·3′W	H	22
Maoile an t-Searraich	Highld	NH0110	57°8·5′	5°16·9′W	X	33
Maoile Choill-mhias	Highld	NH1442	57°26·1′	5°5·5′W	H	25
Maoile Lunndaidh	Highld	NH1345	57°27·7′	5°6·6′W	H	25
Maoile Mhór	Arg & Bt	NR3242	55°36·1′	6°14·9′W	H	60
Maoile nan Gamhnach	Highld	NH2457	57°34·4′	4°56·1′W	H	25
Maoim	N Eil	NB5556	58°25·7′	6°11·3′W	X	8
Maol	Arg & Bt	NM2823	56°19·5′	6°23·5′W	X	48
Maol-a' Bhàird	Arg & Bt	NM6323	56°20·7′	5°49·7′W	X	49
Maol a' Bharra	Arg & Bt	NR4060	55°46·1′	6°8·3′W	X	60
Maola Breac	N Eil	NF7933	57°16·8′	7°19·2′W	H	22
Maol Accurrach	Arg & Bt	NN1119	56°19·8′	5°3·0′W	H	50,56
Maol á Chapuill	Stir	NN3607	56°13·9′	4°38·3′W	H	56
Maol a' Chatadail	Arg & Bt	NR4159	55°45·6′	6°7·3′W	X	60
Maol a' Chreagain	Arg & Bt	NR3268	55°50·1′	6°16·4′W	X	60,61
Maol a' Chreagain	Highld	NG7590	57°50·8′	5°47·0′W	X	19
Maol a' Chuir	Arg & Bt	NR7427	55°29·3′	5°34·2′W	X	68
Maolachy	Arg & Bt	NM8912	56°15·5′	5°24·0′W	X	55
Maoladh Creag nam Fitheach	N Eil	NF8033	57°16·8′	7°18·2′W	H	22
Maoladh Creag nan Druidean	N Eil	NF8036	57°18·4′	7°18·4′W	X	22
Maoladh Mhicearraig	N Eil	NG0994	57°50·7′	6°53·8′W	H	14
Maoladh Mór	Highld	NG4368	57°38·0′	6°17·9′W	X	23
Maoladh na h-Uamha	N Eil	NF8433	57°17·0′	7°14·2′W	H	22
Maoladh nam Feannag	N Eil	NF8230	57°15·3′	7°16·0′W	X	22
Maoladh nan Speireag	N Eil	NF8229	57°14·7′	7°15·9′W	X	22
Maol a' Ghearraidh	Arg & Bt	NM6232	56°25·5′	5°51·1′W	H	49
Maol a' Ghiubhais	Highld	NN7997	57°3·2′	3°59·2′W	H	35
Maol Aird	Highld	NN1289	56°57·5′	5°5·1′W	X	34,41
Maol Airigh o Dhùin	Arg & Bt	NR3752	55°41·7′	6°10·7′W	X	60
Maolanaidh Mór	Highld	NH7296	57°56·4′	4°9·3′W	H	21
Maol an Aonaich	Arg & Bt	NM5225	56°21·4′	6°0·4′W	X	48
Maol an Domhnaich	Arg & Bt	NM4436	56°27·1′	6°8·8′W	X	47,48
Maol an Fheidh	Arg & Bt	NS2693	56°6·1′	4°47·4′W	H	56
Maol an Fhithich	Arg & Bt	NN3413	56°17·1′	4°40·5′W	X	50,56
Maol an Fhithich	Arg & Bt	NR2845	55°37·6′	6°18·8′W	X	60
Maol an Iaruinn	Stir	NS4598	56°9·2′	4°29·3′W	H	57
Maol an Tailleir	Highld	NH8938	57°25·4′	3°50·4′W	H	27
Maol an Tailleir	Stir	NS4798	56°9·3′	4°27·4′W	X	57
Maol an Tairbh	Arg & Bt	NS3353	55°36·6′	6°16·8′W	X	60
Maol an t-Searraich	Arg & Bt	NM7129	56°24·1′	5°42·2′W	X	49
Maol an t-Seilich	Highld	NN7588	56°58·2′	4°2·9′W	X	42
Maol an t-Sidhein	Arg & Bt	NM3619	56°17·7′	6°15·6′W	H	48
Maol'an t-Sornaich	Arg & Bt	NR5480	55°57·3′	5°56·0′W	X	61
Maol an t-Sratha	Arg & Bt	NN2513	56°16·9′	4°49·2′W	H	50,56
Maol an t-Srathain	Highld	NH2855	57°33·4′	4°52·0′W	X	25
Maol an Turamain	Arg & Bt	NM4925	56°21·3′	6°3·3′W	X	48
Maol an Uillt Ghrisinn	Highld	NG7586	57°48·7′	5°46·8′W	X	19
Maol an Uillt Mhóir	Highld	NG7447	57°27·7′	5°45·6′W	X	24
Maol Ardtalla	Arg & Bt	NR4655	55°43·6′	6°2·3′W	X	60
Maol Bàn	Arg & Bt	NM6823	56°20·8′	5°44·8′W	H	49
Maol Bàn	Highld	NG5629	57°17·5′	6°2·5′W	X	32
Maol Beag	Arg & Bt	NN0021	56°20·6′	5°13·7′W	X	50
Maol Beag	Arg & Bt	NR3142	55°36·1′	6°15·8′W	H	60
Maol Beag	Highld	NG8428	57°17·8′	5°34·6′W	H	33
Maol Bhadan an Iochdair	Highld	NG7767	57°38·5′	5°43·7′W	X	19
Maol Bhàn	N Eil	NF9182	57°43·5′	7°11·0′W	X	18
Maol Bhreac-achaidh	Arg & Bt	NM6222	56°20·1′	5°50·6′W	X	49
Maol Bhuidhe	Arg & Bt	NM5841	56°30·2′	5°55·5′W	X	47,48
Maol Bhuidhe	Arg & Bt	NR2667	55°49·4′	6°22·1′W	X	60
Maol-bhuidhe	Highld	NH0535	57°22·1′	5°14·1′W	X	25
Maol Breac	Arg & Bt	NN2515	56°18·0′	4°49·3′W	H	50,56
Maol Breac	Highld	NG7483	57°47·0′	5°47·6′W	X	19
Maol Breac	Highld	NG7589	57°50·3′	5°47·0′W	H	19
Maol Brinigeamaul	N Eil	NB1916	58°2·9′	6°45·3′W	H	13,14
Maolbuidhe	Arg & Bt	NM3123	56°19·6′	6°20·6′W	X	48
Maol Buidhe	Arg & Bt	NM4644	56°31·4′	6°7·4′W	H	47,48
Maol Buidhe	Arg & Bt	NM5430	56°24·2′	5°58·8′W	X	48
Maol Buidhe	Arg & Bt	NM5633	56°25·8′	5°57·0′W	X	47,48
Maol Buidhe	Arg & Bt	NM6241	56°30·3′	5°51·6′W	H	49
Maol Buidhe	Arg & Bt	NM7103	56°10·1′	5°40·9′W	H	55
Maol Buidhe	Arg & Bt	NM7126	56°22·5′	5°42·1′W	X	49
Maol Buidhe	Arg & Bt	NM9319	56°19·4′	5°20·4′W	X	55
Maol Buidhe	Arg & Bt	NR2946	55°38·2′	6°17·9′W	X	60
Maol Buidhe	Highld	NG3747	57°26·5′	6°22·5′W	H	23
Maol Buidhe	Highld	NG6407	57°5·9′	5°53·3′W	H	32
Maol Buidhe	Highld	NG8421	57°14·0′	5°34·3′W	X	33
Maol Buidhe	Highld	NM4662	56°41·1′	6°8·4′W	X	47
Maol Buidhe	Highld	NM7271	56°46·7′	5°43·5′W	X	40
Maol Bun an Uillt	Arg & Bt	NR3268	55°50·1′	6°16·4′W	X	60,61
Maol Calaisceig	Highld	NH1594	57°54·1′	5°6·8′W	H	20
Maol Chean-dearg	Highld	NG9249	57°29·3′	5°27·6′W	H	25
Maol Cheannan	Highld	NG9562	57°36·4′	5°25·4′W	X	19
Maol Chinn-dearg	Highld	NH0408	57°7·5′	5°13·8′W	X	33
Maol Chnoc	Arg & Bt	NR2947	55°38·7′	6°18·0′W	X	60
Maol Chnoc	Highld	NH5821	57°15·7′	4°20·8′W	X	26,35
Maol Coire a' Mhile	Highld	NC6823	58°10·8′	4°14·2′W	H	16
Maol Donn	N Ayr	NS0140	55°37·0′	5°9·2′W	H	69
Maol Dubh	Arg & Bt	NR3851	55°41·2′	6°9·7′W	X	60
Maolearn	Angus	NO5876	56°52·7′	2°40·9′W	H	44
Maol Eilean	Arg & Bt	NM7001	56°9·0′	5°41·7′W	X	55,61
Maol Martaig	N Eil	NF8436	57°18·6′	7°14·4′W	H	22
Maol Meadhonach	Arg & Bt	NN2414	56°17·4′	4°50·2′W	H	50,56
Maol Mheadhoin	Arg & Bt	NR3851	55°41·2′	6°9·7′W	X	60
Maol Mhèadhonach	Arg & Bt	NM4629	56°23·4′	6°6·5′W	H	48
Maol Mheadhonach	Arg & Bt	NM4932	56°25·1′	6°3·7′W	H	48
Maol Mhór	Arg & Bt	NR2944	55°37·1′	6°17·8′W	H	60
Maol Mór	Arg & Bt	NM4353	56°36·2′	6°10·8′W	X	47
Maol Mór	Arg & Bt	NM5327	56°22·5′	5°59·6′W	X	48
Maol Mór	Arg & Bt	NM9920	56°20·0′	5°14·6′W	H	49
Maol Mór	Arg & Bt	NR5676	55°55·2′	5°53·9′W	X	61
Maol Mór	Highld	NG8428	57°17·8′	5°34·6′W	H	33
Maol Mor	Stir	NN3711	56°16·1′	4°37·5′W	H	50,56
Maol Mór Glac nan Cnàmh	Highld	NM7394	56°59·1′	5°43·7′W	H	33,40
Maol na Bruaich	Highld	NG8887	57°49·6′	5°33·8′W	H	19
Maol na Coille	Arg & Bt	NR3068	55°50·0′	6°18·3′W	X	60
Maol na Coille Móire	Arg & Bt	NM4929	56°23·5′	6°3·6′W	X	48
Maol na Croige	Arg & Bt	NM5622	56°19·9′	5°56·4′W	X	48
Maol na Gainmhich	Highld	NG5531	57°18·5′	6°3·6′W	X	24,32
Maol na h-Airde	Highld	NG3455	57°30·7′	6°26·0′W	H	23
Maol na h-Ordaig	N Eil	NF8415	57°7·3′	7°12·8′W	H	31
Maol nam Damh	Arg & Bt	NR6288	56°1·8′	5°48·8′W	H	61
Maol nam Fiadh	Arg & Bt	NM6333	56°26·0′	5°50·2′W	X	49
Maol nam Fineag	Arg & Bt	NR5573	55°53·5′	5°54·7′W	X	61
Maol nan Caorach	Arg & Bt	NR3145	55°37·7′	6°16·0′W	X	60
Maol nan Caorach	Arg & Bt	NR3168	55°50·1′	6°17·3′W	X	60,61
Maol nan Caorach	Arg & Bt	NR3568	55°50·2′	6°13·5′W	X	60,61
Maol nan Caorach	Arg & Bt	NR3854	55°42·8′	6°9·8′W	X	60
Maol nan Damh	Arg & Bt	NM5132	56°25·1′	6°1·8′W	X	48
Maol nan Damh	Arg & Bt	NM6836	56°27·8′	5°45·5′W	X	49
Maol nan Damh	Arg & Bt	NR6999	56°7·9′	5°42·6′W	X	55,61
Maol nan Eun	Arg & Bt	NR3045	55°37·7′	6°16·9′W	X	60
Maol nan Gobhar	Arg & Bt	NR4358	55°45·1′	6°5·3′W	X	60
Maol nan Ròn	Arg & Bt	NR2946	55°38·2′	6°17·9′W	X	60
Maol nan Sgreuch	Arg & Bt	NM5739	56°29·1′	5°56·4′W	X	47,48
Maol nan Uan	Arg & Bt	NM5325	56°21·4′	5°59·5′W	X	48
Maol nan Uan	Arg & Bt	NM7035	56°27·3′	5°43·5′W	H	49
Maol na Readhra	Highld	NM6589	56°56·2′	5°51·3′W	X	40
Maol na Samhna	Arg & Bt	NM5425	56°21·5′	5°58·5′W	X	48
Maol na sgùrra	Arg & Bt	NM4219	56°17·9′	6°9·8′W	X	48
Maol Odhar	Arg & Bt	NM6626	56°22·4′	5°46·9′W	H	49
Maol Odhar	Arg & Bt	NS0591	56°4·6′	5°7·6′W	X	56
Maol Odhar	Highld	NM7876	56°49·6′	5°37·9′W	X	40
Maol Odhar	Highld	NM8857	56°39·7′	5°27·1′W	H	49
Maol Odhar	Stir	NN3610	56°15·5′	4°38·4′W	X	50,56
Maol on Tairbh	Highld	NG4026	57°15·3′	6°18·2′W	X	32
Maol Riabhach	Arg & Bt	NS2286	56°2·3′	4°51·0′W	H	56
Maol Ruadh	Highld	NG7568	57°39·0′	5°45·8′W	X	19,24
Maol Ruadh	Highld	NN2782	56°54·1′	4°50·0′W	H	34,41
Maol Ruadh	Stir	NS4796	56°8·2′	4°27·3′W	H	57
Maol Tarsuinn	Arg & Bt	NM6725	56°21·9′	5°45·9′W	X	49
Maol Tobar Leac an t-Sagairt	Arg & Bt	NM6129	56°23·8′	5°51·9′W	X	49
Maol Uachdarach	Arg & Bt	NM5931	56°24·8′	5°54·0′W	X	48
Maovally	Highld	NC3069	58°34·8′	4°55·0′W	H	9
Maovally	Highld	NC3721	58°9·1′	4°45·7′W	H	16
Maovally Beag	Highld	NC3063	58°31·6′	4°54·7′W	H	9
Maovally More	Highld	NC3163	58°31·6′	4°53·7′W	H	9
Maperton	Somer	ST6726	51°2·2′	2°27·9′W	T	183
Maplebeck	Notts	SK7160	53°8·2′	0°55·9′W	T	120
Maplecroft	Wilts	ST8262	51°21·6′	2°15·1′W	X	173
Maple Croft	Wok	SU7980	51°31·0′	0°51·3′W	X	175
Maple Cross	Herts	TQ0392	51°37·3′	0°30·3′W	T	176
Mapledurham	Oxon	SU6776	51°29·0′	1°1·7′W	T	175
Mapledurham House	Oxon	SU6776	51°29·0′	1°1·7′W	A	175
Mapledurwell	Hants	SU6851	51°15·5′	1°1·1′W	T	185,186
Maple End	Essex	TL5937	52°0·7′	0°19·4′E	T	154
Maple Fm	Hants	SU4358	51°19·4′	1°22·6′W	FM	174
Maple Fm	Northnts	SP7455	52°11·5′	0°54·6′W	FM	152
Maple Grange	Leeds	SE1845	53°54·3′	1°43·1′W	X	104
Maple Hayes	Staffs	SK0909	52°41·0′	1°51·6′W	X	128
Maple Hill	Oxon	SP3316	51°50·7′	1°30·9′W	X	164
Maplehurst	Kent	TQ7942	51°9·2′	0°34·0′E	X	188
Maplehurst	W Susx	TQ1924	51°0·4′	0°17·8′W	T	198
Maplehurst Wood	E Susx	TQ8013	50°53·5′	0°34·0′E	F	199
Maple Lodge Fm	Suff	TM1950	52°6·5′	1°12·3′E	FM	156
Mapleridge	S Glos	ST7584	51°33·5′	2°21·2′W	X	172
Maplescombe	Kent	TQ5564	51°21·5′	0°14·0′E	X	177,188
Maple's Cross Fm	Worcs	SO7956	52°12·3′	2°18·0′W	FM	150
Maplesden	E Susx	TQ6528	51°1·9′	0°21·6′E	X	188,199
Maplesden	Kent	TQ8333	51°4·2′	0°37·1′E	X	188
Maplestone Fm	E Susx	TQ8221	50°57·8′	0°35·9′E	FM	199
Mapleton	Derby	SK1647	53°1·4′	1°45·3′W	T	119,128
Mapleton	Kent	TQ4649	51°13·5′	0°5·8′E	X	188
Mapleton Fm	Lincs	TF1967	53°11·4′	0°12·7′W	FM	122
Maplewell Hall School	Leic	SK5213	52°43·0′	1°13·4′W	X	129
Maplin Sands	Essex	TR0188	51°33·5′	0°54·4′E	X	178
Mappercombe Manor	Dorset	SY5195	50°45·4′	2°41·3′W	X	194
Mapperley	C of Nott	SK5843	52°59·1′	1°7·8′W	T	129
Mapperley	Derby	SK4343	52°59·2′	1°21·2′W	T	129
Mapperley Park	C of Nott	SK5742	52°58·6′	1°8·7′W	T	129
Mapperley Park	Derby	SK4243	52°59·2′	1°22·1′W	X	129
Mapperley Plains	Notts	SK6045	53°0·2′	1°5·9′W	X	129
Mapperley Resr	Derby	SK4343	52°59·2′	1°21·2′W	W	129
Mapperton	Dorset	SY5099	50°47·5′	2°42·2′W	T	194
Mapperton	Dorset	SY9098	50°47·1′	2°8·1′W	T	195
Mapperton Fm	Dorset	SY4999	50°47·5′	2°43·1′W	FM	193,194
Mapperton Hill	Wilts	ST7938	51°8·7′	2°17·6′W	H	183
Mapp Fm	Shrops	SO5599	52°35·5′	2°39·5′W	FM	137,138
Mappleborough Green	Warw	SP0865	52°17·2′	1°52·6′W	T	150
Mappleton	E Yorks	TA2244	53°52·9′	0°8·2′W	T	107
Mappleton Sands	E Yorks	TA2244	53°52·9′	0°8·2′W	X	107
Mapplewell	Barns	SE3209	53°34·8′	1°30·6′W	T	110,111
Mappowder	Dorset	ST7306	50°51·4′	2°22·6′W	T	194
Mappowder Court	Dorset	ST7305	50°50·9′	2°22·6′W	A	194
Mapsons Fm	W Susx	SZ8399	50°47·3′	0°49·0′W	FM	197
Maqueston Hill	D & G	NX7793	55°13·2′	3°55·6′W	H	78
Maragaidh Beag	N Eil	NF8853	57°27·9′	7°11·8′W	X	22
Maragaidh Mòr	N Eil	NF8952	57°27·4′	7°10·7′W	X	22
Maragdubh	Pth & Kin	NN7059	56°42·5′	4°7·0′W	X	42,51,52
Máraig	N Eil	NB2006	57°57·6′	6°43·6′W	T	13,14
Mara Ness	Shetld	HU2649	60°13·7′	1°31·3′W	X	3
Maratz Hill	S Ayr	NS4302	55°17·5′	4°27·9′W	H	77
Maraval	N Eil	NF7915	57°7·1′	7°17·8′W	H	31
Marazanvose	Corn	SW8050	50°18·8′	5°5·0′W	T	200,204
Marazion	Corn	SW5130	50°7·3′	5°28·6′W	T	203
Marbhig	N Eil	NB4118	58°4·8′	6°23·1′W	T	14
Marble Hall	Carm	SN1123	51°52·7′	4°44·4′W	X	145,158
Marble Hill	Rich	TQ1773	51°26·9′	0°18·6′W	X	176
Marble Lodge	Pth & Kin	NN8971	56°49·3′	3°48·7′W	X	43
Marble Steps Pot	N Yks	SD6777	54°11·5′	2°29·9′W	X	98
Marbrack	D & G	NX5993	55°12·9′	4°12·5′W	X	77
Marbrack Burn	D & G	NX6094	55°13·5′	4°11·6′W	W	77
Marbury	Ches	SJ5545	53°0·3′	2°39·8′W	T	117
Marbury Heyes	Ches	SJ5746	53°0·8′	2°38·1′W	X	117
Marbury Home Fm	Ches	SJ6476	53°17·0′	2°32·0′W	FM	118
Marcassie	Moray	NJ0556	57°35·3′	3°34·9′W	X	27
Marcassie Br	Pth & Kin	NO0213	56°18·2′	3°34·6′W	X	58
March	Cambs	TL4196	52°32·8′	0°5·2′E	T	142,143
March	Shetld	HU4666	60°22·8′	1°9·4′W	X	2,3
March	S Lanak	NS9914	55°24·8′	3°35·3′W	T	78
March-Aled	Conwy	SH8669	53°12·6′	3°42·0′W	X	116
Marcham	Oxon	SU4596	51°39·9′	1°20·6′W	T	164
Marchamley	Shrops	SJ5929	52°51·7′	2°36·1′W	T	126
Marchamley Hill	Shrops	SJ5929	52°51·7′	2°36·1′W	X	126
Marchamley Wood	Shrops	SJ5931	52°52·7′	2°36·2′W	T	126
Marcham Mill	Oxon	SU4595	51°39·4′	1°20·6′W	X	164
Marchant's Cross	Devon	SX5466	50°28·8′	4°3·1′W	A	201
Marchants Fm	E Susx	TQ3416	50°55·9′	0°5·2′W	FM	198
Marchants Fm	E Susx	TQ5112	50°53·5′	0°9·2′E	FM	199
Marchant's Fm	Herts	SP9902	51°42·7′	0°33·6′W	FM	165
Marchants Fm	Surrey	SU8738	51°8·3′	0°45·0′W	FM	186
Marchbank	D & G	NY0799	55°16·8′	3°27·4′W	X	78
Marchbank Hotel	C of Edin	NT1664	55°52·0′	3°20·1′W	X	65,66
March Brae	S Lanak	NT0532	55°34·6′	3°30·0′W	H	72
March Burn	Aberd	NH9701	57°5·6′	3°41·5′W	W	36
Marchburn	D & G	NS6713	55°23·8′	4°5·6′W	X	71
March Burn	D & G	NS7208	55°21·2′	4°0·7′W	W	71,77
March Burn	D & G	NS7504	55°19·1′	3°57·8′W	W	78
Marchburn	D & G	NX0571	55°0·0′	5°2·5′W	X	76
March Burn	D & G	NX4886	55°9·0′	4°22·7′W	W	77
March Burn	D & G	NX7597	55°15·3′	3°57·6′W	W	78
March Burn	D & G	NX9468	55°0·0′	3°39·0′W	W	84
March Burn	E Ayr	NS6309	55°21·6′	4°9·2′W	W	71,77
March Burn	E Ayr	NS6611	55°22·7′	4°6·5′W	W	71
March Burn	E Ayr	NS6624	55°29·7′	4°6·8′W	W	71
March Burn	E Ayr	NS7120	55°27·7′	4°2·0′W	W	71
March Burn	Highld	NH5701	57°4·9′	4°21·1′W	W	35
March Burn	N Lanak	NS7082	56°1·1′	4°4·7′W	W	57,64
March Burn	Northum	NY8080	55°7·1′	2°18·4′W	W	80
March Burn	Northum	NY9959	54°55·8′	2°0·5′W	W	87
March Burn	Northum	NZ1377	55°5·6′	1°47·4′W	W	88
March Burn	S Ayr	NS3707	55°20·1′	4°33·8′W	W	70,77
March Burn	S Ayr	NX0773	55°1·1′	5°0·7′W	W	76
March Burn or Allt Mòr	Highld	NJ1122	57°17·1′	3°28·1′W	W	36
Marchcleugh	Scot Bord	NT7321	55°29·2′	2°25·2′W	X	74
March Cote Fm	Brad	SE1037	53°50·0′	1°50·5′W	FM	104
March Cottage	D & G	NY3378	55°5·8′	3°2·6′W	X	85
Marche Hall	Shrops	SJ3310	52°41·3′	2°59·1′W	X	126
Marcheini Fawr	Powys	SN9573	52°20·9′	3°32·1′W	W	136,147
Marche Manor	Shrops	SJ3310	52°41·3′	2°59·1′W	A	126
Marchfield	D & G	NX9877	55°4·9′	3°35·4′W	X	84
Marchfield	Moray	NJ2960	57°37·7′	3°10·9′W	X	28
Marchfield Ho	Wok	SU8371	51°26·1′	0°48·0′W	X	175
March Fm	D & G	NX3949	54°48·9′	4°29·9′W	FM	83
March Fm	E Susx	TQ6925	51°0·2′	0°24·9′E	FM	188,199
Marchfont Brook	Warw	SP1850	52°9·1′	1°43·8′W	W	151
March Ghyll Resr	N Yks	SE1251	53°57·5′	1°48·6′W	W	104
Marchglen	Clackm	NS9096	56°8·9′	3°45·8′W	X	58
March-gwyn	Carm	SN1524	51°53·3′	4°40·9′W	X	145,158
March Haigh	Kirk	SE0113	53°37·1′	1°58·7′W	X	110
March Haigh Resr	Kirk	SE0112	53°36·5′	1°58·7′W	W	110
March Hill	Kirk	SE0012	53°36·5′	1°59·6′W	X	110
March Ho	Leic	SK7315	52°43·9′	0°54·7′W	X	129
March-house	D & G	NT0900	55°17·4′	3°25·5′W	X	78
Marchings Fm	Essex	TQ4695	51°38·3′	0°7·0′E	FM	167,177
Marchington	Staffs	SK1330	52°52·3′	1°48·0′W	T	128
Marchington Cliff	Staffs	SK1328	52°51·2′	1°48·0′W	X	128
Marchington Woodlands	Staffs	SK1128	52°51·2′	1°49·8′W	T	128
Marchlands	Aberd	NJ9061	57°38·6′	2°9·6′W	X	30
Marchlands	Aberd	NK0258	57°37·0′	1°57·5′W	X	30
Marchlands	S Lanak	NS9531	55°33·9′	3°39·5′W	X	72
Marchlyn	Gwyn	SH7200	52°35·2′	3°53·0′W	X	135
Marchlyn Bach Resr	Gwyn	SH6062	53°8·5′	4°5·2′W	W	115
Marchlyn Mawr Resr	Gwyn	SH6161	53°7·9′	4°4·3′W	W	115
Marchmar	Aberd	NJ4823	57°17·9′	2°51·3′W	X	37
Marchmont Ho	Scot Bord	NT7448	55°43·7′	2°24·4′W	X	74
Marchnant	Cered	SN7469	52°18·5′	3°50·5′W	W	135,147
Marchnant	Powys	SN9060	52°13·9′	3°36·2′W	W	147
Marchnear	Aberd	NO6498	57°4·6′	2°35·2′W	X	37,45
Marchogdir	Powys	SN8826	51°55·5′	3°37·3′W	X	160
Marchogllwyn	Carm	SN5010	51°46·4′	4°10·1′W	X	159
Marchouse Hill	E Ayr	NS6627	55°31·4′	4°6·9′W	X	71
March Plantation	Northum	NU1226	55°31·9′	1°48·2′W	F	75
March Sike	D & G	NY2299	55°17·0′	3°13·3′W	W	79
March Sike	Scot Bord	NT2521	55°28·9′	3°10·8′W	W	79
March Sike	Scot Bord	NT3110	55°23·0′	3°4·9′W	W	79
Marchurst	Kent	TQ5751	51°14·4′	0°15·3′E	X	188
Marchweeke	Devon	SS7911	50°53·4′	3°42·8′W	X	191
Marchwell	Midlo	NT2261	55°50·4′	3°14·3′W	X	66
Marchwiel	Wrex	SJ3547	53°1·2′	2°57·7′W	T	117

Marchwood	Hants	SU3810	50°53·5'	1°27·2'W	T	196
Marchwood Inclosure	Hants	SU3907	50°51·9'	1°26·4'W	F	196
Marchwood Park	Hants	SU3909	50°53·0'	1°26·4'W	X	196
Marcle Hill	Heref	SO6332	51°59·4'	2°31·9'W	X	149
Marcle Hill	Heref	SO6335	52°1·0'	2°32·0'W	X	149
Marcombe Lake	Devon	ST0420	50°58·5'	3°21·7'W	W	181
Marcroft Gate Fm	Roch	SD8414	53°37·6'	2°14·1'W	FM	109
Marcross	V of Glam	SS9269	51°24·8'	3°32·8'W	T	170
Marcross Fm	V of Glam	SS9268	51°24·3'	3°32·8'W	FM	170
Marcus	Angus	NO5157	56°42·4'	2°47·6'W	T	54
Mardale Banks	Cumbr	NY4812	54°30·3'	2°47·8'W	X	90
Mardale Common	Cumbr	NY4811	54°29·7'	2°47·8'W	X	90
Mardale Ill Bell	Cumbr	NY4410	54°29·2'	2°51·4'W	H	90
Mardale Waters	Cumbr	NY4510	54°29·2'	2°50·5'W	X	90
Marddwr	Conwy	SH8344	52°59·1'	3°44·2'W	W	124,125
Marden	Heref	SO5247	52°7·4'	2°41·7'W	T	149
Marden	Kent	TQ7444	51°10·3'	0°29·7'E	T	188
Marden	N Tyne	NZ3570	55°1·6'	1°26·7'W	T	88
Marden	Scot Bord	NT8057	55°48·6'	2°18·7'W	X	67,74
Marden	Wilts	SU0857	51°19·0'	1°52·7'W	T	173
Marden Ash	Essex	TL5502	51°41·9'	0°15·0'E	T	167
Marden Ash Ho	Essex	TL5501	51°41·4'	0°14·9'E	X	167
Marden Beech	Kent	TQ7343	51°9·8'	0°28·9'E	T	188
Marden Cowbag	Wilts	SU0855	51°17·9'	1°52·7'W	X	173
Marden Down	Wilts	SU0854	51°17·3'	1°52·7'W	X	184
Marden Hill	Herts	TL2714	51°48·8'	0°9·1'W	X	166
Marden Hillboxes Fm	Surrey	TQ3555	51°16·9'	0°3·5'W	FM	187
Marden Ho	Northum	NU2511	55°23·8'	1°35·9'W	X	81
Marden Park Fm	Surrey	TQ3655	51°16·9'	0°2·6'W	FM	187
Marden Rocks	Northum	NU2611	55°23·8'	1°34·9'W	X	81
Marden's Fm	Essex	TM1826	51°53·6'	1°10·5'E	FM	168,169
Marden's Hill	E Susx	TQ4932	51°4·3'	0°8·0'E	T	188
Marden Thorn	Kent	TQ7542	51°9·3'	0°30·5'E	T	188
Marderby Grange	N Yks	SE4783	54°14·7'	1°16·3'W	X	100
Marderby Hall	N Yks	SE4683	54°14·7'	1°17·2'W	X	100
Mar Dike	Lincs	TF4389	53°22·9'	0°9·4'E	W	113,122
Mardle Ho	Suff	TM4777	52°20·3'	1°38·0'E	X	156
Mardleybury	Herts	TL2618	51°51·0'	0°9·8'W	T	166
Mardley Heath	Herts	TL2418	51°51·0'	0°11·6'W	F	166
Mardocks Fm	Herts	TL3914	51°48·7'	0°1·4'E	FM	166
Mardon	Northum	NT9037	55°37·8'	2°9·1'W	X	74,75
Mardon Down	Devon	SX7787	50°40·4'	3°44·1'W	H	191
Mardu	Shrops	SO2684	52°27·2'	3°4·9'W	T	137
Mardy	Monm	SO3015	51°50·0'	3°0·6'W	T	161
Mardy	Monm	SO4204	51°44·1'	2°50·0'W	X	171
Mardy	Shrops	SJ2833	52°53·6'	3°3·8'W	T	126
Mardy Fm	Monm	SO2615	51°50·0'	3°4·0'W	FM	161
Mar Dyke	Thurr	TQ5679	51°29·5'	0°15·2'E	W	177
Mar Dyke	Thurr	TQ6181	51°30·5'	0°19·6'E	W	177
Mardy's Cleugh	Northum	NY6352	54°51·9'	2°34·2'W	X	86
Mare Brook	Staffs	SK1525	52°49·6'	1°46·2'W	W	128
Mare Burn	E Ayr	NS5331	55°33·3'	4°19·4'W	W	70
Mare & Colt, The	Devon	SS6248	51°13·1'	3°58·2'W	X	180
Mare Fen	Cambs	TL3669	52°18·4'	0°0·1'E	X	154
Mare Fen	Cambs	TL5488	52°28·3'	0°16·4'E	X	143
Marefield	Leic	SK7407	52°39·6'	0°54·0'W	T	141
Mare & Foal	Northum	NY7266	54°59·5'	2°25·8'W	A	86,87
Mareham Gate	Lincs	TF2759	53°7·0'	0°5·7'W	X	122
Mareham Grange	Lincs	TF2868	53°11·9'	0°4·6'W	X	122
Mareham Lane	Lincs	TF0839	52°56·5'	0°23·2'W	X	130
Mareham Lane Fm	Lincs	TF0744	52°59·2'	0°24·0'W	FM	130
Mareham le Fen	Lincs	TF2761	53°8·1'	0°5·7'W	T	122
Mareham Moor	Lincs	TF2660	53°7·6'	0°6·6'W	X	122
Mareham on the Hill	Lincs	TF2868	53°11·9'	0°4·6'W	T	122
Marehay	Derby	SK3948	53°1·9'	1°24·7'W	T	119
Marehay Fm	Derby	SK3849	53°2·5'	1°25·6'W	FM	119
Marehay Hall	Derby	SK3848	53°1·9'	1°25·6'W	X	119
Mare Hill	Suff	TL7348	52°6·4'	0°32·0'E	X	155
Mare Hill	Surrey	SU9340	51°9·3'	0°39·8'W	X	186
Marehill	W Susx	TQ0618	50°57·3'	0°29·1'W	T	197
Marelands	Hants	SU7943	51°11·1'	0°51·8'W	A	186
Marepark Cross	Devon	SX7644	50°17·2'	3°44·1'W	X	202
Marepond Fm	Surrey	SU9839	51°8·7'	0°35·5'W	FM	186
Mare Rock	D & G	NX4735	54°41·5'	4°22·0'W	X	83
Maresfield	E Susx	TQ4624	51°0·0'	0°5·2'E	T	198
Maresfield Park	E Susx	TQ4624	51°0·0'	0°5·2'E	T	198
Mare's Pool	Shetld	HP5003	60°42·7'	1°4·5'W	W	1
Mares, The	Orkney	ND2888	58°46·7'	3°14·2'W	X	7
Mare Tail	Lincs	TF4437	52°54·9'	0°8·9'E	X	131
Mare, The	I Scilly	SV8913	49°56·4'	6°19·7'W	X	203
Mare, The	Pemb	SM7922	51°51·4'	5°12·2'W	X	157
Marfield	Midlo	NT1856	55°47·7'	3°18·0'W	X	65
Marfield	Midlo	NT1856	55°47·7'	3°18·0'W	X	65,66,72
Marfleet	K upon H	TA1329	53°44·9'	0°16·8'W	T	107
Marford	Wrex	SJ3656	53°6·1'	2°56·9'W	T	117
Marfurlong Fm	Glos	SP1938	52°2·6'	1°43·0'W	FM	151
Margadale	Arg & Bt	NR3974	55°53·6'	6°10·0'W	X	60,61
Margadale Hill	Arg & Bt	NR3975	55°54·1'	6°10·1'W	H	60,61
Margadale River	Arg & Bt	NR4074	55°53·6'	6°9·1'W	W	60,61
Margam	Nth Pt Talb	SS7887	51°34·4'	3°45·2'W	T	170
Margam	Swan	SS4586	51°33·3'	4°13·8'W	X	159
Margam Country Park	Nth Pt Talb	SS8186	51°33·9'	3°42·6'W	X	170
Margam Moors	Nth Pt Talb	SS7784	51°32·7'	3°46·0'W	X	170
Margam Sands	Nth Pt Talb	SS7685	51°33·3'	3°46·9'W	X	170
Margaret Marsh	Dorset	ST8218	50°57·9'	2°15·0'W	T	183
Margaret or Tripcock Ness	Gren	TQ4581	51°30·8'	0°5·8'E	X	177
Margaret Roding	Essex	TL5912	51°47·3'	0°18·7'E	T	167
Margaret's Bay	N Som	ST4173	51°27·4'	2°50·6'W	W	171,172
Margaret's Camp	Glos	SO8931	51°58·9'	2°9·2'W	A	150
Margaretsmill Fm	Inverc	NS3369	55°53·4'	4°39·8'W	FM	63
Margaret's Spring	Notts	SK6453	53°4·5'	1°2·3'W	F	120
Margaretta Ho	Norf	TF5919	52°44·9'	0°21·8'E	X	131
Margaretting	Essex	TL6701	51°41·2'	0°25·4'E	T	167
Margaretting Hall	Essex	TL6600	51°40·7'	0°24·5'E	X	167
Margaretting Tye	Essex	TL6800	51°40·6'	0°26·2'E	T	167
Margate	Kent	TR3570	51°23·0'	1°23·0'E	T	179
Margate Caves	Kent	TR3571	51°23·6'	1°23·1'E	X	179
Margate Hook	Kent	TR2572	51°24·4'	1°14·5'E	X	179
Margate Wood	Corn	SX0966	50°28·0'	4°41·1'W	F	200
Margbeg	Stir	NN6736	56°30·1'	4°9·2'W	X	51
Margenaish Fm	N Ayr	NS0222	55°27·4'	5°7·5'W	FM	69
Margery	Surrey	TQ2552	51°15·4'	0°12·1'W	T	187
Margery Cross	Oxon	SP3908	51°46·4'	1°25·7'W	X	164
Margery Hall	Surrey	TQ2552	51°15·4'	0°12·1'W	X	187
Margery Hill	Sheff	SK1895	53°27·3'	1°43·3'W	H	110
Margery Wood	Surrey	TQ2452	51°15·4'	0°13·0'W	F	187
Margetts Fm	Cambs	TL2066	52°17·0'	0°14·1'W	FM	153
Margett's Hill	Warw	SP2934	52°0·5'	1°34·3'W	X	151
Margher-e-Kew	I of M	SC4590	54°17·2'	4°22·5'W	X	95
Margidvnvm (Roman Town)	Notts	SK7041	52°57·9'	0°57·1'W	R	129
Margie	Angus	NO5670	56°49·4'	2°42·8'W	X	44
Margley	D & G	NX7673	55°2·4'	3°56·0'W	X	84
Marglolly Br	D & G	NX8379	55°5·8'	3°49·6'W	X	84
Marglolly Burn	D & G	NX8280	55°6·3'	3°50·5'W	W	78
Margmony	D & G	NX7893	55°13·2'	3°54·6'W	X	78
Margmony Hill	D & G	NX7792	55°12·7'	3°55·6'W	H	78
Margmore	Pth & Kin	NN8547	56°36·3'	3°52·0'W	X	52
Marg na Craige	Highld	NN6297	57°2·9'	4°16·0'W	X	35
Margnaheglish	N Ayr	NR9349	55°41·7'	5°17·2'W	T	62,69
Margnaheglish	N Ayr	NS0331	55°32·2'	5°6·9'W	T	69
Margree	D & G	NX6786	55°9·3'	4°4·8'W	X	77
Margree Burn	D & G	NX6784	55°8·2'	4°4·8'W	W	77
Margree Burn	D & G	NX6886	55°9·3'	4°3·9'W	W	77
Margreig	D & G	NX8378	55°5·2'	3°49·6'W	X	84
Margrie	D & G	NX5950	54°49·8'	4°11·3'W	X	83
Margrove Park	Red & Cl	NZ6515	54°31·8'	0°59·3'W	T	94
Marham	Norf	TF7009	52°39·4'	0°31·2'E	T	143
Marhamchurch	Corn	SS2203	50°48·2'	4°31·2'W	T	190
Marham Fen	Norf	TF7211	52°40·4'	0°33·0'E	F	132,143
Marham Hall	Norf	TF7008	52°38·8'	0°31·2'E	X	143
Marham Ho	Norf	TF7009	52°39·4'	0°31·2'E	X	143
Marhayes Manor	Corn	SS2400	50°46·6'	4°29·4'W	X	190
Marholm	Peterb	TF1402	52°36·5'	0°18·6'W	T	142
Marial Gwyn	Denb	SH9955	53°5·5'	3°30·1'W	H	116
Marian	Conwy	SH8275	53°15·8'	3°45·7'W	X	116
Marian	Flint	SJ0979	53°18·3'	3°21·5'W	T	116
Marian Cottage	Arg & Bt	NM6224	56°21·2'	5°50·7'W	X	49
Marian Cwm	Denb	SJ0777	53°17·2'	3°23·3'W	T	116
Mariandyrys	I of Angl	SH6081	53°18·7'	4°5·7'W	T	114,115
Marian Ffrith	Denb	SJ0777	53°17·2'	3°23·3'W	H	116
Marian-glas	I of Angl	SH5084	53°20·1'	4°14·8'W	T	114,115
Marian Inclosure	Glos	SO5612	51°48·5'	2°37·9'W	F	162
Marian Lodge	Cumbr	NY5736	54°43·3'	2°39·6'W	X	91
Marian Port	D & G	NX0367	54°57·8'	5°4·2'W	W	82
Marian Prysau	Flint	SJ1274	53°15·6'	3°18·7'W	X	116
Mariansleigh	Devon	SS7422	50°59·3'	3°47·3'W	T	180
Marian-y-de or South Beach	Gwyn	SH3734	52°53·0'	4°24·9'W	T	123
Marian-y-mor or West End	Gwyn	SH3634	52°53·0'	4°25·8'W	T	123
Marianywinllan	Gwyn	SH6270	53°12·8'	4°3·6'W	X	115
Marigold Fm	N Yks	SE4293	54°20·1'	1°20·8'W	FM	99
Marine Drive	Conwy	SH7684	53°20·5'	3°51·3'W	X	115
Marine Drive	I of M	SC3773	54°7·9'	4°29·3'W	X	95
Marine Lake	Denb	SH9980	53°18·7'	3°30·6'W	W	116
Marine Lake	N Som	ST3161	51°20·9'	2°59·1'W	W	182
Marine Lake	Sefton	SD3317	53°39·0'	3°0·4'W	W	108
Marine Lake	Sefton	SJ3197	53°28·2'	3°2·0'W	W	108
Marine Lake	Wirral	SJ2186	53°22·1'	3°10·8'W	W	108
Mariner's Copse	Hants	SU6160	51°20·4'	1°7·1'W	F	175
Marine Town	Kent	TQ9274	51°26·2'	0°46·1'E	T	178
Marine Villa	E Loth	NT5085	56°3·6'	2°47·7'W	X	66
Marine Zoo	Lincs	TF5763	53°8·7'	0°21·3'E	X	122
Marionburgh	Aberd	NJ7006	57°8·9'	2°29·3'W	T	38
Marionburgh	Moray	NJ1836	57°24·7'	3°21·4'W	X	28
Marish	Powys	SO1435	52°0·6'	3°14·3'W	X	161
Marishader	Highld	NG4963	57°35·5'	6°11·5'W	T	23
Marishes Lodge Fm	N Yks	SE8879	54°12·2'	0°38·6'W	FM	101
Marish, The	Bucks	TQ0289	51°35·7'	0°31·3'W	X	176
Maristow Ho	Devon	SX4764	50°27·6'	4°9·0'W	X	201
Marjery Cross	Devon	SX6254	50°22·4'	3°56·1'W	X	202
Marjoriebanks	D & G	NY0883	55°8·2'	3°26·2'W	T	78
Mark	Arg & Bt	NS2295	56°7·1'	4°51·4'W	X	56
Mark	D & G	NX1057	54°52·6'	4°57·3'W	X	82
Mark	D & G	NX5060	54°55·0'	4°20·0'W	X	83
Mark	D & G	NX6556	54°53·1'	4°5·8'W	X	83,84
Mark	S Ayr	NX2487	55°9·0'	4°45·3'W	X	76
Mark	Somer	ST3847	51°13·4'	2°52·9'W	T	182
Marka Ber	Orkney	HY5907	58°57·2'	2°42·3'W	X	6
Markadon	Devon	SS2325	51°0·1'	4°31·0'W	X	190
Mark Ash Wood	Hants	SU2407	50°51·9'	1°39·2'W	F	195
Markbeech	Kent	TQ4742	51°9·7'	0°6·5'E	T	188
Mark Broom Moss	D & G	NX2561	54°55·0'	4°43·4'W	X	82
Mark Bushes	Essex	TL4607	51°44·8'	0°7·3'E	F	167
Markby	Lincs	TF4878	53°16·9'	0°13·6'E	T	122
Mark Causeway	Somer	ST3647	51°13·4'	2°54·6'W	T	182
Mark Cross	E Susx	TQ5010	50°52·4'	0°8·3'E	T	199
Mark Cross	E Susx	TQ5831	51°3·6'	0°15·7'E	T	188
Markdhu	D & G	NX1873	55°1·3'	4°50·4'W	X	76
Markeaton	C of Derb	SK3337	52°56·0'	1°30·1'W	T	128
Markeaton Brook	Derby	SK3238	52°56·5'	1°31·0'W	W	128
Markeaton Stones	Derby	SK3238	52°56·5'	1°31·0'W	X	128
Markenfield Hall	N Yks	SE2967	54°6·1'	1°33·0'W	A	99
Marker Point	W Susx	SU7402	50°49·0'	0°56·6'W	X	197
Markeston	C of Derb	SK3237	52°56·0'	1°31·0'W	X	
Market Bosworth	Leic	SK4003	52°37·6'	1°24·1'W	T	140
Market Br	Lincs	TF2377	53°16·8'	0°8·9'W	X	122
Market Deeping	Lincs	TF1310	52°40·8'	0°18·9'W	T	130,142
Market Drayton	Shrops	SJ6734	52°54·4'	2°29·0'W	T	127
Market Fm	Essex	TL6134	51°59·1'	0°21·1'E	FM	154
Market Gate	Cumbr	NY4341	54°45·9'	2°52·7'W	X	85
Market Harborough	Leic	SP7387	52°28·8'	0°55·1'W	T	141
Market Hill	Aberd	NJ4239	57°26·5'	2°57·5'W	X	28
Markethill	Highld	ND1630	58°15·3'	3°25·4'W	X	11,17
Markethill	Highld	ND1954	58°28·3'	3°22·8'W	X	11,12
Markethill	Pth & Kin	NO2239	56°32·4'	3°15·7'W	T	53
Markethill	Renf	NS3760	55°48·6'	4°35·6'W	X	63
Market Ho	Derby	SK2460	53°8·4'	1°38·1'W	X	119
Market Lavington	Wilts	SU0154	51°17·3'	1°58·8'W	T	184
Market Overton	Leic	SK8816	52°44·3'	0°41·4'W	T	130
Market Rasen	Lincs	TF1089	53°23·4'	0°20·3'W	T	113,121
Market Road Fm	Dorset	ST9817	50°57·4'	2°1·3'W	FM	184
Market Stainton	Lincs	TF2279	53°17·9'	0°9·8'W	T	122
Market Stance	Highld	NG6722	57°14·0'	5°51·2'W	X	32
Market Warsop	Notts	SK5667	53°12·1'	1°9·3'W	T	120
Market Weighton	E Yorks	SE8741	53°51·7'	0°40·2'W	T	106
Market Weighton Canal	E Yorks	SE8433	53°47·4'	0°43·1'W	W	106
Market Weston	Suff	TL9877	52°21·5'	0°54·9'E	T	144
Markfast	D & G	NX8168	54°59·8'	3°51·2'W	X	84
Markfield	Leic	SK4810	52°41·4'	1°17·0'W	T	129
Markfield Lodge Fm	Leic	SK4709	52°40·8'	1°17·9'W	FM	140
Mark Fm	Essex	TL9904	51°42·2'	0°53·2'E	FM	168
Mark Hall North	Essex	TL4611	51°46·9'	0°7·4'E	T	167
Mark Hall South	Essex	TL4610	51°46·4'	0°7·4'E	T	167
Markham	Caer	SO1601	51°42·3'	3°12·5'W	T	171
Markham Cross	Devon	SX8989	50°41·6'	3°33·9'W	X	192
Markham Fm	N Som	ST5274	51°28·0'	2°41·1'W	FM	172
Markham Ho	Leic	SK7211	52°41·7'	0°55·7'W	X	129
Markham Moor	Notts	SK7173	53°15·2'	0°55·7'W	T	120
Markham's Hill	Herts	TL1329	51°57·1'	0°20·9'W	X	166
Mark Hill	D & G	NX1270	54°59·6'	4°55·9'W	X	76
Mark Hill	D & G	NX6252	54°50·9'	4°8·5'W	H	83
Mark Hill	D & G	NX8454	54°52·3'	3°48·0'W	H	84
Markie Burn	Highld	NN5796	57°2·2'	4°20·9'W	W	35
Markie Water	Moray	NJ3937	57°25·4'	3°0·5'W	W	28
Markinch	Fife	NO2901	56°12·0'	3°8·2'W	T	59
Marki Ness	Shetld	HU3572	60°26·1'	1°21·3'W	X	2,3
Marking Fold Hill	Lancs	SD6159	54°1·8'	2°35·3'W	X	102,103
Markington	N Yks	SE2965	54°5·0'	1°33·0'W	T	99
Marklach	D & G	NX1772	55°0·8'	4°51·3'W	X	76
Markland Fm	Derby	SK5073	53°15·3'	1°14·6'W	FM	120
Markland Fm	Derby	SK5075	53°16·4'	1°14·6'W	FM	120
Markland Grips	Derby	SK5074	53°15·9'	1°14·6'W	F	120
Markland Hill	Bolton	SD6809	53°34·8'	2°28·6'W	T	109
Markle	E Loth	NT5777	55°59·3'	2°40·9'W	A	67
Markle	E Loth	NT5777	55°59·3'	2°40·9'W	T	67
Markle Mains	E Loth	NT5677	55°59·3'	2°41·9'W	X	67
Marklye	E Susx	TQ6218	50°56·5'	0°18·7'E	X	199
Marklye Fm	E Susx	TQ5822	50°58·8'	0°15·4'E	FM	199
Markly Wood	E Susx	TQ5722	50°58·8'	0°14·6'E	F	199
Mark Moor	Somer	ST3746	51°12·8'	2°53·7'W	X	182
Markna Geo	Shetld	HU4486	60°33·6'	1°11·4'W	X	1,2,3
Mark Oak Gate	Surrey	TQ1356	51°17·7'	0°22·4'W	X	187
Mark of Lochronald	D & G	NX2664	54°56·7'	4°42·6'W	X	82
Mark of Luce	D & G	NX2959	54°54·0'	4°39·6'W	X	82
Mark of Luce Moss	D & G	NX2859	54°54·0'	4°40·5'W	X	82
Mark of Shennanton	D & G	NX3464	54°56·8'	4°35·1'W	X	82
Mark Park	Arg & Bt	NN2014	56°17·3'	4°54·1'W	X	50,56
Markreach Hill	D & G	NX7397	55°15·3'	3°59·5'W	X	77
Marks	D & G	NX7351	54°50·5'	3°58·2'W	X	83,84
Marks Barn	Somer	ST4311	50°54·0'	2°48·3'W	X	193
Marks' Br	Devon	SX6057	50°24·0'	3°57·8'W	X	202
Marksbury	Bath & NE Somer	ST6662	51°21·6'	2°28·9'W	T	172
Marksbury Plain	Bath & NE Somer	ST6661	51°21·1'	2°28·9'W	X	172
Marksbury Vale	Bath & NE Somer	ST6662	51°21·6'	2°28·9'W	X	172
Marksclose Wood	Cumbr	NY6512	54°30·4'	2°32·0'W	F	91
Mark's Corner	I of W	SZ4692	50°43·8'	1°20·5'W	T	196
Mark's Fm	Devon	SX8890	50°42·2'	3°34·8'W	FM	192
Marks Fm	Essex	TL6323	51°53·1'	0°22·5'E	FM	167
Mark's Fm	Essex	TQ7796	51°38·3'	0°33·9'E	FM	167
Marks Gate	Bark & Dag	TQ4890	51°35·6'	0°8·6'E	T	177
Mark's Grave	Cambs	TL5948	52°6·7'	0°19·7'E	X	154
Marks Hall	Essex	TL5614	51°48·4'	0°16·2'E	X	167
Marks Hall	Essex	TL5911	51°46·7'	0°18·7'E	X	167
Markshall	Essex	TL8425	51°53·8'	0°40·9'E	X	168
Markshall	Norf	TG2304	52°35·5'	1°17·9'E	X	134
Markshall Wood	Essex	TL8326	51°54·4'	0°40·0'E	F	168
Marks Hill (Nature Reserve)	Essex	TQ6887	51°33·6'	0°25·8'E	X	177,178
Mark Sike	Scot Bord	NT2120	55°28·3'	3°14·5'W	W	73
Markstakes Common	E Susx	TQ3917	50°56·4'	0°0·9'W	X	198
Markstakes Fm	E Susx	TQ4018	50°56·9'	0°0·0'W	FM	198
Marks Tey	Essex	TL9123	51°52·6'	0°46·9'E	T	168
Markstone Ho	N Yks	NZ2904	54°26·1'	1°32·8'W	X	93
Markswood Fm	Essex	TL6529	51°56·3'	0°24·4'E	FM	167
Markway Hill	Hants	SU2402	50°49·3'	1°39·2'W	X	195
Markway Inclosure	Hants	SU2503	50°49·8'	1°38·3'W	F	195
Markwell	Corn	SX3758	50°24·2'	4°17·3'W	X	201
Markwell's	W Susx	TQ2625	51°0·9'	0°11·8'W	X	187,198
Markwells Wood	W Susx	SU7513	50°54·9'	0°55·6'W	F	197
Markwicks	E Susx	TQ6634	51°5·1'	0°22·6'E	X	188
Mark Wood	Suff	TM0037	51°59·9'	0°55·2'E	F	155
Markyate	Herts	TL0616	51°50·2'	0°27·3'W	T	166
Markyate Cell	Herts	TL0517	51°50·7'	0°28·1'W	X	166
Mark Yeo	Somer	ST3651	51°15·5'	2°54·6'W	W	182
Marlage	S Lanak	NS7848	55°42·9'	3°56·1'W	X	64
Marlake Ho	Oxon	SP5915	51°50·1'	1°8·2'W	X	164
Marland	Roch	SD8711	53°36·0'	2°11·4'W	T	109
Marland Moor	Devon	SS5011	50°53·0'	4°7·6'W	X	191
Marlands	Hants	SU6425	51°1·5'	1°4·9'W	X	185
Marlands	Somer	ST0918	50°57·5'	3°17·4'W	X	181
Marlands	W Susx	TQ1327	51°2·1'	0°22·9'W	X	187,198
Marlands Fm	Kent	TQ8838	51°6·8'	0°41·6'E	FM	189
Marlas	Brig	SS8182	51°31·7'	3°42·5'W	X	170
Marlas	Heref	SO4429	51°57·6'	2°48·5'W	T	149,161
Marl Bank	Worcs	SO7840	52°3·7'	2°18·9'W	T	150
Marl Barn	Lancs	SD7554	53°59·1'	2°22·5'W	X	103
Marl Beck	Durham	NY9529	54°39·6'	2°4·2'W	W	91,92
Marlborough	Monm	SO3724	51°54·9'	2°54·6'W	X	161
Marlborough	Wilts	SU1869	51°25·4'	1°44·1'W	T	173
Marlborough Common	Wilts	SU1870	51°26·0'	1°44·1'W	X	173
Marlborough Downs	Wilts	SU1575	51°28·7'	1°46·7'W	X	173
Marlborough Fm	Devon	SX9892	50°43·4'	3°26·3'W	FM	192
Marlborough Fm	Suff	TM4287	52°25·9'	1°34·0'E	FM	156
Marlborough Grange Fm	V of Glam	SS9773	51°27·0'	3°28·6'W	FM	170
Marlborough Hall	Cumbr	NX9810	54°28·8'	3°34·0'W	X	89

Marl Brook	Heref	SO4954	52°11·2'	2°44·4'W	W	148,149
Marlbrook	Heref	SO5054	52°11·2'	2°43·5'W	T	149
Marlbrook	Shrops	SO6570	52°19·9'	2°30·4'W	X	138
Marlbrook	Worcs	SO9774	52°22·1'	2°2·2'W	T	139
Marlbrook Hall	Heref	SO4370	52°19·7'	2°49·8'W	X	137,148
Marlcliff	Warw	SP0950	52°9·1'	1°51·7'W	T	150
Marlcliff Hill	Warw	SP0950	52°9·1'	1°51·7'W	X	150
Marlcombe Fm	Devon	ST1103	50°49·4'	3°15·4'W	FM	192,193
Marldell Fm	Hants	SU6325	51°1·5'	1°5·7'W	FM	185
Marldon	Devon	SX8663	50°27·6'	3°36·0'W	T	202
Marldown	Northum	NT8739	55°38·9'	2°12·0'W	X	74
Marle	Pemb	SN1020	51°51·0'	4°45·1'W	X	145,158
Marledge	Pemb	SR9897	51°38·4'	4°54·8'W	X	158
Marleehill	Pth & Kin	NO1346	56°36·1'	3°24·6'W	X	53
Marlee Ho	Pth & Kin	NO1444	56°35·1'	3°23·6'W	X	53
Marlee Loch	Shetld	HU2954	60°16·4'	1°28·0'W	W	3
Marlee Mill	Pth & Kin	NO1543	56°34·5'	3°22·6'W	X	53
Marlefield	Pth & Kin	NO0524	56°24·2'	3°31·9'W	X	52,53,58
Marlefield	Scot Bord	NT7325	55°31·3'	2°25·2'W	X	74
Marle Green	E Susx	TQ5816	50°55·5'	0°15·3'E	T	199
Marlehall	Pth & Kin	NO0931	56°28·0'	3°28·2'W	X	52,53
Marle Hill	Glos	SO9523	51°54·6'	2°4·0'W	T	163
Marle Hills, The	S Glos	ST6583	51°32·9'	2°29·9'W	X	172
Marle Place	Kent	TQ6839	51°7·8'	0°24·5'E	X	188
Marles Fm	Essex	TL4505	51°43·7'	0°6·4'E	FM	167
Marlesford	Suff	TM3258	52°10·5'	1°24·0'E	T	156
Marles Wood	Lancs	SD6735	53°48·9'	2°29·7'W	F	103
Marley	Brad	SE0940	53°51·6'	1°51·4'W	X	104
Marley	Devon	SS9516	50°56·3'	3°29·3'W	X	181
Marley	E Susx	TQ8921	50°57·7'	0°41·9'E	X	189
Marley	Kent	TR1850	51°12·7'	1°7·7'E	T	179,189
Marley	Kent	TR3353	51°13·9'	1°20·7'E	T	179
Marleycombe Hill	Wilts	SU0222	51°0·1'	1°57·9'W	H	184
Marley Common	W Susx	SU8831	51°4·5'	0°44·2'W	F	186
Marley Cote Walls	Northum	NY9859	54°55·8'	2°1·4'W	X	87
Marley Court	Kent	TQ8853	51°14·9'	0°42·0'E	X	189
Marley Fm	Cambs	TL3389	52°29·2'	0°2·1'W	FM	142
Marley Fm	Devon	SX7261	50°26·3'	3°47·8'W	FM	202
Marley Fm	Kent	TQ8643	51°9·6'	0°40·0'E	FM	189
Marley Green	Ches	SJ5745	53°0·3'	2°38·0'W	T	117
Marley Hall	Ches	SJ5845	53°0·3'	2°37·1'W	X	117
Marley Hall	Heref	SO6840	52°3·7'	2°27·6'W	X	149
Marley Hayes	Devon	SY0184	50°39·1'	3°23·6'W	X	192
Marley Heights	W Susx	SU8930	51°4·0'	0°43·4'W	T	186
Marley Hill	Ghead	NZ2058	54°55·2'	1°40·9'W	T	88
Marley Ho	E Susx	TQ7616	50°55·2'	0°30·6'E	X	199
Marley Ho	W Susx	SU8831	51°4·5'	0°44·2'W	X	186
Marleyknowe	Northum	NT9332	55°35·1'	2°6·2'W	X	74,75
Marley Pots	Sund	NZ3759	54°55·7'	1°24·9'W	T	88
Marley Wood	Dorset	SY8083	50°39·0'	2°16·6'W	F	194
Marley Wood	Oxon	SP4707	51°45·8'	1°18·7'W	F	164
Marl Field	N Yks	SD9247	53°55·4'	2°6·9'W	X	103
Marlfield	Scot Bord	NT8144	55°41·6'	2°17·7'W	X	74
Marlfields Fm	Ches	SJ9181	53°19·8'	2°7·7'W	FM	109
Marl Hall	Conwy	SH7978	53°17·4'	3°48·5'W	X	115
Marlheath Fm	Ches	SJ8572	53°14·9'	2°13·1'W	FM	118
Marl Hill	Lancs	SD6847	53°55·3'	2°28·8'W	X	103
Marl Hill Moor	Lancs	SD6946	53°54·8'	2°27·9'W	X	103
Marlie Fm	Kent	TR0725	50°59·4'	0°57·4'E	FM	189
Marli Fm	Denb	SJ0073	53°14·9'	3°29·5'W	FM	116
Marlin Chapel Fm	Herts	SP9607	51°45·4'	0°36·2'W	FM	165
Marline Wood	E Susx	TQ7812	50°53·0'	0°32·2'E	F	199
Marlingate Fm	Kent	TQ7235	51°5·5'	0°27·8'E	FM	188
Marlingford	Norf	TG1209	52°38·5'	1°8·4'E	T	144
Marlingford Hall	Norf	TG1208	52°37·9'	1°8·4'E	X	144
Marlish	Northum	NZ0785	55°9·8'	1°53·0'W	X	81
Marlock House Fm	Notts	SK6745	53°0·1'	0°59·7'W	FM	129
Mar Lodge	Aberd	NJ5323	57°18·0'	2°46·3'W	X	37
Mar Lodge	Aberd	NO0989	56°59·3'	3°29·4'W	X	43
Marloes	Pemb	SM7908	51°43·9'	5°11·6'W	T	157
Marloes Court	Pemb	SM7808	51°43·8'	5°12·5'W	X	157
Marloes Mere	Pemb	SM7708	51°43·8'	5°13·4'W	W	157
Marloes Sands	Pemb	SM7807	51°43·3'	5°12·5'W	X	157
Marlow	Bucks	SU8586	51°34·2'	0°46·0'W	T	175
Marlow	Heref	SO3976	52°23·0'	2°53·4'W	T	137,148
Marlow	Orkney	HY4732	59°10·6'	2°55·1'W	X	5,6
Marlow Bottom	Bucks	SU8488	51°35·3'	0°46·9'W	T	175
Marlow Common	Bucks	SU8286	51°34·2'	0°48·6'W	T	175
Marlow Fm	Kent	TQ8953	51°14·9'	0°42·9'E	FM	189
Marlows, The	W Susx	SU8715	50°55·9'	0°45·3'W	F	197
Marlpit Hill	Kent	TQ4447	51°12·5'	0°4·1'E	T	187
Marlpit House Fm	Staffs	SK0928	52°51·2'	1°51·6'W	FM	128
Marlpit Plantn	Northum	NZ0572	55°2·8'	1°54·9'W	F	87
Marlpits	E Susx	TQ4528	51°2·2'	0°4·5'E	X	188,198
Marlpits	E Susx	TQ7013	50°53·7'	0°25·4'E	T	199
Marlpits Fm	E Susx	TQ8216	50°55·1'	0°35·8'E	FM	199
Marl Pits Wood	Dorset	SY7992	50°43·9'	2°17·5'W	F	194
Marl Point	Norf	TG2938	52°53·7'	1°24·7'E	X	133
Marlpool	Derby	SK4345	53°0·3'	1°21·1'W	T	129
Marlpool Fm	Glos	SO7101	51°42·7'	2°24·8'W	FM	162
Marlpost Wood	W Susx	TQ1425	51°1·0'	0°22·1'W	F	187,198
Marlsborough	Pemb	SM8817	51°48·9'	5°4·2'W	X	157
Marls Hall	Suff	TL9447	52°5·5'	0°50·3'E	X	155
Marlston Fm	W Berks	SU5372	51°26·9'	1°13·8'W	FM	174
Marl Well	Cumbr	SD6785	54°15·8'	2°30·0'W	W	98
Marlwood Grange	S Glos	ST6388	51°35·6'	2°31·7'W	X	162,172
Marmansgrave Wood	Suff	TL8480	52°23·5'	0°42·6'E	F	144
Marmouth Scars	Northum	NU2613	55°24·9'	1°34·9'W	X	81
Marnabogs	Aberd	NJ9642	57°28·4'	2°3·5'W	X	30
Marnel Dell	Hants	SU6354	51°17·1'	1°5·4'W	X	185
Marnhoul	D & G	NX7178	55°5·0'	4°0·8'W	X	77,84
Marnhoul Wood	D & G	NX7177	55°4·5'	4°0·8'W	F	77,84
Marnhull	Dorset	ST7718	50°57·9'	2°19·3'W	T	183
Marnhull Ham	Dorset	ST7519	50°58·4'	2°21·0'W	X	183
Marno	Aberd	NJ9460	57°38·1'	2°5·6'W	X	30
Marnoch	Aberd	NJ5950	57°32·6'	2°40·6'W	T	29
Marnoch Hill	D & G	NX8058	54°54·4'	3°51·9'W	H	84
Marnoch Lodge	Moray	NJ6049	57°32·0'	2°39·6'W	X	29
Marnock	N Lanak	NS7168	55°53·5'	4°3·3'W	T	64
Marnonwells	Aberd	NJ7452	57°33·7'	2°25·6'W	X	29
Marnshaw Head	Staffs	SK0664	53°10·6'	1°54·2'W	X	119
Marnwood Hall	Wrekin	SJ6504	52°38·2'	2°30·6'W	X	127
Marown Old Church	I of M	SC3278	54°10·5'	4°34·0'W	A	95
Marple	Stock	SJ9588	53°23·6'	2°4·1'W	T	109
Marple Bridge	Stock	SJ9689	53°24·1'	2°3·2'W	T	109
Marple Dale	Stock	SJ9489	53°24·1'	2°5·0'W	X	109
Marpleridge	Stock	SJ9587	53°23·0'	2°4·1'W	T	109
Marquis Drive	Staffs	SJ9918	52°45·8'	2°0·5'W	X	127
Marquis's Drive	Staffs	SK0215	52°44·2'	1°57·8'W	X	128
Marquis' Well	Highld	NJ0004	57°7·2'	3°38·6'W	W	36
Marr	D & G	NS8401	55°17·6'	3°49·2'W	X	78
Marr	Donc	SE5105	53°32·6'	1°13·4'W	T	111
Marra Flaeshins	Shetld	HU5265	60°22·2'	1°2·9'W	X	2,3
Marramatte	E Yorks	SE9164	54°4·1'	0°36·1'W	X	101
Marram Hills	Norf	TG4426	52°46·8'	1°37·5'E	X	134
Marrams, The	Norf	TG0245	52°58·1'	1°0·9'E	W	133
Marraway	Warw	SP2360	52°14·5'	1°39·4'W	X	151
Marrbottom Plantn	E Yorks	TA0049	53°55·9'	0°28·2'W	F	106,107
Marr Burn	D & G	NX8498	55°16·0'	3°49·1'W	W	78
Marrel	Highld	ND0117	58°8·1'	3°40·4'W	T	17
Marr Grange	Donc	SE5204	53°32·0'	1°12·5'W	X	111
Marr Grange	E Yorks	SE8528	53°44·7'	0°42·3'W	X	106
Marr Green	Wilts	SU2260	51°20·6'	1°40·7'W	T	174
Marr Hall Fm	Donc	SE5105	53°32·6'	1°13·4'W	FM	111
Marr Ho	E Yorks	SE8627	53°44·2'	0°41·4'W	X	106
Marr Ho	N Yks	SE8273	54°9·0'	0°44·3'W	X	100
Marriage Fm	Kent	TR0747	51°11·3'	0°58·1'E	FM	179,189
Marriage Hill	Warw	SP0851	52°9·7'	1°52·6'W	X	150
Marrick	N Yks	SE0798	54°22·9'	1°53·1'W	T	99
Marrick Moor	N Yks	NZ0500	54°24·0'	1°55·0'W	X	92
Marrick Park	N Yks	SE0998	54°22·9'	1°51·3'W	X	99
Marridge Fm	Devon	SX7054	50°22·5'	3°49·3'W	FM	202
Marridge Hill	Wilts	SU2874	51°28·1'	1°35·4'W	X	174
Marriforth Fm	N Yks	SE1987	54°16·9'	1°42·1'W	FM	99
Marriners Fm	Hants	SU6129	51°3·7'	1°7·4'W	FM	185
Marrington	Shrops	SO2796	52°33·7'	3°4·2'W	X	137
Marrington Hall	Shrops	SO2797	52°34·2'	3°4·2'W	A	137
Marriott's Drove Fm	Cambs	TL3091	52°30·3'	0°4·7'W	FM	142
Marriotts Way	Norf	TG1317	52°42·7'	1°9·6'E	X	133
Marrister	Shetld	HU5464	60°21·6'	1°0·8'W	T	2
Marrival	N Eil	NF8070	57°36·6'	7°21·1'W	H	18
Marro Field	Shetld	HU3960	60°19·6'	1°17·1'W	H	2,3
Marrofield Water	Shetld	HU3859	60°19·1'	1°18·2'W	W	2,3
Marrogh	N Eil	NF8269	57°36·2'	7°19·0'W	H	18
Marros	Carm	SN2008	51°44·7'	4°36·1'W	T	158
Marros Beacon	Carm	SN2008	51°44·7'	4°36·1'W	H	158
Marros Mountain	Carm	SN1909	51°45·3'	4°37·0'W	H	158
Marros Sands	Carm	SN2007	51°44·2'	4°36·0'W	X	158
Marrowbones Hill	Hants	SU1907	50°52·0'	1°43·4'W	X	195
Marrow Flatts Fm	N Yks	SE3672	54°8·8'	1°26·5'W	FM	99
Marrs Beck	N Yks	SE6776	54°10·8'	0°58·0'W	W	100
Marrs, The	N Yks	SE8273	54°9·0'	0°44·3'W	X	100
Marr Wood	N Yks	SE6485	54°15·6'	1°0·6'W	F	94,100
Marscalloch	D & G	NX6091	55°11·9'	4°11·5'W	X	77
Marsco	Highld	NG5025	57°15·1'	6°8·2'W	H	32
Marsden	Glos	SP0111	51°48·1'	1°58·7'W	X	163
Marsden	Kirk	SE0411	53°36·0'	1°56·0'W	T	110
Marsden	S Tyne	NZ3964	54°58·4'	1°23·0'W	T	88
Marsden Bay	S Tyne	NZ4065	54°58·9'	1°22·1'W	W	88
Marsden Clough	Kirk	SE0907	53°33·8'	1°51·4'W	X	110
Marsden Hall	Lancs	SD8838	53°50·5'	2°10·5'W	X	103
Marsden Hall	S Tyne	NZ3964	54°58·4'	1°23·0'W	X	88
Marsden Height	Lancs	SD8636	53°49·4'	2°12·3'W	T	103
Marsett	N Yks	SD9086	54°16·4'	2°8·8'W	T	98
Marsh	Brad	SE0235	53°48·9'	1°57·8'W	T	104
Marsh	Bucks	SP8109	51°46·7'	0°49·2'W	T	165
Marsh	Corn	SS2305	50°49·3'	4°30·4'W	X	190
Marsh	Devon	ST2510	50°53·3'	3°3·6'W	T	192,193
Marsh	Kirk	SE1217	53°39·2'	1°48·7'W	T	110
Marshall	Corn	SX3189	50°40·8'	4°23·2'W	X	190
Marshall Fm	Devon	SS3118	50°56·4'	4°24·0'W	FM	190
Marshall Fm	Devon	SX8888	50°41·1'	3°34·7'W	FM	192
Marshall Fm	Lincs	TF3474	53°15·0'	0°0·9'E	FM	122
Marshall Lands Fm	Ghead	NZ2160	54°56·3'	1°39·9'W	FM	88
Marshall Meadows	Northum	NT9756	55°48·1'	2°2·4'W	T	75
Marshall Meadows Bay	Northum	NT9856	55°48·1'	2°1·5'W	W	75
Marshall Moor	Renf	NS3762	55°49·7'	4°35·7'W	X	63
Marshall's	Herts	TL3618	51°50·0'	0°1·1'W	X	166
Marshall's Covert	N Lincs	TA0513	53°36·4'	0°24·4'W	F	112
Marshall's Cross	St Hel	SJ5192	53°25·6'	2°43·8'W	T	108
Marshall's Elm	Somer	ST4834	51°6·4'	2°44·2'W	T	182
Marshall's Fm	Kent	TQ8556	51°16·6'	0°39·5'E	FM	178
Marshall's Fm	Lincs	TF2022	52°47·2'	0°12·8'W	FM	131
Marshall's Fm	Warr	SJ6690	53°24·6'	2°30·3'W	FM	109
Marshall's Fm	W Susx	TQ0124	51°0·6'	0°33·2'W	FM	197
Marshalls Heath	Herts	TL1615	51°49·5'	0°18·6'W	T	166
Marshalls, The	Cumbr	NY2336	54°43·0'	3°11·3'W	X	89,90
Marshalsea	Dorset	ST3800	50°48·0'	2°52·4'W	T	193
Marshalswick	Herts	TL1608	51°45·7'	0°18·8'W	T	166
Marsham	Norf	TG1924	52°46·4'	1°15·2'E	T	133,134
Marsham Heath	Norf	TG1723	52°45·9'	1°13·4'E	X	133,134
Marsham Sewer	E Susx	TQ8813	50°53·4'	0°40·8'E	W	199
Marshaw	Lancs	SD5953	53°58·5'	2°37·1'W	X	102
Marshaw Fell	Lancs	SD6052	53°58·0'	2°36·2'W	X	102,103
Marshaw Wyre	Lancs	SD5853	53°58·5'	2°38·0'W	W	102
Marshay Fm	Devon	SS8809	50°52·4'	3°35·1'W	FM	192
Marsh Baldon	Oxon	SU5699	51°41·4'	1°11·0'W	T	164
Marsh Barn	Shrops	SO4683	52°26·8'	2°47·3'W	X	137,138
Marshbarn Fm	Somer	ST7124	51°1·2'	2°24·4'W	FM	183
Marsh Barn Fm	Staffs	SK0916	52°44·7'	1°51·6'W	FM	128
Marsh Barton	Devon	SX9788	50°41·2'	3°27·1'W	X	192
Marsh Benham	W Berks	SU4267	51°24·3'	1°23·4'W	T	174
Marshborough	Kent	TR3057	51°16·2'	1°18·2'E	T	179
Marsh Br	Dorset	SY9098	50°47·1'	2°8·1'W	X	195
Marshbrook	Shrops	SO4389	52°30·0'	2°50·0'W	T	137
Marshchapel	Lincs	TF3599	53°28·5'	0°2·5'E	T	113
Marshchapel Ings	Lincs	TF3597	53°27·4'	0°2·4'E	X	113
Marsh Common	Dorset	ST8319	50°58·4'	2°14·1'W	X	183
Marsh Common	S Glos	ST5683	51°32·8'	2°37·7'W	T	172
Marsh Common	Worcs	SO8942	52°4·8'	2°9·2'W	X	150
Marsh Cott	E Yorks	TA2324	53°42·1'	0°7·8'W	X	107,113
Marsh Cott	E Yorks	TA3917	53°38·1'	0°6·6'E	X	113
Marsh Court	Dorset	ST6713	50°55·2'	2°27·8'W	X	194
Marsh Court	Hants	SU3533	51°5·9'	1°29·6'W	X	185
Marsh Court	Heref	SO4241	52°4·1'	2°50·4'W	X	148,149,161
Marsh Court	Somer	ST7425	51°1·7'	2°21·9'W	X	183
Marsh Court	Worcs	SO8032	51°59·4'	2°17·1'W	X	150
Marsh Ct	Heref	SO5851	52°9·6'	2°36·4'W	X	149
Marsh End	Worcs	SO8135	52°1·0'	2°16·2'W	T	150
Marsh End Sand	Essex	TQ8583	51°31·2'	0°40·4'E	X	178
Marshes Fm	Bolton	SD6404	53°32·1'	2°32·2'W	FM	109
Marshes Fm	Somer	ST0526	51°1·8'	3°20·9'W	FM	181
Marshes Gill	Durham	NY8232	54°41·2'	2°16·3'W	X	91,92
Marshes Hill Fm	Somer	ST5418	50°57·8'	2°38·9'W	FM	183
Marshes, The	Glos	SO7405	51°44·8'	2°22·2'W	X	162
Marshes, The	Stock on T	NZ4619	54°34·1'	1°16·9'W	X	93
Marshes, The	Wilts	ST8726	51°2·2'	2°10·7'W	X	183
Marsh Farm	Luton	TL0625	51°55·0'	0°27·1'W	FM	166
Marsh Farm East	Lincs	TF5258	53°6·1'	0°16·6'E	X	122
Marsh Farmhouse	Devon	SY2496	50°45·8'	3°4·3'W	X	192,193
Marsh Field	Cumbr	SD2283	54°14·5'	3°11·4'W	X	96
Marshfield	Newp	ST2582	51°32·2'	3°4·5'W	T	171
Marshfield	S Glos	ST7773	51°27·6'	2°19·5'W	T	172
Marshfield Bank	Ches	SJ6755	53°5·7'	2°29·2'W	T	118
Marshfield Bridge	Ches	SJ6755	53°5·7'	2°29·2'W	X	118
Marsh-Field Fm	Bucks	SP6321	51°53·3'	1°4·7'W	FM	164,165
Marsh Flatts	Derby	SK3930	52°52·2'	1°24·8'W	X	128
Marsh Fm	Beds	SP9455	52°11·3'	0°37·1'W	FM	153
Marsh Fm	Bucks	SP7213	51°48·9'	0°56·9'W	FM	165
Marsh Fm	Cambs	TF4515	52°43·0'	0°9·2'E	FM	131
Marsh Fm	Ches	SJ7071	53°14·4'	2°26·6'W	FM	118
Marsh Fm	Ches	SJ7483	53°20·8'	2°23·0'W	FM	109
Marsh Fm	Ches	SJ9474	53°16·0'	2°5·0'W	FM	118
Marsh Fm	Derby	SK4278	53°18·1'	1°21·8'W	FM	120
Marsh Fm	Devon	SS8607	50°51·3'	3°36·8'W	FM	191
Marsh Fm	Devon	SS9415	50°55·7'	3°30·1'W	FM	181
Marsh Fm	Devon	ST0401	50°48·3'	3°21·4'W	FM	192
Marsh Fm	Devon	SY2599	50°47·4'	3°3·5'W	FM	192,193
Marsh Fm	Dorset	ST5000	50°48·1'	2°42·2'W	FM	194
Marsh Fm	Dorset	ST7516	50°56·8'	2°21·0'W	FM	183
Marsh Fm	Dorset	ST7808	50°52·4'	2°18·4'W	FM	194
Marsh Fm	Dorset	SY3597	50°46·4'	2°54·9'W	FM	193
Marsh Fm	Dorset	SY5295	50°45·4'	2°40·4'W	FM	194
Marsh Fm	Dorset	SY6085	50°40·0'	2°33·6'W	FM	194
Marsh Fm	Dorset	SY8797	50°46·6'	2°10·7'W	FM	194
Marsh Fm	Essex	TL5817	51°50·0'	0°18·0'E	FM	167
Marsh Fm	Essex	TM0521	51°51·2'	0°59·0'E	FM	168
Marsh Fm	Essex	TQ7186	51°33·0'	0°28·4'E	FM	178
Marsh Fm	Glos	SP1719	51°52·4'	1°44·8'W	FM	163
Marsh Fm	Hants	SU1117	50°57·4'	1°50·2'W	FM	184
Marsh Fm	Heref	SO5646	52°6·9'	2°38·2'W	FM	149
Marsh Fm	Herts	TL0311	51°47·5'	0°30·0'W	FM	166
Marsh Fm	Lancs	SD3342	53°52·4'	3°0·7'W	FM	102
Marsh Fm	Lancs	SD4023	53°42·2'	2°54·1'W	FM	102
Marsh Fm	Lancs	SD4523	53°42·3'	2°49·6'W	FM	102
Marsh Fm	Lancs	SD4928	53°45·0'	2°46·0'W	FM	102
Marsh Fm	Lincs	TF2434	52°53·6'	0°9·0'W	FM	131
Marsh Fm	Lincs	TF2728	52°50·3'	0°6·5'W	FM	131
Marsh Fm	Lincs	TF3528	52°50·2'	0°0·7'E	FM	131
Marsh Fm	Lincs	TF3529	52°50·7'	0°0·7'E	FM	131
Marsh Fm	Lincs	TF3539	52°56·1'	0°0·9'E	FM	131
Marsh Fm	Lincs	TF3740	52°56·6'	0°2·7'E	FM	131
Marsh Fm	Lincs	TF4450	53°1·9'	0°9·3'E	FM	122
Marsh Fm	Lincs	TF5461	53°7·7'	0°18·5'E	FM	122
Marsh Fm	N Lincs	SE9223	53°42·0'	0°36·0'W	FM	106,112
Marsh Fm	Norf	TF5921	52°46·0'	0°21·8'E	FM	131
Marsh Fm	Norf	TF6225	52°48·1'	0°24·6'E	FM	132
Marsh Fm	Norf	TF6528	52°49·7'	0°27·4'E	FM	132
Marsh Fm	Norf	TG4212	52°39·3'	1°35·1'E	FM	134
Marsh Fm	Oxon	SP4100	51°42·1'	1°24·0'W	FM	164
Marsh Fm	S Glos	ST7076	51°29·2'	2°25·5'W	FM	172
Marsh Fm	Shrops	SO4488	52°29·5'	2°49·1'W	FM	137
Marsh Fm	Shrops	SO5786	52°28·5'	2°37·6'W	FM	137,138
Marsh Fm	Somer	ST2544	51°11·7'	3°4·0'W	FM	182
Marsh Fm	Somer	ST5009	50°52·9'	2°42·3'W	FM	194
Marsh Fm	Somer	ST7845	51°12·5'	2°18·5'W	FM	183
Marsh Fm	Staffs	SJ8031	52°52·8'	2°17·4'W	FM	127
Marsh Fm	Staffs	SK0626	52°50·1'	1°54·3'W	FM	128
Marsh Fm	Suff	TM0236	51°59·4'	0°56·9'E	FM	155
Marsh Fm	Suff	TM3860	52°11·4'	1°29·3'E	FM	156
Marsh Fm	Suff	TM4586	52°25·2'	1°36·6'E	FM	156
Marsh Fm	Warw	SP0752	52°10·2'	1°53·5'W	FM	150
Marsh Fm	Wilts	ST9391	51°37·3'	2°5·7'W	FM	163,173
Marsh Fm	Wilts	ST9658	51°19·5'	2°3·1'W	FM	173
Marsh Fm	Wilts	SU0458	51°19·5'	1°56·2'W	FM	173
Marsh Fm	Wilts	SU0476	51°29·2'	1°56·2'W	FM	173
Marsh Fm	W Susx	SU8802	50°48·9'	0°44·7'W	FM	197
Marsh Fm	W Susx	SU9804	50°49·9'	0°36·1'W	FM	197
Marsh Fm	W Susx	SZ8296	50°45·7'	0°49·9'W	FM	197
Marsh Fm	W Susx	SZ8698	50°46·7'	0°46·4'W	FM	197
Marsh Fm Country Park	Essex	TQ8196	51°38·2'	0°37·3'E	FM	168
Marsh Foot Fm	E Susx	TQ6508	50°51·1'	0°21·0'E	FM	199
Marshford Fm	Devon	SS5301	50°47·6'	4°4·8'W	FM	191
Marshgate	Corn	SX1591	50°41·6'	4°36·8'W	T	190
Marsh Gate	Cumbr	SD6994	54°20·7'	2°28·2'W	X	98
Marsh Gate	W Berks	SU3268	51°24·8'	1°32·0'W	T	174
Marshgate Fm	Ches	SJ5378	53°18·1'	2°41·9'W	FM	117
Marshgate Fm	Halton	SJ5583	53°20·8'	2°40·1'W	FM	108
Marsh Gibbon	Bucks	SP6423	51°54·3'	1°3·8'W	T	164,165
Marsh Grange	Cumbr	SD2279	54°12·3'	3°11·3'W	X	96
Marsh Grange	Lincs	TF4198	53°27·8'	0°7·9'E	X	113
Marsh Green	Ches	SJ5177	53°17·5'	2°43·7'W	T	117
Marsh Green	Derby	SK3463	53°10·0'	1°29·1'W	X	119
Marsh Green	Devon	SY0493	50°44·0'	3°21·2'W	T	192
Marsh Green	Kent	TQ4444	51°10·8'	0°4·0'E	T	187
Marsh Green	Staffs	SJ8859	53°7·9'	2°10·4'W	T	118
Marsh Green	Wigan	SD5506	53°33·2'	2°40·3'W	T	108
Marsh Green	Wrekin	SJ6014	52°43·6'	2°35·1'W	T	127
Marsh Green Fm	I of W	SZ4281	50°37·9'	1°24·0'W	FM	196
Marsh Hall	Derby	SK0479	53°18·7'	1°56·0'W	X	119

Marsh Hall	Heref	SO5065	52°17·1′	2°43·6′W	X	137,138,149
Marsh Hall (Hotel)	Devon	SS7227	51°1·9′	3°49·1′W	X	180
Marsh Hill Fm	Bucks	SP8008	51°46·1′	0°50·0′W	FM	165
Marsh Hill Fm	Donc	SE6417	53°39·0′	1°1·5′W	FM	111
Marsh Hill Ho	Essex	TL3903	51°42·7′	0°1·1′E	X	166
Marsh Hill Ho	Somer	SS9029	51°3·2′	3°33·8′W	X	181
Marsh Ho	Ches	SJ4354	53°5·1′	2°50·7′W	X	117
Marsh Ho	Essex	TM0103	51°41·6′	0°54·9′E	X	168
Marsh Ho	Essex	TM2223	51°51·9′	1°13·9′E	X	169
Marsh Ho	E Yorks	TA2223	53°41·6′	0°8·7′W	X	107,113
Marsh Ho	Hants	SU7944	51°11·6′	0°51·8′W	X	186
Marsh Ho	Heref	SO5045	52°6·3′	2°43·4′W	X	149
Marsh Ho	I of W	SZ6088	50°41·5′	1°8·6′W	X	196
Marsh Ho	Lancs	SD6033	53°47·8′	2°36·0′W	X	102,103
Marsh Ho	Staffs	SJ9640	52°57·7′	2°3·2′W	X	118
Marsh Ho	Staffs	SK0961	53°9·0′	1°51·5′W	X	119
Marsh Ho Fm	Lancs	SD4870	54°7·6′	2°47·3′W	FM	97
Marshhouse Decoy Pond	Essex	TM0104	51°42·1′	0°54·9′E	W	168
Marsh House Fm	Essex	TQ8698	51°39·2′	0°41·7′E	FM	168
Marsh House Fm	Hartpl	NZ5026	54°37·8′	1°13·1′W	FM	93
Marsh House Fm	Heref	SO4237	52°1·9′	2°50·3′W	FM	149,161
Marsh House Fm	Lincs	TF5167	53°10·9′	0°16·0′E	FM	122
Marsh House Fm	Norf	TF8644	52°57·9′	0°46·6′E	FM	132
Marshhouse Outfall	Essex	TM0304	51°42·1′	0°56·7′E	W	168
Marsh Houses	Lancs	SD4551	53°57·4′	2°49·9′W	T	102
Mars Hill	Warw	SP0964	52°16·7′	1°51·7′W	F	150
Marshland	E Yorks	SE7820	53°40·5′	0°48·7′W	X	105,106,112
Marshland	Norf	TF5213	52°41·8′	0°15·4′E	X	131,143
Marshland Fen	Norf	TF5407	52°38·6′	0°17·0′E	X	143
Marshland Green	Wigan	SJ6899	53°29·4′	2°28·5′W	X	109
Marshland St James	Norf	TF5109	52°39·7′	0°14·4′E	T	143
Marshland Wood	Herts	TL4215	51°49·2′	0°4·0′E	F	167
Marsh Lane	Derby	SK4079	53°18·6′	1°23·6′W	T	120
Marsh Lane	Glos	SO5807	51°45·8′	2°36·1′W	T	162
Marsh Lane Fm	Ches	SJ6078	53°18·1′	2°35·6′W	FM	118
Marsh Lane Fm	Ches	SJ7766	53°11·7′	2°20·2′W	FM	118
Marsh Lane Fm	Lincs	TF3990	53°23·5′	0°5·8′E	FM	113
Marsh Leys	Beds	TL0245	52°5·9′	0°30·3′W	X	153
Marsh Mill Fm	Bucks	SP8109	51°46·7′	0°49·2′W	FM	165
Marsh Mills	Somer	ST1938	51°8·4′	3°9·1′W	T	181
Marshmoor	Herts	TL2306	51°44·6′	0°12·7′W	T	166
Marsh Moss Ho	Lancs	SD4313	53°36·9′	2°51·3′W	X	108
Marsh Plantation	Devon	SX8883	50°38·4′	3°34·7′W	F	192
Marsh Quarter Fm	Kent	TQ8026	51°0·5′	0°34·3′E	FM	188,199
Marshside	Kent	TR2266	51°21·2′	1°11·7′E	T	179
Marsh Side	Norf	TF7744	52°58·1′	0°38·6′E	T	132
Marshside	Sefton	SD3619	53°40·1′	2°57·7′W	T	108
Marshside Cotts	Cumbr	SD0890	54°18·1′	3°24·4′W	X	96
Marshside Sands	Sefton	SD3421	53°41·1′	2°59·6′W	X	102
Marsh's Pool	Powys	SN9281	52°25·2′	3°34·9′W	W	136
Marsh Street	Somer	SS9944	51°11·4′	3°26·3′W	T	181
Marsh, The	Essex	TL5417	51°50·0′	0°14·5′E	W	167
Marsh, The	E Yorks	TA2323	53°41·6′	0°7·8′W	X	107,113
Marsh, The	Flint	SJ1978	53°17·8′	3°12·5′W	X	116
Marsh, The	Heref	SO4959	52°13·8′	2°44·4′W	X	148,149
Marsh, The	Powys	SO3197	52°34·2′	3°0·7′W	T	137
Marsh, The	Shrops	SO6499	52°35·5′	2°31·5′W	X	138
Marsh, The	Somer	ST7845	51°12·5′	2°18·5′W	X	183
Marsh, The	Wilts	SU0783	51°33·0′	1°53·6′W	X	173
Marshwood	Dorset	SY3899	50°47·5′	2°52·4′W	T	193
Marshwood Fm	Somer	ST0242	51°10·4′	3°23·7′W	FM	181
Marshwood Fm	Somer	ST3405	50°50·7′	2°55·9′W	FM	193
Marshwood Fm	Wilts	SU0032	51°5·5′	1°59·6′W	FM	184
Marshwood Manor	Dorset	SY3999	50°47·5′	2°51·5′W	X	193
Marshwood Vale	Dorset	SY4097	50°46·4′	2°50·7′W	X	193
Marsh Yard	Lincs	TF4955	53°4·5′	0°13·9′E	X	122
Marskaig	D & G	NX6388	55°10·3′	4°8·6′W	X	77
Marske	N Yks	NZ1000	54°24·0′	1°50·3′W	T	92
Marske Beck	N Yks	NZ0901	54°24·5′	1°51·3′W	W	92
Marske-By-The-Sea	Red & Cl	NZ6322	54°35·6′	1°1·1′W	T	94
Marske Mill	Red & Cl	NZ6620	54°34·5′	0°58·3′W	X	94
Marske Moor	N Yks	NZ1002	54°25·0′	1°50·3′W	X	92
Marske Sands	Red & Cl	NZ6422	54°35·6′	1°0·1′W	X	94
Marsland Cliff	Corn	SS2017	50°55·7′	4°33·3′W	X	190
Marsland Fm	Warw	SP2984	52°27·4′	1°34·0′W	FM	140
Marsland Manor	Corn	SS2116	50°55·2′	4°32·4′W	A	190
Marsland Mouth	Corn	SS2017	50°55·7′	4°33·3′W	W	190
Marsland Water	Devon	SS2317	50°55·8′	4°30·7′W	W	190
Marslauch	D & G	NX0167	54°57·7′	5°6·1′W	X	82
Marsley Fm	Shrops	SJ3902	52°37·0′	2°53·7′W	FM	126
Marstage Fm	Devon	SS4835	51°5·9′	4°9·9′W	FM	180
Marstan Ho	Northnts	SP8270	52°19·5′	0°47·4′W	X	141
Marston	Ches	SJ6675	53°16·5′	2°30·2′W	T	118
Marston	Heref	SO3657	52°12·7′	2°55·8′W	T	148,149
Marston	Lincs	SK8943	52°58·9′	0°40·1′W	T	130
Marston	Oxon	SP5208	51°46·3′	1°14·4′W	T	164
Marston	Staffs	SJ8314	52°43·6′	2°14·7′W	T	127
Marston	Staffs	SJ9227	52°50·7′	2°6·7′W	T	127
Marston	Warw	SP2094	52°32·8′	1°41·9′W	T	139
Marston	Warw	SP4276	52°23·1′	1°22·6′W	T	140
Marston	Wilts	ST9656	51°18·4′	2°3·1′W	T	173
Marston Bigot	Somer	ST7544	51°11·9′	2°21·1′W	T	183
Marston Brook	Derby	SK1236	52°55·5′	1°48·9′W	W	128
Marston Brook	Staffs	SJ9226	52°50·1′	2°6·7′W	W	127
Marston Doles	Warw	SP4658	52°13·3′	1°19·2′W	T	151
Marston Farm Hotel	Warw	SP1995	52°33·4′	1°42·8′W	X	139
Marstonfields Fm	Bucks	SP7823	51°54·2′	0°51·6′W	FM	165
Marston Fm	Staffs	SJ9227	52°50·7′	2°6·7′W	FM	127
Marston Gate	Somer	ST7646	51°13·0′	2°20·2′W	T	183
Marstongate Fm	Staffs	SJ9126	52°50·1′	2°7·6′W	FM	127
Marston Grange	N Yks	SE4852	53°58·0′	1°15·7′W	X	105
Marston Grange	Worcs	SP1546	52°7·0′	1°46·5′W	X	151
Marston Green	Sol	SP1785	52°28·0′	1°44·6′W	T	139
Marston Hall	Ches	SJ6676	53°17·0′	2°30·2′W	X	118
Marston Hill	Warw	SP3148	52°8·0′	1°32·4′W	X	151
Marston Hill	Warw	SP4958	52°13·3′	1°16·6′W	H	151
Marston Hill	Wilts	SU1399	51°41·6′	1°48·3′W	T	163
Marstonhill Fm	Northnts	SP5443	52°5·2′	1°12·3′W	FM	152
Marston Ho	Somer	ST7545	51°12·5′	2°21·1′W	X	183
Marston Jabbett	Warw	SP3788	52°29·6′	1°26·9′W	T	140
Marston Junction	Warw	SP3688	52°29·6′	1°27·8′W	W	140
Marston Lodge	N Yks	SE4949	53°56·3′	1°14·8′W	X	105
Marston Lodge Fm	Northnts	SP6884	52°27·2′	0°59·6′W	FM	141
Marston Magna	Somer	ST5922	51°0·0′	2°34·7′W	T	183
Marston Meysey	Wilts	SU1297	51°40·5′	1°49·2′W	T	163
Marston Montgomery	Derby	SK1337	52°56·1′	1°48·0′W	T	128
Marston Moor	N Yks	SE4953	53°58·5′	1°14·8′W	X	105
Marston Moor Fm	N Yks	SE5053	53°58·5′	1°13·8′W	FM	105
Marston Moretaine	Beds	SP9941	52°3·7′	0°33·0′W	T	153
Marston on Dove	Derby	SK2329	52°51·7′	1°39·1′W	T	128
Marston Park	Derby	SK1339	52°57·1′	1°48·0′W	X	128
Marston Stannett	Heref	SO5655	52°11·7′	2°38·2′W	T	149
Marston St Lawrence	Northnts	SP5342	52°4·7′	1°13·2′W	T	152
Marston Thrift (Nature Reserve)	Beds	SP9741	52°3·8′	0°34·7′W	F	153
Marston Trussell	Northnts	SP6985	52°27·7′	0°58·7′W	T	141
Marston Village	Somer	ST7744	51°11·9′	2°19·4′W	A	183
Marston Wood	Somer	ST7840	51°9·8′	2°18·5′W	F	183
Marston Woodhouse	Derby	SK1336	52°55·5′	1°48·0′W	X	128
Marston Wyes	N Yks	SE4850	53°56·9′	1°15·7′W	X	105
Marstow	Heref	SO5519	51°52·3′	2°38·8′W	T	162
Marsworth	Bucks	SP9214	51°49·3′	0°39·5′W	T	165
Martclose	Cumbr	NY5502	54°24·9′	2°41·2′W	X	90
Mart Crag	Cumbr	NY3004	54°25·8′	3°4·3′W	X	90
Martcrag Moor	Cumbr	NY2608	54°28·0′	3°8·1′W	X	89,90
Martel Fm	Pemb	SM9829	51°55·6′	4°55·9′W	FM	157,158
Martells Hall	Essex	TM0528	51°55·0′	0°59·3′E	X	168
Martels	Essex	TL6319	51°51·0′	0°22·4′E	X	167
Marten	Wilts	SU2860	51°20·5′	1°35·5′W	T	174
Marten Fm	Kent	TR0729	51°1·6′	0°57·5′E	FM	189
Marten Hill	Staffs	SK1447	53°1·4′	1°47·1′W	X	119,128
Marthall	Ches	SJ8075	53°16·5′	2°17·6′W	T	118
Marthall Brook	Ches	SJ7877	53°17·6′	2°19·4′W	W	118
Martham	Norf	TG4518	52°42·5′	1°38·0′E	T	134
Martham Broad	Norf	TG4520	52°43·5′	1°38·1′E	W	134
Martham Ferry	Norf	TG4419	52°43·0′	1°37·2′E	X	134
Martholme	Lancs	SD7533	53°47·8′	2°22·4′W	A	103
Marthrown Hill	D & G	NX9371	55°1·6′	3°40·0′W	H	84
Marthrown of Mabie	D & G	NX9371	55°1·6′	3°40·0′W	X	84
Marthwaite	Cumbr	SD6491	54°19·0′	2°32·8′W	T	97
Martin	Devon	SX6892	50°43·0′	3°51·8′W	X	191
Martin	Hants	SU0619	50°58·5′	1°54·5′W	T	184
Martin	Kent	TR3347	51°10·7′	1°20·4′E	T	179
Martin	Lincs	TF1259	53°7·2′	0°19·2′W	T	121
Martin	Lincs	TF2366	53°10·8′	0°9·2′W	T	122
Martinagap	Cumbr	NY6107	54°27·7′	2°35·7′W	X	91
Martin Beck	Donc	SK6294	53°26·6′	1°3·6′W	W	111
Martin Cleuch	S Lanak	NT0123	55°29·7′	3°33·6′W	X	72
Martin Common Fm	Donc	SK6395	53°27·1′	1°2·7′W	FM	111
Martindale	Cumbr	NY4319	54°34·0′	2°52·5′W	T	90
Martindale Common	Cumbr	NY4317	54°33·0′	2°52·5′W	X	90
Martin Dales	Lincs	TF1761	53°8·2′	0°14·7′W	T	121
Martin Down	Hants	SU0419	50°58·5′	1°56·2′W	X	184
Martin Drove End	Hants	SU0521	50°59·5′	1°55·3′W	T	184
Martin Fen	Lincs	TF1461	53°8·3′	0°17·3′W	X	121
Martin Field Ho	Durham	NZ1527	54°38·5′	1°45·6′W	X	92
Martingirth	D & G	NX9668	55°0·0′	3°37·1′W	X	84
Martin Glen	N Ayr	NS2367	55°52·1′	4°49·3′W	X	63
Martin Grange	Donc	SK6494	53°26·6′	1°1·8′W	X	111
Martin Hall	Lancs	SD4212	53°36·3′	2°52·2′W	X	108
Martin Hill	Pemb	SN0711	51°46·1′	4°47·4′W	X	158
Martin Hill Fm	York	SE5961	54°2·7′	1°5·5′W	FM	100
Martinhoe	Devon	SS6648	51°13·2′	3°54·7′W	T	180
Martinhoe Common	Devon	SS6747	51°12·6′	3°53·9′W	H	180
Martinhoe Cross	Devon	SS6846	51°12·1′	3°53·0′W	T	180
Martinholme Fm	N Yks	SE8260	54°2·0′	0°44·5′W	FM	100
Martin Hussingtree	Worcs	SO8860	52°14·5′	2°10·1′W	T	150
Martinlee Plantn	Scot Bord	NT6507	55°21·6′	2°32·7′W	F	80
Martin Mere	Lancs	SD4214	53°37·4′	2°52·2′W	X	108
Martin Mill	Kent	TR3446	51°10·1′	1°21·2′E	T	179
Martin Moor	Lincs	TF2164	53°9·8′	0°11·0′W	T	122
Martins	Essex	TL9732	51°57·3′	0°52·4′E	X	168
Martin's Ash	Shrops	SJ5742	52°58·7′	2°38·0′W	X	117
Martin's Castle	Heref	SO6460	52°14·5′	2°31·2′W	X	138,149
Martin's Clump	Hants	SU2538	51°8·7′	1°38·2′W	X	184
Martin's Copse	Hants	SZ1799	50°47·6′	1°45·1′W	F	195
Martin's Corner	Hants	SU6112	50°54·5′	1°7·6′W	X	196
Martinscroft	Warr	SJ6589	53°24·0′	2°31·2′W	T	109
Martin's Down	Dorset	SY5790	50°42·7′	2°36·2′W	X	194
Martinsell Hill	Wilts	SU1763	51°22·2′	1°45·0′W	H	173
Martinsell Hill (Fort)	Wilts	SU1763	51°22·2′	1°45·0′W	A	173
Martin's Fm	Essex	TL6838	52°1·1′	0°27·3′E	FM	154
Martins Fm	Lincs	TF2913	52°42·2′	0°5·0′W	FM	131,142
Martin's Fm	Somer	ST2212	50°54·4′	3°6·2′W	FM	193
Martin's Fm	Suff	TM3970	52°16·8′	1°30·6′E	FM	156
Martin's Folly	N Yks	SE3989	54°17·9′	1°23·6′W	X	99
Martin's Glen	Suff	TM1036	51°59·2′	1°3·5′E	X	155,169
Martin's Haven	Pemb	SM7609	51°44·3′	5°14·3′W	W	157
Martinshaw Fm	E Susx	TQ8023	50°58·9′	0°34·3′E	FM	199
Martinshaw Wood	Leic	SK5007	52°39·7′	1°15·2′W	F	140
Martin's Heron	Brackn	SU8968	51°24·5′	0°42·8′W	X	175
Martin's Hill	Glos	SP2125	51°55·6′	1°41·3′W	X	163
Martinshouse	Scot Bord	NT4813	55°24·7′	2°48·8′W	X	79
Martinside	Derby	SK0679	53°18·7′	1°54·2′W	X	119
Martinside	S Lanak	NS7138	55°37·4′	4°2·5′W	H	71
Martinslade	Wilts	ST9561	51°21·1′	2°3·9′W	X	173
Martin's Low	Staffs	SK0752	53°4·2′	1°53·3′W	X	119
Martin's Moss	Ches	SJ8060	53°8·4′	2°17·5′W	T	118
Martin's Plantn	N Yks	SE5974	54°9·7′	1°5·4′W	X	100
Martin's Rigg	Northum	NY7551	54°51·4′	2°22·9′W	X	86,87
Martin's Stone	Angus	NO3737	56°31·5′	3°1·0′W	A	54
Martinsthorpe Village	Rut	SK8604	52°37·8′	0°43·4′W	A	141
Martinstown	Dorset	SY6488	50°41·7′	2°30·2′W	T	194
Martin Tarn	Cumbr	NY2551	54°51·1′	3°9·7′W	W	85
Martin Top	Lancs	SD8245	53°54·3′	2°16·0′W	X	103
Martin Top Fm	Herts	TQ0199	51°41·1′	0°31·9′W	FM	166,176
Martin Wood	Hants	SU0616	50°56·8′	1°54·5′W	F	184
Martland	Somer	ST3441	51°10·1′	2°56·3′W	X	182
Martlesham	Suff	TM2547	52°4·8′	1°17·4′E	T	169
Martlesham Creek	Suff	TM2647	52°4·7′	1°18·3′E	W	169
Martlesham Heath	Suff	TM2445	52°3·7′	1°16·5′E	T	169
Martletwy	Pemb	SN0310	51°45·5′	4°50·9′W	T	157,158
Martley	Worcs	SO7559	52°14·0′	2°21·6′W	T	150
Martley Hall	Suff	TM2859	52°11·1′	1°20·5′E	X	156
Martlin Hill	Staffs	SK0520	52°46·9′	1°55·1′W	X	128
Martnaham Loch	E Ayr	NS3917	55°25·5′	4°32·2′W	W	70
Martnaham Mains	E Ayr	NS3916	55°24·9′	4°32·2′W	X	70
Martock	Somer	ST4619	50°58·3′	2°45·8′W	T	193
Marton	Ches	SJ6267	53°12·2′	2°33·7′W	X	118
Marton	Ches	SJ8568	53°12·8′	2°13·1′W	T	118
Marton	Cumbr	SD2477	54°11·2′	3°9·5′W	T	96
Marton	E Yorks	TA1739	53°50·3′	0°12·9′W	T	107
Marton	E Yorks	TA2069	54°6·4′	0°9·5′W	X	101
Marton	Lincs	SK8381	53°19·4′	0°44·8′W	T	121
Marton	Midd	NZ5115	54°31·9′	1°12·3′W	T	93
Marton	N Yks	SE4162	54°3·4′	1°22·0′W	T	99
Marton	N Yks	SE7383	54°14·5′	0°52·4′W	T	100
Marton	Shrops	SJ2802	52°36·9′	3°3·4′W	T	126
Marton	Shrops	SJ4423	52°48·3′	2°49·4′W	T	126
Marton	Warw	SP4068	52°18·8′	1°24·4′W	T	151
Marton Abbey	N Yks	SE5869	54°7·1′	1°6·3′W	X	100
Marton Abbey (Priory)	N Yks	SE5869	54°7·1′	1°6·3′W	A	100
Marton Brook	Ches	SJ8469	53°13·3′	2°14·0′W	W	118
Marton Common Fm	N Yks	SE7283	54°14·5′	0°53·3′W	FM	100
Marton Cottage Fm	N Yks	SE4161	54°2·8′	1°22·0′W	FM	99
Marton Crest	Shrops	SJ2702	52°36·9′	3°4·3′W	X	126
Marton Grange	N Yks	SE5968	54°6·5′	1°5·4′W	X	100
Marton Grange	Shrops	SJ4424	52°48·9′	2°49·5′W	X	126
Marton Green	Ches	SJ6167	53°12·2′	2°34·6′W	T	118
Marton Grove	Midd	NZ4918	54°33·5′	1°14·1′W	T	93
Marton Hall	Ches	SJ8467	53°12·2′	2°14·0′W	X	118
Marton Hall	N Yks	SD8950	53°57·0′	2°9·6′W	X	103
Martonheath	Ches	SJ8669	53°13·3′	2°12·2′W	X	118
Marton Hill	N Yks	SE7283	54°14·5′	0°53·3′W	X	100
Marton Hill	Shrops	SJ2703	52°37·4′	3°4·3′W	X	126
Marton Ho	Cumbr	NY6625	54°37·4′	2°31·2′W	X	91
Marton Hole	Ches	SJ6167	53°12·2′	2°34·6′W	W	118
Marton House Fm	Ches	SJ6266	53°11·6′	2°33·7′W	FM	118
Marton-in-the-Forest	N Yks	SE5968	54°6·5′	1°5·4′W	T	100
Marton-le-Moor	N Yks	SE3770	54°7·7′	1°25·6′W	T	99
Marton Lodge	E Yorks	TA1969	54°6·4′	0°10·4′W	X	101
Marton Mere	Blackp	SD3435	53°48·7′	2°59·7′W	W	102
Marton Moor	Cumbr	NY6625	54°37·4′	2°31·2′W	X	91
Marton Moor	Warw	SP4068	52°18·8′	1°24·4′W	T	151
Marton Moss Side	Blackp	SD3333	53°47·6′	3°0·6′W	T	102
Marton Park	N Yks	SE5869	54°7·1′	1°6·3′W	X	100
Marton Pool	Shrops	SJ2902	52°36·9′	3°2·5′W	W	126
Marton Pool	Shrops	SJ4423	52°48·3′	2°49·4′W	W	126
Marton Priory	N Yks	SE6068	54°6·5′	1°4·5′W	X	100
Martonsands	Ches	SJ6267	53°12·2′	2°33·7′W	X	118
Marton Scar	N Yks	SD8851	53°57·5′	2°10·6′W	X	103
Martour Hill	D & G	NX6995	55°14·2′	4°3·2′W	H	77
Martyrs' Grave	D & G	NX8175	55°3·6′	3°51·4′W	X	84
Martyr's Grave	E Ayr	NS5414	55°24·1′	4°17·9′W	X	70
Martyr's Grave	E Ayr	NS5919	55°26·9′	4°13·3′W	X	71
Martyr's Grave	E Ayr	NS7331	55°33·6′	4°0·4′W	X	71
Martyr's Green	Surrey	TQ0957	51°18·3′	0°25·8′W	T	187
Martyrs' Monument	D & G	NX6659	54°54·7′	4°5·0′W	X	83,84
Martyrs' Moss	E Ayr	NS5112	55°23·0′	4°20·7′W	X	70
Martyr's Stone	D & G	NX7989	55°11·1′	3°53·6′W	A	78
Martyr's Tomb	D & G	NX3978	55°4·5′	4°30·9′W	X	77
Martyrs' Tomb	D & G	NX9079	55°5·8′	3°43·0′W	X	84
Martyrs Tomb	S Ayr	NX2381	55°5·8′	4°46·0′W	X	76
Martyr Worthy	Hants	SU5132	51°5·3′	1°15·9′W	T	185
Marulaig Bay	N Eil	NF8216	57°7·8′	7°14·9′W	W	31
Marvel Fm	I of W	SZ5087	50°41·1′	1°17·1′W	FM	196
Marvel's Garden	Essex	TL8532	51°57·6′	0°42·0′E	X	168
Marven's Pike	Northum	NY5787	55°10·8′	2°40·1′W	X	80
Marvingston	E Loth	NT5065	55°52·8′	2°47·5′W	X	66
Marwell	Devon	SX6547	50°18·7′	3°53·4′W	X	202
Marwell Hall (Zoological Park)	Hants	SU5021	50°59·4′	1°16·9′W	X	185
Marwell Ho	Hants	SU5121	50°59·4′	1°16·0′W	X	185
Marwell Manor	Hants	SU5020	50°58·9′	1°16·9′W	X	185
Marwhirn	D & G	NX7492	55°12·6′	3°58·4′W	X	77
Marwhirn	D & G	NX7973	55°2·5′	3°53·2′W	X	84
Mar Wick	Orkney	HY2224	59°6·0′	3°21·2′W	W	6
Marwick	Orkney	HY2324	59°6·0′	3°20·2′W	T	6
Marwick Head	Orkney	HY2225	59°6·6′	3°21·2′W	X	6
Marwood	Devon	SS5437	51°7·1′	4°4·8′W	T	180
Marwood Fm	Kent	TR0834	51°4·3′	0°58·5′E	FM	179,189
Marwood Grange	Durham	NZ0622	54°35·8′	1°54·0′W	X	92
Marwood Green	Durham	NZ0522	54°35·8′	1°54·9′W	X	92
Marwood House Fm	Lincs	TF0326	52°49·5′	0°27·9′W	FM	130
Marwoods	Devon	SS9619	50°57·9′	3°28·5′W	X	181
Marwood View	Durham	NY9822	54°35·8′	2°1·4′W	X	92
Mary Arden's House	Warw	SP1658	52°13·4′	1°45·5′W	A	151
Marybank	Highld	NH4853	57°32·8′	4°31·9′W	T	26
Marybank	Highld	NH7476	57°45·6′	4°6·6′W	T	21
Marybank	Pth & Kin	NN9930	56°27·3′	3°37·9′W	X	52,53
Mary Bax's Stone	Kent	TR3656	51°15·5′	1°23·3′E	X	179
Maryborough Fm	Pemb	SM8104	51°41·8′	5°9·8′W	FM	157
Maryburgh	Highld	NH5456	57°34·5′	4°26·0′W	T	26
Maryburgh	Pth & Kin	NT1395	56°8·6′	3°23·6′W	X	58
Mary Cross	Devon	SX6652	50°21·4′	3°52·7′W	X	202
Maryculter Ho	Aberd	NO8499	57°5·2′	2°15·4′W	X	38,45
Maryfield	Aberd	NJ6005	57°8·3′	2°39·2′W	X	37
Maryfield	Aberd	NJ7036	57°25·1′	2°29·5′W	X	29
Maryfield	Aberd	NO5698	57°4·5′	2°43·1′W	X	37,44
Maryfield	Aberd	NO7195	57°3·0′	2°28·2′W	X	38,45
Maryfield	Corn	SX4255	50°22·7′	4°13·0′W	T	201
Maryfield	D & G	NX9378	55°5·3′	3°40·2′W	X	84
Maryfield	D & G	NX9766	54°58·9′	3°36·1′W	X	84
Maryfield	D & G	NY0580	55°6·6′	3°28·9′W	X	78
Maryfield	Fife	NO2608	56°15·8′	3°11·2′W	X	59
Maryfield	Pth & Kin	NO1645	56°35·6′	3°21·6′W	X	53
Maryfield	Scot Bord	NT9757	55°48·6′	2°2·4′W	X	75
Maryfield	Shetld	HU4841	60°9·3′	1°7·6′W	X	4
Maryfield Cott	Aberd	NO7698	57°4·6′	2°23·3′W	X	38,45
Marygarth	Orkney	HY6541	59°15·5′	2°36·3′W	X	5

Mary Glyn's Burn	Stir	NS6890	56°6·3'	4°6·8'W	W	57
Marygold	Scot Bord	NT8160	55°50·2'	2°17·8'W	X	67
Marygoldhill Plantn	Scot Bord	NT8060	55°50·2'	2°18·7'W	F	67
Marygolds	Essex	TL8424	51°53·3'	0°40·8'E	X	168
Mary Hare (Sch)	W Berks	SU4671	51°26·6'	1°19·9'W	X	174
Maryhill	Aberd	NO6865	56°46·8'	2°31·0'W	X	45
Maryhill	C of Glas	NS5668	55°53·3'	4°17·7'W	T	64
Maryhill	Moray	NJ3054	57°34·5'	3°9·8'W	X	28
Maryhill	Moray	NJ3549	57°31·9'	3°4·7'W	X	28
Maryhill	Moray	NJ4561	57°38·4'	2°54·8'W	X	28,29
Maryhill Wood	Aberd	NJ6753	57°34·2'	2°32·6'W	F	29
Marykirk	Aberd	NO6865	56°46·8'	2°31·0'W	X	45
Mary Knoll	Heref	SO4873	52°21·4'	2°45·4'W	X	137,138,148
Mary Knoll Valley	Heref	SO4873	52°21·4'	2°45·4'W	X	137,138,148
Maryland	Dorset	SZ0188	50°41·7'	1°58·8'W	X	195
Mary Land	Lincs	TF2048	53°1·2'	0°12·3'W	X	131
Maryland	Monm	SO5105	51°44·7'	2°42·2'W	T	162
Maryland	W Dunb	NS4177	55°57·8'	4°32·4'W	X	64
Maryland Fm	Cumbr	NY1961	54°56·5'	3°15·4'W	FM	85
Maryland Ho	Devon	SX7856	50°23·7'	3°42·6'W	X	202
Maryland Ho	Lincs	TF2049	53°1·7'	0°12·2'W	X	131
Marylands Fm	Oxon	SU5898	51°40·9'	1°9·3'W	FM	164
Marylands Fm	Somer	ST6429	51°3·8'	2°30·4'W	FM	183
Marylea Fm	Leic	SK4823	52°48·4'	1°16·9'W	FM	129
Marylebone	C of West	TQ2881	51°31·0'	0°8·9'W	T	176
Marylebone	Wigan	SD5807	53°33·7'	2°37·6'W	T	108
Marymead	Devon	SS5202	50°48·2'	4°5·6'W	X	191
Marymere Fm	Wilts	SU2961	51°21·1'	1°34·6'W	FM	174
Mary Moors	Worcs	SO7878	52°24·2'	2°19·0'W	X	138
Mary Mount	Cumbr	NY2619	54°33·9'	3°8·2'W	X	89,90
Mary Newman's Cottage	Corn	SX4258	50°24·3'	4°13·0'W	X	201
Marypark	Moray	NJ1938	57°25·8'	3°20·5'W	T	28
Marypark	Moray	NJ4346	57°30·3'	2°56·6'W	X	28
Maryport	Cumbr	NY0336	54°42·8'	3°29·9'W	T	89
Maryport	D & G	NX1434	54°40·3'	4°52·6'W	X	82
Maryport Bay	D & G	NX1434	54°40·3'	4°52·6'W	W	82
Mary's Grove	Notts	SK6271	53°14·2'	1°3·9'W	F	120
Maryside Hill	Ghead	NZ1365	54°59·0'	1°47·4'W	X	88
Mary's Pillar	Cumbr	NY5317	54°33·0'	2°43·2'W	X	90
Mary's Rocks	Devon	SX6146	50°18·1'	3°56·7'W	X	202
Marystow	Devon	SX4382	50°37·2'	4°12·8'W	X	201
Mary's Valley	Aberd	NJ8755	57°35·3'	2°12·6'W	X	30
Mary Tavy	Devon	SX5079	50°35·7'	4°6·8'W	T	191,201
Maryton	Angus	NO3953	56°40·1'	2°59·3'W	T	54
Maryton	Angus	NO6856	56°41·9'	2°30·9'W	T	54
Maryville	C of Glas	NS6762	55°50·2'	4°7·0'W	X	64
Marywell	Aberd	NJ5603	57°7·2'	2°43·1'W	X	37
Marywell	Aberd	NO5896	57°3·4'	2°41·1'W	T	37,44
Marywell	Aberd	NO9299	57°5·2'	2°7·5'W	T	38,45
Marywell	Angus	NO6544	56°35·5'	2°33·7'W	T	54
Marywood Fm	Suff	TM1456	52°9·9'	1°8·1'E	FM	156
Màs a Chnoic	N Eil	NF7775	57°39·2'	7°24·5'W	X	18
Màs a' Chnuic	N Eil	NF9694	57°50·2'	7°6·9'W	H	18
Màs a' Chnuic-chuairtich	N Eil	NB0614	58°3·3'	6°58·3'W	H	13,14
Masamuile	N Eil	NL6594	56°55·2'	7°29·9'W	X	31
Masbrough	Roth	SK4192	53°25·6'	1°22·6'W	T	111
Mascall Court	Kent	TQ6743	51°9·9'	0°23·7'E	X	188
Mascalls	Essex	TQ5792	51°36·5'	0°16·4'E	X	177
Mascalls	Kent	TQ6644	51°10·5'	0°22·9'E	X	188
Mascallsbury Fm	Essex	TL5612	51°47·3'	0°16·1'E	FM	167
Mascal's Fm	Suff	TL9440	52°1·7'	0°50·1'E	FM	155
Mascle Bridge	Pemb	SM9505	51°42·6'	4°57·7'W	T	157,158
Masey Edge	N Yks	SE1173	54°9·4'	1°49·5'W	X	99
Màs Garbh	N Eil	NB0214	58°1·2'	7°2·3'W	H	13
Màs Garbh	N Eil	NG0487	57°46·8'	6°58·3'W	X	18
Masham	N Yks	SE2280	54°13·2'	1°39·3'W	T	99
Masham Moor	N Yks	SE1079	54°12·6'	1°50·4'W	X	99
Masham Moor	N Yks	SE1676	54°11·0'	1°44·9'W	X	99
Mashbury	Essex	TL6511	51°46·6'	0°23·9'E	T	167
Maskeir	N Eil	NF7167	57°34·7'	7°29·8'W	X	18
Maskell's Hall	Suff	TM0448	52°5·8'	0°59·1'E	X	155
Maskel Point	Cumbr	SD2971	54°8·0'	3°4·8'W	X	96,97
Mask Hall	E Yorks	SE8940	53°51·2'	0°38·4'W	X	106
Màs na Garra	N Eil	NG1998	57°53·2'	6°44·0'W	X	14
Mason	N upon Ty	NZ2073	55°3·3'	1°40·8'W	T	88
Masongill	N Yks	SD6675	54°10·4'	2°30·8'W	T	98
Mason Gill Wood	N Yks	SE5981	54°13·5'	1°5·3'W	F	100
Masonhill	S Ayr	NS3521	55°27·6'	4°36·1'W	T	70
Mason House	Lancs	SD6943	53°53·2'	2°27·9'W	X	103
Masonic School	Herts	TQ0595	51°38·9'	0°28·5'W	X	166,176
Mason Lodge	Aberd	NJ8106	57°8·9'	2°18·4'W	X	38
Mason's Bank	Shrops	SO2287	52°28·8'	3°8·5'W	X	137
Maspie Den	Fife	NO2306	56°14·7'	3°14·1'W	X	58
Massacamber	N Eil	NF9382	57°43·6'	7°9·0'W	X	18
Massetts	W Susx	TQ3823	50°59·6'	0°1·6'W	X	198
Massey Brook	Warr	SJ6585	53°21·9'	2°31·1'W	W	109
Massey Fm	Worcs	SO8533	52°0·0'	2°12·7'W	FM	150
Massey House Fm	Shrops	SJ5136	52°55·4'	2°43·3'W	FM	126
Massey's Lodge	Ches	SJ5869	53°13·2'	2°37·3'W	X	117
Màs Sgeir	N Eil	NB0939	58°14·9'	6°57·1'W	X	13
Màs Sgeir	N Eil	NB1443	58°17·2'	6°52·3'W	X	13
Màs Sgeir	N Eil	NB5166	58°30·9'	6°16·1'W	X	8
Mass Ho	Shrops	SO7082	52°26·3'	2°26·1'W	X	138
Massie Brae	Aberd	NK0247	57°31·0'	1°57·5'W	X	30
Massingham Common	Norf	TF8020	52°45·1'	0°40·4'E	X	132
Massingham Heath	Norf	TF7720	52°45·1'	0°37·8'E	X	132
Massingham St Mary	Norf	TF7824	52°47·3'	0°38·8'E	X	132
Massington Fm	Heref	SO7339	52°3·2'	2°23·2'W	FM	150
Mass John's House	Shetld	HU4595	60°38·4'	1°10·1'W	X	1,2
Masson	Derby	SK2859	53°7·9'	1°34·5'W	X	119
Masson Hill	Derby	SK2858	53°7·3'	1°34·5'W	H	119
Masson Lees Fm	Derby	SK2859	53°7·9'	1°34·5'W	FM	119
Masterfield	Pth & Kin	NO0016	56°19·8'	3°36·6'W	X	58
Master Grain	Scot Bord	NT2311	55°23·5'	3°12·5'W	W	79
Master Johns	Essex	TQ6298	51°39·7'	0°20·9'E	X	167,177
Master Stones	Brad	SD9936	53°49·5'	2°0·5'W	X	103
Mastertown	Fife	NT1284	56°2·7'	3°24·3'W	X	65
Masti Geo	Shetld	HU4523	59°59·6'	1°11·1'W	X	4
Mastiles	N Yks	SD9266	54°5·6'	2°6·9'W	X	98
Mastiles Gate	N Yks	SD9466	54°5·6'	2°5·1'W	X	98
Mastin Moor	Derby	SK4575	53°16·4'	1°19·1'W	T	120
Mastrick	Aberd	NJ6930	57°21·8'	2°30·5'W	X	29
Mastrick	C of Aber	NJ9006	57°8·9'	2°9·5'W	T	38
Matamata Fm	Leic	SK8418	52°45·4'	0°44·9'W	FM	130
Matcham's Ho	Dorset	SU1201	50°48·7'	1°49·4'W	X	195
Matcham's Park	Dorset	SU1201	50°48·7'	1°49·4'W	X	195
Matchborough	Worcs	SP0766	52°17·8'	1°53·4'W	T	150
Matching	Essex	TL5211	51°46·8'	0°12·6'E	T	167
Matching Green	Essex	TL5310	51°46·3'	0°13·4'E	T	167
Matching Park	Essex	TL5111	51°46·9'	0°11·7'E	F	167
Matching Tye	Essex	TL5111	51°46·9'	0°11·7'E	T	167
Matcott	Devon	SS3511	50°52·7'	4°20·3'W	X	190
Mates Fm	Kent	TQ6071	51°25·1'	0°18·5'E	FM	177
Matfen	Northum	NZ0371	55°2·3'	1°56·8'W	T	87
Matfield	Kent	TQ6541	51°8·9'	0°21·9'E	T	188
Mathafarn	Powys	SH8004	52°37·5'	3°46·0'W	X	135,136
Mathair a' Gharbh Uilt	Highld	NC2750	58°24·5'	4°57·2'W	W	9
Mathams Wood	Herts	TL4618	51°50·7'	0°7·6'E	F	167
Mathan Isaf	Gwyn	SH3236	52°54·0'	4°29·5'W	X	123
Mathan Uchaf	Gwyn	SH3136	52°54·0'	4°30·4'W	X	123
Mathayes Fm	Devon	ST1708	50°52·2'	3°10·4'W	FM	192,193
Mathern	Monm	ST5291	51°37·2'	2°41·2'W	X	162,172
Mathern Oaze	Monm	ST5289	51°36·1'	2°41·2'W	X	162,172
Mathern Pill	Monm	ST5389	51°36·1'	2°40·3'W	W	162,172
Mathersgrave	Derby	SK3659	53°7·9'	1°27·3'W	X	119
Mathers Head	Shetld	HZ1970	59°31·2'	1°39·4'W	X	4
Mather Wood	Notts	SK7259	53°7·6'	0°55·0'W	F	120
Mathieside Cairn	Scot Bord	NT1322	55°29·3'	3°22·2'W	H	72
Mathon	Heref	SO7345	52°6·4'	2°23·3'W	T	150
Mathon Court	Heref	SO7445	52°6·4'	2°22·4'W	X	150
Mathon Lodge	Heref	SO7645	52°6·4'	2°20·6'W	X	150
Mathrafal	Powys	SJ1211	52°41·6'	3°17·7'W	X	125
Mathry	Pemb	SM8731	51°56·4'	5°5·5'W	T	157
Mathurst Fm	Kent	TQ7740	51°8·1'	0°32·2'E	FM	188
Math Wood	Lincs	TF0918	52°45·1'	0°22·7'W	F	130
Matlaske	Norf	TG1534	52°51·9'	1°12·1'E	T	133
Matley	Tames	SJ9896	53°27·9'	2°1·4'W	T	109
Matley Heath	Hants	SU3307	50°51·9'	1°31·5'W	X	196
Matley Moor	Derby	SK0290	53°24·6'	1°57·8'W	X	110
Matleymoor Fm	Derby	SK0289	53°24·1'	1°57·8'W	FM	110
Matley Passage	Hants	SU3307	50°51·9'	1°31·5'W	X	196
Matley Wood	Hants	SU3307	50°51·9'	1°31·5'W	F	196
Matlock	Derby	SK2959	53°7·9'	1°33·6'W	T	119
Matlock Bank	Derby	SK2960	53°8·4'	1°33·6'W	T	119
Matlock Bath	Derby	SK2958	53°7·3'	1°33·6'W	T	119
Matlock Bridge	Derby	SK2959	53°7·9'	1°33·6'W	T	119
Matlock Cliff	Derby	SK3159	53°7·9'	1°31·8'W	T	119
Matlock Dale	Derby	SK2958	53°7·3'	1°33·6'W	T	119
Matlock Moor	Derby	SK3062	53°9·5'	1°32·7'W	X	119
Matravers	Dorset	SY5193	50°44·3'	2°41·3'W	X	194
Matrimony Fm	Wilts	SU1625	51°1·7'	1°45·9'W	FM	184
Matshead	Lancs	SD5140	53°51·5'	2°44·3'W	T	102
Matson	Glos	SO8515	51°50·2'	2°12·7'W	T	162
Matson Ground	Cumbr	SD4196	54°21·6'	2°54·1'W	X	96,97
Matson House	Glos	SO8415	51°50·2'	2°13·5'W	A	162
Matta Taing	Shetld	HU1656	60°17·5'	1°42·1'W	X	3
Matterdale Common	Cumbr	NY3421	54°35·0'	3°0·9'W	X	90
Matterdale End	Cumbr	NY3923	54°36·2'	2°56·2'W	T	90
Mattergill Sike	Cumbr	NY7730	54°40·1'	2°21·0'W	W	91
Matterley Fm	Hants	SU5529	51°3·7'	1°12·5'W	FM	185
Mattersey	Notts	SK6889	53°23·8'	0°58·2'W	T	111,120
Mattersey Grange	Notts	SK6789	53°23·9'	0°59·1'W	X	111,120
Mattersey Hill	Notts	SK6888	53°23·3'	0°58·2'W	X	111,120
Mattersey Thorpe	Notts	SK6790	53°24·4'	0°59·1'W	T	111
Mattersey Wood	Notts	SK6689	53°23·9'	1°0·0'W	F	111,120
Matthew's Coppice	Shrops	SJ5421	52°47·3'	2°40·5'W	F	126
Matthewsgreen	Wok	SU8069	51°25·1'	0°50·6'W	T	175
Matthew's Hill	D & G	NY1493	55°13·7'	3°20·7'W	H	78
Matthew's Point	Devon	SX8547	50°18·9'	3°36·5'W	X	202
Matthew's Port	S Ayr	NS1903	55°17·5'	4°50·6'W	W	76
Mattie Brown Wood	York	SE6843	53°53·0'	0°57·5'W	F	105,106
Mattilees Cott	Northum	NT9442	55°40·5'	2°5·3'W	X	74,75
Mattilees Hill	Northum	NT9443	55°41·1'	2°5·3'W	X	74,75
Mattingley	Hants	SU7357	51°18·7'	0°56·8'W	T	175,186
Mattiscombe	Devon	SX8042	50°16·2'	3°40·7'W	X	202
Mattishall	Norf	TG0511	52°39·7'	1°2·3'E	T	133
Mattishall Burgh	Norf	TG0511	52°39·7'	1°2·3'E	T	133
Mattocks Down	Devon	SS6043	51°10·4'	3°59·8'W	H	180
Mattock's Fm	Essex	TL7017	51°49·8'	0°28·4'E	FM	167
Mattram Hall	N Yks	SE5434	53°48·2'	1°10·4'W	X	105
Matts Fm	Powys	SO0953	52°10·3'	3°19·4'W	FM	147
Matts Hill Fm	Medway	TQ8162	51°19·9'	0°36·3'E	FM	178,188
Maubern Hall	Ches	SJ9280	53°19·3'	2°6·8'W	X	109
Mauchline	E Ayr	NS4927	55°31·1'	4°23·1'W	T	70
Mauchline Mains	E Ayr	NS5027	55°31·1'	4°22·1'W	X	70
Maud	Aberd	NJ9247	57°31·0'	2°7·6'W	T	30
Maud Heath's Causeway	Wilts	ST9475	51°28·7'	2°4·8'W	A	173
Maudland Ho	Carm	SN3333	51°58·5'	4°25·5'W	X	145
Maudlin	Corn	SX0862	50°25·8'	4°41·8'W	T	200
Maudlin	Dorset	ST3805	50°50·7'	2°52·5'W	T	193
Maudlin	Northum	NU2405	55°20·6'	1°36·9'W	X	81
Maudlin	W Susx	SU8806	50°51·0'	0°44·6'W	T	197
Maudlin Cross	Dorset	ST3805	50°50·7'	2°52·5'W	T	193
Maudlin Fm	Corn	SX2664	50°27·2'	4°26·7'W	FM	201
Maudlin Fm	W Susx	SU8806	50°51·0'	0°44·6'W	FM	197
Maud Loch	Pth & Kin	NN7265	56°45·8'	4°5·2'W	W	42
Maud's Br	Donc	SE7112	53°36·2'	0°55·2'W	X	112
Maud's Fm	N Yks	SE2063	54°4·0'	1°41·2'W	FM	99
Maugersbury	Glos	SP2025	51°55·6'	1°42·2'W	T	163
Maugersbury Hill	Glos	SP2023	51°54·5'	1°42·2'W	X	163
Maugersbury Manor	Glos	SP1925	51°55·6'	1°43·0'W	X	163
Maughanby Fm	Cumbr	NY5737	54°43·8'	2°39·6'W	FM	91
Maughold	I of M	SC4991	54°17·8'	4°18·8'W	T	95
Maughold Brooghs	I of M	SC4892	54°18·3'	4°19·8'W	X	95
Maughold Head	I of M	SC4991	54°17·8'	4°18·8'W	H	95
Mauld	Highld	NH3938	57°24·5'	4°40·3'W	X	26
Maulden	Beds	TL0538	52°2·1'	0°27·8'W	T	153
Maulden Wood	Beds	TL0638	52°2·0'	0°26·9'W	F	153
Mauldslie	Midlo	NT3053	55°46·2'	3°6·5'W	X	66,73
Mauldslie Hill	Scot Bord	NT3251	55°45·1'	3°4·6'W	H	66,73
Mauldslie Mains	S Lanak	NS8150	55°44·0'	3°53·3'W	X	65,72
Maulds Meaburn	Cumbr	NY6216	54°32·5'	2°34·8'W	T	91
Maulds Meaburn Moor	Cumbr	NY6415	54°32·0'	2°33·0'W	X	91
Mauley Cross	N Yks	SE7994	54°20·4'	0°46·7'W	A	94,100
Maulkin's Hall	Suff	TL9368	52°16·8'	0°50·2'E	X	155
Maul Rigg	Northum	NY7161	54°56·8'	2°26·7'W	X	86,87
Maulscastle	D & G	NY1268	55°0·2'	3°22·1'W	X	85
Maulside	N Ayr	NS3251	55°43·7'	4°40·1'W	X	63
Maumbury Rings	Dorset	SY6989	50°42·2'	2°26·0'W	A	194
Maumhill Wood	Notts	SK7683	53°20·5'	0°51·1'W	F	120
Maunby	N Yks	SE3586	54°16·3'	1°27·3'W	T	99
Maunby Demesne	N Yks	SE3487	54°16·9'	1°28·2'W	X	99
Maund Bryan	Heref	SO5650	52°9·0'	2°38·2'W	T	149
Maunditts Park Fm	Wilts	ST9585	51°34·1'	2°3·9'W	FM	173
Maundown	Somer	ST0628	51°2·9'	3°20·1'W	T	181
Maundown Hill	Somer	ST0628	51°2·9'	3°20·1'W	H	181
Maunsel Ho	Somer	ST3030	51°4·1'	2°59·6'W	X	182
Mauns Hill	Shetld	HU1560	60°19·7'	1°43·2'W	H	3
Maurice's Cleuch	S Lanak	NS9535	55°36·1'	3°39·6'W	X	72
Mauricewood	Midlo	NT2361	55°50·4'	3°13·3'W	T	66
Maurs Cairn	D & G	NX1773	55°1·3'	4°51·3'W	X	76
Mausoleum Woods	Lincs	TA1309	53°34·2'	0°17·2'W	F	113
Mautby	Norf	TG4812	52°39·2'	1°40·4'E	T	134
Mautby Lodge	Norf	TG4812	52°39·2'	1°40·4'E	X	134
Mautby Marsh Fm	Norf	TG4809	52°37·5'	1°40·3'E	FM	134
Maut Craig	Aberd	NK0958	57°37·0'	1°50·5'W	X	30
Maux Hall	Lincs	TA1206	53°32·6'	0°18·2'W	X	113
Mauxhall Fm	NE Lincs	TA1913	53°36·2'	0°11·7'W	FM	113
Maverston	Moray	NJ3063	57°39·3'	3°9·9'W	X	28
Mavesyn Ridware	Staffs	SK0816	52°44·7'	1°52·5'W	T	128
Mavie Mill	W Dunb	NS4584	56°1·7'	4°28·8'W	X	57,64
Mavisbank	Angus	NO5956	56°41·9'	2°39·7'W	X	54
Mavisbank	D & G	NS8731	55°22·4'	3°56·0'W	X	71,78
Mavisbank	Falk	NS8977	55°58·6'	3°46·3'W	X	65
Mavisbank	Pth & Kin	NO1330	56°27·5'	3°24·3'W	X	53
Mavisbank Ho	Midlo	NT2865	55°52·6'	3°8·6'W	X	66
Mavis Enderby	Lincs	TF3666	53°10·7'	0°2·5'E	T	122
Mavis Grind	Shetld	HU3468	60°23·9'	1°22·5'W	X	2,3
Mavishall	E Loth	NT4661	55°50·6'	2°51·3'W	X	66
Maviston	Highld	NH9458	57°36·2'	3°46·0'W	X	27
Mavourn Fm	Beds	TL0757	52°12·3'	0°25·7'W	FM	153
Mawbray	Cumbr	NY0846	54°48·3'	3°25·5'W	T	85
Mawbray Bank	Cumbr	NY0847	54°48·8'	3°25·5'W	X	85
Mawbray Hayrigg	Cumbr	NY0949	54°49·9'	3°24·6'W	X	85
Mawbrook Lodge	Leic	SK7525	52°49·3'	0°52·8'W	X	129
Mawcarr Stells	Scot Bord	NT8869	55°55·1'	2°11·1'W	X	67
Mawcarse	Pth & Kin	NO1405	56°14·0'	3°22·8'W	X	58
Mawdesley	Lancs	SD4914	53°37·4'	2°45·9'W	T	108
Mawdesley Moss	Lancs	SD4815	53°38·0'	2°46·8'W	X	108
Mawdlam	Brig	SS8081	51°31·1'	3°43·4'W	T	170
Mawfield Fm	Heref	SO4536	52°1·4'	2°47·7'W	FM	149,161
Mawfield Spring	N Yks	SE4638	53°50·4'	1°17·6'W	F	105
Mawgan	Corn	SW7025	50°5·1'	5°12·5'W	T	203
Mawgan Porth	Corn	SW8567	50°28·0'	5°1·4'W	T	200
Maw Green	Ches	SJ7157	53°6·8'	2°25·6'W	T	118
Mawgre Fm	E Yorks	SE7920	53°40·5'	0°47·8'W	FM	105,106,112
Mawhill	Pth & Kin	NO0803	56°12·9'	3°28·6'W	X	58
Mawk Hole Moss	Durham	NY8918	54°33·7'	2°9·8'W	X	91,92
Mawla	Corn	SW7045	50°15·8'	5°13·3'W	T	203
Mawley Hall	Shrops	SO6875	52°22·6'	2°27·8'W	A	138
Mawleytown Fm	Shrops	SO6876	52°23·1'	2°27·8'W	FM	138
Maw Loch	Shetld	HU2658	60°18·6'	1°31·3'W	W	3
Mawmill	Pth & Kin	NT0898	56°10·2'	3°28·5'W	X	58
Mawmon Sike	Durham	NY9116	54°32·6'	2°7·9'W	W	91,92
Mawnan	Corn	SW7827	50°6·3'	5°5·9'W	T	204
Mawnan Shear	Corn	SW7826	50°5·8'	5°5·9'W	X	204
Mawnan Smith	Corn	SW7728	50°6·8'	5°6·8'W	T	204
Mawnog	Powys	SN7994	52°32·1'	3°46·6'W	X	135
Mawnog Bryn-glas	Powys	SN9392	52°31·2'	3°34·2'W	X	136
Mawnog Egryn	Denb	SJ0135	52°54·4'	3°27·9'W	X	125
Mawn Pool	Powys	SO1348	52°7·6'	3°15·9'W	W	148
Mawn Pools	Powys	SO1651	52°9·3'	3°13·3'W	W	148
Mawn Pools	Powys	SO1955	52°11·5'	3°10·7'W	X	148
Maw Skelly	Angus	NO6844	56°35·5'	2°30·8'W	X	54
Mawsley Wood	Northnts	SP7975	52°22·3'	0°50·0'W	X	141
Mawson Green	Donc	SE6416	53°38·4'	1°1·5'W	T	111
Mawstone Fm	Derby	SK2163	53°10·1'	1°40·7'W	FM	119
Maw Stones	Brad	SD9840	53°51·6'	2°1·4'W	X	103
Maw Stones Slack	N Yks	SD9741	53°52·2'	2°2·3'W	X	103
Mawthorpe	Lincs	TF4572	53°13·7'	0°10·7'E	T	122
Maw Wyke Hole	N Yks	NZ9408	54°27·8'	0°32·6'W	W	94
Maxey	Peterb	TF1208	52°39·7'	0°20·2'W	T	142
Maxey Cut	Peterb	TF1207	52°39·2'	0°20·3'W	W	142
Maxfield	E Susx	TQ8315	50°54·5'	0°36·6'E	X	199
Maxfield Plain	N Yks	SE1465	54°5·1'	1°46·7'W	X	99
Maxfields Coppice	Shrops	SO7078	52°24·2'	2°26·1'W	F	138
Max House Fm	N Som	ST4057	51°18·8'	2°51·3'W	FM	172,182
Maxie Burn	Aberd	NO7283	56°56·5'	2°27·2'W	W	45
Maxie Well	Aberd	NO7384	56°57·0'	2°26·2'W	W	45
Maxpoffle	Scot Bord	NT5530	55°33·9'	2°42·4'W	X	73
Maxstoke	Warw	SP2386	52°28·5'	1°39·3'W	T	139
Maxstoke Castle	Warw	SP2289	52°30·1'	1°40·2'W	A	139
Maxstoke Fm	Warw	SP2287	52°29·1'	1°40·2'W	FM	139
Maxstoke Hall Fm	Warw	SP2487	52°29·1'	1°38·4'W	FM	139
Maxted Street	Kent	TR1244	51°9·6'	1°2·3'E	T	179,189
Maxton	Kent	TR3040	51°7·0'	1°17·6'E	T	179
Maxton	Scot Bord	NT6130	55°34·0'	2°36·7'W	T	74
Maxwellbank	D & G	NX9869	55°0·6'	3°35·3'W	X	84
Maxwellbank	D & G	NY0783	55°8·2'	3°27·1'W	X	78
Maxwellfield	D & G	NX9756	54°53·5'	3°35·9'W	X	84
Maxwellston Hill	S Ayr	NX2598	55°15·0'	4°44·8'W	H	76
Maxwelltown	D & G	NX8778	55°5·3'	3°45·8'W	X	84
Maxwelltown	D & G	NX9675	55°3·8'	3°37·3'W	T	84
Maxwelston	S Ayr	NS2600	55°16·1'	4°43·9'W	X	76
Maxwelton	D & G	NX8289	55°11·1'	3°50·8'W	A	78
Maxwelton Hill	D & G	NX8290	55°11·7'	3°50·8'W	X	78
Maxwelton Mains	D & G	NX8289	55°11·1'	3°50·8'W	X	78
Maxworthy	Corn	SX2592	50°42·3'	4°28·3'W	T	190
Maxworthy Cross	Corn	SX2693	50°42·9'	4°27·5'W	X	190
Mayals	Swan	SS6090	51°35·7'	4°0·9'W	T	159

Mayar	Angus	NO2473	56°50·8'	3°14·3'W	H	44
Mayar Burn	Angus	NO2373	56°50·8'	3°15·3'W	W	44
Mayback	Orkney	HY4952	59°21·3'	2°53·3'W	X	5
Maybank	Midlo	NT2460	55°49·9'	3°12·4'W	X	66
May Bank	Staffs	SJ8547	53°1·4'	2°13·0'W	T	118
Maybanks Manor	Surrey	TQ0935	51°6·5'	0°26·2'W	X	187
May Beck	N Yks	NZ8902	54°24·6'	0°37·3'W	W	94
Maybole	S Ayr	NS2909	55°21·0'	4°41·4'W	T	70,76
Maybury	Surrey	TQ0158	51°19·0'	0°32·7'W	T	186
Maybury Fm	Surrey	TQ2052	51°15·5'	0°16·4'W	FM	187
Maybush	C of Soton	SU3814	50°55·7'	1°27·2'W	T	196
May Crag	Cumbr	NY2117	54°32·8'	3°12·9'W	X	89,90
May Craig	Aberd	NO9192	57°1·4'	2°8·4'W	X	38,45
May Craig	Aberd	NO9396	57°3·6'	2°6·5'W	X	38,45
Mayday Fm	Suff	TL7983	52°25·2'	0°38·3'E	FM	144
Maydays Fm	Essex	TM0215	51°48·1'	0°56·2'E	FM	168
Maydays Marsh	Essex	TM0315	51°48·0'	0°57·1'E	X	168
Maydencroft Manor	Herts	TL1827	51°56·0'	0°16·6'W	X	166
Maydensole Fm	Kent	TR3147	51°10·8'	1°18·7'E	FM	179
Mayen	Moray	NJ5747	57°30·9'	2°42·6'W	X	29
Mayer's Green	Sand	SP0191	52°31·2'	1°58·7'W	T	139
Mayes	E Susx	TQ3833	51°5·0'	0°1·4'W	X	187
Mayes Fm	Essex	TL7504	51°42·7'	0°32·4'E	FM	167
Mayes Green	Surrey	TQ1239	51°8·6'	0°23·5'W	T	187
Mayeston	Pemb	SN0103	51°41·7'	4°52·4'W	T	157,158
Mayfair	C of West	TQ2880	51°30·5'	0°8·9'W	T	176
Mayfield	Aberd	NJ6114	57°13·2'	2°38·3'W	X	37
Mayfield	Cumbr	NY0627	54°38·0'	3°27·0'W	X	89
Mayfield	D & G	NX7157	54°53·7'	4°0·3'W	X	83,84
Mayfield	D & G	NY0882	55°7·7'	3°26·1'W	X	78
Mayfield	E Ayr	NS4420	55°27·2'	4°27·6'W	X	70
Mayfield	E Susx	TQ5826	51°0·9'	0°15·5'E	T	188,199
Mayfield	Fife	NO3613	56°18·6'	3°1·6'W	X	59
Mayfield	Highld	ND1466	58°34·7'	3°28·3'W	T	11,12
Mayfield	Lincs	TF3611	52°41·0'	0°1·1'E	X	131,142
Mayfield	Midlo	NT3564	55°52·1'	3°1·9'W	T	66
Mayfield	N Ayr	NS2542	55°38·7'	4°46·4'W	X	63,70
Mayfield	Northum	NZ2776	55°4·9'	1°34·2'W	T	88
Mayfield	Orkney	HY2411	58°59·0'	3°18·9'W	X	6
Mayfield	Orkney	HY4943	59°16·5'	2°53·2'W	X	5
Mayfield	Pth & Kin	NO0120	56°22·0'	3°35·7'W	X	52,53,58
Mayfield	Scot Bord	NT8360	55°50·2'	2°15·8'W	X	67
Mayfield	Shetld	HU3448	60°13·2'	1°22·7'W	X	3
Mayfield	S Lanak	NS8335	55°35·9'	3°51·0'W	X	71,72
Mayfield	Staffs	SK1545	53°0·4'	1°46·2'W	T	119,128
Mayfield	W Loth	NS9368	55°53·9'	3°42·2'W	T	65
Mayfield Flat Fm	E Susx	TQ5521	50°58·3'	0°12·9'E	FM	199
Mayfield Fm	Beds	TL1534	51°59·8'	0°19·1'W	FM	153
Mayfield Fm	Norf	TM2191	52°28·6'	1°15·7'E	FM	134
Mayfield Fm	Orkney	HY4509	58°58·1'	2°56·9'W	FM	6,7
Mayfield Fm	W Berks	SU5179	51°30·7'	1°15·5'W	FM	174
Mayfields, Fm	Heref	SO6748	52°8·0'	2°28·5'W	FM	149
Mayflower, The	Norf	TF7728	52°49·5'	0°38·0'E	F	132
May Fm	Cambs	TL5987	52°27·3'	0°20·8'E	FM	143
May Fm	Kent	TQ9535	51°5·1'	0°47·4'E	FM	189
Mayford	Surrey	SU9956	51°17·9'	0°34·4'W	T	175,186
Mayfurlong	Staffs	SK0853	53°4·7'	1°52·4'W	X	119
May Green	Norf	TF9628	52°49·1'	0°54·9'E	X	132
Mayhall Fm	Bucks	SU9599	51°41·1'	0°37·2'W	FM	165,176
Mayhar	D & G	NX0268	54°58·3'	5°5·2'W	X	82
May Hill	Glos	SO6921	51°53·4'	2°26·6'W	H	162
May Hill	I of M	SC4494	54°19·3'	4°23·5'W	X	95
May Hill	Monm	SO5112	51°48·5'	2°42·3'W	T	162
May Hill	Shrops	SO4179	52°24·6'	2°51·6'W	X	137,148
May Hill	Shrops	SO6271	52°20·4'	2°33·1'W	X	138
Mayhill	Swan	SS6494	51°37·9'	3°57·5'W	T	159
Mayhill Fm	Hants	SU5817	50°57·2'	1°10·1'W	FM	185
May Hill Ho	Glos	SO6920	51°52·9'	2°26·6'W	X	162
May House Fm	Shrops	SO7683	52°26·9'	2°20·8'W	FM	138
Mayhouse Fm	Worcs	SO8662	52°15·6'	2°11·9'W	FM	150
Mayish	N Ayr	NS0135	55°34·3'	5°9·0'W	X	69
Mayland	Essex	TL9101	51°40·7'	0°46·2'E	T	168
Mayland Court	Essex	TL9300	51°40·2'	0°47·9'E	X	168
Mayland Creek	Essex	TL9103	51°41·8'	0°46·2'E	W	168
Mayland Hall	Essex	TL9300	51°40·2'	0°47·0'E	X	168
Mayland Lea	Durham	NZ0628	54°39·1'	1°54·0'W	X	92
Maylandsea	Essex	TL9002	51°41·3'	0°45·3'E	T	168
Maylands, The	Ches	SJ6650	53°3·0'	2°30·0'W	X	118
Mayles	Hants	SU5710	50°53·4'	1°11·0'W	X	196
Maylord	Powys	SO1871	52°20·1'	3°11·8'W	X	136,148
Maymore	Arg & Bt	NR9986	56°1·7'	5°13·1'W	X	55
May Moss	N Yks	SE8795	54°20·8'	0°39·3'W	X	94,101
Maynards	Essex	TL6535	51°59·6'	0°24·6'E	X	154
Maynards Fm	Essex	TL4102	51°42·2'	0°2·8'E	FM	167
Maynard's Green	E Susx	TQ5818	50°56·6'	0°15·3'E	T	199
Mayne Ho	Moray	NJ2060	57°37·6'	3°19·9'W	X	28
Maynes Fm	Herts	TL1208	51°45·8'	0°22·7'W	FM	166
Maynes Hill	Bucks	SP7924	51°54·8'	0°50·7'W	X	165
Mayo	Moray	NJ3135	57°24·3'	3°8·4'W	X	28
Mayo Fm	Dorset	ST8722	51°0·1'	2°10·7'W	FM	183
Mayon	Corn	SW3525	50°4·2'	5°41·8'W	T	203
Mayon Cliff	Corn	SW3425	50°4·2'	5°42·7'W	X	203
Mayor House Fm	Surrey	TQ0544	51°11·4'	0°29·5'W	FM	187
Mayortorne Manor	Bucks	SP8704	51°43·9'	0°44·0'W	X	165
Maypole	Brom	TQ4963	51°21·0'	0°8·8'E	T	177,188
Maypole	I Scilly	SV9211	49°55·4'	6°17·1'W	T	203
Maypole	Kent	TQ5173	51°26·4'	0°10·8'E	T	177
Maypole	Kent	TR2064	51°20·2'	1°9·9'E	T	179
Maypole	Monm	SO4716	51°50·6'	2°45·8'W	T	161
Maypole Bank	Shrops	SO5599	52°35·5'	2°39·5'W	X	137,138
Maypole Fm	Essex	TL5935	51°59·7'	0°19·4'E	FM	154
Maypole Green	Essex	TL9822	51°51·9'	0°52·9'E	T	168
Maypole Green	Norf	TM4195	52°30·2'	1°33·5'E	T	134
Maypole Green	Suff	TL9159	52°12·0'	0°48·1'E	T	155
Maypole Green	Suff	TM2767	52°15·5'	1°20·0'E	T	156
Maypool	Devon	SX8754	50°22·7'	3°35·0'W	X	202
Mayridge Fm	W Berks	SU6170	51°25·8'	1°7·0'W	FM	175
Mays Fm	E Susx	TQ5207	50°50·8'	0°9·9'E	FM	199
Mays Fm	Norf	TF5306	52°38·0'	0°16·1'E	FM	143
May's Fm	Oxon	SU6588	51°35·5'	1°3·3'W	FM	175
May's Green	N Som	ST3963	51°22·0'	2°52·2'W	T	182
Mays Green	Oxon	SU7480	51°31·1'	0°55·6'W	T	175
May's Green	Surrey	TQ0957	51°18·3'	0°25·8'W	T	187
Mayshaves	Kent	TQ9538	51°6·7'	0°47·5'E	X	189
Mayshiel	E Loth	NT6264	55°52·3'	2°36·0'W	X	67
Mayshill	S Glos	ST6881	51°31·9'	2°27·3'W	T	172
May's Hill Fm	Warw	SP1465	52°17·2'	1°47·3'W	FM	151
Maysland	Essex	TL6124	51°53·7'	0°20·8'E	X	167
Maysleith	W Susx	SU8228	51°3·0'	0°49·4'W	X	186,197
Maysleith Wood	W Susx	SU8127	51°2·4'	0°50·3'W	F	186,197
May's Rock	Corn	SW9540	50°13·7'	4°52·1'W	X	204
May's Wood	Warw	SP1464	52°16·7'	1°47·3'W	F	151
Maytham Fm	Kent	TQ8628	51°1·5'	0°39·5'E	FM	189,199
Maytham Wharf	Kent	TQ8627	51°1·0'	0°39·5'E	X	189,199
May, The	D & G	NX3051	54°49·8'	4°38·4'W	X	82
Maythorn	Barns	SE1805	53°32·7'	1°43·3'W	T	110
Maythorne	Notts	SK6955	53°5·5'	0°57·8'W	T	120
Maythorne Fm	Brad	SE2031	53°46·7'	1°41·4'W	FM	104
Mayton Fm	Kent	TR1561	51°18·7'	1°5·5'E	FM	179
Mayton Hall	Norf	TG2421	52°44·6'	1°19·5'E	X	133,134
May Wick	Shetld	HU3724	60°0·2'	1°19·7'W	W	4
Maywick	Shetld	HU3724	60°0·2'	1°19·7'W	T	4
Maywood Fm	Kent	TQ9235	51°5·2'	0°44·9'E	FM	189
Maze	N Yks	SD8779	54°12·6'	2°11·5'W	X	98
Maze Fm	Lincs	TF4524	52°47·9'	0°9·4'E	FM	131
Mazelands Fm	W Berks	SU5672	51°26·9'	1°11·3'W	FM	174
Maze Pasture	N Yks	SD8991	54°19·1'	2°9·7'W	X	98
Mazon Wath	Cumbr	NY6808	54°28·2'	2°29·2'W	X	91
M Brae	Highld	NH5260	57°36·6'	4°28·2'W	X	20
McAdam's Burn	D & G	NX5484	55°8·0'	4°17·0'W	W	77
Mc Arthur's Head	Arg & Bt	NR4659	55°45·7'	6°2·5'W	X	60
McCaig's Tower	Arg & Bt	NM8630	56°25·1'	5°27·7'W	X	49
McCaul's Rig	D & G	NX6484	55°8·2'	4°7·6'W	X	77
Mc Cheynston	D & G	NX9084	55°8·5'	3°43·1'W	X	78
Mc Cowans Knowe	E Ayr	NS5605	55°19·3'	4°15·7'W	X	71,77
McCrierick's Cairn	D & G	NS6610	55°22·2'	4°6·4'W	X	71
Mc Cubbington	D & G	NX9083	55°8·0'	3°43·1'W	X	78
Mc Culloch's Castle	D & G	NX9957	54°54·1'	3°34·1'W	X	84
Mc Culloch's Castle (Fort)	D & G	NX9957	54°54·1'	3°34·1'W	A	84
McCulloch's Point	D & G	NX0462	54°55·1'	5°3·1'W	X	82
Mc Dougall's Bay	Arg & Bt	NR4468	55°50·5'	6°4·9'W	W	60,61
McFarlane's Rock	Highld	NG2931	57°17·6'	6°29·4'W	X	32
McFarquhar's Cave	Highld	NH7965	57°39·8'	4°1·2'W	X	21,27
Mc Ghie's Seat	D & G	NX6262	54°56·3'	4°8·8'W	X	83
McGregor's Cave	Pth & Kin	NN7158	56°42·0'	4°6·0'W	X	42,51,52
McInnes Bank	Pth & Kin	NO2520	56°22·2'	3°12·4'W	X	59
Mc Mount	D & G	NX9593	55°13·5'	3°38·6'W	X	78
Mc Murdoston	D & G	NX9083	55°8·0'	3°43·1'W	X	78
Mc Naughton	D & G	NX8778	55°5·3'	3°45·8'W	X	84
Mc Neil	Durham	NZ1332	54°41·2'	1°47·5'W	X	92
McNeil's Bay	Arg & Bt	NM0951	56°33·9'	6°43·8'W	W	46
Mc Orriston	Stir	NS6798	56°9·6'	4°8·1'W	X	57
McPhail's Anvil	Arg & Bt	NM2613	56°14·1'	6°24·9'W	X	48
McQueen's Loch	Highld	NG5141	57°23·7'	6°8·2'W	W	23,24
McQueen's Rock	Highld	NG5140	57°23·2'	6°8·1'W	X	23,24
McRitch	Pth & Kin	NO2550	56°38·4'	3°12·9'W	X	53
Mc Whanns Stone	D & G	NX4980	55°5·7'	4°21·6'W	X	77
Mc Whanrick	D & G	NX9381	55°7·0'	3°40·2'W	X	78
Meaburn Hall	Cumbr	NY6217	54°33·1'	2°34·8'W	A	91
Meachard	Corn	SX0991	50°41·5'	4°41·9'W	X	190
Meacombe Fm	Devon	SX7286	50°39·8'	3°48·3'W	FM	191
Mead	Devon	SS2217	50°55·7'	4°31·6'W	T	190
Mead	Devon	SX7770	50°31·2'	3°43·7'W	T	202
Meadacre Fm	Bucks	SP8008	51°46·1'	0°50·0'W	FM	165
Meadale Burn	Highld	NG3834	57°19·5'	6°20·7'W	W	32
Meade Fm	N Som	ST5565	51°23·2'	2°38·4'W	FM	172,182
Meade Fm	Somer	ST4114	50°55·6'	2°50·0'W	FM	193
Meade Fm	Suff	TL9562	52°13·5'	0°51·7'E	FM	155
Mead End	Hants	SU6611	50°53·9'	1°3·3'W	T	196
Mead End	Hants	SZ2698	50°47·1'	1°37·5'W	T	195
Mead End	Wilts	SU0223	51°0·6'	1°57·9'W	T	184
Mead Fm	Bucks	SP7007	51°45·7'	0°58·7'W	FM	165
Mead Fm	E Susx	TQ5432	51°4·2'	0°12·3'E	FM	188
Mead Fm	Newp	ST4083	51°32·8'	2°51·5'W	FM	171,172
Mead Fm	S Glos	ST5986	51°34·5'	2°35·1'W	FM	172
Meadfoot Beach	Torbay	SX9363	50°27·7'	3°30·1'W	X	202
Meadgate	Bath & NE Somer	ST6858	51°19·4'	2°27·2'W	T	172
Meadgate	Essex	TL3807	51°44·9'	0°0·3'E	X	166
Meadhams Fm	Bucks	SP9801	51°42·2'	0°34·5'W	FM	165
Meadhay	Devon	SX8188	50°41·0'	3°40·7'W	X	191
Meadhayes Fm	Devon	SS9109	50°52·4'	3°32·6'W	FM	192
Meadhurst Fm	Surrey	TQ3743	51°10·4'	0°2·0'W	FM	187
Meadie Burn	Highld	NC5136	58°17·5'	4°32·0'W	W	16
Meadie Ridge	Highld	NC4943	58°21·2'	4°34·4'W	H	9
Meadle	Bucks	SP8005	51°44·5'	0°50·1'W	T	165
Meadley Resr	Cumbr	NY0514	54°31·0'	3°27·6'W	W	89
Meadleys, The	Staffs	SJ8100	52°36·1'	2°16·4'W	X	127
Mead Lodge	Herts	TL4211	51°47·0'	0°3·9'E	X	167
Mead Lodge	Pemb	SM9806	51°43·2'	4°55·1'W	X	157,158
Mead Open Fm	Beds	SP9422	51°53·5'	0°37·6'W	FM	165
Mead Open FM	Beds	SP9522	51°53·5'	0°36·8'W	FM	165
Meadow	Aberd	NJ6006	57°8·8'	2°39·2'W	X	37
Meadow	Derby	SK1173	53°15·5'	1°49·7'W	X	119
Meadow	E Ayr	NS5817	55°25·8'	4°14·2'W	X	71
Meadowbank	Aberd	NJ5125	57°19·0'	2°48·4'W	X	37
Meadowbank	Aberd	NK0947	57°31·0'	1°50·5'W	X	30
Meadow Bank	Ches	SJ4852	53°4·0'	2°46·2'W	X	117
Meadowbank	Ches	SJ6568	53°12·7'	2°31·0'W	T	118
Meadowbank	C of Edin	NT2874	55°57·5'	3°8·8'W	T	66
Meadow Bank	D & G	NX3957	54°53·2'	4°30·2'W	X	83
Meadowbank	Pth & Kin	NO0014	56°18·7'	3°36·5'W	X	58
Meadow Cleuch	Scot Bord	NT6604	55°20·0'	2°31·7'W	X	80
Meadow Cottage	Northum	NY8346	54°48·8'	2°15·4'W	X	86,87
Meadow Cottage	Notts	SK7474	53°15·7'	0°53·0'W	X	120
Meadow Court	Heref	SO6151	52°9·6'	2°33·8'W	X	149
Meadow Court Fm	Warw	SP2459	52°14·0'	1°38·5'W	FM	151
Meadowcroft	Lancs	SD5436	53°49·6'	2°41·9'W	X	102
Meadow Dyke	Norf	TG4321	52°44·1'	1°36·4'E	W	134
Meadowend	Clackm	NS9390	56°5·7'	3°42·8'W	X	58
Meadowend	Devon	SS7902	50°48·5'	3°42·7'W	X	191
Meadowend	Essex	TL7440	52°2·1'	0°32·6'E	T	155
Meadowfield	Aberd	NO8892	57°1·4'	2°11·4'W	X	38,45
Meadow Field	Brad	SE0443	53°53·2'	1°55·9'W	X	104
Meadowfield	Durham	NZ2439	54°45·0'	1°37·2'W	T	93
Meadowfield	Fife	NT2289	56°5·5'	3°14·8'W	X	66
Meadowfield	Highld	NH9255	57°34·6'	3°47·9'W	X	27
Meadowfield	N Lanak	NS8170	55°54·8'	3°53·8'W	X	65
Meadowfield	Stir	NS8690	56°5·6'	3°49·5'W	X	58
Meadowfield Fm	C of Edin	NT1773	55°56·8'	3°19·3'W	FM	65,66
Meadow Flatt	Cumbr	NY7243	54°47·1'	2°25·7'W	X	86,87
Meadowflatt	S Lanak	NS9639	55°38·3'	3°38·7'W	X	72
Meadow Fm	Beds	SP9746	52°6·5'	0°34·6'W	FM	153
Meadow Fm	Cambs	TL2582	52°25·5'	0°9·3'W	FM	142
Meadow Fm	Ches	SJ5553	53°4·6'	2°39·9'W	FM	117
Meadow Fm	Derby	SK1474	53°16·0'	1°47·0'W	FM	119
Meadow Fm	Derby	SK4158	53°7·3'	1°22·8'W	FM	120
Meadow Fm	Glos	SP1823	51°54·5'	1°43·9'W	FM	163
Meadow Fm	Lancs	SD4039	53°50·9'	2°54·3'W	FM	102
Meadow Fm	Norf	TF8606	52°37·4'	0°45·3'E	FM	144
Meadow Fm	Norf	TG1904	52°35·6'	1°14·4'E	FM	134
Meadow Fm	Notts	SK6956	53°6·0'	0°57·8'W	FM	120
Meadow Fm	Notts	SK7747	53°1·1'	0°50·7'W	FM	129
Meadow Fm	Oxon	SP3301	51°42·6'	1°30·9'W	FM	164
Meadow Fm	Warw	SK2805	52°38·8'	1°34·8'W	FM	140
Meadow Fm	Wrex	SJ3459	53°7·7'	2°58·8'W	FM	117
Meadow Fm Ho	Oxon	SU4696	51°39·9'	1°19·7'W	X	164
Meadowfoot	D & G	NS8613	55°24·1'	3°47·6'W	X	71,78
Meadowfoot	N Ayr	NS2147	55°41·3'	4°50·4'W	T	63
Meadowfoot	N Lanak	NS9159	55°49·0'	3°43·9'W	X	65,72
Meadowfoot	S Lanak	NS6139	55°37·7'	4°12·0'W	X	71
Meadowgreen	Angus	NO4846	56°36·4'	2°50·4'W	X	54
Meadow Green	Heref	SO7156	52°12·3'	2°25·1'W	T	149
Meadowgreens	Falk	NS7782	56°1·2'	3°58·0'W	X	57,64
Meadow Hall	Roth	SK3992	53°25·6'	1°24·4'W	T	110,111
Meadowhaugh	Northum	NY8990	55°12·5'	2°9·9'W	X	80
Meadow Haven	Northum	NU0152	55°45·9'	1°58·6'W	W	75
Meadowhead	Aberd	NJ6438	57°26·1'	2°35·5'W	X	29
Meadowhead	Aberd	NJ8915	57°13·8'	2°10·5'W	X	38
Meadow Head	Black w Dar	SD6624	53°42·9'	2°30·5'W	X	103
Meadowhead	D & G	NX5199	55°16·0'	4°20·3'W	X	77
Meadowhead	D & G	NX5553	54°51·3'	4°15·1'W	X	83
Meadowhead	D & G	NX8272	55°2·0'	3°50·3'W	X	84
Meadowhead	E Ayr	NS5143	55°39·7'	4°21·7'W	X	70
Meadowhead	E Ayr	NS5431	55°33·3'	4°18·4'W	X	70
Meadowhead	Fife	NT0396	56°9·1'	3°33·2'W	X	58
Meadow Head	Lancs	SD6135	53°48·8'	2°35·1'W	X	102,103
Meadow Head	Lancs	SD8227	53°44·6'	2°16·0'W	X	103
Meadowhead	N Ayr	NS2146	55°40·7'	4°50·4'W	X	63
Meadowhead	S Ayr	NS4220	55°27·2'	4°29·5'W	X	70
Meadowhead	S Ayr	NS4332	55°33·6'	4°28·9'W	X	70
Meadow Head	Sheff	SK3482	53°20·3'	1°29·0'W	T	110,111
Meadowhead	S Lanak	NS6447	55°42·1'	4°9·4'W	X	64
Meadowhead	S Lanak	NS8349	55°43·5'	3°51·3'W	X	72
Meadowhead	S Lanak	NT1046	55°42·2'	3°25·5'W	X	72
Meadowhead Burn	D & G	NX7651	54°50·6'	3°55·4'W	W	84
Meadowhead Fm	C of Edin	NT2669	55°54·8'	3°10·6'W	FM	66
Meadowhead Fm	E Ayr	NS5428	55°31·7'	4°18·3'W	FM	70
Meadowhill	Aberd	NJ9754	57°34·8'	2°2·6'W	X	30
Meadow Hill	D & G	NX2672	55°1·0'	4°42·9'W	X	76
Meadow Hill	E Ayr	NS5743	55°39·8'	4°16·0'W	X	71
Meadow Hill Ho	Northum	NT9854	55°47·0'	2°1·5'W	X	75
Meadow Ho	Wrex	SJ3856	53°6·1'	2°55·2'W	X	117
Meadow House Fm	Ches	SJ3659	53°7·7'	2°57·0'W	FM	117
Meadow House Mains	Scot Bord	NT9153	55°46·5'	2°8·2'W	X	67,74,75
Meadow Ing Fm	Cumbr	NY6522	54°35·8'	2°32·1'W	FM	91
Meadowlands	Ches	SJ7983	53°20·8'	2°18·5'W	X	109
Meadowlands Fm	E Susx	TQ3522	50°59·1'	0°4·2'W	FM	198
Meadowlands Fm	Glos	SP1006	51°45·4'	1°50·9'W	FM	163
Meadowlea	Aberd	NJ4506	57°8·8'	2°54·1'W	X	37
Meadowley	Shrops	SO6692	52°31·7'	2°29·7'W	T	138
Meadow Lodge	Cumbr	NY1353	54°52·1'	3°20·9'W	X	85
Meadow Lodge	W Susx	SU9905	50°50·4'	0°35·2'W	X	197
Meadow Main	S Ayr	NS2501	55°16·6'	4°44·9'W	X	76
Meadowmill	E Loth	NT4073	55°57·0'	2°57·2'W	T	66
Meadowmore	Pth & Kin	NO0132	56°28·4'	3°36·0'W	X	52,53
Meadown	Devon	SS8718	50°57·3'	3°36·1'W	X	181
Meadownay	S Ayr	NS2812	55°22·6'	4°42·4'W	X	70
Meadow of Fitchin	Shetld	HU3970	60°25·0'	1°17·0'W	X	2,3
Meadow Park	C of Edin	NT2572	55°56·4'	3°11·6'W	X	66
Meadow Park	S Ayr	NX0779	55°4·3'	5°1·0'W	X	76
Meadow Place Grange	Derby	SK2065	53°11·1'	1°41·6'W	X	119
Meadow Point	N Ayr	NS1552	55°43·8'	4°56·3'W	X	63,69
Meadows	Aberd	NJ5357	57°36·3'	2°46·7'W	X	29
Meadows	Angus	NO4454	56°40·7'	2°54·4'W	X	54
Meadows	C of Nott	SK5738	52°56·4'	1°8·7'W	T	129
Meadows	Staffs	SJ9863	53°10·1'	2°1·4'W	X	118
Meadows	Staffs	SK0458	53°7·4'	1°56·0'W	X	119
Meadows	Stock	SJ9989	53°24·1'	2°0·5'W	X	109
Meadows Br	Carm	SN5712	51°47·5'	4°4·0'W	X	159
Meadows Downs	Corn	SX1773	50°31·9'	4°34·6'W	X	201
Meadows Fm	Ches	SJ4548	53°1·8'	2°48·8'W	FM	117
Meadows Fm	Lancs	SD7642	53°52·7'	2°21·5'W	FM	103
Meadowside	N Lanak	NS7579	55°59·5'	3°59·8'W	X	64
Meadowside	Pth & Kin	NO2340	56°33·0'	3°14·7'W	X	53
Meadowside	S Lanak	NS7145	55°41·1'	4°2·7'W	X	64
Meadowside	S Lanak	NT0342	55°40·0'	3°32·1'W	X	72
Meadows Mill	Worcs	SO6967	52°18·3'	2°26·9'W	X	138,149
Meadows of Ballied	Pth & Kin	NO1146	56°36·1'	3°26·5'W	X	53
Meadows, The	Heref	SO5546	52°6·9'	2°39·0'W	X	149
Meadows, The	Norf	TG2328	52°48·4'	1°18·9'E	X	133,134
Meadows, The	Powys	SO2792	52°31·5'	3°4·2'W	X	137
Meadows, The	Warw	SP4857	52°12·8'	1°17·4'W	X	151
Meadows, The	Worcs	SO5966	52°17·7'	2°35·7'W	X	137,138,149
Meadows, The	Wrex	SJ4741	52°58·1'	2°46·9'W	X	117
Meadow, The	Cambs	TL3679	52°23·8'	0°0·3'E	X	142
Meadow Top	Lancs	SD7453	53°58·6'	2°23·4'W	X	103
Meadowtown	Shrops	SJ3101	52°36·4'	3°0·7'W	T	126

Meadow Vale Fm	Somer	ST7325	51°1·7'	2°22·7'W	FM	183
Meadowwells	Fife	NO2713	56°18·5'	3°10·4'W	X	59
Meadow Wood	Kent	TQ5442	51°9·6'	0°12·5'E	F	188
Mead Riding	S Glos	ST7283	51°32·9'	2°23·8'W	X	172
Meads	E Susx	TV6097	50°45·3'	0°16·5'E	T	199
Meads	Somer	SS8243	51°10·7'	3°40·9'W	X	181
Meads Fm	Corn	SX1997	50°44·9'	4°33·6'W	FM	190
Meads Fm	Oxon	SP2926	51°56·1'	1°34·3'W	FM	164
Meadshaw	Scot Bord	NT3809	55°22·5'	2°58·3'W	X	79
Meadside	Oxon	SU5893	51°38·2'	1°9·3'W	T	164,174
Meads of St John	Moray	NJ0155	57°34·7'	3°38·9'W	X	27
Meads, The	Devon	SX5682	50°37·4'	4°1·8'W	X	191
Meads, The	Monm	SO4901	51°42·6'	2°43·9'W	X	162
Meads, The	Somer	ST2835	51°6·8'	3°1·3'W	X	182
Mead, The	Northum	NU0443	55°41·1'	1°55·7'W	X	75
Meadulse	Fife	NT1883	56°2·2'	3°18·5'W	X	65,66
Meadup Ho	Lancs	SD4259	54°1·7'	2°52·7'W	X	102
Mead Vale	Surrey	TQ2649	51°13·8'	0°11·3'W	T	187
Meadwell	Devon	SX4081	50°36·6'	4°15·3'W	T	201
Meaford	Staffs	SJ8835	52°55·0'	2°10·3'W	T	127
Meaford Fm	Staffs	SJ8936	52°55·5'	2°9·4'W	FM	127
Meafordhall Fm	Staffs	SJ8837	52°56·1'	2°10·3'W	FM	127
Meagill	N Yks	SE1755	53°59·7'	1°44·0'W	T	104
Meagill Hall Fm	N Yks	SE1756	54°0·2'	1°44·0'W	FM	104
Meagram Ho	Lincs	TF3978	53°17·1'	0°5·5'E	X	122
Meagram Top	Lincs	TF3978	53°17·1'	0°5·5'E	X	122
Meagre Fm	Cambs	TL1563	52°15·4'	0°18·5'W	FM	153
Meahall	N Eil	NF8788	57°46·6'	7°15·5'W	H	18
Meal	Shetld	HU3735	60°6·1'	1°19·6'W	X	4
Mealabost	N Eil	NB4157	58°25·7'	6°25·7'W	T	8
Mealabost	N Eil	NB4632	58°12·5'	6°19·0'W	T	8
Meal an Driuchain	Highld	NN2586	56°56·2'	4°52·1'W	H	34,41
Meal an Driuchain	Highld	NN2586	56°56·2'	4°52·1'W	H	34,41
Meal an t-Snaim	Pth & Kin	NN4540	56°31·8'	4°30·8'W	H	34
Mealasta	N Eil	NB0022	58°5·4'	7°5·0'W	X	13
Mealasta Island	N Eil	NA9821	58°4·8'	7°6·9'W	X	13
Meal Bank	Cumbr	SD5495	54°21·2'	2°42·0'W	T	97
Mealbank	Lancs	SD6067	54°6·1'	2°36·3'W	X	97
Mealbhach	Arg & Bt	NM0647	56°31·6'	6°46·4'W	X	46
Meal Bhad Chaineamnaich	Highld	NH3157	57°34·6'	4°49·1'W	H	26
Meal Chrò Bheinn	Highld	NM4765	56°42·8'	6°7·6'W	H	47
Mealdarroch Point	Arg & Bt	NR8868	55°51·8'	5°22·8'W	X	62
Meal Fell	Cumbr	NY2833	54°41·5'	3°6·6'W	X	89,90
Meal Hill	Kirk	SE0714	53°37·6'	1°53·2'W	X	110
Meal Hill	Kirk	SE1707	53°33·8'	1°44·2'W	T	110
Mealista	N Eil	NA9924	58°6·4'	7°6·2'W	T	13
Mealisval	N Eil	NB0226	58°7·6'	7°3·3'W	H	13
Meall a' Bhainaiche	Highld	NM8859	56°40·7'	5°27·2'W	H	49
Meall a' Bhainne	Highld	NG7583	57°47·1'	5°46·6'W	H	19
Meall a' Bhainne	Highld	NH1481	57°47·1'	5°7·2'W	H	20
Meall a' Bhainne	Highld	NH1975	57°44·0'	5°1·9'W	H	20
Meall a' Bhainne	Highld	NM9078	56°51·0'	5°26·2'W	H	40
Meall a' Bhainne	Highld	NN3066	56°45·5'	4°46·4'W	H	41
Meall a' Bhaird	Highld	NH4070	57°41·7'	4°40·6'W	H	20
Meall a' Bhàrr	Pth & Kin	NN6750	56°37·6'	4°9·6'W	X	42,51
Meall a' Bhata	Highld	NC6326	58°12·4'	4°19·4'W	H	16
Meall a' Bhàthaich	Pth & Kin	NN6673	56°50·0'	4°11·3'W	X	42
Meall a' Bhealaich	Highld	NC8940	58°20·3'	3°53·3'W	H	10
Meall a' Bhealaich	Highld	NH0121	57°14·5'	5°17·4'W	H	25,33
Meall a' Bhealaich	Pth & Kin	NN4569	56°47·5'	4°31·8'W	H	42
Meall a' Bhiord	Pth & Kin	NN6970	56°48·4'	4°8·3'W	X	42
Meall a' Bhobuir	Pth & Kin	NN5152	56°38·4'	4°25·3'W	H	42,51
Meall a' Bhogair Mór	Highld	NH3352	57°31·9'	4°46·9'W	H	26
Meall a' Bhothain	Highld	NH6605	57°7·2'	4°12·3'W	H	35
Meall a' Bhràghaid	Highld	NM9158	56°40·3'	5°24·2'W	H	49
Meall a' Bhreacain	Highld	NH6281	57°48·1'	4°18·9'W	X	21
Meall a' Bhreac-leathaid	Highld	NC6648	58°24·3'	4°17·1'W	X	10
Meall a' Bhreacraibh	Highld	NH7935	57°23·6'	4°0·3'W	H	27
Meall à Bhrodainn	Highld	NM8779	56°51·5'	5°29·2'W	X	40
Meall a' Bhròin	Highld	NM6860	56°40·7'	5°46·8'W	H	40
Meall a' Bhrollaich	Highld	NC5837	58°18·2'	4°24·9'W	H	16
Meall a' Bhuachaille	Highld	NH9911	57°11·0'	3°39·8'W	H	36
Meall a' Bhuailt	Highld	NH5816	57°13·0'	4°20·6'W	H	35
Meall a' Bhùirich	Highld	NC2305	58°0·2'	4°59·2'W	H	15
Meall a' Bhùirich	Highld	NC3134	58°16·0'	4°52·4'W	H	15
Meall a' Bhùirich	Highld	NC3412	58°4·2'	4°48·4'W	H	15
Meall a' Bhùirich	Highld	NC8338	58°19·2'	3°59·4'W	H	17
Meall a' Bhùirich	Highld	NN2570	56°47·6'	4°51·5'W	H	41
Meall a' Bhùirich Rapaig	Highld	NC2502	57°58·6'	4°57·1'W	H	15
Meall a' Bhùiridh	Highld	NM8554	56°38·0'	5°29·9'W	X	49
Meall a' Bhuiridh	Highld	NN1250	56°36·5'	5°3·3'W	H	41
Meall a' Bhuiridh	Highld	NN2550	56°36·8'	4°50·7'W	H	41
Meall a' Bràghaid	Highld	NC3013	58°4·7'	4°52·5'W	H	15
Mealla Bru	N Eil	NF9074	57°39·2'	7°11·4'W	X	18
Meall Acairseid	Highld	NG6257	57°32·7'	5°58·2'W	H	24
Meall Achadh a' Chùirn	Highld	NM7051	56°35·9'	5°44·4'W	H	49
Meall Achadh Deisteil	Highld	NG8176	57°43·5'	5°40·2'W	H	19
Meall a' Chairn	Highld	NH1585	57°49·2'	5°6·4'W	H	20
Meall a' Chàise	Arg & Bt	NM7517	56°17·8'	5°37·7'W	H	55
Meall a' Chàise	Highld	NC6511	58°4·3'	4°16·9'W	H	16
Meall a' Chàise	Highld	NM7256	56°38·7'	5°42·7'W	H	49
Meall a' Chaisg	Highld	NH1032	57°20·6'	5°9·0'W	X	25
Meall a' Chaisteil	Highld	NG8218	57°12·3'	5°36·1'W	X	33
Meall a' Chait	Highld	NH0600	57°3·3'	5°11·5'W	H	33
Meall a' Chall	Pth & Kin	NN4340	56°31·8'	4°32·7'W	H	51
Meall a Chaochain Duibh	Highld	NH7606	57°8·0'	4°2·5'W	H	35
Meall a' Chaorainn	Highld	NH1360	57°35·7'	5°7·3'W	H	19
Meall a' Chaorainn	Highld	NH3582	57°48·1'	4°46·1'W	H	20
Meall a' Chaorainn	Highld	NH4779	57°46·7'	4°33·9'W	H	20
Meall a' Chaorainn	Highld	NH6997	57°56·8'	4°12·3'W	H	21
Meall a' Chaorainn	Highld	NM7644	56°32·3'	5°38·2'W	H	49
Meall a' Chaorainn	Highld	NN1165	56°44·6'	5°5·0'W	H	41
Meall a' Chaorainn	Highld	NN6477	56°52·1'	4°13·4'W	H	42
Meall a' Chaorainn Beag	Highld	NN4794	57°1·0'	4°30·7'W	H	34
Meall a' Chaorainn Loch Uisge	Highld	NM8054	56°37·8'	5°34·8'W	H	49
Meall a' Chaorainn Mór	Highld	NN4892	56°59·9'	4°29·7'W	H	34
Meall a' Chaoruinn	Highld	NC2604	57°59·7'	4°56·2'W	H	15
Meall a' Chaoruinn	Highld	NC6715	58°6·5'	4°15·0'W	H	16
Meall a' Chapuill	Highld	NH0140	57°24·7'	5°18·3'W	H	25
Meall a' Charra	Highld	NH0115	57°11·2'	5°17·1'W	X	33
Meall a' Charra	Highld	NH0412	57°9·7'	5°14·0'W	X	33
Meall a' Charra	Pth & Kin	NN8957	56°41·8'	3°48·3'W	H	52
Meall a' Chathaidh	Pth & Kin	NN7467	56°46·9'	4°3·3'W	H	42
Meallach Bheag	Highld	NN7792	57°0·4'	4°1·1'W	H	35
Meallach Chaitrine	Highld	NN6591	56°59·7'	4°12·9'W	X	35
Meall a' Cheardaich	Highld	NC3140	58°19·2'	4°52·7'W	H	9
Meall a Chlaignn	Highld	NH0780	57°46·4'	5°14·3'W	H	19
Meall a' Chléirich	Highld	NC4036	58°17·3'	4°43·3'W	H	16
Meallach Mhór	Highld	NN7790	56°59·4'	4°1·0'W	H	35
Meall a' Chnoic	Highld	NC5920	58°9·1'	4°23·3'W	H	16
Meall a' Chòcaire	Highld	NH7607	57°8·5'	4°2·5'W	H	35
Meall a' Choire	Highld	NG8695	57°53·9'	5°36·2'W	H	19
Meall a' Choire	Highld	NH3528	57°19·0'	4°43·9'W	H	26
Meall a' Choire Bheithich	Highld	NM7953	56°37·3'	5°35·7'W	H	49
Meall a' Choire Bhuidhe	Highld	NC6938	58°18·9'	4°13·7'W	H	16
Meall a' Choire Bhuidhe	Highld	NM9999	57°2·6'	5°18·3'W	H	33,40
Meall a' Choire Bhuidhe	Pth & Kin	NO0670	56°49·0'	3°31·9'W	H	43
Meall a' Choire Charnaich	Highld	NM9799	57°2·5'	5°20·3'W	H	33,40
Meall a' Choire Chreagaich	Pth & Kin	NN7941	56°33·0'	3°57·6'W	H	51,52
Meall a' Choire Chruinn	Highld	NM8776	56°49·9'	5°29·0'W	H	40
Meall a' Choire Dhuibh	Highld	NM9198	57°1·8'	5°26·2'W	H	33,40
Meall a' Choire Ghlais	Highld	NG9375	57°43·3'	5°28·1'W	H	19
Meall a' Choire Ghlais	Highld	NN2295	57°1·0'	4°55·5'W	H	34
Meall a' Choirein Luachraich	Highld	NM8959	56°40·8'	5°26·2'W	H	49
Meall a' Choire Leacaich	Highld	NC5253	58°26·7'	4°31·7'W	X	10
Meall a' Choire Leith	Highld	NH0101	57°3·7'	5°16·5'W	H	33
Meall a' Choire Léith	Pth & Kin	NN6143	56°33·8'	4°15·3'W	H	51
Meall a' Choire Mhóir	Arg & Bt	NM6736	56°27·8'	5°46·5'W	X	49
Meall a' Choire Odhair	Highld	NG7986	57°48·8'	5°42·8'W	H	19
Meall a' Choire Odhair	Pth & Kin	NN7914	56°18·4'	3°56·9'W	H	57
Meall a' Choire Riabhaich	Pth & Kin	NN7713	56°17·9'	3°58·8'W	H	57
Meall a' Chòis	Highld	NG6933	57°20·0'	5°49·8'W	H	24,32
Meall a' Cholumain	Highld	NH3604	57°6·1'	4°42·0'W	H	34
Meall a' Chòmhlain	Highld	NN3193	57°0·1'	4°46·5'W	H	34
Meall a' Chrasgaidh	Highld	NH1873	57°42·9'	5°2·9'W	H	20
Meall a' Chràthaich	Highld	NH3622	57°15·8'	4°42·7'W	H	26
Meall a' Chreagain Duibh	Highld	NH1143	57°26·5'	5°8·5'W	X	25
Meall a' Chreamha	Highld	NN1048	56°35·4'	5°5·2'W	H	50
Meall a' Chrimig	Highld	NH5168	57°40·9'	4°29·5'W	H	20
Meall a' Chròm Dhoire	Highld	NH2404	57°5·9'	4°53·9'W	H	34
Meall a' Chròm Dhoire	Highld	NH2704	57°5·9'	4°50·9'W	H	34
Meall a' Chròtha	Highld	NN5384	56°55·7'	4°24·5'W	X	42
Meall a' Chuaille	Highld	NC1902	57°58·5'	5°3·2'W	H	15
Meall a' Chuaille	Highld	NH3482	57°48·1'	4°47·1'W	H	20
Meall a' Chuilinn	Highld	NH2962	57°37·2'	4°51·3'W	H	20
Meall a' Chuilinn	Highld	NM7659	56°40·4'	5°38·9'W	X	49
Meall a Chuilinn	Highld	NM8961	56°41·8'	5°26·3'W	H	40
Meall a' Chùit	Highld	NN4697	57°2·6'	4°31·8'W	H	34
Meall a' Chuna Mór	Highld	NC0826	58°11·1'	5°15·5'W	H	15
Meall a' Churain	Stir	NN4632	56°27·5'	4°29·5'W	H	51
Meall a' Cluith or Cliff Hill	Highld	NG8480	57°45·7'	5°37·4'W	H	19
Meall a' Gharbh Choire	Highld	NH5982	57°48·6'	4°21·9'W	X	21
Meall a' Gharbhgair	Highld	NG7754	57°31·5'	5°43·0'W	H	24
Meall a' Gheur-fheadain	Highld	NH2641	57°25·8'	4°53·4'W	H	25
Meall a' Ghiubhais	Highld	NH1747	57°28·8'	5°2·7'W	X	25
Meall a' Ghiubhais	Pth & Kin	NN5096	57°2·1'	4°27·9'W	H	35
Meall a' Ghlamaidh	Arg & Bt	NR6349	55°40·9'	5°45·8'W	H	62
Meall a' Ghlas Leothaid	Highld	NG8670	57°40·4'	5°34·9'W	H	19
Meall a' Ghob Sheilich	Highld	NM6370	56°45·9'	5°52·2'W	H	40
Meall a' Ghoirtein	Highld	NG4001	57°1·9'	6°16·7'W	X	32,39
Meall a' Ghortain	Arg & Bt	NN3749	56°36·5'	4°38·9'W	H	50
Meall a' Ghraidh	Highld	NH1620	57°14·3'	5°2·5'W	X	25
Meall a' Ghrianain	Highld	NH3677	57°45·4'	4°44·9'W	H	20
Meall a' Ghriuth	Highld	NM8266	56°44·3'	5°33·4'W	X	40
Meall a' Ghrùididh	Highld	NC5304	58°0·3'	4°28·8'W	H	16
Meall a' Ghuail	Highld	NH5164	57°38·7'	4°29·3'W	H	20
Meall a' Ghuibhais	Highld	NG9763	57°36·9'	5°23·5'W	H	19
Meall a' Ghuirmein	Highld	NH5822	57°16·3'	4°20·8'W	H	26,35
Meall a' Giubhas	Highld	NH0061	57°35·9'	5°20·4'W	X	19
Meall Ailein	Arg & Bt	NM8121	56°20·1'	5°32·1'W	H	49
Meall Ailein	Highld	NC6131	58°15·0'	4°21·6'W	H	16
Meall Ailein	Highld	NG8731	57°19·5'	5°31·8'W	H	24
Meall Airigh Mhic Criadh	Highld	NG8377	57°44·1'	5°38·2'W	H	19
Meall Alvie	Aberd	NO2091	57°0·5'	3°18·6'W	H	44
Meall a' Mhadaidh	Highld	NH3037	57°23·8'	4°49·3'W	H	26
Meall a' Mhadaidh	Stir	NN5925	56°24·0'	4°16·6'W	H	51
Meall a' Mhadaidh Beag	Highld	NM7174	56°48·3'	5°44·6'W	H	40
Meall a' Mhadaidh Mór	Highld	NM7275	56°48·9'	5°43·7'W	X	40
Meall a' Mhaoil	Highld	NG5530	57°18·0'	6°3·6'W	H	24,32
Meall a' Mheanbh-chruidh	Highld	NN3989	56°58·1'	4°38·5'W	H	34,41
Meall a' Mhuic	Pth & Kin	NN5750	56°37·5'	4°19·4'W	H	42,51
Meall a' Mhuilt	Pth & Kin	NO0966	56°46·9'	3°28·9'W	H	43
Meall a' Mhuirich	Pth & Kin	NN9775	56°51·6'	3°40·9'W	H	43
Meall a' Mhuthaich	Highld	NC1917	58°6·6'	5°3·9'W	H	15
Meallan a' Bhùtha	Highld	NH2876	57°44·7'	4°52·9'W	X	20
Meall an Achaidh Gharbhgein	Highld	NG9728	57°18·1'	5°21·7'W	X	25,33
Meallan a' Chruidh	Highld	NH0272	57°41·9'	5°18·9'W	X	19
Meallan a' Chuail	Highld	NC3429	58°13·4'	4°49·1'W	H	15
Meallan a' Gharuidhe	Highld	NH3170	57°41·6'	4°49·7'W	H	20
Meall an Aisridh	Highld	NM7766	56°44·2'	5°38·3'W	X	40
Meall an Amairich	Highld	NC4832	58°15·3'	4°34·9'W	H	16
Meallan a' Mhùthaidh Beag	Highld	NH3164	57°38·3'	4°49·4'W	H	20
Meallan a' Mhùthaidh Mór	Highld	NH3166	57°39·4'	4°49·5'W	H	20
Meallan an Laoigh	Highld	NH0774	57°43·1'	5°14·0'W	H	19
Meallan an Lochain-ghiubhais	Highld	NG9189	57°50·8'	5°30·8'W	H	19
Meallanan Odhar	Pth & Kin	NN5467	56°46·6'	4°22·9'W	X	42
Meallanan Odhar	Pth & Kin	NN6753	56°39·3'	4°9·7'W	H	42,51
Meall an Aodainn	Highld	NN0852	56°37·5'	5°7·3'W	H	41
Meall an Aoil	Highld	NM6971	56°46·7'	5°46·4'W	X	40
Meall an Aonaich	Highld	NC3316	58°6·4'	4°49·6'W	H	15
Meall an Araich	Arg & Bt	NN2143	56°33·0'	4°54·3'W	H	50
Meall an Arbhair	Arg & Bt	NR3890	56°2·1'	6°11·9'W	X	61
Meallan Bàn	Highld	NH2980	57°46·9'	4°52·1'W	H	20
Meallan Buidhe	Highld	NH1337	57°23·4'	5°6·2'W	X	25
Meallan Buidhe	Highld	NH2469	57°40·9'	4°56·6'W	H	20
Meallan Buidhe	Highld	NH2863	57°37·7'	4°52·4'W	H	20
Meallan Buidhe	Highld	NH3344	57°27·6'	4°46·6'W	H	26
Meallan Buidhe	Pth & Kin	NN6171	56°48·8'	4°16·2'W	H	42
Meallan Buidhe	Pth & Kin	NN6981	56°54·4'	4°8·6'W	H	42
Meallan Buidhe an Fheadain	Highld	NH1336	57°22·8'	5°6·2'W	X	25
Meallan Caoruinn	Highld	NH3268	57°40·5'	4°48·6'W	H	20
Meall an Ceirileach	Highld	NC4150	58°24·8'	4°42·8'W	H	9
Meallan Chuaich	Highld	NH1168	57°40·0'	5°9·7'W	H	19
Meall an Daimh	Arg & Bt	NN2018	56°19·5'	4°54·2'W	H	50,56
Meall an Daimh	Highld	NG9246	57°27·7'	5°27·6'W	X	25
Meall an Daimh	Highld	NH2522	57°15·6'	4°53·6'W	H	25
Meall an Daimh	Pth & Kin	NN9364	56°45·6'	3°44·6'W	H	43
Meall an Daimh Bhig	Highld	NH3090	57°52·3'	4°51·5'W	H	20
Meall an Daimh Mhòir	Highld	NH3190	57°52·3'	4°50·5'W	H	20
Meall an Damhain	Highld	NM7259	56°40·3'	5°42·8'W	H	49
Meallan Damh Mor	Highld	NH3392	57°53·4'	4°48·6'W	H	20
Meall an Dà Uillt	Highld	NM7866	56°44·2'	5°37·3'W	X	40
Meallan Dearg	Highld	NG4822	57°13·4'	6°10·0'W	H	32
Meallan Dearg Mór	Highld	NG7891	57°51·5'	5°44·1'W	H	19
Meallan Diomhain	Highld	NC1711	58°3·3'	5°5·6'W	H	15
Meall an Doire	Highld	NG8682	57°46·9'	5°35·5'W	H	19
Meall an Doireachain	Highld	NG7349	57°28·7'	5°46·7'W	H	24
Meall an Doire Bheithe	Highld	NH0151	57°30·6'	5°18·9'W	X	25
Meall an Doire Dharaich	Highld	NN2062	56°43·2'	4°56·0'W	H	41
Meall an Doire Dhuibh	Highld	NM8251	56°36·3'	5°32·7'W	H	49
Meall an Doire Dhuinn	Highld	NN0470	56°47·1'	5°12·1'W	X	41
Meall an Doirein	Highld	NG8575	57°43·1'	5°36·1'W	H	19
Meall an Doire Shleaghaich	Highld	NM9873	56°48·5'	5°18·1'W	H	40
Meall an Domhnaich	Highld	NN5395	57°1·6'	4°24·9'W	H	35
Meallan Donn	Highld	NH3674	57°43·8'	4°44·8'W	H	20
Meallan Donn	Highld	NH4370	57°41·8'	4°37·6'W	H	20
Meallan Dubh	Highld	NH6100	57°4·5'	4°17·1'W	H	35
Meallan Dubh	Highld	NM9891	56°58·2'	5°18·9'W	H	33,40
Meall an Dubh-chadha	Highld	NN7890	56°59·4'	4°0·0'W	H	35
Meall an Duibhe	Highld	NH1385	57°49·2'	5°8·4'W	H	19
Meall an Duibhe	Highld	NH6715	57°12·7'	4°11·7'W	H	35
Meall an Eich Ghlais	Highld	NH2097	57°55·8'	5°1·9'W	H	20
Meall an Eòin	Highld	NC5929	58°13·9'	4°23·6'W	H	16
Meall an Eòin	Highld	NH7296	57°56·4'	4°9·3'W	H	21
Meall an Fhamhair	Arg & Bt	NS1283	56°0·4'	5°0·5'W	H	56
Meall an Fharaidh	Arg & Bt	NS0785	56°1·4'	5°5·4'W	X	56
Meall an Fheadain	Highld	NB9910	58°2·3'	5°23·6'W	H	15
Meall an Fheadain	Highld	NC3961	58°30·7'	4°45·3'W	H	9
Meall an Fheidh	Highld	NM9473	56°48·4'	5°22·0'W	H	40
Meall an Fheuraich	Arg & Bt	NN1035	56°28·4'	5°4·6'W	H	50
Meall an Fheur Loch	Highld	NC3631	58°14·5'	4°47·2'W	H	16
Meall an Fhìar Mhàim	Arg & Bt	NM4843	56°31·0'	6°5·3'W	H	47,48
Meall an Fhiodhain	Stir	NN5225	56°23·9'	4°23·4'W	H	51
Meall an Fhìr-eòin	Highld	NM4969	56°45·0'	6°5·9'W	H	47
Meall an Fhìr-eòin	Highld	NM9589	56°57·1'	5°21·8'W	H	40
Meall an Fhliuchaird	Highld	NH0649	57°29·6'	5°13·8'W	H	25
Meall an Fhreiceadain	Highld	NM4866	56°43·3'	6°6·7'W	X	47
Meall an Fhuarain	Highld	NC2802	57°58·7'	4°54·0'W	H	15
Meall an Fhuarain	Highld	NC5130	58°14·3'	4°31·8'W	H	16
Meall an Fhuarain	Highld	NC6123	58°10·7'	4°21·3'W	H	16
Meall an Fhuarain	Highld	NG4535	57°20·3'	6°13·8'W	H	32
Meall an Fhuarain	Pth & Kin	NN5648	56°36·4'	4°20·3'W	X	51
Meall an Fhuarain Mhoir	Highld	NG9919	57°13·3'	5°19·3'W	X	33
Meall an Fhùdair	Arg & Bt	NN2719	56°20·2'	4°47·5'W	H	50,56
Meallan Fulann	Arg & Bt	NM3235	56°26·1'	6°20·4'W	X	46,47,48
Meallan Gainmhich	Highld	NG4435	57°20·3'	6°14·8'W	H	32
Meallan Ghobhar	Highld	NH0264	57°37·6'	5°18·5'W	H	19
Meallan Glaic	Arg & Bt	NS0673	55°54·9'	5°5·8'W	X	63
Meallan Gobhar	Highld	NG8446	57°27·4'	5°35·6'W	H	24
Meall an Iasgaich	N Eil	NF8315	57°7·3'	7°13·8'W	H	31
Meall an Iasgaire	Highld	NH2309	57°8·5'	4°55·1'W	H	34
Meallan Ime	Highld	NH3792	57°53·5'	4°44·5'W	H	20
Meall an Inbhire	Arg & Bt	NM4656	56°37·9'	6°8·1'W	H	47
Meall an Laoigh	Arg & Bt	NN2437	56°29·8'	4°51·1'W	H	50
Meall an Leathaid	Highld	NH5573	57°43·7'	4°25·6'W	H	21
Meall an Leathaid Dharaich	Highld	NG8781	57°46·4'	5°34·4'W	H	19
Meall an Leathaid Mhóir	Highld	NH0054	57°32·2'	5°20·0'W	H	25
Meallan Liath	Highld	NC5150	58°25·0'	4°32·6'W	H	9
Meallan Liath Beag	Highld	NC2320	58°8·3'	4°59·9'W	X	15
Meallan Liath Beag	Highld	NC3637	58°17·7'	4°47·4'W	H	16
Meallan Liath Beag	Highld	NC6616	58°7·0'	4°16·0'W	H	16
Meallan Liath Beag	Highld	NC8815	58°6·9'	3°53·6'W	H	17
Meallan Liath Coire Mhic Dhughaill	Highld	NC3539	58°18·8'	4°48·5'W	H	15
Meallan Liath Mór	Highld	NC2218	58°7·2'	5°0·8'W	H	15
Meallan Liath Mór	Highld	NC4032	58°15·1'	4°43·1'W	H	16
Meallan Liath Mór	Highld	NC6517	58°7·5'	4°17·1'W	H	16
Meallan Liath Mór	Highld	NC8813	58°5·8'	3°53·5'W	H	17
Meall an Lochain	Highld	NC3104	57°59·9'	4°51·1'W	H	15
Meall an Lochain	Pth & Kin	NN8845	56°35·3'	3°49·0'W	H	52
Meall an Lochain Duibh	Arg & Bt	NM4743	56°30·9'	6°6·3'W	X	47,48
Meall an Lochain Ghaineamhaich	Highld	NC4148	58°23·8'	4°42·8'W	X	9
Meall an Lochain Ruaidh	Highld	NC6361	58°31·2'	4°20·7'W	H	10
Meall an Lochain Sgeireich	Highld	NC3845	58°22·1'	4°45·7'W	X	9
Meall an Lundain	Aberd	NO0694	57°1·9'	3°32·5'W	H	36,43
Meallan Mhic Iamhair	Highld	NH0654	57°32·3'	5°14·0'W	H	25
Meall an Mhurchaidh	Highld	NH2478	57°45·7'	4°57·0'W	H	20
Mèallan na Ceardaich	Highld	NH2628	57°18·8'	4°52·9'W	H	25
Meallan na Circe-fraoich	Highld	NH0060	57°35·4'	5°20·3'W	X	19
Meallan nan Duibhre	Highld	NH2218	57°13·4'	4°56·4'W	X	34
Meallan nan Gobhar	Highld	NH0172	57°41·9'	5°19·9'W	H	19
Meallan nan Sac	Highld	NH3081	57°47·4'	4°51·1'W	H	20
Meallan nan Uan	Highld	NH2654	57°32·8'	4°54·0'W	H	25
Meallan Odhar	Highld	NC2304	57°59·7'	4°59·2'W	H	15
Meallan Odhar	Highld	NC2904	57°59·8'	4°53·1'W	H	15
Meallan Odhar	Highld	NG9513	57°10·0'	5°23·0'W	H	33
Meall an Odhar	Highld	NH0224	57°16·1'	5°16·6'W	H	25,33

Meallan Odhar	Highld	NH0767	57°39·4′	5°13·6′W	X	19
Meallan Odhar	Highld	NH1538	57°24·0′	5°4·3′W	H	25
Meallan Odhar	Highld	NH2063	57°37·5′	5°0·4′W	H	20
Meallan Odhar	Highld	NH2117	57°12·8′	4°57·4′W	H	34
Meallan Odhar	Highld	NH2435	57°22·6′	4°55·2′W	H	25
Meallan Odhar	Highld	NH2746	57°28·5′	4°52·7′W	H	25
Meallan Odhar	Highld	NH3596	57°55·6′	4°46·7′W	H	34
Meallan Odhar	Highld	NH3893	57°54·1′	4°43·5′W	H	20
Meallan Odhar	Highld	NH4000	57°4·1′	4°37·9′W	H	34
Meallan Odhar	Highld	NM6083	56°52·8′	5°55·9′W	X	40
Meallan Odhar	Highld	NN2097	57°2·0′	4°57·5′W	X	34
Meallan Odhar	Highld	NN3183	56°54·7′	4°46·1′W	X	34,41
Meallan Odhar	Highld	NN3499	57°3·4′	4°43·8′W	H	34
Meallan Odhar	Highld	NN4077	56°51·7′	4°37·0′W	X	42
Meallan Odhar	Highld	NN4496	57°2·0′	4°33·8′W	H	34
Meallan Odhar	Highld	NN5279	56°53·0′	4°25·3′W	H	42
Meall an Odhar	Pth & Kin	NN4744	56°34·0′	4°29·0′W	H	51
Meallan Odhar Doire nan Gillean	Highld	NH1537	57°23·4′	5°4·2′W	H	25
Meallan Odhar Meadhon	Highld	NN4099	57°3·5′	4°37·8′W	X	34
Meallan Odhar nan Glasa	Highld	NH3592	57°53·5′	4°46·5′W	H	20
Meallan Riabhach	Arg & Bt	NS0575	55°56·0′	5°6·9′W	H	63
Meallan Sidhein	Arg & Bt	NS0674	55°55·5′	5°5·9′W	X	63
Meall an Spardain	Highld	NG8575	57°43·1′	5°36·1′W	H	19
Meall an Spàrdain	Highld	NG9400	57°3·0′	5°23·3′W	X	33
Meall an Spothaidh	Highld	NC6649	58°24·8′	4°17·1′W	X	10
Meall an Stalcair	Pth & Kin	NN5052	56°38·4′	4°26·3′W	H	42,51
Meall an Tagraidh	Highld	NN1994	57°0·4′	4°58·4′W	H	34
Meall an Tairbh	Highld	NH2039	57°24·6′	4°59·3′W	H	25
Meall an Tairbh	Highld	NM9666	56°44·7′	5°19·7′W	X	40
Meall an Tarmachain	Highld	NM4966	56°43·4′	6°5·7′W	H	47
Meall an Tàrmachain	Highld	NM9188	56°56·4′	5°25·7′W	H	40
Meall an Tarsaid	Highld	NH4913	57°11·2′	4°29·5′W	H	34
Meall an Tionail	Aberd	NO2287	56°58·3′	3°16·5′W	H	44
Meall an Torcain	Highld	NH3272	57°42·6′	4°48·7′W	H	20
Meall an Tota	Highld	NC1115	58°5·3′	5°11·9′W	H	15
Meall an Triubhais Dhuibh	Highld	NG8572	57°41·5′	5°36·0′W	X	19
Meall an t-Saighdeir	Highld	NG7400	57°2·4′	5°43·1′W	X	33
Meall an t-Seallaidh	Stir	NN5423	56°22·9′	4°21·4′W	H	51
Meall an t-Seamraig	Highld	NN1587	56°56·5′	5°2·0′W	X	34,41
Meall an t-Seangain	Moray	NJ1705	57°8·0′	3°21·8′W	H	36
Meall an t-Siomlair	Highld	NG7855	57°32·1′	5°42·1′W	H	24
Meall an t-sith	Arg & Bt	NS1290	56°4·2′	5°0·8′W	X	56
Meall an t-Sithe	Highld	NH1476	57°44·4′	5°7·0′W	H	20
Meall an t-Sithein	Highld	NN5492	57°0·0′	4°23·8′W	H	35
Meall an t-Slamain	Highld	NN0774	56°49·3′	5°9·3′W	H	41
Meall an t-Slugain	Aberd	NO1295	57°2·5′	3°26·6′W	H	36,43
Meall an t-Slugain	Aberd	NO1886	56°57·7′	3°20·5′W	H	43
Meall an t-Slugain	Highld	NM7965	56°43·7′	5°36·3′W	X	40
Meall an t-Slugain	Highld	NN4872	56°49·1′	4°29·0′W	H	42
Meall an t-Slugain Duibh	Highld	NH5067	57°40·3′	4°30·4′W	H	20
Meall an t-Slugaite	Highld	NC6917	58°7·6′	4°13·0′W	H	16
Meall an t-Socaich	Highld	NC7632	58°15·8′	4°6·3′W	H	17
Meall an t- Sruith	N Eil	NF8644	57°22·9′	7°13·1′W	X	22
Meall an t-Suidhe	Highld	NN1372	56°48·4′	5°3·3′W	H	41
Meall an Tuim Bhàin	Highld	NH3472	57°42·7′	4°46·7′W	H	20
Meall an Tuim Bhuidhe	Highld	NG8164	57°37·0′	5°39·6′W	H	19,24
Meall an Tuirc	Highld	NH5372	57°43·1′	4°27·6′W	H	20
Meall an Tuirc	Highld	NH5569	57°41·5′	4°25·5′W	H	21
Meallan Udrigill	Highld	NG8992	57°52·3′	5°33·0′W	H	19
Meall an Uillt Bhàin	Highld	NG9705	57°5·7′	5°20·6′W	X	33
Meall an Uillt Chaoil	Highld	NM9384	56°54·3′	5°23·5′W	X	40
Meall an Uillt Chreagaich	Highld	NN8287	56°57·8′	3°56·0′W	H	43
Meall an Uillt-fhearna	Highld	NG8002	57°3·7′	5°37·2′W	X	33
Meall an Ulbhaidh	Highld	NC2149	58°23·8′	5°3·3′W	H	9
Meall Aonghais	Highld	NC3144	58°21·4′	4°52·8′W	H	9
Meall a' Phiobaire	Highld	NC6915	58°6·5′	4°12·9′W	H	16
Meall a' Phiobaire	Highld	NH6214	57°12·0′	4°16·6′W	H	35
Meall a' Phubuill	Highld	NN0285	56°55·1′	5°14·7′W	H	41
Meall a' Phuill	Highld	NH4975	57°44·6′	4°31·7′W	X	20
Meall a' Phuill	Highld	NN3257	56°40·7′	4°44·1′W	H	41
Meall a' Phuill	Pth & Kin	NN5048	56°36·3′	4°26·2′W	H	51
Meall Arachaidh	Highld	NG7549	57°28·8′	5°44·7′W	X	24
Meall Ard	Arg & Bt	NR4145	55°38·0′	6°6·5′W	X	60
Meall Àrd	Highld	NC6629	58°14·0′	4°16·5′W	H	16
Meall Ard Archaidh	Highld	NN2199	57°3·1′	4°56·6′W	H	34
Meall Ardruighe	Highld	NN4480	56°53·4′	4°33·2′W	H	34,42
Meall Aundrary	Highld	NG8472	57°41·4′	5°37·0′W	H	19
Meall Bac a' Chùl-dhoire	Highld	NH1330	57°19·6′	5°5·9′W	H	25
Meall Bad a' Bheithe	Highld	NN2359	56°41·6′	4°53·0′W	H	41
Meall Bad a' Chròtha	Highld	NG7772	57°41·2′	5°44·0′W	H	19
Meall Bad a' Mhartuin	Highld	NC4456	58°28·1′	4°40·0′W	H	9
Meall Bad a' Mhuidhe	Highld	NC4355	58°27·6′	4°41·0′W	H	9
Meall Bad na Ceàrdaich	Highld	NG7345	57°26·6′	5°46·5′W	X	24
Meall Bad na Cuaiche	Highld	NC7646	58°23·4′	4°6·8′W	H	10
Meall Bàn	Arg & Bt	NM9949	56°35·7′	5°16·0′W	H	49
Meall Bàn	Highld	NN0053	56°37·8′	5°15·2′W	H	41
Meall Bàn	Pth & Kin	NN5462	56°43·9′	4°22·7′W	H	42
Meall Bàn	Pth & Kin	NN7164	56°45·2′	4°6·1′W	H	42
Meall Beag	Aberd	NJ3914	57°13·0′	3°0·1′W	X	37
Meall Beag	Angus	NO1860	56°43·7′	3°20·0′W	H	43
Meall Beag	Arg & Bt	NN2313	56°16·8′	4°51·1′W	H	50,56
Meall Beag	Arg & Bt	NR8275	55°55·4′	5°28·9′W	X	62
Meall Beag	Highld	NC1237	58°17·2′	5°11·9′W	X	15
Meall Beag	Highld	NH2427	57°18·2′	4°54·8′W	H	25
Meall Beag	Highld	NH5075	57°44·6′	4°30·7′W	H	20
Meall Beag	Highld	NN2947	56°35·3′	4°46·6′W	H	50
Meall Beag	Highld	NN5577	56°52·0′	4°22·3′W	H	42
Meall Beithe	Arg & Bt	NN1635	56°28·5′	4°58·8′W	H	50
Meall Bhàideanach	Highld	NN3983	56°54·9′	4°38·2′W	H	34,41
Meall Bhalach	Highld	NN2657	56°40·6′	4°50·0′W	H	41
Meall Bhanabhie	Highld	NN1178	56°51·6′	5°5·6′W	H	41
Meall Bhasiter	Highld	NM8497	57°1·1′	5°33·0′W	H	33,40
Meall Bhenneit	Highld	NH5483	57°49·0′	4°27·0′W	H	21
Meall Bhig	N Ayr	NR9046	55°40·0′	5°19·9′W	X	62,69
Meall Bhlàir	Pth & Kin	NN9070	56°48·8′	3°47·7′W	H	43
Meall Biorach	Arg & Bt	NN0237	56°29·3′	5°12·5′W	H	50
Meall Biorach	N Ayr	NR8945	55°39·4′	5°20·8′W	X	62,69
Meall Blair	Highld	NN0795	57°0·6′	5°10·3′W	H	33
Meall Bó	Highld	NH5077	57°45·7′	4°30·8′W	H	20
Meall Brataig	Highld	NG4475	57°41·8′	6°17·3′W	X	23
Meall Breac	Arg & Bt	NN1824	56°22·7′	4°56·4′W	H	50
Meall Breac	Arg & Bt	NS1292	56°5·3′	5°0·9′W	H	56
Meall Breac	Highld	NG7908	57°6·9′	5°38·6′W	H	33
Meall Breac	Highld	NG8149	57°29·0′	5°38·7′W	X	24
Meall Breac	Highld	NG8417	57°11·8′	5°34·1′W	X	33
Meall Breac	Highld	NH1111	57°9·3′	5°7·0′W	H	34
Meall Breac	Highld	NH2275	57°44·0′	4°58·9′W	H	20
Meall Breac	Highld	NM3898	57°0·2′	6°18·4′W	H	39
Meall Breac	Highld	NM9864	56°43·7′	5°17·7′W	X	40
Meall Breac	Highld	NN0675	56°49·8′	5°10·3′W	X	41
Meall Breac	Highld	NN1776	56°50·6′	4°59·6′W	X	41
Meall Breac	Highld	NN1991	56°58·7′	4°58·2′W	H	34
Meall Breac	Highld	NN2889	56°57·9′	4°49·3′W	X	34,41
Meall Breac	N Ayr	NS0041	55°37·5′	5°10·2′W	X	69
Meall Breac	Pth & Kin	NN6454	56°39·7′	4°12·7′W	H	42,51
Meall Breac	Pth & Kin	NN6669	56°47·9′	4°11·2′W	H	42
Meall Breac	Pth & Kin	NN9664	56°45·6′	3°41·6′W	H	43
Meall Breac	Pth & Kin	NN9668	56°47·8′	3°41·7′W	H	43
Meall Buaile nan Caorach	Highld	NG6416	57°10·7′	5°53·8′W	X	32
Meall Buidhe	Arg & Bt	NM8225	56°22·3′	5°31·4′W	H	49
Meall Buidhe	Arg & Bt	NM8407	56°12·7′	5°28·5′W	H	55
Meall Buidhe	Arg & Bt	NN1837	56°29·7′	4°56·9′W	H	50
Meall Buidhe	Arg & Bt	NN3544	56°33·8′	4°40·7′W	X	50
Meall Buidhe	Arg & Bt	NR7332	55°32·0′	5°35·4′W	H	68
Meall Buidhe	Arg & Bt	NR7741	55°36·9′	5°32·0′W	X	62,69
Meall Buidhe	Arg & Bt	NR7868	55°51·5′	5°32·4′W	X	62
Meall Buidhe	Arg & Bt	NS1280	55°58·8′	5°0·4′W	X	63
Meall Buidhe	Highld	NG5531	57°18·5′	6°3·6′W	H	24,32
Meall Buidhe	Highld	NG5901	57°2·5′	5°57·9′W	H	32,39
Meall Buidhe	Highld	NG6713	57°9·2′	5°50·7′W	H	32
Meall Buidhe	Highld	NG8014	57°10·1′	5°37·9′W	H	33
Meall Buidhe	Highld	NG9389	57°50·8′	5°28·8′W	H	19
Meall Buidhe	Highld	NH2250	57°30·6′	4°57·8′W	X	25
Meall Buidhe	Highld	NH4595	57°55·3′	4°36·5′W	H	20
Meall Buidhe	Highld	NM6668	56°45·0′	5°49·2′W	H	40
Meall Buidhe	Highld	NM7567	56°44·7′	5°40·3′W	X	40
Meall Buidhe	Highld	NM8498	57°1·6′	5°33·1′W	H	33,40
Meall Buidhe	Highld	NN5182	56°54·6′	4°26·4′W	H	42
Meall Buidhe	Highld	NN7995	57°2·1′	3°59·2′W	H	35
Meall Buidhe	N Ayr	NR9724	55°28·3′	5°12·3′W	X	69
Meall Buidhe	N Ayr	NS0132	55°32·7′	5°8·8′W	X	69
Meall Buidhe	Pth & Kin	NN4245	56°34·5′	4°33·9′W	H	51
Meall Buidhe	Pth & Kin	NN4949	56°36·8′	4°27·2′W	H	51
Meall Buidhe	Pth & Kin	NN5742	56°33·2′	4°19·1′W	X	51
Meall Buidhe	Stir	NN3431	56°26·8′	4°41·1′W	H	50
Meall Buidhe	Stir	NN5727	56°25·1′	4°18·6′W	H	51
Meall Buidhe Mór	Highld	NM4971	56°46·0′	6°6·0′W	H	39,47
Meall Bun na h-Aibhne	Highld	NM6471	56°46·5′	5°51·3′W	H	40
Meall Caca	Highld	NH4802	57°5·3′	4°30·0′W	H	34
Meall Caca Beag	Highld	NH4803	57°5·8′	4°30·1′W	X	34
Meall Cala	Stir	NN5012	56°16·9′	4°24·9′W	H	57
Meall Caol	Pth & Kin	NN4953	56°38·9′	4°27·3′W	H	42,51
Meall Car nan Ruadhag	Highld	NC4536	58°17·4′	4°38·2′W	H	16
Meall Ceann Loch Strathy	Highld	NC7645	58°22·8′	4°6·8′W	H	10
Meall Ceann na Creige	Highld	NG8059	57°34·3′	5°40·3′W	H	24
Meall Challibost	N Eil	NG2294	57°51·2′	6°40·7′W	X	14
Meall Chaorach	Highld	NN3875	56°50·6′	4°38·9′W	H	41
Meall Chnàimhean	Highld	NG9275	57°43·3′	5°29·1′W	H	19
Meall Choin Bhuidhe	Highld	NC2830	58°13·8′	4°55·3′W	H	15
Meall Chomraidh	Pth & Kin	NN4855	56°40·0′	4°28·4′W	H	42,51
Meall Chrombaig	Pth & Kin	NO0080	56°54·3′	3°38·1′W	H	43
Meall Chuaich	Highld	NN7187	56°57·6′	4°6·8′W	H	42
Meall Chuilc	Highld	NC4344	58°21·6′	4°40·5′W	X	9
Meall Cian Dearg	Highld	NN3375	56°50·4′	4°43·8′W	X	41
Meall Clachach	Stir	NN5432	56°27·7′	4°21·7′W	H	51
Meall Clachach	Stir	NN6812	56°17·2′	4°7·5′W	H	57
Meall Clach a' Cheannaiche	Highld	NN4294	57°0·9′	4°35·7′W	H	34
Meall Clachaig	Highld	NN3783	56°54·8′	4°40·2′W	X	34,41
Meall Clach an Daraich	Highld	NM4669	56°44·9′	6°8·8′W	H	47
Meall Clais Doire	Pth & Kin	NO0282	56°55·4′	3°36·1′W	H	43
Meall Clais nan Each	Highld	NH6999	57°57·9′	4°12·4′W	X	21
Meall Cluainidh	Highld	NH3833	57°21·8′	4°41·1′W	X	26
Meall Coire Aghaisgeig	Highld	NC8205	58°1·4′	3°59·4′W	H	17
Meall Coire an Lochain	Highld	NC2106	58°0·7′	5°1·3′W	H	15
Meall Coire an t-Searraich	Highld	NG7705	57°5·2′	5°40·4′W	H	33
Meall Coire Choille-rais	Highld	NN4386	56°56·6′	4°34·4′W	H	34,42
Meall Coire Each	Highld	NH1800	57°3·6′	4°59·6′W	H	34
Meall Coire Lochain	Highld	NN2191	56°58·8′	4°56·3′W	H	34
Meall Coire Mhic Gugain	Highld	NM8555	56°38·5′	5°29·9′W	X	49
Meall Coire na Creadha	Highld	NH1506	57°6·7′	5°2·9′W	H	34
Meall Coire na Gaoithe'n Ear	Highld	NM8699	57°2·2′	5°31·2′W	H	33,40
Meall Coire nan Laogh	Highld	NH3274	57°43·7′	4°48·8′W	H	20
Meall Coire nan Saobhaidh	Highld	NN1795	57°0·9′	5°0·4′W	H	34
Meall Coire na Saobhaidh	Highld	NM8785	56°54·7′	5°29·5′W	X	40
Meall Coire na Saobhaidhe	Aberd	NO2487	56°58·3′	3°14·6′W	H	44
Meall Copagach	Arg & Bt	NN0532	56°26·7′	5°9·4′W	X	50
Meall Copagach	Arg & Bt	NN1534	56°28·0′	4°59·7′W	H	50
Meall Corranaich	Pth & Kin	NN6141	56°32·7′	4°15·2′W	H	51
Meall Còs Chàrnan	Highld	NN4377	56°51·7′	4°34·1′W	H	42
Meall Crìche	Arg & Bt	NS1080	55°58·8′	5°2·3′W	X	63
Meall Cruaidh	Highld	NH2091	57°52·6′	5°1·7′W	H	20
Meall Cruaidh	Highld	NN5780	56°53·6′	4°20·4′W	H	42
Meall Cruidh	Arg & Bt	NN1241	56°31·7′	5°3·0′W	H	50
Meall Cruinn	Pth & Kin	NN4547	56°35·6′	4°31·0′W	H	51
Meall Crumach	Pth & Kin	NN7350	56°37·7′	4°3·8′W	H	42,51,52
Meall Cuanail	Arg & Bt	NN0629	56°25·1′	5°8·3′W	H	50
Meall Cuileig	Highld	NH2716	57°12·4′	4°51·4′W	H	34
Meall Cumhann	Highld	NN1769	56°46·9′	4°59·3′W	H	41
Meall Dà-bheinn	Highld	NG6212	57°8·5′	5°55·6′W	H	32
Meall Dail-chealach	Pth & Kin	NN7067	56°46·8′	4°7·2′W	H	42
Meall Daill	Pth & Kin	NN4143	56°33·4′	4°34·8′W	H	51
Meall Dail Mìn	Pth & Kin	NN8969	56°48·2′	3°48·6′W	H	43
Meall Daimh	Highld	NH0269	57°40·3′	5°18·7′W	H	19
Meall Daimh	Highld	NH2872	57°42·6′	4°52·8′W	H	20
Meall Daimh	Highld	NM8671	56°47·1′	5°29·8′W	H	40
Meall Daimh	Pth & Kin	NN6630	56°26·8′	4°10·0′W	H	51
Meall Daimheidh	Pth & Kin	NO0268	56°47·9′	3°35·8′W	H	43
Meall Damh	Highld	NH2014	57°11·2′	4°58·2′W	H	34
Meall Damh	Highld	NH2609	57°8·6′	4°52·1′W	H	34
Meall Damh	Highld	NM7348	56°34·4′	5°41·3′W	H	49
Meall Damh	Highld	NM7880	56°51·8′	5°38·1′W	X	40
Meall Damh	Highld	NN4989	56°58·3′	4°28·6′W	H	34,42
Meall Damh Ard	Arg & Bt	NM5142	56°30·5′	6°2·4′W	H	47,48
Meall Damh Iosal	Arg & Bt	NM5143	56°31·0′	6°2·4′W	X	47,48
Meall Daraich	Arg & Bt	NS2293	56°6·1′	4°51·3′W	X	56
Meall Dearg	Arg & Bt	NN0239	56°30·3′	5°12·6′W	H	50
Meall Dearg	Highld	NB9810	58°2·3′	5°24·8′W	H	15
Meall Dearg	Highld	NC1408	58°1·6′	5°8·5′W	H	15
Meall Dearg	Highld	NC2459	58°29·3′	5°0·7′W	H	9
Meall Dearg	Highld	NC2762	58°31·0′	4°57·7′W	H	9
Meall Dearg	Highld	NC3033	58°15·4′	4°53·4′W	X	15
Meall Dearg	Highld	NG4923	57°14·0′	6°9·1′W	H	32
Meall Dearg	Highld	NG7554	57°31·5′	5°45·0′W	H	24
Meall Dearg	Highld	NG9158	57°34·1′	5°29·2′W	H	25
Meall Dearg	Highld	NG9351	57°30·4′	5°26·9′W	H	25
Meall Dearg	Highld	NN1658	56°40·9′	4°59·8′W	H	41
Meall Dearg	Pth & Kin	NN6556	56°40·8′	4°11·8′W	H	42,51
Meall Dearg	Pth & Kin	NN8841	56°33·1′	3°48·9′W	H	52
Meall Dearg	Stir	NN4211	56°16·2′	4°32·6′W	X	56
Meall Dearg Choire nam Muc	Highld	NM9765	56°44·2′	5°18·7′W	X	40
Meall Deise	Highld	NG8179	57°45·1′	5°40·4′W	H	19
Meall Dhamh	Stir	NN3921	56°21·5′	4°35·9′W	H	50,56
Meall Dhearcaig	Highld	NN3974	56°50·0′	4°37·9′W	X	41
Meall Dheirgidh	Highld	NH4794	57°54·8′	4°34·5′W	H	20
Meall Dhonuill	Highld	ND1027	58°13·6′	3°31·5′W	X	17
Meall Dhùin Croisg	Stir	NN5437	56°30·4′	4°21·9′W	H	51
Meall Diamhain	Highld	NC2118	58°7·2′	5°1·9′W	X	15
Meall Diamhain	Highld	NC2914	58°5·2′	4°53·6′W	X	15
Meall Dionach	Highld	NH3684	57°49·2′	4°45·2′W	H	20
Meall Doir' a' Bhainne	Highld	NH1549	57°29·9′	5°4·8′W	H	25
Meall Doir a' Chuilinn	Highld	NH5983	57°49·1′	4°22·0′W	X	21
Meall Doir' an Daimh	Highld	NN1696	57°1·4′	5°1·4′W	H	34
Meall Doire	Highld	NN2981	56°53·6′	4°48·0′W	H	34,41
Meall Doire	Pth & Kin	NN6168	56°47·2′	4°16·1′W	H	42
Meall Doire an t-Sìdhean	Highld	NC0410	58°2·4′	5°18·8′W	H	15
Meall Doire Bhrath	Highld	NH4318	57°13·8′	4°35·6′W	H	34
Meall Doire Fàid	Highld	NH2279	57°46·2′	4°59·1′W	H	20
Meall Doire Meallaich	Pth & Kin	NN4652	56°38·3′	4°30·2′W	H	42,51
Meall Doire na h-Achlais	Highld	NN2468	56°46·5′	4°52·4′W	X	41
Meall Doire na Mnatha	Highld	NM8977	56°50·5′	5°27·1′W	H	40
Meall Doire nan Caorach	Highld	NH2111	57°9·6′	4°57·1′W	H	34
Meall Doire nan Damh	Arg & Bt	NM4952	56°35·8′	6°4·9′W	X	47
Meall Dola	Highld	NC6106	58°1·6′	4°20·7′W	H	16
Meall Donn	Arg & Bt	NM7416	56°17·2′	5°38·7′W	X	55
Meall Donn	Arg & Bt	NR7737	55°34·8′	5°31·8′W	H	68,69
Meall Donn	Arg & Bt	NR8861	55°48·0′	5°22·5′W	X	62
Meall Donn	Highld	NH5721	57°15·7′	4°21·8′W	H	26,35
Meall Donn	N Ayr	NR8944	55°38·9′	5°20·8′W	X	62,69
Meall Droilichean	Pth & Kin	NN6151	56°38·1′	4°15·5′W	X	42,51
Meall Druidhe	Pth & Kin	NN6356	56°40·8′	4°13·7′W	H	42,51
Meall Dubh	Aberd	NO3291	57°0·6′	3°6·7′W	H	44
Meall Dubh	Arg & Bt	NN1843	56°32·9′	4°57·2′W	H	50
Meall Dubh	Arg & Bt	NR8477	55°56·5′	5°27·1′W	H	62
Meall Dubh	Arg & Bt	NS0789	56°3·6′	5°5·5′W	H	56
Meall Dubh	Arg & Bt	NS1190	56°4·2′	5°1·7′W	X	56
Meall Dubh	Arg & Bt	NS1586	56°2·1′	4°57·7′W	X	56
Meall Dubh	Highld	NC0231	58°13·7′	5°21·8′W	X	15
Meall Dubh	Highld	NG8548	57°28·5′	5°34·7′W	X	24
Meall Dubh	Highld	NH0124	57°16·1′	5°17·6′W	H	25,33
Meall Dubh	Highld	NH1074	57°43·2′	5°10·9′W	X	19
Meall Dubh	Highld	NH1683	57°48·2′	5°5·3′W	H	20
Meall Dubh	Highld	NH2089	57°51·5′	5°1·6′W	H	20
Meall Dubh	Highld	NH2322	57°15·5′	4°55·6′W	H	25
Meall Dubh	Highld	NH2352	57°31·7′	4°56·9′W	X	25
Meall Dubh	Highld	NH2407	57°7·5′	4°54·0′W	H	34
Meall Dubh	Highld	NH2539	57°24·7′	4°54·4′W	H	25
Meall Dubh	Highld	NN1881	56°53·3′	4°58·8′W	X	34,41
Meall Dubh	Highld	NN2293	56°59·9′	4°55·4′W	H	34
Meall Dubh	Highld	NN2884	56°55·2′	4°49·1′W	X	34,41
Meall dubh	Highld	NN3185	56°55·8′	4°46·2′W	X	34,41
Meall Dubh	Highld	NN5677	56°52·0′	4°21·3′W	H	42
Meall Dubh	Highld	NN7295	57°2·0′	4°6·1′W	H	35
Meall Dubh	Pth & Kin	NN4943	56°33·5′	4°27·0′W	H	51
Meall Dubh	Pth & Kin	NN6560	56°43·0′	4°11·9′W	H	42
Meall Dubh	Pth & Kin	NN7256	56°41·0′	4°4·9′W	X	42,51,52
Meall Dubh	Pth & Kin	NN7961	56°43·8′	3°58·2′W	H	42
Meall Dubh	Pth & Kin	NN8372	56°49·7′	3°54·6′W	H	43
Meall Dubh	Pth & Kin	NN8541	56°33·1′	3°51·8′W	X	52
Meall Dubh	Pth & Kin	NN8630	56°27·2′	3°50·5′W	X	52
Meall Dubh	Pth & Kin	NO0653	56°39·8′	3°31·6′W	X	52,53
Meall Dubh	Pth & Kin	NO1266	56°46·9′	3°26·0′W	H	43
Meall Dubhag	Highld	NN8895	57°2·2′	3°50·3′W	H	35,36,43
Meall Dubh Ard	Highld	NC0504	57°59·2′	5°17·4′W	H	15
Meall Dubh-chlais	Pth & Kin	NN9279	56°53·6′	3°45·9′W	H	43
Meall Dubh-ghlas	Pth & Kin	NN7670	56°48·6′	4°1·4′W	H	42
Meall Dubh na Caoidhe	Highld	NH1843	57°26·7′	5°1·5′W	H	25
Meall Dubh nan Dearcag	Pth & Kin	NN8475	56°51·4′	3°53·7′W	X	43
Meall Dubh Raffin	Highld	NC0132	58°14·2′	5°22·9′W	X	15
Meall Dùn Dhomhnuill	Pth & Kin	NN8342	56°33·6′	3°53·8′W	H	52
Meall Each	Highld	NH0267	57°39·2′	5°18·6′W	H	19
Meall Each	Highld	NN5285	56°56·2′	4°25·5′W	X	42
Meall Eachainn	Highld	NC6100	57°58·3′	4°20·5′W	H	16
Meall Eachainn	Highld	NH6299	57°57·8′	4°19·5′W	H	21
Meall Eadar an da Chuinneag	Highld	NH4882	57°48·4′	4°33·0′W	X	20
Meall Ear	Stir	NN5302	56°11·5′	4°21·7′W	H	57
Meall Earca	Highld	NC1340	58°18·8′	5°11·1′W	X	9
Meall Easganan	Pth & Kin	NO1264	56°45·8′	3°25·9′W	H	43
Meall Eigin-aig	Highld	NM4770	56°45·4′	6°7·9′W	H	39,47
Meall Eudainn	Highld	NC6045	58°22·5′	4°23·2′W	H	10
Meall Fead	Pth & Kin	NN8759	56°42·8′	3°50·3′W	X	52
Meall Fearna	Highld	NH0161	57°36·0′	5°19·4′W	X	19
Meall Féith Dhiongaig	Highld	NH2677	57°45·2′	4°55·0′W	H	20

Meall Féith na Slataich	Highld	NH2985	57°49·6′	4°52·3′W	H	20
Meall Feith-rabhain	Highld	NG8894	57°53·4′	5°34·1′W	H	19
Meall Fhuaran	Highld	NH0071	57°41·3′	5°20·9′W	H	19
Meall Fuaraidh	Highld	NG8375	57°43·0′	5°38·1′W	H	19
Meall Fuar-mhonaidh	Highld	NH4522	57°16·0′	4°33·8′W	H	26
Meall Gaineamhach	Highld	NG6948	57°28·1′	5°50·7′W	X	24
Meall Gaineimh	Moray	NJ1605	57°8·0′	3°22·8′W	H	36
Meall Gainmheich	Stir	NN5009	56°15·2′	4°24·8′W	H	57
Meall Gainmheineach	Stir	NN4822	56°22·2′	4°27·2′W	X	51
Meall Gaothach	Stir	NN4513	56°17·3′	4°29·8′W	H	57
Meall Gaothar	Highld	NG7405	57°5·1′	5°43·3′W	H	33
Meall Garbh	Arg & Bt	NN0243	56°32·5′	5°12·8′W	H	50
Meall Garbh	Arg & Bt	NN0445	56°33·6′	5°10·9′W	H	50
Meall Garbh	Arg & Bt	NN1636	56°29·1′	4°58·8′W	H	50
Meall Garbh	Arg & Bt	NN2632	56°27·1′	4°49·0′W	H	50
Meall Garbh	Arg & Bt	NN3338	56°30·5′	4°42·4′W	H	50
Meall Garbh	Arg & Bt	NN3338	56°30·5′	4°42·4′W	X	50
Meall Garbh	Highld	NC3640	58°19·3′	4°47·5′W	H	9
Meall Garbh	Highld	NH0472	57°42·0′	5°16·9′W	H	19
Meall Garbh	Highld	NH0886	57°49·6′	5°13·5′W	X	19
Meall Garbh	Highld	NH0997	57°55·6′	5°13·1′W	H	19
Meall Garbh	Highld	NH1435	57°22·3′	5°5·1′W	H	25
Meall Garbh	Highld	NM6755	56°38·0′	5°47·5′W	X	49
Meall Garbh	Highld	NN1459	56°41·4′	5°1·8′W	X	41
Meall Garbh	Highld	NN1948	56°35·6′	4°56·4′W	H	50
Meall Garbh	Highld	NN3772	56°48·9′	4°39·8′W	H	41
Meall Garbh	Pth & Kin	NN5463	56°44·4′	4°22·8′W	H	42
Meall Garbh	Pth & Kin	NN6443	56°33·8′	4°12·3′W	H	51
Meall Garbh	Pth & Kin	NN6449	56°37·0′	4°12·5′W	H	51
Meall Garbh	Pth & Kin	NN6451	56°38·1′	4°12·6′W	H	42,51
Meall Garbh	Pth & Kin	NN9465	56°46·1′	3°43·6′W	H	43
Meall Garbh	Stir	NN4230	56°26·4′	4°33·3′W	X	51
Meall Garbh	Stir	NN5738	56°31·0′	4°19·0′W	X	51
Meall Garbhaig	Highld	NG9069	57°40·0′	5°30·8′W	H	19
Meall Garbh Beag	Highld	NN4597	57°2·5′	4°32·8′W	H	34
Meall Geal	N Eil	NB5660	58°27·9′	6°10·6′W	X	8
Meall Ghaordaidh	Stir	NN5139	56°31·4′	4°24·9′W	H	51
Meall Gharran	Pth & Kin	NN9776	56°52·1′	3°40·9′W	H	43
Meall Ghiubhas	Highld	NN2048	56°35·6′	4°55·5′W	H	50
Meall Ghiuragarstidh	Highld	NG8981	57°46·4′	5°32·4′W	X	19
Meall Ghoirleig	Highld	NN5190	56°58·9′	4°26·7′W	H	35
Meall Gille Pheadair	Highld	NC3635	58°16·7′	4°47·3′W	H	16
Meall Giubhais	Highld	NH2951	57°31·3′	4°50·9′W	X	25
Meall Glac a' Bheithe	Highld	NG7992	57°52·0′	5°43·1′W	H	19
Meall glac Airigh an t-Saoir	Highld	NG8673	57°42·0′	5°35·0′W	H	19
Meall Glac an Ruighe	Highld	NH2686	57°50·0′	4°55·4′W	H	20
Meall Glac na Daraich	Highld	NG7680	57°45·5′	5°45·5′W	H	19
Meall Glac Tigh-fàil	Highld	NH1682	57°47·7′	5°5·3′W	H	20
Meall Glas	Highld	NC4349	58°24·3′	4°40·7′W	X	9
Meall Glas	Pth & Kin	NN5950	56°37·5′	4°17·4′W	H	42,51
Meall Glas	Stir	NN4332	56°27·5′	4°32·4′W	H	51
Meall Glas	Stir	NN5640	56°32·1′	4°20·0′W	H	51
Meall Glasail Beag	Aberd	NO1496	57°3·1′	3°24·6′W	H	36,43
Meall Glasail Mór	Aberd	NO1495	57°2·5′	3°24·6′W	H	36,43
Meall Glas Choire	Highld	NN4372	56°49·0′	4°33·9′W	H	42
Meall Gorm	Aberd	NO1894	57°2·0′	3°20·6′W	H	36,43
Meall Gorm	Aberd	NO2988	56°58·9′	3°9·6′W	H	44
Meall Gorm	Highld	NG7740	57°24·0′	5°42·3′W	H	24
Meall Gorm	Highld	NG8752	57°30·8′	5°32·9′W	X	24
Meall Gorm	Highld	NG9148	57°28·7′	5°28·7′W	X	25
Meall Gorm	Highld	NH2269	57°40·8′	4°58·7′W	H	20
Meall Gorm	Highld	NH3078	57°45·8′	4°51·0′W	H	20
Meall Gorm	Highld	NH4833	57°22·0′	4°31·2′W	H	26
Meall Gorm	Pth & Kin	NN5360	56°42·8′	4°23·6′W	H	42
Meall Gorm	Pth & Kin	NO1474	56°51·2′	3°24·2′W	H	43
Meall Greepa	Highld	NG2642	57°23·4′	6°33·2′W	X	23
Meall Greigh	Pth & Kin	NN6743	56°33·9′	4°9·4′W	H	51
Meall Gruaim	Pth & Kin	NN8868	56°47·7′	3°49·6′W	X	43
Meall Gruamach	Highld	NG8007	57°6·3′	5°37·5′W	H	33
Meall Guibhais	Highld	NH3050	57°30·8′	4°49·8′W	H	26
Meall Horn	Highld	NC3544	58°21·5′	4°48·7′W	H	9
Meall Horn	Highld	NC8107	58°2·4′	4°0·5′W	H	17
Meall Iain	Highld	NM8166	56°44·3′	5°34·4′W	H	40
Meall Imireach	Highld	NG7982	57°46·7′	5°42·5′W	X	19
Meall Inbhir	Arg & Bt	NN0736	56°28·8′	5°7·6′W	H	50
Meall Innis an Loichel	Highld	NH2039	57°24·6′	4°59·3′W	H	25
Meall Innis na Sine	Highld	NH1848	57°29·4′	5°1·7′W	H	25
Meall Laire	Highld	NN3378	56°52·1′	4°43·9′W	H	41
Meall Leacachain	Highld	NH2477	57°45·2′	4°57·0′W	H	20
Meall Leac an Fhireoin	Highld	NM8556	56°39·0′	5°30·0′W	X	49
Meall Leachdann nan Each	Pth & Kin	NN4551	56°37·8′	4°31·2′W	H	42,51
Meall Leac na Sgubaich	Highld	NN5681	56°54·1′	4°21·4′W	X	42
Meall Leathad na Craoibhe	Highld	NC6155	58°27·9′	4°22·5′W	H	10
Meall Leathan Dhail	Stir	NN6611	56°16·6′	4°9·4′W	H	57
Meall Liath	Highld	NN5985	56°56·4′	4°18·6′W	X	42
Meall Liath	Pth & Kin	NN6951	56°38·2′	4°7·7′W	H	42,51
Meall Liath	Stir	NN5836	56°29·9′	4°18·0′W	H	51
Meall Liath-Chloich	Highld	NN4694	57°0·9′	4°31·7′W	H	34
Meall Liath Choire	Highld	NH2296	57°55·3′	4°59·9′W	H	20
Meall Liath na Doire	Pth & Kin	NN3958	56°41·4′	4°37·3′W	H	41
Meall Liath na Doire Mhóir	Pth & Kin	NN4861	56°43·2′	4°28·6′W	H	42
Meall Lighiche	Highld	NN0952	56°37·5′	5°6·4′W	H	41
Meall Loch Airigh Alasdair	Highld	NG7436	57°21·8′	5°45·0′W	X	24
Meall Lochan a' Chleirich	Highld	NG8771	57°41·0′	5°33·9′W	H	19
Meall Loch an Fheòir	Highld	NG7244	57°26·0′	5°47·5′W	X	24
Meall Loch an Fhidhleir	Highld	NG7259	57°34·1′	5°48·3′W	H	24
Meall Loch an Iasgair	Highld	NG8083	57°47·2′	5°41·6′W	H	19
Meall Lochan na Geala	Highld	NG8867	57°38·8′	5°32·7′W	H	19
Meall Lochan nan Dubh Lochan	Highld	NN0894	57°0·1′	5°9·2′W	X	33
Meall Lochan nan Lorg	Highld	NM7056	56°38·6′	5°44·6′W	H	49
Meall Loch nan Gamhna	Highld	NC6458	58°29·6′	4°19·5′W	X	10
Meall Luaidhe	Pth & Kin	NN5843	56°33·7′	4°18·2′W	H	51
Meall Luidh Mór	Highld	NN4180	56°53·3′	4°36·1′W	H	34,42
Meall Meadhoin	Highld	NM4968	56°44·4′	6°5·8′W	H	47
Meall Meadhon	Highld	NC6427	58°12·9′	4°18·4′W	H	16
Meall Meadhonach	Highld	NC1617	58°6·5′	5°6·9′W	H	15
Meall Meadhonach	Highld	NC2658	58°28·8′	4°58·6′W	H	9
Meall Meadhonach	Highld	NC4162	58°31·3′	4°43·3′W	H	9
Meall Meadhonach	Highld	NC5723	58°10·6′	4°25·4′W	H	16
Meall Meadhonach	Highld	NC5931	58°15·0′	4°23·7′W	H	16
Meall Meadhonach	Highld	NC6111	58°4·2′	4°20·9′W	H	16
Meall Meadhonach	Highld	NC6408	58°2·7′	4°17·8′W	H	16
Meall Meadhonach	Highld	NC6700	57°58·4′	4°14·5′W	H	16
Meall Meadhonach	Highld	NC6748	58°24·3′	4°16·1′W	X	10
Meall Meadhonach	Highld	NH6180	57°47·5′	4°19·8′W	X	21
Meall Meadhonach	Stir	NN4108	56°14·5′	4°33·5′W	H	56
Meall Mhèinnidh	Highld	NG9574	57°42·8′	5°26·0′W	H	19
Meall Mhic Chiarain	Highld	NM7466	56°44·1′	5°41·3′W	X	40
Meall Mhic Dhomhnuill	Arg & Bt	NM4247	56°32·9′	6°11·4′W	X	47,48
Meall Mhic Iomhair	Highld	NH3167	57°39·9′	4°49·5′W	H	20
Meall Mhór	Arg & Bt	NR8674	55°54·9′	5°25·0′W	X	62
Meall Mhór Loch	Arg & Bt	NR8573	55°54·4′	5°25·9′W	W	62
Meall Monachyle	Stir	NN4620	56°21·1′	4°29·1′W	H	51,57
Meall Mór	Arg & Bt	NM8311	56°14·8′	5°29·7′W	H	55
Meall Mór	Arg & Bt	NR7317	55°23·9′	5°34·7′W	X	68
Meall Mór	Arg & Bt	NR8374	55°54·9′	5°27·9′W	H	62
Meall Mór	Highld	NC1237	58°17·2′	5°11·9′W	X	15
Meall Mór	Highld	NC1300	57°57·3′	5°9·1′W	H	15
Meall Mór	Highld	NC6060	58°30·6′	4°23·7′W	X	10
Meall Mór	Highld	NG7980	57°45·6′	5°42·4′W	H	19
Meall Mór	Highld	NG8939	57°23·8′	5°30·2′W	X	24
Meall Mór	Highld	NH0840	57°24·9′	5°11·3′W	X	25
Meall Mór	Highld	NH1097	57°55·6′	5°12·0′W	H	19
Meall Mór	Highld	NH2428	57°18·8′	4°54·9′W	H	25
Meall Mór	Highld	NH3203	57°5·5′	4°45·9′W	H	34
Meall Mór	Highld	NH4637	57°24·1′	4°33·3′W	H	26
Meall Mór	Highld	NH5174	57°44·1′	4°29·7′W	H	20
Meall Mór	Highld	NH6596	57°56·2′	4°16·3′W	H	21
Meall Mór	Highld	NH6933	57°22·4′	4°10·2′W	H	26
Meall Mór	Highld	NH7335	57°23·5′	4°6·3′W	H	27
Meall Mór	Highld	NH7440	57°26·2′	4°5·5′W	H	27
Meall Mór	Highld	NM7364	56°43·0′	5°42·1′W	H	40
Meall Mór	Highld	NM8872	56°47·7′	5°27·8′W	H	40
Meall Mór	Highld	NN1055	56°39·2′	5°5·5′W	H	41
Meall Mór	Highld	NN2870	56°47·6′	4°48·5′W	H	41
Meall Mór	Highld	NN5376	56°51·4′	4°24·2′W	H	42
Meall Mór	N Ayr	NR9348	55°41·1′	5°17·1′W	H	62,69
Meall Mór	N Eil	NF7603	57°0·5′	7°19·8′W	H	31
Meall Mór	N Eil	NF8027	57°13·6′	7°17·7′W	H	22
Meall Mór	N Eil	NG1891	57°49·4′	6°44·5′W	H	14
Meall Mór	Pth & Kin	NN8343	56°34·1′	3°53·8′W	X	52
Meall Mór	Pth & Kin	NN8535	56°29·8′	3°51·6′W	X	52
Meall Mór	Pth & Kin	NN9239	56°32·1′	3°44·9′W	H	52
Meall Mór	Pth & Kin	NN9266	56°46·6′	3°45·6′W	H	43
Meall Mor	Pth & Kin	NO0055	56°40·8′	3°37·5′W	H	52,53
Meall Mór	Pth & Kin	NO1760	56°43·7′	3°20·9′W	H	43
Meall Mór	Stir	NN3815	56°18·2′	4°36·7′W	H	50,56
Meall Mór	Stir	NN5815	56°18·6′	4°17·3′W	H	57
Meall Moraig	Highld	NH6694	57°55·2′	4°15·3′W	H	21
Meallmore Lodge	Highld	NH7437	57°24·6′	4°5·4′W	X	27
Meall Mór nan Eag	Stir	NN3318	56°19·8′	4°41·6′W	H	50,56
Meall na Bèiste	Highld	NC0011	58°2·8′	5°22·9′W	H	15
Meall na Boineide	Stir	NN4013	56°17·2′	4°34·7′W	X	56
Meall na Brachdlach	Highld	NN5182	56°54·5′	4°26·4′W	H	42
Meall na Braclaich	Highld	NC1916	58°6·0′	5°3·8′W	H	15
Meall na Bràthain	N Eil	NF8745	57°23·5′	7°12·2′W	X	22
Meall na Caillich	Highld	NC6025	58°11·8′	4°22·4′W	H	16
Meall na Caillich Buidhe	Pth & Kin	NN9980	56°54·3′	3°39·1′W	H	43
Meall na Caiplich Bige	Highld	NH5640	57°25·9′	4°23·5′W	X	26
Meall na Caora	Stir	NN6014	56°18·1′	4°15·3′W	H	57
Meall na Caorach	Arg & Bt	NM5447	56°33·3′	5°59·7′W	X	47,48
Meall na Caorach	Highld	ND0926	58°13·1′	3°32·5′W	H	17
Meall na Ceardaich	Highld	NH6403	57°6·1′	4°14·3′W	H	35
Meall na Ceàrdaich	Highld	NN6188	56°58·0′	4°16·7′W	H	42
Meall na Circe Bog Airigh	Arg & Bt	NM5144	56°31·6′	6°2·5′W	X	47,48
Meall na Cloiche	Highld	NH6706	57°7·8′	4°11·4′W	H	35
Meall na Cloiche	Stir	NN5927	56°25·1′	4°16·7′W	H	51
Meall na Cloiche Bioraiche	Highld	NG7103	57°3·9′	5°46·2′W	X	33
Meall na Coille	Highld	NG7457	57°33·1′	5°46·2′W	H	24
Meall na Coille Duibhe	Highld	NG7608	57°6·8′	5°41·5′W	H	33
Meall na Cradh-lice	Highld	NN2659	56°41·7′	4°50·0′W	X	41
Meall na Creughaich	Highld	NH6505	57°7·2′	4°13·3′W	H	35
Meall na Cruaidhe	Highld	NN2462	56°43·3′	4°52·1′W	X	41
Meall na Cuartaige	Highld	NM9076	56°49·9′	5°26·1′W	X	40
Meall na Cuilce	Highld	NG4820	57°12·4′	6°9·9′W	H	32
Meall na Curraichd	Highld	NC4326	58°12·0′	4°39·8′W	X	16
Meall na Dige	Stir	NN4522	56°22·2′	4°30·1′W	H	51
Meall na Doire	Highld	NH0410	57°8·6′	5°13·9′W	X	33
Meall na Doire	Highld	NH3015	57°11·9′	4°48·4′W	H	34
Meall na Doire Duinne	Highld	NG8597	57°54·9′	5°37·3′W	X	19
Meall na Doire Gairbhe	Highld	NG8982	57°46·9′	5°32·5′W	H	19
Meall na Drochaide	Highld	NH5069	57°41·4′	4°30·5′W	H	20
Meall na Dubh Chlaise	Highld	NG7978	57°44·5′	5°42·3′W	H	19
Meall na Duibhe	Highld	NN2262	56°43·2′	4°54·1′W	H	41
Meall na Faiche	Highld	NH3418	57°13·6′	4°44·5′W	H	34
Meall na Fàire	Highld	NH2845	57°28·0′	4°51·6′W	H	25
Meall na Faochaig	Highld	NH2552	57°31·7′	4°54·9′W	H	25
Meall na Fearna	Pth & Kin	NN6518	56°20·4′	4°10·6′W	X	57
Meall na Fhuaid	Highld	NG7350	57°29·3′	5°46·8′W	H	24
Meall na Fidhle	Highld	NM8050	56°35·7′	5°34·6′W	X	49
Meall na Frean	Stir	NN4923	56°22·8′	4°26·3′W	H	51
Meall na Freumha	Highld	NM9467	56°45·2′	5°21·7′W	X	40
Meall na Fuar-ghlaic	Highld	NH6932	57°21·8′	4°10·1′W	H	26
Meall na Gaisge	Pth & Kin	NN7218	56°20·5′	4°3·8′W	H	57
Meall na Gaoithe	Highld	NC7213	58°5·5′	4°9·8′W	H	16
Meall na Gearra	Highld	NH7105	57°7·3′	4°7·4′W	X	35
Meall na Glaic Bàine	Highld	NH3377	57°45·4′	4°47·9′W	X	20
Meall na Gréine	Highld	NM7952	56°36·7′	5°35·6′W	X	49
Meall na h-Airde	Highld	NG7674	57°42·3′	5°45·1′W	H	19
Meall na h-Airde	Highld	NG8237	57°22·5′	5°37·1′W	H	24
Meall na h-Airigh	Highld	NM9078	56°51·0′	5°26·2′W	H	40
Meall na h-Airighe Riabhaich	Highld	NG8793	57°52·8′	5°35·1′W	H	19
Meall na h-Aisre	Highld	NH5100	57°4·3′	4°27·0′W	H	35
Meall na h-Amaite	Highld	NC7714	58°6·1′	4°4·8′W	H	17
Meall na h-Aodainn Móire	Pth & Kin	NN9462	56°44·5′	3°43·5′W	H	43
Meall na Harraw	Highld	NN3991	56°59·2′	4°38·5′W	H	34
Meall na h-Easaiche	Highld	NM8148	56°34·6′	5°33·5′W	H	49
Meall na h-Eilde	Highld	NN1894	57°0·3′	4°59·4′W	H	34
Meall na h-Eilrig	Highld	NH5332	57°21·5′	4°26·2′W	H	26
Meall na h-Eilrig	Pth & Kin	NN9771	56°49·4′	3°40·8′W	H	43
Meall na h-Imrich	Pth & Kin	NN8462	56°44·3′	3°53·3′W	H	43
Meall na h-Iolaire	Arg & Bt	NM2661	56°39·9′	6°27·9′W	H	46,47
Meall na h-Iolaire	Highld	NM8151	56°36·2′	5°33·6′W	X	49
Meall na h-Iolaire	Pth & Kin	NN8560	56°43·3′	3°52·3′W	H	43,52
Meall na h-Iolaire	Stir	NN6415	56°18·7′	4°11·5′W	H	57
Meall na h-Odhar-aghaidh	Highld	NG8462	57°36·0′	5°36·4′W	H	19,24
Meall na h-Uamh	Highld	NM6973	56°47·7′	5°46·5′W	H	40
Meall na h-Uamha	Highld	NG7536	57°21·8′	5°44·0′W	X	24
Meall na h-Uamha	Highld	NG7765	57°37·5′	5°43·6′W	H	19,24
Meall na h-Uamhaidh	Highld	NG8091	57°51·5′	5°42·0′W	H	19
Meall na h-Uigeig	Highld	NH5585	57°50·1′	4°26·1′W	H	21
Meall na Leitreach	Highld	NC3432	58°15·0′	4°49·2′W	H	15
Meall na Leitreach	Pth & Kin	NN6370	56°48·3′	4°14·2′W	H	42
Meall na Lice	Highld	NN3866	56°45·7′	4°38·6′W	H	41
Meall na Maoile	Pth & Kin	NN7773	56°50·2′	4°0·5′W	H	42
Meall nam Bacan	Highld	NG8871	57°41·0′	5°32·9′W	H	19
Meall nam Bràdhan	Highld	NH2690	57°52·2′	4°55·5′W	H	20
Meall nam Creag Leac	Highld	NM8674	56°48·8′	5°29·9′W	H	40
Meall na Mèine	Highld	NG8869	57°39·9′	5°32·8′W	H	19,24
Meall na Mèine	Highld	NG9081	57°46·4′	5°31·4′W	X	19
Meall na Meoig	Pth & Kin	NN4464	56°44·8′	4°32·6′W	H	42
Meall nam Fairneag	Highld	NH2604	57°5·9′	4°51·9′W	H	34
Meall nam Fiadh	Arg & Bt	NN0847	56°34·8′	5°7·1′W	H	50
Meall nam Fiadh	Highld	NC1112	58°3·7′	5°11·7′W	H	15
Meall nam Fiadh	Highld	NM8046	56°33·5′	5°34·4′W	H	49
Meall nam Fiadh	Pth & Kin	NN6927	56°25·3′	4°7·0′W	H	51
Meall nam Fiasgan	Highld	NM5070	56°45·5′	6°5·0′W	X	39,47
Meall nam Fuaran	Highld	NH3889	57°51·9′	4°43·4′W	H	20
Meall nam Fuaran	Pth & Kin	NN8236	56°30·3′	3°54·6′W	H	52
Meall nam Madadh	Highld	NH3389	57°51·8′	4°48·4′W	H	20
Meall nam Maigheach	Highld	NM9576	56°50·1′	5°21·2′W	H	40
Meall nam Maigheach	Pth & Kin	NN5549	56°36·9′	4°21·3′W	H	51
Meall nam Maigheach	Pth & Kin	NN5843	56°33·7′	4°18·2′W	X	51
Meall nam Meallan	Highld	NG8994	57°53·4′	5°33·1′W	H	19
Meall nam Measagh	Arg & Bt	NN0529	56°25·0′	5°9·2′W	X	50
Meall nam Moine	Stir	NN4930	56°26·5′	4°26·5′W	X	51
Meall nam Muc	Arg & Bt	NM2457	56°37·7′	6°29·6′W	X	46,47
Meall nam Mullach	Highld	NH3875	57°44·4′	4°42·8′W	H	20
Meall na Moch-eirigh	Highld	NH2491	57°52·7′	4°57·6′W	H	20
Meall na Moine	Highld	NC2862	58°31·0′	4°56·7′W	H	9
Meall na Mòine	Highld	NC2956	58°27·8′	4°55·4′W	H	9
Meall na Moine	Pth & Kin	NN7063	56°44·7′	4°7·1′W	X	42
Meall na Moine	Pth & Kin	NN7735	56°29·7′	3°59·4′W	X	51,52
Meall na Mucarach	Pth & Kin	NN4459	56°42·1′	4°32·4′W	H	42,51
Meall nan Aighean	Highld	NC6828	58°13·5′	4°14·4′W	H	16
Meall nan Aighean	Highld	NH3520	57°14·7′	4°43·6′W	X	26
Meall nan Aighean	Pth & Kin	NN4749	56°36·7′	4°29·1′W	H	51
Meall nan Aighean Mór	Highld	NH4910	57°9·6′	4°29·3′W	H	34
Meall nan Allt Beithe	Highld	NM8571	56°47·1′	5°30·7′W	X	40
Meall nan Bradan Leathan	Highld	NH4971	57°42·5′	4°31·6′W	H	20
Meall nan Calman	Highld	NH2806	57°7·0′	4°50·0′W	H	34
Meall nan Caora	Stir	NN2819	56°20·2′	4°46·5′W	H	50,56
Meall nan Caorach	Arg & Bt	NN0143	56°32·5′	5°13·8′W	H	50
Meall nan Caorach	Arg & Bt	NR7763	55°48·8′	5°33·1′W	X	62
Meall nan Caorach	Highld	NC0101	57°57·5′	5°21·3′W	X	15
Meall nan Caorach	Highld	NH4735	57°23·0′	4°32·3′W	H	26
Meall nan Caorach	Highld	NH6706	57°7·8′	4°11·4′W	H	35
Meall nan Caorach	N Eil	NB3814	58°2·5′	6°25·9′W	H	14
Meall nan Caorach	Pth & Kin	NN9233	56°28·9′	3°44·8′W	H	52
Meall nan Capull	Arg & Bt	NM4229	56°23·2′	6°10·4′W	H	48
Meall nan Capull	Arg & Bt	NM6428	56°23·4′	5°49·0′W	X	49
Meall nan Carn	Arg & Bt	NM3225	56°20·7′	6°19·8′W	H	48
Meall nan Carn	Highld	NH0303	57°4·8′	5°14·6′W	X	33
Meall nan Ceapairean	Highld	NG9348	57°28·8′	5°26·7′W	H	25
Meall nan Ceapraichean	Highld	NH2582	57°47·9′	4°56·2′W	H	20
Meall nan Clach	Highld	NG8008	57°6·9′	5°37·6′W	X	33
Meall nan Clach	Highld	NM7845	56°32·9′	5°36·3′W	H	49
Meall nan Clachan	Highld	NC1302	57°58·3′	5°9·2′W	X	15
Meall nan Clach Ruadha	Highld	NC6057	58°29·0′	4°23·6′W	H	10
Meall nan Cléireach	Highld	NN0867	56°45·6′	5°8·0′W	H	41
Meall nan Cnaimhean	Highld	NM6457	56°39·0′	5°50·5′W	X	49
Meall nan Coireachan	Highld	NM5567	56°44·1′	5°59·9′W	H	47
Meall nan Con	Highld	NC5829	58°13·9′	4°24·6′W	H	16
Meall nan Con	Highld	NM5068	56°44·5′	6°4·8′W	H	47
Meall nan Cra	Highld	NC3759	58°29·6′	4°47·3′W	H	9
Meall nan Damh	Highld	NH3552	57°31·9′	4°44·9′W	H	26
Meall nan Damh	Highld	NM9174	56°48·9′	5°25·0′W	H	40
Meall nan Damh	N Ayr	NR9146	55°40·0′	5°19·0′W	H	62,69
Meall nan Dearcag	Highld	NN2595	57°1·0′	4°52·5′W	H	34
Meall nan Dearcag Mór	Highld	NC2006	58°0·7′	5°2·3′W	H	15
Meall nan Doireachan	Highld	NH2278	57°45·6′	4°59·1′W	H	20
Meall nan Each	Arg & Bt	NN0531	56°26·1′	5°9·3′W	H	50
Meall nan Each	Highld	NM6364	56°42·7′	5°52·1′W	H	40
Meall nan Each	Highld	NM8856	56°39·1′	5°27·1′W	H	49
Meall nan Each	Highld	NM8890	56°57·4′	5°28·7′W	H	33,40
Meall nan Eagan	Highld	NN5987	56°57·4′	4°18·7′W	H	42
Meall nan Eanchainn	Pth & Kin	NN7836	56°30·3′	3°58·5′W	H	51,52
Meall nan Eun	Arg & Bt	NN1944	56°33·4′	4°56·3′W	H	50
Meall nan Eun	Highld	NG9005	57°5·5′	5°27·5′W	H	33
Meall nan Eun	Highld	NH4993	57°54·3′	4°32·3′W	H	20
Meall nan Eun	Pth & Kin	NN5942	56°33·2′	4°17·2′W	H	51
Meall nan Eun	Pth & Kin	NN6862	56°44·1′	4°8·5′W	H	42
Meall nan Eun	Pth & Kin	NN7050	56°37·7′	4°6·7′W	H	42,51,52
Meall nan Gabhar	Arg & Bt	NM5242	56°30·5′	6°1·4′W	H	47,48
Meall nan Gabhar	Arg & Bt	NN2324	56°22·8′	4°51·5′W	H	50
Meall nan Gabhar	Highld	NC0205	57°59·7′	5°20·5′W	X	15
Meall nan Garbh Loch	Highld	NC0830	58°13·3′	5°15·7′W	H	15
Meall nan Gearran	Highld	NH2906	57°7·1′	4°49·0′W	X	34
Meall nan Gobhar	Arg & Bt	NN1049	56°35·9′	5°5·3′W	H	50
Meall nan Gobhar	Highld	NN1045	56°33·8′	5°5·1′W	H	50
Meall nan Gobhar	Stir	NN5604	56°12·7′	4°18·9′W	H	57
Meall nan Imrichean	Highld	NC2606	58°0·8′	4°56·3′W	H	15
Meall nan Laogh	Highld	NH6910	57°10·0′	4°9·5′W	H	35
Meall nan Laogh	N Eil	NG2398	57°53·4′	6°40·0′W	X	14

Meall nan Leac Sleamhuinn	N Ayr	NR9147	55°40·5'	5°19·0'W	X	62,69
Meall nan Leapaichean	Highld	NC1419	58°7·5'	5°9·0'W	X	15
Meall nan Loth	Pth & Kin	NN8368	56°47·6'	3°54·5'W	H	43
Meall nan Luath	Highld	NN2483	56°54·6'	4°53·0'W	H	34,41
Meall nan Oighreag	Pth & Kin	NN7034	56°29·1'	4°6·2'W	H	51,52
Meall nan Oighreag	Stir	NN5719	56°20·8'	4°18·4'W	H	57
Meall nan Oighreagan	Highld	NH3622	57°15·8'	4°42·7'W	H	26
Meall nan Reitheachan	Highld	NN2999	57°3·3'	4°48·7'W	H	34
Meall nan Ruadhag	Highld	NH5206	57°7·5'	4°26·2'W	H	35
Meall nan Ruadhag	Highld	NM8067	56°44·8'	5°35·4'W	H	40
Meall nan Ruadhag	Highld	NN1698	57°2·4'	5°1·5'W	H	34
Meall nan Ruadhag	Highld	NN2957	56°40·7'	4°47·0'W	H	41
Meall nan Ruadhag	Highld	NN5098	57°3·2'	4°27·9'W	X	35
Meall nan Ruadhlag	Highld	NM9267	56°45·2'	5°23·7'W	H	40
Meall nan Ruag	Pth & Kin	NN4650	56°37·3'	4°30·1'W	H	42,51
Meall nan Ruaig	Pth & Kin	NN6972	56°49·5'	4°8·3'W	H	42
Meall nan Sac	Highld	NH4073	57°43·4'	4°40·7'W	H	20
Meall nan Sac	Pth & Kin	NN5651	56°38·0'	4°20·4'W	H	42,51
Meall nan Saighead	Highld	NG7405	57°5·1'	5°43·3'W	H	33
Meall nan Slatach	Highld	NH3184	57°49·1'	4°50·2'W	X	20
Meall nan Sleac	Highld	NN8694	57°1·6'	3°52·2'W	X	35,36,43
Meall nan Spardan	Highld	NM9291	56°58·1'	5°24·9'W	H	33,40
Meall nan Sùbh	Pth & Kin	NN4539	56°31·3'	4°30·7'W	H	51
Meall nan Tarmachan	Pth & Kin	NN5838	56°31·0'	4°18·0'W	H	51
Meall nan Tarmachan	Stir	NN3518	56°19·8'	4°39·7'W	X	50,56
Meall nan Tighearn	Arg & Bt	NN2323	56°22·2'	4°51·5'W	H	50
Meall nan Tri Tighearnan	Highld	NN1442	56°32·3'	5°1·0'W	H	50
Meall nan Tunn	Highld	NH4968	57°40·9'	4°31·5'W	H	20
Meall nan Uamh	Stir	NN5820	56°21·3'	4°17·4'W	H	51,57
Meall nan Uan	Arg & Bt	NM2661	56°39·9'	6°27·9'W	H	46,47
Meall nan Uan	Arg & Bt	NM1836	56°29·1'	4°56·9'W	H	50
Meall nan Uan	Highld	NC5629	58°13·8'	4°26·7'W	X	16
Meall nan Uan	Highld	NG9083	57°47·5'	5°31·5'W	H	19
Meall nan Uan	Highld	NH2295	57°54·8'	4°59·8'W	H	20
Meall na Rainich	Highld	NH3884	57°49·3'	4°43·2'W	H	20
Meall na Ruadhaig	Highld	NH3209	57°8·7'	4°46·2'W	H	34
Meall na Samhna	Stir	NN4932	56°27·6'	4°26·6'W	H	51
Meall na Saobhaidhe	Highld	NG8748	57°28·6'	5°32·7'W	H	24
Meall na Seana-chreig	Highld	NG8394	57°53·2'	5°39·2'W	H	19
Meall na Sguabaich	Highld	NN5682	56°54·7'	4°21·5'W	H	42
Meall na Sidhinn	Highld	NC1904	57°59·6'	5°3·3'W	H	15
Meall na Slinngearaich	Highld	NN3972	56°49·0'	4°37·8'W	X	41
Meall na Speireig	Highld	NH3069	57°41·0'	4°50·6'W	H	20
Meall na Speireig	Highld	NH4966	57°39·8'	4°31·4'W	H	20
Meall na Spionaig	Pth & Kin	NO0077	56°52·7'	3°38·0'W	H	43
Meall na Sròine	Arg & Bt	NM9305	56°11·8'	5°19·8'W	H	55
Meall na Sròine	Highld	NH4418	57°13·8'	4°34·6'W	H	34
Meall na Sròine	Highld	NM9194	56°59·7'	5°26·0'W	H	33,40
Meall na Suiramach	Highld	NG4469	57°38·6'	6°16·9'W	H	23
Meall na Targaid	Highld	NH4614	57°11·7'	4°32·5'W	H	34
Meall na Teanga	Highld	NC4834	58°16·4'	4°35·0'W	H	16
Meall na Teanga	Highld	NN2292	56°59·4'	4°55·3'W	H	34
Meall na Teanga Fhiadhaich	Highld	NG9446	57°27·7'	5°25·6'W	X	25
Meall Nathrach	Highld	NN4575	56°50·7'	4°32·0'W	H	42
Meall Nathrach Mór	Highld	NN4368	56°46·9'	4°33·7'W	H	42
Meall na Tulchainn	Highld	NH6599	57°57·9'	4°16·4'W	X	21
Meallneveron	Pth & Kin	NN8528	56°26·1'	3°51·5'W	X	52,58
Meall Odhar	Arg & Bt	NM9416	56°17·8'	5°19·3'W	H	55
Meall Odhar	Arg & Bt	NN1946	56°34·5'	4°56·3'W	H	50
Meall Odhar	Arg & Bt	NR7870	55°52·6'	5°32·5'W	X	62
Meall Odhar	Arg & Bt	NR8074	55°54·8'	5°30·8'W	X	62
Meall Odhar	Highld	NC1907	58°1·2'	5°3·4'W	H	15
Meall Odhar	Highld	NC4424	58°10·9'	4°38·7'W	H	16
Meall Odhar	Highld	NC5721	58°9·6'	4°25·3'W	H	16
Meall Odhar	Highld	NC7806	58°1·8'	4°3·5'W	H	17
Meall Odhar	Highld	NG4626	57°15·5'	6°12·3'W	X	32
Meall Odhar	Highld	NH1706	57°6·8'	5°0·9'W	H	34
Meall Odhar	Highld	NH2767	57°39·8'	4°53·5'W	X	20
Meall Odhar	Highld	NM7869	56°45·8'	5°37·5'W	X	40
Meall Odhar	Highld	NN2092	56°59·3'	4°57·3'W	H	34
Meall Odhar	Highld	NN4679	56°52·9'	4°31·2'W	X	42
Meall Odhar	Pth & Kin	NN6640	56°32·2'	4°10·3'W	X	51
Meall Odhar	Pth & Kin	NN8382	56°55·1'	3°54·9'W	H	43
Meall Odhar	Pth & Kin	NN8542	56°33·6'	3°51·8'W	X	52
Meall Odhar	Pth & Kin	NO1165	56°46·3'	3°26·9'W	H	43
Meall Odhar	Pth & Kin	NO1577	56°52·9'	3°23·2'W	H	43
Meall Odhar	Stir	NN2929	56°25·6'	4°45·9'W	H	50
Meall Odhar	Stir	NN6414	56°18·2'	4°11·4'W	H	57
Meall Odhar a' Chire	Pth & Kin	NN7978	56°52·9'	3°58·7'W	H	42
Meall Odharaich	Highld	NN6890	56°59·2'	4°9·9'W	H	35
Meall Odhar Ailleag	Pth & Kin	NN8079	56°53·5'	3°57·7'W	H	43
Meall Odhar Aillig	Highld	NN7783	56°55·6'	4°0·8'W	H	42
Meall Odhar Beag	Highld	NG4933	57°19·4'	6°9·7'W	H	32
Meall Odhar Loisgte	Highld	NN8082	56°55·1'	3°57·8'W	H	43
Meall Odhar Mór	Highld	NG4832	57°18·8'	6°10·6'W	H	32
Meall Odhar Mór	Highld	NN7284	56°56·0'	4°5·8'W	H	42
Meall Odhar Mór	Pth & Kin	NN6880	56°53·8'	4°9·6'W	H	42
Meall Odhar na Féithe Bige	Pth & Kin	NN5868	56°47·2'	4°19·0'W	H	42
Meall Onfhaidh	Highld	NN0184	56°54·5'	5°15·7'W	H	41
Meallon Odhar	Highld	NH5505	57°7·0'	4°23·2'W	X	35
Meall Phubuill	Pth & Kin	NN4442	56°32·9'	4°31·8'W	X	51
Meall Port Mealary	Highld	NG7416	57°11·0'	5°43·9'W	X	33
Meall Preas a' Chreamha	Highld	NC2108	58°1·8'	5°1·4'W	H	15
Meall Ptarmigan	Highld	NN4290	56°58·7'	4°35·5'W	H	34
Meall Reamhar	Arg & Bt	NM7230	56°24·7'	5°41·3'W	X	49
Meall Reamhar	Arg & Bt	NM8106	56°12·0'	5°31·4'W	H	55
Meall Reamhar	Arg & Bt	NM8320	56°19·6'	5°30·1'W	H	49
Meall Reamhar	Arg & Bt	NM8406	56°12·1'	5°28·5'W	H	55
Meall Reamhar	Arg & Bt	NM8900	56°9·0'	5°23·4'W	H	55
Meall Reamhar	Arg & Bt	NM8928	56°24·1'	5°24·7'W	X	49
Meall Reamhar	Arg & Bt	NN2004	56°11·9'	4°53·6'W	X	56
Meall Reamhar	Arg & Bt	NN2421	56°21·2'	4°50·5'W	X	50,56
Meall Reamhar	Arg & Bt	NR7768	55°51·5'	5°33·4'W	H	62
Meall Reamhar	Arg & Bt	NR8369	55°52·2'	5°27·7'W	H	62
Meall Reamhar	Arg & Bt	NR9298	56°8·0'	5°20·4'W	X	55
Meall Reamhar	Arg & Bt	NR9582	55°59·5'	5°16·8'W	X	55

Meall Reamhar	Arg & Bt	NS0899	56°9·0'	5°5·0'W	X	56
Meall Reamhar	Arg & Bt	NS0997	56°7·9'	5°4·0'W	X	56
Meall Reamhar	Pth & Kin	NN6621	56°22·0'	4°9·7'W	H	51,57
Meall Reamhar	Pth & Kin	NN6727	56°25·2'	4°8·9'W	H	51
Meall Reamhar	Pth & Kin	NN7861	56°43·7'	3°59·2'W	H	42
Meall Reamhar	Pth & Kin	NN8670	56°48·7'	3°51·6'W	H	43
Meall Reamhar	Pth & Kin	NN8732	56°28·3'	3°49·6'W	H	52
Meall Reamhar	Pth & Kin	NN9233	56°28·9'	3°44·9'W	H	52
Meall Reamhar	Pth & Kin	NN9346	56°35·9'	3°44·1'W	H	52
Meall Reamhar	Pth & Kin	NN9975	56°51·6'	3°38·9'W	H	43
Meall Reamhar	Pth & Kin	NO0356	56°41·4'	3°34·6'W	H	52,53
Meall Reamhar	Stir	NN5022	56°22·3'	4°25·3'W	X	51
Meall Reamhar	Stir	NN5724	56°23·5'	4°18·5'W	H	51
Meall Reamhar	Stir	NN6128	56°25·7'	4°14·8'W	X	51
Meall Rèidh	Arg & Bt	NN1011	56°15·5'	5°3·6'W	H	50,56
Meall Reinidh	Highld	NC3537	58°17·7'	4°48·4'W	H	15
Meall Riabhach	Highld	NH0166	57°38·7'	5°19·6'W	H	19
Meall Riabhach	Highld	NH3450	57°30·9'	4°45·8'W	H	26
Meall Riaghain	Arg & Bt	NN0632	56°26·7'	5°8·4'W	H	50
Meall Righ Beag	Arg & Bt	NR5182	55°58·2'	5°59·0'W	X	61
Meall Righ Mór	Arg & Bt	NR5183	55°58·8'	5°59·1'W	X	61
Meall Ruadh	Arg & Bt	NR7980	55°58·0'	5°32·0'W	X	55
Meall Ruadh	Arg & Bt	NR8081	55°58·6'	5°31·1'W	X	55
Meall Ruadh	Highld	NG9736	57°22·4'	5°22·1'W	H	25
Meall Ruadh	Highld	NN0571	56°47·6'	5°11·1'W	H	41
Meall Ruadh	N Eil	NG1188	57°47·6'	6°51·3'W	X	14
Meall Ruigh a' Bhricleathaid	Highld	NN2059	56°41·5'	4°55·9'W	X	41
Meall Ruighe an Fhirich	Highld	NH4162	57°37·5'	4°39·3'W	H	20
Meall Ruigh Mór Thearlaich	Pth & Kin	NO0571	56°49·5'	3°32·9'W	H	43
Meall Ruigh nam Biorag	Highld	NN6590	56°59·2'	4°12·9'W	H	35
Meall Ruigh Uisdein	Highld	NH2917	57°13·0'	4°49·4'W	X	34
Meall Sanna	Highld	NM4568	56°44·3'	6°9·7'W	H	47
Meall Seilich	Highld	NH1645	57°27·7'	5°3·6'W	X	25
Meall Sgallachd	Stir	NN5526	56°24·5'	4°20·6'W	H	51
Meall Sguman	Highld	NH0226	57°17·2'	5°16·7'W	H	25,33
Meall Shuas	Highld	NH0831	57°20·0'	5°10·9'W	H	25
Meall Steidhnoill	N Eil	NB0234	58°11·9'	7°3·9'W	X	13
Meall Sùil a' Chròtha	Highld	NG8885	57°48·5'	5°33·6'W	H	19
Meall Tairbh	Arg & Bt	NN2537	56°29·8'	4°50·1'W	H	50
Meall Tairneachan	Pth & Kin	NN8054	56°40·0'	3°57·0'W	H	52
Meall Tarsuinn	Arg & Bt	NN1744	56°33·4'	4°58·2'W	H	50
Meall Tarsuinn	Highld	NC3947	58°23·2'	4°44·8'W	X	9
Meall Tarsuinn	Highld	NN1696	57°1·4'	5°1·4'W	H	34
Meall Tarsuinn	Pth & Kin	NN8729	56°26·6'	3°49·5'W	H	52,58
Meall Taurnie	Stir	NN4838	56°30·8'	4°27·8'W	H	51
Meall Thailm	Highld	NC6266	58°33·9'	4°21·9'W	X	10
Meall Thairbh	Stir	NN4426	56°24·3'	4°31·2'W	X	51
Meall Thucrabhat	N Eil	NF7836	57°18·3'	7°20·4'W	X	22
Meall Tionail	Aberd	NO0184	56°56·5'	3°37·2'W	H	43
Meall Tionail	Arg & Bt	NN3439	56°31·1'	4°41·4'W	H	50
Meall Tionail	Highld	NH8800	57°4·9'	3°50·4'W	X	35,36
Meall Tionail	Highld	NN2447	56°35·2'	4°51·5'W	H	50
Meall Tionail	Highld	NN8984	56°56·3'	3°49·0'W	H	43
Meall Tionail	Pth & Kin	NN3837	56°30·1'	4°37·8'W	H	50
Meall Tionail	Pth & Kin	NN8373	56°50·3'	3°54·6'W	H	43
Meall Tionail	Pth & Kin	NN9277	56°52·6'	3°45·9'W	H	43
Meall Tionail na Beinne Brice	Pth & Kin	NN8881	56°54·7'	3°49·9'W	H	43
Meall Tionail na Glais Feith	Pth & Kin	NN8983	56°55·8'	3°49·0'W	H	43
Meall Tional	Moray	NJ0903	57°6·8'	3°29·7'W	H	36
Meall Toll a' Choin	Highld	NH5278	57°46·3'	4°28·8'W	H	20
Meall Tom a' Ghanntair	Highld	NM6562	56°41·7'	5°49·8'W	H	40
Meall Tòn Eich	Stir	NN5538	56°31·0'	4°21·0'W	H	51
Meall Tuath	Highld	NG4175	57°41·7'	6°20·3'W	X	23
Meall Tuath	Highld	NG7638	57°22·9'	5°43·1'W	X	24
Meall Tuirslighe	Highld	NC6559	58°30·2'	4°18·5'W	X	10
Meall Uain	Highld	NM8066	56°44·3'	5°35·4'W	X	40
Meall Uaine	Pth & Kin	NN9360	56°43·4'	3°44·5'W	H	43
Meall Uaine	Pth & Kin	NO0360	56°43·6'	3°34·7'W	H	43
Meall Uaine	Pth & Kin	NO1167	56°47·4'	3°27·0'W	H	43
Meall Uaineil	Highld	NC6913	58°5·5'	4°12·9'W	H	16
Meall Unaig	Highld	NH7205	57°7·3'	4°6·4'W	X	35
Meall Voirlich	Arg & Bt	NN1134	56°27·9'	5°3·6'W	H	50
Meall Na Chap-laraich	Pth & Kin	NN4939	56°31·4'	4°26·8'W	H	51
Mealna Letter or Duchray Hill	Pth & Kin	NO1667	56°47·5'	3°22·1'W	H	43
Meal nam Fiannaidhean	Highld	NM6974	56°48·3'	5°46·6'W	H	40
Mealo Hill	Cumbr	NY0841	54°45·6'	3°25·4'W	X	85
Mealo Ho	Cumbr	NY0741	54°45·6'	3°26·3'W	X	85
Mealowther	W Loth	NT0755	55°47·0'	3°28·5'W	X	65,72
Mealrigg	Cumbr	NY1245	54°47·8'	3°21·7'W	T	85
Mealrigg	Cumbr	SD5676	54°10·9'	2°40·0'W	X	97
Meals Fm	Lincs	TF4197	53°27·3'	0°7·8'E	FM	113
Mealsgate	Cumbr	NY2042	54°46·2'	3°14·2'W	T	85
Meals Ho	Norf	TF8845	52°58·4'	0°48·4'E	X	132
Meams	Angus	NO3656	56°41·7'	3°2·3'W	X	54
Meams Hill	Angus	NO3757	56°42·3'	3°1·3'W	H	54
Meanach (Bothy)	Highld	NN2668	56°46·5'	4°50·4'W	X	41
Meanais	N Eil	NF8651	57°26·7'	7°13·6'W	X	22
Mean Burn	Scot Bord	NT4651	55°45·2'	2°51·2'W	W	66,73
Mean Dubh	Stir	NN5334	56°28·8'	4°22·8'W	X	51
Meanecht	Aberd	NJ7506	57°8·9'	2°24·3'W	X	38
Mean Ham	Glos	SO8219	51°52·4'	2°15·3'W	X	162
Meanish	Highld	NG1550	57°27·3'	6°44·6'W	X	23
Meanish	N Eil	NL6590	56°53·1'	7°29·6'W	X	31
Meanley	Lancs	SD7049	53°56·4'	2°27·0'W	X	103
Meanlour Hill	E Ayr	NS6531	55°33·5'	4°8·0'W	H	71
Mean Moor	Cumbr	SD2480	54°12·9'	3°9·5'W	X	96
Mean Muir	E Ayr	NS5533	55°34·4'	4°17·6'W	X	71
Meannan	Highld	NB3635	58°13·7'	6°29·3'W	H	8
Meann Chnoc	Highld	NH5968	57°41·1'	4°21·4'W	H	21
Meanwood	Leeds	SE2837	53°50·0'	1°34·1'W	T	104
Mean Wood	Wilts	SU2525	51°1·7'	1°38·2'W	F	184
Meanygate Fm	Lancs	SD4017	53°39·0'	2°54·1'W	FM	108

Mearbeck	N Yks	SD8160	54°2·4'	2°17·0'W	T	98
Meare	Somer	ST4541	51°10·2'	2°46·8'W	T	182
Meare Court Fm	Somer	ST2921	50°59·3'	3°0·3'W	FM	193
Meare Fm	Somer	ST4541	51°10·2'	2°46·8'W	A	182
Meare Green	Somer	ST2922	50°59·8'	3°0·3'W	T	193
Meare Green	Somer	ST3326	51°2·0'	2°56·9'W	T	193
Meare Heath	Somer	ST4440	51°9·6'	2°47·7'W	X	182
Meare Pool	Somer	ST4542	51°10·7'	2°46·8'W	X	182
Meare, The	Suff	TM4659	52°10·7'	1°36·3'E	W	156
Mear Fm	Devon	SS7809	50°52·3'	3°43·7'W	FM	191
Mearley Hall	Lancs	SD7640	53°51·6'	2°21·5'W	X	103
Mearley Moor	Lancs	SD7840	53°51·6'	2°19·7'W	X	103
Mearness Fm	Cumbr	SD3281	54°13·5'	3°2·2'W	FM	96,97
Mearness Point	Cumbr	SD3281	54°13·5'	3°2·2'W	X	96,97
Mearns	Bath & NE Somer	ST6558	51°19·4'	2°29·8'W	T	172
Mearns	E Renf	NS5455	55°46·2'	4°19·2'W	T	64
Mearns Law	E Renf	NS5053	55°45·1'	4°23·0'W	H	64
Mears Ashby	Northnts	SP8366	52°17·4'	0°46·6'W	T	152
Mearse Fm	Worcs	SO8776	52°23·1'	2°11·1'W	FM	139
Mearse Fm	Worcs	SO9376	52°23·2'	2°5·8'W	FM	139
Mearse Fm	Worcs	SP0358	52°13·4'	1°57·0'W	FM	150
Meary Veg	I of M	SC3371	54°6·7'	4°32·9'W	X	95
Meary Voar	I of M	SC3270	54°6·2'	4°33·8'W	X	95
Meas	Cumbr	SD7790	54°18·6'	2°20·8'W	X	98
Measand Beck	Cumbr	NY4715	54°31·9'	2°48·7'W	W	90
Measand End	Cumbr	NY4715	54°31·9'	2°48·7'W	X	90
Measborough Dike	Barns	SE3605	53°32·7'	1°27·0'W	T	110,111
Measbury Moor	Devon	SS7218	50°57·1'	3°49·0'W	X	180
Measer	Orkney	HY6940	59°15·0'	2°32·1'W	X	5
Measham	Leic	SK3312	52°42·5'	1°30·3'W	T	128
Measham Fields Fm	Leic	SK3411	52°42·0'	1°29·4'W	FM	128
Measham Hall	Leic	SK3511	52°42·0'	1°28·5'W	X	128
Measham House Fm	Leic	SK3412	52°42·5'	1°29·4'W	FM	128
Measham Lodge	Leic	SK3411	52°42·0'	1°29·4'W	X	128
Meashill Fm	Shrops	SJ8208	52°40·4'	2°15·6'W	FM	127
Measured Nautical Mile	Corn	SX2351	50°20·2'	4°28·9'W	X	201
Meathaw Hill	Cumbr	NY6742	54°46·6'	2°30·4'W	X	86,87
Meath Green	Surrey	TQ2744	51°11·1'	0°10·6'W	T	187
Meath Hill	E Ayr	NS6028	55°31·8'	4°12·7'W	X	71
Meathop	Cumbr	SD4380	54°13·0'	2°52·0'W	T	97
Meathop Moss	Cumbr	SD4481	54°13·5'	2°51·1'W	F	97
Meaton	Shrops	SO7177	52°23·7'	2°25·2'W	X	138
Meaul	D & G	NS5802	55°17·8'	4°13·8'W	H	77
Meaul	D & G	NX4382	55°6·7'	4°27·3'W	H	77
Meaul	D & G	NX5090	55°11·1'	4°20·9'W	H	77
Meaux	E Yorks	TA0939	53°50·4'	0°20·2'W	T	107
Meaux Abbey Fm	E Yorks	TA0940	53°50·9'	0°20·2'W	FM	107
Meaval	N Eil	NG0291	57°48·8'	7°0·6'W	H	18
Meaver	Corn	SW6818	50°1·3'	5°14·0'W	T	203
Meavie Point	Aberd	NJ6864	57°40·1'	2°31·7'W	X	29
Meavy	Devon	SX5467	50°29·3'	4°3·1'W	T	201
Meayll Hill	I of M	SC1867	54°4·3'	4°46·5'W	X	95
Mechi	Cumbr	NY1741	54°45·7'	3°17·0'W	X	85
Mecklin Beck	Cumbr	NY1202	54°24·6'	3°20·9'W	W	89
Mecklin Park	Cumbr	NY1302	54°24·6'	3°20·0'W	X	89
Mecknoch	Arg & Bt	NS0459	55°47·3'	5°7·1'W	X	63
Meckphen	Pth & Kin	NO0124	56°24·1'	3°35·8'W	X	52,53,58
Medart	Caer	ST2392	51°37·5'	3°6·4'W	H	171
Medbourne	Leic	SP7993	52°32·0'	0°49·7'W	T	141
Medbourne	Swin	SU2080	51°31·3'	1°42·3'W	X	174
Medbourne Fm	Swin	SU1981	51°31·9'	1°43·2'W	FM	173
Medbourne Grange	Leic	SP8194	52°32·5'	0°47·9'W	X	141
Med Burn	Northum	NZ1170	55°1·7'	1°49·2'W	W	88
Medburn	Northum	NZ1370	55°1·7'	1°47·4'W	T	88
Medbury Fm	Beds	TL0546	52°6·4'	0°27·6'W	FM	153
Meddat	Highld	NH7774	57°44·6'	4°3·5'W	X	21
Meddens	Aberd	NJ8522	57°17·6'	2°14·5'W	X	38
Meddon	Devon	SS2717	50°55·8'	4°27·3'W	T	190
Meddrick Rocks	Devon	SX6245	50°17·6'	3°55·9'W	X	202
Meddygan	Carm	SN3527	51°55·3'	4°23·6'W	X	145
Medelfyw	Carm	SN5304	51°43·2'	4°7·3'W	X	159
Meden Vale	Notts	SK5769	53°13·1'	1°8·4'W	T	120
Medge Hall	N Lincs	SE7412	53°36·2'	0°52·5'W	X	112
Medhone Fm	W Susx	TQ0025	51°1·2'	0°34·1'W	FM	186,197
Medhurst Row	Kent	TQ4647	51°12·4'	0°5·8'E	T	188
Mediobogdvm (Roman Fort)	Cumbr	NY2101	54°24·1'	3°12·6'W	R	89,90
Medlam	Lincs	TF3156	53°5·3'	0°2·2'W	T	122
Medlam Br	Lincs	TF3256	53°5·3'	0°1·3'W	X	122
Medlam Drain	Lincs	TF3151	53°2·6'	0°2·3'W	W	122
Medlam Drain	Lincs	TF3157	53°5·9'	0°2·2'W	W	122
Medlam Fm	Lincs	TF3252	53°3·2'	0°1·4'W	FM	122
Medlam Ho	Lincs	TF3056	53°5·4'	0°3·1'W	X	122
Medlam Manor	Lincs	TF3156	53°5·3'	0°2·2'W	X	122
Medland	Corn	SX1372	50°31·3'	4°37·9'W	X	200
Medland	Devon	SS5401	50°47·6'	4°3·9'W	X	191
Medland Brook	Devon	SX5599	50°46·6'	4°3·0'W	W	191
Medland Manor	Devon	SX7795	50°44·7'	3°44·2'W	X	191
Medlar	Lancs	SD4135	53°48·7'	2°53·4'W	T	102
Medley Fm	Shrops	SJ4619	52°46·2'	2°47·6'W	FM	126
Medley Park Fm	Shrops	SO4782	52°26·2'	2°46·4'W	FM	137,138
Medlicott	Shrops	SO3981	52°25·7'	2°53·4'W	X	137
Medlicott	Shrops	SO4094	52°32·7'	2°52·7'W	T	137
Medlock Vale	Tames	SJ9099	53°29·5'	2°8·6'W	X	109
Medlock Valley Way	Oldham	SD9607	53°33·8'	2°3·2'W	X	109
Medlyn	Corn	SW7033	50°9·4'	5°12·8'W	T	203
Medmenham	Bucks	SU8084	51°33·2'	0°50·4'W	T	175
Medomsley	Durham	NZ1154	54°53·1'	1°49·3'W	T	88
Medros Fm	Corn	SX0556	50°22·5'	4°44·2'W	FM	200
Medstead	Hants	SU6537	51°7·9'	1°3·9'W	T	185,186
Medstead Grange	Hants	SU6538	51°8·5'	1°3·9'W	X	185,186
Medwaledd	Powys	SO1583	52°26·5'	3°14·6'W	X	136
Medway	Medway	TQ8163	51°20·5'	0°36·3'E	X	178
Medway Br	Medway	TQ7267	51°22·8'	0°28·7'E	X	178
Medway Fm	E Susx	TQ5730	51°3·1'	0°14·8'E	FM	188
Medwin Water	S Lanak	NS9744	55°41·0'	3°37·9'W	W	72
Medwin Water	S Lanak	NT0852	55°45·4'	3°27·5'W	W	65,72
Medwyn Cott	Scot Bord	NT1248	55°43·3'	3°23·6'W	X	72
Medwynhead	Scot Bord	NT0951	55°44·9'	3°26·5'W	X	65,72

Medwyn Ho	Scot Bord	NT1452	55°45·5'	3°21·8'W	X	65,72
Medwyn Mains	Scot Bord	NT1349	55°43·9'	3°22·7'W	X	72
Meece Brook	Staffs	SJ8432	52°53·4'	2°13·9'W	W	127
Meeke Wood	N Yks	SE5336	53°49·3'	1°11·3'W	F	105
Meeks Park	Clackm	NS9595	56°8·4'	3°40·9'W	X	58
Meend Fm	Monm	SO5008	51°46·3'	2°43·1'W	FM	162
Men's Fm	Suff	TM3282	52°23·4'	1°25·0'E	FM	156
Meepshole Wood	Essex	TQ7095	51°37·9'	0°27·8'E	F	167
Meer Booth Fm	Lincs	TF2848	53°1·1'	0°5·1'W	FM	131
Meerbrook	Staffs	SJ9960	53°8·5'	2°0·5'W	T	118
Meer Common	Heref	SO3652	52°10·0'	2°55·7'W	T	148,149
Meer Court	Heref	SO4336	52°1·4'	2°49·4'W	X	149,161
Meer End	Sol	SP2474	52°22·0'	1°38·5'W	T	139
Meerhay	Dorset	ST4802	50°49·1'	2°43·9'W	T	193
Meer Hill	Warw	SP2453	52°10·7'	1°38·5'W	X	151
Meerlees	Scot Bord	NT2811	55°23·5'	3°7·8'W	X	79
Meeroak	Shrops	SO3476	52°22·9'	2°57·8'W	X	137,148
Meers Bank	Lincs	TF4885	53°20·7'	0°13·8'E	X	122
Meers Bridge	Lincs	TF4886	53°21·2'	0°13·8'E	X	113,122
Meersbrook	Sheff	SK3584	53°21·3'	1°28·0'W	T	110,111
Meers Place	Heref	SO4250	52°9·0'	2°50·5'W	X	148,149
Meesden	Herts	TL4332	51°58·3'	0°5·3'E	T	167
Meesden Bury	Herts	TL4432	51°58·3'	0°6·2'E	X	167
Meeson	Wrekin	SJ6520	52°46·8'	2°30·7'W	T	127
Meeson Heath	Wrekin	SJ6520	52°46·8'	2°30·7'W	T	127
Meesons	Shrops	SO5479	52°24·7'	2°40·2'W	X	137,138
Meeth	Devon	SS5408	50°51·4'	4°4·1'W	T	191
Meethe	Devon	SS6722	50°59·2'	3°53·3'W	T	180
Meethe Barton	Devon	SS6723	50°59·7'	3°53·3'W	X	180
Meethill	Aberd	NK1145	57°30·0'	1°48·5'W	T	30
Meeting Green	Suff	TL7455	52°10·2'	0°33·1'E	T	155
Meeting Ho	Bucks	SU9791	51°36·8'	0°35·5'W	X	175,176
Meeting House Fm	N Som	ST4863	51°22·1'	2°44·4'W	FM	172,182
Meeting House Hill	Norf	TG3028	52°48·3'	1°25·1'E	T	133,134
Meeting of Three Waters	Highld	NN1756	56°39·9'	4°58·7'W	W	41
Meeting Scar	Cumbr	SD2165	54°4·7'	3°12·0'W	X	96
Meeting's The	Oxon	SP3729	51°57·7'	1°27·3'W	X	164
Meetings, The	S Lanak	NS9744	55°41·0'	3°37·9'W	W	72
Meetlaw	Aberd	NO8181	56°55·5'	2°18·3'W	X	45
Megcrofts	Staffs	SK0250	53°3·1'	1°57·8'W	X	119
Megdale	D & G	NY2995	55°14·9'	3°6·6'W	X	79
Meg Dike	Cald	SE0517	53°39·2'	1°55·0'W	A	110
Megen Burn	Aberd	NO3090	57°0·0'	3°8·7'W	W	44
Meg Gate	N Yks	SE2359	54°1·8'	1°38·5'W	X	104
Meggatland Fm	Pth & Kin	NO2727	56°26·0'	3°10·6'W	FM	53,59
Meggat Water	D & G	NY2993	55°13·8'	3°6·6'W	W	79
Meggerland Pt	D & G	NX5947	54°48·1'	4°11·2'W	X	83
Meggernie Castle	Pth & Kin	NN5546	56°35·3'	4°21·2'W	A	51
Meggeson Ho	N Yks	NZ4505	54°26·5'	1°17·9'W	X	93
Meggethead	Scot Bord	NT1621	55°28·8'	3°19·3'W	X	72
Megget Reservoir	Scot Bord	NT1821	55°28·8'	3°17·4'W	W	72
Megget Stone	Scot Bord	NT1520	55°28·2'	3°20·2'W	X	72
Meggett Fm	Kent	TR2541	51°7·7'	1°13·3'E	FM	179
Megget Water	Scot Bord	NT2122	55°29·4'	3°14·6'W	W	73
Meggie's Burn	Northum	NZ3078	55°6·0'	1°31·4'W	W	88
Megginch Castle	Pth & Kin	NO2424	56°24·4'	3°13·4'W	A	53,59
Megrim's Knowe	Northum	NT9615	55°26·0'	2°3·4'W	H	81
Meggs Hill	Cambs	TL5152	52°9·0'	0°12·8'E	X	154
Meghills	Essex	TL5912	51°47·3'	0°18·7'E	X	167
Megiliggar Rocks	Corn	SW6026	50°5·4'	5°21·0'W	X	203
Megray	Aberd	NO8787	56°58·7'	2°12·4'W	X	45
Meg Rocks	Devon	SX8848	50°19·5'	3°34·0'W	X	202
Meg's Cairn	Cumbr	NY6537	54°43·9'	2°32·2'W	X	91
Meg's Craig	Angus	NO6843	56°34·9'	2°30·8'W	X	54
Meg's Dub	Scot Bord	NT9757	55°48·6'	2°2·4'W	W	75
Megsfield	D & G	NY2781	55°7·3'	3°8·3'W	X	79
Meg's Hill	Scot Bord	NT2922	55°29·5'	3°7·0'W	H	73
Meg's Hill	Scot Bord	NT4102	55°18·8'	2°55·3'W	H	79
Meg's Shank	D & G	NY3492	55°13·3'	3°1·8'W	H	79
Megstone	Northum	NU2037	55°37·8'	1°40·5'W	X	75
Meg Swerie	Angus	NO4070	56°49·3'	2°58·5'W	X	44
Meg, The	Beds	TL1129	51°57·1'	0°22·7'W	X	166
Meickle Daan	Highld	NH6884	57°49·8'	4°12·9'W	X	21
Meidrim	Carm	SN2820	51°51·4'	4°29·5'W	T	145,158
Meifod	Conwy	SH8576	53°16·4'	3°43·1'W	X	116
Meifod	Denb	SJ0359	53°7·4'	3°26·6'W	X	116
Meifod	Powys	SJ1513	52°42·7'	3°15·1'W	T	125
Meifod-uchaf	Gwyn	SH5923	52°47·4'	4°5·1'W	X	124
Meighs Wood	Sol	SP2684	52°27·4'	1°36·6'W	F	140
Meigle	N Ayr	NS1965	55°50·9'	4°53·0'W	T	63
Meigle	Pth & Kin	NO2844	56°35·2'	3°9·9'W	T	53
Meigle	Scot Bord	NT4536	55°37·1'	2°52·0'W	X	73
Meigle Bay	N Ayr	NS1965	55°50·9'	4°53·0'W	W	63
Meigle Hill	Scot Bord	NT4636	55°37·1'	2°51·0'W	H	73
Meikle Aiden	Arg & Bt	NS2281	55°59·6'	4°50·8'W	X	63
Meikle Ardo	Aberd	NJ8439	57°26·7'	2°15·5'W	X	29,30
Meikle Ardrone	Moray	NJ4550	57°32·5'	2°54·7'W	X	28,29
Meikle Auchengibbert	E Ayr	NS5919	55°26·9'	4°13·3'W	X	71
Meikle Auchengree	N Ayr	NS3252	55°44·2'	4°40·1'W	X	63
Meikle Aucheoch	Aberd	NJ9151	57°33·2'	2°8·6'W	X	30
Meikle Auchinstilloch	S Lanak	NS7532	55°34·2'	3°58·5'W	H	71
Meikle Auchlyne	Aberd	NJ5526	57°19·6'	2°44·4'W	X	37
Meikle Auchrae	D & G	NX6494	55°13·5'	4°7·9'W	X	77
Meikle Awfell	Cumbr	NY6337	54°43·8'	2°34·1'W	X	91
Meikle Balloch Hill	Aberd	NJ4749	57°31·9'	2°52·6'W	H	28,29
Meikle Balloch Hill	Moray	NJ3534	57°23·8'	3°4·4'W	H	28
Meikle Balquhomrie	Fife	NO2302	56°12·5'	3°14·0'W	X	58
Meikle Balsmith	D & G	NX4639	54°43·6'	4°23·1'W	X	83
Meikle Barfil	D & G	NX8572	55°2·0'	3°47·5'W	X	84
Meikle Barncleugh	D & G	NX9077	55°4·8'	3°43·0'W	X	84
Meikle Bennan	D & G	NX5461	54°55·6'	4°16·3'W	H	83
Meikle Bennan	D & G	NX6587	55°9·8'	4°6·7'W	H	77
Meikle Bennane Fm	S Ayr	NX0986	55°8·1'	4°59·4'W	FM	76
Meikle Ben Shalag	Moray	NJ1044	57°28·9'	3°29·6'W	H	28
Meikle Beoch	D & G	NX8474	55°3·1'	3°48·5'W	X	84
Meikle Bin	Stir	NS6682	56°1·0'	4°8·5'W	H	57,64
Meikle Blackhills	Aberd	NJ8153	57°34·3'	2°18·6'W	X	29,30
Meikle Black Law	Scot Bord	NT8268	55°54·5'	2°16·8'W	X	67
Meikle Blackton	Aberd	NJ6558	57°36·9'	2°34·7'W	X	29
Meikle Boturich	W Dunb	NS3984	56°1·6'	4°34·6'W	X	56

Meikle Branchill	Moray	NJ0951	57°32·7'	3°30·8'W	X	27
Meikle Brown Hill	Moray	NJ5752	57°33·6'	2°42·7'W	H	29
Meikle Burn	S Lanak	NS9509	55°22·1'	3°39·0'W	W	78
Meikle Busbie	N Ayr	NS2345	55°40·2'	4°48·4'W	X	63
Meikle Cairn	Moray	NJ4125	57°19·0'	2°58·3'W	H	37
Meikle Cairnhill	Aberd	NJ7952	57°33·7'	2°20·6'W	X	29,30
Meikle Caldon	Stir	NS4983	56°1·2'	4°24·9'W	H	57,64
Meikle Calf Hill	Aberd	NO6181	56°55·4'	2°38·0'W	H	45
Meikle Camaloun	Aberd	NJ7540	57°27·2'	2°24·5'W	X	29
Meikle Canglour	Stir	NS7786	56°3·3'	3°58·1'W	X	57
Meikle Cantly	Moray	NJ4750	57°32·5'	2°52·7'W	X	28,29
Meikle Carco	D & G	NS7813	55°24·0'	3°55·2'W	X	71,78
Meikle Carewe Hill	Aberd	NO8292	57°1·4'	2°17·3'W	H	38,45
Meikle Carleith	E Ayr	NS5332	55°33·8'	4°19·4'W	X	70
Meikle Carse	D & G	NX4562	54°56·0'	4°24·7'W	X	83
Meikle Charsk Hill	Aberd	NJ3307	57°9·2'	3°6·0'W	H	37
Meikle Clinterty	C of Aber	NJ8311	57°11·6'	2°16·4'W	X	38
Meikle Cloak	Renf	NS3460	55°48·5'	4°38·5'W	X	63
Meikle Cloak Farm	D & G	NX8558	54°54·5'	3°47·2'W	FM	84
Meikle Colp	Aberd	NJ7448	57°31·5'	2°25·6'W	X	29
Meikle Conval	Moray	NJ2937	57°25·3'	3°10·5'W	H	28
Meikle Corr Riabhach	Aberd	NJ2513	57°12·4'	3°14·0'W	H	37
Meikle Corseford	Renf	NS4060	55°48·7'	4°32·8'W	X	64
Meikle Corsehill	E Ayr	NS4247	55°41·7'	4°30·4'W	X	64
Meikle Coull	Angus	NO4559	56°43·4'	2°53·5'W	X	54
Meikle Craigs		NS3228	55°31·3'	4°39·2'W	X	70
Meikle Craigtarson	D & G	NX4887	55°9·5'	4°22·7'W	X	77
Meikle Creoch	E Ayr	NS6013	55°23·7'	4°12·2'W	X	71
Meikle Culcaigrie Hill	D & G	NX6558	54°54·2'	4°5·9'W	H	83,84
Meikle Cullendoch	D & G	NX5565	54°57·8'	4°15·5'W	X	83
Meikle Cullendoch Moss	D & G	NX5665	54°57·8'	4°14·5'W	X	83
Meikle Culloch	D & G	NX8364	54°57·7'	3°49·2'W	X	84
Meikle Culmain	D & G	NX8369	55°0·4'	3°49·3'W	X	84
Meikle Cutstraw	E Ayr	NS4245	55°40·6'	4°30·3'W	X	64
Meikle Dalbeattie Fm	D & G	NX8261	54°56·0'	3°50·1'W	FM	84
Meikledale	D & G	NY3792	55°13·3'	2°59·0'W	X	79
Meikledale Burn	D & G	NY3694	55°14·4'	3°0·0'W	W	79
Meikledalehaugh	D & G	NY3792	55°13·3'	2°59·0'W	X	79
Meikledams	Aberd	NO7794	57°2·4'	2°22·3'W	X	38,45
Meikle Dens	Aberd	NK0743	57°28·9'	1°52·5'W	X	30
Meikle Dibbin Hill	D & G	NX6897	55°15·2'	4°4·2'W	X	77
Meikledod Hill	E Ayr	NS6503	55°18·4'	4°7·2'W	H	77
Meikle Dornell	D & G	NX6966	54°58·5'	4°2·4'W	H	83,84
Meikle Dripps	S Lanak	NS5755	55°46·3'	4°16·3'W	X	64
Meikle Drumgray	N Lanak	NS7869	55°54·2'	3°56·6'W	X	64
Meikle Dumfin	Arg & Bt	NS3385	56°2·0'	4°40·4'W	X	56
Meikle Dyke	D & G	NY1073	55°2·9'	3°24·1'W	X	85
Meikle Earnock	S Lanak	NS7153	55°45·4'	4°2·9'W	T	64
Meikle Eddieston	C of Aber	NJ7902	57°6·8'	2°20·4'W	X	38
Meikle Eldrig	D & G	NX3467	54°58·5'	4°35·2'W	X	82
Meikle Elrick	Aberd	NO1595	57°2·6'	3°23·6'W	X	36,43
Meikle Endovie	Aberd	NJ5915	57°13·7'	2°40·3'W	X	37
Meikle Ernambrie	D & G	NX7566	54°58·6'	3°56·8'W	X	84
Meikle Fardle	Pth & Kin	NO1332	56°33·4'	3°24·5'W	X	53
Meikle Ferry	Highld	NH7287	57°51·5'	4°9·0'W	X	21
Meikle Ferry Inn	Highld	NH7484	57°49·9'	4°6·8'W	X	21
Meikle Fiddes	Aberd	NO8080	56°54·9'	2°19·3'W	X	45
Meiklefield	Renf	NS4070	55°54·0'	4°33·1'W	X	64
Meikle Fieldie	Pth & Kin	NO1412	56°17·8'	3°22·9'W	X	58
Meikle Findon	Highld	NH6160	57°36·8'	4°19·1'W	X	21
Meikle Findowie	Pth & Kin	NN9539	56°32·1'	3°42·0'W	X	52,53
Meikle Finnery	W Dunb	NS4484	56°1·7'	4°29·8'W	X	57,64
Meikle Firbriggs	Moray	NJ3528	57°20·5'	3°4·3'W	H	37
Meikle Firbriggs Hill	Aberd	NJ3917	57°14·6'	3°0·2'W	H	37
Meikle Firthhead	D & G	NX8264	54°57·7'	3°50·2'W	F	84
Meikle Float	D & G	NX0648	54°47·6'	5°0·6'W	X	82
Meikle Folla	Aberd	NJ7233	57°23·5'	2°27·5'W	X	29
Meikle Forter	Angus	NO1864	56°45·9'	3°20·0'W	X	43
Meikle Galdenoch	D & G	NW9763	54°55·5'	5°9·7'W	X	82
Meikle Garclaugh	E Ayr	NS6424	55°24·3'	4°8·4'W	X	71
Meikle Garronach	Moray	NJ3524	57°18·4'	3°4·3'W	X	37
Meikle Geal Charn	Moray	NJ2005	57°8·0'	3°18·8'W	H	36
Meikle Geddes	Highld	NH8652	57°32·9'	3°53·8'W	X	27
Meiklegen	E Ayr	NS5739	55°37·7'	4°15·8'W	X	71
Meikle Gluich	Highld	NH6883	57°49·3'	4°12·9'W	X	21
Meikle Grenach	Arg & Bt	NS0760	55°47·9'	5°4·3'W	X	63
Meikle Haddo	Aberd	NJ9824	57°18·7'	2°1·5'W	X	38
Meiklehall	Aberd	NO6572	56°50·5'	2°34·0'W	X	45
Meikle Hard Hill	D & G	NX9362	54°56·7'	3°39·8'W	H	84
Meikle Harelaw	Scot Bord	NT6547	55°43·2'	2°33·0'W	X	74
Meiklehaugh	Aberd	NJ6117	57°14·8'	2°38·3'W	X	37
Meikle Heateth	E Ayr	NS5323	55°29·0'	4°19·1'W	X	70
Meikle Hill	D & G	NY0499	55°16·8'	3°30·2'W	X	78
Meikle Hill	E Ayr	NS5307	55°20·4'	4°18·6'W	H	70,77
Meiklehill	E Ayr	NS5308	55°20·9'	4°18·7'W	X	70,77
Meikle Hill	E Ayr	NS6107	55°20·5'	4°11·1'W	X	71,77
Meiklehill	E Dunb	NS6372	55°55·6'	4°11·1'W	X	64
Meikle Hill	Moray	NJ1450	57°32·2'	3°25·7'W	H	28
Meikle Hilton	Aberd	NJ7352	57°33·7'	2°26·6'W	X	29
Meikleholm	D & G	NY0489	55°11·4'	3°30·0'W	X	78
Meikleholm Burn	E Ayr	NS4108	55°20·7'	4°30·0'W	W	70,77
Meikleholmside	D & G	NT0709	55°22·2'	3°27·6'W	X	78
Meikle Isle	D & G	NX6279	55°5·4'	4°9·3'W	X	77
Meikle Ittington	N Ayr	NS2547	55°41·4'	4°46·6'W	X	63
Meikle Kenny	Angus	NO3053	56°40·1'	3°8·1'W	X	53
Meikle Kilchattan	Arg & Bt	NS0957	55°46·4'	5°2·3'W	X	63
Meikle Kilchattan Butts	Arg & Bt	NS0957	55°46·4'	5°2·3'W	T	63
Meikle Kildrummie	Highld	NH8553	57°33·4'	3°54·9'W	X	27
Meikle Killantrae	D & G	NX3545	54°46·6'	4°33·5'W	X	83
Meikle Kilmory	Arg & Bt	NS0561	55°48·4'	5°6·3'W	X	63
Meikle Kilmundie	Angus	NO3943	56°34·8'	2°59·1'W	X	54
Meikle Kilrannoch	Angus	NO2277	56°52·9'	3°16·3'W	X	44
Meikle Kinord	Aberd	NO4498	57°4·4'	2°55·0'W	X	37,44
Meikle Kirkhill	Aberd	NJ9344	57°29·4'	2°6·5'W	X	30
Meikle Kirkland	D & G	NX8269	55°0·3'	3°50·3'W	X	84
Meikle Knox	D & G	NX7962	54°56·5'	3°53·2'W	X	84
Meikle Knypes	D & G	NS7617	55°26·1'	3°57·2'W	X	71,78
Meikle Laight	D & G	NX0670	54°59·5'	5°1·5'W	X	76
Meikle Larg	D & G	NX8273	55°2·5'	3°50·4'W	X	84
Meikle Laught	N Ayr	NS2545	55°40·3'	4°46·5'W	X	63

Meikle Law	Scot Bord	NT6059	55°49·6'	2°37·9'W	H	67,74
Meikle Ley	Aberd	NJ6411	57°11·6'	2°35·3'W	X	37
Meikle Loch	Aberd	NK0230	57°21·9'	1°57·5'W	W	30
Meikle Logie	Pth & Kin	NN9841	56°33·3'	3°39·1'W	X	52,53
Meikle Lump	D & G	NX5283	55°7·4'	4°18·8'W	X	77
Meikle Mackie	Aberd	NK1342	57°28·3'	1°46·5'W	X	30
Meikle Maldron	Aberd	NJ6402	57°6·7'	2°35·2'W	X	37
Meikle Mark	D & G	NX0360	54°54·0'	5°3·9'W	X	82
Meikle Maxwood	E Ayr	NS5136	55°35·9'	4°21·5'W	X	70
Meikle Midmar	Aberd	NJ7007	57°9·4'	2°29·3'W	X	38
Meiklemill	Aberd	NJ9430	57°21·9'	2°5·5'W	X	30
Meikle Millyea	D & G	NX5182	55°6·9'	4°19·7'W	H	77
Meikle Mosside	E Ayr	NS4441	55°38·5'	4°28·3'W	X	70
Meiklemoss Wood	Aberd	NJ6016	57°14·2'	2°39·3'W	F	37
Meikle Multaggart	D & G	NX5167	54°58·8'	4°19·3'W	H	83
Meiklemyre	N Ayr	NS2851	55°43·6'	4°43·9'W	X	63
Meikle Namels Ridge	Scot Bord	NT5958	55°49·1'	2°38·8'W	X	67,73,74
Meikle Obney	Pth & Kin	NO0337	56°31·2'	3°34·1'W	X	52,53
Meikle or South Port of Spittal	D & G	NX0351	54°49·2'	5°3·6'W	X	82
Meikleour	Pth & Kin	NO1539	56°32·4'	3°22·5'W	T	53
Meikleour Beech Hedge	Pth & Kin	NO1638	56°31·8'	3°21·5'W	X	53
Meikleour Ho	Pth & Kin	NO1538	56°31·8'	3°22·5'W	X	53
Meikleour Wood	Pth & Kin	NO1842	56°34·0'	3°19·6'W	F	53
Meikle Pap	Aberd	NO2586	56°57·8'	3°13·6'W	H	44
Meiklepark	Aberd	NJ8227	57°20·2'	2°17·5'W	X	38
Meikle Phoineas	Highld	NH5244	57°28·0'	4°27·6'W	X	26
Meikle Pinkerton	E Loth	NT7075	55°58·3'	2°28·4'W	X	67
Meikle Pinnacle	D & G	NX5946	54°47·6'	4°11·2'W	X	83
Meikle Pittinnan	Aberd	NJ7529	57°21·3'	2°24·5'W	X	38
Meikleplank	Orkney	HY2528	59°8·2'	3°18·2'W	X	6
Meikle Poo Craig	Scot Bord	NT8270	55°55·6'	2°16·8'W	X	67
Meikle Rahane	Arg & Bt	NS2386	56°2·3'	4°50·0'W	X	56
Meikle Rathen	Aberd	NK0060	57°38·1'	1°59·5'W	X	30
Meikle Reive	E Dunb	NS6378	55°58·8'	4°11·3'W	X	64
Meikle Reive (Fort)	E Dunb	NS6378	55°58·8'	4°11·3'W	A	64
Meikle Rhynie	Highld	NH8579	57°47·4'	3°55·6'W	X	21
Meikle Ribrae	Aberd	NJ6850	57°32·6'	2°31·6'W	X	29
Meikle Richorn	D & G	NX8357	54°53·9'	3°49·0'W	X	84
Meiklerig	E Loth	NT6374	55°57·7'	2°35·1'W	X	67
Meiklerig Wood	E Loth	NT6374	55°57·7'	2°35·1'W	F	67
Meikle Ross	D & G	NX6543	54°46·1'	4°5·5'W	X	83,84
Meikleross Bay	Arg & Bt	NS2680	55°59·1'	4°46·9'W	W	63
Meikle Says Law	E Loth	NT5861	55°50·7'	2°39·8'W	H	67
Meikle Score	Highld	ND2175	58°39·6'	3°21·2'W	X	7,12
Meikle Seggie	Pth & Kin	NO1006	56°14·5'	3°26·7'W	X	58
Meikle Shag	S Lanak	NS9308	55°21·5'	3°40·8'W	H	71,78
Meikle Shalloch	S Ayr	NS4202	55°17·5'	4°28·9'W	X	77
Meikle Snout	D & G	NS8409	55°21·9'	3°49·4'W	H	71,78
Meikle Spiker	E Loth	NT6879	56°0·4'	2°30·4'W	X	67
Meikle Strath	Aberd	NO6471	56°50·0'	2°34·9'W	X	45
Meikle Strathvella	Aberd	NO6189	56°59·7'	2°38·1'W	X	45
Meikle Sypland	D & G	NX7151	54°50·5'	4°0·1'W	X	83,84
Meikle Tap	Aberd	NJ7202	57°6·7'	2°27·3'W	H	38
Meikle Tarrel	Highld	NH9081	57°48·6'	3°50·6'W	X	21
Meikle Tarty	Aberd	NJ9927	57°20·3'	2°0·5'W	X	38
Meikle Tillyeve	Aberd	NJ8923	57°18·1'	2°10·5'W	X	38
Meikle Tolly	Aberd	NJ3711	57°11·4'	3°2·1'W	X	37
Meikle Tombane	Pth & Kin	NN9440	56°32·7'	3°43·0'W	X	52,53
Meikleton	Aberd	NJ4543	57°28·7'	2°54·6'W	X	28,29
Meikleton	Aberd	NJ5841	57°27·7'	2°41·5'W	X	29
Meikle Tongue	D & G	NX1162	54°55·3'	4°56·5'W	X	82
Meikle Toux	Aberd	NJ5458	57°36·8'	2°45·7'W	X	29
Meikle Tullo	Angus	NO5772	56°50·5'	2°41·8'W	X	44
Meikle Tulloch	Aberd	NO7894	57°2·5'	2°21·3'W	X	38,45
Meikle Urchany	Highld	NH8850	57°31·8'	3°51·8'W	X	27
Meikle Ussie	Highld	NH5257	57°35·0'	4°28·1'W	X	26
Meikle Wartle	Aberd	NJ7230	57°21·8'	2°27·5'W	T	29
Meikle Watchman	Aberd	NJ4431	57°22·2'	2°55·4'W	X	37
Meikle Water	Orkney	HY6624	59°6·4'	2°35·1'W	W	5
Meikle Weistern	Aberd	NJ5738	57°26·1'	2°42·5'W	X	29
Meikle Westland	E Ayr	NS6513	55°23·8'	4°7·5'W	X	71
Meikle Whitefield	Pth & Kin	NO1734	56°29·7'	3°20·4'W	T	53
Meikle White Hill	W Dunb	NS4478	55°58·4'	4°29·6'W	H	64
Meikle Whitriggs	D & G	NY2083	55°8·3'	3°14·9'W	X	79
Meiklewood	D & G	NX6857	54°53·7'	4°3·1'W	X	83,84
Meiklewood	E Ayr	NS4441	55°38·5'	4°28·3'W	X	70
Meiklewood	Stir	NS7295	56°8·1'	4°3·1'W	X	57
Meikleyard	E Ayr	NS5132	55°33·8'	4°21·3'W	X	70
Meilein	N Eil	NB0014	58°1·1'	7°4·4'W	H	13
Meillionen	Gwyn	SH2937	52°54·4'	4°32·2'W	X	123
Meillionen	Gwyn	SH5748	53°0·9'	4°7·5'W	X	115
Meillionydd	Gwyn	SH2129	52°50·0'	4°39·0'W	X	123
Mein a' Chòis	Moray	NJ1913	57°12·3'	3°20·0'W	W	36
Meinbank	D & G	NY1872	55°2·4'	3°16·6'W	X	85
Meinciau	Carm	SN4610	51°46·3'	4°13·5'W	T	159
Meincyn	Cered	SN7868	52°18·0'	3°47·0'W	X	135,147
Meinek	Corn	SW3225	50°4·1'	5°44·4'W	X	203
Meinfoot	D & G	NY1872	55°2·4'	3°16·6'W	X	85
Meini Duon	Pemb	SM6921	51°50·6'	5°20·8'W	X	157
Meini Gwyn	Carm	SN4526	51°54·9'	4°14·8'W	A	146
Meinigwynion	Cered	SN4550	52°7·8'	4°15·5'W	X	146
Meini-gwynion	Cered	SN6160	52°13·5'	4°1·7'W	X	146
Meini Gwŷr	Carm	SN1426	51°54·3'	4°41·8'W	A	145,158
Meinihirion	Gwyn	SH8635	52°54·3'	3°41·3'W	X	124,125
Meini Llwydion	Carm	SN3715	51°48·8'	4°21·5'W	A	159
Meinir	I of Angl	SH3985	53°20·5'	4°24·7'W	X	114
Meinside	D & G	NY2375	55°4·1'	3°11·9'W	X	85
Mein Water	D & G	NY1973	55°2·9'	3°15·6'W	W	85
Meir	C of Stoke	SJ9342	52°58·8'	2°5·9'W	T	118
Meir Hay	C of Stoke	SJ9243	52°59·3'	2°6·7'W	X	118
Meir Heath	Staffs	SJ9339	52°57·1'	2°5·8'W	T	127
Meiriogen	I of Angl	SH3585	53°20·4'	4°28·3'W	X	114
Meirion Mill	Gwyn	SH8513	52°42·4'	3°41·7'W	X	124,125
Meirland, The	Moray	NJ3840	57°27·0'	3°1·5'W	X	28
Meiros	Rho Cyn Taf	ST0083	51°32·5'	3°26·1'W	X	170
Meith Bheinn	Highld	NM8287	56°55·6'	5°34·5'W	H	40
Meity-fawr	Powys	SN8525	51°54·9'	3°39·9'W	X	160
Meity-isaf	Powys	SN8526	51°55·5'	3°40·0'W	X	160
Mela	Gwyn	SH3438	52°55·1'	4°27·7'W	X	123

Melai	Conwy	SH9067	53°11·6'	3°38·4'W	X	116
Melancoose	Corn	SW8662	50°25·4'	5°0·4'W	X	200
Melandra Castle (Roman Fort)	Derby	SK0095	53°27·3'	1°59·6'W	R	110
Melbecks	Cumbr	NY2431	54°40·3'	3°10·3'W	X	89,90
Melbecks Moor	N Yks	NY9400	54°24·0'	2°5·1'W	X	91,92
Melberry	Orkney	ND2688	58°46·7'	3°16·3'W	X	7
Melbourn	Cambs	TL3844	52°4·9'	0°1·2'E	T	154
Melbourn Bury	Cambs	TL3744	52°4·9'	0°0·4'E	X	154
Melbourne	Derby	SK3825	52°49·5'	1°25·8'W	T	128
Melbourne	E Yorks	SE7544	53°53·4'	0°51·1'W	T	105,106
Melbourne	S Lanak	NT0844	55°41·1'	3°27·4'W	X	72
Melbourne Fm	Derby	SK1967	53°12·2'	1°42·5'W	FM	119
Melbourne Grange	E Yorks	SE7443	53°52·9'	0°52·0'W	X	105,106
Melbourne Hall	E Yorks	SE7543	53°52·9'	0°51·1'W	X	105,106
Melbourne Ho	Cumbr	NY5030	54°40·0'	2°46·1'W	X	90
Melbourne Lodge	Leic	SP5782	52°26·2'	1°9·3'W	X	140
Melbourne Parks	Derby	SK3923	52°48·4'	1°24·9'W	X	128
Melbur	Corn	SW9254	50°21·2'	4°55·1'W	X	200
Melbury Abbas	Dorset	ST8820	50°59·0'	2°9·9'W	T	183
Melbury Bubb	Dorset	ST5906	50°51·4'	2°34·6'W	T	194
Melbury Fm	Devon	SS3719	50°57·1'	4°18·9'W	FM	190
Melbury Hill	Devon	SS3819	50°57·1'	4°18·0'W	H	190
Melbury Hill	Dorset	ST8719	50°58·4'	2°10·7'W	H	183
Melbury Ho	Dorset	ST5706	50°51·3'	2°36·3'W	A	194
Melbury Osmond	Dorset	ST5707	50°51·9'	2°36·3'W	T	194
Melbury Park	Dorset	ST5705	50°50·8'	2°36·3'W	F	194
Melbury Resr	Devon	SS3820	50°57·6'	4°18·0'W	W	190
Melbury Sampford	Dorset	ST5706	50°51·3'	2°36·3'W	T	194
Melbury Wood	Dorset	ST9019	50°58·5'	2°8·2'W	F	184
Melby	Shetld	HU1857	60°18·1'	1°40·0'W	T	3
Melby Ho	Shetld	HU1857	60°18·1'	1°40·0'W	X	3
Melchbourne	Beds	TL0265	52°16·7'	0°29·9'W	T	153
Melchbourne Ho	Beds	TL0365	52°16·6'	0°29·0'W	X	153
Melchbourne Park	Beds	TL0264	52°16·1'	0°29·9'W	X	153
Melchet Court (Sch)	Hants	SU2722	51°0·0'	1°36·5'W	X	184
Melcombe	Somer	ST2833	51°5·7'	3°1·3'W	T	182
Melcombe Bingham	Dorset	ST7602	50°49·3'	2°20·1'W	T	194
Melcombe Park	Dorset	ST7404	50°50·3'	2°21·8'W	F	194
Melcombe Regis	Dorset	SY6880	50°37·4'	2°26·8'W	T	194
Melcombe Wood	Somer	ST7048	51°14·1'	2°25·4'W	F	183
Meldingscale Fm	N Yks	SD7367	54°6·1'	2°24·4'W	FM	98
Meldon	Devon	SX5592	50°42·8'	4°2·9'W	T	191
Meldon	Northum	NZ1183	55°8·7'	1°49·2'W	T	81
Meldon Burn	Scot Bord	NT2142	55°40·2'	3°14·9'W	W	73
Meldon Cottage	Scot Bord	NT2040	55°39·1'	3°15·8'W	X	73
Meldon Hall	Devon	SX6986	50°39·8'	3°50·8'W	X	191
Meldon Hill	Cumbr	NY7729	54°39·6'	2°21·0'W	H	91
Meldon Hill	Devon	SX6986	50°39·8'	3°50·8'W	H	191
Meldon Lane Ho	Northum	NZ1182	55°8·2'	1°49·2'W	X	81
Meldon Park	Northum	NZ1085	55°9·8'	1°50·2'W	X	81
Meldon Quarry	Devon	SX5792	50°42·8'	4°1·2'W	X	191
Meldon Reservoir	Devon	SX5590	50°41·7'	4°2·8'W	W	191
Meldreth	Cambs	TL3746	52°5·9'	0°0·4'E	T	154
Meldreth Sta	Cambs	TL3745	52°5·4'	0°0·4'E	X	154
Meldrum	Stir	NS7199	56°10·2'	4°4·2'W	X	57
Meldrum Ho	Aberd	NJ8129	57°21·3'	2°18·5'W	X	38
Mel Fea	Orkney	ND2197	58°51·5'	3°21·7'W	X	6,7
Melford Hall	Suff	TL8646	52°5·1'	0°43·3'E	A	155
Melford Park Fm	Suff	TL8850	52°7·2'	0°45·2'E	FM	155
Melfort	Arg & Bt	NM8314	56°16·4'	5°29·9'W	T	55
Melfort Ho	Arg & Bt	NM8314	56°16·4'	5°29·9'W	X	55
Melgam Water	Angus	NO2556	56°41·6'	3°13·0'W	W	53
Melgarve	Highld	NN4695	57°1·5'	4°31·8'W	X	34
Melgate	N Yks	SE7074	54°9·7'	0°55·3'W	X	100
Melgum	Aberd	NJ4706	57°8·8'	2°52·1'W	X	37
Melgum Lodge	Aberd	NJ4605	57°8·2'	2°53·1'W	X	37
Melgund Castle	Angus	NO5456	56°41·9'	2°44·6'W	A	54
Melgund Cottage	Angus	NO5356	56°41·9'	2°45·6'W	X	54
Melgund Glen	Scot Bord	NT5619	55°28·0'	2°41·3'W	X	80
Melgund Muir	Angus	NO5554	56°40·8'	2°43·6'W	X	54
Melholme	Lincs	TF3892	53°24·6'	0°5·0'E	X	113
Melhuish Barton	Devon	SX7992	50°43·1'	3°42·5'W	X	191
Meliden (Gallt Melyd)	Denb	SJ0680	53°18·8'	3°24·2'W	T	116
Melinau	Pemb	SN1613	51°47·4'	4°39·7'W	X	158
Melin Bodowyr	I of Angl	SH4668	53°11·5'	4°17·9'W	X	114,115
Melinbyrhedyn	Powys	SN8198	52°34·3'	3°45·0'W	T	135,136
Melin Caiach	Merth Tyd	ST1096	51°39·6'	3°17·7'W	T	171
Melincourt	Nth Pt Talb	SN8101	51°41·9'	3°42·9'W	T	170
Melin Court Brook	Nth Pt Talb	SN8300	51°41·4'	3°41·2'W	W	170
Melincryddan	Nth Pt Talb	SS7496	51°39·2'	3°48·9'W	T	170
Melindwr	Powys	SJ0415	52°43·7'	3°24·9'W	X	125
Melin-llan	Swan	SS6299	51°40·6'	3°59·4'W	X	159
Melin Meredydd	Denb	SJ1058	53°6·9'	3°20·3'W	X	116
Melinsey	Corn	SW9039	50°13·1'	4°56·3'W	T	204
Melin-y-coed	Conwy	SH8160	53°7·7'	3°46·3'W	T	116
Melin-y-ddôl	Powys	SJ0906	52°38·9'	3°20·3'W	X	125
Melinygloch	Powys	SO0694	52°32·4'	3°22·8'W	X	136
Melin-y-grug	Powys	SJ0507	52°39·4'	3°23·9'W	X	125
Melin-y-Wig	Denb	SJ0348	53°1·5'	3°26·4'W	T	116
Melkington	Northum	NT8741	55°40·0'	2°12·0'W	T	74
Melkinthorpe	Cumbr	NY5525	54°37·3'	2°41·4'W	T	90
Melkinthorpe Wood	Cumbr	NY5624	54°36·8'	2°40·5'W	F	90
Melkridge	Northum	NY7364	54°58·4'	2°24·9'W	T	86,87
Melkridge Common	Northum	NY7367	55°0·1'	2°24·9'W	X	86,87
Melksham	Wilts	ST9064	51°22·7'	2°8·2'W	T	173
Melksham Forest	Wilts	ST9164	51°22·7'	2°7·4'W	T	173
Mellanbrae	Aberd	NJ7220	57°16·4'	2°27·4'W	X	38
Mellands	Devon	SX9484	50°39·0'	3°29·6'W	X	192
Mellangaun	Highld	NG8189	57°50·5'	5°40·9'W	X	19
Mellangoose	Corn	SW6428	50°6·5'	5°17·7'W	X	203
Mellangoose	Corn	SW6826	50°5·6'	5°14·3'W	T	203
Mellaston	Pemb	SM9500	51°39·9'	4°57·5'W	X	157,158
Mell Bank Wood	N Yks	SE6688	54°17·2'	0°58·7'W	F	94,100
Mellbreak	Cumbr	NY1419	54°33·8'	3°19·4'W	H	89
Melldalloch	Arg & Bt	NR9274	55°55·1'	5°19·3'W	X	62
Melledgan	I Scilly	SV8606	49°52·5'	6°21·9'W	X	203
Mellendean	Scot Bord	NT7434	55°36·2'	2°24·3'W	X	74
Mellenside	Aberd	NJ6530	57°21·8'	2°34·5'W	X	29
Mellerstain Ho	Scot Bord	NT6439	55°38·8'	2°33·9'W	X	74

Mellerstain Mill	Scot Bord	NT6538	55°38·3'	2°32·9'W	X	74
Mell Fell	Cumbr	NY7422	54°35·8'	2°23·7'W	X	91
Mellfell Ho	Cumbr	NY4323	54°36·2'	2°52·5'W	X	90
Mellfield Wood	Suff	TL9260	52°12·5'	0°49·0'E	F	155
Mell Fm	Essex	TL9609	51°44·9'	0°50·8'E	FM	168
Mell Green	W Berks	SU4577	51°29·6'	1°20·7'W	T	174
Mellguards	Cumbr	NY4419	54°34·0'	2°51·5'W	X	90
Mellguards	Cumbr	NY4445	54°48·1'	2°51·8'W	T	85
Mell Head	Highld	ND3376	58°40·3'	3°8·8'W	X	7,12
Melliker	Kent	TQ6367	51°22·9'	0°20·9'E	X	177
Melling	Lancs	SD5971	54°8·2'	2°37·2'W	T	97
Melling	Sefton	SD3800	53°29·8'	2°55·7'W	T	108
Mellingey	Corn	SW9271	50°30·3'	4°55·6'W	T	200
Melling Ho	Sefton	SD4000	53°29·8'	2°53·9'W	X	108
Melling Mount	Sefton	SD4001	53°30·4'	2°53·9'W	T	108
Mellingshaw Burn	D & G	NT0309	55°22·2'	3°31·4'W	W	78
Mellingshaw Tower	D & G	NT0308	55°21·6'	3°31·4'W	A	78
Mellington Fm	Powys	SO2693	52°32·0'	3°5·1'W	FM	137
Mellington Hall Hotel	Powys	SO2592	52°31·5'	3°5·9'W	X	137
Mellin-y-Grogue	Shrops	SO2376	52°22·8'	3°7·5'W	X	137,148
Mellion Muir	D & G	NY3392	55°13·3'	3°2·8'W	H	79
Mellis	Suff	TM0974	52°19·7'	1°4·4'E	T	144
Mellis Green	Suff	TM0974	52°19·7'	1°4·4'E	T	144
Mellock Hill	Pth & Kin	NO0206	56°14·4'	3°34·4'W	H	58
Mellon Charles	Highld	NG8491	57°51·6'	5°38·0'W	T	19
Mellon Udrigle	Highld	NG8895	57°53·9'	5°34·2'W	T	19
Mellor	Lancs	SD6530	53°46·2'	2°31·4'W	T	102,103
Mellor	Stock	SJ9788	53°23·6'	2°2·3'W	T	109
Mellor Brook	Lancs	SD6431	53°46·7'	2°32·4'W	T	102,103
Mellor Hall	Stock	SJ9889	53°24·1'	2°1·4'W	X	109
Mellor Knoll	Lancs	SD6449	53°56·4'	2°32·5'W	H	102,103
Mellor Moor	Lancs	SD6531	53°46·7'	2°31·5'W	X	102,103
Mellor Moor	Stock	SJ9987	53°23·0'	2°0·5'W	X	109
Mellow Fm	Hants	SU8238	51°8·4'	0°49·3'W	FM	186
Mellow Purgess Fm	Essex	TQ5799	51°40·3'	0°16·6'E	FM	167,177
Mells	Somer	ST7249	51°14·6'	2°23·7'W	T	183
Mells	Suff	TM4076	52°20·0'	1°31·8'E	T	156
Mells Down	Somer	ST7251	51°15·7'	2°23·7'W	X	183
Mells Fm	N Lincs	SE9003	53°31·2'	0°38·1'W	FM	112
Mells Green	Somer	ST7248	51°14·1'	2°23·7'W	T	183
Mells Hill Fm	Suff	TM4076	52°20·0'	1°31·8'E	FM	156
Mells Kirk	Orkney	HY6522	59°5·3'	2°36·2'W	X	5
Mells Park	Somer	ST7148	51°14·1'	2°24·5'W	X	183
Mells River	Somer	ST7749	51°14·6'	2°19·4'W	W	183
Melmannoch	Aberd	NO6888	56°59·2'	2°31·1'W	H	45
Melmerby	Cumbr	NY6137	54°43·8'	2°35·9'W	T	91
Melmerby	N Yks	SE0785	54°15·9'	1°53·1'W	T	99
Melmerby	N Yks	SE3376	54°11·0'	1°29·2'W	T	99
Melmerby Beck	N Yks	SE0786	54°16·4'	1°53·1'W	W	99
Melmerby Fell	Cumbr	NY6538	54°44·4'	2°32·2'W	H	91
Melmerby Green End	N Yks	SE3376	54°11·0'	1°29·2'W	X	99
Melmerby High Scar	Cumbr	NY6437	54°43·8'	2°33·1'W	X	91
Melmerby Low Scar	Cumbr	NY6338	54°44·4'	2°34·1'W	X	91
Melmerby Mire	Cumbr	NY5938	54°44·4'	2°37·8'W	X	91
Melmerby Moor	N Yks	SE0586	54°16·4'	1°55·0'W	X	98
Melmerby Moor	N Yks	SE0686	54°16·4'	1°54·1'W	X	99
Melness	Highld	NC5863	58°32·2'	4°25·9'W	X	10
Melness House	Highld	NC5860	58°30·6'	4°25·8'W	X	10
Melnroy's Point	Inverc	NS2176	55°56·9'	4°51·6'W	X	63
Melon Fm	Kent	TR0328	51°1·2'	0°54·1'E	FM	189
Melon Green	Suff	TL8457	52°11·1'	0°41·9'E	T	155
Melonsplace	Falk	NS9473	55°56·6'	3°41·4'W	X	65
Melowther Hill	E Renf	NS5648	55°42·5'	4°17·1'W	H	64
Melplash	Dorset	SY4898	50°47·0'	2°43·9'W	T	193
Melplash Court	Dorset	SY4898	50°47·0'	2°43·9'W	A	193
Melrose	Aberd	NJ7662	57°39·1'	2°23·7'W	X	29
Melrose	Scot Bord	NT5434	55°36·1'	2°43·4'W	T	73
Melrose Fm	E Yorks	SE7642	53°52·4'	0°50·2'W	FM	105,106
Melrose Ho	N Yks	SE4682	54°14·1'	1°17·2'W	X	100
Melsbury	Somer	ST5143	51°11·3'	2°41·7'W	X	182,183
Melsbury Fm	Somer	ST5143	51°11·3'	2°41·7'W	FM	182,183
Melsetter	Orkney	ND2689	58°47·2'	3°16·3'W	X	7
Melsetter Hill	Orkney	ND2689	58°47·2'	3°16·3'W	H	7
Melsome Wood	Wilts	ST9878	51°30·3'	2°1·3'W	F	173
Melsonby	N Yks	NZ1908	54°28·3'	1°42·1'W	T	92
Melsop Fm	Norf	TF9900	52°33·9'	0°56·6'E	FM	144
Meltham	Kirk	SE0910	53°35·4'	1°51·4'W	T	110
Meltham Cop	Kirk	SE0912	53°36·5'	1°51·4'W	H	110
Meltham Grange	Kirk	SE0811	53°36·0'	1°52·3'W	X	110
Meltham Mills	Kirk	SE1010	53°35·4'	1°50·5'W	T	110
Meltham Moor	Kirk	SE0809	53°34·9'	1°52·3'W	X	110
Melton	E Yorks	SE9726	53°43·5'	0°31·4'W	T	106
Melton	Suff	TM2850	52°6·3'	1°20·2'E	T	156
Melton Brand Fm	Donc	SE5203	53°31·5'	1°12·0'W	FM	111
Meltonby	E Yorks	SE7952	53°57·7'	0°47·3'W	T	105,106
Meltonby Grange	E Yorks	SE8052	53°57·7'	0°46·4'W	X	106
Meltonby Hall	E Yorks	SE8052	53°57·7'	0°46·4'W	X	106
Meltonby Ho Fm	E Yorks	SE8050	53°56·6'	0°46·5'W	FM	106
Melton Constable	Norf	TG0433	52°51·6'	1°2·2'E	T	133
Melton Gallows	N Lincs	TA0410	53°34·8'	0°25·3'W	X	112
Melton Hall	Norf	TG0331	52°50·5'	1°1·3'E	A	133
Melton Hall Fm	Surrey	TQ2039	51°8·5'	0°16·7'W	FM	187
Melton High Wood	N Lincs	TA0612	53°35·9'	0°23·5'W	F	112
Melton Hill	E Yorks	SE9826	53°43·5'	0°30·5'W	X	106
Melton Ho	N Yks	SE2694	54°20·7'	1°35·6'W	X	99
Melton Leys	N Yks	SE5332	53°47·1'	1°11·3'W	X	105
Melton Mowbray	Leic	SK7519	52°46·0'	0°52·9'W	T	129
Melton Paddocks	Norf	TL9382	52°24·3'	0°50·6'E	X	144
Melton Road Fm	N Lincs	TA0309	53°34·3'	0°26·3'W	FM	112
Melton Ross	N Lincs	TA0710	53°34·8'	0°22·6'W	FM	112
Melton Spinney Fm	Leic	SK7622	52°47·6'	0°52·0'W	FM	129
Melton Wood	Donc	SE5103	53°31·5'	1°13·4'W	F	111
Mel Tor	Devon	SX6972	50°32·2'	3°50·5'W	H	191
Meluncart	Aberd	NO6382	56°55·9'	2°36·0'W	H	45
Melvaig	Highld	NG7486	57°48·7'	5°47·8'W	T	19
Melverley	Shrops	SJ3316	52°44·5'	2°59·1'W	T	126
Melverley	Shrops	SJ5840	52°57·6'	2°37·1'W	X	117
Melverley	Wrekin	SJ6119	52°46·3'	2°34·3'W	X	127
Melverley Green	Shrops	SJ3217	52°45·0'	3°0·0'W	T	126
Melverley Hall	Shrops	SJ3218	52°45·6'	3°0·1'W	X	126

Melvich	Highld	NC8864	58°33·2'	3°55·0'W	T	10
Melvich Bay	Highld	NC8865	58°33·8'	3°55·0'W	W	10
Melville Grange	Midlo	NT3067	55°53·7'	3°6·7'W	X	66
Melville Ho	Fife	NO2913	56°18·5'	3°8·4'W	X	59
Melville Home Fm	Fife	NO2913	56°18·5'	3°8·4'W	FM	59
Melville Mains	Midlo	NT3067	55°53·7'	3°6·7'W	X	66
Melvin Hall	Midlo	NT3968	55°54·3'	2°58·1'W	X	66
Melvin Holme	Ches	SJ6972	53°14·9'	2°27·5'W	X	118
Melwood Grange	N Lincs	SE7903	53°31·3'	0°48·1'W	X	112
Melynllyn	Conwy	SH7065	53°10·2'	3°56·3'W	W	115
Membland	Devon	SX5648	50°19·1'	4°1·0'W	T	202
Membury	Devon	ST2703	50°49·6'	3°1·8'W	T	193
Membury	Wilts	SU3074	51°28·1'	1°33·7'W	X	174
Membury	Wilts	SU3075	51°28·6'	1°33·7'W	A	174
Membury Castle	Devon	ST2802	50°49·0'	3°0·9'W	X	193
Membury Castle (Fort)	Devon	ST2802	50°49·0'	3°0·9'W	A	193
Membury Court	Devon	ST2603	50°49·5'	3°2·7'W	A	192,193
Membury Service Area	W Berks	SU3075	51°28·6'	1°33·7'W	X	174
Memorial Hut	Somer	SS9147	51°12·9'	3°33·3'W	X	181
Memsie	Aberd	NJ9762	57°39·1'	2°2·6'W	T	30
Memsie Ho	Aberd	NJ9761	57°38·6'	2°2·6'W	X	30
Memus	Angus	NO4259	56°43·4'	2°56·4'W	T	54
Mena	Corn	SX0462	50°25·7'	4°45·2'W	T	200
Menabilly	Corn	SX0951	50°19·9'	4°40·7'W	X	200,204
Menabilly Barton	Corn	SX0950	50°19·4'	4°40·6'W	X	200,204
Menaburle	Corn	SX1660	50°24·9'	4°35·0'W	X	201
Menachban	Pth & Kin	NO0864	56°45·8'	3°29·8'W	H	43
Menachurch Point	Corn	SS2008	50°50·8'	4°33·0'W	X	190
Menacrin Downs	Corn	SX1474	50°32·4'	4°37·1'W	X	200
Menacuddle	Corn	SX0153	50°20·8'	4°47·5'W	A	200
Menadarva	Corn	SW6141	50°13·5'	5°20·7'W	T	203
Menadews Fm	Corn	SW8444	50°15·6'	5°1·5'W	FM	204
Menagerie Fm	N Yks	SE6340	53°51·4'	1°2·1'W	FM	105,106
Menagerie Pool	Shrops	SJ5728	52°51·1'	2°37·9'W	W	126
Menagerie Wood	Notts	SK5778	53°18·0'	1°8·3'W	F	120
Menagissey	Corn	SW7146	50°16·4'	5°12·5'W	T	203
Menagwins	Corn	SX0150	50°19·2'	4°47·4'W	X	200,204
Menai Bridge or Porthaethwy	I of Angl	SH5572	53°13·8'	4°9·9'W	T	114,115
Menai Bridge (Porthaethwy)	I of Angl	SH5572	53°13·8'	4°9·9'W	T	114,115
Menaifron	I of Angl	SH4563	53°8·7'	4°18·7'W	X	114,115
Menai Strait (Afon Menai)	Gwyn	SH5370	53°12·7'	4°11·7'W	W	114,115
Men-amber Fm	Corn	SW6532	50°8·7'	5°17·0'W	FM	203
Men-An-Tol	Corn	SW4234	50°9·2'	5°36·3'W	A	203
Men-a-vaur	I Scilly	SV8917	49°58·6'	6°19·9'W	X	203
Mên-aver Beach	Corn	SW7925	50°5·3'	5°5·0'W	X	204
Menaway	Aberd	NJ6516	57°14·3'	2°34·3'W	H	38
Menawethan	I Scilly	SV9513	49°56·6'	6°14·7'W	X	203
Menchine	Devon	SS8313	50°54·5'	3°39·5'W	X	181
Mendea	Corn	SX4892	50°42·7'	4°8·8'W	X	191
Mendham	Suff	TM2782	52°23·6'	1°20·6'E	T	156
Mendham Marshes	Suff	TM2681	52°23·0'	1°19·7'E	X	156
Mendham Priory	Suff	TM2681	52°23·0'	1°19·7'E	X	156
Mendick	Scot Bord	NT1350	55°44·4'	3°22·7'W	X	65,72
Mendick Hill	Scot Bord	NT1250	55°44·4'	3°23·7'W	H	65,72
Mendip Fm	Somer	ST5832	51°5·4'	2°35·6'W	FM	182,183
Mendip Fm	Somer	ST5850	51°15·1'	2°35·7'W	FM	182,183
Mendip Forest	Somer	ST5054	51°17·2'	2°42·6'W	X	182,183
Mendip Hills	Somer	ST5352	51°16·1'	2°40·0'W	H	182,183
Mendip Lodge Wood	N Som	ST4758	51°19·4'	2°45·2'W	F	172,182
Mendlesham	Suff	TM1065	52°14·8'	1°5·0'E	T	155
Mendlesham Green	Suff	TM0963	52°13·8'	1°4·0'E	T	155
Menear Fm	Corn	SX0354	50°21·4'	4°45·8'W	FM	200
Menehay	Corn	SW7832	50°9·0'	5°6·1'W	X	204
Menerdue	Corn	SW7235	50°10·5'	5°11·2'W	X	204
Menethorpe	N Yks	SE7667	54°5·8'	0°49·9'W	T	100
Menethorpe Beck	N Yks	SE7767	54°5·8'	0°48·9'W	W	100
Menewenicke Barton	Corn	SX2683	50°37·5'	4°27·2'W	X	201
Mengearne	Corn	SW7029	50°7·2'	5°12·7'W	X	203
Mengham	Hants	SZ7299	50°47·4'	0°58·3'W	T	197
Mengham Salterns	Hants	SZ7399	50°47·4'	0°57·5'W	X	197
Menheniot	Corn	SX2862	50°26·2'	4°25·0'W	T	201
Menherion	Corn	SW7036	50°11·0'	5°12·9'W	X	203
Mên Hyr	Corn	SW7010	49°57·0'	5°12·0'W	X	203
Menie Ho	Aberd	NJ9720	57°16·5'	2°2·5'W	X	38
Menie Links	Aberd	NJ9920	57°16·5'	2°0·5'W	X	38
Menithwood	Worcs	SO7069	52°19·3'	2°26·0'W	T	138
Menkee	Corn	SX0572	50°31·2'	4°44·7'W	X	200
Menmarsh Guide Post	Oxon	SP6010	51°47·4'	1°7·4'W	X	164,165
Menna	Corn	SW9154	50°21·2'	4°55·9'W	T	200
Mennabroom	Corn	SX1670	50°30·3'	4°35·3'W	X	201
Mennock	D & G	NS8008	55°21·3'	3°53·1'W	T	71,78
Mennock Hass	D & G	NS8712	55°23·6'	3°46·6'W	X	71,78
Mennock Pass	D & G	NS8510	55°22·5'	3°48·5'W	X	71,78
Mennock Water	D & G	NS8410	55°22·5'	3°49·4'W	W	71,78
Men of Mey	Highld	ND3175	58°39·7'	3°10·9'W	X	7,12
Mên Scryfa	Corn	SW4235	50°9·8'	5°36·4'W	A	203
Menslaws	Scot Bord	NT5920	55°28·6'	2°38·5'W	X	73,74
Mens, The	W Susx	TQ0223	51°0·1'	0°32·4'W	F	197
Menston	Brad	SE1743	53°53·2'	1°44·1'W	T	104
Menstrie	Clackm	NS8496	56°8·8'	3°51·6'W	T	58
Menstrie Burn	Stir	NS8498	56°9·9'	3°51·6'W	W	58
Mên-te-heul	Corn	SW6516	50°0·1'	5°16·4'W	X	203
Menteith Hills	Stir	NN5502	56°11·6'	4°19·8'W	H	57
Menthorpe	N Yks	SE7034	53°48·1'	0°55·8'W	T	105,106
Mentley Fm	Herts	TL3723	51°53·5'	0°0·1'W	FM	166
Mentmore	Bucks	SP9019	51°52·0'	0°41·2'W	T	165
Mentmore	Bucks	SP9019	51°52·0'	0°41·2'W	X	165
Mentmore Cross Roads	Bucks	SP8820	51°52·5'	0°42·9'W	X	165
Mentmore Park	Bucks	SP9019	51°52·0'	0°41·2'W	X	165
Mentmore Park Fm	Bucks	SP9118	51°51·4'	0°40·3'W	FM	165
Menutton	Shrops	SO3077	52°23·4'	3°1·3'W	X	137,148
Menwinnion	Corn	SW6442	50°14·1'	5°18·2'W	X	203
Menwith Hill	N Yks	SE1957	54°0·8'	1°42·2'W	X	104
Mên-y-grib Point	Corn	SW6619	50°1·7'	5°15·7'W	X	203
Menzieshill	C of Dun	NO3631	56°28·3'	3°1·9'W	X	54
Menzies Wood Fm	W Susx	TQ0827	51°2·2'	0°27·2'W	FM	187,197
Menzion	Scot Bord	NT0923	55°29·8'	3°26·0'W	T	72

Menzion Burn	Scot Bord	NT0922	55°29·3'	3°26·0'W	W	72
Meoble	Highld	NM7987	56°55·6'	5°37·4'W	T	40
Meòir Langwell	Highld	NH4298	57°56·9'	4°39·7'W	W	20
Meoir Veannaich	Aberd	NJ2106	57°8·5'	3°17·9'W	W	36
Meokame Skerry	Shetld	HU3787	60°34·2'	1°19·0'W	X	1,2
Meolbank	Cumbr	NY0802	54°24·6'	3°24·6'W	X	89
Meole Brace	Shrops	SJ4810	52°41·4'	2°45·8'W	T	126
Meols	Wirral	SJ2289	53°23·8'	3°10·0'W	T	108
Meol's Hall	Sefton	SD3618	53°39·5'	2°57·7'W	X	108
Meon	Hants	SU5303	50°49·7'	1°14·5'W	T	196
Meo Ness	Shetld	HU5560	60°19·5'	0°59·8'W	X	2
Meo Ness	Shetld	HZ2069	59°30·7'	1°38·3'W	X	4
Meon Hall	Warw	SP1845	52°6·4'	1°43·8'W	X	151
Meon Hill	Hants	SU3435	51°7·0'	1°30·5'W	X	185
Meon Hill	Warw	SP1745	52°6·4'	1°44·7'W	H	151
Meon Hill (Fort)	Warw	SP1745	52°6·4'	1°44·7'W	A	151
Meon Ho	Glos	SP1644	52°5·9'	1°45·6'W	X	151
Meonstoke	Hants	SU6119	50°58·3'	1°7·5'W	T	185
Meonvale Fm	Hants	SU6220	50°58·8'	1°6·6'W	FM	185
Meon Valley	Hants	SU5915	50°56·1'	1°9·2'W	X	196
Meon Valley	Hants	SU6016	50°56·6'	1°8·4'W	X	185
Meon View Fm	Hants	SU5403	50°49·7'	1°13·6'W	FM	196
Meopham	Kent	TQ6465	51°21·8'	0°21·7'E	T	177
Meopham Bank	Kent	TQ5647	51°12·3'	0°14·4'E	X	188
Meopham Green	Kent	TQ6365	51°21·9'	0°20·9'E	T	177
Meopham Station	Kent	TQ6367	51°22·9'	0°20·9'E	T	177
Meoul	D & G	NX0451	54°49·2'	5°2·6'W	X	82
Meowl of Aldinna	S Ayr	NX3694	55°13·0'	4°34·2'W	H	77
Meowl of Blackrow	S Ayr	NX3695	55°13·6'	4°34·3'W	H	77
Mepal	Cambs	TL4480	52°24·2'	0°7·4'E	T	142,143
Mepal Fen	Cambs	TL4382	52°25·3'	0°6·6'E	X	142,143
Mepham's Fm	E Susx	TQ5718	50°56·6'	0°14·5'E	FM	199
Meppershall	Beds	TL1336	52°0·9'	0°20·8'W	T	153
Meran Licks	Aberd	NJ7664	57°40·2'	2°23·7'W	X	29
Merbach	Heref	SO3045	52°6·2'	3°0·9'W	T	148
Merbach Hill	Heref	SO3044	52°5·6'	3°0·9'W	H	148,161
Mercaston Brook	Derby	SK2842	52°58·7'	1°34·6'W	W	119,128
Mercaston Hall	Derby	SK2741	52°58·2'	1°35·5'W	X	119,128
Mercaton	Derby	SK2643	52°59·3'	1°36·4'W	T	119,128
Mercers Fm	Surrey	TQ3051	51°14·8'	0°7·9'W	FM	187
Merchant Fields	Kirk	SE1926	53°44·0'	1°42·3'W	T	104
Merchanthall	S Lanak	NS8135	55°35·9'	3°52·9'W	X	71,72
Merchant's Croft	Aberd	NO8898	57°4·6'	2°11·4'W	X	38,45
Merchants' Downs	Glos	SP0007	51°45·9'	1°59·6'W	X	163
Merchants Fm	Glos	ST9191	51°37·3'	2°7·4'W	FM	163,173
Merchant Taylors' Sch	Herts	TQ0994	51°38·3'	0°25·1'W	X	166,176
Merchelyton Burn	Scot Bord	NT4515	55°25·8'	2°51·7'W	W	79
Merchiston	C of Edin	NT2472	55°56·4'	3°12·6'W	T	66
Merchlyn	Conwy	SH7673	53°14·6'	3°51·1'W	X	115
Mercombe Wood	Glos	SO9815	51°50·3'	2°1·3'W	F	163
Mercote Mill Fm	Sol	SP2280	52°25·3'	1°40·2'W	FM	139
Mercyfield Wood	Lancs	SD6333	53°47·8'	2°33·3'W	F	102,103
Merddwr	Conwy	SH8950	53°2·4'	3°38·9'W	W	116
Merddwr	Conwy	SJ0043	52°58·7'	3°29·0'W	W	125
Merddyn	Conwy	SH8759	53°7·2'	3°40·9'W	X	116
Merddyn-y-bit	I of Angl	SH3470	53°12·3'	4°28·7'W	X	114
Merdon Castle	Hants	SU4226	51°2·1'	1°23·7'W	A	185
Merdon Manor Fm	Hants	SU4126	51°2·1'	1°24·5'W	FM	185
Mere	Ches	SJ7281	53°19·8'	2°24·8'W	T	109
Mere	Wilts	ST8132	51°5·5'	2°15·9'W	T	183
Merebank	Ches	SJ6174	53°15·9'	2°34·7'W	X	118
Mere Bank Fm	Cumbr	NY7214	54°31·5'	2°25·5'W	FM	91
Mere Barn Fm	Lincs	SK8827	52°50·2'	0°41·2'W	FM	130
Mere Barn Fm	Northnts	SP8258	52°13·1'	0°47·6'W	FM	152
Mere Barn Fm	Warw	SP1551	52°9·7'	1°46·4'W	FM	151
Mere Beck	Cumbr	NY4416	54°32·4'	2°51·5'W	W	90
Mere Beck	D & G	NT0810	55°22·8'	3°26·7'W	W	78
Mere Beck	Durham	NY9418	54°33·7'	2°5·1'W	X	91,92
Mere Brook	Ches	SJ4657	53°6·7'	2°48·0'W	W	117
Mere Brow	Lancs	SD4118	53°39·6'	2°53·2'W	T	108
Mere Burn	Northum	NU0312	55°24·4'	1°56·7'W	W	81
Mere Burn	Northum	NU1903	55°19·5'	1°41·6'W	W	81
Merecleuch Hill	D & G	NT1007	55°21·2'	3°24·7'W	X	78
Mereclough	Lancs	SD8730	53°46·2'	2°11·4'W	T	103
Mere Copse	Staffs	SO8189	52°30·2'	2°16·4'W	F	138
Mere Court	Kent	TQ9264	51°20·8'	0°45·8'E	X	178
Mere Crag	Cumbr	NY5006	54°27·1'	2°45·8'W	X	90
Mere Crags	Cumbr	SD1789	54°17·6'	3°16·1'W	X	96
Meredith	Glos	SO7621	51°53·5'	2°20·5'W	X	162
Mere Down	Devon	SS9917	50°56·9'	3°25·9'W	X	181
Mere Down Fm	Wilts	ST8334	51°6·5'	2°14·2'W	FM	183
Mere Dyke	N Lincs	SE8416	53°38·3'	0°43·4'W	X	112
Mere End Down	Oxon	SU3681	51°31·8'	1°28·5'W	X	174
Merefield	Heref	SO4868	52°18·7'	2°45·4'W	X	137,138,148
Merefield	Northnts	SP7457	52°12·6'	0°54·6'W	X	152
Mere Fm	Cambs	TL3189	52°29·2'	0°3·8'W	FM	142
Mere Fm	Ches	SJ6940	52°57·6'	2°27·3'W	FM	118
Mere Fm	Ches	SJ7382	53°20·3'	2°23·9'W	FM	109
Mere Fm	Derby	SK1762	53°9·5'	1°44·3'W	FM	119
Mere Fm	Heref	SO2953	52°10·5'	3°1·9'W	FM	148
Mere Fm	Lancs	SD4117	53°39·0'	2°53·1'W	FM	108
Mere Fm	Norf	TG1332	52°50·8'	1°10·2'E	FM	133
Mere Fm	Norf	TG3100	52°33·1'	1°24·9'E	FM	134
Mere Fm	Norf	TL9496	52°31·9'	0°52·0'E	FM	144
Mere Fm	Northnts	TL0171	52°19·9'	0°30·7'W	FM	141,153
Mere Fm	Staffs	SO8289	52°30·2'	2°15·5'W	FM	138
Mere Fm	Staffs	SO8289	52°30·2'	2°15·5'W	FM	138
Mere Fm	Suff	TL9067	52°16·3'	0°47·5'E	FM	155
Mere Fm	Suff	TM0262	52°13·4'	0°57·8'E	FM	155
Mere Fm	Wilts	SU2271	51°26·5'	1°40·6'W	FM	174
Meregarth	Cumbr	SD3999	54°23·2'	2°55·9'W	X	96,97
Meregill Beck	Cumbr	NY1021	54°34·8'	3°23·1'W	W	89
Meregill Hole	N Yks	SD7475	54°10·5'	2°23·5'W	X	98
Mere Green	Birm	SP1199	52°35·6'	1°49·9'W	T	139
Mere Green	Worcs	SO9562	52°15·6'	2°4·0'W	T	150
Mere Hall	Ches	SJ7281	53°19·8'	2°24·8'W	X	109
Mere Hall	Lancs	SD4016	53°38·5'	2°54·0'W	X	108
Mere Hall	Lincs	TF0065	53°10·6'	0°29·8'W	X	121
Mere Hall	Worcs	SO9561	52°15·1'	2°4·0'W	A	150
Merehead	Wrex	SJ4538	52°56·4'	2°48·7'W	T	126
Mere Heath	Ches	SJ6670	53°13·8'	2°30·2'W	T	118
Mere Heyes	Ches	SJ7081	53°19·7'	2°26·6'W	X	109
Mere Hill	Leic	SK5620	52°46·7'	1°9·8'W	X	129
Mere Hill	Staffs	SK1052	53°4·1'	1°50·6'W	X	119
Mere Hill Wood	Heref	SO4065	52°17·0'	2°52·4'W	F	137,148,149
Mere Ho	Ches	SJ5950	53°3·0'	2°36·3'W	X	117
Mere Ho	Lincs	SK8881	53°19·4'	0°40·3'W	X	121
Mere Ho	Powys	SO1370	52°19·5'	3°16·2'W	X	136,148
Mere Ho	Shrops	SJ4223	52°48·3'	2°51·2'W	X	126
Merelake	Ches	SJ8153	53°4·7'	2°16·6'W	X	118
Mere Lane Fm	Staffs	SJ9111	52°42·0'	2°7·6'W	FM	127
Meremoor Fm	Ches	SJ7453	53°4·7'	2°22·9'W	FM	118
Meremoor Moss	Ches	SJ7452	53°4·1'	2°22·9'W	F	118
Mere Moss	Ches	SJ8369	53°13·3'	2°14·9'W	F	118
Mere Mouth Fm	Cambs	TL2292	52°31·0'	0°11·7'W	FM	142
Mere Oak	Staffs	SJ8300	52°36·1'	2°14·7'W	X	127
Mere Pits	Staffs	SK2008	52°40·4'	1°41·9'W	X	128
Mere Platt Fm	Ches	SJ7380	53°19·2'	2°23·9'W	FM	109
Mere Plot Fm	Norf	TF6811	52°40·5'	0°29·5'E	FM	132,143
Meres	Corn	SW6719	50°1·8'	5°14·8'W	X	203
Mere Sands Wood	Lancs	SD4415	53°38·0'	2°50·4'W	F	108
Meresborough	Medway	TQ8264	51°21·0'	0°37·2'E	T	178,188
Meres Fm	E Susx	TQ5724	50°59·9'	0°14·6'E	FM	199
Mereside	Blackp	SD3434	53°48·1'	2°59·7'W	T	102
Mere Side	Cambs	TL2989	52°29·2'	0°5·6'W	X	142
Mereside	Cumbr	NY1647	54°48·9'	3°18·0'W	X	85
Mere Side	Lancs	SD4216	53°38·5'	2°52·2'W	X	108
Mere Side Fm	Cambs	TL2989	52°29·2'	0°5·6'W	FM	142
Mereside Fm	Ches	SJ7384	53°21·4'	2°23·9'W	FM	109
Meres, The	Northum	NY7948	54°49·8'	2°19·2'W	X	86,87
Mere Stones	Cald	SD9534	53°48·4'	2°4·1'W	X	103
Mere Syke	Lancs	SD7954	53°59·1'	2°18·8'W	X	103
Mere Tarn	Cumbr	SD2671	54°8·0'	3°7·5'W	W	96,97
Mere, The	Ches	SJ7381	53°19·8'	2°23·9'W	W	109
Mere, The	Norf	TM1179	52°22·3'	1°6·4'E	W	144
Mere, The	N Yks	TA0386	54°15·8'	0°24·7'W	W	101
Mere, The	Shrops	SJ4034	52°54·2'	2°53·1'W	W	126
Meretown	Staffs	SJ7520	52°46·9'	2°21·8'W	T	127
Merevale Fm	Worcs	SO8342	52°4·8'	2°14·5'W	FM	150
Merevale Hall	Warw	SP2997	52°34·4'	1°33·9'W	X	140
Mereview Fm	Ches	SJ6877	53°17·6'	2°28·4'W	FM	118
Mereway Fm	Cambs	TL4663	52°15·0'	0°8·7'E	FM	154
Mereworth	Kent	TQ6653	51°15·3'	0°23·1'E	T	188
Mereworth Castle	Kent	TQ6653	51°15·3'	0°23·1'E	X	188
Mereworth Woods	Kent	TQ6455	51°16·5'	0°21·5'E	F	188
Mergate Hall	Norf	TM1899	52°32·9'	1°13·3'E	X	134
Mergie	Aberd	NO7988	56°59·2'	2°20·3'W	X	45
Meriafel	Gwyn	SH6807	52°38·9'	3°56·5'W	X	124
Meriden	Herts	TQ1199	51°41·0'	0°23·3'W	T	166,176
Meriden	Sol	SP2482	52°26·4'	1°38·4'W	T	139
Meriden Ho	Sol	SP2581	52°25·8'	1°37·5'W	X	140
Meriden Shafts	Sol	SP2683	52°26·9'	1°36·6'W	F	140
Merkadale	Highld	NG3831	57°17·9'	6°20·5'W	T	32
Merk Burn	Arg & Bt	NN2115	56°17·9'	4°53·1'W	W	50,56
Merki Burn	Shetld	HU2753	60°15·9'	1°30·2'W	W	3
Merkinch	Highld	NH6546	57°29·3'	4°14·7'W	T	26
Merkins Fm	W Dunb	NS4482	56°0·6'	4°29·7'W	FM	57,64
Merkins, The	W Dunb	NS4482	56°0·6'	4°29·7'W	X	57,64
Merkland	D & G	NX7473	55°2·4'	3°57·9'W	X	77,84
Merkland	D & G	NX8199	55°16·5'	3°52·0'W	X	78
Merkland	D & G	NX8874	55°3·1'	3°44·8'W	X	84
Merkland	D & G	NX9085	55°9·1'	3°43·1'W	X	78
Merkland	D & G	NY0369	55°0·6'	3°30·6'W	X	84
Merkland	D & G	NY2472	55°2·5'	3°10·9'W	X	85
Merkland	E Ayr	NS5926	55°30·7'	4°13·5'W	X	71
Merkland	E Ayr	NS6513	55°23·8'	4°7·5'W	X	71
Merkland	N Ayr	NS0239	55°36·5'	5°8·2'W	T	69
Merkland	S Ayr	NS2407	55°19·8'	4°46·0'W	X	70,76
Merkland	S Ayr	NS2600	55°16·1'	4°43·9'W	X	76
Merkland	S Ayr	NS3407	55°20·0'	4°36·6'W	X	70,76
Merkland	S Ayr	NX2491	55°11·2'	4°45·4'W	X	76
Merkland	Stir	NS6194	56°7·4'	4°13·7'W	X	57
Merkland Hill	D & G	NS8000	55°17·0'	3°52·9'W	H	78
Merkland Lodge	Highld	NC4029	58°13·5'	4°43·0'W	X	16
Merkland Moss	D & G	NX8871	55°1·5'	3°44·7'W	X	84
Merkland Point	N Ayr	NS0238	55°36·0'	5°8·1'W	X	69
Merkland River	Highld	NC3928	58°13·0'	4°44·0'W	W	16
Merklands Ho	Pth & Kin	NO0956	56°40·5'	3°28·7'W	X	52,53
Merklandwell	D & G	NX8972	55°2·1'	3°43·8'W	X	84
Merkland Wood	N Ayr	NS0138	55°36·0'	5°9·1'W	F	69
Merks Hall	Essex	TL6422	51°52·6'	0°23·3'E	X	167
Merle Common	Surrey	TQ4049	51°13·6'	0°0·7'E	T	187
Merlewood	Cumbr	SD4079	54°12·4'	2°54·8'W	X	96,97
Merlewood Fm	Kent	TQ8755	51°16·0'	0°41·2'E	FM	178
Merley	Poole	SZ0298	50°47·1'	1°57·9'W	T	195
Merley Ho	Poole	SZ0098	50°47·1'	1°59·6'W	X	195
Merlin	Corn	SW8667	50°28·1'	5°0·6'W	X	200
Merlindale	Scot Bord	NT1234	55°35·8'	3°23·4'W	X	72
Merlin's Bridge	Pemb	SM9414	51°47·4'	4°58·8'W	T	157,158
Merlin's Brook	Pemb	SM9213	51°46·9'	5°0·5'W	W	157,158
Merlin's Cross	Pemb	SM9900	51°40·0'	4°54·0'W	T	158
Merlin's Hill	Carm	SN4521	51°52·2'	4°14·7'W	X	159
Merlin's Hill (Fort)	Carm	SN4521	51°52·2'	4°14·7'W	A	159
Merlinwood	N Yks	SD9149	53°56·5'	2°7·8'W	X	103
Merllwyn-gwyn	Gwyn	SJ0041	52°57·7'	3°28·9'W	X	125
Merllyn	Conwy	SH7868	53°12·0'	3°49·2'W	X	115
Merllyn	Denb	SJ0849	53°2·1'	3°21·9'W	X	116
Merllyn	Denb	SJ1356	53°5·9'	3°17·6'W	X	116
Merllyn	Flint	SJ2668	53°12·5'	3°6·1'W	X	117
Merlyn Rock	Corn	SW4625	50°4·5'	5°32·6'W	X	203
Mermaid Inn	I of Angl	SH4764	53°9·3'	4°16·9'W	X	114,115
Mermaid (PH)	Staffs	SK0360	53°8·5'	1°56·9'W	X	119
Mermaid's Chair	Orkney	HY6526	59°7·4'	2°36·2'W	X	5
Mermaid's Head	Norf	TG1724	52°46·4'	1°13·4'E	W	133,134
Mermaid's Pool	Derby	SK0788	53°23·6'	1°53·3'W	W	110
Mermaid's Pool	Devon	SS4128	51°2·0'	4°15·7'W	W	180
Mermaid, The	Norf	TG1924	52°46·4'	1°15·2'E	W	133,134
Mermaid, The	Norf	TG2024	52°46·3'	1°16·1'E	W	133
Merope Rocks	Corn	SW8676	50°32·9'	5°0·9'W	X	200
Merrals Shaw	Medway	TQ7167	51°22·8'	0°27·8'E	F	178
Merriams Fm	Kent	TQ8053	51°15·1'	0°35·2'E	FM	188
Merrick	D & G	NX0054	54°50·7'	5°6·5'W	X	82
Merrick	D & G	NX4185	55°8·3'	4°29·2'W	H	77
Merrick Island	I Scilly	SV8714	49°56·9'	6°21·4'W	X	203
Merricks	Cumbr	NY7712	54°30·4'	2°20·9'W	X	91
Merrick's Fm	Somer	ST4125	51°1·5'	2°50·1'W	FM	193
Merridale	Wolv	SO8998	52°35·0'	2°9·3'W	T	139
Merridale Fm	Lancs	SD4210	53°35·2'	2°52·2'W	FM	108
Merridge	Somer	ST2034	51°6·2'	3°8·2'W	T	182
Merridge Hill	Somer	ST1932	51°5·1'	3°9·0'W	X	181
Merrie Gardens	I of W	SZ5883	50°38·9'	1°10·4'W	T	196
Merries	Corn	SW6823	50°3·9'	5°14·1'W	X	203
Merries Fm	Norf	TF5917	52°43·9'	0°21·7'E	FM	131
Merrie Thought, The	Hants	SU1613	50°55·2'	1°46·0'W	X	195
Merrieweathers	E Susx	TQ6027	51°1·4'	0°17·3'E	X	188,199
Merrifield	Corn	SX1472	50°31·3'	4°37·1'W	X	200
Merrifield	Devon	SS2601	50°47·2'	4°27·7'W	T	190
Merrifield	Devon	SS8401	50°48·1'	3°38·4'W	X	191
Merrifield	Devon	SX6946	50°18·2'	3°50·0'W	X	202
Merrifield	Devon	SX8147	50°18·9'	3°39·9'W	T	202
Merrifieldhayes	Devon	SS8512	50°54·0'	3°37·7'W	X	181
Merrifield's Fm	Lincs	TF5058	53°6·1'	0°14·8'E	FM	122
Merril Grange	Leic	SK4421	52°47·3'	1°20·4'W	X	129
Merril Grove Fm	Staffs	SK0464	53°10·6'	1°56·0'W	FM	119
Merrill Hill	Glos	SP0502	51°43·2'	1°55·3'W	X	163
Merrimans	Glos	SO7420	51°52·9'	2°22·3'W	X	162
Merriments Fm	E Susx	TQ7428	51°1·7'	0°29·3'E	FM	188,199
Merrimoles	Oxon	SU7085	51°33·8'	0°59·0'W	X	175
Merriness	Pth & Kin	NO0223	56°23·6'	3°34·8'W	X	52,53,58
Merrington	Shrops	SJ4720	52°46·7'	2°46·7'W	T	126
Merrington Grange	Durham	NZ2630	54°40·1'	1°35·4'W	X	93
Merrington Green	Shrops	SJ4621	52°47·3'	2°47·6'W	X	126
Merrington Lane Fm	Shrops	SJ4721	52°47·3'	2°46·8'W	FM	126
Merrington Mill Fm	Durham	NZ2729	54°39·6'	1°34·5'W	FM	93
Merrington Place	Kent	TQ8330	51°2·6'	0°37·0'E	X	188
Merrion	Pemb	SR9397	51°38·3'	4°59·1'W	T	158
Merriott	Dorset	SY5195	50°45·4'	2°41·3'W	T	194
Merriott	Somer	ST4412	50°54·5'	2°47·4'W	T	193
Merriottsford	Somer	ST4412	50°54·5'	2°47·4'W	T	193
Merripit Hill	Devon	SX6580	50°36·5'	3°54·1'W	H	191
Merriscourt Fm	Oxon	SP2821	51°53·4'	1°35·2'W	FM	163
Merriscourt Fm	Oxon	SP2921	51°53·4'	1°34·3'W	FM	164
Merrishaw	Shrops	SJ5800	52°36·0'	2°36·8'W	X	126
Merrist Wood	Surrey	SU9653	51°16·3'	0°37·0'W	X	186
Merritown	Dorset	SZ1197	50°46·6'	1°50·3'W	T	195
Merritts Fm	Hants	SU6445	51°12·3'	1°4·6'W	FM	185
Merrivale	Devon	SX5475	50°33·6'	4°3·3'W	T	191,201
Merrivale	Heref	SO6023	51°54·5'	2°34·5'W	T	162
Merrivale Fm	Heref	SO5132	51°59·3'	2°42·4'W	FM	149
Merrivale Range	Devon	SX5779	50°35·8'	4°0·9'W	X	191
Merriville Fm	Donc	SE6514	53°37·3'	1°0·6'W	FM	111
Merrixton	Pemb	SN1408	51°44·6'	4°41·3'W	X	158
Merrow	Surrey	TQ0150	51°14·6'	0°32·8'W	T	186
Merrow Common	Surrey	TQ0251	51°15·2'	0°31·9'W	X	186
Merrow Downs	Surrey	TQ0249	51°14·1'	0°31·9'W	X	186
Merrybent	Darl	NZ2414	54°31·5'	1°37·3'W	T	93
Merrybent Hill	Lancs	SD7056	54°0·2'	2°27·0'W	X	103
Merryborough	Pemb	SM9916	51°48·6'	4°54·6'W	X	157,158
Merry Bower Fm	Derby	SK3329	52°51·7'	1°30·2'W	FM	128
Merry Brook	Worcs	SP0142	52°4·8'	1°58·7'W	W	150
Merryfall	Ches	SJ6278	53°18·1'	2°33·8'W	X	118
Merryfield	Devon	SS3506	50°50·0'	4°20·2'W	X	190
Merryfield	N Yks	SE1166	54°5·6'	1°49·5'W	X	99
Merryfield Fm	Hants	SU6630	51°4·2'	1°3·1'W	FM	185,186
Merryfield Fm	Oxon	SP3611	51°48·0'	1°28·3'W	FM	164
Merry Field Hill	Dorset	SU0201	50°48·7'	1°57·9'W	T	195
Merryfields Fm	Notts	SK7670	53°13·5'	0°51·3'W	FM	120
Merry Fm	Ches	SJ7374	53°16·0'	2°23·9'W	FM	118
Merrygill Beck	Durham	NY8226	54°38·0'	2°16·3'W	W	91,92
Merrygill Moss	Durham	NY8227	54°38·5'	2°16·3'W	X	91,92
Merryhagen	N Ayr	NS3648	55°42·1'	4°36·2'W	X	63
Merryhatton	E Loth	NT4774	55°57·6'	2°50·5'W	X	66
Merryhatton	E Loth	NT5479	56°0·4'	2°43·8'W	X	66
Merry Hill	Dorset	SY5984	50°39·5'	2°34·4'W	X	194
Merry Hill	Herts	TQ1394	51°38·2'	0°21·6'W	T	166,176
Merry Hill	Wolv	SO8897	52°34·5'	2°10·2'W	T	139
Merryhill Fm	Heref	SO4837	52°2·0'	2°45·1'W	FM	149,161
Merryhill Green	Wok	SU7871	51°26·2'	0°52·3'W	T	175
Merryhillock	Aberd	NJ9765	57°40·7'	2°2·6'W	X	30
Merryhills	Pth & Kin	NT0199	56°10·7'	3°35·2'W	X	58
Merry Hills	W Susx	TQ0432	51°4·9'	0°30·5'W	X	186
Merryhill Wood	Heref	SO4345	52°6·3'	2°49·5'W	F	148,149
Merry Holm	Shetld	HU3837	60°7·2'	1°18·5'W	X	4
Merryhue	Corn	SX3368	50°29·5'	4°20·9'W	X	201
Merry Know	Northum	NY6753	54°52·5'	2°30·4'W	X	86,87
Merrylands Fm	Dorset	ST5306	50°51·3'	2°39·7'W	FM	194
Merryland Stream	Devon	SS5603	50°48·8'	4°2·3'W	W	191
Merrylaw	Scot Bord	NT3601	55°18·2'	3°0·1'W	X	79
Merrylaws	E Loth	NT5881	56°1·5'	2°40·0'W	X	67
Merrylee	E Renf	NS5659	55°48·4'	4°17·4'W	T	64
Merry Lees	Leic	SK4705	52°38·7'	1°17·9'W	T	140
Merry Maidens	Corn	SW4324	50°3·9'	5°35·1'W	X	203
Merry Maidens (Stone Circle)	Corn	SW4324	50°3·9'	5°35·1'W	A	203
Merrymead	Bucks	SP8328	51°56·9'	0°47·1'W	X	165
Merry Mead Fm	Kent	TQ7632	51°3·8'	0°31·1'E	FM	188
Merrymeet	Corn	SX2765	50°27·8'	4°25·9'W	T	201
Merry Meeting	Corn	SW6239	50°12·4'	5°19·8'W	X	203
Merry Meeting	Corn	SX0873	50°31·8'	4°42·2'W	T	200
Merrymouth	E Ayr	NS4149	55°42·8'	4°31·4'W	X	64
Merry Naze	Scot Bord	NT3805	55°20·4'	2°58·2'W	H	79
Merry Oak	C of Soton	SU4412	50°54·6'	1°22·1'W	T	196
Merrypath Rig	Scot Bord	NY3799	55°17·1'	2°59·1'W	H	79
Merry's Fm	Cambs	TL3653	52°9·7'	0°0·3'W	FM	154
Merry Shield	Northum	NZ0661	54°56·9'	1°54·0'W	X	87
Merry Shiels	Northum	NZ0081	55°7·6'	1°59·6'W	X	81
Merryton	S Lanak	NS7553	55°45·5'	3°59·1'W	X	64
Merryton Low	Staffs	SK0460	53°8·5'	1°56·0'W	X	119
Merry Vale	Pemb	SM7424	51°52·4'	5°16·6'W	X	157
Merry Vale	Pemb	SN1112	51°46·7'	4°44·0'W	X	158

Merryvale Fm	Heref	SO5166	52°17·6′	2°42·7′W	FM	137,138,149
Merryview Fm	Heref	SO4427	51°56·6′	2°48·5′W	FM	161
Merse	D & G	NY0364	54°57·9′	3°30·5′W	W	84
Merse	Scot Bord	NT8146	55°42·7′	2°17·7′W	X	74
Mersea Flats	Essex	TM0513	51°46·9′	0°58·7′E	X	168
Mersea Fleet	Essex	TL9912	51°46·5′	0°53·5′E	W	168
Mersea Island	Essex	TM0314	51°47·5′	0°57·0′E	X	168
Mersea Quarters	Essex	TL9911	51°46·0′	0°53·4′E	W	168
Mersea Stone	Essex	TM0715	51°47·9′	1°0·5′E	X	168,169
Merse Cott	D & G	NX6852	54°51·0′	4°2·9′W	X	83,84
Mersehead	D & G	NX9255	54°52·9′	3°40·6′W	X	84
Mersehead Plantn	D & G	NX9255	54°52·9′	3°40·6′W	F	84
Mersehead Sands	D & G	NX9253	54°51·9′	3°40·5′W	X	84
Mersey Ho	Traf	SJ7692	53°25·7′	2°21·3′W	X	109
Mersham	Kent	TR0539	51°7·0′	0°56·1′E	T	179,189
Mersham-le-Hatch	Kent	TR0640	51°7·6′	0°57·0′E	A	179,189
Mersington	Scot Bord	NT7744	55°41·6′	2°21·5′W	X	74
Mersington Ho	Scot Bord	NT7744	55°41·6′	2°21·5′W	X	74
Mersingtonmill	Scot Bord	NT7644	55°41·6′	2°22·5′W	X	74
Mersley Down	I of W	SZ5587	50°41·0′	1°12·9′W	X	196
Mersley Fms	I of W	SZ5586	50°40·5′	1°12·9′W	FM	196
Merstham	Surrey	TQ2953	51°15·9′	0°8·7′W	T	187
Merston	W Susx	SU8902	50°48·9′	0°43·8′W	T	197
Merstone	I of W	SZ5285	50°40·0′	1°15·5′W	T	196
Merston Manor	I of W	SZ5285	50°40·0′	1°15·5′W	X	196
Merthen Downs	Corn	SW7227	50°6·2′	5°10·9′W	X	204
Merthen Fm	Corn	SX0652	50°20·4′	4°43·2′W	FM	200,204
Merthen Manor	Corn	SW7226	50°5·7′	5°10·9′W	X	204
Merthen Point	Corn	SW4122	50°2·7′	5°36·7′W	X	203
Merther	Corn	SW8644	50°15·7′	4°59·8′W	T	204
Merther Lane	Corn	SW8542	50°14·6′	5°0·6′W	T	204
Merther Uny	Corn	SW7029	50°7·2′	5°12·7′W	X	203
Merthyr	Carm	SN3520	51°51·5′	4°23·4′W	T	145,159
Merthyr Common	Merth Tyd	SO0704	51°43·9′	3°20·4′W	X	170
Merthyr Common	Merth Tyd	SO0709	51°46·6′	3°20·5′W	X	160
Merthyr Cynog	Powys	SN9837	52°1·6′	3°28·8′W	T	160
Merthyr Dyfan	V of Glam	ST1169	51°25·0′	3°16·4′W	T	171
Merthyr-Fâch	Carm	SN3320	51°51·5′	4°25·1′W	X	145,159
Merthyr Fm	Gwyn	SH6031	52°51·7′	4°4·4′W	FM	124
Merthyr Mawr	Brig	SS8877	51°29·1′	3°36·4′W	T	170
Merthyr-mawr Warren	Brig	SS8676	51°28·5′	3°38·1′W	X	170
Merthyr Tydfil	Merth Tyd	SO0506	51°44·9′	3°22·2′W	T	160
Merthyr Vale	Merth Tyd	ST0799	51°41·2′	3°20·3′W	T	170
Merton	Devon	SS5212	50°53·5′	4°5·9′W	T	180
Merton	Merton	TQ2569	51°24·6′	0°11·8′W	T	176
Merton	Norf	TL9098	52°33·0′	0°48·5′E	T	144
Merton	Oxon	SP5717	51°51·2′	1°10·0′W	T	164
Merton Common	Norf	TL9099	52°33·6′	0°48·6′E	X	144
Merton Fm	Kent	TR1455	51°15·5′	1°4·4′E	FM	179
Merton Fm	Suff	TM2754	52°8·5′	1°19·5′E	FM	156
Merton Grange	Cambs	TL2452	52°9·4′	0°10·8′W	X	153
Merton Grange	Durham	NZ3424	54°36·8′	1°28·0′W	X	93
Merton Grounds	Oxon	SP5719	51°52·2′	1°9·9′W	X	164
Merton Hall	D & G	NX3864	54°56·9′	4°31·3′W	X	83
Merton Hall Moss	D & G	NX3662	54°55·8′	4°33·1′W	X	83
Merton Mill	Devon	SS5312	50°53·6′	4°5·0′W	X	180
Merton Moors	Devon	SS5112	50°53·5′	4°6·7′W	X	180
Merton Park	Merton	TQ2569	51°24·6′	0°11·8′W	T	176
Merton Park	Norf	TL9098	52°33·0′	0°48·5′E	X	144
Mertoun Br	Scot Bord	NT6032	55°35·1′	2°37·6′W	X	74
Mertoun Ho	Scot Bord	NT6131	55°34·5′	2°36·7′W	X	74
Mertoun Newstead	Scot Bord	NT6332	55°35·1′	2°34·8′W	X	74
Mertyn	Flint	SJ1577	53°17·2′	3°16·1′W	X	116
Mertyn Downing	Flint	SJ1678	53°17·8′	3°15·2′W	X	116
Mertyn Hall	Flint	SJ1777	53°17·3′	3°14·3′W	X	116
Mervar	Orkney	HY6533	59°5·8′	2°38·3′W	X	5
Mervins Law	Scot Bord	NT6612	55°24·3′	2°31·8′W	H	80
Mervinslaw	Scot Bord	NT6713	55°24·8′	2°30·8′W	X	80
Mescoed Mawr	Newp	ST2790	51°36·5′	3°2·9′W	F	171
Meshaw	Devon	SS7519	50°57·6′	3°46·4′W	T	180
Meshaw Barton	Devon	SS7619	50°57·7′	3°45·6′W	X	180
Meshaw Moor	Devon	SS7617	50°56·6′	3°45·5′W	X	180
Mesmear Fm	Corn	SW9578	50°34·2′	4°53·3′W	FM	200
Messack Fm	Corn	SW8436	50°11·3′	5°1·2′W	FM	204
Messack Point	Corn	SW8435	50°10·8′	5°1·2′W	X	204
Messengermire Wood	Cumbr	NY2033	54°41·4′	3°14·0′W	F	89,90
Messengers Lodge Fm	Leic	SK6814	52°43·4′	0°59·2′W	FM	129
Messens Fm	E Susx	TQ7111	50°52·6′	0°26·2′E	FM	199
Messigate	Orkney	HY5107	58°57·1′	2°50·6′W	X	6,7
Messing	Essex	TL8918	51°49·9′	0°45·0′E	T	168
Messingham	N Lincs	SE8904	53°31·7′	0°39·0′W	T	112
Messingham Ings	N Lincs	SE8303	53°31·3′	0°44·5′W	X	112
Messing Lodge	Essex	TL9019	51°50·5′	0°45·9′E	X	168
Messing Park	Essex	TL8918	51°49·9′	0°45·0′E	X	168
Messuage Fm	Ches	SJ8267	53°12·2′	2°15·8′W	FM	118
Mesty Croft	Sand	SO9994	52°32·9′	2°0·5′W	T	139
Mesur-y-dorth	Pemb	SM8330	51°55·8′	5°9·0′W	T	157
Metalband Hill	Cumbr	NY7733	54°41·7′	2°21·0′W	X	91
Metal Br	Cumbr	NY3564	54°58·2′	3°0·5′W	X	85
Metal Bridge	Durham	NZ2934	54°42·3′	1°32·6′W	T	93
Metcalf's Wife's Cross	N Yks	SE1968	54°6·7′	1°42·1′W	X	99
Metcombe	Devon	SS5339	51°8·1′	4°5·7′W	X	180
Metcombe	Devon	SY0792	50°43·4′	3°18·7′W	T	192
Metcombe Down	Devon	SS5340	51°8·7′	4°5·7′W	H	180
Mete Ho	Lancs	SD5629	53°45·6′	2°39·6′W	X	102
Metfield	Suff	TM2980	52°22·4′	1°22·3′E	T	156
Metfield Common	Suff	TM2979	52°21·9′	1°22·2′E	X	156
Metfield Hall	Suff	TM2978	52°21·4′	1°22·2′E	X	156
Metham Grange	E Yorks	SE8231	53°46·3′	0°44·9′W	X	106
Metham Hall	E Yorks	SE8024	53°42·6′	0°46·9′W	X	106,112
Metheral Hill	Devon	SX6289	50°41·3′	3°56·8′W	H	191
Metherall	Devon	SX6783	50°38·1′	3°52·5′W	X	191
Metherell	Corn	SX4069	50°30·2′	4°15·0′W	T	201
Metherell	Devon	SX4480	50°36·2′	4°11·9′W	X	201
Metherell Fm	Devon	SX4596	50°44·8′	4°11·4′W	FM	190
Metherin	Corn	SX1174	50°32·4′	4°39·7′W	X	200
Metheringham	Lincs	TF0661	53°8·4′	0°24·5′W	T	121
Metheringham Barff	Lincs	TF0862	53°8·9′	0°22·7′W	X	121
Metheringham Barff Fm	Lincs	TF0962	53°8·9′	0°21·8′W	FM	121
Metheringham Delph	Lincs	TF1363	53°9·4′	0°18·2′W	W	121
Metheringham Fen	Lincs	TF1264	53°9·9′	0°19·1′W	X	121
Metheringham Heath	Lincs	TF0360	53°7·9′	0°27·2′W	X	121
Metheringham Lodge	Lincs	TF0360	53°7·9′	0°27·2′W	X	121
Metheringham Low Fields	Lincs	TF0762	53°8·9′	0°23·6′W	X	121
Methersgate	Suff	TM2846	52°4·1′	1°20·0′E	T	169
Methersham	E Susx	TQ8626	51°0·4′	0°39·5′E	X	189,199
Methil	Fife	NT3699	56°11·0′	3°1·4′W	T	59
Methilhill	Fife	NT3599	56°11·0′	3°2·4′W	T	59
Methill Hall	E Yorks	SE8649	53°56·0′	0°41·0′W	X	106
Methleigh	Corn	SW6226	50°5·4′	5°19·3′W	X	203
Methlem	Gwyn	SH1730	52°50·4′	4°42·6′W	X	123
Methley	Leeds	SE3926	53°44·0′	1°24·1′W	T	104
Methley Br	Leeds	SE4025	53°43·4′	1°23·2′W	X	105
Methley Junction	Leeds	SE3925	53°43·4′	1°24·1′W	T	104
Methley Lanes	Wakf	SE3724	53°43·4′	1°25·9′W	T	104
Methlick	Aberd	NJ8537	57°25·6′	2°14·5′W	T	30
Methrose Fm	Corn	SW9944	50°15·9′	4°48·9′W	FM	204
Methven	Pth & Kin	NO0226	56°25·2′	3°34·9′W	T	52,53,58
Methven Castle	Pth & Kin	NO0426	56°25·2′	3°32·9′W	A	52,53,58
Methven Castle Fm	Pth & Kin	NO0426	56°25·2′	3°32·9′W	FM	52,53,58
Methven Loch	Pth & Kin	NO0525	56°24·7′	3°31·9′W	W	52,53,58
Methven Moss	Pth & Kin	NO0123	56°23·6′	3°35·8′W	X	52,53,58
Methwold	Norf	TL7394	52°31·2′	0°33·4′E	T	143
Methwold Common	Norf	TL6994	52°31·3′	0°29·9′E	X	143
Methwold Fens	Norf	TL6593	52°30·8′	0°26·3′E	X	143
Methwold Hythe	Norf	TL7194	52°31·4′	0°31·6′E	T	143
Methwold Lode	Norf	TL7096	52°32·3′	0°30·8′E	W	143
Methwold Severals	Norf	TL6695	52°31·9′	0°27·2′E	X	143
Methwold Warren	Norf	TL7492	52°30·1′	0°34·2′E	F	143
Metlands	E Yorks	TA2172	54°8·0′	0°8·5′W	X	101
Metley	Devon	SX8170	50°31·3′	3°40·3′W	X	202
Metley Hill	Herts	TL2835	52°0·1′	0°7·7′W	X	153
Metlins, The	Warw	SP2389	52°30·1′	1°39·3′W	X	139
Metro Centre, The	Ghead	NZ2162	54°57·4′	1°39·9′W	X	88
Mettaford Fm	Devon	SS2824	50°59·6′	4°26·7′W	FM	190
Mettingham	Suff	TM3689	52°27·1′	1°28·8′E	T	156
Mettingham Castle	Suff	TM3588	52°26·6′	1°27·9′E	X	156
Mettle Hill	Cambs	TL3645	52°5·4′	0°0·5′W	X	154
Metton	Norf	TG1937	52°53·4′	1°15·7′E	T	133
Metz Lodge	Notts	SK5670	53°13·7′	1°9·3′W	X	120
Meudon	Corn	SW7828	50°6·9′	5°5·9′W	X	204
Meugher	N Yks	SE0470	54°7·8′	1°55·9′W	H	98
Meugher Dike	N Yks	SE0470	54°7·8′	1°55·9′W	W	98
Meulach	Moray	NJ3439	57°26·5′	3°5·5′W	X	28
Meur Bheòil	Highld	NH8440	57°26·4′	3°55·5′W	W	27
Meur Crionach	Moray	NJ2213	57°12·3′	3°17·0′W	W	36
Meur Meadhonach	Highld	NN8288	56°58·4′	3°56·0′W	W	43
Meur Tuath	Highld	NH8340	57°26·4′	3°56·5′W	W	27
Meusydd	Conwy	SH8073	53°14·7′	3°47·5′W	X	116
Meusydd-Brwyn	Denb	SJ0668	53°12·3′	3°24·0′W	X	116
Meusydd Hall	Carm	SN6118	51°50·8′	4°0·7′W	X	159
Meux Decoy	E Yorks	TA0840	53°50·9′	0°21·1′W	X	107
Mevagissey	Corn	SX0145	50°16·5′	4°47·2′W	T	204
Mevagissey Bay	Corn	SX0345	50°16·6′	4°45·5′W	W	204
Mewie Hill	Orkney	HY2409	58°58·0′	3°18·8′W	X	6,7
Mewith Head	N Yks	SD7066	54°5·6′	2°27·1′W	T	98
Mewith Head Hall	N Yks	SD6966	54°5·6′	2°28·0′W	X	98
Mewsford Point	Pemb	SR9493	51°36·1′	4°58·1′W	X	158
Mewsgate	Cumbr	NY5272	55°2·7′	2°44·6′W	X	86
Mewslade Bay	Swan	SS4187	51°33·8′	4°17·3′W	W	159
Mew Stone	Devon	SX7236	50°12·8′	3°47·3′W	X	202
Mew Stone	Devon	SX9049	50°20·1′	3°32·4′W	X	202
Mew Stone	Pemb	SM7208	51°43·7′	5°17·7′W	X	157
Mexborough	Donc	SE4700	53°29·9′	1°17·1′W	T	111
Mexican Br	Lincs	TF3758	53°6·3′	0°3·2′E	X	122
Mexico Towans	Corn	SW5538	50°11·7′	5°25·6′W	X	203
Mey	Highld	ND2872	58°38·1′	3°13·9′W	X	7,12
Meyarth Hall	Denb	SJ0649	53°2·0′	3°23·7′W	X	116
Mey Hill	Highld	ND3174	58°39·2′	3°10·9′W	H	7,12
Meyllteyrn	Gwyn	SH2332	52°51·6′	4°37·4′W	X	123
Meynell Hall	N Yks	NZ5606	54°27·0′	1°7·8′W	X	93
Meynell Langley	Derby	SK2840	52°57·6′	1°34·6′W	X	119,128
Meynell Langley	Derby	SK3039	52°57·1′	1°32·8′W	X	128
Meyrick Park	Bourne	SZ0892	50°43·9′	1°52·8′W	X	195
Meysey Hampton	Glos	SU1199	51°41·6′	1°50·1′W	T	163
Mhor	N Ayr	NS1848	55°41·7′	4°53·3′W	X	63
Mhòr Cottage	Highld	NH9515	57°13·1′	3°43·9′W	X	36
Miabhaig	N Eil	NB0906	57°57·2′	6°54·7′W	T	13,14
Miabhaig	N Eil	NG1596	57°52·0′	6°47·9′W	T	14
Mia Hall	Flint	SJ0780	53°18·8′	3°23·3′W	X	116
Mial	Highld	NG7977	57°44·0′	5°42·3′W	T	19
Mianais	N Eil	NG4296	57°53·3′	6°20·7′W	X	14
Miavaig	N Eil	NB0834	58°12·2′	6°57·8′W	T	13
Michaelchurch	Heref	SO5225	51°55·5′	2°41·5′W	T	162
Michaelchurch Court	Heref	SO3034	52°0·2′	3°0·8′W	X	161
Michaelchurch Escley	Heref	SO3134	52°0·2′	2°59·9′W	T	161
Michaelchurch-on-Arrow	Powys	SO2450	52°8·8′	3°6·2′W	T	148
Michaelmuir	Aberd	NJ9033	57°23·5′	2°9·5′W	X	30
Michael's Nook	Cumbr	NY3408	54°28·0′	3°0·7′W	X	90
Michaelston-le-Pit	V of Glam	ST1572	51°26·7′	3°13·0′W	T	171
Michaelston-super-Ely	Card	ST1176	51°28·8′	3°16·5′W	T	171
Michaelston-y-Fedw	Newp	ST2484	51°33·2′	3°5·4′W	T	171
Michaelstow	Corn	SX0878	50°34·4′	4°42·3′W	T	200
Michaelstow Ho	Corn	SX0778	50°34·4′	4°43·2′W	X	200
Michaelwood Fm	Glos	ST7195	51°39·4′	2°24·8′W	FM	162
Michaelwood Lodge Fm	Glos	ST7194	51°38·9′	2°24·8′W	FM	162,172
Michael Wood Service Area	Glos	ST7095	51°39·4′	2°25·6′W	X	162
Michelcombe	Devon	SX6968	50°30·1′	3°50·5′W	T	202
Micheldever	Hants	SU5139	51°9·1′	1°15·9′W	T	185
Micheldever Station	Hants	SU5142	51°10·7′	1°15·8′W	X	185
Micheldever Wood	Hants	SU5337	51°8·0′	1°14·2′W	F	185
Michelgrove	W Susx	TQ0808	50°51·9′	0°27·5′W	X	197
Michelham Priory	E Susx	TQ5509	50°51·8′	0°12·5′E	A	199
Michelmersh	Hants	SU3426	51°2·2′	1°30·5′W	T	185
Michelmersh Wood	Hants	SU3427	51°2·7′	1°30·5′W	F	185
Mickelden Beck	Sheff	SK1998	53°28·9′	1°42·4′W	W	110
Micker Brook	Stock	SJ8787	53°23·0′	2°11·3′W	W	109
Mickering Fm	Lancs	SD4004	53°32·0′	2°53·9′W	FM	108
Mickfield	Suff	TM1361	52°12·6′	1°7·5′E	T	156
Mickfield Hall	Suff	TM1362	52°13·1′	1°7·5′E	X	156
Mickfield Plantn	E Yorks	SE7346	53°54·5′	0°52·9′W	F	105,106
Micklam	Cumbr	NX9822	54°35·2′	3°34·3′W	X	89
Mickland's Hill	Glos	SP2323	51°54·5′	1°39·5′W	X	163
Micklebarrow Hill	Notts	SK7455	53°5·5′	0°53·3′W	X	120
Mickleberry Hill	Lincs	TF5273	53°14·2′	0°17·1′E	X	122
Mickleborough Hill	Notts	SK5834	52°54·3′	1°7·9′W	X	129
Micklebrack	N Yks	SE2789	54°18·0′	1°34·7′W	X	99
Micklebring	Donc	SK5194	53°26·7′	1°13·5′W	T	111
Mickleburnt Hill	Durham	NY8717	54°33·1′	2°11·6′W	H	91,92
Micklebury Fm	N Yks	SE2081	54°13·7′	1°41·2′W	FM	99
Mickleby	N Yks	NZ8012	54°30·1′	0°45·5′W	T	94
Mickleby Beck	N Yks	NZ8012	54°30·1′	0°45·5′W	X	94
Mickle Corum	Stir	NN8502	56°12·1′	3°50·8′W	H	58
Mickledale	Ches	SJ5175	53°16·4′	2°43·7′W	X	117
Mickleden	Cumbr	NY2606	54°26·9′	3°8·1′W	X	89,90
Mickleden Edge	Sheff	SK1998	53°28·9′	1°42·4′W	X	110
Mickledore	Cumbr	NY2106	54°26·8′	3°12·7′W	X	89,90
Mickle Fell	Durham	NY8124	54°36·9′	2°17·2′W	H	91,92
Mickle Fell Brocks	Durham	NY8223	54°36·4′	2°16·3′W	X	91,92
Micklefield	Bucks	SU8892	51°37·4′	0°43·3′W	T	175
Micklefield	Leeds	SE4433	53°47·7′	1°19·5′W	T	105
Micklefield Green	Herts	TQ0498	51°40·5′	0°29·4′W	T	166,176
Micklefield Hall	Herts	TQ0597	51°39·9′	0°28·5′W	X	166,176
Mickleham	Surrey	TQ1753	51°16·1′	0°19·0′W	T	187
Mickleham Downs	Surrey	TQ1753	51°16·1′	0°19·0′W	X	187
Micklehaugh Fm	Norf	TM0786	52°26·2′	1°3·1′E	FM	144
Micklehead Fm	St Hel	SJ5091	53°25·0′	2°44·7′W	FM	108
Mickle Hill	Cambs	TL0573	52°20·9′	0°27·1′W	X	153
Mickle Hill	Durham	NZ4638	54°44·3′	1°16·7′W	X	93
Mickle Hill	Leic	SP4691	52°31·1′	1°18·9′W	X	140
Mickle Hill	Norf	TL8788	52°27·7′	0°45·6′E	X	144
Mickle Hill	Suff	TL9177	52°21·7′	0°48·7′E	X	144
Mickle Hill Fm	Cambs	TL0572	52°20·4′	0°27·1′W	FM	153
Mickle Hill (Tumulus)	Norf	TL8788	52°27·7′	0°45·6′E	A	144
Mickleholme	Lincs	TF0479	53°18·1′	0°26·0′W	X	121
Mickleholme Fm	N Lincs	SE9516	53°38·1′	0°33·4′W	FM	112
Mickle Howe	N Yks	SE8983	54°14·3′	0°37·6′W	A	101
Micklehurst	Lancs	SD6744	53°53·7′	2°29·7′W	X	103
Micklehurst	Tames	SD9802	53°31·1′	2°1·4′W	T	109
Mickle Mere	Norf	TL9091	52°29·3′	0°48·3′E	W	144
Mickle Mere	Suff	TL9369	52°17·3′	0°50·2′E	X	155
Micklemoor Hill	Norf	TL9785	52°25·9′	0°54·3′E	X	144
Mickleover	C of Derb	SK3034	52°54·4′	1°32·8′W	T	128
Micklepage Fm	W Susx	TQ1925	51°0·9′	0°17·8′W	FM	187,198
Mickle Rigg	Cumbr	NY2736	54°43·1′	3°7·6′W	X	89,90
Micklethwaite	Brad	SE1041	53°52·1′	1°50·5′W	T	104
Micklethwaite	Cumbr	NY2850	54°50·6′	3°6·8′W	T	85
Mickleton	Durham	NY9623	54°36·4′	2°3·3′W	T	91,92
Mickleton	Glos	SP1643	52°5·3′	1°45·6′W	T	151
Mickleton Hills Fm	Glos	SP1640	52°3·7′	1°45·6′W	FM	151
Mickleton Moor	Durham	NY9220	54°34·8′	2°7·0′W	X	91,92
Mickleton Wood Fm	Glos	SP1643	52°5·3′	1°45·6′W	FM	151
Mickletown	Leeds	SE3927	53°44·5′	1°24·1′W	T	104
Mickle Trafford	Ches	SJ4469	53°13·1′	2°49·9′W	T	117
Micklewood	Shrops	SJ4701	52°36·5′	2°46·6′W	X	126
Micklewood	Staffs	SJ9411	52°42·0′	2°4·9′W	X	127
Mickley	Derby	SK3279	53°18·7′	1°30·8′W	T	119
Mickley	N Yks	SE2576	54°11·0′	1°36·6′W	T	99
Mickley	Shrops	SJ6132	52°53·3′	2°34·4′W	T	127
Mickley Grange	Northum	NZ0760	54°56·3′	1°53·0′W	X	88
Mickley Green	Suff	TL8457	52°11·1′	0°41·9′E	T	155
Mickley Hall	Ches	SJ6347	53°1·4′	2°32·7′W	X	118
Mickley Moor	Northum	NZ0861	54°56·9′	1°52·1′W	X	88
Mickley Square	Northum	NZ0762	54°57·4′	1°53·0′W	T	88
Micklow Hill	N Yks	NZ2010	54°29·3′	1°41·1′W	X	93
Micklow Ho	Staffs	SJ8832	52°53·4′	2°10·3′W	X	127
Mick's Gill	N Yks	SE2147	53°55·4′	1°40·4′W	X	104
Midanbury	C of Soton	SU4514	50°55·7′	1°21·2′W	T	196
Mid Anguston	C of Aber	NJ8002	57°6·8′	2°19·4′W	X	38
Mid Ardlaw	Aberd	NJ9463	57°39·7′	2°5·6′W	T	30
Mid Ardyne	Arg & Bt	NS1068	55°52·3′	5°1·8′W	X	63
Mid Ascog	Arg & Bt	NS1062	55°49·1′	5°1·5′W	X	63
Mid Ashgill	Cumbr	NY7640	54°45·5′	2°22·0′W	X	86,87
Midastew	Shetld	HU3686	60°33·6′	1°20·1′W	X	1,2,3
Mid Auchinleck	Inverc	NS3373	55°55·5′	4°39·9′W	T	63
Mid Bank	D & G	NX4852	54°50·6′	4°21·6′W	X	83
Mid Barnaigh	Renf	NS3563	55°50·2′	4°37·6′W	X	63
Midbea	Orkney	HY4444	59°17·0′	2°58·5′W	T	5
Mid Beltie	Aberd	NJ6200	57°5·6′	2°37·2′W	X	37
Midberg	Shetld	HU5988	60°34·5′	0°54·9′W	X	1,2
Midbigging	Orkney	HY5103	58°55·0′	2°50·6′W	X	6,7
Mid Blairs	Aberd	NO7480	56°54·9′	2°25·2′W	X	45
Mid Borland	Stir	NN6400	56°10·7′	4°11·0′W	X	57
Midbrake	Shetld	HP5204	60°43·2′	1°2·3′W	T	1
Mid Breck	Shetld	HU5865	60°22·2′	0°56·4′W	X	2
Mid Breich	W Loth	NT0064	55°51·8′	3°35·4′W	X	65
Mid Burn	D & G	NS8708	55°21·4′	3°46·5′W	W	71,78
Mid Burn	D & G	NX5366	54°58·3′	4°17·4′W	W	83
Mid Burn	D & G	NX5485	55°8·5′	4°17·0′W	W	77
Mid Burn	D & G	NX6173	55°2·2′	4°10·1′W	W	77
Mid Burn	D & G	NX6697	55°15·2′	4°6·1′W	W	77
Mid Burn	S Ayr	NX1681	55°5·6′	4°52·6′W	W	76
Mid Burn	Scot Bord	NT4902	55°18·8′	2°47·8′W	W	79
Midburn	Scot Bord	NT5051	55°45·2′	2°47·4′W	X	66,73
Midburn	Scot Bord	NT5611	55°23·7′	2°41·2′W	X	80
Mid Burn	Scot Bord	NT6353	55°46·4′	2°35·0′W	W	67,74
Mid-Cairneywhing	Aberd	NJ8757	57°36·4′	2°12·6′W	X	30
Mid Calder	W Loth	NT0767	55°53·5′	3°28·8′W	T	65
Mid Cambushinnie	Pth & Kin	NN8006	56°14·1′	3°55·7′W	X	57
Mid Cleuch	D & G	NY4282	55°8·0′	2°54·2′W	W	79
Mid Cloch Forbie	Aberd	NJ7958	57°36·9′	2°20·6′W	X	29,30
Mid Clova	Aberd	NJ4521	57°16·8′	2°54·3′W	X	37
Midclune	Aberd	NO6091	57°0·8′	2°39·1′W	X	45
Mid Clyth	Highld	ND2837	58°19·2′	3°13·3′W	T	11
Mid Coul	Highld	NH7750	57°31·7′	4°2·8′W	X	27
Midcover Plantn	D & G	NX7489	55°11·0′	3°58·3′W	F	77
Mid Craiglands	Highld	NH7157	57°35·3′	4°9·0′W	X	27
Mid Crochail	Highld	NH3734	57°22·3′	4°42·2′W	X	26
Mid Crosswood	W Loth	NT0556	55°47·5′	3°30·5′W	X	65,72

Mid Culbeuchly	Aberd	NJ6562	57°39·1′	2°34·7′W	X	29
Mid Culsh	Aberd	NJ8848	57°31·6′	2°11·6′W	X	30
Mid Curr	Highld	NH9923	57°17·4′	3°40·1′W	X	36
Middale	Cumbr	NY4903	54°25·4′	2°46·7′W	X	90
Mid Dale	Shetld	HU1853	60°15·9′	1°40·0′W	X	3
Mid Danna	Arg & Bt	NR6978	55°56·6′	5°41·5′W	X	61,62
Mid Dargavel	D & G	NY0176	55°4·4′	3°32·6′W	X	84
Middle Ardo	Aberd	NJ9321	57°17·0′	2°6·5′W	X	38
Middle Assendon	Oxon	SU7385	51°33·8′	0°56·4′W	T	175
Middle Aston	Oxon	SP4726	51°56·1′	1°18·6′W	T	164
Middle Back	Devon	SX8456	50°23·8′	3°37·5′W	X	202
Middle Balbeggie	Fife	NT2796	56°9·3′	3°10·1′W	X	59
Middle Ballewan	Stir	NS5480	55°59·7′	4°20·0′W	X	64
Middle Balnald	Pth & Kin	NO0759	56°43·1′	3°30·7′W	X	52,53
Middle Bank		NY1159	54°55·3′	3°22·9′W	X	85
Middlebank	Cumbr	NY0105	54°26·1′	3°31·2′W	X	89
Middle Bank	Cumbr	SD1091	54°18·6′	3°22·6′W	X	96
Middle Bank	Fife	NO4028	56°26·7′	2°57·9′W	X	54,59
Middle Bank	Highld	NH5759	57°36·2′	4°23·1′W	X	26
Middlebank	N Ayr	NS3349	55°42·6′	4°39·1′W	X	63
Middlebank	Pth & Kin	NO2527	56°26·0′	3°12·5′W	T	53,59
Middle Bank End	Cumbr	NY7118	54°33·6′	2°26·5′W	X	91
Middle Banks	Orkney	HY6923	59°5·8′	2°32·0′W	X	5
Middlebar Knowe	Scot Bord	NT3835	55°36·5′	2°58·6′W	H	73
Middle Barlington	Devon	SS5516	50°55·8′	4°3·4′W	X	180
Middle Barn	E Susx	TQ4808	50°51·4′	0°6·6′E	X	198
Middle Barn	Lincs	TF2892	53°24·8′	0°4·0′W	X	113
Middle Barn	N Yks	SD9067	54°6·2′	2°8·8′W	X	98
Middle Barn	Suff	TM3438	51°59·7′	1°24·9′E	X	169
Middle Barn	Wilts	SU0045	51°12·5′	1°59·6′W	X	184
Middle Barn	W Susx	SU9210	50°53·2′	0°41·1′W	X	197
Middle Barnego	Falk	NS7883	56°1·7′	3°57·0′W	X	57,64
Middlebarn Fm	Hants	SU4138	51°8·6′	1°24·4′W	FM	185
Middlebarrow Wood	Cumbr	SD4676	54°10·9′	2°49·2′W	F	97
Middle Barton	Northum	NU0812	55°24·4′	1°52·0′W	X	81
Middle Barton	Oxon	SP4325	51°55·5′	1°22·1′W	T	164
Middle Baxton's Fm	N Yks	SE6086	54°16·2′	1°4·3′W	FM	94,100
Middle Beachin Fm	Ches	SJ4456	53°6·1′	2°49·8′W	FM	117
Middle Beck	Notts	SK7951	53°3·3′	0°48·9′W	W	120,121
Middle Bent	Durham	NY9909	54°28·8′	2°0·5′W	X	92
Middle Bents	Brad	SE0836	53°49·5′	1°52·3′W	X	104
Middlebere Fm	Dorset	SY9686	50°40·6′	2°3·0′W	FM	195
Middlebere Heath	Dorset	SY9584	50°39·6′	2°3·9′W	X	195
Middle Bickenhill	Sol	SP2083	52°26·9′	1°41·9′W	T	139
Middlebie	D & G	NY2176	55°4·6′	3°13·8′W	T	85
Middlebie Burn	D & G	NY2176	55°4·6′	3°13·8′W	W	85
Middlebiehill	D & G	NY2076	55°4·6′	3°14·8′W	X	85
Middlebierig	D & G	NY2077	55°5·1′	3°14·8′W	X	85
Middle Biggin	N Yks	SE2075	54°10·5′	1°41·2′W	X	99
Middle Birks	N Yks	SD7365	54°5·1′	2°24·3′W	X	98
Middle Black Clough	Derby	SK1198	53°29·0′	1°49·6′W	X	110
Middle Blainslie	Scot Bord	NT5444	55°41·5′	2°43·5′W	X	73
Middle Bockhampton	Dorset	SZ1796	50°46·0′	1°45·2′W	T	195
Middleborough Hill	Devon	SS4339	51°8·0′	4°14·3′W	H	180
Middle Bourne	Surrey	SU8444	51°11·6′	0°47·5′W	T	186
Middle Br	Notts	SK7391	53°24·9′	0°53·7′W	X	112
Middle Brackland	Stir	NN6608	56°15·0′	4°9·3′W	X	57
Middle Bradley	Devon	SS8913	50°54·6′	3°34·3′W	X	181
Middle Bramble	Devon	SX8683	50°38·4′	3°36·4′W	X	191
Middle Bridge	E Susx	TQ6606	50°50·0′	0°21·8′E	X	199
Middle Bridge	Northnts	SP8894	52°32·4′	0°41·7′W	X	141
Middle Bridge	N Som	ST4775	51°28·5′	2°45·4′W	T	171,172
Middlebridge	Pth & Kin	NN8766	56°46·6′	3°50·5′W	T	43
Middlebridge Fm	E Yorks	SE8750	53°56·6′	0°40·1′W	FM	106
Middle Brighty	Angus	NO4438	56°32·1′	2°54·2′W	T	54
Middle Brookend Fm	Oxon	SP2330	51°58·3′	1°39·5′W	FM	151
Middlebrooks	Somer	ST1830	51°4·0′	3°9·8′W	X	181
Middle Broomhill	Aberd	NJ7208	57°10·0′	2°27·3′W	X	38
Middle Brow	W Susx	TQ1310	50°52·9′	0°23·2′W	X	198
Middle Brow Top	Lancs	SD5258	54°1·2′	2°43·5′W	X	102
Middle Brunton	N upon Ty	NZ2270	55°1·7′	1°38·9′W	X	88
Middle Burn	Northum	NY7774	55°3·8′	2°21·2′W	W	86,87
Middleburn	Northum	NY7975	55°4·4′	2°19·3′W	X	86,87
Middleburn	Pth & Kin	NT1898	56°10·3′	3°18·8′W	X	58
Middle Burn	Scot Bord	NT2250	55°44·5′	3°14·1′W	W	66,73
Middle Burnham	Somer	ST3149	51°14·4′	2°58·9′W	T	182
Middle Busk	Cumbr	NY6809	54°28·8′	2°29·2′W	X	91
Middle Cairncake	Aberd	NJ8249	57°32·1′	2°17·6′W	X	29,30
Middlecale Fm	Ches	SJ9584	53°21·4′	2°4·1′W	FM	109
Middle Cardney	Pth & Kin	NO0545	56°35·5′	3°32·4′W	X	52,53
Middlecave	N Yks	SE7771	54°8·0′	0°48·9′W	T	100
Middle Caves	N Yks	NZ2108	54°28·3′	1°40·1′W	X	93
Middle Cawledge Park	Northum	NU1910	55°23·3′	1°41·6′W	X	81
Middle Chase Fm	Wilts	SU0020	50°59·0′	1°59·6′W	FM	184
Middle Chinnock	Somer	ST4713	50°55·1′	2°44·9′W	T	193
Middle Claydon	Bucks	SP7225	51°55·4′	0°56·8′W	T	165
Middle Cliff	Staffs	SK0054	53°5·2′	1°59·6′W	T	119
Middlecliffe	Barns	SE4205	53°32·6′	1°21·6′W	T	111
Middlecombe Fm	Devon	SX8139	50°14·6′	3°39·8′W	FM	202
Middle Common	Cambs	TL5072	52°19·8′	0°12·5′E	X	154
Middle Common	Worcs	SO5962	52°15·5′	2°35·6′W	X	137,138,149
Middle Conholt Fm	Wilts	SU3255	51°17·8′	1°32·1′W	FM	174,185
Middle Coppice	Staffs	SJ7736	52°55·5′	2°20·1′W	F	127
Middlecot Ho	Hants	SU2543	51°11·4′	1°38·1′W	X	184
Middlecott	Devon	SS4105	50°49·6′	4°15·1′W	T	190
Middlecott	Devon	SS6106	50°50·4′	3°58·1′W	X	191
Middlecott	Devon	SS6732	51°4·6′	3°53·5′W	X	180
Middlecott	Devon	SS7507	50°51·2′	3°46·2′W	T	191
Middlecott	Devon	SS8618	50°57·2′	3°37·0′W	X	181
Middlecott	Devon	SX7186	50°39·8′	3°49·1′W	T	191
Middlecott Fm	Devon	SX3893	50°43·1′	4°17·3′W	FM	190
Middle Coul	Angus	NO2757	56°42·2′	3°11·1′W	X	53
Middle Covert	Cambs	TL2188	52°28·8′	0°12·7′W	F	142
Middle Cowden	Northum	NY9178	55°6·0′	2°8·0′W	X	87
Middle Crackington	Corn	SX1595	50°43·7′	4°36·9′W	T	190
Middle Crag	Cumbr	NY2815	54°31·8′	3°6·3′W	X	89,90
Middle Crag	Cumbr	NY5881	55°7·5′	2°39·1′W	X	80
Middle Crag	Lancs	SD5155	53°59·6′	2°44·4′W	X	102
Middle Cragabus	Arg & Bt	NR3245	55°37·7′	6°15·0′W	X	60
Middle Craigs	C of Edin	NT2777	55°59·1′	3°9·8′W	X	66
Middlecroft	Derby	SK4273	53°15·4′	1°21·8′W	T	120
Middlecroft	Devon	SS3700	50°46·8′	4°18·4′W	X	190
Middle Croft	S Lanak	NS6538	55°37·3′	4°8·2′W	X	71
Middlecross	V of Glam	ST0469	51°25·0′	3°22·4′W	X	170
Middle Culham Fm	Wok	SU7982	51°32·1′	0°51·3′W	FM	175
Middle Cuts	Cambs	TL4872	52°19·8′	0°10·7′E	X	154
Middle Dairy	Dorset	ST9101	50°48·7′	2°7·3′W	X	195
Middledale	E Yorks	TA0465	54°4·5′	0°24·2′W	X	101
Middle Dale Park	Cumbr	SD3592	54°19·4′	2°59·5′W	X	96,97
Middledean Burn	Northum	NU0115	55°26·0′	1°58·6′W	W	81
Middle Dean Fm	Devon	SS6133	51°5·0′	3°58·7′W	FM	180
Middle Deepdale	N Yks	TA0485	54°15·2′	0°23·8′W	X	101
Middle Ditchford	Glos	SP2137	52°2·1′	1°41·2′W	X	151
Middle Dod	Scot Bord	NT1222	55°29·3′	3°23·1′W	H	72
Middle Dodd	Cumbr	NY3909	54°28·6′	2°56·1′W	H	90
Middle Down	Wilts	ST9725	51°1·7′	2°2·2′W	X	184
Middledown Ho	S Glos	ST7574	51°28·1′	2°21·2′W	X	172
Middle Drift	Corn	SX1364	50°27·0′	4°37·7′W	X	200
Middle Drimmie	Pth & Kin	NO1750	56°38·3′	3°20·7′W	X	53
Middle Drums	Angus	NO5957	56°42·4′	2°39·7′W	X	54
Middle Duddo	Northum	NZ1879	55°6·6′	1°42·6′W	X	88
Middle Duntisbourne	Glos	SO9806	51°45·4′	2°1·3′W	T	163
Middle Edge	Northum	NY7953	54°52·5′	2°19·2′W	X	86,87
Middle Edge	Staffs	SK0065	53°11·2′	1°59·6′W	X	119
Middle Edge Moss	Oldham	SE0504	53°32·2′	1°55·1′W	X	110
Middle Ehenside	Cumbr	NY0007	54°27·2′	3°32·1′W	X	89
Middle Ellick Fm	Somer	ST4957	51°18·8′	2°43·5′W	FM	172,182
Middle End Fm	Durham	NY9828	54°39·1′	2°1·4′W	FM	92
Middle End Plantn	Durham	NY9829	54°39·6′	2°1·4′W	F	92
Middle Essie	Aberd	NK0854	57°34·8′	1°51·5′W	X	30
Middle Fell	Cumbr	NY1018	54°33·2′	3°23·1′W	X	89
Middle Fell	Cumbr	NY1507	54°27·3′	3°18·2′W	H	89
Middle Fell	Cumbr	NY7444	54°47·7′	2°23·8′W	H	86,87
Middle Fell	Cumbr	NY7445	54°48·2′	2°23·8′W	H	86,87
Middle Fell	Cumbr	NY7718	54°33·6′	2°20·9′W	X	91
Middle Fell	Cumbr	NY8511	54°29·9′	2°13·5′W	X	91,92
Middle Fell Fm	Cumbr	NY2806	54°26·9′	3°6·2′W	FM	89,90
Middle Fell Gate	Cumbr	SD3977	54°11·4′	2°55·7′W	X	96,97
Middle Fell Ho	Cumbr	SD5885	54°15·8′	2°38·3′W	X	97
Middle Fen	Cambs	TL4071	52°19·4′	0°3·7′E	X	154
Middle Fen	Cambs	TL5679	52°23·4′	0°18·0′E	X	143
Middle Fen	Norf	TM0479	52°22·5′	1°0·2′E	W	144
Middle Fen Fm	Lincs	TF1329	52°51·0′	0°18·9′W	FM	130
Middlefield	Aberd	NJ9514	57°13·3′	2°4·5′W	X	38
Middlefield	Cambs	TL4752	52°9·0′	0°9·3′E	X	154
Middlefield	C of Aber	NJ9008	57°10·0′	2°9·5′W	T	38
Middlefield	E Ayr	NS5434	55°34·9′	4°18·5′W	X	70
Middlefield	E Ayr	NS6829	55°32·5′	4°5·1′W	X	71
Middlefield	Falk	NS8980	56°0·3′	3°46·4′W	T	65
Middlefield	Fife	NO3206	56°14·8′	3°5·4′W	X	59
Middlefield	Fife	NO3815	56°19·7′	2°59·7′W	X	59
Middlefield	Moray	NJ0360	57°37·4′	3°37·0′W	X	27
Middle Field	N Yks	SE5015	53°38·0′	1°14·2′W	X	111
Middle Field	N Yks	SE5766	54°5·4′	1°7·3′W	X	100
Middlefield	Scot Bord	NT7851	55°45·4′	2°20·6′W	X	67,74
Middlefield	S Lanak	NS8234	55°35·4′	3°51·9′W	X	71,72
Middlefield Fm	Leeds	SE3445	53°54·2′	1°28·5′W	FM	104
Middlefield Fm	Lincs	SK9993	53°25·7′	0°30·2′W	FM	112
Middlefield Fm	Oxon	SP3611	51°48·0′	1°28·3′W	FM	164
Middlefield Fm	Stock on T	NZ4123	54°36·3′	1°21·5′W	FM	93
Middlefield Law	E Ayr	NS6830	55°33·0′	4°5·1′W	H	71
Middlefield Rig	D & G	NT0913	55°24·4′	3°25·8′W	X	78
Middlefields Fm	Corn	SS2314	50°54·1′	4°30·7′W	FM	190
Middlefields Fm	N Yks	SE1590	54°18·6′	1°45·7′W	FM	99
Middle Flat	N Yks	SE8978	54°11·6′	0°37·7′W	X	101
Middle Fm	Beds	SP9256	52°11·9′	0°38·8′W	FM	152
Middle Fm	Beds	TL1147	52°6·8′	0°22·3′W	FM	153
Middle Fm	Bucks	SP6414	51°49·5′	1°3·9′W	FM	164,165
Middle Fm	Bucks	SP6817	51°51·1′	1°0·4′W	FM	164,165
Middle Fm	Bucks	SP7423	51°54·3′	0°55·1′W	FM	165
Middle Fm	Cambs	TL2185	52°27·2′	0°12·8′W	FM	142
Middle Fm	Cumbr	NY5160	54°56·2′	2°45·5′W	FM	86
Middle Fm	Dorset	ST8604	50°50·4′	2°11·5′W	FM	194
Middle Fm	Dorset	SY6790	50°42·8′	2°27·7′W	FM	194
Middle Fm	E Susx	TQ4807	50°50·8′	0°6·5′E	FM	198
Middle Fm	E Yorks	SE9836	53°48·9′	0°30·3′W	FM	106
Middle Fm	E Yorks	TA2718	53°38·8′	0°4·3′W	FM	113
Middle Fm	Hants	SU5929	51°3·7′	1°9·1′W	FM	185
Middle Fm	Hants	SU6459	51°19·8′	1°4·5′W	FM	175
Middle Fm	Herts	TL3430	51°57·4′	0°2·6′W	FM	166
Middle Fm	Leic	SK6019	52°46·2′	1°6·2′W	FM	129
Middle Fm	Leic	SP5684	52°27·3′	1°10·2′W	FM	140
Middle Fm	Lincs	SK8246	53°0·5′	0°46·3′W	FM	130
Middle Fm	Lincs	SK8769	53°12·9′	0°41·4′W	FM	121
Middle Fm	Lincs	TF1325	52°48·9′	0°19·0′W	FM	130
Middle Fm	Lincs	TF2171	53°13·6′	0°10·8′W	FM	122
Middle Fm	Lincs	TF2577	53°16·7′	0°7·1′W	FM	122
Middle Fm	Lincs	TF3161	53°8·0′	0°2·1′W	FM	122
Middle Fm	Lincs	TF3798	53°27·9′	0°4·2′E	FM	113
Middle Fm	Norf	TL5897	52°33·1′	0°20·2′E	FM	143
Middle Fm	Norf	TL6789	52°28·6′	0°27·9′E	FM	143
Middle Fm	Northum	NY9473	55°3·3′	2°5·2′W	FM	87
Middle Fm	Northum	NZ2875	55°4·4′	1°33·3′W	FM	88
Middle Fm	N Yks	NZ3807	54°27·7′	1°24·4′W	FM	93
Middle Fm	N Yks	SE1950	53°57·0′	1°42·2′W	FM	104
Middle Fm	N Yks	SE6388	54°17·3′	1°1·5′W	FM	94,100
Middle Fm	N Yks	SE8067	54°5·8′	0°46·2′W	FM	100
Middle Fm	N Yks	SE8576	54°10·6′	0°41·4′W	FM	100
Middle Fm	Oxon	SP5112	51°48·5′	1°15·2′W	FM	164
Middle Fm	Oxon	SP6032	51°59·2′	1°7·2′W	FM	152,165
Middle Fm	Powys	SJ2914	52°43·4′	3°2·7′W	FM	126
Middle Fm	Stock	SJ9290	53°24·6′	2°6·8′W	FM	109
Middle Fm	Suff	TM0552	52°7·9′	1°0·1′E	FM	155
Middle Fm	Warw	SP3160	52°14·5′	1°32·4′W	FM	151
Middle Fm	W Berks	SU4774	51°28·0′	1°19·0′W	FM	174
Middle Fm	W Berks	SU6267	51°24·1′	1°6·1′W	FM	175
Middle Fm	Wilts	SU0844	51°11·9′	1°52·7′W	FM	184
Middlefoodie	Fife	NO4017	56°20·7′	2°57·8′W	X	59
Middlefoot	Cumbr	NY4772	55°2·6′	2°49·3′W	X	86
Middleforth Green	Lancs	SD5227	53°44·5′	2°43·3′W	T	102
Middle Foulshaw	Cumbr	SD4782	54°14·1′	2°48·4′W	X	97
Middle Garland	Devon	SS7118	50°57·1′	3°49·8′W	X	180
Middle Garth	Powys	SO0994	52°32·4′	3°20·1′W	X	136
Middlegate	N Lincs	TA0214	53°37·0′	0°27·1′W	X	112
Middlegate Fm	Suff	TM0668	52°16·5′	1°1·6′E	FM	155
Middlegill	D & G	NT0406	55°20·6′	3°30·4′W	X	78
Middle Gill	Lancs	SD6661	54°2·9′	2°30·7′W	W	98
Middle Gill Fm	Cumbr	NX9921	54°34·7′	3°33·3′W	FM	89
Middlegill Sike	Cumbr	NY8507	54°27·7′	2°13·5′W	W	91,92
Middle Gourdie	Pth & Kin	NO1142	56°33·9′	3°26·5′W	X	53
Middle Grange	Aberd	NK1146	57°30·5′	1°48·5′W	T	30
Middle Grange	Fife	NS9889	56°5·2′	3°37·9′W	X	65
Middle Green	Bucks	TQ0080	51°30·8′	0°33·1′W	T	176
Middle Green	Somer	ST1319	50°58·1′	3°14·0′W	T	181,193
Middle Green	Suff	TL7465	52°15·6′	0°33·4′E	T	155
Middle Green	Suff	TM4582	52°23·1′	1°36·4′E	X	156
Middle Grounds,	Newp	ST3576	51°29·0′	2°55·8′W	X	171
Middle Grove	Cumbr	NY3905	54°26·5′	2°56·0′W	X	90
Middlegrove Fm	Bucks	SP9101	51°42·3′	0°40·6′W	FM	165
Middlehall	Clackm	NN9900	56°11·2′	3°37·2′W	X	58
Middle Hall	Powys	SO0649	52°8·1′	3°22·0′W	X	147
Middleham	E Susx	TQ4412	50°53·6′	0°3·2′E	X	198
Middleham	N Yks	SE1287	54°17·0′	1°48·5′W	T	99
Middleham Br	N Yks	SE1188	54°17·5′	1°49·4′W	X	99
Middleham High Moor	N Yks	SE0787	54°17·0′	1°53·1′W	X	99
Middleham Low Moor	N Yks	SE1087	54°17·0′	1°50·4′W	X	99
Middle Handley	Derby	SK4077	53°17·5′	1°23·6′W	T	120
Middle Hare Head	N Yks	SE0455	53°59·7′	1°55·9′W	X	104
Middle Harling	Norf	TL9885	52°25·9′	0°55·2′E	T	144
Middle Head	N Yks	NZ6201	54°24·3′	1°2·3′W	X	94
Middle Head	N Yks	SE8092	54°19·3′	0°45·8′W	X	94,100
Middle Head	Scot Bord	NT0930	55°33·6′	3°26·1′W	H	72
Middle Head	Swan	SS6387	51°34·2′	3°58·2′W	X	159
Middle Heads	Durham	NZ0948	54°49·9′	1°51·2′W	X	88
Middle Heads Fm	N Yks	SE5886	54°16·2′	1°6·1′W	FM	100
Middle Heads Wood	N Yks	SE5985	54°15·7′	1°5·2′W	F	100
Middle Heldre	Powys	SJ2810	52°41·2′	3°3·5′W	X	126
Middle Herrington	Sund	NZ3553	54°52·5′	1°26·8′W	T	88
Middleheugh	Northum	NZ1198	55°16·8′	1°49·2′W	X	81
Middle Highfield	Lancs	SD5366	54°5·5′	2°42·7′W	X	97
Middlehill	Aberd	NJ7237	57°25·6′	2°27·5′W	X	29
Middlehill	Aberd	NJ8349	57°32·1′	2°16·6′W	X	29,30
Middlehill	Aberd	NJ8759	57°37·5′	2°12·6′W	X	30
Middlehill	Angus	NO3763	56°45·5′	3°1·4′W	X	44
Middle Hill	Cambs	TL5762	52°14·3′	0°18·4′E	X	154
Middlehill	Corn	SX2869	50°30·0′	4°25·1′W	T	201
Middle Hill	Derby	SK1077	53°17·6′	1°50·6′W	H	119
Middle Hill	Derby	SK1182	53°20·3′	1°49·7′W	X	110
Middlehill	Devon	SS6631	51°4·0′	3°54·4′W	X	180
Middle Hill	Devon	SS7545	51°11·7′	3°47·0′W	X	180
Middlehill	Devon	SX7993	50°43·7′	3°42·5′W	X	191
Middle Hill	D & G	NT2606	55°20·8′	3°9·6′W	X	79
Middle Hill	Heref	SO4753	52°10·6′	2°46·1′W	X	148,149
Middle Hill	Northum	NT8712	55°24·4′	2°11·9′W	H	80
Middle Hill	Northum	NY9490	55°12·5′	2°5·2′W	H	80
Middlehill	Pemb	SM8801	51°40·3′	5°3·6′W	X	157,158
Middle Hill	Pemb	SM9511	51°45·9′	4°57·9′W	T	157,158
Middle Hill	Pth & Kin	NN9202	56°12·2′	3°44·0′W	H	58
Middle Hill	Pth & Kin	NN9433	56°28·9′	3°42·8′W	H	52,53
Middle Hill	Scot Bord	NT1529	55°33·1′	3°20·4′W	H	72
Middle Hill	Scot Bord	NT2018	55°27·2′	3°15·5′W	H	79
Middle Hill	Scot Bord	NT2432	55°34·8′	3°11·9′W	H	73
Middle Hill	Scot Bord	NT3346	55°42·4′	3°3·5′W	H	73
Middle Hill	Scot Bord	NT3833	55°35·5′	2°58·6′W	H	73
Middle Hill	Shrops	SO4893	52°32·2′	2°45·6′W	X	137,138
Middle Hill	Somer	ST1734	51°6·2′	3°10·7′W	X	181
Middle Hill	Staffs	SJ9607	52°39·9′	2°3·1′W	T	127,139
Middlehill	V of Glam	ST0570	51°25·5′	3°21·6′W	X	170
Middlehill	Wilts	ST8168	51°24·9′	2°16·0′W	T	173
Middle Hill	Wilts	ST9044	51°11·9′	2°8·2′W	H	184
Middle Hill	Worcs	SO9662	52°15·6′	2°3·1′W	X	150
Middle Hill	W Susx	TQ2133	51°5·2′	0°15·9′W	X	187
Middle Hill Fm	Devon	SS8522	50°59·4′	3°37·9′W	FM	181
Middle Hill Fm	Warw	SP2857	52°12·9′	1°35·0′W	FM	151
Middlehill Fm	Wilts	SU0478	51°30·3′	1°56·2′W	FM	173
Middle Hill Ho	Worcs	SP1135	52°1·0′	1°50·0′W	X	150
Middle Hills	Staffs	SK0363	53°10·1′	1°56·9′W	X	119
Middle Hills	Wilts	SU0134	51°6·5′	1°58·8′W	X	184
Middlehills Fm	Staffs	SK0849	53°2·5′	1°52·4′W	FM	119
Middle Ho	Ches	SJ7883	53°20·8′	2°19·4′W	X	109
Middle Ho	Northum	NY8469	55°1·2′	2°14·6′W	X	86,87
Middle Ho	N Yks	SD9068	54°6·7′	2°8·8′W	X	98
Middle Ho	Powys	SO1599	52°35·2′	3°14·9′W	X	136
Middleholm	D & G	NY3782	55°8·0′	2°58·9′W	X	79
Middleholm Hill	D & G	NY3682	55°7·9′	2°59·8′W	X	79
Middle Hook Fm	Pemb	SN0916	51°48·8′	4°45·9′W	FM	158
Middle Hope	N Som	ST3366	51°23·6′	2°57·4′W	X	171,182
Middlehope	Shrops	SO4988	52°29·5′	2°44·7′W	T	137,138
Middlehope Burn	Durham	NY8841	54°46·1′	2°10·8′W	W	87
Middlehope Fm	S Lanak	NS8951	55°44·6′	3°45·7′W	FM	65,72
Middlehope Lodge	Durham	NY8940	54°45·5′	2°9·8′W	X	87
Middlehope Moor	Durham	NY8742	54°46·6′	2°11·7′W	X	87
Middlehope Moor	Northum	NY8244	54°47·7′	2°16·4′W	X	86
Middle Hos	Cumbr	NY7442	54°46·6′	2°23·8′W	X	86,87
Middlehouse	S Lanak	NS8951	55°44·6′	3°45·7′W	X	65,72
Middle House Fm	N Yks	SD9067	54°6·2′	2°8·8′W	FM	98
Middle Hulme	Staffs	SJ9960	53°8·5′	2°0·5′W	X	118
Middlehurst Fm	Warw	SP2439	52°3·2′	1°38·6′W	FM	151
Middle Hythie	Aberd	NK0151	57°33·2′	1°58·5′W	X	30
Middle Ivy Thorn Fm	Somer	ST4634	51°6·4′	2°45·9′W	FM	182
Middle Kames	Arg & Bt	NR9189	56°3·2′	5°20·9′W	T	55
Middle Kerse	Stir	NS6595	56°8·0′	4°9·9′W	X	57
Middle Kilburn Park	N Yks	SE4978	54°12·0′	1°14·5′W	X	100
Middle Kinleith	C of Edin	NT1867	55°53·6′	3°18·2′W	X	65,66
Middle Knoll	Lancs	SD6554	53°59·1′	2°31·6′W	H	102,103
Middleknowes	Scot Bord	NT7414	55°25·4′	2°24·2′W	X	80
Middle Knox	Aberd	NO8170	56°49·5′	2°18·2′W	X	45
Middle Knuck	Shrops	SO2686	52°28·3′	3°5·0′W	X	137
Middle Lane Fm	N Som	ST3967	51°24·2′	2°52·2′W	FM	171,182
Middle Lathe	N Yks	SE0851	53°57·5′	1°52·3′W	X	104

Middle Leading Drain	Norf	TL5693	52°31·0'	0°18·3'E	W	143
Middle Leaze Fm	Oxon	SU2394	51°38·9'	1°39·7'W	FM	163,174
Middle Level Main Drain	Norf	TF5506	52°38·0'	0°17·8'E	W	143
Middle Level Main Drain	Norf	TF5711	52°40·7'	0°19·7'E	W	131,143
Middle Ley	Staffs	SJ7900	52°36·1'	2°18·2'W	X	127
Middle Littleton	Worcs	SP0746	52°7·0'	1°53·5'W	T	150
Middle Lix	Stir	NN5530	56°26·7'	4°20·7'W	X	51
Middle Lodge	Northnts	SP8580	52°24·9'	0°44·6'W	X	141
Middle Lodge	Northnts	TL0793	52°31·7'	0°25·0'W	X	142
Middle Lodge Buildings	Beds	TL0664	52°16·1'	0°26·4'W	X	153
Middle Lodge Fm	Wilts	ST9371	51°26·5'	2°5·7'W	FM	173
Middle Low Wood	Cumbr	SD4286	54°16·2'	2°53·0'W	F	96,97
Middle Luxton	Devon	ST2010	50°53·3'	3°7·9'W	T	192,193
Middle Lypiatt	Glos	SO8704	51°44·3'	2°10·9'W	X	162
Middle Madeley	Staffs	SJ7745	53°0·3'	2°20·2'W	T	118
Middle Maes-coed	Heref	SO3333	51°59·7'	2°58·2'W	T	149,161
Middlemains	E Loth	NT4768	55°54·4'	2°50·4'W	X	66
Middle Mains	S Lanak	NT0541	55°39·4'	3°30·2'W	X	72
Middle Manton	N Lincs	SE9303	53°31·2'	0°35·4'W	X	112
Middle Marchup Fm	Brad	SE0449	53°56·5'	1°55·9'W	FM	104
Middlemarsh	Dorset	ST6707	50°51·9'	2°27·8'W	T	194
Middle Marsh	Norf	TG3623	52°45·4'	1°30·3'E	W	133,134
Middlemarsh Common	Dorset	ST6508	50°52·5'	2°29·5'W	F	194
Middlemarsh Fm	Cambs	TL1684	52°26·7'	0°17·2'W	FM	142
Middle Marsh Fm	Lincs	TF3332	52°52·4'	0°1·0'W	FM	131
Middlemarsh Fm	Lincs	TF5263	53°8·8'	0°16·8'E	FM	122
Middle Marsh Ho	Lincs	TF3629	52°50·7'	0°1·6'E	X	131
Middle Marwood	Devon	SS5338	51°7·6'	4°5·7'W	T	180
Middle Mause	Pth & Kin	NO1648	56°37·2'	3°21·7'W	X	53
Middle Mayfield	Staffs	SK1444	52°59·8'	1°47·1'W	T	119,128
Middle Mill	Pemb	SM8025	51°53·1'	5°11·4'W	T	157
Middle Mill Fm	Glos	ST6995	51°39·4'	2°26·5'W	FM	162
Middle Monynut	Scot Bord	NT7264	55°52·4'	2°26·4'W	X	67
Middle Moor	Cald	SD9834	53°48·4'	2°1·4'W	X	103
Middle Moor	Cambs	TL2689	52°29·3'	0°8·3'W	X	142
Middle Moor	Cumbr	NY5745	54°48·1'	2°39·7'W	X	86
Middle Moor	Derby	SK0488	53°23·6'	1°56·0'W	X	110
Middle Moor	Derby	SK3163	53°10·0'	1°31·8'W	X	119
Middlemoor	Devon	SX4972	50°31·9'	4°7·5'W	T	191,201
Middlemoor	Devon	SX4972	50°31·9'	4°7·5'W	T	191,201
Middle Moor	D & G	NS8610	55°22·5'	3°47·5'W	X	71,78
Middlemoor	Heref	SO3264	52°16·4'	2°59·4'W	X	137,148
Middle Moor	Northum	NT9008	55°22·2'	2°9·0'W	X	80
Middle Moor	Northum	NU1423	55°30·3'	1°46·3'W	X	75
Middle Moor	Northum	NZ2389	55°11·9'	1°37·9'W	X	81
Middle Moor	N Yks	SD9174	54°9·9'	2°7·9'W	X	98
Middle Moor	Somer	ST4028	51°3·1'	2°51·0'W	X	193
Middlemoor Br	Somer	ST3231	51°4·7'	2°57·9'W	X	182
Middlemoor Cross	Devon	SS6016	50°55·8'	3°59·2'W	X	180
Middlemoor Fm	Cambs	TL2788	52°28·7'	0°7·4'W	FM	142
Middlemoor Fm	Derby	SK1756	53°6·3'	1°44·4'W	FM	119
Middle Moor Fm	Lincs	SE8501	53°30·2'	0°42·7'W	FM	112
Middlemoor Fm	N Yks	SE1499	54°23·4'	1°46·6'W	FM	99
Middlemoor House	Cumbr	NY2451	54°51·1'	3°10·6'W	X	85
Middlemore Fm	Northnts	SP5665	52°17·1'	1°10·3'W	FM	152
Middle Morrey	Shrops	SJ6240	52°57·6'	2°33·5'W	X	118
Middlemoss	D & G	NY4085	55°9·6'	2°56·1'W	X	79
Middle Moss	Sheff	SK2094	53°26·8'	1°41·5'W	X	110
Middlemoss Head	D & G	NY3985	55°9·6'	2°57·0'W	H	79
Middle Mount Barrow	Cumbr	SD2875	54°10·2'	3°5·8'W	X	96,97
Middle Mouse or Yngs Badrig	I of Angl	SH3895	53°25·9'	4°25·9'W	X	114
Middle Mown Meadows	Durham	NZ1535	54°42·8'	1°45·6'W	X	92
Middlemuir	Aberd	NJ5410	57°11·0'	2°45·2'W	X	37
Middlemuir	Aberd	NJ8643	57°28·9'	2°13·6'W	T	30
Middlemuir	Aberd	NJ9057	57°36·4'	2°9·6'W	T	30
Middlemuir	Aberd	NJ9420	57°16·5'	2°5·5'W	X	38
Middlemuir	Aberd	NK0461	57°38·6'	1°55·5'W	X	30
Middle Muir	S Lanak	NS8525	55°30·6'	3°48·8'W	X	71,72
Middlemuir Croft	Aberd	NJ9320	57°16·5'	2°6·5'W	X	38
Middle Newham	Northum	NZ1076	55°4·9'	1°50·2'W	X	88
Middle Norton	C of Edin	NT1472	55°56·3'	3°22·2'W	X	65
Middle Norton Fm	Glos	SP1541	52°4·3'	1°46·5'W	FM	151
Middle Old Park	Surrey	SU8247	51°13·2'	0°49·2'W	X	186
Middle Ord	Northum	NT9650	55°44·9'	2°3·4'W	X	74,75
Middle Park Fm	Kent	TR0836	51°5·4'	0°58·6'E	FM	179,189
Middle Park Fm	Oxon	SP5711	51°47·9'	1°10·0'W	FM	164
Middlepark of Cloquhat	Pth & Kin	NO1452	56°39·4'	3°23·7'W	X	53
Middle Parks Fm	N Yks	SE3075	54°10·4'	1°32·0'W	FM	99
Middlepart	N Ayr	NS2543	55°39·2'	4°46·5'W	X	63,70
Middlepart	Northum	NZ0880	55°7·1'	1°52·0'W	X	81
Middle Pasture	N Yks	SD8075	54°10·5'	2°18·0'W	X	98
Middle Pasture	N Yks	SD9380	54°13·2'	2°6·0'W	X	98
Middlepeak	Derby	SK2855	53°5·7'	1°34·5'W	X	119
Middle Plantn	E Yorks	TA0669	54°6·6'	0°22·3'W	F	101
Middle Plantn	N Yks	SD9255	53°59·7'	2°6·9'W	F	103
Middle Point	Glos	SO7105	51°44·8'	2°24·8'W	X	162
Middleport	C of Stoke	SJ8649	53°2·5'	2°12·1'W	T	118
Middle Poultney Fm	Leic	SP5885	52°27·8'	1°8·4'W	FM	140
Middle Quarter	Kent	TQ8938	51°6·8'	0°42·4'E	T	189
Middlequarter	N Eil	NF8074	57°38·8'	7°21·4'W	T	18
Middle Rainton	Sund	NZ3347	54°49·2'	1°28·8'W	T	88
Middle Rasen	Lincs	TF0889	53°23·4'	0°22·1'W	T	112,121
Middle Rasen Plantn	Lincs	TF1091	53°24·5'	0°20·3'W	F	113
Middleridge	S Ayr	NS2607	55°19·8'	4°44·2'W	X	70,76
Middle Ridge Down	Wilts	ST9149	51°14·6'	2°7·3'W	X	184
Middlerig	Falk	NS9177	55°58·7'	3°44·4'W	T	65
Middle Rig	Scot Bord	NT3733	55°35·4'	2°59·5'W	X	73
Middle Rig	S Lanak	NS7139	55°37·9'	4°2·5'W	H	71
Middle Rig	S Lanak	NT0115	55°25·4'	3°33·4'W	X	78
Middle Rig	S Lanak	NT0431	55°34·0'	3°30·9'W	H	72
Middlerig	W Loth	NS9568	55°53·9'	3°40·3'W	X	65
Middle Rigg	Durham	NY8539	54°45·0'	2°13·6'W	X	91,92
Middlerigg	Falk	NS8472	55°55·9'	3°51·0'W	X	65
Middle Rigg	Northum	NY7847	54°49·3'	2°20·1'W	X	86,87
Middle Rigg	N Yks	SE7997	54°22·0'	0°46·6'W	X	94,100
Middle Rigg	Pth & Kin	NO0608	56°15·6'	3°30·6'W	X	58
Middlerigg Fm	N Yks	SE2367	54°6·1'	1°38·5'W	FM	99
Middle Road Fm	Warw	SP3561	52°15·0'	1°28·8'W	FM	151
Middle Rocombe	Devon	SX9069	50°30·9'	3°32·7'W	T	202
Middle Row	Cumbr	NY5862	54°57·3'	2°38·9'W	X	86
Middle Row	Northum	NY7049	54°50·3'	2°27·6'W	X	86,87
Middles	Durham	NY9847	54°49·3'	2°1·4'W	X	87
Middle Salter	Lancs	SD6063	54°3·9'	2°36·3'W	X	97
Middlesber	N Yks	SD7666	54°5·6'	2°21·6'W	X	98
Middlesbrough	Midd	NZ5118	54°33·5'	1°12·3'W	T	93
Middlesceugh	Cumbr	NY4041	54°45·9'	2°55·5'W	T	85
Middlesceugh Hall	Cumbr	NY4040	54°45·3'	2°55·5'W	X	85
Middle Seal Clough	Derby	SK1089	53°24·1'	1°50·6'W	X	110
Middles Fm	Durham	NZ0646	54°48·8'	1°54·0'W	FM	87
Middles Fm	Durham	NZ1048	54°49·8'	1°50·2'W	FM	88
Middle Shadymoor	Shrops	SJ4502	52°37·0'	2°48·3'W	X	126
Middle Shank	Northum	NT7305	55°20·5'	2°25·1'W	X	80
Middleshaw	Cumbr	SD5589	54°17·9'	2°41·1'W	T	97
Middleshaw	D & G	NY1475	55°4·0'	3°20·4'W	T	85
Middle Shield Beck	Cumbr	NY6171	55°2·2'	2°36·2'W	W	86
Middle Shield Park	Cumbr	NY6070	55°1·6'	2°37·1'W	X	86
Middle Shield Rigg	Cumbr	NY6270	55°1·6'	2°35·2'W	X	86
Middle Side	Durham	NY9326	54°38·0'	2°6·1'W	T	91,92
Middle Skerr	Northum	NU0348	55°43·8'	1°56·7'W	X	75
Middle Skerry	Orkney	HY2405	58°55·8'	3°18·7'W	X	6,7
Middle Skyreholme	N Yks	SE0660	54°2·4'	1°54·1'W	X	99
Middlesmoor	N Yks	SD7063	54°4·0'	2°27·1'W	X	98
Middlesmoor	N Yks	SE0974	54°9·9'	1°51·3'W	T	99
Middlesmoor Pasture	N Yks	SD9571	54°8·3'	2°4·2'W	X	98
Middle Softlaw	Scot Bord	NT7430	55°34·0'	2°24·3'W	X	74
Middle Sontley	Wrex	SJ3246	53°0·7'	3°0·4'W	X	117
Middle South Fm	N Yks	SE2265	54°5·1'	1°39·4'W	FM	99
Middlestead	Scot Bord	NT4526	55°31·7'	2°51·8'W	X	73
Middlesteads Fm	Northum	NZ2590	55°12·5'	1°36·0'W	FM	81
Middles, The	Wilts	ST8432	51°5·5'	2°13·3'W	X	183
Middle Stoford	Somer	ST1821	50°59·2'	3°9·7'W	T	181,193
Middle Stoke	Cov	SP3579	52°24·7'	1°28·7'W	T	140
Middle Stoke	Medway	TQ8375	51°26·9'	0°38·4'E	T	178
Middle Stone	Corn	SW9236	50°11·5'	4°54·5'W	X	204
Middlestone	Durham	NZ2531	54°40·7'	1°36·3'W	T	93
Middle Stone Fm	Somer	ST0931	51°4·5'	3°17·6'W	FM	181
Middlestone Moor	Durham	NZ2432	54°41·2'	1°37·2'W	T	93
Middle Stotfold	Hartpl	NZ4529	54°39·5'	1°17·7'W	X	93
Middlestots	Scot Bord	NT8250	55°44·8'	2°16·8'W	X	67,74
Middle Stoughton	Somer	ST4249	51°14·5'	2°49·5'W	T	182
Middlestown	Wakf	SE2617	53°39·2'	1°36·0'W	T	110
Middle Strath	W Loth	NS9272	55°56·0'	3°43·3'W	X	65
Middle Strath	W Loth	NS9272	55°56·0'	3°43·3'W	X	65
Middle Street	Glos	SO7704	51°44·3'	2°19·6'W	T	162
Middlestye Ho	N Yks	SE4697	54°22·2'	1°17·1'W	X	100
Middle Swainston	Durham	NZ4129	54°39·5'	1°21·4'W	X	93
Middle Swan Beck	Cumbr	NY3819	54°34·0'	2°57·1'W	W	90
Middletack	Aberd	NJ8146	57°30·5'	2°18·6'W	X	29,30
Middletack	Aberd	NJ9960	57°38·1'	2°0·5'W	X	30
Middle Taphouse	Corn	SX1763	50°26·5'	4°34·3'W	T	201
Middlethird	Aberd	NJ8741	57°27·8'	2°12·5'W	X	30
Middlethird	Aberd	NJ9653	57°34·3'	2°3·6'W	X	30
Middlethird	Aberd	NJ9845	57°30·0'	2°1·5'W	X	30
Middle Third	E Ayr	NS5235	55°35·4'	4°20·5'W	X	70
Middle Third	Pth & Kin	NO0312	56°17·7'	3°33·6'W	X	58
Middlethird	Scot Bord	NT6743	55°41·0'	2°31·1'W	X	74
Middlethorpe	York	SE5948	53°55·7'	1°5·7'W	T	105
Middlethorpe Fm	E Yorks	SE8945	53°53·8'	0°38·3'W	FM	106
Middlethorpe Fm	Hartpl	NZ4736	54°43·3'	1°15·8'W	FM	93
Middlethorpe Grange	Notts	SK7558	53°7·1'	0°52·4'W	X	120
Middlethorpe Grange	York	SE5948	53°55·7'	1°5·7'W	X	105
Middlethorpe Ings	York	SE6048	53°55·7'	1°4·8'W	X	105
Middle Threave	D & G	NX3658	54°53·6'	4°33·0'W	X	83
Middleton	Aberd	NJ7322	57°17·5'	2°26·4'W	X	38
Middleton	Aberd	NJ8264	57°40·2'	2°17·6'W	X	29,30
Middleton	Aberd	NJ8419	57°15·9'	2°15·5'W	X	38
Middleton	Aberd	NJ9514	57°13·3'	2°4·5'W	X	38
Middleton	Aberd	NO6673	56°51·1'	2°33·0'W	X	45
Middleton	Aberd	NO7373	56°51·1'	2°26·1'W	X	45
Middleton	Angus	NO2455	56°41·1'	3°14·0'W	X	53
Middleton	Angus	NO5848	56°37·6'	2°40·6'W	T	54
Middleton	Arg & Bt	NL9443	56°29·0'	6°57·8'W	T	46
Middleton	C of Dun	NO4234	56°29·9'	2°56·1'W	X	54
Middleton	Cumbr	NY6501	54°24·4'	2°31·9'W	X	91
Middleton	Cumbr	SD6286	54°16·3'	2°34·6'W	T	97
Middleton	Derby	SK1963	53°10·1'	1°42·5'W	T	119
Middleton	Derby	SK2756	53°6·3'	1°35·4'W	T	119
Middleton	E Renf	NS4457	55°47·1'	4°28·8'W	X	64
Middleton	E Renf	NS4954	55°45·6'	4°24·0'W	X	64
Middleton	Essex	TL8739	52°1·3'	0°43·9'E	T	155
Middleton	Hants	SU4244	51°11·9'	1°23·5'W	T	185
Middleton	Hartpl	NZ5233	54°41·6'	1°11·2'W	T	93
Middleton	Heref	SO5469	52°19·3'	2°41·1'W	T	137,138
Middleton	Highld	NN6293	57°0·7'	4°15·9'W	X	35
Middleton	I of W	SZ3386	50°40·6'	1°31·6'W	T	196
Middleton	Lancs	SD4258	54°1·1'	2°52·7'W	T	102
Middleton	Leeds	SE2927	53°44·6'	1°33·2'W	T	104
Middleton	Midlo	NT3657	55°48·4'	3°0·8'W	T	66,73
Middleton	Mil Key	SP8839	52°2·8'	0°42·6'W	X	152
Middleton	Moray	NJ2054	57°34·4'	3°19·8'W	X	28
Middleton	N Ayr	NS2162	55°49·3'	4°51·0'W	X	63
Middleton	N Ayr	NS3641	55°38·4'	4°35·9'W	X	70
Middleton	N Ayr	NS3952	55°44·3'	4°33·4'W	X	63
Middleton	Norf	TF6616	52°43·2'	0°27·9'E	T	132
Middleton	Northnts	SP8390	52°30·3'	0°46·2'W	T	141
Middleton	Northum	NU1035	55°36·8'	1°50·0'W	T	75
Middleton	Northum	NZ0685	55°9·8'	1°53·9'W	T	81
Middleton	N Yks	SD9643	53°53·2'	2°3·2'W	T	103
Middleton	N Yks	SE1249	53°56·5'	1°48·6'W	T	104
Middleton	N Yks	SE7885	54°15·5'	0°47·7'W	T	94,100
Middleton	Pth & Kin	NN7817	56°20·0'	3°58·0'W	X	57
Middleton	Pth & Kin	NN8714	56°18·6'	3°49·1'W	X	58
Middleton	Pth & Kin	NN9054	56°40·1'	3°47·2'W	X	52
Middleton	Pth & Kin	NO0839	56°32·3'	3°29·3'W	X	52,53
Middleton	Pth & Kin	NO1206	56°14·6'	3°24·8'W	X	58
Middleton	Pth & Kin	NO1447	56°36·7'	3°23·6'W	X	53
Middleton	Pth & Kin	NO1728	56°26·5'	3°20·3'W	X	53,58
Middleton	Renf	NS4565	55°51·5'	4°28·1'W	X	64
Middleton	Roch	SD8706	53°33·3'	2°11·4'W	T	109
Middleton	Shrops	SJ3129	52°51·5'	3°1·1'W	T	126
Middleton	Shrops	SO5377	52°23·6'	2°41·0'W	T	137,138
Middleton	Stir	NS6095	56°7·9'	4°14·7'W	X	57
Middleton	Suff	TM4367	52°15·1'	1°34·0'E	T	156
Middleton	Swan	SS4287	51°33·8'	4°16·4'W	T	159
Middleton	Warw	SP1798	52°35·0'	1°44·5'W	T	139
Middleton	W Dunb	NS4275	55°56·8'	4°31·4'W	X	64
Middleton Baggot	Shrops	SO6290	52°30·6'	2°33·2'W	T	138
Middleton Bank Top	Northum	NZ0583	55°8·7'	1°54·9'W	X	81
Middleton Barton	Devon	ST1811	50°53·8'	3°9·6'W	X	192,193
Middleton Bottom	Somer	ST0132	51°5·0'	3°24·4'W	F	181
Middleton Carr	N Yks	SE7683	54°14·5'	0°49·6'W	X	100
Middleton Cheney	Northnts	SP5041	52°4·1'	1°15·8'W	T	151
Middleton Common	Derby	SK1763	53°10·1'	1°44·3'W	X	119
Middleton Common	Durham	NY9531	54°40·7'	2°4·2'W	X	91,92
Middleton Court	Shrops	SO5477	52°23·6'	2°40·2'W	X	137,138
Middleton Court	Somer	ST0132	51°5·0'	3°24·4'W	X	181
Middleton Crags	Northum	NT9721	55°29·2'	2°2·4'W	X	75
Middleton Dale	Derby	SK2175	53°16·5'	1°40·7'W	X	119
Middleton Dean	Northum	NT9922	55°29·8'	2°0·5'W	X	75
Middleton Down	Wilts	ST9246	51°13·0'	2°6·5'W	X	184
Middleton Fell	Cumbr	SD6586	54°16·4'	2°31·8'W	X	97
Middleton Fm	Hants	SU4144	51°11·9'	1°24·4'W	FM	185
Middleton Fm	Kent	TQ6266	51°22·4'	0°20·0'E	FM	177
Middleton Fm	Kent	TQ8036	51°5·9'	0°34·6'E	FM	188
Middleton Fm	Pemb	SN1411	51°46·2'	4°41·4'W	FM	158
Middleton Fossoway	Pth & Kin	NO0202	56°12·3'	3°34·3'W	X	58
Middleton Grange	E Yorks	SE9149	53°56·0'	0°36·4'W	X	106
Middleton Grange	N Yks	NZ4608	54°28·2'	1°17·0'W	X	93
Middleton Green	Staffs	SJ9935	52°55·0'	2°0·5'W	T	127
Middle Tongue	Cumbr	NY3227	54°38·3'	3°2·8'W	X	90
Middle Tongue	Cumbr	NY6932	54°41·2'	2°28·4'W	X	91
Middle Tongue	Cumbr	NY7324	54°36·9'	2°24·7'W	X	91
Middle Tongue	Cumbr	SD6795	54°21·2'	2°30·0'W	X	98
Middle Tongue	N Yks	SD9181	54°13·7'	2°7·9'W	X	98
Middle Tongue	N Yks	SD9495	54°21·3'	2°5·1'W	X	98
Middle Tongue	N Yks	SE0958	54°1·3'	1°51·3'W	X	104
Middle Tongue Tarn	N Yks	SD9081	54°13·7'	2°8·8'W	W	98
Middleton Hall	Carm	SN5218	51°50·7'	4°8·5'W	X	159
Middleton Hall	Cumbr	SD6287	54°16·9'	2°34·6'W	A	97
Middleton Hall	Darl	NZ3513	54°30·9'	1°27·1'W	X	93
Middleton Hall	Lancs	SD5537	53°49·9'	2°40·6'W	X	102
Middleton Hall	Midlo	NT3658	55°48·9'	3°0·8'W	X	66,73
Middleton Hall	Northum	NT9825	55°31·4'	2°1·5'W	T	75
Middleton Hall	Suff	TM2883	52°24·1'	1°21·5'E	X	156
Middleton Hall	Warw	SP1998	52°35·0'	1°42·8'W	A	139
Middleton Hall Fm	Shrops	SO2999	52°35·3'	3°2·5'W	FM	137
Middletonhill	S Ayr	NS4627	55°31·0'	4°25·9'W	X	70
Middleton Hill	Wilts	SU0423	51°0·6'	1°56·2'W	X	184
Middleton Ho	Durham	NZ1719	54°34·2'	1°43·8'W	X	92
Middleton Ho	Pth & Kin	NT1395	56°8·6'	3°23·6'W	X	58
Middleton House Fm	Hartpl	NZ4432	54°41·1'	1°18·6'W	FM	93
Middleton House Fm	Warw	SP1896	52°33·9'	1°43·7'W	FM	139
Middleton in Teesdale	Durham	NY9425	54°37·5'	2°5·2'W	T	91,92
Middleton Junction	Oldham	SD8804	53°32·2'	2°10·5'W	T	109
Middleton Lodge	E Yorks	SE9249	53°56·0'	0°35·5'W	X	106
Middleton Lodge	N Yks	NZ2206	54°27·2'	1°39·2'W	X	93
Middleton Lodge	N Yks	NZ4710	54°29·2'	1°16·0'W	X	93
Middleton Lodge Fm	Northnts	SP5040	52°3·6'	1°15·8'W	FM	151
Middleton Lodge Fm	Northnts	SP8588	52°29·2'	0°44·5'W	FM	141
Middleton Mains	Midlo	NT3858	55°48·9'	2°58·9'W	X	66,73
Middleton Manor	E Susx	TQ3414	50°54·8'	0°5·2'W	X	198
Middleton Mill	Northum	NZ0584	55°9·3'	1°54·9'W	X	81
Middletonmoor	Angus	NO5951	56°39·2'	2°39·7'W	X	54
Middleton Moor	Derby	SK2074	53°16·0'	1°41·6'W	X	119
Middleton Moor	Midlo	NT3857	55°48·4'	2°58·9'W	X	66,73
Middleton Moor	N Yks	SE1151	53°57·5'	1°49·5'W	X	104
Middleton Moor	Suff	TM4167	52°15·1'	1°32·3'E	T	156
Middleton Moor Enclosure	N Yks	SE1152	53°58·1'	1°49·5'W	X	104
Middleton Mount	Norf	TF6616	52°43·2'	0°27·9'E	A	132
Middleton North Burn	Midlo	NT3557	55°48·4'	3°1·8'W	W	66,73
Middleton of Aberarder	Aberd	NO2093	57°1·5'	3°18·6'W	X	36,44
Middleton of Aldie	Pth & Kin	NT0599	56°10·7'	3°31·4'W	X	58
Middleton of Blackford	Aberd	NJ7035	57°24·5'	2°29·5'W	X	29
Middleton of Dalrulzian	Pth & Kin	NO1358	56°42·6'	3°24·8'W	T	53
Middleton of Fonab	Pth & Kin	NN9357	56°41·8'	3°44·4'W	X	52
Middleton of Lonmay	Aberd	NK0560	57°38·1'	1°54·5'W	X	30
Middleton of Potterton	Aberd	NJ9315	57°13·8'	2°6·5'W	X	38
Middleton of Rattray	Aberd	NK0956	57°35·9'	1°50·5'W	X	30
Middleton of Rora	Aberd	NK0649	57°32·1'	1°53·5'W	X	30
Middleton Old Town	Northum	NT9923	55°30·3'	2°0·5'W	A	75
Middleton One Row	Darl	NZ3512	54°30·4'	1°27·1'W	T	93
Middleton-on-Leven	N Yks	NZ4609	54°28·7'	1°17·0'W	T	93
Middleton-on-Sea	W Susx	SU9700	50°47·7'	0°37·0'W	T	197
Middleton on the Hill	Heref	SO5464	52°16·6'	2°40·1'W	T	137,138,149
Middleton on-the-Wolds	E Yorks	SE9449	53°56·0'	0°33·7'W	T	106
Middleton Park	C of Aber	NJ9211	57°11·6'	2°7·5'W	T	38
Middleton Park	Derby	SK1837	52°56·0'	1°43·5'W	X	128
Middleton Park	Leeds	SE3029	53°45·6'	1°32·3'W	X	104
Middleton Park	Oxon	SP5223	51°54·4'	1°14·3'W	X	164
Middleton Place	Cumbr	SD0992	54°19·2'	3°23·5'W	T	96
Middleton Priors	Shrops	SO6290	52°30·6'	2°33·2'W	T	138
Middleton Quernhow	N Yks	SE3378	54°12·0'	1°29·2'W	T	99
Middleton Sands	Lancs	SD3958	54°1·1'	2°55·4'W	X	102
Middleton Scriven	Shrops	SO6887	52°29·0'	2°27·9'W	T	138
Middleton South	Northum	NZ0483	55°8·7'	1°55·8'W	X	81
Middleton South Burn	Midlo	NT3557	55°48·4'	3°1·8'W	W	66,73
Middleton St George	Darl	NZ3413	54°30·9'	1°28·1'W	T	93
Middleton Stoney	Oxon	SP5323	51°54·4'	1°13·4'W	T	164
Middleton Top Visitor's Centre	Derby	SK2755	53°5·7'	1°35·4'W	X	119
Middleton Towers	Norf	TF6617	52°43·7'	0°27·9'E	A	132
Middleton Tyas	N Yks	NZ2205	54°26·6'	1°39·2'W	T	93
Middleton Wold	E Yorks	SE9248	53°55·4'	0°35·5'W	X	106
Middleton Wood	Derby	SK2756	53°6·3'	1°35·4'W	F	119
Middleton Wood	N Yks	NZ4509	54°28·7'	1°17·9'W	F	93
Middleton Wood	V of Glam	ST0868	51°24·5'	3°19·0'W	F	170
Middleton Woods	Brad	SE1148	53°55·9'	1°49·5'W	F	104
Middle Top	Cumbr	NY5852	54°51·9'	2°38·8'W	H	86

Middle Tor	Devon	SX6685	50°39·2'	3°53·4'W	H	191
Middle Toucks	Aberd	NO8484	56°57·1'	2°15·3'W	X	45
Middletoun	Scot Bord	NT4450	55°44·7'	2°53·1'W	X	66,73
Middletown	Cumbr	NX9908	54°27·7'	3°33·1'W	T	89
Middletown	Devon	SX7992	50°43·1'	3°42·5'W	X	191
Middletown	Glos	SO7626	51°56·2'	2°20·6'W	X	162
Middle Town	I Scilly	SV9216	49°58·1'	6°17·4'W	T	203
Middletown	N Som	ST4571	51°25·1'	2°47·1'W	T	171,172
Middletown	Powys	SJ3012	52°42·3'	3°1·8'W	T	126
Middletown	Warw	SP0662	52°15·6'	1°54·3'W	T	150
Middletown Fm	Powys	SJ2911	52°41·8'	3°2·6'W	FM	126
Middletown Hill	Powys	SJ3013	52°42·8'	3°1·8'W	H	126
Middle Trewern	Heref	SO3231	51°58·6'	2°59·0'W	X	161
Middle Tysoe	Warw	SP3344	52°5·8'	1°30·7'W	T	151
Middle Wallop	Hants	SU2937	51°8·1'	1°34·7'W	T	185
Middle Walton	Shrops	SJ2905	52°38·5'	3°2·6'W	X	126
Middle Warren	Hartpl	NZ4934	54°42·2'	1°14·0'W	X	93
Middle Warren Fm	Norf	TL7593	52°30·6'	0°35·1'E	FM	143
Middleway	Carm	SN2015	51°48·5'	4°36·3'W	X	158
Middleway, The	Essex	TQ9690	51°34·7'	0°50·1'E	W	178
Middle Weald	Mil Key	SP7938	52°2·3'	0°50·5'W	T	152
Middle West Fm	Peterb	TF2504	52°37·4'	0°8·8'W	FM	142
Middle Wheatley	Corn	SX2494	50°43·4'	4°29·2'W	X	190
Middle Whitstone	Devon	SS7818	50°57·1'	3°43·8'W	X	180
Middlewich	Ches	SJ7066	53°11·7'	2°26·5'W	T	118
Middlewick	Devon	SS8213	50°54·5'	3°40·3'W	X	181
Middle Wick	Essex	TR0198	51°38·9'	0°54·7'E	X	168
Middle Wick	Glos	ST7196	51°40·0'	2°24·8'W	T	162
Middlewick	Wilts	ST8571	51°26·5'	2°12·6'W	T	173
Middle Winterslow	Wilts	SU2332	51°5·4'	1°39·9'W	T	184
Middle Wood	Bath & NE Somer	ST7261	51°21·1'	2°23·7'W	F	172
Middlewood	Ches	SJ9484	53°21·4'	2°5·0'W	T	109
Middlewood	Corn	SX2775	50°33·2'	4°26·2'W	T	201
Middlewood	Devon	SS6121	50°58·5'	3°58·4'W	X	180
Middlewood	Heref	SO2844	52°5·6'	3°2·7'W	X	148,161
Middlewood	Lancs	SD7643	53°53·2'	2°21·5'W	X	103
Middlewood	Lancs	SD8440	53°51·6'	2°14·2'W	X	103
Middle Wood	Oxon	SU2882	51°32·4'	1°35·4'W	F	174
Middle Wood	Powys	SJ1114	52°43·2'	3°18·7'W	F	125
Middlewood	Sheff	SK3191	53°25·1'	1°31·6'W	T	110,111
Middlewood	Sheff	SK3192	53°25·7'	1°31·6'W	T	110,111
Middle Wood	Suff	TM0649	52°6·3'	1°0·9'E	F	155
Middlewood Fm	Durham	NZ1546	54°48·8'	1°45·6'W	FM	88
Middle Wood Fm	Notts	SK6996	53°27·6'	0°57·2'W	FM	111
Middlewood Fm	Powys	SO1323	51°54·2'	3°15·5'W	FM	161
Middle Woodford	Wilts	SU1136	51°7·6'	1°50·2'W	T	184
Middlewood Green	Suff	TM0961	52°12·7'	1°4·0'E	T	155
Middlewood Hall	Barns	SE4204	53°32·1'	1°21·6'W	X	111
Middlewood Way	Ches	SJ9482	53°20·3'	2°5·0'W	X	109
Middle Wyke Fm	Hants	SU4049	51°14·6'	1°25·2'W	FM	185
Middleyard	Glos	SO8203	51°43·8'	2°15·2'W	T	162
Middle Yeo Fm	Devon	SS7304	50°49·5'	3°47·8'W	FM	191
Middlezoy	Somer	ST3732	51°5·3'	2°53·6'W	T	182
Middlington Ho	Hants	SU6017	50°57·2'	1°8·4'W	X	185
Mid Dod	Angus	NO4949	56°38·1'	2°49·4'W	X	54
Middop Hall	Lancs	SD8345	53°54·3'	2°15·1'W	X	103
Middop Wood	Lancs	SD8344	53°53·8'	2°15·1'W	F	103
Middridge	Durham	NZ2526	54°38·0'	1°36·3'W	T	93
Middridge Grange	Darl	NZ2424	54°36·9'	1°37·3'W	X	93
Mid Drumloch	S Lanak	NS6751	55°44·3'	4°6·7'W	X	64
Mid Dublin	Shetld	HU5136	60°6·6'	1°4·5'W	X	4
Mid Duloch	Fife	NT1385	56°3·3'	3°23·4'W	X	65
Midelney	Somer	ST4122	50°59·9'	2°50·1'W	T	193
Midelney Place	Somer	ST4025	51°1·5'	2°50·9'W	X	193
Mid Fell	Northum	NY6398	55°16·7'	2°34·5'W	H	80
Mid Fiddes	Aberd	NO8181	56°55·5'	2°18·3'W	X	45
Midfield	Cambs	TL4163	52°15·1'	0°4·3'E	X	154
Midfield	Cumbr	NY6505	54°26·6'	2°32·0'W	X	91
Midfield	Fife	NT0391	56°6·4'	3°33·1'W	X	58
Midfield	Highld	NC5864	58°32·7'	4°25·9'W	T	10
Mid Field	Shetld	HP6201	60°41·5'	0°51·4'W	X	1
Mid Field	Shetld	HU2579	60°29·9'	1°32·2'W	X	3
Mid Field	Shetld	HU3149	60°13·7'	1°25·9'W	H	3
Mid Field	Shetld	HU3163	60°21·3'	1°25·8'W	H	3
Mid Field	Shetld	HU3183	60°32·0'	1°25·6'W	H	1,3
Mid Field	Shetld	HU3632	60°4·5'	1°20·7'W	H	4
Mid Field	Shetld	HU3970	60°25·0'	1°17·0'W	X	2,3
Midfield	Shetld	HU4566	60°22·8'	1°10·5'W	X	2,3
Mid Field	Shetld	HU4624	60°0·2'	1°10·0'W	H	4
Midfield Ho	Midlo	NT2964	55°52·1'	3°7·6'W	X	66
Midfleenas	Highld	NH9049	57°31·3'	3°49·7'W	X	27
Midford	Bath & NE Somer	ST7560	51°20·5'	2°21·1'W	T	172
Midford Brook	Bath & NE Somer	ST7661	51°21·1'	2°20·3'W	W	172
Midford Cas	Bath & NE Somer	ST7561	51°21·1'	2°21·2'W	X	172
Mid Fordun	Pth & Kin	NN9415	56°19·2'	3°42·4'W	X	58
Mid Forest	N Lanak	NS7874	55°56·9'	3°56·8'W	X	64
Mid Foulshiels	W Loth	NS9764	55°51·7'	3°38·3'W	X	65
Midgard	Scot Bord	NT5415	55°25·9'	2°43·2'W	X	79
Midgard	Scot Bord	NT5516	55°26·4'	2°42·2'W	T	80
Mid Garrary	D & G	NX5378	55°4·7'	4°17·7'W	X	77
Midgarth	Orkney	HY3922	59°5·1'	3°3·4'W	X	6
Mid Garth	Orkney	HY4329	59°8·9'	2°59·3'W	X	5,6
Mid Garth	Orkney	HY6328	59°8·5'	2°38·3'W	X	5
Midgarth	Shetld	HU4940	60°8·8'	1°6·6'W	X	4
Midgarth	Shetld	HU5285	60°33·0'	1°2·6'W	X	1,2,3
Mid-Gavin Fm	Renf	NS3859	55°48·1'	4°34·6'W	FM	63
Midga Water	Shetld	HP6307	60°44·7'	0°50·2'W	W	1
Midge Brook	Ches	SJ8167	53°12·2'	2°16·7'W	W	118
Midgebrook Fm	Ches	SJ8266	53°11·7'	2°15·8'W	FM	118
Midge Hall	Lancs	SD5123	53°42·3'	2°44·1'W	T	102
Midge Hall	Lancs	SD6632	53°47·2'	2°30·6'W	X	103
Midge Hall	N Yks	NZ7616	54°32·3'	0°49·1'W	X	94
Midge Hall	Swin	SU1677	51°29·7'	1°45·8'W	X	173
Midge Hall	Wilts	SU0883	51°33·0'	1°52·7'W	X	173
Midgehall Copse	Wilts	SU0684	51°33·5'	1°54·4'W	F	173
Midge Hall Fms	Lancs	SD3916	53°38·5'	2°54·9'W	FM	108
Midge Hill	S Lanak	NT0021	55°28·6'	3°34·5'W	H	72
Midgehole	Cald	SD9928	53°45·1'	2°0·5'W	T	103
Midgeholm	Northum	NY7861	54°56·8'	2°20·2'W	X	86,87
Midgeholme	Cumbr	NY6358	54°55·2'	2°34·2'W	T	86
Midgeholme and Haltonlea West Fell	Cumbr	NY6357	54°54·6'	2°34·2'W	X	86
Midgeholme Moss	Cumbr	NY6066	54°59·5'	2°37·1'W	X	86
Midgehope	Scot Bord	NT2713	55°24·6'	3°8·7'W	X	79
Midgelden	Cald	SD9024	53°43·0'	2°8·7'W	X	103
Midgell Fm	N Som	ST4668	51°24·7'	2°46·2'W	FM	171,172,182
Midger Wood	Glos	ST7989	51°36·2'	2°17·8'W	F	162,172
Midgham	W Berks	SU5567	51°24·2'	1°12·2'W	T	174
Midgham Fm	Hants	SU1312	50°54·7'	1°48·5'W	FM	195
Midgham Green	W Berks	SU5667	51°24·2'	1°11·3'W	T	174
Midgham Ho	W Berks	SU5667	51°24·2'	1°11·3'W	X	174
Midgham Park	W Berks	SU5667	51°24·2'	1°11·3'W	X	174
Midgham Sta	W Berks	SU5766	51°23·6'	1°10·5'W	X	174
Mid Glasslaw	Aberd	NJ8560	57°38·0'	2°14·6'W	X	30
Mid Glen	D & G	NX9565	54°58·4'	3°38·0'W	X	84
Mid Glen	Renf	NS3870	55°54·0'	4°35·0'W	X	63
Mid Gleniron	D & G	NX1861	54°54·9'	4°49·9'W	X	82
Midgley	Cald	SE0226	53°44·1'	1°57·8'W	T	104
Midgley	Wakf	SE2714	53°37·6'	1°35·1'W	T	110
Midgley Fm	Ches	SJ9766	53°11·7'	2°2·3'W	FM	118
Midgley Fm	Leeds	SE2245	53°54·3'	1°39·5'W	FM	104
Midgley Moor	Cald	SE0129	53°45·7'	1°58·7'W	X	104
Mid Grain	Angus	NO4687	56°58·5'	2°52·8'W	W	44
Mid Grain	D & G	NS6604	55°19·0'	4°6·3'W	W	77
Mid Grange Burn	Scot Bord	NT8566	55°53·5'	2°14·0'W	W	67
Midgy Ha	Northum	NY9698	55°16·8'	2°3·3'W	X	81
Mid Haddo	Aberd	NJ7538	57°26·2'	2°24·5'W	X	29
Mid Hangingshaw	S Lanak	NT0032	55°34·5'	3°34·7'W	X	72
Mid Hartfield	Renf	NS4258	55°47·6'	4°30·8'W	X	64
Mid Hartwood	W Loth	NT0160	55°49·6'	3°34·4'W	X	65
Mid Height	D & G	NS9802	55°18·3'	3°36·0'W	H	78
Mid Height	D & G	NT1801	55°18·0'	3°17·1'W	H	79
Mid Height	D & G	NY2489	55°11·6'	3°11·2'W	H	79
Mid Height	D & G	NY4292	55°13·4'	2°54·3'W	H	79
Mid Height	S Lanak	NS9711	55°23·2'	3°37·1'W	H	78
Mid Hill	Aberd	NJ3514	57°13·0'	3°4·1'W	H	37
Mid Hill	Aberd	NO7185	56°57·6'	2°28·2'W	X	45
Mid Hill	Aberd	NO7885	56°57·6'	2°21·3'W	X	45
Mid Hill	Angus	NO2270	56°49·2'	3°16·2'W	H	44
Mid Hill	Arg & Bt	NS0980	55°58·8'	5°3·2'W	X	63
Mid Hill	Arg & Bt	NS3295	56°7·4'	4°41·7'W	H	56
Mid Hill	C of Edin	NT1360	55°49·8'	3°22·9'W	X	65
Mid Hill	D & G	NS6907	55°20·6'	4°3·5'W	H	71,77
Mid Hill	D & G	NS7904	55°19·2'	3°54·0'W	X	78
Mid Hill	D & G	NT0010	55°22·7'	3°34·3'W	H	78
Mid Hill	D & G	NX1674	55°1·8'	4°52·3'W	H	76
Mid Hill	D & G	NX5384	55°8·0'	4°17·9'W	X	77
Mid Hill	D & G	NX7754	54°52·2'	3°54·6'W	H	84
Mid Hill	D & G	NY1588	55°11·0'	3°19·7'W	H	79
Mid Hill	D & G	NY2484	55°8·9'	3°11·1'W	X	79
Mid Hill	D & G	NY2784	55°8·9'	3°8·3'W	H	79
Mid Hill	D & G	NY3485	55°9·5'	3°1·7'W	H	79
Mid Hill	D & G	NY3490	55°12·3'	3°1·8'W	X	79
Mid Hill	E Ayr	NS5112	55°23·0'	4°20·7'W	X	70
Mid Hill	E Ayr	NS5830	55°32·8'	4°14·6'W	H	71
Mid Hill	E Loth	NT6169	55°55·0'	2°37·0'W	X	67
Mid Hill	Highld	NC8324	58°11·6'	3°58·9'W	X	17
Mid Hill	Highld	NC9757	58°29·6'	3°45·5'W	H	11
Mid Hill	Highld	ND0223	58°11·4'	3°39·5'W	H	17
Mid Hill	Northum	NT8829	55°33·5'	2°11·0'W	H	74
Mid Hill	Northum	NT8912	55°24·4'	2°10·0'W	H	80
Mid Hill	Northum	NT9021	55°29·2'	2°9·1'W	H	74,75
Mid Hill	Orkney	HY3308	58°57·5'	3°9·4'W	H	6,7
Mid Hill	Orkney	HY3324	59°6·1'	3°9·7'W	H	6
Mid Hill	S Ayr	NX2889	55°10·2'	4°41·6'W	H	76
Mid Hill	Scot Bord	NT1538	55°37·9'	3°20·6'W	H	72
Mid Hill	Scot Bord	NT2013	55°24·5'	3°15·4'W	X	79
Mid Hill	Scot Bord	NT2215	55°25·6'	3°13·5'W	X	79
Mid Hill	Scot Bord	NT2612	55°24·0'	3°9·7'W	H	79
Mid Hill	Scot Bord	NT3708	55°22·0'	2°59·2'W	H	79
Mid Hill	Scot Bord	NT3813	55°24·7'	2°58·3'W	H	79
Mid Hill	Scot Bord	NT5601	55°18·3'	2°41·2'W	H	80
Mid Hill	Scot Bord	NT8216	55°26·5'	2°16·6'W	H	80
Mid Hill	Scot Bord	NY4295	55°15·0'	2°54·3'W	H	79
Mid Hill	S Lanak	NS6044	55°40·4'	4°13·1'W	H	71
Mid Hill	S Lanak	NS6044	55°40·4'	4°13·1'W	H	71
Mid Hill	S Lanak	NS7422	55°28·8'	3°59·2'W	X	71
Mid Hill	S Lanak	NS9419	55°27·5'	3°40·1'W	H	71,78
Mid Hill	S Lanak	NT0018	55°27·0'	3°34·4'W	H	78
Mid Hill	S Lanak	NT0649	55°43·8'	3°29·4'W	H	72
Mid Hill	Stir	NN5332	56°27·7'	4°22·7'W	H	51
Midhill Fm	S Lanak	NT0342	55°40·0'	3°32·1'W	FM	72
Mid Hill of Glenhead	D & G	NX6399	55°16·2'	4°9·0'W	H	77
Mid Hill or Choc Meadhonach	Highld	NC9820	58°9·7'	3°43·5'W	X	17
Mid Ho	Orkney	HY4603	58°54·9'	2°55·8'W	X	6,7
Mid Ho	Orkney	HY6622	59°5·3'	2°35·1'W	X	5
Mid Ho	Shetld	HU5496	60°38·9'	1°0·2'W	T	1
Mid Holm	Orkney	HY6842	59°16·1'	2°33·2'W	X	5
Mid Holmwood	Surrey	TQ1646	51°12·3'	0°20·0'W	T	187
Midhope	W Loth	NT0778	55°59·4'	3°29·0'W	A	65
Midhope Burn	W Loth	NT0678	55°59·4'	3°30·0'W	W	65
Midhopelaw Pike	Northum	NY8287	55°10·9'	2°16·5'W	H	80
Midhope Moors	Sheff	SK1998	53°28·9'	1°42·4'W	X	110
Midhope Resr	Sheff	SK2299	53°29·5'	1°39·7'W	W	110
Midhopestones	Sheff	SK2399	53°29·5'	1°38·8'W	T	110
Midhops Fm	Warr	SJ6292	53°25·6'	2°33·9'W	FM	109
Midhouse	Orkney	HY2626	59°7·1'	3°17·1'W	X	6
Mid House	Orkney	HY2716	59°1·8'	3°15·8'W	X	6
Midhouse	Orkney	HY2726	59°7·1'	3°16·0'W	X	6
Midhouse	Orkney	HY2823	59°5·5'	3°14·9'W	X	6
Midhouse	Orkney	HY3229	59°8·8'	3°10·8'W	X	6
Midhouse	Orkney	HY3318	59°2·9'	3°9·6'W	X	6
Midhouse	Renf	NS3563	55°50·2'	4°37·6'W	X	63
Midhouse	Shetld	HU3471	60°25·6'	1°22·4'W	X	2,3
Mid Howe	Orkney	HY3730	59°9·4'	3°5·6'W	X	6
Mid Howe (Chambered Cairn)	Orkney	HY3730	59°9·4'	3°5·6'W	A	6
Midhurst	W Susx	SU8821	50°59·1'	0°44·4'W	T	197
Midhurst Common	W Susx	SU8721	50°59·1'	0°45·2'W	X	197
Midhurst & Harting Cycle Route	W Susx	SU8019	50°58·1'	0°51·3'W	X	197
Midi Field	Shetld	HU3823	59°59·7'	1°18·6'W	H	4
Midisi	Shetld	HU5089	60°35·1'	1°4·7'W	X	1,2
Mid Kame	Shetld	HU3891	60°36·3'	1°17·9'W	X	1,2
Mid Kame	Shetld	HU4058	60°18·5'	1°16·1'W	H	2,3
Mid Kelton	D & G	NX7660	54°55·4'	3°55·7'W	X	84
Mid Kinmonth	Aberd	NO7781	56°55·4'	2°22·2'W	X	45
Mid Knock	D & G	NY2990	55°12·2'	3°6·5'W	X	79
Mid Lairgs	Highld	NH7136	57°24·0'	4°8·3'W	X	27
Midlairgs Burn	Highld	NH7235	57°23·5'	4°7·3'W	W	27
Midlake Swatch	I of Angl	SH6581	53°18·8'	4°1·2'W	W	114,115
Mid Lambrook	Somer	ST4218	50°57·7'	2°49·2'W	T	193
Mid Lambroughton	N Ayr	NS3943	55°39·5'	4°33·1'W	X	63,70
Midland	E Ayr	NS4742	55°39·1'	4°25·5'W	X	70
Midland	Orkney	HY3204	58°55·3'	3°10·4'W	T	6,7
Midland	Orkney	HY3923	59°5·6'	3°3·4'W	X	6
Midland	Pemb	SM7022	51°51·2'	5°20·0'W	X	157
Midland Isle	Pemb	SM7409	51°44·3'	5°16·0'W	X	157
Midland Ness	Orkney	HY3203	58°54·8'	3°10·4'W	X	6,7
Midland Railway Centre	Derby	SK4052	53°4·1'	1°23·8'W	X	120
Midlands	Devon	SX5179	50°35·7'	4°5·9'W	X	191,201
Midlands	D & G	NY3474	55°3·6'	3°1·6'W	X	85
Midlands	Essex	TM0002	51°41·1'	0°54·0'E	X	168
Midlands Fm	Traf	SJ7290	53°24·6'	2°24·9'W	FM	109
Mid Lavant	W Susx	SU8508	50°52·1'	0°47·1'W	T	197
Midlaw Burn	D & G	NT1615	55°25·6'	3°19·2'W	W	79
Midlem	Scot Bord	NT5227	55°32·3'	2°45·2'W	T	73
Midlem Burn	Scot Bord	NT5227	55°32·3'	2°45·2'W	W	73
Mid Lenshie	Aberd	NJ6741	57°27·7'	2°32·5'W	X	29
Mid Letter	Arg & Bt	NN0700	56°9·5'	5°6·0'W	X	56
Mid Lettrick	S Lanak	NS6657	55°47·5'	4°7·8'W	X	64
Midley Cottages	Kent	TR0123	50°58·5'	0°52·2'E	X	189
Midlinbank Fm	S Lanak	NS6640	55°38·4'	4°7·3'W	FM	71
Midlock	S Lanak	NS9521	55°28·5'	3°39·2'W	T	72
Midlock Water	S Lanak	NS9820	55°28·0'	3°36·4'W	W	72
Midloe Grange	Cambs	TL1664	52°15·9'	0°17·6'W	X	153
Midloe Wood	Cambs	TL1564	52°16·0'	0°18·5'W	F	153
Mid Lump	D & G	NX4579	55°5·1'	4°25·3'W	X	77
Mid Lundie	Stir	NN7204	56°12·9'	4°3·4'W	X	57
Mid Main	Corn	SX2552	50°20·8'	4°27·2'W	X	201
Mid Main	Highld	NH4239	57°25·1'	4°37·4'W	X	26
Mid Mains	E Loth	NT4871	55°56·0'	2°49·5'W	X	66
Mid Mains	Moray	NJ1966	57°40·9'	3°21·0'W	X	28
Midmar	Aberd	NJ6807	57°9·4'	2°31·3'W	X	38
Midmar Castle	Aberd	NJ7005	57°8·4'	2°29·3'W	A	38
Midmar Forest	Aberd	NJ6904	57°7·8'	2°30·3'W	F	38
Midmar Moss	Aberd	NJ6804	57°7·8'	2°31·3'W	F	38
Mid Mill	Aberd	NJ5515	57°13·7'	2°44·3'W	X	37
Mid Mill	Aberd	NJ7914	57°13·2'	2°20·4'W	X	38
Midmill	Aberd	NK0637	57°25·7'	1°53·5'W	X	30
Mid Moile	D & G	NX0971	55°0·1'	4°58·8'W	X	76
Mid Moncur	N Ayr	NS3243	55°39·3'	4°39·8'W	X	63,70
Midmore	Aberd	NJ5653	57°34·2'	2°43·7'W	X	29
Mid Morile	Highld	NH7926	57°18·8'	4°0·1'W	X	35
Mid Moss	Orkney	HY3108	58°57·5'	3°11·5'W	X	6,7
Mid Mossdale	N Yks	SD8391	54°19·1'	2°15·3'W	X	98
Midmuir	Arg & Bt	NM9523	56°21·6'	5°18·7'W	X	49
Mid Muir	E Ayr	NS5532	55°33·9'	4°17·5'W	X	71
Mid Muntloch	D & G	NX1133	54°39·7'	4°55·4'W	X	82
Mid Murthat	D & G	NY0999	55°16·9'	3°25·5'W	T	78
Midnell Fm	Somer	ST3807	50°51·8'	2°52·5'W	FM	193
Mid Ness	Shetld	HP5205	60°43·7'	1°2·3'W	X	1
Midney	Somer	ST4927	51°2·6'	2°43·3'W	X	183,193
Midnight Fm	N Yks	NZ5803	54°25·4'	1°5·9'W	FM	93
Midoxgate	Highld	NH8278	57°46·8'	3°58·6'W	X	21
Midpark	Aberd	NK0262	57°39·1'	1°57·5'W	X	30
Midpark	Arg & Bt	NS0259	55°47·3'	5°9·0'W	X	63
Midpark	D & G	NX7260	54°55·4'	3°59·4'W	X	83,84
Midpark	D & G	NX7563	54°57·0'	3°56·7'W	X	84
Mid Peebles	Angus	NO6144	56°35·4'	2°37·7'W	X	54
Mid Pitglassie	Aberd	NJ6943	57°28·8'	2°30·6'W	X	29
Midplough	Aberd	NJ5346	57°30·4'	2°46·6'W	X	29
Mid Port	Highld	NJ0629	57°20·8'	3°33·3'W	X	36
Mid Raeburn	D & G	NT2600	55°17·6'	3°9·5'W	X	79
Mid Rig	D & G	NS6400	55°16·8'	4°8·0'W	X	77
Mid Rig	D & G	NS7305	55°19·6'	3°59·7'W	H	71,77
Mid Rig	D & G	NT2014	55°25·1'	3°15·4'W	H	79
Midrig	D & G	NX8878	55°5·3'	3°44·9'W	X	84
Mid Rig	Scot Bord	NT3404	55°19·8'	3°2·0'W	H	79
Mid Rig	Scot Bord	NT3512	55°24·1'	3°1·2'W	H	79
Mid Rig	S Lanak	NS8627	55°31·7'	3°47·9'W	X	71,72
Mid Rigg	N Yks	SD8296	54°21·8'	2°16·2'W	X	98
Mid Ringuinea	D & G	NX0747	54°47·1'	4°59·7'W	X	82
Midrips	E Susx	TR0018	50°55·8'	0°51·2'E	X	189
Midross	Arg & Bt	NS3585	56°2·0'	4°38·5'W	X	56
Mid Savock	Aberd	NJ9523	57°18·1'	2°4·5'W	X	38
Mid Setter	Shetld	HU1760	60°19·7'	1°41·0'W	X	3
Midshade	Aberd	NJ8109	57°10·5'	2°18·4'W	X	38
Mid Shandon	Stir	NS4789	56°4·4'	4°27·0'W	X	57
Midshiels	Scot Bord	NT5317	55°26·9'	2°44·2'W	X	79
Midshires Way	Derby	SK1661	53°9·0'	1°45·2'W	X	119
Mid Skeith	Moray	NJ5059	57°37·4'	2°49·8'W	X	29
Midsomer Norton	Bath & NE Somer	ST6654	51°17·3'	2°28·9'W	T	183
Mid Standard (Cairn)	D & G	NX6981	55°6·6'	4°2·8'W	X	77
Mid Strathore	Fife	NT2897	56°9·9'	3°9·1'W	X	59
Mid Strome	Highld	NG8636	57°22·1'	5°33·1'W	T	24
Midsummer Hill	Heref	SO7637	52°2·1'	2°20·6'W	H	150
Midsummer Hill (Fort)	Heref	SO7637	52°2·1'	2°20·6'W	A	150
Mid Taing	Orkney	HY4307	58°57·1'	2°59·0'W	X	6,7
Mid Tartraven	W Loth	NT0072	55°56·1'	3°35·6'W	X	65
Midthird	Moray	NJ3643	57°28·6'	3°3·6'W	X	28
Midthorpe Fm	Lincs	TF2673	53°14·6'	0°6·3'W	FM	122
Mid Todhills	Cumbr	NY5277	55°5·4'	2°44·7'W	X	86
Midton	Inverc	NS2376	55°56·9'	4°49·6'W	T	63

Midton	S Ayr	NS4130	55°32·5′	4°30·8′W	X	70
Midton of Balgray	E Ayr	NS4434	55°34·7′	4°28·0′W	X	70
Mid Tooin	Orkney	HY3520	59°4·0′	3°7·5′W	H	6
Mid Torrie Fm	Stir	NN6504	56°12·8′	4°10·2′W	FM	57
Mid Torrs	D & G	NX1355	54°51·5′	4°54·4′W	X	82
Midtown	Aberd	NJ4944	57°29·3′	2°50·6′W	X	28,29
Midtown	Aberd	NJ8043	57°28·9′	2°19·6′W	X	29,30
Midtown	Aberd	NO7190	57°0·3′	2°28·2′W	X	38,45
Midtown	Angus	NO4262	56°45·0′	2°56·5′W	X	44
Midtown	Clackm	NS8494	56°7·7′	3°51·5′W	X	58
Midtown	Cumbr	NY0321	54°34·7′	3°29·6′W	X	89
Midtown	D & G	NX8676	55°4·2′	3°46·7′W	X	84
Midtown	D & G	NX9761	54°56·2′	3°36·0′W	X	84
Midtown	D & G	NY1165	54°58·6′	3°23·0′W	X	85
Midtown	Highld	NC5861	58°31·1′	4°25·8′W	T	10
Midtown	Highld	NG8285	57°48·4′	5°39·7′W	T	19
Midtown	Highld	NH6233	57°22·3′	4°17·2′W	X	26
Midtown	Highld	NH6339	57°25·5′	4°16·4′W	X	26
Midtown	Highld	NJ1219	57°15·5′	3°27·1′W	X	36
Midtown	Moray	NJ1965	57°40·3′	3°21·0′W	X	28
Midtown	N Lanak	NS8068	55°53·7′	3°54·7′W	X	65
Midtown	Orkney	ND4191	58°48·4′	3°0·8′W	X	7
Midtown	S Lanak	NS7841	55°39·1′	3°55·9′W	X	71
Midtown	S Lanak	NS8234	55°35·4′	3°51·9′W	X	71,72
Midtown	S Lanak	NS8329	55°32·7′	3°50·8′W	X	71,72
Midtown	S Lanak	NS9336	55°36·6′	3°41·5′W	X	71,72
Midtown of Badenspink	Aberd	NJ5860	57°37·9′	2°41·7′W	X	29
Midtown of Barras	Aberd	NO8480	56°54·9′	2°15·3′W	X	45
Midtown of Bellyhack	Moray	NJ3942	57°28·1′	3°0·6′W	X	28
Midtown of Buchromb	Moray	NJ3143	57°28·6′	3°8·6′W	X	28
Midtown of Glass	Aberd	NJ4042	57°28·1′	2°59·6′W	X	28
Midtown of Haddo	Aberd	NJ6246	57°30·4′	2°37·6′W	X	29
Midtown of Hatton	Aberd	NK0438	57°26·2′	1°55·5′W	X	30
Midtown of Urr	D & G	NX8067	54°59·2′	3°52·1′W	X	84
Mid Uplaw	E Renf	NS4455	55°46·0′	4°28·8′W	X	64
Mid Urchany	Highld	NH8849	57°31·3′	3°51·7′W	X	27
Midville	Lincs	TF3856	53°5·2′	0°4·0′E	T	122
Midville House Fm	Lincs	TF3756	53°5·2′	0°3·1′E	FM	122
Mid Walls	Shetld	HU2050	60°14·3′	1°37·8′W	T	3
Mid Ward	Shetld	HU2245	60°11·6′	1°35·7′W	H	4
Mid Ward	Shetld	HU3265	60°22·3′	1°24·7′W	H	3
Midwath Stead	Cumbr	NY5804	54°26·0′	2°38·4′W	X	91
Midway	Ches	SJ9182	53°20·3′	2°7·7′W	T	109
Midway	Corn	SX2480	50°35·8′	4°28·8′W	X	201
Midway	Somer	ST6546	51°13·0′	2°30·2′W	T	183
Midway Fm	Suff	TL8852	52°8·3′	0°45·2′E	FM	155
Midway Ho Fm	Ches	SJ8565	53°11·2′	2°13·1′W	FM	118
Midway Manor	Wilts	ST8158	51°19·5′	2°16·0′W	X	173
Midwellwood Fm	E Ayr	NS6626	55°30·8′	4°6·9′W	FM	71
Mid Widdale	N Yks	SD8086	54°16·4′	2°18·0′W	X	98
Mid Yell	Shetld	HU5190	60°35·7′	1°3·6′W	T	1,2
Mid Yell Voe	Shetld	HU5191	60°36·2′	1°3·6′W	W	1,2
Mien's Plantation	Scot Bord	NT6435	55°36·7′	2°33·9′W	F	74
Miffia	Orkney	HY2313	59°0·1′	3°19·9′W	X	6
Migdale	Highld	NH6292	57°54·0′	4°19·2′W	T	21
Migdale	Inverc	NS3571	55°54·5′	4°37·9′W	X	63
Migdale Rock	Highld	NH6490	57°53·0′	4°17·1′W	X	21
Migga Ness	Shetld	HP5305	60°43·7′	1°1·2′W	X	1
Migneint	Conwy	SH7842	52°57·9′	3°48·6′W	X	124
Migovie	Highld	NH5318	57°14·0′	4°25·7′W	X	35
Migram's Brook	Powys	SO1076	52°22·7′	3°18·9′W	W	136,148
Migvie	Aberd	NJ4306	57°8·7′	2°56·1′W	T	37
Milaid	Powys	SO2421	51°53·2′	3°5·9′W	X	161
Milarrochy	Stir	NS4092	56°5·9′	4°33·9′W	X	56
Milber	Devon	SX8770	50°31·4′	3°35·3′W	T	202
Milbethill	Aberd	NJ6156	57°35·8′	2°38·7′W	X	29
Milborne Down	Somer	ST6521	50°59·5′	2°29·5′W	X	183
Milborne Port	Somer	ST6718	50°57·9′	2°27·8′W	T	183
Milborne St Andrew	Dorset	SY8097	50°46·6′	2°16·6′W	T	194
Milborne Wick	Somer	ST6620	50°58·9′	2°28·7′W	T	183
Milborne Wood	Dorset	SY7897	50°46·6′	2°18·3′W	F	194
Milborne Wood Fm	Dorset	SY7896	50°46·0′	2°18·3′W	FM	194
Milbourne	Northum	NZ1175	55°4·4′	1°49·2′W	T	88
Milbourne	Wilts	ST9487	51°35·1′	2°4·8′W	T	173
Milbourne Grange	Northum	NZ1175	55°4·4′	1°49·2′W	X	88
Milbourne Hall	Northum	NZ1174	55°3·9′	1°49·2′W	X	88
Milbuie	Arg & Bt	NR3893	56°3·7′	6°12·1′W	X	61
Milburn	Cumbr	NY6529	54°39·5′	2°32·1′W	T	91
Milburn Beck	Cumbr	NY6628	54°39·0′	2°31·2′W	W	91
Milburn Fm	N Yks	SE4179	54°12·5′	1°21·9′W	FM	99
Milburn Forest	Cumbr	NY7232	54°41·2′	2°25·6′W	X	91
Milburn Grange	Cumbr	NY6728	54°39·0′	2°30·3′W	X	91
Milbury Heath	S Glos	ST6690	51°36·7′	2°29·1′W	T	162,172
Milby	N Yks	SE4067	54°6·1′	1°22·9′W	T	99
Milby Fm	Cambs	TL2294	52°32·0′	0°11·7′W	FM	142
Milch Hill	Essex	TL7220	51°51·3′	0°30·3′E	T	167
Milcombe	Corn	SX2355	50°22·3′	4°29·0′W	T	201
Milcombe	Oxon	SP4134	52°0·4′	1°23·8′W	T	151
Milcote Hall Fm	Warw	SP1952	52°10·2′	1°42·9′W	FM	151
Milcote Manor Fm	Warw	SP1752	52°10·2′	1°44·7′W	FM	151
Milden	Suff	TL9546	52°4·9′	0°51·2′E	T	155
Mildenhall	Suff	TL7175	52°21·0′	0°31·0′E	T	143
Milden Hall	Suff	TL9446	52°4·9′	0°50·3′E	X	155
Mildenhall	Wilts	SU2069	51°25·4′	1°42·4′W	T	174
Mildenhall Airfield	Suff	TL6976	52°21·6′	0°29·3′E	X	143
Mildenhall Borders	Wilts	SU2270	51°25·9′	1°40·6′W	F	174
Mildenhall Drain	Suff	TL6582	52°24·9′	0°26·0′E	W	143
Mildenhall Fen	Suff	TL6678	52°22·7′	0°26·7′E	X	143
Mildenhall Woods	Suff	TL7375	52°21·0′	0°32·8′E	F	143
Mildon	Devon	SS8822	50°59·4′	3°35·4′W	X	181
Mildridge Fm	Win & Maid	TQ0177	51°29·2′	0°32·3′W	FM	176
Mile Ball	Wilts	SU1650	51°15·2′	1°45·9′W	X	184
Milebarn Fm	Beds	TL0014	51°49·2′	0°32·6′W	FM	166
Milebridge Fm	Norf	TG1302	52°34·7′	1°9·0′E	FM	144
Milebrook	Powys	SO3172	52°20·7′	3°0·4′W	T	137,148
Milebush	Kent	TQ7545	51°10·9′	0°30·6′E	T	188
Mile Bush Fm	N Yks	SE9183	54°14·3′	0°35·8′W	FM	101
Mile Cairn	Angus	NO5180	56°54·8′	2°47·8′W	A	44
Mile Cross	Norf	TG2110	52°38·8′	1°16·4′E	T	133,134
Mile Dorcha	Highld	NN1888	56°57·1′	4°59·1′W	X	34,41

Mile Drive, The	Glos	SP1338	52°2·6′	1°48·2′W	X	151
Mile Dubh	Highld	NH1154	57°32·5′	5°9·0′W	X	25
Mile Elm	Wilts	ST9969	51°25·4′	2°0·5′W	T	173
Mile End	Cambs	TL6083	52°25·5′	0°21·6′E	T	143
Mile End	Devon	SX8372	50°32·4′	3°38·7′W	T	191
Mile-end	D & G	NX6349	54°49·3′	4°7·5′W	X	83
Mile End	Essex	TL9927	51°54·6′	0°54·0′E	T	168
Mile End	Glos	SO5811	51°48·0′	2°36·2′W	T	162
Mile End	Suff	TL8252	52°8·4′	0°40·0′E	T	155
Mile End	T Ham	TQ3682	51°31·5′	0°2·0′W	T	177
Mile End	W Berks	SU3380	51°31·3′	1°31·1′W	X	174
Mile End Fm	Ches	SJ6554	53°5·2′	2°30·9′W	FM	118
Mile End Fm	Herts	TL3538	52°1·7′	0°1·5′W	FM	154
Mile End Fm	Northum	NU0513	55°24·9′	1°54·8′W	FM	81
Mile End Hill	Oxon	SU6283	51°32·8′	1°6·0′W	X	175
Mileham	Norf	TF9119	52°44·3′	0°50·2′E	T	132
Milehead	Highld	NH8306	57°8·1′	3°55·5′W	X	35
Mile Hill	Angus	NO3157	56°42·2′	3°7·2′W	H	53
Mile Hill	Angus	NO3760	56°43·9′	3°1·3′W	H	44
Mile Hill	Northum	NZ3277	55°5·4′	1°29·5′W	X	88
Mile Hill	N Yks	SE4734	53°48·2′	1°16·8′W	X	105
Mile Ho	Ches	SJ6857	53°6·8′	2°28·3′W	X	118
Mile Ho	E Yorks	SE8640	53°51·2′	0°41·1′W	X	106
Mile Ho	E Yorks	TA3223	53°41·4′	0°0·4′E	X	107,113
Mile Ho	Lincs	TF1644	52°59·1′	0°15·9′W	X	130
Mile Ho	N Yks	SD9770	54°7·8′	2°2·3′W	X	98
Mile Ho	N Yks	SE4480	54°13·1′	1°19·1′W	X	99
Mile Ho	Shrops	SJ3028	52°50·9′	3°2·0′W	X	126
Milehope Head	Scot Bord	NT2325	55°31·0′	3°12·7′W	H	73
Milehouse	Highld	NH8304	57°7·0′	3°55·5′W	X	35
Mile House Fm	N Yks	SE2182	54°14·2′	1°40·2′W	FM	99
Mile House Fm	N Yks	SE2586	54°16·4′	1°36·5′W	FM	99
Milehouse Fm	W Berks	SU6269	51°25·2′	1°6·1′W	FM	175
Milehouse of Nuide	Highld	NN7498	57°3·6′	4°4·2′W	X	35
Mile Moor	Northum	NU0413	55°24·9′	1°55·8′W	X	81
Milens-houllan	Shetld	HZ2173	59°32·8′	1°37·2′W	X	4
Mile Oak	Bri & Hov	TQ2507	50°51·2′	0°13·1′W	T	198
Mile Oak	Kent	TQ6843	51°9·9′	0°24·6′E	T	188
Mile Oak	Shrops	SJ3027	52°50·4′	3°2·0′W	T	126
Mile Oak	Staffs	SK1802	52°37·2′	1°43·6′W	T	139
Mile Oak Fm	Bri & Hov	TQ2408	50°51·7′	0°13·9′W	FM	198
Mileoak Fm	Northnts	SP6747	52°7·3′	1°0·9′W	FM	152
Mileplain Plantn	Norf	TG1416	52°42·2′	1°10·5′E	F	133
Mile Plantn	Northum	NZ0370	55°1·7′	1°56·8′W	F	87
Miles Cross	Dorset	SY4493	50°44·3′	2°47·2′W	T	193
Miles Cross Hill	Lincs	TF4374	53°14·9′	0°9·0′E	X	122
Milesfield	Bucks	SP8907	51°45·5′	0°42·2′W	X	165
Miles Fm	E Susx	TQ7821	50°57·9′	0°32·5′E	FM	199
Mile-sgeir	W Eil	NG0182	57°44·0′	7°1·0′W	X	18
Miles Green	Staffs	SJ8049	53°2·5′	2°17·5′W	T	118
Miles Green	Surrey	SU9558	51°19·0′	0°37·8′W	T	175,186
Mileshiggins	Heref	SO4829	51°57·7′	2°45·0′W	X	149,161
Miles Hill	Hants	SU8352	51°15·9′	0°48·2′W	X	186
Miles Hill	Lancs	SD7234	53°48·3′	2°25·1′W	X	103
Miles Hill	Leeds	SE2936	53°49·4′	1°33·2′W	T	104
Miles Hope	Heref	SO5764	52°16·6′	2°37·4′W	X	137,138,149
Miles Knoll	Staffs	SK1049	53°2·5′	1°50·6′W	X	119
Milesmark	Fife	NT0788	56°4·8′	3°29·2′W	T	65
Miles Platting	Man	SJ8699	53°29·5′	2°12·3′W	T	109
Miles's Green	W Berks	SU5469	51°25·3′	1°13·0′W	T	174
Milestone	Kent	TR1755	51°15·4′	1°7·0′E	X	179
Milestone	Pth & Kin	NO1835	56°30·3′	3°19·5′W	X	53
Milestone Cross	Devon	SX8781	50°37·3′	3°35·5′W	X	192
Milestone Fm	Cambs	TL2983	52°26·0′	0°5·7′W	FM	142
Mile Stone Hill	N Yks	SD9882	54°14·3′	2°1·4′W	X	98
Milestone Ho	Cumbr	NY5032	54°41·1′	2°46·1′W	X	90
Milestone Ho	Durham	NZ0014	54°31·5′	1°59·6′W	X	92
Milestone Ho	Northum	NY7266	54°59·5′	2°25·8′W	X	86,87
Milethorne Fm	Warw	SP4285	52°27·9′	1°22·5′W	FM	140
Mile Town	Kent	TQ9174	51°26·2′	0°45·3′E	T	178
Miletree Clump	Oxon	SP2115	51°50·2′	1°41·3′W	F	163
Miletree Fm	Beds	SP9427	51°56·2′	0°37·6′W	FM	165
Miley Howe	N Yks	SE5497	54°22·2′	1°9·7′W	A	100
Miley Pike	N Yks	SE4896	54°21·7′	1°15·3′W	X	100
Miley Pike (Tumulus)	N Yks	SE4896	54°21·7′	1°15·3′W	A	100
Milfield	Northum	NT9333	55°35·7′	2°6·2′W	T	74,75
Milfield Hill	Northum	NT9234	55°36·2′	2°7·2′W	X	74,75
Milford	Derby	SK3545	53°0·3′	1°28·3′W	T	119,128
Milford	Devon	SS2322	50°58·5′	4°30·9′W	T	190
Milford	Devon	SS4017	50°56·1′	4°16·2′W	X	180,190
Milford	Devon	SX4086	50°39·3′	4°15·4′W	X	201
Milford	Powys	SO0990	52°30·3′	3°20·0′W	T	136
Milford	Shrops	SJ4121	52°47·2′	2°52·1′W	X	126
Milford	Staffs	SJ9621	52°47·4′	2°3·2′W	T	127
Milford	Surrey	SU9442	51°10·4′	0°38·9′W	T	186
Milford	Wilts	SU1529	51°3·8′	1°46·8′W	T	184
Milford Hagg Fm	N Yks	SE5232	53°47·1′	1°12·2′W	FM	105
Milford Haven	Pemb	SM8804	51°41·9′	5°3·7′W	W	157
Milford Haven (Aberdaugleddau)	Pemb	SM9005	51°42·5′	5°2·0′W	T	157,158
Milford Lake	Hants	SU4560	51°20·5′	1°20·8′W	W	174
Milford Leys Fm	Mil Key	SP7844	52°5·6′	0°51·3′W	FM	152
Milford Lodge	N Yks	SE5131	53°46·6′	1°13·2′W	X	105
Milford Lodge	Shrops	SO5086	52°28·4′	2°43·8′W	X	137,138
Milford on Sea	Hants	SZ2891	50°43·3′	1°35·8′W	T	195
Milford Sta	Surrey	SU9541	51°9·8′	0°38·1′W	X	186
Milgarva	S Ayr	NX0876	55°2·7′	4°59·9′W	H	76
Milgate Ho	Kent	TQ8054	51°15·6′	0°35·2′E	X	188
Milharay Hill	D & G	NX7974	55°3·0′	3°53·2′W	H	84
Milifiach	Highld	NH5443	57°27·5′	4°25·6′W	X	26
Milkhall Pond	Midlo	NT2457	55°48·3′	3°12·3′W	W	66,73
Milkham Inclosure	Hants	SU2009	50°53·0′	1°42·6′W	F	195
Milk Hill	Staffs	SK0949	53°2·5′	1°51·5′W	H	119
Milk Hill	Wilts	SU1063	51°22·2′	1°51·0′W	H	173
Milkhill Fm	W Berks	SU5277	51°29·6′	1°14·7′W	FM	174
Milkhope	Northum	NT9211	55°23·8′	2°7·1′W	X	80
Milkhope	Northum	NZ2176	55°4·9′	1°39·8′W	X	88
Milkhouse Barn	S Ayr	NX2790	55°10·7′	4°42·6′W	W	76
Milkhouse Water	Wilts	SU1761	51°21·1′	1°45·0′W	T	173
Milkieston	Scot Bord	NT2445	55°41·8′	3°12·1′W	T	73

Milkieston Rings	Scot Bord	NT2445	55°41·8′	3°12·1′W	X	73
Milking Burn	S Lanak	NS8931	55°33·9′	3°45·2′W	W	71,72
Milking Hills Corner	Cambs	TL4171	52°19·4′	0°4·5′E	X	154
Milking Nook	Peterb	TF1805	52°38·0′	0°15·0′W	X	142
Milking Oak	Northnts	SP8051	52°9·3′	0°49·4′W	X	152
Milkingstead	Cumbr	SD1599	54°23·0′	3°18·1′W	X	96
Milknob Hill	Bucks	SP7625	51°55·3′	0°53·3′W	X	165
Milkup Bank	Durham	NZ1936	54°43·4′	1°41·9′W	X	92
Milkvale	D & G	NY1475	55°4·0′	3°20·4′W	X	85
Milkwall	Glos	SO5809	51°46·9′	2°36·1′W	T	162
Milkwell	Wilts	ST9123	51°0·6′	2°7·3′W	T	184
Milkwell Burn	Northum	NZ1057	54°54·7′	1°50·2′W	W	88
Milkwellburn Wood	Northum	NZ1057	54°54·7′	1°50·2′W	F	88
Milkwell Covert	Glos	SP0918	51°51·9′	1°51·8′W	F	163
Milky Law	Scot Bord	NT2647	55°42·9′	3°10·2′W	X	73
Mill	Devon	SS4509	50°51·8′	4°11·8′W	X	190
Millae	D & G	NX6362	54°56·3′	4°7·9′W	X	83
Mill Affleck	E Ayr	NS5220	55°27·3′	4°20·0′W	X	70
Milla Geo	Shetld	HU4436	60°6·6′	1°12·0′W	X	4
Millairies	D & G	NX4148	54°48·4′	4°28·0′W	X	83
Millan	Aberd	NJ5804	57°7·8′	2°41·2′W	X	37
Milland	Corn	SX1469	50°29·7′	4°37·0′W	X	200
Milland	W Susx	SU8326	51°1·9′	0°48·6′W	T	186,197
Milland Ho	W Susx	SU8328	51°2·9′	0°48·6′W	X	186,197
Millands	E Ayr	NS4935	55°35·4′	4°23·3′W	X	70
Millands	Pth & Kin	NN9816	56°19·8′	3°38·5′W	X	58
Millands Fm	Devon	SY2695	50°45·2′	3°2·6′W	FM	192,193
Millaneoch Hill	E Ayr	NS6202	55°17·8′	4°10·0′W	H	77
Millans Wood	E Yorks	SE7851	53°57·2′	0°48·3′W	F	105,106
Millantae	D & G	NY1580	55°6·7′	3°19·5′W	X	79
Millards	Pemb	SN0707	51°44·0′	4°47·3′W	X	158
Millards Hill Ho	Somer	ST7442	51°10·8′	2°21·9′W	X	183
Millar's Moss Resr	Scot Bord	NT9068	55°54·6′	2°9·2′W	W	67
Millarston	Renf	NS4663	55°50·4′	4°27·1′W	T	64
Millaton Ho	Devon	SX5089	50°41·1′	4°7·0′W	X	191
Millaway Fm	Oxon	SU3692	51°37·8′	1°28·4′W	FM	164,174
Millbank	Aberd	NJ8924	57°18·6′	2°10·5′W	X	38
Millbank	Aberd	NK0449	57°32·1′	1°55·5′W	X	30
Millbank	Aberd	NK1242	57°28·3′	1°47·5′W	X	30
Millbank	Aberd	NO8599	57°5·2′	2°14·4′W	T	38,45
Mill Bank	Cald	SE0321	53°41·4′	1°56·9′W	T	104
Millbank	D & G	NX9257	54°54·0′	3°40·6′W	X	84
Millbank	D & G	NY1385	55°9·4′	3°21·5′W	X	78
Millbank	D & G	NY1476	55°4·5′	3°20·4′W	X	85
Millbank	Highld	ND1167	58°35·2′	3°31·4′W	T	11,12
Millbank	Kent	TR0330	51°2·2′	0°54·1′E	X	189
Millbank	Kent	TR2065	51°20·7′	1°9·9′E	T	179
Mill Bank	N Yks	SE3077	54°11·5′	1°32·0′W	X	99
Millbank	Pth & Kin	NO1840	56°32·9′	3°19·6′W	X	53
Millbank	Renf	NS3357	55°46·9′	4°39·3′W	X	63
Millbank	Scot Bord	NT4336	55°37·1′	2°53·9′W	X	73
Millbank	Scot Bord	NT9362	55°51·3′	2°6·3′W	X	67
Millbank	S Lanak	NS8632	55°34·4′	3°48·0′W	X	71,72
Millbank	Stock	SJ9185	53°21·9′	2°7·7′W	X	109
Millbank Fm	Ches	SJ7572	53°14·9′	2°22·1′W	FM	118
Millbank Fm	Ches	SJ7770	53°13·8′	2°20·3′W	FM	118
Millbank Fm	Lincs	TF3622	52°46·9′	0°1·4′E	FM	131
Millbank Hill	D & G	NX9157	54°54·0′	3°41·6′W	H	84
Millbank Ho	Midlo	NT3361	55°50·5′	3°3·8′W	X	66
Millbank Ho	N Yks	SE8673	54°9·0′	0°40·6′W	X	101
Mill Bank Wood	Kent	TQ5153	51°15·6′	0°10·2′E	F	188
Mill Bank Wood	N Yks	NZ5909	54°28·6′	1°4·9′W	F	93
Millbarn Cross	Devon	SS8113	50°54·5′	3°41·2′W	X	181
Mill Barn Fm	Cambs	TL2877	52°22·8′	0°6·8′W	FM	142
Mill Barrows	Hants	SU5724	51°1·0′	1°10·9′W	A	185
Mill Barton	Devon	SS8112	50°53·9′	3°41·2′W	X	181
Mill Basin	Norf	TF5712	52°41·2′	0°19·8′E	W	131,143
Mill Bay	Devon	SX7438	50°13·9′	3°45·6′W	W	202
Mill Bay	Orkney	HY5735	59°12·2′	2°44·7′W	W	5,6
Mill Bay	Orkney	HY6726	59°7·4′	2°34·1′W	W	5
Mill Bay	Orkney	ND3095	58°50·5′	3°12·3′W	W	7
Mill Bay	Pemb	SM8003	51°41·2′	5°10·6′W	W	157
Mill Bay	Pemb	SN0005	51°42·7′	4°53·3′W	W	157,158
Mill Bay Cove	Devon	SX8950	50°20·6′	3°33·2′W	W	202
Mill Bay or Nanjizal	Corn	SW3523	50°3·1′	5°41·8′W	W	203
Mill Beach	Essex	TL8807	51°44·0′	0°43·8′E	X	168
Millbeck	Cumbr	NY1623	54°36·0′	3°17·6′W	X	89
Millbeck	Cumbr	NY2526	54°37·7′	3°9·3′W	T	89,90
Millbeck	Cumbr	NY2906	54°26·9′	3°5·3′W	X	89,90
Mill Beck	Cumbr	NY3657	54°54·5′	2°59·5′W	X	85
Mill Beck	Cumbr	NY5556	54°54·1′	2°41·7′W	W	86
Mill Beck	Cumbr	NY5767	55°0·0′	2°39·9′W	W	86
Millbeck	Cumbr	SD6285	54°15·8′	2°34·6′W	X	97
Mill Beck	Cumbr	SD7086	54°16·4′	2°27·2′W	X	98
Mill Beck	E Yorks	SE9029	53°45·2′	0°37·7′W	W	106
Mill Beck	N Yks	NZ9403	54°25·1′	0°32·7′W	W	94
Mill Beck	N Yks	SE2993	54°20·1′	1°32·8′W	W	99
Mill Beck	N Yks	SE7765	54°4·7′	0°49·0′W	W	100
Mill Beck	N Yks	SE8265	54°4·7′	0°44·4′W	W	100
Mill Belt	Suff	TL7771	52°18·7′	0°36·2′E	F	144,155
Mill Bottom	N Yks	NY9900	54°24·0′	2°0·5′W	X	92
Millbounds	Orkney	HY5635	59°12·2′	2°45·7′W	T	5,6
Mill Br	N Yks	SD8357	54°0·8′	2°15·1′W	X	103
Mill Br	N Yks	SE5061	54°2·8′	1°13·8′W	X	100
Millbrae	D & G	NX7575	55°3·5′	3°57·0′W	X	84
Millbreck	Aberd	NK0045	57°30·0′	1°59·5′W	T	30
Millbridge	Surrey	SU8442	51°10·5′	0°47·5′W	T	186
Millbrook	Beds	TL0138	52°2·1′	0°31·3′W	T	153
Millbrook	Ches	SJ4372	53°14·8′	2°50·8′W	W	117
Millbrook	C of Soton	SU3813	50°55·1′	1°27·2′W	T	196
Millbrook	Corn	SX4252	50°21·0′	4°12·9′W	T	201
Mill Brook	Derby	SK1889	53°24·1′	1°43·3′W	W	110
Millbrook	Devon	SS7530	51°3·6′	3°46·6′W	T	180
Millbrook	Devon	SY3098	50°46·9′	2°59·2′W	T	193
Millbrook	Monm	SO3910	51°47·4′	2°52·7′W	X	161
Millbrook	Newp	ST4392	51°37·7′	2°49·0′W	X	171,172
Mill Brook	Oxon	SU4893	51°38·3′	1°18·0′W	W	164,174
Mill Brook	Oxon	SU5487	51°35·0′	1°12·8′W	W	174
Mill Brook	Oxon	SU5788	51°35·6′	1°10·2′W	W	174
Millbrook	Powys	SO0827	51°56·3′	3°19·9′W	X	160

Mill Brook	Shrops	SO6473	52°21·5'	2°31·3'W	W	138
Millbrook	Somer	ST6245	51°12·4'	2°32·3'W	X	183
Millbrook	Surrey	SU9760	51°20·1'	0°36·1'W	X	175,176,186
Millbrook	Tames	SJ9899	53°29·5'	2°1·4'W	T	109
Millbrook	Wrex	SJ3943	52°59·1'	2°54·1'W	X	117
Millbrook Br	Shrops	SO6572	52°20·9'	2°30·4'W	X	138
Millbrook Lake	Corn	SX4352	50°21·1'	4°12·0'W	W	201
Millbrooks Fm	Essex	TL8629	51°55·9'	0°42·7'E	FM	168
Millbrook Sta	Beds	TL0040	52°3·2'	0°32·1'W	X	153
Mill Brow	Cumbr	NY3403	54°25·3'	3°0·6'W	X	90
Millbrow	Cumbr	SD1892	54°19·3'	3°15·2'W	X	96
Mill Brow	Stock	SJ9789	53°24·1'	2°2·3'W	T	109
Millbuie	Highld	NH6458	57°35·8'	4°16·1'W	X	26
Mill Buie	Moray	NJ0950	57°32·1'	3°30·7'W	H	27
Mill Buie	Moray	NJ1651	57°32·7'	3°23·7'W	H	28
Millbuie Fm	Aberd	NJ7909	57°10·5'	2°20·4'W	FM	38
Millbuies Country Park	Moray	NJ2456	57°35·5'	3°15·8'W	X	28
Millburn	Aberd	NJ5544	57°29·3'	2°44·6'W	X	29
Millburn	Aberd	NJ5722	57°17·5'	2°42·3'W	X	37
Millburn	Aberd	NJ6236	57°25·0'	2°37·5'W	X	29
Mill Burn	Angus	NO4773	56°51·0'	2°51·7'W	W	44
Mill Burn	D & G	NX4766	54°58·2'	4°23·0'W	W	83
Mill Burn	D & G	NX7367	54°59·1'	3°58·7'W	W	83,84
Mill Burn	D & G	NX7461	54°55·9'	3°57·6'W	W	83,84
Mill Burn	D & G	NX8653	54°51·8'	3°46·1'W	W	84
Millburn	D & G	NY1770	55°1·3'	3°17·5'W	X	85
Mill Burn	E Loth	NT5802	56°2·0'	2°47·7'W	W	66
Mill Burn	E Loth	NT5280	56°0·9'	2°45·8'W	W	66
Millburn	Highld	NC8855	58°28·4'	3°54·7'W	X	10
Mill Burn	Inverc	NS3165	55°51·2'	4°41·6'W	W	63
Mill Burn	Northum	NU0940	55°39·5'	1°51·0'W	W	75
Mill Burn	Northum	NZ1075	55°4·4'	1°50·2'W	W	88
Millburn	S Ayr	NS4429	55°32·0'	4°27·9'W	X	70
Mill Burn	Scot Bord	NT7457	55°48·6'	2°24·5'W	W	67,74
Millburn	Shetld	HU4173	60°26·6'	1°14·8'W	X	2,3
Mill Burn	Shetld	HU6194	60°37·7'	0°52·6'W	W	1,2
Millburn	S Lanak	NS7747	55°42·3'	3°57·0'W	X	64
Mill Burn	S Lanak	NS9027	55°31·7'	3°44·1'W	W	71,72
Millburn	W Dunb	NS3879	55°58·9'	4°35·4'W	X	63
Millburn Bay	Orkney	HY4521	59°4·6'	2°57·1'W	W	5,6
Millburn Bay	Shetld	HU3833	60°5·1'	1°18·5'W	W	4
Millburn Bridge	Scot Bord	NT7657	55°48·6'	2°22·5'W	X	67,74
Millburn Cott	S Lanak	NT0945	55°41·7'	3°26·4'W	X	72
Millburn Cottage	Highld	NM6485	56°54·0'	5°52·1'W	X	40
Millburn Geo	Shetld	HU4012	59°53·7'	1°16·6'W	X	4
Millburn Geo	Shetld	HU5239	60°8·2'	1°3·3'W	X	4
Millburn Grange	Warw	SP3073	52°21·5'	1°33·2'W	X	140
Millburn Ho	S Lanak	NS7950	55°44·0'	3°55·2'W	X	64
Mill Burn of Stovabreck	Shetld	HU2779	60°29·9'	1°30·0'W	W	3
Millburn Tower	C of Edin	NT1771	55°55·7'	3°19·3'W	X	65,66
Mill Close	N Yks	SE2392	54°19·6'	1°38·4'W	X	99
Millcombe	Corn	SX3173	50°32·2'	4°22·7'W	X	201
Millcombe	Devon	SX8049	50°20·0'	3°40·8'W	X	202
Mill Common	Norf	TG3201	52°33·7'	1°25·8'E	T	134
Mill Common	Norf	TG3226	52°47·1'	1°26·8'E	X	133,134
Mill Common	Norf	TG3432	52°50·3'	1°28·9'E	X	133
Mill Common	Norf	TL9890	52°28·5'	0°55·3'E	X	144
Mill Common	Suff	TM4181	52°22·7'	1°32·9'E	X	156
Mill Corner	E Susx	TQ8223	50°58·9'	0°36·0'E	T	199
Mill Cott	Arg & Bt	NR2768	55°49·9'	6°21·2'W	X	60
Mill Cott	Arg & Bt	NR9986	56°1·7'	5°13·1'W	X	55
Mill Cott	Highld	NH8404	57°7·0'	3°54·5'W	X	35
Mill Cottage	N Yks	SE5441	53°52·0'	1°10·3'W	X	105
Mill Cottages	E Yorks	SE9263	54°3·5'	0°35·3'W	X	101
Mill Court	Hants	SU7541	51°10·0'	0°55·2'W	X	186
Mill Court	Oxon	SU6087	51°35·0'	1°7·6'W	X	175
Mill Court	Scot Bord	NT5416	55°26·4'	2°43·2'W	X	79
Mill Covert	Norf	TF8724	52°47·1'	0°46·8'E	F	132
Mill Covert	Oxon	SP3927	51°56·6'	1°25·6'W	F	164
Millcraig	Highld	NH6571	57°42·8'	4°15·5'W	T	21
Mill Creek	Essex	TL9708	51°44·4'	0°51·6'E	W	168
Millcrest	Cumbr	SD5294	54°20·6'	2°43·9'W	X	97
Millcroft Fm	Devon	SX9578	50°35·8'	3°28·6'W	FM	192
Millcroon	S Ayr	NX1277	55°3·4'	4°56·2'W	X	76
Mill Cross	Devon	SX7361	50°26·3'	3°46·9'W	X	202
Mill Cross	Somer	ST2228	51°3·0'	3°6·4'W	X	193
Milldale	Staffs	SK1354	53°5·2'	1°47·9'W	T	119
Milldale Burn	Shetld	HP5914	60°48·5'	0°54·4'W	W	1
Milldam	Cumbr	SD4494	54°20·6'	2°51·3'W	X	97
Mill Dam	N Yks	SD6867	54°6·1'	2°28·9'W	T	98
Milldam	Orkney	HY5105	58°56·0'	2°50·6'W	X	6,7
Mill Dam	Pth & Kin	NO0346	56°36·0'	3°34·3'W	W	52,53
Mill Dam	S Tyne	NZ3566	54°59·5'	1°26·8'W	T	88
Mill Dam Lake	Essex	TM1115	51°47·9'	1°4·0'E	W	168,169
Mill Dam of Rango	Orkney	HY2618	59°2·8'	3°16·9'W	W	6
Milldeans	Fife	NO2300	56°11·4'	3°14·0'W	X	58
Milldeans	Fife	NO3305	56°14·2'	3°4·4'W	X	59
Millden	Aberd	NJ9616	57°14·3'	2°3·5'W	T	38
Millden Links	Aberd	NJ9615	57°13·8'	2°3·5'W	X	38
Millden Lodge	Angus	NO5478	56°53·7'	2°44·9'W	X	44
Milldens	Angus	NO5450	56°38·6'	2°44·6'W	T	54
Millder Ness	Shetld	HU2859	60°19·1'	1°29·1'W	X	3
Milldewan Hill	Angus	NO2762	56°44·9'	3°11·2'W	H	44
Mill Dike	Norf	TG3503	52°34·7'	1°28·5'E	W	134
Mill Dike	N Yks	SE4832	53°47·2'	1°15·9'W	W	105
Milldoe	Orkney	HY3520	59°4·0'	3°7·5'W	X	6
Mill Door	Fife	NT6599	56°11·2'	2°33·4'W	X	59
Milldown	D & G	NX5183	55°7·4'	4°19·8'W	H	77
Milldown	Scot Bord	NT9166	55°53·5'	2°8·2'W	X	67
Milldown Rig	D & G	NX4077	55°4·0'	4°29·9'W	X	77
Mill Downs	Corn	SW4636	50°10·4'	5°33·1'W	X	203
Milldown Well	D & G	NX6273	55°2·2'	4°9·1'W	W	77
Milldowrie	Aberd	NJ6618	57°15·3'	2°33·4'W	X	38
Millearne	Pth & Kin	NN9317	56°20·3'	3°43·4'W	X	58
Millees	Cumbr	NY3872	55°2·6'	2°57·8'W	X	85
Millegan	Moray	NJ5151	57°33·0'	2°48·7'W	X	29
Millen Burn	Pth & Kin	NN9119	56°21·3'	3°45·4'W	W	58
Mill End	Beds	TL1157	52°12·2'	0°22·1'W	X	153
Mill End	Bucks	SU7885	51°33·7'	0°52·1'W	T	175
Mill End	Cambs	TL6956	52°10·8'	0°28·7'E	T	154

Mill End	Essex	TL6833	51°58·4'	0°27·2'E	X	167
Millend	Glos	SO5609	51°46·9'	2°37·9'W	T	162
Millend	Glos	SO7805	51°44·8'	2°18·7'W	T	162
Mill End	Glos	SP1114	51°49·7'	1°50·0'W	T	163
Millend	Glos	ST7596	51°40·0'	2°21·3'W	T	162
Mill End	Herts	TL3332	51°58·5'	0°3·4'W	T	166
Mill End	Herts	TQ0494	51°38·3'	0°29·4'W	T	166,176
Millend	Oxon	SP3222	51°54·0'	1°31·7'W	T	164
Mill End	Worcs	SO9237	52°2·1'	2°6·6'W	X	150
Millenderdale	S Ayr	NX1790	55°10·5'	4°52·0'W	X	76
Mill End Fm	Ches	SJ8769	53°13·3'	2°11·3'W	FM	118
Millend Fm	Heref	SO6545	52°6·4'	2°30·3'W	FM	149
Mill End Green	Essex	TL6126	51°54·8'	0°20·8'E	T	167
Millendreath	Corn	SX2654	50°21·8'	4°26·4'W	T	201
Millendreath Beach	Corn	SX2653	50°21·3'	4°26·4'W	X	201
Millenheath	Shrops	SJ5735	52°54·9'	2°38·0'W	X	126
Millennium Coastal Park	Carm	SN5298	52°33·8'	4°10·6'W	X	159
Millennium Way	I of M	SC3684	54°13·8'	4°30·5'W	X	95
Miller Bridge Ho	Cumbr	NY3704	54°25·9'	2°57·9'W	X	90
Miller Burn	Northum	NY8791	55°13·0'	2°11·8'W	W	80
Millergill Beck	Cumbr	SD1085	54°15·4'	3°22·5'W	W	96
Millerground Landing	Cumbr	SD4098	54°22·7'	2°55·0'W	X	96,97
Miller Hill	Cumbr	NY5966	54°59·5'	2°38·0'W	X	86
Miller Hill	Cumbr	SD0890	54°18·1'	3°24·4'W	X	96
Millerhill	Midlo	NT3269	55°54·8'	3°4·8'W	T	66
Miller Moss	Cumbr	NY3033	54°41·5'	3°4·7'W	X	90
Miller Place	Cumbr	NY1623	54°36·0'	3°17·6'W	X	89
Millers	Essex	TL5521	51°52·2'	0°15·5'E	X	167
Miller's Bay	Arg & Bt	NR7067	55°50·7'	5°40·0'W	W	61,62
Miller's Bog	Aberd	NO6386	56°58·1'	2°36·1'W	X	45
Miller's Causeway	Northum	NU1022	55°29·7'	1°50·1'W	X	75
Miller's Court	Worcs	SO7936	52°1·6'	2°18·0'W	X	150
Miller's Dale	Derby	SK1473	53°15·5'	1°47·0'W	T	119
Miller's Dale	Derby	SK1573	53°15·5'	1°46·1'W	X	119
Millers Fm	E Susx	TQ7413	50°53·6'	0°28·8'E	FM	199
Millers Fm	Somer	ST7239	51°9·2'	2°23·6'W	FM	183
Millersford Bottom	Hants	SU1916	50°56·8'	1°43·4'W	X	184
Millersford Plantn	Hants	SU1917	50°57·4'	1°43·4'W	F	184
Millers Green	Derby	SK2852	53°4·1'	1°34·5'W	T	119
Miller's Green	Essex	TL5907	51°44·6'	0°18·6'E	T	167
Millers House	Lancs	SD6255	53°59·6'	2°34·4'W	X	102,103
Miller's Loch	Fife	NO2106	56°14·7'	3°16·0'W	W	58
Miller's Moss	Northum	NY9696	55°15·7'	2°3·3'W	X	81
Miller's Moss	W Loth	NS9558	55°48·5'	3°40·1'W	X	65,72
Millersneuk	E Dunb	NS6671	55°55·1'	4°8·2'W	T	64
Miller's Place	Highld	NH8181	57°48·4'	3°59·7'W	X	21
Miller's pond	Derby	SK4564	53°10·5'	1°19·2'W	W	120
Miller's Port	Arg & Bt	NM8137	56°28·7'	5°32·9'W	W	49
Millerston	C of Glas	NS6467	55°52·9'	4°10·0'W	T	64
Millerston	E Ayr	NS4824	55°29·4'	4°23·9'W	X	70
Millerston	E Renf	NS5755	55°46·3'	4°16·3'W	X	64
Millerton Hill	Scot Bord	NT9159	55°49·7'	2°8·2'W	H	67,74,75
Milles Fm	Essex	TL7923	51°52·8'	0°36·4'E	FM	167
Millets	Lancs	SD5003	53°31·5'	2°44·8'W	X	108
Millets Fm	Oxon	SU4396	51°39·9'	1°22·3'W	FM	164
Milleur Point	D & G	NX0173	55°1·0'	5°6·3'W	X	76,82
Millewarne	Corn	SW6722	50°3·4'	5°14·9'W	X	203
Millfaid	Stir	NS4585	56°2·2'	4°28·8'W	X	57
Mill Farm	Aberd	NJ8864	57°40·2'	2°11·6'W	FM	30
Mill Farm	Red & Cl	NZ5616	54°32·4'	1°7·6'W	FM	93
Mill Fiel	Shetld	HP5915	60°49·1'	0°54·4'W	X	1
Millfield	Aberd	NJ5624	57°18·5'	2°43·4'W	X	37
Millfield	Aberd	NJ8152	57°33·7'	2°18·6'W	X	29,30
Millfield	Aberd	NO4896	57°3·4'	2°51·0'W	T	37,44
Millfield	Angus	NO5850	56°38·7'	2°40·6'W	X	54
Millfield	Angus	NO6348	56°37·6'	2°35·7'W	X	54
Mill Field	Notts	SK7166	53°11·4'	0°55·8'W	X	120
Millfield	Orkney	HY2510	58°58·5'	3°17·8'W	X	6
Millfield	Orkney	HY2511	58°59·0'	3°17·8'W	X	6
Millfield	Orkney	HY6524	59°6·4'	2°36·2'W	X	5
Millfield	Peterb	TF1800	52°35·3'	0°15·1'W	T	142
Millfield	Scot Bord	NT6533	55°35·6'	2°32·9'W	X	74
Millfield	Shetld	HP6513	60°47·9'	0°47·8'W	X	1
Millfield	Sund	NZ3857	54°54·6'	1°24·0'W	T	88
Millfield Fm	Beds	TL0518	51°51·3'	0°28·1'W	FM	166
Millfield Fm	Cambs	TL4747	52°6·3'	0°9·2'E	FM	154
Millfield Fm	Derby	SK2264	53°10·6'	1°39·8'W	FM	119
Millfield Fm	Leeds	SE3141	53°52·1'	1°31·3'W	FM	104
Mill Field Fm	N Yks	SE6433	53°47·6'	1°1·3'W	FM	105,106
Millfield Fm	York	SE6744	53°53·5'	0°58·4'W	FM	105,106
Millfield Ho	Angus	NO6142	56°34·4'	2°37·6'W	X	54
Millfield Lodge	Cumbr	NY3834	54°42·1'	2°57·3'W	X	90
Millfield Moss	Orkney	HY6122	59°5·3'	2°40·3'W	X	5
Millfields	Cambs	TL6358	52°12·0'	0°23·5'E	X	154
Millfield School	Somer	ST4936	51°7·5'	2°43·3'W	X	182,183
Millfields (Inn)	Derby	SK2449	53°2·5'	1°38·1'W	X	119,128
Millfire	D & G	NX5084	55°7·9'	4°20·7'W	X	77
Mill Fleam	Staffs	SK2228	52°51·2'	1°40·0'W	W	128
Mill Fm	Aberd	NJ5502	57°6·7'	2°44·1'W	FM	37
Mill Fm	Aberd	NJ7317	57°14·8'	2°26·4'W	FM	38
Mill Fm	Aberd	NJ9960	57°38·1'	2°0·5'W	FM	30
Mill Fm	Bath & NE Somer	ST6157	51°18·9'	2°33·2'W	FM	172
Mill Fm	Beds	SP9832	51°58·9'	0°34·0'W	FM	165
Mill Fm	Beds	TL0849	52°8·0'	0°24·9'W	FM	153
Mill Fm	Bucks	SP7738	52°2·3'	0°52·2'W	FM	152
Mill Fm	Bucks	TQ0198	51°40·5'	0°32·0'W	FM	166,176
Mill Fm	Cambs	TL3681	52°24·8'	0°0·4'E	FM	142
Mill Fm	Ches	SJ5060	53°8·3'	2°44·4'W	FM	117
Mill Fm	Ches	SJ6966	53°11·7'	2°27·4'W	FM	118
Mill Fm	Ches	SJ7653	53°4·7'	2°21·1'W	FM	118
Mill Fm	Ches	SJ7960	53°8·4'	2°18·4'W	FM	118
Mill Fm	Ches	SJ8880	53°19·2'	2°10·4'W	FM	109
Mill Fm	Derby	SK4565	53°11·0'	1°19·2'W	FM	120
Mill Fm	Devon	SS6546	51°12·1'	3°55·6'W	FM	180
Mill Fm	Devon	SS7022	50°59·2'	3°50·7'W	FM	180
Mill Fm	Devon	SX6992	50°43·0'	3°51·0'W	FM	191
Mill Fm	Devon	SX7842	50°16·2'	3°42·3'W	FM	202
Mill Fm	Donc	SK5797	53°28·2'	1°8·1'W	FM	111
Mill Fm	Dorset	ST8111	50°54·1'	2°15·8'W	FM	194

Mill Fm	Essex	TL7035	51°59·5'	0°29·0'E	FM	154
Mill Fm	Essex	TL7644	52°4·2'	0°34·5'E	FM	155
Mill Fm	Essex	TL8133	51°58·2'	0°38·5'E	FM	168
Mill Fm	Essex	TM0724	51°52·8'	1°0·9'E	FM	168,169
Mill Fm	Essex	TM2130	51°55·7'	1°13·3'E	FM	169
Mill Fm	E Susx	TQ4222	50°59·0'	0°1·8'E	FM	198
Mill Fm	E Yorks	SE6722	53°41·6'	0°58·7'W	FM	105,106
Mill Fm	E Yorks	SE8030	53°45·8'	0°46·8'W	FM	106
Mill Fm	E Yorks	SE8151	53°57·2'	0°45·5'W	FM	106
Mill Fm	E Yorks	SE8755	53°59·3'	0°40·0'W	FM	106
Mill Fm	E Yorks	SE9029	53°45·2'	0°37·7'W	FM	106
Mill Fm	E Yorks	SE9164	54°4·1'	0°36·1'W	FM	101
Mill Fm	E Yorks	SE9842	53°52·1'	0°30·2'W	FM	106
Mill Fm	Flint	SJ3765	53°10·9'	2°56·2'W	FM	117
Mill Fm	Glos	SP0330	51°58·3'	1°57·0'W	FM	150
Mill Fm	Glos	SP0335	52°1·0'	1°57·0'W	FM	150
Mill Fm	Hants	SU6957	51°18·7'	1°0·2'W	FM	175,186
Mill Fm	Hants	SU7630	51°4·1'	0°54·5'W	FM	186
Mill Fm	Hants	SU8161	51°20·8'	0°49·8'W	FM	175,186
Mill Fm	Heref	SO5017	51°51·2'	2°43·2'W	FM	162
Mill Fm	Herts	TL3424	51°54·1'	0°2·7'W	FM	166
Mill Fm	I of W	SZ6387	50°41·0'	1°6·1'W	FM	196
Mill Fm	Kent	TQ4946	51°11·9'	0°8·3'E	FM	188
Mill Fm	Kent	TQ9340	51°7·8'	0°45·9'E	FM	189
Mill Fm	Lancs	SD3837	53°49·8'	2°56·1'W	FM	102
Mill Fm	Lancs	SD3841	53°51·9'	2°56·2'W	FM	102
Mill Fm	Lancs	SD7245	53°54·3'	2°25·2'W	FM	103
Mill Fm	Leeds	SE2645	53°54·3'	1°35·8'W	FM	104
Mill Fm	Leic	SK6912	52°42·3'	0°58·3'W	FM	129
Mill Fm	Leic	SK7226	52°49·8'	0°55·5'W	FM	129
Mill Fm	Leic	SP7394	52°32·6'	0°55·0'W	FM	141
Mill Fm	Lincs	SK8448	53°1·6'	0°44·4'W	FM	130
Mill Fm	Lincs	SK8691	53°24·8'	0°42·0'W	FM	112
Mill Fm	Lincs	SK9043	52°58·8'	0°39·2'W	FM	130
Mill Fm	Lincs	SK9749	53°2·0'	0°32·8'W	FM	130
Mill Fm	Lincs	TF0015	52°43·6'	0°30·7'W	FM	130
Mill Fm	Lincs	TF0593	53°25·6'	0°24·8'W	FM	112
Mill Fm	Lincs	TF2791	53°24·3'	0°5·0'W	FM	113
Mill Fm	Lincs	TF2957	53°5·9'	0°4·0'W	FM	122
Mill Fm	Lincs	TF3676	53°16·0'	0°2·8'E	FM	122
Mill Fm	Lincs	TF4067	53°11·1'	0°6·1'E	FM	122
Mill Fm	Mil Key	SP8545	52°6·0'	0°45·1'W	FM	152
Mill Fm	N Ayr	NS2344	55°39·7'	4°48·4'W	FM	63,70
Mill Fm	N Lincs	SE9413	53°36·5'	0°34·3'W	FM	112
Mill Fm	Norf	TF6604	52°36·7'	0°27·5'E	FM	143
Mill Fm	Norf	TF6615	52°42·7'	0°27·8'E	FM	132
Mill Fm	Norf	TF6907	52°38·3'	0°30·3'E	FM	143
Mill Fm	Norf	TF8442	52°56·9'	0°44·7'E	FM	132
Mill Fm	Norf	TF9407	52°37·8'	0°52·4'E	FM	144
Mill Fm	Norf	TG0921	52°45·0'	1°6·2'E	FM	133
Mill Fm	Norf	TG3929	52°48·6'	1°33·2'E	FM	133,134
Mill Fm	Norf	TG4918	52°42·4'	1°41·6'E	FM	134
Mill Fm	Norf	TL7887	52°27·3'	0°37·6'E	FM	144
Mill Fm	Norf	TM0498	52°32·7'	1°0·9'E	FM	144
Mill Fm	Norf	TM0787	52°26·7'	1°3·2'E	FM	144
Mill Fm	Norf	TM2094	52°30·2'	1°14·9'E	FM	134
Mill Fm	Northnts	SP8277	52°23·3'	0°47·3'W	FM	141
Mill Fm	Northum	NT9852	55°45·9'	2°1·5'W	FM	75
Mill Fm	Notts	SK4548	53°1·9'	1°19·3'W	FM	129
Mill Fm	Notts	SK6846	53°0·7'	0°58·9'W	FM	129
Mill Fm	Notts	SK7044	52°59·6'	0°57·0'W	FM	129
Mill Fm	Notts	SK7867	53°11·9'	0°49·5'W	FM	120,121
Mill Fm	Notts	SK7874	53°15·7'	0°49·4'W	FM	120,121
Mill Fm	N Som	ST4761	51°21·0'	2°45·3'W	FM	172,182
Mill Fm	N Yks	NZ4801	54°24·4'	1°15·2'W	FM	93
Mill Fm	N Yks	SE2859	54°1·8'	1°33·9'W	FM	104
Mill Fm	N Yks	SE3651	53°57·5'	1°26·7'W	FM	104
Mill Fm	N Yks	SE4754	53°59·0'	1°16·6'W	FM	105
Mill Fm	N Yks	SE4970	54°7·7'	1°14·6'W	FM	100
Mill Fm	N Yks	SE5872	54°8·7'	1°6·3'W	FM	100
Mill Fm	N Yks	SE6779	54°12·4'	0°57·9'W	FM	100
Mill Fm	N Yks	SE7394	54°20·4'	0°52·2'W	FM	94,100
Mill Fm	N Yks	SE8266	54°5·2'	0°44·4'W	FM	100
Mill Fm	N Yks	TA1079	54°11·9'	0°18·4'W	FM	101
Mill Fm	Oxon	SP2904	51°44·3'	1°34·4'W	FM	164
Mill Fm	Oxon	SP4313	51°49·1'	1°22·2'W	FM	164
Mill Fm	Oxon	SP4447	52°7·4'	1°21·0'W	FM	151
Mill Fm	Oxon	SP5213	51°49·0'	1°14·3'W	FM	164
Mill Fm	Oxon	SU3492	51°37·8'	1°30·1'W	FM	164,174
Mill Fm	Oxon	SU6777	51°29·5'	1°1·7'W	FM	175
Mill Fm	Peterb	TF0602	52°36·6'	0°25·7'W	FM	142
Mill Fm	Rut	SK9508	52°39·9'	0°35·3'W	FM	141
Mill Fm	Shrops	SO5194	52°32·7'	2°43·0'W	FM	137,138
Mill Fm	Shrops	SO5983	52°26·8'	2°35·8'W	FM	137,138
Mill Fm	Shrops	SO6287	52°29·0'	2°33·2'W	FM	138
Mill Fm	Somer	ST3246	51°12·8'	2°58·0'W	FM	182
Mill Fm	Somer	ST4113	50°55·0'	2°50·0'W	FM	193
Mill Fm	Staffs	SK2511	52°42·0'	1°37·4'W	FM	128
Mill Fm	Suff	TL8268	52°17·0'	0°40·5'E	FM	155
Mill Fm	Suff	TL9336	51°59·6'	0°49·1'E	FM	155
Mill Fm	Suff	TL9374	52°20·0'	0°50·4'E	FM	144
Mill Fm	Suff	TM0668	52°16·5'	1°1·6'E	FM	155
Mill Fm	Suff	TM1871	52°17·9'	1°12·2'E	FM	156
Mill Fm	Suff	TM2580	52°22·5'	1°18·7'E	FM	156
Mill Fm	Suff	TM3482	52°23·4'	1°26·7'E	FM	156
Mill Fm	Suff	TM3764	52°13·6'	1°28·6'E	FM	156
Mill Fm	Surrey	TQ0337	51°7·6'	0°31·3'W	FM	186
Mill Fm	Warw	SP2733	51°59·9'	1°36·0'W	FM	151
Mill Fm	Warw	SP3157	52°12·9'	1°32·4'W	FM	151
Mill Fm	Wilts	ST8141	51°10·3'	2°15·9'W	FM	183
Mill Fm	Wilts	ST8862	51°21·6'	2°10·0'W	FM	173
Mill Fm	Wilts	ST9557	51°19·0'	2°3·9'W	FM	173
Mill Fm	Wilts	ST9856	51°18·4'	2°1·3'W	FM	173
Mill Fm	Wilts	SU0030	51°4·4'	1°59·6'W	FM	184
Mill Fm	Wilts	SU0860	51°20·6'	1°52·7'W	FM	173
Mill Fm	Worcs	SO7837	52°2·1'	2°18·8'W	FM	150
Mill Fm	W Susx	SU8327	51°2·4'	0°48·6'W	FM	186,197
Mill Fm	W Susx	SU9425	51°1·2'	0°39·2'W	FM	186,197
Mill Fm	W Susx	TQ2029	51°3·1'	0°16·9'W	FM	187,198
Mill Fm, The	Warw	SP2183	52°26·9'	1°41·1'W	FM	139

Mill Fold	N Yks	SD9348	53°55·9'	2°6·0'W	X	103
Millfordhope Marsh	Kent	TQ8669	51°23·6'	0°40·8'E	W	178
Millfore	D & G	NX4775	55°3·0'	4°23·3'W	H	77
Millfore Hill	D & G	NX5070	55°0·4'	4°20·3'W	H	77
Millgate	Lancs	SD8819	53°40·3'	2°10·5'W	T	109
Millgate	Norf	TG1927	52°48·0'	1°15·3'E	T	133,134
Millgate Fm	Ches	SJ7273	53°15·4'	2°24·8'W	FM	118
Millgate Fm	Lincs	TF3219	52°45·4'	0°2·2'W	FM	131
Millgate Ho	Lincs	TF3219	52°45·4'	0°2·2'W	X	131
Millgeo	Orkney	HY3222	59°5·0'	3°10·7'W	X	6
Mill Geos	Shetld	HU3071	60°25·6'	1°26·8'W	X	3
Mill Gill	Cumbr	NY3219	54°33·9'	3°2·7'W	W	90
Millgill Burn	D & G	NY2990	55°12·2'	3°6·5'W	W	79
Millgillhead	Cumbr	NY0720	54°34·3'	3°25·9'W	T	89
Mill Glen	Clackm	NS9198	56°10·0'	3°44·9'W	X	58
Mill Glen Resr	N Ayr	NS2344	55°39·7'	4°48·4'W	W	63,70
Millgrane Hill	D & G	NX3465	54°57·4'	4°35·1'W	H	82
Mill Green	Cambs	TL6245	52°5·0'	0°22·3'E	T	154
Mill Green	Essex	TL6401	51°41·3'	0°22·8'E	T	167
Mill Green	Essex	TM1225	51°53·2'	1°5·2'E	X	168,169
Mill Green	Hants	SU5263	51°22·1'	1°14·8'W	T	174
Mill Green	Herts	TL2409	51°46·2'	0°11·8'W	T	166
Mill Green	Norf	TM1384	52°25·0'	1°8·3'E	T	144,156
Mill Green	N Yks	SE5671	54°8·1'	1°8·2'W	X	100
Mill Green	Shrops	SJ6828	52°51·2'	2°28·1'W	T	127
Mill Green	Staffs	SK0701	52°36·6'	1°53·4'W	T	139
Mill Green	Staffs	SK0823	52°48·5'	1°52·5'W	X	128
Mill Green	Suff	TL9542	52°2·7'	0°51·0'E	T	155
Mill Green	Suff	TL9957	52°10·7'	0°55·0'E	T	155
Mill Green	Suff	TM1360	52°12·0'	1°7·4'E	T	156
Mill Green	Suff	TM3161	52°12·1'	1°23·2'E	X	156
Mill Green Fm	Ches	SJ5288	53°23·4'	2°42·9'W	FM	108
Mill Green Fm	Halton	SJ5288	53°23·4'	2°42·9'W	FM	108
Mill Green Fm	Lincs	TF1947	53°0·7'	0°13·2'W	FM	130
Millgreen Fm	Suff	TM1460	52°12·0'	1°8·3'E	FM	156
Mill Green Ho	Lincs	TF2223	52°47·7'	0°11·0'W	X	131
Mill Green Park	Essex	TL6301	51°41·3'	0°21·9'E	X	167
Mill Greens	Northum	NZ0882	55°9·3'	1°52·0'W	X	81
Millgrip	Orkney	HY6123	59°5·8'	2°40·4'W	X	5
Mill Haft	Staffs	SJ7922	52°47·9'	2°18·3'W	X	127
Millhalf	Heref	SO2748	52°7·8'	3°3·6'W	T	148
Millhall	Angus	NO3235	56°30·4'	3°5·8'W	X	53
Mill Hall	D & G	NX6548	54°48·8'	4°5·6'W	X	83,84
Millhall	E Renf	NS5851	55°44·2'	4°15·3'W	X	64
Millhall	Kent	TQ7259	51°18·5'	0°28·5'E	T	178,188
Millhall Fm	Essex	TL6332	51°58·0'	0°22·8'E	FM	167
Mill Ham	Devon	SS6347	51°12·6'	3°57·3'W	X	180
Millham Fm	Corn	SX1160	50°24·8'	4°39·2'W	FM	200
Millham Fm	Worcs	SO7551	52°9·6'	2°21·5'W	FM	150
Millhampost Fm	Glos	SP0430	51°58·3'	1°56·1'W	FM	150
Millhaugh	Pth & Kin	NO0014	56°18·7'	3°36·5'W	X	58
Millhaugh	Pth & Kin	NO0029	56°26·8'	3°36·9'W	X	52,53,58
Mill Haven	Pemb	SM8112	51°46·1'	5°10·1'W	W	157
Millhayes	Devon	ST1314	50°55·4'	3°13·9'W	T	181,193
Millhayes	Devon	ST2303	50°49·5'	3°5·2'W	T	192,193
Mill Hayes	Staffs	SJ8855	53°5·8'	2°10·3'W	X	118
Millhead	Aberd	NJ4705	57°8·2'	2°52·1'W	X	37
Millhead	Lancs	SD4971	54°8·2'	2°46·4'W	T	97
Mill Heath	Suff	TL7771	52°18·7'	0°36·2'E	X	144,155
Mill Heath	Suff	TL9164	52°14·7'	0°48·3'E	X	155
Mill Heath	Suff	TM4176	52°20·0'	1°32·6'E	X	156
Millheugh	Scot Bord	NT6919	55°28·1'	2°29·0'W	X	80
Millheugh	S Lanak	NS7551	55°44·4'	3°59·0'W	T	64
Millhill	Aberd	NJ5234	57°23·9'	2°47·5'W	X	29
Millhill	Aberd	NJ5718	57°15·3'	2°42·3'W	X	37
Millhill	Aberd	NJ6249	57°32·0'	2°37·6'W	X	29
Mill Hill	Aberd	NK0144	57°29·4'	1°58·5'W	H	30
Mill Hill	Aberd	NK0144	57°29·4'	1°58·5'W	X	30
Millhill	Aberd	NK0458	57°37·0'	1°55·5'W	X	30
Millhill	Aberd	NO8677	56°53·3'	2°13·3'W	X	45
Mill Hill	Barnet	TQ2292	51°37·0'	0°13·9'W	T	176
Mill Hill	Black w Dar	SD6626	53°44·0'	2°30·5'W	T	103
Mill Hill	Bolton	SD7209	53°34·9'	2°25·0'W	T	109
Mill Hill	Bucks	SP6821	51°53·2'	1°0·3'W	X	164,165
Mill Hill	Cambs	TL2351	52°8·8'	0°11·7'W	X	153
Mill Hill	Cambs	TL2944	52°5·0'	0°6·6'W	X	153
Mill Hill	Cambs	TL5155	52°10·6'	0°12·9'E	X	154
Mill Hill	Cumbr	NY3467	54°59·8'	3°1·5'W	X	85
Mill Hill	Cumbr	NY7313	54°30·9'	2°24·6'W	X	91
Mill Hill	Derby	SK0690	53°24·6'	1°54·2'W	H	110
Millhill	Devon	SX4574	50°32·9'	4°10·9'W	T	201
Millhill	D & G	NX9275	55°3·7'	3°41·0'W	X	84
Millhill	D & G	NX9568	55°0·0'	3°38·1'W	X	84
Millhill	D & G	NY1181	55°7·2'	3°23·3'W	X	78
Mill Hill	Dorset	ST9908	50°52·5'	2°0·5'W	X	195
Mill Hill	Durham	NZ0810	54°29·4'	1°52·2'W	X	92
Mill Hill	Durham	NZ4237	54°43·8'	1°20·4'W	X	93
Mill Hill	Essex	TL7627	51°55·0'	0°34·0'E	A	167
Mill Hill	Essex	TQ7998	51°39·4'	0°35·7'E	X	167
Mill Hill	Essex	TQ8293	51°36·6'	0°38·1'E	T	178
Mill Hill	E Susx	TQ4105	50°49·9'	0°0·5'E	X	198
Mill Hill	E Susx	TQ6205	50°49·5'	0°18·4'E	T	199
Mill Hill	Glos	SO5401	51°42·6'	2°39·6'W	X	162
Mill Hill	Glos	SO6006	51°45·3'	2°34·4'W	T	162
Mill Hill	Herts	TL2025	51°54·9'	0°14·9'W	X	166
Mill Hill	Herts	TL3432	51°58·4'	0°2·5'W	X	166
Millhill	Highld	NH9156	57°35·1'	3°48·9'W	X	27
Mill Hill	Kent	TQ9672	51°25·0'	0°49·5'E	X	178
Mill Hill	Kent	TR3651	51°12·8'	1°23·1'E	T	179
Mill Hill	Lancs	SD4521	53°41·2'	2°49·6'W	X	102
Mill Hill	Leic	SP7087	52°28·8'	0°57·8'W	X	141
Mill Hill	Lincs	TF0033	52°53·3'	0°30·4'W	X	130
Mill Hill	Lincs	TF0090	53°24·1'	0°29·3'W	X	112
Mill Hill	Lincs	TF1587	53°22·3'	0°15·9'W	X	113,121
Mill Hill	Lincs	TF3171	53°24·2'	0°1·4'W	X	113
Mill Hill	Lincs	TF4880	53°18·0'	0°13·7'E	X	122
Mill Hill	Lincs	TF5073	53°14·2'	0°15·3'E	X	122
Mill Hill	Lincs	TF5365	53°9·8'	0°17·7'E	T	122
Millhill	Moray	NJ3158	57°36·7'	3°8·8'W	X	28

Mill Hill	N Lincs	SE7907	53°33·5'	0°48·0'W	X	112
Mill Hill	Norf	TG4701	52°33·3'	1°39·0'E	X	134
Mill Hill	Norf	TL9096	52°31·9'	0°48·5'E	X	144
Mill Hill	Northnts	SP6879	52°24·5'	0°59·6'W	X	141
Mill Hill	Northnts	SP7679	52°24·5'	0°52·6'W	X	141
Mill Hill	Notts	SK5333	52°53·7'	1°12·3'W	H	129
Mill Hill	Notts	SK6661	53°8·8'	1°0·4'W	X	120
Mill Hill	Notts	SK7577	53°17·3'	0°52·1'W	X	120
Mill Hill	N upon Ty	NZ2172	55°2·8'	1°39·9'W	X	88
Mill Hill	N Yks	SE4058	54°1·2'	1°23·0'W	X	105
Mill Hill	N Yks	SE4590	54°18·5'	1°18·1'W	X	99
Millhill	Pth & Kin	NN9309	56°15·9'	3°43·2'W	X	58
Millhill	Pth & Kin	NO2931	56°28·2'	3°8·7'W	X	53
Mill Hill	Rut	SK8309	52°40·6'	0°45·9'W	X	141
Millhill	S Lanak	NS9241	55°39·3'	3°42·6'W	X	71,72
Millhill	S Lanak	NS9852	55°45·3'	3°37·1'W	X	65,72
Mill Hill	Somer	SS8245	51°11·8'	3°40·9'W	X	181
Mill Hill	Stock on T	NZ3715	54°32·0'	1°25·3'W	X	93
Mill Hill	Suff	TL8551	52°7·8'	0°42·6'E	T	155
Mill Hill	Suff	TL9759	52°11·9'	0°53·4'E	X	155
Mill Hill	Suff	TL9767	52°16·2'	0°53·6'E	A	155
Mill Hill	Wakf	SE3921	53°41·3'	1°24·2'W	X	104
Mill Hill	Warw	SP4252	52°10·1'	1°22·8'W	X	151
Mill Hill	W Susx	TQ2106	50°50·7'	0°16·5'W	X	198
Mill Hill	York	SE6753	53°58·4'	0°58·3'W	X	105,106
Millhill Burn	S Lanak	NS9340	55°38·8'	3°41·6'W	W	71,72
Mill Hill East Sta	Barnet	TQ2491	51°36·5'	0°12·2'W	X	176
Mill Hill Fm	Ches	SJ9184	53°21·4'	2°7·7'W	FM	109
Millhill Fm	Essex	TL5931	51°57·5'	0°19·2'E	FM	167
Millhill Fm	Essex	TQ7597	51°38·9'	0°32·2'E	FM	167
Millhill Fm	Kent	TR1642	51°8·4'	1°5·7'E	FM	179,189
Mill Hill Fm	Norf	TG3812	52°39·4'	1°31·6'E	FM	133,134
Mill Hill Fm	Northnts	SP6885	52°27·8'	0°59·5'W	FM	141
Mill Hill Fm	N Yks	NZ3601	54°24·4'	1°26·3'W	FM	93
Mill Hill Fm	N Yks	SE6366	54°5·4'	1°1·8'W	FM	100
Millhill Fm	Suff	TM0054	52°9·1'	0°55·8'E	FM	155
Millhill Fm	Suff	TM1068	52°16·4'	1°5·1'E	FM	155
Millhill Ho	Midlo	NT3365	55°52·7'	3°3·8'W	X	66
Millhill Ho	Suff	TL8256	52°10·6'	0°40·1'E	X	155
Millhills	Pth & Kin	NN8919	56°21·3'	3°47·3'W	X	58
Mill Hills	Suff	TM2749	52°5·8'	1°19·3'E	T	169
Millhills Cott	Pth & Kin	NN8610	56°16·4'	3°50·0'W	X	58
Mill Hill (Tumulus)	Norf	TG4701	52°33·3'	1°39·0'E	A	134
Millhill Wood	Suff	TL8380	52°23·5'	0°41·8'E	F	144
Mill Hirst	N Yks	SE1960	54°2·4'	1°42·2'W	T	99
Mill Ho	Bucks	SP8700	51°41·7'	0°44·1'W	X	165
Mill Ho	Cambs	TL6050	52°7·7'	0°20·7'E	X	154
Mill Ho	Ches	SJ9079	53°18·7'	2°8·6'W	X	118
Mill Ho	Cumbr	SD6385	54°15·8'	2°33·7'W	X	97
Mill Ho	Dorset	SY7787	50°41·2'	2°19·2'W	X	194
Mill Ho	Durham	NZ2647	54°49·3'	1°35·3'W	X	88
Mill Ho	Durham	NZ3731	54°40·6'	1°25·1'W	X	93
Mill Ho	Essex	TL6915	51°48·7'	0°27·5'E	X	167
Mill Ho	Essex	TL9227	51°54·7'	0°47·9'E	X	168
Mill Ho	Essex	TQ7798	51°39·4'	0°33·9'E	X	167
Mill Ho	E Yorks	SE7141	53°51·9'	0°54·8'W	X	105,106
Mill Ho	E Yorks	SE7644	53°53·4'	0°50·2'W	X	105,106
Mill Ho	E Yorks	TA1443	53°52·5'	0°15·5'W	X	107
Mill Ho	Kent	TQ9845	51°10·4'	0°50·3'E	X	189
Mill Ho	Lancs	SD4349	53°56·3'	2°51·7'W	X	102
Mill Ho	Monm	SO4314	51°49·5'	2°49·2'W	X	161
Mill Ho	Norf	TF6931	52°51·2'	0°31·0'E	X	132
Mill Ho	Norf	TF7814	52°41·9'	0°38·5'E	X	132
Mill Ho	Northnts	SP5232	51°59·3'	1°14·2'W	X	151
Mill Ho	Northum	NY7864	54°58·5'	2°20·2'W	X	86,87
Mill Ho	N Yks	SE1965	54°5·1'	1°42·2'W	X	99
Mill Ho	N Yks	SE5060	54°2·3'	1°13·8'W	X	100
Mill Ho	N Yks	SE5139	53°50·9'	1°13·1'W	X	105
Mill Ho	N Yks	SE6967	54°5·9'	0°56·3'W	X	100
Mill Ho	Shrops	SJ4021	52°47·2'	2°53·0'W	X	126
Mill Ho	Shrops	SJ6530	52°52·2'	2°30·8'W	X	127
Mill Ho	Somer	ST1723	51°0·3'	3°10·6'W	X	181,193
Mill Ho	Stir	NN6022	56°22·4'	4°15·6'W	X	51
Mill Ho	Suff	TM0236	51°59·4'	0°56·9'E	X	155
Mill Ho	Thurr	TQ6578	51°28·8'	0°23·2'E	X	177,178
Mill Ho	W Susx	SZ8198	50°46·8'	0°50·7'W	X	197
Mill Ho	York	SE6951	53°57·3'	0°56·5'W	X	105,106
Millhockie Hill	Aberd	NJ5620	57°16·4'	2°43·3'W	H	37
Millhole	Angus	NO3139	56°32·5'	3°6·9'W	X	53
Millhole	Pth & Kin	NO0430	56°27·4'	3°33·0'W	X	52,53
Millhole	Pth & Kin	NO1041	56°33·4'	3°27·4'W	X	53
Millhole	Pth & Kin	NO1347	56°36·7'	3°24·6'W	X	53
Millholm Cross	Scot Bord	NY4786	55°10·2'	2°49·5'W	A	79
Millholme	Cumbr	NY4870	55°1·6'	2°48·4'W	X	86
Millholme	Cumbr	SD5690	54°18·5'	2°40·2'W	T	97
Mill Holme	N Yks	SE0053	53°58·6'	1°59·6'W	X	104
Millholme Fm	Red & Cl	NZ6719	54°33·9'	0°57·4'W	FM	94
Millhorn	Pth & Kin	NO2243	56°34·6'	3°15·7'W	X	53
Mill Ho, The	Essex	TL5427	51°55·4'	0°14·8'E	X	167
Mill Ho, The	Hants	SU2909	50°53·0'	1°34·9'W	X	196
Mill Ho, The	Kent	TQ5466	51°22·6'	0°13·2'E	X	177
Mill Ho, The	Suff	TL8867	52°16·4'	0°45·7'E	X	155
Mill Ho, The	Worcs	SO8664	52°16·7'	2°11·9'W	X	150
Millhouse	Arg & Bt	NR9570	55°53·0'	5°16·2'W	T	62
Millhouse	Cumbr	NY3637	54°43·7'	2°59·2'W	T	90
Millhouse	Orkney	HY3918	59°2·9'	3°3·3'W	X	6
Millhouse	Orkney	HY4802	58°54·4'	2°53·7'W	X	6,7
Millhouse	Orkney	ND3095	58°50·5'	3°12·3'W	X	7
Millhouse	S Lanak	NS6050	55°43·6'	4°13·3'W	X	64
Millhousebridge	D & G	NY1085	55°9·3'	3°24·3'W	T	78
Mill House Fm	Ches	SJ8560	53°8·5'	2°13·0'W	FM	118
Mill House Fm	Ches	SJ8770	53°13·9'	2°11·3'W	FM	118
Mill House Fm	Cumbr	SD1199	54°23·0'	3°21·3'W	FM	96
Mill House Fm	E Susx	TQ4623	50°59·5'	0°5·2'E	FM	198
Millhouse Fm	Herts	TL1003	51°43·1'	0°24·1'W	FM	166
Mill House Fm	Lincs	TF1782	53°19·6'	0°14·2'W	FM	121
Mill House Fm	N Lincs	SE7800	53°29·7'	0°49·0'W	FM	112
Mill House Fm	Northnts	SP4934	52°0·4'	1°16·8'W	FM	151
Mill House Fm	Northum	NZ1185	55°9·8'	1°49·2'W	FM	81
Mill House Fm	Oxon	SP6120	51°52·7'	1°6·4'W	FM	164,165

Millhouse Fm	Shrops	SJ4209	52°40·8'	2°51·1'W	FM	126
Millhouse Green	Barns	SE2103	53°31·6'	1°40·6'W	T	110
Millhouses	Barns	SE4204	53°32·1'	1°21·6'W	T	111
Mill Houses	Lancs	SD6267	54°6·1'	2°34·5'W	X	97
Millhouses	Sheff	SK3283	53°20·8'	1°30·7'W	T	110,111
Mill Howfe	Red & Cl	NZ6224	54°36·7'	1°2·0'W	X	94
Millhuie Hill	Aberd	NJ4016	57°14·1'	2°59·2'W	H	37
Milliagord	Shetld	HU5891	60°36·2'	0°55·9'W	X	1,2
Millichen	C of Glas	NS5772	55°55·4'	4°16·9'W	X	64
Millichope Park	Shrops	SO5288	52°29·5'	2°42·0'W	A	137,138
Millichope Park	Shrops	SO5288	52°29·5'	2°42·0'W	X	137,138
Millie Burn	Moray	NJ1166	57°40·8'	3°29·1'W	W	28
Milligansbush	D & G	NY3171	55°2·0'	3°4·3'W	X	85
Milligansbushfield	D & G	NY3272	55°2·5'	3°3·4'W	X	85
Milliganton	D & G	NX8483	55°7·9'	3°48·7'W	X	78
Milliganton	D & G	NX9183	55°8·0'	3°42·2'W	X	78
Millikenpark	Renf	NS4162	55°49·8'	4°31·9'W	T	64
Millin Brook	Pemb	SN0016	51°48·7'	4°53·7'W	W	157,158
Millin Cross	Pemb	SM9913	51°47·0'	4°54·5'W	T	157,158
Millinder Ho	N Yks	NZ6706	54°26·9'	0°57·6'W	X	94
Millingdale Fm	E Yorks	TA0858	54°0·6'	0°20·7'W	FM	107
Millington	E Yorks	SE8351	53°57·1'	0°43·7'W	T	106
Millington Beck	E Yorks	SE8251	53°57·2'	0°44·6'W	W	106
Millington Grange	E Yorks	SE8354	53°58·8'	0°43·6'W	X	106
Millington Green	Derby	SK2647	53°1·4'	1°36·3'W	T	119,128
Millington Hall	Ches	SJ7284	53°21·4'	2°24·8'W	X	109
Millington Heights	E Yorks	SE8354	53°58·8'	0°43·6'W	X	106
Millington Pasture	E Yorks	SE8454	53°58·8'	0°42·7'W	X	106
Millington Springs	Notts	SK4852	53°4·0'	1°16·6'W	F	120
Millington Wood	E Yorks	SE8353	53°58·2'	0°43·7'W	F	106
Millingwood Fell	Scot Bord	NY4294	55°14·5'	2°54·3'W	H	79
Million, The	Staffs	SO8486	52°28·5'	2°13·7'W	F	138
Millisle	D & G	NX4646	54°47·4'	4°23·3'W	X	83
Millison's Wood	Sol	SP2681	52°25·8'	1°36·7'W	F	140
Milljoan Hill	S Ayr	NX1177	55°3·3'	4°57·1'W	H	76
Mill Knock	D & G	NX5554	54°51·8'	4°15·1'W	H	83
Mill Knowe	Arg & Bt	NR7121	55°26·0'	5°36·8'W	T	68
Millknowe	E Loth	NT6564	55°52·3'	2°33·1'W	X	67
Millknowe Burn	Scot Bord	NT6850	55°44·8'	2°30·1'W	W	67,74
Mill Lands	D & G	NY0285	55°9·2'	3°31·8'W	X	78
Mill Lane	Hants	SU7850	51°14·9'	0°52·6'W	T	186
Mill Lane Fm	Cambs	TL4464	52°15·5'	0°7·0'E	FM	154
Mill Lane Fm	Lincs	SK9054	53°4·8'	0°39·0'W	FM	121
Mill Lane Fm	Lincs	TF4192	53°24·6'	0°7·7'E	FM	113
Mill Lane House Farm	Ches	SJ5674	53°15·9'	2°39·2'W	FM	117
Mill Loch	Arg & Bt	NR6450	55°41·4'	5°44·9'W	W	62
Mill Loch	D & G	NY0783	55°8·2'	3°27·1'W	W	78
Mill Loch	Orkney	HY5636	59°12·8'	2°45·8'W	W	5
Mill Loch	S Ayr	NX2384	55°7·4'	4°46·1'W	W	76
Mill Loch	Shetld	HT9638	60°7·9'	2°3·8'W	W	4
Mill Loch	Shetld	HU2478	60°29·4'	1°33·3'W	W	3
Mill Loch	Shetld	HU2756	60°17·5'	1°30·2'W	W	3
Mill Loch	Shetld	HU2855	60°17·0'	1°29·1'W	W	3
Mill Loch	Shetld	HU3165	60°22·3'	1°25·8'W	W	3
Mill Loch	Shetld	HU3251	60°14·8'	1°24·8'W	W	3
Mill Loch	Shetld	HU3390	60°35·8'	1°23·3'W	W	1,2
Mill Loch	Shetld	HU3766	60°22·8'	1°19·2'W	W	2,3
Mill Loch	Shetld	HU4469	60°24·4'	1°11·6'W	W	2,3
Mill Loch	Shetld	HU4490	60°35·7'	1°11·3'W	W	1,2
Mill Loch	Shetld	HU4591	60°36·3'	1°10·2'W	W	1,2
Mill Loch	Shetld	HU5066	60°22·8'	1°5·1'W	W	2,3
Mill Loch	Shetld	HU5070	60°24·9'	1°5·0'W	W	2,3
Mill Loch	Shetld	HU5173	60°26·5'	1°3·9'W	W	2,3
Mill Loch	Shetld	HU5388	60°34·6'	1°1·5'W	W	1,2
Mill Loch of Gunnister	Shetld	HU3274	60°27·2'	1°24·6'W	W	3
Mill Lochs	Shetld	HU2481	60°31·0'	1°33·3'W	W	3
Mill Lochs	Shetld	HU3163	60°21·3'	1°25·8'W	W	3
Mill Lochs of Ockran	Shetld	HU2484	60°32·6'	1°33·2'W	W	3
Mill Lochs of Sandvoe	Shetld	HU3488	60°34·7'	1°22·3'W	W	1,2
Mill Lochs of Stovabreck	Shetld	HU2779	60°29·9'	1°30·0'W	W	3
Millmannoch	S Ayr	NS4318	55°26·1'	4°28·5'W	X	70
Mill Maud	Aberd	NJ5706	57°8·8'	2°42·2'W	H	37
Mill Meads	Newham	TQ3883	51°32·0'	0°0·2'W	T	177
Millmeece	Staffs	SJ8333	52°53·9'	2°14·8'W	T	127
Millminnoch	D & G	NX6272	55°1·7'	4°9·1'W	X	77
Millmoan Hill	S Ayr	NX0974	55°1·7'	4°58·9'W	H	76
Millmoor	Devon	ST1014	50°55·3'	3°16·4'W	T	181,193
Mill Moor	N Yks	NZ8401	54°24·1'	0°41·9'W	X	94
Millmoor	S Lanak	NS9039	55°38·2'	3°44·4'W	X	71,72
Millmoor Fm	Ches	SJ5147	53°1·3'	2°43·4'W	FM	117
Millmoor Rig	Scot Bord	NT6306	55°21·0'	2°34·6'W	X	80
Millmore	D & G	NX4388	55°9·9'	4°27·5'W	X	77
Millmore	S Ayr	NX1480	55°5·0'	4°54·4'W	H	76
Millmoss	Aberd	NJ7348	57°31·5'	2°26·6'W	X	29
Mill Mound	Hants	SU7129	51°3·6'	0°58·8'W	A	186,197
Mill Mound	Somer	ST1143	51°11·0'	3°16·0'W	A	181
Mill Mound	Somer	ST3248	51°13·9'	2°58·1'W	A	182
Mill Mound	Wilts	SU2524	51°1·1'	1°38·2'W	A	184
Mill Mound	Wilts	SU2623	51°0·6'	1°37·4'W	A	184
Mill Mound	York	SE6951	53°57·3'	0°56·5'W	A	105,106
Millmount	Scot Bord	NT5534	55°36·1'	2°42·4'W	X	73
Mill Mount	Suff	TM2879	52°21·9'	1°21·3'E	X	156
Mill Mount (Castle Mound)	Suff	TM3983	52°23·8'	1°31·2'E	A	156
Millnain	Highld	NH5059	57°36·0'	4°30·1'W	T	26
Millness	Cumbr	SD5382	54°14·1'	2°42·8'W	T	97
Millness	Highld	NH3831	57°20·7'	4°41·1'W	X	26
Mill of Aden	Aberd	NJ9846	57°30·5'	2°1·5'W	X	30
Mill of Air Cott	Aberd	NJ7705	57°8·4'	2°22·3'W	X	38
Mill of Airntully	Pth & Kin	NO1034	56°29·6'	3°27·3'W	X	53
Mill of Allardice	Aberd	NO8174	56°51·7'	2°18·2'W	X	45
Mill of Allathan	Aberd	NJ8927	57°20·3'	2°10·5'W	X	38
Mill of Alvah	Aberd	NJ6760	57°38·0'	2°32·7'W	X	29
Mill of Ardo	Aberd	NJ8438	57°26·2'	2°15·5'W	X	29,30
Mill of Ardoch	Pth & Kin	NN8311	56°16·9'	3°52·9'W	X	57
Mill of Argaty	Stir	NN7401	56°11·4'	4°1·4'W	X	57
Mill of Ashogle	Aberd	NJ7052	57°33·7'	2°29·6'W	X	29
Mill of Auchedly	Aberd	NJ9033	57°23·5'	2°9·5'W	X	30
Mill of Aucheen	Angus	NO5379	56°54·3'	2°45·9'W	X	44
Mill of Auchenhuive	Aberd	NJ8425	57°19·2'	2°15·5'W	X	38
Mill of Auchintoul	Aberd	NJ6151	57°33·1'	2°38·6'W	X	29

Mill of Auchlin	Aberd	NJ9163	57°39·7'	2°8·6'W	X	30
Mill of Auchmar	Aberd	NJ5625	57°19·1'	2°43·4'W	X	37
Mill of Auchreddie	Aberd	NJ8946	57°30·5'	2°10·6'W	X	30
Mill of Balcairn	Aberd	NJ7829	57°21·3'	2°21·5'W	X	38
Mill of Balmaud	Aberd	NJ7456	57°35·9'	2°25·6'W	X	29
Mill of Balrownie	Angus	NO5763	56°45·7'	2°41·8'W	X	44
Mill of Bandley	Aberd	NJ6116	57°14·2'	2°38·3'W	X	37
Mill of Barnes	Aberd	NO6869	56°48·9'	2°31·0'W	X	45
Mill of Barns	Aberd	NJ6425	57°19·1'	2°35·4'W	X	37
Mill of Barras	Aberd	NO8579	56°54·4'	2°14·3'W	X	45
Mill of Birsack	Aberd	NJ8310	57°11·1'	2°16·4'W	X	38
Mill of Blackford	Aberd	NJ7035	57°24·5'	2°29·5'W	X	29
Mill of Blairshinnoch	Aberd	NJ6462	57°39·0'	2°35·7'W	X	29
Mill of Blairton	Aberd	NJ9719	57°16·0'	2°2·5'W	X	38
Mill of Bonnyton	Aberd	NJ6829	57°21·3'	2°31·5'W	X	38
Mill of Botary	Aberd	NJ4645	57°29·8'	2°53·6'W	X	28,29
Mill of Bourtie	Aberd	NJ7725	57°19·2'	2°22·5'W	X	38
Mill of Braco	Aberd	NJ7121	57°17·0'	2°28·4'W	X	38
Mill of Brathinch	Angus	NO5863	56°45·7'	2°40·8'W	X	44
Mill of Brighty	Angus	NO4438	56°32·1'	2°54·2'W	T	54
Mill of Brux	Aberd	NJ4814	57°13·1'	2°51·2'W	X	37
Mill of Brydock	Aberd	NJ6558	57°36·9'	2°34·7'W	X	29
Mill of Buckie	Moray	NJ4264	57°40·0'	2°57·9'W	X	28
Mill of Burns Fm	Aberd	NJ7434	57°24·0'	2°25·5'W	FM	29
Mill of Cammie	Aberd	NO6892	57°1·3'	2°31·2'W	X	38,45
Mill of Camno	Pth & Kin	NO2642	56°34·1'	3°11·8'W	X	53
Mill of Camsail	Arg & Bt	NS2581	55°59·7'	4°47·9'W	X	63
Mill of Carden	Aberd	NJ6925	57°19·1'	2°30·4'W	X	38
Mill of Cattie	Aberd	NO6095	57°2·9'	2°39·1'W	X	37,45
Mill of Chon	Stir	NN4502	56°11·4'	4°29·4'W	X	57
Mill of Clinter	Aberd	NO6192	57°1·3'	2°38·1'W	X	45
Mill of Collieston	Aberd	NK0130	57°21·9'	1°58·5'W	X	30
Mill of Colp	Aberd	NJ7447	57°31·0'	2°25·6'W	X	29
Mill of Conveth	Aberd	NO7274	56°51·7'	2°27·1'W	X	45
Mill of Craigievar	Aberd	NJ5710	57°11·0'	2°42·2'W	X	37
Mill of Craigston	Aberd	NJ7755	57°35·3'	2°22·6'W	X	29,30
Mill of Crichie	Aberd	NJ7636	57°25·1'	2°23·5'W	X	29
Mill of Criggie	Aberd	NO7265	56°46·8'	2°27·0'W	X	45
Mill of Cruick	Angus	NO5662	56°45·1'	2°42·7'W	X	44
Mill of Culfork	Aberd	NJ4411	57°11·4'	2°55·1'W	X	37
Mill of Cullen	Aberd	NJ7464	57°40·2'	2°25·7'W	X	29
Mill of Delgaty	Aberd	NJ7549	57°32·1'	2°24·6'W	X	29
Mill of Dess	Aberd	NO5699	57°5·1'	2°43·1'W	X	37,44
Mill of Dinnet	Aberd	NO4698	57°4·5'	2°53·0'W	X	37,44
Mill of Drummond	Pth & Kin	NN8315	56°19·0'	3°53·1'W	X	57
Mill of Durn	Aberd	NJ5863	57°39·6'	2°41·8'W	X	29
Mill of Durno	Aberd	NJ7125	57°19·1'	2°28·4'W	X	38
Mill of Easterton	Aberd	NJ7730	57°21·9'	2°22·5'W	X	29,30
Mill of Echt	Aberd	NJ7305	57°8·4'	2°26·3'W	T	38
Mill of Elrick	Aberd	NJ9340	57°27·3'	2°6·5'W	X	30
Mill of Fechel	Aberd	NJ8625	57°19·2'	2°13·5'W	X	38
Mill of Fedderate	Aberd	NJ8850	57°32·7'	2°11·6'W	X	30
Mill of Fiddes	Aberd	NJ9524	57°18·6'	2°4·5'W	X	38
Mill of Findon	Aberd	NO9297	57°4·1'	2°7·5'W	X	38,45
Mill of Fintray	Aberd	NJ8316	57°14·3'	2°16·4'W	X	38
Mill of Fintry	Aberd	NJ7554	57°34·8'	2°24·6'W	X	29
Mill of Forest	Aberd	NO8685	56°57·6'	2°13·4'W	X	45
Mill of Forgue	Aberd	NJ6245	57°29·9'	2°37·6'W	X	29
Mill of Forneth	Pth & Kin	NO0945	56°35·5'	3°28·5'W	X	52,53
Mill of Fortrie	Aberd	NJ9540	57°27·3'	2°4·5'W	X	30
Mill of Fortune	Pth & Kin	NN7820	56°21·7'	3°58·0'W	X	51,52,57
Mill of Fowlis	Aberd	NJ5512	57°12·1'	2°44·2'W	X	37
Mill of Garvock	Aberd	NO7774	56°51·7'	2°22·2'W	X	45
Mill of Gask	Pth & Kin	NN9817	56°20·3'	3°38·6'W	X	58
Mill of Gaval	Aberd	NJ9951	57°33·2'	2°0·5'W	X	30
Mill of Gellan	Aberd	NJ5101	57°6·1'	2°48·1'W	X	37
Mill of Glenbervie	Aberd	NO7680	56°54·9'	2°23·2'W	X	45
Mill of Glen Burn	D & G	NX8157	54°53·9'	3°50·9'W	W	84
Mill of Grange	Moray	NJ0460	57°37·4'	3°36·0'W	X	27
Mill of Haldane	W Dunb	NS4081	56°0·0'	4°33·5'W	T	64
Mill of Haughs	Aberd	NO6691	57°0·8'	2°33·1'W	X	38,45
Mill of Haulkerton	Aberd	NO7173	56°51·1'	2°28·1'W	X	45
Mill of Hirn	Aberd	NO7299	57°5·1'	2°27·3'W	X	38,45
Mill of Hole	Aberd	NJ7105	57°8·4'	2°28·3'W	X	38
Mill of Inverarity	Angus	NO4544	56°35·3'	2°53·3'W	X	54
Mill of Johnston	Aberd	NJ5724	57°18·5'	2°42·4'W	X	37
Mill of Kair	Aberd	NO7677	56°53·3'	2°23·2'W	X	45
Mill of Keithfield	Aberd	NJ8333	57°23·5'	2°16·5'W	X	29,30
Mill of Kincardine	Aberd	NO6775	56°52·2'	2°32·0'W	T	45
Mill of Kincraigie	Aberd	NJ5003	57°7·2'	2°49·1'W	X	37
Mill of Kingoodie	Aberd	NJ8325	57°19·2'	2°16·5'W	X	38
Mill of Kinmuck	Aberd	NJ9936	57°25·1'	2°0·5'W	X	30
Mill of Kintocher	Aberd	NJ5709	57°10·4'	2°42·2'W	X	37
Mill of Knockenbaird	Aberd	NJ6330	57°21·8'	2°36·4'W	X	29,37
Mill of Laithers	Aberd	NJ6949	57°32·1'	2°30·6'W	X	29
Mill of Leask	Aberd	NK0131	57°22·4'	1°58·5'W	X	30
Mill of Leslie	Aberd	NJ5924	57°18·5'	2°40·4'W	X	37
Mill of Lethnot	Angus	NO5368	56°48·3'	2°45·7'W	X	44
Mill of Lumphart	Aberd	NJ7727	57°20·2'	2°22·5'W	X	38
Mill of Lyne	Aberd	NJ7008	57°10·0'	2°29·3'W	X	38
Mill of Lynebain	Aberd	NJ4135	57°24·4'	2°58·5'W	X	28
Mill of Marcus	Angus	NO5159	56°43·5'	2°47·6'W	T	54
Mill of Meaggie	Aberd	NJ6649	57°32·1'	2°33·6'W	X	29
Mill of Melrose	Aberd	NJ7364	57°40·2'	2°26·7'W	X	29
Mill of Menie	Aberd	NJ9820	57°16·5'	2°1·5'W	X	38
Mill of Minnes	Aberd	NJ9423	57°18·1'	2°5·5'W	X	38
Mill of Mondynes	Aberd	NO7779	56°54·4'	2°22·2'W	X	45
Mill of Monquich	Aberd	NO8595	57°3·0'	2°14·4'W	T	38,45
Mill of Morphie	Aberd	NO7162	56°45·2'	2°28·0'W	X	45
Mill of Morphie	Aberd	NO7162	56°45·2'	2°28·0'W	X	45
Mill of Muckly	Pth & Kin	NO0641	56°33·4'	3°31·3'W	X	52,53
Mill of Muiresk	Aberd	NJ6948	57°31·5'	2°30·6'W	X	29
Mill of Newburgh	Aberd	NJ9924	57°18·7'	2°0·5'W	X	38
Mill of Peattie	Pth & Kin	NO2236	56°30·8'	3°15·6'W	X	53
Mill of Pert	Angus	NO6466	56°47·3'	2°34·9'W	X	45
Mill of Pitcaple	Aberd	NJ7326	57°19·7'	2°26·4'W	T	38
Mill of Pitmedden	Aberd	NJ6727	57°20·2'	2°32·4'W	X	38
Mill of Plunton	D & G	NX6251	54°50·3'	4°8·5'W	X	83
Mill of Pot	Aberd	NJ7950	57°32·6'	2°20·6'W	X	29,30
Mill of Raemoir	Aberd	NO6998	57°4·6'	2°30·2'W	X	38,45

Mill of Rango	Orkney	HY2618	59°2·8'	3°16·9'W	T	6
Mill of Rannieston	Aberd	NJ9425	57°19·2'	2°5·5'W	X	38
Mill of Ribrae	Aberd	NJ6851	57°33·1'	2°31·6'W	X	29
Mill of Rora	Aberd	NK0449	57°32·1'	1°55·5'W	X	30
Mill of Ryland	Aberd	NJ6658	57°36·9'	2°33·7'W	X	29
Mill of Saphock	Aberd	NJ7629	57°21·3'	2°23·5'W	X	38
Mill of Sessnie	Aberd	NJ8737	57°25·6'	2°12·5'W	X	30
Mill of Sterin	Aberd	NO3492	57°1·1'	3°4·8'W	X	44
Mill of Tarty	Aberd	NJ9726	57°19·7'	2°2·5'W	X	38
Mill of Thornton	Aberd	NJ8224	57°18·6'	2°17·5'W	X	38
Mill of Thornton	Aberd	NO6870	56°49·5'	2°31·0'W	X	45
Mill of Tillieroure	Aberd	NJ6520	57°16·4'	2°34·4'W	X	38
Mill of Tolquhon	Aberd	NJ8629	57°21·3'	2°13·5'W	X	38
Mill of Tommore	Moray	NJ1935	57°24·2'	3°20·4'W	X	28
Mill of Torr	Stir	NS7498	56°9·7'	4°1·3'W	X	57
Mill of Torry	Aberd	NJ9127	57°20·3'	2°8·5'W	X	38
Mill of Towie	Aberd	NJ5264	57°40·1'	2°47·8'W	X	29
Mill of Towie	Aberd	NJ9337	57°25·7'	2°6·5'W	X	30
Mill of Towie Fm	Moray	NJ4047	57°30·8'	2°59·6'W	FM	28
Mill of Uras	Aberd	NO8680	56°54·9'	2°13·3'W	X	45
Mill of Wartle	Aberd	NJ7229	57°21·3'	2°27·5'W	X	38
Mill of Waterton	Aberd	NJ9831	57°22·4'	2°1·5'W	X	30
Mill of Wester Coull	Aberd	NJ4803	57°7·2'	2°51·1'W	X	37
Mill of Whitehill	Aberd	NJ8950	57°32·7'	2°10·6'W	X	30
Millom	Cumbr	SD1780	54°12·8'	3°15·9'W	T	96
Millom Castle	Cumbr	SD1781	54°13·3'	3°16·0'W	A	96
Millom Marsh	Cumbr	SD1882	54°13·9'	3°15·1'W	X	96
Millom Park	Cumbr	SD1682	54°13·9'	3°16·9'W	F	96
Millook	Corn	SX1899	50°46·0'	4°34·5'W	T	190
Millook Common	Corn	SX1899	50°46·0'	4°34·5'W	F	190
Millook Haven	Corn	SS1800	50°46·5'	4°34·5'W	W	190
Mill O'Shiel	E Ayr	NS4317	55°25·6'	4°28·4'W	X	70
Millour	D & G	NX9559	54°55·1'	3°37·9'W	X	84
Mill Our	Moray	NJ1952	57°33·3'	3°20·8'W	X	28
Millow	Beds	TL2243	52°4·5'	0°12·8'W	T	153
Millowbury Fm	Beds	TL2342	52°4·0'	0°11·9'W	FM	153
Millow Hall Fm	Beds	TL2343	52°4·5'	0°11·9'W	FM	153
Mill Park	Arg & Bt	NR7009	55°19·5'	5°37·1'W	T	68
Mill Pit Fm	Warw	SP4057	52°12·8'	1°24·5'W	FM	151
Mill Place	Cumbr	NY1001	54°24·0'	3°22·8'W	X	89
Mill Place	N Lincs	SE9806	53°32·7'	0°30·8'W	T	112
Mill Place	W Susx	TQ3734	51°5·6'	0°2·2'W	X	187
Mill Place Fm	Kent	TQ6948	51°12·6'	0°25·6'E	FM	188
Millplough	Aberd	NO8174	56°51·7'	2°18·2'W	X	45
Mill Point	Essex	TL9608	51°44·4'	0°50·7'E	X	168
Mill Point	Kent	TR2235	51°4·5'	1°10·5'E	X	179,189
Mill Point	Orkney	HY5051	59°20·8'	2°52·3'W	X	5
Mill Pond	I of W	SZ5491	50°43·2'	1°13·7'W	W	196
Mill Pond	Shetld	HU3833	60°5·1'	1°18·5'W	W	4
Mill Pond	W Susx	SU9326	51°1·8'	0°40·0'W	W	186,197
Millpond Fm	Essex	TM2029	51°55·2'	1°12·4'E	FM	169
Millpool	Corn	SW5730	50°7·5'	5°23·6'W	T	203
Millpool	Corn	SX1270	50°30·2'	4°38·7'W	T	200
Millport	N Ayr	NS1655	55°45·5'	4°55·5'W	T	63
Millport Bay	N Ayr	NS1654	55°44·9'	4°55·5'W	W	63
Millquarter	D & G	NX6283	55°7·6'	4°9·4'W	X	77
Millquoy	Orkney	HY2910	58°58·5'	3°13·6'W	X	6
Mill Race or Water Cut	N Yks	SD6776	54°11·0'	2°29·9'W	W	98
Millridge Fm	S Lanak	NT0044	55°41·0'	3°35·0'W	FM	72
Mill Rig	E Ayr	NS5940	55°38·2'	4°14·0'W	X	71
Millrig	N Ayr	NS1964	55°50·4'	4°53·0'W	X	63
Mill Rig	Scot Bord	NT3140	55°39·2'	3°5·4'W	H	73
Mill Rig	S Lanak	NS6334	55°35·1'	4°10·0'W	H	71
Millrig	S Lanak	NS9532	55°34·5'	3°39·5'W	X	72
Millrigg	Cumbr	SD5691	54°19·0'	2°40·2'W	X	97
Millrigg Fm	Cumbr	NY2358	54°54·9'	3°11·6'W	FM	85
Millrigg Fm	Cumbr	NY4429	54°39·4'	2°51·7'W	FM	90
Mill Rigg Fm	Cumbr	NY6028	54°39·0'	2°36·8'W	FM	91
Millrigg Knott	Cumbr	NY4601	54°24·3'	2°49·5'W	H	90
Millriggs	Cumbr	NY4502	54°24·9'	2°50·4'W	X	90
Millriggs	D & G	NY0879	55°6·1'	3°26·1'W	X	85
Millriggs	D & G	NY1690	55°12·1'	3°18·8'W	X	79
Mill Rithe	Hants	SU7400	50°47·9'	0°56·6'W	W	197
Mill River	Cambs	TL3145	52°5·5'	0°4·9'W	W	153
Mill River	Suff	TM2243	52°2·7'	1°14·6'E	W	169
Mill Rock		NS3132	55°33·4'	4°40·3'W	X	70
Mill Rock	Devon	SS4543	51°10·2'	4°12·6'W	X	180
Millrodgie	Pth & Kin	NO2229	56°26·7'	3°44·7'W	X	52,58
Mills	Fife	NO3413	56°18·5'	3°3·6'W	T	59
Mill Sand	Orkney	HY5107	58°57·1'	2°50·6'W	X	6,7
Millsburn	Aberd	NO8089	56°59·8'	2°19·3'W	X	45
Mill Scar	Cumbr	SD1668	54°6·3'	3°16·7'W	X	96
Mill Scar	S Lanak	NS8822	55°29·0'	3°45·9'W	X	71,72
Millseat	Aberd	NJ7855	57°35·3'	2°21·6'W	X	29,30
Mills Farmhouse	Suff	TM2970	52°17·0'	1°21·9'E	X	156
Mills' Fm	Suff	TM1164	52°14·2'	1°5·8'E	FM	155
Mill's Fm	Suff	TM4184	52°24·3'	1°33·0'E	FM	156
Mill Shaw	Leeds	SE2830	53°46·2'	1°34·1'W	T	104
Millshield	Northum	NZ0153	54°52·6'	1°58·6'W	X	87
Mill Shoulder	D & G	NX8196	55°14·9'	3°51·9'W	X	78
Millside	Arg & Bt	NN1123	56°22·0'	5°3·1'W	X	50
Mill Side	Cumbr	SD4484	54°15·2'	2°51·2'W	T	97
Millside	E Ayr	NS5033	55°34·3'	4°22·3'W	X	70
Millside	Scot Bord	NT1244	55°41·1'	3°23·5'W	X	72
Millside Plantn	D & G	NY1670	55°1·3'	3°18·4'W	F	85
Millsike Beck	E Yorks	SE7154	53°58·9'	0°54·6'W	W	105,106
Millslade Fm	Somer	ST4437	51°8·0'	2°47·6'W	FM	182
Mills of Earn	Pth & Kin	NN9216	56°19·7'	3°44·4'W	X	58
Mills of the Ord	Shetld	HU5036	60°6·6'	1°5·5'W	X	4
Millsome	Devon	SS6605	50°50·0'	3°53·8'W	X	191
Mill's Br	Lincs	TF2755	53°4·9'	0°5·8'W	X	122
Millstone Band	Northum	NY7155	54°53·6'	2°26·7'W	X	86,87
Millstone Burn	Northum	NU1204	55°20·0'	1°48·2'W	W	81
Millstone Burn	Stir	NN8403	56°12·6'	3°51·8'W	W	58
Millstone Cairn	Aberd	NO1688	56°58·8'	3°22·5'W	H	43
Millstone Crag	Northum	NY6892	55°13·5'	2°29·8'W	H	80
Millstone Edge	Scot Bord	NT4300	55°17·7'	2°53·4'W	H	79
Millstone Edge	Sheff	SK2480	53°19·2'	1°38·0'W	X	110
Millstone Hill	Aberd	NJ6720	57°16·4'	2°32·4'W	H	38
Millstone Hill	Moray	NJ4257	57°36·2'	2°57·8'W	H	28

Millstone Howe	Cumbr	NY8512	54°30·4'	2°13·5'W	X	91,92
Millstone How Hill	Durham	NY8825	54°37·4'	2°10·7'W	X	91,92
Millstone Knowe	E Ayr	NS6416	55°25·4'	4°8·5'W	X	71
Millstone Moor	Cumbr	NY1335	54°42·4'	3°20·6'W	X	89
Mill Stone Neuk	E Loth	NT7078	55°59·9'	2°28·4'W	X	67
Millstone Point	N Ayr	NR9950	55°42·4'	5°11·5'W	X	62,69
Millstone Rig	Scot Bord	NT0854	55°46·5'	3°27·6'W	X	65,72
Millstone Rig	S Lanak	NS6833	55°34·6'	4°5·2'W	X	71
Millstone Rigg	Durham	NZ0041	54°46·1'	1°59·6'W	X	87
Millstone Rocks	Derby	SK0599	53°29·5'	1°55·1'W	X	110
Millstone Sick	Derby	SK3067	53°12·2'	1°32·6'W	W	119
Millstone Wood	Stir	NS5686	56°3·0'	4°18·3'W	F	57
Millstonford	N Ayr	NS2050	55°42·9'	4°51·5'W	X	63
Mill Street	Kent	TQ6957	51°17·4'	0°25·8'E	T	178,188
Mill Street	Norf	TG0517	52°42·9'	1°2·5'E	T	133
Mill Street	Suff	TL9837	52°0·0'	0°53·5'E	T	155
Milltack	Aberd	NJ7357	57°36·4'	2°26·6'W	X	29
Mill, The	Angus	NO1963	56°45·4'	3°19·0'W	X	43
Mill, The	Ches	SJ8366	53°11·7'	2°14·9'W	X	118
Mill, The	Denb	SJ0757	53°6·4'	3°22·9'W	X	116
Mill, The	Durham	NZ1820	54°34·7'	1°42·9'W	X	92
Mill, The	Essex	TM1423	51°52·1'	1°6·9'E	X	168,169
Mill, The	Lincs	SK9238	52°56·1'	0°37·5'W	X	130
Mill, The	Newp	ST2385	51°33·8'	3°6·3'W	X	171
Mill, The	Nth Pt Talb	SN7403	51°42·9'	3°49·0'W	X	170
Mill, The	W Susx	TQ0101	50°48·2'	0°33·6'W	X	197
Millthorpe	Derby	SK3176	53°17·0'	1°31·7'W	T	119
Millthorpe	Lincs	TF1130	52°51·6'	0°20·7'W	T	130
Mill Throop	Bourne	SZ1095	50°45·5'	1°51·1'W	T	195
Millthrop	Cumbr	SD6691	54°19·1'	2°30·9'W	T	98
Milltim	D & G	NX2072	55°0·9'	4°48·5'W	X	76
Miltimber	C of Aber	NJ8501	57°6·2'	2°14·4'W	T	38
Milltir Gerrig	Powys	SJ0230	52°51·8'	3°26·9'W	X	125
Millton	Highld	ND2353	58°27·8'	3°18·7'W	X	11,12
Millton	Highld	NJ1032	57°22·4'	3°29·3'W	X	36
Millton	Pth & Kin	NO1460	56°43·7'	3°23·9'W	X	43
Millton of Corsindae	Aberd	NJ6809	57°10·5'	2°31·3'W	X	38
Milltown	Aberd	NJ2609	57°10·2'	3°13·0'W	X	37
Milltown	Aberd	NK0163	57°39·7'	1°58·5'W	X	30
Milltown	Aberd	NK0736	57°25·1'	1°52·6'W	X	30
Milltown	Corn	SX1057	50°23·2'	4°40·0'W	T	200
Milltown	Corn	SX1168	50°29·1'	4°39·5'W	T	200
Milltown	Cumbr	NY4267	54°59·9'	2°54·0'W	X	85
Milltown	Derby	SK3561	53°8·9'	1°28·2'W	T	119
Milltown	Devon	SS5000	50°47·0'	4°7·3'W	X	191
Milltown	Devon	SS5538	51°7·6'	4°3·9'W	T	180
Milltown	Devon	SS6547	51°12·6'	3°55·6'W	X	180
Milltown	Devon	SS7520	50°58·2'	3°46·4'W	X	180
Milltown	D & G	NY3375	55°4·1'	3°2·5'W	X	85
Milltown	Highld	ND3764	58°33·8'	3°4·5'W	X	12
Milltown	Highld	NH9441	57°27·1'	3°45·5'W	X	27
Milltown	Moray	NJ2758	57°36·6'	3°12·8'W	X	28
Milltown	Moray	NJ3726	57°19·5'	3°2·3'W	X	37
Milltown	Moray	NJ3831	57°22·2'	3°1·4'W	X	37
Milltown	Somer	ST0431	51°4·5'	3°21·8'W	X	181
Milltown Burn	Aberd	NJ2610	57°10·8'	3°13·0'W	W	37
Milltown of Aberdalgie	Pth & Kin	NO0720	56°22·0'	3°29·9'W	T	52,53,58
Milltown of Auchindoun	Moray	NJ3540	57°27·0'	3°4·5'W	T	28
Milltown of Birness	Aberd	NJ9634	57°24·0'	2°3·5'W	X	30
Milltown of Craigston	Aberd	NJ7655	57°35·3'	2°23·6'W	X	29
Milltown of Dunnideer	Aberd	NJ6028	57°20·7'	2°39·4'W	X	37
Milltown of Edinvillie	Moray	NJ2640	57°26·9'	3°13·5'W	T	28
Milltown of Gaval	Aberd	NK0050	57°32·7'	1°59·5'W	X	30
Milltown of Kellas	Moray	NJ1754	57°34·4'	3°22·8'W	X	28
Milltown of Kildrummy	Aberd	NJ4616	57°14·2'	2°53·2'W	T	37
Milltown of Laggan	Moray	NJ2834	57°23·7'	3°11·4'W	X	28
Milltown of Learney	Aberd	NJ6303	57°7·2'	2°36·2'W	X	37
Milltown of Leask	Aberd	NK0132	57°23·0'	1°58·5'W	X	30
Milltown of Phingask	Aberd	NJ9766	57°41·3'	2°2·6'W	X	30
Milltown of Rothiemay	Moray	NJ5448	57°31·4'	2°45·6'W	T	29
Milltown of Towie	Aberd	NJ4612	57°12·0'	2°53·2'W	X	37
Milltown of Ythsie	Aberd	NJ8831	57°22·4'	2°11·5'W	X	30
Mill Vale	N Yks	NZ5408	54°28·1'	1°9·6'W	X	93
Millwall	T Ham	TQ3779	51°29·8'	0°1·2'W	T	177
Millward's Park	Herts	TL2306	51°44·6'	0°12·7'W	F	166
Millway Fm	Suff	TM1078	52°21·8'	1°5·5'E	FM	144
Millway Rise	Devon	SY3099	50°47·4'	2°59·2'W	T	193
Millwell	S Lanak	NS6549	55°43·2'	4°8·5'W	X	64
Millwood	Cumbr	SD2172	54°8·5'	3°12·1'W	X	96
Mill Wood	E Susx	TQ4328	51°2·2'	0°2·8'E	F	187,198
Mill Wood	E Susx	TQ6922	50°58·6'	0°24·8'E	F	199
Mill Wood	N Yks	SE6176	54°10·8'	1°3·5'W	F	100
Mill Wood	N Yks	SE6473	54°9·2'	1°0·8'W	X	100
Mill Wood	N Yks	SE6574	54°9·7'	0°59·9'W	F	100
Mill Wood	Oxon	SP4114	51°49·6'	1°23·9'W	F	164
Mill Wood	Shrops	SJ4137	52°55·9'	2°52·3'W	F	126
Millwood	S Lanak	NS8447	55°42·4'	3°50·3'W	X	72
Millwood Brook	Notts	SK5575	53°16·4'	1°10·1'W	W	120
Millwood Fm	Oxon	SP4114	51°49·6'	1°23·9'W	FM	164
Millyeat	Cumbr	NY0217	54°32·6'	3°30·5'W	X	89
Millyford Br	Hants	SU2607	50°51·9'	1°37·4'W	X	195
Milnacraig	Angus	NO2453	56°40·0'	3°14·0'W	X	53
Milnafua	Highld	NH6770	57°42·3'	4°13·5'W	T	21
Milnathort	Pth & Kin	NO1204	56°13·5'	3°24·7'W	T	58
Milnbank	Aberd	NJ6848	57°31·5'	2°31·6'W	X	29
Milncraig	S Ayr	NS4020	55°27·1'	4°31·4'W	X	70
Milncroft	N Lanak	NS7571	55°55·2'	3°59·6'W	X	64
Milne	D & G	NY1397	55°15·8'	3°21·7'W	X	78
Milne Fell	D & G	NY1497	55°15·8'	3°20·8'W	X	78
Milne Graden	Scot Bord	NT8744	55°41·6'	2°12·0'W	X	74
Milne Graden East Mains	Scot Bord	NT8745	55°42·1'	2°12·0'W	X	74
Milne Graden West Mains	Scot Bord	NT8644	55°41·6'	2°12·9'W	X	74
Milne Height	D & G	NY1597	55°15·8'	3°19·8'W	H	79
Milners Heath	Ches	SJ4663	53°9·9'	2°48·1'W	T	117
Milnesfield	Moray	NJ4560	57°37·9'	2°54·8'W	X	28,29
Milngate	D & G	NY0586	55°9·8'	3°29·0'W	X	78
Milngavie	E Dunb	NS5574	55°56·5'	4°18·9'W	T	64
Milnhay Fm	Derby	SK3250	53°3·0'	1°31·0'W	FM	119
Milnhead	D & G	NX9781	55°7·0'	3°36·5'W	X	78
Milnholm	D & G	NY3587	55°10·6'	3°0·8'W	X	79

Milnholm	Stir	NS7887	56°3·9′	3°57·1′W	X	57
Milnmark	D & G	NX6582	55°7·1′	4°6·6′W	X	77
Milnmark Hill	D & G	NX6683	55°7·6′	4°5·7′W	X	77
Milnquarter	Falk	NS8179	55°59·6′	3°54·0′W	T	65
Milnrow	Roch	SD9212	53°36·5′	2°6·8′W	T	109
Milnsbridge	Kirk	SE1115	53°38·1′	1°49·6′W	T	110
Milnshaw	Lancs	SD7529	53°45·6′	2°22·3′W	T	103
Milnthird	D & G	NX7156	54°53·2′	4°0·2′W	X	83,84
Milnthird	E Renf	NS4557	55°47·1′	4°27·9′W	X	64
Milnthorpe	Cumbr	SD4981	54°13·6′	2°46·5′W	T	97
Milnthorpe	Wakf	SE3317	53°39·1′	1°29·6′W	T	110,111
Milnthorpe Sands	Cumbr	SD4680	54°13·0′	2°49·3′W	X	97
Milnton	D & G	NX8192	55°12·7′	3°51·8′W	X	78
Milntown	I of M	SC4394	54°19·3′	4°24·4′W	X	95
Milntown Cott	I of M	SC4394	54°19·3′	4°24·4′W	X	95
Milnwood	N Lanak	NS7459	55°48·7′	4°0·2′W	T	64
Milo	Carm	SN5917	51°50·3′	4°2·4′W	T	159
Milo Brook	Powys	SO0950	52°8·7′	3°19·4′W	W	147
Milquhanzie Hill	Pth & Kin	NN8924	56°24·0′	3°47·5′W	H	52,58
Milray Hill	E Ayr	NS5905	55°19·4′	4°12·9′W	H	71,77
Milrig	C of Edin	NT1173	55°56·8′	3°25·1′W	X	65
Milrig	E Ayr	NS5034	55°34·9′	4°22·3′W	X	70
Milrig	W Loth	NT1067	55°53·5′	3°25·9′W	X	65
Milrighall	Scot Bord	NT5327	55°32·3′	2°44·3′W	X	73
Milsey Bay	E Loth	NT5685	56°3·6′	2°42·0′W	W	67
Milsey Burn	Scot Bord	NT3014	55°25·1′	3°5·9′W	W	79
Milsington	Scot Bord	NT4012	55°24·1′	2°56·4′W	X	79
Milson	Shrops	SO6372	52°20·9′	2°32·2′W	T	138
Milstead	Kent	TQ9058	51°17·6′	0°43·9′E	T	178
Milstead Manor Fm	Kent	TQ9058	51°17·6′	0°43·9′E	FM	178
Milston	Wilts	SU1645	51°12·5′	1°45·9′W	T	184
Milston Down	Wilts	SU2046	51°13·0′	1°42·4′W	X	184
Milthorpe	Northnts	SP5946	52°6·8′	1°7·9′W	T	152
Milton	Aberd	NJ3311	57°11·4′	3°6·1′W	X	37
Milton	Aberd	NJ3815	57°13·6′	3°1·2′W	X	37
Milton	Aberd	NJ5140	57°27·1′	2°48·5′W	X	29
Milton	Aberd	NJ6948	57°31·5′	2°30·6′W	X	29
Milton	Aberd	NJ7215	57°13·8′	2°27·4′W	X	38
Milton	Aberd	NJ8621	57°17·0′	2°13·5′W	X	38
Milton	Aberd	NO5795	57°2·9′	2°42·1′W	X	37,44
Milton	Aberd	NO7496	57°3·5′	2°25·3′W	X	38,45
Milton	Aberd	NO7695	57°3·0′	2°23·3′W	X	38,45
Milton	Angus	NO4880	56°54·8′	2°50·8′W	X	44
Milton	Arg & Bt	NS0563	55°49·5′	5°6·3′W	X	63
Milton	Barns	SE3700	53°30·0′	1°26·1′W	T	110,111
Milton	Cambs	TL4762	52°14·4′	0°9·6′E	T	154
Milton	C of Edin	NT1276	55°58·4′	3°24·2′W	X	65
Milton	C of Glas	NS5969	55°53·9′	4°14·9′W	T	64
Milton	C of Port	SZ6699	50°47·4′	1°3·4′W	T	196
Milton	C of Stoke	SJ9050	53°3·1′	2°8·5′W	T	118
Milton	Corn	SS2414	50°54·2′	4°29·8′W	X	190
Milton	Corn	SS2501	50°47·2′	4°28·6′W	X	190
Milton	Cumbr	NY5560	54°56·2′	2°41·7′W	T	86
Milton	Cumbr	SD5383	54°14·7′	2°42·9′W	T	97
Milton	Derby	SK3226	52°50·1′	1°31·1′W	T	128
Milton	Devon	ST0800	50°47·8′	3°17·9′W	X	192
Milton	Devon	SX8650	50°20·6′	3°35·8′W	X	202
Milton	D & G	NT0900	55°17·4′	3°25·5′W	X	78
Milton	D & G	NX0166	54°57·2′	5°6·0′W	X	82
Milton	D & G	NX2154	54°51·2′	4°46·9′W	X	82
Milton	D & G	NX7046	54°47·8′	4°0·9′W	X	83,84
Milton	D & G	NX8470	55°0·9′	3°48·4′W	T	84
Milton	E Ayr	NS4737	55°36·4′	4°25·3′W	X	70
Milton	Fife	NO4420	56°22·4′	2°54·0′W	X	54,59
Milton	Highld	NC9764	58°33·4′	3°45·7′W	X	11
Milton	Highld	ND2059	58°31·0′	3°21·9′W	X	11,12
Milton	Highld	ND3450	58°26·3′	3°7·4′W	X	12
Milton	Highld	NG7043	57°25·4′	5°49·4′W	T	24
Milton	Highld	NH3055	57°33·5′	4°50·0′W	T	26
Milton	Highld	NH4930	57°20·4′	4°30·1′W	T	26
Milton	Highld	NH5849	57°30·8′	4°21·8′W	T	26
Milton	Highld	NH6426	57°18·5′	4°15·0′W	X	26,35
Milton	Highld	NH7046	57°29·4′	4°9·7′W	X	27
Milton	Highld	NH7082	57°48·8′	4°10·8′W	X	21
Milton	Highld	NH7674	57°44·6′	4°4·5′W	T	21
Milton	Highld	NH8913	57°11·9′	3°49·8′W	X	35,36
Milton	Highld	NH9314	57°12·5′	3°45·8′W	X	36
Milton	Highld	NH9419	57°15·2′	3°45·0′W	X	36
Milton	Highld	NJ0021	57°16·4′	3°39·0′W	X	36
Milton	Inverc	NS3568	55°52·9′	4°37·8′W	X	63
Milton	Kent	TQ6574	51°26·7′	0°22·9′E	T	177,178
Milton	Moray	NJ1424	57°18·2′	3°25·2′W	X	36
Milton	Moray	NJ1719	57°15·5′	3°22·1′W	X	36
Milton	Moray	NJ5163	57°39·5′	2°48·8′W	T	29
Milton	Newp	ST3688	51°35·5′	2°55·0′W	T	171
Milton	Notts	SK7173	53°15·2′	0°55·7′W	T	120
Milton	N Som	ST3462	51°21·4′	2°56·5′W	T	182
Milton	Oxon	SP4535	52°0·9′	1°20·3′W	T	151
Milton	Oxon	SU4892	51°37·7′	1°18·0′W	T	164,174
Milton	Pemb	SN0303	51°41·7′	4°50·6′W	T	157,158
Milton	Pemb	SN0823	51°52·6′	4°47·0′W	X	145,158
Milton	Powys	SO2450	52°8·8′	3°6·2′W	T	148
Milton	Pth & Kin	NN7039	56°31·8′	4°6·4′W	X	51,52
Milton	Pth & Kin	NN9138	56°31·5′	3°45·9′W	X	52
Milton	Pth & Kin	NN9512	56°17·6′	3°41·3′W	T	58
Milton	Pth & Kin	NO0434	56°29·6′	3°33·1′W	X	52,53
Milton	Pth & Kin	NO0761	56°44·1′	3°30·8′W	X	43
Milton	Pth & Kin	NO2630	56°27·6′	3°11·6′W	X	53
Milton	S Ayr	NS3705	55°19·0′	4°33·7′W	X	70,77
Milton	S Ayr	NS4323	55°28·8′	4°28·6′W	X	70
Milton	S Ayr	NX2996	55°14·0′	4°40·9′W	X	76
Milton	Somer	ST4621	50°59·4′	2°45·8′W	T	193
Milton	Stir	NN5001	56°10·9′	4°24·6′W	T	57
Milton	W Dunb	NS4274	55°56·2′	4°31·3′W	T	64
Milton	Wilts	ST8731	51°4·9′	2°10·7′W	T	183
Milton Abbas	Dorset	ST8001	50°48·7′	2°16·6′W	T	194
Milton Abbey (Sch)	Dorset	ST7902	50°49·3′	2°17·5′W	X	194
Milton Abbot	Devon	SX4079	50°35·2′	4°15·3′W	T	201
Miltonbank	Angus	NO4457	56°42·3′	2°54·4′W	X	54
Miltonbank	Highld	NC7303	58°0·1′	4°8·5′W	X	16
Milton Bank	Midlo	NT2462	55°51·0′	3°12·4′W	X	66
Milton Br	S Ayr	NX2895	55°13·4′	4°41·8′W	X	76
Miltonbrae	Moray	NJ1760	57°37·6′	3°22·9′W	X	28
Milton Bridge	Midlo	NT2562	55°51·0′	3°11·4′W	T	66
Milton Brodie Ho	Moray	NJ0962	57°38·6′	3°31·0′W	X	27
Milton Bryan	Beds	SP9730	51°57·8′	0°34·9′W	T	165
Milton Burn	Arg & Bt	NS0375	55°55·9′	5°8·8′W	W	63
Milton Burn	D & G	NX2154	54°51·2′	4°46·9′W	W	82
Milton Burn	D & G	NX8569	55°0·4′	3°47·5′W	W	84
Milton Burn	Highld	NH8714	57°12·4′	3°51·8′W	W	35,36
Milton Burn	Highld	NH9413	57°12·0′	3°44·8′W	W	36
Milton Burn	Highld	NN7398	57°3·6′	4°5·2′W	W	35
Milton Burn	Moray	NJ1225	57°18·7′	3°27·2′W	W	36
Milton Burn	Pth & Kin	NN9532	56°28·4′	3°41·8′W	W	52,53
Milton Burn	S Ayr	NS2105	55°18·6′	4°48·8′W	W	70,76
Milton Clevedon	Somer	ST6637	51°8·1′	2°28·8′W	T	183
Milton Common	Oxon	SP6503	51°43·5′	1°3·1′W	T	164,165
Milton Coombe	Devon	SX4865	50°28·1′	4°8·1′W	T	201
Milton Cott	Angus	NO4780	56°54·8′	2°51·8′W	X	44
Milton Coullie	Aberd	NJ8725	57°19·2′	2°12·5′W	X	38
Milton Country Park	Cambs	TL4762	52°14·4′	0°9·6′E	X	154
Milton Court	Carm	SN5521	51°52·4′	4°6·0′W	X	159
Milton Court	Surrey	TQ1549	51°13·9′	0°20·8′W	X	187
Milton Court Fm	E Susx	TQ5203	50°48·6′	0°9·8′E	FM	199
Milton Creek	Kent	TQ9265	51°21·3′	0°45·8′E	W	178
Milton Croft	Aberd	NJ9029	57°21·3′	2°9·5′W	X	38
Milton Cross	Heref	SO3860	52°14·3′	2°54·1′W	X	137,148,149
Milton Damerel	Devon	SS3810	50°52·2′	4°17·8′W	T	190
Milton Downs Fm	Oxon	SP2515	51°50·2′	1°37·8′W	FM	163
Miltonduff	Moray	NJ1860	57°37·6′	3°21·9′W	T	28
Milton End	Glos	SO7110	51°47·5′	2°24·8′W	T	162
Milton End	Glos	SP1400	51°42·1′	1°47·5′W	T	163
Milton Eonan	Pth & Kin	NN5746	56°35·3′	4°19·3′W	X	51
Milton Ernest	Beds	TL0156	52°11·8′	0°30·9′W	T	153
Milton Fell	D & G	NX3147	54°47·6′	4°37·3′W	H	82
Milton Fm	Carm	SN2911	51°46·5′	4°28·3′W	FM	159
Milton Fm	Ches	SJ5974	53°15·9′	2°36·5′W	FM	117
Milton Fm	Dorset	ST7928	51°3·3′	2°17·6′W	FM	183
Milton Fm	Fife	NT0193	56°7·4′	3°35·1′W	FM	58
Milton Fm	Highld	NH9725	57°18·5′	3°42·1′W	FM	36
Milton Fm	Pemb	SM9606	51°43·2′	4°56·8′W	FM	157,158
Milton Fm	Pth & Kin	NN9729	56°26·8′	3°39·8′W	FM	52,53,58
Milton Fm	Somer	ST1733	51°5·7′	3°10·7′W	FM	181
Milton Fm	Somer	ST6637	51°8·1′	2°28·8′W	FM	183
Milton Glen Burn	Stir	NN5607	56°14·3′	4°19·0′W	W	57
Milton Green	Ches	SJ4658	53°7·2′	2°48·0′W	T	117
Milton Green	Devon	SX4078	50°35·0′	4°15·2′W	T	201
Milton Hall	Cumbr	NY5460	54°56·2′	2°42·7′W	X	86
Milton Ham	Northnts	SP7257	52°12·6′	0°56·4′W	X	152
Milton Heath	Surrey	TQ1548	51°13·4′	0°20·8′W	X	187
Milton Heights	Oxon	SU4891	51°37·2′	1°18·0′W	T	164,174
Milton Hide	E Susx	TQ5608	50°51·2′	0°13·4′E	X	199
Milton Hill	Cumbr	NY5560	54°56·2′	2°41·7′W	X	86
Milton Hill	Devon	SX9278	50°35·7′	3°31·2′W	T	192
Miltonhill	Moray	NJ0963	57°39·1′	3°31·0′W	X	27
Milton Hill	Oxon	SU4790	51°36·6′	1°18·9′W	X	164,174
Milton Hill	Powys	SO2449	52°8·3′	3°6·2′W	H	148
Milton Hill	S Ayr	NX2996	55°14·0′	4°40·9′W	X	76
Milton Hill Clump	Wilts	SU1958	51°19·5′	1°43·3′W	F	173
Milton Hill Fm	Wilts	SU1957	51°18·9′	1°43·3′W	FM	173
Milton Ho	Beds	TL0255	52°11·3′	0°30·1′W	X	153
Milton Ho	Devon	SS3811	50°52·8′	4°17·8′W	X	190
Milton Ho	D & G	NY2384	55°8·9′	3°12·1′W	X	79
Milton Ho	E Loth	NT4567	55°53·8′	2°52·3′W	X	66
Milton Ho	Heref	SO3860	52°14·3′	2°54·1′W	X	137,148,149
Milton I	Renf	NS4273	55°55·7′	4°31·3′W	X	64
Miltonise	D & G	NX1873	55°1·3′	4°50·4′W	X	76
Milton Keynes	Mil Key	SP8537	52°1·7′	0°45·3′W	T	152
Milton Keynes Bowl	Mil Key	SP8536	52°1·2′	0°45·3′W	X	152
Milton Keynes Village	Mil Key	SP8939	52°2·8′	0°41·7′W	T	152
Milton Knowe	Pth & Kin	NO1060	56°43·6′	3°27·8′W	H	43
Milton Lilbourne	Wilts	SU1860	51°20·6′	1°44·1′W	T	173
Milton Loch	D & G	NX8371	55°1·4′	3°49·4′W	W	84
Milton-Lockhart	S Lanak	NS8149	55°43·4′	3°53·2′W	X	72
Milton Lodge	Beds	SP9630	51°57·8′	0°35·8′W	X	165
Milton Lodge	Highld	NH5665	57°39·4′	4°24·3′W	X	21
Milton Lodge	Somer	ST5446	51°12·9′	2°39·1′W	X	182,183
Milton Mains	D & G	NX8470	55°0·9′	3°48·4′W	X	84
Milton Malsor	Northnts	SP7355	52°11·5′	0°55·5′W	T	152
Milton Manor	Oxon	SU4892	51°37·7′	1°18·0′W	X	164,174
Milton Manor Fm	Kent	TR1255	51°15·5′	1°2·7′E	FM	179
Milton Mill	Oxon	SU4892	51°37·7′	1°18·0′W	X	164,174
Milton Moor	Cumbr	SD5283	54°14·7′	2°43·8′W	X	97
Milton Morenish	Pth & Kin	NN6135	56°29·5′	4°15·0′W	T	51
Milton Moss	Highld	NC9862	58°32·3′	3°44·6′W	X	11
Milton Ness	Aberd	NO7764	56°46·3′	2°22·1′W	X	45
Milton of Abercairny	Pth & Kin	NN9023	56°23·4′	3°46·5′W	X	52,58
Milton of Ardlethen	Aberd	NJ9130	57°21·9′	2°8·5′W	X	30
Milton of Auchinhove	Aberd	NJ5503	57°7·2′	2°44·1′W	X	37
Milton of Auchlossan	Aberd	NJ5702	57°6·7′	2°42·1′W	X	37
Milton of Auchorthie	Aberd	NJ9151	57°33·2′	2°8·6′W	X	30
Milton of Balgonie	Fife	NO3200	56°11·5′	3°5·3′W	T	59
Milton of Balhall	Angus	NO5162	56°45·1′	2°47·6′W	X	44
Milton of Balnagowan	Highld	NH8155	57°34·4′	3°58·9′W	X	27
Milton of Blebo	Fife	NO4113	56°18·6′	2°56·8′W	X	59
Milton of Brogan	Aberd	NK0030	57°21·9′	1°59·5′W	X	30
Milton of Buchanan	Stir	NS4490	56°4·9′	4°30·0′W	T	57
Milton of Buittle	D & G	NX8164	54°57·6′	3°51·1′W	X	84
Milton of Cairnborrow	Aberd	NJ4740	57°27·1′	2°52·5′W	X	28,29
Milton of Callander	Stir	NN5706	56°13·8′	4°18·0′W	X	57
Milton of Cambus	Stir	NN7004	56°12·9′	4°5·3′W	X	57
Milton of Campfield	Aberd	NJ6400	57°5·6′	2°35·2′W	T	37
Milton of Campsie	E Dunb	NS6576	55°57·7′	4°9·3′W	T	64
Milton of Carmyllie	Angus	NO5542	56°34·3′	2°43·5′W	X	54
Milton of Clola	Aberd	NJ9944	57°29·4′	2°0·5′W	X	30
Milton of Clunie	Pth & Kin	NO1044	56°35·0′	3°27·5′W	X	53
Milton of Coldwells	Aberd	NJ9538	57°26·2′	2°4·5′W	X	30
Milton of Collace	Pth & Kin	NO1934	56°29·7′	3°18·5′W	X	53
Milton of Collieston	Aberd	NK0129	57°21·3′	1°58·5′W	X	38
Milton of Conon	Angus	NO5743	56°34·9′	2°41·6′W	X	54
Milton of Cullerlie	Aberd	NJ7602	57°6·8′	2°23·3′W	X	38
Milton of Cultoquhey	Pth & Kin	NN8922	56°22·9′	3°47·4′W	T	52,58
Milton of Cushnie	Aberd	NJ5211	57°11·5′	2°47·2′W	T	37
Milton of Dalcapon	Pth & Kin	NN9754	56°40·2′	3°40·4′W	T	52,53
Milton of Dellavaird	Aberd	NO7381	56°55·4′	2°26·2′W	T	45
Milton of Drimmie	Pth & Kin	NO1651	56°38·9′	3°21·7′W	X	53
Milton of Drum	C of Aber	NJ7901	57°6·2′	2°20·3′W	X	38
Milton of Dryfe	D & G	NY1389	55°11·5′	3°21·6′W	X	78
Milton of Dumbreck	Aberd	NJ9029	57°21·3′	2°9·5′W	X	38
Milton of Edradour	Pth & Kin	NN9557	56°41·8′	3°42·4′W	T	52,53
Milton of Farr	Highld	NH6832	57°21·8′	4°11·2′W	X	26
Milton of Finavon	Angus	NO4956	56°41·8′	2°49·5′W	T	54
Milton of Finnercy	Aberd	NJ7503	57°7·3′	2°24·3′W	X	38
Milton of Fintray	Aberd	NJ8216	57°14·3′	2°17·4′W	X	38
Milton of Fisherie	Aberd	NJ7558	57°36·9′	2°24·6′W	X	29
Milton of Forteviot	Pth & Kin	NO0418	56°20·9′	3°32·8′W	X	58
Milton of Garlogie	Aberd	NJ7806	57°8·9′	2°21·4′W	X	38
Milton of Gight	Aberd	NJ8340	57°27·3′	2°16·5′W	X	29,30
Milton of Gollanfield	Highld	NH7852	57°32·8′	4°1·8′W	X	27
Milton of Grange	Moray	NJ0460	57°37·4′	3°36·0′W	X	27
Milton Of Inkorn	Aberd	NJ9338	57°26·2′	2°6·5′W	X	30
Milton of Inveramsay	Aberd	NJ7424	57°18·6′	2°25·4′W	X	38
Milton of Katewell	Highld	NH5965	57°39·4′	4°21·3′W	X	21
Milton of Kilravock	Highld	NH8350	57°31·8′	3°56·8′W	X	27
Milton of Kincraigie	Pth & Kin	NN9948	56°37·0′	3°38·3′W	X	52,53
Milton of Larg	D & G	NX1663	54°55·9′	4°51·9′W	X	82
Milton of Lesmore	Aberd	NJ4628	57°20·6′	2°53·4′W	X	37
Milton of Leys	Highld	NH6941	57°26·7′	4°10·5′W	X	26
Milton of Logie	Aberd	NJ4402	57°6·6′	2°55·0′W	X	37
Milton of Machany	Pth & Kin	NN9115	56°19·1′	3°45·3′W	X	58
Milton of Mathers	Aberd	NO7765	56°46·8′	2°22·1′W	X	45
Milton of Migvie	Aberd	NJ4406	57°8·7′	2°55·1′W	X	37
Milton of Minnes	Aberd	NJ9423	57°18·1′	2°5·5′W	X	38
Milton of Moy	Highld	NH8032	57°22·0′	3°59·3′W	X	27
Milton of Murtle	C of Aber	NJ8702	57°6·8′	2°12·4′W	X	38
Milton of Noth	Aberd	NJ5028	57°20·6′	2°49·4′W	X	37
Milton of Nuide	Highld	NN7398	57°3·6′	4°5·2′W	X	35
Milton of Ogil	Angus	NO4561	56°44·5′	2°53·5′W	X	44
Milton of Ogilvie	Angus	NO3843	56°34·7′	3°0·1′W	T	54
Milton of Panholes	Pth & Kin	NN8909	56°15·9′	3°47·1′W	X	58
Milton of Philorth	Aberd	NJ9964	57°40·2′	2°0·5′W	X	30
Milton of Potterton	Aberd	NJ9416	57°14·3′	2°5·5′W	X	38
Milton of Rattray	Pth & Kin	NO1944	56°35·1′	3°18·7′W	X	53
Milton of Tolmauds	Aberd	NJ6107	57°9·4′	2°38·2′W	X	37
Milton of Tullich	Aberd	NO3897	57°3·9′	3°0·9′W	X	37,44
Milton of Whitehouse	Aberd	NJ4104	57°7·6′	2°58·0′W	X	37
Milton on Stour	Dorset	ST8028	51°3·3′	2°17·6′W	T	183
Milton Park	Aberd	NO7780	56°54·9′	2°22·2′W	X	45
Milton Park	D & G	NX8065	54°58·2′	3°52·0′W	X	84
Milton Park	Oxon	SU4991	51°37·2′	1°17·1′W	X	164,174
Milton Park	Peterb	TL1499	52°34·8′	0°18·6′W	X	142
Milton Park	Surrey	TQ0169	51°24·9′	0°32·5′W	X	176
Milton Park Fm	Dorset	ST8102	50°49·3′	2°15·8′W	FM	194
Milton Park Wood	Dorset	ST8102	50°49·3′	2°15·8′W	F	194
Milton Point	D & G	NX3146	54°47·1′	4°37·3′W	X	82
Milton Regis	Kent	TQ8964	51°20·8′	0°43·2′E	T	178
Miltonrigg Wood	Cumbr	NY5561	54°56·7′	2°41·7′W	F	86
Miltons	Somer	SS9232	51°4·9′	3°32·1′W	X	181
Milton Sands	D & G	NX6646	54°47·7′	4°4·6′W	X	83,84
Milton's Cottage	Bucks	SU9893	51°37·9′	0°34·6′W	X	175,176
Milton Street	E Susx	TQ5304	50°49·1′	0°10·7′E	T	199
Milton, The	Pth & Kin	NN7822	56°22·7′	3°58·1′W	X	51,52
Milton under Wychwood	Oxon	SP2618	51°51·8′	1°37·0′W	T	163
Milton Wood	Beds	SP9731	51°58·4′	0°34·9′W	F	165
Milton Wood	Essex	TM1319	51°50·0′	1°5·9′E	F	168,169
Milverton	Somer	ST1225	51°1·3′	3°14·9′W	T	181,193
Milverton	Warw	SP3066	52°17·7′	1°33·2′W	T	151
Milward's Fm	E Susx	TQ5112	50°53·5′	0°9·2′E	FM	199
Milwharran Hill	S Ayr	NX1785	55°7·8′	4°51·8′W	X	76
Milwich	Staffs	SJ9732	52°53·4′	2°2·3′W	T	127
Milwr	Flint	SJ1974	53°15·7′	3°12·5′W	T	116
Milzeoch	E Ayr	NS5417	55°25·8′	4°18·0′W	X	70
Mimbridge	Surrey	SU9861	51°20·6′	0°35·2′W	T	175,176,186
Mi-mheall Breac	Arg & Bt	NR5689	56°2·2′	5°54·6′W	X	61
Mi-mheall Dubh	Arg & Bt	NR5589	56°2·1′	5°55·5′W	X	61
Mimmshall Brook	Herts	TL2302	51°42·4′	0°12·8′W	W	166
Minacre Fm	Kent	TR3048	51°11·3′	1°17·9′E	FM	179
Minard	Arg & Bt	NM8223	56°21·2′	5°31·3′W	X	49
Minard	Arg & Bt	NR9796	56°7·1′	5°15·5′W	T	55
Minard	Corn	SX3256	50°23·0′	4°21·4′W	X	201
Minard Bay	Arg & Bt	NR9794	56°6·0′	5°15·4′W	W	55
Minard Castle	Arg & Bt	NR9794	56°6·0′	5°15·4′W	T	55
Minard Point	Arg & Bt	NM8123	56°21·2′	5°32·2′W	X	49
Mina Stac	N Eil	NA1000	57°49·4′	8°33·8′W	X	18
Mincarlo	I Scilly	SV8512	49°55·7′	6°23·0′W	X	203
Minchams	Essex	TL5618	51°50·6′	0°16·3′E	X	167
Min Charn	Highld	NH1451	57°30·9′	5°5·9′W	X	25
Minchington	Dorset	ST9614	50°55·8′	2°3·0′W	T	195
Minchington Down	Dorset	ST9516	50°56·8′	2°3·9′W	X	184
Minchinhampton	Glos	SO8600	51°42·1′	2°11·8′W	T	162
Minchinhampton Common	Glos	SO8501	51°42·7′	2°12·6′W	X	162
Minchins	Essex	TL6120	51°51·5′	0°20·7′E	X	167
Minch Moor	Scot Bord	NT3533	55°35·4′	3°1·4′W	H	73
Minchmoor Road	Scot Bord	NT3831	55°34·4′	2°58·6′W	X	73
Min Choire	Highld	NH4201	57°4·6′	4°35·9′W	X	34
Min Choire	Highld	NN4490	56°58·8′	4°33·6′W	H	34
Min Choire	Highld	NN4799	57°3·7′	4°30·9′W	X	34
Minch, The		NB5645	58°19·8′	6°9·6′W	W	8
Minch, The		NG8699	57°56·0′	5°36·4′W	W	19
Minch,The	Highld	NB9610	58°2·2′	5°26·9′W	W	15
Mincingfield Fm	Hants	SU5216	50°56·7′	1°15·2′W	FM	185
Mindork Fell	D & G	NX3258	54°53·6′	4°36·8′W	H	82
Mindork Moss	D & G	NX3057	54°53·0′	4°38·6′W	X	82
Mindrum	Northum	NT8432	55°35·1′	2°14·8′W	T	74
Mindrum Mill	Northum	NT8433	55°35·7′	2°14·8′W	X	74
Mindrum Station	Northum	NT8533	55°35·7′	2°13·8′W	X	74
Minduff	Moray	NJ4360	57°37·8′	2°56·8′W	X	28
Mine	Clackm	NS9894	56°7·9′	3°38·0′W	X	58
Mine	E Ayr	NS5316	55°25·2′	4°18·9′W	X	70
Minehead	Somer	SS9646	51°12·5′	3°28·9′W	T	181

Minehead Bluff	Somer	SS9149	51°14·0′	3°33·3′W	X	181
Minehill	Orkney	HY2410	58°58·5′	3°18·8′W	X	6
Mine Hill	S Lanak	NS8813	55°24·1′	3°45·7′W	H	71,78
Mine Hill Ho	Warw	SP3137	52°2·1′	1°32·5′W	X	151
Mine Ho	D & G	NX7752	54°51·1′	3°54·5′W	X	84
Minen	Arg & Bt	NR7552	55°42·8′	5°34·5′W	X	62,69
Minepit Copse	W Susx	SU8728	51°2·9′	0°45·1′W	F	186,197
Minera	Wrex	SJ2751	53°3·3′	3°4·9′W	T	117
Miners Br	Conwy	SH7856	53°5·5′	3°48·9′W	X	115
Miners Track	Gwyn	SH6254	53°4·2′	4°3·2′W	X	115
Minerton Fm	Pemb	SN0802	51°41·3′	4°46·3′W	FM	158
Mineshope	Corn	SX1596	50°44·3′	4°36·9′W	T	190
Mines Ho, The	I of M	SC4489	54°16·6′	4°23·3′W	X	95
Minety	Wilts	SU0290	51°36·8′	1°57·9′W	T	163,173
Minew	Aberd	NJ5902	57°6·7′	2°40·2′W	X	37
Minffordd	Conwy	SH7251	53°2·7′	3°54·2′W	X	115
Minffordd	Conwy	SH9668	53°12·2′	3°33·0′W	X	116
Minffordd	Flint	SJ2666	53°11·4′	3°6·0′W	X	117
Minffordd	Gwyn	SH5770	53°12·7′	4°8·1′W	T	114,115
Minffordd	Gwyn	SH5938	52°55·5′	4°5·4′W	T	124
Minffordd	Gwyn	SH7311	52°41·2′	3°52·3′W	T	124
Minffordd Path	Gwyn	SH7111	52°41·1′	3°54·1′W	X	124
Minffrwd	Brig	SS9682	51°31·9′	3°29·6′W	X	170
Minffrwd	Powys	SJ0523	52°48·0′	3°24·1′W	X	125
Mingarry	Highld	NM6870	56°46·1′	5°47·3′W	X	40
Mingarry Burn	Highld	NM6970	56°46·1′	5°46·4′W	W	40
Mingarrypark	Highld	NM6869	56°45·6′	5°47·3′W	T	40
Mingary	Arg & Bt	NM4155	56°37·2′	6°12·9′W	X	47
Mingary	Arg & Bt	NR6419	55°24·7′	5°43·3′W	X	68
Mingary	Highld	NM5063	56°41·8′	6°4·6′W	X	47
Mingary Aird	Arg & Bt	NM4156	56°37·7′	6°12·9′W	X	47
Mingary Burn	Arg & Bt	NM4453	56°36·2′	6°9·8′W	W	47
Mingary Castle	Highld	NM5063	56°41·8′	6°4·6′W	A	47
Mingary Pier	Highld	NM4962	56°41·2′	6°5·5′W	X	47
Mingay	Highld	NG2257	57°31·3′	6°38·1′W	X	23
Mingearraidh	N Eil	NF7426	57°12·8′	7°23·6′W	T	22
Minges	Herts	TL4316	51°49·7′	0°4·9′E	X	167
Mingledale Plantn	E Yorks	SE8254	53°58·8′	0°44·6′W	F	106
Mingoose	Corn	SW7148	50°17·5′	5°12·5′W	T	203
Mingulay	N Eil	NL5683	56°48·9′	7°37·9′W	X	31
Mingulay Bay	N Eil	NL5683	56°48·9′	7°37·9′W	W	31
Min-gwern	Powys	SJ1514	52°43·3′	3°15·1′W	X	125
Minigaig	Pth & Kin	NN8184	56°56·2′	3°56·9′W	X	43
Mining Mus	Torf	SO2308	51°46·2′	3°6·6′W	X	161
Miningsby	Lincs	TF3264	53°9·6′	0°1·1′W	T	122
Miningsby Ho	Lincs	TF3263	53°9·1′	0°1·2′W	X	122
Minions	Corn	SX2671	50°31·0′	4°26·9′W	T	201
Minishal	Highld	NG3500	57°1·2′	6°21·5′W	H	32,39
Minishant	S Ayr	NS3314	55°23·7′	4°37·8′W	T	70
Minish Island	N Eil	NF9070	57°37·1′	7°11·1′W	X	18
Minister's Flag	Orkney	HY4849	59°19·7′	2°54·3′W	X	5
Minister's Moss	D & G	NY0190	55°11·9′	3°32·9′W	X	78
Mink Fm	Essex	TQ8793	51°36·5′	0°42·4′E	FM	178
Minley Manor	Hants	SU8258	51°19·1′	0°49·0′W	X	175,186
Minley Wood	Hants	SU8157	51°18·6′	0°49·9′W	F	175,186
Minllyn	Gwyn	SH8514	52°42·9′	3°41·7′W	T	124,125
Minmanueth	I Scilly	SV8508	49°55·3′	6°22·8′W	X	203
Minn	Shetld	HU3368	60°23·9′	1°23·6′W	X	2,3
Minn	Shetld	HU3630	60°3·5′	1°20·7′W	X	4
Minnbank	Staffs	SJ7540	52°57·6′	2°21·9′W	X	118
Minnett Fm	Heref	SO5524	51°55·0′	2°38·9′W	FM	162
Minnett's Hill	Lincs	SK9341	52°57·7′	0°36·5′W	X	130
Minnetts, The	Monm	ST4489	51°36·1′	2°48·1′W	X	171,172
Minnickfold	Surrey	TQ1643	51°10·7′	0°20·0′W	X	187
Minnie Fm	Staffs	SJ7948	53°2·0′	2°18·4′W	FM	118
Minnigaff	D & G	NX4166	54°58·1′	4°28·6′W	T	83
Minnigall Lane	D & G	NX5381	55°6·4′	4°17·8′W	W	77
Minni Loch	Shetld	HU4459	60°19·0′	1°11·7′W	W	2,3
Minnin Burn	D & G	NX9072	55°2·1′	3°42·8′W	W	84
Minningdale Fm	E Yorks	SE8752	53°57·6′	0°40·0′W	FM	106
Minninglow Hill	Derby	SK2157	53°6·8′	1°40·8′W	H	119
Minni of Aith	Shetld	HU5143	60°10·4′	1°4·4′W	X	4
Minnis Bay	Kent	TR2869	51°22·7′	1°17·0′E	W	179
Minnis, The	Kent	TR2743	51°8·7′	1°15·1′E	X	179
Minnivey	E Ayr	NS4607	55°20·2′	4°25·3′W	X	70,77
Minniwick	D & G	NX3777	55°3·9′	4°32·7′W	X	77
Minniwick Moss	D & G	NX3677	55°3·9′	4°33·7′W	X	77
Minnonie	Aberd	NJ7760	57°38·0′	2°22·6′W	X	29,30
Minnow End	Essex	TL7012	51°47·1′	0°28·3′E	T	167
Minnows Islands	Corn	SW8572	50°30·7′	5°1·6′W	X	200
Minnybae	S Ayr	NS2306	55°19·2′	4°46·9′W	X	70,76
Minny E'Hill	D & G	NS7904	55°19·2′	3°54·0′W	H	78
Minnygap	D & G	NY0496	55°15·2′	3°30·2′W	X	78
Minnygap Height	D & G	NY0296	55°15·2′	3°32·1′W	H	78
Minnygryle	D & G	NX7188	55°10·4′	4°1·1′W	X	77
Minnygryle Burn	D & G	NX7188	55°10·4′	4°1·1′W	W	77
Minnygryle Hill	D & G	NX7189	55°11·0′	4°1·1′W	X	77
Minorca	Caer	ST2486	51°34·3′	3°5·4′W	X	171
Minorca	I of M	SC4384	54°13·9′	4°24·1′W	T	95
Minor Pt	Swan	SS4093	51°37·0′	4°18·3′W	X	159
Minor's Park	Heref	SO4745	52°6·3′	2°46·0′W	X	148,149
Minsbury Hill	Herts	TL1527	51°56·0′	0°19·2′W	X	166
Minsca	D & G	NY2281	55°7·3′	3°13·0′W	X	79
Minsden Chapel	Herts	TL1924	51°54·3′	0°15·8′W	A	166
Minshull Hall	Ches	SJ6561	53°8·9′	2°31·0′W	X	118
Minskip	N Yks	SE3864	54°4·5′	1°24·7′W	T	99
Minsmere Cliffs	Suff	TM4768	52°15·5′	1°37·6′E	X	156
Minsmere Haven	Suff	TM4765	52°13·9′	1°37·4′E	W	156
Minsmere Level	Suff	TM4666	52°14·5′	1°36·6′E	X	156
Minsmere River	Suff	TM4367	52°15·1′	1°34·0′E	W	156
Minson's Hill	Devon	ST2009	50°52·7′	3°7·8′W	X	192,193
Minstead	Hants	SU2811	50°54·1′	1°35·7′W	T	195
Minstead Lodge	Hants	SU2811	50°54·1′	1°35·7′W	X	195
Minsted	W Susx	SU8521	50°59·2′	0°47·0′W	T	197
Minster	Kent	TQ9573	51°25·6′	0°48·7′E	T	178
Minster	Kent	TR3064	51°19·9′	1°18·5′E	T	179
Minster Abbey	Kent	TQ9572	51°25·0′	0°48·7′E	X	178
Minsteracres	Northum	NZ0255	54°53·6′	1°57·7′W	X	87
Minster Fm	Lincs	TF4169	53°12·2′	0°7·1′E	FM	122
Minster Hag	N Yks	SE4451	53°57·4′	1°19·4′W	F	105

Minster Hill	N Yks	SE7668	54°6·4′	0°49·8′W	X	100
Minsterley	Shrops	SJ3705	52°38·6′	2°55·5′W	T	126
Minsterley Park	Shrops	SJ3604	52°38·1′	2°56·3′W	X	126
Minster Lovell	Oxon	SP3110	51°47·5′	1°32·6′W	T	164
Minster Marshes	Kent	TQ9270	51°24·0′	0°46·0′E	X	178
Minster Marshes	Kent	TQ9274	51°26·2′	0°46·1′E	X	178
Minster Marshes	Kent	TR3163	51°19·4′	1°19·3′E	X	179
Minster, The	E Yorks	TA0339	53°50·5′	0°25·7′W	X	107
Minster, The	York	SE6052	53°57·9′	1°4·7′W	X	105
Minster Way	E Yorks	SE8854	53°58·7′	0°39·1′W	X	106
Minster Way	E Yorks	TA0345	53°53·7′	0°25·5′W	X	107
Minster Way	York	SE7053	53°58·3′	0°55·6′W	X	105,106
Minsterworth	Glos	SO7716	51°50·8′	2°19·6′W	T	162
Minsterworth Ham	Glos	SO7916	51°50·8′	2°17·9′W	X	162
Minsthorpe	Wakf	SE4712	53°36·4′	1°17·0′W	T	111
Mintching Wood	Kent	TQ9158	51°17·6′	0°44·8′E	F	178
Minterne Ho	Dorset	ST6504	50°50·3′	2°29·4′W	X	194
Minterne Magna	Dorset	ST6504	50°50·3′	2°29·4′W	T	194
Minterne Parva	Dorset	ST6603	50°49·8′	2°28·6′W	T	194
Mintern's Hill	Dorset	ST4803	50°49·7′	2°43·9′W	X	193
Mintfield Fm	Powys	SO1336	52°1·2′	3°15·7′W	FM	161
Mint Fm	Surrey	TQ2659	51°19·2′	0°11·1′W	FM	187
Minting	Lincs	TF1873	53°14·7′	0°13·5′W	T	122
Minting Ho	Lincs	TF1874	53°15·2′	0°13·5′W	X	122
Minting Park	Lincs	TF1573	53°14·7′	0°16·2′W	F	121
Minting Park Fm	Lincs	TF1573	53°14·7′	0°16·2′W	FM	121
Minting Wood	Lincs	TF1674	53°15·3′	0°15·3′W	F	121
Mintlaw	Aberd	NK0048	57°31·6′	1°59·5′W	T	30
Mintlaw Station	Aberd	NJ9848	57°31·6′	2°1·5′W	T	30
Mintlyn Fm	Norf	TF6519	52°44·8′	0°27·1′E	FM	132
Mintlyn Wood	Norf	TF6619	52°44·8′	0°28·0′E	F	132
Minto	Scot Bord	NT5620	55°28·6′	2°41·3′W	T	73
Minto Hills	Scot Bord	NT5621	55°29·1′	2°41·3′W	H	73
Minto House	Scot Bord	NT5720	55°28·6′	2°40·4′W	X	73,74
Minto Kames	Scot Bord	NT5522	55°29·6′	2°42·3′W	X	73
Minton	Shrops	SO4390	52°30·5′	2°50·0′W	T	137
Minton Batch	Shrops	SO4191	52°31·1′	2°51·8′W	X	137
Mintridge	Heref	SO6352	52°10·1′	2°32·1′W	X	149
Mintsfeet	Cumbr	SD5194	54°20·6′	2°44·8′W	T	97
Minuntion	S Ayr	NX2291	55°11·1′	4°47·3′W	X	76
Minwear	Pemb	SN0313	51°47·1′	4°51·0′W	T	157,158
Minwear Wood	Pemb	SN0513	51°47·1′	4°49·2′W	F	158
Minworth	Birm	SP1592	52°31·8′	1°46·3′W	T	139
Min-yr-afon	Wrex	SJ3542	52°58·5′	2°57·7′W	X	117
Minzies Downs	Corn	SX1775	50°33·0′	4°34·6′W	X	201
Miodar	Arg & Bt	NM0749	56°32·8′	6°45·6′W	X	46
Mio Ness	Shetld	HU4279	60°29·8′	1°13·6′W	X	2,3
Mio Ness	Shetld	HU6670	60°24·8′	0°47·6′W	X	2
Miotag	Highld	NG9693	57°53·1′	5°26·0′W	X	19
Mio Tong	Shetld	HP5714	60°48·6′	0°56·6′W	X	1
Mirabels Fm	Glos	SO6934	52°0·5′	2°26·7′W	FM	149
Miramar Ho	Lincs	TF3841	52°57·1′	0°3·7′E	X	131
Mirbister	Orkney	HY3019	59°3·4′	3°12·7′W	T	6
Mirdesgill	Shetld	HU1856	60°17·5′	1°40·0′W	W	3
Mire	Orkney	ND4390	58°47·9′	2°58·7′W	X	7
Mire Barf Fm	N Yks	SE3078	54°12·1′	1°32·0′W	FM	99
Mire Beck	Leeds	SE1742	53°52·7′	1°44·1′W	W	104
Mire Close	N Yks	SD9645	53°54·3′	2°3·2′W	X	103
Mire Cottages	Cumbr	NY2646	54°48·5′	3°8·7′W	X	85
Mire End	Fife	NT0585	56°3·2′	3°31·1′W	X	65
Mire Fold	Lancs	SD6633	53°47·8′	2°30·6′W	X	103
Mirefold Fm	N Yks	SE2589	54°18·0′	1°36·5′W	FM	99
Mire Garth	Cumbr	SD7283	54°14·8′	2°25·4′W	X	98
Mire Head	Cumbr	SD6297	54°22·3′	2°34·7′W	X	97
Mire Ho	Cumbr	NY3123	54°36·1′	3°3·7′W	X	90
Mire Ho	Cumbr	SD1684	54°14·9′	3°16·9′W	X	96
Mire Ho	Cumbr	SD6789	54°18·0′	2°30·0′W	X	98
Mire Ho	Cumbr	SD6994	54°20·7′	2°28·2′W	X	98
Mire Ho	Northum	NY9257	54°54·7′	2°7·1′W	X	87
Mire Ho	N Yks	SD8951	53°57·5′	2°9·6′W	X	103
Mirehouse	Cumbr	NX9815	54°31·5′	3°34·1′W	T	89
Mirehouse	Cumbr	NY2328	54°38·7′	3°11·2′W	X	89,90
Mireland	Highld	ND3160	58°31·6′	3°10·6′W	X	11,12
Mire Loch	Scot Bord	NT9168	55°54·6′	2°8·2′W	W	67
Mire of Midgates	Aberd	NJ5122	57°17·4′	2°48·3′W	H	37
Mires	Orkney	HY6339	59°14·4′	2°38·4′W	X	5
Mires Barn	N Yks	SE4072	54°8·8′	1°22·8′W	X	99
Mires Fm	N Yks	SE2884	54°15·3′	1°33·8′W	FM	99
Mireside	Cumbr	NY1016	54°32·1′	3°23·0′W	X	89
Mire Side	Cumbr	NY2230	54°39·8′	3°12·1′W	X	89,90
Mireside	Cumbr	NY4762	54°57·2′	2°49·2′W	X	86
Mireside	Cumbr	SD2288	54°17·1′	3°11·5′W	X	96
Mireside	Cumbr	SD4390	54°18·4′	2°52·1′W	X	97
Mireside	Cumbr	SD5983	54°14·7′	2°37·3′W	X	97
Mires of Helliersness	Shetld	HU6088	60°34·5′	0°53·8′W	X	1,2
Mires of Linksetter	Shetld	HU6092	60°36·7′	0°53·7′W	X	1,2
Mires of Oddsetter	Shetld	HU5992	60°36·7′	0°54·8′W	X	1,2
Mires of Ramnageo	Shetld	HP6100	60°41·0′	0°52·5′W	X	1
Mire Spring	Glos	SP1928	51°57·2′	1°43·0′W	W	163
Mires, The	Derby	SK2071	53°14·4′	1°41·6′W	X	119
Mires, The	Fife	NO3101	56°12·1′	3°6·3′W	X	59
Mires, The	N Yks	SE3360	54°2·3′	1°29·3′W	X	99
Mirfield	Kirk	SE2019	53°40·3′	1°41·4′W	T	110
Mirfield	Kirk	SE2020	53°40·8′	1°41·4′W	T	104
Mirfield Fm	Leic	SP4897	52°34·4′	1°17·1′W	FM	140
Mirfield Moor	Kirk	SE1921	53°41·3′	1°42·3′W	X	104
Mirgill Hearne Brocks	Durham	NY8916	54°32·6′	2°9·8′W	X	91,92
Mirianog Ganot	Pemb	SN1334	51°58·6′	4°43·0′W	X	145
Mirkady	Orkney	HY5406	58°56·6′	2°47·5′W	X	6,7
Mirkady Point	Orkney	HY5306	58°56·6′	2°48·5′W	X	6,7
Mirka Water	Shetld	HU4999	60°40·5′	1°5·7′W	W	1
Mirka Water	Shetld	HU5065	60°22·2′	1°5·1′W	W	2,3
Mirkbooths	Cumbr	NY3942	54°46·4′	2°56·5′W	X	85
Mirk Fell	N Yks	NY9106	54°27·2′	2°7·9′W	X	91,92
Mirk Fell Gill	N Yks	NY9107	54°27·7′	2°7·9′W	W	91,92
Mirk Hills	York	SE6754	53°58·9′	0°58·3′W	X	105,106
Mirkholme	Cumbr	NY2532	54°40·9′	3°9·4′W	X	89,90
Mirk Howe	Cumbr	SD4391	54°18·9′	2°52·2′W	X	97
Mirk Pot	N Yks	SD8287	54°16·9′	2°16·2′W	X	98
Mirk Side	D & G	NT1813	55°24·5′	3°17·3′W	X	79

Mirkslair Hill	D & G	NY3085	55°9·5′	3°5·5′W	H	79
Mirky Hole	Orkney	HY4245	59°17·5′	3°0·6′W	X	5
Mirlaw Ho	Northum	NZ0281	55°7·6′	1°57·7′W	X	81
Mirth Hilly	Orkney	ND5198	58°52·3′	2°50·5′W	X	6,7
Miry Ellis	Lancs	SD6250	53°56·9′	2°34·3′W	X	102,103
Miry Wood	S Glos	ST7888	51°35·7′	2°18·7′W	F	172
Misarden Park	Glos	SO9408	51°46·5′	2°4·8′W	A	163
Misbister Geo	Orkney	ND3388	58°46·7′	3°9·0′W	X	7
Misbourne Farms	E Susx	TQ4527	51°1·7′	0°4·5′E	FM	188,198
Misbourne Fm	Bucks	SU9894	51°38·4′	0°34·6′W	FM	175,176
Miserden	Glos	SO9308	51°46·5′	2°5·7′W	T	163
Misery Corner	Norf	TM2689	52°27·4′	1°20·0′E	T	156
Mishnish	Arg & Bt	NM4656	56°37·9′	6°8·1′W	X	47
Misk Hill	Notts	SK5049	53°2·4′	1°14·8′W	X	129
Miskin	Rho Cyn Taf	ST0480	51°30·9′	3°22·6′W	T	170
Miskin	Rho Cyn Taf	ST0498	51°40·6′	3°22·9′W	T	170
Miskin Manor	Rho Cyn Taf	ST0580	51°30·9′	3°21·8′W	X	170
Misleham	Kent	TQ9926	51°0·2′	0°50·6′E	X	189
Mislet	Cumbr	SD4399	54°23·2′	2°52·2′W	X	97
Misling Fm	Kent	TR1345	51°10·1′	1°3·2′E	FM	179,189
Mislingford	Hants	SU5814	50°55·6′	1°10·1′W	X	196
Misselfore	Wilts	SU0122	51°0·1′	1°58·9′W	T	184
Missies Fm	N Yks	SE2272	54°8·8′	1°39·4′W	FM	99
Misson	Notts	SK6894	53°26·5′	0°58·2′W	T	111
Misson Bank	Donc	SE7000	53°29·8′	0°56·3′W	X	112
Misson Grange	Notts	SK6897	53°28·2′	0°58·1′W	X	111
Miste Fm	Lancs	SD7830	53°46·2′	2°19·6′W	FM	103
Misterton	Leic	SP5583	52°26·8′	1°11·0′W	T	140
Misterton	Notts	SK7694	53°26·5′	0°50·9′W	T	112
Misterton	Somer	ST4508	50°52·4′	2°46·5′W	T	193
Misterton Carr	Notts	SK7394	53°26·5′	0°53·6′W	X	112
Misterton Carr Fm	Notts	SK7396	53°27·6′	0°53·6′W	FM	112
Misterton Grange	Leic	SP5582	52°26·2′	1°11·1′W	X	140
Misterton Soss	Notts	SK7795	53°27·0′	0°50·0′W	T	112
Mistlaw Muir	Renf	NS3061	55°49·0′	4°42·4′W	X	63
Mistletoe Oak	Heref	SO3967	52°18·1′	2°53·3′W	X	137,148,149
Mistley	Essex	TM1131	51°56·5′	1°4·6′E	T	168,169
Mistley Hall	Essex	TM1030	51°56·0′	1°3·7′E	X	168,169
Mistley Heath	Essex	TM1230	51°55·9′	1°5·4′E	T	168,169
Misty Law	Renf	NS2961	55°49·0′	4°43·3′W	H	63
Miswell Fm	Herts	SP9112	51°48·2′	0°40·4′W	FM	165
Miswells Ho	W Susx	TQ3336	51°6·7′	0°5·6′W	X	187
Mitcham	Merton	TQ2868	51°24·0′	0°9·2′W	T	176
Mitcham Common	Merton	TQ2867	51°23·5′	0°9·2′W	X	176
Mitcheldean	Glos	SO6618	51°51·8′	2°29·2′W	T	162
Mitchel Head	Suff	TL7370	52°18·3′	0°32·6′E	X	155
Mitchelhill Rings	Scot Bord	NT0634	55°35·7′	3°29·1′W	X	72
Mitchelhill Rings (Fort and Settlement)	Scot Bord	NT0634	55°35·7′	3°29·1′W	A	72
Mitchell	Corn	SW8654	50°21·1′	5°0·1′W	T	200
Mitchelland	Cumbr	SD4395	54°21·1′	2°52·2′W	X	97
Mitchelland	Hants	SU6209	50°52·9′	1°6·7′W	X	196
Mitchell Copse	W Berks	SU4079	51°30·7′	1°25·0′W	F	174
Mitchell Field	Derby	SK2481	53°19·8′	1°38·0′W	X	110
Mitchell Fm	Kent	TQ9644	51°9·9′	0°48·6′E	FM	189
Mitchell Fold	Ches	SJ9482	53°20·3′	2°5·0′W	X	109
Mitchell Hagg	N Yks	SE6392	54°19·4′	1°1·5′W	X	94,100
Mitchell Hall	E Loth	NT5372	55°56·6′	2°44·7′W	X	66
Mitchellhill	Aberd	NJ8944	57°29·4′	2°10·6′W	X	30
Mitchell Hill	D & G	NT2208	55°21·8′	3°13·4′W	H	79
Mitchell Hill	Herts	TL2736	52°0·7′	0°8·6′W	X	153
Mitchell Hill	Scot Bord	NT0633	55°35·1′	3°29·0′W	T	72
Mitchell Hill Common	Cambs	TL4770	52°18·7′	0°9·8′E	X	154
Mitchell Hill Fm	Cambs	TL4769	52°18·2′	0°9·8′E	FM	154
Mitchell Park Fm	W Susx	SU9629	51°3·4′	0°37·4′W	FM	186,197
Mitchells	Essex	TL5542	52°3·5′	0°16·1′E	X	154
Mitchell's Elm Fm	Somer	ST6942	51°10·8′	2°26·2′W	FM	183
Mitchell's Fm	Cambs	TL4873	52°20·3′	0°10·7′E	FM	154
Mitchells Fm	Essex	TQ5198	51°39·9′	0°11·4′E	FM	167,177
Mitchell's Fm	Somer	ST7428	51°3·3′	2°21·9′W	FM	183
Mitchell's Fold	Shrops	SO3098	52°34·8′	3°1·6′W	X	137
Mitchell's Fold (Stone Circle)	Shrops	SO3098	52°34·8′	3°1·6′W	A	137
Mitchell's House Reservoirs	Lancs	SD7827	53°44·6′	2°19·6′W	W	103
Mitchellslacks	D & G	NX9696	55°15·1′	3°37·7′W	X	78
Mitchelston	Scot Bord	NT4648	55°43·6′	2°51·2′W	T	73
Mitchel Troy	Monm	SO4910	51°47·4′	2°44·0′W	T	162
Mitchen Hall	Surrey	SU9245	51°12·0′	0°40·6′W	X	186
Mitcheson's Gill	Ghead	NZ2357	54°54·7′	1°38·0′W	W	88
Mitchin Hole Cave	Swan	SS5586	51°33·5′	4°5·1′W	A	159
Mitchley Wood	Croy	TQ3360	51°19·6′	0°5·1′W	F	176,177,187
Mitchmore Fm	Heref	SO5435	52°0·9′	2°39·8′W	FM	149
Mite Houses	Cumbr	SD0897	54°21·9′	3°24·5′W	T	96
Miterdale	Cumbr	NY1501	54°24·1′	3°18·1′W	X	89
Miterdale Forest	Cumbr	NY1301	54°24·1′	3°20·0′W	F	89
Miteside	Cumbr	SD1098	54°22·4′	3°22·7′W	X	96
Mitford	Northum	NZ1786	55°10·3′	1°43·6′W	T	81
Mitford Br	Warw	SP2637	52°2·1′	1°36·9′W	X	151
Mitford Castle	Northum	NZ1785	55°9·8′	1°43·6′W	A	81
Mitford Steads	Northum	NZ1784	55°9·2′	1°43·6′W	X	81
Mither Tap	Aberd	NJ6822	57°17·5′	2°31·4′W	H	38
Mithian	Corn	SW7450	50°18·6′	5°10·1′W	T	204
Mithian Downs	Corn	SW7449	50°18·1′	5°10·0′W	T	204
Mithil Brook	Powys	SO1561	52°14·7′	3°14·3′W	W	148
Mithraeum	Northum	NY8571	55°2·2′	2°13·7′W	R	87
Mitley Spinney	Northnts	SP7175	52°22·3′	0°57·0′W	F	141
Mitney Cottage	Cumbr	NY3334	54°42·0′	3°2·0′W	H	90
Mitten	Shetld	HU4550	60°14·2′	1°10·7′W	X	3
Mitten Hill Beck	N Yks	NZ9206	54°26·7′	0°34·5′W	W	94
Mitten Hill Fm	N Yks	NZ9207	54°27·2′	0°34·4′W	FM	94
Mitton	Glos	SO9033	52°0·0′	2°8·3′W	T	150
Mitton	Staffs	SJ8815	52°44·2′	2°10·3′W	T	127
Mitton Green	Lancs	SD7139	53°51·0′	2°26·0′W	X	103
Mitton Hall	Lancs	SD7138	53°50·5′	2°26·0′W	X	103
Mitton Ho	N Yks	SD9346	53°54·8′	2°6·0′W	X	103
Mitton Ho	N Yks	SD9449	53°56·5′	2°5·1′W	X	103
Mitton Lodge	Staffs	SJ8614	52°43·6′	2°12·0′W	X	127
Mitton Lodge	Worcs	SO9034	52°0·5′	2°8·3′W	X	150
Mitton Manor	Staffs	SJ8814	52°43·6′	2°10·3′W	X	127

Mitton of Barras	Aberd	NO8379	56°54·4′	2°16·3′W	X	45
Mitton Wood	Lancs	SD7137	53°50·0′	2°26·0′W	F	103
Mixbury	Oxon	SP6033	51°59·8′	1°7·2′W	T	152,165
Mixbury Ho	Oxon	SP6034	52°0·3′	1°7·2′W	X	152,165
Mixbury Lodge	Oxon	SP6133	51°59·8′	1°6·3′W	X	152,165
Mixbury Plantation	Oxon	SP6132	51°59·2′	1°6·3′W	F	152,165
Mixenden	Cald	SE0628	53°45·1′	1°54·1′W	T	104
Mixenden Resr	Cald	SE0528	53°45·1′	1°55·0′W	W	104
Mixon	Staffs	SK0457	53°6·8′	1°56·0′W	X	119
Mixon, The	W Susx	SZ8690	50°42·4′	0°46·5′W	X	197
Mixtow	Corn	SX1253	50°21·1′	4°38·2′W	T	200
Mixtow Pill	Corn	SX1352	50°20·5′	4°37·3′W	W	200
Mizbrook Fm	Surrey	TQ1841	51°9·6′	0°18·4′W	FM	187
Mizbrook's Fm	W Susx	TQ2926	51°1·4′	0°9·2′W	FM	187,198
Miz Maze	Dorset	ST6108	50°52·4′	2°32·9′W	A	194
Mo	N Eil	NF9989	57°47·6′	7°3·5′W	H	18
Moa	Orkney	HY3113	59°0·2′	3°11·6′W	X	6
Moa	Orkney	HY4219	59°3·5′	3°0·2′W	X	6
Moa	Orkney	HY4942	59°16·0′	2°53·2′W	X	5
Moak Hill	S Ayr	NX1388	55°9·3′	4°55·7′W	H	76
Moan	Orkney	HY3615	59°1·3′	3°6·4′W	X	6
Moan	Orkney	HY3833	59°11·0′	3°4·6′W	X	6
Moa Ness	Orkney	HY3729	59°8·9′	3°5·6′W	X	6
Moaness	Orkney	ND3192	58°48·9′	3°11·2′W	X	7
Moar	Pth & Kin	NN5344	56°34·2′	4°23·1′W	X	51
Moarfield	Shetld	HP5303	60°42·7′	1°1·2′W	T	1
Moast	Shetld	HU3810	59°52·7′	1°18·8′W	X	4
Moasta	Shetld	HU4569	60°24·4′	1°10·5′W	X	2,3
Moat	Carm	SN4305	51°43·5′	4°16·0′W	X	159
Moat	Cumbr	NY4173	55°3·1′	2°55·0′W	T	85
Moat	D & G	NX8985	55°9·1′	3°44·1′W	X	78
Moat	S Lanak	NS8439	55°38·1′	3°50·1′W	X	71,72
Moat	S Lanak	NS9427	55°31·8′	3°40·3′W	X	71,72
Moat Bank	Shrops	SJ5727	52°50·6′	2°37·9′W	X	126
Moat Bank	Staffs	SK0806	52°39·3′	1°52·5′W	X	139
Moated Grange	Lincs	TF3296	53°26·9′	0°0·3′W	X	113
Moated House Fm	W Susx	TQ1833	51°5·3′	0°18·5′W	FM	187
Moatenden Fm	Kent	TQ8146	51°11·3′	0°35·8′E	FM	188
Moat Flow	D & G	NY0789	55°11·4′	3°27·2′W	X	78
Moat Fm	Beds	SP9643	52°4·9′	0°35·5′W	FM	153
Moat Fm	Beds	SP9752	52°9·7′	0°34·5′W	FM	153
Moat Fm	Beds	SP9941	52°3·7′	0°33·0′W	FM	153
Moat Fm	Bucks	SP6917	51°51·1′	0°59·5′W	FM	165
Moat Fm	Bucks	SP7709	51°46·7′	0°52·6′W	FM	165
Moat Fm	Bucks	SP8210	51°47·2′	0°48·3′W	FM	165
Moat Fm	Bucks	SP8701	51°42·3′	0°44·1′W	FM	165
Moat Fm	Bucks	SU9788	51°35·2′	0°35·6′W	FM	175,176
Moat Fm	Cambs	TL2282	52°25·6′	0°11·9′W	FM	142
Moat Fm	Cambs	TL6342	52°3·4′	0°23·0′E	FM	154
Moat Fm	Ches	SJ3660	53°8·2′	2°57·0′W	FM	117
Moat Fm	Ches	SJ3963	53°9·9′	2°54·3′W	FM	117
Moat Fm	Ches	SJ6860	53°8·4′	2°28·3′W	FM	118
Moat Fm	Cumbr	SD2770	54°7·5′	3°6·6′W	FM	96,97
Moat Fm	Essex	TL8136	51°59·8′	0°38·6′E	FM	155
Moat Fm	Essex	TL9324	51°53·1′	0°48·7′E	FM	168
Moat Fm	E Susx	TQ5318	50°56·7′	0°11·1′E	FM	199
Moat Fm	E Susx	TQ7524	50°59·5′	0°30·0′E	FM	199
Moat Fm	E Susx	TQ8924	50°59·3′	0°42·0′E	FM	189
Moat Fm	E Yorks	TA2534	53°47·5′	0°5·7′W	FM	107
Moat Fm	Glos	SO7523	51°54·5′	2°21·4′W	FM	162
Moat Fm	Glos	SO8322	51°54·0′	2°14·4′W	FM	162
Moat Fm	Kent	TQ6445	51°11·1′	0°21·2′E	FM	188
Moat Fm	Kent	TQ7947	51°11·9′	0°34·1′E	FM	188
Moat Fm	Kent	TQ9736	51°5·6′	0°49·2′E	FM	189
Moat Fm	Lincs	TF4266	53°10·6′	0°7·9′E	FM	122
Moat Fm	Lincs	TF4764	53°9·4′	0°12·3′E	FM	122
Moat Fm	Lincs	TF4776	53°15·9′	0°12·7′E	FM	122
Moat Fm	Medway	TQ8076	51°27·5′	0°35·9′E	FM	178
Moat Fm	Mil Key	SP9245	52°6·0′	0°39·0′W	FM	152
Moat Fm	Norf	TF8703	52°35·8′	0°46·1′E	FM	144
Moat Fm	Norf	TL9592	52°29·7′	0°52·8′E	FM	144
Moat Fm	Norf	TM3096	52°31·0′	1°23·8′E	FM	134
Moat Fm	N Yks	NZ4005	54°26·6′	1°22·6′W	FM	93
Moat Fm	Oxon	SP6427	51°56·5′	1°3·7′W	FM	164,165
Moat Fm	Powys	SJ1102	52°36·8′	3°18·5′W	FM	136
Moat Fm	Powys	SJ2712	52°42·3′	3°4·4′W	FM	126
Moat Fm	Roth	SK4890	53°24·5′	1°16·3′W	FM	111
Moat Fm	Shrops	SJ4503	52°37·6′	2°48·4′W	FM	126
Moat Fm	Staffs	SJ7851	53°3·6′	2°19·3′W	FM	118
Moat Fm	Staffs	SK1530	52°52·3′	1°46·2′W	FM	128
Moat Fm	Suff	TM0152	52°8·0′	0°56·6′E	FM	155
Moat Fm	Suff	TM0168	52°16·6′	0°57·2′E	FM	155
Moat Fm	Suff	TM0254	52°9·1′	0°57·6′E	FM	155
Moat Fm	Suff	TM0551	52°7·4′	1°0·1′E	FM	155
Moat Fm	Suff	TM1052	52°7·8′	1°4·5′E	FM	155
Moat Fm	Suff	TM1061	52°12·7′	1°4·8′E	FM	155
Moat Fm	Suff	TM1469	52°16·9′	1°8·6′E	FM	156
Moat Fm	Suff	TM1656	52°9·8′	1°9·9′E	FM	156
Moat Fm	Suff	TM1866	52°15·2′	1°12·0′E	FM	156
Moat Fm	Suff	TM2071	52°17·8′	1°14·0′E	FM	156
Moat Fm	Suff	TM2159	52°11·3′	1°14·4′E	FM	156
Moat Fm	Suff	TM2256	52°9·7′	1°15·2′E	FM	156
Moat Fm	Suff	TM2361	52°12·3′	1°16·2′E	FM	156
Moat Fm	Suff	TM2452	52°7·5′	1°16·7′E	FM	156
Moat Fm	Suff	TM2463	52°13·4′	1°17·2′E	FM	156
Moat Fm	Suff	TM2571	52°17·7′	1°18·4′E	FM	156
Moat Fm	Suff	TM2754	52°8·5′	1°19·5′E	FM	156
Moat Fm	Suff	TM2769	52°16·6′	1°20·1′E	FM	156
Moat Fm	Suff	TM2963	52°13·3′	1°21·6′E	FM	156
Moat Fm	Suff	TM3358	52°10·5′	1°24·9′E	FM	156
Moat Fm	Suff	TM3370	52°16·9′	1°25·4′E	FM	156
Moat Fm	Suff	TM3482	52°23·4′	1°26·7′E	FM	156
Moat Fm	Suff	TM3581	52°22·8′	1°27·6′E	FM	156
Moat Fm	Suff	TM4385	52°24·8′	1°34·8′E	FM	156
Moat Fm	Suff	TM4884	52°24·1′	1°39·2′E	FM	156
Moat Fm	Worcs	SO9040	52°3·7′	2°8·4′W	FM	150
Moat Fm	Worcs	SO9857	52°12·9′	2°1·4′W	FM	150
Moat Fm, The	Powys	SJ2104	52°37·9′	3°9·6′W	FM	126
Moat Fm, The	Suff	TM2965	52°14·4′	1°21·6′E	FM	156
Moat Fm, The	Surrey	TQ4250	51°14·1′	0°2·4′E	FM	187

Moat Grange	Pemb	SN0522	51°52·0′	4°49·6′W	X	145,158
Moat Hall	Ches	SJ8075	53°16·5′	2°17·6′W	X	118
Moat Hall	Derby	SK1260	53°8·5′	1°48·8′W	X	119
Moat Hall	Essex	TL9228	51°55·3′	0°47·9′E	X	168
Moat Hall	Shrops	SJ4408	52°40·2′	2°49·3′W	X	126
Moat Hall	Suff	TM0239	52°1·0′	0°57·0′E	X	155
Moat Hall	Suff	TM2255	52°9·1′	1°15·1′E	X	156
Moat Hall Farm	Suff	TM3159	52°11·1′	1°23·2′E	FM	156
Moat Hall Fm	Ches	SJ9376	53°17·1′	2°5·9′W	FM	118
Moathill	Aberd	NO7970	56°49·5′	2°20·2′W	X	45
Moat Hill	D & G	NX7969	55°0·3′	3°53·1′W	H	84
Moat Hill	Donc	SE5815	53°37·9′	1°7·0′W	A	111
Moat Hill	Leic	SK5521	52°47·3′	1°10·7′W	X	129
Moat Hill	Shrops	SO2989	52°29·9′	3°2·4′W	X	137
Moat Hill	Staffs	SK1324	52°49·0′	1°48·0′W	X	128
Moat Hill Fm	Donc	SE5815	53°37·9′	1°7·0′W	FM	111
Moat Ho	Essex	TL7041	52°2·7′	0°29·1′E	X	154
Moat Ho	Kent	TR0228	51°1·2′	0°53·2′E	X	189
Moat Ho	Lincs	TF1572	53°14·2′	0°16·2′W	X	121
Moat Ho	Lincs	TF4149	53°1·4′	0°6·5′E	X	131
Moat Ho	Lincs	TF4876	53°15·9′	0°13·6′E	X	122
Moat Ho	Norf	TF6805	52°37·2′	0°29·3′E	X	143
Moat Ho	Shrops	SJ4900	52°36·0′	2°44·8′W	X	126
Moat Ho	Shrops	SJ5327	52°50·5′	2°41·5′W	X	126
Moat Ho	Suff	TM4365	52°14·0′	1°33·9′E	X	156
Moat Ho	Worcs	SO8336	52°1·6′	2°14·5′W	A	150
Moat Ho Fm	Warw	SP2785	52°28·0′	1°35·8′W	FM	140
Moat House	Sol	SP2080	52°25·3′	1°42·0′W	A	139
Moathouse	Staffs	SJ8042	52°58·7′	2°17·5′W	X	118
Moat House	Suff	TM0169	52°17·2′	0°57·2′E	X	155
Moathouse Fm	Ches	SJ5358	53°7·3′	2°41·7′W	FM	117
Moathouse Fm	Essex	TL6127	51°55·3′	0°20·9′E	FM	167
Moat House Fm	Lincs	TF4466	53°10·5′	0°9·7′E	FM	122
Moat House Fm	N Som	ST4873	51°27·5′	2°44·5′W	FM	171,172
Moat House Fm	Sol	SP2577	52°23·7′	1°37·6′W	FM	140
Moat House Fm	Surrey	TQ2048	51°13·3′	0°16·5′W	FM	187
Moat House Fm	Warw	SP2186	52°28·5′	1°41·0′W	FM	139
Moat House Fm	Warw	SP2390	52°30·7′	1°39·3′W	FM	139
Moat Knowe	S Lanak	NS6143	55°39·9′	4°12·2′W	X	71
Moatlands	Kent	TQ6743	51°9·9′	0°23·7′E	X	188
Moatlaw	Northum	NZ0075	55°4·4′	1°59·6′W	X	87
Moat Low	Derby	SK1554	53°5·2′	1°46·2′W	A	119
Moat Mains	S Lanak	NS8439	55°38·1′	3°50·1′W	X	71,72
Moatmill	Angus	NO4036	56°31·0′	2°58·1′W	T	54
Moat Mill Fm	E Susx	TQ5924	50°59·8′	0°16·3′E	FM	199
Moat Mount	Barnet	TQ2194	51°38·1′	0°14·7′W	X	166,176
Moatpark Fm	E Susx	TQ4616	50°55·7′	0°5·0′E	FM	198
Moat Scar	Cumbr	SD2769	54°6·9′	3°6·6′W	X	96,97
Moats, The	Cambs	TL2958	52°12·5′	0°6·3′W	A	153
Moats Tye	Suff	TM0455	52°9·6′	0°59·4′E	T	155
Moat, The	Glos	SO7224	51°55·1′	2°24·0′W	X	162
Moat, The	Glos	SO7829	51°57·8′	2°18·8′W	X	150
Moat, The	Kent	TQ4840	51°8·6′	0°7·3′E	X	188
Moat, The	Kent	TQ7833	51°4·3′	0°32·8′E	X	188
Moat, The	Oxon	SP5911	51°47·9′	1°8·3′W	X	164
Moat, The	Shrops	SO1880	52°25·0′	3°11·9′W	X	136
Moat, The	Sol	SP2579	52°24·7′	1°37·5′W	X	140
Moat, The	Surrey	SU8941	51°9·9′	0°43·2′W	W	186
Moat, The	Wilts	SU1628	51°3·3′	1°45·9′W	X	184
Moat Wood	Kent	TQ6751	51°14·2′	0°23·9′E	F	188
Moat Yards	Suff	TM4081	52°22·7′	1°32·0′E	A	156
Moatyett	S Lanak	NS8439	55°38·1′	3°50·1′W	X	71,72
Mobberley	Ches	SJ7879	53°18·7′	2°19·4′W	T	118
Mobberley	Staffs	SK0041	52°58·2′	1°59·6′W	T	119,128
Mobberley Brook	Ches	SJ7782	53°20·3′	2°20·3′W	W	109
Mobberley Sta	Ches	SJ7781	53°19·8′	2°20·3′W	X	109
Mobb's Hole	Herts	TL2643	52°4·5′	0°9·3′W	X	153
Mobb's Hole Fm	Herts	TL2643	52°4·5′	0°9·3′W	FM	153
Mobbs Wood Fm	Warw	SP4282	52°26·3′	1°22·5′W	FM	140
Mò Bhiogadail	N Eil	NB1610	57°59·6′	6°47·9′W	H	13,14
Moblake	Ches	SJ6743	52°59·2′	2°29·1′W	T	118
Mobley	Glos	ST6999	51°41·6′	2°26·5′W	X	162
Mò Buidhe	N Eil	NB1306	57°57·3′	6°50·6′W	H	13,14
Mobwell	Bucks	SP8901	51°42·3′	0°42·3′W	T	165
Moccas	Heref	SO3542	52°4·6′	2°56·5′W	T	148,149,161
Moccas Court	Heref	SO3543	52°5·1′	2°56·5′W	X	148,149,161
Moccas Park	Heref	SO3342	52°4·6′	2°58·3′W	X	148,149,161
Mochdre	Conwy	SH8278	53°17·4′	3°45·8′W	T	116
Mochdre	Powys	SO0788	52°29·2′	3°21·8′W	T	136
Mochdre Brook	Powys	SO0686	52°28·1′	3°22·6′W	W	136
Mochnant	Powys	SJ0825	52°49·1′	3°21·5′W	X	125
Mochowgryn	Gwyn	SH8040	52°56·9′	3°46·8′W	H	124,125
Mochras	Gwyn	SH3036	52°53·9′	4°31·2′W	X	123
Mochrie	Angus	NO4465	56°46·6′	2°54·5′W	X	44
Mochrum	D & G	NX3446	54°47·1′	4°34·5′W	T	82
Mochrum	D & G	NX7274	55°2·9′	3°59·8′W	X	77,84
Mochrum	S Ayr	NS2609	55°20·9′	4°44·2′W	X	70,76
Mochrum Fell	D & G	NX3050	54°49·2′	4°38·3′W	H	82
Mochrum Fell	D & G	NX7275	55°3·4′	3°59·8′W	H	77,84
Mochrum Loch	D & G	NX3053	54°50·8′	4°38·4′W	W	82
Mochrum Loch	S Ayr	NS2709	55°20·9′	4°43·3′W	W	70,76
Mochrum Park	D & G	NX3657	54°53·1′	4°33·0′W	X	83
Mochrum Wood	S Ayr	NS2610	55°21·4′	4°44·3′W	F	70
Mockbeggar	E Susx	TQ9122	50°58·2′	0°43·6′E	X	189
Mockbeggar	Hants	SU1609	50°53·0′	1°46·0′W	T	195
Mockbeggar	Kent	TQ7146	51°11·5′	0°27·2′E	X	188
Mockbeggar	Kent	TQ9762	51°19·6′	0°50·1′E	X	178
Mockbeggar	Kent	TR1443	51°9·0′	1°4·0′E	T	179,189
Mockbeggar	Medway	TQ7372	51°25·5′	0°29·7′E	T	178
Mockbeggars Hall	Suff	TM1348	52°5·6′	1°7·0′E	A	169
Mockbeggar Wharf	Wirral	SJ2692	53°25·4′	3°6·4′W	X	108
Mockerkin	Cumbr	NY0923	54°35·9′	3°24·1′W	T	89
Mockerkin How	Cumbr	NY0922	54°35·4′	3°24·1′W	H	89
Mockerkin Tarn	Cumbr	NY0823	54°35·9′	3°25·0′W	W	89
Mocketts	Kent	TR0166	51°21·7′	0°53·6′E	X	178
Mockford	W Susx	TQ2020	50°58·2′	0°17·1′W	X	198
Mock Hall	Shrops	SJ4318	52°45·6′	2°50·3′W	X	126
Mockham Barton	Devon	SS6735	51°6·2′	3°53·6′W	X	180
Mockham Down	Devon	SS6635	51°6·2′	3°54·5′W	H	180
Mockham Down Gate	Devon	SS6636	51°6·7′	3°54·5′W	X	180

Mockley Manor	Warw	SP1168	52°18·8′	1°49·9′W	X	139
Mockley Wood	Warw	SP1268	52°18·8′	1°49·0′W	F	139
Mocktree	Heref	SO4276	52°23·0′	2°50·7′W	X	137,148
Mocktree Hays	Heref	SO4176	52°23·0′	2°51·6′W	F	137,148
Mocleitean	N Eil	NB0020	58°4·3′	7°4·8′W	H	13
Moclett	Orkney	HY4949	59°19·7′	2°53·3′W	X	5
Moco Fm	Bucks	SP7928	51°56·9′	0°50·6′W	FM	165
Modbury	Devon	SX6551	50°20·8′	3°53·5′W	T	202
Modbury Fm	Dorset	SY5189	50°42·1′	2°41·3′W	FM	194
Modbury Village	Dorset	SY5189	50°42·1′	2°41·3′W	A	194
Moddershall	Staffs	SJ9236	52°55·5′	2°6·7′W	T	127
Moddershall Grange	Staffs	SJ9337	52°56·1′	2°5·8′W	X	127
Mode Hill	Ches	SJ9276	53°17·1′	2°6·8′W	X	118
Model Fm	Bath & NE Somer	ST5965	51°23·2′	2°35·0′W	FM	172,182
Model Fm	Bath & NE Somer	ST5965	51°23·2′	2°35·0′W	FM	172,182
Model Fm	Beds	TL0436	52°1·0′	0°28·7′W	FM	153
Model Fm	Bucks	SP7413	51°48·9′	0°55·2′W	FM	165
Model Fm	Bucks	TQ0193	51°37·8′	0°32·0′W	FM	176
Model Fm	Cambs	TL1667	52°17·6′	0°17·5′W	FM	153
Model Fm	Cambs	TL2753	52°9·9′	0°8·2′W	FM	153
Model Fm	Cambs	TL3167	52°17·4′	0°4·4′W	FM	153
Model Fm	C of Aber	NJ9603	57°7·3′	2°3·5′W	FM	38
Model Fm	E Yorks	TA0436	53°48·8′	0°24·8′W	FM	107
Model Fm	Flint	SJ3161	53°8·7′	3°1·5′W	FM	117
Model Fm	Herts	TL0600	51°41·6′	0°27·6′W	FM	166
Model Fm	Leeds	SE2936	53°49·4′	1°33·2′W	FM	104
Model Fm	Lincs	TF4167	53°11·1′	0°7·0′E	FM	122
Model Fm	Monm	SO4912	51°48·5′	2°44·0′W	FM	162
Model Fm	Monm	ST4498	51°40·9′	2°48·2′W	FM	171
Model Fm	Norf	TM1894	52°30·2′	1°13·1′E	FM	134
Model Fm	N Yks	SE3563	54°3·9′	1°27·5′W	FM	99
Model Fm	N Yks	SE5635	53°48·7′	1°8·6′W	FM	105
Model Fm	Oxon	SP3820	51°52·9′	1°26·5′W	FM	164
Model Fm	Oxon	SU6997	51°40·3′	0°59·7′W	FM	165
Model Fm	Staffs	SJ8340	52°57·7′	2°14·8′W	FM	118
Model Fm	Suff	TM0456	52°10·1′	0°59·4′E	FM	155
Model Fm	Suff	TM3077	52°20·8′	1°23·0′E	FM	156
Model Fm	V of Glam	ST0767	51°23·9′	3°19·8′W	FM	170
Model Village	Derby	SK5273	53°15·3′	1°12·8′W	T	120
Model Village	Warw	SP4164	52°16·6′	1°23·5′W	T	151
Modest Corner	Kent	TQ5742	51°9·6′	0°15·1′E	T	188
Moditonham Quay	Corn	SX4161	50°25·9′	4°14·0′W	X	201
Modney Br	Norf	TL6196	52°32·5′	0°22·9′E	X	143
Modney Hall	Norf	TL6096	52°32·5′	0°22·0′E	X	143
Modrydd	Powys	SO0025	51°55·1′	3°26·9′W	X	160
Modsarie	Highld	NC6561	58°31·2′	4°18·6′W	T	10
Moel Achles	Powys	SJ0016	52°44·2′	3°28·5′W	H	125
Moel-aden	Denb	SJ0344	52°59·3′	3°26·3′W	X	125
Moel Arthur	Flint	SJ1466	53°11·3′	3°16·8′W	H	116
Moel Bengam	Conwy	SH9359	53°7·3′	3°35·5′W	H	116
Moel Bentyrch	Powys	SJ0509	52°40·5′	3°23·9′W	H	125
Moel Berfedd	Gwyn	SH6555	53°4·8′	4°0·5′W	H	115
Moel Bowydd	Gwyn	SH7147	53°0·5′	3°55·0′W	X	115
Moel Bronmiod	Gwyn	SH4145	52°59·0′	4°21·7′W	H	115,123
Moel Caerau	Gwyn	SH2935	52°53·4′	4°32·1′W	H	115
Moel Caetwpa	Powys	SH9201	52°36·0′	3°35·3′W	H	136
Moelcerni	Cered	SN5986	52°27·5′	4°4·1′W	X	135
Moel Cors-y-garnedd	Gwyn	SH7723	52°47·7′	3°49·1′W	H	124
Moel Crychion	Powys	SN8873	52°20·9′	3°38·3′W	X	135,136,147
Moel Cynghorion	Gwyn	SH5856	53°5·2′	4°6·8′W	H	115
Moel Cynhordy	Brig	SS8890	51°36·1′	3°36·6′W	H	170
Moel Cynnedd	Powys	SN8488	52°28·9′	3°42·1′W	X	135,136
Moel Darren	Gwyn	SH9541	52°57·6′	3°33·4′W	H	125
Moel Ddolwen	Powys	SH9807	52°39·3′	3°30·1′W	X	125
Moel-ddu	Gwyn	SH5744	52°58·7′	4°7·4′W	H	124
Moel Ddu	Gwyn	SH7232	52°52·5′	3°53·7′W	H	124
Moel Ddu	Gwyn	SH8727	52°50·0′	3°40·2′W	H	124,125
Moel Derwydd	Conwy	SH8856	53°5·6′	3°39·9′W	X	116
Moel Dimoel	Powys	SJ0225	52°49·1′	3°26·9′W	X	125
Moel Dod	Powys	SO0776	52°22·7′	3°21·6′W	H	136,147
Moel Dowel	Conwy	SH9266	53°11·1′	3°36·6′W	H	116
Moel Druman	Gwyn	SH6747	53°0·5′	3°58·5′W	H	115
Moel Dyrnogydd	Conwy	SH6949	53°1·6′	3°56·8′W	H	115
Moel Dywyll	Denb	SJ1563	53°9·7′	3°15·9′W	H	116
Moel Eaban	Gwyn	SH6368	53°11·7′	4°2·6′W	H	115
Moel Eglwys	Conwy	SH9047	53°0·8′	3°38·0′W	H	116
Moel Eiddew	Powys	SH8605	52°38·1′	3°40·7′W	H	124,125
Moel Eilio	Conwy	SH7465	53°10·3′	3°52·7′W	H	115
Moel Eilio	Gwyn	SH5557	53°5·7′	4°9·5′W	H	115
Moel Eithinen	Denb	SJ1659	53°7·5′	3°14·9′W	H	116
Moel Emoel	Gwyn	SH9340	52°57·0′	3°35·2′W	H	125
Moel Emwnt	Conwy	SH9368	53°12·1′	3°35·7′W	H	116
Moel Famau	Flint	SJ1662	53°9·2′	3°15·0′W	H	116
Moel Famau Country Park	Denb	SJ1463	53°9·7′	3°16·8′W	X	116
Moel Farlwyd	Conwy	SH7048	53°1·1′	3°55·9′W	H	115
Moel Fechan	Denb	SH9963	53°9·5′	3°30·2′W	H	116
Moel Feity	Powys	SN8422	51°53·3′	3°40·7′W	H	160
Moel-feliarth	Powys	SH9913	52°42·6′	3°29·3′W	H	125
Moel Fferm	Cered	SN7089	52°29·2′	3°54·5′W	X	135
Moel Fferna	Denb	SJ1139	52°56·7′	3°19·1′W	H	125
Moel Findeg	Denb	SJ2061	53°8·7′	3°11·4′W	H	117
Moel Fleiddiau	Conwy	SH6749	53°1·6′	3°58·6′W	X	115
Moel Fodiar	Conwy	SH9768	53°12·2′	3°32·1′W	H	116
Moel Fodig	Denb	SJ0945	52°59·9′	3°21·0′W	A	116
Moelfre	Carm	SN3235	51°59·5′	4°26·4′W	H	145
Moelfre	Carm	SN3415	51°48·8′	4°24·1′W	X	159
Moelfre	Carm	SN6234	51°59·5′	4°0·2′W	H	146
Moelfre	Carm	SN7840	52°2·9′	3°46·4′W	X	146,147,160
Moelfre	Cered	SN2146	52°5·2′	4°36·4′W	X	145
Moelfre	Cered	SN5056	52°11·2′	4°11·3′W	H	146
Moelfre	Cered	SN5348	52°6·9′	4°8·4′W	X	146
Moelfre	Conwy	SH7174	53°15·1′	3°55·6′W	H	115
Moelfre	Conwy	SH9574	53°15·4′	3°34·0′W	T	116
Moelfre	Gwyn	SH3944	52°58·4′	4°23·5′W	H	123
Moelfre	Gwyn	SH6224	52°48·0′	4°2·4′W	H	124
Moelfre	I of Angl	SH5186	53°21·2′	4°13·9′W	T	114
Moelfre	Powys	SJ1828	52°50·8′	3°12·7′W	T	125
Moelfre	Powys	SN8498	52°34·3′	3°42·3′W	X	135,136

Moelfre	Powys	SN9982	52°25·8′	3°28·7′W	H	136
Moelfre	Powys	SO0074	52°21·5′	3°27·7′W	H	136,147
Moelfre	Powys	SO0148	52°7·5′	3°26·4′W	H	147
Moelfre City	Powys	SO1175	52°22·2′	3°18·0′W	X	136,148
Moelfre Hill	Powys	SO1276	52°22·7′	3°17·2′W	X	136,148
Moelfre Isaf	Carm	SN4017	51°50·0′	4°18·9′W	X	159
Moelfre Isaf	Conwy	SH9573	53°14·9′	3°34·0′W	H	116
Moelfre Mâwr	Gwyn	SH3944	52°58·4′	4°23·5′W	X	123
Moelfre Newydd	Conwy	SH9547	53°0·8′	3°33·5′W	X	116
Moelfre Uchaf	Carm	SN4116	51°49·4′	4°18·0′W	X	159
Moelfre Uchaf	Conwy	SH8971	53°13·7′	3°39·4′W	H	116
Moel Frochas	Powys	SJ1122	52°47·5′	3°18·8′W	X	125
Moelfronllwyd	Powys	SJ1117	52°44·8′	3°18·7′W	X	125
Moelfryn	Cered	SN5762	52°14·5′	4°5·3′W	H	146
Moelfryn	Cered	SN6882	52°25·4′	3°56·1′W	X	135
Moelfryn	Gwyn	SH5651	53°2·5′	4°8·5′W	X	115
Moelfryn	Gwyn	SH6836	52°54·6′	3°57·4′W	X	124
Moelfryn	Gwyn	SH9432	52°52·7′	3°34·1′W	X	125
Moelfryn	Powys	SN8966	52°17·1′	3°37·2′W	X	135,136,147
Moelfryn	Powys	SN9372	52°20·4′	3°33·8′W	H	136,147
Moelfryn-mawr	Cered	SN5762	52°14·5′	4°5·3′W	X	146
Moelfryn-Serw	Conwy	SH8144	52°59·1′	3°46·0′W	X	124,125
Moel Gallt-y-cwm	Nth Pt Talb	SS8190	51°36·0′	3°42·7′W	H	170
Moel Garegog	Denb	SJ2152	53°3·8′	3°10·3′W	H	117
Moel Geufron	Powys	SN9171	52°19·8′	3°35·6′W	X	136,147
Moel Gîd	Conwy	SH6954	53°4·3′	3°56·9′W	X	115
Moelgiliau	Brig	SS9088	51°35·0′	3°34·9′W	X	170
Moel-glo	Gwyn	SH6234	52°53·4′	4°2·7′W	X	124
Moel Goch	Conwy	SH9060	53°7·8′	3°38·2′W	H	116
Moel Goedog	Gwyn	SH6132	52°52·3′	4°3·5′W	H	124
Moelgolomen	Cered	SN6987	52°28·2′	3°55·3′W	X	135
Moel Golomen	Cered	SN7087	52°28·2′	3°54·4′W	H	135
Moel Gornach	Carm	SN7418	51°51·0′	3°49·4′W	X	160
Moel Grugoer	Conwy	SH9662	53°8·9′	3°32·9′W	H	116
Moel Gwynus	Gwyn	SH3442	52°57·2′	4°27·9′W	H	123
Moel Gydia	Conwy	SH8659	53°7·2′	3°41·8′W	X	116
Moel Gyffylog	Conwy	SH8271	53°13·6′	3°45·7′W	H	116
Moel Gyw	Denb	SJ1757	53°6·5′	3°14·0′W	H	116
Moel Hafodowen	Gwyn	SH7526	52°49·3′	3°50·9′W	H	124
Moel Hafod-y-wŷn	Gwyn	SH8432	52°52·6′	3°43·0′W	H	124,125
Moel Hebog	Gwyn	SH5646	52°59·8′	4°8·3′W	H	115
Moelhedog	Cered	SN4446	52°5·7′	4°16·2′W	X	146
Moel Hen-fache	Powys	SJ1128	52°50·8′	3°18·9′W	H	125
Moel Heulen	Powys	SH7708	52°39·6′	3°48·7′W	H	124
Moel Heulog	Gwyn	SH9835	52°54·4′	3°30·6′W	H	125
Moel Hiraddug	Denb	SJ0678	53°17·7′	3°24·2′W	H	116
Moel Hyrddod	Cered	SN7295	52°32·5′	3°52·9′W	H	135
Moel Hywel	Powys	SO0071	52°19·9′	3°27·7′W	H	136,147
Moel Iago	Conwy	SH9469	53°12·7′	3°34·8′W	H	116
Moel Iart	Powys	SO0488	52°29·1′	3°24·4′W	H	136
Moelifor	Cered	SN4353	52°9·4′	4°17·3′W	X	146
Moelifor	Cered	SN5470	52°18·8′	4°8·1′W	X	135
Moel-is-y-goedwig	Denb	SJ0437	52°55·6′	3°25·3′W	X	125
Moeliwrch	Powys	SJ2028	52°50·9′	3°10·9′W	X	126
Moel Lefn	Gwyn	SH5548	53°0·8′	4°9·3′W	H	115
Moel Llaethbwlch	Powys	SJ1016	52°44·3′	3°19·6′W	X	125
Moel Llanfair	Denb	SJ1656	53°5·9′	3°14·9′W	H	116
Moel Llechwedd Hafod	Conwy	SH7548	53°1·1′	3°51·4′W	X	115
Moel Lledr	Conwy	SH6849	53°1·6′	3°57·7′W	X	115
Moel Lloran	Powys	SJ1527	52°50·3′	3°15·3′W	H	125
Moel Llyfnant	Gwyn	SH8035	52°54·2′	3°46·6′W	H	124,125
Moel Llyn	Conwy	SH8957	53°6·2′	3°39·1′W	H	116
Moel Llys-y-coed	Flint	SJ1565	53°10·8′	3°15·9′W	H	116
Moel Maelogen	Conwy	SH8461	53°8·3′	3°43·6′W	H	116
Moel Maenefa	Denb	SJ0874	53°15·5′	3°22·3′W	H	116
Moel Maes-y-wern-goch	Gwyn	SH7103	52°36·8′	3°53·9′W	X	135
Moel Main	Powys	SJ1715	52°43·8′	3°13·3′W	H	125
Moel Marchyria	Conwy	SH7546	53°0·0′	3°51·4′W	X	115
Moel Meirch	Gwyn	SH6650	53°2·1′	3°59·5′W	H	115
Moel Morfydd	Denb	SJ1545	53°0·0′	3°15·6′W	H	116
Moel Oernant	Gwyn	SH7434	52°53·6′	3°52·0′W	H	124
Moel Pearce	Denb	SJ0635	52°54·5′	3°23·5′W	H	125
Moel Penamnen	Gwyn	SH7148	53°1·1′	3°55·0′W	H	115
Moel Penderyn	Rho Cyn Taf	SN9308	51°45·9′	3°32·6′W	H	160
Moel-Pen-llechog	Gwyn	SH3846	52°59·5′	4°24·4′W	H	123
Moel Pentre-wern	Conwy	SH8867	53°11·5′	3°40·2′W	H	116
Moel Pen-y-bryn	Conwy	SH7749	53°1·7′	3°49·6′W	H	115
Moel Phylip	Gwyn	SH8740	52°57·0′	3°40·5′W	X	124,125
Moel Plas-yw	Flint	SJ1566	53°11·3′	3°15·9′W	H	116
Moel Prion	Denb	SJ0461	53°8·5′	3°25·7′W	H	116
Moel-prysgau	Cered	SN8061	52°14·3′	3°45·0′W	X	147
Moel Prysgau	Cered	SN8161	52°14·3′	3°44·2′W	F	147
Moel Rhiwen	Gwyn	SH5864	53°9·5′	4°7·0′W	H	114,115
Moel Rhiwlug	Conwy	SH8855	53°5·1′	3°39·9′W	H	116
Moel Seisiog	Conwy	SH8657	53°6·1′	3°41·8′W	H	116
Moel Siabod	Conwy	SH7054	53°4·3′	3°56·0′W	H	115
Moel Smytho	Gwyn	SH5257	53°5·6′	4°12·2′W	H	115
Moel Sych	Powys	SJ0631	52°52·3′	3°23·4′W	H	125
Moel Sychbant	Brig	SS8489	51°35·5′	3°40·1′W	X	170
Moel Ton-mawr	Nth Pt Talb	SS8387	51°34·4′	3°40·9′W	H	170
Moel Troed-y-Rhiw	Brig	SS8589	51°35·5′	3°39·2′W	H	170
Moel Truan	Denb	SJ1146	53°0·5′	3°19·2′W	H	116
Moel Trwyn-swch	Conwy	SH8044	52°59·0′	3°46·8′W	H	124,125
Moel Tryfan	Gwyn	SH5156	53°5·1′	4°13·1′W	T	115
Moel Ty-gwyn	Gwyn	SH3341	52°56·7′	4°28·7′W	H	123
Moel Tywysog	Conwy	SH9865	53°10·6′	3°31·2′W	H	116
Moel Unben	Conwy	SH9067	53°11·6′	3°38·4′W	H	116
Moel Wilym	Powys	SO1177	52°23·3′	3°18·1′W	H	136,148
Moel Wnion	Gwyn	SH6469	53°12·3′	4°1·8′W	H	115
Moelwyn	Cered	SN6471	52°19·5′	3°59·3′W	X	135
Moelwyn Bach	Gwyn	SH6643	52°58·3′	3°59·3′W	H	124
Moelwyn Mawr	Gwyn	SH6544	52°58·8′	4°0·2′W	H	124
Moelyblithcwm	Gwyn	SH6425	52°48·6′	4°0·7′W	H	124
Moel y Bryn	Powys	SH9722	52°47·4′	3°31·2′W	X	125
Moel y Bryniau	Conwy	SH9158	53°6·7′	3°37·3′W	H	116
Moel y Cerrig Duon	Powys	SH9224	52°48·4′	3°35·7′W	H	125
Moel y Ci	Gwyn	SH5966	53°10·6′	4°6·2′W	H	114,115
Moel-y-crio	Flint	SJ1969	53°13·0′	3°12·4′W	T	116
Moel y Croesau	Gwyn	SH7438	52°55·7′	3°52·1′W	H	124
Moelydd	Powys	SH8909	52°40·3′	3°38·1′W	X	124,125
Moelydd	Powys	SN9255	52°11·2′	3°34·4′W	X	147
Moelydd	Shrops	SJ2425	52°49·3′	3°7·3′W	X	126
Moel-y-don	I of Angl	SH5167	53°11·0′	4°13·4′W	X	114,115
Moel y Dyniewyd	Gwyn	SH6147	53°0·4′	4°3·9′W	H	115
Moel y Faen	Denb	SJ1847	53°1·1′	3°12·9′W	H	116
Moel y Feidiog	Gwyn	SH7832	52°52·5′	3°48·4′W	H	124
Moel y Fen	Nth Pt Talb	SS8093	51°37·6′	3°43·6′W	H	170
Moel y Fronllwyd	Powys	SJ1117	52°44·8′	3°18·7′W	X	125
Moel y Gaer	Denb	SJ0970	53°13·4′	3°21·4′W	A	116
Moel y Gaer	Denb	SJ1461	53°8·6′	3°16·7′W	A	116
Moel y Gaer	Denb	SJ1646	53°0·5′	3°14·7′W	A	116
Moel y Gaer	Flint	SJ2169	53°13·0′	3°10·6′W	A	117
Moel y Gamelin	Denb	SJ1746	53°0·5′	3°13·8′W	H	116
Moel y Garn	Cered	SN6991	52°30·3′	3°55·4′W	H	135
Moel-y-garnedd	Gwyn	SH9035	52°54·3′	3°37·7′W	X	125
Moel-y-garth	Powys	SJ1910	52°41·1′	3°11·5′W	X	125
Moel y Garth	Powys	SJ2010	52°41·1′	3°10·6′W	X	126
Moel y Gaseg-wen	Conwy	SH9058	53°6·7′	3°38·2′W	H	116
Moel-y-geifr	Gwyn	SH6334	52°53·4′	4°1·8′W	X	124
Moel y Gerddi	Gwyn	SH6231	52°51·8′	4°2·6′W	H	124
Moel-y-Gest	Gwyn	SH5538	52°55·4′	4°9·0′W	H	124
Moel y Gôd	Powys	SJ0716	52°44·3′	3°22·2′W	H	125
Moel y Golfa	Powys	SJ2912	52°42·3′	3°2·6′W	H	126
Moel-y Gwelltyn	Powys	SJ1727	52°50·3′	3°13·5′W	H	125
Moel y Gwynt	Nth Pt Talb	SS8598	51°40·4′	3°39·4′W	X	170
Moel y Gydros	Gwyn	SH9145	52°59·7′	3°37·0′W	H	116
Moel y Llyn	Cered	SN7191	52°30·3′	3°53·6′W	H	135
Moel y Llyn	Powys	SH9415	52°43·6′	3°33·8′W	H	125
Moel y Mab	Powys	SJ2405	52°38·5′	3°7·0′W	X	126
Moel Ymenyn	Gwyn	SH8334	52°53·7′	3°44·0′W	H	124,125
Moel y Mor	Cered	SN4146	52°5·6′	4°18·9′W	H	146
Moelyn	Pemb	SM6623	51°51·6′	5°23·5′W	X	157
Moel y Parc	Denb	SJ1169	53°12·9′	3°19·6′W	H	116
Moelypenmaen	Gwyn	SH3338	52°55·1′	4°28·6′W	H	123
Moel y Plâs	Denb	SJ1755	53°5·4′	3°14·0′W	H	116
Moel yr Accre	Denb	SJ1752	53°3·8′	3°13·9′W	H	116
Moel yr Ewig	Powys	SJ0732	52°52·9′	3°22·5′W	H	125
Moel yr Henfaes	Denb	SJ0738	52°56·1′	3°22·6′W	H	125
Moel-yr-hydd	Gwyn	SH6745	52°59·4′	3°58·5′W	H	115
Moel yr Hyrddod	Nth Pt Talb	SN8500	51°41·5′	3°39·4′W	X	170
Moel yr Iwrch	Conwy	SH8354	53°4·5′	3°44·4′W	H	116
Moel yr Ogof	Gwyn	SH5547	53°0·3′	4°9·3′W	H	115
Moel yr Wden	Gwyn	SH7735	52°54·1′	3°49·3′W	H	124
Moel y Sant	Powys	SJ1510	52°41·1′	3°15·0′W	X	125
Moel Ysgyfarnogod	Gwyn	SH6534	52°53·4′	4°0·0′W	H	124
Moel y Slates	Gwyn	SH7836	52°54·7′	3°48·5′W	H	124
Moel Ystradau	Gwyn	SH6843	52°58·3′	3°57·5′W	H	124
Moel y Tryfel	Powys	SH9715	52°43·6′	3°31·1′W	H	125
Moel Ytta	Denb	SJ0259	53°7·4′	3°27·5′W	H	116
Moel y Waun	Denb	SJ1653	53°4·3′	3°14·8′W	H	116
Moelywigoedd	Powys	SO1299	52°35·1′	3°17·5′W	X	136
Moffat	D & G	NT0805	55°20·1′	3°26·6′W	T	78
Moffat Dale	D & G	NT1306	55°20·7′	3°21·9′W	X	78
Moffat Hills	N Lanak	NS8167	55°53·1′	3°53·7′W	X	65
Moffat Mills	N Lanak	NS7964	55°51·5′	3°55·6′W	T	64
Moffat Water	D & G	NT1104	55°19·6′	3°23·7′W	W	78
Moffat Water	D & G	NT1510	55°22·9′	3°20·1′W	W	79
Moffat Well	D & G	NT0907	55°21·2′	3°25·7′W	W	78
Moffinber Fm	N Yks	SD6574	54°9·9′	2°31·7′W	FM	97
Mogador	Surrey	TQ2352	51°15·5′	0°13·8′W	T	187
Mo Geo	Shetld	HU1659	60°19·2′	1°42·1′W	X	3
Mogerhanger	Beds	TL1449	52°7·9′	0°19·7′W	T	153
Mogg Forest	Shrops	SO5593	52°32·2′	2°39·4′W	F	137,138
Moggforest	Shrops	SO5693	52°32·2′	2°38·5′W	X	137,138
Moggs Eye	Lincs	TF5477	53°16·3′	0°19·0′E	X	122
Mogridge Fm	Devon	SS9311	50°53·6′	3°30·9′W	FM	192
Mogshade Hill	Hants	SU2409	50°53·0′	1°39·1′W	X	195
Mogworthy	Devon	SS8517	50°56·7′	3°37·8′W	T	181
Mohope Burn	Northum	NY7649	54°50·4′	2°22·0′W	W	86,87
Mohope Head	Northum	NY7650	54°50·9′	2°22·0′W	X	86,87
Mohope Moor	Northum	NY7549	54°50·4′	2°22·9′W	X	86,87
Mohun Castle	Dorset	ST4606	50°51·3′	2°45·6′W	A	193
Mohun's Ottery	Devon	ST1805	50°50·6′	3°9·5′W	A	192,193
Mohuns Park	Somer	ST7321	50°59·5′	2°22·7′W	X	183
Moidach More	Moray	NJ0342	57°27·7′	3°36·6′W	X	27
Moidart	Highld	NM7472	56°47·3′	5°41·6′W	X	40
Moie Lodge	Arg & Bt	NM6225	56°21·7′	5°50·7′W	X	49
Moi Fea	Orkney	ND2895	58°50·5′	3°14·4′W	X	7
Moi Geo	Orkney	ND4093	58°49·5′	3°1·9′W	X	7
Moi Geo	Orkney	ND4191	58°48·4′	3°0·8′W	X	7
Moigne Combe	Dorset	SY7787	50°41·2′	2°19·2′W	X	194
Moigne Court	Dorset	SY7785	50°40·1′	2°19·1′W	A	194
Moigns Down	Dorset	SY7583	50°39·0′	2°20·8′W	X	194
Moim	N Eil	NB4151	58°22·5′	6°25·3′W	X	8
Moineach Cainish	N Eil	NF8965	57°34·3′	7°11·7′W	X	18
Mòineach Loch Portain	N Eil	NF9272	57°38·2′	7°9·2′W	X	18
Moineach Mararaulin	Highld	NG4227	57°15·9′	6°16·3′W	X	32
Mòine an t-Saraiche	Arg & Bt	NR8078	55°56·9′	5°31·0′W	X	62
Moine Bheag	Pth & Kin	NN7831	56°27·6′	3°58·3′W	X	51,52
Mòine Bhealaidh	Aberd	NO0599	57°4·6′	3°33·6′W	X	36,43
Mòine Bhuide	Highld	NH5996	57°56·1′	4°22·4′W	X	21
Mòine Bhuidhe	Aberd	NJ2903	57°7·0′	3°9·9′W	X	37
Mòine Chruinn	Aberd	NO2291	57°0·5′	3°16·6′W	X	44
Mòine Dhaor	Highld	NH6992	57°54·2′	4°12·2′W	X	21
Moine Folaich	Pth & Kin	NN9936	56°30·6′	3°38·0′W	X	52,53
Mòine Ghlas	Arg & Bt	NR9294	56°5·9′	5°20·2′W	X	55
Moine House	Highld	NC5160	58°30·4′	4°33·0′W	X	9
Moin Eich	Stir	NN3800	56°10·2′	4°36·1′W	X	56
Mòine Liath	Arg & Bt	NR3171	55°51·7′	6°17·5′W	X	60,61
Moine Loisgte	Arg & Bt	NR7661	55°47·7′	5°34·0′W	X	62
Mòine Mhór	Arg & Bt	NR8293	56°5·1′	5°29·8′W	X	55
Mòine Mhór	Highld	NG8646	57°27·5′	5°33·6′W	X	24
Mòine Mhór	Highld	NH0555	57°32·9′	5°15·1′W	X	25
Mòine Mhór	Highld	NH1964	57°38·0′	5°1·4′W	X	20
Mòine Mhór	Highld	NN8995	57°2·2′	3°49·3′W	X	35,36,43
Mòine na h-Airde	Arg & Bt	NM8321	56°20·2′	5°30·2′W	X	49
Mòine nam Faoileann	Arg & Bt	NR2567	55°49·3′	6°23·0′W	X	60
Moine nan Each	Stir	NN5013	56°17·4′	4°25·0′W	X	57
Mòine na Surdaig	Arg & Bt	NR3849	55°40·1′	6°9·6′W	X	60
Moine Odhar	Highld	NN1477	56°51·1′	5°2·6′W	X	41
Moine Path	Highld	NC4853	58°26·6′	4°35·8′W	X	9
Moine Path	Highld	NC5354	58°27·2′	4°30·7′W	X	10
Mòine Riabhach	Arg & Bt	NR4065	55°48·8′	6°8·6′W	X	60,61
Moineruadh	Arg & Bt	NR7938	55°35·4′	5°30·0′W	X	68,69
Mòinteach a' Bhreamanaich	Highld	NH0862	57°36·7′	5°12·4′W	X	19
Mointeach Airinis	N Eil	NB4029	58°10·7′	6°24·9′W	X	8
Mòinteach a' Lòin	N Eil	NB1120	58°4·8′	6°53·7′W	X	13,14
Mointeach Bharabhais	N Eil	NB3645	58°19·1′	6°30·0′W	X	8
Mòinteach Dubh	Highld	NN2079	56°52·3′	4°56·8′W	X	41
Mointeach Leacaidh	Highld	NH0966	57°38·9′	5°11·6′W	X	19
Mointeach Mhór	Highld	NM6689	56°56·3′	5°50·3′W	X	40
Mointeach Mhòr	N Eil	NF7633	57°16·6′	7°22·1′W	X	22
Mòinteach na Dubh Chlaise	Highld	NC1322	58°9·1′	5°10·2′W	X	15
Mointeach nan Tarbh	Highld	NG1348	57°26·2′	6°46·5′W	X	23
Mòinteach na Totaig	Highld	NC2510	58°2·9′	4°57·4′W	X	15
Mòinteach Toll a' Choin	Highld	NH1443	57°26·6′	5°5·5′W	X	25
Mòinteach Uineval	N Eil	NF7867	57°35·0′	7°22·8′W	X	18
Moira	Leic	SK3115	52°44·1′	1°32·0′W	T	128
Moithan Moor	Pemb	SN0208	51°44·4′	4°51·7′W	F	157,158
Moity	Powys	SO1842	52°4·5′	3°11·4′W	T	148,161
Moke Hill Fm	N Yks	SE2159	54°1·8′	1°40·3′W	FM	104
Mol a' Chaolais	N Eil	NG2297	57°52·8′	6°40·9′W	X	14
Mol a' Gharaidh	N Eil	NB1337	58°14·0′	6°52·9′W	X	13
Mol a' Mhaide Mhóir	N Eil	NF8788	57°46·6′	7°15·5′W	X	18
Mol an Droighinn	N Eil	NB1736	58°13·6′	6°48·8′W	H	8,13
Molands Br	Sol	SP2281	52°25·8′	1°40·2′W	X	139
Mol an Eich	N Eil	NB4215	58°3·2′	6°21·9′W	X	14
Molash	Kent	TR0251	51°13·6′	0°54·0′E	T	189
Mol a' Tuath	N Eil	NF8535	57°18·1′	7°13·4′W	W	22
Mol Bàn	N Eil	NG1289	57°48·1′	6°50·4′W	X	14
Mol Bàn	N Eil	NG1590	57°48·8′	6°47·5′W	X	14
Mol Bheag	Highld	NB9607	58°0·6′	5°26·7′W	X	15
Molchenydd	V of Glam	SS9478	51°29·7′	3°31·2′W	X	170
Mol-chlach	Highld	NG4513	57°8·5′	6°12·5′W	T	32
Moldgreen	Kirk	SE1516	53°38·7′	1°46·0′W	T	110
Mold or Yr Wyddgrug	Flint	SJ2363	53°9·8′	3°8·7′W	T	117
Mole Br	Devon	SS7225	51°0·8′	3°49·1′W	X	180
Molecomb	W Susx	SU8910	50°53·2′	0°43·7′W	X	197
Mole Drove Fm	Lincs	TF3513	52°42·1′	0°0·3′E	FM	131,142
Mole Hall	Essex	TL5431	51°57·6′	0°14·9′E	A	167
Molehill Common	Essex	TL6801	51°41·2′	0°26·2′E	X	167
Molehill Green	Essex	TL5624	51°53·8′	0°16·4′E	T	167
Molehill Green	Essex	TL7120	51°51·4′	0°29·4′E	T	167
Moleigh	Arg & Bt	NM8726	56°23·0′	5°26·6′W	X	49
Mol Eire	N Eil	NB3754	58°24·0′	6°29·6′W	X	8
Mole Lodge	E Yorks	SE8928	53°44·7′	0°38·6′W	X	106
Molemount Fm	E Ayr	NS5135	55°35·4′	4°21·4′W	FM	70
Molenick	Corn	SX3361	50°25·7′	4°20·7′W	X	201
Mole's Chamber	Somer	SS7139	51°8·4′	3°50·3′W	X	180
Molescombe	Devon	SX7841	50°15·6′	3°42·3′W	X	202
Molescroft	E Yorks	TA0240	53°51·0′	0°26·6′W	T	106,107
Molescroft Carr Fm	E Yorks	TA0341	53°51·5′	0°25·6′W	FM	107
Molescroft Grange	E Yorks	TA0341	53°51·5′	0°25·6′W	X	107
Moles Cross	Devon	SX8765	50°28·7′	3°35·2′W	X	202
Molesden	Northum	NZ1484	55°9·3′	1°46·4′W	T	81
Molesden Burn	Northum	NZ1483	55°8·7′	1°46·4′W	W	81
Molesey Lock	Surrey	TQ1568	51°24·2′	0°20·4′W	X	176
Molesey Reservoirs	Surrey	TQ1268	51°24·2′	0°23·0′W	W	176
Moles Fm	Herts	TL3616	51°49·8′	0°1·2′W	FM	166
Moles Fm	Herts	TL3731	51°57·9′	0°0·0′E	FM	166
Moleside Moor	Lancs	SD7828	53°45·1′	2°19·6′W	X	103
Moleskin	Beds	TL0630	51°57·7′	0°27·0′W	X	166
Molesworth	Cambs	TL0775	52°22·0′	0°25·3′W	T	142
Molesworth Lodge Fm	Cambs	TL0673	52°20·9′	0°26·2′W	FM	153
Mol Forsgeo	N Eil	NA9924	58°6·4′	7°6·2′W	X	13
Molingeanais	N Eil	NB2100	57°54·4′	6°42·1′W	X	14
Molingey	Corn	SX0050	50°19·2′	4°48·2′W	X	200,204
Molinnis	Corn	SX0159	50°24·1′	4°47·6′W	T	200
Moll	Highld	NG5630	57°18·0′	6°2·6′W	T	24,32
Mollan	Stir	NN6500	56°10·7′	4°10·0′W	X	57
Mollance	D & G	NX7159	54°54·8′	4°0·3′W	X	83,84
Mollance	D & G	NX7765	54°58·1′	3°54·9′W	X	84
Molland	Devon	SS7416	50°56·0′	3°47·2′W	X	180
Molland	Devon	SS8028	51°2·6′	3°42·3′W	T	181
Molland Common	Devon	SS8130	51°3·7′	3°41·5′W	X	181
Molland Cross	Devon	SS7133	51°5·1′	3°50·1′W	X	180
Mollandhu	Arg & Bt	NS3378	55°58·2′	4°40·1′W	X	63
Mollands	Stir	NN6206	56°13·9′	4°13·1′W	X	57
Mollards, The	Ches	SJ8769	53°13·3′	2°11·3′W	X	118
Mollen Wood	Cumbr	NY5670	55°1·6′	2°40·9′W	F	86
Mollersteads	Northum	NY9258	54°55·2′	2°7·1′W	X	87
Molleston Back	Pemb	SN0913	51°47·2′	4°45·8′W	X	158
Molleston Cross	Pemb	SN0912	51°46·7′	4°45·7′W	X	158
Mollin	D & G	NY0593	55°13·6′	3°29·2′W	X	78
Mollin Burn	D & G	NY0592	55°13·0′	3°29·2′W	W	78
Mollinburn	D & G	NY0592	55°13·0′	3°29·2′W	X	78
Mollington	Ches	SJ3870	53°13·6′	2°55·3′W	T	117
Mollington	Oxon	SP4447	52°7·4′	1°21·0′W	T	151
Mollington Grange	Ches	SJ3869	53°13·1′	2°55·3′W	X	117
Mollington Hill	Warw	SP3262	52°15·5′	1°31·5′W	X	151
Mollin Moor	D & G	NY0494	55°14·1′	3°30·1′W	X	78
Mollinsburn	N Lanak	NS7171	55°55·1′	4°3·4′W	T	64
Moll River	Highld	NG5529	57°17·4′	6°3·5′W	W	32
Molls Cleuch	Scot Bord	NT1519	55°27·7′	3°20·2′W	X	79
Molls Cleuch Dod	Scot Bord	NT1518	55°27·2′	3°20·2′W	H	79
Molly Quirk's Glen	I of M	SC4078	54°10·6′	4°26·7′W	X	95
Mol Mhór	Highld	NC4968	58°34·7′	4°35·3′W	X	9
Molmontend	E Ayr	NS5235	55°35·4′	4°20·5′W	X	70
Mol Mór	Highld	NB9806	58°0·1′	5°24·6′W	X	15
Mol Mór	Highld	NC6365	58°33·4′	4°20·8′W	X	10
Mol Mór	N Eil	NA9713	58°0·4′	7°7·3′W	X	13
Mol Mór	N Eil	NB1335	58°12·9′	6°52·8′W	X	13
Mol Mór	N Eil	NB1533	58°11·9′	6°50·6′W	X	13
Mol Mór	N Eil	NF8481	57°42·7′	7°17·9′W	X	18
Mol Mòr Bhatasgeir	N Eil	NB4939	58°16·3′	6°16·4′W	X	8
Mol na Coinnle	Highld	NC6465	58°33·4′	4°19·8′W	X	10
Mol na Cùile	N Eil	NB3611	58°0·8′	6°27·7′W	X	14
Mol nam Braithrean	N Eil	NB4118	58°4·8′	6°23·1′W	X	14

Mol na Muic	N Eil	NB0019	58°3·8′	7°4·8′W	X	13
Mol nan Clachan Gairbh	N Eil	NB2205	57°57·1′	6°41·5′W	X	13,14
Mol nan Stòp	N Eil	NB0601	57°54·4′	6°57·3′W	X	14,18
Mol Shanndabhaig	N Eil	NB4332	58°12·4′	6°22·0′W	X	8
Mol Shilldinis	N Eil	NB4630	58°11·4′	6°18·8′W	X	8
Mol Stiogh' a' Chragain	N Eil	NB4111	58°1·0′	6°22·7′W	X	14
Mol Tealasavay	N Eil	NB0318	58°3·4′	7°1·6′W	X	13
Mol Teiltein	N Eil	NF9363	57°33·4′	7°7·5′W	X	18
Mol Tiacanish	N Eil	NA9824	58°6·4′	7°7·2′W	X	13
Mol Truisg	N Eil	NB3505	57°57·6′	6°28·3′W	W	14
Mompesson's Well	Derby	SK2277	53°17·6′	1°39·8′W	A	119
Mona	I of Angl	SH4274	53°14·6′	4°21·7′W	X	114,115
Mona Airfield	I of Angl	SH4176	53°15·7′	4°22·6′W	X	114
Monach	Aberd	NJ5422	57°17·4′	2°45·3′W	H	37
Monach or Heisker Islands	Highld	NG6262	57°35·4′	5°58·5′W	X	24
Monachty	Cered	SN5062	52°14·4′	4°11·4′W	X	146
Monachty bach	Cered	SN5062	52°14·4′	4°11·4′W	X	146
Monachyle	Stir	NN4719	56°20·6′	4°28·1′W	X	57
Monachyle Burn	Stir	NN4722	56°22·2′	4°28·2′W	W	51
Monachyle Glen	Stir	NN4722	56°22·2′	4°28·2′W	X	51
Monadh a' Bhràighe	Highld	NM4886	56°54·1′	6°7·9′W	X	39
Monadh a' Choilich	Arg & Bt	NR3958	55°45·0′	6°9·1′W	X	60
Monadh a' Ghiuthais	Moray	NJ2120	57°16·1′	3°18·1′W	X	36
Monadh ant-Stuichd Leith	Aberd	NJ2617	57°14·5′	3°13·1′W	X	37
Monadh Beag	Arg & Bt	NM6232	56°25·5′	5°51·1′W	X	49
Monadh Beag	Highld	NN0486	56°55·7′	5°12·8′W	H	41
Monadh Beag	Highld	NN1585	56°55·4′	5°1·9′W	X	34,41
Monadh Ceann Lochairceig	Highld	NM9990	56°57·7′	5°17·9′W	H	33,40
Monadh Ceann Lochairceig	Highld	NN0090	56°57·7′	5°16·9′W	X	33
Monadh Choisleadar	Highld	NG3249	57°27·4′	6°27·6′W	X	23
Monadh Driseig	Arg & Bt	NN1128	56°24·6′	5°3·4′W	H	50
Monadh Dubh	Highld	NG3402	57°2·2′	6°22·6′W	X	32,39
Monadh Dubh Knockie	Highld	NH4412	57°10·6′	4°34·4′W	X	34
Monadh Fergie	Moray	NJ1914	57°12·8′	3°20·0′W	H	36
Monadh Gleann Uige	Highld	NM6676	56°49·3′	5°49·6′W	X	40
Monadh Gorm	Highld	NM9691	56°58·2′	5°20·9′W	H	33,40
Monadh Liath	Arg & Bt	NN1038	56°30·0′	5°4·8′W	H	50
Monadhliath Mountains	Highld	NH6610	57°9·9′	4°12·5′W	H	35
Monadh Meadale	Highld	NG4036	57°20·7′	6°18·8′W	H	23,32
Monadh Meadhoin	Highld	NM7153	56°37·0′	5°43·5′W	H	49
Monadh Meadhonach	Arg & Bt	NM9108	56°13·4′	5°21·8′W	X	55
Monadh Meadhonach	Highld	NM6252	56°36·2′	5°52·2′W	X	49
Monadh Mhiltich	Highld	NM3599	57°0·6′	6°21·5′W	X	39
Monadh Mór	Highld	NH5853	57°33·0′	4°21·9′W	X	26
Monadh Mór	Highld	NN9394	57°1·7′	3°45·3′W	H	36,43
Monadh Morsaig	Highld	NG6514	57°9·7′	5°52·7′W	X	32
Monadh na Ceapaich	Highld	NM6487	56°55·1′	5°52·2′W	H	40
Monadh nam Mial	Pth & Kin	NN8644	56°34·7′	3°50·9′W	H	52
Monadh nan Carn	Highld	ND0458	58°30·2′	3°38·4′W	X	11,12
Monadh nan Còrr	Highld	NM7146	56°33·3′	5°43·1′W	X	49
Monadh nan Eun	Moray	NJ1007	57°9·0′	3°28·8′W	H	36
Monadh nan Lochan	Highld	NG7915	57°10·6′	5°38·9′W	X	33
Monadh na Sròine Duibhe	Highld	NM7392	56°58·1′	5°43·6′W	H	33,40
Monadh Odhar	Pth & Kin	NN6814	56°18·3′	4°7·6′W	H	57
Monadh Rahuaidh	Highld	NM6357	56°38·9′	5°51·5′W	X	49
Monadh Seann-talaimh	Highld	NH3001	57°4·4′	4°47·8′W	H	34
Monadh Slochd Chaimbeil	Aberd	NJ2716	57°14·0′	3°12·1′W	X	37
Monadh Stairneach	Highld	NC6626	58°12·4′	4°16·4′W	X	16
Monadh Uisge Mhuilinn	Highld	NN1484	56°54·9′	5°2·9′W	X	34,41
Mona Fm	Norf	TF8909	52°39·0′	0°48·0′E	FM	144
Mona Gowan	Aberd	NJ3305	57°8·1′	3°6·0′W	H	37
Mona Hill	Norf	TF8908	52°38·4′	0°48·0′E	A	144
Monahoudie Moss	Moray	NJ2243	57°28·5′	3°17·6′W	X	28
Monaltrie Ho	Aberd	NO3796	57°3·3′	3°1·9′W	X	37,44
Monaltrie Moss	Aberd	NO2198	57°4·2′	3°17·7′W	X	36,44
Monamenach	Angus	NO1770	56°49·1′	3°21·1′W	H	43
Monamore Br	N Ayr	NS0130	55°31·6′	5°8·7′W	X	69
Monamore Glen	N Ayr	NS0029	55°31·1′	5°9·6′W	X	69
Mònan	N Eil	NB1304	57°56·2′	6°50·5′W	H	13,14
Monandavan	Aberd	NJ4500	57°5·5′	2°54·0′W	X	37
Monarch's Way	Hants	SU4924	51°1·0′	1°17·7′W	X	185
Monarch's Way	Warw	SP1649	52°8·6′	1°45·6′W	X	151
Monarch's Way	W Susx	TQ2608	50°51·7′	0°12·2′W	X	197,198
Monar Lodge	Highld	NH2040	57°25·1′	4°59·4′W	X	25
Monastery Fm	Dorset	SY8680	50°37·4′	2°11·5′W	FM	194
Monastery, The	Powys	SO2531	51°58·6′	3°5·1′W	X	161
Monaughty	Moray	NJ1260	57°37·5′	3°27·9′W	X	28
Monaughty	Powys	SO2368	52°18·5′	3°7·4′W	A	137,148
Monaughty	Powys	SO2368	52°18·5′	3°7·4′W	T	137,148
Monaughty Poeth	Shrops	SO2574	52°21·8′	3°5·7′W	X	137,148
Monaughty Wood	Moray	NJ1359	57°37·0′	3°26·9′W	F	28
Monawee	Angus	NO4080	56°54·7′	2°58·7′W	H	44
Monboddo	Aberd	NO7478	56°53·8′	2°25·2′W	T	45
Monboys	Aberd	NO8589	56°59·8′	2°14·4′W	X	45
Monck's Hall	Norf	TG0707	52°37·5′	1°3·9′E	X	144
Monckton Hook	Surrey	TQ0533	51°5·4′	0°29·7′W	X	187
Monckton Walk	E Yorks	SE9436	53°48·9′	0°33·9′W	X	106
Moncreiffe	Pth & Kin	NO1121	56°22·6′	3°26·0′W	T	53,58
Moncreiffe Hill	Pth & Kin	NO1319	56°21·6′	3°24·0′W	X	58
Moncreiffe Ho	Pth & Kin	NO1319	56°21·6′	3°24·0′W	X	58
Moncur	Pth & Kin	NO2829	56°27·1′	3°9·6′W	X	53,59
Mondaytown	Shrops	SJ3407	52°39·6′	2°58·1′W	T	126
Mondhuie	Highld	NH9920	57°15·8′	3°40·0′W	X	36
Monedie	Aberd	NJ6052	57°33·6′	2°39·7′W	X	29
Monega Hill	Angus	NO1875	56°51·8′	3°20·2′W	H	43
Monellie	Aberd	NJ5940	57°27·2′	2°40·5′W	X	29
Monelpie Moss	Aberd	NO2783	56°56·2′	3°11·5′W	X	44
Monemore	Stir	NN5632	56°27·7′	4°19·8′W	T	51
Moness	Orkney	HY2403	58°54·7′	3°18·7′W	X	6,7
Moness	Pth & Kin	NN8748	56°36·9′	3°50·0′W	X	52
Monessie	Highld	NN2980	56°53·1′	4°47·9′W	X	34,41
Monevechadan	Arg & Bt	NN1805	56°12·4′	4°55·6′W	X	56
Monewden	Suff	TM2358	52°10·7′	1°16·1′E	T	156
Monewden Hall	Suff	TM2459	52°11·2′	1°17·0′E	X	156
Money Acre Cross	Devon	SY1696	50°45·7′	3°11·1′W	X	192,193
Moneyacres	E Ayr	NS4250	55°43·3′	4°30·5′W	T	64
Money Br	Lincs	TF2125	52°48·8′	0°11·9′W	X	131
Money Burgh	E Susx	TQ4203	50°48·8′	0°1·3′E	X	198
Money Burgh (Long Barrow)	E Susx	TQ4203	50°48·8′	0°1·3′E	A	198
Moneybury Hill	Bucks	SP9713	51°48·7′	0°35·2′W	X	165
Moneydie	Pth & Kin	NO0629	56°26·9′	3°31·1′W	T	52,53,58
Moneydie Ho	Pth & Kin	NO0629	56°26·9′	3°31·1′W	X	52,53,58
Moneydie Roger	Pth & Kin	NO0528	56°26·3′	3°32·0′W	X	52,53,58
Moneydown Bottom	Wilts	SU0849	51°14·6′	1°52·7′W	X	184
Money Head	D & G	NX0448	54°47·6′	5°2·5′W	X	82
Money Hill	Cambs	TL4051	52°8·6′	0°3·2′E	X	154
Money Hill	E Yorks	SE9245	53°53·8′	0°35·6′W	X	106
Moneyhill	Herts	TQ0494	51°38·3′	0°29·4′W	T	166,176
Money Hill	Leic	SK3517	52°45·2′	1°28·5′W	T	128
Moneyhill Fm	Norf	TG0200	52°33·8′	0°59·2′E	FM	144
Money Hill (Tumulus)	Cambs	TL4051	52°8·6′	0°3·2′E	A	154
Money Hill (Tumulus)	E Yorks	SE9245	53°53·8′	0°35·6′W	A	106
Moneyhole Corner	Suff	TL9250	52°7·1′	0°48·7′E	X	155
Money Howe	N Yks	SE5995	54°21·1′	1°5·1′W	A	100
Moneylaws Covert	Northum	NT8835	55°36·8′	2°11·0′W	F	74
Moneylaws Hill	Northum	NT8734	55°36·2′	2°11·9′W	H	74
Moneymore	Staffs	SK1302	52°37·2′	1°48·1′W	X	139
Moneypenny	E Susx	TQ9421	50°57·6′	0°46·1′E	X	189
Moneypool Burn	D & G	NX5161	54°55·5′	4°19·1′W	W	83
Moneypot Hill	Beds	TL0037	52°1·6′	0°32·2′W	X	153
Moneypot Hill	Suff	TM0478	52°21·9′	1°0·2′E	X	144
Moneypot Hill Fm	E Yorks	SE9346	53°54·3′	0°34·6′W	FM	106
Moneyrow Green	Win & Maid	SU8977	51°29·3′	0°42·7′W	T	175
Moneystone	Staffs	SK0546	53°0·9′	1°55·1′W	T	119,128
Moneystones	Derby	SK1561	53°9·0′	1°46·1′W	X	119
Money Tump	Glos	SO9004	51°44·3′	2°8·3′W	A	163
Mongewell Park	Oxon	SU6187	51°34·9′	1°6·8′W	X	175
Mongewell Woods	Oxon	SU6586	51°34·4′	1°3·3′W	F	175
Mongleath	Corn	SW7832	50°9·0′	5°6·1′W	T	204
Mongour	Aberd	NO7590	57°0·3′	2°24·2′W	H	38,45
Moniabrock	Renf	NS3563	55°50·2′	4°37·6′W	X	63
Moniack Burn	Highld	NH5542	57°27·0′	4°24·5′W	W	26
Moniack Castle	Highld	NH5543	57°27·5′	4°24·6′W	X	26
Moniaive	D & G	NX7790	55°11·6′	3°55·5′W	T	78
Moniemouies	Moray	NJ2756	57°35·5′	3°12·8′W	X	28
Monifieth	Angus	NO4932	56°28·9′	2°49·2′W	T	54
Monifieth Links	Angus	NO5032	56°28·9′	2°48·3′W	X	54
Monifieth Sands	Angus	NO4931	56°28·4′	2°49·2′W	X	54
Monikie	Angus	NO4938	56°32·1′	2°49·3′W	T	54
Monikie Burn	Angus	NO5437	56°31·6′	2°44·4′W	W	54
Monikie Reservoir	Angus	NO5038	56°32·1′	2°48·3′W	W	54
Monimail	Fife	NO2914	56°19·0′	3°8·4′W	T	59
Monington	Pemb	SN1343	52°3·5′	4°43·3′W	T	145
Monivey	Orkney	HY4048	59°19·1′	3°2·8′W	W	5
Monk	Northum	NY7856	54°54·1′	2°20·2′W	X	86,87
Monk Br	Lancs	SD8549	53°56·5′	2°13·3′W	X	103
Monk Bretton	Barns	SE3607	53°33·7′	1°27·0′W	T	110,111
Monkcastle	Cumbr	NY4246	54°48·6′	2°53·7′W	X	85
Monkcastle	N Ayr	NS2946	55°40·9′	4°42·8′W	X	63
Monk Castle	N Ayr	NS2947	55°41·4′	4°42·8′W	A	63
Monk Coniston	Cumbr	SD3198	54°22·6′	3°3·3′W	X	96,97
Monk Coniston Moor	Cumbr	SD3296	54°21·5′	3°2·4′W	X	96,97
Monk Cott	Northum	NY7855	54°53·6′	2°20·2′W	X	86,87
Monk Dike	E Yorks	TA1042	53°52·0′	0°19·2′W	W	107
Monk Downs Fm	Essex	TL8623	51°52·7′	0°42·5′E	FM	168
Monkdown Wood	Kent	TQ7960	51°18·9′	0°34·5′E	F	178,188
Monk End	N Yks	NZ2809	54°28·8′	1°33·7′W	T	93
Monk End Fm	N Yks	NZ2809	54°28·8′	1°33·7′W	FM	93
Monk End Wood	N Yks	NZ2710	54°29·3′	1°34·6′W	F	93
Monken Hadley	Barnet	TQ2497	51°39·7′	0°12·0′W	T	166,176
Monken Hadley Common	Barnet	TQ2597	51°39·7′	0°11·2′W	F	166,176
Monkenshaw	D & G	NT2200	55°17·5′	3°13·3′W	X	79
Monkerton	Devon	SX9693	50°43·9′	3°28·0′W	T	192
Monkery Fm	Kent	TQ9751	51°13·7′	0°49·7′E	FM	189
Monket Ho	N Yks	SE6697	54°22·1′	0°58·6′W	X	94,100
Monkeybeck Grains	Cumbr	SD7787	54°16·9′	2°20·8′W	X	98
Monkey Island	Win & Maid	SU9178	51°29·8′	0°41·0′W	X	175
Monkfield	Durham	NZ1134	54°42·3′	1°49·3′W	X	92
Monkfield Fm	Cambs	TL3259	52°13·0′	0°3·7′W	FM	153
Monk Foss Fm	Cumbr	SD1185	54°15·4′	3°21·6′W	FM	96
Monk Fryston	N Yks	SE5029	53°45·5′	1°14·1′W	T	105
Monk Fryston Lodge	N Yks	SE4829	53°45·5′	1°15·9′W	X	105
Monk Hall	Lancs	SD8834	53°48·4′	2°10·5′W	X	103
Monkhall	Shrops	SO6193	52°32·2′	2°34·1′W	X	138
Monkhall Fm	Heref	SO4733	51°59·8′	2°45·9′W	FM	149,161
Monkhall Grange	Shrops	SO6194	52°32·8′	2°34·1′W	X	138
Monkham Down	Somer	ST3406	50°51·2′	2°55·9′W	X	193
Monkham Hill	Somer	SS9838	51°8·2′	3°27·1′W	X	181
Monkhams Hall	Essex	TL3802	51°42·2′	0°0·2′E	X	166
Monkham Wood	Glos	SP0112	51°48·6′	1°58·7′W	F	163
Monk Haven	Pemb	SM8206	51°42·9′	5°9·0′W	W	157
Monk Hesleden	Durham	NZ4537	54°43·8′	1°17·6′W	T	93
Monkhide	Heref	SO6143	52°5·3′	2°33·8′W	T	149
Monkhill	Cumbr	NY3458	54°55·0′	3°1·4′W	T	85
Monkhill	Wakf	SE4522	53°41·8′	1°18·7′W	T	105
Monk Hill Fm	Glos	SO6916	51°50·7′	2°26·6′W	FM	162
Monkhill Lough	Cumbr	NY3358	54°55·0′	3°2·3′W	W	85
Monk Holme Wood	N Yks	SE6284	54°15·1′	1°2·5′W	F	100
Monkhopton	Shrops	SO6293	52°32·3′	2°33·2′W	T	138
Monkhopton Ho	Shrops	SO6293	52°32·3′	2°33·2′W	X	138
Monkhouse Hill	Cumbr	NY3442	54°46·4′	3°1·1′W	X	85
Monk Ing	N Yks	SE1761	54°2·9′	1°44·0′W	X	99
Monkland	E Ayr	NS4639	55°37·5′	4°26·3′W	X	70
Monkland	Heref	SO4557	52°12·7′	2°47·9′W	T	148,149
Monkland	Renf	NS3963	55°50·3′	4°33·8′W	X	63
Monklaw	Scot Bord	NT6422	55°29·7′	2°33·8′W	X	74
Monkleigh	Devon	SS4520	50°57·8′	4°12·1′W	T	180,190
Monkley Gill	Lancs	SD5266	54°5·5′	2°43·6′W	X	97
Monkmains Cottage	E Loth	NT5273	55°57·1′	2°45·7′W	X	66
Monkmoor	Shrops	SJ5113	52°43·0′	2°43·1′W	T	126
Monk Moor	Somer	ST4549	51°14·5′	2°46·9′W	X	182
Monk Moors	Cumbr	SD0892	54°19·2′	3°24·4′W	X	96
Monk Myre	Pth & Kin	NO2042	56°34·0′	3°17·7′W	W	53
Monknash	V of Glam	SS9170	51°25·3′	3°33·7′W	T	170
Monkokehampton	Devon	SS5805	50°49·9′	4°0·6′W	T	191
Monkomb Fm	Bucks	SP7426	51°55·9′	0°55·0′W	FM	165
Monk Park	N Yks	SE4781	54°13·6′	1°16·3′W	X	100
Monkredding House	N Ayr	NS3245	55°40·4′	4°39·9′W	A	63
Monkridge	Northum	NY9191	55°13·0′	2°8·1′W	X	80
Monkridge Hall	Northum	NY9092	55°13·6′	2°9·0′W	X	80
Monkrigg	E Loth	NT5272	55°56·6′	2°45·7′W	X	66
Monkrigg Fm	E Loth	NT5272	55°56·6′	2°45·7′W	FM	66
Monkroyd	Lancs	SD9341	53°52·2′	2°6·0′W	X	103
Monkroyd Fm	Wakf	SE4320	53°40·7′	1°20·5′W	FM	105
Monks	Devon	SS2902	50°47·8′	4°25·2′W	X	190
Monks	Surrey	TQ1236	51°7·0′	0°23·6′W	X	187
Monks	Worcs	SO8875	52°22·6′	2°10·2′W	X	139
Monks	W Susx	TQ3133	51°5·1′	0°7·4′W	X	187
Monk's Barn	Warw	SP2051	52°9·6′	1°42·1′W	X	151
Monksbarn Fm	Notts	SK5354	53°5·1′	1°12·1′W	FM	120
Monk's & Barrow's Fm	Essex	TL6302	51°41·8′	0°21·9′E	FM	167
Monks Bay	I of W	SZ5877	50°35·6′	1°10·5′W	W	196
Monk's Br	Worcs	SO6168	52°18·8′	2°33·9′W	X	138
Monks Bridge	Cumbr	NY0610	54°28·8′	3°26·6′W	A	89
Monks' Bridge	I of M	SC2870	54°6·1′	4°37·4′W	A	95
Monks Brook	Hants	SU4417	50°57·3′	1°22·0′W	W	185
Monks Burn	Midlo	NT1759	55°49·3′	3°19·0′W	W	65,66,72
Monk's Cally	Pth & Kin	NO1252	56°39·3′	3°25·7′W	X	53
Monk's Court	Heref	SO4158	52°13·3′	2°51·4′W	A	148,149
Monkscroft	Pth & Kin	NN9314	56°18·6′	3°43·3′W	X	58
Monkscross	Corn	SX3871	50°31·2′	4°16·7′W	T	201
Monks Cross	York	SE6255	53°59·5′	1°2·8′W	X	105
Monk's Dale	Derby	SK1374	53°16·0′	1°47·9′W	X	119
Monksdale Ho	Derby	SK1375	53°16·5′	1°47·9′W	X	119
Monks Dike	Lincs	TF3588	53°22·5′	0°2·2′E	W	113,122
Monk's Down	Wilts	ST9420	50°59·0′	2°4·7′W	X	184
Monkseaton	N Tyne	NZ3472	55°2·7′	1°27·6′W	T	88
Monks Eleigh	Suff	TL9647	52°5·4′	0°52·1′E	T	155
Monks Eleigh Tye	Suff	TL9548	52°6·0′	0°51·2′E	X	155
Monksfield	Worcs	SO8050	52°9·1′	2°17·1′W	X	150
Monksfields	Powys	SJ2908	52°40·1′	3°2·6′W	X	126
Monks Fm	Essex	TL5323	51°53·3′	0°13·8′E	FM	167
Monk's Fm	Essex	TL5731	51°57·5′	0°17·5′E	FM	167
Monk's Fm	Essex	TL8520	51°51·1′	0°41·6′E	FM	168
Monks Fm	Hav	TQ6087	51°33·8′	0°18·9′E	FM	177
Monks Fm	Kent	TQ9559	51°18·0′	0°48·2′E	FM	178
Monk's Fm	Norf	TM2098	52°32·3′	1°15·1′E	FM	134
Monks Fm	Oxon	SU3990	51°36·7′	1°25·8′W	FM	164,174
Monk's Fm	W Susx	SU7508	50°52·2′	0°55·7′W	FM	197
Monks Fm	W Susx	TQ1335	51°6·4′	0°22·8′W	FM	187
Monksfoot	S Lanak	NS7828	55°32·1′	3°55·6′W	X	71
Monksford	Scot Bord	NT5832	55°35·0′	2°39·5′W	X	73,74
Monks Forest	W Susx	TQ3032	51°4·6′	0°8·3′W	F	187
Monk's Gate	W Susx	TQ2027	51°2·0′	0°16·9′W	T	187,198
Monks Green	Herts	TL3308	51°45·5′	0°4·0′W	X	166
Monk's Hall	Essex	TL5543	52°4·0′	0°16·1′E	X	154
Monks Hall	Lincs	TF2332	52°52·5′	0°9·9′W	X	131
Monks Hall	Suff	TL8348	52°6·2′	0°40·7′E	A	155
Monk's Hall	Suff	TM2078	52°21·6′	1°14·3′E	X	156
Monks Hall Fm	Ches	SJ6545	53°0·3′	2°30·9′W	FM	118
Monksham Fm	Somer	ST7642	51°10·8′	2°20·2′W	FM	183
Monks Hardwick	Cambs	TL2161	52°14·3′	0°13·3′W	X	153
Monkshead	S Lanak	NS7636	55°36·4′	3°57·7′W	X	71
Monkshead	S Lanak	NS7730	55°33·1′	3°56·6′W	X	71
Monk's Heath	Ches	SJ8474	53°16·0′	2°14·0′W	T	118
Monksheath Hall Fm	Ches	SJ8474	53°16·0′	2°14·0′W	FM	118
Monk Sherborne	Hants	SU6056	51°18·2′	1°8·0′W	T	175
Monkshill	Aberd	NJ7940	57°27·2′	2°20·5′W	T	29,30
Monkshill	Aberd	NJ9125	57°19·2′	2°8·5′W	X	38
Monks Hill	Glos	SO7713	51°49·1′	2°19·6′W	H	162
Monks Hill	Kent	TQ8641	51°8·5′	0°39·9′E	T	189
Monks Hill	Surrey	SU8844	51°11·5′	0°44·1′W	X	186
Monkshill Fm	Kent	TR0662	51°19·4′	0°57·8′E	FM	179
Monks Ho	Cumbr	NY4937	54°43·8′	2°47·1′W	X	90
Monk's Ho	Lincs	TF2222	52°47·1′	0°11·1′W	A	131
Monks Ho	Northum	NU2033	55°35·7′	1°40·5′W	X	75
Monksholm	Fife	NO4617	56°20·8′	2°52·0′W	X	59
Monks Horton Manor	Kent	TR1239	51°6·9′	1°2·1′E	X	179,189
Monks House Rocks	Northum	NU2033	55°35·7′	1°40·5′W	X	75
Monkside	Northum	NY6894	55°14·6′	2°29·8′W	H	80
Monksilver	Somer	ST0737	51°7·7′	3°19·4′W	T	181
Monks Kirby	Warw	SP4683	52°26·8′	1°19·0′W	T	140
Monks Kirby Lodge	Warw	SP4684	52°27·4′	1°19·0′W	X	140
Monksland	Swan	SS4587	51°33·9′	4°13·8′W	X	159
Monk's Lode	Cambs	TL2084	52°26·7′	0°13·7′W	W	142
Monks Lodge	Essex	TL8035	51°59·3′	0°37·7′E	X	155
Monk's Moor	Durham	NY9628	54°39·1′	2°3·3′W	H	91,92
Monksmoor Fm	Northnts	SP5864	52°16·5′	1°8·6′W	FM	152
Monk Soham	Suff	TM2165	52°14·5′	1°14·6′E	T	156
Monks Orchard	Croy	TQ3567	51°23·4′	0°3·2′W	T	177
Monks Park	E Susx	TQ6434	51°5·1′	0°20·9′E	X	188
Monk's Park	Wilts	ST8768	51°24·9′	2°10·8′W	T	173
Monks Park Wood	Warw	SP2996	52°33·9′	1°33·9′W	F	140
Monkspath	Sol	SP1476	52°23·1′	1°47·3′W	T	139
Monkspath Hill Fm	Sol	SP1475	52°22·6′	1°47·3′W	FM	139
Monks Risborough	Bucks	SP8004	51°44·0′	0°50·1′W	T	165
Monk's Road	Derby	SK0291	53°25·2′	1°57·8′W	X	110
Monkstadt	Highld	NG3767	57°37·2′	6°23·8′W	X	23
Monksthorpe	Lincs	TF4465	53°10·0′	0°9·7′E	T	122
Monkston	Mil Key	SP8938	52°2·2′	0°41·8′W	X	152
Monkstone	Devon	SX4681	50°36·7′	4°10·2′W	X	201
Monkstone,	V of Glam	ST2369	51°25·1′	3°6·1′W	X	171,182
Monkstone Point	Pemb	SN1503	51°42·0′	4°40·2′W	X	158
Monkston Park	Mil Key	SP8838	52°2·2′	0°42·6′W	T	152
Monkstown	Fife	NO3009	56°16·4′	3°7·4′W	T	59
Monk Stray	York	SE6253	53°58·4′	1°2·9′W	X	105
Monk Street	Essex	TL6128	51°55·9′	0°20·9′E	T	167
Monks Wall	Devon	SY0984	50°39·1′	3°16·9′W	X	192
Monks Wall, The	Kent	TR3259	51°17·2′	1°20·0′E	A	179
Monks Water	S Lanak	NS7729	55°32·6′	3°56·5′W	W	71
Monkswell	Aberd	NJ8860	57°38·0′	2°11·6′W	X	30
Monk's Well	Ches	SJ6469	53°13·3′	2°31·9′W	X	118
Monk's Wood	Cambs	TL1980	52°24·5′	0°14·6′W	F	142
Monk's Wood	Essex	TL5217	51°50·1′	0°12·8′E	F	167
Monkswood	Leeds	SE3437	53°49·9′	1°28·6′W	T	104
Monk's Wood	Lincs	TF0414	52°43·1′	0°27·2′W	F	130

Monkswood	Midlo	NT3363	55°51·6'	3°3·8'W	T	66
Monkswood	Monm	SO3402	51°43·0'	2°56·9'W	T	171
Monk's Wood	Northnts	SP6543	52°5·1'	1°2·7'W	F	152
Monks' Wood Fm	Cambs	TL1879	52°24·0'	0°15·5'W	FM	142
Monkswood Resr	S Glos	ST7571	51°26·5'	2°21·2'W	W	172
Monkton	Devon	ST1803	50°49·5'	3°9·5'W	T	192,193
Monkton	Heref	SO4926	51°56·0'	2°44·1'W	X	162
Monkton	Heref	SO5745	52°6·3'	2°37·3'W	X	149
Monkton	Kent	TR2865	51°20·5'	1°16·8'E	T	179
Monkton	Pemb	SM9701	51°40·5'	4°55·8'W	T	157,158
Monkton	S Ayr	NS3527	55°30·8'	4°36·4'W	T	70
Monkton	S Tyne	NZ3263	54°57·9'	1°29·6'W	T	88
Monkton	V of Glam	SS9271	51°25·9'	3°32·8'W	T	170
Monkton Barn	Essex	TQ9993	51°36·3'	0°52·8'E	X	178
Monkton Barton	Devon	ST1903	50°49·5'	3°8·6'W	X	192,193
Monkton Combe	Bath & NE Somer	ST7762	51°21·6'	2°19·4'W	T	172
Monkton Deverill	Wilts	ST8537	51°8·2'	2°12·5'W	T	183
Monkton Down	Dorset	ST9208	50°52·5'	2°6·4'W	X	195
Monkton Down	Wilts	SU1272	51°27·0'	1°49·2'W	X	173
Monkton Elm	Somer	ST2627	51°2·5'	3°2·9'W	X	193
Monkton Farleigh	Wilts	ST8065	51°23·3'	2°16·9'W	T	173
Monkton Field	Wilts	SU0872	51°27·0'	1°52·7'W	X	173
Monkton Fm	Bucks	SP8400	51°41·8'	0°46·7'W	FM	165
Monkton Fm	Bucks	SU8589	51°35·8'	0°46·0'W	FM	175
Monkton Fm	W Susx	SU8216	50°56·5'	0°49·6'W	FM	197
Monkton Fms	Somer	ST2142	51°10·5'	3°7·4'W	FM	182
Monktonhall	E Loth	NT3471	55°55·9'	3°2·9'W	T	66
Monktonhead	S Ayr	NS3528	55°31·3'	4°36·4'W	X	70
Monkton Heathfield	Somer	ST2526	51°1·9'	3°3·8'W	T	193
Monktonhill	S Ayr	NS3429	55°31·8'	4°37·4'W	X	70
Monkton Ho	E Loth	NT3370	55°55·4'	3°3·9'W	X	66
Monkton Ho	Somer	ST2628	51°3·0'	3°3·0'W	X	193
Monkton Ho	Wilts	ST8862	51°21·6'	2°10·0'W	A	173
Monkton Ho	Wilts	ST9273	51°27·6'	2°6·5'W	X	173
Monkton Ho	W Susx	SU8317	50°57·0'	0°48·7'W	X	197
Monkton Mains	N Yks	SE3164	54°4·5'	1°31·2'W	X	99
Monkton Marshes	Kent	TR2764	51°20·0'	1°15·9'E	X	179
Monkton Road Fm	Kent	TR2967	51°21·6'	1°17·8'E	FM	179
Monkton Up Wimborne	Dorset	SU0113	50°55·2'	1°58·8'W	T	195
Monkton Wood	Bucks	SP8301	51°42·3'	0°47·5'W	F	165
Monkton Wyld	Dorset	SY3396	50°45·8'	2°56·6'W	T	193
Monkton Wyld Cross	Devon	SY3296	50°45·8'	2°57·5'W	X	193
Monk Wall	N Yks	SE2667	54°6·1'	1°35·7'W	A	99
Monkwearmouth	Sund	NZ3958	54°55·2'	1°23·1'W	T	88
Monkwith	E Yorks	TA3032	53°46·3'	0°1·2'W	X	107
Monkwood	Dorset	SY4298	50°47·0'	2°49·0'W	T	193
Monkwood	Hants	SU6630	51°4·2'	1°3·1'W	T	185,186
Monk Wood	Hants	SU7439	51°9·0'	0°56·1'W	F	186
Monk Wood	Kent	TQ7364	51°21·1'	0°29·5'E	F	178,188
Monkwood	S Ayr	NS3313	55°23·2'	4°37·8'W	X	70
Monkwood	S Ayr	NS3314	55°23·7'	4°37·8'W	X	70
Monk Wood	Somer	ST6942	51°10·8'	2°26·2'W	F	183
Monk Wood	Worcs	SO8061	52°15·0'	2°17·2'W	F	138,150
Monkwood Fm	Derby	SK3575	53°16·5'	1°28·1'W	FM	119
Monkwood Green	Worcs	SO8060	52°14·5'	2°17·2'W	T	138,150
Monkwood Hill Fm	Dorset	ST7304	50°50·3'	2°22·6'W	FM	194
Monkwood Mains	S Ayr	NS3314	55°23·7'	4°37·8'W	X	70
Monkwood Mill	S Ayr	NS3313	55°23·2'	4°37·8'W	X	70
Monkyn Pyn	E Susx	TQ5405	50°49·7'	0°11·6'E	X	199
Monlettie	Aberd	NJ8739	57°26·7'	2°12·5'W	X	30
Monluth Hill	Aberd	NO7387	56°58·7'	2°26·2'W	H	45
Monmarsh	Heref	SO5249	52°8·5'	2°41·7'W	T	149
Monmore Green	Wolv	SO9397	52°34·5'	2°5·8'W	T	139
Monmouth Cap	Monm	SO3926	51°56·0'	2°52·8'W	T	161
Monmouth Ho	Lincs	TF4424	52°47·9'	0°8·6'E	X	131
Monmouth or Trefynwy	Monm	SO5012	51°48·5'	2°43·1'W	T	162
Monmouth's Ash	Dorset	SU0607	50°52·0'	1°54·5'W	X	195
Monmouth's Hill	Dorset	ST7902	50°49·3'	2°17·5'W	X	194
Monmouthshire and Brecon Canal	Powys	SO1819	51°52·1'	3°11·1'W	W	161
Monmouthshire & Brecon Canal	Newp	ST2689	51°35·9'	3°3·7'W	W	171
Monneley Fm	Ches	SJ7553	53°4·7'	2°22·0'W	FM	118
Monnington Court	Heref	SO3836	52°1·4'	2°53·8'W	X	149,161
Monnington on Wye	Heref	SO3743	52°5·1'	2°54·8'W	T	148,149,161
Monorgan	Pth & Kin	NO3228	56°26·6'	3°5·7'W	X	53,59
Monquhill	E Ayr	NS5906	55°19·9'	4°12·9'W	X	71,77
Monreith	D & G	NX3641	54°44·5'	4°32·4'W	T	83
Monreith Bay	D & G	NX3540	54°43·9'	4°33·3'W	W	83
Monreith Burn	D & G	NX3843	54°45·6'	4°30·6'W	W	83
Monreith Ho	D & G	NX3542	54°45·0'	4°33·4'W	X	83
Monreith Mains	D & G	NX3643	54°45·6'	4°32·5'W	X	83
Monsal Dale	Derby	SK1771	53°14·4'	1°44·3'W	X	119
Monsal Head	Derby	SK1871	53°14·4'	1°43·4'W	X	119
Mons Hill	C of Edin	NT1578	55°59·5'	3°21·3'W	H	65
Mons Hill	Dudley	SO9392	52°31·8'	2°5·8'W	X	139
Monson Fm	Lincs	SK9270	53°13·4'	0°36·9'W	FM	121
Monson's Wood	Norf	TG1227	52°48·2'	1°9·1'E	F	133
Monstay Fm	Heref	SO4673	52°21·4'	2°47·2'W	FM	137,138,148
Montacute	Somer	ST4916	50°56·7'	2°43·2'W	T	183,193
Montacute Ho	Somer	ST4917	50°57·2'	2°43·2'W	A	183,193
Montague	E Susx	TQ6205	50°49·5'	0°18·4'E	X	199
Montague	Pth & Kin	NO1828	56°26·5'	3°19·4'W	X	53,58
Montague's Fm	Essex	TL8633	51°58·1'	0°42·9'E	FM	168
Montagu Steps	Devon	SS1343	51°9·6'	4°40·1'W	X	180
Montalt	Pth & Kin	NO0613	56°18·3'	3°30·7'W	X	58
Montammo	Aberd	NJ9722	57°17·6'	2°2·5'W	X	38
Montana Park Fm	Devon	ST1412	50°54·3'	3°13·0'W	FM	181,193
Montbletton	Aberd	NJ7261	57°38·5'	2°27·7'W	X	29
Montboy	Angus	NO5361	56°44·6'	2°45·7'W	X	44
Montcliffe	Bolton	SD6512	53°36·4'	2°31·3'W	T	109
Montcoffer Ho	Aberd	NJ6861	57°38·5'	2°31·7'W	X	29
Montcoffer Wood	Aberd	NJ6862	57°39·1'	2°31·7'W	F	29
Monteach	Aberd	NJ8640	57°27·3'	2°13·5'W	X	30
Monteith Ho	S Lanak	NS9444	55°40·9'	3°40·7'W	X	71,72
Monteith Houses	Midlo	NT3561	55°50·5'	3°1·8'W	X	66
Monteviot Ho	Scot Bord	NT6424	55°30·8'	2°33·8'W	X	74
Montfode	N Ayr	NS2244	55°39·7'	4°49·3'W	X	63,70

Montford	Arg & Bt	NS1064	55°50·2'	5°1·6'W	T	63
Montford	Lancs	SD8336	53°49·4'	2°15·1'W	X	103
Montford	Shrops	SJ4114	52°43·5'	2°52·0'W	T	126
Montford Bridge	Shrops	SJ4315	52°44·0'	2°50·2'W	T	126
Montfothie	Aberd	NJ9841	57°27·8'	2°1·5'W	X	30
Montgarrie	Aberd	NJ5717	57°14·8'	2°42·3'W	T	37
Montgarswood	E Ayr	NS5227	55°31·1'	4°20·2'W	X	70
Montgatehead	Aberd	NO8891	57°0·9'	2°11·4'W	X	38,45
Montgoldrum	Aberd	NO8177	56°53·3'	2°18·3'W	X	45
Montgomerieston	S Ayr	NS3612	55°22·7'	4°34·9'W	X	70
Montgomery	Powys	SO2296	52°33·6'	3°8·6'W	T	137
Montgomery Castle	Powys	SO2296	52°33·6'	3°8·6'W	A	137
Montgomery Lines	Hants	SU8651	51°15·3'	0°45·7'W	T	186
Montgomery's Fm	Hants	SU7846	51°12·7'	0°52·6'W	FM	186
Montgreenan	N Ayr	NS3444	55°39·9'	4°37·9'W	X	63,70
Montgrew	Moray	NJ4551	57°33·0'	2°54·7'W	X	28,29
Montgrew Br	Moray	NJ4451	57°33·0'	2°55·7'W	X	28
Monthammock	Aberd	NO7994	57°2·5'	2°20·3'W	X	38,45
Monthrey	Angus	NO3162	56°44·9'	3°7·2'W	X	44
Monton	Salf	SJ7699	53°29·5'	2°21·3'W	T	109
Montpelier	C of Bris	ST5974	51°28·0'	2°35·0'W	T	172
Montpelier's Fm	Essex	TL6704	51°42·8'	0°25·4'E	FM	167
Montquey	Fife	NT2087	56°4·4'	3°16·7'W	X	66
Montquhir	Angus	NO5441	56°33·8'	2°44·5'W	X	54
Montrave	Fife	NO3706	56°14·8'	3°0·6'W	X	59
Montrave Home Fm	Fife	NO3706	56°14·8'	3°0·6'W	FM	59
Montraw Burn	E Ayr	NS6403	55°18·4'	4°8·1'W	W	77
Montreal	Heref	SO6059	52°13·9'	2°34·7'W	X	149
Montreal	Pth & Kin	NN9931	56°27·9'	3°37·9'W	X	52,53
Montreal Fm	N Yks	SE6374	54°9·7'	1°1·7'W	FM	100
Montreathmont Forest	Angus	NO5654	56°40·8'	2°42·6'W	F	54
Montreathmont Moor	Angus	NO5954	56°40·8'	2°39·7'W	X	54
Montreux Fm	N Som	ST4563	51°22·0'	2°47·0'W	FM	172,182
Montrose	Angus	NO7157	56°42·5'	2°28·0'W	T	54
Montrose Basin	Angus	NO6957	56°43·0'	2°29·9'W	W	54
Montrose Bay	Angus	NO7358	56°43·0'	2°26·0'W	W	54
Montrose Bay	Angus	NO7461	56°44·7'	2°25·1'W	W	45
Montrose Fm	Suff	TL9873	52°19·4'	0°54·7'E	FM	144,155
Montrose's Camp	Aberd	NJ7739	57°26·7'	2°22·5'W	A	29,30
Montsale	Essex	TR0097	51°38·4'	0°53·8'E	T	168
Montsnaught	Aberd	NO8293	57°1·9'	2°17·3'W	X	38,45
Monturpie	Fife	NO4303	56°13·2'	2°54·7'W	X	59
Montys Court	Somer	ST1726	51°1·9'	3°10·6'W	X	181,193
Monubent	Lancs	SD7951	53°57·5'	2°18·8'W	X	103
Monubent Head	Lancs	SD8051	53°57·5'	2°17·9'W	X	103
Monument Fm	Suff	TM2243	52°2·7'	1°14·6'E	FM	169
Monument on Birthplace of James Hogg	Scot Bord	NT2614	55°25·1'	3°9·7'W	X	79
Monument to Flora Macdonald	Highld	NG4071	57°39·5'	6°21·1'W	X	23
Monwode House Fm	Warw	SP2691	52°31·2'	1°36·6'W	FM	140
Monwode Lea	Warw	SP2691	52°31·2'	1°36·6'W	T	140
Monxton	Hants	SU3144	51°11·9'	1°33·0'W	T	185
Monxton Fm	Hants	SU3042	51°10·8'	1°33·9'W	FM	185
Monyash	Derby	SK1566	53°11·7'	1°46·1'W	T	119
Monybachach	Arg & Bt	NR9058	55°46·4'	5°20·5'W	X	62
Monybuie	D & G	NX7382	55°7·2'	3°59·1'W	X	77
Monybuie Burn	D & G	NX7381	55°6·7'	3°59·0'W	W	77
Monybuie Flow	D & G	NX7481	55°6·7'	3°58·1'W	X	77
Monybuie Hill	D & G	NX7283	55°7·7'	4°0·0'W	X	77
Monydrain	Arg & Bt	NR8689	56°3·0'	5°25·7'W	X	55
Monykebbuck	Aberd	NJ8718	57°15·4'	2°12·5'W	X	38
Monymusk	Aberd	NJ6815	57°13·7'	2°31·3'W	T	38
Monynut Edge	E Loth	NT7067	55°54·0'	2°28·3'W	H	67
Monynut Water	Scot Bord	NT7165	55°52·9'	2°27·4'W	W	67
Monynut Water	Scot Bord	NT7165	55°52·9'	2°27·4'W	W	67
Monyquil	N Ayr	NR9335	55°34·1'	5°16·6'W	X	68,69
Monyroads	Aberd	NJ6712	57°12·1'	2°32·3'W	X	38
Monyruy	Aberd	NK0547	57°31·0'	1°54·5'W	X	30
Mony's Stone	Highld	NH3730	57°20·1'	4°42·0'W	A	26
Monzie	Pth & Kin	NN8725	56°24·5'	3°49·4'W	T	52,58
Monzie	Pth & Kin	NN9067	56°47·2'	3°47·6'W	X	43
Monzie Castle	Pth & Kin	NN8724	56°23·9'	3°49·4'W	A	52,58
Monziehall	Fife	NT1687	56°4·4'	3°20·5'W	X	65,66
Mooa	Shetld	HU6064	60°21·6'	0°54·2'W	X	2
Mooa Clett	Shetld	HU5767	60°23·2'	0°57·5'W	X	2
Mooa Stack	Shetld	HP6611	60°46·9'	0°46·8'W	X	1
Moo Burn	Shetld	HU4587	60°34·1'	1°10·2'W	W	1,2
Moodersley	Derby	SK2941	52°58·2'	1°33·7'W	X	119,128
Moodiesburn	N Lanak	NS6870	55°54·6'	4°6·3'W	T	64
Moodlaw	D & G	NT2501	55°18·1'	3°10·5'W	X	79
Mood Law	D & G	NT2601	55°18·1'	3°9·5'W	H	79
Moodlaw Burn	D & G	NT2501	55°18·1'	3°10·5'W	W	79
Moodlaw Loch	D & G	NT2907	55°21·4'	3°6·8'W	W	79
Moody's Down Fm	Hants	SU4338	51°8·6'	1°22·7'W	FM	185
Moodystreet	Staffs	SJ8757	53°6·8'	2°11·2'W	X	118
Moo Field	Shetld	HU3072	60°26·1'	1°26·8'W	X	3
Moo Field	Shetld	HU4357	60°18·0'	1°12·8'W	X	2,3
Moolham	Somer	ST3613	50°55·0'	2°54·2'W	T	193
Mool Hill	Highld	ND3672	58°38·1'	3°5·7'W	X	7,12
Moolie	Orkney	HY3831	59°9·9'	3°4·6'W	X	6
Moon	Shetld	HU3561	60°20·2'	1°21·5'W	X	2,3
Moon Cottage	Stir	NN7600	56°10·8'	3°59·4'W	X	57
Moonen Bay	Highld	NG1346	57°25·1'	6°46·4'W	W	23
Mooness	Orkney	HY4802	58°54·4'	2°53·7'W	X	6,7
Moo Ness	Shetld	HU2965	60°22·3'	1°27·9'W	X	3
Moo Ness	Shetld	HU3260	60°19·6'	1°24·7'W	X	3
Moonhaugh	Aberd	NJ6017	57°14·8'	2°39·3'W	X	37
Moonhayes	Devon	ST2009	50°52·7'	3°7·8'W	X	192,193
Moon Hill	Hants	SU3502	50°49·2'	1°29·8'W	F	196
Moonhills Copse	Hants	SU4002	50°49·2'	1°25·5'W	F	196
Moonhouse Plantn	Devon	SX3984	50°38·2'	4°16·2'W	F	201
Moonlight Barn	W Berks	SU4282	51°32·4'	1°23·3'W	X	174
Moon's Cross	Devon	SX6594	50°44·0'	3°54·4'W	X	191
Moon's Fm	Essex	TQ8694	51°37·1'	0°41·6'E	FM	168,178
Moon's Fm	E Susx	TQ4421	50°58·4'	0°3·5'E	FM	198
Moon's Green	Kent	TQ8827	51°0·9'	0°41·2'E	T	189,199
Moons Hill Fm	Somer	ST6647	51°13·5'	2°28·8'W	FM	183
Moonshine Fm	Herts	TL0200	51°41·6'	0°31·1'W	FM	166
Moonshine Gap	Cambs	TL1286	52°27·9'	0°20·7'W	X	142

Moon & Sixpence	Suff	TM2645	52°3·7'	1°18·2'E	X	169
Moonsleaze Fm	Wilts	SU0387	51°35·1'	1°57·0'W	FM	173
Moon's Moat	Worcs	SP0768	52°18·8'	1°53·4'W	A	139
Moon's Moat	Worcs	SP0768	52°18·8'	1°53·4'W	T	139
Moon's Park	Corn	SX0683	50°37·1'	4°44·2'W	X	200
Moon Wood	Lincs	TF4471	53°13·2'	0°9·8'E	F	122
Moonzie	Fife	NO3317	56°20·7'	3°4·6'W	T	59
Moonzie Burn	Fife	NO3917	56°20·7'	2°58·8'W	W	59
Moonzie Mill	Fife	NO4219	56°21·8'	2°55·9'W	X	59
Moor	Carm	SN2316	51°49·1'	4°33·7'W	X	158
Moor	Cumbr	NY2822	54°35·5'	3°6·4'W	X	89,90
Moor	Devon	SS2626	51°0·7'	4°28·4'W	X	190
Moor	Devon	SX4294	50°43·7'	4°13·9'W	X	190
Moor	D & G	NS5603	55°18·3'	4°15·7'W	X	77
Moor	E Ayr	NS5048	55°42·4'	4°22·8'W	X	64
Moor	Pemb	SR9297	51°38·2'	5°0·0'W	X	158
Moor	Somer	ST4216	50°56·7'	2°49·2'W	T	193
Moor Abbey	Heref	SO5463	52°16·0'	2°40·0'W	X	137,138,149
Mooradale	Shetld	HU4970	60°24·9'	1°6·1'W	X	2,3
Mooragh, The	I of M	SC4594	54°19·3'	4°22·6'W	T	95
Moorahill Fm	Cumbr	NY4918	54°33·5'	2°46·9'W	FM	90
Moor Allerton	Leeds	SE3039	53°51·0'	1°32·2'W	T	104
Moora Waters	Shetld	HU3272	60°26·1'	1°24·6'W	W	3
Mooray	Wilts	ST9732	51°5·5'	2°2·2'W	T	184
Moorbank	Cumbr	SD5697	54°22·2'	2°40·2'W	X	97
Moor Bank Fm	Wrekin	SJ6418	52°45·7'	2°31·6'W	FM	127
Moor Barn	Derby	SK1551	53°3·6'	1°46·2'W	X	119
Moor Barn	Lincs	SK9147	53°1·0'	0°38·2'W	X	130
Moor Barn	Newp	ST3685	51°33·9'	2°55·0'W	X	171
Moor Barn	Shrops	SO6493	52°32·3'	2°31·4'W	X	138
Moorbarns	Leic	SP5282	52°26·2'	1°13·7'W	X	140
Moor Barns Fm	Cambs	TL4159	52°12·9'	0°4·2'E	FM	154
Moorbarns Fm	Leic	SK3002	52°37·1'	1°33·0'W	FM	140
Moorbarns Fm	Leic	SP5283	52°26·8'	1°13·7'W	FM	140
Moor Barton	Devon	SX8183	50°38·3'	3°40·6'W	X	191
Moor Barton Fm	Devon	SS8413	50°54·5'	3°38·6'W	FM	181
Moorbath	Dorset	SY4395	50°45·3'	2°48·1'W	T	193
Moor Beck	E Yorks	SE9944	53°53·2'	0°29·2'W	W	106
Moor Beck	N Yks	SE7762	54°3·1'	0°49·0'W	W	100
Moorber Hill	N Yks	SD9252	53°58·1'	2°6·9'W	H	103
Moorbrae	Shetld	HU4587	60°34·1'	1°10·2'W	X	1,2
Moorbridge Brook	Oxon	SP5910	51°47·4'	1°8·3'W	W	164
Moorbridge Fm	Suff	TM0161	52°12·9'	0°56·9'E	FM	155
Moorbrock	D & G	NX6296	55°14·6'	4°9·8'W	X	77
Moorbrock Gairy	D & G	NX6298	55°15·7'	4°9·9'W	X	77
Moorbrock Hill	D & G	NX6197	55°15·1'	4°10·8'W	H	77
Moor Brook	Devon	SX5993	50°43·4'	3°59·5'W	W	191
Moor Brook	Devon	SX9076	50°34·6'	3°32·8'W	W	192
Moor Brook	Heref	SO4458	52°13·3'	2°48·8'W	W	148,149
Moor Brook	Shrops	SO6483	52°26·9'	2°31·4'W	W	138
Moorbrook Fm	Shrops	SO6483	52°26·9'	2°31·4'W	FM	138
Moorby	Lincs	TF2964	53°9·7'	0°3·8'W	T	122
Moorclose	Cumbr	NX9927	54°37·9'	3°33·5'W	T	89
Moor Close	Lancs	SD8646	53°54·8'	2°12·4'W	X	103
Moor Close	N Yks	SD8798	54°22·9'	2°11·6'W	X	98
Moorclose	Roch	SD8805	53°32·7'	2°10·5'W	T	109
Moor Close Fm	N Yks	SE8279	54°12·2'	0°44·2'W	FM	100
Moor Close Gill	N Yks	SD9364	54°4·6'	2°6·0'W	W	98
Moor Close Holt	Lincs	TF4468	53°11·6'	0°9·7'E	F	122
Moor Close Plantation	Notts	SK6742	52°58·5'	0°59·7'W	F	129
Moor Cock	Lancs	SD6764	54°4·5'	2°29·8'W	X	98
Moorcock Fm	Brad	SE0843	53°53·2'	1°52·3'W	FM	104
Moorcock Hall	Cumbr	SD4583	54°14·6'	2°50·2'W	X	97
Moorcock Hall	Cumbr	SD6094	54°20·6'	2°36·5'W	X	97
Moorcock Hall	E Loth	NT6170	55°55·5'	2°37·0'W	X	67
Moorcock Inn	Lancs	SD7146	53°54·8'	2°26·1'W	X	103
Moorcock Inn	N Yks	SD7992	54°19·6'	2°19·0'W	X	98
Moorcock Plantn	Cumbr	NY4262	54°57·2'	2°53·9'W	F	85
Moorcocks	Kent	TQ6554	51°15·9'	0°22·3'E	X	188
Moor Common	Bucks	SU8090	51°36·4'	0°50·3'W	T	175
Moor Copse	Wok	SU7366	51°23·5'	0°56·7'W	F	175
Moor Corner Fm	Swan	SS4686	51°33·4'	4°12·9'W	FM	159
Moorcot	Heref	SO3555	52°11·6'	2°56·7'W	T	148,149
Moor Cote	N Yks	SE1683	54°14·8'	1°44·8'W	X	99
Moor Cottage	Cumbr	NY3562	54°57·2'	3°0·5'W	X	85
Moor Cottage Fm	E Yorks	TA1350	53°56·3'	0°16·3'W	FM	107
Moor Cottage Fm	N Yks	SE9696	54°21·3'	0°30·9'W	FM	94,101
Moor Cottages	Notts	SK4940	52°57·5'	1°15·8'W	X	129
Moorcourt	Hants	SU3416	50°56·8'	1°30·6'W	X	185
Moor Court	Heref	SO3556	52°12·1'	2°56·7'W	X	148,149
Moor Court	Oxon	SU7097	51°40·3'	0°58·9'W	A	165
Moorcourt Copse	Hants	SU3417	50°57·3'	1°30·6'W	F	185
Moorcourt Fm	Dorset	ST9300	50°48·2'	2°5·6'W	FM	195
Moor Court Fm	Hants	SU4331	51°4·8'	1°22·8'W	FM	185
Moor Court Fm	Heref	SO5450	52°9·0'	2°39·9'W	FM	149
Moor Covert	E Yorks	SE8444	53°53·4'	0°42·9'W	F	106
Moor Covert	Staffs	SJ8825	52°49·6'	2°10·3'W	F	127
Moorcox	Devon	SY2299	50°47·4'	3°6·0'W	X	192,193
Moor Croft	Corn	SW4224	50°3·8'	5°35·9'W	X	203
Moorcroft	D & G	NX0057	54°52·3'	5°6·6'W	X	82
Moorcroft	Monm	SO5109	51°46·9'	2°42·2'W	X	162
Moorcroft	N Yks	SE0950	53°57·0'	1°51·4'W	X	104
Moorcroft Ho	Glos	SO7917	51°51·3'	2°17·9'W	X	162
Moor Cross	Devon	SX6158	50°24·6'	3°57·0'W	T	202
Moordales Plantn	E Yorks	SE8247	53°55·0'	0°44·7'W	F	106
Moorden	Kent	TQ5246	51°11·8'	0°10·9'E	X	188
Moor Dike	N Yks	SE9586	54°15·9'	0°32·1'W	A	94,101
Moor Dike	N Yks	SE9687	54°16·4'	0°31·1'W	A	94,101
Moor Dingle	Shrops	SO6493	52°32·3'	2°31·4'W	X	138
Moor Ditch	Oxon	SU5292	51°37·7'	1°14·5'W	W	164,174
Moor Divock	Cumbr	NY4822	54°35·7'	2°47·9'W	X	90
Moordown	Bourne	SZ0994	50°45·0'	1°52·0'W	T	195
Moordown Fm	Wilts	SU3259	51°20·0'	1°32·1'W	FM	174
Moor Drain	Lincs	SK8245	53°0·0'	0°46·3'W	W	130
Moor Drain or New Cut	N Yks	SE5151	53°57·4'	1°13·0'W	W	105
Moor Drain or Old Cut	N Yks	SE5151	53°57·4'	1°13·0'W	W	105
Moordyke	Cumbr	NY2754	54°52·8'	3°7·8'W	X	85
Moordyke	Cumbr	NY3948	54°49·6'	2°56·5'W	X	85
Moor Dyke	Notts	SK7537	52°55·7'	0°52·6'W	W	129
Moore	Devon	SX7458	50°24·7'	3°46·0'W	X	202

Moore	Halton	SJ5884	53°21·3'	2°37·5'W	T	108
Moor Edge	Brad	SE0838	53°50·5'	1°52·3'W	T	104
Mooredge	Derby	SK3360	53°8·4'	1°30·0'W	X	119
Moor Edge	Northum	NZ1692	55°13·6'	1°44·5'W	X	81
Moor Edge Fm	Derby	SK2978	53°18·1'	1°33·5'W	FM	119
Moor Edge Fm	E Yorks	TA1149	53°55·7'	0°18·1'W	FM	107
Moor Edge Fm	N Tyne	NZ3171	55°2·2'	1°30·5'W	FM	88
Moore Fm	Devon	SS9524	51°0·6'	3°29·4'W	FM	181
Moor End	Barns	SE2904	53°32·2'	1°33·3'W	T	110
Moor End	Beds	SP9720	51°52·4'	0°35·1'W	T	165
Moor End	Beds	TL0058	52°12·9'	0°31·8'W	X	153
Moor End	Bucks	SU8090	51°36·4'	0°50·3'W	T	175
Moor End	Cald	SE0528	53°45·1'	1°55·0'W	T	104
Moor End	Cambs	TL3847	52°6·5'	0°1·3'E	T	154
Moorend	Cumbr	NY0715	54°31·6'	3°25·8'W	X	89
Moorend	Cumbr	NY3250	54°50·7'	3°3·1'W	T	85
Moorend	Cumbr	NY4725	54°37·3'	2°48·8'W	X	90
Moor End	Cumbr	NY7605	54°26·6'	2°21·8'W	X	91
Moor End	Cumbr	SD0899	54°22·9'	3°24·6'W	X	96
Moor End	Cumbr	SD5677	54°11·5'	2°40·0'W	X	97
Moorend	Derby	SK2145	53°0·4'	1°40·8'W	T	119,128
Moorend	Devon	SS6608	50°51·6'	3°53·9'W	X	191
Moorend	D & G	NY2570	55°1·4'	3°10·0'W	T	85
Moor End	Durham	NZ3043	54°47·1'	1°31·6'W	T	88
Moor End	E Yorks	SE8137	53°49·6'	0°45·7'W	T	106
Moorend	Glos	SO7302	51°43·2'	2°23·1'W	T	162
Moor End	Glos	SO7923	51°54·5'	2°17·9'W	X	162
Moorend	Glos	SO8613	51°49·2'	2°11·8'W	T	162
Moor End	Glos	SO9620	51°52·9'	2°3·1'W	T	163
Moor End	Lancs	SD3744	53°53·5'	2°57·1'W	T	102
Moor End	Lancs	SD5167	54°6·0'	2°44·5'W	X	97
Moor End	Lancs	SD6750	53°56·9'	2°29·8'W	X	103
Moor End	Leeds	SE4145	53°54·2'	1°22·1'W	T	105
Moor End	Northnts	SP7544	52°5·6'	0°53·9'W	X	152
Moor End	N Yks	SD9573	54°9·4'	2°4·2'W	X	98
Moor End	N Yks	SE3047	53°55·3'	1°32·2'W	X	104
Moor End	N Yks	SE3662	54°3·4'	1°26·6'W	T	99
Moor End	N Yks	SE4479	54°12·5'	1°19·1'W	X	99
Moor End	N Yks	SE5938	53°50·3'	1°5·8'W	T	105
Moorend	S Glos	ST6578	51°30·2'	2°29·9'W	T	172
Moorend	Staffs	SK0649	53°2·5'	1°54·2'W	X	119
Moorend	Stock	SJ9988	53°23·6'	2°0·5'W	T	109
Moor End	Worcs	SO9056	52°12·4'	2°8·4'W	T	150
Moor End	York	SE6656	54°0·0'	0°59·2'W	T	105,106
Moorend Cross	Heref	SO7245	52°6·4'	2°24·1'W	T	149
Moor End Fell	N Yks	SD9374	54°9·9'	2°6·0'W	X	98
Moor End Field	N Yks	SE4469	54°7·1'	1°19·2'W	T	99
Moorend Fm	Ches	SJ3561	53°8·8'	2°57·9'W	FM	117
Moorend Fm	Cumbr	NY4023	54°36·2'	2°55·3'W	FM	90
Moorend Fm	Devon	SS6304	50°49·4'	3°56·3'W	FM	191
Moor End Fm	Essex	TL5825	51°54·3'	0°18·2'E	FM	167
Moorend Fm	E Yorks	SE7818	53°39·4'	0°48·8'W	FM	112
Moorend Fm	Heref	SO5742	52°4·7'	2°37·3'W	FM	149
Moorend Fm	Heref	SO6541	52°4·2'	2°30·2'W	FM	149
Moorend Fm	Notts	SK5631	52°52·6'	1°9·7'W	FM	129
Moor End Fm	N Yks	SE3167	54°6·1'	1°31·1'W	FM	99
Moor End Fm	Staffs	SJ8322	52°48·0'	2°14·7'W	FM	127
Moorend Fms	Heref	SO6446	52°6·9'	2°31·1'W	FM	149
Moor End Game Fm	N Yks	NZ8605	54°26·2'	0°40·0'W	FM	94
Moorends	Donc	SE6915	53°37·9'	0°57·0'W	T	111
Moor Ends	Donc	SE6917	53°38·9'	0°57·0'W	X	111
Mooresbarrow Fms	Ches	SJ7465	53°11·1'	2°22·9'W	FM	118
Moore's Ditch	Essex	TL6401	51°41·3'	0°22·8'E	X	167
Moores Fm	Peterb	TF1907	52°39·1'	0°14·0'W	FM	142
Moore's Fm	Somer	ST6750	51°15·1'	2°28·0'W	FM	183
Moore's Fm	Suff	TL9556	52°10·3'	0°51·5'E	FM	155
Moore's Wood	Wilts	SU2273	51°27·6'	1°40·6'W	F	174
Moore Wood	Peterb	TF1100	52°35·4'	0°21·3'W	F	142
Moor Fea	Orkney	ND1999	58°52·5'	3°23·8'W	H	7
Moorfea	Orkney	ND1999	58°52·5'	3°23·8'W	X	7
Moorfield	Cumbr	NY5465	54°58·9'	2°42·7'W	X	86
Moorfield	Derby	SK0492	53°25·7'	1°56·0'W	T	110
Moorfield	E Ayr	NS3937	55°36·3'	4°32·9'W	X	70
Moorfield	Lancs	SD4532	53°47·1'	2°49·7'W	X	102
Moorfield	Northum	NY7165	54°59·0'	2°26·8'W	X	86,87
Moorfield	Peterb	TF1807	52°39·1'	0°14·9'W	X	142
Moor Field	Shetld	HU2954	60°16·4'	1°28·0'W	H	3
Moor Field	Shetld	HU3151	60°14·8'	1°25·9'W	X	3
Moorfield	Shetld	HU4272	60°26·0'	1°13·7'W	X	2,3
Moorfield Common	Herts	TL3421	51°52·5'	0°2·8'W	X	166
Moorfield Fm	E Yorks	SE7151	53°57·3'	0°54·7'W	FM	105,106
Moorfield Fm	E Yorks	SE9845	53°53·8'	0°30·0'W	FM	106
Moorfield Fm	Worcs	SP0672	52°21·0'	1°54·3'W	FM	139
Moorfield Hill	Staffs	SK2227	52°50·6'	1°40·0'W	X	128
Moorfield Ho	Sefton	SD3901	53°30·3'	2°54·8'W	X	108
Moorfield Lodge	Northnts	SP8472	52°20·6'	0°45·6'W	X	141
Moor Fields	Kirk	SE2227	53°44·6'	1°39·6'W	X	104
Moorfields	Staffs	SJ8335	52°55·0'	2°14·8'W	X	127
Moorfields	Staffs	SJ9156	53°6·3'	2°7·7'W	X	118
Moorfields Fm	E Yorks	SE7321	53°41·1'	0°53·3'W	FM	105,106,112
Moorfields Fm	Notts	SK6253	53°4·5'	1°4·1'W	FM	120
Moor Fm	Beds	TL0333	51°59·4'	0°29·6'W	FM	166
Moor Fm	Brig	SS9479	51°30·2'	3°31·2'W	FM	170
Moor Fm	Bucks	SU8090	51°36·4'	0°50·3'W	FM	175
Moor Fm	Cambs	TL2556	52°11·5'	0°9·9'W	FM	153
Moor Fm	Cambs	TL6173	52°20·1'	0°22·2'E	FM	154
Moor Fm	Carm	SN2714	51°48·1'	4°30·2'W	FM	158
Moor Fm	Cumbr	SD2893	54°19·9'	3°6·0'W	FM	96,97
Moor Fm	Derby	SK2559	53°7·9'	1°37·2'W	FM	119
Moor Fm	Derby	SK3564	53°10·6'	1°28·2'W	FM	119
Moor Fm	Derby	SK3938	52°56·5'	1°24·8'W	FM	128
Moor Fm	Devon	SS7906	50°50·7'	3°42·7'W	FM	191
Moor Fm	Devon	SS8601	50°48·1'	3°36·7'W	FM	191
Moor Fm	Devon	SX7737	50°13·4'	3°43·1'W	FM	202
Moor Fm	Devon	SX8090	50°42·1'	3°41·6'W	FM	191
Moor Fm	Devon	SX8199	50°46·9'	3°40·9'W	FM	191
Moor Fm	Donc	SE6908	53°34·1'	0°57·1'W	FM	111
Moor Fm	Dorset	SY6381	50°37·9'	2°31·0'W	FM	194
Moor Fm	Essex	TL8925	51°53·7'	0°45·2'E	FM	168
Moor Fm	Essex	TM0016	51°48·6'	0°54·5'E	FM	168

Moor Fm	E Yorks	SE8445	53°53·9'	0°42·9'W	FM	106
Moor Fm	E Yorks	SE8936	53°49·0'	0°38·5'W	FM	106
Moor Fm	E Yorks	SE9848	53°55·4'	0°30·0'W	FM	106
Moor Fm	E Yorks	TA2035	53°48·1'	0°10·3'W	FM	107
Moor Fm	Glos	SO7610	51°47·5'	2°20·5'W	FM	162
Moor Fm	Glos	SP0710	51°47·6'	1°53·5'W	FM	163
Moor Fm	Highld	NH7680	57°47·8'	4°4·7'W	FM	21
Moor Fm	I of W	SZ5382	50°38·3'	1°14·6'W	FM	196
Moor Fm	Leeds	SE1943	53°53·2'	1°42·2'W	FM	104
Moor Fm	Lincs	SK8657	53°6·4'	0°42·5'W	FM	121
Moor Fm	Lincs	SK8848	53°1·6'	0°40·9'W	FM	130
Moor Fm	Lincs	SK9169	53°12·9'	0°37·8'W	FM	121
Moor Fm	Lincs	TF0652	53°3·5'	0°24·7'W	FM	121
Moor Fm	Lincs	TF0747	53°0·8'	0°23·9'W	FM	130
Moor Fm	Lincs	TF0849	53°1·9'	0°23·0'W	FM	130
Moor Fm	Lincs	TF1479	53°18·0'	0°17·0'W	FM	121
Moor Fm	Lincs	TF1670	53°13·1'	0°15·4'W	FM	121
Moor Fm	Lincs	TF1990	53°23·8'	0°12·2'W	FM	113
Moor Fm	Lincs	TF2263	53°9·2'	0°10·1'W	FM	122
Moor Fm	N Lincs	SE9405	53°32·2'	0°34·5'W	FM	112
Moor Fm	N Lincs	TA0411	53°35·4'	0°25·3'W	FM	112
Moor Fm	Norf	TF7632	52°51·6'	0°37·3'E	FM	132
Moor Fm	Norf	TM2191	52°28·6'	1°15·7'E	FM	134
Moor Fm	Northnts	SP6565	52°17·0'	1°2·4'W	FM	152
Moor Fm	Notts	SK6657	53°6·6'	1°0·4'W	FM	120
Moor Fm	Notts	SK8371	53°14·0'	0°45·0'W	FM	121
Moor Fm	Notts	SK8571	53°14·0'	0°43·2'W	FM	121
Moor Fm	N Yks	NZ9506	54°26·7'	0°31·7'W	FM	94
Moor Fm	N Yks	SE0992	54°19·7'	1°51·3'W	FM	99
Moor Fm	N Yks	SE3364	54°4·5'	1°29·3'W	FM	99
Moor Fm	N Yks	SE4459	54°1·7'	1°19·3'W	FM	105
Moor Fm	N Yks	SE5146	53°54·7'	1°13·0'W	FM	105
Moor Fm	N Yks	SE6139	53°50·9'	1°4·0'W	FM	105
Moor Fm	N Yks	SE6364	54°4·3'	1°1·8'W	FM	100
Moor Fm	N Yks	SE9472	54°8·4'	0°33·2'W	FM	101
Moor Fm	N Yks	TA1276	54°10·3'	0°16·6'W	FM	101
Moor Fm	N Yks	TA1375	54°9·7'	0°15·7'W	FM	101
Moor Fm	Pemb	SM8810	51°45·2'	5°3·9'W	FM	157
Moor Fm	Pemb	SN0708	51°44·5'	4°47·3'W	FM	158
Moor Fm	Sefton	SD3103	53°31·4'	3°2·0'W	FM	108
Moor Fm	Somer	ST2315	50°56·0'	3°5·4'W	FM	193
Moor Fm	Staffs	SK2205	52°38·8'	1°40·1'W	FM	139
Moor Fm	S Tyne	NZ3961	54°56·8'	1°23·0'W	FM	88
Moor Fm	Suff	TM4061	52°11·9'	1°31·1'E	FM	156
Moor Fm	Win & Maid	SU8978	51°29·9'	0°42·7'W	FM	175
Moor Fm	Worcs	SO6968	52°18·8'	2°26·9'W	FM	138
Moor Fm	W Susx	SU9121	50°59·1'	0°41·8'W	FM	197
Moor Fm	W Susx	SU9823	51°0·1'	0°35·8'W	FM	197
Moor Fm	York	SE5958	54°1·1'	1°5·6'W	FM	105
Moor Fms	Pemb	SS0498	51°39·0'	4°49·6'W	FM	158
Moor Fm, The	Heref	SO3364	52°16·4'	2°58·5'W	FM	137,148,149
Moorfoot	Midlo	NT2952	55°45·6'	3°7·4'W	X	66,73
Moorfoot Hills	Scot Bord	NT3251	55°45·1'	3°4·6'W	H	66,73
Moor Game	Northum	NZ0253	54°52·6'	1°57·7'W	X	87
Moor Game Fm	St Hel	SJ4699	53°29·3'	2°48·4'W	FM	108
Moorgarth	Lancs	SD5463	54°3·9'	2°41·8'W	X	97
Moorgarth Hall	N Yks	SD6972	54°8·8'	2°28·1'W	X	98
Moor Gate	Brad	SE0249	53°56·5'	1°57·8'W	X	104
Moorgate	Corn	SX1182	50°36·7'	4°39·9'W	X	200
Moorgate	Cumbr	SD0998	54°22·4'	3°23·6'W	X	96
Moor Gate	Devon	SX7083	50°38·2'	3°49·9'W	X	191
Moorgate	Lancs	SD5166	54°5·5'	2°44·5'W	X	97
Moorgate	Norf	TG1730	52°49·7'	1°13·7'E	T	133
Moor Gate	N Yks	SE5491	54°18·9'	1°9·8'W	X	100
Moorgate	Roth	SK4490	53°24·5'	1°19·9'W	T	111
Moorgate Fm	Devon	SX5993	50°43·4'	3°59·5'W	FM	191
Moorgate Fm	Notts	SK7082	53°20·1'	0°56·5'W	FM	120
Moorgate Fm	N Yks	NZ8209	54°28·4'	0°43·7'W	FM	94
Moorgate Fm	Somer	ST4139	51°9·1'	2°50·2'W	FM	182
Moorgate Fm	Worcs	SO9666	52°17·8'	2°3·1'W	FM	150
Moorgates	N Yks	SE8499	54°23·0'	0°42·0'W	X	94,100
Moorgill	Cumbr	NY1039	54°44·5'	3°23·5'W	X	89
Moor Grange	Derby	SK3459	53°7·9'	1°29·1'W	X	119
Moor Grange	E Yorks	TA1451	53°56·8'	0°15·4'W	X	107
Moor Green	Birm	SP0682	52°26·4'	1°54·3'W	T	139
Moorgreen	Hants	SU4715	50°56·2'	1°19·5'W	T	196
Moor Green	Herts	TL3226	51°55·2'	0°4·4'W	T	166
Moorgreen	Notts	SK4847	53°1·3'	1°16·7'W	T	129
Moor Green	Staffs	SJ9641	52°58·2'	2°3·2'W	T	118
Moor Green	Wilts	ST8568	51°24·9'	2°12·6'W	T	173
Moorgreen Fm	Hants	SU4715	50°56·2'	1°19·5'W	FM	196
Moor Green Fm	Wok	SU8062	51°21·3'	0°50·7'W	FM	175,186
Moorgreen Hall	Worcs	SP0574	52°22·1'	1°55·2'W	X	139
Moorgreen Resr	Notts	SK4849	53°2·4'	1°16·6'W	W	129
Moorguards	Cumbr	NY5867	55°0·0'	2°39·0'W	X	86
Moorhaigh	Notts	SK5063	53°9·9'	1°14·7'W	T	120
Moor Hall	Birm	SP1298	52°35·0'	1°49·0'W	T	139
Moorhall	Derby	SK3074	53°16·0'	1°32·6'W	T	119
Moor Hall	Essex	TL6506	51°43·9'	0°23·8'E	A	167
Moor Hall	Essex	TL6631	51°57·4'	0°25·4'E	X	167
Moor Hall	Hav	TQ5581	51°30·6'	0°14·4'E	X	177
Moorhall	Heref	SO7156	52°12·3'	2°25·1'W	X	149
Moor Hall	Herts	TL3226	51°55·2'	0°4·4'W	X	166
Moor Hall	Herts	TL4618	51°50·7'	0°7·6'E	X	167
Moor Hall	Lancs	SD4105	53°32·5'	2°53·0'W	A	108
Moor Hall	Lancs	SD4143	53°53·0'	2°53·4'W	X	102
Moor Hall	Lancs	SD9145	53°54·3'	2°7·8'W	X	103
Moor Hall	Norf	TG0930	52°49·8'	1°6·6'E	X	133
Moor Hall	Shrops	SO2181	52°25·5'	3°9·3'W	X	137
Moor Hall	Staffs	SJ7644	52°59·8'	2°21·1'W	X	118
Moor Hall	Staffs	SJ9450	53°3·1'	2°5·0'W	X	118
Moor Hall	Suff	TL7444	52°4·2'	0°32·7'E	X	155
Moor Hall	Suff	TM1473	52°19·0'	1°8·8'E	X	144,156
Moor Hall	Warw	SP0853	52°10·7'	1°52·6'W	X	150
Moor Hall	Win & Maid	SU8985	51°33·6'	0°42·6'W	X	175
Moorhall Fm	Cald	SD9428	53°45·1'	2°5·0'W	FM	103
Moorhall Fm	Ches	SJ6145	53°0·3'	2°34·5'W	FM	118
Moorhall Fm	Worcs	SO9378	52°24·2'	2°5·8'W	FM	139
Moor Hall Hotel	E Susx	TQ6912	50°53·2'	0°24·6'E	X	199
Moorham Hill	Lancs	SD3942	53°52·5'	2°55·3'W	X	102

Moorhampton	Heref	SO3846	52°6·8'	2°53·9'W	T	148,149
Moorhams Fm	Hants	SU6751	51°15·5'	1°2·0'W	FM	185,186
Moorhaye Fm	Devon	SS3801	50°47·4'	4°17·5'W	FM	190
Moorhayes	Devon	SS9316	50°56·2'	3°31·0'W	X	181
Moorhayes	Devon	SS9613	50°54·7'	3°28·4'W	X	181
Moorhayes	Devon	ST0408	50°52·0'	3°21·5'W	X	192
Moorhayes Fm	Somer	ST6930	51°4·3'	2°26·2'W	FM	183
Moorhay Fm	Derby	SK3172	53°14·9'	1°31·7'W	FM	119
Moorhayne	Devon	ST2407	50°51·7'	3°4·4'W	T	192,193
Moorhead	Brad	SE1337	53°50·0'	1°47·7'W	T	104
Moorhead	Corn	SX1684	50°37·8'	4°35·7'W	X	201
Moor Head	Cumbr	NY4203	54°25·4'	2°53·2'W	H	90
Moorhead	Devon	SS4223	50°59·3'	4°14·7'W	X	180,190
Moor Head	Kirk	SE2212	53°36·5'	1°39·6'W	T	110
Moor Head	Leeds	SE2429	53°45·6'	1°37·7'W	T	104
Moor Head	Scot Bord	NT7211	55°23·8'	2°26·1'W	X	80
Moorhead Cottage	N Yks	SE1477	54°11·6'	1°46·7'W	X	99
Moor Head Cottages	Cumbr	SD2368	54°6·4'	3°10·2'W	X	96
Moorhead Fm	Ches	SJ5345	53°0·3'	2°41·6'W	FM	117
Moorhead Fm	Ches	SJ7963	53°10·1'	2°18·4'W	FM	118
Moorhead of Glenturk	D & G	NX4156	54°52·7'	4°28·3'W	X	83
Moor Head, The	Shrops	SJ5231	52°52·7'	2°42·4'W	X	126
Moor Hey	Lancs	SD4036	53°49·3'	2°54·3'W	X	102
Moor Hey	Lancs	SD6438	53°50·5'	2°32·4'W	X	102,103
Moorhey	Oldham	SD9304	53°32·2'	2°5·9'W	T	109
Moorhill	Devon	SS5113	50°54·1'	4°6·8'W	X	180
Moor Hill	D & G	NX6453	54°51·5'	4°6·7'W	H	83
Moor Hill	E Yorks	SE6420	53°40·6'	1°1·5'W	X	105,106
Moor Hill Fm	Leeds	SE3244	53°53·7'	1°30·4'W	FM	104
Moorhill Plantn	N Yks	SE7868	54°6·4'	0°48·0'W	F	100
Moorhills	D & G	NY2276	55°4·6'	3°12·9'W	X	85
Moorhills	Warw	SP1967	52°18·3'	1°42·9'W	X	151
Moor Hill Spinneys	Leic	SP7798	52°34·7'	0°51·4'W	F	141
Moor Ho	Brad	SE1545	53°54·3'	1°45·9'W	X	104
Moor Ho	C of Bris	ST5479	51°30·7'	2°39·4'W	X	172
Moor Ho	Cumbr	NY3763	54°57·7'	2°58·6'W	X	85
Moor Ho	Cumbr	NY4157	54°54·5'	2°54·8'W	X	85
Moor Ho	Cumbr	NY5354	54°53·0'	2°43·5'W	X	86
Moor Ho	Cumbr	NY6007	54°27·7'	2°36·6'W	X	91
Moor Ho	Cumbr	NY7417	54°33·1'	2°23·7'W	X	91
Moor Ho	Cumbr	NY7532	54°41·2'	2°22·8'W	X	91
Moor Ho	Cumbr	SD2095	54°20·9'	3°13·4'W	X	96
Moor Ho	Cumbr	SD2682	54°13·9'	3°7·7'W	X	96,97
Moor Ho	Darl	NZ2123	54°36·3'	1°40·1'W	X	93
Moor Ho	Darl	NZ3219	54°34·2'	1°29·9'W	X	93
Moor Ho	Durham	NY9129	54°39·6'	2°7·9'W	X	91,92
Moor Ho	Durham	NZ3145	54°48·2'	1°30·6'W	X	88
Moor Ho	E Yorks	TA1349	53°55·7'	0°16·3'W	X	107
Moor Ho	Glos	SO9211	51°48·1'	2°6·6'W	X	163
Moor Ho	Heref	SO5946	52°6·9'	2°35·5'W	X	149
Moor Ho	Lancs	SD4638	53°50·4'	2°48·8'W	X	102
Moor Ho	Lincs	SK8385	53°21·6'	0°44·8'W	X	112,121
Moor Ho	NE Lincs	TA2401	53°29·7'	0°7·4'W	X	113
Moor Ho	Northum	NU2203	55°19·5'	1°38·8'W	X	81
Moor Ho	Notts	SK7858	53°7·0'	0°49·7'W	X	120,121
Moor Ho	N Yks	NZ9501	54°24·5'	2°4·2'W	X	91,92
Moor Ho	N Yks	NZ0801	54°24·5'	1°52·2'W	X	92
Moor Ho	N Yks	NZ2507	54°27·7'	1°36·4'W	X	93
Moor Ho	N Yks	NZ3907	54°27·7'	1°23·5'W	X	93
Moor Ho	N Yks	NZ4704	54°26·0'	1°16·1'W	X	93
Moor Ho	N Yks	SE0872	54°8·9'	1°52·2'W	X	99
Moor Ho	N Yks	SE3097	54°22·3'	1°31·9'W	X	99
Moor Ho	N Yks	SE3294	54°20·7'	1°30·0'W	X	99
Moor Ho	N Yks	SE3573	54°9·3'	1°27·4'W	X	99
Moor Ho	N Yks	SE3799	54°23·4'	1°25·4'W	X	99
Moor Ho	N Yks	SE4582	54°14·1'	1°18·2'W	X	99
Moor Ho	N Yks	SE4693	54°20·1'	1°17·1'W	X	100
Moor Ho	N Yks	TA1176	54°10·3'	0°17·6'W	X	101
Moor Ho	N Yks	TA1376	54°10·3'	0°15·7'W	X	101
Moor Ho	Scot Bord	NT8467	55°54·0'	2°14·9'W	X	67
Moor Ho	Shrops	SO7485	52°28·0'	2°22·6'W	X	138
Moor Ho	Wakf	SE4516	53°38·6'	1°18·7'W	X	111
Moorhole	Sheff	SK4182	53°20·2'	1°22·6'W	T	111,120
Moor Hospl	Lancs	SD4961	54°2·8'	2°46·3'W	X	97
Moorhouse	Cumbr	NY2551	54°51·1'	3°9·7'W	T	85
Moorhouse	Cumbr	NY3356	54°53·9'	3°2·3'W	T	85
Moorhouse	Devon	SS7422	50°59·3'	3°47·3'W	X	180
Moorhouse	Donc	SE4810	53°35·3'	1°16·1'W	T	111
Moorhouse	Northum	NU0238	55°38·4'	1°57·7'W	X	75
Moorhouse	Northum	NU1509	55°22·7'	1°45·4'W	X	81
Moorhouse	Notts	SK7566	53°11·4'	0°52·2'W	T	120
Moorhouse	Scot Bord	NT7762	55°51·3'	2°21·6'W	X	67
Moorhouse	Shrops	SO3993	52°32·1'	2°53·6'W	X	137
Moorhouse	Somer	ST5234	51°6·4'	2°40·8'W	X	182,183
Moorhouse	Staffs	SK1061	53°9·0'	1°50·6'W	X	119
Moorhouse	Surrey	TQ4353	51°15·7'	0°3·4'E	X	187
Moorhouse Bank	Surrey	TQ4253	51°15·7'	0°2·5'E	T	187
Moorhouse Common	Donc	SE4809	53°34·8'	1°16·1'W	X	111
Moor House Cott	Durham	NZ0511	54°29·9'	1°54·9'W	X	92
Moorhouse Ellers	Cumbr	NY2751	54°51·2'	3°7·8'W	X	85
Moor House Fm	Bucks	TQ0287	51°34·6'	0°31·3'W	FM	176
Moorhouse Fm	Cumbr	NY0125	54°36·9'	3°31·6'W	FM	89
Moorhouse Fm	Cumbr	NY0407	54°27·2'	3°28·4'W	FM	89
Moorhouse Fm	Donc	SK6092	53°25·5'	1°5·4'W	FM	111
Moorhouse Fm	Durham	NZ0511	54°29·9'	1°54·9'W	FM	92
Moorhouse Fm	Durham	NZ4042	54°46·5'	1°22·3'W	FM	88
Moorhouse Fm	Lancs	SD8151	53°57·5'	2°17·0'W	FM	103
Moorhouse Fm	Northum	NU2603	55°19·5'	1°35·0'W	FM	81
Moorhouse Fm	N Yks	NZ7909	54°28·5'	0°46·4'W	FM	94
Moorhouse Fm	N Yks	NZ8805	54°26·2'	0°38·2'W	FM	94
Moorhouse Fm	N Yks	SE4570	54°7·7'	1°18·3'W	FM	99
Moor House Fm	N Yks	SE4871	54°8·2'	1°15·5'W	FM	100
Moor House Fm	N Yks	SE6394	54°20·5'	1°1·4'W	FM	94,100
Moorhouse Fm	N Yks	SE6673	54°9·2'	0°58·9'W	FM	100
Moorhouse Fm	N Yks	TA0285	54°15·3'	0°25·6'W	FM	101
Moorhouse Fm	Shrops	SO5692	52°31·7'	2°38·5'W	FM	137,138
Moorhouse Fm	Somer	ST0029	51°3·3'	3°25·2'W	FM	181
Moorhouse Fm	Somer	ST1642	51°10·5'	3°11·7'W	FM	181
Moorhouse Fm	Stock on T	NZ4208	54°28·2'	1°20·7'W	FM	93
Moorhouse Fm	Stock on T	NZ4216	54°32·5'	1°20·6'W	FM	93

Moorhouse Fm	Suff	TL8251	52°7.9'	0°39.9'E	FM	155
Moorhouse Fm	Wilts	ST9864	51°22.7'	2°1.3'W	FM	173
Moorhouse Gate	Northum	NY8456	54°54.2'	2°14.5'W	X	86,87
Moorhouse Hall	Cumbr	NY2651	54°51.2'	3°8.7'W	X	85
Moorhouse Hall	Cumbr	NY4656	54°54.0'	2°50.1'W	X	86
Moorhouse Ridge	Devon	SS8231	51°4.2'	3°40.7'W	X	181
Moorhouses	Cumbr	NY5428	54°38.9'	2°42.4'W	X	90
Moorhouses	Lincs	TF2756	53°5.4'	0°5.8'W	T	122
Moor How	Cumbr	SD3990	54°18.4'	2°55.8'W	X	96,97
Mooring Head	N Yks	SD9077	54°11.6'	2°8.8'W	X	98
Moorings, The	Lincs	TF3397	53°27.4'	0°0.6'E	X	113
Moorins	Shetld	HU6393	60°37.2'	0°50.4'W	X	1,2
Moor Isles	Lancs	SD8236	53°49.4'	2°16.0'W	X	103
Moor Laithe	Lancs	SD8348	53°55.9'	2°15.1'W	X	103
Moorlake	Devon	SX8199	50°46.9'	3°40.9'W	X	191
Moorlakes Wood	Swan	SS5690	51°35.7'	4°4.3'W	F	159
Moorland	Beds	TL0049	52°8.0'	0°31.9'W	X	153
Moorland	Devon	SS9802	50°48.7'	3°26.5'W	X	192
Moorland	Pemb	SM9622	51°51.8'	4°57.4'W	X	157,158
Moorland Close	Cumbr	NY1028	54°38.6'	3°23.3'W	X	89
Moorland Cott	N Yks	SD8092	54°19.6'	2°18.0'W	X	98
Moorland Court Fm	Somer	ST3333	51°5.8'	2°57.0'W	FM	182
Moorland Fm	E Susx	TQ4611	50°53.0'	0°4.9'E	FM	198
Moorland Fm	Somer	ST3332	51°5.2'	2°57.0'W	FM	182
Moorland Fm	W Susx	SU9221	50°59.1'	0°41.0'W	FM	197
Moorland House Fm	Somer	ST3431	51°4.7'	2°56.1'W	FM	182
Moorland or Northmoor Green	Somer	ST3332	51°5.2'	2°57.0'W	T	182
Moorlands	Cumbr	NY7509	54°28.8'	2°22.7'W	X	91
Moorlands	Highld	NG6623	57°14.5'	5°52.2'W	X	32
Moorlands	Lancs	SD6666	54°5.6'	2°30.8'W	X	98
Moorlands	Lincs	TF0467	53°11.6'	0°26.2'W	X	121
Moorlands	Newp	ST3583	51°32.8'	2°55.9'W	X	171
Moorlands	Warw	SP3348	52°8.0'	1°30.7'W	X	151
Moorlands	York	SE5758	54°1.1'	1°7.4'W	X	105
Moorlands Farm Park, The	Staffs	SK0451	53°3.6'	1°56.0'W	X	119
Moorlands Fm	Devon	SX6273	50°32.7'	3°56.5'W	FM	191
Moorlands Fm	V of Glam	SS9569	51°24.9'	3°30.2'W	FM	170
Moorlands Head	Cumbr	NY6328	54°39.0'	2°34.0'W	X	91
Moorlands Plantn	Cumbr	NY5931	54°40.6'	2°37.7'W	F	91
Moorland Stud	Suff	TL7067	52°16.7'	0°29.9'E	X	154
Moorlands Wood	Kent	TQ6557	51°17.5'	0°22.4'E	F	178,188
Moor Lane Fm	N Yks	NZ8404	54°25.7'	0°41.9'W	FM	94
Moorlaw Coppice	Derby	SK3468	53°12.7'	1°29.0'W	F	119
Moorlaws	Northum	NU1313	55°24.9'	1°47.2'W	X	81
Moorlaw Strips	Scot Bord	NT7060	55°50.2'	2°28.3'W	F	67,74
Moor Leas	N Yks	NZ8410	54°28.9'	0°41.8'W	X	94
Moorleaze	S Glos	ST6687	51°35.1'	2°29.1'W	X	172
Moor Leaze	Swin	SU1982	51°32.4'	1°43.2'W	X	173
Moorleaze Fm	Somer	ST7440	51°9.8'	2°21.9'W	FM	183
Moor Leazes	Durham	NZ1748	54°49.8'	1°43.7'W	X	88
Moorledge	Bath & NE Somer	ST5862	51°21.6'	2°35.8'W	T	172,182
Moor Leys Fm	Staffs	SJ9828	52°51.2'	2°1.4'W	FM	127
Moorlinch	Somer	ST3936	51°7.4'	2°51.9'W	T	182
Moor Loch	Fife	NS9488	56°4.6'	3°41.7'W	W	65
Moor Lodge	Derby	SK0285	53°22.0'	1°57.8'W	X	110
Moor Lodge	Sheff	SK2389	53°24.1'	1°38.8'W	X	110
Moor Lodge Fm	Brad	SD9737	53°50.0'	2°2.3'W	FM	103
Moormains	D & G	NX3544	54°46.1'	4°33.5'W	X	83
Moorman's Down	Devon	SS7133	51°5.1'	3°50.1'W	X	180
Moormill	Devon	SS5110	50°52.5'	4°6.7'W	X	191
Moor Mill Fm	Ghead	NZ2557	54°54.7'	1°36.2'W	FM	88
Moor Mill Fm	Oxon	SU3090	51°36.7'	1°33.6'W	FM	164,174
Moor Mill Fm	Somer	ST1030	51°4.0'	3°16.7'W	FM	181
Moor Monkton	N Yks	SE5056	54°0.1'	1°13.8'W	T	105
Moor Monkton Grange	N Yks	SE5054	53°59.0'	1°13.8'W	X	105
Moor Monkton Moor	N Yks	SE5155	53°59.6'	1°12.9'W	X	105
Moormore	Highld	NH9311	57°10.9'	3°45.8'W	X	36
Moor Nook	Lancs	SD6538	53°50.5'	2°31.5'W	X	102,103
Moor of Alvie	Highld	NH8507	57°8.6'	3°53.6'W	X	35,36
Moor of Auchanacie	Moray	NJ3848	57°31.3'	3°1.6'W	X	28
Moor of Auchendreich	Aberd	NO8376	56°52.8'	2°16.3'W	X	45
Moor of Balvack	Aberd	NJ6713	57°12.7'	2°32.3'W	X	38
Moor of Barclye	D & G	NX3969	54°59.6'	4°30.6'W	X	83
Moor of Drumwalt	D & G	NX3054	54°51.4'	4°38.5'W	X	82
Moor of Feshie	Highld	NH8605	57°7.6'	3°52.5'W	X	35,36
Moor of Findochty	Moray	NJ4667	57°41.6'	2°53.9'W	X	28,29
Moor of Granary	Moray	NJ0755	57°34.8'	3°32.9'W	T	27
Moor of Knockchoilum	Highld	NH4814	57°11.8'	4°30.5'W	X	34
Moor of Ravenstone	D & G	NX3942	54°45.1'	4°29.7'W	X	83
Moor of Tore	Moray	NJ1054	57°34.3'	3°29.8'W	X	28
Moor Park	Cumbr	NY0638	54°43.9'	3°27.2'W	T	89
Moorpark	Cumbr	NY3256	54°53.9'	3°3.2'W	X	85
Moorpark	D & G	NX0849	54°48.2'	4°58.8'W	X	82
Moorpark	D & G	NX9887	55°10.3'	3°35.7'W	X	78
Moor Park	Heref	SO4940	52°3.6'	2°44.2'W	T	148,149
Moor Park	Herts	TQ0893	51°37.8'	0°26.0'W	T	176
Moor Park	Lancs	SD5330	53°46.1'	2°42.4'W	X	102
Moorpark	N Ayr	NS3155	55°45.8'	4°41.2'W	X	63
Moor Park	N Yks	SE2553	53°58.6'	1°36.7'W	X	104
Moor Park	Powys	SO2319	51°52.1'	3°6.7'W	X	161
Moorpark	Scot Bord	NT9257	55°48.6'	2°7.7'W	X	67,74,75
Moorpark	Stir	NS4592	56°6.0'	4°29.1'W	X	57
Moor Park	Stir	NS4792	56°6.0'	4°27.1'W	X	57
Moor Park	Surrey	SU8646	51°12.6'	0°45.7'W	T	186
Moorpark Fm	Somer	ST7539	51°9.2'	2°21.1'W	FM	183
Moorpark of Baldoon	D & G	NX4153	54°51.0'	4°28.2'W	X	83
Moor Park of Barr	D & G	NX4063	54°56.4'	4°29.4'W	X	83
Moor Park Sch	Shrops	SO5071	52°20.3'	2°43.6'W	X	137,138
Moorpit Fm	Devon	ST2507	50°51.7'	3°3.6'W	FM	192,193
Moor Place	Herts	TL4218	51°50.8'	0°4.1'E	X	167
Moor Plantation	Scot Bord	NT7158	55°49.1'	2°27.3'W	F	67,74
Moor Plantn	Norf	TL7897	52°32.7'	0°37.9'E	F	144
Moor Plantn	Northum	NZ2376	55°4.9'	1°38.0'W	F	88
Moor Plantn	N Yks	NZ3609	54°28.7'	1°26.2'W	F	93
Moor Plantn	N Yks	SE1849	53°56.4'	1°43.1'W	F	104
Moorplash Fm	Devon	SY2094	50°44.6'	3°7.7'W	FM	192,193
Moor Platt	Cumbr	NX9810	54°28.8'	3°34.0'W	X	89
Moor Pot	Cumbr	NY7602	54°25.0'	2°21.8'W	X	91
Moor Rig	Durham	NY9934	54°42.3'	2°0.5'W	X	92
Moor Rigg	Cumbr	SD7793	54°20.2'	2°20.8'W	X	98
Moor Rigg	Durham	NY9424	54°36.9'	2°5.2'W	X	91,92
Moor Riggs	Durham	NY8729	54°39.6'	2°11.7'W	X	91,92
Moor Row	Cumbr	NY0014	54°30.9'	3°32.3'W	T	89
Moor Row	Cumbr	NY2149	54°50.0'	3°13.4'W	T	85
Moor Row	Durham	NZ1515	54°32.0'	1°45.7'W	X	92
Moor Row	Somer	ST3545	51°12.3'	2°55.4'W	X	182
Moors	Cumbr	SD6195	54°21.2'	2°35.6'W	X	97
Moors	Shetld	HU4224	60°0.2'	1°14.3'W	X	4
Moor's Brook	Ches	SJ4972	53°14.8'	2°45.5'W	W	117
Moorseek Fm	Somer	ST2513	50°54.9'	3°3.6'W	FM	193
Moor's Fm	Bucks	SP9903	51°43.2'	0°33.6'W	FM	165
Moor's Fm	Ches	SJ8258	53°7.4'	2°15.7'W	FM	118
Moor's Fm	Essex	TL7123	51°53.0'	0°29.5'E	FM	167
Moor's Fm	Essex	TL8811	51°46.2'	0°43.9'E	FM	168
Moors Fm	E Yorks	SE7717	53°38.9'	0°49.7'W	FM	112
Moor's Fm	Glos	SP1506	51°45.4'	1°46.6'W	FM	163
Moors Fm	Glos	SP1721	51°53.5'	1°44.8'W	FM	163
Moors Fm	Kent	TQ7045	51°11.0'	0°26.3'E	FM	188
Moors Fm	Lancs	SD3741	53°51.9'	2°57.1'W	FM	102
Moor's Fm	Peterb	TF2306	52°38.5'	0°10.5'W	FM	142
Moors Fm	Staffs	SJ8604	52°38.3'	2°12.0'W	FM	127,139
Moors Fm	Staffs	SK0926	52°50.1'	1°51.6'W	FM	128
Moor's Fm	Suff	TL9236	51°59.6'	0°48.2'E	FM	155
Moor's Fm	Suff	TM3544	52°2.9'	1°26.0'E	FM	169
Moor's Fm	Wilts	ST8630	51°4.4'	2°11.6'W	FM	183
Moor's Gorse	Staffs	SK0215	52°44.2'	1°57.8'W	X	128
Moorshall Fm	Wilts	ST8978	51°30.3'	2°9.1'W	FM	173
Moorshead Fm	V of Glam	SS9772	51°26.5'	3°28.5'W	FM	170
Moorsholm	E Susx	TQ8219	50°56.7'	0°35.8'E	X	199
Moorsholm	Red & Cl	NZ6814	54°31.2'	0°56.5'W	T	94
Moorsholm Mill	Red & Cl	NZ6814	54°31.2'	0°56.5'W	X	94
Moorsholm Moor	Red & Cl	NZ6711	54°29.6'	0°57.5'W	H	94
Moorshop	Devon	SX5174	50°33.0'	4°5.8'W	X	191,201
Moor Side	Brad	SE0235	53°49.7'	1°57.7'W	T	104
Moor Side	Brad	SE1528	53°45.1'	1°45.9'W	T	104
Moorside	Ches	SJ2877	53°17.3'	3°4.4'W	T	117
Moorside	Cumbr	NY5127	54°38.4'	2°45.1'W	X	90
Moorside	Cumbr	NY5622	54°35.7'	2°40.4'W	X	90
Moorside	Cumbr	NY5930	54°40.1'	2°37.7'W	X	91
Moor Side	Cumbr	SD2278	54°11.8'	3°11.3'W	X	96
Moorside	Derby	SK0091	53°25.2'	1°59.6'W	X	110
Moorside	Derby	SK0495	53°27.3'	1°56.0'W	X	110
Moorside	Derby	SK2650	53°3.0'	1°36.3'W	X	119
Moorside	Derby	SK2956	53°6.3'	1°33.6'W	X	119
Moorside	Dorset	ST7919	50°58.4'	2°17.6'W	T	183
Moorside	Durham	NZ0849	54°50.4'	1°52.1'W	T	88
Moorside	Durham	NZ1550	54°50.9'	1°45.6'W	X	88
Moor Side	Lancs	SD4334	53°48.2'	2°51.5'W	T	102
Moor Side	Lancs	SD4935	53°48.8'	2°46.1'W	T	102
Moor Side	Lancs	SD5063	54°3.9'	2°45.4'W	X	97
Moorside	Lancs	SD7842	53°52.7'	2°19.7'W	X	103
Moorside	Lancs	SD8745	53°54.3'	2°11.5'W	X	103
Moorside	Leeds	SE2228	53°45.1'	1°39.6'W	T	104
Moor Side	Leeds	SE2341	53°52.1'	1°38.6'W	X	104
Moor Side	Leeds	SE2435	53°48.9'	1°37.7'W	T	104
Moor Side	Lincs	TF2457	53°6.0'	0°8.5'W	T	122
Moor Side	N Yks	SE1363	54°4.0'	1°47.7'W	X	99
Moor Side	N Yks	SE4452	53°58.0'	1°19.3'W	X	105
Moorside	Oldham	SD9507	53°33.8'	2°4.1'W	T	109
Moorside	Salf	SD7701	53°30.6'	2°20.4'W	T	109
Moorside	Shrops	SJ3224	52°48.8'	3°0.1'W	X	126
Moorside	Staffs	SK0454	53°5.2'	1°56.0'W	X	119
Moor Side	Staffs	SK0566	53°11.7'	1°55.1'W	X	119
Moorside	Staffs	SK0647	53°1.5'	1°54.2'W	X	119,128
Moorside Edge	Kirk	SE0715	53°38.1'	1°53.2'W	X	110
Moorside Fm	Ches	SJ5346	53°0.8'	2°41.6'W	FM	117
Moorside Fm	Cumbr	NY0602	54°24.5'	3°26.5'W	FM	89
Moorside Fm	Derby	SK2772	53°14.9'	1°35.3'W	FM	119
Moorside Fm	E Yorks	TA1249	53°55.7'	0°17.2'W	FM	107
Moorside Fm	Lancs	SD5464	54°4.4'	2°41.8'W	FM	97
Moorside Fm	Lincs	TF1864	53°9.8'	0°13.7'W	FM	122
Moor Side Fm	N Yks	NZ7907	54°27.4'	0°46.5'W	FM	94
Moorside Fm	N Yks	SE1450	53°57.0'	1°46.8'W	FM	104
Moorside Fm	N Yks	SE1649	53°56.5'	1°45.0'W	FM	104
Moorside Fm	N Yks	SE2450	53°57.0'	1°37.6'W	FM	104
Moorside Fm	Red & Cl	NZ6913	54°30.7'	0°55.6'W	FM	94
Moorside Fm	Sheff	SK3082	53°20.3'	1°32.6'W	FM	110,111
Moorside Fm	Staffs	SK0759	53°7.9'	1°53.3'W	FM	119
Moorside Fm	Tames	SJ9997	53°28.4'	2°0.5'W	FM	109
Moor Side Ho	Lancs	SD4935	53°48.8'	2°46.1'W	X	102
Moorside Parks	Cumbr	NY0520	54°34.2'	3°27.7'W	X	89
Moorside Plantn	Scot Bord	NT8867	55°54.0'	2°11.1'W	F	67
Moorslade	S Glos	ST6794	51°38.9'	2°28.2'W	X	162,172
Moorslane Fm	Ches	SJ6463	53°10.0'	2°31.9'W	FM	118
Moors Lodge Fm	Norf	TF5105	52°37.5'	0°14.3'E	FM	143
Moorsome Fm	N Yks	SE9185	54°15.4'	0°35.8'W	FM	94,101
Moors River	Dorset	SZ1199	50°47.7'	1°50.3'W	W	195
Moors, The	Cumbr	SD2074	54°9.6'	3°13.1'W	X	96
Moors, The	Dorset	SY9487	50°41.2'	2°4.7'W	X	195
Moors, The	E Yorks	TA1837	53°49.2'	0°12.0'W	F	107
Moors, The	Glos	SO7203	51°43.7'	2°23.9'W	X	162
Moors, The	Heref	SO4364	52°16.5'	2°49.7'W	X	137,148,149
Moors, The	Heref	SO5432	51°59.3'	2°39.8'W	T	149
Moors, The	Oxon	SP3508	51°46.4'	1°29.2'W	X	164
Moors, The	Powys	SJ2409	52°40.6'	3°7.0'W	X	126
Moors, The	Shrops	SJ6505	52°38.7'	2°30.6'W	X	127
Moorstock	Kent	TR1038	51°6.4'	1°0.4'E	T	179,189
Moorston	S Ayr	NS2802	55°17.2'	4°42.1'W	X	76
Moorstone Barton	Devon	ST0109	50°52.6'	3°24.0'W	X	192
Moor Street	Medway	TQ8265	51°21.5'	0°37.2'E	T	178
Moors Valley Country Park	Dorset	SU1005	50°50.9'	1°51.1'W	X	195
Moorswater	Corn	SX2364	50°27.2'	4°29.2'W	T	201
Moorswood Fm	Lincs	TF4020	52°45.8'	0°4.9'E	FM	131
Moor Syke	Lancs	SD7055	53°59.7'	2°27.0'W	W	103
Moor, The	Cambs	TL3845	52°5.4'	0°1.3'E	X	154
Moor, The	E Susx	TQ8115	50°54.6'	0°34.9'E	X	199
Moor, The	Flint	SJ1877	53°17.3'	3°13.4'W	X	116
Moor, The	Lincs	TF3575	53°15.5'	0°1.8'E	X	122
Moor, The	N Yks	SE8171	54°7.9'	0°45.2'W	X	100
Moor, The	Shrops	SO5679	52°24.7'	2°38.4'W	X	137,138
Moor, The	S Lanak	NS9722	55°29.1'	3°37.4'W	X	72
Moor, The	Wrex	SJ4841	52°58.1'	2°46.1'W	X	117
Moorthorpe	Wakf	SE4611	53°35.9'	1°17.9'W	T	111
Moorthwaite	Cumbr	NY2948	54°49.6'	3°5.9'W	X	85
Moorthwaite	Cumbr	NY5050	54°50.8'	2°46.3'W	X	86
Moorthwaite Lough	Cumbr	NY2948	54°49.6'	3°5.9'W	W	85
Moorthwaite Moss	Cumbr	NY5151	54°51.3'	2°45.4'W	X	86
Moor Top	Kirk	SE1921	53°41.3'	1°42.3'W	T	104
Moortop	Staffs	SJ9157	53°6.8'	2°7.7'W	X	118
Moor Top	Staffs	SK0354	53°5.2'	1°56.9'W	X	119
Moortop Fm	Derby	SK3878	53°18.1'	1°25.4'W	FM	119
Moortown	Devon	SS4312	50°53.4'	4°13.6'W	X	180,190
Moortown	Devon	SS4800	50°47.0'	4°9.0'W	X	191
Moortown	Devon	SS5120	50°57.8'	4°6.9'W	T	180
Moortown	Devon	SS6913	50°54.3'	3°51.4'W	X	180
Moortown	Devon	SX3396	50°44.6'	4°21.6'W	T	190
Moortown	Devon	SX5273	50°32.5'	4°4.9'W	T	191,201
Moortown	Devon	SX6689	50°41.3'	3°53.4'W	X	191
Moortown	Hants	SU1504	50°50.3'	1°46.8'W	T	195
Moortown	I of W	SZ4283	50°38.9'	1°24.0'W	T	196
Moortown	Leeds	SE3038	53°50.5'	1°32.2'W	T	104
Moortown	Lincs	TF0799	53°28.8'	0°22.8'W	T	112
Moortown	Wrekin	SJ6118	52°45.7'	2°34.3'W	T	127
Moortown Barton	Devon	SS8321	50°58.8'	3°39.6'W	X	181
Moortown Brook	Devon	SX6688	50°40.8'	3°53.4'W	W	191
Moortown Fm	Poole	SZ0397	50°46.6'	1°57.1'W	FM	195
Moortown Fm	Somer	ST3723	51°0.4'	2°53.5'W	FM	193
Moortown House Fm	Lincs	TF0699	53°28.9'	0°23.7'W	FM	112
Moortown Pasture	E Yorks	TA1250	53°56.3'	0°17.2'W	X	107
Moortown Plantn	Devon	SX3396	50°44.6'	4°21.6'W	F	190
Moorville Hall (Hotel)	Staffs	SJ9546	53°0.9'	2°4.1'W	X	118
Moorwards	Bucks	TQ0382	51°31.9'	0°30.5'W	X	176
Moor Wood	Bucks	SU8190	51°36.4'	0°49.4'W	F	175
Moor Wood	Glos	SO9908	51°46.5'	2°0.5'W	F	163
Moor Wood	Kent	TQ8031	51°3.2'	0°34.5'E	F	188
Moor Wood	Lincs	TF0152	53°3.6'	0°29.2'W	F	121
Moor Wood	Somer	SS9547	51°13.0'	3°29.8'W	F	181
Moorwood Fm	Derby	SK3655	53°5.7'	1°27.3'W	FM	119
Moorwood Moor	Derby	SK3656	53°6.2'	1°27.3'W	X	119
Moorwood's Hall Fm	Derby	SK3078	53°18.1'	1°32.6'W	FM	119
Moory	Angus	NO3964	56°46.1'	2°59.4'W	X	44
Moor Yeat	Cumbr	NY4655	54°53.5'	2°50.1'W	X	86
Moory Hass	Scot Bord	NT2721	55°28.9'	3°8.9'W	X	73
Moory Lea	Durham	NZ0423	54°36.4'	1°55.9'W	X	92
Moory Spot	Durham	NZ1733	54°41.7'	1°43.8'W	X	92
Moory Spot	N upon Ty	NZ1973	55°3.3'	1°41.7'W	X	88
Moosa Water	Shetld	HU3389	60°35.3'	1°23.4'W	W	1,2
Mooseheart	N Som	ST4157	51°18.8'	2°50.4'W	X	172,182
Moo Stack	Shetld	HU2079	60°29.9'	1°37.7'W	X	3
Moo Stack	Shetld	HU2940	60°8.9'	1°28.2'W	X	4
Moo Stack	Shetld	HU2971	60°25.6'	1°27.9'W	X	3
Moo Stack	Shetld	HU3090	60°35.8'	1°26.6'W	X	1
Moota Hill	Cumbr	NY1436	54°42.9'	3°19.7'W	H	89
Moo Taing	Orkney	HY2907	58°56.9'	3°13.6'W	X	6,7
Moota Motel	Cumbr	NY1636	54°43.0'	3°17.8'W	X	89
Moot Hill	Norf	TG1201	52°34.2'	1°8.1'E	A	144
Moothill Cross	Devon	SX7964	50°28.0'	3°41.9'W	X	202
Moots Copse	Dorset	ST7704	50°50.3'	2°19.2'W	F	194
Moo Water	Shetld	HU4555	60°16.9'	1°10.7'W	W	3
Moo Wick	Shetld	HU6287	60°34.0'	0°51.6'W	W	1,2
Mop End	Bucks	SU9297	51°40.1'	0°39.8'W	X	165
Mopes Fm	Bucks	TQ0190	51°36.2'	0°32.1'W	FM	176
Mopley Pond	Hants	SU4501	50°48.6'	1°21.3'W	W	196
Mopper's Barn	Hants	SU4356	51°18.3'	1°22.6'W	X	174
Mopul	Shetld	HZ2273	59°32.8'	1°36.2'W	X	4
Morah or Maen Chynoweth	Corn	SW8121	50°3.2'	5°3.2'W	X	204
Moralees	Northum	NZ0474	55°3.9'	1°55.8'W	X	87
Morangie	Highld	NH7683	57°49.4'	4°4.8'W	T	21
Morangie Forest	Highld	NH7480	57°47.8'	4°6.7'W	F	21
Morants Court	Kent	TQ5057	51°17.8'	0°9.5'E	X	188
Morants Court Fm	Kent	TQ4958	51°18.3'	0°8.6'E	FM	188
Morar	Highld	NM6793	56°58.4'	5°49.6'W	T	40
Morar Lodge	Highld	NM6993	56°58.5'	5°47.6'W	X	40
Moraston Ho	Heref	SO5725	51°55.5'	2°37.1'W	X	162
Moravian Settlement	Derby	SK4235	52°54.9'	1°22.1'W	T	129
Morawel	Pemb	SN0843	52°3.4'	4°47.6'W	X	145
Môrawelon	I of Angl	SH2582	53°18.6'	4°37.2'W	T	114
Morawelon	Pemb	SN1245	52°4.5'	4°44.2'W	X	145
Moray Firth		NH7960	57°37.1'	4°1.1'W	W	21,27
Morayhill	Highld	NH7549	57°31.2'	4°4.8'W	X	27
Morayscairn	Moray	NJ1060	57°37.5'	3°30.0'W	X	28
Morayston	Highld	NH7548	57°30.6'	4°4.7'W	X	27
Morbec Fm	Essex	TQ7790	51°35.1'	0°33.7'E	FM	178
Morben Hall	Powys	SN7199	52°34.7'	3°53.8'W	X	135
Morben-isaf	Powys	SN7098	52°34.1'	3°54.7'W	X	135
Mór Bheinn	Pth & Kin	NN7121	56°22.1'	4°4.9'W	H	51,52,57
Morborne	Cambs	TL1391	52°30.5'	0°19.7'W	T	142
Morborne Hill	Cambs	TL1291	52°30.6'	0°20.6'W	X	142
Mor Brook	Shrops	SO6694	52°32.8'	2°29.7'W	W	138
Morcar Grange	N Yks	SE2867	54°6.1'	1°33.9'W	X	99
Morcar Hill Fm	N Yks	SE3347	53°55.3'	1°29.4'W	FM	104
Morcar Ho	N Yks	SE2866	54°5.6'	1°33.9'W	X	99
Morchard Bishop	Devon	SS7607	50°51.2'	3°45.3'W	T	191
Morchard Road	Devon	SS7504	50°49.6'	3°46.1'W	T	191
Morcombe	Glos	SO9310	51°47.6'	2°5.7'W	X	163
Morcombelake	Dorset	SY3994	50°44.8'	2°51.5'W	T	193
Morcombe Plantation	Devon	SS4101	50°47.4'	4°15.0'W	F	190
Morcott	Rut	SK9200	52°35.6'	0°38.1'W	T	141
Morda	Shrops	SJ2827	52°50.4'	3°3.7'W	T	126
Morden	Dorset	SY9195	50°45.5'	2°7.3'W	T	195
Morden	Merton	TQ2568	51°24.1'	0°11.8'W	T	176
Morden Fm	Corn	SX4168	50°29.6'	4°14.1'W	FM	201
Morden Grange Fm	Cambs	TL3040	52°2.8'	0°5.9'W	FM	153
Morden Grange Plantation	Cambs	TL3039	52°2.3'	0°5.9'W	F	153
Morden Green	Cambs	TL2942	52°3.9'	0°6.7'W	T	153
Morden Hall Park	Merton	TQ2668	51°24.0'	0°10.9'W	X	176
Morden Ho	Cambs	TL2843	52°4.5'	0°7.5'W	X	153

Morden Mill	Dorset	SY9093	50°44·4'	2°8·1'W	X	195
Morden Park	Dorset	SY9093	50°44·4'	2°8·1'W	F	195
Morden Park	Merton	TQ2366	51°23·0'	0°13·6'W	T	176
Mordiford	Heref	SO5737	52°2·0'	2°37·2'W	T	149
Mordington Ho	Scot Bord	NT9556	55°48·1'	2°4·3'W	X	67,74,75
Mordington Holdings	Scot Bord	NT9456	55°48·1'	2°5·3'W	T	67,74,75
Mordon	Durham	NZ3226	54°37·9'	1°29·8'W	T	93
Mordon Carrs	Durham	NZ3225	54°37·4'	1°29·8'W	X	93
Mordon Moor	Durham	NZ3427	54°38·5'	1°28·0'W	X	93
Mordon Southside Fm	Durham	NZ3325	54°37·4'	1°28·9'W	FM	93
Mordun Top	Pth & Kin	NO1320	56°22·1'	3°24·1'W	H	53,58
More	Shrops	SO3491	52°31·0'	2°58·0'W	T	137
Morebath	Devon	SS9524	51°0·6'	3°29·4'W	T	181
Morebath Manor	Devon	SS9625	51°1·1'	3°28·6'W	X	181
Morebattle	Scot Bord	NT7724	55°30·8'	2°21·4'W	T	74
Morebattle Hill	Scot Bord	NT7723	55°30·3'	2°21·4'W	H	74
Morebattle Mains	Scot Bord	NT7624	55°30·8'	2°22·4'W	X	74
Morebattle Tofts	Scot Bord	NT7725	55°31·3'	2°21·4'W	X	74
Moreb Fm	Carm	SN4601	51°41·4'	4°13·3'W	FM	159
Moreby Grange Fm	N Yks	SE5941	53°52·0'	1°5·8'W	FM	105
Moreby Hall	N Yks	SE5943	53°53·0'	1°5·7'W	X	105
Moreby Wood	N Yks	SE6042	53°52·5'	1°4·8'W	F	105
Morecambe	Lancs	SD4263	54°3·8'	2°52·8'W	T	97
Morecambe Bay	Cumbr	SD3669	54°7·0'	2°58·3'W	W	96,97
Morecambe Lodge	Lancs	SD4767	54°6·0'	2°48·2'W	X	97
Morecombe Fm	Devon	SX7549	50°19·9'	3°45·0'W	FM	202
More Crichel	Dorset	ST9908	50°52·5'	2°0·5'W	T	195
Moredon	Somer	ST3226	51°2·0'	2°57·8'W	X	193
Moredon	Swin	SU1387	51°35·1'	1°48·4'W	T	173
Moredun	C of Edin	NT2969	55°54·8'	3°7·7'W	T	66
Morefield	Highld	NH1195	57°54·5'	5°10·9'W	T	19
More Fm	Shrops	SO3492	52°31·6'	2°58·0'W	FM	137
Moregrove	Norf	TG4519	52°43·0'	1°38·1'E	X	134
Morehall	Kent	TR2036	51°5·1'	1°8·9'E	T	179,189
More Hall	Shrops	SO5792	52°31·7'	2°37·6'W	X	137,138
More Hall Resr	Sheff	SK2895	53°27·3'	1°34·3'W	W	110
Morehampton Park Fm	Heref	SO3734	52°0·3'	2°54·7'W	FM	149,161
Morehams Hall	Essex	TM0823	51°52·2'	1°1·7'E	X	168,169
Morehay Lawn	Northnts	TL0094	52°32·3'	0°31·1'W	X	141
More Head	Aberd	NJ7865	57°40·7'	2°21·7'W	X	29,30
More Ho	E Susx	TQ3420	50°58·1'	0°5·1'W	X	198
Morehouse, The	Shrops	SO5792	52°31·7'	2°37·6'W	X	137,138
Morelaggan	Arg & Bt	NN2701	56°10·5'	4°46·8'W	X	56
Moreland	Pth & Kin	NT0496	56°9·1'	3°32·3'W	X	58
Moreland's	Essex	TL8831	51°57·0'	0°44·5'E	X	168
Morelands Fm	Pth & Kin	NT0596	56°9·1'	3°31·3'W	FM	58
Moreleigh	Devon	SX7652	50°21·5'	3°44·2'W	T	202
Moreleigh Hill Brake	Devon	SX7551	50°21·0'	3°45·0'W	X	202
Moreleigh Mount	Devon	SX7452	50°21·5'	3°45·9'W	X	202
Moreless	Aberd	NJ7657	57°36·4'	2°23·6'W	X	29
Morells Fm	W Susx	SU9000	50°47·8'	0°43·0'W	FM	197
Moren	Shetld	HU4664	60°21·7'	1°9·5'W	X	2,3
Morendy Wood	Fife	NO4224	56°24·5'	2°56·0'W	F	54,59
Morenish	Pth & Kin	NN5935	56°29·4'	4°17·0'W	X	51
Moresby Moss	Cumbr	NY0020	54°34·2'	3°32·4'W	X	89
Moresby Parks	Cumbr	NX9919	54°33·6'	3°33·3'W	T	89
Moresdale Gill	N Yks	NZ0404	54°26·1'	1°55·9'W	W	92
Moresdale Hall	Cumbr	SD5895	54°21·2'	2°38·4'W	X	97
Moresdale Ridge	N Yks	NZ0404	54°26·1'	1°55·9'W	X	92
Moreseat	Aberd	NK0540	57°27·3'	1°54·5'W	X	30
Morestead	Hants	SU5025	51°1·6'	1°16·8'W	T	185
Morestead Down	Hants	SU5026	51°2·1'	1°16·8'W	X	185
Morestead Fm	Hants	SU5026	51°2·1'	1°16·8'W	FM	185
Morestead Ho	Hants	SU5124	51°1·0'	1°16·0'W	X	185
Mores, The	Essex	TQ5696	51°38·7'	0°15·7'E	F	167,177
Moreston	Pemb	SM9300	51°39·9'	4°59·2'W	X	157,158
Moreswood	Shrops	SO3293	52°32·1'	2°59·8'W	X	137
Moreton	Dorset	SY8089	50°42·2'	2°16·6'W	T	194
Moreton	Essex	TL5307	51°44·7'	0°13·4'E	T	167
Moreton	Heref	SO5064	52°16·6'	2°43·6'W	T	137,138,149
Moreton	Oxon	SP4101	51°42·6'	1°24·0'W	T	164
Moreton	Oxon	SP6904	51°44·1'	0°59·7'W	T	165
Moreton	Staffs	SJ7917	52°45·3'	2°18·3'W	T	127
Moreton	Staffs	SK1429	52°51·7'	1°47·1'W	T	128
Moreton	Wirral	SJ2690	53°24·3'	3°6·4'W	T	108
Moreton Below	Wrex	SJ3244	52°59·6'	3°0·4'W	X	117
Moreton Br	Heref	SO5145	52°6·3'	2°42·5'W	X	149
Moreton Corbet	Shrops	SJ5523	52°48·4'	2°39·7'W	T	126
Moreton Corbet Castle	Shrops	SJ5623	52°48·4'	2°38·8'W	A	126
Moreton Cotts	Ches	SJ8360	53°8·5'	2°14·8'W	X	118
Moreton Field Fm	Oxon	SP6903	51°43·5'	0°59·7'W	FM	165
Moreton Fm	Bucks	SP7909	51°46·7'	0°50·9'W	FM	165
Moreton Fm	Shrops	SJ5603	52°37·6'	2°38·6'W	FM	126
Moreton Fm	Staffs	SK0223	52°48·5'	1°57·8'W	FM	128
Moreton Fm	Wrex	SJ3244	52°59·6'	3°0·4'W	FM	117
Moreton Hall	Shrops	SJ2935	52°54·7'	3°2·9'W	X	126
Moreton Hall	Shrops	SJ6334	52°54·4'	2°32·6'W	X	127
Moreton Hall Fm	Lancs	SD7434	53°48·3'	2°23·3'W	FM	103
Moreton Hall (Sch)	Suff	TL8764	52°14·8'	0°44·8'E	X	155
Moretonhampstead	Devon	SX7586	50°39·9'	3°45·7'W	T	191
Moreton Ho	Dorset	SY8089	50°42·2'	2°16·6'W	A	194
Moreton Ho (Coll)	Devon	SS4326	51°1·0'	4°13·9'W	X	180,190
Moreton-in-Marsh	Glos	SP2032	51°59·4'	1°42·1'W	T	151
Moreton Jeffries	Heref	SO6048	52°8·0'	2°34·7'W	T	149
Moreton Mill	Corn	SS2808	50°51·0'	4°26·2'W	X	190
Moreton Mill	Essex	TL5308	51°45·2'	0°13·4'E	X	167
Moreton Morrell	Warw	SP3156	52°12·3'	1°32·4'W	T	151
Moreton on Lugg	Heref	SO5045	52°6·3'	2°43·4'W	T	149
Moreton Paddox	Warw	SP3054	52°11·2'	1°33·3'W	T	151
Moreton Park	Staffs	SJ7817	52°45·2'	2°19·2'W	X	127
Moreton Pinkney	Northnts	SP5749	52°8·4'	1°9·6'W	T	152
Moreton Plantation	Dorset	SY8191	50°43·3'	2°15·8'W	F	194
Moreton Pound Fm	Corn	SS2708	50°51·0'	4°27·1'W	FM	190
Moreton Say	Shrops	SJ6234	52°54·4'	2°33·5'W	T	127
Moreton Sta	Dorset	SY7789	50°42·2'	2°19·2'W	X	194
Moreton Sta	Wirral	SJ2690	53°24·3'	3°6·4'W	X	108
Moreton Valence	Glos	SO7809	51°47·0'	2°18·7'W	T	162
Moreton Village	Bucks	SP7909	51°46·7'	0°50·9'W	A	165
Moretonwood	Shrops	SJ6234	52°54·4'	2°33·5'W	T	127
Moreton Wood	Warw	SP2955	52°11·8'	1°34·1'W	F	151

More Wood	W Berks	SU4166	51°23·7'	1°24·3'W	F	174
Morfa	Carm	SN5314	51°48·6'	4°7·6'W	X	159
Morfa	Carm	SN5712	51°47·5'	4°4·0'W	T	159
Morfa	Carm	SS5198	51°39·9'	4°8·9'W	T	159
Morfa	Cered	SN3052	52°8·7'	4°28·7'W	T	145
Morfa	Cered	SN5269	52°18·2'	4°9·8'W	X	135
Morfa	Gwyn	SH1933	52°52·1'	4°40·9'W	T	123
Morfa	Gwyn	SH3647	53°0·0'	4°26·2'W	X	123
Morfa	Gwyn	SH6111	52°41·0'	4°3·0'W	X	124
Morfa	Pemb	SM8733	51°57·5'	5°5·6'W	X	157
Morfa	Pemb	SN0541	52°2·2'	4°50·2'W	X	145
Morfa Abererch	Gwyn	SH4136	52°54·1'	4°21·4'W	X	123
Morfa Bacas	Carm	SS5497	51°39·4'	4°6·3'W	X	159
Morfa Bach	Carm	SN3613	51°47·7'	4°22·3'W	T	159
Morfa-Bach	Carm	SN4306	51°44·1'	4°16·0'W	X	159
Morfa Bychan	Cered	SN5677	52°22·6'	4°6·5'W	X	135
Morfa Bychan	Gwyn	SH5437	52°54·9'	4°9·9'W	T	124
Morfa Camp	Gwyn	SH5701	52°35·5'	4°6·3'W	X	135
Morfa Common	Pemb	SM7824	51°52·5'	5°13·1'W	X	157
Morfa-cwybr	Denb	SJ0179	53°18·2'	3°28·7'W	X	116
Morfa Dinlle	Gwyn	SH4358	53°6·0'	4°20·3'W	X	115,123
Morfa-du	Cered	SN5967	52°17·2'	4°3·6'W	X	135
Morfa Dyffryn	Gwyn	SH5624	52°47·9'	4°7·8'W	X	124
Morfa Fm	Gwyn	SH1730	52°50·4'	4°42·6'W	FM	123
Morfa Fm	V of Glam	SS9570	51°25·4'	3°30·2'W	FM	170
Morfa Glas	Nth Pt Talb	SN8706	51°44·7'	3°37·8'W	T	160
Morfa Gors	Gwyn	SH3127	52°49·1'	4°30·1'W	X	123
Morfa Gwyllt	Gwyn	SH5702	52°36·1'	4°6·3'W	X	135
Morfa Gwyllt	Gwyn	SH6041	52°57·1'	4°4·6'W	X	124
Morfa Harlech	Gwyn	SH5833	52°52·8'	4°6·2'W	X	124
Morfa Lodge	Gwyn	SH4458	53°6·0'	4°19·4'W	X	115,123
Morfa Mawddach Sta	Gwyn	SH6214	52°42·6'	4°2·2'W	X	124
Morfa Mawr	Carm	SN4205	51°43·5'	4°16·9'W	X	159
Morfa Mawr	Swan	SN5701	51°41·6'	4°3·8'W	X	159
Morfa Mawr Fm	Cered	SN5065	52°16·0'	4°11·5'W	FM	135
Morfa Nefyn	Gwyn	SH2840	52°56·0'	4°33·2'W	T	123
Morfa Rhuddlan	Conwy	SH9778	53°17·6'	3°32·3'W	X	116
Morfa Uchaf	Carm	SN3712	51°47·2'	4°21·4'W	X	159
Morfe Hall Fm	Staffs	SO8287	52°29·1'	2°15·5'W	FM	138
Morfe House Fm	Staffs	SO8288	52°29·6'	2°15·5'W	FM	138
Morfevalley	Shrops	SO7690	52°30·7'	2°20·8'W	X	138
Morfodion	Powys	SN9785	52°27·4'	3°30·6'W	X	136
Morfydd	Denb	SJ1145	52°59·9'	3°19·2'W	T	116
Morganhayes	Devon	SY2193	50°44·1'	3°6·8'W	X	192,193
Morganhayes Covert	Devon	SY2192	50°43·6'	3°6·8'W	F	192,193
Morgans	Bath & NE Somer	ST5654	51°17·2'	2°37·5'W	X	182,183
Morgan's Hill	Wilts	SU0267	51°24·4'	1°57·9'W	H	173
Morganston	Pth & Kin	NO1649	56°37·8'	3°21·7'W	X	53
Morganstown	Card	ST1281	51°31·5'	3°15·7'W	T	171
Morgans Tynings	Wilts	ST9595	51°39·5'	2°3·9'W	X	163
Morgan's Vale	Wilts	SU1921	50°59·5'	1°43·4'W	T	184
Morgan's Walk	Herts	TL3210	51°46·6'	0°4·8'W	X	166
Morgastor Wood	Hants	SU6257	51°18·8'	1°6·2'W	F	175
Morghew	Kent	TQ8832	51°3·6'	0°41·4'E	X	189
Morghew Fm	Kent	TQ8731	51°3·1'	0°40·5'E	FM	189
Morgrove Coppice	Warw	SP0962	52°15·6'	1°51·7'W	F	150
Morham Bank	E Loth	NT5470	55°55·5'	2°43·7'W	X	66
Morham Loanhead	E Loth	NT5571	55°56·1'	2°42·8'W	X	66
Morham Mains	E Loth	NT5571	55°56·1'	2°42·8'W	X	66
Moriah	Cered	SN6279	52°23·7'	4°1·3'W	T	135
Moricambe	Cumbr	NY1656	54°53·8'	3°18·2'W	X	85
Moridvnvm (Roman Town)	Carm	SN4120	51°51·6'	4°18·2'W	R	159
Morilemore	Highld	NH8028	57°19·9'	3°59·1'W	X	35
Morins Hill	D & G	NX9794	55°14·0'	3°36·7'W	H	78
Mork	Glos	SO5505	51°44·7'	2°38·7'W	T	162
Morkery Wood	Lincs	SK9518	52°45·3'	0°35·1'W	F	130
Mork Hill	Glos	SO5505	51°44·7'	2°38·7'W	X	162
Morlais Hill	Merth Tyd	SO0509	51°46·5'	3°22·2'W	H	160
Morlais River	Swan	SS5494	51°37·8'	4°6·2'W	W	159
Morland	Cumbr	NY5922	54°35·7'	2°37·7'W	T	91
Morland Moor	Cumbr	NY6121	54°35·2'	2°35·8'W	X	91
Morlands Fm	Bucks	SU8097	51°40·2'	0°50·2'W	FM	165
Morlanga	V of Glam	ST0977	51°29·3'	3°18·3'W	X	171
Morlas Brook	Shrops	SJ2935	52°54·7'	3°2·9'W	W	126
Morley	Ches	SJ8282	53°20·3'	2°15·8'W	T	109
Morley	Derby	SK3940	52°57·6'	1°24·8'W	T	119,128
Morley	Devon	SX8271	50°31·8'	3°39·5'W	X	202
Morley	Durham	NZ1227	54°38·5'	1°48·4'W	T	92
Morley	Durham	NZ2239	54°45·0'	1°39·1'W	X	93
Morley	Leeds	SE2627	53°44·6'	1°35·9'W	T	104
Morley	W Susx	TQ2019	50°57·7'	0°17·1'W	X	198
Morley Br	Ches	SJ4671	53°14·2'	2°48·1'W	X	117
Morley Carr	Stock on T	NZ4110	54°29·3'	1°21·6'W	X	93
Morley Fm	Durham	NZ1228	54°39·1'	1°48·4'W	FM	92
Morley Fm	E Susx	TQ8222	50°58·3'	0°35·9'E	FM	199
Morley Fm	Leic	SK4717	52°45·1'	1°17·8'W	FM	129
Morley Fm	W Susx	TQ2317	50°56·6'	0°14·6'W	FM	198
Morley Green	Ches	SJ8282	53°20·3'	2°15·8'W	T	109
Morley Hall	Ches	SJ4670	53°13·7'	2°48·1'W	X	117
Morley Hall	Herts	TL3815	51°49·2'	0°0·5'E	X	166
Morley Hall	Norf	TM0798	52°32·7'	1°3·6'E	X	144
Morley Hill	Cumbr	NY5053	54°52·4'	2°46·3'W	X	86
Morley Hill	Northum	NY7654	54°53·1'	2°22·0'W	X	86,87
Morleyhill Fell	Northum	NY7452	54°52·0'	2°23·9'W	X	86,87
Morley Hill Fm	N upon Ty	NZ2272	55°2·8'	1°38·9'W	FM	88
Morley Manor	Norf	TM0599	52°33·2'	1°1·8'E	X	144
Morleymoor	Derby	SK3841	52°58·1'	1°25·6'W	T	119,128
Morleymoor Fm	Derby	SK3942	52°58·7'	1°24·7'W	FM	119,128
Morley Park	Derby	SK3848	53°1·9'	1°25·6'W	T	119
Morley Pond	Roth	SK3996	53°27·8'	1°24·3'W	W	110,111
Morleys	Essex	TL5118	51°50·6'	0°11·9'E	X	167
Morley's Fm	Cambs	TL3587	52°28·1'	0°0·4'W	FM	142
Morley Smithy	Derby	SK3941	52°58·1'	1°24·8'W	T	119,128
Morley St Botolph	Norf	TG0600	52°33·8'	1°2·8'E	X	144
Morley St Botolph	Norf	TM0799	52°33·2'	1°3·6'E	T	144
Morlogws-isaf	Pemb	SN2933	51°58·4'	4°29·0'W	X	145
Mòr-mheall	Arg & Bt	NL9649	56°32·3'	6°56·3'W	X	46
Mòr Mhonadh	N Eil	NB2713	58°1·6'	6°37·0'W	H	13,14
Mormondfoot	Aberd	NJ9656	57°35·9'	2°3·6'W	X	30

Mormond Hill	Aberd	NJ9757	57°36·4'	2°2·6'W	H	30
Mormond Prop	Aberd	NJ8853	57°34·3'	2°11·6'W	X	30
Mormondside	Aberd	NJ9855	57°35·4'	2°1·5'W	X	30
Mornacott	Devon	SS7627	51°2·0'	3°45·7'W	X	180
Morness	Highld	NC7105	58°1·2'	4°10·6'W	X	16
Mornick	Corn	SX3172	50°31·6'	4°22·7'W	T	201
Morningbank	Scot Bord	NT8347	55°43·2'	2°15·8'W	X	74
Morning Dawn	Kent	TQ8655	51°16·0'	0°40·4'E	X	178
Morningside	C of Edin	NT2471	55°55·8'	3°12·5'W	T	66
Morningside	D & G	NY2167	54°59·7'	3°13·7'W	X	85
Morningside	N Lanak	NS8355	55°46·7'	3°51·5'W	T	65,72
Morningside	Pth & Kin	NN9630	56°27·3'	3°40·8'W	X	52,53
Mornings Mill Fm	E Susx	TQ5804	50°49·1'	0°15·0'E	FM	199
Morning Springs	Notts	SK4949	53°2·4'	1°15·7'W	F	129
Morningthorpe	Norf	TM2192	52°29·1'	1°15·7'E	T	134
Morningthorpe Fm	Norf	TM2190	52°28·0'	1°15·6'E	FM	134
Morningthorpe Green	Norf	TM2191	52°28·6'	1°15·7'E	X	134
Mornington House Fm	Lincs	TF1731	52°52·1'	0°15·3'W	FM	130
Morpeth	Northum	NZ2085	55°9·8'	1°40·7'W	T	81
Morphany Hall	Ches	SJ5980	53°19·2'	2°36·5'W	X	108
Morphie	Aberd	NO7164	56°46·3'	2°28·0'W	X	45
Morrach	D & G	NX4635	54°41·4'	4°22·9'W	X	83
Morralee	Northum	NY8064	54°58·5'	2°18·3'W	X	86,87
Morraston	Heref	SO5331	51°58·8'	2°40·7'W	X	149
Morrelhirst	Northum	NZ0596	55°15·7'	1°54·8'W	X	81
Morrell Hill	Cumbr	NY4864	54°58·3'	2°48·3'W	X	86
Morrell's Fm	Devon	ST0119	50°58·0'	3°24·2'W	FM	181
Morrell's Wood Fm	Shrops	SJ6206	52°39·3'	2°33·3'W	FM	127
Morrell Wood Fm	Derby	SK3748	53°1·9'	1°26·5'W	FM	119
Morrey	Staffs	SK1218	52°45·8'	1°48·9'W	T	128
Morrice Green	Herts	TL4135	52°0·0'	0°3·6'E	X	154
Morrich More	Highld	NH8384	57°50·1'	3°57·8'W	X	21
Morridge	Staffs	SK0257	53°6·8'	1°57·8'W	X	119
Morridge	Staffs	SK0362	53°9·5'	1°56·9'W	X	119
Morridgehall	Scot Bord	NT6129	55°33·4'	2°36·7'W	X	74
Morridge Side	Staffs	SK0254	53°5·2'	1°57·8'W	T	119
Morridge Top	Staffs	SK0365	53°11·2'	1°56·9'W	X	119
Morrilow Heath	Staffs	SJ9835	52°55·0'	2°1·4'W	T	127
Morrington	D & G	NX8781	55°6·9'	3°45·9'W	X	78
Morris Croft	Derby	SK2418	52°45·8'	1°38·3'W	X	128
Morris Ct	Kent	TQ9262	51°19·7'	0°45·8'E	X	178
Morris Dancer's Plantn	Notts	SK6472	53°14·7'	1°2·0'W	F	120
Morris Fen	Peterb	TF2806	52°38·4'	0°6·1'W	X	142
Morris Fm	Essex	TQ8298	51°39·3'	0°38·3'E	FM	168
Morris Fm	Lancs	SD6118	53°39·7'	2°35·0'W	FM	109
Morris Grange	N Yks	NZ2204	54°26·1'	1°39·2'W	X	93
Morris Green	Essex	TL7433	51°58·3'	0°32·4'E	X	167
Morris Hall	Northum	NT9147	55°43·2'	2°8·2'W	X	74,75
Morrishall Fm	Northum	NT9147	55°43·2'	2°8·2'W	FM	74,75
Morris Hill	Lancs	SD4748	53°55·8'	2°48·0'W	X	102
Morrisholt Fm	Wilts	SU2723	51°0·6'	1°36·5'W	FM	184
Morrispark	D & G	NY2166	54°59·2'	3°13·6'W	X	85
Morris's Fm	Warr	SJ6295	53°27·3'	2°33·9'W	FM	109
Morriston	S Ayr	NS2308	55°20·3'	4°47·0'W	X	70,76
Morriston	Swan	SS6698	51°40·1'	3°55·9'W	T	159
Morriston Cott	Scot Bord	NT5942	55°40·4'	2°38·7'W	X	73,74
Morristown	V of Glam	ST1770	51°25·6'	3°11·2'W	T	171
Morroch	D & G	NX0152	54°49·7'	5°5·5'W	X	82
Morroch	Highld	NM6686	56°54·6'	5°50·2'W	X	40
Morroch Bay	D & G	NX0152	54°49·7'	5°5·5'W	W	82
Morroch Point	Highld	NM6585	56°54·1'	5°51·1'W	X	40
Morrone Birkwood	Aberd	NO1390	56°59·8'	3°25·5'W	F	43
Morrone or Morven	Aberd	NO1388	56°58·8'	3°25·4'W	H	43
Morro Ness	Shetld	HU4962	60°20·6'	1°6·2'W	X	2,3
Morrow Edge Fm	Durham	NZ1849	54°50·4'	1°42·8'W	FM	88
Morrowfield Fm	Northum	NZ0855	54°53·6'	1°52·1'W	FM	88
Morry Ho	Kent	TQ8349	51°12·9'	0°37·6'E	X	188
Morses	Essex	TM0818	51°49·5'	1°1·5'E	X	168,169
Morse's Fm	Glos	SO7420	51°52·9'	2°22·3'W	FM	162
Morsgail Forest or Frith Mhorsgail	N Eil	NB1117	58°3·1'	6°53·5'W	F	13,14
Morson Fm	Devon	SX4590	50°41·6'	4°11·3'W	FM	190
Mor Stein	Orkney	HY5216	59°2·0'	2°49·7'W	X	6
Mor Stein (Standing Stone)	Orkney	HY5216	59°2·0'	2°49·7'W	A	6
Morston	Norf	TG0043	52°57·1'	0°59·0'E	T	133
Morston Creek	Norf	TG0044	52°57·6'	0°59·1'E	W	133
Morston Hall	Suff	TM2538	51°59·9'	1°17·1'E	X	169
Morston Salt Marshes	Norf	TG0144	52°57·6'	1°0·0'E	W	133
Mortar Crag	Cumbr	NY4017	54°32·9'	2°55·2'W	X	90
Mortar Pit Fm	N Yks	NZ9006	54°26·7'	0°36·3'W	FM	94
Mort Bank	Cumbr	SD3067	54°5·9'	3°3·8'W	X	96,97
Morte Bay	Devon	SS4342	51°9·6'	4°14·3'W	W	180
Mortehoe	Devon	SS4545	51°11·2'	4°12·7'W	T	180
Morte Point	Devon	SS4445	51°11·2'	4°13·6'W	X	180
Morte Stone	Devon	SS4345	51°11·2'	4°14·4'W	X	180
Mortgrove Fm	Herts	TL1028	51°56·6'	0°23·6'W	FM	166
Morth	Devon	SX5099	50°46·5'	4°7·3'W	X	191
Mortham Tower	Durham	NZ0814	54°31·5'	1°52·2'W	A	92
Mortham Wood	Durham	NZ0813	54°31·0'	1°52·2'W	F	92
Morthen	Roth	SK4789	53°24·0'	1°17·2'W	T	111,120
Mortice Hill	Norf	TF9421	52°45·3'	0°52·9'E	X	132
Mortimer	W Berks	SU6564	51°22·5'	1°3·6'W	T	175,186
Mortimer Ho	W Berks	SU6765	51°23·0'	1°1·8'W	X	175
Mortimer Lodge	W Berks	SU6664	51°22·5'	1°2·7'W	X	175,186
Mortimer's Cross	Heref	SO4263	52°16·0'	2°50·6'W	T	137,148,149
Mortimer's Deep	Fife	NT1883	56°2·2'	3°18·5'W	W	65,66
Mortimers Fm	Devon	ST0809	50°52·6'	3°18·1'W	FM	192
Mortimer's Fm	Essex	TL7237	52°0·5'	0°30·8'E	FM	154
Mortimers Fm	Hants	SU5018	50°57·8'	1°16·9'W	FM	185
Mortimer's Fm	Norf	TL8994	52°30·9'	0°47·5'E	FM	144
Mortimer's Fm	Suff	TL9451	52°7·6'	0°50·5'E	FM	155
Mortimer's Rock	Heref	SO4163	52°16·0'	2°51·5'W	X	137,148,149
Mortimer West End	Hants	SU6363	51°22·0'	1°5·3'W	T	175
Mortlake	Rich	TQ2075	51°27·9'	0°16·0'W	T	176
Mortley	Northum	NY8277	55°5·5'	2°16·5'W	X	86,87
Mortlich	Aberd	NJ5301	57°6·1'	2°46·1'W	H	37
Mortomley	Sheff	SK3497	53°28·4'	1°28·9'W	T	110,111
Morton	Cumbr	NY3854	54°52·9'	2°57·6'W	T	85

Morton	Cumbr	NY4439	54°44·8'	2°51·8'W	T	90
Morton	Derby	SK4060	53°8·4'	1°23·7'W	T	120
Morton	Fife	NO4626	56°25·6'	2°52·1'W	X	54,59
Morton	Fife	NO5812	56°18·2'	2°40·3'W	X	59
Morton	I of W	SZ6086	50°40·5'	1°8·7'W	T	196
Morton	Lincs	SK8091	53°24·8'	0°47·4'W	T	112
Morton	Lincs	SK8863	53°9·6'	0°40·6'W	T	121
Morton	Lincs	TF0924	52°48·4'	0°22·6'W	T	130
Morton	Norf	TG1217	52°42·8'	1°8·7'E	T	133
Morton	Notts	SK6880	53°19·0'	0°58·3'W	X	111,120
Morton	Notts	SK7251	53°3·3'	0°55·1'W	T	120
Morton	S Glos	ST6490	51°36·7'	2°30·8'W	T	162,172
Morton	Shrops	SJ2924	52°48·8'	3°2·8'W	T	126
Morton	W Loth	NT0763	55°51·3'	3°28·7'W	X	65
Morton Bagot	Warw	SP1164	52°16·7'	1°49·9'W	T	150
Morton Bagot Manor	Warw	SP1065	52°17·2'	1°50·8'W	X	150
Morton Burn	W Loth	NT0863	55°51·3'	3°27·7'W	W	65
Morton Carr	Red & Cl	NZ5514	54°31·3'	1°8·6'W	X	93
Morton Castle	D & G	NX8999	55°16·6'	3°44·4'W	A	78
Morton Close	N Yks	NZ8203	54°25·2'	0°43·8'W	X	94
Morton Common	Shrops	SJ2924	52°48·8'	3°2·8'W	T	126
Morton Common Fm	Warw	SP0963	52°16·1'	1°51·7'W	FM	150
Morton Fen	Lincs	TF1423	52°47·8'	0°18·1'W	X	130
Morton Flatts	N Yks	SE3191	54°19·1'	1°31·0'W	X	99
Morton Fm	S Glos	ST6691	51°37·2'	2°29·1'W	FM	162,172
Morton Fm	Shrops	SJ2924	52°48·8'	3°2·8'W	FM	126
Morton Grange	Darl	NZ3213	54°30·9'	1°29·9'W	X	93
Morton Grange	Notts	SK6878	53°17·9'	0°58·4'W	X	120
Morton Grange	N Yks	SE3291	54°19·1'	1°30·1'W	X	99
Morton Grange	Red & Cl	NZ5514	54°31·3'	1°8·6'W	X	93
Morton Grange Fm	Durham	NZ3049	54°50·3'	1°31·5'W	FM	88
Morton Grange Fm	N Yks	SE4299	54°23·3'	1°20·8'W	FM	99
Mortonhall	C of Edin	NT2668	55°54·2'	3°10·6'W	X	66
Morton Hall	Norf	TG1215	52°41·7'	1°8·6'E	X	133
Morton Hall	Notts	SK6580	53°19·0'	1°1·0'W	X	111,120
Morton Hall	Shrops	SJ3023	52°48·2'	3°1·9'W	X	126
Morton Hall	Worcs	SP0259	52°14·0'	1°57·8'W	X	150
Mortonhill	W Loth	NT0663	55°51·3'	3°29·7'W	X	65
Morton Hill	W Loth	NT0761	55°50·3'	3°28·7'W	X	65
Morton Hill Fm	Notts	SK6578	53°17·9'	1°1·1'W	FM	120
Morton Ho	C of Edin	NT2567	55°53·7'	3°11·5'W	X	66
Morton Ho	Durham	NZ1120	54°34·7'	1°49·4'W	X	92
Morton Ho	Durham	NZ3149	54°50·3'	1°30·6'W	X	88
Morton Holm	D & G	NX8693	55°13·3'	3°47·1'W	X	78
Morton Links	Fife	NO4626	56°25·6'	2°52·1'W	X	54,59
Morton Loch	D & G	NX8999	55°16·6'	3°44·4'W	W	78
Morton Lochs	Fife	NO4626	56°25·6'	2°52·1'W	W	54,59
Morton Mains	D & G	NX8899	55°16·6'	3°45·4'W	T	78
Morton Mill	D & G	NX8697	55°15·5'	3°47·2'W	X	78
Morton Mill	Shrops	SJ5722	52°47·9'	2°37·9'W	T	126
Morton Mill Fm	Shrops	SJ6235	52°54·9'	2°33·5'W	FM	127
Morton Moor	Brad	SE0944	53°53·8'	1°51·4'W	X	104
Morton of Blebo	Fife	NO4314	56°19·2'	2°54·8'W	X	59
Morton-on-Swale	N Yks	SE3291	54°19·1'	1°30·1'W	T	99
Morton Palms Fm	Darl	NZ3314	54°31·5'	1°29·0'W	FM	93
Morton Pool	Shrops	SJ3023	52°48·2'	3°1·9'W	W	126
Morton Reservoir	W Loth	NT0763	55°51·3'	3°28·7'W	W	65
Morton's Br	Norf	TF5404	52°36·9'	0°16·9'E	X	143
Morton's Leam	Cambs	TF3400	52°35·1'	0°0·9'W	A	142
Morton's Leam	Cambs	TL3099	52°34·6'	0°4·5'W	A	142
Morton Spirt	Worcs	SP0454	52°11·3'	1°56·1'W	T	150
Morton's Way	Moray	NJ2829	57°21·0'	3°11·3'W	X	37
Morton Tinmouth	Durham	NZ1821	54°35·3'	1°42·9'W	T	92
Morton Underhill	Worcs	SP0159	52°14·0'	1°58·7'W	T	150
Morton Wood	D & G	NX8898	55°16·1'	3°45·3'W	F	78
Morton Wood Fm	Worcs	SP0353	52°10·8'	1°57·0'W	FM	150
Moruisg	Highld	NH1049	57°29·7'	5°9·8'W	H	25
Morvah	Corn	SW4035	50°9·7'	5°38·1'W	T	203
Morval	Corn	SX2656	50°22·9'	4°26·5'W	T	201
Morval Ho	Corn	SX2556	50°22·9'	4°27·3'W	A	201
Morven	Aberd	NJ3704	57°7·6'	3°2·0'W	H	37
Morven	Highld	ND0028	58°14·0'	3°41·7'W	H	17
Morven	N Eil	NB3651	58°17·6'	6°30·4'W	X	8
Morven	Scot Bord	NT6249	55°44·2'	2°35·9'W	X	74
Morven Burn	Aberd	NJ3403	57°7·1'	3°4·9'W	W	37
Morven Lodge	Aberd	NJ3302	57°6·5'	3°5·9'W	X	37
Morven or Morrone	Aberd	NO1388	56°58·8'	3°25·4'W	H	43
Morvern	Highld	NM6654	56°37·4'	5°48·4'W	X	49
Morvich	Highld	NC7500	57°58·6'	4°6·3'W	X	16
Morvich	Highld	NG9621	57°14·3'	5°22·4'W	X	25,33
Morvil	Pemb	SN0330	51°56·3'	4°51·6'W	X	145,157
Morville	Shrops	SO6694	52°32·8'	2°29·7'W	T	138
Morville Hall	Shrops	SO6694	52°32·8'	2°29·7'W	A	138
Morville Heath	Shrops	SO6893	52°32·3'	2°27·9'W	T	138
Morwell Barton	Devon	SX4470	50°30·8'	4°11·6'W	X	201
Morwelldown Plantn	Devon	SX4571	50°31·3'	4°10·8'W	X	201
Morwellham Quay	Devon	SX4469	50°30·2'	4°11·6'W	T	201
Morwell Wood	Devon	SX4470	50°30·8'	4°11·6'W	F	201
Morwenstow	Corn	SS2015	50°54·6'	4°33·2'W	T	190
Morwents Fm	Glos	SO7215	51°50·2'	2°24·0'W	FM	162
Morwick	Northum	NU2303	55°19·5'	1°37·8'W	X	81
Morwick Hall	Leeds	SE3737	53°49·9'	1°25·9'W	X	104
Morwood	Northum	NY7967	55°0·1'	2°19·3'W	X	86,87
Morwood	Shrops	SO4585	52°27·9'	2°48·2'W	X	137,138
Mosborough	Sheff	SK4280	53°19·2'	1°21·8'W	T	111,120
Moscar Cross	Sheff	SK2388	53°23·5'	1°38·8'W	X	110
Moscar Fields	Derby	SK2287	53°23·0'	1°39·7'W	X	110
Moscar Fm	Derby	SK1464	53°10·6'	1°47·0'W	FM	119
Moscar Ho	Derby	SK2288	53°23·5'	1°39·7'W	X	110
Moscar Lodge	Derby	SK2388	53°23·5'	1°38·8'W	X	110
Moscar Moor	Derby	SK2286	53°22·5'	1°39·7'W	X	110
Moscow	Cumbr	NY6268	55°0·6'	2°35·2'W	X	86
Moscow	Cumbr	NY7350	54°50·9'	2°24·8'W	X	86,87
Moscow	E Ayr	NS4840	55°38·1'	4°24·4'W	T	70
Moscow Fm	Derby	SK3444	52°59·8'	1°29·2'W	FM	119,128
Moscow Fm	Leic	SK7512	52°42·3'	0°53·0'W	FM	129
Mose	Shrops	SO7590	52°30·7'	2°21·7'W	T	138
Mosedale	Cumbr	NY1417	54°32·7'	3°19·3'W	X	89
Mosedale	Cumbr	NY1710	54°29·0'	3°16·4'W	X	89,90
Mosedale	Cumbr	NY2402	54°24·7'	3°9·8'W	X	89,90
Mosedale	Cumbr	NY3532	54°41·0'	3°0·1'W	T	90
Mosedale	Cumbr	NY4909	54°28·7'	2°46·8'W	X	90
Mosedale Beck	Cumbr	NY1318	54°33·2'	3°20·3'W	W	89
Mosedale Beck	Cumbr	NY1710	54°29·0'	3°16·4'W	W	89,90
Mosedale Beck	Cumbr	NY3524	54°36·7'	3°0·0'W	W	90
Mosedale Beck	Cumbr	NY5010	54°29·2'	2°45·9'W	W	90
Mosedale Cottage	Cumbr	NY4909	54°28·7'	2°46·8'W	X	90
Moseham	E Susx	TQ6431	51°3·5'	0°20·8'E	X	188
Moselden Height	Kirk	SE0416	53°38·7'	1°56·0'W	X	110
Moseley	Birm	SP0883	52°26·9'	1°52·5'W	T	139
Moseley	Staffs	SK0466	53°11·7'	1°56·0'W	X	119
Moseley	Wolv	SJ9303	52°37·7'	2°5·8'W	X	127,139
Moseley	Wolv	SO9398	52°35·0'	2°5·8'W	T	139
Moseley	Worcs	SO8159	52°14·0'	2°16·3'W	T	150
Moseley Common	Heref	SO3758	52°13·2'	2°54·9'W	X	148,149
Moseley Grange	Donc	SE6014	53°37·4'	1°5·2'W	X	111
Moseley Green	Glos	SO6308	51°46·4'	2°31·8'W	X	162
Moseley Hall	Ches	SJ7677	53°17·6'	2°21·2'W	X	118
Mosely Old Hall	Staffs	SJ9304	52°38·3'	2°5·8'W	A	127,139
Mosergh Fm	Cumbr	SD5299	54°23·3'	2°43·9'W	FM	97
Moser Hill	Cumbr	SD6690	54°18·5'	2°30·9'W	X	98
Moses Cocker's	Lancs	SD6315	53°38·1'	2°33·2'W	X	109
Moses Fm	Lincs	TF2581	53°18·9'	0°7·0'W	FM	122
Moses Gate	Bolton	SD7306	53°33·2'	2°24·0'W	T	109
Moses Gate Country Park	Bolton	SD7407	53°33·8'	2°23·1'W	X	109
Moses Lee	Lancs	SD8745	53°54·3'	2°11·5'W	X	103
Mosey Br	N Yks	SE5161	54°2·8'	1°12·8'W	X	100
Moseyley	Derby	SK3044	52°59·8'	1°32·8'W	X	119,128
Mosey Low	Derby	SK1264	53°10·6'	1°48·8'W	X	119
Moshella Lochs	Shetld	HU3186	60°33·6'	1°25·6'W	W	1,3
Mosklyns	Essex	TL8203	51°42·0'	0°38·4'E	X	168
Mosley Bank	Derby	SK1695	53°27·3'	1°45·1'W	X	110
Mosley Common	Wigan	SD7101	53°30·5'	2°25·8'W	T	109
Mosley Hall Fm	Derby	SK0181	53°19·8'	1°58·7'W	FM	110
Mosley Hills	Notts	SK5255	53°5·6'	1°13·0'W	X	120
Moss	Arg & Bt	NL9644	56°29·7'	6°55·9'W	T	46
Moss	Arg & Bt	NM8940	56°30·5'	5°25·3'W	X	49
Moss	Cumbr	NY6904	54°26·1'	2°28·3'W	X	91
Moss	Donc	SE5914	53°37·4'	1°6·1'W	T	111
Moss	Highld	NM6868	56°45·0'	5°47·2'W	T	40
Moss	Lancs	SD9037	53°50·0'	2°8·7'W	X	103
Moss	Orkney	ND1999	58°52·5'	3°23·8'W	X	7
Moss	Stir	NS5183	56°1·3'	4°23·0'W	X	57,64
Moss	Wrex	SJ3053	53°4·4'	3°2·3'W	T	117
Mossa Grange	N Yks	SE3296	54°21·8'	1°30·0'W	X	99
Mossat	Aberd	NJ4719	57°15·8'	2°52·3'W	X	37
Mossat Burn	Aberd	NJ4519	57°15·8'	2°54·3'W	W	37
Mossback	E Ayr	NS5517	55°25·8'	4°17·1'W	X	71
Mossband	N Lanak	NS7960	55°49·3'	3°55·4'W	X	64
Mossband Hall	Cumbr	NY3465	54°58·8'	3°1·4'W	X	85
Mossband Hall Marsh	Cumbr	NY3364	54°58·2'	3°2·4'W	W	85
Mossband Ho	Cumbr	NY3565	54°58·8'	3°0·5'W	X	85
Moss Bank	Ches	SJ8667	53°12·2'	2°12·2'W	X	118
Moss Bank	Halton	SJ5285	53°21·8'	2°42·9'W	T	108
Mossbank	Highld	NG4841	57°23·6'	6°11·2'W	X	23
Mossbank	Highld	NJ0421	57°16·4'	3°35·1'W	X	36
Mossbank	Orkney	HY4109	58°58·1'	3°1·1'W	X	6,7
Mossbank	Shetld	HU4475	60°27·6'	1°11·5'W	T	2,3
Mossbank	S Lanak	NS8522	55°29·0'	3°48·8'W	X	71,72
Moss Bank	St Hel	SJ5197	53°28·3'	2°43·9'W	T	108
Moss Bank Fm	Ches	SJ7676	53°17·1'	2°21·2'W	FM	118
Mossbank Fm	Fife	NT1789	56°5·5'	3°19·6'W	FM	65,66
Moss Bank Fm	Wigan	SJ7097	53°28·4'	2°26·7'W	FM	109
Moss Bank Park	Bolton	SD6911	53°35·9'	2°27·7'W	X	109
Moss Barns	Northum	NY9978	55°6·0'	2°0·5'W	X	87
Moss Bay	Cumbr	NX9826	54°37·4'	3°34·4'W	W	89
Mossbay	Cumbr	NX9827	54°37·9'	3°34·4'W	T	89
Mossblown	S Ayr	NS4024	55°29·3'	4°31·5'W	T	70
Mossblown Fm	S Ayr	NS3924	55°29·3'	4°32·5'W	FM	70
Mossbog	S Ayr	NS4629	55°32·1'	4°26·0'W	X	70
Mossborough Hall	St Hel	SJ4699	53°29·3'	2°48·4'W	A	108
Moss Br	Ches	SJ6958	53°7·3'	2°27·4'W	X	118
Mossbrae	Orkney	HY4745	59°17·6'	2°55·3'W	X	5
Mossbrae Height	Scot Bord	NT3419	55°27·9'	3°2·2'W	H	79
Moss Brook	Brad	SE1745	53°54·3'	1°44·1'W	X	104
Moss Brook	Salf	SJ6898	53°28·9'	2°28·5'W	W	109
Mossbrow	Traf	SJ7189	53°24·1'	2°25·8'W	T	109
Moss Burn	Cumbr	NY7532	54°41·2'	2°22·8'W	W	91
Mossburn	D & G	NY0878	55°5·5'	3°26·1'W	X	85
Moss Burn	Scot Bord	NT5240	55°39·3'	2°45·3'W	W	73
Moss Burn	S Lanak	NS8327	55°31·6'	3°50·8'W	W	71,72
Mossburnford	Scot Bord	NT6616	55°26·5'	2°31·8'W	T	80
Mossburnford Bank	Scot Bord	NT6615	55°25·9'	2°31·8'W	X	80
Mossbury Manor	Beds	TL1754	52°10·5'	0°16·9'W	X	153
Moss Carr	Leeds	SE3626	53°44·0'	1°26·8'W	X	104
Mosscarr	N Yks	SE1466	54°5·6'	1°46·7'W	X	99
Moss Carr	Staffs	SK0765	53°11·2'	1°53·3'W	X	119
Moss Carrs Fm	N Yks	SE4349	53°56·4'	1°20·3'W	FM	105
Moss Castle	Derby	SK0791	53°25·2'	1°53·3'W	X	110
Mosscastle	S Lanak	NS8422	55°28·9'	3°49·7'W	X	71,72
Mosscastle Hill	S Lanak	NS8423	55°29·5'	3°49·7'W	H	71,72
Moss Chain	Derby	SK0270	53°13·9'	1°57·8'W	X	119
Moss Close	Durham	NZ0221	54°35·3'	1°57·7'W	X	92
Moss Cottage	Ches	SJ7280	53°19·2'	2°24·8'W	X	109
Moss Cottage	Cumbr	NY2559	54°55·5'	3°9·8'W	X	85
Moss Cottage	Cumbr	SD2885	54°15·6'	3°5·9'W	X	96,97
Moss Cottage	Renf	NS4466	55°52·0'	4°29·1'W	X	64
Moss Cotts	Ches	SJ7556	53°6·3'	2°22·0'W	X	118
Moss Cotts	Shrops	SJ5036	52°55·4'	2°44·2'W	X	126
Moss Croft	Aberd	NK0056	57°35·9'	1°59·5'W	X	30
Mosscroft	D & G	NX0955	54°51·5'	4°58·1'W	X	82
Mosscroft	D & G	NX6574	55°2·8'	4°6·4'W	X	77,84
Mossdale	D & G	NX6670	55°0·6'	4°5·3'W	T	77,84
Mossdale	E Ayr	NS4904	55°18·7'	4°22·3'W	X	77
Mossdale Beck	N Yks	SE0270	54°7·8'	1°57·7'W	W	98
Mossdale Burn	E Ayr	NS5005	55°19·2'	4°21·4'W	W	70,77
Mossdale Head	N Yks	SD8291	54°19·1'	2°16·2'W	X	98
Mossdale Loch	D & G	NX6571	55°1·2'	4°6·3'W	W	77,84
Mossdale Moor	N Yks	SD8090	54°18·6'	2°18·0'W	X	98
Mossdale Scar	N Yks	SE0169	54°7·3'	1°58·7'W	X	98
Moss Dalts	Cumbr	NY0210	54°28·8'	3°30·3'W	X	89
Moss Dam	N Yks	NY9200	54°24·0'	2°7·0'W	W	91,92
Moss Dyke	Cumbr	NY3631	54°40·4'	2°59·1'W	X	90
Moss Eccles Tarn	Cumbr	SD3796	54°21·6'	2°57·8'W	W	96,97
Mossedge	Cumbr	NY4768	55°0·5'	2°49·3'W	T	86
Moss Edge	Lancs	SD4243	53°53·0'	2°52·5'W	T	102
Moss Edge	Lancs	SD4349	53°56·3'	2°51·7'W	T	102
Mossend	Aberd	NJ6115	57°13·7'	2°38·3'W	X	37
Mossend	Aberd	NK0438	57°26·2'	1°55·5'W	X	30
Mossend	Angus	NO3749	56°38·0'	3°1·2'W	X	54
Moss-end	Angus	NO5242	56°34·3'	2°46·4'W	X	54
Moss End	Brackn	SU8672	51°26·7'	0°45·4'W	T	175
Moss End	Ches	SJ6778	53°18·1'	2°29·3'W	T	118
Mossend	Ches	SJ8062	53°9·5'	2°17·5'W	X	118
Moss End	Cumbr	NY2354	54°52·7'	3°11·6'W	X	85
Moss End	Cumbr	NY3645	54°48·0'	2°59·3'W	X	85
Moss End	Cumbr	SD5382	54°14·1'	2°42·8'W	X	97
Mossend	D & G	NX7457	54°53·8'	3°57·5'W	X	83,84
Mossend	Highld	NH5854	57°33·5'	4°21·9'W	X	26
Moss End	Lancs	SD4105	53°32·5'	2°53·0'W	X	108
Mossend	Midlo	NT3561	55°50·5'	3°1·8'W	X	66
Mossend	Moray	NJ1553	57°33·2'	3°24·8'W	X	28
Mossend	Moray	NJ4046	57°30·3'	2°59·6'W	X	28
Mossend	N Ayr	NS3052	55°44·2'	4°42·0'W	X	63
Mossend	N Lanak	NS7560	55°49·3'	3°59·3'W	T	64
Mossend	S Ayr	NS3509	55°21·1'	4°35·7'W	X	70,77
Mossend	S Ayr	NS3817	55°25·5'	4°33·2'W	X	70
Mossend	W Loth	NT0060	55°49·6'	3°35·3'W	X	65
Mossend Croft	Moray	NJ3652	57°33·5'	3°3·7'W	X	28
Moss End Fm	N Yks	SE5366	54°5·5'	1°11·0'W	FM	100
Mosser	Cumbr	NY1124	54°36·4'	3°22·3'W	T	89
Mosser Fell	Cumbr	NY1223	54°35·9'	3°21·3'W	X	89
Mossergate Fm	Cumbr	NY1124	54°36·4'	3°22·3'W	FM	89
Mosser Mains	Cumbr	NY1125	54°37·0'	3°22·3'W	T	89
Mosses	Cumbr	NY0621	54°34·8'	3°26·8'W	X	89
Mosses Fm	Essex	TM1927	51°54·1'	1°11·4'E	FM	168,169
Mossetter	Orkney	ND4486	58°45·7'	2°57·6'W	X	7
Mosseye	Aberd	NJ8326	57°19·7'	2°16·5'W	X	38
Mossfennan	Scot Bord	NT1131	55°34·1'	3°24·2'W	X	72
Mossfield	Aberd	NJ7327	57°20·2'	2°26·5'W	X	38
Mossfields Fm	Wrex	SJ4638	52°56·4'	2°47·8'W	FM	126
Moss Fm	Aberd	NK0234	57°24·0'	1°57·5'W	FM	30
Moss Fm	Bury	SD7813	53°37·0'	2°19·5'W	FM	109
Moss Fm	Ches	SJ5054	53°5·1'	2°44·4'W	FM	117
Moss Fm	Ches	SJ6171	53°14·3'	2°34·7'W	FM	118
Moss Fm	Ches	SJ6473	53°15·4'	2°32·0'W	FM	118
Moss Fm	Ches	SJ6958	53°7·3'	2°27·4'W	FM	118
Moss Fm	Ches	SJ7059	53°7·9'	2°26·5'W	FM	118
Moss Fm	Ches	SJ7184	53°21·4'	2°25·7'W	FM	109
Moss Fm	Ches	SJ7274	53°16·0'	2°24·8'W	FM	118
Moss Fm	Ches	SJ7379	53°18·7'	2°23·9'W	FM	118
Moss Fm	Ches	SJ7755	53°5·7'	2°20·2'W	FM	118
Moss Fm	Ches	SJ7875	53°16·5'	2°19·4'W	FM	118
Moss Fm	Ches	SJ7974	53°16·0'	2°18·5'W	FM	118
Moss Fm	Ches	SJ8064	53°10·6'	2°17·5'W	FM	118
Moss Fm	Lancs	SD3514	53°37·4'	2°58·6'W	FM	108
Moss Fm	Lancs	SD4501	53°30·4'	2°49·3'W	FM	108
Moss Fm	Lancs	SD7854	53°59·1'	2°19·7'W	FM	103
Moss Fm	Lincs	SE8601	53°30·2'	0°41·8'W	FM	112
Moss Fm	Salf	SJ7196	53°27·8'	2°25·8'W	FM	109
Moss Fm	Sefton	SD3002	53°30·8'	3°2·9'W	FM	108
Moss Fm	Shrops	SJ4935	52°54·8'	2°45·1'W	FM	126
Moss Fm	Wrekin	SJ6022	52°47·9'	2°35·2'W	FM	127
Mossfoot	D & G	NY2172	55°2·4'	3°13·7'W	X	85
Moss Force	Cumbr	NY1917	54°32·8'	3°14·7'W	W	89,90
Mossford	Aberd	NJ5750	57°32·5'	2°42·6'W	X	29
Mossgate	Staffs	SJ9437	52°56·1'	2°5·0'W	T	127
Mossgavel	S Ayr	NX1085	55°7·6'	4°58·4'W	X	76
Mossgerrie	Aberd	NJ9064	57°40·2'	2°9·6'W	X	30
Mossgiel	E Ayr	NS4828	55°31·6'	4°24·0'W	X	70
Mossgirl	Aberd	NK0462	57°39·1'	1°55·5'W	X	30
Mossgrain Burn	D & G	NT1109	55°22·3'	3°23·8'W	W	78
Mossgrove	Cumbr	NY5169	55°1·0'	2°45·6'W	X	86
Mossgrove	D & G	NY0879	55°6·1'	3°26·1'W	X	85
Moss Hagg	N Yks	SE5633	53°47·7'	1°8·6'W	F	105
Moss Hall	Ches	SJ6544	52°59·8'	2°30·9'W	A	118
Mosshall	Highld	NH8554	57°34·0'	3°54·9'W	X	27
Moss Hall	Northum	NU0039	55°38·9'	1°59·6'W	X	75
Moss Hall	Warr	SJ6382	53°20·3'	2°32·9'W	X	109
Mosshall	W Loth	NS9764	55°51·7'	3°38·3'W	X	65
Moss Hall Fm	Bolton	SD6607	53°33·8'	2°30·4'W	FM	109
Moss Hall Fm	Ches	SJ6883	53°20·8'	2°28·4'W	FM	109
Moss Hall Fm	Lancs	SD3529	53°45·4'	2°58·7'W	FM	102
Moss Hall Fm	Lancs	SD4034	53°48·2'	2°54·3'W	FM	102
Mosshall Fm	Traf	SJ7289	53°24·1'	2°24·9'W	FM	109
Moss Hall Spinney	Northnts	SP7174	52°21·8'	0°57·0'W	F	141
Mosshayne	Devon	SX9894	50°44·4'	3°26·4'W	X	192
Mosshead	Aberd	NJ5327	57°20·1'	2°46·4'W	X	37
Mosshead	Aberd	NJ5639	57°26·6'	2°43·5'W	X	29
Mosshead	Aberd	NJ6114	57°13·2'	2°38·3'W	X	37
Mosshead	Aberd	NJ6150	57°32·6'	2°38·6'W	X	29
Mosshead	Aberd	NJ6439	57°26·7'	2°35·5'W	X	29
Mosshead	Aberd	NJ8029	57°21·3'	2°19·5'W	X	38
Mosshead	Aberd	NJ9026	57°19·7'	2°9·5'W	X	38
Mosshead	Aberd	NJ9839	57°26·7'	2°1·5'W	X	30
Moss Head	Cumbr	SD5590	54°18·5'	2°41·1'W	X	97
Mosshead	D & G	NY1780	55°6·7'	3°17·6'W	X	79
Mosshead	E Ayr	NS4233	55°34·2'	4°29·9'W	X	70
Mosshead	E Ayr	NS4826	55°30·5'	4°24·0'W	X	70
Mosshead	Pth & Kin	NN9814	56°18·7'	3°38·5'W	X	58
Mosshead of Keithfield	Aberd	NJ8432	57°22·9'	2°15·5'W	X	29,30
Moss Heyes	Ches	SJ5066	53°11·6'	2°44·5'W	X	117
Moss Hill	Aberd	NJ3117	57°14·6'	3°8·1'W	H	37
Moss Hill	Cumbr	NY5760	54°56·2'	2°39·8'W	X	86
Moss Hill	Heref	SO4357	52°12·7'	2°49·7'W	X	148,149
Moss Hill Fm	N Yks	SE4758	54°1·2'	1°16·5'W	FM	105
Moss Ho	Ches	SJ8355	53°5·8'	2°14·8'W	X	118
Moss Ho	Cumbr	NY4674	55°3·7'	2°50·3'W	X	86
Moss Ho	Cumbr	SD2468	54°6·4'	3°9·3'W	X	96
Moss Ho	Cumbr	SD5177	54°11·4'	2°44·6'W	X	97

Moss Ho	Lancs	SD3745	53°54·1′	2°57·1′W	X	102
Moss Ho	Lancs	SD3936	53°49·2′	2°55·2′W	X	102
Moss Ho	Lancs	SD4341	53°52·0′	2°51·6′W	X	102
Moss Ho	Lancs	SD4922	53°41·8′	2°45·9′W	X	102
Moss Ho	Lancs	SD6270	54°7·7′	2°34·5′W	X	97
Moss Ho	Leeds	SE2339	53°51·0′	1°38·6′W	X	104
Moss Ho	Northum	NY6859	54°55·7′	2°29·5′W	X	86,87
Moss Ho	Staffs	SJ8732	52°53·4′	2°11·2′W	X	127
Moss Ho	Staffs	SJ9452	53°4·2′	2°5·0′W	X	118
Mossholm	D & G	NS8012	55°23·5′	3°53·2′W	X	71,78
Mosshope	D & G	NT0206	55°20·5′	3°32·3′W	X	78
Mosshope Bank	D & G	NT0109	55°22·2′	3°33·3′W	H	78
Mosshope Fell	D & G	NT0007	55°21·1′	3°34·2′W	H	78
Moss Houll	Shetld	HP5201	60°41·6′	1°2·4′W	H	1
Moss Houll	Shetld	HU4587	60°34·1′	1°10·2′W	X	1,2
Moss Houll	Shetld	HU5181	60°30·8′	1°3·8′W	X	1,2,3
Moss House	N Yks	SD7264	54°4·5′	2°25·3′W	X	98
Mosshouse	Orkney	HY4703	58°54·9′	2°54·7′W	X	6,7
Mosshouse	Shetld	HU3251	60°14·8′	1°24·8′W	X	3
Mosshouse	Staffs	SJ8053	53°4·7′	2°17·5′W	X	118
Mosshouse	W Loth	NS8866	55°52·7′	3°47·0′W	X	65
Moss House Fm	Ches	SJ4672	53°14·8′	2°48·1′W	FM	117
Moss House Fm	Ches	SJ7284	53°21·4′	2°24·8′W	FM	109
Moss House Fm	Derby	SK0475	53°16·6′	1°56·0′W	FM	119
Moss House Fm	Lancs	SD3633	53°47·6′	2°57·9′W	FM	102
Moss House Fm	Lancs	SD4533	53°47·7′	2°49·7′W	FM	102
Moss House Fm	Lancs	SD5311	53°35·9′	2°42·2′W	FM	108
Moss House Fm	Salf	SJ6795	53°27·3′	2°29·4′W	FM	109
Moss Houses	Ches	SJ8970	53°13·9′	2°9·5′W	T	118
Moss Houses	Cumbr	SD2283	54°14·5′	3°11·4′W	X	96
Mosshouses	Midlo	NT2456	55°47·7′	3°12·3′W	X	66,73
Mosshouses	Scot Bord	NT5339	55°38·8′	2°44·4′W	T	73
Mosshouses Moor	Scot Bord	NT5340	55°39·3′	2°44·4′W	X	73
Mosshouse Wood	Nth Pt Talb	SS7797	51°39·7′	3°46·3′W	F	170
Mosside	Aberd	NJ6531	57°22·3′	2°34·5′W	X	29
Mosside	Aberd	NJ9222	57°17·6′	2°7·5′W	X	38
Mosside	Angus	NO4947	56°37·0′	2°49·4′W	X	54
Mosside	D & G	NX8265	54°58·2′	3°50·2′W	X	84
Mosside	E Ayr	NS4248	55°42·2′	4°30·4′W	X	64
Mosside	E Ayr	NS6139	55°37·7′	4°12·0′W	X	71
Mosside	N Ayr	NS2749	55°42·5′	4°44·8′W	X	63
Mosside	N Lanak	NS7465	55°52·0′	4°0·4′W	X	64
Mosside	S Ayr	NS2608	55°20·4′	4°44·2′W	X	70,76
Mosside	S Ayr	NS4532	55°33·7′	4°27·0′W	X	70
Mosside Fm	W Loth	NS9767	55°53·4′	3°38·4′W	FM	65
Mosside of Ballinshoe	Angus	NO4352	56°39·6′	2°55·3′W	X	54
Mossie Mire	N Yks	SE2172	54°8·8′	1°40·3′W	X	99
Mossilee	Scot Bord	NT4735	55°36·6′	2°50·0′W	X	73
Mossilee Hill	Scot Bord	NT4635	55°36·6′	2°51·0′W	H	73
Moss Kennels	Northum	NY8069	55°1·2′	2°18·3′W	X	86,87
Moss Knowe	Cumbr	NY5054	54°52·9′	2°46·3′W	X	86
Mossknowe	D & G	NY2869	55°0·9′	3°7·1′W	X	85
Mossknowe	D & G	NY3677	55°5·2′	2°59·7′W	X	85
Moss Knowe	Scot Bord	NT4618	55°27·4′	2°50·8′W	X	79
Moss Laithe	N Yks	SD7855	53°59·7′	2°19·7′W	X	103
Mosslands	D & G	NY0797	55°15·8′	3°27·4′W	X	78
Moss Lane	Ches	SJ9071	53°14·4′	2°8·6′W	T	118
Mosslane	Staffs	SJ9536	52°55·5′	2°4·1′W	X	127
Mosslane Fm	Ches	SJ7073	53°15·4′	2°26·6′W	FM	118
Moss Law	E Loth	NT6065	55°52·8′	2°37·9′W	X	67
Moss Law	S Lanak	NT0527	55°31·9′	3°29·9′W	H	72
Moss Leask Croft	Aberd	NK0333	57°23·5′	1°56·5′W	X	30
Mosslee Fm	Ches	SJ9471	53°14·4′	2°5·0′W	FM	118
Mosslee Hall	Staffs	SK0050	53°3·1′	1°59·6′W	X	119
Mossley	Ches	SJ8761	53°9·0′	2°11·3′W	T	118
Mossley	Tames	SD9701	53°30·6′	2°2·3′W	T	109
Mossley Brow	Tames	SD9702	53°31·1′	2°2·3′W	T	109
Mossley Hall	Ches	SJ8861	53°9·0′	2°10·4′W	X	118
Mossley Hall	Wigan	SJ6299	53°29·4′	2°34·0′W	X	109
Mossley Hill	Liv	SJ3887	53°22·8′	2°55·5′W	T	108
Moss Maud	Aberd	NO6299	57°5·1′	2°37·2′W	X	37,45
Moss Mire	Durham	NZ0221	54°35·3′	1°57·7′W	X	92
Moss Moor	Cald	SD9914	53°37·6′	2°0·5′W	X	109
Moss Moor	Cald	SE0014	53°37·6′	1°59·6′W	X	110
Moss Moor	Durham	NY8340	54°45·5′	2°15·4′W	X	86,87
Moss Morran	Fife	NT1790	56°6·0′	3°19·6′W	X	58
Mossmulloch	S Lanak	NS6341	55°38·9′	4°10·2′W	X	71
Mossneuk	Stir	NS8786	56°3·5′	3°48·4′W	X	65
Mossneuk Fm	Aberd	NJ9433	57°23·5′	2°5·5′W	FM	30
Mossneuk Fm	E Renf	NS4558	55°47·7′	4°27·9′W	FM	64
Moss Nook	Cumbr	NY5054	54°52·9′	2°46·3′W	X	86
Moss Nook	Man	SJ8385	53°21·9′	2°14·9′W	T	109
Moss Nook	St Hel	SJ5394	53°26·7′	2°42·0′W	T	108
Moss of Achnacree	Arg & Bt	NM9135	56°27·9′	5°23·1′W	X	49
Moss of Air	Aberd	NJ7706	57°8·9′	2°22·4′W	X	38
Moss of Auchleuchries	Aberd	NK0037	57°25·7′	1°59·5′W	X	30
Moss of Auquharney	Aberd	NK0239	57°26·7′	1°57·5′W	F	30
Moss of Badarclay	Highld	ND2452	58°27·2′	3°17·7′W	X	11,12
Moss of Barmuckity	Moray	NJ2461	57°38·2′	3°15·9′W	T	28
Moss of Bednawinny	Moray	NJ1147	57°30·5′	3°28·7′W	X	28
Moss of Belnagoak	Aberd	NJ8742	57°28·3′	2°12·5′W	X	30
Moss of Birnie	Moray	NJ2051	57°32·8′	3°19·7′W	X	28
Moss of Blackhillock	Aberd	NJ8242	57°28·3′	2°17·5′W	X	29,30
Moss of Catagreen	Orkney	HY4031	59°10·0′	3°2·5′W	X	5,6
Moss of Cree	D & G	NX4360	54°54·9′	4°26·5′W	X	83
Moss of Crombie	Aberd	NJ5752	57°33·6′	2°42·7′W	X	29
Moss of Cruden	Aberd	NK0340	57°27·3′	1°56·5′W	X	30
Moss of Delnahaugh	Moray	NJ1351	57°32·7′	3°26·7′W	X	28
Moss of Dunnet	Highld	ND2073	58°38·5′	3°22·2′W	X	7,12
Moss of Essie	Aberd	NJ4327	57°20·1′	2°56·4′W	X	37
Moss of Faebuie	Moray	NJ0447	57°30·4′	3°35·7′W	X	27
Moss of Fishrie	Aberd	NJ8259	57°37·5′	2°17·6′W	X	29,30
Moss of Forse	Highld	ND2136	58°18·6′	3°20·4′W	X	11
Moss of Geise	Highld	ND0864	58°33·5′	3°34·4′W	X	11,12
Moss of Glanny	Angus	NO2563	56°45·4′	3°13·1′W	X	44
Moss of Greenland	Highld	ND2465	58°34·2′	3°17·9′W	X	11,12
Moss of Killimster	Highld	ND2956	58°29·5′	3°12·6′W	X	11,12
Moss of Kinmundy	Aberd	NK0543	57°28·9′	1°54·5′W	X	30
Moss of Kirk	Highld	ND2959	58°31·1′	3°12·7′W	X	11,12
Moss of Longhillock	Moray	NJ1751	57°32·8′	3°22·7′W	X	28
Moss of Loomachun	Orkney	HY3931	59°9·9′	3°3·5′W	X	6
Moss of Meft	Moray	NJ2663	57°39·3′	3°13·9′W	X	28
Moss of Quintfall	Highld	ND3162	58°32·7′	3°10·6′W	X	11,12
Moss of Redhills	Aberd	NJ6835	57°24·5′	2°31·5′W	X	29
Moss of Reid Plantn	Aberd	NJ5760	57°37·9′	2°42·7′W	F	29
Moss of Rothes	Moray	NJ2351	57°32·8′	3°16·7′W	X	28
Moss of Savock	Aberd	NK0542	57°28·4′	1°54·5′W	X	30
Moss of Sheepal	Orkney	HY4229	59°8·9′	3°0·3′W	X	5,6
Moss of Swanford	Aberd	NJ8244	57°29·4′	2°17·6′W	X	29,30
Moss of Tain	Highld	ND2365	58°34·2′	3°19·0′W	X	11,12
Moss of the Whitestanes	Orkney	ND2199	58°52·5′	3°21·7′W	X	6,7
Moss of Toftingall	Highld	ND1852	58°27·2′	3°23·8′W	X	11,12
Moss of Wester	Highld	ND3158	58°30·5′	3°10·6′W	X	11,12
Moss of Whilk	Highld	ND2940	58°20·8′	3°12·3′W	X	11,12
Moss of Windyhill	Aberd	NJ8040	57°27·2′	2°19·5′W	X	29,30
Mosspark	Clackm	NO0100	56°11·2′	3°35·3′W	X	58
Mosspark	C of Glas	NS5463	55°50·5′	4°19·5′W	T	64
Moss Park	D & G	NX4143	54°45·7′	4°27·8′W	X	83
Mosspaul Burn	D & G	NY3997	55°16·1′	2°57·2′W	W	79
Mosspaul Hotel	Scot Bord	NY4099	55°17·1′	2°56·3′W	X	79
Mosspeeble	D & G	NY3893	55°13·9′	2°58·1′W	X	79
Mosspeeble Burn	D & G	NY3993	55°13·9′	2°57·1′W	W	79
Moss Peteral	Northum	NY6768	55°0·6′	2°30·5′W	X	86,87
Moss Pit	Staffs	SJ9220	52°46·9′	2°6·7′W	T	127
Moss Plantn	D & G	NY0692	55°13·1′	3°28·2′W	F	78
Mossplatt	S Lanak	NS9151	55°44·7′	3°43·7′W	X	65,72
Mossquoy	Orkney	HY5505	58°56·1′	2°46·4′W	X	6
Moss Rake	Derby	SK1480	53°19·2′	1°47·0′W	X	110
Moss Rigg Wood	Cumbr	NY3102	54°24·8′	3°3·4′W	F	90
Moss Rise Fm	Staffs	SK0327	52°50·7′	1°56·9′W	FM	128
Moss Road Plantn	Scot Bord	NT7047	55°43·2′	2°28·2′W	F	74
Moss Roddock Loch	D & G	NX6381	55°6·5′	4°8·4′W	W	77
Mosssfield	Highld	NH6770	57°42·3′	4°13·5′W	X	21
Moss's Fm	Essex	TL6337	52°0·7′	0°22·9′E	FM	154
Moss-side	Aberd	NJ5806	57°8·8′	2°41·2′W	X	37
Moss-side	Aberd	NJ6500	57°5·6′	2°34·2′W	X	38
Moss-side	Aberd	NJ6813	57°12·7′	2°31·3′W	X	38
Moss-side	Aberd	NJ7117	57°14·8′	2°28·4′W	X	38
Moss Side	Aberd	NJ7161	57°38·5′	2°28·7′W	X	29
Moss-side	Aberd	NJ8149	57°32·1′	2°18·6′W	X	29,30
Moss-side	Aberd	NJ8332	57°22·9′	2°16·5′W	X	29,30
Moss-side	Aberd	NJ8745	57°30·0′	2°12·6′W	X	30
Moss-side	Aberd	NJ9115	57°13·8′	2°8·5′W	X	38
Moss-side	Aberd	NJ9164	57°40·2′	2°8·6′W	X	30
Moss-side	Aberd	NJ9465	57°40·7′	2°5·6′W	X	30
Moss-side	Aberd	NJ9557	57°36·4′	2°4·6′W	X	30
Moss-side	Aberd	NJ9633	57°23·5′	2°3·5′W	X	30
Moss-side	Aberd	NJ9841	57°27·8′	2°1·5′W	X	30
Moss-side	Aberd	NK0556	57°35·9′	1°54·5′W	X	30
Moss-side	Aberd	NO6991	57°0·8′	2°30·2′W	X	38,45
Moss-side	Aberd	NO8098	57°4·6′	2°19·3′W	X	38,45
Moss-side	Angus	NO5242	56°34·3′	2°46·4′W	X	54
Moss-side	C of Aber	NO9399	57°5·2′	2°6·5′W	X	38,45
Moss Side	Cumbr	NY0602	54°24·5′	3°26·5′W	X	89
Moss Side	Cumbr	NY1952	54°51·6′	3°15·3′W	T	85
Moss Side	Cumbr	NY3470	55°1·5′	3°1·5′W	X	85
Moss Side	Cumbr	NY4772	55°2·6′	2°49·3′W	X	86
Moss Side	Cumbr	SD2468	54°6·4′	3°9·3′W	X	96
Moss Side	Cumbr	SD4490	54°18·4′	2°51·2′W	X	97
Moss Side	Cumbr	SD4895	54°21·1′	2°47·6′W	X	97
Moss-side	D & G	NX9380	55°6·4′	3°40·2′W	X	78
Moss-side	D & G	NX9472	55°2·1′	3°39·1′W	X	84
Moss-side	D & G	NY1365	54°58·6′	3°21·1′W	X	85
Moss-side	Highld	NH8554	57°34·0′	3°54·9′W	X	27
Moss-side	Highld	NH8555	57°34·5′	3°54·9′W	T	27
Moss Side	Know	SJ4497	53°28·2′	2°50·2′W	T	108
Moss Side	Lancs	SD3830	53°46·0′	2°56·0′W	T	102
Moss Side	Lancs	SD5122	53°41·8′	2°44·1′W	T	102
Moss Side	Man	SJ8395	53°27·3′	2°14·9′W	T	109
Moss-side	Moray	NJ2863	57°39·3′	3°11·9′W	X	28
Moss-side	Moray	NJ5062	57°39·0′	2°49·8′W	X	29
Moss-side	Moray	NJ5550	57°32·5′	2°44·6′W	T	29
Moss-side	Pth & Kin	NO0224	56°24·1′	3°34·8′W	X	52,53,58
Moss Side	Sefton	SD3903	53°31·5′	2°54·8′W	T	108
Moss-side	S Lanak	NS8651	55°44·6′	3°48·5′W	X	65,72
Moss Side	Warr	SJ5685	53°21·8′	2°39·3′W	X	108
Moss Side	Wigan	SJ6998	53°28·9′	2°27·6′W	X	109
Moss Side Fm	Cumbr	SD2289	54°17·7′	3°11·5′W	FM	96
Moss Side Fm	Cumbr	SD4983	54°14·7′	2°46·5′W	FM	97
Moss Side Fm	Lancs	SD4119	53°40·1′	2°53·2′W	FM	108
Moss Side Fm	Lancs	SD4361	54°2·8′	2°51·8′W	FM	97
Moss Side Fm	Lancs	SD4418	53°39·6′	2°50·4′W	FM	108
Moss Side Fm	N Yks	SD8055	53°59·7′	2°17·9′W	FM	103
Moss Side Fm	Warr	SJ6693	53°26·2′	2°30·3′W	FM	109
Moss-side of Boquhapple	Stir	NS6598	56°9·6′	4°10·0′W	X	57
Moss-side of Coullie	Aberd	NJ6916	57°14·3′	2°30·4′W	X	38
Moss-side of Esslie	Aberd	NO6470	56°49·5′	2°34·9′W	X	45
Moss-side of Gight	Aberd	NJ8139	57°26·7′	2°18·5′W	X	29,30
Moss-side of Kirkbuddo	Angus	NO5042	56°34·3′	2°48·4′W	X	54
Moss-side of Monellie	Aberd	NJ6039	57°26·6′	2°39·5′W	T	29
Moss-side of Rathen	Aberd	NK0263	57°39·7′	1°57·5′W	X	30
Moss Side Stables	Lancs	SD4549	53°56·3′	2°49·9′W	X	102
Moss Sike	Durham	NY8337	54°43·9′	2°15·4′W	W	91,92
Moss, The	Ches	SJ4946	53°0·8′	2°45·2′W	X	117
Moss, The	Ches	SJ5064	53°10·5′	2°44·5′W	X	117
Moss, The	Ches	SJ8277	53°17·6′	2°15·8′W	X	118
Moss, The	Derby	SK4180	53°19·2′	1°22·7′W	W	111,120
Moss, The	Highld	NN2747	56°35·2′	4°48·6′W	X	50
Moss, The	N Yks	SE2359	54°1·8′	1°38·5′W	X	104
Moss, The	Sheff	SK3082	53°20·3′	1°32·6′W	X	110,111
Moss, The	Shrops	SJ5642	52°58·7′	2°38·9′W	X	117
Mossthorns	Cumbr	NY4730	54°40·0′	2°48·9′W	X	90
Mossthwaite	Lancs	SD6750	53°56·9′	2°29·8′W	X	103
Mosstodloch	Moray	NJ3360	57°37·8′	3°6·9′W	T	28
Mosston	Angus	NO5444	56°35·4′	2°44·5′W	X	54
Mosstonmuir	Angus	NO5753	56°40·3′	2°41·7′W	X	54
Moss Top	N Yks	SD9076	54°11·0′	2°8·8′W	X	98
Mosstower	Scot Bord	NT7126	55°31·9′	2°27·1′W	X	74
Mosstowie	Moray	NJ1560	57°37·6′	3°24·9′W	X	28
Mosstown	Aberd	NJ4204	57°7·7′	2°57·0′W	X	37
Mosstown	Aberd	NJ4404	57°7·7′	2°55·0′W	X	37
Mosstown	Aberd	NJ5328	57°20·7′	2°46·4′W	X	29
Mosstown	Aberd	NJ5542	57°28·2′	2°44·6′W	X	29
Mosstown	Aberd	NJ5957	57°36·3′	2°40·7′W	X	29
Mosstown	Aberd	NK0335	57°24·6′	1°56·5′W	X	30
Mosstown	Aberd	NK0360	57°38·1′	1°56·5′W	X	30
Mosstown	Aberd	NK0362	57°39·1′	1°56·5′W	X	30
Mosstown	Aberd	NK0559	57°37·5′	1°54·5′W	X	30
Moss Villa	Shrops	SJ5440	52°57·6′	2°40·7′W	X	117
Moss Well	Northum	NY8657	54°54·7′	2°12·7′W	X	87
Moss Wood	Fife	NT3097	56°9·9′	3°7·2′W	F	59
Moss Wood	Northum	NT9939	55°38·9′	2°0·5′W	F	75
Mosswood	Northum	NZ0650	54°50·9′	1°54·0′W	X	87
Moss Wood	N Yks	SE1369	54°7·2′	1°47·6′W	F	99
Moss Wood	Sefton	SD3202	53°30·9′	3°1·1′W	F	108
Mosswood Grange	N Lincs	SE7809	53°34·5′	0°48·9′W	X	112
Mosswood Hall	Warr	SJ6282	53°20·3′	2°33·8′W	X	109
Mosswood Ho	N Yks	SE5670	54°7·6′	1°8·2′W	X	100
Mossyard	D & G	NX5451	54°50·2′	4°16·0′W	X	83
Mossyard Bay	D & G	NX5551	54°50·2′	4°15·0′W	W	83
Mossyards	Moray	NJ1566	57°40·8′	3°25·1′W	X	28
Mossy Beck	Cumbr	NY4821	54°35·1′	2°47·9′W	W	90
Mossy Bottom	Cumbr	SD7783	54°14·8′	2°20·8′W	F	98
Mossy Burn	E Loth	NT6569	55°55·0′	2°33·2′W	W	67
Mossy Burn	S Lanak	NS7623	55°29·4′	3°57·3′W	W	71
Mossy Dod	S Lanak	NS9821	55°28·6′	3°36·4′W	X	72
Mossy Hill	Shetld	HU4260	60°19·6′	1°13·9′W	H	2,3
Mossy Hill	Shetld	HU4340	60°8·8′	1°13·0′W	H	4
Mossy Hill	Shetld	HU4783	60°31·9′	1°8·1′W	X	1,2,3
Mossy Hill	Shetld	HU5137	60°7·1′	1°4·4′W	H	4
Mossy Hill	Shetld	HU5181	60°30·8′	1°3·8′W	X	1,2,3
Mossy Law	Northum	NT9511	55°23·8′	2°4·3′W	X	81
Mossy Law	Scot Bord	NT8315	55°26·0′	2°15·7′W	X	80
Mossy Lea	Lancs	SD5312	53°36·4′	2°42·2′W	T	108
Mossy Lea Fm	Derby	SK0594	53°26·8′	1°55·1′W	FM	110
Mossymere Wood	Norf	TG1331	52°50·3′	1°10·2′E	F	133
Mossy Moor Reservoir	N Yks	SE0264	54°4·6′	1°57·7′W	W	98
Mossy Rig	Scot Bord	NT3843	55°40·8′	2°58·7′W	H	73
Mossywood	N Lanak	NS7570	55°54·7′	3°59·5′W	X	64
Mosterley	Shrops	SJ5602	52°37·1′	2°38·6′W	X	126
Mosterton	Dorset	ST4505	50°50·7′	2°46·5′W	T	193
Mosterton Down	Dorset	ST4406	50°51·3′	2°47·4′W	X	193
Moston	Ches	SJ4070	53°13·7′	2°53·5′W	T	117
Moston	Man	SD8701	53°30·6′	2°11·4′W	T	109
Moston	Shrops	SJ5626	52°50·0′	2°38·8′W	T	126
Moston Brook	Oldham	SD8801	53°30·6′	2°10·4′W	W	109
Moston Green	Ches	SJ7261	53°9·0′	2°24·7′W	T	118
Moston Manor	Ches	SJ7261	53°9·0′	2°24·7′W	X	118
Moston Park	Shrops	SJ5527	52°50·6′	2°39·7′W	X	126
Mostyn	Conwy	SH9467	53°11·6′	3°34·8′W	X	116
Mostyn	Flint	SJ1580	53°18·9′	3°16·1′W	T	116
Mostyn Bank	Flint	SJ1482	53°19·9′	3°17·1′W	X	116
Mostyn Quay	Flint	SJ1581	53°19·4′	3°16·2′W	X	116
Motcombe	Dorset	ST8425	51°1·7′	2°13·3′W	T	183
Mote Fm	Glos	SO7221	51°53·4′	2°24·0′W	FM	162
Mote Hill	D & G	NS7901	55°17·5′	3°53·9′W	X	78
Mote Hill	N Yks	SE5539	53°50·9′	1°9·4′W	A	105
Mote Ho	Kent	TQ7855	51°16·2′	0°33·5′E	X	178,188
Mote Knowe	S Ayr	NS2900	55°16·1′	4°41·1′W	A	76
Mote of Mark	D & G	NX8453	54°51·8′	3°48·0′W	X	84
Mote of Mark (Fort)	D & G	NX8453	54°51·8′	3°48·0′W	A	84
Mote of Urr	D & G	NX8164	54°57·6′	3°51·1′W	A	84
Mote Park	Kent	TQ7754	51°15·7′	0°32·6′E	X	188
Mote Slap	D & G	NX0950	54°48·8′	4°57·9′W	X	82
Mote Toll	E Ayr	NS4920	55°27·3′	4°22·8′W	X	70
Mothecombe	Devon	SX6047	50°18·6′	3°57·6′W	T	202
Mother Anthony's Well	Wilts	ST9964	51°22·7′	2°0·5′W	W	173
Motherby	Cumbr	NY4228	54°38·9′	2°53·5′W	T	90
Mother Cap	Sheff	SK2580	53°19·2′	1°37·1′W	X	110
Mother Drain	Notts	SK7396	53°27·6′	0°53·6′W	W	112
Mother Drain	Notts	SK8184	53°21·0′	0°46·6′W	W	121
Mother Ivey's or Polventon Bay	Corn	SW8676	50°32·9′	5°0·9′W	W	200
Mother Shipton's Cave	N Yks	SE3456	54°0·2′	1°28·5′W	X	104
Mothersome Village	Leeds	SE4042	53°52·6′	1°23·1′W	A	105
Motherwell	N Lanak	NS7556	55°47·1′	3°59·2′W	T	64
Mother Wood	Lincs	TF4378	53°17·0′	0°9·1′E	F	122
Motney Hill	Medway	TQ8268	51°23·1′	0°37·3′E	X	178
Motor Sports Centre	Carm	SN4003	51°42·4′	4°18·6′W	X	159
Motray Water	Fife	NO3720	56°22·3′	3°0·8′W	W	54,59
Motray Water	Fife	NO4223	56°24·0′	2°55·9′W	W	54,59
Motspur Park	King	TQ2167	51°23·6′	0°15·3′W	T	176
Mottingham	Lew	TQ4172	51°26·0′	0°2·1′E	T	177
Mottisfont	Hants	SU3226	51°2·2′	1°32·2′W	T	185
Mottisfont Abbey (Priory)	Hants	SU3227	51°2·7′	1°32·2′W	A	185
Mottistone	I of W	SZ4083	50°38·9′	1°25·7′W	T	196
Mottram Cross	Ches	SJ8878	53°18·2′	2°10·4′W	X	118
Mottram Hall (Hotel)	Ches	SJ8879	53°18·7′	2°10·4′W	X	118
Mottram in Longdendale	Tames	SJ9995	53°27·3′	2°0·5′W	T	109
Mottram Old Hall	Ches	SJ8879	53°18·7′	2°10·4′W	A	118
Mottram Old Hall	Tames	SJ9996	53°27·9′	2°0·5′W	X	109
Mottram Rise	Tames	SJ9897	53°28·4′	2°1·4′W	T	109
Mottram St Andrew	Ches	SJ8778	53°18·2′	2°11·3′W	T	118
Mott's Fm	Essex	TL9504	51°42·3′	0°49·7′E	FM	168
Mott's Fm	E Susx	TQ5334	51°5·3′	0°11·5′E	FM	188
Mott's Green	Essex	TL5116	51°49·6′	0°11·9′E	T	167
Mott's Green	Essex	TL6112	51°47·2′	0°20·5′E	X	167
Mott's Hall	Essex	TL5425	51°54·4′	0°14·7′E	X	167
Mott's Mill	E Susx	TQ5135	51°5·9′	0°9·8′E	T	188
Mott's Road	Shrops	SO4295	52°33·2′	2°50·9′W	X	137
Mottynsden	E Susx	TQ6625	51°0·2′	0°22·4′E	X	188,199
Motygido	Cered	SN4057	52°11·5′	4°20·1′W	X	146
Moudy Mea	Cumbr	NY8711	54°29·9′	2°11·6′W	H	91,92
Moughton	N Yks	SD7971	54°8·3′	2°18·9′W	X	98
Moughton Nab	N Yks	SD7969	54°7·2′	2°18·9′W	X	98
Moughton Scars	N Yks	SD7872	54°8·8′	2°19·8′W	X	98
Moulden's Wood	Oxon	SP3407	51°45·9′	1°30·0′W	F	164
Mouldridge Grange	Derby	SK2059	53°7·9′	1°41·7′W	X	119
Mouldron	N Yks	NZ1603	54°25·6′	1°44·8′W	X	92
Mouldshaugh	Northum	NU1901	55°18·4′	1°41·6′W	X	81

Mouldsworth	Ches	SJ5171	53°14·3′	2°43·6′W	T	117
Mouldy Hill	Shetld	HU3246	60°12·1′	1°24·9′W	X	4
Mouldyhills	D & G	NY3775	55°4·2′	2°58·8′W	X	85
Moulie Loch	Shetld	HU3040	60°8·9′	1°27·1′W	W	4
Moulin	Pth & Kin	NN9459	56°42·9′	3°43·5′W	T	52,53
Moulinard	Highld	NH7779	57°47·3′	4°3·7′W	X	21
Moulinearn	Aberd	NJ6305	57°8·3′	2°36·2′W	X	37
Moulinearn	Pth & Kin	NN9654	56°40·2′	3°41·4′W	X	52,53
Moul of Eswick	Shetld	HU4953	60°15·8′	1°6·4′W	X	3
Mouls	I Scilly	SV9514	49°57·1′	6°14·8′W	X	203
Moulsecomb	Bri & Hov	TQ3306	50°50·5′	0°6·3′W	T	198
Moulsford	Oxon	SU5883	51°32·8′	1°9·4′W	T	174
Moulsford Bottom	Oxon	SU5783	51°32·8′	1°10·3′W	X	174
Moulsford Downs	Oxon	SU5782	51°32·3′	1°10·3′W	X	174
Moulsham	Essex	TL7005	51°43·3′	0°28·1′E	T	167
Moulsham Hall	Essex	TL7218	51°50·3′	0°30·2′E	X	167
Moulsham's Fm	Essex	TL9615	51°48·2′	0°51·0′E	FM	168
Moulshay Fm	Hants	SU6755	51°17·6′	1°2·0′W	FM	175,185,186
Moulsoe	Mil Key	SP9041	52°3·8′	0°40·8′W	T	152
Moulsoe Old Wood	Mil Key	SP9242	52°4·4′	0°39·1′W	F	152
Mouls, The	Corn	SW9381	50°35·8′	4°55·1′W	X	200
Moultavie	Highld	NH6371	57°42·7′	4°17·5′W	X	21
Moulter Hill	Notts	SK5226	52°50·0′	1°13·3′W	X	129
Moult Hill	Leic	SK4617	52°45·2′	1°18·7′W	X	129
Moulton	Ches	SJ6569	53°13·3′	2°31·0′W	T	118
Moulton	Lincs	TF3024	52°48·1′	0°3·9′W	T	131
Moulton	Northnts	SP7866	52°17·4′	0°51·0′W	T	152
Moulton	N Yks	NZ2303	54°25·6′	1°38·3′W	T	93
Moulton	Suff	TL6964	52°15·1′	0°29·0′E	T	154
Moulton	V of Glam	ST0770	51°25·5′	3°19·9′W	T	170
Moulton Chantry Ho	Lincs	TF3949	53°1·4′	0°4·8′E	X	131
Moulton Chapel	Lincs	TF2918	52°44·9′	0°4·9′W	T	131
Moulton Common	Lincs	TF3228	52°50·2′	0°2·0′W	X	131
Moulton East Fen	Lincs	TF3014	52°42·7′	0°4·1′W	X	131
Moulton Eaugate	Lincs	TF3016	52°43·8′	0°4·1′W	T	131
Moulton Fen	Lincs	TF2917	52°44·3′	0°4·9′W	X	131
Moulton Grange	Northnts	SP7668	52°18·5′	0°52·7′W	X	152
Moulton Grange Fm	Northnts	SP7769	52°19·1′	0°51·8′W	FM	152
Moulton Hall	N Yks	NZ2303	54°25·6′	1°38·3′W	A	93
Moulton Hills	Cambs	TL3257	52°12·0′	0°3·7′W	A	153
Moulton Lodge	Northnts	SP7767	52°18·0′	0°51·8′W	X	152
Moulton Marsh	Lincs	TF3131	52°51·9′	0°2·8′W	X	131
Moulton Mere Drain	Lincs	TF2924	52°48·1′	0°4·8′W	W	131
Moulton Park	Northnts	SP7764	52°16·4′	0°51·9′W	T	152
Moulton River	Lincs	TF3126	52°49·2′	0°3·0′W	W	131
Moulton Seas End	Lincs	TF3227	52°49·7′	0°2·0′W	T	131
Moulton St Mary	Norf	TG3907	52°36·7′	1°32·2′E	T	134
Moulton West Fen	Lincs	TF2814	52°42·7′	0°5·9′W	X	131
Moulzie	Angus	NO2877	56°53·0′	3°10·4′W	T	44
Moulzie Burn	Angus	NO2878	56°53·5′	3°10·5′W	W	44
Mound Rock	Highld	NH7798	57°57·5′	4°4·3′W	X	21
Moundsley Fm	Worcs	SP0677	52°23·7′	1°54·3′W	FM	139
Moundsley Hall	Worcs	SP0677	52°23·7′	1°54·3′W	X	139
Moundsmere Manor	Hants	SU6243	51°11·2′	1°6·4′W	X	185
Mound, The	Highld	NH7798	57°57·0′	4°4·2′W	X	21
Mound, The	Somer	SS8843	51°10·8′	3°35·8′W	X	181
Mou Ness	Orkney	HY3917	59°2·4′	3°3·3′W	X	6
Mounie Castle	Aberd	NJ7628	57°20·8′	2°23·5′W	X	38
Mounseybank	Cumbr	NY5035	54°42·7′	2°46·1′W	X	90
Mounsey Castle	Somer	SS8829	51°3·2′	3°35·5′W	X	181
Mounsey Castle (Fort)	Somer	SS8829	51°3·2′	3°35·5′W	A	181
Mounsey Hill	Somer	SS8831	51°4·3′	3°35·5′W	H	181
Mounstephen Ho	Devon	ST0412	50°54·2′	3°21·5′W	X	181
Mount	Carm	SN6127	51°55·7′	4°0·9′W	X	146
Mount	Ches	SJ9277	53°17·6′	2°6·8′W	X	118
Mount	Corn	SW7856	50°22·0′	5°6·9′W	T	200
Mount	Corn	SX1467	50°28·6′	4°36·9′W	T	200
Mount	Highld	NH9745	57°29·3′	3°42·6′W	X	27
Mount	Kent	TR1643	51°8·9′	1°5·7′E	X	179,189
Mount	Kirk	SE0918	53°39·7′	1°51·4′W	T	110
Mount	Powys	SO2194	52°32·5′	3°9·5′W	X	137
Mount	S Lanak	NS6140	55°38·3′	4°12·1′W	X	71
Mount	Stir	NS5886	56°3·0′	4°16·4′W	X	57
Mountain	Brad	SE0930	53°46·2′	1°51·4′W	T	104
Mountain	I of Angl	SH2382	53°18·5′	4°39·9′W	T	114
Mountain	Northum	NU0513	55°24·9′	1°54·8′W	X	81
Mountain Air	Blae Gw	SO1509	51°46·6′	3°13·5′W	T	161
Mountain Ash / Aberpennar	Rho Cyn Taf	ST0499	51°41·1′	3°22·9′W	T	170
Mountain Ash Fm	Derby	SK1957	53°6·8′	1°42·6′W	FM	119
Mountainblaw Fm	S Lanak	NS9756	55°47·4′	3°38·1′W	FM	65,72
Mountainblow	D & G	NT0810	55°22·8′	3°26·7′W	X	78
Mountain Bower	Wilts	ST8075	51°28·7′	2°16·9′W	T	173
Mountain Box	I of M	SC4189	54°16·6′	4°26·1′W	X	95
Mountain Cott	Pemb	SM9123	51°52·2′	5°1·8′W	X	157,158
Mountain Cross	Scot Bord	NT1446	55°42·2′	3°21·7′W	T	72
Mountain Cross Steading	Scot Bord	NT1447	55°42·8′	3°21·7′W	X	72
Mountain Fm	Kent	TQ7644	51°10·3′	0°31·5′E	FM	188
Mountain Fm	Kent	TR0032	51°3·4′	0°51·6′E	FM	189
Mountain Fm	Lancs	SD8342	53°52·7′	2°15·1′W	FM	103
Mountain Fm	Shrops	SJ3109	52°40·7′	3°0·8′W	FM	126
Mountain Fm	Warr	SJ6286	53°22·4′	2°33·9′W	FM	109
Mountain Hall	Carm	SN3836	52°0·2′	4°21·2′W	X	145
Mountain Lodge	V of Glam	ST0377	51°29·3′	3°23·4′W	X	170
Mountain Lodge	Wrex	SJ2547	53°1·1′	3°6·7′W	X	117
Mountain Park	Pemb	SM9027	51°54·4′	5°2·8′W	X	157,158
Mountain Park Fm	Pemb	SN0208	51°44·4′	4°51·7′W	FM	157,158
Mountains	Essex	TL8612	51°46·8′	0°42·2′E	X	168
Mountains Fm	Essex	TL6219	51°51·0′	0°21·5′E	FM	167
Mountain Street	Kent	TR0652	51°14·0′	0°57·4′E	T	179,189
Mountain, The	Corn	SX0484	50°37·6′	4°45·9′W	X	200
Mountain, The	Derby	SK2649	53°2·5′	1°36·3′W	H	119
Mountaintop	D & G	NX7367	54°59·1′	3°58·7′W	X	83,84
Mountain View	Cumbr	NY0532	54°40·7′	3°28·0′W	X	89
Mountain View	Cumbr	SD0899	54°22·9′	3°24·6′W	X	96
Mountain View	Cumbr	SD6197	54°22·3′	2°35·6′W	X	97
Mountain View	Cumbr	SD6998	54°22·8′	2°28·2′W	X	98
Mountain View	Scot Bord	NY5392	55°13·4′	2°43·9′W	X	79
Mountain Water	Pemb	SM9224	51°52·8′	5°0·9′W	W	157,158
Mountain Wood	Nth Pt Talb	SN7200	51°41·3′	3°50·7′W	F	170

Mountain Wood	Surrey	TQ0950	51°14·6′	0°25·9′W	F	187
Mount Airy Fm	E Yorks	SE9331	53°46·3′	0°34·9′W	FM	106
Mount Alban	Scot Bord	NT8563	55°51·8′	2°13·9′W	X	67
Mount Alvernia	Surrey	SU8734	51°6·1′	0°45·1′W	X	186
Mount Alyn	Wrex	SJ3456	53°6·1′	2°58·7′W	X	117
Mount Ambrose	Corn	SW7043	50°14·8′	5°13·2′W	T	203
Mount Annan	D & G	NY1969	55°0·8′	3°15·6′W	X	85
Mount Ararat	Corn	SX4065	50°28·0′	4°14·9′W	X	201
Mount Ararat	Dorset	SU0910	50°53·6′	1°51·9′W	X	195
Mount Ararat	Kent	TR2641	51°7·6′	1°14·2′E	X	179
Mount Ballan	Monm	ST4989	51°36·1′	2°43·8′W	T	162,172
Mount Bank	Shrops	SO2584	52°27·2′	3°5·8′W	X	137
Mount Bark	N Yks	SE1956	54°0·2′	1°42·2′W	X	104
Mount Barnard	Cumbr	SD3678	54°11·9′	2°58·4′W	H	96,97
Mount Barton	Devon	SX8064	50°28·0′	3°41·1′W	X	202
Mount Batten Point	C of Plym	SX4853	50°21·7′	4°7·8′W	X	201
Mount Battock	Angus	NO5484	56°57·0′	2°44·9′W	H	44
Mountbenger	Scot Bord	NT3025	55°31·1′	3°6·1′W	T	73
Mountbenger Burn	Scot Bord	NT3026	55°31·6′	3°6·1′W	W	73
Mountbengerburn	Scot Bord	NT3125	55°31·1′	3°5·1′W	T	73
Mountbengerhope	Scot Bord	NT3027	55°32·2′	3°6·1′W	X	73
Mountbenger Law	Scot Bord	NT3127	55°32·2′	3°5·2′W	H	73
Mount Blair	Pth & Kin	NO1663	56°45·3′	3°22·0′W	H	43
Mount Blair Lodge	Pth & Kin	NO1462	56°44·8′	3°23·9′W	X	43
Mountblairy Home Fm	Aberd	NJ6954	57°34·8′	2°30·6′W	FM	29
Mountblow	W Dunb	NS4771	55°54·7′	4°26·4′W	T	64
Mount Bouie	Angus	NO3070	56°49·2′	3°8·4′W	H	44
Mount Bovers	Essex	TQ8491	51°35·5′	0°39·8′E	T	178
Mountboy	Angus	NO6653	56°40·3′	2°32·8′W	X	54
Mount Bures	Essex	TL9032	51°57·5′	0°46·3′E	T	168
Mount Caburn	E Susx	TQ4408	50°51·4′	0°3·1′E	X	198
Mount Caburn (Fort)	E Susx	TQ4408	50°51·4′	0°3·1′E	A	198
Mount Canisp	Highld	NH7970	57°42·5′	4°1·4′W	X	21
Mount Carmel	Northum	NT9247	55°43·2′	2°7·2′W	X	74,75
Mount Carvey	W Susx	TQ1307	50°51·3′	0°23·3′W	X	198
Mount Charles	Corn	SX0252	50°20·3′	4°46·6′W	T	200,204
Mount Charles	Corn	SX0468	50°29·0′	4°45·4′W	T	200
Mountcharles	S Ayr	NS3218	55°25·9′	4°38·9′W	X	70
Mount Clifton	Cumbr	NY5325	54°37·3′	2°43·3′W	X	90
Mount Close Batch	Somer	ST3536	51°7·4′	2°55·3′W	X	182
Mount Common	Northum	NY6493	55°14·0′	2°33·5′W	H	80
Mountcommon Hill	Scot Bord	NT2812	55°24·1′	3°7·8′W	H	79
Mount Cottage	Pth & Kin	NN9616	56°19·8′	3°40·5′W	X	58
Mountcow	N Lanak	NS8264	55°51·5′	3°52·7′W	X	65
Mount Cowdown	Wilts	SU2854	51°17·3′	1°35·5′W	T	184
Mount Dam	E Dunb	NS6477	55°58·3′	4°10·3′W	W	64
Mount Douglas	Corn	SW5237	50°11·1′	5°28·1′W	X	203
Mount Down	Hants	SU4028	51°3·2′	1°25·4′W	X	185
Mount Eagle	Highld	NH6459	57°36·3′	4°16·1′W	H	26
Mounteagle	Highld	NH8378	57°46·8′	3°57·6′W	X	21
Mount Edgcumbe Country Park	Corn	SX4552	50°21·1′	4°10·4′W	X	201
Mount Een	Angus	NO5281	56°55·3′	2°46·9′W	X	44
Mount Eff	Durham	NZ0716	54°32·6′	1°53·1′W	X	92
Mount End	Essex	TL4801	51°41·5′	0°8·9′E	T	167
Mounteney's Fm	Glos	ST7489	51°36·2′	2°22·1′W	FM	162,172
Mount Ephraim	E Susx	TQ4819	50°57·3′	0°6·8′E	T	198
Mount Ephraim	E Yorks	TA1250	53°56·3′	0°17·2′W	X	107
Mount Ephraim	Kent	TQ7735	51°5·4′	0°32·0′E	X	188
Mount Ephraim	Kent	TR0659	51°17·8′	0°57·7′E	X	179
Mount Ephraim	Norf	TL7791	52°29·5′	0°36·8′E	X	144
Mounters	Dorset	ST7718	50°57·9′	2°19·3′W	T	183
Mount Escob	Ghead	NZ2354	54°53·1′	1°38·1′W	X	88
Mountfair	Scot Bord	NT8648	55°43·8′	2°12·9′W	X	74
Mount Famine	Derby	SK0584	53°21·4′	1°55·1′W	H	110
Mount Fancy Fm	Somer	ST2516	50°56·5′	3°3·7′W	FM	193
Mount Farm	Essex	TL4901	51°41·5′	0°9·7′E	FM	167
Mount Farm	Mil Key	SP8735	52°0·6′	0°43·5′W	FM	152
Mount Ferguson	S Ayr	NS3617	55°25·4′	4°35·1′W	X	70
Mount Ferrant Fm	N Yks	SE8063	54°3·6′	0°46·2′W	FM	100
Mountfield	E Susx	TQ7320	50°57·4′	0°28·2′E	T	199
Mountfield Court	E Susx	TQ7320	50°57·4′	0°28·2′E	X	199
Mountfield Park Fm	E Susx	TQ7121	50°58·0′	0°26·5′E	FM	199
Mount Flatts Fm	N Yks	NZ4306	54°27·1′	1°19·8′W	FM	93
Mount Flirt	Shrops	SO4892	52°31·6′	2°45·6′W	X	137,138
Mount Fm	Carm	SN6442	52°3·8′	3°58·6′W	FM	146
Mount Fm	Ches	SJ4072	53°14·7′	2°53·5′W	FM	117
Mount Fm	Ches	SJ8676	53°17·1′	2°12·2′W	FM	118
Mount Fm	Derby	SK2643	52°59·3′	1°36·4′W	FM	119,128
Mount Fm	E Susx	TQ4715	50°55·2′	0°5·9′E	FM	198
Mount Fm	Flint	SJ2655	53°5·5′	3°5·9′W	FM	117
Mount Fm	Flint	SJ3262	53°9·3′	3°0·6′W	FM	117
Mount Fm	Hants	SU3125	51°1·6′	1°33·1′W	FM	185
Mount Fm	Lincs	TF0453	53°4·1′	0°26·5′W	FM	121
Mount Fm	N Lincs	SE9807	53°33·3′	0°30·8′W	FM	112
Mount Fm	N Yks	SE6140	53°51·4′	1°3·9′W	FM	105
Mount Fm	Oxon	SU5796	51°39·8′	1°10·2′W	FM	164
Mount Fm	Pemb	SM8224	51°52·6′	5°9·6′W	FM	157
Mount Fm	Powys	SJ1804	52°37·9′	3°12·3′W	FM	136
Mount Fm	Shrops	SJ5342	52°58·6′	2°41·6′W	FM	117
Mount Fm	Shrops	SJ6422	52°47·9′	2°31·6′W	FM	127
Mount Fm	Shrops	SJ6839	52°57·1′	2°28·2′W	FM	127
Mount Fm	Suff	TL8550	52°7·3′	0°42·5′E	FM	155
Mount Fm	Suff	TL9252	52°8·2′	0°48·7′E	FM	155
Mount Fm	Win & Maid	SU8683	51°32·6′	0°45·2′W	FM	175
Mount Fm, The	Cumbr	NY4062	54°57·2′	2°55·8′W	FM	85
Mount Fm, The	Powys	SO2970	52°19·6′	3°2·1′W	FM	137,148
Mount Fm, The	Scot Bord	NT1042	55°40·0′	3°25·4′W	FM	72
Mount Folly	Devon	SX6644	50°17·1′	3°52·5′W	X	202
Mountford Fm	Warw	SP1671	52°20·4′	1°45·5′W	FM	139
Mountgerald	Highld	NH5661	57°37·2′	4°24·2′W	T	21
Mount Glass	D & G	NS9900	55°17·3′	3°35·0′W	X	78
Mount Gould	C of Plym	SX4955	50°22·8′	4°7·1′W	T	201
Mount Grace Priory	N Yks	SE4598	54°22·8′	1°18·0′W	A	99
Mount Grace Wood	N Yks	SE4498	54°22·8′	1°18·9′W	F	99
Mounthalie	Highld	ND2567	58°35·3′	3°16·9′W	X	11,12
Mount Hall	Essex	TL6534	51°59·0′	0°24·6′E	X	167
Mount Hall	Essex	TL9631	51°56·8′	0°51·5′E	X	168
Mount Hall	Essex	TQ4999	51°40·4′	0°9·7′E	A	167,177
Mount Hall Fm	Kent	TQ8233	51°4·3′	0°36·3′E	FM	188

Mount Harry	E Susx	TQ3812	50°53·7′	0°1·9′W	H	198
Mount Haul	D & G	NY0298	55°16·2′	3°32·1′W	H	78
Mount Hawke	Corn	SW7147	50°16·9′	5°12·5′W	T	203
Mount Hazel	Gwyn	SH4656	53°5·0′	4°17·6′W	X	115,123
Mountheathie	Aberd	NJ8755	57°35·3′	2°12·6′W	X	30
Mount Hermon	Corn	SW7015	49°59·7′	5°12·2′W	T	203
Mount Hermon	Surrey	TQ0057	51°18·4′	0°33·5′W	T	186
Mountherrick	S Lanak	NS8522	55°29·0′	3°48·8′W	X	71,72
Mountherrick Hill	S Lanak	NS8623	55°29·5′	3°47·8′W	H	71,72
Mount High	Highld	NH6963	57°38·5′	4°11·2′W	T	21,27
Mount Hill	Fife	NO3316	56°20·2′	3°4·6′W	H	59
Mount Hill	Heref	SO3929	51°57·6′	2°52·9′W	X	149,161
Mount Hill	Herts	TL3136	52°0·6′	0°5·1′W	X	153
Mount Hill	S Glos	ST6572	51°27·0′	2°29·8′W	T	172
Mount Hill	W Berks	SU4470	51°25·9′	1°21·6′W	X	174
Mount Hill	Win & Maid	SU8684	51°33·1′	0°45·2′W	X	175
Mounthill Fm	Devon	SY2594	50°44·7′	3°3·4′W	FM	192,193
Mount Ho	E Ayr	NS4037	55°36·3′	4°32·0′W	X	70
Mount Ho	Kent	TQ7959	51°18·3′	0°34·5′E	X	178,188
Mount Ho	N Yks	SE4397	54°22·2′	1°19·9′W	X	99
Mount Ho	N Yks	SE5575	54°10·3′	1°9·0′W	X	100
Mount Ho	Somer	ST1327	51°2·4′	3°14·1′W	X	181,193
Mount Ho	Sund	NZ2857	54°54·7′	1°33·4′W	X	88
Mount Hooley	Northum	NU0541	55°40·0′	1°54·8′W	X	75
Mount Hooley	Northum	NU0811	55°23·8′	1°52·0′W	X	81
Mounthoolie	D & G	NY1481	55°7·2′	3°20·5′W	H	78
Mounthoolie Br	D & G	NX7894	55°13·8′	3°54·7′W	X	78
Mounthooly	Aberd	NJ9266	57°41·3′	2°7·6′W	X	30
Mounthooly	Northum	NT8822	55°29·7′	2°11·0′W	X	74
Mounthooly	Orkney	HY5215	59°1·4′	2°49·7′W	X	6
Mounthooly	Scot Bord	NT6624	55°30·8′	2°31·9′W	X	74
Mounthooly	W Loth	NT0676	55°58·3′	3°29·9′W	X	65
Mounthope	E Ayr	NS6315	55°24·8′	4°9·4′W	X	71
Mount House Fm	Red & Cl	NZ5813	54°30·8′	1°5·8′W	FM	93
Mount Howe	Devon	SX9787	50°40·6′	3°27·1′W	X	192
Mounth Road	Aberd	NO4088	56°59·0′	2°58·8′W	X	44
Mount Huley	Durham	NZ2735	54°42·8′	1°34·4′W	X	93
Mount Huly	Northum	NZ0477	55°5·5′	1°55·8′W	X	87
Mount Huly	Northum	NZ0864	54°58·5′	1°52·1′W	X	88
Mounticombe	Devon	SS7214	50°54·9′	3°48·9′W	X	180
Mount Joe	D & G	NT0008	55°21·6′	3°34·2′W	H	78
Mountjoy	C of Aber	NJ8511	57°11·6′	2°14·4′W	X	38
Mountjoy	Corn	SW8760	50°24·3′	4°59·5′W	T	200
Mountjoy	Cumbr	SD4693	54°20·0′	2°49·4′W	X	97
Mountjoy Fm	Kent	TQ5147	51°12·4′	0°10·1′E	FM	188
Mountjoy Fm	Pemb	SN0121	51°51·4′	4°53·0′W	FM	145,157,158
Mount Karrin	I of M	SC3791	54°17·6′	4°29·9′W	H	95
Mount Kedar	D & G	NY0771	55°1·7′	3°26·9′W	X	85
Mount Keen	Angus	NO4086	56°57·9′	2°58·8′W	H	44
Mount Lane	Devon	SX3595	50°44·1′	4°19·9′W	T	190
Mount Lane Fm	Lincs	TF0945	52°59·7′	0°22·1′W	FM	130
Mount Le Hoe	Kent	TQ8233	51°4·3′	0°36·3′E	X	188
Mount Leven	Stock on T	NZ4412	54°30·3′	1°18·8′W	X	93
Mount Lodge	Corn	SX3869	50°30·1′	4°16·7′W	X	201
Mount Lodge Fm	N Yks	SE4498	54°22·8′	1°18·9′W	FM	99
Mount Lothian	Midlo	NT2756	55°47·8′	3°9·4′W	X	66,73
Mount Maesry	Orkney	HY7843	59°16·6′	2°22·7′W	X	5
Mount Maesry (Chambered Cairn)	Orkney	HY7843	59°16·6′	2°22·7′W	A	5
Mount Main	Scot Bord	NT3848	55°43·5′	2°58·8′W	H	73
Mount Manisty	Ches	SJ3978	53°18·0′	2°54·5′W	X	117
Mountmarle	Midlo	NT2863	55°51·5′	3°8·6′W	X	66
Mount Mascal Fm	Bexley	TQ4972	51°25·9′	0°9·0′E	FM	177
Mount Maskall	Essex	TL7411	51°46·5′	0°31·7′E	X	167
Mount Maw	Scot Bord	NT1455	55°47·1′	3°21·8′W	H	65,72
Mount Meddin	Moray	NJ4021	57°16·8′	2°59·3′W	H	37
Mountmill	Scot Bord	NT4854	55°46·8′	2°49·3′W	X	66,73
Mount Mill Fm	Northnts	SP7637	52°1·8′	0°53·1′W	FM	152
Mount Misery	N Yks	SE9489	54°17·5′	0°32·9′W	X	94,101
Mount Misery	Orkney	HY2427	59°7·7′	3°19·2′W	X	6
Mountnessing	Essex	TQ6297	51°39·1′	0°20·9′E	T	167,177
Mountnessing Hall	Essex	TQ6496	51°38·6′	0°22·6′E	X	167,177
Mountney Level	E Susx	TQ6303	50°48·4′	0°19·2′E	X	199
Mountneys	Essex	TL6209	51°45·6′	0°21·2′E	X	167
Mount Noddy	W Susx	SU9307	50°51·5′	0°40·3′W	X	197
Mount of Haddoch	Moray	NJ4128	57°20·6′	2°58·4′W	H	37
Mount Oliphant	S Ayr	NS3517	55°25·4′	4°36·0′W	X	70
Mounton	Monm	ST5193	51°38·3′	2°42·1′W	T	162,172
Mounton Brook	Monm	ST4795	51°39·3′	2°45·6′W	W	171
Mounton Fm	Pemb	SN0812	51°46·7′	4°46·6′W	FM	158
Mounton Hill	Pemb	SN0812	51°46·7′	4°46·6′W	H	158
Mountop	Renf	NS4259	55°48·2′	4°30·8′W	X	64
Mount Orleans Fm	Wilts	SU2553	51°16·8′	1°38·1′W	FM	184
Mountover Fm	Dorset	ST5503	50°49·7′	2°38·0′W	FM	194
Mount Owen Fm	Oxon	SP3204	51°44·3′	1°31·8′W	FM	164
Mount Park Fm	N Yks	SE0888	54°17·5′	1°52·2′W	FM	99
Mount Plantation	Suff	TL7366	52°16·1′	0°32·5′E	F	155
Mountpleasant	Aberd	NJ9940	57°27·3′	2°0·5′W	X	30
Mountpleasant	Aberd	NK0842	57°28·3′	1°51·5′W	X	30
Mount Pleasant	Aberd	NK1047	57°31·0′	1°49·5′W	X	30
Mount Pleasant	Arg & Bt	NM8430	56°25·0′	5°29·7′W	X	49
Mount Pleasant	Beds	SP9750	52°8·6′	0°34·5′W	X	153
Mount Pleasant	Beds	TL0759	52°13·4′	0°25·6′W	X	153
Mount Pleasant	Brad	SE0739	53°51·1′	1°53·2′W	X	104
Mount Pleasant	Bri & Hov	TQ3504	50°49·4′	0°4·6′W	X	198
Mount Pleasant	Bucks	SP6933	51°59·7′	0°59·3′W	T	152,165
Mount Pleasant	Bucks	SP7010	51°47·3′	0°58·7′W	X	165
Mount Pleasant	Bucks	SP8723	51°54·2′	0°43·7′W	X	165
Mount Pleasant	Caer	SO1405	51°44·5′	3°14·3′W	X	161
Mount Pleasant	Cambs	TL4289	52°29·1′	0°5·9′E	X	142,143
Mount Pleasant	Carm	SN7133	51°59·1′	3°52·3′W	X	146,160
Mount Pleasant	Cered	SN5352	52°9·0′	4°8·5′W	X	146
Mount Pleasant	Ches	SJ6244	52°59·8′	2°33·6′W	X	118
Mountpleasant	Ches	SJ7569	53°13·3′	2°22·1′W	X	118
Mount Pleasant	Ches	SJ8456	53°6·3′	2°13·9′W	T	118
Mount Pleasant	C of Stoke	SJ8844	52°59·8′	2°10·3′W	T	118
Mount Pleasant	Corn	SX0062	50°25·7′	4°48·6′W	T	200
Mount Pleasant	Cumbr	NY4631	54°40·5′	2°49·8′W	X	90
Mount Pleasant	Cumbr	NY4954	54°52·9′	2°47·3′W	X	86
Mount Pleasant	Cumbr	NY7640	54°45·5′	2°22·0′W	X	86,87

Mount Pleasant	Darl	NZ2616	54°32·6'	1°35·5'W	X	93
Mount Pleasant	Denb	SJ1960	53°8·1'	3°12·2'W	X	116
Mount Pleasant	Denb	SJ2255	53°5·4'	3°9·5'W	X	117
Mount Pleasant	Derby	SK2233	52°53·9'	1°40·0'W	X	128
Mount Pleasant	Derby	SK2817	52°45·2'	1°34·7'W	T	128
Mount Pleasant	Derby	SK3126	52°50·1'	1°32·0'W	T	128
Mount Pleasant	Derby	SK3448	53°1·9'	1°29·2'W	T	119
Mount Pleasant	Devon	ST0303	50°49·3'	3°22·2'W	X	192
Mount Pleasant	Devon	ST1900	50°47·9'	3°8·6'W	T	192,193
Mount Pleasant	Devon	SX4797	50°45·4'	4°9·8'W	X	191
Mount Pleasant	Devon	SX5856	50°23·4'	3°59·5'W	X	202
Mount Pleasant	D & G	NX0657	54°52·5'	5°1·0'W	X	82
Mount Pleasant	Dorset	SY5498	50°47·0'	2°38·8'W	X	194
Mount Pleasant	Durham	NY8341	54°46·1'	2°15·4'W	X	86,87
Mount Pleasant	Durham	NY9640	54°45·5'	2°3·3'W	X	87
Mount Pleasant	Durham	NZ2634	54°42·3'	1°35·4'W	T	93
Mount Pleasant	E Ayr	NS5337	55°36·5'	4°19·6'W	X	70
Mount Pleasant	Essex	TL4727	51°55·6'	0°8·7'E	X	167
Mount Pleasant	E Susx	TQ3715	50°55·3'	0°2·7'W	X	198
Mount Pleasant	E Susx	TQ4216	50°55·8'	0°1·6'E	T	198
Mount Pleasant	E Susx	TQ4502	50°48·2'	0°3·9'E	T	198
Mount Pleasant	E Yorks	SE7533	53°47·5'	0°51·3'W	X	105,106
Mount Pleasant	E Yorks	SE7719	53°39·9'	0°49·7'W	X	112
Mount Pleasant	E Yorks	SE8840	53°51·2'	0°39·3'W	X	106
Mount Pleasant	E Yorks	SE9649	53°55·9'	0°31·9'W	X	106
Mount Pleasant	E Yorks	TA0040	53°51·0'	0°28·4'W	X	106,107
Mount Pleasant	E Yorks	TA0764	54°3·9'	0°21·5'W	X	101
Mount Pleasant	E Yorks	TA2042	53°51·9'	0°10·1'W	X	107
Mount Pleasant	E Yorks	TA2539	53°50·2'	0°5·6'W	X	107
Mount Pleasant	Fife	NO4601	56°12·2'	2°51·8'W	X	59
Mount Pleasant	Flint	SJ2372	53°14·6'	3°8·8'W	T	117
Mount Pleasant	Ghead	NZ2661	54°56·8'	1°35·2'W	T	88
Mount Pleasant	Gwyn	SH3543	52°57·8'	4°27·0'W	X	123
Mount Pleasant	Hants	SZ2997	50°46·5'	1°34·9'W	X	196
Mountpleasant	Highld	ND1268	58°35·7'	3°30·4'W	T	11,12
Mount Pleasant	Highld	NH7156	57°34·8'	4°9·0'W	X	27
Mount Pleasant	Hill	TQ0490	51°36·2'	0°29·5'W	T	176
Mount Pleasant	Kent	TQ6251	51°14·3'	0°19·6'E	X	188
Mount Pleasant	Kent	TQ6636	51°6·2'	0°22·7'E	X	188
Mount Pleasant	Kent	TR3065	51°20·5'	1°18·5'E	T	179
Mount Pleasant	Kirk	SE2323	53°42·4'	1°38·7'W	T	104
Mount Pleasant	Lancs	SD4969	54°7·1'	2°46·4'W	X	97
Mount Pleasant	Lancs	SD5342	53°52·6'	2°42·5'W	X	102
Mount Pleasant	Leic	SK7428	52°50·9'	0°53·7'W	X	129
Mount Pleasant	Lincs	TF0697	53°27·8'	0°23·8'W	X	112
Mount Pleasant	Lincs	TF0988	53°22·9'	0°21·3'W	X	112,121
Mount Pleasant	Lincs	TF1397	53°27·7'	0°17·5'W	X	113
Mount Pleasant	Lincs	TF3369	53°12·3'	0°0·1'W	X	122
Mount Pleasant	Merth Tyd	ST0798	51°40·6'	3°20·3'W	T	170
Mount Pleasant	Midd	NZ5114	54°31·4'	1°12·3'W	X	93
Mount Pleasant	Monm	SO3411	51°47·9'	2°57·0'W	X	161
Mount Pleasant	Moray	NJ3548	57°31·3'	3°4·7'W	F	28
Mount Pleasant	Newp	ST2689	51°35·9'	3°3·7'W	X	171
Mount Pleasant	N Lincs	SE9300	53°29·5'	0°35·5'W	X	112
Mount Pleasant	Norf	TL9994	52°30·7'	0°56·4'E	T	144
Mount Pleasant	Northnts	SP6072	52°20·8'	1°6·8'W	X	140
Mount Pleasant	Northum	NT9237	55°37·8'	2°7·2'W	X	74,75
Mount Pleasant	Northum	NT9550	55°44·9'	2°4·3'W	X	67,74,75
Mount Pleasant	Northum	NY7286	55°10·3'	2°25·9'W	X	80
Mount Pleasant	Northum	NY7854	54°53·1'	2°20·2'W	X	86,87
Mount Pleasant	Northum	NY9766	54°59·6'	2°2·4'W	X	87
Mount Pleasant	Nth Pt Talb	SS7596	51°39·2'	3°48·0'W	T	170
Mount Pleasant	N Yks	SE0483	54°14·8'	1°55·9'W	X	98
Mount Pleasant	N Yks	SE2047	53°55·4'	1°41·3'W	X	104
Mount Pleasant	N Yks	SE2196	54°21·8'	1°40·2'W	X	99
Mount Pleasant	N Yks	SE2272	54°8·8'	1°39·4'W	X	99
Mount Pleasant	N Yks	SE3997	54°22·3'	1°23·6'W	X	99
Mount Pleasant	N Yks	SE4568	54°6·6'	1°18·3'W	X	99
Mount Pleasant	N Yks	SE5373	54°9·2'	1°10·9'W	X	100
Mount Pleasant	N Yks	SE6466	54°5·4'	1°0·9'W	X	100
Mount Pleasant	N Yks	SE7863	54°3·7'	0°48·1'W	X	100
Mount Pleasant	N Yks	SE8591	54°18·7'	0°41·2'W	X	94,100
Mount Pleasant	N Yks	SE9784	54°14·8'	0°30·3'W	X	101
Mount Pleasant	Orkney	HY2512	58°59·6'	3°17·8'W	X	6
Mount Pleasant	Orkney	HY6324	59°6·3'	2°38·3'W	X	5
Mount Pleasant	Pemb	SN0027	51°54·8'	4°54·1'W	X	145,157,158
Mount Pleasant	Pemb	SN0105	51°42·7'	4°52·4'W	T	157,158
Mount Pleasant	Powys	SJ0905	52°38·3'	3°20·3'W	X	125
Mount Pleasant	Powys	SO0664	52°16·2'	3°22·3'W	X	147
Mount Pleasant	Scot Bord	NT8049	55°44·3'	2°18·7'W	X	74
Mount Pleasant	Shrops	SJ3820	52°46·7'	2°54·7'W	X	126
Mount Pleasant	Shrops	SJ4914	52°43·5'	2°44·9'W	T	126
Mount Pleasant	Shrops	SJ6829	52°51·7'	2°28·1'W	X	127
Mount Pleasant	Shrops	SO2377	52°23·4'	3°7·5'W	H	137,148
Mount Pleasant	Staffs	SJ8859	53°7·9'	2°10·4'W	X	118
Mount Pleasant	Staffs	SJ8907	52°39·9'	2°9·4'W	X	127,139
Mount Pleasant	Staffs	SJ9637	52°56·1'	2°3·2'W	X	127
Mount Pleasant	Staffs	SJ9741	52°58·2'	2°2·4'W	X	118
Mount Pleasant	Stock on T	NZ4420	54°34·6'	1°18·7'W	T	93
Mount Pleasant	S Tyne	NZ3460	54°56·3'	1°27·7'W	X	88
Mount Pleasant	Suff	TL7347	52°5·9'	0°31·9'E	T	155
Mount Pleasant	Suff	TM0559	52°11·7'	1°0·4'E	X	155
Mount Pleasant	Suff	TM4085	52°24·8'	1°32·2'E	X	156
Mount Pleasant	Suff	TM4669	52°16·1'	1°36·7'E	X	156
Mount Pleasant	V of Glam	SS9174	51°27·5'	3°33·7'W	X	170
Mount Pleasant	Warw	SP1153	52°10·7'	1°50·0'W	X	150
Mount Pleasant	Warw	SP2457	52°12·9'	1°38·5'W	X	151
Mount Pleasant	Warw	SP3587	52°29·0'	1°28·7'W	T	140
Mount Pleasant	Warw	SP4575	52°22·5'	1°19·9'W	X	140
Mount Pleasant	Worcs	SO8073	52°21·5'	2°17·2'W	X	138
Mount Pleasant	Worcs	SP0064	52°16·7'	1°59·6'W	T	150
Mount Pleasant	Worcs	SP0439	52°3·2'	1°56·1'W	T	150
Mount Pleasant	York	SE6945	53°54·0'	0°56·6'W	X	105,106
Mount Pleasant Fm	Brad	SE0436	53°49·5'	1°55·9'W	FM	104
Mount Pleasant Fm	Brig	SS8379	51°30·1'	3°40·8'W	FM	170
Mount Pleasant Fm	Bucks	SP7226	51°55·9'	0°56·8'W	FM	165
Mount Pleasant Fm	Bucks	SP8424	51°54·7'	0°46·3'W	FM	165
Mount Pleasant Fm	Bucks	SP8829	51°57·4'	0°42·8'W	FM	165
Mountpleasant Fm	Ches	SJ7977	53°17·6'	2°18·5'W	FM	118
Mountpleasant Fm	Ches	SJ8564	53°10·6'	2°13·1'W	FM	118

Mount Pleasant Fm	Cumbr	NY8014	54°31·5'	2°18·1'W	FM	91,92
Mount Pleasant Fm	Darl	NZ3320	54°34·7'	1°28·9'W	FM	93
Mount Pleasant Fm	Derby	SK1961	53°9·0'	1°42·5'W	FM	119
Mount Pleasant Fm	Dorset	ST7708	50°52·5'	2°19·2'W	FM	194
Mount Pleasant Fm	Dorset	SU0608	50°52·5'	1°54·5'W	FM	195
Mount Pleasant Fm	Durham	NZ0846	54°48·8'	1°52·1'W	FM	88
Mount Pleasant Fm	E Susx	TQ5310	50°52·4'	0°10·9'E	FM	199
Mount Pleasant Fm	E Yorks	TA1052	53°57·4'	0°19·0'W	FM	107
Mount Pleasant Fm	Kent	TQ6651	51°14·3'	0°23·1'E	FM	188
Mount Pleasant Fm	Kent	TQ7851	51°14·0'	0°33·4'E	FM	188
Mount Pleasant Fm	Kent	TQ8434	51°4·8'	0°38·0'E	FM	188
Mount Pleasant Fm	Lancs	SD5239	53°50·9'	2°43·4'W	FM	102
Mount Pleasant Fm	Leic	SK8519	52°45·9'	0°44·0'W	FM	130
Mount Pleasant Fm	Lincs	SK8797	53°28·0'	0°41·0'W	FM	112
Mount Pleasant Fm	Lincs	SK9896	53°27·3'	0°31·0'W	FM	112
Mount Pleasant Fm	Northum	NZ2982	55°8·1'	1°32·3'W	FM	81
Mount Pleasant Fm	N Yks	NZ4104	54°26·0'	1°21·7'W	FM	93
Mount Pleasant Fm	N Yks	NZ4106	54°27·1'	1°21·6'W	FM	93
Mount Pleasant Fm	N Yks	SE5486	54°16·2'	1°9·8'W	FM	100
Mount Pleasant Fm	N Yks	SE5570	54°7·6'	1°9·1'W	FM	100
Mount Pleasant Fm	N Yks	SE5839	53°50·9'	1°6·7'W	FM	105
Mount Pleasant Fm	N Yks	SE6541	53°51·9'	1°0·3'W	FM	105,106
Mount Pleasant Fm	N Yks	SE7060	54°2·1'	0°55·5'W	FM	100
Mount Pleasant Fm	N Yks	SE7366	54°5·3'	0°52·6'W	FM	100
Mount Pleasant Fm	N Yks	SE9483	54°14·3'	0°33·0'W	FM	101
Mount Pleasant Fm	N Yks	TA0783	54°14·1'	0°21·1'W	FM	101
Mount Pleasant Fm	Oxon	SU3497	51°40·5'	1°31·1'W	FM	164
Mount Pleasant Fm	Somer	ST7655	51°17·9'	2°20·3'W	FM	172
Mount Pleasant Fm	Suff	TM3478	52°21·2'	1°26·6'E	FM	156
Mount Pleasant Fm	Swin	SU2185	51°34·0'	1°41·4'W	FM	174
Mount Pleasant Fm	Warw	SP2751	52°9·6'	1°35·9'W	FM	151
Mountpleasant Fm	Worcs	SO8668	52°18·8'	2°11·9'W	FM	139
Mount Pleasant Fm	W Susx	TQ2833	51°5·1'	0°10·0'W	FM	187
Mount Pleasant Mill	N Lincs	SK9399	53°29·0'	0°35·5'W	X	112
Mountpleasant Plantn	Glos	ST9598	51°41·1'	2°3·9'W	F	163
Mount Plesant	Cumbr	NY6617	54°33·1'	2°31·1'W	X	91
Mount Prosperous	Wilts	SU3364	51°22·7'	1°31·2'W	X	174
Mountquhanie Ho	Fife	NO3421	56°22·9'	3°3·7'W	X	54,59
Mountquharry	Pth & Kin	NO1814	56°18·9'	3°19·1'W	X	58
Mountrich	Highld	NH5660	57°36·7'	4°24·2'W	X	21
Mount Rule	I of M	SC3579	54°11·1'	4°31·3'W	X	95
Mount's Bay	Corn	SW5626	50°5·3'	5°24·3'W	W	203
Mounts Court Fm	Kent	TR1842	51°8·4'	1°7·4'E	FM	179,189
Mount Segg	Worcs	SO8676	52°23·1'	2°11·9'W	X	139
Mount Severn	Powys	SN9484	52°26·9'	3°33·2'W	X	136
Mount's Fm	Essex	TL7125	51°54·1'	0°29·5'E	FM	167
Mount's Fm	Kent	TQ7933	51°4·3'	0°33·7'E	FM	188
Mount Shade	Aberd	NO6287	56°58·6'	2°37·1'W	H	45
Mount Shellie	S Ayr	NX3690	55°10·9'	4°34·1'W	X	77
Mount's Hill	Herts	SP9905	51°44·3'	0°33·6'W	X	165
Mount Sion	Wrex	SJ2953	53°4·4'	3°3·2'W	T	117
Mount Sion Down	Pemb	SR9195	51°37·1'	5°0·3'W	X	158
Mount Skep	Scot Bord	NT4733	55°35·5'	2°50·0'W	H	73
Mount Skip	Derby	SE0300	53°30·0'	1°56·9'W	X	110
Mountskip Farm	Midlo	NT3661	55°50·5'	3°0·9'W	FM	66
Mount Skippett	Oxon	SP3520	51°50·2'	1°29·1'W	T	164
Mount Skippetts Fm	Win & Maid	SU8975	51°28·2'	0°42·7'W	FM	175
Mountsland	Devon	SX7574	50°33·4'	3°45·5'W	X	191
Mounts Lodge	Rut	TF0010	52°40·9'	0°30·8'W	X	130
Mount Sned	Angus	NO4469	56°48·8'	2°54·6'W	X	44
Mountsolie	Aberd	NJ9359	57°37·5'	2°6·6'W	T	30
Mountsorrel	Leic	SK5814	52°43·5'	1°8·1'W	T	129
Mount Sorrel	Wilts	SU0324	51°1·2'	1°57·0'W	T	184
Mount Sorrell	Glos	SP2434	52°0·5'	1°38·6'W	X	151
Mount St Bernard Abbey (Monastery)	Leic	SK4516	52°44·6'	1°19·6'W	X	129
Mount Stewart	Pth & Kin	NO1017	56°20·5'	3°26·9'W	X	58
Mountstewart	S Lanak	NS8833	55°34·9'	3°46·2'W	X	71,72
Mounts, The	Devon	SX7548	50°19·4'	3°45·1'W	X	202
Mounts, The	Surrey	TQ1557	51°18·3'	0°20·6'W	X	187
Mount St John	N Yks	SE4784	54°15·2'	1°16·3'W	X	100
Mountstuart	Arg & Bt	NS1059	55°47·5'	5°1·4'W	X	63
Mount Stuart	Clackm	NO0002	56°12·3'	3°36·3'W	X	58
Mount Stuart	D & G	NS7519	55°27·2'	3°58·2'W	H	71,78
Mount Tabor	Cald	SE0527	53°44·6'	1°55·0'W	T	104
Mount Tamar	Devon	SX4567	50°29·2'	4°10·7'W	X	201
Mount, The	Bath & NE Somer	ST7868	51°24·9'	2°18·6'W	X	172
Mount, The	Bucks	SP8003	51°43·4'	0°50·1'W	A	165
Mount, The	Bucks	SU9590	51°36·3'	0°37·3'W	X	175,176
Mount, The	Ches	SJ8774	53°16·0'	2°11·3'W	X	118
Mount, The	Corn	SW7123	50°4·0'	5°11·6'W	X	203
Mount, The	Cumbr	NY4174	55°3·7'	2°55·0'W	X	85
Mount, The	Derby	SK2143	52°59·3'	1°40·8'W	X	119,128
Mount, The	Devon	SX8059	50°25·4'	3°41·0'W	X	202
Mount, The	D & G	NY0896	55°15·2'	3°26·4'W	X	78
Mount, The	Essex	TL6524	51°53·6'	0°24·3'E	A	167
Mount, The	E Susx	TQ6132	51°4·1'	0°18·3'E	X	188
Mount, The	Fife	NO3316	56°20·2'	3°4·6'W	X	59
Mount, The	Glos	SO8010	51°47·5'	2°17·0'W	A	162
Mount, The	Herts	TL3234	51°59·6'	0°4·2'W	A	153
Mount, The	I of M	SC3275	54°8·9'	4°33·9'W	H	95
Mount, The	Kent	TQ4658	51°18·4'	0°6·1'E	X	188
Mount, The	Kent	TQ9672	51°25·0'	0°49·5'E	X	178
Mount, The	Kent	TR0454	51°15·1'	0°55·8'E	X	179,189
Mount, The	Leic	SK6505	52°38·6'	1°2·0'W	X	141
Mount, The	Lincs	SK9392	53°25·2'	0°35·6'W	X	112
Mount, The	Lincs	TF1383	53°20·1'	0°17·8'W	X	121
Mount, The	Medway	TQ7472	51°25·4'	0°30·6'E	X	178
Mount, The	Norf	TG0834	52°52·0'	1°5·8'E	X	133
Mount, The	N Som	ST5074	51°28·0'	2°42·8'W	X	172
Mount, The	N Yks	SD9247	53°55·4'	2°6·9'W	X	103
Mount, The	N Yks	SE0888	54°17·5'	1°52·2'W	X	99
Mount, The	N Yks	SE1995	54°21·3'	1°42·1'W	X	99
Mount, The	N Yks	SE2079	54°12·6'	1°41·2'W	X	99
Mount, The	N Yks	SE3170	54°7·7'	1°31·1'W	X	99
Mount, The	Oxon	SP2723	51°54·5'	1°36·1'W	A	163
Mount, The	Oxon	SU7583	51°32·7'	0°54·7'W	X	175
Mount, The	Powys	SO0175	52°22·1'	3°26·8'W	A	136,147
Mount, The	Powys	SO1154	52°10·9'	3°17·7'W	A	148

Mount, The	Scot Bord	NT0942	55°40·0'	3°26·4'W	H	72
Mount, The	Scot Bord	NT1457	55°48·2'	3°21·9'W	H	65,72
Mount, The	Scot Bord	NT8141	55°40·0'	2°17·7'W	X	74
Mount, The	Scot Bord	NT9166	55°53·5'	2°8·2'W	X	67
Mount, The	S Glos	ST8083	51°33·0'	2°16·9'W	X	173
Mount, The	Shrops	SJ2730	52°52·0'	3°4·7'W	X	126
Mount, The	Shrops	SJ5629	52°51·6'	2°38·8'W	A	126
Mount, The	Shrops	SJ6528	52°51·1'	2°30·8'W	X	127
Mount, The	Staffs	SJ8925	52°49·6'	2°9·4'W	X	127
Mount, The	Suff	TL9766	52°15·6'	0°53·6'E	A	155
Mount, The	Suff	TM3687	52°26·0'	1°28·7'E	A	156
Mount, The	Surrey	TQ3647	51°12·6'	0°2·8'W	X	187
Mount, The	Surrey	TQ3752	51°15·3'	0°1·8'W	A	187
Mount, The	Thurr	TQ6083	51°31·6'	0°18·8'E	A	177
Mount, The	Warw	SK2802	52°37·1'	1°34·8'W	X	140
Mount, The	Worcs	SO9664	52°16·7'	2°3·1'W	X	150
Mount, The	Worcs	SP0669	52°19·4'	1°54·3'W	A	139
Mount, The	Wrex	SJ2435	52°54·7'	3°7·4'W	X	126
Mount, The	W Susx	TQ2238	51°7·9'	0°15·0'W	X	187
Mount, The (Earthwork)	Oxon	SU3799	51°41·5'	1°27·5'W	A	164
Mount, The (Motte)	Scot Bord	NT8141	55°40·0'	2°17·7'W	A	74
Mount, The (Tumulus)	Bucks	SU9590	51°36·3'	0°37·3'W	A	175,176
Mount Thrift	Essex	TQ6391	51°35·9'	0°21·6'E	X	177
Mount Tree	Oxon	SU6796	51°39·8'	1°1·5'W	X	164,165
Mount Ulston	Scot Bord	NT6622	55°29·7'	2°31·9'W	X	74
Mount Vernon	C of Glas	NS6563	55°50·7'	4°8·9'W	T	64
Mount Vernon	Lancs	SD5058	54°1·2'	2°45·4'W	X	102
Mount View	Corn	SW7227	50°6·2'	5°10·9'W	X	204
Mount Wise	C of Plym	SX4553	50°21·6'	4°10·4'W	T	201
Mount Wood	Bucks	TQ0298	51°40·5'	0°31·1'W	F	166,176
Mount Wood	Shrops	SJ2535	52°54·7'	3°6·5'W	F	126
Mountwood Fm	Bucks	TQ0298	51°40·5'	0°31·1'W	FM	166,176
Mour	Orkney	HY7445	59°17·7'	2°26·9'W	X	5
Mousa	Shetld	HU4624	60°0·2'	1°10·0'W	X	4
Mousa Ness	Shetld	HU3945	60°11·5'	1°17·3'W	X	4
Mousa Sound	Shetld	HU4424	60°0·2'	1°12·2'W	W	4
Mousavord Loch	Shetld	HU2255	60°17·0'	1°35·6'W	W	3
Mousa Vords	Shetld	HU2254	60°16·4'	1°35·6'W	H	3
Mousa Water	Shetld	HU2551	60°14·8'	1°32·4'W	W	3
Mouseberry	Devon	SS7616	50°56·0'	3°45·5'W	X	180
Mouse Castle	Heref	SO2442	52°4·5'	3°6·1'W	X	148,161
Mouse Castle (Motte and Bailey)	Heref	SO2442	52°4·5'	3°6·1'W	A	148,161
Mouseden	Kent	TQ6139	51°7·9'	0°18·5'E	X	188
Mousefield Fm	W Berks	SU4869	51°25·3'	1°18·2'W	FM	174
Mouse Hall	Norf	TF6301	52°35·2'	0°24·8'E	X	143
Mousehill	Surrey	SU9441	51°9·9'	0°38·9'W	T	186
Mousehill Down	Surrey	SU9342	51°10·4'	0°39·8'W	X	186
Mousehold Fm	Norf	TG2913	52°40·2'	1°23·6'E	FM	133,134
Mousehold Heath	Norf	TG2410	52°38·7'	1°19·1'E	X	133,134
Mouseholdheath Fm	Norf	TG3213	52°40·1'	1°26·3'E	FM	133,134
Mousehold Plantn	Norf	TG3312	52°39·6'	1°27·1'E	F	133,134
Mousehole	Corn	SW4626	50°5·0'	5°32·7'W	T	203
Mouse Hole	Devon	ST0902	50°48·9'	3°17·1'W	X	192
Mousehole Bridge	Worcs	SO7351	52°9·6'	2°23·3'W	X	150
Mousehole, The	Corn	SW4625	50°4·5'	5°32·6'W	W	203
Mousehole & Trap	Devon	SS1346	51°11·2'	4°40·2'W	X	180
Mousells Wood	Bucks	SU7890	51°36·4'	0°52·0'W	F	175
Mousen	Northum	NU1232	55°35·1'	1°48·1'W	X	75
Mousenatch	Heref	SO4660	52°14·4'	2°47·1'W	X	137,138,148
Mousen Burn	Northum	NU1131	55°34·6'	1°49·1'W	W	75
Mouse Syke	Cumbr	SD7792	54°19·6'	2°20·8'W	X	98
Mouse Water	S Lanak	NS9347	55°42·5'	3°41·7'W	W	72
Mousland	Orkney	HY2212	58°59·5'	3°21·0'W	X	6
Mouslee Hill	Shetld	HP6015	60°49·1'	0°53·3'W	X	1
Mousley End	Warw	SP2169	52°19·4'	1°41·1'W	T	139,151
Mousley Hill Fm	Warw	SP2170	52°19·9'	1°41·1'W	FM	139
Mouster Head	Orkney	ND4688	58°46·8'	2°55·6'W	X	7
Mousthwaite Comb	Cumbr	NY3427	54°38·3'	3°0·9'W	X	90
Mouswald	D & G	NY0672	55°2·3'	3°27·8'W	T	85
Mouswald Banks	D & G	NY0674	55°3·3'	3°27·9'W	X	85
Mouswald Burn	D & G	NY0371	55°1·7'	3°30·6'W	W	84
Mouswald Grange	D & G	NY0573	55°2·8'	3°28·8'W	X	85
Mouswell Fm	S Glos	ST7280	51°31·3'	2°23·8'W	FM	172
Mouthlock	Cumbr	NY8412	54°30·4'	2°14·4'W	X	91,92
Mouth Mill	Devon	SS2926	51°0·7'	4°25·9'W	T	190
Mouth Of The Humber		TA3709	53°33·8'	0°4·5'E	W	113
Mouth of the Severn		ST3273	51°27·4'	2°58·3'W	W	171
Mouthstone Point	Devon	SX5247	50°18·5'	4°4·3'W	X	201
Mouzel Fm	Cumbr	SD2375	54°10·1'	3°10·4'W	FM	96
Moverons	Essex	TM0618	51°49·6'	0°59·8'E	X	168
Mowatseat	Aberd	NJ5509	57°10·4'	2°44·2'W	X	37
Mowat's Seat	Angus	NO4767	56°47·7'	2°51·6'W	X	44
Mowbage Fm	Heref	SO3439	52°3·0'	2°57·4'W	FM	149,161
Mowbray	Cumbr	NY0316	54°32·0'	3°29·5'W	X	89
Mowbray Hall	N Yks	SE2376	54°11·0'	1°38·4'W	X	99
Mowbray Hill	N Yks	SE2681	54°13·7'	1°35·7'W	X	99
Mowbray Ho	N Yks	SE2374	54°9·9'	1°38·4'W	X	99
Mowbray Ho	N Yks	SE5568	54°6·5'	1°9·1'W	X	100
Mowbreck	Lancs	SD4233	53°47·6'	2°52·4'W	T	102
Mow Cop	Staffs	SJ8557	53°6·8'	2°13·0'W	T	118
Mow Cop	Wrekin	SJ7224	52°49·0'	2°24·5'W	X	127
Mow Cop Trail	Staffs	SJ8860	53°8·5'	2°10·4'W	X	118
Mow Creek	Norf	TF7844	52°58·1'	0°39·4'E	W	132
Mowden	Darl	NZ2615	54°32·0'	1°35·5'W	T	93
Mowden	Essex	TL7710	51°45·9'	0°34·3'E	T	167
Mowden Hall (School)	Northum	NZ0465	54°59·0'	1°55·8'W	X	87
Mow Fen	Cambs	TL5788	52°28·3'	0°19·1'E	X	143
Mow Fen	Norf	TF6610	52°40·0'	0°27·7'E	X	132,143
Mowhaugh	Scot Bord	NT8120	55°28·7'	2°17·6'W	T	74
Mo Wick	Shetld	HU2956	60°17·5'	1°28·0'W	W	3
Mowingword	Pemb	SR9994	51°36·8'	4°53·8'W	X	158
Mow Law	Scot Bord	NT8120	55°28·7'	2°17·6'W	H	74
Mow Law	Scot Bord	NT8218	55°27·6'	2°16·6'W	H	80
Mowles Manor	Norf	TG0214	52°41·4'	0°59·7'E	X	133
Mowley	Heref	SO3360	52°14·3'	2°58·5'W	X	137,148,149
Mowley Wood	Heref	SO3459	52°13·8'	2°57·6'W	F	148,149
Mowlish Manor	Devon	SX9581	50°37·4'	3°28·7'W	X	192
Mowmacre Hill	C of Leic	SK5708	52°40·2'	1°9·0'W	T	140
Mowness Hall	Suff	TM1259	52°11·5'	1°6·5'E	X	155

Mown Fen	Norf	TG3427	52°47·6′	1°28·7′E	W	133,134
Mowsbury Hill	Beds	TL0653	52°10·1′	0°26·6′W	X	153
Mowsbury Park	Beds	TL0652	52°9·6′	0°26·6′W	X	153
Mows Hill Fm	Warw	SP1469	52°19·4′	1°47·3′W	FM	139,151
Mowshurst	Kent	TQ4547	51°12·5′	0°4·9′E	T	188
Mowsley	Leic	SP6489	52°29·9′	1°3·0′W	T	140
Mowsley Hills	Leic	SP6487	52°28·9′	1°3·1′W	X	140
Mowthorpe	N Yks	SE6868	54°6·4′	0°57·2′W	X	100
Mowthorpe Dale	N Yks	SE6869	54°7·0′	0°57·2′W	X	100
Mowthorpe Fm	N Yks	SE9888	54°16·9′	0°29·3′W	FM	94,101
Mowthorpe Hill Fm	N Yks	SE6769	54°7·0′	0°58·1′W	FM	100
Mowthorpe Wold	N Yks	SE8967	54°5·7′	0°37·9′W	X	101
Moxby	N Yks	SE5966	54°5·4′	1°5·5′W	T	100
Moxby Hall Fm	N Yks	SE5966	54°5·4′	1°5·5′W	FM	100
Moxby Moor	N Yks	SE5866	54°5·4′	1°6·4′W	X	100
Moxby Moor Fm	N Yks	SE5966	54°5·4′	1°5·5′W	FM	100
Moxhayes	Devon	ST2506	50°51·2′	3°3·5′W	X	192,193
Mox Hill	Beds	TL1246	52°6·3′	0°21·5′W	X	153
Moxhill Fm	Beds	TL1246	52°6·3′	0°21·5′W	FM	153
Moxhull Hall (Hotel)	Warw	SP1696	52°33·9′	1°45·4′W	X	139
Moxley	Wals	SO9695	52°33·4′	2°3·1′W	T	139
Moxon's Fm	Warw	SP4092	52°31·7′	1°24·2′W	FM	140
Moxon's Hill	Derby	SK3121	52°47·4′	1°32·0′W	X	128
Moy	Arg & Bt	NR7020	55°25·5′	5°37·7′W	X	68
Moy	Highld	NH7634	57°23·0′	4°3·3′W	T	27
Moy	Highld	NN1682	56°53·8′	5°0·8′W	X	34,41
Moy	Highld	NN4282	56°54·4′	4°35·2′W	X	34,42
Moy Br	Highld	NH4854	57°33·3′	4°32·0′W	X	26
Moy Burn	Highld	NH7736	57°24·1′	4°2·4′W	W	27
Moy Burn	Highld	NN4184	56°55·5′	4°36·3′W	W	34,42
Moy Burn or Allt á Mhaigh	Highld	NN4983	56°55·1′	4°28·4′W	W	34,42
Moy Castle	Arg & Bt	NM6124	56°21·1′	5°51·7′W	A	49
Moy Corrie	Highld	NN4386	56°56·6′	4°34·4′W	X	34,42
Moycroft	Moray	NJ2362	57°38·7′	3°16·9′W	T	28
Moyddin Fawr	Cered	SN4852	52°9·0′	4°12·9′W	X	146
Moydog Fawr	Powys	SJ1607	52°39·5′	3°14·1′W	X	125
Moy Forest	Highld	NN4385	56°56·0′	4°34·4′W	X	34,42
Moy Hall	Highld	NH7635	57°23·6′	4°3·3′W	T	27
Moy House	Moray	NJ0159	57°36·9′	3°39·0′W	X	27
Moyl	D & G	NX8351	54°50·7′	3°48·9′W	H	84
Moyle	Highld	NG8818	57°12·5′	5°30·2′W	X	33
Moyle Hill	D & G	NX8457	54°53·9′	3°48·1′W	H	84
Moyles Court	Hants	SU1608	50°52·5′	1°46·0′W	X	195
Moylgrove	Pemb	SN1144	52°4·0′	4°45·1′W	T	145
Moy Lodge	Highld	NN4483	56°55·0′	4°33·3′W	X	34,42
Moyne Fm	E Renf	NS4753	55°45·0′	4°25·8′W	FM	64
Moyne Moor	E Renf	NS4752	55°44·5′	4°25·8′W	X	64
Moynes Ct	Monm	ST5190	51°36·6′	2°42·1′W	A	162,172
Moynes Fm	Essex	TL9602	51°41·2′	0°50·5′E	FM	168
Moynes Fm	Essex	TM1220	51°50·5′	1°5·1′E	FM	168,169
Moyn's Park	Essex	TL6940	52°2·2′	0°28·2′E	A	154
Moyse's Fm	E Susx	TQ4225	51°0·6′	0°1·8′E	FM	187,198
Moys Hill Fm	Glos	SO7113	51°49·1′	2°24·9′W	FM	162
Moyson	Devon	SX8040	50°15·1′	3°40·6′W	X	202
Moy Wood	Highld	NH4955	57°33·9′	4°31·0′W	F	26
Moze Cross	Essex	TM1926	51°53·6′	1°11·4′E	X	168,169
Moze Hall	Essex	TM0327	51°54·5′	0°57·5′E	X	168
Mozens, The	Corn	SW3936	50°10·2′	5°38·9′W	X	203
Mozergh Ho	Cumbr	SD5597	54°22·2′	2°41·1′W	X	97
Mozie Law	Scot Bord	NT8215	55°26·0′	2°16·6′W	H	80
Mt Florida	C of Glas	NS5961	55°49·6′	4°14·6′W	T	64
Mt Pleasant	Orkney	HY4444	59°17·0′	2°58·5′W	X	5
Muaitheabhal	N Eil	NB2511	58°0·5′	6°38·9′W	H	13,14
Mualichbeg	Pth & Kin	NN8967	56°47·1′	3°48·6′W	X	43
Muasdale	Arg & Bt	NR6740	55°36·1′	5°41·5′W	T	62
Muce	Orkney	HY2323	59°5·5′	3°20·1′W	X	6
Muchalls	Aberd	NO9092	57°1·4′	2°9·4′W	T	38,45
Muchalls Castle	Aberd	NO8991	57°0·9′	2°10·4′W	A	38,45
Much Birch	Heref	SO5030	51°58·2′	2°43·3′W	T	149
Much Cowardne	Heref	SO6247	52°7·4′	2°32·9′W	T	149
Much Dewchurch	Heref	SO4831	51°58·7′	2°45·0′W	T	149,161
Muchelney	Somer	ST4324	51°1·0′	2°48·4′W	T	193
Muchelney Ham	Somer	ST4323	51°0·4′	2°48·4′W	T	193
Muchelney Level	Somer	ST4325	51°1·5′	2°48·4′W	X	193
Much Hadham	Herts	TL4219	51°51·3′	0°4·1′E	T	167
Much Hoole	Lancs	SD4723	53°42·3′	2°47·8′W	T	102
Much Hoole Moss Houses	Lancs	SD4822	53°41·8′	2°46·8′W	T	102
Much Hoole Town	Lancs	SD4722	53°41·7′	2°47·8′W	T	102
Muchlarnick	Corn	SX2156	50°22·8′	4°30·7′W	T	201
Much Marcle	Heref	SO6532	51°59·4′	2°30·2′W	T	149
Muchra	Scot Bord	NT2217	55°26·7′	3°13·6′W	X	79
Muchrachd	Highld	NH2833	57°21·6′	4°51·1′W	X	25
Much Wenlock	Shrops	SO6299	52°35·5′	2°33·3′W	T	138
Muck	Highld	NM4179	56°50·1′	6°14·3′W	X	39
Muckairn	Arg & Bt	NM9733	56°27·0′	5°17·2′W	X	49
Muckelborough Lodge Fm	Leic	SP8298	52°34·7′	0°47·0′W	FM	141
Muckerach	Highld	NJ0617	57°14·3′	3°33·0′W	X	36
Muckernich	Highld	NH5952	57°32·4′	4°20·9′W	X	26
Mucketlands	Pth & Kin	NO2847	56°36·8′	3°9·9′W	X	53
Muck Fleet	Norf	TG4212	52°39·3′	1°35·1′E	W	134
Muckford	Devon	SS7924	51°0·4′	3°43·1′W	X	180
Muckhart Mill	Clackm	NS9998	56°10·1′	3°37·2′W	X	58
Mucking	Thurr	TQ6881	51°30·4′	0°25·6′E	T	177,178
Muckinger Wood	Suff	TM0552	52°7·9′	1°0·1′E	F	155
Mucking Flats	Thurr	TQ7080	51°29·8′	0°27·3′E	X	178
Mucking Hall	Essex	TQ9189	51°34·3′	0°45·8′E	X	178
Mucking Marshes	Thurr	TQ6880	51°29·9′	0°25·6′E	X	177,178
Muckla Billan	Shetld	HU5456	60°17·3′	1°0·9′W	X	2
Muckla Field	Shetld	HU3063	60°21·3′	1°26·9′W	H	3
Muckla Moor	Shetld	HU4367	60°23·3′	1°12·7′W	X	2,3
Mucklands Wood	Peterb	TF1501	52°35·9′	0°17·7′W	F	142
Mucklarie	Pth & Kin	NO0742	56°33·9′	3°30·4′W	X	52,53
Muckla Water	Shetld	HU2278	60°29·4′	1°35·5′W	W	3
Muckla Water	Shetld	HU3063	60°21·3′	1°26·9′W	W	3
Muckle Allt Venney	Moray	NJ3837	57°25·4′	3°1·5′W	W	28
Muckle Ayre	Shetld	HU4444	60°10·9′	1°11·9′W	X	4
Muckle Ballia Clett	Shetld	HU3182	60°31·5′	1°25·6′W	X	1,3
Muckle Bard	Shetld	HU4623	59°59·6′	1°10·0′W	X	4
Muckle Billia Fiold	Orkney	HY3523	59°5·6′	3°7·6′W	X	6
Muckle Birriers Geo	Shetld	HU6688	60°34·5′	0°47·2′W	X	1,2

Muckle Black Hill	Aberd	NJ4434	57°23·8′	2°55·4′W	X	28
Muckle Bratt-houll	Shetld	HP5101	60°41·6′	1°3·5′W	X	1
Muckle Breck	Shetld	HU5865	60°22·2′	0°56·4′W	X	2
Muckle Brei Geo	Shetld	HU4421	59°58·6′	1°12·2′W	X	4
Mucklebrick's Wick	Shetld	HT9438	60°7·9′	2°6·0′W	W	4
Muckle Brig	Orkney	HY4431	59°10·0′	2°58·3′W	X	5,6
Muckleburgh Collection, The	Norf	TG1043	52°56·8′	1°8·0′E	X	133
Muckleburgh Hill	Norf	TG1043	52°56·8′	1°8·0′E	X	133
Muckleburgh Hill (Tumulus)	Norf	TG1043	52°56·8′	1°8·0′E	A	133
Muckle Burn	Angus	NO2164	56°45·9′	3°17·1′W	W	44
Muckle Burn	Highld	NH9452	57°33·0′	3°45·8′W	W	27
Muckle Burn	Stir	NN7807	56°14·7′	3°57·7′W	W	57
Muckle Burn of Kilrie	Angus	NO5573	56°51·0′	2°43·8′W	W	44
Muckle Cairn	Angus	NO3582	56°55·7′	3°3·6′W	X	44
Muckle Cairn	Angus	NO3776	56°52·5′	3°1·6′W	H	44
Muckle Castle	Orkney	HY5603	58°55·0′	2°45·4′W	X	6
Muckle Cauldron Burn	D & G	NT2108	55°21·8′	3°14·3′W	W	79
Muckle Dod	Scot Bord	NT4119	55°27·9′	2°55·6′W	H	79
Muckle Dodd Hill	Northum	NY7179	55°6·5′	2°26·8′W	H	86,87
Muckle Eriff Hill	E Ayr	NS4801	55°17·0′	4°23·2′W	H	77
Muckle Eskadale	Orkney	HY3416	59°1·8′	3°8·5′W	X	6
Muckle Falloch	Angus	NO4074	56°51·5′	2°58·6′W	W	44
Muckle Fergie Burn	Moray	NJ1813	57°12·3′	3°21·0′W	W	36
Muckle Fladdicap	Shetld	HU5658	60°18·4′	0°58·7′W	X	2
Muckle Flaes	Shetld	HU2445	60°11·6′	1°33·5′W	X	4
Muckle Flugga	Shetld	HP6019	60°51·2′	0°53·2′W	X	1
Muckleford	Dorset	SY6493	50°44·4′	2°30·2′W	T	194
Muckle Geo	Orkney	ND4996	58°51·2′	2°52·6′W	X	6,7
Muckle Geo of Hoini	Shetld	HZ1971	59°31·7′	1°39·4′W	X	4
Muckle Green Holm	Orkney	HY5227	59°7·9′	2°49·8′W	X	5,6
Muckle Greens	Moray	NJ0650	57°32·1′	3°33·7′W	X	27
Mucklegrind	Shetld	HT9540	60°8·9′	2°4·9′W	X	4
Muckle Hallitie	Shetld	HU3411	59°53·2′	1°23·1′W	X	4
Muckle Head	Orkney	HY2105	58°55·8′	3°21·9′W	X	6,7
Muckle Head	Shetld	HP6608	60°45·2′	0°46·8′W	X	1
Muckle Head	Shetld	HU4860	60°19·5′	1°7·4′W	X	2,3
Mucklehead Knowe	D & G	NY2399	55°17·0′	3°12·3′W	H	79
Muckle Hell	Shetld	HU5239	60°8·2′	1°3·3′W	X	4
Muckle Heog	Shetld	HP6310	60°46·3′	0°50·1′W	H	1
Muckle Hill	Norf	TG2042	52°56·0′	1°16·8′E	X	133
Muckle Hill	Shetld	HU4358	60°18·5′	1°12·8′W	H	2,3
Muckle Ho	Orkney	ND3299	58°52·6′	3°10·3′W	X	6,7
Muckle Holm	Orkney	HY3127	59°7·7′	3°11·8′W	X	6
Muckle Holm (Nature Reserve)	Shetld	HU4088	60°34·7′	1°15·7′W	X	1,2
Mucklehouse	Orkney	ND4389	58°47·4′	2°58·7′W	X	7
Muckle Hunclett	Orkney	HY4705	58°56·0′	2°54·8′W	X	6,7
Muckle Kiln	Orkney	HY6544	59°17·1′	2°36·4′W	X	5
Muckle Knees	Scot Bord	NT1919	55°27·7′	3°16·4′W	H	79
Muckle Knock	Scot Bord	NT1156	55°47·6′	3°24·7′W	H	65,72
Muckle Knowe	D & G	NT2506	55°20·8′	3°10·5′W	H	79
Muckle Knowe	D & G	NY2897	55°16·0′	3°7·6′W	H	79
Muckle Knowe	D & G	NY3298	55°16·5′	3°3·8′W	H	79
Muckle Knowe	D & G	NY3886	55°10·1′	2°58·0′W	H	79
Muckle Knowe	Northum	NY6285	55°9·7′	2°35·4′W	X	80
Muckle Knowe	Scot Bord	NT1021	55°28·7′	3°25·0′W	H	72
Muckle Knowe	Scot Bord	NT3207	55°21·4′	3°3·9′W	H	79
Muckle Land Knowe	Scot Bord	NY4699	55°17·2′	2°50·6′W	H	79
Muckle Lapprach	Moray	NJ2729	57°21·0′	3°12·3′W	H	37
Muckle Law	Pth & Kin	NN9809	56°16·0′	3°38·4′W	X	58
Muckle Lochs	Orkney	ND2696	58°51·0′	3°16·5′W	W	6,7
Muckle Long Hill	Aberd	NJ4536	57°24·9′	2°54·5′W	X	28,29
Muckle Lunga Water	Shetld	HU3288	60°34·7′	1°24·5′W	W	1
Muckle Lyne	Highld	NH9745	57°29·3′	3°42·6′W	X	27
Muckle Moss	Northum	NY7966	54°59·5′	2°19·3′W	H	86,87
Muckle Ness	Shetld	HU4661	60°20·1′	1°9·5′W	X	2,3
Muckle Ocklester	Orkney	HY5102	58°54·4′	2°50·6′W	X	6,7
Muckle Ord	Aberd	NO6295	57°2·9′	2°37·1′W	H	37,45
Muckle Ossa	Shetld	HU2185	60°33·1′	1°36·5′W	X	3
Muckle Quoy	Orkney	HY4851	59°20·8′	2°54·4′W	X	5
Muckleridge	Northum	NZ0373	55°3·3′	1°56·8′W	X	87
Muckle Rig	Pth & Kin	NO0207	56°15·0′	3°34·5′W	X	58
Muckle Roe	Shetld	HU3165	60°22·3′	1°25·8′W	X	3
Muckle Rysa	Orkney	ND3096	58°51·0′	3°12·3′W	X	6,7
Muckle Samuel's Crags	Northum	NY6878	55°6·0′	2°29·7′W	X	86,87
Muckle Scord	Shetld	HU6292	60°36·7′	0°51·5′W	X	1,2
Muckle Shank	Moray	NJ2434	57°23·7′	3°15·4′W	X	28
Muckle Side	Scot Bord	NT1321	55°28·8′	3°22·2′W	H	72
Muckle Skerry	Orkney	ND4678	58°41·4′	2°55·4′W	X	7
Muckle Skerry	Shetld	HU6273	60°26·4′	0°51·9′W	X	2
Muckle Skerry of Neapaback	Shetld	HU5378	60°29·2′	1°1·6′W	X	2,3
Muckle Snab	D & G	NY2683	55°8·4′	3°9·2′W	X	79
Muckle Sound	Shetld	HU3518	59°57·0′	1°21·9′W	W	4
Mucklestone	Staffs	SJ7237	52°56·0′	2°24·6′W	T	127
Mucklestone Wood Fm	Staffs	SJ7336	52°55·5′	2°23·7′W	FM	127
Muckle Swart Houll	Shetld	HU4894	60°37·9′	1°6·9′W	H	1,2
Muckleton	Norf	TF8139	52°55·3′	0°42·0′E	T	132
Muckleton	Shrops	SJ5921	52°47·3′	2°36·1′W	T	126
Muckleton Bank Fm	Shrops	SJ5921	52°47·3′	2°36·1′W	FM	126
Muckleton Moss	Shrops	SJ5922	52°47·9′	2°36·1′W	X	126
Muckletown	Aberd	NJ5721	57°16·9′	2°42·3′W	X	37
Muckletown	Aberd	NJ5758	57°36·9′	2°42·7′W	X	29
Muckle Twiness	Orkney	HY5206	58°56·6′	2°49·6′W	X	6,7
Muckle Vandra Water	Shetld	HU4989	60°35·2′	1°5·8′W	W	1,2
Muckle Ward	Shetld	HU2961	60°20·2′	1°28·0′W	H	3
Muckle Ward	Shetld	HU3246	60°12·1′	1°24·9′W	H	4
Muckle Water	Orkney	HY3930	59°9·4′	3°3·5′W	W	6
Muckle Water	Orkney	HY4343	59°16·4′	2°59·5′W	W	5
Muckle White Hope	D & G	NT1900	55°17·5′	3°16·1′W	X	79
Mucklewick Hill	Shrops	SO3397	52°34·2′	2°58·9′W	H	137
Muckle Wirawil	Shetld	HU6690	60°35·5′	0°47·2′W	H	1,2
Muckle Wood	D & G	NX8097	55°15·4′	3°52·9′W	F	78
Muckley	Northum	NZ1393	55°14·1′	1°47·3′W	X	81
Muckley	Shrops	SO6495	52°33·3′	2°31·5′W	T	138
Muckley Corner	Staffs	SK0806	52°39·3′	1°52·5′W	T	139
Muckley Cross	Shrops	SO6495	52°33·3′	2°31·5′W	T	138

Mucklow Hill	Dudley	SO9784	52°27·5′	2°2·2′W	X	139
Mucklure	Shetld	HU2147	60°12·7′	1°36·8′W	X	3
Mucknell Fm	Worcs	SO9051	52°9·7′	2°8·4′W	FM	150
Muckquoy	Orkney	ND4589	58°47·4′	2°56·6′W	X	7
Muckrach Farm	Highld	NH9825	57°18·5′	3°41·1′W	FM	36
Muckraw	W Loth	NS9271	55°55·5′	3°43·3′W	X	65
Mucks Water	E Ayr	NS5540	55°38·2′	4°17·8′W	W	71
Muckton	Lincs	TF3781	53°18·7′	0°3·8′E	T	122
Muckton Bottom	Lincs	TF3682	53°19·3′	0°2·9′E	T	122
Muckton Wood	Lincs	TF3881	53°18·7′	0°4·7′E	F	122
Muck Water	E Ayr	NS4903	55°18·1′	4°22·3′W	W	77
Muck Water	S Ayr	NX2588	55°9·6′	4°44·4′W	W	76
Muckwell	Devon	SX8039	50°14·6′	3°40·6′W	X	202
Muckworthy	Devon	SS4001	50°47·4′	4°15·8′W	X	190
Mucky Park	N Yks	SE0457	54°0·8′	1°55·9′W	X	104
Muclich Hill	Arg & Bt	NS0072	55°54·2′	5°11·5′W	H	63
Mucomir Fm	Highld	NN1883	56°54·4′	4°58·9′W	FM	34,41
Mucraidh	Arg & Bt	NR4565	55°48·9′	6°3·8′W	X	60,61
Mudalach	Highld	NG7624	57°15·4′	5°42·4′W	X	33
Mudale	Highld	NC5335	58°17·0′	4°30·0′W	X	16
Mudbeck	N Yks	NY9507	54°27·7′	2°4·2′W	X	91,92
Mud Beck	N Yks	NY9608	54°28·3′	2°3·3′W	W	91,92
Mud Becks	Cumbr	SD7892	54°19·6′	2°19·9′W	X	98
Mudd	Tames	SJ9994	53°26·8′	2°0·5′W	T	109
Muddiford	Devon	SS5638	51°7·6′	4°3·1′W	T	180
Muddifords Fm	Devon	ST0212	50°54·2′	3°23·2′W	FM	181
Muddioch Rock	D & G	NX0937	54°41·8′	4°57·4′W	X	82
Muddisdale	Orkney	HY4310	58°58·7′	2°59·0′W	X	6
Muddlebridge	Devon	SS5232	51°4·3′	4°6·4′W	T	180
Muddlescwm	Carm	SN4205	51°43·5′	4°16·9′W	X	159
Muddles Green	E Susx	TQ5413	50°54·0′	0°11·8′E	T	199
Muddleswood	W Susx	TQ2614	50°54·9′	0°12·1′W	X	198
Muddox Barrow Fm	Dorset	SY8496	50°46·0′	2°13·2′W	FM	194
Muddy Brook	Kirk	SE0610	53°35·4′	1°54·1′W	W	110
Muddygill Plain	Cumbr	NY6710	54°29·3′	2°30·1′W	X	91
Muddyloch	Shetld	HU4768	60°23·9′	1°8·3′W	X	2,3
Mudeford	Dorset	SZ1892	50°43·9′	1°44·3′W	T	195
Mudfields Fm	N Yks	SE2389	54°18·0′	1°38·4′W	FM	99
Mud Fm	Hants	SU5231	51°4·8′	1°15·1′W	FM	185
Mudford	Somer	ST5719	50°58·4′	2°36·4′W	T	183
Mudford Gates	Devon	SS8612	50°54·0′	3°36·9′W	X	181
Mudford Sock	Somer	ST5519	50°58·4′	2°38·1′W	T	183
Mudgedown Fm	S Glos	ST6885	51°34·0′	2°27·3′W	FM	172
Mudgeley Hill	Somer	ST4445	51°12·3′	2°47·7′W	H	182
Mudgeon Fm	Corn	SW7324	50°4·6′	5°10·0′W	FM	204
Mudge's Fm	Somer	ST3518	50°57·7′	2°55·2′W	FM	193
Mudginwell Fm	Oxon	SP5027	51°56·6′	1°16·0′W	FM	164
Mudgley	Somer	ST4445	51°12·3′	2°47·7′W	T	182
Mudhall	Pth & Kin	NO2242	56°34·1′	3°15·7′W	X	53
Mudhouse	Aberd	NJ9423	57°18·1′	2°5·5′W	X	38
Mudlee Bracks	Angus	NO5185	56°57·5′	2°47·9′W	H	44
Mudless Copse	I of W	SZ4487	50°41·1′	1°22·2′W	F	196
Mudloch Cott	Angus	NO5278	56°53·7′	2°46·8′W	X	44
Mudwall	Essex	TL6217	51°49·9′	0°21·5′E	X	167
Mudwalls Fm	Warw	SP0653	52°10·7′	1°54·3′W	FM	150
Muffy's Platt Fm	Lancs	SD3748	53°55·7′	2°57·2′W	FM	102
Mugdock	Stir	NS5576	55°57·6′	4°18·9′W	T	64
Mugdock Country Park	Stir	NS5577	55°58·1′	4°19·0′W	X	64
Mugdock Loch	Stir	NS5577	55°58·1′	4°19·0′W	W	64
Mugdock Resr	E Dunb	NS5575	55°57·0′	4°18·9′W	W	64
Mugdock Wood	Stir	NS5476	55°57·5′	4°19·9′W	F	64
Mugdrum	Fife	NO2218	56°21·1′	3°15·3′W	X	58
Mugdrum Island	Fife	NO2218	56°21·1′	3°15·3′W	X	58
Mugeary	Highld	NG4438	57°21·9′	6°15·0′W	T	23,32
Mu Geos	Orkney	HY5736	59°12·8′	2°44·7′W	X	5
Muggerslandburn	E Ayr	NS4433	55°34·2′	4°28·0′W	X	70
Mugginton	Derby	SK2843	52°59·3′	1°34·6′W	T	119,128
Muggintonlane End	Derby	SK2844	52°59·8′	1°34·6′W	T	119,128
Muggleswick	Durham	NZ0450	54°50·9′	1°55·8′W	T	87
Muggleswick Common	Durham	NZ0146	54°48·8′	1°58·6′W	X	87
Muggleswick Park	Durham	NZ0349	54°50·4′	1°56·8′W	X	87
Mugswell	Surrey	TQ2654	51°16·5′	0°11·2′W	T	187
Muie	Highld	NC6704	58°0·6′	4°14·6′W	T	16
Muiemore Lochs	Highld	NC7619	58°8·8′	4°5·9′W	W	17
Muil	D & G	NX8180	55°6·3′	3°51·5′W	X	78
Muil Burn	D & G	NX8279	55°5·7′	3°50·5′W	W	84
Muileann Dhail	N Eil	NB4961	58°28·2′	6°17·8′W	X	8
Muileann Eiteag Bàgh	Arg & Bt	NR7173	55°54·0′	5°39·4′W	W	62
Muileann Gaoithe	N Ayr	NR9835	55°34·3′	5°11·8′W	X	69
Muil Fm	D & G	NX2860	54°54·6′	4°40·6′W	FM	82
Muil Hill	D & G	NX8280	55°6·3′	3°50·5′W	H	78
Muillbane Hill	S Ayr	NX0874	55°1·7′	4°59·8′W	X	76
Muillichinn	N Eil	NF7941	57°21·0′	7°19·8′W	X	22
Muil, The	D & G	NX1970	54°59·8′	4°49·3′W	X	76
Muir	Aberd	NO0689	56°59·2′	3°32·4′W	T	43
Muir	E Ayr	NS4826	55°30·5′	4°24·0′W	X	70
Muirake	Aberd	NJ5657	57°36·3′	2°43·7′W	X	29
Muirale Ho	Pth & Kin	NO1739	56°32·4′	3°20·5′W	X	53
Muiralehouse	Highld	NH6955	57°34·2′	4°11·0′W	X	26
Muiralehouse	Stir	NS8189	56°5·0′	3°54·3′W	X	57,65
Muiravonside Country Park	Falk	NS9675	55°57·7′	3°39·5′W	X	65
Muir Burn	D & G	NY4581	55°7·5′	2°51·3′W	W	79
Muirburn	Scot Bord	NT0941	55°39·5′	3°26·3′W	X	72
Muir Burn	Scot Bord	NT1336	55°36·8′	3°22·4′W	W	72
Muirburn	S Lanak	NS8135	55°35·9′	3°52·9′W	X	71,72
Muirburnhead Plantation	D & G	NY4482	55°8·0′	2°52·3′W	F	79
Muircambus	Fife	NO4602	56°12·7′	2°51·8′W	X	59
Muircleuch	D & G	NS8805	55°19·8′	3°45·5′W	X	71,78
Muircleugh	Scot Bord	NT5145	55°42·0′	2°46·3′W	T	73
Muircleugh Stell	Scot Bord	NT5045	55°42·0′	2°47·3′W	X	73
Muircockhall	Fife	NT1190	56°5·9′	3°25·4′W	X	58
Muir Cottage	Aberd	NO0789	56°59·2′	3°31·4′W	X	43
Muircraigs	Fife	NO3723	56°24·0′	3°0·8′W	X	54,59
Muircroft	Arg & Bt	NM8729	56°24·6′	5°26·7′W	X	49
Muir Dam	Stir	NN6602	56°11·8′	4°9·1′W	W	57
Muirden	Aberd	NJ7053	57°34·2′	2°29·6′W	X	29
Muir Dens	Fife	NO3422	56°23·4′	3°3·7′W	X	54,59
Muirdrochwood	D & G	NX6191	55°11·9′	4°10·6′W	X	77
Muirdrum	Angus	NO5637	56°31·6′	2°42·5′W	T	54

Muirdyke	E Ayr	NS5616	55°25·3'	4°16·1'W	X	71
Muirdykes	Renf	NS3959	55°48·1'	4°33·7'W	X	63
Muir-edge	Angus	NO5443	56°34·9'	2°44·5'W	X	54
Muiredge	Fife	NT3598	56°10·5'	3°2·4'W	T	59
Muiredge	Pth & Kin	NN9012	56°17·5'	3°46·2'W	X	58
Muiredge	Pth & Kin	NO2323	56°23·8'	3°14·4'W	X	53,58
Muirend	Aberd	NJ4520	57°16·3'	2°54·3'W	X	37
Muirend	Aberd	NK0542	57°28·4'	1°54·5'W	X	30
Muirend	C of Glas	NS5760	55°49·0'	4°16·5'W	T	64
Muirend	Fife	NO3107	56°15·3'	3°6·4'W	X	59
Muirend	N Lanak	NS7371	55°55·2'	4°1·5'W	X	64
Muirend	Pth & Kin	NN7821	56°22·2'	3°58·1'W	X	51,52,57
Muirend	Pth & Kin	NN9921	56°22·5'	3°37·7'W	X	52,53,58
Muirend	Pth & Kin	NO1625	56°24·8'	3°21·2'W	X	53,58
Muirend	Renf	NS3857	55°47·0'	4°34·6'W	X	63
Muirend	W Loth	NT0970	55°55·1'	3°26·9'W	X	65
Muiresk Ho	Aberd	NJ7049	57°32·1'	2°29·6'W	X	29
Muirfad	D & G	NX4562	54°56·0'	4°24·7'W	X	83
Muirfad Flow	D & G	NX4562	54°56·0'	4°24·7'W	X	83
Muirfauldhouse	Renf	NS3360	55°48·5'	4°39·5'W	X	63
Muirfield	D & G	NY0879	55°6·1'	3°26·1'W	X	85
Muirfield	E Loth	NT4883	56°2·5'	2°49·6'W	X	66
Muirfield	Pth & Kin	NO0400	56°11·2'	3°32·4'W	X	58
Muirfield	Pth & Kin	NO1510	56°16·7'	3°21·9'W	X	58
Muirfield	Scot Bord	NT5120	55°28·5'	2°46·1'W	X	73
Muir Fm	S Lanak	NS6157	55°47·4'	4°12·6'W	FM	64
Muirfoot	S Lanak	NS9149	55°43·6'	3°43·7'W	X	72
Muirfoot Burn	E Ayr	NS6216	55°25·4'	4°10·4'W	W	71
Muirhall	Pth & Kin	NO1424	56°24·3'	3°23·2'W	X	53,58
Muirhall	S Lanak	NS9952	55°45·3'	3°36·1'W	X	65,72
Muirhead	Aberd	NJ5611	57°11·5'	2°43·2'W	X	37
Muirhead	Aberd	NO7266	56°47·3'	2°27·1'W	X	45
Muirhead	Angus	NO3434	56°29·9'	3°3·9'W	T	54
Muirhead	Angus	NO5441	56°33·8'	2°44·5'W	X	54
Muirhead	C of Glas	NS6763	55°50·8'	4°7·0'W	X	64
Muirhead	D & G	NS8210	55°23·2'	3°51·3'W	X	71,78
Muirhead	D & G	NX6555	54°52·5'	4°5·8'W	X	83,84
Muirhead	E Ayr	NS5534	55°34·9'	4°17·6'W	X	71
Muirhead	E Ayr	NS5731	55°33·4'	4°15·6'W	X	71
Muirhead	E Dunb	NS6176	55°57·7'	4°13·2'W	X	64
Muirhead	E Renf	NS4555	55°46·1'	4°27·8'W	X	64
Muirhead	E Renf	NS4855	55°46·1'	4°24·9'W	X	64
Muirhead	Falk	NS7682	56°1·2'	3°58·9'W	X	57,64
Muirhead	Fife	NO2805	56°14·2'	3°9·3'W	T	59
Muirhead	Fife	NO3708	56°15·9'	3°0·6'W	X	59
Muirhead	Fife	NO4118	56°21·3'	2°56·8'W	X	59
Muirhead	Fife	NO5708	56°16·0'	2°41·2'W	X	59
Muirhead	Fife	NS9887	56°4·2'	3°37·9'W	X	65
Muirhead	Fife	NT2193	56°7·6'	3°15·8'W	X	58
Muirhead	Highld	NH7562	57°38·1'	4°5·2'W	X	21,27
Muirhead	Moray	NJ0863	57°39·1'	3°32·0'W	X	27
Muirhead	N Lanak	NS6869	55°54·0'	4°6·2'W	T	64
Muirhead	N Lanak	NS7576	55°57·9'	3°59·7'W	X	64
Muirhead	N Lanak	NS7671	55°55·2'	3°58·6'W	X	64
Muirhead	Pth & Kin	NN8513	56°18·0'	3°51·1'W	X	58
Muirhead	Pth & Kin	NN9410	56°16·5'	3°42·3'W	X	58
Muirhead	Pth & Kin	NO0315	56°19·3'	3°33·7'W	X	58
Muirhead	S Ayr	NS3331	55°32·9'	4°38·4'W	T	70
Muirhead	S Lanak	NS6344	55°40·5'	4°10·3'W	X	71
Muirhead	S Lanak	NS9048	55°43·0'	3°44·6'W	X	72
Muirhead	S Lanak	NS9330	55°33·4'	3°41·3'W	X	71,72
Muirhead Fm	Fife	NO2905	56°14·2'	3°8·3'W	FM	59
Muirhead Fm	N Lanak	NS8963	55°51·1'	3°45·9'W	FM	65
Muirhead of Balgray	N Ayr	NS3643	55°39·4'	4°36·0'W	X	63,70
Muirhead Resr	N Ayr	NS2556	55°46·2'	4°46·9'W	W	63
Muirheads	Angus	NO6044	56°35·4'	2°38·6'W	X	54
Muirheadston	Pth & Kin	NO0438	56°31·7'	3°33·2'W	X	52,53
Muir Hill	D & G	NY0096	55°15·1'	3°34·0'W	H	78
Muir Hill	S Lanak	NS5944	55°40·4'	4°14·1'W	H	71
Muirhouse	C of Edin	NT2176	55°58·5'	3°15·5'W	T	66
Muirhouse	D & G	NY1284	55°8·8'	3°22·4'W	X	78
Muirhouse	D & G	NY2566	54°59·2'	3°9·9'W	X	85
Muirhouse	E Ayr	NS3837	55°36·2'	4°33·9'W	X	70
Muirhouse	E Renf	NS4256	55°46·5'	4°30·7'W	X	64
Muirhouse	Inverc	NS3168	55°52·8'	4°41·7'W	X	63
Muirhouse	N Lanak	NS7655	55°46·6'	3°58·2'W	T	64
Muirhouse	S Ayr	NS4032	55°33·6'	4°31·8'W	X	70
Muirhouse	Scot Bord	NT4744	55°41·4'	2°50·1'W	X	73
Muirhouse	S Lanak	NS7740	55°38·5'	3°56·8'W	X	71
Muirhouse	S Lanak	NS8242	55°39·7'	3°52·1'W	X	71,72
Muirhouse	S Lanak	NS9349	55°43·6'	3°41·8'W	X	72
Muirhouse	S Lanak	NS9836	55°36·7'	3°36·7'W	X	72
Muirhouse	S Lanak	NS9843	55°40·4'	3°36·9'W	X	72
Muirhouse	Stir	NS5678	55°58·7'	4°18·0'W	X	64
Muirhouse	W Loth	NT0362	55°50·7'	3°32·5'W	X	65
Muirhousehead	D & G	NY1184	55°8·8'	3°23·4'W	X	78
Muirhouselaw	Scot Bord	NT6228	55°32·9'	2°35·7'W	X	74
Muirhouses	Angus	NO3251	56°39·0'	3°6·1'W	X	53
Muirhouses	Angus	NO3956	56°41·8'	2°59·3'W	T	54
Muirhouses	Angus	NO4436	56°31·0'	2°54·2'W	X	54
Muirhouses	Falk	NT0180	56°0·4'	3°34·8'W	T	65
Muirhouses	Pth & Kin	NO2724	56°24·4'	3°10·5'W	T	53,59
Muirhouses	S Lanak	NS6753	55°45·4'	4°6·7'W	X	64
Muirhouses	W Dunb	NS5075	55°56·9'	4°23·7'W	X	64
Muirkirk	E Ayr	NS6927	55°31·4'	4°4·1'W	T	71
Muirlaggan	Stir	NN5119	56°20·7'	4°24·2'W	X	57
Muirlands	Pth & Kin	NO0537	56°31·2'	3°32·2'W	X	52,53
Muirlaught Fm	N Ayr	NS2646	55°40·8'	4°45·6'W	FM	63
Muirlea Fm	S Lanak	NT0341	55°39·4'	3°32·1'W	FM	72
Muirloch	Angus	NO3134	56°29·8'	3°6·8'W	X	53
Muirmailing	Stir	NS8286	56°3·4'	3°53·3'W	X	57,65
Muirmains Fm	S Lanak	NS6854	55°45·9'	4°5·8'W	FM	64
Muirmealing	Fife	NS9992	56°6·9'	3°37·0'W	X	58
Muirmill	Pth & Kin	NS9995	56°8·5'	3°37·1'W	X	58
Muirmill	S Ayr	NS3833	55°34·1'	4°33·7'W	X	70
Muirmill	Stir	NS7283	56°1·6'	4°2·8'W	X	57
Muirmill	Stir	NS7283	56°1·6'	4°2·8'W	X	64
Muirmills	Angus	NO6154	56°40·8'	2°37·7'W	X	54
Muirmouth	Pth & Kin	NN9319	56°21·3'	3°43·5'W	X	58
Muirneag	N Eil	NB4748	58°21·1'	6°19·0'W	H	8

Mùirnemeall	Arg & Bt	NR2672	55°52·1'	6°22·4'W	X	60
Muir of Alford	Aberd	NJ5415	57°13·7'	2°45·3'W	T	37
Muir o' Fauld	Pth & Kin	NN9719	56°21·4'	3°39·6'W	X	58
Muir of Balnagowan	Highld	NH8155	57°34·4'	3°58·9'W	X	27
Muir of Blackiemuir	Aberd	NO7071	56°50·0'	2°29·0'W	X	45
Muir of Dess	Aberd	NJ5501	57°6·1'	2°44·1'W	X	37
Muir of Dinnet	Aberd	NO4397	57°3·9'	2°55·9'W	X	37,44
Muir of Drumlochy	Pth & Kin	NO1548	56°37·2'	3°22·7'W	X	53
Muir of Drumshade or Cabbylatch	Angus	NO3850	56°38·5'	3°0·2'W	X	54
Muir of Fairburn	Highld	NH4852	57°32·2'	4°31·9'W	X	26
Muir of Fowlis	Aberd	NJ5612	57°12·1'	2°43·2'W	T	37
Muir of Gormack	Pth & Kin	NO1247	56°36·7'	3°25·6'W	X	53
Muir of Holm	Angus	NO3155	56°41·2'	3°7·1'W	X	53
Muir of Holmie	Moray	NJ4161	57°38·4'	2°58·8'W	X	28
Muir of Kinellar	Aberd	NJ8013	57°12·7'	2°19·4'W	X	38
Muir of Kinnoir	Aberd	NJ5545	57°29·8'	2°44·6'W	X	29
Muir of Lochs	Moray	NJ3062	57°38·8'	3°9·9'W	T	28
Muir of Logie	Moray	NJ0151	57°32·6'	3°38·8'W	X	27
Muir of Lour	Angus	NO4844	56°35·4'	2°50·4'W	X	54
Muir of Merklands	Pth & Kin	NO1056	56°41·5'	3°27·7'W	X	53
Muir of Miltonduff	Moray	NJ1859	57°37·1'	3°21·9'W	X	28
Muir of Orchil	Pth & Kin	NN8512	56°17·4'	3°51·0'W	X	58
Muir of Ord	Highld	NH5250	57°31·2'	4°27·8'W	T	26
Muir of Pearsie	Angus	NO3661	56°44·4'	3°2·3'W	X	44
Muir of Pert	Angus	NO4136	56°31·0'	2°57·1'W	T	54
Muir of Pert	Angus	NO6563	56°45·7'	2°33·9'W	F	45
Muir of Tarradale	Highld	NH5450	57°31·3'	4°25·8'W	T	26
Muir of the Clans	Highld	NH8352	57°32·8'	3°56·8'W	X	27
Muir of Thorn	Pth & Kin	NO0737	56°31·2'	3°30·2'W	X	52,53
Muir of Turtory	Moray	NJ5948	57°31·5'	2°40·6'W	X	29
Muir o' Lea	Pth & Kin	NN9217	56°20·2'	3°44·4'W	X	58
Muirpark	Clackm	NS8695	56°8·3'	3°49·6'W	X	58
Muirpark	E Loth	NT4172	55°56·5'	2°56·2'W	X	66
Muir Park	Fife	NO5113	56°18·7'	2°47·1'W	X	59
Muirpark	Stir	NS7587	56°3·8'	4°0·0'W	X	57
Muir Park Resr	Stir	NS4892	56°6·1'	4°26·2'W	W	57
Muirs	Orkney	ND2991	58°48·3'	3°13·3'W	X	7
Muirshearlich	Highld	NN1380	56°52·7'	5°3·7'W	T	34,41
Muirshiel	E Ayr	NS4351	55°43·9'	4°29·6'W	X	64
Muirshiel Country Park	Renf	NS3163	55°50·1'	4°41·5'W	X	63
Muirside	Aberd	NJ5136	57°25·0'	2°48·5'W	X	29
Muirside	Angus	NO4243	56°34·8'	2°56·2'W	X	54
Muirside	D & G	NX9481	55°7·0'	3°39·3'W	X	78
Muirside	E Ayr	NS5040	55°38·1'	4°22·5'W	X	70
Muirside	Fife	NO3416	56°20·2'	3°3·6'W	X	59
Muirside	Fife	NT0485	56°3·2'	3°32·0'W	X	65
Muirside	Fife	NT0990	56°5·9'	3°27·3'W	X	58
Muirside	Moray	NH9758	57°36·3'	3°43·0'W	X	27
Muirside	Pth & Kin	NN8416	56°19·6'	3°52·1'W	X	58
Muirside Fm	Clackm	NS8695	56°8·3'	3°49·6'W	FM	58
Muirside of Aldbar	Angus	NO5756	56°41·9'	2°41·7'W	X	54
Muirside of Craigo	Angus	NO6864	56°46·2'	2°31·0'W	X	45
Muirside of Kinneddar	Fife	NT0290	56°5·8'	3°34·1'W	X	58
Muirside of Kinnell	Angus	NO6052	56°39·7'	2°38·7'W	X	54
Muirside of Melgund	Angus	NO5454	56°40·8'	2°44·6'W	X	54
Muirskeith	Angus	NO3859	56°43·4'	3°0·3'W	X	54
Muirs of Kildrummy	Aberd	NJ4619	57°15·8'	2°53·3'W	X	37
Muirs of Kinnesswood	Pth & Kin	NO1605	56°14·1'	3°20·9'W	X	58
Muirston	E Ayr	NS4616	55°25·1'	4°25·5'W	X	70
Muirston	E Ayr	NS4723	55°28·9'	4°24·8'W	X	70
Muirstone	Aberd	NJ9360	57°38·1'	2°6·6'W	X	30
Muirstone Croft	Aberd	NJ9260	57°38·1'	2°7·6'W	X	30
Muirtack	Aberd	NJ8146	57°30·5'	2°18·6'W	X	29,30
Muirtack	Aberd	NJ9937	57°25·7'	2°0·5'W	T	30
Muir, The	E Ayr	NS5216	55°25·2'	4°19·9'W	X	70
Muir Toll	Stir	NS6382	56°0·9'	4°11·4'W	X	57,64
Muirton	Aberd	NJ5608	57°9·9'	2°43·2'W	X	37
Muirton	Aberd	NJ6708	57°10·0'	2°32·3'W	X	38
Muirton	Aberd	NJ7128	57°20·8'	2°28·5'W	X	38
Muirton	Aberd	NJ7358	57°36·9'	2°26·7'W	X	29
Muirton	Aberd	NJ7726	57°19·7'	2°22·5'W	X	38
Muirton	Aberd	NJ9316	57°14·3'	2°6·5'W	X	38
Muirton	Aberd	NO7768	56°48·4'	2°22·2'W	X	45
Muirton	E Loth	NT5180	56°0·9'	2°46·7'W	X	66
Muirton	Fife	NT1492	56°7·0'	3°22·5'W	X	58
Muirton	Highld	NH6254	57°33·6'	4°17·9'W	X	26
Muirton	Highld	NH7463	57°38·6'	4°6·2'W	X	21,27
Muirton	Moray	NJ2268	57°42·0'	3°18·1'W	X	28
Muirton	Pth & Kin	NN9211	56°17·0'	3°44·2'W	T	58
Muirton	Pth & Kin	NO1025	56°24·8'	3°27·1'W	T	53,58
Muirton	Pth & Kin	NO2247	56°36·8'	3°15·8'W	X	53
Muirton	Scot Bord	NT7058	55°49·1'	2°28·3'W	X	67,74
Muirton	Stir	NS8192	56°6·6'	3°54·4'W	X	57
Muirton Fm	Fife	NT2495	56°8·8'	3°13·0'W	FM	59
Muirton Hill	Arg & Bt	NS0468	55°52·2'	5°7·5'W	H	63
Muirton Home Fm	Aberd	NJ9317	57°14·9'	2°6·5'W	FM	38
Muirton Mains	Highld	NH4553	57°32·7'	4°34·9'W	X	26
Muirton of Ardblair	Pth & Kin	NO1643	56°34·5'	3°21·6'W	T	53
Muirton of Ballochy	Angus	NO6462	56°45·2'	2°34·9'W	X	45
Muirton of Drumlochy	Pth & Kin	NO1547	56°36·7'	3°22·6'W	X	53
Muirton of Memsie	Aberd	NJ9662	57°39·1'	2°3·6'W	X	30
Muirton of Sauchen	Aberd	NJ6811	57°11·6'	2°31·3'W	X	38
Muirton Wood	Aberd	NJ4804	57°7·7'	2°51·1'W	F	37
Muirton Wood	Highld	NH4453	57°32·7'	4°35·9'W	F	26
Muirtown	Aberd	NJ6045	57°29·9'	2°39·6'W	X	29
Muirtown	Moray	NH9959	57°36·8'	3°41·0'W	X	27
Muirtown Basin	Highld	NH6546	57°29·3'	4°14·7'W	W	26
Muirtown of Barras	Aberd	NO8381	56°55·5'	2°16·3'W	X	45
Muirward Wood	Pth & Kin	NO1428	56°26·4'	3°23·2'W	F	53,58
Muiryard	D & G	NX6454	54°52·0'	4°6·7'W	X	83
Muiryden	Highld	NH7059	57°36·4'	4°10·1'W	X	27
Muiryfaulds	Angus	NO4342	56°34·2'	2°55·2'W	X	54
Muiryfield	Aberd	NJ6351	57°33·1'	2°36·6'W	X	29
Muiryfold	Aberd	NJ7651	57°33·2'	2°23·6'W	X	29
Muiryfold	Aberd	NJ8427	57°20·3'	2°15·5'W	X	38
Muiryfold	Aberd	NJ8816	57°14·3'	2°11·5'W	X	38
Muiryfold	Moray	NJ4852	57°33·6'	2°51·6'W	X	28,29
Muiryhall	Moray	NJ1860	57°37·6'	3°21·9'W	X	28
Muiryhall	Moray	NJ2862	57°38·8'	3°11·9'W	X	28

Muiryhaugh	Aberd	NO6691	57°0·8'	2°33·1'W	X	38,45
Muiryhill	Aberd	NJ6458	57°36·9'	2°35·7'W	X	29
Muiryhill	D & G	NS8703	55°18·7'	3°46·4'W	X	78
Muker	N Yks	SD9097	54°22·3'	2°8·8'W	T	98
Muker Common	N Yks	SD8995	54°21·3'	2°9·7'W	X	98
Muker Edge	N Yks	SD8996	54°21·8'	2°9·7'W	X	98
Muker Side	N Yks	SD8997	54°22·3'	2°9·7'W	X	98
Mula	N Eil	NB0322	58°5·5'	7°1·9'W	H	13
Mùla	N Eil	NG0290	57°48·3'	7°0·5'W	H	18
Mula Chaolartan	N Eil	NB0524	58°6·7'	7°0·1'W	H	13,14
Muladail	N Eil	NB0812	58°0·3'	6°56·1'W	H	13,14
Mula Mac Sgiathain	N Eil	NB0227	58°8·2'	7°3·3'W	X	13
Mula na Caillich	N Eil	NB2507	57°58·3'	6°38·6'W	H	13,14
Mulan an t- Sagairt	Stir	NN4103	56°11·8'	4°33·3'W	X	56
Mulbarton	Norf	TG1900	52°33·4'	1°14·3'E	T	134
Mulben	Moray	NJ3550	57°32·4'	3°4·7'W	T	28
Mulberry	Corn	SX0265	50°27·3'	4°47·0'W	T	200
Mulberry Fm	N Yks	SE6135	53°48·7'	1°4·0'W	FM	105
Mulberry Middle	Suff	TM1840	52°1·2'	1°11·0'E	X	169
Mulbrooks Fm	E Susx	TQ5807	50°50·7'	0°15·0'E	FM	199
Muldaddie	D & G	NX0940	54°43·4'	4°57·5'W	X	82
Muldearie Mains	Moray	NJ3950	57°32·4'	3°0·7'W	X	28
Mulderg	Highld	NH8378	57°46·8'	3°57·6'W	X	21
Muldoanich	N Eil	NL6893	56°54·8'	7°26·9'W	X	31
Muldron	W Loth	NS9258	55°48·4'	3°43·0'W	X	65,72
Mulea Plantation	Arg & Bt	NS3489	56°4·2'	4°39·6'W	F	56
Mule Hill	E Ayr	NS5934	55°35·0'	4°13·8'W	H	71
Mule, The	Powys	SO1790	52°30·3'	3°13·0'W	W	136
Mulfra	Corn	SW4534	50°9·3'	5°33·8'W	T	203
Mulfra Hill	Corn	SW4535	50°9·8'	5°33·9'W	H	203
Mulfran	Blae Gw	SO2010	51°47·2'	3°9·2'W	H	161
Mulfra Quoit	Corn	SW4535	50°9·8'	5°33·9'W	A	203
Mulgrave Castle	N Yks	NZ8412	54°30·0'	0°41·8'W	X	94
Mulgrave Cottage	N Yks	NZ8512	54°30·0'	0°40·8'W	X	94
Mulgrave Fm	N Yks	NZ8110	54°29·0'	0°44·6'W	FM	94
Mulgrave Woods	N Yks	NZ8411	54°29·5'	0°41·8'W	F	94
Mulindry	Arg & Bt	NR3559	55°45·4'	6°13·0'W	X	60
Mull	Arg & Bt	NR5808	55°18·7'	5°48·4'W	X	68
Mulla	N Eil	NB2202	57°55·5'	6°41·3'W	H	14
Mulla	Shetld	HU4064	60°21·7'	1°16·0'W	X	2,3
Mullach	D & G	NX9386	55°9·7'	3°40·3'W	X	78
Mullach a' Bhrian Léitir	Highld	NH2793	57°53·8'	4°54·7'W	H	20
Mullach a' Chadha Bhuidhe	Highld	NH3095	57°55·0'	4°51·7'W	H	20
Mullach a' Charnain	N Eil	NF7604	57°1·1'	7°19·9'W	H	31
Mullach a' Chùirn	Arg & Bt	NS1799	56°9·2'	4°56·3'W	X	56
Mullach a' Gharbh-leathaid	Highld	NH1744	57°27·2'	5°2·6'W	X	25
Mullach a' Ghlas-thuill	Highld	NH1631	57°20·2'	5°3·0'W	H	25
Mullach a' Ghlinne	Highld	NH3601	57°4·5'	4°41·9'W	H	34
Mullach a' Ghlinn-mhòir	N Eil	NF8125	57°12·5'	7°16·6'W	H	22
Mullach Airisprìdh	N Eil	NB0716	58°2·4'	6°57·4'W	X	13,14
Mullach a' Lusgan	N Eil	NL5579	56°46·7'	7°38·5'W	X	31
Mullach an Achaidh Mhòir	Highld	NG6716	57°10·8'	5°50·9'W	H	32
Mullach an Langa	N Eil	NB1409	57°59·0'	6°49·8'W	H	13,14
Mullach an Leathaid Riabhaich	Highld	NC2924	58°10·6'	4°54·0'W	H	15
Mullach an Rathain	Highld	NG9157	57°33·6'	5°29·2'W	H	25
Mullach an Ròin	N Eil	NB0716	58°2·4'	6°57·4'W	H	13,14
Mullach a' Ruisg	N Eil	NB1612	58°0·6'	6°48·0'W	H	13,14
Mullach Bàn	Arg & Bt	NM3920	56°18·3'	6°12·7'W	H	48
Mullach Bàn	Arg & Bt	NR4651	55°41·4'	6°2·1'W	X	60
Mullach Beag	N Ayr	NS0530	55°31·7'	5°4·9'W	H	69
Mullach Ben Sca	Highld	NG3348	57°26·9'	6°26·6'W	X	23
Mullach Bhiogadail	N Eil	NB1712	58°0·7'	6°47·0'W	H	13,14
Mullach Bi	N Eil	NF0899	57°48·8'	8°35·7'W	H	18
Mullach Breac Mhalasgair	N Eil	NB3016	58°3·3'	6°34·1'W	H	13,14
Mullach Buidhe	N Ayr	NR9042	55°37·8'	5°19·7'W	H	62,69
Mullach Buidhe	N Ayr	NR9942	55°38·1'	5°11·2'W	X	62,69
Mullach Buidhe	Highld	NG1099	57°53·4'	6°53·2'W	X	14
Mullach Chàrlabhaigh	N Eil	NB2043	58°17·5'	6°46·2'W	T	8
Mullach Chonachair	Highld	NC3402	57°58·8'	4°48·0'W	H	15
Mullach Clach à Bhlàir	Highld	NN8892	57°0·6'	3°50·2'W	A	35,43
Mullach Coire a' Chuir	Arg & Bt	NN1703	56°11·3'	4°56·5'W	H	56
Mullach Coire Ardachaidh	Highld	NH2004	57°5·8'	4°57·8'W	H	34
Mullach Coire Mhic Fhearchair	Highld	NH0573	57°42·5'	5°15·9'W	H	19
Mullach Coire na Gaoitheag	Highld	NH4681	57°47·8'	4°35·0'W	H	20
Mullach Coire nan Dearcag	Highld	NN7786	56°57·2'	4°0·9'W	H	42
Mullach Coire nan Guer-oirean	Highld	NN0489	56°57·3'	5°12·9'W	H	41
Mullach Coire nan Nead	Highld	NN4273	56°49·6'	4°34·9'W	H	42
Mullach Coire Preas nan Seana-char	Highld	NH4380	57°47·2'	4°38·0'W	H	20
Mullach Creag Riaraidh	Highld	NH4684	57°49·4'	4°35·1'W	X	20
Mullachdubh	Aberd	NJ3506	57°8·7'	3°4·0'W	H	37
Mullach Dubh	Arg & Bt	NM8007	56°12·5'	5°32·4'W	H	55
Mullach Dubh	Arg & Bt	NR4064	55°48·2'	6°8·5'W	X	60,61
Mullach Dubh	Arg & Bt	NR7855	55°44·5'	5°31·8'W	H	62
Mullach Fraoch-choire	Highld	NH0917	57°12·5'	5°9·3'W	H	33
Mullach Gàraidh Dhuibhe	Highld	NG3340	57°22·6'	6°26·1'W	X	23
Mullach Glac an t-Sneachda	Arg & Bt	NM4922	56°19·7'	6°3·2'W	X	48
Mullach Glen Ullinish	Highld	NG3342	57°23·7'	6°26·2'W	X	23
Mulla Chleiseabhal	N Eil	NB0707	57°57·6'	6°56·8'W	X	13,14
Mullach Li	Highld	NG8106	57°5·8'	5°36·5'W	H	33
Mullach Lochan nan Gabhar	Moray	NJ1402	57°6·3'	3°24·7'W	X	36
Mullach Mór	Arg & Bt	NR1856	55°43·2'	6°29·0'W	X	60
Mullach Mór	Highld	NG3801	57°1·8'	6°18·6'W	H	32,39
Mullach Mór	N Ayr	NS0629	55°31·2'	5°4·0'W	H	69
Mullach Mór	N Eil	NA0900	57°49·4'	8°34·8'W	H	18
Mullach Mór	N Eil	NF8481	57°42·7'	7°17·9'W	H	18
Mullach na Briobaig	Highld	NN1089	56°57·5'	5°7·0'W	X	34,41
Mullach na Càrn	Highld	NG6029	57°17·6'	5°58·5'W	H	32
Mullach na Creige Deirge	Highld	NC1747	58°22·7'	5°7·3'W	X	9

Mullach na Dheiragain	Highld	NH0825	57°16·8′	5°10·7′W	H	25,33
Mullach na Dubh-chlaise	Highld	NH2513	57°10·7′	4°53·3′W	H	34
Mullach na Maoile	Highld	NH1832	57°20·8′	5°1·0′W	H	25
Mullach nam Faochag	Highld	NH2433	57°21·5′	4°55·1′W	X	25
Mullach nam Maol	Arg & Bt	NN0716	56°18·1′	5°6·7′W	H	50,56
Mullach nan Cadhaichean	Highld	NG8269	57°39·8′	5°38·8′W	H	19,24
Mullach nan Coirean	Highld	NN1266	56°45·1′	5°4·0′W	H	41
Mullach nan Gàll	Arg & Bt	NM0948	56°32·3′	6°43·6′W	X	46
Mullach nan ròn	N Eil	NB3509	57°59·7′	6°28·6′W	H	14
Mullach na Reidheachd	N Eil	NB0914	58°1·5′	6°55·3′W	H	13,14
Mullach na Stùghadh	N Eil	NG0484	57°45·1′	6°58·1′W	X	18
Mullach Neachel	N Eil	NF7308	57°3·1′	7°23·2′W	H	31
Mullach Sgar	N Eil	NF0999	57°48·8′	8°34·7′W	H	18
Mullach Sithidh	Highld	NH0826	57°17·3′	5°10·7′W	X	25,33
Mullach Tarsuinn	Highld	NH2333	57°21·5′	4°56·1′W	H	25
Mullacott	Devon	SS5145	51°11·3′	4°7·5′W	X	180
Mullacott Cross	Devon	SS5144	51°10·8′	4°7·5′W	X	180
Mulla-fo-Dheas	N Eil	NB1407	57°57·9′	6°49·7′W	H	13,14
Mulla-Fo-Thuath	N Eil	NB1308	57°58·4′	6°50·8′W	X	13,14
Mullagh Ouyr	I of M	SC3986	54°14·9′	4°27·9′W	H	95
Mullaghouyr	I of M	SC4085	54°14·4′	4°26·9′W	X	95
Mullairidh	Arg & Bt	NR3796	56°5·3′	6°13·2′W	X	61
Mullardoch House	Highld	NH2331	57°20·4′	4°56·0′W	X	25
Mullbuie	Highld	ND1535	58°18·0′	3°26·5′W	X	11,17
Mull Burn	S Ayr	NX1677	55°3·5′	4°52·4′W	W	76
Mulldonoch	D & G	NX4278	55°4·5′	4°28·1′W	H	77
Mullens Fm	Wilts	SU1258	51°19·5′	1°49·3′W	FM	173
Mullensgrove Fm	Warw	SP1993	52°32·3′	1°42·8′W	FM	139
Mullenspond	Hants	SU2945	51°12·4′	1°34·7′W	T	185
Muller Taing	Orkney	HY6230	59°9·6′	2°39·4′W	X	5
Mullett's Fm	Suff	TL9856	52°10·2′	0°54·1′E	FM	155
Mulley's Fm	Essex	TM1027	51°54·3′	1°3·6′E	FM	168,169
Mulley's Grove	Suff	TL9771	52°18·3′	0°53·8′E	F	144,155
Mullgibbon	D & G	NX5673	55°2·1′	4°14·8′W	X	77
Mullhampton Fm	Heref	SO6427	51°56·7′	2°31·0′W	FM	162
Mull Head	Orkney	HY4955	59°23·0′	2°53·4′W	X	5
Mull Head	Orkney	HY5909	58°58·2′	2°42·3′W	X	6
Mullhill	D & G	NX0842	54°44·4′	4°58·5′W	X	82
Mull Hill	I of M	SC1867	54°4·3′	4°46·5′W	H	95
Mull Hill	Pth & Kin	NN8827	56°25·6′	3°48·5′W	X	52,58
Mullicourt Aqueduct	Norf	TF5302	52°35·9′	0°15·9′E	X	143
Mullinaragher	I of M	SC3073	54°7·7′	4°35·7′W	X	95
Mullinavadie	Pth & Kin	NN7161	56°43·6′	4°6·0′W	X	42
Mulliner's Rough	Warw	SP2285	52°28·0′	1°40·2′W	F	139
Mullingarroch Farm	Highld	NH9518	57°14·7′	3°43·9′W	FM	36
Mullins' Fm	Dorset	ST7514	50°55·7′	2°21·0′W	FM	194
Mullion	Corn	SW6719	50°1·8′	5°14·8′W	T	203
Mullion	Pth & Kin	NN9933	56°29·0′	3°38·0′W	X	52,53
Mullion Cliff	Corn	SW6617	50°0·7′	5°15·6′W	X	203
Mullion Cove	Corn	SW6617	50°0·7′	5°15·6′W	T	203
Mullion Island	Corn	SW6617	50°0·7′	5°15·6′W	X	203
Mullmein Hill	D & G	NX3581	55°6·0′	4°34·7′W	H	77
Mulloch	D & G	NX3762	54°55·8′	4°32·2′W	X	83
Mulloch	D & G	NX6377	55°4·4′	4°8·3′W	X	77
Mulloch an Aird	Highld	NC7564	58°33·0′	4°8·4′W	H	10
Mullochard	Highld	NH9423	57°17·4′	3°45·1′W	X	36
Mullochard	Moray	NJ2230	57°21·5′	3°17·3′W	X	36
Mullochbuie	Highld	NM7282	56°52·7′	5°44·1′W	X	40
Mullochdhu	Aberd	NJ4600	57°5·5′	2°53·0′W	X	37
Mulloch Gorm	Highld	NG9211	57°8·8′	5°25·8′W	X	33
Mulloch Hill	Aberd	NO7391	57°0·8′	2°26·2′W	X	38,45
Mullock	D & G	NX7144	54°46·7′	3°59·9′W	X	83,84
Mullock	Pemb	SM8108	51°43·9′	5°9·9′W	X	157
Mullock Bay	D & G	NX7143	54°46·2′	3°59·9′W	W	83,84
Mull of Cara	Arg & Bt	NR6343	55°37·6′	5°45·5′W	X	62
Mull of Galloway	D & G	NX1530	54°38·1′	4°51·6′W	X	82
Mull of Galloway Fm	D & G	NX1331	54°38·6′	4°53·5′W	FM	82
Mull of Kintyre	Arg & Bt	NR5906	55°17·6′	5°47·3′W	X	68
Mull of Logan	D & G	NX0741	54°43·9′	4°59·4′W	X	82
Mull of Miljoan	S Ayr	NX2796	55°13·9′	4°42·8′W	H	76
Mull of Oa	Arg & Bt	NR2641	55°35·4′	6°20·5′W	X	60
Mull of Ross	D & G	NX6344	54°46·6′	4°7·4′W	H	83
Mull of Sinniness	D & G	NX2251	54°49·6′	4°45·8′W	X	82
Mull Point	D & G	NX6344	54°46·6′	4°7·4′W	X	83
Mull, The	D & G	NX8589	55°11·2′	3°47·9′W	H	78
Mullwhanny	D & G	NX7197	55°15·3′	4°1·3′W	H	77
Mullwharchar	E Ayr	NX4586	55°8·9′	4°25·5′W	H	77
Mullwhilley	S Ayr	NX2277	55°3·6′	4°46·8′W	X	76
Mully Brook	Devon	SS6315	50°55·3′	3°56·6′W	W	180
Mulmein Moss	D & G	NX4276	55°3·5′	4°28·0′W	X	77
Mulniegarroch or Purgatory Burn	D & G	NX2168	54°58·7′	4°47·4′W	W	82
Mulrea Burn	D & G	NX1035	54°40·7′	4°56·4′W	W	82
Mulreesh	Arg & Bt	NR4068	55°50·4′	6°8·7′W	X	60,61
Mulsey Fm	W Susx	TQ0621	50°58·9′	0°29·0′W	FM	197
Mulsford	Wrex	SJ4244	52°59·7′	2°51·4′W	X	117
Mulsford Hall	Wrex	SJ4343	52°59·1′	2°50·5′W	X	117
Mulsop Fm	Powys	SJ2605	52°38·5′	3°5·2′W	FM	126
Mul Thàgaraidh	N Eil	NB3606	57°58·2′	6°27·4′W	X	14
Mulvin	Corn	SW6911	49°57·5′	5°12·9′W	X	203
Mulvra	Corn	SX0050	50°19·2′	4°48·2′W	X	200,204
Mulwith Fm	N Yks	SE3666	54°5·6′	1°26·6′W	FM	99
Mumbie Cottages	D & G	NY3780	55°6·9′	2°58·8′W	X	79
Mumbles Head	Swan	SS6387	51°34·2′	3°58·2′W	X	159
Mumbles Hill	Swan	SS6287	51°34·1′	3°59·1′W	T	159
Mumbles, The	Swan	SS6187	51°34·1′	3°59·9′W	T	159
Mumby	Lincs	TF5174	53°14·7′	0°16·2′E	T	122
Mumfords Fm	Bucks	SU9889	51°35·7′	0°34·7′W	FM	175,176
Mumford's Wood	Suff	TL9138	52°0·7′	0°47·4′E	F	155
Mumps	Oldham	SD9305	53°32·7′	2°5·9′W	T	109
Mumpumps	E Susx	TQ7129	51°2·3′	0°26·7′E	X	188,199
Muncaster Castle	Cumbr	SD1096	54°21·3′	3°22·7′W	A	96
Muncaster Fell	Cumbr	SD1198	54°22·4′	3°21·8′W	X	96
Muncaster Head	Cumbr	SD1498	54°22·5′	3°19·0′W	X	96
Muncey's Fm	Cambs	TL3842	52°3·8′	0°1·2′E	FM	154
Munches	D & G	NX8358	54°54·4′	3°49·1′W	X	84
Munches Wood	Herts	TL2931	51°58·0′	0°6·9′W	F	166
Muncombe Hill	Somer	ST5131	51°4·8′	2°41·6′W	X	182,183
Muncoy	I Scilly	SV8506	49°52·5′	6°22·7′W	X	203
Muncoy Neck	I Scilly	SV8606	49°52·5′	6°21·9′W	W	203

Muncraig	D & G	NX6046	54°47·6′	4°10·2′W	X	83
Muncraig Hill	D & G	NX6147	54°48·2′	4°9·3′W	X	83
Munday	Pth & Kin	NO0720	56°22·0′	3°29·9′W	X	52,53,58
Mundaydean Bottom	Bucks	SU8288	51°35·3′	0°48·6′W	X	175
Munday Fm	Kent	TQ9245	51°10·5′	0°45·2′E	FM	189
Munden Ho	Herts	TL1300	51°41·5′	0°21·5′W	X	166
Munderfield Harold	Heref	SO6254	52°11·2′	2°33·0′W	X	149
Munderfield Row	Heref	SO6451	52°9·6′	2°31·2′W	T	149
Munderfield Stocks	Heref	SO6550	52°9·1′	2°30·3′W	T	149
Mundernal	Aberd	NO7893	57°1·9′	2°21·3′W	H	38,45
Mundesley	Norf	TG3136	52°52·5′	1°26·4′E	T	133
Mundford	Norf	TL8093	52°30·5′	0°39·5′E	T	144
Mundham	Norf	TM3398	52°32·0′	1°26·5′E	T	134
Mundham Grange	Norf	TM3296	52°31·0′	1°25·6′E	X	134
Mundham Ho	Norf	TM3397	52°31·5′	1°26·5′E	X	134
Mundles	S Tyne	NZ3660	54°56·2′	1°25·9′W	X	88
Mundole	Moray	NJ0156	57°35·3′	3°38·9′W	X	27
Mundon	Essex	TL8702	51°41·4′	0°42·7′E	T	168
Mundon Creek	Essex	TL9002	51°41·3′	0°45·3′E	W	168
Mundon Hall	Essex	TL8702	51°41·4′	0°42·7′E	X	168
Mundon Stone Point	Essex	TL9104	51°42·4′	0°46·3′E	X	168
Mundon Wash	Essex	TL8703	51°41·9′	0°42·8′E	W	168
Munduff Hill	Pth & Kin	NO1903	56°13·0′	3°17·9′W	X	58
Mundurno	C of Aber	NJ9413	57°12·7′	2°5·5′W	X	38
Mundy Bois	Kent	TQ9045	51°10·6′	0°43·5′E	T	189
Munerigie	Highld	NH2602	57°4·8′	4°51·8′W	X	34
Munerigie Wood	Highld	NH2702	57°4·9′	4°50·8′W	F	34
Mu Ness	Shetld	HP6301	60°41·5′	0°50·3′W	X	1
Muness	Shetld	HP6301	60°41·5′	0°50·3′W	T	1
Mu Ness	Shetld	HU1652	60°15·4′	1°42·2′W	X	3
Muness Castle	Shetld	HP6201	60°41·5′	0°51·4′W	A	1
Mungal Fm	Falk	NS8781	56°0·8′	3°48·3′W	FM	65
Mungasdale	Highld	NG9693	57°53·1′	5°26·0′W	X	19
Munga Skerries	Shetld	HU2987	60°34·2′	1°27·8′W	X	1
Munger Skerries	Shetld	HU4739	60°8·2′	1°8·7′W	X	4
Mungosdail	Highld	NM5653	56°36·6′	5°58·1′W	X	47
Mungo's Walls	Scot Bord	NT8052	55°45·9′	2°18·7′W	X	67,74
Mungoswells	E Loth	NT4978	55°59·8′	2°48·6′W	X	66
Mungrisdale	Cumbr	NY3630	54°39·9′	2°59·1′W	T	90
Mungrisdale Common	Cumbr	NY3129	54°39·3′	3°3·7′W	X	90
Munkins Fm	Essex	TM0207	51°43·7′	0°55·9′E	FM	168
Munlochy	Highld	NH6453	57°33·1′	4°15·9′W	T	26
Munlochy Bay	Highld	NH6752	57°32·6′	4°12·9′W	W	26
Munn End	N Yks	NZ0702	54°25·0′	1°53·1′W	H	92
Munnieston	Stir	NN6700	56°10·7′	4°8·1′W	X	57
Munnoch	N Ayr	NS2548	55°41·9′	4°46·6′W	X	63
Munnoch Burn	N Ayr	NS2448	55°41·9′	4°47·6′W	W	63
Munnoch Resr	N Ayr	NS2547	55°41·4′	4°46·6′W	W	63
Munsary	Highld	ND2145	58°23·4′	3°20·6′W	X	11,12
Munsary Cottage	Highld	ND2145	58°23·4′	3°20·6′W	X	11,12
Munsary Dubh Lochs	Highld	ND2146	58°24·0′	3°20·6′W	W	11,12
Munsgore Fm	Kent	TQ8762	51°19·8′	0°41·4′E	FM	178
Munshiel Hill	D & G	NY3195	55°14·9′	3°4·7′W	H	79
Munsley	Heref	SO6640	52°3·7′	2°29·4′W	T	149
Munslow	Shrops	SO5287	52°29·0′	2°42·0′W	T	137,138
Munson Fm	Devon	SS7621	50°58·7′	3°45·6′W	FM	180
Munstead Heath	Surrey	SU9842	51°10·4′	0°35·5′W	X	186
Munstone	Heref	SO5142	52°4·7′	2°42·5′W	T	149
Muntham Fm	W Susx	TQ1010	50°53·0′	0°25·8′W	FM	198
Muntham Ho (Sch)	W Susx	TQ1227	51°2·1′	0°23·8′W	X	187,198
Munwhall	D & G	NX6357	54°53·6′	4°7·7′W	H	83
Munwhul	D & G	NX4975	55°3·0′	4°21·4′W	H	77
Munzie Burn	E Renf	NS5848	55°42·5′	4°15·2′W	W	64
Mupe Bay	Dorset	SY8479	50°36·9′	2°13·2′W	W	194
Mupe Rocks	Dorset	SY8479	50°36·9′	2°13·2′W	X	194
Muran a' Mhachaire	Arg & Bt	NR3249	55°39·9′	6°15·3′W	X	60
Murbie Stacks	Shetld	HU3062	60°20·7′	1°26·9′W	X	3
Murch	V of Glam	ST1671	51°26·1′	3°12·1′W	T	171
Murchadh Breac	Highld	NG7061	57°35·1′	5°50·4′W	X	24
Murchan Hill	N Ayr	NS2960	55°48·4′	4°43·3′W	X	63
Murchington	Devon	SX6888	50°40·8′	3°51·7′W	T	191
Murcot	Worcs	SP0640	52°3·7′	1°54·4′W	T	150
Murcott	Oxon	SP5815	51°50·1′	1°9·1′W	T	164
Murcott	Wilts	ST9591	51°37·3′	2°3·9′W	T	163,173
Mur-cwymp	Gwyn	SH3941	52°56·8′	4°23·4′W	X	123
Murcyplau	Gwyn	SH4142	52°57·4′	4°21·6′W	X	123
Murder Combe	Somer	ST7448	51°14·1′	2°22·0′W	X	183
Murder Hole	D & G	NX4382	55°6·7′	4°27·3′W	W	77
Murder Loch	D & G	NY0285	55°9·2′	3°31·8′W	W	78
Murdieston	Stir	NS6798	56°9·6′	4°8·1′W	T	57
Murdishaw	Halton	SJ5580	53°19·1′	2°40·1′W	T	108
Murdochcairnie	Fife	NO3519	56°21·8′	3°2·7′W	X	59
Murdochcairnie Hill	Fife	NO3519	56°21·8′	3°2·7′W	H	59
Murdoch Head	Aberd	NK1239	57°26·7′	1°47·5′W	X	30
Murdostoun Castle	N Lanak	NS8257	55°47·8′	3°52·5′W	X	65,72
Murhill	Wilts	ST7960	51°20·6′	2°17·7′W	X	172
Muriau	Gwyn	SH3130	52°50·7′	4°30·2′W	X	123
Muriau	Gwyn	SH4837	52°54·8′	4°15·2′W	X	123
Muriau	Gwyn	SH4841	52°56·9′	4°15·3′W	X	123
Murie Gardens	Pth & Kin	NO2322	56°23·3′	3°14·4′W	X	53,58
Muriel's Fm	Norf	TL7292	52°30·2′	0°32·5′E	FM	143
Murieston	W Loth	NT0664	55°51·9′	3°29·7′W	T	65
Murieston Castle Fm	W Loth	NT0463	55°51·3′	3°31·6′W	FM	65
Murieston Water	W Loth	NT0564	55°51·8′	3°30·6′W	W	65
Murk Esk	N Yks	NZ8103	54°25·0′	0°44·7′W	W	94
Murk Head	N Yks	SE9595	54°20·7′	0°31·9′W	X	94,101
Murkle	Highld	ND1668	58°35·8′	3°26·2′W	X	11,12
Murkle Bay	Highld	ND1669	58°36·3′	3°26·3′W	W	12
Murk Mire Moor	N Yks	NZ7902	54°24·7′	0°46·5′W	X	94
Murkside Ho	N Yks	NZ8103	54°25·2′	0°44·7′W	X	94
Murky Hill	N Yks	NZ2405	54°26·6′	1°37·4′W	X	93
Murlaganmore	Stir	NN5434	56°28·8′	4°21·8′W	X	51
Murlaggan	Highld	NN0192	56°58·8′	5°16·0′W	X	33
Murlaggan	Highld	NN3181	56°53·6′	4°46·0′W	X	34,41
Murley	Aberd	NO3280	56°54·6′	3°6·6′W	H	44
Murley	Aberd	NO5693	57°1·8′	2°43·0′W	X	37,44
Murley	Devon	ST0216	50°56·3′	3°23·3′W	X	181
Murleywell	Angus	NO3545	56°35·8′	3°3·1′W	X	54
Murligan Hill	Highld	NH4110	57°9·5′	4°37·3′W	H	34
Murlingden	Angus	NO5962	56°45·1′	2°39·8′W	X	44

Murmannoch	Angus	NO5879	56°54·3′	2°40·9′W	H	44
Mur-mawr	Gwyn	SH2231	52°51·1′	4°38·2′W	X	123
Mur Melyn	Gwyn	SH1728	52°49·4′	4°42·6′W	X	123
Mur-moch	Gwyn	SH5562	53°8·4′	4°9·7′W	X	114,115
Murra	Orkney	HY2104	58°55·2′	3°21·8′W	X	6,7
Murrah	Cumbr	NY3831	54°40·5′	2°57·3′W	X	90
Murrah Hall	Cumbr	NY3731	54°40·5′	2°58·2′W	X	90
Murrayfield	C of Edin	NT2173	55°56·9′	3°15·5′W	T	66
Murrayfield	D & G	NY1581	55°7·2′	3°19·5′W	X	79
Murrayfield	Pth & Kin	NN8716	56°19·6′	3°49·2′W	X	58
Murrayfield	Pth & Kin	NO0330	56°27·4′	3°34·0′W	X	52,53
Murrayfield Ho	W Susx	SU9306	50°51·0′	0°40·3′W	X	197
Murrayhill	Aberd	NJ8540	57°27·3′	2°14·5′W	X	30
Murray Holme	Cumbr	NY5477	55°5·4′	2°42·8′W	X	86
Murray's Burn	D & G	NS5402	55°17·7′	4°17·5′W	W	77
Murrayshall	Pth & Kin	NO1526	56°25·4′	3°22·2′W	X	53,58
Murrayshall	Stir	NS7691	56°6·0′	3°59·2′W	X	57
Murray's Hill	Pth & Kin	NN9325	56°24·6′	3°43·6′W	H	52,58
Murray's Isles	D & G	NX5650	54°49·7′	4°14·1′W	X	83
Murray's Monument	D & G	NX4871	55°0·9′	4°22·2′W	X	77
Murrays Plantation	Highld	NH7790	57°53·2′	4°4·0′W	F	21
Murray's Rock	Devon	SX6543	50°16·5′	3°53·3′W	X	202
Murrays, The	E Loth	NT4166	55°53·3′	2°56·2′W	X	66
Murraythwaite	D & G	NY1272	55°2·3′	3°22·2′W	T	85
Murrayton	D & G	NX5761	54°55·6′	4°13·5′W	X	83
Murrell Green	Hants	SU7455	51°17·6′	0°55·9′W	T	175,186
Murrell's End	Glos	SO7430	51°58·3′	2°22·3′W	T	150
Murrell's End	Glos	SO7822	51°54·0′	2°18·8′W	T	162
Murrells Fm	Essex	TQ5299	51°40·4′	0°12·3′E	FM	167,177
Murrel, The	Fife	NT1886	56°3·8′	3°18·6′W	X	65,66
Murren	Orkney	HY3734	59°11·5′	3°5·7′W	X	6
Murrial	Aberd	NJ6126	57°19·6′	2°38·4′W	X	37
Murrion	Shetld	HU2479	60°29·9′	1°33·3′W	X	3
Murrister	Shetld	HP6001	60°41·5′	0°53·6′W	X	1
Murrister	Shetld	HU2751	60°14·8′	1°30·2′W	X	3
Murroch	W Dunb	NS4077	55°57·8′	4°33·4′W	X	64
Murroch Burn	W Dunb	NS4178	55°58·4′	4°32·4′W	W	64
Murroes	Angus	NO4635	56°30·5′	2°52·2′W	T	54
Murrow	Cambs	TF3707	52°38·8′	0°1·9′E	T	142,143
Murr Rock	I Scilly	SV9316	49°58·1′	6°16·5′W	X	203
Murrystone Hill	Aberd	NO8277	56°53·3′	2°17·3′W	X	45
Mursley	Bucks	SP8128	51°56·9′	0°48·9′W	T	165
Murston	Kent	TQ9264	51°20·8′	0°45·8′E	T	178
Murt	Cumbr	NY1304	54°25·7′	3°20·0′W	X	89
Murt Grain	Scot Bord	NT3026	55°31·6′	3°6·1′W	W	73
Murthat Burn	D & G	NY1994	55°14·3′	3°16·0′W	W	79
Murthill	Angus	NO4657	56°42·4′	2°52·5′W	X	54
Murthly	Pth & Kin	NO0938	56°31·8′	3°28·3′W	T	52,53
Murthly Castle	Pth & Kin	NO0739	56°32·3′	3°30·3′W	A	52,53
Murtholm	D & G	NY3683	55°8·5′	2°59·8′W	X	79
Murthwaite	Cumbr	NY5100	54°23·8′	2°44·9′W	X	90
Murthwaite	Cumbr	SD7198	54°22·8′	2°26·4′W	X	98
Murtland's Fm	Mil Key	SP9343	52°4·9′	0°38·2′W	FM	153
Murtle Ho	C of Aber	NJ8701	57°6·2′	2°12·4′W	X	38
Murton	Angus	NO4951	56°39·1′	2°49·5′W	X	54
Murton	Cumbr	NY0720	54°34·3′	3°25·9′W	X	89
Murton	Cumbr	NY7221	54°35·3′	2°25·6′W	T	91
Murton	Durham	NZ3947	54°49·2′	1°23·2′W	T	88
Murton	Northum	NT9648	55°43·8′	2°3·4′W	X	74,75
Murton	N Tyne	NZ3270	55°1·7′	1°29·5′W	T	88
Murton	Orkney	HY5409	58°58·2′	2°47·5′W	X	6,7
Murton	Swan	SS5889	51°35·2′	4°2·6′W	T	159
Murton	York	SE6552	53°57·8′	1°0·1′W	T	105,106
Murton Blue Ho	Durham	NZ4032	54°41·1′	1°22·3′W	X	93
Murton Common	N Yks	SE5188	54°17·3′	1°12·6′W	X	100
Murton Craggy Bog	Northum	NT9548	55°43·8′	2°4·3′W	X	74,75
Murton Fell	Cumbr	NY0918	54°33·2′	3°24·0′W	H	89
Murton Fell	Cumbr	NY7524	54°36·9′	2°22·8′W	H	91
Murton Grange	N Yks	SE5388	54°17·3′	1°10·7′W	T	100
Murton Grange	York	SE6453	53°58·4′	1°1·0′W	X	105,106
Murton Hall Fm	Durham	NZ4131	54°40·6′	1°21·4′W	FM	93
Murton Herds	Cumbr	NY7526	54°38·0′	2°22·8′W	X	91
Murton High Crags	Northum	NT9649	55°44·3′	2°3·4′W	X	74,75
Murton Moor	Durham	NZ3746	54°48·7′	1°25·0′W	X	88
Murton Moor	York	SE6553	53°58·4′	1°0·1′W	X	105,106
Murton Moor Fm	Durham	NZ3746	54°48·7′	1°25·0′W	FM	88
Murton of Ardovie	Angus	NO5855	56°41·3′	2°40·7′W	X	54
Murton Pike	Cumbr	NY7323	54°36·3′	2°24·7′W	H	91
Murton White Ho	Northum	NT9748	55°43·8′	2°2·4′W	X	75
Murt Rig	Scot Bord	NT2926	55°31·6′	3°7·0′W	H	73
Murtry Hill	Somer	ST7650	51°15·2′	2°20·2′W	H	183
Murtwell	Devon	SX7556	50°23·7′	3°45·1′W	T	202
Murza	Highld	ND2463	58°33·2′	3°17·9′W	X	11,12
Murzie Fm	Kent	TQ7346	51°11·4′	0°28·9′E	FM	188
Musbatch	Shrops	SO6777	52°23·6′	2°28·7′W	X	138
Musbury	Devon	SY2794	50°44·7′	3°1·7′W	T	193
Musbury Castle	Devon	SY2894	50°44·7′	3°0·8′W	X	193
Musbury Castle (Fort)	Devon	SY2894	50°44·7′	3°0·8′W	A	193
Musbury Heights	Lancs	SD7521	53°41·3′	2°22·3′W	X	103
Musbury Ho	Devon	SY2693	50°44·1′	3°2·5′W	X	192,193
Muscar House Fm	Darl	NZ3117	54°33·1′	1°30·8′W	FM	93
Muscliff	Bourne	SZ0995	50°45·5′	1°52·0′W	T	195
Muscoates	N Yks	SE6880	54°12·9′	0°57·0′W	T	100
Muscoates Grange	N Yks	SE6880	54°12·9′	0°57·0′W	X	100
Muscombs	Essex	TL5925	51°54·3′	0°19·1′E	X	167
Muscott	Northnts	SP6263	52°15·9′	1°5·1′W	T	152
Musdale	Arg & Bt	NM9322	56°21·0′	5°20·6′W	X	49
Musden Grange	Staffs	SK1251	53°3·6′	1°48·9′W	X	119
Musden Head Moor	Lancs	SD7520	53°40·8′	2°22·3′W	X	103
Musden Low	Staffs	SK1150	53°3·1′	1°49·7′W	H	119
Musden Wood	Staffs	SK1151	53°3·6′	1°49·7′W	F	119
Musehill	Devon	SX4587	50°40·0′	4°11·2′W	X	190
Muselee	Scot Bord	NT3911	55°23·6′	2°57·4′W	X	79
Museum of Army Flying	Hants	SU3039	51°9·2′	1°33·9′W	X	185
Musgrave Fell	Cumbr	NY7918	54°33·7′	2°19·1′W	X	91
Musgrove Fm	Devon	ST1411	50°53·8′	3°13·0′W	FM	192,193
Musgrove or Cleaburn Pasture	N Yks	NZ0800	54°24·0′	1°52·2′W	X	92
Mushroom Green	Dudley	SO9386	52°28·6′	2°5·8′W	T	139
Mushton	Corn	SX3765	50°28·0′	4°17·4′W	X	201

Muska Hill	Cumbr	NY6535	54°42·8'	2°32·2'W	H	91
Muskham Woodhouse Fm	Notts	SK7457	53°6·5'	0°53·3'W	FM	120
Musk Hill Fm	Bucks	SP7213	51°48·9'	0°56·9'W	FM	165
Muskna Field	Shetld	HU4032	60°4·5'	1°16·4'W	H	4
Muskra Loch	Shetld	HP5202	60°42·1'	1°2·3'W	W	1
Musland	Orkney	HY4843	59°16·5'	2°54·3'W	X	5
Muslandale	Orkney	HY4844	59°17·0'	2°54·3'W	X	5
Musland Fm	Pemb	SM9427	51°54·4'	4°59·3'W	FM	157,158
Musley	Wrex	SJ3740	52°57·5'	2°55·9'W	X	117
Musley Bank	N Yks	SE7670	54°7·5'	0°49·8'W	X	100
Mussaquay	Orkney	HY5603	58°55·0'	2°45·4'W	X	6
Mussel Brook	Devon	SS4710	50°52·4'	4°10·1'W	W	191
Musselburgh	E Loth	NT3573	55°57·0'	3°2·0'W	T	66
Mussel Loch	Shetld	HU4778	60°29·2'	1°8·2'W	W	2,3
Mussel Point	Corn	SW4640	50°12·6'	5°33·2'W	X	203
Mussel Rock	Torbay	SX9355	50°23·3'	3°29·9'W	X	202
Mussel Scalp	Highld	NG4120	57°12·1'	6°16·8'W	X	32
Mussel Scalps	Highld	NH7883	57°49·5'	4°2·8'W	X	21
Musselwick	Pemb	SM8106	51°42·8'	5°9·8'W	T	157
Musselwick Fm	Pemb	SM7909	51°44·4'	5°11·7'W	FM	157
Musselwick Sands	Corn	SM7809	51°44·4'	5°12·5'W	X	157
Mussenden Fm	Kent	TQ5667	51°23·1'	0°14·9'E	FM	177
Mustard Hyrn	Norf	TG4418	52°42·5'	1°37·1'E	T	134
Mustards	Kent	TR0171	51°24·4'	0°53·8'E	X	178
Muster Brook	Derby	SK4267	53°12·1'	1°21·9'W	W	120
Musterfield	N Yks	SE2776	54°11·0'	1°34·8'W	X	99
Must Fm	Cambs	TL2396	52°33·1'	0°10·7'W	FM	142
Must Hill	Cumbr	SD5195	54°21·1'	2°44·8'W	X	97
Muston	Leic	SK8237	52°55·7'	0°46·4'W	T	130
Muston	N Yks	TA0979	54°11·9'	0°19·3'W	T	101
Muston Cottage Fm	N Yks	TA0981	54°13·0'	0°19·3'W	FM	101
Muston Down	Dorset	ST8600	50°48·2'	2°11·5'W	X	194
Muston Fm	Dorset	SY7295	50°45·5'	2°23·4'W	FM	194
Muston Gorse	Leic	SK8235	52°54·6'	0°46·4'W	F	130
Muston Gorse Fm	Leic	SK8135	52°54·6'	0°47·3'W	FM	130
Muston Grange	N Yks	TA1179	54°11·9'	0°17·5'W	X	101
Muston Sands	N Yks	TA1279	54°11·9'	0°16·6'W	X	101
Muston Wold Fm	N Yks	TA0778	54°11·4'	0°21·2'W	FM	101
Mustow Green	Worcs	SO8674	52°22·1'	2°11·9'W	T	139
Muswell Fm	Bucks	SU8091	51°37·0'	0°50·3'W	FM	175
Muswell Hill	Bucks	SP6415	51°50·0'	1°3·9'W	H	164,165
Muswell Hill	Hargy	TQ2890	51°35·9'	0°8·7'W	T	176
Muswellhill Fm	Oxon	SP6415	51°50·0'	1°3·9'W	FM	164,165
Muswell Leys	Warw	SP4983	52°26·8'	1°16·3'W	X	140
Muswell Manor	Kent	TR0469	51°23·2'	0°56·3'E	X	178,179
Mus Wells	Shetld	HU2583	60°32·1'	1°32·2'W	X	3
Mutehill	D & G	NX6848	54°48·8'	4°2·8'W	T	83,84
Mutford	Suff	TM4888	52°26·2'	1°39·3'E	T	156
Mutford Big Wood	Suff	TM4989	52°26·8'	1°40·3'E	F	156
Mutford Hall	Suff	TM4887	52°25·7'	1°39·3'E	A	156
Mutford Little Wood	Suff	TM4988	52°26·2'	1°40·2'E	F	156
Mutfords	Herts	TL4028	51°56·2'	0°2·6'E	X	167
Muthill	Pth & Kin	NN8616	56°19·6'	3°50·2'W	T	58
Mutiny Stones	Scot Bord	NT6259	55°49·6'	2°36·0'W	X	67,74
Mutiny Stones (Long Cairn)	Scot Bord	NT6259	55°49·6'	2°36·0'W	A	67,74
Mutley	C of Plym	SX4855	50°22·8'	4°7·9'W	T	201
Mutlow Fm	Ches	SJ8567	53°12·2'	2°13·1'W	FM	118
Mutlow Hill	Cambs	TL5454	52°10·0'	0°15·5'E	X	154
Mutlow Hill (Tumulus)	Cambs	TL5454	52°10·0'	0°15·5'E	A	154
Mutter's Moor	Devon	SY1087	50°40·8'	3°16·1'W	X	192
Mutterton	Devon	ST0305	50°50·4'	3°22·3'W	T	192
Muttonbrae	Aberd	NJ8517	57°14·9'	2°14·5'W	X	38
Mutton Cove	C of Plym	SX4553	50°21·6'	4°10·4'W	W	201
Mutton Hall	Cumbr	SD5990	54°18·5'	2°37·4'W	X	97
Mutton Hall	E Susx	TQ5821	50°58·2'	0°15·4'E	T	199
Muttonhall	Scot Bord	NT2528	55°32·7'	3°10·9'W	X	73
Mutton Hall	Suff	TM0063	52°14·0'	0°56·1'E	X	155
Mutton Hall	Worcs	SP0261	52°15·1'	1°57·8'W	X	150
Mutton Hall	Wrex	SJ2749	53°2·2'	3°4·9'W	X	117
Mutton Hill	Pemb	SN0002	51°41·1'	4°53·2'W	H	157,158
Mutton Marsh Fm	Wilts	ST8354	51°17·3'	2°14·2'W	FM	183
Mutton's Downs	Corn	SX1969	50°29·8'	4°32·8'W	H	201
Mutton's Fm	W Susx	TQ1114	50°55·1'	0°24·9'W	FM	198
Muxlow Hill	Notts	SK6826	52°49·9'	0°59·0'W	X	129
Muxton	Wrekin	SJ7114	52°43·6'	2°25·4'W	T	127
Muxwell Fm	Bucks	SP7124	51°54·8'	0°57·7'W	FM	165
Muxworthy	Devon	SS7037	51°7·3'	3°51·1'W	X	180
Mwccwd	Flint	SJ1770	53°13·5'	3°14·2'W	X	116
Mwche	Carm	SN3211	51°46·6'	4°25·7'W	X	159
Mwdwl Eithin	Conwy	SH8268	53°12·0'	3°45·6'W	H	116
Mwdwl-eithin	Conwy	SH9154	53°4·6'	3°37·2'W	H	116
Mwdwl-eithin	Conwy	SH9266	53°11·1'	3°36·6'W	H	116
Mwdwl-eithin	Conwy	SH9846	53°0·3'	3°30·8'W	H	116
Mwdwl-eithin	Flint	SJ1676	53°16·7'	3°15·2'W	T	116
Mwdwl Fm	Cered	SN4660	52°13·2'	4°14·9'W	FM	146
Mwmffri	Carm	SN8036	52°0·8'	3°44·5'W	H	160
Mwnt	Cered	SN1951	52°7·9'	4°38·3'W	X	145
Mwyars	Powys	SH8702	52°36·5'	3°39·7'W	X	135,136
Mwynbwll	Flint	SJ1867	53°11·9'	3°13·2'W	T	116
Mwyndy	Rho Cyn Taf	ST0581	51°31·4'	3°21·8'W	X	170
Myarth	Powys	SO1720	51°52·6'	3°12·0'W	H	161
Mybster	Highld	ND1652	58°27·2'	3°25·9'W	T	11,12
Myddelton Ho	Enf	TQ3499	51°40·7'	0°3·3'W	X	166,176,177
Myddelton Lodge	Brad	SE1149	53°56·5'	1°49·5'W	X	104
Myddfai	Carm	SN7730	51°57·5'	3°47·0'W	T	146,160
Myddle	Shrops	SJ4723	52°48·4'	2°46·8'W	T	126
Myddle Hill	Shrops	SJ4723	52°48·4'	2°46·8'W	X	126
Myddleton Lodge	Brad	SE1149	53°56·5'	1°49·5'W	A	104
Myddlewood	Shrops	SJ4523	52°48·3'	2°48·6'W	T	126
Myddlewood Fm	Shrops	SJ4524	52°48·9'	2°48·6'W	FM	126
Myddyn-fych	Carm	SN6213	51°48·2'	3°59·7'W	T	159
Mydroilyn	Cered	SN4555	52°10·5'	4°15·6'W	T	146
Mydub	Falk	NS8182	56°1·2'	3°54·1'W	X	57,65
Myers	Cumbr	SD5693	54°20·1'	2°40·2'W	X	97
Myers	Orkney	HY6524	59°6·4'	2°36·2'W	X	5
Myerscough Cottage	Lancs	SD5138	53°50·4'	2°44·3'W	X	102
Myerscough Ho	Lancs	SD4841	53°52·0'	2°47·0'W	X	102
Myerscough Lodge	Lancs	SD4939	53°50·9'	2°46·1'W	X	102
Myerscough Smithy	Lancs	SD6131	53°46·7'	2°35·1'W	T	102,103
Myers Garth	N Yks	SD9683	54°14·8'	2°3·3'W	X	98
Myers Gill	N Yks	SE0085	54°15·9'	1°59·6'W	W	98
Myer's Green	N Yks	SE2758	54°1·3'	1°34·9'W	X	104
Myers Hill Fm	Beds	TL0858	52°12·8'	0°24·8'W	FM	153
Myers's Fm	Lancs	SD6339	53°51·0'	2°33·3'W	FM	102,103
Myfoniog	Conwy	SH9971	53°13·8'	3°30·4'W	X	116
Myfyr	Gwyn	SH2534	52°52·7'	4°35·6'W	X	123
Myfyrian-isaf	I of Angl	SH4770	53°12·5'	4°17·1'W	X	114,115
Myfyrian-uchaf	I of Angl	SH4770	53°12·5'	4°17·1'W	X	114,115
My Lady's Farm	Staffs	SO8489	52°30·2'	2°13·7'W	FM	138
My Lady's Seat	Oxon	SP4607	51°45·8'	1°19·6'W	X	164
Mylah	Lancs	SD8146	53°54·8'	2°16·9'W	X	103
Myles Fm	E Loth	NT3971	55°55·9'	2°58·1'W	FM	66
Mylett	Carm	SN2714	51°48·1'	4°30·2'W	X	158
Mylnefield	Pth & Kin	NO3330	56°27·7'	3°4·8'W	X	53
Mylor Bridge	Corn	SW8036	50°11·2'	5°4·5'W	T	204
Mylor Churchtown	Corn	SW8235	50°10·7'	5°2·8'W	T	204
Mylor Creek	Corn	SW8035	50°10·7'	5°4·5'W	W	204
My Lord's Bank	C of Dun	NO3828	56°26·7'	2°59·9'W	X	54,59
My Lord's Rock	E Susx	TQ7507	50°50·4'	0°29·5'E	X	199
My Lord's Throat	Aberd	NJ6319	57°15·9'	2°36·3'W	X	37
My Lord's Wood	Norf	TL7499	52°33·9'	0°34·4'E	F	143
Myme	Stir	NS6697	56°9·1'	4°9·0'W	X	57
Mymms Hall	Herts	TL2302	51°42·4'	0°12·8'W	X	166
Mymmshall Wood	Herts	TL2202	51°42·4'	0°13·7'W	F	166
Mynach	Cered	SN7576	52°22·3'	3°49·8'W	W	135,147
Mynachdy	Card	ST1678	51°29·9'	3°12·2'W	T	171
Mynachdy	Carm	SN5022	51°52·8'	4°10·4'W	X	159
Mynachdy	I of Angl	SH3092	53°24·1'	4°33·0'W	X	114
Mynachdy	Powys	SN7995	52°32·6'	3°46·7'W	X	135
Mynachdy	Rho Cyn Taf	ST0495	51°39·0'	3°22·9'W	T	170
Mynachdy Bach	Gwyn	SH4343	52°57·9'	4°19·9'W	X	123
Mynachdy Fm	Monm	SO3414	51°49·5'	2°57·1'W	FM	161
Mynachdy Gwyn	Gwyn	SH4445	52°59·0'	4°19·0'W	X	115,123
Mynach Falls	Cered	SN7477	52°22·8'	3°50·7'W	W	135,147
Mynachlog	Cered	SN4152	52°8·8'	4°19·0'W	X	146
Mynachlog	Flint	SJ2367	53°11·9'	3°8·8'W	X	117
Mynachlog-ddu	Pemb	SN1430	51°56·5'	4°42·0'W	T	145
Mynd	Powys	SO1859	52°13·6'	3°11·6'W	H	148
Mynd	Shrops	SO3574	52°21·9'	2°56·9'W	T	137,148
Myndd Llandegai	Gwyn	SH6065	53°10·1'	4°5·3'W	T	115
Mynde Fm	Heref	SO3567	52°18·1'	2°56·8'W	FM	137,148,149
Mynde, The	Heref	SO4729	51°57·7'	2°45·9'W	X	149,161
Mynde Wood	Heref	SO4729	51°57·7'	2°45·9'W	F	149,161
Myndmill Fm	Shrops	SO3888	52°29·4'	2°54·4'W	FM	137
Mynd Scrubs	Shrops	SO3575	52°22·4'	2°56·9'W	F	137,148
Myndtown	Shrops	SO3989	52°30·0'	2°53·5'W	T	137
Mynogau	Gwyn	SH8316	52°44·0'	3°43·6'W	X	124,125
Mynte Fm	Wilts	ST8871	51°26·5'	2°10·0'W	FM	173
Mynthurst	Surrey	TQ2245	51°11·7'	0°14·8'W	X	187
Mynwhirr Hill	D & G	NS6909	55°21·7'	4°3·6'W	H	71,77
Mynydd	Conwy	SH8377	53°16·9'	3°44·9'W	X	116
Mynydd Abercorris	Gwyn	SH7509	52°40·1'	3°50·5'W	X	124
Mynydd Aberdar	Rho Cyn Taf	SO0105	51°44·3'	3°25·6'W	H	160
Mynydd Abergwynfi	Nth Pt Talb	SS8897	51°39·3'	3°36·8'W	X	170
Mynydd Aberysgir	Powys	SN9932	51°58·9'	3°27·8'W	H	160
Mynydd Alltir-fach	Newp	ST4293	51°38·2'	2°49·9'W	H	171,172
Mynydd Allt-y-grug	Nth Pt Talb	SN7507	51°45·1'	3°48·3'W	H	160
Mynydd Anelog	Gwyn	SH1527	52°48·8'	4°44·3'W	H	123
Mynydd Bach	Brig	SS8692	51°37·2'	3°38·4'W	H	170
Mynydd Bach	Cered	SN6166	52°16·7'	4°1·9'W	X	135
Mynydd Bach	Cered	SN7070	52°19·0'	3°54·0'W	H	135,147
Mynydd Bach	Cered	SN7176	52°22·3'	3°53·3'W	T	135,147
Mynydd Bach	Gwyn	SH6009	52°39·9'	4°3·8'W	H	124
Mynydd Bach	Gwyn	SH7431	52°51·9'	3°51·9'W	X	124
Mynydd-bach	Monm	ST4894	51°38·8'	2°44·7'W	T	171,172
Mynydd Bâch	Nth Pt Talb	SN7510	51°46·7'	3°48·3'W	X	160
Mynydd Bach	Nth Pt Talb	SS8290	51°36·0'	3°41·8'W	H	170
Mynydd Bâch	Pemb	SN1029	51°55·9'	4°45·4'W	H	145,158
Mynydd-bach	Pemb	SN1132	51°57·5'	4°44·7'W	X	145
Mynydd Bach	Powys	SN9935	52°0·5'	3°27·9'W	H	160
Mynydd-Bach	Swan	SS6597	51°39·6'	3°56·7'W	T	159
Mynydd Bâch	Wrex	SJ1533	52°53·5'	3°15·4'W	H	125
Mynydd Bach Trecastell	Powys	SN8330	51°57·6'	3°41·8'W	H	160
Mynydd-Bach-y-Cocs	Swan	SS5593	51°37·3'	4°5·3'W	H	159
Mynydd-bach-y-glo	Swan	SS6195	51°38·4'	4°0·1'W	T	159
Mynydd Baedan	Brig	SS8785	51°33·4'	3°37·4'W	H	170
Mynydd Bedwellte	Blae Gw	SO1406	51°45·0'	3°14·4'W	H	161
Mynydd Beili-glas	Rho Cyn Taf	SN9202	51°42·6'	3°33·4'W	H	170
Mynydd Blaenafan	Nth Pt Talb	SS9096	51°39·4'	3°35·0'W	X	170
Mynydd Blaenafon	Nth Pt Talb	SS8097	51°39·8'	3°43·7'W	H	170
Mynydd Blaengwynfi	Nth Pt Talb	SS9097	51°39·9'	3°35·0'W	H	170
Mynydd Blaen-nant-du	Nth Pt Talb	SS8699	51°40·9'	3°38·5'W	H	170
Mynydd Blaenrhondda	Rho Cyn Taf	SN9100	51°41·5'	3°34·2'W	H	170
Mynydd-blewog	I of Angl	SH3587	53°21·5'	4°28·4'W	X	114
Mynydd Bodafon	I of Angl	SH4685	53°20·6'	4°18·4'W	T	114
Mynydd Bodran	Conwy	SH9470	53°13·2'	3°34·9'W	H	116
Mynydd Bodrochwyn	Conwy	SH9372	53°14·3'	3°35·8'W	H	116
Mynydd Braich-gôch	Gwyn	SH7407	52°39·0'	3°51·4'W	H	124
Mynydd Branar	Conwy	SH8771	53°13·7'	3°41·2'W	H	116
Mynydd-brith	Cered	SN6365	52°16·2'	4°0·1'W	X	135
Mynydd Brith	Heref	SO2740	52°3·5'	3°3·5'W	X	148,161
Mynydd-brith	Powys	SJ0717	52°44·8'	3°22·3'W	X	125
Mynydd Brith-weunydd	Rho Cyn Taf	ST0092	51°37·3'	3°26·3'W	H	170
Mynyddbrydd	Heref	SO2841	52°4·0'	3°2·6'W	X	148,161
Mynydd Bryn-llech	Gwyn	SH8031	52°52·0'	3°46·6'W	H	124,125
Mynydd Bwlch-y-Groes	Powys	SN8635	52°0·3'	3°39·3'W	H	160
Mynydd Bwllfa	Rho Cyn Taf	SN9502	51°42·7'	3°30·8'W	H	170
Mynydd Bwllfa	Rho Cyn Taf	SS9693	51°37·8'	3°29·8'W	H	170
Mynydd Bychan	Nth Pt Talb	SS7992	51°37·1'	3°44·5'W	H	170
Mynydd Bychan	Powys	SN7792	52°31·0'	3°48·4'W	H	135
Mynydd Bychan	Powys	SO1932	51°59·1'	3°10·4'W	X	161
Mynydd Bychan	V of Glam	SS9675	51°28·1'	3°29·4'W	X	170
Mynydd Caerau	Brig	SS8894	51°38·3'	3°36·7'W	H	170
Mynydd Canol	Nth Pt Talb	SS8297	51°39·8'	3°42·0'W	X	170
Mynydd Carn-ingli	Pemb	SN0436	51°59·5'	4°50·9'W	H	145,157
Mynydd Carnedd Hywel	Gwyn	SH9227	52°50·0'	3°35·8'W	X	125
Mynydd Carnguwch	Gwyn	SH3742	52°57·3'	4°25·2'W	H	123
Mynydd Carningli	Pemb	SN0537	52°0·1'	4°50·1'W	H	145
Mynydd Carnllechart	Nth Pt Talb	SN6907	51°45·0'	3°53·5'W	H	160
Mynydd-Carn-y-cefn	Blae Gw	SO1808	51°46·1'	3°10·9'W	H	161
Mynydd Carreg	Gwyn	SH1629	52°49·9'	4°43·5'W	H	123
Mynydd Castlebythe	Pemb	SN0229	51°55·7'	4°52·4'W	H	145,157,158
Mynydd Cedris	Gwyn	SH7007	52°39·0'	3°54·9'W	H	124
Mynydd Cefnamwlch	Gwyn	SH2233	52°52·1'	4°38·3'W	H	123
Mynydd Cefn-caer	Gwyn	SH7003	52°36·8'	3°54·8'W	H	135
Mynydd Cefn-y-gyngon	Rho Cyn Taf	SN9503	51°43·2'	3°30·8'W	H	170
Mynydd Ceiswyn	Gwyn	SH7713	52°42·3'	3°48·8'W	H	124
Mynydd Cennin	Gwyn	SH4545	52°59·0'	4°18·1'W	H	115,123
Mynydd Cerrig	Carm	SN5013	51°48·0'	4°10·1'W	H	159
Mynydd Cerrigllwydion	Powys	SO0298	52°34·5'	3°26·4'W	X	136
Mynydd Cilciffeth	Pemb	SN0132	51°57·3'	4°53·4'W	H	145,157
Mynydd Cil-cwm	Powys	SN8596	52°33·2'	3°41·4'W	H	135,136
Mynydd Cilfach-yr-encil	Merth Tyd	SO0703	51°43·3'	3°20·4'W	H	170
Mynydd Clogau	Powys	SO0399	52°35·1'	3°25·5'W	X	136
Mynydd Clywedog	Gwyn	SH9014	52°43·0'	3°37·3'W	H	125
Mynydd Coch	Powys	SH9319	52°45·7'	3°34·7'W	H	125
Mynydd Coedbychan	Rho Cyn Taf	SS9984	51°33·0'	3°27·0'W	X	170
Mynydd Copog	Gwyn	SH8814	52°43·0'	3°39·1'W	H	124,125
Mynydd Coronwen	Cered	SN7093	52°31·4'	3°54·6'W	H	135
Mynydd Corrwg Fechan	Nth Pt Talb	SN8800	51°41·5'	3°36·8'W	H	170
Mynydd Cribau	Conwy	SH7555	53°4·9'	3°51·6'W	H	115
Mynydd Cricor	Denb	SJ1450	53°2·7'	3°16·6'W	H	116
Mynydd Crogwy	Pemb	SN1839	52°1·4'	4°38·8'W	X	145
Mynydd Crwn	Pemb	SN0929	51°55·8'	4°46·3'W	X	145,158
Mynydd Cwmcelli	Gwyn	SH7910	52°40·7'	3°47·0'W	H	124
Mynydd Cwmgerwyn	Gwyn	SH8010	52°40·7'	3°46·1'W	H	124,125
Mynydd Cwm-mynach	Gwyn	SH6722	52°47·0'	3°57·9'W	H	124
Mynydd Cynros	Carm	SN6232	51°58·4'	4°0·2'W	H	146
Mynydd Deulyn	Conwy	SH7561	53°8·1'	3°51·7'W	H	115
Mynydd Dimlaith	Caer	ST1590	51°36·4'	3°13·3'W	H	171
Mynydd Dinas	Nth Pt Talb	SS7691	51°36·5'	3°47·1'W	H	170
Mynydd Dinas	Pemb	SN0137	52°0·0'	4°53·6'W	X	145,157
Mynydd Dinas	Rho Cyn Taf	ST0090	51°36·2'	3°26·2'W	H	170
Mynydd-dir	Conwy	SH9171	53°13·7'	3°37·6'W	H	116
Mynydd Dolgoed	Gwyn	SH7913	52°42·3'	3°47·1'W	H	124
Mynydd Drum	Powys	SN8210	51°46·8'	3°42·2'W	H	160
Mynydd Drumau	Nth Pt Talb	SN7200	51°41·3'	3°50·7'W	H	170
Mynydd Drws-y-coed	Gwyn	SH5451	53°2·4'	4°10·3'W	X	115
Mynydd Du	Cered	SN7295	52°32·5'	3°52·9'W	H	135
Mynydd Du	Denb	SJ2157	53°6·5'	3°10·4'W	X	117
Mynydd Du	Gwyn	SH6564	53°9·6'	4°0·7'W	X	115
Mynydd du	Pemb	SM7626	51°53·5'	5°14·9'W	X	157
Mynydd Du	Powys	SH8008	52°39·6'	3°46·1'W	H	124,125
Mynydd-du Commin	Pemb	SN0731	51°56·9'	4°48·1'W	X	145
Mynydd Du Forest	Powys	SO2426	51°55·9'	3°5·9'W	F	161
Mynydd Dwyriw	Powys	SJ0000	52°35·6'	3°28·2'W	X	136
Mynydd Dyfnant	Powys	SH9816	52°44·2'	3°30·2'W	H	125
Mynydd Ednyfed	Gwyn	SH5039	52°55·9'	4°13·5'W	X	124
Mynydd Eglwysilan	Caer	ST1292	51°37·4'	3°15·9'W	H	171
Mynydd Egryn	Gwyn	SH6120	52°45·8'	4°3·2'W	H	124
Mynydd Eilian	I of Angl	SH4791	53°23·9'	4°17·7'W	H	114
Mynydd Eithaf	Powys	SN7497	52°33·6'	3°51·1'W	H	135
Mynydd Emroch	Nth Pt Talb	SS7890	51°36·0'	3°45·3'W	X	170
Mynydd Enlli	Gwyn	SH1221	52°45·5'	4°46·8'W	H	123
Mynydd Eppynt	Powys	SN9543	52°4·8'	3°31·5'W	H	147,160
Mynydd Esgair	Powys	SN8998	52°34·4'	3°37·9'W	H	135,136
Mynydd Esgair-Ebrill	Conwy	SH8368	53°12·0'	3°44·7'W	H	116
Mynydd Esgair-Ebrill	I of Angl	SH3868	53°11·3'	4°25·1'W	H	114
Mynydd Esgairneiriau	Powys	SH7809	52°40·1'	3°47·9'W	H	124
Mynydd Esgairweddon	Gwyn	SH6702	52°36·2'	3°57·4'W	H	135
Mynydd Farteg Fach	Torf	SO2506	51°45·1'	3°4·8'W	X	161
Mynydd Farteg Fawr	Torf	SO2506	51°45·1'	3°4·8'W	H	161
Mynydd Fforch-dwm	Nth Pt Talb	SS8297	51°39·8'	3°42·0'W	H	170
Mynydd Fforest	Powys	SO0939	52°2·8'	3°19·2'W	H	161
Mynydd Figyn	Carm	SN5930	51°57·3'	4°2·7'W	H	146
Mynydd Fochriw	Merth Tyd	SO0904	51°43·9'	3°18·7'W	H	171
Mynydd Fron-felen	Powys	SH7607	52°39·0'	3°49·6'W	H	124
Mynydd Fron-fraith	Gwyn	SH7512	52°41·7'	3°50·6'W	H	124
Mynydd Garnclochdy	Torf	SO2805	51°44·6'	3°2·2'W	X	161
Mynydd Garn-fach	Swan	SN6506	51°44·4'	3°56·9'W	H	159
Mynydd Garn-wen	Torf	SO2804	51°44·0'	3°2·2'W	H	171
Mynydd Gartheiniog	Gwyn	SH8113	52°42·3'	3°45·3'W	H	124,125
Mynydd Garthmaelwg	Rho Cyn Taf	ST0184	51°33·0'	3°25·3'W	H	170
Mynydd Garth-pwt	Powys	SN9894	52°32·3'	3°29·8'W	H	136
Mynydd Gellionnen	Nth Pt Talb	SN7004	51°43·4'	3°52·5'W	H	170
Mynydd Gelliwastad	Swan	SN6701	51°41·8'	3°55·1'W	H	159
Mynydd Gellwion	Rho Cyn Taf	ST0590	51°36·3'	3°21·9'W	X	170
Mynydd Gilan	Gwyn	SH2924	52°47·4'	4°31·8'W	T	123
Mynydd Glandulas	Powys	SH7503	52°36·9'	3°50·4'W	H	135
Mynydd Glan-llyn-y-forwyn	Gwyn	SH6824	52°48·1'	3°57·1'W	H	124
Mynydd Glyn-Lws	Conwy	SH8872	53°14·2'	3°40·3'W	H	116
Mynydd Gorddu	Cered	SN6786	52°27·6'	3°57·1'W	X	135
Mynydd Gorllwyn	Gwyn	SH5742	52°57·6'	4°7·3'W	X	124
Mynydd Graig	Gwyn	SH2227	52°48·9'	4°38·1'W	H	123
Mynydd Graig Goch	Gwyn	SH4948	53°0·7'	4°14·6'W	H	115,123
Mynydd Gwerngraig	Gwyn	SH7514	52°42·8'	3°50·6'W	H	124
Mynydd Hafotty	Gwyn	SH7410	52°40·6'	3°51·4'W	H	124
Mynydd Hendre-ddu	Gwyn	SH8012	52°41·8'	3°46·1'W	H	124,125
Mynydd Henllys	Torf	ST2593	51°38·1'	3°4·6'W	X	171
Mynydd-hir	Powys	SJ0519	52°45·9'	3°24·1'W	X	125
Mynydd Hiraethog	Conwy	SH9455	53°5·1'	3°34·6'W	H	116
Mynydd Illtud	Powys	SN9726	51°55·6'	3°29·5'W	X	160
Mynydd Isa	Flint	SJ2564	53°10·3'	3°6·9'W	T	117
Mynydd Isaf	Carm	SN6615	51°49·3'	3°56·3'W	H	159
Mynyddislwyn	Caer	ST1994	51°38·6'	3°9·8'W	T	171
Mynydd James	Blae Gw	SO2108	51°46·1'	3°8·3'W	H	161
Mynydd Jaram	Powys	SJ1821	52°47·1'	3°12·5'W	H	125
Mynydd Lan	Caer	ST2092	51°37·5'	3°9·0'W	H	171
Mynydd-llan	Flint	SJ1572	53°14·5'	3°16·0'W	T	116
Mynydd Llanbedr	Gwyn	SH6227	52°49·6'	4°2·5'W	H	124
Mynydd Llanelian	Conwy	SH8474	53°15·3'	3°43·9'W	H	116
Mynydd Llanfihangel-rhos-y-corn	Carm	SN5035	51°59·8'	4°10·7'W	H	146
Mynydd Llangatwg	Powys	SO1814	51°49·4'	3°11·0'W	H	161
Mynydd Llangeinwyr	Brig	SS9192	51°37·2'	3°34·1'W	H	170
Mynydd Llangorse	Powys	SO1526	51°55·8'	3°13·8'W	H	161
Mynydd Llangyndeyrn	Carm	SN4813	51°47·9'	4°11·9'W	H	159
Mynydd Llangynidr	Blae Gw	SO1214	51°49·3'	3°16·2'W	H	161
Mynydd Llanhilleth	Blae Gw	SO2302	51°42·9'	3°6·5'W	X	171

Mynydd Llanllwni	Carm	SN5038	52°1·5'	4°10·8'W	X	146
Mynydd Llansadwrn	Carm	SN6835	52°0·1'	3°55·0'W	H	146
Mynydd Llanwenarth	Monm	SO2617	51°51·0'	3°4·1'W	X	161
Mynydd Llanybyther	Carm	SN5439	52°2·1'	4°7·3'W	H	146
Mynydd-llêch	Denb	SJ0861	53°8·5'	3°22·1'W	X	116
Mynydd Lledrod	Powys	SJ2130	52°51·9'	3°10·0'W	H	126
Mynydd Lluest Fach	Powys	SH9008	52°39·8'	3°37·2'W	H	125
Mynydd Lluest-y-graig	Powys	SH9904	52°37·7'	3°29·1'W	X	136
Mynydd Llwyd	Caer	ST2598	51°40·8'	3°4·7'W	H	171
Mynydd Llwydiarth	I of Angl	SH5479	53°17·5'	4°11·0'W	H	114,115
Mynydd Llwyn-gwern	Powys	SH7604	52°37·4'	3°49·5'W	H	135
Mynydd Llwytgoed	Powys	SO0396	52°33·4'	3°25·5'W	X	136
Mynydd Llyn Coch-hwyad	Powys	SH9110	52°40·8'	3°36·3'W	X	125
Mynydd Llyndy	Gwyn	SH6148	53°0·9'	4°3·9'W	X	115
Mynydd-llys	Powys	SO0675	52°22·1'	3°22·4'W	X	136,147
Mynydd Llysiau	Powys	SO2027	51°56·4'	3°9·4'W	H	161
Mynydd Machen	Caer	ST2290	51°36·4'	3°7·2'W	H	171
Mynydd Maen	Caer	ST2596	51°39·7'	3°4·7'W	H	171
Mynydd Maendy	Brig	SS9689	51°35·7'	3°29·7'W	X	170
Mynydd Maendy	Rho Cyn Taf	SS9495	51°38·9'	3°31·5'W	X	170
Mynydd Maendy	Rho Cyn Taf	SS9886	51°34·1'	3°27·9'W	H	170
Mynydd Maentwrog	Gwyn	SH7139	52°56·2'	3°54·8'W	X	124
Mynydd Maerdy	Rho Cyn Taf	SS9697	51°40·0'	3°29·8'W	X	170
Mynydd Maes-teg	Brig	SS9690	51°36·2'	3°29·7'W	X	170
Mynydd Mallaen	Carm	SN7344	52°5·0'	3°50·8'W	H	146,147,160
Mynydd Marchywel	Nth Pt Talb	SN7603	51°43·0'	3°47·3'W	H	170
Mynydd Marchywel	Nth Pt Talb	SN7605	51°44·0'	3°47·4'W	F	160
Mynydd Margam	Nth Pt Talb	SS8188	51°34·9'	3°42·7'W	H	170
Mynydd Marian	Conwy	SH8977	53°16·9'	3°39·5'W	T	116
Mynydd Mawr	Gwyn	SH1325	52°47·7'	4°46·0'W	H	123
Mynydd-mawr	Gwyn	SH3640	52°56·2'	4°26·0'W	X	123
Mynydd Mawr	Gwyn	SH5354	53°4·0'	4°11·2'W	H	115
Mynydd Mawr	Powys	SJ1328	52°50·8'	3°17·1'W	H	125
Mynydd Mawr	Powys	SJ1521	52°47·0'	3°15·2'W	H	125
Mynydd Mechell	I of Angl	SH3589	53°22·6'	4°28·4'W	T	114
Mynydd Meio	Caer	ST1188	51°35·3'	3°16·7'W	H	171
Mynydd Meiros	Rho Cyn Taf	ST0184	51°33·0'	3°25·3'W	X	170
Mynydd Melyn	Pemb	SN0135	51°58·9'	4°53·5'W	X	145,157
Mynydd Melyn	Pemb	SN0236	51°59·5'	4°52·6'W	H	145,157
Mynydd Merddin	Heref	SO3327	51°56·5'	2°58·1'W	X	161
Mynydd Merthyr	Rho Cyn Taf	SO0402	51°42·7'	3°23·0'W	H	170
Mynydd Moel	Gwyn	SH7213	52°42·2'	3°53·3'W	H	124
Mynydd Moelgeila	Brig	SS8989	51°35·6'	3°35·8'W	H	170
Mynydd Morfa	Pemb	SM8734	51°58·1'	5°5·7'W	H	157
Mynydd Morvil	Pemb	SN0331	51°56·8'	4°51·6'W	X	145,157
Mynydd Mostyn	Flint	SJ1279	53°18·3'	3°18·8'W	X	116
Mynydd-Mwyn	I of Angl	SH4081	53°18·4'	4°23·7'W	X	114,115
Mynydd Mwyn Mawr	I of Angl	SH4082	53°18·9'	4°23·7'W	X	114,115
Mynydd Myddfai	Carm	SN8029	51°57·0'	3°44·4'W	H	160
Mynydd Myfyr	Shrops	SJ2427	52°50·4'	3°7·3'W	H	126
Mynydd Mynyllod	Gwyn	SJ0039	52°56·6'	3°28·9'W	H	125
Mynydd Nant-y-bar	Nth Pt Talb	SS8396	51°39·3'	3°41·1'W	H	170
Mynydd Nefyn	Gwyn	SH3240	52°56·1'	4°29·6'W	H	123
Mynydd Nodol	Gwyn	SH8639	52°56·4'	3°41·4'W	H	124,125
Mynydd Pant-côch	Powys	SH7705	52°38·0'	3°48·7'W	H	124
Mynydd Penarfynydd	Gwyn	SH2126	52°48·4'	4°38·9'W	H	123
Mynydd Pen-banc	Pemb	SN0232	51°57·3'	4°52·5'W	X	145,157
Mynydd Pen-bre	Carm	SN4503	51°42·5'	4°14·2'W	H	159
Mynydd Pencarreg	Carm	SN5742	52°3·7'	4°4·8'W	H	146
Mynydd Pencoed	Gwyn	SH6911	52°41·1'	3°55·9'W	H	124
Mynydd Pen-cyrn	Powys	SO1814	51°49·4'	3°11·0'W	X	161
Mynydd Penhydd	Nth Pt Talb	SS8193	51°37·6'	3°42·8'W	H	170
Mynydd Pen-lan	Powys	SH7808	52°39·6'	3°47·8'W	H	124
Mynydd Pennant	Gwyn	SH6610	52°40·5'	3°58·5'W	H	124
Mynydd Pen-rhiw	Gwyn	SH6409	52°39·9'	4°0·3'W	H	124
Mynydd Pen-rhys	Nth Pt Talb	SS8094	51°38·2'	3°43·7'W	H	170
Mynydd Pentre	Gwyn	SH6605	52°37·8'	3°58·4'W	H	124
Mynydd Pentre	Gwyn	SH7110	52°40·6'	3°54·1'W	H	124
Mynydd Pen-y-cae	Nth Pt Talb	SN8803	51°43·1'	3°36·9'W	H	170
Mynydd Pen-y-fâl	Powys	SO2619	51°52·1'	3°4·1'W	X	161
Mynydd Pen-y-fan	Caer	SO1902	51°42·9'	3°10·0'W	H	171
Mynydd Pen-y-graig	Rho Cyn Taf	SS9890	51°36·2'	3°28·0'W	H	170
Mynydd Penypistyll	Powys	SN8996	52°33·3'	3°37·8'W	H	135,136
Mynydd Perfedd	Gwyn	SH6261	53°7·9'	4°3·4'W	H	115
Mynydd Pistyll-du	Powys	SH9900	52°35·5'	3°29·1'W	X	136
Mynydd Poeth	Conwy	SH9551	53°3·0'	3°33·6'W	H	116
Mynydd Pont-erwyd	Cered	SN7381	52°25·0'	3°51·6'W	X	135
Mynydd Portref	Rho Cyn Taf	SS9985	51°33·5'	3°27·0'W	H	170
Mynydd Preseli	Pemb	SN1032	51°57·5'	4°45·5'W	H	145
Mynydd Pwllyrhebog	Rho Cyn Taf	SS9691	51°36·7'	3°29·7'W	X	170
Mynydd Pysgodlyn	Swan	SN6304	51°43·3'	3°58·6'W	H	159
Mynydd Resolfen	Nth Pt Talb	SN8503	51°43·1'	3°39·5'W	H	170
Mynydd Rhiw	Gwyn	SH2229	52°50·0'	4°38·1'W	H	123
Mynydd Rhiwgregen	Nth Pt Talb	SS8496	51°39·3'	3°40·2'W	X	170
Mynydd Rhiw-Saeson	Powys	SH9006	52°38·7'	3°37·2'W	H	125
Mynydd Rhos-wen	Carm	SN4833	51°58·7'	4°12·4'W	X	146
Mynydd Rhŷd ddu	Denb	SJ0547	53°1·0'	3°24·6'W	H	116
Mynydd Rhyd-galed	Gwyn	SH7004	52°37·3'	3°54·8'W	H	124
Mynydd Rudry	Caer	ST1886	51°34·3'	3°10·6'W	H	171
Mynydd Rugog	Gwyn	SH7209	52°40·1'	3°53·2'W	H	124
Mynydd St John or Cefn Tre-ysbyty	Powys	SH9720	52°46·3'	3°31·2'W	H	125
Mynydd Sylen	Carm	SN5108	51°45·3'	4°9·1'W	H	159
Mynydd Talyglannau	Powys	SH9011	52°41·3'	3°36·2'W	H	125
Mynydd Tal-y-mignedd	Gwyn	SH5351	53°2·4'	4°11·2'W	H	115
Mynydd Tan-y-coed	Gwyn	SH6604	52°37·3'	3°58·4'W	H	135
Mynydd Tarw	Powys	SJ1132	52°52·9'	3°19·0'W	H	125
Mynydd Tir-y-cwmwd	Gwyn	SH3230	52°50·7'	4°29·3'W	H	123
Mynydd Ton	Rho Cyn Taf	SS9594	51°38·3'	3°30·7'W	X	170
Mynydd Trawsnant	Powys	SN8248	52°7·3'	3°43·0'W	H	147
Mynydd Tre-beddau	Carm	SN4834	51°59·3'	4°12·4'W	X	146
Mynydd Tre-newydd	Pemb	SN0231	51°56·8'	4°52·5'W	X	145,157
Mynydd Tri Arglwydd	Powys	SH8109	52°40·2'	3°45·2'W	H	124,125
Mynydd Troed	Powys	SO1728	51°56·9'	3°12·1'W	H	161
Mynydd Troed-y-rhiw	Rho Cyn Taf	ST0192	51°37·3'	3°25·4'W	H	170
Mynydd Tryfan	Conwy	SH9765	53°10·6'	3°32·1'W	H	116
Mynydd Twyn-glas	Torf	ST2697	51°40·3'	3°3·8'W	X	171
Mynydd Ty-isaf	Rho Cyn Taf	SS9197	51°39·9'	3°34·2'W	X	170
Mynydd Tyle-coch	Rho Cyn Taf	SS9396	51°39·4'	3°32·4'W	H	170
Mynydd Tŷ-mawr	Gwyn	SH6604	52°37·3'	3°58·4'W	H	135

Mynydd Ty-mawr	Powys	SH7607	52°39·0'	3°49·6'W	H	124
Mynydd Tynewydd	Rho Cyn Taf	SN9400	51°41·6'	3°31·6'W	H	170
Mynydd Ty'n-tyle	Rho Cyn Taf	SS9995	51°38·9'	3°27·2'W	H	170
Mynydd Ty'n-y-ceunant	Gwyn	SH7308	52°39·5'	3°52·3'W	H	124
Mynydd Tyn-y-fach	Gwyn	SH6809	52°40·0'	3°56·7'W	H	124
Mynydd Tŷ'r-sais	Powys	SH8500	52°35·4'	3°41·5'W	H	135,136
Mynydd Ty-talwyn	Brig	SS8586	51°33·9'	3°39·2'W	X	170
Mynydd Uchaf	Nth Pt Talb	SN7110	51°46·7'	3°51·8'W	H	160
Mynydd Waun Fawr	Powys	SJ0105	52°38·3'	3°27·4'W	X	125
Mynydd William Meyrick	Rho Cyn Taf	SS9593	51°37·8'	3°30·6'W	H	170
Mynydd Wysg	Powys	SN8226	51°55·4'	3°42·6'W	F	160
Mynydd y Betws	Carm	SN6710	51°46·6'	3°55·3'W	H	159
Mynydd-y-briw	Powys	SJ1726	52°49·8'	3°13·5'W	X	125
Mynydd y Bryn	Powys	SJ2126	52°49·8'	3°10·0'W	H	126
Mynydd y Bwlch	Caer	ST2087	51°34·8'	3°8·9'W	X	171
Mynydd y Castell	Nth Pt Talb	SS8086	51°33·8'	3°43·5'W	X	170
Mynydd y Castell (Fort)	Nth Pt Talb	SS8086	51°33·8'	3°43·5'W	A	170
Mynydd y Cemais	Powys	SH8607	52°39·2'	3°40·7'W	H	124,125
Mynydd y Cilgwyn	Gwyn	SH4954	53°4·0'	4°14·8'W	H	115,123
Mynydd y Cymmer	Rho Cyn Taf	ST0190	51°36·2'	3°25·4'W	H	170
Mynydd y Defaid	Powys	SN8478	52°23·5'	3°41·9'W	X	135,136,147
Mynydd y Dref or Conwy Mountain	Conwy	SH7677	53°16·8'	3°51·2'W	H	115
Mynydd y Ffaldau	Rho Cyn Taf	SS9898	51°40·5'	3°28·1'W	H	170
Mynydd y Fforest	V of Glam	ST0078	51°29·8'	3°26·0'W	H	170
Mynydd y Gadfa	Powys	SH9914	52°43·1'	3°29·3'W	H	125
Mynydd y Gaer	Brig	SS9585	51°33·5'	3°30·5'W	H	170
Mynydd y Gaer	Conwy	SH9771	53°13·8'	3°32·2'W	A	116
Mynydd-y-Gaer	Nth Pt Talb	SS7693	51°37·6'	3°47·1'W	H	170
Mynydd y Garn	I of Angl	SH3190	53°23·0'	4°32·1'W	H	114
Mynydd y Garn	Powys	SN9514	51°49·1'	3°31·0'W	H	160
Mynydd-y-garn-fawr	Torf	SO2709	51°46·7'	3°3·1'W	X	161
Mynyddygarreg	Carm	SN4208	51°45·1'	4°17·0'W	T	159
Mynydd y Garreg	Carm	SN4409	51°45·7'	4°15·2'W	H	159
Mynydd y Garth	Nth Pt Talb	SN7108	51°45·6'	3°51·8'W	H	160
Mynydd y Gelli	Nth Pt Talb	SS8995	51°38·8'	3°35·9'W	X	170
Mynydd y Gelli	Rho Cyn Taf	SS9794	51°38·4'	3°28·9'W	X	170
Mynydd y Gilfach	Rho Cyn Taf	SS9889	51°35·7'	3°28·0'W	X	170
Mynydd y glew	V of Glam	ST0376	51°28·7'	3°23·4'W	X	170
Mynydd-y-glog	Rho Cyn Taf	SN9709	51°46·5'	3°29·2'W	H	160
Mynydd y Glyn	Powys	SJ1522	52°47·6'	3°15·2'W	X	125
Mynydd y Glyn	Rho Cyn Taf	ST0389	51°35·7'	3°23·6'W	H	170
Mynydd-y-gôf	I of Angl	SH3281	53°18·2'	4°30·9'W	X	114
Mynydd y Gribin	Powys	SJ0102	52°36·6'	3°27·3'W	X	136
Mynydd y Groes	Powys	SN8787	52°28·4'	3°39·4'W	H	135,136
Mynydd y Grug	Caer	ST1790	51°36·4'	3°11·5'W	H	171
Mynydd y Gwair	Brig	SS9489	51°35·6'	3°31·4'W	X	170
Mynydd y Gwair	Swan	SN6507	51°45·0'	3°57·0'W	H	159
Mynydd y Gyrt	Conwy	SH9669	53°12·7'	3°33·0'W	H	116
Mynydd y Llan	Carm	SN7924	51°54·3'	3°45·1'W	H	160
Mynydd y Llyn	Gwyn	SN6598	52°34·0'	3°59·1'W	H	135
Mynydd Ynyscorrwg	Nth Pt Talb	SS8898	51°40·4'	3°36·8'W	H	170
Mynydd yr Aber	Brig	SS9491	51°36·7'	3°31·5'W	H	170
Mynydd yr Eglwys	Rho Cyn Taf	SS9796	51°39·4'	3°29·0'W	X	170
Mynydd-yr-eithin	I of Angl	SH3182	53°18·7'	4°31·8'W	X	114
Mynydd yr Esgyrn	Powys	SJ0818	52°45·3'	3°21·4'W	X	125
Mynydd yr Hendre	Powys	SH9901	52°36·1'	3°29·1'W	X	136
Mynyddyrheol	Powys	SO1060	52°14·1'	3°18·7'W	H	148
Mynydd yr Ychen	Cered	SN7679	52°23·9'	3°49·0'W	X	135,147
Mynydd Ystradffernol	Rho Cyn Taf	SN9301	51°42·1'	3°32·5'W	H	170
Mynydd Ystum	Gwyn	SH1828	52°49·4'	4°41·7'W	H	123
Mynydd y Waun	Gwyn	SH7613	52°42·3'	3°49·7'W	H	124
Mynytho	Gwyn	SH3030	52°50·7'	4°31·1'W	T	123
Mynytho Common	Gwyn	SH2931	52°51·2'	4°32·0'W	X	123
Myot Hill	Falk	NS7882	56°1·2'	3°57·0'W	H	57,64
Myothill	Falk	NS7882	56°1·2'	3°57·0'W	X	57,64
Myot Hill (Fort)	Falk	NS7882	56°1·2'	3°57·0'W	A	57,64
Myott's Wood	Staffs	SJ9933	52°53·9'	2°0·5'W	F	127
Myrddin's Quoit	Carm	SN3716	51°49·4'	4°21·5'W	A	159
Myre	Cumbr	NY5477	55°5·4'	2°42·8'W	X	86
Myre	Orkney	HY3204	58°55·3'	3°10·4'W	X	6,7
Myre	W Loth	NT0875	55°57·8'	3°28·0'W	X	65
Myre Bay	Orkney	ND3291	58°48·3'	3°10·1'W	W	7
Myrebird	Aberd	NO7499	57°5·1'	2°25·3'W	X	38,45
Myrecairnie	Fife	NO3717	56°20·7'	3°0·7'W	X	59
Myrecairnie Hill	Fife	NO3618	56°21·3'	3°1·7'W	H	59
Myredykes	Scot Bord	NY5998	55°16·7'	2°38·3'W	X	80
Myredykes Plantn	Scot Bord	NY6098	55°16·7'	2°37·4'W	F	80
Myreground	Cumbr	SD1191	54°18·7'	3°21·7'W	X	96
Myrehaugh	Pth & Kin	NO0105	56°13·9'	3°35·4'W	X	58
Myrehaugh Hill	Pth & Kin	NO0105	56°13·9'	3°35·4'W	X	58
Myrehead	Falk	NS9677	55°58·7'	3°39·6'W	X	65
Myre Keld Fm	Durham	NZ0013	54°31·0'	1°59·6'W	FM	92
Myrelandhorn	Highld	ND2858	58°30·5'	3°13·7'W	T	11,12
Myremill	S Ayr	NS3110	55°21·6'	4°39·5'W	X	70
Myre of Bedlam	Aberd	NJ8745	57°30·0'	2°12·6'W	X	30
Myre Point	Orkney	ND3291	58°48·3'	3°10·1'W	X	7
Myrepole Fm	Lancs	SD4837	53°49·8'	2°47·0'W	FM	102
Myres	Aberd	NK0838	57°26·2'	1°51·5'W	X	30
Myres	Orkney	HY2927	59°7·7'	3°13·9'W	X	6
Myres	Orkney	HY4432	59°10·5'	2°58·3'W	X	5,6
Myres	Stir	NS7886	56°3·3'	3°57·1'W	X	57
Myres Castle	Fife	NO2411	56°17·4'	3°13·2'W	A	59
Myres Hill	E Renf	NS5646	55°41·4'	4°17·0'W	X	64
Myreside	Aberd	NJ6050	57°32·6'	2°39·6'W	X	29
Myreside	Aberd	NJ7000	57°5·7'	2°29·3'W	X	38
Myreside	Aberd	NO6866	56°47·3'	2°31·0'W	X	45
Myreside	Aberd	NO7379	56°54·3'	2°26·1'W	X	45
Myreside	Angus	NO4852	56°39·7'	2°50·5'W	X	54
Myreside	Angus	NO6648	56°37·6'	2°32·8'W	X	54
Myreside	E Loth	NT5369	55°55·0'	2°44·7'W	X	66
Myreside	E Loth	NT6677	55°59·3'	2°32·3'W	X	67
Myreside	Fife	NO2607	56°15·2'	3°11·2'W	X	59
Myreside	Moray	NJ2164	57°39·8'	3°19·0'W	X	28
Myreside	Moray	NJ4857	57°36·3'	2°51·7'W	X	28,29
Myreside	Pth & Kin	NO0425	56°24·7'	3°32·9'W	X	52,53,58
Myreside	Pth & Kin	NO1434	56°29·7'	3°23·4'W	X	53
Myreside	Pth & Kin	NO1644	56°35·1'	3°21·6'W	X	53
Myreside	Pth & Kin	NO2224	56°24·4'	3°15·4'W	X	53,58
Myrestone	Angus	NO4853	56°40·2'	2°50·5'W	X	54

Myreton	Aberd	NJ6029	57°21·2'	2°39·4'W	X	37
Myreton	Angus	NO4337	56°31·6'	2°55·1'W	X	54
Myreton	Moray	NJ4956	57°35·7'	2°50·7'W	X	28,29
Myreton	Pth & Kin	NN9932	56°28·4'	3°37·9'W	X	52,53
Myreton Fm	Stir	NS6794	56°7·5'	4°7·9'W	FM	57
Myreton Hill	Clackm	NS8598	56°9·9'	3°50·7'W	H	58
Myreton of Claverhouse	Angus	NO3936	56°31·0'	2°59·0'W	X	54
Myretoun, The	Clackm	NS8597	56°9·4'	3°50·6'W	X	58
Myriedale	Aberd	NJ6526	57°19·7'	2°34·4'W	X	38
Myrie Hall	Fife	NT0491	56°6·4'	3°32·2'W	X	58
Myrie Hill	Aberd	NJ7000	57°5·7'	2°29·3'W	H	38
Myriewells	Aberd	NJ7406	57°8·9'	2°25·3'W	X	38
Myrobella Fm	Norf	TF5322	52°46·7'	0°16·5'E	FM	131
Myroch Point	D & G	NX1241	54°44·0'	4°54·8'W	X	82
Myrtleberry Cleave	Devon	SS7348	51°13·3'	3°48·7'W	X	180
Myrtle Cott	Devon	SS5130	51°3·2'	4°7·2'W	X	180
Myrtle Fm	Somer	ST2918	50°57·7'	3°0·3'W	FM	193
Myrtle Grove Fm	W Susx	TQ0908	50°51·9'	0°26·7'W	FM	198
Myrtle Hill	Carm	SN5006	51°44·2'	4°10·0'W	X	159
Myrtle Hill	Carm	SN7630	51°57·5'	3°47·9'W	T	146,160
Myrtle House Fm	N Som	ST5363	51°22·1'	2°40·1'W	FM	172,182
Myrtlelane	Orkney	HY6841	59°15·5'	2°33·2'W	X	5
Mysevin	Denb	SJ0062	53°9·0'	3°29·3'W	X	116
Myskyns	E Susx	TQ6828	51°1·8'	0°24·1'E	X	188,199
Mystole Ho	Kent	TR0953	51°14·5'	1°0·1'E	X	179,189
Mytchett	Surrey	SU8855	51°17·5'	0°43·9'W	T	175,186
Mytchett Lake	Surrey	SU8954	51°16·9'	0°43·0'W	W	186
Mytchett Place	Surrey	SU8954	51°16·9'	0°43·0'W	T	186
Mythe Hill	Dorset	SY4998	50°47·0'	2°43·0'W	H	193,194
Mytholm	Cald	SD9827	53°44·6'	2°1·4'W	T	103
Mytholmes	Brad	SE0338	53°50·5'	1°56·9'W	T	104
Mytholmroyd	Cald	SE0126	53°44·1'	1°58·7'W	T	104
Mythop	Lancs	SD3634	53°48·1'	2°57·9'W	T	102
Mytice	Aberd	NJ4730	57°21·7'	2°52·4'W	X	29,37
Myton	Warw	SP3064	52°16·6'	1°33·2'W	T	151
Myton Field	N Yks	SE4468	54°6·6'	1°19·2'W	F	99
Myton Grange	N Yks	SE4467	54°6·1'	1°19·2'W	X	99
Myton Hall	N Yks	SE4466	54°5·5'	1°19·2'W	T	99
Myton Home Fm	N Yks	SE4567	54°6·1'	1°18·3'W	FM	99
Myton House Fm	Stock on T	NZ4413	54°30·9'	1°18·8'W	FM	93
Myton Ings	N Yks	SE4465	54°5·0'	1°19·2'W	X	99
Myton Moor	N Yks	SE4566	54°5·5'	1°18·3'W	X	99
Myton-on-Swale	N Yks	SE4366	54°5·5'	1°20·1'W	T	99
Mytten Hall	Lancs	SD5048	53°55·8'	2°45·3'W	X	102
Mytton	Shrops	SJ4417	52°45·1'	2°49·4'W	T	126
Mytton Dingle	Shrops	SJ3600	52°35·9'	2°56·3'W	F	126
Mytton Ho	Shrops	SJ4416	52°44·6'	2°49·4'W	X	126
Mytton Mill	Shrops	SJ4417	52°45·1'	2°49·4'W	X	126
Mytton's Coppice	Wrekin	SJ5517	52°45·2'	2°39·6'W	F	126
Myze Fm	Bucks	SU8294	51°38·6'	0°48·5'W	FM	175

N

Naas Court	Glos	SO6402	51°43·2'	2°30·9'W	X	162
Naas Fm	Glos	SO8212	51°48·6'	2°15·3'W	FM	162
Naas House	Glos	SO6401	51°42·6'	2°30·9'W	A	162
Naast	Highld	NG8283	57°47·3'	5°39·6'W	X	19
Nab	Cumbr	SD6494	54°20·7'	2°32·8'W	X	97
Nab	I of M	SC3480	54°11·6'	4°32·3'W	X	95
Nab	N Yks	NZ6403	54°25·3'	1°0·4'W	X	94
Na Bachdanan	Arg & Bt	NM5839	56°29·1'	5°55·4'W	X	47,48
Na Badagan	Arg & Bt	NR2975	55°53·8'	6°19·7'W	W	60
Na Badain	Arg & Bt	NM7034	56°26·8'	5°43·5'W	X	49
Na Bàighe-dubha	N Eil	NF7729	57°14·5'	7°20·8'W	W	22
Nabb Fm	Durham	NZ0015	54°32·1'	1°59·6'W	FM	92
Nabb Fm	Lancs	SD8426	53°44·1'	2°14·1'W	FM	103
Nabb Fm	Staffs	SK0840	52°57·7'	1°52·4'W	FM	119,128
Nabbotts Fm	Essex	TL7209	51°45·4'	0°29·9'E	FM	167
Nab Brow	Derby	SK0588	53°23·6'	1°55·1'W	X	110
Nabbs, The	Notts	SK7349	53°2·2'	0°54·3'W	X	129
Nab Cottage	Cumbr	NY3506	54°27·0'	2°59·7'W	X	90
Nab Crags	Cumbr	NY3112	54°30·2'	3°3·5'W	X	90
Nabdean	Scot Bord	NT9252	55°45·9'	2°7·2'W	X	67,74,75
Nab End	Brad	SE0647	53°55·4'	1°54·1'W	X	104
Nab End	Ches	SJ9478	53°18·2'	2°5·0'W	H	118
Nabend	Cumbr	NY4125	54°37·3'	2°54·4'W	X	90
Nab End	Lancs	SD5952	53°58·0'	2°37·1'W	X	102
Nab End	N Yks	NZ7502	54°24·7'	0°50·2'W	X	94
Nab End	N Yks	SD9070	54°7·8'	2°8·8'W	X	98
Nabend	Staffs	SK0766	53°11·7'	1°53·3'W	X	119
Nab End Moor	N Yks	SE5798	54°22·7'	1°6·9'W	X	100
Nab Fm	E Yorks	SE9161	54°2·5'	0°36·2'W	FM	101
Nab Fm	N Yks	SE4792	54°19·5'	1°16·2'W	FM	100
Nab Fm	N Yks	SE8695	54°20·8'	0°40·2'W	FM	94,101
Nab Head	Ches	SJ9478	53°18·2'	2°5·0'W	H	118
Nab Head, The	Pemb	SM7911	51°45·5'	5°11·8'W	X	157
Nab Hill	Cald	SE0332	53°47·3'	1°56·9'W	H	104
Nab Hill	Kirk	SE1718	53°39·7'	1°44·2'W	T	110
Nab Hill	Lancs	SD7423	53°42·4'	2°23·2'W	X	103
Nab Hill	Lincs	TF3074	53°15·1'	0°2·7'W	X	122
Nabhill	Northum	NU0046	55°42·7'	1°59·6'W	X	75
Nab Hill	N Yks	SE2949	53°56·4'	1°33·1'W	X	104
Na Binneinean	Arg & Bt	NM5838	56°28·6'	5°55·3'W	H	47,48
Nables Fm	Wilts	ST9380	51°31·4'	2°5·7'W	FM	173
Nabor Pt	Devon	SS2120	50°57·3'	4°32·5'W	X	190
Nab Point	Cumbr	SD3180	54°12·9'	3°3·1'W	X	96,97
Nab Ridge	N Yks	SE5797	54°22·2'	1°6·9'W	X	100
Nabs	N Yks	SE1265	54°5·1'	1°48·6'W	X	99
Nab Scar	Cumbr	NY3506	54°27·0'	2°59·7'W	X	90
Nab's Head	Lancs	SD6229	53°45·6'	2°34·2'W	T	102,103
Nab Side Fm	Lancs	SD7235	53°48·9'	2°25·1'W	FM	103
Nabs Moor	Cumbr	NY5011	54°29·8'	2°45·9'W	H	90
Nabs, The	Derby	SK1453	53°4·7'	1°47·1'W	X	119

Nabs Wood	Derby	SK1689	53°24·1′	1°45·2′W	F	110
Nab, The	Cumbr	NY4315	54°31·9′	2°52·4′W	H	90
Nab, The	Cumbr	NY5713	54°30·9′	2°39·4′W	X	91
Nab, The	Cumbr	SD7699	54°23·4′	2°21·8′W	X	98
Nab, The	Derby	SK1286	53°22·5′	1°48·8′W	X	110
Nab, The	Norf	TG4413	52°39·8′	1°36·9′E	W	134
Nab, The	Shetld	HU2148	60°13·2′	1°36·8′W	X	3
Naburn	York	SE5945	53°54·1′	1°5·7′W	T	105
Naburn Grange	York	SE5944	53°53·6′	1°5·7′W	X	105
Naburn Hill Fm	York	SE6246	53°54·6′	1°3·0′W	FM	105
Naburn Lodge	York	SE6046	53°54·6′	1°4·8′W	X	105
Naburn Moor	York	SE6045	53°54·1′	1°4·8′W	X	105
Naburn Wood	York	SE6043	53°53·0′	1°4·8′W	F	105
Nab Wood	Brad	SE1237	53°50·0′	1°48·6′W	T	104
Naby	Durham	NZ0018	54°33·7′	1°59·6′W	X	92
Na Caol Lochan	Highld	NC6955	58°28·1′	4°14·3′W	W	10
Naccolt	Kent	TR0444	51°9·8′	0°55·5′E	T	179,189
Naccolt Fm	Kent	TR0642	51°8·6′	0°57·1′E	FM	179,189
Na Ciochan	Highld	NG7942	57°25·1′	5°40·4′W	X	24
Nacka Skerry	Shetld	HU6166	60°22·7′	0°53·1′W	X	2
Nacker Hole	Northum	NU2329	55°33·5′	1°37·7′W	W	75
Nackerye End	Herts	TL1515	51°49·5′	0°19·5′W	A	166
Nackington	Kent	TR1554	51°14·9′	1°5·2′E	T	179,189
Nackshivan Fm	Durham	NZ1836	54°43·4′	1°42·8′W	FM	92
Na Cléirich	N Eil	NB1332	58°11·3′	6°52·5′W	X	13
Na Cluasnadh	Highld	NC1957	58°28·1′	5°5·7′W	X	9
Na Cnapain	Highld	NH1720	57°14·3′	5°1·5′W	X	25
Na Cnapanan	Highld	NN4788	56°57·7′	4°30·5′W	H	34,42
Na Coireachan	Arg & Bt	NN0503	56°11·0′	5°8·1′W	X	56
Na Coireachan	Highld	NM5467	56°44·0′	6°0·9′W	X	47
Na Creagan	N Eil	NF7936	57°18·4′	7°19·4′W	H	22
Na Cruachan	Arg & Bt	NN1830	56°25·9′	4°56·7′W	X	50
Na Cruachan	Highld	NG7707	57°6·3′	5°40·5′W	H	33
Nacton	Suff	TM2140	52°1·1′	1°13·7′E	T	169
Nacton Heath	Suff	TM2041	52°1·6′	1°12·8′E	X	169
Na Cùiltean	Arg & Bt	NR5464	55°45·3′	5°55·1′W	X	61
Nadbury	Warw	SP3948	52°8·0′	1°25·4′W	A	151
Nadbury Ho	Warw	SP3947	52°7·4′	1°25·4′W	X	151
Nadder Brook	Devon	SX8992	50°43·3′	3°34·0′W	W	192
Nadderwater	Devon	SX8993	50°43·8′	3°34·0′W	T	192
Naddle Beck	Cumbr	NY2923	54°36·1′	3°5·5′W	W	89,90
Naddle Fm	Cumbr	NY5015	54°31·9′	2°45·9′W	FM	90
Naddle Forest	Cumbr	NY4914	54°31·4′	2°46·9′W	F	90
Naddles Beck	Cumbr	NY3828	54°38·8′	2°57·2′W	W	90
Naddles Crags	Cumbr	NY3829	54°39·4′	2°57·2′W	X	90
Na Doireachan	Highld	NH2200	57°3·7′	4°55·7′W	X	34
Nadrid Fm	Devon	SS7029	51°3·0′	3°50·9′W	FM	180
Nadrid Water	Devon	SS6824	51°0·3′	3°52·5′W	W	180
Na Dromannan	Highld	NC2101	57°58·0′	5°1·1′W	X	15
Na Dubh-lochan	Highld	NC8604	58°0·9′	3°55·3′W	W	17
Na Dubh-sgeireagan	Arg & Bt	NR6655	55°44·2′	5°43·2′W	X	62
Naemoor	Clackm	NO0101	56°11·7′	3°35·3′W	X	58
Na Faing Arda	Arg & Bt	NM7328	56°23·6′	5°40·2′W	X	49
Na Fairchean	Arg & Bt	NM3924	56°20·4′	6°13·0′W	X	48
Na Famhairean	Highld	NG5258	57°32·9′	6°8·2′W	X	23,24
Na Fasreidhnean	Highld	NG8659	57°34·5′	5°34·3′W	X	24
Na Feamindean	Arg & Bt	NR4270	55°51·5′	6°6·9′W	X	60,61
Nafferton	Durham	NZ2438	54°44·4′	1°37·2′W	X	93
Nafferton	E Yorks	TA0559	54°1·2′	0°23·4′W	T	107
Nafferton Fm	Northum	NZ0665	54°59·0′	1°53·9′W	FM	87
Nafferton Grange	E Yorks	TA0460	54°1·8′	0°24·3′W	X	101
Nafferton Kesters	E Yorks	TA0462	54°2·8′	0°24·3′W	X	101
Nafferton Wold	E Yorks	TA0461	54°2·3′	0°24·3′W	X	101
Naffit's Fm	N Yks	SE5862	54°3·3′	1°6·4′W	FM	100
Nafford	Worcs	SO9441	52°4·3′	2°4·9′W	X	150
Na Gamhnachain	Highld	NG6363	57°36·0′	5°57·5′W	X	24
Na Gamhnaichean	Highld	NG4312	57°7·9′	6°14·4′W	X	32
Na Gamhnaichean	Highld	NG9495	57°54·1′	5°28·1′W	X	19
Na Garbh-lochanan	Arg & Bt	NR4974	55°53·9′	6°0·5′W	W	60,61
Nagden	Kent	TR0363	51°20·0′	0°55·2′E	X	178,179
Nagden Marshes	Kent	TR0264	51°20·6′	0°54·4′E	X	178
Na Gearrannan	N Eil	NB1944	58°17·9′	6°47·3′W	T	8
Naggyfauld	Stir	NN8005	56°13·6′	3°55·7′W	X	57
Naginton Grange	Shrops	SJ6725	52°49·5′	2°29·0′W	X	127
Na Glas-coire	Highld	NC5930	58°14·4′	4°23·6′W	X	16
Na Glas Leacan	Highld	NC3471	58°36·0′	4°50·9′W	X	9
Na Gruagaichean	Highld	NN2065	56°44·8′	4°56·2′W	H	41
Nag's Fold Fm	Durham	NZ2746	54°48·7′	1°34·4′W	FM	88
Nags Hall	Surrey	TQ3651	51°14·7′	0°2·7′W	X	187
Nag's Head	Cumbr	NY7941	54°46·1′	2°19·2′W	H	86,87
Nag's Head	Glos	ST8998	51°41·1′	2°9·2′W	T	163
Nag's Head Fm	Darl	NZ2711	54°29·9′	1°34·6′W	FM	93
Nagshead Knowe	Northum	NT9116	55°26·5′	2°8·1′W	X	80
Nagshead Plantation	Glos	SO5909	51°46·9′	2°35·3′W	F	162
Na h-Airichean	Arg & Bt	NM6122	56°20·1′	5°51·6′W	X	49
Na h-Amaranan	N Eil	NB3144	58°18·4′	6°35·1′W	X	8
Na h-Athanan Dubha	N Eil	NF8669	57°36·4′	7°15·0′W	X	18
Na h-Iseanan	Arg & Bt	NM0143	56°29·3′	6°51·0′W	X	46
Na h-Uaighean	Highld	NH1835	57°22·4′	5°1·2′W	X	25
Na h'-uamhachan	Highld	NM9684	56°54·4′	5°20·6′W	X	40
Na h-Uillt Chonnaidh	Highld	NC2201	57°58·0′	5°0·1′W	W	15
Na Huranan	Highld	NG3430	57°17·3′	6°24·4′W	X	32
Na h- Urrachann	Arg & Bt	NM6704	56°10·6′	5°44·8′W	X	55
Na h-Ursainnan	Arg & Bt	NR5284	55°59·4′	5°58·1′W	X	61
Naidevala Muigh	N Eil	NB0222	58°5·5′	7°3·0′W	H	13
Naideval a Stigh	N Eil	NB0123	58°6·0′	7°4·0′W	X	13
Naid-y-march	Flint	SJ1675	53°16·2′	3°15·2′W	T	116
Nail Bourne	Kent	TR1845	51°10·0′	1°7·5′E	W	179,189
Nailbridge	Glos	SO6416	51°50·7′	2°31·0′W	T	162
Nailcote Hall	Sol	SP2677	52°23·7′	1°36·7′W	X	140
Nailey Fm	S Glos	ST7771	51°26·5′	2°19·5′W	FM	172
Nailsbourne	Somer	ST2128	51°3·0′	3°7·2′W	T	193
Nailsea	N Som	ST4669	51°25·3′	2°46·2′W	T	171,172,182
Nailsea Court	N Som	ST4568	51°24·7′	2°47·1′W	A	171,172,182
Nailsea Moor	N Som	ST4470	51°25·8′	2°47·9′W	X	171,172
Nailstone	Leic	SK4107	52°39·8′	1°23·2′W	T	140
Nailstone Gorse	Leic	SK4007	52°39·8′	1°24·1′W	F	140
Nailstone Grange	Leic	SK4108	52°40·3′	1°23·2′W	X	140
Nailsworth	Glos	ST8499	51°41·6′	2°13·5′W	T	162
Nailwell	Bath & NE Somer	ST7060	51°20·5′	2°25·5′W	T	172
Nairdwood Fm	Bucks	SU8899	51°41·2′	0°43·2′W	FM	165
Nairn	Highld	NH8856	57°35·1′	3°51·9′W	T	27
Nairnside	Highld	NH8250	57°31·7′	3°57·8′W	X	27
Nairnside Ho	Highld	NH7442	57°27·3′	4°5·5′W	X	27
Nairns Mains	E Loth	NT4672	55°56·5′	2°51·4′W	X	66
Naisberry	Hartpl	NZ4733	54°41·6′	1°15·8′W	X	93
Naishes Fm	Wilts	SU0329	51°3·9′	1°57·0′W	FM	184
Naish Hill Fm	Wilts	ST9369	51°25·4′	2°5·7′W	FM	173
Naish Ho	N Som	ST4773	51°27·4′	2°45·4′W	X	171,172
Naked Hill	Angus	NO4487	56°58·5′	2°54·8′W	H	44
Naked Man	Hants	SU2401	50°48·7′	1°39·2′W	X	195
Naked Tam	Angus	NO4264	56°46·1′	2°56·5′W	H	44
Naker's Hill	Devon	SX6468	50°30·0′	3°54·7′W	X	202
Nalderhill Ho	W Berks	SU4168	51°24·8′	1°24·2′W	X	174
Nalderswood	Surrey	TQ2345	51°11·7′	0°14·0′W	T	187
Naldretts	W Susx	TQ2719	50°57·6′	0°11·1′W	X	198
Naldretts Court	W Susx	TQ0527	51°2·2′	0°29·8′W	X	187,197
Naldretts Fm	W Susx	TQ0832	51°4·9′	0°27·1′W	FM	187
Naldretts Fm	W Susx	TQ2339	51°8·4′	0°14·1′W	FM	187
Na Leacanan	Highld	NM8369	56°46·0′	5°32·6′W	X	40
Na Leitrichean	Highld	NC1812	58°3·9′	5°4·6′W	X	15
Na Liathanaich	Arg & Bt	NM3525	56°20·8′	6°16·9′W	X	48
Nallers Fm	Dorset	SY5492	50°43·8′	2°38·7′W	FM	194
Na Luirgean	Highld	NC2211	58°3·4′	5°0·5′W	W	15
Na Maoilean	Arg & Bt	NM9736	56°28·6′	5°17·3′W	H	49
Na Maoilean	Arg & Bt	NR4865	55°49·0′	6°0·9′W	X	60,61
Na Maoil Mhòra	Arg & Bt	NM3316	56°15·9′	6°18·3′W	X	48
Nambol	Corn	SW7721	50°3·1′	5°6·5′W	X	204
Na Meallanan Buidhe	Highld	NH0647	57°28·6′	5°13·7′W	X	25
Namen's Leases	N Yks	NZ2012	54°30·4′	1°41·0′W	X	93
Na Mill Ghlasa	Highld	NH0170	57°40·8′	5°19·8′W	H	19
Na Minn	Arg & Bt	NM3818	56°17·2′	6°13·6′W	X	48
Na Minnean	Arg & Bt	NR4766	55°49·5′	6°1·9′W	X	60,61
Namor Fm	Denb	SJ1555	53°5·4′	3°15·7′W	FM	116
Namprathic	Corn	SW8743	50°15·2′	4°58·9′W	X	204
NA Mulcaneann	Highld	NG9150	57°29·8′	5°28·8′W	X	25
Na Mullaichean	N Eil	NF9087	57°46·2′	7°12·4′W	X	18
Nan Bield Pass	Cumbr	NY4509	54°28·7′	2°50·5′W	X	90
Nancarrow	Corn	SW8641	50°14·1′	4°59·7′W	X	204
Nance	Corn	SW5137	50°11·1′	5°28·9′W	X	203
Nance	Corn	SW6644	50°15·2′	5°16·6′W	T	203
Nanceddan	Corn	SW5033	50°8·9′	5°29·6′W	T	203
Nancegollan	Corn	SW6332	50°8·7′	5°18·7′W	T	203
Nancekuke Common	Corn	SW6846	50°16·3′	5°15·0′W	X	203
Nancemellin	Corn	SW6041	50°13·5′	5°21·5′W	T	203
Nancemere	Corn	SW8246	50°16·7′	5°3·2′W	X	204
Nancemerrin	Corn	SW6725	50°5·0′	5°15·1′W	X	203
Nancenoy	Corn	SW7328	50°6·8′	5°10·1′W	T	204
Nancewidden	Corn	SW6525	50°5·0′	5°16·7′W	X	203
Nancewrath	Corn	SW7847	50°17·1′	5°6·6′W	X	204
Nancledra	Corn	SW4935	50°10·0′	5°30·5′W	T	203
Nancolleth	Corn	SW8656	50°22·1′	5°0·2′W	X	200
Nancor	Corn	SW9448	50°18·0′	4°53·2′W	X	204
Naneby Hall Fm	Leic	SK4302	52°37·1′	1°21·5′W	FM	140
Nanfan	Corn	SW6820	50°2·3′	5°14·0′W	X	203
Nangreaves	Bury	SD8115	53°38·1′	2°16·8′W	T	109
Nanhellan	Corn	SW8355	50°21·5′	5°2·7′W	X	200
Nan Hill	Cumbr	NY5706	54°27·1′	2°39·4′W	X	91
Nanhoron	Gwyn	SH2831	52°51·2′	4°32·9′W	X	123
Nanhurst	Surrey	TQ0338	51°8·1′	0°31·3′W	X	186
Nanjizal or Mill Bay	Corn	SW3523	50°3·1′	5°41·8′W	W	203
Nankelly	Corn	SW9061	50°24·9′	4°57·0′W	X	200
Nankervis	Corn	SW9053	50°20·6′	4°56·7′W	X	200,204
Nankilly	Corn	SW8648	50°17·8′	4°59·9′W	X	204
Nankilly	Corn	SW9051	50°19·5′	4°56·7′W	X	200,204
Nan King's Fm	Lancs	SD6144	53°53·7′	2°35·2′W	FM	102,103
Nanmor	Gwyn	SH6145	52°59·3′	4°3·8′W	W	115
Nannau	Gwyn	SH7420	52°46·0′	3°51·7′W	T	124
Nannau-is-afon	Gwyn	SH7022	52°47·0′	3°55·3′W	X	124
Nannau-is-afon	Gwyn	SH7525	52°48·7′	3°50·9′W	X	124
Nannau-uwch-afon	Gwyn	SH7822	52°47·2′	3°48·1′W	X	124
Nanner	I of Angl	SH3392	53°24·2′	4°30·3′W	X	114
Nannerch	Flint	SJ1669	53°12·9′	3°15·1′W	T	116
Nannerth	Powys	SN9471	52°19·9′	3°32·9′W	X	136,147
Nanny Crag	N Yks	SE0758	54°1·3′	1°53·2′W	X	104
Nanny Felton's Cairn	Northum	NU1207	55°21·7′	1°48·2′W	X	81
Nanny Hall	Cumbr	SD5777	54°11·5′	2°39·1′W	X	97
Nanny's Rock	Staffs	SO8382	52°26·4′	2°14·6′W	X	138
Nanpantan	Leic	SK5017	52°45·1′	1°15·1′W	T	129
Nanpean	Corn	SW8955	50°21·7′	4°57·6′W	X	200
Nanpean	Corn	SW9656	50°22·3′	4°51·8′W	T	200
Nanphysick Barton	Corn	SW9851	50°19·7′	4°49·9′W	X	200,204
Nanpusker	Corn	SW5837	50°11·3′	5°23·0′W	X	203
Nanquidno	Corn	SW3629	50°6·4′	5°41·2′W	T	203
Nansalsa	Corn	SW8748	50°17·8′	4°59·1′W	X	204
Nansavallan	Corn	SW8143	50°15·0′	5°4·0′W	X	204
Nan Scar	Brad	SE0333	53°47·8′	1°56·9′W	X	104
Nanscow	Corn	SW9670	50°29·9′	4°52·2′W	X	200
Nansen Hill	I of W	SZ5778	50°36·2′	1°11·3′W	X	196
Nansfield	Scot Bord	NT9152	55°45·9′	2°8·2′W	X	67,74,75
Nanskeval	Corn	SW8864	50°26·5′	4°58·8′W	X	200
Nansladron	Corn	SX0048	50°18·1′	4°48·1′W	X	204
Nansloe	Corn	SW6526	50°5·5′	5°16·8′W	X	203
Nansmerrow	Corn	SW8547	50°17·3′	5°0·7′W	X	204
Nansough	Corn	SW8750	50°18·9′	4°59·1′W	X	200,204
Nanstallon	Corn	SX0367	50°28·4′	4°46·2′W	T	200
Nanswhyden	Corn	SW8762	50°25·4′	4°59·6′W	X	200
Nant	Carm	SN4319	51°51·1′	4°16·4′W	T	159
Nant	Conwy	SH7860	53°7·6′	3°49·0′W	X	115
Nant	Conwy	SH8164	53°9·8′	3°46·4′W	X	116
Nant	Conwy	SH8669	53°12·6′	3°42·0′W	X	116
Nant	Conwy	SH9964	53°10·1′	3°30·2′W	X	116
Nant	Denb	SJ0462	53°9·0′	3°25·7′W	X	116
Nant	Denb	SJ1247	53°1·0′	3°18·3′W	X	116
Nant	Denb	SJ1441	52°57·8′	3°16·4′W	X	125
Nant	Denb	SJ1957	53°6·5′	3°12·2′W	T	116
Nant	Gwyn	SH2127	52°48·9′	4°39·0′W	X	123
Nant	Gwyn	SH2929	52°50·1′	4°31·9′W	X	123
Nant	Gwyn	SH6671	53°13·4′	4°0·0′W	X	115
Nant	I of Angl	SH4873	53°14·2′	4°16·2′W	X	114,115
Nant	I of Angl	SH5977	53°16·5′	4°6·5′W	X	114,115
Nant	Monm	SO4316	51°50·6′	2°49·3′W	X	161
Nant	Powys	SJ1932	52°53·0′	3°11·8′W	X	125
Nant	Powys	SO1258	52°13·0′	3°16·9′W	X	148
Nant	Shrops	SJ2634	52°54·1′	3°5·6′W	X	126
Nant	Wrex	SJ3942	52°58·6′	2°54·1′W	X	117
Nant Aberbleiddyn	Gwyn	SH8938	52°55·9′	3°38·7′W	W	124,125
Nant Aberdeuddwr	Powys	SN8298	52°34·3′	3°44·1′W	W	135,136
Nant Aberduldog	Gwyn	SH8937	52°55·4′	3°38·7′W	W	124,125
Nant Achlas	Powys	SJ0026	52°49·6′	3°28·6′W	W	125
Nant Adwy'r-llan	Conwy	SH8546	53°0·2′	3°42·4′W	W	116
Nant Aerau	Carm	SN4530	51°57·1′	4°14·9′W	W	146
Nant Aeron	Carm	SN4130	51°57·0′	4°18·4′W	W	146
Nant Alan	Powys	SJ1119	52°45·9′	3°18·7′W	W	125
Nant Alltwalis	Carm	SN4330	51°57·0′	4°16·7′W	W	146
Nant Alyn	Flint	SJ1966	53°11·3′	3°12·3′W	T	116
Nant Aman Fâch	Rho Cyn Taf	SN9900	51°41·6′	3°27·3′W	W	170
Nantanog	I of Angl	SH3883	53°19·4′	4°25·5′W	X	114
Nant Arberth	Cered	SN2247	52°5·8′	4°35·5′W	W	145
Nant Bach	Conwy	SH9058	53°6·7′	3°38·2′W	W	116
Nant Bach	Conwy	SH9168	53°12·1′	3°37·5′W	W	116
Nant Bach	Denb	SH9873	53°14·9′	3°31·3′W	W	116
Nant Bach	Denb	SJ0558	53°6·9′	3°24·8′W	W	116
Nant Bach	Gwyn	SH2634	52°52·8′	4°34·7′W	X	123
Nant Bai	Carm	SN7844	52°5·1′	3°46·4′W	W	146,147,160
Nant Bargod	Carm	SN3636	52°0·1′	4°23·0′W	W	145
Nant Bargod Rhymni	Caer	SO1104	51°43·9′	3°16·9′W	W	171
Nant Barrog	Conwy	SH9268	53°12·1′	3°36·6′W	W	116
Nantbendigaid	Carm	SN3928	51°55·9′	4°20·1′W	X	145
Nant Blaenogwr	Brig	SS9493	51°37·8′	3°31·5′W	W	170
Nant Blaenpelenna	Nth Pt Talb	SS8298	51°40·3′	3°42·0′W	W	170
Nant Boeth	Nth Pt Talb	SS8897	51°39·9′	3°36·8′W	W	170
Nant Braich-y-ceunant	Gwyn	SH7636	52°54·7′	3°50·2′W	W	124
Nant Braich-y-rhiw	Gwyn	SH6300	52°35·1′	4°0·9′W	W	135
Nant Bran	Powys	SN9532	51°58·8′	3°31·3′W	W	160
Nant Brân	Swan	SS7099	51°40·7′	3°52·4′W	W	170
Nant-brân	V of Glam	ST1072	51°26·6′	3°17·3′W	X	171
Nant Brechfa	Carm	SN4225	51°54·3′	4°17·4′W	W	146
Nant Brwynog	Cered	SN8164	52°15·9′	3°44·2′W	W	147
Nant Bryn-llefrith	Gwyn	SH7233	52°53·0′	3°53·7′W	W	124
Nant Bryn-maen	Cered	SN6356	52°11·4′	3°59·9′W	W	146
Nant Bryn-yr-ieir	Powys	SN8472	52°20·3′	3°41·8′W	W	135,136,147
Nant Budr	Gwyn	SH7435	52°54·1′	3°52·0′W	W	124
Nant Bwch	Powys	SO0144	52°5·4′	3°26·3′W	W	147,160
Nant Bwch	Powys	SO2332	51°59·1′	3°6·9′W	W	161
Nant Bwlch-glas	Cered	SN7087	52°28·2′	3°54·4′W	W	135
Nant Bwrefwr	Powys	SO0518	51°51·4′	3°22·4′W	W	160
Nant Bychan	I of Angl	SH5185	53°20·7′	4°13·9′W	X	114
Nant Byfre	Powys	SN8516	51°50·1′	3°39·8′W	W	160
Nant-byr	Cered	SN6970	52°19·0′	3°54·9′W	X	135
Nant Caeach	Merth Tyd	ST1197	51°40·1′	3°16·8′W	W	171
Nant Cae-dudwg	Rho Cyn Taf	ST0992	51°37·4′	3°18·5′W	W	171
Nantcaerio	Cered	SN6180	52°24·3′	4°2·2′W	X	135
Nant Caledfryn	Conwy	SH8857	53°6·2′	3°40·0′W	W	116
Nant Car	Merth Tyd	SO0112	51°48·1′	3°25·8′W	W	160
Nant-Carfan	Powys	SH8907	52°39·2′	3°38·1′W	X	124,125
Nant Carn	Caer	ST2494	51°38·6′	3°5·5′W	W	171
Nant-Caw	Gwyn	SH6509	52°40·0′	3°59·4′W	X	124
Nant Cawrddu	Denb	SJ0741	52°57·7′	3°22·7′W	W	125
Nant Cefn-coch	Gwyn	SH9440	52°57·1′	3°34·3′W	W	125
Nant Ceiliog	Powys	SN8114	51°49·0′	3°43·2′W	W	160
Nant Ceiswyn	Gwyn	SH7813	52°42·3′	3°47·9′W	W	124
Nantcellan	Cered	SN5984	52°26·4′	4°4·1′W	X	135
Nant Cerdin	Powys	SN8749	52°7·9′	3°38·7′W	W	147
Nant Cerrig-y-groes	Powys	SH9414	52°43·0′	3°33·8′W	W	125
Nant Cil-y-fforch	Powys	SN9120	51°52·3′	3°34·6′W	W	160
Nant Ciwc	Rho Cyn Taf	SS9883	51°32·4′	3°27·9′W	W	170
Nant Clawdd	Carm	SN6646	52°6·0′	3°57·0′W	W	146
Nant-clawdd-isaf	Carm	SN3731	51°57·5′	4°21·9′W	X	145
Nant Cledlyn	Cered	SN4944	52°4·7′	4°11·8′W	W	146
Nant Cletwr	Powys	SN8768	52°18·2′	3°39·0′W	W	135,136,147
Nantclimbers	Wrex	SJ3938	52°56·4′	2°54·1′W	X	126
Nantclimbers Wood	Shrops	SJ3938	52°56·4′	2°54·1′W	F	126
Nant Clwyd	Nth Pt Talb	SN8405	51°44·1′	3°40·4′W	W	160
Nantclwyd Hall	Denb	SJ1151	53°3·2′	3°19·3′W	A	116
Nantclwyd Uchaf	Denb	SJ1252	53°3·7′	3°18·4′W	X	116
Nant Clydach	Powys	SN8931	51°58·2′	3°36·6′W	W	160
Nant Clydach	Rho Cyn Taf	ST0693	51°37·9′	3°21·1′W	W	170
Nant Clywedog-ganol	Cered	SN6550	52°8·2′	3°58·0′W	W	146
Nant Clywedog-isaf	Cered	SN6350	52°8·1′	3°59·7′W	W	146
Nant Clywedog-uchaf	Cered	SN6551	52°8·7′	3°58·0′W	W	146
Nantcoch	Carm	SN3531	51°57·4′	4°23·7′W	X	145
Nantcoch	Powys	SN9222	51°53·4′	3°33·8′W	X	160
Nant Coed-y-mynydd	Flint	SJ1269	53°12·9′	3°18·7′W	W	116
Nant Coegen	Powys	SH8505	52°38·1′	3°41·6′W	W	124,125
Nantcol	Gwyn	SH6427	52°49·6′	4°0·7′W	X	124
Nant Colwyn	Gwyn	SH5749	53°1·4′	4°7·5′W	X	115
Nant Corrwg	Carm	SN4527	51°55·4′	4°14·9′W	W	146
Nantcoy	Cered	SN5663	52°15·0′	4°6·2′W	X	146
Nant Craigyfrân	Powys	SH9608	52°39·8′	3°31·9′W	W	125
Nant Craigyraber	Nth Pt Talb	SS8585	51°33·4′	3°39·1′W	W	170
Nant Crechwyl	Denb	SJ0232	52°52·8′	3°27·0′W	W	125
Nant Cregan	Nth Pt Talb	SS8598	51°40·4′	3°39·1′W	W	170
Nant Creuddyn	Cered	SN5550	52°8·0′	4°6·7′W	W	146
Nant Crew	Powys	SO0018	51°51·3′	3°26·7′W	W	160
Nantcribba	Powys	SJ2301	52°36·3′	3°7·8′W	X	126
Nant Cringae	Powys	SJ0413	52°42·6′	3°24·9′W	W	125
Nant Croes-y-wernen	Denb	SJ0939	52°56·7′	3°20·9′W	W	125
Nant Crychiau	Carm	SN4424	51°53·8′	4°15·6′W	W	159
Nantcrymanau	Cered	SN2044	52°4·2′	4°37·2′W	X	145
Nant Crymlyn	Brig	SS9483	51°32·4′	3°31·3′W	W	170
Nant Crysan	Powys	SN8641	52°3·6′	3°39·4′W	W	147,160
Nant Cwm-breichiau	Gwyn	SH7103	52°36·8′	3°53·9′W	W	135
Nant Cwm bychan	Gwyn	SH9728	52°50·6′	3°31·4′W	W	125
Nant Cwm-bys	Powys	SN8150	52°8·4′	3°43·9′W	W	147
Nant Cwm-cas	Nth Pt Talb	SS8999	51°41·0′	3°35·9′W	W	170
Nant Cwm-ceir	Carm	SN4527	51°55·4′	4°14·9′W	W	146
Nant Cwm-da	Gwyn	SH9641	52°57·6′	3°32·5′W	W	125

Nant Cwm-du	Brig	SS8789	51°35·5'	3°37·5'W	W	170
Nant Cwm-du	Cered	SN7955	52°11·0'	3°45·8'W	W	146,147
Nant Cwm-du	Powys	SN9421	51°52·9'	3°32·0'W	W	160
Nant Cwm-ffernol	Gwyn	SH6601	52°35·7'	3°58·3'W	W	135
Nant Cwmffrwd	Carm	SN4316	51°49·5'	4°16·3'W	X	159
Nant Cwmgwernog	Powys	SN9292	52°31·2'	3°35·1'W	W	136
Nantcwmgwili	Carm	SN4528	51°56·0'	4°14·9'W	X	146
Nant Cwm-llawenog	Wrex	SJ1234	52°54·0'	3°18·1'W	W	125
Nant Cwm-lloi	Powys	SH9526	52°49·5'	3°33·1'W	W	125
Nant Cwm Llwch	Powys	SO0024	51°54·6'	3°26·8'W	W	160
Nant Cwm-marydd	Carm	SN5031	51°57·7'	4°10·6'W	W	146
Nant Cwm-moel	Merth Tyd	SO0311	51°47·6'	3°24·0'W	W	160
Nant Cwmnewydion	Cered	SN7074	52°21·2'	3°54·1'W	W	135,147
Nant Cwm Pydew	Denb	SJ0132	52°52·8'	3°27·9'W	W	125
Nantcwmrhys	Carm	SN3430	51°56·9'	4°24·5'W	X	145
Nant Cwm-sarn	Caer	ST1390	51°36·4'	3°15·0'W	W	171
Nant Cwm-sylwi	Gwyn	SN6798	52°34·1'	3°57·3'W	W	135
Nant Cwm Tywyll	Denb	SJ0433	52°53·4'	3°25·2'W	W	125
Nant Cwm y Geifr	Wrex	SJ1233	52°53·5'	3°18·1'W	W	125
Nant Cwmyrwden	Powys	SH7703	52°36·9'	3°48·6'W	W	135
Nantcwtta	Cered	SN5969	52°18·3'	4°3·7'W	X	135
Nant Cwy	Powys	SO1428	51°56·9'	3°14·7'W	W	161
Nant Cydros	Powys	SN9979	52°24·2'	3°28·7'W	W	136,147
Nant Cyfyng	Powys	SN9257	52°12·3'	3°34·4'W	W	147
Nant Cymdu	Powys	SN8297	52°33·7'	3°44·0'W	W	135,136
Nant Cymrun	Powys	SN9661	52°14·5'	3°31·0'W	W	147
Nant Cynafon	Powys	SO0718	51°51·4'	3°20·6'W	W	160
Nant Cynfal	Gwyn	SH6100	52°35·0'	4°2·7'W	W	135
Nant Cynnen	Carm	SN3622	51°52·6'	4°22·6'W	W	145,159
Nant Cynnyd	Gwyn	SH6554	53°4·2'	4°0·5'W	W	115
Nant Cyw	Powys	SN7913	51°48·4'	3°44·9'W	W	160
Nant Dâr	Carm	SN7044	52°5·0'	3°53·4'W	W	146,147,160
Nant Ddu	Gwyn	SH6664	53°9·6'	3°59·9'W	W	115
Nant Ddu	Gwyn	SH6743	52°58·3'	3°58·4'W	W	124
Nant Ddu	Gwyn	SH7933	52°53·1'	3°47·5'W	W	124
Nant Ddu	Gwyn	SH8038	52°55·8'	3°46·7'W	X	124,125
Nant-ddu	Powys	SO0015	51°49·7'	3°26·7'W	T	160
Nant Ddu	Powys	SO0116	51°50·3'	3°25·8'W	W	160
Nantddu	Powys	SO1161	52°14·6'	3°17·8'W	X	148
Nant Derbyniad	Conwy	SH7741	52°57·4'	3°49·5'W	W	124
Nant Dol-gôch	Gwyn	SH6603	52°36·7'	3°58·3'W	W	135
Nant Dowlais	Rho Cyn Taf	ST0784	51°33·1'	3°20·1'W	W	170
Nant Du	Cered	SN7286	52°27·7'	3°52·6'W	W	135
Nant Du	Nth Pt Talb	SS8699	51°40·9'	3°38·5'W	W	170
Nant Duad	Pemb	SN1340	52°1·9'	4°43·2'W	W	145
Nant Dyfrgi	V of Glam	ST0278	51°29·8'	3°24·3'W	W	170
Nant Dyniewyd	Wrex	SJ1133	52°53·5'	3°19·0'W	W	125
Nant Dyrys	Nth Pt Talb	SS8995	51°38·8'	3°35·9'W	W	170
Nanteague Fm	Corn	SW7949	50°18·2'	5°5·8'W	FM	204
Nant Egnant	Cered	SN7865	52°16·4'	3°46·9'W	W	135,147
Nantego	Carm	SN3315	51°48·8'	4°25·0'W	X	159
Nantegryd	Cered	SN4442	52°3·5'	4°16·1'W	X	146
Nant Eiddig	Carm	SN5845	52°5·3'	4°4·0'W	W	146
Nant Eiddon	Gwyn	SH1729	52°49·9'	4°42·6'W	W	123
Nant Einon	Powys	SN9050	52°8·5'	3°36·1'W	W	147
Nant Eithrim	Powys	SN8934	51°59·8'	3°36·6'W	W	160
Nantellan	Corn	SW9449	50°18·5'	4°53·2'W	X	204
Nanteos	Cered	SN6278	52°23·2'	4°1·3'W	X	135
Nanteos	Powys	SO0176	52°22·6'	3°26·9'W	X	136,147
Nanternis	Cered	SN3756	52°10·9'	4°22·7'W	T	145
Nanterrow	Corn	SW5941	50°13·4'	5°22·4'W	X	203
Nant Esgair-neiriau	Powys	SH7809	52°40·1'	3°47·9'W	W	124
Nant Esgeiriau	Denb	SJ0433	52°53·4'	3°25·2'W	W	125
Nant Ewyn	Powys	SJ0227	52°50·1'	3°26·9'W	W	125
Nant Fach	Conwy	SH6763	53°9·1'	3°58·9'W	W	115
Nant-fach	Gwyn	SH9046	53°0·2'	3°38·0'W	X	116
Nant Fawr	Conwy	SH9275	53°15·9'	3°36·8'W	X	116
Nant Fawr	Denb	SJ0844	52°59·4'	3°21·8'W	X	125
Nant Fawr	Powys	SO0338	52°2·2'	3°24·5'W	W	160
Nant Felin-blwm	Flint	SJ1380	53°18·8'	3°17·9'W	W	116
Nant Felys	Carm	SN4224	51°53·8'	4°17·4'W	W	159
Nant Ffin	Cered	SN7671	52°19·6'	3°48·8'W	W	135,147
Nant Ffornwg	Brig	SS8681	51°31·2'	3°38·2'W	W	170
Nant Ffrancon	Gwyn	SH6363	53°9·0'	4°2·5'W	X	115
Nant Ffriddisel	Denb	SJ1241	52°57·8'	3°18·2'W	W	125
Nant Ffridd y Castell	Powys	SH9708	52°39·8'	3°31·0'W	W	125
Nant Ffrydlan	Powys	SH7703	52°36·9'	3°48·6'W	W	135
Nant-figillt Wood	Flint	SJ2068	53°12·4'	3°11·5'W	F	117
Nant Fm	Flint	SJ2172	53°14·6'	3°10·6'W	FM	117
Nant Fm	Gwyn	SH2925	52°48·0'	4°31·8'W	FM	123
Nant Fridd-fawr	Gwyn	SH7716	52°43·9'	3°48·9'W	X	124
Nant Fydd	Carm	SN7314	51°48·9'	3°50·2'W	W	160
Nant Fyllon	Powys	SJ1220	52°46·5'	3°17·9'W	W	125
Nant Ganol	Gwyn	SH7632	52°52·5'	3°50·1'W	W	124
Nantgaredig	Carm	SN4921	51°52·3'	4°11·2'W	T	159
Nant Garenig	Carm	SN6712	51°47·7'	3°55·3'W	W	159
Nant Garw	Carm	SN7216	51°49·9'	3°51·1'W	W	160
Nantgarw	Rho Cyn Taf	ST1285	51°33·7'	3°15·8'W	T	171
Nant Gau	Cered	SN7772	52°20·2'	3°47·9'W	W	135,147
Nant-gau	Gwyn	SH9141	52°57·6'	3°37·0'W	X	125
Nantgerdinen	Carm	SN3831	51°57·5'	4°21·1'W	X	145
Nant-geseiliog	Gwyn	SH5808	52°39·3'	4°5·6'W	X	124
Nant Gewyn	Powys	SN8856	52°11·7'	3°37·9'W	W	147
Nant Gihirych	Powys	SN8820	51°52·3'	3°37·2'W	W	160
Nant Gladur	Denb	SJ0556	53°5·8'	3°24·7'W	W	116
Nant-glâs	Carm	SN3129	51°56·3'	4°27·1'W	X	145
Nantglas	Cered	SN6054	52°10·2'	4°2·4'W	X	146
Nant-glas	Powys	SN9965	52°16·7'	3°28·4'W	T	136,147
Nant Gledyr	Caer	ST1486	51°34·2'	3°14·1'W	W	171
Nantglyn	Denb	SJ0062	53°9·0'	3°29·3'W	T	116
Nant-goch	Cered	SN3550	52°7·7'	4°24·2'W	X	145
Nant-goch	Gwyn	SH8443	52°58·6'	3°43·3'W	W	124,125
Nant Goch	Powys	SJ2124	52°48·7'	3°9·9'W	X	126
Nant Goch	Powys	SN7791	52°30·4'	3°48·3'W	W	135
Nant Gochen	Carm	SN3529	51°56·3'	4°23·6'W	W	145
Nant Gorffen	Cered	SN7262	52°14·7'	3°52·1'W	W	146,147
Nant Gou	Cered	SN6048	52°7·0'	4°2·3'W	W	146
Nantgwared	Powys	SN8731	51°58·2'	3°38·3'W	X	160
Nant Gwastadedd	Gwyn	SJ0037	52°55·5'	3°28·9'W	W	125
Nant Gwdi	Powys	SO0225	51°55·1'	3°25·1'W	W	160
Nant Gweinion	Powys	SH8811	52°41·3'	3°39·0'W	W	124,125
Nant Gwen	Carm	SN4435	51°59·7'	4°15·9'W	W	146
Nant Gwennol	Carm	SN8435	52°0·3'	3°41·0'W	W	160
Nant Gwernog	Cered	SN7452	52°9·4'	3°50·1'W	X	146,147
Nant Gwernol	Gwyn	SH6806	52°38·4'	3°56·6'W	W	124
Nant Gwernol Sta	Gwyn	SH6806	52°38·4'	3°56·6'W	X	124
Nant Gwern y Gof	Conwy	SH6759	53°6·9'	3°58·8'W	W	115
Nantgwilym	Denb	SJ0871	53°13·9'	3°22·3'W	X	116
Nant Gwilym	Powys	SN9557	52°12·3'	3°31·8'W	W	147
Nant Gwinau	Cered	SN7862	52°14·8'	3°46·8'W	W	146,147
Nant Gwinau	Merth Tyd	SO0113	51°48·7'	3°25·8'W	W	160
Nant Gwnfel	Powys	SN9254	52°10·7'	3°34·4'W	W	147
Nant Gwnfi	Nth Pt Talb	SS8997	51°39·9'	3°35·9'W	W	170
Nant Gwrangon	Rho Cyn Taf	SN9204	51°43·7'	3°33·4'W	W	170
Nant Gwrtheyrn	Gwyn	SH3545	52°58·9'	4°27·1'W	W	123
Nant Gwydderig	Powys	SN8732	51°58·7'	3°38·3'W	W	160
Nant Gwyddon	Caer	ST2395	51°39·1'	3°6·4'W	W	171
Nantgwylan	Cered	SN3445	52°5·0'	4°25·0'W	X	145
Nant Gwyllt	Powys	SN9062	52°15·0'	3°36·3'W	W	147
Nantgwyn	Carm	SN7022	51°53·1'	3°52·9'W	X	160
Nant Gwyn	Carm	SN7944	52°5·1'	3°45·6'W	H	146,147,160
Nant Gwyn	Denb	SJ0737	52°55·6'	3°22·6'W	W	125
Nant Gwyn	Gwyn	SH8041	52°57·4'	3°46·8'W	W	124,125
Nant Gwyn	Pemb	SN1637	52°0·3'	4°40·5'W	X	145
Nantgwyn	Powys	SN9776	52°22·6'	3°30·4'W	T	136,147
Nantgwyn	Powys	SN9858	52°12·9'	3°29·2'W	X	147
Nant Gwyn	Powys	SO0247	52°7·0'	3°25·5'W	W	147
Nantgwynant	Gwyn	SH6250	53°2·0'	4°3·1'W	X	115
Nantgwynfaen	Cered	SN3744	52°4·5'	4°22·3'W	X	145
Nantgwyn Fm	Cered	SN7175	52°21·7'	3°53·3'W	FM	135,147
Nantgwynfynydd	Cered	SN4558	52°12·1'	4°15·7'W	X	146
Nant-gwynne	Carm	SN7424	51°54·3'	3°49·5'W	X	160
Nant Gwys	Powys	SN7712	51°47·8'	3°46·6'W	W	160
Nant Gwythwch	Carm	SN6717	51°50·4'	3°55·4'W	W	159
Nant Gyrawd	Merth Tyd	SO0805	51°44·4'	3°19·6'W	W	160
Nant Gyrawd	Pemb	SN0805	51°42·9'	4°46·4'W	W	158
Nant Gyrnant	Powys	SN8547	52°6·8'	3°40·4'W	W	147
Nant Hafhesp	Gwyn	SH9337	52°55·4'	3°35·1'W	W	125
Nant Hawen	Cered	SN3453	52°9·3'	4°25·2'W	W	145
Nant Heilyn	Conwy	SH9255	53°5·1'	3°36·3'W	W	116
Nant Helygog	Gwyn	SH7919	52°45·5'	3°47·2'W	W	124
Nanthenfoel	Cered	SN5451	52°8·5'	4°7·6'W	X	146
Nant Henog	Powys	SN8448	52°7·3'	3°41·3'W	W	147
Nant Henwen	Powys	SN8329	51°57·1'	3°41·8'W	W	160
Nant Hesgog	Powys	SN9168	52°18·2'	3°35·5'W	W	136,147
Nant Heulog	Gwyn	SJ0143	52°58·8'	3°28·1'W	W	125
Nant Hir	Carm	SN3132	51°57·9'	4°27·2'W	W	145
Nant Hir	Carm	SN3823	51°53·2'	4°20·8'W	W	145,159
Nant Hîr	Gwyn	SH7531	52°52·0'	3°51·0'W	W	124
Nant-hir	Gwyn	SH8111	52°41·3'	3°45·2'W	X	124,125
Nant-hir	Gwyn	SH8436	52°54·8'	3°43·1'W	W	124,125
Nant-hir	Gwyn	SH9025	52°48·9'	3°37·5'W	X	125
Nant Hir	Gwyn	SH9041	52°57·5'	3°37·9'W	X	125
Nant Hir	Gwyn	SH9730	52°51·7'	3°31·4'W	W	125
Nant Hir	Nth Pt Talb	SN8208	51°45·7'	3°42·2'W	W	160
Nant-hir	Powys	SH8908	52°39·7'	3°38·1'W	X	124,125
Nant Hir	Powys	SN8354	52°10·6'	3°42·3'W	W	147
Nant Hir	Powys	SN8810	51°46·9'	3°37·0'W	W	160
Nant Hîr	Rho Cyn Taf	SN9806	51°44·8'	3°28·3'W	W	160
Nant Hirgwm	Carm	SN8341	52°3·5'	3°42·0'W	W	147,160
Nant Hirin	Powys	SN8671	52°19·8'	3°40·0'W	W	135,136,147
Nanthirwen	Powys	SJ1729	52°51·4'	3°13·6'W	X	125
Nant Hust	Carm	SN5241	52°3·1'	4°9·1'W	W	146
Nant Iago	Gwyn	SH7007	52°39·0'	3°54·9'W	W	124
Nant Iechyd	Brig	SS9488	51°35·1'	3°31·4'W	W	170
Nant-ifan-fach	Pemb	SN2534	51°58·9'	4°32·5'W	X	145
Nantillio	Corn	SW8654	50°21·1'	5°0·1'W	X	200
Nant Isaf	Conwy	SH8157	53°6·1'	3°46·2'W	X	116
Nant-isaf	Denb	SJ0456	53°5·8'	3°25·6'W	X	116
Nant Isaf	I of Angl	SH4782	53°19·0'	4°17·4'W	X	114,115
Nant Isaf Fm	Conwy	SH9269	53°12·7'	3°36·6'W	FM	116
Nant Islyn	Gwyn	SH7237	52°55·2'	3°53·8'W	W	124
Nant Issa	Wrex	SJ2643	52°59·0'	3°5·7'W	X	117
Nantithet	Corn	SW6822	50°3·4'	5°14·1'W	T	203
Nantiwrch	Carm	SN7039	52°2·3'	3°53·3'W	X	146,160
Nant Las	Gwyn	SH7123	52°47·6'	3°54·4'W	W	124
Nantleach	Powys	SO1166	52°17·3'	3°17·9'W	X	136,148
Nant-Lewis-Alyn	Denb	SJ0967	53°11·8'	3°21·3'W	X	116
Nantllanerch	Powys	SO0821	51°53·0'	3°19·8'W	X	160
Nant Llan-gwrach	Conwy	SH8647	53°0·7'	3°41·6'W	W	116
Nant Llaniestyn	Gwyn	SH2635	52°53·3'	4°34·8'W	X	123
Nantlle	Gwyn	SH5053	53°3·4'	4°13·9'W	T	115
Nant-llêch	Carm	SN4236	52°0·2'	4°17·7'W	X	146
Nant Llech	Powys	SN8412	51°47·9'	3°40·5'W	W	160
Nant Llechog	Denb	SJ0941	52°57·8'	3°20·9'W	W	125
Nant Llech Pellaf	Powys	SN8612	51°47·9'	3°38·8'W	W	160
Nant Lleidiog	Gwyn	SH9841	52°57·6'	3°30·7'W	W	125
Nant Lletgwial	Powys	SN8447	52°6·8'	3°41·2'W	W	147
Nant Lliwdy	Gwyn	SH7205	52°37·9'	3°53·1'W	W	124
Nant Lliwdy	Gwyn	SH7304	52°37·4'	3°52·2'W	W	135
Nant-llo	Cered	SN3452	52°8·7'	4°25·2'W	X	145
Nant Lluest	Cered	SN7467	52°17·4'	3°50·5'W	W	135,147
Nant Llwch	Powys	SN9615	51°49·7'	3°30·2'W	W	160
Nant-llwyd	Cered	SN7852	52°9·4'	3°46·6'W	X	146,147
Nant Llwydiarth	Powys	SJ0415	52°43·7'	3°24·9'W	W	125
Nant Llwyngwrgi	Powys	SH9927	52°50·1'	3°29·6'W	W	125
Nant Llyfarddu	Denb	SJ0253	53°4·2'	3°27·4'W	W	116
Nantllyndir	Carm	SN8239	52°2·5'	3°42·8'W	X	160
Nant Llynfell	Carm	SN7515	51°49·4'	3°48·4'W	W	160
Nant Llyn Mynyllod	Denb	SJ0239	52°56·6'	3°27·1'W	W	125
Nant Lwyd	Cered	SN6987	52°28·2'	3°55·3'W	W	135
Nantlys	Denb	SJ0871	53°13·9'	3°22·3'W	X	116
Nant-maden	Rho Cyn Taf	SN9610	51°47·0'	3°30·1'W	X	160
Nantmadog	Powys	SN9125	51°55·0'	3°34·7'W	X	160
Nant Maes y gamfa	Gwyn	SH8112	52°41·8'	3°45·3'W	W	124,125
Nant Magwr	Cered	SN6774	52°21·1'	3°56·8'W	W	135
Nantmawr	Cered	SN2151	52°7·9'	4°36·5'W	X	145
Nant Mawr	Conwy	SH8969	53°12·6'	3°39·3'W	X	116
Nant Mawr	Denb	SJ0661	53°8·5'	3°23·9'W	W	116
Nant Mawr	Flint	SJ2763	53°9·8'	3°5·1'W	T	117
Nant Mawr	Powys	SN9519	51°51·8'	3°31·1'W	W	160
Nantmawr	Shrops	SJ2424	52°48·7'	3°7·3'W	T	126
Nantmeddal Fach	Cered	SN4354	52°10·0'	4°17·3'W	X	146
Nantmeddal Fawr	Cered	SN4255	52°10·5'	4°18·2'W	X	146
Nant Meifod	Conwy	SH9773	53°14·9'	3°32·2'W	X	116
Nant Meirch	Cered	SN7880	52°24·5'	3°47·2'W	W	135
Nantmel	Powys	SO0366	52°17·3'	3°24·9'W	T	136,147
Nant Melai	Conwy	SH9062	53°8·9'	3°38·3'W	X	116
Nant Melai	Conwy	SH9065	53°10·5'	3°38·3'W	W	116
Nant Melyn	Carm	SN7115	51°49·4'	3°51·9'W	W	160
Nant Melyn	Carm	SN7346	52°6·1'	3°50·9'W	W	146,147
Nant-melyn	Nth Pt Talb	SN6909	51°46·1'	3°53·5'W	X	160
Nant Melyn	Nth Pt Talb	SN8309	51°46·3'	3°41·4'W	W	160
Nant Melyn	Powys	SN8757	52°12·2'	3°38·8'W	W	147
Nant Melyn Fm	Rho Cyn Taf	SN9703	51°43·2'	3°29·1'W	FM	170
Nant Menasgin	Powys	SO0523	51°54·1'	3°22·5'W	W	160
Nant Menial	Powys	SJ0208	52°39·9'	3°26·5'W	W	125
Nant Methan	Powys	SN8965	52°16·6'	3°37·2'W	W	135,136,147
Nant Meurig	Cered	SN5856	52°11·3'	4°4·2'W	W	146
Nant Milwyn	Cered	SN7972	52°20·2'	3°46·2'W	W	135,147
Nant-moel	Swan	SN6807	51°45·0'	3°54·3'W	X	159
Nant-moel Resr	Rho Cyn Taf	SN9807	51°45·4'	3°28·3'W	W	160
Nantmor	Gwyn	SH6046	52°59·8'	4°4·8'W	T	115
Nant Muchudd	Rho Cyn Taf	ST0386	51°34·1'	3°23·6'W	W	170
Nant Mwth Fm	Brig	SS8986	51°34·0'	3°35·7'W	FM	170
Nant Myddlyn	Rho Cyn Taf	ST0783	51°32·5'	3°20·1'W	W	170
Nant Mynach	Cered	SN5250	52°8·0'	4°9·3'W	W	146
Nant Mynian	Denb	SJ0851	53°3·1'	3°22·0'W	W	116
Nant Nadroedd Fawr	Powys	SH9326	52°49·5'	3°34·9'W	W	125
Nant Neel	Pemb	SN2534	51°58·9'	4°32·5'W	X	145
Nant Newydd	I of Angl	SH4474	53°14·7'	4°19·9'W	X	114,115
Nant Newydd	I of Angl	SH4881	53°18·5'	4°16·5'W	X	114,115
Nant Nodwydd	Powys	SH9909	52°40·4'	3°29·2'W	W	125
Nant-oer	Monm	SO3012	51°48·4'	3°0·5'W	X	161
Nan Tow's Tump	Glos	ST8089	51°36·2'	2°16·9'W	A	162,173
Nant Padrig	Denb	SJ0571	53°13·9'	3°25·0'W	W	116
Nant Paith	Cered	SN6178	52°23·2'	4°2·2'W	W	135
Nant Paradwys	Powys	SN8960	52°13·9'	3°37·1'W	W	147
Nant-Pasgan	Gwyn	SH6536	52°54·5'	4°0·0'W	X	124
Nant Pedol	Carm	SN6915	51°49·3'	3°53·7'W	W	160
Nantpelau	Cered	SN3757	52°11·5'	4°22·7'W	X	145
Nant Pennig	Powys	SN9818	51°51·3'	3°28·5'W	W	160
Nant Penycnwc	Carm	SN4623	51°53·3'	4°13·9'W	W	159
Nant Perfedd	Cered	SN7086	52°27·6'	3°54·4'W	W	135
Nant Peris or Old Llanberis	Gwyn	SH6058	53°6·3'	4°5·1'W	T	115
Nant Pibwr	Carm	SN4418	51°50·6'	4°15·5'W	W	159
Nantremenyn	Cered	SN4247	52°6·2'	4°18·0'W	X	146
Nant Rhaeadr	Powys	SH9408	52°39·8'	3°33·6'W	W	125
Nant Rhiw-afallen	Cered	SN5558	52°12·3'	4°6·9'W	W	146
Nant Rhiw-y-llyn	Gwyn	SH9531	52°52·2'	3°33·2'W	W	125
Nantrhos-ddu	Gwyn	SH8140	52°56·9'	3°45·9'W	W	124,125
Nant Rhos-goch	Gwyn	SH8525	52°48·9'	3°42·0'W	W	124,125
Nant Rhuddnant	Cered	SN7877	52°22·9'	3°47·2'W	W	135,147
Nant Rhyd-goch	Powys	SN8351	52°8·9'	3°42·2'W	W	147
Nant Rhyd-goch	Powys	SN9161	52°14·4'	3°35·4'W	W	147
Nant Rhydol	Cered	SN7767	52°17·5'	3°47·8'W	W	135,147
Nant Rhydroser	Cered	SN5767	52°17·2'	4°5·4'W	W	135
Nant Rhyd-ros-lan	Powys	SO0595	52°32·9'	3°23·7'W	W	136
Nantrhydw	Carm	SN4314	51°48·4'	4°16·2'W	W	159
Nant Rhyd-wen	Gwyn	SH9130	52°51·6'	3°36·7'W	W	125
Nant Rhydwilym	Wrex	SJ1235	52°54·6'	3°18·1'W	W	125
Nant Rhydyfedw	Powys	SO1585	52°27·6'	3°14·7'W	W	136
Nant Rhyd-y-môch	Conwy	SJ0045	52°59·8'	3°29·0'W	W	116
Nant Rhyd-y-moch	Powys	SJ2211	52°41·7'	3°8·8'W	W	126
Nant Rhyd-y-saeson	Denb	SJ0442	52°58·2'	3°25·4'W	W	125
Nant Rhŷs	Cered	SN7881	52°25·0'	3°47·2'W	W	135
Nant Rhys	Cered	SN8379	52°24·0'	3°42·8'W	X	135,136,147
Nant Rhysgog	Cered	SN6853	52°9·8'	3°55·4'W	W	146
Nantricket	Carm	SN6910	51°46·6'	3°53·5'W	X	160
Nant Ring	Carm	SN3626	51°54·7'	4°22·7'W	W	145
Nan Trodds Hill	Hants	SU4326	51°2·1'	1°22·8'W	X	185
Nant Saeson	Powys	SH9212	52°41·9'	3°35·5'W	W	125
Nant Sarffle	Wrex	SJ1432	52°53·0'	3°16·3'W	W	125
Nantsebon	Powys	SN9033	51°59·3'	3°35·7'W	X	160
Nant Sere	Powys	SO0223	51°54·1'	3°25·1'W	W	160
Nantserth	Powys	SN9670	52°19·3'	3°31·2'W	T	136,147
Nant Sgrin	Denb	SJ0131	52°52·3'	3°27·8'W	W	125
Nant-Sidyll	Cered	SN4654	52°10·0'	4°14·7'W	X	146
Nant Silo	Cered	SN6583	52°25·9'	3°58·7'W	W	135
Nantsiriol	Cered	SN6184	52°26·4'	4°2·3'W	X	135
Nantsyddion	Cered	SN7779	52°24·0'	3°48·1'W	X	135,147
Nant Tarren-fedw-ddu	Powys	SN7893	52°31·5'	3°47·5'W	W	135
Nant Tarthwynni	Powys	SO0819	51°52·0'	3°19·8'W	W	160
Nant Tarw	Powys	SN8225	51°54·9'	3°42·5'W	W	160
Nant Tawe	Carm	SN6041	52°3·2'	4°2·1'W	W	146
Nant Tawelan	Powys	SN9775	52°22·0'	3°30·4'W	W	136,147
Nant Thames	Carm	SN6141	52°3·2'	4°1·2'W	W	146
Nant, The	Flint	SJ2067	53°11·9'	3°11·4'W	X	117
Nant Trefil	Blae Gw	SO1113	51°48·8'	3°17·1'W	W	161
Nant Treflyn	Powys	SO0064	52°16·1'	3°27·5'W	W	147
Nant Tre-gof	V of Glam	ST0270	51°25·5'	3°24·2'W	W	170
Nant Tridwr	Carm	SN8438	52°1·9'	3°41·1'W	W	160
Nant Troedyresgair	Powys	SN8779	52°24·1'	3°39·3'W	W	135,136,147
Nant Troyddyn	Carm	SN6342	52°3·8'	3°59·5'W	W	146
Nant Twll-y-cwm	Gwyn	SH7238	52°55·7'	3°53·9'W	W	124
Nant Tŷ-nant	Gwyn	SH8542	52°58·0'	3°42·3'W	W	124,125
Nant Tywynni	Powys	SN8618	51°51·2'	3°38·9'W	W	160
Nantuchaf	Conwy	SH8476	53°16·3'	3°44·0'W	X	116
Nant Uchaf	Conwy	SH9268	53°12·1'	3°36·6'W	X	116
Nant Uchaf	Denb	SJ0255	53°5·2'	3°27·4'W	X	116
Nant-uchaf	Denb	SJ1349	53°2·1'	3°17·4'W	X	116
Nant-uchaf	I of Angl	SH4881	53°18·5'	4°16·5'W	X	114,115
Nant Uchaf Fm	Wrex	SJ2543	52°59·0'	3°6·6'W	FM	117
Nant Wechan	Monm	SO4312	51°48·5'	2°49·2'W	W	161
Nant Wern-ddu	Powys	SO0115	51°49·7'	3°25·8'W	W	160
Nant Wgan	Powys	SJ0211	52°41·5'	3°26·6'W	W	125
Nant Whitton	V of Glam	ST0672	51°26·6'	3°20·8'W	W	170
Nantwich	Ches	SJ6552	53°4·1'	2°30·9'W	T	118
Nant Wysg	Cered	SN5555	52°10·7'	4°6·8'W	W	146

Nant Wythan	Powys	SH9803	52°37·2′	3°30·0′W	W	136
Nanty	Powys	SN8581	52°25·1′	3°41·1′W	X	135,136
Nant y Bache	Denb	SJ1840	52°57·3′	3°12·8′W	W	125
Nant y Bachws	Powys	SN9489	52°29·6′	3°33·3′W	W	136
Nant-y-Bai	Carm	SN7744	52°5·1′	3°47·3′W	T	146,147,160
Nant-y-banw	Monm	ST4097	51°40·4′	2°51·7′W	X	171
Nant-y-Bar	Heref	SO2840	52°3·5′	3°2·6′W	X	148,161
Nant y Baracs	Cered	SN7588	52°28·8′	3°50·0′W	W	135
Nant-y-barcut	Gwyn	SH8825	52°48·9′	3°39·3′W	X	124,125
Nantybedd	Powys	SO2526	51°55·9′	3°5·1′W	X	161
Nantybeddau	Powys	SN8566	52°17·0′	3°40·8′W	X	135,136,147
Nantybelan	Wrex	SJ3041	52°58·0′	3°2·1′W	X	117
Nantybenglog	Cered	SN6478	52°23·2′	3°59·5′W	X	135
Nant y Betws	Gwyn	SH5459	53°6·7′	4°10·5′W	W	115
Nant y Betws	Gwyn	SH5555	53°4·6′	4°9·5′W	X	115
Nant-y-big	Gwyn	SH3025	52°48·0′	4°30·9′W	X	123
Nant y Bont	Cered	SN7959	52°13·2′	3°45·9′W	W	146,147
Nant-y-brain	Powys	SN8451	52°8·9′	3°41·3′W	X	147
Nant-y-brenni	Cered	SN3348	52°6·5′	4°25·9′W	X	145
Nant y Brithyll	Powys	SJ0722	52°47·5′	3°22·3′W	W	125
Nant y Brwyn	Conwy	SH7945	52°59·6′	3°47·8′W	W	115
Nant y Bryn	Powys	SN8611	51°47·4′	3°38·8′W	W	160
Nant y Bugail	Pemb	SM9632	51°57·2′	4°57·7′W	W	157
Nant y Bustach	Powys	SN8153	52°10·0′	3°44·0′W	W	147
Nant-y-Bwch	Blae Gw	SO1210	51°47·1′	3°16·2′W	T	161
Nantybwla	Carm	SN3821	51°52·1′	4°20·8′W	X	145,159
Nant-y-bwla	Cered	SN6682	52°25·4′	3°57·8′W	X	135
Nant y Caerhedyn	Cered	SN7582	52°25·5′	3°49·9′W	X	135
Nant y Cafn	Gwyn	SH8920	52°46·2′	3°38·3′W	W	124,125
Nant-y-cafn	Nth Pt Talb	SN8107	51°45·2′	3°43·1′W	T	160
Nant y Capel	Swan	SN6803	51°42·9′	3°54·3′W	W	159
Nant y Capel	Swan	SN6903	51°42·9′	3°53·4′W	W	170
Nantycastell	Carm	SN3429	51°56·3′	4°24·5′W	X	145
Nant y Castell	Cered	SN7396	52°33·1′	3°52·0′W	W	135
Nantycaws	Carm	SN4518	51°50·6′	4°14·6′W	T	159
Nant y Caws	Shrops	SJ2826	52°49·8′	3°3·7′W	T	126
Nant-y-ceisiad	Caer	ST2089	51°35·9′	3°8·9′W	T	171
Nant-y-cerdin	Powys	SN8750	52°8·4′	3°38·7′W	X	147
Nantycerrig	Carm	SN3231	51°57·4′	4°26·3′W	X	145
Nant-y-cerrig	Conwy	SH8269	53°12·5′	3°45·6′W	X	116
Nant y Ceunant	Gwyn	SH7216	52°43·8′	3°53·3′W	W	124
Nant y ci	Brig	SS9288	51°35·1′	3°33·1′W	W	170
Nantyci	Carm	SN3719	51°51·0′	4°21·6′W	X	159
Nantyci	Carm	SN3721	51°52·1′	4°21·7′W	X	145,159
Nant y Cloddiad	Powys	SN8256	52°11·6′	3°43·2′W	W	147
Nantycnidiw	Gwyn	SH7720	52°46·1′	3°49·0′W	X	124
Nant y Cnwch	Cered	SN7650	52°8·3′	3°48·3′W	W	146,147
Nant y Coed	Gwyn	SH8743	52°58·6′	3°40·6′W	W	124,125
Nantycoedwr	Powys	SJ0121	52°46·9′	3°27·7′W	X	125
Nant-y-corddi	Powys	SO2267	52°18·0′	3°8·2′W	X	137,148
Nant-y-coy	Powys	SO2325	51°55·3′	3°6·8′W	W	161
Nant-y-coy Brook	Pemb	SM9324	51°52·8′	5°0·1′W	W	157,158
Nant y Craflwyn	Powys	SN8150	52°8·4′	3°43·9′W	W	147
Nant-y-creau	Conwy	SH8751	53°2·9′	3°40·7′W	X	116
Nantycroy	Cered	SN1851	52°7·9′	4°39·2′W	X	145
Nant-y-cwm	Denb	SJ0737	52°55·6′	3°22·6′W	W	125
Nant-y-cwm	Flint	SJ1468	53°12·4′	3°16·9′W	X	116
Nantycwnstabl	Cered	SN3948	52°6·7′	4°20·7′W	X	145
Nant y Cwrier	Powys	SN9716	51°50·2′	3°29·3′W	W	160
Nant y Cyffed	Gwyn	SH8826	52°49·4′	3°39·3′W	X	124,125
Nant y Cyllyll	Denb	SJ0736	52°55·0′	3°22·6′W	W	125
Nantycynnog	Cered	SN6299	52°34·5′	4°1·8′W	X	135
Nantycynog	Gwyn	SH5804	52°37·2′	4°5·5′W	X	135
Nant-y-cyrtiau	Gwyn	SH9142	52°58·1′	3°37·0′W	X	125
Nantycyw	Carm	SN2831	51°57·3′	4°29·8′W	X	145
Nant-y-cywarch	Conwy	SH8173	53°14·7′	3°46·6′W	X	116
Nant y Darren	Gwyn	SH7305	52°37·9′	3°52·2′W	W	124
Nant y Dderwen	Cered	SN6656	52°11·4′	3°57·2′W	X	146
Nantydeilie	Gwyn	SH8631	52°52·1′	3°41·2′W	X	124,125
Nant y Dernol	Powys	SN9074	52°21·4′	3°36·5′W	W	136,147
Nantyderri Fm	Monm	SO4014	51°49·5′	2°51·8′W	FM	161
Nant-y-derry	Monm	SO3306	51°45·2′	2°57·8′W	T	161
Nant-y-draenog Resr	Caer	ST1893	51°38·0′	3°10·7′W	W	171
Nant y Dresglen	Powys	SN8534	51°59·8′	3°40·1′W	W	160
Nant-y-dugoed	Powys	SH9113	52°42·5′	3°36·4′W	X	125
Nant y Dwyslyn	Powys	SH9715	52°43·6′	3°31·1′W	W	125
Nant y Fannog	Powys	SN8152	52°9·4′	3°44·0′W	W	147
Nant-y-fedw	Conwy	SH9073	53°14·8′	3°38·5′W	X	116
Nant y Fedw	Nth Pt Talb	SS8895	51°38·8′	3°36·7′W	W	170
Nant y Fedw	Powys	SN8456	52°11·6′	3°41·4′W	W	147
Nant y Fedwen	Powys	SN8711	51°47·4′	3°37·9′W	W	160
Nant-y-felin	Conwy	SH6874	53°15·0′	3°58·3′W	T	115
Nant y Felin	Gwyn	SH9648	53°1·4′	3°32·6′W	W	116
Nant y Felin	Nth Pt Talb	SN8501	51°42·0′	3°39·5′W	W	170
Nant-y-Felin	Powys	SO1424	51°54·7′	3°14·6′W	X	161
Nantyfen	Carm	SN3832	51°58·0′	4°21·1′W	X	145
Nant-y-fendrod	Swan	SS6898	51°40·2′	3°54·1′W	W	159
Nant y Feni	Gwyn	SH9733	52°53·3′	3°31·5′W	W	125
Nant y Fergi	Cered	SN5458	52°12·3′	4°7·8′W	W	146
Nant-y-ffin	Carm	SN5532	51°58·3′	4°6·3′W	T	146
Nant-y-ffin	Carm	SN5532	51°58·3′	4°6·3′W	X	146
Nant y Ffin	Carm	SN5535	51°59·9′	4°6·3′W	W	146
Nantyffin	Carm	SN6028	51°56·2′	4°1·8′W	X	146
Nant y Ffin	Cered	SN6768	52°17·9′	3°56·6′W	W	135
Nant-y-ffin	Merth Tyd	SO0904	51°43·9′	3°18·7′W	X	171
Nant-y-ffridd	Denb	SJ0660	53°8·0′	3°23·9′W	X	116
Nant y Ffrith	Wrex	SJ2754	53°4·9′	3°5·0′W	W	117
Nant-y-Ffrith Reservoir	Denb	SJ2453	53°4·4′	3°7·7′W	W	117
Nantyffyllon	Brig	SS8592	51°37·1′	3°39·3′W	T	170
Nant y Fign	Gwyn	SH8329	52°51·0′	3°43·8′W	W	124,125
Nant y Fleiddiast	Conwy	SH9561	53°8·4′	3°33·8′W	W	116
Nant-y-Flint	Flint	SJ2171	53°14·1′	3°10·6′W	W	117
Nant y Foel	Conwy	SH8753	53°4·0′	3°40·8′W	W	116
Nant y Foel	Conwy	SH9450	53°2·5′	3°34·5′W	W	116
Nant-y-frân	I of Angl	SH3892	53°24·2′	4°25·8′W	X	114
Nantyfyda	Powys	SN8196	52°33·2′	3°44·9′W	X	135,136
Nant y Gadair	Powys	SN8665	52°16·5′	3°39·9′W	W	135,136,147
Nant y Gadair	Powys	SO2128	51°56·9′	3°8·6′W	W	161
Nant y Gadlys	Brig	SS8787	51°34·5′	3°37·5′W	W	170
Nant y Galen	Powys	SH9725	52°49·0′	3°31·3′W	W	125
Nant y Garn	Cered	SN7052	52°9·3′	3°53·6′W	W	146,147
Nant-y-garreg	Conwy	SH9662	53°8·9′	3°32·9′W	H	116
Nant-y-garth	Cered	SN5763	52°15·0′	4°5·3′W	X	146
Nant y Garth Pass	Denb	SJ1651	53°3·2′	3°14·8′W	X	116
Nantygaseg	Powys	SH8101	52°35·9′	3°45·0′W	X	135,136
Nant y Gaseg	Powys	SN9420	51°52·3′	3°32·0′W	W	160
Nant-y-gaseg-uchaf	Nth Pt Talb	SN7008	51°45·6′	3°52·6′W	X	160
Nant y Gath	Powys	SN9057	52°12·3′	3°36·2′W	W	147
Nant-y-gedd	Brig	SS8784	51°32·9′	3°37·4′W	W	170
Nantygeifr	Powys	SN9183	52°26·3′	3°35·8′W	X	136
Nant-y-geifr-fawr	Pemb	SN2032	51°57·7′	4°36·8′W	X	145
Nantygelli	Carm	SN3830	51°56·9′	4°21·0′W	X	145
Nantygelli Fm	Monm	ST4499	51°41·5′	2°48·2′W	FM	171
Nant-y-gern	Monm	SO4616	51°50·6′	2°46·6′W	X	161
Nant y Gerwyn	Cered	SN7857	52°12·1′	3°46·7′W	W	146,147
Nant-y-geuryd	Conwy	SJ0047	53°0·9′	3°29·0′W	X	116
Nantyglo	Blae Gw	SO1910	51°47·2′	3°10·1′W	T	161
Nant-y-Glyn	Conwy	SH8062	53°8·7′	3°47·2′W	X	116
Nant y Goedwig	Gwyn	SH7406	52°38·5′	3°51·3′W	W	124
Nant-y-gof	Pemb	SN0924	51°53·2′	4°46·1′W	X	145,158
Nant y Gog	Powys	SN7594	52°32·0′	3°50·2′W	W	135
Nantygoitre	Carm	SN3912	51°47·3′	4°19·7′W	X	159
Nant-y-gollen	Shrops	SJ2428	52°50·9′	3°7·3′W	T	126
Nant y Gors	Conwy	SH6958	53°6·4′	3°57·0′W	W	115
Nant y Graean	Gwyn	SH7430	52°51·4′	3°51·9′W	W	124
Nantygragen	Carm	SN4234	51°59·2′	4°17·7′W	X	146
Nant y Graig-wen	Gwyn	SH8217	52°44·5′	3°44·5′W	W	124,125
Nant y Gro	Powys	SN9262	52°15·0′	3°34·5′W	W	147
Nant y Groes	Conwy	SH8476	53°16·3′	3°44·0′W	W	116
Nant y Groes	Gwyn	SH7541	52°57·4′	3°51·2′W	W	124
Nant-y-groes	Powys	SO2667	52°18·0′	3°4·7′W	X	137,148
Nant y Groes-fagl	Gwyn	SH9729	52°51·2′	3°31·4′W	W	125
Nantygronw	Carm	SN3632	51°58·0′	4°22·8′W	X	145
Nantygwair	Carm	SN4135	51°59·7′	4°18·6′W	X	146
Nant y Gwair	Nth Pt Talb	SS9098	51°40·4′	3°35·1′W	W	170
Nant y Gwair	Powys	SN9520	51°52·4′	3°31·1′W	W	160
Nant y Gwrdu	Powys	SN8688	52°28·9′	3°40·3′W	X	135,136
Nant-y-gwrdy	Cered	SN4456	52°11·1′	4°16·5′W	X	146
Nantygwreiddyn	Powys	SO0035	52°0·5′	3°27·0′W	X	160
Nantygwryd	Conwy	SH6856	53°5·3′	3°57·9′W	W	115
Nant y gwyddau	Cered	SN4449	52°7·3′	4°16·3′W	X	146
Nantygwyddel	Monm	SO2728	51°57·0′	3°3·3′W	X	161
Nant-y-gwyrddail	Gwyn	SH6714	52°42·7′	3°57·7′W	X	124
Nant y Gylchedd	Conwy	SH8646	53°0·2′	3°41·5′W	W	116
Nant-y-Lladron	Conwy	SH9661	53°8·4′	3°32·9′W	X	116
Nant y Lladron	Conwy	SH9662	53°8·9′	3°32·9′W	W	116
Nant y Lladron	Denb	SJ0938	52°56·1′	3°20·8′W	W	125
Nant-y-Lladron	Wrex	SJ3543	52°59·1′	2°57·7′W	X	117
Nant-y-llan	Cered	SN2448	52°6·4′	4°33·8′W	X	145
Nant-y-llyn	Carm	SN6749	52°7·6′	3°56·2′W	X	146
Nant y Llyn	Carm	SN7717	51°50·5′	3°46·7′W	W	160
Nant y Llyn	Cered	SN7888	52°28·8′	3°47·4′W	W	135
Nant-y-llyn	Gwyn	SH8342	52°58·0′	3°44·1′W	X	124,125
Nant y Llyn	Powys	SJ0730	52°51·8′	3°22·5′W	W	125
Nant y Llyn	Powys	SN8420	51°52·2′	3°40·7′W	W	160
Nant y Llyn Mawr	Powys	SO0199	52°35·0′	3°27·3′W	W	136
Nant-y-llys	Gwyn	SH6655	53°4·8′	3°59·6′W	W	115
Nantymab	Carm	SN5322	51°52·9′	4°7·8′W	X	159
Nantymadwen	Denb	SJ1245	52°59·9′	3°18·3′W	X	116
Nant y Maen	Cered	SN7658	52°12·6′	3°48·5′W	W	146,147
Nantymaen	Cered	SN7658	52°12·6′	3°48·5′W	X	146,147
Nantymair	Monm	SO3224	51°54·9′	2°58·9′W	X	161
Nant y March	Powys	SN7689	52°29·3′	3°49·2′W	W	135
Nantymark	Monm	ST4299	51°41·4′	2°50·0′W	X	171
Nanty-mawr	Cered	SN3252	52°8·7′	4°26·9′W	X	145
Nant-y-medd	Cered	SN6150	52°8·1′	4°1·5′W	X	146
Nantymeichiaid	Powys	SJ1517	52°44·9′	3°15·2′W	X	125
Nant-y-Merddyn	Conwy	SH9261	53°8·4′	3°36·5′W	X	116
Nant-y-moch	Cered	SN7786	52°27·7′	3°48·2′W	W	135
Nant-y-moch	Powys	SN8917	51°50·7′	3°36·3′W	W	160
Nant-y-moch Reservoir	Cered	SN7586	52°27·7′	3°50·0′W	W	135
Nant-y-moel	Brig	SS9392	51°37·3′	3°32·3′W	T	170
Nant-y-mynach	Gwyn	SH6404	52°37·2′	4°0·1′W	X	135
Nantymynach	Powys	SO0166	52°17·2′	3°26·7′W	X	136,147
Nantymynach	Powys	SO0639	52°2·7′	3°21·8′W	X	160
Nant-y-Neuadd	Powys	SN8052	52°9·4′	3°44·9′W	X	147
Nant-y-pair	Carm	SN3422	51°52·6′	4°24·3′W	X	145,159
Nant-y-pandy	Conwy	SH6974	53°15·1′	3°57·4′W	T	115
Nant y Pandy	Denb	SJ1441	52°57·8′	3°16·4′W	W	125
Nant y Pandy	Torf	ST2691	51°37·0′	3°3·7′W	W	171
Nantypaun	Carm	SN5123	51°53·4′	4°9·5′W	X	159
Nantyperchyll	Carm	SN5336	52°0·4′	4°8·1′W	X	146
Nant y Pistyll-gwyn	Gwyn	SH7543	52°58·4′	3°51·3′W	W	124
Nant-y-pyd	Conwy	SH9444	52°59·2′	3°34·3′W	X	125
Nantypyllau	Shrops	SO1883	52°26·6′	3°12·0′W	X	136
Nant yr Aber	Caer	ST1388	51°35·3′	3°15·0′W	W	171
Nant yr Allor	Nth Pt Talb	SS8899	51°41·0′	3°36·8′W	W	170
Nant yr Annell	Powys	SN9051	52°9·0′	3°36·1′W	W	147
Nantyrarian	Cered	SN7181	52°24·9′	3°53·4′W	X	135
Nant-yr-arian	Powys	SO0938	52°2·2′	3°19·2′W	X	161
Nantyrast	Carm	SN7048	52°7·1′	3°53·5′W	X	146,147
Nant-yr-efail	Cered	SN4557	52°11·6′	4°15·7′W	X	146
Nant yr Efail	Cered	SN6664	52°15·7′	3°57·4′W	W	146
Nantyreglwys	Carm	SN2422	51°52·4′	4°33·0′W	X	145,158
Nant-yr-eira	Gwyn	SH6808	52°39·5′	3°56·7′W	X	124
Nant yr Eira	Powys	SH9606	52°38·7′	3°31·8′W	X	125
Nant yr Eira	Powys	SN9817	51°50·8′	3°28·5′W	W	160
Nant yr Esgob	Powys	SN9654	52°10·7′	3°30·9′W	W	147
Nant yr Esgyrn	Powys	SN9416	51°50·2′	3°32·0′W	W	160
Nant y Rhaeadr	Carm	SN7543	52°4·5′	3°49·0′W	W	146,147,160
Nant yr Hafod	Gwyn	SH8924	52°48·4′	3°38·4′W	W	124,125
Nant-yr-hafod	Powys	SN8791	52°30·6′	3°39·5′W	X	135,136
Nant-yr-haidd	Powys	SN9366	52°17·1′	3°33·7′W	X	136,147
Nantyrharn	Powys	SN8926	51°55·5′	3°36·5′W	X	160
Nantyrhawl	Carm	SN2838	52°1·1′	4°30·0′W	X	145
Nantyrhebog	Carm	SN3518	51°50·4′	4°23·3′W	X	159
Nant yr Helyg	Gwyn	SH7927	52°49·9′	3°47·4′W	W	124
Nantyrhelygen	Pemb	SN1437	52°0·3′	4°42·2′W	X	145
Nant-yr-hendre	Carm	SN4938	52°1·4′	4°11·7′W	X	146
Nantyrhendy	Powys	SN9077	52°23·0′	3°36·6′W	X	136,147
Nant-yr-hengoed	Conwy	SJ0064	53°10·1′	3°29·4′W	H	116
Nantyrherwydd	Carm	SN3631	51°57·4′	4°22·8′W	X	145
Nant yr Rhestr	Powys	SN8358	52°12·7′	3°42·4′W	W	147
Nantyrhibo	Carm	SN6223	51°53·5′	3°59·9′W	X	159
Nant yr Hillwyn	Denb	SJ0838	52°56·1′	3°21·7′W	W	125
Nant-y-Rhiw	Conwy	SH8258	53°6·6′	3°45·4′W	T	116
Nantyrhwch	Powys	SN8056	52°11·6′	3°44·9′W	X	147
Nant yr Hwch	Powys	SN8854	52°10·6′	3°37·9′W	X	147
Nantyrhydd	Cered	SN6378	52°23·2′	4°0·4′W	X	135
Nantyrhynau	Powys	SO1685	52°27·6′	3°13·8′W	X	136
Nant yr Iau	Powys	SN8462	52°14·9′	3°41·6′W	W	147
Nant-yr-Nele	Powys	SH8007	52°39·1′	3°46·0′W	X	124,125
Nant yr Odyn	Conwy	SH9848	53°1·4′	3°30·8′W	W	116
Nant yr Offeiriad	Powys	SO0343	52°4·9′	3°24·5′W	W	147,160
Nantyroffeiriad-fawr	Powys	SO0343	52°4·9′	3°24·5′W	X	147,160
Nant yr Ogof	Conwy	SH6859	53°7·0′	3°57·9′W	W	115
Nantyrolchfa	Carm	SN3328	51°55·8′	4°25·3′W	X	145
Nantyronen Station	Cered	SN6778	52°23·3′	3°56·9′W	T	135
Nant-yr-onog	Gwyn	SH8916	52°44·1′	3°38·2′W	X	124,125
Nant yr Wydd	Powys	SN8717	51°50·6′	3°38·0′W	W	160
Nantyrychain	Powys	SO2324	51°54·8′	3°6·8′W	X	161
Nant yr Ysfa	Rho Cyn Taf	ST0397	51°40·0′	3°23·8′W	W	170
Nant y Sarn	Gwyn	SH9831	52°52·3′	3°30·5′W	W	125
Nant y Sarn	Powys	SN9271	52°19·8′	3°34·7′W	W	136,147
Nant Ysguthan	Powys	SH9411	52°41·4′	3°33·7′W	W	125
Nant-ystalwyn	Powys	SN8057	52°12·1′	3°45·0′W	X	147
Nant-y-Stepsau	V of Glam	ST0069	51°24·9′	3°25·9′W	W	170
Nant Ystradau	Gwyn	SH6742	52°57·8′	3°58·4′W	W	124
Nant Ystrad-y-groes	Gwyn	SH9630	52°51·7′	3°32·3′W	W	125
Nant y Terfyn	Conwy	SH9666	53°11·1′	3°33·0′W	W	116
Nant y Tryfal	Gwyn	SH9028	52°50·5′	3°37·6′W	W	125
Nant y Waun	Denb	SJ0332	52°52·8′	3°26·1′W	W	125
Nant y Waun Fraith	Powys	SH9716	52°44·2′	3°31·1′W	W	125
Nantyweirglodd	Pemb	SN2332	51°57·7′	4°34·2′W	X	145
Nantywellan	Powys	SO1568	52°18·5′	3°14·4′W	X	136,148
Nant-y-wrach	Conwy	SH8464	53°9·9′	3°43·7′W	X	116
Nap Bridge	S Lanak	NS9329	55°32·8′	3°41·3′W	X	71,72
Napchester	Kent	TR3147	51°10·8′	1°18·7′E	T	179
Na Peileirean	Arg & Bt	NR2976	55°54·3′	6°19·7′W	W	60
Napes Needle	Cumbr	NY2009	54°28·5′	3°13·7′W	X	89,90
Naphene Downs	Corn	SW7127	50°6·2′	5°11·8′W	X	203
Nap Hill	Bath & NE Somer	ST6359	51°20·0′	2°31·5′W	X	172
Naphill	Bucks	SU8497	51°40·2′	0°46·7′W	T	165
Nap Hill	S Lanak	NT0015	55°25·4′	3°34·4′W	H	78
Naphill Common	Bucks	SU8397	51°40·2′	0°47·6′W	F	165
Napleton	Worcs	SO8548	52°8·0′	2°12·8′W	T	150
Napleton Lodge Fm	Northnts	TL0173	52°21·0′	0°30·6′W	FM	141,153
Napley	Staffs	SJ7137	52°56·0′	2°25·5′W	T	127
Napley Fm	Staffs	SJ7138	52°56·6′	2°25·5′W	FM	127
Napley Heath	Staffs	SJ7238	52°56·6′	2°24·6′W	T	127
Nappa	N Yks	SD8553	53°58·6′	2°13·3′W	T	103
Nappa Flats	Lancs	SD8553	53°58·6′	2°13·3′W	X	103
Nappa Hall	N Yks	SD9690	54°18·6′	2°3·3′W	A	98
Nappa Mill	N Yks	SD9690	54°18·6′	2°3·3′W	T	98
Nappa Scar	N Yks	SD9691	54°19·1′	2°3·3′W	T	98
Nappers Cott	D & G	NX4071	55°0·7′	4°29·7′W	X	77
Napps	Corn	SX2185	50°38·5′	4°31·5′W	X	201
Napp's Moor	Corn	SX2185	50°38·5′	4°31·5′W	X	201
Nappyfaulds Ho	Falk	NS8674	55°57·0′	3°49·1′W	X	65
Napsbury	Herts	TL1604	51°43·6′	0°18·8′W	X	166
Naptha Cott	Lancs	SD5224	53°42·9′	2°43·2′W	X	102
Napthen's Fm	Suff	TL7779	52°23·1′	0°36·5′E	FM	144
Napton Fields	Warw	SP4461	52°15·0′	1°20·9′W	X	151
Napton Hill	Warw	SP4561	52°15·0′	1°20·1′W	H	151
Napton Holt	Warw	SP4559	52°13·9′	1°20·1′W	X	151
Napton Junction	Warw	SP4662	52°15·5′	1°19·2′W	X	151
Napton on the Hill	Warw	SP4661	52°14·9′	1°19·2′W	T	151
Napton Road Fm	Warw	SP4361	52°15·0′	1°21·8′W	FM	151
Nap Wood	E Susx	TQ5832	51°4·2′	0°15·7′E	F	188
Narachan	Arg & Bt	NR7646	55°39·6′	5°33·2′W	X	62,69
Narachan Burn	Arg & Bt	NR7748	55°40·7′	5°32·4′W	W	62,69
Narachan Hill	Arg & Bt	NR7547	55°40·1′	5°34·2′W	H	62,69
Na Rathanan	Highld	NG8761	57°35·6′	5°33·4′W	H	19
Narberth (Arberth)	Pemb	SN1014	51°47·8′	4°44·9′W	T	158
Narberth Bridge	Pemb	SN1014	51°47·8′	4°44·9′W	T	158
Narberth Mountain	Pemb	SN1013	51°47·2′	4°44·9′W	T	158
Narberth Sta	Pemb	SN1214	51°47·8′	4°43·2′W	X	158
Narborough	Leic	SP5497	52°34·3′	1°11·8′W	T	140
Narborough	Norf	TF7412	52°40·9′	0°34·8′E	T	132,143
Narborough Common	Norf	TF7311	52°40·4′	0°33·9′E	X	132,143
Narborough Field	Norf	TF7510	52°39·8′	0°35·7′E	X	132,143
Nare Cove	Corn	SW7924	50°4·7′	5°5·0′W	W	204
Nare Head	Corn	SW8024	50°4·8′	5°4·1′W	X	204
Nare Head	Corn	SW9136	50°11·5′	4°55·3′W	X	204
Nare Point	Corn	SW8025	50°5·3′	5°4·2′W	X	204
Narford Hall	Norf	TF7613	52°41·4′	0°36·7′E	A	132,143
Narfords	Devon	ST2906	50°51·2′	3°0·1′W	T	193
Narkurs	Corn	SX3255	50°22·5′	4°21·4′W	T	201
Narlwood Rocks	S Glos	ST5895	51°39·4′	2°36·0′W	X	162
Narnain Boulders	Arg & Bt	NN2705	56°12·6′	4°46·9′W	X	56
Narnell's Rock	Shrops	SO4293	52°32·1′	2°50·9′W	X	137
Narrachan	Arg & Bt	NM9114	56°16·6′	5°22·1′W	T	55
Narrachan	Arg & Bt	NN1136	56°29·0′	5°3·7′W	X	50
Narracombe	Devon	SX7876	50°34·5′	3°43·0′W	X	191
Narracott	Devon	SS3617	50°56·0′	4°19·7′W	T	190
Narracott	Devon	SS4504	50°49·1′	4°11·6′W	X	190
Narracott	Devon	SS6003	50°48·8′	3°58·9′W	X	191
Narracott	Devon	SS6123	50°59·6′	3°58·5′W	X	180
Narracott	Devon	SS6212	50°53·7′	3°57·4′W	X	180
Narracott	Devon	SS6439	51°8·3′	3°56·3′W	X	180
Narracott	Devon	SS7024	51°0·3′	3°50·8′W	X	180
Narracott	Devon	SS7619	50°57·7′	3°45·6′W	X	180
Narracott	Devon	SX4280	50°36·1′	4°13·6′W	X	201
Narracott	Devon	SX7591	50°42·5′	3°45·8′W	X	191
Narracott Fm	Devon	SS5300	50°47·1′	4°4·7′W	FM	191
Narradale	I of M	SC4093	54°18·7′	4°27·2′W	X	95
Narramore Fm	Devon	SX7584	50°38·8′	3°45·7′W	FM	191
Narraton	Devon	SX5696	50°45·0′	4°2·1′W	X	191
Narr Lodge	Lancs	SD5159	54°1·7′	2°44·5′W	X	102

Narr Ness	Orkney	HY4349	59°19·7'	2°59·6'W	X	5
Narrowdale	Staffs	SK1257	53°6·8'	1°48·8'W	X	119
Narrowdale Hill	Staffs	SK1257	53°6·8'	1°48·8'W	H	119
Narrowgate Beacon	Cumbr	NY7326	54°38·0'	2°24·7'W	X	91
Narrowgate Corner	Norf	TG4415	52°40·9'	1°37·0'E	T	134
Narrowgate Fm	Norf	TF8916	52°42·7'	0°48·3'E	FM	132
Narrow Meadow Fm	Worcs	SP0241	52°4·3'	1°57·9'W	FM	150
Narrow Moor	Cumbr	NY2317	54°32·8'	3°11·0'W	X	89,90
Narrows	Aberd	NO7866	56°47·4'	2°21·2'W	X	45
Narrows of Rassay	Highld	NG5435	57°20·6'	6°4·9'W	W	24,32
Narrows, The	Corn	SW9178	50°34·1'	4°56·7'W	W	200
Narrows, The	Devon	SX8137	50°13·5'	3°39·7'W	X	202
Narrows, The	Highld	NN0776	56°50·4'	5°9·4'W	W	41
Narrows, The	Suff	TM4147	52°4·4'	1°31·4'E	W	169
Narstay	N Eil	NF9776	57°40·6'	7°4·5'W	X	18
Narthwaite	Cumbr	SD7097	54°22·3'	2°27·3'W	X	98
Nar Valley Way	Norf	TF7111	52°40·4'	0°32·2'E	X	132,143
Nasareth	Gwyn	SH4750	53°1·8'	4°16·5'W	T	115,123
Naseby	Northnts	SP6877	52°23·4'	0°59·6'W	T	141
Naseby Covert	Northnts	SP6979	52°24·5'	0°58·7'W	F	141
Naseby Field	Northnts	SP6779	52°24·5'	1°0·5'W	X	141
Naseby Hall	Northnts	SP6679	52°24·5'	1°1·4'W	X	141
Naseby Resr	Northnts	SP6677	52°23·5'	1°1·4'W	W	141
Nase Wick	Essex	TR0093	51°36·2'	0°53·7'E	X	178
Na Sgeirean Móra	Arg & Bt	NM0048	56°32·0'	6°52·3'W	X	46
Nash	Brom	TQ4063	51°21·2'	0°1·0'E	T	177,187
Nash	Bucks	SP7834	52°0·2'	0°51·4'W	T	152,165
Nash	Heref	SO3062	52°15·3'	3°1·1'W	T	137,148
Nash	Kent	TR2658	51°16·8'	1°14·8'E	T	179
Nash	Newp	ST3483	51°32·8'	2°56·7'W	T	171
Nash	Pemb	SM9710	51°45·4'	4°56·1'W	X	157,158
Nash	Shrops	SO6071	52°20·4'	2°34·8'W	T	138
Nash	Somer	ST5313	50°55·1'	2°39·7'W	T	194
Nash Barn	Glos	SP0222	51°54·0'	1°57·9'W	X	163
Nash Court	Dorset	ST7819	50°58·4'	2°18·4'W	A	183
Nash Court	Kent	TQ9846	51°11·0'	0°50·4'E	X	189
Nash Court	Kent	TR0459	51°17·8'	0°56·0'E	X	178,179
Nash Court	Kent	TR3568	51°22·0'	1°23·0'E	X	179
Nash Court Fm	Kent	TR2659	51°17·3'	1°14·9'E	FM	179
Nash Court Fm	Shrops	SO6071	52°20·4'	2°34·8'W	FM	138
Nash Elm	Worcs	SO7781	52°25·8'	2°19·9'W	X	138
Nashend	Glos	SO8905	51°44·9'	2°9·2'W	T	163
Nash End	Worcs	SO7781	52°25·8'	2°19·9'W	T	138
Nashenden Fm	Medway	TQ7365	51°21·7'	0°29·5'E	FM	178
Nashend Fm	Worcs	SO8231	51°58·9'	2°15·3'W	FM	150
Nashes Fm	E Susx	TQ7411	50°52·6'	0°28·8'E	FM	199
Nashe's Fm	Herts	TL1709	51°46·3'	0°17·9'W	FM	166
Nashes Fm	Kent	TQ5242	51°9·6'	0°10·8'E	FM	188
Nashes Green	Hants	SU6745	51°12·2'	1°2·1'W	T	185,186
Nash Fm	Beds	TL0218	51°51·3'	0°30·7'W	FM	166
Nash Fm	Dorset	SY3798	50°46·9'	2°53·2'W	FM	193
Nash Fm	Kent	TR3668	51°21·9'	1°23·8'E	FM	179
Nash Fm	Pemb	SN0412	51°46·6'	4°50·1'W	FM	157,158
Nash Fm	W Susx	TQ3723	50°59·6'	0°2·5'W	FM	198
Nash Hall	Essex	TL5603	51°42·5'	0°15·9'E	X	167
Nash Hill	Heref	SO5348	52°7·9'	2°40·8'W	X	149
Nashick	Aberd	NJ7605	57°8·4'	2°23·3'W	X	38
Nashland Fm	W Susx	TQ2530	51°3·6'	0°12·6'W	FM	187
Nash Lee	Bucks	SP8408	51°46·1'	0°46·6'W	T	165
Nashleigh Fm	Bucks	SP9603	51°43·3'	0°36·2'W	FM	165
Nash Manor	V of Glam	SS9672	51°26·5'	3°29·4'W	X	170
Nash Mills	Herts	TL0604	51°43·7'	0°27·5'W	T	166
Nash Point	V of Glam	SS9168	51°24·3'	3°33·6'W	X	170
Nash Scar	Heref	SO3062	52°15·3'	3°1·1'W	X	137,148
Nash's Fm	Kent	TQ9962	51°19·6'	0°51·8'E	FM	178
Nash's Fm	Surrey	TQ3549	51°13·7'	0°3·6'W	FM	187
Nash Street	E Susx	TQ5412	50°53·4'	0°11·8'E	T	199
Nash Street	Kent	TQ6469	51°24·0'	0°21·9'E	T	177
Nash, The	Heref	SO5754	52°11·2'	2°37·3'W	X	149
Nashway Fm	Bucks	SP6413	51°48·9'	1°3·9'W	FM	164,165
Nash Wood	Heref	SO3062	52°15·3'	3°1·1'W	F	137,148
Nash Wood	Heref	SO4146	52°6·8'	2°51·3'W	F	148,149
Nask	N Eil	NL6598	56°57·4'	7°30·2'W	T	31
Na Socachan	Highld	NM9884	56°54·5'	5°18·6'W	X	40
Nassington	Northnts	TL0696	52°33·3'	0°25·8'W	T	142
Nass, The	Essex	TM0010	51°45·4'	0°54·3'E	X	168
Na Stacain	Highld	NC1760	58°29·7'	5°7·9'W	X	9
Nastend	Glos	SO7906	51°45·4'	2°17·9'W	T	162
Nastfield Fm	Glos	SO7506	51°45·4'	2°21·3'W	FM	162
Nast Hyde	Herts	TL2107	51°45·1'	0°14·4'W	T	166
Nasty	Herts	TL3524	51°54·1'	0°1·9'W	T	166
Natal Barn	Shrops	SO5794	52°32·8'	2°37·6'W	X	137,138
Natcott	Devon	SS2723	50°59·1'	4°27·5'W	T	190
Nateby	Cumbr	NY7706	54°27·2'	2°20·9'W	T	91
Nateby	Lancs	SD4644	53°53·6'	2°48·9'W	T	102
Nateby Common	Cumbr	NY7905	54°26·6'	2°19·0'W	X	91
Nateby Cow Close	Cumbr	NY7906	54°27·2'	2°19·0'W	X	91
Nateby Hall	Lancs	SD4746	53°54·7'	2°48·0'W	X	102
Nateby Ho	Lancs	SD4846	53°54·7'	2°47·1'W	X	102
Nately Scures	Hants	SU7053	51°16·5'	0°59·4'W	T	186
Nate Wood	E Susx	TQ5706	50°50·2'	0°14·2'E	F	199
Nath Point	Dorset	SY9886	50°40·6'	2°1·3'W	X	195
Nathro	Angus	NO5069	56°48·8'	2°48·7'W	X	44
Nathro Hill	Angus	NO4969	56°48·8'	2°49·7'W	H	44
Nathro Lodge	Angus	NO4968	56°48·3'	2°49·7'W	X	44
National Agricultural Centre	Warw	SP3271	52°20·4'	1°31·4'W	X	140
National Badminton Centre	Mil Key	SP8338	52°2·3'	0°47·0'W	X	152
National Bowl, The	Mil Key	SP8536	52°1·2'	0°45·3'W	X	152
National Exhibition Centre	Sol	SP1883	52°26·9'	1°43·7'W	X	139
National Film Archive	Bucks	SP9806	51°44·9'	0°34·4'W	X	165
National Gallery	C of West	TQ3080	51°30·5'	0°7·2'W	X	176,177
National Motor Museum, The	Hants	SU3802	50°49·2'	1°27·2'W	X	196
National Physical Laboratory	Rich	TQ1570	51°25·3'	0°20·4'W	X	176
National Railway Museum	York	SE5951	53°57·3'	1°5·6'W	X	105
National Stadium	Card	ST1876	51°28·9'	3°10·5'W	X	171
National Stud	Cambs	TL5961	52°13·7'	0°20·1'E	X	154
National Theatre	Lam	TQ3180	51°30·5'	0°6·3'W	X	176,177

National Tramway Museum	Derby	SK3454	53°5·2'	1°29·1'W	X	119
National Water Sports Centre	Notts	SK6139	52°56·9'	1°5·1'W	X	129
Nation's Fm	Hants	SU5414	50°55·6'	1°13·5'W	FM	196
Natland	Cumbr	SD5289	54°17·9'	2°43·8'W	T	97
Natland Park	Cumbr	SD5289	54°17·9'	2°43·8'W	X	97
Na Tònan	Arg & Bt	NM4557	56°38·4'	6°9·1'W	X	47
Na Torrain	Arg & Bt	NM2614	56°14·6'	6°24·9'W	X	48
Na Torranan	Arg & Bt	NM4541	56°29·8'	6°8·1'W	X	47,48
Na Tri Lochan	Highld	NC1316	58°5·9'	5°9·9'W	W	15
Natsley	Devon	SS6938	51°7·8'	3°52·0'W	X	180
Natson	Devon	SS7100	50°47·3'	3°49·4'W	X	191
Natsworthy Manor	Devon	SX7279	50°36·0'	3°48·1'W	X	191
Nattadon Common	Devon	SX7086	50°39·8'	3°50·0'W	X	191
Nattles	Cumbr	SD8293	54°20·2'	2°16·2'W	X	144
Natton	Glos	SO9232	51°59·4'	2°6·6'W	T	150
Nattonhall	Devon	SX7091	50°42·5'	3°50·1'W	X	191
Nat Tor	Devon	SX5482	50°37·4'	4°3·5'W	X	191,201
Nattor	Devon	SX5767	50°29·4'	4°0·6'W	X	202
Nattor Down	Devon	SX5482	50°37·4'	4°3·5'W	X	191,201
Nattshook Fm	Pemb	SM8913	51°46·8'	5°3·1'W	FM	157,158
Natty Cross	Devon	SS5818	50°56·9'	4°0·9'W	X	180
Naughtberry Hill	N Yks	SD9781	54°13·7'	2°2·3'W	H	98
Naughton	Suff	TM0248	52°5·8'	0°57·3'E	T	155
Naughton Bank	Fife	NO3827	56°26·1'	2°59·9'W	X	54,59
Naughton Ho	Fife	NO3724	56°24·5'	3°0·8'W	X	54,59
Naunton	Glos	SP1123	51°54·6'	1°50·0'W	T	163
Naunton	Worcs	SO8739	52°3·2'	2°11·0'W	T	150
Naunton Beauchamp	Worcs	SO9652	52°10·2'	2°3·1'W	T	150
Naunton Court	Worcs	SO9552	52°10·2'	2°4·0'W	A	150
Naunton Downs	Glos	SP0822	51°54·0'	1°52·6'W	X	163
Naunton Fm	Glos	SP0133	52°0·0'	1°58·7'W	FM	150
Naunton Fm	Worcs	SO8262	52°15·6'	2°15·4'W	FM	138,150
Naunton Hall Fm	Suff	TM3253	52°7·8'	1°23·8'E	FM	156
Naunton House Fm	Worcs	SO9652	52°10·2'	2°3·1'W	FM	150
Navages Wood	Powys	SO2659	52°13·7'	3°4·6'W	F	148
Naval Temple	Monm	SO5212	51°48·5'	2°41·4'W	X	162
Navant Hill	W Susx	SU9428	51°2·8'	0°39·2'W	T	186,197
Navarino	Corn	SX2889	50°40·8'	4°25·7'W	T	190
Navax Point	Corn	SW5943	50°14·5'	5°22·4'W	X	203
Nave Island	Arg & Bt	NR2875	55°53·7'	6°20·6'W	X	60
Navenby	Lincs	SK9857	53°6·3'	0°31·6'W	T	121
Navenby Heath	Lincs	TF0057	53°6·3'	0°30·0'W	X	121
Navenby Low Fields	Lincs	SK9557	53°6·3'	0°34·4'W	X	121
Naver Forest	Highld	NC6841	58°20·5'	4°14·8'W	F	10
Naver Forest	Highld	NC7038	58°18·9'	4°12·7'W	F	16
Naver Rock	Highld	NC7059	58°30·3'	4°13·4'W	H	10
Naversdale	Orkney	HY3409	58°58·1'	3°8·4'W	X	6,7
Navershaw	Orkney	HY2609	58°58·0'	3°16·7'W	X	6,7
Navestock Common	Essex	TQ5395	51°38·2'	0°13·1'E	X	167,177
Navestock Hall Fm	Essex	TQ5498	51°39·8'	0°14·0'E	FM	167,177
Navestock Heath	Essex	TQ5397	51°39·3'	0°13·1'E	T	167,177
Navestock Side	Essex	TQ5697	51°39·2'	0°15·7'E	T	167,177
Navidale	Highld	ND0316	58°7·6'	3°38·3'W	T	17
Navidale Fm	Highld	ND0416	58°7·6'	3°37·3'W	FM	17
Navio (Roman Fort)	Derby	SK1782	53°20·3'	1°44·3'W	R	110
Navitie Fm	Fife	NT1798	56°10·3'	3°19·8'W	FM	58
Navitie Hill	Fife	NT1798	56°10·3'	3°19·8'W	X	58
Navity	Highld	NH7864	57°39·2'	4°2·2'W	X	21,27
Navo	Orkney	HY6037	59°13·3'	2°41·6'W	X	5
Navy Hall	Cered	SN6368	52°17·8'	4°0·1'W	X	135
Nawlyn	Powys	SH7300	52°35·2'	3°52·1'W	X	135
Naworth Park	Cumbr	NY5662	54°57·6'	2°40·8'W	X	86
Nawton	N Yks	SE6584	54°15·1'	0°59·7'W	T	100
Nawton Tower	N Yks	SE6488	54°17·3'	1°0·6'W	X	94,100
Naychurch	Staffs	SK0161	53°9·0'	1°58·7'W	X	119
Nayland	Suff	TL9734	51°58·4'	0°52·5'E	T	155
Nayland End Wood	Suff	TL9334	51°58·5'	0°49·0'E	F	155
Nayland Fm	Suff	TM0253	52°8·5'	0°57·5'E	FM	155
Nayland Hall	Suff	TL9636	51°59·5'	0°51·7'E	X	155
Nayland Rock	Kent	TR3470	51°23·1'	1°22·2'E	X	179
Naylinghurst	Essex	TL7322	51°52·4'	0°31·2'E	X	167
Naylor's Hills	Lincs	SK8375	53°16·2'	0°44·9'W	X	121
Nay, The	I of M	SC1870	54°5·9'	4°46·6'W	X	95
Nazareth Ho	Halton	SJ4985	53°21·8'	2°45·6'W	X	108
Nazareth Ho	Midlo	NT3066	55°53·2'	3°6·7'W	X	66
Naze Hill	D & G	NY3385	55°9·5'	3°2·7'W	H	79
Nazeing	Essex	TL4106	51°44·3'	0°2·9'E	T	167
Nazeing Gate	Essex	TL4105	51°43·8'	0°2·9'E	T	167
Nazeing Long Green	Essex	TL4004	51°43·3'	0°2·0'E	T	167
Nazeing Marsh	Herts	TL3705	51°43·8'	0°0·6'W	X	166
Nazeing Mead	Essex	TL3806	51°44·4'	0°0·3'E	T	166
Nazeing Park (Sch)	Essex	TL4106	51°44·3'	0°2·9'E	X	167
Nazeingwood Common	Essex	TL4205	51°43·8'	0°3·8'E	X	167
Naze Mount	Lancs	SD4327	53°44·4'	2°51·4'W	X	102
Naze, The	Essex	TM2623	51°51·8'	1°17·3'E	X	169
N Burn of Gremista	Shetld	HU4543	60°10·4'	1°10·8'W	W	4
Neach Hill	Shrops	SJ7806	52°39·3'	2°19·1'W	X	127
Neachley Hall	Shrops	SJ7806	52°39·3'	2°19·1'W	X	127
Neachley Ho	Shrops	SJ7806	52°39·3'	2°19·1'W	X	127
Neach's Fm	Norf	TG2430	52°49·5'	1°19·9'E	FM	133
Neacroft	Hants	SZ1896	50°46·0'	1°44·3'W	T	195
Nead an Fhir-eoin	Highld	NG5519	57°12·0'	6°2·9'W	H	32
Nead an Fhitich	Arg & Bt	NR8677	55°56·6'	5°25·2'W	X	62
Nead na h-Iolaire	Highld	NG4827	57°16·1'	6°10·3'W	X	32
Neadon Cleave	Devon	SX7581	50°37·2'	3°45·6'W	X	191
Neadon Fm	Devon	SX8287	50°40·5'	3°39·8'W	FM	191
Neale's Barrow	Wilts	SU0828	51°3·3'	1°52·8'W	A	184
Neale's Covert	Notts	SK6490	53°24·4'	1°1·8'W	F	111
Nealhouse	Cumbr	NY3351	54°51·2'	3°2·2'W	T	85
Neal Point	Corn	SX4361	50°25·9'	4°12·3'W	X	201
Neals	E Susx	TQ7726	51°0·6'	0°31·8'E	X	188,199
Neal's Fm	Oxon	SU6882	51°32·2'	1°0·8'W	FM	175
Neal's Green	Warw	SP3384	52°27·4'	1°30·5'W	T	140
Neals Ing	N Yks	SD8469	54°7·2'	2°14·3'W	X	98
Neames Forstal	Kent	TR0557	51°16·7'	0°56·8'E	T	179
Nean Howe	N Yks	NZ7210	54°29·1'	0°52·9'W	A	94
Neap	Shetld	HP5916	60°20·1'	0°52·5'W	X	1
Neap	Shetld	HU5058	60°18·4'	1°5·2'W	X	2,3

Neapabhal	N Eil	NB2328	58°9·5'	6°42·1'W	H	8,13
Neapabhal	N Eil	NB2926	58°8·7'	6°35·8'W	H	8,13
Neapack, The	Shetld	HU3621	59°58·6'	1°20·8'W	X	4
Neap Ho	N Lincs	SE8613	53°36·6'	0°41·6'W	X	112
Neapna Field	Shetld	HU5991	60°36·1'	0°54·9'W	X	1,2
Neap of Foraness	Shetld	HU4571	60°25·5'	1°10·5'W	X	2,3
Neap of Norby	Shetld	HU1958	60°18·6'	1°38·9'W	X	3
Neap of Skea	Shetld	HU3783	60°32·0'	1°19·0'W	X	1,2,3
Neap, The	Shetld	HU2577	60°28·8'	1°32·2'W	X	3
Neap, The	Shetld	HU3678	60°29·3'	1°20·2'W	H	2,3
Neap, The	Shetld	HU3890	60°35·8'	1°17·9'W	X	1,2
Near Bank	Cumbr	SD1091	54°18·6'	3°22·6'W	X	96
Near Beck	N Yks	SE1767	54°6·2'	1°44·0'W	W	99
Near Black Clough	Derby	SK1098	53°29·0'	1°50·5'W	X	110
Near Bleaklow Stones	Derby	SK1096	53°27·9'	1°50·6'W	X	110
Near Broadslate	Derby	SE0502	53°31·1'	1°55·1'W	X	110
Near Cairn	D & G	NX2174	55°2·0'	4°47·6'W	X	76
Near Cat Clough	Barns	SK1798	53°28·9'	1°44·2'W	X	110
Near Costy Clough	Lancs	SD6957	54°0·7'	2°28·0'W	X	103
Near Down	W Berks	SU2979	51°30·8'	1°34·5'W	X	174
Near Drain	E Yorks	SE7927	53°44·2'	0°47·7'W	W	105,106
Nearer Light Ash	Lancs	SD4840	53°51·5'	2°47·0'W	X	102
Near Eyes Stanks	S Ayr	NX2584	55°7·4'	4°44·2'W	W	76
Nearfield Fm	N Yks	SE7563	54°3·7'	0°50·8'W	FM	100
Near Gill Laids	Cumbr	SD7192	54°19·6'	2°26·3'W	W	98
Near Gulf	Cumbr	NY3162	54°57·1'	3°4·2'W	W	85
Near Hardcastle	N Yks	SE1165	54°5·1'	1°49·5'W	T	99
Near Hearkening Rock	Monm	SO5413	51°49·1'	2°39·6'W	X	162
Nearhouse	Orkney	HY3215	59°1·3'	3°10·6'W	X	6
Nearhouse	Orkney	HY3919	59°3·5'	3°3·3'W	X	6
Nearhouse	Orkney	HY4127	59°7·8'	3°1·4'W	X	5,6
Nearhouse Hill	Orkney	HY3609	58°58·1'	3°6·3'W	X	6,7
Near Howe	Cumbr	NY3728	54°38·8'	2°58·2'W	X	90
Nearmarsh Fm	E Yorks	TA2522	53°41·0'	0°6·0'W	FM	107,113
Near Meadow Fm	Derby	SK4534	52°54·3'	1°19·5'W	FM	129
Near Moon Fm	Wakf	SE3012	53°36·5'	1°32·4'W	FM	110,111
Near Moor	N Yks	SE4799	54°23·3'	1°16·2'W	X	100
Near Naze	Lancs	SD4060	54°2·2'	2°54·6'W	X	96,97
Near Old Park	Cumbr	SD2277	54°11·2'	3°11·3'W	X	96
Near Orrest	Cumbr	NY4100	54°23·8'	2°54·1'W	X	90
Near Sawrey	Cumbr	SD3795	54°21·0'	2°57·7'W	T	96,97
Near Skerrs	Northum	NU0248	55°43·8'	1°57·7'W	X	75
Near Slack	Derby	SK0190	53°24·6'	1°58·7'W	X	110
Nearton End	Bucks	SP8026	51°55·8'	0°49·8'W	T	165
Near Tongue Gill	Cumbr	NY2216	54°32·2'	3°11·9'W	W	89,90
Neasden	Brent	TQ2185	51°33·3'	0°14·9'W	T	176
Neasham	Darl	NZ3210	54°29·3'	1°29·9'W	T	93
Neasham Hall	Darl	NZ3309	54°28·8'	1°29·0'W	X	93
Neasham Springs	Darl	NZ3211	54°29·8'	1°29·9'W	X	93
Neasless Fm	Durham	NZ3627	54°38·5'	1°26·1'W	FM	93
Neate Burn	Northum	NY5888	55°11·3'	2°39·2'W	W	80
Neat Enstone	Oxon	SP3724	51°55·0'	1°27·3'W	T	164
Neath	Pemb	SM9001	51°40·4'	5°1·8'W	X	157,158
Neath Abbey	Nth Pt Talb	SS7398	51°40·2'	3°49·8'W	T	170
Neatham	Hants	SU7440	51°9·5'	0°56·1'W	T	186
Neatham Down	Hants	SU7339	51°9·0'	0°57·0'W	X	186
Neath Canal	Nth Pt Talb	SN8504	51°43·6'	3°39·5'W	W	170
Neath Canal	Nth Pt Talb	SS7395	51°38·6'	3°49·7'W	W	170
Neath / Castell-Nedd	Nth Pt Talb	SS7396	51°39·1'	3°49·8'W	T	170
Neath (Castell-Nedd)	Nth Pt Talb	SS7497	51°39·7'	3°48·9'W	T	170
Neath Hill	D & G	NT0403	55°19·0'	3°30·3'W	X	78
Neath Hill	Mil Key	SP8540	52°3·3'	0°45·2'W	T	152
Neathwood	Devon	SX4088	50°40·4'	4°15·5'W	X	190
Neathwood Fm	Glos	ST7391	51°37·3'	2°23·0'W	FM	162,172
Neatishead	Norf	TG3420	52°43·8'	1°28·4'E	T	133,134
Neatishead Hall	Norf	TG3518	52°42·7'	1°29·2'E	X	133,134
Neat Marsh	E Yorks	TA1531	53°46·0'	0°14·9'W	T	107
Neatmoor Hall Fm	Norf	TL5398	52°33·7'	0°15·8'E	FM	143
Neaton	Norf	TF9101	52°34·6'	0°49·5'E	T	144
Neat's Close	Norf	TG0032	52°51·1'	0°58·6'E	F	133
Neats Court	Kent	TQ9271	51°24·6'	0°46·0'E	X	178
Neatscourt Marshes	Kent	TQ9170	51°24·0'	0°45·1'E	X	178
Neat's Ling	Norf	TF7139	52°55·5'	0°33·0'E	X	132
Neaty Burn	Highld	NH3541	57°26·0'	4°44·5'W	W	26
Neave or Coomb Island	Highld	NC6664	58°32·9'	4°17·7'W	X	10
Neavy Downs	Kent	TR2456	51°15·8'	1°13·0'E	X	179
Neback, The	Highld	ND1976	58°40·1'	3°23·3'W	X	7,12
Neban Point	Orkney	HY2113	59°0·1'	3°22·0'W	X	6
Nebbifield	Shetld	HT9339	60°8·4'	2°7·1'W	X	4
Nebit, The	Clackm	NS8898	56°9·9'	3°47·8'W	H	58
Neblonga	Orkney	HY2111	58°59·0'	3°22·0'W	X	6
Nebo	Cered	SN5465	52°16·1'	4°8·0'W	T	135
Nebo	Conwy	SH8356	53°5·5'	3°44·4'W	T	116
Nebo	Gwyn	SH4750	53°1·8'	4°16·5'W	T	115,123
Nebo	I of Angl	SH4690	53°23·3'	4°18·5'W	T	114
Nebo Fm	Wilts	SU0776	51°29·2'	1°53·6'W	FM	173
Nebo Geo	Orkney	HY2220	59°3·9'	3°21·1'W	X	6
Nebsworth	Warw	SP1942	52°4·8'	1°43·0'W	T	151
Nechells	Birm	SP0989	52°30·2'	1°51·6'W	T	139
Neck, The	Devon	SS4532	51°4·2'	4°12·4'W	X	180
Neck, The	Pemb	SM7309	51°44·3'	5°16·9'W	X	157
Necton	Norf	TF8709	52°39·0'	0°46·3'E	T	144
Necton Common	Norf	TF8908	52°38·4'	0°48·0'E	F	144
Necton Wood	Norf	TF9010	52°39·5'	0°49·0'E	F	132
Nedd	Highld	NC1331	58°14·0'	5°10·6'W	T	15
Nedderton	Northum	NZ2381	55°7·6'	1°37·9'W	T	81
Nedd Fechan	Powys	SN9112	51°48·0'	3°34·5'W	W	160
Nedern Brook	Monm	ST4889	51°36·1'	2°44·7'W	W	171,172
Nedge Hill	Somer	ST5851	51°15·6'	2°35·7'W	T	182,183
Nedge Hill	Wrekin	SJ7107	52°39·8'	2°25·3'W	T	127
Nedging	Suff	TL9948	52°5·9'	0°54·7'E	T	155
Nedging Mill	Suff	TL9947	52°5·4'	0°54·7'E	X	155
Nedging Tye	Suff	TM0149	52°6·4'	0°56·5'E	T	155
Neeans	Shetld	HU2758	60°18·6'	1°30·2'W	X	3
Neean Skerry	Shetld	HU2659	60°19·1'	1°31·3'W	X	3
Neeans Neap	Shetld	HU2759	60°19·1'	1°30·2'W	X	3
Needham	Norf	TM2281	52°23·1'	1°16·1'E	T	156
Needham Green	Essex	TL5515	51°49·0'	0°15·3'E	T	167
Needham Hall	Cambs	TF4704	52°37·1'	0°10·6'E	X	143
Needham Hall	Suff	TL7265	52°15·6'	0°31·6'E	X	154

Needham Lake	Suff	TM0954	52°8·9′	1°3·7′E	W	155
Needham Lodge Fm	Cambs	TF4904	52°37·0′	0°12·5′E	FM	143
Needham Market	Suff	TM0855	52°9·5′	1°2·9′E	T	155
Needham Plantation	Suff	TM1254	52°8·8′	1°6·3′E	F	155
Needham Street	Suff	TL7265	52°15·6′	0°31·6′E	T	154
Needingworth	Cambs	TL3472	52°20·0′	0°1·6′W	T	154
Needle E'e	Angus	NO6641	56°33·8′	2°32·7′W	X	54
Needle Hill	E Loth	NT7071	55°56·1′	2°28·4′W	X	67
Needle Ho	Cumbr	SD7296	54°21·8′	2°25·4′W	X	98
Needlehole	Glos	SO9816	51°50·8′	2°1·3′W	X	163
Needle Point	N Yks	SE8495	54°20·9′	0°42·0′W	X	94,100
Needle Point	Orkney	ND4494	58°50·1′	2°57·7′W	X	7
Needle Rock	Devon	SS1245	51°10·6′	4°41·0′W	X	180
Needle Rock	Pemb	SN0140	52°1·6′	4°53·7′W	X	145,157
Needles Eye	D & G	NX8954	54°52·4′	3°43·4′W	X	84
Needles Eye	D & G	NX9156	54°53·5′	3°41·5′W	X	84
Needles Eye	Northum	NT9955	55°47·5′	2°0·5′W	X	75
Needle's Eye	Shrops	SJ6207	52°39·8′	2°33·3′W	X	127
Needless	E Loth	NT5377	55°59·3′	2°44·8′W	X	66
Needless Hall	Durham	NZ1930	54°40·1′	1°41·9′W	X	92
Needless Hall	Northum	NZ1186	55°10·3′	1°49·2′W	X	81
Needless Hall Moor	Northum	NZ1087	55°10·9′	1°50·1′W	X	81
Needles, The	I of W	SZ2984	50°39·5′	1°35·0′W	X	196
Needle, The	Highld	ND0819	58°9·3′	3°33·3′W	X	17
Needle, The	Highld	NG4569	57°38·6′	6°15·9′W	H	23
Needle, The	Orkney	ND2490	58°47·7′	3°18·4′W	X	7
Needs	Angus	NO2358	56°42·7′	3°15·0′W	X	53
Needs Law	Scot Bord	NT6002	55°18·9′	2°37·4′W	H	80
Needs Ore Point	Hants	SZ4297	50°46·5′	1°23·9′W	X	196
Needwood	Staffs	SK1824	52°49·0′	1°43·6′W	T	128
Needwood Forest	Staffs	SK1624	52°49·0′	1°45·4′W	X	128
Needwood Ho	Staffs	SK1825	52°49·6′	1°43·6′W	X	128
Neegirth	Shetld	HU5171	60°25·4′	1°3·9′W	X	2,3
Neeham	Corn	SW8257	50°22·6′	5°3·6′W	X	200
Neen Savage	Shrops	SO6777	52°23·6′	2°28·7′W	T	138
Neens Hill	Shrops	SO6671	52°20·4′	2°29·5′W	X	138
Neen Sollars	Shrops	SO6572	52°20·9′	2°30·4′W	T	138
Neenton	Shrops	SO6387	52°29·0′	2°32·3′W	T	138
Neenton Heath	Shrops	SO6489	52°30·1′	2°31·4′W	X	138
Neep's Br	Norf	TF5506	52°38·0′	0°17·8′E	X	143
Nefod	Shrops	SJ3036	52°55·3′	3°2·1′W	T	126
Nefyn	Gwyn	SH3040	52°56·1′	4°31·4′W	T	123
Neidpath Hill	Scot Bord	NT4634	55°36·0′	2°51·0′W	H	73
Neigarth	Orkney	HY3722	59°5·1′	3°5·5′W	X	6
Neigarth	Orkney	HY6644	59°17·1′	2°35·3′W	X	5
Neigarth	Orkney	HY6940	59°15·0′	2°32·1′W	X	5
Neigarth	Shetld	HU4864	60°21·7′	1°7·3′W	X	2,3
Neighbour Moor	Durham	NZ0228	54°39·1′	1°57·7′W	X	92
Neighbourne	Somer	ST6448	51°14·0′	2°30·6′W	T	183
Neighbourway Fm	Ches	SJ9878	53°18·2′	2°1·4′W	FM	118
Neigh Bridge Country Park	Glos	SU0194	51°38·9′	1°58·7′W	X	163,173
Neighbrook	Glos	SP2036	52°1·6′	1°42·1′W	X	151
Neight Hill	Worcs	SO9458	52°13·4′	2°4·9′W	T	150
Neigwl Ganol	Gwyn	SH2729	52°50·1′	4°33·7′W	X	123
Neigwl Plâs	Gwyn	SH2728	52°49·6′	4°33·7′W	X	123
Neigwl Uchaf	Gwyn	SH2529	52°50·1′	4°35·5′W	X	123
Neild's Fm	Staffs	SJ9663	53°10·1′	2°3·2′W	FM	118
Neilsbrae	Aberd	NJ8318	57°15·4′	2°16·5′W	X	38
Neil's Helly	Orkney	HY5054	59°22·4′	2°52·3′W	X	5
Neilshill Fm	S Ayr	NS4026	55°30·4′	4°31·6′W	FM	70
Neilshill Ho	S Ayr	NS4026	55°30·4′	4°31·6′W	X	70
Neilston	E Renf	NS4757	55°47·2′	4°26·0′W	T	64
Neilston Ho	E Renf	NS4856	55°46·7′	4°25·0′W	X	64
Neilston Pad	E Renf	NS4755	55°46·1′	4°25·9′W	H	64
Neilstonside	E Renf	NS4655	55°46·1′	4°26·9′W	X	64
Neint	Cered	SN8375	52°21·9′	3°42·7′W	X	135,136,147
Neinthirion	Powys	SH9606	52°38·7′	3°31·8′W	X	125
Neis Hill	D & G	NX7290	55°11·5′	4°0·2′W	H	77
Neist	Highld	NG1247	57°25·6′	6°47·4′W	X	23
Neithrop	Oxon	SP4440	52°3·6′	1°21·1′W	T	151
Neive of the Spit	D & G	NX4184	55°7·7′	4°29·2′W	X	77
Nelfields	Glos	SO7325	51°55·6′	2°23·2′W	X	162
Nell Bank Centre	Brad	SE1248	53°55·9′	1°48·6′W	X	104
Nell Br	Oxon	SP4934	52°0·4′	1°16·8′W	X	151
Nellbridge Fm	Northnts	SP4933	51°59·8′	1°16·8′W	FM	151
Nellfield Ho	S Lanak	NS8548	55°43·0′	3°49·4′W	X	72
Nell Fm	Swin	SU1793	51°38·4′	1°44·9′W	FM	163,173
Nello	Orkney	HY3716	59°1·9′	3°5·4′W	X	6
Nell's Pike	Derby	SK0497	53°28·4′	1°56·0′W	X	110
Nell's Point	V of Glam	ST1266	51°23·4′	3°15·5′W	X	171
Nell Stones	N Yks	SE1459	54°1·9′	1°46·8′W	X	104
Nelly Andrews Green	Powys	SJ2609	52°40·7′	3°5·3′W	X	126
Nelly Ayre Foss	N Yks	SE8199	54°23·0′	0°44·7′W	W	94,100
Nelly Burdon's Beck	Stock on T	NZ4013	54°30·9′	1°22·5′W	W	93
Nelly Park Wood	N Yks	SE0458	54°1·3′	1°55·9′W	F	104
Nelly's Moss Lakes	Northum	NU0802	55°19·0′	1°52·0′W	W	81
Nelmes, The	Heref	SO6741	52°4·2′	2°28·5′W	X	149
Nelson	Caer	ST1195	51°39·0′	3°16·8′W	T	171
Nelson	Hartpl	NZ4735	54°42·7′	1°15·8′W	X	93
Nelson	Lancs	SD8637	53°50·0′	2°12·3′W	T	103
Nelson Hill	Cumbr	NY4946	54°48·6′	2°47·2′W	X	86
Nelson Hill Fm	Cumbr	NY4936	54°43·2′	2°47·1′W	FM	90
Nelson House Fm	N Yks	NZ8507	54°27·3′	0°40·9′W	FM	94
Nelson's Grove	Notts	SK6270	53°13·6′	1°3·9′W	F	120
Nelson's Monument	Derby	SK2773	53°15·4′	1°35·3′W	X	119
Nelson's Monument	Hants	SU6107	50°51·8′	1°7·6′W	X	196
Nelson's Monument	Norf	TG5305	52°35·3′	1°44·5′E	X	134
Nelson's Nursery	N Yks	SE2798	54°22·8′	1°34·6′W	F	99
Nelson's Place	Hants	SU4700	50°48·1′	1°19·6′W	X	196
Nelson Villa	Lincs	TF5573	53°14·1′	0°19·8′E	X	122
Nelson Village	Northum	NZ2577	55°5·5′	1°36·1′W	T	88
Nemphlar	S Lanak	NS8544	55°40·8′	3°49·3′W	T	71,72
Nempnett Fm	Bath & NE Somer	ST5261	51°21·0′	2°41·0′W	FM	172,182
Nempnett Thrubwell	Bath & NE Somer	ST5360	51°20·5′	2°40·1′W	T	172,182
Nene Lodge Fm	Lincs	TF4923	52°47·3′	0°13·0′E	FM	131
Nene Outfall Cut	Lincs	TF4823	52°47·3′	0°12·1′E	W	131
Nene Terrace	Lincs	TF2507	52°39·0′	0°8·7′W	T	142
Nene Valley Railway	Peterb	TL1397	52°33·8′	0°19·6′W	X	142
Nene Way	Northnts	SP7359	52°13·7′	0°55·5′W	X	152
Nene Way	Northnts	TL0587	52°28·5′	0°26·8′W	X	142
Nenthall	Cumbr	NY7545	54°48·2′	2°22·9′W	T	86,87
Nenthead	Cumbr	NY7843	54°47·1′	2°20·1′W	T	86,87
Nenthorn	Scot Bord	NT6737	55°37·8′	2°31·0′W	T	74
Nenthorn Ho	Scot Bord	NT6737	55°37·8′	2°31·0′W	X	74
Nentsberry	Cumbr	NY7545	54°48·2′	2°22·9′W	X	86,87
Nentydd	Pemb	SN1932	51°57·7′	4°37·7′W	X	145
Neopardy	Devon	SX7999	50°46·9′	3°42·6′W	T	191
Nepcote	W Susx	TQ1208	50°51·9′	0°24·1′W	T	198
Nepgill	Cumbr	NY0629	54°39·1′	3°27·0′W	T	89
Nepicar Fm	Kent	TQ6258	51°18·1′	0°19·8′E	FM	188
Nep Town	W Susx	TQ2115	50°55·5′	0°16·3′W	T	198
Neptune Hall	Gwyn	SN5899	52°34·5′	4°5·3′W	X	135
Neptune's Staircase	Highld	NN1177	56°51·0′	5°5·5′W	X	41
Nerabus	Arg & Bt	NR2255	55°42·8′	6°25·1′W	T	60
Nercwys	Flint	SJ2361	53°8·7′	3°8·7′W	T	117
Nercwys Mountain	Flint	SJ2158	53°7·0′	3°10·4′W	X	117
Nerdpath Castle	Scot Bord	NT2340	55°39·1′	3°13·0′W	A	73
Neriby	Arg & Bt	NR3660	55°45·9′	6°12·1′W	X	60
Nerston	S Lanak	NS6456	55°46·9′	4°9·7′W	T	64
Nervelstone	Renf	NS3256	55°46·3′	4°40·3′W	X	63
Nesbister	Shetld	HU3945	60°11·5′	1°17·3′W	X	4
Nesbister Hill	Shetld	HU4045	60°11·5′	1°16·2′W	H	4
Nesbit	Northum	NT9833	55°35·7′	2°1·5′W	X	75
Nesbitt Dene	Durham	NZ4636	54°43·3′	1°16·7′W	F	93
Nesbitt Hall	Durham	NZ4536	54°43·3′	1°17·7′W	X	93
Nesbitt Hill Head	Northum	NZ0869	55°1·2′	1°52·1′W	X	88
Nesfield	N Yks	SE0949	53°56·5′	1°51·4′W	X	104
Neshion Water	Shetld	HU4275	60°27·7′	1°13·7′W	W	2,3
Neslam Br	Lincs	TF1632	52°52·6′	0°16·2′W	X	130
Neslam Fm	Lincs	TF1432	52°52·6′	0°18·0′W	FM	130
Nesley Fm	Glos	ST8592	51°37·8′	2°12·6′W	FM	162,173
Ness	Ches	SJ3076	53°16·8′	3°2·6′W	T	117
Ness	Orkney	HY2507	58°56·9′	3°17·7′W	X	6,7
Ness	Orkney	HY2525	59°6·6′	3°18·1′W	X	6
Ness	Orkney	HY2815	59°1·2′	3°14·8′W	X	6
Ness	Orkney	HY2908	58°57·5′	3°13·6′W	X	6,7
Ness	Orkney	HY3014	59°0·7′	3°12·6′W	X	6
Ness	Orkney	HY4939	59°14·3′	2°53·1′W	X	5
Ness	Orkney	HY4953	59°21·9′	2°53·3′W	X	5
Ness	Orkney	HY5321	59°4·7′	2°48·7′W	X	5,6
Ness	Orkney	HY5335	59°12·2′	2°48·9′W	X	5,6
Ness	Orkney	ND4996	58°51·2′	2°52·6′W	X	6,7
Ness	Shetld	HU2158	60°18·6′	1°36·7′W	X	3
Nessbreck	Orkney	HY3219	59°3·4′	3°10·7′W	X	6
Ness Castle	Highld	NH6541	57°26·6′	4°14·5′W	X	26
Nesscliffe	Shrops	SJ3819	52°46·1′	2°54·7′W	T	126
Nesscliffe Hill Country Park	Shrops	SJ3919	52°46·2′	2°53·8′W	X	126
Nessfield Court	N Yks	SE0949	53°56·5′	1°51·4′W	X	104
Nessfield Ho	N Lincs	SE8419	53°39·9′	0°43·3′W	X	112
Ness Fm	Cambs	TL6069	52°18·0′	0°21·2′E	FM	154
Ness Fm	Suff	TM2133	51°57·3′	1°13·4′E	FM	169
Ness Glen	E Ayr	NS4702	55°17·6′	4°24·1′W	X	77
Ness Hag Wood	Red & Cl	NZ6916	54°32·3′	0°55·6′W	F	94
Ness Head	Highld	ND3866	58°34·9′	3°3·5′W	X	12
Ness Head	N Yks	SE8288	54°17·1′	0°44·0′W	X	94,100
Ness Ho	Highld	NH7356	57°34·8′	4°7·0′W	X	27
Ness Ho	Suff	TM4761	52°11·7′	1°37·3′E	X	156
Nessholt	Ches	SJ3076	53°16·8′	3°2·6′W	T	117
Ness Ho, The	Devon	SX9471	50°32·0′	3°29·4′W	X	202
Nessit Hill	Ches	SJ9670	53°13·9′	2°3·2′W	X	118
Ness of Bakka	Shetld	HU1651	60°14·8′	1°42·2′W	X	3
Ness of Bardister	Shetld	HU3676	60°28·2′	1°20·2′W	X	2,3
Ness of Beosetter	Shetld	HU4944	60°10·9′	1°6·5′W	X	4
Ness of Bixter	Shetld	HU3351	60°14·8′	1°23·7′W	X	3
Ness of Boray	Orkney	HY4421	59°4·6′	2°58·1′W	X	5,6
Ness of Brodgar	Orkney	HY2913	59°0·2′	3°13·7′W	X	6
Ness of Brough	Orkney	HY4548	59°19·2′	2°57·5′W	X	5
Ness of Brough	Orkney	HY6542	59°16·1′	2°36·4′W	X	5
Ness of Brough	Shetld	HU5792	60°36·7′	0°57·0′W	X	1,2
Ness of Burgi	Shetld	HU3808	59°51·6′	1°18·8′W	X	4
Ness of Burravoe	Shetld	HU3890	60°35·8′	1°17·9′W	X	1,2
Ness of Burwick	Shetld	HU3840	60°8·8′	1°18·4′W	X	4
Ness of Campston	Orkney	HY5304	58°55·5′	2°48·5′W	X	6,7
Ness of Clousta	Shetld	HU3057	60°18·0′	1°26·9′W	X	3
Ness of Collaster	Shetld	HP5707	60°44·8′	0°56·8′W	X	1
Ness of Copister	Shetld	HU4978	60°29·2′	1°6·0′W	X	2,3
Ness of Culsetter	Shetld	HU3367	60°23·4′	1°23·6′W	X	2,3
Ness of Duncansby	Highld	ND3873	58°38·7′	3°3·6′W	X	7,12
Ness of Gairsay	Orkney	HY4521	59°4·6′	2°57·1′W	X	5,6
Ness of Galtagarth	Shetld	HU4979	60°29·8′	1°6·0′W	X	2,3
Ness of Gillarona	Shetld	HU3262	60°20·7′	1°24·7′W	X	3
Ness of Gossabrough	Shetld	HU5383	60°31·9′	1°1·6′W	X	1,2,3
Ness of Gruting	Shetld	HU6591	60°36·1′	0°48·3′W	X	1,2
Ness of Haggrister	Shetld	HU3570	60°25·0′	1°21·4′W	X	2,3
Ness of Hamar	Shetld	HU3075	60°27·7′	1°26·8′W	X	3
Ness of Hillswick	Shetld	HU2775	60°27·7′	1°30·0′W	X	3
Ness of Hoswick	Shetld	HU4123	59°59·7′	1°15·4′W	X	4
Ness of Houll	Shetld	HU3267	60°23·4′	1°24·7′W	X	3
Ness of Houlland	Shetld	HP5205	60°43·7′	1°2·3′W	X	1
Ness of Houlland	Shetld	HU3788	60°34·7′	1°19·0′W	X	1,2
Ness of Housetter	Shetld	HU3684	60°32·5′	1°20·1′W	X	1,2,3
Ness of Howe	Orkney	HY5115	59°1·4′	2°50·7′W	X	6
Ness of Huna	Highld	ND3673	58°38·7′	3°5·7′W	X	7,12
Ness of Ireland	Shetld	HU3723	59°59·7′	1°19·7′W	X	4
Ness of Kaywick	Shetld	HU5392	60°36·7′	1°1·4′W	X	1,2
Ness of Litter	Highld	ND0771	58°37·3′	3°35·6′W	X	12
Ness of Little-ayre	Shetld	HU3262	60°20·7′	1°24·7′W	X	3
Ness of Lussetter	Shetld	HU5390	60°35·7′	1°1·4′W	X	1,2
Ness of Melby	Shetld	HU1857	60°18·1′	1°40·0′W	X	3
Ness of Noonsbrough	Shetld	HU2957	60°18·0′	1°28·0′W	H	3
Ness of Olnesfirth	Shetld	HU3076	60°28·3′	1°26·8′W	X	3
Ness of Ork	Orkney	HY5422	59°5·2′	2°47·7′W	X	5,6
Ness of Portnaculter	Highld	NH7385	57°50·5′	4°7·9′W	X	21
Ness of Queyfirth	Shetld	HU3582	60°31·5′	1°21·2′W	X	1,2,3
Ness of Queyhoose	Shetld	HP6012	60°47·5′	0°53·4′W	H	1
Ness of Queyon	Shetld	HU5485	60°33·0′	1°0·4′W	X	1,2,3
Ness of Quoys	Highld	ND3473	58°38·7′	3°7·7′W	X	7,12
Ness of Ramnageo	Orkney	HY2217	59°2·2′	3°21·1′W	X	6
Ness of Ramnageo	Shetld	HU6299	60°40·4′	0°51·4′W	X	1
Ness of Rerwick	Shetld	HU3719	59°57·5′	1°19·8′W	X	4
Ness of Seatter	Orkney	HY2712	58°59·6′	3°15·7′W	X	6
Ness of Setter	Shetld	HU4437	60°7·2′	1°12·0′W	X	4
Ness of Setter	Shetld	HU4870	60°24·9′	1°7·2′W	X	2,3
Ness of Sheenareef	Shetld	HU5264	60°21·7′	1°2·9′W	X	2,3
Ness of Skellister	Shetld	HU4755	60°16·9′	1°8·5′W	X	3
Ness of Snabrough	Shetld	HU5793	60°37·2′	0°57·0′W	X	1,2
Ness of Sound	Shetld	HU4482	60°31·4′	1°11·4′W	X	1,2,3
Ness of Sound	Shetld	HU4638	60°7·7′	1°9·8′W	X	4
Ness of Tenston	Orkney	HY2816	59°1·8′	3°14·8′W	X	6
Ness of Trebister	Shetld	HU4538	60°7·7′	1°10·9′W	X	4
Ness of Tuquoy	Orkney	HY4543	59°16·5′	2°57·4′W	X	5
Ness of Vatsetter	Shetld	HU5489	60°35·1′	1°0·4′W	X	1,2
Ness of Wadbister	Shetld	HP5601	60°41·6′	0°58·0′W	X	1
Ness of West Sandwick	Shetld	HU4387	60°34·1′	1°12·4′W	X	1,2
Ness of Westshore	Shetld	HU3939	60°8·3′	1°17·4′W	H	4
Ness of Woodwick	Orkney	HY4024	59°6·2′	3°2·4′W	X	5,6
Ness Point or North Cheek	N Yks	NZ9606	54°26·7′	0°30·8′W	X	94
Ness-side	Highld	NH6442	57°27·1′	4°15·5′W	X	26
Ness-side Ho	Highld	NH6442	57°27·1′	4°15·5′W	X	26
Ness, The	Notts	SK8060	53°8·1′	0°47·8′W	X	121
Ness, The	Orkney	HY2514	59°0·7′	3°17·9′W	X	6
Ness, The	Orkney	HY5408	58°57·7′	2°47·5′W	X	6,7
Ness, The	Orkney	HY6630	59°9·6′	2°35·2′W	X	5
Ness, The	Orkney	ND3885	58°45·2′	3°3·8′W	X	7
Ness, The	Shetld	HP6114	60°48·5′	0°52·2′W	X	1
Ness, The	Shetld	HU3192	60°36·9′	1°25·5′W	X	1
Ness, The	Shetld	HU3626	60°1·3′	1°20·8′W	X	4
Ness, The	Shetld	HU3786	60°33·6′	1°19·0′W	X	1,2,3
Nesstoun	Orkney	HY7652	59°21·5′	2°24·8′W	T	5
Ness Vird	Shetld	HU3375	60°27·7′	1°23·5′W	X	2,3
Nest	Cumbr	NY2922	54°35·5′	3°5·5′W	X	89,90
Nest	Cumbr	NY7144	54°47·7′	2°26·6′W	X	86,87
Nest	Shetld	HU3688	60°34·7′	1°20·1′W	X	1,2
Nestends	Scot Bord	NT9564	55°52·4′	2°4·4′W	X	67
Nesti Voe	Shetld	HU5340	60°8·7′	1°2·2′W	W	4
Nestley Point	Devon	SX8237	50°13·5′	3°38·9′W	X	202
Nest of Fannich	Highld	NH1470	57°41·1′	5°6·7′W	X	20
Neston	Ches	SJ2877	53°17·3′	3°4·4′W	T	117
Neston	Wilts	ST8668	51°24·9′	2°11·7′W	T	173
Neston Park	Wilts	ST8667	51°24·3′	2°11·7′W	X	173
Nest, The	Northum	NU1626	55°31·9′	1°44·4′W	X	75
Nest, The	Scot Bord	NT4335	55°36·6′	2°53·9′W	X	73
Nest, The	Shrops	SO6171	52°20·4′	2°33·9′W	X	138
Neswick Fm	E Yorks	SE9852	53°57·5′	0°30·0′W	FM	106
Neswick Low Fm	E Yorks	SE9754	53°58·6′	0°30·8′W	FM	106
Netchells Green	Birm	SP0887	52°29·1′	1°52·5′W	T	139
Netchwood Common	Shrops	SO6191	52°31·2′	2°34·1′W	X	138
Netchwood Fm	Shrops	SO6192	52°31·7′	2°34·1′W	FM	138
Netham	C of Bris	ST6172	51°27·0′	2°33·3′W	T	172
Nethanfoot	S Lanak	NS8247	55°42·4′	3°52·2′W	T	72
Nether Abber Village (site of)	Somer	ST5821	50°59·4′	2°35·5′W	A	183
Nether Abington	S Lanak	NS9324	55°30·1′	3°41·2′W	X	71,72
Nether Achie	D & G	NX6277	55°4·4′	4°9·3′W	X	77
Nether Aden	Aberd	NJ9947	57°31·0′	2°0·5′W	X	30
Nether Affleck	S Lanak	NS8442	55°39·7′	3°50·2′W	X	71,72
Nether Affloch	Aberd	NJ7708	57°10·0′	2°22·4′W	X	38
Nether Aird	Pth & Kin	NO1340	56°32·9′	3°24·5′W	X	53
Nether Alderley	Ches	SJ8476	53°17·1′	2°14·0′W	T	118
Netherall Fm	E Susx	TQ4122	50°59·0′	0°0·9′E	FM	198
Nether Anguston	C of Aber	NJ8101	57°6·2′	2°18·4′W	X	38
Nether Ardgrain	Aberd	NJ9533	57°23·5′	2°4·5′W	X	30
Nether Ardroscadale	Arg & Bt	NS0362	55°48·9′	5°8·2′W	X	63
Nether Arniefoul	Angus	NO3945	56°35·8′	2°59·2′W	X	54
Nether Arthrath	Aberd	NJ9637	57°25·7′	2°3·5′W	X	30
Nether Ascreavie	Angus	NO3356	56°41·7′	3°5·2′W	X	53
Nether Ashentilly	Aberd	NO8297	57°4·1′	2°17·4′W	X	38,45
Nether Auchendrane	S Ayr	NS3316	55°24·8′	4°37·9′W	X	70
Nether Auchlinsky	Pth & Kin	NO0002	56°12·3′	3°36·3′W	X	58
Nether Auquhollie	Aberd	NO8290	57°0·3′	2°17·3′W	X	38,45
Netheravon	Wilts	SU1448	51°14·1′	1°47·6′W	T	184
Netheravon Down	Wilts	SU1147	51°13·6′	1°50·2′W	X	184
Nether Backhill	Aberd	NK0039	57°26·7′	1°59·5′W	X	30
Nether Balfour	Aberd	NJ5317	57°14·7′	2°46·3′W	X	37
Nether Balgillo	Angus	NO4858	56°42·9′	2°50·5′W	X	54
Nether Balgray	Angus	NO3558	56°42·8′	3°3·3′W	X	54
Nether Ballunie	Pth & Kin	NO2540	56°33·0′	3°12·8′W	X	53
Nether Barfod	Renf	NS3657	55°47·0′	4°36·5′W	X	63
Nether Barr	D & G	NX4263	54°56·5′	4°27·6′W	X	83
Nether Barr	D & G	NX7676	55°4·0′	3°56·1′W	X	84
Nether Barr	S Ayr	NX2894	55°12·9′	4°41·8′W	X	76
Netherbarrow Fm	Wigan	SJ6898	53°28·9′	2°28·5′W	FM	109
Nether Baulk	Aberd	NO8185	56°57·6′	2°18·3′W	X	45
Nether Beanshill	C of Aber	NJ8402	57°6·8′	2°15·4′W	X	38
Nether Beck	Cumbr	NY1508	54°27·9′	3°18·3′W	W	89
Nether Bellandy	Moray	NJ2833	57°23·2′	3°11·4′W	X	28
Nether Belliehill	Angus	NO5763	56°45·7′	2°41·8′W	X	44
Nether Benchil	Pth & Kin	NO0930	56°27·5′	3°28·2′W	X	52,53
Nether Benholm	Aberd	NO8069	56°49·0′	2°19·2′W	X	45
Nether Bigging	Orkney	HY2911	58°59·1′	3°13·6′W	X	6
Nether Birchy Law	Scot Bord	NT3849	55°44·1′	2°58·8′W	X	73
Nether Birnie	Aberd	NO8068	56°48·4′	2°19·2′W	X	45
Nether Birnie	Moray	NJ2059	57°37·1′	3°19·9′W	X	28
Nether Black Law	E Ayr	NS7219	55°27·1′	4°1·0′W	X	71
Nether Blainslie	Scot Bord	NT5443	55°41·0′	2°43·5′W	T	73
Nether Blairmaud	Aberd	NJ6160	57°38·0′	2°38·7′W	X	29
Nether Blairock	Moray	NJ5063	57°39·5′	2°49·8′W	X	29
Nether Boddam	Aberd	NJ6229	57°21·3′	2°37·4′W	X	37
Nether Bogside	Moray	NJ1957	57°36·0′	3°20·9′W	X	28
Nether Booth	Derby	SK1486	53°22·5′	1°47·0′W	T	110
Nether Borlum	Moray	NJ1942	57°27·9′	3°20·6′W	X	28
Nether Bouprie	Fife	NT1885	56°3·3′	3°18·6′W	X	65,66
Nether Bow	Angus	NO4352	56°39·6′	2°55·3′W	X	54
Nether Boyndlie	Aberd	NJ9263	57°39·7′	2°7·6′W	X	30
Nether Bracco	N Lanak	NS8366	55°52·6′	3°51·8′W	X	65
Nether Braco	Pth & Kin	NN8310	56°16·3′	3°52·9′W	X	57
Netherbrae	Aberd	NJ7959	57°37·5′	2°20·6′W	T	29,30

Nether Braehead	Orkney	ND4590	58°47·9'	2°56·6'W	X	7
Nether Bridge	Corn	SX3486	50°39·2'	4°20·5'W	X	201
Netherbridge	Devon	SX3587	50°39·8'	4°19·7'W	X	190
Nether Broadfield	Renf	NS4058	55°47·6'	4°32·7'W	X	64
Nether Broadmuir	Aberd	NK0632	57°23·0'	1°53·6'W	X	30
Nether Brotherstone	Scot Bord	NT4354	55°46·8'	2°54·1'W	X	66,73
Netherbrough	Orkney	HY3016	59°1·8'	3°12·7'W	T	6
Nether Broughton	Leic	SK6925	52°49·3'	0°58·2'W	T	129
Nether Brownhill	Aberd	NK0432	57°23·0'	1°55·6'W	X	30
Netherburn	S Lanak	NS7947	55°42·3'	3°55·1'W	X	64
Netherburn	S Lanak	NS8047	55°42·4'	3°54·1'W	T	72
Nether Burn	S Lanak	NS9308	55°21·5'	3°40·8'W	W	71,78
Nether Burnhaugh	Aberd	NO8395	57°3·0'	2°16·4'W	X	38,45
Nether Burnside	Aberd	NJ6510	57°11·0'	2°34·3'W	X	38
Nether Burrow	Lancs	SD6175	54°10·4'	2°35·4'W	T	97
Nether Burrows	Derby	SK2739	52°57·1'	1°35·5'W	T	128
Netherbury	Dorset	SY4699	50°47·5'	2°45·6'W	T	193
Nether button	Orkney	HY4504	58°55·5'	2°56·8'W	X	6,7
Netherby	Cumbr	NY3971	55°2·0'	2°56·8'W	T	85
Netherby	Devon	SS5330	51°3·3'	4°5·5'W	X	180
Netherby	N Yks	SE3346	53°54·8'	1°29·4'W	T	104
Netherby Dale	N Yks	SE9083	54°14·3'	0°36·7'W	X	101
Netherbyre	Moray	NJ1557	57°36·0'	3°24·9'W	X	28
Netherbyres	Scot Bord	NT9463	55°51·9'	2°5·3'W	X	67
Nether Cabra	Aberd	NJ9752	57°33·7'	2°2·5'W	X	30
Nether Cairn	D & G	NS6912	55°23·3'	4°3·7'W	X	71
Nether Cairn	E Renf	NS4951	55°44·0'	4°23·9'W	X	64
Nether Cairn	Scot Bord	NT1050	55°44·4'	3°25·6'W	A	65,72
Nether Cairnhill	Aberd	NO8993	57°1·9'	2°10·4'W	X	38,45
Nether Cambushinnie	Pth & Kin	NN8006	56°14·1'	3°55·7'W	X	57
Nether Careston	Angus	NO5258	56°42·9'	2°46·6'W	X	54
Nethercarr	N Yks	SE4553	53°58·5'	1°18·4'W	X	105
Nether Carse	Stir	NS6996	56°8·6'	4°6·1'W	X	57
Nether Carswell	E Renf	NS4653	55°45·0'	4°26·8'W	X	64
Nether Cassock	D & G	NT2303	55°19·2'	3°12·4'W	T	79
Nether Cerne	Dorset	SY6698	50°47·1'	2°28·6'W	T	194
Netherclay	Somer	ST2520	50°58·7'	3°3·7'W	T	193
Nethercleave	Devon	SS6124	51°0·2'	3°58·5'W	X	180
Nethercleave	Devon	SS9012	50°54·1'	3°33·5'W	X	181
Nethercleuch	D & G	NY1286	55°9·9'	3°22·5'W	X	78
Nether Cleugh	D & G	NX6186	55°9·2'	4°10·5'W	X	77
Nethercleugh Burn	D & G	NY1085	55°9·3'	3°24·3'W	W	78
Nether Clifton	D & G	NX9156	54°53·5'	3°41·5'W	T	84
Netherclose	Cumbr	NY1421	54°34·9'	3°19·4'W	X	89
Nether Cluny	Moray	NJ3137	57°25·3'	3°8·5'W	X	28
Nether Cog	D & G	NS8015	55°25·1'	3°53·3'W	X	71,78
Nether Collinhirst	D & G	NY1775	55°4·0'	3°17·6'W	X	85
Nether Comisty	Aberd	NJ5942	57°28·2'	2°40·6'W	X	29
Nether Compton	Dorset	ST5917	50°57·3'	2°34·6'W	T	183
Nether Contlaw	C of Aber	NJ8402	57°6·8'	2°15·4'W	X	38
Nether Coomb Craig	D & G	NT1311	55°23·4'	3°22·0'W	X	78
Nether Corsock	D & G	NX7572	55°1·9'	3°56·9'W	X	84
Nether Cortes	Aberd	NK0058	57°37·0'	1°59·5'W	X	30
Nethercote	Oxon	SP4741	52°4·2'	1°18·5'W	T	151
Nethercote	Oxon	SU7098	51°40·8'	0°58·9'W	X	165
Nethercote	Somer	SS8736	51°7·0'	3°36·5'W	X	181
Nethercote	Warw	SP2534	52°0·5'	1°37·8'W	X	151
Nethercote	Warw	SP5164	52°16·5'	1°14·8'W	T	151
Nethercote Brook	Warw	SP2536	52°1·5'	1°37·7'W	W	151
Nethercott	Devon	SS3721	50°58·2'	4°18·9'W	X	190
Nethercott	Devon	SS4839	51°8·0'	4°10·0'W	T	180
Nethercott	Devon	SS5324	51°0·0'	4°5·3'W	X	180
Nethercott	Devon	SS6912	50°53·8'	3°51·4'W	X	180
Nethercott	Devon	SX3596	50°44·6'	4°19·9'W	T	190
Nethercott	Devon	SX5495	50°44·4'	4°3·8'W	X	191
Nethercott	Devon	SX6995	50°44·6'	3°51·0'W	X	191
Nethercott	Oxon	SP4820	51°52·8'	1°17·8'W	T	164
Nethercott	Shrops	SO6778	52°24·2'	2°28·7'W	X	138
Nethercott	Somer	ST1432	51°5·1'	3°13·3'W	T	181
Nethercott Barton	Devon	SS5606	50°50·4'	4°2·3'W	X	191
Nethercott Fm	Devon	SS9020	50°58·4'	3°33·6'W	FM	181
Nethercott Ho	Devon	SS5606	50°50·4'	4°2·3'W	X	191
Nethercott Manor Fm	Devon	SS7920	50°58·2'	3°43·0'W	FM	180
Nether Coul	Moray	NJ2130	57°21·5'	3°18·3'W	X	36
Nether Coul	Pth & Kin	NN9613	56°18·1'	3°40·4'W	X	58
Nether Coullie	Aberd	NJ7115	57°13·7'	2°28·4'W	X	38
Nether Coullie	Aberd	NO7176	56°52·7'	2°28·1'W	X	45
Nether Court Fm	Leic	SK7204	52°38·0'	0°55·8'W	FM	141
Nether Crae	D & G	NX6667	54°59·0'	4°5·2'W	X	83,84
Nether Craig	Angus	NO2652	56°39·5'	3°12·0'W	X	53
Nether Craig	E Ayr	NS3737	55°36·2'	4°34·8'W	X	70
Nethercraig	E Renf	NS5950	55°43·6'	4°14·3'W	X	64
Nether Craig	Pth & Kin	NO1661	56°44·2'	3°21·9'W	H	43
Nether Craig	Scot Bord	NT2410	55°22·9'	3°11·5'W	H	79
Nether Craigenputtock	D & G	NX7883	55°7·8'	3°54·4'W	X	78
Nether Craighill	Aberd	NO8077	56°53·3'	2°19·2'W	X	45
Nether Craigwell	Aberd	NO8494	57°2·5'	2°15·4'W	X	38,45
Nether Criggie	Aberd	NO8382	56°56·0'	2°16·3'W	X	45
Nether Crimond	Aberd	NJ8222	57°17·6'	2°17·5'W	X	38
Nether Cule Burn	Scot Bord	NT0625	55°30·8'	3°28·9'W	W	72
Nether Culzean	S Ayr	NS3111	55°22·1'	4°39·6'W	X	70
Nether Cuttlehill	Aberd	NJ4947	57°30·9'	2°50·6'W	X	28,29
Netherdale	Shetld	HU1752	60°15·4'	1°41·1'W	X	3
Netherdale Ho	Aberd	NJ6548	57°31·5'	2°34·6'W	X	29
Nether Dalgliesh	Scot Bord	NT2709	55°22·4'	3°8·7'W	X	79
Nether Dalgliesh Burn	Scot Bord	NT2510	55°22·9'	3°10·6'W	W	79
Nether Dalgliesh Hope	Scot Bord	NT2609	55°22·4'	3°9·6'W	X	79
Nether Dallachy	Aberd	NJ6464	57°40·1'	2°35·7'W	X	29
Nether Dallachy	Moray	NJ3663	57°39·4'	3°3·9'W	T	28
Nether Dargavel	D & G	NY0175	55°3·8'	3°32·6'W	X	84
Nether Darley	Aberd	NJ7239	57°26·7'	2°27·5'W	X	29
Nether Daugh	Aberd	NJ8015	57°13·8'	2°19·4'W	X	38
Nether Dechmont	W Loth	NT0369	55°54·5'	3°32·7'W	X	65
Nether Denend	Aberd	NJ9953	57°34·3'	2°0·5'W	X	30
Nether Dod	D & G	NX9796	55°15·1'	3°36·8'W	H	78
Netherdowns	Devon	SS4723	50°59·4'	4°10·4'W	X	180
Nether Drumallochie	Aberd	NJ4714	57°13·1'	2°52·2'W	X	37
Nether Drumgley	Angus	NO4250	56°38·6'	2°56·3'W	X	54
Nether Drumhead	Angus	NO2155	56°41·1'	3°16·9'W	X	53
Nether Drums	Fife	NO2706	56°14·7'	3°10·2'W	X	59

Nether Dullarg	D & G	NX6873	55°2·3'	4°3·5'W	X	77,84
Nether Durdie	Pth & Kin	NO2124	56°24·4'	3°16·4'W	X	53,58
Nether Dysart	Angus	NO6953	56°40·3'	2°29·9'W	T	54
Nether Easter Offerance	Stir	NS5896	56°8·4'	4°16·7'W	X	57
Nether Edge	Sheff	SK3384	53°21·3'	1°29·8'W	T	110,111
Nether End	Derby	SK2572	53°14·9'	1°37·1'W	T	119
Netherend	Glos	SO5900	51°42·1'	2°35·2'W	T	162
Nether End	Kirk	SE2407	53°33·8'	1°37·8'W	T	110
Nether End	Leic	SK7414	52°43·3'	0°53·9'W	T	129
Nether Enoch	E Renf	NS5850	55°43·6'	4°15·2'W	X	64
Nether Ernambrie	D & G	NX7665	54°58·1'	3°55·8'W	X	84
Nether Ervie	D & G	NX6772	55°1·7'	4°4·4'W	X	77,84
Nether Exe	Devon	SS9300	50°47·6'	3°30·7'W	T	192
Netherexe	Devon	ST0212	50°54·2'	3°23·2'W	X	181
Nether Falla	Scot Bord	NT2451	55°45·0'	3°12·2'W	X	66,73
Netherfield	D & G	NX9070	55°1·0'	3°42·8'W	X	84
Netherfield	D & G	NY0580	55°6·6'	3°28·9'W	X	78
Netherfield	E Susx	TQ7118	50°56·4'	0°26·4'E	T	199
Netherfield	Mil Key	SP8736	52°1·2'	0°43·5'W	T	152
Netherfield	Notts	SK6140	52°57·5'	1°5·1'W	T	129
Nether Field	Notts	SK6351	53°3·4'	1°3·2'W	X	120
Netherfield	Renf	NS4467	55°52·5'	4°29·2'W	X	64
Netherfield Court	E Susx	TQ7118	50°56·4'	0°26·4'E	X	199
Netherfield Fm	Derby	SK2841	52°58·2'	1°34·6'W	FM	119,128
Netherfield Fm	Notts	SK6648	53°1·7'	1°0·5'W	FM	129
Netherfield Ho	Herts	TL3911	51°47·0'	0°1·3'E	X	166
Netherfield Ho	S Lanak	NS7145	55°41·1'	4°2·7'W	X	64
Nether Fieldhouse	S Lanak	NS8435	55°35·9'	3°50·0'W	X	71,72
Netherfield Place	E Susx	TQ7217	50°55·8'	0°27·3'E	X	199
Nether Fingland	S Lanak	NS9310	55°22·6'	3°40·9'W	X	71,78
Nether Finlarg	Angus	NO4241	56°33·7'	2°56·2'W	X	54
Nether Fordun	Pth & Kin	NN9516	56°19·7'	3°41·4'W	X	58
Nether Garrel	D & G	NY0588	55°10·9'	3°29·1'W	X	78
Nether Garvock	Pth & Kin	NO0315	56°19·3'	3°33·7'W	X	58
Nethergate	Norf	TG0529	52°49·4'	1°3·0'E	T	133
Nethergill	N Yks	SD8682	54°14·3'	2°12·5'W	X	98
Nether Glaisters	D & G	NX7679	55°5·6'	3°56·2'W	X	84
Nether Glanlair	D & G	NX7571	55°1·3'	3°56·9'W	X	84
Nether Glasslaw	Aberd	NJ8659	57°37·5'	2°13·6'W	X	30
Nether Glastry	Stir	NN7404	56°13·0'	4°1·5'W	X	57
Netherglen	Moray	NJ2454	57°34·4'	3°15·8'W	X	28
Nether Glenny	Stir	NN5701	56°11·1'	4°17·8'W	X	57
Nether Glensone	D & G	NX9159	54°55·1'	3°41·6'W	X	84
Nether Glenton	Aberd	NJ6612	57°12·1'	2°33·3'W	X	38
Nether Glinns Fm	Stir	NS6088	56°4·1'	4°14·5'W	FM	57
Nethergong Fm	Kent	TR2263	51°19·6'	1°11·6'E	FM	179
Nether Gothens	Pth & Kin	NO1740	56°32·9'	3°20·6'W	X	53
Nether Gree	N Ayr	NS3850	55°43·2'	4°34·3'W	X	63
Nether Gribton	D & G	NX9280	55°6·4'	3°41·1'W	X	78
Nethergrove	Devon	SS6020	50°58·0'	3°59·2'W	X	180
Nether Hailes	E Loth	NT5675	55°58·2'	2°41·9'W	X	67
Nether Hall	C of Leic	SK6306	52°39·1'	1°3·7'W	T	140
Netherhall	Cumbr	NY0436	54°42·8'	3°29·0'W	A	89
Nether Hall	Cumbr	SD4384	54°15·2'	2°52·1'W	X	97
Nether Hall	Cumbr	SD6082	54°14·2'	2°36·4'W	X	97
Nether Hall	Derby	SK2281	53°19·8'	1°39·8'W	X	110
Nether Hall	Derby	SK3121	52°47·4'	1°32·0'W	X	128
Netherhall	D & G	NX7360	54°55·4'	3°58·5'W	X	83,84
Netherhall	D & G	NY1287	55°10·4'	3°22·5'W	X	78
Nether Hall	Essex	TL3908	51°45·4'	0°1·2'E	A	166
Nether Hall	Essex	TL5306	51°44·1'	0°13·3'E	X	167
Nether Hall	Essex	TL8039	52°1·4'	0°37·8'E	X	155
Nether Hall	Essex	TM1331	51°56·4'	1°6·3'E	X	168,169
Nether Hall	Leic	SK6606	52°39·1'	1°1·1'W	X	141
Netherhall	N Ayr	NS2060	55°48·2'	4°51·9'W	X	63
Netherhall	N Lanak	NS8657	55°47·8'	3°48·7'W	X	65,72
Netherhall	Pth & Kin	NO1005	56°14·0'	3°26·7'W	X	58
Netherhall	S Lanak	NS8838	55°37·6'	3°46·3'W	X	71,72
Nether Hall	Suff	TL9246	52°5·0'	0°48·5'E	X	155
Nether Hall	Suff	TL9249	52°6·6'	0°48·6'E	X	155
Nether Hall	Suff	TL9266	52°15·7'	0°49·2'E	X	155
Nether Hall	Suff	TM1933	51°57·4'	1°11·6'E	X	168,169
Netherhall Fm	Cambs	TL4755	52°10·4'	0°9·4'E	FM	154
Netherhampton	Wilts	SU1029	51°3·8'	1°51·1'W	T	184
Nether Handley	Derby	SK4077	53°17·5'	1°23·6'W	T	120
Nether Handwick	Angus	NO3641	56°33·7'	3°2·0'W	T	54
Nether Hangingshaw	S Lanak	NT0033	55°35·1'	3°34·8'W	X	72
Nether Haresceugh	Cumbr	NY5742	54°46·5'	2°39·7'W	A	86
Nether Harsley	Northum	NY7849	54°50·4'	2°20·1'W	X	86,87
Nether Haugh	Roth	SK4196	53°27·8'	1°22·5'W	T	111
Nether Hawkhillock	Aberd	NK0137	57°25·7'	1°58·5'W	X	30
Nether Hay	Staffs	SK0060	53°8·5'	1°59·6'W	X	119
Nether Hayston	Angus	NO4146	56°36·4'	2°57·2'W	X	54
Nether Hazelfield	D & G	NX7848	54°49·0'	3°53·5'W	X	84
Nether Headon	Notts	SK7477	53°17·3'	0°53·0'W	T	120
Nether Heage	Derby	SK3650	53°3·0'	1°27·4'W	T	119
Nether Heilar	E Ayr	NS5825	55°30·1'	4°14·5'W	X	71
Nether Hesleden	N Yks	SD8874	54°9·9'	2°10·6'W	X	98
Nether Hey	Sheff	SK1793	53°26·2'	1°44·2'W	H	110
Nether Heyford	Northnts	SP6658	52°13·2'	1°1·6'W	T	152
Netherhill	Aberd	NK0852	57°33·7'	1°51·5'W	X	30
Nether Hill	Cumbr	NY5075	55°4·3'	2°46·6'W	X	86
Nether Hill	D & G	NS9002	55°18·2'	3°43·5'W	H	78
Nether Hill	D & G	NX8561	54°56·1'	3°47·3'W	H	84
Netherhill	E Ayr	NS3948	55°42·2'	4°33·3'W	X	63
Netherhill	Orkney	HY5007	58°57·1'	2°51·7'W	X	6,7
Nether Hill	Scot Bord	NT3624	55°30·6'	3°0·4'W	X	73
Nether Hill	Scot Bord	NT4040	55°39·2'	2°56·8'W	H	73
Netherhill	S Lanak	NS8421	55°28·4'	3°49·7'W	X	71,72
Nether Hillhouse	W Loth	NS9269	55°54·4'	3°43·2'W	X	65
Netherhills	Aberd	NJ7859	57°37·5'	2°21·6'W	X	29,30
Nether Hilton	Aberd	NJ4240	57°27·1'	2°57·5'W	X	28
Nether Hindhope	Scot Bord	NT7610	55°23·3'	2°22·3'W	X	80
Netherhirst	Cumbr	NY4473	55°3·2'	2°52·2'W	X	85
Nether Ho	Brad	SE0539	53°51·1'	1°55·0'W	X	104
Nether Ho	Orkney	HY4343	59°16·4'	2°59·5'W	X	5
Nether Hoff	Cumbr	NY6620	54°34·7'	2°31·1'W	X	91
Netherholm	D & G	NX9681	55°7·0'	3°37·4'W	X	78
Netherholm	Pth & Kin	NO0616	56°19·9'	3°30·8'W	X	58
Netherholm	S Lanak	NS6842	55°39·5'	4°5·5'W	X	71

Nether Holm of Dalquhain	D & G	NX6599	55°16·3'	4°7·1'W	X	77
Nether Horsburgh	Scot Bord	NT3039	55°38·6'	3°6·3'W	T	73
Netherhouse	C of Glas	NS6965	55°51·9'	4°5·2'W	X	64
Netherhouse	Orkney	HY3417	59°2·4'	3°8·5'W	X	6
Netherhouse	Orkney	HY3718	59°2·9'	3°5·4'W	X	6
Netherhouse	S Lanak	NS8038	55°37·5'	3°53·9'W	X	71,72
Nether House Fm	Cumbr	NY5100	54°23·8'	2°44·9'W	FM	90
Nether House Fm	Essex	TL8336	51°59·8'	0°40·3'E	FM	155
Netherhouses	Cumbr	SD2782	54°14·0'	3°6·8'W	X	96,97
Netherhouses	E Dunb	NS6771	55°55·1'	4°7·3'W	X	64
Nether Houses	Northum	NY8397	55°16·3'	2°15·6'W	X	80
Netherhouses	Renf	NS3556	55°46·4'	4°37·4'W	X	63
Netherhouses	W Loth	NS9366	55°52·8'	3°42·2'W	X	65
Nether Howbog	Moray	NJ4025	57°19·0'	2°59·3'W	X	37
Netherhowden	Scot Bord	NT5053	55°46·3'	2°47·4'W	X	66,73
Nether Howecleuch	S Lanak	NT0312	55°23·8'	3°31·5'W	X	78
Nether Hurst	Derby	SK2282	53°20·3'	1°39·8'W	X	110
Nether Hutton	D & G	NY1689	55°11·5'	3°18·7'W	X	79
Nether Hythie	Aberd	NK0150	57°32·7'	1°58·5'W	X	30
Netherinch	N Lanak	NS6876	55°57·8'	4°6·4'W	X	64
Nether Inver	Aberd	NJ7013	57°12·7'	2°29·3'W	X	38
Nether Keir	D & G	NX8790	55°11·7'	3°46·1'W	X	78
Nether Keith	E Loth	NT4564	55°52·2'	2°52·3'W	X	66
Nether Kellet	Lancs	SD5068	54°6·6'	2°45·5'W	T	97
Nether Kelly	Angus	NO5938	56°32·2'	2°39·6'W	X	54
Nether Kidston	Scot Bord	NT2343	55°40·6'	3°13·0'W	T	73
Nether Kildrummy	Aberd	NJ4616	57°14·2'	2°53·2'W	X	37
Nether Kinknockie	Aberd	NK0040	57°27·3'	1°59·5'W	X	30
Nether Kinmundy	Aberd	NK0443	57°28·9'	1°55·5'W	T	30
Nether Kinneddar	Fife	NT0291	56°6·4'	3°34·1'W	X	58
Nether Kinneil	Falk	NS9780	56°0·4'	3°38·7'W	X	65
Nether Kirkton	Aberd	NJ8134	57°24·0'	2°18·5'W	X	29,30
Nether Kirkton	E Renf	NS4857	55°47·2'	4°25·0'W	T	64
Nether Knock	D & G	NY3090	55°12·2'	3°5·6'W	X	79
Nether Knox	Aberd	NO8169	56°49·0'	2°18·2'W	X	45
Nether Kypeside	S Lanak	NS7541	55°39·0'	3°58·8'W	X	71
Nether Laggan	D & G	NX7171	55°1·3'	4°0·6'W	X	77,84
Netherland Green	Staffs	SK1030	52°52·3'	1°50·7'W	T	128
Netherlands	Aberd	NJ6404	57°7·8'	2°35·2'W	X	37
Netherlands	N Yks	SE4552	53°58·0'	1°18·4'W	X	105
Netherlands	Surrey	TQ0549	51°14·1'	0°29·4'W	F	187
Netherlands Fm	E Ayr	NS4733	55°34·3'	4°25·2'W	FM	70
Netherlands Fm	W Susx	SU9321	50°59·1'	0°40·1'W	FM	197
Nether Langwith	Notts	SK5370	53°13·7'	1°12·0'W	T	120
Nether Lauchentilly	Aberd	NJ7411	57°11·6'	2°25·4'W	X	38
Netherlaw	D & G	NX7445	54°47·3'	3°57·1'W	X	83,84
Nether Law	S Lanak	NS9705	55°19·9'	3°37·0'W	H	78
Netherlaw Burn	D & G	NX7344	54°46·7'	3°58·1'W	W	83,84
Netherlaw Ho	D & G	NX7444	54°46·8'	3°57·1'W	X	83,84
Netherlaw Point	D & G	NX7143	54°46·2'	3°59·9'W	X	83,84
Netherlay	Dorset	ST4105	50°50·7'	2°49·9'W	T	193
Nether Leask	Aberd	NK0232	57°23·0'	1°57·5'W	X	30
Netherlee	E Renf	NS5758	55°47·9'	4°16·4'W	T	64
Nether Lennie	C of Edin	NT1675	55°57·9'	3°20·3'W	X	65,66
Nether Lenshie	Aberd	NJ6840	57°27·2'	2°31·5'W	X	29
Nether Lethame	S Lanak	NS6844	55°40·5'	4°5·5'W	X	71
Netherley	Aberd	NO8493	57°1·9'	2°15·4'W	T	38,45
Netherley	Kirk	SE0410	53°35·4'	1°56·0'W	T	110
Netherley	Liv	SJ4488	53°23·4'	2°50·1'W	T	108
Netherley Fm	Hants	SU7215	50°56·0'	0°58·1'W	FM	197
Netherley Ho	Aberd	NO8493	57°1·9'	2°15·4'W	X	38,45
Nether Linkins	D & G	NX7454	54°52·1'	3°57·4'W	X	83,84
Nether Linklater	Orkney	HY2621	59°4·4'	3°17·0'W	X	6
Nether Loads	Derby	SK3269	53°13·3'	1°30·8'W	T	119
Nether Locharwoods	D & G	NY0567	54°59·6'	3°28·7'W	X	85
Nether Lochty	Fife	NO5208	56°16·0'	2°46·1'W	X	59
Nether Lodge	N Yks	SD7977	54°11·5'	2°18·9'W	X	98
Nether Logie	Pth & Kin	NO3246	56°36·3'	3°6·0'W	X	53
Nether Longford	W Loth	NS9861	55°50·1'	3°37·3'W	X	65
Nether Low	Derby	SK1069	53°13·3'	1°50·6'W	X	119
Netherlow Fm	Derby	SK1069	53°13·3'	1°50·6'W	FM	119
Nether Lypiatt Manor	Glos	SO8703	51°43·8'	2°10·9'W	A	162
Nether Magask	Fife	NO4415	56°19·7'	2°53·9'W	X	59
Nether Mains	Aberd	NJ6200	57°5·6'	2°37·2'W	X	37
Nether Mains	Aberd	NJ7014	57°13·2'	2°29·4'W	X	38
Nethermains	D & G	NY1869	55°0·8'	3°16·5'W	X	85
Nether Mains	Pth & Kin	NO2019	56°21·7'	3°17·2'W	X	58
Nether Mains	Scot Bord	NT8855	55°47·6'	2°11·0'W	X	67,74
Nethermains of Gorthy	Pth & Kin	NN9623	56°23·5'	3°40·6'W	X	52,53,58
Nether Meft	Moray	NJ2764	57°39·9'	3°13·0'W	X	28
Nether Middleton	Angus	NO3743	56°34·7'	3°1·1'W	X	54
Nether Migvie	Angus	NO3954	56°40·7'	2°59·3'W	X	54
Nethermill	Aberd	NJ7144	57°29·4'	2°28·6'W	X	29
Nethermill	Aberd	NJ7914	57°13·2'	2°20·4'W	X	38
Nether Mill	Aberd	NJ9334	57°24·0'	2°6·5'W	X	30
Nethermill	Aberd	NK0836	57°25·1'	1°51·6'W	X	30
Nethermill	D & G	NX9858	54°54·6'	3°35·0'W	X	84
Nethermill	D & G	NY0487	55°10·3'	3°30·0'W	T	78
Nethermill	Pth & Kin	NO2036	56°30·8'	3°17·6'W	X	53
Nether Mill of Birness	Aberd	NJ9832	57°23·0'	2°1·5'W	X	30
Nethermill of Tillyhilt	Aberd	NJ8531	57°22·4'	2°14·5'W	X	30
Nether Mills	Aberd	NJ5757	57°36·3'	2°42·7'W	X	29
Nethermills	Moray	NJ5050	57°32·5'	2°49·7'W	T	29
Nether Mills of Crathes	Aberd	NO7596	57°3·5'	2°24·3'W	X	38,45
Nether Minmore	Aberd	NJ4913	57°12·6'	2°50·2'W	X	37
Nether Monynut	Scot Bord	NT7264	55°52·4'	2°26·4'W	X	67
Nether Moor	Derby	SK1487	53°23·0'	1°47·0'W	X	110
Nether Moor	Derby	SK3866	53°11·6'	1°25·5'W	T	119
Nether Moor	Somer	ST3732	51°5·3'	2°53·6'W	X	182
Nethermoor House	Derby	SK4260	53°8·4'	1°21·9'W	X	120
Nethermore Fm	Wilts	ST9469	51°25·4'	2°4·8'W	FM	173
Nethermost Cove	Cumbr	NY3414	54°31·3'	3°0·8'W	X	90
Nethermost Pike	Cumbr	NY3414	54°31·3'	3°0·8'W	H	90
Nethermuir	Aberd	NJ7208	57°10·0'	2°27·3'W	X	38
Nethermuir	Aberd	NJ9044	57°29·4'	2°9·6'W	T	30
Nethermuir	Angus	NO5252	56°39·7'	2°46·5'W	X	54
Nethermuir	S Ayr	NS3528	55°31·3'	4°36·4'W	X	70
Nethermuir	W Loth	NS9570	55°55·0'	3°40·4'W	X	65
Nether Muirskie	Aberd	NO8395	57°3·0'	2°16·4'W	X	38,45
Nether Mumbie	D & G	NY3779	55°6·3'	2°58·8'W	X	85

Nether Murthat	D & G	NY1098	55°16·3′	3°24·6′W	X	78
Nethermyers	Fife	NO2410	56°16·8′	3°13·2′W	X	59
Nether Newton	E Ayr	NS5039	55°37·5′	4°22·5′W	X	70
Nether Obney	Pth & Kin	NO0336	56°30·6′	3°34·1′W	X	52,53
Nether Oldhall	E Ayr	NS3949	55°42·7′	4°33·3′W	X	63
Nether Oliver Dod	Scot Bord	NT0926	55°31·4′	3°26·1′W	H	72
Nether Ord	Aberd	NJ4927	57°20·1′	2°50·4′W	X	37
Netheroyd Hill	Kirk	SE1419	53°40·3′	1°46·9′W	T	110
Nether Padley	Derby	SK2578	53°18·1′	1°37·1′W	T	119
Nether Park	Aberd	NK0056	57°35·9′	1°59·5′W	X	30
Nether Park	Aberd	NO7797	57°4·1′	2°22·3′W	X	38,45
Nether Park	N Yks	SE4981	54°13·6′	1°14·5′W	X	100
Netherpark Fm	Derby	SK3251	53°3·6′	1°30·9′W	FM	119
Netherpaths	Heref	SO7540	52°3·7′	2°21·5′W	X	150
Nether Phawhope	Scot Bord	NT2111	55°23·4′	3°14·4′W	X	79
Nether Pirn	Scot Bord	NT3437	55°37·6′	3°2·5′W	X	73
Nether Pitforthie	Aberd	NO8079	56°54·4′	2°19·3′W	X	45
Netherplace	E Renf	NS5255	55°46·2′	4°21·1′W	T	64
Nether Poppleton	York	SE5654	53°59·0′	1°8·3′W	T	105
Nether Port	Highld	NJ0628	57°20·2′	3°33·2′W	X	36
Nether Pratis	Fife	NO3805	56°14·3′	2°59·6′W	X	59
Netherraith Fm	E Ayr	NS4641	55°38·5′	4°26·4′W	FM	70
Netherraw	Scot Bord	NT5523	55°30·2′	2°42·3′W	T	73
Netherraw	Scot Bord	NY5093	55°14·0′	2°46·7′W	X	79
Nether Reddale Clough	Derby	SK1192	53°25·7′	1°49·7′W	X	110
Nether Rig	D & G	NX9190	55°11·8′	3°42·3′W	X	78
Nether Ringorm	Moray	NJ2644	57°29·1′	3°13·6′W	X	28
Nether Rodnoll Fm	Derby	SK3070	53°13·8′	1°32·6′W	FM	119
Nether Ross	Arg & Bt	NS3585	56°2·0′	4°38·5′W	X	56
Nether Row	Cumbr	NY3237	54°43·7′	3°2·9′W	T	90
Nether Rusko	D & G	NX5860	54°55·1′	4°12·5′W	X	83
Nether Ruthven	Aberd	NJ4602	57°6·6′	2°53·0′W	X	37
Nether Sauchen	Aberd	NJ6710	57°11·0′	2°32·3′W	X	38
Nether Savock	Aberd	NK0643	57°28·9′	1°53·5′W	X	30
Netherscale	Cumbr	NY1730	54°39·7′	3°16·8′W	X	89,90
Netherscales	Cumbr	NY4438	54°44·3′	2°51·8′W	X	90
Nether Scarsick	Corn	SX2088	50°40·1′	4°32·5′W	X	190
Nether Scythie	Angus	NO2457	56°42·2′	3°14·0′W	X	53
Netherseal	Derby	SK2813	52°43·1′	1°34·7′W	T	128
Netherset Hey	Staffs	SJ7843	52°59·3′	2°19·3′W	X	118
Nethershaugh Fm	Devon	SX5362	50°26·6′	4°3·8′W	FM	201
Nethershiel	W Loth	NT0969	55°54·6′	3°26·9′W	X	65
Nethershield	E Ayr	NS5826	55°30·7′	4°14·5′W	X	71
Nethershields	S Lanak	NS6948	55°42·7′	4°4·7′W	X	64
Nethershields	S Lanak	NS7048	55°42·7′	4°3·7′W	X	64
Nether Shiels	Aberd	NJ6509	57°10·5′	2°34·3′W	X	38
Nether Shiels	Scot Bord	NT4146	55°42·5′	2°55·9′W	T	73
Nether Shiels Burn	Scot Bord	NT4144	55°41·4′	2°55·9′W	W	73
Netherside	Highld	ND2058	58°30·4′	3°21·9′W	X	11,12
Netherside	S Lanak	NS7143	55°40·1′	4°2·6′W	X	71
Netherside Hall School	N Yks	SD9864	54°4·6′	2°1·4′W	X	98
Nether Silton	N Yks	SE4592	54°19·5′	1°18·1′W	T	99
Netherskaill	Orkney	HY2324	59°6·0′	3°20·2′W	X	6
Nether Skyborry	Shrops	SO2773	52°21·3′	3°3·9′W	T	137,148
Nether Southbar	Renf	NS4568	55°53·1′	4°28·2′W	X	64
Nether St	Suff	TL9261	52°13·0′	0°49·0′E	T	155
Nether Stainton	Cumbr	SD1195	54°20·8′	3°21·7′W	X	96
Netherstead	Warw	SP1063	52°16·1′	1°50·8′W	X	150
Nether Stenries	D & G	NY1270	55°1·3′	3°22·2′W	X	85
Nether Stenton	Fife	NT2699	56°10·9′	3°11·1′W	X	59
Netherstoke	Dorset	ST5409	50°53·0′	2°38·9′W	T	194
Netherstove	Orkney	HY2419	59°3·3′	3°19·0′W	X	6
Nether Stowe	Staffs	SK1210	52°41·5′	1°48·9′W	T	128
Nether Stowey	Somer	ST1939	51°8·9′	3°9·1′W	T	181
Nether Strathkinness	Fife	NO4715	56°19·7′	2°51·0′W	X	59
Nether Stravannan	Arg & Bt	NS0757	55°46·3′	5°4·2′W	X	63
Nether Street	Essex	TL5812	51°47·3′	0°17·8′E	T	167
Nether Street	Herts	TL4216	51°49·7′	0°4·0′E	T	167
Netherstreet Fm	Wilts	ST9865	51°23·3′	2°1·3′W	FM	173
Nether Sturston	Derby	SK1946	53°0·9′	1°42·6′W	X	119,128
Nether Swanley	Aberd	NO8287	56°58·7′	2°17·3′W	X	45
Nether Swell Manor	Glos	SP1824	51°55·1′	1°43·9′W	X	163
Nether Terryvale	Aberd	NJ7809	57°10·5′	2°21·4′W	X	38
Nether Thainston	Aberd	NO6374	56°51·6′	2°36·0′W	X	45
Netherthird	Aberd	NJ6839	57°26·7′	2°31·5′W	X	29
Netherthird	D & G	NX7155	54°52·6′	4°0·2′W	X	83,84
Netherthird	E Ayr	NS5718	55°26·4′	4°15·2′W	T	71
Netherthong	Kirk	SE1309	53°34·9′	1°47·8′W	T	110
Netherthorpe	Derby	SK4474	53°15·9′	1°20·0′W	T	120
Netherthorpe	Roth	SK5380	53°19·1′	1°11·9′W	X	111,120
Nether Tillygarmond	Aberd	NO6293	57°1·8′	2°37·1′W	X	37,45
Nether Tillylair	Aberd	NJ5402	57°6·7′	2°45·1′W	X	37
Nether Tillymauld	Aberd	NJ8154	57°34·8′	2°18·6′W	X	29,30
Nether Tillyrie	Pth & Kin	NO1105	56°14·0′	3°25·7′W	X	58
Nether Timble	N Yks	SE1852	53°58·1′	1°43·1′W	X	104
Nether Toes	Kent	TQ8965	51°21·4′	0°43·3′E	X	178
Nether Tofts	Scot Bord	NT5514	55°25·3′	2°42·2′W	X	80
Nether Tomdow	Moray	NJ1841	57°27·4′	3°21·5′W	X	28
Netherton	Aberd	NJ3517	57°14·6′	3°4·2′W	X	37
Netherton	Aberd	NJ4237	57°25·4′	2°57·5′W	X	28
Netherton	Aberd	NJ4604	57°7·7′	2°53·1′W	X	37
Netherton	Aberd	NJ5048	57°31·4′	2°49·6′W	X	29
Netherton	Aberd	NJ5425	57°19·1′	2°45·4′W	X	37
Netherton	Aberd	NJ6030	57°21·8′	2°39·4′W	X	29,37
Netherton	Aberd	NJ6419	57°15·9′	2°35·4′W	X	37
Netherton	Aberd	NJ6736	57°25·0′	2°32·5′W	X	29
Netherton	Aberd	NJ7116	57°14·3′	2°28·4′W	X	38
Netherton	Aberd	NJ7911	57°11·6′	2°20·4′W	X	38
Netherton	Aberd	NJ8142	57°28·3′	2°18·5′W	X	29,30
Netherton	Aberd	NJ8757	57°36·4′	2°12·6′W	X	30
Netherton	Aberd	NK0457	57°36·4′	1°55·5′W	X	30
Netherton	Aberd	NK0545	57°30·0′	1°54·5′W	X	30
Netherton	Aberd	NO4597	57°3·9′	2°54·0′W	X	37,44
Netherton	Angus	NO5457	56°42·4′	2°44·6′W	T	54
Netherton	Ches	SJ5176	53°17·0′	2°43·7′W	T	117
Netherton	Corn	SX1558	50°23·8′	4°35·8′W	X	201
Netherton	Corn	SX2872	50°31·6′	4°25·2′W	T	201
Netherton	Cumbr	NY0335	54°42·3′	3°29·9′W	T	89
Netherton	Cumbr	NY4151	54°51·3′	2°54·7′W	X	85
Netherton	Cumbr	NY5357	54°54·6′	2°43·6′W	X	86

Netherton	Devon	SX7746	50°18·3′	3°43·3′W	X	202
Netherton	Devon	SX8262	50°27·0′	3°39·3′W	X	202
Netherton	Devon	SX8971	50°31·9′	3°33·6′W	T	202
Netherton	D & G	NS7013	55°23·9′	4°2·7′W	X	71
Netherton	Dudley	SO9488	52°29·6′	2°4·9′W	T	139
Netherton	E Ayr	NS4254	55°45·5′	4°30·6′W	X	64
Netherton	E Ayr	NS5020	55°27·3′	4°21·9′W	X	70
Netherton	E Renf	NS5057	55°47·2′	4°23·1′W	X	64
Netherton	E Renf	NS5749	55°43·1′	4°16·2′W	X	64
Netherton	Glos	SP1504	51°44·3′	1°46·6′W	T	163
Netherton	Hants	SU3757	51°18·9′	1°27·8′W	T	174
Netherton	Heref	SO5226	51°56·1′	2°41·5′W	T	162
Netherton	Heref	SO5925	51°55·6′	2°35·4′W	X	162
Netherton	Highld	NC5001	57°58·6′	4°31·7′W	X	16
Netherton	Highld	ND2952	58°27·3′	3°12·5′W	X	11,12
Netherton	Kirk	SE1213	53°37·0′	1°48·7′W	T	110
Netherton	Moray	NJ0361	57°38·0′	3°37·0′W	X	27
Netherton	Moray	NJ3245	57°29·7′	3°7·6′W	X	28
Netherton	Moray	NJ5452	57°33·6′	2°45·7′W	X	29
Netherton	N Lanak	NS7854	55°46·1′	3°56·2′W	T	64
Netherton	Northum	NT9807	55°21·7′	2°1·5′W	T	81
Netherton	Orkney	HY4902	58°54·4′	2°52·6′W	X	6,7
Netherton	Oxon	SU4199	51°41·5′	1°24·0′W	T	164
Netherton	Pth & Kin	NN8659	56°42·8′	3°51·3′W	X	43,52
Netherton	Pth & Kin	NN8708	56°15·3′	3°49·0′W	X	58
Netherton	Pth & Kin	NO1306	56°14·6′	3°23·8′W	X	58
Netherton	Pth & Kin	NO1452	56°39·4′	3°23·7′W	T	53
Netherton	Pth & Kin	NO1616	56°20·0′	3°21·1′W	X	58
Netherton	Pth & Kin	NO2646	56°36·3′	3°11·9′W	X	53
Netherton	Renf	NS3972	55°55·1′	4°34·1′W	X	63
Netherton	Renf	NS4967	55°52·6′	4°24·4′W	X	64
Netherton	S Ayr	NS3713	55°23·3′	4°34·0′W	X	70
Netherton	Sefton	SD3500	53°29·8′	2°58·4′W	T	108
Netherton	Shetld	HU4121	59°58·6′	1°15·4′W	X	4
Netherton	Shrops	SO7382	52°26·4′	2°23·4′W	T	138
Netherton	S Lanak	NS9240	55°38·7′	3°42·5′W	X	71,72
Netherton	S Lanak	NS9250	55°44·1′	3°42·8′W	X	65,72
Netherton	S Lanak	NT0136	55°36·7′	3°33·9′W	X	72
Netherton	Somer	ST5511	50°54·0′	2°38·0′W	X	194
Netherton	Stir	NN7402	56°11·9′	4°1·4′W	X	57
Netherton	Stir	NS5579	55°59·2′	4°19·0′W	T	64
Netherton	Stir	NS5988	56°4·1′	4°15·5′W	X	57
Netherton	Stir	NS6699	56°10·1′	4°9·0′W	X	57
Netherton	Stir	NS7896	56°8·7′	3°57·4′W	X	57
Netherton	Wakf	SE2716	53°38·6′	1°35·1′W	T	110
Netherton	Worcs	SO9941	52°4·3′	2°0·5′W	T	150
Netherton Barton	Devon	SY1895	50°45·2′	3°9·4′W	X	192,193
Netherton Burn	Northum	NT9707	55°21·7′	2°2·4′W	W	81
Netherton Burn	S Lanak	NS9051	55°44·6′	3°44·7′W	W	65,72
Netherton Burnfoot	Northum	NT9907	55°21·7′	2°0·5′W	X	81
Netherton Fields	Worcs	SO9840	52°3·7′	2°1·4′W	X	150
Netherton Fm	Devon	SS4909	50°51·9′	4°8·4′W	FM	191
Netherton Fm	Heref	SO7439	52°3·2′	2°22·4′W	FM	150
Netherton Fm	Moray	NJ4447	57°30·8′	2°55·6′W	FM	28
Netherton Fm	N Lanak	NS9065	55°52·2′	3°45·0′W	FM	65
Netherton Fm	S Lanak	NS9025	55°30·6′	3°44·1′W	FM	71,72
Netherton Hall	Derby	SK2252	53°4·1′	1°39·9′W	X	119
Netherton Ho	Devon	SX7391	50°42·5′	3°47·5′W	X	191
Netherton Ho	Devon	SX8972	50°32·5′	3°33·6′W	X	192,202
Netherton Ho	Worcs	SO7668	52°18·8′	2°20·7′W	X	138
Netherton House	Hants	SU3757	51°18·9′	1°27·8′W	A	174
Netherton Moor Fm	Northum	NZ2380	55°7·1′	1°37·9′W	FM	81
Netherton Northside	Northum	NT9907	55°21·7′	2°0·5′W	X	81
Netherton of Balquhain	Aberd	NJ7322	57°17·5′	2°26·4′W	X	38
Netherton of Dalcapon	Pth & Kin	NN9754	56°40·2′	3°40·4′W	X	52,53
Netherton of Garlogie	Aberd	NJ7806	57°8·9′	2°21·4′W	X	38
Netherton of Lethenty	Aberd	NJ7625	57°19·2′	2°23·5′W	X	38
Netherton of Lonmay	Aberd	NK0560	57°38·1′	1°54·5′W	X	30
Netherton of Mounie	Aberd	NJ7628	57°20·8′	2°23·5′W	X	38
Netherton Park	Northum	NZ2180	55°7·1′	1°39·8′W	X	81
Netherton Tunnel	Sand	SO9689	52°30·2′	2°3·1′W	X	139
Netherton Wood	Northum	NZ2281	55°7·6′	1°38·9′W	F	81
Netherton Wood	N Som	ST4568	51°24·7′	2°47·1′W	X	171,172,182
Nether Tor	Derby	SK1287	53°23·0′	1°48·8′W	X	110
Nether Toucks	Aberd	NO8584	56°57·1′	2°14·3′W	X	45
Nethertoun	Scot Bord	NT4450	55°44·7′	2°53·1′W	X	66,73
Nether Towie	Aberd	NJ4412	57°12·0′	2°55·2′W	X	37
Nethertown	Cumbr	NX9807	54°27·1′	3°34·0′W	T	89
Nethertown	D & G	NX7365	54°58·1′	3°58·6′W	X	83,84
Nethertown	D & G	NX8284	55°8·4′	3°50·6′W	X	78
Nethertown	D & G	NX8475	55°3·6′	3°48·5′W	X	84
Nethertown	D & G	NX9672	55°2·2′	3°37·2′W	X	84
Nethertown	D & G	NY1265	54°58·6′	3°22·1′W	X	85
Nethertown	D & G	NY3575	55°4·2′	3°0·6′W	X	85
Nethertown	Highld	ND3578	58°41·4′	3°6·8′W	T	7,12
Nethertown	Lancs	SD7236	53°49·4′	2°25·1′W	T	103
Nethertown	Moray	NJ1829	57°20·9′	3°21·3′W	X	36
Nethertown	Moray	NJ4957	57°36·3′	2°50·7′W	X	28,29
Nethertown	S Lanak	NS8143	55°40·2′	3°53·1′W	X	71,72
Nethertown	Staffs	SK1017	52°45·3′	1°50·7′W	T	128
Nethertown Burn	Scot Bord	NT4449	55°44·1′	2°53·1′W	W	73
Nether Town Hill	Pth & Kin	NO0204	56°13·4′	3°34·4′W	H	58
Nethertown Moor	D & G	NX8283	55°7·9′	3°50·6′W	X	78
Nethertown of Croys	D & G	NX7768	54°59·7′	3°54·9′W	X	84
Nethertown of Poniel	S Lanak	NS8234	55°35·4′	3°51·9′W	X	71,72
Nether Tulloch	Aberd	NJ8131	57°22·4′	2°18·5′W	X	29,30
Nether Tulloch	Aberd	NO7771	56°50·0′	2°22·2′W	X	45
Nether Tulloes	Angus	NO5045	56°35·9′	2°48·4′W	X	54
Nether Turin	Angus	NO5352	56°39·7′	2°45·6′W	X	54
Nether Unthank	Moray	NJ2966	57°41·0′	3°11·0′W	X	28
Netherurd	Scot Bord	NT1144	55°41·1′	3°24·5′W	X	72
Netherurd Mains	Scot Bord	NT1044	55°41·1′	3°25·5′W	X	72
Nether Urquhart	Fife	NO1808	56°15·7′	3°19·0′W	X	58
Nether Wallop	Hants	SU3036	51°7·6′	1°33·9′W	T	185
Nether Warburton	Aberd	NO7363	56°45·7′	2°26·0′W	X	45
Nether Warden	Northum	NY9167	55°0·1′	2°8·0′W	T	87
Nether Wasdale	Cumbr	NY1204	54°25·7′	3°21·0′W	T	89
Nether Wasdale Common	Cumbr	NY1307	54°27·3′	3°20·1′W	X	89
Nether Water Fm	Derby	SK1779	53°18·7′	1°44·3′W	FM	119
Netherwell	Devon	SS8327	51°2·1′	3°39·7′W	X	181

Nether Wells	Cumbr	SD4988	54°17·4′	2°46·6′W	X	97
Netherwells	Scot Bord	NT6820	55°28·6′	2°29·9′W	X	74
Nether Wellwood	E Ayr	NS6525	55°30·3′	4°7·8′W	X	71
Nether Welton	Cumbr	NY3545	54°48·0′	3°0·2′W	T	85
Nether Westcote	Glos	SP2220	51°52·9′	1°40·4′W	T	163
Nether Wheal	Derby	SK1569	53°13·3′	1°46·1′W	X	119
Nether Whitacre	Warw	SP2392	52°31·8′	1°39·3′W	T	139
Nether Whitecleuch	S Lanak	NS8319	55°27·3′	3°50·6′W	X	71,78
Nether Whitehaugh	E Ayr	NS6129	55°32·4′	4°11·7′W	X	71
Nether Whiteside Moor	D & G	NX8183	55°7·9′	3°51·6′W	X	78
Nether Whitlaw	Scot Bord	NT5129	55°33·4′	2°46·2′W	X	73
Nether Williamston	W Loth	NT0665	55°52·4′	3°29·7′W	X	65
Nether Winchendon Ho	Bucks	SP7311	51°47·8′	0°56·1′W	X	165
Nether Winchendon or Lower Winchendon	Bucks	SP7312	51°48·3′	0°56·1′W	T	165
Netherwitton	Northum	NZ0990	55°12·5′	1°51·1′W	T	81
Netherwitton Hall	Northum	NZ1090	55°12·5′	1°50·1′W	A	81
Netherwood	Aberd	NJ7160	57°38·0′	2°28·7′W	X	29
Netherwood	D & G	NX9872	55°2·2′	3°35·3′W	X	84
Netherwood	E Ayr	NS6628	55°31·9′	4°7·0′W	X	71
Nether Wood	Heref	SO5233	51°59·8′	2°41·6′W	F	149
Netherwood	Heref	SO6360	52°14·5′	2°32·1′W	A	138,149
Netherwood	Inverc	NS3469	55°53·4′	4°38·8′W	X	63
Netherwood	N Lanak	NS7778	55°59·0′	3°57·8′W	X	64
Netherwood	W Susx	TQ1325	51°1·0′	0°23·0′W	X	187,198
Netherwood Bank	D & G	NX9972	55°2·2′	3°34·4′W	X	84
Nether Woodburn	Devon	SS8723	51°0·0′	3°36·2′W	X	181
Netherwood Coppice	Shrops	SO5398	52°34·9′	2°41·2′W	F	137,138
Netherwood Dairy	NE Lincs	TA2404	53°31·3′	0°7·4′W	X	113
Netherwood Fm	Worcs	SO9158	52°13·4′	2°7·5′W	FM	150
Netherwood Heath	Warw	SP1973	52°21·5′	1°42·9′W	X	139
Netherwoodhill	Aberd	NJ8332	57°22·9′	2°16·5′W	X	29,30
Netherwood Ho	Brad	SE0847	53°55·4′	1°52·3′W	X	104
Nether Woodhouse	D & G	NY2671	55°1·9′	3°9·0′W	X	85
Nether Woodhouse Fm	Derby	SK4671	53°14·3′	1°18·2′W	FM	120
Netherwood Mains	D & G	NX9872	55°2·2′	3°35·3′W	X	84
Nether Woodston	Aberd	NO7565	56°46·8′	2°24·1′W	X	45
Nether Worton	Oxon	SP4230	51°58·2′	1°22·9′W	T	151
Netherwyde Fm	Herts	TL1501	51°42·0′	0°19·8′W	FM	166
Nether Wyndings	Aberd	NO8185	56°57·6′	2°18·3′W	X	45
Nether Yeadon	Leeds	SE2040	53°51·6′	1°41·3′W	T	104
Netheryett	D & G	NX8164	54°57·6′	3°51·1′W	X	84
Neth Hill, The	Scot Bord	NT3143	55°40·8′	3°5·4′W	X	73
Nethway Ho	Devon	SX9052	50°21·7′	3°32·4′W	X	202
Nethy Bridge	Highld	NJ0020	57°15·8′	3°39·0′W	T	36
Netley	Hants	SU4508	50°52·4′	1°21·2′W	T	196
Netley Hall	Shrops	SJ4701	52°36·5′	2°46·6′W	X	126
Netley Heath	Surrey	TQ0849	51°14·0′	0°26·8′W	F	187
Netley Hill	Hants	SU4711	50°54·0′	1°19·5′W	T	196
Netley Ho	Surrey	TQ0748	51°13·5′	0°27·7′W	X	187
Netley Marsh	Hants	SU3312	50°54·6′	1°31·5′W	T	196
Netley Old Hall Fm	Shrops	SJ4601	52°36·5′	2°47·4′W	FM	126
Nettacott	Devon	SX9099	50°47·0′	3°33·2′W	T	192
Netter's Hall Fm	Kent	TQ7733	51°4·4′	0°32·0′E	FM	188
Netteswell	Essex	TL4510	51°46·4′	0°6·5′E	T	167
Nettlebed	Oxon	SU6986	51°34·3′	0°59·9′W	T	175
Nettlebed Fm	Hants	SU6035	51°6·9′	1°8·2′W	FM	185
Nettlebed Ho	N Yks	SD9697	54°22·4′	2°3·3′W	X	98
Nettlebed Woods	Oxon	SU7185	51°33·8′	0°58·1′W	F	175
Nettlebridge	Somer	ST6448	51°14·0′	2°30·6′W	T	183
Nettle Brow	Cumbr	SD7694	54°20·7′	2°21·7′W	X	98
Nettlecombe	Dorset	SY5195	50°45·4′	2°41·3′W	T	194
Nettlecombe	I of W	SZ5278	50°36·2′	1°15·5′W	T	196
Nettlecombe Court	Somer	ST0537	51°7·7′	3°21·1′W	X	181
Nettlecombe Fm	Dorset	ST7401	50°48·7′	2°21·8′W	FM	194
Nettlecombe Tout	Dorset	ST7303	50°49·8′	2°22·6′W	X	194
Nettle Dale Wood	N Yks	SE5485	54°15·7′	1°9·8′W	F	100
Nettleden	Herts	TL0110	51°47·0′	0°31·8′W	T	166
Nettleden Lodge	Herts	TL0010	51°47·0′	0°32·6′W	X	166
Nettleford	Devon	SS8018	50°57·2′	3°42·1′W	X	181
Nettleford Wood	Ches	SJ5369	53°13·2′	2°41·8′W	F	117
Nettle Hall	Cumbr	NY7544	54°47·7′	2°22·9′W	X	86,87
Nettleham	Lincs	TF0075	53°16·0′	0°29·6′W	T	121
Nettleham Field	Lincs	SK9974	53°15·5′	0°30·5′W	X	121
Nettleham Hall	Lincs	SK9976	53°16·5′	0°30·5′W	X	121
Nettleham Well Fm	Notts	SK6995	53°27·1′	0°57·2′W	FM	111
Nettle Hill	Cumbr	NY7107	54°27·7′	2°26·4′W	H	91
Nettle Hill	Northum	NY8254	54°53·1′	2°16·4′W	X	86,87
Nettle Hill	Suff	TM2945	52°3·6′	1°20·8′E	X	169
Nettle Hill	Warw	SP4182	52°26·3′	1°23·4′W	X	140
Nettlehirst	N Ayr	NS3650	55°43·2′	4°36·2′W	X	63
Nettlehole Wood	N Yks	SD9856	54°0·2′	2°1·4′W	F	103
Nettlehope Hill	Northum	NT8911	55°23·8′	2°10·0′W	H	80
Nettlepot	Durham	NY9222	54°35·8′	2°7·0′W	X	91,92
Nettleslack	Cumbr	NY4218	54°33·5′	2°53·4′W	X	90
Nettleslack	Cumbr	SD2883	54°14·5′	3°5·9′W	X	96,97
Nettlestead	Kent	TQ6852	51°14·8′	0°24·8′E	T	188
Nettlestead	Suff	TM0849	52°6·2′	1°2·6′E	T	155,169
Nettlestead Green	Kent	TQ6850	51°13·7′	0°24·8′E	T	188
Nettlestone	I of W	SZ6290	50°42·6′	1°6·9′W	T	196
Nettlestone Allotment	N Yks	SD8284	54°15·3′	2°16·2′W	X	98
Nettlestone Point	I of W	SZ6291	50°43·1′	1°6·9′W	X	196
Nettlesworth	Durham	NZ2547	54°49·3′	1°36·2′W	T	88
Nettlesworth Place	E Susx	TQ5918	50°56·6′	0°16·2′E	X	199
Nettlesworth West Ho	Durham	NZ2448	54°49·8′	1°37·2′W	X	88
Nettleton	Glos	SO9413	51°49·2′	2°4·8′W	T	163
Nettleton	Lincs	TA1000	53°29·3′	0°20·1′W	T	113
Nettleton	Wilts	ST8178	51°30·3′	2°16·0′W	T	173
Nettleton Beck	Lincs	TF1199	53°28·8′	0°19·2′W	W	113
Nettleton Bleak Ho	Lincs	TA1100	53°29·3′	0°19·2′W	X	113
Nettleton Green	Wilts	ST8178	51°30·3′	2°16·0′W	T	173
Nettleton Hill	Kirk	SE0917	53°39·2′	1°51·4′W	T	110
Nettleton Hill	Lincs	TF1099	53°28·8′	0°20·1′W	X	113
Nettleton Ho	Lincs	TA1100	53°29·3′	0°19·2′W	X	113
Nettleton Lodge	Lincs	TA0900	53°29·4′	0°21·0′W	X	112
Nettleton Manor	Lincs	TA0900	53°29·4′	0°21·0′W	X	112
Nettleton Moor	Lincs	TF0999	53°28·8′	0°21·0′W	X	112
Nettleton Shrub	Wilts	ST8277	51°29·7′	2°15·2′W	T	173
Nettleton Top	Lincs	TF1198	53°28·3′	0°19·3′W	T	113
Nettleworth Manor	Notts	SK5465	53°11·0′	1°11·1′W	X	120

Nettlingflat	Scot Bord	NT4055	55°47·3'	2°57·0'W	X	66,73
Netty Burn	Fife	NT0794	56°8·0'	3°29·3'W	W	58
Netty Knowe	Derby	SK1556	53°6·3'	1°46·2'W	A	119
Netton	Wilts	SU1236	51°7·6'	1°49·3'W	X	184
Netton	Wilts	SU1336	51°7·6'	1°48·5'W	T	184
Netton Down	Wilts	SU0627	51°2·8'	1°54·5'W	X	184
Netton Fm	Devon	SX5546	50°18·0'	4°1·8'W	FM	202
Netton Fm	Devon	SX8282	50°37·8'	3°39·7'W	FM	191
Netton Island	Devon	SX5545	50°17·5'	4°1·8'W	X	202
Nettwood Fm	Somer	ST5653	51°16·7'	2°37·5'W	FM	182,183
Netty Hill	Aberd	NO6384	56°57·0'	2°36·0'W	X	45
Neuadd	Carm	SN2925	51°54·1'	4°28·7'W	X	145
Neuadd	Carm	SN6921	51°52·6'	3°53·8'W	T	160
Neuadd	Cered	SN3655	52°10·4'	4°23·5'W	X	145
Neuadd	Cered	SN4458	52°12·1'	4°16·6'W	X	146
Neuadd	I of Angl	SH3373	53°13·9'	4°29·7'W	X	114
Neuadd	I of Angl	SH3392	53°24·2'	4°30·3'W	X	114
Neuadd	I of Angl	SH3893	53°24·8'	4°25·8'W	X	114
Neuadd	I of Angl	SH4280	53°17·9'	4°21·8'W	X	114,115
Neuadd	Monm	SO2923	51°54·3'	3°1·5'W	X	161
Neuadd	Monm	SO3308	51°46·2'	2°57·9'W	X	161
Neuadd	Pemb	SN1737	52°0·3'	4°39·6'W	X	145
Neuadd	Powys	SJ0807	52°39·4'	3°21·2'W	X	125
Neuadd	Powys	SN9033	51°59·3'	3°35·7'W	X	160
Neuadd	Powys	SN9222	51°53·4'	3°33·8'W	X	160
Neuadd	Powys	SN9511	51°47·5'	3°31·0'W	X	160
Neuadd	Powys	SN9566	52°17·2'	3°32·0'W	X	136,147
Neuadd	Powys	SN9756	52°11·8'	3°30·0'W	X	147
Neuadd	Powys	SN9835	52°0·5'	3°28·8'W	X	160
Neuadd	Powys	SN9947	52°7·0'	3°28·1'W	X	147
Neuadd	Powys	SO0355	52°11·3'	3°24·7'W	X	147
Neuadd	Powys	SO0424	51°54·6'	3°23·3'W	X	160
Neuadd	Powys	SO0961	52°14·6'	3°19·6'W	X	147
Neuadd	Powys	SO1450	52°8·7'	3°15·0'W	X	148
Neuadd	Powys	SO2034	52°0·2'	3°9·5'W	X	161
Neuadd	Powys	SO2067	52°18·0'	3°10·0'W	X	137,148
Neuadd	Powys	SO2320	51°52·6'	3°6·7'W	X	161
Neuadd	Powys	SO2820	51°52·7'	3°2·4'W	X	161
Neuadd Cwmcamlais	Powys	SN9526	51°55·6'	3°31·2'W	X	160
Neuadd-ddu	Powys	SN9175	52°22·0'	3°35·7'W	X	136,147
Neuaddfach	Powys	SO1825	51°55·3'	3°11·2'W	X	161
Neuadd-Fadog	Powys	SO0146	52°6·4'	3°26·3'W	X	147
Neuadd-fawr	Cered	SN5348	52°6·9'	4°8·4'W	X	146
Neuadd-fawr	Powys	SO2322	51°53·7'	3°6·7'W	X	161
Neuadd Fm	Powys	SO1128	51°56·8'	3°17·3'W	FM	161
Neuadd Fm	Powys	SO1325	51°55·2'	3°15·5'W	FM	161
Neuadd-fry	Powys	SO1622	51°53·7'	3°12·9'W	X	161
Neuadd-goch	Powys	SJ0602	52°36·7'	3°22·9'W	X	136
Neuadd-goch Bank	Powys	SO1083	52°26·5'	3°19·0'W	X	136
Neuadd-lwyd	Cered	SN4759	52°12·7'	4°14·0'W	X	146
Neuaddlwyd	Powys	SJ1007	52°39·4'	3°19·4'W	X	125
Neuadd-lwyd	Powys	SN7912	51°47·9'	3°44·9'W	X	160
Neuadd-lwyd	Powys	SO0898	52°34·6'	3°21·1'W	X	136
Neuadd Parc	Cered	SN6879	52°23·8'	3°56·0'W	X	135
Neuadd Reservoir	Powys	SO0218	51°51·4'	3°25·0'W	W	160
Neuadd Wen	I of Angl	SH4786	53°21·2'	4°17·5'W	X	114
Neuadd-wen	Powys	SJ0411	52°41·5'	3°24·8'W	X	125
Neuadd-yr-ynys	Cered	SN6591	52°30·3'	3°58·9'W	X	135
Neuck	S Lanak	NS8137	55°37·0'	3°52·9'W	X	71,72
Neucks Cotts	Falk	NS8872	55°55·9'	3°47·1'W	X	65
Neuk	Aberd	NJ4602	57°6·6'	2°53·0'W	X	37
Neuk	D & G	NX0451	54°49·2'	5°2·6'W	X	82
Neuk	D & G	NX7063	54°56·9'	4°1·4'W	X	83,84
Neuk	S Lanak	NS7544	55°40·7'	3°58·8'W	X	71
Neuk Fm	Scot Bord	NT7770	55°55·6'	2°21·6'W	FM	67
Neuk, The	Aberd	NO6071	56°50·0'	2°38·9'W	X	45
Neuk, The	Aberd	NO7397	57°4·1'	2°26·3'W	T	38,45
Neuk, The	Angus	NO3038	56°32·0'	3°7·8'W	X	53
Neutral Fm	Suff	TM3751	52°6·6'	1°28·1'E	FM	156
Nevay Park	Angus	NO3243	56°34·7'	3°6·0'W	X	53
Neven Craig	Orkney	HY3949	59°19·6'	3°3·8'W	X	5
Nevendon	Essex	TQ7591	51°35·7'	0°32·0'E	T	178
Neven o'Grinni	Orkney	HY4146	59°18·0'	3°1·7'W	X	5
Neven Point	Orkney	HY5429	59°9·0'	2°47·8'W	X	5,6
Nevergood Fm	Kent	TQ7039	51°7·7'	0°26·2'E	FM	188
Nevern	Pemb	SN0839	52°1·2'	4°47·5'W	T	145
Neves Castle	Shrops	SJ6107	52°39·8'	2°34·2'W	X	127
Nev Hill	Orkney	ND4289	58°47·3'	2°59·7'W	X	7
Nevie	Moray	NJ2127	57°19·3'	3°18·3'W	X	36
Nevie Hill	Moray	NJ2126	57°19·3'	3°18·3'W	X	36
Neville House Fm	Suff	TL8573	52°19·7'	0°43·3'E	FM	144,155
Nevilles Cross	Durham	NZ2541	54°46·0'	1°36·3'W	T	88
Nevilles Fm	E Susx	TQ5819	50°57·1'	0°15·4'E	FM	199
Nevilles Fm	E Yorks	TA3625	53°42·5'	0°4·0'E	FM	107,113
Neville's Fm	Oxon	SU4290	51°36·7'	1°23·2'W	FM	164,174
Neville Wood	Lincs	TF0665	53°10·5'	0°24·4'W	F	121
Nevill Holt	Leic	SP8193	52°32·0'	0°48·0'W	X	141
Nevilthorne	N Yks	SE6733	53°47·6'	0°58·6'W	X	105,106
Nevis Br	Highld	NN1174	56°49·4'	5°5·4'W	X	41
Nevis Forest	Highld	NN1270	56°47·3'	5°4·2'W	F	41
Nevi Skerry	Orkney	ND3995	58°50·6'	3°2·9'W	X	7
Nevi,The	Orkney	HY2704	58°55·3'	3°15·6'W	X	6,7
Nev of Stuis	Shetld	HU4697	60°39·5'	1°9·0'W	X	1
Nev, The	Orkney	HY4452	59°21·3'	2°58·6'W	X	5
Nev, The	Orkney	HY5336	59°12·7'	2°48·9'W	X	5
Nev, The	Orkney	ND4289	58°47·3'	2°59·7'W	X	7
Nev, The	Shetld	HP5504	60°43·2'	0°59·0'W	X	1
Nev, The	Shetld	HP6410	60°46·3'	0°49·0'W	X	1
Nev, The	Shetld	HP6611	60°46·9'	0°46·8'W	X	1
Nev, The	Shetld	HU2543	60°10·5'	1°32·5'W	X	4
Nev, The	Shetld	HU2742	60°10·0'	1°30·3'W	X	4
Nev, The	Shetld	HU3414	59°54·8'	1°23·0'W	X	4
Nev, The	Shetld	HU3442	60°9·9'	1°22·7'W	X	4
Nev, The	Shetld	HU3551	60°14·8'	1°21·6'W	X	3
New Abbey	D & G	NX9666	54°58·9'	3°37·1'W	T	84
New Abbey Pow	D & G	NX9666	54°58·9'	3°37·1'W	W	84
New Aberdour	Aberd	NJ8863	57°39·7'	2°11·6'W	T	30
New Achamore	Highld	NH9048	57°30·8'	3°49·7'W	X	27
Newacott	Devon	SS2602	50°47·7'	4°27·8'W	X	190
New Acres	Durham	NZ1950	54°50·9'	1°41·8'W	X	88
New Addington	Croy	TQ3862	51°20·6'	0°0·7'W	T	177,187
Newall	Leeds	SE2046	53°54·8'	1°41·3'W	T	104
Newall Carr Side	N Yks	SE2047	53°55·4'	1°41·3'W	X	104
Newall Fm	Ches	SJ7070	53°13·8'	2°26·6'W	FM	118
Newall Green	Man	SJ8187	53°23·0'	2°16·7'W	T	109
Newall Hall Fm	Suff	TM3376	52°20·2'	1°25·6'E	FM	156
New Allotments	Derby	SK0384	53°21·4'	1°56·9'W	X	110
New Allotment, The	Brad	SD9941	53°52·2'	2°0·5'W	X	103
New Alresford	Hants	SU5832	51°5·3'	1°9·9'W	T	185
New Alston	Northum	NY8466	54°59·5'	2°14·6'W	X	86,87
New Alves	Moray	NJ1460	57°37·6'	3°25·9'W	X	28
New Alyth	Pth & Kin	NO2447	56°36·8'	3°13·8'W	T	53
New Amberden Hall	Essex	TL5630	51°57·0'	0°16·6'E	X	167
Newan	Orkney	HY2627	59°7·7'	3°17·1'W	X	6
New Ardonachie	Pth & Kin	NO0834	56°29·6'	3°29·2'W	X	52,53
Newark	Aberd	NK0357	57°36·4'	1°56·5'W	X	30
Newark	D & G	NS7809	55°21·8'	3°55·1'W	X	71,78
Newark	D & G	NX8470	55°0·9'	3°48·4'W	X	84
Newark	Fife	NO5101	56°12·2'	2°46·9'W	X	59
Newark	Glos	SO8117	51°51·3'	2°16·2'W	X	162
Newark	Orkney	HY3921	59°4·6'	3°3·4'W	X	6
Newark	Orkney	HY4944	59°17·0'	2°53·2'W	X	5
Newark	Orkney	HY5704	58°55·5'	2°44·3'W	X	6
Newark	Orkney	HY7242	59°16·1'	2°29·0'W	T	5
Newark	Peterb	TF2100	52°35·3'	0°12·4'W	T	142
Newark	S Ayr	NS3216	55°24·8'	4°38·8'W	X	70
Newark Bay	Orkney	HY5704	58°55·5'	2°44·3'W	W	6
Newark Bay	Orkney	ND4689	58°47·4'	2°55·6'W	W	7
Newark Castle	Inverc	NS3374	55°56·1'	4°40·0'W	A	63
Newark Castle	Scot Bord	NT4229	55°33·3'	2°54·7'W	A	73
Newark Farm	Orkney	HY7242	59°16·1'	2°29·0'W	FM	5
Newark Hill	S Ayr	NS3116	55°24·8'	4°39·8'W	X	70
Newark Hill	Scot Bord	NT4028	55°32·8'	2°56·6'W	H	73
Newark-on-Trent	Notts	SK7953	53°4·3'	0°48·8'W	T	120,121
Newark Park	Glos	ST7893	51°38·4'	2°18·7'W	X	162,172
Newark Priory	Surrey	TQ0457	51°18·4'	0°30·1'W	A	186
New Arley	Warw	SP2989	52°30·1'	1°34·0'W	T	140
New Arngrove Fm	Bucks	SP6113	51°49·0'	1°6·5'W	FM	164,165
New Arr	Highld	NH9151	57°32·4'	3°48·8'W	X	27
New Arram	E Yorks	TA0344	53°53·2'	0°25·6'W	T	107
Newarthill	N Lanak	NS7859	55°48·8'	3°56·4'W	T	64
New Ash Green	Kent	TQ6065	51°21·9'	0°18·3'E	T	177
New Ashley	Lancs	SD5836	53°49·4'	2°37·9'W	X	102
New Balderton	Notts	SK8152	53°3·8'	0°47·1'W	T	121
Newbald Lodge	E Yorks	SE9439	53°50·6'	0°33·9'W	X	106
Newbald Wold	E Yorks	SE9237	53°49·5'	0°35·7'W	X	106
Newball	Lincs	TF0776	53°16·4'	0°23·3'W	T	121
Newball Common	Lincs	TF0874	53°15·4'	0°22·5'W	X	121
Newball Grange	Lincs	TF0777	53°17·0'	0°23·3'W	X	121
Newball Wood	Lincs	TF0876	53°16·4'	0°22·4'W	F	121
New Bampton Fm	Cumbr	NY2554	54°52·8'	3°9·7'W	FM	85
Newbank	D & G	NY0698	55°16·3'	3°28·3'W	X	78
New Barn	Black w Dar	SD6620	53°40·8'	2°30·5'W	X	103
Newbarn	Bucks	SU9792	51°37·3'	0°35·5'W	X	175,176
Newbarn	Ches	SJ8870	53°13·9'	2°10·4'W	X	118
New Barn	Derby	SK2158	53°7·4'	1°40·8'W	X	119
New Barn	Dorset	ST9817	50°57·4'	2°1·3'W	X	184
New Barn	Dorset	SY5983	50°38·9'	2°34·4'W	X	194
New Barn	Dorset	SY6198	50°47·0'	2°32·8'W	X	194
New Barn	Dorset	SY6692	50°43·8'	2°29·4'W	X	194
New Barn	Dorset	SZ0079	50°36·9'	1°59·6'W	X	195
New Barn	E Susx	TQ3111	50°53·2'	0°7·9'W	X	198
New Barn	E Susx	TQ3608	50°51·6'	0°3·7'W	X	198
New Barn	E Susx	TQ5104	50°49·2'	0°9·0'E	X	199
New Barn	Glos	ST9495	51°39·5'	2°4·8'W	X	163
New Barn	Hants	SU3841	51°10·2'	1°27·0'W	X	185
New Barn	Hants	SU4335	51°7·0'	1°22·8'W	X	185
New Barn	Hants	SU4951	51°15·6'	1°17·5'W	X	185
New Barn	Kent	TQ6268	51°23·5'	0°20·1'E	T	177
New Barn	Kent	TQ8527	51°1·0'	0°38·6'E	X	189,199
Newbarn	Kent	TR0731	51°2·7'	0°57·6'E	X	189
Newbarn	Kent	TR1539	51°6·8'	1°4·7'E	T	179,189
New Barn	Lancs	SD8130	53°46·2'	2°16·9'W	X	103
New Barn	Leic	SP3999	52°35·5'	1°25·1'W	X	140
New Barn	Medway	TQ7574	51°26·5'	0°31·5'E	X	178
New Barn	Powys	SO2152	52°9·9'	3°8·9'W	X	148
New Barn	Shrops	SJ2426	52°49·8'	3°7·3'W	X	126
New Barn	Somer	ST2924	51°0·9'	3°0·3'W	X	193
New Barn	Suff	TL9142	52°2·8'	0°47·5'E	X	155
New Barn	V of Glam	ST0070	51°25·4'	3°25·9'W	X	170
New Barn	W Berks	SU3280	51°31·3'	1°31·9'W	X	174
New Barn	Wilts	SU2576	51°29·2'	1°38·0'W	X	174
New Barn	Wilts	SU3054	51°17·3'	1°33·8'W	X	185
Newbarn	Worcs	SO8232	51°59·4'	2°15·3'W	X	150
New Barn	W Susx	SU7802	50°49·0'	0°53·2'W	X	197
New Barn	W Susx	SU8301	50°48·4'	0°48·9'W	X	197
New Barn	W Susx	TQ1009	50°52·4'	0°25·8'W	X	198
New Barn	W Susx	TQ1314	50°55·1'	0°23·2'W	X	198
New Barn	W Susx	TQ3017	50°56·5'	0°8·6'W	X	198
New Barn Cotts	Hants	SU4946	51°12·9'	1°17·5'W	X	185
Newbarn Down	I of W	SZ4385	50°40·0'	1°23·1'W	X	196
Newbarn Down	I of W	SZ4784	50°39·5'	1°19·7'W	X	196
New Barnes	Heref	SO6655	52°11·8'	2°29·5'W	X	149
New Barnet	Barnet	TQ2695	51°38·6'	0°10·3'W	T	166,176
New Barnetby	N Lincs	TA0710	53°34·8'	0°22·6'W	T	112
New Barn Fm	Bath & NE Somer	ST6065	51°23·2'	2°34·1'W	FM	172
New Barn Fm	Brom	TQ4458	51°18·4'	0°4·3'E	FM	187
New Barn Fm	Bucks	SP6518	51°51·6'	1°3·0'W	FM	164,165
Newbarn Fm	Derby	SK3252	53°4·1'	1°30·9'W	FM	119
Newbarn Fm	Devon	ST2510	50°53·3'	3°3·6'W	FM	192,193
New Barn Fm	Devon	SX4462	50°26·5'	4°11·4'W	FM	201
New Barn Fm	Devon	SX9087	50°40·6'	3°33·0'W	FM	192
New Barn Fm	Devon	SY0698	50°46·7'	3°19·6'W	FM	192
New Barn Fm	Dorset	ST9501	50°48·7'	2°3·9'W	FM	195
New Barn Fm	E Susx	TQ6708	50°51·1'	0°22·7'E	FM	199
New Barn Fm	E Susx	TQ7311	50°52·6'	0°27·9'E	FM	199
New Barn Fm	E Susx	TQ8713	50°53·4'	0°39·9'E	FM	199
Newbarn Fm	Glos	SO7327	51°56·7'	2°23·2'W	FM	162
New Barn Fm	Glos	SO9707	51°45·9'	2°2·2'W	FM	163
New Barn Fm	Glos	SP1414	51°49·7'	1°47·4'W	FM	163
New Barn Fm	Hants	SU4449	51°14·5'	1°21·8'W	FM	185
New Barn Fm	Hants	SU4825	51°1·6'	1°18·5'W	FM	185
New Barn Fm	Hants	SU4945	51°12·4'	1°17·5'W	FM	185
New Barn Fm	Hants	SU7114	50°55·5'	0°59·0'W	FM	197
New Barn Fm	Hants	SU7533	51°5·7'	0°55·3'W	FM	186
Newbarn Fm	I of W	SZ4386	50°40·6'	1°23·1'W	FM	196
New Barn Fm	I of W	SZ4683	50°38·9'	1°20·6'W	FM	196
New Barn Fm	Kent	TQ8045	51°10·8'	0°34·9'E	FM	188
New Barn Fm	Kent	TQ8633	51°4·2'	0°39·7'E	FM	189
New Barn Fm	Kent	TR0530	51°2·2'	0°55·8'E	FM	189
New Barn Fm	Kent	TR1249	51°12·3'	1°2·5'E	FM	179,189
Newbarn Fm	Lincs	SK8735	52°54·6'	0°42·0'W	FM	130
New Barn Fm	Notts	SK6637	52°55·8'	1°0·7'W	FM	129
New Barn Fm	Oxon	SP3437	52°2·1'	1°29·9'W	FM	151
New Barn Fm	Oxon	SP4311	51°48·0'	1°22·2'W	FM	164
Newbarn Fm	Oxon	SP4523	51°54·5'	1°20·4'W	FM	164
New Barn Fm	Oxon	SP5420	51°52·8'	1°12·5'W	FM	164
New Barn Fm	Suff	TL9053	52°8·8'	0°47·0'E	FM	155
New Barn Fm	Suff	TM0439	52°0·9'	0°58·8'E	FM	155
New Barn Fm	Warw	SP2462	52°15·6'	1°38·5'W	FM	151
New Barn Fm	Warw	SP3138	52°2·6'	1°32·5'W	FM	151
Newbarn Fm	W Berks	SU3280	51°31·3'	1°31·9'W	FM	174
New Barn Fm	W Berks	SU5571	51°26·3'	1°12·1'W	FM	174
New Barn Fm	Wilts	SU1873	51°27·6'	1°44·1'W	FM	173
New Barn Fm	W Susx	SU8226	51°1·9'	0°49·4'W	FM	186,197
New Barn Fm	W Susx	SU9810	50°53·1'	0°36·0'W	FM	197
New Barn Fm	W Susx	TQ1520	50°58·3'	0°21·3'W	FM	198
New Barn Fm	W Susx	TQ1937	51°7·4'	0°17·6'W	FM	187
New Barn Fm	W Susx	TQ2114	50°55·0'	0°16·3'W	FM	198
New Barn Fm	W Susx	TQ3012	50°53·8'	0°8·7'W	FM	198
New Barn Fm	W Susx	TQ3928	51°2·3'	0°0·7'W	FM	187,198
New Barnham Slip	Suff	TL8379	52°22·9'	0°41·7'E	X	144
Newbarns	Angus	NO4355	56°41·3'	2°55·4'W	X	54
Newbarns	Angus	NO6849	56°38·2'	2°30·9'W	X	54
Newbarns	Cumbr	SD2170	54°7·4'	3°12·1'W	T	96
New Barns	Cumbr	SD4477	54°11·4'	2°51·1'W	X	97
Newbarns	D & G	NX8755	54°52·9'	3°45·3'W	X	84
New Barns	Essex	TL6708	51°45·0'	0°25·6'E	X	167
New Barns	Essex	TL7432	51°57·8'	0°32·4'E	X	167
New Barns	Hants	SU6307	50°51·8'	1°5·9'W	X	196
Newbarns	Herts	TL3633	51°59·0'	0°0·8'W	X	166
New Barns	Herts	TL3931	51°57·8'	0°1·8'E	X	166
New Barns	Herts	TL4119	51°51·3'	0°3·2'E	X	167
New Barns	Kent	TQ6856	51°16·9'	0°24·9'E	X	178,188
New Barns	Northum	NU2404	55°20·0'	1°36·9'W	X	81
New Barns	Shrops	SO6274	52°22·0'	2°33·1'W	X	138
New Barns	Staffs	SK0803	52°37·7'	1°52·5'W	X	139
New Barns Fm	Beds	SP9654	52°10·8'	0°35·4'W	FM	153
New Barns Fm	Cambs	TL3366	52°16·8'	0°2·6'W	FM	154
New Barns Fm	Essex	TQ4293	51°37·3'	0°3·5'E	FM	177
Newbarns Fm	Heref	SO3835	52°0·8'	2°53·8'W	FM	149,161
New Barns Fm	Heref	SO4438	52°2·5'	2°48·6'W	FM	149,161
New Barns Fm	Kent	TQ4343	51°10·3'	0°3·1'E	FM	187
New Barton	Devon	SX5248	50°19·0'	4°4·4'W	X	201
New Barton	Northnts	SP8564	52°16·3'	0°44·9'W	X	152
New Basford	C of Nott	SK5542	52°58·6'	1°10·4'W	T	129
Newbattle	Midlo	NT3365	55°52·7'	3°3·8'W	T	66
Newbattle Abbey	Midlo	NT3366	55°53·2'	3°3·8'W	X	66
New Beaupre	V of Glam	ST0073	51°27·1'	3°26·0'W	T	170
New Beckenham	Brom	TQ3670	51°25·0'	0°2·3'W	T	177
New Bedford River or Hundred Foot Drain	Cambs	TL4178	52°23·1'	0°4·7'E	W	142,143
New Bedford River or Hundred Foot Drain	Cambs	TL5088	52°28·4'	0°12·9'E	W	143
New Beechenhurst Inclosure	Glos	SO6112	51°48·6'	2°33·5'W	F	162
New Bells Fm	Suff	TM0364	52°14·4'	0°58·8'E	FM	155
New Belses	Scot Bord	NT5725	55°31·3'	2°40·4'W	X	73,74
Newberryside	Cumbr	NY7344	54°47·7'	2°24·8'W	X	86,87
New Bewick	Northum	NU0620	55°28·7'	1°53·9'W	T	75
New Bewley	Cumbr	NY6421	54°35·2'	2°33·0'W	A	91
New Bewley Castle	Cumbr	NY6521	54°35·2'	2°32·1'W	X	91
Newbie	D & G	NY1865	54°58·6'	3°16·4'W	T	85
Newbie	D & G	NY3777	55°5·3'	2°58·8'W	X	85
Newbiebarns	D & G	NY1764	54°58·1'	3°17·4'W	X	85
Newbie Cottages	D & G	NY1664	54°58·1'	3°18·3'W	X	85
Newbie Mains	D & G	NY1764	54°58·1'	3°17·4'W	X	85
Newbie Mill	D & G	NY1967	54°59·7'	3°15·5'W	X	85
Newbiggen Hall	N Yks	NZ8406	54°26·8'	0°41·9'W	X	94
Newbiggen Ho	Northum	NZ0386	55°10·3'	1°56·7'W	X	81
Newbiggin	Cumbr	NY4265	54°58·8'	2°53·9'W	X	85
Newbiggin	Cumbr	NY4729	54°39·4'	2°48·9'W	T	90
Newbiggin	Cumbr	NY5549	54°50·3'	2°41·6'W	T	86
Newbiggin	Cumbr	NY6228	54°39·0'	2°34·9'W	T	91
Newbiggin	Cumbr	SD0994	54°20·3'	3°23·6'W	T	96
Newbiggin	Cumbr	SD2669	54°6·9'	3°7·5'W	T	96,97
Newbiggin	Cumbr	SD2780	54°12·9'	3°6·7'W	X	96,97
Newbiggin	Cumbr	SD5579	54°12·5'	2°41·0'W	T	97
Newbiggin	Darl	NZ2124	54°36·9'	1°40·1'W	X	93
Newbiggin	Durham	NY9127	54°38·5'	2°7·9'W	T	91,92
Newbiggin	Durham	NZ1447	54°49·3'	1°46·5'W	T	88
New Biggin	Lancs	SD6852	53°58·0'	2°28·9'W	X	103
Newbiggin	Northum	NY9460	54°56·3'	2°5·2'W	X	87
Newbiggin	Northum	NY9549	54°50·4'	2°4·2'W	T	87
Newbiggin	N Yks	SD9591	54°19·1'	2°4·2'W	T	98
Newbiggin	N Yks	SD9985	54°15·9'	2°0·5'W	T	98
Newbiggin	N Yks	TA1081	54°13·0'	0°18·4'W	X	101
Newbiggin Bay	Northum	NZ3187	55°10·8'	1°30·4'W	W	81
Newbiggin Burn	Northum	NZ0195	55°15·2'	1°58·6'W	W	81
Newbiggin-by-the-Sea	Northum	NZ3087	55°10·8'	1°31·3'W	T	81
Newbiggin Common	Durham	NY9131	54°40·7'	2°8·0'W	X	91,92
Newbiggin Crags	Cumbr	SD5479	54°12·5'	2°41·9'W	X	97
Newbiggin Fell	Cumbr	NY5849	54°50·3'	2°38·8'W	H	86
Newbiggin Fell	Northum	NY9250	54°50·9'	2°7·1'W	X	87
Newbiggin Fm	Northum	NZ0394	55°14·7'	1°56·7'W	FM	81
Newbigging	Aberd	NJ4502	57°6·6'	2°54·0'W	X	37
Newbigging	Aberd	NJ5326	57°19·6'	2°46·4'W	X	37
Newbigging	Aberd	NJ5358	57°36·8'	2°46·7'W	X	29

Newbigging	Aberd	NJ6025	57°19·1'	2°39·4'W	X	37
Newbigging	Aberd	NJ6108	57°9·9'	2°38·2'W	X	37
Newbigging	Aberd	NJ6115	57°13·7'	2°38·3'W	X	37
Newbigging	Aberd	NJ6631	57°22·3'	2°33·5'W	X	29
Newbigging	Aberd	NJ7022	57°17·5'	2°29·4'W	X	38
Newbigging	Aberd	NJ7321	57°17·0'	2°26·4'W	X	38
Newbigging	Aberd	NJ7736	57°25·1'	2°22·5'W	X	29,30
Newbigging	Aberd	NO1485	56°57·2'	3°24·4'W	X	43
Newbigging	Aberd	NO8389	56°59·8'	2°16·3'W	X	45
Newbigging	Aberd	NO8591	57°0·8'	2°14·4'W	X	38,45
Newbigging	Angus	NO2842	56°34·1'	3°9·9'W	X	53
Newbigging	Angus	NO3471	56°49·8'	3°4·4'W	X	44
Newbigging	Angus	NO4237	56°31·5'	2°56·1'W	T	54
Newbigging	Angus	NO4935	56°30·5'	2°49·3'W	T	54
Newbigging	Angus	NO5468	56°48·3'	2°44·7'W	X	44
Newbigging	Angus	NO6344	56°35·4'	2°35·7'W	X	54
Newbigging	Angus	NO6450	56°38·7'	2°34·8'W	X	54
Newbigging	C of Edin	NT1277	55°58·9'	3°24·2'W	T	65
Newbigging	D & G	NY1198	55°16·3'	3°23·6'W	X	78
Newbigging	D & G	NY1389	55°11·5'	3°21·6'W	X	78
Newbigging	Fife	NT0489	56°5·3'	3°32·1'W	X	65
Newbigging	Fife	NT2186	56°3·9'	3°15·7'W	X	66
Newbigging	Fife	NT2290	56°6·0'	3°14·8'W	X	58
Newbigging	Midlo	NT2760	55°49·9'	3°9·5'W	X	66
Newbigging	Moray	NJ4060	57°37·8'	2°59·8'W	X	28
Newbigging	Orkney	HY4707	58°57·1'	2°54·8'W	X	6,7
Newbigging	Orkney	HY4953	59°21·9'	2°53·3'W	X	5
Newbigging	Orkney	HY5107	58°57·1'	2°50·6'W	X	6,7
Newbigging	Orkney	HY5431	59°10·1'	2°47·8'W	X	5,6
Newbigging	Orkney	HY7644	59°17·2'	2°24·8'W	X	5
Newbigging	Orkney	ND3390	58°47·8'	3°9·1'W	X	7
Newbigging	Orkney	ND4290	58°47·9'	2°59·7'W	X	7
Newbigging	Pth & Kin	NN8420	56°21·7'	3°52·2'W	X	52,58
Newbigging	Pth & Kin	NN9514	56°18·7'	3°41·4'W	X	58
Newbigging	Pth & Kin	NO0301	56°11·8'	3°33·4'W	X	58
Newbigging	Pth & Kin	NO0422	56°23·1'	3°32·8'W	X	52,53,58
Newbigging	Pth & Kin	NO1236	56°30·7'	3°25·4'W	X	53
Newbigging	Pth & Kin	NO1515	56°19·4'	3°22·0'W	X	58
Newbigging	Pth & Kin	NO1535	56°30·2'	3°22·4'W	X	53
Newbigging	Pth & Kin	NO1642	56°34·0'	3°21·6'W	X	53
Newbigging	Pth & Kin	NO2625	56°24·9'	3°11·5'W	X	53,59
Newbigging	Scot Bord	NT5350	55°44·7'	2°44·5'W	X	66,73
Newbigging	Scot Bord	NT7015	55°25·9'	2°28·0'W	T	80
Newbigging	S Lanak	NT0145	55°41·6'	3°34·1'W	T	72
Newbigging	W Loth	NT0673	55°56·7'	3°29·9'W	X	65
Newbigging Birks	Scot Bord	NT7016	55°26·5'	2°28·0'W	X	80
Newbigging Burn	Scot Bord	NT7114	55°25·4'	2°27·1'W	W	80
Newbigging Bush	Scot Bord	NT6915	55°25·9'	2°29·0'W	X	80
Newbigging Fm	Angus	NO6959	56°43·6'	2°29·9'W	FM	54
Newbigging Fm	Pth & Kin	NN9424	56°24·0'	3°42·6'W	FM	52,53,58
Newbiggingmill	S Lanak	NT0244	55°41·0'	3°33·1'W	X	72
Newbigging of Blebo	Fife	NO4313	56°18·6'	2°54·8'W	X	59
Newbigging of Ceres	Fife	NO4011	56°17·5'	2°57·7'W	X	59
Newbigging of Craighall	Fife	NO4110	56°17·0'	2°56·7'W	X	59
Newbiggin Grange	Cumbr	NY2140	54°45·2'	3°13·2'W	X	85
Newbigging Rig	Scot Bord	NT5756	55°48·0'	2°40·7'W	X	67,73,74
Newbiggings	Orkney	HY6641	59°15·5'	2°35·3'W	T	5
Newbigging Walls	Scot Bord	NT5350	55°44·7'	2°44·5'W	X	66,73
Newbiggin Hall	Cumbr	NY4350	54°50·7'	2°52·8'W	A	85
Newbiggin Hall Estate	N upon Ty	NZ2067	55°0·1'	1°40·8'W	T	88
Newbiggin Moor	Cumbr	NY6329	54°39·5'	2°34·0'W	X	91
Newbiggin-on-Lune	Cumbr	NY7005	54°26·6'	2°27·3'W	T	91
Newbiggin Pasture	N Yks	SD9592	54°19·7'	2°4·2'W	X	98
Newbiggin Pasture	N Yks	SD9985	54°15·3'	2°0·5'W	X	98
Newbiggin Point	Northum	NZ3187	55°10·8'	1°30·4'W	X	81
Newbiggins	Aberd	NK0238	57°26·2'	1°57·5'W	X	30
Newbiggin Scar	Cumbr	SD2769	54°6·9'	3°6·6'W	X	96,97
New Bilbo	Heref	SO3628	51°57·0'	2°55·5'W	X	149,161
New Bilton	Warw	SP4975	52°22·5'	1°16·4'W	T	140
New Bingfield	Northum	NY9873	55°3·3'	2°1·5'W	X	87
New Black Fen	Leeds	SE4240	53°51·5'	1°21·3'W	F	105
New Blainslie	Scot Bord	NT5444	55°41·5'	2°43·5'W	X	73
New Bldgs	Norf	TL8689	52°28·3'	0°44·7'E	X	144
New Boghead	Aberd	NJ7432	57°22·9'	2°25·5'W	X	29
Newbold	Ches	SJ8760	53°7·8'	2°49·8'W	X	117
Newbold	Derby	SK3773	53°15·4'	1°26·3'W	T	119
Newbold	Leic	SK4019	52°46·3'	1°24·0'W	T	129
Newbold	Leic	SK7609	52°40·6'	0°52·1'W	T	141
Newbold	Roch	SD9113	53°37·0'	2°7·8'W	T	109
Newbold Comyn Park	Warw	SP3365	52°17·2'	1°30·6'W	X	151
Newbold Fields	Derby	SK3574	53°15·9'	1°28·1'W	X	119
Newbold Grange Fm	Leic	SK7509	52°40·6'	0°53·0'W	FM	141
Newbold Grounds	Northnts	SP5160	52°14·4'	1°14·8'W	X	151
Newbold Heath	Leic	SK4405	52°38·7'	1°20·6'W	T	140
Newbold Manor Fm	Staffs	SK2019	52°46·3'	1°41·8'W	FM	128
Newbold on Avon	Warw	SP4976	52°23·0'	1°16·4'W	T	140
Newbold-on-Stour	Warw	SP2446	52°6·9'	1°38·6'W	T	151
Newbold Pacey	Warw	SP2957	52°12·9'	1°34·1'W	T	151
Newbolds	Wolv	SJ9300	52°36·1'	2°5·8'W	T	127,139
Newbold's Fm	Monm	SO4813	51°49·0'	2°44·9'W	FM	161
Newbold Verdon	Leic	SK4403	52°37·6'	1°20·6'W	T	140
New Bolingbroke	Lincs	TF3057	53°5·9'	0°3·1'W	T	122
New Bolsover	Derby	SK4670	53°13·7'	1°18·2'W	T	120
Newbon	Essex	TL8241	52°2·5'	0°39·6'E	X	155
Newborns Fm	Kent	TR2261	51°18·5'	1°11·5'E	FM	179
Newborough	Peterb	TF2005	52°38·0'	0°13·2'W	T	142
Newborough	Staffs	SK1325	52°49·6'	1°48·0'W	T	128
Newborough Fen	Peterb	TF1904	52°37·5'	0°14·1'W	X	142
Newborough Fm	Warw	SP3147	52°7·5'	1°32·4'W	FM	151
Newborough Forest	I of Angl	SH4064	53°9·2'	4°23·2'W	F	114,115
Newborough or Niwbwrch	I of Angl	SH4265	53°9·8'	4°21·4'W	T	114,115
Newborough Warren (Tywyn Niwbwrch)	I of Angl	SH4263	53°8·7'	4°21·3'W	X	114,115
New Boston	St Hel	SJ5697	53°28·3'	2°39·4'W	T	108
New Botley	Oxon	SP4906	51°45·3'	1°17·0'W	T	164
Newbottle	Northnts	SP5236	52°1·4'	1°14·1'W	T	151
Newbottle	Sund	NZ3351	54°51·4'	1°28·7'W	T	88
Newbottle Br	Northnts	SP7881	52°25·5'	0°50·8'W	X	141
Newbottle Fm	Northnts	SP5135	52°0·9'	1°15·0'W	FM	151
Newbottle Spinney	Northnts	SP5136	52°1·4'	1°15·0'W	F	151

New Boultham	Lincs	SK9670	53°13·3'	0°33·3'W	T	121
Newbound Fm	Notts	SK4963	53°9·9'	1°15·6'W	FM	120
Newboundmill Fm	Notts	SK4963	53°9·9'	1°15·6'W	FM	120
Newbourne	Suff	TM2742	52°2·0'	1°19·0'E	T	169
Newbourne Hall	Suff	TM2742	52°2·0'	1°19·0'E	X	169
Newbourne Hill	Worcs	SP0471	52°20·5'	1°56·1'W	H	139
New Bourtreebush	Aberd	NO9095	57°3·0'	2°9·4'W	X	38,45
New Br	Devon	SX7147	50°18·8'	3°48·3'W	X	202
New Br	Devon	SX7170	50°31·2'	3°48·8'W	A	202
New Br	Devon	SX8476	50°34·6'	3°37·9'W	X	191
New Br	E Yorks	SE6620	53°40·6'	0°59·6'W	X	105,106
New Br	Lancs	SD5240	53°51·5'	2°43·4'W	X	102
New Br	Somer	ST3126	51°2·0'	2°58·7'W	X	193
New Br	W Susx	TQ0625	51°1·1'	0°28·9'W	X	187,197
New Bradwell	Mil Key	SP8241	52°3·9'	0°47·8'W	T	152
Newbraes	Aberd	NJ5411	57°11·5'	2°45·2'W	X	37
New Brakes Fm	E Yorks	SE8020	53°40·5'	0°46·9'W	FM	106,112
New Brancepeth	Durham	NZ2241	54°46·1'	1°39·1'W	T	88
New Breach Fm	V of Glam	SS9773	51°27·0'	3°28·6'W	FM	170
Newbreck	Orkney	HY3820	59°4·0'	3°4·4'W	X	6
Newbreck	Orkney	HY3920	59°4·0'	3°3·3'W	X	6
Newbridge	Bath & NE Somer	ST7265	51°23·2'	2°23·8'W	T	172
Newbridge	Cered	SN5059	52°12·8'	4°11·3'W	X	146
Newbridge	C of Edin	NT1272	55°56·2'	3°24·1'W	T	65
Newbridge	Corn	SW4231	50°7·6'	5°36·2'W	T	203
Newbridge	Corn	SW7944	50°15·5'	5°5·7'W	T	204
Newbridge	Corn	SX3468	50°29·5'	4°20·0'W	T	201
New Bridge	Devon	SS5411	50°53·0'	4°4·2'W	X	191
New Bridge	Devon	SS5628	51°2·2'	4°2·9'W	X	180
New Bridge	Devon	SS7914	50°55·0'	3°42·9'W	X	180
New Bridge	Devon	SX5990	50°41·8'	3°59·4'W	X	191
New Bridge	D & G	NX9479	55°5·9'	3°39·0'W	T	84
Newbridge	E Susx	TQ4532	51°4·4'	0°4·6'E	T	188
New Bridge	E Susx	TQ6209	50°51·7'	0°18·5'E	X	199
New Bridge	Glos	SP1717	51°51·3'	1°44·8'W	A	163
Newbridge	Hants	SU2915	50°56·3'	1°34·9'W	T	196
New Bridge	Highld	NN2287	56°56·7'	4°55·1'W	X	34,41
Newbridge	I of W	SZ4187	50°41·1'	1°24·8'W	T	196
Newbridge	Lancs	SD8538	53°50·5'	2°13·3'W	T	103
New Bridge	N Yks	SD9942	53°52·7'	2°0·5'W	X	103
New Bridge	N Yks	SE8085	54°15·5'	0°45·9'W	T	94,100
Newbridge	Oxon	SP4001	51°42·6'	1°24·9'W	T	164
Newbridge	Pemb	SM9431	51°56·6'	4°59·4'W	X	157
Newbridge	Powys	SJ1411	52°41·6'	3°16·0'W	X	125
Newbridge	Shrops	SJ3025	52°49·3'	3°1·9'W	T	126
Newbridge	Wolv	SO8999	52°35·6'	2°9·3'W	T	139
Newbridge	Wrex	SJ2841	52°57·9'	3°3·9'W	T	117
Newbridge Fm	Ches	SJ6245	53°0·3'	2°33·6'W	FM	118
Newbridge Fm	Derby	SK2872	53°14·9'	1°34·4'W	FM	119
Newbridge Fm	D & G	NX9578	55°5·4'	3°38·3'W	FM	84
Newbridge Fm	Heref	SO6637	52°2·1'	2°29·3'W	FM	149
Newbridge Fm	Kent	TQ9125	50°59·8'	0°43·7'E	FM	189
Newbridge Fm	Lincs	TF4459	53°6·8'	0°9·5'E	FM	122
Newbridge Fm	Norf	TF5504	52°36·9'	0°17·8'E	FM	143
Newbridge Fm	Oxon	SP4001	51°42·6'	1°24·9'W	FM	164
Newbridge Fm	Oxon	SP5218	51°51·7'	1°14·8'W	FM	164
Newbridge Green	Worcs	SO8439	52°3·2'	2°13·6'W	T	150
Newbridge on Usk	Monm	ST3894	51°38·7'	2°53·4'W	T	171
Newbridge-on-Wye	Powys	SO0158	52°12·9'	3°26·6'W	T	147
Newbridge or Cefn Bychan	Caer	ST2197	51°40·2'	3°8·2'W	T	171
New Bridges Fm	Warw	SP2343	52°5·3'	1°39·5'W	FM	151
Newbridge Wood	Corn	SX1164	50°27·0'	4°39·4'W	F	200
Newbridge Wood	E Susx	TQ6427	51°1·4'	0°20·7'E	F	188,199
New Brighton	Brad	SE1236	53°49·4'	1°48·6'W	T	104
New Brighton	Flint	SJ2565	53°10·9'	3°6·9'W	T	117
New Brighton	Hants	SU7506	50°51·1'	0°55·7'W	T	197
New Brighton	Leeds	SE2627	53°44·6'	1°35·9'W	T	104
New Brighton	N Yks	SD9253	53°58·6'	2°6·9'W	X	103
New Brighton	Wirral	SJ3093	53°26·0'	3°2·8'W	T	108
New Brighton	Wrex	SJ2750	53°2·8'	3°4·9'W	T	117
New Brimington	Derby	SK4074	53°15·9'	1°23·6'W	T	120
New Brinsley	Notts	SK4550	53°3·0'	1°19·3'W	T	120
Newbrook Fm	Heref	SO4033	51°59·8'	2°52·0'W	FM	149,161
Newbrook Fm	Worcs	SO9779	52°24·8'	2°2·2'W	FM	139
New Broomielaw	Durham	NZ0619	54°34·2'	1°54·0'W	X	92
New Brotton	Red & Cl	NZ6820	54°34·5'	0°56·5'W	T	94
Newbrough	Northum	NY8767	55°0·1'	2°11·8'W	T	87
Newbrough Lodge	Northum	NY8668	55°0·6'	2°12·7'W	X	87
New Broughton	Wrex	SJ3151	53°3·4'	3°1·4'W	T	117
New Buckenham	Norf	TM0890	52°28·3'	1°4·2'E	T	144
New Building	Powys	SO2045	52°6·1'	3°9·7'W	X	148
New Building Fm	Shrops	SJ8006	52°39·3'	2°17·3'W	FM	127
New Buildings	Bath & NE Somer	ST6957	51°18·9'	2°26·3'W	T	172
New Buildings	Beds	SP9457	52°12·4'	0°37·1'W	X	153
New Buildings	Cumbr	SD1183	54°14·3'	3°21·5'W	X	96
Newbuildings	Devon	SS7903	50°49·1'	3°42·7'W	T	191
New Buildings	Devon	SX3797	50°45·2'	4°18·3'W	X	190
New Buildings	Dorset	SY6996	50°46·0'	2°26·0'W	X	194
New Buildings	Dorset	SY8485	50°40·1'	2°13·2'W	X	194
New Buildings	Dorset	SY9980	50°37·4'	2°0·5'W	T	195
New Buildings	Lincs	TF2683	53°20·0'	0°6·1'W	X	122
New Buildings	Mil Key	SP8144	52°5·5'	0°48·7'W	X	152
New Buildings	Norf	TF8129	52°49·9'	0°41·6'E	X	132
New Buildings	Norf	TM0891	52°28·9'	1°4·2'E	X	144
New Buildings	Northnts	SP5432	51°59·3'	1°12·4'W	X	152
New Buildings	Oxon	SU5185	51°33·9'	1°15·5'W	X	174
New Buildings	Red & Cl	NZ6120	54°34·5'	1°3·0'W	X	94
New Buildings	Shrops	SO5789	52°30·1'	2°37·6'W	X	137,138
New Buildings	Staffs	SJ9636	52°55·5'	2°3·2'W	X	127
New Buildings	Suff	TM2147	52°4·9'	1°13·9'E	X	169
New Buildings	Wilts	SU1966	51°23·8'	1°43·2'W	X	173
New Buildings	Wilts	SU3260	51°20·5'	1°32·0'W	X	174
New Buildings Fm	Cambs	TL4140	52°2·7'	0°3·8'E	FM	154
Newbuildings Fm	Ches	SJ9574	53°16·0'	2°4·1'W	FM	118
New Buildings Fm	Derby	SK1743	52°59·1'	1°44·4'W	FM	119,128
New Buildings Fm	Derby	SK2932	52°53·3'	1°33·7'W	FM	128
New Buildings Fm	Derby	SK2951	53°3·6'	1°33·6'W	FM	119

Newbuildings Fm	Derby	SK3048	53°1·9'	1°32·8'W	FM	119
New Buildings Fm	E Susx	TQ6815	50°54·8'	0°23·8'E	FM	199
New Buildings Fm	Kent	TQ9624	50°59·1'	0°47·9'E	FM	189
New Buildings Fm	N Yks	SE4847	53°55·3'	1°15·7'W	FM	105
New Buildings Fm	Shrops	SJ5903	52°37·6'	2°35·9'W	FM	126
Newbuildings Fm	Staffs	SJ9226	52°50·1'	2°6·7'W	FM	127
Newbuildings Fm	Staffs	SK0325	52°49·6'	1°56·9'W	FM	128
New Buildings Fm	Staffs	SK0329	52°51·7'	1°56·9'W	FM	128
Newbuildings Place	W Susx	TQ1424	51°0·5'	0°22·1'W	A	198
Newburgh	Aberd	NJ9659	57°37·5'	2°3·6'W	X	30
Newburgh	Aberd	NJ9925	57°19·2'	2°0·5'W	T	38
Newburgh	Fife	NO2218	56°21·1'	3°15·3'W	T	58
Newburgh	Fife	NO2318	56°21·1'	3°14·3'W	T	58
Newburgh	Lancs	SD4810	53°35·3'	2°46·7'W	T	108
Newburgh	Moray	NJ3944	57°29·2'	3°0·6'W	X	28
Newburgh	Orkney	HY2512	58°59·6'	3°17·8'W	X	6
Newburgh	Scot Bord	NT3220	55°28·4'	3°4·1'W	X	73
Newburgh Bar	Aberd	NK0123	57°18·1'	1°58·5'W	X	38
Newburgh Fm	Dorset	SY8285	50°40·1'	2°14·9'W	FM	194
Newburgh Grange	N Yks	SE5475	54°10·3'	1°9·9'W	X	100
Newburgh Priory	N Yks	SE5476	54°10·9'	1°9·9'W	A	100
Newburn	Northum	NT9246	55°42·7'	2°7·2'W	X	74,75
New Burn	Northum	NT9422	55°29·8'	2°5·3'W	W	74,75
Newburn	N upon Ty	NZ1765	54°59·0'	1°43·6'W	T	88
Newburn	Stir	NS6195	56°7·9'	4°13·7'W	X	57
New Burnshot	C of Edin	NT1776	55°58·4'	3°19·4'W	X	65,66
New Bursea Fm	E Yorks	SE8135	53°48·5'	0°45·8'W	FM	106
New Bury	Bolton	SD7305	53°32·7'	2°24·0'W	T	109
Newbury	Devon	SX7597	50°45·8'	3°46·0'W	X	191
Newbury	Kent	TQ9259	51°18·1'	0°45·7'E	T	178
Newbury	Somer	ST6950	51°15·1'	2°26·3'W	T	183
Newbury	W Berks	SU4767	51°24·2'	1°19·1'W	T	174
Newbury	Wilts	ST8241	51°10·3'	2°15·1'W	T	183
Newbury Fm	Heref	SO5955	52°11·7'	2°35·6'W	FM	149
Newbury Hill	Oxon	SU6197	51°40·3'	1°6·7'W	X	164,165
Newbury Hill	Somer	ST7349	51°14·6'	2°22·8'W	H	183
Newbury Ho	Somer	ST6950	51°15·1'	2°26·3'W	T	183
Newbury Park	Redbr	TQ4488	51°34·6'	0°5·1'E	T	177
Newbus Grange (Hotel)	Darl	NZ3109	54°28·8'	1°30·9'W	X	93
New Butt	N Yks	SD7069	54°7·2'	2°27·1'W	X	98
Newby	Cumbr	NY5921	54°35·2'	2°37·6'W	T	91
Newby	Lancs	SD8145	53°54·3'	2°16·9'W	T	103
Newby	N Yks	NZ5012	54°30·3'	1°13·2'W	T	93
Newby	N Yks	SD7270	54°7·8'	2°25·3'W	T	98
Newby	N Yks	SE2647	53°55·4'	1°35·8'W	T	104
Newby	N Yks	SE3567	54°6·1'	1°27·5'W	T	99
Newby	N Yks	TA0190	54°18·0'	0°26·5'W	T	101
Newby Bridge	Cumbr	SD3786	54°16·2'	2°57·6'W	T	96,97
Newby Cote	N Yks	SD7370	54°7·8'	2°24·4'W	T	98
Newby Cross	Cumbr	NY3653	54°52·3'	2°59·4'W	X	85
Newby East	Cumbr	NY4758	54°55·1'	2°49·2'W	T	86
Newby End	Cumbr	NY5921	54°35·2'	2°37·6'W	X	91
Newbygill	N Yks	SE4587	54°16·8'	1°18·1'W	X	99
Newby Grange	N Yks	NZ5111	54°29·7'	1°12·3'W	X	93
Newby Grange (Hotel)	Cumbr	NY4658	54°55·1'	2°50·1'W	X	86
Newby Hall	N Yks	SE3467	54°6·1'	1°28·4'W	A	99
Newby Head	Cumbr	NY5821	54°35·2'	2°38·6'W	T	91
Newby Head Fm	N Yks	SD7984	54°15·3'	2°18·9'W	FM	98
Newby Head Moss	N Yks	SD7983	54°14·8'	2°18·9'W	X	98
Newby Hills	Lancs	SD8245	53°54·3'	2°16·0'W	X	103
Newby Kipps	Scot Bord	NT2536	55°37·0'	3°11·0'W	X	73
Newby Moor	N Yks	SD7169	54°7·2'	2°26·2'W	X	98
Newby Moss	N Yks	SD7472	54°8·8'	2°23·5'W	X	98
Newbyre	E Ayr	NS4734	55°34·8'	4°25·2'W	X	70
New Byth	Aberd	NJ8254	57°34·8'	2°17·6'W	T	29,30
Newbyth	E Loth	NT5880	56°0·9'	2°40·0'W	X	67
Newby West	Cumbr	NY3653	54°52·3'	2°59·4'W	T	85
Newby Wiske	N Yks	SE3687	54°16·9'	1°26·4'W	T	99
Newcairnie	Fife	NO3519	56°21·8'	3°2·7'W	X	59
New Cample	D & G	NX8894	55°13·9'	3°45·2'W	X	78
New Carden	Fife	NT2295	56°8·7'	3°14·9'W	X	58
Newcastle	Brig	SS9079	51°30·2'	3°34·7'W	T	170
Newcastle	Monm	SO4417	51°51·2'	2°48·4'W	T	161
Newcastle	Shrops	SO2482	52°26·1'	3°6·7'W	T	137
Newcastle Court	Powys	SO2563	52°15·8'	3°5·5'W	X	137,148
Newcastle Emlyn	Carm	SN3040	52°2·2'	4°28·3'W	T	145
New Castle Fm	E Susx	TQ6418	50°56·5'	0°20·5'E	FM	199
Newcastle Fm	Kent	TQ8539	51°7·4'	0°39·0'E	FM	189
Newcastle International Airport	N upon Ty	NZ1971	55°2·2'	1°41·7'W	X	88
Newcastleton Forest	Scot Bord	NY5287	55°10·7'	2°44·8'W	F	79
Newcastleton or Copshaw Holm	Scot Bord	NY4887	55°10·7'	2°48·6'W	T	79
Newcastle-under-Lyme	Staffs	SJ8546	53°0·9'	2°13·0'W	T	118
Newcastle upon Tyne	N upon Ty	NZ2564	54°58·4'	1°36·1'W	T	88
New Catton	Norf	TG2310	52°38·7'	1°18·2'E	T	133,134
New-Caynton Mill	Wrekin	SJ6922	52°47·9'	2°27·2'W	X	127
New Channel	Suff	TM1741	52°1·7'	1°10·2'E	W	169
New Channelkirk	Scot Bord	NT4855	55°47·4'	2°49·3'W	X	66,73
Newchapel	Pemb	SN2239	52°1·5'	4°35·3'W	T	145
Newchapel	Powys	SN9883	52°26·4'	3°29·6'W	T	136
Newchapel	Staffs	SJ8654	53°5·2'	2°12·1'W	T	118
Newchapel	Surrey	TQ3642	51°9·9'	0°2·9'W	T	187
New Charlton	Gren	TQ4078	51°29·2'	0°1·4'E	T	177
New Cheltenham	S Glos	ST6574	51°28·1'	2°29·8'W	T	172
New Cheriton	Hants	SU5828	51°3·1'	1°10·0'W	T	185
New Chingle Hall	Lancs	SD5534	53°48·3'	2°40·6'W	X	102
Newchurch	Blae Gw	SO1610	51°47·2'	3°12·7'W	T	161
Newchurch	Carm	SN3824	51°53·7'	4°20·9'W	T	145,159
Newchurch	Heref	SO3550	52°8·9'	2°56·6'W	T	148,149
Newchurch	I of W	SZ5585	50°40·0'	1°12·9'W	T	196
Newchurch	Kent	TR0531	51°2·7'	0°55·9'E	T	189
Newchurch	Lancs	SD8222	53°41·9'	2°15·9'W	T	103
Newchurch	Monm	ST4597	51°40·4'	2°47·3'W	T	171
Newchurch	Powys	SO2150	52°8·8'	3°8·9'W	T	148
Newchurch	Staffs	SK1423	52°48·5'	1°47·1'W	T	128
Newchurch Common	Ches	SJ6069	53°13·2'	2°35·5'W	X	118
Newchurches	Corn	SX3085	50°38·6'	4°23·9'W	X	201
New Church Fm	Lincs	SK8890	53°24·2'	0°40·2'W	FM	112
New Church Fm	Norf	TF9511	52°39·9'	0°53·4'E	FM	132

Newchurch Hill	Powys	SO2050	52°8·8'	3°9·8'W	H	148
Newchurch in Pendle	Lancs	SD8239	53°51·1'	2°16·0'W	T	103
New Clee Sta	NE Lincs	TA2810	53°34·5'	0°3·6'W	X	113
Newcliff Ho	N Yks	SE7485	54°15·6'	0°51·4'W	X	94,100
New Clingre Fm	Glos	ST7299	51°41·6'	2°23·9'W	FM	162
Newclochtow	Aberd	NK0631	57°22·4'	1°53·6'W	X	30
New Close	Brad	SE1236	53°49·4'	1°48·6'W	X	104
New Close	Durham	NZ9036	54°43·4'	2°8·9'W	X	91,92
New Close	N Yks	SD8884	54°15·3'	2°10·6'W	X	98
New Close	N Yks	SD8961	54°2·9'	2°9·7'W	X	98
New Close Allotments	N Yks	SD8290	54°18·6'	2°16·2'W	X	98
New Close Allotments	N Yks	SD9969	54°7·3'	2°0·5'W	X	98
Newclosefield	Staffs	SJ9843	52°59·3'	2°1·4'W	X	118
New Close Fm	Bolton	SD6409	53°34·8'	2°32·2'W	FM	109
New Close Fm	Cambs	TL3864	52°15·6'	0°1·7'E	FM	154
New Close Fm	Cambs	TL4663	52°15·0'	0°8·7'E	FM	154
New Close Fm	Cumbr	SD2371	54°8·0'	3°10·3'W	FM	96
New Close Fm	Derby	SK2066	53°11·7'	1°41·6'W	FM	119
New Close Fm	Derby	SK2831	52°52·8'	1°34·6'W	FM	128
New Close Fm	N Yks	NZ4504	54°26·0'	1°18·0'W	FM	93
Newclose Fm	N Yks	SE0583	54°14·8'	1°55·0'W	FM	98
New Close Fm	Oxon	SP7504	51°44·0'	0°54·4'W	FM	165
New Close Fm	Somer	ST7451	51°15·7'	2°22·0'W	FM	183
New Close Fm	Somer	ST7544	51°11·9'	2°21·1'W	FM	183
New Close Fm	W Susx	TQ3017	50°56·5'	0°8·6'W	FM	198
New Close Ho	I of W	SZ4987	50°41·1'	1°18·0'W	X	196
New Close Plantn	Lincs	SK9991	53°24·6'	0°30·2'W	F	112
New Close Plantn	N Yks	SD7467	54°6·1'	2°23·4'W	F	98
New Closes	Corn	SX2071	50°30·9'	4°32·0'W	X	201
New Close Wood	Lincs	TA1504	53°31·4'	0°15·5'W	F	113
New Close Wood	Warw	SP4077	52°23·6'	1°24·3'W	F	140
Newcombe Fm	Somer	SS9737	51°7·6'	3°27·9'W	FM	181
New Coombe Fm	W Susx	TQ3733	51°5·0'	0°2·2'W	FM	187
New Coppy	Lancs	SD6661	54°2·9'	2°30·7'W	X	98
New Copse	Oxon	SU6980	51°31·1'	0°59·9'W	F	175
New Copse	Wilts	SU0250	51°15·2'	1°57·9'W	F	184
New Copse Down	Wilts	SU0350	51°15·2'	1°57·0'W	X	184
New Copse Inclosure	Hants	SU3202	50°49·2'	1°32·4'W	F	196
New Costessey	Norf	TG1810	52°38·9'	1°13·8'E	T	133,134
Newcott	Devon	ST2308	50°52·2'	3°5·3'W	T	192,193
Newcott	Devon	SX7399	50°46·8'	3°47·7'W	X	191
Newcott	Orkney	HY3008	58°57·5'	3°12·5'W	X	6,7
New Cottage Fm	Enf	TL2700	51°41·3'	0°9·4'W	FM	166
New Coundon	Durham	NZ2230	54°40·1'	1°39·1'W	T	93
Newcourt	Devon	SS3305	50°49·5'	4°21·9'W	X	190
New Court	Heref	SO3444	52°5·7'	2°57·4'W	X	148,149,161
New Court	Heref	SO5441	52°4·2'	2°39·9'W	X	149
Newcourt	Powys	SO1936	52°1·2'	3°10·4'W	X	161
Newcourt Barton	Devon	SS4907	50°50·8'	4°8·3'W	X	191
Newcourt Barton	Devon	SX9690	50°42·3'	3°28·0'W	X	192
New Court Down	Wilts	SU1422	51°0·1'	1°47·6'W	X	184
New Court Down Barn	Wilts	SU1522	51°0·1'	1°46·8'W	X	184
Newcourt Fm	Heref	SO3733	51°59·8'	2°54·7'W	FM	149,161
New Court Fm	Wilts	SU1722	51°0·1'	1°45·1'W	FM	184
New Covert	Ches	SJ3571	53°14·2'	2°58·0'W	F	117
New Covert	Denb	SJ0345	52°59·9'	3°26·3'W	F	116
New Covert	Glos	SP0920	51°52·9'	1°51·8'W	F	163
New Covert	Lincs	TF0291	53°24·6'	0°27·5'W	F	112
New Covert	Mil Key	SP9039	52°2·8'	0°40·9'W	F	152
New Covert	Norf	TG1132	52°50·9'	1°8·4'E	F	133
New Covert	Norf	TL9582	52°24·3'	0°52·4'E	F	144
New Covert	Northnts	SP7075	52°22·3'	0°57·9'W	F	141
New Cowper	Cumbr	NY1245	54°47·8'	3°21·7'W	T	85
New Craig	Aberd	NJ7429	57°21·3'	2°25·5'W	X	38
New Craig	Aberd	NJ9024	57°18·6'	2°9·5'W	X	38
New Craig	Pth & Kin	NO2452	56°39·5'	3°13·9'W	X	53
Newcraig Cottage	Falk	NS8475	55°57·5'	3°51·0'W	X	65
Newcraighall	C of Edin	NT3271	55°55·9'	3°4·9'W	T	66
New Cranes Fm	Norf	TM1998	52°32·4'	1°14·2'E	FM	134
New Crickett	Shrops	SJ3635	52°54·8'	2°56·7'W	X	126
Newcroft	Aberd	NJ8004	57°7·8'	2°19·4'W	X	38
New Crofton	Wakf	SE3817	53°39·1'	1°25·1'W	T	110,111
New Crook	Orkney	HY5201	58°53·9'	2°49·5'W	X	6,7
New Cross	Cered	SN6377	52°22·7'	4°0·4'W	X	135
New Cross	Devon	SX8674	50°33·5'	3°36·2'W	X	191
New Cross	Lew	TQ3676	51°28·2'	0°2·1'W	T	177
New Cross	Oxon	SU7678	51°30·0'	0°53·9'W	T	175
New Cross	Sheff	SK2192	53°25·7'	1°40·6'W	A	110
New Cross	Somer	ST4119	50°58·3'	2°50·0'W	T	193
New Cross Gate	Dorset	ST8112	50°54·7'	2°15·8'W	X	194
New Cross Gate	Lew	TQ3576	51°28·2'	0°3·0'W	T	177
New Cumnock	E Ayr	NS6113	55°23·7'	4°11·3'W	T	71
New Cut	Beds	TL0749	52°8·0'	0°25·8'W	W	153
New Cut	E Susx	TQ8115	50°54·6'	0°34·9'E	X	199
New Cut	Norf	TG0744	52°57·4'	1°5·3'E	W	133
New Cut	Norf	TG2508	52°37·6'	1°19·9'E	W	134
New Cut	Norf	TG4325	52°46·3'	1°36·6'E	W	134
New Cut	Norf	TG4400	52°32·8'	1°36·3'E	W	134
New Cut	Powys	SJ2615	52°43·9'	3°5·4'W	W	126
New Cut or Moor Drain	N Yks	SE5151	53°57·4'	1°13·0'W	W	105
New Cwmceste	Powys	SO1754	52°10·9'	3°12·4'W	X	148
New Dairy	D & G	NX7160	54°55·3'	4°0·3'W	X	83,84
New Danna	Arg & Bt	NR6979	55°57·2'	5°41·6'W	T	61,62
New Deanham	Northum	NZ0382	55°8·2'	1°56·7'W	X	81
New Decoy	Norf	TL9290	52°28·7'	0°50·0'E	X	144
New Decoy	N Yks	SE2393	54°20·2'	1°38·4'W	W	99
New Decoy Fm	Cambs	TL2288	52°28·8'	0°11·8'W	FM	142
New Deer	Aberd	NJ8846	57°30·5'	2°11·6'W	T	30
New Delaval	Northum	NZ2979	55°6·5'	1°32·3'W	T	88
New Delight	Leic	SK4528	52°51·1'	1°19·5'W	X	129
Newdelight Covert	Suff	TM4573	52°18·2'	1°36·0'E	F	156
New Delights	Lincs	TA3300	53°29·0'	0°0·7'E	X	113
Newdelight Walks	Suff	TM4572	52°17·7'	1°36·0'E	X	156
New Delph	Oldham	SD9807	53°33·8'	2°1·4'W	T	109
New Denham	Bucks	TQ0484	51°32·9'	0°29·6'W	T	176
New Derrings	N Yks	SE4768	54°6·6'	1°16·4'W	X	100
Newdigate	Surrey	TQ1942	51°10·1'	0°17·5'W	T	187
New Dike	Lincs	TF3299	53°28·5'	0°0·3'W	W	113
New Ditch	Somer	ST5033	51°5·9'	2°42·5'W	A	182,183
New Down	Corn	SX3565	50°27·9'	4°19·1'W	X	201
Newdown	N Lincs	SE8606	53°32·9'	0°41·7'W	X	112
New Down	W Susx	TQ0508	50°51·9'	0°30·1'W	X	197
Newdown Copse	Hants	SU2648	51°14·1'	1°37·3'W	F	184
Newdown Fm	Hants	SU5136	51°7·5'	1°15·9'W	FM	185
New Downie	Angus	NO5236	56°31·1'	2°46·4'W	X	54
New Downs	Corn	SW3631	50°7·5'	5°41·3'W	T	203
New Downs	Corn	SW7051	50°19·1'	5°13·5'W	T	203
Newdowns Fm	Corn	SX0266	50°27·9'	4°47·0'W	FM	200
New Downs Fm	Kent	TR3458	51°16·6'	1°21·7'E	FM	179
Newdowns Head	Corn	SW7051	50°19·1'	5°13·5'W	X	203
New Drain	E Yorks	TA1146	53°54·1'	0°18·2'W	W	107
New Draught Br	Lancs	SD4740	53°51·5'	2°47·9'W	X	102
Newdrop Inn (PH)	Lancs	SD6439	53°51·0'	2°32·4'W	X	102,103
New Duston	Northnts	SP7162	52°15·3'	0°57·2'W	T	152
Newdyke	Angus	NO4848	56°37·5'	2°50·4'W	X	54
New Dyke	Cambs	TL2186	52°27·7'	0°12·7'W	W	142
New Dyke	Suff	TM3691	52°28·2'	1°28·9'E	W	134
Newe	Aberd	NJ3712	57°11·9'	3°2·1'W	X	37
New Earnstrey Park	Shrops	SO5787	52°29·0'	2°37·6'W	X	137,138
New Earswick	York	SE6055	53°59·5'	1°4·7'W	T	105
New East Fm	Northum	NT9756	55°48·1'	2°2·4'W	FM	75
New Eastwood	Notts	SK4646	53°0·8'	1°18·5'W	T	129
New Edlington	Donc	SK5398	53°28·8'	1°11·7'W	T	111
Newe Ho	Suff	TL9367	52°16·3'	0°50·1'E	A	155
New Elgin	Moray	NJ2261	57°38·2'	3°17·9'W	T	28
New Ellerby	E Yorks	TA1639	53°50·3'	0°13·8'W	T	107
Newell Green	Brackn	SU8771	51°26·1'	0°44·5'W	T	175
Newells	Aberd	NJ8129	57°21·3'	2°18·5'W	X	38
Newells	W Susx	TQ2126	51°1·5'	0°16·1'W	X	187,198
Newells Fm	W Susx	TQ2026	51°1·5'	0°16·9'W	FM	187,198
Newell Wood	Rut	TF0014	52°43·1'	0°30·8'W	F	130
Newelm	E Susx	TQ4607	50°50·9'	0°4·8'E	X	198
New Eltham	Gren	TQ4472	51°25·9'	0°4·7'E	T	177
Newel Tor	Corn	SX2374	50°32·6'	4°29·5'W	X	201
New End	Lincs	TF2374	53°15·2'	0°9·0'W	T	122
New End	Warw	SP1060	52°14·5'	1°50·8'W	T	150
New End	Worcs	SP0560	52°14·5'	1°55·2'W	T	150
Newenden	Kent	TQ8327	51°1·0'	0°36·9'E	T	188,199
New England	Essex	TL7042	52°3·2'	0°29·2'E	T	154
New England	E Yorks	TA1437	53°49·2'	0°15·7'W	X	107
New England	Lancs	SD3747	53°55·2'	2°57·1'W	X	102
New England	Lincs	TF5059	53°6·7'	0°14·9'E	T	122
New England	Pemb	SN0637	52°0·1'	4°49·2'W	X	145
New England	Peterb	TF1801	52°35·9'	0°15·1'W	T	142
New England	Somer	ST3210	50°53·4'	2°57·6'W	T	193
New England	Surrey	SU9361	51°20·7'	0°39·5'W	X	175,186
New England	W Susx	TQ2830	51°3·5'	0°10·0'W	X	187
New England Bay	D & G	NX1242	54°44·5'	4°54·8'W	W	82
New England Cottage	Lincs	SK9932	52°52·8'	0°31·3'W	X	130
New England Creek	Essex	TQ9789	51°34·1'	0°51·0'E	W	178
New England Fm	Cambs	TL2748	52°7·2'	0°8·3'W	FM	153
New England Fm	Lincs	TF2822	52°47·1'	0°5·7'W	FM	131
New England Fm	Northnts	TL0170	52°19·4'	0°30·7'W	FM	141,153
New England Island	Essex	TQ9789	51°34·1'	0°51·0'E	X	178
New England Stud Fm	Cambs	TL5861	52°13·7'	0°19·2'E	FM	154
Newenham Abbey	Devon	SY2897	50°46·3'	3°0·9'W	A	193
New Enson Fm	Staffs	SJ9228	52°51·2'	2°6·7'W	FM	127
Newent	Glos	SO7225	51°55·6'	2°24·0'W	T	162
Newent Woods	Glos	SO7022	51°54·0'	2°25·8'W	F	162
Newerne	Glos	SO6303	51°43·7'	2°31·8'W	T	162
New Erringham Fm	W Susx	TQ2108	50°51·8'	0°16·4'W	FM	198
New Eskham	Lancs	SD4343	53°53·0'	2°51·6'W	X	102
New Etal	Northum	NT9239	55°38·9'	2°7·2'W	X	74,75
New Fairlee Fm	I of W	SZ5189	50°42·1'	1°16·3'W	FM	196
New Fancy View	Glos	SO6209	51°46·9'	2°32·7'W	X	162
New Fargie Ho	Pth & Kin	NO1512	56°17·8'	3°22·0'W	X	58
New Farm	Aberd	NJ6217	57°14·8'	2°37·3'W	FM	37
New Farm	D & G	NX9058	54°54·5'	3°42·5'W	FM	84
Newfarm	D & G	NY0998	55°16·3'	3°25·5'W	X	78
New Farm	E Ayr	NS4438	55°36·9'	4°28·2'W	FM	70
New Farm	Essex	TL4334	51°59·4'	0°5·4'E	FM	154
New Farm	Essex	TL5306	51°44·1'	0°13·3'E	FM	167
Newfarm	Midlo	NT3468	55°54·3'	3°2·9'W	X	66
New Farm	Pth & Kin	NO2623	56°23·9'	3°11·5'W	FM	53,59
New Farm	Scot Bord	NT9256	55°48·1'	2°7·2'W	FM	67,74,75
New Farm Cotts	Suff	TL8273	52°19·7'	0°40·7'E	X	144,155
Newfarm Plantation	W Susx	SU8516	50°56·5'	0°47·0'W	F	197
New Farnley	Leeds	SE2431	53°46·7'	1°37·7'W	T	104
Newfaulds	Renf	NS3356	55°46·4'	4°39·3'W	X	63
New Fen	Cambs	TL2686	52°27·7'	0°8·3'W	X	142
New Fen	Suff	TL7085	52°26·4'	0°30·5'E	X	143
New Ferry	Wirral	SJ3485	53°21·7'	2°59·1'W	T	108
Newfield	Aberd	NJ7403	57°7·3'	2°25·3'W	X	38
Newfield	Aberd	NJ9938	57°26·2'	2°0·5'W	X	30
Newfield	Aberd	NK1043	57°28·9'	1°49·5'W	X	30
Newfield	Ches	SJ6861	53°9·0'	2°28·3'W	X	118
Newfield	C of Stoke	SJ8552	53°4·1'	2°13·0'W	T	118
Newfield	Cumbr	NY5567	55°0·0'	2°41·8'W	X	86
New Field	Cumbr	SD6292	54°19·6'	2°34·6'W	X	97
Newfield	D & G	NX0359	54°53·5'	5°3·9'W	X	82
Newfield	D & G	NX6251	54°50·3'	4°8·5'W	X	83
Newfield	D & G	NX8464	54°57·7'	3°48·3'W	X	84
Newfield	D & G	NY1168	55°0·2'	3°23·1'W	X	85
Newfield	D & G	NY1485	55°9·4'	3°20·6'W	X	78
Newfield	D & G	NY1776	55°4·5'	3°17·6'W	X	85
New Field	Durham	NZ1027	54°38·5'	1°50·3'W	X	92
Newfield	Durham	NZ2033	54°41·7'	1°41·0'W	T	93
Newfield	Durham	NZ2452	54°52·0'	1°37·1'W	T	88
Newfield	E Ayr	NS5434	55°34·9'	4°18·5'W	X	70
Newfield	Highld	ND3351	58°26·8'	3°8·4'W	X	12
Newfield	Highld	NH7877	57°46·2'	4°2·6'W	T	21
Newfield	Moray	NJ2659	57°37·2'	3°13·9'W	X	28
Newfield	Northum	NY8158	54°55·1'	2°17·4'W	X	86,87
Newfield	Northum	NZ0355	54°53·6'	1°56·8'W	X	87
Newfield	Notts	SK7245	53°0·1'	0°55·2'W	X	129
Newfield	N Yks	SE2675	54°10·4'	1°35·7'W	X	99
Newfield	Orkney	HY5117	59°2·5'	2°50·8'W	X	6
Newfield	Orkney	HY6723	59°5·8'	2°34·1'W	X	5
Newfield	S Ayr	NS3734	55°34·6'	4°34·7'W	X	70
Newfield	S Lanak	NS6754	55°45·9'	4°6·8'W	X	64
Newfield Cott	Orkney	HY5217	59°2·5'	2°49·7'W	X	6
Newfield Edge Hall Fm	Lancs	SD8445	53°54·3'	2°14·2'W	FM	103
Newfield Fm	Ches	SJ6963	53°10·0'	2°27·4'W	FM	118
Newfield Fm	Dorset	ST9011	50°54·1'	2°8·1'W	FM	195
Newfield Fm	E Yorks	SE7649	53°56·1'	0°50·1'W	FM	105,106
Newfield Fm	Leeds	SE4528	53°45·0'	1°18·6'W	FM	105
Newfield Fm	Mil Key	SP9044	52°5·5'	0°40·8'W	FM	152
Newfield Fm	Notts	SK6632	52°53·1'	1°0·7'W	FM	129
Newfield Fm	Notts	SK7257	53°6·6'	0°55·1'W	FM	120
Newfield Hall (Youth Centre)	N Yks	SD9158	54°1·3'	2°7·8'W	X	103
Newfield Hill	Herts	TL2632	51°58·6'	0°9·5'W	X	166
Newfield Moor	D & G	NY1585	55°9·4'	3°19·6'W	X	79
Newfield Plantn	D & G	NY1169	55°0·7'	3°23·1'W	F	85
Newfields	Cambs	TF4010	52°40·4'	0°4·6'E	X	131,142,143
Newfields	Staffs	SJ9334	52°54·4'	2°5·8'W	X	127
Newfields	Staffs	SJ9449	53°2·5'	2°5·0'W	X	118
Newfields	Warw	SP4066	52°17·7'	1°24·4'W	X	151
Newfields Fm	E Yorks	SE7629	53°45·3'	0°50·4'W	FM	105,106
Newfields Fm	N Yks	SE3664	54°4·5'	1°26·6'W	FM	99
Newfield Wood	Cumbr	SD2295	54°20·9'	3°11·6'W	F	96
New Fleenas	Highld	NH9051	57°32·4'	3°49·8'W	X	27
New Fletton	Peterb	TL1997	52°33·7'	0°14·3'W	T	142
New Flinder	Aberd	NJ5828	57°20·7'	2°41·4'W	X	37
New Fm	Arg & Bt	NS0959	55°47·5'	5°2·4'W	FM	63
New Fm	Beds	TL0827	51°56·1'	0°25·3'W	FM	166
New Fm	Beds	TL1064	52°16·0'	0°22·9'W	FM	153
New Fm	Bucks	SP6112	51°48·4'	1°6·5'W	FM	164,165
New Fm	Bucks	SU8889	51°35·8'	0°43·4'W	FM	175
New Fm	Cambs	TL2154	52°10·5'	0°13·4'W	FM	153
New Fm	Cambs	TL2865	52°16·3'	0°7·0'W	FM	153
New Fm	Cambs	TL3155	52°10·9'	0°4·6'W	FM	153
New Fm	Cambs	TL3352	52°9·2'	0°3·0'W	FM	154
New Fm	Cambs	TL3642	52°3·8'	0°0·6'W	FM	154
New Fm	Cambs	TL3961	52°14·0'	0°2·5'E	FM	154
New Fm	Cambs	TL4068	52°17·8'	0°3·6'E	FM	154
New Fm	Cambs	TL4268	52°17·7'	0°5·3'E	FM	154
New Fm	Cambs	TL4548	52°6·9'	0°7·5'E	FM	154
New Fm	Cambs	TL5067	52°17·1'	0°12·3'E	FM	154
New Fm	Cambs	TL6272	52°19·6'	0°23·0'E	FM	154
New Fm	Ches	SJ4546	53°0·8'	2°48·8'W	FM	117
New Fm	Ches	SJ6160	53°8·4'	2°34·6'W	FM	118
New Fm	Ches	SJ6246	53°0·8'	2°33·6'W	FM	118
New Fm	Ches	SJ6254	53°5·2'	2°33·6'W	FM	118
New Fm	Ches	SJ6879	53°18·7'	2°28·4'W	FM	118
New Fm	Ches	SJ6943	52°59·2'	2°27·3'W	FM	118
New Fm	Ches	SJ7264	53°10·6'	2°24·7'W	FM	118
New Fm	Ches	SJ7386	53°22·5'	2°23·9'W	FM	109
New Fm	Derby	SK1478	53°18·2'	1°47·0'W	FM	119
New Fm	Essex	TL4401	51°41·6'	0°5·4'E	FM	167
New Fm	Essex	TL4837	52°0·9'	0°9·8'E	FM	154
New Fm	E Yorks	SE8130	53°45·8'	0°45·9'W	FM	106
New Fm	Fife	NT1993	56°7·6'	3°17·7'W	FM	58
New Fm	Glos	SO9716	51°50·8'	2°2·2'W	FM	163
New Fm	Glos	SP2425	51°55·6'	1°38·7'W	FM	163
New Fm	Hants	SU3608	50°52·5'	1°28·9'W	FM	196
New Fm	Hants	SU3936	51°7·5'	1°26·2'W	FM	185
New Fm	Hants	SU5339	51°9·1'	1°14·1'W	FM	185
New Fm	Hants	SU6945	51°12·2'	1°0·4'W	FM	186
New Fm	Hants	SU7245	51°12·2'	0°57·8'W	FM	186
New Fm	I of W	SZ5987	50°41·0'	1°9·5'W	FM	196
New Fm	Leic	SK4201	52°36·5'	1°22·4'W	FM	140
New Fm	Leic	SK7629	52°51·4'	0°51·9'W	FM	129
New Fm	Lincs	SK9574	53°15·5'	0°34·1'W	FM	121
New Fm	Lincs	TF1097	53°27·7'	0°20·2'W	FM	113
New Fm	Lincs	TF1874	53°15·2'	0°13·5'W	FM	122
New Fm	Lincs	TF2534	52°53·6'	0°8·1'W	FM	131
New Fm	Lincs	TF3798	53°27·9'	0°4·2'E	FM	113
New Fm	Lincs	TF4251	53°2·5'	0°7·5'E	FM	122
New Fm	Mil Key	SP7747	52°7·2'	0°52·1'W	FM	152
New Fm	NE Lincs	TA1512	53°35·8'	0°15·3'W	FM	113
New Fm	NE Lincs	TA2105	53°31·9'	0°10·1'W	FM	113
New Fm	NE Lincs	TA2203	53°30·8'	0°9·2'W	FM	113
New Fm	Norf	TF8914	52°41·7'	0°48·2'E	FM	132
New Fm	Norf	TL6792	52°30·2'	0°28·0'E	FM	143
New Fm	Norf	TL6793	52°30·8'	0°28·1'E	FM	143
New Fm	Northnts	SP5856	52°12·2'	1°8·7'W	FM	152
New Fm	Notts	SK5145	53°0·2'	1°14·0'W	FM	129
New Fm	Notts	SK5576	53°16·9'	1°10·1'W	FM	120
New Fm	Notts	SK5746	53°0·7'	1°8·6'W	FM	129
New Fm	N Som	ST4673	51°27·4'	2°46·2'W	FM	171,172
New Fm	N Yks	SE4863	54°3·9'	1°15·6'W	FM	100
New Fm	Oxon	SP6218	51°51·7'	1°5·6'W	FM	164,165
New Fm	Oxon	SU4991	51°37·2'	1°17·1'W	FM	164,174
New Fm	Oxon	SU6775	51°28·4'	1°1·7'W	FM	175
New Fm	Oxon	SU7383	51°32·7'	0°56·4'W	FM	175
New Fm	Pemb	SM9628	51°55·0'	4°57·6'W	FM	157,158
New Fm	Shrops	SJ4131	52°52·6'	2°52·2'W	FM	126
New Fm	Shrops	SO6389	52°30·1'	2°32·3'W	FM	138
New Fm	Staffs	SK0541	52°58·2'	1°55·1'W	FM	119,128
New Fm	Staffs	SK1112	52°42·6'	1°49·8'W	FM	128
New Fm	Suff	TL6764	52°15·2'	0°27·2'E	FM	154
New Fm	Suff	TM0059	52°11·8'	0°56·0'E	FM	155
New Fm	Swin	SU1979	51°30·8'	1°43·2'W	FM	173
New Fm	Warr	SJ6482	53°20·3'	2°32·0'W	FM	109
New Fm	Warr	SJ6993	53°26·2'	2°27·6'W	FM	109
New Fm	Warw	SP3551	52°9·6'	1°28·9'W	FM	151
New Fm	Warw	SP4275	52°22·5'	1°22·6'W	FM	140
New Fm	W Berks	SU5278	51°30·1'	1°14·7'W	FM	174
New Fm	Wilts	SU0889	51°36·2'	1°52·7'W	FM	173
New Fm	Worcs	SO8770	52°19·9'	2°11·0'W	FM	139
New Fm	Worcs	SO9046	52°7·0'	2°8·4'W	FM	150
New Fm	Wrekin	SJ5615	52°44·1'	2°38·7'W	FM	126
New Fm	York	SE5455	53°59·5'	1°10·2'W	FM	105
New Fm	York	SE5656	54°0·1'	1°8·3'W	FM	105
Newfold Ho	Northum	NY8552	54°52·0'	2°13·6'W	X	87
Newfolds	Aberd	NJ6514	57°13·2'	2°34·3'W	X	38
New Forebank	Angus	NO6057	56°42·4'	2°38·8'W	X	54
New Forest	Hants	SU2605	50°50·9'	1°37·5'W	F	195

New Forest	Hants	SU3405	50°50·8′	1°30·6′W	F	196
New Forest	Powys	SO2439	52°2·9′	3°6·1′W	X	161
New Forest Fm	N Yks	SE4154	53°59·1′	1°22·1′W	FM	105
Newforest House Fm	V of Glam	ST0078	51°29·8′	3°26·0′W	FM	170
New Forest Plantation	N Lincs	SE9406	53°32·8′	0°34·5′W	F	112
New Fosse Fm	Somer	ST5934	51°6·5′	2°34·8′W	FM	182,183
Newfound	Hants	SU5851	51°15·5′	1°9·7′W	T	185
Newfound England	N Yks	SE1595	54°21·3′	1°45·7′W	X	99
Newfound Fm	Norf	TG1806	52°36·7′	1°13·6′E	FM	134
Newfoundland Cove	Devon	SX9049	50°20·1′	3°32·4′W	W	202
Newfoundland Fm	Carm	SN6229	51°56·8′	4°0·1′W	FM	146
Newfoundland Point	I Scilly	SV9210	49°54·9′	6°17·1′W	X	203
New Fowlis	Pth & Kin	NN9223	56°23·5′	3°44·5′W	X	52,58
New Fryston	Wakf	SE4527	53°44·5′	1°18·6′W	T	105
Newgale	Pemb	SM8422	51°51·5′	5°7·8′W	T	157
Newgale Fm	Pemb	SM8522	51°51·6′	5°7·0′W	FM	157
Newgale Sands	Pemb	SM8421	51°51·0′	5°7·8′W	X	157
New Galloway	D & G	NX6377	55°4·4′	4°8·3′W	T	77
New Garth	Cumbr	NY5760	54°56·2′	2°39·8′W	X	86
Newgarth	Orkney	HY2519	59°3·4′	3°18·0′W	T	6
Newgate	Corn	SX0362	50°25·7′	4°46·1′W	X	200
Newgate	Derby	SK3374	53°16·0′	1°29·9′W	X	119
New Gate	E Susx	TQ9016	50°55·0′	0°42·6′E	A	189
Newgate	Lancs	SD5105	53°32·6′	2°44·0′W	T	108
Newgate	Norf	TG0543	52°56·9′	1°3·5′E	T	133
Newgate	N Yks	SE9592	54°19·1′	0°31·9′W	X	94,101
Newgate	Powys	SO2048	52°7·7′	3°9·7′W	X	148
Newgate Bank	N Yks	SE5689	54°17·9′	1°8·0′W	X	100
Newgate Corner	Norf	TG4413	52°39·8′	1°36·9′E	T	134
Newgate Fm	Notts	SK6939	52°56·9′	0°58·0′W	FM	129
Newgate Foot	N Yks	SE6290	54°18·4′	1°2·4′W	X	94,100
Newgate Foot	N Yks	SE8693	54°19·8′	0°40·2′W	X	94,101
Newgate Street	Herts	TL3004	51°43·4′	0°6·7′W	T	166
Newgate Wood	Herts	TL3913	51°48·1′	0°1·4′E	F	166
New Gawdy Hall	E Yorks	TA0153	53°58·0′	0°27·2′W	X	106,107
New Geanies	Highld	NH8881	57°48·5′	3°52·6′W	X	21
New Ghant Fm	Cambs	TL4588	52°28·5′	0°8·5′E	FM	143
New Gill	N Yks	SD9783	54°14·8′	2°2·3′W	X	98
Newgord	Shetld	HP5706	60°44·2′	0°56·8′W	X	1
New Gorse	Dorset	ST7110	50°53·6′	2°24·4′W	F	194
New Gout	Newp	ST3183	51°32·7′	2°59·3′W	X	171
New Grange	Angus	NO4443	56°34·8′	2°54·2′W	X	54
New Grange	Cumbr	NY0936	54°42·9′	3°24·3′W	X	89
New Grange Fm	E Yorks	SE8455	53°59·3′	0°42·7′W	FM	106
New Grange Fm	N Yks	SE5270	54°7·6′	1°11·8′W	FM	100
New Grange Fm	N Yks	SE5769	54°7·1′	1°7·3′W	FM	100
New Grange, The	Glos	SO6829	51°57·8′	2°27·6′W	X	149
New Green	N Lincs	TA1224	53°42·3′	0°17·8′W	X	107,113
New Green Fm	Essex	TL6827	51°55·2′	0°27·0′E	FM	167
New Greenhill	Scot Bord	NT4825	55°31·2′	2°49·0′W	X	73
New Greens	Herts	TL1409	51°46·3′	0°20·5′W	T	166
New Grimsby	I Scilly	SV8815	49°57·5′	6°20·7′W	T	203
New Ground	Cambs	TL6663	52°14·6′	0°26·3′E	X	154
New Ground	Herts	SP9510	51°47·1′	0°37·0′W	T	165
New Grounds	Glos	SO6300	51°42·1′	2°31·7′W	X	162
New Grounds	Glos	SO7205	51°44·8′	2°23·9′W	X	162
Newgrounds	Hants	SU1714	50°55·7′	1°45·1′W	T	195
Newgrounds Fm	Wilts	ST9255	51°17·9′	2°6·5′W	FM	173
New Grunasound	Shetld	HU3733	60°5·1′	1°19·6′W	X	4
New Guadaloupe	Leic	SK7417	52°45·0′	0°53·8′W	X	129
New Guild	Staffs	SJ7720	52°46·9′	2°20·1′W	X	127
New Gullet Br	Pth & Kin	NT1899	56°10·9′	3°18·8′W	X	58
New Haggerston	Northum	NU0243	55°41·1′	1°57·7′W	X	75
Newhailes	E Loth	NT3272	55°56·4′	3°4·9′W	T	66
New Hainford	Norf	TG2118	52°43·1′	1°16·7′E	T	133,134
Newhall	Aberd	NJ7700	57°5·7′	2°22·3′W	X	38
Newhall	Aberd	NO8894	57°2·5′	2°11·4′W	X	38,45
New Hall	Birm	SP1394	52°32·9′	1°48·1′W	A	139
Newhall	Ches	SJ6045	53°0·3′	2°35·4′W	T	118
New Hall	Ches	SJ8969	53°13·3′	2°9·5′W	X	118
New Hall	Cumbr	NY7117	54°33·1′	2°26·5′W	X	91
New Hall	Cumbr	NY8310	54°29·3′	2°15·3′W	X	91,92
New Hall	Cumbr	SD1779	54°12·2′	3°15·9′W	X	96
New Hall	Cumbr	SD4697	54°22·2′	2°49·5′W	X	97
Newhall	Derby	SK2820	52°46·8′	1°34·7′W	T	128
Newhall	D & G	NX8889	55°11·2′	3°45·1′W	X	78
Newhall	D & G	NY2383	55°8·4′	3°12·0′W	X	79
New Hall	Essex	TL5816	51°49·4′	0°18·0′E	X	167
New Hall	Essex	TL8302	51°41·4′	0°39·3′E	X	168
New Hall	Essex	TL9815	51°48·1′	0°52·7′E	X	168
New Hall	Essex	TM0529	51°55·5′	0°59·3′E	X	168
New Hall	Essex	TM1128	51°54·9′	1°4·5′E	X	168,169
New Hall	Essex	TM1423	51°52·1′	1°6·9′E	X	168,169
New Hall	Essex	TM1923	51°52·0′	1°11·3′E	X	168,169
New Hall	Essex	TQ8889	51°34·3′	0°43·2′E	X	178
New Hall	Essex	TQ9094	51°37·0′	0°45·1′E	X	168,178
Newhall	Fife	NO3307	56°15·3′	3°4·4′W	X	59
New Hall	Glos	SO7722	51°54·0′	2°19·7′W	X	162
New Hall	Lancs	SD4738	53°50·4′	2°47·9′W	X	102
New Hall	Lancs	SD6635	53°48·9′	2°30·6′W	X	103
New Hall	Lancs	SD7635	53°48·9′	2°21·5′W	X	103
New Hall	Lancs	SD8019	53°40·3′	2°17·8′W	X	109
Newhall	Midlo	NT1756	55°47·7′	3°19·0′W	X	65,66,72
New Hall	Monm	ST5192	51°37·7′	2°42·1′W	X	162,172
New Hall	Norf	TG3826	52°47·0′	1°32·2′E	X	133,134
Newhall	Northum	NU0328	55°33·0′	1°56·7′W	X	75
New Hall	Northum	NU2503	55°19·5′	1°35·9′W	X	81
New Hall	N Yks	SD7961	54°2·9′	2°18·8′W	X	98
New Hall	N Yks	SE0853	53°58·6′	1°52·3′W	X	104
New Hall	N Yks	SE5390	54°18·4′	1°10·7′W	X	100
Newhall	Orkney	HY2525	59°6·6′	3°18·1′W	X	6
Newhall	Orkney	HY2613	59°0·1′	3°16·8′W	X	6
Newhall	Orkney	HY2622	59°5·0′	3°17·0′W	X	6
Newhall	Orkney	HY5806	58°56·6′	2°43·3′W	X	6
New Hall	Powys	SJ2917	52°45·0′	3°2·7′W	X	126
Newhall	Pth & Kin	NN7946	56°35·7′	3°57·8′W	X	51,52
Newhall	Pth & Kin	NO1831	56°28·1′	3°19·4′W	X	53
Newhall	Pth & Kin	NO2339	56°32·5′	3°14·7′W	X	53
Newhall	Pth & Kin	NS9895	56°8·5′	3°38·0′W	X	58
Newhall	Scot Bord	NT3132	55°34·9′	3°5·2′W	X	73

Newhall	Scot Bord	NT4237	55°37·6′	2°54·8′W	X	73
Newhall	Scot Bord	NT5627	55°32·3′	2°41·4′W	X	73
New Hall	Shrops	SJ3436	52°55·3′	2°58·5′W	X	126
New Hall	Shrops	SJ4501	52°36·5′	2°48·3′W	X	126
New Hall	Shrops	SO4889	52°30·0′	2°45·6′W	X	137,138
New Hall	Shrops	SO5699	52°35·5′	2°38·6′W	X	137,138
New Hall	Suff	TM1658	52°10·9′	1°10·0′E	X	156
New Hall	Warr	SJ5889	53°24·0′	2°37·5′W	X	108
New Hall	Wilts	SU1626	51°2·2′	1°45·9′W	X	184
New Hall	Wirral	SJ2980	53°19·0′	3°3·5′W	X	108
New Hall	Wrex	SJ2738	52°56·3′	3°4·8′W	X	126
New Hall	Wrex	SJ3045	53°0·1′	3°2·2′W	A	117
New Hall	Wrex	SJ4541	52°58·1′	2°48·7′W	X	117
Newhall Burn	E Loth	NT5167	55°53·9′	2°46·6′W	W	66
Newhall Burn	Highld	NH6964	57°39·1′	4°11·2′W	W	21
New Hall (Convent)	Essex	TL7310	51°45·9′	0°30·8′E	A	167
Newhall Covert	Suff	TL9164	52°14·7′	0°48·3′E	F	155
New Hall Fm	Ches	SJ6670	53°13·8′	2°30·2′W	FM	118
New Hall Fm	Ches	SJ7071	53°14·4′	2°26·6′W	FM	118
New Hall Fm	Ches	SJ7384	53°21·4′	2°23·9′W	FM	109
Newhall Fm	Ches	SJ7774	53°16·0′	2°20·3′W	FM	118
Newhall Fm	Corn	SX1080	50°35·6′	4°40·7′W	FM	200
Newhall Fm	Devon	SX9899	50°47·1′	3°26·4′W	FM	192
Newhall Fm	Durham	NZ1031	54°40·7′	1°50·3′W	FM	92
Newhall Fm	Durham	NZ1037	54°43·9′	1°50·3′W	FM	92
New Hall Fm	Essex	TL4710	51°46·4′	0°8·2′E	FM	167
New Hall Fm	Essex	TL9801	51°40·6′	0°52·2′E	FM	168
New Hall Fm	Flint	SJ3360	53°8·2′	2°59·7′W	FM	117
New Hall Fm	Herts	TL3816	51°49·8′	0°0·6′E	FM	166
Newhall Fm	Herts	TQ0599	51°41·0′	0°28·5′W	FM	166,176
New Hall Fm	Kirk	SE2515	53°38·1′	1°36·9′W	FM	110
New Hall Fm	Lancs	SD4648	53°55·8′	2°48·9′W	FM	102
New Hall Fm	Lancs	SD5045	53°54·2′	2°45·2′W	FM	102
Newhall Fm	Medway	TQ8276	51°27·4′	0°37·6′E	FM	178
New Hall Fm	Notts	SK6554	53°5·0′	1°1·4′W	FM	120
Newhall Fm	Suff	TL8556	52°10·5′	0°42·7′E	FM	155
New Hall Fm	Wrex	SJ4839	52°57·0′	2°46·0′W	FM	126
Newhall Fm	W Susx	TQ2013	50°54·5′	0°17·2′W	FM	198
Newhall Grange	Roth	SK5091	53°25·0′	1°14·5′W	X	111
Newhall Green	Warw	SP2686	52°28·5′	1°36·6′W	T	140
New Hall Hey	Lancs	SD8022	53°41·9′	2°17·8′W	T	103
New Hall Ho	Highld	NH6965	57°39·6′	4°11·3′W	X	21
Newhall Manor	Corn	SX0682	50°36·6′	4°44·1′W	X	200
Newhall Park Fm	Leic	SK5000	52°36·0′	1°15·3′W	FM	140
Newhall Point	Highld	NH7067	57°40·7′	4°10·3′W	X	21,27
Newhall Wood	Norf	TG1226	52°47·6′	1°9·1′E	F	133
New Hall Wood	Wakf	SE2615	53°38·1′	1°36·0′W	F	110
Newham	Lincs	TF2850	53°2·1′	0°5·1′W	T	122
Newham	Northum	NU1728	55°33·0′	1°43·4′W	T	75
New Hambleton Fm	N Yks	SE8086	54°16·0′	0°45·9′W	FM	94,100
Newham Buildings	Northum	NU1626	55°31·9′	1°44·4′W	X	75
Newham Drain	Lincs	TF2756	53°5·4′	0°5·8′W	W	122
Newham Drain	Lincs	TF2851	53°2·7′	0°5·0′W	W	122
Newham Fm	Corn	SX1157	50°23·2′	4°39·2′W	FM	200
Newham Fm	Lincs	TF2850	53°2·1′	0°5·1′W	FM	122
Newham Hagg	Northum	NU1527	55°32·4′	1°45·3′W	X	75
Newham Hall	Northum	NU1729	55°33·5′	1°43·4′W	X	75
Newham Hall	N Yks	NZ5113	54°30·8′	1°12·3′W	X	93
Newham Lodge Fm	Warw	SP4884	52°27·3′	1°17·2′W	FM	140
Newham Manor	Corn	SX3583	50°37·6′	4°19·6′W	X	201
New Hammond Beck	Lincs	TF2742	52°57·9′	0°6·1′W	W	131
Newhampton Fm	Heref	SO5857	52°12·8′	2°36·5′W	FM	149
New Harboro' Fm	Derby	SK2455	53°5·7′	1°38·1′W	FM	119
New Harbour	I of Angl	SH2483	53°19·1′	4°38·1′W	X	114
New Hartley	Northum	NZ3076	55°4·9′	1°31·4′W	T	88
Newhaven	C of Edin	NT2577	55°59·1′	3°11·7′W	T	66
Newhaven	Derby	SK1660	53°8·5′	1°45·2′W	T	119
Newhaven	Devon	SS3922	50°58·7′	4°17·2′W	T	190
Newhaven	E Susx	TQ4401	50°47·7′	0°3·0′E	T	198
Newhaven Cottage	Derby	SK1561	53°9·0′	1°46·1′W	X	119
Newhaven Fm	Derby	SK1760	53°8·5′	1°44·3′W	FM	119
Newhaven Lodge	Derby	SK1562	53°9·5′	1°46·1′W	X	119
New Haw	Surrey	TQ0563	51°21·6′	0°29·1′W	T	176,187
Newhay	Corn	SX2481	50°36·4′	4°28·9′W	X	201
Newhay	N Yks	SE6630	53°46·0′	0°59·5′W	T	105,106
New Hayes	Staffs	SK0312	52°42·6′	1°56·9′W	X	128
New Hayes Fm	Leic	SK4807	52°39·8′	1°17·0′W	FM	140
New Hayes Fm	Somer	ST3408	50°52·3′	2°55·9′W	FM	193
New Hayes Fm	Staffs	SJ8341	52°58·2′	2°14·8′W	FM	118
New Hay Fm	Lancs	SD6449	53°56·4′	2°32·5′W	FM	102,103
New Hay Fm	Northnts	SP8555	52°11·4′	0°45·0′W	FM	152
New Hayward Fm	W Berks	SU3470	51°25·9′	1°30·3′W	FM	174
New Headington	Oxon	SP5506	51°45·2′	1°11·8′W	T	164
New Headshaw	Scot Bord	NT4622	55°29·6′	2°50·8′W	X	73
New Heaton	Northum	NT8840	55°39·5′	2°11·0′W	T	74
New Hedges	Pemb	SN1302	51°41·4′	4°41·9′W	T	158
New Heritage	E Susx	TQ3922	50°59·1′	0°0·8′W	X	198
New Herrington	Sund	NZ3352	54°51·9′	1°28·7′W	T	88
Newhey	Roch	SD9311	53°36·0′	2°5·9′W	T	109
New Hey Fm	Ches	SJ9677	53°17·6′	2°3·2′W	FM	118
New Heys Fm	Lancs	SD3547	53°55·1′	2°59·0′W	FM	102
Newhill	Fife	NO2113	56°18·4′	3°16·2′W	X	58
Newhill	Pth & Kin	NO1108	56°15·6′	3°25·8′W	X	58
Newhill	Roth	SK4399	53°29·4′	1°20·7′W	T	111
New Hill	Worcs	SP1344	52°5·9′	1°48·2′W	X	151
New Hill Barn	W Susx	TQ1609	50°52·4′	0°20·7′W	X	198
Newhills	C of Aber	NJ8709	57°10·6′	2°12·4′W	T	38
New Hinksey	Oxon	SP5104	51°44·2′	1°15·3′W	T	164
New Ho	Card	ST2478	51°30·0′	3°4·3′W	X	171
New Ho	Cumbr	NY0950	54°50·4′	3°24·6′W	X	85
New Ho	Cumbr	NY3542	54°46·4′	3°0·2′W	X	85
New Ho	Cumbr	NY4674	55°3·7′	2°50·3′W	X	86
New Ho	Cumbr	NY5675	55°4·3′	2°40·9′W	X	86
New Ho	Cumbr	NY6108	54°28·2′	2°35·7′W	X	91
New Ho	Cumbr	NY6407	54°27·7′	2°32·9′W	X	91
New Ho	Cumbr	SD6393	54°20·1′	2°33·7′W	X	97
New Ho	Darl	NZ2324	54°36·9′	1°38·2′W	X	93
New Ho	Darl	NZ2520	54°34·7′	1°36·4′W	X	93
New Ho	Derby	SK2742	52°58·7′	1°35·5′W	X	119,128
New Ho	D & G	NX9798	55°16·2′	3°36·8′W	X	78

New Ho	Dorset	ST4504	50°50·2′	2°46·5′W	X	193
New Ho	Durham	NY8530	54°40·1′	2°13·5′W	X	91,92
New Ho	Durham	NY8738	54°44·5′	2°11·7′W	T	91,92
New Ho	E Susx	TQ7725	51°0·1′	0°31·8′E	X	188,199
New Ho	Heref	SO2640	52°3·4′	3°4·4′W	X	148,161
New Ho	Heref	SO3151	52°9·4′	3°0·1′W	X	148
New Ho	Heref	SO3466	52°17·5′	2°57·7′W	X	137,148,149
New Ho	Heref	SO3565	52°17·0′	2°56·8′W	X	137,148,149
New Ho	Heref	SO4572	52°20·8′	2°48·0′W	X	137,138,148
New Ho	Heref	SO4621	51°53·3′	2°46·7′W	X	161
New Ho	Lancs	SD6242	53°52·6′	2°34·3′W	X	102,103
New Ho	Lancs	SD6433	53°47·8′	2°32·4′W	X	102,103
New Ho	Lancs	SD7158	54°1·3′	2°26·1′W	X	103
New Ho	Lancs	SD8641	53°52·1′	2°12·4′W	X	103
New Ho	Lincs	TF4523	52°47·3′	0°9·4′E	X	131
New Ho	Monm	SO3616	51°50·6′	2°55·3′W	X	161
New Ho	Monm	SO4403	51°43·6′	2°48·3′W	X	171
New Ho	Monm	SO4418	51°51·7′	2°48·4′W	X	161
New Ho	Monm	ST4398	51°40·9′	2°49·1′W	X	171
New Ho	Newp	ST2780	51°31·1′	3°2·7′W	X	171
New Ho	Newp	ST3083	51°32·7′	3°0·2′W	X	171
New Ho	Northum	NY7848	54°49·8′	2°20·1′W	X	86,87
New Ho	Northum	NY9152	54°52·0′	2°8·0′W	X	87
New Ho	N Yks	NZ1511	54°29·9′	1°45·7′W	X	92
New Ho	N Yks	NZ6504	54°25·9′	0°59·5′W	X	94
New Ho	N Yks	NZ7603	54°25·2′	0°49·3′W	X	94
New Ho	N Yks	SD6867	54°6·1′	2°28·9′W	X	98
New Ho	N Yks	SD7957	54°0·8′	2°18·8′W	X	103
New Ho	N Yks	SD8353	53°58·6′	2°15·1′W	X	103
New Ho	N Yks	SD8457	54°0·8′	2°14·2′W	X	103
New Ho	N Yks	SD9364	54°4·6′	2°6·0′W	X	98
New Ho	N Yks	SD9683	54°14·8′	2°3·3′W	X	98
New Ho	N Yks	SE0149	53°56·5′	1°58·7′W	X	104
New Ho	N Yks	SE5792	54°19·5′	1°7·0′W	X	100
New Ho	Pemb	SM9113	51°46·8′	5°1·4′W	X	157,158
New Ho	Powys	SJ2303	52°37·4′	3°7·9′W	X	126
New Ho	Powys	SN9667	52°17·7′	3°31·1′W	X	136,147
New Ho	Powys	SO0495	52°32·9′	3°24·5′W	X	136
New Ho	Powys	SO1471	52°20·1′	3°15·3′W	X	136,148
New Ho	Powys	SO1594	52°32·5′	3°14·8′W	X	136
New Ho	Powys	SO1798	52°34·7′	3°13·1′W	X	136
New Ho	Powys	SO2293	52°32·0′	3°8·6′W	X	137
New Ho	Shrops	SJ3239	52°56·9′	3°0·3′W	X	126
New Ho	Shrops	SJ3905	52°38·6′	2°53·7′W	X	126
New Ho	Shrops	SJ4732	52°53·2′	2°46·9′W	X	126
New Ho	Shrops	SJ5030	52°52·2′	2°44·2′W	X	126
New Ho	Shrops	SJ5321	52°47·3′	2°41·4′W	X	126
New Ho	Shrops	SJ7301	52°36·6′	2°23·5′W	X	127
New Ho	Shrops	SO2786	52°28·3′	3°4·1′W	X	137
New Ho	Shrops	SO2875	52°22·3′	3°3·1′W	X	137,148
New Ho	Shrops	SO2897	52°34·2′	3°3·3′W	X	137
New Ho	Shrops	SO3378	52°24·0′	2°58·7′W	X	137,148
New Ho	Shrops	SO3581	52°25·6′	2°57·0′W	X	137
New Ho	Shrops	SO3895	52°33·2′	2°54·5′W	X	137
New Ho	Shrops	SO4389	52°30·0′	2°50·0′W	X	137
New Ho	Shrops	SO4883	52°26·8′	2°45·5′W	X	137,138
New Ho	Shrops	SO5281	52°25·7′	2°42·0′W	X	137,138
New Ho	Shrops	SO5384	52°27·4′	2°41·1′W	X	137,138
New Ho	Shrops	SO5490	52°30·6′	2°40·3′W	X	137,138
New Ho	Shrops	SO5782	52°26·3′	2°37·6′W	X	137,138
New Ho	Shrops	SO5786	52°28·5′	2°37·6′W	X	137,138
New Ho	Staffs	SJ9837	52°56·1′	2°1·4′W	X	127
New Ho	Worcs	SO7669	52°19·4′	2°20·7′W	X	138
New Ho	Wrekin	SJ7221	52°47·4′	2°24·5′W	X	127
New Ho Fm	Shrops	SO3691	52°31·0′	2°56·2′W	FM	137
New Ho Fm	Shrops	SO4580	52°25·2′	2°48·1′W	FM	137,138
New Ho Fm	Shrops	SO6492	52°31·7′	2°31·4′W	FM	138
New Holbeck Fm	Notts	SK6553	53°4·5′	1°1·4′W	FM	120
New Holkham	Norf	TF8839	52°55·2′	0°48·2′E	T	132
New Holland	Brad	SE0835	53°48·9′	1°52·3′W	T	104
New Holland	N Lincs	TA0823	53°41·8′	0°21·4′W	T	107,112
New Holland	Orkney	HY4903	58°54·9′	2°52·7′W	X	6,7
Newholm	N Yks	NZ8610	54°28·9′	0°39·9′W	T	94
Newholm	S Lanak	NT0847	55°42·7′	3°27·4′W	X	72
Newholm Cairns Hill	Scot Bord	NT1628	55°32·6′	3°19·4′W	H	72
Newholme	Lincs	TF3592	53°24·7′	0°2·3′E	X	113
Newholme Fm	N Yks	SE2375	54°10·5′	1°38·4′W	FM	99
New Homer Carr Plantn	Durham	NZ3726	54°37·9′	1°25·2′W	F	93
New Homestead Fm	Lincs	TF0251	53°3·0′	0°28·3′W	FM	121
New Homestead Fm	Somer	ST3750	51°15·0′	2°53·8′W	FM	182
New Hook Fm	Kent	TQ9670	51°23·9′	0°49·5′E	FM	178
New Horndean	Scot Bord	NT8949	55°44·3′	2°10·1′W	X	74
New Horwich	Derby	SK0180	53°19·3′	1°58·7′W	T	110
New Hos	Northum	NY8645	54°48·2′	2°12·6′W	X	87
New Hos	Northum	NZ0381	55°7·6′	1°56·7′W	X	81
New Hotel	Cumbr	NY2906	54°26·9′	3°5·3′W	X	89,90
New Houghton	Derby	SK4965	53°11·0′	1°15·6′W	T	120
New Houghton	Norf	TF7927	52°48·9′	0°39·8′E	T	132
Newhouse	Arg & Bt	NR7461	55°47·6′	5°35·9′W	X	62
Newhouse	C of Edin	NT1567	55°53·6′	3°21·1′W	X	65
Newhouse	Corn	SX3185	50°38·6′	4°23·0′W	X	201
Newhouse	Devon	SS8015	50°55·6′	3°42·1′W	X	181
Newhouse	Devon	SX4666	50°28·7′	4°9·9′W	X	201
Newhouse	Devon	SX7453	50°22·0′	3°45·9′W	X	202
Newhouse	Devon	SX7954	50°22·6′	3°41·7′W	X	202
Newhouse	D & G	NX9081	55°6·9′	3°43·0′W	X	78
New House	Durham	NZ1842	54°46·6′	1°42·8′W	X	88
Newhouse	E Ayr	NS3737	55°36·2′	4°34·8′W	X	70
Newhouse	E Ayr	NS4250	55°43·3′	4°30·5′W	X	64
Newhouse	E Ayr	NS4538	55°36·9′	4°27·2′W	X	70
Newhouse	E Ayr	NS5432	55°33·8′	4°18·5′W	X	70
Newhouse	E Loth	NT5383	56°2·5′	2°44·8′W	X	66
Newhouse	E Renf	NS4957	55°47·2′	4°24·1′W	X	64
Newhouse	Essex	TL4913	51°48·0′	0°10·1′E	X	167
Newhouse	Essex	TL5408	51°45·2′	0°14·3′E	X	167
Newhouse	Essex	TM0727	51°54·4′	1°1·0′E	X	168,169
New House	Kent	TQ6372	51°25·6′	0°21·1′E	X	177
New House	Kent	TR0169	51°23·3′	0°55·7′E	X	178
New House	Kirk	SE2007	53°33·8′	1°41·5′W	X	110
New House	Monm	SO3202	51°43·0′	2°58·7′W	X	171

New House	Monm	SO3822	51°53·8'	2°53·7'W	X	161
Newhouse	Monm	ST4095	51°39·3'	2°51·7'W	X	171
Newhouse	N Ayr	NS3549	55°42·6'	4°37·1'W	X	63
Newhouse	N Lanak	NS7961	55°49·9'	3°55·5'W	T	64
Newhouse	Orkney	HY2513	59°0·1'	3°17·8'W	X	6
Newhouse	Orkney	HY3021	59°4·5'	3°12·8'W	X	6
Newhouse	Orkney	HY3928	59°8·3'	3°3·5'W	X	6
Newhouse	Orkney	HY5202	58°54·4'	2°49·5'W	X	6,7
Newhouse	Orkney	HY5605	58°56·1'	2°45·4'W	X	6
Newhouse	Orkney	ND3593	58°49·4'	3°7·1'W	X	7
New House	Pemb	SM9912	51°46·5'	4°54·4'W	X	157,158
Newhouse	Pemb	SM9927	51°54·6'	4°54·9'W	X	157,158
New House	Pemb	SN1511	51°46·3'	4°40·5'W	X	158
Newhouse	Powys	SO0476	52°22·7'	3°24·2'W	X	136,147
Newhouse	Powys	SO0968	52°18·4'	3°19·7'W	X	136,147
Newhouse	Powys	SO2254	52°11·0'	3°8·1'W	X	148
Newhouse	Pth & Kin	NO0824	56°24·2'	3°29·0'W	X	52,53,58
Newhouse	Scot Bord	NT5223	55°30·2'	2°45·2'W	T	73
Newhouse	Shetld	HU4062	60°20·7'	1°16·0'W	X	2,3
Newhouse	S Lanak	NS5952	55°44·7'	4°14·3'W	X	64
Newhouse	S Lanak	NS6755	55°46·5'	4°6·8'W	X	64
Newhouse	S Lanak	NS7449	55°43·3'	3°59·9'W	X	64
Newhouse	S Lanak	NS9245	55°41·4'	3°42·6'W	X	72
Newhouse	Wilts	SU2121	50°59·5'	1°41·7'W	A	184
Newhouse	W Loth	NS9861	55°50·1'	3°37·3'W	X	65
New House	W Susx	TQ2519	50°57·6'	0°12·8'W	X	198
Newhouse Barton	Devon	SX8265	50°28·6'	3°39·4'W	X	202
Newhouse Copse	Hants	SZ3799	50°47·6'	1°28·1'W	F	196
Newhouse Cottages	Essex	TL8636	51°59·7'	0°43·0'E	X	155
New House Fm	Bucks	SP7117	51°51·1'	0°57·8'W	FM	165
New House Fm	Bucks	SU8699	51°41·2'	0°45·0'W	FM	165
New House Fm	Bucks	TQ0196	51°39·5'	0°32·0'W	FM	166,176
New House Fm	Bucks	TQ0385	51°33·5'	0°30·5'W	FM	176
New House Fm	Cambs	TL3685	52°27·0'	0°0·5'E	FM	142
New House Fm	Ches	SJ8477	53°17·6'	2°14·0'W	FM	118
New House Fm	Ches	SJ9484	53°21·4'	2°5·0'W	FM	109
New House Fm	Cumbr	NY0234	54°41·7'	3°30·8'W	FM	89
New House Fm	Cumbr	NY1523	54°36·0'	3°18·5'W	FM	89
New House Fm	Cumbr	NY3754	54°52·9'	2°58·5'W	FM	85
New House Fm	Derby	SK0683	53°20·9'	1°54·2'W	FM	110
Newhouse Fm	Derby	SK2151	53°3·6'	1°40·8'W	FM	119
New House Fm	Devon	SS8507	50°51·3'	3°37·6'W	FM	191
New House Fm	Devon	ST1605	50°50·5'	3°11·2'W	FM	192,193
New House Fm	Devon	ST3401	50°48·5'	2°55·8'W	FM	193
New House Fm	Devon	SX8392	50°43·2'	3°39·1'W	FM	191
New House Fm	Devon	SX9480	50°36·8'	3°29·5'W	FM	192
New House Fm	Donc	SE6414	53°37·4'	1°1·5'W	FM	111
New House Fm	Dorset	ST7412	50°54·6'	2°21·8'W	FM	194
New House Fm	Dorset	SY4297	50°46·4'	2°49·0'W	FM	193
New House Fm	Durham	NZ1147	54°49·3'	1°49·3'W	FM	88
New House Fm	Essex	TL5005	51°43·6'	0°10·7'E	FM	167
New House Fm	Essex	TL5534	51°59·2'	0°15·8'E	FM	154
New House Fm	Essex	TL5635	51°59·7'	0°16·7'E	FM	154
New House Fm	Essex	TL5712	51°47·3'	0°17·0'E	FM	167
Newhouse Fm	Essex	TL5937	52°0·7'	0°19·4'E	FM	154
New House Fm	Essex	TL5939	52°1·8'	0°19·5'E	FM	154
New House Fm	Essex	TL7837	52°0·4'	0°36·0'E	FM	155
New House Fm	Essex	TL8236	51°59·8'	0°39·5'E	FM	155
New House Fm	Essex	TR0293	51°36·2'	0°55·4'E	FM	178
New House Fm	E Susx	TQ3620	50°58·0'	0°3·4'W	FM	198
New House Fm	E Susx	TQ4418	50°56·8'	0°3·4'E	FM	198
Newhouse Fm	E Susx	TQ4708	50°51·4'	0°5·7'E	FM	198
New House Fm	E Susx	TQ4924	51°0·0'	0°7·8'E	FM	199
New House Fm	E Susx	TQ5210	50°52·4'	0°10·0'E	FM	199
New House Fm	E Susx	TQ6407	50°50·6'	0°20·2'E	FM	199
New House Fm	E Susx	TQ7022	50°58·6'	0°25·7'E	FM	199
New House Fm	E Susx	TQ7027	51°1·3'	0°25·8'E	FM	188,199
New House Fm	E Susx	TQ8022	50°58·4'	0°34·2'E	FM	199
New House Fm	E Susx	TQ8740	50°59·3'	0°41·1'E	FM	189,199
New House Fm	E Yorks	TA2122	53°41·1'	0°9·7'W	FM	107,113
Newhouse Fm	Hants	SU3700	50°48·1'	1°28·1'W	FM	196
New House Fm	Hants	SU5436	51°7·5'	1°13·3'W	FM	185
New House Fm	Hants	SU6859	51°19·8'	1°1·0'W	FM	175,186
New House Fm	Heref	SO2838	52°2·4'	3°2·6'W	FM	161
New House Fm	Heref	SO3035	52°0·8'	3°0·8'W	FM	161
New House Fm	Heref	SO3354	52°11·0'	2°58·4'W	FM	148,149
Newhouse Fm	Heref	SO4343	52°5·2'	2°49·5'W	FM	148,149,161
New House Fm	Heref	SO4529	51°57·6'	2°47·6'W	FM	149,161
New House Fm	Heref	SO5554	52°11·2'	2°39·1'W	FM	149
Newhouse Fm	Heref	SO5648	52°8·0'	2°38·2'W	FM	149
Newhouse Fm	Heref	SO6152	52°10·1'	2°33·8'W	FM	149
New House Fm	Heref	SO6432	51°59·4'	2°31·1'W	FM	149
New House Fm	Heref	SO6657	52°12·8'	2°29·5'W	FM	149
New House Fm	Heref	SO6822	51°54·0'	2°27·5'W	FM	162
New House Fm	Heref	SO7159	52°13·9'	2°25·1'W	FM	149
Newhouse Fm	Herts	TL4717	51°50·2'	0°8·4'E	FM	167
New House Fm	Kent	TQ5250	51°14·0'	0°11·0'E	FM	188
New House Fm	Kent	TQ5959	51°18·7'	0°17·3'E	FM	188
New House Fm	Kent	TQ8343	51°9·6'	0°37·4'E	FM	188
New House Fm	Kent	TQ8842	51°9·0'	0°41·7'E	FM	189
Newhouse Fm	Kent	TQ9142	51°8·9'	0°44·2'E	FM	189
New House Fm	Kent	TR0028	51°1·2'	0°51·5'E	FM	189
New House Fm	Kent	TR0135	51°5·0'	0°52·6'E	FM	189
New House Fm	Kent	TR0257	51°16·8'	0°54·2'E	FM	178
New House Fm	Kent	TR1354	51°14·9'	1°3·5'E	FM	179,189
New House Fm	Kent	TR2562	51°19·0'	1°14·1'E	FM	179
New House Fm	Lancs	SD3930	53°46·0'	2°55·1'W	FM	102
New House Fm	Lancs	SD4740	53°51·5'	2°47·9'W	FM	102
New House Fm	Lancs	SD4747	53°55·2'	2°48·0'W	FM	102
New House Fm	Leic	SK5301	52°36·5'	1°12·6'W	FM	140
New House Fm	Lincs	TF1324	52°48·3'	0°19·0'W	FM	130
New House Fm	Monm	SO4204	51°44·1'	2°50·0'W	FM	171
New House Fm	Monm	SO4410	51°47·4'	2°48·3'W	FM	161
New House Fm	N Ayr	NS2946	55°40·9'	4°42·8'W	FM	63
New House Fm	Norf	TM0987	52°26·7'	1°4·9'E	FM	144
New-house Fm	Northnts	SP7079	52°24·5'	0°57·9'W	FM	141
New House Fm	Northum	NZ0353	54°52·6'	1°56·8'W	FM	87
New House Fm	N Yks	SE6666	54°5·4'	0°59·0'W	FM	100
New House Fm	Oxon	SP3405	51°44·8'	1°30·1'W	FM	164
Newhouse Fm	Oxon	SP4329	51°57·7'	1°22·1'W	FM	164

New House Fm	Oxon	SP5416	51°50·6'	1°12·6'W	FM	164
Newhouse Fm	Oxon	SU3997	51°40·5'	1°25·8'W	FM	164
Newhouse Fm	Powys	SO0652	52°9·7'	3°22·1'W	FM	147
Newhouse Fm	Powys	SO1669	52°19·0'	3°13·5'W	FM	136,148
Newhouse Fm	S Glos	ST7290	51°36·7'	2°23·9'W	FM	162,172
Newhouse Fm	S Glos	ST7587	51°35·1'	2°21·3'W	FM	172
Newhouse Fm	S Glos	ST7880	51°31·3'	2°18·6'W	FM	172
Newhouse Fm	Shrops	SJ3704	52°38·0'	2°55·5'W	FM	126
New House Fm	Shrops	SJ4238	52°56·4'	2°51·4'W	FM	126
New House Fm	Shrops	SJ5627	52°50·6'	2°38·8'W	FM	126
Newhouse Fm	Shrops	SJ6130	52°52·2'	2°34·4'W	FM	127
New House Fm	Shrops	SJ6401	52°36·6'	2°31·5'W	FM	127
New House Fm	Shrops	SJ6626	52°50·1'	2°29·9'W	FM	127
New House Fm	Shrops	SJ6636	52°55·5'	2°29·9'W	FM	127
New House Fm	Shrops	SO4694	52°32·7'	2°47·4'W	FM	137,138
New House Fm	Shrops	SO5784	52°27·4'	2°37·6'W	FM	137,138
New House Fm	Shrops	SO6388	52°29·6'	2°32·3'W	FM	138
New House Fm	Shrops	SO6681	52°25·8'	2°29·6'W	FM	138
Newhouse Fm	Somer	ST3015	50°56·0'	2°59·4'W	FM	193
New House Fm	Somer	ST3233	51°5·8'	2°57·9'W	FM	182
New House Fm	Somer	ST3331	51°4·7'	2°57·0'W	FM	182
New House Fm	Somer	ST7341	51°10·3'	2°22·8'W	FM	183
Newhouse Fm	Staffs	SJ7932	52°53·3'	2°18·3'W	FM	127
New House Fm	Staffs	SJ8114	52°43·6'	2°16·5'W	FM	127
New House Fm	Staffs	SJ8140	52°57·7'	2°16·6'W	FM	118
New House Fm	Staffs	SJ9350	53°3·1'	2°5·9'W	FM	118
New House Fm	Staffs	SJ9637	52°56·1'	2°3·2'W	FM	127
New House Fm	Staffs	SK0356	53°6·3'	1°56·9'W	FM	119
New House Fm	Staffs	SO8087	52°29·1'	2°17·3'W	FM	138
New House Fm	Suff	TL7748	52°6·3'	0°35·5'E	FM	155
New House Fm	Suff	TL8653	52°8·9'	0°43·5'E	FM	155
New House Fm	Suff	TM0038	52°0·5'	0°55·2'E	FM	155
New House Fm	Suff	TM4386	52°25·3'	1°34·8'E	FM	156
New House Fm	Surrey	TQ0636	51°7·0'	0°28·7'W	FM	187
New House Fm	Surrey	TQ2040	51°9·0'	0°16·7'W	FM	187
New House Fm	Surrey	TQ3140	51°8·9'	0°7·2'W	FM	187
New House Fm	Surrey	TQ3749	51°13·6'	0°1·9'W	FM	187
New House Fm	V of Glam	SS9973	51°27·1'	3°26·8'W	FM	170
New House Fm	Warw	SP1998	52°35·0'	1°42·8'W	FM	139
New House Fm	Warw	SP2592	52°31·8'	1°37·5'W	FM	140
New House Fm	Warw	SP3038	52°2·6'	1°33·4'W	FM	151
New House Fm	Warw	SP3062	52°15·6'	1°33·2'W	FM	151
New House Fm	Warw	SP3954	52°11·2'	1°25·4'W	FM	151
New House Fm	Warw	SP4257	52°12·8'	1°22·7'W	FM	151
New House Fm	Warw	SP4355	52°11·7'	1°21·9'W	FM	151
New House Fm	Wilts	ST8664	51°22·7'	2°11·7'W	FM	173
New House Fm	Worcs	SO6465	52°17·2'	2°31·3'W	FM	138,149
New House Fm	Worcs	SO6766	52°17·7'	2°28·6'W	FM	138,149
New House Fm	Worcs	SO8670	52°19·9'	2°11·9'W	FM	139
New House Fm	Worcs	SO8974	52°22·1'	2°9·3'W	FM	139
Newhouse Fm	Worcs	SP0375	52°22·6'	1°57·0'W	FM	139
New House Fm	Wrex	SJ4534	52°54·3'	2°48·7'W	FM	126
New House Fm	Wrex	SJ4740	52°57·5'	2°46·9'W	FM	117
New House Fm	W Susx	SU8319	50°58·1'	0°48·7'W	FM	197
Newhouse Fm	W Susx	SU9014	50°55·3'	0°42·8'W	FM	197
Newhouse Fm	W Susx	SU9731	51°4·4'	0°36·5'W	FM	186
New House Fm	W Susx	TQ1115	50°55·7'	0°24·8'W	FM	198
Newhouse Fm	W Susx	TQ2033	51°5·3'	0°16·8'W	FM	187
Newhouse Fm	W Susx	TQ2718	50°57·1'	0°11·1'W	FM	198
New House Fm	W Susx	TQ3332	51°4·5'	0°5·7'W	FM	187
New House Gill	N Yks	SE0980	54°13·2'	1°51·3'W	W	99
New House Grange	Leic	SK3102	52°37·1'	1°32·1'W	X	140
Newhouse Hill	Powys	SO1476	52°22·8'	3°15·4'W	X	136,148
Newhouse Industrial Estate	N Lanak	NS7761	55°49·9'	3°57·4'W	X	64
Newhouse Kip	Scot Bord	NT3623	55°30·0'	3°0·4'W	X	73
Newhousemill	S Lanak	NS6553	55°45·3'	4°8·6'W	T	64
Newhouse Moor	Durham	NY8739	54°45·0'	2°11·7'W	X	91,92
Newhouse Moor	Durham	NY8740	54°45·5'	2°11·7'W	X	87
Newhouse Plantation	D & G	NX8598	55°16·0'	3°48·2'W	F	78
New Houses	Derby	SK1673	53°15·5'	1°45·2'W	X	119
New Houses	Durham	NY9419	54°34·2'	2°5·1'W	X	91,92
Newhouses	Northum	NU1630	55°34·1'	1°44·3'W	X	75
Newhouses	Northum	NZ0083	55°8·7'	1°59·6'W	X	81
New Houses	N Yks	SD8073	54°9·4'	2°18·0'W	T	98
New Houses	N Yks	SE0976	54°11·0'	1°51·3'W	X	99
Newhouses	Scot Bord	NT5118	55°27·5'	2°46·1'W	X	79
Newhouses	Scot Bord	NT5144	55°41·5'	2°46·3'W	T	73
Newhouses	Scot Bord	NT6814	55°25·4'	2°29·9'W	X	80
New Houses	Shrops	SJ8103	52°37·7'	2°16·4'W	X	127
New Houses	Wigan	SD5502	53°31·0'	2°40·3'W	T	108
New Houses Fm	Durham	NZ1548	54°49·8'	1°45·6'W	FM	88
New Houses Fm	Northum	NZ1893	55°14·1'	1°42·6'W	FM	81
Newhouses Fm	S Lanak	NS6843	55°40·0'	4°5·5'W	FM	71
New House Wood	Heref	SO2639	52°2·9'	3°4·4'W	F	161
New Hunwick	Durham	NZ1832	54°41·2'	1°42·8'W	T	92
Newhurst Fm	Kent	TQ9635	51°5·1'	0°48·3'E	FM	189
New Hutton	Cumbr	SD5691	54°19·0'	2°40·2'W	T	97
New Hythe	Kent	TQ7059	51°18·5'	0°26·7'E	T	178,188
Newick	E Susx	TQ4121	50°58·5'	0°0·9'E	T	198
Newick Fm	E Susx	TQ5922	50°58·7'	0°16·3'E	FM	199
Newick Park	E Susx	TQ4219	50°57·4'	0°1·7'E	X	198
New Ing	Lancs	SD7850	53°57·0'	2°19·7'W	X	103
New Ing	Lancs	SD8347	53°55·4'	2°15·1'W	X	103
Newing	Shetld	HU4656	60°17·4'	1°9·6'W	X	2,3
New Ingarsby Fm	Leic	SK6604	52°38·0'	1°1·1'W	FM	141
Newingreen	Kent	TR1236	51°5·3'	1°2·0'E	T	179,189
New Ings	Donc	SE6517	53°39·0'	1°0·6'W	X	111
New Ings	E Yorks	TA0634	53°47·7'	0°23·0'W	X	107
New Ings Plantn	N Yks	SE9780	54°12·6'	0°30·3'W	F	101
Newington	C of Edin	NT2671	55°55·8'	3°10·6'W	T	66
Newington	D & G	NX9480	55°6·4'	3°39·3'W	X	78
Newington	Fife	NO3419	56°21·8'	3°3·7'W	X	59
Newington	Kent	TQ8564	51°20·9'	0°39·8'E	T	178
Newington	Kent	TR1737	51°5·7'	1°6·3'E	T	179,189
Newington	Kent	TR3666	51°20·9'	1°23·7'E	T	179
Newington	Notts	SK6693	53°26·0'	1°0·0'W	T	111
Newington	Oxon	SU6096	51°39·8'	1°7·6'W	T	164,165
Newington	Shrops	SO4383	52°26·8'	2°49·9'W	T	137
Newington	Sthwk	TQ3279	51°29·9'	0°5·5'W	T	176,177

Newington Bagpath	Glos	ST8194	51°38·9'	2°16·1'W	T	162,173
Newington Grounds Fm	Oxon	SP4140	52°3·6'	1°23·7'W	FM	151
Newington Ho	Oxon	SU6096	51°39·8'	1°7·6'W	A	164,165
Newington Manor	Kent	TQ8564	51°20·9'	0°39·8'E	X	178
New Inn	Carm	SN4736	52°0·3'	4°13·4'W	T	146
New Inn	Carm	SN6325	51°54·6'	3°59·1'W	X	146
New Inn	Devon	SS4408	50°51·3'	4°12·6'W	T	190
New Inn	Fife	NO2804	56°13·6'	3°9·2'W	X	59
New Inn	Leic	SP7299	52°35·3'	0°55·8'W	X	141
New Inn	Monm	SO4800	51°42·0'	2°44·8'W	T	171
New Inn	Torf	ST3099	51°41·4'	3°0·4'W	T	171
New Inn Bridge Fm	Flint	SJ2967	53°12·0'	3°3·4'W	FM	117
New Inn Fm	Beds	TL0833	51°59·3'	0°25·2'W	FM	166
New Inn Fm	Bucks	SP6836	52°1·3'	1°0·1'W	FM	152
New Inn Fm	Cambs	TL3260	52°13·6'	0°3·6'W	FM	153
New Inn Fm	N Yks	SE3284	54°15·3'	1°30·1'W	FM	99
New Inn Fm	N Yks	SE4156	54°0·1'	1°22·1'W	FM	105
New Inn Fm	Oxon	SP5610	51°47·4'	1°10·9'W	FM	164
New Inn Fm	Pemb	SN0802	51°41·3'	4°46·3'W	FM	158
Newinn of Gorthy	Pth & Kin	NN9724	56°24·1'	3°39·7'W	X	52,53,58
New Inns	Lancs	SD7031	53°46·7'	2°26·9'W	X	103
New Intax	E Ayr	NS5039	55°37·5'	4°22·5'W	X	70
New Invention	Shrops	SO2976	52°22·9'	3°2·2'W	T	137,148
New Invention	Somer	SS9029	51°3·2'	3°33·8'W	X	181
New Invention	Wals	SJ9701	52°36·6'	2°2·3'W	T	127,139
New Ivesley	Durham	NZ1741	54°46·1'	1°43·7'W	X	88
New Jerome Cottage	Herts	TL1109	51°46·3'	0°23·1'W	X	166
New Jersey Fm	Essex	TL4740	52°2·6'	0°9·0'E	FM	154
New Junction Canal	Donc	SE6315	53°37·9'	1°2·4'W	W	111
New Keig	Aberd	NJ5919	57°15·8'	2°40·3'W	X	37
New Kelso	Highld	NG9342	57°25·5'	5°26·4'W	X	25
New Kendal	Aberd	NJ8323	57°18·1'	2°16·5'W	X	38
New Kennels	Northum	NZ2178	55°6·0'	1°39·8'W	X	88
New Kilrie	Angus	NO3851	56°39·1'	3°0·2'W	X	54
New Kingston	Notts	SK5128	52°51·1'	1°14·2'W	T	129
New Kinord	Aberd	NO4499	57°5·0'	2°55·0'W	X	37,44
New Kyo	Durham	NZ1751	54°51·5'	1°43·7'W	T	88
New Ladykirk	Scot Bord	NT8948	55°43·8'	2°10·1'W	T	74
New Laith	Lancs	SD9038	53°50·5'	2°8·7'W	X	103
New Laith	Lancs	SD9139	53°51·1'	2°7·8'W	X	103
New Laithe	Lancs	SD6948	53°55·9'	2°27·9'W	X	103
New Laithe	Lancs	SD8128	53°45·1'	2°16·9'W	X	103
New Laithe	N Yks	SD8865	54°5·1'	2°10·6'W	X	98
New Laithe	N Yks	SD9359	54°1·9'	2°6·0'W	X	103
New Laithe	N Yks	SD9760	54°2·4'	2°2·3'W	X	98
New Laithe Fm	Leeds	SE3344	53°53·7'	1°29·5'W	FM	104
New Laithe Moor	Cald	SD9631	53°46·8'	2°3·2'W	X	103
New Lambton	Durham	NZ3150	54°50·9'	1°30·6'W	X	88
New Lanark	S Lanak	NS8842	55°39·8'	3°46·4'W	T	71,72
Newland	Corn	SW9181	50°35·7'	4°56·8'W	X	200
Newland	Cumbr	SD3079	54°12·4'	3°4·0'W	T	96,97
Newland	Devon	SS8509	50°52·4'	3°37·7'W	X	191
Newland	E Yorks	SE8029	53°45·3'	0°46·8'W	T	106
Newland	Glos	SO5509	51°46·9'	2°38·7'W	T	162
Newland	Kent	TR0122	50°58·0'	0°52·1'E	X	189
Newland	K upon H	TA0831	53°46·1'	0°21·3'W	T	107
Newland	Nth Pt Talb	SS8083	51°32·2'	3°43·4'W	X	170
Newland	N Yks	SE6924	53°42·7'	0°56·9'W	T	105,106
Newland	Oxon	SP3610	51°47·5'	1°28·3'W	T	164
Newland	Somer	SS8238	51°8·0'	3°40·8'W	X	181
Newland	Somer	SS8335	51°6·4'	3°39·9'W	X	181
Newland	V of Glam	SS9477	51°29·2'	3°31·2'W	X	170
Newland	Worcs	SO7948	52°8·0'	2°18·0'W	T	150
Newland Beck	Cumbr	SD3080	54°12·9'	3°4·0'W	W	96,97
Newland Bottom	Cumbr	SD2980	54°12·9'	3°4·9'W	T	96,97
Newland Brook	Essex	TL6309	51°45·6'	0°22·1'E	W	167
Newlandburn Fm	Midlo	NT3662	55°51·1'	3°0·9'W	FM	66
Newlandburn Ho	Midlo	NT3662	55°51·1'	3°0·9'W	X	66
Newland Common	Worcs	SO9060	52°14·5'	2°8·4'W	T	150
Newland Court	Worcs	SO8049	52°8·6'	2°17·1'W	X	150
Newland End	Essex	TL4735	51°59·9'	0°8·9'E	X	154
Newland Fm	Devon	SS8316	50°56·1'	3°39·5'W	FM	181
Newland Fm	Devon	ST0407	50°51·5'	3°21·5'W	FM	192
Newland Fm	Kent	TR0222	50°57·9'	0°53·0'E	FM	189
Newland Fm	Lincs	TF1020	52°46·2'	0°21·8'W	FM	130
Newland Green	Kent	TQ9045	51°10·6'	0°43·5'E	T	189
Newland Hall	Essex	TL6309	51°45·6'	0°22·1'E	X	167
Newland Hall	Lancs	SD5054	53°59·0'	2°45·3'W	X	102
Newland Hall	Wakf	SE3622	53°41·8'	1°26·9'W	X	104
Newland Hall Fm	Warw	SP3285	52°28·0'	1°31·3'W	FM	140
Newlandhead	Angus	NO3738	56°32·0'	3°1·0'W	X	54
Newlandhead	Angus	NO4840	56°33·2'	2°50·3'W	T	54
Newlandhill	Aberd	NJ9351	57°33·2'	2°6·6'W	X	30
Newland Hill	D & G	NY2586	55°10·0'	3°10·2'W	H	79
Newland Ho	Cumbr	SD8271	54°8·3'	2°16·1'W	X	98
Newland House Fm	Warw	SP3285	52°28·0'	1°31·3'W	FM	140
Newland Mill	Devon	SS6500	50°47·3'	3°54·5'W	X	191
Newland Park	Bucks	TQ0193	51°37·8'	0°32·0'W	X	176
Newlandrig	Midlo	NT3662	55°51·1'	3°0·9'W	T	66
Newlands	Aberd	NJ8317	57°14·9'	2°16·4'W	X	38
Newlands	Aberd	NO7280	56°54·9'	2°27·1'W	X	45
Newlands	Aberd	NO7467	56°47·9'	2°25·1'W	X	45
Newlands	Aberd	NO8483	56°56·5'	2°15·3'W	X	45
Newlands	Angus	NO4447	56°36·9'	2°54·3'W	X	54
Newlands	C of Glas	NS5760	55°49·0'	4°16·5'W	T	64
Newlands	Cumbr	NY2320	54°34·4'	3°11·0'W	T	89,90
Newlands	Cumbr	NY3439	54°44·7'	3°1·1'W	T	90
Newlands	Cumbr	NY4352	54°51·8'	2°52·9'W	X	85
Newlands	Cumbr	NY6715	54°32·0'	2°30·2'W	X	91
Newlands	Cumbr	SD5188	54°17·4'	2°44·7'W	X	97
Newlands	Derby	SK3143	52°59·2'	1°31·9'W	X	119,128
Newlands	Derby	SK4446	53°0·8'	1°20·2'W	T	129
Newlands	Devon	SS3012	50°53·2'	4°24·6'W	X	190
Newlands	Devon	SS6521	50°58·6'	3°55·0'W	X	180
Newlands	Devon	SX6355	50°23·0'	3°55·2'W	X	202
Newlands	Devon	SY0097	50°46·1'	3°24·7'W	X	192
Newlands	D & G	NX8798	55°16·0'	3°46·3'W	X	78
Newlands	D & G	NX9685	55°9·2'	3°37·5'W	T	78
Newlands	D & G	NY2374	55°3·5'	3°11·9'W	X	85
Newlands	Durham	NZ1055	54°53·6'	1°50·2'W	T	88

Newlands	E Ayr	NS4142	55°39·0′	4°31·2′W	X	70
Newlands	E Ayr	NS6037	55°36·6′	4°12·9′W	X	71
Newlands	E Dunb	NS6076	55°57·7′	4°14·1′W	X	64
Newlands	E Loth	NT5766	55°53·4′	2°40·8′W	X	67
Newlands	Essex	TL6020	51°51·6′	0°19·8′E	X	167
Newlands	E Yorks	TA3119	53°39·3′	0°0·7′W	X	113
Newlands	Hants	SZ3798	50°47·1′	1°28·1′W	X	196
Newlands	Heref	SO2955	52°11·6′	3°1·9′W	X	148
Newlands	Herts	TL3912	51°47·6′	0°1·3′E	X	166
Newlands	Highld	ND2173	58°38·5′	3°21·2′W	X	7,12
Newlands	Highld	ND3249	58°25·7′	3°9·4′W	X	12
Newlands	Highld	NH5622	57°16·2′	4°22·8′W	X	26,35
Newlands	Highld	NH7545	57°28·9′	4°4·6′W	T	27
New Lands	Lincs	TF3991	53°24·1′	0°5·9′E	X	113
Newlands	Mil Key	SP8739	52°2·8′	0°43·5′W	X	152
Newlands	Moray	NJ2156	57°35·5′	3°18·8′W	X	28
Newlands	Moray	NJ2951	57°32·9′	3°10·7′W	X	28
Newlands	N Lincs	SE8103	53°31·3′	0°46·3′W	X	112
Newlands	N Lincs	SE9402	53°30·6′	0°34·5′W	X	112
Newlands	Northum	NU1132	55°35·1′	1°49·1′W	X	75
Newlands	Notts	SK5762	53°9·4′	1°8·4′W	T	120
Newlands	Notts	SK6837	52°55·8′	0°58·9′W	X	129
Newlands	Notts	SK7133	52°53·6′	0°56·3′W	X	129
Newlands	Notts	SK7289	53°23·8′	0°54·6′W	X	112,120
Newlands	N Yks	NZ3906	54°27·1′	1°23·5′W	X	93
Newlands	Pth & Kin	NO1505	56°14·1′	3°21·8′W	X	58
Newlands	Pth & Kin	NO1527	56°25·9′	3°22·3′W	X	53,58
Newlands	Pth & Kin	NO1532	56°28·6′	3°22·4′W	X	53
Newlands	Pth & Kin	NO1919	56°21·6′	3°18·2′W	X	58
Newlands	S Ayr	NS2704	55°18·2′	4°43·1′W	X	76
Newlands	S Ayr	NS3827	55°30·9′	4°33·5′W	X	70
Newlands	Scot Bord	NT5321	55°29·1′	2°44·2′W	T	73
Newlands	Scot Bord	NY5094	55°14·5′	2°46·8′W	X	79
Newlands	Staffs	SK0721	52°47·4′	1°53·4′W	T	128
Newlands	Wok	SU7668	51°24·6′	0°54·0′W	X	175
Newlands	Worcs	SP0772	52°21·0′	1°53·4′W	X	139
Newlands Beck	Cumbr	NY2318	54°33·3′	3°11·0′W	W	89,90
Newlands Burn	E Loth	NT5766	55°53·4′	2°40·8′W	W	67
Newlands Burn	Northum	NU1332	55°35·1′	1°47·2′W	W	75
Newlands Copse	Hants	SU3200	50°48·1′	1°32·4′W	F	196
Newlands Corner	Surrey	TQ0449	51°14·1′	0°30·2′W	T	186
Newlands Cottages	W Susx	TQ3631	51°4·0′	0°3·2′W	X	187
Newlands Fm	Beds	TL0918	51°51·2′	0°24·6′W	FM	166
Newlands Fm	Corn	SX2772	50°31·6′	4°26·1′W	FM	201
Newlands Fm	Cumbr	NY2539	54°44·7′	3°9·5′W	FM	89,90
Newlands Fm	Devon	SS2716	50°55·3′	4°27·3′W	FM	190
Newland's Fm	Donc	SK5395	53°27·2′	1°11·7′W	FM	111
Newlands Fm	Dorset	ST6105	50°50·8′	2°32·9′W	FM	194
Newlands Fm	Dorset	ST6908	50°52·5′	2°26·1′W	FM	194
Newlands Fm	Dorset	SY8181	50°37·9′	2°15·7′W	FM	194
Newlands Fm	Hants	SU5604	50°50·2′	1°11·9′W	FM	196
Newlands Fm	Hants	SU6608	50°52·3′	1°3·3′W	FM	196
Newlands Fm	Hants	SU7548	51°13·8′	0°55·2′W	FM	186
Newlands Fm	Kent	TQ9851	51°13·7′	0°50·5′E	FM	189
Newlands Fm	Kent	TR2144	51°9·4′	1°10·0′E	FM	179,189
Newlands Fm	Kent	TR3766	51°20·8′	1°24·6′E	FM	179
Newlands Fm	Lincs	TF2528	52°50·3′	0°8·2′W	FM	131
Newlands Fm	Medway	TQ7976	51°27·5′	0°35·0′E	FM	178
Newlands Fm	N Lanak	NS6962	55°50·3′	4°5·1′W	FM	64
Newlands Fm	Northnts	SP9259	52°13·5′	0°38·8′W	FM	152
Newland's Fm	Notts	SK5762	53°9·4′	1°8·4′W	FM	120
Newlands Fm	Notts	SK7098	53°28·7′	0°56·3′W	FM	112
Newlands Fm	N Yks	SE5660	54°2·2′	1°8·3′W	FM	100
Newlands Fm	N Yks	SE6431	53°46·5′	1°1·3′W	FM	105,106
Newlands Fm	S Lanak	NS6052	55°44·7′	4°13·4′W	FM	64
Newlands Fm	Swin	SU1391	51°37·3′	1°48·3′W	FM	163,173
Newlands Fm	Warw	SP1992	52°31·8′	1°42·8′W	FM	139
Newlands Fm	Wilts	ST8680	51°31·4′	2°11·7′W	FM	173
Newlands Grange	Northum	NZ0654	54°53·1′	1°54·0′W	X	87
Newlands Hall	Durham	NZ0437	54°43·9′	1°55·8′W	X	92
Newlands Hause	Cumbr	NY1917	54°32·8′	3°14·7′W	X	89,90
Newlands Hill	Cumbr	NY4537	54°43·7′	2°50·8′W	X	90
Newlands Hill	E Loth	NT5865	55°52·8′	2°39·8′W	H	67
Newlands Ho	N Yks	SE1975	54°10·5′	1°42·1′W	X	99
Newlandside Fm	Durham	NY9737	54°43·9′	2°2·4′W	FM	92
Newlands Manor	Hants	SZ2893	50°44·4′	1°35·8′W	X	195
Newlandsmuir	S Lanak	NS6153	55°45·3′	4°12·5′W	T	64
Newlands North Moor	Northum	NU0931	55°34·6′	1°51·0′W	X	75
Newlands of Broomhill	Highld	NH8750	57°31·8′	3°52·8′W	X	27
Newlands of Budgate	Highld	NH8147	57°30·1′	3°58·7′W	X	27
Newlands of Ferintosh	Highld	NH5954	57°33·5′	4°20·9′W	X	26
Newlands of Fleenas Wood	Highld	NH9146	57°29·7′	3°48·7′W	F	27
Newlands of Forse	Highld	ND2135	58°18·1′	3°20·4′W	X	11
Newlands of Geise	Highld	ND0865	58°34·1′	3°34·4′W	T	11,12
Newlands of Inchnacaorach	Highld	NH8549	57°31·3′	3°54·7′W	X	27
Newlands of Knockaneorn	Highld	NH9145	57°29·2′	3°48·6′W	X	27
Newlands of Knockaneorn	Highld	NH9146	57°29·7′	3°48·7′W	X	27
Newlands of Moyness	Highld	NH9652	57°33·0′	3°43·8′W	X	27
Newlands of Oyne	Aberd	NJ6925	57°19·1′	2°30·4′W	X	38
Newlands of Tynet	Moray	NJ3761	57°38·3′	3°2·9′W	T	28
Newlands of Urchany	Highld	NH8949	57°31·3′	3°50·7′W	X	27
Newlands Park	I of Angl	SH2980	53°17·6′	4°33·5′W	T	114
Newlands Plantation	Hants	SZ3798	50°47·1′	1°28·1′W	F	196
Newlands Stud	Kent	TQ9348	51°12·1′	0°46·2′E	X	189
Newlands Warren	Dorset	SY8080	50°37·4′	2°16·6′W	X	194
Newlands Wood	Kent	TQ8060	51°18·9′	0°35·4′E	F	178,188
Newlands Wood	Staffs	SJ9513	52°43·1′	2°4·0′W	F	127
Newland Wood	Warw	SP2268	52°18·8′	1°40·2′W	F	139,151
New Lane	Lancs	SD4212	53°36·3′	2°52·2′W	T	108
New Lane End	Warr	SJ6394	53°26·7′	2°33·0′W	T	109
New Langholm	D & G	NY3584	55°9·0′	3°0·8′W	T	79
New Laund	Lancs	SD6547	53°55·3′	2°31·6′W	X	102,103
New Laund	Lancs	SD8336	53°49·4′	2°15·1′W	X	103
New Laund Hill	Lancs	SD6546	53°54·8′	2°31·6′W	X	102,103
Newlaw	D & G	NX7448	54°48·9′	3°57·2′W	X	83,84
Newlaw Hill	D & G	NX7348	54°48·9′	3°58·2′W	H	83,84
Newlay	Leeds	SE2436	53°49·4′	1°37·7′W	X	104
New Lea Hall	Lancs	SD4929	53°45·5′	2°46·0′W	X	102
New Leake	Lincs	TF4056	53°5·2′	0°5·8′E	T	122
New Lease Fm	Hants	SU3732	51°5·4′	1°27·9′W	FM	185
New Leasowes Fm	Shrops	SO4099	52°35·4′	2°52·7′W	FM	137
New Leaze	S Glos	ST5987	51°35·1′	2°35·1′W	X	172
New Leaze Fm	Wilts	ST8529	51°3·8′	2°12·5′W	FM	183
New Leaze Fm	Wilts	ST9373	51°27·6′	2°5·7′W	FM	173
New Leeds	Aberd	NJ9954	57°34·8′	2°0·5′W	T	30
Newlees Fm	Falk	NS9273	55°56·5′	3°43·3′W	FM	65
New Leslie	Aberd	NJ5825	57°19·1′	2°41·4′W	X	37
Newleuchar	C of Aber	NJ7904	57°7·8′	2°20·4′W	X	38
Newley	Moray	NJ3740	57°27·0′	3°2·5′W	X	28
Newleycombe Lake	Devon	SX5869	50°30·5′	3°59·8′W	W	202
New Leys Fm	N Yks	SE5886	54°16·2′	1°6·1′W	FM	100
Newliston	C of Edin	NT1073	55°56·8′	3°26·0′W	T	65
Newliston	Fife	NT2592	56°7·1′	3°11·9′W	T	59
New Littlewood Fm	Dorset	SY6293	50°44·4′	2°31·9′W	FM	194
New Lodge	Barns	SE3409	53°34·8′	1°28·8′W	T	110,111
New Lodge	Donc	SK6296	53°27·7′	1°3·6′W	X	111
New Lodge	Essex	TL7606	51°43·7′	0°33·3′E	X	167
New Lodge	Leic	SP8295	52°33·0′	0°47·0′W	X	141
New Lodge	Northnts	SP8176	52°22·8′	0°48·2′W	X	141
New Lodge	Northnts	SP9581	52°25·4′	0°35·8′W	X	141
New Lodge	Win & Maid	SU9174	51°27·7′	0°41·0′W	X	175
New Lodge	Wrekin	SJ7312	52°42·5′	2°23·6′W	X	127
New Lodge Fm	E Susx	TQ4532	51°4·4′	0°4·6′E	FM	188
New Lodge Fm	E Susx	TQ6808	50°51·0′	0°23·6′E	FM	199
New Lodge Fm	Heref	SO3039	52°2·9′	3°0·9′W	FM	161
New Lodge Fm	Northnts	SP8173	52°21·2′	0°48·2′W	FM	141
New Lodge Fm	Staffs	SK0368	53°12·8′	1°56·9′W	FM	119
New Lodge Fm	Win & Maid	SU9075	51°28·2′	0°41·9′W	FM	175
New Lodge Ho	Kent	TQ7347	51°12·0′	0°29·0′E	X	188
New Longton	Lancs	SD5025	53°43·4′	2°45·1′W	T	102
Newlot	Orkney	HY5215	59°1·4′	2°49·7′W	X	6
New Luce	D & G	NX1764	54°56·5′	4°51·0′W	T	82
Newlyn	Corn	SW4628	50°6·1′	5°32·8′W	T	203
Newlyn Downs	Corn	SW8354	50°21·0′	5°2·6′W	X	200
Newmachar	Aberd	NJ8819	57°15·9′	2°11·5′W	T	38
Newmains	Aberd	NJ6724	57°18·6′	2°32·4′W	X	38
Newmains	D & G	NX8592	55°12·8′	3°48·0′W	X	78
Newmains	D & G	NX8875	55°3·7′	3°44·8′W	X	84
Newmains	D & G	NX9683	55°8·1′	3°37·5′W	X	78
Newmains	D & G	NX9757	54°54·1′	3°36·0′W	X	84
Newmains	D & G	NY0466	54°59·0′	3°29·6′W	X	84
Newmains	E Ayr	NS7528	55°32·0′	3°58·4′W	X	71
New Mains	E Loth	NT4563	55°51·7′	2°52·3′W	X	66
New Mains	E Loth	NT5081	56°1·4′	2°47·7′W	X	66
New Mains	E Loth	NT5184	56°3·0′	2°46·8′W	X	66
Newmains	E Loth	NT6071	55°56·1′	2°38·0′W	X	67
New Mains	E Loth	NT6082	56°2·0′	2°38·1′W	X	67
New Mains	Moray	NJ3262	57°38·8′	3°7·9′W	X	28
Newmains	N Lanak	NS8256	55°47·2′	3°52·5′W	T	65,72
New Mains	Pth & Kin	NO1427	56°25·9′	3°23·2′W	X	53,58
New Mains	Pth & Kin	NO1723	56°23·8′	3°20·2′W	X	53,58
New Mains	Pth & Kin	NO2728	56°26·6′	3°10·6′W	X	53,59
New Mains	Renf	NS4668	55°53·1′	4°27·3′W	X	64
Newmains	Scot Bord	NT8761	55°50·8′	2°12·0′W	X	67
New Mains	S Lanak	NS7040	55°38·4′	4°3·5′W	X	71
New Mains	S Lanak	NS8431	55°33·8′	3°49·9′W	X	71,72
Newmains	S Lanak	NS9150	55°44·1′	3°43·7′W	X	65,72
Newmains Ho	E Loth	NT5178	55°59·8′	2°46·7′W	X	66
New Mains of Edingarioch	Aberd	NJ6024	57°18·5′	2°39·4′W	X	37
New Mains of Fingask	Pth & Kin	NO2227	56°26·0′	3°15·4′W	X	53,58
New Mains of Ury	Aberd	NO8787	56°58·7′	2°12·4′W	X	45
New Malden	King	TQ2168	51°24·1′	0°15·2′W	T	176
Newman	I Scilly	SV8910	49°54·8′	6°19·6′W	X	203
New Manor Fm	Halton	SJ5880	53°19·2′	2°37·4′W	FM	108
New Manor Fm	N Yks	SE5076	54°10·9′	1°13·6′W	FM	100
New Manor Fm	Warw	SP3467	52°18·2′	1°29·7′W	FM	151
New Manor Fm	Wilts	SU2233	51°6·0′	1°40·3′W	FM	184
Newman's End	Essex	TL5112	51°47·4′	0°11·8′E	T	167
Newman's Fm	Dorset	SU0704	50°50·4′	1°53·7′W	FM	195
Newman's Fm	Essex	TQ9697	51°38·5′	0°50·4′E	FM	168
Newman's Fm	E Susx	TQ8519	50°56·7′	0°38·4′E	FM	189,199
Newmans Fm	Hants	SU7018	50°57·7′	0°59·8′W	FM	197
Newman's Fm	Norf	TG2811	52°39·1′	1°22·7′E	FM	133,134
Newman's Green	Suff	TL8843	52°3·4′	0°44·9′E	T	155
Newman's Place	Heref	SO2949	52°8·3′	3°1·9′W	T	148
Newman Street	Somer	ST6444	51°11·9′	2°30·5′W	X	183
Newmarket	Derby	SK3863	53°10·0′	1°25·5′W	X	119
Newmarket	Glos	ST8499	51°41·6′	2°13·5′W	T	162
Newmarket	N Eil	NB4235	58°14·0′	6°23·2′W	T	8
Newmarket	Suff	TL6463	52°14·7′	0°24·5′E	T	154
Newmarket Cycle Way	Cambs	TL5761	52°13·7′	0°18·3′E	X	154
Newmarket Cycle Way	Suff	TL7164	52°15·1′	0°30·7′E	X	154
Newmarket Cycle Way	Suff	TL7671	52°18·8′	0°35·3′E	X	155
Newmarket Heath	Suff	TL6162	52°14·2′	0°21·9′E	X	154
Newmarket Hill	E Susx	TQ3607	50°51·0′	0°3·7′W	X	198
New Marsh	Lincs	TF4954	53°4·0′	0°13·8′E	X	122
New Marsh	Somer	ST1233	51°5·6′	3°15·0′W	X	181
Newmarsh Fm	Surrey	TQ1056	51°17·8′	0°24·9′W	FM	187
New Marske	Red & Cl	NZ6220	54°34·5′	1°2·0′W	T	94
New Marston	Oxon	SP5207	51°45·8′	1°14·4′W	T	164
New Marton	Shrops	SJ3334	52°54·2′	2°59·4′W	T	126
New May Beck	N Yks	NZ8903	54°25·1′	0°37·3′W	X	94
Newmead Fm	Powys	SO0258	52°12·9′	3°25·7′W	FM	147
Newmead Fm	Powys	SO0554	52°10·8′	3°23·0′W	FM	147
Newmead Fm	Wilts	ST8138	51°8·7′	2°15·9′W	FM	183
New Meadows	Durham	NY8939	54°45·0′	2°9·8′W	X	91,92
New Meads	V of Glam	SS9975	51°28·1′	3°26·9′W	X	170
New Merdrum	Aberd	NJ4628	57°20·6′	2°53·4′W	X	37
Newmer Fm	Hants	SU6237	51°8·0′	1°6·4′W	FM	185
New Micklefield	Leeds	SE4432	53°47·2′	1°19·5′W	T	105
Newmill	Aberd	NJ4520	57°16·3′	2°54·3′W	X	37
Newmill	Aberd	NJ7141	57°27·8′	2°28·5′W	X	29
Newmill	Aberd	NJ8122	57°17·6′	2°18·5′W	X	38
Newmill	Aberd	NJ8201	57°6·2′	2°17·4′W	X	38
Newmill	Aberd	NJ8515	57°13·8′	2°14·5′W	X	38
Newmill	Aberd	NJ8543	57°28·9′	2°14·6′W	X	30
Newmill	Aberd	NJ9354	57°34·8′	2°6·6′W	X	30
Newmill	Aberd	NK0061	57°38·6′	1°59·5′W	X	30
Newmill	Aberd	NK0345	57°30·0′	1°56·5′W	X	30
Newmill	Aberd	NO5495	57°2·9′	2°45·0′W	X	37,44
Newmill	Aberd	NO7399	57°5·1′	2°26·3′W	X	38,45
Newmill	Aberd	NO7883	56°56·5′	2°21·2′W	X	45
Newmill	Angus	NO3245	56°35·8′	3°6·0′W	X	53
Newmill	Angus	NO3657	56°42·3′	3°2·3′W	X	54
Newmill	Angus	NO5250	56°38·6′	2°46·5′W	X	54
New Mill	Angus	NO6848	56°37·6′	2°30·8′W	X	54
New Mill	Carm	SN2613	51°47·6′	4°31·0′W	X	158
New Mill	Cered	SN1847	52°5·7′	4°39·0′W	X	145
New Mill	Corn	SW4534	50°9·3′	5°33·8′W	T	203
New Mill	Corn	SW8045	50°16·1′	5°4·9′W	T	204
Newmill	Corn	SX2198	50°45·5′	4°31·9′W	X	190
New Mill	Cumbr	NY0504	54°25·6′	3°27·4′W	T	89
New Mill	Cumbr	NY2045	54°47·9′	3°14·2′W	X	85
New Mill	Cumbr	SD5277	54°11·4′	2°43·7′W	X	97
Newmill	E Dunb	NS6476	55°57·7′	4°10·3′W	X	64
Newmill	Fife	NO3915	56°19·7′	2°58·7′W	X	59
New Mill	Herts	SP9212	51°48·2′	0°39·5′W	T	165
Newmill	Highld	NH9154	57°34·0′	3°48·9′W	X	27
New Mill	Kirk	SE1608	53°34·3′	1°45·1′W	T	110
Newmill	Moray	NJ0960	57°37·5′	3°31·0′W	X	27
Newmill	Moray	NJ4352	57°33·5′	2°56·7′W	T	28
Newmill	Oxon	SP3411	51°48·0′	1°30·0′W	X	164
New Mill	Pemb	SN0521	51°51·5′	4°49·5′W	X	145,158
Newmill	Pth & Kin	NO0832	56°28·5′	3°29·2′W	X	52,53
Newmill	Pth & Kin	NO2035	56°30·3′	3°17·5′W	X	53
Newmill	Scot Bord	NT4510	55°23·1′	2°51·7′W	T	79
New Mill	Scot Bord	NT5010	55°23·1′	2°46·9′W	T	79
Newmill	S Lanak	NS9145	55°41·4′	3°43·6′W	X	72
Newmill	S Lanak	NT1146	55°42·2′	3°24·5′W	X	72
New Mill	W Berks	SU3864	51°22·7′	1°26·9′W	X	174
New Mill	Wilts	SU1861	51°21·1′	1°44·1′W	T	173
New Mill	Wok	SU7662	51°21·3′	0°54·1′W	X	175,186
Newmill Beck	Cumbr	NY0404	54°25·6′	3°28·4′W	W	89
New Mill Br	Worcs	SO7262	52°15·6′	2°24·2′W	X	138,149
Newmill Burn	Scot Bord	NT4411	55°23·6′	2°52·6′W	W	79
Newmill Channel	Kent	TQ8729	51°2·0′	0°40·4′E	W	189,199
Newmill Cotts	Pth & Kin	NO0832	56°28·5′	3°29·2′W	X	52,53
Newmill Creek	Suff	TM1332	51°57·0′	1°6·4′E	W	168,169
New Mill End	Beds	TL1217	51°50·6′	0°22·1′W	X	166
Newmillerdam	Wakf	SE3215	53°38·1′	1°30·6′W	T	110,111
Newmillerdam Country Park	Wakf	SE3314	53°37·5′	1°29·6′W	X	110,111
New Mill Flatt	Cumbr	NY5919	54°34·1′	2°37·6′W	X	91
New Mill Fm	Scot Bord	NT6522	55°29·7′	2°32·8′W	FM	74
Newmill Hill	Aberd	NJ8200	57°5·7′	2°17·4′W	H	38
Newmill of Inshewan	Angus	NO4260	56°43·9′	2°56·4′W	X	44
Newmill of Pitfancy	Aberd	NJ5943	57°28·8′	2°40·6′W	X	29
New Mills	Ches	SJ7781	53°19·8′	2°20·3′W	T	109
New Mills	Corn	SW9052	50°20·1′	4°56·7′W	T	200,204
Newmills	Corn	SX1191	50°41·5′	4°40·2′W	X	190
New Mills	Derby	SJ9985	53°22·0′	2°0·5′W	T	109
New Mills	D & G	NT0902	55°18·5′	3°25·6′W	X	78
Newmills	Fife	NT0186	56°3·7′	3°35·0′W	T	65
New Mills	Glos	SO6304	51°44·2′	2°31·8′W	T	162
New Mills	Glos	SP0301	51°42·7′	1°57·0′W	X	163
New Mills	Heref	SO7038	52°2·6′	2°25·9′W	T	149
Newmills	Highld	NH6764	57°39·0′	4°13·3′W	T	21
Newmills	Monm	SO5107	51°45·8′	2°42·2′W	X	162
New Mills	Northum	NT9552	55°45·9′	2°4·3′W	X	67,74,75
New Mills	N Yks	SE4473	54°9·3′	1°19·2′W	X	99
New Mills	Powys	SJ0901	52°36·2′	3°20·2′W	X	136
New Mills	Powys	SJ1319	52°45·9′	3°17·0′W	X	125
New Mills	Scot Bord	NT5249	55°44·2′	2°45·4′W	T	73
Newmills	Stir	NS8290	56°5·6′	3°53·4′W	X	57
Newmills Fm	Glos	ST7790	51°36·7′	2°19·5′W	FM	162,172
New Mills Fm	Heref	SO5230	51°58·2′	2°41·5′W	FM	149
New Mills Heath	Dorset	SY9584	50°39·6′	2°3·9′W	X	195
Newmills of Boyne	Aberd	NJ5759	57°37·4′	2°42·7′W	X	29
Newmiln	Pth & Kin	NO0122	56°23·1′	3°35·8′W	X	52,53,58
Newmiln	Pth & Kin	NO1230	56°27·5′	3°25·2′W	T	53
Newmilne	Pth & Kin	NN9223	56°23·5′	3°44·5′W	X	52,58
Newmilns	D & G	NX4055	54°52·1′	4°29·2′W	X	83
Newmilns	E Ayr	NS5237	55°36·5′	4°20·5′W	T	70
New Milton	Hants	SZ2395	50°45·5′	1°40·1′W	T	195
New Milton	Midlo	NT2562	55°51·0′	3°11·4′W	X	66
Newminster Abbey	Northum	NZ1885	55°9·8′	1°42·6′W	A	81
New Mistley	Essex	TM1231	51°56·4′	1°5·5′E	T	168,169
New Mixon Hay	Staffs	SK0357	53°6·8′	1°56·9′W	X	119
New Moat	Pemb	SN0625	51°53·6′	4°48·8′W	T	145,158
New Monkwray	Cumbr	NX9917	54°32·5′	3°33·3′W	X	89
Newmoor	Essex	TL9600	51°40·1′	0°50·5′E	X	168
New Moor Fm	Darl	NZ2319	54°34·2′	1°38·2′W	FM	93
New Moor Fm	York	SE5254	53°59·0′	1°12·0′W	FM	105
Newmoor Hall	Northum	NU1403	55°19·5′	1°46·3′W	X	81
New Moor Ho	Northum	NU0906	55°21·1′	1°51·1′W	X	81
New Moors	Durham	NZ1724	54°36·9′	1°43·8′W	X	92
Newmore	Highld	NH5452	57°32·3′	4°25·9′W	T	26
Newmore Ho	Highld	NH6872	57°43·4′	4°12·5′W	X	21
Newmore Mains	Highld	NH6872	57°43·4′	4°12·5′W	X	21
New Moreton Fm	Glos	SO7908	51°46·5′	2°17·9′W	FM	162
Newmore Wood	Highld	NH6873	57°43·9′	4°12·5′W	F	21
New Morlich	Aberd	NJ4414	57°13·1′	2°55·2′W	X	37
New Moss	Angus	NO4566	56°47·2′	2°53·6′W	H	44
New Moss	Midlo	NT3049	55°44·0′	3°6·4′W	X	73
New Moss	Midlo	NT3049	55°44·0′	3°6·4′W	X	73
New Moston	Man	SD8902	53°31·1′	2°9·5′W	T	109
New Moze Hall	Essex	TM1925	51°53·1′	1°11·3′E	X	168,169
Newnant	Carm	SN2730	51°56·7′	4°30·6′W	X	145
Newnes	Shrops	SJ3834	52°54·2′	2°54·9′W	T	126
Newnes Brook	Shrops	SJ3735	52°54·8′	2°55·8′W	W	126
Newney Green	Essex	TL6507	51°44·5′	0°23·8′E	T	167
Newnham	Cambs	TL4457	52°11·8′	0°6·8′E	T	154
Newnham	Glos	SO6911	51°48·0′	2°26·6′W	T	162
Newnham	Hants	SU7053	51°16·5′	0°59·4′W	T	186
Newnham	Herts	TL2437	52°1·3′	0°11·2′W	T	153
Newnham	Kent	TQ9557	51°16·9′	0°48·2′E	T	178
Newnham	Northnts	SP5759	52°13·8′	1°9·5′W	T	152
Newnham	Warw	SP1560	52°14·5′	1°46·4′W	T	151

Newnham Barton Fm	Devon	SS6617	50°56·4′	3°54·1′W	FM	180
Newnham Bridge	Worcs	SO6469	52°19·3′	2°31·3′W	T	138
Newnham Court	Worcs	SO6468	52°18·8′	2°31·3′W	X	138
Newnham Court Fm	Kent	TQ7857	51°17·3′	0°33·6′E	FM	178,188
Newnham Fields Fm	Warw	SP4883	52°26·8′	1°17·2′W	FM	140
Newnham Fm	I of W	SZ5691	50°43·2′	1°12·0′W	FM	196
Newnham Fm	Oxon	SU6188	51°35·5′	1°6·8′W	FM	175
Newnham Fm	Shrops	SJ4109	52°40·8′	2°52·0′W	FM	126
Newnham Fms	Dorset	ST4101	50°48·6′	2°49·9′W	FM	193
Newnham Grange	Northnts	SP5961	52°14·9′	1°7·7′W	X	152
Newnham Grounds	Northnts	SP5960	52°14·3′	1°7·8′W	X	152
Newnham Hall	Warw	SP4477	52°23·6′	1°20·8′W	X	140
Newnham Hall Fm	Essex	TL5842	52°3·5′	0°18·7′E	FM	154
Newnham Hill	Herts	TL2539	52°2·3′	0°10·3′W	X	153
Newnham Hill	Northnts	SP5760	52°14·3′	1°9·5′W	H	152
Newnham Hill	Oxon	SU6885	51°33·8′	1°0·7′W	X	175
Newnham Lodge	Northnts	SP5758	52°13·3′	1°9·5′W	X	152
Newnham Lodge	Northnts	SP5959	52°13·8′	1°7·8′W	X	152
Newnham Paddox	Warw	SP4783	52°26·8′	1°18·1′W	X	140
Newnham Park	Devon	SX5557	50°23·9′	4°2·0′W	X	202
Newnham Park Wood	E Susx	TQ4928	51°2·1′	0°7·9′E	F	188,199
Newnham's Wood	E Susx	TQ4029	51°2·8′	0°0·2′E	F	187,198
Newnoth	Aberd	NJ5130	57°21·7′	2°48·4′W	X	29,37
Newnton Ho	Glos	ST9191	51°37·3′	2°7·4′W	X	163,173
New Ollerton	Notts	SK6668	53°12·5′	1°0·3′W	T	120
Newon Fell	Northum	NY7253	54°52·5′	2°25·8′W	X	86,87
New-o-Nook	Lancs	SD7146	53°54·8′	2°26·1′W	X	103
Newonstead Fm	Northum	NY9779	55°6·6′	2°2·4′W	FM	87
Newordden Fm	Monm	SO3816	51°50·6′	2°53·6′W	FM	161
New Orleans	Arg & Bt	NR7517	55°24·0′	5°32·8′W	X	68,69
New or North Western Cut	Cambs	TL2291	52°30·4′	0°11·7′W	W	142
New Oscott	Birm	SP1094	52°32·9′	1°50·8′W	T	139
New Pale	Ches	SJ5272	53°14·8′	2°42·8′W	T	117
New Pallyards	Cumbr	NY4671	55°2·1′	2°50·3′W	X	86
Newpans	Fife	NS9486	56°3·6′	3°41·7′W	X	65
Newpark	Aberd	NJ5462	57°39·0′	2°45·8′W	X	29
Newpark	Aberd	NJ5755	57°35·2′	2°42·7′W	X	29
Newpark	Aberd	NJ9015	57°13·8′	2°9·5′W	X	38
Newpark	C of Aber	NJ8706	57°8·9′	2°12·4′W	X	38
Newpark	Corn	SX2597	50°45·0′	4°28·5′W	X	190
New Park	Cumbr	NY2238	54°44·1′	3°12·3′W	X	89,90
New Park	Cumbr	SD6091	54°19·0′	2°36·5′W	X	97
New Park	Devon	SY3298	50°46·9′	2°57·5′W	X	193
Newpark	D & G	NY1871	55°1·9′	3°16·5′W	X	85
New Park	Hants	SU2904	50°50·3′	1°34·9′W	X	196
New Park	Hants	SU6651	51°15·5′	1°2·9′W	X	185,186
New Park	Lancs	SD5776	54°10·9′	2°39·1′W	F	97
New Park	Leic	SP7498	52°34·7′	0°54·1′W	X	141
New Park	Newp	ST2584	51°33·2′	3°4·5′W	X	171
New Park	N Yks	SE2956	54°0·2′	1°33·0′W	T	104
New Park	Oxon	SP3721	51°53·4′	1°27·3′W	X	164
New Park	Oxon	SP7203	51°43·5′	0°57·1′W	X	165
New Park	Pemb	SN0211	51°46·0′	4°51·8′W	X	157,158
New Park	Pemb	SN0406	51°43·4′	4°49·9′W	X	157,158
Newpark	Shetld	HU5464	60°21·6′	1°0·8′W	X	2
New Park	Surrey	TQ0451	51°15·1′	0°30·2′W	X	186
New Park	Surrey	TQ0738	51°8·1′	0°27·8′W	X	187
Newpark	W Loth	NT0464	55°51·8′	3°31·6′W	X	65
New Park Fm	Bucks	SP6015	51°50·1′	1°7·4′W	FM	164,165
New Park FM	Corn	SX1783	50°37·3′	4°34·9′W	FM	201
New Park Fm	Devon	SS8326	51°1·5′	3°39·7′W	FM	181
New Park Fm	Devon	SX4463	50°27·0′	4°11·5′W	FM	201
Newpark Fm	Glos	ST6694	51°38·9′	2°29·1′W	FM	162,172
New Park Fm	Herts	TL2905	51°44·0′	0°7·5′W	FM	166
Newpark Fm	I of W	SZ4688	50°41·6′	1°20·5′W	FM	196
New Park Fm	Leic	SK4400	52°36·0′	1°20·6′W	FM	140
New Park Fm	Somer	ST7432	51°5·4′	2°21·9′W	FM	183
New Park Plantn	Hants	SU2905	50°50·9′	1°34·9′W	F	196
New Parks	C of Leic	SK5505	52°38·6′	1°10·8′W	T	140
New Parks	N Yks	SE5562	54°3·3′	1°9·2′W	X	100
New Parks	Worcs	SO7475	52°22·6′	2°22·5′W	X	138
New Parkside Fm	Lancs	SD5164	54°4·4′	2°44·5′W	FM	97
New Park Spring	Barns	SE4107	53°33·7′	1°22·4′W	X	111
Newpark Waste	Devon	SX5961	50°26·2′	3°58·8′W	F	202
Newpark Wood	Kent	TQ5238	51°7·5′	0°10·7′E	F	188
New Park Wood	Lincs	TF1570	53°13·1′	0°16·2′W	F	121
Newpark Wood	Northum	NZ0991	55°13·0′	1°51·1′W	F	81
New Park Wood	Notts	SK6564	53°10·4′	1°1·2′W	F	120
Newpark Wood	Somer	ST7432	51°5·4′	2°21·9′W	F	183
New Park Wood	Warw	SP1598	52°35·0′	1°46·3′W	F	139
New Passage	S Glos	ST5486	51°34·5′	2°39·4′W	T	172
New Pasture	N Yks	SD8571	54°8·3′	2°13·4′W	X	98
New Pasture	N Yks	SD9990	54°18·6′	2°0·5′W	X	98
New Pasture Allotments	N Yks	SD9483	54°14·8′	2°5·1′W	X	98
New Pastures Fm	Lincs	TF1286	53°21·8′	0°18·6′W	FM	113,121
New Pastures Fm	Mil Key	SP8955	52°11·4′	0°41·5′W	FM	152
New Pieces	Powys	SJ2913	52°42·8′	3°2·7′W	X	126
New Piece Wood	Derby	SK2468	53°12·7′	1°38·0′W	F	119
New Pier	Gwyn	SH5873	53°14·3′	4°7·3′W	X	114,115
New Pilfit	N Yks	SE5677	54°11·4′	1°8·1′W	X	100
New Pitsligo	Aberd	NJ8855	57°35·4′	2°11·6′W	T	30
Newplace	Aberd	NJ8220	57°16·5′	2°17·5′W	X	38
Newplace	Orkney	HY3507	58°57·0′	3°7·3′W	X	6,7
New Place	W Susx	TQ0519	50°57·9′	0°29·9′W	A	197
Newplace Fm	E Susx	TQ5019	50°57·3′	0°8·5′E	FM	199
Newplace Fm	W Susx	TQ0605	50°50·3′	0°29·3′W	FM	197
New Plantation	Lincs	SK9184	53°20·9′	0°37·6′W	F	121
New Plantation	Northnts	SP8266	52°17·4′	0°47·5′W	F	152
New Plantation	N Yks	SE4890	54°18·4′	1°15·3′W	F	100
New Plantation	Somer	ST4910	50°53·5′	2°43·1′W	F	193,194
New Plantn	Essex	TL8716	51°48·9′	0°43·2′E	F	168
New Plantn	Notts	SK6342	52°58·5′	1°3·3′W	F	129
New Plantn	Notts	SK6780	53°19·0′	0°59·2′W	F	111,120
New Plantn	N Yks	SE4678	54°12·0′	1°17·3′W	F	100
New Plantn	N Yks	SE5244	53°53·6′	1°12·1′W	F	105
Newplatt Fm	Ches	SJ7570	53°13·8′	2°22·1′W	FM	118
New Polzeath	Corn	SW9379	50°34·7′	4°55·1′W	T	200
New Pond	W Susx	TQ2225	51°0·9′	0°15·3′W	W	187,198
Newpond Fm	Cambs	TL1064	52°16·0′	0°22·9′W	FM	153
Newpond Fm	E Susx	TQ7521	50°57·9′	0°29·9′E	FM	199
New Pond Fm	Surrey	SU9746	51°12·5′	0°36·3′W	FM	186
New Pool	Cered	SN7492	52°30·9′	3°51·0′W	W	135
Newpool	Staffs	SJ8756	53°6·3′	2°11·2′W	T	118
New Pool	Worcs	SO7843	52°5·3′	2°18·9′W	W	150
Newpool Fm	Ches	SJ5771	53°14·3′	2°38·3′W	FM	117
New Pools Fm	Cambs	TL5489	52°28·9′	0°16·5′E	FM	143
Newport	Corn	SX3285	50°38·7′	4°22·2′W	T	201
Newport	Devon	SS5632	51°4·4′	4°2·9′W	T	180
Newport	Dorset	SY8894	50°45·0′	2°9·8′W	T	194
Newport	Essex	TL5233	51°58·7′	0°13·2′E	T	167
Newport	Essex	TL5234	51°59·2′	0°13·2′E	T	154
Newport	E Yorks	SE8530	53°45·8′	0°42·2′W	T	106
Newport	Glos	ST6997	51°40·5′	2°26·5′W	T	162
Newport	Highld	ND1224	58°12·0′	3°29·4′W	T	17
Newport	I of W	SZ4988	50°41·6′	1°18·0′W	T	196
Newport	Norf	TG5016	52°41·3′	1°42·4′E	T	134
Newport	Pemb	SN0539	52°1·2′	4°50·1′W	T	145
Newport	Somer	ST3123	51°0·4′	2°58·6′W	T	193
Newport	Wrekin	SJ7419	52°46·3′	2°22·7′W	T	127
Newport Bay	Pemb	SN0340	52°1·6′	4°51·9′W	W	145,157
Newport Castle	Pemb	SN0538	52°0·6′	4°50·1′W	A	145
Newport Fm	Glos	SP0412	51°48·6′	1°56·1′W	FM	163
Newporth Head	Corn	SW7930	50°8·0′	5°5·2′W	X	204
Newport-on-Tay	Fife	NO4127	56°26·1′	2°57·0′W	T	54,59
Newport or Casnewydd	Newp	ST3188	51°35·4′	2°59·4′W	T	171
Newport Pagnell	Mil Key	SP8743	52°4·9′	0°43·4′W	T	152
Newport Sands	Pemb	SN0539	52°1·2′	4°50·1′W	X	145
Newport Stables	Mil Key	SP8842	52°4·4′	0°42·6′W	X	152
Newpots	Essex	TL9915	51°48·1′	0°53·6′E	X	168
New Pound	Kent	TQ6554	51°15·9′	0°22·3′E	X	188
Newpound Common	W Susx	TQ0627	51°2·2′	0°28·9′W	T	187,197
New Precipice Walk	Gwyn	SH7019	52°45·4′	3°55·2′W	X	124
New Pudsey Sta	Leeds	SE2134	53°48·4′	1°40·5′W	X	104
New Quarry Ho	Rut	SK9815	52°43·7′	0°32·5′W	X	130
Newquay	Corn	SW8161	50°24·7′	5°4·6′W	T	200
Newquay	Devon	SX4569	50°30·3′	4°10·8′W	X	201
Newquay Airport	Corn	SW8665	50°27·0′	5°0·5′W	X	200
New Quay Bay	Cered	SN3959	52°12·6′	4°21·0′W	W	145,146
Newquay Bay	Corn	SW8162	50°25·3′	5°4·6′W	W	200
New Quay (Ceinewydd)	Cered	SN3859	52°12·6′	4°21·9′W	T	145
New Quay Head	Cered	SN3860	52°13·1′	4°21·9′W	X	145
Newra	Pth & Kin	NN8516	56°19·6′	3°51·1′W	X	58
New Rackheath	Norf	TG2812	52°39·7′	1°22·7′E	T	133,134
New Radley Fm	Notts	SK6752	53°3·9′	0°59·6′W	FM	120
New Radnor	Powys	SO2160	52°14·2′	3°9·0′W	T	137,148
New Ramerwick Fm	Herts	TL1733	51°59·2′	0°17·4′W	FM	166
Newraw	Pth & Kin	NN9521	56°22·4′	3°41·6′W	X	52,53,58
New Rd Fm	Beds	TL0957	52°12·3′	0°23·9′W	FM	153
New Rent	Cumbr	NY4536	54°43·2′	2°50·8′W	X	90
New Rides	Kent	TQ9970	51°23·9′	0°52·0′E	X	178
New Ridley	Northum	NZ0559	54°55·8′	1°54·9′W	T	87
New Rift	Northum	NY9467	55°0·1′	2°5·2′W	X	87
New River	Cambs	TL5869	52°18·0′	0°19·4′E	W	154
New River	Herts	TL3504	51°43·3′	0°2·3′W	W	166
New River	Lincs	TF2313	52°42·3′	0°10·4′W	W	131,142
New River	Lincs	TF2518	52°44·9′	0°8·5′W	W	131
New River Ancholme	N Lincs	SE9904	53°31·6′	0°30·0′W	W	112
New River Ray	Oxon	SP5615	51°50·1′	1°10·8′W	W	164
New Road Fm	Wilts	ST9264	51°22·7′	2°6·5′W	FM	173
New Road Side	Brad	SE1527	53°44·6′	1°45·9′W	T	104
New Road Side	N Yks	SD9742	53°52·7′	2°2·3′W	T	103
New Rock	Glos	SO6830	51°58·3′	2°27·6′W	X	149
New Rocklands	Wirral	SJ3181	53°19·5′	3°1·8′W	X	108
New Rollestons Fm	Essex	TL6705	51°43·4′	0°25·5′E	FM	167
New Romney	Kent	TR0624	50°58·9′	0°56·5′E	T	189
New Rossington	Donc	SK6197	53°28·2′	1°4·5′W	T	111
New Row	Cered	SN7273	52°20·7′	3°52·3′W	T	135,147
New Row	Durham	NZ1029	54°39·6′	1°50·3′W	X	92
New Row	Durham	NZ1038	54°44·5′	1°50·3′W	X	92
New Row	Lancs	SD6438	53°50·5′	2°32·4′W	T	102,103
New Row	N Yks	NZ6110	54°29·1′	1°3·1′W	X	94
Newrow Lodge	Pth & Kin	NN9723	56°23·5′	3°39·7′W	X	52,53,58
New Rowney Fm	Beds	TL1240	52°3·1′	0°21·6′W	FM	153
New Russia Hall	Ches	SJ4760	53°8·3′	2°47·1′W	X	117
Newsam Green	Leeds	SE3630	53°46·1′	1°26·8′W	T	104
New Sandsfield	Cumbr	NY3361	54°56·6′	3°2·3′W	X	85
New Sawley	Derby	SK4732	52°53·2′	1°17·7′W	T	129
Newsbank	Ches	SJ8366	53°11·7′	2°14·9′W	T	118
New Scarbro	Leeds	SE2434	53°48·3′	1°37·7′W	T	104
New Scone	Pth & Kin	NO1326	56°25·3′	3°24·2′W	T	53,58
Newseat	Aberd	NJ3419	57°15·7′	3°5·2′W	X	37
Newseat	Aberd	NJ4828	57°20·6′	2°51·4′W	X	37
Newseat	Aberd	NJ4911	57°11·5′	2°50·2′W	X	37
Newseat	Aberd	NJ6635	57°24·5′	2°33·5′W	X	29
Newseat	Aberd	NJ6938	57°26·1′	2°30·5′W	X	29
Newseat	Aberd	NJ7033	57°23·4′	2°29·5′W	X	29
Newseat	Aberd	NJ7420	57°16·5′	2°25·4′W	X	38
Newseat	Aberd	NJ9036	57°25·1′	2°9·5′W	X	30
Newseat	Aberd	NJ9462	57°39·1′	2°5·6′W	X	30
Newseat	Aberd	NK0748	57°31·6′	1°52·5′W	X	30
Newseat	Aberd	NK0853	57°34·3′	1°51·5′W	X	30
Newseat	Moray	NJ5254	57°34·7′	2°47·7′W	X	29
Newseat of Ardo	Aberd	NJ8538	57°26·2′	2°14·5′W	X	30
Newseat of Dumbreck	Aberd	NJ8929	57°21·3′	2°10·5′W	X	38
Newseat of Tolquhon	Aberd	NJ8729	57°21·3′	2°12·5′W	X	38
Newsells	Herts	TL3837	52°1·1′	0°1·1′E	T	154
Newsells Fm	Herts	TL3838	52°1·6′	0°1·1′E	FM	154
Newsells Park	Herts	TL3936	52°0·5′	0°1·9′E	X	154
New Sewer	Kent	TR0426	51°0·1′	0°54·8′E	W	189
Newsham	Cumbr	NY3324	54°36·7′	3°1·8′W	X	90
Newsham	Cumbr	NY3935	54°42·6′	2°56·4′W	X	90
Newsham	Lancs	SD5136	53°49·3′	2°44·2′W	T	102
Newsham	Northum	NZ3079	55°6·5′	1°31·4′W	T	88
Newsham	Northum	NZ3080	55°7·1′	1°31·4′W	T	81
Newsham	N Yks	NZ1010	54°29·4′	1°50·3′W	T	92
Newsham	N Yks	SE3784	54°15·3′	1°25·5′W	T	99
Newsham	N Yks	SE3885	54°15·8′	1°24·6′W	X	99
Newsham Br	Lincs	TA1313	53°36·3′	0°17·1′W	X	113
Newsham Br	N Yks	SE7476	54°10·7′	0°51·6′W	X	100
Newsham Field	E Yorks	TA1871	54°7·5′	0°11·2′W	X	101
Newsham Grange	Durham	NZ1218	54°33·7′	1°48·4′W	X	92
Newsham Grange	N Yks	NZ1011	54°29·9′	1°50·3′W	X	92
Newsham Grange	N Yks	SE3592	54°19·6′	1°27·3′W	X	99
Newsham Grange	N Yks	SE3688	54°17·4′	1°26·4′W	X	99
Newsham Grange	N Yks	SE3895	54°21·2′	1°24·5′W	X	99
Newsham Grange	Stock on T	NZ3710	54°29·3′	1°25·3′W	X	93
Newsham Hall	Lancs	SD5135	53°48·8′	2°44·2′W	X	102
Newsham Hall	Stock on T	NZ3811	54°29·8′	1°24·4′W	X	93
Newsham Lodge	Lancs	SD5035	53°48·8′	2°45·2′W	X	102
Newsham Lodge	Lincs	TA1212	53°35·8′	0°18·0′W	X	113
Newsham Lodge	N Yks	NZ1010	54°29·4′	1°50·3′W	X	92
Newsham Moor	N Yks	NZ0607	54°27·7′	1°54·0′W	X	92
Newsham Park	Liv	SJ3791	53°25·0′	2°56·5′W	X	108
Newsham Village	Stock on T	NZ3811	54°29·8′	1°24·4′W	A	93
New Shardelowes Fm	Cambs	TL5354	52°10·0′	0°14·6′E	FM	154
New Sharlston	Wakf	SE3820	53°40·7′	1°25·1′W	T	104
New Shelve Fm	Kent	TQ9151	51°13·8′	0°44·5′E	FM	189
Newshield	Cumbr	NY7148	54°49·8′	2°26·7′W	X	86,87
New Shield	Northum	NY8352	54°52·0′	2°15·5′W	X	86,87
Newshield Moss	Cumbr	NY7348	54°49·8′	2°24·8′W	H	86,87
New Shifford Fm	Oxon	SP3703	51°43·7′	1°27·5′W	FM	164
News Hill	Suff	TM2946	52°4·1′	1°20·9′E	X	169
New Shipping Point	Pemb	SN0304	51°42·3′	4°50·7′W	X	157,158
New Shipton Fm	Birm	SP1394	52°32·9′	1°48·1′W	FM	139
Newsholme	Brad	SE0239	53°51·1′	1°57·8′W	T	104
Newsholme	E Yorks	SE7129	53°45·4′	0°55·0′W	T	105,106
Newsholme	Lancs	SD8451	53°57·5′	2°14·2′W	T	103
Newsholme Dean	Brad	SE0140	53°51·6′	1°58·7′W	X	104
Newsholme Fm	E Yorks	SE7333	53°47·5′	0°53·1′W	FM	105,106
Newsholme Fm	N Yks	SE3751	53°57·5′	1°25·8′W	FM	104
Newsholme Parks	E Yorks	SE7329	53°45·4′	0°53·2′W	X	105,106
New Shoreston	Northum	NU1932	55°35·1′	1°41·5′W	X	75
Newshot Island	Renf	NS4870	55°54·2′	4°25·4′W	X	64
Newside	N Ayr	NS2851	55°43·6′	4°43·9′W	X	63
New Silksworth	Sund	NZ3753	54°52·5′	1°25·0′W	T	88
New Skelton	Red & Cl	NZ6618	54°33·4′	0°58·3′W	T	94
New Smailholm	Scot Bord	NT6236	55°37·2′	2°35·8′W	X	74
New Smithy	Derby	SK0582	53°20·3′	1°55·1′W	T	110
Newsole Fm	Kent	TR2846	51°10·3′	1°16·1′E	FM	179
Newsome	Kirk	SE1414	53°37·6′	1°46·9′W	T	110
New South Eau	Peterb	TF2808	52°39·5′	0°6·0′W	W	142
New Southgate	Enf	TQ2992	51°36·9′	0°7·8′W	T	176
New Spa	N Yks	NZ2809	54°28·8′	1°33·7′W	X	93
Newspring Fm	Beds	TL2141	52°3·5′	0°13·7′W	FM	153
New Springs	Staffs	SJ8153	53°4·7′	2°16·6′W	X	118
New Springs	Wigan	SD6007	53°33·7′	2°35·8′W	T	109
New Spring Wood	N Yks	SE7570	54°7·5′	0°50·7′W	F	100
New Sprowston	Norf	TG2311	52°39·3′	1°18·2′E	T	133,134
New Sta	Birm	SP0686	52°28·6′	1°54·3′W	X	139
New Stanton	Derby	SK4639	52°57·0′	1°18·5′W	T	129
Newstead	Aberd	NJ8150	57°32·6′	2°18·6′W	X	29,30
Newstead	C of Stoke	SJ8940	52°57·7′	2°9·4′W	T	118
Newstead	Lincs	TF0408	52°39·8′	0°27·3′W	X	141
Newstead	Midlo	NT2355	55°47·2′	3°13·2′W	X	66,73
Newstead	N Lincs	SE8703	53°31·2′	0°40·9′W	X	112
Newstead	Northum	NU1527	55°32·4′	1°45·3′W	X	75
Newstead	Notts	SK5152	53°4·0′	1°13·9′W	T	120
Newstead	Scot Bord	NT5634	55°36·1′	2°41·5′W	T	73
Newstead	Scot Bord	NT8456	55°48·1′	2°14·9′W	X	67,74
Newstead	Wakf	SE3914	53°37·5′	1°24·2′W	T	110,111
Newstead Abbey	Notts	SK5453	53°4·5′	1°11·2′W	X	120
Newstead Fm	Darl	NZ3520	54°34·7′	1°27·1′W	FM	93
Newstead Fm	Kent	TQ7945	51°10·8′	0°34·1′E	FM	188
Newstead Fm	Leic	SP6194	52°32·7′	1°5·6′W	FM	140
Newstead Fm	Lincs	TF1665	53°10·4′	0°15·5′W	FM	121
Newstead Fm	NE Lincs	TA1711	53°35·2′	0°13·5′W	FM	113
Newstead Fm	N Yks	SE4638	53°50·4′	1°17·6′W	FM	105
Newstead Fm	W Susx	TQ2430	51°3·6′	0°13·4′W	FM	187
Newstead Ghyll	W Susx	TQ2331	51°4·1′	0°14·3′W	X	187
Newstead Grange	N Yks	SE3798	54°22·8′	1°25·4′W	X	99
Newstead Grange	N Yks	SE8379	54°12·2′	0°43·2′W	X	100
Newstead Grange	N Yks	SE8679	54°12·2′	0°40·5′W	X	101
Newstead Grange Fm	Notts	SK5552	53°4·0′	1°10·3′W	FM	120
Newstead Ho	N Yks	SE8070	54°7·4′	0°46·1′W	X	100
Newsteadings	S Lanak	NS8745	55°41·4′	3°47·4′W	X	72
Newstead Priory Fm	N Lincs	SE9904	53°31·6′	0°30·0′W	FM	112
New Stevenston	N Lanak	NS7659	55°48·8′	3°58·3′W	T	64
Newstone Fm	Staffs	SK0163	53°10·1′	1°58·7′W	FM	119
New Street	Heref	SO3356	52°12·1′	2°58·4′W	X	148,149
New Street	Kent	TQ6264	51°21·3′	0°20·0′E	T	177,188
New Street	Staffs	SK0552	53°4·2′	1°55·1′W	T	119
New Street Fm	Kent	TQ9740	51°7·7′	0°49·3′E	FM	189
New Street Fm	Suff	TL8148	52°6·3′	0°39·0′E	FM	155
New Street Fm	Suff	TM2663	52°13·4′	1°18·9′E	FM	156
Newstreet Lane	Shrops	SJ6237	52°56·0′	2°33·5′W	T	127
New Stynie	Moray	NJ3261	57°38·3′	3°7·9′W	X	28
New Sulehay	Northnts	TL0596	52°33·3′	0°26·7′W	X	142
New Sutch House Fm	Lancs	SD4512	53°36·3′	2°49·5′W	FM	108
New Swanage	Dorset	SZ0280	50°37·4′	1°57·9′W	T	195
New Swannington	Leic	SK4215	52°44·1′	1°22·3′W	T	129
News Wood	Heref	SO7538	52°2·6′	2°21·5′W	F	150
Newtack	Moray	NJ3354	57°34·5′	3°6·8′W	X	28
Newtack	Moray	NJ4446	57°30·3′	2°55·6′W	X	28
Newtack	Moray	NJ4654	57°34·6′	2°53·7′W	X	28,29
Newtake	Devon	SX7964	50°28·0′	3°41·9′W	X	202
Newtake	Devon	SX8870	50°31·4′	3°34·4′W	T	202
New Terrace	Staffs	SJ7542	52°58·7′	2°21·9′W	X	118
Newte's Hill	Devon	SS9711	50°53·6′	3°27·5′W	H	192
New Thirsk	N Yks	SE4281	54°13·6′	1°20·9′W	T	99
Newthorpe	Notts	SK4846	53°0·8′	1°16·7′W	T	129
Newthorpe	N Yks	SE4732	53°47·2′	1°16·8′W	T	105
Newthorpe Barrack	Leeds	SE4532	53°47·2′	1°18·6′W	X	105
Newthorpe Common	Notts	SK4745	53°0·3′	1°17·6′W	T	129
New Thundersley	Essex	TQ7789	51°34·5′	0°33·7′E	T	178
Newtimber Hill	W Susx	TQ2712	50°53·8′	0°11·3′W	X	198
Newtimber Place	W Susx	TQ2613	50°54·4′	0°12·1′W	A	198
Newtoft	Lincs	TF0486	53°21·9′	0°25·8′W	T	112,121
Newtoft	Pth & Kin	NO0810	56°16·7′	3°28·7′W	X	58
Newton	Aberd	NJ3715	57°13·5′	3°2·1′W	X	37
Newton	Aberd	NJ4311	57°11·4′	2°56·1′W	X	37

Newton	Aberd	NJ4443	57°28·7'	2°55·6'W	X	28
Newton	Aberd	NJ4745	57°29·8'	2°52·6'W	X	28,29
Newton	Aberd	NJ4815	57°13·6'	2°51·2'W	X	37
Newton	Aberd	NJ5461	57°38·5'	2°45·8'W	X	29
Newton	Aberd	NJ5802	57°6·7'	2°41·2'W	X	37
Newton	Aberd	NJ5821	57°16·9'	2°41·3'W	X	37
Newton	Aberd	NJ5829	57°21·2'	2°41·4'W	X	37
Newton	Aberd	NJ5934	57°23·9'	2°40·5'W	X	29
Newton	Aberd	NJ6118	57°15·3'	2°38·3'W	X	37
Newton	Aberd	NJ6324	57°18·6'	2°36·4'W	X	37
Newton	Aberd	NJ7118	57°15·4'	2°28·4'W	X	38
Newton	Aberd	NJ7147	57°31·0'	2°28·6'W	X	29
Newton	Aberd	NJ7717	57°14·8'	2°22·4'W	X	38
Newton	Aberd	NJ8127	57°20·2'	2°18·5'W	X	38
Newton	Aberd	NJ8217	57°14·9'	2°17·4'W	X	38
Newton	Aberd	NJ8220	57°16·5'	2°17·5'W	X	38
Newton	Aberd	NJ8247	57°31·0'	2°17·6'W	X	29,30
Newton	Aberd	NJ8326	57°19·7'	2°16·5'W	X	38
Newton	Aberd	NJ8837	57°25·6'	2°11·5'W	X	30
Newton	Aberd	NJ9554	57°34·8'	2°4·6'W	X	30
Newton	Aberd	NK0142	57°28·4'	1°58·5'W	X	30
Newton	Aberd	NK0549	57°32·1'	1°54·5'W	X	30
Newton	Aberd	NK0641	57°27·8'	1°53·5'W	X	30
Newton	Aberd	NK0951	57°33·2'	1°50·5'W	X	30
Newton	Aberd	NK1143	57°28·9'	1°48·5'W	X	30
Newton	Aberd	NO2595	57°2·7'	3°13·7'W	X	37,44
Newton	Aberd	NO4697	57°3·9'	2°53·0'W	X	37,44
Newton	Aberd	NO6099	57°5·1'	2°39·1'W	X	37,45
Newton	Aberd	NO7099	57°5·1'	2°29·2'W	X	38,45
Newton	Aberd	NO7494	57°2·4'	2°25·3'W	X	38,45
Newton	Angus	NO2360	56°43·8'	3°15·1'W	X	44
Newton	Angus	NO2857	56°42·2'	3°10·1'W	X	53
Newton	Angus	NO3138	56°32·0'	3°6·9'W	X	53
Newton	Angus	NO4541	56°33·7'	2°53·2'W	X	54
Newton	Angus	NO5543	56°34·9'	2°43·5'W	X	54
Newton	Angus	NO5964	56°46·2'	2°39·8'W	X	44
Newton	Arg & Bt	NS0498	56°8·3'	5°8·8'W	X	56
Newton	Arg & Bt	NS0572	55°54·4'	5°6·7'W	X	63
Newton	Beds	TL2244	52°5·1'	0°12·8'W	T	153
Newton	Brig	SS8377	51°29·0'	3°40·7'W	T	170
Newton	Cambs	TF4314	52°42·5'	0°7·4'E	T	131
Newton	Cambs	TL4349	52°7·5'	0°5·7'E	T	154
Newton	Card	ST2378	51°30·0'	3°6·2'W	T	171
Newton	Carm	SN2612	51°47·0'	4°31·0'W	X	158
Newton	Ches	SJ4168	53°12·6'	2°52·6'W	T	117
Newton	Ches	SJ5057	53°6·7'	2°44·4'W	X	117
Newton	Ches	SJ5059	53°7·8'	2°44·4'W	T	117
Newton	Ches	SJ5275	53°16·4'	2°42·8'W	T	117
Newton	C of Aber	NJ8609	57°10·6'	2°13·4'W	X	38
Newton	C of Aber	NJ8611	57°11·6'	2°13·4'W	X	38
Newton	Corn	SW9445	50°16·4'	4°53·1'W	X	204
Newton	Corn	SX0963	50°26·4'	4°41·0'W	T	200
Newton	Corn	SX1079	50°35·0'	4°40·7'W	X	200
Newton	Corn	SX1273	50°31·8'	4°38·8'W	X	200
Newton	Corn	SX2586	50°39·1'	4°28·2'W	X	201
Newton	Corn	SX4168	50°29·6'	4°14·1'W	X	201
Newton	Cumbr	SD2271	54°8·0'	3°11·2'W	T	96
Newton	Derby	SK4459	53°7·8'	1°20·1'W	T	120
Newton	Devon	SS2423	50°59·0'	4°30·1'W	X	190
Newton	Devon	SX4573	50°32·4'	4°10·9'W	X	201
Newton	Devon	SX8048	50°19·4'	3°40·8'W	X	202
Newton	D & G	NT0710	55°22·8'	3°27·6'W	X	78
Newton	D & G	NX5553	54°51·3'	4°15·1'W	X	83
Newton	D & G	NX6550	54°49·9'	4°5·7'W	X	83,84
Newton	D & G	NX9096	55°15·0'	3°43·4'W	X	78
Newton	D & G	NY1075	55°3·9'	3°24·1'W	X	85
Newton	D & G	NY1194	55°14·2'	3°23·5'W	T	78
Newton	D & G	NY2670	55°1·4'	3°9·0'W	T	85
Newton	Donc	SE5602	53°30·9'	1°8·9'W	T	111
Newton	Dorset	ST7713	50°55·2'	2°19·2'W	T	194
Newton	Dorset	SZ0085	50°40·1'	1°59·6'W	X	195
Newton	E Yorks	SE8429	53°45·3'	0°43·1'W	X	106
Newton	Fife	NO2202	56°12·5'	3°15·0'W	X	58
Newton	Fife	NO2212	56°17·9'	3°15·2'W	X	58
Newton	Fife	NO2902	56°12·6'	3°8·2'W	X	59
Newton	Fife	NO2912	56°18·0'	3°8·4'W	X	59
Newton	Fife	NO4024	56°24·5'	2°57·9'W	X	54,59
Newton	Fife	NT1792	56°7·1'	3°19·7'W	X	58
Newton	Fife	NT3396	56°9·4'	3°4·3'W	X	59
Newton	Heref	SO2943	52°5·1'	3°1·8'W	T	148,161
Newton	Heref	SO3349	52°8·4'	2°58·3'W	X	148,149
Newton	Heref	SO3432	51°59·2'	2°57·3'W	T	149,161
Newton	Heref	SO3769	52°19·2'	2°55·1'W	T	137,148
Newton	Heref	SO5053	52°10·6'	2°43·5'W	T	149
Newton	Highld	NC2331	58°14·2'	5°0·4'W	X	15
Newton	Highld	ND1861	58°32·0'	3°24·0'W	X	11,12
Newton	Highld	ND2153	58°27·8'	3°20·8'W	X	11,12
Newton	Highld	ND3449	58°25·7'	3°7·3'W	T	12
Newton	Highld	NH5850	57°31·3'	4°21·8'W	X	26
Newton	Highld	NH7055	57°34·2'	4°10·0'W	X	27
Newton	Highld	NH7448	57°30·5'	4°5·7'W	T	27
Newton	Highld	NH7866	57°40·3'	4°2·3'W	X	21,27
Newton	Highld	NH8450	57°31·8'	3°55·8'W	X	27
Newton	Highld	NH8481	57°48·5'	3°56·7'W	X	21
Newton	Inverc	NS3367	55°52·3'	4°39·7'W	X	63
Newton	Lancs	SD3436	53°49·2'	2°59·7'W	T	102
Newton	Lancs	SD5974	54°9·9'	2°37·3'W	T	97
Newton	Lancs	SD6950	53°57·0'	2°27·9'W	T	103
Newton	Lincs	TF0436	52°54·9'	0°26·8'W	T	130
Newton	Midlo	NT3369	55°54·8'	3°3·9'W	X	66
Newton	Moray	NJ1663	57°39·2'	3°24·0'W	T	28
Newton	Moray	NJ2759	57°37·2'	3°12·9'W	X	28
Newton	Moray	NJ3362	57°38·8'	3°6·9'W	X	28
Newton	Moray	NJ3931	57°22·2'	3°0·4'W	X	37
Newton	Moray	NJ4147	57°30·8'	2°58·6'W	X	28
Newton	N Ayr	NR9351	55°42·8'	5°17·3'W	T	62,69
Newton	N Eil	NF8877	57°40·7'	7°13·6'W	X	18
Newton	Norf	TF8315	52°42·3'	0°42·9'E	T	132
Newton	Northnts	SP8883	52°26·5'	0°41·9'W	T	141
Newton	Northum	NT9407	55°21·7'	2°5·2'W	X	80
Newton	Northum	NY7984	55°9·2'	2°19·3'W	X	80
Newton	Northum	NZ0364	54°58·5'	1°56·8'W	T	87
Newton	Notts	SK6841	52°58·0'	0°58·8'W	T	129
Newton	Orkney	HY3228	59°8·3'	3°10·8'W	X	6
Newton	Pemb	SM9000	51°39·8'	5°1·8'W	X	157,158
Newton	Pemb	SM9820	51°50·8'	4°55·6'W	X	157,158
Newton	Pemb	SM9907	51°43·8'	4°54·3'W	X	157,158
Newton	Powys	SO1124	51°54·7'	3°17·2'W	X	161
Newton	Pth & Kin	NN8831	56°27·7'	3°48·6'W	X	52
Newton	Sand	SP0393	52°32·3'	1°56·9'W	T	139
Newton	Scot Bord	NT5017	55°26·9'	2°47·0'W	T	79
Newton	Scot Bord	NT5920	55°28·6'	2°38·5'W	X	73,74
Newton	Scot Bord	NT6020	55°28·6'	2°37·5'W	T	74
Newton	S Glos	ST6492	51°37·8'	2°30·8'W	T	162,172
Newton	Shetld	HU2755	60°17·0'	1°30·2'W	X	3
Newton	Shetld	HU3731	60°4·0'	1°19·6'W	X	4
Newton	Shetld	HU3785	60°33·1'	1°19·0'W	X	1,2,3
Newton	Shrops	SJ4234	52°54·3'	2°51·3'W	T	126
Newton	Shrops	SJ4817	52°45·1'	2°45·8'W	X	126
Newton	Shrops	SO3491	52°31·0'	2°58·0'W	X	137
Newton	Shrops	SO5882	52°26·3'	2°36·7'W	X	137,138
Newton	Shrops	SO7397	52°34·4'	2°23·5'W	T	138
Newton	S Lanak	NS6760	55°49·2'	4°6·9'W	T	64
Newton	S Lanak	NS7043	55°40·0'	4°3·6'W	X	71
Newton	S Lanak	NS9331	55°33·9'	3°41·4'W	T	71,72
Newton	Somer	ST1038	51°8·3'	3°16·8'W	T	181
Newton	Staffs	SJ9838	52°56·6'	2°1·4'W	X	127
Newton	Staffs	SK0325	52°49·6'	1°56·9'W	T	128
Newton	Stir	NN6101	56°11·1'	4°13·9'W	X	57
Newton	Suff	TL9140	52°1·8'	0°47·5'E	T	155
Newton	Swan	SS6088	51°34·6'	4°0·8'W	T	159
Newton	Tames	SJ9596	53°27·9'	2°4·1'W	T	109
Newton	Warw	SP5378	52°24·1'	1°12·9'W	T	140
Newton	Wilts	SU2322	51°0·0'	1°39·9'W	T	184
Newton	Wirral	SJ2387	53°22·7'	3°9·0'W	T	108
Newton	W Loth	NT0977	55°58·9'	3°27·1'W	T	65
Newton Abbot	Devon	SX8671	50°31·9'	3°36·1'W	T	202
Newtonairds	D & G	NX8880	55°6·4'	3°44·9'W	X	78
Newtonairds Wood	D & G	NX8880	55°6·4'	3°44·9'W	F	78
Newton Arlosh	Cumbr	NY2055	54°53·3'	3°14·4'W	T	85
Newton Auchaber	Aberd	NJ6240	57°27·2'	2°37·5'W	X	29
Newton Aycliffe	Durham	NZ2724	54°36·9'	1°34·5'W	T	93
Newton Bank	Pth & Kin	NO2632	56°28·7'	3°11·6'W	X	53
Newtonbank Fm	Halton	SJ5781	53°19·7'	2°38·3'W	FM	108
Newton Bar	Lincs	TF0437	52°55·5'	0°26·8'W	X	130
Newtonbarns	Northum	NU2224	55°30·8'	1°38·7'W	X	75
Newton Barrow	Wilts	SU1035	51°7·1'	1°51·0'W	A	184
Newton Barton	Devon	SX7192	50°43·0'	3°49·3'W	X	191
Newton Bay	Arg & Bt	NS0498	56°8·3'	5°8·8'W	W	56
Newton Bay	Dorset	SZ0085	50°40·1'	1°59·6'W	W	195
Newton Beck	N Yks	SE1990	54°18·6'	1°42·1'W	W	99
Newton Bewley	Hartpl	NZ4626	54°37·9'	1°16·8'W	T	93
Newton Blossomville	Mil Key	SP9251	52°9·2'	0°38·9'W	T	152
Newton Br	N Yks	SD9152	53°58·1'	2°7·8'W	X	103
Newton Br	Pth & Kin	NN8831	56°27·7'	3°48·6'W	X	52
Newtonbrae	Moray	NJ4256	57°35·7'	2°57·8'W	X	28
Newton Bromswold	Northnts	SP9965	52°16·7'	0°32·5'W	T	153
Newton Brow	N Yks	NZ7814	54°31·2'	0°47·3'W	X	94
Newton Burgoland	Leic	SK3709	52°40·9'	1°26·8'W	T	128,140
Newton Burn	Angus	NO2361	56°44·3'	3°15·1'W	W	44
Newton Burn	Northum	NU1506	55°21·1'	1°45·4'W	W	81
Newton by Toft	Lincs	TF0587	53°22·4'	0°24·9'W	T	112,121
Newton Carnaveron	Aberd	NJ5612	57°12·1'	2°43·2'W	X	37
Newton Carr	E Yorks	SE7449	53°56·1'	0°52·0'W	X	105,106
Newton Castle	Pth & Kin	NO1745	56°35·6'	3°20·7'W	A	53
Newton Cliff	Swan	SS6087	51°34·1'	4°0·8'W	X	159
Newton Common	Hants	SU6933	51°5·8'	1°0·5'W	F	186
Newton Common	St Hel	SJ5595	53°27·2'	2°40·3'W	X	108
Newton Cott	Aberd	NK0352	57°33·7'	1°56·5'W	X	30
Newton Court	Monm	SO5214	51°49·6'	2°41·4'W	X	162
Newton Cross	Devon	SS5227	51°1·6'	4°6·2'W	X	180
Newton Cross	Devon	SX8048	50°19·4'	3°40·8'W	X	202
Newton Cross	Pemb	SM8927	51°54·3'	5°3·7'W	T	157,158
Newton Ct	Heref	SO3953	52°10·6'	2°53·1'W	X	148,149
Newton Dale	N Yks	SE8190	54°18·2'	0°44·9'W	X	94,100
Newtondale Halt	N Yks	SE8394	54°20·3'	0°43·0'W	X	94,100
Newton Dee	C of Aber	NJ8801	57°6·2'	2°11·4'W	X	38
Newton Dingel	Shrops	SO5781	52°25·8'	2°37·5'W	X	137,138
Newton Don	Scot Bord	NT7037	55°37·8'	2°28·2'W	X	74
Newton Down	Brig	SS8479	51°30·1'	3°39·9'W	X	170
Newton Down Fm	Hants	SU4239	51°9·2'	1°23·6'W	FM	185
Newton Downs	Devon	SX5549	50°19·6'	4°1·9'W	X	202
Newton East	Pemb	SM9326	51°53·9'	4°59·5'W	X	157,158
Newton Farm	Heref	SO4938	52°2·5'	2°44·2'W	FM	149
Newton Fell	Cumbr	SD4182	54°14·1'	2°53·9'W	H	96,97
Newton Fell Ho	Northum	NZ0366	54°59·6'	1°56·8'W	X	87
Newton Fells	Lancs	SD7148	53°55·9'	2°26·1'W	X	103
Newton Fen	Cambs	TF4012	52°41·5'	0°4·7'E	X	131,142,143
Newton Ferrers	Corn	SX3466	50°28·5'	4°20·0'W	X	201
Newton Ferrers	Devon	SX5448	50°19·1'	4°2·7'W	T	201
Newtonferry	N Eil	NF8978	57°41·3'	7°12·7'W	T	18
Newton Field	Cumbr	NY1043	54°46·7'	3°23·5'W	X	85
Newton Field	Warw	SK2809	52°40·9'	1°34·7'W	X	128,140
Newton Flotman	Norf	TM2198	52°32·3'	1°15·9'E	T	134
Newton Fm	Ches	SJ6342	52°58·7'	2°32·7'W	FM	118
Newton Fm	Corn	SW6719	50°1·8'	5°14·8'W	FM	203
Newton Fm	Corn	SX1393	50°42·6'	4°38·5'W	FM	190
Newton Fm	Corn	SX2768	50°29·4'	4°26·0'W	FM	201
Newton Fm	Corn	SX3292	50°42·4'	4°22·4'W	FM	190
Newton Fm	Corn	SX3482	50°37·1'	4°20·4'W	FM	201
Newton Fm	Dorset	ST7701	50°48·7'	2°19·2'W	FM	194
Newton Fm	Dorset	SY9393	50°44·4'	2°5·6'W	FM	195
Newton Fm	Fife	NT2089	56°5·5'	3°16·7'W	FM	66
Newton Fm	Heref	SO4725	51°55·6'	2°45·9'W	FM	161
Newton Fm	Heref	SO6251	52°9·6'	2°32·9'W	FM	149
Newton Fm	Leeds	SE4427	53°44·5'	1°19·6'W	FM	105
Newton Fm	Pemb	SN0307	51°43·9'	4°50·8'W	FM	157,158
Newton Fm	Pemb	SN0613	51°47·2'	4°48·4'W	FM	158
Newton Fm	Shrops	SO6585	52°27·9'	2°30·5'W	FM	138
Newton Fm	S Lanak	NS6661	55°49·7'	4°7·9'W	FM	64
Newton Fm	Suff	TM4150	52°6·0'	1°31·5'E	FM	156
Newtongarry Hill	Aberd	NJ5740	57°27·2'	2°42·5'W	H	29
Newton Garth	Cumbr	NY8214	54°31·5'	2°16·3'W	X	91,92
Newton Garth	E Yorks	TA1827	53°43·8'	0°12·3'W	X	107
Newton Gorse	Beds	TL0065	52°16·7'	0°31·7'W	F	153
Newton Gorse	Warw	SK2807	52°39·8'	1°34·8'W	F	140
Newton Grange	Derby	SK1653	53°4·7'	1°45·3'W	X	119
Newton Grange	Durham	NZ2745	54°48·2'	1°34·4'W	X	88
Newton Grange	Lincs	TF0586	53°21·9'	0°24·9'W	X	112,121
Newtongrange	Midlo	NT3464	55°52·1'	3°2·8'W	T	66
Newton Grange	N Yks	SE5262	54°3·3'	1°11·9'W	X	100
Newton Grange Fm	Darl	NZ3516	54°32·5'	1°27·1'W	FM	93
Newton Grange Fm	N Yks	SD9152	53°58·1'	2°7·8'W	FM	103
Newton Grange Fm	N Yks	SE6280	54°13·0'	1°2·5'W	FM	100
Newton Gray	Pth & Kin	NO2632	56°28·7'	3°11·6'W	X	53
Newton Green	Lancs	SD5974	54°9·9'	2°37·3'W	X	97
Newton Green	Monm	ST5191	51°37·2'	2°42·1'W	T	162,172
Newton Greens	Northum	NU1605	55°20·6'	1°44·4'W	X	81
Newton Greenways	Norf	TM2099	52°32·9'	1°15·1'E	X	134
Newton Hall	Ches	SJ4645	53°0·2'	2°47·9'W	X	117
Newton Hall	Ches	SJ4960	53°8·3'	2°45·3'W	X	117
Newton Hall	Ches	SJ5375	53°16·4'	2°41·9'W	X	117
Newton Hall	Ches	SJ8079	53°18·7'	2°17·6'W	X	118
Newton Hall	Durham	NZ2745	54°48·2'	1°34·4'W	T	88
Newton Hall	E Loth	NT5265	55°52·8'	2°45·6'W	X	66
Newton Hall	Essex	TL6122	51°52·6'	0°20·7'E	X	167
Newton Hall	Fife	NO3302	56°12·6'	3°4·4'W	X	59
Newton Hall	Northum	NU2324	55°30·8'	1°37·7'W	X	75
Newton Hall	Northum	NZ0365	54°59·0'	1°56·8'W	T	87
Newton Hall	N Yks	SD9053	53°58·6'	2°8·7'W	X	103
Newton Hall	N Yks	SE2861	54°2·9'	1°33·9'W	X	99
Newton Hall	Suff	TM1555	52°9·3'	1°9·0'E	X	156
Newton Hall	Suff	TM1951	52°7·1'	1°12·3'E	X	156
Newton Hall Fm	Ches	SJ8780	53°19·2'	2°11·3'W	FM	109
Newton Hanzard	Durham	NZ4227	54°38·4'	1°20·5'W	X	93
Newton Hanzard Plantns	Hartpl	NZ4228	54°39·0'	1°20·5'W	F	93
Newton Harcourt	Leic	SP6396	52°33·7'	1°3·8'W	T	140
Newtonhead	N Ayr	NS3741	55°38·4'	4°35·0'W	X	70
Newtonhead	S Lanak	NS8634	55°35·4'	3°48·1'W	X	71,72
Newton Heath	Dorset	SZ0084	50°39·6'	1°59·6'W	F	195
Newton Heath	Man	SD8800	53°30·0'	2°10·4'W	T	109
Newton High Ho	Northum	NZ0365	54°59·0'	1°56·8'W	X	87
Newton Hill	Aberd	NJ4541	57°27·6'	2°54·5'W	H	28,29
Newtonhill	Aberd	NJ5524	57°18·5'	2°44·4'W	X	37
Newtonhill	Aberd	NJ9215	57°13·8'	2°7·5'W	X	38
Newtonhill	Aberd	NO9193	57°1·9'	2°8·4'W	T	38,45
Newton Hill	Angus	NO6042	56°34·4'	2°38·6'W	H	54
Newton Hill	Arg & Bt	NN2116	56°18·4'	4°53·2'W	H	50,56
Newtonhill	D & G	NX4052	54°50·5'	4°29·1'W	X	83
Newton Hill	Fife	NO3923	56°24·0'	2°58·9'W	H	54,59
Newtonhill	Highld	NH5743	57°27·5'	4°22·6'W	T	26
Newton Hill	Northnts	TL0595	52°32·8'	0°26·7'W	X	142
Newtonhill	Orkney	HY2412	58°59·6'	3°18·9'W	X	6
Newton Hill	Wakf	SE3322	53°41·8'	1°29·6'W	T	104
Newton Ho	Aberd	NJ6629	57°21·3'	2°33·4'W	X	38
Newton Ho	Arg & Bt	NR3462	55°46·9'	6°14·1'W	X	60,61
Newton Ho	Devon	SX8798	50°46·5'	3°35·8'W	X	192
Newton Ho	Highld	NH5645	57°28·6'	4°23·6'W	X	26
Newton Ho	Moray	NJ1663	57°39·2'	3°24·0'W	X	28
Newton Ho	N Yks	NZ8803	54°25·1'	0°38·2'W	X	94
Newton Ho	Oxon	SU3698	51°41·0'	1°28·4'W	X	164
Newton Ho	V of Glam	ST0076	51°28·7'	3°26·0'W	X	170
Newtonholme	Cumbr	NY2056	54°53·8'	3°14·4'W	X	85
Newton House	Carm	SN6122	51°53·0'	4°0·8'W	X	159
Newton Hurst	Staffs	SK0525	52°49·6'	1°55·1'W	T	128
Newtonia	Ches	SJ6966	53°11·7'	2°27·4'W	T	118
Newton Ings	Leeds	SE4427	53°44·5'	1°19·6'W	X	105
Newton Ings Fm	Lincs	TF0586	53°21·9'	0°24·9'W	FM	112,121
Newton Ketton	Darl	NZ3120	54°34·7'	1°30·8'W	T	93
Newton Kyme	N Yks	SE4644	53°53·6'	1°17·6'W	T	105
Newton Lane Fm	Derby	SK2924	52°49·0'	1°33·8'W	FM	128
Newtonlees	E Loth	NT6877	55°59·3'	2°30·3'W	X	67
Newtonlees	Scot Bord	NT7237	55°37·8'	2°26·2'W	X	74
Newton-le-Willows	N Yks	SE2189	54°18·0'	1°40·2'W	T	99
Newton-Le-Willows	St Hel	SJ5895	53°27·2'	2°37·5'W	T	108
Newton-Le-Willows Sta	St Hel	SJ5995	53°27·3'	2°36·6'W	X	108
Newton Leys	Suff	TL9140	52°1·8'	0°47·5'E	X	155
Newton Links	Northum	NU2326	55°31·9'	1°37·7'W	X	75
Newton Links Ho	Northum	NU2326	55°31·9'	1°37·7'W	X	75
Newtonloan	Midlo	NT3363	55°51·6'	3°3·8'W	X	66
Newton Lodge	E Yorks	SE7250	53°56·7'	0°53·8'W	X	105,106
Newton Lodge	Northnts	SP9966	52°17·2'	0°32·5'W	X	153
Newton Lodge Fm	Mil Key	SP9051	52°9·2'	0°40·7'W	FM	152
Newton Longville	Bucks	SP8431	51°58·5'	0°46·2'W	T	152,165
Newton Low Hall	Northum	NU1706	55°21·1'	1°43·5'W	X	81
Newton Lowsteads Fm	Northum	NU1606	55°21·1'	1°44·4'W	FM	81
Newton Manor	Cumbr	NY0403	54°25·1'	3°28·3'W	X	89
Newton Manor Ho	Warw	SP5277	52°23·5'	1°13·8'W	X	140
Newton Marsh	Cumbr	NY1855	54°53·2'	3°16·3'W	W	85
Newton Mearns	E Renf	NS5355	55°46·2'	4°20·2'W	T	64
Newton Mere	Shrops	SJ4234	52°54·3'	2°51·3'W	W	126
Newtonmill	Angus	NO6064	56°46·2'	2°38·8'W	T	45
Newton Mill	Northum	NU0423	55°30·3'	1°55·8'W	X	75
Newton Mill	Northum	NZ1586	55°10·3'	1°45·4'W	X	81
Newton Moor	N Yks	SD8558	54°1·3'	2°13·3'W	H	103
Newton Moor	Red & Cl	NZ5912	54°30·2'	1°4·9'W	X	93
Newton Moor	V of Glam	SS9976	51°28·7'	3°26·9'W	X	170
Newtonmore	Highld	NN7199	57°4·1'	4°7·2'W	T	35
Newton Morrell	N Yks	NZ2309	54°28·8'	1°38·3'W	T	93
Newton Morrell	Oxon	SP6129	51°57·6'	1°6·3'W	T	164,165
Newton Moss	Highld	ND3449	58°25·7'	3°7·3'W	X	12
Newton Mount	Derby	SK2823	52°48·5'	1°34·7'W	X	128
Newton Mulgrave	N Yks	NZ7815	54°31·7'	0°47·3'W	T	94
Newton Mulgrave Moor	N Yks	NZ7713	54°30·6'	0°48·2'W	X	94
Newton Noyes	Pemb	SM9205	51°42·6'	5°0·3'W	X	157,158
Newton of Abirlot	Angus	NO6041	56°33·8'	2°38·6'W	X	54
Newton of Affleck	Aberd	NJ8623	57°18·1'	2°13·5'W	X	38
Newton of Affleck	Angus	NO4838	56°32·1'	2°50·3'W	X	54
Newton of Airlie	Angus	NO3250	56°38·5'	3°6·1'W	X	53
Newton of Ardoyne	Aberd	NJ6428	57°20·7'	2°35·4'W	X	37

Newton of Ardtoe	Highld	NM6470	56°46·0′	5°51·3′W	T	40
Newton of Auchintoul	Aberd	NJ6152	57°33·6′	2°38·6′W	X	29
Newton of Balcanquhal	Pth & Kin	NO1510	56°16·7′	3°21·9′W	X	58
Newton of Balcormo	Fife	NO5104	56°13·8′	2°47·0′W	T	59
Newton of Balhary	Pth & Kin	NO2547	56°36·8′	3°12·9′W	X	53
Newton of Ballunie	Pth & Kin	NO2539	56°32·5′	3°12·7′W	X	53
Newton of Balquhain	Aberd	NJ7224	57°18·6′	2°27·4′W	X	38
Newton of Bamff	Pth & Kin	NO2351	56°38·9′	3°14·9′W	X	53
Newton of Barras	Aberd	NO8681	56°55·5′	2°13·3′W	X	45
Newton of Begshill	Aberd	NJ5937	57°25·5′	2°40·5′W	X	29
Newton of Beltrees	Renf	NS3758	55°47·5′	4°35·6′W	X	63
Newton of Bogenlea	Aberd	NJ8252	57°33·7′	2°17·6′W	X	29,30
Newton of Boysack	Angus	NO6047	56°37·0′	2°38·7′W	T	54
Newton of Braco	Aberd	NJ7020	57°16·4′	2°29·4′W	X	38
Newton of Budgate	Highld	NH8249	57°31·2′	3°57·7′W	X	27
Newton of Carnousie	Aberd	NJ6650	57°32·6′	2°33·6′W	X	29
Newton of Clunie	Aberd	NJ6349	57°32·0′	2°36·6′W	X	29
Newton of Coldwells	Aberd	NJ9638	57°26·2′	2°3·5′W	X	30
Newton of Corsegight	Aberd	NJ8549	57°32·1′	2°14·6′W	X	30
Newton of Corsindae	Aberd	NJ6907	57°9·4′	2°30·3′W	X	38
Newton of Craigston	Aberd	NJ7556	57°35·9′	2°24·6′W	X	29
Newton of Culvie	Aberd	NJ5854	57°34·7′	2°41·7′W	X	29
Newton of Dalvey	Moray	NJ0057	57°35·8′	3°39·9′W	X	27
Newton of Darnaway	Moray	NH9853	57°33·6′	3°41·8′W	X	27
Newton of Deershaw	Aberd	NJ6357	57°36·3′	2°36·7′W	X	29
Newton of Drum	Aberd	NO7999	57°5·1′	2°20·3′W	X	38,45
Newton of Drumgesk	Aberd	NO5699	57°5·1′	2°43·1′W	X	37,44
Newton of Edingight	Moray	NJ5256	57°35·7′	2°47·7′W	X	29
Newton of Falkland	Fife	NO2607	56°15·2′	3°11·2′W	T	59
Newton of Ferintosh	Highld	NH5653	57°32·9′	4°23·9′W	X	26
Newton of Forbes	Aberd	NJ5517	57°14·7′	2°44·3′W	X	37
Newton of Forgie	Moray	NJ3953	57°34·0′	3°0·7′W	X	28
Newton of Fortrie	Aberd	NJ6745	57°29·9′	2°32·6′W	X	29
Newton of Foulzie	Aberd	NJ7359	57°37·5′	2°26·7′W	X	29
Newton of Glamis	Angus	NO3747	56°36·9′	3°1·1′W	X	54
Newton of Gorthy	Pth & Kin	NN9524	56°24·1′	3°41·6′W	X	52,53,58
Newton of Greenness	Aberd	NJ7848	57°31·6′	2°21·6′W	X	29,30
Newton of Guthrie	Angus	NO5750	56°38·6′	2°41·6′W	X	54
Newton of Haddo	Aberd	NJ6147	57°30·9′	2°38·6′W	X	29
Newton of Hythie	Aberd	NK0151	57°33·2′	1°58·5′W	X	30
Newton of Innes	Moray	NJ2866	57°40·9′	3°12·0′W	X	28
Newton of Inshewan	Angus	NO4159	56°43·4′	2°57·4′W	X	54
Newton of Kingsdale	Fife	NO3302	56°12·6′	3°4·4′W	X	59
Newton of Kinkell	Highld	NH5652	57°32·4′	4°23·9′W	X	26
Newton of Kirkbuddo	Angus	NO5143	56°34·8′	2°47·4′W	X	54
Newton of Lathrisk	Fife	NO2707	56°15·3′	3°10·3′W	X	59
Newton of Letterfourie	Moray	NJ4360	57°37·8′	2°56·8′W	X	28
Newton of Lewesk	Aberd	NJ6927	57°20·2′	2°30·4′W	X	38
Newton of Leys	Aberd	NO6897	57°4·0′	2°31·2′W	X	38,45
Newton of Leys	Highld	NH6739	57°25·6′	4°12·4′W	X	26
Newton of Litterty	Aberd	NJ7954	57°34·8′	2°20·6′W	X	29,30
Newton of Ludquharn	Aberd	NK0243	57°28·9′	1°57·5′W	X	30
Newton of Melrose	Aberd	NJ7563	57°39·6′	2°24·7′W	X	29
Newton of Menie	Aberd	NJ9520	57°16·5′	2°4·5′W	X	38
Newton of Millfield	Aberd	NJ8251	57°33·2′	2°17·6′W	X	29,30
Newton of Mounie	Aberd	NJ7528	57°20·8′	2°24·5′W	X	38
Newton of Mountblairy	Aberd	NJ6855	57°35·3′	2°31·7′W	X	29
Newton of Mundurno	C of Aber	NJ9413	57°12·7′	2°5·5′W	X	38
Newton of Nydie	Fife	NO4417	56°20·8′	2°53·9′W	X	59
Newton of Ochtow	Highld	NC4700	57°58·0′	4°34·7′W	X	16
Newton of Park	Highld	NH9054	57°34·0′	3°49·9′W	X	27
Newton of Pitcairns	Pth & Kin	NO0214	56°18·8′	3°34·6′W	T	58
Newton of Rainnieshill	Aberd	NJ8920	57°16·5′	2°10·5′W	X	38
Newton of Rothmaise	Aberd	NJ6733	57°23·4′	2°32·5′W	X	29
Newton of Saphock	Aberd	NJ7728	57°20·8′	2°22·5′W	X	38
Newton of Shielhill	C of Aber	NJ9314	57°13·3′	2°6·5′W	X	38
Newton of Struthers	Moray	NJ0861	57°38·0′	3°32·0′W	X	27
Newton of Teuchar	Aberd	NJ8049	57°32·1′	2°19·6′W	X	29,30
Newton of Tollo	Aberd	NJ6544	57°29·4′	2°34·6′W	X	29
Newton of Tornaveen	Aberd	NJ6206	57°8·9′	2°37·2′W	X	37
Newton of Tullich	Aberd	NO3997	57°3·9′	2°59·9′W	X	37,44
Newton of Tulloch	Aberd	NJ7732	57°22·9′	2°22·5′W	X	29,30
Newton on Ayr	S Ayr	NS3423	55°28·6′	4°37·2′W	T	70
Newton-on-Ouse	N Yks	SE5159	54°1·7′	1°12·9′W	T	105
Newton-on-Rawcliffe	N Yks	SE8190	54°18·2′	0°44·9′W	T	94,100
Newton on the Hill	Shrops	SJ4823	52°48·4′	2°45·9′W	T	126
Newton on the Moor	Northum	NU1605	55°20·6′	1°44·4′W	T	81
Newton on Trent	Lincs	SK8374	53°15·6′	0°44·9′W	T	121
Newton-out-Field	Cumbr	NY1143	54°46·7′	3°22·6′W	X	85
Newton Park	Arg & Bt	NS1469	55°53·0′	4°58·0′W	T	63
Newton Park	Carm	SN3628	51°55·8′	4°22·7′W	X	145
Newton Park	Mil Key	SP9350	52°8·7′	0°38·1′W	X	153
Newton Park	Northum	NZ1586	55°10·3′	1°45·4′W	X	81
Newton Park	St Hel	SJ5994	53°26·7′	2°36·6′W	T	108
Newton Park College	Bath & NE Somer	ST6964	51°22·7′	2°26·3′W	X	172
Newton Peveril	Dorset	SY9399	50°47·7′	2°5·6′W	T	195
Newton Point	Brig	SS8376	51°28·5′	3°40·7′W	X	170
Newton Point	Highld	NH7187	57°51·5′	4°10·0′W	X	21
Newton Point	N Ayr	NR9351	55°42·8′	5°17·3′W	X	62,69
Newton Point	Northum	NU2425	55°31·3′	1°36·8′W	X	75
Newton Poppleford	Devon	SY0889	50°41·8′	3°17·8′W	T	192
Newton Purcell	Oxon	SP6230	51°58·1′	1°5·5′W	T	152,165
Newton Red Ho	Northum	NZ1485	55°9·8′	1°46·4′W	X	81
Newton Regis	Warw	SK2707	52°39·8′	1°35·6′W	T	140
Newton Reigny	Cumbr	NY4731	54°40·5′	2°48·9′W	T	90
Newtonrig	D & G	NX9480	55°6·4′	3°39·3′W	X	78
Newton Rigg	Cumbr	NY4931	54°40·5′	2°47·0′W	T	90
Newtonrigg	Northum	NY8375	55°4·4′	2°15·5′W	X	86,87
Newton's Corner	Derby	SK4026	52°50·0′	1°24·0′W	X	129
Newtons Fm	Cambs	TL3484	52°26·5′	0°1·3′W	FM	142
Newtons Fm	E Susx	TQ3315	50°55·4′	0°6·1′W	FM	198
Newton's Fm	Lincs	SK8661	53°8·6′	0°42·4′W	FM	121
Newton's Hill	E Susx	TQ4735	51°6·0′	0°6·4′E	X	188
Newton Skene	Aberd	NJ7710	57°11·1′	2°22·4′W	X	38
Newton Solney	Derby	SK2825	52°49·5′	1°34·7′W	T	128
Newton South Wold Ho	N Yks	SE8870	54°7·3′	0°38·8′W	X	101
Newton Spinney	Northnts	TL0495	52°32·8′	0°27·6′W	F	141
Newton Stacey	Hants	SU4140	51°9·7′	1°24·4′W	T	185
Newton St Boswells	Scot Bord	NT5731	55°34·5′	2°40·5′W	T	73,74

Newton St Cyres	Devon	SX8798	50°46·5′	3°35·8′W	T	192
Newton Stewart	D & G	NX4065	54°57·5′	4°29·5′W	T	83
Newton St Faith	Norf	TG2217	52°42·5′	1°17·6′E	T	133,134
Newton St Loe	Bath & NE Somer	ST7064	51°22·7′	2°25·5′W	T	172
Newton St Petrock	Devon	SS4112	50°53·4′	4°15·3′W	T	180,190
Newton Surmaville	Somer	ST5615	50°56·2′	2°37·2′W	A	183
Newton's Wood	Suff	TM3874	52°19·0′	1°29·9′E	F	156
Newton Thorneybank	Aberd	NJ6740	57°27·2′	2°32·5′W	X	29
Newton Tony	Wilts	SU2140	51°9·8′	1°41·6′W	T	184
Newton Tors	Northum	NT9026	55°31·9′	2°9·1′W	H	74,75
Newton Tracey	Devon	SS5226	51°1·1′	4°6·2′W	T	180
Newton Tump	Heref	SO2944	52°5·6′	3°1·8′W	A	148,161
Newton under Roseberry	Red & Cl	NZ5613	54°30·8′	1°7·7′W	T	93
Newton Underwood	Northum	NZ1486	55°10·3′	1°46·4′W	T	81
Newton upon Derwent	E Yorks	SE7249	53°56·2′	0°53·8′W	T	105,106
Newton Valence	Hants	SU7232	51°5·2′	0°57·9′W	T	186
Newton Valence Place	Hants	SU7233	51°5·7′	0°57·9′W	X	186
Newton West Fm	Pemb	SM8926	51°53·8′	5°3·6′W	FM	157,158
Newton with Scales	Lancs	SD4430	53°46·0′	2°50·6′W	T	102
Newton Wood	Devon	SX8795	50°44·9′	3°35·7′W	F	192
Newton Wood	Herts	TL2222	51°53·2′	0°13·2′W	F	166
Newton Wood	Mil Key	SP9250	52°8·7′	0°38·9′W	F	152
Newton Wood	Red & Cl	NZ5712	54°30·2′	1°6·8′W	F	93
Newton Wood	Tames	SJ9396	53°27·9′	2°5·9′W	T	109
New Totley	Sheff	SK3179	53°18·7′	1°31·7′W	T	119
New Totterdown	Wilts	SU1372	51°27·0′	1°48·4′W	X	173
Newtown	Aberd	NJ4707	57°9·3′	2°52·1′W	X	37
Newtown	Aberd	NJ9958	57°37·0′	2°0·5′W	X	30
Newtown	Arg & Bt	NN0907	56°13·3′	5°4·4′W	T	56
New Town	Bath & NE Somer	ST5861	51°21·0′	2°35·8′W	T	172,182
New Town	Bath & NE Somer	ST7757	51°18·9′	2°19·4′W	T	172
Newtown	Birm	SP0688	52°29·6′	1°54·3′W	T	139
Newtown	Blae Gw	SO1710	51°47·2′	3°11·8′W	T	161
Newtown	Bucks	SP9602	51°42·7′	0°36·2′W	T	165
Newtown	Caer	ST2191	51°37·0′	3°8·1′W	T	171
Newtown	Cambs	TL0968	52°18·2′	0°23·7′W	T	153
Newtown	Ches	SJ5278	53°18·0′	2°42·8′W	T	117
Newtown	Ches	SJ9383	53°20·9′	2°5·9′W	T	109
New Town	C of Edin	NT2474	55°57·4′	3°12·6′W	T	66
New Town	C of Edin	NT2674	55°57·5′	3°10·7′W	T	66
New Town	C of Soton	SU4510	50°53·5′	1°21·2′W	T	196
Newtown	Corn	SW5729	50°6·9′	5°23·6′W	T	203
Newtown	Corn	SX1052	50°20·5′	4°39·8′W	X	200,204
Newtown	Corn	SX2978	50°34·8′	4°24·5′W	T	201
Newtown	Cumbr	NY0948	54°49·4′	3°24·6′W	T	85
Newtown	Cumbr	NY3855	54°53·4′	2°57·6′W	T	85
Newtown	Cumbr	NY4962	54°57·3′	2°47·4′W	T	86
Newtown	Cumbr	NY5224	54°36·8′	2°44·2′W	X	90
Newtown	Cumbr	NY6032	54°41·1′	2°36·8′W	X	91
Newtown	Cumbr	SD0995	54°20·8′	3°23·6′W	X	96
Newtown	Derby	SJ9984	53°21·4′	2°0·5′W	T	109
Newtown	Devon	SS6031	51°3·9′	3°59·5′W	X	180
Newtown	Devon	SS7625	51°0·9′	3°45·7′W	T	180
Newtown	Devon	SY0699	50°47·2′	3°19·6′W	T	192
Newtown	Dorset	ST4802	50°49·1′	2°43·9′W	T	193
New Town	Dorset	ST7622	51°0·0′	2°20·1′W	T	183
New Town	Dorset	ST9415	50°56·3′	2°4·7′W	T	184
New Town	Dorset	ST9818	50°57·9′	2°1·3′W	T	184
New Town	Dorset	ST9907	50°52·0′	2°0·5′W	T	195
New Town	Durham	NZ2434	54°42·3′	1°37·2′W	X	93
New Town	E Loth	NT4470	55°55·4′	2°53·3′W	T	66
New Town	E Susx	TQ4720	50°57·9′	0°6·0′E	T	198
Newtown	Falk	NS9980	56°0·4′	3°36·7′W	T	65
Newtown	Flint	SJ3266	53°11·4′	3°0·7′W	X	117
Newtown	Glos	SO6701	51°42·6′	2°28·3′W	T	162
Newtown	Glos	SO7905	51°44·8′	2°17·9′W	T	162
Newtown	Glos	SO9032	51°59·4′	2°8·3′W	T	150
New Town	Glos	SP0432	51°59·4′	1°56·1′W	T	150
Newtown	Hants	SU2710	50°53·6′	1°36·6′W	T	195
Newtown	Hants	SU3023	51°0·6′	1°34·0′W	T	185
Newtown	Hants	SU4763	51°22·1′	1°19·1′W	T	174
Newtown	Hants	SU4905	50°50·8′	1°17·9′W	T	196
Newtown	Hants	SU5417	50°57·2′	1°13·5′W	T	185
Newtown	Hants	SU6112	50°54·5′	1°7·6′W	T	196
Newtown	Hants	SU7138	51°8·4′	0°58·7′W	T	186
Newtown	Hants	SU8430	51°4·0′	0°47·7′W	T	186
Newtown	Hants	SZ6199	50°47·5′	1°7·7′W	T	196
Newtown	Heref	SO4757	52°12·8′	2°46·1′W	X	148,149
Newtown	Heref	SO5333	51°59·8′	2°40·7′W	T	149
Newtown	Heref	SO6144	52°5·8′	2°33·8′W	T	149
Newtown	Heref	SO6319	51°52·3′	2°31·9′W	X	162
Newtown	Highld	NH3504	57°6·1′	4°43·0′W	X	34
Newtown	I of M	SC3273	54°7·8′	4°33·9′W	T	95
Newtown	I of W	SZ4290	50°42·7′	1°23·9′W	T	196
Newtown	Kent	TQ5474	51°26·9′	0°13·4′E	T	177
New Town	Kent	TQ6757	51°17·5′	0°24·1′E	T	178,188
Newtown	Lancs	SD5118	53°39·6′	2°44·1′W	T	108
New Town	Lancs	SD6036	53°49·4′	2°36·0′W	T	102,103
New Town	Luton	TL0920	51°52·3′	0°24·6′W	T	166
New Town	Medway	TQ7064	51°21·2′	0°26·9′E	T	178,188
New Town	Norf	TG5209	52°37·4′	1°43·8′E	T	134
Newtown	Northum	NU0300	55°17·9′	1°56·7′W	T	81
Newtown	Northum	NU0425	55°31·4′	1°55·8′W	T	75
Newtown	Northum	NU1008	55°22·2′	1°50·1′W	X	81
Newtown	Northum	NU1635	55°36·7′	1°44·3′W	X	75
New Town	Oxon	SP2529	51°57·8′	1°37·8′W	T	163
New Town	Oxon	SU7681	51°31·6′	0°53·9′W	T	175
Newtown	Poole	SZ0493	50°44·4′	1°56·2′W	T	195
Newtown	Powys	SJ3114	52°43·4′	3°0·9′W	X	126
Newtown	Powys	SO1191	52°30·8′	3°18·3′W	T	136
Newtown	Read	SU7373	51°27·3′	0°56·6′W	T	175
Newtown	Rho Cyn Taf	ST0598	51°40·6′	3°22·0′W	T	170
Newtown	Salf	SD7702	53°31·1′	2°20·4′W	T	109
Newtown	Sand	SO9791	52°31·2′	2°2·3′W	T	139
Newtown	Shetld	HU4582	60°31·4′	1°10·3′W	X	1,2,3
Newtown	Shrops	SJ4222	52°47·8′	2°51·2′W	T	126
Newtown	Shrops	SJ4831	52°52·7′	2°46·0′W	T	126

Newtown	Shrops	SJ6200	52°36·0′	2°33·3′W	T	127,138
Newtown	Somer	ST2712	50°54·4′	3°1·9′W	T	193
Newtown	Somer	ST2937	51°7·9′	3°0·5′W	T	182
New Town	Somer	ST4645	51°12·3′	2°46·0′W	T	182
New Town	Somer	ST5616	50°57·9′	2°37·2′W	T	183
New Town	Somer	ST6618	50°57·9′	2°28·7′W	T	183
Newtown	Staffs	SJ9060	53°8·5′	2°8·6′W	T	118
Newtown	Staffs	SJ9514	52°43·7′	2°4·0′W	X	127
Newtown	Staffs	SJ9904	52°38·3′	2°0·5′W	T	127,139
Newtown	Staffs	SK0663	53°10·1′	1°54·2′W	T	119
Newtown	St Hel	SJ4995	53°27·2′	2°45·7′W	T	108
New Town	S Tyne	NZ3461	54°56·8′	1°27·7′W	T	88
Newtown	Suff	TM2168	52°16·2′	1°14·7′E	X	156
New Town	Sund	NZ3449	54°50·3′	1°27·8′W	T	88
New Town	Swin	SU1584	51°33·5′	1°46·6′W	T	173
New Town	Wakf	SE4523	53°42·3′	1°18·7′W	T	105
New Town	Wals	SK0506	52°39·3′	1°55·2′W	T	139
New Town	W Berks	SU6075	51°28·5′	1°7·8′W	T	175
Newtown	Wigan	SD5605	53°32·6′	2°39·4′W	T	108
Newtown	Wilts	ST9129	51°3·8′	2°7·3′W	T	184
New Town	Wilts	SU1164	51°22·7′	1°50·1′W	X	173
New Town	Wilts	SU1450	51°15·2′	1°47·6′W	T	184
New Town	Wilts	SU2871	51°26·5′	1°35·4′W	T	174
New Town	Wilts	SU3063	51°22·1′	1°33·8′W	T	174
Newtown	Worcs	SO7557	52°12·9′	2°21·6′W	T	150
Newtown	Worcs	SO8863	52°16·1′	2°10·2′W	T	150
New Town	W Susx	TQ1829	51°3·1′	0°18·6′W	T	187,198
Newtown Bay	Arg & Bt	NN0908	56°13·8′	5°4·4′W	W	56
Newtown Bay	I of W	SZ4192	50°43·8′	1°24·8′W	W	196
Newtown Bridge	Devon	SS6932	51°4·6′	3°51·8′W	X	180
Newtown Common	Hants	SU4762	51°21·5′	1°19·1′W	X	174
Newtown Fm	Cumbr	SD2467	54°5·8′	3°9·3′W	FM	96
Newtown Fm	Somer	ST2817	50°57·1′	3°1·1′W	FM	193
Newtown Fm	Wilts	ST9060	51°20·6′	2°8·2′W	FM	173
Newtown Fm	Wilts	ST9555	51°17·9′	2°3·9′W	FM	173
Newtown Fm	Worcs	SO5962	52°15·5′	2°35·6′W	FM	137,138,149
Newtown Fm	Worcs	SO9778	52°24·2′	2°2·2′W	FM	139
Newtown Ho	Hants	SU4763	51°22·1′	1°19·1′W	X	174
Newtown-in-St Martin	Corn	SW7423	50°4·1′	5°9·1′W	T	204
Newtown Linford	Leic	SK5109	52°40·8′	1°14·3′W	T	140
Newtown Linford	Leic	SK5110	52°41·4′	1°14·3′W	T	129
Newtown Moor	Northum	NU0326	55°31·9′	1°56·7′W	X	75
Newtown Mountain	Wrex	SJ2545	53°0·1′	3°6·7′W	H	117
Newtown of Covington	S Lanak	NS9739	55°38·3′	3°37·7′W	X	72
Newtown of Glenmarkie	Moray	NJ3838	57°25·9′	3°1·5′W	X	28
Newtown of Rockcliffe	Cumbr	NY3862	54°57·2′	2°57·7′W	X	85
Newtown Park	Hants	SZ3496	50°46·0′	1°30·7′W	X	196
Newtown Park	Northum	NZ0399	55°17·4′	1°56·7′W	F	81
Newtown River	I of W	SZ4191	50°43·3′	1°24·8′W	W	196
Newtown Unthank	Leic	SK4904	52°38·1′	1°16·2′W	T	140
Newtrain Bay	Corn	SW8875	50°32·4′	4°59·1′W	W	200
New Tredegar	Caer	SO1403	51°43·4′	3°14·3′W	T	171
New Trows	S Lanak	NS8038	55°37·5′	3°53·9′W	T	71,72
Newtyle	Aberd	NJ9822	57°17·6′	2°1·5′W	X	38
Newtyle	Angus	NO2941	56°33·6′	3°8·9′W	T	53
Newtyle	Pth & Kin	NO0440	56°32·8′	3°33·2′W	X	52,53
Newtyle Forest	Moray	NJ0552	57°33·2′	3°34·8′W	F	27
Newtyle Hill	Angus	NO2939	56°32·5′	3°8·8′W	H	53
Newtyle Hill	Pth & Kin	NO0442	56°33·9′	3°33·3′W	H	52,53
Newtyle Ho	Aberd	NJ9722	57°17·6′	2°2·5′W	X	38
New Ulva	Arg & Bt	NR7080	55°57·7′	5°40·7′W	T	55,61
New Union Fm	Lancs	SD4145	53°54·1′	2°53·5′W	FM	102
New Velzian	Orkney	HY2821	59°4·5′	3°14·9′W	X	6
New Village	Donc	SE5606	53°33·1′	1°8·9′W	T	111
New Village	E Yorks	TA0532	53°46·7′	0°24·0′W	T	107
New Village Grange	E Yorks	SE8529	53°45·3′	0°42·2′W	X	106
New Village Ho	E Yorks	SE8629	53°45·3′	0°41·3′W	X	106
Newville Fm	Lincs	SK8193	53°25·9′	0°46·4′W	FM	112
New Wallace	V of Glam	ST1070	51°25·5′	3°17·3′W	X	171
Newwall Nook	Derby	SK1680	53°19·2′	1°45·2′W	X	110
New Waltham	NE Lincs	TA2804	53°31·3′	0°3·7′W	T	113
New Warren Fm	Hants	SU5426	51°2·1′	1°13·4′W	FM	185
New Waste	Devon	SX6261	50°26·2′	3°56·2′W	X	202
New Water	Cumbr	NY5951	54°51·4′	2°37·9′W	W	86
New Water Haugh	Northum	NT9752	55°45·9′	2°2·4′W	X	75
New Waters	Warw	SP2963	52°16·1′	1°34·1′W	W	151
New Waters Fm	Suff	TM0676	52°20·8′	1°1·9′E	FM	144
New Wavendon Heath	Beds	SP9233	51°59·5′	0°39·2′W	F	152,165
New Way	Essex	TL5009	51°45·8′	0°10·8′E	X	167
New Well	Powys	SO0776	52°22·7′	3°21·6′W	T	136,147
New Wellbury	Herts	TL1329	51°57·1′	0°20·9′W	X	166
New Wells	Powys	SO1595	52°33·0′	3°14·8′W	T	136
New Wester Echt	Aberd	NJ7308	57°10·0′	2°26·3′W	X	38
New Whitchurch Fm	Somer	ST6352	51°16·2′	2°31·4′W	FM	183
New Whitcombe Fm	Somer	ST4722	50°59·9′	2°44·9′W	FM	193
New Whittington	Derby	SK3975	53°16·5′	1°24·5′W	T	119
New Wimpole	Cambs	TL3449	52°7·6′	0°2·1′W	T	154
New Wintles Fm	Oxon	SP4310	51°47·5′	1°22·2′W	FM	164
New Winton	E Loth	NT4271	55°56·0′	2°55·3′W	T	66
New Wiseton	Notts	SK7188	53°23·3′	0°55·5′W	X	112,120
New Woll	Scot Bord	NT4621	55°29·0′	2°50·8′W	X	73
New Wood	Herts	TL2319	51°51·6′	0°12·4′W	F	166
New Wood	Midlo	NT3963	55°51·6′	2°58·0′W	F	66
New Wood	Monm	ST4998	51°40·9′	2°43·9′W	F	162
New Wood	Newp	ST3691	51°37·1′	2°55·1′W	F	171
New Wood	Norf	TF8419	52°44·5′	0°44·0′E	F	132
New Wood	N Yks	NZ2311	54°29·9′	1°38·3′W	F	93
New Wood	Rut	SK9506	52°38·8′	0°35·3′W	F	141
New Wood	Staffs	SO8885	52°28·0′	2°10·2′W	F	139
New Wood	Suff	TM0970	52°17·5′	1°4·3′E	F	144,155
New Woodcroft	Durham	NZ0037	54°43·9′	1°59·6′W	X	92
New Woodhouses	Shrops	SJ5941	52°58·1′	2°36·2′W	T	117
New Works	Wrekin	SJ6608	52°40·4′	2°29·8′W	T	127
New Wortley	Leeds	SE2832	53°47·3′	1°34·1′W	T	104
New Wrights Fm	Herts	TL1532	51°58·7′	0°19·1′W	FM	166
New Wryde Drain	Peterb	TF3403	52°36·7′	0°0·8′W	W	142
New Yard Fm	Lincs	TF5359	53°6·6′	0°17·6′E	FM	122
New Yatt	Oxon	SP3713	51°49·1′	1°27·4′W	T	164
Newydd Fynyddog	Powys	SH9100	52°35·5′	3°36·1′W	X	136
Newyearfield	W Loth	NT0368	55°54·0′	3°32·6′W	X	65

New Years Bridge Resr	Oldham	SD9810	53°35·4'	2°1·4'W	W	109
Newyears Green	Hill	TQ0788	51°35·1'	0°26·9'W	T	176
Newyears Wood	Brom	TQ4560	51°19·5'	0°5·3'E	F	177,188
New Yetts Resr	Inverc	NS2673	55°55·4'	4°46·6'W	W	63
Newyork	Arg & Bt	NM9611	56°15·1'	5°17·1'W	X	55
New York	E Yorks	TA2031	53°45·9'	0°10·4'W	X	107
New York	Kent	TQ9856	51°16·3'	0°50·7'E	X	178
New York	Lincs	TF2455	53°4·9'	0°8·5'W	T	122
New York	N Tyne	NZ3270	55°1·7'	1°29·5'W	T	88
New York	N Yks	SE1962	54°3·5'	1°42·2'W	T	99
New York	Staffs	SK0459	53°7·9'	1°56·0'W	X	119
New York Fm	Leeds	SE4342	53°52·6'	1°20·3'W	FM	105
New York Fm	Leic	SK6610	52°41·3'	1°1·0'W	FM	129
New York Fm	N Yks	SE2949	53°56·4'	1°33·1'W	FM	104
New Zealand	Wilts	SU0177	51°29·7'	1°58·7'W	T	173
New Zealand	Wilts	SU2855	51°17·8'	1°35·5'W	X	174
New Zealand Cotts	Suff	TL8576	52°21·3'	0°43·4'E	X	144
New Zealand Farm Camp	Wilts	ST9750	51°15·2'	2°2·2'W	X	184
Nex Common	Monm	ST4898	51°40·9'	2°44·7'W	X	171
Nextend	Heref	SO3357	52°12·7'	2°58·4'W	T	148,149
Next Ness	Cumbr	SD3078	54°11·8'	3°4·0'W	X	96,97
Ney Gill	N Yks	NY8402	54°25·0'	2°14·4'W	W	91,92
Neyland	Pemb	SM9605	51°42·6'	4°56·8'W	T	157,158
Neylands Fm	E Susx	TQ3834	51°5·5'	0°1·4'W	FM	187
Nhadog Isaf	Conwy	SH6850	53°2·1'	3°57·7'W	X	115
Nhare	Highld	NC8954	58°27·9'	3°53·7'W	X	10
Niag-àrd	Highld	NG7406	57°5·6'	5°43·4'W	X	33
Niandt	Highld	ND2133	58°17·0'	3°20·4'W	X	11
Niarbyl	I of M	SC2077	54°9·7'	4°45·0'W	X	95
Niarbyl Bay	I of M	SC2176	54°9·2'	4°44·1'W	W	95
Niatts, The	S Glos	ST5985	51°34·0'	2°35·1'W	X	172
Nibbetstane	Aberd	NO7995	57°3·0'	2°20·3'W	X	38,45
Nib Green Farm	Worcs	SO7579	52°24·7'	2°21·7'W	FM	
Nib Heath	Shrops	SJ4118	52°45·6'	2°52·1'W	T	126
Nibley	Glos	SO6606	51°45·3'	2°29·2'W	T	162
Nibley	S Glos	ST6982	51°32·4'	2°26·4'W	T	172
Nibley Green	Glos	ST7396	51°40·0'	2°23·0'W	T	162
Nibley Knoll	Glos	ST7495	51°39·4'	2°22·2'W	X	162
Nibon	Shetld	HU3073	60°26·6'	1°26·8'W	T	3
Nibs End Fm	Staffs	SK1146	53°0·9'	1°49·8'W	FM	119,128
Nibthwaite Grange	Cumbr	SD2988	54°17·2'	3°5·0'W	X	96,97
Nicco Wood	Shrops	SJ5928	52°51·1'	2°36·1'W	F	126
Nicholas Fm	Beds	SP9554	52°10·8'	0°36·2'W	FM	153
Nicholashayne	Devon	ST1016	50°56·4'	3°16·5'W	T	181,193
Nicholas Pike	Roch	SD9513	53°37·1'	2°4·1'W	X	109
Nicholaston	Swan	SS5288	51°34·5'	4°7·8'W	T	159
Nicholaston Burrows	Swan	SS5288	51°34·5'	4°7·8'W	X	159
Nicholaston Woods	Swan	SS5188	51°34·5'	4°8·6'W	F	159
Nichol End	Cumbr	NY2522	54°35·5'	3°9·2'W	X	89,90
Nichol Hopple	Durham	NY8525	54°37·4'	2°13·5'W	X	91,92
Nicholls Fm	Herts	TL0913	51°48·5'	0°24·7'W	FM	166
Nicholl's Loch	Angus	NO6453	56°40·3'	2°34·8'W	W	54
Nichol's Fm	Essex	TL7228	51°55·7'	0°30·5'E	FM	167
Nichols Nymet Ho	Devon	SS6902	50°48·4'	3°51·2'W	X	191
Nichols Nymett Cross	Devon	SS6901	50°47·9'	3°51·2'W	X	191
Nicholson	Heref	SO5858	52°13·4'	2°36·5'W	X	149
Nicholson Park	Aberd	NJ5564	57°40·1'	2°44·8'W	X	29
Nicholson Wood	Cumbr	SD4282	54°14·1'	2°53·0'W	F	96,97
Nick Burn	D & G	NX5772	55°1·6'	4°13·8'W	W	77
Nickelodeon	Warw	SP3158	52°13·4'	1°32·4'W	X	151
Nickerbush Plantn	Notts	SK6970	53°13·6'	0°57·6'W	F	120
Nickerlands	Essex	TL5001	51°41·5'	0°10·6'E	X	167
Nickerwood Fm	Roth	SK4784	53°21·3'	1°17·2'W	FM	111,120
Nickie's Hill	Cumbr	NY5367	55°0·0'	2°43·7'W	X	86
Nickies Knowe	Scot Bord	NT1619	55°27·7'	3°19·3'W	H	79
Nick i'th' Hill	Staffs	SJ8759	53°7·9'	2°11·3'W	X	118
Nick Knolls	Shrops	SJ3400	52°35·9'	2°58·1'W	H	126
Nickle Fm	Kent	TR0956	51°16·1'	1°0·2'E	FM	179
Nick of Carclach	S Ayr	NX4089	55°10·4'	4°30·3'W	X	77
Nick of Curleywee	D & G	NX4576	55°3·5'	4°25·2'W	X	77
Nick of Kindram	D & G	NX1132	54°39·1'	4°55·4'W	X	82
Nick of Orchars	D & G	NX5871	55°1·1'	4°12·8'W	X	77
Nick of Pendle	Lancs	SD7738	53°50·5'	2°20·6'W	X	103
Nick of the Balloch	S Ayr	NX3492	55°11·9'	4°36·1'W	X	76
Nick of the Lochans	D & G	NX4278	55°4·5'	4°28·1'W	X	77
Nick of the Loup	E Ayr	NX4596	55°14·3'	4°25·8'W	X	77
Nick Pot	N Yks	SD7773	54°9·4'	2°20·7'W	X	98
Nick's Hill	Suff	TL9479	52°22·7'	0°51·4'E	X	144
Nicky Nook	Lancs	SD5148	53°55·8'	2°44·4'W	H	102
Nicky Way	Herts	TL1011	51°47·4'	0°23·9'W	X	166
Nicolfield	Shetld	HU3448	60°13·2'	1°22·7'W	X	3
Nicol Point	Orkney	HY2625	59°6·6'	3°17·0'W	X	6
Nicolson's Leap	N Eil	NF8633	57°17·0'	7°12·2'W	W	22
Nicolswalls	Falk	NS7684	56°2·2'	3°59·0'W	X	57,64
Nidd	N Yks	SE3059	54°1·8'	1°32·1'W	T	104
Nidd	N Yks	SE3060	54°2·3'	1°32·1'W	T	99
Nidderdale	N Yks	SE0976	54°11·0'	1°51·3'W	X	99
Nidderdale Way	N Yks	SE1367	54°6·2'	1°47·7'W	X	99
Nidderdale Way	N Yks	SE2558	54°1·3'	1°36·7'W	X	104
Nidderdale Way	N Yks	SE2558	54°1·3'	1°36·7'W	X	104
Nidd Gorge	N Yks	SE3258	54°1·3'	1°30·3'W	X	104
Nidd Head	N Yks	SE0075	54°10·5'	1°59·6'W	X	98
Nidd Heads	N Yks	SE1073	54°9·4'	1°50·4'W	X	99
Nidd Moor Fm	N Yks	SE3058	54°1·3'	1°32·1'W	FM	104
Niddrie	C of Edin	NT2971	55°55·9'	3°7·7'W	T	66
Niddry	W Loth	NT0973	55°56·7'	3°27·0'W	X	65
Niddry Burn	W Loth	NT0673	55°56·7'	3°29·9'W	W	65
Niddry Burn	W Loth	NT1074	55°57·3'	3°26·0'W	W	65
Niddry Castle	W Loth	NT0974	55°57·3'	3°27·0'W	A	65
Niddry Mains	W Loth	NT0975	55°57·8'	3°27·0'W	X	65
Nidd Valley	N Yks	SE2159	54°1·8'	1°40·3'W	X	104
Nidd Valley	N Yks	SE2260	54°2·4'	1°39·4'W	X	99
Nidd Viaduct	N Yks	SE3058	54°1·3'	1°32·1'W	X	104
Niden Manor	Northnts	SP5748	52°7·9'	1°9·6'W	X	152
Nidgarth	Orkney	HY3526	59°7·2'	3°7·6'W	X	6
Nidons	Somer	ST3840	51°9·6'	2°52·8'W	X	182
Nidvm (Neath)(Castell-Nedd)	Nth Pt Talb	SS7497	51°39·7'	3°48·9'W	R	170
Nield Bank	Staffs	SK0367	53°12·2'	1°56·9'W	X	119
Nielston	Highld	NH7766	57°40·3'	4°3·3'W	X	21,27

Nieuport Ho	Heref	SO3152	52°10·0'	3°0·1'W	X	148
Nigg	C of Aber	NJ9402	57°6·8'	2°5·5'W	T	38
Nigg	Highld	NH8071	57°43·0'	4°0·4'W	T	21
Niggards	Shetld	HT9637	60°7·3'	2°3·8'W	X	4
Nigg Bay	C of Aber	NJ9604	57°7·9'	2°3·5'W	W	38
Nigg Bay	Highld	NH7772	57°43·5'	4°3·5'W	W	21
Nigg Ferry	Highld	NH7968	57°41·4'	4°1·3'W	T	21,27
Nigg Ho	Highld	NH8071	57°43·0'	4°0·4'W	X	21
Nigh-no-place	N Yks	SE3099	54°23·4'	1°31·9'W	X	99
Nightcott	Somer	SS8925	51°1·1'	3°34·6'W	X	181
Nightfield Burn	S Lanak	NT0125	55°30·8'	3°33·6'W	W	72
Nightfield Gate	Lancs	SD6332	53°47·2'	2°33·3'W	X	102,103
Nightfold Ridge	Northum	NY8977	55°5·5'	2°9·9'W	X	87
Nightingale Fm	Essex	TM0232	51°57·2'	0°56·8'E	FM	168
Nightingale Fm	E Susx	TQ5806	50°50·1'	0°15·0'E	FM	199
Nightingale Fm	Kent	TQ5843	51°10·1'	0°16·0'E	FM	188
Nightingale Fm	Oxon	SU2891	51°37·3'	1°35·3'W	FM	163,174
Nightingale Fm	Swin	SU1681	51°31·9'	1°45·8'W	FM	173
Nightingale Fm	Swin	SU2088	51°35·7'	1°42·3'W	FM	174
Nightingale Hall	Essex	TL8328	51°55·4'	0°40·1'E	X	168
Nightingale Plantn	Lincs	TF0137	52°55·5'	0°29·4'W	F	130
Nightingale Plantn	Notts	SK5972	53°14·7'	1°6·5'W	F	120
Nightingale's Corner	Cambs	TL2487	52°28·2'	0°10·1'W	X	142
Nightingale's Fm	Warw	SP2694	52°32·8'	1°36·6'W	FM	140
Nightingale Valley	N Som	ST5573	51°27·5'	2°38·5'W	X	172
Nightingale Wood	Hants	SU3717	50°57·3'	1°28·0'W	F	185
Nightlayer's Fen	Cambs	TL4087	52°28·0'	0°4·1'E	X	142,143
Nightwood Copse	Wilts	SU2128	51°3·3'	1°41·6'W	F	184
Nigley	Orkney	HY5103	58°55·0'	2°50·6'W	X	6,7
Nikka Vord	Shetld	HP6210	60°46·4'	0°51·2'W	X	1
Nilig	Denb	SJ0254	53°4·7'	3°27·4'W	X	116
Nill Fm	Oxon	SP3634	52°0·4'	1°28·1'W	FM	151
Nillgreen	Shrops	SJ4126	52°49·9'	2°52·1'W	X	126
Nills Hill	Shrops	SJ3905	52°38·6'	2°53·7'W	X	126
Nill Well (Chalybeate)	Cambs	TL2662	52°14·7'	0°8·9'W	W	153
Nilston Rigg	Northum	NY8260	54°56·3'	2°16·4'W	X	86,87
Nimble Nook	Oldham	SD9004	53°32·2'	2°8·6'W	T	109
Nimlet	S Glos	ST7471	51°26·5'	2°22·1'W	T	172
Nimlet Hill	S Glos	ST7471	51°26·5'	2°22·1'W	X	172
Nimmer	Somer	ST3210	50°53·4'	2°57·6'W	T	193
Nimney Bourne	Herts	TL4018	51°50·8'	0°2·3'E	W	167
Nimpwll	Carm	SN3908	51°45·1'	4°19·6'W	X	159
Nimrod Rocks	I of Angl	SH2682	53°18·6'	4°36·3'W	X	114
Nind	Shrops	SO3396	52°33·7'	2°58·9'W	X	137
Nind Fm	Glos	ST7591	51°37·3'	2°21·3'W	FM	162,172
Nine Acre Plantn	E Yorks	SE7826	53°43·7'	0°48·6'W	F	105,106
Nine Ashes	Essex	TL5902	51°41·9'	0°18·4'E	T	167
Ninebanks	Northum	NY7853	54°52·5'	2°20·1'W	T	86,87
Nine Barrow Down	Dorset	SZ0081	50°38·0'	1°59·6'W	X	195
Nine Bridges	Peterb	TF1507	52°39·1'	0°17·6'W	X	142
Nine Elms	Swin	SU1185	51°34·1'	1°50·1'W	T	173
Nine Elms	Wan	TQ2977	51°28·9'	0°8·1'W	T	176
Nine Elms Fm	W Berks	SU5770	51°25·8'	1°10·4'W	FM	174
Nine Ladies	Derby	SK2563	53°10·0'	1°37·2'W	X	119
Nine Ladies (Stone Circle)	Derby	SK2563	53°10·0'	1°37·2'W	A	119
Nine Maidens	Corn	SW4335	50°9·8'	5°35·5'W	X	203
Nine Maidens	Corn	SW6836	50°11·0'	5°14·6'W	A	203
Nine Maidens	Corn	SW9367	50°28·2'	4°54·7'W	A	200
Nine Maidens	Corn	SW9367	50°28·2'	4°54·7'W	X	200
Nine Maidens Downs	Corn	SW6736	50°10·9'	5°15·5'W	T	203
Nine Maidens (Stone Circle)	Corn	SW4335	50°9·8'	5°35·5'W	A	203
Ninemile Bar or Crocketford	D & G	NX8372	55°2·0'	3°49·4'W	T	84
Nine Mile Burn	Midlo	NT1757	55°48·2'	3°19·0'W	X	65,66,72
Nine Mile Ride	Wok	SU8265	51°22·9'	0°48·9'W	X	175
Nine Mile River	Wilts	SU1945	51°12·5'	1°43·3'W	W	184
Nine Mile Water Fm	Hants	SU3034	51°6·5'	1°33·9'W	FM	185
Nine Oaks	Devon	SY0290	50°42·3'	3°22·9'W	T	192
Ninescores Fm	Donc	SE7001	53°30·3'	0°56·3'W	FM	112
Nine Springs	Somer	ST5515	50°56·2'	2°38·0'W	X	183
Nine Standards	Cumbr	NY8206	54°27·2'	2°16·2'W	X	91,92
Nine Standards Rigg	Cumbr	NY8206	54°27·2'	2°16·2'W	H	91,92
Nine Stanes, The	Aberd	NO7291	57°0·8'	2°27·2'W	X	38,45
Nine Stone Rig	E Loth	NT6265	55°52·9'	2°36·0'W	X	67
Ninestone Rig	Scot Bord	NY5197	55°16·1'	2°45·8'W	X	79
Nine Stones	Corn	SX2378	50°34·7'	4°29·6'W	A	201
Nine Stones	Devon	SX6192	50°42·9'	3°57·8'W	A	191
Nine Stones	Devon	SX6692	50°43·0'	3°54·4'W	A	191
Nine Stones	Dorset	SY6190	50°42·7'	2°32·8'W	A	194
Nine Stones	E Loth	NT6265	55°52·9'	2°36·0'W	X	67
Ninestones Fm	Corn	SX2174	50°32·5'	4°31·2'W	FM	201
Nine Stones (Stone Circle)	E Loth	NT6265	55°52·9'	2°36·0'W	A	67
Nineteen Acre Wood	Wilts	SU0188	51°35·7'	1°58·7'W	F	173
Nineteen Lands	N Yks	NZ8312	54°30·0'	0°42·7'W	X	94
Ninevah	N Yks	SE2767	54°6·1'	1°34·8'W	X	99
Ninevah Fm	N Lincs	SE7404	53°31·9'	0°52·6'W	FM	112
Nineveh	Corn	SW3633	50°8·5'	5°41·3'W	X	203
Nineveh	N Yks	SE4060	54°2·3'	1°22·9'W	X	99
Nineveh	N Yks	SE5170	54°7·6'	1°12·8'W	X	100
Nineveh	Worcs	SO6264	52°16·6'	2°33·0'W	T	138,149
Nineveh	Worcs	SO6873	52°21·5'	2°27·8'W	T	138
Nineveh Fm	Oxon	SP5500	51°42·0'	1°11·9'W	FM	164
Nineveh Fm	Warw	SP3043	52°5·3'	1°33·3'W	FM	151
Ninewar	E Loth	NT6277	55°59·3'	2°36·1'W	X	67
Ninewar	Scot Bord	NT8055	55°47·5'	2°18·7'W	X	67,74
Nine Wells	Cambs	TL4654	52°10·1'	0°8·5'E	X	154
Ninewells	C of Dun	NO3629	56°27·2'	3°1·9'W	T	54,59
Nine Wells	Fife	NO2409	56°16·3'	3°13·2'W	X	59
Ninewells	Glos	SO5812	51°48·5'	2°36·2'W	T	162
Ninewells	Monm	SO5202	51°43·1'	2°41·3'W	X	162
Nine Wells	Monm	ST4294	51°38·7'	2°49·9'W	X	171,172
Nine Wells	Pemb	SM7824	51°52·5'	5°13·1'W	T	157
Ninewells	Pth & Kin	NO0743	56°34·4'	3°30·4'W	X	52,53
Nine Wells	Pth & Kin	NO2217	56°20·6'	3°15·3'W	X	58
Ninewells	Fife	NO2216	56°20·1'	3°15·3'W	FM	58
Ninewells Wood	Monm	SO5003	51°43·6'	2°43·0'W	F	162
Nine Yews	Dorset	SU0015	50°56·2'	1°57·1'W	X	184
Ninezergh	Cumbr	SD4984	54°15·2'	2°46·5'W	X	97
Ninfield	E Susx	TQ7012	50°53·2'	0°25·4'E	T	199

Ningwood	I of W	SZ4088	50°41·6'	1°25·6'W	T	196
Ningwood Common	I of W	SZ3989	50°42·2'	1°26·5'W	T	196
Ningwood Manor Fm	I of W	SZ3988	50°41·6'	1°26·5'W	FM	196
Ninham	I of W	SZ5782	50°38·3'	1°11·3'W	X	196
Ninian Brae	N Ayr	NS1755	55°45·5'	4°54·6'W	X	63
Ninnage Lodge	Glos	SO7414	51°49·7'	2°22·2'W	X	162
Ninnes	Corn	SW4534	50°9·3'	5°33·8'W	T	203
Ninnes Bridge	Corn	SW5135	50°10·0'	5°28·8'W	T	203
Ninneywood Fm	Bucks	SU8798	51°40·7'	0°44·1'W	FM	165
Ninnis	Corn	SW7242	50°14·3'	5°11·5'W	X	204
Ninnis	Corn	SW8049	50°18·2'	5°5·0'W	X	204
Ninnis Fm	Corn	SW9750	50°19·1'	4°50·7'W	FM	200,204
Ninn Lodge Fm	Kent	TQ9742	51°8·8'	0°49·4'E	FM	189
Nipes	D & G	NS7319	55°27·2'	4°0·1'W	X	71
Nippers Grove	Oxon	SU6781	51°31·7'	1°1·7'W	F	175
Nipsells Fm	Essex	TL9102	51°41·3'	0°46·2'E	FM	168
Nipster	Highld	ND2158	58°30·4'	3°20·9'W	X	11,12
Nipstone Rock	Shrops	SO3596	52°33·7'	2°57·1'W	X	137
Nisa Mhòr	N Eil	NB0935	58°12·7'	6°56·8'W	H	13
Nisam Point	N Eil	NL5779	56°46·8'	7°36·6'W	X	31
Nisbet	E Loth	NT4669	55°54·9'	2°51·4'W	X	66
Nisbet	Scot Bord	NT6725	55°31·3'	2°30·9'W	T	74
Nisbet	S Lanak	NT0332	55°34·6'	3°31·9'W	X	72
Nisbet Burn	S Lanak	NT0431	55°34·0'	3°30·9'W	W	72
Nisbet Hill	Scot Bord	NT7950	55°44·8'	2°19·6'W	X	67,74
Nisbet Hillhead	Scot Bord	NT6626	55°31·8'	2°31·9'W	X	74
Nisbet House	Scot Bord	NT7951	55°45·4'	2°19·6'W	A	67,74
Nisbet Loanhead	E Loth	NT4570	55°55·4'	2°52·4'W	X	66
Nisbetmill	Scot Bord	NT6625	55°31·3'	2°31·9'W	X	74
Nisbet Rhodes	Scot Bord	NT7851	55°45·4'	2°20·6'W	X	67,74
Nisreabhal	N Eil	NB3426	58°8·8'	6°30·8'W	H	8,13
Nissetter	Shetld	HU3577	60°28·8'	1°21·3'W	X	2,3
Nista	Shetld	HU6165	60°22·1'	0°53·1'W	X	2
Nistaben	Orkney	HY3017	59°2·3'	3°12·7'W	X	6
Nistaben	Orkney	HY3311	58°59·1'	3°9·5'W	X	6
Nista Skerries	Shetld	HU3292	60°36·9'	1°24·4'W	X	1
Nisthouse	Orkney	HY2926	59°7·2'	3°13·9'W	X	6
Nisthouse	Orkney	HY3119	59°3·4'	3°11·7'W	X	6
Nisthouse	Orkney	HY3411	58°59·1'	3°8·4'W	X	6
Nisthouse	Shetld	HU5864	60°21·6'	0°56·4'W	T	2
Nistigar	Orkney	HY4445	59°17·5'	2°58·5'W	X	5
Nithbank	D & G	NX8796	55°15·0'	3°46·2'W	T	78
Nith Lodge	E Ayr	NS5309	55°21·4'	4°18·7'W	X	70,77
Nithsdale	D & G	NX8990	55°11·8'	3°44·2'W	X	78
Nithside	D & G	NX8890	55°11·7'	3°45·1'W	X	78
Nithside	D & G	NX9676	55°4·3'	3°37·3'W	T	84
Niton	I of W	SZ5076	50°35·1'	1°17·2'W	T	196
Nitshiel Sike	Scot Bord	NT3710	55°23·0'	2°59·2'W	W	79
Nitshill	C of Glas	NS5160	55°48·9'	4°22·2'W	T	64
Nitticar Fm	Derby	SK4878	53°18·0'	1°16·4'W	FM	120
Nitting Haws	Cumbr	NY2416	54°32·3'	3°10·1'W	X	89,90
Nittings Down	Corn	SX3577	50°34·4'	4°19·4'W	X	201
Nivenhill	D & G	NY2866	54°59·3'	3°7·1'W	X	85
Niven's Knowe	Midlo	NT2665	55°52·6'	3°10·5'W	X	66
Niver Hill	Somer	ST5653	51°16·7'	2°37·5'W	H	182,183
Niveveh Fm	Glos	SP1542	52°4·8'	1°46·5'W	FM	151
Nivingston	Pth & Kin	NT1097	56°9·7'	3°26·5'W	X	58
Nivingston Craigs	Pth & Kin	NT1097	56°9·7'	3°26·5'W	X	58
Niviston	D & G	NS6913	55°23·9'	4°3·7'W	X	71
Niviston Hill	D & G	NS6815	55°24·9'	4°4·7'W	H	71
Niv, The	Shetld	HU4481	60°30·9'	1°11·4'W	X	1,2,3
Niwbwrch	Gwyn	SH5767	53°11·1'	4°8·0'W	X	114,115
Niwbwrch or Newborough	I of Angl	SH4265	53°9·8'	4°21·4'W	T	114,115
Nix Green Fm	Suff	TL8968	52°16·9'	0°46·6'E	FM	155
Nixhill Fm	Cambs	TL4191	52°30·1'	0°5·0'E	FM	142,143
Nixon Head	Cumbr	NY5453	54°52·4'	2°42·6'W	X	86
Nixon Hillock	Lancs	SD5419	53°40·2'	2°41·4'W	X	108
Nixonstown	Cumbr	NY5475	55°4·3'	2°42·8'W	X	86
Nizels	Kent	TQ5450	51°13·9'	0°12·7'E	X	188
Nizz, The	Shetld	HU4637	60°7·2'	1°9·8'W	X	4
Nizz, The	Shetld	HZ2274	59°33·3'	1°36·2'W	X	4
Njugals Water	Shetld	HU4241	60°9·3'	1°14·1'W	W	4
Noad Fm	Heref	SO7134	52°0·5'	2°25·0'W	FM	149
Noad's Copse	Hants	SU2532	51°5·4'	1°38·2'W	F	184
Noads, The	Hants	SU3905	50°50·8'	1°26·4'W	F	196
Noah Dale	Cald	SD9328	53°45·1'	2°6·0'W	X	103
Noah's Arc	Pth & Kin	NO0823	56°23·7'	3°29·0'W	FM	52,53,58
Noah's Ark	Herts	TL3715	51°49·2'	0°0·3'W	X	166
Noah's Ark Fm	York	SE6746	53°54·6'	0°58·4'W	FM	105,106
Noah's Arks	Kent	TQ5557	51°17·7'	0°13·8'E	T	188
Noah's Farm Yard Nature Trail	W Susx	SU9421	50°59·1'	0°39·3'W	X	197
Noah's Green	Worcs	SP0061	52°15·1'	1°59·6'W	T	150
Noah's Hill	Somer	ST2528	51°3·0'	3°3·8'W	X	193
Noak Bridge	Essex	TQ6990	51°35·2'	0°26·8'E	T	177,178
Noake Fm	Dorset	ST7104	50°50·3'	2°24·3'W	FM	194
Noake Mill	Herts	TL0409	51°46·4'	0°29·2'W	X	166
Noake's Fm	Essex	TL7414	51°48·1'	0°31·8'E	FM	167
Noakes Fm	Heref	SO6355	52°11·8'	2°32·1'W	FM	149
Noakes Fm	Kent	TR0233	51°3·9'	0°53·4'E	FM	189
Noak Fm	Worcs	SO7360	52°14·5'	2°23·3'W	FM	138,150
Noak Fm	Worcs	SO7560	52°14·5'	2°21·6'W	FM	138,150
Noak Hill	Essex	TQ6891	51°35·8'	0°25·9'E	T	177,178
Noak Hill	Hav	TQ5493	51°37·1'	0°13·9'E	T	177
Noak's Cross	Essex	TL8514	51°47·9'	0°41·4'E	X	168
Noaks Tye Fm	Suff	TM0043	52°3·2'	0°55·4'E	FM	155
Noar Hill	Hants	SU7431	51°4·6'	0°56·2'W	H	186
Nob End	Bolton	SD7506	53°33·2'	2°22·2'W	T	109
Nob Hill	Lincs	TF2482	53°19·5'	0°7·9'W	X	122
Nobland Green	Herts	TL4017	51°50·3'	0°2·3'E	T	167
Noblehall	Scot Bord	NT1647	55°42·8'	3°19·8'W	X	72
Noblehill	D & G	NX9976	55°4·3'	3°34·5'W	X	84
Noble Hindrance	Devon	ST0113	50°54·7'	3°24·1'W	X	181
Noblehouse	Scot Bord	NT1850	55°44·4'	3°17·9'W	X	65,66,72
Noble lands	Northum	NT9829	55°33·5'	2°1·5'W	X	75
Nobles Fm	Bucks	SU8196	51°39·6'	0°49·3'W	FM	165
Nobles Fm	Cumbr	NY4029	54°39·4'	2°55·4'W	FM	90
Nobles Fm	Herts	TL3624	51°54·1'	0°1·0'W	FM	166
Nobleston Wood	W Dunb	NS4179	55°58·9'	4°32·5'W	F	64
Noblestown	Cumbr	NY5474	55°3·8'	2°42·8'W	X	86

Noblethorpe	Barns	SE2805	53°32·7′	1°34·2′W	T	110
Noble Wood	N Yks	SE2286	54°16·4′	1°39·3′W	F	99
Nobold	Shrops	SJ4710	52°41·3′	2°46·6′W	T	126
Noborough Fm	Northnts	SP6062	52°15·4′	1°6·9′W	FM	152
Noborough Lodge	Northnts	SP6163	52°15·9′	1°6·0′W	X	152
Nobottle	Northnts	SP6763	52°15·9′	1°0·7′W	T	152
Nobottle Belt	Northnts	SP6862	52°15·4′	0°59·8′W	F	152
Nobottle Ho	Northnts	SP6762	52°15·4′	1°0·7′W	X	152
Nobottle Wood	Northnts	SP6763	52°15·9′	1°0·7′W	F	152
Nobridge	Shrops	SJ6436	52°55·5′	2°31·7′W	X	127
Nob's Crook	Hants	SU4821	50°59·4′	1°18·6′W	T	185
Nobut Hall	Staffs	SK0435	52°55·0′	1°56·0′W	X	128
Nochnarie	Fife	NO2012	56°17·9′	3°17·1′W	X	58
Nochnary	Fife	NO2609	56°16·3′	3°11·3′W	X	59
Nocketts Hill	Wilts	ST9469	51°25·4′	2°4·8′W	X	173
Nocton	Lincs	TF0564	53°10·0′	0°25·4′W	T	121
Nocton Delph	Lincs	TF1065	53°10·5′	0°20·8′W	W	121
Nocton Fen	Lincs	TF1066	53°11·0′	0°20·8′W	X	121
Nocton Grange	Lincs	TF0364	53°10·0′	0°27·1′W	X	121
Nocton Heath	Lincs	TF0263	53°9·5′	0°28·1′W	X	121
Nocton Rise	Lincs	TF0464	53°10·0′	0°26·2′W	X	121
Nocton Wood	Lincs	TF0863	53°9·4′	0°22·7′W	F	121
Noctorum	Wirral	SJ2887	53°22·7′	3°4·5′W	T	108
Nodden Gate	Devon	SX5386	50°39·5′	4°4·4′W	X	191,201
Noddings Fm	Surrey	SU9537	51°7·7′	0°38·2′W	FM	186
Noddle Fm	Norf	TM0380	52°23·0′	0°59·4′E	FM	144
Noddle Hill	Dorset	SU0614	50°55·8′	1°54·5′W	X	195
Noddsdale	N Ayr	NS2161	55°48·8′	4°51·0′W	X	63
Noddsdale Water	N Ayr	NS2264	55°50·4′	4°50·1′W	W	63
Nodes Fm	I of W	SZ4893	50°44·3′	1°18·8′W	FM	196
Node's Point	I of W	SZ6390	50°42·6′	1°6·1′W	X	196
Nodes, The	I of W	SZ3285	50°40·1′	1°32·4′W	X	196
Nodewell Fm	I of W	SZ3285	50°40·1′	1°32·4′W	FM	196
Nod Hill	N Yks	SE7469	54°6·9′	0°51·7′W	X	100
Nodic Ski Centre	Aberd	NJ5420	57°16·4′	2°45·3′W	X	29
Nodmans Bowda	Corn	SX2675	50°33·2′	4°27·0′W	X	201
Nodmore	W Berks	SU4177	51°29·7′	1°24·2′W	T	174
Nodmore Corner	W Berks	SU4275	51°28·6′	1°23·3′W	X	174
Nods Nook	Notts	SK6156	53°6·1′	1°4·9′W	X	120
Noel Park	Hargy	TQ3190	51°35·8′	0°6·1′W	T	176,177
Noe Stool	Derby	SK0786	53°22·5′	1°53·3′W	X	110
Noethgrug	Carm	SN8337	52°1·4′	3°41·9′W	H	160
Nogdam End	Norf	TG3900	52°32·9′	1°31·9′E	T	134
Noggin	Heref	SO6334	52°0·4′	2°31·9′W	X	149
Nog Tow	Lancs	SD5033	53°47·7′	2°45·1′W	T	102
Nohome Fm	Surrey	TQ2156	51°17·6′	0°15·5′W	FM	187
Noke	Oxon	SP5413	51°49·0′	1°12·6′W	T	164
Noke Fm	Herts	TL1203	51°43·1′	0°22·3′W	FM	166
Noke Fm	I of W	SZ4891	50°43·2′	1°18·8′W	FM	196
Noke Fm	Surrey	TQ2756	51°17·6′	0°10·3′W	FM	187
Noke Hall Fm	Thurr	TQ6486	51°33·2′	0°22·3′E	FM	177
Noke Street	Medway	TQ7471	51°24·9′	0°30·5′E	T	178
Noke Wood	Oxon	SP5511	51°47·9′	1°11·8′W	F	164
Noke Wood	Wilts	SU2667	51°24·3′	1°37·2′W	F	174
Nolands Fm	Wilts	SU0571	51°26·5′	1°55·3′W	FM	173
Noleham Brook	Warw	SP1448	52°8·0′	1°47·3′W	W	151
Noller's Fm	Suff	TM3880	52°22·2′	1°30·2′E	FM	156
Noltland	Orkney	HY4248	59°19·1′	3°0·7′W	X	5
Nolton	Pemb	SM8618	51°49·4′	5°5·9′W	T	157
Nolton Croft Fm	Pemb	SM9807	51°43·8′	4°55·1′W	FM	157,158
Nolton Cross	Pemb	SM8717	51°48·9′	5°5·0′W	X	157
Nolton Haven	Pemb	SM8518	51°49·4′	5°6·8′W	T	157
Nolton Haven	Pemb	SM8518	51°49·4′	5°6·8′W	W	157
No Man's Friend Fm	Lincs	TF2656	53°5·4′	0°6·7′W	FM	122
No Man's Green	Shrops	SO8084	52°27·5′	2°17·3′W	X	138
No Mans Heath	Ches	SJ5148	53°1·9′	2°43·4′W	T	117
No Man's Heath	Warw	SK2808	52°40·4′	1°34·8′W	T	128,140
No Man's Hill	Oxon	SU7584	51°33·2′	0°54·7′W	X	175
Nomanshill Wood	Notts	SK5456	53°6·1′	1°11·2′W	F	120
No Man's Land	Corn	SX2756	50°22·9′	4°25·6′W	T	201
No Man's Land	Devon	SS5438	51°7·6′	4°4·8′W	X	180
Nomansland	Devon	SS8313	50°54·5′	3°39·5′W	T	181
No Man's Land	Devon	ST0513	50°54·8′	3°20·7′W	X	181
No Man's Land	Devon	SX9070	50°31·4′	3°32·7′W	X	202
No Man's Land	Hants	SU5029	51°3·7′	1°16·8′W	T	185
Nomansland	Herts	TL1712	51°47·9′	0°17·8′W	T	166
Nomansland	Wilts	SU2517	50°57·3′	1°38·3′W	T	184
No Man's Land	W Susx	TQ1409	50°52·4′	0°22·4′W	X	198
Nomansland Common	Herts	TL1712	51°47·9′	0°17·8′W	X	166
Nomansland Fm	Herts	TL1812	51°47·9′	0°16·9′W	FM	166
No Man's Land Fort	I of W	SZ6393	50°44·2′	1°6·0′W	A	196
No Man's Land Plantation	Glos	SP1908	51°46·5′	1°43·1′W	F	163
Nonach Lodge	Highld	NG9330	57°19·1′	5°25·8′W	X	25
None-Go-Bye Fm	Leeds	SE2341	53°52·1′	1°38·6′W	FM	104
None-Go-Bye Fm	N Yks	SD9754	53°59·2′	2°2·3′W	FM	103
Noneley	Shrops	SJ4827	52°50·5′	2°45·9′W	T	126
No Ness	Shetld	HU2377	60°28·8′	1°34·4′W	X	3
No Ness	Shetld	HU4421	59°58·6′	1°12·2′W	X	4
Noness	Shetld	HU4422	59°59·1′	1°12·2′W	X	4
Noness Head	Shetld	HU4570	60°24·9′	1°10·5′W	X	2,3
Nonesuch	Wilts	SU0776	51°29·2′	1°53·6′W	X	173
Nonikiln	Highld	NH6671	57°42·8′	4°14·5′W	T	21
Nonington	Kent	TR2552	51°13·6′	1°13·7′E	T	179
Nonsuch Palace	Surrey	TQ2263	51°21·4′	0°14·5′W	A	176,187
Nonsuch Park	Surrey	TQ2363	51°21·4′	0°13·6′W	X	176,187
Nook	Aberd	NK0336	57°25·1′	1°56·5′W	X	30
Nook	Cumbr	NY3648	54°49·6′	2°59·3′W	X	85
Nook	Cumbr	NY4679	55°6·4′	2°50·4′W	X	86
Nook	Cumbr	NY5278	55°5·9′	2°44·7′W	X	86
Nook	Cumbr	NY5864	54°58·4′	2°38·9′W	X	86
Nook	Cumbr	SD2195	54°20·9′	3°12·5′W	X	96
Nook	Cumbr	SD5481	54°13·6′	2°41·9′W	T	97
Nook	Lancs	SD4843	53°53·1′	2°47·1′W	X	102
Nook	N Yks	SD9967	54°6·2′	2°0·5′W	X	98
Nook Beach	E Susx	TQ9217	50°55·4′	0°44·3′E	X	189
Nookdales Ho	N Yks	SD6870	54°7·7′	2°29·0′W	X	98
Nook End Fm	Cumbr	NY3705	54°26·4′	2°57·9′W	FM	90
Nook Flatt Wood	Notts	SK6289	53°23·9′	1°3·6′W	F	111,120
Nook Fm	Cumbr	NY0112	54°29·9′	3°31·3′W	FM	89
Nook Fm	Lancs	SD4838	53°50·4′	2°47·0′W	FM	102
Nook Fm	Lancs	SD5016	53°38·5′	2°45·0′W	FM	108
Nook Fm, The	Staffs	SJ7332	52°53·3′	2°23·7′W	FM	127
Nookfoot	Cumbr	NY4579	55°6·4′	2°51·3′W	X	86
Nook Ho	Lancs	SD6633	53°47·8′	2°30·6′W	X	103
Nook Ho	N Yks	NZ6803	54°25·3′	0°56·7′W	X	94
Nooklane Foot	Cumbr	NY3649	54°50·2′	2°59·4′W	X	85
Nooks, The	Leic	SP6395	52°33·2′	1°3·8′W	X	140
Nook, The	Cumbr	NY0948	54°49·4′	3°24·6′W	X	85
Nook, The	Cumbr	NY3539	54°44·8′	3°0·2′W	X	90
Nook, The	Cumbr	NY4463	54°57·8′	2°52·1′W	X	85
Nook, The	Cumbr	NY4504	54°26·0′	2°50·5′W	X	90
Nook, The	Cumbr	SD0990	54°18·1′	3°23·5′W	X	96
Nook, The	Derby	SK1957	53°6·8′	1°42·6′W	X	119
Nook, The	Moray	NJ4266	57°41·1′	2°57·9′W	W	28
Nook, The	Northum	NY7849	54°50·4′	2°20·1′W	X	86,87
Nookton	Durham	NY9247	54°49·3′	2°7·0′W	X	87
Nookton Back Fell	Durham	NY9148	54°49·9′	2°8·0′W	X	87
Nookton Burn	Durham	NY9247	54°49·3′	2°7·0′W	W	87
Nookton East Park	Durham	NY9248	54°49·9′	2°7·0′W	X	87
Nookton Edge	Northum	NY8946	54°48·8′	2°9·8′W	X	87
Nookton Fell	Durham	NY9148	54°49·9′	2°8·0′W	X	87
Nookton West Fell	Durham	NY9047	54°49·3′	2°8·9′W	X	87
Noon Folly Fm	Cambs	TL3864	52°15·6′	0°1·7′E	FM	154
Noongallas	Corn	SW4633	50°8·8′	5°33·0′W	X	203
Noon Hill	Cald	SD9220	53°40·8′	2°6·9′W	H	103
Noon Hill	Dorset	SU1008	50°52·5′	1°51·1′W	X	195
Noon Hill	Durham	NY8527	54°38·5′	2°13·5′W	X	91,92
Noon Hill	Durham	NY8535	54°42·8′	2°13·5′W	X	91,92
Noonhill Fm	Warw	SP3983	52°26·8′	1°25·2′W	FM	140
Noon Nick	Brad	SE1136	53°49·5′	1°49·6′W	T	104
Noonsbrough	Shetld	HU2957	60°18·0′	1°28·0′W	T	3
Noon's Fm	Wilts	SU3060	51°20·5′	1°33·8′W	FM	174
Noon's Folly Fm	Cambs	TL3941	52°3·2′	0°2·0′E	FM	154
Noon Stone	Brad	SE0847	53°55·4′	1°52·3′W	X	104
Noonstone Fm	N Yks	SE1463	54°4·0′	1°46·7′W	FM	99
Noonstones Hill	Cumbr	NY7438	54°44·4′	2°23·8′W	X	91
Noonsun	Ches	SJ8078	53°18·2′	2°17·6′W	T	118
Noonsun Common	Staffs	SK0049	53°2·5′	1°59·6′W	X	119
Noonsun Hill	Oldham	SD9802	53°31·1′	2°1·4′W	H	109
Noons Water	Shetld	HU4686	60°33·6′	1°9·2′W	W	1,2,3
Noonvares	Corn	SW5932	50°8·6′	5°22·0′W	T	203
Noor Fm	Dorset	ST5916	50°56·8′	2°34·6′W	FM	183
Noose, The	Glos	SO7207	51°45·9′	2°24·0′W	X	162
Noranbank	Angus	NO5059	56°43·5′	2°48·6′W	X	54
Noran Bank Fm	Cumbr	NY3915	54°31·8′	2°56·1′W	FM	90
Noranside	Angus	NO4760	56°44·0′	2°51·5′W	T	44
Noran Water	Angus	NO4563	56°45·6′	2°53·5′W	W	44
Noran Water	Angus	NO4566	56°47·2′	2°53·6′W	W	44
Noran Water	Angus	NO5159	56°43·5′	2°47·6′W	W	54
Nor Beck	Durham	NZ0911	54°29·9′	1°51·2′W	W	92
Nor Beck	N Yks	SE2850	53°57·0′	1°34·0′W	W	104
Norber	N Yks	SD7669	54°7·2′	2°21·6′W	X	98
Norbin Barton Fm	Wilts	ST8266	51°23·8′	2°15·1′W	FM	173
Norbin Fm	Wilts	ST8366	51°23·8′	2°14·3′W	FM	173
Norbin's Wood	W Berks	SU3672	51°27·0′	1°28·5′W	F	174
Norbister	Shetld	HU3732	60°4·5′	1°19·6′W	X	4
Norbiton	King	TQ1969	51°24·7′	0°16·9′W	T	176
Norbreck	Blackp	SD3141	53°51·9′	3°2·5′W	T	102
Norbreck Fm	Lancs	SD4553	53°58·5′	2°49·9′W	FM	102
Norbridge	Heref	SO7145	52°6·4′	2°25·0′W	T	149
Nor Brook	Oxon	SU4395	51°39·4′	1°22·3′W	W	164
Norbury	Bucks	SP7130	51°58·1′	0°57·6′W	A	152,165
Norbury	Ches	SJ5547	53°1·3′	2°39·8′W	T	117
Norbury	Croy	TQ3169	51°24·5′	0°6·6′W	T	176,177
Norbury	Derby	SK1242	52°58·8′	1°48·9′W	T	119,128
Norbury	Glos	SO9915	51°50·3′	2°0·5′W	A	163
Norbury	Glos	SP1215	51°50·2′	1°49·2′W	A	163
Norbury	Shrops	SO3692	52°31·6′	2°56·2′W	T	137
Norbury	Staffs	SJ7823	52°48·5′	2°19·2′W	T	127
Norbury Brook	Ches	SJ9285	53°21·9′	2°6·8′W	W	109
Norbury Common	Ches	SJ5548	53°1·9′	2°39·9′W	T	117
Norbury Coppice	Bucks	SP8031	51°58·5′	0°49·7′W	F	152,165
Norbury Hill	Shrops	SO3594	52°32·6′	2°57·1′W	H	137
Norbury Hills	Lincs	SK8385	53°21·6′	0°44·8′W	F	112,121
Norbury Hollow	Ches	SJ9384	53°21·4′	2°5·9′W	X	109
Norbury House Fm	Stock	SJ9185	53°21·9′	2°7·7′W	FM	109
Norbury Junction	Staffs	SJ7922	52°47·9′	2°18·3′W	T	127
Norbury Meres	Ches	SJ5549	53°2·4′	2°39·9′W	W	117
Norbury Moor	Stock	SJ9186	53°22·5′	2°7·7′W	T	109
Norbury Park	Staffs	SJ8022	52°48·0′	2°17·4′W	X	127
Norbury Park	Surrey	TQ1653	51°16·1′	0°19·8′W	X	187
Norby	N Yks	SE4282	54°14·2′	1°20·9′W	T	99
Norby	Shetld	HU1957	60°18·1′	1°38·9′W	T	3
Norchard	Pemb	SM9813	51°47·0′	4°55·3′W	X	157,158
Norchard	Worcs	SO8468	52°18·8′	2°13·7′W	T	138
Norchard Fm	Dorset	SY4093	50°44·2′	2°50·6′W	FM	193
Norchard Fm	Pemb	SN0804	51°42·4′	4°46·3′W	FM	158
Norchard Fm	Pemb	SS0899	51°39·7′	4°46·2′W	FM	158
Norchard Fm	Worcs	SO9450	52°9·1′	2°4·9′W	FM	150
Norchard Fms	Worcs	SO7669	52°19·4′	2°20·7′W	FM	138
Norcliffe	Cald	SE1125	53°43·5′	1°49·6′W	X	104
Norcliffe Hall	Ches	SJ8283	53°20·9′	2°15·8′W	X	109
Norcote	Glos	SP0402	51°43·2′	1°56·1′W	T	163
Norcote Wood	Surrey	TQ0552	51°15·7′	0°29·3′W	F	187
Norcott Brook	Ches	SJ6180	53°19·2′	2°34·7′W	T	109
Norcott Court	Herts	SP9610	51°47·1′	0°36·1′W	A	165
Norcott Hall Fm	Herts	SP9610	51°47·1′	0°36·1′W	FM	165
Norcroft	Barns	SE2806	53°33·2′	1°34·2′W	X	110
Norcroft Fm	Ches	SJ6964	53°10·6′	2°27·4′W	FM	118
Norcross	Lancs	SD3241	53°51·9′	3°1·6′W	T	102
Norcross	Lancs	SD6134	53°48·3′	2°35·1′W	X	102,103
Nordan Hall	Heref	SO4961	52°14·9′	2°44·4′W	X	137,138,148
Nordelph	Norf	TF5500	52°34·8′	0°17·7′E	T	143
Nordelph Corner	Norf	TG0303	52°35·4′	1°0·2′E	T	144
Nordelph Fm	Norf	TL5599	52°34·2′	0°17·6′E	FM	143
Norden	Dorset	SY9483	50°39·0′	2°4·7′W	T	195
Norden	Roch	SD8514	53°37·6′	2°13·2′W	T	109
Norden Fm	Devon	SX8169	50°30·8′	3°40·3′W	FM	202
Norden Fm	Dorset	SY9482	50°38·5′	2°4·7′W	FM	195
Norden Hill	Dorset	SY5998	50°47·0′	2°34·5′W	X	194
Norden Station	Dorset	SY9582	50°38·5′	2°3·9′W	X	195
Nordley	Shrops	SO6996	52°33·9′	2°27·0′W	T	138
Nordon Hill	Dorset	ST7402	50°49·2′	2°21·8′W	X	194
Nordown	Glos	SP0308	51°46·5′	1°57·0′W	X	163
Norduck Fm	Bucks	SP8320	51°52·6′	0°47·3′W	FM	165
Nord Vue Fm	Cumbr	NY4944	54°47·5′	2°47·2′W	FM	86
Nordy Bank	Shrops	SO5784	52°27·4′	2°37·6′W	X	137,138
Nordy Bank (Fort)	Shrops	SO5784	52°27·4′	2°37·6′W	A	137,138
Nore	Surrey	TQ0138	51°8·2′	0°33·0′W	X	186
Nore Down	E Susx	TQ4302	50°48·2′	0°2·2′E	X	198
Nore Down	W Susx	SU7712	50°54·4′	0°53·9′W	X	197
Nore Hill	Surrey	TQ3757	51°18·0′	0°1·7′W	X	187
Nore Hill	W Susx	SU9510	50°53·1′	0°38·6′W	H	197
Norfolk Cycle Way -	Norf	TF5118	52°44·5′	0°14·6′E	X	131
Norfolk Cycle Way	Norf	TL5996	52°32·5′	0°21·1′E	X	143
Norfolk Fm	Win & Maid	SU9670	51°25·5′	0°36·8′W	FM	175,176
Norfolk Ho	W Susx	TQ0706	50°50·8′	0°28·4′W	X	197
Norfolk House Fm	Lincs	TF4428	52°50·0′	0°8·7′E	FM	131
Norfolk Island	Cumbr	NY3918	54°33·5′	2°56·2′W	X	90
Nor Gill	Cumbr	SD7094	54°20·7′	2°27·3′W	W	98
Norgrove Court	Worcs	SP0065	52°17·2′	1°59·6′W	X	150
Norham	Aberd	NJ5308	57°9·9′	2°46·2′W	X	37
Norham	northum	NT8947	55°43·2′	2°10·1′W	T	74
Norham	Northum	NT9047	55°43·2′	2°9·1′W	T	74,75
Norham Castle	Northum	NT9047	55°43·2′	2°9·1′W	A	74,75
Norham East Mains	Northum	NT9248	55°43·8′	2°7·2′W	X	74,75
Norham West Mains	Northum	NT9148	55°43·8′	2°8·2′W	T	74,75
Norham Wood	Aberd	NJ5308	57°9·9′	2°46·2′W	F	37
Norheads Fm	Brom	TQ4059	51°19·0′	0°0·9′E	FM	187
Nor Hill Well	N Yks	SE0250	53°57·0′	1°57·8′W	W	104
Nork	Surrey	TQ2359	51°19·2′	0°13·7′W	T	187
Nork	Surrey	TQ2460	51°19·8′	0°12·8′W	T	176,187
Norland Moor	Cald	SE0621	53°41·4′	1°54·1′W	X	104
Norlands	E Yorks	TA1770	54°7·0′	0°12·2′W	X	101
Norland Town	Cald	SE0722	53°41·9′	1°53·2′W	T	104
Norleaze	Wilts	ST8653	51°16·8′	2°11·7′W	T	183
Norleigh Barton	Devon	SS5400	50°47·1′	4°3·9′W	X	191
Norley	Ches	SJ5672	53°14·8′	2°39·2′W	T	117
Norley	Devon	SS5000	50°47·0′	4°7·3′W	T	191
Norley Bank	Ches	SJ5772	53°14·8′	2°38·3′W	X	117
Norley Common	Surrey	TQ0244	51°11·4′	0°32·0′W	T	186
Norley Fm	Hants	SZ3598	50°47·1′	1°29·8′W	FM	196
Norley Inclosure	Hants	SZ3598	50°47·1′	1°29·8′W	F	196
Norley Moat Ho	Suff	TL7052	52°8·6′	0°29·5′E	X	154
Norleywood	Hants	SZ3597	50°46·5′	1°29·8′W	T	196
Norlington	E Susx	TQ4413	50°54·1′	0°3·3′E	T	198
Norlynn	Moray	NJ1729	57°20·9′	3°22·3′W	X	36
Normacot	C of Stoke	SJ9242	52°58·8′	2°6·7′W	T	118
Norman	Cumbr	NY2736	54°43·1′	3°7·6′W	X	89,90
Normanby	N Lincs	SE8816	53°38·2′	0°39·7′W	T	112
Normanby	N Yks	NZ9206	54°26·7′	0°34·5′W	X	94
Normanby	N Yks	SE7381	54°13·4′	0°52·4′W	T	100
Normanby	Red & Cl	NZ5518	54°33·5′	1°8·5′W	T	93
Normanby-by-Spital	Lincs	TF0088	53°23·0′	0°29·4′W	T	112,121
Normanby by Stow	Lincs	SK8883	53°20·4′	0°40·3′W	T	121
Normanby Cliff	Lincs	SK9787	53°22·5′	0°32·1′W	X	112,121
Normanby Gorse	Lincs	SK8983	53°20·4′	0°39·4′W	F	121
Normanby Grange	N Yks	SE7581	54°13·4′	0°50·6′W	X	100
Normanby Hall Country Park	N Lincs	SE8816	53°38·2′	0°39·7′W	X	112
Normanby le Wold	Lincs	TF1295	53°26·6′	0°18·4′W	T	113
Normanby Lodge	Lincs	TF1195	53°26·6′	0°19·3′W	X	113
Normanby Lodge	N Yks	SE7581	54°13·4′	0°50·6′W	X	100
Normanby Manor	N Yks	SE7582	54°13·9′	0°50·5′W	X	100
Norman Corner	NE Lincs	TA2503	53°30·8′	0°6·5′W	X	113
Norman Court Fm	Hants	SU3543	51°11·3′	1°29·6′W	FM	185
Norman Crag	Cumbr	NY3634	54°42·1′	2°59·2′W	X	90
Norman Cross	Cambs	TL1590	52°30·0′	0°17·9′W	T	142
Normandale Fm	Essex	TL5018	51°50·7′	0°11·0′E	FM	167
Normandy	Hants	SZ3294	50°44·9′	1°32·4′W	X	196
Normandy	Surrey	SU9251	51°15·3′	0°40·5′W	T	186
Normandy Common	Surrey	SU9251	51°15·3′	0°40·5′W	F	186
Normandy Fm	Dorset	ST8405	50°50·9′	2°13·3′W	FM	194
Normandy Hill	Surrey	SU9051	51°15·3′	0°42·2′W	X	186
Norman Fm	Hants	SU4760	51°20·5′	1°19·1′W	FM	174
Normangill	S Lanak	NS9722	55°29·1′	3°37·4′W	X	72
Normangill Burn	S Lanak	NS9723	55°29·7′	3°37·4′W	W	72
Normangill Rig	S Lanak	NS9721	55°28·6′	3°37·3′W	X	72
Norman Hill	Donc	SE4907	53°33·7′	1°15·2′W	X	111
Norman Hill	Glos	ST7599	51°41·6′	2°21·3′W	T	162
Norman Hill Resr	Roch	SD9613	53°37·1′	2°3·2′W	W	109
Norman Ho	Essex	TL5126	51°54·9′	0°12·1′E	X	167
Norman Norris	E Susx	TQ5916	50°55·5′	0°16·1′E	X	199
Normann's Ruh	Arg & Bt	NM4144	56°31·3′	6°12·2′W	X	47,48
Normans	Glos	SO7223	51°54·5′	2°24·0′W	X	162
Normans	Kent	TQ7048	51°12·6′	0°26·4′E	A	188
Normans	N Yks	SE5247	53°55·2′	1°12·1′W	X	105
Normans	W Susx	TQ2137	51°7·4′	0°15·9′W	X	187
Norman's Bay	E Susx	TQ6805	50°49·4′	0°23·5′E	T	199
Norman's Burrow Wood	Norf	TF8823	52°46·5′	0°47·6′E	F	132
Normans Fm	Derby	SK1685	53°21·9′	1°45·2′W	FM	110
Norman's Fm	Essex	TM0828	51°54·9′	1°1·9′E	FM	168,169
Norman's Fm	Heref	SO5255	52°11·7′	2°41·7′W	FM	149
Norman's Fm	Somer	ST0423	51°0·1′	3°21·7′W	FM	181
Norman's Green	Devon	ST0503	50°49·4′	3°20·5′W	T	192
Norman's Grove	Oxon	SP3721	51°53·4′	1°27·3′W	X	164
Norman's Hall Fm	Ches	SJ9380	53°19·3′	2°5·9′W	FM	109
Normans Land Fm	Glos	SO6930	51°58·3′	2°26·7′W	FM	149
Norman's Law	Fife	NO3020	56°22·3′	3°7·6′W	H	53,59
Norman's Riding Fm	Ghead	NZ1661	54°56·8′	1°44·6′W	FM	88
Normanston	Suff	TM5393	52°28·8′	1°44·0′E	T	134
Normanswood	Surrey	SU8844	51°11·5′	0°44·1′W	X	186
Normanton	C of Derb	SK3433	52°53·8′	1°29·3′W	T	128
Normanton	Leic	SK8140	52°57·3′	0°47·2′W	T	130
Normanton	Leic	SP4998	52°34·9′	1°16·2′W	X	140
Normanton	Lincs	SK9446	53°0·4′	0°35·5′W	T	130
Normanton	Notts	SK7054	53°5·0′	0°56·9′W	T	120
Normanton	Rut	SK9306	52°38·9′	0°37·1′W	T	141
Normanton	Wakf	SE3822	53°41·8′	1°25·1′W	T	104
Normanton	Wilts	SU1340	51°9·8′	1°48·5′W	T	184

Normanton Brook	Derby	SK4357	53°6·7′	1°21·0′W	W	120
Normanton Down	Wilts	SU1140	51°9·8′	1°50·2′W	X	184
Normanton Hill	Lincs	SK9546	53°0·4′	0°34·6′W	X	130
Normanton Hill	Notts	SK6674	53°15·8′	1°0·2′W	X	120
Normanton Holme	Notts	SK8167	53°11·9′	0°46·8′W	X	121
Normanton Larches Fm	Notts	SK6574	53°15·8′	1°1·1′W	FM	120
Normanton le Heath	Leic	SK3712	52°42·5′	1°26·7′W	T	128
Normanton Lodge	Leic	SK8142	52°58·4′	0°47·2′W	X	130
Normanton Lodge Fm	Leic	SK3612	52°42·5′	1°27·6′W	FM	128
Normanton Lodge Fm	Rut	SK9406	52°38·8′	0°36·2′W	FM	141
Normanton on Soar	Notts	SK5123	52°48·4′	1°14·2′W	T	129
Normanton-on-the-Wolds	Notts	SK6233	52°53·7′	1°4·3′W	T	129
Normanton on Trent	Notts	SK7968	53°12·4′	0°48·6′W	T	120,121
Normanton Spring	Sheff	SK4084	53°21·3′	1°23·5′W	T	111,120
Normanton Turville	Leic	SP4998	52°34·9′	1°16·2′W	T	140
Normanton Wolds	Notts	SK6231	52°52·6′	1°4·3′W	X	129
Normanview	Fife	NO4811	56°17·6′	2°50·0′W	X	59
Normanwood	Derby	SK0078	53°18·2′	1°59·6′W	X	119
Nor Marsh	Medway	TQ8169	51°23·7′	0°36·5′E	W	178
Normill Terrace	Bucks	SP8612	51°48·2′	0°44·8′W	X	165
Normoor	Cambs	TL4188	52°28·5′	0°5·0′E	X	142,143
Normoor Common	Worcs	SO8647	52°7·5′	2°11·9′W	X	150
Normoss	Cumbr	SD1092	54°19·2′	3°22·6′W	X	96
Normoss	Lancs	SD3437	53°49·8′	2°59·8′W	T	102
Nornay	Notts	SK6287	53°22·8′	1°3·7′W	X	111,120
Nornea Fm	Cambs	TL5778	52°22·9′	0°18·8′E	FM	143
Norney	Surrey	SU9444	51°11·5′	0°38·9′W	T	186
Norney Br	Wilts	ST9657	51°19·0′	2°3·1′W	X	173
Norney Plantn	Suff	TL6647	52°6·0′	0°25·8′E	F	154
Nornour	I Scilly	SV9414	49°57·1′	6°15·6′W	X	203
Norr	Brad	SE0936	53°49·5′	1°51·4′W	T	104
Norrard or Northern Rocks	I Scilly	SV8613	49°56·3′	6°22·2′W	X	203
Norrells, The	Oxon	SP2821	51°53·4′	1°35·2′W	F	163
Norrest, The	Worcs	SO7550	52°9·1′	2°21·5′W	X	150
Norr Hill	Brad	SE1036	53°49·5′	1°50·5′W	H	104
Norridge Fm	Wilts	ST8547	51°13·6′	2°12·5′W	FM	183
Norridge Wood	Wilts	ST8545	51°12·5′	2°12·5′W	F	183
Norrie's Law	Fife	NO4007	56°15·4′	2°57·7′W	A	59
Norrieston	Stir	NS6699	56°10·1′	4°9·0′W	X	57
Norrington	Wilts	ST9623	51°0·6′	2°3·0′W	A	184
Norrington Common	Wilts	ST8864	51°22·7′	2°10·0′W	T	173
Norringtonend Fm	Herts	TL0914	51°49·1′	0°24·7′W	FM	166
Norris Br	Hants	SU8353	51°16·4′	0°48·2′W	X	186
Norris Castle	I of W	SZ5196	50°45·9′	1°16·2′W	X	196
Norris Fm	Cambs	TL4370	52°18·8′	0°6·3′E	FM	154
Norris Green	Corn	SX4169	50°30·2′	4°14·2′W	T	201
Norris Green	Liv	SJ3994	53°26·6′	2°54·7′W	T	108
Norris Hill	Leic	SK3216	52°44·7′	1°31·2′W	T	128
Norris Hill Fm	Wilts	ST8352	51°16·2′	2°14·2′W	FM	183
Norris Hill West	Hants	SU8353	51°16·4′	0°48·2′W	X	186
Norris Mill Fm	Dorset	SY7391	50°43·3′	2°22·6′W	FM	194
Norristhorpe	Kirk	SE2022	53°41·9′	1°41·4′W	T	104
Norrold's Fm	Norf	TM0096	52°31·7′	0°57·3′E	FM	144
Norry Hill	Aberd	NJ4342	57°28·1′	2°56·6′W	H	28
Norsebury Ho	Hants	SU4939	51°9·1′	1°17·6′W	X	185
Norsebury Ring	Hants	SU4940	51°9·7′	1°17·6′W	A	185
Norsey Wood (Nature Reserve)	Essex	TQ6895	51°37·9′	0°26·0′E	F	167,177
Norsted Manor Fm	Brom	TQ4661	51°20·0′	0°6·1′E	FM	177,188
North Acomb	Northum	NZ0464	54°58·5′	1°55·8′W	X	87
Northacre	Norf	TL9598	52°32·9′	0°53·0′E	T	144
North Acres	E Susx	TQ3515	50°55·3′	0°4·4′W	X	198
North Acton	Ealing	TQ2082	51°31·7′	0°15·8′W	T	176
North Ailey	Arg & Bt	NS2281	55°59·6′	4°50·8′W	X	63
North Airmyn Grange	E Yorks	SE7124	53°42·7′	0°55·0′W	X	105,106,112
North Aittit	Orkney	HY4220	59°4·0′	3°0·2′W	X	5,6
North Aldie	Aberd	NK0740	57°27·3′	1°52·5′W	X	30
North Alfordon	Devon	SX6196	50°45·1′	3°57·8′W	X	191
Northall	Bucks	SP9520	51°52·5′	0°36·8′W	T	165
North Allenford Fm	Hants	SU0818	50°57·9′	1°52·8′W	FM	184
North Aller	Devon	SS6928	51°2·4′	3°51·7′W	X	180
Northallerton	N Yks	SE3794	54°20·7′	1°25·4′W	T	99
North Allerton	S Lanak	NS5951	55°44·2′	4°14·3′W	X	64
Northall Green	Norf	TF9914	52°41·5′	0°57·1′E	T	132
Northall Green	Norf	TG0015	52°42·0′	0°58·0′E	X	133
North Altens	C of Aber	NJ9603	57°7·3′	2°3·5′W	X	38
North Alves	Moray	NJ1263	57°39·2′	3°28·0′W	X	28
Northam	C of Soton	SU4312	50°54·6′	1°22·9′W	T	196
Northam	Devon	SS4429	51°2·6′	4°13·1′W	T	180
Northam Br	C of Soton	SU4312	50°54·6′	1°22·9′W	X	196
Northam Burrows Country Park	Devon	SS4430	51°3·1′	4°13·2′W	X	180
North America	E Yorks	SE8431	53°46·4′	0°43·1′W	X	106
North America Fm	E Susx	TQ3418	50°57·0′	0°5·2′W	FM	198
Northam Fm	Somer	ST3054	51°17·1′	2°59·8′W	FM	182
Northampton	Northnts	SP7561	52°14·8′	0°53·7′W	T	152
Northampton	Worcs	SO8365	52°17·2′	2°14·6′W	X	138,150
Northampton & Lamport Rly	Northnts	SP7366	52°17·5′	0°55·4′W	X	152
Northampton Stadium	Northnts	SP8156	52°12·0′	0°48·5′W	X	152
Northampton (Sywell) Airport	Northnts	SP8268	52°18·5′	0°47·4′W	X	152
Northam's Fm	Devon	ST2310	50°53·3′	3°5·3′W	FM	192,193
North Anston	Roth	SK5284	53°21·3′	1°12·7′W	T	111,120
North Appleford	I of W	SZ5081	50°37·8′	1°17·2′W	X	196
North Ardbeg	Arg & Bt	NR7184	55°59·9′	5°39·9′W	X	55
North Ardgrain	Aberd	NJ9534	57°24·0′	2°4·5′W	X	30
North Ardittie	Pth & Kin	NO0029	56°26·8′	3°36·9′W	X	52,53,58
North Ardo	Aberd	NJ8440	57°27·3′	2°15·5′W	X	29,30
North Ardoyne	Aberd	NJ6528	57°20·7′	2°34·4′W	X	38
North Arnybogs	Aberd	NJ8639	57°26·7′	2°13·5′W	X	30
North Artrochie	Aberd	NK0032	57°23·0′	1°59·5′W	X	30
North Ascot	Brackn	SU9069	51°25·0′	0°42·0′W	T	175
North Aston	Oxon	SP4729	51°57·7′	1°18·6′W	T	164
North Auchenbrain	E Ayr	NS5131	55°33·2′	4°21·3′W	X	70
North Auchenharvie	E Ayr	NS3644	55°40·0′	4°36·0′W	X	63,70
North Auchmachar	Aberd	NJ9550	57°32·7′	2°4·6′W	X	30
North Auchray	Angus	NO3535	56°30·4′	3°2·9′W	X	54
North Auchtylair	Aberd	NJ9843	57°28·9′	2°1·5′W	X	30
North a Voe	Shetld	HU5292	60°36·7′	1°2·5′W	X	1,2

Northaw	Herts	TL2802	51°42·4′	0°8·5′W	T	166
Northaw Place	Herts	TL2602	51°42·4′	0°10·2′W	X	166
Northaw School	Hants	SU2630	51°4·4′	1°37·3′W	X	184
Northay	Devon	ST3600	50°48·0′	2°54·1′W	T	193
Northay	Somer	ST2811	50°53·9′	3°1·0′W	T	193
Northay Barrow	Somer	ST2811	50°53·9′	3°1·0′W	A	193
Northay Fm	Dorset	SY3797	50°46·4′	2°53·2′W	FM	193
Northayne Fm	Devon	ST0023	51°0·1′	3°25·1′W	FM	181
North Ayre	Orkney	HY5538	59°13·8′	2°46·8′W	X	5
North Ayre	Shetld	HU4572	60°26·0′	1°10·4′W	X	2,3
North Aywick	Shetld	HU5387	60°34·0′	1°1·5′W	T	1,2
North Backstone	Devon	SS8320	50°58·3′	3°39·6′W	X	181
North Baddesley	Hants	SU3919	50°58·4′	1°26·3′W	T	185
North Baldutho	Fife	NO4907	56°15·4′	2°48·9′W	X	59
North Balfern	D & G	NX4351	54°50·0′	4°26·2′W	X	83
North Balkeith	Highld	NH7981	57°48·4′	4°1·7′W	X	21
North Ballachulish	Highld	NN0560	56°41·7′	5°10·6′W	T	41
North Ballaird	S Ayr	NX1287	55°8·8′	4°56·6′W	X	76
North Ballo	Pth & Kin	NO2436	56°30·9′	3°13·7′W	X	53
North Balloch	S Ayr	NX3295	55°13·5′	4°38·1′W	X	76
Northballo Hill	Pth & Kin	NO2535	56°30·3′	3°12·7′W	H	53
North Balluderon	Angus	NO3738	56°32·0′	3°1·0′W	X	54
North Balnakettle	Aberd	NJ8921	57°17·0′	2°10·5′W	X	38
North Bank	Aberd	NJ7909	57°10·5′	2°20·4′W	X	38
North Bank	Falk	NT0180	56°0·4′	3°34·8′W	X	65
Northbank	Fife	NO4810	56°17·0′	2°50·0′W	X	59
North Bank	Gwyn	SH5435	52°53·8′	4°9·8′W	X	124
North Bank	Gwyn	SH6014	52°42·6′	4°3·9′W	X	124
North Bank	Pth & Kin	NO3130	56°27·7′	3°6·7′W	X	53
Northbank	Scot Bord	NT6509	55°22·7′	2°32·7′W	X	80
North Bankend	S Lanak	NS7835	55°35·9′	3°55·7′W	X	71
North Bank Fm	Aberd	NJ5518	57°15·3′	2°44·3′W	FM	37
Northbank Fm	Fife	NO4816	56°20·3′	2°50·0′W	FM	59
Northbank Fm	Lancs	SD8734	53°48·4′	2°11·4′W	FM	103
North Bankhead	Falk	NS8973	55°56·5′	3°46·2′W	X	65
Northbanks Hill	Shetld	HU4959	60°19·0′	1°6·3′W	H	2,3
North Bardowie	E Dunb	NS5874	55°56·5′	4°16·0′W	X	64
Northbar Ho	Renf	NS4869	55°53·7′	4°25·4′W	X	64
North Barn	Essex	TM0615	51°48·0′	0°59·7′E	X	168
North Barn	Wilts	ST9925	51°1·7′	2°0·5′W	X	184
North Barnes Fm	E Susx	TQ3716	50°55·9′	0°2·6′W	FM	198
North Barneystead	Northum	NY8180	55°7·1′	2°17·4′W	X	80
North Barn Fm	Dorset	ST8105	50°50·9′	2°15·8′W	FM	194
North Barn Fm	Dorset	SY5691	50°43·2′	2°37·0′W	FM	194
North Barnkirk	D & G	NX3966	54°58·0′	4°30·5′W	X	83
North Barns	Pth & Kin	NO0735	56°30·1′	3°30·2′W	X	52,53
North Barrow	Somer	ST6029	51°3·8′	2°33·9′W	T	183
North Barrule	I of M	SC4490	54°17·2′	4°23·4′W	H	95
North Barsalloch	D & G	NX3441	54°44·4′	4°34·3′W	X	82
North Barsham	Norf	TF9134	52°52·4′	0°50·7′E	T	132
North Barsham Fm	Norf	TF9035	52°53·0′	0°49·8′E	FM	132
North Bay	Arg & Bt	NR8671	55°53·3′	5°24·9′W	W	62
North Bay	N Ayr	NS2242	55°38·6′	4°49·3′W	W	63,70
North Bay	N Eil	NF7202	56°59·8′	7°23·7′W	W	31
North Bay	N Yks	TA0490	54°17·9′	0°23·7′W	W	101
North Bay	Orkney	HY6001	58°53·9′	2°41·2′W	W	6
North Bay	Orkney	HY6542	59°16·1′	2°36·4′W	W	5
North Bay	Orkney	ND2890	58°47·8′	3°14·3′W	W	7
North Bay	S Ayr	NS3132	55°33·4′	4°40·3′W	W	70
North Beach	Norf	TG5309	52°37·4′	1°44·7′E	X	134
North Beach	Suff	TM5594	52°29·3′	1°45·8′E	X	134
North Beachmore	Arg & Bt	NR6841	55°36·7′	5°40·6′W	X	62
North Beck	Brad	SE0440	53°51·6′	1°55·9′W	W	104
Northbeck	Lincs	TF0941	52°57·5′	0°22·2′W	T	130
North Beck	Lincs	TF1040	52°57·0′	0°21·4′W	W	130
North Beck	Notts	SK7775	53°16·2′	0°50·3′W	W	120
North Bedlam	Aberd	NJ8746	57°30·5′	2°12·6′W	X	30
North Beer	Corn	SX3092	50°42·4′	4°24·1′W	T	190
North Beer	Devon	SX3698	50°45·7′	4°19·1′W	X	190
North Beer Fm	Devon	SX7097	50°45·7′	3°50·2′W	FM	191
North Belton	E Loth	NT6377	55°59·3′	2°35·1′W	X	67
North Benelip	Shetld	HU6669	60°24·2′	0°47·6′W	X	2
North Benfleet	Essex	TQ7589	51°34·6′	0°31·9′E	T	178
North Benfleet Hall	Essex	TQ7690	51°35·1′	0°32·8′E	X	178
North Bentley Inclosure	Hants	SU2313	50°55·2′	1°40·0′W	F	195
North Bersted	W Susx	SU9200	50°47·8′	0°41·3′W	T	197
North Berwick	E Loth	NT5585	56°3·6′	2°42·9′W	T	66
North Berwick Bay	E Loth	NT5585	56°3·6′	2°42·9′W	W	66
North Berwick Law	E Loth	NT5584	56°3·1′	2°42·9′W	H	66
North Berwick Law (Fort)	E Loth	NT5584	56°3·1′	2°42·9′W	A	66
North Bethelnie	Aberd	NJ7831	57°22·4′	2°21·5′W	X	29,30
North Biggart	N Ayr	NS4053	55°44·9′	4°32·5′W	X	64
North Bigging	Orkney	HY3020	59°3·9′	3°12·8′W	X	6
North Binn	Angus	NO2934	56°29·8′	3°8·8′W	X	53
North Binness Island	Hants	SU6904	50°50·1′	1°0·8′W	X	197
North Birny Fell	Scot Bord	NY4791	55°12·9′	2°49·5′W	H	79
North Bishop	Pemb	SM6727	51°53·8′	5°22·8′W	X	157
North Bishopden Wood	Kent	TR0960	51°18·3′	1°0·3′E	F	179
North Bitchburn	Durham	NZ1732	54°41·2′	1°43·8′W	T	92
North Bitts	Durham	NZ0413	54°31·0′	1°55·9′W	X	92
North Blachrie	Aberd	NJ7743	57°28·9′	2°22·6′W	X	29,30
North Blackbog	Aberd	NJ7833	57°23·5′	2°21·5′W	X	29,30
North Black Burn	N Ayr	NS2565	55°51·0′	4°47·3′W	W	63
North Black Dod	S Lanak	NT0421	55°28·7′	3°30·7′W	H	72
North Blackruthven	Pth & Kin	NO0624	56°24·2′	3°30·9′W	X	52,53,58
North Blackstocks	Aberd	NJ8136	57°25·1′	2°18·5′W	X	29,30
North Blairs	Aberd	NO7480	56°54·9′	2°25·2′W	X	45
North Blochairn	E Dunb	NS5876	55°57·6′	4°16·0′W	X	64
North Blyth	Northum	NZ3182	55°8·1′	1°30·5′W	T	81
North Boarhunt	Hants	SU6010	50°53·4′	1°8·4′W	T	196
North Bockhampton	Dorset	SZ1797	50°46·6′	1°45·1′W	T	195
Northbog	Aberd	NJ8319	57°15·9′	2°16·5′W	X	38
North Bogbain	Moray	NJ3952	57°33·5′	3°0·7′W	X	28
North Bogside	S Ayr	NS3828	55°31·4′	4°33·5′W	X	70
North Boig	E Ayr	NS6013	55°23·7′	4°12·2′W	X	71
North Boisdale	N Eil	NF7417	57°8·0′	7°22·9′W	T	31
North Booth	Shetld	HU5599	60°40·5′	0°59·1′W	X	1
Northborough	Peterb	TF1507	52°39·1′	0°17·6′W	T	142
North Bottom	S Lanak	NS7523	55°29·3′	3°58·3′W	X	71
North Boundary Fm	Suff	TM3971	52°17·3′	1°30·7′E	FM	156

Northbourne	Bourne	SZ0895	50°45·5′	1°52·8′W	T	195
Northbourne	Kent	TR3352	51°13·4′	1°20·6′E	T	179
Northbourne Court	Kent	TR3352	51°13·4′	1°20·6′E	X	179
Northbourne Park (Sch)	Kent	TR3052	51°13·5′	1°18·0′E	X	179
North Bovey	Devon	SX7383	50°38·2′	3°47·4′W	T	191
North Bowda	Corn	SX2477	50°34·2′	4°28·8′W	X	201
North Bowerhouses	D & G	NY0670	55°1·2′	3°27·8′W	X	85
North Bowood	Dorset	SY4499	50°47·5′	2°47·3′W	T	193
North Brackenridge	S Lanak	NS7639	55°38·0′	3°57·7′W	X	71
North Braco	Aberd	NK0638	57°26·2′	1°53·5′W	X	30
North Bradbury	Devon	SS6626	51°1·3′	3°54·3′W	X	180
North Bradley	Wilts	ST8555	51°17·9′	2°12·5′W	T	173
North Bradon	Somer	ST3620	50°58·8′	2°54·3′W	X	193
Northbrae	Aberd	NJ6300	57°5·6′	2°36·2′W	X	37
Northbrae	Aberd	NO5797	57°4·0′	2°42·1′W	X	37,44
Northbrae	Aberd	NO7394	57°2·4′	2°26·2′W	X	38,45
North Brae	E Renf	NS5158	55°47·8′	4°22·2′W	X	64
Northbrae	Shetld	HU3568	60°23·9′	1°21·4′W	X	2,3
North Braehead	Aberd	NJ5936	57°25·0′	2°40·5′W	X	29
Northbrae Plantation	Aberd	NO7294	57°2·4′	2°27·2′W	F	38,45
North Braeside	Aberd	NJ6251	57°33·1′	2°37·6′W	X	29
North Branchal	Inverc	NS3466	55°51·8′	4°38·7′W	X	63
North Breach	Bath & NE Somer	ST6865	51°23·2′	2°27·2′W	X	172
North Breache Manor	Surrey	TQ1040	51°9·1′	0°25·2′W	X	187
North Breckenholme	N Yks	SE8359	54°1·5′	0°43·6′W	X	106
North Brentor	Devon	SX4881	50°36·8′	4°8·5′W	T	191,201
North Brewham	Somer	ST7236	51°7·6′	2°23·6′W	T	183
North Brideswell	Aberd	NJ5110	57°11·0′	2°48·2′W	X	37
Northbridge	Surrey	SU9636	51°7·1′	0°37·3′W	X	186
Northbridge Street	E Susx	TQ7324	50°59·6′	0°28·3′E	T	199
North Briggs	Aberd	NJ6552	57°33·7′	2°34·6′W	X	29
North Brittain	Derby	SK3065	53°11·1′	1°32·7′W	X	119
North Broad Haven	Aberd	NK0327	57°20·3′	1°56·6′W	W	38
Northbrook	Cumbr	NY3842	54°46·4′	2°57·4′W	X	85
Northbrook	Dorset	SY7594	50°44·9′	2°20·9′W	T	194
Northbrook	Hants	SU5139	51°9·1′	1°15·9′W	T	185
Northbrook	Hants	SU5518	50°57·8′	1°12·6′W	T	185
Northbrook	Hants	SU8044	51°11·6′	0°50·9′W	X	186
Northbrook	Oxon	SP4922	51°53·9′	1°16·9′W	T	164
North Brook	Rut	SK9511	52°41·5′	0°35·3′W	W	130
Northbrook	Warw	SP2461	52°15·0′	1°38·5′W	X	151
Northbrook	Wilts	SU0154	51°17·3′	1°58·8′W	T	184
North Brook End	Cambs	TL2944	52°5·0′	0°6·6′W	T	153
Northbrook Fm	Hants	SU5142	51°10·7′	1°15·8′W	FM	185
Northbrook Fm	Somer	ST4339	51°9·1′	2°48·5′W	FM	182
Northbrook Fm	W Susx	SU8007	50°51·6′	0°51·4′W	FM	197
Northbrook Ho	Hants	SU5040	51°9·7′	1°16·7′W	X	185
North Broomage	Falk	NS8583	56°1·8′	3°50·3′W	T	65
North Broomhill	Aberd	NJ5835	57°24·5′	2°41·5′W	X	29
North Brora Muir	Highld	NC8804	58°0·9′	3°53·3′W	X	17
North Brownhill	S Lanak	NS6442	55°39·4′	4°9·3′W	X	71
North Brunton	N upon Ty	NZ2371	55°2·2′	1°38·0′W	X	88
North Buckinghamshire Way	Bucks	SP7418	51°51·6′	0°55·1′W	X	165
North Buckinghamshire Way	Bucks	SP7733	51°59·6′	0°52·3′W	X	152,165
North Buckinghamshire Way	Mil Key	SP8136	52°1·2′	0°48·8′W	X	152
North Buckland	Devon	SS4740	51°8·6′	4°10·9′W	T	180
North Bulcombe	Devon	ST0122	50°59·6′	3°24·3′W	X	181
North Burlingham	Norf	TG3710	52°38·4′	1°30·6′E	T	133,134
Northburn	D & G	NY1881	55°7·2′	3°16·7′W	X	79
North Burn	Hartpl	NZ4627	54°38·4′	1°16·8′W	W	93
North Burn	Highld	NC9448	58°24·7′	3°48·4′W	W	11
North Burn	N Ayr	NS2654	55°45·1′	4°45·9′W	W	63
North Burn	Shetld	HU3862	60°20·7′	1°18·2′W	W	2,3
North Burn	Shetld	HU4173	60°26·6′	1°14·8′W	W	2,3
North Burn	Shetld	HU4683	60°31·9′	1°9·2′W	W	1,2,3
Northburnhill	Aberd	NJ8147	57°31·0′	2°18·6′W	X	29,30
North Burn of Murrion	Shetld	HU2580	60°30·4′	1°32·2′W	W	3
North Burn of Vigon	Shetld	HP4804	60°43·2′	1°6·7′W	W	1
North Burnside	Aberd	NJ9037	57°25·7′	2°9·5′W	X	30
North Burnt Hill	N Ayr	NS2566	55°51·6′	4°47·3′W	H	63
North Burreldales Croft	Aberd	NJ6754	57°34·8′	2°32·6′W	X	29
Northbury Fm	Wok	SU7976	51°28·9′	0°51·3′W	FM	175
North Cadboll	Highld	NH8778	57°46·9′	3°53·6′W	X	21
North Cadbury	Somer	ST6327	51°2·7′	2°31·3′W	T	183
North Cadbury Court	Somer	ST6327	51°2·7′	2°31·3′W	X	183
North Cairn	D & G	NW9770	54°59·2′	5°10·0′W	X	76,82
North Calder	Highld	ND1161	58°31·9′	3°31·2′W	X	11,12
North Calder Water	N Lanak	NS7463	55°50·9′	4°0·3′W	W	64
North Calder Water	N Lanak	NS8668	55°53·8′	3°48·9′W	W	65
North Califf	Shetld	HU4446	60°12·0′	1°11·9′W	X	4
North Callange	Fife	NO4212	56°18·1′	2°55·8′W	X	59
North Camalour	Aberd	NJ7540	57°27·2′	2°24·5′W	X	29
North Camp	Hants	SU8753	51°16·4′	0°44·8′W	T	186
North Carlton	Lincs	SK9477	53°17·1′	0°35·0′W	T	121
North Carlton	Notts	SK5984	53°21·2′	1°6·4′W	T	111,120
North Carlton Covert	Lincs	SK9278	53°17·7′	0°36·8′W	F	121
North Carr	K upon H	TA1134	53°47·7′	0°18·5′W	X	107
North Carr	N Lincs	SE7600	53°29·7′	0°50·9′W	X	112
North Carr Beacon	Fife	NO6411	56°17·7′	2°34·5′W	X	59
North Carr Fm	E Yorks	SE8633	53°47·4′	0°41·3′W	FM	106
North Carr Fm	Lincs	SK7993	53°25·9′	0°48·2′W	FM	112
North Carr Fm	Notts	SK7295	53°27·0′	0°54·5′W	FM	112
North Carrine	Arg & Bt	NR6609	55°19·4′	5°40·9′W	X	68
North Carr Wood	Durham	NZ1233	54°41·8′	1°48·4′W	F	92
North Carthat	D & G	NY0577	55°5·0′	3°28·9′W	X	85
North Cassingray	Fife	NO4808	56°16·0′	2°49·9′W	X	59
North Castlewalls	Renf	NS4159	55°48·1′	4°31·8′W	X	64
North Cave	E Yorks	SE8932	53°46·8′	0°38·5′W	T	106
North Cerney	Glos	SP0207	51°45·9′	1°57·9′W	T	163
North Cerney Downs	Glos	SP0307	51°45·9′	1°57·0′W	X	163
North Chailey	E Susx	TQ3921	50°58·5′	0°0·8′W	T	198
North Channel		NW9556	54°51·7′	5°11·2′W	W	82
North Channel	Essex	TL9811	51°46·0′	0°52·6′E	W	168
North Channel	E Yorks	TA2621	53°40·5′	0°5·1′W	W	107,113
North Channel	Highld	NM6287	56°55·1′	5°54·2′W	W	40
North Channel	Highld	NM6574	56°48·2′	5°50·5′W	W	40

Northchapel	W Susx	SU9529	51°3·4'	0°38·3'W	T	186,197
North Charford	Hants	SU1919	50°58·4'	1°43·4'W	T	184
North Charford Down Fm	Hants	SU1520	50°59·0'	1°46·8'W	FM	184
North Charford Manor Ho	Hants	SU1719	50°58·4'	1°45·1'W	X	184
North Charlton	Northum	NU1622	55°29·7'	1°44·4'W	T	75
North Charlton Moor	Northum	NU1422	55°29·7'	1°46·3'W	X	75
North Cheam	Sutton	TQ2465	51°22·5'	0°12·7'W	T	176
North Cheek or Ness Point	N Yks	NZ9606	54°26·7'	0°30·8'W	X	94
North Cheriton	Somer	ST6925	51°1·6'	2°26·1'W	T	183
North Chideock	Dorset	SY4294	50°44·8'	2°48·9'W	T	193
North Choppington	Northum	NZ2385	55°9·8'	1°37·9'W	X	81
Northchurch	Herts	SP9708	51°46·0'	0°35·3'W	T	165
Northchurch Common	Herts	SP9710	51°47·0'	0°35·2'W	X	165
Northchurch Fm	Herts	SP9809	51°46·5'	0°34·4'W	FM	165
North Clays	E Susx	TQ4536	51°6·5'	0°4·7'E	X	188
North Cleave	Devon	SS6348	51°13·1'	3°57·3'W	X	180
North Clettraval	N Eil	NF7472	57°37·5'	7°27·2'W	H	18
North Cliff	E Yorks	TA2049	53°55·6'	0°9·9'W	X	107
North Cliff	E Yorks	TA2372	54°8·0'	0°6·6'W	X	101
North Cliff	N Yks	TA1182	54°13·5'	0°17·4'W	X	101
Northcliff	V of Glam	ST0870	51°25·5'	3°19·0'W	X	170
North Cliffe	E Yorks	SE8737	53°49·6'	0°40·3'W	T	106
North Cliffe Wood	E Yorks	SE8637	53°49·6'	0°41·2'W	F	106
Northcliff Fm	E Yorks	TA2471	54°7·4'	0°5·7'W	FM	101
North Cliffs	Corn	SW6243	50°14·6'	5°19·9'W	X	203
North Cliftbog	Aberd	NJ6946	57°30·4'	2°30·6'W	X	29
North Clifton	Notts	SK8272	53°14·6'	0°45·9'W	T	121
North Close	Durham	NZ2632	54°41·2'	1°35·4'W	T	93
North Close Fm	N Yks	SE2474	54°9·9'	1°37·5'W	FM	99
North Clutag	D & G	NX3853	54°51·0'	4°31·0'W	X	83
Northcoates Point	Lincs	TA3703	53°30·6'	0°4·4'E	X	113
North Cobbinshaw	W Loth	NT0157	55°48·0'	3°34·3'W	X	65,72
North Cockerham	Devon	SS7128	51°2·4'	3°50·0'W	X	180
North Cockerington	Lincs	TF3790	53°23·6'	0°4·0'E	T	113
North Coker	Somer	ST5313	50°55·1'	2°39·7'W	T	194
North Coldstream	Aberd	NJ7800	57°5·7'	2°21·3'W	X	38
North Collafirth	Shetld	HU3483	60°32·0'	1°22·3'W	T	1,2,3
North Collielaw	Aberd	NK0943	57°28·9'	1°50·5'W	X	30
North Combe	Devon	SS8217	50°56·7'	3°40·4'W	X	181
Northcombe	Devon	SX4595	50°44·3'	4°11·4'W	X	190
Northcombe	Somer	SS9129	51°3·2'	3°32·9'W	X	181
North Combe	Somer	ST0428	51°2·8'	3°21·8'W	X	181
Northcombe Plantation	Devon	SX4696	50°44·8'	4°10·6'W	F	190
North Common	Devon	ST2511	50°53·9'	3°3·6'W	X	192,193
North Common	Donc	SE6814	53°37·3'	0°57·9'W	X	111
North Common	E Susx	TQ3821	50°58·5'	0°1·7'W	T	198
North Common	S Glos	ST6772	51°27·0'	2°28·1'W	T	172
North Common	Somer	SS8147	51°12·8'	3°41·8'W	X	181
North Common	Suff	TL9775	52°20·5'	0°53·9'E	T	144
North Common Fm	Beds	SP9639	52°2·7'	0°35·6'W	FM	153
North Common Fm	Wilts	SU2420	50°59·0'	1°39·1'W	FM	184
North Commonside	Renf	NS4568	55°53·1'	4°28·2'W	X	64
North Commonty	Aberd	NJ8648	57°31·6'	2°13·6'W	X	30
North Common Wood	Suff	TM5182	52°22·9'	1°41·7'E	F	156
North Connel	Arg & Bt	NM9134	56°27·4'	5°23·1'W	T	49
North Coombe	Devon	SS8704	50°49·7'	3°35·9'W	X	192
North Coombe	Devon	SS8815	50°55·7'	3°35·2'W	X	181
North Coombe Fm	Corn	SX2974	50°32·7'	4°24·4'W	FM	201
North Coos	Shetld	HP6715	60°49·0'	0°45·6'W	X	1
North Copse	Hants	SU6461	51°20·9'	1°4·5'W	F	175
North Corbelly	D & G	NX9863	54°57·3'	3°35·1'W	X	84
North Cornelly	Brig	SS8181	51°31·2'	3°42·5'W	T	170
North Corner	Corn	SW7818	50°1·5'	5°5·6'W	T	204
North Corner	S Glos	ST6582	51°32·4'	2°29·9'W	T	172
North Corriegills	N Ayr	NS0335	55°34·4'	5°7·1'W	T	69
North Corrielaw	D & G	NY1784	55°9·9'	3°17·7'W	X	79
North Corry	Highld	NM8352	56°36·8'	5°31·7'W	X	49
North Corse	Shetld	HU4543	60°10·4'	1°10·8'W	X	4
North Corston	Pth & Kin	NO2338	56°31·6'	3°14·7'W	X	53
North Cortiecram	Aberd	NJ9741	57°27·8'	2°2·5'W	X	30
Northcote	Devon	SS8613	50°54·5'	3°36·9'W	X	181
Northcote	Devon	ST1701	50°48·4'	3°10·3'W	T	192,193
North Cote	N Yks	SD9768	54°6·7'	2°2·3'W	X	98
Northcote Fm	Devon	SS6042	51°9·8'	3°59·8'W	FM	180
North Cote Fm	N Yks	SE2381	54°13·7'	1°38·4'W	FM	99
North Cote Fm	Red & Cl	NZ6017	54°32·9'	1°3·9'W	FM	94
Northcote Fm	Surrey	TQ0344	51°11·4'	0°31·2'W	FM	186
Northcote Manor (Hotel)	Devon	SS6218	50°56·9'	3°57·5'W	X	180
North Cotes	Lincs	TA3400	53°29·0'	0°1·6'E	T	113
North Cotes Plantn	E Yorks	TA0574	54°9·3'	0°23·1'W	F	101
North Cotes Road	E Yorks	TA0474	54°9·3'	0°24·0'W	X	101
Northcott	Corn	SS2108	50°50·9'	4°32·2'W	T	190
Northcott	Devon	SS3313	50°53·8'	4°22·1'W	X	190
Northcott	Devon	ST0912	50°54·3'	3°17·3'W	T	181
Northcott	Devon	ST1109	50°52·7'	3°15·5'W	T	192,193
Northcott	Devon	SX3392	50°42·5'	4°21·5'W	T	190
North Cottage	Northum	NY9859	54°55·8'	2°1·4'W	X	87
Northcott Barton	Devon	SS5914	50°54·7'	4°0·0'W	X	180
Northcott Fms	Somer	ST0423	51°0·1'	3°21·7'W	FM	181
Northcott Mouth	Corn	SS2008	50°50·8'	4°33·0'W	W	190
North Coullie	Aberd	NJ8726	57°19·7'	2°12·5'W	X	38
North Country	Corn	SW6943	50°14·7'	5°14·0'W	T	203
North Court	I of W	SZ4583	50°38·9'	1°21·4'W	A	196
North Court	Kent	TQ9657	51°16·9'	0°49·0'E	X	178
North Court	Kent	TR2343	51°8·8'	1°11·7'E	X	179,189
North Court	Kent	TR3051	51°12·9'	1°18·0'E	X	179
Northcourt	Oxon	SU5098	51°40·9'	1°16·2'W	T	164
North Court	Suff	TL7584	52°25·8'	0°34·8'E	X	143
North Court	Wok	SU7963	51°21·9'	0°51·5'W	X	175,186
North Court Fm	Pemb	SN0024	51°53·0'	4°54·0'W	FM	145,157,158
North Couston	W Loth	NS9571	55°55·5'	3°40·4'W	X	65
North Cove	Suff	TM4689	52°26·8'	1°37·6'E	T	134,156
North Covert	E Yorks	SE7435	53°48·6'	0°52·2'W	F	105,106
North Cowfords	Aberd	NJ8761	57°38·6'	2°12·6'W	X	30
North Cowshaw	D & G	NY0284	55°8·7'	3°31·8'W	X	78
North Cowton	N Yks	NZ2803	54°25·5'	1°33·7'W	T	93
Northcraig	E Ayr	NS4341	55°38·5'	4°29·2'W	X	70
North Craighead	Aberd	NJ9840	57°27·3'	2°1·5'W	X	30
North Craighill	Aberd	NJ9384	57°37·0'	2°6·6'W	X	30
North Craigo	Angus	NO6863	56°45·7'	2°31·0'W	T	45
North Craig Resr	E Ayr	NS4341	55°38·5'	4°29·2'W	W	70
North Craleckan	Arg & Bt	NN0202	56°10·4'	5°10·9'W	X	55
North Crane Row	Durham	NZ1028	54°39·1'	1°50·3'W	X	92
North Cranna	Aberd	NJ6353	57°34·2'	2°36·7'W	X	29
North Crawley	Mil Key	SP9244	52°5·4'	0°39·0'W	T	152
North Cray	Bexley	TQ4972	51°25·9'	0°9·0'E	T	177
North Creake	Norf	TF8538	52°54·7'	0°45·5'E	T	132
North Creedy	Devon	SS8304	50°49·7'	3°39·3'W	X	191
Northcroft Fm	W Berks	SU3664	51°22·7'	1°28·6'W	FM	174
North Croo	Shetld	HU5441	60°9·3'	1°1·1'W	X	4
North Crookedstone	S Lanak	NS7250	55°43·8'	4°1·9'W	X	64
North Crowlea Plantn	Scot Bord	NT9257	55°48·6'	2°7·2'W	F	67,74,75
North Cubbington Wood	Warw	SP3569	52°19·3'	1°28·8'W	F	151
North Culdigo	Orkney	HY4730	59°9·5'	2°55·1'W	X	5,6
North Cult	Fife	NT0296	56°9·1'	3°34·2'W	X	58
North Curry	Somer	ST3225	51°1·5'	2°57·8'W	T	193
North Dalchork	Highld	NC5420	58°9·0'	4°28·4'W	F	16
North Dale	E Yorks	TA0475	54°9·9'	0°24·0'W	X	101
North Dale	E Yorks	TA1572	54°8·1'	0°14·0'W	X	101
North Dale	Orkney	HY3733	59°11·0'	3°5·7'W	X	6
North Dale	Orkney	ND2697	58°51·5'	3°16·5'W	X	6,7
Northdale	Shetld	HP6413	60°48·0'	0°48·9'W	T	1
Northdale	Shetld	HU6091	60°36·1'	0°53·8'W	X	1,2
Northdale Beck	N Yks	SE7298	54°22·6'	0°53·1'W	W	94,100
Northdale Fm	N Yks	SE7298	54°22·6'	0°53·1'W	FM	94,100
Northdale Rigg	N Yks	SE7397	54°22·0'	0°52·2'W	X	94,100
North Dales	Orkney	HY3028	58°57·5'	3°10·4'W	X	6,7
Northdale Scar	N Yks	SE8397	54°21·9'	0°42·9'W	X	94,100
North Dallens	Arg & Bt	NM9248	56°34·9'	5°22·8'W	X	49
North Dalton	E Yorks	SE9352	53°57·6'	0°34·5'W	T	106
North Darley	Corn	SX2773	50°32·1'	4°26·1'W	T	201
North Dawn	Orkney	HY4703	58°54·9'	2°54·7'W	X	6,7
North Deep	Fife	NO2119	56°21·7'	3°16·3'W	W	58
North Deighton	N Yks	SE3951	53°57·5'	1°23·9'W	T	104
North Demesne	Northum	NU1914	55°25·4'	1°41·6'W	X	81
North Denes	Norf	TG5210	52°38·0'	1°43·9'E	T	134
North Denford Fm	W Berks	SU3671	51°26·4'	1°28·5'W	FM	174
North Denmore	Aberd	NJ9040	57°27·3'	2°9·5'W	X	30
North Dennetys	Aberd	NO7187	56°58·7'	2°28·2'W	X	45
North Denniston	Inverc	NS3668	55°52·9'	4°36·9'W	X	63
North District	Norf	TF5101	52°35·4'	0°14·1'E	X	143
North Docken Bush	N Yks	SE3161	54°2·9'	1°31·2'W	X	99
North Dodd	Durham	NY9314	54°31·5'	2°6·1'W	X	91,92
North Dog	E Loth	NT5187	56°4·7'	2°46·8'W	X	66
North Doll	Stir	NS8788	56°4·5'	3°48·5'W	X	65
North Down	Corn	SX3676	50°33·9'	4°18·6'W	X	201
North Down	Devon	SS3400	50°46·8'	4°20·9'W	X	190
Northdown	Devon	SX4788	50°40·5'	4°9·5'W	X	191
North Down	Devon	SX7798	50°46·3'	3°44·3'W	X	191
North Down	Dorset	SY8599	50°47·7'	2°12·4'W	X	194
Northdown	Kent	TR3770	51°23·0'	1°24·8'E	T	179
North Down	Pemb	SN0001	51°40·6'	4°53·2'W	X	157,158
North Down	Somer	ST2215	50°56·0'	3°6·2'W	X	193
North Down	Wilts	SU0467	51°24·4'	1°56·2'W	X	173
North Down	W Susx	SU8914	50°55·3'	0°43·6'W	X	197
North Down Fm	Somer	ST0626	51°1·8'	3°20·0'W	FM	181
North Down Fm	Somer	ST4712	50°54·5'	2°44·8'W	FM	193
North Downs	Corn	SW7144	50°15·3'	5°12·4'W	X	203
North Downs	Devon	SS4941	51°9·1'	4°9·2'W	X	180
North Downs	Hants	SU7847	51°13·2'	0°52·6'W	H	186
North Downs	Kent	TQ5260	51°19·4'	0°11·3'E	X	177,188
North Downs	Kent	TR0250	51°13·0'	0°53·9'E	X	189
North Downs	Surrey	TQ1851	51°15·0'	0°18·2'W	H	187
North Downs Steam Rly	Kent	TQ5674	51°26·8'	0°15·1'E	X	177
North Downs Way	Kent	TQ4657	51°17·8'	0°6·0'E	X	188
North Downs Way	Kent	TQ6059	51°18·7'	0°18·1'E	X	188
North Downs Way	Kent	TQ6762	51°20·2'	0°24·2'E	X	177,178,188
North Downs Way	Kent	TR2338	51°6·1'	1°11·5'E	X	179,189
North Downs Way	Surrey	SU9647	51°13·1'	0°37·1'W	X	186
North Downs Way	Surrey	TQ2551	51°14·9'	0°12·1'W	X	187
North Drain	Lincs	TF5268	53°11·5'	0°16·9'E	W	122
North Drain	Somer	ST4245	51°12·3'	2°49·4'W	W	182
North Dronley	Angus	NO3336	56°30·9'	3°4·9'W	T	53
North Drove Drain	Lincs	TF1717	52°44·5'	0°15·6'W	W	130
North Druimachro	Arg & Bt	NR6447	55°39·8'	5°44·7'W	X	62
North Drumboy	E Ayr	NS4948	55°42·4'	4°23·8'W	X	64
North Drumochter Lodge	Highld	NN6379	56°53·2'	4°14·5'W	X	42
North Duffield	N Yks	SE6837	53°49·7'	0°57·6'W	T	105,106
North Duffield Lodge	N Yks	SE6939	53°50·8'	0°56·7'W	X	105,106
North Dun	Angus	NO6661	56°44·6'	2°32·9'W	X	45
North Dunslaw Holm	Northum	NZ0866	54°59·6'	1°52·1'W	X	88
North Durieshill	Stir	NS8186	56°3·4'	3°54·2'W	X	57,65
Northdyke	Orkney	HY2320	59°3·9'	3°20·1'W	T	6
North Dykes	Cumbr	NY5437	54°43·8'	2°42·4'W	T	90
North Dykes	N Ayr	NS3055	55°45·8'	4°42·1'W	X	63
Northease Fm	E Susx	TQ4106	50°50·4'	0°0·5'E	FM	198
North Eastling	Kent	TQ9657	51°16·9'	0°49·0'E	T	178
North East Mason Fm	N upon Ty	NZ2274	55°3·8'	1°38·9'W	FM	88
North East Mouth	Shetld	HU6971	60°25·3'	0°44·3'W	W	2
North East Point	Cumbr	SD2362	54°3·1'	3°10·2'W	X	96
North East Point	Devon	SS1348	51°12·3'	4°40·2'W	X	180
North Ecchinswell Fm	Hants	SU5061	51°21·0'	1°16·5'W	FM	174
North Eddieston	C of Aber	NJ7802	57°6·8'	2°21·3'W	X	38
Northedge	Derby	SK3665	53°11·1'	1°27·3'W	T	119
North Egliston	Dorset	SY8980	50°37·4'	2°8·9'W	X	195
North Elham	Kent	TR1844	51°9·4'	1°7·5'E	T	179,189
North Elkington	Lincs	TF2890	53°23·7'	0°4·1'W	T	113
North Elmham	Norf	TF9820	52°44·7'	0°56·4'E	T	132
North Elmsall	Wakf	SE4712	53°36·4'	1°17·0'W	T	111
North Elmsall Hall	Wakf	SE4713	53°36·9'	1°17·0'W	X	111
North Elphinstone	E Loth	NT3970	55°55·4'	2°58·1'W	T	66
Northenby	Hants	SU4062	51°21·6'	1°25·1'W	X	174
North End	Bath & NE Somer	ST6260	51°20·5'	2°32·3'W	T	172
Northend	Bath & NE Somer	ST7868	51°24·9'	2°18·6'W	T	172
North End	Beds	SP9749	52°8·1'	0°34·6'W	T	153
North End	Beds	TL0259	52°13·4'	0°30·0'W	T	153
North End	Bexley	TQ5176	51°28·0'	0°10·8'E	T	177
North End	Bucks	SP7027	51°56·5'	0°58·5'W	T	165
North End	Bucks	SP8427	51°56·3'	0°46·3'W	T	165
Northend	Bucks	SU7392	51°37·6'	0°56·3'W	T	175
North End	Camden	TQ2687	51°34·3'	0°10·5'W	T	176
North End	C of Port	SU6502	50°49·1'	1°4·3'W	T	196
North End	Cumbr	NY3259	54°55·5'	3°3·2'W	T	85
North End	Devon	SS1347	51°11·7'	4°40·2'W	X	180
North End	Devon	ST1016	50°56·4'	3°16·5'W	T	181,193
North End	Dorset	ST8427	51°2·8'	2°13·3'W	T	183
North End	Durham	NZ2643	54°47·1'	1°35·3'W	T	88
Northend	Essex	TL5239	52°1·9'	0°13·3'E	T	154
North End	Essex	TL6618	51°50·4'	0°25·0'E	T	167
North End	Essex	TL7839	52°1·5'	0°36·1'E	T	155
Northend	Essex	TL9500	51°40·1'	0°49·6'E	T	168
North End	E Susx	TQ4113	50°54·2'	0°0·7'E	X	198
North End	E Yorks	SE9449	53°56·0'	0°33·7'W	X	106
North End	E Yorks	TA1650	53°56·2'	0°13·6'W	T	107
North End	E Yorks	TA1941	53°51·3'	0°11·0'W	T	107
North End	E Yorks	TA2831	53°45·8'	0°3·1'W	T	107
North End	Hants	SU1016	50°56·8'	1°51·1'W	T	184
North End	Hants	SU4063	51°22·1'	1°25·1'W	T	174
North End	Hants	SU5829	51°3·7'	1°10·0'W	T	185
Northend	Kent	TQ6071	51°25·1'	0°18·5'E	X	177
North End	Leic	SK5715	52°44·0'	1°8·9'W	T	129
North End	Lincs	TA3101	53°29·6'	0°1·1'W	T	113
North End	Lincs	TF0499	53°28·9'	0°25·6'W	T	112
North End	Lincs	TF2341	52°57·4'	0°9·7'W	T	131
North End	Lincs	TF3592	53°24·7'	0°2·3'E	T	113
North End	Lincs	TF4289	53°23·0'	0°8·5'E	T	113,122
North End	Lincs	TF4987	53°21·8'	0°14·8'E	T	113,122
North End	N Lincs	TA1022	53°41·2'	0°19·6'W	T	107,113
North End	Norf	TM0092	52°29·6'	0°57·2'E	T	144
North End	Northum	NU1301	55°18·4'	1°47·3'W	T	81
North End	N Som	ST4167	51°24·2'	2°50·5'W	T	171,172,182
North End	Sefton	SD3004	53°31·9'	3°3·0'W	X	108
North End	Somer	ST2726	51°2·0'	3°2·1'W	T	193
Northend	Warw	SP3952	52°10·1'	1°25·4'W	T	151
North End	Wilts	SU0494	51°38·9'	1°56·1'W	T	163,173
North End	W Susx	SU9804	50°49·9'	0°36·1'W	T	197
North End	W Susx	TQ1109	50°52·4'	0°25·0'W	T	198
North End	W Susx	TQ3739	51°8·3'	0°2·1'W	T	187
Northenden	Man	SJ8290	53°24·6'	2°15·8'W	T	109
North End Fm	Brom	TQ4363	51°21·1'	0°3·6'E	FM	177,187
North End Fm	Dorset	SY4294	50°44·8'	2°48·9'W	FM	193
North End Fm	E Yorks	TA2426	53°43·2'	0°6·8'W	FM	107
North End Fm	E Yorks	TA2725	53°42·6'	0°4·1'W	FM	107,113
Northend Fm	Glos	SO7220	51°52·9'	2°24·0'W	FM	162
North End Fm	Hants	SU1411	50°54·1'	1°47·7'W	FM	195
North End Fm	Herts	TL3933	51°58·9'	0°1·8'E	FM	166
North End Fm	N Yks	NZ7006	54°26·9'	0°54·8'W	FM	94
North End Fm	Surrey	SU9636	51°7·1'	0°37·3'W	FM	186
North End Fm	Wilts	ST8384	51°33·5'	2°14·3'W	FM	173
Northend Fm	Worcs	SO8343	52°5·3'	2°14·5'W	FM	150
Northend Fm	W Susx	SU8527	51°2·4'	0°46·9'W	FM	186,197
North End Haws	Cumbr	SD1773	54°9·0'	3°15·8'W	X	96
North End Marsh	Cumbr	SD1772	54°8·5'	3°15·8'W	W	96
North End Scar	N Yks	SD6876	54°11·0'	2°29·0'W	X	98
Norther Geo	Shetld	HU4495	60°38·4'	1°11·2'W	X	1,2
Norther House	Shetld	HU4067	60°23·4'	1°16·0'W	X	2,3
Northern Gate Ho	Highld	ND2071	58°37·4'	3°22·2'W	X	7,12
Northern Hares	Northum	NU2439	55°38·9'	1°36·7'W	X	75
Northern Moor	Man	SJ8190	53°24·6'	2°16·7'W	T	109
Northern Ness	Shetld	HU3618	59°57·0'	1°20·8'W	X	4
Northern or Norrard Rocks	Scilly	SV8613	49°56·3'	6°22·2'W	X	203
Northern Erradale	Highld	NG7481	57°46·0'	5°47·5'W	T	19
Northerwood Grange	Northnts	SP7990	52°30·4'	0°49·8'W	X	141
Northerwood Ho	Hants	SU2908	50°52·5'	1°34·9'W	X	196
North Esk Resr	Scot Bord	NT1558	55°48·7'	3°20·9'W	W	65,72
North Essie	Aberd	NK0755	57°35·4'	1°52·5'W	X	30
North Esworthy	Devon	SS8722	50°59·4'	3°36·2'W	X	181
North Everton	Aberd	NJ7952	57°33·7'	2°20·6'W	X	29,30
North Evington	C of Leic	SK6104	52°38·1'	1°5·5'W	T	140
North Ewster	N Lincs	SE8303	53°31·3'	0°44·5'W	T	112
Northey	Peterb	TL2399	52°34·7'	0°10·7'W	X	142
Northeye Village	E Susx	TQ6807	50°50·5'	0°23·6'E	A	199
Northey Fm	Beds	SP9554	52°10·8'	0°36·2'W	FM	153
Northey Fm	Mil Key	SP9055	52°11·4'	0°40·6'W	FM	152
Northey Island	Essex	TL8806	51°43·5'	0°43·7'E	X	168
Northey Wood	Suff	TL7950	52°7·4'	0°37·3'E	F	155
North Faddonhill	Aberd	NJ8343	57°28·9'	2°16·6'W	X	29,30
North Fairlee Fm	I of W	SZ5191	50°43·2'	1°16·3'W	FM	196
North Falaknowe	Scot Bord	NT8766	55°53·5'	2°12·0'W	X	67
North Fambridge	Essex	TQ8597	51°38·3'	0°40·8'E	T	168
North Fareham Fm	Hants	SU5807	50°51·8'	1°10·2'W	FM	196
North Farm Ho	Somer	ST3455	51°17·7'	2°56·4'W	X	182
Northfaulds	S Lanak	NS9044	55°40·9'	3°44·5'W	X	71,72
North Fawr	Cered	SN3250	52°7·6'	4°26·9'W	X	145
North Fearns	Highld	NG5936	57°21·3'	5°59·9'W	X	24,32
North Featherstone	Wakf	SE4222	53°41·8'	1°21·4'W	T	105
North Fellsigeo	Shetld	HZ2073	59°32·8'	1°38·3'W	X	4
North Feltham	Houns	TQ1074	51°27·5'	0°24·6'W	T	176
North Fen	Cambs	TL4081	52°24·8'	0°3·9'E	X	142,143
North Fen	Cambs	TL4477	52°22·6'	0°7·3'E	X	142,143
North Fen	Cambs	TL5169	52°18·1'	0°13·3'E	X	154
North Fen	Peterb	TF1508	52°39·8'	0°17·6'W	X	142
North Fen	Peterb	TF2909	52°40·0'	0°5·1'W	X	142
North Fen	Peterb	TL2599	52°34·7'	0°8·9'W	X	142
North Fen	Suff	TL7284	52°25·8'	0°32·2'E	X	143
North Fen Fm	Cambs	TL3579	52°23·8'	0°0·5'W	FM	142
North Fen Fm	Cambs	TL4367	52°17·2'	0°6·2'E	FM	154
North Fen Fm	Cambs	TL5384	52°26·2'	0°15·4'E	FM	143
North Fen Fm	Lincs	TF4094	53°25·7'	0°6·8'E	FM	113
North Fens	Northum	NZ0574	55°3·9'	1°54·9'W	X	87
North Feorline	N Ayr	NR9028	55°30·3'	5°19·1'W	X	68,69
North Fergushill	N Ayr	NS3343	55°39·4'	4°38·8'W	X	63,70
North Ferriby	E Yorks	SE9825	53°43·0'	0°30·5'W	T	106
Northfield	Aberd	NJ7132	57°22·9'	2°28·5'W	X	29
Northfield	Aberd	NJ8266	57°41·3'	2°17·7'W	X	29,30
Northfield	Aberd	NJ8659	57°37·5'	2°13·6'W	X	30
Northfield	Aberd	NJ9123	57°18·1'	2°8·5'W	X	38

Northfield	Bath & NE Somer	ST6759	51°20·0'	2°28·0'W	X	172
Northfield	Birm	SP0279	52°24·8'	1°57·8'W	T	139
North Field	Cambs	TL5975	52°21·2'	0°20·5'E	X	143
Northfield	C of Aber	NJ9008	57°10·0'	2°9·5'W	T	38
Northfield	C of Edin	NT2973	55°56·9'	3°7·8'W	T	66
Northfield	D & G	NX8987	55°10·1'	3°44·1'W	X	78
Northfield	D & G	NY1968	55°0·2'	3°15·6'W	X	85
North Field	Durham	NZ0115	54°32·1'	1°58·7'W	X	92
North Field	E Yorks	SE8957	54°0·3'	0°38·1'W	X	106
North Field	E Yorks	SE9360	54°1·9'	0°34·4'W	X	101
Northfield	E Yorks	TA0326	53°43·4'	0°25·9'W	T	107
North Field	E Yorks	TA2433	53°46·9'	0°6·7'W	X	107
Northfield	Fife	NO4328	56°26·7'	2°55·0'W	X	54,59
Northfield	Highld	ND3548	58°25·2'	3°6·3'W	X	12
Northfield	Highld	NH7071	57°42·9'	4°10·5'W	X	21
Northfield	Mil Key	SP8840	52°3·3'	0°42·6'W	T	152
North Field	N Lincs	TA1116	53°38·0'	0°18·9'W	X	113
Northfield	Northnts	SP8993	52°31·9'	0°40·9'W	T	141
Northfield	Northum	NU2407	55°21·6'	1°36·9'W	X	81
Northfield	Orkney	HY5707	58°57·1'	2°44·4'W	X	6
Northfield	Orkney	ND4898	58°52·2'	2°53·6'W	X	6,7
Northfield	Scot Bord	NT5629	55°33·4'	2°41·4'W	T	73
Northfield	Scot Bord	NT9167	55°54·0'	2°8·2'W	T	67
Northfield	Somer	ST2836	51°7·4'	3°1·3'W	T	182
Northfield	W Loth	NS9461	55°50·1'	3°41·1'W	X	65
Northfield Barn	Glos	SP1715	51°50·2'	1°44·8'W	X	163
North Field Barn	Wilts	SU2677	51°29·7'	1°37·1'W	X	174
Northfield Brook	Oxon	SP5603	51°43·6'	1°11·0'W	W	164
Northfield Cott	W Dunb	NS4079	55°58·9'	4°33·4'W	X	64
Northfield Fm	Beds	TL0840	52°3·1'	0°25·1'W	FM	153
Northfield Fm	Beds	TL1153	52°10·1'	0°22·2'W	FM	153
Northfield Fm	Cambs	TF3102	52°29·4'	0°13·8'E	FM	143
Northfield Fm	Cambs	TL5361	52°13·8'	0°14·8'E	FM	154
Northfield Fm	Cov	SP3081	52°25·8'	1°33·1'W	FM	140
Northfield Fm	E Yorks	SE7950	53°56·6'	0°47·4'W	FM	105,106
Northfield Fm	E Yorks	TA1848	53°55·1'	0°11·8'W	FM	107
Northfield Fm	Glos	SO9822	51°54·0'	2°1·4'W	FM	163
Northfield Fm	Glos	SP0217	51°51·3'	1°57·9'W	FM	163
Northfield Fm	Leic	SK8112	52°42·2'	0°47·7'W	FM	130
Northfield Fm	Lincs	SK8592	53°25·3'	0°42·8'W	FM	112
North Field Fm	Lincs	SK9161	53°8·5'	0°38·0'W	FM	121
Northfield Fm	Lincs	TF3188	53°22·6'	0°1·4'W	FM	113,122
Northfield Fm	Lincs	TF3567	53°11·2'	0°1·6'E	FM	122
Northfield Fm	Lincs	TF3687	53°22·0'	0°3·0'E	FM	113,122
North Field Fm	N Lincs	SE8905	53°32·3'	0°39·0'W	FM	112
Northfield Fm	Norf	TL6195	52°32·0'	0°22·8'E	FM	143
Northfield Fm	Notts	SK7236	52°55·2'	0°55·3'W	FM	129
North Field Fm	N Yks	SE2291	54°19·1'	1°39·3'W	FM	99
Northfield Fm	N Yks	SE3899	54°23·3'	1°24·5'W	FM	99
Northfield Fm	N Yks	SE5227	53°44·4'	1°12·3'W	FM	105
Northfield Fm	N Yks	SE6968	54°6·4'	0°56·3'W	FM	100
Northfield Fm	N Yks	SE9890	54°18·0'	0°29·2'W	FM	94,101
Northfield Fm	Oxon	SP5113	51°49·0'	1°15·2'W	FM	164
Northfield Fm	Oxon	SP5603	51°43·6'	1°11·0'W	FM	164
Northfield Fm	Oxon	SU2797	51°40·5'	1°36·2'W	FM	163
Northfield Fm	Oxon	SU3490	51°36·7'	1°30·1'W	FM	164,174
Northfield Fm	Oxon	SU4099	51°41·5'	1°24·9'W	FM	164
Northfield Fm	Oxon	SU5595	51°39·3'	1°11·9'W	FM	164
Northfield Fm	W Berks	SU3976	51°29·1'	1°25·9'W	FM	174
Northfield Fm	Worcs	SO8443	52°5·3'	2°13·6'W	FM	150
Northfieldhead	Northum	NT9811	55°23·8'	2°1·5'W	X	81
North Fieldhead	S Lanak	NS6543	55°40·0'	4°8·3'W	X	71
Northfieldhead Hill	Northum	NT9811	55°23·8'	2°1·5'W	H	81
North Field Hill	Dorset	ST6200	50°48·1'	2°32·0'W	X	194
Northfield Ho	D & G	NY1967	54°59·7'	3°15·5'W	X	85
Northfield Ho	E Yorks	SE8727	53°44·2'	0°40·4'W	X	106
Northfield Ho	E Yorks	SE8856	53°59·8'	0°39·0'W	X	106
Northfield Ho	E Yorks	TA1849	53°55·7'	0°11·8'W	X	107
Northfield Ho	E Yorks	TA2435	53°48·0'	0°6·6'W	X	107
Northfield Ho	E Yorks	TA3328	53°44·1'	0°1·4'E	X	107
Northfield Ho	Notts	SK7662	53°9·2'	0°51·4'W	X	120
Northfield Ho	N Yks	SE3899	54°23·3'	1°24·5'W	X	99
Northfield Ho	N Yks	SE3991	54°19·0'	1°23·6'W	X	99
Northfield Ho	Somer	ST5431	51°4·8'	2°39·0'W	X	182,183
Northfield Lodge	Northnts	SP8478	52°23·8'	0°45·5'W	X	141
Northfields	Hants	SU4825	51°1·6'	1°18·5'W	T	185
Northfields	Northnts	SP7639	52°2·9'	0°53·1'W	X	152
Northfields	Northnts	SP7869	52°19·0'	0°50·9'W	X	152
Northfields Fm	Cambs	TL5165	52°16·0'	0°13·2'E	FM	154
Northfields Fm	Hants	SU5712	50°54·5'	1°11·0'W	FM	196
Northfields Fm	N Yks	NZ8014	54°31·1'	0°45·4'W	FM	94
Northfields Fm	N Yks	SE7580	54°12·9'	0°50·6'W	FM	100
Northfields Fm	Rut	TF0208	52°39·8'	0°29·1'W	FM	141
Northfields Fm	W Susx	SU9406	50°51·0'	0°39·5'W	FM	197
Northfields Fms	Warw	SP4859	52°13·9'	1°17·4'W	FM	151
Northfield Wood	Suff	TM0260	52°12·3'	0°57·8'E	F	155
North Finchley	Barnet	TQ2692	51°37·0'	0°10·4'W	T	176
North Flats	Norf	TG4907	52°36·4'	1°41·1'E	X	134
Northflatt	S Lanak	NS9740	55°38·8'	3°37·8'W	X	72
Northfleet	Kent	TQ6274	51°26·7'	0°20·3'E	T	177
Northfleet Green	Kent	TQ6271	51°25·1'	0°20·2'E	T	177
Northfleet Hope	Kent	TQ6176	51°27·8'	0°19·5'E	W	177
North Flobbets	Aberd	NJ7934	57°24·0'	2°20·5'W	T	29,30
North Fm	Bucks	SP7120	51°52·7'	0°57·7'W	FM	165
North Fm	Bucks	SP8325	51°55·3'	0°47·2'W	FM	165
North Fm	Cambs	TL2360	52°13·7'	0°11·5'W	FM	153
North Fm	Cambs	TL2557	52°12·1'	0°9·9'W	FM	153
North Fm	Cambs	TL4181	52°24·8'	0°4·8'E	FM	142,143
North Fm	Cambs	TL4950	52°7·9'	0°11·0'E	FM	154
North Fm	Dorset	ST8902	50°49·3'	2°9·0'W	FM	195
North Fm	Dorset	ST9713	50°55·2'	2°2·2'W	FM	195
North Fm	Dorset	SU0208	50°52·5'	1°57·9'W	FM	195
North Fm	Durham	NZ1944	54°47·7'	1°41·8'W	FM	88
North Fm	E Yorks	TA1542	53°51·9'	0°14·7'W	FM	107
North Fm	E Yorks	TA1932	53°46·5'	0°11·2'W	FM	107
North Fm	E Yorks	TA3129	53°44·7'	0°0·4'W	FM	107
North Fm	E Yorks	TA3522	53°40·9'	0°3·1'E	FM	107,113
North Fm	Ghead	NZ2558	54°55·2'	1°36·2'W	FM	88
North Fm	Hants	SU6817	50°57·1'	1°1·5'W	FM	185

North Fm	Lancs	SD3730	53°46·0'	2°56·9'W	FM	102
North Fm	Lancs	SD4361	54°2·8'	2°51·8'W	FM	97
North Fm	Leic	SK6119	52°46·1'	1°5·3'W	FM	129
North Fm	Lincs	TF2784	53°20·5'	0°5·1'W	FM	122
North Fm	Monm	SO3712	51°48·4'	2°54·4'W	FM	161
North Fm	Norf	TF6607	52°38·3'	0°27·6'E	FM	143
North Fm	Norf	TG2325	52°46·8'	1°18·8'E	FM	133,134
North Fm	Norf	TG3218	52°42·8'	1°26·5'E	FM	133,134
North Fm	Norf	TM2186	52°25·9'	1°15·5'E	FM	156
North Fm	Norf	TM4097	52°31·3'	1°32·7'E	FM	134
North Fm	Northnts	SP7868	52°18·5'	0°51·0'W	FM	152
North Fm	Northum	NU2223	55°30·3'	1°38·7'W	FM	75
North Fm	Northum	NZ1282	55°8·2'	1°48·3'W	FM	81
North Fm	Notts	SK6437	52°55·8'	1°2·5'W	FM	129
North Fm	N Yks	SE3399	54°23·4'	1°29·1'W	FM	99
North Fm	N Yks	SE4587	54°16·8'	1°18·1'W	FM	99
North Fm	N Yks	SE7877	54°11·2'	0°47·9'W	FM	100
North Fm	N Yks	SE9692	54°19·1'	0°31·0'W	FM	94,101
North Fm	Oxon	SU5892	51°37·7'	1°9·3'W	FM	164,174
North Fm	Pemb	SM9924	51°52·9'	4°54·8'W	FM	157,158
North Fm	Peterb	TF3003	52°36·8'	0°4·4'W	FM	142
North Fm	Somer	ST3042	51°10·6'	2°59·7'W	FM	182
North Fm	Suff	TL8579	52°22·9'	0°43·5'E	FM	144
North Fm	Warw	SP2838	52°2·6'	1°35·1'W	FM	151
North Fm	W Berks	SU3379	51°30·8'	1°31·1'W	FM	174
North Fm	Wilts	ST9144	51°11·9'	2°7·3'W	FM	184
North Fm	Wilts	SU1368	51°24·9'	1°48·4'W	FM	173
North Fm	Wilts	SU1395	51°39·5'	1°48·3'W	FM	163
North Fm	Wilts	SU2578	51°30·3'	1°38·0'W	FM	174
North Fm	Worcs	SP0351	52°9·7'	1°57·0'W	FM	150
North Fm	W Susx	TQ1211	50°53·5'	0°24·1'W	FM	198
North Fms	Derby	SK2543	52°59·3'	1°37·2'W	FM	119,128
North Footie	Aberd	NJ6101	57°6·2'	2°38·2'W	X	37
North Fording Bungalow	Kent	TR0528	51°1·1'	0°55·8'E	X	189
North Fordon Fm	E Yorks	TA0475	54°9·9'	0°24·0'W	FM	101
North Foreland	Kent	TR4069	51°22·4'	1°27·3'E	T	179
North Foreland Lodge	Hants	SU6857	51°18·7'	1°1·1'W	X	175,186
North Fornet	Aberd	NJ7811	57°11·6'	2°21·4'W	X	38
North Forty Foot Drain	Lincs	TF2645	52°59·5'	0°7·0'W	W	131
North Fosse Fm	Warw	SP3663	52°16·1'	1°27·9'W	FM	151
North Frith	Kent	TQ6050	51°13·8'	0°17·9'E	X	188
North Frodingham	E Yorks	TA1053	53°57·9'	0°19·0'W	T	107
North Frodingham Carrs	E Yorks	TA0951	53°56·9'	0°19·9'W	X	107
North Furze	Devon	SS4410	50°52·3'	4°12·7'W	X	190
North Gairy Top	D & G	NX5186	55°9·0'	4°19·9'W	X	77
North Gap	Norf	TG4128	52°48·0'	1°34·9'E	X	134
North Gardie	Shetld	HU3356	60°17·5'	1°23·7'W	H	2,3
Northgardin	Shetld	HU3785	60°33·1'	1°19·0'W	X	1,2,3
North Gare Breakwater	Hartpl	NZ5428	54°38·9'	1°9·4'W	X	93
North Gare Sands	Hartpl	NZ5427	54°38·4'	1°9·4'W	X	93
North Garmond	Aberd	NJ8053	57°34·3'	2°19·6'W	X	29,30
North Garngour	S Lanak	NS8040	55°38·6'	3°54·0'W	X	71,72
North Garphar	S Ayr	NX1183	55°6·6'	4°57·4'W	X	76
North Garvan River	Highld	NM9675	56°49·6'	5°20·1'W	W	40
Northgate	Aberd	NO6367	56°47·8'	2°35·9'W	X	45
Northgate	Durham	NY9340	54°45·5'	2°6·1'W	X	87
North Gate	Hants	SU3804	50°50·3'	1°27·2'W	X	196
Northgate	Lincs	TF1926	52°49·3'	0°13·6'W	T	130
Northgate	Somer	ST0828	51°2·9'	3°18·4'W	T	181
Northgate	W Susx	TQ2738	51°7·9'	0°10·7'W	T	187
Northgate Fell	Durham	NY9240	54°45·5'	2°7·0'W	X	87
Northgate Fm	Hants	SU6346	51°12·8'	1°5·5'W	FM	185
North Gate Fm	Lincs	TF2026	52°49·3'	0°12·7'W	FM	131
Northgate Hall Fm	Norf	TF9442	52°56·2'	0°53·6'E	FM	132
Northgates,The	Heref	SO4624	51°55·0'	2°46·7'W	X	161
North Gaulton	Orkney	HY2113	59°0·1'	3°22·0'W	X	6
North Gavel	Shetld	HZ2272	59°32·3'	1°36·2'W	X	4
North Gellan	Aberd	NJ4902	57°6·6'	2°50·1'W	X	37
North Geo of Brough	Shetld	HP5712	60°47·5'	0°56·7'W	X	1
North Gill Beck	N Yks	SE1672	54°8·9'	1°44·9'W	W	99
North Gill Head	N Yks	NZ5900	54°23·8'	1°5·1'W	X	93
North Gill Ho	Durham	NY9917	54°33·1'	2°0·5'W	X	92
North Gill Ho	N Yks	SE6798	54°22·6'	0°57·7'W	X	94,100
North Glassmount	Fife	NT2488	56°5·0'	3°12·8'W	X	66
North Glen	D & G	NX8256	54°53·3'	3°50·0'W	X	84
North Glendale	N Eil	NF7917	57°8·2'	7°17·9'W	T	31
North Glen Dale	N Eil	NF8016	57°7·7'	7°16·9'W	X	31
North Glen Fm	Renf	NS3871	55°54·5'	4°35·1'W	FM	63
North Glen Sannox	N Ayr	NR9846	55°40·2'	5°12·3'W	X	62,69
North Glenton	Aberd	NO8288	56°59·2'	2°17·3'W	X	45
North Gluss	Shetld	HU3477	60°28·8'	1°22·4'W	T	2,3
North Goatfell	N Ayr	NR9842	55°38·0'	5°12·1'W	X	62,69
North Gorley	Hants	SU1611	50°54·1'	1°46·0'W	T	195
North Grain	Angus	NO4076	56°52·5'	2°58·6'W	W	44
Northgrain	Durham	NY8440	54°45·5'	2°14·5'W	X	86,87
North Grain	Scot Bord	NT2019	55°27·8'	3°15·5'W	W	79
North Grain	Scot Bord	NT3934	55°36·0'	2°57·7'W	W	73
North Grain Beck	Durham	NZ0432	54°41·2'	1°55·9'W	W	92
North Grane Burn	N Ayr	NS2563	55°50·0'	4°47·2'W	W	63
North Grange	E Yorks	SE7139	53°50·8'	0°54·8'W	X	105,106
North Grange	E Yorks	SE9253	53°58·1'	0°35·4'W	X	106
North Grange	E Yorks	TA0940	53°50·9'	0°20·2'W	X	107
North Grange	Pth & Kin	NO2626	56°25·5'	3°11·5'W	X	53,59
North Grange Fm	N Lincs	SE8508	53°33·9'	0°42·6'W	FM	112
North Grange Fm	Suff	TM3670	52°16·9'	1°28·0'E	FM	156
North Green	Norf	TG0206	52°37·1'	0°59·4'E	T	144
North Green	Norf	TM2288	52°26·9'	1°16·4'E	T	156
North Green	Suff	TM3076	52°20·3'	1°23·0'E	T	156
North Green	Suff	TM3162	52°12·7'	1°23·3'E	T	156
North Green	Suff	TM3966	52°14·6'	1°30·5'E	T	156
North Green	Suff	TM4483	52°23·7'	1°35·6'E	X	156
North Greenhill	Cumbr	NY5171	55°2·1'	2°45·6'W	X	86
North Green of Huesbreck	Shetld	HU3914	59°54·8'	1°17·7'W	X	4
North Greens	Falk	NS8987	56°4·0'	3°46·5'W	X	65
North Greens	Moray	NJ2070	57°43·0'	3°20·1'W	X	28
North Greetwell	Lincs	TF0173	53°14·9'	0°28·8'W	T	121
North Grimston	N Yks	SE8467	54°5·8'	0°42·5'W	T	100
North Grimston Ho	N Yks	SE8467	54°5·8'	0°42·5'W	X	100
Northground Dairy	Dorset	SY7783	50°39·0'	2°19·1'W	X	194
North Grounds	I of W	SZ4880	50°37·3'	1°18·9'W	X	196

North Gulham	Lincs	TF0495	53°26·7'	0°25·6'W	X	112
North Gulham Lodge	Lincs	TF0595	53°26·7'	0°24·7'W	X	112
North Gut	Pemb	SM5909	51°43·9'	5°29·0'W	X	157
North Haa	Shetld	HU4487	60°34·1'	1°11·3'W	X	1,2
North Haddo	Aberd	NJ7539	57°26·7'	2°24·5'W	X	29
North Hall	E Susx	TQ3716	50°55·9'	0°2·6'W	X	198
North Hall	E Yorks	SE8527	53°44·2'	0°42·3'W	X	106
Northhall	Fife	NO3002	56°12·6'	3°7·3'W	X	59
North Hall	W Susx	TQ2727	51°1·9'	0°10·9'W	X	187,198
North Halley	Orkney	HY5507	58°57·1'	2°46·4'W	X	6
North Hall Fm	Cambs	TL4041	52°3·2'	0°2·9'E	FM	154
North Hall Fm	E Yorks	SE6219	53°40·1'	1°3·3'W	FM	111
North Hall Fm	N Yks	SE5542	53°52·5'	1°9·4'W	FM	105
North Hall Fm	Suff	TL9876	52°21·0'	0°54·8'E	FM	144
North Hall Fm	Suff	TM4984	52°24·1'	1°40·0'E	FM	156
North Halling	Medway	TQ7065	51°21·7'	0°26·9'E	T	178
North Hall Moor	York	SE5759	54°1·7'	1°7·4'W	X	105
North Halls	S Lanak	NS6437	55°36·7'	4°9·1'W	X	71
North Ham	Shetld	HU3066	60°22·9'	1°26·9'W	X	3
North Hamarsland	Shetld	HU4448	60°13·1'	1°11·9'W	X	3
North Happas	Angus	NO4441	56°33·7'	2°54·2'W	X	54
North Harby	Notts	SK8872	53°14·5'	0°40·5'W	X	121
North Harris or Ceann a Tuath na Hearadh	N Eil	NB1207	57°57·8'	6°51·7'W	X	13,14
North Harrow	Harrow	TQ1388	51°35·0'	0°21·7'W	T	176
North Hart Fm	Hartpl	NZ4635	54°42·7'	1°16·7'W	FM	93
North Hart Law	Scot Bord	NT5658	55°49·0'	2°41·7'W	X	67,73
North Harton	Devon	SX7682	50°37·7'	3°44·8'W	X	191
North Hatton	Aberd	NJ6427	57°20·2'	2°35·4'W	X	37
North Haven	Aberd	NK1138	57°26·2'	1°48·5'W	W	30
North Haven	Pemb	SM7309	51°44·3'	5°16·9'W	W	157
North Haven	Pemb	SM7405	51°42·1'	5°15·9'W	W	157
North Haven	Shetld	HZ2272	59°32·3'	1°36·2'W	W	4
North Haven Point	Dorset	SZ0387	50°41·2'	1°57·1'W	X	195
North Havra	Shetld	HU3642	60°9·9'	1°20·6'W	X	4
North Hawkshaw Rig	Scot Bord	NT2727	55°32·1'	3°9·0'W	X	73
North Hawkwell	Somer	SS9240	51°9·2'	3°32·3'W	X	181
North Hayes Fm	Dorset	ST8626	51°2·2'	2°11·6'W	FM	183
North Hayling	Hants	SU7303	50°49·5'	0°57·4'W	T	197
North Hayne	Devon	SS7725	51°0·9'	3°44·8'W	X	180
North Hazelrigg	Northum	NU0533	55°35·7'	1°54·8'W	X	75
North Head	Cumbr	NX9314	54°30·9'	3°38·8'W	X	89
North Head	Highld	ND3850	58°26·3'	3°3·2'W	X	12
North Head	N Yks	SE9291	54°18·6'	0°34·7'W	X	94,101
North Head	Orkney	HY4423	59°5·7'	2°58·2'W	X	5,6
North Head	Shetld	HU2383	60°32·1'	1°34·3'W	X	3
North Head	Shetld	HU4281	60°30·9'	1°13·6'W	X	1,2,3
North Head, The	Orkney	ND3985	58°45·2'	3°2·8'W	X	7
North Healand	Devon	SS5117	50°56·2'	4°6·9'W	X	180
North Heale	Devon	SS5721	50°58·5'	4°1·8'W	X	180
North Heasley	Devon	SS7333	51°5·2'	3°48·4'W	T	180
North Heath	Norf	TM0093	52°30·1'	0°57·2'E	X	144
North Heath	W Berks	SU4574	51°28·0'	1°20·7'W	T	174
North Heath	W Susx	SU8924	51°0·7'	0°43·5'W	F	197
North Heath	W Susx	TQ0621	50°58·9'	0°29·0'W	T	197
North Heatherybank	Aberd	NJ8036	57°25·1'	2°19·5'W	X	29,30
North Heath Fm	W Berks	SU4574	51°28·0'	1°20·7'W	FM	174
North Hele	Devon	ST0223	51°0·1'	3°23·4'W	X	181
North Hessary Tor	Devon	SX5774	50°33·1'	4°0·7'W	H	191
North Heugh	Northum	NY9580	55°7·1'	2°4·3'W	X	81
North Hidden Fm	W Berks	SU3572	51°27·0'	1°29·4'W	FM	174
North Highcraig	E Renf	NS5950	55°43·6'	4°14·3'W	X	64
North Hill	Cambs	TL4476	52°22·0'	0°7·3'E	X	142,143
North Hill	Corn	SX2776	50°33·7'	4°26·2'W	T	201
North Hill	Devon	SS5736	51°6·6'	4°2·2'W	X	180
North Hill	Devon	ST0906	50°51·0'	3°17·2'W	X	192
North Hill	Devon	SY0892	50°43·5'	3°17·8'W	X	192
North Hill	Dorset	SY4890	50°42·7'	2°43·8'W	H	193
North Hill	Dorset	SY5699	50°47·6'	2°37·1'W	H	194
North Hill	Dorset	SY6290	50°42·7'	2°31·9'W	X	194
North Hill	E Yorks	SE7656	53°59·9'	0°50·0'W	X	105,106
North Hill	Fife	NO3621	56°22·9'	3°1·7'W	H	54,59
North Hill	I Scilly	SV8713	49°56·3'	6°21·4'W	H	203
North Hill	Lincs	TF0141	52°57·6'	0°29·4'W	X	130
North Hill	Orkney	HY2213	59°0·1'	3°21·0'W	X	6
North Hill	Orkney	HY4048	59°19·1'	3°2·8'W	H	5
North Hill	Orkney	HY4954	59°22·4'	2°53·4'W	H	5
North-hill	Orkney	HY6941	59°15·5'	2°32·1'W	X	5
North Hill	Pemb	SM8603	51°41·3'	5°5·4'W	H	157
North Hill	Pemb	SM9324	51°52·8'	5°0·1'W	X	157,158
North Hill	Pth & Kin	NO0508	56°15·6'	3°31·6'W	H	58
North Hill	Shetld	HU3391	60°36·3'	1°23·3'W	X	1,2
North-hill	Shetld	HU4866	60°22·8'	1°7·3'W	X	2,3
North Hill	Shetld	HU6772	60°25·8'	0°46·5'W	H	2
North Hill	Somer	SS9447	51°13·0'	3°30·7'W	X	181
North Hill	Somer	ST5451	51°15·6'	2°39·2'W	H	182,183
North Hill	Wilts	SU2961	51°21·1'	1°34·6'W	X	174
North Hill	Worcs	SO7646	52°6·9'	2°20·6'W	H	150
North Hill	Worcs	SO8954	52°11·3'	2°9·3'W	X	150
North Hill Covert	Suff	TL8862	52°13·7'	0°45·6'E	F	155
North Hillend	S Lanak	NS8245	55°41·3'	3°52·2'W	X	72
North Hill Fm	Bucks	SP7826	51°55·9'	0°51·5'W	FM	165
North Hill Fm	Devon	ST2305	50°50·6'	3°5·2'W	FM	192,193
North Hill Fm	Leic	SK6318	52°45·6'	1°3·6'W	FM	129
North Hill Fm	N Yks	SE3971	54°8·2'	1°23·8'W	FM	99
North Hill Fm	Swan	SS4593	51°37·1'	4°13·9'W	FM	159
North Hill Fm	Wilts	ST9824	51°1·2'	2°1·3'W	FM	184
North Hillingdon	Hill	TQ0884	51°32·9'	0°26·2'W	T	176
North Hill of Bullochreg	Arg & Bt	NS0371	55°53·8'	5°8·6'W	H	63
North Hill of Craigo	Angus	NO6763	56°45·7'	2°31·9'W	X	45
North Hill of Dripps	S Lanak	NS5854	55°45·8'	4°15·4'W	X	64
North Hills	Lincs	TF0952	53°3·5'	0°22·0'W	X	121
North Hillswood	Staffs	SJ9859	53°7·9'	2°1·4'W	X	118
North Hill Tor	Swan	SS4593	51°37·1'	4°13·9'W	X	159
North Hill Wood	Corn	SX0656	50°22·6'	4°43·3'W	F	200
North Hinksey Village	Oxon	SP4905	51°44·7'	1°17·0'W	T	164
North Hinton Fm	Hants	SZ2197	50°46·6'	1°41·7'W	FM	195
North Ho	N Yks	SE2670	54°7·8'	1°35·7'W	X	99
North Ho	N Yks	SE5361	54°2·8'	1°11·0'W	X	100
North Ho	Orkney	HY4049	59°19·7'	3°2·8'W	X	5

North Ho	Shetld	HU3244	60°11·0′	1°24·9′W	X	4
North Ho	Shetld	HU3731	60°4·0′	1°19·6′W	X	4
North Hole	Devon	SS4539	51°8·0′	4°12·5′W	X	180
North Hollow	Lancs	SD3029	53°45·4′	3°3·3′W	X	102
North Hollymill	Aberd	NJ7156	57°35·8′	2°28·7′W	X	29
North Holm	Shetld	HU4955	60°16·8′	1°6·3′W	X	3
North Holme	Notts	SK8066	53°11·3′	0°47·8′W	X	121
North Holme Wood	N Yks	NZ4409	54°28·7′	1°18·8′W	F	93
North Holm of Burravoe	Shetld	HU3889	60°35·2′	1°17·9′W	X	1,2
North Holms	Shetld	HP5611	60°46·9′	0°57·8′W	X	1
North Holmwood	Surrey	TQ1647	51°12·9′	0°20·0′W	T	187
Northhope Burn	Scot Bord	NT3207	55°21·4′	3°3·9′W	W	79
North Houghton	Hants	SU3433	51°5·9′	1°30·5′W	T	185
North Houlann	Shetld	HU2955	60°17·0′	1°28·0′W	X	3
North Hourat	N Ayr	NS2854	55°45·2′	4°44·0′W	X	63
North House	Orkney	HY4907	58°57·1′	2°52·7′W	X	6,7
Northhouse	Scot Bord	NT4307	55°21·5′	2°53·5′W	X	79
North-house	Shetld	HU1860	60°19·7′	1°39·9′W	X	3
Northhouse Burn	Scot Bord	NT4406	55°20·9′	2°52·6′W	W	79
North House Fm	York	SE6347	53°55·2′	1°2·0′W	FM	105,106
North Howden	E Yorks	SE7530	53°45·9′	0°51·3′W	T	105,106
North Howe	Orkney	HY3730	59°9·4′	3°5·6′W	X	6
North Howe (Brocks)	Orkney	HY3730	59°9·4′	3°5·6′W	A	6
North Huckham	Somer	SS9335	51°6·5′	3°31·3′W	X	181
North Huish	Devon	SX7156	50°23·6′	3°48·5′W	T	202
North Hush	N Yks	NY9301	54°24·5′	2°6·1′W	X	91,92
North Hyde	Houns	TQ1278	51°29·6′	0°22·8′W	T	176
North Hykeham	Lincs	SK9466	53°11·2′	0°35·2′W	T	121
North Hylton	Sund	NZ3457	54°54·6′	1°27·8′W	T	88
Northiam	E Susx	TQ8224	50°59·4′	0°36·0′E	T	199
Northiam Fm	Kent	TQ7241	51°8·8′	0°27·9′E	FM	188
North Idle Drain	N Lincs	SE7407	53°33·5′	0°52·6′W	W	112
Northill	Beds	TL1446	52°6·3′	0°19·7′W	T	153
Northill Fm	Devon	ST0905	50°50·5′	3°17·2′W	FM	192
North Inch	Pth & Kin	NO1124	56°24·2′	3°26·1′W	T	53,58
North Inchmichael	Pth & Kin	NO2426	56°25·5′	3°13·5′W	X	53,59
North Ing	Lincs	TF1837	52°55·3′	0°14·3′W	X	130
North Ings	Donc	SE4801	53°30·4′	1°16·2′W	W	111
North Ings	Durham	NY9013	54°31·0′	2°8·8′W	X	91,92
North Ings	N Yks	NZ6411	54°29·7′	1°0·3′W	X	94
North Ings Fm	N Yks	SE6570	54°7·5′	0°59·9′W	FM	100
North Ings Moor	N Yks	NZ6411	54°29·7′	1°0·3′W	X	94
Northington	Glos	SO7008	51°46·4′	2°25·7′W	T	162
Northington	Hants	SU5637	51°8·0′	1°11·6′W	T	185
Northington Down Fm	Hants	SU5537	51°8·0′	1°12·4′W	FM	185
Northingtown Fm	Worcs	SO8161	52°15·0′	2°16·3′W	FM	138,150
North Isle	Shetld	HU4524	60°0·2′	1°11·1′W	X	4
North Isle of Gletness	Shetld	HU4751	60°14·7′	1°8·6′W	X	3
North Ives	Brad	SE0335	53°48·9′	1°56·9′W	X	104
North Kaim	Renf	NS3461	55°49·1′	4°38·5′W	X	63
North Keanchulish	Highld	NC1100	57°57·2′	5°11·2′W	X	15
North Keig	Aberd	NJ5920	57°16·4′	2°40·3′W	X	37
North Kelsey	Lincs	TA0401	53°30·0′	0°25·5′W	T	112
North Kelsey Beck	Lincs	TA0202	53°30·5′	0°27·3′W	W	112
North Kelsey Carrs	Lincs	TA0100	53°29·5′	0°28·2′W	X	112
North Kelsey Moor	Lincs	TA0702	53°30·5′	0°22·8′W	T	112
North Kensington	Ken & Ch	TQ2381	51°31·1′	0°13·2′W	T	176
North Kenwood	Devon	SX9182	50°37·9′	3°32·1′W	X	192
North Kersebonny	Stir	NS7794	56°7·6′	3°58·3′W	X	57
North Kessock	Highld	NH6548	57°30·4′	4°14·7′W	T	26
North Kildarroch	D & G	NX3850	54°49·4′	4°30·9′W	X	83
North Kilduff	Pth & Kin	NO0601	56°11·8′	3°30·5′W	X	58
North Killimster	Highld	ND3255	58°28·9′	3°9·5′W	X	12
North Killingholme	N Lincs	TA1417	53°38·5′	0°16·1′W	T	113
North Killingholme Haven	N Lincs	TA1620	53°40·1′	0°14·2′W	W	107,113
North Kilrusken	N Ayr	NS2050	55°42·9′	4°51·5′W	X	63
North Kilvington	N Yks	SE4285	54°15·8′	1°20·9′W	T	99
North Kilworth	Leic	SP6183	52°26·7′	1°5·7′W	T	140
North Kilworth Ho	Leic	SP6083	52°26·7′	1°6·6′W	X	140
North Kilworth Mill Fm	Leic	SP6182	52°26·2′	1°5·8′W	FM	140
North Kingsfield	E Yorks	TA1462	54°2·7′	0°15·1′W	X	101
North Kingston	Hants	SU1602	50°49·3′	1°46·0′W	T	195
North Kingwell	Devon	SX7686	50°39·9′	3°44·9′W	X	191
North Kinkell	Pth & Kin	NN9316	56°19·7′	3°43·4′W	X	58
North Kirk Geo	Shetld	HU4483	60°32·0′	1°11·4′W	X	1,2,3
North Kirkton	Aberd	NK1050	57°32·7′	1°49·5′W	X	30
North Kirktonmoor	E Renf	NS5551	55°44·1′	4°18·1′W	X	64
North Kiscadale	N Ayr	NS0426	55°29·6′	5°5·7′W	T	69
North Knockandoch	Aberd	NJ5611	57°11·5′	2°43·2′W	X	37
North Knowe of Bodwell	Shetld	HU4149	60°13·7′	1°15·1′W	X	3
North Kyme	Lincs	TF1552	53°3·4′	0°16·6′W	T	121
North Kyme Common	Lincs	TF1554	53°4·5′	0°16·6′W	X	121
North Kyme Fen	Lincs	TF1653	53°3·9′	0°15·7′W	X	121
Northlade	Kent	TR0622	50°57·9′	0°56·4′E	X	189
North Laggan	Highld	NN2998	57°2·7′	4°48·7′W	X	34
North Laithes	Notts	SK6664	53°10·4′	1°0·3′W	X	120
North Lake Fm	Devon	SS7511	50°53·3′	3°46·3′W	FM	191
North Lambhill	Cumbr	NY4172	55°2·6′	2°55·0′W	X	85
North Lambielethan	Fife	NO5013	56°18·7′	2°48·0′W	X	59
North Lancing	W Susx	TQ1805	50°50·2′	0°19·1′W	T	198
Northland Corner	Devon	SS6739	51°8·3′	3°53·7′W	X	180
Northland Cross	Devon	SS7030	51°3·5′	3°50·9′W	X	180
Northlands	E Susx	TQ7727	51°1·1′	0°31·8′E	X	188,199
Northlands	E Yorks	SE9938	53°50·0′	0°29·3′W	X	106
Northlands	Lincs	TF3453	53°3·7′	0°0·4′E	T	122
Northlands	N Lincs	SE9220	53°40·3′	0°36·0′W	X	106,112
Northlands	Suff	TM0744	52°3·6′	1°1·6′E	X	155,169
Northlands	Wilts	SU2520	50°59·0′	1°38·2′W	X	184
Northlands	W Susx	SU8306	50°51·1′	0°48·9′W	X	197
Northlands	W Susx	TQ1335	51°6·4′	0°22·8′W	X	187
Northlands Fm	E Susx	TQ3925	51°0·7′	0°0·7′W	FM	198
Northlands Fm	Lincs	SK9388	53°23·1′	0°35·7′W	FM	112,121
Northlands Fm	N Yks	SE4254	53°59·1′	1°21·2′W	FM	105
Northlands Fm	W Susx	TQ2929	51°3·0′	0°9·2′W	FM	187,198
Northlands Fm	W Susx	TQ3927	51°1·8′	0°0·7′W	FM	187,198
North Lane	Devon	SS3312	50°53·2′	4°22·1′W	X	190
North Lane Fm	Red & Cl	NZ6914	54°31·2′	0°55·6′W	FM	94
North Lasts	C of Aber	NJ8304	57°7·9′	2°16·4′W	X	38
North Lauves	Aberd	NJ8759	57°37·5′	2°12·6′W	X	30
Northlea	Durham	NZ4150	54°50·8′	1°21·3′W	T	88
North Lea	Shetld	HU3051	60°14·8′	1°27·0′W	X	3
Northleach	Glos	SP1114	51°49·7′	1°50·0′W	T	163
Northleach Downs	Glos	SP1216	51°50·8′	1°49·2′W	X	163
North Leasow	Warw	SP3135	52°1·0′	1°32·5′W	X	151
North Leaze Fm	Somer	ST6128	51°3·2′	2°33·0′W	FM	183
North Leaze Fm	Swin	SU1995	51°39·4′	1°43·1′W	FM	163
North Leazes	Durham	NZ1727	54°38·5′	1°43·8′W	X	92
North Leckaway	Angus	NO4349	56°38·0′	2°55·3′W	X	54
North Ledaig	Arg & Bt	NM9036	56°28·4′	5°24·1′W	X	49
North Lee	Bucks	SP8308	51°46·1′	0°47·4′W	T	165
North Lee	N Eil	NF9366	57°35·0′	7°7·8′W	H	18
North Lee Fm	Devon	SS7129	51°3·0′	3°50·0′W	FM	180
North Lees	Derby	SK2383	53°20·8′	1°38·9′W	X	110
North Lees	N Yks	SE3073	54°9·4′	1°32·0′W	T	99
Northlees	Pth & Kin	NO1623	56°23·8′	3°21·2′W	X	53,58
North Lees	Shetld	HU3076	60°28·3′	1°26·8′W	X	3
North Lees Grange	N Yks	SE2974	54°9·9′	1°32·9′W	X	99
Northleigh	Devon	SS6034	51°5·5′	3°59·6′W	T	180
Northleigh	Devon	SY1996	50°45·7′	3°8·5′W	T	192,193
North Leigh	Kent	TR1347	51°11·2′	1°3·3′E	T	179,189
North Leigh	Oxon	SP3812	51°48·6′	1°26·5′W	T	164
Northleigh Cross	Devon	SS6035	51°6·1′	3°59·6′W	X	180
North Lethans	Fife	NT0595	56°8·6′	3°31·3′W	X	58
North Level	Medway	TQ8678	51°28·4′	0°41·1′E	X	178
North Level Main Drain	Cambs	TF3912	52°41·5′	0°3·8′E	W	131,142,143
North Leverton with Habblesthorpe	Notts	SK7882	53°20·0′	0°49·3′W	T	120,121
Northlew	Devon	SX5099	50°46·5′	4°7·3′W	T	191
Northlew Manor	Devon	SS4800	50°47·0′	4°9·0′W	X	191
Northleys	Pth & Kin	NO0830	56°27·4′	3°29·1′W	X	52,53
North Limbersey Fm	Beds	TL0539	52°2·6′	0°27·7′W	FM	153
North Links	Orkney	ND4897	58°51·7′	2°53·6′W	X	6,7
North Linn	C of Aber	NJ8203	57°7·3′	2°17·4′W	X	38
North Linrigg	N Lanak	NS8061	55°49·9′	3°54·5′W	X	65
North Linton Fm	Northum	NZ2592	55°13·5′	1°36·0′W	FM	81
North Lissens	N Ayr	NS3247	55°41·6′	4°39·9′W	X	63
North Littleton	Pth & Kin	NO1945	56°35·7′	3°18·7′W	X	53
North Littleton	Worcs	SP0847	52°7·5′	1°52·6′W	T	150
Northload Fm	Somer	ST4646	51°12·9′	2°46·0′W	FM	182
North Lobb	Devon	SS4738	51°7·5′	4°10·8′W	X	180
North Lobers	Orkney	ND4289	58°47·3′	2°59·7′W	X	7
North Loch	Orkney	HY7545	59°17·7′	2°25·8′W	W	5
North Loch	Shetld	HU4766	60°22·8′	1°8·4′W	W	2,3
North Lochboisdale	N Eil	NF7720	57°9·7′	7°20·1′W	T	31
North Lochbrowmoor	D & G	NY0889	55°11·5′	3°26·3′W	X	78
North Lodge	Beds	SP9663	52°15·6′	0°35·2′W	X	153
North Lodge	Cumbr	NY0843	54°46·7′	3°25·4′W	X	85
North Lodge	Cumbr	SD4287	54°16·8′	2°53·0′W	X	96,97
North Lodge	Lincs	SK8734	52°54·0′	0°42·0′W	X	130
North Lodge	Northnts	SP8773	52°21·1′	0°43·0′W	X	141
North Lodge	N Yks	SE3878	54°12·0′	1°24·6′W	X	99
North Lodge	Scot Bord	NT5622	55°29·6′	2°41·4′W	X	73
North Lodge Fm	Cambs	TL1176	52°22·5′	0°21·8′W	FM	142
North Lodge Fm	Enf	TQ2899	51°40·7′	0°8·5′W	FM	166,176
North Lodge Fm	Lincs	SK9835	52°54·4′	0°32·2′W	FM	130
North Lodge Fm	Northnts	TL0784	52°26·8′	0°25·1′W	FM	142
North Lodge Fm	Notts	SK5264	53°10·5′	1°12·9′W	FM	120
North Lodge Fm	Notts	SK6228	52°51·0′	1°4·4′W	FM	129
North Lodge Fm	Notts	SK7159	53°7·6′	0°55·9′W	FM	120
North Looe	Surrey	TQ2260	51°19·8′	0°14·5′W	T	176,187
North Lopham	Norf	TM0383	52°24·7′	0°59·5′E	T	144
North Lord's Land	Cumbr	SD7088	54°17·5′	2°27·2′W	X	98
North Lough Ho	Northum	NZ0671	55°2·3′	1°53·9′W	X	87
North Low	Northum	NU0445	55°42·2′	1°55·7′W	W	75
North Lowfields	N Yks	SE2995	54°21·2′	1°32·8′W	X	99
North Low Ho	Northum	NZ1480	55°7·1′	1°46·4′W	X	81
North Luffenham	Rut	SK9303	52°37·2′	0°37·2′W	T	141
North Lyham	Northum	NU0631	55°34·6′	1°53·9′W	X	75
North Lyne	Highld	NH5320	57°15·1′	4°25·7′W	X	26,35
North Lynn Fm	Norf	TF6121	52°46·0′	0°23·6′E	FM	132
North Mains	Aberd	NJ7406	57°8·9′	2°25·3′W	X	38
North Mains	Aberd	NJ7656	57°35·9′	2°23·6′W	X	29
North Mains	Aberd	NJ8828	57°20·8′	2°11·5′W	X	38
North Mains	Angus	NO4551	56°39·1′	2°53·4′W	X	54
North Mains	Angus	NO5452	56°39·7′	2°44·6′W	X	54
North Mains	Angus	NO6451	56°39·2′	2°34·8′W	X	54
North Mains	Angus	NO6947	56°37·1′	2°29·9′W	X	54
North Mains	E Loth	NT4170	55°55·4′	2°56·2′W	X	66
North Mains	Fife	NO3303	56°13·1′	3°4·4′W	X	59
North Mains	Pth & Kin	NN9216	56°19·7′	3°44·4′W	X	58
North Mains	Renf	NS4267	55°52·5′	4°31·1′W	X	64
North Mains	S Ayr	NS2708	55°20·4′	4°43·2′W	X	70,76
North Mains	W Loth	NT0173	55°56·6′	3°34·7′W	X	65
North Mains of Auchmaliddie	Aberd	NJ8845	57°30·0′	2°11·6′W	X	30
North Mains of Baldovan	Angus	NO3836	56°31·0′	3°0·0′W	X	54
North Mains of Barra	Aberd	NJ7926	57°19·7′	2°20·5′W	X	38
North Mains of Cononsyth	Angus	NO5746	56°36·5′	2°41·6′W	X	54
North Mains of Culsh	Aberd	NJ8749	57°32·1′	2°12·6′W	X	30
North Mains of Dun	Angus	NO6561	56°44·6′	2°33·9′W	X	45
North Mains of Invereigh	Angus	NO4446	56°36·4′	2°54·3′W	X	54
North Mains of Kinnettles	Angus	NO4346	56°36·4′	2°55·3′W	X	54
North Mains of Logie	Angus	NO3852	56°39·6′	3°0·2′W	X	54
North Mains of Turin	Angus	NO5253	56°40·2′	2°46·5′W	X	54
Northmanse	Orkney	HY7554	59°22·6′	2°25·9′W	X	5
North Marden	W Susx	SU8016	50°56·5′	0°51·3′W	T	197
North Marden Down	W Susx	SU8016	50°56·5′	0°51·3′W	X	197
North Marston	Bucks	SP7722	51°53·7′	0°52·5′W	T	165
Northmead Fm	S Glos	ST6875	51°28·6′	2°27·3′W	FM	172
North Meadow	Wilts	SU0994	51°38·9′	1°51·8′W	X	163,173
North Medburn Fm	Herts	TQ1797	51°39·8′	0°18·1′W	FM	166,176
North Medrox	N Lanak	NS7271	55°55·2′	4°2·5′W	X	64
North Medwin	S Lanak	NT0148	55°43·2′	3°34·1′W	W	72
North Middlemuir	Aberd	NJ8644	57°29·4′	2°13·6′W	X	30
North Middleton	Midlo	NT3559	55°49·4′	3°1·8′W	T	66,73
North Middleton	Northum	NT9924	55°30·8′	2°0·5′W	T	75
North Mid Field	Shetld	HU3755	60°16·9′	1°19·4′W	X	3
North Mid Frew	Stir	NS6797	56°9·1′	4°8·0′W	X	57
North Mid Hill	Scot Bord	NT4500	55°17·7′	2°51·5′W	X	79
North Milford Grange	N Yks	SE5038	53°50·4′	1°14·0′W	X	105
North Milford Hall	N Yks	SE5039	53°50·9′	1°14·0′W	X	105
North Mill	Devon	ST2504	50°50·1′	3°3·5′W	X	192,193
North Millbrex	Aberd	NJ8243	57°28·9′	2°17·6′W	X	29,30
North Millhill	Aberd	NJ6349	57°32·0′	2°36·6′W	X	29
North Milmain	D & G	NX0852	54°49·8′	4°58·9′W	T	82
North Milton	D & G	NX7047	54°48·3′	4°0·9′W	X	83,84
North Mire	Orkney	HY6237	59°13·3′	2°39·5′W	X	5
North Molton	Devon	SS7329	51°3·0′	3°48·3′W	T	180
North Molton Ridge	Devon	SS7732	51°4·7′	3°45·0′W	H	180
North Monecht	Aberd	NJ7406	57°8·9′	2°25·3′W	X	38
Northmoor	Devon	SS3016	50°55·3′	4°24·7′W	T	190
Northmoor	Devon	SX7588	50°41·0′	3°45·8′W	X	191
North Moor	E Yorks	TA2471	54°7·4′	0°5·7′W	X	101
Northmoor	Glos	SU0598	51°41·1′	1°55·3′W	X	163
North Moor	Kirk	SE1819	53°40·3′	1°43·2′W	X	110
North Moor	Lancs	SD3810	53°35·2′	2°55·8′W	X	108
North Moor	N Lincs	SE7909	53°34·5′	0°48·0′W	X	112
North Moor	N Yks	SD9878	54°12·1′	2°1·4′W	X	98
North Moor	N Yks	SE0778	54°12·1′	1°53·1′W	X	99
North Moor	N Yks	SE5191	54°19·0′	1°12·5′W	X	100
North Moor	N Yks	SE9586	54°15·9′	0°32·1′W	X	94,101
Northmoor	Oxon	SP4202	51°43·1′	1°23·1′W	T	164
Northmoor	Somer	SS9028	51°2·7′	3°33·8′W	X	181
North Moor	Somer	ST2145	51°12·2′	3°7·5′W	X	182
North Moor	Somer	ST3231	51°4·7′	2°57·9′W	X	182
North Moor	Somer	ST3830	51°4·2′	2°52·7′W	X	182
North Moor	Somer	ST5043	51°11·3′	2°42·5′W	X	182,183
North Moor	York	SE5846	53°54·7′	1°6·6′W	X	105
North Moor	York	SE6356	54°0·0′	1°1·9′W	X	105,106
Northmoor Corner	Somer	ST3130	51°4·1′	2°58·7′W	T	182
North Moor Fm	Lincs	TF0991	53°24·5′	0°21·2′W	FM	112
North Moor Fm	N Lincs	SE8212	53°36·1′	0°45·2′W	FM	112
North Moor Fm	Northum	NZ2877	55°5·4′	1°33·2′W	FM	88
North Moor Fm	N Yks	SE5171	54°8·2′	1°12·7′W	FM	100
North Moor Fm	N Yks	TA1078	54°11·4′	0°18·4′W	FM	101
North Moor Fm	Sund	NZ3359	54°55·7′	1°28·7′W	FM	88
Northmoor Green or Moorland	Somer	ST3332	51°5·2′	2°57·0′W	T	182
North Moor Ho	Lincs	TF1160	53°8·0′	0°20·1′W	X	121
North Moorhouse	E Renf	NS5252	55°44·6′	4°21·0′W	X	64
Northmoor Main Drain	Somer	ST3231	51°4·7′	2°57·9′W	W	182
North Moor Wood	N Yks	SE5191	54°19·0′	1°12·5′W	F	100
North Morar	Highld	NM7592	56°58·1′	5°41·6′W	X	33,40
Northmore Fm	Suff	TL6166	52°16·3′	0°22·0′E	FM	154
North Moreton	Oxon	SU5689	51°36·1′	1°11·1′W	T	174
North Morte Fm	Devon	SS4546	51°11·8′	4°12·7′W	FM	180
North Mosstown	Aberd	NK0656	57°35·9′	1°53·5′W	X	30
Northmostown	Devon	SY0989	50°41·7′	3°16·9′W	T	192
North Motherwell	N Lanak	NS7457	55°47·6′	4°0·1′W	T	64
North Moulsecoomb	Bri & Hov	TQ3307	50°51·1′	0°6·2′W	T	198
North Mount	E Yorks	TA1770	54°7·0′	0°12·2′W	X	101
North Mouth	Shetld	HU6872	60°25·8′	0°45·4′W	W	2
North Muasdale	Arg & Bt	NR6839	55°35·6′	5°40·5′W	X	68
Northmuir	Aberd	NJ7229	57°21·3′	2°27·5′W	X	38
Northmuir	Angus	NO3855	56°41·2′	3°0·2′W	T	54
North Muir	Scot Bord	NT1051	55°44·9′	3°25·6′W	H	65,72
North Mundham	W Susx	SU8702	50°48·9′	0°45·5′W	T	197
North Munstead	Surrey	SU9842	51°10·4′	0°35·5′W	X	186
North Murie	Pth & Kin	NO2224	56°24·4′	3°15·4′W	X	53,58
North Murnich	Highld	NH5220	57°15·1′	4°26·7′W	X	26,35
North Muskham	Notts	SK7958	53°7·0′	0°48·8′W	T	120,121
North Mymms Park	Herts	TL2104	51°43·5′	0°14·5′W	A	166
North Myvot	N Lanak	NS7372	55°55·7′	4°1·5′W	X	64
North Naaversgill	Shetld	HZ2072	59°32·3′	1°38·3′W	X	4
North Nab	N Yks	SE0856	54°0·2′	1°52·3′W	X	104
North Neaps	Shetld	HP4805	60°43·8′	1°6·7′W	X	1
North Ness	Fife	NO6500	56°11·7′	2°33·4′W	X	59
North Ness	Orkney	ND3091	58°48·3′	3°12·2′W	T	7
North Ness	Shetld	HU1861	60°20·2′	1°39·9′W	X	3
Northness	Shetld	HU4573	60°26·6′	1°10·4′W	X	2,3
North Ness	Shetld	HU4741	60°9·3′	1°8·7′W	X	4
North Nesting	Shetld	HU4559	60°19·0′	1°10·6′W	X	2,3
North Nevay	Angus	NO3244	56°35·2′	3°6·0′W	T	53
North Nevi	Orkney	HY6101	58°53·9′	2°40·1′W	X	6
North Newbald	E Yorks	SE9136	53°49·0′	0°36·7′W	T	106
North Newington	Oxon	SP4239	52°3·1′	1°22·9′W	T	151
North Newmill	Aberd	NJ8544	57°29·4′	2°14·6′W	X	30
North Newnton	Wilts	SU1257	51°19·0′	1°49·3′W	T	173
North Newton	Aberd	NJ5508	57°9·9′	2°44·2′W	X	37
North Newton	Aberd	NJ6930	57°21·8′	2°30·5′W	X	29
North Newton	Aberd	NJ8838	57°26·2′	2°11·5′W	X	30
North Newton	Shetld	HU2856	60°17·5′	1°29·1′W	X	3
North Newton	Somer	ST3031	51°4·7′	2°59·6′W	T	182
Northney	Hants	SU7303	50°49·5′	0°57·4′W	T	197
North Nib	Aberd	NJ5513	57°12·6′	2°44·2′W	X	37
North Nibley	Glos	ST7395	51°39·4′	2°23·0′W	T	162
North Nittanshead	Aberd	NJ8654	57°34·8′	2°13·6′W	X	30
North Norfolk Railway	Norf	TG1343	52°56·8′	1°10·6′E	X	133
North Northlands Fm	E Susx	TQ4027	51°1·7′	0°0·2′E	FM	187,198
North Oakley	Hants	SU5354	51°17·2′	1°14·0′W	T	185
North Oakley Inclosure	Hants	SU2307	50°52·0′	1°40·0′W	F	195
North Oaks	N Yks	SE1867	54°6·2′	1°43·1′W	X	99
North Ockendon	Hav	TQ5985	51°32·7′	0°18·0′E	T	177
Northolme	Lincs	TF3514	52°42·6′	0°0·3′E	X	131
Northolm Fm	Peterb	TF2304	52°37·4′	0°10·6′W	FM	142
Northolt	Ealing	TQ1384	51°32·8′	0°21·8′W	T	176
Northolt Aerodrome	Hill	TQ0984	51°32·9′	0°25·3′W	X	176
Northop	I of M	SC3080	54°11·5′	4°35·9′W	X	95
Northop Brook	Flint	SJ2468	53°12·5′	3°7·9′W	W	117
Northop Hall	Flint	SJ2767	53°11·9′	3°5·2′W	T	117
Northophall Fm	Flint	SJ2668	53°12·5′	3°6·1′W	FM	117
Northop or Llan-eurgain	Flint	SJ2468	53°12·5′	3°7·9′W	T	117
North or Little Port of Spittal	D & G	NX0253	54°50·2′	5°4·6′W	X	82
North Ormesby	Midd	NZ5119	54°34·1′	1°12·2′W	T	93
North Ormsby	Lincs	TF2893	53°25·3′	0°4·0′W	T	113
Northorpe	Barns	SE3000	53°30·0′	1°32·5′W	X	110,111
Northorpe	Kirk	SE2120	53°40·8′	1°40·5′W	T	104
Northorpe	Lincs	SK8997	53°28·0′	0°39·1′W	T	112
Northorpe	Lincs	TF0917	52°44·6′	0°22·7′W	T	130

Northorpe	Lincs	TF2036	52°54·7'	0°12·5'W	T	131
Northorpe Beck	Lincs	SK8897	53°28·0'	0°40·1'W	W	112
Northorpe Fen	Lincs	TF1218	52°45·1'	0°20·0'W	X	130
Northorpe Fm	Lincs	TF4166	53°10·6'	0°7·0'E	FM	122
Northorpe Ho	Lincs	TF1936	52°54·7'	0°13·4'W	X	130
Northorpe Lodge	Lincs	TF0918	52°45·1'	0°22·7'W	X	130
North Orrock	Aberd	NJ9519	57°16·0'	2°4·5'W	X	38
North Otterington	N Yks	SE3689	54°18·0'	1°26·4'W	X	99
Northover	Somer	ST4838	51°8·6'	2°44·2'W	T	182
Northover	Somer	ST5223	51°0·5'	2°40·7'W	T	183
Northover Fm	E Susx	TQ5624	50°59·9'	0°13·8'E	FM	199
Northover Fm	W Susx	TQ1814	50°55·0'	0°18·9'W	FM	198
North Owersby	Lincs	TF0694	53°26·2'	0°23·8'W	T	112
North Owl	N Yks	SE2265	54°5·1'	1°39·4'W	X	99
Northowram	Cald	SE1126	53°44·1'	1°49·6'W	T	104
North Oxen-le-Fields	Darl	NZ2811	54°29·9'	1°33·6'W	X	93
North Palmerston	E Ayr	NS5020	55°27·3'	4°21·9'W	X	70
Northpark	Aberd	NK0057	57°36·4'	1°59·5'W	X	30
Northpark	Arg & Bt	NS0260	55°47·8'	5°9·1'W	X	63
North Park	D & G	NW9872	55°0·3'	5°9·1'W	X	76,82
Northpark	D & G	NX9074	55°3·2'	3°42·9'W	X	84
Northpark	D & G	NY0366	54°59·0'	3°30·5'W	X	84
North Park	E Yorks	TA2131	53°45·9'	0°9·4'W	X	107
North Park	Leeds	SE3145	53°54·3'	1°31·3'W	X	104
Northpark Copse	W Susx	SU8826	51°1·8'	0°44·3'W	F	186,197
North Park Fm	Hants	SU3733	51°5·9'	1°27·9'W	FM	185
North Park Fm	Notts	SK7566	53°11·4'	0°52·2'W	FM	120
North Park Fm	Suff	TM1858	52°10·9'	1°11·7'E	FM	156
North Park Fm	Surrey	TQ3452	51°15·3'	0°4·4'W	FM	187
North Parks Fms	N Yks	SE3076	54°11·0'	1°32·0'W	FM	99
Northpark Wood	Devon	SX3981	50°36·6'	4°16·2'W	F	201
North Park Wood	Hants	SU3733	51°5·9'	1°27·9'W	F	185
Northpark Wood	W Susx	TQ0515	50°55·7'	0°30·0'W	F	197
North Pasture	N Yks	SE2065	54°5·1'	1°41·2'W	X	99
Northpasture Fm	E Yorks	TA1156	53°59·5'	0°18·0'W	FM	107
North Peat Geo	Orkney	HY4943	59°16·5'	2°53·2'W	X	5
North Perrott	Somer	ST4709	50°52·9'	2°44·8'W	T	193
North Petherton	Somer	ST2933	51°5·7'	3°0·5'W	T	182
North Petherwin	Corn	SX2889	50°40·8'	4°25·7'W	T	190
North Pickenham	Norf	TF8606	52°37·4'	0°45·3'E	T	144
North Pickenham Warren	Norf	TF8405	52°36·9'	0°43·5'E	X	144
North Piddle	Worcs	SO9654	52°11·3'	2°3·1'W	T	150
North Pier	Blackp	SD3036	53°49·2'	3°3·4'W	X	102
North Pier	N Tyne	NZ3769	55°1·1'	1°24·9'W	X	88
North Pike	Northum	NT9713	55°24·9'	2°2·4'W	X	81
North Pirehill Fm	Staffs	SJ8931	52°52·8'	2°9·4'W	FM	127
North Piteadie	Fife	NT2589	56°5·5'	3°11·9'W	X	66
North Pit Fm	Sund	NZ3348	54°49·8'	1°28·8'W	FM	88
North Pitglassie	Aberd	NJ6944	57°29·4'	2°30·6'W	X	29
North Plain	Cumbr	NY1961	54°56·5'	3°15·4'W	X	85
North Planks	Lancs	SD5139	53°50·9'	2°44·3'W	X	102
North Plantation	Staffs	SK0240	52°57·7'	1°57·8'W	F	119,128
North Plantn	E Yorks	SE8351	53°57·1'	0°43·7'W	F	106
North Plantn	E Yorks	TA0463	54°3·4'	0°24·3'W	F	101
North Plantn	E Yorks	TA1738	53°49·7'	0°12·9'W	F	107
North Plantn	Northum	NU0225	55°31·4'	1°57·7'W	F	75
North Plantn	N Yks	SE8462	54°3·1'	0°42·6'W	F	100
North Plantn	N Yks	SE8562	54°3·1'	0°41·7'W	F	100
North Plumley Fm	Hants	SU1210	50°53·6'	1°49·4'W	FM	195
North Point	Orkney	ND3297	58°51·6'	3°10·2'W	X	6,7
North Point	Shetld	HU3982	60°31·4'	1°16·9'W	X	1,2,3
North Point	Shetld	HU5463	60°21·1'	1°0·8'W	X	2
Northpoint Beach	E Susx	TQ9319	50°56·5'	0°45·2'E	X	189
North Point of Toabsgeo	Shetld	HU3811	59°53·2'	1°18·8'W	X	4
North Polduie	Moray	NJ2739	57°26·4'	3°12·5'W	X	28
North Pole Fm	Norf	TF8029	52°49·9'	0°40·7'E	FM	132
North Pool	Devon	SX7741	50°15·6'	3°43·2'W	X	202
North Poorton	Dorset	SY5198	50°47·0'	2°41·3'W	T	194
North Port	Arg & Bt	NN0421	56°20·7'	5°9·8'W	X	50,56
Northport	Dorset	SY9288	50°41·7'	2°6·4'W	T	195
Northport Heath	Dorset	SY9189	50°42·3'	2°7·3'W	F	195
North Porton	Renf	NS4471	55°54·7'	4°29·3'W	X	64
North Poulner	Hants	SU1606	50°51·4'	1°46·0'W	T	195
North Pourie	Angus	NO4135	56°30·5'	2°57·1'W	X	54
North Priorhill	S Lanak	NS7540	55°38·5'	3°58·7'W	X	71
Northpund	Shetld	HU3556	60°17·5'	1°21·5'W	X	2,3
Northpunds	Shetld	HU4022	59°59·1'	1°16·5'W	T	4
North Quarme	Somer	SS9236	51°7·0'	3°32·2'W	X	181
North Quarter	Fife	NO5711	56°17·6'	2°41·2'W	X	59
North Queensferry	Fife	NT1380	56°0·6'	3°23·3'W	T	65
North Queich	Pth & Kin	NO0804	56°13·4'	3°28·6'W	W	58
North Quilkoe	Angus	NO4553	56°40·2'	2°53·4'W	X	54
Northquoy	Orkney	HY5307	58°57·1'	2°48·5'W	X	6,7
Northquoy Point	Orkney	HY5507	58°57·1'	2°46·4'W	X	6
North Radworthy	Devon	SS7534	51°5·7'	3°46·7'W	T	180
North Rauceby	Lincs	TF0246	53°0·3'	0°28·4'W	T	130
North Rauceby Heath	Lincs	TF0047	53°0·9'	0°30·2'W	X	130
Northra Voe	Shetld	HU2961	60°20·2'	1°28·0'W	W	3
North Rayne	Aberd	NJ6831	57°22·4'	2°31·5'W	T	29
North Redbog	Aberd	NJ9955	57°35·4'	2°0·5'W	X	30
North Redbriggs	Aberd	NJ7946	57°30·5'	2°20·6'W	X	29,30
North Reddish	Stock	SJ8994	53°26·8'	2°9·5'W	T	109
North Reins	Northum	NU2713	55°24·9'	1°34·0'W	X	81
Northrepps	Norf	TG2439	52°54·3'	1°20·3'E	T	133
Northrepps Hall	Norf	TG2339	52°54·4'	1°19·4'E	X	133
North Reston	Lincs	TF3883	53°19·8'	0°4·7'E	T	122
North Riccalton	Scot Bord	NT7313	55°24·9'	2°25·2'W	X	80
North Riddingwood	D & G	NX9785	55°9·2'	3°36·6'W	X	78
Northridge	Devon	SX8696	50°45·4'	3°36·3'W	X	191
North Ridge Common	Devon	SS7141	51°9·5'	3°50·3'W	H	180
North Riding	Northum	NY9495	55°15·2'	2°5·2'W	X	80
Northrig	E Loth	NT5472	55°56·6'	2°43·8'W	X	66
Northrigg Fm	N Lanak	NS9166	55°52·7'	3°44·1'W	FM	65
Northrigg Fm	W Loth	NS9166	55°52·7'	3°44·1'W	FM	65
Northrigg Hill	Cumbr	NY5765	54°58·9'	2°39·9'W	X	86
North Riggins	Aberd	NJ4847	57°30·9'	2°51·6'W	X	28,29
Northri Gill	Shetld	HU3513	59°54·3'	1°22·0'W	X	4
North Rigton	N Yks	SE2749	53°56·4'	1°34·9'W	T	104
North Ripley	Hants	SZ1699	50°47·7'	1°46·0'W	T	195
North River	W Susx	TQ1436	51°6·9'	0°21·9'W	W	187

North Rode	Ches	SJ8866	53°11·7'	2°10·4'W	T	118
North Roe	Shetld	HU3487	60°34·2'	1°22·3'W	X	1,2
North Roe	Shetld	HU3689	60°35·2'	1°20·1'W	T	1,2
North Ronaldsay	Orkney	HY7553	59°22·0'	2°25·9'W	X	5
North Ronaldsay Firth	Orkney	HY7549	59°19·9'	2°25·9'W	W	5
North Ross Fm	E Yorks	SE7241	53°51·9'	0°53·9'W	FM	105,106
North Rotten Burn	N Ayr	NS2667	55°52·1'	4°46·4'W	W	63
North Row	Cumbr	NY2232	54°40·9'	3°12·2'W	T	89,90
North Rowens	Shrops	SJ2907	52°39·6'	3°2·6'W	X	126
North Row Fm	Newp	ST4084	51°33·3'	2°51·5'W	FM	171,172
North Runcton	Norf	TF6415	52°42·7'	0°26·1'E	T	132
North Russell	Devon	SX5092	50°42·7'	4°7·1'W	X	191
North Rye Ho	Glos	SP2028	51°57·2'	1°42·1'W	X	163
North Saltwick	Northum	NZ1781	55°7·6'	1°43·6'W	X	81
North Sand	Orkney	HY4533	59°11·1'	2°57·3'W	X	5,6
North Sandlaw	Aberd	NJ6960	57°38·0'	2°30·7'W	X	29
North Sands	E Yorks	TA1967	54°5·3'	0°10·4'W	X	101
North Sands	Hartpl	NZ5035	54°42·7'	1°13·0'W	X	93
North Sands	S Ayr	NS3231	55°32·9'	4°39·3'W	X	70
North Sandwick	Shetld	HU5496	60°38·9'	1°0·2'W	X	1
North Sannox	N Ayr	NS0046	55°40·2'	5°10·4'W	X	63,69
North Scale	Cumbr	SD1870	54°7·4'	3°14·9'W	T	96
North Scales	Cumbr	NY5154	54°53·0'	2°45·4'W	X	86
North Scar	Cumbr	SD1670	54°7·4'	3°16·7'W	X	96
North Scarle	Lincs	SK8466	53°11·3'	0°44·2'W	T	121
North Scoo	Shetld	HU4330	60°3·4'	1°13·2'W	H	4
North Score Holm	Shetld	HU3443	60°10·5'	1°22·7'W	X	4
North Scotstarvit	Fife	NO3510	56°16·9'	3°2·5'W	X	59
North Screapadal	Highld	NG5744	57°25·5'	6°2·4'W	X	24
North Sea Camp	Lincs	TF3739	52°56·1'	0°2·7'E	X	131
Northseat	Aberd	NJ8933	57°23·5'	2°10·5'W	X	30
Northseat	Aberd	NJ9340	57°27·3'	2°6·5'W	X	30
North Seat	E Susx	TQ8412	50°52·9'	0°37·3'E	X	199
North Seaton	Northum	NZ2986	55°10·3'	1°32·3'W	T	81
North Seaton Colliery	Northum	NZ2985	55°9·8'	1°32·3'W	T	81
North Selby Mine	York	SE6444	53°53·5'	1°1·2'W	X	105,106
North Setter	Shetld	HU4143	60°10·4'	1°15·2'W	X	4
North Sheen	Rich	TQ1976	51°28·5'	0°16·8'W	T	176
North Shian	Arg & Bt	NM9143	56°32·2'	5°23·5'W	T	49
Northshield Rings	Scot Bord	NT2549	55°44·0'	3°11·2'W	X	73
Northshields	Falk	NS7783	56°1·7'	3°58·0'W	X	57,64
North Shields	N Tyne	NZ3568	55°0·6'	1°26·7'W	T	88
North Ship Channel	Dorset	SY6977	50°35·7'	2°25·9'W	W	194
North Shoebury	Sou-on-Sea	TQ9286	51°32·6'	0°46·5'E	T	178
North Shore	Blackp	SD3038	53°50·3'	3°3·4'W	T	102
North Shortcleugh	S Lanak	NS9217	55°26·4'	3°42·0'W	X	71,78
North Shun	Shetld	HU3861	60°20·1'	1°18·2'W	W	2,3
Northside	Aberd	NJ7231	57°22·4'	2°27·5'W	X	29
Northside	Aberd	NJ8106	57°8·9'	2°18·4'W	X	38
Northside	Aberd	NJ8554	57°34·8'	2°14·6'W	X	30
North Side	Cumbr	NY0029	54°39·0'	3°32·6'W	T	89
North Side	Cumbr	NY5805	54°26·6'	2°38·4'W	X	91
North Side	Durham	NZ0214	54°31·5'	1°57·7'W	X	92
North Side	Durham	NZ1438	54°44·5'	1°46·5'W	X	92
North Side	Durham	NZ3735	54°42·8'	1°25·1'W	X	93
North Side	Norf	TG0145	52°58·1'	1°0·0'E	X	133
Northside	Northum	NY9882	55°8·2'	2°1·5'W	X	81
North Side	Northum	NZ1185	55°9·8'	1°49·2'W	X	81
North Side	N Yks	SE9292	54°19·2'	0°34·7'W	X	94,101
Northside	Orkney	HY2528	59°8·2'	3°18·2'W	T	6
North Side	Peterb	TL2799	52°34·7'	0°7·1'W	T	142
North Side	W Susx	SU9214	50°55·3'	0°41·1'W	X	197
Northside Fm	E Yorks	SE8026	53°43·7'	0°46·8'W	FM	106
Northside Fm	E Yorks	TA0664	54°3·9'	0°22·4'W	FM	101
Northside Fm	Hants	SU6132	51°5·3'	1°7·4'W	FM	185
North Side Fm	Northum	NZ0867	55°0·1'	1°52·1'W	FM	88
Northside Head	N Yks	SE0975	54°10·5'	1°51·3'W	X	99
North Side Ho	N Yks	SE9292	54°19·2'	0°34·7'W	X	94,101
North Side Moss	N Yks	SE0964	54°4·6'	1°51·3'W	X	99
North Side Wood	Somer	ST6922	51°0·0'	2°26·1'W	F	183
Northskaill	Orkney	HY6844	59°17·1'	2°33·2'W	X	5
North Skelmanae	Aberd	NJ9159	57°37·5'	2°8·6'W	X	30
North Skelmanae	Aberd	NJ8840	57°27·3'	2°11·5'W	X	30
North Skelton	Red & Cl	NZ6718	54°33·4'	0°57·4'W	T	94
North Skerry	Shetld	HU1065	60°22·4'	1°48·6'W	X	3
North Slipperfield	Scot Bord	NT1251	55°44·9'	3°23·7'W	X	65,72
North Snods	Northum	NZ0651	54°51·5'	1°54·0'W	X	87
North Somercotes	Lincs	TF4296	53°26·5'	0°8·7'E	T	113
North Sound	Shetld	HP5606	60°44·3'	0°57·9'W	W	1
North Sound	Shetld	HU3073	60°26·6'	1°26·8'W	W	3
North Sound	Shetld	HU3170	60°25·0'	1°25·7'W	W	3
North Sound, The	Orkney	HY5645	59°17·6'	2°45·9'W	W	5
North Spinney	Northnts	SP9999	52°35·0'	0°31·9'W	F	141
North Stack (Ynys Arw)	I of Angl	SH2183	53°19·1'	4°40·8'W	X	114
North Stainley	N Yks	SE2876	54°11·0'	1°33·8'W	T	99
North Stainley	N Yks	SE2975	54°10·4'	1°32·9'W	X	99
North Stainmore	Cumbr	NY8315	54°32·0'	2°15·3'W	T	91,92
North Standen Ho	W Berks	SU3167	51°24·3'	1°32·9'W	X	174
North Stane	Shetld	HP6613	60°47·9'	0°46·7'W	X	1
North Stank Fm	Cumbr	SD2371	54°8·0'	3°10·3'W	FM	96
North Stany Hill	Shetld	HU4641	60°9·3'	1°9·8'W	X	4
North Star	Devon	SY0885	50°39·7'	3°17·7'W	T	192
North Steel	Northum	NU2904	55°20·0'	1°32·1'W	X	81
North Steinmanhill	Aberd	NJ7643	57°28·9'	2°23·6'W	X	29
North Stifford	Thurr	TQ6080	51°30·0'	0°18·7'E	T	177
North Stoke	Bath & NE Somer	ST7069	51°25·4'	2°25·5'W	T	172
North Stoke	Oxon	SU6186	51°34·4'	1°6·8'W	T	175
North Stoke	W Susx	TQ0210	50°53·1'	0°32·6'W	T	197
North Stole	Shetld	HU2077	60°28·8'	1°37·7'W	X	3
North Stoneham	Hants	SU4317	50°57·3'	1°22·9'W	T	185
Northstow	Shetld	HU2179	60°29·9'	1°36·6'W	X	3
North Stow Hall	Suff	TL8175	52°20·8'	0°39·8'E	X	144
North Straiton	Fife	NO4223	56°24·0'	2°55·9'W	X	54,59
North Stream	Kent	TR2266	51°21·2'	1°11·7'E	W	179
North Stream	Kent	TR3556	51°15·5'	1°22·5'E	W	179
North Street	Hants	SU1518	50°57·9'	1°46·8'W	T	184
North Street	Hants	SU6433	51°5·8'	1°4·8'W	T	185
North Street	Kent	TR0158	51°17·5'	0°52·4'E	T	178,179
North Street	Medway	TQ8174	51°26·4'	0°36·7'E	T	178

North Street	W Berks	SU6372	51°26·8'	1°5·2'W	T	175
North Stroud Fm	Hants	SU7123	51°0·3'	0°58·9'W	FM	197
North Studdock	Pemb	SM8502	51°40·8'	5°6·2'W	X	157
North Sunderland	Northum	NU2131	55°34·6'	1°39·6'W	T	75
North Sutor	Highld	NH8168	57°41·4'	3°59·3'W	X	21,27
North Sweeming	N Yks	SE5333	53°47·7'	1°11·3'W	X	105
North Sydmonton Ho	Hants	SU4962	51°21·5'	1°17·4'W	X	174
North Synton	Scot Bord	NT4823	55°30·1'	2°49·0'W	T	73
North Taing	Orkney	HY6125	59°6·9'	2°40·4'W	X	5
North Taing	Orkney	HY6128	59°8·5'	2°40·4'W	X	5
North Taing	Orkney	HY6717	59°2·6'	2°34·0'W	X	5
North Taing	Orkney	ND3691	58°48·4'	3°6·0'W	X	7
North Taing	Orkney	ND4784	58°44·7'	2°54·5'W	X	7
North Taing	Shetld	HU4640	60°8·8'	1°9·8'W	X	4
North Taing	Shetld	HU5379	60°29·7'	1°1·6'W	X	2,3
North Tamerton	Corn	SX3197	50°45·1'	4°23·4'W	T	190
North Tanfield	N Yks	SE2680	54°13·1'	1°35·7'W	X	99
North Tanton Fm	N Yks	NZ5211	54°29·7'	1°11·4'W	FM	93
North Tararet	Shetld	HU4463	60°21·2'	1°11·7'W	X	2,3
North Tarbothill	Aberd	NJ9513	57°12·7'	2°4·5'W	X	38
North Tarbrax	Angus	NO4342	56°34·2'	2°55·2'W	X	54
North Tarrel	Highld	NH8981	57°48·6'	3°51·6'W	X	21
North Tarwathie	Aberd	NJ9559	57°37·5'	2°4·6'W	X	30
North Tawton	Devon	SS6601	50°47·8'	3°53·7'W	T	191
North Techmuiry	Aberd	NJ9560	57°38·1'	2°4·6'W	X	30
North Teign River	Devon	SX6486	50°39·7'	3°55·1'W	W	191
North Terminal	W Susx	TQ2741	51°9·5'	0°10·6'W	X	187
North Teuchan Croft	Aberd	NK0839	57°26·7'	1°51·5'W	X	30
North Third Resr	Stir	NS7589	56°4·9'	4°0·1'W	W	57
North Thoresby	Lincs	TF2998	53°28·0'	0°3·0'W	T	113
North Thornber	N Yks	SD8154	53°59·1'	2°17·0'W	X	103
North Thornberry	Durham	NZ0115	54°32·1'	1°58·7'W	X	92
North Thorne	Devon	SS6441	51°9·4'	3°56·3'W	X	180
North Thorne	Devon	SX4095	50°44·2'	4°15·7'W	X	190
North Thorne Village	Devon	SS6441	51°9·4'	3°56·3'W	A	180
North Threave	S Ayr	NS2404	55°18·2'	4°45·9'W	X	76
North Thundergay or Lenimore	N Ayr	NR8847	55°40·5'	5°21·9'W	X	62,69
North Tidworth	Wilts	SU2348	51°14·1'	1°39·8'W	T	184
North Tifty	Aberd	NJ7841	57°27·8'	2°21·5'W	X	29,30
North Tilbouries	Aberd	NO8298	57°4·6'	2°17·4'W	X	38,45
North Tillydaff	Aberd	NJ7107	57°9·4'	2°28·3'W	X	38
North Toft	N Yks	SE6835	53°48·6'	0°57·6'W	X	105,106
North Toft	Orkney	HY4630	59°9·5'	2°56·2'W	X	5,6
North Togston	Northum	NU2502	55°18·9'	1°35·9'W	T	81
Northton	Aberd	NJ7703	57°7·3'	2°22·3'W	X	38
Northton	N Eil	NF9989	57°47·6'	7°3·5'W	T	18
North Top	Aberd	NJ0900	57°5·2'	3°29·6'W	H	36
North Touxhill	Aberd	NJ9041	57°27·8'	2°9·5'W	X	30
Northtown	Aberd	NJ8449	57°32·1'	2°15·6'W	X	29,30
North Town	Devon	SS5109	50°51·9'	4°6·7'W	T	191
North Town	Hants	SU8750	51°14·8'	0°44·8'W	T	186
Northtown	Orkney	ND4797	58°51·7'	2°54·6'W	T	6,7
North Town	Shetld	HU3912	59°53·7'	1°17·7'W	T	4
North Town	Somer	ST5642	51°10·8'	2°37·4'W	T	182,183
North Town	Somer	ST6328	51°3·2'	2°31·3'W	T	183
North Town	Win & Maid	SU8882	51°32·0'	0°43·5'W	T	175
Northtown of Falfield	Fife	NO4509	56°16·5'	2°52·8'W	X	59
North Tregeare	Corn	SX2288	50°40·1'	4°30·8'W	X	190
North Trekeive	Corn	SX2270	50°30·4'	4°30·2'W	X	201
North Treviddo	Corn	SX2762	50°26·2'	4°25·8'W	X	201
North Trewick	Northum	NZ1080	55°7·1'	1°50·2'W	X	81
North Trigon Fm	Dorset	SY8990	50°42·8'	2°9·0'W	FM	195
North Tuddenham	Norf	TG0413	52°40·8'	1°1·5'E	T	133
North Two Mark	D & G	NX0752	54°49·8'	4°59·9'W	X	82
North Ugie Water	Aberd	NJ9256	57°35·9'	2°7·6'W	W	30
North Uist	N Eil	NF8369	57°36·2'	7°18·0'W	X	18
North Uist (Uibhist a Tuath)	N Eil	NF8661	57°32·1'	7°14·4'W	X	22
Northumberland Fm	Pemb	SM9918	51°49·7'	4°54·6'W	FM	157,158
Northumberland Heath	Bexley	TQ5077	51°28·5'	0°10·0'E	T	177
North Unigarth	Orkney	HY2521	59°4·4'	3°18·0'W	X	6
North Upton	Devon	SX6844	50°17·1'	3°50·8'W	X	202
North Urn Fm	Hartpl	NZ4633	54°41·6'	1°16·8'W	FM	93
North Uya Taing	Shetld	HU5365	60°22·2'	1°1·8'W	X	2,3
North Vatson Fm	Pemb	SN1104	51°42·4'	4°43·7'W	FM	158
Northville	Torf	ST2996	51°39·7'	3°1·2'W	T	171
North Voe	Shetld	HU3060	60°19·6'	1°26·9'W	W	3
North Voe	Shetld	HU3637	60°7·2'	1°20·6'W	W	4
North Voe	Shetld	HU5462	60°20·6'	1°0·8'W	W	2
North Voe of Clousta	Shetld	HU3058	60°18·6'	1°26·9'W	W	3
North Voe of Gletness	Shetld	HU4752	60°15·2'	1°8·6'W	W	3
North Voxter	Shetld	HU4328	60°2·3'	1°13·2'W	X	4
North Walbottle	N upon Ty	NZ1767	55°0·1'	1°43·6'W	T	88
North Wald	Orkney	HY3817	59°2·4'	3°4·3'W	X	6
North Wales Path	Gwyn	SH5971	53°13·3'	4°6·3'W	X	114,115
North Walk Fm	Lincs	TF2085	53°21·1'	0°11·4'W	FM	122
North Walks	Suff	TM4667	52°15·0'	1°36·6'E	X	156
Northwall	Orkney	HY7444	59°17·2'	2°26·9'W	X	5
North Walney	Cumbr	SD1769	54°6·9'	3°15·8'W	T	96
North Walsham	Norf	TG2830	52°49·4'	1°23·5'E	T	133
North Walsham Wood	Norf	TG2528	52°48·4'	1°20·7'E	F	133,134
North Waltham	Hants	SU5646	51°12·9'	1°11·5'W	T	185
North Wamses	Northum	NU2338	55°38·3'	1°37·6'W	X	75
Northward	I Scilly	SV8915	49°57·5'	6°19·8'W	T	203
North Ward	Shetld	HU2958	60°18·6'	1°28·0'W	H	3
North Ward	Shetld	HU3165	60°22·3'	1°25·8'W	H	3
North Ward	Shetld	HU3361	60°20·2'	1°23·6'W	H	2,3
North Ward	Shetld	HU3671	60°25·5'	1°20·3'W	H	2,3
North Ward Fm	Devon	SX4268	50°29·7'	4°13·3'W	FM	201
Northward Hill	Medway	TQ7876	51°27·5'	0°34·1'E	F	178
North Ward of Reafirth	Shetld	HU5088	60°34·6'	1°4·8'W	X	1,2
North Warnborough	Hants	SU7351	51°15·4'	0°56·8'W	T	186
North Warrackston	Aberd	NJ5521	57°16·9'	2°44·3'W	X	37
North Warren	Suff	TM4558	52°10·2'	1°35·4'E	X	156
North Warren Hill	Dorset	SY4899	50°47·5'	2°43·9'W	X	193
North Water	Shetld	HP5813	60°48·0'	0°55·6'W	W	1
North Water Bridge	Angus	NO6566	56°47·3'	2°33·9'W	T	45
North Waterhayne	Devon	ST2508	50°52·2'	3°3·6'W	T	192,193

North Water of Wormadale	Shetld	HU4045	60°11·5′	1°16·2′W	W	4
North Watford	Herts	TQ1098	51°40·4′	0°24·2′W	T	166,176
North Watten	Highld	ND2458	58°30·5′	3°17·8′W	X	11,12
North Watten Moss	Highld	ND2459	58°31·0′	3°17·8′W	X	11,12
Northway	Devon	SS3823	50°59·3′	4°18·1′W	T	190
Northway	Devon	SX7276	50°34·4′	3°48·1′W	X	191
Northway	Glos	SO9233	52°0·0′	2°6·6′W	T	150
Northway	Somer	ST1329	51°3·5′	3°14·1′W	T	181,193
Northway	Swan	SS5889	51°35·2′	4°2·6′W	T	159
North Weald Bassett	Essex	TL4904	51°43·1′	0°9·8′E	T	167
Northweek	Devon	SS6402	50°48·3′	3°55·4′W	X	191
North Weir Point	Suff	TM3743	52°2·3′	1°27·7′E	X	169
North Weirs	Hants	SU2802	50°49·2′	1°35·8′W	T	195
North Wells	Aberd	NJ7138	57°26·1′	2°28·5′W	X	29
North Wembley	Brent	TQ1786	51°33·9′	0°18·3′W	T	176
North Westerhouse	Shetld	HU5289	60°35·1′	1°2·6′W	X	1,2
North Western or New Cut	Cambs	TL2291	52°30·4′	0°11·7′W	W	142
North Westfield	C of Aber	NJ8403	57°7·3′	2°15·4′W	X	38
Northwest Fm	Northnts	SP5652	52°10·0′	1°10·5′W	FM	152
North Weston	N Som	ST4675	51°28·5′	2°46·3′W	T	171,172
North Weston	Oxon	SP6805	51°44·6′	1°0·5′W	T	164,165
North West Passage	Devon	SX5982	50°37·5′	3°59·2′W	X	191
North West Passage	I Scilly	SV8411	49°55·2′	6°23·8′W	W	203
North West Point	Devon	SS1248	51°12·3′	4°41·1′W	X	180
North West Point	V of Glam	ST2164	51°22·4′	3°7·7′W	X	171,182
Northwethel	I Scilly	SV8916	49°58·0′	6°19·9′W	X	203
North Wharf	Lancs	SD3149	53°56·2′	3°2·6′W	X	102
North Wheatley	Notts	SK7585	53°21·6′	0°52·0′W	T	112,120
North Whilborough	Devon	SX8766	50°29·2′	3°35·2′W	T	202
North Whilk	Shetld	HU3073	60°26·6′	1°26·8′W	X	3
North Whitehouse	Essex	TL7418	51°50·2′	0°31·9′E	X	167
North Whitehouse Fm	Northum	NZ1981	55°7·6′	1°41·7′W	FM	81
North Whiteley	Moray	NJ4347	57°30·8′	2°56·6′W	X	28
Northwich	Ches	SJ6573	53°15·4′	2°31·1′W	T	118
North Wick	Bath & NE Somer	ST5865	51°23·2′	2°35·8′W	T	172,182
Northwick	Essex	TQ7583	51°31·4′	0°31·7′E	X	178
North Wick	Orkney	HY5093	59°21·9′	2°52·3′W	W	5
Northwick	S Glos	ST5686	51°34·5′	2°37·7′W	T	172
North Wick	Shetld	HU3292	60°36·9′	1°24·4′W	W	1
Northwick	Somer	ST3548	51°13·9′	2°55·5′W	T	182
Northwick	Worcs	SO8457	52°12·9′	2°13·7′W	T	150
Northwick Hill	Glos	SP1435	52°1·0′	1°47·4′W	X	151
Northwick Oaze	S Glos	ST5587	51°35·0′	2°38·6′W	X	172
Northwick Oaze	S Glos	ST5588	51°35·6′	2°38·6′W	X	162,172
North Wick of Sound	Shetld	HU4582	60°31·4′	1°10·3′W	W	1,2,3
Northwick Park	Glos	SP1636	52°1·6′	1°45·6′W	X	151
Northwick Park Sta	Brent	TQ1687	51°34·4′	0°19·2′W	X	176
North Widcombe	Bath & NE Somer	ST5758	51°19·4′	2°36·6′W	T	172,182
Northwilds	Highld	NH8181	57°48·4′	3°59·7′W	X	21
North Willingham	Lincs	TF1688	53°22·8′	0°15·0′W	T	113,121
North Wingfield	Derby	SK4165	53°11·1′	1°22·8′W	T	120
North Wirral Coastal Path	Wirral	SJ2591	53°24·9′	3°7·3′W	X	108
North Witham	Lincs	SK9221	52°47·0′	0°37·8′W	T	130
Northwold	Norf	TL7597	52°32·8′	0°35·3′E	T	143
Northwold Common	Norf	TL7597	52°32·8′	0°35·3′E	X	143
Northwold Fen	Norf	TL7097	52°32·9′	0°30·8′E	X	143
North Wold Fm	Lincs	TF1591	53°24·4′	0°15·8′W	FM	113
North Wold Fm	N Lincs	TA0019	53°39·7′	0°28·8′W	FM	112
Northwold Fm	N Lincs	TA0215	53°37·5′	0°27·0′W	FM	112
North Wold Fm	N Yks	TA0678	54°11·4′	0°22·1′W	FM	101
Northwold Lodge	Norf	TL7696	52°32·2′	0°36·1′E	X	143
North Wolds Walk	E Yorks	SE8452	53°57·7′	0°42·8′W	X	106
North Wolds Walk	N Yks	SE8361	54°2·5′	0°43·5′W	X	100
North Wood	Angus	NO5261	56°44·5′	2°46·6′W	F	44
Northwood	C of Stoke	SJ8948	53°2·0′	2°9·4′W	T	118
Northwood	Corn	SX2069	50°29·8′	4°31·9′W	X	201
Northwood	Derby	SK2664	53°10·6′	1°36·3′W	T	119
Northwood	Devon	SS6121	50°58·5′	3°58·4′W	X	180
Northwood	Devon	SS7708	50°51·7′	3°44·5′W	X	191
North Wood	Devon	SX5464	50°27·7′	4°3·0′W	F	201
Northwood	Devon	SX5599	50°46·6′	4°3·0′W	X	191
North Wood	Devon	SX8688	50°41·1′	3°36·4′W	F	191
North Wood	Durham	NZ0711	54°29·9′	1°53·1′W	F	92
North Wood	Durham	NZ1223	54°36·4′	1°48·4′W	F	92
North Wood	E Yorks	TA1169	54°6·5′	0°17·7′W	F	101
North Wood	E Yorks	TA1368	54°6·0′	0°15·9′W	F	101
Northwood	Hill	TQ0991	51°36·7′	0°25·2′W	T	176
Northwood	I of W	SZ4893	50°44·3′	1°18·8′W	T	196
Northwood	Kent	TR3767	51°21·4′	1°24·6′E	T	179
Northwood	Know	SJ4299	53°29·3′	2°52·0′W	T	108
Northwood	Lancs	SD8036	53°49·4′	2°17·8′W	X	103
North Wood	Medway	TQ6966	51°22·3′	0°26·1′E	F	177,178
North Wood	Northum	NU1229	55°33·5′	1°48·2′W	F	75
Northwood	Northum	NZ2177	55°5·5′	1°39·8′W	F	88
North Wood	Notts	SK7465	53°10·9′	0°53·2′W	F	120
North Wood	N Yks	SE1478	54°12·1′	1°46·7′W	F	99
North Wood	N Yks	SE2470	54°7·8′	1°37·5′W	F	99
North Wood	N Yks	SE5290	54°18·4′	1°11·6′W	F	100
North Wood	Pemb	SN0110	51°45·4′	4°52·6′W	F	157,158
North Wood	Pth & Kin	NO1640	56°32·9′	3°21·5′W	F	53
North Wood	Scot Bord	NT9063	55°51·9′	2°9·1′W	F	67
Northwood	Shrops	SJ4633	52°53·7′	2°47·8′W	T	126
Northwood	Shrops	SO6784	52°27·4′	2°28·7′W	X	138
Northwood	Staffs	SJ8542	52°58·7′	2°13·0′W	T	118
North Wood	Warw	SP1995	52°33·4′	1°42·8′W	F	139
North Wood	Worcs	SO7877	52°23·7′	2°19·0′W	F	138
North Wood	W Susx	SU9511	50°53·7′	0°38·6′W	F	197
Northwood	W Susx	TQ3731	51°3·9′	0°2·3′W	X	187
North Woodend	Falk	NS8078	55°59·1′	3°55·0′W	X	65
Northwood Fm	Ches	SJ8469	53°13·3′	2°14·0′W	FM	118
Northwood Fm	Devon	SX8580	50°36·7′	3°37·1′W	FM	191
Northwood Fm	Dorset	ST8116	50°56·8′	2°15·8′W	FM	183
Northwood Fm	Lancs	SD7935	53°48·9′	2°18·7′W	FM	103
Northwood Fm	N Lincs	SE9600	53°29·5′	0°32·8′W	FM	112
Northwood Fm	Shrops	SJ6031	52°52·7′	2°35·3′W	FM	127
Northwood Fm	Somer	ST5435	51°7·0′	2°39·0′W	FM	182,183
Northwood Fm	Staffs	SJ8542	52°58·7′	2°13·0′W	FM	118
Northwood Fm	Staffs	SK1243	52°59·3′	1°48·9′W	FM	119,128
Northwood Fm	W Susx	SU7512	50°54·4′	0°55·6′W	FM	197
Northwood Fm	W Susx	SU9318	50°57·5′	0°40·2′W	FM	197
Northwood Fm	W Susx	TQ0523	51°0·0′	0°29·8′W	FM	197
Northwood Grange	Shrops	SJ6032	52°53·3′	2°35·3′W	X	127
Northwood Green	Glos	SO7116	51°50·7′	2°24·9′W	T	162
Northwood Hall	Ches	SJ5168	53°12·7′	2°43·6′W	X	117
Northwood Hall	Shrops	SJ4931	52°52·7′	2°45·1′W	X	126
Northwood Hall Fm	Ches	SJ6981	53°19·7′	2°27·5′W	FM	109
North Woodhill	E Ayr	NS4139	55°37·4′	4°31·1′W	X	70
Northwood Hills	Hill	TQ0990	51°36·1′	0°25·2′W	T	176
Northwood Ho	Ches	SJ6882	53°20·3′	2°28·4′W	X	109
Northwood Ho	I of W	SZ4996	50°45·9′	1°17·9′W	X	196
Northwood Ho	Kent	TR1666	51°21·3′	1°6·5′E	X	179
Northwood Ho	Shrops	SJ4038	52°56·4′	2°53·2′W	X	126
Northwood Ho	Worcs	SO7876	52°23·1′	2°19·0′W	X	138
North Wood Moor	Devon	SX6699	50°46·7′	3°53·7′W	X	191
Northwood Park	Hants	SU4432	51°5·4′	1°21·9′W	X	185
North Woods	N Yks	NZ5601	54°24·3′	1°7·8′W	X	93
Northwoods	N Yks	SE1862	54°3·5′	1°43·1′W	X	99
North Woods	S Glos	ST6382	51°32·4′	2°31·6′W	X	172
Northwood's Fm	Ches	SJ6440	52°57·6′	2°31·8′W	FM	118
North Wood's Hill Fm	Lancs	SD4445	53°54·1′	2°50·7′W	FM	102
Northwood Villa	Shrops	SJ4931	52°52·7′	2°45·1′W	X	126
Northwood Woolley Fm	Devon	SS6039	51°8·2′	3°59·7′W	FM	180
North Woolwich	T Ham	TQ4379	51°29·7′	0°4·0′E	T	177
North Wootton	Dorset	ST6514	50°55·7′	2°29·5′W	T	194
North Wootton	Norf	TF6424	52°47·5′	0°26·3′E	T	132
North Wootton	Somer	ST5641	51°10·2′	2°37·4′W	T	182,183
North Worcestershire Path	Worcs	SO8381	52°25·8′	2°14·6′W	X	138
North Worcestershire Path	Worcs	SO8980	52°25·3′	2°9·3′W	X	139
North Worden	Devon	SS4407	50°50·7′	4°12·6′W	X	190
North Wraxall	Wilts	ST8175	51°28·7′	2°16·0′W	T	173
North Wrixhill	Devon	SX4691	50°42·1′	4°10·5′W	X	190
North Wroughton	Swin	SU1481	51°31·9′	1°47·5′W	T	173
North Wycke	Essex	TL9700	51°40·1′	0°51·3′E	X	168
North Wyke	Devon	SX6698	50°46·2′	3°53·6′W	A	191
North Yardhope	Northum	NT9201	55°18·4′	2°7·1′W	X	80
Northycote Fm	Wolv	SJ9203	52°37·7′	2°6·7′W	FM	127,139
North Yeo Fm	Somer	ST3654	51°17·1′	2°54·7′W	FM	182
North Yorkshire Moors Railway	N Yks	SE8499	54°23·0′	0°42·0′W	X	94,100
North Ythsie	Aberd	NJ8830	57°21·9′	2°11·5′W	X	30
Nortoft Grange	Northnts	SP6773	52°21·3′	1°0·6′W	X	141
Nortoft Lodge	Northnts	SP6774	52°21·8′	1°0·6′W	X	141
Nortofts	Essex	TL7031	51°57·3′	0°28·8′E	X	167
Norton	Corn	SX0869	50°29·6′	4°42·0′W	X	200
Norton	Corn	SX3575	50°33·3′	4°19·4′W	X	201
Norton	Devon	SS2625	51°0·1′	4°28·4′W	T	190
Norton	Devon	SS2803	50°48·3′	4°26·1′W	X	190
Norton	Devon	SX7245	50°17·7′	3°47·5′W	X	202
Norton	Devon	SX7847	50°18·9′	3°42·4′W	X	202
Norton	Devon	SX8551	50°21·1′	3°36·6′W	T	202
Norton	Donc	SE5415	53°38·0′	1°10·6′W	T	111
Norton	Dudley	SO8982	52°26·4′	2°9·3′W	T	139
Norton	E Susx	TQ4701	50°47·6′	0°5·5′E	T	198
Norton	Glos	SO8524	51°55·1′	2°12·7′W	T	162
Norton	Halton	SJ5582	53°20·2′	2°40·1′W	X	108
Norton	Herts	TL2334	51°59·7′	0°12·1′W	T	153
Norton	I of W	SZ3489	50°42·2′	1°30·7′W	T	196
Norton	Monm	SO4420	51°52·8′	2°48·4′W	T	161
Norton	Northnts	SP6063	52°15·9′	1°6·8′W	T	152
Norton	Notts	SK5772	53°14·8′	1°8·3′W	T	120
Norton	N Som	ST3463	51°22·0′	2°56·5′W	T	182
Norton	Orkney	HY2822	59°5·0′	3°14·9′W	X	6
Norton	Orkney	HY2908	58°57·5′	3°13·6′W	X	6,7
Norton	Pemb	SM9507	51°43·7′	4°57·7′W	X	157,158
Norton	Powys	SO3067	52°18·0′	3°1·2′W	T	137,148
Norton	Scot Bord	NT5348	55°43·6′	2°44·5′W	X	73
Norton	Sheff	SK3582	53°20·3′	1°28·1′W	T	110,111
Norton	Shrops	SJ5609	52°40·9′	2°38·7′W	T	126
Norton	Shrops	SJ7200	52°36·1′	2°24·4′W	T	127
Norton	Shrops	SO4681	52°25·7′	2°47·3′W	T	137,138
Norton	Shrops	SO6382	52°26·3′	2°32·3′W	X	138
Norton	Stock on T	NZ4421	54°35·2′	1°18·7′W	T	93
Norton	Suff	TL9565	52°15·1′	0°51·8′E	T	155
Norton	Swan	SS4986	51°33·4′	4°10·3′W	T	159
Norton	Swan	SS6188	51°34·7′	4°0·0′W	T	159
Norton	V of Glam	SS8775	51°28·0′	3°37·2′W	X	170
Norton	Wilts	ST8884	51°33·5′	2°10·0′W	T	173
Norton	Worcs	SO8850	52°9·1′	2°10·1′W	T	150
Norton	Worcs	SP0347	52°7·5′	1°57·0′W	T	150
Norton	W Susx	SU9206	50°51·0′	0°41·2′W	T	197
Norton	W Susx	SZ8695	50°45·1′	0°46·5′W	T	197
Norton Ash	Kent	TQ9761	51°19·1′	0°50·0′E	T	178
Norton Barn Fm	Leic	SK3307	52°39·8′	1°30·3′W	FM	140
Norton Barton	Corn	SS2508	50°50·9′	4°28·8′W	X	190
Norton Barton Manor	Devon	SX4092	50°42·6′	4°15·6′W	X	190
Norton Bavant	Wilts	ST9043	51°11·4′	2°8·2′W	T	184
Norton Big Wood	Lincs	SK8860	53°8·0′	0°40·7′W	F	121
Norton Bridge	Staffs	SJ8730	52°52·3′	2°11·2′W	T	127
Norton Brook	Heref	SO5036	52°1·4′	2°43·3′W	W	149
Norton Brook Fm	Heref	SO5035	52°0·9′	2°43·3′W	FM	149
Norton Bury	Herts	TL2334	51°59·7′	0°12·1′W	X	153
Norton Camp	Shrops	SO4481	52°25·7′	2°49·0′W	A	137
Nortoncamp Wood	Shrops	SO4481	52°25·7′	2°49·0′W	F	137
Norton Canes	Staffs	SK0107	52°39·9′	1°58·7′W	T	139
Norton Canon	Heref	SO3847	52°7·3′	2°53·9′W	T	148,149
Norton Common	Herts	TL2133	51°59·2′	0°13·9′W	X	166
Norton Common Fm	Donc	SE5615	53°37·9′	1°8·8′W	FM	111
Norton Conyers	N Yks	SE3176	54°11·0′	1°31·1′W	A	99
Norton Corner	Norf	TG0928	52°48·8′	1°6·5′E	T	133
Norton Court	Bath & NE Somer	ST5965	51°23·2′	2°35·0′W	X	172,182
Norton Court	Kent	TQ9661	51°19·1′	0°49·2′E	A	178
Norton Court Fm	Glos	SO8624	51°55·1′	2°11·8′W	FM	162
Norton Coverts	Leic	SK3306	52°39·3′	1°30·3′W	F	140
Norton Creek	Norf	TF8245	52°58·5′	0°43·0′E	W	132
Norton Curlieu	Warw	SP2263	52°16·1′	1°40·3′W	X	151
Norton Disney	Lincs	SK8859	53°7·5′	0°40·7′W	T	121
Norton Disney Hall	Lincs	SK8760	53°8·0′	0°41·6′W	X	121
Norton Ditch	Oxon	SP3106	51°45·3′	1°32·7′W	W	164
Norton Down	Wilts	ST9246	51°13·0′	2°6·5′W	X	184
Norton East	Staffs	SK0208	52°40·4′	1°57·8′W	T	128
Norton Ferris	Wilts	ST7936	51°7·6′	2°17·6′W	T	183
Norton Fine Beck	Durham	NZ1627	54°38·5′	1°44·7′W	W	92
Norton Fine Fm	Durham	NZ1626	54°38·0′	1°44·7′W	FM	92
Norton Fitzwarren	Somer	ST1925	51°1·4′	3°8·9′W	T	181,193
Norton Fm	Devon	SX4665	50°28·1′	4°9·8′W	FM	201
Norton Fm	Devon	SX8899	50°47·0′	3°34·9′W	FM	192
Norton Fm	Fife	NT1193	56°7·5′	3°25·5′W	FM	58
Norton Fm	Hants	SU7335	51°6·8′	0°57·0′W	FM	186
Norton Fm	Shrops	SJ4907	52°39·7′	2°44·8′W	FM	126
Norton Fm	Staffs	SJ8830	52°52·3′	2°10·3′W	FM	127
Norton Fm	Surrey	SU9654	51°16·9′	0°37·0′W	FM	186
Norton Forge	Shrops	SJ7037	52°56·0′	2°26·4′W	X	127
Norton Gorse	Leic	SK6801	52°36·4′	0°59·3′W	F	141
Norton Green	C of Stoke	SJ9052	53°4·1′	2°8·5′W	T	118
Norton Green	Herts	TL2223	51°53·8′	0°13·2′W	T	166
Norton Green	I of W	SZ3488	50°41·7′	1°30·7′W	T	196
Norton Green	Kent	TQ8560	51°18·8′	0°39·7′E	X	178
Norton Green	Sol	SP1774	52°22·1′	1°44·6′W	T	139
Norton Grounds Fm	Glos	SP1442	52°4·8′	1°47·3′W	FM	151
Norton Grove Stud	N Yks	SE8071	54°8·0′	0°46·1′W	X	100
Norton Hall	Essex	TQ8599	51°39·8′	0°40·9′E	X	168
Norton Hall	Glos	SP1443	52°5·3′	1°47·3′W	X	151
Norton Hall	Norf	TG0127	52°48·4′	0°59·3′E	X	133
Norton Hall	Suff	TL9765	52°15·1′	0°53·6′E	X	155
Norton Hall Fm	Essex	TL9029	51°55·8′	0°46·2′E	FM	168
Norton Hall Fm	Glos	SP1444	52°5·9′	1°47·3′W	FM	151
Norton Hawkfield	Bath & NE Somer	ST5964	51°22·6′	2°35·0′W	T	172,182
Norton Hayes	Somer	ST1723	51°0·3′	3°10·6′W	X	181,193
Norton Heath	Essex	TL6004	51°42·9′	0°19·4′E	T	167
Norton Hill	Bath & NE Somer	ST6653	51°16·7′	2°28·9′W	T	183
Norton Ho	Warr	SJ5883	53°20·8′	2°37·4′W	X	108
Norton House Fm	Leic	SK3106	52°39·3′	1°32·1′W	FM	140
Norton House Hotel	C of Edin	NT1371	55°55·7′	3°23·1′W	X	65
Norton in Hales	Shrops	SJ7038	52°56·6′	2°26·4′W	T	127
Norton-in-the-Moors	C of Stoke	SJ8951	53°3·6′	2°9·4′W	T	118
Norton-Juxta-Twycross	Leic	SK3206	52°39·3′	1°31·2′W	T	140
Norton Lane Fm	Bath & NE Somer	ST7457	51°18·9′	2°22·0′W	FM	172
Norton-le-Clay	N Yks	SE4071	54°8·2′	1°22·8′W	T	99
Norton Lindsey	Warw	SP2263	52°16·1′	1°40·3′W	T	151
Norton Little Green	Suff	TL9766	52°15·6′	0°53·6′E	T	155
Norton Lodge	N Yks	SE8070	54°7·4′	0°46·1′W	X	100
Norton Low Wood	Lincs	SK8860	53°8·0′	0°40·7′W	F	121
Norton Mains	C of Edin	NT1472	55°56·3′	3°22·2′W	X	65
Norton Malreward	Bath & NE Somer	ST6065	51°23·2′	2°34·1′W	T	172
Norton Mandeville	Essex	TL5804	51°43·0′	0°17·6′E	T	167
Norton Manor	Essex	TL6004	51°42·9′	0°19·4′E	X	167
Norton Manor	Hants	SU4740	51°9·7′	1°19·3′W	A	185
Norton Manor	Powys	SO2966	52°17·5′	3°2·1′W	X	137,148
Norton Manor	Wilts	ST8884	51°33·5′	2°10·0′W	X	173
Norton Manor Camp	Somer	ST1927	51°2·4′	3°8·9′W	X	181,193
Norton Marsh	Norf	TF8244	52°58·0′	0°43·0′E	X	132
Norton Marsh	Warr	SJ5685	53°21·8′	2°39·3′W	X	108
Norton Marshes	Norf	TG4100	52°32·9′	1°33·7′E	X	134
Norton Mere	Shrops	SJ7908	52°40·4′	2°18·2′W	W	127
Norton-on-Derwent	N Yks	SE7971	54°8·0′	0°47·0′W	T	100
Norton Park	Worcs	SO9339	52°3·2′	2°5·7′W	X	150
Norton Parks	N Yks	SE8172	54°8·5′	0°45·2′W	X	100
Norton Place	Lincs	SK9790	53°24·1′	0°32·0′W	X	112
Norton Priory	Donc	SE5415	53°38·0′	1°10·6′W	X	111
Nortons	Devon	SX9299	50°47·1′	3°31·5′W	X	192
Nortons	Essex	TL6937	52°0·6′	0°28·1′E	X	154
Norton Sandhays Fm	Lincs	TF0093	53°25·7′	0°29·3′W	FM	112
Norton School	Warw	SP3350	52°9·1′	1°30·7′W	X	151
Nortons End Fm	Shrops	SO7182	52°26·4′	2°25·2′W	FM	138
Nortons Fm	Essex	TL9031	51°56·9′	0°46·3′E	FM	168
Norton's Fm	E Susx	TQ7815	50°54·6′	0°32·3′E	FM	199
Norton Staithe	Norf	TG4001	52°33·5′	1°32·8′E	X	134
Norton St Philip	Somer	ST7755	51°17·9′	2°19·4′W	T	172
Norton Subcourse	Norf	TM4198	52°31·8′	1°33·6′E	T	134
Norton Sub Hamdon	Somer	ST4715	50°56·2′	2°44·9′W	T	193
Norton's Wood	Hants	SU6245	51°12·3′	1°6·4′W	F	185
Norton's Wood	N Som	ST4372	51°26·9′	2°48·8′W	T	171,172
Norton Tower	N Yks	SD9757	54°0·8′	2°2·3′W	A	103
Norton Villa	Pemb	SN1514	51°47·9′	4°40·6′W	X	158
Norton Wood	Dorset	ST8408	50°52·5′	2°13·3′W	F	194
Norton Wood	Heref	SO3648	52°7·8′	2°55·7′W	X	148,149
Norton Wood	Suff	TL9764	52°14·6′	0°53·5′E	F	155
Norton Wood Fm	Shrops	SJ6840	52°57·6′	2°28·2′W	FM	118
Norton Woodseats	Sheff	SK3582	53°20·3′	1°28·1′W	T	110,111
Nort Veedal	Shetld	HT9740	60°8·9′	2°2·7′W	X	4
Norval Fm	Worcs	SP0946	52°7·0′	1°51·7′W	FM	150
Norway Fm	Devon	SX8694	50°44·3′	3°36·6′W	FM	191
Norwell	Notts	SK7761	53°8·7′	0°50·5′W	T	120
Norwell Woodhouse	Notts	SK7462	53°9·2′	0°53·2′W	T	120
Norwich	Norf	TG2308	52°37·7′	1°18·1′E	T	134
Norwich Airport	Norf	TG2213	52°40·4′	1°17·4′E	X	133,134
Norwich Gap	Norf	TM1191	52°28·8′	1°6·8′E	X	144
Norwick	Shetld	HP6514	60°48·5′	0°47·8′W	T	1
Nor Wick	Shetld	HP6614	60°48·5′	0°46·7′W	W	1
Nor Wick	Shetld	HU3681	60°30·9′	1°20·2′W	W	1,2,3
Norwick Hevda	Shetld	HP6217	60°50·1′	0°51·1′W	X	1
Norwith Hill	Notts	SK6794	53°26·5′	0°59·1′W	X	111
Norwood	Derby	SK4681	53°19·7′	1°18·1′W	T	111,120
Norwood	D & G	NY1579	55°6·1′	3°19·5′W	X	85
Norwood	Dorset	ST5305	50°50·8′	2°39·7′W	T	194
Norwood	E Yorks	TA1837	53°49·2′	0°12·0′W	X	107
Norwood	Kent	TQ8858	51°17·6′	0°42·2′E	X	178
Norwood	Lincs	TF0325	52°49·0′	0°27·9′W	F	130
Nor Wood	Wilts	ST7932	51°5·4′	2°17·6′W	F	183
Norwood Bottom	N Yks	SE2050	53°57·0′	1°41·3′W	X	104
Norwood Bottoms	Leeds	SE3841	53°52·1′	1°24·9′W	X	104

Norwood End	Essex	TL5608	51°45·2'	0°16·0'E	T	167
Norwood Fm	Devon	SS4920	50°57·8'	4°8·6'W	FM	180
Norwood Fm	Devon	SS9818	50°57·4'	3°26·8'W	FM	181
Norwood Fm	Kent	TR0430	51°2·2'	0°55·0'E	FM	189
Norwood Fm	Notts	SK5272	53°14·8'	1°12·8'W	FM	120
Norwood Fm	Notts	SK6551	53°3·4'	1°1·4'W	FM	120
Norwood Fm	Peterb	TF1903	52°36·9'	0°14·1'W	FM	142
Norwood Fm	Somer	ST7757	51°18·9'	2°19·4'W	FM	172
Norwood Fm	Surrey	TQ1055	51°17·2'	0°25·0'W	FM	187
Norwood Fm	Surrey	TQ1062	51°21·0'	0°24·8'W	FM	176,187
Norwood Fm	Warw	SP4885	52°27·9'	1°17·2'W	FM	140
Norwood Green	Cald	SE1326	53°44·1'	1°47·8'W	T	104
Norwood Green	Ealing	TQ1378	51°29·6'	0°21·9'W	T	176
Norwood Hall	N Yks	SE2150	53°57·0'	1°40·4'W	X	104
Norwood Hill	Surrey	TQ2443	51°10·6'	0°13·2'W	T	187
Norwood Ho	Leeds	SE3841	53°52·1'	1°24·9'W	X	104
Norwood Ho	Northnts	SP7061	52°14·8'	0°58·1'W	X	152
Norwood Lodge	Essex	TM1420	51°50·5'	1°6·8'E	X	168,169
Norwood Lodge	E Yorks	TA0234	53°47·8'	0°26·7'W	X	106,107
Norwood Lodge	Notts	SK4763	53°10·0'	1°17·4'W	X	120
Norwood Manor	Kent	TQ9771	51°24·4'	0°50·4'E	X	178
Norwood New Town	Croy	TQ3270	51°25·0'	0°5·7'W	T	176,177
Norwood Park	Notts	SK6854	53°5·0'	0°58·7'W	X	120
Norwood Park	Somer	ST5239	51°9·1'	2°40·8'W	X	182,183
Norwood Place Fm	Surrey	TQ2344	51°11·1'	0°14·0'W	FM	187
Norwoods Fm	Northum	NZ2393	55°14·1'	1°37·9'W	FM	81
Norwoodside	Cambs	TL4198	52°33·9'	0°5·2'E	T	142,143
Noseley	Leic	SP7398	52°34·7'	0°55·0'W	T	141
Noseley Village	Leic	SP7398	52°34·7'	0°55·0'W	A	141
Nosely Wood	Leic	SP7397	52°34·2'	0°55·0'W	F	141
Nose of the Bring	Orkney	HY2702	58°54·2'	3°15·5'W	X	6,7
Nose's Point	Durham	NZ4347	54°49·2'	1°19·4'W	X	88
Noska	N Yks	SE0855	53°59·7'	1°52·3'W	X	104
Noska Brow	N Yks	SE0955	53°59·7'	1°51·3'W	X	104
Noss	Highld	ND3754	58°28·4'	3°4·3'W	T	12
Noss	Shetld	HU3516	59°55·9'	1°21·9'W	T	4
Noss Head	Highld	ND3855	58°28·9'	3°3·3'W	X	12
Noss Head	Shetld	HU5539	60°8·2'	1°0·1'W	X	4
Noss Hill	Shetld	HU3615	59°55·4'	1°20·9'W	H	4
Nossill Scars	N Yks	SE0488	54°17·5'	1°55·9'W	X	98
Noss Mayo	Devon	SX5447	50°18·5'	4°2·7'W	T	201
Noss Sound	Shetld	HU5241	60°9·3'	1°3·3'W	W	4
Nostell Park	Wakf	SE4017	53°39·1'	1°23·3'W	X	111
Nostell Priory	Wakf	SE4017	53°39·1'	1°23·3'W	X	111
Noster	N Eil	NB2203	57°56·0'	6°41·3'W	X	13,14
Nosterfield	N Yks	SE2780	54°13·1'	1°34·7'W	T	99
Nosterfield End	Cambs	TL6344	52°4·4'	0°23·1'E	T	154
Nostie	Highld	NG8527	57°17·2'	5°33·6'W	T	33
Nostie Bay	Highld	NG8526	57°16·7'	5°33·5'W	W	33
Nostie Br	Highld	NG8527	57°17·2'	5°33·6'W	X	33
Notcliffe	Devon	SS7420	50°58·2'	3°47·3'W	X	180
Notcliffe Ho	Glos	SO8828	51°57·3'	2°10·1'W	X	150
Note o' the Gate	Scot Bord	NT5802	55°18·9'	2°39·3'W	X	80
Notgrove	Glos	SP1020	51°52·9'	1°50·9'W	T	163
Nothe Fort	Dorset	SY6878	50°36·3'	2°26·8'W	X	194
Nothill Fm	Staffs	SK0737	52°56·1'	1°53·3'W	FM	128
Nothing Hill	Hants	SU5058	51°19·4'	1°16·6'W	X	174
Notley Abbey	Bucks	SP7109	51°46·7'	0°57·9'W	A	165
Notley Enterprise Park	Suff	TM0639	52°0·9'	1°0·5'E	X	155
Notman Law	Scot Bord	NT1826	55°31·5'	3°17·5'W	H	72
Notoaks Wood	Oxon	SP4016	51°50·7'	1°24·8'W	F	164
Noton Barn Fm	Derby	SK2166	53°11·7'	1°40·7'W	FM	119
Notster	Orkney	HY5301	58°53·9'	2°48·5'W	X	6,7
Nottage	Brig	SS8178	51°29·5'	3°42·5'W	T	170
Nottage Court	Brig	SS8278	51°29·6'	3°41·6'W	A	170
Notter	Corn	SX3960	50°25·3'	4°15·6'W	T	201
Notter Br	Corn	SX3960	50°25·3'	4°16·5'W	X	201
Notter Tor	Corn	SX2773	50°32·1'	4°26·1'W	H	201
Nottingham	C of Nott	SK5641	52°58·0'	1°9·6'W	T	129
Nottingham	Fife	NO2905	56°14·2'	3°8·3'W	X	59
Nottingham	Highld	ND2135	58°18·1'	3°20·4'W	X	11
Nottingham Airport	Notts	SK6136	52°55·3'	1°5·2'W	X	129
Nottingham Canal	Derby	SK4742	52°58·6'	1°17·6'W	W	129
Nottingham Hill	Glos	SO9828	51°57·3'	2°1·4'W	H	150,163
Nottingham Hill (Fort)	Glos	SO9828	51°57·3'	2°1·4'W	A	150,163
Notting Hill	Dorset	SY9597	50°46·6'	2°3·9'W	X	195
Notting Hill	Ken & Ch	TQ2480	51°30·5'	0°12·4'W	T	176
Nottington	Dorset	SY6682	50°38·4'	2°28·5'W	T	194
Nottiston	Devon	SS5329	51°2·7'	4°5·4'W	X	180
Notton	Dorset	SY6095	50°45·4'	2°33·6'W	X	194
Notton	Wakf	SE3413	53°37·0'	1°28·7'W	T	110,111
Notton	Wilts	ST9169	51°25·4'	2°7·4'W	T	173
Notton Grange	Wakf	SE3513	53°37·0'	1°27·8'W	X	110,111
Notton Hill Barn	Dorset	SY5994	50°44·9'	2°34·5'W	X	194
Notton Park	Wakf	SE3411	53°35·9'	1°28·8'W	F	110,111
Notts Pot	Lancs	SD6777	54°11·5'	2°29·9'W	X	98
Nott Wood	Oxon	SU6985	51°33·8'	0°59·9'W	F	175
Nottwood Hill	Glos	SO7018	51°51·8'	2°25·7'W	X	162
Nottylees	Scot Bord	NT7936	55°37·3'	2°19·6'W	X	74
Nouds	Kent	TQ9561	51°19·1'	0°48·3'E	X	178
Nouds Fm	Kent	TQ9561	51°19·1'	0°48·3'E	FM	178
Nounsie	Shetld	HU2942	60°10·0'	1°28·2'W	X	4
Nounsley	Essex	TL7910	51°45·8'	0°36·0'E	T	167
Noup	Orkney	HY4148	59°19·1'	3°1·7'W	X	5
Noup	Shetld	HU3512	59°53·8'	1°22·0'W	X	4
Noup Geo	Shetld	HP6318	60°50·7'	0°49·9'W	X	1
Noup Head	Orkney	HY3950	59°20·2'	3°3·8'W	X	5
Noup Hill	Orkney	HY5639	59°14·4'	2°45·8'W	H	5
Noup Noss	Shetld	HU3516	59°55·9'	1°21·9'W	X	4
Noup of Noss	Shetld	HU5539	60°8·2'	1°0·1'W	X	4
Noup, The	Shetld	HP6318	60°50·7'	0°49·9'W	X	1
Noup, The	Shetld	HT9537	60°7·3'	2°4·9'W	H	4
Noup, The	Shetld	HU4120	59°58·0'	1°15·4'W	X	4
Noup, The	Shetld	HU4853	60°15·8'	1°7·5'W	H	3
Nousta Ness	Shetld	HU6689	60°35·0'	0°47·2'W	X	1,2
Nouster	Orkney	HY7552	59°21·5'	2°25·9'W	X	5
Noust Geo	Orkney	HY5420	59°4·1'	2°47·7'W	X	5,6
Noust Geo	Orkney	HY5630	59°9·5'	2°45·7'W	X	5,6
Noustiger	Orkney	HY4431	59°10·0'	2°58·3'W	X	5,6
Noust of Ayre	Orkney	HY6541	59°15·5'	2°36·3'W	X	5

Noust of Boloquoy	Orkney	HY6239	59°14·4'	2°39·5'W	X	5
Noust of Burraland	Shetld	HU3775	60°27·7'	1°19·1'W	X	2,3
Noust of Erraby	Orkney	HY5321	59°4·7'	2°48·7'W	X	5,6
Noust of Helliersness	Shetld	HU5988	60°34·5'	0°54·9'W	X	1,2
Noust of Nethertown	Orkney	HY2407	58°56·9'	3°18·8'W	X	6,7
Noust of Switha	Orkney	ND3691	58°48·4'	3°6·0'W	X	7
Noust of the Pund	Shetld	HU3075	60°27·7'	1°26·8'W	X	3
Noust of Treawick	Shetld	HU5762	60°20·5'	0°57·5'W	X	2
Nousty Sand	Orkney	HY4033	59°11·0'	3°2·5'W	X	5,6
Noutard's Green	Worcs	SO7966	52°17·7'	2°18·1'W	T	138,150
Nouthill	D & G	NY2969	55°0·9'	3°6·2'W	X	85
Nout Hill	Scot Bord	NT3528	55°32·7'	3°1·4'W	H	73
Nout Rig	Scot Bord	NT3228	55°32·7'	3°4·2'W	X	73
Nova	N Yks	SE5368	54°6·5'	1°10·9'W	X	100
Nova Lodge	N Yks	SE7987	54°16·6'	0°46·8'W	X	94,100
Novan	Orkney	HY3930	59°9·4'	3°3·5'W	X	6
Novar Ho	Highld	NH6167	57°40·5'	4°19·4'W	X	21
Nova Scotia	Ches	SJ6168	53°12·7'	2°34·6'W	T	118
Nova Scotia	Cumbr	NY2749	54°50·1'	3°7·8'W	X	85
Nova Scotia	Durham	NY9815	54°32·1'	2°1·4'W	X	92
Nova Scotia	E Yorks	SE7829	53°45·3'	0°48·6'W	X	105,106
Nova Scotia	E Yorks	TA2142	53°51·8'	0°9·2'W	X	107
Nova Scotia	Leeds	SE3940	53°51·5'	1°24·0'W	X	104
Nova Scotia	Northum	NU0418	55°27·6'	1°55·8'W	H	81
Nova Scotia	N Yks	SE0099	54°23·4'	1°59·6'W	X	98
Nova Scotia	York	SE6357	54°0·5'	1°1·9'W	X	105,106
Nova Scotia Fm	Norf	TG5013	52°39·6'	1°42·2'E	FM	134
Nova Scotia Fm	York	SE6554	53°58·9'	1°0·1'W	FM	105,106
Nova Scotia Wood	N Yks	SE4849	53°56·3'	1°15·7'W	F	105
Novay Farm	N Yks	SE6069	54°7·0'	1°4·5'W	FM	100
Nover's Hill	Shrops	SO4595	52°33·2'	2°48·3'W	H	137,138
Novers Park	C of Bris	ST5869	51°25·3'	2°35·9'W	T	172,182
Noverton	Glos	SO9723	51°54·6'	2°2·2'W	T	163
Noverton Fm	Worcs	SO7064	52°16·2'	2°26·0'W	FM	138,149
Novia Fm	Leeds	SE2142	53°52·7'	1°40·4'W	FM	104
Novia Plantn	Leeds	SE2142	53°52·7'	1°40·4'W	F	104
Novington Fm	E Susx	TQ3713	50°54·2'	0°2·7'W	FM	198
Novington Manor	E Susx	TQ3614	50°54·8'	0°3·5'W	X	198
Noviomagvs (Chichester)	W Susx	SU8604	50°50·0'	0°46·3'W	R	197
Nower Fm	Devon	ST2500	50°47·9'	3°3·5'W	FM	192,193
Nower Hill	Harrow	TQ1289	51°35·5'	0°22·6'W	X	176
Nower's Copse	Wilts	ST9225	51°1·7'	2°6·5'W	F	184
Nower, The	Surrey	TQ1548	51°13·4'	0°20·8'W	X	187
Nower Wood	Surrey	TQ1954	51°16·6'	0°17·2'W	F	187
Nowhurst Fm	W Susx	TQ1232	51°4·8'	0°23·7'W	FM	187
Nowt Bield	Orkney	HY2301	58°53·6'	3°19·7'W	X	6,7
Nowton	Suff	TL8660	52°12·6'	0°43·7'E	T	155
Nowton Lodge Fm	Suff	TL8661	52°13·2'	0°43·8'E	FM	155
Nowton Park	Suff	TL8661	52°13·2'	0°43·8'E	X	155
Nox	Shrops	SJ4110	52°41·3'	2°52·0'W	T	126
Noxon Fm	Glos	SO5806	51°45·3'	2°36·1'W	FM	162
Noxon Park	Glos	SO5906	51°45·3'	2°35·2'W	X	162
Noyadd	Powys	SO0661	52°14·6'	3°22·2'W	X	147
Noyadde	Powys	SO1842	52°4·5'	3°11·4'W	X	148,161
Noyadd Fach	Powys	SO0270	52°19·4'	3°25·9'W	X	136,147
Noyadd Fm	Powys	SO1241	52°3·9'	3°16·6'W	FM	148,161
Noyaddllwyd	Monm	SO2825	51°55·4'	3°2·4'W	X	161
Noyaddllwyd	Powys	SO0651	52°9·2'	3°22·0'W	X	147
Noyadd Sharmon	Powys	SO0147	52°7·0'	3°26·4'W	X	147
Noyadd Trefawr	Cered	SN2546	52°5·3'	4°32·9'W	T	145
Noyadd Wilym	Cered	SN2044	52°4·2'	4°37·2'W	T	145
Noyes Fm	Suff	TM3071	52°17·6'	1°22·8'E	FM	156
Noyna Bottom	Lancs	SD9042	53°52·7'	2°8·7'W	X	103
Noyna Hall	Lancs	SD9041	53°52·1'	2°8·7'W	X	103
Nuckro Water	Shetld	HU5663	60°21·1'	0°58·6'W	W	2
Nuck's Wood	Lancs	SD4116	53°38·5'	2°53·1'W	F	108
Nuckwell Fm	Devon	SX7046	50°18·2'	3°49·2'W	FM	202
Nuda	Shetld	HP6203	60°42·6'	0°51·3'W	X	1
Nudge Hill	Brad	SE0648	53°55·9'	1°54·1'W	X	104
Nudge Hill Fm	Brad	SE0649	53°56·5'	1°54·1'W	FM	104
Nuffield	Oxon	SU6687	51°34·9'	1°2·5'W	T	175
Nuffield Common	Oxon	SU6787	51°34·9'	1°1·6'W	X	175
Nuffield Fm	Herts	TL0303	51°43·2'	0°30·1'W	FM	166
Nuffield Hill	Oxon	SU6687	51°34·9'	1°2·5'W	X	175
Nuffield Place	Oxon	SU6787	51°34·9'	1°1·6'W	X	175
Nufwith Cote	N Yks	SE2378	54°12·1'	1°38·4'W	X	99
Nuide Farm	Highld	NN7298	57°3·6'	4°6·2'W	FM	35
Nuide Moss	Highld	NN7196	57°2·5'	4°7·1'W	X	35
Numbers Fm	Durham	NZ1030	54°40·1'	1°50·3'W	FM	92
Numbers Fm	Herts	TL0802	51°42·6'	0°25·8'W	FM	166
Numberstones End	N Yks	SE0260	54°2·4'	1°57·8'W	X	98
Numphra	Corn	SW3829	50°6·4'	5°39·5'W	X	203
Nun Appleton	N Yks	SE5539	53°50·9'	1°9·4'W	T	105
Nun Brook	Shrops	SO7998	52°35·0'	2°18·2'W	W	138
Nun Burn	Northum	NZ1287	55°10·9'	1°48·3'W	W	81
Nunburnholme	E Yorks	SE8548	53°55·5'	0°41·9'W	T	106
Nunburnholme Wold	E Yorks	SE8747	53°54·9'	0°40·1'W	X	106
Nuncargate	Notts	SK5054	53°5·1'	1°14·8'W	T	120
Nunclose	Cumbr	NY4945	54°48·1'	2°47·2'W	T	86
Nun Cote Nook	N Yks	SE0898	54°22·9'	1°52·2'W	X	99
Nuneaton	Warw	SP3691	52°31·2'	1°27·8'W	T	140
Nuneham Courtenay	Oxon	SU5599	51°41·5'	1°11·9'W	T	164
Nuneham Ho	Oxon	SU5498	51°40·9'	1°12·7'W	X	164
Nuneham Park	Oxon	SU5497	51°40·4'	1°12·8'W	X	164
Nuney Green	Oxon	SU6779	51°30·6'	1°1·7'W	T	175
Nunfield	Cumbr	NY5051	54°51·3'	2°46·3'W	X	86
Nunford Dairy	Devon	SY2594	50°44·7'	3°3·4'W	X	192,193
Nunhead	Sthwk	TQ3575	51°27·7'	0°3·0'W	T	177
Nunhide Fm	W Berks	SU6472	51°26·8'	1°4·4'W	FM	175
Nun Hill	Northum	NZ1277	55°5·5'	1°48·3'W	X	88
Nun Hills	Lancs	SD8521	53°41·4'	2°13·2'W	T	103
Nun Ho	N Yks	SE4494	54°20·6'	1°19·0'W	X	99
Nunhold Fm	Warw	SP2365	52°17·2'	1°39·4'W	FM	151
Nunhold Grange	Warw	SP2265	52°17·2'	1°40·3'W	X	151
Nunholm	D & G	NX9777	55°4·9'	3°36·4'W	T	84
Nunkeeling	E Yorks	TA1449	53°55·7'	0°15·4'W	X	107
Nunland	D & G	NX9280	55°3·2'	3°40·9'W	X	84
Nunlands	Scot Bord	NT9356	55°48·1'	2°6·3'W	X	67,74,75
Nunley Fm	Warw	SP2273	52°21·5'	1°40·2'W	FM	139
Nun Mill	D & G	NX6548	54°48·8'	4°5·6'W	X	83,84

Nun Monkton	N Yks	SE5057	54°0·6'	1°13·8'W	T	105
Nun Moors	Donc	SE7112	53°36·2'	0°55·2'W	X	112
Nunnerie	S Lanak	NS9512	55°23·7'	3°39·0'W	X	78
Nunnerley Ho	Lincs	TF1724	52°48·3'	0°15·5'W	X	130
Nunnery Br	Essex	TL7735	51°59·3'	0°35·1'E	X	155
Nunnery Burn	S Lanak	NS9612	55°23·7'	3°38·1'W	W	78
Nunnery Fm	Northnts	SP8080	52°25·0'	0°49·0'W	FM	141
Nunnery Grove	Dorset	SY5884	50°39·5'	2°35·3'W	F	194
Nunnery Hill	Corn	SW9948	50°18·1'	4°49·0'W	X	204
Nunnery Hill	Cumbr	NY7642	54°46·6'	2°22·0'W	H	86,87
Nunnery House Hotel	Cumbr	NY5342	54°46·5'	2°43·4'W	X	86
Nunnery Howe	I of M	SC3674	54°8·4'	4°30·2'W	X	95
Nunnery, The	I of M	SC3775	54°8·9'	4°29·3'W	X	95
Nunnery, The	Leeds	SE2845	53°54·3'	1°34·0'W	X	104
Nunnery, The	W Susx	TQ1836	51°6·9'	0°18·5'W	X	187
Nunnery Walks	Cumbr	NY5342	54°46·5'	2°43·4'W	X	86
Nunnery Wood	Worcs	SO8754	52°11·3'	2°11·0'W	F	150
Nunney	Somer	ST7345	51°12·4'	2°22·8'W	T	183
Nunney Brook	Somer	ST7346	51°13·0'	2°22·8'W	W	183
Nunney Catch	Somer	ST7344	51°11·9'	2°22·8'W	T	183
Nunneys Wood	I of W	SZ4089	50°42·2'	1°25·6'W	F	196
Nunningham Fm	E Susx	TQ6313	50°53·8'	0°19·5'E	FM	199
Nunningham Stream	E Susx	TQ6612	50°53·2'	0°22·0'E	W	199
Nunnington	Heref	SO5543	52°5·2'	2°39·0'W	X	149
Nunnington	N Yks	SE6679	54°12·4'	0°58·9'W	T	100
Nunnington Fm	W Susx	TQ7898	50°46·8'	0°53·2'W	FM	197
Nunnington Park Fm	Somer	ST0826	51°1·8'	3°18·3'W	FM	181
Nunn's Br	Lincs	TF3641	52°57·2'	0°1·9'E	X	131
Nunnykirk	Northum	NZ0892	55°13·6'	1°52·0'W	T	81
Nunraw	E Loth	NT5970	55°55·5'	2°38·9'W	X	67
Nunraw Abbey	E Loth	NT5970	55°55·5'	2°38·9'W	X	67
Nunraw Barns	E Loth	NT5870	55°55·5'	2°39·9'W	X	67
Nunriding Hall	Northum	NZ1387	55°10·9'	1°47·3'W	X	81
Nunriding Moor	Northum	NZ1487	55°10·9'	1°46·4'W	X	81
Nun Rig	Scot Bord	NT5953	55°46·4'	2°38·8'W	X	67,73,74
Nun's Bridge	Cambs	TL2271	52°19·6'	0°12·2'W	X	153
Nuns Bridges	Norf	TL8782	52°24·5'	0°45·4'E	X	144
Nunscleugh	Cumbr	NY5374	55°3·7'	2°43·7'W	X	86
Nun's Cross Fm	Devon	SX6069	50°30·5'	3°58·1'W	FM	202
Nunsfield	Derby	SK2538	52°56·6'	1°37·3'W	X	128
Nunsland	Heref	SO3753	52°10·5'	2°54·9'W	X	148,149
Nunsmere	Ches	SJ5968	53°12·7'	2°36·4'W	X	117
Nuns Moor	N upon Ty	NZ2266	54°59·5'	1°38·9'W	X	88
Nuns' Pass	Arg & Bt	NM5220	56°18·7'	6°0·2'W	X	48
Nunstainton East	Durham	NZ3129	54°39·6'	1°30·7'W	X	93
Nunstainton Grange	Durham	NZ3028	54°39·0'	1°31·7'W	X	93
Nunsthorpe	NE Lincs	TA2507	53°32·9'	0°6·4'W	T	113
Nun's Well	N Yks	SE5190	54°18·4'	1°12·6'W	A	100
Nunthorpe	Midd	NZ5314	54°31·4'	1°10·4'W	T	93
Nunthorpe	York	SE5949	53°56·3'	1°5·7'W	T	105
Nunthorpe Hall	Midd	NZ5413	54°30·8'	1°9·5'W	X	93
Nunthorpe Stell	Midd	NZ5413	54°30·8'	1°9·5'W	W	93
Nunton	Wilts	SU1526	51°2·2'	1°46·8'W	T	184
Nunton Lodge Fm	Peterb	TF1107	52°39·2'	0°21·1'W	FM	142
Nun Upton	Heref	SO5466	52°17·7'	2°40·1'W	A	137,138,149
Nunwell Fm	I of W	SZ5987	50°41·0'	1°9·5'W	FM	196
Nunwell House	I of W	SZ5987	50°41·0'	1°9·5'W	X	196
Nunwell Trail	I of W	SZ5886	50°40·5'	1°10·4'W	X	196
Nunwick	Northum	NY8774	55°3·9'	2°11·8'W	X	87
Nunwick	N Yks	SE3274	54°9·9'	1°30·2'W	T	99
Nunwick Beck	N Yks	SE3275	54°10·4'	1°30·2'W	W	99
Nunwick Fm	Suff	TL8258	52°11·6'	0°40·2'E	FM	155
Nunwick Hall	Cumbr	NY5535	54°42·7'	2°41·5'W	X	90
Nunwick Mill	Northum	NY8974	55°3·9'	2°9·9'W	X	87
Nun Wood	Beds	SP9155	52°11·4'	0°39·7'W	F	152
Nunwood	D & G	NX9478	55°5·4'	3°39·2'W	X	84
Nun Wood	Northnts	SP7251	52°9·4'	0°56·5'W	F	152
Nupdown	S Glos	ST6395	51°39·4'	2°31·7'W	T	162
Nup End	Bucks	SP8619	51°52·0'	0°44·7'W	T	165
Nupend	Glos	SO7806	51°45·4'	2°18·7'W	T	162
Nupend	Glos	ST8398	51°41·1'	2°14·4'W	T	162
Nup End	Herts	TL2219	51°51·6'	0°13·3'W	T	166
Nupend Fm	Heref	SO7248	52°8·0'	2°24·1'W	FM	149
Nuper's Hatch	Essex	TQ5194	51°37·7'	0°11·3'E	T	167,177
Nuppend	Glos	SO6001	51°42·6'	2°34·3'W	T	162
Nupton	Heref	SO4548	52°7·9'	2°47·8'W	X	148,149
Nupton Hill	Heref	SO4447	52°7·3'	2°48·7'W	H	148,149
Nuptown	Brackn	SU8873	51°27·2'	0°43·6'W	T	175
N Uquhart	Fife	NO0787	56°4·3'	3°29·2'W	X	65
Nurcott Fm	Somer	SS9638	51°8·1'	3°28·8'W	FM	181
Nurnburnholme Wold	E Yorks	SE8648	53°55·5'	0°41·0'W	X	106
Nurscombe Fm	Surrey	SU9943	51°10·9'	0°34·6'W	FM	186
Nursebatch Fm	N Som	ST4569	51°25·3'	2°47·1'W	FM	171,172,182
Nurse Gellidywyll	Gwyn	SH6841	52°57·3'	3°57·5'W	F	124
Nurse Gron	Denb	SJ0334	52°53·9'	3°26·1'W	X	125
Nursery Cott	N Yks	SE7863	54°3·7'	0°48·1'W	X	100
Nursery Cottage	Aberd	NJ6724	57°18·6'	2°32·4'W	X	38
Nursery Fm	Derby	SK2964	53°10·6'	1°33·6'W	FM	119
Nursery Fm	Essex	TL8104	51°42·6'	0°37·9'E	FM	168
Nursery Fm	Lincs	TF2559	53°7·0'	0°7·5'W	FM	122
Nursery Hill Cottage	N Yks	SE4354	53°59·1'	1°20·2'W	X	105
Nursery, The	Northum	NY9075	55°4·4'	2°9·0'W	X	87
Nursery Wood	Suff	TM2941	52°1·4'	1°20·7'E	F	169
Nursery Wood	Warw	SP2963	52°16·1'	1°34·1'W	F	151
Nursling	Hants	SU3716	50°56·8'	1°28·0'W	T	185
Nursling Ho	Hants	SU3516	50°56·8'	1°29·7'W	X	185
Nursling Mill	Hants	SU3515	50°56·2'	1°29·7'W	X	196
Nurstead Court	Kent	TQ6468	51°23·5'	0°21·8'E	A	177
Nurstead Hill Fm	Kent	TQ6268	51°23·5'	0°20·1'E	FM	177
Nursted	Hants	SU7621	50°59·2'	0°54·6'W	T	197
Nursted Ho	Hants	SU7421	50°59·2'	0°56·4'W	X	197
Nursteed	Wilts	SU0260	51°20·6'	1°57·9'W	T	173
Nurston	Devon	SX7164	50°27·9'	3°48·7'W	X	202
Nurston	V of Glam	ST0567	51°23·9'	3°21·5'W	T	170
Nurton	Shrops	SO3593	52°32·1'	2°57·1'W	X	137
Nurton	Staffs	SO8399	52°35·6'	2°14·7'W	T	138
Nurton Court	Heref	SO5464	52°16·6'	2°40·1'W	X	137,138,149
Nurton Hill	Staffs	SO8399	52°35·6'	2°14·7'W	X	138
Nurton's Fm	Worcs	SO7467	52°18·3'	2°22·5'W	FM	138,150
Nussey House Fm	N Yks	SE0763	54°4·0'	1°53·2'W	FM	99

Nussteads, The	Suff	TL9738	52°0·6′	0°52·6′E	X	155
Nutbane	Hants	SU3249	51°14·6′	1°32·1′W	X	185
Nutbeam Fm	Glos	SO9707	51°45·9′	2°2·2′W	FM	163
Nutberry	D & G	NY2668	55°0·3′	3°9·0′W	X	85
Nutberry Hill	S Lanak	NS7433	55°34·7′	3°59·5′W	H	71
Nutberry Moss	D & G	NY2668	55°0·3′	3°9·0′W	X	85
Nutbourne	W Susx	SU7805	50°50·6′	0°53·1′W	T	197
Nutbourne	W Susx	TQ0718	50°57·3′	0°28·2′W	T	197
Nutbourne Common	W Susx	TQ0718	50°57·3′	0°28·2′W	T	197
Nut Brown Fm	E Susx	TQ6709	50°51·6′	0°22·8′E	FM	199
Nutburn	Hants	SU3920	50°58·9′	1°26·3′W	T	185
Nutcombe	Surrey	SU8834	51°6·1′	0°44·2′W	T	186
Nutcombe Fm	Devon	SS6145	51°11·5′	3°59·0′W	FM	180
Nutcombe Fm	Devon	SS8021	50°58·8′	3°42·2′W	FM	181
Nutcombe Fm	Devon	SX7648	50°19·4′	3°44·1′W	FM	202
Nutcombe Manor	Devon	ST0123	51°0·1′	3°24·3′W	X	181
Nutcott	Devon	SS8418	50°57·2′	3°38·7′W	X	181
Nut Crackers	Devon	SX7681	50°37·2′	3°44·8′W	X	191
Nutfield	Surrey	TQ3050	51°14·3′	0°7·9′W	T	187
Nutfield Down	W Berks	SU4879	51°30·7′	1°18·1′W	X	174
Nutfield Marsh	Surrey	TQ3051	51°14·8′	0°7·9′W	X	187
Nutfield Priory (Hotel)	Surrey	TQ2950	51°14·3′	0°8·7′W	X	187
Nutford Fm	Dorset	ST8708	50°52·5′	2°10·7′W	FM	194
Nutgill Fm	N Yks	SD6970	54°7·7′	2°28·0′W	FM	98
Nut Grove	St Hel	SJ4992	53°25·6′	2°45·6′W	T	108
Nuthall	Notts	SK5144	52°59·7′	1°14·0′W	T	129
Nuthampstead	Herts	TL4034	51°59·4′	0°2·7′E	T	154
Nuthampstead Bury	Herts	TL4034	51°59·4′	0°2·7′E	X	154
Nuthanger Fm	Hants	SU4958	51°19·4′	1°17·4′W	FM	174
Nuthill	E Yorks	TA2129	53°44·8′	0°9·5′W	X	107
Nut Hill	Leeds	SE4339	53°51·0′	1°20·4′W	X	105
Nut Hill	Somer	ST5227	51°2·7′	2°40·7′W	X	183
Nuthill Fm	Surrey	TQ0253	51°16·2′	0°31·9′W	FM	186
Nutholm	D & G	NY1276	55°4·5′	3°22·3′W	X	85
Nutholmhill	D & G	NY1276	55°4·5′	3°22·3′W	X	85
Nuthurst	Lancs	SD4954	53°59·0′	2°46·2′W	X	102
Nuthurst	Warw	SP1571	52°20·4′	1°46·4′W	T	139
Nuthurst	W Susx	TQ1926	51°1·5′	0°17·8′W	T	187,198
Nuthurst Fm	Warw	SP1570	52°19·9′	1°46·4′W	FM	139
Nuthurst Grange	Warw	SP1571	52°20·4′	1°46·4′W	X	139
Nuthurst Heath Fm	Warw	SP3090	52°30·7′	1°33·1′W	FM	140
Nutley	E Susx	TQ4427	51°1·7′	0°3·6′E	T	187,198
Nutley	Hants	SU6044	51°11·8′	1°8·1′W	T	185
Nutley Dean Fm	Surrey	TQ2444	51°11·1′	0°13·2′W	FM	187
Nutley Down	Hants	SU6244	51°11·7′	1°6·4′W	X	185
Nutley Fm	Devon	SX5075	50°33·6′	4°6·7′W	FM	191,201
Nutley Wood	Hants	SU6045	51°12·3′	1°8·1′W	F	185
Nutnells Wood	Worcs	SO9273	52°21·5′	2°6·7′W	F	139
Nut Rock	I Scilly	SV8812	49°55·8′	6°20·5′W	X	203
Nutscale Reservoir	Somer	SS8643	51°10·7′	3°37·5′W	W	181
Nutscale Water	Somer	SS8643	51°10·7′	3°37·5′W	W	181
Nutsgrove Fm	Peterb	TF3205	52°37·8′	0°2·6′W	FM	142
Nutshaw Hill	Lancs	SD8228	53°45·1′	2°16·0′W	H	103
Nutson	Devon	SS7211	50°53·3′	3°48·8′W	X	191
Nutstile	N Yks	SD6971	54°8·3′	2°28·1′W	X	98
Nutta Fm	N Yks	SD7368	54°6·7′	2°24·4′W	FM	98
Nuttal	Heref	SO6333	51°59·9′	2°31·9′W	X	149
Nuttall	Bury	SD7915	53°38·1′	2°18·6′W	T	109
Nutter's Platt	Lancs	SD5226	53°43·9′	2°43·2′W	X	102
Nutterswood	Glos	SO9825	51°55·6′	2°1·4′W	X	163
Nuttles Hall Fm	E Yorks	TA2032	53°46·5′	0°10·3′W	FM	107
Nutton Fm	Devon	SS3518	50°56·5′	4°20·5′W	FM	190
Nut Tree Fm	Norf	TM2488	52°26·9′	1°18·2′E	FM	156
Nuttree Fm	Shrops	SJ2724	52°48·8′	3°4·6′W	FM	126
Nutt's Fm	Essex	TL5740	52°2·4′	0°17·7′E	FM	154
Nuttys Fm	Essex	TQ6188	51°34·3′	0°19·8′E	FM	177
Nutwalls	Devon	SY0490	50°42·3′	3°21·2′W	X	192
Nutwell	Donc	SE6304	53°32·0′	1°2·6′W	T	111
Nutwell Court	Devon	SX9885	50°39·6′	3°26·2′W	A	192
Nutwell Fm	Somer	ST0227	51°2·3′	3°23·5′W	FM	181
Nutwith Common	N Yks	SE2178	54°12·1′	1°40·3′W	F	99
Nut Wood	Notts	SK6859	53°7·7′	0°58·6′W	F	120
Nut Wood	Staffs	SJ8122	52°48·0′	2°16·5′W	F	127
Nutwood Down	Oxon	SU3682	51°32·4′	1°28·5′W	X	174
Nyadd	Stir	NS7497	56°9·2′	4°1·3′W	X	57
Nybster	Highld	ND3663	58°33·3′	3°5·5′W	T	12
Nydie Mains	Fife	NO4317	56°20·8′	2°54·9′W	X	59
Nydie Mill	Fife	NO4316	56°20·2′	2°54·9′W	X	59
Nye	N Som	ST4161	51°20·9′	2°50·4′W	T	172,182
Nye, The	E Susx	TQ3314	50°54·8′	0°6·1′W	X	198
Nyetimber	W Susx	SZ8998	50°46·7′	0°43·9′W	T	197
Nyetimber Fm	W Susx	TQ0819	50°57·8′	0°27·3′W	FM	197
Nyewood	W Susx	SU8021	50°59·2′	0°51·2′W	T	197
Nyffryn	Gwyn	SH2637	52°54·4′	4°34·8′W	X	123
Nyland	Somer	ST4550	51°15·0′	2°46·9′W	T	182
Nyland Hill	Somer	ST4550	51°15·0′	2°46·9′W	H	182
Nyland Manor	Somer	ST4652	51°16·1′	2°46·1′W	X	182
Nymans Fm	W Susx	TQ2118	50°57·1′	0°16·3′W	FM	198
Nymet Bridge	Devon	SS7109	50°52·2′	3°49·6′W	X	191
Nymet Ho	Devon	SS7108	50°51·7′	3°49·6′W	X	191
Nymet Rowland	Devon	SS7108	50°51·7′	3°49·6′W	T	191
Nymet Tracey	Devon	SS7200	50°47·4′	3°48·6′W	T	191
Nymetwood	Devon	SX7397	50°45·8′	3°47·7′W	X	191
Nymphayes	Devon	SS7205	50°50·1′	3°48·7′W	X	191
Nympsfield	Glos	SO8000	51°42·1′	2°17·0′W	T	162
Nynehead	Somer	ST1322	50°59·7′	3°14·0′W	T	181,193
Nyn Park	Herts	TL2702	51°42·4′	0°9·3′W	F	166
Nyth-brân Ho	Rho Cyn Taf	ST0391	51°36·8′	3°23·7′W	X	170
Nythe	Somer	ST4234	51°6·4′	2°49·3′W	T	182
Nythe	Swin	SU1885	51°34·0′	1°44·0′W	T	173
Nythe Fm	Somer	ST3224	51°0·9′	2°57·8′W	FM	193
Nythe Fm	Swin	SU1985	51°34·0′	1°43·2′W	FM	173
Nyth-grug	Powys	SO1760	52°14·2′	3°12·5′W	H	148
Nyton	W Susx	SU9305	50°50·4′	0°40·4′W	T	197

O

Oadby	Leic	SK6200	52°35·9′	1°4·7′W	T	140
Oadby Lodge Fm	Leic	SK6400	52°35·9′	1°2·9′W	FM	140
Oad Street	Kent	TQ8662	51°19·8′	0°40·6′E	T	178
Oaf's Orchard	Wrex	SJ4836	52°55·4′	2°46·0′W	X	126
Oak	Devon	SS8626	51°1·6′	3°37·2′W	X	181
Oak	Somer	ST0040	51°9·3′	3°25·4′W	X	181
Oakall Green	Worcs	SO8160	52°14·5′	2°16·3′W	T	138,150
Oakamoor	Staffs	SK0544	52°59·8′	1°55·1′W	T	119,128
Oak Ash Fm	W Berks	SU4277	51°29·7′	1°23·3′W	FM	174
Oakbank	Aberd	NJ6118	57°15·3′	2°38·3′W	X	37
Oakbank	Arg & Bt	NM7232	56°25·8′	5°41·4′W	X	49
Oak Bank	Bury	SD8105	53°32·7′	2°16·8′W	T	109
Oakbank	Cumbr	NY1422	54°35·4′	3°19·4′W	X	89
Oakbank	Cumbr	NY3670	55°1·5′	2°59·6′W	X	85
Oakbank	Cumbr	NY4455	54°53·4′	2°52·0′W	X	85
Oak Bank	Cumbr	NY4746	54°48·6′	2°49·1′W	X	86
Oakbank	Cumbr	NY8311	54°29·9′	2°15·3′W	X	91,92
Oakbank	Cumbr	SD4795	54°21·5′	2°48·5′W	X	97
Oakbank	Cumbr	SD5196	54°21·7′	2°44·8′W	X	97
Oakbank	Cumbr	SD6294	54°20·7′	2°34·7′W	X	97
Oakbank	D & G	NY1171	55°1·8′	3°23·1′W	X	85
Oak Bank	Lancs	SD6467	54°6·1′	2°32·6′W	X	97
Oak Bank	N Yks	SE2277	54°11·5′	1°39·4′W	X	99
Oakbank	W Loth	NT0766	55°52·9′	3°28·8′W	T	65
Oakbank Fm	Ches	SJ5056	53°6·2′	2°44·4′W	FM	117
Oak Bank (SCH)	Kent	TQ5655	51°16·6′	0°14·6′E	X	188
Oak Beck	N Yks	SE2855	53°59·7′	1°34·0′W	W	104
Oak Belt	Norf	TG2724	52°46·2′	1°22·3′E	F	133,134
Oak Br	Lincs	TF5061	53°7·7′	0°14·9′E	X	122
Oak Burn	Moray	NJ1646	57°30·0′	3°23·6′W	W	28
Oak Burn	Scot Bord	NT3940	55°39·2′	2°57·7′W	W	73
Oakbutts Fm	York	SE6259	54°1·6′	1°2·8′W	FM	105
Oak Cott	Derby	SK1532	52°53·4′	1°46·2′W	X	128
Oak Cott	W Berks	SU5563	51°22·0′	1°12·2′W	X	174
Oak Covert	Glos	ST9091	51°37·3′	2°8·3′W	F	163,173
Oak Covert	Norf	TL7797	52°32·8′	0°37·0′E	F	144
Oak Cragg	N Yks	SE6796	54°21·5′	0°57·7′W	X	94,100
Oakcroft Fm	Heref	SO3159	52°13·7′	3°0·2′W	FM	148
Oakcroft Fm	Oxon	SP6315	51°50·0′	1°4·7′W	FM	164,165
Oak Cross	Devon	SX5399	50°46·6′	4°4·7′W	T	191
Oakdale	Caer	ST1898	51°40·7′	3°10·8′W	T	171
Oakdale	N Yks	SE2855	53°59·7′	1°34·0′W	T	104
Oak Dale	N Yks	SE4696	54°21·7′	1°17·1′W	X	100
Oakdale	Poole	SZ0292	50°43·9′	1°57·9′W	T	195
Oakdale	Surrey	TQ1745	51°11·8′	0°19·1′W	X	187
Oakdale Fm	N Yks	SE2854	53°59·1′	1°34·0′W	FM	104
Oakdale Fm	Surrey	TQ1537	51°7·5′	0°21·0′W	FM	187
Oakdene	V of Glam	ST1569	51°25·1′	3°13·0′W	X	171
Oakdene	W Susx	TQ0923	51°0·0′	0°26·4′W	X	198
Oakdene Fm	Derby	SK2832	52°53·3′	1°34·6′W	FM	128
Oakdene Fm	Kent	TQ9341	51°8·4′	0°45·9′E	FM	189
Oak Dene Fm	N Yks	SE5571	54°8·2′	1°9·1′W	FM	100
Oak Dene Grange	Northum	NU1401	55°18·4′	1°46·3′W	X	81
Oakdown	E Susx	TQ6323	50°59·2′	0°19·7′E	X	199
Oake	Somer	ST1525	51°1·3′	3°12·3′W	T	181,193
Oakedene Manor	W Susx	TQ2222	50°59·3′	0°15·3′W	X	198
Oakedge Park	Staffs	SK0019	52°46·4′	1°59·6′W	X	128
Oake Green	Somer	ST1525	51°1·3′	3°12·3′W	T	181,193
Oakeley Fm	Shrops	SO3388	52°29·4′	2°58·8′W	FM	137
Oakeley Mynd	Shrops	SO3487	52°28·9′	2°57·9′W	H	137
Oaken	Staffs	SJ8502	52°37·2′	2°12·9′W	T	127,139
Oaken Bank	Lancs	SD9137	53°50·0′	2°7·8′W	X	103
Oakenclough	Ches	SJ9669	53°13·3′	2°3·2′W	X	118
Oaken Clough	Derby	SE0501	53°30·6′	1°55·1′W	X	110
Oaken Clough	Derby	SK0685	53°22·0′	1°54·2′W	X	110
Oakenclough	Lancs	SD5447	53°55·3′	2°41·6′W	T	102
Oakenclough Fell	Lancs	SD5547	53°55·3′	2°40·7′W	X	102
Oakenclough Hall	Staffs	SK0563	53°10·1′	1°55·1′W	X	119
Oaken Coppice	Heref	SO7549	52°8·6′	2°21·5′W	F	150
Oaken Coppice	Wilts	SU3072	51°27·0′	1°33·7′W	F	174
Oaken Copse	W Berks	SU3569	51°25·4′	1°29·4′W	F	174
Oakendean Ho	Scot Bord	NT5633	55°35·6′	2°41·5′W	X	73
Oakenden	Kent	TQ5042	51°9·7′	0°9·1′E	X	188
Oakenden	Kent	TQ6666	51°22·3′	0°23·5′E	X	177,178
Oakend Wood	Bucks	TQ0188	51°35·1′	0°32·1′W	F	176
Oakenford Fm	Somer	ST2634	51°6·3′	3°3·0′W	FM	182
Oakengates	Wrekin	SJ7011	52°42·0′	2°26·2′W	T	127
Oakengrove	Bucks	SP9108	51°46·0′	0°40·5′W	X	165
Oaken Grove	Bucks	SU7685	51°33·8′	0°53·8′W	F	175
Oaken Grove	Surrey	TQ1049	51°14·0′	0°25·1′W	F	187
Oakenhayes	Corn	SX4370	50°30·8′	4°12·5′W	X	201
Oaken Head	Lancs	SD5367	54°6·1′	2°42·7′W	X	97
Oakenhead	Moray	NJ2468	57°42·0′	3°16·0′W	X	28
Oakenhead	Moray	NJ4152	57°33·5′	2°58·7′W	X	28
Oakenhill Hall	Suff	TM3066	52°14·9′	1°22·6′E	X	156
Oakenhill Wood	Glos	SO6207	51°45·9′	2°32·6′W	F	162
Oakenholt	Flint	SJ2671	53°14·1′	3°6·1′W	T	117
Oaken Holt	Oxon	SP4606	51°45·3′	1°19·6′W	X	164
Oakenknowes	Moray	NJ5154	57°34·7′	2°48·7′W	X	29
Oaken Lawn	Staffs	SJ8403	52°37·7′	2°13·8′W	X	127
Oaken Park Fm	Staffs	SJ8303	52°37·7′	2°14·7′W	FM	127
Oakenpole Wood	Kent	TQ9254	51°15·4′	0°45·5′E	F	189
Oakenshaw	Durham	NZ1937	54°43·9′	1°41·9′W	T	92
Oakenshaw	Durham	NZ2036	54°43·4′	1°40·9′W	T	93
Oakenshaw	Kirk	SE1727	53°44·6′	1°44·1′W	T	104
Oakenshaw	Lancs	SD7431	53°46·7′	2°23·3′W	T	103
Oaken Wood	Kent	TQ7155	51°16·3′	0°27·5′E	F	178,188
Oaken Wood	Surrey	SU9933	51°5·5′	0°34·8′W	F	186
Oaker	Shrops	SO3881	52°25·6′	2°54·3′W	X	137
Oaker Bank	N Yks	SE2756	54°0·2′	1°34·9′W	X	104
Oaker Coppice	Heref	SO4667	52°18·1′	2°47·1′W	F	137,138,148
Oaker Fm	Derby	SK1685	53°21·9′	1°45·2′W	FM	110
Oaker Hill	Essex	TL7439	52°1·6′	0°32·6′E	X	155
Oakerland	Northum	NY9462	54°57·4′	2°5·2′W	X	87
Oaker Lodge	Cumbr	NY3940	54°45·3′	2°56·4′W	X	85
Oakersdykes	Falk	NS8474	55°57·0′	3°51·0′W	X	65
Oaker's Hill	Heref	SO3446	52°6·7′	2°57·4′W	H	148,149
Oakers Wood	Dorset	SY8091	50°43·3′	2°16·6′W	F	194
Oakerthorpe	Derby	SK3854	53°5·1′	1°25·6′W	T	119
Oaker Wood	Heref	SO4663	52°16·0′	2°47·1′W	F	137,138,148
Oaker Wood	Shrops	SO3781	52°25·6′	2°55·2′W	F	137
Oakes	Kirk	SE1117	53°39·2′	1°49·6′W	T	110
Oakes Fm	N Som	ST3756	51°18·2′	2°53·8′W	FM	182
Oakeydean Burn	Northum	NY8155	54°53·6′	2°17·3′W	W	86,87
Oakey Fm	Glos	SO7711	51°48·1′	2°19·6′W	FM	162
Oakfield	Arg & Bt	NR8588	56°2·5′	5°26·7′W	X	55
Oakfield	Ches	SJ6749	53°2·5′	2°29·1′W	X	118
Oakfield	Hants	SU3927	51°2·7′	1°26·2′W	X	185
Oakfield	Herts	TL1928	51°56·5′	0°15·7′W	T	166
Oakfield	I of W	SZ5991	50°43·2′	1°9·5′W	T	196
Oakfield	Kent	TQ5242	51°9·6′	0°10·8′E	X	188
Oakfield	Kent	TQ8354	51°15·6′	0°37·8′E	X	188
Oakfield	Powys	SO1127	51°56·3′	3°17·3′W	X	161
Oakfield	Powys	SO2241	52°4·0′	3°7·9′W	X	148,161
Oakfield	Shrops	SJ4018	52°45·6′	2°52·9′W	X	126
Oakfield	Shrops	SO3883	52°26·7′	2°54·3′W	X	137
Oakfield	Somer	ST1425	51°1·3′	3°13·2′W	X	181,193
Oakfield	Torf	ST2993	51°38·1′	3°1·2′W	T	171
Oakfield	W Berks	SU6766	51°23·6′	1°1·8′W	X	175
Oakfield Fm	Ches	SJ5059	53°7·8′	2°44·4′W	FM	117
Oakfield Fm	Flint	SJ2859	53°7·6′	3°4·2′W	FM	117
Oakfield Fm	Worcs	SO8871	52°20·5′	2°10·2′W	FM	139
Oakfield House	Cumbr	NY2526	54°37·7′	3°9·3′W	X	89,90
Oakfields	Shrops	SJ5134	52°54·3′	2°43·3′W	X	126
Oakfields	Staffs	SK0423	52°48·5′	1°56·0′W	X	128
Oak Fm	Cambs	TL6756	52°10·8′	0°27·0′E	FM	154
Oak Fm	Ches	SJ5856	53°6·2′	2°37·2′W	FM	117
Oak Fm	Ches	SJ7761	53°9·0′	2°20·2′W	FM	118
Oak Fm	Ches	SJ8081	53°19·8′	2°17·6′W	FM	109
Oak Fm	Ches	SJ8459	53°7·9′	2°13·9′W	FM	118
Oak Fm	Devon	SS6805	50°50·0′	3°52·1′W	FM	191
Oak Fm	Devon	SX8193	50°43·7′	3°40·8′W	FM	191
Oak Fm	Devon	SX9382	50°37·9′	3°30·4′W	FM	192
Oak Fm	Essex	TL7520	51°51·3′	0°32·9′E	FM	167
Oak Fm	Essex	TL7917	51°49·6′	0°36·3′E	FM	167
Oak Fm	Essex	TL8106	51°43·6′	0°37·6′E	FM	168
Oak Fm	Essex	TL8433	51°58·1′	0°41·1′E	FM	168
Oak Fm	E Yorks	SE7639	53°50·7′	0°50·3′W	FM	105,106
Oak Fm	Glos	SP0131	51°58·9′	1°58·7′W	FM	150
Oak Fm	Herts	TL1808	51°45·7′	0°17·0′W	FM	166
Oak Fm	Kent	TR0432	51°3·3′	0°55·0′E	FM	189
Oak Fm	Kent	TR0733	51°3·8′	0°57·6′E	FM	179,189
Oak Fm	Man	SJ8084	53°21·4′	2°17·6′W	FM	109
Oak Fm	Monm	SO3903	51°43·6′	2°52·6′W	FM	171
Oak Fm	Norf	TF6604	52°36·7′	0°27·5′E	FM	143
Oak Fm	Norf	TG5100	52°32·6′	1°42·5′E	FM	134
Oak Fm	Norf	TL8391	52°29·4′	0°42·1′E	FM	144
Oak Fm	Norf	TM1284	52°25·0′	1°7·5′E	FM	144
Oak Fm	Norf	TM1882	52°23·8′	1°12·7′E	FM	156
Oak Fm	Notts	SK6928	52°50·9′	0°58·1′W	FM	129
Oak Fm	Notts	SK7858	53°7·0′	0°49·7′W	FM	120,121
Oak Fm	Oxon	SU7188	51°35·4′	0°58·1′W	FM	175
Oak Fm	Shrops	SJ3525	52°49·4′	2°57·5′W	FM	126
Oak Fm	Shrops	SJ4425	52°49·4′	2°49·5′W	FM	126
Oak Fm	Shrops	SO6373	52°21·5′	2°32·2′W	FM	138
Oak Fm	Staffs	SJ9409	52°41·0′	2°4·9′W	FM	127
Oak Fm	Staffs	SK1700	52°36·1′	1°44·5′W	FM	139
Oak Fm	Suff	TL8953	52°8·8′	0°46·1′E	FM	155
Oak Fm	Suff	TM0968	52°16·4′	1°4·2′E	FM	155
Oak Fm	Suff	TM1079	52°22·3′	1°5·5′E	FM	144
Oak Fm	Suff	TM1164	52°14·2′	1°5·8′E	FM	155
Oak Fm	Suff	TM2279	52°22·1′	1°16·1′E	FM	156
Oak Fm	Suff	TM2361	52°12·3′	1°16·2′E	FM	156
Oak Fm	Suff	TM2466	52°15·0′	1°17·3′E	FM	156
Oak Fm	Suff	TM2765	52°14·4′	1°19·9′E	FM	156
Oak Fm	Suff	TM3162	52°12·7′	1°23·3′E	FM	156
Oak Fm	Thurr	TQ7082	51°30·9′	0°27·4′E	FM	178
Oak Fm	Warw	SP1858	52°13·4′	1°43·8′W	FM	151
Oak Fm	Warw	SP2060	52°14·5′	1°42·0′W	FM	151
Oak Fm	Wilts	SU1361	51°21·1′	1°48·4′W	FM	173
Oak Fms	Ches	SJ9169	53°13·3′	2°7·7′W	FM	118
Oakford	Cered	SN4558	52°12·1′	4°15·7′W	T	146
Oakford	Devon	SS7229	51°3·0′	3°49·2′W	X	180
Oakford	Devon	SS9021	50°58·9′	3°33·6′W	T	181
Oakfordbridge	Devon	SS9121	50°58·9′	3°32·8′W	T	181
Oakford Fm	Devon	SX9096	50°45·4′	3°33·2′W	FM	192
Oakford Fm	Dorset	SY4098	50°46·9′	2°50·7′W	FM	193
Oakford Fm	S Glos	ST7870	51°25·9′	2°18·6′W	FM	172
Oakfrith Wood	Wilts	SU0257	51°19·0′	1°57·9′W	F	173
Oak Grange	N Yks	SE1894	54°20·7′	1°43·0′W	X	99
Oakgrove	Ches	SJ9169	53°13·3′	2°7·7′W	T	118
Oakgrove	Mil Key	SP8738	52°2·2′	0°43·5′W	T	152
Oakgrove	Monm	ST5195	51°39·3′	2°42·1′W	X	162
Oak Grove	Norf	TG1028	52°48·7′	1°7·4′E	F	133
Oak Grove	Suff	TL9172	52°19·0′	0°48·5′E	F	144,155
Oak Hall	Essex	TL6714	51°48·2′	0°25·7′E	X	167
Oakhall	Northum	NT9237	55°37·8′	2°7·2′W	X	74,75
Oak Hall (Sch)	E Susx	TQ6122	50°58·7′	0°18·0′E	X	199
Oakham	Rut	SK8509	52°40·6′	0°44·2′W	T	141
Oakham	Sand	SO9689	52°30·2′	2°3·1′W	T	139
Oakham	Shrops	SO5494	52°32·8′	2°40·3′W	X	137,138
Oakham	Warw	SP2730	51°58·3′	1°36·0′W	X	151
Oakham Bottom	Hants	SU7418	50°57·6′	0°56·4′W	F	197
Oakham Fm	Bucks	SP7825	51°55·3′	0°51·6′W	FM	165
Oakham Fm	Warw	SP2651	52°9·6′	1°36·8′W	FM	151
Oakham Marsh	Medway	TQ8372	51°25·3′	0°38·3′E	W	178
Oakham Ness	Medway	TQ8371	51°24·7′	0°38·3′E	X	178
Oakham Ness Jetty	Medway	TQ8372	51°25·3′	0°38·3′E	X	178
Oakhampton	Worcs	SO7969	52°19·4′	2°18·1′W	X	138
Oakhampton Fm	Somer	ST0929	51°3·4′	3°17·5′W	FM	181

Oakhanger	Ches	SJ7654	53°5·2'	2°21·1'W	T	118
Oakhanger	Hants	SU7635	51°6·8'	0°54·5'W	T	186
Oakhanger Hall	Ches	SJ7655	53°5·7'	2°21·1'W	X	118
Oakhanger Ho	W Berks	SU3873	51°27·5'	1°26·8'W	X	174
Oakhanger Moss	Ches	SJ7654	53°5·2'	2°21·1'W	X	118
Oakhanger Stream	Hants	SU7534	51°6·3'	0°55·3'W	W	186
Oakhay Barton	Devon	SX9398	50°46·5'	3°30·7'W	X	192
Oak Head	Cumbr	SD3883	54°14·6'	2°56·7'W	X	96,97
Oakhead	Lancs	SD6567	54°6·1'	2°31·7'W	X	97
Oakhedge Copse	W Berks	SU3778	51°30·2'	1°27·6'W	F	174
Oakhill	Aberd	NJ8227	57°20·2'	2°17·5'W	X	38
Oak Hill	C of Stoke	SJ8644	52°59·8'	2°12·1'W	T	118
Oak Hill	Cumbr	NY1526	54°37·6'	3°18·6'W	X	89
Oak Hill	Dorset	SY8893	50°44·4'	2°9·8'W	X	194
Oakhill	I of M	SC3574	54°8·4'	4°31·1'W	X	95
Oak Hill	Kent	TQ8665	51°21·4'	0°40·7'E	X	178
Oak Hill	Lancs	SD7336	53°49·4'	2°24·2'W	X	103
Oakhill	Leeds	SE3339	53°51·0'	1°29·5'W	X	104
Oak Hill	Pemb	SN0407	51°43·9'	4°49·9'W	X	157,158
Oak Hill	Pemb	SN0507	51°43·9'	4°49·0'W	X	158
Oak Hill	Shrops	SJ3600	52°35·9'	2°56·3'W	H	126
Oak Hill	Somer	ST3818	50°57·7'	2°52·6'W	X	193
Oakhill	Somer	ST6347	51°13·5'	2°31·4'W	T	183
Oakhill	Staffs	SK0039	52°57·1'	1°59·6'W	X	128
Oak Hill	Suff	TM3146	52°4·1'	1°22·6'E	X	169
Oak Hill	Suff	TM3645	52°3·4'	1°27·0'E	T	169
Oak Hill	Wilts	ST9380	51°31·4'	2°5·7'W	X	173
Oak Hill	Wilts	SU3067	51°24·3'	1°33·7'W	X	174
Oakhill	W Susx	TQ1830	51°3·7'	0°18·6'W	T	187
Oakhill Fm	Ches	SJ5775	53°16·5'	2°38·3'W	FM	117
Oakhill Fm	Lincs	SK8761	53°8·6'	0°41·6'W	FM	121
Oak Hill Fm	Suff	TM2464	52°13·9'	1°17·2'E	FM	156
Oak Hill Fm	Suff	TM2880	52°22·5'	1°21·4'E	FM	156
Oakhill Fm	Suff	TM2882	52°23·5'	1°21·5'E	FM	156
Oak Hill Park	Barnet	TQ2794	51°38·1'	0°9·5'W	X	166,176
Oakhill Wood	Glos	SO5500	51°42·1'	2°38·7'W	F	162
Oakhill Wood	Mil Key	SP8135	52°0·7'	0°48·8'W	F	152
Oakhill Wood	Wilts	SU3257	51°18·9'	1°32·1'W	F	174
Oak Ho	Lincs	TF3645	52°59·3'	0°2·0'E	X	131
Oak Ho	N Yks	SE5690	54°18·4'	1°7·9'W	X	100
Oak Ho	N Yks	SE5797	54°22·2'	1°6·9'W	X	100
Oak Ho	N Yks	SE6598	54°22·6'	0°59·5'W	X	94,100
Oak House	Hants	SU5860	51°20·4'	1°9·6'W	X	174
Oak House	Wrekin	SJ6122	52°47·9'	2°34·3'W	X	127
Oak House Fm	Essex	TM1818	51°49·3'	1°10·2'E	FM	168,169
Oak House Fm	Norf	TL9788	52°27·5'	0°54·4'E	FM	144
Oakhouse Fm	W Berks	SU5076	51°29·1'	1°16·4'W	FM	174
Oak Howe	Cumbr	NY3005	54°26·4'	3°4·3'W	X	90
Oakhowe Crag	Cumbr	NY3005	54°26·4'	3°4·3'W	X	90
Oakhunger Fm	Glos	SO6600	51°42·1'	2°29·1'W	FM	162
Oak Hurst	Derby	SK3352	53°4·1'	1°30·0'W	X	119
Oakhurst	Hants	SU4262	51°21·6'	1°23·4'W	X	174
Oakhurst	Kent	TQ5450	51°13·9'	0°12·7'E	T	188
Oakhurst	Shrops	SJ2831	52°52·5'	3°3·8'W	X	126
Oakhurst Fm	Peterb	TF2304	52°37·4'	0°10·6'W	FM	142
Oakhurst Fm	W Susx	SZ8496	50°45·7'	0°48·2'W	FM	197
Oakhurst Fm	W Susx	TQ0332	51°4·9'	0°31·4'W	FM	186
Oakington	Cambs	TL4164	52°15·6'	0°4·4'E	T	154
Oakland	Cumbr	SD4199	54°23·2'	2°54·1'W	X	96,97
Oakland Ho	Cumbr	NY4151	54°51·3'	2°54·7'W	X	85
Oaklands	Carm	SN4216	51°49·5'	4°17·2'W	T	159
Oaklands	Ches	SJ5657	53°6·7'	2°39·0'W	X	117
Oaklands	Conwy	SH8158	53°6·6'	3°46·3'W	X	116
Oaklands	Devon	SS7547	51°12·7'	3°47·0'W	X	180
Oaklands	Devon	SX5895	50°44·5'	4°0·4'W	X	191
Oaklands	Devon	SX6798	50°46·2'	3°52·8'W	X	191
Oaklands	Essex	TL8827	51°54·8'	0°44·4'E	X	168
Oaklands	Flint	SJ2174	53°15·7'	3°10·7'W	X	117
Oaklands	Herts	TL1807	51°45·2'	0°17·0'W	X	166
Oaklands	Herts	TL2417	51°50·5'	0°11·6'W	T	166
Oaklands	Kent	TQ8844	51°10·1'	0°41·7'E	X	189
Oak Lands	Kent	TQ9431	51°3·0'	0°46·5'E	X	189
Oaklands	Kirk	SE2012	53°36·5'	1°41·5'W	X	110
Oaklands	Lancs	SD8539	53°51·1'	2°13·3'W	X	103
Oaklands	Leic	SP4096	52°33·9'	1°24·2'W	X	140
Oaklands	Monm	ST3592	51°37·6'	2°56·0'W	X	171
Oaklands	N Yks	SD7068	54°6·7'	2°27·1'W	X	98
Oaklands	N Yks	SE5155	53°59·6'	1°12·9'W	X	105
Oaklands	Powys	SO0631	51°58·4'	3°21·7'W	X	160
Oaklands	Shrops	SJ3836	52°55·3'	2°54·9'W	X	126
Oaklands	Shrops	SJ5127	52°50·5'	2°43·2'W	X	126
Oaklands	Shrops	SJ5731	52°52·7'	2°37·9'W	X	126
Oaklands	Shrops	SO3792	52°31·6'	2°55·3'W	X	137
Oaklands	Surrey	TQ0538	51°8·1'	0°29·6'W	X	187
Oaklands	W Susx	SU8920	50°58·6'	0°43·5'W	X	197
Oaklands (Cheshire Home)	Lancs	SD5044	53°53·6'	2°45·2'W	X	102
Oaklands Fm	Cov	SP2883	52°26·9'	1°34·9'W	FM	140
Oaklands Fm	Derby	SK2216	52°44·7'	1°40·2'W	FM	128
Oaklands Fm	Hants	SU7637	51°7·9'	0°54·4'W	FM	186
Oaklands Fm	Heref	SO4622	51°53·9'	2°46·7'W	FM	161
Oaklands Fm	Lincs	TF2454	53°4·4'	0°8·5'W	FM	122
Oaklands Fm	Lincs	TF3321	52°46·4'	0°1·3'W	FM	131
Oaklands Fm	Norf	TF8818	52°43·8'	0°47·5'E	FM	132
Oaklands Fm	Norf	TF9604	52°36·1'	0°54·1'E	FM	144
Oaklands Fm	Norf	TM2486	52°25·8'	1°18·1'E	FM	156
Oaklands Fm	Norf	TM3495	52°30·4'	1°27·3'E	FM	134
Oaklands Fm	Norf	TM4692	52°28·4'	1°37·7'E	FM	134
Oaklands Fm	N Yks	SE4562	54°3·4'	1°18·3'W	FM	99
Oaklands Fm	Oxon	SP3816	51°50·7'	1°26·5'W	FM	164
Oaklands Fm	Shrops	SJ5305	52°38·7'	2°41·3'W	FM	126
Oaklands Fm	Somer	ST4111	50°54·0'	2°50·0'W	FM	193
Oaklands Fm	Suff	TM1969	52°16·8'	1°13·0'E	FM	156
Oaklands Fm	Worcs	SO9744	52°5·9'	2°2·2'W	FM	150
Oaklands Fm	W Susx	TQ2220	50°58·3'	0°15·4'W	FM	198
Oaklands Fm	W Susx	TQ2800	50°47·4'	0°10·7'W	FM	198
Oaklands Ho	Hants	SU4716	50°56·7'	1°19·5'W	X	185
Oaklands (Hotel)	NE Lincs	TA2005	53°31·9'	0°11·0'W	X	113
Oaklands Park	E Susx	TQ4515	50°55·2'	0°5·1'E	X	198
Oaklands Park	Glos	SO6709	51°47·0'	2°28·3'W	X	162
Oaklands Park	Surrey	TQ2139	51°8·5'	0°15·8'W	X	187
Oaklands Park	W Susx	TQ2819	50°57·6'	0°10·3'W	X	198
Oaklands, The	Ches	SJ3577	53°17·4'	2°58·1'W	X	117
Oaklands, The	Shrops	SJ5132	52°53·2'	2°43·3'W	X	126
Oaklands, The	Shrops	SO8096	52°33·9'	2°17·3'W	X	138
Oak Lane Fm	Sol	SP2078	52°24·2'	1°42·0'W	FM	139
Oak Lawn	Suff	TM1675	52°20·1'	1°10·6'E	X	144,156
Oaklawn Fm	Suff	TM1674	52°19·5'	1°10·6'E	FM	144,156
Oaklea Fm	Hants	SU8333	51°5·6'	0°48·5'W	FM	186
Oakleaze	S Glos	ST6286	51°34·5'	2°32·5'W	X	172
Oakleaze Fm	Glos	ST6997	51°40·5'	2°26·5'W	FM	162
Oakleigh	Kent	TQ7274	51°26·6'	0°28·9'E	X	178
Oakleigh Park	Barnet	TQ2694	51°38·1'	0°10·4'W	T	166,176
Oakle Street	Glos	SO7517	51°51·3'	2°21·4'W	T	162
Oakley	Beds	TL0153	52°10·2'	0°31·0'W	T	153
Oakley	Bucks	SP6312	51°48·4'	1°4·8'W	T	164,165
Oakley	Fife	NT0388	56°4·8'	3°33·1'W	T	65
Oakley	Glos	SO9722	51°54·0'	2°2·2'W	T	163
Oakley	Hants	SU5650	51°15·0'	1°11·5'W	T	185
Oakley	Oxon	SP7400	51°41·9'	0°55·4'W	T	165
Oakley	Poole	SZ0198	50°47·1'	1°58·8'W	T	195
Oakley	Staffs	SJ7036	52°55·5'	2°26·4'W	T	127
Oakley	Staffs	SJ8608	52°40·4'	2°12·0'W	X	127
Oakley	Suff	TM1677	52°21·1'	1°10·7'E	T	144,156
Oakley	Worcs	SO8960	52°14·5'	2°9·3'W	X	150
Oakley Bank	Northnts	SP6048	52°7·9'	1°7·0'W	X	152
Oakley Brook	Somer	ST5320	50°58·9'	2°39·8'W	W	182,183
Oakley Court	Win & Maid	SU9277	51°29·3'	0°40·1'W	X	175
Oakley Creek	Essex	TM2126	51°53·5'	1°13·1'E	W	169
Oakley Cross Beck	Durham	NZ1725	54°37·4'	1°43·8'W	W	92
Oakley Down	Dorset	SU0117	50°57·4'	1°58·8'W	X	184
Oakley Fm	Devon	SX5273	50°32·5'	4°4·9'W	FM	191,201
Oakley Fm	Dorset	SU0018	50°57·9'	1°59·6'W	FM	184
Oakley Fm	Hants	SU3327	51°2·7'	1°31·4'W	FM	185
Oakley Fm	Staffs	SJ9402	52°37·2'	2°4·9'W	FM	127,139
Oakley Fm	Staffs	SK1913	52°43·1'	1°42·7'W	FM	128
Oakley Fm	Wilts	ST9265	51°23·3'	2°6·5'W	FM	173
Oakley Fm	Wilts	SU0034	51°6·5'	1°59·6'W	FM	184
Oakley Fm	Wok	SU8072	51°26·7'	0°50·5'W	FM	175
Oakley Fms	Somer	ST5320	50°58·9'	2°39·8'W	FM	183
Oakley Grange	Northnts	SP8786	52°28·1'	0°42·8'W	X	141
Oakley Grange Fm	Leic	SK4922	52°47·8'	1°16·0'W	FM	129
Oakley Green	Win & Maid	SU9276	51°28·8'	0°40·1'W	T	175
Oakley Hall	Hants	SU5649	51°14·5'	1°11·5'W	X	185
Oakley Hill	Beds	TL0254	52°10·7'	0°30·1'W	X	153
Oakley Ho	Beds	TL0053	52°10·2'	0°31·9'W	X	153
Oakley Ho	Brom	TQ4166	51°22·8'	0°2·0'E	X	177
Oakley Ho	Devon	SS6007	50°51·0'	3°58·9'W	X	191
Oakley Ho	Suff	TM1677	52°21·1'	1°10·7'E	X	144,156
Oakley Park	Oxon	SU4598	51°41·0'	1°20·6'W	X	164
Oakley Park	Powys	SN9886	52°28·0'	3°29·7'W	X	136
Oakley Park	Suff	TM1777	52°21·1'	1°11·6'E	T	156
Oakley Side	N Yks	NZ7208	54°28·0'	0°52·9'W	X	94
Oakley Walls Fm	N Yks	NZ7208	54°28·0'	0°52·0'W	FM	94
Oakley Wood	Bucks	SP6111	51°47·9'	1°6·5'W	F	164,165
Oakley Wood	Glos	SO9702	51°43·2'	2°2·2'W	F	163
Oakley Wood	Leic	SK4821	52°47·3'	1°16·9'W	F	129
Oakley Wood	Oxon	SU6488	51°35·5'	1°4·2'W	T	175
Oakley Wood	Warw	SP3059	52°13·9'	1°33·2'W	F	151
Oakley Wood Fm	Warw	SP3060	52°14·5'	1°33·2'W	FM	151
Oak Lodge	Barnet	TQ2294	51°38·1'	0°13·8'W	X	166,176
Oak Lodge	Lincs	TF3823	52°47·4'	0°3·2'E	X	131
Oak Lodge	Sol	SP1474	52°22·1'	1°47·3'W	X	139
Oak Lodge Fm	Kent	TQ4849	51°13·5'	0°7·6'E	FM	188
Oak Lodge Fm	Leic	SP4995	52°33·3'	1°16·2'W	FM	140
Oak Lodge Fm	Norf	TG2412	52°39·8'	1°19·2'E	FM	133,134
Oakly Park	Shrops	SO4875	52°22·5'	2°45·4'W	X	137,138,148
Oak Mere	Ches	SJ5767	53°12·1'	2°38·2'W	W	117
Oakmere	Ches	SJ5769	53°13·2'	2°38·2'W	T	117
Oakmere Hall	Ches	SJ5870	53°13·8'	2°37·3'W	X	117
Oakmoor Sch	Hants	SU5016	50°56·7'	1°16·9'W	X	185
Oaknowe	S Ayr	NX1585	55°7·7'	4°53·7'W	X	76
Oakover	E Susx	TQ6829	51°2·4'	0°24·2'E	X	188,199
Oak Plantation	Norf	TL9489	52°28·1'	0°51·8'E	F	144
Oak Plantation	Powys	SJ2608	52°40·1'	3°5·3'W	F	126
Oak Plantn	Suff	TL7671	52°18·8'	0°35·3'E	F	155
Oakpool	Northum	NY8057	54°54·7'	2°18·3'W	X	86,87
Oakreeds Wood	W Susx	SU8829	51°3·4'	0°44·3'W	F	186,197
Oakridge	Glos	SO9103	51°43·8'	2°7·4'W	T	163
Oakridge	Hants	SU6353	51°16·6'	1°5·4'W	T	185
Oakridge	N Som	ST4356	51°18·3'	2°48·7'W	X	172,182
Oak Ridge Fm	Corn	SW7952	50°19·8'	5°5·9'W	FM	200,204
Oakridge Fm	Devon	SS5245	51°11·3'	4°6·7'W	FM	180
Oakrigg	D & G	NT0903	55°19·0'	3°25·6'W	X	78
Oakrigside	D & G	NT0902	55°18·5'	3°25·6'W	X	78
Oakrigg Wood	N Yks	NZ7816	54°32·2'	0°47·2'W	F	94
Oaks	Cumbr	NY3404	54°25·9'	3°0·6'W	X	90
Oaks	Shrops	SJ4204	52°38·1'	2°51·0'W	T	126
Oaks Bottom	Glos	SP0714	51°49·7'	1°53·5'W	X	163
Oaksey	Wilts	ST9993	51°38·4'	2°0·5'W	T	163,173
Oaksey Moor Fm	Wilts	SU0094	51°38·9'	1°59·6'W	FM	163,173
Oaksey Nursery	Wilts	ST9991	51°37·3'	2°0·5'W	F	163,173
Oaksey Wood	Wilts	ST9793	51°38·4'	2°2·2'W	F	163,173
Oaks Fm	Ches	SJ3476	53°16·9'	2°59·0'W	FM	117
Oaks Fm	Derby	SK2079	53°18·7'	1°41·6'W	FM	119
Oaks Fm	Flint	SJ2765	53°10·9'	3°5·1'W	FM	117
Oaks Fm	Flint	SJ3065	53°10·9'	3°2·4'W	FM	117
Oaks Fm	Leeds	SE1844	53°53·8'	1°43·2'W	FM	104
Oaks Fm	Leeds	SE2341	53°52·1'	1°38·6'W	FM	104
Oaks Fm	Leic	SK4716	52°44·6'	1°17·8'W	FM	129
Oaks Fm	Leic	SK5103	52°37·6'	1°14·4'W	FM	140
Oaks Fm	Norf	TF5402	52°35·9'	0°16·8'E	FM	143
Oaks Fm	Norf	TG0622	52°45·6'	1°3·6'E	FM	133
Oaks Fm	Norf	TG2606	52°36·5'	1°20·7'E	FM	134
Oaks Fm	Norf	TG2810	52°38·6'	1°22·6'E	FM	133,134
Oaks Fm	Norf	TM0994	52°30·5'	1°5·2'E	FM	144
Oaks Fm	Norf	TM2795	52°30·6'	1°21·1'E	FM	134
Oaks Fm	Notts	SK4749	53°2·4'	1°17·5'W	FM	129
Oaks Fm	N Yks	NZ7716	54°32·2'	0°48·2'W	FM	94
Oaks Fm	N Yks	SE6565	54°4·8'	1°0·0'W	FM	100
Oaks Fm	Suff	TM0636	51°59·3'	1°0·4'E	FM	155
Oaks Fm	Warw	SP2771	52°20·4'	1°35·8'W	FM	140
Oaks Fm, The	Cumbr	SD1784	54°14·9'	3°16·0'W	FM	96
Oaks Fm, The	Leic	SK6420	52°46·7'	1°2·7'W	FM	129
Oaks Fm, The	Shrops	SJ3209	52°40·7'	2°59·9'W	FM	126
Oaks Green	Derby	SK1533	52°53·9'	1°46·2'W	T	128
Oakshaw	Cumbr	NY5275	55°4·3'	2°44·7'W	X	86
Oakshaw Ford	Cumbr	NY5176	55°4·8'	2°45·6'W	T	86
Oakshaw Hill	Cumbr	NY4171	55°2·1'	2°55·0'W	X	85
Oakshott	Hants	SU7327	51°2·5'	0°57·1'W	T	186,197
Oakshott Fm	Hants	SU7328	51°3·0'	0°57·1'W	FM	186,197
Oakshott Stream	Hants	SU7528	51°3·0'	0°55·4'W	W	186,197
Oaksike Clough	Derby	SE0900	53°30·0'	1°51·4'W	X	110
Oaks in Charnwood	Leic	SK4716	52°44·6'	1°17·8'W	T	129
Oakslade Fm	Warw	SP2266	52°17·7'	1°40·2'W	FM	151
Oaksmere	Suff	TM1376	52°20·7'	1°8·0'E	X	144,156
Oaks Park	Croy	TQ2761	51°20·3'	0°10·2'W	X	176,187
Oak Spinney	Leic	SP5590	52°30·5'	1°11·0'W	F	140
Oaks, The	Bath & NE Somer	ST5662	51°21·6'	2°37·5'W	X	172,182
Oaks, The	Bucks	SP7935	52°0·7'	0°50·5'W	X	152
Oaks, The	Derby	SK3344	52°59·8'	1°30·1'W	X	119,128
Oaks, The	Derby	SK4472	53°14·8'	1°20·0'W	X	120
Oaks, The	Derby	SK5173	53°15·3'	1°13·7'W	X	120
Oaks, The	Essex	TM1125	51°53·2'	1°4·4'E	X	168,169
Oaks, The	Flint	SJ3060	53°8·2'	3°2·4'W	X	117
Oaks, The	Kent	TQ9959	51°17·9'	0°51·7'E	X	178
Oaks, The	Leic	SK4808	52°40·3'	1°17·0'W	X	140
Oaks, The	Lincs	TF0323	52°47·9'	0°27·9'W	F	130
Oaks, The	Monm	SO5101	51°42·6'	2°42·2'W	F	162
Oaks, The	N Lincs	SE9817	53°38·7'	0°30·6'W	F	112
Oaks, The	Norf	TG0831	52°50·4'	1°5·7'E	X	133
Oaks, The	Norf	TG3804	52°35·1'	1°31·2'E	X	134
Oaks, The	Norf	TM0883	52°24·6'	1°3·9'E	X	144
Oaks, The	Northum	NT9301	55°18·4'	2°6·2'W	F	80
Oaks, The	Shrops	SJ3928	52°51·0'	2°53·9'W	X	126
Oaks, The	Surrey	SU9560	51°20·1'	0°37·8'W	X	175,176,186
Oaks, The	Warw	SP3448	52°8·0'	1°29·8'W	F	151
Oaks, The	W Susx	TQ3231	51°4·0'	0°6·6'W	X	187
Oakstock	Cumbr	NY5774	55°3·8'	2°40·0'W	X	86
Oaks Wood	Derby	SK3754	53°5·2'	1°26·4'W	F	119
Oaks Wood	Shrops	SJ4104	52°38·1'	2°51·9'W	F	126
Oak, The	Essex	TM1725	51°53·1'	1°9·6'E	X	168,169
Oak, The	Shrops	SJ4512	52°42·4'	2°48·4'W	X	126
Oakthorpe	Leic	SK3213	52°43·1'	1°31·2'W	T	128
Oak Tree	Darl	NZ3513	54°30·9'	1°27·1'W	T	93
Oak Tree	Lancs	SD5838	53°50·4'	2°37·9'W	X	102
Oak Tree	N Yks	SE3184	54°15·3'	1°31·0'W	X	99
Oaktree Fm	Cambs	TF4115	52°43·1'	0°5·7'E	FM	131
Oak Tree Fm	Ches	SJ5365	53°11·0'	2°41·8'W	FM	117
Oak Tree Fm	Ches	SJ5963	53°10·0'	2°36·4'W	FM	117
Oaktree Fm	Ches	SJ7158	53°7·3'	2°25·6'W	FM	118
Oak Tree Fm	Devon	SS7303	50°49·0'	3°47·8'W	FM	191
Oak Tree Fm	E Yorks	SE7633	53°47·5'	0°50·4'W	FM	105,106
Oak Tree Fm	Hants	SU4050	51°15·1'	1°25·2'W	FM	185
Oaktree Fm	Kent	TQ9137	51°6·2'	0°44·1'E	FM	189
Oak Tree Fm	Lincs	SK8588	53°23·2'	0°42·9'W	FM	112,121
Oak Tree Fm	Lincs	TF0118	52°45·2'	0°29·8'W	FM	130
Oak Tree Fm	Lincs	TF1712	52°41·8'	0°15·7'W	FM	130,142
Oak Tree Fm	Notts	SK6025	52°49·4'	1°6·2'W	FM	129
Oak Tree Fm	Notts	SK8068	53°12·4'	0°47·7'W	FM	121
Oak Tree Fm	N Yks	SE0588	54°17·5'	1°55·0'W	FM	98
Oak Tree Fm	N Yks	SE2782	54°14·2'	1°34·7'W	FM	99
Oaktree Fm	N Yks	SE3977	54°11·5'	1°23·7'W	FM	99
Oak Tree Fm	N Yks	SE5733	53°47·6'	1°7·7'W	FM	105
Oak Tree Fm	N Yks	SE8087	54°16·6'	0°45·9'W	FM	94,100
Oaktree Fm	Suff	TL9145	52°4·4'	0°47·6'E	FM	155
Oaktree Fm	Suff	TL9765	52°15·1'	0°53·6'E	FM	155
Oak Tree Fm	Suff	TM0861	52°12·7'	1°3·1'E	FM	155
Oaktree Fm	Suff	TM1964	52°14·1'	1°12·8'E	FM	156
Oak Tree Fm	Suff	TM3869	52°16·3'	1°29·7'E	FM	156
Oak Tree Fm	Suff	TM4064	52°13·5'	1°31·3'E	FM	156
Oak Tree Fm	Win & Maid	SU8473	51°27·2'	0°47·1'W	FM	175
Oaktree Hall	Cumbr	NY5354	54°53·0'	2°43·5'W	X	86
Oaktree Hill	N Yks	SE3698	54°22·8'	1°26·3'W	X	99
Oaktree Ho	N Yks	SE2892	54°19·6'	1°33·7'W	X	99
Oaktree Ho	N Yks	SE4094	54°20·6'	1°22·7'W	X	99
Oak Trees	N Yks	SE5572	54°8·7'	1°9·1'W	X	100
Oaktrow Fm	Somer	SS9440	51°9·2'	3°30·6'W	FM	181
Oaktrow Wood	Somer	SS9440	51°9·2'	3°30·6'W	F	181
Oak View Fm	N Yks	SE3453	53°58·6'	1°28·5'W	FM	104
Oak Villa Fm	Warr	SJ7087	53°23·0'	2°26·7'W	FM	109
Oakwell	Kirk	SE2127	53°44·6'	1°40·5'W	T	104
Oakwood	C of Derb	SK3838	52°56·5'	1°25·7'W	T	128
Oak Wood	Corn	SW6342	50°14·1'	5°19·0'W	F	203
Oak Wood	E Loth	NT5879	56°0·4'	2°40·0'W	F	67
Oakwood	Enf	TQ2995	51°38·6'	0°7·7'W	T	166,176
Oak Wood	E Susx	TQ8215	50°54·6'	0°35·7'E	F	199
Oakwood	Leeds	SE3236	53°49·4'	1°30·4'W	T	104
Oakwood	Moray	NJ1554	57°34·3'	3°24·8'W	X	28
Oakwood	Moray	NJ1862	57°38·7'	3°22·0'W	X	28
Oak Wood	Norf	TG1342	52°56·2'	1°10·6'E	F	133
Oak Wood	Norf	TL8799	52°33·6'	0°45·9'E	F	144
Oak Wood	Norf	TL9082	52°24·4'	0°48·0'E	F	144
Oakwood	Northum	NY9465	54°59·0'	2°5·2'W	T	87
Oak Wood	N Yks	NZ9203	54°25·1'	0°34·5'W	F	94
Oak Wood	Oxon	SU2695	51°39·4'	1°37·1'W	F	163
Oakwood	Pth & Kin	NO2537	56°31·4'	3°12·7'W	X	53
Oakwood	Scot Bord	NT4225	55°31·2'	2°54·7'W	X	73
Oakwood	Scot Bord	NT8653	55°46·5'	2°13·0'W	X	67,74
Oakwood	Shrops	SO4490	52°30·5'	2°49·1'W	X	137
Oak Wood	Suff	TM1352	52°7·7'	1°7·1'E	F	156
Oak Wood	Suff	TM3748	52°5·0'	1°28·0'E	F	169
Oakwood	Warr	SJ6591	53°25·1'	2°31·2'W	T	109
Oakwood	W Susx	TQ1318	50°57·2'	0°23·1'W	X	198
Oak Wood	York	SE6261	54°2·7'	1°2·8'W	F	100
Oakwood Fm	Ches	SJ8271	53°14·4'	2°15·8'W	FM	118
Oakwood Fm	Kent	TQ8960	51°18·7'	0°43·1'E	FM	178
Oakwood Fm	N Yks	SE3251	53°57·5'	1°30·3'W	FM	104
Oakwood Fm	N Yks	SE3757	54°0·7'	1°25·7'W	FM	104
Oakwood Fm	Shrops	SO6187	52°29·0'	2°34·1'W	FM	138
Oakwoodhill	D & G	NY3174	55°3·6'	3°4·4'W	X	85

Oakwoodhill	Surrey	TQ1337	51°7·5′	0°22·7′W	T	187
Oakwood Ho	Norf	TF6312	52°41·1′	0°25·1′E	X	132,143
Oakwood Ho	Northum	NZ1165	54°59·0′	1°49·3′W	X	88
Oakwood (Hotel)	Cumbr	NY5261	54°56·7′	2°44·5′W	X	86
Oakwood Lodge	Kent	TQ4850	51°14·0′	0°7·6′E	X	188
Oakwood Mill	Scot Bord	NT4426	55°31·7′	2°52·8′W	X	73
Oakwood Mill Fm	Surrey	TQ1338	51°8·0′	0°22·7′W	FM	187
Oakwood Park	Enf	TQ3095	51°38·6′	0°6·9′W	X	166,176,177
Oakwood Park	Kent	TQ7455	51°16·3′	0°30·1′E	X	178,188
Oakwood (Sch)	W Susx	SU8206	50°51·1′	0°49·7′W	X	197
Oakworth	Brad	SE0338	53°50·5′	1°56·9′W	T	104
Oakworth Moor	Brad	SD9938	53°50·5′	2°0·5′W	X	103
Oans	Highld	NG2859	57°32·6′	6°32·3′W	X	23
Oape	Highld	NC4500	57°58·0′	4°36·7′W	T	16
Oare	Kent	TR0062	51°19·5′	0°52·6′E	T	178
Oare	Somer	SS8047	51°12·8′	3°42·7′W	T	181
Oare	W Berks	SU5074	51°28·0′	1°16·4′W	T	174
Oare	Wilts	SU1563	51°22·2′	1°46·7′W	T	173
Oareborough Hill	W Berks	SU4975	51°28·5′	1°17·3′W	H	174
Oare Common	Somer	SS7946	51°12·3′	3°43·5′W	X	180
Oareford	Somer	SS8146	51°12·3′	3°41·8′W	T	181
Oare Hill	Wilts	SU1664	51°22·7′	1°45·8′W	X	173
Oare Ho	Wilts	SU1562	51°21·6′	1°46·7′W	X	173
Oare Post	Somer	SS8346	51°12·3′	3°40·1′W	X	181
Oare Water	Somer	SS8046	51°12·3′	3°42·7′W	W	181
Oar Fm	Kent	TR2268	51°22·3′	1°11·8′E	FM	179
Oasby	Lincs	TF0039	52°56·6′	0°30·3′W	T	130
Oatclose Wood	Dorset	ST8302	50°49·3′	2°14·1′W	F	194
Oat Eddish Fm	Ches	SJ6848	53°1·9′	2°28·2′W	FM	118
Oaters Wood	W Susx	SU9023	51°0·2′	0°42·6′W	F	197
Oates Wood	N Yks	SE4251	53°57·4′	1°21·2′W	F	105
Oatfield	Arg & Bt	NR6817	55°23·8′	5°39·4′W	X	68
Oatfield	E Loth	NT5184	56°3·0′	2°46·8′W	X	66
Oatfield	Glos	SO7508	51°46·4′	2°21·3′W	X	162
Oatfield Fm	Glos	SO6705	51°44·8′	2°28·3′W	FM	162
Oatfield Ho	Arg & Bt	NR6818	55°24·3′	5°39·4′W	X	68
Oath	Somer	ST3827	51°2·6′	2°52·7′W	T	193
Oa, The	Arg & Bt	NR3144	55°37·2′	6°15·9′W	X	60
Oath Hill	Somer	ST3827	51°2·6′	2°52·7′W	H	193
Oat Hill	Ches	SJ4848	53°1·8′	2°46·1′W	H	117
Oathill	Dorset	ST4005	50°50·7′	2°50·8′W	T	193
Oat Hill	Glos	SP0933	52°0·0′	1°51·7′W	X	150
Oat Hill	Staffs	SJ9720	52°46·9′	2°2·3′W	H	127
Oathill Fm	Kent	TR0251	51°13·6′	0°54·0′E	FM	189
Oathill Fm	Oxon	SP4124	51°55·0′	1°23·8′W	FM	164
Oathill Fm	Oxon	SP4648	52°7·9′	1°19·3′W	FM	151
Oathillock	Moray	NJ5161	57°38·4′	2°48·8′W	X	29
Oathlaw	Angus	NO4756	56°41·8′	2°51·5′W	T	54
Oath Lock	Somer	ST3827	51°2·6′	2°52·7′W	X	193
Oatlands	C of Glas	NS5963	55°50·6′	4°14·7′W	T	64
Oatlands	Cumbr	NY0221	54°34·7′	3°30·6′W	X	89
Oatlands	I of M	SC3272	54°7·2′	4°33·8′W	X	95
Oatlands	N Som	ST4764	51°22·6′	2°45·3′W	X	172,182
Oatlands	N Yks	SE3053	53°58·6′	1°32·1′W	T	104
Oatlands Fm	Devon	ST2806	50°51·2′	3°1·0′W	FM	193
Oatlands Fm	Notts	SK7293	53°26·0′	0°54·6′W	FM	112
Oatlands Fm	N Yks	SE4055	53°59·6′	1°23·0′W	FM	105
Oatlands Hill	Wilts	SU0940	51°9·8′	1°51·9′W	X	184
Oatlands Park	Surrey	TQ0964	51°22·1′	0°25·7′W	T	176,187
Oatlee Hill	Scot Bord	NT8869	55°55·1′	2°11·1′W	X	67
Oatleycleugh	Scot Bord	NT7558	55°49·1′	2°23·5′W	X	67,74
Oatley Fm	Heref	SO3237	52°1·9′	2°59·1′W	FM	161
Oatley Hill Fm	Oxon	SP3334	52°0·4′	1°30·8′W	FM	151
Oatleys Fm	Bucks	SP6137	52°1·9′	1°6·3′W	FM	152
Oatleys Hall	Bucks	SP6037	52°1·9′	1°7·1′W	X	152
Oatley Vineyard	Somer	ST2339	51°8·9′	3°5·7′W	X	182
Oatnell	Devon	SX5192	50°42·7′	4°6·3′W	X	191
Oatridge	W Loth	NT0473	55°56·7′	3°31·8′W	X	65
Oatscroft	W Susx	SU8919	50°58·0′	0°43·6′W	X	197
Oatslie	Midlo	NT2662	55°51·0′	3°10·5′W	X	66
Oatway	Somer	SS9330	51°3·8′	3°31·2′W	X	181
Oatyhill	Aberd	NO6969	56°48·9′	2°30·0′W	X	45
Oaze, The	Kent	TR0865	51°21·0′	0°59·6′E	X	179
Ob a' Bhràighe	Highld	NG8257	57°33·3′	5°38·2′W	W	24
Ob a' Choir'-uidhe	Highld	NG8875	57°43·2′	5°33·1′W	W	19
Oback	Orkney	HY3510	58°58·6′	3°7·4′W	X	6
Oback	Orkney	ND4391	58°48·4′	2°58·7′W	X	7
Oback Fm	Leic	SP5685	52°27·8′	1°10·1′W	FM	140
Ob a' Ghibhte	N Eil	NF8564	57°33·6′	7°15·6′W	W	18
Ob Allt an Daraich	Highld	NG7125	57°15·8′	5°47·4′W	W	33
Oban	Arg & Bt	NM8630	56°25·1′	5°27·7′W	T	49
Oban	Highld	NM8690	56°57·4′	5°30·7′W	X	33,40
Oban	N Eil	NB1600	57°54·2′	6°47·2′W	T	14
Oban a' Chlachain	N Eil	NF8264	57°33·5′	7°18·6′W	W	18
Oban an Innseanaich	N Eil	NF8659	57°31·0′	7°14·2′W	W	22
Oban Bay	Arg & Bt	NM8530	56°25·1′	5°28·7′W	W	49
Ob an Dreallaire	Highld	NG6260	57°34·3′	5°58·4′W	W	24
Oban Irpeig	N Eil	NF8063	57°32·9′	7°20·5′W	W	18
Oban Lionacleit	N Eil	NF7850	57°25·8′	7°21·5′W	W	22
Oban na Buail'-uachdraich	N Eil	NF7746	57°23·6′	7°22·2′W	W	22
Oban na Curra	N Eil	NF8263	57°33·0′	7°18·5′W	W	18
Oban nam Fiadh	N Eil	NF8462	57°32·5′	7°16·4′W	X	22
Oban nam Muca-mara	N Eil	NF8759	57°31·0′	7°13·2′W	W	22
Oban nan Forsanan	N Eil	NF8550	57°26·1′	7°14·5′W	W	22
Oban Seil	Arg & Bt	NM7718	56°18·4′	5°35·9′W	T	55
Oban Skibinish	N Eil	NF8374	57°38·9′	7°18·4′W	W	18
Oban Sponish	N Eil	NF8864	57°33·8′	7°12·6′W	W	18
Oban THaca	N Eil	NF8452	57°27·2′	7°15·7′W	W	22
Oban Trumisgarry	N Eil	NF8774	57°39·1′	7°14·4′W	W	18
Oban Uaine	N Eil	NF8447	57°24·5′	7°15·3′W	W	22
Oban Uaine	N Eil	NF8553	57°27·7′	7°14·8′W	W	22
Ob Apoldoire	Highld	NG6026	57°16·0′	5°58·4′W	W	32
Obbe, The	N Eil	NG0186	57°46·1′	7°1·3′W	W	18
Ob Breakish	Highld	NG6824	57°15·1′	5°50·3′W	W	32
Ob Ceann a' Ghàraidh	N Eil	NG2098	57°53·3′	6°43·0′W	W	14
Ob Chuaig	Highld	NG7059	57°34·0′	5°50·3′W	W	24
Ob Dubh	Highld	NG2348	57°26·5′	6°36·5′W	W	23
Obeden Fm	Kent	TQ8641	51°8·5′	0°39·9′E	FM	189
Obelisk	Scot Bord	NT7336	55°37·3′	2°25·3′W	X	74
Obelisk Pond	Surrey	SU9770	51°25·5′	0°35·9′W	W	175,176

Ober Heath	Hants	SU2803	50°49·8′	1°35·8′W	X	195
Ober Ho	Hants	SU2802	50°49·2′	1°35·8′W	X	195
Ober Water	Hants	SU2603	50°49·8′	1°37·5′W	W	195
Ob Gauscavaig	Highld	NG5911	57°7·9′	5°58·5′W	W	32
Ob Gorm Beag	Highld	NG8654	57°31·8′	5°34·0′W	W	24
Ob Gorm Mór	Highld	NG8654	57°31·8′	5°34·0′W	W	24
Ob Leasaid	N Eil	NG1188	57°47·6′	6°51·3′W	W	14
Obley	Shrops	SO3277	52°23·4′	2°59·6′W	T	137,148
Ob Liceasto	N Eil	NG1698	57°53·1′	6°47·0′W	W	14
Ob Lusa	Highld	NG7024	57°15·2′	5°48·3′W	W	33
Ob Mheallaidh	Highld	NG8354	57°31·7′	5°37·0′W	W	24
Ob Mhiabhaig	N Eil	NG1596	57°52·0′	6°47·9′W	W	14
Ob na Bà Ruaidhe	Highld	NG8683	57°47·4′	5°35·6′W	W	19
Ob na h-Uamha	Highld	NG7160	57°34·6′	5°49·3′W	W	24
Ob nam Feusgan	Highld	NG6160	57°34·3′	5°59·4′W	W	24
Ob nam Muc	Highld	NG9470	57°40·6′	5°26·8′W	W	19
Ob nan Ròn	Highld	NG4968	57°38·2′	6°11·9′W	W	23
Obney Hills	Pth & Kin	NO0238	56°31·7′	3°35·1′W	H	52,53
Oborne	Dorset	ST6518	50°57·9′	2°29·5′W	T	183
Obourne's Fm	Essex	TL6934	51°58·9′	0°28·1′E	FM	154
Obriss Fm	Kent	TQ4650	51°14·1′	0°5·9′E	FM	188
O Brook	Devon	SX6571	50°31·6′	3°53·9′W	W	202
Ob Saile	N Eil	NF8148	57°24·9′	7°18·3′W	W	22
Ob Scalla	N Eil	NG1188	57°47·6′	6°51·3′W	W	14
Obsdale Park	Highld	NH6769	57°41·7′	4°13·4′W	T	21
Ob Snaosaig	Highld	NG6910	57°7·6′	5°48·5′W	W	32
Obthorpe	Lincs	TF0915	52°43·5′	0°22·8′W	X	130
Obthorpe Lodge	Lincs	TF1015	52°43·5′	0°21·9′W	T	130
Oburnford	Devon	SS9809	50°52·5′	3°26·6′W	X	192
Occaney	N Yks	SE3561	54°2·9′	1°27·5′W	X	99
Occlestone Green	Ches	SJ6962	53°9·5′	2°27·4′W	T	118
Occold	Suff	TM1570	52°17·4′	1°9·6′E	T	144,156
Occombe	Devon	SX8763	50°27·6′	3°35·1′W	X	202
Occumster	Highld	ND2635	58°18·1′	3°15·3′W	X	11
Ocean View Fm	E Yorks	TA2370	54°6·9′	0°6·7′W	FM	101
Ocean Village	C of Soton	SU4210	50°53·5′	1°23·8′W	T	196
Ochil Hills	Pth & Kin	NO0409	56°16·1′	3°32·6′W	H	58
Ochiltree	D & G	NX3274	55°2·2′	4°37·3′W	X	76
Ochiltree Mains	E Ayr	NS5120	55°27·3′	4°20·9′W	X	70
Ochiltree Mill	W Loth	NT0373	55°56·7′	3°32·7′W	X	65
Ochor	Cered	SN6659	52°13·0′	3°57·3′W	X	146
Ochram Fm	Monm	SO3009	51°46·8′	3°0·5′W	FM	161
Ochr Cefn	Conwy	SH8449	53°1·8′	3°43·4′W	X	116
Ochr-cefn	Powys	SN9468	52°18·2′	3°32·9′W	X	136,147
Ochre Fm	N Yks	SE8977	54°11·1′	0°37·8′W	FM	101
Ochre Plantns	N Yks	SE8876	54°10·6′	0°38·7′W	F	101
Ochr Fawr	Cered	SN7455	52°11·0′	3°50·2′W	H	146,147
Ochr Garth	Cered	SN6456	52°11·4′	3°59·0′W	X	146
Ochr-glan-hafon	Powys	SJ0626	52°49·6′	3°23·3′W	X	125
Ochr Hen-fache	Powys	SJ1127	52°50·2′	3°18·9′W	X	125
Ochr Lwyd	Cered	SN7972	52°20·2′	3°46·2′W	X	135,147
Ochr-lwyd	Cered	SN8373	52°20·8′	3°42·7′W	X	135,136,147
Ochr y Bwlch	Gwyn	SH8017	52°44·5′	3°46·3′W	X	124,125
Ochr-y-cefn	Conwy	SH9162	53°8·9′	3°37·4′W	X	116
Ochr-y-fforest	Carm	SN7739	52°2·4′	3°47·2′W	X	146,160
Ochr-y-foel	Denb	SJ0578	53°17·7′	3°25·1′W	T	116
Ochr y Foel	Gwyn	SH7519	52°45·5′	3°50·7′W	X	124
Ochtermuthill	Pth & Kin	NN8316	56°19·6′	3°53·1′W	T	57
Ochtertyre	Pth & Kin	NN8323	56°23·3′	3°53·3′W	T	52
Ochtertyre	Stir	NS7597	56°9·2′	4°0·3′W	X	57
Ochtow	Highld	NC4600	57°58·0′	4°35·7′W	X	16
Ochtrelure	D & G	NX0559	54°53·5′	5°2·0′W	X	82
Ockbrook	Derby	SK4236	52°55·4′	1°22·1′W	T	129
Ockendon Sta	Thurr	TQ5882	51°31·1′	0°17·0′E	X	177
Ocker Hill	Sand	SO9793	52°32·3′	2°2·3′W	T	139
Ockeridge	Worcs	SO7762	52°15·6′	2°19·8′W	T	138,150
Ockeridge Fm	Heref	SO7439	52°3·2′	2°22·4′W	FM	150
Ockeridge Wood	Worcs	SO7962	52°15·6′	2°18·1′W	F	138,150
Ockerton Court	Devon	SX6086	50°39·6′	3°58·5′W	W	191
Ockford Ridge	Surrey	SU9542	51°10·4′	0°38·1′W	T	186
Ockham	E Susx	TQ7824	50°59·5′	0°32·6′E	X	199
Ockham	Surrey	TQ0756	51°17·8′	0°27·5′W	T	187
Ockham Common	Surrey	TQ0858	51°18·9′	0°26·6′W	F	187
Ockham Ho	E Susx	TQ7225	51°0·1′	0°27·5′E	X	188,199
Ockham Mill	Surrey	TQ0557	51°18·4′	0°29·2′W	X	187
Ockham Park	Surrey	TQ0656	51°17·8′	0°28·4′W	X	187
Ockhams	Kent	TQ4443	51°10·3′	0°4·0′E	X	187
Ockington	Glos	SO7132	51°59·4′	2°24·9′W	X	149
Ockington Fm	Glos	SO7032	51°59·4′	2°25·8′W	FM	149
Ockle	Highld	NM5570	56°45·7′	6°0·1′W	T	39,47
Ockle Point	Highld	NM5471	56°46·2′	6°1·1′W	X	39,47
Ocklester	Orkney	HY5102	58°54·4′	2°50·6′W	X	6,7
Ockley	Kent	TQ7631	51°3·3′	0°31·1′E	X	188
Ockley	Surrey	TQ1440	51°9·1′	0°21·8′W	T	187
Ockley Brook	Oxon	SP5431	51°58·7′	1°12·4′W	W	152
Ockley Common	Surrey	SU9141	51°9·9′	0°41·5′W	X	186
Ockley Court	Surrey	TQ1540	51°9·1′	0°21·0′W	X	187
Ockley Fm	Derby	SK3680	53°19·2′	1°27·2′W	FM	110,111
Ockley Lodge	Surrey	TQ2040	51°9·0′	0°16·7′W	X	187
Ockley Manor	W Susx	TQ3116	50°55·9′	0°7·8′W	X	198
Ockley Sta	Surrey	TQ1640	51°9·1′	0°20·1′W	X	187
Ocknell Inclosure	Hants	SU2411	50°54·1′	1°39·1′W	F	195
Ocknell Plain	Hants	SU2311	50°54·1′	1°40·0′W	X	195
Ockran Head	Shetld	HU2484	60°32·6′	1°33·2′W	X	3
Ockwells Manor	Win & Maid	SU8778	51°29·9′	0°44·4′W	A	175
Ocle Court	Heref	SO5946	52°6·9′	2°35·5′W	X	149
Ocle Pychard	Heref	SO5946	52°6·9′	2°35·5′W	T	149
Octagon Fm	Beds	TL0949	52°7·9′	0°24·1′W	FM	153
Octofad	Arg & Bt	NR2254	55°42·2′	6°25·1′W	X	60
Octomore	Arg & Bt	NR2458	55°44·5′	6°23·4′W	X	60
Octomore Hill	Arg & Bt	NR2459	55°45·0′	6°23·5′W	H	60
Octon	E Yorks	TA0369	54°6·6′	0°25·0′W	X	101
Octon Cross Roads	E Yorks	TA0169	54°6·7′	0°26·9′W	X	101
Octon Grange	E Yorks	TA0271	54°7·7′	0°25·9′W	X	101
Octon Lodge	E Yorks	TA0169	54°6·7′	0°26·9′W	X	101
Octon Manor	E Yorks	TA0370	54°7·2′	0°25·0′W	X	101
Octon Village	E Yorks	TA0370	54°7·2′	0°25·0′W	A	101
Octovullin	Arg & Bt	NR3464	55°48·0′	6°14·2′W	X	60,61
Odam Barton	Devon	SS7419	50°57·7′	3°47·3′W	T	180
Odam Br	Devon	SS7420	50°58·2′	3°47·3′W	X	180

Odarum	N Eil	NF5963	57°32·0′	7°41·5′W	X	22
Oday Hill	Oxon	SU4895	51°39·3′	1°18·0′W	X	164
Odcombe	Somer	ST5015	50°56·2′	2°42·3′W	T	183
Oddacres	N Yks	SD9953	53°58·6′	2°0·5′W	X	103
Odda's Chapel	Glos	SO8629	51°57·8′	2°11·8′W	A	150
Odd Down	Bath & NE Somer	ST7362	51°21·6′	2°22·9′W	T	172
Oddendale	Cumbr	NY5913	54°30·9′	2°37·6′W	X	91
Odder	Lincs	SK9174	53°15·5′	0°37·7′W	X	121
Odd Ho	Lancs	SD4624	53°42·8′	2°48·7′W	X	102
Odd House Fm	Leic	SP4297	52°34·4′	1°22·4′W	FM	140
Oddhouse Fm	Notts	SK6832	52°53·1′	0°59·0′W	FM	129
Oddi-ar-y-llyn	Powys	SJ1628	52°50·8′	3°14·4′W	X	125
Oddicombe Beach	Torbay	SX9265	50°28·7′	3°31·0′W	X	202
Oddingley	Worcs	SO9059	52°14·0′	2°8·4′W	T	150
Oddington	Oxon	SP5514	51°49·5′	1°11·7′W	T	164
Oddington Grange	Oxon	SP5416	51°50·6′	1°12·6′W	X	164
Odd Mill	Corn	SX2499	50°46·1′	4°29·4′W	X	190
Oddo	Derby	SK2360	53°8·4′	1°39·0′W	X	119
Oddo House Fm	Derby	SK2160	53°8·4′	1°40·8′W	FM	119
Odds Fm	Bucks	SU9287	51°34·7′	0°39·9′W	FM	175
Odell	Beds	SP9657	52°12·4′	0°35·3′W	T	153
Odell and Harrold Country Park	Beds	SP9657	52°12·4′	0°35·3′W	X	153
Odell Great Wood	Beds	SP9558	52°13·0′	0°36·2′W	F	153
Odell Lodge	Beds	SP9758	52°12·9′	0°34·4′W	X	153
Odells, The	Notts	SK5229	52°51·6′	1°13·3′W	X	129
Odessa	NE Lincs	TA1903	53°30·8′	0°11·9′W	X	113
Odessa	Norf	TG0726	52°47·7′	1°4·6′E	X	133
Odewells	Essex	TL8136	51°59·8′	0°38·6′E	X	155
Odham	Devon	SS4702	50°48·1′	4°9·9′W	T	191
Odham Moor	Devon	SS4702	50°48·1′	4°9·9′W	X	191
Odiam Fm	Kent	TQ9228	51°1·4′	0°44·7′E	FM	189
Odie	Orkney	HY6229	59°9·0′	2°39·4′W	X	5
Odiham	Hants	SU7451	51°15·4′	0°56·0′W	T	186
Odiham Airfield	Hants	SU7349	51°14·4′	0°56·9′W	X	186
Odiham Castle	Hants	SU7251	51°15·4′	0°57·7′W	A	186
Odiham Common	Hants	SU7552	51°16·0′	0°55·1′W	F	186
Odiham Firs	Hants	SU7350	51°14·9′	0°56·9′W	F	186
Odin Bay	Orkney	HY6824	59°6·4′	2°33·0′W	W	5
Odiness	Orkney	HY6825	59°6·9′	2°33·0′W	X	5
Odin Ness	Orkney	HY4322	59°5·1′	2°59·2′W	X	5,6
Odinsgarth	Orkney	HY6741	59°15·5′	2°34·2′W	X	5
Odin Sitch	Derby	SK1483	53°20·9′	1°47·0′W	W	110
Odinstone	Orkney	HY5018	59°3·0′	2°51·8′W	X	6
Odle Fm	Devon	ST1906	50°51·1′	3°8·7′W	FM	192,193
Odmoston	Aberd	NO6876	56°52·7′	2°31·1′W	X	45
Odness	Orkney	HY6926	59°7·4′	2°32·0′W	X	5
Odsal	Brad	SE1529	53°45·7′	1°45·9′W	T	104
Odsey	Cambs	TL2938	52°1·8′	0°6·8′W	T	153
Odstock	Wilts	SU1426	51°2·2′	1°47·6′W	T	184
Odstock Down	Wilts	SU1324	51°1·1′	1°48·5′W	X	184
Odstone	Leic	SK3907	52°39·8′	1°25·0′W	T	140
Odstone Barn	Oxon	SU2884	51°33·5′	1°35·4′W	X	174
Odstone Down	Oxon	SU2883	51°32·9′	1°35·4′W	X	174
Odstone Fm	Oxon	SU2786	51°34·6′	1°36·2′W	FM	174
Odstone Hill	Oxon	SU2785	51°34·0′	1°36·2′W	X	174
Odstone Hill Fm	Leic	SK3808	52°40·3′	1°25·9′W	FM	128,140
Odstone Lands	Oxon	SU2687	51°35·1′	1°37·1′W	X	174
Odstone Marsh	Oxon	SU2687	51°35·1′	1°37·1′W	X	174
Odyn-fâch	Cered	SN6487	52°28·1′	3°59·7′W	X	135
Odyn-fach	Powys	SO0912	51°48·2′	3°18·8′W	X	161
Oerddwr	Gwyn	SH3130	52°50·7′	4°30·2′W	X	123
Oerddwr-uchaf	Gwyn	SH5845	52°59·3′	4°6·5′W	X	115
Oerfa	Conwy	SH8359	53°7·2′	3°44·5′W	X	116
Oerffrwd	Powys	SN9995	52°32·9′	3°29·0′W	X	136
Oerle	Powys	SN9792	52°31·2′	3°30·7′W	X	136
Oerley Hall	Shrops	SJ2629	52°51·4′	3°5·5′W	X	126
Oernant	Cered	SN4260	52°13·2′	4°18·4′W	X	146
Oernant	Denb	SJ1846	53°0·5′	3°12·9′W	X	116
Oessen Skerry	Orkney	HY6616	59°2·0′	2°35·1′W	X	5
Oe Stack	Shetld	HU2972	60°26·1′	1°27·9′W	X	3
Offa's Dyke	Flint	SJ1079	53°18·3′	3°20·6′W	A	116
Offa's Dyke	Flint	SJ2757	53°6·6′	3°5·0′W	A	117
Offa's Dyke	Flint	SJ2856	53°6·0′	3°4·1′W	A	117
Offa's Dyke	Glos	SO5407	51°45·8′	2°39·6′W	A	162
Offa's Dyke	Glos	ST5492	51°37·7′	2°39·5′W	A	162,172
Offa's Dyke	Heref	SO3355	52°11·6′	2°58·4′W	A	148,149
Offa's Dyke	Heref	SO4043	52°5·2′	2°52·1′W	A	148,149,161
Offa's Dyke	Powys	SJ2622	52°47·7′	3°5·4′W	A	126
Offa's Dyke	Shrops	SO2589	52°29·9′	3°5·9′W	A	137
Offa's Dyke	Wrex	SJ2949	53°2·3′	3°3·1′W	A	117
Offa's Dyke	Wrex	SJ3044	52°59·6′	3°2·2′W	A	117
Offa's Dyke Path	Denb	SJ0675	53°16·1′	3°24·2′W	X	116
Offa's Dyke Path	Denb	SJ2150	53°2·8′	3°10·3′W	X	117
Offa's Dyke Path	Denb	SJ2246	53°0·6′	3°9·3′W	X	117
Offa's Dyke Path	Monm	SO3027	51°56·5′	3°0·7′W	X	161
Offa's Dyke Path	Monm	SO5311	51°48·0′	2°40·5′W	X	162
Offa's Dyke Path	Powys	SJ2716	52°44·4′	3°4·5′W	X	126
Offa's Dyke Path	Shrops	SO2578	52°23·9′	3°5·7′W	X	137,148
Offchurch	Warw	SP3665	52°17·2′	1°27·9′W	T	151
Offchurch Bury	Warw	SP3466	52°17·7′	1°29·7′W	A	151
Offcote Grange	Derby	SK2048	53°2·0′	1°41·7′W	X	119
Offcote Ho	Derby	SK1948	53°2·0′	1°42·6′W	X	119
Off Cove	Devon	SX7136	50°12·8′	3°48·1′W	W	202
Offenham	Worcs	SP0546	52°7·0′	1°55·2′W	T	150
Offenham Cross	Worcs	SP0645	52°6·4′	1°54·3′W	T	150
Offen's Fm	E Susx	TQ9523	50°58·6′	0°47·1′E	FM	189
Offerance	Stir	NS5496	56°8·3′	4°20·5′W	X	57
Offers	Stir	NS7195	56°8·1′	4°4·1′W	X	57
Offerton	Stock	SJ9188	53°23·6′	2°7·7′W	T	109
Offerton	Sund	NZ3455	54°53·6′	1°27·8′W	T	88
Offerton Fm	Worcs	SO8958	52°13·4′	2°9·3′W	FM	150
Offerton Green	Stock	SJ9388	53°23·6′	2°5·9′W	T	109
Offerton Hall	Derby	SK2181	53°19·8′	1°40·7′W	X	110
Offerton Moor	Derby	SK2080	53°19·2′	1°41·6′W	X	110
Offham	E Susx	TQ4012	50°53·7′	0°0·2′W	T	198
Offham	Kent	TQ6557	51°17·5′	0°22·4′E	T	178,188
Offham	W Susx	TQ0208	50°52·0′	0°32·6′W	T	197
Offham Hill	E Susx	TQ3911	50°53·1′	0°1·0′W	X	198

Office Fm	Essex	TL8812	51°46·7'	0°43·9'E	FM	168
Office Fm	Suff	TM3079	52°21·9'	1°23·1'E	FM	156
Officer's Croft	D & G	NX1958	54°53·3'	4°48·9'W	X	82
Offin's Cottages	Essex	TL5905	51°43·5'	0°18·5'E	X	167
Offlands Fm	Oxon	SU5884	51°33·3'	1°9·4'W	FM	174
Offley Bottom	Herts	TL1628	51°56·5'	0°18·3'W	X	166
Offleybrook	Staffs	SJ7830	52°52·3'	2°19·2'W	X	127
Offley Chase	Herts	TL1324	51°54·4'	0°21·0'W	X	166
Offley Cross	Herts	TL1628	51°56·5'	0°18·3'W	X	166
Offley Grange	Herts	TL1528	51°56·5'	0°19·2'W	X	166
Offley Grove Fm	Staffs	SJ7627	52°50·6'	2°21·0'W	FM	127
Offleyhay	Staffs	SJ7929	52°51·7'	2°18·3'W	T	127
Offleyholes Fm	Herts	TL1626	51°55·5'	0°18·4'W	FM	166
Offley Hoo	Herts	TL1426	51°55·5'	0°20·1'W	X	166
Offleymarsh	Staffs	SJ7829	52°51·7'	2°19·2'W	T	127
Offley Place	Derby	SK3371	53°14·3'	1°29·9'W	X	119
Offley Place	Herts	TL1427	51°56·0'	0°20·1'W	X	166
Offleyrock	Staffs	SJ7829	52°51·7'	2°19·2'W	T	127
Offmore Fm	Worcs	SO8576	52°23·1'	2°12·8'W	FM	139
Offord Cluny	Cambs	TL2167	52°17·5'	0°13·1'W	T	153
Offord D'Arcy	Cambs	TL2166	52°17·0'	0°13·2'W	T	153
Offord Hill	Cambs	TL2368	52°18·0'	0°11·4'W	X	153
Offoxey Fm	Shrops	SJ8108	52°40·4'	2°16·5'W	FM	127
Offton	Suff	TM0649	52°6·3'	1°0·9'E	T	155
Offton Pl	Suff	TM0748	52°5·7'	1°1·7'E	X	155,169
Offwell	Devon	SY1999	50°47·3'	3°8·6'W	T	192,193
Offwell Brook	Devon	SY2097	50°46·3'	3°7·7'W	W	192,193
Offwell Fm	Hants	SU6207	50°51·8'	1°6·8'W	FM	196
Offwell Ho	Devon	SY1999	50°47·3'	3°8·6'W	X	192,193
Ogbeare	Devon	SX4474	50°32·9'	4°11·7'W	X	201
Ogbeare Hall	Corn	SX3095	50°44·0'	4°24·2'W	X	190
Ogbourne Down	Wilts	SU1774	51°28·1'	1°44·9'W	X	173
Ogbourne Maizey	Wilts	SU1871	51°26·5'	1°44·1'W	T	173
Ogbourne St Andrew	Wilts	SU1872	51°27·0'	1°44·1'W	T	173
Ogbourne St George	Wilts	SU2074	51°28·1'	1°42·3'W	T	174
Ogbury	Wilts	SU1438	51°8·7'	1°47·6'W	A	184
Ogden	Cald	SE0631	53°46·8'	1°54·1'W	T	104
Ogden	Roch	SD9512	53°36·5'	2°4·1'W	X	109
Ogden Brook	Tames	SK0199	53°29·5'	1°58·7'W	W	110
Ogden Clough	Derby	SK0496	53°27·9'	1°56·0'W	X	110
Ogden Down Fm	Dorset	ST9713	50°55·2'	2°2·2'W	FM	195
Ogden Hill	Lancs	SD8040	53°51·6'	2°17·8'W	X	103
Ogden Resr	Cald	SE0630	53°46·2'	1°54·1'W	W	104
Ogden Resr	Lancs	SD7622	53°41·9'	2°21·4'W	W	103
Ogden Resr	Roch	SD9512	53°36·5'	2°4·1'W	W	109
Ogden Resrs	Lancs	SD8039	53°51·1'	2°17·8'W	W	103
Ogdens	Hants	SU1812	50°54·7'	1°44·3'W	T	195
Ogdens Fm	Hants	SU1812	50°54·7'	1°44·3'W	FM	195
Ogden's Purlieu	Hants	SU1811	50°54·1'	1°44·3'W	X	195
Ogdown Ho	W Berks	SU4673	51°27·5'	1°19·9'W	X	174
Oggshole Fm	Somer	ST2430	51°4·1'	3°4·7'W	FM	182
Ogle	Northum	NZ1378	55°6·0'	1°47·3'W	T	88
Oglebird Plantn	Cumbr	NY6027	54°38·4'	2°36·8'W	F	91
Ogle Burn	E Loth	NT7272	55°56·7'	2°26·5'W	W	67
Ogle Burn	Northum	NZ1478	55°6·0'	1°46·4'W	W	88
Ogle Dene Ho	Northum	NZ1279	55°6·6'	1°48·3'W	X	88
Ogle Hill Head	Northum	NZ1278	55°6·0'	1°49·2'W	X	88
Ogle Linn	D & G	NY0495	55°14·6'	3°30·2'W	W	78
Ogle South Fm	Northum	NZ1477	55°5·5'	1°46·4'W	FM	88
Oglet	Liv	SJ4381	53°19·6'	2°50·9'W	X	108
Oglethorpe Hall Fm	Leeds	SE4444	53°53·7'	1°19·4'W	FM	105
Oglethorpe Hills	Leeds	SE4443	53°53·1'	1°19·4'W	X	105
Oglethorpe Whin Covert	Leeds	SE4443	53°53·1'	1°19·4'W	F	105
Ogle Well Ho	Northum	NZ1278	55°6·0'	1°48·3'W	X	88
Ogmore	V of Glam	SS8876	51°28·6'	3°36·4'W	T	170
Ogmore-by-Sea	V of Glam	SS8674	51°27·4'	3°38·1'W	T	170
Ogmore Down	V of Glam	SS8876	51°28·6'	3°36·4'W	X	170
Ogmore Forest	Brig	SS9489	51°35·6'	3°31·4'W	F	170
Ogmore River / Afon Ogwr	Brig	SS8979	51°30·2'	3°35·6'W	W	170
Ogmore Vale	Brig	SS9390	51°36·2'	3°32·3'W	T	170
Ogmore Valley (Cwm Ogwr)	Brig	SS9084	51°32·9'	3°34·8'W	X	170
Ogo-dour Cove	Corn	SW6615	49°59·6'	5°15·5'W	W	203
Ogof	Gwyn	SH1020	52°44·9'	4°48·5'W	X	123
Ogof Ddeuddrws	Gwyn	SH1825	52°47·8'	4°41·6'W	X	123
Ogof Ddu	Gwyn	SH8921	52°46·8'	3°38·3'W	H	124,125
Ogof Diban	Gwyn	SH1120	52°44·9'	4°47·6'W	X	123
Ogof Lladron	Gwyn	SH1020	52°44·9'	4°48·5'W	X	123
Ogof Llechwyn	Gwyn	SH6342	52°57·7'	4°2·0'W	X	124
Ogof Lwyd	Gwyn	SH1925	52°47·8'	4°40·7'W	X	123
Ogof Owain Glyndŵr	Gwyn	SH5647	53°0·3'	4°8·4'W	X	115
Ogof y Cae	Pemb	SM8222	51°51·5'	5°9·6'W	X	157
Ogof-yr-esgyrn	Powys	SN8316	51°50·1'	3°41·5'W	A	160
Ogre Hill	Northum	NT7706	55°21·1'	2°21·3'W	H	80
Ogscastle	S Lanak	NT0344	55°41·0'	3°32·1'W	X	72
Ogston	Aberd	NK0632	57°23·0'	1°53·6'W	X	30
Ogston	Derby	SK3859	53°7·8'	1°25·5'W	X	119
Ogston Carr	Derby	SK3659	53°7·9'	1°27·3'W	X	119
Ogston Resr	Derby	SK3760	53°8·4'	1°26·4'W	W	119
Ogwen Bank	Gwyn	SH6265	53°10·1'	4°3·5'W	X	115
Ogwr Fach	Brig	SS9788	51°35·1'	3°28·8'W	W	170
Ogwr Fawr	Brig	SS9388	51°35·1'	3°32·3'W	W	170
Ogwr Ridgeway Walk	Brig	SS8785	51°33·4'	3°37·4'W	X	170
Ohio Plantn	I of M	SC3993	54°18·7'	4°28·1'W	F	95
Ohirnie	Arg & Bt	NM6220	56°19·0'	5°50·5'W	X	49
Oh Me Edge	Northum	NY7099	55°17·3'	2°27·9'W	X	80
Oidreabhal	N Eil	NB3227	58°9·3'	6°32·9'W	H	8,13
Oigh-sgeir	Highld	NM1596	56°58·3'	6°40·9'W	X	39
Oigin's Geo	Highld	NC9968	58°35·4'	3°43·8'W	X	11
Oils Heath	Staffs	SK0758	53°7·4'	1°53·3'W	X	119
Oireabhal	N Eil	NB0809	57°58·7'	6°55·9'W	H	13,14
Oiseval	N Eil	NF1099	57°48·9'	8°33·7'W	H	18
Oisgill Bay	Highld	NG1349	57°26·7'	6°46·6'W	W	23
Oitir	Arg & Bt	NR9184	56°0·5'	5°20·7'W	X	55
Oitir an t-Sàmhla	N Eil	NF7963	57°32·9'	7°21·5'W	X	18
Oitir Bheag	N Eil	NF8147	57°24·3'	7°18·3'W	X	22
Oitir Fhiadhaich	N Eil	NF7465	57°33·7'	7°26·7'W	X	18
Oitir Mhór	Arg & Bt	NM8230	56°25·0'	5°31·6'W	X	49
Oitir Mhór	N Eil	NF7305	57°1·5'	7°22·9'W	W	31
Oitir Mhór	N Eil	NF7566	57°34·3'	7°25·7'W	X	18

Oitir Mhòr	N Eil	NF8157	57°29·7'	7°19·1'W	X	22
Oitir Mhór	N Eil	NF8979	57°41·9'	7°12·8'W	X	18
Oitir Mór	Arg & Bt	NR7409	55°19·6'	5°33·3'W	X	68
Oitir na Cudaig	N Eil	NF8315	57°7·3'	7°13·8'W	X	31
Oitir nam Bó	Arg & Bt	NR2869	55°50·5'	6°20·3'W	X	60
Okeford Common	Dorset	ST7811	50°54·1'	2°18·4'W	F	194
Okeford Fitzpaine	Dorset	ST8010	50°53·6'	2°16·7'W	T	194
Okeford Hill	Dorset	ST8109	50°53·0'	2°15·8'W	X	194
Okehampton	Devon	SX5895	50°44·5'	4°0·4'W	T	191
Okehampton Common	Devon	SX5790	50°41·8'	4°1·1'W	X	191
Okehampton Range	Devon	SX5987	50°40·2'	3°59·3'W	X	191
Okehills	Somer	ST2227	51°2·5'	3°6·4'W	X	193
Okehurst	W Susx	TQ0727	51°2·2'	0°28·0'W	X	187,197
Okement Hill	Devon	SX6087	50°40·2'	3°58·5'W	H	191
Okenbury	Devon	SX6447	50°18·7'	3°54·2'W	X	202
Okeover Hall	Staffs	SK1548	53°2·0'	1°46·2'W	X	119
Oker	Derby	SK2761	53°9·0'	1°35·4'W	T	119
Okers Wood Ho	Dorset	SY8191	50°43·3'	2°15·8'W	X	194
Oke Tor	Devon	SX6189	50°41·3'	3°57·7'W	H	191
Okewill	Devon	SS5839	51°8·2'	4°1·4'W	X	180
Okewill Cross	Devon	SS5839	51°8·2'	4°1·4'W	X	180
Oklahoma Fm	Hants	SU2940	51°9·7'	1°34·7'W	FM	185
Okle Clifford	Glos	SO7425	51°55·6'	2°22·3'W	X	162
Okle Green	Glos	SO7525	51°55·6'	2°21·4'W	T	162
Okraquoy	Shetld	HU4331	60°4·0'	1°13·2'W	X	4
Okus	Swin	SU1483	51°33·0'	1°47·5'W	T	173
Olantigh	Kent	TR0548	51°11·9'	0°56·4'E	X	179,189
Ola's Ness	Shetld	HU3583	60°32·0'	1°21·2'W	X	1,2,3
Olas Voe	Shetld	HU2846	60°12·1'	1°29·2'W	W	4
Olchard	Devon	SX8777	50°35·1'	3°35·4'W	T	192
Olchfa	Carm	SN7327	51°55·9'	3°50·4'W	X	146,160
Olchon Brook	Heref	SO2832	51°59·1'	3°2·5'W	W	161
Olchon Court	Heref	SO2732	51°59·1'	3°3·4'W	X	161
Olchon Ho	Heref	SO3029	51°57·5'	3°0·7'W	X	161
Olchon Valley	Heref	SO3030	51°58·1'	3°0·7'W	X	161
Old	Northnts	SP7873	52°21·2'	0°50·9'W	T	141
Old Abbey	Suff	TM4564	52°13·4'	1°35·6'E	X	156
Old Abbey Fm	Cered	SN7164	52°15·8'	3°53·0'W	FM	146,147
Old Aberdeen	C of Aber	NJ9408	57°10·0'	2°5·5'W	T	38
Old Aberlosk	D & G	NT2605	55°20·3'	3°9·6'W	X	79
Old Acres Hall Fm	Durham	NZ3928	54°39·0'	1°23·3'W	FM	93
Old Acres Lodge Fm	Durham	NZ3829	54°39·5'	1°24·2'W	FM	93
Old Alresford	Hants	SU5834	51°6·4'	1°9·9'W	T	185
Old Alresford Pond	Hants	SU5933	51°5·8'	1°9·1'W	W	185
Oldany	Highld	NC0932	58°14·4'	5°14·8'W	X	15
Oldany Island	Highld	NC0834	58°15·4'	5°15·9'W	X	15
Oldany River	Highld	NC1032	58°14·4'	5°13·7'W	W	15
Oldaport	Devon	SX6349	50°19·7'	3°55·1'W	X	202
Old Arley	Warw	SP2890	52°30·7'	1°34·8'W	T	140
Old Arngrove	Bucks	SP6113	51°49·0'	1°6·5'W	X	164,165
Old Ash	Lincs	TF3167	53°11·3'	0°2·0'W	X	122
Old Ashway	Somer	SS8832	51°4·8'	3°35·6'W	X	181
Old Auchenbrack	D & G	NX7597	55°15·3'	3°57·6'W	X	78
Oldaway Fm	Devon	SX7142	50°16·1'	3°48·2'W	FM	202
Old Backbarrow	Cumbr	SD3685	54°15·6'	2°58·5'W	X	96,97
Old Balgove	Aberd	NJ8132	57°22·9'	2°18·5'W	X	29,30
Old Balgowan	Aberd	NJ6020	57°16·4'	2°39·3'W	X	37
Old Balkello	Angus	NO3638	56°32·0'	3°2·0'W	T	54
Old Ballikinrain	Stir	NS5587	56°3·5'	4°19·3'W	X	57
Old Balornock	C of Glas	NS6167	55°52·8'	4°12·9'W	T	64
Old Bank End Fm	Donc	SE6800	53°29·8'	0°58·1'W	FM	111
Old Bargains Wood	Glos	SO6003	51°43·7'	2°34·4'W	F	162
Old Barn	E Renf	NS4255	55°46·0'	4°30·7'W	X	64
Oldbarn	Essex	TL6901	51°41·2'	0°27·1'E	X	167
Old Barn	E Susx	TQ4812	50°53·5'	0°6·7'E	X	198
Old Barn	Lancs	SD8030	53°46·2'	2°17·8'W	X	103
Old Barn	Northum	NU2405	55°20·6'	1°36·9'W	X	81
Old Barn	W Susx	TQ1737	51°7·4'	0°19·3'W	X	187
Old Barn Fm	Kent	TQ4544	51°10·8'	0°4·9'E	FM	188
Old Barn Fm	Norf	TF9539	52°55·0'	0°54·4'E	FM	132
Oldbarn Fm	Norf	TG3726	52°47·0'	1°31·3'E	FM	133,134
Old Barn Fm	Northnts	SP8255	52°11·5'	0°47·6'W	FM	152
Old Barn Fm	Oxon	SP4436	52°1·5'	1°21·1'W	FM	151
Old Barn Fm	Warw	SP4058	52°13·4'	1°24·5'W	FM	151
Old Barnham Slip	Suff	TL8377	52°21·9'	0°41·7'E	X	144
Old Barns	Essex	TL6203	51°42·4'	0°21·1'E	X	167
Old Barns	Fife	NO5906	56°14·9'	2°39·3'W	X	59
Old Barns Fm	E Susx	TQ3816	50°55·8'	0°1·8'W	FM	198
Old Barn, The	Kent	TQ5548	51°12·8'	0°13·5'E	X	188
Old Barr	D & G	NS7608	55°21·3'	3°56·9'W	X	71,78
Old Barrow	Somer	SS8432	51°4·8'	3°39·0'W	A	181
Old Barskimming	E Ayr	NS4825	55°30·0'	4°23·9'W	X	70
Old Basford	C of Nott	SK5543	52°59·1'	1°10·4'W	T	129
Old Basing	Hants	SU6652	51°16·0'	1°2·8'W	T	185,186
Old Beachin Fm	Ches	SJ4457	53°6·7'	2°49·8'W	FM	117
Old Beat	Devon	ST0815	50°55·9'	3°18·2'W	X	181
Old Beck	Lincs	SK8636	52°55·1'	0°42·8'W	W	130
Old Beck	Lincs	TF1127	52°50·0'	0°20·7'W	W	130
Old Bedford River	Cambs	TL4178	52°23·1'	0°4·7'E	W	142,143
Old Bedford River	Norf	TL5394	52°31·6'	0°15·7'E	W	143
Old Beetley	Norf	TF9718	52°43·7'	0°55·5'E	X	132
Old Bell Fm	Devon	SS8518	50°57·2'	3°37·9'W	FM	181
Old Bell Middle	Lincs	TF5935	52°53·6'	0°22·2'E	X	131
Old Bells Fm	Suff	TM0464	52°14·4'	0°59·7'E	FM	155
Old Belses	Scot Bord	NT5624	55°30·7'	2°41·4'W	T	73
Old Belton	E Loth	NT6576	55°58·8'	2°33·2'W	X	67
Oldberrow	Warw	SP1265	52°17·2'	1°49·0'W	T	150
Oldberrow Hill Fm	Warw	SP1067	52°18·3'	1°50·8'W	FM	150
Oldberry Castle	Somer	SS9028	51°2·7'	3°33·8'W	A	181
Old Berry Fm	Somer	SS9028	51°2·7'	3°33·8'W	FM	181
Old Bess	Brad	SD9738	53°50·5'	2°2·3'W	X	103
Old Bewick	Northum	NU0621	55°29·2'	1°53·9'W	X	75
Old Bexley	Bexley	TQ4973	51°26·4'	0°9·0'E	T	177
Old Blair	Pth & Kin	NN8666	56°46·6'	3°51·5'W	T	43
Old Blairs	Moray	NJ0255	57°34·7'	3°37·9'W	X	27
Old Blairshinnoch	D & G	NX8768	54°59·9'	3°45·6'W	X	84
Old Boghead	Aberd	NJ7432	57°22·9'	2°25·5'W	X	29
Old Bolingbroke	Lincs	TF3564	53°9·6'	0°1·6'E	T	122
Old Boon	Scot Bord	NT5845	55°42·1'	2°39·7'W	X	73,74
Oldborough	Devon	SS7706	50°50·7'	3°44·4'W	T	191

Oldborough Fm	Glos	SP2235	52°1·0'	1°40·4'W	FM	151
Oldborough Fm	Warw	SP2453	52°10·7'	1°38·5'W	FM	151
Old Boston	St Hel	SJ5797	53°28·3'	2°38·5'W	T	108
Old Bottom	Norf	TF7827	52°48·9'	0°38·9'E	X	132
Old Bottom Fm	Lancs	SD6168	54°6·6'	2°35·4'W	FM	97
Old Bourne, The	Herts	TL3223	51°53·6'	0°4·5'W	W	166
Old Bourtie	Aberd	NJ7923	57°18·1'	2°20·5'W	X	38
Old Bourtreebush	Aberd	NO9095	57°3·0'	2°9·4'W	X	38,45
Old Boyland Hall	Norf	TM0884	52°25·1'	1°3·9'E	X	144
Old Boywood Fm	Dorset	ST7309	50°53·0'	2°22·6'W	FM	194
Old Braidlie	Scot Bord	NY4797	55°16·1'	2°49·6'W	X	79
Old Brake	Leic	SK4901	52°36·5'	1°16·2'W	F	140
Old Bramhope	Leeds	SE2343	53°53·2'	1°38·6'W	T	104
Old Brampton	Derby	SK3371	53°14·3'	1°29·9'W	T	119
Old Brandelhow	Cumbr	NY2520	54°34·4'	3°9·2'W	X	89,90
Old Braxton	E Loth	NT7372	55°56·7'	2°25·5'W	X	67
Old Breach Fm	V of Glam	SS9773	51°27·0'	3°28·6'W	FM	170
Old Brick Fm	E Susx	TQ6823	50°59·1'	0°24·0'E	FM	199
Oldbridge	Cumbr	NY0730	54°39·6'	3°26·1'W	X	89
Old Bridge End	Northum	NY9265	54°59·0'	2°7·1'W	X	87
Old Bridge Fm	Devon	ST0503	50°49·4'	3°20·5'W	FM	192
Old Bridge of Tilt	Pth & Kin	NN8766	56°46·6'	3°50·5'W	T	43
Old Bridge of Urr	D & G	NX7767	54°59·2'	3°54·9'W	T	84
Oldbridge River	N Som	ST4163	51°22·0'	2°50·5'W	W	172,182
Oldbrook	Mil Key	SP8537	52°1·7'	0°45·3'W	T	152
Old Brook Hall	St Hel	SJ5189	53°24·0'	2°43·8'W	X	108
Old Broomhill	D & G	NY0983	55°8·2'	3°25·2'W	X	78
Old Buckenham	Norf	TM0691	52°28·9'	1°2·4'E	T	144
Old Buckenham Fen	Norf	TM0491	52°29·0'	1°0·7'E	W	144
Old Buckenham Hall	Norf	TM0690	52°28·4'	1°2·4'E	X	144
Old Buckenham Hall (Sch)	Suff	TL9552	52°8·1'	0°51·4'E	X	155
Old Buckholm	Scot Bord	NT4837	55°37·7'	2°49·1'W	X	73
Old Buckley	Lancs	SD6437	53°49·9'	2°32·4'W	X	102,103
Old Burdon	Sund	NZ3850	54°50·8'	1°24·1'W	T	88
Old Burghclere	Hants	SU4657	51°18·8'	1°20·0'W	T	174
Old Burn	Scot Bord	NT0420	55°28·1'	3°30·7'W	W	72
Old Burrow Hill	Devon	SS7849	51°13·9'	3°44·5'W	H	180
Oldbury	Heref	SO6332	51°59·4'	2°31·9'W	A	149
Oldbury	Kent	TQ5856	51°17·1'	0°16·3'E	A	188
Oldbury	Kent	TQ5856	51°17·1'	0°16·3'E	T	188
Oldbury	Sand	SO9888	52°29·6'	2°1·4'W	T	139
Oldbury	Shrops	SO7091	52°31·2'	2°26·1'W	T	138
Oldbury	Warw	SP3194	52°32·8'	1°32·2'W	A	140
Oldbury	Warw	SP3194	52°32·8'	1°32·2'W	T	140
Oldbury	Wilts	SU0469	51°25·4'	1°56·2'W	A	173
Oldbury Fm	Essex	TQ9287	51°33·2'	0°46·6'E	FM	178
Oldbury Fm	Warw	SP3095	52°33·4'	1°33·0'W	FM	140
Oldbury Fm	Worcs	SO8155	52°11·8'	2°16·3'W	FM	150
Oldbury Fm	W Susx	SU9206	50°51·0'	0°41·2'W	FM	197
Oldbury Hill	Kent	TQ5856	51°17·1'	0°16·3'E	X	188
Oldbury Ho	S Glos	ST6192	51°37·8'	2°33·4'W	X	162,172
Oldbury Lake	S Glos	ST5892	51°37·8'	2°36·0'W	W	162,172
Oldbury Naite	S Glos	ST6293	51°38·3'	2°32·6'W	T	162,172
Oldbury-on-Severn	S Glos	ST6192	51°37·8'	2°33·4'W	T	162,172
Oldbury on the Hill	Glos	ST8188	51°35·7'	2°16·1'W	T	162,173
Oldbury Resr	Warw	SP3095	52°33·4'	1°33·0'W	W	140
Oldbury Sands	S Glos	ST5893	51°38·3'	2°36·0'W	X	162,172
Old Byland	N Yks	SE5485	54°15·7'	1°9·8'W	T	100
Old Byre, The	Arg & Bt	NM4350	56°34·6'	6°10·6'W	X	47
Old Caberston	Scot Bord	NT3637	55°37·6'	3°0·5'W	X	73
Oldcake	Aberd	NO7777	56°53·3'	2°22·2'W	X	45
Old Cambus	Scot Bord	NT8069	55°55·1'	2°18·8'W	T	67
Old Cambus East Mains	Scot Bord	NT8169	55°55·1'	2°17·8'W	X	67
Old Cambus Townhead	Scot Bord	NT8069	55°55·1'	2°18·8'W	X	67
Old Cambus West Mains	Scot Bord	NT8070	55°55·6'	2°18·8'W	X	67
Old Cambus Wood	Scot Bord	NT8368	55°54·5'	2°15·9'W	F	67
Old Camp Fm	W Susx	TQ2027	51°2·0'	0°16·9'W	FM	187,198
Old Cardinham Castle	Corn	SX1267	50°28·6'	4°38·6'W	T	200
Old Carlisle	Cumbr	NY2646	54°48·5'	3°8·7'W	T	85
Old Carlton Fm	N Yks	SE6756	54°0·0'	0°58·3'W	FM	105,106
Old Carlton Fm	York	SE6656	54°0·0'	0°59·2'W	FM	105,106
Old Carr	Norf	TF9614	52°41·5'	0°54·4'E	X	132
Old Carr Grange	N Yks	SE4293	54°20·1'	1°20·8'W	X	99
Old Carr Head	N Yks	SD9744	53°53·8'	2°2·3'W	X	103
Old Cassop	Durham	NZ3339	54°44·9'	1°28·8'W	T	93
Old Castle	E Susx	TQ6519	50°57·0'	0°21·3'E	X	199
Oldcastle	Heref	SO3252	52°10·0'	2°59·3'W	X	148
Old Castle	Lancs	SD3939	53°50·9'	2°55·2'W	X	102
Oldcastle	Monm	SO3224	51°54·9'	2°58·9'W	T	161
Old Castle	Swan	SS4088	51°34·3'	4°18·1'W	X	159
Old Castle Down	V of Glam	SS9075	51°28·0'	3°34·6'W	X	170
Old Castle Fm	Cered	SN1646	52°5·1'	4°40·7'W	FM	145
Oldcastle Fm	Heref	SO7540	52°3·7'	2°21·5'W	FM	150
Oldcastle Fm	Somer	ST2715	50°56·0'	3°1·9'W	FM	193
Old Castle (Fort)	Swan	SS4088	51°34·3'	4°18·1'W	A	159
Old Castle Head	Pemb	SS0796	51°38·0'	4°46·9'W	X	158
Oldcastle Heath	Ches	SJ4745	53°0·2'	2°47·0'W	T	117
Oldcastle Mill	Ches	SJ4644	52°59·7'	2°47·9'W	X	117
Old Castle Point	I of W	SZ5196	50°45·9'	1°16·2'W	X	196
Oldcastles	Scot Bord	NT8658	55°49·2'	2°13·0'W	X	67,74
Old Castleton	Scot Bord	NY5190	55°12·4'	2°45·8'W	X	79
Old Catton	Norf	TG2312	52°39·8'	1°18·3'E	T	133,134
Old Caunton Lodge	Notts	SK7361	53°8·7'	0°54·1'W	X	120
Old Caverton	Scot Bord	NT7427	55°32·4'	2°24·3'W	X	74
Old Chalford	Oxon	SP3425	51°55·6'	1°29·9'W	T	164
Old Chamber	Cald	SD9926	53°44·1'	2°0·5'W	X	103
Oldchapel Hill	Powys	SN9780	52°24·7'	3°30·5'W	H	136
Old Cheyne Court	Kent	TQ9923	50°58·5'	0°50·5'E	X	189
Oldchurch	Cumbr	NY4421	54°35·1'	2°51·6'W	X	90
Old Church Fm	Cumbr	NY5161	54°56·7'	2°45·5'W	FM	86
Old Church Stoke	Powys	SO2894	52°32·6'	3°3·3'W	T	137
Old Churn Oak	Notts	SK5765	53°11·0'	1°8·4'W	X	120
Old Cilgwyn	Cered	SN3141	52°2·7'	4°27·5'W	X	145
Old Clapperton Hall	W Loth	NT0868	55°54·0'	3°27·8'W	X	65
Old Claypits Fm	Herts	TL3106	51°44·5'	0°5·8'W	FM	166
Old Clee	NE Lincs	TA2908	53°33·4'	0°2·7'W	T	113
Old Cleeve	Somer	ST0341	51°9·8'	3°22·9'W	T	181
Old Cleeve	Wilts	SU1254	51°17·3'	1°49·3'W	F	184
Old Cliff Fm	N Lincs	SE9118	53°39·3'	0°37·0'W	FM	112
Old Clipstone	Notts	SK5964	53°10·4'	1°6·6'W	T	120

Old Close Bottom	Devon	SS7040	51°8·9'	3°51·1'W	X	180
Oldclose Fm	S Glos	ST6987	51°35·1'	2°26·5'W	FM	172
Old Cloth Hall	Kent	TQ7935	51°5·4'	0°33·8'E	X	188
Old Cluden	D & G	NX8877	55°4·7'	3°44·8'W	X	84
Old Clune Ho	Highld	NH6035	57°23·3'	4°19·3'W	X	26
Old Coach Road	Cumbr	NY3423	54°36·1'	3°0·9'W	X	90
Old Coalburn	E Ayr	NS5613	55°23·6'	4°16·0'W	X	71
Old Cogan Hall Fm	V of Glam	ST1670	51°25·6'	3°12·1'W	FM	171
Old Coghurst Fm	E Susx	TQ8313	50°53·5'	0°36·5'E	FM	199
Old Colwall	Heref	SO7341	52°4·2'	2°23·2'W	X	150
Old Colwyn	Conwy	SH8678	53°17·4'	3°42·2'W	T	116
Old Combe	Somer	ST2318	50°57·6'	3°5·4'W	X	193
Old Common Plantn	Norf	TF9041	52°56·2'	0°50·0'E	F	132
Old Coppice	Heref	SO5652	52°10·1'	2°38·2'W	F	149
Old Coppice	Shrops	SJ4607	52°39·7'	2°47·5'W	T	126
Old Coppice	Shrops	SJ5627	52°50·6'	2°38·8'W	F	126
Old Coppice	Shrops	SO7182	52°26·4'	2°25·2'W	F	138
Old Copse	Wilts	SU0289	51°36·2'	1°57·9'W	F	173
Old Corner Common	Norf	TG3128	52°48·2'	1°26·0'E	X	133,134
Old Cornhill	Aberd	NJ5756	57°35·8'	2°42·7'W	T	29
Old Corpse Road	Cumbr	NY4912	54°30·3'	2°46·8'W	X	90
Old Corry	Highld	NG6223	57°14·4'	5°56·2'W	X	32
Old Cote High Moor	N Yks	SD9373	54°9·4'	2°6·0'W	X	98
Old Cote Little Moor	N Yks	SD9472	54°8·9'	2°5·1'W	X	98
Old Cote Low Moor	N Yks	SD9272	54°8·9'	2°6·9'W	X	98
Old Cote Moor	N Yks	SD9373	54°9·4'	2°6·0'W	X	98
Old Cote Moor Top	N Yks	SD9374	54°9·9'	2°6·0'W	X	98
Oldcotes	Notts	SK5888	53°23·4'	1°7·3'W	T	111,120
Old Coulsdon	Croy	TQ3157	51°18·0'	0°6·9'W	T	187
Old Country	Heref	SO7144	52°5·9'	2°25·0'W	T	149
Old Country Ho	Heref	SO7244	52°5·9'	2°24·1'W	X	149
Old Course of the River Derwent	N Yks	SE9578	54°11·6'	0°32·2'W	W	101
Old Court	Heref	SO3344	52°5·7'	2°58·3'W	X	148,149,161
Old Court	Monm	SO3619	51°52·2'	2°55·4'W	X	161
Oldcourt Fm	Heref	SO3330	51°58·1'	2°58·1'W	FM	149,161
Old Court Fm	Kent	TR2453	51°14·1'	1°12·9'E	FM	179,189
Old Court Fm	S Glos	ST7093	51°38·3'	2°25·6'W	FM	162,172
Old Covert	Derby	SK2843	52°59·3'	1°34·6'W	F	119,128
Old Covert	Leic	SK4101	52°36·5'	1°23·3'W	F	140
Old Covert	Mil Key	SP9140	52°3·3'	0°40·0'W	F	152
Old Covert	Norf	TG1132	52°50·9'	1°8·4'E	F	133
Old Covert	Northnts	SP7075	52°22·3'	0°57·9'W	F	141
Old Covert	N Yks	SE2785	54°15·8'	1°34·7'W	F	99
Old Covert	Oxon	SP5322	51°53·9'	1°13·4'W	F	164
Old Covert	Suff	TM4773	52°18·2'	1°37·8'E	F	156
Old Covert	Warw	SP2433	51°59·9'	1°38·6'W	F	151
Old Craig	Aberd	NJ9025	57°19·2'	2°9·5'W	X	38
Old Craig	Angus	NO2769	56°48·7'	3°11·3'W	X	44
Old Craig Fm	Aberd	NJ7329	57°21·3'	2°26·5'W	FM	38
Old Craighall	E Loth	NT3370	55°55·4'	3°3·9'W	X	66
Old Craighouse	D & G	NY1884	55°8·9'	3°16·8'W	X	79
Old Crawfordton	D & G	NX8188	55°10·6'	3°51·7'W	X	78
Oldcroft	Glos	SO6406	51°45·3'	2°30·9'W	T	162
Old Croft River	Cambs	TL5690	52°29·4'	0°18·3'E	W	143
Old Croft River	Norf	TL5096	52°32·7'	0°13·1'E	W	143
Old Crombie	Aberd	NJ5951	57°33·1'	2°40·6'W	X	29
Old Cryals	Kent	TQ6640	51°8·3'	0°22·8'E	T	188
Old Crymbles	Wrex	SJ3243	52°59·0'	3°0·4'W	X	117
Old Cullen	Moray	NJ5066	57°41·1'	2°49·9'W	X	29
Old Cut or Moor Drain	N Yks	SE5151	53°57·4'	1°13·0'W	W	105
Old Dailly	S Ayr	NX2299	55°15·4'	4°47·6'W	T	76
Old Dairy Fm	Brackn	SU9173	51°27·1'	0°41·0'W	FM	175
Old Dairy Fm	Northnts	SP6456	52°12·1'	1°3·4'W	FM	152
Old Dalby	Leic	SK6723	52°48·3'	1°0·0'W	T	129
Old Dalby Grange	Leic	SK6622	52°47·7'	1°0·9'W	X	129
Old Dalby Lodge	Leic	SK6522	52°47·7'	1°1·8'W	X	129
Old Dalby Wood	Leic	SK6822	52°47·7'	0°59·1'W	F	129
Old Dale Plantn	E Yorks	SE9344	53°53·3'	0°34·7'W	F	106
Old Dam	Derby	SK1179	53°18·7'	1°49·7'W	T	119
Old Dane	Corn	SW8062	50°25·2'	5°5·5'W	X	200
Olddean Common	Surrey	SU8862	51°21·2'	0°43·8'W	F	175,186
Old Deanham	Northum	NZ0383	55°8·7'	1°56·7'W	X	81
Old Decoy Fm	Cambs	TL2389	52°29·3'	0°10·9'W	FM	142
Old Decoy Fm	Lincs	TF1329	52°51·0'	0°18·9'W	FM	130
Old Decoy Fm	Suff	TL6685	52°26·5'	0°26·9'E	FM	143
Old Deer	Aberd	NJ9747	57°31·0'	2°2·5'W	T	30
Old Deer Park	Rich	TQ1775	51°27·9'	0°18·5'W	X	176
Old Den	E Yorks	TA4012	53°35·4'	0°7·3'E	X	113
Old Denaby	Donc	SK4899	53°29·4'	1°16·2'W	T	111
Old Derwent	E Yorks	SE7228	53°44·8'	0°54·1'W	W	105,106
Old Dilton	Wilts	ST8649	51°14·6'	2°11·6'W	T	183
Old Ditch	Somer	ST5049	51°14·5'	2°42·6'W	T	182,183
Old Ditcham	Hants	SU7620	50°58·7'	0°54·7'W	X	197
Old Dolphin	Brad	SE1130	53°46·2'	1°49·6'W	T	104
Old Dornie	Highld	NB9811	58°2·8'	5°24·9'W	X	15
Old Douganhill	D & G	NX8155	54°52·8'	3°50·9'W	X	84
Old Down	Hants	SU5325	51°1·5'	1°14·3'W	X	185
Old Down	Hants	SU6725	51°1·5'	1°2·3'W	H	185,186
Old Down	S Glos	ST6187	51°35·1'	2°33·4'W	T	172
Old Down	S Glos	ST6187	51°35·1'	2°33·4'W	X	172
Old Down	Somer	ST6251	51°15·6'	2°32·3'W	T	183
Old Down	W Berks	SU4582	51°32·3'	1°20·7'W	X	174
Old Down Fm	Hants	SU6725	51°1·5'	1°2·3'W	FM	185,186
Old Downie	Angus	NO5136	56°31·1'	2°47·3'W	X	54
Old Downs, The	Kent	TR3249	51°11·8'	1°19·6'E	X	179
Old Down Wood	Hants	SU6533	51°5·8'	1°3·9'W	F	185,186
Old Drive	Suff	TM0971	52°18·1'	1°4·3'E	F	144,155
Old Drove Road	Scot Bord	NT1157	55°48·1'	3°24·8'W	X	65,72
Old Drove Road	Scot Bord	NT3932	55°34·9'	2°57·6'W	X	73
Old Dryburn	Northum	NU0041	55°40·0'	1°59·6'W	X	75
Old Dry Hills	Northnts	SP9486	52°28·1'	0°36·6'W	F	141
Old Duffus	Moray	NJ1867	57°41·4'	3°22·1'W	X	28
Old Duncrahill	E Loth	NT4565	55°52·8'	2°52·3'W	X	66
Old Dunwear Ho	Somer	ST3236	51°7·4'	2°57·9'W	X	182
Old Durham	Durham	NZ2841	54°46·0'	1°33·5'W	X	88
Old Eagle	Wilts	SU1671	51°26·5'	1°45·8'W	X	173
Oldeamere	Cambs	TL3096	52°33·0'	0°4·6'W	X	142
Old East End Hall	Suff	TM1560	52°12·0'	1°9·2'E	X	156
Old & East Harbours	N Yks	TA0488	54°16·9'	0°23·7'W	X	101
Old Echt	Aberd	NJ7305	57°8·4'	2°26·3'W	X	38
Old Edinburgh Road	D & G	NX5274	55°2·6'	4°18·6'W	X	77
Old Edlington	Donc	SK5397	53°28·3'	1°11·7'W	T	111
Olde Fm	Warw	SP5168	52°18·7'	1°14·7'W	FM	151
Olde Fm, The	Oxon	SP3012	51°48·6'	1°33·5'W	FM	164
Old Eldon	Durham	NZ2427	54°38·5'	1°37·3'W	T	93
Old Ellerby	E Yorks	TA1637	53°49·2'	0°13·9'W	T	107
Oldend	Glos	SO7905	51°44·8'	2°17·9'W	T	162
Olden Fm	Heref	SO5461	52°15·0'	2°40·0'W	FM	137,138,149
Old England	Pth & Kin	NO1237	56°31·3'	3°25·4'W	X	53
Old Englands Fm	Thurr	TQ6087	51°33·8'	0°18·9'E	FM	177
Older Hill	W Susx	SU8626	51°1·8'	0°46·0'W	X	186,197
Old Erringham Fm	W Susx	TQ2007	50°51·2'	0°17·3'W	FM	198
Oldershaw Fm	Lincs	TF4529	52°50·6'	0°9·6'E	FM	131
Olderwood Plantn	Devon	SX5266	50°28·7'	4°4·8'W	F	201
Old Eye	N Yks	SE5226	53°43·9'	1°12·3'W	W	105
Old Fallings	Wolv	SJ9201	52°36·6'	2°6·7'W	T	127,139
Oldfallow	Staffs	SJ9711	52°42·0'	2°2·3'W	T	127
Old Fallow Fm	Worcs	SO9743	52°5·4'	2°2·2'W	FM	150
Old Fall Plantn	E Yorks	TA2470	54°6·9'	0°5·8'W	F	101
Old Fargie	Pth & Kin	NO1511	56°17·3'	3°21·9'W	X	58
Old Farm	NE Lincs	TA2201	53°29·7'	0°9·2'W	FM	113
Old Farm Clump	Wilts	SU1048	51°14·1'	1°51·0'W	F	184
Old Farmhouse, The	E Susx	TQ5311	50°52·9'	0°10·9'E	X	199
Old Farmhouse, The	Kent	TQ9762	51°19·6'	0°50·1'E	X	178
Old Farm Park	Mil Key	SP9036	52°1·1'	0°40·9'W	T	152
Old Fawdon Hill	Northum	NU0214	55°25·4'	1°57·7'W	H	81
Old Felixstowe	Suff	TM3135	51°58·1'	1°22·2'E	T	169
Old Felton	Northum	NU1702	55°19·0'	1°43·5'W	X	81
Old Fen Fm	Lincs	TF2255	53°4·9'	0°10·3'W	FM	122
Oldfield	Brad	SE0037	53°50·0'	1°59·6'W	T	104
Oldfield	Cumbr	NY0527	54°38·0'	3°27·9'W	T	89
Oldfield	Derby	SK0077	53°17·6'	1°59·6'W	X	119
Oldfield	Kirk	SE1310	53°35·4'	1°47·8'W	T	110
Old Field	N Yks	SD6667	54°6·1'	2°30·8'W	X	98
Oldfield	Shrops	SO4083	52°26·7'	2°52·6'W	X	137
Old Field	Shrops	SO4977	52°23·6'	2°44·6'W	T	137,138,148
Oldfield	Shrops	SO6788	52°29·6'	2°28·8'W	T	138
Oldfield	Wirral	SJ2582	53°20·0'	3°7·2'W	X	108
Oldfield	Worcs	SO8464	52°16·7'	2°13·7'W	T	138,150
Oldfield Brow	Traf	SJ7588	53°23·5'	2°22·1'W	T	109
Old Field Carr	Lancs	SD3538	53°50·3'	2°58·9'W	X	102
Old Field End	Cumbr	SD5596	54°21·7'	2°41·1'W	X	97
Oldfield Fm	Beds	TL1735	52°0·3'	0°17·3'W	FM	153
Oldfield Fm	Cambs	TL4664	52°15·5'	0°8·8'E	FM	154
Oldfield Fm	Heref	SO4523	51°54·4'	2°47·6'W	FM	161
Oldfield Fm	Heref	SO4669	52°19·2'	2°47·1'W	FM	137,138,148
Oldfield Fm	Oxon	SP6328	51°57·0'	1°4·6'W	FM	164,165
Oldfield Fm	Oxon	SU2596	51°40·0'	1°37·9'W	FM	163
Oldfield Fm	Oxon	SU3391	51°37·2'	1°31·0'W	FM	164,174
Oldfield Fm	Oxon	SU4787	51°35·0'	1°18·9'W	FM	174
Oldfield Fm	S Glos	ST6484	51°33·5'	2°30·8'W	FM	172
Oldfield Fm	S Glos	ST7573	51°27·6'	2°21·2'W	FM	172
Oldfield Fm	Warw	SP2168	52°18·8'	1°41·1'W	FM	139,151
Oldfield Ho	Highld	ND1267	58°35·2'	3°30·3'W	X	11,12
Oldfield Manor Fm	Wirral	SJ2488	53°23·2'	3°8·2'W	FM	108
Oldfield Mill	Cumbr	NY0527	54°38·0'	3°27·9'W	X	89
Oldfield Park	Bath & NE Somer	ST7364	51°22·7'	2°22·9'W	T	172
Oldfield Plantn	Notts	SK7739	52°56·8'	0°50·8'W	F	129
Oldfield Pond	Peterb	TF1300	52°35·4'	0°19·5'W	W	142
Oldfields	Glos	SO6835	52°1·0'	2°27·6'W	X	149
Oldfields	Shrops	SJ6236	52°55·4'	2°33·5'W	X	127
Oldfields Fm	Bucks	SU9592	51°37·4'	0°37·3'W	FM	175,176
Oldfields Fm	Ches	SJ3760	53°8·2'	2°56·1'W	FM	117
Oldfields Fm	Ches	SJ6564	53°10·6'	2°31·0'W	FM	118
Oldfields Fm	Staffs	SK0853	53°4·7'	1°52·4'W	FM	119
Old Field Top	Glos	SO7827	51°56·7'	2°18·8'W	X	162
Old Fir Hill	Moray	NJ4658	57°36·8'	2°53·8'W	H	28,29
Oldflat Wood	E Yorks	SE8241	53°51·8'	0°44·8'W	F	106
Old Fleet	Essex	TQ9195	51°37·5'	0°46·0'E	W	168
Old Fletton	Peterb	TL1996	52°33·2'	0°14·3'W	T	142
Old Flinder	Aberd	NJ5927	57°20·2'	2°40·4'W	X	37
Old Flue	Northum	NY8154	54°53·1'	2°17·3'W	A	86,87
Old Flue	N Yks	SE0692	54°19·7'	1°54·0'W	X	99
Old Fm	Beds	SP9530	51°57·9'	0°36·6'W	FM	165
Old Fm	Cumbr	SD3577	54°11·3'	2°59·4'W	FM	96,97
Old Fm	E Susx	TQ4617	50°56·3'	0°5·1'E	FM	198
Old Fm	Hants	SU5362	51°21·5'	1°13·9'W	FM	174
Old Fm	Hants	SU7316	50°56·6'	0°57·3'W	FM	197
Old Fm	Kent	TQ6539	51°7·8'	0°21·9'E	FM	188
Old Fm	Kent	TQ9726	51°0·2'	0°48·9'E	FM	189
Old Fm	Lincs	SK8768	53°12·4'	0°41·4'W	FM	121
Old Fm	Lincs	TF4754	53°4·0'	0°12·0'E	FM	122
Old Fm	N Lincs	SE8008	53°34·0'	0°47·1'W	FM	112
Old Fm	Norf	TG3123	52°45·5'	1°25·8'E	FM	133,134
Old Fm	Norf	TL5298	52°33·7'	0°15·0'E	FM	143
Old Fm	Peterb	TF2307	52°39·0'	0°10·5'W	FM	142
Old Fm	S Glos	ST7578	51°30·3'	2°21·2'W	FM	172
Old Fm	Somer	ST3310	50°53·4'	2°56·8'W	FM	193
Old Fm	Suff	TM4186	52°25·4'	1°33·1'E	FM	156
Old Fm	Warr	SJ6483	53°20·8'	2°32·0'W	FM	109
Old Fm	W Berks	SU6166	51°23·6'	1°7·0'W	FM	175
Old Fm	Worcs	SP0671	52°20·5'	1°54·3'W	FM	139
Old Fm	W Susx	TQ0425	51°1·1'	0°30·6'W	FM	186,197
Old Fm, The	E Susx	TQ4421	50°58·4'	0°3·5'E	FM	198
Old Fodderlee	Scot Bord	NT6015	55°25·9'	2°37·5'W	X	80
Old Fold	Ghead	NZ2762	54°57·4'	1°34·3'W	T	88
Old Folds	Durham	NY8531	54°40·7'	2°13·5'W	X	91,92
Oldford	Somer	ST7850	51°15·2'	2°18·5'W	T	183
Old Ford	T Ham	TQ3683	51°32·0'	0°2·0'W	T	177
Old Fordey Ho	Cambs	TL5474	52°20·8'	0°16·1'E	X	143
Old Ford Ho	Devon	SS8911	50°53·5'	3°34·3'W	X	192
Old Forest	Aberd	NJ4429	57°21·1'	2°55·4'W	X	37
Old Forge	Heref	SO5518	51°51·8'	2°38·8'W	T	162
Old Forge Fm	Kent	TQ5942	51°9·5'	0°16·8'E	FM	188
Old Forge Fm	Kent	TQ8459	51°18·2'	0°38·8'E	FM	178,188
Old Forge, The	Shrops	SJ4801	52°36·5'	2°45·7'W	X	126
Old Fort	Pemb	SM9637	51°59·9'	4°57·9'W	X	157
Old Foss Beck	York	SE6455	53°59·5'	1°1·0'W	W	105,106
Old Fox Covert Plantn	E Yorks	TA0154	53°58·6'	0°27·2'W	F	106,107
Old Froodvale	Carm	SN6438	52°1·7'	3°58·5'W	X	146
Old Furnace	Heref	SO4923	51°54·4'	2°44·1'W	X	162
Old Furnace	Monm	SO5100	51°42·0'	2°42·2'W	X	162
Oldfurnace	Staffs	SK0443	52°59·3'	1°56·0'W	T	119,128
Old Furnace	Torf	SO2600	51°41·9'	3°3·9'W	T	171
Old Garroch	D & G	NX5882	55°7·0'	4°13·2'W	X	77
Old Garswood Hall Fm	St Hel	SJ5398	53°28·8'	2°42·1'W	FM	108
Old Garwaldshiels	D & G	NY1999	55°17·0'	3°16·1'W	X	79
Old Gate	Lincs	TF4120	52°45·8'	0°5·8'E	T	131
Oldgate Nick	Ches	SJ9976	53°17·1'	2°0·5'W	X	118
Old Gawdy Hall	E Yorks	TA0153	53°58·0'	0°27·2'W	X	106,107
Old Glanrhyd	Powys	SN9824	51°54·6'	3°28·6'W	X	160
Old Glasson	Lancs	SD4455	53°59·5'	2°50·8'W	X	102
Old Glebe Fm	Northnts	SP5838	52°2·5'	1°8·9'W	FM	152
Old Glenlee	D & G	NX5980	55°5·9'	4°12·2'W	X	77
Old Glossop	Derby	SK0494	53°26·8'	1°56·0'W	T	110
Old Goginan	Cered	SN6881	52°24·9'	3°56·1'W	T	135
Old Goole	E Yorks	SE7422	53°41·6'	0°52·3'W	T	105,106,112
Old Gore	Heref	SO6228	51°57·2'	2°32·8'W	T	149
Old Graden	Scot Bord	NT7929	55°33·5'	2°19·5'W	X	74
Old Graitney	D & G	NY3166	54°59·3'	3°4·3'W	T	85
Old Grange	Bucks	SP8205	51°44·5'	0°48·3'W	X	165
Old Grange	Lancs	SD4627	53°44·4'	2°48·7'W	X	102
Old Greenlaw	Scot Bord	NT7144	55°41·6'	2°27·2'W	X	74
Old Grimsby	I Scilly	SV8915	49°57·5'	6°19·8'W	T	203
Oldgrit	Shrops	SO3298	52°34·8'	2°59·8'W	X	137
Old Grove	Norf	TM4193	52°29·1'	1°33·4'E	F	134
Old Grove	Warw	SP1272	52°21·0'	1°49·0'W	X	139
Old Guadaloupe	Leic	SK7416	52°44·4'	0°53·8'W	X	129
Old Gwernyfed	Powys	SO1836	52°1·2'	3°11·3'W	A	161
Old Ha	S Ayr	NS4021	55°27·7'	4°31·4'W	A	70
Old Haa	Shetld	HU5279	60°29·7'	1°2·7'W	A	2,3
Old Hag	Staffs	SJ9763	53°10·1'	2°2·3'W	X	118
Old Hag Wood	Lincs	SK9071	53°13·9'	0°38·7'W	F	121
Oldhall	Aberd	NO4698	57°4·5'	2°53·0'W	X	37,44
Old Hall	Black w Dar	SD6325	53°43·4'	2°33·2'W	X	102,103
Old Hall	Bury	SD7805	53°32·7'	2°19·5'W	X	109
Old Hall	Ches	SJ3273	53°15·2'	3°0·7'W	A	117
Old Hall	Ches	SJ4263	53°9·9'	2°51·6'W	X	117
Old Hall	Ches	SJ5049	53°2·4'	2°44·3'W	A	117
Old Hall	Ches	SJ5164	53°10·5'	2°43·6'W	X	117
Old Hall	Ches	SJ6065	53°11·1'	2°35·5'W	X	118
Old Hall	Ches	SJ6546	53°0·9'	2°30·9'W	X	118
Old Hall	Ches	SJ7582	53°20·3'	2°22·1'W	X	109
Old Hall	Ches	SJ7979	53°18·7'	2°18·5'W	A	118
Old Hall	Ches	SJ8266	53°11·7'	2°15·8'W	X	118
Old Hall	Ches	SJ8465	53°11·2'	2°14·0'W	X	118
Old Hall	Ches	SJ8674	53°16·0'	2°12·2'W	X	118
Old Hall	Cumbr	NY4579	55°6·4'	2°51·3'W	X	86
Old Hall	Cumbr	SD5384	54°15·2'	2°42·9'W	X	97
Old Hall	Derby	SK2049	53°2·5'	1°41·7'W	X	119
Old Hall	Derby	SK3178	53°18·1'	1°31·7'W	X	119
Old Hall	Derby	SK4663	53°10·0'	1°18·3'W	A	120
Old Hall	Devon	ST0814	50°55·3'	3°18·2'W	X	181
Old Hall	D & G	NX1459	54°53·7'	4°53·6'W	X	82
Old Hall	D & G	NX4066	54°58·0'	4°29·5'W	X	83
Old Hall	Durham	NZ2034	54°42·3'	1°41·0'W	X	93
Oldhall	E Ayr	NS3950	55°43·3'	4°33·4'W	X	63
Oldhall	E Ayr	NS4444	55°40·1'	4°28·4'W	X	70
Old Hall	Essex	TL6840	52°2·2'	0°27·4'E	X	154
Old Hall	Essex	TL7124	51°53·5'	0°29·5'E	X	167
Old Hall	Essex	TL7509	51°45·4'	0°32·5'E	X	167
Old Hall	E Yorks	SE7328	53°44·8'	0°53·2'W	A	105,106
Old Hall	E Yorks	TA0436	53°48·8'	0°24·8'W	X	107
Old Hall	E Yorks	TA1244	53°53·0'	0°17·3'W	X	107
Old Hall	E Yorks	TA1558	54°0·5'	0°14·3'W	A	107
Old Hall	E Yorks	TA2826	53°43·1'	0°3·2'W	X	107
Old Hall	Flint	SJ2071	53°14·0'	3°11·5'W	X	117
Old Hall	Gwyn	SH5369	53°12·1'	4°11·6'W	A	114,115
Old Hall	Heref	SO4661	52°14·9'	2°47·1'W	X	137,138,148
Oldhall	Inverc	NS3670	55°54·0'	4°36·9'W	X	63
Old Hall	Lancs	SD4255	53°59·5'	2°52·7'W	X	102
Old Hall	Lancs	SD5335	53°48·8'	2°42·4'W	X	102
Old Hall	Lancs	SD5416	53°38·6'	2°41·3'W	X	108
Old Hall	Lancs	SD5713	53°37·0'	2°38·6'W	X	108
Old Hall	Leic	SK6412	52°42·3'	1°2·8'W	A	129
Old Hall	Leic	SP5791	52°31·1'	1°9·2'W	X	140
Old Hall	Lincs	SK8190	53°24·3'	0°46·5'W	A	112
Old Hall	Lincs	SK9240	52°57·2'	0°37·4'W	X	130
Old Hall	Lincs	SK9552	53°3·6'	0°34·5'W	X	121
Old Hall	Lincs	TF0810	52°40·8'	0°23·7'W	A	130,142
Old Hall	Lincs	TF3870	53°12·8'	0°4·4'E	X	122
Old Hall	Norf	TF5618	52°44·5'	0°19·1'E	X	131
Old Hall	Norf	TF9011	52°40·0'	0°49·0'E	X	132
Old Hall	Norf	TF9406	52°37·3'	0°52·4'E	X	144
Old Hall	Norf	TF9718	52°43·7'	0°55·5'E	X	132
Old Hall	Norf	TG0106	52°37·1'	0°58·6'E	X	144
Old Hall	Norf	TG0304	52°36·0'	1°0·3'E	X	144
Old Hall	Norf	TG0627	52°48·3'	1°3·8'E	X	133
Old Hall	Norf	TG0811	52°39·6'	1°4·9'E	X	133
Old Hall	Norf	TG1901	52°34·0'	1°14·3'E	X	134
Old Hall	Norf	TG1942	52°56·1'	1°15·9'E	X	133
Old Hall	Norf	TG2303	52°35·0'	1°17·9'E	X	134
Old Hall	Norf	TG2720	52°44·0'	1°22·1'E	X	133,134
Old Hall	Norf	TG2917	52°42·4'	1°23·8'E	X	133,134
Old Hall	Norf	TG3204	52°35·3'	1°25·9'E	X	134
Old Hall	Norf	TG3216	52°41·7'	1°26·4'E	X	133,134
Old Hall	Norf	TG3230	52°49·3'	1°27·0'E	X	133
Old Hall	Norf	TG3402	52°34·1'	1°27·6'E	A	134
Old Hall	Norf	TG3415	52°41·1'	1°28·1'E	X	133,134
Old Hall	Norf	TG3926	52°46·9'	1°33·1'E	X	133,134
Old Hall	Norf	TG4202	52°33·9'	1°34·8'E	X	134
Old Hall	Norf	TM0598	52°32·7'	1°1·8'E	A	144
Old Hall	Norf	TM0791	52°28·9'	1°3·3'E	X	144
Old Hall	Norf	TM1290	52°28·2'	1°7·7'E	X	144
Old Hall	Norf	TM1485	52°25·5'	1°9·3'E	X	144,156
Old Hall	Norf	TM2397	52°31·7'	1°17·7'E	A	134
Old Hall	Norf	TM2398	52°32·3'	1°17·7'E	X	134

Old Hall	Norf	TM2995	52°30·5′	1°22·9′E	X	134
Old Hall	Northum	NU1501	55°18·4′	1°45·4′W	A	81
Old Hall	Northum	NY7686	55°10·3′	2°22·2′W	X	80
Old Hall	Notts	SK7243	52°59·0′	0°55·2′W	X	129
Old Hall	Notts	SK8258	53°7·0′	0°46·1′W	X	121
Old Hall	N Yks	NZ3209	54°28·8′	1°29·9′W	X	93
Old Hall	N Yks	NZ4407	54°27·6′	1°18·9′W	X	93
Old Hall	N Yks	SD8454	53°59·2′	2°14·2′W	X	103
Old Hall	N Yks	SE2369	54°7·2′	1°38·5′W	X	99
Old Hall	N Yks	SE3259	54°1·8′	1°30·3′W	X	104
Old Hall	N Yks	SE4366	54°5·5′	1°20·1′W	A	99
Old Hall	Orkney	HY2412	58°59·6′	3°18·9′W	X	6
Old Hall	Powys	SJ1101	52°36·2′	3°18·5′W	X	136
Old Hall	Powys	SN9084	52°26·8′	3°36·7′W	T	136
Old Hall	Powys	SO1666	52°17·4′	3°13·5′W	X	136,148
Old Hall	Powys	SO2090	52°30·4′	3°10·3′W	X	137
Oldhall	Renf	NS5064	55°51·0′	4°23·3′W	T	64
Old Hall	Roth	SK4984	53°21·3′	1°15·4′W	X	111,120
Old Hall	Rut	SK9211	52°41·6′	0°37·9′W	A	130
Old Hall	Scot Bord	NT6921	55°29·2′	2°29·0′W	X	74
Oldhall	Shetld	HU4472	60°26·0′	1°11·5′W	X	2,3
Old Hall	Staffs	SJ7744	52°59·8′	2°20·2′W	A	118
Old Hall	Staffs	SJ9849	53°2·5′	2°1·4′W	X	118
Old Hall	Staffs	SK0816	52°44·7′	1°52·5′W	A	128
Old Hall	Staffs	SK1820	52°46·9′	1°43·6′W	X	128
Old Hall	Stock on T	NZ4213	54°30·9′	1°20·7′W	X	93
Old Hall	Suff	TL9268	52°16·8′	0°49·3′E	X	155
Old Hall	Suff	TM0271	52°18·2′	0°58·2′E	X	144,155
Old Hall	Suff	TM0364	52°14·4′	0°58·8′E	X	155
Old Hall	Suff	TM0734	51°58·2′	1°1·2′E	X	155,169
Old Hall	Suff	TM1564	52°14·2′	1°9·3′E	X	156
Old Hall	Suff	TM2758	52°10·6′	1°19·6′E	X	156
Old Hall	Suff	TM4369	52°16·1′	1°34·1′E	X	156
Old Hall	Suff	TM5195	52°29·9′	1°42·3′E	X	134
Old Hall	Thurr	TQ7082	51°30·9′	0°27·4′E	X	178
Old Hall	Wals	SP0596	52°33·9′	1°55·2′W	X	139
Old Hall	Warr	SJ5889	53°24·0′	2°37·5′W	A	108
Old Hall	Warw	SP2384	52°27·4′	1°39·3′W	A	139
Old Hall	Wrekin	SJ7214	52°43·6′	2°24·5′W	X	127
Old Hall	Wrex	SJ3443	52°59·1′	2°58·6′W	X	117
Old Hall	W Susx	TQ2828	51°2·4′	0°10·1′W	X	187,198
Old Hall Austerson	Ches	SJ6549	53°2·5′	2°30·9′W	X	118
Oldhall Bank	Powys	SO1766	52°17·4′	3°12·6′W	H	136,148
Old Hall Bay	Aberd	NO8883	56°56·5′	2°11·4′W	W	45
Old Hall Creek	Essex	TL9611	51°46·0′	0°50·8′E	W	168
Old Hall Farm	Derby	SK2144	52°59·8′	1°40·8′W	FM	119,128
Old Hall Fm	Ches	SJ3773	53°15·3′	2°56·3′W	FM	117
Oldhall Fm	Ches	SJ6867	53°12·2′	2°28·3′W	FM	118
Old Hall Fm	Cumbr	SD2879	54°12·3′	3°5·8′W	FM	96,97
Old Hall Fm	Cumbr	SD3285	54°15·6′	3°2·2′W	FM	96,97
Old Hall Fm	Derby	SK2144	52°59·8′	1°40·8′W	FM	119,128
Old Hall Fm	Essex	TL9512	51°46·6′	0°50·0′E	FM	168
Old Hall Fm	E Yorks	SE7533	53°47·5′	0°51·3′W	FM	105,106
Old Hall Fm	E Yorks	TA1534	53°47·6′	0°14·8′W	FM	107
Old Hall Fm	E Yorks	TA2229	53°44·8′	0°8·6′W	FM	107
Old Hall Fm	E Yorks	TA3719	53°39·2′	0°4·8′E	FM	113
Old Hall Fm	Heref	SO4625	51°55·5′	2°46·7′W	FM	161
Old Hall Fm	Kent	TQ9926	51°0·2′	0°50·6′E	FM	189
Old Hall Fm	Lancs	SD5163	54°3·9′	2°44·5′W	FM	97
Old Hall Fm	Lincs	TF0649	53°1·9′	0°24·8′W	FM	130
Old Hall Fm	Lincs	TF1862	53°8·8′	0°13·7′W	FM	122
Old Hall Fm	Norf	TF9520	52°44·8′	0°53·8′E	FM	132
Old Hall Fm	Norf	TF9610	52°39·4′	0°54·3′E	FM	132
Old Hall Fm	Norf	TF9932	52°51·1′	0°57·7′E	FM	132
Old Hall Fm	Norf	TG0107	52°37·6′	0°58·6′E	FM	144
Old Hall Fm	Norf	TG0112	52°40·3′	0°58·8′E	FM	133
Old Hall Fm	Norf	TG0310	52°39·2′	1°0·5′E	FM	133
Old Hall Fm	Norf	TG0418	52°43·5′	1°1·7′E	FM	133
Old Hall Fm	Norf	TG0514	52°41·3′	1°2·4′E	FM	133
Old Hall Fm	Norf	TG0524	52°46·7′	1°2·8′E	FM	133
Old Hall Fm	Norf	TG0824	52°46·6′	1°5·4′E	FM	133
Old Hall Fm	Norf	TG2616	52°41·9′	1°21·1′E	FM	133,134
Old Hall Fm	Norf	TG2914	52°40·7′	1°23·7′E	FM	133,134
Old Hall Fm	Norf	TG3707	52°36·8′	1°30·5′E	FM	134
Old Hall Fm	Norf	TM0196	52°31·7′	0°58·2′E	FM	144
Old Hall Fm	Norf	TM1093	52°29·9′	1°6·0′E	FM	144
Old Hall Fm	Norf	TM1579	52°22·2′	1°9·9′E	FM	144,156
Old Hall Fm	Notts	SK6555	53°5·5′	1°1·4′W	FM	120
Old Hall Fm	N Yks	SD9986	54°16·4′	2°0·5′W	FM	98
Old Hall Fm	N Yks	SE1488	54°17·5′	1°46·7′W	FM	99
Old Hall Fm	N Yks	SE3387	54°16·9′	1°29·2′W	FM	99
Old Hall Fm	N Yks	SE4190	54°18·5′	1°21·8′W	FM	99
Old Hall Fm	Peterb	TF2707	52°39·0′	0°7·0′W	FM	142
Old Hall Fm	Stock	SJ8881	53°19·8′	2°10·4′W	FM	109
Old Hall Fm	Suff	TL7371	52°18·8′	0°32·7′E	FM	155
Old Hall Fm	Suff	TM1553	52°8·2′	1°8·9′E	FM	156
Old Hall Fm	Suff	TM1856	52°9·8′	1°11·7′E	FM	156
Old Hall Fm	Suff	TM3684	52°24·4′	1°28·6′E	FM	156
Old Hall Fm	Suff	TM4088	52°26·5′	1°32·3′E	FM	156
Old Hall Fm	Suff	TM4174	52°18·9′	1°32·6′E	FM	156
Old Hall Fm	Suff	TM4877	52°20·3′	1°38·8′E	FM	156
Old Hall Fm	Surrey	TQ3244	51°11·0′	0°6·3′W	FM	187
Old Hall Fm	Warw	SP2382	52°26·4′	1°39·3′W	FM	139
Old Hall Fm	Wrex	SJ3547	53°1·2′	2°57·7′W	FM	117
Old Hall Fm	York	SE7049	53°56·2′	0°55·6′W	FM	105,106
Old Hall Green	Herts	TL3722	51°53·0′	0°0·2′W	T	166
Oldhall Green	Suff	TL8956	52°10·4′	0°46·2′E	T	155
Oldhall Ho	Highld	ND2056	58°29·4′	3°21·9′W	X	11,12
Old Hall Marshes	Essex	TL9712	51°46·5′	0°51·7′E	X	168
Oldhall Murray Fm	E Ayr	NS3849	55°42·7′	4°34·3′W	FM	63
Old Hall School	Norf	TG1504	52°35·7′	1°10·9′E	X	144
Old Hall Street	Norf	TG3033	52°50·9′	1°25·4′E	T	133
Old Hall, The	E Yorks	TA2717	53°38·3′	0°4·3′W	X	113
Old Hall, The	Norf	TF6617	52°43·7′	0°27·9′E	X	132
Old Hall,The	Norf	TG0708	52°38·0′	1°3·9′E	A	144
Old Hall, The	Norf	TG1309	52°38·4′	1°9·3′E	X	144
Old Hall, The	N Yks	NZ5907	54°27·5′	1°5·0′W	X	93
Old Hall Wood	Suff	TM1239	52°0·8′	1°5·8′E	F	155,169
Old Halterburnhead	Scot Bord	NT8525	55°31·4′	2°13·8′W	X	74
Old Halves	Cambs	TL3881	52°24·8′	0°2·1′E	X	142,143

Old Halves Fm	Cambs	TL3881	52°24·8′	0°2·1′E	FM	142,143
Oldham	Oldham	SD9204	53°32·2′	2°6·8′W	T	109
Oldham Edge	Oldham	SD9206	53°33·3′	2°6·8′W	T	109
Old Hammond Beck	Lincs	TF2941	52°57·3′	0°4·4′W	W	131
Oldhams, The	Derby	SK1761	53°9·0′	1°44·3′W	X	119
Oldhamstocks	E Loth	NT7470	55°55·6′	2°24·5′W	T	67
Oldhamstocks Burn	E Loth	NT7170	55°55·6′	2°27·4′W	W	67
Oldhamstocks Mains	E Loth	NT7471	55°56·1′	2°24·5′W	X	67
Old Hangy Burn	Aberd	NO6281	56°55·4′	2°37·0′W	W	45
Old Harden	Scot Bord	NT4416	55°26·3′	2°52·7′W	X	79
Old Harlow	Essex	TL4711	51°46·9′	0°8·3′E	T	167
Old Harry	Dorset	SZ0582	50°38·5′	1°55·4′W	X	195
Old Harry's Wife	Dorset	SZ0582	50°38·5′	1°55·4′W	X	195
Old Harts Fm	Bolton	SD6711	53°35·9′	2°29·5′W	FM	109
Oldhat Barrow	Wilts	SU2056	51°18·4′	1°42·4′W	A	174
Old Hatfield	Herts	TL2308	51°45·7′	0°12·7′W	T	166
Old Haven	Aberd	NJ7364	57°40·2′	2°26·7′W	W	29
Old Haven	E Susx	TQ6506	50°50·0′	0°21·0′E	W	199
Old Hawkhill	Northum	NU2112	55°24·3′	1°39·7′W	X	81
Oldhay	Corn	SX2382	50°36·9′	4°29·7′W	X	201
Old Hays Fm	Leic	SK4906	52°39·2′	1°16·1′W	FM	140
Oldhay Top	Staffs	SJ9762	53°9·5′	2°2·3′W	X	118
Old Hayward Fm	W Berks	SU3371	51°26·5′	1°31·1′W	FM	174
Old Hazelrigg	Northum	NU0533	55°35·7′	1°54·8′W	X	75
Old Hazeltonrig	Northum	NT9710	55°23·3′	2°2·4′W	X	81
Old Head	Orkney	ND4783	58°44·2′	2°54·5′W	X	7
Old Head Wood	Northnts	SP9282	52°25·9′	0°38·4′W	F	141
Old Heath	Essex	TM0123	51°52·4′	0°55·6′E	T	168
Old Heathfield	E Susx	TQ5920	50°57·7′	0°16·2′E	T	199
Old Heath Fm	Essex	TQ9498	51°39·1′	0°48·7′E	FM	168
Old Heath Lodge	Rut	SK9706	52°38·8′	0°33·6′W	X	141
Old Heazille Fm	Devon	SS9500	50°47·6′	3°29·0′W	FM	192
Old Hendre	Heref	SO4926	51°56·0′	2°44·1′W	X	162
Old Heritage	E Susx	TQ3821	50°58·5′	0°1·7′W	X	198
Old Hertsfield	Kent	TQ7647	51°11·9′	0°31·5′E	X	188
Old High	Cumbr	NY5601	54°24·4′	2°40·3′W	H	90
Old Higham	Fife	NO2719	56°21·7′	3°10·4′W	X	59
Old Highwood	Devon	ST1406	50°51·1′	3°12·9′W	X	192,193
Old Hill	Devon	SX6662	50°26·8′	3°52·9′W	X	202
Old Hill	D & G	NY3887	55°10·7′	2°58·0′W	H	79
Old Hill	Heref	SO4762	52°15·5′	2°46·2′W	X	137,138,148
Old Hill	Leic	SK7102	52°36·9′	0°56·7′W	X	141
Old Hill	N Eil	NB1143	58°17·1′	6°55·4′W	X	13
Old Hill	Notts	SK6944	52°59·6′	0°57·9′W	X	129
Old Hill	N Som	ST5073	51°27·5′	2°42·8′W	X	172
Old Hill	N Som	ST5364	51°22·6′	2°40·1′W	X	172,182
Old Hill	Sand	SO9586	52°28·6′	2°4·0′W	T	139
Old Hill	Scot Bord	NT3729	55°33·3′	2°59·5′W	H	73
Oldhill	S Lanak	NS8348	55°42·9′	3°51·3′W	X	72
Old Hill	Worcs	SO8161	52°15·0′	2°16·3′W	X	138,150
Oldhill Barn	Glos	SP1014	51°49·7′	1°50·9′W	X	163
Oldhill Bridge	Staffs	SJ9721	52°47·4′	2°2·3′W	X	127
Old Hill Court	Heref	SO5821	51°53·4′	2°36·2′W	X	162
Old Hillock	Aberd	NO8494	57°2·5′	2°15·4′W	X	38,45
Old Hills	Leic	SK7422	52°47·7′	0°53·7′W	X	129
Old Hills	Worcs	SO8348	52°8·0′	2°14·5′W	T	150
Oldhill Wood	Beds	TL0216	51°50·2′	0°30·8′W	F	166
Old Hive	E Yorks	TA3823	53°41·3′	0°5·8′E	X	107,113
Old Ho	Derby	SK0497	53°28·4′	1°56·0′W	X	110
Old Ho	Derby	SK1660	53°8·5′	1°45·2′W	X	119
Old Ho	Essex	TL9729	51°55·7′	0°52·3′E	X	168
Old Ho	Hants	SU2206	50°51·4′	1°40·9′W	X	195
Old Ho	Surrey	TQ0938	51°8·1′	0°26·1′W	X	187
Old Ho	W Susx	TQ3433	51°5·1′	0°4·8′W	X	187
Old Holbeck	Cumbr	SD2369	54°6·9′	3°10·3′W	X	96
Old Hollinside	Ghead	NZ1859	54°55·8′	1°42·7′W	A	88
Old Hollow	Cambs	TL6663	52°14·6′	0°26·3′E	F	154
Old Hollow Fm	Lancs	SD3922	53°41·7′	2°55·0′W	FM	102
Old Home Fm	Aberd	NJ7639	57°26·7′	2°23·5′W	FM	29
Old Hook Fm	Kent	TQ9670	51°23·9′	0°49·5′E	FM	178
Old Hoolgrave	Ches	SJ6659	53°7·9′	2°30·1′W	X	118
Old Hopsrig	D & G	NY3188	55°11·1′	3°4·6′W	X	79
Old Horse Rocks	N Yks	TA1083	54°14·1′	0°18·3′W	X	101
Old Horton Grange	Northum	NZ1975	55°4·4′	1°41·7′W	X	88
Old Hotel	Cumbr	NY2806	54°26·9′	3°6·2′W	X	89,90
Old Ho, The	Bucks	SP8102	51°42·9′	0°49·3′W	X	165
Old Ho, The	Norf	TG1342	52°56·2′	1°10·6′E	X	133
Old Ho, The	Shrops	SJ4629	52°51·6′	2°47·7′W	X	126
Old Ho, The	Worcs	SP0557	52°12·9′	1°55·2′W	X	150
Old Hough	Ches	SJ6962	53°9·5′	2°27·4′W	X	118
Old House	Essex	TL6323	51°53·1′	0°22·5′E	X	167
Old House	Essex	TL8235	51°59·2′	0°39·4′E	X	155
Old House	Suff	TM0644	52°3·6′	1°0·7′E	X	155
Oldhouse	W Susx	TQ2729	51°3·0′	0°10·9′W	X	187,198
Old House Beck	Durham	NZ2235	54°42·8′	1°39·1′W	W	93
Old House Fm	Bucks	SU8490	51°36·4′	0°46·8′W	FM	175
Oldhouse Fm	Ches	SJ7659	53°7·9′	2°21·1′W	FM	118
Old House Fm	Essex	TL5522	51°52·7′	0°15·5′E	FM	167
Old House Fm	Essex	TL6635	51°59·5′	0°25·5′E	FM	154
Oldhouse Fm	Essex	TL8929	51°55·9′	0°45·3′E	FM	168
Oldhouse Fm	Essex	TM0030	51°56·2′	0°55·0′E	FM	168
Oldhouse Fm	Essex	TM1825	51°53·1′	1°10·5′E	FM	168,169
Oldhouse Fm	E Susx	TQ4511	50°53·0′	0°4·1′E	FM	198
Old House Fm	E Susx	TQ8923	50°58·7′	0°41·9′E	FM	189
Oldhouse Fm	Heref	SO2937	52°1·9′	3°1·7′W	FM	161
Old House Fm	Heref	SO4227	51°56·5′	2°50·2′W	FM	161
Old House Fm	Kent	TQ5150	51°14·0′	0°10·2′E	FM	188
Old House Fm	Norf	TM2797	52°31·6′	1°21·2′E	A	134
Old House Fm	Staffs	SJ7927	52°50·6′	2°18·3′W	FM	127
Oldhouse Fm	Surrey	TQ4047	51°12·5′	0°0·6′E	FM	187
Old House Fm	Worcs	SO8952	52°10·2′	2°9·3′W	FM	150
Oldhouse Fm	W Susx	SU8000	50°47·9′	0°51·5′W	FM	197
Oldhouse Fm	W Susx	TQ1022	50°59·4′	0°25·6′W	FM	198
Oldhouse Fm, The	Bucks	TQ0086	51°34·1′	0°33·0′W	FM	176
Old House Green	Ches	SJ8458	53°7·4′	2°13·9′W	X	118
Old House of Carpow	Pth & Kin	NO2017	56°20·6′	3°17·2′W	X	58
Old House Point	D & G	NX0569	54°58·9′	5°2·4′W	X	82
Oldhouse Sike	Northum	NY7556	54°54·1′	2°23·0′W	W	86,87
Oldhouse Spinney	Bucks	SP6115	51°50·0′	1°6·5′W	F	164,165
Old House, The	Hants	SU5458	51°19·3′	1°13·1′W	X	174

Old House, The	Hants	SU7055	51°17·6′	0°59·4′W	X	175,186
Oldhouse Warren	W Susx	TQ2934	51°5·7′	0°9·1′W	F	187
Old Howe	E Yorks	TA1054	53°58·5′	0°19·0′W	W	107
Old Howford	Scot Bord	NT3036	55°37·0′	3°6·3′W	X	73
Old Howpasley	Scot Bord	NT3406	55°20·9′	3°2·0′W	X	79
Old Hundred Fm	Norf	TL5597	52°33·2′	0°17·6′E	FM	143
Old Hundred Lane Fm	Suff	TM0863	52°13·8′	1°3·1′E	FM	155
Old Hunstanton	Norf	TF6842	52°57·2′	0°30·5′E	T	132
Old Hurst	Cambs	TL3077	52°22·8′	0°5·0′W	T	142
Old Hurst Fm	Glos	SO7202	51°43·2′	2°23·9′W	FM	162
Old Hutton	Cumbr	SD5688	54°17·4′	2°40·1′W	T	97
Old Hutton	Lancs	SD6270	54°7·7′	2°34·5′W	X	97
Old Hyndhope	Scot Bord	NT3620	55°28·4′	3°0·3′W	X	73
Old Hyton	Cumbr	SD0987	54°16·5′	3°23·4′W	X	96
Oldicote Fm	Derby	SK2822	52°47·9′	1°34·7′W	FM	128
Old Idsworth	Hants	SU7413	50°54·9′	0°56·5′W	X	197
Old Idsworth Fm	Hants	SU7414	50°55·5′	0°56·4′W	FM	197
Old Inclosed Marsh	Norf	TF4918	52°44·6′	0°12·8′E	X	131
Old Ing	Lancs	SD7458	54°1·3′	2°23·4′W	X	103
Old Ing	N Yks	SD8077	54°11·5′	2°18·0′W	X	98
Old Ingarsby	Leic	SK6805	52°38·5′	0°59·3′W	X	141
Old Ing Moor	N Yks	SD8178	54°12·1′	2°17·1′W	X	98
Oldington	Shrops	SO7397	52°34·4′	2°23·5′W	T	138
Old Inn Fm	Aberd	NJ6431	57°22·3′	2°35·5′W	FM	29,37
Old Inzievar House	Fife	NT0287	56°4·2′	3°34·0′W	X	65
Old Irvine	D & G	NY3681	55°7·4′	2°59·8′W	X	79
Oldiscleave Fm	Devon	SS4724	50°59·9′	4°10·4′W	FM	180
Old Ivesley Fm	Durham	NZ1741	54°46·1′	1°43·7′W	FM	88
Old Jeddart	Scot Bord	NT6614	55°25·4′	2°31·8′W	X	80
Old Jeromes	Herts	TL1008	51°45·8′	0°24·0′W	X	166
Old Johnstone	D & G	NY2499	55°17·0′	3°11·4′W	T	79
Old John's Wood	Norf	TG2235	52°52·2′	1°18·3′E	F	133
Old John Tower	Leic	SK5211	52°41·9′	1°13·4′W	X	129
Old Kea	Corn	SW8441	50°14·0′	5°1·4′W	T	204
Old Keig	Aberd	NJ5919	57°15·8′	2°40·3′W	X	37
Old Keir	Stir	NS7697	56°9·2′	3°59·3′W	X	57
Old Kendal	Aberd	NJ8322	57°17·6′	2°16·5′W	X	38
Old Kennels, The	Moray	NJ1719	57°15·5′	3°22·1′W	X	36
Old Kennels, The	Staffs	SO8382	52°26·4′	2°14·6′W	X	138
Old Kennels, The	W Susx	TQ2827	51°1·9′	0°10·1′W	X	187,198
Oldkiln	Cumbr	NY0744	54°47·2′	3°26·3′W	X	85
Old Kiln	N Yks	SE6092	54°19·4′	1°4·2′W	X	94,100
Old Kiln	Oxon	SU7086	51°34·3′	0°59·0′W	X	175
Old Kilpatrick	W Dunb	NS4673	55°55·8′	4°27·5′W	T	64
Old Kinnernie	Aberd	NJ7209	57°10·5′	2°27·3′W	T	38
Old Kinord	Aberd	NJ4400	57°5·5′	2°55·0′W	X	37
Oldkirk	Aberd	NJ7831	57°22·4′	2°21·5′W	X	29,30
Old Kirk	W Dunb	NS4083	56°1·1′	4°33·6′W	X	56,64
Old Kirkhope	Scot Bord	NT1830	55°33·7′	3°17·6′W	X	72
Old Kirkhope	Scot Bord	NT3724	55°30·6′	2°59·4′W	X	73
Old Kirkland	D & G	NS7214	55°24·4′	4°0·9′W	X	71
Old Kirkstead	Scot Bord	NT2524	55°30·5′	3°10·8′W	X	73
Old Knebworth	Herts	TL2320	51°52·1′	0°12·4′W	T	166
Old Knockwood	Kent	TQ8934	51°4·7′	0°42·3′E	X	189
Old Knoll	Derby	SK2554	53°5·2′	1°37·2′W	X	119
Old Knowle	Dorset	SY7987	50°41·2′	2°17·5′W	X	194
Old Lagg	S Ayr	NS2817	55°25·3′	4°42·6′W	X	70
Old Laith Ho	Donc	SE6911	53°35·7′	0°57·0′W	X	111
Oldland	D & G	NX3261	54°55·2′	4°36·9′W	X	82
Old Land	D & G	NX5553	54°51·3′	4°15·1′W	X	83
Oldland	S Glos	ST6671	51°26·5′	2°29·0′W	T	172
Oldland	W Susx	TQ3216	50°55·9′	0°6·9′W	X	198
Oldland Common	S Glos	ST6771	51°26·5′	2°28·1′W	T	172
Oldlands Fm	Glos	SO6901	51°42·6′	2°26·5′W	FM	162
Oldlands Fm	W Susx	SU9401	50°48·3′	0°39·6′W	FM	197
Oldlands Hall	E Susx	TQ4727	51°1·6′	0°6·2′E	X	188,198
Oldlands Wood	Surrey	TQ1051	51°15·1′	0°25·0′W	F	187
Oldlands Wood	Wilts	ST8480	51°31·4′	2°13·4′W	F	173
Old Langho	Lancs	SD7035	53°48·9′	2°26·9′W	T	103
Old Langtonlees	Scot Bord	NT7352	55°45·9′	2°25·4′W	X	67,74
Old Law	Northum	NU1339	55°38·9′	1°47·2′W	X	75
Old Lawn Fm	Dorset	ST9804	50°50·4′	2°1·3′W	FM	195
Old Laxey	I of M	SC4483	54°13·4′	4°23·2′W	T	95
Old Lea	Staffs	SJ7725	52°49·6′	2°20·1′W	X	127
Old Leake	Lincs	TF4050	53°2·0′	0°5·7′E	T	122
Old Leam Fm	Lincs	TF4525	52°48·4′	0°9·5′E	FM	131
Old Leckie	Stir	NS6894	56°7·5′	4°7·0′W	A	57
Old Lees Fm	Derby	SK2081	53°19·8′	1°41·6′W	FM	110
Old Leslie	Aberd	NJ5925	57°19·1′	2°40·4′W	X	37
Old Leven Wood	N Yks	NZ4506	54°27·1′	1°17·9′W	F	93
Old Ley Court	Glos	SO7417	51°51·3′	2°22·3′W	X	162
Old Leys	Lincs	SK9592	53°25·2′	0°33·8′W	X	112
Old Lilly Hall	Heref	SO6836	52°1·5′	2°27·6′W	X	149
Old Lindley	Cald	SE0919	53°40·3′	1°51·4′W	T	110
Old Linslade	Beds	SP9126	51°55·7′	0°40·2′W	T	165
Old Linthill	Scot Bord	NT9362	55°51·3′	2°6·3′W	X	67
Old Little Humber	E Yorks	TA2023	53°41·6′	0°10·5′W	X	107,113
Old Llanberis or Nant Peris	Gwyn	SH6058	53°6·3′	4°5·1′W	T	115
Old Llanishen Fm	Monm	SO4404	51°44·2′	2°48·3′W	FM	171
Old Llwyn Onn Fm	Wrex	SJ3648	53°1·8′	2°56·9′W	FM	117
Old Lodge	Durham	NZ0922	54°35·8′	1°51·2′W	X	92
Old Lodge	E Susx	TQ4529	51°2·7′	0°4·5′E	X	188,198
Old Lodge	E Yorks	TA1735	53°48·1′	0°13·0′W	X	107
Old Lodge	Northnts	SP7975	52°22·3′	0°50·0′W	X	141
Old Lodge	Northnts	SP8276	52°22·8′	0°47·3′W	X	141
Old Lodge	Suff	TM3662	52°12·6′	1°27·7′E	X	156
Old Lodge Fm	Essex	TL7209	51°45·4′	0°29·9′E	FM	167
Old Lodge Fm	Northnts	SP9283	52°26·5′	0°38·4′W	FM	141
Old Lodge Fm	Shrops	SO6083	52°26·8′	2°34·9′W	FM	138
Old Lodge Fm	Surrey	TQ4241	51°9·3′	0°2·2′E	FM	187
Old Lodge Fm	Warw	SP3544	52°5·8′	1°28·9′W	FM	151
Old Lodge Fm	Warw	SP3978	52°24·2′	1°25·2′W	FM	140
Old Lodge Hill	Warw	SP3544	52°5·8′	1°28·9′W	X	151
Old Lodge, The	Northnts	SP8862	52°15·2′	0°42·3′W	X	152
Old Lodge, The	N Yks	SE5274	54°9·8′	1°11·8′W	X	100
Old Lodge Warren Fm	E Susx	TQ5430	51°3·1′	0°12·2′E	FM	188
Oldlord	Fife	NO3809	56°16·4′	2°59·6′W	X	59
Old Lyham	Northum	NU0631	55°34·6′	1°53·9′W	X	75
Old Lynn Channel		TF5133	52°52·6′	0°15·0′E	W	131

Old Lynn Roads	Norf	TF5231	52°51·5'	0°15·9'E	W	131
Old Madeley Manor	Staffs	SJ7742	52°58·7'	2°20·1'W	A	118
Old Maids Fm	N Yks	NZ2100	54°23·9'	1°40·2'W	FM	93
Old Mains	N Ayr	NS3444	55°39·9'	4°37·9'W	X	63,70
Old Mains	Renf	NS4968	55°53·1'	4°24·4'W	X	64
Old Malden	King	TQ2166	51°23·0'	0°15·3'W	T	176
Old Malling Fm	E Susx	TQ4011	50°53·1'	0°0·2'W	FM	198
Old Malt Ho, The	Kent	TQ6062	51°20·3'	0°18·2'E	X	177,188
Old Malton	N Yks	SE7972	54°8·5'	0°47·0'W	T	100
Old Malton Moor	N Yks	SE7974	54°9·6'	0°47·0'W	X	100
Old Man	Angus	NO4866	56°47·2'	2°50·6'W	X	44
Old Man	I Scilly	SV9016	49°58·1'	6°19·0'W	X	203
Old Man Leys	Oxon	SP4620	51°52·8'	1°19·5'W	X	164
Old Man Of Coniston, The	Cumbr	SD2797	54°22·0'	3°7·0'W	H	96,97
Old Man of Hoy	Orkney	HY1700	58°53·0'	3°25·9'W	X	7
Old Man of Mow	Ches	SJ8557	53°6·8'	2°13·0'W	X	118
Old Man of Stoer	Highld	NC0135	58°15·8'	5°23·1'W	X	15
Old Man of Storr	Highld	NG5053	57°30·2'	6°9·9'W	H	23,24
Old Manor	Devon	SX8063	50°27·5'	3°41·1'W	A	202
Old Manor	Dorset	SY6681	50°37·9'	2°28·5'W	A	194
Old Manor	Wilts	ST9065	51°23·3'	2°8·2'W	A	173
Old Manor Fm	Beds	TL1737	52°1·4'	0°17·3'W	FM	153
Old Manor Fm	Bucks	SP8413	51°48·8'	0°46·5'W	FM	165
Old Manor Fm	Warw	SP2368	52°18·8'	1°39·4'W	FM	139,151
Old Manor, The	Hants	SU3908	50°52·4'	1°26·4'W	X	196
Old Manor, The	Somer	SS9944	51°11·4'	3°26·3'W	A	181
Old Manor, The	Somer	ST2813	50°55·0'	3°1·1'W	X	193
Old Man's Br	Oxon	SP2900	51°42·1'	1°34·4'W	X	164
Old Manse	Shetld	HU4869	60°24·4'	1°7·2'W	X	2,3
Oldmanse Fm	Aberd	NJ4340	57°27·1'	2°56·5'W	FM	28
Old Man's Head Spring	Lincs	SK9979	53°18·2'	0°30·5'W	W	121
Old Man's Hill	Black w Dar	SD6618	53°39·7'	2°30·5'W	X	109
Old Man's Sheel	Northum	NY8083	55°8·7'	2°18·4'W	X	80
Old Man's Stack	Shetld	HU6971	60°25·3'	0°44·3'W	X	2
Old Man, The	Angus	NO4967	56°47·8'	2°49·6'W	X	44
Oldman Wood	Aberd	NO8598	57°4·6'	2°14·4'W	F	38,45
Old Marlborough Road, The	Wilts	SU2048	51°14·1'	1°42·4'W	X	184
Old Marsh Fm	Flint	SJ3369	53°13·1'	2°59·8'W	FM	117
Old Marshfoot Fm	E Susx	TQ6009	50°51·7'	0°16·8'E	FM	199
Old Marton	Shrops	SJ3434	52°54·2'	2°58·5'W	T	126
Old Maud	Aberd	NJ9146	57°30·5'	2°8·6'W	X	30
Old May Beck	N Yks	NZ8902	54°24·6'	0°37·3'W	X	94
Old Mead	Essex	TL5327	51°55·5'	0°13·9'E	T	167
Oldmeldrum	Aberd	NJ8027	57°20·2'	2°19·5'W	T	38
Old Melrose	Scot Bord	NT5834	55°36·1'	2°39·6'W	X	73,74
Old Merdrum	Aberd	NJ4629	57°21·2'	2°53·4'W	X	37
Old Merrose Fm	Corn	SW6543	50°14·7'	5°17·4'W	FM	203
Old Micklefield	Leeds	SE4433	53°47·7'	1°19·5'W	T	105
Old Middlegouch Plantn	Suff	TL8278	52°22·4'	0°40·8'E	F	144
Old Middlemoor	Northum	NU1523	55°30·3'	1°45·3'W	X	75
Old Military Road	Pth & Kin	NN9941	56°33·3'	3°38·1'W	X	52,53
Oldmill	Aberd	NJ4706	57°8·8'	2°52·1'W	X	37
Oldmill	Aberd	NJ5307	57°9·3'	2°46·2'W	X	37
Oldmill	Aberd	NJ8122	57°17·6'	2°18·5'W	X	38
Oldmill	Aberd	NJ8719	57°15·9'	2°12·5'W	X	38
Oldmill	Aberd	NJ9356	57°35·9'	2°6·6'W	X	30
Oldmill	Aberd	NJ9724	57°18·7'	2°2·5'W	X	38
Oldmill	Aberd	NK0244	57°29·4'	1°57·5'W	X	30
Old Mill	Corn	SX3673	50°32·3'	4°18·5'W	T	201
Old Mill	Cumbr	NY7843	54°47·1'	2°20·1'W	X	86,87
Oldmill	Highld	NH5352	57°32·3'	4°26·9'W	X	26
Old Mill	Highld	NM8252	56°36·8'	5°32·7'W	X	49
Old Mill	W Berks	SU5966	51°23·6'	1°8·7'W	X	174
Old Mill	Wilts	SU1329	51°3·8'	1°48·5'W	A	184
Old Mill Burn	D & G	NX3246	54°47·1'	4°36·3'W	W	82
Old Mill Cott	Devon	SX8651	50°21·1'	3°35·8'W	X	202
Old Mill Creek	Devon	SX8652	50°21·6'	3°35·8'W	W	202
Oldmill Fm	Ches	SJ6279	53°18·6'	2°33·8'W	FM	118
Old Mill Fm	E Susx	TQ5824	50°59·8'	0°15·5'E	FM	199
Oldmill Fm	Heref	SO2835	52°0·8'	3°2·6'W	FM	161
Old Mill Fm	Shrops	SO4599	52°35·4'	2°48·3'W	FM	137,138
Old Mill Fm	W Susx	SU9426	51°1·8'	0°39·2'W	FM	186,197
Old Mill Hill	Lincs	SK9477	53°17·1'	0°35·0'W	X	121
Old Mill Ho	Bucks	SP7134	52°0·2'	0°57·5'W	X	152,165
Old Mill Ho	E Susx	TQ4830	51°3·2'	0°7·1'E	X	188
Old Mill Ho, The	E Susx	TQ3615	50°55·3'	0°3·5'W	X	198
Oldmill of Allathan	Aberd	NJ8347	57°31·0'	2°16·6'W	X	29,30
Old Mills	Moray	NJ2063	57°39·3'	3°20·0'W	X	28
Old Mills	Powys	SJ2712	52°42·3'	3°4·4'W	X	126
Old Mills Fm	Stir	NS7795	56°8·2'	3°58·3'W	FM	57
Old Mills Hill	Powys	SJ2813	52°42·8'	3°3·5'W	X	126
Old Mill, The	Bucks	SP8721	51°53·1'	0°43·8'W	X	165
Old Mill, The	N Yks	SE5372	54°8·7'	1°10·9'W	X	100
Old Mill, The	N Yks	TA0093	54°19·6'	0°27·3'W	X	101
Old Mill, The	Oxon	SP6228	51°57·1'	1°5·5'W	X	164,165
Old Milton	Hants	SZ2394	50°44·9'	1°40·1'W	T	195
Old Milton	Highld	NH7900	57°4·8'	3°59·3'W	X	35
Old Milverton	Warw	SP3067	52°18·3'	1°33·2'W	T	151
Old Mint Ho	Surrey	TQ2653	51°16·0'	0°11·2'W	X	187
Old Mint House	E Susx	TQ6404	50°49·0'	0°20·1'E	X	199
Oldmixon	N Som	ST3358	51°19·3'	2°57·3'W	T	182
Old Mixon Hay	Staffs	SK0257	53°6·8'	1°57·8'W	X	119
Old Monkland	N Lanak	NS7263	55°50·9'	4°2·2'W	T	64
Old Montrose	Angus	NO6757	56°42·5'	2°31·9'W	T	54
Old Moor	Derby	SK1073	53°15·5'	1°50·6'W	X	119
Old Moor	Derby	SK1380	53°19·2'	1°47·9'W	X	110
Oldmoor	Essex	TL9600	51°40·1'	0°50·5'E	X	168
Old Moor	Northum	NZ2489	55°11·9'	1°36·9'W	X	81
Oldmoor Wood	Notts	SK4941	52°58·1'	1°15·8'W	F	129
Oldmoss	Aberd	NJ8140	57°27·3'	2°18·5'W	X	29,30
Old Moss	Ches	SJ4965	53°11·0'	2°45·4'W	X	117
Old Moss	Lancs	SD7935	53°48·9'	2°18·7'W	X	103
Old Moss Fm	Ches	SJ4964	53°10·5'	2°45·4'W	FM	117
Old Moss, The	Durham	NY9714	54°31·5'	2°2·4'W	X	92
Old Mousen	Northum	NU1131	55°34·6'	1°49·1'W	X	75
Old Moze Hall	Essex	TM2026	51°53·6'	1°12·2'E	X	169
Old Nab	N Yks	NZ7918	54°33·3'	0°46·3'W	X	94
Old Nafferton	Northum	NZ0565	54°59·0'	1°54·9'W	X	87
Old Nenthorn	Scot Bord	NT6736	55°37·2'	2°31·0'W	T	74
Oldner Ho	Oxon	SP3225	51°55·6'	1°31·7'W	X	164
Old Netley	Hants	SU4710	50°53·5'	1°19·5'W	T	196
Old Neuadd	Powys	SO0886	52°28·1'	3°20·9'W	T	136
Old Neuadd Bank	Powys	SO0984	52°27·0'	3°19·9'W	X	136
Old Newbyth	E Loth	NT5880	56°0·9'	2°40·0'W	X	67
Old Newham	Corn	SX1792	50°42·2'	4°35·1'W	X	190
Old Newnham	Devon	SX5557	50°23·9'	4°2·0'W	A	202
Old Newton	Highld	NH8249	57°31·2'	3°57·7'W	X	27
Old Newton	Suff	TM0562	52°13·3'	1°0·5'E	T	155
Old Newton Hall	Suff	TM0661	52°12·7'	1°1·3'E	X	155
Oldnoth	Aberd	NJ5230	57°21·7'	2°47·4'W	X	29,37
Old Oak Common	Ham & Ful	TQ2182	51°31·7'	0°14·9'W	T	176
Old Oak Fm	Bucks	SP9705	51°44·3'	0°35·3'W	FM	165
Old Orchard	Lincs	SK9069	53°12·9'	0°38·7'W	F	121
Old Oswestry	Shrops	SJ2931	52°52·5'	3°2·9'W	X	126
Old Oswestry (Fort)	Shrops	SJ2931	52°52·5'	3°2·9'W	A	126
Oldown	Glos	ST8692	51°37·8'	2°11·7'W	X	162,173
Oldown Country Park	S Glos	ST6087	51°35·1'	2°34·2'W	X	172
Old Paddock	Oxon	SP6704	51°44·1'	1°1·4'W	F	164,165
Old Pale	Carm	SN2314	51°48·0'	4°33·6'W	X	158
Old Pale	Ches	SJ5469	53°13·2'	2°40·9'W	X	117
Old Park	Bucks	SP8722	51°53·6'	0°43·7'W	X	165
Oldpark	Corn	SX1682	50°36·8'	4°35·7'W	X	201
Old Park	Corn	SX2465	50°27·7'	4°28·4'W	T	201
Old Park	Cumbr	NY4123	54°36·2'	2°54·4'W	X	90
Old Park	Cumbr	NY8313	54°31·0'	2°15·3'W	X	91,92
Old Park	Cumbr	SD3478	54°11·9'	3°0·3'W	X	96,97
Old Park	Cumbr	SD6089	54°17·9'	2°36·5'W	F	97
Old Park	Devon	SY3097	50°46·3'	2°59·2'W	X	193
Old Park	Dorset	SY9295	50°45·5'	2°6·4'W	X	195
Old Park	Glos	SP0109	51°47·0'	1°58·7'W	F	163
Old Park	Herts	TL4416	51°49·7'	0°5·8'E	X	167
Old Park	I of W	SZ5276	50°35·1'	1°15·5'W	X	196
Old Park	Leic	SP7398	52°34·7'	0°55·0'W	X	141
Oldpark	Nth Pt Talb	SS8085	51°33·3'	3°43·5'W	X	170
Old Park	N Yks	SD9852	53°58·1'	2°1·4'W	X	103
Old Park	Staffs	SJ8000	52°35·6'	2°17·3'W	X	127
Old Park	Wilts	ST9960	51°20·6'	2°0·5'W	X	173
Old Park	Wrekin	SJ6809	52°40·9'	2°28·0'W	T	127
Old Park	W Susx	SU8204	50°50·0'	0°49·7'W	X	197
Old Park	W Susx	SU9417	50°56·9'	0°39·3'W	X	197
Old Parkbury	Herts	TL1502	51°42·5'	0°19·7'W	X	166
Old Park Fm	Beds	TL0229	51°57·2'	0°30·5'W	FM	166
Old Park Fm	Devon	SY3097	50°46·3'	2°59·2'W	FM	193
Oldpark Fm	Essex	TL6616	51°49·3'	0°24·9'E	FM	167
Old Park Fm	Hants	SU6710	50°53·4'	1°2·5'W	FM	196
Old Park Fm	Hants	SU6837	51°7·9'	1°1·3'W	FM	185,186
Old Park Fm	Leic	SK6320	52°46·7'	1°3·6'W	FM	129
Old Park Fm	Monm	SO5001	51°42·6'	2°43·0'W	FM	162
Old Park Fm	Northnts	SP6243	52°5·1'	1°5·3'W	FM	152
Old Park Fm	Oxon	SP6007	51°45·7'	1°7·4'W	FM	164,165
Old Park Fm	Red & Cl	NZ6315	54°31·8'	1°1·2'W	FM	94
Old Park Fm	Shrops	SJ7100	52°36·1'	2°25·3'W	FM	127
Old Park Fm	Suff	TM2657	52°10·1'	1°18·7'E	FM	156
Old Park Fm	Wilts	SU0482	51°32·4'	1°56·1'W	FM	173
Old Park Fm	W Susx	SU8203	50°49·5'	0°49·8'W	FM	197
Old Park Fm	W Susx	TQ1924	51°0·4'	0°17·8'W	FM	198
Old Park Fm	W Susx	TQ2527	51°2·0'	0°12·6'W	FM	187,198
Old Park Hall Fm	Durham	NZ2333	54°41·7'	1°38·2'W	FM	93
Oldpark Hill	Staffs	SK1053	53°4·7'	1°50·6'W	X	119
Old Park Ho	N Yks	SE2192	54°19·6'	1°40·2'W	X	99
Old Park Laithe	Lancs	SD8549	53°56·5'	2°13·3'W	X	103
Old Park Lodge	Herts	SP9812	51°48·1'	0°34·3'W	X	165
Old Park Lodge Fm	Durham	NZ2232	54°41·2'	1°39·1'W	FM	93
Old Parks	Cumbr	NY5740	54°45·4'	2°39·7'W	X	86
Old Parks	Leic	SK3619	52°46·3'	1°27·6'W	X	128
Old Parks Fm	Ches	SJ8770	53°13·9'	2°11·3'W	FM	118
Old Parks Ho	Leic	SK3518	52°45·7'	1°28·5'W	X	128
Old Parkside Fm	Lancs	SD5063	54°3·9'	2°45·4'W	FM	97
Old Park, The	Barns	SE3301	53°30·5'	1°29·7'W	F	110,111
Old Park, The	Worcs	SO8746	52°7·0'	2°11·0'W	X	150
Old Park Wood	Cumbr	SD3378	54°11·9'	3°1·2'W	F	96,97
Oldpark Wood	E Susx	TQ4118	50°56·9'	0°0·8'E	F	198
Old Park Wood	Glos	SO6103	51°43·7'	2°33·5'W	F	162
Old Park Wood	Hants	SU6229	51°3·6'	1°6·5'W	F	185
Old Park Wood	Kent	TQ7438	51°7·1'	0°29·6'E	F	188
Old Park Wood	Lancs	SD6534	53°48·3'	2°31·5'W	F	102,103
Old Park Wood	Leic	SK8032	52°53·0'	0°48·3'W	F	130
Old Park Wood	Lincs	TF0126	52°49·6'	0°29·7'W	F	130
Oldpark Wood	Northum	NZ0989	55°12·0'	1°51·1'W	F	81
Old Park Wood	Warw	SP0657	52°12·9'	1°54·3'W	F	150
Oldpark Wood	W Susx	SU8202	50°48·9'	0°49·8'W	F	197
Old Parsonage Fm	Suff	TM4281	52°22·6'	1°33·7'E	FM	156
Old Partick Water	E Renf	NS4357	55°47·1'	4°29·8'W	W	64
Old Passage	S Glos	ST5688	51°35·6'	2°37·7'W	T	162,172
Old Pasture	N Yks	SD8192	54°19·6'	2°17·1'W	X	98
Old Pasture	N Yks	SD9867	54°6·2'	2°1·4'W	X	98
Old Pasture Fm	Warw	SP2456	52°12·3'	1°38·5'W	FM	151
Old Pastures	Northnts	SP8855	52°11·4'	0°42·4'W	F	152
Old Peak or South Cheek	N Yks	NZ9802	54°24·5'	0°29·0'W	X	94
Old Peel	Staffs	SJ7850	53°3·0'	2°19·3'W	X	118
Old Pengoyffordd	Powys	SO1131	51°58·5'	3°17·3'W	X	161
Old Pentland	Midlo	NT2666	55°53·1'	3°10·5'W	X	66
Old Perton	Staffs	SO8598	52°35·0'	2°12·9'W	T	139
Old Perton	Staffs	SO8598	52°35·0'	2°12·9'W	X	139
Old Philpstoun	W Loth	NT0577	55°58·9'	3°30·9'W	T	65
Old Pike	Heref	SO5425	51°55·5'	2°39·7'W	X	162
Old Pike, The	N Yks	SE1052	53°58·1'	1°50·4'W	X	104
Old Pinzarie	D & G	NX7895	55°14·3'	3°54·7'W	X	78
Old Pit	N Yks	SE1080	54°13·2'	1°50·4'W	X	99
Oldpits Plantn	Derby	SK0487	53°23·0'	1°56·0'W	F	110
Old Place	E Susx	TQ5827	51°1·5'	0°15·6'E	X	188,199
Old Place	N Lanak	NS6977	55°58·3'	4°5·5'W	X	64
Old Place	Oxon	SU7380	51°31·1'	0°56·5'W	X	175
Old Place	W Susx	TQ0419	50°57·9'	0°30·7'W	A	197
Old Place Fm	Hants	SU7032	51°5·2'	0°59·6'W	FM	186
Old Place Fm	Kent	TQ7926	51°0·6'	0°33·5'E	FM	188,199
Oldplace Fm	W Susx	SU8706	50°51·0'	0°45·5'W	FM	197
Old Place Fm	W Susx	TQ0604	50°49·8'	0°29·3'W	FM	197
Old Place of Mochrum	D & G	NX3054	54°51·4'	4°38·5'W	A	82
Old Plantn	Scot Bord	NT6654	55°46·9'	2°32·1'W	F	67,74
Old Pole Fm	Ches	SJ6579	53°18·6'	2°31·1'W	FM	118
Old Polquhairn	E Ayr	NS4715	55°24·6'	4°24·6'W	X	70
Old Poltalloch	Arg & Bt	NM8000	56°8·8'	5°32·1'W	X	55
Old Pond Close	Northnts	SP8754	52°10·9'	0°43·3'W	F	152
Oldpool	Shrops	SJ5822	52°47·9'	2°37·0'W	X	126
Old Poor's Gorse	Northnts	SP8075	52°22·3'	0°49·1'W	F	141
Old Portsmouth	C of Port	SZ6399	50°47·5'	1°6·0'W	T	196
Old Post Office	Corn	SX0588	50°39·8'	4°45·2'W	X	200
Oldpots	Highld	NH9751	57°32·5'	3°42·8'W	X	27
Old Pound	Hants	SU3944	51°11·9'	1°26·1'W	X	185
Old Pound (Earthwork)	Hants	SU3944	51°11·9'	1°26·1'W	A	185
Old Prieston	Scot Bord	NT5328	55°32·9'	2°44·3'W	X	73
Old Priory, The	E Yorks	SE8042	53°52·3'	0°46·6'W	X	106
Old Quarrington	Durham	NZ3237	54°43·9'	1°29·8'W	T	93
Old Quarry Fm	N Som	ST4056	51°18·2'	2°51·3'W	FM	172,182
Old Quay	N Ayr	NS0137	55°35·4'	5°9·0'W	X	69
Old Radley Fm	Notts	SK6552	53°3·9'	1°1·4'W	FM	120
Old Radnor	Powys	SO2559	52°13·7'	3°5·5'W	T	148
Old Radnor Hill	Powys	SO2559	52°13·7'	3°5·5'W	H	148
Old Rail Fm	Warw	SP2396	52°33·9'	1°39·2'W	FM	139
Old Ramerick	Herts	TL1734	51°59·8'	0°17·4'W	X	153
Old Rattray	Aberd	NK0857	57°36·4'	1°51·5'W	X	30
Old Ravensworth	Ghead	NZ2357	54°54·7'	1°38·0'W	X	88
Old Rayne	Aberd	NJ6728	57°20·7'	2°32·4'W	T	38
Old Rectory	N Lincs	SE7803	53°31·3'	0°49·0'W	X	112
Old Rectory	N Yks	SE5972	54°8·7'	1°5·4'W	A	100
Old Rectory Fm	Devon	SX6193	50°43·4'	3°57·8'W	FM	191
Old Rectory Fm	Worcs	SO8261	52°15·0'	2°15·4'W	FM	138,150
Old Rectory, The	Devon	SS6833	51°5·1'	3°52·7'W	X	180
Old Rectory, The	Devon	SS8813	50°54·6'	3°35·2'W	X	181
Old Rectory, The	Dorset	ST8204	50°50·3'	2°15·0'W	X	194
Old Rectory, The	Essex	TL5200	51°40·9'	0°12·3'E	X	167
Old Rectory, The	Kent	TR1942	51°8·3'	1°8·2'E	X	179,189
Old Rectory, The	Norf	TF9800	52°33·9'	0°55·7'E	X	144
Old Rectory, The	Somer	ST1625	51°1·3'	3°11·5'W	X	181,193
Old Rectory, The	Suff	TM3167	52°15·4'	1°23·5'E	X	156
Old Rectory, The	W Berks	SU5972	51°26·9'	1°8·7'W	X	174
Old Rectory, The	W Berks	SU6165	51°23·1'	1°7·0'W	X	175
Old Rectory, The	Wilts	ST9378	51°30·3'	2°5·7'W	X	173
Old Redgate Fm	Essex	TL8600	51°40·3'	0°41·8'E	FM	168
Old Redhead	Scot Bord	NT4337	55°37·6'	2°53·9'W	X	73
Oldrey	Somer	SS9037	51°7·5'	3°33·9'W	X	181
Old Rhodes	Lancs	SD6138	53°50·5'	2°35·1'W	X	102,103
Old Rhyne	Somer	ST3127	51°2·5'	2°58·7'W	W	193
Old Rides Fm	Kent	TR0070	51°23·4'	0°52·9'E	FM	178
Oldridge	Devon	SX8296	50°45·3'	3°40·0'W	X	191
Oldridge	Staffs	SK0448	53°2·0'	1°56·0'W	X	119
Old Ridgeway	Swin	SU1777	51°29·7'	1°44·9'W	X	173
Oldridge Wood	Devon	SX8295	50°44·8'	3°40·0'W	F	191
Oldridge Wood	Kent	TR1958	51°17·0'	1°8·8'E	F	179
Old Ridley	Northum	NZ0560	54°56·3'	1°54·9'W	X	87
Old Riggs	Cumbr	NY4829	54°39·5'	2°47·9'W	X	90
Old Rise Rocks	Leic	SK4612	52°42·5'	1°18·7'W	X	129
Old River Ancholme	N Lincs	SE9714	53°37·0'	0°31·6'W	W	112
Old River Axe	Somer	ST3753	51°16·6'	2°53·8'W	W	182
Old River Bain	Lincs	TF2566	53°10·8'	0°7·4'W	W	122
Old River Don	N Lincs	SE7512	53°36·2'	0°51·6'W	W	112
Old River Lea or Lee	Essex	TL3701	51°41·7'	0°0·7'W	W	166
Old River Slea	Lincs	TF0948	53°1·3'	0°22·1'W	W	130
Old River Tees	STock on T	NZ4717	54°33·0'	1°16·0'W	W	93
Old River Witham	Lincs	TF1070	53°13·2'	0°20·7'W	W	121
Old Road Fm	E Susx	TQ6807	50°50·5'	0°23·6'E	FM	199
Old Roan Sta	Sefton	SJ3799	53°29·3'	2°56·6'W	X	108
Old Rock, The	Glos	SO6830	51°58·3'	2°27·6'W	X	149
Old Rome	S Ayr	NS3936	55°35·7'	4°32·9'W	X	70
Old Romney	Kent	TR0325	50°59·5'	0°54·0'E	T	189
Old Rookery Ho	Suff	TM3251	52°6·7'	1°23·7'E	X	156
Old Rookland	Northum	NT9308	55°22·2'	2°6·2'W	X	80
Old Rowfant	W Susx	TQ3137	51°7·3'	0°7·3'W	X	187
Old Rowney Fm	Beds	TL1241	52°3·6'	0°21·6'W	FM	153
Old Rush	E Yorks	TA0248	53°55·3'	0°26·4'W	F	106,107
Old Ryes	Essex	TL6822	51°52·5'	0°26·8'E	X	167
Old Sandsfield	Cumbr	NY3361	54°56·6'	3°2·4'W	X	85
Old Sarum	Wilts	SU1332	51°5·5'	1°48·5'W	A	184
Old Sauchie	Stir	NS7788	56°4·4'	3°58·1'W	A	57
Old Savage	Kent	TQ7350	51°13·6'	0°29·1'E	X	188
Old Scales	Cumbr	NY1928	54°38·7'	3°14·9'W	X	89,90
Old School	Aberd	NJ5603	57°7·2'	2°43·1'W	X	37
Old School Ho	Shrops	SO5596	52°33·8'	2°39·4'W	X	137,138
Old Scone	Pth & Kin	NO1126	56°25·3'	3°26·1'W	T	53,58
Old Scotland Fm	Surrey	TQ0650	51°14·6'	0°28·5'W	FM	187
Old Semeil	Aberd	NJ3811	57°11·4'	3°1·1'W	X	37
Old Shandwick	Highld	NH8574	57°44·7'	3°55·5'W	X	21
Old Shaw's Fm	Essex	TL7016	51°49·2'	0°28·4'E	FM	167
Old Sheepfold Fm	N Yks	NZ5903	54°25·4'	1°5·0'W	FM	93
Old Shelve	Kent	TQ9251	51°13·8'	0°45·4'E	X	189
Old Shields	N Lanak	NS8175	55°57·5'	3°53·9'W	X	65
Old Shields Fm	Essex	TM0628	51°55·0'	1°0·1'E	FM	168
Oldshields Wood	D & G	NY0795	55°14·7'	3°27·3'W	F	78
Oldshiel Knowe	D & G	NX9594	55°14·0'	3°38·6'W	X	78
Old Shipyard	Notts	SK8090	53°24·3'	0°47·4'W	X	112
Old Shirley	C of Soton	SU3914	50°55·7'	1°26·3'W	T	196
Old Shop	Corn	SX2996	50°44·5'	4°25·0'W	X	190
Old Shop	Heref	SO3966	52°17·6'	2°53·3'W	X	137,148,149
Oldshop	Heref	SO4916	51°50·7'	2°44·0'W	X	162
Oldshore Beg	Highld	NC1959	58°29·2'	5°5·8'W	T	9
Old Shoreham	W Susx	TQ2006	50°50·7'	0°17·3'W	T	198
Oldshoremore	Highld	NC2058	58°28·7'	5°4·7'W	T	9
Old Shoyswell Manor	E Susx	TQ6827	51°1·3'	0°24·1'E	X	188,199
Old Shute	Somer	SS9028	51°2·7'	3°33·8'W	X	181
Old Skerries	Orkney	ND4783	58°44·2'	2°54·5'W	X	7
Old Sleningford Hall	N Yks	SE2676	54°11·0'	1°35·7'W	X	99
Old Smithston	E Ayr	NS4112	55°22·8'	4°30·1'W	X	70
Old Smithy	D & G	NY3268	55°0·4'	3°3·4'W	X	85
Old Smithy	Staffs	SJ9763	53°10·1'	2°2·3'W	X	118
Old Smokedown Cottages	Oxon	SU2998	51°41·0'	1°34·4'W	X	164
Old Snap	Brad	SD9837	53°50·0'	2°1·4'W	X	103
Old Snydale	Wakf	SE4021	53°41·3'	1°23·2'W	T	105

Old Soar Manor	Kent	TQ6154	51°16·0′	0°18·9′E	A	188
Old Sodbury	S Glos	ST7581	51°31·9′	2°21·2′W	T	172
Old Softlaw	Scot Bord	NT7531	55°34·6′	2°23·4′W	X	74
Old Somerby	Lincs	SK9633	52°53·4′	0°34·0′W	T	130
Old Songhurst Fm	W Susx	TQ0432	51°4·9′	0°30·5′W	FM	186
Old Sontly	Wrex	SJ3346	53°0·7′	2°59·5′W	X	117
Old South	Lincs	TF4635	52°53·8′	0°10·6′E	X	131
Old South Eau	Peterb	TF2709	52°40·1′	0°6·9′W	W	142
Old South Middle	Lincs	TF4637	52°54·9′	0°10·7′E	X	131
Old Spa Fm	N Yks	NZ2809	54°28·8′	1°33·7′W	FM	93
Old Spital	Durham	NY9112	54°30·4′	2°7·9′W	X	91,92
Old Splott Rhine	S Glos	ST5788	51°35·6′	2°36·9′W	W	162,172
Old Springs	Staffs	SJ9764	53°10·6′	2°2·3′W	X	118
Old SPrings Fm	Staffs	SJ7032	52°53·3′	2°26·3′W	FM	127
Old Springs Hall	Staffs	SJ7032	52°53·3′	2°26·3′W	X	127
Old Spring Wood	N Yks	SE2063	54°4·0′	1°41·2′W	F	99
Old Spring Wood	Roth	SK5381	53°19·6′	1°11·8′W	F	111,120
Oldstairs Bay	Kent	TR3847	51°10·6′	1°24·7′E	W	179
Old Standen	Kent	TQ8030	51°2·7′	0°34·5′E	X	188
Old Star	Staffs	SK0645	53°0·4′	1°54·2′W	X	119,128
Old Station	Monm	SO5300	51°42·0′	2°40·4′W	X	162
Oldstead	N Yks	SE5380	54°13·0′	1°10·8′W	T	100
Oldstead Grange	N Yks	SE5379	54°12·5′	1°10·8′W	X	100
Oldstead Moor	N Yks	SE5382	54°14·1′	1°10·8′W	X	100
Old Stell	N Yks	SE2985	54°15·8′	1°32·9′W	W	99
Old Stillington	Stock on T	NZ3622	54°35·8′	1°26·1′W	T	93
Old Stirkoke	Highld	ND3249	58°25·5′	3°9·4′W	X	12
Old Stobswood	Scot Bord	NT7255	55°47·5′	2°26·4′W	X	67,74
Old Stoke	Hants	SU4837	51°8·0′	1°18·4′W	X	185
Oldstone	Devon	SX8151	50°21·0′	3°40·0′W	X	202
Oldstone Fm	Heref	SO5833	51°59·9′	2°36·3′W	FM	149
Old Stonelaws	E Loth	NT5781	56°1·5′	2°41·0′W	X	67
Old Stone Trough	Lancs	SD9043	53°53·2′	2°8·7′W	X	103
Old Stork Vein	N Yks	SE0695	54°21·3′	1°54·0′W	X	99
Old Storridge Common	Worcs	SO7451	52°9·6′	2°22·4′W	T	150
Old Stowey	Somer	SS9538	51°8·1′	3°29·7′W	X	181
Old Stratford	Northnts	SP7741	52°4·0′	0°52·2′W	T	152
Old Strathlunach	Aberd	NJ5418	57°15·3′	2°45·3′W	X	37
Old Street Fm	Lincs	SK9591	53°24·7′	0°33·8′W	FM	112
Old Street Fm	N Yks	SE5045	53°54·2′	1°13·9′W	FM	105
Old Struan	Pth & Kin	NN8065	56°45·9′	3°57·3′W	T	43
Old Sufton	Heref	SO5738	52°2·6′	2°37·2′W	X	149
Old Sulby Village	Northnts	SP6581	52°25·6′	1°2·2′W	A	141
Old Sulehay Forest	Northnts	TL0698	52°34·4′	0°25·7′W	F	142
Old Sulehay Lodge	Northnts	TL0598	52°34·4′	0°26·6′W	X	142
Old Sunderlandwick	E Yorks	TA0154	53°58·6′	0°27·2′W	X	106,107
Old Surrenden Manor	Kent	TQ9540	51°7·8′	0°47·6′E	X	189
Old Surrey Hall	Surrey	TQ4240	51°8·7′	0°2·2′E	A	187
Old Swan	Liv	SJ3991	53°25·0′	2°54·7′W	T	108
Old Swarland	Northum	NU1601	55°18·4′	1°44·4′W	T	81
Old Swaylands	Kent	TQ5342	51°9·6′	0°11·7′E	X	188
Old Swinford	Dudley	SO9083	52°26·9′	2°8·4′W	T	139
Old Tame	Oldham	SD9609	53°34·9′	2°3·2′W	T	109
Oldtay Fm	Heref	SO3138	52°2·4′	3°0·0′W	FM	161
Old Tebay	Cumbr	NY6105	54°26·6′	2°35·7′W	T	91
Old Thirsk	N Yks	SE4382	54°14·2′	1°20·0′W	T	99
Old Thornville	N Yks	SE4554	53°59·0′	1°18·4′W	A	105
Old Tinnis	Scot Bord	NT3829	55°33·3′	2°58·5′W	T	73
Old Toll	S Ayr	NS3620	55°27·0′	4°35·2′W	T	70
Old Tong Fm	Kent	TQ6739	51°7·8′	0°23·6′E	FM	188
Old Torbeckhill	D & G	NY2379	55°6·2′	3°12·0′W	X	85
Old Tottingworth Fm	E Susx	TQ6121	50°58·2′	0°18·0′E	FM	199
Old Tower	Brad	SE0448	53°55·9′	1°55·9′W	X	104
Old Tower	Conwy	SH8081	53°19·0′	3°47·7′W	X	116
Oldtown	Aberd	NJ5004	57°7·7′	2°49·1′W	X	37
Oldtown	Aberd	NJ5108	57°9·9′	2°48·2′W	X	37
Oldtown	Aberd	NJ5702	57°6·7′	2°42·1′W	X	37
Oldtown	Aberd	NJ5829	57°21·2′	2°41·4′W	X	37
Oldtown	Aberd	NJ8037	57°31·0′	2°16·6′W	X	29,30
Oldtown	Aberd	NK0138	57°26·2′	1°58·5′W	X	30
Oldtown	Aberd	NO5598	57°4·5′	2°44·1′W	X	37,44
Oldtown	Angus	NO5470	56°49·4′	2°44·8′W	X	44
Old Town	Cald	SD9928	53°45·1′	2°0·5′W	T	103
Oldtown	C of Aber	NO8399	57°5·2′	2°16·4′W	X	38,45
Old Town	C of Edin	NT2573	55°56·9′	3°11·6′W	T	66
Oldtown	Corn	SW9373	50°31·4′	4°54·9′W	X	200
Old Town	Cumbr	NY4743	54°47·0′	2°49·0′W	T	86
Old Town	Cumbr	SD5983	54°14·3′	2°37·3′W	T	97
Old Town	E Susx	TQ7408	50°50·9′	0°28·7′E	T	199
Old Town	E Susx	TQ8209	50°51·3′	0°35·5′E	T	199
Old Town	E Susx	TV5999	50°46·3′	0°15·7′E	T	199
Old Town	E Yorks	TA1867	54°5·4′	0°11·3′W	T	101
Old Town	Herts	TL2325	51°54·8′	0°12·3′W	T	166
Oldtown	Highld	NC8508	58°3·0′	3°56·4′W	X	17
Oldtown	Highld	NH5524	57°17·3′	4°23·9′W	X	26,35
Oldtown	Highld	NH5989	57°52·4′	4°22·2′W	T	21
Old Town	I Scilly	SV9110	49°54·9′	6°17·9′W	T	203
Oldtown	Moray	NJ1367	57°41·3′	3°27·1′W	X	28
Oldtown	Moray	NJ3932	57°22·7′	3°0·4′W	X	37
Old Town	Northum	NY7858	54°55·2′	2°20·2′W	X	86,87
Old Town	Northum	NY8158	54°55·2′	2°17·4′W	X	86,87
Oldtown	S Lanak	NS9451	55°44·7′	3°40·9′W	X	65,72
Old Town	Swin	SU1583	51°33·0′	1°46·6′W	T	173
Old Town Burn	S Lanak	NS9508	55°21·5′	3°38·9′W	W	78
Oldtown Cove	Corn	SW9373	50°31·4′	4°54·9′W	W	200
Old Town Covert	Scot Bord	NT8648	55°43·8′	2°12·9′W	F	74
Old Town Fm	Northum	NY8891	55°13·0′	2°10·9′W	FM	80
Old Town Fm	Warw	SP3956	52°12·3′	1°25·4′W	FM	151
Old Town Hall	I of W	SZ4290	50°42·7′	1°23·9′W	X	196
Old Townhead	Scot Bord	NT8069	55°55·1′	2°18·8′W	X	67
Oldtownleys	Aberd	NJ8936	57°25·1′	2°10·5′W	X	30
Oldtown of Aigas	Highld	NH4540	57°25·7′	4°34·4′W	X	26
Oldtown of Carnaveron	Aberd	NJ5612	57°12·1′	2°43·2′W	X	37
Oldtown of Leys	Highld	NH6641	57°26·6′	4°13·5′W	X	26
Oldtown of Meikle Dens	Aberd	NK0743	57°28·9′	1°52·5′W	X	30
Oldtown of Newmill	Aberd	NK0062	57°39·1′	1°59·5′W	X	30
Oldtown of Ord	Aberd	NJ6259	57°37·4′	2°37·7′W	X	29
Old Town or King's Links	C of Aber	NJ9508	57°10·0′	2°4·5′W	X	38
Old Trafford	Traf	SJ8295	53°27·3′	2°15·9′W	T	109
Old Tree	Kent	TR2064	51°20·2′	1°9·9′E	T	179

Old Tree Ho	Corn	SX3084	50°38·1′	4°23·9′W	X	201
Old Trees	S Ayr	NS2711	55°22·0′	4°43·4′W	X	70
Old Trent Dyke	Notts	SK7853	53°4·3′	0°49·7′W	W	120,121
Old Tulchan Wood	Highld	NJ1032	57°22·4′	3°29·3′W	X	36
Old Tun Copse	Northnts	SP7143	52°5·1′	0°57·4′W	F	152
Old Tupton	Derby	SK3865	53°11·1′	1°25·5′W	T	119
Old Turncole	Essex	TQ9997	51°38·4′	0°53·0′E	X	168
Old Ulva	Arg & Bt	NR7181	55°58·3′	5°39·8′W	X	55
Old Urray	Highld	NH5052	57°32·3′	4°29·9′W	X	26
Old Vicarage, The	Devon	SY2497	50°46·3′	3°4·3′W	X	192,193
Old Vicarage, The	N Yks	SE1073	54°9·4′	1°50·4′W	X	99
Old Vicarage, The	Oldham	SE0005	53°32·7′	1°59·6′W	A	110
Old Vicarage, The	Oxon	SP4005	51°44·8′	1°24·8′W	X	164
Old Vicarage, The	Suff	TM2981	52°23·0′	1°22·3′E	X	156
Old Vole Fm	Somer	ST3649	51°14·4′	2°54·6′W	FM	182
Oldwall	Cumbr	NY4761	54°56·7′	2°49·2′W	X	86
Old Wallace	V of Glam	ST0970	51°25·5′	3°18·1′W	X	171
Oldwalls	Swan	SS4891	51°36·1′	4°11·3′W	T	159
Oldwalls Fm	Glos	SP1109	51°47·0′	1°50·0′W	FM	163
Old Warden	Beds	TL1343	52°4·7′	0°20·7′W	T	153
Old Wardour Castle	Wilts	ST9326	51°2·2′	2°5·6′W	A	184
Old Warren	Dorset	SY5888	50°41·6′	2°35·3′W	X	194
Old Warren	Flint	SJ3263	53°9·8′	3°0·6′W	T	117
Old Warren	S Glos	ST7979	51°30·8′	2°17·8′W	X	172
Old Warren	W Berks	SU3780	51°31·3′	1°27·6′W	X	174
Old Warren Fm	Leic	SK5302	52°37·0′	1°12·6′W	FM	140
Old Warren Hill	Dorset	SY4494	50°44·8′	2°47·2′W	X	193
Old Warren Plantation	Dorset	ST8605	50°50·9′	2°11·5′W	F	194
Old Warren Wood	Suff	TL8164	52°14·9′	0°39·5′E	X	155
Old Water	Cumbr	NY5953	54°52·5′	2°37·9′W	W	86
Old Water	D & G	NX8776	55°4·2′	3°45·8′W	W	84
Old Wavendon Heath	Beds	SP9234	52°0·0′	0°39·2′W	X	152,165
Old Wavendon Heath	Beds	SP9334	52°0·0′	0°38·3′W	F	153,165
Old Way	Somer	ST3617	50°57·2′	2°54·3′W	T	193
Oldway	Swan	SS5888	51°34·6′	4°2·6′W	T	159
Oldway	Torbay	SX8861	50°26·5′	3°34·3′W	T	202
Oldway Mansion	Torbay	SX8861	50°26·5′	3°34·3′W	X	202
Oldways End	Devon	SS8624	51°0·5′	3°37·1′W	T	181
Old Wellbury	Herts	TL1429	51°57·1′	0°20·1′W	X	166
Old Well Fm	Worcs	SP0739	52°3·2′	1°53·5′W	FM	150
Old Wester Echt	Aberd	NJ7308	57°10·0′	2°26·3′W	X	38
Old Westhall	Aberd	NJ6725	57°19·1′	2°32·4′W	T	38
Old Weston	Cambs	TL0977	52°23·0′	0°23·5′W	T	142
Old Wharf	Heref	SO7036	52°1·5′	2°25·8′W	T	149
Old Wharf Fm	Northnts	SP7645	52°6·1′	0°53·0′W	FM	152
Old Wharry Burn	Stir	NN8501	56°11·5′	3°50·7′W	W	58
Oldwhat	Aberd	NJ8651	57°33·2′	2°13·6′W	T	30
Old Whitehill	Fife	NT1786	56°3·8′	3°19·5′W	X	65,66
Old Whitehill Fm	Oxon	SP4819	51°52·3′	1°17·8′W	FM	164
Old White Ho	Lincs	TF3927	52°49·6′	0°4·2′E	X	131
Old Whittington	Derby	SK3874	53°15·9′	1°25·4′W	T	119
Old Whyly	E Susx	TQ5116	50°55·6′	0°9·3′E	X	199
Oldwich Lane	Sol	SP2174	52°22·1′	1°41·1′W	T	139
Old Wick	Highld	ND3649	58°25·7′	3°5·3′W	X	7,12
Old Wick	Highld	ND3649	58°25·7′	3°5·3′W	X	12
Oldwick Fm	W Susx	SU8407	50°51·6′	0°48·0′W	FM	197
Old Widdale Head	N Yks	SD7984	54°15·3′	2°18·9′W	X	98
Old Will's Fm	Essex	TL8721	51°51·6′	0°43·3′E	FM	168
Old Wilsley	Kent	TQ7736	51°6·0′	0°32·1′E	A	188
Old Wimpole	Cambs	TL3451	52°8·7′	0°2·1′W	T	154
Old Winchester Hill	Hants	SU6420	50°58·8′	1°4·9′W	H	185
Old Windmill Hill	Surrey	SU9156	51°18·0′	0°41·3′W	X	175,186
Old Windsor	Win & Maid	SU9874	51°27·6′	0°35·0′W	T	175,176
Old Windy Mains	E Loth	NT4464	55°52·2′	2°53·3′W	X	66
Old Wingate	Durham	NZ3737	54°43·8′	1°25·1′W	T	93
Old Wives Lees	Kent	TR0754	51°15·1′	0°58·4′E	T	179,189
Old Wive's Well	N Yks	SE7994	54°20·4′	0°46·7′W	X	94,100
Old Woking	Surrey	TQ0157	51°18·4′	0°32·7′W	T	186
Old Wolverton	Mil Key	SP8141	52°3·9′	0°48·7′W	T	152
Old Woman	Derby	SK0993	53°26·3′	1°51·5′W	X	110
Old Wood	Devon	SS4108	50°51·2′	4°15·2′W	F	190
Old Wood	Leic	SK5109	52°40·8′	1°14·3′W	F	140
Old Wood	Leic	SK5821	52°47·2′	1°8·0′W	F	129
Old Wood	Lincs	SK9072	53°14·5′	0°38·7′W	F	121
Old Wood	Notts	SK5828	52°51·0′	1°7·9′W	F	129
Oldwood	Pth & Kin	NO2325	56°24·9′	3°14·4′W	X	53,58
Old Wood	Shrops	SJ4620	52°46·7′	2°47·6′W	F	126
Oldwood	Worcs	SO5966	52°17·7′	2°36·7′W	T	137,138,149
Old Woodbury	Beds	TL2152	52°9·4′	0°13·5′W	X	153
Oldwood Common	Worcs	SO5866	52°17·7′	2°36·6′W	X	137,138,149
Oldwood Coppice	Shrops	SJ4520	52°46·7′	2°48·5′W	F	126
Old Wood Fm	Staffs	SK0619	52°46·4′	1°54·3′W	FM	128
Old Woodhall	Lincs	TF2167	53°11·4′	0°10·9′W	T	122
Old Woodhouselee Castle	Midlo	NT2561	55°50·4′	3°11·4′W	A	66
Old Woodhouses	Shrops	SJ5842	52°58·7′	2°37·1′W	T	117
Old Woods	Shrops	SJ4520	52°46·7′	2°48·5′W	X	126
Old Woodstock	Oxon	SP4417	51°51·2′	1°21·3′W	T	164
Old Yarr	Worcs	SP0162	52°15·6′	1°58·7′W	X	150
Old Yeavering	Northum	NT9230	55°34·1′	2°7·2′W	X	74,75
Old Yew Hill Wood	Worcs	SP0252	52°10·2′	1°57·8′W	F	150
Oldyleiper	Aberd	NO5596	57°3·4′	2°44·1′W	X	37,44
Olgrinbeg	Highld	ND1053	58°27·6′	3°32·1′W	X	11,12
Olgrinmore	Highld	ND0955	58°28·7′	3°33·2′W	X	11,12
Oliclate	Highld	ND3045	58°23·5′	3°11·4′W	X	11,12
Olies Burn	Pth & Kin	NO1852	56°39·4′	3°19·8′W	W	53
Olistadh	Arg & Bt	NR2158	55°44·4′	6°26·3′W	X	60
Olive Bush Fm	N Yks	SE5933	53°47·6′	1°5·8′W	FM	105
Olive Green	Staffs	SK1118	52°45·8′	1°49·8′W	T	128
Olive Ho	N Yks	SE2272	54°8·8′	1°39·4′W	X	99
Olive Ho	N Yks	SE6794	54°20·5′	0°57·7′W	X	94,100
Olivemead Fm	Wilts	SU0182	51°32·4′	1°58·7′W	FM	173
Olive Mount Fm	Salf	SJ6996	53°27·8′	2°27·6′W	FM	109
Oliver	Scot Bord	NT0924	55°30·3′	3°26·0′W	X	72
Oliverburn	Pth & Kin	NO1825	56°24·9′	3°19·5′W	X	53,58
Oliver Cromwell Ho	Cambs	TL5380	52°24·0′	0°15·3′E	X	143
Oliver Cromwell's Battery	Hants	SU4527	51°2·7′	1°21·1′W	A	185
Oliver Fold	Wigan	SD6903	53°31·6′	2°27·6′W	X	109
Oliver Ford	Durham	NZ0947	54°49·3′	1°51·2′W	X	88
Oliver Hill	Staffs	SK0267	53°12·2′	1°57·8′W	H	119
Oliver's	Essex	TL9621	51°51·4′	0°51·2′E	X	168

Olivers	Glos	SO8711	51°48·1′	2°10·9′W	X	162
Olivers	N Yks	SD7756	54°0·2′	2°20·6′W	X	103
Oliver's Battery	Hants	SU4527	51°2·7′	1°21·1′W	T	185
Oliver's Battery	Hants	SU5836	51°7·4′	1°9·9′W	X	185
Oliver's Battery	Hants	SU6653	51°16·6′	1°2·8′W	X	185,186
Oliver's Battery (Motte & Bailey)	Hants	SU6653	51°16·6′	1°2·8′W	A	185,186
Oliver's Battery (Settlement)	Hants	SU5836	51°7·4′	1°9·9′W	A	185
Oliver's Castle	Wilts	SU0064	51°22·7′	1°59·6′W	X	173
Oliver's Castle (Fort)	Wilts	SU0064	51°22·7′	1°59·6′W	A	173
Oliver's Fm	Essex	TL7436	51°59·9′	0°32·5′E	FM	155
Oliver's Fm	Essex	TL8212	51°46·8′	0°38·7′E	FM	168
Oliver's Fm	Hants	SU6659	51°19·8′	1°2·8′W	FM	175,186
Oliver's Mount	N Yks	TA0386	54°15·8′	0°24·7′W	X	101
Oliver's Point	Shrops	SJ3819	52°46·1′	2°54·7′W	X	126
Oliver's Stray	N Yks	SE2774	54°9·9′	1°34·8′W	X	99
Oliver's Wood	Norf	TM2081	52°23·2′	1°14·4′E	F	156
Olives Fm	Herts	TL4012	51°47·6′	0°2·2′E	FM	167
Olives or Shingle Hall	Essex	TL6220	51°51·5′	0°21·5′E	X	167
Olives, The	E Susx	TQ6529	51°2·4′	0°21·6′E	X	188,199
Ollaberry	Shetld	HU3680	60°30·4′	1°20·2′W	T	1,2,3
Ollag	N Eil	NF7845	57°23·1′	7°21·1′W	T	22
Ollands Fm	Norf	TG1326	52°47·6′	1°10·0′E	FM	133
Ollashal	N Eil	NB1030	58°10·1′	6°55·4′W	H	13
Ollas Water	Shetld	HU4964	60°21·7′	1°6·2′W	W	2,3
Oller Brook	Derby	SK1286	53°22·5′	1°48·8′W	W	110
Ollerbrook Booth	Derby	SK1285	53°21·9′	1°48·8′W	T	110
Ollerenshaw Hall	Derby	SK0280	53°19·3′	1°57·8′W	X	110
Ollersett	Derby	SK0385	53°22·0′	1°56·9′W	X	110
Ollerton	Ches	SJ7776	53°17·1′	2°20·3′W	T	118
Ollerton	Notts	SK6567	53°12·0′	1°1·2′W	T	120
Ollerton	Shrops	SJ6425	52°49·5′	2°31·7′W	T	127
Ollerton Corner	Notts	SK6468	53°12·5′	1°2·1′W	F	120
Ollerton Fold	Lancs	SD6123	53°42·4′	2°35·0′W	T	102,103
Ollerton Grange	Ches	SJ7777	53°17·6′	2°20·3′W	X	118
Ollerton Hall	Ches	SJ7876	53°17·1′	2°19·4′W	X	118
Ollerton Hills	Notts	SK6566	53°11·5′	1°1·2′W	F	120
Ollerton Lane	Shrops	SJ6525	52°49·5′	2°30·8′W	T	127
Ollerton Park	Shrops	SJ6424	52°49·0′	2°31·6′W	X	127
Olleys Fm	Norf	TL8381	52°24·0′	0°41·8′E	FM	144
Ollinsgarth	Shetld	HU4430	60°3·4′	1°12·1′W	X	4
Ollisdal Geo	Highld	NG2038	57°21·1′	6°38·6′W	X	23
Ollisdal Lochs	Highld	NG2240	57°22·2′	6°37·0′W	W	23
Olliver	N Yks	NZ1803	54°25·6′	1°42·9′W	X	92
Olmarch	Cered	SN6255	52°10·8′	4°0·7′W	X	146
Olmstead Green	Cambs	TL6341	52°2·8′	0°23·0′E	T	154
Olmstead Hall	Cambs	TL6240	52°2·3′	0°22·1′E	X	154
Olna Firth	Shetld	HU3764	60°21·8′	1°19·3′W	W	2,3
Olney	Mil Key	SP8851	52°9·2′	0°42·4′W	T	152
Olney Hyde	Mil Key	SP8853	52°10·3′	0°42·4′W	X	152
Olney Lane End	Northnts	SP8654	52°10·9′	0°44·1′W	X	152
Olney Park Fm	Mil Key	SP8753	52°10·3′	0°43·3′W	FM	152
Olrig Croft	Aberd	NK0242	57°28·4′	1°57·5′W	X	30
Olrig Ho	Highld	ND1866	58°34·7′	3°24·1′W	X	11,12
Olton	Sol	SP1382	52°26·4′	1°48·1′W	T	139
Olton Resr	Sol	SP1381	52°25·8′	1°48·1′W	W	139
Olverston House Fm	Lancs	SD3512	53°36·3′	2°58·5′W	FM	108
Olveston	S Glos	ST6087	51°35·1′	2°34·2′W	T	172
Olveston Common	S Glos	ST5987	51°35·1′	2°35·1′W	X	172
Olway Brook	Monm	SO4102	51°43·1′	2°50·9′W	W	171
Olwen	Cered	SN5849	52°7·5′	4°4·1′W	X	146
Olympia	Ham & Ful	TQ2479	51°30·0′	0°12·4′W	X	176
Omachie	Angus	NO4835	56°30·5′	2°50·2′W	X	54
Omand's Dale	Shetld	HP5002	60°42·1′	1°4·5′W	X	1
Omans Geo	Shetld	HU4863	60°21·2′	1°7·3′W	X	2,3
Ombersley	Worcs	SO8463	52°16·1′	2°13·7′W	T	138,150
Omoa	N Lanak	NS7959	55°48·8′	3°55·4′W	X	64
Ompton	Notts	SK6865	53°10·9′	0°58·5′W	T	120
Omrod Fm	Warr	SJ6892	53°25·7′	2°28·5′W	FM	109
Omunsgarth	Shetld	HU3548	60°13·2′	1°21·6′W	T	3
Once Brewed	Northum	NY7567	55°0·1′	2°23·0′W	X	86,87
Onchan	I of M	SC3978	54°10·6′	4°27·6′W	T	95
Onchan Head	I of M	SC4077	54°10·1′	4°26·6′W	X	95
Onchor's Fm	Essex	TL7024	51°53·5′	0°28·6′E	FM	167
One Ash Grange Fm	Derby	SK1665	53°11·1′	1°45·2′W	FM	119
One Barrow Lodge	Leic	SK4616	52°44·6′	1°18·7′W	X	129
Onecote	Staffs	SK0455	53°5·8′	1°56·0′W	T	119
Onecote Grange	Staffs	SK0555	53°5·8′	1°55·1′W	X	119
Onecote Lane Head	Staffs	SK0355	53°5·8′	1°56·9′W	X	119
Onecote Old Hall	Staffs	SK0555	53°5·8′	1°55·1′W	X	119
One Gun Point	Devon	SX8850	50°20·6′	3°34·1′W	X	202
Oneholmes	N Yks	NZ5008	54°28·1′	1°13·3′W	X	93
Onehouse	Suff	TM0259	52°11·8′	0°57·7′E	T	155
Onen	Monm	SO4314	51°49·5′	2°49·2′W	T	161
Onen-fawr	Carm	SN5928	51°56·2′	4°2·7′W	X	146
Onen-fawr	Carm	SN6419	51°51·4′	3°58·1′W	X	159
Onen Fawr Fm	Wrex	SJ2747	53°1·2′	3°4·9′W	FM	117
Onesacre	Sheff	SK2993	53°26·2′	1°33·4′W	T	110
Onesmoor	Sheff	SK2892	53°25·7′	1°34·3′W	T	110
One Tree Hill	Essex	TQ6986	51°33·1′	0°26·7′E	H	177,178
One Tree Hill	Kent	TQ5653	51°15·5′	0°14·5′E	X	188
Ongar Hall Fm	Thurr	TQ6584	51°32·1′	0°23·1′E	FM	177,178
Ongar Hill	Norf	TF5724	52°47·7′	0°20·1′E	X	131
Ongar Hill Fm	Bucks	SU9594	51°38·4′	0°37·2′W	FM	175,176
Ongar Park Hall	Essex	TL5103	51°42·5′	0°11·5′E	X	167
Ongars	Essex	TL5215	51°49·0′	0°12·7′E	X	167
Ongar Street	Heref	SO3967	52°18·1′	2°53·3′W	X	137,148,149
Ongers Fm	Glos	SO8412	51°48·6′	2°13·5′W	FM	162
Ongley	Kent	TQ8339	51°7·5′	0°37·3′E	X	188
Ongutein Manor Fm	Cambs	TL1289	52°29·5′	0°20·6′W	FM	142
Onibury	Shrops	SO4579	52°24·6′	2°48·1′W	T	137,138,148
Onich	Highld	NN0261	56°42·2′	5°13·6′W	T	41
Onley	Northnts	SP5171	52°20·3′	1°14·7′W	X	140
Onley Fields	Northnts	SP5271	52°20·3′	1°13·8′W	X	140
Onley Fields Fm	Northnts	SP5169	52°19·2′	1°14·7′W	FM	151
Onley Grounds	Northnts	SP5070	52°19·8′	1°15·6′W	X	140
Onllwyn	Nth Pt Talb	SN8410	51°46·8′	3°40·5′W	T	160
Onllwyn	Rho Cyn Taf	SN9908	51°45·9′	3°27·4′W	H	160
Only Grange Fm	Derby	SK1484	53°21·4′	1°47·0′W	FM	110

Onneley	Staffs	SJ7543	52°59·3'	2°21·9'W	T	118
Onnvm (Roman Fort)	Northum	NY9968	55°0·6'	2°0·5'W	R	87
Onslow	Shrops	SJ4312	52°42·4'	2°50·2'W	X	126
Onslow Fm	Lincs	TF4221	52°46·3'	0°6·7'E	FM	131
Onslow Fm	Lincs	TF4628	52°50·0'	0°10·4'E	FM	131
Onslow Green	Essex	TL6518	51°50·4'	0°24·1'E	T	167
Onslow Village	Surrey	SU9749	51°14·1'	0°36·2'W	T	186
Onston	Ches	SJ5974	53°15·9'	2°36·5'W	X	117
Onston	Shrops	SJ3832	52°53·2'	2°54·9'W	X	126
Onthank	E Ayr	NS4240	55°37·9'	4°30·2'W	T	70
Onweather Hill	Scot Bord	NT0617	55°26·5'	3°28·7'W	H	78
Onziebust	Orkney	HY4526	59°7·3'	2°57·2'W	X	5,6
Onziebust	Orkney	HY4728	59°8·4'	2°55·1'W	X	5,6
Ooig Mooar	I of M	SC2988	54°15·8'	4°37·1'W	X	95
Ool, The	Orkney	ND3690	58°47·8'	3°6·0'W	X	7
Oorlair	Kent	TQ8856	51°16·5'	0°42·1'E	X	178
Oozedam	Thurr	TQ7383	51°31·4'	0°30·0'E	X	178
Ooze Rocks	Moray	NJ2371	57°43·6'	3°17·1'W	X	28
Open Basenose	Oxon	SP5605	51°44·7'	1°10·9'W	X	164
Open Dale	N Yks	SE8060	54°2·0'	0°46·3'W	X	100
Open Dale	N Yks	SE8159	54°1·5'	0°45·4'W	X	106
Opendale Plantn	N Yks	SE8060	54°2·0'	0°46·3'W	F	100
Open Fm	Wilts	ST9832	51°5·5'	2°1·3'W	FM	184
Open Pits	Kent	TR0718	50°55·7'	0°57·1'E	W	189
Openshaw	Man	SJ8897	53°28·4'	2°10·4'W	T	109
Open University Walton Hall, The	Mil Key	SP8837	52°1·7'	0°42·6'W	X	152
Open Winkins	W Susx	SU9011	50°53·7'	0°42·8'W	F	197
Openwoodgate	Derby	SK3647	53°1·4'	1°27·4'W	T	119,128
Opinan	Highld	NG7472	57°41·1'	5°47·0'W	T	19
Opinan	Highld	NG8796	57°54·4'	5°35·2'W	X	19
Opsay	N Eil	NF9876	57°40·6'	7°3·5'W	X	18
Oragaig	Arg & Bt	NR8554	55°44·2'	5°25·0'W	X	62
Ora Hill	Devon	SS4439	51°8·0'	4°13·4'W	H	180
Orakirk	Orkney	HY3004	58°55·3'	3°12·5'W	X	6,7
Oran	Moray	NJ4161	57°38·4'	2°58·8'W	T	28
Oran	N Yks	SE2596	54°21·8'	1°36·5'W	X	99
Orange End	Herts	TL3325	51°54·7'	0°3·6'W	X	166
Orange Grove	Surrey	SU9847	51°13·1'	0°35·4'W	X	186
Orange Hayes, The	Staffs	SJ9232	52°53·4'	2°6·7'W	F	127
Orange Hill	Derby	SK3224	52°49·0'	1°31·1'W	X	128
Orange Lane	Scot Bord	NT7742	55°40·5'	2°21·5'W	X	74
Orange Row	Norf	TF5420	52°45·6'	0°17·3'E	T	131
Oranges Fm, The	Glos	SP1514	51°49·7'	1°46·5'W	FM	163
Oransaigh	N Eil	NB3612	58°1·4'	6°27·8'W	T	14
Orasaigh	N Eil	NF8243	57°22·2'	7°17·0'W	X	22
Orasaigh	N Eil	NF8451	57°26·6'	7°15·6'W	X	22
Orasaigh	N Eil	NF8652	57°27·2'	7°13·7'W	X	22
Orasaigh Uisgeabhagh	N Eil	NF8650	57°26·2'	7°13·5'W	X	22
Orasay	N Eil	NF8364	57°33·6'	7°17·6'W	X	18
Orasay	N Eil	NF9473	57°38·8'	7°7·3'W	X	18
Orasay	N Eil	NF9673	57°38·9'	7°5·3'W	X	18
Orasay Bay	N Eil	NF8364	57°33·6'	7°17·6'W	W	18
Orbister	Shetld	HU3176	60°28·3'	1°25·7'W	X	3
Orbiston	N Lanak	NS7359	55°48·7'	4°1·2'W	T	64
Orbliston	Moray	NJ3057	57°36·1'	3°9·8'W	X	28
Orbost	Highld	NG2543	57°23·9'	6°34·2'W	X	23
Orbost House	Highld	NG2543	57°23·9'	6°34·2'W	X	23
Orby	Lincs	TF4967	53°11·0'	0°14·2'E	T	122
Orby Beck	Lincs	TF4968	53°11·5'	0°14·2'E	W	122
Orby Drain	Lincs	TF5450	53°1·7'	0°18·2'E	W	122
Orby Marsh	Lincs	TF5167	53°10·9'	0°16·0'E	X	122
Orchan House Fm	Cald	SD9226	53°44·1'	2°6·9'W	FM	103
Orchard	Arg & Bt	NS1582	56°0·0'	4°57·6'W	X	56
Orchard	Clackm	NS8693	56°7·2'	3°49·6'W	X	58
Orchard	Devon	SS4929	51°2·7'	4°8·9'W	X	180
Orchard	D & G	NS7812	55°23·5'	3°55·1'W	X	71,78
Orchard	D & G	NY1096	55°15·3'	3°24·5'W	X	78
Orchard	D & G	NY1976	55°4·6'	3°15·7'W	X	85
Orchard	D & G	NY4080	55°6·9'	2°56·0'W	X	79
Orchard	Falk	NS7679	55°59·5'	3°58·8'W	X	64
Orchard	Pth & Kin	NN9817	56°20·3'	3°38·6'W	X	58
Orchard	Scot Bord	NT5215	55°25·8'	2°45·1'W	X	79
Orchardbank	Angus	NO4350	56°38·6'	2°55·3'W	X	54
Orchardbank	Angus	NO4450	56°38·6'	2°54·3'W	X	54
Orchard Barton	Devon	SX4689	50°41·1'	4°10·4'W	X	190
Orchard Copse	Hants	SU5910	50°53·4'	1°9·3'W	F	196
Orchardfield	Moray	NJ1665	57°40·3'	3°24·0'W	X	28
Orchard Field	Northum	NZ0751	54°51·5'	1°53·0'W	X	88
Orchard Fm	Cambs	TL2396	52°33·1'	0°10·7'W	FM	142
Orchard Fm	Devon	SS4421	50°58·3'	4°12·9'W	FM	180,190
Orchard Fm	Devon	SS5522	50°59·0'	4°3·6'W	FM	180
Orchard Fm	Devon	SX5952	50°21·3'	3°58·6'W	FM	202
Orchard Fm	Dorset	ST4706	50°51·3'	2°44·8'W	FM	193
Orchard Fm	Essex	TL4605	51°43·7'	0°7·2'E	FM	167
Orchard Fm	Kent	TQ8867	51°22·5'	0°42·5'E	FM	178
Orchard Fm	Leic	SP4591	52°31·1'	1°19·8'W	FM	140
Orchard Fm	Lincs	TF0685	53°21·3'	0°24·0'W	FM	112,121
Orchard Fm	Lincs	TF2911	52°41·1'	0°5·1'W	FM	131,142
Orchard Fm	Lincs	TF2911	52°41·1'	0°5·1'W	FM	131,142
Orchard Fm	Lincs	TF3448	53°1·0'	0°0·3'E	FM	131
Orchard Fm	Newp	ST2881	51°31·6'	3°1·9'W	FM	171
Orchard Fm	N Lanak	NS7462	55°50·3'	4°0·3'W	FM	64
Orchard Fm	Norf	TG3002	52°34·3'	1°24·1'E	FM	134
Orchard Fm	Norf	TM1088	52°27·2'	1°5·8'E	FM	144
Orchard Fm	N Yks	SE2799	54°23·4'	1°34·6'W	FM	99
Orchard Fm	Oxon	SU4492	51°37·7'	1°21·5'W	FM	164,174
Orchard Fm	S Ayr	NS3509	55°21·1'	4°35·7'W	FM	70,77
Orchard Fm	Shrops	SJ3611	52°41·8'	2°56·4'W	FM	126
Orchard Fm	Staffs	SK0268	53°12·8'	1°57·8'W	FM	119
Orchard Fm	Suff	TM4064	52°13·5'	1°31·3'E	FM	156
Orchard Fm	Surrey	TQ2440	51°9·0'	0°13·2'W	FM	187
Orchard Fm	Surrey	TQ3045	51°11·6'	0°8·0'W	FM	187
Orchard Fm	Wrex	SJ4044	52°59·6'	2°53·2'W	FM	117
Orchard Fm	York	SE6644	53°53·5'	0°59·3'W	FM	105,106
Orchard Head	Cumbr	SD2286	54°16·1'	3°11·4'W	X	96
Orchardhead	Falk	NS9184	56°2·4'	3°44·5'W	X	65
Orchard Hill	Devon	SS4527	51°1·5'	4°12·2'W	T	180
Orchard Hill	Oxon	SP3441	52°4·2'	1°29·8'W	X	151
Orchard Hill Fm	Dorset	SY9479	50°36·9'	2°4·7'W	FM	195

Orchard Hill Fm	Warw	SP2052	52°10·2'	1°42·1'W	FM	151
Orchard Ho	Cumbr	NY1252	54°51·6'	3°21·8'W	X	85
Orchard Ho	Cumbr	NY4454	54°52·9'	2°51·9'W	X	85
Orchard Ho	Cumbr	NY6366	54°59·5'	2°34·3'W	X	86
Orchard Ho	E Susx	TQ5822	50°58·8'	0°15·4'E	X	199
Orchard Ho	Lincs	TF4056	53°5·2'	0°5·8'E	X	122
Orchard Ho	Norf	TL6388	52°28·2'	0°24·4'E	X	143
Orchard Ho	S Lanak	NS8247	55°42·4'	3°52·2'W	X	72
Orchard Knowes	D & G	NX8356	54°53·4'	3°49·0'W	X	84
Orchard Ledges	Card	ST2174	51°27·8'	3°7·8'W	X	171
Orchard Leigh	Bucks	SP9803	51°43·3'	0°34·5'W	T	165
Orchardleigh Park	Somer	ST7751	51°15·7'	2°19·4'W	X	183
Orchardleigh Stones	Somer	ST7650	51°15·2'	2°20·2'W	A	183
Orchard Mains	Scot Bord	NT3133	55°35·4'	3°5·3'W	X	73
Orchard Portman	Somer	ST2421	50°59·2'	3°4·6'W	T	193
Orchard Rig	Scot Bord	NT2934	55°35·9'	3°7·2'W	H	73
Orchards	W Susx	TQ4139	51°8·2'	0°1·3'E	X	187
Orchards, The	Ches	SJ7768	53°12·8'	2°20·3'W	X	118
Orchards, The	Hants	SU4850	51°15·1'	1°18·3'W	X	185
Orchards, The	Norf	TM3996	52°30·8'	1°31·7'E	X	134
Orchards, The	Staffs	SK1547	53°1·4'	1°46·2'W	X	119,128
Orchard, The	Bucks	SP8525	51°55·3'	0°45·4'W	X	165
Orchard, The	Essex	TL6003	51°42·4'	0°19·3'E	X	167
Orchard, The	I of W	SZ5176	50°35·1'	1°16·4'W	X	196
Orchardton	E Ayr	NS5219	55°26·8'	4°20·0'W	X	70
Orchardton Bay	D & G	NX8152	54°51·2'	3°50·8'W	W	84
Orchardton Burn	D & G	NX8154	54°52·2'	3°50·8'W	W	84
Orchardton Fm	D & G	NX4549	54°49·0'	4°24·3'W	FM	83
Orchardton Ho	D & G	NX8153	54°51·7'	3°50·8'W	X	84
Orchardton Mains	D & G	NX8155	54°52·8'	3°50·9'W	X	84
Orchard Wood Fm	Notts	SK6959	53°7·7'	0°57·7'W	FM	120
Orchard Wyndham	Somer	ST0740	51°9·3'	3°19·4'W	X	181
Orchars	D & G	NX5773	55°2·1'	4°13·8'W	X	77
Orcheston	Wilts	SU0545	51°12·5'	1°55·3'W	T	184
Orcheston Down	Wilts	SU0446	51°13·0'	1°56·2'W	X	184
Orcheston Down	Wilts	SU0748	51°14·1'	1°53·6'W	X	184
Orchid Centre	Norf	TF5519	52°45·0'	0°18·2'E	X	131
Orchill Home Fm	Pth & Kin	NN8711	56°16·9'	3°49·1'W	FM	58
Orchilmore	Pth & Kin	NN9163	56°45·0'	3°46·5'W	X	43
Orchin	Orkney	HY4728	59°8·4'	2°55·1'W	X	5,6
Orchleit	N Eil	NB0829	58°9·5'	6°57·4'W	H	13
Orcombe Rocks	Devon	SY0279	50°36·4'	3°22·7'W	X	192
Orcop	Heref	SO4726	51°56·0'	2°45·9'W	T	161
Orcop Hill	Heref	SO4728	51°57·1'	2°45·9'W	T	149,161
Ord	Highld	NG6113	57°9·0'	5°56·6'W	T	32
Ord	Highld	NH7170	57°42·3'	4°9·4'W	T	21
Ordaal Ho	Shetld	HP6308	60°45·3'	0°50·1'W	X	1
Ordachoy	Aberd	NJ2707	57°9·1'	3°11·9'W	X	37
Ordale	Shetld	HP6307	60°44·7'	0°50·2'W	T	1
Ordan Shios	Highld	NN7196	57°2·5'	4°7·1'W	H	35
Ord Bàn	Highld	NH8908	57°9·2'	3°49·6'W	H	35,36
Ordbrae	Aberd	NJ5042	57°28·2'	2°49·6'W	X	29
Ordbreck	Highld	NH8747	57°30·2'	3°52·7'W	X	27
Ord Burn	Aberd	NJ4826	57°19·6'	2°51·4'W	W	37
Ord Burn	C of Aber	NJ8304	57°7·9'	2°16·4'W	X	38
Orddu	Gwyn	SH9642	52°58·2'	3°32·5'W	X	125
Ordens	Moray	NJ5160	57°37·9'	2°48·8'W	X	29
Ordens Fm	Aberd	NJ6161	57°38·5'	2°38·7'W	FM	29
Ord Fundlie	Aberd	NJ6100	57°5·6'	2°38·2'W	H	37
Ordgarff	Aberd	NJ2608	57°9·7'	3°13·0'W	X	37
Ordhead	Aberd	NJ6610	57°11·0'	2°33·5'W	T	38
Ordhead	Moray	NJ1934	57°23·6'	3°20·4'W	X	28
Ord Hill	Aberd	NJ4827	57°20·1'	2°51·4'W	H	37
Ordhill	Aberd	NJ8200	57°5·7'	2°17·4'W	X	38
Ordhill	Aberd	NJ8631	57°22·4'	2°13·5'W	X	30
Ord Hill	Highld	NH6649	57°30·9'	4°13·8'W	H	26
Ordhill	Highld	NH7058	57°35·9'	4°10·0'W	X	27
Ordhill	Highld	NH8949	57°31·3'	3°50·7'W	X	27
Ordhill	Moray	NJ2557	57°36·1'	3°14·8'W	X	28
Ordhill	Northum	NT9850	55°44·9'	2°1·5'W	X	75
Ord Ho	Highld	NH5150	57°31·2'	4°28·8'W	X	26
Ordie	Aberd	NJ4501	57°6·1'	2°54·0'W	T	37
Ordie	Aberd	NO6191	57°0·8'	2°38·1'W	X	45
Ordie	Angus	NO4757	56°42·4'	2°51·5'W	X	54
Ordie Burn	Pth & Kin	NO0533	56°29·0'	3°32·1'W	W	52,53
Ordie Caber	Aberd	NJ6405	57°8·3'	2°35·2'W	X	37
Ordiefauld	Aberd	NJ8022	57°17·5'	2°19·5'W	X	38
Ordie Moss	Aberd	NJ4501	57°6·1'	2°54·0'W	X	37
Ordiequish Hill	Moray	NJ3456	57°35·6'	3°5·8'W	X	28
Ordies	Moray	NJ1061	57°38·1'	3°30·0'W	X	28
Ordies Hill	Angus	NO4872	56°50·5'	2°50·7'W	X	44
Ordiquhill	Aberd	NJ5243	57°28·7'	2°47·6'W	H	29
Ordiquhill	Aberd	NJ5655	57°35·2'	2°43·7'W	T	29
Ordiquish	Moray	NJ3357	57°36·1'	3°6·8'W	X	28
Orditeach	Aberd	NJ4427	57°20·1'	2°55·4'W	X	37
Ordley	Aberd	NJ7244	57°29·4'	2°27·6'W	X	29
Ordley	Northum	NY9459	54°55·8'	2°5·2'W	T	87
Ord Loch	Highld	NH9050	57°31·9'	3°49·8'W	W	27
Ord Mains	Highld	NH5150	57°31·2'	4°28·8'W	X	26
Ord Mains	Northum	NT9750	55°44·9'	2°2·4'W	X	75
Ord Mill	Aberd	NJ6717	57°14·8'	2°32·4'W	T	38
Ord More	Aberd	NO6198	57°4·5'	2°38·1'W	H	37,45
Ord Muir	Highld	NH5451	57°31·8'	4°25·8'W	X	26
Ordnance Place	E Susx	TQ5626	51°1·0'	0°13·8'E	X	188,199
Ordnance Survey Office	C of Soton	SU3814	50°55·7'	1°27·2'W	X	196
Ord of Caithness	Highld	ND0517	58°8·2'	3°36·3'W	X	17
Ord of Cardno	Aberd	NJ9663	57°39·7'	2°3·6'W	X	30
Ord of Elrick	Aberd	NJ8817	57°14·9'	2°11·5'W	X	38
Ord of Tillyfumerie	Aberd	NO6589	56°59·8'	2°34·1'W	H	45
Ord Point	Highld	ND0617	58°8·2'	3°35·3'W	X	17
Ord River	Highld	NG6212	57°8·5'	5°55·6'W	W	32
Ordsall	Notts	SK6980	53°19·0'	0°57·4'W	T	111,120
Ordsall	Salf	SJ8197	53°28·4'	2°16·8'W	T	109
Ordsall Hill	Notts	SK7280	53°19·0'	0°54·7'W	X	120
Ord Skerries	Shetld	HU3413	59°54·3'	1°23·0'W	X	4
Ords, The	Shetld	HU3413	59°54·3'	1°23·0'W	X	4
Ord, The	Aberd	NO7491	57°0·8'	2°25·2'W	H	38,45
Ord, The	Highld	NC5705	58°0·9'	4°24·8'W	H	16
Ord, The	Highld	NH8849	57°31·3'	3°51·7'W	X	27
Ord, The	Shetld	HU4936	60°6·6'	1°6·6'W	X	4

Ore	E Susx	TQ8311	50°52·4'	0°36·5'E	T	199
Ore Bay	Orkney	ND3194	58°49·9'	3°11·2'W	W	7
Ore Bridge	Fife	NT2996	56°9·3'	3°8·1'W	X	59
Ore Carr	Durham	NY8727	54°38·5'	2°11·7'W	X	91,92
Ore Farm	Orkney	ND3093	58°49·4'	3°12·3'W	FM	7
Ore Gap	Cumbr	NY2307	54°27·4'	3°10·8'W	X	89,90
Oreham Common	W Susx	TQ2214	50°55·0'	0°15·5'W	X	198
Oreham Manor	W Susx	TQ2213	50°54·4'	0°15·5'W	X	198
Or Eilean	N Eil	NF9475	57°39·9'	7°7·4'W	X	18
Or Eilean	N Eil	NG2194	57°51·2'	6°41·7'W	X	14
Orell Water Park	Wigan	SD5303	53°31·5'	2°42·1'W	X	108
Ore Mills	Fife	NT3097	56°9·9'	3°7·2'W	X	59
Orepool	Glos	SO5707	51°45·8'	2°37·0'W	X	162
Ore Sta	E Susx	TQ8210	50°51·9'	0°35·6'E	X	199
Orestan Fm	Surrey	TQ1153	51°16·1'	0°24·1'W	FM	187
Oreston	C of Plym	SX5053	50°21·7'	4°6·2'W	T	201
Ore Stone	Torbay	SX9562	50°27·1'	3°28·4'W	X	202
Oreton	Shrops	SO6580	52°25·3'	2°30·5'W	T	138
Oreval	N Eil	NB0111	57°59·5'	7°3·1'W	H	13
Oreval	N Eil	NF7473	57°38·0'	7°27·3'W	X	18
Ore Wick	Shetld	HP6000	60°41·0'	0°53·6'W	X	1
Orfasay	Shetld	HU4977	60°28·7'	1°6·0'W	X	2,3
Orfold Fm	W Susx	TQ0525	51°1·1'	0°29·8'W	FM	187,197
Orford	Suff	TM4249	52°5·4'	1°32·4'E	T	169
Orford	Suff	TM4250	52°5·9'	1°32·4'E	T	156
Orford	Warr	SJ6190	53°24·6'	2°34·8'W	T	109
Orford Beach	Suff	TM4146	52°3·8'	1°31·4'E	X	169
Orford Haven	Suff	TM3744	52°2·8'	1°27·8'E	W	169
Orford Ho	Essex	TL5127	51°55·5'	0°12·2'E	X	167
Orford Ho	Lincs	TF2094	53°26·0'	0°11·2'W	X	113
Orford Manor	Kent	TQ5559	51°18·8'	0°13·8'E	X	188
Orford Ness	Suff	TM4549	52°5·3'	1°35·0'E	X	169
Organford	Dorset	SY9392	50°43·9'	2°5·6'W	T	195
Organ Ho	Shrops	SJ5336	52°55·4'	2°41·5'W	X	126
Organsdale Ho	Ches	SJ5468	53°12·7'	2°40·9'W	X	117
Orgarswick Fm	Kent	TR0930	51°2·1'	0°59·3'E	FM	189
Orgarth Hill Fm	Lincs	TF3281	53°18·8'	0°0·7'W	FM	122
Orgate	N Yks	NZ0901	54°24·5'	1°51·3'W	X	92
Orgil	Orkney	HY2303	58°54·7'	3°19·7'W	X	6,7
Orgill	Shetld	HU4865	60°22·2'	1°7·3'W	X	2,3
Orgreave	Roth	SK4187	53°22·9'	1°22·6'W	T	111,120
Orgreave	Staffs	SK1416	52°44·7'	1°47·2'W	T	128
Oridge Street	Glos	SO7827	51°56·7'	2°18·8'W	T	162
Orielton Field Centre	Pemb	SR9598	51°38·8'	4°57·4'W	X	158
Oris Field	Shetld	HU2775	60°27·7'	1°30·0'W	X	3
Orisgal	Arg & Bt	NM0145	56°30·4'	6°51·2'W	X	46
Orka Voe	Shetld	HU4077	60°28·7'	1°15·8'W	W	2,3
Orkie	Fife	NO2907	56°15·3'	3°8·3'W	X	59
Orknagable	Shetld	HP5713	60°48·0'	0°56·7'W	X	1
Orkney Islands	Orkney	HY3615	59°1·3'	3°6·4'W	X	6
Orlandon	Pemb	SM8109	51°44·5'	5°9·9'W	T	157
Orleigh Court	Devon	SS4222	50°58·8'	4°14·7'W	A	180,190
Orleigh Mills	Devon	SS4322	50°58·8'	4°13·8'W	X	180,190
Orleigh's Hill	Devon	SY1589	50°41·9'	3°11·8'W	X	192
Orlestone	Kent	TQ9934	51°4·5'	0°50·8'E	X	189
Orles Wood	Monm	SO5115	51°50·1'	2°42·3'W	F	162
Orleton	Heref	SO4967	52°18·2'	2°44·5'W	T	137,138,148
Orleton	Worcs	SO6967	52°18·3'	2°26·9'W	T	138,149
Orleton Common	Heref	SO4768	52°18·7'	2°46·2'W	T	137,138,148
Orleton Court	Worcs	SO7066	52°17·7'	2°26·0'W	X	138,149
Orleton Hall	Wrekin	SJ6311	52°42·0'	2°32·5'W	X	127
Orley Common	Devon	SX8266	50°29·2'	3°39·4'W	F	202
Orlham Fm	Heref	SO6935	52°1·0'	2°26·7'W	FM	149
Orlingbury	Northnts	SP8672	52°20·6'	0°43·9'W	T	141
Orlingbury Hold	Northnts	SP8372	52°20·6'	0°46·5'W	X	141
Orltons	W Susx	TQ2138	51°7·9'	0°15·8'W	X	187
Ormacleit	N Eil	NF7431	57°15·5'	7°24·0'W	T	22
Ormaig	Arg & Bt	NM4138	56°28·0'	6°11·9'W	X	47,48
Ormàig	Arg & Bt	NM8203	56°10·4'	5°30·3'W	X	55
Ormal	Shetld	HU1065	60°22·4'	1°48·6'W	X	3
Ormathwaite	Cumbr	NY2625	54°37·1'	3°8·3'W	T	89,90
Orme House	Surrey	TQ3549	51°13·7'	0°3·6'W	X	187
Ormerod Ho	Lancs	SD8731	53°46·8'	2°11·4'W	X	103
Ormersfield Fm	Hants	SU7852	51°15·9'	0°52·5'W	FM	186
Ormes Bay or Llandudno Bay	Conwy	SH7983	53°20·1'	3°48·6'W	W	115
Ormes Bay or Llandudno Bay	Conwy	SH8082	53°19·5'	3°47·7'W	W	116
Ormesby	Red & Cl	NZ5317	54°33·0'	1°10·4'W	T	93
Ormesby Broad	Norf	TG4616	52°41·4'	1°38·8'E	W	134
Ormesby Grange	Midd	NZ5216	54°32·4'	1°11·4'W	X	93
Ormesby Hall	Midd	NZ5216	54°32·4'	1°11·4'W	X	93
Ormesby St Margaret	Norf	TG4915	52°40·7'	1°41·4'E	T	134
Ormesby St Michael	Norf	TG4814	52°40·2'	1°40·5'E	T	134
Ormes Moor	Derby	SE0200	53°30·0'	1°57·8'W	X	110
Ormidale	Arg & Bt	NS0081	55°59·1'	5°11·9'W	X	55,63
Ormiscaig	Highld	NG8590	57°51·1'	5°36·9'W	T	19
Ormiston	E Loth	NT4169	55°54·9'	2°56·2'W	T	66
Ormiston	Fife	NO2416	56°20·1'	3°13·3'W	X	59
Ormiston	Scot Bord	NT5213	55°24·8'	2°45·1'W	T	79
Ormiston	W Loth	NT0966	55°53·0'	3°26·8'W	X	65
Ormiston Hill	Fife	NO2317	56°20·6'	3°14·3'W	H	58
Ormiston Ho	Scot Bord	NT6926	55°31·9'	2°29·0'W	X	74
Ormiston Mains	E Loth	NT4166	55°53·3'	2°56·2'W	X	66
Ormiston Mains	Scot Bord	NT7027	55°32·4'	2°28·1'W	X	74
Ormlie	Highld	ND1067	58°35·2'	3°32·4'W	X	11,12
Ormond Castle	Highld	NH6953	57°33·2'	4°10·9'W	A	26
Ormonde Fields	Derby	SK4249	53°2·4'	1°22·0'W	X	129
Ormonde Hall	W Susx	TQ2522	50°59·3'	0°12·8'W	X	198
Ormsa	Arg & Bt	NM7111	56°14·4'	5°41·3'W	X	55
Ormsaig	Arg & Bt	NM4423	56°20·1'	6°8·1'W	X	48
Ormsaigbeg	Highld	NM4763	56°41·7'	6°7·5'W	T	47
Ormsaigmore	Highld	NM4763	56°41·7'	6°7·5'W	T	47
Ormsary	Arg & Bt	NR6610	55°20·0'	5°40·9'W	X	68
Ormsary	Arg & Bt	NR7472	55°53·5'	5°36·4'W	T	62
Ormsary Water	Arg & Bt	NR7471	55°53·0'	5°36·4'W	W	62
Ormsgill	Cumbr	SD1971	54°8·0'	3°14·0'W	T	96
Orms Gill Green	N Yks	SD8759	54°1·9'	2°11·5'W	X	103
Ormskirk	Lancs	SD4108	53°34·2'	2°53·0'W	T	108
Ornais	N Eil	NF8537	57°19·1'	7°13·5'W	X	22

Ornella Fm	Durham	NY9724	54°36·9'	2°2·4'W	FM	92
Ornhams Hall	N Yks	SE4063	54°3·9'	1°22·9'W	X	99
Ornockenoch	D & G	NX5759	54°54·6'	4°13·4'W	X	83
Ornsay	Highld	NG7012	57°8·7'	5°47·7'W	X	32,33
Ornsby Hill	Durham	NZ1648	54°49·8'	1°44·6'W	T	88
Oronsay	Arg & Bt	NR3588	56°1·0'	6°14·7'W	X	61
Oronsay	Highld	NG3136	57°20·4'	6°27·8'W	X	23,32
Oronsay	Highld	NM5959	56°39·9'	5°55·5'W	X	47
Oronsay	N Eil	NF7777	57°40·3'	7°24·6'W	X	18
Oronsay	N Eil	NF8475	57°39·5'	7°17·5'W	X	18
Oronsay Fm	Arg & Bt	NR3488	56°0·9'	6°15·6'W	FM	61
Oror	Denb	SJ0847	53°1·0'	3°21·9'W	X	116
Orosay	N Eil	NF7106	57°1·9'	7°25·0'W	X	31
Orosay	N Eil	NF7217	57°7·9'	7°24·8'W	X	31
Orosay	N Eil	NL6497	56°56·8'	7°31·1'W	X	31
Orosay	N Eil	NL6697	56°56·9'	7°29·2'W	X	31
Orosay	N Eil	NL7099	56°58·1'	7°25·4'W	X	31
Orpenham Fm	W Berks	SU3870	51°25·9'	1°26·8'W	FM	174
Orphir	Orkney	HY3405	58°55·9'	3°8·3'W	X	6,7
Orphir Bay	Orkney	HY3304	58°55·3'	3°9·3'W	W	6,7
Orpington	Brom	TQ4565	51°22·2'	0°5·4'E	T	177
Orplands	Essex	TL9906	51°43·3'	0°53·3'E	X	168
Orpwoods Fm	Oxon	SP6403	51°43·6'	1°4·0'W	FM	164,165
Orquil	Orkney	HY4021	59°4·6'	3°2·3'W	X	5,6
Orquil	Orkney	HY4209	58°58·1'	3°0·0'W	X	6,7
Orra Wick	Shetld	HU5067	60°23·3'	1°5·1'W	W	2,3
Orrell	Sefton	SJ3496	53°27·6'	2°59·2'W	T	108
Orrell	Wigan	SD5305	53°32·6'	2°42·1'W	T	108
Orrell Cote Fm	Black w Dar	SD7319	53°40·2'	2°24·1'W	FM	109
Orrell House Fm	Ches	SJ8081	53°19·8'	2°17·6'W	FM	109
Orrell Post	Wigan	SD5304	53°32·1'	2°42·1'W	T	108
Orrells Well	Ches	SJ8278	53°18·2'	2°15·8'W	X	118
Orrest Head	Cumbr	SD4199	54°23·2'	2°54·1'W	H	96,97
Orrin Reservoir	Highld	NH3749	57°30·4'	4°42·8'W	W	26
Orrinside	Highld	NH4851	57°31·7'	4°31·8'W	X	26
Orrisdale	I of M	SC2971	54°6·6'	4°36·5'W	X	95
Orrisdale	I of M	SC3293	54°18·5'	4°34·5'W	T	95
Orrisdale Head	I of M	SC3192	54°18·0'	4°35·4'W	X	95
Orrock	Fife	NT2288	56°5·0'	3°14·8'W	T	66
Orrok Ho	Aberd	NJ9619	57°16·0'	2°3·5'W	X	38
Orroland	D & G	NX7746	54°47·9'	3°54·4'W	X	84
Orroland Heugh	D & G	NX7745	54°47·3'	3°54·4'W	X	84
Orroland Lodge	D & G	NX7746	54°47·9'	3°54·4'W	X	84
Orr Shun	Orkney	HY2820	59°3·7'	3°14·9'W	W	6
Orr Wick	Shetld	HU3381	60°30·9'	1°23·4'W	W	1,2,3
Orsay	Arg & Bt	NR1651	55°40·4'	6°30·6'W	X	60
Orsedd Fawr	Gwyn	SH4041	52°56·8'	4°22·5'W	X	123
Orsedd Goch	I of Angl	SH3090	53°23·0'	4°33·0'W	X	114
Orsedd-lâs	Gwyn	SH7031	52°51·9'	3°55·5'W	X	124
Orseddwen	Wrex	SJ2533	52°53·6'	3°6·5'W	X	126
Orsett	Thurr	TQ6481	51°30·5'	0°22·2'E	T	177
Orsett Fen	Thurr	TQ6283	51°31·6'	0°20·5'E	X	177
Orsett Hall (Hotel)	Thurr	TQ6582	51°31·0'	0°23·1'E	X	177,178
Orsett Heath	Thurr	TQ6379	51°29·4'	0°21·3'E	T	177
Orsett Ho	Thurr	TQ6382	51°31·0'	0°21·4'E	X	177
Orsgates Plantn	Norf	TF6908	52°38·8'	0°30·3'E	F	143
Orslow	Staffs	SJ8015	52°44·2'	2°17·4'W	T	127
Orston	Notts	SK7740	52°57·3'	0°50·8'W	T	129
Orston Grange	Notts	SK7838	52°56·2'	0°50·0'W	X	129
Orswell	Devon	SS6435	51°6·1'	3°56·2'W	X	180
Orterley Fms	N Yks	SE5598	54°22·7'	1°8·8'W	FM	100
Orthwaite	Cumbr	NY2534	54°42·0'	3°9·4'W	T	89,90
Ortie	Orkney	HY6845	59°17·7'	2°33·2'W	X	5
Ortner	Lancs	SD5354	53°59·0'	2°42·6'W	T	102
Orton	Cumbr	NY6208	54°28·2'	2°34·8'W	T	91
Orton	Moray	NJ3153	57°34·0'	3°8·7'W	T	28
Orton	Northnts	SP8079	52°24·4'	0°49·0'W	T	141
Orton	Pemb	SN0020	51°50·8'	4°53·8'W	X	145,157,158
Orton	Staffs	SO8695	52°33·4'	2°12·0'W	T	139
Orton Brimbles	Peterb	TL1596	52°33·2'	0°17·8'W	T	142
Orton Goldhay	Peterb	TL1595	52°32·7'	0°17·8'W	T	142
Orton Grange Fm	Cumbr	NY3552	54°51·8'	3°0·3'W	FM	85
Orton Hill	Leic	SK3105	52°38·7'	1°32·1'W	X	140
Orton Ho	Moray	NJ3153	57°34·0'	3°8·7'W	X	28
Orton House Fm	Leic	SK3105	52°38·7'	1°32·1'W	FM	140
Orton Lodge	Northnts	SP8179	52°24·4'	0°48·2'W	X	141
Orton Longueville	Peterb	TL1696	52°33·2'	0°16·9'W	T	142
Orton Malbourne	Cambs	TL1795	52°32·6'	0°16·1'W	T	142
Orton Moss	Cumbr	NY3354	54°52·8'	3°2·2'W	F	85
Orton-on-the-Hill	Leic	SK3003	52°37·7'	1°33·0'W	T	140
Orton Park	Cumbr	NY3552	54°51·8'	3°0·3'W	X	85
Orton Park Fm	Cumbr	NY3553	54°52·3'	3°0·3'W	FM	85
Orton Rigg	Cumbr	NY3352	54°51·7'	3°2·2'W	T	85
Orton Scar	Cumbr	NY6209	54°28·7'	2°34·8'W	X	91
Orton Southgate	Peterb	TL1494	52°32·1'	0°18·8'W	T	142
Orton Water	Peterb	TL1696	52°33·2'	0°16·9'W	W	142
Orton Waterville	Peterb	TL1596	52°33·2'	0°17·8'W	T	142
Orton Wistow	Peterb	TL1496	52°33·2'	0°18·7'W	T	142
Orton Wood	Leic	SK3205	52°38·7'	1°31·2'W	F	140
Orval	Highld	NM3399	57°0·6'	6°23·4'W	H	39
Orvis Fm	Suff	TM0833	51°57·6'	1°2·0'E	FM	168,169
Orway	Devon	ST0807	50°51·5'	3°18·0'W	X	192
Orwell	Cambs	TL3650	52°8·1'	0°0·4'W	T	154
Orwell	Pth & Kin	NO1404	56°13·5'	3°22·8'W	X	58
Orwell Br	Suff	TM1741	52°1·7'	1°10·2'E	X	169
Orwell Park Ho	Suff	TM2039	52°0·6'	1°12·7'E	X	169
Orwell Park Sch	Suff	TM2139	52°0·5'	1°13·6'E	X	169
Orwell Pit Fm	Cambs	TL5382	52°25·1'	0°15·4'E	FM	143
Orwick	Orkney	HY5411	58°59·3'	2°47·5'W	X	6
Orwick Water	Shetld	HU3364	60°21·8'	1°23·6'W	W	2,3
Orznash Fm	E Susx	TQ5233	51°4·8'	0°10·6'E	FM	188
Ósa Losgaintir	N Eil	NG0699	57°53·3'	6°57·2'W	W	14,18
Osbaldeston	Lancs	SD6431	53°46·7'	2°32·4'W	T	102,103
Osbaldeston Green	Lancs	SD6432	53°47·2'	2°32·4'W	T	102,103
Osbaldeston Hall	Lancs	SD6434	53°48·3'	2°32·4'W	X	102,103
Osbaldwick	York	SE6351	53°57·3'	1°2·0'W	T	105,106
Osbaldwick Beck	York	SE6452	53°57·8'	1°1·1'W	W	105,106
Osbaston	Leic	SK4204	52°38·2'	1°22·4'W	T	140
Osbaston	Monm	SO5014	51°49·6'	2°43·1'W	X	162
Osbaston	Shrops	SJ3222	52°47·7'	3°0·1'W	T	126
Osbaston	Wrekin	SJ5918	52°45·7'	2°36·1'W	T	126
Osbaston Hollow	Leic	SK4106	52°39·3'	1°23·2'W	T	140
Osbaston Lodge Fm	Leic	SK4104	52°38·2'	1°23·2'W	FM	140
Osbaston Toll Gate	Leic	SK4105	52°38·7'	1°23·2'W	X	140
Osberton Grange	Notts	SK6379	53°18·5'	1°2·9'W	X	120
Osberton Hall	Notts	SK6279	53°18·5'	1°3·8'W	X	120
Osberton Mill	Notts	SK6480	53°19·0'	1°1·9'W	X	111,120
Osbonall Wood	Rut	SK9614	52°43·1'	0°34·3'W	F	130
Osborne Bay	I of W	SZ5395	50°45·4'	1°14·5'W	W	196
Osborne Ho	Glos	SO7804	51°44·3'	2°18·7'W	X	162
Osborne Ho	I of W	SZ5194	50°44·8'	1°16·2'W	X	196
Osborne Ho	Lincs	TF2030	52°51·5'	0°12·7'W	X	131
Osborne Lodge	N Yks	SE9886	54°15·9'	0°29·3'W	X	94,101
Osborne Newton	Devon	SX6945	50°17·7'	3°50·0'W	X	202
Osborne's	Kent	TQ7533	51°4·4'	0°30·3'E	X	188
Osbornes Fm	Devon	SX8892	50°43·2'	3°34·8'W	FM	192
Osbournby	Lincs	TF0638	52°56·0'	0°25·0'W	T	130
Osbourne Ho	Lincs	TF3626	52°49·1'	0°1·5'E	X	131
Osbrooks	Surrey	TQ1638	51°8·0'	0°20·1'W	X	187
Oscar Br	Notts	SK7742	52°58·4'	0°50·8'W	X	129
Oscar Hill	N Yks	SE2486	54°16·4'	1°37·5'W	X	99
Oscar Park Fm	N Yks	SE5787	54°16·8'	1°7·1'W	FM	100
Osclay	Highld	ND2238	58°19·7'	3°19·4'W	X	11
Oscroft	Ches	SJ5066	53°11·6'	2°44·5'W	T	117
Oscroft Ho	Ches	SJ5066	53°11·6'	2°44·5'W	X	117
Osdal	Highld	NG4241	57°23·1'	6°27·1'W	X	23
Osdale	Highld	NG2445	57°25·0'	6°35·3'W	X	23
Osdale River	Highld	NG2445	57°25·0'	6°35·3'W	W	23
Ose	Highld	NG3141	57°23·1'	6°28·1'W	T	23
Ose	N Eil	NF8787	57°46·1'	7°15·4'W	X	18
Osea Fm	Essex	TL9106	51°43·4'	0°46·3'E	FM	168
Osea Island	Essex	TL9106	51°43·4'	0°46·3'E	T	168
Osehill Green	Dorset	ST6609	50°53·0'	2°28·6'W	T	194
Ose Point	Highld	NG3041	57°23·0'	6°29·1'W	X	23
Ose Point	N Eil	NF8787	57°46·1'	7°15·4'W	X	18
Osgathorpe	Leic	SK4319	52°46·2'	1°21·4'W	T	129
Osgodby	Lincs	TF0792	53°25·1'	0°23·0'W	T	112
Osgodby	N Yks	SE6433	53°47·6'	1°1·3'W	T	105,106
Osgodby	N Yks	TA0584	54°14·7'	0°22·9'W	X	101
Osgodby Common	N Yks	SE6435	53°48·7'	1°1·3'W	T	105,106
Osgodby Coppice	Lincs	SK9928	52°50·7'	0°31·4'W	F	130
Osgodby Manor Fm	Lincs	TF0128	52°50·6'	0°29·6'W	FM	130
Osgodby Moor	Lincs	TF0891	53°24·5'	0°22·1'W	X	112
Osgodby Point	N Yks	TA0685	54°15·2'	0°22·0'W	X	101
Osgoodby Hall	N Yks	SE4980	54°13·0'	1°14·5'W	A	100
Osidge	Barnet	TQ2894	51°38·0'	0°8·6'W	T	166,176
Osier Fen	Cambs	TL2092	52°31·0'	0°13·5'W	X	142
Osier Holt	Norf	TL6687	52°27·6'	0°27·0'E	F	143
Osier Holts	Beds	SP9855	52°11·3'	0°33·6'W	X	153
Osiers Fm	Kent	TQ9663	51°20·2'	0°49·2'E	FM	178
Osiers Fm	W Susx	SU9625	51°1·2'	0°37·5'W	FM	186,197
Oskaig	Highld	NG5438	57°22·2'	6°5·0'W	T	24,32
Oskaig Point	Highld	NG5438	57°22·2'	6°5·0'W	X	24,32
Oskamull	Arg & Bt	NM4540	56°29·2'	6°8·1'W	X	47,48
Osland Wood	Notts	SK6271	53°14·2'	1°3·9'W	F	120
Osleston	Derby	SK2436	52°55·5'	1°38·2'W	T	128
Osleston Village	Derby	SK2437	52°56·0'	1°38·2'W	A	128
Osliebrae	E Ayr	NS4346	55°41·2'	4°29·4'W	X	64
Osmanthorpe Manor	Notts	SK6756	53°6·1'	0°59·6'W	X	120
Osmaston	C of Derb	SK3633	52°53·8'	1°27·5'W	T	128
Osmaston	Derby	SK2043	52°59·3'	1°41·7'W	T	119,128
Osmaston Fields Fm	Derby	SK1844	52°59·8'	1°43·5'W	FM	119,128
Osmaston Park	Derby	SK2043	52°59·3'	1°41·7'W	X	119,128
Osmaston Pastures	Derby	SK1843	52°59·3'	1°43·5'W	X	119,128
Osmigarry	Highld	NG3971	57°39·5'	6°22·1'W	X	23
Osmington	Dorset	SY7283	50°39·0'	2°23·4'W	T	194
Osmington Hill	Dorset	SY7182	50°38·4'	2°24·2'W	H	194
Osmington Ho	Dorset	SY7283	50°39·0'	2°23·4'W	X	194
Osmington Mills	Dorset	SY7381	50°37·9'	2°22·5'W	T	194
Osmond Croft	Durham	NZ1215	54°32·1'	1°48·5'W	X	92
Osmond Flatt	Durham	NZ0216	54°32·6'	1°57·7'W	X	92
Osmondthorpe	Leeds	SE3233	53°47·8'	1°30·4'W	T	104
Osmondwall	Orkney	ND3289	58°47·3'	3°10·1'W	X	7
Osmore Fm	Devon	ST2604	50°50·1'	3°2·7'W	FM	192,193
Osmotherley	N Yks	SE4597	54°22·2'	1°18·0'W	T	99
Osmotherley Moor	Cumbr	SD2681	54°13·4'	3°7·7'W	X	96,97
Osmotherley Moor	N Yks	SE4797	54°22·2'	1°16·2'W	X	100
Osnaburgh or Dairsie	Fife	NO4117	56°20·8'	2°56·8'W	T	59
Osney	Oxon	SP5006	51°45·3'	1°16·1'W	T	164
Osney Hill Fm	Oxon	SP3711	51°48·0'	1°27·4'W	FM	164
Ospisdale	Highld	NH7189	57°52·6'	4°10·0'W	T	21
Osprey, The	Wilts	ST9670	51°26·0'	2°3·1'W	X	173
Ospringe	Kent	TR0060	51°18·5'	0°52·6'E	T	178
Osquoy	Orkney	ND4485	58°45·2'	2°57·6'W	X	7
Ossage	Glos	SP0119	51°52·4'	1°58·7'W	X	163
Ossajoie	D & G	NX1173	55°1·2'	4°57·0'W	X	76
Ossemsley	Hants	SZ2398	50°47·1'	1°40·0'W	T	195
Ossemsley Manor	Hants	SZ2296	50°46·0'	1°40·9'W	X	195
Osset Spa	Wakf	SE2919	53°40·2'	1°33·3'W	T	110
Ossett	Wakf	SE2820	53°40·8'	1°34·2'W	T	104
Ossett Street Side	Wakf	SE2721	53°41·3'	1°35·1'W	T	104
Ossian's Cave	Highld	NN1556	56°39·8'	5°0·7'W	X	41
Ossian's Cave	N Ayr	NR9651	55°42·8'	5°14·4'W	A	62,69
Ossin	Orkney	HY4729	59°8·9'	2°55·1'W	X	5,6
Ossington	Notts	SK7564	53°10·3'	0°52·3'W	T	120
Ossi Taing	Orkney	ND4686	58°45·8'	2°55·5'W	X	7
Oss Mere	Shrops	SJ5643	52°59·2'	2°38·9'W	W	117
Ossoms Hill	Staffs	SK0955	53°5·8'	1°51·5'W	H	119
Ostaig Ho	Highld	NG6405	57°4·8'	5°53·2'W	X	32
Ostbridge Manor Fm	S Glos	ST5785	51°34·0'	2°36·8'W	FM	172
Ostem	N Eil	NA9617	58°2·5'	7°8·7'W	X	13
Ostend	Essex	TQ9397	51°38·5'	0°47·8'E	T	168
Ostend	Norf	TG3632	52°50·2'	1°30·6'E	T	133
Osterley	Houns	TQ1477	51°29·1'	0°21·1'W	T	176
Osterley Park	Houns	TQ1478	51°29·6'	0°21·1'W	X	176
Ostler's Plantn	Lincs	TF2162	53°8·7'	0°11·0'W	F	122
Oswald Beck	Notts	SK7785	53°21·6'	0°50·2'W	W	112,120
Oswaldkirk	N Yks	SE6278	54°11·9'	1°2·6'W	T	100
Oswaldkirk Bank Top	N Yks	SE6279	54°12·4'	1°2·5'W	X	100
Oswaldkirk Hag	N Yks	SE6078	54°11·9'	1°4·4'W	X	100
Oswald's Br	S Ayr	NS3823	55°28·7'	4°33·4'W	X	70
Oswalds Well	Shrops	SJ2829	52°51·5'	3°3·8'W	A	126
Oswaldtwistle	Lancs	SD7327	53°44·6'	2°24·2'W	T	103
Oswaldtwistle Moor	Lancs	SD7424	53°42·9'	2°23·2'W	X	103
Oswestry or Croeswallt	Shrops	SJ2929	52°51·5'	3°2·9'W	T	126
Otby	Lincs	TF1393	53°25·5'	0°17·6'W	T	113
Otby Top	Lincs	TF1495	53°26·6'	0°16·6'W	X	113
Oteley	Shrops	SJ4134	52°54·3'	2°52·2'W	T	126
Otervik	Shetld	HU3666	60°22·8'	1°20·3'W	X	2,3
Otford	Kent	TQ5159	51°18·8'	0°10·4'E	T	188
Otford Court	Kent	TQ5459	51°18·8'	0°13·0'E	X	188
Otford Mount	Kent	TQ5359	51°18·8'	0°12·1'E	X	188
Otham	Kent	TQ7953	51°15·1'	0°34·3'E	T	188
Otham Hole	Kent	TQ8052	51°14·5'	0°35·1'E	T	188
Otherton	Staffs	SJ9212	52°42·6'	2°6·7'W	T	127
Othery	Somer	ST3831	51°4·7'	2°52·7'W	T	182
Othona	Dorset	SY5188	50°41·6'	2°41·2'W	X	194
Othona (Roman Fort)	Essex	TM0308	51°44·3'	0°56·8'E	R	168
Othorpe Ho	Leic	SP7795	52°33·1'	0°51·5'W	X	141
Othorpe Village	Leic	SP7795	52°33·1'	0°51·5'W	A	141
Otley	Leeds	SE2045	53°54·3'	1°41·3'W	T	104
Otley	Suff	TM2055	52°9·2'	1°13·4'E	T	156
Otley Bottom	Suff	TM2054	52°8·6'	1°13·3'E	X	156
Otley Plantn	N Yks	SE2146	53°54·8'	1°40·4'W	F	104
Ot Moor	Oxon	SP5614	51°49·5'	1°10·9'W	X	164
Otney	Oxon	SU4994	51°38·8'	1°17·1'W	X	164,174
Otteham Court	E Susx	TQ5805	50°49·6'	0°15·0'E	X	199
Otter Ayre	Shetld	HU3266	60°22·9'	1°24·7'W	X	3
Otter Bank	Cumbr	SD5397	54°22·2'	2°43·0'W	X	97
Otterbourne	Hants	SU4623	51°0·5'	1°20·3'W	T	185
Otterbourne Hill	Hants	SU4522	51°0·0'	1°21·1'W	X	185
Otterburn	Northum	NY8793	55°14·1'	2°11·8'W	A	80
Otterburn	Northum	NY8893	55°14·1'	2°10·9'W	T	80
Otter Burn	Northum	NY8895	55°15·2'	2°10·9'W	W	80
Otterburn	N Yks	SD8857	54°0·8'	2°10·6'W	T	103
Otterburn	Scot Bord	NT7524	55°30·8'	2°23·3'W	X	74
Otter Burn	Scot Bord	NT7861	55°50·8'	2°20·6'W	W	67
Otterburn Beck	N Yks	SD8857	54°0·8'	2°10·6'W	W	103
Otterburn Camp	Northum	NY8995	55°15·2'	2°10·0'W	T	80
Otterburn Hall	Northum	NY8894	55°14·7'	2°10·9'W	X	80
Otterburn Moor	N Yks	SD8758	54°1·3'	2°11·5'W	H	103
Otter Bush Fm	Cambs	TL5083	52°25·7'	0°12·8'E	FM	143
Otter Channel	E Susx	TQ8726	51°0·4'	0°40·3'E	W	189,199
Ottercops	Northum	NY9588	55°11·4'	2°4·3'W	X	81
Ottercops Burn	Northum	NY9688	55°11·4'	2°3·3'W	W	81
Ottercops Moss	Northum	NY9589	55°12·0'	2°4·3'W	X	81
Otter Cove	Devon	SY0479	50°36·4'	3°21·0'W	W	192
Otterden Ho	S Ayr	NS3014	55°23·7'	4°40·6'W	X	70
Otterden Place	Kent	TQ9454	51°15·3'	0°47·2'E	T	189
Otter Ferry	Arg & Bt	NR9384	56°0·5'	5°18·8'W	T	55
Otterford	Somer	ST2214	50°55·4'	3°6·2'W	T	193
Otter Had	Shetld	HU3981	60°30·9'	1°16·9'W	X	1,2,3
Otter Hadd	Shetld	HU3780	60°30·4'	1°19·1'W	X	1,2,3
Otterham	Corn	SX1690	50°41·1'	4°35·9'W	T	190
Otterham Creek	Medway	TQ8267	51°22·6'	0°37·3'E	W	178
Otterham Down	Corn	SX1590	50°41·1'	4°36·8'W	X	190
Otterham Ho	Kent	TQ8367	51°22·6'	0°38·2'E	X	178
Otterham Mill	Corn	SX1790	50°41·1'	4°35·1'W	X	190
Otterhampton	Somer	ST2443	51°11·1'	3°4·9'W	T	182
Otterham Quay	Kent	TQ8366	51°22·0'	0°38·1'E	T	178
Otterham Station	Corn	SX1589	50°40·5'	4°36·7'W	T	190
Otter Haven	Highld	NG7822	57°14·4'	5°40·3'W	X	33
Otterhill Common	N Yks	SE6390	54°18·3'	1°1·5'W	X	94,100
Otterhills	N Yks	SE6491	54°18·9'	1°0·6'W	X	94,100
Otter Hills Beck	N Yks	NZ5808	54°28·1'	1°5·9'W	W	93
Otter Hole	Orkney	HY6737	59°13·4'	2°34·2'W	X	5
Otter Holts Fm	Cambs	TL3797	52°33·4'	0°1·7'E	FM	142,143
Otter House	Arg & Bt	NR9278	55°57·3'	5°19·5'W	X	62
Otterington Hall	N Yks	SE3788	54°17·4'	1°25·5'W	X	99
Otterington Hall Fm	N Yks	SE3788	54°17·4'	1°25·5'W	FM	99
Otterington Ho	N Yks	SE3691	54°19·0'	1°26·4'W	X	99
Otter Loch	Shetld	HU3772	60°26·1'	1°19·2'W	W	2,3
Otternish	N Eil	NF9885	57°45·4'	7°4·2'W	X	18
Otter Point	Shetld	HU4448	60°13·1'	1°11·9'W	X	3
Otterpool Manor	Kent	TR1036	51°5·3'	1°0·3'E	X	179,189
Otter Pool, The	D & G	NX5973	55°2·1'	4°12·0'W	W	77
Ottersbank Fm	Ches	SJ5667	53°12·1'	2°39·1'W	FM	117
Otters Geo	Shetld	HP5503	60°42·6'	0°59·0'W	X	1
Ottershaw	Surrey	TQ0263	51°21·6'	0°31·7'W	T	176,186
Otterspool	Herts	TQ1298	51°40·4'	0°22·4'W	X	166,176
Otterspool	Liv	SJ3785	53°21·7'	2°56·4'W	T	108
Otters Pool	Orkney	HY5227	59°7·9'	2°49·8'W	W	5,6
Otters Pool	Orkney	HY5640	59°14·9'	2°45·8'W	W	5
Otterston Loch	Fife	NT1685	56°3·3'	3°20·5'W	W	65,66
Otterswick	Orkney	HY6741	59°15·5'	2°34·2'W	X	5
Otters Wick	Orkney	HY7044	59°17·2'	2°31·1'W	W	5
Otters Wick	Shetld	HU5285	60°33·0'	1°2·6'W	W	1,2,3
Otterswick	Shetld	HU5285	60°33·0'	1°2·6'W	T	1,2,3
Otterton	Devon	SY0885	50°39·7'	3°17·7'W	T	192
Otterton Ledge	Devon	SY0781	50°37·5'	3°18·5'W	X	192
Otter Trust, The	Norf	TM3188	52°26·7'	1°24·4'E	X	156
Otterwood	Hants	SU4102	50°49·2'	1°24·7'W	T	196
Otterwood Gate	Hants	SU4102	50°49·2'	1°24·7'W	X	196
Ottery	Devon	SX4475	50°33·5'	4°11·8'W	X	201
Ottery St Mary	Devon	SY1095	50°45·1'	3°16·2'W	T	192,193
Ottinge	Kent	TR1642	51°8·4'	1°5·7'E	T	179,189
Ottringham	E Yorks	TA2624	53°42·1'	0°5·1'W	T	107,113
Ottringham Drain	E Yorks	TA2521	53°40·5'	0°6·0'W	W	107,113
Ottringham Grange	E Yorks	TA2622	53°41·0'	0°5·1'W	X	107,113
Otty Bottom	Kent	TR3746	51°10·1'	1°23·8'E	X	179
Otway Ho	Lincs	TF2425	52°48·7'	0°9·2'W	X	131
Oubas Hill	Cumbr	SD2979	54°12·4'	3°4·9'W	H	96,97
Oubrough	E Yorks	TA1536	53°48·7'	0°14·8'W	X	107
Ouchnoire	Highld	NH9621	57°16·3'	3°43·0'W	X	36
Ouchtriemakain	D & G	NW9956	54°51·8'	5°7·5'W	X	82
Oudenard	Pth & Kin	NO1418	56°21·0'	3°23·1'W	X	58
Oughterby	Cumbr	NY2955	54°53·3'	3°6·0'W	T	85
Oughtershaw	N Yks	SD8681	54°13·7'	2°12·5'W	T	98
Oughtershaw Beck	N Yks	SD8482	54°14·3'	2°14·3'W	W	98

Oughtershaw Moss	N Yks	SD8581	54°13·7′	2°13·4′W	X	98
Oughtershaw Side	N Yks	SD8483	54°14·8′	2°14·3′W	X	98
Oughtershaw Tarn	N Yks	SD8882	54°14·3′	2°10·6′W	W	98
Oughterside	Cumbr	NY1140	54°45·1′	3°22·5′W	T	85
Oughterside Mill	Cumbr	NY1139	54°44·5′	3°22·5′W	X	89
Oughtibridge	Sheff	SK3093	53°26·2′	1°32·5′W	T	110,111
Oughton Head	Herts	TL1629	51°57·1′	0°18·3′W	W	166
Oughtonhead Common	Herts	TL1630	51°57·6′	0°18·3′W	X	166
Oughton Head Fm	Herts	TL1629	51°57·1′	0°18·3′W	FM	166
Oughtrington	Warr	SJ6987	53°23·0′	2°27·6′W	T	109
Ouglassy Parks	Highld	ND1856	58°29·3′	3°23·9′W	X	11,12
Ouharity Burn	Angus	NO3758	56°42·8′	3°1·3′W	W	54
Ouldray Fm	N Yks	SE5986	54°16·2′	1°5·2′W	FM	100
Ouldray Wood	N Yks	SE5986	54°16·2′	1°5·2′W	F	100
Oulmsdale Burn	Highld	NC9616	58°7·5′	3°45·5′W	W	17
Oulsclough	Staffs	SK0545	53°0·4′	1°55·1′W	X	119,128
Oulston	N Yks	SE5474	54°9·8′	1°10·0′W	T	100
Oulston Reservoir	N Yks	SE5674	54°9·8′	1°8·1′W	W	100
Oulton	Cumbr	NY2450	54°50·6′	3°10·6′W	T	85
Oulton	Leeds	SE3628	53°45·1′	1°26·8′W	T	104
Oulton	Norf	TG1328	52°48·7′	1°10·0′E	T	133
Oulton	Staffs	SJ7822	52°47·9′	2°19·2′W	T	127
Oulton	Staffs	SJ9135	52°55·0′	2°7·6′W	T	127
Oulton	Staffs	SJ9262	53°9·5′	2°6·8′W	X	118
Oulton	Suff	TM5294	52°29·4′	1°43·1′E	T	134
Oulton Broad	Suff	TM5192	52°28·3′	1°42·2′E	T	134
Oultoncross	Staffs	SJ9034	52°54·4′	2°8·5′W	T	127
Oulton Dyke	Suff	TM5093	52°28·9′	1°41·3′E	W	134
Oulton Grange	Staffs	SJ9035	52°55·0′	2°8·5′W	T	127
Oulton Heath	Staffs	SJ9036	52°55·5′	2°8·5′W	T	127
Oulton Hill	Norf	TG0341	52°55·9′	1°1·6′E	X	133
Oulton Ho	Cumbr	NY2350	54°50·6′	3°11·5′W	X	85
Oulton Ho	Staffs	SJ9633	52°53·9′	2°3·2′W	X	127
Oulton Lodge	Norf	TG1528	52°48·6′	1°11·8′E	X	133
Oultonlowe Fm	Ches	SJ5963	53°10·0′	2°36·4′W	FM	117
Oultonlowe Green	Ches	SJ6162	53°9·5′	2°34·6′W	X	118
Oulton Marsh	Suff	TM5094	52°29·4′	1°41·4′E	W	134
Oulton Park	Ches	SJ5864	53°10·5′	2°37·3′W	X	117
Oulton's Fm	Ches	SJ3669	53°13·1′	2°57·1′W	FM	117
Oulton Stret	Norf	TG1527	52°48·1′	1°11·8′E	T	133
Oundle	Northnts	TL0388	52°29·0′	0°28·6′W	T	141
Oundle Lodge	Northnts	TL0287	52°28·5′	0°29·5′W	X	141
Oundle Marina	Northnts	TL0387	52°28·5′	0°28·6′W	X	141
Oundle Wood	Northnts	TL0187	52°28·5′	0°30·4′W	F	141
Ounsdale	Staffs	SO8693	52°32·3′	2°12·0′W	T	139
Ourack Burn	Highld	NJ0440	57°26·7′	3°35·5′W	W	27
Ouraquoy	Orkney	HY3512	58°59·7′	3°7·4′W	X	6
Our Ness	Orkney	HY4149	59°19·7′	3°1·7′W	X	5
Ousbacky	Highld	ND2936	58°18·7′	3°12·2′W	X	11
Ousby	Cumbr	NY6234	54°42·2′	2°35·0′W	T	91
Ousby Fell	Cumbr	NY6837	54°43·9′	2°29·4′W	X	91
Ousby Moor	Cumbr	NY5935	54°42·7′	2°37·8′W	X	91
Ousdale	Highld	ND0720	58°9·8′	3°34·4′W	X	17
Ousdale Burn	Highld	ND0520	58°9·8′	3°36·4′W	W	17
Ousden	Suff	TL7459	52°12·3′	0°33·2′E	T	155
Ouse Ber	Orkney	HY3835	59°12·1′	3°4·6′W	X	6
Ouse Br	Cumbr	NY1932	54°40·8′	3°15·0′W	X	89,90
Ouse Bridge Fm	Norf	TL5899	52°34·2′	0°20·3′E	FM	143
Ouse Burn	N upon Ty	NZ2369	55°1·1′	1°38·0′W	W	88
Ouse Fen	Cambs	TL3773	52°20·5′	0°1·1′E	X	154
Ousefleet	E Yorks	SE8223	53°42·1′	0°45·1′W	T	106,112
Ouse Gill	N Yks	SE6394	54°20·5′	1°1·4′W	W	94,100
Ouse Gill Beck	N Yks	SE4461	54°2·8′	1°19·3′W	W	99
Ouse Gill Head	N Yks	SE6397	54°22·1′	1°1·4′W	X	94,100
Ouseley Barn	Oxon	SU6383	51°32·8′	1°5·1′W	X	175
Ouseley Fm	Kent	TR0442	51°8·7′	0°55·4′E	FM	179,189
Ousel Hole	Brad	SE1042	53°52·7′	1°50·5′W	T	104
Ouse Manor	Beds	SP9959	52°13·4′	0°32·6′W	X	153
Ouse Ness	Orkney	HY4549	59°19·7′	2°57·5′W	X	5
Ouseness	Orkney	HY4550	59°20·2′	2°57·5′W	X	5
Ousen Stand	Cumbr	NY6125	54°37·4′	2°35·8′W	X	91
Ouse Point	Orkney	HY6739	59°14·4′	2°34·2′W	X	5
Ouse, The	Orkney	HY3514	59°0·8′	3°7·4′W	W	6
Ouse, The	Orkney	HY4550	59°20·2′	2°57·5′W	W	5
Ouse, The	Orkney	HY5019	59°3·6′	2°51·8′W	W	6
Ouse, The	Orkney	HY6639	59°14·4′	2°35·3′W	W	5
Ousethorpe Fm	E Yorks	SE8151	53°57·2′	0°45·5′W	FM	106
Ouse Valley Park	Mil Key	SP8041	52°3·9′	0°49·6′W	X	152
Ousley Fm	Shrops	SO6494	52°32·8′	2°31·5′W	FM	138
Ousley Wood	Staffs	SK1244	52°59·8′	1°48·9′W	F	119,128
Oust	Highld	ND0665	58°34·0′	3°36·5′W	X	11,12
Ouster Bank	N Yks	SE1275	54°10·5′	1°48·6′W	H	99
Ouster Gill	N Yks	SD7982	54°14·2′	2°18·9′W	W	98
Ousterley	Durham	NZ2050	54°50·9′	1°40·9′W	X	88
Ouston	Durham	NZ2554	54°53·1′	1°36·2′W	T	88
Ouston	Northum	NY7752	54°52·0′	2°21·1′W	T	86,87
Ouston	Northum	NZ0770	55°1·7′	1°53·0′W	T	88
Ouston Fell	Northum	NY7551	54°51·4′	2°22·9′W	X	86,87
Ouston Fm	N Yks	SE5042	53°52·5′	1°14·0′W	FM	105
Ouston Moor	Northum	NZ0670	55°1·7′	1°53·9′W	X	87
Ouston Moor	Stock on T	NZ3919	54°34·1′	1°23·4′W	X	93
Oust Rocks	D & G	NW9771	54°59·8′	5°10·0′W	X	76,82
Outawell	Moray	NJ0152	57°33·1′	3°38·8′W	X	27
Outback Fm	E Susx	TQ4428	51°2·2′	0°3·6′E	FM	187,198
Outberry Plain	Durham	NY9332	54°41·2′	2°6·1′W	H	91,92
Outbrecks	Orkney	HY2810	58°58·5′	3°14·7′W	X	6
Out Carr	Northum	NU2524	55°30·8′	1°35·8′W	X	75
Outcast	Cumbr	SD3077	54°11·3′	3°3·9′W	T	96,97
Outcast	Shrops	SJ4030	52°52·1′	2°53·1′W	X	126
Outchester	Northum	NU1433	55°35·7′	1°46·2′W	X	75
Out Dubs Tarn	Cumbr	SD3694	54°20·5′	2°58·6′W	W	96,97
Out Elmstead	Kent	TR2050	51°12·6′	1°9·4′E	T	179,189
Outer Alscott	Somer	SS8244	51°11·2′	3°40·9′W	X	181
Outer Ardoch	N Ayr	NS3145	55°40·4′	4°40·8′W	X	63
Outer Blair	D & G	NX0855	54°51·4′	4°59·1′W	X	82
Outer Booth	Shetld	HU3795	60°38·5′	1°18·9′W	X	1,2
Outer Brough	Shetld	HU6793	60°37·2′	0°46·0′W	X	1,2
Outer Brough (Settlement)	Shetld	HU6793	60°37·2′	0°46·0′W	A	1,2
Outer Carrs	Northum	NZ3288	55°11·4′	1°29·4′W	X	81
Outer Edge	Sheff	SK1797	53°28·4′	1°44·2′W	H	110
Outer Flaess	Shetld	HP6617	60°50·1′	0°46·7′W	X	1
Outerford	D & G	NY1669	55°0·8′	3°18·4′W	X	85
Outer Froward Point	Devon	SX9049	50°20·1′	3°32·4′W	X	202
Outer Gat		TF4837	52°54·8′	0°12·5′E	X	131
Outer Head	I Scilly	SV9109	49°54·3′	6°17·9′W	X	203
Outer Heath	Dorset	SY7587	50°41·2′	2°20·9′W	X	194
Outer Hebrides	N Eil	NB1735	58°13·0′	6°48·7′W	X	8,13
Outer Hebrides	N Eil	NB2022	58°6·2′	6°44·7′W	X	13,14
Outer Hebrides	N Eil	NF6903	57°0·2′	7°26·7′W	X	31
Outer Hebrides	N Eil	NF7942	57°21·6′	7°19·9′W	X	22
Outer Hebrides	N Eil	NF8982	57°43·5′	7°13·0′W	X	18
Outer Heisker	N Eil	NL5786	56°50·6′	7°37·1′W	X	31
Outer Hill	D & G	NY3378	55°5·8′	3°2·6′W	H	85
Outer Hole	Shetld	HU2685	60°33·1′	1°31·1′W	X	3
Outer Holm	Orkney	HY2508	58°57·4′	3°17·7′W	X	6,7
Outer Holm of Skaw	Shetld	HU6067	60°23·2′	0°54·2′W	X	2
Outer Hope	Devon	SX6740	50°14·9′	3°51·6′W	T	202
Outer Huccaby Ring	Devon	SX6574	50°33·2′	3°54·0′W	A	191
Outer Huntly	Scot Bord	NT4422	55°29·6′	2°52·7′W	X	73
Outer Knowe Head	Scot Bord	NT5402	55°18·8′	2°43·1′W	X	79
Outerland	D & G	NY2576	55°4·6′	3°10·1′W	X	85
Outer Narracott Fm	Devon	SS5443	51°10·3′	4°4·9′W	FM	180
Outer Nebbock	N Ayr	NS2440	55°37·6′	4°47·3′W	X	70
Outer Retallick	Corn	SW9266	50°27·7′	4°55·5′W	X	200
Outer Road	I of Angl	SH6481	53°18·8′	4°2·1′W	W	114,115
Outer Score	Shetld	HU5145	60°11·4′	1°4·3′W	X	4
Outerside	Cumbr	NY2121	54°34·9′	3°12·9′W	X	89,90
Outerside	Scot Bord	NT3810	55°23·1′	2°58·3′W	X	79
Outerside Rig	Scot Bord	NT3810	55°23·1′	2°58·3′W	H	79
Outer Sillock	Shetld	HU3414	59°54·8′	1°23·0′W	X	4
Outer Skerry	Shetld	HU3885	60°33·1′	1°17·9′W	X	1,2,3
Outer Sound	Orkney	HY6446	59°18·2′	2°37·4′W	W	5
Outer Stack	Shetld	HU3797	60°39·5′	1°18·9′W	X	1
Outerston	Midlo	NT3357	55°48·4′	3°3·7′W	X	66,73
Outer Stone	Corn	SW9236	50°11·5′	4°54·5′W	X	204
Outerston Hill	Midlo	NT3355	55°47·3′	3°3·7′W	X	66,73
Outerthwaite	Cumbr	SD3775	54°10·3′	2°57·5′W	X	96,97
Outertown	D & G	NY2068	55°0·3′	3°14·6′W	X	85
Outertown	Orkney	HY2310	58°58·5′	3°19·9′W	T	6
Outerwards	N Ayr	NS2366	55°51·5′	4°49·2′W	X	63
Outerwards Resr	N Ayr	NS2365	55°51·0′	4°49·2′W	W	63
Outer Westmark Knock		TF5032	52°52·1′	0°14·1′E	X	131
Outer Woodhead	D & G	NY4079	55°6·4′	2°56·0′W	X	85
Outfalls, The	Devon	SS5148	51°12·9′	4°7·6′W	X	180
Out Fell	N Yks	SD8569	54°7·2′	2°13·4′W	X	98
Out Fell	N Yks	SD9957	54°0·8′	2°0·5′W	X	103
Outfield	Pth & Kin	NO2430	56°27·6′	3°13·6′W	X	53
Outfield Fm	Lancs	SD5874	54°9·9′	2°38·2′W	FM	97
Outfields Fm	Beds	TL0455	52°11·2′	0°28·3′W	FM	153
Out Gang	N Yks	SD9061	54°2·9′	2°8·7′W	X	98
Out Gang	York	SE6349	53°56·2′	1°2·0′W	X	105,106
Outgang Hill	N Yks	SD9766	54°5·6′	2°2·3′W	X	98
Outgate	Cumbr	SD3599	54°23·2′	2°59·6′W	T	96,97
Outgate Fm	E Yorks	TA0859	54°1·2′	0°20·7′W	FM	107
Outh	Fife	NT0694	56°8·0′	3°30·3′W	X	58
Out Head	Fife	NO4919	56°21·9′	2°49·1′W	X	59
Outhgill	Cumbr	NY7801	54°24·5′	2°19·9′W	T	91
Outh Hill	Fife	NT0695	56°8·6′	3°30·3′W	H	58
Outhill	Aberd	NK0552	57°33·7′	1°54·5′W	X	30
Outhill	Warw	SP1066	52°17·8′	1°50·8′W	T	150
Outh Muir	Fife	NT0795	56°8·6′	3°29·4′W	X	58
Outholme Fm	Lincs	TA3200	53°29·0′	0°0·2′W	FM	113
Outhwaite	Cumbr	NY6043	54°47·1′	2°36·9′W	X	86
Outhwaite	Lancs	SD6165	54°5·0′	2°35·4′W	X	97
Outhwaite Wood	Lancs	SD6165	54°5·0′	2°35·4′W	F	97
Out Ings	Notts	SK8185	53°21·6′	0°46·6′W	X	112,121
Outlands	Staffs	SJ7730	52°52·3′	2°20·1′W	T	127
Outlands, The	Ches	SJ6558	53°7·3′	2°31·0′W	X	118
Outlands Wood	Corn	SX0569	50°29·5′	4°44·6′W	F	200
Outlane	Kirk	SE0818	53°39·7′	1°52·3′W	T	110
Outlane Moor	Kirk	SE0717	53°39·2′	1°53·2′W	T	110
Outlanes Fm	Ches	SJ5257	53°6·7′	2°42·6′W	FM	117
Outlanes Fm	Ches	SJ6559	53°7·9′	2°31·0′W	FM	118
Outlaw Crag	Cumbr	NY5112	54°30·3′	2°45·0′W	H	90
Outlaw Gill Syke	N Yks	SD7063	54°4·0′	2°27·1′W	W	98
Outlet Farm	Lancs	SD4102	53°30·9′	2°53·0′W	FM	108
Outlet Village	Ches	SJ4174	53°15·8′	2°52·7′W	T	117
Outmains	S Ayr	NS4425	55°29·9′	4°27·7′W	X	70
Out Marsh	Cumbr	SD3874	54°9·7′	2°56·6′W	W	96,97
Outmarsh	Wilts	ST8961	51°21·1′	2°9·1′W	T	173
Outmarsh Yard	Lincs	TF5257	53°5·5′	0°16·6′E	X	122
Out Moor	N Yks	SD9175	54°10·5′	2°7·9′W	X	98
Out Moor	N Yks	SD9578	54°12·1′	2°4·2′W	X	98
Out Newton	E Yorks	TA3821	53°40·3′	0°5·8′E	T	107,113
Outney Common	Suff	TM3290	52°27·7′	1°25·3′E	X	134
Outovercott	Devon	SS7046	51°12·1′	3°51·3′W	X	180
Out Park	Cumbr	SD2481	54°13·4′	3°9·5′W	H	96
Out Pasture	N Yks	SD9068	54°6·7′	2°8·8′W	X	98
Outrabister	Shetld	HU5072	60°26·0′	1°5·0′W	X	2,3
Outrack	Shrops	SO4182	52°26·2′	2°51·7′W	X	137
Outrake Foot	Cumbr	SD7284	54°15·3′	2°25·4′W	X	98
Outrake, The	Derby	SK1871	53°14·4′	1°43·4′W	X	119
Outra Loch	Shetld	HU3529	60°2·9′	1°21·8′W	W	4
Outram	Arg & Bt	NR4648	55°39·8′	6°1·9′W	X	60
Outra Neap	Shetld	HU5966	60°22·7′	0°55·3′W	X	2
Out Rawcliffe	Lancs	SD4041	53°52·0′	2°54·3′W	T	102
Outridden Copse	Hants	SU8351	51°15·4′	0°48·2′W	F	186
Outrun Nook	Cumbr	SD4396	54°21·6′	2°52·2′W	X	97
Out Scar	Cumbr	NY5418	54°33·6′	2°42·3′W	X	90
Outseat	Aberd	NJ7361	57°38·5′	2°26·7′W	X	29
Outshore Point	Orkney	HY2222	59°4·9′	3°21·2′W	X	6
Out Shuna Stack	Shetld	HU3092	60°36·9′	1°26·6′W	X	1
Outside	N Yks	SD8665	54°5·1′	2°12·4′W	X	98
Outside Fm	Ches	SJ6066	53°11·6′	2°35·5′W	FM	118
Out Skerries	Shetld	HU6871	60°25·3′	0°45·4′W	X	2
Out Sleets	N Yks	SD8772	54°8·9′	2°11·5′W	H	98
Out Stack	Shetld	HP6120	60°51·8′	0°52·1′W	X	1
Outsta Ness	Shetld	HP5205	60°43·7′	1°2·3′W	X	1
Outstray Fm	E Yorks	TA3219	53°39·3′	0°0·3′E	FM	113
Out Taings	Orkney	HY2205	58°55·8′	3°20·8′W	X	6,7
Outtle Well Plantn	D & G	NX4648	54°48·4′	4°23·3′W	F	83
Outvoe	Shetld	HU3915	59°55·4′	1°17·7′W	X	4
Outwell	Norf	TF5103	52°36·5′	0°14·2′E	T	143
Outwick	Hants	SU1417	50°57·4′	1°47·7′W	T	184
Outwood	Bury	SD7705	53°32·7′	2°20·4′W	T	109
Out Wood	Cambs	TL6554	52°9·8′	0°25·1′E	F	154
Out Wood	Oxon	SP4020	51°52·9′	1°24·7′W	F	164
Outwood	Somer	ST3028	51°3·1′	2°59·5′W	T	193
Outwood	Surrey	TQ3245	51°11·6′	0°6·3′W	T	187
Outwood	Wakf	SE3223	53°42·4′	1°30·5′W	T	104
Outwood	Worcs	SO9072	52°21·0′	2°8·4′W	X	139
Outwood Common	Surrey	TQ3246	51°12·1′	0°6·2′W	X	187
Outwood Fm	Essex	TQ6994	51°37·4′	0°26·9′E	FM	167,177,178
Outwood Ho	Somer	ST3028	51°3·1′	2°59·5′W	X	193
Outwoods	Derby	SK3542	52°58·7′	1°28·3′W	X	119,128
Outwoods	Leic	SK4018	52°45·7′	1°24·0′W	T	129
Out Woods	Leic	SK5116	52°44·6′	1°14·3′W	F	129
Outwoods	Staffs	SJ7818	52°45·8′	2°19·2′W	T	127
Outwoods	Staffs	SK2324	52°49·0′	1°39·1′W	T	128
Outwoods	Warw	SP2484	52°27·4′	1°38·4′W	T	139
Outwoods Fm	Leic	SK5116	52°44·6′	1°14·3′W	FM	129
Outwoods Fm	Warw	SP2484	52°27·4′	1°38·4′W	FM	139
Outwoods Ho	N Yks	SE5833	53°47·6′	1°6·8′W	X	105
Outwoods, The	Warw	SP3096	52°33·9′	1°33·0′W	X	140
Ouvaig	Highld	NH7192	57°54·2′	4°10·1′W	X	21
Ouvrafandal	Shetld	HT9539	60°8·4′	2°4·9′W	X	4
Ouvrafandal Loch	Shetld	HT9639	60°8·4′	2°3·8′W	W	4
Ouzelden Clough	Derby	SK1590	53°24·6′	1°46·1′W	X	110
Ouzel Hall Br	Lancs	SD7749	53°56·4′	2°20·6′W	X	103
Ouzel Thorn	Lancs	SD5855	53°59·6′	2°38·0′W	X	102
Ouzlewell Green	Leeds	SE3326	53°44·0′	1°29·6′W	T	104
Oval, The	Lam	TQ3177	51°28·8′	0°6·4′W	X	176,177
Oven Back Fm	Warr	SJ6194	53°26·7′	2°34·8′W	FM	109
Oven Bottom	Oxon	SU5383	51°32·8′	1°13·7′W	X	174
Ovenden	Cald	SE0727	53°44·6′	1°53·2′W	T	104
Ovenden Moor	Cald	SE0431	53°46·8′	1°55·9′W	X	104
Ovenden Wood	Cald	SE0627	53°44·6′	1°54·1′W	X	104
Ovenscloss	Scot Bord	NT4730	55°33·9′	2°50·0′W	X	73
Oven's Fm	Lincs	TF3772	53°13·9′	0°3·6′E	FM	122
Ovenshank	Scot Bord	NY5089	55°11·8′	2°46·7′W	X	79
Ovenstone	Angus	NO4743	56°34·8′	2°51·3′W	X	54
Ovenstone	Fife	NO5305	56°14·4′	2°45·1′W	X	59
Oven, The	Notts	SK8060	53°8·1′	0°47·8′W	W	121
Over	Cambs	TL3770	52°18·9′	0°1·0′E	T	154
Over	Ches	SJ6365	53°11·1′	2°32·8′W	T	118
Over	Glos	SO8119	51°52·4′	2°16·2′W	T	162
Over	S Glos	ST5882	51°32·4′	2°35·9′W	T	172
Over Abington	S Lanak	NS9223	55°29·6′	3°42·1′W	X	71,72
Overabist	Orkney	HY3223	59°5·6′	3°10·7′W	X	6
Overacres	Northum	NY9093	55°14·1′	2°9·0′W	X	80
Overa House Fm	Norf	TL9888	52°27·5′	0°55·3′E	FM	144
Over Airies	D & G	NX3948	54°48·3′	4°29·9′W	X	83
Over Ardoch	Pth & Kin	NN8311	56°16·9′	3°52·9′W	X	57
Over Auchentiber	E Ayr	NS4449	55°42·8′	4°28·6′W	X	64
Over Baldinnie	Fife	NO4311	56°17·5′	2°54·8′W	X	59
Over Balgray	S Lanak	NS8824	55°30·1′	3°46·0′W	X	71,72
Over Balloch	W Dunb	NS3983	56°1·0′	4°34·5′W	X	56
Overbank Fm	Ches	SJ8871	53°14·4′	2°10·4′W	FM	118
Over Barskeoch	D & G	NX5882	55°7·0′	4°13·2′W	X	77
Over Beck	Cumbr	NY1608	54°27·9′	3°17·3′W	W	89
Over Benchil	Pth & Kin	NO0932	56°28·5′	3°28·2′W	X	52,53
Overbister	Orkney	HY6840	59°15·0′	2°33·2′W	T	5
Over Blelock	Pth & Kin	NO0534	56°29·6′	3°32·1′W	X	52,53
Over Bohespic	Pth & Kin	NN7361	56°43·7′	4°4·1′W	X	42
Over Boothlow	Staffs	SK0963	53°10·1′	1°51·5′W	X	119
Over Bow	Angus	NO4353	56°40·2′	2°55·4′W	X	54
Overbrae	Aberd	NJ8059	57°37·5′	2°19·6′W	X	29,30
Overbrent	Devon	SX6962	50°26·8′	3°50·3′W	X	202
Overbridge Fm	Kent	TQ7644	51°10·3′	0°31·5′E	FM	188
Overbrook Fm	Cambs	TL4766	52°16·6′	0°9·7′E	FM	154
Over Broomrigg Fm	D & G	NX9679	55°5·9′	3°37·4′W	FM	84
Overburns	S Lanak	NS9932	55°34·5′	3°35·7′W	X	72
Over Burrow	Lancs	SD6176	54°10·9′	2°35·4′W	T	97
Over Burrows	Derby	SK2639	52°57·1′	1°36·4′W	T	128
Overbury	Worcs	SO9537	52°2·1′	2°4·0′W	T	150
Overbury Hall	Suff	TM0240	52°1·5′	0°57·1′E	X	155
Overbury Park	Worcs	SO9537	52°2·1′	2°4·0′W	X	150
Over Buttergask	Pth & Kin	NO2134	56°29·7′	3°16·5′W	X	53
Overby	Cumbr	NY1146	54°48·3′	3°22·7′W	X	85
Over Cairn	E Ayr	NS6612	55°23·3′	4°6·5′W	X	71
Over Carden	Aberd	NJ6826	57°19·7′	2°31·4′W	X	38
Over Carnbee	Fife	NO5307	56°15·4′	2°45·1′W	X	59
Over Carswell	E Renf	NS4552	55°44·5′	4°27·7′W	X	64
Over Cassock	D & G	NT2304	55°19·7′	3°12·4′W	X	79
Over Cave	Cumbr	NY4308	54°28·1′	2°52·3′W	X	90
Overclose	N Yks	SD8466	54°5·6′	2°14·3′W	X	98
Overcombe	Dorset	SY6982	50°38·4′	2°25·9′W	T	194
Over Compton	Dorset	ST5916	50°56·8′	2°34·6′W	T	183
Overcote Fm	Cambs	TL3571	52°19·5′	0°0·7′W	FM	154
Overcott	Devon	SS7921	50°58·8′	3°43·0′W	X	180
Overcourt Fm	Wilts	ST8352	51°16·2′	2°14·2′W	FM	183
Over Craig	Pth & Kin	NO1661	56°44·2′	3°21·9′W	H	43
Overcraig Hill	Highld	ND0231	58°15·7′	3°39·7′W	X	11,17
Over Cross	Norf	TM0588	52°27·3′	1°1·4′E	X	144
Overdale	Carm	SN6627	51°55·8′	3°56·5′W	X	146
Over Dale	Derby	SK1880	53°19·2′	1°43·4′W	X	110
Overdale	N Yks	SD8370	54°7·8′	2°15·2′W	X	98
Overdale Fm	N Yks	NZ8414	54°31·1′	0°41·7′W	FM	94
Overdale Wyke	N Yks	NZ8514	54°31·1′	0°40·8′W	W	94
Over Dalgliesh	Scot Bord	NT2608	55°21·9′	3°9·6′W	X	79
Over Dalgliesh Burn	Scot Bord	NT2409	55°22·4′	3°11·5′W	W	79
Over Dalgliesh Hope	Scot Bord	NT2508	55°21·9′	3°10·6′W	X	79
Over Dalserf	S Lanak	NS7949	55°43·4′	3°55·2′W	X	64
Overday Fm	Devon	ST1607	50°51·6′	3°11·2′W	FM	192,193
Over Dean	N Yks	SD9741	53°52·2′	2°2·3′W	X	103
Overdene	Northum	NZ0664	54°58·5′	1°53·9′W	X	87
Overdine	Heref	SO5933	51°59·9′	2°35·4′W	X	149
Over Dinsdale Grange	N Yks	NZ3411	54°29·8′	1°28·1′W	X	93
Over Dinsdale Hall	N Yks	NZ3411	54°29·8′	1°28·1′W	X	93
Over Dumfedling	D & G	NT2402	55°18·6′	3°11·4′W	X	79

Over Durdie	Pth & Kin	NO2024	56°24·3'	3°17·3'W	X	53,58
Over Easter Offerance	Stir	NS5897	56°8·9'	4°16·7'W	X	57
Overedge	Ches	SJ8862	53°9·5'	2°10·4'W	X	118
Over End	Cambs	TL0993	52°31·7'	0°23·2'W	T	142
Overend	Cumbr	NY0729	54°39·1'	3°26·1'W	X	89
Overend	Cumbr	NY4605	54°26·5'	2°49·5'W	X	90
Over End	Derby	SK2572	53°14·9'	1°37·1'W	T	119
Overend	Derby	SK3264	53°10·6'	1°30·9'W	X	119
Overend	Sand	SO9584	52°27·5'	2°4·0'W	T	139
Overendgreen Fm	Beds	SP9328	51°56·8'	0°38·4'W	FM	165
Over Enoch	E Renf	NS5850	55°43·6'	4°15·2'W	X	64
Overfield	E Loth	NT5972	55°56·6'	2°38·9'W	X	67
Overfield Fm	Leic	SK3302	52°37·1'	1°30·4'W	FM	140
Overfields Fm	Derby	SK2315	52°44·2'	1°39·2'W	FM	128
Over Fingask	Pth & Kin	NO2228	56°26·5'	3°15·5'W	X	53,58
Over Fingland	S Lanak	NS9209	55°22·0'	3°41·8'W	H	71,78
Over Finlarg	Angus	NO4141	56°33·7'	2°57·2'W	T	54
Over Fold, The	Derby	SK0683	53°20·9'	1°54·2'W	X	110
Overfole	Staffs	SK0536	52°55·5'	1°55·1'W	X	128
Over Forneth	Pth & Kin	NO1046	56°36·1'	3°27·5'W	X	53
Over Foulzie	Aberd	NJ7159	57°37·5'	2°28·7'W	X	29
Over Garrel	D & G	NY0590	55°12·0'	3°29·1'W	X	78
Overgate	Orkney	ND3492	58°48·9'	3°8·1'W	X	7
Overgates	Cumbr	NY1839	54°44·6'	3°16·0'W	X	89,90
Over Glaisnock	E Ayr	NS5716	55°25·3'	4°15·1'W	X	71
Overglinns	Stir	NS6088	56°4·1'	4°14·5'W	X	57
Overgrass	Northum	NU1403	55°19·5'	1°46·3'W	X	81
Over Green	Birm	SP1694	52°32·9'	1°45·4'W	T	139
Overgreen	Derby	SK3273	53°15·4'	1°30·8'W	X	119
Over Greens	N Yks	TA0093	54°19·6'	0°27·3'W	X	101
Over Guelt	E Ayr	NS6517	55°26·0'	4°7·6'W	X	71
Over Hacking	Lancs	SD6939	53°51·0'	2°27·9'W	X	103
Over Haddon	Derby	SK2066	53°11·7'	1°41·6'W	T	119
Overhailes	E Loth	NT5776	55°58·8'	2°40·9'W	X	67
Overhall	Aberd	NJ5048	57°31·4'	2°49·6'W	X	29
Overhall	Aberd	NJ6325	57°19·1'	2°36·4'W	X	37
Overhall	Aberd	NJ7842	57°28·3'	2°21·5'W	X	29,30
Over Hall	Essex	TL8038	52°0·9'	0°37·8'E	X	155
Over Hall	Essex	TL8630	51°56·5'	0°42·8'E	X	168
Over Hall	Lancs	SD6575	54°10·4'	2°31·8'W	X	97
Overhall	Scot Bord	NT4814	55°25·3'	2°48·9'W	X	79
Overhall	S Lanak	NS7143	55°40·1'	4°2·6'W	X	71
Overhall	S Lanak	NS8642	55°39·7'	3°48·3'W	X	71,72
Over Hall	Suff	TM2434	51°57·8'	1°16·0'E	X	169
Overhall Fm	Herts	TL4413	51°48·1'	0°5·7'E	FM	167
Over Hall Fm	Staffs	SJ8960	53°8·5'	2°9·5'W	FM	118
Over Hall Fm	Suff	TL9234	51°58·5'	0°48·1'E	FM	155
Overhall Fm	Suff	TM0652	52°7·9'	1°1·0'E	FM	155
Over Hazelfield	D & G	NX7749	54°49·5'	3°54·5'W	X	84
Over Hessilhead	N Ayr	NS3853	55°44·9'	4°34·4'W	X	63
Overhill	Aberd	NJ6834	57°24·0'	2°31·5'W	X	29
Overhill	Aberd	NJ8853	57°34·3'	2°11·6'W	T	30
Overhill	Aberd	NJ9417	57°14·9'	2°5·5'W	X	38
Overhill	Aberd	NJ9623	57°18·1'	2°3·5'W	X	38
Overhill	E Ayr	NS4547	55°41·8'	4°27·5'W	X	64
Over Hill	E Ayr	NS5011	55°22·5'	4°21·6'W	X	70
Overhill	Pth & Kin	NN8515	56°19·1'	3°51·1'W	X	58
Overhill Fm	Derby	SK0278	53°18·2'	1°57·8'W	FM	119
Over Hillhouse	W Loth	NS9270	55°54·9'	3°43·2'W	X	65
Overhills	C of Aber	NJ8708	57°10·0'	2°12·4'W	X	38
Over Ho	N Yks	SD9644	53°53·8'	2°3·2'W	X	103
Overhouse	S Lanak	NS6336	55°36·2'	4°10·0'W	X	71
Overhouse Fm	Warw	SP2499	52°35·5'	1°38·3'W	FM	139
Over Houses	Lancs	SD6365	54°5·0'	2°33·5'W	X	97
Over Houses	Lancs	SD8240	53°51·6'	2°16·0'W	X	103
Overhouses Fm	Staffs	SJ9562	53°9·5'	2°4·1'W	FM	118
Overhowden	Scot Bord	NT4852	55°45·8'	2°49·3'W	X	66,73
Over Hulton	Bolton	SD6805	53°32·7'	2°28·6'W	T	109
Over Inzievar	Fife	NT0188	56°4·7'	3°35·0'W	X	65
Over Kellet	Lancs	SD5269	54°7·1'	2°43·6'W	T	97
Over Kellie	Fife	NO5006	56°14·9'	2°48·0'W	X	59
Over Kiddington	Oxon	SP4022	51°53·9'	1°24·7'W	T	164
Over Kirkhope	Scot Bord	NT2111	55°23·4'	3°14·4'W	X	79
Over Knutsford	Ches	SJ7678	53°18·1'	2°21·2'W	T	118
Over Kypeside	S Lanak	NS7540	55°38·5'	3°58·7'W	X	71
Overlaggan	D & G	NX7072	55°1·8'	4°1·6'W	X	77,84
Overland	E Ayr	NS4833	55°34·3'	4°24·2'W	X	70
Overland Fm	Kent	TR2759	51°17·3'	1°15·7'E	FM	179
Over Langshaw	Scot Bord	NT5240	55°39·3'	2°45·3'W	T	73
Overlaw	D & G	NX7247	54°48·3'	3°59·1'W	X	83,84
Over Law	S Lanak	NS9704	55°19·4'	3°37·0'W	H	78
Over Leck	Lancs	SD6577	54°11·5'	2°31·8'W	X	97
Over Lee Fm	Derby	SK0186	53°22·5'	1°58·7'W	FM	110
Over Lee Ho	Cumbr	NY7539	54°45·0'	2°22·9'W	X	91
Overleigh	Devon	SS9508	50°52·0'	3°29·1'W	X	192
Overleigh	Somer	ST4835	51°7·0'	2°44·2'W	T	182
Overley	Staffs	SK1615	52°44·2'	1°45·4'W	T	128
Overley	Wrekin	SJ6111	52°42·0'	2°34·2'W	X	127
Overley Fm	Glos	SO9804	51°44·3'	2°1·3'W	FM	163
Overley Hill	Wrekin	SJ6110	52°41·4'	2°34·2'W	H	127
Overley Ride	Glos	SO9603	51°43·8'	2°3·1'W	X	163
Overley Wood	Glos	SO9705	51°44·9'	2°2·2'W	F	163
Over Linkins	D & G	NX7555	54°52·7'	3°56·5'W	X	84
Over Lochridge	E Ayr	NS4344	55°40·1'	4°29·3'W	X	70
Over Low	Staffs	SK1146	53°0·9'	1°49·8'W	A	119,128
Over Menzion	Scot Bord	NT1020	55°28·2'	3°25·0'W	X	72
Over Migvie	Angus	NO3955	56°41·2'	2°59·3'W	X	54
Over Monnow	Monm	SO5012	51°48·5'	2°43·1'W	T	162
Overmoor	Staffs	SJ9647	53°1·5'	2°3·2'W	T	118
Overmoor Fm	Derby	SK4561	53°8·9'	1°19·2'W	FM	120
Over Newton	E Loth	NT5264	55°52·3'	2°45·6'W	X	66
Overnoons	W Susx	SU9125	51°1·3'	0°41·8'W	X	186,197
Over Norton	Oxon	SP3128	51°57·2'	1°32·5'W	T	164
Over Norton Common	Oxon	SP3329	51°57·7'	1°30·8'W	X	164
Over Norton Ho	Oxon	SP3128	51°57·2'	1°32·5'W	X	164
Over Ornscleuch	S Lanak	NS9805	55°20·0'	3°36·0'W	X	78
Over Owler Tor	Sheff	SK2580	53°19·2'	1°37·1'W	X	110
Over Peover	Ches	SJ7873	53°15·5'	2°19·4'W	T	118
Over Phawhope	Scot Bord	NT1808	55°21·8'	3°17·2'W	X	79
Overpool	Ches	SJ3877	53°17·4'	2°55·4'W	T	117
Over Rankeilour	Fife	NO3213	56°18·5'	3°5·5'W	X	59
Over Raygill	N Yks	SD6770	54°7·7'	2°29·9'W	X	98
Over Ridge	Cumbr	SD3680	54°13·0'	2°58·5'W	X	96,97
Over Rig	D & G	NY2493	55°13·8'	3°11·3'W	X	79
Over Roxburgh	Scot Bord	NT6930	55°34·0'	2°29·1'W	X	74
Overs	Shrops	SO3996	52°33·7'	2°53·6'W	T	137
Overscaig Hotel	Highld	NC4123	58°10·3'	4°41·7'W	X	16
Overseal	Derby	SK2915	52°44·1'	1°33·8'W	T	128
Over's Fm	Bucks	SU9288	51°35·2'	0°39·9'W	FM	175
Overshiel	W Loth	NT0968	55°54·0'	3°26·9'W	X	65
Over Shiels	Scot Bord	NT4046	55°42·5'	2°56·9'W	X	73
Overshot Br	Essex	TL7803	51°42·1'	0°35·0'E	X	167
Overside	Aberd	NK0654	57°34·8'	1°53·5'W	X	30
Over Silton	N Yks	SE4593	54°20·1'	1°18·1'W	T	99
Over Silton Moor	N Yks	SE4694	54°20·6'	1°17·1'W	X	100
Overskibo	Highld	NH7389	57°52·6'	4°8·0'W	X	21
Overslade	Warw	SP4973	52°21·4'	1°16·4'W	T	140
Oversland	Kent	TR0557	51°16·7'	0°56·8'E	T	179
Oversley Castle	Warw	SP0955	52°11·8'	1°51·7'W	X	150
Oversley Fm	Ches	SJ8183	53°20·9'	2°16·7'W	FM	109
Oversley Green	Warw	SP0956	52°12·4'	1°51·7'W	T	150
Oversley Hill Fm	Warw	SP1056	52°12·4'	1°50·8'W	FM	150
Oversley Wood	Warw	SP1056	52°12·4'	1°50·8'W	F	150
Over Stenton	Fife	NT2799	56°10·9'	3°10·1'W	X	59
Over Stockbriggs	S Lanak	NS7935	55°35·9'	3°54·8'W	X	71
Overstone	Northnts	SP8066	52°17·4'	0°49·2'W	T	152
Overstone Grange	Northnts	SP7967	52°18·0'	0°50·1'W	X	152
Overstone Park	Northnts	SP8065	52°16·9'	0°49·2'W	X	152
Overstones Fm	Derby	SK2482	53°20·3'	1°38·0'W	FM	110
Overstone Solarium	Northnts	SP8265	52°16·9'	0°47·5'W	X	152
Over Stowey	Somer	ST1838	51°8·4'	3°9·9'W	T	181
Overstrand	Norf	TG2440	52°54·9'	1°20·3'E	T	133
Over Stratton	Somer	ST4315	50°56·1'	2°48·3'W	T	193
Over Tabley	Ches	SJ7280	53°19·2'	2°24·8'W	T	109
Over the Hill Fm	Sund	NZ3451	54°51·4'	1°27·8'W	FM	88
Overthorpe	Kirk	SE2418	53°39·7'	1°37·8'W	T	110
Overthorpe	Northnts	SP4840	52°3·6'	1°17·6'W	T	151
Overthorpe Hall (Sch)	Northnts	SP4841	52°4·1'	1°17·6'W	X	151
Overthwaite	Cumbr	SD5181	54°13·6'	2°44·7'W	X	97
Overthwarts	Northum	NU1210	55°23·3'	1°48·2'W	X	81
Over Tocher	Aberd	NJ6932	57°22·9'	2°30·5'W	X	29
Overton	Aberd	NJ6519	57°15·9'	2°34·4'W	X	38
Overton	Aberd	NJ7118	57°15·4'	2°28·4'W	X	38
Overton	Aberd	NJ9734	57°24·0'	2°2·5'W	X	30
Overton	Aberd	NO8477	56°53·3'	2°15·3'W	X	45
Overton	Ches	SJ5277	53°17·5'	2°42·8'W	T	117
Overton	C of Aber	NJ8714	57°13·3'	2°12·5'W	T	38
Overton	C of Edin	NT1074	55°57·3'	3°26·0'W	X	65
Overton	Devon	SS5729	51°2·8'	4°2·0'W	X	180
Overton	D & G	NX6378	55°4·9'	4°8·3'W	X	77
Overton	D & G	NX9864	54°57·9'	3°35·2'W	X	84
Overton	Falk	NS7783	56°1·7'	3°58·0'W	X	57,64
Overton	Fife	NS9989	56°5·2'	3°36·9'W	X	65
Overton	Glos	SO7210	51°47·5'	2°24·0'W	T	162
Overton	Glos	SO8022	51°54·0'	2°17·0'W	X	162
Overton	Hants	SU5149	51°14·5'	1°15·8'W	T	185
Overton	Highld	ND2836	58°18·7'	3°13·3'W	X	11
Overton	Inverc	NS2674	55°55·9'	4°46·7'W	T	63
Overton	Lancs	SD4358	54°1·1'	2°51·8'W	T	102
Overton	Moray	NJ2745	57°29·6'	3°12·6'W	X	28
Overton	N Ayr	NS3753	55°44·8'	4°35·4'W	X	63
Overton	N Yks	SE5555	53°59·5'	1°9·2'W	T	105
Overton	S Ayr	NS4116	55°25·0'	4°30·3'W	X	70
Overton	Shrops	SO5072	52°20·9'	2°43·6'W	T	137,138
Overton	Shrops	SO6686	52°28·5'	2°29·6'W	X	138
Overton	Somer	ST2628	51°3·0'	3°3·0'W	X	193
Overton	Staffs	SK0438	52°56·6'	1°56·0'W	T	128
Overton	Stir	NS5987	56°3·6'	4°15·4'W	X	57
Overton	Swan	SS4685	51°32·8'	4°12·9'W	T	159
Overton	Wakf	SE2616	53°38·6'	1°36·0'W	T	110
Overton	W Dunb	NS3879	55°58·9'	4°35·4'W	X	63
Overton Bridge	Wrex	SJ3542	52°58·5'	2°57·7'W	T	117
Overton Burn	W Dunb	NS4277	55°57·9'	4°31·4'W	W	64
Overton Bush	Scot Bord	NT6813	55°24·8'	2°29·9'W	X	80
Overton Cliff	Swan	SS4584	51°32·3'	4°13·7'W	X	159
Overton Down	Wilts	SU1370	51°26·0'	1°48·4'W	X	173
Overton Fm	Aberd	NJ8622	57°17·6'	2°13·5'W	FM	38
Overton Fm	Glos	SO7209	51°47·0'	2°24·0'W	FM	162
Overton Fm	Heref	SO4866	52°17·6'	2°45·4'W	FM	137,138,148
Overton Fm	Heref	SO6026	51°56·1'	2°34·5'W	FM	162
Overton Fm	Lincs	SK9854	53°4·7'	0°31·8'W	X	121
Overton Fm	N Ayr	NS3640	55°37·8'	4°35·9'W	FM	70
Overton Fm	Renf	NS3862	55°49·7'	4°34·7'W	FM	63
Overton Fm	S Lanak	NS8148	55°42·9'	3°53·2'W	FM	72
Overton Fm	W Loth	NT1066	55°53·0'	3°25·9'W	FM	65
Overton Grange	N Yks	SE5556	54°0·1'	1°9·2'W	X	105
Overton Grange Hotel	Shrops	SO5171	52°20·3'	2°42·8'W	X	137,138
Overton Hall	Ches	SJ4748	53°1·8'	2°47·0'W	X	117
Overton Hall	Derby	SK3462	53°9·5'	1°29·1'W	X	119
Overton Hall	Staffs	SJ8961	53°9·0'	2°9·5'W	X	118
Overton Hall Fm	Ches	SJ8060	53°8·4'	2°17·5'W	FM	118
Overton Hall Fm	Derby	SK0078	53°18·2'	1°59·6'W	FM	119
Overton Heath	Ches	SJ4747	53°1·3'	2°47·0'W	X	117
Overton Hill	Wilts	SU1168	51°24·9'	1°50·1'W	X	173
Overton Lodge	Wrex	SJ3642	52°58·5'	2°56·8'W	X	117
Overton Mere	Swan	SS4684	51°32·3'	4°12·8'W	X	159
Overton Muir	W Dunb	NS3779	55°58·8'	4°36·3'W	H	63
Overton of Auchnagatt	Aberd	NJ9140	57°27·3'	2°8·5'W	X	30
Overton of Bruxie	Aberd	NJ9348	57°31·6'	2°6·6'W	X	30
Overton of Keithfield	Aberd	NJ8434	57°24·0'	2°15·5'W	X	29,30
Overton of Knaven	Aberd	NJ8943	57°28·9'	2°10·5'W	X	30
Overton or Owrtyn	Wrex	SJ3741	52°58·0'	2°55·9'W	T	117
Overton Scar	Ches	SJ4749	53°2·4'	2°47·0'W	X	117
Overton Station	Hants	SU5150	51°15·0'	1°15·8'W	X	185
Overton Wood	N Yks	SE5457	54°0·6'	1°10·1'W	F	105
Overtoun	S Ayr	NS4728	55°31·6'	4°25·0'W	X	70
Overtoun	W Dunb	NS4276	55°57·3'	4°31·4'W	X	64
Overtown	Aberd	NJ9661	57°38·6'	2°3·6'W	X	30
Overtown	D & G	NS8107	55°20·8'	3°52·2'W	X	71,78
Overtown	D & G	NY2272	55°2·4'	3°12·8'W	X	85
Overtown	Glos	SO8912	51°48·6'	2°9·2'W	X	163
Overtown	Lancs	SD6276	54°10·9'	2°34·5'W	T	97
Over Town	Lancs	SD8729	53°45·7'	2°11·4'W	T	103
Overtown	N Lanak	NS8052	55°45·0'	3°54·3'W	T	65,72
Overtown	Swin	SU1579	51°30·8'	1°46·6'W	T	173
Overtown	Wakf	SE3516	53°38·6'	1°27·8'W	T	110,111
Overtown Hackpen	Swin	SU1577	51°29·7'	1°46·6'W	X	173
Overtown Ho	Swin	SU1579	51°30·8'	1°46·6'W	X	173
Over Wallop	Hants	SU2838	51°8·7'	1°35·6'W	T	184
Over Water	Cumbr	NY2535	54°42·5'	3°9·4'W	W	89,90
Overwater Hall (Hotel)	Cumbr	NY2434	54°42·0'	3°10·3'W	X	89,90
Overwells	Scot Bord	NT6820	55°28·6'	2°29·9'W	X	74
Overwells Cott	Scot Bord	NT6720	55°28·6'	2°30·9'W	X	74
Over Wheal	Derby	SK1569	53°13·3'	1°46·1'W	X	119
Over Whitacre	Warw	SP2590	52°30·7'	1°37·5'W	T	140
Over Whitacre Ho	Warw	SP2690	52°30·7'	1°36·6'W	X	140
Over Whitlaw Fm	Scot Bord	NT5130	55°33·9'	2°46·2'W	FM	73
Over Whitton	Scot Bord	NT7519	55°28·1'	2°23·3'W	X	80
Over Williamston	W Loth	NT0561	55°50·2'	3°30·6'W	X	65
Over Windyhills	Moray	NJ4956	57°35·7'	2°50·7'W	X	28,29
Over Wood	Cambs	TL6348	52°6·6'	0°23·2'E	F	154
Overwood	Corn	SX3087	50°39·7'	4°23·9'W	X	190
Overwood	S Lanak	NS7745	55°41·2'	3°57·0'W	X	64
Overwood Common	Shrops	SO6879	52°24·7'	2°27·8'W	X	138
Overwood Fm	Shrops	SO6879	52°24·7'	2°27·8'W	FM	138
Overwoodhill	Aberd	NJ8333	57°23·5'	2°16·5'W	X	29,30
Over Wood Moss	Derby	SK1194	53°26·8'	1°49·7'W	X	110
Over Worton	Oxon	SP4329	51°57·7'	1°22·1'W	T	164
Overy	Oxon	SU5893	51°38·2'	1°9·3'W	X	164,174
Overyards	Pth & Kin	NO3128	56°26·6'	3°6·7'W	X	53,59
Overy Fm	Norf	TM0088	52°27·4'	0°57·0'E	FM	144
Overy Marsh	Norf	TF8444	52°57·9'	0°44·8'E	W	132
Overy Marshes	Norf	TF8644	52°57·9'	0°46·6'E	X	132
Overy's Fm	E Susx	TQ6931	51°3·4'	0°25·1'E	FM	188
Oving	Bucks	SP7821	51°53·2'	0°51·6'W	T	165
Oving	W Susx	SU9004	50°49·9'	0°42·9'W	T	197
Ovingdean	Bri & Hov	TQ3503	50°48·9'	0°4·6'W	T	198
Ovingham	Northum	NZ0863	54°57·9'	1°52·1'W	T	88
Oving Hill Fm	Bucks	SP7019	51°52·1'	0°58·6'W	FM	165
Oving Ho	Bucks	SP7821	51°53·2'	0°51·6'W	X	165
Ovington	Durham	NZ1314	54°31·5'	1°47·5'W	T	92
Ovington	Essex	TL7642	52°3·1'	0°34·4'E	T	155
Ovington	Hants	SU5631	51°4·8'	1°11·6'W	T	185
Ovington	Norf	TF9202	52°35·1'	0°50·5'E	T	144
Ovington	Northum	NZ0663	54°57·9'	1°54·0'W	T	87
Ovington Down Fm	Hants	SU5528	51°3·2'	1°12·5'W	FM	185
Ovington Grange	Durham	NZ1414	54°31·5'	1°46·6'W	X	92
Ovington Hall	Essex	TL7642	52°3·1'	0°34·4'E	X	155
Ovington Ho	Hants	SU5631	51°4·8'	1°11·6'W	X	185
Ovis	Devon	SS6737	51°7·2'	3°53·6'W	X	180
Ovluss	Shetld	HU4837	60°7·1'	1°7·7'W	X	4
Owday Wood	Notts	SK5782	53°20·1'	1°8·2'W	F	111,120
Owen Glyndwr's Mount	Denb	SJ1243	52°58·9'	3°18·2'W	A	125
Owen's Bank	Staffs	SK2028	52°51·2'	1°41·8'W	T	128
Owens Barn Fm	Lincs	TF0532	52°52·7'	0°26·0'W	FM	130
Owens Court	Kent	TR0257	51°16·8'	0°54·2'E	X	178
Owen's Fm	Hants	SU7154	51°17·1'	0°58·5'W	FM	186
Owen's Fm	Lincs	TF2018	52°45·0'	0°12·9'W	FM	131
Owen's Hill	Devon	SX6147	50°18·6'	3°56·8'W	X	202
Ower	Hants	SU3216	50°56·8'	1°32·3'W	T	185
Ower	Hants	SU4701	50°48·6'	1°19·6'W	X	196
Ower Bay	Dorset	SY9986	50°40·6'	2°0·5'W	W	195
Ower Fm	Dorset	SY9985	50°40·1'	2°0·5'W	FM	195
Ower Fm	Hants	SU5521	50°59·4'	1°12·6'W	FM	185
Owermoigne	Dorset	SY7685	50°40·1'	2°20·0'W	T	194
Owersby Moor	Lincs	TF0895	53°26·7'	0°22·0'W	X	112
Owersby Top	Lincs	TF0793	53°25·6'	0°23·0'W	X	112
Owery Fm	Somer	ST3833	51°5·8'	2°52·7'W	FM	182
Owlaborough	Devon	SS8323	50°59·9'	3°39·7'W	X	181
Owlacombe	Devon	SS5716	50°55·8'	4°1·7'W	X	180
Owlacombe Cross	Devon	SX7672	50°32·3'	3°44·6'W	X	191
Owlands Ho	N Yks	NZ0501	54°24·5'	1°55·0'W	X	92
Owlbury Hall	Shrops	SO3191	52°31·0'	3°0·6'W	X	137
Owlcotes	Derby	SK4467	53°12·1'	1°20·1'W	T	120
Owl End	Cambs	TL2275	52°21·8'	0°12·1'W	T	142
Owler Bar	Derby	SK2978	53°18·1'	1°33·5'W	T	119
Owler Hall	Ches	SJ5058	53°7·3'	2°44·4'W	X	117
Owler Lea	Derby	SK3178	53°18·1'	1°31·7'W	X	119
Owlers Plantn	N Yks	SE6970	54°7·5'	0°56·2'W	F	100
Owlerton	Sheff	SK3389	53°24·0'	1°29·8'W	T	110,111
Owler Tor	Derby	SK2580	53°19·2'	1°37·1'W	X	110
Owles Hall	Herts	TL3728	51°56·2'	0°0·0'W	X	166
Owleshayes Fm	Devon	SY0390	50°42·3'	3°22·0'W	FM	192
Owlet	Brad	SE1536	53°49·4'	1°45·9'W	T	104
Owlet Hall	Leeds	SE3042	53°52·6'	1°32·2'W	X	104
Owlet Hall	N Yks	SD7667	54°6·1'	2°21·6'W	X	98
Owlet Hall	N Yks	SE5331	53°46·6'	1°11·3'W	X	105
Owlet Hall	Wakf	SE4218	53°39·6'	1°21·5'W	X	111
Owlethirst	Cumbr	NY4573	55°3·2'	2°51·2'W	X	86
Owlet Ho	N Yks	SD9754	53°59·2'	2°2·3'W	X	103
Owlet Hurst	Kirk	SE2022	53°41·9'	1°41·4'W	X	104
Owlet Moor	N Yks	SE7597	54°22·0'	0°50·3'W	X	94,100
Owlet Plantn	Lincs	SK8295	53°27·0'	0°45·5'W	F	112
Owletts	Kent	TQ6668	51°23·4'	0°23·5'E	A	177,178
Owlett's Fm	E Susx	TQ4337	51°7·1'	0°3·0'E	FM	187
Owletts Hall Fm	Staffs	SK0904	52°38·3'	1°51·6'W	FM	139
Owley	Devon	SX6759	50°25·2'	3°52·0'W	X	202
Owley	Kent	TQ9028	51°1·4'	0°42·9'E	X	189
Owlgreave Fm	Derby	SK0479	53°18·7'	1°56·0'W	FM	119
Owlhayes Fm	Somer	ST2314	50°55·5'	3°5·4'W	FM	193
Owl Hill Fm	Somer	ST2331	51°4·6'	3°5·6'W	FM	182
Owl Ho	Kent	TQ6637	51°6·7'	0°22·7'E	X	188
Owlpen	Glos	ST8098	51°41·1'	2°17·0'W	T	162
Owlsbury Fm	E Susx	TQ4620	50°57·9'	0°5·1'E	FM	198
Owlsbury Fm	E Susx	TQ5228	51°2·1'	0°10·5'E	FM	188,199
Owls Castle Fm	Kent	TQ6634	51°5·1'	0°22·6'E	FM	188
Owlscastle Fm	W Susx	TQ2033	51°5·3'	0°16·8'W	FM	187
Owls Court	Kent	TQ4747	51°12·4'	0°6·7'E	X	188
Owl's Fm	Suff	TL9544	52°3·8'	0°51·1'E	FM	155
Owl's Green	Suff	TM2869	52°16·5'	1°20·9'E	X	156

Owlshatch	Surrey	SU8946	51°12·6'	0°43·2'W	X	186
Owlshaw	N Yks	SD7659	54°1·8'	2°21·6'W	X	103
Owlsmoor	Brackn	SU8562	51°21·3'	0°46·4'W	T	175,186
Owl's Nest	Halton	SJ5981	53°19·7'	2°36·5'W	X	108
Owlsnest Fm	S Glos	ST6587	51°35·1'	2°29·9'W	FM	172
Owl Spring	Derby	SK5170	53°13·7'	1°13·8'W	W	120
Owlswick	Bucks	SP7806	51°45·1'	0°51·8'W	T	165
Owlthorpe	Sheff	SK4182	53°20·2'	1°22·6'W	T	111,120
Owl Wood	Scot Bord	NT7257	55°48·6'	2°26·4'W	F	67,74
Owmby	Lincs	TA0704	53°31·5'	0°22·7'W	T	112
Owmby-by-Spital	Lincs	TF0087	53°22·5'	0°29·4'W	T	112,121
Owmby Cliff	Lincs	SK9786	53°22·0'	0°32·1'W	X	112,121
Owmby Cliff Fm	Lincs	SK9786	53°22·0'	0°32·1'W	FM	112,121
Owmby Mount	Lincs	TA0705	53°32·1'	0°22·7'W	X	112
Owmby Vale	Lincs	TA0604	53°31·6'	0°23·6'W	X	112
Ownham	W Berks	SU4270	51°25·9'	1°23·4'W	T	174
Owrtyn or Overton	Wrex	SJ3741	52°58·0'	2°55·9'W	T	117
Owsen Fell	Cumbr	NY1020	54°34·3'	3°23·1'W	H	89
Owsen Hill	E Dunb	NS5782	56°0·8'	4°17·2'W	X	57,64
Owsen Wood	N Yks	NZ7903	54°25·2'	0°46·5'W	F	94
Owset Well	N Yks	SE1673	54°9·4'	1°44·9'W	W	99
Owshaw Hill	Cumbr	SD6092	54°19·6'	2°36·5'W	X	97
Owslebury	Hants	SU5123	51°0·5'	1°16·0'W	T	185
Owslin	N Yks	SD9558	54°1·3'	2°4·2'W	X	103
Owslow Fm	Derby	SK2352	53°4·1'	1°39·0'W	FM	119
Owster Hill Fm	N Yks	SE2573	54°9·4'	1°36·6'W	FM	99
Owsthill Ho	E Yorks	TA2436	53°48·6'	0°6·6'W	X	107
Owsthorpe	E Yorks	SE8131	53°46·4'	0°45·8'W	X	106
Owston	Donc	SE5511	53°35·8'	1°9·7'W	T	111
Owston	Leic	SK7707	52°39·5'	0°51·3'W	T	141
Owston Ferry	N Lincs	SE8000	53°29·7'	0°47·2'W	T	112
Owston Grange	Donc	SE5710	53°35·2'	1°7·9'W	X	111
Owston Grange	Leic	SK7607	52°39·6'	0°52·2'W	X	141
Owston Grange	N Lincs	SK7998	53°28·6'	0°48·2'W	X	112
Owston Lodge	Leic	SK7607	52°39·6'	0°52·2'W	X	141
Owston Lodge Fm	Leic	SK7508	52°40·1'	0°53·1'W	FM	141
Owston Wood	Donc	SE5710	53°35·2'	1°7·9'W	F	111
Owston Woods	Leic	SK7806	52°39·0'	0°50·4'W	F	141
Owstwick	E Yorks	TA2732	53°46·4'	0°4·0'W	T	107
Owthorne	E Yorks	TA3328	53°44·1'	0°1·4'E	T	107
Owthorpe	Notts	SK6733	52°53·7'	0°59·8'W	T	129
Owthorpe Hill	Notts	SK6633	52°53·7'	1°0·7'W	X	129
Owthorpe Lodge	Notts	SK6531	52°52·6'	1°1·6'W	X	129
Owthorpe Wolds	Notts	SK6532	52°53·1'	1°1·6'W	X	129
Owton Grange	Hartpl	NZ4729	54°39·5'	1°15·9'W	X	93
Owton Manor	Hartpl	NZ4929	54°39·5'	1°14·0'W	T	93
Ox Bank	N Yks	SE4392	54°19·5'	1°19·9'W	X	99
Oxbank Wood	N Yks	NZ9301	54°24·0'	0°33·6'W	F	94
Oxbatch	Staffs	SK0461	53°9·0'	1°56·0'W	X	119
Oxbind Coppice	Worcs	SO7474	52°22·0'	2°22·5'W	F	138
Oxborough	Norf	TF7401	52°35·0'	0°34·5'E	T	143
Oxborough Wood	Norf	TF7201	52°35·0'	0°32·7'E	F	143
Oxbottom	E Susx	TQ4020	50°58·0'	0°0·0'E	X	198
Oxbridge	Dorset	SY4797	50°46·4'	2°44·7'W	T	193
Ox Brook	Leic	SK6517	52°45·0'	1°1·8'W	W	129
Oxburgh Hall	Norf	TF4707	52°38·7'	0°10·8'E	X	143
Oxcars	C of Edin	NT2081	56°1·2'	3°16·6'W	X	66
Ox Cleuch	Scot Bord	NT2320	55°28·3'	3°12·7'W	X	73
Oxcleuch Rig	Scot Bord	NT2220	55°28·3'	3°13·6'W	X	73
Oxcliffe Hill	Lancs	SD4461	54°2·8'	2°50·9'W	X	97
Ox Close	Derby	SK2047	53°1·4'	1°41·7'W	X	119,128
Ox Close	Durham	NZ3540	54°45·5'	1°26·9'W	X	88
Ox Close	Lancs	SD8145	53°54·3'	2°16·9'W	X	103
Ox Close	Leeds	SE3646	53°54·8'	1°26·7'W	X	104
Ox Close	N Yks	NZ4105	54°26·6'	1°21·6'W	X	93
Ox Close	N Yks	SE3368	54°6·7'	1°29·3'W	X	99
Ox Close	N Yks	SE7088	54°17·2'	0°55·1'W	X	94,100
Oxclose	Sheff	SK4380	53°19·1'	1°20·9'W	T	111,120
Oxclose	Sund	NZ2956	54°54·1'	1°32·4'W	T	88
Oxclose Fm	Derby	SK3862	53°9·5'	1°25·5'W	FM	119
Ox Close Fm	Durham	NZ2136	54°43·4'	1°40·0'W	FM	93
Ox Close Fm	N Yks	SE4673	54°9·3'	1°17·3'W	FM	100
Oxclose Fm	N Yks	SE6387	54°16·7'	1°1·5'W	FM	94,100
Ox Close Fm	York	SE6449	53°56·2'	1°1·1'W	FM	105,106
Ox Close Ho	N Yks	SE4052	53°58·0'	1°23·0'W	X	105
Ox Close Plantation	N Yks	SE1579	54°12·6'	1°45·8'W	F	99
Ox Closes	N Yks	SE3764	54°4·5'	1°25·7'W	X	99
Ox Close Wood	E Yorks	SE8644	53°53·3'	0°41·1'W	F	106
Oxclose Wood	N Yks	SE6080	54°13·0'	1°4·4'W	F	100
Oxcombe	Lincs	TF3177	53°16·7'	0°1·7'W	T	122
Oxcroft	Derby	SK4873	53°15·3'	1°16·4'W	T	120
Oxcroft Estate	Derby	SK4873	53°15·3'	1°16·4'W	T	120
Oxcroft Fm	Cambs	TL5951	52°8·3'	0°19·8'E	FM	154
Oxcroft Ho	Lincs	TF3119	52°45·4'	0°3·1'W	X	131
Ox Dale	N Yks	SE8884	54°14·9'	0°38·5'W	X	101
Oxdales Fm	Derby	SK1656	53°6·3'	1°45·3'W	FM	119
Ox Drove	Wilts	ST9821	50°59·5'	2°1·3'W	X	184
Ox Drove, The	Hants	SU6139	51°9·0'	1°7·3'W	X	185
Oxe Eye Fm	Stock on T	NZ3819	54°34·1'	1°24·3'W	FM	93
Oxenards	Lancs	SD9043	53°53·2'	2°8·7'W	X	103
Oxenber Wood	N Yks	SD7868	54°6·7'	2°19·8'W	F	98
Oxenbourne Down	Hants	SU7119	50°58·2'	0°58·9'W	X	197
Oxenbourne Ho	Hants	SU6921	50°59·3'	1°0·6'W	X	197
Oxenbows	Cumbr	SD1679	54°12·2'	3°16·9'W	X	96
Oxenbridge	E Susx	TQ8725	50°59·9'	0°40·3'E	X	189,199
Oxenbridge	E Susx	TQ9124	50°59·2'	0°43·7'E	X	189
Oxen Close	N Yks	SD9351	53°57·5'	2°6·0'W	X	103
Oxen Close	N Yks	SE1859	54°1·8'	1°43·1'W	X	104
Oxencombe Fm	Devon	SX8882	50°37·9'	3°34·6'W	FM	192
Oxen Craig	Aberd	NJ6622	57°17·5'	2°33·4'W	H	38
Oxendale	Cumbr	NY2605	54°26·4'	3°8·0'W	X	89,90
Oxendean	E Susx	TQ5600	50°46·9'	0°13·2'E	X	199
Oxendean Tower	Scot Bord	NT7756	55°48·1'	2°21·6'W	X	67,74
Oxenden	Kent	TQ9327	51°0·8'	0°45·5'E	X	189
Oxen Down	W Susx	SU9213	50°54·8'	0°41·1'W	X	197
Oxen End	Essex	TL6629	51°56·3'	0°25·3'E	T	167
Oxen Fell	Cumbr	NY3202	54°24·8'	3°2·4'W	X	90
Oxenfoord Castle School	Midlo	NT3865	55°52·7'	2°59·0'W	X	66
Oxenfoord Home Fm	Midlo	NT3865	55°52·7'	2°59·0'W	FM	66
Oxenfoord Mains	Midlo	NT3967	55°53·8'	2°58·1'W	X	66

Oxenford Fm	Somer	ST3612	50°54·5'	2°54·2'W	FM	193
Oxenford Grange	Surrey	SU9343	51°10·9'	0°39·8'W	X	186
Oxenforth Green	Lancs	SD6468	54°6·6'	2°32·6'W	X	97
Oxenhall	Glos	SO7126	51°56·1'	2°24·9'W	T	162
Oxenhall Wood	Glos	SO6828	51°57·2'	2°27·5'W	F	149
Oxenham Fm	Essex	TQ9688	51°33·6'	0°50·1'E	FM	178
Oxenham Manor	Devon	SX6694	50°44·0'	3°53·6'W	X	191
Oxenholme	Cumbr	SD5389	54°17·9'	2°42·9'W	T	97
Oxenhope	Brad	SE0335	53°48·9'	1°56·9'W	T	104
Oxenhope Moor	Cald	SE0232	53°47·3'	1°57·8'W	X	104
Oxenhope Stoop Hill	Brad	SD9934	53°48·4'	2°0·5'W	X	103
Oxen House Bay	Cumbr	SD2992	54°19·4'	3°5·1'W	W	96,97
Oxenhurst	Lancs	SD6751	53°57·5'	2°29·8'W	X	103
Oxen Law	Durham	NZ0745	54°48·2'	1°53·0'W	X	88
Oxenlears	Devon	SY2796	50°45·8'	3°1·7'W	X	193
Oxenleaze Fm	Somer	ST0127	51°2·3'	3°24·3'W	FM	181
Oxen Leaze Fm	Wilts	ST8762	51°21·6'	2°10·8'W	FM	173
Oxen-le-Fields	Darl	NZ2810	54°29·3'	1°33·6'W	X	93
Oxenloan	Aberd	NJ6830	57°21·8'	2°31·5'W	X	29
Oxen Park	Cumbr	SD3187	54°16·7'	3°3·2'W	T	96,97
Oxenpark	Devon	SS4109	50°51·8'	4°15·2'W	X	190
Oxenpark	Devon	SS7907	50°51·2'	3°42·8'W	X	191
Oxenpark Fm	Devon	ST1312	50°54·3'	3°13·9'W	FM	181,193
Oxenpill	Somer	ST4441	51°10·2'	2°47·7'W	T	182
Oxenrig	Scot Bord	NT8441	55°40·0'	2°14·8'W	X	74
Oxenriggs	Cumbr	NY0210	54°28·8'	3°30·3'W	X	89
Oxensetter	Shetld	HU3482	60°31·5'	1°22·3'W	X	1,2,3
Oxenshaw	E Ayr	NS5228	55°31·7'	4°20·2'W	X	70
Oxen, The	Corn	SW7817	50°0·9'	5°5·6'W	X	204
Oxenthwaite	Cumbr	NY8212	54°30·4'	2°16·3'W	X	91,92
Oxenton	Glos	SO9531	51°58·9'	2°4·0'W	T	150
Oxenton Hill	Glos	SO9632	51°59·4'	2°3·1'W	H	150
Oxen Wood	Northnts	SP9882	52°25·9'	0°33·1'W	F	141
Oxen Wood	Northum	NU1311	55°23·8'	1°47·3'W	F	81
Oxenwood	Wilts	SU3059	51°20·0'	1°33·8'W	T	174
Ox Eye	Shetld	HU3518	59°57·0'	1°21·9'W	X	4
Oxey Fm	Leic	SK7703	52°37·4'	0°51·3'W	FM	141
Oxey Mead	Oxon	SP4710	51°47·4'	1°18·7'W	X	164
Oxfield Fm	Cambs	TF4212	52°41·5'	0°6·5'E	FM	131,142,143
Oxfield Fm	N Yks	SE4583	54°14·7'	1°18·1'W	FM	99
Oxfield Fm	N Yks	SE7462	54°3·2'	0°51·8'W	FM	100
Oxfield Ho	N Yks	NZ5504	54°25·9'	1°8·7'W	X	93
Oxfootstone Fm	Norf	TM0580	52°23·0'	1°1·1'E	FM	144
Oxford	C of Stoke	SJ8753	53°4·7'	2°11·2'W	T	118
Oxford	Northum	NU0046	55°42·7'	1°59·6'W	X	75
Oxford	Oxon	SP5106	51°45·3'	1°15·3'W	T	164
Oxford Airport	Oxon	SP4615	51°50·1'	1°19·5'W	X	164
Oxford Canal	Northnts	SP5366	52°17·6'	1°13·0'W	W	152
Oxford Canal	Oxon	SP4747	52°7·4'	1°18·4'W	W	151
Oxford Canal	Oxon	SP4820	51°52·8'	1°17·8'W	W	164
Oxford Canal	Warw	SP4281	52°25·8'	1°22·5'W	W	140
Oxford Canal	Warw	SP5268	52°18·7'	1°13·8'W	W	151
Oxford Canal Walk	Oxon	SP4745	52°6·3'	1°18·4'W	X	151
Oxford Cross	Devon	SS4640	51°8·6'	4°11·7'W	X	180
Oxford Down	Devon	SS6628	51°2·4'	3°54·3'W	H	180
Oxford Grange Fm	N Lincs	TA0723	53°41·8'	0°22·3'W	FM	107,112
Oxford Ho	N Yks	NZ5306	54°27·0'	1°10·5'W	X	93
Oxfordshire Circular Walks	Oxon	SP3011	51°48·0'	1°33·5'W	X	164
Oxfordshire Circular Walks	Oxon	SP4044	52°5·8'	1°24·6'W	X	151
Oxfordshire Circular Walks	Oxon	SP4509	51°46·9'	1°20·5'W	X	164
Oxfordshire Circular Walks	Oxon	SP5001	51°42·6'	1°16·2'W	X	164
Oxfordshire Circular Walks	Oxon	SU4485	51°34·0'	1°21·5'W	X	174
Oxfordshire Circular Walks	Oxon	SU5892	51°37·7'	1°9·3'W	X	164,174
Oxfordshire Circular Walks	Oxon	SU6090	51°36·6'	1°7·6'W	X	164,175
Oxfordshire Cycle Way	Oxon	SP4137	52°2·0'	1°23·7'W	X	151
Oxfordshire Way	Glos	SP2322	51°54·0'	1°39·5'W	X	163
Oxfordshire Way	Oxon	SP5316	51°50·6'	1°13·4'W	X	164
Oxfordshire Way	Oxon	SU7287	51°34·9'	0°57·3'W	X	175
Oxford Water	Bucks	SP6636	52°1·3'	1°1·9'W	W	152
Oxgang	E Dunb	NS6673	55°56·1'	4°8·3'W	T	64
Oxgang Fm	D & G	NY0375	55°3·9'	3°30·7'W	FM	84
Oxgangs	C of Edin	NT2368	55°54·2'	3°13·5'W	T	66
Ox Geo	Shetld	HU4088	60°34·7'	1°15·7'W	X	1,2
Oxgoddes Fm	E Yorks	TA1925	53°42·7'	0°11·4'W	FM	107,113
Oxgrove	Somer	SS9329	51°3·3'	3°31·2'W	X	181
Oxhall	Worcs	SO7159	52°13·9'	2°25·1'W	X	149
Ox Hay	Staffs	SJ9260	53°8·5'	2°6·8'W	X	118
Oxhay	Staffs	SJ9860	53°8·5'	2°1·4'W	X	118
Ox Hayes Fm	Warw	SP2993	52°32·3'	1°33·9'W	FM	140
Ox Hey	Derby	SK1694	53°26·8'	1°45·1'W	X	110
Oxhey	Herts	TQ1295	51°38·8'	0°22·5'W	T	166,176
Ox Hey	Lancs	SD6235	53°48·8'	2°34·2'W	X	102,103
Oxhey Fm	Stock	SJ9486	53°22·5'	2°5·0'W	FM	109
Oxhey Grange	Herts	TQ1294	51°38·2'	0°22·5'W	X	166,176
Oxhey Hall	Herts	TQ1094	51°38·3'	0°24·2'W	X	166,176
Oxheylane Fm	Harrow	TQ1392	51°37·2'	0°21·7'W	FM	176
Oxheys	Ches	SJ5862	53°9·5'	2°37·3'W	X	117
Oxheys Fm	Warr	SJ6685	53°21·9'	2°30·2'W	FM	109
Oxhey Warren	Herts	TQ1193	51°37·7'	0°23·4'W	X	176
Oxhey Woods	Herts	TQ1092	51°37·2'	0°24·3'W	F	176
Ox Hill	Devon	SY2393	50°44·1'	3°5·1'W	X	192,193
Ox Hill	D & G	NS7102	55°18·0'	4°1·5'W	H	77
Ox Hill	D & G	NS7200	55°16·9'	4°0·5'W	H	77
Oxhill	Durham	NZ1852	54°52·0'	1°42·7'W	T	88
Oxhill	Stir	NS5793	56°6·8'	4°17·5'W	X	57
Oxhill	Warw	SP3145	52°6·4'	1°32·4'W	T	151
Ox Hill Fm	N Yks	NZ4501	54°24·4'	1°18·0'W	FM	93
Oxhill Hill	Warw	SP3045	52°6·4'	1°33·3'W	X	151
Ox House Fm	Heref	SO4061	52°14·9'	2°52·3'W	FM	137,148,149
Oxhouse Fm	Northnts	SP6461	52°14·8'	1°3·4'W	FM	152
Ox House Fm	Wilts	SU1092	51°37·8'	1°50·9'W	FM	163,173
Oxlands Plantn	E Yorks	SE8955	53°59·2'	0°38·1'W	F	106
Oxlease	Herts	TL2207	51°45·1'	0°13·6'W	T	166
Ox Leas Fm	N Yks	SE7762	54°3·1'	0°49·0'W	FM	100
Oxleasows	Staffs	SJ8530	52°52·3'	2°13·0'W	X	127
Oxleasows Fm	Worcs	SP0070	52°19·9'	1°59·6'W	FM	139
Oxleas Wood	Gren	TQ4476	51°28·1'	0°4·8'E	F	177
Oxleaze	Glos	SP0522	51°54·0'	1°55·2'W	X	163
Oxleaze Fm	Glos	SP2024	51°55·1'	1°42·2'W	FM	163
Oxleaze Fm	Glos	SP2105	51°44·8'	1°41·4'W	FM	163

Oxleaze Fm	Oxon	SU2989	51°36·2'	1°34·5'W	FM	174
Oxleaze Fm	S Glos	ST7688	51°35·7'	2°20·4'W	FM	162,172
Oxley	Wolv	SJ9101	52°36·6'	2°7·6'W	T	127,139
Oxley Dairy	Suff	TM3643	52°2·3'	1°26·9'E	X	169
Oxley Green	Essex	TL9114	51°47·7'	0°46·6'E	T	168
Oxley Marshes	Suff	TM3643	52°2·3'	1°26·9'E	X	169
Oxleys Copse	Hants	SU3901	50°48·7'	1°26·4'W	F	196
Oxleys Fm	Beds	TL0739	52°2·6'	0°26·0'W	FM	153
Ox Leys Fm	Birm	SP1595	52°33·4'	1°46·3'W	FM	139
Oxley's Fm	Bucks	SP8620	51°52·5'	0°44·6'W	FM	165
Oxley's Green	E Susx	TQ6921	50°58·0'	0°24·8'E	T	199
Oxley Wood	Essex	TL8332	51°57·6'	0°40·2'E	F	168
Oxlode	Cambs	TL4886	52°27·3'	0°11·1'E	T	143
Ox Low	Derby	SK1280	53°19·2'	1°48·8'W	X	110
Oxlow Ho	Derby	SK1282	53°20·3'	1°48·8'W	X	110
Oxlow Rake	Derby	SK1279	53°18·7'	1°48·8'W	X	119
Oxlow Rake	Derby	SK1280	53°19·2'	1°48·8'W	X	110
Oxlynch	Glos	SO8207	51°45·9'	2°15·3'W	X	162
Oxmardyke Crossing	E Yorks	SE8428	53°44·7'	0°43·2'W	X	106
Oxmardyke Grange	E Yorks	SE8528	53°44·7'	0°42·3'W	X	106
Ox Moor	N Yks	SE4279	54°12·5'	1°20·9'W	X	99
Ox Moor	N Yks	SE5468	54°6·5'	1°10·0'W	X	100
Oxmoor	Somer	ST4450	51°15·0'	2°47·8'W	X	182
Oxmoor Dikes	N Yks	SE8987	54°16·5'	0°37·6'W	A	94,101
Ox Moor Plantn	N Yks	SE4379	54°12·5'	1°20·0'W	F	99
Oxmoor Wood	V of Glam	ST0268	51°24·4'	3°24·2'W	F	170
Oxmuir	Scot Bord	NT7141	55°40·0'	2°27·2'W	X	74
Oxna	Shetld	HU3537	60°7·2'	1°21·7'W	X	4
Oxna Field	Shetld	HU2758	60°18·6'	1°30·2'W	X	3
Oxna Geo	Orkney	HY6127	59°7·9'	2°40·4'W	X	5
Oxna Leog	Shetld	HU3386	60°33·6'	1°23·4'W	X	1,2,3
Oxnam	Scot Bord	NT6918	55°27·5'	2°29·0'W	T	80
Oxnam Neuk	Scot Bord	NT6918	55°27·5'	2°29·0'W	X	80
Oxnam Row	Scot Bord	NT7017	55°27·0'	2°28·0'W	X	80
Oxnamrow Hill	Scot Bord	NT7117	55°27·0'	2°27·1'W	H	80
Oxnam Water	Scot Bord	NT7017	55°27·0'	2°28·0'W	W	80
Oxnead	Norf	TG2324	52°46·3'	1°18·8'E	T	133,134
Oxney Flatt	Darl	NZ2711	54°29·9'	1°34·6'W	X	93
Oxney Fm	Hants	SU7837	51°7·8'	0°52·7'W	FM	186
Oxney Ho	Peterb	TF2200	52°35·3'	0°11·5'W	X	142
Oxnop Beck	N Yks	SD9396	54°21·8'	2°6·0'W	W	98
Oxnop Beck Head	N Yks	SD9394	54°20·7'	2°6·0'W	X	98
Oxnop Common	N Yks	SD9295	54°21·3'	2°7·0'W	X	98
Oxnop Ghyll	N Yks	SD9396	54°21·8'	2°6·0'W	X	98
Oxnop Scar	N Yks	SD9395	54°21·3'	2°6·0'W	X	98
Oxnop Side	N Yks	SD9196	54°21·8'	2°7·9'W	X	98
Oxon Hall	Shrops	SJ4513	52°43·0'	2°48·5'W	X	126
Oxon Hoath	Kent	TQ6352	51°14·9'	0°20·5'E	X	188
Oxpasture	Derby	SK2372	53°14·9'	1°38·9'W	X	119
Ox Pasture	Donc	SE5102	53°31·0'	1°13·4'W	X	111
Oxpasture	Heref	SO5149	52°8·5'	2°42·6'W	X	149
Ox Pasture Fm	Lincs	TF2267	53°11·4'	0°10·0'W	FM	122
Ox Pasture Fm	N Yks	SE9989	54°17·5'	0°28·3'W	FM	94,101
Ox Pastures	N Yks	SD9668	54°6·7'	2°3·3'W	X	98
Oxpasture Wood	E Susx	TQ6137	51°6·8'	0°18·4'E	F	188
Ox Pasture Wood	Lancs	SD7952	53°58·1'	2°18·8'W	F	103
Ox Pasture Wood	N Yks	SE6968	54°6·4'	0°56·3'W	F	100
Oxpasture Wood	N Yks	SE8364	54°4·2'	0°43·5'W	F	100
Oxpens Fm	Glos	SP0814	51°49·7'	1°52·6'W	FM	163
Oxrigg	Cumbr	NY2845	54°47·9'	3°6·8'W	X	85
Oxroad Fm	Kent	TR1945	51°10·0'	1°8·3'E	FM	179,189
Ox Rock	Highld	NC1338	58°17·7'	5°11·0'W	X	15
Ox Rocks	E Loth	NT3874	55°57·6'	2°59·1'W	X	66
Oxscar or South Goldstone	Northum	NU2137	55°37·8'	1°39·6'W	X	75
Oxshott	Surrey	TQ1460	51°19·9'	0°21·4'W	T	176,187
Oxshott Heath	Surrey	TQ1361	51°20·4'	0°22·3'W	X	176,187
Oxspring	Barns	SE2602	53°31·1'	1°36·1'W	T	110
Oxstalls Fm	Warw	SP2156	52°12·3'	1°41·2'W	FM	151
Ox Stones	Sheff	SK2783	53°20·8'	1°35·3'W	X	110
Oxted	Surrey	TQ3852	51°15·3'	0°1·0'W	T	187
Oxton	Notts	SK6351	53°3·4'	1°3·2'W	T	120
Oxton	N Yks	SE5043	53°53·1'	1°13·9'W	T	105
Oxton	Scot Bord	NT4953	55°46·3'	2°48·3'W	T	66,73
Oxton	Wirral	SJ2987	53°22·7'	3°3·6'W	T	108
Oxton Bogs	Notts	SK6151	53°3·4'	1°5·0'W	W	120
Oxton Ditch	Worcs	SO9845	52°6·4'	2°1·4'W	W	150
Oxton Dumble	Notts	SK6452	53°3·9'	1°2·3'W	W	120
Oxton Grange	Notts	SK6254	53°5·0'	1°4·1'W	X	120
Oxton Hall	N Yks	SE4943	53°53·1'	1°14·9'W	X	105
Oxton Hill Fm	Notts	SK6452	53°3·9'	1°2·3'W	FM	120
Oxton Ho	Devon	SX9282	50°37·9'	3°31·2'W	X	192
Oxton Rakes	Derby	SK3273	53°15·4'	1°30·8'W	T	119
Oxtro	Orkney	HY2526	59°7·1'	3°18·1'W	X	6
Oxtro (Brock)	Orkney	HY2526	59°7·1'	3°18·1'W	A	6
Oxwell	Moray	NJ4154	57°34·6'	2°58·7'W	X	28
Oxwich	Swan	SS4986	51°33·4'	4°10·3'W	T	159
Oxwich Bay	Swan	SS5186	51°33·4'	4°8·6'W	W	159
Oxwich Burrows	Swan	SS5087	51°34·0'	4°9·5'W	X	159
Oxwich Green	Swan	SS4986	51°33·4'	4°10·3'W	T	159
Oxwich Point	Swan	SS5185	51°32·9'	4°8·6'W	X	159
Oxwick	Norf	TF9124	52°47·0'	0°50·3'E	T	132
Oxwick Fm	S Glos	ST7285	51°34·0'	2°23·8'W	FM	172
Oxwold Ho	Glos	SP0706	51°45·4'	1°53·5'W	X	163
Oxygrains Old Bridge	Cald	SE0015	53°38·1'	1°59·6'W	A	110
Oyce	Orkney	HY2829	59°8·8'	3°15·0'W	X	6
Oyce	Orkney	HY6744	59°17·1'	2°34·3'W	X	5
Oyce of Herston	Orkney	ND4291	58°48·4'	2°59·8'W	W	7
Oyce of Huip	Orkney	HY6429	59°9·0'	2°37·3'W	W	5
Oyce of Isbister	Orkney	HY3918	59°2·9'	3°3·3'W	W	6
Oyce of Quindry	Orkney	ND4392	58°49·0'	2°58·7'W	W	7
Oykel Bridge	Highld	NC3800	57°57·9'	4°43·8'W	X	16
Oyne	Aberd	NJ6725	57°19·1'	2°32·4'W	T	38
Oyster Clough	Derby	SK1190	53°24·6'	1°49·7'W	X	110
Oyster Hill	Heref	SO7241	52°4·2'	2°24·1'W	X	149
Oystermouth	Swan	SS6188	51°34·7'	4°0·0'W	T	159
Oyster Skerries	Orkney	HY5305	58°56·0'	2°48·5'W	X	6,7
Ozendyke Grange	N Yks	SE5438	53°50·4'	1°10·3'W	X	105
Ozendyke House Fm	N Yks	SE5339	53°50·9'	1°11·2'W	FM	105
Ozendyke Ings	N Yks	SE5440	53°51·4'	1°10·3'W	X	105
Ozleworth	Glos	ST7993	51°38·4'	2°17·8'W	T	162,172

Ozleworth Bottom	Glos	ST7992	51°37·8′	2°17·8′W	X	162,172
Ozleworth Park	Glos	ST7993	51°38·4′	2°17·8′W	X	162,172

P

Paa Farm	Lancs	SD8352	53°58·1′	2°15·1′W	FM	103
Pabail Iarach	N Eil	NB5131	58°12·1′	6°13·8′W	T	8
Pabay	Highld	NG6727	57°16·7′	5°51·5′W	X	32
Pabay Beag	N Eil	NB0938	58°14·3′	6°57·1′W	X	13
Pabay Mór	N Eil	NB1038	58°14·4′	6°56·0′W	X	13
Pabbay	N Eil	NF7719	57°9·2′	7°20·1′W	X	31
Pabbay	N Eil	NL6087	56°51·3′	7°34·3′W	X	31
Pabo	Conwy	SH8078	53°17·4′	3°47·6′W	T	116
Pabyer Point	Corn	SX0242	50°14·9′	4°46·3′W	X	204
Paccombe Fm	Devon	SY1590	50°42·4′	3°11·8′W	FM	192,193
Paccombe Hill	Devon	SY1690	50°42·4′	3°11·0′W	X	192,193
Pace Gate	N Yks	SE1154	53°59·2′	1°49·5′W	X	104
Pace Hill	Northum	NT9137	55°37·8′	2°8·1′W	X	74,75
Pace's Ho	N Yks	NZ1106	54°27·2′	1°49·4′W	X	92
Pachesham Park	Surrey	TQ1659	51°19·3′	0°19·7′W	T	187
Pachington Fm	Hants	SU4142	51°10·8′	1°24·4′W	FM	185
Pacific Hall Fm	Sund	NZ3850	54°50·8′	1°24·1′W	FM	88
Packards	Essex	TM0004	51°42·2′	0°54·1′E	X	168
Packers Hill	Dorset	ST7110	50°53·6′	2°24·4′W	T	194
Packet House Fm	Lincs	TF2354	53°4·4′	0°9·4′W	FM	122
Packetstone Hill	Shrops	SO4291	52°31·1′	2°50·9′W	X	137
Packhorse	Derby	SK3152	53°4·1′	1°31·8′W	X	119
Packhorse	Pth & Kin	NN9723	56°23·5′	3°39·7′W	X	52,53,58
Packhorse Bridge	Somer	SS8945	51°11·8′	3°34·9′W	A	181
Packhorse Bridge	Somer	SS8946	51°12·4′	3°35·0′W	A	181
Pack Horse (PH)	Cald	SD9531	53°46·8′	2°4·1′W	X	103
Packington	Leic	SK3614	52°43·6′	1°27·6′W	T	128
Packington Fm	Staffs	SK1604	52°38·2′	1°45·4′W	FM	139
Packington Hall	Staffs	SK1606	52°39·3′	1°45·4′W	X	139
Packington Hall	Warw	SP2283	52°26·9′	1°40·2′W	X	139
Packington Lane Fm	Warw	SP2087	52°29·1′	1°41·9′W	FM	139
Packington Moor	Staffs	SK1405	52°38·8′	1°47·2′W	X	139
Packington Park	Warw	SP2284	52°27·4′	1°40·2′W	X	139
Packman's Burn	Scot Bord	NT5636	55°37·2′	2°41·5′W	W	73
Packmoor	C of Stoke	SJ8654	53°5·2′	2°12·1′W	T	118
Packmores	Warw	SP2865	52°17·2′	1°35·0′W	T	151
Packover Ho	Cambs	TF4509	52°39·8′	0°9·1′E	X	143
Pack Saddle	Tames	SK0098	53°29·0′	1°59·6′W	X	110
Packsfield	I of W	SZ5391	50°43·2′	1°14·6′W	X	196
Packthorne Fm	Glos	SO7609	51°47·0′	2°20·5′W	FM	162
Packway Fm	Suff	TM3772	52°17·9′	1°29·0′E	FM	156
Packway Fm	Suff	TM4166	52°14·6′	1°32·2′E	FM	156
Packwood	Sol	SP1773	52°21·5′	1°44·6′W	T	139
Packwood Gullet	Sol	SP1674	52°22·1′	1°45·5′W	T	139
Packwood Haugh	Shrops	SJ3923	52°48·3′	2°53·9′W	X	126
Packwood House	Warw	SP1772	52°21·0′	1°44·6′W	A	139
Packwood Towers	Warw	SP1673	52°21·5′	1°45·5′W	X	139
Padanaram	Angus	NO4251	56°39·1′	2°56·3′W	T	54
Padarn Country Park	Gwyn	SH5860	53°7·4′	4°6·9′W	X	114,115
Padarn Country Park	Gwyn	SH5861	53°7·9′	4°6·9′W	X	114,115
Padbrook Hill	Devon	ST0106	50°50·9′	3°24·0′W	X	192
Padbury	Bucks	SP7230	51°58·1′	0°56·7′W	T	152,165
Padbury Br	Bucks	SP7131	51°58·6′	0°57·6′W	X	152,165
Padbury Brook (The Twins)	Bucks	SP7132	51°59·1′	0°57·6′W	W	152,165
Padbury Brook (Twins, The)	Bucks	SP7132	51°59·1′	0°57·6′W	W	152,165
Padburyhill Fm	Bucks	SP7229	51°57·5′	0°56·7′W	FM	165
Pad Cote	N Yks	SD9541	53°52·2′	2°4·1′W	X	103
Paddaburn	Cumbr	NY6377	55°5·4′	2°34·4′W	X	86
Padda Burn	Northum	NY6478	55°6·0′	2°33·4′W	W	86
Paddaburn	Northum	NY6478	55°6·0′	2°33·4′W	F	86
Padderbury	Corn	SX3161	50°25·7′	4°22·4′W	X	201
Paddigill	Cumbr	NY3040	54°45·3′	3°4·8′W	X	85
Paddingham Ho	N Som	ST4357	51°18·8′	2°48·7′W	X	172,182
Paddington	C of West	TQ2681	51°31·1′	0°10·6′W	T	176
Paddington	Warr	SJ6389	53°24·0′	2°33·0′W	T	109
Paddington Fm	Surrey	TQ1047	51°12·9′	0°25·1′W	FM	187
Paddington Sike	Scot Bord	NY5193	55°14·0′	2°45·8′W	W	79
Paddington Sta	C of West	TQ2681	51°31·1′	0°10·6′W	X	176
Paddle Brook	Glos	SP2137	52°2·1′	1°41·2′W	W	151
Paddlesworth	Kent	TQ6862	51°20·2′	0°25·1′E	T	177,178,188
Paddlesworth	Kent	TR1939	51°6·7′	1°8·1′E	T	179,189
Paddlesworth Court Fm	Kent	TR1940	51°7·3′	1°8·2′E	FM	179,189
Paddock	Kent	TQ9950	51°13·1′	0°51·4′E	T	189
Paddock	Kirk	SE1216	53°38·7′	1°48·7′W	T	110
Paddock	Shrops	SO4282	52°26·2′	2°50·8′W	X	137
Paddock	Staffs	SJ9765	53°11·2′	2°2·3′W	X	118
Paddock Barn	Surrey	TQ3554	51°16·4′	0°3·5′W	X	187
Paddock Burn	Scot Bord	NT3130	55°33·8′	3°5·2′W	W	73
Paddock Fm	Wilts	ST9966	51°23·8′	2°0·5′W	FM	173
Paddock-ha'	Aberd	NJ8326	57°19·7′	2°16·5′W	X	38
Paddockhall	Falk	NT0378	55°59·4′	3°32·9′W	X	65
Paddock Hall Fm	Northum	NZ2385	55°9·8′	1°37·9′W	FM	81
Paddockhaugh	Moray	NJ2058	57°36·6′	3°19·9′W	T	28
Paddockhill	Ches	SJ8179	53°18·7′	2°16·7′W	T	118
Paddock Hill	N Yks	SE2052	53°58·1′	1°41·3′W	X	104
Paddock Ho	N Yks	SE3547	53°55·3′	1°27·6′W	X	104
Paddockhole	D & G	NY2383	55°8·4′	3°12·0′W	X	79
Paddock House Fm	Staffs	SK1057	53°6·8′	1°50·6′W	FM	119
Paddockhurst Park	W Susx	TQ3233	51°5·1′	0°6·5′W	X	187
Paddocklaw	Aberd	NJ6661	57°38·5′	2°33·7′W	X	29
Paddocklaw	N Ayr	NS3740	55°37·8′	4°34·9′W	X	70
Paddock Mire	Durham	NZ1523	54°36·4′	1°45·6′W	X	92
Paddockmuir Wood	Pth & Kin	NO2120	56°22·2′	3°16·3′W	F	53,58
Paddock's Cross	Dorset	SY4297	50°46·4′	2°49·0′W	X	193
Paddocks Fm, The	Leic	SP6795	52°33·2′	1°0·3′W	FM	141
Paddock Slack	Scot Bord	NT3128	55°32·7′	3°5·2′W	X	73
Paddocks, The	Ches	SJ5174	53°15·9′	2°43·7′W	X	117
Paddocks, The	Enf	TL3100	51°41·2′	0°5·9′W	X	166
Paddocks, The	Essex	TL5414	51°48·4′	0°14·4′E	X	167
Paddocks, The	Kent	TR0639	51°7·0′	0°57·0′E	X	179,189
Paddocks, The	Lincs	TA1410	53°34·7′	0°16·3′W	X	113
Paddocks,The	Powys	SO2140	52°3·4′	3°8·7′W	X	148,161
Paddocks, The	V of Glam	SS9377	51°29·1′	3°32·1′W	X	170
Paddock, The	Glos	SO6600	51°42·1′	2°29·1′W	X	162
Paddock Wood	Durham	NZ0422	54°35·8′	1°55·9′W	F	92
Paddock Wood	Kent	TQ6744	51°10·5′	0°23·7′E	T	188
Paddock Wood	W Susx	SU8618	50°57·5′	0°46·1′W	F	197
Paddock Wray	Cumbr	NY1801	54°24·1′	3°15·4′W	X	89,90
Paddolgreen	Shrops	SJ5032	52°53·2′	2°44·2′W	T	126
Paddon	Devon	SS3509	50°51·7′	4°20·3′W	X	190
Paddon	Devon	SS4411	50°52·9′	4°12·7′W	X	190
Pademoor	N Lincs	SE8014	53°37·2′	0°47·0′W	X	112
Pad End Fm	Lancs	SD4638	53°50·4′	2°48·8′W	FM	102
Padeswood	Flint	SJ2762	53°9·3′	3°5·1′W	X	117
Padeswood Hall	Flint	SJ2962	53°9·3′	3°3·3′W	X	117
Padfield	Derby	SK0296	53°27·9′	1°57·8′W	T	110
Padgate	Warr	SJ6390	53°24·6′	2°33·0′W	T	109
Padgham	E Susx	TQ8025	51°0·0′	0°34·3′E	X	188,199
Padgham Down Fm	E Susx	TQ6517	50°56·0′	0°21·3′E	FM	199
Padham's Green	Essex	TQ6497	51°39·1′	0°22·6′E	T	167,177
Padiham	Lancs	SD7933	53°47·8′	2°18·7′W	T	103
Padiham Heights	Lancs	SD7836	53°49·4′	2°19·6′W	X	103
Padley Common	Devon	SX6987	50°40·3′	3°50·9′W	X	191
Padleywater	Suff	TM3751	52°6·6′	1°28·1′E	X	156
Padley Wood	Derby	SK4061	53°8·9′	1°23·7′W	F	120
Padleywood Fm	Derby	SK4161	53°8·9′	1°22·8′W	FM	120
Padmoor Fm	Lincs	SK8586	53°22·1′	0°42·9′W	FM	112,121
Padnal Fen	Cambs	TL5785	52°26·7′	0°19·0′E	X	143
Padnal Fen	Cambs	TL5883	52°25·6′	0°19·8′E	X	143
Padney	Cambs	TL5473	52°20·2′	0°16·0′E	X	154
Padneyhill Fm	Cambs	TL5574	52°20·8′	0°16·9′E	FM	143
Padnoller Ho	Somer	ST2239	51°8·9′	3°6·5′W	X	182
Padog	Conwy	SH8451	53°2·9′	3°43·4′W	T	116
Padon Hill	Northum	NY8192	55°13·6′	2°17·5′W	H	80
Padside	N Yks	SE1260	54°2·4′	1°48·6′W	X	99
Padside	N Yks	SE1659	54°1·8′	1°44·9′W	T	104
Padside Green	N Yks	SE1659	54°1·8′	1°44·9′W	T	104
Padside Hall	N Yks	SE1460	54°2·4′	1°46·8′W	X	99
Padson	Devon	SX5697	50°45·5′	4°2·1′W	T	191
Padstow	Corn	SW9175	50°32·5′	4°56·6′W	T	200
Padstow Bay	Corn	SW9279	50°34·7′	4°55·9′W	W	200
Pads Wood	W Susx	SU7816	50°56·5′	0°53·0′W	F	197
Paduff Burn	N Ayr	NS2956	55°46·3′	4°43·1′W	W	63
Padworth	W Berks	SU6266	51°23·6′	1°6·1′W	T	175
Padworth Common	W Berks	SU6264	51°22·5′	1°6·2′W	T	175
Padworth Ho	W Berks	SU6166	51°23·6′	1°7·0′W	X	175
Paganhill	Glos	SO8405	51°44·8′	2°13·5′W	T	162
Pagans Hill	Bath & NE Somer	ST5562	51°21·6′	2°38·4′W	X	172,182
Page Bank	Durham	NZ2335	54°42·8′	1°38·2′W	T	93
Page Bank Fm	Cumbr	SD2468	54°6·4′	3°9·3′W	FM	96
Page Croft	Northum	NY8465	54°59·0′	2°14·6′W	X	86,87
Page Fold	Lancs	SD7143	53°53·2′	2°26·1′W	X	103
Page Hill	Bucks	SP7034	52°0·2′	0°58·4′W	X	152,165
Pagehurst	Kent	TQ7743	51°9·8′	0°32·3′E	X	188
Page Moss	Know	SJ4291	53°25·0′	2°52·0′W	T	108
Pages	Lancs	SD7052	53°58·0′	2°27·0′W	X	103
Page's Fm	Essex	TL6627	51°55·2′	0°25·2′E	FM	167
Pages Fm	E Susx	TQ5727	51°1·5′	0°14·7′E	FM	188,199
Page's Fm	Norf	TG0727	52°48·3′	1°4·7′E	FM	133
Pages Fm	Oxon	SU7187	51°34·9′	0°58·1′W	FM	175
Page's Green	Suff	TM1465	52°14·7′	1°8·5′E	T	156
Pages Lodge Fm	Northnts	SP6177	52°23·5′	1°5·8′W	FM	140
Page's Place	Norf	TF8902	52°35·2′	0°47·8′E	X	144
Page's Wood	Ches	SJ5961	53°8·9′	2°36·4′W	F	117
Pagham	W Susx	SZ8897	50°46·2′	0°44·7′W	T	197
Pagham Fm	I of W	SZ5184	50°39·4′	1°16·3′W	FM	196
Pagham Harbour (Nature Reserve)	W Susx	SZ8796	50°45·6′	0°45·6′W	W	197
Pagham Rife	W Susx	SZ8899	50°47·3′	0°44·7′W	W	197
Pagie Hill	S Lanak	NS8428	55°32·2′	3°49·9′W	H	71,72
Paglesham Churchend	Essex	TQ9293	51°36·4′	0°46·8′E	T	178
Paglesham Creek	Essex	TQ9394	51°36·9′	0°47·7′E	W	168,178
Paglesham Eastend	Essex	TQ9492	51°35·8′	0°48·5′E	T	178
Paglesham Pool	Essex	TQ9493	51°36·4′	0°48·5′E	W	178
Paglesham Reach	Essex	TQ9491	51°35·3′	0°48·4′E	W	178
Paible	N Eil	NF7368	57°35·3′	7°27·9′W	X	18
Paible	N Eil	NG0399	57°53·2′	7°0·2′W	X	18
Paiblesgarry	N Eil	NF7368	57°35·3′	7°27·9′W	X	18
Paidland Vird	Shetld	HU3184	60°32·6′	1°25·6′W	X	1,3
Paignton	Torbay	SX8960	50°26·0′	3°33·4′W	T	202
Pailton	Warw	SP4781	52°25·7′	1°18·1′W	T	140
Pailton Fields Fm	Warw	SP4782	52°26·3′	1°18·1′W	FM	140
Pailton Ho	Warw	SP4682	52°26·3′	1°19·0′W	X	140
Pailton Pastures	Warw	SP4882	52°26·3′	1°17·2′W	X	140
Paine's Corner	E Susx	TQ6223	50°59·5′	0°18·9′E	X	199
Paine's Manor	Essex	TL7944	52°4·2′	0°37·1′E	X	155
Paine's Wood	W Susx	SU9907	50°51·5′	0°35·2′W	F	197
Paington & Dartmouth Rly	Devon	SX8753	50°22·2′	3°35·0′W	X	202
Pain Hill	Lancs	SD6952	53°58·0′	2°27·9′W	X	103
Painley Fm	Lancs	SD8450	53°57·0′	2°14·2′W	FM	103
Painleyhill	Staffs	SK0333	52°53·9′	1°56·9′W	T	128
Pains Br	Wilts	SU1661	51°21·1′	1°45·8′W	X	173
Painsbrook	Shrops	SJ5321	52°47·3′	2°41·4′W	X	126
Painscastle	Powys	SO1646	52°6·6′	3°13·2′W	T	148
Painsdale Burn	Northum	NY6864	54°58·4′	2°29·6′W	W	86,87
Painsend Fm	Bucks	SP9009	51°46·6′	0°41·3′W	FM	165
Painsford	Devon	SX8056	50°23·7′	3°40·9′W	X	202
Painshawfield	Northum	NZ0660	54°56·3′	1°54·0′W	T	87
Pains Hill	Suff	TM1159	52°11·6′	1°5·6′E	X	155
Pains Hill	Surrey	TQ0960	51°19·9′	0°25·7′W	X	176,187
Pains Hill	Surrey	TQ4151	51°14·7′	0°1·6′E	T	187
Painshill Fm	Hants	SU2825	51°1·7′	1°35·7′W	FM	184
Painshill Fm	Surrey	TQ0238	51°8·2′	0°32·1′W	FM	186
Painslack Fm	E Yorks	SE9057	54°0·3′	0°37·2′W	FM	106
Pains Rock	Pemb	SM7110	51°44·8′	5°18·7′W	X	157
Painsthorpe	E Yorks	SE8158	54°0·9′	0°45·4′W	T	106
Painsthorpe Field	E Yorks	SE8158	54°0·9′	0°45·4′W	X	106
Painsthorpe Wold Fm	E Yorks	SE8258	54°0·9′	0°44·5′W	FM	106
Painswhin Fm	Norf	TF8526	52°48·2′	0°45·1′E	FM	132
Painswick	Glos	SO8609	51°47·0′	2°11·8′W	T	162
Painswick Hill	Glos	SO8612	51°48·6′	2°11·8′W	H	162
Painswick Ho	Glos	SO8610	51°47·5′	2°11·8′W	X	162
Painswick Lodge	Glos	SO8810	51°47·5′	2°10·0′W	A	162
Painswick Valley	Glos	SO8507	51°45·9′	2°12·6′W	X	162
Painter's Forstal	Kent	TQ9958	51°17·4′	0°51·6′E	T	178
Painter's Green	Herts	TL2718	51°51·0′	0°9·0′W	T	166
Painters Green	Wrex	SJ5040	52°57·5′	2°44·3′W	T	117
Painters Way Fm	Derby	SK2460	53°8·4′	1°38·1′W	FM	119
Painter Wood Fm	Lancs	SD7335	53°48·9′	2°24·2′W	FM	103
Painthorpe	Wakf	SE3115	53°38·1′	1°31·5′W	T	110,111
Paintmoor	Somer	ST3409	50°52·8′	2°55·9′W	T	193
Pàirc Dhubh	Arg & Bt	NR3365	55°48·5′	6°15·2′W	X	60,61
Pàirce nan Each	Arg & Bt	NR4864	55°48·5′	6°0·9′W	X	60,61
Pairc Gharbh	Arg & Bt	NR4097	56°6·0′	6°10·4′W	X	61
Pairc Mhor	Arg & Bt	NR3668	55°50·2′	6°12·6′W	X	60,61
Pairc nan Each	Arg & Bt	NR4554	55°43·0′	6°3·2′W	X	60
Pairc or Park	N Eil	NB3112	58°1·2′	6°32·9′W	X	13,14
Pairc Shiaboist	N Eil	NB2646	58°19·3′	6°40·3′W	T	8
Pairney	Pth & Kin	NN9713	56°18·2′	3°39·4′W	X	58
Pairney Burn	Pth & Kin	NN9810	56°16·5′	3°38·4′W	W	58
Paise, The	Northum	NY8861	54°56·9′	2°10·8′W	X	87
Paisley	Renf	NS4863	55°50·4′	4°25·2′W	T	64
Paisley Mead	Devon	SX5176	50°34·1′	4°5·9′W	X	191,201
Pait Forest	Highld	NH1035	57°22·2′	5°9·1′W	F	25
Paithnick	Moray	NJ4753	57°34·1′	2°52·7′W	X	28,29
Pait Lodge	Highld	NH1239	57°24·4′	5°7·3′W	X	25
Paits Hill	Scot Bord	NT7467	55°54·0′	2°24·5′W	X	67
Paize	Corn	SS2107	50°50·3′	4°32·2′W	X	190
Paize	Devon	SS6200	50°47·2′	3°57·1′W	X	191
Pakefield	Suff	TM5289	52°26·7′	1°42·9′E	T	156
Pakefield	Suff	TM5390	52°27·2′	1°43·8′E	T	134
Pakefield Cliffs	Suff	TM5389	52°26·6′	1°43·8′E	X	156
Pakefield Hall	Suff	TM5388	52°26·1′	1°43·7′E	X	156
Pakenham	Suff	TL9267	52°16·3′	0°49·2′E	T	155
Pakenham Fen	Suff	TL9368	52°16·8′	0°50·2′E	X	155
Pakenham Manor	Suff	TL9267	52°16·3′	0°49·2′E	X	155
Pakenham Wood	Suff	TL9367	52°16·3′	0°50·1′E	F	155
Pakes	Essex	TL6831	51°57·4′	0°27·1′E	X	167
Pakington Fm	Worcs	SO8665	52°17·2′	2°11·9′W	FM	150
Palace	N Lanak	NS7367	55°53·0′	4°1·4′W	X	64
Palace	Scot Bord	NT6724	55°30·8′	2°30·9′W	X	74
Palacecraig	N Lanak	NS7563	55°50·9′	3°59·4′W	X	64
Palacefields	Halton	SJ5480	53°19·1′	2°41·0′W	T	108
Palace Fm	Aberd	NJ7961	57°38·6′	2°20·6′W	FM	29,30
Palace Hill	Leic	SK6903	52°37·5′	0°58·4′W	X	141
Palacehill	Scot Bord	NT6026	55°31·8′	2°37·6′W	X	74
Palace Ho	Hants	SU3802	50°49·2′	1°27·2′W	X	196
Palace How	Cumbr	NY1027	54°38·1′	3°23·2′W	X	89
Palace Land Fm	W Susx	TQ1220	50°58·3′	0°23·9′W	FM	198
Palace of Spynie	Moray	NJ2365	57°40·4′	3°17·0′W	A	28
Palace Pier	Bri & Hov	TQ3103	50°48·9′	0°8·0′W	X	198
Palacerigg Country Park	N Lanak	NS7873	55°56·3′	3°56·8′W	X	64
Palace, The	Pemb	SS0898	51°39·1′	4°46·1′W	A	158
Palace, The	York	SE5947	53°55·2′	1°5·7′W	A	105
Palaceyard Wood	Beds	TL1354	52°10·6′	0°20·4′W	F	153
Pal a' Chaitainich	N Eil	HW6230	59°5·7′	6°8·8′W	X	8
Pal a' Chléirich	N Eil	HW8133	59°7·9′	5°49·2′W	X	8
Paldy Fair	Aberd	NO7281	56°55·4′	2°27·1′W	X	45
Pale	Ches	SJ8673	53°15·5′	2°12·2′W	X	118
Pale Flatts Fm	Staffs	SK0737	52°56·1′	1°53·3′W	FM	128
Pale Fm	Lancs	SD6241	53°52·1′	2°34·3′W	FM	102,103
Palegate Fm	Lancs	SD5539	53°51·0′	2°40·6′W	FM	102
Palegates Fm	Essex	TL5627	51°55·4′	0°16·5′E	FM	167
Pale Green	Essex	TL6542	52°3·3′	0°24·8′E	T	154
Pale Heights	Ches	SJ5469	53°13·2′	2°40·9′W	H	117
Pale (Hotel)	Gwyn	SH9836	52°54·9′	3°30·6′W	X	125
Palehouse Common	E Susx	TQ4918	50°56·8′	0°7·7′E	T	199
Palelane Fm	Hants	SU7855	51°17·6′	0°52·5′W	FM	175,186
Pale Park	Kent	TQ6969	51°23·9′	0°26·2′E	X	177,178
Palerow Fm	Derby	SK3151	53°3·6′	1°31·8′W	FM	119
Pales, The	Powys	SO1364	52°16·3′	3°16·1′W	X	148
Palestine	Hants	SU2640	51°9·7′	1°37·3′W	T	184
Paley Fm	Kent	TQ7740	51°8·1′	0°32·2′E	FM	188
Paley Street	Win & Maid	SU8676	51°28·8′	0°45·3′W	T	175
Palfern Burn	D & G	NX5172	55°1·5′	4°19·4′W	W	77
Palfrey	Wals	SP0197	52°34·5′	1°58·7′W	T	139
Palfrey Fm	W Susx	SU9725	51°1·2′	0°36·6′W	FM	186,197
Palfrey's Barton	Devon	SS9618	50°57·4′	3°28·5′W	X	181
Palgowan	D & G	NX3783	55°7·1′	4°32·9′W	X	77
Palgrave	Suff	TM1178	52°21·8′	1°6·3′E	T	144
Palgrave Fm	Suff	TM0862	52°13·2′	1°3·1′E	FM	155
Palgrave Hall	Norf	TF8311	52°40·2′	0°42·8′E	X	132
Palladian Br	Bucks	SP6837	52°1·9′	1°0·1′W	X	152
Pallaflat	Cumbr	NX9912	54°29·8′	3°33·2′W	T	89
Palla Fm	V of Glam	ST0877	51°29·3′	3°19·1′W	FM	170
Pallance Fm	I of W	SZ4893	50°44·3′	1°18·8′W	FM	196
Pallancegate	I of W	SZ4792	50°43·8′	1°19·7′W	X	196
Pallastreet	Devon	SX3780	50°36·1′	4°17·8′W	X	201
Pallathorpe Fm	N Yks	SE5142	53°52·5′	1°13·0′W	FM	105
Palle Fm	Pemb	SN1440	52°1·9′	4°42·3′W	FM	145
Pallet Crag Ho	Durham	NZ0122	54°35·8′	1°58·6′W	X	92
Pallet Hill	Cumbr	NY4730	54°40·2′	2°48·9′W	X	90
Pallet Hill	N Yks	SE4786	54°16·3′	1°16·3′W	X	100
Pallet Stone Ho	Durham	NZ0322	54°35·8′	1°56·8′W	X	92
Palleys Crags	N Yks	SE1461	54°2·9′	1°46·8′W	X	99
Palliard	Cumbr	NY8613	54°31·0′	2°12·6′W	X	91,92

Palling Burn	D & G	NY3078	55°5·7'	3°5·4'W	W	85
Pallingham Manor Fm	W Susx	TQ0422	50°59·5'	0°30·7'W	FM	197
Pallingham Quay Fm	W Susx	TQ0321	50°59·0'	0°31·6'W	FM	197
Pallinghurst Fm	Surrey	TQ0534	51°6·0'	0°29·6'W	FM	187
Pallington	Dorset	SY7891	50°43·3'	2°18·3'W	T	194
Pallington Heath	Dorset	SY7991	50°43·3'	2°17·5'W	X	194
Pallinsburn	Northum	NT9138	55°38·4'	2°8·1'W	X	74,75
Pallinsburn Ho	Northum	NT8939	55°38·9'	2°10·1'W	X	74
Pallion	Sund	NZ3757	54°54·6'	1°24·9'W	T	88
Pallister	Midd	NZ5119	54°34·1'	1°12·2'W	T	93
Pall Mall	Gwyn	SH5901	52°35·6'	4°4·5'W	X	135
Pallotti Hall	Ches	SJ8671	53°14·4'	2°12·2'W	X	118
Palmallet	D & G	NX4742	54°45·2'	4°22·2'W	X	83
Palmallet Point	D & G	NX4842	54°45·3'	4°21·3'W	X	83
Palmarsh	Kent	TR1333	51°3·6'	1°2·8'E	T	179,189
Palm Bay	Kent	TR3771	51°23·5'	1°24·8'E	W	179
Palmer Hill	Cumbr	NY5868	55°0·5'	2°39·0'W	X	86
Palmer Moor	Derby	SK1333	52°53·9'	1°48·0'W	T	128
Palmer Mount	S Ayr	NS3735	55°35·1'	4°34·7'W	X	70
Palmers	Corn	SX1077	50°33·9'	4°40·6'W	X	200
Palmers	Devon	SS9314	50°55·2'	3°31·0'W	X	181
Palmers	Hants	SU7928	51°3·0'	0°52·0'W	X	186,197
Palmer's Ball	Hants	SU7830	51°4·1'	0°52·8'W	X	186
Palmersbridge	Corn	SX1977	50°34·1'	4°33·0'W	T	201
Palmer's Brook	I of W	SZ5292	50°43·7'	1°15·4'W	W	196
Palmerscross	Moray	NJ2061	57°38·2'	3°19·9'W	X	28
Palmers Cross	Surrey	TQ0240	51°9·2'	0°32·1'W	T	186
Palmers Cross	Wolv	SJ8801	52°36·6'	2°10·2'W	T	127,139
Palmer's End	Worcs	SO8231	51°58·9'	2°15·3'W	X	150
Palmer's Flat	Glos	SO5809	51°46·9'	2°36·1'W	T	162
Palmers Flat	Heref	SO6320	51°52·9'	2°31·9'W	X	162
Palmer's Fm	Devon	ST1513	50°54·8'	3°12·2'W	FM	181,193
Palmer's Fm	Essex	TL8624	51°53·2'	0°42·6'E	FM	168
Palmer's Fm	Essex	TL9219	51°50·4'	0°47·6'E	FM	168
Palmer's Fm	Essex	TQ6096	51°37·6'	0°19·1'E	FM	167,177
Palmers Fm	Kent	TQ5340	51°8·6'	0°11·6'E	FM	188
Palmers Fm	Kent	TQ6038	51°7·4'	0°17·6'E	FM	188
Palmers Fm	Suff	TL9154	52°9·3'	0°47·9'E	FM	155
Palmer's Fm	W Susx	TQ1024	51°0·5'	0°25·5'W	FM	198
Palmers Green	Enf	TQ3093	51°37·5'	0°6·9'W	T	176,177
Palmer's Green	Kent	TQ6841	51°8·8'	0°24·5'E	T	188
Palmers Heath	Suff	TL7484	52°25·8'	0°34·0'E	X	143
Palmer's Hill Ho	Hants	SU4761	51°21·0'	1°19·1'W	X	174
Palmerslake Fm	Pemb	SN0900	51°40·2'	4°45·3'W	FM	158
Palmer's Shrubs	Beds	SP9831	51°58·4'	0°34·0'W	F	165
Palmerstown	V of Glam	ST1369	51°25·0'	3°14·7'W	T	171
Palmersville	N Tyne	NZ2970	55°1·7'	1°32·4'W	T	88
Palmers Wood	Beds	TL1244	52°5·2'	0°21·5'W	F	153
Palm Ho	Rich	TQ1876	51°28·5'	0°17·7'W	X	176
Palmire	Shetld	HU2778	60°29·4'	1°30·0'W	X	3
Palm Loch	Highld	NC7041	58°20·6'	4°12·8'W	W	10
Palms Hall Fm	N Yks	NZ3600	54°23·9'	1°26·3'W	FM	93
Palms Hill	Shrops	SJ5227	52°50·5'	2°42·4'W	X	126
Palmstead	Kent	TR1647	51°11·1'	1°5·8'E	T	179,189
Palm Strothers	Northum	NY9557	54°54·7'	2°4·3'W	X	87
Palmullan Burn	S Ayr	NS3600	55°16·3'	4°34·5'W	W	77
Palnackie	D & G	NX8256	54°53·2'	3°50·0'W	T	84
Palnure	D & G	NX4563	54°56·5'	4°24·8'W	X	83
Palnure Burn	D & G	NX4666	54°58·1'	4°23·9'W	W	83
Palnure Burn	D & G	NX5072	55°1·4'	4°20·4'W	W	77
Palstone	Devon	SX7060	50°25·8'	3°49·4'W	X	202
Palterton	Derby	SK4768	53°12·7'	1°17·4'W	T	120
Paltry Fm	Suff	TL9069	52°17·4'	0°47·6'E	FM	155
Pamber End	Hants	SU6158	51°19·3'	1°7·1'W	T	175
Pamber Fm	Hants	SU6258	51°19·3'	1°6·2'W	FM	175
Pamber Forest	Hants	SU6161	51°20·9'	1°7·1'W	F	175
Pamber Green	Hants	SU6059	51°19·8'	1°7·9'W	T	175
Pamber Heath	Hants	SU6162	51°21·5'	1°7·0'W	T	175
Pamflete Ho	Devon	SX6148	50°19·2'	3°56·8'W	X	202
Pamington	Glos	SO9433	52°0·0'	2°4·8'W	T	150
Pamos Fm	Devon	ST2110	50°53·3'	3°7·0'W	FM	192,193
Pampard Kennels	Herts	TL0312	51°48·1'	0°30·0'W	X	166
Pamperdale Moor	N Yks	SE4798	54°22·8'	1°16·2'W	X	100
Pamphill	Dorset	ST9900	50°48·2'	2°0·5'W	T	195
Pamphillions	Essex	TL5535	51°59·7'	0°15·9'E	X	154
Pamphry	Angus	NO6452	56°39·8'	2°34·8'W	X	54
Pampisford	Cambs	TL4948	52°6·8'	0°11·0'E	T	154
Pan	I of W	SZ5088	50°41·6'	1°17·1'W	T	196
Pan	Orkney	ND3794	58°50·0'	3°5·0'W	X	7
Panborough	Somer	ST4745	51°12·3'	2°45·1'W	T	182
Panborough Moor	Somer	ST4746	51°12·9'	2°45·1'W	X	182
Panbreck Burn	S Lanak	NS7422	55°28·8'	3°59·2'W	W	71
Panbreck Hill	E Ayr	NS7222	55°28·8'	4°1·1'W	X	71
Panbride	Angus	NO5735	56°30·6'	2°41·5'W	T	54
Panbride Ho	Angus	NO5735	56°30·6'	2°41·5'W	X	54
Pan Burn	Durham	NZ1343	54°47·1'	1°47·4'W	W	88
Pancakehill	Glos	SP0611	51°48·1'	1°54·4'W	T	163
Pancake Stone	Brad	SE1346	53°54·8'	1°47·7'W	A	104
Pan Castle (Motte & Bailey)	Shrops	SJ5240	52°57·6'	2°42·5'W	A	117
Pancrasweek	Devon	SS2905	50°49·4'	4°25·3'W	T	190
Pancross	V of Glam	ST0469	51°25·0'	3°22·4'W	T	170
Pandewen	Angus	NO4184	56°56·9'	2°57·7'W	X	44
Pandora Sand	Norf	TF5931	52°51·4'	0°22·1'E	X	131
Pandown Fm	Wilts	ST8868	51°24·9'	2°10·0'W	FM	173
Pandy	Caer	ST2288	51°35·4'	3°7·2'W	X	171
Pandy	Cered	SN4860	52°13·3'	4°13·1'W	X	146
Pandy	Conwy	SH9566	53°11·1'	3°33·9'W	X	116
Pandy	Conwy	SJ0264	53°10·1'	3°27·6'W	X	116
Pandy	Gwyn	SH2832	52°51·7'	4°32·9'W	X	123
Pandy	Gwyn	SH6202	52°36·1'	4°1·9'W	T	135
Pandy	Gwyn	SH7217	52°44·4'	3°53·4'W	T	124
Pandy	Gwyn	SH8729	52°51·0'	3°40·3'W	T	124,125
Pandy	I of Angl	SH4185	53°20·5'	4°22·9'W	X	114
Pandy	Monm	SO3322	51°53·8'	2°58·0'W	T	161
Pandy	Powys	SH9004	52°37·6'	3°37·1'W	T	136
Pandy	Wrex	SJ1935	52°54·6'	3°11·9'W	T	125
Pandy	Wrex	SJ4243	52°59·1'	2°51·4'W	T	117
Pandy-bâch	Gwyn	SH7319	52°45·5'	3°52·5'W	X	124
Pandy Cott	Denb	SJ1171	53°14·0'	3°19·6'W	X	116
Pandy'r Capel	Denb	SJ0850	53°2·6'	3°21·9'W	T	116
Pandy Treban	I of Angl	SH3677	53°16·1'	4°27·1'W	X	114
Pandy Tudur	Conwy	SH8564	53°9·9'	3°42·8'W	T	116
Pandy Uchaf	Conwy	SH8448	53°1·2'	3°43·4'W	X	116
Panfield	Essex	TL7325	51°54·0'	0°31·3'E	T	167
Panford Beck	Norf	TF9620	52°44·7'	0°54·6'E	W	132
Pangbourne	W Berks	SU6376	51°29·0'	1°5·2'W	T	175
Pangbourne College	W Berks	SU6175	51°28·5'	1°6·9'W	X	175
Pangdean Fm	W Susx	TQ2911	50°53·3'	0°9·6'W	FM	198
Pangfield Fm	W Berks	SU5671	51°26·3'	1°11·3'W	FM	174
Pangkor Ho	Devon	SS5204	50°49·2'	4°5·7'W	X	191
Panhall	Fife	NT3092	56°7·2'	3°7·1'W	T	59
Pan Hope	Orkney	ND3794	58°50·0'	3°5·0'W	W	7
Pankridge Fm	Bucks	SP8701	51°42·3'	0°44·1'W	FM	165
Panks Bridge	Heref	SO6248	52°8·0'	2°32·9'W	T	149
Pank's Fm	Peterb	TF2106	52°38·5'	0°12·3'W	FM	142
Panlands	D & G	NY0989	55°11·5'	3°25·3'W	X	78
Panlathy	Angus	NO5738	56°32·2'	2°41·5'W	X	54
Panlathy Mill	Angus	NO5637	56°31·6'	2°42·5'W	X	54
Panmure Gardens	Angus	NO5437	56°31·6'	2°44·4'W	X	54
Panmure Testimonial	Angus	NO5137	56°31·6'	2°47·3'W	X	54
Pannal	N Yks	SE3051	53°57·5'	1°32·2'W	T	104
Pannal Ash	N Yks	SE2952	53°58·0'	1°33·1'W	T	104
Pannanich Hill	Aberd	NO3994	57°2·2'	2°59·9'W	H	37,44
Pannel Fm	E Susx	TQ8814	50°53·9'	0°40·8'E	FM	199
Pannel Fm	E Susx	TQ8815	50°54·5'	0°40·8'E	FM	189,199
Pannell Fm	Renf	NS4064	55°50·8'	4°32·9'W	FM	64
Pannell's Ash	Essex	TL7944	52°4·2'	0°37·1'E	X	155
Pannells Ash Fm	Essex	TL8036	51°59·8'	0°37·7'E	FM	155
Pannelridge Wood	E Susx	TQ6818	50°56·4'	0°23·9'E	F	199
Pannel's Ash	Essex	TL7542	52°3·1'	0°33·5'E	T	155
Pannel Sewer	E Susx	TQ8815	50°54·5'	0°40·8'E	W	189,199
Pannington Hall	Suff	TM1440	52°1·2'	1°7·5'E	X	169
Panope	Cumbr	NY0501	54°24·0'	3°27·4'W	X	89
Panorama Walk	Gwyn	SH6216	52°43·7'	4°2·2'W	X	124
Pan Point	Northum	NU2704	55°20·0'	1°34·0'W	X	81
Panpudding Hill	Shrops	SO7192	52°31·7'	2°25·2'W	A	138
Panpunton	Powys	SO2872	52°20·7'	3°3·0'W	T	137,148
Panpunton Hill	Shrops	SO2873	52°21·3'	3°3·0'W	H	137,148
Pan Rocks	S Ayr	NS3131	55°32·9'	4°40·3'W	X	70
Pans Goat	Fife	NO5301	56°12·2'	2°45·0'W	X	59
Panshanger	Herts	TL2513	51°48·3'	0°10·8'W	T	166
Panshanger Aerodrome	Herts	TL2612	51°47·8'	0°10·0'W	X	166
Panshield	Northum	NZ0954	54°53·1'	1°51·2'W	X	88
Pans Hill	Bucks	SP6114	51°49·5'	1°6·5'W	X	164,165
Pans Hill	Pth & Kin	NO1821	56°22·7'	3°19·2'W	H	53,58
Panshill Fms	Bucks	SP6015	51°50·1'	1°7·4'W	FM	164,165
Pansington Fm	Worcs	SO8270	52°19·9'	2°15·5'W	FM	138
Panson Wood	Devon	SX3693	50°43·0'	4°19·0'W	F	190
Pans, The	Fife	NO6006	56°14·9'	2°38·3'W	X	59
Panstones Fm	Lancs	SD6637	53°49·9'	2°30·6'W	FM	103
Pant	Carm	SN4702	51°42·0'	4°12·5'W	X	159
Pant	Cered	SN6656	52°11·4'	3°57·2'W	X	146
Pant	Conwy	SH8275	53°15·8'	3°45·7'W	X	116
Pant	Denb	SJ2052	53°3·8'	3°11·2'W	T	117
Pant,	E Ayr	NS4624	55°29·4'	4°25·8'W	X	70
Pant	Flint	SJ1374	53°15·6'	3°17·8'W	T	116
Pant	Gwyn	SH2131	52°51·1'	4°39·1'W	T	123
Pant	Gwyn	SH2638	52°54·9'	4°34·9'W	X	123
Pant	Gwyn	SH5803	52°36·6'	4°5·4'W	X	135
Pant	Merth Tyd	SO0608	51°46·0'	3°21·3'W	T	160
Pant	Monm	SO2911	51°47·8'	3°1·4'W	X	161
Pant	Monm	SO3516	51°50·6'	2°56·2'W	X	161
Pant	Powys	SJ0500	52°35·6'	3°23·7'W	T	136
Pant	Powys	SJ1613	52°42·7'	3°14·2'W	X	125
Pant	Powys	SJ1710	52°41·1'	3°13·3'W	X	125
Pant	Powys	SN9789	52°29·6'	3°30·6'W	X	136
Pant	Powys	SO1394	52°32·5'	3°16·6'W	X	136
Pant	Powys	SO1863	52°15·8'	3°11·7'W	X	148
Pant	Shrops	SJ2722	52°47·7'	3°4·6'W	T	126
Pant	Wrex	SJ2945	53°0·1'	3°3·1'W	T	117
Pant	Wrex	SJ3555	53°5·5'	2°57·8'W	T	117
Pant	Wrex	SJ4340	52°57·5'	2°50·5'W	X	117
Pantacridge	Devon	SS9015	50°55·7'	3°33·5'W	X	181
Panta Fm	Monm	ST4999	51°41·5'	2°43·9'W	FM	162
Pant Afon	Gwyn	SH5261	53°7·8'	4°12·3'W	X	114,115
Pantanamlwg	Cered	SN5466	52°16·6'	4°8·0'W	X	135
Pantaquesta	Rho Cyn Taf	ST0480	51°30·9'	3°22·6'W	X	170
Pantasaph	Flint	SJ1675	53°16·2'	3°15·2'W	T	116
Pantau	Carm	SN6422	51°53·0'	3°58·2'W	X	159
Pantau	Powys	SO0633	51°59·5'	3°21·7'W	X	160
Pantau	Powys	SO0846	52°6·5'	3°20·2'W	X	147
Pantau'r Brywyn	Cered	SN7989	52°29·4'	3°46·5'W	X	135
Pantawel	Card	ST1180	51°31·0'	3°16·6'W	X	171
Pant-bach	Cered	SN4049	52°7·1'	4°19·8'W	X	146
Pant Blaenhirwr	Brig	SS9190	51°36·1'	3°34·0'W	X	170
Pant Brook	Monm	SO3512	51°48·4'	2°56·2'W	W	161
Pant Cefn	Cered	SN4357	52°11·6'	4°17·4'W	X	146
Pant Clyd	Gwyn	SH8425	52°48·8'	3°42·9'W	X	124,125
Pantcoy	Cered	SN5650	52°8·0'	4°5·8'W	X	146
Pantcrafog Fawr	Powys	SN8827	51°56·1'	3°37·4'W	X	160
Pantcynghorior	Cered	SN5965	52°16·1'	4°3·6'W	X	135
Pantdafydd	Cered	SN3443	52°3·9'	4°24·9'W	X	145
Pant-Dafydd-gôch	Wrex	SJ2439	52°56·8'	3°7·5'W	X	126
Pantdaniel	Cered	SN2947	52°5·9'	4°29·4'W	X	145
Pant Derw	Cered	SN3756	52°10·9'	4°22·7'W	X	145
Pant-du	Denb	SJ2059	53°7·6'	3°11·3'W	X	117
Pantdu	Nth Pt Talb	SS7791	51°36·5'	3°46·2'W	T	170
Pant-du	Wrex	SJ2539	52°56·8'	3°6·6'W	X	126
Pant-dwfn	Carm	SN2815	51°48·7'	4°29·3'W	X	158
Pante	Carm	SN4123	51°53·2'	4°18·2'W	X	159
Pant Ednyfed	I of Angl	SH3086	53°20·9'	4°32·8'W	X	114
Panteg	Carm	SN3911	51°46·7'	4°19·6'W	X	159
Panteg	Carm	SN4433	51°58·7'	4°15·9'W	X	146
Panteg	Cered	SN3958	52°12·0'	4°21·0'W	X	146
Panteg	Cered	SN4562	52°14·3'	4°15·8'W	T	146
Panteg	Pemb	SM9234	51°58·2'	5°1·3'W	X	157
Panteg	Pemb	SN1516	51°49·0'	4°40·7'W	X	158
Panteg	Powys	SO1729	51°57·4'	3°12·1'W	X	161
Panteg	Torf	ST3199	51°41·4'	2°59·5'W	T	171
Pant Einion Hall	Gwyn	SH6212	52°41·5'	4°2·1'W	X	124
Panteinon	Cered	SN2944	52°4·3'	4°29·3'W	X	145
Pant End	Cumbr	SD5782	54°14·2'	2°39·2'W	X	97
Panters	Wilts	ST9829	51°3·9'	2°1·3'W	X	184
Pantersbridge	Corn	SX1568	50°29·2'	4°36·1'W	T	201
Panteryrod	Cered	SN4360	52°13·2'	4°17·5'W	X	146
Panteth Hill	D & G	NY0771	55°1·7'	3°26·9'W	X	85
Panteurig	Pemb	SM9038	52°0·3'	5°3·2'W	X	157
Pant Fm	Brig	SS8882	51°31·8'	3°36·5'W	FM	170
Pant Fm	Carm	SN2820	51°51·4'	4°29·5'W	FM	145,158
Pant Fm	Flint	SJ2858	53°7·1'	3°4·1'W	FM	117
Pant Fm	Gwyn	SH3125	52°48·0'	4°30·0'W	FM	123
Pant Fm	Powys	SO1465	52°16·8'	3°15·2'W	FM	136,148
Pant Fm	Wrex	SJ2036	52°55·2'	3°11·0'W	FM	126
Pant Fm,The	Monm	SO3918	51°51·7'	2°52·8'W	FM	161
Pant Gilfach-wen	Powys	SN9518	51°51·3'	3°31·1'W	X	160
Pant-glas	Caer	ST1993	51°38·0'	3°9·8'W	X	171
Pantglas	Carm	SN2126	51°54·5'	4°35·7'W	X	145,158
Pantglas	Carm	SN2820	51°51·4'	4°29·5'W	X	145,158
Pantglas	Carm	SN4226	51°54·8'	4°17·4'W	X	146
Pantglas	Carm	SN4736	52°0·3'	4°13·4'W	X	146
Pantglas	Carm	SN5719	51°51·3'	4°4·2'W	X	159
Pantglas	Carm	SN7838	52°1·9'	3°46·3'W	X	146,160
Pantglas	Cered	SN4450	52°7·8'	4°16·4'W	X	146
Pant-glas	Cered	SN6958	52°12·5'	3°54·6'W	X	146
Pant-glas	Conwy	SH9462	53°8·9'	3°34·7'W	X	116
Pant Glas	Denb	SJ0973	53°15·0'	3°21·4'W	X	116
Pant-glas	Flint	SJ1080	53°18·8'	3°20·6'W	X	116
Pant Glas	Flint	SJ1176	53°16·7'	3°19·7'W	X	116
Pant-glas	Flint	SJ2064	53°10·3'	3°11·4'W	X	117
Pant Glâs	Gwyn	SH4747	53°0·2'	4°16·4'W	T	115,123
Pant Glas	Gwyn	SH7529	52°50·9'	3°51·0'W	X	124
Pant-glâs	Monm	SO4804	51°44·2'	2°44·8'W	X	171
Pantglas	Powys	SH9301	52°36·0'	3°34·4'W	X	136
Pantglas	Powys	SJ0417	52°44·8'	3°24·9'W	X	125
Pantglas	Powys	SJ0605	52°38·3'	3°22·9'W	X	125
Pant-glas	Powys	SJ1812	52°42·2'	3°12·4'W	X	125
Pant-glas	Powys	SN7798	52°34·2'	3°48·5'W	X	135
Pant Glas	Powys	SN8659	52°13·3'	3°39·7'W	X	147
Pantglas	Powys	SN9325	51°55·0'	3°33·0'W	X	160
Pant-glas	Powys	SO1855	52°11·5'	3°11·6'W	X	148
Pant-glas	Shrops	SJ2732	52°53·1'	3°4·7'W	T	126
Pantglas	Shrops	SO2489	52°29·9'	3°6·8'W	X	137
Pant-glas	Torf	ST2992	51°37·6'	3°1·2'W	X	171
Pant Glas Fm	Caer	ST1885	51°33·7'	3°10·6'W	FM	171
Pant Glas Hall	Carm	SN5425	51°54·5'	4°7·0'W	X	146
Pant Glas Isaf	Denb	SJ0959	53°7·5'	3°21·2'W	A	116
Pantglas Isaf	Powys	SJ1729	52°51·4'	3°13·6'W	X	125
Pantglas Ucha	Powys	SJ1729	52°51·4'	3°13·6'W	X	125
Pant-glâs-uchaf	Gwyn	SH4747	53°0·2'	4°16·4'W	A	115,123
Pantgwyn	Carm	SN2019	51°50·7'	4°36·4'W	X	158
Pantgwyn	Carm	SN5925	51°54·6'	4°2·6'W	X	146
Pantgwyn	Cered	SN2446	52°5·3'	4°33·7'W	X	145
Pant-gwyn	Cered	SN2750	52°7·5'	4°31·2'W	X	145
Pantgwyn	Cered	SN3852	52°8·8'	4°21·7'W	X	145
Pant-gwyn	Cered	SN4143	52°4·0'	4°18·8'W	X	146
Pantgwyn	Cered	SN4455	52°10·5'	4°16·5'W	X	146
Pantgwyn	Cered	SN6654	52°10·3'	3°57·2'W	X	146
Pant Gwyn	Gwyn	SH2438	52°54·9'	4°36·7'W	X	123
Pant-gwyn	Gwyn	SH5807	52°38·8'	4°5·5'W	X	124
Pant Gwyn	Gwyn	SH8426	52°49·4'	3°42·9'W	X	124,125
Pant-gwyn	Pemb	SM9934	51°58·3'	4°55·2'W	X	157
Pantgwyn	Powys	SN9939	52°2·7'	3°28·0'W	X	160
Pant Gwyn Bach	Flint	SJ1572	53°14·5'	3°16·0'W	X	116
Pant-gwyn Hill	Powys	SN8978	52°23·6'	3°37·5'W	H	135,136,147
Pantgwyn Mawr	Pemb	SN1242	52°2·9'	4°44·1'W	X	145
Pantgwyn-mawr	Pemb	SN2432	51°57·8'	4°33·3'W	X	145
Pant-gwyyn	Powys	SJ0708	52°39·9'	3°22·1'W	X	125
Panther's Lodge	Northnts	SP6366	52°17·5'	1°4·2'W	X	152
Pant Hill	Powys	SO2289	52°29·8'	3°8·5'W	X	137
Panthir	Shrops	SJ2328	52°50·9'	3°8·2'W	X	126
Pant Howel	I of Angl	SH5674	53°14·9'	4°9·1'W	X	114,115
Pant-Howel-Ddu	Nth Pt Talb	SS7594	51°38·1'	3°48·0'W	X	170
Panthowell	Carm	SN2725	51°54·0'	4°30·5'W	X	145,158
Panthurst Fm	Kent	TQ5351	51°14·5'	0°11·9'E	FM	188
Panthwdog	Carm	SN3628	51°55·8'	4°22·7'W	X	145
Pant-Hywel	Carm	SN4801	51°41·5'	4°11·6'W	X	159
Pant-Hywel	Carm	SN7425	51°54·8'	3°49·5'W	X	146,160
Pantiau	Powys	SH9817	52°44·7'	3°30·3'W	X	125
Pantiauau	Carm	SN6034	51°59·4'	4°1·9'W	X	146
Pant Idda	Conwy	SH9275	53°15·9'	3°36·8'W	X	116
Pantile Fm	Essex	TM0017	51°49·2'	0°54·6'E	FM	168
Pantile Fm	Essex	TQ7591	51°35·7'	0°32·0'E	FM	178
Pantinker	Cered	SN2345	52°4·7'	4°34·6'W	X	145
Pantiouar	Cered	SN4127	51°55·4'	4°18·3'W	X	146
Pantirion	Pemb	SN1346	52°5·1'	4°43·4'W	X	145
Pantithel	Pemb	SN1230	51°56·4'	4°43·7'W	X	145
Pant-lasau	Swan	SN6500	51°41·2'	3°56·8'W	X	159
Pantle	Powys	SN9296	52°33·3'	3°35·2'W	X	136
Pantlaethdy	Carm	SN4942	52°3·6'	4°11·8'W	X	146
Pantllan	Carm	SN5016	51°49·6'	4°10·2'W	X	159
Pantllechddu	Carm	SN7841	52°3·5'	3°46·4'W	X	146,147,160
Pantllefrith	Powys	SO0824	51°54·7'	3°19·9'W	X	160
Pantlleinau	Cered	SN5965	52°16·1'	4°3·6'W	X	135
Pant Llin Bach	Conwy	SH8163	53°9·3'	3°46·4'W	X	116
Pant Llin Mawr	Conwy	SH8163	53°9·3'	3°46·4'W	X	116
Pantlludw	Gwyn	SH7301	52°35·8'	3°52·1'W	X	135
Pant-llwyd	Powys	SN8370	52°19·2'	3°42·6'W	X	135,136,147
Pantllwyd	Powys	SO1417	51°50·9'	3°15·4'W	X	161
Pantllwyni	Gwyn	SH8340	52°56·9'	3°44·1'W	X	124,125
Pantllydu	Carm	SN5003	51°42·6'	4°9·9'W	X	159
Pant-maenog	Pemb	SN0831	51°56·9'	4°47·2'W	X	145
Pantmaenog Forest	Pemb	SN0830	51°56·4'	4°47·2'W	F	145
Pantmawr	Card	ST1481	51°31·5'	3°14·0'W	T	171
Pantmawr	Carm	SN6239	52°2·2'	4°0·3'W	X	146
Pantmawr	Cered	SN6878	52°23·3'	3°56·0'W	X	135
Pant-mawr	Gwyn	SH7136	52°54·6'	3°54·7'W	X	124
Pant Mawr	Powys	SJ1218	52°45·4'	3°17·8'W	X	125
Pant-mawr	Powys	SJ1611	52°41·7'	3°14·2'W	X	125
Pant Mawr	Powys	SN8482	52°25·7'	3°42·0'W	T	135,136

Pant Mawr	Powys	SN8914	51°49·1'	3°36·2'W	X	160
Pant-meddyg	Cered	SN4846	52°5·7'	4°12·7'W	X	146
Pantmeinog	Carm	SN7326	51°55·8'	3°50·4'W	X	146,160
Pantmelyn	Carm	SN2726	51°54·6'	4°30·5'W	X	145,158
Pant-Meredith	Carm	SN6925	51°54·7'	3°53·9'W	X	146,160
Pantmoch	Cered	SN4345	52°5·1'	4°17·1'W	X	146
Pant Myharan	Denb	SJ1654	53°4·8'	3°14·8'W	X	116
Pant Nant-fforchog	Carm	SN6918	51°51·0'	3°53·7'W	X	160
Pant-Olwen	Cered	SN4142	52°3·5'	4°18·8'W	X	146
Panton	Lincs	TF1778	53°17·4'	0°14·3'W	T	121
Panton Hall	Lincs	TF1880	53°18·5'	0°13·3'W	X	122
Panton House Fm	Lincs	TF2229	52°50·9'	0°10·9'W	FM	131
Pant-pastynog	Denb	SJ0461	53°8·5'	3°25·7'W	T	116
Pant Perthog	Gwyn	SH7305	52°37·9'	3°52·2'W	H	124
Pantperthog	Gwyn	SH7404	52°37·4'	3°51·3'W	T	135
Pant-Phylip	Gwyn	SH6414	52°42·6'	4°0·4'W	X	124
Pant-poeth Hill	Powys	SN9981	52°25·3'	3°28·7'W	H	136
Pantpurlais	Powys	SO0760	52°14·1'	3°21·3'W	X	147
Pantrhiwddulais	Cered	SN4152	52°8·8'	4°19·0'W	X	146
Pantroity	Carm	SN3528	51°55·8'	4°23·6'W	X	145
Pantruthyn	V of Glam	SS9680	51°30·8'	3°29·5'W	X	170
Pantry Br	Wilts	ST9358	51°19·5'	2°5·6'W	X	173
Pantsaeson	Pemb	SN1344	52°4·0'	4°43·3'W	X	145
Pantscawen	Cered	SN4447	52°6·2'	4°16·3'W	X	146
Pantscythan	Cered	SN3943	52°4·0'	4°20·5'W	X	145
Pantseiri	Cered	SN3048	52°6·5'	4°28·6'W	X	145
Pantside	Caer	ST2197	51°40·2'	3°8·2'W	T	171
Pant-sod	Cered	SN4053	52°9·4'	4°19·9'W	X	146
Pant St Bride's	V of Glam	SS8975	51°28·0'	3°35·5'W	X	170
Pantstreimon	Cered	SN4544	52°4·6'	4°15·3'W	X	146
Pant Sychbant	Rho Cyn Taf	SN9809	51°46·5'	3°28·3'W	X	160
Pant-teg	Carm	SN4613	51°47·9'	4°13·6'W	X	159
Pant-têg	Carm	SN4825	51°54·4'	4°12·2'W	X	146
Pantteg	Cered	SN3744	52°4·5'	4°22·3'W	X	145
Pant-têg	Denb	SJ0241	52°57·7'	3°27·1'W	X	125
Pant-têg	Powys	SN9050	52°8·5'	3°36·1'W	X	147
Pant, The	Monm	SO2821	51°53·2'	3°2·4'W	X	161
Pant,The	Monm	SO4213	51°49·0'	2°50·1'W	X	161
Pant, The	Powys	SO1649	52°8·2'	3°13·2'W	X	148
Pant, The	Shrops	SJ3539	52°56·9'	2°57·6'W	X	126
Pant Tyle Gwyn	Carm	SN7822	51°53·2'	3°46·0'W	X	160
Pantunos	Carm	SN5441	52°3·1'	4°7·4'W	X	146
Pant-y-beili	Powys	SO1521	51°53·1'	3°13·7'W	X	161
Pantybeiliau	Monm	SO2314	51°49·4'	3°6·6'W	X	161
Pantybettws	Cered	SN3047	52°6·0'	4°28·5'W	X	145
Pant-y-Bettws	Flint	SJ2260	53°8·1'	3°9·6'W	X	117
Pantyblodau	Powys	SN9949	52°8·0'	3°28·1'W	X	147
Pant-y-brâd	Rho Cyn Taf	ST0287	51°34·6'	3°24·5'W	X	170
Pant-y-briallu	Powys	SJ1405	52°38·4'	3°15·9'W	X	125
Pant y Brwyn	Powys	SO0072	52°20·5'	3°27·7'W	X	136,147
Pant-y-bryn	Carm	SN6514	51°48·7'	3°57·1'W	X	159
Pantybryn	Carm	SN7539	52°2·4'	3°49·0'W	X	146,160
Pantybryn	Cered	SN4349	52°7·3'	4°17·2'W	X	146
Pant-y-buarth	Flint	SJ2063	53°9·7'	3°11·4'W	X	117
Pant-y-bwch	Powys	SJ2505	52°38·5'	3°6·1'W	X	126
Pant-y-bwla	Cered	SN3144	52°4·4'	4°27·6'W	X	145
Pant-y-cabal	Pemb	SN0327	51°54·6'	4°51·5'W	X	145,157,158
Pant-y-cae	Gwyn	SN6199	52°34·5'	4°2·7'W	X	135
Pantycaragle	Powys	SO1979	52°24·4'	3°11·0'W	X	136,148
Pant-y-carw	Conwy	SH7862	53°8·7'	3°49·0'W	X	115
Pant-y-Caws	Carm	SN1426	51°54·3'	4°41·8'W	T	145,158
Pant-y-cefn	Conwy	SH9462	53°8·9'	3°34·7'W	F	116
Pantycelyn	Carm	SN8235	52°0·3'	3°42·8'W	X	160
Pantycelyn	Powys	SN9941	52°3·7'	3°28·0'W	X	147,160
Pantycelyn Fm	Carm	SN6143	52°4·3'	4°1·3'W	FM	146
Pant-y-Cendy Hall	Carm	SN3423	51°53·1'	4°24·3'W	X	145,159
Pantycerrig	Carm	SN5431	51°57·7'	4°7·1'W	X	146
Pant-y-clyd	Conwy	SH8972	53°14·3'	3°39·4'W	X	116
Pantyclynhir	Cered	SN3856	52°11·0'	4°21·8'W	X	145
Pantycoch	Pemb	SM9133	51°57·6'	5°2·1'W	X	157
Pantycolin	Monm	SO3603	51°43·6'	2°55·2'W	X	171
Pant-y-Colly	Powys	SO0640	52°3·3'	3°21·9'W	X	147,160
Pantycollyn Fm	Monm	SO3716	51°50·6'	2°54·5'W	FM	161
Pant-y-cored	Powys	SO0432	51°58·9'	3°23·5'W	X	160
Pantycornant	Brig	SS9688	51°35·1'	3°29·7'W	X	170
Pant-y-cosyn	Monm	ST4695	51°39·3'	2°46·4'W	X	171
Pant-y-coubal	Carm	SN5333	51°58·8'	4°8·0'W	X	146
Pantycraf	Cered	SN7161	52°14·2'	3°53·0'W	X	146,147
Pantycrai	Powys	SJ0600	52°35·6'	3°22·9'W	X	136
Pant y Creigiau	Powys	SO0516	51°50·3'	3°22·3'W	H	160
Pant-y-crûg	Cered	SN6578	52°23·2'	3°58·6'W	T	135
Pantyddafad	Cered	SN6768	52°17·9'	3°56·6'W	X	135
Pant-y-dderwen	Carm	SN5730	51°57·2'	4°4·5'W	X	146
Pantydderwen	Carm	SN6437	52°1·1'	3°58·5'W	X	146
Pantyddrainan	Rho Cyn Taf	ST0386	51°34·1'	3°23·6'W	X	170
Pant-y-defaid	Cered	SN4344	52°4·6'	4°17·1'W	X	146
Pantyderi	Carm	SN3119	51°50·9'	4°26·8'W	X	159
Pant-y-Deri	Pemb	SN1637	52°0·3'	4°40·5'W	X	145
Pant-y-drain	Powys	SN9176	52°22·5'	3°35·7'W	X	136,147
Pant-y-dulath	Denb	SJ0976	53°16·6'	3°21·5'W	X	116
Pant-y-dwn	Cered	SN6289	52°29·1'	4°1·5'W	X	135
Pantydwr	Carm	SN5806	51°44·3'	4°3·0'W	X	159
Pant-y-dŵr	Powys	SN9874	52°21·5'	3°29·5'W	T	136,147
Pantyfallen	Swan	SN6503	51°42·8'	3°56·9'W	X	159
Pant-y-fedw	Powys	SJ1020	52°46·4'	3°19·6'W	X	125
Pantyfedwen	Cered	SN7565	52°16·4'	3°49·5'W	X	135,147
Pantyfen	Carm	SN4639	52°1·9'	4°14·3'W	X	146
Pant-y-fen	Carm	SN5643	52°4·2'	4°5·7'W	X	146
Pant y Ffald	Brig	SS8792	51°37·2'	3°37·5'W	X	170
Pant-y-ffordd	Denb	SJ1954	53°4·9'	3°12·2'W	X	116
Pantyffordd	Flint	SJ2457	53°6·5'	3°7·7'W	X	117
Pant-y-ffordd	Powys	SN9223	51°53·9'	3°33·8'W	X	160
Pant-y-ffridd	Powys	SJ1502	52°36·8'	3°14·9'W	T	136
Pant-y-ffuon	Flint	SJ1769	53°12·9'	3°14·2'W	X	116
Pantyffynnon	Carm	SN4917	51°50·1'	4°11·1'W	T	159
Pant-y-ffynnon	Carm	SN5829	51°56·7'	4°3·6'W	X	146
Pantyffynnon	Carm	SN6210	51°46·5'	3°59·6'W	T	159
Pantyffynnon	Carm	SN6915	51°49·3'	3°53·7'W	X	160
Pant-y-ffynnon	Cered	SN5049	52°7·4'	4°11·1'W	H	146
Pantyffynnon	Cered	SN6886	52°27·6'	3°56·2'W	X	135

Pantyffynnon	Powys	SJ0019	52°45·8'	3°28·5'W	X	125
Pantyffynnon	Carm	SN1920	51°51·2'	4°37·3'W	X	145,158
Pant-y-fithel	Powys	SO2240	52°3·4'	3°7·9'W	X	148,161
Pant-y-fotty	Conwy	SH8859	53°7·2'	3°40·0'W	X	116
Pant y Gadair	Rho Cyn Taf	SN9812	51°48·1'	3°28·4'W	X	160
Pantygarn	Pemb	SN1338	52°0·8'	4°43·1'W	X	145
Pantygasseg	Torf	ST2599	51°41·3'	3°4·7'W	T	171
Pant-y-gelli	Carm	SN2029	51°56·1'	4°36·7'W	X	145,158
Pantygelli	Monm	SO3018	51°51·6'	3°0·6'W	X	161
Pantygesail	Powys	SN9897	52°33·9'	3°29·9'W	X	136
Pantyglien	Carm	SN4522	51°52·7'	4°14·7'W	X	159
Pantygof	Carm	SN4429	51°56·5'	4°15·8'W	X	146
Pant-y-gof	Flint	SJ2170	53°13·5'	3°10·6'W	X	117
Pantygoida	Monm	SO4116	51°50·6'	2°51·0'W	X	161
Pant-y-Goitre	Monm	SO3408	51°46·2'	2°57·0'W	X	161
Pant-y-griafolen	Conwy	SH9149	53°1·9'	3°37·1'W	X	116
Pantygroes	Carm	SN2121	51°51·8'	4°35·6'W	X	145,158
Pantygroes	Pemb	SN1042	52°2·9'	4°45·9'W	X	145
Pant-y-Gronw	Carm	SN3124	51°53·6'	4°27·0'W	X	145,159
Pantygronw	Cered	SN3150	52°7·6'	4°27·7'W	X	145
Pantygrug	Carm	SN2218	51°50·2'	4°34·6'W	X	158
Pantygrwndy	Pemb	SN1643	52°3·5'	4°40·6'W	X	145
Pant-y-gwair	Cered	SN6067	52°17·2'	4°2·8'W	X	135
Pantygwenith	Cered	SN3343	52°3·9'	4°25·8'W	X	145
Pant-y-gwiail	Cered	SN4953	52°9·5'	4°12·1'W	X	146
Pant-y-gwlanod	Denb	SJ2057	53°6·5'	3°11·3'W	X	117
Pantygwyddel	Pemb	SN2130	51°56·6'	4°35·9'W	X	145
Pantygwyfol	Cered	SN6275	52°21·6'	4°1·2'W	X	135
Pant-y-gynt	Brig	SS9487	51°34·6'	3°31·4'W	X	170
Panty Hill	Powys	SO1383	52°26·5'	3°16·4'W	X	136
Pantylladron	V of Glam	ST0374	51°27·6'	3°23·4'W	X	170
Pant-y-llan	Gwyn	SH6513	52°42·1'	3°59·5'W	X	124
Pant-y-lliwydd Fm	V of Glam	SS9779	51°30·3'	3°28·7'W	FM	170
Pantyllyn	Carm	SN3425	51°54·2'	4°24·4'W	X	145
Pant-y-llyn	Carm	SN6016	51°49·7'	4°1·5'W	X	159
Pant-y-llyn	Denb	SJ0234	52°53·9'	3°27·0'W	X	125
Pant y Llyn	Powys	SO0346	52°6·5'	3°24·6'W	W	147
Pant-y-llyn Hill	Powys	SO0447	52°7·0'	3°23·7'W	H	147
Pant-y-maen	Carm	SN2725	51°54·0'	4°30·5'W	X	145,158
Pant-y-maen	Denb	SH9758	53°6·8'	3°31·9'W	X	116
Pant-y-maen	Powys	SJ1530	52°51·9'	3°15·4'W	X	125
Pantymaes	Powys	SN9126	51°55·6'	3°34·7'W	X	160
Pant-y-mel	Conwy	SJ0047	53°0·9'	3°29·0'W	X	116
Pant-y-milwyr	Powys	SJ0404	52°37·8'	3°24·7'W	X	136
Pantymwyn	Flint	SJ1964	53°10·3'	3°12·3'W	T	116
Pantyneuadd	Gwyn	SH5900	52°35·0'	4°4·5'W	X	135
Pant-y-Phillip	Pemb	SM9433	51°57·7'	4°59·5'W	X	157
Pant-y-pistyll	Carm	SN6347	52°6·5'	3°59·6'W	X	146
Pantypistyll	Carm	SN6733	51°59·0'	3°55·8'W	X	146
Pant-y-pyllau	Brig	SS9282	51°31·8'	3°33·0'W	T	170
Pantypyllau	Powys	SO0548	52°7·6'	3°22·9'W	X	147
Pantyrallad	Cered	SN5675	52°21·5'	4°6·5'W	X	135
Pant Yr Athro	Carm	SN3613	51°47·7'	4°22·3'W	X	159
Pant-yr-awel	Brig	SS9287	51°34·5'	3°33·1'W	T	170
Pant-yr-eglwys	I of Angl	SH2992	53°24·1'	4°33·9'W	X	114
Pantyreos Brook	Newp	ST2690	51°36·5'	3°3·7'W	W	171
Pant-yr-eos Resr	Newp	ST2591	51°37·0'	3°4·6'W	W	171
Pant-yr-esgair	Carm	SN6431	51°57·9'	3°58·4'W	X	146
Pant-yr-haiarn	Conwy	SH8175	53°15·8'	3°46·6'W	X	116
Pantyrhas	Carm	SN2220	51°51·3'	4°34·7'W	X	145,158
Pantyrheddwch	Pemb	SN2533	51°58·3'	4°32·5'W	X	145
Pantyrhedyn	Carm	SN2823	51°53·0'	4°29·6'W	X	145,158
Pant-y-rhedyn	Carm	SN8140	52°3·0'	3°43·7'W	X	147,160
Pant-y-rhedyn	Conwy	SH8466	53°11·0'	3°43·7'W	X	116
Pant-y-rhedynen	Cered	SN3943	52°4·0'	4°20·5'W	X	145
Pantyrhen	Cered	SN4956	52°11·1'	4°12·1'W	X	146
Pantyrhendre	Powys	SO0107	52°39·3'	3°27·4'W	X	125
Pantyrhendy	Cered	SN4356	52°11·0'	4°17·4'W	X	146
Pant-y-rhiw	Powys	SO2015	51°49·9'	3°9·3'W	X	161
Pantyrhogfaen	Cered	SN5666	52°16·6'	4°6·3'W	X	135
Pant yr Holiad	Cered	SN3350	52°7·6'	4°26·0'W	X	145
Pantyrhuad	Carm	SN2311	51°46·4'	4°33·5'W	X	158
Pantyrhufen	Powys	SO0540	52°3·3'	3°21·9'W	X	147,160
Pant yr Hyl	Brig	SS8379	51°30·1'	3°40·8'W	X	170
Pant-yr-ochain	Wrex	SJ3453	53°4·5'	2°58·7'W	X	117
Pantyrodyn	Carm	SN1524	51°53·3'	4°40·9'W	X	145,158
Pantyrodyn	Carm	SN5732	51°58·3'	4°4·5'W	X	146
Pantyrodyn	Carm	SN6116	51°49·8'	4°0·6'W	X	159
Pantyrodyn	Cered	SN3145	52°4·9'	4°27·6'W	X	145
Pantyrodyn	Pemb	SN1235	51°59·1'	4°43·9'W	X	145
Pantyronen	Cered	SN3144	52°4·4'	4°27·6'W	X	145
Pantyronen	Cered	SN4862	52°14·4'	4°13·2'W	X	146
Pant-yr-ych	Conwy	SH7967	53°11·4'	3°48·3'W	X	115
Pantyrynn	Carm	SN5506	51°44·3'	4°5·6'W	X	159
Pant-yr-yrfa	Torf	ST2593	51°38·1'	3°4·6'W	X	171
Pant-y-Sais	Nth Pt Talb	SS7194	51°38·0'	3°51·5'W	X	170
Pantysgallog	Powys	SN9028	51°56·6'	3°35·6'W	X	160
Pantyspydded	Gwyn	SH7204	52°37·4'	3°53·1'W	X	135
Pant y Wacco	Flint	SJ1476	53°16·7'	3°17·0'W	T	116
Pant-y-wal	Powys	SN8414	51°49·0'	3°40·6'W	X	160
Pant y Waun	Powys	SN9816	51°50·2'	3°28·4'W	X	160
Pantywenallt	Powys	SO1120	51°52·5'	3°17·2'W	X	161
Pant y Wern	Rho Cyn Taf	SN9914	51°49·2'	3°27·5'W	X	160
Pant-y-Wheel	Carm	SN7434	51°59·7'	3°49·7'W	X	146,160
Pantywilco	Cered	SN5147	52°6·3'	4°10·1'W	X	146
Pantywrach	Pemb	SM9634	51°58·3'	4°57·8'W	X	157
Pant-y-wynthrew	Powys	SJ1401	52°36·2'	3°15·8'W	X	136
Panty-y-Falog	Powys	SO1888	52°29·3'	3°12·1'W	X	136
Panty-yr-esgair	Powys	SN8784	52°26·8'	3°39·4'W	X	135,136
Panwaun Pen-y-coetgae	Nth Pt Talb	SN9000	51°41·5'	3°35·1'W	X	170
Panwen Garreg-wen	Rho Cyn Taf	SN9600	51°41·6'	3°29·9'W	X	170
Panworth Hall	Norf	TF8905	52°36·8'	0°47·9'E	X	144
Panxworth	Norf	TG3413	52°40·1'	1°28·1'E	T	133,134
Panylau Gwynion	Powys	SH9306	52°38·7'	3°34·5'W	H	125
Papa	Shetld	HU3637	60°7·2'	1°20·6'W	X	4
Papadil Lodge	Highld	NM3692	56°56·9'	6°20·0'W	X	39
Papa Little	Shetld	HU3361	60°20·2'	1°23·6'W	X	2,3
Papana Water	E Loth	NT5868	55°54·4'	2°39·9'W	W	67
Papa Skerry	Shetld	HU3738	60°7·8'	1°19·5'W	X	4
Papa Sound	Orkney	HY4752	59°21·3'	2°55·4'W	W	5

Papa Stronsay	Orkney	HY6629	59°9·1'	2°35·2'W	X	5
Papa Westray	Orkney	HY4952	59°21·3'	2°53·3'W	X	5
Papcastle	Cumbr	NY1031	54°40·2'	3°23·3'W	T	89
Pap Craig	S Lanak	NS9533	55°35·0'	3°39·5'W	X	72
Paper Cave	Arg & Bt	NS1389	56°3·7'	4°59·8'W	X	56
Papercourt Fm	Surrey	TQ0356	51°17·9'	0°31·0'W	FM	186
Paper Hall Fm	Norf	TF6733	52°52·3'	0°29·3'E	FM	132
Paper Hill	Cumbr	NY7438	54°44·4'	2°23·8'W	H	91
Paper Hill	Scot Bord	NT2117	55°26·7'	3°14·5'W	H	79
Paper House Fm	N Yks	SE5727	53°44·4'	1°7·7'W	FM	105
Paper Mill	Bucks	SP8929	51°57·4'	0°41·9'W	X	165
Papermill Bank	Shrops	SJ5525	52°49·5'	2°39·7'W	T	126
Paper Mill Br	Essex	TL7709	51°45·3'	0°34·3'E	X	167
Papermill Fm	Glos	SP0732	51°59·4'	1°53·5'W	FM	150
Paper Mill Fm	Hants	SU4445	51°12·4'	1°21·8'W	FM	185
Paper Mill Fms	N Yks	SE8484	54°14·9'	0°42·2'W	FM	100
Paper Mill, The	Kent	TQ7831	51°3·3'	0°32·8'E	X	188
Paphle	Pth & Kin	NT0997	56°9·7'	3°27·5'W	X	58
Paphrie Burn	Angus	NO5166	56°47·2'	2°47·7'W	W	44
Papigoe	Highld	ND3851	58°26·8'	3°3·3'W	T	12
Papil	Shetld	HU3631	60°4·0'	1°20·7'W	T	4
Papil Bay	Shetld	HP5403	60°42·7'	1°0·1'W	W	1
Papil Geo	Shetld	HU5341	60°9·3'	1°2·2'W	X	4
Papillon Hall Fm	Leic	SP6886	52°28·3'	0°59·5'W	FM	141
Papil Ness	Shetld	HP5404	60°43·2'	1°0·1'W	X	1
Papil Water	Shetld	HU6090	60°35·6'	0°53·8'W	W	1,2
Paplands Fm	W Susx	TQ0627	51°2·2'	0°28·9'W	FM	187,197
Papley	Northnts	TL1089	52°29·5'	0°22·4'W	T	142
Papley Fm	Northnts	TL1088	52°29·0'	0°22·4'W	FM	142
Papley Grove Fm	Cambs	TL2761	52°14·2'	0°8·0'W	FM	153
Papley Hollow	Cambs	TL2761	52°14·2'	0°8·0'W	X	153
Pap of Glencoe or Sgorr na Ciche	Highld	NN1259	56°41·4'	5°3·7'W	H	41
Pappert Hill	W Dunb	NS4280	55°59·5'	4°31·5'W	H	64
Papperthill Craigs	N Lanak	NS8565	55°52·1'	3°49·8'W	X	65
Papple	E Loth	NT5972	55°56·6'	2°38·9'W	X	67
Papplewick	Notts	SK5451	53°3·4'	1°11·3'W	T	120
Paprill's Fm	Essex	TL7700	51°40·5'	0°34·0'E	FM	167
Paps of Jura	Arg & Bt	NR4973	55°53·3'	6°0·4'W	X	60,61
Paps of Jura	Arg & Bt	NR5074	55°53·9'	5°59·5'W	X	61
Paps, The	Arg & Bt	NS3392	56°5·8'	4°40·6'W	X	56
Papworth Everard	Cambs	TL2863	52°15·2'	0°7·1'W	T	153
Papworth St Agnes	Cambs	TL2664	52°15·8'	0°8·8'W	T	153
Papworth Village Settlement	Cambs	TL2862	52°14·7'	0°7·1'W	X	153
Par	Corn	SX0753	50°21·0'	4°42·4'W	T	200,204
Paradise	Aberd	NJ7627	57°20·2'	2°23·5'W	X	38
Paradise	Corn	SX0990	50°40·9'	4°41·8'W	X	190
Paradise	Durham	NZ4343	54°47·0'	1°19·5'W	X	88
Paradise	Fife	NO3608	56°15·9'	3°1·6'W	X	59
Paradise	Glos	SO8711	51°48·1'	2°10·9'W	T	162
Paradise	Hants	SU0821	50°59·5'	1°52·8'W	X	184
Paradise	Somer	ST4228	51°3·1'	2°49·3'W	X	193
Paradise Copse	Devon	ST0101	50°48·2'	3°23·9'W	F	192
Paradise Cottages	N Yks	SE8561	54°2·5'	0°41·7'W	X	100
Paradise Fm	Cambs	TL5278	52°23·0'	0°14·4'E	FM	143
Paradise Fm	Ches	SJ6461	53°8·9'	2°31·9'W	FM	118
Paradise Fm	Ches	SJ8168	53°12·8'	2°16·7'W	FM	118
Paradise Fm	Corn	SW6819	50°1·8'	5°14·0'W	FM	203
Paradise Fm	Glos	SU2399	51°41·6'	1°39·6'W	FM	163
Paradise Fm	Leeds	SE4341	53°52·0'	1°20·4'W	FM	105
Paradise Fm	Norf	TF4809	52°39·7'	0°11·7'E	FM	143
Paradise Fm	N Yks	NZ2708	54°28·2'	1°34·6'W	FM	93
Paradise Fm	N Yks	SE4277	54°11·5'	1°21·0'W	FM	99
Paradise Fm	N Yks	SE4687	54°16·8'	1°17·2'W	FM	100
Paradise Fm	N Yks	SE7361	54°2·6'	0°52·7'W	FM	100
Paradise Fm	Oxon	SP3932	51°59·3'	1°25·5'W	FM	151
Paradise Fm	Powys	SO2964	52°16·4'	3°2·0'W	FM	137,148
Paradise Fm	Somer	ST1238	51°8·3'	3°15·1'W	FM	181
Paradise Fm	Suff	TL6648	52°6·5'	0°25·8'E	FM	154
Paradise Fm	Suff	TM3678	52°21·2'	1°28·3'E	FM	156
Paradise Fm	Wigan	SD5409	53°34·8'	2°41·3'W	FM	108
Paradise Green	Ches	SJ6560	53°8·4'	2°31·0'W	X	118
Paradise Green	Heref	SO5247	52°7·4'	2°41·7'W	T	149
Paradise Lodge	Notts	SK5930	52°52·1'	1°7·0'W	X	129
Paradise Lodge	N Yks	SE5437	53°49·8'	1°10·4'W	X	105
Paradise Wood	Aberd	NJ6718	57°15·3'	2°32·4'W	F	38
Paradise Wood	N Yks	SE5437	53°49·8'	1°10·4'W	F	105
Paradwys	I of Angl	SH4271	53°13·0'	4°21·6'W	X	114,115
Paramoor	Corn	SW9749	50°18·6'	4°50·7'W	T	204
Paramoor Wood	Corn	SW9848	50°18·1'	4°49·8'W	F	204
Paramour Street	Kent	TR2861	51°18·4'	1°16·7'E	T	179
Paran	Pemb	SM8326	51°53·7'	5°8·8'W	X	157
Parbeth	E Ayr	NS5936	55°36·1'	4°13·8'W	X	71
Parbold	Lancs	SD4911	53°35·8'	2°45·8'W	T	108
Parbold Hall	Lancs	SD5110	53°35·3'	2°44·0'W	X	108
Parbroath	Fife	NO3217	56°20·7'	3°5·6'W	T	59
Parbrook	Somer	ST5636	51°7·5'	2°37·3'W	T	182,183
Parbrook	W Susx	TQ0825	51°1·1'	0°27·2'W	T	187,197
Parbrook Ho	Medway	TQ7974	51°26·4'	0°34·9'E	X	178
Parc	Card	ST1683	51°32·6'	3°12·3'W	X	171
Parc	Carm	SN5428	51°56·1'	4°7·0'W	H	146
Parc	Conwy	SH8050	53°2·3'	3°47·0'W	X	116
Parc	Denb	SJ0756	53°5·8'	3°22·9'W	X	116
Parc	Gwyn	SH4357	53°5·5'	4°20·3'W	X	115,123
Parc	Gwyn	SH4758	53°6·1'	4°16·7'W	X	115,123
Parc	Gwyn	SH5862	53°8·4'	4°7·0'W	X	114,115
Parc	Gwyn	SH6243	52°58·2'	4°2·9'W	X	124
Parc	Gwyn	SH6367	53°11·2'	4°2·6'W	X	115
Parc	Gwyn	SH8733	52°53·2'	3°40·4'W	T	124,125
Parc	I of Angl	SH3678	53°16·7'	4°27·2'W	X	114
Parc	Powys	SJ0210	52°41·0'	3°26·6'W	X	125
Parc	Powys	SJ0924	52°48·6'	3°20·6'W	X	125
Parc	Powys	SN7599	52°34·7'	3°50·3'W	H	135
Parc	Powys	SN9554	52°10·7'	3°31·7'W	X	147
Parcau Fm	V of Glam	SS9375	51°28·1'	3°32·0'W	FM	170
Parcau-gwynion	Cered	SN6362	52°14·6'	4°0·0'W	X	146
Parcau Isaf	Brig	SS8579	51°30·1'	3°39·0'W	X	170
Parc Bach	Powys	SO2434	52°0·2'	3°6·0'W	X	161
Parc Behan	Corn	SW9139	50°13·1'	4°55·4'W	X	204

Parc Cae-cra	Gwyn	SH5650	53°1·9′	4°8·4′W	X	115
Parc Cae-mawr	Gwyn	SH5650	53°1·9′	4°8·4′W	X	115
Parc Caletwr	Gwyn	SH9635	52°54·4′	3°32·4′W	X	125
Parc Caragloose Rock	Corn	SW9238	50°12·6′	4°54·5′W	X	204
Parc Cefn Onn Country Park	Card	ST1784	51°33·2′	3°11·4′W	X	171
Parc-clement	Pemb	SN2337	52°0·4′	4°34·3′W	X	145
Parc-coed-machen	V of Glam	ST0878	51°29·8′	3°19·1′W	X	170
Parc Cwm Darran Country Park	Caer	SO1203	51°43·4′	3°16·1′W	X	171
Parcelstown	Cumbr	NY3965	54°58·8′	2°56·8′W	X	85
Parc Erissey	Corn	SW6944	50°15·3′	5°14·1′W	T	203
Parcevall Hall	N Yks	SE0661	54°2·9′	1°54·1′W	X	99
Parc Fm	Brig	SS9282	51°31·8′	3°33·0′W	FM	170
Parc Fm	Conwy	SH9049	53°1·9′	3°38·0′W	FM	116
Parc Fm	Powys	SJ1628	52°50·8′	3°14·4′W	FM	125
Parc Fm	V of Glam	SS9368	51°24·3′	3°31·9′W	FM	170
Parc-glâs	Carm	SN6829	51°56·9′	3°54·8′W	X	146
Parc Glas	I of Angl	SH4070	53°12·4′	4°23·3′W	X	114,115
Parc Glasfryn	Gwyn	SH3941	52°56·8′	4°23·4′W	X	123
Parc-Grace Dieu	Monm	SO4412	51°48·5′	2°48·3′W	X	161
Parcgwyn	Carm	SN3909	51°45·6′	4°19·6′W	X	159
Parcgwyn	Cered	SN7580	52°24·5′	3°49·9′W	X	135
Parc-gwyn	Denb	SJ1557	53°6·4′	3°15·8′W	X	116
Parc-gwyn	Monm	SO3515	51°50·0′	2°56·2′W	X	161
Parc-henfy	Swan	SS5495	51°38·3′	4°6·2′W	T	159
Parc-Henri	Carm	SN5523	51°53·4′	4°6·0′W	X	159
Parchey	Somer	ST3437	51°7·9′	2°56·2′W	T	182
Parchfield Ho	Staffs	SK0519	52°46·4′	1°55·2′W	X	128
Parciau	Carm	SN1719	51°50·6′	4°39·0′W	X	158
Parciau	Carm	SN2313	51°47·5′	4°33·6′W	X	158
Parciau	Conwy	SH8677	53°16·9′	3°42·2′W	X	116
Parciau	Gwyn	SH5065	53°9·9′	4°14·2′W	X	114,115
Parciau	I of Angl	SH4984	53°20·1′	4°15·7′W	T	114,115
Parciau	Powys	SO2043	52°5·0′	3°9·7′W	X	148,161
Parci Gill	N Yks	SE5395	54°21·1′	1°10·7′W	X	100
Parc Isa	Powys	SJ1425	52°49·2′	3°16·2′W	X	125
Parc le Breos	Swan	SS5289	51°35·1′	4°7·8′W	X	159
Parc Llettis	Monm	SO3210	51°47·3′	2°58·8′W	X	161
Parc Llwydiarth	Powys	SJ0215	52°43·7′	3°26·7′W	X	125
Parcllyn	Cered	SN2451	52°8·0′	4°33·9′W	T	145
Parc Lodge Fm	Monm	SO2818	51°51·6′	3°2·3′W	FM	161
Parc Mawr	Caer	ST1191	51°36·9′	3°16·7′W	T	171
Parc-mawr	Carm	SN6329	51°56·8′	3°59·2′W	X	146
Parcmawr	Carm	SN6434	51°59·5′	3°58·5′W	X	146
Parc-mawr	Carm	SN6645	52°5·5′	3°57·0′W	X	146
Parc-mawr	Cered	SN3748	52°6·6′	4°22·4′W	X	145
Parc-mawr	Pemb	SN0336	51°59·5′	4°51·8′W	X	145,157
Parc-mawr	Swan	SS6198	51°40·1′	4°0·2′W	X	159
Parc-nest	Carm	SN3039	52°1·6′	4°28·3′W	X	145
Parc-neuadd	Cered	SN4959	52°12·8′	4°12·2′W	X	146
Parc-newydd	Gwyn	SH5157	53°5·6′	4°13·1′W	X	115
Parc Newydd	I of Angl	SH3983	53°19·4′	4°24·6′W	X	114
Parc Newydd	Powys	SJ0214	52°43·1′	3°26·7′W	X	125
Parc Newydd Fm	Brig	SS8179	51°30·1′	3°42·5′W	FM	170
Parc-Owen	Carm	SN6819	51°51·5′	3°54·6′W	X	159
Parc Postyn	Denb	SJ0661	53°8·5′	3°23·9′W	X	116
Parcrhydderch	Cered	SN6058	52°12·4′	4°2·5′W	X	146
Parc-Seymour	Newp	ST4091	51°37·1′	2°51·6′W	T	171,172
Parc Sycharth	Powys	SJ2026	52°49·8′	3°10·8′W	F	126
Parc Trwyn-du	I of Angl	SH6381	53°18·7′	4°3·0′W	X	114,115
Parctwad	Cered	SN2444	52°4·2′	4°33·7′W	X	145
Parc Ucha	Denb	SJ0345	52°59·9′	3°26·3′W	X	116
Parc Uchaf	Shrops	SJ2630	52°52·0′	3°5·6′W	X	126
Parc Uchaf Gwydyr	Conwy	SH7959	53°7·1′	3°48·1′W	X	115
Parcummin	Carm	SN2211	51°46·4′	4°34·4′W	X	158
Parcwilws	Carm	SN4703	51°42·5′	4°12·5′W	X	159
Parcyberllan	Carm	SN3420	51°51·5′	4°24·2′W	X	145,159
Parc y Bryn	Nth Pt Talb	SS8293	51°37·6′	3°41·9′W	X	170
Parcybwla	Cered	SN2847	52°5·9′	4°30·3′W	X	145
Parcycastell	Cered	SN2842	52°3·2′	4°30·1′W	A	145
Parc y Derwgoed	Gwyn	SH9738	52°56·0′	3°31·5′W	X	125
Parcydilfa	Carm	SN6333	51°59·0′	3°59·3′W	X	146
Parcygadair	Gwyn	SH5651	53°2·5′	4°8·5′W	X	115
Parc-y-Gors	Cered	SN2446	52°5·3′	4°33·7′W	X	145
Parc-y-Justice	Card	ST0980	51°30·9′	3°18·3′W	X	171
Parc-y-llyn	Pemb	SM9826	51°54·0′	4°55·8′W	X	157,158
Parcymarchog	Carm	SN4818	51°50·6′	4°12·0′W	X	159
Parc-y-marl	Pemb	SN0424	51°53·0′	4°50·5′W	X	145,157,158
Parc y Meirch	Heref	SO2637	52°1·8′	3°4·3′W	X	161
Parcymynydd	Carm	SN3230	51°56·8′	4°26·3′W	X	145
Parcymynydd	Carm	SN4408	51°45·2′	4°15·2′W	X	159
Parc-y-neithw	Pemb	SN2141	52°2·6′	4°36·2′W	X	145
Parc-y-nole	Pemb	SM8833	51°57·5′	5°4·7′W	X	157
Parc-y-prat	Cered	SN1744	52°4·1′	4°39·8′W	X	145
Parc-y-pwll	Pemb	SM9727	51°54·5′	4°56·7′W	X	157,158
Parc-yr-eithan	Pemb	SM8729	51°55·4′	5°5·5′W	X	157
Parcyreithin	Pemb	SN0524	51°53·1′	4°49·6′W	X	145,158
Parc-y-rhedyn	Swan	SS5092	51°36·7′	4°9·6′W	X	159
Parc-y-rhiw	Powys	SJ0706	52°38·9′	3°22·1′W	X	125
Parc-y-rhiw	Powys	SN9996	52°33·4′	3°29·0′W	X	136
Parc y Rhos	Carm	SN3517	51°49·9′	4°23·3′W	X	159
Parc-y-rhôs	Carm	SN5745	52°5·3′	4°4·8′W	X	146
Parc-yr-ynn	Cered	SN6361	52°14·1′	4°0·0′W	X	146
Pardes of Glack	Aberd	NJ7329	57°21·3′	2°26·5′W	X	38
Pard House Fm	Worcs	SO7264	52°16·6′	2°24·2′W	FM	138,149
Pardlestone Fm	Somer	ST1442	51°10·5′	3°13·4′W	FM	181
Pardlestone Hill	Somer	ST1441	51°9·9′	3°13·4′W	X	181
Pardovan Ho	W Loth	NT0477	55°58·8′	3°31·9′W	X	65
Pardown	Hants	SU5749	51°14·5′	1°10·6′W	T	185
Pardshaw	Cumbr	NY0924	54°36·4′	3°24·1′W	T	89
Pardshaw Hall	Cumbr	NY1025	54°37·0′	3°23·2′W	T	89
Parduvine	Midlo	NT3061	55°50·5′	3°6·6′W	X	66
Pared-mawr	Gwyn	SH3024	52°47·5′	4°30·9′W	X	123
Pared y Cefn-hîr	Gwyn	SH6615	52°43·2′	3°58·6′W	H	124
Pared yr Ychain	Gwyn	SH8422	52°47·2′	3°42·8′W	X	124,125
Parehayne Fm	Devon	SY2296	50°45·7′	3°6·0′W	FM	192,193
Parehayne Fm	Devon	SY2396	50°45·7′	3°5·1′W	FM	192,193
Parehayne Hill	Devon	SY2296	50°45·7′	3°6·0′W	H	192,193
Parenwell Cotts	Pth & Kin	NT1396	56°9·2′	3°23·6′W	X	58

Pare's Br	Leic	SK3408	52°40·4′	1°29·4′W	X	128,140
Parfin	D & G	NX7997	55°15·4′	3°53·8′W	H	78
Parford	Devon	SX7189	50°41·4′	3°49·2′W	X	191
Parham	Suff	TM3060	52°11·6′	1°22·3′E	T	156
Parham Ho	Suff	TM2961	52°12·2′	1°21·5′E	X	156
Parham Ho	W Susx	TQ0614	50°55·2′	0°29·1′W	A	197
Parham Old Hall	Suff	TM3059	52°11·1′	1°22·3′E	X	156
Parham Wood	Suff	TM3061	52°12·2′	1°22·4′E	F	156
Parham Wood	Wilts	SU0055	51°17·9′	1°59·6′W	F	173
Par Hill	D & G	NS9000	55°17·2′	3°43·5′W	X	78
Paris Fm	Suff	TM1757	52°10·3′	1°10·8′E	FM	156
Paris Hall	Essex	TL4807	51°44·8′	0°9·0′E	X	167
Parish Brook	N Som	ST4570	51°25·8′	2°47·1′W	W	171,172
Parish Fm	Norf	TM1988	52°27·0′	1°13·8′E	FM	156
Parish Holm	S Lanak	NS7627	55°31·5′	3°57·4′W	X	71
Parishholm Hill	S Lanak	NS7727	55°31·5′	3°56·5′W	H	71
Park	Aberd	NJ5857	57°36·3′	2°41·7′W	X	29
Park	Aberd	NJ6912	57°12·1′	2°30·3′W	X	38
Park	Arg & Bt	NM8320	56°19·6′	5°30·1′W	X	49
Park	Cald	SD9329	53°45·7′	2°6·0′W	X	103
Park	Clackm	NS9090	56°5·7′	3°45·6′W	X	58
Park	Conwy	SH9445	52°59·8′	3°34·4′W	X	116
Park	Corn	SX0370	50°30·0′	4°46·3′W	T	200
Park	Cumbr	NY5575	55°4·3′	2°41·9′W	X	86
Park	Cumbr	NY6109	54°28·7′	2°35·7′W	X	91
Park	Devon	SS4822	50°58·9′	4°9·5′W	X	180
Park	Devon	SS6829	51°2·9′	3°52·6′W	X	180
Park	Devon	SS7523	50°59·8′	3°46·5′W	X	180
Park	Devon	SS8408	50°51·8′	3°38·5′W	X	191
Park	Devon	SX8399	50°47·0′	3°39·2′W	T	191
Park	D & G	NX8875	55°3·7′	3°44·8′W	X	84
Park	D & G	NX9091	55°12·3′	3°43·3′W	X	78
Park	D & G	NY1869	55°0·8′	3°16·5′W	X	85
Park	Dorset	ST4403	50°49·7′	2°47·3′W	X	193
Park	Highld	NH5933	57°22·2′	4°20·2′W	X	26
Park	Highld	NH6056	57°34·6′	4°20·0′W	X	26
Park	Highld	NH9053	57°33·5′	3°49·8′W	X	27
Park	Moray	NJ1453	57°33·8′	3°25·8′W	X	28
Park	N Lincs	SE7400	53°29·7′	0°52·7′W	X	112
Park	Northum	NY8353	54°52·5′	2°15·5′W	X	86,87
Park	N Yks	SD9542	53°52·7′	2°4·1′W	X	103
Park	Powys	SJ1426	52°49·7′	3°16·2′W	X	125
Park	Powys	SN9446	52°6·4′	3°32·5′W	X	147
Park	Powys	SN9879	52°24·2′	3°29·6′W	X	136,147
Park	Powys	SO0171	52°19·9′	3°26·8′W	X	136,147
Park	Powys	SO0192	52°31·3′	3°27·1′W	A	136
Park	S Lanak	NS9845	55°41·5′	3°36·9′W	X	72
Park	Somer	ST4530	51°4·2′	2°46·7′W	T	182
Park	Swin	SU1783	51°33·0′	1°44·9′W	T	173
Park Attwood	Worcs	SO7979	52°24·8′	2°18·1′W	X	138
Park Banks	Staffs	SK0842	52°58·8′	1°52·4′W	X	119,128
Park Bank Wood	Powys	SO3372	52°20·8′	2°58·6′W	F	137,148
Park Barn	N Yks	SE3877	54°11·5′	1°24·6′W	X	99
Park Barn	Somer	ST3217	50°57·1′	2°57·7′W	X	193
Park Barn	Surrey	SU9750	51°14·7′	0°36·2′W	T	186
Park Barn	W Susx	TQ1116	50°56·2′	0°24·8′W	X	198
Park Barn Fm	E Susx	TQ3214	50°54·8′	0°6·9′W	FM	198
Park Barn Fm	Kent	TQ8352	51°14·5′	0°37·7′E	FM	188
Park Barn Fm	Kent	TR0246	51°10·9′	0°53·8′E	FM	189
Park Barn Fm	Staffs	SK0621	52°47·4′	1°54·3′W	FM	128
Park Barns	Cumbr	NY5059	54°55·6′	2°46·4′W	X	86
Park Beck	Cumbr	NY4402	54°24·9′	2°51·4′W	W	90
Park Bernisdale	Highld	NG4051	57°28·7′	6°19·8′W	T	23
Park Bottom	Corn	SW6642	50°14·1′	5°16·5′W	T	203
Park Bottom	Glos	ST8593	51°38·4′	2°12·6′W	F	162,173
Park Bottom	Wilts	ST9537	51°8·2′	2°3·9′W	X	184
Park Br	N Yks	NY8801	54°24·5′	2°10·7′W	X	91,92
Parkbrae	Aberd	NJ6525	57°19·1′	2°34·4′W	X	38
Park Bridge	Tames	SD9402	53°31·1′	2°5·0′W	T	109
Park Brook	Lancs	SD6834	53°48·3′	2°28·7′W	W	103
Park Broom	Cumbr	NY4358	54°55·1′	2°52·9′W	T	85
Park Brow	W Susx	TQ1509	50°52·4′	0°21·5′W	X	198
Parkburn	Aberd	NJ7739	57°26·7′	2°22·5′W	X	29,30
Parkburn	D & G	NX9882	55°7·6′	3°35·5′W	X	78
Park Burn	D & G	NX9883	55°8·1′	3°35·6′W	W	78
Park Burn	E Loth	NT5765	55°52·8′	2°40·8′W	W	67
Park Burn	Midlo	NT3167	55°53·7′	3°5·8′W	W	66
Park Burn	Northum	NY7059	54°55·8′	2°27·7′W	W	86,87
Park Burnfoot	Northum	NY6862	54°57·3′	2°29·6′W	X	86,87
Park Bushes	Northnts	SP9696	52°33·4′	0°34·6′W	F	141
Park Close	Lancs	SD8844	53°53·8′	2°10·5′W	T	103
Park Common	Norf	TM0586	52°26·2′	1°1·4′E	X	144
Parkconon	Angus	NO5845	56°36·0′	2°40·6′W	X	54
Park Coppice	Cumbr	SD2995	54°21·0′	3°5·1′W	F	96,97
Park Coppice	Heref	SO6237	52°2·0′	2°32·8′W	F	149
Park Coppice	Lancs	SD4756	54°0·1′	2°48·1′W	F	102
Park Coppice	Shrops	SJ5802	52°37·1′	2°36·8′W	F	126
Park Coppice	Wilts	SU2870	51°25·9′	1°35·4′W	F	174
Park Copse	Northnts	SP7338	52°2·4′	0°55·7′W	F	152
Park Copse	Surrey	SU9237	51°7·7′	0°40·7′W	F	186
Park Copse	W Berks	SU4777	51°29·6′	1°19·0′W	F	174
Park Copse	Wilts	ST9989	51°36·2′	2°0·5′W	F	173
Park Copse	Wilts	SU0885	51°34·1′	1°52·7′W	F	173
Park Copse	Wilts	SU1462	51°21·6′	1°47·5′W	F	173
Park Copse	Wilts	SU2529	51°3·8′	1°38·2′W	F	184
Park Corner	Bath & NE Somer	ST7859	51°20·0′	2°18·6′W	T	172
Park Corner	Dorset	SY9193	50°44·4′	2°7·3′W	X	195
Park Corner	E Susx	TQ5114	50°54·6′	0°9·3′E	T	199
Park Corner	E Susx	TQ5336	51°6·4′	0°11·5′E	T	188
Park Corner	Glos	SO9604	51°44·3′	2°3·1′W	X	163
Park Corner	Hants	SU7162	51°21·4′	0°58·4′W	X	175,186
Park Corner	Herts	TL1905	51°44·1′	0°16·2′W	X	166
Park Corner	Oxon	SU6988	51°35·4′	0°59·8′W	T	175
Park Corner	Sol	SP2075	52°22·6′	1°42·0′W	X	139
Park Corner Fm	Hants	SU7648	51°13·8′	0°54·3′W	FM	186
Parkcorner Fm	Oxon	SU6889	51°36·0′	1°0·7′W	FM	175
Park Corner Fm	Wilts	ST8430	51°4·4′	2°13·3′W	FM	183
Park Cott	Northum	NU1713	55°24·9′	1°43·5′W	X	81
Park Cott	Shrops	SJ3724	52°48·8′	2°55·7′W	X	126

Park Cottage	Angus	NO3761	56°44·4′	3°1·3′W	X	44
Park Cottage	Lancs	SD3646	53°54·6′	2°58·0′W	X	102
Park Cottage	Stir	NN8201	56°11·5′	3°53·6′W	X	57
Park Cotts	Shrops	SO5486	52°28·4′	2°40·2′W	X	137,138
Park Cwm Darren Country Park	Caer	SO1202	51°42·8′	3°16·0′W	X	171
Park Dairy	Herts	TL2407	51°45·1′	0°11·8′W	X	166
Park Dam	Northum	NY8569	55°1·2′	2°13·6′W	W	87
Parkdargue	Aberd	NJ6044	57°29·3′	2°39·6′W	X	29
Park Downs	Surrey	TQ2658	51°18·7′	0°11·1′W	X	187
Parke	Cered	SN3641	52°2·8′	4°23·1′W	X	145
Parke	Devon	SX8078	50°35·6′	3°41·3′W	X	191
Parke	Pemb	SN0237	52°0·0′	4°52·7′W	X	145,157
Parke	Pemb	SN1242	52°2·9′	4°44·1′W	X	145
Parke	Pemb	SN2337	52°0·4′	4°34·3′W	X	145
Park East	Pemb	SN0624	51°53·1′	4°48·7′W	X	145,158
Parkend	Angus	NO5962	56°45·1′	2°39·8′W	X	44
Park End	Beds	SP9953	52°10·2′	0°32·7′W	T	153
Park End	Cambs	TL5561	52°13·7′	0°16·6′E	T	154
Parkend	Cumbr	NY3038	54°44·2′	3°4·8′W	X	90
Parkend	Cumbr	NY4572	55°2·6′	2°51·2′W	X	86
Parkend	D & G	NY0979	55°6·1′	3°25·1′W	X	85
Park End	Durham	NY9225	54°37·5′	2°7·0′W	X	91,92
Parkend	E Loth	NT5071	55°56·0′	2°47·6′W	X	66
Parkend	Fife	NT1686	56°3·8′	3°20·5′W	X	65,66
Parkend	Glos	SO6108	51°46·4′	2°33·5′W	T	162
Parkend	Glos	SO7810	51°47·5′	2°18·7′W	T	162
Park End	Midd	NZ5217	54°33·0′	1°11·3′W	T	93
Park End	Northum	NY8775	55°4·4′	2°11·8′W	T	87
Park End	N Yks	NZ6908	54°28·0′	0°55·7′W	X	94
Park End	S Ayr	NX0883	55°6·5′	5°0·2′W	T	76
Parkend	Scot Bord	NT1951	55°45·0′	3°17·0′W	X	65,66,72
Parkend	Scot Bord	NT6938	55°38·3′	2°29·1′W	X	74
Parkend	S Glos	ST6991	51°37·3′	2°26·5′W	X	162,172
Parkend	S Lanak	NS9222	55°29·0′	3°42·1′W	X	71,72
Park End	Somer	ST1833	51°5·7′	3°9·9′W	T	181
Park End	Staffs	SJ7851	53°3·6′	2°19·3′W	T	118
Park End	Worcs	SO7673	52°21·5′	2°20·7′W	T	138
Parkend Br	Glos	SO7710	51°47·5′	2°19·6′W	X	162
Parkenden	Kent	TQ8046	51°11·3′	0°34·9′E	X	188
Park End Fm	Beds	TL0657	52°12·3′	0°26·5′W	FM	153
Park End Fm	Cumbr	SD4888	54°17·3′	2°47·5′W	FM	97
Park End Fm	Somer	ST4537	51°8·0′	2°46·8′W	FM	182
Parkend Lodge	Glos	SO7810	51°47·5′	2°18·7′W	X	162
Parkend Walk	Glos	SO6007	51°45·9′	2°34·4′W	F	162
Park End Wood	Durham	NY9226	54°38·0′	2°7·0′W	X	91,92
Parkengear	Corn	SW9047	50°17·4′	4°56·5′W	T	204
Parkergate	Cumbr	NY2230	54°39·8′	3°12·1′W	X	89,90
Parker's Corner	W Berks	SU6271	51°26·3′	1°6·1′W	T	175
Parkers Fm	Essex	TM1827	51°54·2′	1°10·5′E	FM	168,169
Parker's Green	Herts	TL3225	51°54·7′	0°4·5′W	T	166
Parker's Green	Kent	TQ6148	51°12·7′	0°18·7′E	T	188
Parker's Grove	Suff	TL9867	52°16·2′	0°54·5′E	F	155
Parkerston	E Ayr	NS5336	55°36·0′	4°19·6′W	X	70
Parke's Fm	Suff	TM1476	52°20·6′	1°8·9′E	FM	144,156
Parkes, The	Ches	SJ6644	52°59·8′	2°30·0′W	X	118
Parkeston	Essex	TM2332	51°56·7′	1°15·1′E	T	169
Parkeston Quay	Essex	TM2332	51°56·7′	1°15·1′E	X	169
Parkey	Wrex	SJ3848	53°1·8′	2°55·1′W	X	117
Parkey Fm	Wrex	SJ3747	53°1·2′	2°55·9′W	FM	117
Park Eyton	Wrex	SJ3343	52°59·1′	2°59·5′W	X	117
Parkfairn	S Ayr	NS3306	55°19·4′	4°37·5′W	X	70,76
Park Farm	Inverc	NS3473	55°55·5′	4°39·0′W	FM	63
Park Farm	Worcs	SP0665	52°17·2′	1°54·3′W	FM	150
Parkfarm Down	W Berks	SU2981	51°31·9′	1°34·5′W	X	174
Park Farm Ho	Staffs	SJ8226	52°50·1′	2°15·6′W	X	127
Park Farms	Northnts	SP8668	52°18·4′	0°43·9′W	X	152
Park Fauld	Cumbr	NY3951	54°51·3′	2°56·6′W	X	85
Park Fell	Cumbr	NY3302	54°24·8′	3°1·5′W	H	90
Park Fell	Cumbr	NY6945	54°48·2′	2°28·5′W	H	86,87
Park Fell	N Yks	SD7676	54°11·0′	2°21·6′W	X	98
Park Fell Head	Cumbr	NY4209	54°28·6′	2°53·3′W	X	90
Parkfield	Aberd	NJ8127	57°20·2′	2°18·5′W	X	38
Parkfield	Ches	SJ6960	53°8·4′	2°27·4′W	X	118
Parkfield	Corn	SX3167	50°28·9′	4°22·6′W	T	201
Parkfield	Devon	SX7668	50°30·2′	3°44·5′W	X	202
Parkfield	S Glos	ST6977	51°29·7′	2°26·4′W	T	172
Parkfield	Sol	SP1774	52°22·1′	1°44·6′W	X	139
Parkfield	Wolv	SO9296	52°33·9′	2°6·7′W	T	139
Parkfield Fm	Mil Key	SP8351	52°9·3′	0°46·8′W	FM	152
Park Field Fm	Norf	TF5203	52°36·4′	0°15·1′E	FM	143
Parkfield Fm	Pth & Kin	NO1425	56°24·8′	3°23·2′W	FM	53,58
Parkfield Ho	N Yks	SE3278	54°12·0′	1°30·1′W	X	99
Parkfield Ho	Pth & Kin	NO1425	56°24·8′	3°23·2′W	X	53,58
Parkfield Ho	Wirral	SJ2491	53°24·9′	3°8·2′W	X	108
Parkfield House Fm	Ches	SJ6058	53°7·3′	2°35·5′W	FM	118
Parkfield House Fm	Warw	SP0761	52°15·1′	1°53·4′W	FM	150
Parkfield Loch	S Lanak	NS6442	55°39·4′	4°9·7′W	W	71
Parkfields	Bucks	SP6639	52°3·0′	1°1·9′W	X	152
Parkfields	Ches	SJ7043	52°59·3′	2°26·4′W	X	118
Parkfields	Heref	SO6221	51°53·4′	2°32·7′W	X	162
Parkfields	Staffs	SK0244	52°59·8′	1°57·8′W	X	119,128
Park Fields	Staffs	SK0733	52°53·9′	1°53·4′W	X	128
Parkfields	Wirral	SJ2490	53°24·3′	3°8·2′W	X	108
Parkfields Ho	Staffs	SJ8738	52°56·6′	2°11·2′W	X	127
Park Fm	Bath & NE Somer	ST6963	51°22·1′	2°26·3′W	FM	172
Park Fm	Beds	SP9533	51°59·5′	0°36·6′W	FM	165
Park Fm	Beds	SP9621	51°53·0′	0°35·9′W	FM	165
Park Fm	Beds	TL0134	51°59·9′	0°31·3′W	FM	153
Park Fm	Beds	TL0360	52°13·9′	0°29·1′W	FM	153
Park Fm	Beds	TL0662	52°15·0′	0°26·4′W	FM	153
Park Fm	Birm	SP0391	52°31·2′	1°56·9′W	FM	139
Park Fm	Brackn	SU8470	51°25·6′	0°47·1′W	FM	175
Park Fm	Brig	SS8784	51°32·9′	3°37·4′W	FM	170
Park Fm	Bucks	SP9131	51°58·4′	0°40·1′W	FM	152,165
Park Fm	Cambs	TL0866	52°17·1′	0°24·6′W	FM	153
Park Fm	Cambs	TL1675	52°21·9′	0°17·4′W	FM	142
Park Fm	Cambs	TL1888	52°28·9′	0°15·3′W	FM	142
Park Fm	Cambs	TL1968	52°18·1′	0°14·9′W	FM	153

Park Fm	Cambs	TL2178	52°23·4'	0°12·9'W	FM 142
Park Fm	Cambs	TL3085	52°27·1'	0°4·8'W	FM 142
Park Fm	Cambs	TL3094	52°31·9'	0°4·6'W	FM 142
Park Fm	Cambs	TL3859	52°12·9'	0°1·6'E	FM 154
Park Fm	Cambs	TL6568	52°17·3'	0°25·6'E	FM 154
Park Fm	Ches	SJ4471	53°14·2'	2°49·9'W	FM 117
Park Fm	Ches	SJ5450	53°3·0'	2°40·8'W	FM 117
Park Fm	Ches	SJ5454	53°5·1'	2°40·8'W	FM 117
Park Fm	Ches	SJ6254	53°5·2'	2°33·6'W	FM 118
Park Fm	Ches	SJ6682	53°20·3'	2°30·2'W	FM 109
Park Fm	Ches	SJ6865	53°11·1'	2°28·3'W	FM 118
Park Fm	Ches	SJ7083	53°20·8'	2°26·6'W	FM 109
Park Fm	Ches	SJ7354	53°5·2'	2°23·8'W	FM 118
Park Fm	Ches	SJ7681	53°19·8'	2°21·2'W	FM 109
Park Fm	Ches	SJ8372	53°14·9'	2°14·9'W	FM 118
Park Fm	Ches	SJ8483	53°20·9'	2°14·0'W	FM 109
Park Fm	Corn	SS2101	50°47·1'	4°32·0'W	FM 190
Park Fm	Corn	SW8443	50°15·1'	5°1·4'W	FM 204
Park Fm	Derby	SK1840	52°57·7'	1°43·5'W	FM 119,128
Park Fm	Derby	SK2171	53°14·4'	1°40·7'W	FM 119
Park Fm	Derby	SK2532	52°53·3'	1°37·3'W	FM 128
Park Fm	Derby	SK2544	52°59·8'	1°37·2'W	FM 119,128
Park Fm	Derby	SK2615	52°44·2'	1°36·5'W	FM 128
Park Fm	Derby	SK2744	52°59·8'	1°35·5'W	FM 119,128
Park Fm	Derby	SK2769	53°13·3'	1°35·3'W	FM 119
Park Fm	Derby	SK4041	52°58·1'	1°23·9'W	FM 129
Park Fm	Derby	SK4437	52°56·0'	1°20·3'W	FM 129
Park Fm	Derby	SK4448	53°1·9'	1°20·2'W	FM 129
Park Fm	Devon	SS4019	50°57·1'	4°16·3'W	FM 180,190
Park Fm	Devon	SS4936	51°6·4'	4°9·0'W	FM 180
Park Fm	Devon	SS5127	51°1·6'	4°7·1'W	FM 180
Park Fm	Devon	SS5409	50°52·0'	4°4·1'W	FM 191
Park Fm	Devon	SS6221	50°58·6'	3°57·6'W	FM 180
Park Fm	Devon	ST1012	50°54·3'	3°16·4'W	FM 181,193
Park Fm	Devon	ST1409	50°52·7'	3°13·0'W	FM 192,193
Park Fm	Devon	SX7342	50°16·1'	3°46·5'W	FM 202
Park Fm	Devon	SX9695	50°45·0'	3°28·1'W	FM 192
Park Fm	Devon	SY2995	50°45·2'	3°0·0'W	FM 193
Park Fm	D & G	NX4160	54°54·8'	4°28·4'W	FM 83
Park Fm	D & G	NX8362	54°56·6'	3°49·2'W	FM 84
Park Fm	Dorset	ST8513	50°55·2'	2°12·4'W	FM 194
Park Fm	Dorset	SY7793	50°44·4'	2°19·2'W	FM 194
Park Fm	Enf	TQ2998	51°40·2'	0°7·7'W	FM 166,176
Park Fm	E Renf	NS5750	55°43·6'	4°16·2'W	FM 64
Park Fm	Essex	TL5245	52°5·2'	0°13·5'E	FM 154
Park Fm	Essex	TL5443	52°4·1'	0°15·2'E	FM 154
Park Fm	Essex	TL6000	51°40·8'	0°19·3'E	FM 167
Park Fm	Essex	TL6239	52°1·8'	0°22·1'E	FM 154
Park Fm	Essex	TL6615	51°48·8'	0°24·9'E	FM 167
Park Fm	Essex	TL7014	51°48·2'	0°28·3'E	FM 167
Park Fm	Essex	TL7134	51°58·9'	0°29·8'E	FM 154
Park Fm	Essex	TL7311	51°46·5'	0°30·9'E	FM 167
Park Fm	Essex	TL7424	51°53·5'	0°32·1'E	FM 167
Park Fm	Essex	TL7641	52°2·6'	0°34·4'E	FM 155
Park Fm	Essex	TL8335	51°59·2'	0°40·3'E	FM 155
Park Fm	Essex	TL8519	51°50·6'	0°41·5'E	FM 168
Park Fm	Essex	TL8718	51°50·0'	0°43·2'E	FM 168
Park Fm	Essex	TL9115	51°48·3'	0°46·6'E	FM 168
Park Fm	Essex	TL9401	51°40·7'	0°48·8'E	FM 168
Park Fm	Essex	TL9920	51°50·8'	0°53·7'E	FM 168
Park Fm	Essex	TM0424	51°52·9'	0°58·2'E	FM 168
Park Fm	Essex	TM0527	51°54·4'	0°59·2'E	FM 168
Park Fm	Essex	TM0623	51°52·3'	0°59·9'E	FM 168
Park Fm	Essex	TM1025	51°53·3'	1°3·5'E	FM 168,169
Park Fm	Essex	TM1316	51°48·3'	1°5·8'E	FM 168,169
Park Fm	Essex	TQ5998	51°39·7'	0°18·3'E	FM 167,177
Park Fm	Essex	TQ6490	51°35·3'	0°22·4'E	FM 177
Park Fm	E Susx	TQ3418	50°57·0'	0°5·2'W	FM 198
Park Fm	E Susx	TQ4623	50°59·5'	0°5·2'E	FM 198
Park Fm	E Susx	TQ5728	51°2·0'	0°14·7'E	FM 188,199
Park Fm	E Susx	TQ5911	50°52·8'	0°16·0'E	FM 199
Park Fm	E Susx	TQ6623	50°59·2'	0°22·3'E	FM 199
Park Fm	E Susx	TQ7523	50°59·0'	0°30·0'E	FM 199
Park Fm	E Susx	TQ7712	50°53·0'	0°31·4'E	FM 199
Park Fm	E Susx	TQ7725	51°0·1'	0°31·8'E	FM 188,199
Park Fm	E Yorks	SE6419	53°40·1'	1°1·5'W	FM 111
Park Fm	E Yorks	SE7420	53°40·5'	0°52·4'W	FM 105,106,112
Park Fm	E Yorks	SE7429	53°45·4'	0°52·2'W	FM 105,106
Park Fm	E Yorks	SE7542	53°52·4'	0°51·1'W	FM 105,106
Park Fm	E Yorks	SE7740	53°51·3'	0°49·3'W	FM 105,106
Park Fm	E Yorks	SE8139	53°50·7'	0°45·7'W	FM 106
Park Fm	E Yorks	SE8241	53°51·8'	0°44·8'W	FM 106
Park Fm	E Yorks	SE8746	53°54·4'	0°40·1'W	FM 106
Park Fm	E Yorks	SE9968	54°6·1'	0°28·7'W	FM 101
Park Fm	E Yorks	TA0036	53°48·9'	0°28·5'W	FM 106,107
Park Fm	E Yorks	TA0036	53°48·9'	0°28·5'W	FM 106,107
Park Fm	E Yorks	TA0848	53°55·2'	0°20·9'W	FM 107
Park Fm	E Yorks	TA1454	53°58·4'	0°15·3'W	FM 107
Park Fm	Flint	SJ3264	53°10·4'	3°0·6'W	FM 117
Park Fm	Glos	SO5603	51°43·7'	2°37·8'W	FM 162
Park Fm	Glos	SO5901	51°42·6'	2°35·2'W	FM 162
Park Fm	Glos	SO6202	51°43·2'	2°32·6'W	FM 162
Park Fm	Glos	SO7632	51°59·4'	2°20·6'W	FM 150
Park Fm	Glos	SO8309	51°47·0'	2°14·4'W	FM 162
Park Fm	Glos	SO8730	51°58·3'	2°11·0'W	FM 150
Park Fm	Glos	SO9309	51°47·0'	2°5·7'W	FM 163
Park Fm	Glos	SP0131	51°58·9'	1°58·7'W	FM 150
Park Fm	Glos	SP0602	51°43·2'	1°54·4'W	FM 163
Park Fm	Glos	SP1239	52°3·2'	1°49·1'W	FM 150
Park Fm	Glos	SP1634	52°0·5'	1°45·6'W	FM 151
Park Fm	Glos	ST6797	51°40·5'	2°28·2'W	FM 162
Park Fm	Glos	ST7497	51°40·5'	2°22·2'W	FM 162
Park Fm	Glos	ST7691	51°37·3'	2°20·4'W	FM 162,172
Park Fm	Glos	ST8693	51°38·4'	2°11·7'W	FM 162,173
Park Fm	Hants	SU2627	51°2·7'	1°37·4'W	FM 184
Park Fm	Hants	SU2810	50°53·6'	1°35·7'W	FM 195
Park Fm	Hants	SU2939	51°9·2'	1°34·7'W	FM 185
Park Fm	Hants	SU3427	51°2·7'	1°30·5'W	FM 185
Park Fm	Hants	SU3942	51°10·8'	1°26·1'W	FM 185
Park Fm	Hants	SU5307	50°51·8'	1°14·4'W	FM 196
Park Fm	Hants	SU5432	51°5·3'	1°13·3'W	FM 185
Park Fm	Hants	SU6746	51°12·8'	1°2·1'W	FM 185,186
Park Fm	Hants	SU6823	51°0·4'	1°1·5'W	FM 185
Park Fm	Hants	SU7361	51°20·8'	0°56·7'W	FM 175,186
Park Fm	Hants	SZ3996	50°46·0'	1°26·4'W	FM 196
Park Fm	Hav	TQ4993	51°37·2'	0°9·5'E	FM 177
Park Fm	Heref	SO3039	52°2·9'	3°0·9'W	FM 161
Park Fm	Heref	SO5062	52°15·5'	2°43·6'W	FM 137,138,149
Park Fm	Heref	SO5353	52°10·6'	2°40·8'W	FM 149
Park Fm	Heref	SO6127	51°56·6'	2°33·6'W	FM 162
Park Fm	Heref	SO6137	52°2·0'	2°33·7'W	FM 149
Park Fm	Heref	SO6664	52°16·6'	2°29·5'W	FM 138,149
Park Fm	Herts	SP9410	51°47·1'	0°37·8'W	FM 165
Park Fm	Herts	TL2801	51°41·8'	0°8·5'W	FM 166
Park Fm	Herts	TL3337	52°1·2'	0°3·3'W	FM 154
Park Fm	I of M	SC3274	54°8·3'	4°33·9'W	FM 95
Park Fm	I of W	SZ6190	50°42·6'	1°7·8'W	FM 196
Park Fm	Kent	TQ4655	51°16·7'	0°6·0'E	FM 188
Park Fm	Kent	TQ4860	51°19·4'	0°7·8'E	FM 177,188
Park Fm	Kent	TQ6158	51°18·1'	0°19·0'E	FM 188
Park Fm	Kent	TQ6351	51°14·3'	0°20·5'E	FM 188
Park Fm	Kent	TQ6844	51°10·5'	0°24·6'E	FM 188
Park Fm	Kent	TQ7731	51°3·3'	0°31·9'E	FM 188
Park Fm	Kent	TQ8039	51°7·5'	0°34·7'E	FM 188
Park Fm	Kent	TQ8844	51°10·1'	0°41·7'E	FM 189
Park Fm	Kent	TQ8856	51°16·5'	0°42·1'E	FM 178
Park Fm	Kent	TQ9430	51°2·4'	0°46·4'E	FM 189
Park Fm	Kent	TQ9460	51°18·6'	0°47·4'E	FM 178
Park Fm	Kent	TQ9855	51°15·8'	0°50·7'E	FM 178
Park Fm	Kent	TR0139	51°7·1'	0°52·7'E	FM 189
Park Fm	Kent	TR0940	51°7·5'	0°59·6'E	FM 179,189
Park Fm	Kent	TR1242	51°8·5'	1°2·2'E	FM 179,189
Park Fm	King	TQ1862	51°20·9'	0°17·9'W	FM 176,187
Park Fm	Kirk	SE2122	53°41·9'	1°40·5'W	FM 104
Park Fm	Lancs	SD7438	53°50·5'	2°23·3'W	FM 103
Park Fm	Leic	SK2911	52°42·0'	1°33·8'W	FM 128
Park Fm	Leic	SK4108	52°40·3'	1°23·2'W	FM 140
Park Fm	Leic	SK5521	52°47·3'	1°10·7'W	FM 129
Park Fm	Leic	SK6920	52°46·6'	0°58·2'W	FM 129
Park Fm	Leic	SK7302	52°36·9'	0°54·9'W	FM 141
Park Fm	Leic	SP8395	52°33·0'	0°46·2'W	FM 141
Park Fm	Lincs	SK8574	53°15·6'	0°43·1'W	FM 121
Park Fm	Lincs	SK8684	53°21·0'	0°42·1'W	FM 121
Park Fm	Lincs	SK9427	52°50·2'	0°35·9'W	FM 130
Park Fm	Lincs	SK9584	53°20·9'	0°34·0'W	FM 121
Park Fm	Lincs	TF0222	52°47·4'	0°28·8'W	FM 130
Park Fm	Lincs	TF1313	52°42·4'	0°19·2'W	FM 130,142
Park Fm	Lincs	TF1876	53°16·3'	0°13·4'W	FM 122
Park Fm	Lincs	TF2059	53°7·1'	0°12·0'W	FM 122
Park Fm	Lincs	TF2118	52°45·0'	0°12·0'W	FM 131
Park Fm	Lincs	TF2797	53°27·5'	0°4·8'W	FM 113
Park Fm	Lincs	TF3261	53°8·0'	0°1·2'W	FM 122
Park Fm	Lincs	TF3770	53°12·8'	0°3·5'E	FM 122
Park Fm	Lincs	TF3779	53°17·6'	0°3·8'E	FM 122
Park Fm	Lincs	TF4281	53°18·6'	0°8·3'E	FM 122
Park Fm	Mil Key	SP8246	52°6·6'	0°47·8'W	FM 152
Park Fm	Mil Key	SP8547	52°7·1'	0°45·1'W	FM 152
Park Fm	Mil Key	SP9154	52°10·8'	0°39·7'W	FM 152
Park Fm	Monm	SO3915	51°50·1'	2°52·7'W	FM 161
Park Fm	Newp	ST3191	51°37·1'	2°59·4'W	FM 171
Park Fm	Norf	TF6405	52°37·3'	0°25·8'E	FM 143
Park Fm	Norf	TF6712	52°41·0'	0°28·6'E	FM 132,143
Park Fm	Norf	TF6933	52°52·3'	0°31·1'E	FM 132
Park Fm	Norf	TF7015	52°42·6'	0°31·4'E	FM 132
Park Fm	Norf	TF9105	52°36·8'	0°49·7'E	FM 144
Park Fm	Norf	TF9411	52°39·9'	0°52·5'E	FM 144
Park Fm	Norf	TF9622	52°45·8'	0°54·7'E	FM 132
Park Fm	Norf	TF9807	52°37·7'	0°55·9'E	FM 144
Park Fm	Norf	TF9908	52°38·2'	0°56·9'E	FM 144
Park Fm	Norf	TG0114	52°41·4'	0°58·9'E	FM 133
Park Fm	Norf	TG0216	52°42·5'	0°59·8'E	FM 133
Park Fm	Norf	TG0229	52°49·5'	1°0·3'E	FM 133
Park Fm	Norf	TG0332	52°51·1'	1°1·3'E	FM 133
Park Fm	Norf	TG0420	52°44·6'	1°1·7'E	FM 133
Park Fm	Norf	TG0704	52°35·9'	1°3·8'E	FM 144
Park Fm	Norf	TG1403	52°35·2'	1°10·0'E	FM 144
Park Fm	Norf	TG1532	52°50·8'	1°12·0'E	FM 133
Park Fm	Norf	TG1829	52°49·1'	1°14·5'E	FM 133,134
Park Fm	Norf	TG2016	52°42·0'	1°15·8'E	FM 133,134
Park Fm	Norf	TG2505	52°36·0'	1°19·8'E	FM 134
Park Fm	Norf	TG2934	52°51·5'	1°24·5'E	FM 133
Park Fm	Norf	TG3332	52°50·3'	1°28·0'E	FM 133
Park Fm	Norf	TL9498	52°32·9'	0°52·1'E	FM 144
Park Fm	Norf	TM0483	52°24·6'	1°0·4'E	FM 144
Park Fm	Norf	TM0892	52°29·4'	1°4·2'E	FM 144
Park Fm	Norf	TM1186	52°26·1'	1°6·6'E	FM 144
Park Fm	Norf	TM1199	52°33·1'	1°7·1'E	FM 144
Park Fm	Norf	TM1891	52°28·6'	1°13·0'E	FM 134
Park Fm	Norf	TM2298	52°32·3'	1°16·8'E	FM 134
Park Fm	Norf	TM2591	52°28·5'	1°19·2'E	FM 134
Park Fm	Northnts	SP6178	52°24·0'	1°5·8'W	FM 140
Park Fm	Northnts	SP6581	52°25·6'	1°2·2'W	FM 141
Park Fm	Northnts	SP6747	52°7·3'	1°0·9'W	FM 152
Park Fm	Northnts	SP7144	52°5·6'	0°57·4'W	FM 152
Park Fm	Northnts	SP7749	52°8·3'	0°52·1'W	FM 152
Park Fm	Northnts	SP7854	52°11·0'	0°51·2'W	FM 152
Park Fm	Northnts	SP8187	52°28·7'	0°48·0'W	FM 141
Park Fm	Northnts	SP9384	52°27·0'	0°37·5'W	FM 141
Park Fm	Northum	NU1614	55°25·4'	1°44·4'W	FM 81
Park Fm	Notts	SK6450	53°2·8'	1°2·3'W	FM 120
Park Fm	Notts	SK7063	53°9·8'	0°56·8'W	FM 120
Park Fm	Notts	SK7191	53°24·9'	0°55·5'W	FM 112
Park Fm	N Som	ST3860	51°20·4'	2°53·0'W	FM 182
Park Fm	N Yks	NZ1904	54°26·1'	1°42·0'W	FM 92
Park Fm	N Yks	NZ4705	54°26·5'	1°16·1'W	FM 93
Park Fm	N Yks	NZ6008	54°28·1'	1°4·0'W	FM 94
Park Fm	N Yks	SE1087	54°17·0'	1°50·4'W	FM 99
Park Fm	N Yks	SE4064	54°4·5'	1°22·9'W	FM 99
Park Fm	N Yks	SE5256	54°0·1'	1°12·0'W	FM 105
Park Fm	N Yks	SE6792	54°19·4'	0°57·8'W	FM 94,100
Park Fm	N Yks	SE6838	53°50·3'	0°57·6'W	FM 105,106
Park Fm	N Yks	SE7070	54°7·5'	0°55·3'W	FM 100
Park Fm	N Yks	SE7776	54°10·7'	0°48·8'W	FM 100
Park Fm	N Yks	SE9386	54°15·9'	0°33·9'W	FM 94,101
Park Fm	Oxon	SP2727	51°56·7'	1°36·0'W	FM 163
Park Fm	Oxon	SP3427	51°56·7'	1°29·9'W	FM 164
Park Fm	Oxon	SP3632	51°59·4'	1°28·1'W	FM 151
Park Fm	Oxon	SP4217	51°51·2'	1°23·0'W	FM 164
Park Fm	Oxon	SP4734	52°0·4'	1°18·5'W	FM 151
Park Fm	Oxon	SP5120	51°52·8'	1°15·1'W	FM 164
Park Fm	Oxon	SP5224	51°55·0'	1°14·2'W	FM 164
Park Fm	Oxon	SP5530	51°58·2'	1°11·6'W	FM 152
Park Fm	Oxon	SP6108	51°46·3'	1°6·6'W	FM 164,165
Park Fm	Oxon	SU5299	51°41·5'	1°14·5'W	FM 164
Park Fm	Oxon	SU6776	51°29·0'	1°1·7'W	FM 175
Park Fm	Pemb	SS0698	51°39·1'	4°47·9'W	FM 158
Park Fm	Peterb	TF1500	52°35·4'	0°17·7'W	FM 142
Park Fm	Peterb	TF2903	52°36·8'	0°5·3'W	FM 142
Park Fm	Powys	SJ2011	52°41·7'	3°10·6'W	FM 126
Park Fm	Powys	SN9429	51°57·2'	3°32·2'W	FM 160
Park Fm	Powys	SO1671	52°20·1'	3°13·6'W	FM 136,148
Park Fm	Powys	SO1919	51°52·1'	3°10·2'W	FM 161
Park Fm	Powys	SO2117	51°51·0'	3°8·4'W	FM 161
Park Fm	Red & Cl	NZ6019	54°34·0'	1°3·9'W	FM 94
Park Fm	Renf	NS3555	55°45·9'	4°37·4'W	FM 63
Park Fm	Rut	SK8301	52°36·3'	0°46·1'W	FM 141
Park Fm	Rut	TF0512	52°42·0'	0°26·4'W	FM 130,142
Park Fm	S Glos	ST6391	51°37·2'	2°31·7'W	FM 162,172
Park Fm	Shrops	SJ3910	52°41·3'	2°53·7'W	FM 126
Park Fm	Shrops	SJ5100	52°36·0'	2°43·0'W	FM 126
Park Fm	Shrops	SJ5132	52°53·2'	2°43·3'W	FM 126
Park Fm	Shrops	SJ5903	52°37·6'	2°35·9'W	FM 126
Park Fm	Shrops	SJ6541	52°58·2'	2°30·9'W	FM 118
Park Fm	Shrops	SO4480	52°25·1'	2°49·0'W	FM 137
Park Fm	Shrops	SO6388	52°29·6'	2°32·3'W	FM 138
Park Fm	Shrops	SO6595	52°33·3'	2°30·6'W	FM 138
Park Fm	Shrops	SO7179	52°24·7'	2°25·2'W	FM 138
Park Fm	Shrops	SO7487	52°29·1'	2°22·6'W	FM 138
Park Fm	S Lanak	NS6349	55°43·2'	4°10·4'W	FM 64
Park Fm	Sol	SP2084	52°27·5'	1°41·9'W	FM 139
Park Fm	Sol	SP2380	52°25·3'	1°39·3'W	FM 139
Park Fm	Somer	ST1317	50°57·0'	3°13·9'W	FM 181,193
Park Fm	Somer	ST1620	50°58·6'	3°11·4'W	FM 181,193
Park Fm	Somer	ST1645	51°12·1'	3°11·8'W	FM 181
Park Fm	Somer	ST2129	51°3·5'	3°7·3'W	FM 193
Park Fm	Somer	ST2719	50°58·2'	3°2·0'W	FM 193
Park Fm	Somer	ST3922	50°59·9'	2°51·8'W	FM 193
Park Fm	Somer	ST4529	51°3·7'	2°46·7'W	FM 193
Park Fm	Somer	ST7952	51°16·2'	2°17·7'W	FM 183
Park Fm	Staffs	SJ7718	52°45·8'	2°20·0'W	FM 127
Park Fm	Staffs	SJ8051	53°3·6'	2°17·5'W	FM 118
Park Fm	Staffs	SJ9128	52°51·2'	2°7·6'W	FM 127
Park Fm	Staffs	SJ9525	52°49·6'	2°4·0'W	FM 127
Park Fm	Staffs	SJ9831	52°52·8'	2°1·4'W	FM 127
Park Fm	Staffs	SK0229	52°51·7'	1°57·8'W	FM 128
Park Fm	Staffs	SK1811	52°42·0'	1°43·6'W	FM 128
Park Fm	Staffs	SO8892	52°31·8'	2°10·2'W	FM 139
Park Fm	Suff	TL7170	52°18·3'	0°30·9'E	FM 154
Park Fm	Suff	TL7259	52°12·4'	0°31·4'E	FM 154
Park Fm	Suff	TL8350	52°7·3'	0°40·8'E	FM 155
Park Fm	Suff	TL8468	52°17·0'	0°42·3'E	FM 155
Park Fm	Suff	TL8871	52°18·5'	0°45·9'E	FM 144,155
Park Fm	Suff	TL9342	52°2·8'	0°49·3'E	FM 155
Park Fm	Suff	TL9653	52°8·7'	0°52·3'E	FM 155
Park Fm	Suff	TL9772	52°18·9'	0°53·8'E	FM 144,155
Park Fm	Suff	TL9956	52°10·2'	0°55·0'E	FM 155
Park Fm	Suff	TM0142	52°2·6'	0°56·3'E	FM 155
Park Fm	Suff	TM0345	52°4·2'	0°58·1'E	FM 155
Park Fm	Suff	TM0468	52°16·6'	0°59·8'E	FM 155
Park Fm	Suff	TM0744	52°3·6'	1°1·6'E	FM 155,169
Park Fm	Suff	TM0759	52°11·6'	1°2·1'E	FM 155
Park Fm	Suff	TM0847	52°5·2'	1°2·6'E	FM 155,169
Park Fm	Suff	TM1472	52°18·5'	1°8·8'E	FM 144,156
Park Fm	Suff	TM1660	52°12·0'	1°10·1'E	FM 156
Park Fm	Suff	TM1869	52°16·8'	1°12·2'E	FM 156
Park Fm	Suff	TM1977	52°21·1'	1°13·3'E	FM 156
Park Fm	Suff	TM2039	52°0·6'	1°12·7'E	FM 169
Park Fm	Suff	TM2075	52°20·0'	1°14·1'E	FM 156
Park Fm	Suff	TM2456	52°9·6'	1°16·9'E	FM 156
Park Fm	Suff	TM2781	52°23·0'	1°20·5'E	FM 156
Park Fm	Suff	TM3136	51°58·7'	1°22·2'E	FM 169
Park Fm	Suff	TM3154	52°8·4'	1°23·0'E	FM 156
Park Fm	Suff	TM3161	52°12·1'	1°23·2'E	FM 156
Park Fm	Suff	TM3280	52°22·4'	1°24·9'E	FM 156
Park Fm	Suff	TM4259	52°10·8'	1°32·8'E	FM 156
Park Fm	Suff	TM4384	52°24·2'	1°34·8'E	FM 156
Park Fm	Suff	TM4577	52°20·4'	1°36·2'E	FM 156
Park Fm	Suff	TM5083	52°23·5'	1°40·9'E	FM 156
Park Fm	Suff	TM5098	52°31·6'	1°41·5'E	FM 134
Park Fm	Surrey	TQ0037	51°7·6'	0°33·9'W	FM 186
Park Fm	Surrey	TQ1248	51°13·4'	0°23·4'W	FM 187
Park Fm	Surrey	TQ1849	51°13·9'	0°18·2'W	FM 187
Park Fm	Surrey	TQ2754	51°16·5'	0°10·4'W	FM 187
Park Fm	Surrey	TQ3640	51°8·8'	0°2·9'W	FM 187
Park Fm	Surrey	TQ3944	51°10·9'	0°0·3'W	FM 187
Park Fm	Surrey	TQ4054	51°16·3'	0°0·8'E	FM 187
Park Fm	Swin	SU1789	51°36·2'	1°44·9'W	FM 173
Park Fm	Wakf	SE4222	53°41·8'	1°21·4'W	FM 105
Park Fm	Warw	SP1462	52°15·6'	1°47·3'W	FM 151
Park Fm	Warw	SP1957	52°12·9'	1°42·9'W	FM 151
Park Fm	Warw	SP2259	52°14·0'	1°40·3'W	FM 151
Park Fm	Warw	SP2646	52°6·9'	1°36·8'W	FM 151
Park Fm	Warw	SP2962	52°15·6'	1°34·1'W	FM 151
Park Fm	Warw	SP3052	52°10·2'	1°33·3'W	FM 151
Park Fm	Warw	SP3884	52°27·4'	1°26·0'W	FM 140
Park Fm	Warw	SP4071	52°20·4'	1°24·4'W	FM 140
Park Fm	Warw	SP4960	52°14·4'	1°16·5'W	FM 151
Park Fm	W Berks	SU2981	51°31·9'	1°34·5'W	FM 174
Park Fm	W Berks	SU3567	51°24·3'	1°29·4'W	FM 174
Park Fm	W Berks	SU5269	51°25·3'	1°14·7'W	FM 174

Park Fm	W Berks	SU6177	51°29·5′	1°6·9′W	FM	175
Park Fm	Wilts	ST8255	51°17·9′	2°15·1′W	FM	173
Park Fm	Wilts	ST8677	51°29·7′	2°11·7′W	FM	173
Park Fm	Wilts	ST9787	51°35·1′	2°2·2′W	FM	173
Park Fm	Wilts	ST9892	51°37·8′	2°1·3′W	FM	163,173
Park Fm	Wilts	SU0080	51°31·4′	1°59·6′W	FM	173
Park Fm	Wilts	SU1084	51°33·5′	1°51·0′W	FM	173
Park Fm	Wilts	SU1665	51°23·3′	1°45·8′W	FM	173
Park Fm	Wilts	SU2065	51°23·3′	1°42·4′W	FM	174
Park Fm	Wilts	SU2569	51°25·4′	1°38·0′W	FM	174
Park Fm	Win & Maid	SU8273	51°27·2′	0°48·8′W	FM	175
Park Fm	Win & Maid	SU8584	51°33·1′	0°46·0′W	FM	175
Park Fm	W Loth	NT0277	55°58·8′	3°33·8′W	FM	65
Park Fm	Worcs	SO7663	52°16·1′	2°20·7′W	FM	138,150
Park Fm	Worcs	SO7774	52°22·1′	2°19·9′W	FM	138
Park Fm	Worcs	SO8462	52°15·6′	2°13·7′W	FM	138,150
Park Fm	Worcs	SO8647	52°7·5′	2°11·9′W	FM	150
Park Fm	Worcs	SO8965	52°17·2′	2°9·3′W	FM	150
Park Fm	Worcs	SO9160	52°14·5′	2°7·5′W	FM	150
Park Fm	Worcs	SO9371	52°20·5′	2°5·8′W	FM	139
Park Fm	Worcs	SO9639	52°3·2′	2°3·1′W	FM	150
Park Fm	Wrex	SJ2451	53°3·3′	3°7·6′W	FM	117
Park Fm	Wrex	SJ3141	52°58·0′	3°1·2′W	FM	117
Park Fm	W Susx	SU9001	50°48·3′	0°43·0′W	FM	197
Park Fm	W Susx	SU9204	50°49·9′	0°41·2′W	FM	197
Park Fm	W Susx	SU9308	50°52·1′	0°40·3′W	FM	197
Park Fm	W Susx	SU9327	51°2·3′	0°40·0′W	FM	186,197
Park Fm	W Susx	SZ8694	50°44·6′	0°46·5′W	FM	197
Park Fm	W Susx	TQ0007	50°51·5′	0°34·4′W	FM	197
Park Fm	W Susx	TQ0931	51°4·3′	0°26·3′W	FM	187
Park Fm	W Susx	TQ1622	50°59·4′	0°20·4′W	FM	198
Park Fm	W Susx	TQ2217	50°56·6′	0°15·4′W	FM	198
Park Fm	W Susx	TQ2519	50°57·6′	0°12·8′W	FM	198
Park Fm	W Susx	TQ2624	51°0·3′	0°11·9′W	FM	198
Park Fm	York	SE5745	53°54·1′	1°7·5′W	FM	105
Park Fm	York	SE5757	54°0·6′	1°7·4′W	FM	105
Park Fms	Lancs	SD6330	53°46·1′	2°33·3′W	FM	102,103
Park Fm, The	Norf	TF9809	52°38·8′	0°56·0′E	FM	144
Park Foot	Cumbr	NY4623	54°36·2′	2°49·7′W	X	90
Parkfoot	D & G	NY0681	55°7·1′	3°28·0′W	X	78
Parkfoot	Falk	NS8079	55°59·6′	3°55·0′W	T	65
Parkfoot	Moray	NJ3751	57°32·9′	3°2·7′W	X	28
Park Foot	N Yks	SD6771	54°8·3′	2°29·9′W	X	98
Parkford	Angus	NO4754	56°40·7′	2°51·5′W	X	54
Parkgate	Ches	SJ2778	53°17·9′	3°5·3′W	T	117
Parkgate	Ches	SJ7873	53°15·5′	2°19·4′W	T	118
Parkgate	Ches	SJ9684	53°21·4′	2°3·2′W	X	109
Parkgate	Cumbr	NY1100	54°23·5′	3°21·8′W	X	89
Parkgate	Cumbr	NY2146	54°48·4′	3°13·3′W	T	85
Parkgate	Derby	SK2771	53°14·4′	1°35·3′W	X	119
Park Gate	Devon	SS5529	51°2·8′	4°3·7′W	X	180
Parkgate	D & G	NX6746	54°47·7′	4°3·7′W	X	83,84
Parkgate	D & G	NY0187	55°10·3′	3°32·8′W	T	78
Parkgate	D & G	NY1971	55°1·9′	3°15·6′W	X	85
Park Gate	Dorset	ST7407	50°51·9′	2°21·8′W	T	194
Parkgate	Essex	TL6621	51°49·8′	0°24·9′E	T	167
Parkgate	Essex	TL6829	51°56·3′	0°27·0′E	X	167
Park Gate	E Susx	TQ4313	50°54·1′	0°2·4′E	X	198
Park Gate	Hants	SU5108	50°52·4′	1°16·1′W	T	196
Park Gate	Heref	SO4755	52°11·7′	2°46·1′W	X	148,149
Parkgate	Kent	TQ8534	51°4·7′	0°38·9′E	T	189
Park Gate	Kent	TR1745	51°10·0′	1°6·6′E	T	179,189
Park Gate	Kirk	SE2311	53°35·9′	1°38·7′W	T	110
Park Gate	Lancs	SD5049	53°56·3′	2°45·3′W	X	102
Park Gate	Lancs	SD6245	53°54·2′	2°34·3′W	X	102,103
Park Gate	Lancs	SD6433	53°47·8′	2°32·4′W	X	102,103
Park Gate	N Yks	NZ9304	54°25·6′	0°33·6′W	X	94
Park Gate	N Yks	SE0788	54°17·5′	1°53·1′W	X	99
Park Gate	N Yks	SE8085	54°15·5′	0°45·9′W	X	94,100
Parkgate	Roth	SK4395	53°27·2′	1°20·7′W	T	111
Parkgate	Staffs	SK1044	52°59·8′	1°50·7′W	X	119,128
Parkgate	Staffs	SK1225	52°49·6′	1°48·9′W	X	128
Park Gate	Suff	TL7456	52°10·7′	0°33·1′E	T	155
Parkgate	Surrey	TQ2043	51°10·6′	0°16·6′W	T	187
Park Gate	Worcs	SO9371	52°20·5′	2°5·8′W	T	139
Parkgate Cottages	Cumbr	NY5570	55°1·6′	2°41·8′W	X	86
Parkgate Fm	Ches	SJ7083	53°20·8′	2°26·6′W	FM	109
Parkgate Fm	Ches	SJ7377	53°17·6′	2°23·9′W	FM	118
Parkgate Fm	Ches	SJ9385	53°22·0′	2°5·9′W	FM	109
Parkgate Fm	Cumbr	NY3921	54°35·1′	2°56·2′W	FM	90
Parkgate Fm	Derby	SK3844	52°59·8′	1°25·6′W	FM	119,128
Parkgate Fm	Derby	SK4076	53°17·0′	1°23·6′W	FM	120
Parkgate Fm	Essex	TL8037	52°0·4′	0°37·8′E	FM	155
Parkgate Fm	Essex	TL8219	51°50·6′	0°38·9′E	FM	168
Parkgate Fm	Essex	TM1819	51°49·8′	1°10·2′E	FM	168,169
Park Gate Fm	Hants	SU6359	51°19·8′	1°5·4′W	FM	175
Parkgate Fm	Suff	TM2866	52°14·9′	1°20·8′E	FM	156
Parkgate Fm	Suff	TM3559	52°11·0′	1°26·7′E	FM	156
Park Gate Fm	Suff	TM3866	52°14·7′	1°29·6′E	FM	156
Park Gate Fm	Wilts	ST9225	51°1·7′	2°6·5′W	FM	184
Parkgate Fm	Wilts	SU0788	51°35·7′	1°53·5′W	FM	173
Parkgate Ho	Ches	SJ3670	53°13·6′	2°57·1′W	X	117
Park Gate Ho	Kent	TQ5064	51°21·5′	0°9·7′E	X	177,188
Parkgate Ho	Rich	TQ1871	51°25·8′	0°17·8′W	X	176
Parkgate Manor	E Susx	TQ7214	50°54·2′	0°27·2′E	X	199
Parkgate Rough	W Susx	SU8629	51°3·5′	0°46·0′W	F	186,197
Parkgates	Northum	NY8454	54°53·1′	2°14·5′W	X	86,87
Parkgatestone	Scot Bord	NT0936	55°36·8′	3°26·2′W	X	72
Parkgate Tarn	Cumbr	NY1100	54°23·5′	3°21·8′W	W	89
Park Gill	Northum	NY8154	54°53·1′	2°17·3′W	X	86,87
Park Gill Beck	N Yks	SD9874	54°10·0′	2°1·4′W	W	98
Park Grange	Leic	SK5316	52°44·6′	1°12·5′W	X	129
Park Grange	N Yks	SE1291	54°19·1′	1°48·5′W	X	99
Parkgrange Fm	Oxon	SP7003	51°43·5′	0°58·8′W	FM	165
Park Green	Essex	TL4628	51°56·1′	0°7·8′E	T	167
Park Green	N Yks	SE3267	54°6·1′	1°30·2′W	X	99
Park Green	Suff	TM1364	52°14·2′	1°7·6′E	X	156
Park Green Fm	I of W	SZ4689	50°42·2′	1°20·5′W	FM	196
Park Ground	Cumbr	SD2893	54°19·9′	3°6·0′W	X	96,97
Park Ground Inclosure	Hants	SU3006	50°51·4′	1°34·0′W	F	196
Park Grounds	Lincs	SK9720	52°46·4′	0°33·3′W	X	130
Park Grounds Fm	E Yorks	SE7919	53°39·9′	0°47·8′W	FM	112
Parkgrounds Fm	Lincs	SK9721	52°46·9′	0°33·3′W	FM	130
Park Grounds Fm	Wilts	SU0584	51°33·5′	1°55·3′W	FM	173
Park Grove	E Susx	TQ5133	51°4·8′	0°9·7′E	X	188
Park Grove	Suff	TL9276	52°21·1′	0°49·6′E	F	144
Parkhall	Aberd	NJ4440	57°27·1′	2°55·5′W	X	28
Park Hall	Ches	SJ4868	53°12·6′	2°46·3′W	X	117
Park Hall	Ches	SJ6961	53°9·0′	2°27·4′W	X	118
Park Hall	Derby	SK0388	53°23·6′	1°56·9′W	X	110
Park Hall	Derby	SK3847	53°1·4′	1°25·6′W	A	119,128
Park Hall	Essex	TL7028	51°55·7′	0°28·8′E	X	167
Park Hall	Lancs	SD5415	53°38·0′	2°41·3′W	X	108
Park Hall	Notts	SK5465	53°11·0′	1°11·1′W	X	120
Park Hall	N Yks	NZ1407	54°27·7′	1°46·6′W	A	92
Park Hall	N Yks	SE0098	54°22·9′	1°59·6′W	X	98
Parkhall	Orkney	HY4918	59°3·0′	2°52·9′W	X	6
Park Hall	Shetld	HU3152	60°15·3′	1°25·9′W	X	3
Park Hall	Shrops	SJ3031	52°52·6′	3°2·0′W	T	126
Park Hall	Shrops	SJ3938	52°56·4′	2°54·1′W	X	126
Parkhall	S Lanak	NS8633	55°34·9′	3°48·1′W	X	71,72
Park Hall	Staffs	SK0236	52°55·5′	1°57·8′W	X	128
Parkhall	Stir	NS5387	56°3·5′	4°21·2′W	X	57
Park Hall	Warw	SP0651	52°9·7′	1°54·3′W	X	150
Parkhall	W Dunb	NS4972	55°55·3′	4°24·5′W	T	64
Parkhall	W Loth	NT0362	55°50·7′	3°32·5′W	X	65
Park Hall	Worcs	SO8677	52°23·7′	2°11·9′W	X	139
Parkhall Burn	S Lanak	NS8631	55°33·8′	3°48·0′W	W	71,72
Park Hall Fm	Bolton	SD6209	53°34·8′	2°34·0′W	FM	109
Parkhall Fm	Essex	TL7629	51°56·1′	0°34·0′E	FM	167
Park Hall Fm	Staffs	SJ7926	52°50·1′	2°18·3′W	FM	127
Park Hall (Hotel)	Derby	SK4678	53°18·1′	1°18·2′W	A	120
Parkhall Wood	Essex	TL7528	51°55·6′	0°33·1′E	F	167
Parkham	Devon	SS3821	50°58·2′	4°18·1′W	T	190
Parkham Ash	Devon	SS3620	50°57·6′	4°19·7′W	T	190
Park Hatch	Surrey	TQ0138	51°8·2′	0°33·0′W	X	186
Parkhead	Aberd	NJ5720	57°16·4′	2°42·3′W	X	37
Parkhead	Aberd	NO7867	56°47·9′	2°21·2′W	X	45
Parkhead	Aberd	NO8599	57°5·2′	2°14·4′W	T	38,45
Parkhead	Angus	NO2453	56°40·0′	3°14·0′W	X	53
Parkhead	Arg & Bt	NS2681	55°59·7′	4°47·0′W	X	63
Parkhead	C of Aber	NJ8606	57°8·9′	2°13·4′W	X	38
Parkhead	C of Aber	NJ8610	57°11·1′	2°13·4′W	X	38
Parkhead	C of Glas	NS6263	55°50·7′	4°11·8′W	T	64
Park Head	Corn	SW8470	50°29·6′	5°2·4′W	X	200
Park Head	Cumbr	NY1351	54°51·0′	3°20·9′W	X	85
Parkhead	Cumbr	NY3340	54°45·3′	3°2·0′W	T	85
Park Head	Cumbr	NY5676	55°4·8′	2°40·9′W	X	86
Park Head	Cumbr	NY5841	54°46·0′	2°38·7′W	T	86
Park Head	Cumbr	SD3378	54°11·9′	3°1·2′W	X	96,97
Park Head	Cumbr	SD5493	54°20·1′	2°42·0′W	X	97
Park Head	Derby	SK3654	53°5·2′	1°27·3′W	T	119
Parkhead	D & G	NX9060	54°55·6′	3°42·6′W	X	84
Parkhead	D & G	NY3275	55°4·1′	3°3·5′W	X	85
Park Head	Durham	NZ1650	54°50·9′	1°44·6′W	X	88
Park Head	Durham	NZ2330	54°40·1′	1°38·2′W	X	93
Parkhead	E Ayr	NS4943	55°39·7′	4°23·6′W	X	70
Parkhead	Falk	NS8373	55°56·4′	3°52·0′W	X	65
Park Head	Kirk	SE1908	53°34·3′	1°42·4′W	T	110
Park Head	Lancs	SD5037	53°49·9′	2°45·2′W	X	102
Park Head	Lancs	SD5439	53°51·0′	2°41·5′W	X	102
Park Head	Lancs	SD7434	53°48·3′	2°23·3′W	X	103
Parkhead	Moray	NJ2038	57°25·8′	3°19·5′W	X	28
Parkhead	Moray	NJ3437	57°25·4′	3°5·5′W	X	28
Park Head	Northum	NY7656	54°54·1′	2°22·0′W	X	86,87
Park Head	Northum	NY7665	54°59·0′	2°22·1′W	X	86,87
Parkhead	Northum	NY9085	55°9·8′	2°9·0′W	X	80
Park Head	Northum	NZ0381	55°7·6′	1°56·7′W	X	81
Park Head	N Yks	NY9606	54°27·2′	2°3·3′W	X	91,92
Parkhead	Pth & Kin	NN8917	56°20·2′	3°47·3′W	X	58
Parkhead	Pth & Kin	NO1434	56°29·7′	3°23·4′W	X	53
Parkhead	Scot Bord	NT4006	55°20·9′	2°56·3′W	X	79
Park Head	Sheff	SK3283	53°20·8′	1°30·7′W	T	110,111
Parkhead	S Lanak	NS6552	55°44·8′	4°8·6′W	X	64
Parkhead	S Lanak	NS8630	55°33·3′	3°48·0′W	X	71,72
Parkhead	S Lanak	NS8740	55°38·7′	3°47·3′W	X	71,72
Parkhead	Stir	NS8197	56°9·3′	3°54·5′W	X	57
Parkhead	W Loth	NS9977	55°58·8′	3°36·7′W	X	65
Parkhead	W Loth	NT0878	55°59·4′	3°28·0′W	X	65
Parkhead Fell	Northum	NY7456	54°54·1′	2°23·9′W	X	86,87
Parkhead Fm	Lancs	SD5045	53°54·2′	2°45·2′W	FM	102
Park Head Fm	Northum	NZ1091	55°13·0′	1°50·1′W	FM	81
Parkhead Hill	S Lanak	NS8530	55°33·3′	3°49·0′W	H	71,72
Park Head Plantn	Durham	NZ0643	54°47·2′	1°54·0′W	F	87
Park Heath	Norf	TL8589	52°28·3′	0°43·8′E	F	144
Park Heath	Shrops	SJ7326	52°50·1′	2°23·6′W	X	127
Parkhill	Aberd	NJ7315	57°13·8′	2°26·4′W	X	38
Parkhill	Aberd	NJ8246	57°30·5′	2°17·6′W	X	29,30
Parkhill	Aberd	NK0645	57°30·0′	1°53·5′W	X	30
Parkhill	Aberd	NK0646	57°30·5′	1°53·5′W	X	30
Parkhill	Angus	NO2360	56°43·8′	3°15·1′W	X	44
Parkhill	Angus	NO6445	56°36·0′	2°34·7′W	X	54
Park Hill	Cumbr	SD4982	54°14·1′	2°46·5′W	H	97
Park Hill	Cumbr	SD6087	54°16·9′	2°36·4′W	H	97
Park Hill	Derby	SK2629	52°51·7′	1°36·4′W	X	128
Park Hill	D & G	NX8066	54°58·7′	3°52·1′W	H	84
Park Hill	D & G	NX8255	54°52·8′	3°49·9′W	H	84
Park Hill	Dorset	SY7797	50°46·6′	2°19·2′W	X	194
Parkhill	Fife	NO2418	56°21·2′	3°13·3′W	T	59
Park Hill	Fife	NT0695	56°8·6′	3°30·3′W	H	58
Park Hill	Glos	ST5699	51°41·5′	2°37·8′W	T	162
Park Hill	Hants	SU3106	50°51·4′	1°33·2′W	X	196
Parkhill	Hants	SU3107	50°51·9′	1°33·2′W	X	196
Park Hill	Hants	SU6822	50°59·8′	1°1·5′W	H	185
Parkhill	Inverc	NS3573	55°55·6′	4°38·0′W	T	63
Park Hill	Kent	TQ9531	51°2·9′	0°47·3′E	T	189
Park Hill	Kent	TR2741	51°7·6′	1°15·0′E	X	179
Park Hill	Lancs	SD8639	53°51·1′	2°12·4′W	A	103
Park Hill	Leic	SK6217	52°45·1′	1°4·5′W	X	129
Park Hill	Lincs	TF2976	53°16·1′	0°3·5′W	X	122
Park Hill	Notts	SK7052	53°3·9′	0°56·9′W	X	120
Park Hill	N Yks	SE9497	54°21·8′	0°32·8′W	X	94,101
Park Hill	Oxon	SU4588	51°35·6′	1°20·6′W	X	174
Parkhill	Pth & Kin	NO1846	56°36·2′	3°19·7′W	X	53
Parkhill	S Ayr	NS4528	55°31·5′	4°26·9′W	X	70
Park Hill	S Ayr	NX1777	55°3·5′	4°51·5′W	X	76
Parkhill	Scot Bord	NT4212	55°24·2′	2°54·5′W	X	79
Park Hill	Scot Bord	NY4687	55°10·7′	2°50·4′W	H	79
Park Hill	Sheff	SK3687	53°23·0′	1°27·1′W	T	110,111
Park Hill	St Hel	SD4602	53°31·0′	2°48·5′W	T	108
Parkhill	Suff	TM5395	52°29·9′	1°44·1′E	X	134
Park Hill	Warw	SP4962	52°15·5′	1°16·5′W	X	151
Park Hill	Wilts	ST8243	51°11·4′	2°15·1′W	H	183
Park Hill	Wolv	SO9195	52°33·4′	2°7·6′W	X	139
Parkhill Fm	Bucks	SP7932	51°59·1′	0°50·6′W	FM	152,165
Park Hill Fm	Devon	SX8467	50°29·7′	3°37·8′W	FM	202
Parkhill Fm	Hants	SU5341	51°10·2′	1°14·1′W	FM	185
Parkhill Fm	Herts	SP9413	51°48·7′	0°37·8′W	FM	165
Park Hill Fm	Leeds	SE4147	53°55·3′	1°22·1′W	FM	105
Park Hill Fm	Northnts	SP7784	52°27·1′	0°51·6′W	FM	141
Parkhill Fm	Northnts	SP8759	52°13·6′	0°43·2′W	FM	152
Park Hill Fm	Roth	SK5688	53°23·4′	1°9·1′W	FM	111,120
Parkhill Fm	Warw	SP2644	52°5·9′	1°36·8′W	FM	151
Park Hill Grange	Donc	SE6208	53°34·1′	1°3·4′W	X	111
Park Hill Hales	Staffs	SJ7334	52°54·4′	2°23·7′W	X	127
Parkhillhead	N Lanak	NS6470	55°54·5′	4°10·1′W	X	64
Parkhill Ho	Aberd	NJ8913	57°12·7′	2°10·5′W	X	38
Parkhill Ho	Fife	NO2518	56°21·2′	3°12·4′W	X	59
Park Hill Ho	N Yks	SE3268	54°6·7′	1°30·2′W	X	99
Parkhill Inclosure	Glos	SO6107	51°45·9′	2°33·5′W	F	162
Parkhill Inclosure	Hants	SU3105	50°50·9′	1°33·2′W	F	196
Park Hills	E Loth	NT4980	56°0·9′	2°48·6′W	X	66
Park Hills Wood	Hants	SU5019	50°58·3′	1°16·9′W	F	185
Park Ho	Aberd	NO7797	57°4·1′	2°22·3′W	X	38,45
Park Ho	Brad	SE0340	53°51·6′	1°56·8′W	X	104
Park Ho	Bury	SD8015	53°38·1′	2°17·7′W	X	109
Park Ho	Cambs	TF4016	52°43·6′	0°4·8′E	X	131
Park Ho	Cambs	TF4310	52°40·4′	0°7·3′E	X	131,142,143
Park Ho	Carm	SN5602	51°42·1′	4°4·6′W	X	159
Park Ho	Ches	SJ4654	53°5·1′	2°48·0′W	X	117
Park Ho	Ches	SJ6961	53°9·0′	2°27·4′W	X	118
Park Ho	Ches	SJ7661	53°9·0′	2°21·1′W	X	118
Park Ho	Cumbr	NX9823	54°35·8′	3°34·3′W	X	89
Park Ho	Cumbr	NY2140	54°45·2′	3°13·2′W	X	85
Park Ho	Cumbr	NY2954	54°52·8′	3°6·0′W	X	85
Park Ho	Cumbr	NY3303	54°25·3′	3°1·5′W	X	90
Park Ho	Cumbr	NY3645	54°48·0′	2°59·3′W	X	85
Park Ho	Cumbr	NY4449	54°52·5′	2°51·9′W	X	85
Park Ho	Cumbr	NY4700	54°23·8′	2°48·6′W	X	90
Park Ho	Cumbr	NY4727	54°38·4′	2°48·8′W	X	90
Park Ho	Cumbr	NY5154	54°53·0′	2°45·4′W	X	86
Park Ho	Cumbr	NY6724	54°36·9′	2°30·2′W	X	91
Park Ho	Cumbr	SD1682	54°13·9′	3°16·9′W	X	96
Park Ho	Cumbr	SD4982	54°14·1′	2°46·5′W	X	97
Park Ho	Darl	NZ2322	54°35·8′	1°38·2′W	X	93
Park Ho	Derby	SK2931	52°52·8′	1°33·7′W	X	128
Park Ho	D & G	NX6850	54°49·9′	4°2·9′W	X	83,84
Park Ho	D & G	NY3976	55°4·7′	2°56·9′W	X	85
Park Ho	Durham	NY9238	54°44·5′	2°7·0′W	X	91,92
Park Ho	Durham	NZ0520	54°34·8′	1°54·9′W	X	92
Park Ho	Durham	NZ1232	54°41·2′	1°48·4′W	X	92
Park Ho	Durham	NZ1523	54°36·4′	1°45·6′W	X	92
Park Ho	Durham	NZ2036	54°43·4′	1°40·9′W	X	93
Park Ho	Durham	NZ3834	54°42·2′	1°24·2′W	X	93
Park Ho	Essex	TL8022	51°52·3′	0°37·3′E	X	168
Park Ho	Essex	TQ6390	51°35·3′	0°21·6′E	X	177
Park Ho	E Yorks	TA1158	54°0·6′	0°18·0′W	X	107
Park Ho	Glos	ST6697	51°40·5′	2°29·1′W	X	162
Park Ho	Hants	SU2343	51°11·4′	1°39·9′W	X	184
Park Ho	Hants	SU6516	50°56·6′	1°4·1′W	X	185
Park Ho	Kent	TQ5464	51°21·5′	0°13·1′E	X	177,188
Park Ho	Kent	TQ7233	51°4·5′	0°27·7′E	X	188
Park Ho	Kent	TQ7643	51°9·8′	0°31·4′E	X	188
Park Ho	Kent	TQ7758	51°17·8′	0°32·7′E	X	178,188
Park Ho	Kent	TQ8747	51°11·7′	0°41·0′E	X	189
Park Ho	Lancs	SD5338	53°50·4′	2°42·4′W	X	102
Park Ho	Lancs	SD6069	54°7·2′	2°36·3′W	X	97
Park Ho	Lancs	SD6366	54°5·6′	2°33·5′W	X	97
Park Ho	Leic	SP4494	52°32·8′	1°20·7′W	X	140
Park Ho	Lincs	SK8388	53°23·2′	0°44·7′W	X	112,121
Park Ho	Lincs	TF0583	53°20·2′	0°25·0′W	X	121
Park Ho	Lincs	TF1539	52°56·4′	0°16·9′W	X	130
Park Ho	Lincs	TF1550	53°2·3′	0°16·7′W	X	121
Park Ho	Mil Key	SP8145	52°6·1′	0°48·6′W	X	152
Park Ho	Moray	NJ3639	57°26·5′	3°3·5′W	X	28
Park Ho	Newp	ST2486	51°34·3′	3°5·4′W	X	171
Park Ho	Norf	TF6828	52°49·6′	0°30·0′E	X	132
Park Ho	Norf	TF9621	52°45·3′	0°54·7′E	X	132
Park Ho	Northnts	SP6470	52°19·7′	1°3·3′W	X	140
Park Ho	Northum	NT9205	55°20·6′	2°7·1′W	X	80
Park Ho	Northum	NY7750	54°50·9′	2°21·1′W	X	86,87
Park Ho	Northum	NY9253	54°52·5′	2°7·1′W	X	87
Park Ho	Northum	NZ1774	55°3·9′	1°43·6′W	X	88
Park Ho	Northum	NZ2185	55°9·8′	1°39·8′W	X	81
Park Ho	Notts	SK5989	53°23·9′	1°6·3′W	X	111,120
Park Ho	N Yks	NZ0809	54°28·8′	1°52·2′W	X	92
Park Ho	N Yks	NZ1810	54°29·3′	1°42·9′W	X	92
Park Ho	N Yks	NZ4407	54°27·6′	1°18·9′W	X	93
Park Ho	N Yks	NZ7208	54°28·0′	0°52·9′W	X	94
Park Ho	N Yks	NZ7515	54°31·7′	0°50·0′W	X	94
Park Ho	N Yks	SD8859	54°1·9′	2°10·6′W	X	103
Park Ho	N Yks	SD9363	54°4·0′	2°6·0′W	X	98
Park Ho	N Yks	SE2263	54°4·0′	1°39·4′W	X	99
Park Ho	N Yks	SE2585	54°15·8′	1°36·6′W	X	99
Park Ho	N Yks	SE2667	54°6·1′	1°35·7′W	X	99
Park Ho	N Yks	SE3164	54°4·5′	1°31·2′W	X	99
Park Ho	N Yks	SE3875	54°10·4′	1°24·7′W	X	99
Park Ho	N Yks	SE3954	53°59·1′	1°23·9′W	X	104
Park Ho	N Yks	SE4770	54°7·7′	1°16·4′W	X	100
Park Ho	N Yks	SE5226	53°43·9′	1°12·3′W	X	105

Park Ho	N Yks	SE5259	54°1·7'	1°12·0'W	X	105
Park Ho	N Yks	SE5569	54°7·1'	1°9·1'W	X	100
Park Ho	N Yks	SE5675	54°10·3'	1°8·1'W	X	100
Park Ho	N Yks	SE5976	54°10·8'	1°5·3'W	X	100
Park Ho	N Yks	SE7065	54°4·8'	0°55·4'W	X	100
Park Ho	N Yks	SE7371	54°8·0'	0°52·5'W	X	100
Park Ho	Pemb	SN0416	51°48·7'	4°50·2'W	X	157,158
Park Ho	Red & Cl	NZ6418	54°33·4'	1°0·2'W	X	94
Park Ho	Red & Cl	NZ7016	54°32·3'	0°54·7'W	X	94
Park Ho	Shrops	SJ3724	52°48·8'	2°55·7'W	X	126
Park Ho	Shrops	SJ4028	52°51·0'	2°53·1'W	X	126
Park Ho	Shrops	SJ6822	52°47·9'	2°28·1'W	X	127
Park Ho	Somer	ST1938	51°8·4'	3°9·1'W	X	181
Park Ho	Somer	ST7148	51°14·1'	2°24·5'W	X	183
Park Ho	Staffs	SJ7532	52°53·3'	2°21·9'W	X	127
Park Ho	Staffs	SJ7538	52°56·6'	2°21·9'W	X	127
Park Ho	Staffs	SJ8520	52°46·9'	2°12·9'W	X	127
Park Ho	Staffs	SJ9749	53°2·5'	2°2·3'W	X	118
Park Ho	Staffs	SJ9859	53°7·9'	2°1·4'W	X	118
Park Ho	Suff	TM0934	51°58·1'	1°3·0'E	X	155,169
Park Ho	Suff	TM1439	52°0·7'	1°7·5'E	X	169
Park Ho	Warw	SP2786	52°28·5'	1°35·7'W	X	140
Park Ho	W Berks	SU3862	51°21·6'	1°26·9'W	X	174
Park Ho	Wilts	ST9027	51°2·8'	2°8·2'W	X	184
Park Ho (Hotel)	Devon	SS7226	51°1·4'	3°49·1'W	X	180
Park Ho (Hotel)	W Susx	SU8618	50°57·5'	0°46·1'W	X	197
Park Hole Wood	N Yks	NZ7903	54°25·2'	0°46·5'W	F	94
Park Hoskyn	Corn	SW7549	50°18·1'	5°9·2'W	X	204
Park Hospl	Beds	TL1348	52°7·4'	0°20·6'W	X	153
Parkhouse	Aberd	NJ9546	57°30·5'	2°4·5'W	X	30
Parkhouse	Ches	SJ8969	53°13·3'	2°9·5'W	X	118
Parkhouse	Cumbr	NY1352	54°51·6'	3°20·9'W	X	85
Park House	Cumbr	NY4572	55°2·6'	2°51·2'W	X	86
Parkhouse	D & G	NY4379	55°6·4'	2°53·2'W	X	85
Park House	Durham	NZ2627	54°38·5'	1°35·4'W	X	93
Parkhouse	E Yorks	TA0141	53°51·6'	0°27·4'W	X	106,107
Parkhouse	Highld	NH6045	57°28·7'	4°19·6'W	X	26
Park House	Kent	TR1444	51°9·5'	1°4·0'E	X	179,189
Park House	Lancs	SD8149	53°56·4'	2°17·0'W	X	103
Parkhouse	Monm	SO4902	51°43·1'	2°43·9'W	T	162
Parkhouse	Orkney	HY7654	59°22·6'	2°24·9'W	X	5
Parkhouse	S Lanak	NS9839	55°38·3'	3°36·8'W	X	72
Park House	Staffs	SJ7037	52°56·0'	2°26·4'W	X	127
Parkhouse	Suff	TM0839	52°0·8'	1°2·3'E	X	155,169
Park House Fm	Cambs	TL2293	52°31·5'	0°11·7'W	FM	142
Park House Fm	Ches	SJ6444	52°59·8'	2°31·8'W	FM	118
Park House Fm	Ches	SJ8773	53°15·5'	2°11·3'W	FM	118
Park House Fm	Ches	SJ9077	53°17·6'	2°8·6'W	FM	118
Park House Fm	Ches	SJ9184	53°21·4'	2°7·7'W	FM	109
Parkhouse Fm	Cumbr	NX9913	54°30·4'	3°33·2'W	FM	89
Park House Fm	Cumbr	NY1331	54°40·2'	3°20·5'W	FM	89
Park House Fm	Cumbr	SD2271	54°8·0'	3°11·2'W	FM	96
Park House Fm	Derby	SK4163	53°10·0'	1°22·8'W	FM	120
Park House Fm	Durham	NY9620	54°34·8'	2°3·3'W	FM	91,92
Park House Fm	E Yorks	SE7243	53°52·9'	0°53·9'W	FM	105,106
Park House Fm	Kent	TQ9847	51°11·5'	0°50·4'E	FM	189
Park House Fm	Lancs	SD3509	53°34·7'	2°58·5'W	FM	108
Park House Fm	Leeds	SE4235	53°48·8'	1°21·3'W	FM	105
Park House Fm	Leeds	SE4429	53°45·6'	1°19·5'W	FM	105
Park House Fm	Leic	SK4903	52°37·6'	1°16·2'W	FM	140
Park House Fm	Lincs	SK8697	53°28·0'	0°41·9'W	FM	112
Park House Fm	Lincs	SK9620	52°46·4'	0°34·2'W	FM	130
Parkhouse Fm	Northum	NY8776	55°4·9'	2°11·8'W	FM	87
Park House Fm	Notts	SK5570	53°13·7'	1°10·2'W	FM	120
Park House Fm	N Yks	NZ3300	54°23·9'	1°29·1'W	FM	93
Park House Fm	N Yks	SE1591	54°19·1'	1°45·7'W	FM	99
Park House Fm	N Yks	SE3450	53°56·9'	1°28·5'W	FM	104
Park House Fm	N Yks	SE3582	54°14·2'	1°27·4'W	FM	99
Park House Fm	N Yks	SE4585	54°15·8'	1°18·1'W	FM	99
Parkhouse Fm	Somer	ST1443	51°11·0'	3°13·4'W	FM	181
Park House Fm	Staffs	SJ8226	52°50·1'	2°15·6'W	FM	127
Park House Fm	Staffs	SK0253	53°4·7'	1°57·8'W	FM	119
Parkhouse Fm	Surrey	TQ2144	51°11·2'	0°15·7'W	FM	187
Park House Fm	Wigan	SD5702	53°31·0'	2°38·5'W	FM	108
Parkhouse Green	Derby	SK4163	53°10·0'	1°22·8'W	T	120
Parkhouse Hill	Aberd	NJ9547	57°31·0'	2°4·5'W	X	30
Parkhouse Hill	Derby	SK0867	53°12·2'	1°52·4'W	H	119
Park House Lodge	Ches	SJ7765	53°11·1'	2°20·2'W	X	118
Park House Stables	Hants	SU5257	51°18·8'	1°14·8'W	X	174
Parkhurst	E Susx	TQ4925	51°0·5'	0°7·8'E	X	188,199
Parkhurst	I of W	SZ4990	50°42·7'	1°18·0'W	T	196
Parkhurst	Surrey	TQ1244	51°11·3'	0°23·4'W	X	187
Parkhurst Fm	W Susx	SU9524	51°0·7'	0°38·4'W	FM	197
Parkhurst Forest	I of W	SZ4791	50°43·2'	1°19·7'W	F	196
Parkhurst Hill	Hants	SU8250	51°14·8'	0°49·1'W	X	186
Parkhurst Prison	I of W	SZ4890	50°42·7'	1°18·8'W	X	196
Parkia	Gwyn	SH4964	53°9·4'	4°15·1'W	X	114,115
Park Ings Fm	N Lincs	SE8713	53°36·6'	0°40·7'W	FM	112
Parkinhill	Cumbr	NY6819	54°34·2'	2°29·3'W	X	91
Park Issa	Shrops	SJ3131	52°52·6'	3°1·1'W	X	126
Park Knowe	S Lanak	NS9736	55°36·7'	3°37·7'W	X	72
Parkland Farmhouse	Surrey	TQ1339	51°8·6'	0°22·7'W	X	187
Parkland Grange	N Yks	SE3981	54°13·6'	1°23·7'W	X	99
Parklands	Leeds	SE3535	53°48·8'	1°27·7'W	T	104
Parklands	Surrey	TQ1239	51°8·6'	0°23·5'W	X	187
Parklands	Traf	SJ7587	53°23·0'	2°22·1'W	X	109
Parklands	Wilts	SU0159	51°20·0'	1°58·8'W	X	173
Park Lands Fm	Hants	SU7629	51°3·5'	0°54·5'W	FM	186,197
Park Lane	Staffs	SJ8806	52°39·3'	2°10·2'W	T	127,139
Park Lane	Wrex	SJ4239	52°57·0'	2°51·4'W	T	126
Parklane Fm	Carm	SN6119	51°51·4'	4°0·7'W	FM	159
Park Lane Fm	Essex	TM0231	51°56·7'	0°56·7'E	FM	168
Park Langley	Brom	TQ3867	51°23·3'	0°0·6'W	T	177
Park Law	Scot Bord	NT7608	55°22·2'	2°22·3'W	X	80
Parklea	Inverc	NS3574	55°56·1'	4°38·1'W	X	63
Parklea Fm	C of Glas	NS6056	55°46·9'	4°13·5'W	FM	64
Park Lewellyn	I of M	SC4390	54°17·1'	4°24·3'W	X	95
Parkley Craigs	W Loth	NT0175	55°57·7'	3°34·7'W	X	65
Parkley Fm	Wrex	SJ4942	52°58·6'	2°45·2'W	FM	117
Parkley Place	W Loth	NT0176	55°58·3'	3°34·7'W	X	65
Park Leys	Notts	SK7357	53°6·5'	0°54·2'W	X	120
Park Leys	Warw	SP2450	52°9·1'	1°38·6'W	X	151
Park Lidget	Notts	SK7663	53°9·8'	0°51·4'W	X	120
Park Lodge	Bucks	TQ0183	51°32·4'	0°32·2'W	X	176
Park Lodge	Cambs	TL0967	52°17·6'	0°23·7'W	X	153
Park Lodge	Derby	SK2672	53°14·9'	1°36·2'W	X	119
Park Lodge	Dorset	SY8583	50°39·0'	2°12·3'W	X	194
Park Lodge	Northnts	TL0694	52°32·2'	0°25·8'W	X	142
Park Lodge	Notts	SK6463	53°9·9'	1°2·2'W	X	120
Park Lodge	N Yks	SE3877	54°11·5'	1°24·6'W	X	99
Park Lodge	Staffs	SJ8907	52°39·9'	2°9·4'W	X	127,139
Park Lodge	Staffs	SK1027	52°50·7'	1°50·7'W	X	128
Park Lodge Fm	Hill	TQ0589	51°35·6'	0°28·7'W	FM	176
Park Lodge Fm	Wakf	SE4321	53°41·3'	1°20·5'W	FM	105
Parkmaclurg	D & G	NX4363	54°56·5'	4°26·6'W	X	83
Park Mains	Renf	NS4670	55°54·2'	4°27·4'W	T	64
Park Manor Fm	Staffs	SJ7952	53°4·1'	2°18·4'W	FM	118
Park Meads	Somer	ST3527	51°2·6'	2°55·2'W	X	193
Park Mill	Fife	NO5613	56°18·7'	2°42·2'W	X	59
Park Mill	Kirk	SE2511	53°35·9'	1°36·9'W	T	110
Parkmill	S Ayr	NS4427	55°31·0'	4°27·8'W	X	70
Park Mill	Staffs	SJ7926	52°50·1'	2°18·3'W	X	127
Parkmill	Swan	SS5489	51°35·1'	4°6·1'W	T	159
Parkmill Burn	S Ayr	NS4527	55°31·0'	4°26·9'W	W	70
Parkmill Fm	Ches	SJ7766	53°11·7'	2°20·2'W	FM	118
Parkmill Fm	S Glos	ST6291	51°37·2'	2°32·5'W	FM	162,172
Park Mill Fm	W Susx	SU9730	51°3·9'	0°36·6'W	FM	186
Parkminster Fm	W Susx	TQ2020	50°58·2'	0°17·1'W	FM	198
Park Moor	Ches	SJ9680	53°19·3'	2°3·2'W	X	109
Parkmore	Moray	NJ3341	57°27·5'	3°6·5'W	X	28
Park Moss Fm	Ches	SJ6581	53°19·7'	2°31·1'W	FM	109
Park-ne-Earkan	I of M	SC4192	54°18·2'	4°26·2'W	X	95
Parkneuk	Aberd	NJ4722	57°17·4'	2°52·3'W	X	37
Parkneuk	Aberd	NO7975	56°52·2'	2°20·2'W	X	45
Parkneuk	D & G	NY1769	55°0·8'	3°17·5'W	X	85
Parkneuk	Fife	NT0888	56°4·8'	3°28·3'W	T	65
Parkneuk	Pth & Kin	NO1833	56°29·2'	3°19·4'W	X	53
Parkneuk	Scot Bord	NT1446	55°42·2'	3°21·7'W	X	72
Parkneuk Cottage	Pth & Kin	NN9118	56°20·8'	3°45·4'W	X	58
Park Nook	Cald	SE1022	53°41·9'	1°50·5'W	X	104
Parknook	Cumbr	NY0803	54°25·1'	3°24·6'W	X	89
Park Nook	Cumbr	NY1649	54°50·0'	3°18·0'W	X	85
Parknook	Cumbr	NY5676	55°4·8'	2°40·9'W	X	86
Park Nook	Cumbr	NY5866	54°59·5'	2°39·0'W	X	86
Park Nook	Cumbr	SD1093	54°19·7'	3°22·6'W	X	96
Park Nook	Derby	SK3241	52°58·2'	1°31·0'W	X	119,128
Park Nook	Lancs	SD7850	53°57·0'	2°19·7'W	X	103
Park Nook	N Yks	NZ6808	54°28·0'	0°56·6'W	X	94
Parknook	Staffs	SJ8423	52°48·5'	2°13·8'W	X	127
Parknook	Staffs	SK0449	53°2·5'	1°56·0'W	X	119
Parknowe	Fife	NO4019	56°21·8'	2°57·8'W	X	59
Parknoweth	Corn	SW8256	50°22·0'	5°3·6'W	X	200
Park of Auchentroig	Stir	NS5293	56°6·7'	4°22·4'W	X	57
Park of Bandley	Aberd	NJ6016	57°14·2'	2°39·3'W	X	37
Park of Brux	Aberd	NJ4720	57°16·3'	2°52·3'W	X	37
Park of Drumquhassle	Stir	NS4886	56°2·8'	4°26·0'W	F	57
Park of Dykeside	Moray	NJ1158	57°36·5'	3°28·9'W	X	28
Park of Keir	Stir	NS7899	56°10·3'	3°57·5'W	F	57
Park of Logie	Aberd	NK0255	57°35·4'	1°57·5'W	X	30
Park of Tongland	D & G	NX7055	54°52·6'	4°1·1'W	X	83,84
Park or Pairc	N Eil	NB3112	58°1·2'	6°32·9'W	X	13,14
Park Pale	Essex	TL6434	51°59·0'	0°23·7'E	X	154
Park Pale	E Susx	TQ7121	50°58·0'	0°26·5'E	X	199
Park Pale	Heref	SO6059	52°13·9'	2°34·7'W	A	149
Park Pale	Somer	ST2121	50°59·2'	3°7·1'W	A	193
Park Pale	Wilts	SU1730	51°4·4'	1°45·1'W	A	184
Parkpale Fm	Bucks	SP6612	51°48·4'	1°2·2'W	FM	164,165
Park Pitham Copse	Hants	SU7060	51°20·3'	0°59·3'W	F	175,186
Park Place	Ches	SJ5865	53°11·1'	2°37·3'W	X	117
Park Place	Hants	SU5611	50°54·0'	1°11·8'W	X	196
Park Place	Heref	SO6160	52°14·4'	2°33·9'W	A	138,149
Park Place	Swan	SS5489	51°35·1'	4°6·1'W	X	159
Park Place	Wok	SU7782	51°32·1'	0°53·0'W	X	175
Park Place Fm	I of W	SZ4687	50°41·1'	1°20·5'W	FM	196
Park Plantation	Durham	NY9741	54°46·1'	2°2·4'W	F	87
Park Plantn	Cumbr	SD3295	54°21·0'	3°2·4'W	F	96,97
Park Plantn	Lincs	SK8384	53°21·0'	0°44·8'W	F	121
Park Plantn	N Yks	SE0656	54°0·2'	1°54·1'W	F	104
Park Rash	N Yks	SD9774	54°10·0'	2°2·3'W	X	98
Park Rigg	Cumbr	NY4672	55°2·6'	2°50·3'W	X	86
Park Royal	Brent	TQ1982	51°31·7'	0°16·7'W	T	176
Parks	Aberd	NJ4205	57°8·2'	2°57·0'W	X	37
Parks	Ches	SJ9967	53°12·2'	2°0·5'W	X	118
Parks	Cumbr	SD4791	54°19·0'	2°48·5'W	X	97
Parks	D & G	NY0697	55°15·7'	3°28·3'W	X	78
Parks	Donc	SE6410	53°35·2'	1°1·6'W	X	111
Parks	Highld	NH6035	57°23·2'	4°11·5'W	X	26
Parks	N Eil	NF7910	57°4·4'	7°17·4'W	T	31
Parks	Shrops	SO5876	52°23·1'	2°36·6'W	X	137,138
Park's Dairy Fm	Dorset	SY5588	50°41·6'	2°37·8'W	FM	194
Parkseat	Aberd	NJ5642	57°28·2'	2°43·6'W	X	29
Park's Fm	Essex	TL8334	51°58·7'	0°40·3'E	FM	155
Park's Fm	E Yorks	SE7229	53°45·4'	0°54·1'W	FM	105,106
Park's Fm	Glos	SO7505	51°44·8'	2°21·3'W	FM	162
Parks Fm	Glos	SP0426	51°56·2'	1°56·1'W	FM	163
Park's Fm	Lincs	TF2439	52°56·3'	0°8·9'W	FM	131
Parks Fm	Lincs	TF3138	52°55·6'	0°2·7'W	FM	131
Park's Fm	N Yks	SE3349	53°56·4'	1°29·4'W	FM	104
Park's Fm	S Glos	ST7382	51°32·4'	2°23·0'W	FM	172
Parks Fm	S Glos	ST7879	51°30·8'	2°18·6'W	FM	172
Parks Fm	Worcs	SP0544	52°5·9'	1°55·2'W	FM	150
Park's Fm	York	SE6143	53°53·0'	1°3·9'W	FM	105
Park Shield	Northum	NY8969	55°1·2'	2°9·9'W	X	87
Park Shore	Hants	SZ4096	50°46·0'	1°25·6'W	X	196
Parkside	Aberd	NJ4724	57°18·5'	2°52·3'W	X	37
Parkside	Aberd	NJ8028	57°20·8'	2°19·5'W	X	38
Parkside	Aberd	NO5297	57°4·0'	2°47·0'W	X	37,44
Parkside	Angus	NO3961	56°44·5'	2°59·4'W	X	44
Parkside	Angus	NO5762	56°45·1'	2°42·6'W	X	44
Parkside	Beds	TL0224	51°54·5'	0°30·6'W	T	166
Parkside	Cumbr	NY0315	54°31·5'	3°29·5'W	T	89
Park Side	Cumbr	SD4981	54°13·6'	2°46·5'W	X	97
Parkside	Durham	NZ4248	54°49·7'	1°20·3'W	T	88
Parkside	Lancs	SD6168	54°6·6'	2°35·4'W	X	97
Parkside	Lincs	SK9096	53°27·4'	0°38·3'W	X	112
Parkside	N Lanak	NS8058	55°48·3'	3°54·4'W	T	65,72
Parkside	Northum	NY7764	54°58·5'	2°21·1'W	X	86,87
Parkside	Northum	NY8254	54°53·1'	2°16·4'W	X	86,87
Parkside	Northum	NY8774	55°3·9'	2°11·8'W	X	87
Parkside	Pth & Kin	NO1626	56°25·4'	3°21·3'W	X	53,58
Parkside	Staffs	SJ9125	52°49·6'	2°7·6'W	T	127
Parkside	Staffs	SK0844	52°59·8'	1°52·4'W	X	119,128
Parkside	Wrex	SJ3855	53°5·6'	2°55·1'W	T	117
Parkside Fm	Ches	SJ5577	53°17·5'	2°40·1'W	FM	117
Parkside Fm	Ches	SJ5649	53°2·4'	2°39·0'W	FM	117
Parkside Fm	Ches	SJ7365	53°11·1'	2°23·8'W	FM	118
Parkside Fm	Ches	SJ7376	53°17·1'	2°23·9'W	FM	118
Parkside Fm	Ches	SJ7781	53°19·8'	2°20·3'W	FM	109
Parkside Fm	Ches	SJ8979	53°18·7'	2°9·5'W	FM	118
Parkside Fm	Enf	TQ3098	51°40·2'	0°6·8'W	FM	166,176,177
Parkside Fm	Lancs	SD4655	53°59·5'	2°49·0'W	FM	102
Parkside Fm	Lancs	SD6275	54°10·4'	2°34·5'W	FM	97
Parkside Fm	Staffs	SJ9829	52°51·7'	2°1·4'W	FM	127
Parkside Fm	Warr	SJ6094	53°26·7'	2°35·7'W	FM	109
Parkside Ho	Surrey	SU9770	51°25·5'	0°35·9'W	X	175,176
Parkside of Craig	Pth & Kin	NN9419	56°21·3'	3°42·5'W	X	58
Park Slade Fm	Warw	SP3049	52°8·5'	1°33·3'W	FM	151
Parks of Aldie	Pth & Kin	NT0498	56°10·2'	3°32·3'W	X	58
Parks of Garden	Stir	NS6096	56°8·4'	4°14·7'W	X	57
Parks of Innes	Moray	NJ2763	57°39·3'	3°12·9'W	X	28
Parks of Keillour	Pth & Kin	NN9726	56°25·2'	3°39·7'W	X	52,53,58
Park Spinney	Northnts	TL0594	52°32·3'	0°26·7'W	F	142
Parks Plantn	N Yks	SE4670	54°7·7'	1°17·3'W	F	100
Park Springs	Staffs	SJ7233	52°53·9'	2°24·6'W	F	127
Park Springs Fm	Lincs	SK8388	53°23·2'	0°44·7'W	FM	112,121
Parkspring Wood	Cumbr	SD4892	54°19·5'	2°47·6'W	F	97
Park Spring Wood	Notts	SK7258	53°7·1'	0°55·0'W	F	120
Park Sta	Wirral	SJ3089	53°23·8'	3°2·8'W	X	108
Parks, The	Cambs	TL3577	52°22·7'	0°0·6'W	X	142
Parks, The	Devon	ST3003	50°49·6'	2°59·3'W	X	193
Parks, The	Glos	SO7128	51°57·2'	2°24·9'W	X	149
Parks, The	Heref	SO3549	52°8·4'	2°56·6'W	X	148,149
Parks, The	Heref	SO4747	52°7·4'	2°46·1'W	X	148,149
Parks,The	Moray	NJ5350	57°32·5'	2°46·6'W	X	29
Parks, The	N Yks	SE1188	54°17·5'	1°49·4'W	X	99
Parks, The	N Yks	SE4770	54°7·7'	1°16·4'W	X	100
Parks, The	Somer	SS8746	51°12·4'	3°36·7'W	F	181
Parks, The	Wrex	SJ3754	53°5·0'	2°56·0'W	X	117
Parkstile	Staffs	SK0928	52°51·2'	1°51·6'W	X	128
Park Stone	Pemb	SN0522	51°52·0'	4°49·6'W	X	145,158
Parkstone	Poole	SZ0391	50°43·3'	1°57·1'W	T	195
Parkstone Bay	Poole	SZ0290	50°42·8'	1°57·9'W	W	195
Park Street	Herts	TL1404	51°43·6'	0°20·6'W	T	166
Park Street	W Susx	TQ1131	51°4·3'	0°24·5'W	T	187
Parkstyle	Aberd	NJ6519	57°15·9'	2°34·4'W	X	38
Park Style	Lancs	SD6345	53°54·2'	2°33·4'W	X	102,103
Park Style Fm	Derby	SK2039	52°57·1'	1°41·7'W	FM	128
Parkswadog	Carm	SN3738	52°1·2'	4°22·1'W	X	145
Park,The	Aberd	NJ7556	57°35·9'	2°24·6'W	X	29
Park, The	Cumbr	NY5858	54°55·1'	2°38·9'W	X	86
Park, The	Cumbr	SD3193	54°19·9'	3°3·2'W	X	96,97
Park, The	Derby	SK4033	52°53·8'	1°23·9'W	X	129
Park, The	D & G	NX9867	54°59·5'	3°35·2'W	X	84
Park, The	E Yorks	SE8449	53°56·1'	0°42·8'W	X	106
Park, The	Glos	SO8710	51°47·5'	2°10·9'W	X	162
Park, The	Glos	SO9327	51°56·7'	2°5·7'W	X	163
Park, The	Glos	ST5599	51°41·5'	2°38·7'W	F	162
Park, The	Heref	SO5434	52°0·4'	2°39·8'W	X	149
Park, The	Leic	SP5499	52°35·4'	1°11·8'W	X	140
Park, The	Norf	TF7636	52°53·8'	0°37·4'E	X	132
Park, The	Notts	SK6848	53°1·7'	0°58·8'W	X	129
Park, The	Notts	SK7345	53°0·1'	0°54·3'W	X	129
Park, The	N Yks	SE5540	53°51·4'	1°9·4'W	X	105
Park, The	N Yks	SE6671	54°8·1'	0°59·0'W	X	100
Park, The	N Yks	SE9582	54°13·7'	0°32·1'W	X	101
Park, The	Powys	SO1634	52°0·1'	3°13·0'W	X	161
Park, The	Scot Bord	NT5936	55°37·2'	2°38·6'W	X	73,74
Park, The	Shrops	SJ5237	52°55·9'	2°42·4'W	X	126
Park, The	Shrops	SO5876	52°23·1'	2°36·6'W	X	137,138
Park, The	Somer	ST5545	51°12·4'	2°38·3'W	X	182,183
Park, The	Wilts	ST8336	51°7·6'	2°14·2'W	X	183
Park, The	Worcs	SO8442	52°4·8'	2°13·6'W	X	150
Park Thorns	Oxon	SP6132	51°59·2'	1°6·3'W	F	152,165
Parkton	Highld	NH5950	57°31·4'	4°20·8'W	X	26
Park Top	N Yks	NZ1202	54°25·0'	1°48·5'W	X	92
Park Town	Luton	TL0920	51°52·3'	0°24·6'W	T	166
Park Town	Oxon	SP5107	51°45·8'	1°15·3'W	T	164
Park Vale	Oxon	SU2980	51°31·3'	1°34·5'W	A	174
Parkview Fm	Ches	SJ6044	52°59·8'	2°35·4'W	FM	118
Park View Fm	Hants	SU8338	51°8·3'	0°48·4'W	FM	186
Park View Fm	Wilts	SU0486	51°34·6'	1°56·1'W	FM	173
Park Village	Northum	NY6861	54°56·8'	2°29·5'W	T	86,87
Park Village	Wolv	SJ9200	52°36·1'	2°6·7'W	T	127,139
Park Villas	Leeds	SE3238	53°50·5'	1°30·4'W	T	104
Park Wall	Durham	NZ1337	54°43·9'	1°47·5'W	X	92
Park Wall	Pemb	SN0600	51°40·2'	4°47·9'W	X	158
Parkwall Fm	Monm	ST5090	51°36·6'	2°42·9'W	FM	162,172
Parkwalls	Corn	SX1183	50°37·2'	4°39·9'W	X	200
Parkway	Heref	SO4137	52°1·9'	2°51·2'W	X	149,161
Parkway	Heref	SO7135	52°1·0'	2°25·0'W	T	149
Parkway	Somer	ST5921	50°59·4'	2°34·7'W	T	183
Park Wells	Powys	SO0251	52°9·2'	3°25·6'W	X	147
Park Wood	Beds	SP9358	52°13·0'	0°37·9'W	F	153
Park Wood	Brad	SE0640	53°51·6'	1°54·1'W	F	104
Park Wood	Brad	SE2131	53°46·7'	1°40·5'W	F	104
Park Wood	Bucks	SU8298	51°40·7'	0°48·4'W	F	165
Park Wood	Cambs	TL6454	52°9·8'	0°24·3'E	F	154
Park Wood	Corn	SX0569	50°29·5'	4°44·6'W	F	200
Park Wood	Corn	SX3466	50°28·5'	4°20·0'W	F	201
Park Wood	Cov	SP2877	52°23·7'	1°34·9'W	F	140

Park Wood	Cumbr	NY1634	54°41·9'	3°17·8'W	F	89
Park Wood	Cumbr	NY2332	54°40·9'	3°11·2'W	F	89,90
Park Wood	Cumbr	NY2944	54°47·4'	3°5·8'W	F	85
Park Wood	Cumbr	SD3087	54°16·7'	3°4·1'W	F	96,97
Park Wood	Cumbr	SD4387	54°16·8'	2°52·1'W	F	97
Park Wood	Cumbr	SD6085	54°15·8'	2°36·4'W	F	97
Park Wood	Devon	SS6619	50°57·5'	3°54·1'W	F	180
Park Wood	Donc	SK6196	53°27·7'	1°4·5'W	F	111
Park Wood	Donc	SK6198	53°28·7'	1°4·4'W	F	111
Park Wood	Dorset	ST7904	50°50·3'	2°17·5'W	F	194
Park Wood	Dorset	SY8382	50°38·5'	2°14·0'W	F	194
Park Wood	Essex	TL4538	52°1·5'	0°7·2'E	F	154
Park Wood	Essex	TL5500	51°40·9'	0°14·9'E	F	167
Park Wood	Essex	TL7039	52°1·6'	0°29·1'E	F	154
Park Wood	Essex	TQ5997	51°39·2'	0°18·3'E	F	167,177
Park Wood	E Susx	TQ4522	50°59·0'	0°4·3'E	F	198
Park Wood	E Susx	TQ5431	51°3·7'	0°12·3'E	F	188
Park Wood	E Susx	TQ6012	50°53·3'	0°16·9'E	F	199
Park Wood	E Susx	TQ6825	51°0·2'	0°24·1'E	F	188,199
Park Wood	E Susx	TQ7311	50°52·6'	0°27·9'E	F	199
Park Wood	E Susx	TQ8118	50°56·2'	0°35·0'E	F	199
Park Wood	Glos	ST8189	51°36·2'	2°16·1'W	F	162,173
Park Wood	Heref	SO2856	52°12·1'	3°2·8'W	F	148
Park Wood	Heref	SO3533	51°59·7'	2°56·4'W	F	149,161
Park Wood	Herts	TL2319	51°51·6'	0°12·4'W	F	166
Park Wood	Herts	TL2815	51°49·4'	0°8·2'W	F	166
Park Wood	Hill	TQ0988	51°35·0'	0°25·2'W	F	176
Park Wood	Kent	TQ7757	51°17·3'	0°32·7'E	F	178,188
Park Wood	Kent	TQ7851	51°14·0'	0°33·4'E	T	188
Park Wood	Kent	TR0436	51°5·4'	0°55·2'E	F	179,189
Park Wood	Kent	TR0452	51°14·1'	0°55·7'E	F	179,189
Park Wood	Kent	TR1444	51°9·5'	1°4·0'E	F	179,189
Park Wood	Leic	SP8297	52°34·1'	0°47·0'W	F	141
Park Wood	Lincs	TF1016	52°44·1'	0°21·8'W	F	130
Park Wood	Medway	TQ8063	51°20·5'	0°35·5'E	T	178,188
Park Wood	Monm	SO3802	51°43·0'	2°53·5'W	F	171
Park Wood	Newp	ST2486	51°34·3'	3°5·4'W	F	171
Park Wood	N Lincs	TA0505	53°32·1'	0°24·5'W	F	112
Park Wood	Northnts	TL0288	52°29·1'	0°29·5'W	F	141
Park Wood	Northum	NZ0956	54°54·2'	1°51·2'W	F	88
Park Wood	Northum	NZ2294	55°14·6'	1°38·8'W	F	81
Park Wood	Notts	SK7561	53°8·7'	0°52·3'W	F	120
Park Wood	N Yks	NZ1206	54°27·2'	1°48·5'W	F	92
Park Wood	N Yks	NZ4408	54°28·2'	1°18·8'W	F	93
Park Wood	N Yks	NZ7508	54°27·9'	0°50·1'W	F	94
Park Wood	N Yks	SE1899	54°23·4'	1°42·9'W	F	99
Park Wood	N Yks	SE5976	54°10·8'	1°5·3'W	F	100
Park Wood	Oxon	SU6281	51°31·7'	1°6·0'W	F	175
Park Wood	Powys	SO1634	52°0·1'	3°13·0'W	F	161
Park Wood	Red & Cl	NZ5916	54°32·4'	1°4·9'W	F	93
Park Wood	Shrops	SJ5301	52°36·5'	2°41·2'W	F	126
Park Wood	Somer	ST5333	51°5·9'	2°39·9'W	F	182,183
Park Wood	Somer	ST5544	51°11·8'	2°38·3'W	F	182,183
Park Wood	Somer	ST5733	51°5·9'	2°36·5'W	F	182,183
Park Wood	Suff	TL7861	52°3·3'	0°36·8'E	F	155
Park Wood	Suff	TL9242	52°2·8'	0°48·4'E	F	155
Parkwood	Surrey	TQ3545	51°11·5'	0°3·7'W	X	187
Park Wood	W Berks	SU6077	51°29·6'	1°7·8'W	F	175
Park Wood	Win & Maid	SU8583	51°32·6'	0°46·1'W	F	175
Park Wood	Worcs	SO7644	52°5·9'	2°20·6'W	F	150
Park Wood	W Susx	TQ2613	50°54·4'	0°12·1'W	F	198
Parkwood Fm	E Susx	TQ5409	50°51·8'	0°11·7'E	FM	199
Parkwood Hall	Kent	TQ5268	51°23·7'	0°11·5'E	X	177
Park Woods	Swan	SS5390	51°35·6'	4°6·9'W	F	159
Parkwood Springs	Sheff	SK3489	53°24·0'	1°28·9'W	T	110,111
Parkyns	Devon	SS5916	50°55·8'	4°0·0'W	X	180
Parky-vicar	Carm	SN3411	51°46·8'	4°24·0'W	X	159
Parlan Hill	Stir	NN3517	56°19·3'	4°39·6'W	H	50,56
Parletts Fm	W Susx	SU9810	50°53·1'	0°36·0'W	FM	197
Parley Beans Fm	Essex	TL8329	51°56·0'	0°40·1'E	FM	168
Parley Common	Dorset	SZ0999	50°47·7'	1°52·0'W	X	195
Parley Cross	Dorset	SZ0898	50°47·1'	1°52·8'W	X	195
Parley Green	Dorset	SZ0997	50°46·6'	1°52·0'W	T	195
Parliament	Devon	SX8359	50°25·4'	3°38·4'W	A	202
Parliament Clump	Suff	TL9178	52°22·2'	0°48·7'E	F	144
Parliament Heath	Suff	TL9643	52°3·3'	0°51·9'E	T	155
Parliament Hill	Camden	TQ2786	51°33·7'	0°9·7'W	X	176
Parliament Oak	Notts	SK5765	53°11·0'	1°8·4'W	X	120
Parliament Sq	I of M	SC4494	54°19·3'	4°23·5'W	X	95
Parlick	Lancs	SD5945	53°54·2'	2°37·0'W	H	102
Parlington	Leeds	SE4235	53°48·8'	1°21·3'W	T	105
Parlington Hollins	Leeds	SE4135	53°48·8'	1°22·2'W	F	105
Parlour Fm	Glos	SO8906	51°45·4'	2°9·2'W	FM	163
Parlour Fm	Monm	SO4412	51°48·5'	2°48·3'W	FM	161
Parme Fm	Ches	SJ7464	53°10·5'	2°22·9'W	FM	118
Parmentley Cottage	Northum	NY7754	54°53·1'	2°21·1'W	X	86,87
Parmentley Hall	Northum	NY7855	54°53·6'	2°20·2'W	X	86,87
Parmoor	Bucks	SU7989	51°35·9'	0°51·2'W	T	175
Parnacott	Devon	SS3105	50°49·4'	4°23·6'W	T	190
Parndon Wood	Essex	TL4406	51°44·3'	0°5·5'E	F	167
Parney Heath	Essex	TM0431	51°56·6'	0°58·5'E	T	168
Parnham Fm	N Yks	SE7776	54°10·7'	0°48·8'W	FM	100
Parnham Ho	Dorset	ST4700	50°48·1'	2°44·7'W	A	193
Parnholt Wood	Hants	SU3828	51°3·2'	1°27·1'W	F	185
Parr	St Hel	SJ5394	53°26·7'	2°42·0'W	T	108
Parracombe	Devon	SS6644	51°11·0'	3°54·7'W	T	180
Parracombe Common	Devon	SS6844	51°11·0'	3°52·9'W	X	180
Parr Brow	Wigan	SD7101	53°30·5'	2°25·8'W	T	109
Parr Grange	Ches	SJ4449	53°2·4'	2°49·7'W	X	117
Parr Green Hall	Ches	SJ4449	53°2·4'	2°49·7'W	X	117
Parrick Ho	Durham	NZ0220	54°34·8'	1°57·7'W	X	92
Parrie Burn	E Ayr	NS4905	55°19·2'	4°22·4'W	W	70,77
Parrock	Moray	NJ5350	57°32·5'	2°46·6'W	X	29
Parrock Farm	Kent	TQ6572	51°25·6'	0°22·8'E	FM	177,178
Parrock Head	Lancs	SD6952	53°58·0'	2°27·9'W	X	103
Parrog	Pemb	SN0439	52°1·1'	4°51·0'W	T	145,157
Parrot Fm	Wok	SU7367	51°24·1'	0°56·6'W	FM	175
Parrott's Fm	Bucks	SP9207	51°45·5'	0°39·6'W	FM	165
Parrox Hall	Lancs	SD3647	53°55·2'	2°58·1'W	X	102
Parr's Warren	Staffs	SJ9916	52°44·7'	2°0·5'W	F	127

Parruten Burn	D & G	NX9359	54°55·1'	3°39·7'W	W	84
Parry's Castle	Carm	SN4114	51°48·4'	4°18·0'W	X	159
Parry's Field Barn	Wilts	SU0039	51°9·2'	1°59·6'W	X	184
Par Sands	Corn	SX0852	50°20·4'	4°41·5'W	X	200,204
Parselle	Pemb	SM9028	51°54·9'	5°2·8'W	X	157,158
Parsley Barn	Lancs	SD7738	53°50·5'	2°20·6'W	X	103
Parsley Beck	N Yks	NZ8703	54°25·1'	0°39·1'W	W	94
Parsley Hay	Derby	SK1463	53°10·1'	1°47·0'W	X	119
Parslow's Hillock	Bucks	SP8201	51°42·3'	0°48·4'W	T	165
Parsonage	Worcs	SO8363	52°16·1'	2°14·6'W	X	138,150
Parsonage Cross	Devon	SS8118	50°57·2'	3°41·3'W	X	181
Parsonage Down	Somer	SS8432	51°4·8'	3°39·0'W	X	181
Parsonage Down	Wilts	ST8939	51°9·2'	2°9·1'W	X	184
Parsonage Down	Wilts	SU0541	51°10·3'	1°55·3'W	X	184
Parsonage Fm	Bucks	SU9192	51°37·4'	0°40·7'W	FM	175
Parsonage Fm	Bucks	TQ0180	51°30·8'	0°32·3'W	FM	176
Parsonage Fm	Cambs	TL6856	52°10·8'	0°27·8'E	FM	154
Parsonage Fm	Devon	SS5812	50°53·6'	4°0·8'W	FM	180
Parsonage Fm	Devon	SS6915	50°55·4'	3°51·5'W	FM	180
Parsonage Fm	Devon	SS6923	50°59·7'	3°51·6'W	FM	180
Parsonage Fm	Devon	SS7308	50°51·7'	3°47·9'W	FM	191
Parsonage Fm	Devon	SS7624	51°0·4'	3°45·7'W	FM	180
Parsonage Fm	Dorset	ST7307	50°51·9'	2°22·6'W	FM	194
Parsonage Fm	Dorset	SY7897	50°46·6'	2°18·3'W	FM	194
Parsonage Fm	Essex	TL4826	51°55·0'	0°9·5'E	FM	167
Parsonage Fm	Essex	TL5123	51°53·3'	0°12·1'E	FM	167
Parsonage Fm	Essex	TL5128	51°56·0'	0°12·2'E	FM	167
Parsonage Fm	Essex	TL5735	51°59·7'	0°17·6'E	FM	154
Parsonage Fm	Essex	TL6536	52°0·1'	0°24·6'E	FM	154
Parsonage Fm	Essex	TL7127	51°55·1'	0°29·6'E	FM	167
Parsonage Fm	Essex	TL8601	51°40·8'	0°41·8'E	FM	168
Parsonage Fm	Essex	TL8818	51°50·0'	0°44·1'E	FM	168
Parsonage Fm	Essex	TM0625	51°53·4'	1°0·0'E	FM	168
Parsonage Fm	E Susx	TQ4323	50°59·5'	0°2·6'E	FM	198
Parsonage Fm	E Susx	TQ5414	50°54·5'	0°11·8'E	FM	199
Parsonage Fm	Hants	SZ1698	50°47·1'	1°46·0'W	FM	195
Parsonage Fm	Heref	SO3049	52°8·3'	3°1·0'W	FM	148
Parsonage Fm	Herts	TL1624	51°54·4'	0°18·4'W	FM	166
Parsonage Fm	Herts	TL4816	51°49·6'	0°9·3'E	FM	167
Parsonage Fm	Kent	TQ8361	51°19·3'	0°38·0'E	FM	178,188
Parsonage Fm	Kent	TQ8859	51°18·2'	0°42·2'E	FM	178
Parsonage Fm	Kent	TQ9552	51°14·3'	0°48·0'E	FM	189
Parsonage Fm	Kent	TQ9734	51°4·5'	0°49·1'E	FM	189
Parsonage Fm	Kent	TQ9870	51°23·9'	0°51·2'E	FM	178
Parsonage Fm	Kent	TQ9955	51°15·8'	0°51·5'E	FM	178
Parsonage Fm	Kent	TR0534	51°4·3'	0°56·0'E	FM	179,189
Parsonage Fm	Kent	TR1061	51°18·8'	1°1·2'E	FM	179
Parsonage Fm	Lancs	SD6435	53°48·8'	2°32·4'W	FM	102,103
Parsonage Fm	Lincs	TF2392	53°24·9'	0°8·5'W	FM	113
Parsonage Fm	Lincs	TF4218	52°44·7'	0°6·6'E	FM	131
Parsonage Fm	Monm	SO3405	51°44·6'	2°57·0'W	FM	161
Parsonage Fm	Monm	SO3416	51°50·6'	2°57·1'W	FM	161
Parsonage Fm	Norf	TF5609	52°39·6'	0°18·8'E	FM	143
Parsonage Fm	Somer	SS8532	51°4·8'	3°38·1'W	FM	181
Parsonage Fm	Somer	ST0430	51°3·9'	3°21·8'W	FM	181
Parsonage Fm	Somer	ST2129	51°3·5'	3°7·3'W	FM	193
Parsonage Fm	Somer	ST3216	50°56·6'	2°57·7'W	FM	193
Parsonage Fm	Somer	ST3228	51°3·1'	2°57·8'W	FM	193
Parsonage Fm	Somer	ST3528	51°3·1'	2°55·3'W	FM	193
Parsonage Fm	Somer	ST5928	51°3·2'	2°34·7'W	FM	183
Parsonage Fm	Suff	TL7347	52°5·9'	0°31·9'E	FM	155
Parsonage Fm	Suff	TL8447	52°5·7'	0°41·6'E	FM	155
Parsonage Fm	Wilts	ST8240	51°9·8'	2°15·1'W	FM	183
Parsonage Fm	Wilts	ST8846	51°13·0'	2°9·9'W	FM	183
Parsonage Fm	Wilts	SU0778	51°30·3'	1°53·6'W	FM	173
Parsonage Fm	W Susx	TQ0026	51°1·7'	0°34·1'W	FM	186,197
Parsonage Fm	W Susx	TQ2016	50°56·1'	0°17·1'W	FM	198
Parsonage Green	Essex	TL7010	51°46·0'	0°28·2'E	T	167
Parsonage Heath	Suff	TL8081	52°24·1'	0°39·2'E	F	144
Parsonagehill Barn	Oxon	SU3783	51°32·9'	1°27·6'W	X	174
Parsonage Resr	Lancs	SD7032	53°47·3'	2°26·9'W	W	103
Parsonage, The	Essex	TL6223	51°53·1'	0°21·6'E	X	167
Parsonage Wood	Devon	SS3101	50°47·3'	4°23·5'W	F	190
Parson and Clerk, The	Devon	SX9674	50°33·6'	3°27·7'W	X	192
Parsonbridge	Cumbr	NY2444	54°47·4'	3°10·5'W	X	85
Parsonby	Cumbr	NY1438	54°44·0'	3°19·7'W	T	89
Parson Byers	Durham	NZ0037	54°43·9'	1°59·6'W	X	92
Parson Cross	Sheff	SK3592	53°25·7'	1°28·0'W	T	110,111
Parson Drove	Cambs	TF3708	52°39·4'	0°1·9'E	T	142,143
Parson Lee	Lancs	SD9438	53°50·5'	2°5·1'W	X	103
Parsonnage Fm	Surrey	SU9338	51°8·2'	0°39·9'W	FM	186
Parson's Beach	Corn	SW7826	50°5·8'	5°5·9'W	X	204
Parson's Br	Cered	SN7479	52°23·9'	3°50·7'W	X	135,147
Parson's Brake	Staffs	SK1526	52°50·1'	1°46·2'W	F	128
Parsons Close	N Yks	SD7863	54°4·0'	2°19·8'W	X	98
Parson's Cottage	Devon	SX6175	50°33·7'	3°57·4'W	X	191
Parson's Fm	Oxon	SP6108	51°46·3'	1°6·6'W	FM	164,165
Parsons Fm	Wok	SU7565	51°23·0'	0°54·9'W	FM	175
Parsons Green	Ham & Ful	TQ2576	51°28·4'	0°11·6'W	T	176
Parson's Heath	Essex	TM0126	51°54·0'	0°55·7'E	T	168
Parson Shields	Northum	NY6853	54°52·5'	2°29·5'W	X	86,87
Parson's Hill	Glos	SO9407	51°45·9'	2°4·8'W	X	163
Parson's Hill	Notts	SK7040	52°57·4'	0°57·1'W	X	129
Parson's Hills	Derby	SK2926	52°50·1'	1°33·8'W	X	128
Parson's House Fm	Sheff	SK2780	53°19·2'	1°35·3'W	FM	110
Parson's Park	Cumbr	NY3340	54°45·3'	3°2·0'W	F	85
Parson's Park Wood	Cumbr	NY4437	54°43·7'	2°51·8'W	F	90
Parson's Pightle	Croy	TQ3157	51°18·0'	0°6·9'W	X	187
Parson's Pitch	Glos	SO9314	51°49·7'	2°5·7'W	X	163
Parson's Pulpit	N Yks	SD9168	54°6·7'	2°7·8'W	X	98
Parsonsquarry Bay	Pemb	SM8401	51°40·2'	5°7·0'W	W	157
Parson's Rig	D & G	NY3590	55°12·3'	3°0·9'W	H	79
Parson's Rocks	Sund	NZ4059	54°55·7'	1°22·1'W	X	88
Parsons Spring	Essex	TL6202	51°41·8'	0°21·0'E	F	167
Parson's Steeple	Somer	ST5725	51°1·6'	2°36·4'W	X	183
Par Sta	Corn	SX0754	50°21·5'	4°42·4'W	X	200
Parswell	Devon	SX4673	50°32·4'	4°10·0'W	X	201
Partabies Fm	Suff	TM4660	52°11·2'	1°36·3'E	FM	156
Partachal	N Eil	NF9466	57°35·1'	7°6·8'W	X	18
Partan Cleugh	E Loth	NT7167	55°54·0'	2°27·4'W	X	67

Partan Craig	Fife	NO5201	56°12·2'	2°46·0'W	X	59
Partanhall	Scot Bord	NT9561	55°50·8'	2°4·4'W	X	67
Partan Taing	Orkney	HY6126	59°7·4'	2°40·4'W	X	5
Parthings	W Susx	TQ1529	51°3·2'	0°21·2'W	X	187,198
Parth-y-gwyddwch	Gwyn	SH5910	52°40·4'	4°4·7'W	X	124
Partick	C of Glas	NS5566	55°52·2'	4°18·6'W	T	64
Partington	Traf	SJ7191	53°25·1'	2°25·8'W	T	109
Partition Belt	Suff	TL7778	52°22·5'	0°36·4'E	F	144
Partney	Lincs	TF4168	53°11·7'	0°7·0'E	T	122
Partney Br	Lincs	TF4067	53°11·1'	0°6·1'E	X	122
Parton	Cumbr	NX9720	54°34·1'	3°35·2'W	T	89
Parton	Cumbr	NY2750	54°50·6'	3°7·8'W	T	85
Parton	D & G	NX6970	55°0·7'	4°2·5'W	T	77,84
Parton	Heref	SO3148	52°7·8'	3°0·1'W	T	148
Parton Bay	Cumbr	NX9720	54°34·1'	3°35·2'W	W	89
Parton Ho	D & G	NX7169	55°0·2'	4°0·6'W	X	83,84
Parton Rocks	Hartpl	NZ5234	54°42·1'	1°11·2'W	X	93
Parton Stiel	Northum	NU1440	55°39·4'	1°46·2'W	X	75
Partonwood	Shrops	SJ3311	52°41·8'	2°59·1'W	X	126
Partridge Close	Durham	NZ1344	54°47·7'	1°47·4'W	X	88
Partridge Fm	Devon	SS8813	50°54·6'	3°35·2'W	FM	181
Partridge Fm	E Susx	TQ8620	50°57·2'	0°39·3'E	FM	189,199
Partridge Fm	Kent	TR0837	51°5·9'	0°58·6'E	FM	179,189
Partridge Fm	Shrops	SO3592	52°31·6'	2°57·1'W	FM	137
Partridge Fm	Worcs	SO8056	52°12·3'	2°17·2'W	FM	150
Partridgegreen	Essex	TL6911	51°46·6'	0°27·4'E	X	167
Partridge Green	W Susx	TQ1919	50°57·7'	0°17·9'W	T	198
Partridge Hall	E Yorks	SE8546	53°54·4'	0°42·0'W	X	106
Partridge Hall Fm	Herts	TL3234	51°59·6'	0°4·2'W	FM	153
Partridge Hill	Bucks	SP8929	51°57·4'	0°41·9'W	X	165
Partridge Hill	N Yks	NZ8400	54°23·6'	0°42·0'W	X	94
Partridge Hill	N Yks	NZ8807	54°27·3'	0°38·1'W	X	94
Partridge Hill Fm	Donc	SK6596	53°27·6'	1°0·8'W	FM	111
Partridge Hill Fm	N Yks	SE5336	53°49·3'	1°11·3'W	FM	105
Partridge Hole	Devon	SS8308	50°51·8'	3°39·4'W	X	191
Partridge Nest	Northum	NY7764	54°58·5'	2°21·1'W	X	86,87
Partridge Walls	Devon	SS6708	50°51·6'	3°53·0'W	X	191
Partrishow	Powys	SO2722	51°53·7'	3°3·3'W	T	161
Partrishow Hill	Powys	SO2721	51°53·2'	3°3·2'W	X	161
Part-y-seal	Monm	SO4223	51°54·4'	2°50·2'W	X	161
Parvilles	Essex	TL5313	51°47·9'	0°13·5'E	X	167
Parvills Fm	Essex	TL4203	51°42·7'	0°3·7'E	FM	167
Parwich	Derby	SK1854	53°5·2'	1°43·5'W	T	119
Parwich Hill	Derby	SK1855	53°5·8'	1°43·5'W	H	119
Parwich Lees	Derby	SK1754	53°5·2'	1°44·4'W	X	119
Parwyd	Gwyn	SH1524	52°47·2'	4°44·2'W	W	123
Parys Fm	I of Angl	SH4390	53°23·3'	4°21·2'W	FM	114
Parys Mountain	I of Angl	SH4490	53°23·3'	4°20·3'W	H	114
Paschoe	Devon	SS7501	50°47·9'	3°46·0'W	X	191
Pasford	Staffs	SO8099	52°35·5'	2°17·3'W	T	138
Pashley Fm	E Susx	TQ7011	50°52·6'	0°25·4'E	FM	199
Pashley Manor	E Susx	TQ7029	51°2·3'	0°25·9'E	X	188,199
Paskeston	Pemb	SN0203	51°41·7'	4°51·5'W	X	157,158
Paslow Hall	Essex	TL5703	51°42·5'	0°16·7'E	X	167
Paslow Wood Common	Essex	TL5801	51°41·4'	0°17·5'E	X	167
Passaford	Devon	SS5403	50°48·7'	4°4·0'W	X	191
Passaford Fm	Devon	SY0987	50°40·8'	3°16·9'W	A	192
Pass Bye	Carm	SN1918	51°50·1'	4°37·2'W	X	158
Passenham	Northnts	SP7839	52°2·9'	0°51·4'W	T	152
Passfield	Hants	SU8234	51°6·2'	0°49·3'W	T	186
Passfield Common	Hants	SU8133	51°5·7'	0°50·2'W	F	186
Passford	E Ayr	NS5837	55°36·6'	4°14·8'W	X	71
Passingford Bridge	Essex	TQ5097	51°39·3'	0°10·5'E	T	167,177
Passmores	Essex	TL4408	51°45·4'	0°5·6'E	T	167
Pass of Aberglaslyn	Gwyn	SH5946	52°59·8'	4°5·7'W	X	115
Pass of Ballater	Aberd	NO3696	57°3·3'	3°2·9'W	X	37,44
Pass of Balmaha	Stir	NS4191	56°5·4'	4°32·9'W	X	56
Pass of Birnam	Pth & Kin	NO0539	56°32·3'	3°32·2'W	X	52,53
Pass of Brander	Arg & Bt	NN0527	56°24·0'	5°9·1'W	X	50
Pass of Drumochter	Pth & Kin	NN6276	56°51·6'	4°15·3'W	X	42
Pass of Glencoe	Highld	NN1756	56°39·9'	4°58·7'W	X	41
Pass of Inverfarigaig	Highld	NH5223	57°16·7'	4°26·8'W	X	26,35
Pass of Killiecrankie	Pth & Kin	NN9162	56°43·9'	3°46·4'W	X	43
Pass of Leny	Stir	NN5908	56°14·9'	4°16·1'W	X	57
Pass of Llanberis	Gwyn	SH6256	53°5·2'	4°3·2'W	X	115
Pass of Melfort	Arg & Bt	NM8415	56°17·0'	5°29·8'W	X	55
Pastheap	Kent	TQ6340	51°8·4'	0°20·2'E	X	188
Paston	Norf	TG3234	52°51·4'	1°27·2'E	T	133
Paston	Peterb	TF1902	52°36·4'	0°14·2'W	T	142
Paston Green	Norf	TG3134	52°51·5'	1°26·3'E	T	133
Pastoral Centre	Herts	TL1702	51°42·5'	0°18·0'W	X	166
Pastor's Hill	Glos	SO6105	51°44·8'	2°33·5'W	X	162
Pasture	Lancs	SD9242	53°52·7'	2°6·9'W	X	103
Pasture Barn	Lancs	SD4234	53°48·2'	2°52·4'W	X	102
Pasture Beck	Cumbr	NY4112	54°30·2'	2°54·2'W	W	90
Pasture Cross	Devon	SX7849	50°19·9'	3°42·5'W	X	202
Pasture End	Durham	NY9512	54°30·4'	2°4·2'W	X	91,92
Pasture End Fm	E Yorks	TA1449	53°55·7'	0°15·4'W	X	107
Pasturefields	Staffs	SJ9925	52°49·6'	2°0·5'W	T	127
Pasture Fm	Beds	TL0946	52°6·3'	0°24·1'W	FM	153
Pasture Fm	Bucks	SP6112	51°48·4'	1°6·5'W	FM	164,165
Pasture Fm	Bucks	SP7706	51°45·1'	0°52·7'W	FM	165
Pasture Fm	Devon	SX7849	50°19·9'	3°42·5'W	FM	202
Pasture Fm	E Yorks	SE7624	53°42·7'	0°50·5'W	FM	105,106,112
Pasture Fm	E Yorks	SE7958	54°1·0'	0°47·2'W	FM	105,106
Pasture Fm	E Yorks	SE8119	53°39·9'	0°46·0'W	FM	112
Pasture Fm	Glos	SP1734	52°0·5'	1°44·7'W	FM	151
Pasture Fm	Lincs	SK8739	52°56·7'	0°41·9'W	FM	130
Pasture Fm	Lincs	SK8928	52°50·8'	0°40·3'W	FM	130
Pasture Fm	Lincs	SK9329	52°51·3'	0°35·8'W	FM	130
Pasture Fm	Lincs	TF3187	53°22·0'	0°1·5'W	FM	113,122
Pasture Fm	N Lincs	SE8314	53°37·2'	0°44·3'W	FM	112
Pasture Fm	Notts	SK6892	53°25·5'	0°58·2'W	FM	111
Pasture Fm	N Yks	SE3383	54°14·7'	1°29·2'W	FM	99
Pasture Fm	N Yks	SE4383	54°14·7'	1°20·0'W	FM	99
Pasture Fm	N Yks	SE4469	54°7·1'	1°19·2'W	FM	99
Pasture Fm	N Yks	SE6959	54°1·6'	0°56·4'W	FM	105,106
Pasture Fm	N Yks	SE7559	54°1·5'	0°50·9'W	FM	105,106
Pasture Fm	N Yks	SE9767	54°5·6'	0°30·6'W	FM	101
Pasture Fm	Sol	SP2082	52°26·4'	1°41·9'W	FM	139

Pasture Foot	Durham	NY8727	54°38·5'	2°11·7'W	X	91,92
Pasture Gill	Cumbr	SD7798	54°22·9'	2°20·8'W	W	98
Pasture Head	Lancs	SD8642	53°52·7'	2°12·4'W	X	103
Pasturehill	Northum	NU1930	55°34·0'	1°41·5'W	X	75
Pasture Hill Fm	Lincs	TF0620	52°46·3'	0°25·3'W	FM	130
Pasture Hill Fm	Notts	SK5470	53°13·7'	1°11·1'W	FM	120
Pasture Ho	Black w Dar	SD6717	53°39·2'	2°29·5'W	X	109
Pasture Ho	Cumbr	NY1443	54°46·7'	3°19·8'W	X	85
Pasture Ho	Cumbr	NY1860	54°55·9'	3°16·4'W	X	85
Pasture Ho	Cumbr	NY7538	54°44·4'	2°22·9'W	X	91
Pasture Ho	Derby	SK4159	53°7·8'	1°22·8'W	X	120
Pasture Ho	Durham	NY9441	54°46·1'	2°5·2'W	X	87
Pasture Ho	E Yorks	TA1337	53°49·3'	0°16·6'W	X	107
Pasture Ho	E Yorks	TA1444	53°53·0'	0°15·5'W	X	107
Pasture Ho	E Yorks	TA1935	53°48·1'	0°11·2'W	X	107
Pasture Ho	Lancs	SD8540	53°51·6'	2°13·3'W	X	103
Pasture Ho	Lancs	SD8750	53°57·0'	2°11·5'W	X	103
Pasture Ho	Northum	NU2317	55°27·0'	1°37·7'W	X	81
Pasture Ho	Northum	NY8577	55°5·5'	2°13·7'W	X	87
Pasture Ho	Northum	NY9359	54°55·8'	2°6·1'W	X	87
Pasture Ho	N Yks	SD9252	53°58·1'	2°6·9'W	X	103
Pasture Ho	N Yks	SD9550	53°57·0'	2°4·2'W	X	103
Pasture Ho	N Yks	SE2286	54°16·4'	1°39·3'W	X	99
Pasture Ho	N Yks	SE4088	54°17·4'	1°22·7'W	X	99
Pasture Ho	N Yks	SE6487	54°16·7'	1°0·6'W	X	94,100
Pasture Ho	N Yks	SE7164	54°4·3'	0°54·5'W	X	100
Pasture House Fm	Lancs	SD3848	53°55·7'	2°56·2'W	FM	102
Pasture Houses	Cumbr	NY2355	54°53·3'	3°11·6'W	X	85
Pasture Houses	Cumbr	NY7441	54°46·0'	2°23·8'W	X	86,87
Pasture Lodge	Leic	SK6423	52°48·3'	1°2·6'W	X	129
Pasture Lodge	Lincs	SK9524	52°48·5'	0°35·0'W	X	130
Pasture Lodge Fm	Lincs	SK8246	53°0·5'	0°46·3'W	FM	130
Pasture Plantation	N Yks	SE9868	54°6·2'	0°29·7'W	F	101
Pastures	Ches	SJ8767	53°12·2'	2°11·3'W	X	118
Pastures Fm	Beds	SP9749	52°8·1'	0°34·6'W	FM	153
Pastures Fm	Cambs	TL1463	52°15·4'	0°19·4'W	FM	153
Pastures Fm	Cambs	TL2960	52°13·6'	0°6·3'W	FM	153
Pastures Fm	Mil Key	SP8754	52°10·9'	0°43·3'W	FM	152
Pastures Fm	Northnts	SP6971	52°20·2'	0°58·8'W	FM	141
Pastures Fm	Warw	SP2452	52°10·2'	1°38·5'W	FM	151
Pastures Lodge Fm	Northnts	SP9970	52°19·4'	0°32·4'W	FM	141,153
Pastures, The	Derby	SK2838	52°56·6'	1°34·6'W	X	128
Pastures, The	Northnts	SP8755	52°11·4'	0°43·2'W	X	152
Pastures, The	Notts	SK6230	52°52·1'	1°4·3'W	X	129
Pasture Tops	Derby	SK1849	53°2·5'	1°43·5'W	X	119
Pasture Wood	Leic	SK4221	52°47·3'	1°22·2'W	F	129
Pasture Wood	Surrey	TQ1143	51°10·8'	0°24·3'W	F	187
Patchacott	Devon	SX4798	50°45·9'	4°9·8'W	T	191
Patcham	Bri & Hov	TQ3008	50°51·6'	0°8·8'W	T	198
Patcham Place	Bri & Hov	TQ3008	50°51·6'	0°8·8'W	X	198
Patchendon Fm	Herts	TL3017	51°50·4'	0°6·4'W	FM	166
Patchett's Cliff	Lincs	SK9392	53°25·2'	0°35·6'W	X	112
Patchetts Fm	Worcs	SO9868	52°18·8'	2°1·4'W	FM	139
Patchetts Green	Herts	TQ1497	51°39·8'	0°20·7'W	T	166,176
Patch Hill	Oxon	SP3416	51°50·7'	1°30·0'W	X	164
Patch Ho	Shrops	SO5283	52°26·8'	2°42·0'W	X	137,138
Patchill	Devon	SX4589	50°41·0'	4°11·3'W	X	190
Patching	W Susx	TQ0806	50°50·8'	0°27·6'W	T	197
Patching Hill	W Susx	TQ0807	50°51·4'	0°27·5'W	X	197
Patching's Fm	Notts	SK5949	53°2·3'	1°6·8'W	FM	129
Patchins Point	Dorset	SY9889	50°42·3'	2°1·3'W	X	195
Patch Lodge	Northnts	SP9474	52°21·6'	0°36·8'W	X	141
Patchole	Devon	SS6142	51°9·9'	3°58·6'W	T	180
Patch Park	Essex	TQ4896	51°38·8'	0°8·7'E	X	167,177
Patch Pit Creek	Norf	TF9745	52°58·2'	0°56·4'E	W	132
Patchway	S Glos	ST6082	51°32·4'	2°34·2'W	T	172
Patcombe Hill	Wilts	ST9251	51°15·7'	2°6·5'W	X	184
Patcott	Devon	SS9311	50°53·6'	3°30·9'W	X	192
Patefield Wood	N Yks	SE4938	53°50·4'	1°14·9'W	F	105
Pategill	Cumbr	NY5229	54°39·5'	2°44·2'W	T	90
Pateley Bridge	N Yks	SE1565	54°5·1'	1°45·8'W	T	99
Pateley Moor	N Yks	SE1967	54°6·2'	1°42·1'W	X	99
Paterland	Aberd	NJ6205	57°8·3'	2°37·2'W	X	37
Paternoster Fm	Essex	TL7704	51°42·6'	0°34·1'E	FM	167
Paternoster Heath	Essex	TL9115	51°48·3'	0°46·6'E	T	168
Paterson's Rock	Arg & Bt	NR7504	55°17·0'	5°32·2'W	X	68
Patervan Fm	Scot Bord	NT1128	55°32·5'	3°24·2'W	FM	72
Pateshall	Heref	SO5262	52°15·5'	2°41·8'W	X	137,138,149
Pateshill	Cumbr	NY4862	54°57·2'	2°48·3'W	X	86
Pate's Hill	W Loth	NS9959	55°49·1'	3°36·3'W	X	65,72
Patford Br	Northnts	SP6466	52°17·5'	1°3·3'W	X	152
Pathada Wood	Corn	SX3262	50°26·3'	4°21·6'W	F	201
Pathcondie	Fife	NO2914	56°19·0'	3°8·4'W	X	59
Pathe	Somer	ST3730	51°4·2'	2°53·6'W	T	182
Pather	N Lanak	NS7954	55°46·1'	3°55·3'W	T	64
Pathfinder Village	Devon	SX8493	50°43·7'	3°38·2'W	T	191
Path-head	Aberd	NK1037	57°25·7'	1°49·6'W	X	30
Pathhead	Aberd	NO7263	56°45·7'	2°27·0'W	X	45
Pathhead	D & G	NY1475	55°4·0'	3°20·4'W	X	85
Pathhead	E Ayr	NS6114	55°24·3'	4°11·3'W	T	71
Pathhead	E Loth	NT6473	55°57·2'	2°34·2'W	X	67
Pathhead	Fife	NO5311	56°17·6'	2°45·1'W	X	59
Pathhead	Fife	NT2892	56°6·7'	3°9·0'W	T	59
Path Head	Ghead	NZ1763	54°57·9'	1°43·6'W	T	88
Pathhead	Midlo	NT3964	55°52·2'	2°58·1'W	T	66
Pathhead	S Ayr	NS2803	55°17·7'	4°42·1'W	X	76
Pathhead Muir	Fife	NT2894	56°8·3'	3°9·1'W	X	59
Path Hill	Devon	SY1393	50°44·0'	3°13·6'W	X	192,193
Path Hill	Oxon	SU6478	51°30·1'	1°4·3'W	X	175
Pathlow	Warw	SP1758	52°13·4'	1°44·7'W	T	151
Path of Condie	Pth & Kin	NO0711	56°17·2'	3°29·7'W	T	58
Pathside	Moray	NJ3855	57°35·1'	3°1·8'W	X	28
Pathstruie	Pth & Kin	NO0712	56°17·7'	3°29·7'W	T	58
Patience Bridge	Essex	TL6307	51°44·5'	0°22·1'E	X	167
Patient End	Herts	TL4227	51°55·6'	0°4·3'E	T	167
Patieshill	Midlo	NT1656	55°47·7'	3°19·9'W	H	66
Patie's Hill	Midlo	NT1657	55°48·2'	3°20·0'W	H	65,66,72
Patiesmill	Aberd	NJ8319	57°15·9'	2°16·5'W	X	38
Patman's Fm	W Susx	TQ1122	50°59·4'	0°24·7'W	FM	198
Patmarsh	Shrops	SO7498	52°35·0'	2°22·6'W	X	138
Patmore	Notts	SK6774	53°15·8'	0°59·3'W	F	120
Patmore Hall	Herts	TL4525	51°54·5'	0°6·9'E	X	167
Patmore Heath	Herts	TL4425	51°54·5'	0°6·0'E	T	167
Patna	E Ayr	NS4110	55°21·8'	4°30·1'W	T	70
Patna Hill	E Ayr	NS4011	55°22·3'	4°31·1'W	H	70
Patney	Wilts	SU0758	51°19·5'	1°53·6'W	T	173
Patowl Burn	E Ayr	NS6818	55°26·5'	4°4·8'W	W	71
Patrick	I of M	SC2481	54°11·9'	4°41·5'W	T	95
Patrick Br	Sol	SP2181	52°25·8'	1°41·1'W	X	139
Patrick Brompton	N Yks	SE2290	54°18·6'	1°39·3'W	T	99
Patrick Burn	E Ayr	NS7131	55°33·6'	4°2·3'W	W	71
Patrickgill Flow	S Lanak	NS7438	55°37·4'	3°59·6'W	X	71
Patrickholm	S Lanak	NS7549	55°43·4'	3°59·0'W	A	64
Patrickston	Stir	NS6996	56°8·6'	4°6·1'W	X	57
Patricroft	Salf	SJ7698	53°28·9'	2°21·3'W	T	109
Patrieda Barton	Corn	SX3073	50°32·2'	4°23·6'W	X	201
Patrington	E Yorks	TA3122	53°40·9'	0°0·6'W	T	107,113
Patrington Channel	E Yorks	TA3417	53°38·2'	0°2·0'E	W	113
Patrington Fm	E Yorks	TA2820	53°39·9'	0°3·3'W	FM	107,113
Patrington Haven	E Yorks	TA3021	53°40·4'	0°1·5'W	T	107,113
Patrixbourne	Kent	TR1855	51°15·4'	1°7·9'E	T	179
Patsford	Devon	SS5339	51°8·1'	4°5·7'W	T	180
Patshull Hall	Staffs	SJ8000	52°36·1'	2°17·3'W	X	127
Patson Hill	Dorset	ST6219	50°58·4'	2°32·1'W	H	183
Pattacott Fm	Corn	SX2492	50°42·3'	4°29·2'W	FM	190
Pattard	Devon	SS2525	51°0·1'	4°29·3'W	X	190
Pattard Cross	Devon	SS2525	51°0·1'	4°29·3'W	X	190
Pattenden Fm	Kent	TQ7136	51°6·1'	0°26·9'E	FM	188
Pattendens Fm	E Susx	TQ8319	50°56·7'	0°36·7'E	FM	199
Patten's Fm	Essex	TL7400	51°40·5'	0°31·4'E	FM	167
Patten's Fm	Essex	TL7431	51°57·2'	0°32·3'E	FM	167
Patterdale	Cumbr	NY3915	54°31·8'	2°56·1'W	T	90
Patterdale Common	Cumbr	NY3615	54°31·8'	2°58·9'W	X	90
Patterdown Fm	Wilts	ST9071	51°26·5'	2°8·2'W	FM	173
Patter Farm	Pth & Kin	NO1037	56°31·2'	3°27·3'W	FM	53
Patterton Sta	E Renf	NS5357	55°47·3'	4°20·2'W	X	64
Pattesley Ho	Norf	TF8924	52°47·1'	0°48·6'E	X	132
Patteson's Cross	Devon	SY0997	50°46·2'	3°17·0'W	X	192
Patties Hill	Cumbr	NY5070	55°1·6'	2°46·5'W	X	86
Pattiesmuir	Fife	NT0983	56°2·1'	3°27·2'W	T	65
Pattingden Ho	Lincs	TF1848	53°1·2'	0°14·0'W	X	130
Pattingham	Staffs	SO8299	52°35·5'	2°15·5'W	T	138
Pattinson's Allotment	Cumbr	NY7917	54°33·1'	2°19·1'W	X	91
Pattishall	Northnts	SP6754	52°11·0'	1°0·8'W	T	152
Pattison	Kent	TR0339	51°7·1'	0°54·4'E	X	179,189
Pattison's Fm	Kent	TR0635	51°4·9'	0°56·9'E	FM	179,189
Pattiston	E Renf	NS4556	55°46·6'	4°27·8'W	X	64
Pattiswick	Essex	TL8124	51°53·3'	0°38·2'E	T	168
Pattiswick Hall	Essex	TL8124	51°53·3'	0°38·2'E	X	168
Pattle's Fm	Suff	TM4162	52°12·4'	1°32·0'E	FM	156
Pattleton's Fm	E Susx	TQ8216	50°55·1'	0°35·8'E	FM	199
Pattock's Fm	Essex	TL8826	51°54·3'	0°44·4'E	FM	168
Patton	Shrops	SO5894	52°32·8'	2°36·8'W	T	137,138
Patton Bridge	Cumbr	SD5597	54°22·2'	2°41·1'W	T	97
Patton Grange	Shrops	SO5895	52°33·3'	2°36·8'W	X	137,138
Patton Hall Fm	Cumbr	SD5496	54°21·7'	2°42·1'W	FM	97
Pattys Fm	Lancs	SD4552	53°57·9'	2°49·9'W	FM	102
Paudy Cross Roads	Leic	SK6018	52°45·6'	1°6·2'W	X	129
Paul	Corn	SW4627	50°5·6'	5°32·7'W	T	203
Paulerspury	Northnts	SP7145	52°6·2'	0°57·4'W	T	152
Paulfield	Highld	NH6549	57°30·9'	4°14·8'W	X	26
Paulith Bank	Shrops	SJ4000	52°35·9'	2°52·8'W	H	126
Paul Jones Cott	D & G	NX9857	54°54·1'	3°35·0'W	X	84
Paul Jone's Point	D & G	NX6748	54°48·8'	4°3·8'W	X	83,84
Paull	E Yorks	TA1626	53°43·3'	0°14·1'W	T	107
Paullet Hill	Devon	ST0214	50°55·3'	3°23·3'W	X	181
Paull Holme	E Yorks	TA1824	53°42·2'	0°12·3'W	X	107,113
Paull Holme Sands	E Yorks	TA1823	53°41·6'	0°12·4'W	X	107,113
Paull Roads	E Yorks	TA1624	53°42·2'	0°14·2'W	W	107,113
Paul Matthew Hill	Aberd	NO7769	56°49·0'	2°22·2'W	H	45
Paul's Copse	Hants	SU4254	51°17·2'	1°23·5'W	F	185
Pauls Cray Hill	Brom	TQ4868	51°23·6'	0°8·0'E	X	177
Paul's Fm	Essex	TL6630	51°56·8'	0°25·3'E	FM	167
Paul's Fm	Kent	TQ5446	51°11·8'	0°12·6'E	FM	188
Paul's Fm	Kent	TQ7631	51°3·3'	0°31·1'E	FM	188
Paul's Ford	Warw	SP3891	52°31·2'	1°26·0'W	X	140
Paul's Green	Corn	SW6033	50°9·1'	5°21·2'W	T	203
Paulsgrove	C of Port	SU6306	50°51·2'	1°5·9'W	T	196
Paul's Grove Fm	Suff	TM3261	52°12·1'	1°24·1'E	FM	156
Paul's Hall	Essex	TL7943	52°3·6'	0°37·1'E	X	155
Paul's Hill	Moray	NJ1140	57°26·8'	3°28·5'W	H	28
Paulsland	D & G	NY1976	55°4·6'	3°15·7'W	X	85
Paulsland Fm	Devon	ST0108	50°52·0'	3°24·0'W	FM	192
Paul's Moor	Devon	SS5822	50°59·0'	4°1·0'W	X	180
Paul's Moor	Devon	SS8024	51°0·4'	3°42·2'W	X	181
Paulswell	Scot Bord	NT1549	55°43·9'	3°20·8'W	X	72
Paulton	Bath & NE Somer	ST6556	51°18·4'	2°29·7'W	T	172
Paultons Park	Hants	SU3116	50°56·8'	1°33·1'W	X	185
Paulville	W Loth	NS9768	55°53·9'	3°38·4'W	T	65
Pauncefoot Ho	Hants	SU3420	50°58·9'	1°30·6'W	X	185
Pauncefoot Court	Heref	SO6740	52°3·7'	2°28·5'W	X	149
Paunch Beck	Lincs	TF0089	53°23·5'	0°29·4'W	W	112,121
Paunt Ho	Glos	SO7229	51°57·8'	2°24·1'W	X	149
Pauntley Court	Glos	SO7429	51°57·8'	2°22·3'W	X	150
Paunton Court	Heref	SO6749	52°8·5'	2°28·5'W	X	149
Pauperhaugh	Northum	NZ1099	55°17·3'	1°50·1'W	X	81
Pauper's Drain	N Lincs	SE8114	53°37·2'	0°46·1'W	W	112
Pave Lane	Wrekin	SJ7516	52°44·7'	2°21·8'W	T	127
Pavement Lane Fm	Ches	SJ7779	53°18·7'	2°20·3'W	FM	118
Pavenham	Beds	SP9955	52°11·3'	0°32·7'W	T	153
Paven Hill	Wilts	SU0887	51°35·1'	1°52·7'W	X	173
Pavey Ark	Cumbr	NY2808	54°28·0'	3°6·2'W	H	89,90
Paviland Cave	Swan	SS4385	51°32·8'	4°15·5'W	A	159
Paviland Manor	Swan	SS4486	51°33·3'	4°14·6'W	X	159
Pavilion Fm	Scot Bord	NT5235	55°36·6'	2°45·3'W	FM	73
Pavilion, The	Bucks	SP7613	51°48·9'	0°53·5'W	X	165
Pavington	Devon	SS6216	50°55·9'	3°57·4'W	X	180
Pavyotts Fm	Somer	ST5513	50°55·1'	2°38·0'W	FM	194
Pawdy Fm	Leic	SK5917	52°45·1'	1°7·1'W	FM	129
Pawlaw Pike	Durham	NZ0032	54°41·2'	1°59·6'W	X	92
Pawlett	Somer	ST2942	51°10·6'	3°0·6'W	T	182
Pawlett Hams	Somer	ST2742	51°10·6'	3°2·3'W	X	182
Pawlett Hill	Somer	ST2943	51°11·1'	3°0·6'W	T	182
Pawlett Level	Somer	ST3044	51°11·7'	2°59·7'W	X	182
Pawl-hir	Powys	SO1059	52°13·6'	3°18·7'W	X	148
Pawston	Northum	NT8532	55°35·1'	2°13·8'W	T	74
Pawston Hill	Northum	NT8531	55°34·6'	2°13·8'W	H	74
Pawston Lake	Northum	NT8531	55°34·6'	2°13·8'W	W	74
Pawton Gate Fm	Corn	SW9568	50°28·8'	4°53·0'W	FM	200
Pawton Hill Fm	Hartpl	NZ4332	54°41·1'	1°19·6'W	FM	93
Pawton Manor Fm	Corn	SW9570	50°29·9'	4°53·1'W	FM	200
Pawton Springs	Corn	SW9668	50°28·8'	4°52·2'W	FM	200
Paxcroft Brook	Wilts	ST8758	51°19·5'	2°10·8'W	W	173
Paxcroft Fms	Wilts	ST8858	51°19·5'	2°9·9'W	FM	173
Paxford	Glos	SP1837	52°2·1'	1°43·9'W	T	151
Pax Hill	Hants	SU7744	51°11·6'	0°53·5'W	X	186
Paxhill	Northum	NY8446	54°48·8'	2°14·5'W	X	86,87
Paxhill Park	W Susx	TQ3526	51°1·3'	0°4·1'W	X	187,198
Paxtane	N Lanak	NS9063	55°51·1'	3°45·0'W	X	65
Paxton	Scot Bord	NT9353	55°46·5'	2°6·3'W	T	67,74,75
Paxton Dean	Northum	NZ1694	55°14·6'	1°44·5'W	X	81
Paxtondean Burn	Northum	NZ1593	55°14·1'	1°45·4'W	W	81
Paxton Dene	Northum	NZ1695	55°15·2'	1°44·5'W	X	81
Paxton Hill Ho	Cambs	TL2062	52°14·8'	0°14·1'W	X	153
Paxton Ho	Scot Bord	NT9352	55°45·9'	2°6·3'W	X	67,74,75
Paxton North Mains	Scot Bord	NT9353	55°46·5'	2°6·3'W	X	67,74,75
Paxton South Mains	Scot Bord	NT9352	55°45·9'	2°6·3'W	X	67,74,75
Payables Fm	Oxon	SU6582	51°32·2'	1°3·4'W	FM	175
Paycocke's Ho	Essex	TL8422	51°52·2'	0°40·8'E	A	168
Payden Street	Kent	TQ9254	51°15·4'	0°45·5'E	T	189
Paye Fm	Somer	ST1813	50°54·9'	3°9·6'W	FM	181,193
Payford Br	Glos	SO7429	51°57·8'	2°22·3'W	X	150
Payhembury	Devon	ST0801	50°48·3'	3°18·0'W	T	192
Payne's Down	Dorset	ST3801	50°48·5'	2°52·4'W	X	193
Paynes Fm	Ches	SJ6481	53°19·7'	2°32·0'W	FM	109
Paynes Fm	Devon	SX9996	50°45·5'	3°25·5'W	FM	192
Paynes Fm	Essex	TM1023	51°52·2'	1°3·4'E	FM	168,169
Paynes Fm	Oxon	SP2813	51°49·1'	1°35·2'W	FM	163
Paynes Green	Surrey	TQ1437	51°7·5'	0°21·9'W	T	187
Paynes Hall	Herts	TL3316	51°49·8'	0°3·8'W	X	166
Paynes Hay Fm	Hants	SU3625	51°1·6'	1°28·8'W	FM	185
Paynes Place Fm	W Susx	TQ2921	50°58·7'	0°9·4'W	FM	198
Paynsley Hall	Staffs	SJ9838	52°56·6'	2°1·4'W	X	127
Paynter's Cross	Corn	SX3964	50°27·5'	4°15·7'W	T	201
Paynter's Lane End	Corn	SW6743	50°14·7'	5°15·7'W	T	203
Paynthouse Fm	Dorset	ST8321	50°59·5'	2°14·1'W	FM	183
Pay Street Fm	Kent	TR2040	51°7·2'	1°9·0'E	FM	179,189
Paythorne	Lancs	SD8351	53°57·5'	2°15·1'W	T	103
Paythorne Br	Lancs	SD8351	53°57·5'	2°15·1'W	X	103
Paythorne Moor	Lancs	SD8353	53°58·6'	2°15·1'W	X	103
Paytoe Hall	Heref	SO4171	52°20·3'	2°51·6'W	X	137,148
Payton	Somer	ST1120	50°58·6'	3°15·7'W	T	181,193
Paywell Fm	Somer	ST5056	51°18·3'	2°42·6'W	FM	172,182
Peacehaven	Aberd	NJ8641	57°27·8'	2°13·5'W	X	30
Peacehaven	E Susx	TQ4101	50°47·7'	0°0·4'E	T	198
Peacehaven Fm	Bucks	SP6507	51°45·7'	1°3·1'W	FM	164,165
Peacehaven Heights	E Susx	TQ4200	50°47·2'	0°1·3'E	T	198
Peacehill	Fife	NO3825	56°25·0'	2°59·9'W	X	54,59
Peacemarsh	Dorset	ST8027	51°2·8'	2°16·7'W	T	183
Peaches Fm	Glos	SO8900	51°42·2'	2°9·2'W	FM	163
Peacock	Ches	SJ8579	53°18·7'	2°13·1'W	X	118
Peacock Fm	Essex	TM0425	51°53·4'	0°58·3'E	FM	168
Peacock Fm	E Yorks	SE7550	53°56·7'	0°51·0'W	FM	105,106
Peacock Fm	Norf	TF9406	52°37·3'	0°52·4'E	FM	144
Peacock Fm	Norf	TF9818	52°43·6'	0°56·3'E	FM	132
Peacock Fm	N Yks	SE2570	54°7·8'	1°36·6'W	FM	99
Peacock Fm	N Yks	SE8672	54°8·4'	0°40·6'W	FM	101
Peacock Fm	Somer	ST4443	51°11·2'	2°47·7'W	FM	182
Peacock Fm	Suff	TM4171	52°17·3'	1°32·4'E	FM	156
Peacock Hey Fm	Lancs	SD6144	53°53·7'	2°35·2'W	FM	102,103
Peacock Hill	Lancs	SD5445	53°54·2'	2°41·6'W	X	102
Peacock Lodge	Lincs	TF0453	53°4·1'	0°26·5'W	X	121
Peacocks	Essex	TL6701	51°41·2'	0°25·4'E	X	167
Peacock's Fm	Cambs	TL6284	52°26·0'	0°21·7'E	FM	143
Peacocks Fm	Lincs	SK9656	53°5·8'	0°33·6'W	FM	121
Peacock's Fm	Lincs	TF2948	53°1·1'	0°4·2'W	FM	131
Peacock's Fm	Suff	TL7353	52°9·1'	0°32·1'E	FM	155
Peadhill	Devon	SS9714	50°55·2'	3°27·5'W	X	181
Peadon Fm	Somer	ST2041	51°10·0'	3°8·3'W	FM	182
Pea Down	E Susx	TV5798	50°45·8'	0°14·0'E	X	199
Peafield Fm	Notts	SK5664	53°10·4'	1°9·3'W	FM	120
Peagham Barton	Devon	SS5220	50°57·9'	4°6·1'W	X	180
Peagill	Cumbr	NY1004	54°25·7'	3°22·8'W	X	89
Pea Hill	Staffs	SJ9428	52°51·2'	2°4·9'W	X	127
Peak Cavern	Derby	SK1482	53°20·3'	1°47·0'W	X	110
Peak Clumps	N Yks	SE9976	54°10·5'	0°28·6'W	X	101
Peak Coppice	Dorset	SY7095	50°45·5'	2°25·1'W	F	194
Peak Cross	Devon	SX7859	50°25·3'	3°42·7'W	X	202
Peak Dale	Derby	SK0976	53°17·1'	1°51·5'W	T	119
Peaked Down	Glos	ST7699	51°41·6'	2°20·4'W	X	162
Peaked Rock	I Scilly	SV8511	49°55·2'	6°23·0'W	X	203
Peaked Tor Cove	Torbay	SX9262	50°27·1'	3°30·9'W	W	202
Peake Fm	Hants	SU6321	50°59·3'	1°5·8'W	FM	185
Peak End Hill	Dorset	SY6299	50°47·6'	2°32·0'W	X	194
Peake's Covert	Leic	SK7609	52°40·6'	0°51·7'W	F	141
Peake's Fm	Dorset	ST8626	51°2·2'	2°11·6'W	FM	183
Peakes Fm	Essex	TQ4899	51°40·4'	0°8·8'E	FM	167,177
Peak Field	Durham	NZ0136	54°43·4'	1°58·6'W	X	92
Peak Fm	Hants	SU6625	51°1·5'	1°3·1'W	FM	185,186
Peak Forest	Derby	SK1179	53°18·7'	1°49·7'W	T	119
Peak Forest Canal	Stock	SJ9685	53°22·0'	2°3·2'W	W	109
Peak Hill	Devon	SY1087	50°40·8'	3°16·1'W	X	192
Peak Hill	Lincs	TF2616	52°43·8'	0°7·6'W	T	131
Peak Hill	Notts	SK5982	53°20·1'	1°6·4'W	F	111,120
Peak Ho	Devon	SY1187	50°40·8'	3°15·2'W	X	192
Peak Hole	Durham	NZ0309	54°28·8'	1°56·8'W	X	92
Peakins	Essex	TL6216	51°49·4'	0°21·4'E	X	167
Peakirk	Peterb	TF1606	52°38·6'	0°16·7'W	T	142

Peakley Hill	Derby	SK3376	53°17·0′	1°29·9′W	X	119
Peak Naze	Derby	SK0496	53°27·9′	1°56·0′W	X	110
Peaknaze Moor	Derby	SK0597	53°28·4′	1°55·1′W	X	110
Peak Pasture	Derby	SK2373	53°15·4′	1°38·9′W	X	119
Peak Railway	Derby	SK2861	53°9·0′	1°34·5′W	X	119
Peak Scar	N Yks	SE5288	54°17·3′	1°11·7′W	H	100
Peaks Downs	Wilts	SU2679	51°30·8′	1°37·1′W	X	174
Peakshill	Derby	SK1182	53°20·3′	1°49·7′W	X	110
Peakshill Fm	Staffs	SJ9433	52°53·9′	2°4·9′W	FM	127
Peakshole Water	Derby	SK1683	53°20·9′	1°45·2′W	W	110
Peaks Tunnel Fm	NE Lincs	TA2806	53°32·3′	0°3·7′W	FM	113
Peakswater	Corn	SX1654	50°21·7′	4°34·8′W	X	201
Peak, The	Glos	SO9215	51°50·2′	2°6·6′W	X	163
Peak, The	N Yks	SE8567	54°5·8′	0°41·6′W	X	100
Peak, The	Shetld	HU2047	60°12·7′	1°37·8′W	X	3
Peak Tor	Derby	SK2565	53°11·1′	1°37·1′W	X	119
Peakway	Derby	SK1754	53°5·2′	1°44·4′W	X	119
Peal Hill	D & G	NX6176	55°3·8′	4°10·2′W	H	77
Pea Low	Staffs	SK1356	53°6·3′	1°47·9′W	A	119
Peal, The	Corn	SW3425	50°4·2′	5°42·7′W	X	203
Peamore Ho (Hotel)	Devon	SX9188	50°41·1′	3°32·2′W	X	192
Pean Hill	Kent	TR1062	51°19·3′	1°1·2′E	T	179
Peanmeanach	Highld	NM7180	56°51·6′	5°44·9′W	X	40
Peans	E Susx	TQ7123	50°59·1′	0°26·6′E	X	199
Pear Ash	Somer	ST7531	51°4·9′	2°21·0′W	T	183
Pearcelands	W Susx	TQ3432	51°4·5′	0°4·8′W	X	187
Pearce's Fm	Wilts	SU3158	51°19·4′	1°32·9′W	FM	174
Pearchay Fm	Devon	SS7822	50°59·3′	3°43·9′W	FM	180
Pearhill	Shrops	SJ4817	52°45·1′	2°45·8′W	X	126
Pearie Law	W Loth	NT0058	55°48·6′	3°35·3′W	H	65
Pearith Fm	Oxon	SU5392	51°37·7′	1°13·7′W	FM	164,174
Pearl Fm	Ches	SJ5245	53°0·3′	2°42·5′W	FM	117
Pearls	Ches	SJ9866	53°11·7′	2°1·4′W	X	118
Pearls Fm	Suff	TM1855	52°9·2′	1°11·6′E	FM	156
Pearsby Hall	D & G	NY2384	55°8·9′	3°12·1′W	X	79
Pearse Hay Fm	Staffs	SJ8408	52°40·4′	2°13·8′W	FM	127
Pears Gill	Cumbr	NY4940	54°45·4′	2°47·1′W	X	86
Pearsie	Angus	NO3659	56°43·4′	3°2·3′W	X	54
Pears Lodge Fm	Leic	SK8316	52°44·3′	0°45·8′W	FM	130
Pearson	Devon	SS5515	50°55·2′	4°3·4′W	X	180
Pearson Fm	Pemb	SM8110	51°45·0′	5°10·0′W	FM	157
Pearson Ho	Durham	NZ0721	54°35·3′	1°53·1′W	X	92
Pearsons	Lancs	SD8829	53°45·7′	2°10·5′W	X	103
Pearson's Flash	Wigan	SD5803	53°31·6′	2°37·6′W	W	108
Pearsons Fm	Derby	SK2555	53°5·7′	1°37·2′W	FM	119
Pearson's Green	Kent	TQ6943	51°9·9′	0°25·4′E	T	188
Pearson's Rigg	N Yks	NZ7811	54°29·5′	0°47·3′W	X	94
Pearson's Wood	Warw	SP0655	52°11·8′	1°54·3′W	F	150
Pearson Wood	N Yks	SE5572	54°8·7′	1°9·1′W	F	100
Peart Fm	Somer	ST7754	51°17·3′	2°19·4′W	FM	183
Pear Tree	C of Derb	SK3533	52°53·8′	1°28·4′W	T	128
Peartree	Herts	TL2412	51°47·8′	0°11·7′W	T	166
Peartree	Shrops	SO4992	52°31·6′	2°44·7′W	X	137,138
Pear Tree Corner	Norf	TF8923	52°46·5′	0°48·5′E	X	132
Peartree Cottage	Peterb	TF3110	52°40·5′	0°3·3′W	X	131,142
Peartree Fm	Ches	SJ5755	53°5·7′	2°38·1′W	FM	117
Peartree Fm	Ches	SJ7368	53°12·7′	2°23·9′W	FM	118
Pear Tree Fm	Ches	SJ7759	53°7·9′	2°20·2′W	FM	118
Pear Tree Fm	E Susx	TQ4817	50°56·2′	0°6·8′E	FM	198
Pear Tree Fm	E Susx	TQ6515	50°54·9′	0°21·2′E	FM	199
Pear Tree Fm	Kent	TR0432	51°3·3′	0°55·0′E	FM	189
Peartree Fm	Norf	TM2684	52°24·7′	1°19·8′E	FM	156
Peartree Fm	N Yks	SE6533	53°47·6′	1°0·4′W	FM	105,106
Pear Tree Fm	S Glos	ST5885	51°34·0′	2°36·0′W	FM	172
Pear Tree Fm	Suff	TL6577	52°22·2′	0°25·8′E	FM	143
Peartree Fm	Suff	TM0173	52°19·3′	0°57·4′E	FM	144,155
Peartree Fm	Suff	TM2236	51°58·9′	1°14·4′E	FM	169
Peartree Fm	Suff	TM3680	52°22·3′	1°28·4′E	FM	156
Peartree Fm	Suff	TM4161	52°11·9′	1°32·0′E	FM	156
Peartree Fm Cotts	Ches	SJ6871	53°14·3′	2°28·4′W	X	118
Peartree Green	C of Soton	SU4311	50°54·0′	1°22·9′W	T	196
Peartree Green	Essex	TQ5998	51°39·7′	0°18·3′E	T	167,177
Peartree Green	Heref	SO5932	51°59·3′	2°35·4′W	T	149
Peartree Green	Surrey	SU9937	51°7·6′	0°34·7′W	T	186
Peartree Hill	D & G	NX8476	55°4·1′	3°48·6′W	H	84
Pear Tree Hill	Notts	SK7790	53°24·3′	0°50·1′W	X	112
Peartree Hill	Oxon	SP4910	51°47·4′	1°17·0′W	X	164
Peartree Ho	Lincs	TF2125	52°48·8′	0°11·9′W	X	131
Pear Tree Ho	Suff	TM2774	52°19·2′	1°20·3′E	X	156
Peartree Ho	Wrex	SJ4341	52°58·0′	2°50·5′W	X	117
Pear Tree Ho	Wrex	SJ5040	52°57·5′	2°44·3′W	X	117
Peartree House Fm	N Yks	SE3798	54°22·8′	1°25·4′W	FM	99
Pear Tree Lake Fm	Staffs	SJ7550	53°3·0′	2°22·0′W	FM	118
Peas Acre	Brad	SE1041	53°52·1′	1°50·5′W	T	104
Peasash Fm	Hants	SU1416	50°56·8′	1°47·7′W	FM	184
Peascliff Tunnel	Lincs	SK9139	52°56·7′	0°38·3′W	X	130
Pease Bay	Scot Bord	NT7971	55°56·1′	2°19·7′W	W	67
Peasebrook Fm	Worcs	SP0737	52°2·1′	1°53·5′W	FM	150
Pease Burn	Scot Bord	NT7867	55°54·0′	2°20·7′W	W	67
Peasedown St John	Bath & NE Somer	ST7057	51°18·9′	2°25·4′W	T	172
Peasefield	Herts	TL3525	51°54·7′	0°1·8′W	X	166
Peasehill	Derby	SK4049	53°2·4′	1°23·8′W	T	129
Peaseland Green	Norf	TG0516	52°42·4′	1°2·5′E	T	133
Pease Lane	Shrops	SJ4300	52°35·9′	2°50·1′W	X	126
Peasemore	W Berks	SU4577	51°29·6′	1°20·7′W	T	174
Pease Myres	Durham	NY9740	54°45·5′	2°2·4′W	X	87
Peasenhall	Suff	TM3569	52°16·4′	1°27·1′E	T	156
Pease Pottage	W Susx	TQ2532	51°4·6′	0°12·5′W	T	187
Pease Pottage Forest	W Susx	TQ2533	51°5·2′	0°12·5′W	F	187
Peasewell Wood	Glos	SP2428	51°57·2′	1°38·7′W	F	163
Peasey Beck	Cumbr	SD5486	54°16·3′	2°42·0′W	W	97
Peashell Fm	Oxon	SP3209	51°47·0′	1°31·8′W	FM	164
Peas Hill	Cambs	TL4097	52°33·4′	0°4·3′E	T	142,143
Peashill Fm	Leic	SP6490	52°30·5′	1°3·0′W	FM	140
Peashill Fm	Notts	SK6336	52°55·3′	1°3·4′W	FM	129
Peasholmes Fms	Cumbr	SD2467	54°5·8′	3°9·3′W	FM	96
Peasholm Park	N Yks	TA0389	54°17·4′	0°24·6′W	X	101
Peasiehill	Angus	NO6140	56°33·3′	2°37·6′W	X	54

Peaslake	Surrey	TQ0844	51°11·3′	0°26·9′W	T	187
Peaslands	Cumbr	NY6319	54°34·1′	2°33·9′W	X	91
Peaslands Fm	Leic	SK5924	52°48·9′	1°7·1′W	FM	129
Peasley Bank	Staffs	SJ9029	52°51·7′	2°8·5′W	H	127
Peasley Cross	St Hel	SJ5293	53°26·1′	2°42·9′W	T	108
Peasmarsh	E Susx	TQ8723	50°58·8′	0°40·2′E	T	189,199
Peasmarsh	Somer	ST3412	50°54·5′	2°55·9′W	T	193
Peasmarsh	Surrey	SU9946	51°12·5′	0°34·6′W	T	186
Peasmarsh Place	E Susx	TQ8821	50°57·7′	0°41·0′E	X	189,199
Peasmeadows	Northum	NY8547	54°49·3′	2°13·6′W	X	87
Peasridge Fm	Kent	TQ8241	51°8·6′	0°36·5′E	FM	188
Peaston	E Loth	NT4265	55°52·7′	2°55·2′W	X	66
Peastonbank	E Loth	NT4466	55°53·3′	2°53·3′W	X	66
Peastree	Cumbr	NY3951	54°51·3′	2°56·6′W	X	85
Peasunhurst	Derby	SK3166	53°11·6′	1°31·8′W	X	119
Peasy Fm	Somer	ST3338	51°8·5′	2°57·1′W	FM	182
Peat Bay	Orkney	ND3296	58°51·0′	3°10·2′W	W	6,7
Peat Burn	D & G	NX6697	55°15·2′	4°6·1′W	W	77
Peat Carr	Donc	SE7000	53°29·8′	0°56·3′W	X	112
Peat Cot	Devon	SX6071	50°31·6′	3°58·1′W	X	202
Peat Craig	D & G	NS7502	55°18·0′	3°57·7′W	X	78
Peatdraught Bay	C of Edin	NT1579	56°0·0′	3°21·3′W	W	65
Peat Fell	N Yks	SE0895	54°21·3′	1°52·2′W	X	99
Peatfold	Aberd	NJ3518	57°15·1′	3°4·2′W	X	37
Peatgap	Northum	NY7750	54°50·9′	2°21·1′W	X	86,87
Peatgate	Cumbr	NY6124	54°36·8′	2°35·8′W	X	91
Peat Gate	Northum	NY6661	54°56·8′	2°31·4′W	X	86
Peat Gate Head	N Yks	SD9998	54°22·9′	2°0·5′W	X	98
Peat Geo	Shetld	HU5966	60°22·7′	0°55·3′W	X	2
Peat Gill Head	N Yks	SD9747	53°55·4′	2°2·3′W	X	103
Peathead Rigg	N Yks	SE8890	54°18·1′	0°38·4′W	X	94,101
Peat Hill	Aberd	NJ4119	57°15·7′	2°58·2′W	H	37
Peathill	Aberd	NJ8218	57°15·4′	2°17·4′W	X	38
Peathill	Aberd	NJ9366	57°41·3′	2°6·6′W	T	30
Peat Hill	Angus	NO5067	56°47·8′	2°48·7′W	H	44
Peathill	Angus	NO5360	56°44·0′	2°45·6′W	X	44
Peat Hill	D & G	NS7402	55°18·0′	3°58·7′W	H	77
Peat Hill	D & G	NS7704	55°19·1′	3°55·9′W	X	78
Peat Hill	D & G	NT0101	55°17·8′	3°33·1′W	H	78
Peat Hill	D & G	NT1511	55°23·4′	3°20·1′W	H	79
Peat Hill	D & G	NX6257	54°53·6′	4°8·7′W	H	83
Peathill	D & G	NX7269	55°0·2′	3°59·6′W	X	83,84
Peat Hill	D & G	NY1793	55°13·7′	3°17·9′W	H	79
Peat Hill	D & G	NY1799	55°16·9′	3°18·0′W	X	79
Peat Hill	E Ayr	NS5509	55°21·5′	4°16·8′W	H	71,77
Peat Hill	E Ayr	NS6324	55°29·7′	4°9·7′W	X	71
Peat Hill	N Ayr	NS2364	55°50·5′	4°49·2′W	X	63
Peat Hill	Northum	NY7459	54°55·7′	2°23·9′W	X	86,87
Peat Hill	S Ayr	NX1677	55°3·5′	4°52·4′W	X	76
Peat Hill	Scot Bord	NT0619	55°27·6′	3°28·8′W	H	78
Peat Hill	Scot Bord	NT2048	55°43·4′	3°16·0′W	H	73
Peat Hill	Scot Bord	NT2418	55°27·3′	3°11·7′W	H	79
Peat Hill	Scot Bord	NT2730	55°33·7′	3°9·0′W	X	73
Peat Hill	Scot Bord	NT3552	55°45·7′	3°1·7′W	X	66,73
Peat Hill	S Lanak	NS9117	55°26·3′	3°42·9′W	H	71,78
Peathillock	Moray	NJ0150	57°32·0′	3°38·7′W	X	27
Peat Hill, The	Aberd	NJ2913	57°12·4′	3°10·1′W	H	37
Peathrow	Durham	NZ1024	54°36·9′	1°50·3′W	X	92
Peat Inn	Fife	NO4509	56°16·5′	2°52·8′W	T	59
Peatland	S Ayr	NS3835	55°35·2′	4°33·8′W	X	70
Peat Law	Northum	NT9010	55°23·3′	2°9·0′W	H	80
Peat Law	Scot Bord	NT2528	55°32·7′	3°10·9′W	X	73
Peat Law	Scot Bord	NT2621	55°28·9′	3°9·8′W	H	73
Peat Law	Scot Bord	NT3326	55°31·6′	3°3·2′W	H	73
Peat Law	Scot Bord	NT4430	55°33·9′	2°52·8′W	H	73
Peat Law	Scot Bord	NT5308	55°22·1′	2°44·1′W	H	79
Peat Law	Scot Bord	NT5454	55°46·9′	2°43·6′W	X	66,73
Peat Law	Scot Bord	NT5850	55°44·7′	2°39·7′W	X	67,73,74
Peat Law	Scot Bord	NT6964	55°52·3′	2°29·3′W	X	67
Peatling Hall	Leic	SP5889	52°30·0′	1°8·3′W	X	140
Peatling Lo	Leic	SP5989	52°30·0′	1°7·5′W	X	140
Peatling Lodge Fm	Leic	SP5893	52°32·1′	1°8·3′W	FM	140
Peatling Magna	Leic	SP5992	52°31·6′	1°7·4′W	T	140
Peatling Parva	Leic	SP5889	52°30·0′	1°8·3′W	T	140
Peat Loch	D & G	NX2655	54°51·8′	4°42·2′W	W	82
Peat Moors Visitor Centre	Somer	ST4241	51°10·2′	2°49·4′W	X	182
Peatmoss Plantn	Derby	SK2440	52°57·6′	1°38·2′W	F	119,128
Peaton	Shrops	SO5384	52°27·4′	2°41·1′W	T	137,138
Peaton Ho	Arg & Bt	NS2186	56°2·3′	4°52·0′W	X	56
Peaton Layo	Arg & Bt	NS2185	56°1·7′	4°51·9′W	X	56
Peatonstrand	Shrops	SO5384	52°27·4′	2°41·1′W	T	137,138
Peat Pits Fm	Sheff	SK2793	53°26·2′	1°35·2′W	FM	110
Peat Point	Orkney	ND3296	58°51·0′	3°10·2′W	X	6,7
Peatpots	N Lanak	NS8162	55°50·4′	3°53·6′W	X	65
Peat Rig	D & G	NS7513	55°24·0′	3°58·0′W	H	71,78
Peat Rig	D & G	NS8017	55°26·2′	3°53·4′W	X	71,78
Peat Rig	D & G	NX7298	55°15·8′	4°0·4′W	X	77
Peat Rig	D & G	NY3495	55°14·9′	3°1·9′W	H	79
Peat Rig	S Ayr	NX3099	55°15·6′	4°40·1′W	X	76
Peat Rig	Scot Bord	NT3523	55°30·0′	3°1·3′W	H	73
Peat Rig	Scot Bord	NT3603	55°19·3′	3°0·1′W	X	79
Peat Rigg	Northum	NY6670	55°1·7′	2°31·5′W	X	86
Peatrigg	Northum	NY7568	55°0·6′	2°23·0′W	X	86,87
Peat Rigg	N Yks	SE7790	54°18·2′	0°48·6′W	X	94,100
Peatrig Hill	Scot Bord	NT3648	55°43·5′	3°0·7′W	H	73
Peat Rig Strand	D & G	NX4269	54°59·7′	4°27·8′W	W	83
Peats Corner	Suff	TM1960	52°11·9′	1°12·7′E	X	156
Peat Shank	Angus	NO3261	56°44·4′	3°6·3′W	X	44
Peat Shank	Scot Bord	NT7407	55°21·6′	2°24·2′W	X	80
Peatshank Head	Scot Bord	NT3529	55°33·3′	3°1·4′W	H	73
Peat Sike	Northum	NY6188	55°11·3′	2°36·3′W	W	80
Peat Sike	Northum	NY7478	55°6·0′	2°24·0′W	X	86,87
Peatsteel crags	Northum	NY6865	54°59·0′	2°29·6′W	X	86,87
Peatswood	Staffs	SJ6933	52°53·9′	2°27·2′W	X	127
Peattie	Aberd	NO8073	56°51·1′	2°19·2′W	X	45
Peattie	Pth & Kin	NO2236	56°30·8′	3°15·6′W	X	53
Peattieshill	Fife	NO4308	56°15·9′	2°54·8′W	X	59
Peatworth	Orkney	HY6021	59°4·7′	2°41·4′W	X	5,6
Pebble Coombe	Surrey	TQ2152	51°15·5′	0°15·6′W	X	187
Pebble Hill	Oxon	SU5699	51°41·4′	1°11·0′W	X	164

Pebble Ho	Lincs	TF2920	52°46·0′	0°4·9′W	X	131
Pebble Ridge	Devon	SS4330	51°3·1′	4°14·0′W	X	180
Pebbly Hill Fm	Glos	SP2323	51°54·5′	1°39·5′W	FM	163
Pebleygrove Fm	Derby	SK4879	53°18·6′	1°16·4′W	FM	120
Pebley Resr	Derby	SK4879	53°18·6′	1°16·4′W	W	120
Pebmarsh	Essex	TL8533	51°58·1′	0°42·0′E	T	168
Pebsham	E Susx	TQ7608	50°50·9′	0°30·4′E	T	199
Pebsham Fm	E Susx	TQ7609	50°51·4′	0°30·4′E	FM	199
Pebworth	Worcs	SP1346	52°7·0′	1°48·2′W	T	151
Pebworth Downs	Worcs	SP1248	52°8·0′	1°49·1′W	X	150
Pebworth Fields Fm	Worcs	SP1345	52°6·4′	1°48·2′W	FM	151
Pebyll	Nth Pt Talb	SS9197	51°39·9′	3°34·2′W	A	170
Pecca Falls	N Yks	SD6974	54°9·9′	2°28·1′W	W	98
Pecket Well	Cald	SD9929	53°45·7′	2°0·5′W	T	103
Peckfield Bar	Leeds	SE4331	53°46·7′	1°20·4′W	X	105
Peckfield Lodge	N Yks	SE4630	53°46·1′	1°17·7′W	X	105
Peck Fm	Devon	SX7582	50°37·7′	3°45·7′W	FM	191
Peckforton	Ches	SJ5356	53°6·2′	2°41·7′W	T	117
Peckforton Castle	Ches	SJ5358	53°7·3′	2°41·7′W	X	117
Peckforton Hills	Ches	SJ5256	53°6·2′	2°42·6′W	H	117
Peckforton Mere	Ches	SJ5457	53°6·7′	2°40·8′W	W	117
Peckforton Moss	Ches	SJ5455	53°5·7′	2°40·8′W	X	117
Peckham	Sthwk	TQ3476	51°28·3′	0°3·8′W	T	176,177
Peckham Bush	Kent	TQ6649	51°13·2′	0°23·0′E	T	188
Peckham Fm	Kent	TQ8346	51°11·3′	0°37·5′E	FM	188
Peckham Place Fm	Kent	TQ6550	51°13·7′	0°22·2′E	FM	188
Peckham Rye Park	Sthwk	TQ3474	51°27·2′	0°3·9′W	X	176,177
Peckhams	E Susx	TQ4916	50°55·7′	0°7·6′E	X	199
Peckhams	W Susx	TQ0405	50°50·3′	0°31·0′W	X	197
Peckingell	Wilts	ST9374	51°28·1′	2°5·7′W	T	173
Pecking Mill	Somer	ST6337	51°8·1′	2°31·3′W	T	183
Peckledy	Shrops	SO5584	52°27·4′	2°39·3′W	X	137,138
Peckleton	Leic	SK4600	52°36·0′	1°18·8′W	T	140
Peckleton Ho	Leic	SK4601	52°36·5′	1°18·8′W	X	140
Peckmill Brook	Ches	SJ4873	53°15·3′	2°46·4′W	W	117
Peck Mill Fm	Ches	SJ4873	53°15·3′	2°46·4′W	FM	117
Peck Mill Fm	Ches	SJ8175	53°16·5′	2°16·7′W	FM	118
Pecknall	Powys	SJ3414	52°43·4′	2°58·2′W	X	126
Pecknell	Durham	NZ0217	54°33·1′	1°57·7′W	X	92
Peck's Ho	Staffs	SJ9263	53°10·1′	2°6·8′W	X	118
Pecks Lodge	Northnts	TL0074	52°21·5′	0°31·5′W	X	141
Pedair-ffordd	Powys	SJ1124	52°48·6′	3°18·8′W	T	125
Pedair Onnen	V of Glam	SS9778	51°29·7′	3°28·6′W	X	170
Pedam's Oak	Durham	NY9848	54°49·9′	2°1·4′W	X	87
Peddars Way and Norfolk Coast Path	Norf	TG0944	52°57·4′	1°7·1′E	X	133
Peddars Way and Norfolk Coast Path	Norf	TL9194	52°30·8′	0°49·3′E	X	144
Peddars Way & Norfolk Coast Path	Norf	TF7626	52°48·4′	0°37·1′E	X	132
Peddars Way (Roman Road)	Norf	TF7627	52°48·9′	0°37·1′E	R	132
Peddars Way (Roman Road)	Norf	TL9388	52°27·6′	0°50·9′E	R	144
Pedderhill	Cumbr	NY4273	55°3·1′	2°54·0′W	X	85
Pedder Potts Resr	Lancs	SD5370	54°7·7′	2°42·7′W	W	97
Pedder's Wood	Lancs	SD5147	53°55·3′	2°44·4′W	F	102
Peddie's Hill	Aberd	NJ4424	57°18·4′	2°55·3′W	H	37
Peddieston	Highld	NH7464	57°39·2′	4°6·2′W	X	21,27
Peddimore Hall	Birm	SP1593	52°32·3′	1°46·3′W	X	139
Peddinnan Burn	E Ayr	NS5408	55°20·9′	4°17·7′W	W	70,77
Peddirie Dod	Scot Bord	NT0521	55°28·7′	3°29·8′W	H	72
Peden	S Lanak	NS9412	55°23·7′	3°40·0′W	X	71,78
Peden Burn	S Lanak	NS9312	55°23·7′	3°40·9′W	W	71,78
Peden Head	S Lanak	NS9012	55°23·6′	3°43·8′W	X	71,78
Peden's Cave	E Ayr	NS4823	55°28·9′	4°23·9′W	X	70
Peden's Cleuch	Scot Bord	NT6207	55°21·6′	2°35·5′W	X	80
Peden's Stone	Scot Bord	NY4692	55°13·4′	2°50·5′W	X	79
Pedestal	Heref	SO4361	52°14·9′	2°49·7′W	X	137,148,149
Pedge Croft	Cumbr	SD6692	54°19·6′	2°30·9′W	X	98
Pedham	Norf	TG3312	52°39·6′	1°27·1′E	T	133,134
Pedington Elm	Glos	ST6796	51°39·9′	2°28·2′W	X	162
Pedington Fm	Glos	ST6796	51°39·9′	2°28·2′W	FM	162
Pedlars End	Essex	TL5306	51°44·1′	0°13·2′E	T	167
Pedlar's Rest	Shrops	SO4884	52°27·3′	2°45·5′W	T	137,138
Pedlar's Stone	Northum	NT9300	55°17·9′	2°6·2′W	X	80
Pedlersburgh	E Susx	TQ3902	50°48·3′	0°1·2′W	X	198
Pedlersburgh (Tumulus)	E Susx	TQ3902	50°48·3′	0°1·2′W	A	198
Pedley Barton	Devon	SS7712	50°53·9′	3°44·6′W	X	180
Pedley Brook	Ches	SJ7878	53°18·2′	2°19·4′W	W	118
Pedley House Fm	Ches	SJ7977	53°17·6′	2°18·5′W	FM	118
Pedley Wood Fm	Beds	TL0939	52°2·5′	0°24·2′W	FM	153
Pedlicote Fm	Derby	SK1079	53°18·7′	1°50·6′W	FM	119
Pedlinge	Kent	TR1335	51°4·7′	1°2·8′E	T	179,189
Pedmore	Dudley	SO9182	52°26·4′	2°7·5′W	T	139
Pedmyre	C of Glas	NS5957	55°47·4′	4°14·5′W	X	64
Pednathise Head	I Scilly	SV8305	49°51·9′	6°24·3′W	X	203
Pednavounder	Corn	SW7617	50°0·9′	5°7·2′W	X	204
Pedn Boar	Corn	SW7716	50°0·4′	5°6·4′W	X	204
Pednbrose	I Scilly	SV9116	49°58·1′	6°18·2′W	X	203
Pedn Crifton	Corn	SW6516	50°0·1′	5°16·4′W	X	203
Pedngwinian	Corn	SW6520	50°2·3′	5°16·5′W	W	203
Pedn-mên-an-mere	Corn	SW3821	50°2·1′	5°39·2′W	X	203
Pedn-mên-du	Corn	SW3426	50°4·7′	5°42·7′W	X	203
Pedn-myin	Corn	SW7919	50°2·0′	5°4·8′W	X	204
Pedn Olva	Corn	SW5240	50°12·7′	5°28·2′W	X	203
Pednor Bottom	Bucks	SP9303	51°43·3′	0°38·8′W	T	165
Pednormead End	Bucks	SP9501	51°42·2′	0°37·1′W	T	165
Pednvadan	Corn	SW8835	50°10·9′	4°57·8′W	X	204
Pedsmore Fm	Shrops	SJ6136	52°55·4′	2°34·4′W	FM	127
Pedwardine	Heref	SO3670	52°19·7′	2°56·0′W	X	137,148
Pedwardine Wood	Heref	SO3570	52°19·7′	2°56·8′W	F	137,148
Pedwell	Somer	ST4236	51°7·5′	2°49·3′W	T	182
Pedwell Hill	Somer	ST4336	51°7·5′	2°48·5′W	H	182
Peebles	Angus	NO6244	56°35·4′	2°36·7′W	X	54
Peebles	Scot Bord	NT2540	55°39·1′	3°11·1′W	T	73
Peekhill	Devon	SX5469	50°30·4′	4°3·2′W	X	201
Peek Hill	Devon	SX5569	50°30·4′	4°2·3′W	H	202
Peekie	Fife	NO5512	56°18·2′	2°43·2′W	X	59
Peel	Angus	NO2654	56°40·6′	3°12·0′W	X	53

Peel	Cumbr	NY1941	54°45·7'	3°15·1'W	A	85
Peel	I of M	SC2484	54°13·5'	4°41·6'W	T	95
Peel	Lancs	SD3531	53°46·5'	2°58·8'W	T	102
Peel	Scot Bord	NT4335	55°36·6'	2°53·9'W	T	73
Peel	Scot Bord	NY6099	55°17·3'	2°37·4'W	X	80
Peel Acres	Darl	NZ2418	54°33·6'	1°37·3'W	X	93
Peel Bay	I of M	SC2484	54°13·5'	4°41·6'W	W	95
Peelbraehope	Scot Bord	NT4804	55°19·9'	2°48·7'W	X	79
Peel Burn	Scot Bord	NT6000	55°17·8'	2°37·4'W	W	80
Peel Castle	I of M	SC2484	54°13·5'	4°41·6'W	A	95
Peel Common	Hants	SU5702	50°49·1'	1°11·1'W	T	196
Peel Dod	Cumbr	NY6047	54°49·2'	2°36·9'W	X	86
Peel Fell	Scot Bord	NY6299	55°17·3'	2°35·5'W	H	80
Peel Flatt	Northum	NY9858	54°55·2'	2°1·4'W	X	87
Peel Fm	Ches	SJ8561	53°9·0'	2°13·1'W	FM	118
Peel Green	Salf	SJ7497	53°28·4'	2°23·1'W	T	109
Peel Hall	Ches	SJ4969	53°13·2'	2°45·4'W	A	117
Peel Hall	Man	SJ8387	53°23·0'	2°14·9'W	T	109
Peel Hall	Warr	SJ6191	53°25·1'	2°34·8'W	X	109
Peel Hall Fm	N Yks	SE6438	53°50·3'	1°1·2'W	FM	105,106
Peel Hill	Hants	SU3508	50°52·5'	1°29·8'W	X	196
Peel Hill	Lancs	SD3533	53°47·6'	2°58·8'W	T	102
Peel Hill	Scot Bord	NT4234	55°36·0'	2°54·8'W	H	73
Peelhill	S Lanak	NS6436	55°36·2'	4°9·1'W	X	71
Peel Hill Br	Lancs	SD3632	53°47·1'	2°57·9'W	X	102
Peel Ho	E Susx	TQ5807	50°50·7'	0°15·0'E	X	199
Peel Ho	Staffs	SJ7850	53°3·0'	2°19·3'W	X	118
Peelhouses	D & G	NY1484	55°8·8'	3°20·5'W	X	78
Peel I	Cumbr	SD2991	54°18·8'	3°5·1'W	X	96,97
Peelings	E Susx	TQ6104	50°49·0'	0°17·5'E	X	199
Peelinick	Scot Bord	NT7914	55°25·4'	2°19·5'W	X	80
Peel Moat	Stock	SJ8792	53°25·7'	2°11·3'W	A	109
Peel of Lumphanan	Aberd	NJ5703	57°7·2'	2°42·2'W	A	37
Peel O'Hill	Cumbr	NY5575	55°4·3'	2°41·9'W	X	86
Peel Park	Brad	SE1634	53°48·4'	1°45·0'W	X	104
Peel Park	N Yks	SE5872	54°8·7'	1°6·3'W	X	100
Peel Park	S Lanak	NS6054	55°45·8'	4°13·4'W	T	64
Peel Place	Cumbr	NY0701	54°24·0'	3°25·5'W	X	89
Peelrig	Scot Bord	NT7952	55°45·9'	2°19·6'W	X	67,74
Peels Fm	Norf	TL9795	52°31·3'	0°54·6'E	FM	144
Peels, The	Northum	NT9404	55°20·0'	2°5·2'W	X	80
Peel, The	Pth & Kin	NO0523	56°23·6'	3°31·9'W	X	52,53,58
Peelton Hill	D & G	NX8091	55°12·2'	3°52·7'W	H	78
Peel Tower	Bury	SD7716	53°38·6'	2°20·5'W	X	109
Peelwalls Fm	Scot Bord	NT9259	55°49·7'	2°7·2'W	FM	67,74,75
Peelwalls Ho	Scot Bord	NT9260	55°50·2'	2°7·2'W	X	67
Peelwell	Northum	NY8364	54°58·5'	2°15·5'W	X	86,87
Peel Wood	N Yks	NZ8110	54°29·0'	0°44·6'W	F	94
Peel Wood	N Yks	SE5873	54°9·2'	1°6·3'W	F	100
Peene	Kent	TR1837	51°5·7'	1°7·2'E	T	179,189
Peening Quarter	Kent	TQ8828	51°1·5'	0°41·2'E	T	189,199
Peeping Hill	Cumbr	NY7225	54°37·4'	2°25·6'W	X	91
Peep O' Day	N Yks	SE5372	54°8·7'	1°10·9'W	X	100
Peep O' Sea	Northum	NU2418	55°27·6'	1°36·8'W	X	81
Peepy	Northum	NZ0362	54°57·4'	1°56·8'W	X	87
Peepy Plantation	Sund	NZ3357	54°54·6'	1°28·7'W	F	88
Peerie Breast	Orkney	HY4145	59°17·5'	3°1·7'W	X	5
Peerie Castle	Orkney	HY5603	58°55·0'	2°45·4'W	X	6
Peerie Hill	Orkney	HY2312	58°59·6'	3°19·9'W	H	6
Peerie Water	Orkney	HY3327	59°7·7'	3°9·8'W	W	6
Peerie Water	Orkney	HY3929	59°8·9'	3°3·5'W	W	6
Peesweep Bank	Fife	NO2519	56°21·7'	3°12·4'W	X	59
Peewit Fm	Oxon	SP4745	52°6·3'	1°18·4'W	FM	151
Peewits Hill	Glos	SP0105	51°44·9'	1°58·7'W	X	163
Peffer Burn	E Loth	NT5080	56°0·9'	2°47·7'W	W	66
Peffer Burn	E Loth	NT5577	55°59·3'	2°42·8'W	W	66
Peffer Burn	E Loth	NT6082	56°2·0'	2°38·1'W	W	67
Peffermill House	C of Edin	NT2871	55°55·9'	3°8·7'W	A	66
Peffer Sands	E Loth	NT6282	56°2·0'	2°36·1'W	X	67
Pefferside	E Loth	NT6182	56°2·0'	2°37·1'W	X	67
Pefham Plantn	N Yks	SE8658	54°0·9'	0°40·8'W	F	106
Pegal Bay	Orkney	ND3097	58°51·6'	3°12·3'W	W	6,7
Pegal Burn	Orkney	ND2798	58°52·1'	3°15·5'W	W	6,7
Pegal Head	Orkney	ND3098	58°52·1'	3°12·3'W	X	6,7
Pegal Hill	Orkney	ND2898	58°52·1'	3°14·4'W	H	6,7
Pegden	W Susx	TQ3723	50°59·6'	0°2·5'W	X	198
Peg Fleet	Kent	TQ9666	51°21·8'	0°49·3'E	W	178
Pegglesworth	Glos	SO9818	51°51·9'	2°1·3'W	X	163
Pegg's Fm	Dorset	ST8515	50°56·3'	2°12·4'W	FM	183
Peggs Fm	Oxon	SP6500	51°41·9'	1°3·2'W	FM	164,165
Peggs Green	Leic	SK4117	52°45·2'	1°23·1'W	T	129
Peggy's Bridge	Cumbr	NY1814	54°31·1'	3°15·6'W	X	89,90
Peggyslea	Midlo	NT1757	55°48·2'	3°19·0'W	X	65,66,72
Peggy Wests Well	N Yks	SE0157	54°0·8'	1°58·7'W	W	104
Peghorn Lodge	Durham	NY8331	54°40·7'	2°15·4'W	X	91,92
Peghorn Sike	Durham	NY8231	54°40·7'	2°16·3'W	W	91,92
Peghouse Fm	Worcs	SO7657	52°12·9'	2°20·7'W	FM	150
Peglar's Fm	Glos	SO6914	51°49·7'	2°26·6'W	FM	162
Peg Law	Scot Bord	NT7414	55°25·4'	2°24·2'W	H	80
Pegsdon	Beds	TL1230	51°57·7'	0°21·8'W	T	166
Pegsdon Common Fm	Beds	TL1230	51°57·7'	0°21·8'W	FM	166
Peg's Fm	Heref	SO7041	52°4·2'	2°25·9'W	FM	149
Pegswood	Northum	NZ2287	55°10·9'	1°38·8'W	T	81
Pegswood Moor	Northum	NZ2087	55°10·9'	1°40·7'W	X	81
Pegwell	Kent	TR3664	51°19·8'	1°23·7'E	T	179
Pegwell Bay	Kent	TR3563	51°19·3'	1°22·8'E	W	179
Pegwhistle Burn	Northum	NZ2380	55°7·1'	1°37·9'W	W	81
Pegwn Bach	Powys	SO0180	52°24·8'	3°26·9'W	H	136
Pegwn Mawr	Powys	SO0281	52°25·3'	3°26·1'W	H	136
Pegwyn-y-bwlch	Caer	ST2392	51°37·5'	3°6·4'W	X	171
Peibron	I of Angl	SH4093	53°24·8'	4°24·0'W	X	114
Peigh Hills	Northum	NZ2094	55°14·6'	1°40·7'W	X	81
Peighinn a Bhaile	N Eil	NF7652	57°26·8'	7°23·6'W	X	22
Peighinn Lodain	N Eil	NF7754	57°27·9'	7°22·8'W	X	22
Peighinn nan Aoireann	N Eil	NF7434	57°17·1'	7°24·2'W	X	22
Pein a' Chleibh	Highld	NG4847	57°26·9'	6°11·6'W	H	23
Peinaha	Highld	NG4258	57°32·6'	6°18·2'W	T	23
Pein Borve	Highld	NG4648	57°27·3'	6°13·6'W	X	23
Peinchorran	Highld	NG5233	57°19·5'	6°6·7'W	T	24,32
Peiness	Highld	NG4246	57°26·1'	6°17·5'W	T	23

Peingown	Highld	NG4071	57°39·5'	6°21·1'W	X	23
Peinlich	Highld	NG4158	57°32·5'	6°19·2'W	T	23
Peinmore	Highld	NG4248	57°27·2'	6°17·6'W	T	23
Peinmore	Highld	NG4840	57°23·1'	6°11·1'W	T	23
Peipards Fm	Bath & NE Somer	ST7760	51°20·6'	2°19·4'W	FM	172
Peirk, The	Aberd	NJ4727	57°20·1'	2°52·4'W	H	37
Peithyll	Cered	SN6382	52°25·4'	4°0·5'W	X	135
Peithyn	Carm	SN5542	52°3·7'	4°6·5'W	X	146
Pekes Ho	E Susx	TQ5513	50°54·0'	0°12·6'E	X	199
Pelaig	Highld	NH5662	57°37·8'	4°24·2'W	X	21
Pelaw	Ghead	NZ2862	54°57·4'	1°33·3'W	T	88
Pelaw Ho	Durham	NZ2752	54°52·0'	1°34·3'W	X	88
Pel Beggar	Shrops	SO5682	52°26·3'	2°38·4'W	X	137,138
Pelcomb	Pemb	SM9218	51°49·6'	5°0·7'W	T	157,158
Pelcomb Bridge	Pemb	SM9317	51°49·0'	4°59·8'W	T	157,158
Pelcomb Cross	Pemb	SM9117	51°49·0'	5°1·6'W	T	157,158
Pelcomb Fm	Pemb	SM9317	51°49·0'	4°59·8'W	FM	157,158
Peldon	Essex	TL9816	51°48·7'	0°52·7'E	T	168
Peldon Lodge	Essex	TL9817	51°49·2'	0°52·8'E	X	168
Pelhamfield	I of W	SZ5892	50°43·7'	1°10·3'W	T	196
Pelham Fm	Staffs	SK0451	53°3·6'	1°56·0'W	FM	119
Pelham House Fm	NE Lincs	TA1414	53°36·8'	0°16·2'W	FM	113
Pelham House Sch	Cumbr	NY0305	54°26·1'	3°29·3'W	X	89
Pelham Place	Hants	SU7033	51°5·7'	0°59·6'W	X	186
Pelham's Lands Fm	Lincs	TF2250	53°2·2'	0°10·4'W	FM	122
Pelham's Pillar	Lincs	TA1203	53°30·9'	0°18·2'W	X	113
Pelican Fm	Cambs	TL2980	52°24·4'	0°5·8'W	FM	142
Pelican House Fm	Suff	TL6848	52°6·5'	0°27·6'E	FM	154
Pelistry Bay	I Scilly	SV9311	49°55·5'	6°16·3'W	W	203
Pellagenna	Corn	SX2166	50°28·2'	4°31·0'W	X	201
Pellew's Redoubt	I Scilly	SV9312	49°56·0'	6°16·3'W	A	203
Pell Green	E Susx	TQ6432	51°4·1'	0°20·8'E	T	188
Pellingbridge Fm	W Susx	TQ3722	50°59·1'	0°2·5'W	FM	198
Pellon	Cald	SE0725	53°43·5'	1°53·2'W	T	104
Pells Fm	Kent	TQ5861	51°19·8'	0°16·5'E	FM	177,188
Pellsyeat	Cumbr	SD5979	54°12·6'	2°37·3'W	X	97
Pell Wall	Shrops	SJ6733	52°53·8'	2°29·0'W	X	127
Pellynwartha	Corn	SW7638	50°12·2'	5°8·0'W	X	204
Peloe Dairy Fm	Corn	SW6536	50°10·9'	5°17·1'W	FM	203
Pelsall	Wals	SK0203	52°37·7'	1°57·8'W	T	139
Pelsall Wood	Wals	SK0103	52°37·7'	1°58·7'W	T	139
Pelsham	E Susx	TQ8720	50°57·2'	0°40·1'E	X	189,199
Pelsham Fm	Dorset	ST7423	51°0·6'	2°21·9'W	FM	183
Pelton	Durham	NZ2553	54°52·5'	1°36·2'W	T	88
Pelton Fell	Durham	NZ2551	54°51·4'	1°36·2'W	T	88
Pelutho	Cumbr	NY1249	54°49·9'	3°21·8'W	T	85
Pelutho Grange	Cumbr	NY1150	54°50·5'	3°22·7'W	X	85
Pelutho Park	Cumbr	NY1150	54°50·5'	3°22·7'W	X	85
Pelyn	Corn	SX0958	50°23·7'	4°40·9'W	X	200
Pelyne	Corn	SX1759	50°24·4'	4°34·1'W	X	201
Pelynt	Corn	SX2055	50°22·3'	4°31·5'W	T	201
Pemberton	Carm	SN5300	51°41·0'	4°7·2'W	T	159
Pemberton	Wigan	SD5504	53°32·1'	2°40·3'W	T	108
Pemberton Well	N Yks	SE1053	53°58·6'	1°50·4'W	W	104
Pembles Cross	Kent	TQ8847	51°11·7'	0°41·8'E	T	189
Pemboa Fm	Corn	SW6826	50°5·6'	5°14·3'W	FM	203
Pembrey	Carm	SN4201	51°41·4'	4°16·8'W	T	159
Pembrey Burrows	Carm	SN4100	51°40·8'	4°17·6'W	X	159
Pembrey Forest	Carm	SN3803	51°42·4'	4°20·3'W	F	159
Pembridge	Heref	SO3958	52°13·2'	2°53·2'W	T	148,149
Pembridge Castle	Heref	SO4819	51°52·3'	2°44·9'W	A	161
Pembroke Dock (Doc Penfro)	Pemb	SM9603	51°41·6'	4°56·7'W	T	157,158
Pembroke Ferry	Pemb	SM9704	51°42·1'	4°55·9'W	T	157,158
Pembroke Fm	Cambs	TL2860	52°13·6'	0°7·2'W	FM	153
Pembroke Fm	Herts	TL2737	52°1·2'	0°8·5'W	FM	153
Pembroke Ho	Cumbr	NY5328	54°38·9'	2°43·3'W	X	90
Pembroke Lodge	Rich	TQ1872	51°26·3'	0°17·7'W	X	176
Pembroke Manor	E Susx	TQ5119	50°57·3'	0°9·4'E	X	199
Pembroke (Penfro)	Pemb	SM9801	51°40·5'	4°54·9'W	T	157,158
Pembroke River	Pemb	SM9502	51°41·0'	4°57·5'W	W	157,158
Pembrokeshire Coast Path	Pemb	SM8423	51°52·1'	5°7·9'W	X	157
Pembrokeshire Coast Path	Pemb	SN0743	52°3·3'	4°48·5'W	X	145
Pembrokeshire Coast Path	Pemb	SN1147	52°5·6'	4°45·2'W	X	145
Pembrokeshire Coast Path	Pemb	SS1098	51°39·2'	4°44·4'W	X	158
Pembury	Kent	TQ6240	51°8·4'	0°19·3'E	T	188
Pembury Hall	Kent	TQ6242	51°9·5'	0°19·4'E	X	188
Pembury Walks	Kent	TQ6142	51°9·5'	0°18·5'E	X	188
Pemprys	Cered	SN7194	52°32·0'	3°53·7'W	X	135
Pempwell	Corn	SX3775	50°33·4'	4°17·7'W	T	201
Penadlake	Corn	SX1758	50°23·8'	4°34·1'W	X	201
Penair	Corn	SW8445	50°16·2'	5°1·5'W	X	204
Penalbanach	Arg & Bt	NM4657	56°38·4'	6°8·1'W	X	47
Penaligon Downs	Corn	SX0368	50°29·0'	4°46·2'W	X	200
Penallt	Carm	SN5318	51°50·7'	4°7·7'W	X	159
Pen-allt	Heref	SO5729	51°57·7'	2°37·2'W	T	149
Penallt	Monm	SO5210	51°47·4'	2°41·4'W	T	162
Penalltfangor	Carm	SN3327	51°55·2'	4°25·3'W	X	145
Penallt Fm	Carm	SN3807	51°44·5'	4°20·4'W	FM	159
Pen Allt-mawr	Powys	SO2024	51°54·8'	3°9·4'W	H	161
Penalltygwin	Cered	SN3046	52°5·4'	4°28·5'W	X	145
Penally Hill	Corn	SX0991	50°41·5'	4°41·9'W	H	190
Penally Ho	Corn	SX1091	50°41·5'	4°41·0'W	X	190
Penally (Penalum)	Pemb	SS1199	51°39·7'	4°43·6'W	T	158
Penally Pt	Corn	SX0991	50°41·5'	4°41·9'W	X	190
Penaluna	Corn	SW4526	50°5·0'	5°33·5'W	X	203
Pen-a-maen or Maenease Point	Corn	SX0141	50°14·4'	4°47·1'W	X	204
Penamser	Gwyn	SH5539	52°56·0'	4°9·0'W	X	124
Pen Anglas	Pemb	SM9440	52°1·5'	4°59·8'W	X	157
Penanheath	Shrops	SO3087	52°28·8'	3°1·4'W	X	137
Penans	Corn	SW9548	50°18·0'	4°52·3'W	X	204
Penantigi Uchaf	Gwyn	SH8116	52°44·0'	3°45·3'W	X	124,125
Penanty	Pemb	SN0934	51°58·5'	4°46·5'W	X	145
Penaran	Gwyn	SH8326	52°49·4'	3°43·8'W	X	124,125
Penard Pill	Swan	SS5488	51°34·6'	4°6·0'W	W	159
Penare	Corn	SW9940	50°13·8'	4°48·7'W	T	204
Penare Ho	Corn	SW7924	50°4·7'	5°5·0'W	X	204
Penare Point	Corn	SX0245	50°16·5'	4°46·4'W	X	204

Penarfynydd	Gwyn	SH2126	52°48·4'	4°38·9'W	X	123
Penarfynydd	Gwyn	SH4037	52°54·6'	4°22·4'W	X	123
Penarlâg or Hararden	Flint	SJ3165	53°10·9'	3°1·5'W	T	117
Penarnewydd	Cered	SN2451	52°8·0'	4°33·9'W	X	145
Penarron	Powys	SO1388	52°29·2'	3°16·5'W	T	136
Penarrow Point	Corn	SW8234	50°10·2'	5°2·8'W	X	204
Penarth	Corn	SW8344	50°15·6'	5°2·3'W	X	204
Penarth	Denb	SJ1142	52°58·3'	3°19·1'W	X	125
Penarth	Gwyn	SH5928	52°50·1'	4°5·2'W	X	124
Penarth	Powys	SJ0903	52°37·3'	3°20·3'W	X	136
Penarth	Powys	SO1492	52°31·4'	3°15·7'W	A	136
Penarth	V of Glam	ST1871	51°26·2'	3°10·4'W	T	171
Penarth Bach	Gwyn	SH4238	52°55·2'	4°20·6'W	X	123
Penarth Fawr	Gwyn	SH4137	52°54·7'	4°21·5'W	A	123
Penarth Flats	Card	ST1873	51°27·2'	3°10·4'W	X	171
Penarth Head	V of Glam	ST1971	51°26·2'	3°9·5'W	X	171
Penarth Ho	Monm	ST3796	51°39·8'	2°54·3'W	X	171
Penarth-isaf	Carm	SN6439	52°2·2'	3°58·6'W	X	146
Penarth Moors	Card	ST1773	51°27·2'	3°11·3'W	T	171
Penarth Mount	Powys	SO1252	52°9·8'	3°16·8'W	A	148
Penarth Tack	Powys	SO1391	52°30·8'	3°16·5'W	X	136
Penarthtown	Corn	SX2556	50°22·9'	4°27·3'W	X	201
Penarth-uchaf	Carm	SN6540	52°2·8'	3°57·7'W	X	146
Penarth Uchaf	Gwyn	SH4039	52°55·7'	4°22·4'W	X	123
Pen-Arthur	Carm	SN7123	51°53·7'	3°52·1'W	X	160
Penarthur Farm	Pemb	SM7426	51°53·4'	5°16·7'W	FM	157
Pen-Arthur-isaf	Carm	SN7224	51°54·2'	3°51·2'W	X	160
Penarwel	Gwyn	SH3232	52°51·8'	4°29·3'W	X	123
Penback Fm	Carm	SN2321	51°51·8'	4°33·9'W	FM	145,158
Pen banc	Carm	SN6543	52°4·4'	3°57·8'W	X	146
Penbanc	Cered	SN6249	52°7·6'	4°0·6'W	X	146
Penbanc	Cered	SN6568	52°17·9'	3°58·4'W	X	135
Penbanc	Cered	SN6876	52°22·2'	3°55·9'W	X	135
Penbanc	Pemb	SN1342	52°2·9'	4°43·2'W	X	145
Pen-banc	Pemb	SN2334	51°58·8'	4°34·3'W	X	145
Penbane	D & G	NS9005	55°19·9'	3°43·6'W	H	71,78
Pen Barn Fm	Dorset	SY6388	50°41·7'	2°31·0'W	FM	194
Pen Bars	Kent	TR0617	50°55·2'	0°56·2'E	X	189
Penbeagle	Corn	SW5039	50°12·1'	5°29·8'W	T	203
Pen bedw	Denb	SJ1647	53°1·1'	3°14·7'W	X	116
Penbedw	Flint	SJ1668	53°12·4'	3°15·1'W	T	116
Pen-bedw	Pemb	SN2039	52°1·5'	4°37·0'W	T	145
Penbedw	Powys	SO0394	52°32·4'	3°25·4'W	X	136
Penbedw	Powys	SO1347	52°7·1'	3°15·8'W	X	148
Penbedw-uchaf	Flint	SJ1568	53°12·4'	3°16·0'W	A	116
Penbeili-mawr	Cered	SN3643	52°3·9'	4°23·2'W	X	145
Penbennar	Gwyn	SH3128	52°49·6'	4°30·1'W	X	123
Penberlan Fm	Corn	SW9748	50°18·1'	4°50·7'W	FM	204
Penberry	Pemb	SM7629	51°55·1'	5°15·1'W	H	157
Penberth	Corn	SW4022	50°2·7'	5°37·5'W	T	203
Penberth	Powys	SO1049	52°8·2'	3°18·5'W	X	148
Penberth Cove	Corn	SW4022	50°2·7'	5°37·5'W	W	203
Penberthy Cross	Corn	SW5532	50°8·5'	5°25·4'W	X	203
Penbidwal	Monm	SO3322	51°53·8'	2°58·0'W	T	161
Penbigwrn	Carm	SN3020	51°51·4'	4°27·7'W	X	145,159
Pen-blaen	Powys	SO1050	52°8·7'	3°18·5'W	X	148
Penblaith Fm	Heref	SO4919	51°52·3'	2°44·1'W	FM	162
Penblewin	Pemb	SN1216	51°48·9'	4°43·3'W	X	158
Penblodeuyn	Cered	SN6155	52°10·8'	4°1·6'W	X	146
Penbodlas	Gwyn	SH2833	52°52·3'	4°32·9'W	T	123
Penbol	I of Angl	SH4088	53°22·1'	4°23·9'W	X	114
Penbol Uchaf	I of Angl	SH3987	53°21·6'	4°24·8'W	X	114
Penbontbren	Cered	SN3149	52°7·1'	4°27·7'W	X	145
Pen-bont Rhydybeddau	Cered	SN6783	52°26·0'	3°57·0'W	T	135
Penbontrhydyfothair	Cered	SN3554	52°9·8'	4°24·4'W	X	145
Penboyr	Carm	SN3536	52°0·1'	4°23·8'W	T	145
Penbreck	D & G	NS9800	55°17·3'	3°35·9'W	H	78
Penbreck Rig	E Ayr	NS7220	55°27·7'	4°1·0'W	X	71
Pen Brilley	Heref	SO2348	52°7·7'	3°7·1'W	X	148
Penbro Fm	Corn	SW6228	50°6·5'	5°19·4'W	FM	203
Pen Brush	Pemb	SM8839	52°0·8'	5°5·0'W	X	157
Penbrycoch	Gwyn	SH8733	52°53·2'	3°40·4'W	X	124,125
Penbryn	Carm	SN4722	51°52·8'	4°13·0'W	X	159
Penbryn	Cered	SN2952	52°8·6'	4°29·6'W	T	145
Pen-bryn	Cered	SN5151	52°8·5'	4°10·3'W	X	146
Penbryn	Cered	SN5971	52°19·4'	4°3·7'W	X	135
Pen-bryn	Cered	SN6864	52°15·7'	3°55·7'W	X	146
Penbryn	Cered	SN6880	52°24·4'	3°56·0'W	X	135
Penbryn	Denb	SJ0341	52°57·7'	3°26·2'W	X	125
Penbryn	Gwyn	SH4440	52°56·3'	4°18·9'W	X	123
Penbryn	Powys	SJ2009	52°40·6'	3°10·6'W	X	126
Penbryn	Powys	SN9630	51°57·8'	3°30·4'W	X	160
Penbryn	Shrops	SJ3340	52°57·4'	2°59·4'W	X	117
Pen-bryn-brwynog	Conwy	SH7464	53°9·7'	3°52·7'W	X	115
Penbryn-ci	Conwy	SH8756	53°5·6'	3°40·8'W	H	116
Pen Bryn-du	Gwyn	SH6971	53°13·4'	3°57·3'W	X	115
Pen Bryn Llan	Conwy	SH9770	53°13·3'	3°32·2'W	X	116
Pen-bryn-llŵyn	Denb	SJ0764	53°10·1'	3°23·1'W	X	116
Penbryn-Mawr	Cered	SN5454	52°10·1'	4°7·7'W	X	146
Penbryn Mawr	Gwyn	SH4553	53°3·4'	4°18·4'W	X	115,123
Pen Bryn-y-fawnog	Powys	SH9527	52°50·1'	3°33·1'W	X	125
Penbrynyreglwys	I of Angl	SH2992	53°24·1'	4°33·9'W	X	114
Penbuarth	Carm	SN3138	52°1·1'	4°27·4'W	X	145
Penbugle	Corn	SX0768	50°29·0'	4°42·9'W	X	200
Penbugle	Corn	SX2260	50°25·0'	4°30·0'W	X	201
Penburth	Powys	SO0665	52°16·7'	3°22·3'W	X	136,147
Penbury Grove	Bucks	SU9292	51°37·4'	0°39·9'W	X	175
Penbury Knoll	Dorset	SU0317	50°57·4'	1°57·1'W	X	184
Penbwchdy	Pemb	SM8737	51°59·7'	5°5·8'W	X	157
Penbwch Isaf	Rho Cyn Taf	ST0586	51°34·1'	3°21·9'W	X	170
Penbwch Uchaf	Rho Cyn Taf	ST0587	51°34·7'	3°21·9'W	X	170
Penbwlcha	Merth Tyd	ST0897	51°40·1'	3°19·4'W	X	170
Penbwlch Mawr	Cered	SN5957	52°11·8'	4°3·4'W	X	146
Pen Bwlchycloddiau	Powys	SN8578	52°23·5'	3°41·0'W	X	135,136,147
Pen Bwlch y Garnedd	Conwy	SH9054	53°4·6'	3°38·1'W	X	116
Pen Bwlch-y-groes	Powys	SN9082	52°25·7'	3°36·7'W	H	136
Penbwliaid	Cered	SN2944	52°4·3'	4°29·3'W	X	145
Pencabe	Corn	SW8735	50°10·8'	4°58·6'W	X	204
Pencader	Carm	SN4436	52°0·3'	4°16·0'W	T	146
Pen-cae	Cered	SN4356	52°11·0'	4°17·4'W	X	146

Pen-cae	Powys	SN8955	52°11·2′	3°37·0′W	X	147
Pencaeau	Cered	SN3149	52°7·1′	4°27·7′W	X	145
Pencaeau Fm	Powys	SO1725	51°55·3′	3°12·0′W	FM	161
Pen-cae-cwm	Conwy	SH9461	53°8·4′	3°34·7′W	X	116
Pencaedu	Powys	SJ1009	52°40·5′	3°19·5′W	X	125
Pen-cae-du Fm	Denb	SJ0469	53°12·8′	3°25·9′W	FM	116
Pencaefadog	Powys	SO0425	51°55·2′	3°23·4′W	X	160
Pencaelyfri	Cered	SN5056	52°11·2′	4°11·3′W	X	146
Pencaemelyn	Powys	SO0534	52°0·0′	3°22·6′W	X	160
Pencaenewydd	Gwyn	SH4040	52°56·3′	4°22·5′W	T	123
Pencaenewydd	Powys	SO1245	52°6·0′	3°16·7′W	X	148
Pen-cae-newydd	Wrex	SJ1331	52°52·4′	3°17·2′W	X	125
Pen Caer	Pemb	SM9041	52°1·9′	5°3·3′W	X	157
Pen Caer	Pemb	SM9140	52°1·4′	5°2·4′W	X	157
Pencaerau	Nth Pt Talb	SS7495	51°38·6′	3°48·9′W	T	170
Pencaerau Mawr	Carm	SN3327	51°55·2′	4°25·3′W	X	145
Pen-caer-fenny	Swan	SS5295	51°38·3′	4°7·9′W	T	159
Pencaerhelem	Powys	SN9953	52°10·2′	3°28·2′W	X	147
Pencaerodyn	Cered	SN6252	52°9·2′	4°0·6′W	X	146
Pencaitland	E Loth	NT4468	55°54·4′	2°53·3′W	T	66
Pencalenick	Corn	SW8545	50°16·2′	5°0·7′W	X	204
Pencannow Point	Corn	SX1397	50°44·8′	4°38·7′W	X	190
Pen-carn	Newp	ST2884	51°33·3′	3°1·9′W	X	171
Pencarnan	Pemb	SM7225	51°52·9′	5°18·4′W	X	157
Pencarniced	Cered	SN4143	52°4·0′	4°18·8′W	X	146
Pencarnisiog	I of Angl	SH3573	53°14·0′	4°27·9′W	T	114
Pencarreg	Carm	SN5345	52°5·3′	4°8·3′W	T	146
Pencarreg	Carm	SN7824	51°54·3′	3°46·0′W	X	160
Pen Carreg-dân	Powys	SN8654	52°10·6′	3°39·6′W	H	147
Pencarreg Fm	Monm	SO4206	51°45·2′	2°50·0′W	FM	161
Pencarreg Fm	Monm	ST3898	51°40·9′	2°53·4′W	FM	171
Pen Carreg Gopa	Powys	SN7299	52°34·7′	3°52·9′W	X	135
Pencarrow	Corn	SX0371	50°30·6′	4°46·3′W	X	200
Pencarrow	Corn	SX1082	50°36·6′	4°40·8′W	T	200
Pencarrow Head	Corn	SX1550	50°19·5′	4°35·6′W	X	201
Pencarrow Rounds	Corn	SX0370	50°30·0′	4°46·3′W	A	200
Pencarrow Wood	Corn	SX0569	50°29·5′	4°44·6′W	F	200
Pen-carth	Gwyn	SH4539	52°55·8′	4°18·0′W	X	123
Pencastell	Carm	SN2528	51°55·6′	4°32·3′W	A	145,158
Pencastell	Carm	SN4037	52°0·7′	4°19·5′W	A	146
Pencefn	I of Angl	SH4678	53°16·8′	4°18·2′W	X	114,115
Pencefn Drysgol	Cered	SN6857	52°12·0′	3°55·5′W	X	146
Pen-cefn-mawr	I of Angl	SH4283	53°19·5′	4°21·9′W	X	114,115
Penceiliogi	Carm	SN5300	51°41·0′	4°7·2′W	T	159
Pencelli	Powys	SO0925	51°55·2′	3°19·0′W	T	161
Pencelli Fm	Carm	SN4413	51°47·9′	4°15·4′W	FM	159
Pencelly	Pemb	SN1240	52°1·8′	4°44·0′W	X	145
Pencelly Forest	Pemb	SN1339	52°1·3′	4°43·1′W	F	145
Pen Cerrig	Cered	SN7385	52°27·1′	3°51·7′W	X	135
Pen Cerrig-calch	Powys	SO2122	51°53·7′	3°8·5′W	H	161
Pen Cerrigdiddos	Carm	SN7143	52°4·5′	3°52·5′W	X	146,147,160
Pen Cerrig-mwyn	Carm	SN7944	52°5·1′	3°45·6′W	X	146,147,160
Pen Cerrig Tewion	Cered	SN7988	52°28·8′	3°46·5′W	H	135
Pen-cerrigyffynnon	Powys	SN8993	52°31·7′	3°37·8′W	X	135,136
Pencestyll	Cered	SN2052	52°8·5′	4°37·4′W	X	145
Penchrise	Scot Bord	NT4906	55°21·0′	2°47·8′W	X	79
Penchrise Burn	Scot Bord	NT4905	55°20·4′	2°47·8′W	W	79
Penchrise Peel	Scot Bord	NT5105	55°20·4′	2°45·9′W	X	79
Penciau	I of Angl	SH4783	53°19·6′	4°17·4′W	X	114,115
Pencilau	Powys	SO1816	51°50·4′	3°11·0′W	X	161
Penclacwydd	Carm	SS5398	51°39·9′	4°7·1′W	X	159
Pen-clawdd	Pemb	SN0040	52°1·6′	4°54·5′W	X	145,157
Pen-clawdd	Swan	SS5495	51°38·3′	4°6·2′W	T	159
Pen-clawdd-mawr	Cered	SN5555	52°10·7′	4°6·8′W	A	146
Penclawdd Uchaf	Carm	SN3735	51°59·6′	4°22·1′W	X	145
Pencleden	Conwy	SH9365	53°10·5′	3°35·7′W	X	116
Penclegyr	Pemb	SM7629	51°55·1′	5°15·1′W	X	157
Penclegyr	Pemb	SM8032	51°56·8′	5°11·7′W	X	157
Penclippin	Carm	SN1621	51°51·7′	4°39·9′W	X	145,158
Pencloddiau	Powys	SN8779	52°24·1′	3°39·3′W	X	135,136,147
Pencloe	E Ayr	NS6109	55°21·6′	4°11·1′W	X	71,77
Penclose Fm	W Berks	SU4473	51°27·5′	1°21·6′W	FM	174
Penclose Wood	W Berks	SU4474	51°28·0′	1°21·6′W	F	174
Pencnwc	Carm	SN2222	51°52·3′	4°34·8′W	X	145,158
Pencnwc	Carm	SN4623	51°53·3′	4°13·9′W	X	159
Pencobben	Corn	SW5942	50°14·0′	5°22·4′W	X	203
Pencoed	Brig	SS9581	51°31·3′	3°30·4′W	T	170
Pencoed	Carm	SN1627	51°54·9′	4°40·1′W	X	145,158
Pencoed	Carm	SN2412	51°47·0′	4°32·7′W	X	158
Pencoed	Carm	SN2819	51°50·8′	4°29·4′W	X	158
Pencoed	Carm	SS5599	51°40·5′	4°5·4′W	X	159
Pencoed	Gwyn	SH6811	52°41·1′	3°56·8′W	X	124
Pencoed	Pemb	SN0407	51°43·9′	4°49·9′W	X	157,158
Pen Coed	Powys	SH9808	52°39·8′	3°30·1′W	H	125
Pen-coed Castle	Newp	ST4089	51°36·0′	2°51·6′W	A	171,172
Pencoed Fm	Denb	SJ1053	53°4·2′	3°20·2′W	FM	116
Pencoed Fm	Monm	SO4317	51°51·2′	2°49·3′W	FM	161
Pencoed-y-foel	Cered	SN4242	52°3·5′	4°17·9′W	A	146
Pencoetre Wood	V of Glam	ST1270	51°25·6′	3°15·6′W	F	171
Pencombe	Heref	SO5952	52°10·1′	2°35·6′W	T	149
Pencombe Cross	Heref	SO5952	52°10·1′	2°35·6′W	X	149
Pencombe Hall	Heref	SO6052	52°10·1′	2°34·7′W	X	149
Pen-common	Powys	SN9008	51°45·8′	3°35·2′W	T	160
Pencoose	Corn	SW8547	50°17·3′	5°0·7′W	X	204
Pencoose	Corn	SW9444	50°15·8′	4°53·1′W	X	204
Pencorse	Corn	SW8756	50°22·2′	4°59·3′W	X	200
Pencot	N Ayr	NS3248	55°42·0′	4°40·0′W	X	63
Pencoyd	Heref	SO5126	51°56·1′	2°42·4′W	X	162
Pencoys	Corn	SW6838	50°12·0′	5°14·7′W	T	203
Pencra Head	Corn	SW8022	50°3·7′	5°4·1′W	X	204
Pencraig	Carm	SN2425	51°54·0′	4°33·1′W	X	145,158
Pencraig	Cered	SN6276	52°22·1′	4°1·2′W	X	135
Pencraig	Conwy	SH7658	53°6·5′	3°50·7′W	X	115
Pencraig	Conwy	SH8673	53°14·8′	3°42·1′W	X	116
Pencraig	Gwyn	SH4139	52°55·7′	4°21·5′W	X	123
Pencraig	Heref	SO5620	51°52·8′	2°38·0′W	T	162
Pencraig	I of Angl	SH4675	53°15·2′	4°18·1′W	T	114,115
Pencraig	Pemb	SN1226	51°54·3′	4°43·6′W	X	145,158
Pencraig	Powys	SJ0427	52°50·2′	3°25·1′W	T	125
Pencraig	Powys	SJ0604	52°37·8′	3°22·9′W	X	136
Pencraig Arthur	Conwy	SH8164	53°9·8′	3°46·4′W	X	116
Pencraig-fawr	Conwy	SH9365	53°10·5′	3°35·7′W	X	116
Pencraig Fawr	Denb	SJ0148	53°1·5′	3°28·2′W	X	116
Pencraig Fm	Monm	ST3592	51°37·6′	2°56·0′W	FM	171
Pencraig Isaf	Nth Pt Talb	SS8597	51°39·8′	3°39·4′W	X	170
Pencraig-Peris	Cered	SN5666	52°16·6′	4°6·3′W	X	135
Pencraig Rocks	Powys	SO0785	52°27·5′	3°21·7′W	X	136
Pencraig Uchaf	Carm	SN1424	51°53·3′	4°41·8′W	X	145,158
Pencraig Wood	E Loth	NT5776	55°58·8′	2°40·9′W	F	67
Pencrebar	Corn	SX3568	50°29·6′	4°19·2′W	X	201
Pen Creigiau'r Barcut	Denb	SJ1039	52°56·7′	3°20·0′W	X	125
Pen Creigiau'r Llan	Cered	SN7494	52°32·0′	3°51·1′W	H	135
Pencrennys	Corn	SW9066	50°27·6′	4°57·2′W	X	200
Pencribach	Cered	SN2552	52°8·6′	4°33·1′W	X	145
Pencringoed	Powys	SH9905	52°38·2′	3°29·2′W	X	125
Pen Cristin	Gwyn	SH1220	52°44·9′	4°46·7′W	X	123
Pencroeslan	Powys	SO1818	51°51·5′	3°11·1′W	X	161
Pencroesoped	Monm	SO3107	51°45·7′	2°59·6′W	T	161
Pen Cross	Devon	ST1314	50°55·4′	3°13·9′W	X	181,193
Pen crug	Carm	SN7423	51°53·7′	3°49·5′W	X	160
Pencrug	Powys	SO0329	51°57·3′	3°24·3′W	X	160
Pen-crug-mawr	I of Angl	SH4270	53°12·5′	4°21·5′W	X	114,115
Pencuke	Corn	SX1694	50°43·2′	4°36·0′W	T	190
Pen-cw	Pemb	SM9539	52°0·9′	4°58·9′W	X	157
Pencwarre	Pemb	SN2033	51°58·2′	4°36·8′W	X	145
Pencwm	Carm	SN5307	51°44·8′	4°7·4′W	X	159
Pen-cwm	Cered	SN5659	52°12·9′	4°6·1′W	X	146
Pencwm	Cered	SN5670	52°18·8′	4°6·4′W	X	135
Pen-cwm	Pemb	SN1640	52°1·9′	4°40·6′W	X	145
Pencwm-Mawr	Cered	SN5572	52°19·9′	4°7·3′W	X	135
Pen Cwmyrhafod	Powys	SN9068	52°18·2′	3°36·4′W	H	136,147
Pencyrn	V of Glam	ST0077	51°29·2′	3°26·0′W	X	170
Pen Dal-aderyn	Pemb	SM7123	51°51·8′	5°19·2′W	X	157
Pendale	Corn	SW7648	50°17·6′	5°8·3′W	X	204
Pendalog	Powys	SJ1420	52°46·5′	3°16·1′W	X	125
Pendared	Conwy	SH8876	53°16·4′	3°40·4′W	X	116
Pendarren Ho	Powys	SO2418	51°51·6′	3°5·8′W	X	161
Pendarves	Corn	SW6437	50°11·4′	5°18·0′W	X	203
Pendarves Island	Corn	SW8469	50°29·1′	5°2·3′W	X	200
Pendas Fields	Leeds	SE3735	53°48·8′	1°25·9′W	T	104
Pendavey	Corn	SX0071	50°30·5′	4°48·9′W	X	200
Penddaulwyn	Carm	SN4619	51°51·1′	4°13·8′W	X	159
Pen-ddôl	Carm	SN3627	51°55·3′	4°22·7′W	X	145
Penddol	Cered	SN6353	52°9·7′	3°59·8′W	X	146
Pendeen	Corn	SW3834	50°9·1′	5°39·7′W	T	203
Pendeen House	Corn	SW3835	50°9·7′	5°39·7′W	A	203
Pendeen Watch	Corn	SW3735	50°9·6′	5°40·6′W	X	203
Pendeford	Wolv	SJ8902	52°37·2′	2°9·3′W	T	127,139
Pendeilo	Pemb	SN1609	51°45·2′	4°39·6′W	X	158
Pendell	Surrey	TQ3151	51°14·8′	0°7·0′W	X	187
Pendennis Castle	Corn	SW8231	50°8·6′	5°2·7′W	A	204
Pendennis Point	Corn	SW8231	50°8·6′	5°2·7′W	X	204
Pen-deri	Carm	SN1518	51°50·0′	4°40·7′W	X	158
Penderi	Carm	SN5306	51°44·2′	4°7·3′W	X	159
Penderi	Pemb	SN1638	52°0·8′	4°40·5′W	X	145
Penderi Fm	Caer	SO1800	51°41·8′	3°10·8′W	FM	171
Penderleath	Corn	SW4937	50°11·0′	5°30·6′W	X	203
Pen Derlwyn	Powys	SN8445	52°5·7′	3°41·2′W	X	147
Penderry Hill	S Ayr	NX0675	55°2·2′	5°1·7′W	H	76
Penderyn	Rho Cyn Taf	SN9408	51°45·9′	3°31·8′W	T	160
Penderyn Resr	Rho Cyn Taf	SN9307	51°45·3′	3°32·6′W	W	160
Pen Diban	Gwyn	SH1120	52°44·9′	4°47·6′W	X	123
Pendicles of Collymoon	Stir	NS5896	56°8·4′	4°16·7′W	X	57
Pen Dihewyd	Cered	SN7779	52°24·0′	3°48·1′W	X	135,147
Pendinas	Cered	SN5880	52°24·2′	4°4·8′W	X	135
Pen Dinas	Cered	SN6787	52°28·1′	3°57·1′W	A	135
Pendinas	Denb	SJ2251	53°3·3′	3°9·4′W	X	117
Pen Dinas	Gwyn	SH5565	53°10·0′	4°9·7′W	X	114,115
Pendinaslochdyn	Cered	SN3154	52°9·7′	4°27·9′W	A	145
Pendinas Reservoir	Denb	SJ2351	53°3·3′	3°8·5′W	W	117
Pendine	Corn	SW9560	50°24·5′	4°52·7′W	X	200
Pendine Burrows	Carm	SN2607	51°44·3′	4°30·8′W	X	158
Pendine (Pentywyn)	Carm	SN2308	51°44·8′	4°33·5′W	T	158
Pendine Sands	Carm	SN2607	51°44·3′	4°30·8′W	X	158
Pen Disgwylfa	Nth Pt Talb	SS8293	51°37·6′	3°41·9′W	H	170
Pen Disgwylfa	Powys	SN8750	52°8·4′	3°38·7′W	X	147
Pendlebury	Salf	SD7801	53°30·6′	2°19·5′W	T	109
Pendle Hall	Lancs	SD8135	53°48·9′	2°16·9′W	X	103
Pendle Heritage Centre	Lancs	SD8639	53°51·1′	2°12·4′W	X	103
Pendle Hill	Lancs	SD7941	53°52·1′	2°18·7′W	H	103
Pendle Ho	Lancs	SD8041	53°52·1′	2°17·8′W	X	103
Pendle Moor	Lancs	SD7840	53°51·6′	2°19·7′W	X	103
Pendle Side	Lancs	SD8141	53°52·1′	2°16·9′W	X	103
Pendleton	Lancs	SD7539	53°51·0′	2°22·4′W	T	103
Pendleton	Salf	SJ8199	53°29·5′	2°16·8′W	T	109
Pendleton Hall	Lancs	SD7640	53°51·6′	2°21·5′W	X	103
Pendleton Moor	Lancs	SD7739	53°51·0′	2°20·6′W	X	103
Pendle Water	Lancs	SD8437	53°50·0′	2°14·2′W	W	103
Pendle Water	Lancs	SD8541	53°52·1′	2°13·3′W	W	103
Pendle Way	Lancs	SD8139	53°51·1′	2°16·9′W	X	103
Pendley Manor (Hotel)	Herts	SP9411	51°47·6′	0°37·8′W	X	165
Pendock	Worcs	SO7832	51°59·4′	2°18·8′W	T	150
Pendock Moor	Worcs	SO8134	52°0·5′	2°16·2′W	X	150
Pendoggett	Corn	SX0279	50°34·9′	4°47·4′W	T	200
Pendomer	Somer	ST5210	50°53·5′	2°40·6′W	T	194
Pendon Hill	Somer	ST3538	51°8·5′	2°55·4′W	H	182
Pendouble	Pemb	SM9732	51°57·2′	4°56·9′W	X	157
Pendour Cove	Corn	SW4439	50°12·0′	5°34·9′W	W	203
Pendower Beach	Corn	SW8938	50°12·5′	4°57·1′W	X	204
Pendower Coves	Corn	SW3522	50°2·6′	5°41·7′W	W	203
Pendower Ho	Corn	SX1551	50°20·0′	4°35·6′W	X	201
Pendown	Corn	SW7648	50°17·6′	5°8·3′W	X	204
Pendown Hill	Bath & NE Somer	ST6861	51°21·1′	2°27·2′W	X	172
Pendoylan	V of Glam	ST0676	51°28·7′	3°20·8′W	T	170
Pendragon Castle	Cumbr	NY7802	54°25·0′	2°19·9′W	A	91
Pen-draw	Gwyn	SH5561	53°7·8′	4°9·6′W	X	114,115
Pendre	Brig	SS9081	51°31·3′	3°34·7′W	T	170
Pendre	Cered	SN7673	52°20·8′	3°48·8′W	X	135,147
Pendre	Denb	SJ1844	52°59·5′	3°12·9′W	X	125
Pendre	Gwyn	SH5900	52°35·0′	4°4·5′W	T	135
Pendre	Powys	SO0429	51°57·3′	3°23·4′W	T	160
Pendre	Powys	SO1328	51°56·9′	3°15·6′W	X	161
Pendre	Powys	SO1423	51°54·2′	3°14·6′W	X	161
Pendre	Powys	SO1532	51°59·0′	3°13·9′W	X	161
Pendref	Gwyn	SH1726	52°48·3′	4°42·5′W	X	123
Pendrê-fawr	Denb	SJ0349	53°2·0′	3°26·4′W	X	116
Pendre-gwehelydd	I of Angl	SH3482	53°18·8′	4°29·1′W	X	114
Pendreich	Stir	NS8099	56°10·4′	3°55·5′W	X	57
Pendrell Hall (College)	Staffs	SJ8504	52°38·3′	2°12·9′W	X	127,139
Pendriffey	Corn	SX2056	50°22·8′	4°31·5′W	X	201
Pendrift	Corn	SX1074	50°32·3′	4°40·5′W	T	200
Pendriscott	Corn	SX2057	50°23·4′	4°31·6′W	X	201
Pendruffle	Corn	SX2059	50°24·4′	4°31·6′W	X	201
Pendruffle Wood	Corn	SX2159	50°24·5′	4°30·8′W	F	201
Pendugwm	Powys	SJ1014	52°43·2′	3°19·5′W	X	125
Pendyffryn Hall	Conwy	SH7477	53°16·7′	3°53·0′W	X	115
Penearth	Corn	SX3162	50°26·2′	4°22·4′W	X	201
Penegoes	Powys	SH7700	52°35·3′	3°48·5′W	T	135
Penelewey	Corn	SW8140	50°13·4′	5°3·8′W	T	204
Penelopefield	Aberd	NJ6649	57°32·1′	2°33·6′W	X	29
Penenden Heath	Kent	TQ7657	51°17·3′	0°31·8′E	T	178,188
Pen Enys Point	Corn	SW4841	50°13·2′	5°31·6′W	X	203
Penerley Fm	Hants	SU3703	50°49·7′	1°28·1′W	FM	196
Penerley Lodge	Hants	SU3703	50°49·7′	1°28·1′W	X	196
Penfai	Cered	SN2542	52°3·2′	4°32·7′W	X	145
Penfarch	Carm	SN5327	51°55·6′	4°7·9′W	X	146
Penfarteg	Cered	SN5162	52°14·4′	4°10·5′W	X	146
Penfathach	Pemb	SM9440	52°1·5′	4°59·8′W	X	157
Pen-fathor	Powys	SN9415	51°49·7′	3°31·9′W	X	160
Penfedi	Swan	SN6402	51°42·3′	3°57·7′W	X	159
Penfedw	Powys	SN8949	52°7·9′	3°36·9′W	X	147
Penfedw	Swan	SN6601	51°41·7′	3°55·9′W	X	159
Penfedw Fawr	Carm	SN7641	52°3·5′	3°48·1′W	X	146,147,160
Penfeidir	Pemb	SM8930	51°56·0′	5°3·8′W	X	157
Penffordd	Cered	SN1750	52°7·3′	4°40·0′W	X	145
Penffordd	Carm	SN4844	52°4·7′	4°12·7′W	X	146
Penffordd	Cered	SN7061	52°14·2′	3°53·8′W	X	146,147
Penffordd	Pemb	SN0032	51°57·3′	4°54·2′W	X	145,157
Penffordd	Pemb	SN0722	51°52·0′	4°47·8′W	T	145,158
Pen-ffordd-goch Pond	Monm	SO2510	51°47·3′	3°4·9′W	W	161
Penffordwen	Powys	SJ1227	52°50·2′	3°18·0′W	X	125
Pen Ffridd-sarn	Conwy	SH8446	53°0·2′	3°43·3′W	H	116
Pen-ffynnon	Carm	SN3639	52°1·8′	4°23·0′W	X	145
Pen Ffynnon	Carm	SN3829	51°56·4′	4°21·0′W	X	145
Penffynnon	Cered	SN3940	52°2·3′	4°20·5′W	X	145
Penfield	Kent	TQ5557	51°17·7′	0°13·8′E	X	188
Penfield Ho	Kent	TQ9159	51°18·1′	0°44·8′E	X	178
Penfillan	D & G	NX8592	55°12·8′	3°48·0′W	X	78
Penfillan Moor	D & G	NX8492	55°12·8′	3°49·0′W	H	78
Pen Fm	Essex	TL5544	52°4·6′	0°16·1′E	FM	154
Pen Fm	Staffs	SK0755	53°5·8′	1°53·3′W	FM	119
Penfoel	Cered	SN3957	52°11·5′	4°20·9′W	X	145
Pen Foel Aman	Rho Cyn Taf	SN9800	51°41·6′	3°28·2′W	X	170
Penfoelcaru	Carm	SN3828	51°55·9′	4°21·0′W	X	145
Penfoot	Corn	SX3082	50°37·0′	4°23·8′W	X	201
Penfor	Cered	SN5367	52°17·1′	4°8·9′W	X	135
Pen-forial	Cered	SN6261	52°14·0′	4°0·9′W	X	146
Penfound Manor	Corn	SX2299	50°46·0′	4°31·1′W	A	190
Penfrane Fm	Corn	SX2062	50°26·1′	4°31·7′W	FM	201
Penfras-uchaf	Gwyn	SH3741	52°56·7′	4°25·2′W	X	123
Pengaer	Cered	SN3648	52°6·6′	4°23·3′W	X	145
Pengaer	Pemb	SN1541	52°2·4′	4°41·5′W	X	145
Pengallt	Cered	SN3643	52°3·9′	4°23·2′W	X	145
Pengalltegfa	Denb	SJ0855	53°5·3′	3°22·0′W	H	116
Pengam	Caer	ST1597	51°40·2′	3°13·4′W	T	171
Pengam	Newp	ST2679	51°30·5′	3°3·6′W	X	171
Pengarn	Pemb	SN1348	52°6·2′	4°43·4′W	X	145
Pengarnddu	Merth Tyd	SO0708	51°46·0′	3°20·5′W	X	160
Pen Garreg	Powys	SO2326	51°55·9′	3°6·8′W	X	161
Pengawse	Pemb	SN1716	51°49·0′	4°38·9′W	X	158
Pengay Fm	Carm	SN3708	51°45·1′	4°21·3′W	FM	159
Penge	Brom	TQ3470	51°25·0′	0°4·0′W	T	176,177
Pen-gegin	Pemb	SN0334	51°58·4′	4°51·7′W	X	145,157
Pengegon	Corn	SW6639	50°12·5′	5°16·4′W	T	203
Pengelli	Carm	SN2939	52°1·6′	4°29·2′W	X	145
Pengelli	Carm	SN6137	52°1·1′	4°1·1′W	X	146
Pengelli	Cered	SN3243	52°3·8′	4°26·7′W	X	145
Pengelli	Powys	SO1790	52°30·3′	3°13·0′W	X	136
Pengelli	V of Glam	ST0576	51°28·7′	3°21·7′W	X	170
Pengelli-fach	Carm	SN2940	52°2·2′	4°29·2′W	X	145
Pengellifawr	Merth Tyd	SO0511	51°47·6′	3°22·3′W	X	160
Pengelly	Corn	SW8551	50°19·4′	5°0·9′W	X	200,204
Pengelly	Corn	SW9564	50°26·6′	4°52·9′W	X	200
Pengelly	Corn	SW9649	50°18·6′	4°51·5′W	X	204
Pengelly	Corn	SX0783	50°37·1′	4°43·3′W	T	200
Pengelly	Corn	SX1765	50°27·6′	4°34·3′W	X	201
Pengelly	Corn	SX3174	50°32·7′	4°22·7′W	X	201
Pengelly	Swan	SN5800	51°41·1′	4°2·9′W	X	159
Pengelly Barton	Corn	SW6132	50°8·6′	5°20·3′W	X	203
Pengelly Fm	Corn	SW6432	50°8·7′	5°17·8′W	FM	203
Pengelly Fm	Corn	SW9970	50°30·0′	4°49·7′W	FM	200
Pengenffordd	Powys	SO1730	51°58·0′	3°12·1′W	T	161
Pengenna	Corn	SX0578	50°34·4′	4°44·9′W	A	200
Pengersick	Corn	SW5828	50°6·4′	5°22·7′W	T	203
Pengethley	Heref	SO5425	51°55·5′	2°39·7′W	X	162
Pengethley	Powys	SO1949	52°8·2′	3°10·6′W	X	148
Pen-gilfach	Gwyn	SH5661	53°7·8′	4°8·7′W	T	114,115
Pengilfach	Powys	SO2418	51°51·6′	3°5·8′W	X	161
Penglaise	Cered	SN5982	52°25·3′	4°4·0′W	X	135
Penglanowen	Cered	SN6170	52°18·9′	4°2·0′W	X	135
Penglaze	Corn	SW8253	50°20·4′	5°3·5′W	X	200,204
Pen Gloch-y-pibwr	Powys	SO2023	51°54·2′	3°9·4′W	X	161
Pen Glôg	Cered	SN5573	52°20·4′	4°7·3′W	X	135
Penglogor	Conwy	SH9665	53°10·6′	3°33·0′W	X	116
Penglogue	Carm	SN2219	51°50·7′	4°34·7′W	X	158
Pengoiallt	Carm	SN5026	51°55·0′	4°10·5′W	X	146
Pengold	Corn	SX1394	50°43·2′	4°38·6′W	T	190
Pengorffwysfa	I of Angl	SH4692	53°24·4′	4°18·6′W	T	114
Pengover Green	Corn	SX2765	50°27·8′	4°25·9′W	T	201

Pengraig	Carm	SN2528	51°55·6'	4°32·3'W	X	145,158
Pen-graig	Cered	SN4856	52°11·1'	4°13·0'W	X	146
Pengraigfawr	Carm	SN3328	51°55·8'	4°25·3'W	X	145
Pen-graig-wen	Carm	SN4139	52°1·8'	4°18·7'W	X	146
Pengrain	D & G	NT1905	55°20·2'	3°16·2'W	X	79
Pengreep	Corn	SW7438	50°12·2'	5°9·7'W	X	204
Pengribyn	Pemb	SN2835	51°59·5'	4°29·9'W	X	145
Pengrugla	Corn	SW9947	50°17·6'	4°48·9'W	X	204
Penguithal	Heref	SO5020	51°52·8'	2°43·2'W	T	162
Pengwedna	Corn	SW6231	50°8·1'	5°19·5'W	X	203
Pengwern	Carm	SN2619	51°50·8'	4°31·2'W	X	158
Pengwern	Carm	SN2739	52°1·6'	4°30·9'W	X	145
Pengwern	Conwy	SH7960	53°7·7'	3°48·1'W	X	115
Pengwern	Conwy	SH9667	53°11·7'	3°33·0'W	X	116
Pengwern	Conwy	SH9767	53°11·7'	3°32·1'W	H	116
Pengwern	Denb	SJ0176	53°16·5'	3°28·7'W	T	116
Pengwern	Gwyn	SH4558	53°6·0'	4°18·5'W	X	115,123
Pengwern	Powys	SH8510	52°40·8'	3°41·7'W	X	124,125
Pengwern	Powys	SJ0425	52°49·1'	3°25·1'W	X	125
Pengwern	Swan	SS5391	51°36·2'	4°7·0'W	X	159
Pengwern Common	Swan	SS5491	51°36·2'	4°6·1'W	X	159
Pengwern Hall	Denb	SJ2241	52°57·9'	3°9·3'W	X	117
Pengwern-isaf	Carm	SN2739	52°1·6'	4°30·9'W	X	145
Pengwern Old Hall Fm	Gwyn	SH6943	52°58·3'	3°56·6'W	FM	124
Pengwmryn	Cered	SN6382	52°25·4'	4°0·5'W	X	135
Pengwndwn	Pemb	SN0235	51°58·9'	4°52·6'W	X	145,157
Pen Gwyllt Meirch	Powys	SO2424	51°54·8'	3°5·9'W	X	161
Pengymill	Essex	TL6609	51°45·5'	0°24·7'E	X	167
Penhale	Corn	SW4232	50°8·2'	5°36·3'W	X	203
Penhale	Corn	SW6918	50°1·3'	5°13·1'W	T	203
Penhale	Corn	SW8551	50°19·4'	5°0·9'W	X	200,204
Penhale	Corn	SW8851	50°19·5'	4°58·3'W	X	200,204
Penhale	Corn	SW9057	50°22·8'	4°56·9'W	T	200
Penhale	Corn	SW9572	50°31·0'	4°53·1'W	X	200
Penhale	Corn	SX0774	50°32·3'	4°43·0'W	X	200
Penhale	Corn	SX0860	50°24·7'	4°41·8'W	X	200
Penhale	Corn	SX1691	50°41·6'	4°35·9'W	X	190
Penhale	Corn	SX2261	50°25·5'	4°30·0'W	X	201
Penhale	Corn	SX4153	50°21·6'	4°13·7'W	X	201
Penhale-an-drea	Corn	SW6231	50°8·1'	5°19·5'W	X	203
Penhale Camp	Corn	SW7658	50°23·0'	5°8·7'W	X	200
Penhale Fm	Corn	SW9252	50°20·1'	4°55·0'W	FM	200,204
Penhale Fm	Corn	SX1052	50°20·5'	4°39·8'W	FM	200,204
Penhale Fm	Corn	SX2264	50°27·2'	4°30·1'W	FM	201
Penhale Fm	Corn	SX2954	50°21·9'	4°23·9'W	FM	201
Penhale Jakes	Corn	SW6028	50°6·5'	5°21·0'W	T	203
Penhale Moor	Corn	SW6237	50°11·3'	5°19·7'W	X	203
Penhale Point	Corn	SW7559	50°23·5'	5°9·6'W	X	200
Penhale Sands	Corn	SW7656	50°21·9'	5°8·6'W	X	200
Penhallick	Corn	SW6740	50°13·1'	5°15·6'W	T	203
Penhallick	Corn	SW7618	50°1·4'	5°7·3'W	T	204
Penhallic Point	Corn	SX0487	50°39·2'	4°46·0'W	X	200
Penhallow	Corn	SW7651	50°19·2'	5°8·4'W	T	200,204
Penhallow	Corn	SW8839	50°13·0'	4°57·9'W	X	204
Penhallow Fm	Corn	SW7247	50°17·0'	5°11·7'W	FM	204
Penhallow Moor	Corn	SW8255	50°21·5'	5°3·5'W	X	200
Penhallym	Corn	SX2197	50°44·9'	4°31·9'W	X	190
Penhalt Cliff	Corn	SS1900	50°46·5'	4°33·7'W	X	190
Penhalt Fm	Corn	SS1900	50°46·5'	4°33·7'W	FM	190
Penhalurick	Corn	SW7038	50°12·1'	5°13·0'W	T	203
Penhalvean	Corn	SW7137	50°11·6'	5°12·1'W	T	203
Penhalveor	Corn	SW7037	50°11·5'	5°13·0'W	X	203
Penhargard	Corn	SX0669	50°29·6'	4°43·7'W	X	200
Penhargard Castle	Corn	SX0569	50°29·5'	4°44·6'W	A	200
Penharget	Corn	SX2970	50°30·5'	4°24·3'W	X	201
Penhawger Fm	Corn	SX2866	50°28·4'	4°25·1'W	FM	201
Penhay	Devon	SS8408	50°51·8'	3°38·5'W	X	191
Penheale Manor	Corn	SX2688	50°40·2'	4°27·4'W	A	190
Penhein	Monm	ST4493	51°38·2'	2°48·2'W	X	171,172
Penhelig	Gwyn	SN6296	52°32·9'	4°1·7'W	T	135
Penhellick	Corn	SW9464	50°26·6'	4°53·7'W	X	200
Penhempen	Powys	SO1088	52°29·2'	3°19·1'W	X	136
Penhen	Carm	SN3915	51°48·9'	4°19·8'W	X	159
Penhenallt	Powys	SO2339	52°2·9'	3°7·0'W	X	161
Penhenllan	Heref	SO2541	52°4·0'	3°5·3'W	X	148,161
Penhenllys	I of Angl	SH3571	53°12·9'	4°27·9'W	X	114
Penhenrhiw	Carm	SN2624	51°53·5'	4°31·3'W	X	145,158
Penhenwernfach	Powys	SN8847	52°6·8'	3°37·7'W	X	147
Pen-heol-Adam	Caer	ST1298	51°40·7'	3°16·0'W	X	171
Pen-heol-machen	Caer	ST1990	51°36·4'	3°9·8'W	X	171
Penhesgyn	I of Angl	SH5374	53°14·8'	4°11·8'W	X	114,115
Penhesken	Corn	SW9142	50°14·7'	4°55·5'W	X	204
Pen-hill	Carm	SN3908	51°45·1'	4°19·6'W	X	159
Pen-hill	Carm	SN4228	51°55·9'	4°17·5'W	X	146
Penhill	Carm	SN5725	51°54·6'	4°4·3'W	X	146
Penhill	Carm	SN6526	51°55·2'	3°57·4'W	X	146
Penhill	Corn	SW8661	50°24·8'	5°0·4'W	X	200
Penhill	Devon	SS5233	51°4·9'	4°6·4'W	T	180
Pen Hill	Devon	SY1493	50°44·0'	3°12·7'W	X	192,193
Pen Hill	Dorset	ST8516	50°56·8'	2°12·4'W	H	183
Pen Hill	Glos	SO8102	51°43·2'	2°16·1'W	X	162
Pen Hill	Glos	SO9912	51°48·6'	2°0·5'W	H	163
Pen Hill	Kent	TQ8635	51°5·3'	0°39·7'E	X	189
Pen Hill	Notts	SK7130	52°52·0'	0°56·3'W	X	129
Penhill	N Yks	SE0486	54°16·4'	1°55·9'W	X	98
Pen Hill	Somer	ST5648	51°14·0'	2°37·4'W	H	182,183
Pen Hill	Somer	ST6424	51°1·1'	2°30·4'W	H	183
Penhill	Swin	SU1588	51°35·7'	1°46·6'W	T	173
Penhill	Wilts	ST8736	51°7·6'	2°10·8'W	X	183
Penhill Beacon	N Yks	SE0586	54°16·4'	1°55·0'W	A	98
Penhill Fm	Carm	SN6619	51°51·5'	3°56·4'W	FM	159
Penhill Fm	Glos	SO9813	51°49·2'	2°1·3'W	FM	163
Penhill Fm	Glos	SP0619	51°52·4'	1°54·3'W	FM	163
Penhill Fm	Norf	TM0096	52°31·7'	0°57·3'E	FM	144
Penhill Fm	N Yks	SE0687	54°17·0'	1°54·1'W	FM	99
Pen Hill Fm	Somer	ST5111	50°54·0'	2°41·4'W	FM	194
Pen Hill Fm	Somer	ST5548	51°14·0'	2°38·3'W	FM	182,183
Penhill Park	N Yks	SE0586	54°16·4'	1°55·0'W	X	98
Penhill Park	N Yks	SE0686	54°16·4'	1°54·1'W	X	99
Penhill Plantation	Glos	SP0012	51°48·6'	1°59·6'W	F	163
Penhill Point	Devon	SS5134	51°5·4'	4°7·3'W	X	180
Pen Hills	Herts	TL3339	52°2·2'	0°3·3'W	X	154
Penhoelmeirch	Powys	SO2322	51°53·7'	3°6·7'W	X	161
Penhole	Corn	SX1861	50°25·5'	4°33·4'W	X	201
Penhole	Corn	SX2876	50°33·7'	4°25·3'W	X	201
Penhow	Caer	ST2087	51°34·8'	3°8·9'W	X	171
Penhow	Newp	ST4290	51°36·6'	2°49·9'W	T	171,172
Pen Howe	N Yks	NZ8503	54°25·2'	0°41·0'W	A	94
Penhriwfer	Rho Cyn Taf	ST0089	51°35·7'	3°26·2'W	X	170
Penhurst	E Susx	TQ6916	50°55·3'	0°24·7'E	T	199
Penhwnllys	I of Angl	SH5980	53°18·1'	4°6·6'W	X	114,115
Penhydd Fawr	Nth Pt Talb	SS8093	51°37·6'	3°43·6'W	X	170
Penhyddgan	Gwyn	SH3038	52°55·0'	4°31·3'W	A	123
Penhydd-waelod	Nth Pt Talb	SS8092	51°37·1'	3°43·6'W	X	170
Pen-hyle-mawr	Powys	SN9180	52°24·7'	3°35·8'W	X	136
Penial Dowyn	I of Angl	SH2983	53°19·2'	4°33·6'W	X	114
Peniarth	Gwyn	SH6105	52°37·7'	4°2·8'W	X	124
Peniarth	Powys	SJ0724	52°48·6'	3°22·4'W	X	125
Peniarth	Powys	SJ1415	52°43·8'	3°16·0'W	X	125
Peniarth	Powys	SJ1616	52°44·3'	3°14·3'W	X	125
Peniarth Fawr	Conwy	SH9074	53°15·3'	3°38·5'W	X	116
Peniarth-uchaf	Gwyn	SH6307	52°38·9'	4°1·1'W	X	124
Peniarthy Bach	Conwy	SH9273	53°14·8'	3°36·7'W	X	116
Penick	Highld	NH9356	57°35·1'	3°46·9'W	X	27
Penicuik	Midlo	NT2360	55°49·9'	3°13·3'W	T	66
Penicuik Ho	Midlo	NT2159	55°49·3'	3°15·2'W	X	66,73
Peniel	Carm	SN4324	51°53·8'	4°16·5'W	T	159
Peniel	Denb	SJ0362	53°9·0'	3°26·6'W	T	116
Peniel Heugh	Scot Bord	NT6526	55°31·8'	2°32·8'W	H	74
Peniestone Knowe	Scot Bord	NT2316	55°26·2'	3°12·6'W	H	79
Penifiler	Highld	NG4841	57°23·6'	6°11·2'W	T	23
Penimble	Corn	SX3559	50°24·7'	4°19·0'W	X	201
Peninnis Head	I Scilly	SV9109	49°54·3'	6°17·9'W	X	203
Peninver Br	Arg & Bt	NR7625	55°28·3'	5°32·2'W	X	68,69
Peninver	Arg & Bt	NR7524	55°27·7'	5°33·1'W	T	68,69
Penisacyffin	Powys	SJ0513	52°42·6'	3°24·0'W	X	125
Pen-Isa-Dre	Conwy	SH8572	53°14·2'	3°43·0'W	X	116
Pen Isaf	Conwy	SH8865	53°10·5'	3°40·1'W	X	116
Penisa'r	Denb	SJ0977	53°17·2'	3°21·5'W	X	116
Pen-isa'r-cwm	Gwyn	SH6126	52°49·1'	4°3·4'W	X	124
Penisarcwm	Powys	SJ0018	52°45·3'	3°28·5'W	X	125
Penisa'r Glyn	Wrex	SJ2537	52°55·8'	3°6·5'W	X	126
Pen-isa'r-llan	Shrops	SJ2523	52°48·2'	3°6·4'W	X	126
Penisarplwyf	Powys	SO1144	52°5·5'	3°17·6'W	X	148,161
Penisar Waen	Conwy	SH8171	53°13·6'	3°46·6'W	X	116
Penisa'r Waun	Gwyn	SH5563	53°8·9'	4°9·7'W	T	114,115
Penishapentre	Powys	SO0128	51°56·7'	3°26·0'W	X	160
Penishapentre	Powys	SO1233	51°59·5'	3°16·5'W	X	161
Penishaplwydd	Monm	SO3422	51°53·8'	2°57·2'W	X	161
Penishawain	Powys	SO0832	51°59·0'	3°20·0'W	X	160
Penisker Fm	Corn	SW9954	50°21·3'	4°49·2'W	FM	200
Penistone	Barns	SE2403	53°31·6'	1°37·9'W	T	110
Penistone Hill	Brad	SE0236	53°49·5'	1°57·8'W	X	104
Penistone Stile	Sheff	SK1894	53°26·8'	1°43·3'W	X	110
Pen Ithon Hall	Powys	SO0781	52°25·4'	3°21·7'W	X	136
Penjerrick	Corn	SW7730	50°7·9'	5°6·9'W	X	204
Penkelly	Corn	SX1853	50°21·2'	4°33·1'W	X	201
Penkelly Castle	Powys	SO0924	51°54·7'	3°19·0'W	A	161
Penkestle	Corn	SX1463	50°26·5'	4°36·8'W	X	200
Penkestle	Corn	SX1769	50°29·8'	4°34·4'W	X	201
Penkestle Downs	Corn	SX1464	50°27·0'	4°36·8'W	X	200
Penkestle Moor	Corn	SX1770	50°30·3'	4°34·5'W	X	201
Penketh	Warr	SJ5687	53°22·9'	2°39·3'W	T	108
Penkevel	Corn	SW8640	50°13·5'	4°59·6'W	X	204
Penkhull	C of Stoke	SJ8644	52°59·8'	2°12·1'W	T	118
Penkill	S Ayr	NX2398	55°14·9'	4°46·6'W	X	76
Penkiln	D & G	NX4847	54°47·9'	4°21·5'W	X	83
Penkiln Burn	D & G	NX4268	54°59·1'	4°27·7'W	W	83
Penkiln Burn	D & G	NX4473	55°1·9'	4°26·0'W	W	77
Penknap	Wilts	ST8549	51°14·6'	2°12·5'W	T	183
Penknight	Corn	SX0959	50°24·2'	4°40·9'W	X	200
Penkridge	Staffs	SJ9213	52°43·1'	2°6·7'W	T	127
Penkridge Bank	Staffs	SK0016	52°44·7'	1°59·6'W	X	128
Penkridge Hall	Shrops	SO4897	52°34·3'	2°45·6'W	A	137,138
Penkridge Lake Fm	Halton	SJ5981	53°19·7'	2°36·5'W	FM	108
Penlan	Carm	SN1723	51°52·8'	4°39·1'W	X	145,158
Penlan	Carm	SN2028	51°55·5'	4°36·7'W	X	145,158
Penlan	Carm	SN2413	51°47·5'	4°32·7'W	X	158
Penlan	Carm	SN2521	51°51·9'	4°32·1'W	X	145,158
Penlan	Carm	SN3216	51°49·3'	4°25·9'W	X	159
Pen-lan	Carm	SN3429	51°56·3'	4°24·5'W	X	145
Pen-lan	Carm	SN3818	51°50·5'	4°20·7'W	X	159
Penlan	Carm	SN4239	52°1·9'	4°17·8'W	X	146
Penlan	Carm	SN4410	51°46·3'	4°15·3'W	X	159
Penlan	Carm	SN4618	51°50·6'	4°13·7'W	X	159
Pen-lan	Carm	SN5112	51°47·4'	4°9·2'W	X	159
Penlan	Carm	SN5343	52°4·2'	4°8·3'W	X	146
Penlan	Carm	SN6235	52°0·0'	4°0·2'W	X	146
Pen-Lan	Cered	SN1946	52°5·2'	4°38·1'W	X	145
Pen-lan	Cered	SN2043	52°3·6'	4°37·2'W	X	145
Pen-lan	Cered	SN3551	52°8·2'	4°24·3'W	X	145
Pen-lan	Cered	SN3844	52°4·5'	4°21·4'W	X	145
Penlan	Cered	SN4746	52°5·7'	4°13·6'W	X	146
Penlan	Cered	SN5458	52°12·3'	4°7·8'W	X	146
Pen-lan	Cered	SN5953	52°9·7'	4°3·3'W	X	146
Penlan	Cered	SN6351	52°8·7'	3°59·7'W	X	146
Penlan	Cered	SN6569	52°18·4'	3°58·4'W	X	135
Penlan	Cered	SN6765	52°16·3'	3°56·6'W	X	135
Penlan	Cered	SN6869	52°18·4'	3°55·8'W	X	135
Pen-lan	Conwy	SH8370	53°13·1'	3°44·7'W	X	116
Penlan	Conwy	SH8751	53°2·9'	3°40·7'W	X	116
Pen-lan	Denb	SJ2140	52°57·3'	3°10·2'W	X	117
Penlan	Gwyn	SH9135	52°54·3'	3°36·8'W	X	125
Penlan	Pemb	SM7425	51°52·9'	5°16·6'W	X	157
Penlan	Pemb	SM8431	51°56·4'	5°8·2'W	X	157
Penlan	Pemb	SM8829	51°55·4'	5°4·6'W	X	157
Pen-lan	Pemb	SN0525	51°53·6'	4°49·7'W	X	145,158
Penlan	Pemb	SN1043	52°3·4'	4°45·9'W	X	145
Penlan	Powys	SN9451	52°9·1'	3°32·6'W	X	147
Penlan	Powys	SN9753	52°10·2'	3°30·0'W	X	147
Penlan	Powys	SO1267	52°17·9'	3°17·0'W	X	136,148
Penlan	Powys	SO1623	51°54·2'	3°12·9'W	X	161
Penlan	Powys	SO2239	52°2·9'	3°7·9'W	X	161
Penlan	Swan	SN6006	51°44·4'	4°1·3'W	X	159
Pen-lan	Swan	SS6496	51°39·0'	3°57·6'W	T	159
Penlan	Wrex	SJ1834	52°54·1'	3°12·7'W	X	125
Penlanau	Nth Pt Talb	SN6709	51°46·1'	3°55·3'W	X	159
Penlanbridell	Pemb	SN1739	52°1·4'	4°39·6'W	X	145
Penlan-Cenarth	Carm	SN2541	52°2·6'	4°32·7'W	X	145
Penlan Centre, The	Carm	SN2819	51°50·8'	4°29·4'W	X	158
Penlancwnlle	Cered	SN5658	52°12·3'	4°6·0'W	X	146
Pen Lan-dalau	Cered	SN6642	52°3·9'	3°56·9'W	H	146
Penlanfach	Cered	SN2544	52°4·2'	4°32·8'W	X	145
Penlan-fâch	Cered	SN4753	52°9·5'	4°13·8'W	X	146
Penlanfawr	Carm	SN3537	52°0·7'	4°23·9'W	X	145
Pen Lan-fawr	Cered	SN7975	52°21·8'	3°46·2'W	H	135,147
Pen Lan-fawr	Powys	SN8974	52°21·4'	3°37·4'W	X	135,136,147
Penlanfeigan	Pemb	SN1738	52°0·9'	4°39·6'W	X	145
Penlan Fm	Carm	SN5703	51°42·7'	4°3·8'W	FM	159
Penlan Fm	Cered	SN5065	52°16·0'	4°11·5'W	X	135
Penlan Fm	Heref	SO2940	52°3·5'	3°1·7'W	FM	148,161
Pen-lan Fm	Pemb	SN1413	51°47·3'	4°41·4'W	FM	158
Penlangarreg	Carm	SN2738	52°1·0'	4°30·9'W	X	145
Penlangrug	Powys	SO0549	52°8·1'	3°22·9'W	X	147
Penlan Hall	Essex	TL9128	51°55·3'	0°47·1'E	X	168
Penlan-Isaf	Carm	SN4008	51°45·1'	4°18·7'W	X	159
Penlan-isaf	Cered	SN6575	52°21·6'	3°58·6'W	X	135
Penlanisaf	Pemb	SN0435	51°59·0'	4°50·9'W	X	145,157
Penlanlas	Cered	SN5457	52°11·8'	4°7·8'W	X	146
Penlanlas	Cered	SN6076	52°22·1'	4°3·0'W	X	135
Penlanlwyd	Powys	SN8843	52°4·7'	3°37·7'W	X	147,160
Pen-Lan-mabws	Pemb	SM8829	51°55·4'	5°4·6'W	T	157
Penlanmedd	Cered	SN6050	52°8·1'	4°2·3'W	X	146
Penlan-noeth	Cered	SN4751	52°8·4'	4°13·8'W	X	146
Penlanole	Powys	SN9863	52°15·6'	3°29·3'W	X	147
Penlan Oleu	Cered	SN6681	52°24·9'	3°57·8'W	X	135
Penlan Oleu	Pemb	SM9933	51°57·8'	4°55·2'W	X	157
Penlantelych	Carm	SN7833	51°59·2'	3°46·2'W	X	146,160
Penlan Uchaf	Carm	SN4008	51°45·1'	4°18·7'W	X	159
Penlan-uchaf	Pemb	SN2034	51°58·8'	4°36·9'W	X	145
Penlan Voss	Carm	SN4122	51°52·7'	4°18·2'W	X	159
Penlanwen	Cered	SN6554	52°10·3'	3°58·1'W	X	146
Penlanwen	Powys	SN8941	52°3·6'	3°36·8'W	X	147,160
Penlanwynt	Pemb	SN0533	51°57·9'	4°49·9'W	X	145
Penlanymor	Cered	SN4159	52°12·6'	4°19·2'W	X	146
Penlasgarn Ho	Torf	SO2803	51°43·5'	3°2·2'W	X	171
Pen-las Rock	I of Angl	SH2081	53°18·0'	4°41·4'W	X	114
Penlaw	D & G	NY1985	55°9·4'	3°15·8'W	X	79
Penlean	Corn	SX2098	50°45·5'	4°32·7'W	X	190
Penlee Fm	Devon	SX6578	50°35·4'	3°54·1'W	FM	191
Penlee Point	Corn	SW4726	50°5·1'	5°31·8'W	X	203
Penlee Point	Corn	SX4448	50°18·9'	4°11·1'W	X	201
Penley	Wrex	SJ4139	52°57·0'	2°52·3'W	T	126
Penley	Wrex	SJ4140	52°57·5'	2°52·3'W	T	117
Penley Fm	Bucks	SU7694	51°38·6'	0°53·7'W	FM	175
Penley Hall	Wrex	SJ4140	52°57·5'	2°52·3'W	X	117
Penley Hollies	Bucks	SU7794	51°38·6'	0°52·8'W	X	175
Penley Wood	Bucks	SU7693	51°38·1'	0°53·7'W	F	175
Penllan	Cered	SN5470	52°18·8'	4°8·1'W	X	135
Pen Llifau	Carm	SN7239	52°2·3'	3°51·6'W	H	146,160
Penllan	Heref	SO2552	52°9·9'	3°5·4'W	X	148
Penllan	Powys	SJ2128	52°50·9'	3°10·0'W	X	126
Penllan	Powys	SO0365	52°16·7'	3°24·9'W	X	136,147
Penllan	Powys	SO1346	52°6·6'	3°15·8'W	X	148
Penllanafel	Powys	SO1529	51°57·4'	3°13·8'W	X	161
Pen Llanerch	Cered	SN6962	52°14·7'	3°54·7'W	X	146
Penllanerch	Powys	SO1352	52°9·8'	3°15·9'W	X	148
Pen-Llan-y-gwr	Flint	SJ2654	53°4·9'	3°5·9'W	H	117
Penllech	Gwyn	SH2234	52°52·7'	4°38·3'W	T	123
Penllech	Powys	SO0147	52°7·0'	3°26·4'W	X	147
Penllech Bach	Gwyn	SH2135	52°53·2'	4°39·2'W	X	123
Penllechog	Gwyn	SH3945	52°58·9'	4°23·5'W	X	123
Penllech Uchaf	Gwyn	SH2033	52°52·1'	4°40·0'W	X	123
Penllechwen	Pemb	SM7329	51°55·0'	5°17·7'W	X	157
Penllededwen	Pemb	SM7227	51°53·9'	5°18·5'W	X	157
Penlle'r Bebyll	Swan	SN6304	51°43·3'	3°58·6'W	A	159
Penlle'r-Castell	Swan	SN6609	51°46·1'	3°56·1'W	A	159
Penlle'rfedwen	Nth Pt Talb	SN7211	51°47·2'	3°51·0'W	X	160
Penllergaer	Swan	SS6198	51°40·1'	4°0·2'W	T	159
Penllergaer Forest	Swan	SN6200	51°41·1'	3°59·4'W	F	159
Pen Llithrig y Wrach	Conwy	SH7162	53°8·6'	3°55·3'W	H	115
Penlloegr	I of Angl	SH3290	53°23·1'	4°30·4'W	X	114
Pen Lluest-y-carn	Powys	SN8086	52°27·8'	3°45·6'W	X	135,136
Penllwybr	Cered	SN4057	52°11·5'	4°20·1'W	X	146
Pen-llwydcoed	Carm	SN4532	51°58·1'	4°15·0'W	X	146
Penllwyn	Caer	ST1795	51°39·1'	3°11·6'W	T	171
Penllwyn	Card	ST0981	51°31·5'	3°18·3'W	X	171
Penllwyn	Carm	SN3339	52°1·7'	4°25·7'W	X	145
Penllwyn	Carm	SN5208	51°45·3'	4°8·3'W	X	159
Penllwyn	Cered	SN3656	52°10·9'	4°23·5'W	X	145
Pen Llwyn	Denb	SJ0456	53°5·8'	3°25·6'W	X	116
Pen-llŵyn	Denb	SJ1166	53°11·3'	3°19·5'W	X	116
Penllwyn	Gwyn	SH3536	52°54·0'	4°26·8'W	X	123
Pen-llŵyn	Powys	SJ1418	52°45·4'	3°16·1'W	X	125
Penllwyn	Powys	SO1344	52°5·5'	3°15·8'W	X	148,161
Penllwyn	Wrex	SJ2236	52°55·2'	3°9·2'W	X	126
Penllwynau	Carm	SN4922	51°52·8'	4°11·2'W	X	159
Penllwynbedw	Cered	SN6561	52°14·1'	3°58·2'W	X	146
Penllwyncoch-fawr	Carm	SN3438	52°1·2'	4°24·8'W	X	145
Penllwyn-Einon	Powys	SN9213	51°48·6'	3°33·6'W	X	160
Penllwyn Ho	Pemb	SN0817	51°49·4'	4°46·8'W	X	158
Penllwyn Isaf	Carm	SN4202	51°41·9'	4°16·8'W	X	159
Penllwyn Robert Fm	Swan	SS5393	51°37·2'	4°7·0'W	FM	159
Penllwyn Uchaf	Carm	SN4302	51°41·9'	4°15·9'W	X	159
Penllwynuchel	Carm	SN4027	51°55·4'	4°19·2'W	X	146
Pen Llwyn-uchel	Carm	SN5138	52°1·5'	4°9·9'W	H	146
Pen Llyn	Gwyn	SH5537	52°54·9'	4°9·0'W	X	124
Pen-Llyn	Gwyn	SH5662	53°8·4'	4°8·8'W	X	114,115
Penllyn	Gwyn	SN5899	52°34·5'	4°5·3'W	X	135
Pen-llyn	I of Angl	SH3582	53°18·8'	4°28·2'W	T	114

Penllyn	V of Glam	SS9776	51°28·7'	3°28·6'W	T	170
Penllyn Castle	V of Glam	SS9776	51°28·7'	3°28·6'W	X	170
Penllyn Court	V of Glam	SS9776	51°28·7'	3°28·6'W	X	170
Penllyn Forest	Gwyn	SH9630	52°51·7'	3°32·3'W	F	125
Pen Llyn-gloyw	Wrex	SJ1635	52°54·6'	3°14·5'W	W	125
Penllyn Moor	V of Glam	SS9876	51°28·7'	3°27·7'W	X	170
Penllyn Station	Gwyn	SH5662	53°8·4'	4°8·8'W	X	114,115
Penlon	Carm	SN3139	52°1·7'	4°27·4'W	X	145
Penlon	Carm	SN3737	52°0·7'	4°22·1'W	X	145
Penlon	Cered	SN3955	52°10·4'	4°20·9'W	X	145
Pen lôn	I of Angl	SH3372	53°13·4'	4°29·7'W	X	114
Pen-lôn	I of Angl	SH4264	53°9·2'	4°21·4'W	T	114,115
Penlon Betws	Cered	SN2948	52°6·5'	4°29·4'W	X	145
Penlone	Cered	SN6457	52°11·9'	3°59·0'W	X	146
Penmachno	Conwy	SH7950	53°2·3'	3°47·9'W	T	115
Penmaen	Caer	ST1897	51°40·2'	3°10·8'W	T	171
Penmaen	Carm	SN7522	51°53·2'	3°48·6'W	X	160
Penmaen	Gwyn	SH3338	52°55·1'	4°28·6'W	X	123
Penmaen	Gwyn	SH3634	52°53·0'	4°25·8'W	X	123
Penmaen	Gwyn	SH7229	52°50·8'	3°53·6'W	X	124
Penmaen	Gwyn	SH9339	52°56·5'	3°35·1'W	X	125
Pen-maen	I of Angl	SH5981	53°18·7'	4°6·6'W	X	114,115
Penmaen	Swan	SS5388	51°34·5'	4°6·9'W	T	159
Penmaenan	Conwy	SH7175	53°15·6'	3°55·6'W	T	115
Penmaenau	Powys	SO0352	52°9·7'	3°24·7'W	X	147
Penmaen-bach	Conwy	SH7478	53°17·3'	3°53·0'W	H	115
Penmaen Bach	Gwyn	SN6899	52°34·6'	3°56·5'W	X	135
Penmaen-bach Point	Conwy	SH7478	53°17·3'	3°53·0'W	X	115
Penmaen-brith	Gwyn	SH6451	53°2·6'	4°1·3'W	X	115
Penmaen Isa	Gwyn	SN6898	52°34·1'	3°56·5'W	X	135
Penmaenllwyd	Powys	SN8646	52°6·3'	3°39·5'W	X	147
Penmaen Mawr	Conwy	SH7075	53°15·6'	3°56·5'W	X	115
Penmaenmawr	Conwy	SH7176	53°16·2'	3°55·7'W	T	115
Penmaenpool	Gwyn	SH6918	52°44·9'	3°56·0'W	T	124
Penmaenpool-Morfa Mawddach Walk	Gwyn	SH6516	52°43·7'	3°59·6'W	X	124
Penmaen Rhôs	Conwy	SH8778	53°17·5'	3°41·3'W	T	116
Penmaen Swatch	Conwy	SH6577	53°16·6'	4°1·1'W	W	114,115
Pen Maen-wern	Powys	SN8661	52°14·4'	3°39·8'W	H	147
Penmaes	Powys	SO1233	51°59·5'	3°16·5'W	X	161
Penman's Green	Herts	TL0300	51°41·6'	0°30·2'W	X	166
Penmanshiel	Scot Bord	NT8067	55°54·0'	2°18·8'W	X	67
Penmanshiel Cott	Scot Bord	NT7967	55°54·0'	2°19·7'W	X	67
Penmanshiel Moor	Scot Bord	NT8268	55°54·5'	2°16·8'W	X	67
Penmanshiel Wood	Scot Bord	NT7968	55°54·5'	2°19·7'W	F	67
Pen March	Merth Tyd	SO0810	51°47·1'	3°19·6'W	X	160
Penmark	V of Glam	ST0568	51°24·4'	3°21·6'W	T	170
Penmarth	Corn	SW7035	50°10·5'	5°12·9'W	T	203
Penmayne	Corn	SW9476	50°33·1'	4°54·1'W	T	200
Penmeiddyn	Pemb	SM9235	51°58·7'	5°1·3'W	X	157
Penmenor	Corn	SW4225	50°4·4'	5°36·0'W	X	203
Pen Milan	Powys	SN9923	51°54·0'	3°27·7'W	X	160
Pen Mill	Somer	ST5616	50°56·7'	2°37·2'W	T	183
Penmincae	Powys	SO0054	52°10·8'	3°27·4'W	X	147
Penmire Brook	Warw	SP2599	52°35·5'	1°37·5'W	W	140
Penmoelallt	Rho Cyn Taf	SO0109	51°46·5'	3°25·7'W	H	160
Penmoelciliau	Cered	SN3455	52°10·3'	4°25·3'W	H	145
Pen Moelhedog	Cered	SN4546	52°5·7'	4°15·4'W	H	146
Penmon	I of Angl	SH6380	53°18·2'	4°3·0'W	T	114,115
Pen Moor	Somer	ST5210	50°53·5'	2°40·6'W	X	194
Penmore Ho	Arg & Bt	NM4052	56°35·5'	6°13·7'W	X	47
Penmore Mill	Arg & Bt	NM4052	56°35·5'	6°13·7'W	X	47
Penmorfa	Cered	SN3052	52°8·7'	4°28·7'W	T	145
Penmorfa	Gwyn	SH5440	52°56·5'	4°10·0'W	T	124
Penmorfa	Pemb	SM8734	51°58·1'	5°5·7'W	X	157
Penmount	Corn	SW8247	50°17·2'	5°3·2'W	X	204
Penmyarth	Powys	SO1820	51°52·6'	3°11·1'W	X	161
Penmynydd	Conwy	SH7783	53°20·0'	3°50·4'W	X	115
Penmynydd	Conwy	SH8369	53°12·6'	3°44·7'W	X	116
Penmynydd	I of Angl	SH5074	53°14·8'	4°14·5'W	T	114,115
Penmynydd	Swan	SS4492	51°36·6'	4°14·8'W	X	159
Penn	Bucks	SU9193	51°37·9'	0°40·7'W	T	175
Penn	Cumbr	SD1890	54°18·2'	3°15·2'W	H	96
Penn	Dorset	SY3495	50°45·3'	2°55·8'W	T	193
Penn	Wolv	SO8996	52°33·9'	2°9·3'W	T	139
Pennal	Gwyn	SH6900	52°35·2'	3°55·6'W	T	135
Pennal-isaf	Gwyn	SH7001	52°35·7'	3°54·8'W	X	135
Pennal Towers	Gwyn	SH7001	52°35·7'	3°54·8'W	X	135
Pennal-uchaf	Gwyn	SH7304	52°37·4'	3°52·2'W	X	135
Pennan	Aberd	NJ8465	57°40·7'	2°15·6'W	T	29,30
Pennan Bay	Aberd	NJ8465	57°40·7'	2°15·6'W	W	29,30
Pennance	Corn	SW4437	50°10·9'	5°34·8'W	X	203
Pennance	Corn	SW7140	50°13·2'	5°12·2'W	T	203
Pennance	Corn	SW7930	50°8·0'	5°5·2'W	X	204
Pennance	Corn	SW9253	50°20·6'	4°55·0'W	X	200,204
Pennance Point	Corn	SW8030	50°8·0'	5°4·3'W	X	204
Pennan Farm	Aberd	NJ8565	57°40·7'	2°14·6'W	FM	30
Pennan Head	Aberd	NJ8565	57°40·7'	2°14·6'W	X	30
Pennant	Cered	SN5163	52°14·9'	4°10·6'W	T	146
Pennant	Conwy	SH8167	53°11·5'	3°46·5'W	X	116
Pennant	Conwy	SH8247	53°0·7'	3°45·1'W	X	116
Pennant	Conwy	SH8759	53°7·2'	3°40·9'W	T	116
Pennant	Corn	SX1964	50°27·1'	4°32·6'W	X	201
Pennant	Denb	SJ0334	52°53·9'	3°26·1'W	X	125
Pennant	Denb	SJ0354	53°4·7'	3°26·5'W	X	116
Pennant	Denb	SJ0533	52°53·4'	3°24·3'W	X	125
Pennant	Denb	SJ0755	53°5·3'	3°22·9'W	X	116
Pennant	Gwyn	SH9020	52°46·2'	3°37·4'W	X	125
Pennant	Powys	SN8795	52°32·7'	3°39·6'W	X	135,136
Pennant	Powys	SN8797	52°33·8'	3°39·6'W	X	135,136
Pennant	Powys	SO0229	51°57·3'	3°25·2'W	X	160
Pennant	Powys	SO1696	52°33·6'	3°13·9'W	X	136
Pennant	Powys	SO2235	52°0·7'	3°7·8'W	X	161
Pennant	Wrex	SJ2439	52°56·8'	3°7·5'W	X	126
Pennant Canol	Conwy	SH8266	53°10·9'	3°45·5'W	X	116
Pennant Fm	Corn	SW9979	50°34·8'	4°50·0'W	FM	200
Pennant-isaf	Denb	SJ1750	53°2·7'	3°13·9'W	X	116
Pennant-Lliw	Gwyn	SH8132	52°52·6'	3°45·7'W	X	124,125
Pennant Melangell	Powys	SJ0226	52°49·6'	3°26·9'W	X	125
Pennant Pound	Powys	SO2177	52°23·4'	3°9·3'W	X	137,148
Pennant Twrch	Powys	SH9615	52°43·6'	3°32·0'W	X	125
Pennant Ucha	Conwy	SH8266	53°10·9'	3°45·5'W	X	116
Pennant Uchaf	Denb	SH9959	53°7·4'	3°30·2'W	X	116
Pennant-y-priddbwll	Conwy	SH8260	53°7·7'	3°45·4'W	X	116
Pennar	Cered	SN3753	52°9·3'	4°22·6'W	X	145
Pennar	Pemb	SM9502	51°41·0'	4°57·5'W	T	157,158
Pennar Cants	Pemb	SM9203	51°41·5'	5°0·2'W	X	157,158
Pennard	Swan	SS5688	51°34·6'	4°4·3'W	T	159
Pennard Burrows	Swan	SS5488	51°34·6'	4°6·0'W	X	159
Pennard Castle	Swan	SS5488	51°34·6'	4°6·0'W	A	159
Pennard Hill	Somer	ST5738	51°8·6'	2°36·5'W	H	182,183
Pennard Ho	Somer	ST5937	51°8·1'	2°34·8'W	X	182,183
Pennare	Corn	SW8149	50°18·3'	5°4·2'W	X	204
Pennare	Corn	SW9238	50°12·6'	4°54·5'W	X	204
Pennar Fm	Caer	ST1995	51°39·1'	3°9·9'W	FM	171
Pennar Mouth	Pemb	SM9403	51°41·5'	4°58·4'W	W	157,158
Pennar Park	Pemb	SM9402	51°41·0'	4°58·4'W	T	157,158
Pennatillie	Corn	SW9166	50°27·6'	4°56·3'W	X	200
Pennau	Powys	SN9547	52°6·9'	3°31·6'W	H	147
Penn Beacon	Devon	SX5962	50°26·7'	3°58·8'W	X	202
Penn Bottom	Bucks	SU9294	51°38·5'	0°39·8'W	T	175
Penn Common	Hants	SU2716	50°56·8'	1°36·6'W	X	184
Penn Common	Staffs	SO9094	52°32·9'	2°8·4'W	X	139
Penn Croft Fm	Hants	SU7848	51°13·8'	0°52·6'W	FM	186
Penn Cross	Dorset	SY3494	50°44·7'	2°55·7'W	X	193
Penneilly Wood	D & G	NX7485	55°8·9'	3°58·2'W	F	77
Pennel Burn	E Ayr	NS6029	55°32·3'	4°12·7'W	W	71
Pennellick	Corn	SX1863	50°26·6'	4°33·4'W	X	201
Pennerley	Shrops	SO3599	52°35·3'	2°57·2'W	T	137
Pennersaughs	D & G	NY2174	55°3·5'	3°13·8'W	X	85
Pennett's Fm	Essex	TL7719	51°50·7'	0°34·6'E	FM	167
Penn Fm	Hants	SU2716	50°56·8'	1°36·6'W	FM	184
Penn Fm	Kent	TQ4853	51°15·6'	0°7·7'E	FM	188
Penn Fm	Oxon	SP7404	51°44·0'	0°55·3'W	FM	165
Penn Hall	Worcs	SO7168	52°18·8'	2°25·1'W	X	138
Penn Hill	Dorset	SY6492	50°43·8'	2°30·2'W	X	194
Penn Ho	Bucks	SU9294	51°38·5'	0°39·8'W	X	175
Pennicknold	Devon	SS4410	50°52·3'	4°12·7'W	X	190
Pennicott	Devon	SS8701	50°48·1'	3°35·8'W	X	192
Pennicott's Fm	W Susx	SU8900	50°47·8'	0°43·8'W	FM	197
Penniment Fms	Notts	SK5162	53°9·4'	1°13·8'W	FM	120
Pennine Way	Cumbr	NY7129	54°39·6'	2°26·5'W	X	91
Pennine Way	Derby	SK0796	53°27·9'	1°53·3'W	X	110
Pennine Way	Durham	NY9316	54°32·6'	2°6·1'W	X	91,92
Pennine Way	Northum	NT7800	55°17·9'	2°20·4'W	X	80
Pennine Way	Northum	NY6462	54°57·3'	2°33·3'W	X	86
Pennine Way	Northum	NY8178	55°6·0'	2°17·4'W	X	86,87
Pennine Way	N Yks	SD8078	54°12·1'	2°18·0'W	X	98
Pennine Way	N Yks	SD8790	54°18·6'	2°11·6'W	X	98
Pennine Way	N Yks	SD9641	53°52·2'	2°3·2'W	X	103
Pennine Way	Roch	SD9717	53°39·2'	2°2·3'W	X	109
Penning	Wilts	ST9235	51°7·1'	2°6·5'W	X	184
Penning Bottom	Wilts	SU0135	51°7·1'	1°58·8'W	X	184
Penning Down	Wilts	SU0454	51°17·3'	1°56·2'W	X	184
Penninghame Ho	D & G	NX3869	54°59·6'	4°31·5'W	X	83
Penninghame Home Farm	D & G	NX3869	54°59·6'	4°31·5'W	FM	83
Pennings Barn	Wilts	SU2250	51°15·2'	1°40·7'W	X	184
Pennings Fm	Wilts	SU1123	51°0·6'	1°50·2'W	FM	184
Pennings, The	Wilts	SU1741	51°10·3'	1°45·0'W	X	184
Pennington	Cumbr	SD2677	54°11·3'	3°7·6'W	T	96,97
Pennington	Devon	SX5072	50°31·9'	4°6·6'W	X	191,201
Pennington	Hants	SZ3194	50°44·9'	1°33·3'W	T	196
Pennington	Wigan	SJ6599	53°29·4'	2°31·2'W	T	109
Pennington Cott	Durham	NZ0427	54°38·5'	1°55·9'W	X	92
Pennington Flash Country Park	Wigan	SJ6399	53°29·4'	2°33·1'W	X	109
Pennington Green	Wigan	SD6106	53°33·2'	2°34·9'W	T	109
Pennington Hall	Essex	TL5426	51°54·9'	0°14·7'E	X	167
Pennington Ho	Cumbr	SD2677	54°11·3'	3°7·6'W	X	96,97
Pennington Ho	Hants	SZ3193	50°44·4'	1°33·3'W	X	196
Pennington Marshes	Hants	SZ3292	50°43·8'	1°32·4'W	X	196
Pennington Plantn	Durham	NZ0327	54°38·5'	1°56·8'W	F	92
Pennington Resr	Cumbr	SD2578	54°11·8'	3°8·6'W	W	96
Pennlands Fm	Bucks	SU9587	51°34·7'	0°37·3'W	FM	175,176
Penn Moor	Devon	SX6063	50°27·2'	3°58·0'W	X	202
Pennorth	Powys	SO1126	51°55·8'	3°17·3'W	T	161
Pennoxstone	Heref	SO5528	51°57·2'	2°38·9'W	X	149
Penns in the Rocks	E Susx	TQ5234	51°5·3'	0°10·6'E	X	188
Penn's Lodge Fm	Wilts	SU0286	51°34·6'	1°57·9'W	FM	173
Penn Street	Bucks	SU9296	51°39·5'	0°39·8'W	T	165
Pennsylvania	Devon	SX9294	50°44·4'	3°31·5'W	T	192
Pennsylvania	S Glos	ST7473	51°27·6'	2°22·1'W	T	172
Pennsylvania Fm	Bath & NE Somer	ST7063	51°22·2'	2°25·5'W	FM	172
Penn Wood	Beds	TL0164	52°16·1'	0°30·8'W	F	153
Penn Wood	Bucks	SU9196	51°39·6'	0°40·7'W	F	165
Pennyarthur Rigg	E Ayr	NS4803	55°18·1'	4°23·2'W	X	77
Penny Bridge	Cumbr	SD3183	54°14·5'	3°3·1'W	T	96,97
Pennybridge	E Susx	TQ6130	51°3·0'	0°18·2'E	X	188
Penny Bridge	Pemb	SN0002	51°41·1'	4°53·2'W	X	157,158
Pennybridge Fm	E Susx	TQ5928	51°2·0'	0°16·5'E	FM	188,199
Penny Burn	N Ayr	NS2843	55°39·3'	4°43·6'W	W	63,70
Pennycombe Fm	Devon	SX9384	50°39·0'	3°30·4'W	FM	192
Pennycombe Water	Somer	SS8337	51°7·5'	3°39·9'W	W	181
Pennycomequick	Devon	SX5174	50°33·0'	4°5·8'W	X	191,201
Pennycotts	Devon	SS7206	50°50·6'	3°48·7'W	X	191
Pennycross	Arg & Bt	NM5026	56°21·9'	6°2·4'W	X	48
Pennycross	C of Plym	SX4757	50°23·8'	4°8·8'W	T	201
Pennydevern	Corn	SX1782	50°36·8'	4°34·8'W	X	201
Pennyfadzeoch	E Ayr	NS5220	55°27·3'	4°20·0'W	X	70
Pennyfeathers Fm	Essex	TL5506	51°44·1'	0°15·1'E	FM	167
Pennyflats Fm	N Yks	SE5767	54°6·0'	1°7·3'W	FM	100
Pennyford Hall	Warw	SP1561	52°15·1'	1°46·4'W	X	151
Pennyfuir	Arg & Bt	NM8732	56°26·2'	5°26·9'W	X	49
Pennygant Hill	Scot Bord	NY4499	55°17·2'	2°52·5'W	H	79
Pennygate	Norf	TG3422	52°44·9'	1°28·4'E	T	133,134
Pennyghael	Arg & Bt	NM5126	56°21·9'	6°1·5'W	X	48
Penny Gill	D & G	NS9902	55°18·4'	3°35·0'W	W	78
Pennyglen	S Ayr	NS2610	55°21·4'	4°44·3'W	X	70
Pennygown	Arg & Bt	NM5942	56°30·8'	5°54·6'W	X	47,48
Pennygown	Arg & Bt	NR6914	55°22·2'	5°38·3'W	X	68
Penny Green	Derby	SK5475	53°16·4'	1°11·0'W	T	120
Penny Hill	Brackn	SU8865	51°22·9'	0°43·7'W	X	175
Penny Hill	Cald	SE0618	53°39·7'	1°54·1'W	T	110
Penny Hill	Cumbr	NY6520	54°34·7'	2°32·1'W	X	91
Penny Hill	Durham	NZ0823	54°36·4'	1°52·1'W	X	92
Penny Hill	Lincs	TF3526	52°49·1'	0°0·6'E	T	131
Penny Hill	Northum	NZ1283	55°8·7'	1°48·3'W	X	81
Penny Hill	Somer	SS9744	51°11·4'	3°28·1'W	X	181
Penny Hill	Worcs	SO7561	52°15·0'	2°21·6'W	X	138,150
Penny Hill Fm	Cumbr	NY1900	54°23·6'	3°14·4'W	FM	89,90
Pennyhole Bay	Essex	TM2526	51°53·4'	1°16·6'E	W	169
Pennyhole Fleet	Essex	TL9812	51°46·5'	0°52·6'E	W	168
Penny Holme	N Yks	SE6491	54°18·9'	1°0·6'W	X	94,100
Pennyhooks Fm	Oxon	SU2390	51°36·7'	1°39·7'W	FM	163,174
Penny Howe	N Yks	SE9699	54°22·9'	0°30·9'W	A	94,101
Pennyland	Arg & Bt	NR7109	55°19·6'	5°36·2'W	X	68
Pennyland	Devon	SX7798	50°46·3'	3°44·3'W	X	191
Pennyland	D & G	NX9387	55°10·2'	3°40·4'W	X	78
Pennyland	Highld	ND1068	58°35·7'	3°32·4'W	X	11,12
Pennyland	Highld	ND2453	58°27·8'	3°17·7'W	X	11,12
Pennyland	Mil Key	SP8641	52°3·9'	0°44·3'W	X	152
Pennyland Burn	D & G	NX9386	55°9·7'	3°40·3'W	W	78
Pennyland Moor	D & G	NX9489	55°11·3'	3°39·5'W	X	78
Pennylands	Lancs	SD4706	53°33·1'	2°47·6'W	T	108
Pennymoor	Devon	SS8611	50°53·5'	3°36·9'W	T	191
Pennymore	Arg & Bt	NN0400	56°9·4'	5°8·9'W	X	56
Pennymore	E Ayr	NS4821	55°27·8'	4°23·8'W	X	70
Pennymore Point	Arg & Bt	NN0400	56°9·4'	5°8·9'W	X	56
Pennymuir	D & G	NX6245	54°47·1'	4°8·3'W	X	83
Pennymuir	Scot Bord	NT7514	55°25·4'	2°23·3'W	X	80
Pennypie Fell	Northum	NY9551	54°51·5'	2°4·2'W	X	87
Pennypie Ho	Northum	NY9551	54°51·5'	2°4·2'W	X	87
Pennypleck Ho	Ches	SJ6682	53°20·3'	2°30·2'W	X	109
Penny Pot	Essex	TL7928	51°55·5'	0°36·6'E	X	167
Pennypot	Kent	TR1434	51°4·1'	1°3·7'E	T	179,189
Penny Pot	Surrey	SU9661	51°20·6'	0°36·9'W	X	175,176,186
Pennyrush	Shrops	SJ4126	52°49·9'	2°52·1'W	X	126
Pennyseorach	Arg & Bt	NR7107	55°18·5'	5°36·1'W	X	68
Penny's Green	Norf	TM1599	52°33·0'	1°10·7'E	T	144
Penny Spot Beck	Norf	TG0315	52°41·9'	1°0·7'E	W	133
Pennyswick Fm	Oxon	SU2295	51°39·4'	1°40·5'W	FM	163
Pennytersal	Inverc	NS3371	55°54·4'	4°39·9'W	X	63
Pennython Hill	Brad	SE1440	53°51·6'	1°46·8'W	X	104
Pennytinney	Corn	SX0177	50°33·8'	4°48·2'W	T	200
Pennyvenie	E Ayr	NS4906	55°19·7'	4°22·4'W	X	70,77
Pennywell	Sund	NZ3555	54°53·6'	1°26·8'W	T	88
Penoben Burn	D & G	NY2578	55°5·7'	3°10·1'W	W	85
Pen Offa	Powys	SO2663	52°15·9'	3°4·7'W	X	137,148
Pen Olver	Corn	SW7111	49°57·6'	5°11·2'W	X	203
Pen-onn	V of Glam	ST0569	51°25·0'	3°21·6'W	T	170
Penoros	Conwy	SH8573	53°14·7'	3°43·0'W	X	116
Penowern	Gwyn	SH6003	52°36·6'	4°3·7'W	X	135
Penoyre	Powys	SO0131	51°58·4'	3°26·1'W	X	160
Penoyre	Powys	SO1170	52°19·5'	3°18·0'W	X	136,148
Pen Padrig	I of Angl	SH3887	53°21·6'	4°25·7'W	X	114
Pen-pâl	Carm	SN5418	51°50·7'	4°6·8'W	X	159
Penpalmant	Denb	SJ0668	53°12·3'	3°24·0'W	X	116
Pen-parc	Carm	SN1218	51°50·0'	4°43·3'W	X	158
Penparc	Carm	SN2417	51°49·7'	4°32·9'W	X	158
Penparc	Cered	SN2148	52°6·3'	4°36·4'W	T	145
Pen-parc	Cered	SN5851	52°8·6'	4°4·1'W	X	146
Penparc	Pemb	SM8431	51°56·4'	5°8·2'W	T	157
Penparcau	Cered	SN5880	52°24·2'	4°4·8'W	T	135
Penparceithin	Pemb	SN2342	52°3·1'	4°34·5'W	X	145
Pen Parc Llwyd	Conwy	SJ0067	53°11·7'	3°29·4'W	X	116
Penpark	Carm	SN3833	51°58·6'	4°21·1'W	X	145
Penpedairheol	Caer	ST1497	51°40·1'	3°14·2'W	T	171
Penpedairheol	Monm	SO3303	51°43·5'	2°57·8'W	T	171
Pen-pedair-heol	Powys	SO2216	51°50·5'	3°7·5'W	X	161
Penpegws	Cered	SN6975	52°21·7'	3°55·0'W	X	135
Pen-Peles	Cered	SN2152	52°8·5'	4°36·6'W	X	145
Penpergym	Monm	SO3310	51°47·3'	2°57·9'W	T	161
Penperlleni	Monm	SO3204	51°44·1'	2°58·7'W	T	171
Penperth	Corn	SW8538	50°12·4'	5°0·4'W	X	204
Penpethy	Corn	SX0886	50°38·8'	4°42·6'W	T	200
Penpeugh	Northum	NY7662	54°57·4'	2°22·1'W	X	86,87
Penpill Fm	Corn	SX3475	50°34·3'	4°20·2'W	FM	201
Penpillick	Corn	SX0856	50°22·6'	4°41·6'W	T	200
Penpistyll	Carm	SN4138	52°1·3'	4°18·6'W	X	146
Pen Pits	Somer	ST7631	51°4·9'	2°20·2'W	A	183
Pen-plaenau	Wrex	SJ1136	52°55·1'	3°19·0'W	H	125
Penplas	Carm	SN3517	51°49·9'	4°23·3'W	T	159
Pen plas	Swan	SS6497	51°39·6'	3°57·6'W	X	159
Penpleidiau	Pemb	SM7623	51°51·9'	5°14·8'W	X	157
Penpol	Corn	SW7960	50°24·1'	5°6·2'W	X	200
Penpol	Corn	SW8139	50°12·9'	5°3·7'W	T	204
Penpol	Corn	SX1390	50°41·0'	4°38·5'W	X	190
Penpoll	Corn	SW7628	50°6·8'	5°7·6'W	X	204
Penpoll	Corn	SX1454	50°21·6'	4°36·5'W	T	200
Penpoll	Corn	SX3363	50°26·8'	4°20·8'W	X	201
Penpoll Creek	Corn	SX1354	50°21·6'	4°37·4'W	W	200
Penpoll Fm	Corn	SX1269	50°29·7'	4°38·7'W	FM	200
Penpompren	Cered	SN6968	52°17·9'	3°54·9'W	X	135
Penpompren Hall	Cered	SN6689	52°29·2'	3°58·0'W	X	135
Penponds	Corn	SW6339	50°12·5'	5°18·9'W	T	203
Pen Ponds	Rich	TQ1972	51°26·3'	0°16·9'W	W	176
Penpont	Corn	SX0874	50°32·3'	4°42·2'W	T	200
Penpont	D & G	NX8494	55°13·8'	3°49·0'W	T	78
Penpont	Powys	SN9728	51°56·7'	3°29·5'W	X	160
Pen-pontbren	Carm	SN3319	51°50·9'	4°25·1'W	X	159
Penpont Burn	D & G	NX8495	55°14·4'	3°49·0'W	W	78
Penpont Fm	Corn	SW9975	50°32·6'	4°49·8'W	FM	200
Penpont Water	Corn	SX2382	50°36·9'	4°29·7'W	W	201
Penporchell	Conwy	SH9967	53°11·7'	3°30·3'W	X	116
Penprisk	Powys	SO2318	51°51·6'	3°6·7'W	X	161
Penprysg	Brig	SS9682	51°31·9'	3°29·6'W	T	170
Pen Pumlumon Arwystli	Powys	SN8187	52°28·3'	3°44·7'W	X	135,136
Pen-pych	Rho Cyn Taf	SS9299	51°41·0'	3°33·3'W	X	170
Penquean	Corn	SW9573	50°31·5'	4°53·2'W	X	200

Penquit	Devon	SX6454	50°22·4'	3°54·4'W	T	202
Penquite	Corn	SX0768	50°29·0'	4°42·9'W	X	200
Penquite	Corn	SX1075	50°32·9'	4°40·5'W	X	200
Penquite	Corn	SX1155	50°22·1'	4°39·1'W	X	200
Penquite	Corn	SX3661	50°25·8'	4°16·2'W	X	201
Penquite Fm	Corn	SX2157	50°23·4'	4°30·7'W	FM	201
Penrallt	Carm	SN1524	51°53·3'	4°40·9'W	X	145,158
Penrallt	Carm	SN1723	51°52·8'	4°39·1'W	X	145,158
Penrallt	Cered	SN2245	52°4·7'	4°35·5'W	X	145
Penrallt	Cered	SN2550	52°7·5'	4°33·0'W	X	145
Penrallt	Cered	SN3253	52°9·2'	4°27·0'W	X	145
Penrallt	Cered	SN5874	52°21·0'	4°4·7'W	X	135
Penrallt	Conwy	SH7662	53°8·7'	3°50·8'W	X	115
Penrallt	Conwy	SH8158	53°6·6'	3°46·3'W	X	116
Penrallt	Gwyn	SH2136	52°53·7'	4°39·3'W	X	123
Penrallt	Gwyn	SH3735	52°53·5'	4°25·0'W	T	123
Pen Rallt	I of Angl	SH5074	53°14·8'	4°14·5'W	X	114,115
Penrallt	Powys	SN9586	52°28·0'	3°32·3'W	T	136
Penrallt-ceri	Cered	SN3042	52°3·2'	4°28·4'W	X	145
Penralltcych	Pemb	SN2636	52°0·0'	4°31·7'W	X	145
Penralltcych	Pemb	SN2736	52°0·0'	4°30·8'W	X	145
Penrallt-dafen	Carm	SN3530	51°56·9'	4°23·7'W	X	145
Penrallt Ddu	Carm	SN3730	51°56·9'	4°21·9'W	X	145
Penralltddu	Pemb	SN0433	51°57·9'	4°50·8'W	X	145,157
Penralltddu	Pemb	SN1742	52°3·0'	4°39·7'W	X	145
Penrallt Fach	Pemb	SN1942	52°3·1'	4°38·0'W	X	145
Penrallt-Fachnog	Cered	SN3740	52°2·3'	4°22·2'W	X	145
Penrallt Fm	Carm	SN3336	52°0·1'	4°25·6'W	FM	145
Penrallt Gillo	Carm	SN2840	52°2·1'	4°30·1'W	X	145
Penralltgochel	Carm	SN2430	51°56·7'	4°33·3'W	X	145
Penrallt Howel	Pemb	SN1841	52°2·5'	4°38·8'W	X	145
Penralltllyn	Pemb	SN2141	52°2·6'	4°36·2'W	X	145
Penrallt Trawscoed	Carm	SN3324	51°53·6'	4°25·2'W	X	145,159
Penrallty	Pemb	SN2237	52°0·4'	4°35·2'W	X	145
Penrallt-y-Bie Fm	Cered	SN2644	52°4·3'	4°31·9'W	FM	145
Penrest	Corn	SX3377	50°34·4'	4°21·1'W	X	201
Penrhengoed	Denb	SJ0958	53°6·9'	3°21·2'W	X	116
Penrheol	Carm	SN2915	51°48·7'	4°28·4'W	X	159
Penrheol	Carm	SN3020	51°51·4'	4°27·7'W	X	145,159
Penrheol	Powys	SO0739	52°2·7'	3°21·0'W	X	160
Penrherber	Carm	SN2839	52°1·6'	4°30·0'W	X	145
Penrhewr	Heref	SO3127	51°56·5'	2°59·8'W	X	161
Pen-rhip	Cered	SN3054	52°9·7'	4°28·7'W	X	145
Penrhiw	Caer	ST2491	51°37·0'	3°5·5'W	T	171
Penrhiw	Carm	SN1924	51°53·4'	4°37·4'W	X	145,158
Penrhiw	Carm	SN3219	51°50·9'	4°26·0'W	X	159
Penrhiw	Carm	SN4817	51°50·1'	4°12·0'W	X	159
Penrhiw	Carm	SN7335	52°0·2'	3°50·6'W	X	146,160
Penrhiw	Carm	SN8335	52°0·3'	3°41·9'W	X	160
Pen-rhiw	Cered	SN2249	52°6·9'	4°35·6'W	X	145
Pen-rhiw	Cered	SN4341	52°3·0'	4°17·0'W	X	146
Pen-rhiw	Cered	SN4659	52°12·7'	4°14·8'W	X	146
Penrhiw	Cered	SN4864	52°15·4'	4°13·2'W	X	146
Penrhiw	Cered	SN4952	52°9·0'	4°12·0'W	X	146
Pen-rhiw	Cered	SN6677	52°22·7'	3°57·7'W	X	135
Penrhiw	Conwy	SH8274	53°15·2'	3°45·7'W	X	116
Pen-rhiw	Denb	SJ1443	52°58·9'	3°16·5'W	X	125
Penrhiw	Flint	SJ2856	53°6·0'	3°4·1'W	X	117
Penrhiw	I of Angl	SH3578	53°16·6'	4°28·1'W	X	114
Penrhiw	Merth Tyd	ST1098	51°40·7'	3°17·7'W	X	171
Pen-rhiw	Nth Pt Talb	SN8906	51°44·7'	3°36·1'W	X	160
Penrhiw	Pemb	SN0234	51°58·4'	4°52·6'W	X	145,157
Pen-rhiw	Pemb	SN0635	51°59·0'	4°49·1'W	X	145
Pen-rhiw	Powys	SJ1004	52°37·8'	3°19·4'W	X	136
Penrhiw	Powys	SN8628	51°56·6'	3°39·1'W	X	160
Penrhiw	Powys	SN9246	52°6·3'	3°34·2'W	X	147
Penrhiw	Powys	SO0041	52°3·7'	3°27·1'W	X	147,160
Pen-Rhiw	Powys	SO1916	51°50·4'	3°10·2'W	X	161
Penrhiwau	Gwyn	SH4049	53°1·1'	4°22·7'W	X	115,123
Pen-rhiw-bâch	Denb	SJ0658	53°6·9'	3°23·9'W	X	116
Pen Rhiwbie	Cered	SN7748	52°7·2'	3°47·4'W	H	146,147
Pen Rhiw-calch	Powys	SO1017	51°50·9'	3°18·0'W	X	161
Penrhiwceiber	Rho Cyn Taf	ST0597	51°40·1'	3°22·0'W	T	170
Pen Rhiwclochdy	Cered	SN7551	52°8·8'	3°49·2'W	X	146,147
Penrhiw Cradoc	Rho Cyn Taf	ST0497	51°40·1'	3°22·9'W	X	170
Penrhiw-fach	Cered	SN3446	52°5·5'	4°25·0'W	X	145
Pen-Rhiw-fawr	Nth Pt Talb	SN7411	51°47·2'	3°49·2'W	T	160
Penrhiwgarreg	Blae Gw	SO2104	51°44·0'	3°8·2'W	T	171
Penrhiwgoch	Carm	SN5518	51°50·7'	4°5·9'W	T	159
Pen-Rhiw-goch	Carm	SN7721	51°52·7'	3°46·8'W	H	160
Penrhiwgoch	Powys	SN9049	52°7·9'	3°36·0'W	X	147
Penrhiwgoleu	Carm	SN5126	51°55·0'	4°9·6'W	X	146
Penrhiwgwiail	Carm	SN3530	51°56·9'	4°23·7'W	X	145
Pen Rhiwiar	Carm	SN7548	52°7·2'	3°49·2'W	F	146,147
Pen-rhiwiau	Carm	SN5025	51°54·4'	4°10·4'W	X	146
Penrhiwlas	Carm	SN3226	51°54·7'	4°26·2'W	X	145
Pen Rhiwlas	Cered	SN7570	52°19·1'	3°49·6'W	X	135,147
Penrhiw-llan	Cered	SN3641	52°2·8'	4°23·1'W	T	145
Penrhiwlodd	Powys	SO1442	52°4·4'	3°14·9'W	X	148,161
Pen Rhiw-mwyn	Powys	SH8600	52°35·4'	3°40·6'W	H	135,136
Pen-rhiw-newydd	Cered	SN6684	52°26·5'	3°57·9'W	X	135
Penrhiw-pal	Cered	SN3445	52°5·0'	4°25·0'W	T	145
Penrhiwronw	Carm	SN3928	51°55·9'	4°20·1'W	X	145
Pen-rhiw-trefan	Powys	SN9252	52°9·6'	3°34·3'W	X	147
Penrhiwtyn	Nth Pt Talb	SS7495	51°38·6'	3°48·9'W	T	170
Penrhiwtywarch	Carm	SN7144	52°5·0'	3°52·6'W	X	146,147,160
Penrhiw Uchaf	Carm	SN7827	51°55·9'	3°46·1'W	X	146,160
Pen-rhiw Warren	Caer	ST2189	51°35·9'	3°8·0'W	X	171
Pen Rhiw-wen	Carm	SN7318	51°50·9'	3°50·2'W	X	160
Penrhiw-wen	Powys	SN9270	52°19·3'	3°34·7'W	X	136,147
Penrhoel	Powys	SO2146	52°6·6'	3°8·8'W	X	148
Penrhos	Cered	SN5569	52°18·2'	4°7·2'W	X	135
Penrhos	Gwyn	SH3434	52°52·9'	4°27·6'W	T	123
Pen-rhos	Gwyn	SH3639	52°55·6'	4°26·0'W	X	123
Penrhôs	Gwyn	SH4961	53°7·7'	4°15·0'W	X	114,115
Pen-rhos	Gwyn	SH6730	52°51·3'	3°58·1'W	X	124
Penrhôs	Gwyn	SH7323	52°47·6'	3°52·6'W	X	124
Penrhos	Heref	SO3156	52°12·1'	3°0·2'W	T	148
Penrhos	I of Angl	SH2781	53°18·1'	4°34·3'W	T	114
Pen-rhôs	Monm	SO3519	51°52·2'	2°56·3'W	X	161

Penrhos	Monm	SO4111	51°47·9'	2°50·9'W	T	161
Penrhos	Pemb	SN1025	51°53·7'	4°45·3'W	X	145,158
Penrhos	Powys	SN8011	51°47·3'	3°44·0'W	T	160
Penrhos	Powys	SN9724	51°54·5'	3°29·4'W	X	160
Pen-rhôs	Powys	SO1341	52°3·9'	3°15·8'W	X	148,161
Pen-rhos	Wrex	SJ2853	53°4·4'	3°4·1'W	T	117
Pen Rhos Dirion	Powys	SO2033	51°59·6'	3°9·5'W	X	161
Penrhosfeilw	I of Angl	SH2280	53°17·5'	4°39·8'W	X	114
Penrhôs Fm	Monm	SO4013	51°49·0'	2°51·8'W	FM	161
Penrhos Fm	Newp	ST3491	51°37·1'	2°56·8'W	FM	171
Penrhos Fm	Powys	SJ2316	52°44·4'	3°8·0'W	FM	126
Penrhos-garnedd	Gwyn	SH5570	53°12·7'	4°9·9'W	T	114,115
Penrhosgoch	Powys	SN9963	52°15·6'	3°28·4'W	X	147
Penrhos Isaf	Carm	SN5626	51°55·1'	4°5·2'W	X	146
Penrhosmawr	Powys	SH7600	52°35·3'	3°49·4'W	X	135
Pen Rhosser	Cered	SN5468	52°17·7'	4°8·1'W	X	135
Penrhyd	Conwy	SH7971	53°13·6'	3°48·3'W	X	115
Penrhyddion	Conwy	SH8153	53°3·9'	3°46·2'W	X	116
Penrhyd Lastra	I of Angl	SH4291	53°23·8'	4°22·2'W	T	114
Penrhydlyniog	Gwyn	SH3634	52°53·0'	4°25·8'W	X	123
Penrhyn	Carm	SN7742	52°4·0'	3°47·3'W	X	146,147,160
Penrhyn	Cered	SN3759	52°12·6'	4°22·7'W	X	145
Penrhyn	Cered	SN4659	52°12·7'	4°14·8'W	X	146
Penrhyn	Conwy	SH8950	53°2·4'	3°38·9'W	X	116
Penrhyn	Gwyn	SH1826	52°48·3'	4°41·6'W	X	123
Penrhyn	Gwyn	SH2633	52°52·2'	4°34·7'W	X	123
Penrhyn	Gwyn	SH4335	52°53·6'	4°19·6'W	X	123
Penrhyn	I of Angl	SH2884	53°19·7'	4°34·6'W	X	114
Penrhyn	I of Angl	SH3468	53°11·2'	4°28·7'W	X	114
Penrhyn	I of Angl	SH3693	53°24·7'	4°27·6'W	X	114
Penrhyn	I of Angl	SH4187	53°21·6'	4°23·0'W	X	114
Penrhyn	I of Angl	SH4888	53°22·3'	4°16·7'W	X	114
Penrhyn	I of Angl	SH5077	53°16·4'	4°14·6'W	X	114,115
Penrhyn	I of Angl	SH5184	53°20·2'	4°13·9'W	X	114,115
Penrhyn	Pemb	SM8023	51°52·0'	5°11·3'W	X	157
Penrhyn	Pemb	SM9140	52°1·4'	5°2·4'W	X	157
Penrhyn	Pemb	SM9838	52°0·5'	4°56·2'W	X	157
Penrhyn Bay (Bae-Penrhyn)	Conwy	SH8281	53°19·0'	3°45·9'W	T	116
Penrhyn Bodeilas	Gwyn	SH3142	52°57·2'	4°30·5'W	X	123
Penrhyn Castle	Gwyn	SH6071	53°13·3'	4°5·4'W	X	115
Penrhyn Castle	Pemb	SN1449	52°6·7'	4°42·6'W	T	145
Penrhyn-coch	Cered	SN6484	52°26·5'	3°59·7'W	T	135
Penrhyn Colmon	Gwyn	SH1934	52°52·6'	4°41·0'W	X	123
Penrhyn Cwmistir	Gwyn	SH2439	52°55·4'	4°36·7'W	X	123
Penrhyndeudraeth	Gwyn	SH6139	52°56·1'	4°3·7'W	T	124
Penrhyn Dû	Gwyn	SH3226	52°48·6'	4°29·2'W	X	123
Penrhyn Dyfi	Gwyn	SN7301	52°35·8'	3°52·1'W	X	135
Penrhyn Erw-goch	Pemb	SM9938	52°0·5'	4°55·3'W	X	157
Penrhyn Ffynnon-las	Pemb	SM7529	51°55·1'	5°15·9'W	X	157
Penrhyn Fm	Gwyn	SH4559	53°6·6'	4°18·5'W	FM	115,123
Penrhyn-gerwin	Cered	SN6694	52°31·9'	3°58·1'W	X	135
Penrhyn Glas	Gwyn	SH3343	52°57·7'	4°28·8'W	X	123
Penrhyn Glas	I of Angl	SH4991	53°23·9'	4°15·9'W	X	114
Penrhyn Gwyn	Carm	SS5197	51°39·4'	4°8·9'W	X	159
Penrhynhalen	I of Angl	SH3767	53°10·8'	4°25·9'W	X	114
Penrhyn-isaf	Gwyn	SH5837	52°54·9'	4°6·3'W	X	124
Penrhyn Mawr	Gwyn	SH1632	52°51·5'	4°43·6'W	X	123
Penrhyn Mawr	I of Angl	SH2179	53°16·9'	4°40·7'W	X	114
Penrhyn Melyn	Gwyn	SH2035	52°53·2'	4°40·1'W	X	123
Penrhyn Nefyn	Gwyn	SH2941	52°56·6'	4°32·3'W	X	123
Penrhyn-oer	I of Angl	SH4279	53°17·3'	4°21·8'W	X	114,115
Penrhyn Quarries	Gwyn	SH6164	53°9·5'	4°4·3'W	X	115
Penrhyn side	Conwy	SH8181	53°19·0'	3°46·8'W	T	116
Penrhyn Twll	Pemb	SM7022	51°51·2'	5°20·0'W	X	157
Penrhyn Ychen	Pemb	SM9838	52°0·5'	4°56·2'W	X	157
Penrhynydyn	Gwyn	SH3234	52°52·9'	4°29·4'W	X	123
Penrhys	Rho Cyn Taf	ST0095	51°38·9'	3°26·3'W	T	170
Penrhys Isaf	Rho Cyn Taf	ST0093	51°37·9'	3°26·3'W	X	170
Penrice	Corn	SX0249	50°18·7'	4°46·5'W	X	204
Penrice	Swan	SS4987	51°33·9'	4°10·3'W	T	159
Penrice Castle	Swan	SS4988	51°34·5'	4°10·4'W	X	159
Pen Ridge Fm	Somer	ST7532	51°5·4'	2°21·0'W	FM	183
Penrith	Cumbr	NY5130	54°40·0'	2°45·2'W	T	90
Penrock	Carm	SN7532	51°58·6'	3°48·8'W	X	146,160
Penrose	Corn	SW3725	50°4·3'	5°40·2'W	A	203
Penrose	Corn	SW6425	50°4·9'	5°17·6'W	X	203
Penrose	Corn	SW8462	50°25·3'	5°2·1'W	X	200
Penrose	Corn	SW8770	50°29·7'	4°59·8'W	T	200
Penrose	Corn	SW9472	50°30·9'	4°54·0'W	X	200
Penrose	Corn	SW9558	50°23·4'	4°52·7'W	X	200
Penrose	Corn	SX0876	50°33·4'	4°42·3'W	T	200
Penrose	Corn	SX0972	50°31·2'	4°41·3'W	X	200
Penrose	Corn	SX2589	50°40·7'	4°28·2'W	X	190
Penrose	Heref	SO4821	51°53·3'	2°44·9'W	X	161
Penrose Fm	Corn	SW7930	50°8·0'	5°5·2'W	FM	204
Penrose Fm	Corn	SX0457	50°23·1'	4°45·1'W	FM	200
Penrose Fm	Swan	SS5291	51°36·1'	4°7·8'W	FM	159
Penrose Hill	Corn	SW6326	50°5·4'	5°18·4'W	T	203
Penrose Walks	Corn	SW6525	50°5·0'	5°16·7'W	X	203
Penruddock	Cumbr	NY4227	54°38·3'	2°53·5'W	T	90
Penruddock Hall	Cumbr	NY4328	54°38·9'	2°52·6'W	X	90
Penry Bay	V of Glam	ST0066	51°23·3'	3°25·8'W	W	170
Penryn	Corn	SW7834	50°10·1'	5°6·2'W	T	204
Pensagillas Fm	Corn	SW9746	50°17·0'	4°50·6'W	FM	204
Pensarn	Carm	SN1923	51°52·8'	4°37·4'W	X	145,158
Pensarn	Carm	SN4119	51°51·1'	4°18·1'W	T	159
Pensarn	Conwy	SH9578	53°17·6'	3°34·1'W	T	116
Pen-sarn	Gwyn	SH4344	52°58·5'	4°19·9'W	X	115,123
Pen-sarn	Gwyn	SH4644	52°58·6'	4°17·2'W	X	123
Pen-sarn	Gwyn	SH5828	52°50·1'	4°6·1'W	X	124
Pensarn	Cered	SN1235	51°59·1'	4°43·9'W	X	145
Pensarn	Powys	SJ1832	52°53·0'	3°12·7'W	X	125
Pensarnau	Cered	SN3957	52°11·5'	4°20·9'W	X	145
Pensarnfawr	Cered	SN5054	52°10·1'	4°11·2'W	X	146
Pensarn Fm	Gwyn	SH3535	52°53·5'	4°26·8'W	FM	123
Pensax	Worcs	SO7269	52°19·3'	2°24·3'W	T	138
Pensax Common	Worcs	SO7268	52°18·8'	2°24·2'W	X	138
Pensby	Wirral	SJ2683	53°20·6'	3°6·3'W	T	108
Pens Close	Northum	NZ0874	55°3·9'	1°52·1'W	X	88

Penscombe	Corn	SX3479	50°35·5'	4°20·3'W	X	201
Penselwood	Somer	ST7531	51°4·9'	2°21·0'W	T	183
Penseri	I of Angl	SH3372	53°13·4'	4°29·7'W	X	114
Pensford	Bath & NE Somer	ST6263	51°22·1'	2°32·4'W	T	172
Pensham	Worcs	SO9444	52°5·9'	2°4·9'W	T	150
Pensham Fields Fm	Worcs	SO9443	52°5·4'	2°4·9'W	FM	150
Penshaw	Sund	NZ3253	54°52·5'	1°29·7'W	T	88
Penshiel	E Loth	NT6463	55°51·8'	2°34·1'W	X	67
Penshiel Hill	E Loth	NT6362	55°51·2'	2°35·0'W	H	67
Penshurst	Kent	TQ5243	51°10·2'	0°10·8'E	T	188
Penshurst Park	Kent	TQ5244	51°10·7'	0°10·9'E	X	188
Penshurst Place	Kent	TQ5243	51°10·2'	0°10·8'E	A	188
Penshurst Sta	Kent	TQ5146	51°11·8'	0°10·1'E	X	188
Pensilva	Corn	SX2969	50°30·0'	4°24·3'W	T	201
Pensipple	Corn	SX2659	50°24·5'	4°26·6'W	X	201
Pensnett	Dudley	SO9189	52°30·2'	2°7·6'W	T	139
Penson	Devon	SX7254	50°22·6'	3°47·6'W	X	202
Penson Fm	Devon	SS6505	50°50·0'	3°54·6'W	FM	191
Pensport Rock	Devon	SS4746	51°11·8'	4°11·0'W	X	180
Pensthorpe Hall	Norf	TF9429	52°49·6'	0°53·2'E	X	132
Pensthorpe Water Fowl Park	Norf	TF9429	52°49·6'	0°53·2'E	X	132
Penstock Hall	Kent	TR0941	51°8·0'	0°59·6'E	X	179,189
Penston	E Loth	NT4472	55°56·5'	2°53·4'W	T	66
Penstone	Devon	SS7700	50°47·4'	3°44·3'W	T	191
Penstones Wood	Wilts	ST7839	51°9·2'	2°18·5'W	F	183
Penstrasse Barton	Corn	SW9849	50°18·6'	4°49·9'W	X	204
Penstraze	Corn	SW7546	50°16·5'	5°9·1'W	T	204
Pensychnant	Conwy	SH7576	53°16·2'	3°52·1'W	X	115
Pensyflog	Gwyn	SH5639	52°56·0'	4°8·2'W	X	124
Pentargon	Corn	SX1091	50°41·5'	4°41·0'W	X	190
Pen Tas-eithin	Carm	SN5743	52°4·3'	4°4·8'W	H	146
Pentecox	C of Edin	NT2970	55°55·3'	3°7·7'W	X	66
Penterry Fm	Monm	ST5299	51°41·5'	2°41·3'W	FM	162
Pen Tew	Cered	SN1751	52°7·9'	4°40·0'W	X	145
Pentewan	Corn	SX0147	50°17·6'	4°47·3'W	T	204
Pentewan Beach	Corn	SX0146	50°17·1'	4°47·2'W	X	204
Pent Fm	Kent	TR1439	51°6·8'	1°3·8'E	FM	179,189
Pen, The	Cumbr	NY4718	54°33·5'	2°48·8'W	X	90
Penthryn	Conwy	SH8170	53°13·1'	3°46·5'W	X	116
Penthryn	Powys	SJ1400	52°35·7'	3°15·8'W	X	136
Penthryn	Powys	SJ2717	52°45·0'	3°4·5'W	X	126
Penthryn	Powys	SO0686	52°28·1'	3°22·6'W	X	136
Penthryn Fechan	Powys	SJ2416	52°44·4'	3°7·1'W	X	126
Pentico Wood	Wilts	SU2573	51°27·6'	1°38·0'W	F	174
Pentiken	Shrops	SO2183	52°26·6'	3°9·3'W	T	137
Pentillie Castle	Corn	SX4064	50°27·5'	4°14·9'W	X	201
Pentimore Wood	Northnts	SP6641	52°4·0'	1°1·8'W	F	152
Pentir	Gwyn	SH5766	53°10·6'	4°8·0'W	T	114,115
Pentir	I of Angl	SH6281	53°18·7'	4°3·9'W	X	114,115
Pen Tir	Powys	SO1725	51°55·3'	3°12·0'W	H	161
Pentir-bâch	Carm	SN7330	51°57·5'	3°50·5'W	H	146,160
Pentire	Corn	SW7961	50°24·7'	5°6·3'W	T	200
Pentire Fm	Corn	SW8570	50°29·7'	5°1·5'W	FM	200
Pentire Fm	Corn	SW9380	50°35·2'	4°55·1'W	FM	200
Pentireglaze	Corn	SW9479	50°34·7'	4°54·2'W	X	200
Pentireglaze Haven	Corn	SW9379	50°34·7'	4°55·1'W	W	200
Pentire Point	Corn	SW9280	50°35·2'	4°55·9'W	X	200
Pentire Point East	Corn	SW7861	50°24·7'	5°7·1'W	X	200
Pentire Point West	Corn	SW7761	50°24·6'	5°7·9'W	X	200
Pentire Steps	Corn	SW8470	50°29·6'	5°2·4'W	X	200
Pentirvin	Shrops	SJ3301	52°36·4'	2°59·0'W	T	126
Pentitla	Nth Pt Talb	SS8585	51°33·4'	3°39·1'W	X	170
Pentland Firth		ND3276	58°40·3'	3°9·9'W	W	7,12
Pentland Firth		ND3581	58°43·0'	3°6·9'W	W	7
Pentland Grove	Midlo	NT2564	55°52·1'	3°11·5'W	X	66
Pentland Hill	D & G	NT2408	55°21·9'	3°11·5'W	H	79
Pentland Hills	Scot Bord	NT1056	55°47·6'	3°25·7'W	H	65,72
Pentland Hills Regional Park	C of Edin	NT1661	55°50·3'	3°20·0'W	X	65,66
Pentland Mains	Midlo	NT2665	55°52·6'	3°10·5'W	X	66
Pentland Skerries	Orkney	ND4777	58°40·9'	2°54·4'W	X	7
Pentle Bay	I Scilly	SV9014	49°57·0'	6°18·9'W	W	203
Pentlepoir	Pemb	SN1105	51°43·0'	4°43·8'W	T	158
Pentlow	Essex	TL8144	52°4·1'	0°38·8'E	T	155
Pentlow	Essex	TL8146	52°5·2'	0°38·8'E	X	155
Pentlow Street	Essex	TL8245	52°4·6'	0°39·8'E	T	155
Pentney	Norf	TF7213	52°41·5'	0°33·1'E	T	132,143
Pentney Lakes Leisure Park	Norf	TF7013	52°41·5'	0°31·3'E	X	132,143
Penton	Cumbr	NY4577	55°5·3'	2°51·3'W	X	86
Penton Copse	Hants	SU3348	51°14·0'	1°31·3'W	F	185
Penton Corner	Hants	SU3346	51°13·0'	1°31·3'W	T	185
Penton Grafton	Hants	SU3247	51°13·5'	1°32·1'W	T	185
Penton Ho	Cumbr	NY4376	55°4·8'	2°53·1'W	X	85
Penton Hook	Surrey	TQ0469	51°24·9'	0°29·9'W	X	176
Penton Lodge (Sch)	Hants	SU3347	51°13·5'	1°31·3'W	X	185
Penton Mewsey	Hants	SU3347	51°13·5'	1°31·3'W	T	185
Pentonville	Isling	TQ3183	51°32·1'	0°6·3'W	T	176,177
Pentood-uchaf	Cered	SN1744	52°4·1'	4°39·8'W	X	145
Pentop	Carm	SN3136	52°0·0'	4°27·3'W	X	145
Pentopyn	Monm	ST3393	51°38·1'	2°57·7'W	X	171
Pen-tor	Denb	SJ0959	53°7·5'	3°21·2'W	X	116
Pentowin	Carm	SN2918	51°50·3'	4°28·5'W	X	159
Pentowyn	Carm	SN3210	51°46·0'	4°25·7'W	X	159
Pentraeth	I of Angl	SH5278	53°16·9'	4°12·8'W	T	114,115
Pentrapeod	Caer	SO1901	51°42·4'	3°9·9'W	T	171
Pentre	Carm	SN4310	51°46·2'	4°16·1'W	X	159
Pentre	Carm	SN5010	51°46·4'	4°10·1'W	T	159
Pentre	Cered	SN4762	52°14·3'	4°14·1'W	X	146
Pentre	Cered	SN5568	52°17·7'	4°7·2'W	X	135
Pentre	Cered	SN5675	52°21·5'	4°6·5'W	X	135
Pentre	Cered	SN6250	52°8·1'	4°0·6'W	X	146
Pentre	Conwy	SH8872	53°14·2'	3°40·3'W	X	116
Pentre	Conwy	SH9963	53°9·5'	3°30·2'W	X	116
Pentre	Denb	SJ0336	52°55·0'	3°26·2'W	X	125
Pentre	Denb	SJ0348	53°1·5'	3°26·4'W	X	116
Pentre	Denb	SJ0376	53°16·6'	3°26·9'W	X	116

Pentre	Denb	SJ0379	53°18·2'	3°26·9'W	X	116
Pentre	Denb	SJ0755	53°5·3'	3°22·9'W	X	116
Pentre	Denb	SJ1049	53°2·1'	3°20·1'W	X	116
Pentre	Denb	SJ1458	53°7·0'	3°16·7'W	T	116
Pentre	Flint	SJ1671	53°14·0'	3°15·1'W	X	116
Pentre	Flint	SJ1764	53°10·2'	3°14·1'W	T	116
Pentre	Flint	SJ1778	53°17·8'	3°14·3'W	X	116
Pentre	Flint	SJ2459	53°7·6'	3°7·7'W	T	117
Pentre	Flint	SJ2463	53°9·8'	3°7·8'W	T	117
Pentre	Flint	SJ3267	53°12·0'	3°0·7'W	T	117
Pentre	Gwyn	SH6361	53°8·0'	4°2·5'W	X	115
Pentre	Gwyn	SH9042	52°58·1'	3°37·9'W	X	125
Pentre	Heref	SO3343	52°5·1'	2°58·3'W	X	148,149,161
Pentre	Monm	SO3006	51°45·1'	3°0·5'W	X	161
Pentre	Monm	SO4200	51°42·0'	2°50·0'W	X	171
Pentre	Monm	SO4401	51°42·5'	2°48·2'W	X	171
Pentre	Pemb	SM9729	51°55·6'	4°56·8'W	X	157,158
Pentre	Pemb	SN2340	52°2·1'	4°34·4'W	X	145
Pentre	Powys	SJ0515	52°43·7'	3°24·0'W	X	125
Pentre	Powys	SJ0525	52°49·1'	3°24·2'W	T	125
Pentre	Powys	SJ0907	52°39·4'	3°20·3'W	X	125
Pentre	Powys	SJ1015	52°43·8'	3°19·6'W	X	125
Pentre	Powys	SJ1109	52°40·5'	3°18·6'W	X	125
Pentre	Powys	SJ1513	52°42·7'	3°15·1'W	T	125
Pentre	Powys	SJ1719	52°46·0'	3°13·4'W	X	125
Pentre	Powys	SJ1928	52°50·8'	3°11·8'W	X	125
Pentre	Powys	SJ2405	52°38·5'	3°7·0'W	T	126
Pentre	Powys	SN9582	52°25·8'	3°32·3'W	X	136
Pentre	Powys	SN9595	52°32·8'	3°32·5'W	X	136
Pentre	Powys	SN9858	52°12·9'	3°29·2'W	X	147
Pentre	Powys	SO0686	52°28·1'	3°22·6'W	T	136
Pentre	Powys	SO0753	52°10·3'	3°21·2'W	X	147
Pentre	Powys	SO0867	52°17·8'	3°20·6'W	X	136,147
Pentre	Powys	SO1450	52°8·7'	3°15·0'W	X	148
Pentre	Powys	SO1545	52°6·0'	3°14·1'W	X	148
Pentre	Powys	SO1588	52°29·2'	3°14·7'W	X	136
Pentre	Powys	SO1641	52°3·9'	3°13·1'W	X	148,161
Pentre	Powys	SO1947	52°7·2'	3°10·6'W	X	148
Pentre	Powys	SO2157	52°12·6'	3°9·0'W	X	148
Pentre	Powys	SO2466	52°17·5'	3°6·5'W	X	137,148
Pentre	Powys	SO2792	52°31·5'	3°4·2'W	T	137
Pentre	Rho Cyn Taf	SS9696	51°39·4'	3°29·8'W	T	170
Pentre	Shrops	SJ2326	52°49·8'	3°8·2'W	T	126
Pentre	Shrops	SJ3237	52°55·8'	3°0·3'W	T	126
Pentre	Shrops	SJ3617	52°45·1'	2°56·5'W	T	126
Pentre	Shrops	SO3076	52°22·9'	3°1·3'W	X	137,148
Pentre	Wrex	SJ1334	52°54·0'	3°17·2'W	X	125
Pentre	Wrex	SJ2840	52°57·4'	3°3·9'W	T	117
Pentre	Wrex	SJ3141	52°58·0'	3°1·2'W	T	117
Pentre Aaron	Shrops	SJ2935	52°54·7'	3°2·9'W	X	126
Pentreath	Corn	SW5728	50°6·4'	5°23·5'W	X	203
Pentreath Beach	Corn	SW6912	49°58·0'	5°12·9'W	X	203
Pentrebach	Carm	SN8233	51°59·2'	3°42·7'W	T	160
Pentre-bâch	Cered	SN5547	52°6·4'	4°6·6'W	X	146
Pentre-bach	Cered	SN6490	52°29·7'	3°59·8'W	X	135
Pentre-bach	Conwy	SH8156	53°5·5'	3°46·2'W	X	116
Pentre-bâch	Flint	SJ2261	53°8·7'	3°9·6'W	X	117
Pentre-bach	Gwyn	SH3944	52°58·4'	4°23·5'W	X	123
Pentrebach	Merth Tyd	SO0603	51°43·3'	3°21·3'W	T	170
Pentre Bach	Powys	SH9812	52°42·0'	3°30·2'W	X	125
Pentre-bach	Powys	SN9033	51°59·3'	3°35·7'W	T	160
Pentrebach	Powys	SN9753	52°10·2'	3°30·0'W	X	147
Pentrebach	Powys	SO1825	51°55·3'	3°11·2'W	X	161
Pentrebach	Rho Cyn Taf	ST0889	51°35·8'	3°19·3'W	T	170
Pentrebach	Swan	SN6005	51°43·8'	4°1·2'W	T	159
Pentre-bach	Torf	ST2892	51°37·6'	3°2·0'W	X	171
Pentrebane	Card	ST1278	51°29·9'	3°15·7'W	T	171
Pentre-beidiog	Conwy	SH9264	53°10·0'	3°36·5'W	X	116
Pentre Berw	I of Angl	SH4772	53°13·6'	4°17·1'W	T	114,115
Pentre-bont	Conwy	SH7352	53°3·3'	3°53·3'W	T	115
Pentre Brook	Powys	SO0463	52°15·6'	3°24·0'W	W	147
Pentre Broughton	Wrex	SJ3052	53°3·9'	3°2·3'W	T	117
Pentre-bwlch	Denb	SJ1949	53°2·2'	3°12·1'W	X	116
Pentre Bychan	Wrex	SJ3047	53°1·2'	3°2·2'W	T	117
Pentre-caeau	Powys	SO0844	52°5·4'	3°20·2'W	X	147,160
Pentrecagal	Carm	SN2830	51°56·8'	4°29·8'W	X	145
Pentrecagal	Carm	SN3340	52°2·2'	4°25·7'W	X	145
Pentre-cefn	Shrops	SJ2327	52°50·3'	3°8·2'W	T	126
Pentre-celyn	Denb	SJ1453	53°4·3'	3°16·6'W	T	116
Pentre-celyn	Powys	SH8905	52°38·1'	3°38·0'W	X	124,125
Pentre-cerrig	Denb	SJ1960	53°8·1'	3°12·2'W	X	116
Pentre-chwyth	Swan	SS6795	51°38·5'	3°54·9'W	T	159
Pentre Cilgwyn	Wrex	SJ2236	52°55·2'	3°9·2'W	T	126
Pentre-clawdd	Shrops	SJ2932	52°53·1'	3°2·9'W	T	126
Pentre-clawdd	Wrex	SJ3144	52°59·6'	3°1·3'W	X	117
Pentreclwydau	Nth Pt Talb	SN8405	51°44·1'	3°40·4'W	X	160
Pentre Cöch	Denb	SJ1555	53°5·4'	3°15·7'W	X	116
Pentre Coch Manor	Denb	SJ1556	53°5·9'	3°15·8'W	X	116
Pentre Coed	Heref	SO2849	52°8·3'	3°2·7'W	X	148
Pentre-coed	Shrops	SJ3026	52°49·9'	3°1·9'W	X	126
Pentre-coed	Shrops	SJ3538	52°56·4'	2°57·6'W	T	126
Pentre Coed Dingle	Heref	SO2850	52°8·9'	3°2·7'W	X	148
Pentre-cwm	Conwy	SH8946	53°0·2'	3°38·8'W	X	116
Pentre Cwm	Denb	SJ0677	53°17·1'	3°24·2'W	X	116
Pentrecwm	Powys	SJ2026	52°49·8'	3°10·8'W	X	126
Pentre-cŵm	Powys	SO2891	52°31·0'	3°3·3'W	X	137
Pentre-cwrt	Carm	SN3838	52°1·2'	4°21·3'W	T	145
Pentre-cyffin	Powys	SJ0314	52°43·1'	3°25·8'W	X	125
Pentre-Dafydd	Shrops	SJ2832	52°53·1'	3°3·8'W	X	126
Pentre-Davis	Carm	SN5720	51°51·9'	4°4·2'W	X	159
Pentre Dolau Honddu	Powys	SN9943	52°4·8'	3°28·0'W	T	147,160
Pentre-draen	Powys	SO2351	52°9·4'	3°7·1'W	X	148
Pentre-du	Cered	SN6567	52°17·3'	3°58·4'W	X	135
Pentre-du	Conwy	SH7756	53°5·5'	3°49·8'W	X	115
Pentre-du	Conwy	SH9369	53°12·7'	3°35·7'W	X	116
Pentre-du	Conwy	SJ0169	53°12·8'	3°28·5'W	X	116
Pentre-duldog	Gwyn	SH8937	52°55·4'	3°38·7'W	X	124,125
Pentredwr	Denb	SJ1946	53°0·6'	3°12·0'W	T	116
Pentre-dwr	Swan	SS6996	51°39·1'	3°53·2'W	T	170
Pentre Eirianell	I of Angl	SH4787	53°21·7'	4°17·5'W	X	114

Pentre Evan	Carm	SN5434	51°59·4'	4°7·2'W	X	146
Pentref	Powys	SJ2520	52°46·6'	3°6·3'W	X	126
Pentrefelen	Cered	SN4458	52°12·1'	4°16·6'W	X	146
Pentrefelin	Carm	SN5923	51°53·5'	4°2·6'W	T	159
Pentrefelin	Cered	SN6149	52°7·6'	4°1·4'W	T	146
Pentrefelin	Conwy	SH8074	53°15·2'	3°47·5'W	T	116
Pentrefelin	Denb	SJ2043	52°58·9'	3°11·1'W	T	117
Pentrefelin	Gwyn	SH5239	52°55·9'	4°11·7'W	T	124
Pentrefelin	I of Angl	SH4392	53°24·3'	4°21·3'W	T	114
Pentrefelin	Powys	SJ1524	52°48·7'	3°15·3'W	X	125
Pentre-Ffwrndan	Flint	SJ2572	53°14·6'	3°7·0'W	T	117
Pentre-ffynnon Hall	Flint	SJ1379	53°18·3'	3°17·9'W	X	116
Pentre Fm	Denb	SJ0862	53°9·1'	3°22·1'W	FM	116
Pentre Fm	Denb	SJ1264	53°10·2'	3°18·6'W	FM	116
Pentre Fm	Flint	SJ2755	53°5·5'	3°5·0'W	FM	117
Pentre Fm	Gwyn	SH7110	52°40·6'	3°54·1'W	FM	124
Pentre Fm	Monm	SO3218	51°51·6'	2°58·9'W	FM	161
Pentre Fm	Monm	SO3317	51°51·1'	2°58·0'W	FM	161
Pentre Fm	Monm	SO3412	51°48·4'	2°57·0'W	FM	161
Pentre Fm	Nth Pt Talb	SS8485	51°33·4'	3°40·0'W	FM	170
Pentre Fm	Powys	SJ3415	52°44·0'	2°58·2'W	FM	126
Pentre Fm	Shrops	SJ2626	52°49·8'	3°5·5'W	FM	126
Pentre Fm	V of Glam	ST0473	51°27·1'	3°22·5'W	FM	170
Pentrefoelas	Conwy	SH8751	53°2·9'	3°40·7'W	T	116
Pentref-y-groes	Caer	ST1998	51°40·7'	3°9·9'W	T	171
Pentrefynys	Carm	SN4225	51°54·3'	4°17·4'W	X	146
Pentregaer	Shrops	SJ2328	52°50·9'	3°8·2'W	X	126
Pentre Galar	Pemb	SN1731	51°57·1'	4°39·4'W	T	145
Pentregat	Cered	SN3551	52°8·2'	4°24·3'W	X	145
Pentre Glas	Pemb	SN1529	51°56·0'	4°41·1'W	X	145,158
Pentregof	I of Angl	SH3692	53°24·2'	4°27·6'W	X	114
Pentregrove	Heref	SO2348	52°7·7'	3°7·1'W	X	148
Pentre-Gwenlais	Carm	SN6016	51°49·7'	4°1·5'W	T	159
Pentregwine	Cered	SN2543	52°3·7'	4°32·8'W	X	145
Pentre-gwnnws	Cered	SN6869	52°18·4'	3°55·8'W	X	135
Pentre Gwyddel	I of Angl	SH2875	53°14·9'	4°34·3'W	X	114
Pentregwyn	Powys	SN9533	51°59·4'	3°31·4'W	X	160
Pentre Gwynfryn	Gwyn	SH5927	52°49·6'	4°5·2'W	T	124
Pentrehaearn Fm	Nth Pt Talb	SN7402	51°42·4'	3°49·0'W	FM	170
Pentre Halkyn	Flint	SJ1972	53°14·6'	3°12·4'W	X	116
Pentre Halkyn	Flint	SJ2072	53°14·6'	3°11·5'W	T	117
Pentre-hardd	Carm	SN5907	51°44·9'	4°2·2'W	X	159
Pentreheulyn	I of Angl	SH3890	53°23·2'	4°25·7'W	X	114
Pentreheylin	Shrops	SJ3636	52°55·3'	2°56·7'W	X	126
Pentreheyling	Shrops	SO2493	52°32·0'	3°6·8'W	T	137
Pentreheylin Hall	Powys	SJ2519	52°46·0'	3°6·3'W	X	126
Pentreheylin Hall	Shrops	SJ3019	52°46·1'	3°1·8'W	X	126
Pentre-Higgen	Heref	SO2539	52°2·9'	3°5·2'W	X	161
Pentrehobin	Flint	SJ2562	53°9·2'	3°6·9'W	A	117
Pentre Hodre	Shrops	SO3276	52°22·9'	2°59·5'W	T	137,148
Pentrehowell	Carm	SN2414	51°48·1'	4°32·8'W	X	158
Pentrehwnt	V of Glam	SS9275	51°28·1'	3°32·9'W	X	170
Pentre Ifan	Pemb	SN0938	52°0·7'	4°46·6'W	X	145
Pentre Ifan (Burial Chamber)	Pemb	SN0936	51°59·6'	4°46·5'W	A	145
Pentre-Isaf	Carm	SN2936	52°0·0'	4°29·1'W	X	145
Pentre Isaf	Conwy	SH8768	53°12·1'	3°41·1'W	T	116
Pentre Isaf	Conwy	SH9871	53°13·8'	3°31·3'W	X	116
Pentre Isaf	Denb	SJ1347	53°1·0'	3°17·4'W	X	116
Pentre Isaf	Denb	SJ1949	53°2·2'	3°12·1'W	X	116
Pentre-isaf	Powys	SJ2021	52°47·1'	3°10·8'W	X	126
Pentre-isaf	Wrex	SJ3041	52°58·0'	3°2·1'W	X	117
Pentrejack	Heref	SO2850	52°8·9'	3°2·7'W	X	148
Pentrekendrick	Shrops	SJ2834	52°54·2'	3°3·8'W	X	126
Pentre Llanrhaeadr	Denb	SJ0862	53°9·1'	3°22·1'W	T	116
Pentre llawen	Conwy	SJ0042	52°58·2'	3°28·9'W	X	125
Pentre Llifior	Powys	SO1498	52°34·6'	3°15·7'W	T	136
Pentre-Lloegr	Powys	SN9833	51°59·4'	3°28·7'W	X	160
Pentre-lludw	Powys	SH9403	52°37·1'	3°33·5'W	X	136
Pentrellwyn	Cered	SN4142	52°3·5'	4°18·8'W	T	146
Pentrellwyn	I of Angl	SH5781	53°18·6'	4°8·4'W	X	114,115
Pentre-llwyn-llwyd	Powys	SN9654	52°10·7'	3°30·9'W	T	147
Pentre-llyn	Cered	SN6175	52°21·6'	4°2·1'W	X	135
Pentre-llyn-cymmer	Conwy	SH9752	53°3·6'	3°31·8'W	T	116
Pentre Madoc	Shrops	SJ3436	52°55·3'	2°58·5'W	X	126
Pentre Maelor	Wrex	SJ3749	53°2·3'	2°56·0'W	T	117
Pentre Mailyn	Wrex	SJ3546	53°0·7'	2°57·7'W	X	117
Pentremawr	Carm	SN4326	51°54·9'	4°16·6'W	X	146
Pentre-mawr	Denb	SJ0073	53°14·9'	3°29·5'W	X	116
Pentre-mawr	Denb	SJ1066	53°11·3'	3°20·4'W	X	116
Pentre-mawr	Flint	SJ0979	53°18·3'	3°21·5'W	X	116
Pentre-mawr	Gwyn	SH5822	52°46·9'	4°5·9'W	X	124
Pentremawr	Powys	SH8903	52°37·0'	3°38·0'W	X	135,136
Pentre Meyrick	V of Glam	SS9675	51°28·1'	3°29·4'W	T	170
Pentremeiley	Heref	SO2449	52°8·3'	3°6·2'W	X	148
Pentre-moel	Powys	SO0741	52°3·8'	3°21·0'W	X	147,160
Pentre Morgan	Shrops	SJ3336	52°55·3'	2°59·4'W	X	126
Pentrenant Hall	Powys	SO2391	52°30·9'	3°7·7'W	X	137
Pentrenewbury	Powys	SO0836	52°1·1'	3°20·0'W	X	160
Pentrenewydd	Carm	SN3213	51°47·7'	4°25·8'W	X	159
Pentre-newydd	Shrops	SJ2636	52°55·2'	3°5·6'W	T	126
Pentre-pant	Shrops	SJ2831	52°52·5'	3°3·8'W	X	126
Pentre Pant	Wrex	SJ1434	52°54·0'	3°16·3'W	X	125
Pentre Parr	Carm	SN6523	51°53·6'	3°57·3'W	X	159
Pentre perfa	Shrops	SJ3020	52°46·6'	3°1·9'W	X	126
Pentre-piod	Gwyn	SH8930	52°51·6'	3°38·5'W	X	124,125
Pentre-poeth	Carm	SN4115	51°48·9'	4°18·0'W	X	159
Pentre-Poeth	Carm	SN5001	51°41·5'	4°9·8'W	T	159
Pentre-poeth	Newp	ST2686	51°34·3'	3°3·7'W	T	171
Pentre-Poid	Torf	SO2602	51°42·9'	3°3·9'W	T	171
Pentre-potes	Denb	SJ0556	53°5·8'	3°24·7'W	X	116
Pentre'r beirdd	Powys	SJ1813	52°42·7'	3°12·4'W	T	125
Pentre'r Felin	Conwy	SH8069	53°12·5'	3°47·4'W	T	116
Pentre'r-felin	Denb	SJ1165	53°10·7'	3°19·5'W	T	116
Pentre'r-felin	Powys	SN9130	51°57·7'	3°34·8'W	T	160
Pentre'r-gof	Powys	SJ1812	52°42·2'	3°12·4'W	X	125
Pentre-rhew	Cered	SN6654	52°10·3'	3°57·2'W	X	146
Pentre'rhydd	Carm	SN3821	51°52·1'	4°20·8'W	X	145,159
Pentre-shannel	Shrops	SJ2527	52°50·4'	3°6·0'W	X	126
Pentresite	Carm	SN4525	51°54·4'	4°14·8'W	X	146

Pentre-Sollars	Powys	SO1436	52°1·2'	3°14·8'W	X	161
Pentre-tafarn-y-fedw	Conwy	SH8162	53°8·8'	3°46·4'W	X	116
Pentre-tai-yn-y-cwm	Gwyn	SH9540	52°57·1'	3°33·4'W	X	125
Pentre-tân	Swan	SN6208	51°45·5'	3°59·6'W	X	159
Pentre, The	Monm	SO2815	51°50·0'	3°2·3'W	X	161
Pentre-traeth	I of Angl	SH3374	53°14·5'	4°29·8'W	X	114
Pentretrewyn	Denb	SJ0843	52°58·8'	3°21·8'W	X	125
Pentre Tump	Powys	SO1957	52°12·6'	3°10·7'W	H	148
Pentre-ty-gwyn	Carm	SN8135	52°0·3'	3°43·6'W	T	160
Pentre-uchaf	Conwy	SH8777	53°16·9'	3°41·3'W	T	116
Pentre-Uchaf	Denb	SJ1071	53°13·9'	3°20·5'W	X	116
Pentreuchaf	Gwyn	SH3539	52°55·6'	4°26·9'W	T	123
Pentre Uchaf	Powys	SJ0209	52°40·4'	3°26·6'W	X	125
Pentre-uchaf	Shrops	SJ2921	52°47·2'	3°2·8'W	X	126
Pentrewain-Ho	Monm	ST3399	51°41·4'	2°57·8'W	X	171
Pentrewern	Gwyn	SH8216	52°44·0'	3°44·5'W	X	124,125
Pentre-Willy	Powys	SO2791	52°31·0'	3°4·1'W	X	137
Pentre-wyman	Carm	SN3714	51°48·3'	4°21·5'W	X	159
Pentrewyn	Carm	SN3212	51°47·1'	4°25·8'W	X	159
Pentrich	Derby	SK3852	53°4·1'	1°25·6'W	T	119
Pentrichlane-end	Derby	SK3751	53°3·5'	1°26·5'W	X	119
Pentridge	Dorset	SU0317	50°57·4'	1°57·1'W	T	184
Pentridge Hill	Dorset	SU0417	50°57·4'	1°56·2'W	X	184
Pentrisil	Pemb	SN0634	51°58·5'	4°49·1'W	X	145
Pentrobin Fm	Flint	SJ3063	53°9·8'	3°2·4'W	FM	117
Pen-troydin	Pemb	SN1417	51°49·5'	4°41·6'W	X	158
Pen Trumau	Powys	SO2029	51°57·5'	3°9·5'W	X	161
Pen Trum-gwr	Gwyn	SH6502	52°36·2'	3°59·2'W	H	135
Pentruse Fm	Corn	SW9070	50°29·8'	4°57·3'W	FM	200
Pen-trwyn	Conwy	SH7883	53°20·0'	3°49·5'W	X	115
Pentwd Isaf	Cered	SN1845	52°4·7'	4°39·0'W	X	145
Pen-twyn	Brig	SS8886	51°33·9'	3°36·6'W	X	170
Pentwyn	Caer	SO1004	51°43·9'	3°17·8'W	T	171
Pen-twyn	Caer	SO2000	51°41·8'	3°9·1'W	T	171
Pen-twyn	Caer	ST2185	51°33·7'	3°8·0'W	X	171
Pentwyn	Card	ST0981	51°31·5'	3°18·3'W	X	171
Pentwyn	Card	ST2081	51°31·6'	3°8·8'W	T	171
Pen-twyn	Carm	SN5611	51°47·0'	4°4·9'W	T	159
Pentwyn	Carm	SN5706	51°44·3'	4°3·9'W	X	159
Pen-twyn	Carm	SN6943	52°4·4'	3°54·3'W	X	146,160
Pen-twyn	Carm	SN7830	51°57·5'	3°46·1'W	X	146,160
Pentwyn	Carm	SN8134	51°59·7'	3°43·6'W	X	160
Pentwyn	Heref	SO2736	52°1·3'	3°3·4'W	X	161
Pentwyn	Monm	SO2821	51°53·2'	3°2·4'W	X	161
Pentwyn	Monm	SO3724	51°54·9'	2°54·6'W	X	161
Pen-twyn	Monm	SO4112	51°48·4'	2°51·0'W	X	161
Pen-twyn	Monm	SO5210	51°47·4'	2°41·4'W	X	162
Pentwyn	Monm	ST3999	51°41·4'	2°52·6'W	A	171
Pentwyn	Powys	SN9434	51°59·9'	3°32·2'W	X	160
Pentwyn	Powys	SO0231	51°58·4'	3°25·2'W	X	160
Pen-twyn	Powys	SO0624	51°54·6'	3°21·6'W	X	160
Pentwyn	Powys	SO0731	51°58·4'	3°20·8'W	X	160
Pentwyn	Powys	SO0824	51°54·7'	3°19·9'W	X	160
Pentwyn	Powys	SO1048	52°7·6'	3°18·5'W	X	148
Pentwyn	Powys	SO1129	51°57·4'	3°17·3'W	X	161
Pentwyn	Powys	SO1251	52°9·3'	3°16·8'W	X	148
Pen-twyn	Powys	SO1822	51°53·7'	3°11·1'W	X	161
Pentwyn	Powys	SO1872	52°20·6'	3°11·8'W	X	136,148
Pentwyn	Powys	SO1949	52°8·2'	3°10·6'W	X	148
Pentwyn	Powys	SO2323	51°54·3'	3°6·8'W	X	161
Pen-twyn	Powys	SO2454	52°11·0'	3°6·3'W	X	148
Pen-twyn	Powys	SO2518	51°51·6'	3°5·0'W	X	161
Pen-twyn	Rho Cyn Taf	ST0696	51°39·5'	3°21·1'W	X	170
Pen-twyn	Torf	SO2603	51°43·5'	3°3·9'W	T	171
Pentwyn Berthlwyd	Merth Tyd	ST1096	51°39·6'	3°17·7'W	T	171
Pen-twyn Camp	Heref	SO2248	52°7·7'	3°8·0'W	A	148
Pentwyn Fm	Carm	SN5608	51°45·4'	4°4·8'W	FM	159
Pentwyn Fm	Heref	SO2942	52°4·5'	3°1·8'W	FM	148,161
Pentwyn Fm	Monm	SO3203	51°43·5'	2°58·7'W	FM	171
Pentwyn Fm	Monm	SO3306	51°45·2'	2°57·8'W	FM	161
Pen Twyn Glas	Powys	SO2125	51°55·3'	3°8·5'W	X	161
Pentwyn House Fm	Monm	ST4199	51°41·4'	2°50·8'W	FM	171
Pen-twyn-isaf	Rho Cyn Taf	SO0010	51°47·0'	3°26·6'W	X	160
Pentwyn-mawr	Caer	ST1996	51°39·7'	3°9·9'W	T	171
Pen Twyn Mawr	Powys	SO2426	51°55·9'	3°5·9'W	H	161
Pentwyn Mawr	Swan	SN6408	51°45·5'	3°57·8'W	H	159
Pentwyn Reservoir	Powys	SO0515	51°49·8'	3°22·3'W	W	160
Penty	N Lanak	NS8358	55°48·3'	3°51·6'W	X	65,72
Pentylands Fm	Swin	SU1894	51°38·6'	1°44·0'W	FM	163,173
Pentyparc	Cered	SN5166	52°16·6'	4°10·6'W	X	135
Penty Park	Pemb	SN0122	51°51·9'	4°53·0'W	X	145,157,158
Pentyrch	Card	ST1082	51°32·0'	3°17·5'W	T	171
Pentyrch	Powys	SJ0608	52°39·9'	3°23·0'W	X	125
Pentyrch	Powys	SJ0708	52°39·9'	3°22·1'W	X	125
Pentyrch-isaf	Gwyn	SH4141	52°56·8'	4°21·6'W	X	123
Pentyrch-uchaf	Gwyn	SH4341	52°56·9'	4°19·8'W	X	123
Penucha	Flint	SJ1073	53°15·0'	3°20·5'W	X	116
Penuchadre	V of Glam	SS8973	51°26·9'	3°35·5'W	X	170
Pen-uchaf	Flint	SJ1172	53°14·5'	3°19·6'W	X	116
Penuchagreen Fm	Denb	SJ0370	53°13·3'	3°26·8'W	FM	116
Pen-ucha'r-cwm	Flint	SJ1468	53°12·4'	3°16·9'W	X	116
Pen-Uchar Plwyf	Flint	SJ1772	53°14·6'	3°14·2'W	T	116
Penuwch	Carm	SN2718	51°50·3'	4°30·3'W	X	158
Penuwch	Cered	SN5962	52°14·5'	4°3·5'W	X	146
Penuwch	Cered	SN6577	52°22·7'	3°58·6'W	X	135
Penvalla	Scot Bord	NT1539	55°38·5'	3°20·6'W	H	72
Penvay	Powys	SN8929	51°57·1'	3°36·5'W	X	160
Penventinue	Corn	SX1153	50°21·0'	4°39·5'W	X	200,204
Penventon	Corn	SX1662	50°26·0'	4°35·1'W	X	201
Penventon Fm	Corn	SW6426	50°5·5'	5°17·6'W	FM	203
Penveny	Scot Bord	NT1639	55°38·5'	3°19·6'W	H	72
Penveor Point	Corn	SX0039	50°13·3'	4°47·9'W	X	204
Penvith	Corn	SX2855	50°22·4'	4°24·8'W	X	201
Penvorder	Corn	SX0976	50°33·4'	4°41·4'W	X	200
Penvose	Corn	SW8943	50°15·2'	4°57·2'W	X	204
Penvose	Corn	SW9441	50°14·2'	4°53·0'W	X	204
Penvose Fm	Corn	SW8564	50°26·4'	5°1·3'W	FM	200
Penvose Fm	Corn	SX0577	50°33·9'	4°44·8'W	FM	200
Penwar	Powys	SN9286	52°27·9'	3°35·0'W	X	136
Penwarden	Corn	SX3269	50°30·0'	4°21·8'W	X	201

Penwarne	Corn	SW7730	50°7·9'	5°6·9'W	X	204
Penwarne	Corn	SX0144	50°16·0'	4°47·2'W	X	204
Penwartha	Corn	SW7552	50°19·7'	5°9·3'W	T	200,204
Penwartha Coombe	Corn	SW7652	50°19·8'	5°8·5'W	T	200,204
Penwartha Ho	Corn	SW7549	50°18·1'	5°9·2'W	X	204
Penwaun	Cered	SN1544	52°4·1'	4°41·6'W	X	145
Penwaundwr	Powys	SN9022	51°53·4'	3°35·5'W	X	160
Penwaun Fm	Carm	SN3033	51°58·4'	4°28·1'W	FM	145
Penweathers	Corn	SW8043	50°15·0'	5°4·8'W	T	204
Penwell Ho	N Yks	SE2893	54°20·2'	1°33·7'W	X	99
Penwenallt	Cered	SN2841	52°2·7'	4°30·1'W	X	145
Penwenallt	Cered	SN4763	52°14·9'	4°14·1'W	X	146
Penwenallt Fm	Pemb	SN2041	52°2·5'	4°37·1'W	FM	145
Penwenham	Corn	SX1890	50°41·1'	4°34·2'W	X	190
Penwern	Cered	SN4256	52°11·0'	4°18·3'W	X	146
Penwern	Cered	SN4543	52°4·1'	4°15·3'W	X	146
Pen-wern	Cered	SN5160	52°13·3'	4°10·5'W	X	146
Penwern	Pemb	SN1037	52°0·2'	4°45·7'W	X	145
Penwern	Pemb	SN1345	52°4·6'	4°43·3'W	X	145
Penwern	Powys	SO0028	51°56·7'	3°26·9'W	X	160
Penwernddu	Pemb	SN2440	52°2·1'	4°33·6'W	X	145
Penwernfach	Cered	SN2643	52°3·7'	4°31·9'W	X	145
Penwernfawr	Cered	SN2643	52°3·7'	4°31·9'W	X	145
Penwhaile	D & G	NX5663	54°56·7'	4°14·5'W	X	83
Penwhapple Burn	S Ayr	NX2397	55°14·4'	4°46·6'W	W	76
Penwhapple Reservoir	S Ayr	NX2697	55°14·4'	4°43·8'W	W	76
Penwhirn Burn	D & G	NX1170	54°59·6'	4°56·8'W	W	76
Penwhirn Reservoir	D & G	NX1269	54°59·1'	4°55·9'W	W	82
Penwine	Corn	SX0673	50°31·7'	4°43·9'W	X	200
Penwithick	Corn	SX0256	50°22·5'	4°46·7'W	T	200
Penwood	Hants	SU4461	51°21·0'	1°21·7'W	T	174
Pen Wood	Somer	ST5109	50°52·9'	2°41·4'W	F	194
Penwood Fm	Shrops	SJ6223	52°48·4'	2°33·4'W	FM	127
Penwood Ho	Corn	SX1176	50°33·4'	4°39·7'W	X	200
Penwortham Lane	Lancs	SD5326	53°43·9'	2°42·3'W	T	102
Penwyllt	Powys	SN8515	51°49·5'	3°39·7'W	T	160
Penwyrlod	Powys	SO2525	51°55·3'	3°5·0'W	X	161
Penyard Park	Heref	SO6122	51°53·9'	2°33·6'W	F	162
Pen-y-back	Carm	SN1914	51°48·0'	4°37·1'W	X	158
Pen-y-bair	Powys	SO2721	51°53·2'	3°3·2'W	X	161
Pen-y-bal	Pemb	SN0441	52°2·2'	4°51·1'W	X	145
Pen-y-Ball Top	Flint	SJ1775	53°16·2'	3°14·3'W	T	116
Pen-y-banc	Carm	SN4321	51°52·2'	4°16·4'W	T	159
Pen-y-banc	Carm	SN4437	52°0·8'	4°16·0'W	X	146
Penybanc	Carm	SN6111	51°47·1'	4°0·5'W	T	159
Pen-y-banc	Carm	SN6124	51°54·1'	4°0·8'W	X	159
Pen-y-banc	Carm	SN7026	51°55·3'	3°53·0'W	X	146,160
Pen-y-banc	Carm	SN7338	52°1·8'	3°50·7'W	X	146,160
Pen-y-banc	Cered	SN3146	52°5·4'	4°27·6'W	X	145
Pen-y-banc	Cered	SN4460	52°13·2'	4°16·6'W	X	146
Pen-y-banc	Conwy	SH9850	53°2·5'	3°30·9'W	X	116
Pen-y-banc	Denb	SJ0749	53°2·1'	3°22·8'W	X	116
Pen-y-banc	Monm	ST3494	51°38·7'	2°56·8'W	X	171
Pen-y-banc	Powys	SN8648	52°7·4'	3°39·5'W	X	147
Pen-y-banc	Powys	SN8987	52°28·4'	3°37·7'W	X	135,136
Penybanc	Powys	SN9176	52°22·5'	3°35·7'W	X	136,147
Pen-y-banc	Powys	SN9884	52°26·9'	3°29·7'W	X	136
Pen-y-banc	Powys	SO1151	52°9·2'	3°17·7'W	X	148
Pen-y-bank	Caer	SO1103	51°43·4'	3°16·9'W	T	171
Penybank	Carm	SN3121	51°52·0'	4°26·9'W	X	145,159
Pen y bank	Pemb	SM8929	51°55·4'	5°3·7'W	X	157,158
Pen-y-Bank	Powys	SJ1802	52°36·8'	3°12·3'W	X	136
Penybank	Powys	SO1079	52°24·3'	3°19·0'W	X	136,148
Pen y Bannau	Cered	SN7466	52°16·9'	3°50·4'W	H	135,147
Penybedd	Carm	SN4102	51°41·9'	4°17·7'W	T	159
Pen y Bedw	Conwy	SH7847	53°0·6'	3°48·7'W	H	115
Pen-y-bedw	Conwy	SH7848	53°1·2'	3°48·7'W	X	115
Pen-y-bedw	Wrex	SJ1737	52°55·7'	3°13·7'W	X	125
Pen-y-belan	Powys	SJ1204	52°37·8'	3°17·6'W	X	136
Pen y Benar	Conwy	SH7350	53°2·2'	3°53·2'W	H	115
Pen-y-benglog	Pemb	SN1138	52°0·7'	4°44·9'W	X	145
Pen y Berth	Powys	SJ0812	52°42·1'	3°21·3'W	X	125
Pen-y-bonc	I of Angl	SH2181	53°18·0'	4°40·8'W	X	114
Pen y Boncyn Trefeilw	Gwyn	SH9628	52°50·6'	3°32·2'W	H	125
Pen y Boncyn Trefeilw	Gwyn	SH9628	52°50·6'	3°32·2'W	H	125
Pen-y-Bont	Blae Gw	SO2105	51°44·5'	3°8·3'W	T	161
Pen-y-bont	Carm	SN3027	51°55·2'	4°27·9'W	T	145
Pen-y-bont	Carm	SN7836	52°0·8'	3°46·3'W	X	146,160
Penybont	Cered	SN6288	52°28·6'	4°1·5'W	T	135
Pen-y-bont	Cered	SN6661	52°14·1'	3°57·3'W	X	146
Pen-y-bont	Cered	SN6871	52°19·5'	3°55·8'W	X	135
Pen-y-bont	Conwy	SH7848	53°1·2'	3°48·7'W	X	115
Pen-y-bont	Conwy	SH8280	53°18·5'	3°45·9'W	X	116
Pen-y-bont	Denb	SJ0443	52°58·8'	3°25·4'W	X	125
Pen-y-Bont	Gwyn	SH2928	52°49·6'	4°31·9'W	X	123
Pen-y-bont	Gwyn	SH6028	52°50·1'	4°4·3'W	T	124
Pen-y-bont	Gwyn	SH7401	52°35·8'	3°51·2'W	X	135
Pen-y-bont	Gwyn	SH8730	52°51·6'	3°40·3'W	X	124,125
Pen-y-bont	I of Angl	SH2878	53°16·5'	4°34·4'W	X	114
Pen-y-bont	Powys	SJ0110	52°41·0'	3°27·5'W	X	125
Penybont	Powys	SO1164	52°16·3'	3°17·9'W	T	148
Pen y bont	Wrex	SJ1834	52°54·1'	3°12·7'W	X	125
Pen-y-bont	Wrex	SJ2841	52°57·9'	3°3·9'W	X	117
Pen-y-bontbren-uchaf	Cered	SN6688	52°28·7'	3°58·0'W	X	135
Pen-y-Bont Fm	I of Angl	SH4168	53°11·4'	4°22·4'W	FM	114,115
Pen-y-Bont Fm	I of Angl	SH4168	53°11·4'	4°22·4'W	FM	114,115
Pen-y-bont Hall	Powys	SJ2123	52°48·2'	3°9·9'W	X	126
Pen-y-bont Llanerch Emrys	Powys	SJ2123	52°48·2'	3°9·9'W	T	126
Penybont Sta	Powys	SO0964	52°16·2'	3°19·6'W	X	147
Penybont Uchaf	Powys	SN8550	52°8·4'	3°40·4'W	X	147
Pen-y-braich	Powys	SJ0316	52°44·2'	3°25·8'W	X	125
Penybryn	Caer	ST1396	51°39·6'	3°15·1'W	T	171
Pen-y-Bryn	Carm	SN4437	52°0·8'	4°16·0'W	X	146
Pen-y-bryn	Carm	SN6044	52°4·8'	4°2·2'W	X	146
Pen y Bryn	Cered	SN7173	52°20·6'	3°53·2'W	H	135,147
Pen-y-bryn	Conwy	SH8170	53°13·1'	3°46·5'W	X	116
Pen-y-bryn	Conwy	SH8249	53°1·8'	3°45·2'W	X	116
Pen-y-Bryn	Conwy	SH8471	53°13·6'	3°43·9'W	X	116
Pen-y-bryn	Conwy	SH8866	53°11·0'	3°40·2'W	X	116
Pen-y-bryn	Conwy	SH9274	53°15·4'	3°36·7'W	X	116

Pen-y-bryn	Denb	SJ0264	53°10·1'	3°27·6'W	X	116
Pen-y-Bryn	Denb	SJ0375	53°16·0'	3°26·9'W	X	116
Pen-y-bryn	Denb	SJ0762	53°9·1'	3°23·0'W	X	116
Pen-y bryn	Denb	SJ0963	53°9·6'	3°21·3'W	X	116
Pen-y-Bryn	Denb	SJ1642	52°58·4'	3°14·7'W	X	125
Pen-y-bryn	Denb	SJ1961	53°8·6'	3°12·3'W	X	116
Pen-y-Bryn	Denb	SJ2052	53°3·8'	3°11·2'W	X	117
Pen-y-Bryn	Flint	SJ1468	53°12·4'	3°16·9'W	X	116
Pen-y-bryn	Gwyn	SH1525	52°47·7'	4°44·2'W	X	123
Pen-y-bryn	Gwyn	SH2132	52°51·6'	4°39·1'W	X	123
Penybryn	Gwyn	SH2434	52°52·7'	4°36·5'W	X	123
Pen-y-bryn	Gwyn	SH4338	52°55·2'	4°19·7'W	X	123
Pen y bryn	Gwyn	SH4538	52°55·3'	4°17·9'W	X	123
Pen-y-Bryn	Gwyn	SH4938	52°55·3'	4°14·4'W	T	123
Pen-y-bryn	Gwyn	SH5825	52°48·5'	4°6·0'W	X	124
Pen-y-bryn	Gwyn	SH6169	53°12·2'	4°4·5'W	X	115
Pen-y-bryn	Gwyn	SH6572	53°13·9'	4°0·9'W	X	115
Pen-y-bryn	Gwyn	SH6919	52°45·4'	3°56·1'W	T	124
Pen-y-bryn	Gwyn	SH7525	52°48·7'	3°50·9'W	X	124
Pen-y-bryn	Gwyn	SH9940	52°57·1'	3°29·8'W	X	125
Pen-y-bryn	Gwyn	SJ0142	52°58·2'	3°28·0'W	X	125
Pen-y-bryn	I of Angl	SH4977	53°16·4'	4°15·5'W	X	114,115
Pen-y-bryn	I of Angl	SH5979	53°17·6'	4°6·5'W	X	114,115
Pen-y-bryn	Nth Pt Talb	SS8384	51°32·8'	3°40·9'W	X	170
Pen-y-Bryn	Pemb	SN1742	52°3·0'	4°39·7'W	T	145
Pen-y-Bryn	Powys	SJ1604	52°37·9'	3°14·1'W	T	136
Pen-y-bryn	Powys	SJ1824	52°48·7'	3°12·6'W	X	126
Pen-y-bryn	Powys	SJ2221	52°47·1'	3°9·0'W	X	126
Pen-y-bryn	Powys	SN8199	52°34·8'	3°45·0'W	X	135,136
Pen-y-bryn	Powys	SO0789	52°29·7'	3°21·8'W	X	136
Pen y bryn	Powys	SO1832	51°59·1'	3°11·3'W	X	161
Pen-y-bryn	Shrops	SJ3235	52°54·7'	3°0·3'W	X	126
Pen-y-Bryn	Shrops	SJ3238	52°56·3'	3°0·3'W	T	126
Pen-y-Bryn	V of Glam	SS9871	51°26·0'	3°27·7'W	X	170
Pen-y-bryn	Wrex	SJ1533	52°53·5'	3°15·4'W	X	125
Pen-y-bryn	Wrex	SJ1834	52°54·1'	3°12·7'W	X	125
Pen-y-bryn	Wrex	SJ2438	52°56·3'	3°7·4'W	X	126
Pen-y-bryn	Wrex	SJ2644	52°59·5'	3°5·7'W	T	117
Pen-y-bryn	Wrex	SJ4843	52°59·2'	2°46·1'W	A	117
Penybryn Fm	Denb	SJ0274	53°15·5'	3°27·7'W	FM	116
Pen-y-bryn Hall	Powys	SO2494	52°32·6'	3°6·8'W	X	137
Pen-y-bryniau	Denb	SJ0147	53°0·9'	3°28·1'W	X	116
Pen-y-Bryn Uchaf	Conwy	SH8376	53°16·3'	3°44·9'W	X	116
Penybwlch	Cered	SN5878	52°23·1'	4°4·8'W	X	135
Pen-y-bwlch	Cered	SN7863	52°15·3'	3°46·8'W	H	146,147
Pen-y-bwlch	Gwyn	SH5560	53°7·3'	4°9·6'W	X	114,115
Pen-y-bwlch	Gwyn	SH5965	53°10·1'	4°6·2'W	X	114,115
Pen y Bwlch	Powys	SN9367	52°17·7'	3°34·2'W	X	136,147
Pen y Bwlch Gwyn	Gwyn	SH9341	52°57·6'	3°35·2'W	X	125
Pen y Bylchau	Powys	SJ0519	52°45·9'	3°24·1'W	H	125
Pen-y-Bythod	Gwyn	SH4455	53°4·4'	4°19·3'W	X	115,123
Pen-y-cae	Brig	SS9082	51°31·8'	3°34·8'W	T	170
Pen-y-cae	Denb	SJ0662	53°9·1'	3°23·9'W	X	116
Pen-y-cae	Nth Pt Talb	SN8804	51°43·7'	3°36·9'W	X	170
Pen-y-cae	Nth Pt Talb	SS7789	51°35·4'	3°46·1'W	T	170
Pen-y-cae	Powys	SN8413	51°48·5'	3°40·6'W	T	160
Penycae	Powys	SO2146	52°6·6'	3°8·8'W	X	148
Pen-y-cae	Rho Cyn Taf	SN9507	51°45·4'	3°30·9'W	X	160
Penycae	Wrex	SJ2745	53°0·1'	3°4·9'W	T	117
Pen-y-caeau	Caer	ST2398	51°40·8'	3°6·4'W	X	171
Pen-y-Cae Fm	V of Glam	SS9269	51°24·8'	3°32·8'W	FM	170
Pen-y-cae-mawr	Monm	ST4195	51°39·3'	2°50·8'W	T	171
Penycaerau	Gwyn	SH1927	52°48·9'	4°40·7'W	T	123
Pen-y-castell	Brig	SS8482	51°31·7'	3°39·9'W	X	170
Pen-y-castell	Cered	SN5368	52°17·7'	4°8·9'W	X	135
Pen y Castell	Cered	SN6375	52°21·6'	4°0·3'W	X	135
Penycastell	Cered	SN6667	52°17·3'	3°57·5'W	A	135
Pen y Castell	Cered	SN6884	52°26·5'	3°56·1'W	X	135
Pen y Castell	Conwy	SH7268	53°11·9'	3°54·6'W	H	115
Pen y Castell	Nth Pt Talb	SS7891	51°36·5'	3°45·3'W	X	170
Pen-y-castell	Powys	SN9888	52°29·1'	3°29·7'W	X	136
Penycastell	Powys	SO1387	52°28·7'	3°16·5'W	A	136
Penycefn	Cered	SN6585	52°27·0'	3°58·8'W	X	135
Pen-y-cefn	Cered	SN6960	52°13·6'	3°54·7'W	X	146
Pen-y-cefn	Conwy	SH8763	53°9·4'	3°41·0'W	X	116
Pen-y-cefn	Flint	SJ1175	53°16·1'	3°19·7'W	T	116
Pen-y-Cefn-Isaf	Flint	SJ0878	53°17·7'	3°22·4'W	X	116
Pen y Cerrig Duon	Gwyn	SH9527	52°50·1'	3°33·1'W	H	125
Pen-y-ceunant	Powys	SJ0823	52°48·0'	3°21·5'W	X	125
Penychain	Gwyn	SH4236	52°54·1'	4°20·6'W	X	123
Pen-ychain	Gwyn	SH4335	52°53·6'	4°19·6'W	X	123
Pen y Cil	Gwyn	SH1523	52°46·6'	4°44·2'W	X	123
Penyclawdd	Monm	SO3120	51°52·7'	2°59·8'W	X	161
Pen-y-clawdd	Monm	SO4507	51°45·8'	2°47·4'W	T	161
Pen-y-clawdd	Powys	SO1870	52°19·6'	3°11·8'W	X	136,148
Pen-y-clawdd Fm	Denb	SJ2045	53°0·0'	3°11·1'W	FM	117
Pen y Clipiau	Gwyn	SH8410	52°40·8'	3°42·6'W	H	124,125
Penycloddiau	Flint	SJ1267	53°11·9'	3°18·6'W	H	116
Pen-y-cnap	Carm	SN5121	51°52·3'	4°9·5'W	A	159
Pen y Cnwc	Powys	SN8256	52°11·6'	3°43·2'W	X	147
Penycoed	Caer	ST1698	51°40·7'	3°12·5'W	X	171
Pen-y-coed	Carm	SN2117	51°49·6'	4°35·5'W	X	158
Pen-y-coed	Carm	SN2718	51°50·3'	4°30·3'W	X	158
Penycoed	Carm	SN3514	51°48·3'	4°23·2'W	X	159
Pen-y-coed	Carm	SN3623	51°53·1'	4°22·6'W	X	145,159
Penycoed	Carm	SN4418	51°50·6'	4°15·5'W	X	159
Penycoed	Carm	SN6221	51°52·5'	3°59·9'W	X	159
Pen-y-Coed	Conwy	SH9671	53°13·8'	3°33·1'W	X	116
Pen-y-coed	Denb	SJ0461	53°8·5'	3°25·7'W	X	116
Pen-y-coed	Denb	SJ0545	52°59·9'	3°24·5'W	X	116
Pen-y-coed	Denb	SJ2058	53°7·0'	3°11·3'W	X	117
Pen-y-coed	Gwyn	SH7218	52°44·9'	3°53·4'W	X	124
Penycoed	Pemb	SN1338	52°0·8'	4°43·1'W	X	145
Pen-y-coed	Powys	SH8105	52°38·0'	3°45·1'W	X	124,125
Pen-y-coed	Powys	SH9714	52°43·1'	3°31·1'W	X	125
Pen-y-coed	Powys	SJ1407	52°39·5'	3°15·9'W	X	125
Pen-y-coed	Powys	SJ2414	52°43·3'	3°7·1'W	X	126
Pen y Coed	Powys	SN9989	52°29·6'	3°28·9'W	X	136
Pen-y-coed	Shrops	SJ2723	52°48·2'	3°4·6'W	T	126
Pen-y-coedcae	Rho Cyn Taf	ST0687	51°34·7'	3°21·0'W	X	170

Pen-y-coed Fm	Powys	SO1497	52°34·1'	3°15·7'W	FM	136
Pen-y-coed-uchaf	Cered	SN5852	52°9·1'	4°4·1'W	X	146
Pen-y-corddyn-mawr	Conwy	SH9176	53°16·4'	3°37·7'W	H	116
Pen-y-corddyn-mawr (Fort)	Conwy	SH9176	53°16·4'	3°37·7'W	A	116
Penycraig	Powys	SO1149	52°8·2'	3°17·6'W	X	148
Pen y Craig-Lâs	Powys	SJ0324	52°48·5'	3°25·9'W	X	125
Pen-y-creigiau	Powys	SJ0711	52°41·6'	3°22·2'W	X	125
Penycrocbren	Powys	SN8593	52°31·6'	3°41·3'W	H	135,136
Penycrocbren (Roman Fortlet)	Powys	SN8593	52°31·6'	3°41·3'W	R	135,136
Pen-y-crug	Gwyn	SH6109	52°39·9'	4°2·9'W	H	124
Pen-y-crug	Powys	SO0230	51°57·8'	3°25·2'W	A	160
Pen y Cwar	Swan	SN6308	51°45·5'	3°58·7'W	X	159
Pen-y-cwarl Fm	Caer	ST1793	51°38·0'	3°11·6'W	FM	171
Pen-y-cwm	Cered	SN6485	52°27·0'	3°59·7'W	X	135
Pen y Cwm	Gwyn	SH7630	52°51·4'	3°50·1'W	H	124
Penycwm	Pemb	SM8523	51°52·1'	5°7·0'W	T	157
Pen-y-cwm	Shrops	SO3179	52°24·5'	3°0·5'W	X	137,148
Pen y Cyfrwy	Pemb	SM7524	51°52·4'	5°15·7'W	X	157
Pen y Darren	Carm	SN7845	52°5·6'	3°46·5'W	X	146,147
Pen-y-Darren	Merth Tyd	SO0507	51°45·5'	3°22·2'W	T	160
Penydarren Fm	Nth Pt Talb	SN7407	51°45·1'	3°49·1'W	FM	160
Pen-y-dderi	Nth Pt Talb	SN7410	51°46·7'	3°49·2'W	X	160
Pen y Ddinas	Carm	SN6235	52°0·0'	4°0·2'W	H	146
Pen y Ddinas	Powys	SN8648	52°7·4'	3°39·5'W	H	147
Pen-y-ddôl	Powys	SN9791	52°30·7'	3°30·7'W	X	136
Pen y dinas	Gwyn	SH6020	52°45·8'	4°4·1'W	A	124
Penydre	Swan	SN6902	51°42·3'	3°53·4'W	T	170
Pen-y-fai	Brig	SS8982	51°31·8'	3°35·6'W	T	170
Pen-y-fai	Carm	SN4901	51°41·5'	4°10·7'W	T	159
Pen-y-fan	Carm	SS5199	51°40·4'	4°8·9'W	T	159
Pen-y-fan	Monm	SO5305	51°44·7'	2°40·5'W	T	162
Pen y Fan	Powys	SO0121	51°53·0'	3°25·9'W	X	160
Pen-y-fan Bellaf	I of Angl	SH4878	53°16·9'	4°16·4'W	X	114,115
Pen-y-fan Pond	Caer	SO1900	51°41·8'	3°9·9'W	W	171
Penyfedw	Carm	SN4012	51°47·3'	4°18·8'W	X	159
Penyfeidr	Pemb	SM8726	51°53·8'	5°5·4'W	T	157
Pen-y-felin	Denb	SJ0640	52°57·2'	3°23·5'W	X	125
Pen-y-felin	Flint	SJ1569	53°12·9'	3°16·0'W	T	116
Penyffordd	Powys	SJ0112	52°42·0'	3°27·5'W	X	125
Pen-y-ffordd	Conwy	SH9677	53°17·0'	3°33·2'W	X	116
Pen-y-ffordd	Denb	SJ0278	53°17·6'	3°27·8'W	T	116
Pen-y-ffordd	Flint	SJ1381	53°19·4'	3°18·0'W	T	116
Penyffordd	Flint	SJ3061	53°8·7'	3°2·4'W	T	117
Pen-y-fforest	Powys	SO1943	52°5·0'	3°10·5'W	X	148,161
Pen-y-ffridd	Conwy	SH8769	53°12·6'	3°41·1'W	X	116
Pen-y-Ffridd	Denb	SJ2154	53°4·9'	3°10·4'W	X	117
Penyffridd	Gwyn	SH5056	53°5·1'	4°14·0'W	T	115
Penyffridd	Gwyn	SH9734	52°53·9'	3°31·5'W	X	125
Pen-y-ffridd	Powys	SJ1129	52°51·3'	3°18·9'W	H	125
Pen y Ffridd Cownwy	Powys	SH9717	52°44·7'	3°31·2'W	X	125
Pen-y-Ffrith	Conwy	SH8772	53°14·2'	3°41·2'W	X	116
Pen-y-ffrith	Conwy	SH9368	53°12·1'	3°35·7'W	X	116
Pen-y-ffrith	Denb	SH9355	53°5·1'	3°35·5'W	X	116
Pen-y-ffynnon	Powys	SN9865	52°16·7'	3°29·3'W	X	136,147
Pen-y-fodau-fawr	Swan	SS6097	51°39·5'	4°1·1'W	X	159
Pen y Foel	Brig	SS9189	51°35·6'	3°34·0'W	H	170
Pen-y-Foel	Denb	SJ2156	53°6·0'	3°10·4'W	X	117
Pen y Foel	Gwyn	SH6639	52°56·1'	3°59·2'W	H	124
Pen-y-foel	I of Angl	SH3089	53°22·5'	4°32·9'W	X	114
Pen-y-foel	Powys	SJ1414	52°43·3'	3°16·0'W	H	125
Pen-y-foel	Powys	SJ1705	52°38·4'	3°13·2'W	X	125
Pen y Foel	Powys	SJ2621	52°47·1'	3°5·4'W	T	126
Pen y Foel	Powys	SN8350	52°8·4'	3°42·2'W	X	147
Pen y Foel	Powys	SN8981	52°25·2'	3°37·5'W	X	135,136
Pen-y-fron	Conwy	SH8371	53°13·6'	3°44·8'W	X	116
Pen-y-fron	Conwy	SH8662	53°8·8'	3°41·9'W	X	116
Pen-y-fyddin	Conwy	SH8870	53°13·2'	3°40·2'W	X	116
Penyfynwent	I of Angl	SH4388	53°22·2'	4°21·2'W	A	114
Penygadair	Conwy	SH7369	53°12·4'	3°53·7'W	X	115
Penygadair	Gwyn	SH7113	52°42·2'	3°54·2'W	H	124
Pen y Gadair Fawr	Powys	SO2228	51°56·9'	3°7·7'W	H	161
Pen-y-gaer	Carm	SN5243	52°4·2'	4°9·2'W	A	146
Pen Y Gaer	Carm	SN7838	52°1·9'	3°46·3'W	X	146,160
Pen-y-gaer	Cered	SN2949	52°7·0'	4°29·5'W	X	145
Pen-y-gaer	Cered	SN5156	52°11·2'	4°10·4'W	A	146
Pen-y-gaer	Cered	SN5758	52°12·3'	4°5·2'W	A	146
Pen-y-Gaer	Cered	SN6360	52°13·5'	4°0·0'W	A	146
Pen-y-gaer	Conwy	SH7569	53°12·4'	3°51·9'W	A	115
Pen-y-gaer	Conwy	SH9647	53°0·9'	3°32·6'W	X	116
Pen y gaer	Denb	SJ1054	53°4·8'	3°20·2'W	A	116
Pen-y-gaer	Gwyn	SH2928	52°49·6'	4°31·9'W	A	123
Pen-y-gaer	Gwyn	SH4245	52°59·0'	4°20·8'W	A	115,123
Pen-y-gaer	Gwyn	SH5845	52°59·3'	4°6·5'W	A	115
Pen-y-gaer	Gwyn	SH6267	53°11·2'	4°3·5'W	A	115
Pen-y-gaer	Powys	SN9086	52°27·9'	3°36·8'W	A	136
Pen y Gaer	Powys	SO0615	51°49·8'	3°21·5'W	X	160
Pen-y-gaer	Powys	SO1397	52°34·1'	3°16·6'W	A	136
Pen-y-gaer	Powys	SO1497	52°34·1'	3°15·7'W	A	136
Pen-y-gaer	Powys	SO1621	51°53·1'	3°12·8'W	X	161
Pen-y-gaer	Swan	SS5395	51°38·3'	4°7·1'W	A	159
Pen-y-gaer (Roman Fort)	Powys	SO1621	51°53·1'	3°12·8'W	R	161
Pen-y-Garfan	Cered	SN7251	52°8·8'	3°51·8'W	H	146,147
Pen y Garn	Carm	SN3137	52°0·6'	4°27·4'W	H	145
Pen-y-garn	Carm	SN5731	51°57·8'	4°4·5'W	X	146
Pen-y-garn	Cered	SN6285	52°27·0'	4°1·4'W	T	135
Pen y Garn	Cered	SN7977	52°22·9'	3°46·3'W	H	135,147
Pen y Garn	Gwyn	SH6210	52°40·5'	4°2·1'W	H	124
Pen y Garn	Powys	SN8450	52°8·4'	3°41·3'W	X	147
Penygarn	Torf	SO2801	51°42·4'	3°2·1'W	T	171
Pen-y-garnedd	Conwy	SH8456	53°5·6'	3°43·5'W	X	116
Pen-y-garnedd	I of Angl	SH5376	53°15·9'	4°11·8'W	T	114,115
Penygarnedd	Powys	SJ1023	52°48·1'	3°19·7'W	T	125
Penygarn Fm	Monm	SO5109	51°46·9'	2°42·2'W	FM	162
Pen y Garn-goch	Powys	SN8850	52°8·5'	3°37·8'W	H	147
Penygarreg	Carm	SN5235	51°59·9'	4°9·0'W	X	146
Pen y Garreg	Gwyn	SH4245	52°59·0'	4°20·8'W	X	115,123
Pen-y-garreg	Gwyn	SH7309	52°40·1'	3°52·3'W	X	124
Pen-y-garreg	Powys	SO0246	52°6·5'	3°25·7'W	X	147
Pen-y-garreg Fm	Caer	SO1300	51°41·8'	3°15·1'W	FM	171

Penygarreg Resr	Powys	SN9067	52°17·6′	3°36·4′W	W	136,147
Pen-y-garth	Conwy	SH8164	53°9·8′	3°46·4′W	X	116
Pen-y-garth	Denb	SJ0859	53°7·5′	3°22·1′W	X	116
Pen-y-garth	Flint	SJ2165	53°10·8′	3°10·5′W	X	117
Pen-y-Garth	Gwyn	SH9334	52°53·8′	3°35·0′W	X	125
Pen y Garth	Powys	SJ1213	52°42·7′	3°17·8′W	H	125
Penygarth	Powys	SJ1418	52°45·4′	3°16·1′W	X	125
Pen-y-gelli	Flint	SJ1868	53°12·4′	3°13·3′W	X	116
Pen-y-Gelli	Gwyn	SH5064	53°9·4′	4°14·2′W	X	114,115
Pen-y-gelli	Gwyn	SH8839	52°56·4′	3°39·6′W	X	124,125
Pen-y-gelli	Gwyn	SH9119	52°45·7′	3°36·5′W	X	125
Penygelli	Powys	SO1291	52°30·8′	3°17·4′W	T	136
Pen-y-gelli	Wrex	SJ2437	52°55·7′	3°7·4′W	X	126
Penygenhill	Powys	SO1939	52°2·8′	3°10·5′W	X	161
Pen-y-gerddi	Denb	SJ0363	53°9·6′	3°26·6′W	X	116
Pen y-geulan	Conwy	SH8350	53°2·3′	3°44·3′W	X	116
Pen-y-ghent	N Yks	SD8373	54°9·4′	2°15·2′W	H	98
Pen-y-ghent Fell	N Yks	SD8573	54°9·4′	2°13·4′W	X	98
Pen-y-ghent Gill	N Yks	SD8674	54°9·9′	2°12·4′W	X	98
Pen-y-ghent Ho	N Yks	SD8673	54°9·4′	2°12·4′W	X	98
Penyghent Pot	N Yks	SD8273	54°9·4′	2°16·1′W	X	98
Pen-y-ghent Side	N Yks	SD8374	54°9·9′	2°15·2′W	X	98
Penyglôg	Powys	SN8097	52°33·7′	3°45·8′W	X	135,136
Pen-y-Gogarth or Great Ormes Head	Conwy	SH7683	53°20·0′	3°51·3′W	X	115
Pen y Gop	Conwy	SH9444	52°59·2′	3°34·3′W	X	125
Penygorddyn	Powys	SJ0814	52°43·2′	3°21·3′W	A	125
Penygoron	Powys	SJ1501	52°36·2′	3°14·9′W	X	136
Pen-y-gors	Pemb	SM8625	51°53·2′	5°6·2′W	X	157
Pen-y-gors	Swan	SN6208	51°45·5′	3°59·6′W	X	159
Penygraig	Carm	SN2824	51°53·5′	4°29·6′W	X	145,158
Penygraig	Carm	SN3630	51°56·9′	4°22·8′W	X	145
Pen-y-Graig	Cered	SN2151	52°7·9′	4°36·5′W	X	145
Pen-y-graig	Cered	SN2741	52°2·7′	4°31·0′W	X	145
Pen-y-graig	Cered	SN3946	52°5·6′	4°20·6′W	X	145
Penygraig	Cered	SN5572	52°19·9′	4°7·3′W	X	135
Pen-y-graig	Cered	SN5778	52°23·1′	4°5·7′W	X	135
Penygraig	Cered	SN5878	52°23·1′	4°4·8′W	X	135
Pen-y-graig	Cered	SN7067	52°17·4′	3°54·0′W	X	135,147
Pen-y-graig	Denb	SJ2640	52°57·4′	3°5·7′W	X	117
Pen-y-graig	Gwyn	SH2033	52°52·1′	4°40·1′W	T	123
Pen-y-graig	Gwyn	SH8713	52°42·4′	3°40·0′W	X	124,125
Pen y Graig	I of Angl	SH3974	53°14·6′	4°24·4′W	X	114
Pen-y-graig	Monm	SO2215	51°49·9′	3°7·5′W	X	161
Pen-y-graig	Monm	SO2516	51°50·5′	3°4·9′W	X	161
Pen-y-graig	Powys	SJ0512	52°42·1′	3°24·0′W	H	125
Pen-y-graig	Powys	SJ1228	52°50·8′	3°18·0′W	X	125
Pen-y-graig	Powys	SJ1528	52°50·8′	3°15·3′W	X	125
Pen-y-graig	Powys	SO1045	52°6·0′	3°18·4′W	X	148
Pen-y-graig	Powys	SO1138	52°2·2′	3°17·5′W	X	161
Penygraig	Rho Cyn Taf	SS9991	51°36·8′	3°27·1′W	T	170
Pen y Graig-ddu	Cered	SN7082	52°25·5′	3°54·3′W	X	135
Pen-y-graig Fm	Monm	SO2713	51°48·9′	3°3·1′W	FM	161
Pen y Graig Gron	Conwy	SH7462	53°8·7′	3°52·6′W	X	115
Pen-y-graig-isaf	Powys	SJ2125	52°49·2′	3°9·9′W	X	126
Penygraigwen	I of Angl	SH4487	53°21·7′	4°20·3′W	T	114
Pen-y-graig y Rhystud	Carm	SN3826	51°54·8′	4°20·9′W	X	145
Pen-y-gribin	Conwy	SH9772	53°14·3′	3°32·2′W	X	116
Pen-y-groes	Carm	SN5813	51°48·1′	4°3·2′W	T	159
Penygroes	Gwyn	SH4653	53°3·4′	4°17·5′W	T	115,123
Penygroes	Pemb	SN1535	51°59·2′	4°41·3′W	T	145
Pen-y-groes	Rho Cyn Taf	ST1187	51°34·7′	3°16·7′W	X	171
Pen-y-groeslon	Gwyn	SH2130	52°50·5′	4°39·1′W	T	123
Pen y Gurnos	Cered	SN7751	52°8·9′	3°47·5′W	H	146,147
Pen-y-gwaith	Conwy	SH7760	53°7·6′	3°49·9′W	X	115
Pen y Gwely	Powys	SJ2133	52°53·6′	3°10·1′W	X	126
Pen-y-gwely Resr	Powys	SJ2232	52°53·0′	3°9·1′W	W	126
Penygwernydd	Cered	SN7273	52°20·7′	3°52·3′W	X	135,147
Pen-y-Gwryd Hotel	Gwyn	SH6655	53°4·8′	3°59·6′W	X	115
Pen-y-gyrn	Powys	SH8304	52°37·5′	3°43·3′W	X	135,136
Pen-y-holt Bay	Pemb	SR8995	51°37·1′	5°2·5′W	W	158
Pen-y-lan	Brig	SS8493	51°37·7′	3°40·2′W	X	170
Pen-y-lan	Brig	SS9582	51°31·9′	3°30·4′W	X	170
Pen-y-lan	Brig	SS9684	51°33·0′	3°29·6′W	X	170
Pen-y-lan	Card	ST1978	51°29·9′	3°9·6′W	T	171
Penylan	Cered	SN2343	52°3·7′	4°34·5′W	X	145
Pen-y-lan	Heref	SO2743	52°5·1′	3°3·5′W	X	148,161
Pen-y-lan	Heref	SO3327	51°56·5′	2°58·1′W	X	161
Pen-y-lan	Monm	SO4416	51°50·6′	2°48·4′W	X	161
Pen-y-lan	Monm	ST3497	51°40·3′	2°56·9′W	X	171
Pen-y-lan	Monm	ST4290	51°36·6′	2°49·9′W	X	171,172
Pen-y-lan	Newp	ST2585	51°33·8′	3°4·5′W	T	171
Pen-y-lan	Powys	SJ1512	52°42·2′	3°15·1′W	X	125
Pen-y-lan	Powys	SJ2201	52°36·3′	3°8·7′W	X	126
Pen-y-lan	Powys	SN8932	51°58·8′	3°36·6′W	X	160
Pen-y-lan	Powys	SO0041	52°3·7′	3°27·1′W	X	147,160
Pen-y-lan	Powys	SO1921	51°53·1′	3°10·2′W	X	161
Pen y Lan	Rho Cyn Taf	ST0494	51°38·4′	3°22·9′W	X	170
Pen-y-lan	V of Glam	SS9976	51°28·7′	3°26·9′W	T	170
Pen-y-lan	Wrex	SJ3241	52°58·0′	3°0·3′W	X	117
Pen-y-lan Fm	Brig	SS8983	51°32·3′	3°35·6′W	FM	170
Pen-y-lan Fm	Heref	SO3826	51°56·0′	2°53·7′W	FM	161
Penylan Fm	Newp	ST2584	51°33·2′	3°4·5′W	FM	171
Pen-y-lan Hill	Merth Tyd	SO0403	51°43·3′	3°23·0′W	X	170
Penylan Home Fm	Carm	SN5525	51°54·5′	4°6·1′W	FM	146
Pen-y-lan Home Fm	Wrex	SJ3241	52°58·0′	3°0·3′W	FM	117
Pen-y-llan	Shrops	SJ2828	52°50·9′	3°3·7′W	X	126
Pen-y-llan	Wrex	SJ3547	53°1·2′	2°57·7′W	X	117
Pen-y-lôn	Denb	SH9961	53°8·4′	3°30·2′W	X	116
Pen-y-maen Berthgoed	Cered	SN7664	52°15·9′	3°48·6′W	X	146,147
Pen-y-maes	Carm	SN4213	51°47·8′	4°17·1′W	X	159
Pen-y-maes	Denb	SJ0765	53°10·7′	3°23·1′W	X	116
Pen-y-maes	Denb	SJ0855	53°5·3′	3°22·0′W	X	116
Pen-y-maes	Flint	SJ1976	53°16·7′	3°12·5′W	T	116
Pen-y-maes	Powys	SO2141	52°3·9′	3°8·8′W	X	148,161
Pen y Manllwyn	Powys	SO2031	51°58·5′	3°9·5′W	X	161
Pen-y-moor Fm	Heref	SO3143	52°5·1′	3°0·0′W	FM	148,161
Pen y Mwdwl	Conwy	SH9266	53°11·1′	3°36·6′W	H	116
Penymynydd	Brig	SS8080	51°30·6′	3°43·4′W	X	170
Pen-y-mynydd	Denb	SJ0876	53°16·6′	3°22·4′W	X	116
Penymynydd	Flint	SJ3062	53°9·3′	3°2·4′W	T	117
Pen-y-mynydd	Pemb	SM9936	51°59·4′	4°55·3′W	X	157
Penymynydd	V of Glam	SS9679	51°30·3′	3°29·5′W	X	170
Penymynydd Mawr	Pemb	SN0231	51°56·8′	4°52·5′W	X	145,157
Pen-y-nant	Powys	SJ1722	52°47·6′	3°13·5′W	X	125
Penynant	Wrex	SJ3041	52°58·0′	3°2·1′W	X	117
Pen-y-Palmant	Denb	SJ0475	53°16·0′	3°26·0′W	X	116
Pen-y-parc	Carm	SN3435	51°59·6′	4°24·7′W	X	145
Pen y parc	Cered	SN3556	52°10·9′	4°24·4′W	X	145
Pen-y-parc	Conwy	SH7960	53°7·7′	3°48·1′W	X	115
Pen-y-parc	Flint	SJ1376	53°16·7′	3°17·9′W	X	116
Pen-y-parc	Flint	SJ2169	53°13·0′	3°10·6′W	X	117
Pen-y-Parc	Flint	SJ2759	53°7·6′	3°5·1′W	X	117
Pen-y-parc	I of Angl	SH3664	53°9·1′	4°26·7′W	X	114
Pen-y-parc	I of Angl	SH5874	53°14·9′	4°7·3′W	X	114,115
Pen-y-parc	Monm	SO3319	51°52·2′	2°58·0′W	X	161
Pen-y-Parc	Monm	SO4008	51°46·3′	2°51·8′W	X	161
Pen-y-Parc	Monm	ST3596	51°39·8′	2°56·0′W	X	171
Pen-y-parc	Monm	ST5097	51°40·4′	2°43·0′W	X	162
Pen-y-parc	Powys	SJ0310	52°41·0′	3°25·7′W	X	125
Pen-y-Parc	Powys	SJ0916	52°44·3′	3°20·5′W	X	125
Penyparc	Powys	SJ1619	52°46·0′	3°14·3′W	X	125
Pen-y-parc	Powys	SN9727	51°56·2′	3°29·5′W	X	160
Pen-y-parc	Rho Cyn Taf	ST0793	51°37·9′	3°20·2′W	X	170
Pen-y-parc	Rho Cyn Taf	ST0795	51°39·0′	3°20·3′W	X	170
Pen-y-Parc	Shrops	SJ3121	52°47·2′	3°1·0′W	X	126
Pen-y-parc Wood	Powys	SJ1700	52°35·7′	3°13·1′W	F	136
Pen-y-Park	Heref	SO2744	52°5·6′	3°3·5′W	T	148,161
Pen-y-Pass	Gwyn	SH6455	53°4·7′	4°1·4′W	X	115
Pen y Pigyns	Powys	SN9397	52°33·9′	3°34·3′W	X	136
Pen-y-pound	Monm	SO2914	51°49·4′	3°1·4′W	X	161
Penyraber	Pemb	SM9537	51°59·9′	4°58·8′W	T	157
Pen yr Afr	Pemb	SN1148	52°6·1′	4°45·2′W	X	145
Pen-y-raglan-wynt	Carm	SN7449	52°7·7′	3°50·1′W	X	146,147
Pen-yr-allt	Carm	SN2525	51°54·0′	4°32·2′W	X	145,158
Penyrallt	Carm	SN3837	52°0·7′	4°21·2′W	X	145
Pen-yr-allt	Carm	SN4821	51°52·3′	4°12·1′W	X	159
Pen-yr-allt	Cered	SN4347	52°6·2′	4°17·1′W	X	146
Pen-yr-allt	Conwy	SH7857	53°6·0′	3°48·9′W	X	115
Pen-yr-allt	Flint	SJ2861	53°8·7′	3°4·2′W	X	117
Pen-yr-allt	Gwyn	SH9142	52°58·1′	3°37·0′W	X	125
Pen-yr-allt	Gwyn	SH9640	52°57·1′	3°32·5′W	X	125
Pen-yr-allt	I of Angl	SH4375	53°15·2′	4°20·8′W	X	114,115
Pen-yr-allt	Pemb	SN1429	51°55·9′	4°41·9′W	X	145,158
Pen-yr-allt	Powys	SJ0216	52°44·2′	3°26·7′W	X	125
Pen-yr-allt	Powys	SJ1623	52°48·1′	3°14·4′W	X	125
Penyrallt	Powys	SO1032	51°59·0′	3°18·2′W	X	161
Penyrargae	I of Angl	SH3284	53°19·8′	4°31·0′W	X	114
Pen-yr-englyn	Rho Cyn Taf	SS9497	51°39·9′	3°31·6′W	T	170
Pen-yr-eryr	Wrex	SJ1135	52°54·5′	3°19·0′W	H	125
Pen-yr-estyn	Shrops	SJ3527	52°50·4′	2°57·5′W	X	126
Pen yr Helgi Du	Conwy	SH6962	53°8·6′	3°57·1′W	H	115
Pen yr Helyg	Carm	SN7616	51°50·0′	3°47·6′W	X	160
Pen yr Henblas	Flint	SJ1872	53°14·6′	3°13·3′W	X	116
Pen-yr-heol	Brig	SS9282	51°31·8′	3°33·0′W	T	170
Pen-yr-heol	Brig	SS9686	51°34·0′	3°29·6′W	X	170
Penyrheol	Caer	ST1488	51°35·3′	3°14·1′W	T	171
Pen-yr-heol	Monm	SO4311	51°47·9′	2°49·2′W	T	161
Pen-yr-heol	Monm	ST4195	51°39·3′	2°50·8′W	X	171
Pen-yr-heol	Rho Cyn Taf	ST0195	51°38·9′	3°25·5′W	X	170
Penyrheol	Swan	SS5594	51°37·8′	4°5·3′W	X	159
Penyrheol	Swan	SS5899	51°40·5′	4°2·8′W	T	159
Penyrheol	Torf	ST2899	51°41·3′	3°2·1′W	T	171
Pen-yr-heol	V of Glam	SS9673	51°27·0′	3°29·4′W	X	170
Pen-yr-heol	V of Glam	SS9971	51°26·0′	3°26·8′W	X	170
Penyrheolddu	Carm	SN6615	51°49·3′	3°56·3′W	X	159
Pen-yr-heol-lâs	Merth Tyd	SO1702	51°42·9′	3°11·7′W	X	171
Pen y Rhestr	Powys	SN9258	52°12·8′	3°34·5′W	X	147
Pen-y-rhiw	Rho Cyn Taf	ST0688	51°35·2′	3°21·0′W	T	170
Pen yr Hwbyn	Cered	SN1851	52°7·9′	4°39·2′W	X	145
Pen-yr-ochr	Powys	SN9173	52°20·9′	3°35·6′W	X	136,147
Pen yr Ole Wen	Conwy	SH6561	53°8·0′	4°0·7′W	H	115
Pen yr Orsedd	Conwy	SH8955	53°5·1′	3°39·0′W	H	116
Pen-yr-Orsedd	Flint	SJ2167	53°11·9′	3°10·6′W	X	117
Pen-yr-orsedd	I of Angl	SH3183	53°19·3′	4°31·8′W	X	114
Penyrorsedd	I of Angl	SH3292	53°24·1′	4°31·2′W	X	114
Pen-yr-orsedd	I of Angl	SH3390	53°23·1′	4°30·3′W	X	114
Penyrorsedd	I of Angl	SH3879	53°17·2′	4°25·4′W	X	114
Penyrorsedd	I of Angl	SH4569	53°12·0′	4°18·8′W	X	114,115
Penyrwrlodd	Powys	SO1531	51°58·5′	3°13·9′W	X	161
Penyrwrlodd	Powys	SO2239	52°2·9′	3°7·9′W	X	161
Pen-yr-wyrlod	Powys	SO1828	51°56·9′	3°11·2′W	X	161
Penysarn	I of Angl	SH4590	53°23·3′	4°19·4′W	T	114
Penysgwarne	Pemb	SM9138	52°0·3′	5°2·3′W	X	157
Penysgwarne Fm	Pemb	SM8430	51°55·8′	5°8·1′W	FM	157
Pen-y-stryt	Denb	SJ1951	53°3·3′	3°12·1′W	T	116
Pen-y-trwyn	Caer	ST1991	51°37·0′	3°9·8′W	X	171
Pen-y-wal	Rho Cyn Taf	ST0592	51°37·4′	3°22·0′W	X	170
Penywaun	Caer	ST1294	51°38·5′	3°15·9′W	X	171
Pen-y-waun	Caer	ST1690	51°36·4′	3°12·4′W	X	171
Pen-y-waun	Carm	SN4034	51°59·1′	4°19·4′W	X	146
Penywaun	Carm	SN6519	51°51·4′	3°57·2′W	X	159
Penywaun	Carm	SN8436	52°0·9′	3°41·0′W	X	160
Penywaun	Rho Cyn Taf	SN9704	51°43·8′	3°29·1′W	T	170
Penywaun-wen	Conwy	SH6863	53°9·1′	3°58·0′W	X	115
Pen-y-wern	Cered	SN6287	52°28·1′	4°1·5′W	X	135
Pen-y-wern	Cered	SN6376	52°22·1′	4°0·3′W	X	135
Pen-y-wern	Cered	SN6389	52°29·1′	4°0·7′W	X	135
Pen-y-wern	Flint	SJ2959	53°7·6′	3°3·3′W	X	117
Pen-y-wern	Powys	SN7613	51°48·4′	3°47·5′W	X	160
Pen-y-wern	Powys	SO1189	52°29·7′	3°18·3′W	X	136
Pen-y-wern	Powys	SO1728	51°56·9′	3°12·1′W	X	161
Pen-y-wern	Shrops	SO3078	52°24·0′	3°1·3′W	T	137,148
Pen-y-wern-hir	Cered	SN7367	52°17·4′	3°51·3′W	X	135,147
Penywingon	Powys	SN8727	51°56·0′	3°38·2′W	X	160
Penyworlod	Heref	SO3626	51°56·0′	2°55·5′W	X	161
Penyworlod	Powys	SO0840	52°3·3′	3°20·1′W	X	147,160
Penyworlod Fm	Monm	SO2630	51°58·1′	3°4·2′W	FM	161
Penyworlod Fm	Newp	ST4191	51°37·1′	2°50·7′W	FM	171,172
Penywyrlod	Monm	SO3125	51°55·4′	2°59·8′W	X	161
Peny-y-banc	Powys	SO0989	52°29·7′	3°20·0′W	X	136
Penzance	Corn	SW4630	50°7·2′	5°32·8′W	T	203
Penzer Point	Corn	SW4624	50°3·9′	5°32·6′W	X	203
Penzoy Fm	Somer	ST3335	51°6·9′	2°57·0′W	FM	182
Peockstone Fm	Renf	NS3560	55°48·6′	4°37·5′W	FM	63
Peopleton	Worcs	SO9350	52°9·1′	2°5·7′W	T	150
Peover Eye	Ches	SJ7175	53°16·5′	2°25·7′W	W	118
Peover Hall	Ches	SJ7773	53°15·5′	2°20·3′W	A	118
Peover Heath	Ches	SJ7973	53°15·5′	2°18·5′W	T	118
Peper Harow	Surrey	SU9344	51°11·5′	0°39·8′W	T	186
Peplow	Shrops	SJ6324	52°49·0′	2°32·5′W	X	127
Peppard Common	Oxon	SU7081	51°31·6′	0°59·1′W	X	175
Pepper Arden	N Yks	NZ2901	54°24·5′	1°32·8′W	X	93
Pepperbox Hill	Wilts	SU2125	51°1·7′	1°41·6′W	H	184
Pepperbox, The	Wilts	SU2124	51°1·1′	1°41·6′W	A	184
Peppercombe	Devon	SS3823	50°59·3′	4°18·1′W	T	190
Peppercombe Cas	Devon	SS3724	50°59·8′	4°19·0′W	A	190
Pepper Cove	Corn	SW8573	50°31·3′	5°1·6′W	W	200
Pepperdale Fm	Lincs	TF0097	53°27·8′	0°29·2′W	FM	112
Pepperdale Fm	N Lincs	TA0305	53°32·1′	0°26·3′W	FM	112
Pepperdon Fm	Devon	SX7785	50°39·3′	3°44·0′W	FM	191
Pepperfield Fm	N Yks	NZ2907	54°27·7′	1°32·7′W	FM	93
Pepper Hill	Cald	SE1128	53°45·1′	1°49·6′W	T	104
Pepper Hill	E Ayr	NS7121	55°28·2′	4°2·0′W	X	71
Pepper Hill	Lancs	SD4733	53°47·7′	2°47·9′W	X	102
Pepperhill	Shrops	SJ6437	52°56·0′	2°31·7′W	X	127
Pepperhill	Shrops	SJ8202	52°37·2′	2°15·6′W	X	127
Pepper Hill Fm	Lincs	TF1918	52°45·0′	0°13·8′W	FM	130
Pepperhill Fm	Somer	ST1937	51°7·8′	3°9·1′W	FM	181
Pepper Hole	Corn	SW9078	50°34·1′	4°57·6′W	X	200
Peppering Eye Fm	E Susx	TQ7413	50°53·6′	0°28·8′E	FM	199
Peppering Fm	W Susx	TQ0309	50°52·5′	0°31·8′W	FM	197
Peppering High Barn	W Susx	TQ0410	50°53·0′	0°30·9′W	X	197
Pepper Knowe	E Ayr	NS5829	55°32·3′	4°14·6′W	X	71
Pepperknowes	S Lanak	NS9138	55°37·7′	3°43·4′W	X	71,72
Pepper Lake	Devon	SS7506	50°50·6′	3°46·1′W	W	191
Pepperly Hill	Notts	SK6875	53°16·3′	0°58·4′W	X	120
Pepper Mill	Glos	SO7334	52°0·5′	2°23·2′W	X	150
Peppermill Dam	Fife	NS9489	56°5·2′	3°41·8′W	W	65
Peppermoor	Northum	NU2215	55°26·0′	1°38·7′W	T	81
Peppermoss	Cumbr	NY4777	55°5·3′	2°49·4′W	X	86
Pepper's	W Susx	TQ1715	50°55·6′	0°19·7′W	A	198
Pepperscoombe	W Susx	TQ1610	50°52·9′	0°20·7′W	X	198
Peppersgate	W Susx	TQ2224	51°0·4′	0°15·3′W	X	198
Pepper's Green	Essex	TL6210	51°46·1′	0°21·3′E	T	167
Peppers Hall	Suff	TL8955	52°9·9′	0°46·2′E	X	155
Peppershill	Bucks	SP6608	51°46·2′	1°2·2′W	X	164,165
Peppershill	Corn	SX3188	50°40·3′	4°23·1′W	X	190
Pepper Side	Northum	NT7906	55°21·1′	2°19·4′W	X	80
Pepper Slade	Staffs	SJ9917	52°45·3′	2°0·5′W	F	127
Pepperstock	Beds	TL0818	51°51·2′	0°25·5′W	T	166
Pepperthorpe Hall	Lincs	TF4857	53°5·6′	0°13·0′E	X	122
Pepperton Hill	Cambs	TL4744	52°4·7′	0°9·1′E	H	154
Pepperwell Fm	Warw	SP2634	52°0·5′	1°36·9′W	FM	151
Pepper Wood	Worcs	SO9374	52°22·1′	2°5·8′W	F	139
Pepples Fm	Essex	TL5833	51°58·6′	0°18·4′E	FM	167
Pepsal End	Herts	TL0817	51°50·7′	0°25·5′W	X	166
Pepys House	Cambs	TL2170	52°19·1′	0°13·1′W	A	153
Peradon Fm	Devon	ST0501	50°48·3′	3°20·5′W	FM	192
Peraidd Fynydd	Cered	SN8182	52°25·6′	3°44·6′W	X	135,136
Perbargus Point	Corn	SW9541	50°14·2′	4°52·1′W	X	204
Perborough Castle	W Berks	SU5277	51°29·6′	1°14·7′W	X	174
Perborough Castle (fort)	W Berks	SU5277	51°29·6′	1°14·7′W	A	174
Perces	Essex	TL8227	51°54·9′	0°39·2′E	X	168
Perceton	N Ayr	NS3540	55°37·8′	4°36·8′W	T	70
Perceton Ho	N Ayr	NS3540	55°37·8′	4°36·8′W	A	70
Perceton Mains	N Ayr	NS3540	55°37·8′	4°36·8′W	X	70
Perch Hill Fm	E Susx	TQ6622	50°58·6′	0°22·3′E	FM	199
Perching Hill	W Susx	TQ2410	50°52·8′	0°13·9′W	X	198
Perching Manor Fm	W Susx	TQ2411	50°53·3′	0°13·8′W	FM	198
Perching Sands Fm	W Susx	TQ2412	50°53·9′	0°13·8′W	FM	198
Perch Lake Plantation	Norf	TG2727	52°47·8′	1°22·4′E	F	133,134
Perch Rock	Arg & Bt	NS2780	55°59·2′	4°46·0′W	X	63
Perch Rock	I of Angl	SH6481	53°18·8′	4°2·1′W	X	114,115
Perch Rock	Wirral	SJ3194	53°26·5′	3°1·9′W	X	108
Perch, The	N Ayr	NS1853	55°44·4′	4°53·5′W	X	63
Perch, The	Somer	ST4555	51°17·7′	2°46·9′W	X	172,182
Percie	Aberd	NO5992	57°1·3′	2°40·1′W	X	44
Percival	Fife	NT3498	56°10·5′	3°3·3′W	X	59
Percival Fm	Cambs	TF4302	52°36·0′	0°7·1′E	FM	142,143
Percoed Reen	Newp	ST2883	51°32·7′	3°1·9′W	W	171
Percuil	Corn	SW8534	50°10·3′	5°0·3′W	T	204
Percuil River	Corn	SW8533	50°9·7′	5°0·3′W	W	204
Percy Baldinnie	Fife	NO4311	56°17·5′	2°54·8′W	X	59
Percy Hill	Cumbr	NY2243	54°46·8′	3°12·3′W	X	85
Percy Hill	D & G	NY2587	55°10·5′	3°10·2′W	H	79
Percyhorner	Aberd	NJ9565	57°40·7′	2°4·6′W	X	30
Percy Law	Scot Bord	NT8123	55°30·3′	2°17·6′W	H	74
Percylieu	Aberd	NJ5326	57°19·6′	2°46·4′W	X	37
Percy Lodge	E Yorks	SE7122	53°41·6′	0°55·1′W	X	105,106,112
Percy Main	N Tyne	NZ3467	55°0·0′	1°27·7′W	T	88
Percy Rigg Fm	N Yks	NZ6210	54°29·1′	1°2·2′W	FM	94
Percy's Cross	Northum	NU0519	55°28·1′	1°54·8′W	A	81
Percy's Cross	Northum	NY8793	55°14·1′	2°11·8′W	X	80
Percy's Leap	Northum	NU0419	55°28·1′	1°55·8′W	A	81
Percy's Moss	Northum	NY8587	55°10·9′	2°13·7′W	X	80
Perdredda Wood	Corn	SX3456	50°23·1′	4°19·7′W	F	201
Pereer's Hills	Norf	TG0739	52°54·7′	1°5·1′E	X	133
Perfeddgoed	Gwyn	SH5769	53°12·2′	4°8·1′W	X	114,115
Perfeddnant	Gwyn	SH6205	52°37·8′	4°1·9′W	X	124
Per-ffordd-llan	Flint	SJ1377	53°17·2′	3°17·9′W	T	116
Pergins Island	Poole	SY9992	50°43·9′	2°0·5′W	X	195
Perham Down	Wilts	SU2549	51°14·6′	1°38·1′W	T	184
Perie Bard	Shetld	HU4723	59°59·6′	1°9·0′W	X	4
Perimead	Essex	TL4830	51°57·2′	0°9·6′E	X	167
Perio Mill	Northnts	TL0492	52°31·2′	0°27·6′W	X	141
Periton	Somer	SS9645	51°11·9′	3°28·9′W	T	181
Periton Hill	Somer	SS9544	51°11·4′	3°29·8′W	X	181
Periton Ho	Somer	SS9545	51°11·9′	3°29·8′W	X	181
Perivale	Ealing	TQ1683	51°32·3′	0°19·3′W	T	176

Periwinkle Hill	Herts	TL3736	52°0·6'	0°0·2'E	H	154
Perkhill	Aberd	NJ5705	57°8·3'	2°42·2'W	T	37
Perkins Beach	Shrops	SJ3600	52°35·9'	2°56·3'W	X	126
Perkins Beach	Shrops	SO3698	52°34·8'	2°56·3'W	X	137
Perkins Beach	Shrops	SO3699	52°35·3'	2°56·3'W	X	137
Perkin's Lodge	Northnts	SP6365	52°17·0'	1°4·2'W	X	152
Perkin's Village	Devon	SY0291	50°42·9'	3°22·9'W	T	192
Perkinsville	Durham	NZ2553	54°52·5'	1°36·2'W	T	88
Perkley	Shrops	SO6198	52°34·9'	2°34·1'W	X	138
Perlees Fm	Corn	SW9773	50°31·5'	4°51·5'W	FM	200
Perlethorpe	Notts	SK6471	53°14·2'	1°2·1'W	T	120
Perllan	Gwyn	SH5806	52°38·2'	4°5·5'W	X	124
Pernagie Isle	I Scilly	SV9117	49°58·6'	6°18·2'W	X	203
Pernassie Hill	Scot Bord	NT4127	55°32·2'	2°55·7'W	X	73
Peronne	Denb	SJ0367	53°11·7'	3°26·7'W	X	116
Perprean Cove	Corn	SW7817	50°0·9'	5°5·6'W	W	204
Perranarworthal	Corn	SW7738	50°12·2'	5°7·1'W	T	204
Perran Beach	Corn	SW7556	50°21·9'	5°9·5'W	X	200
Perrancoombe	Corn	SW7552	50°19·7'	5°9·3'W	T	200,204
Perran Downs	Corn	SW5530	50°7·4'	5°25·3'W	T	203
Perran or Ligger Bay	Corn	SW7556	50°21·9'	5°9·5'W	W	200
Perranporth	Corn	SW7554	50°20·8'	5°9·4'W	T	200,204
Perran Sands	Corn	SW5429	50°6·8'	5°26·1'W	X	203
Perranuthnoe	Corn	SW5329	50°6·8'	5°26·9'W	T	203
Perranwell	Corn	SW7739	50°12·8'	5°7·2'W	T	204
Perranwell	Corn	SW7752	50°19·8'	5°7·6'W	T	200,204
Perranwell Station	Corn	SW7839	50°12·8'	5°6·3'W	T	204
Perran Wharf	Corn	SW7738	50°12·2'	5°7·1'W	T	204
Perranzabuloe	Corn	SW7752	50°19·8'	5°7·6'W	T	200,204
Perren's Hill Fm	Somer	ST4918	50°57·8'	2°43·2'W	FM	183,193
Perreton Fm	I of W	SZ5385	50°40·0'	1°14·6'W	FM	196
Perrett's Fm	W Susx	TQ0816	50°56·2'	0°27·4'W	FM	197
Perridge Ho	Devon	SX8690	50°42·1'	3°36·5'W	X	191
Perridge Ho	Somer	ST5740	51°9·7'	2°36·5'W	X	182,183
Perrills	Essex	TL5204	51°43·1'	0°12·4'E	X	167
Perrinpit Fm	S Glos	ST6582	51°32·4'	2°29·9'W	FM	172
Perrins Fm	W Berks	SU6863	51°21·9'	1°1·0'W	FM	175,186
Perriswood	Swan	SS5088	51°34·5'	4°9·5'W	X	159
Perrose Fm	Corn	SW8858	50°23·3'	4°58·6'W	FM	200
Perrott Hill School	Somer	ST4609	50°52·9'	2°45·7'W	X	193
Perrott's Brook	Glos	SP0106	51°45·4'	1°58·7'W	T	163
Perrott's Fm	Devon	SS9819	50°57·9'	3°26·8'W	FM	181
Perrotts Fm	Surrey	TQ2557	51°18·1'	0°12·0'W	FM	187
Perrotts Hill Fm	Oxon	SP3913	51°49·1'	1°25·7'W	FM	164
Perrow Fm	Somer	ST4351	51°15·6'	2°48·6'W	FM	182
Perry	Birm	SP0792	52°31·8'	1°53·4'W	T	139
Perry	Devon	SS8605	50°50·2'	3°36·8'W	T	191
Perry	Kent	TR2559	51°17·4'	1°14·0'E	T	179
Perry Barr	Birm	SP0692	52°31·8'	1°54·3'W	T	139
Perry Beeches	Birm	SP0593	52°32·3'	1°55·2'W	T	139
Perry Br	N Som	ST4861	51°21·0'	2°44·4'W	X	172,182
Perry Bridges	Birm	SP0791	52°31·2'	1°53·4'W	X	139
Perry Childs Fm	Essex	TL7224	51°53·5'	0°30·4'E	FM	167
Perry Common	Birm	SP0993	52°32·3'	1°51·6'W	T	139
Perry Court	Kent	TR0160	51°18·4'	0°53·4'E	X	178
Perry Court	Kent	TR1153	51°14·4'	1°1·8'E	X	179,189
Perry Court Fm	Kent	TR0347	51°11·4'	0°54·7'E	FM	179,189
Perry Court Fm	Somer	ST2739	51°9·0'	3°2·2'W	FM	182
Perry Crofts	Staffs	SK2104	52°38·2'	1°41·0'W	T	139
Perry Dale	Derby	SK1080	53°19·2'	1°50·6'W	X	110
Perrydown Fm	Suff	TL9154	52°9·3'	0°47·9'E	FM	155
Perry Elm	Somer	ST1119	50°58·0'	3°15·7'W	X	181,193
Perryfields	Essex	TL5924	51°54·2'	0°19·0'E	X	167
Perryfields	Worcs	SO9471	52°20·5'	2°4·9'W	T	139
Perryflatts	S Lanak	NS9538	55°37·7'	3°39·6'W	X	72
Perry Fm	Devon	SS9205	50°50·3'	3°31·6'W	FM	192
Perry Fm	Shrops	SJ3430	52°52·0'	2°58·4'W	FM	126
Perry Fm	Somer	SS9325	51°1·1'	3°31·1'W	FM	181
Perry Fm	Somer	ST0530	51°3·9'	3°21·0'W	FM	181
Perry Fm	Somer	ST1143	51°11·0'	3°16·0'W	FM	181
Perry Fm	Somer	ST1718	50°57·6'	3°10·5'W	FM	181,193
Perry Fm	Somer	ST3848	51°13·9'	2°52·9'W	FM	182
Perry Fm	Surrey	TQ3440	51°8·8'	0°4·7'W	FM	187
Perry Fm	Wilts	ST8039	51°9·2'	2°16·8'W	FM	183
Perry Fm	Worcs	SO6262	52°15·5'	2°33·0'W	FM	138,149
Perry Fm	Worcs	SO8571	52°20·4'	2°12·8'W	FM	139
Perryfoot	Derby	SK1081	53°19·8'	1°50·6'W	T	110
Perry Green	Essex	TL8022	51°52·3'	0°37·3'E	T	168
Perry Green	Herts	TL4317	51°50·2'	0°4·9'E	T	167
Perry Green	Somer	ST2738	51°8·4'	3°2·2'W	T	182
Perry Green	Wilts	ST9689	51°36·2'	2°3·1'W	T	173
Perry Hall	Somer	ST2717	50°57·1'	3°2·0'W	X	193
Perry Hill	Essex	TL3905	51°43·8'	0°1·2'E	X	166
Perry Hill	Heref	SO4638	52°2·5'	2°46·8'W	X	149,161
Perry Hill	W Susx	TQ0509	50°52·5'	0°30·1'W	X	197
Perry Hill Fm	Beds	SP9643	52°4·9'	0°35·5'W	FM	153
Perryhill Fm	E Susx	TQ4837	51°7·0'	0°7·3'E	FM	188
Perry Hill Fm	Medway	TQ7474	51°26·5'	0°30·6'E	FM	178
Perryland	Hants	SU7944	51°11·6'	0°51·6'W	X	186
Perryland Fm	E Susx	TQ5612	50°53·4'	0°13·5'E	FM	199
Perryland Fm	W Susx	TQ1418	50°57·2'	0°22·2'W	FM	198
Perryman's Fm	E Susx	TQ6822	50°58·6'	0°24·0'E	FM	199
Perrymead	Bath & NE Somer	ST7563	51°22·2'	2°21·2'W	T	172
Perry Mill Fm	Somer	ST1840	51°9·4'	3°10·0'W	FM	181
Perry Mill Fm	Worcs	SP0058	52°13·4'	1°59·6'W	FM	150
Perry Moor	Lancs	SD6268	54°6·6'	2°34·5'W	X	97
Perry Moor	Somer	ST2739	51°9·0'	3°2·2'W	X	182
Perrymoor Fm	Shrops	SJ3430	52°52·0'	2°58·4'W	FM	126
Perry Park	Birm	SP0692	52°31·8'	1°54·3'W	X	139
Perry's Dam	Cumbr	NY7841	54°46·1'	2°20·1'W	W	86,87
Perrysfield	Surrey	TQ3950	51°14·2'	0°0·1'W	X	187
Perrysfield Fm	Surrey	TQ3850	51°14·2'	0°1·0'W	FM	187
Perry's Fm	Medway	TQ8776	51°27·3'	0°41·9'E	FM	178
Perrystone	Heref	SO6229	51°57·7'	2°32·8'W	X	149
Perrystone Hill	Heref	SO6329	51°57·7'	2°31·9'W	T	149
Perryston Fm	S Ayr	NS2917	55°25·3'	4°41·7'W	FM	70
Perry Street	Kent	TQ6373	51°26·2'	0°21·1'E	T	177
Perry Street	Somer	ST3305	50°50·7'	2°56·7'W	T	193
Perry West Wood	Cambs	TL1366	52°17·1'	0°20·2'W	F	153

Perrywood	Kent	TR0455	51°15·7'	0°55·8'E	T	178,179
Perrywood Fm	Herts	TL2917	51°50·4'	0°7·3'W	FM	166
Perrywood Haseley Inclosure	Hants	SU3203	50°49·8'	1°32·4'W	F	196
Perrywood Ironshill Inclosure	Hants	SU3202	50°49·2'	1°32·4'W	F	196
Persabus	Arg & Bt	NR4168	55°50·4'	6°7·8'W	X	60,61
Persehall Manor Fm	Norf	TM1391	52°28·7'	1°8·6'E	FM	144
Pershall	Staffs	SJ8129	52°51·7'	2°16·5'W	T	127
Persh Fm	Glos	SO8120	51°52·9'	2°16·2'W	FM	162
Pershore	Worcs	SO9445	52°6·4'	2°4·9'W	T	150
Pershore Airfield (disused)	Worcs	SO9749	52°8·6'	2°2·2'W	X	150
Pershore Bridge	Worcs	SO9545	52°6·4'	2°4·0'W	A	150
Pershore Hall	Worcs	SO9446	52°7·0'	2°4·9'W	X	150
Pershore Sta	Worcs	SO9548	52°8·1'	2°4·0'W	X	150
Persie Ho	Pth & Kin	NO1354	56°40·4'	3°24·7'W	X	53
Persilands	S Lanak	NT0339	55°38·3'	3°32·0'W	X	72
Persley	C of Aber	NJ9010	57°11·1'	2°9·5'W	X	38
Pert	Angus	NO6565	56°46·8'	2°33·9'W	X	45
Pertenhall	Beds	TL0865	52°16·6'	0°24·6'W	T	153
Perterburn	D & G	NY4084	55°9·1'	2°56·1'W	X	79
Perter Burn	D & G	NY4185	55°9·6'	2°55·1'W	W	79
Perter Hill	D & G	NY4285	55°9·6'	2°54·2'W	X	79
Perter Rig	D & G	NY4186	55°10·1'	2°55·1'W	H	79
Perth	Orkney	HY5040	59°14·9'	2°52·1'W	X	5
Perth	Pth & Kin	NO1123	56°23·7'	3°26·1'W	T	53,58
Perth Aerodrome	Pth & Kin	NO1528	56°26·4'	3°22·3'W	X	53,58
Perth Celyn	Brig	SS9582	51°31·9'	3°30·4'W	X	170
Perthcelyn	Rho Cyn Taf	ST0597	51°40·1'	3°22·0'W	T	170
Perthellic Fm	Monm	ST3295	51°39·2'	2°58·6'W	FM	171
Perthewig	Denb	SJ0671	53°13·9'	3°24·1'W	X	116
Perthi	Gwyn	SH5848	53°0·9'	4°6·6'W	X	115
Perthichwareu	Denb	SJ1853	53°4·3'	3°13·0'W	X	116
Perthi Common	Powys	SO0954	52°10·8'	3°19·5'W	X	147
Perthi-crwm	Monm	SO3023	51°54·3'	3°0·7'W	X	161
Perthi-mawr	Cered	SN5258	52°12·3'	4°9·6'W	X	146
Perthudden	Aberd	NK0327	57°20·3'	1°56·6'W	W	38
Perthumie Bay	Aberd	NO8988	56°59·2'	2°10·4'W	W	45
Perthy	Shrops	SJ3633	52°53·7'	2°56·7'W	T	126
Perthybu	Powys	SO2192	52°31·5'	3°9·5'W	X	137
Perthycollie	Powys	SO1742	52°4·4'	3°12·3'W	X	148,161
Perthycolly	Powys	SO1649	52°8·2'	3°13·2'W	X	148
Perthyduon	Powys	SO1038	52°2·2'	3°18·3'W	X	161
Perth-y-felin	Gwyn	SH8518	52°45·1'	3°41·8'W	X	124,125
Perthygleision	Merth Tyd	ST0699	51°41·2'	3°21·2'W	X	170
Perthygopa	Cered	SN3350	52°7·6'	4°26·0'W	X	145
Perthyre Fm	Monm	SO4815	51°50·1'	2°44·9'W	FM	161
Perthyreglwys	Cered	SN4554	52°10·0'	4°15·6'W	X	146
Perth-yr-onen	Cered	SN4043	52°4·0'	4°19·7'W	X	146
Perton	Heref	SO5940	52°3·6'	2°35·5'W	T	149
Perton	Staffs	SO8699	52°35·6'	2°12·0'W	T	139
Pertwood Down	Wilts	ST8837	51°8·2'	2°9·9'W	X	183
Peruppa Fm	Corn	SX0046	50°17·0'	4°48·1'W	FM	204
Pervin	Heref	SO4954	52°11·2'	2°44·4'W	X	148,149
Pervin	Shrops	SO5572	52°20·9'	2°39·2'W	X	137,138
Perwick Bay	I of M	SC2066	54°3·8'	4°44·6'W	W	95
Perwinnes Moss	C of Aber	NJ9312	57°12·2'	2°6·5'W	X	38
Perwinness	C of Aber	NJ9212	57°12·2'	2°7·5'W	X	38
Pespool Hall	Durham	NZ3843	54°47·1'	1°24·1'W	X	88
Pessac Plantation	N Yks	SE4254	53°59·1'	1°21·2'W	F	105
Pessall Brook	Staffs	SK2213	52°43·1'	1°40·1'W	W	128
Pessall Fm	Staffs	SK2113	52°43·1'	1°40·9'W	FM	128
Pestalozzi Children's Village	E Susx	TQ7817	50°55·7'	0°32·4'E	T	199
Pested	Kent	TR0051	51°13·6'	0°52·3'E	T	189
Pested Fm	Kent	TR0051	51°13·6'	0°52·3'E	FM	189
Pest Ho	W Susx	TQ1210	50°52·9'	0°24·1'W	X	198
Pesthouse Wood	Northnts	SP5233	51°59·8'	1°14·2'W	F	151
Pestles Hall	Essex	TM1423	51°52·1'	1°6·9'E	X	168,169
Pestol Fm	Herts	TL1833	51°59·2'	0°16·5'W	FM	166
Petard Point	N Yks	TA0098	54°22·3'	0°27·2'W	X	101
Petches	Essex	TL6931	51°57·3'	0°28·0'E	X	167
Pete Hall	Essex	TM0017	51°49·2'	0°54·5'E	X	168
Peter Black Sand	Norf	TF6230	52°50·8'	0°24·7'E	X	132
Peterborough	Peterb	TL1999	52°34·8'	0°14·2'W	T	142
Peterborough Airport (Conington)	Cambs	TL1886	52°27·8'	0°15·4'W	X	142
Peterbrook	Worcs	SP0978	52°24·2'	1°51·7'W	X	139
Peterburn	Highld	NG7483	57°47·0'	5°47·6'W	X	19
Peterchurch	Heref	SO3438	52°2·4'	2°57·3'W	T	149,161
Peterculter	C of Aber	NJ8401	57°6·2'	2°15·4'W	T	38
Peter Dale	Derby	SK1275	53°16·6'	1°48·8'W	X	119
Peterden	Aberd	NJ6056	57°35·8'	2°39·7'W	X	29
Peterel Field	Northum	NY9261	54°56·9'	2°7·1'W	X	87
Peterfair	Moray	NJ1937	57°25·2'	3°20·5'W	X	28
Peterfield's Fm	Essex	TL7828	51°55·5'	0°35·7'E	FM	167
Peter Hall	Warw	SP4180	52°25·2'	1°23·4'W	X	140
Peterhayes Fm	Devon	ST2406	50°51·1'	3°4·4'W	FM	192,193
Peterhead	Aberd	NK1346	57°30·5'	1°46·5'W	T	30
Peterhead	Fife	NO3211	56°17·5'	3°5·5'W	X	59
Peterhead	Pth & Kin	NN9209	56°15·9'	3°44·2'W	X	58
Peterhead Bay	Aberd	NK1345	57°30·0'	1°46·5'W	W	30
Peter Hill	Aberd	NO5788	56°59·1'	2°42·0'W	H	44
Peter House Fm	Cumbr	NY2432	54°40·9'	3°10·3'W	FM	89,90
Peterhouse Fm	Suff	TL6980	52°23·7'	0°29·4'E	FM	143
Peterhouse Fm	Traf	SJ7289	53°24·1'	2°24·9'W	FM	109
Peterlee	Durham	NZ4240	54°45·4'	1°20·4'W	T	88
Peterley Manor	Bucks	SU8899	51°41·2'	0°43·2'W	X	165
Petersbank	Kent	TQ5442	51°9·6'	0°12·5'E	X	188
Petersburgh	Cumbr	NY0205	54°26·1'	3°30·2'W	X	89
Petersburn	N Lanak	NS7764	55°51·5'	3°57·5'W	T	64
Peter Scott Walk, The	Norf	TF5425	52°48·3'	0°17·5'E	X	131
Peter's Crag	N Yks	SD9959	54°1·9'	2°0·5'W	X	103
Peter's Crook	Cumbr	NY4477	55°5·3'	2°52·2'W	X	85
Peter's Drove Br	Norf	TF5812	52°41·2'	0°20·7'E	X	131,143
Peterseat	C of Aber	NJ9603	57°7·3'	2°3·5'W	X	38
Petersfield	Hants	SU7423	51°0·3'	0°56·3'W	T	197
Petersfield Fm	E Yorks	SE7942	53°52·3'	0°47·5'W	FM	105,106
Petersfield Fm	Surrey	TQ1844	51°11·2'	0°18·3'W	FM	187
Peter's Finger	Devon	SX3588	50°40·3'	4°19·7'W	T	190

Petersfinger	Wilts	SU1629	51°3·8'	1°45·9'W	X	184
Peter's Fm	Glos	SO7027	51°56·7'	2°25·8'W	FM	162
Peter's Fm	Glos	SP1236	52°1·6'	1°49·1'W	FM	150
Peter's Fm	Northnts	SP5744	52°5·7'	1°9·7'W	FM	152
Peters Green	Herts	TL1419	51°51·7'	0°20·3'W	T	166
Petersham	Rich	TQ1773	51°26·9'	0°18·6'W	T	176
Petersham Fm	Dorset	SU0204	50°50·4'	1°57·9'W	FM	195
Peter's Hill	Aberd	NJ3600	57°5·5'	3°2·9'W	H	37
Peters Marland	Devon	SS4713	50°54·0'	4°10·2'W	T	180
Petersmuir Wood	E Loth	NT4866	55°53·3'	2°49·4'W	F	66
Peter's Platn	Northum	NT8540	55°39·4'	2°13·9'W	F	74
Peter's Point	Corn	SW5741	50°13·4'	5°24·0'W	X	203
Peterspoint Fm	Lincs	TF4720	52°45·7'	0°11·1'E	FM	131
Peter's Rock	Highld	NN3966	56°45·7'	4°37·6'W	X	41
Peter's Stone	Derby	SK1775	53°16·5'	1°44·3'W	H	119
Peterstone Ct	Powys	SO0826	51°55·7'	3°19·9'W	X	160
Peterstone Fm	Norf	TF8643	52°57·4'	0°46·5'E	FM	132
Peterstone Gout	Newp	ST2780	51°31·1'	3°2·7'W	X	171
Peterstone Great Wharf	Newp	ST2679	51°30·5'	3°3·6'W	X	171
Peterstone Wentlooge	Newp	ST2680	51°31·1'	3°3·6'W	T	171
Peterston Moors	V of Glam	ST0776	51°28·8'	3°20·0'W	X	170
Peterston-super-Ely	V of Glam	ST0876	51°28·8'	3°19·1'W	T	170
Peterstow	Heref	SO5624	51°55·0'	2°38·0'W	T	162
Peters Water	Shetld	HU2456	60°17·5'	1°33·5'W	W	3
Petersyke	Cumbr	NY5167	55°0·0'	2°45·5'W	X	86
Peter Tavy	Devon	SX5177	50°34·7'	4°5·9'W	T	191,201
Petertavy Great Common	Devon	SX5577	50°34·7'	4°2·5'W	X	191
Petertavy Great Common	Devon	SX5578	50°35·3'	4°2·5'W	X	191,201
Petertown	Orkney	HY3004	58°55·3'	3°12·5'W	T	6,7
Peterville	Corn	SW7250	50°18·6'	5°11·8'W	T	204
Peterwell	Cered	SN5747	52°6·4'	4°4·9'W	A	146
Peter Wood	N Yks	SE2578	54°12·1'	1°36·6'W	F	99
Pete's Shank	Northum	NT7910	55°23·3'	2°19·5'W	X	80
Petester	Shetld	HP5912	60°47·5'	0°54·5'W	X	1
Pete Tye Common	Essex	TM0018	51°49·7'	0°54·5'E	X	168
Petham	Kent	TR1351	51°13·3'	1°3·4'E	T	179,189
Petham Court	Kent	TQ5167	51°23·1'	0°10·6'E	X	177
Petham Ho	Kent	TR1251	51°13·3'	1°2·6'E	X	179,189
Petherton Br	Somer	ST4516	50°56·7'	2°46·6'W	X	193
Petherton Park Fm	Somer	ST3132	51°5·2'	2°58·7'W	FM	182
Petherwin Gate	Corn	SX2889	50°40·8'	4°25·7'W	T	190
Peth Foot	Northum	NY9458	54°55·2'	2°5·2'W	X	87
Pethills	Ches	SJ9468	53°12·8'	2°5·0'W	X	118
Pethills	Derby	SK2048	53°2·0'	1°41·7'W	X	119
Pethills	Staffs	SK0652	53°4·2'	1°54·2'W	X	119
Pethillshead Fm	Staffs	SK0552	53°4·2'	1°55·1'W	FM	119
Petillery Hill	D & G	NS5702	55°17·7'	4°14·7'W	X	77
Petit Tor Point	Torbay	SX9266	50°29·3'	3°31·0'W	X	202
Petley	Highld	NH9082	57°49·1'	3°50·6'W	X	21
Petley Wood	E Susx	TQ7617	50°55·8'	0°30·7'E	F	199
Petmethen	Aberd	NJ6626	57°19·7'	2°33·4'W	X	38
Peto's Marsh	Suff	TM4993	52°28·9'	1°40·4'E	X	134
Petre's Bound Stone	Devon	SX6569	50°30·5'	3°53·9'W	X	202
Petre's Cross	Devon	SX6565	50°28·4'	3°53·8'W	A	202
Petrifying Spring	Scot Bord	NT1456	55°47·6'	3°21·9'W	W	65,72
Petrockstowe	Devon	SS5109	50°51·9'	4°6·7'W	T	191
Petsey	Shrops	SJ6327	52°50·6'	2°32·6'W	A	127
Petsoe End	Mil Key	SP8949	52°8·2'	0°41·6'W	T	152
Petsoe Manor	Mil Key	SP9149	52°8·1'	0°39·8'W	X	152
Petsoe Manor Fm	Mil Key	SP9149	52°8·1'	0°39·8'W	FM	152
Pett	Aberd	NJ4906	57°8·8'	2°50·1'W	X	37
Pett	E Susx	TQ8713	50°53·4'	0°39·9'E	T	199
Pett	Pth & Kin	NN8615	56°19·1'	3°50·1'W	X	58
Petta Dale	Shetld	HU4157	60°18·0'	1°15·0'W	X	2,3
Pettadale Burn	Shetld	HU3491	60°36·3'	1°22·2'W	W	1,2
Pettadale Water	Shetld	HU3489	60°35·2'	1°22·3'W	W	1,2
Pettals Wood	Darl	NZ3309	54°28·8'	1°29·0'W	F	93
Pettaugh	Suff	TM1659	52°11·4'	1°10·0'E	T	156
Pettaugh Hall	Suff	TM1658	52°10·9'	1°10·0'E	X	156
Petta Water	Shetld	HU4159	60°19·0'	1°15·0'W	W	2,3
Pett Bottom	Kent	TR1143	51°9·1'	1°1·4'E	T	179,189
Pett Bottom	Kent	TR1652	51°13·8'	1°6·0'E	T	179,189
Pett Dane	Kent	TQ9756	51°16·4'	0°49·9'E	X	178
Pettens	Aberd	NJ9719	57°16·0'	2°2·5'W	X	38
Pettens Links	Aberd	NJ9819	57°16·0'	2°1·5'W	X	38
Petterden	Angus	NO4239	56°32·6'	2°56·1'W	X	54
Petterhills	NE Lincs	TF2398	53°28·1'	0°8·4'W	X	113
Petteridge	Kent	TQ6641	51°8·9'	0°22·8'E	T	188
Petteril Crook's Mill	Cumbr	NY4447	54°49·1'	2°51·9'W	X	85
Petteril Green	Cumbr	NY4741	54°45·9'	2°49·0'W	X	86
Petterilgreen Cottages	Cumbr	NY4742	54°46·5'	2°49·0'W	X	86
Petteril Hill	Cumbr	NY4543	54°47·0'	2°50·9'W	X	86
Pett Fm	Kent	TQ8561	51°19·3'	0°39·7'E	FM	178
Pett Fms	Kent	TR1653	51°14·3'	1°6·1'E	FM	179
Pett Fms	Kent	TR1653	51°14·3'	1°6·1'E	FM	179,189
Petticombe Manor	Devon	SS4521	50°58·3'	4°12·1'W	X	180,190
Pettico Wick	Scot Bord	NT9069	55°55·1'	2°9·2'W	X	67
Pettifirth	Shetld	HU5040	60°8·8'	1°5·5'W	X	4
Pettinain	S Lanak	NS9542	55°39·9'	3°39·7'W	T	72
Pettings	Kent	TQ6163	51°20·8'	0°19·1'E	T	177,188
Pettiphers Fm	Worcs	SP1448	52°8·0'	1°47·3'W	FM	151
Pettistree	Suff	TM2954	52°8·4'	1°21·2'E	T	156
Pettistree Hall	Suff	TM3044	52°3·0'	1°21·7'E	X	169
Pettistree Ho	Suff	TM2954	52°8·4'	1°21·2'E	X	156
Pettits Fm	Essex	TQ5998	51°39·7'	0°18·3'E	FM	167,177
Pettitts Hall	Essex	TQ4594	51°37·8'	0°6·1'E	X	167,177
Pett Level	E Susx	TQ8813	50°53·4'	0°40·8'E	T	199
Pett Level	E Susx	TQ9015	50°54·4'	0°42·5'E	X	189
Petton	Devon	ST0024	51°0·6'	3°25·1'W	T	181
Petton	Shrops	SJ4326	52°50·0'	2°50·4'W	T	126
Petton Hall Sch	Shrops	SJ4326	52°50·0'	2°50·4'W	X	126
Pett Place	Kent	TQ9649	51°12·6'	0°48·8'E	X	189
Pett Street Fm	Kent	TR0847	51°11·3'	0°59·0'E	FM	179,189
Petts Wood	Brom	TQ4467	51°23·3'	0°4·6'E	T	177
Petts Wood	Brom	TQ4468	51°23·8'	0°4·6'E	F	177
Petty	Aberd	NJ7636	57°25·1'	2°23·5'W	X	29
Pettycur	Fife	NT2786	56°3·9'	3°9·9'W	X	66
Petty France	Heref	SO7240	52°3·7'	2°24·1'W	X	149
Petty France	Kent	TR1057	51°16·6'	1°1·1'E	X	179
Petty France	S Glos	ST7885	51°34·0'	2°18·7'W	T	172

Pettylung	D & G	NS8906	55°20·4′	3°44·6′W	H	71,78
Pettymuick	Aberd	NJ9024	57°18·6′	2°9·5′W	X	38
Petty Pool	Ches	SJ6170	53°13·8′	2°34·6′W	W	118
Pettypool Fm	Ches	SJ6169	53°13·2′	2°34·6′W	FM	118
Pettypool Wood	Ches	SJ6169	53°13·2′	2°34·6′W	F	118
Petty's Nook	Darl	NZ3318	54°33·6′	1°29·0′W	X	93
Pettyvaich	Highld	NH5340	57°25·9′	4°26·4′W	X	26
Pettywell	Norf	TG0823	52°46·1′	1°5·4′E	T	133
Pettywood Fm	Ches	SJ7063	53°10·0′	2°26·5′W	FM	118
Pettywood Fm	Lincs	SK9915	52°43·6′	0°31·6′W	FM	130
Petwick Fm	Oxon	SU3590	51°36·7′	1°29·3′W	FM	164,174
Petwick Stud Fm	Oxon	SU3589	51°36·2′	1°29·3′W	FM	174
Petworth	W Susx	SU9721	50°59·0′	0°36·7′W	T	197
Petworth House	W Susx	SU9721	50°59·0′	0°36·7′W	A	197
Petworth Park	W Susx	SU9622	50°59·6′	0°37·5′W	X	197
Petygards	Norf	TF8508	52°38·5′	0°44·5′E	X	144
Pevensey	E Susx	TQ6404	50°49·0′	0°20·1′E	T	199
Pevensey Bay	E Susx	TQ6504	50°48·9′	0°20·9′E	T	199
Pevensey Bay	E Susx	TQ6603	50°48·4′	0°21·8′E	W	199
Pevensey Haven	E Susx	TQ6405	50°49·5′	0°20·1′E	W	199
Pevensey Levels	E Susx	TQ6307	50°50·6′	0°19·3′E	X	199
Peverall's Fm	Essex	TL8531	51°57·0′	0°41·9′E	FM	168
Peverel Court	Bucks	SP7911	51°47·8′	0°50·9′W	X	165
Peverell	C of Plym	SX4756	50°23·3′	4°8·8′W	T	201
Peverell	Dorset	SY6492	50°43·8′	2°30·2′W	X	194
Peverell's Cross	Corn	SX1272	50°31·3′	4°38·8′W	A	200
Peverel's Fm	Essex	TL7212	51°47·0′	0°30·0′E	FM	167
Peverel's Wood	Essex	TL5535	51°59·7′	0°15·9′E	F	154
Peveril Castle	Derby	SK1482	53°20·3′	1°47·0′W	A	110
Peveril Hall	Essex	TL7201	51°41·1′	0°29·7′E	X	167
Peveril Point	Dorset	SZ0478	50°36·3′	1°56·2′W	X	195
Pever's Fm	Norf	TM2996	52°31·0′	1°22·9′E	FM	134
Peverstone Fm	Devon	ST0205	50°50·4′	3°23·1′W	FM	192
Peveryl Ho	Pth & Kin	NN8920	56°21·8′	3°47·4′W	X	52,58
Pevor's Fm	Essex	TL7632	51°57·7′	0°34·1′E	FM	167
Pewet Island	Essex	TL9908	51°44·3′	0°53·3′E	X	168
Pewit Covert	Ches	SJ7665	53°11·1′	2°21·1′W	F	118
Pewit Fm	Ches	SJ7665	53°11·1′	2°21·1′W	FM	118
Pewit Fm	Oxon	SU4084	51°33·4′	1°25·0′W	FM	174
Pewit Hall	Ches	SJ7044	52°59·8′	2°26·4′W	X	118
Pewit Hall	Staffs	SK0453	53°4·7′	1°56·0′W	X	119
Pewit Island	Essex	TM0516	51°48·5′	0°58·8′E	X	168
Pewit Island	Essex	TM2226	51°53·5′	1°14·0′E	X	169
Pewit Island	Hants	SU6003	50°49·6′	1°8·5′W	X	196
Pewits, The	Cumbr	NY2817	54°32·8′	3°6·4′W	X	89,90
Pewitt Fm	Northnts	SP5547	52°7·3′	1°11·4′W	FM	152
Pewlands Burn	D & G	NY0698	55°16·3′	3°28·3′W	W	78
Pewley Down	Surrey	TQ0048	51°13·6′	0°33·7′W	X	186
Pewsen Barton	Devon	SS5809	50°52·0′	4°0·7′W	X	191
Pewsey	Wilts	SU1660	51°20·6′	1°45·8′W	T	173
Pewsey Down	Wilts	SU1757	51°18·9′	1°45·0′W	X	173
Pewsey Hill	Wilts	SU1757	51°18·9′	1°45·0′W	X	173
Pewsey Hill Fm	Wilts	SU1657	51°18·9′	1°45·8′W	FM	173
Pewsey Wharf	Wilts	SU1561	51°21·1′	1°46·7′W	T	173
Pewsham Ho	Wilts	ST9470	51°26·0′	2°4·8′W	X	173
Pew's Hill	Wilts	ST8574	51°28·1′	2°12·6′W	X	173
Pewter Hill	Norf	TM3793	52°29·2′	1°29·9′E	X	134
Pewterspear	Warr	SJ6283	53°20·8′	2°33·8′W	T	109
Pew Tor	Devon	SX5373	50°32·5′	4°4·1′W	X	191,201
Pex Hill	Know	SJ5088	53°23·4′	2°44·7′W	X	108
Pexhill Fm	Ches	SJ8772	53°14·9′	2°11·3′W	FM	118
Pexton Moor Fm	N Yks	SE8485	54°15·5′	0°42·2′W	FM	94,100
Peyton Hall	Essex	TL4828	51°56·1′	0°9·6′E	X	167
Peyton Hall	Essex	TL8733	51°58·1′	0°43·7′E	X	168
Peyton Hall	Suff	TL9638	52°0·6′	0°51·8′E	A	155
Peyton Hall	Suff	TM0243	52°3·1′	0°57·2′E	X	155
Peyton Hall	Suff	TM3141	52°1·4′	1°22·4′E	X	169
Pfera Hall	Glos	SO7532	51°59·4′	2°21·5′W	X	150
Phantassie	E Loth	NT5977	55°59·3′	2°39·0′W	T	67
Phantassie	Fife	NT3096	56°9·3′	3°7·2′W	X	59
Pharays Park	Orkney	HY4346	59°18·1′	2°59·6′W	X	5
Pharisee Green	Essex	TL6120	51°51·5′	0°20·7′E	T	167
Pharisee Ho	Essex	TL6119	51°51·0′	0°20·7′E	X	167
Phaup	Scot Bord	NT4103	55°19·3′	2°55·4′W	X	79
Phaup Burn	Scot Bord	NT4103	55°19·3′	2°55·4′W	W	79
Phawhope Burn	Scot Bord	NT2110	55°22·9′	3°14·4′W	W	79
Phawhope Hill	Scot Bord	NT2110	55°22·9′	3°14·4′W	H	79
Phawhope Kips	Scot Bord	NT2009	55°22·4′	3°15·3′W	H	79
Pheasant Clough	Staffs	SJ9962	53°9·5′	2°0·5′W	X	118
Pheasant Copse	W Susx	SU9624	51°0·7′	0°37·5′W	F	197
Pheasant Court Fm	W Susx	SU9528	51°2·8′	0°38·3′W	FM	186,197
Pheasantfield	D & G	NY0591	55°12·5′	3°29·1′W	X	78
Pheasant Fm	Kent	TQ8966	51°21·9′	0°43·3′E	FM	178
Pheasant Hall	Staffs	SJ7848	53°2·0′	2°19·3′W	X	118
Pheasant Hill	N Yks	SE8985	54°15·4′	0°37·6′W	X	94,101
Pheasant Hotel, The	Wilts	SU2334	51°6·5′	1°39·9′W	X	184
Pheasant Inn	Cumbr	NY1930	54°39·8′	3°14·9′W	X	89,90
Pheasant Lodge	N Yks	SE9882	54°13·7′	0°29·4′W	X	101
Pheasants	Bucks	SU7988	51°35·3′	0°51·2′W	T	175
Pheasant's Hill	Bucks	SU7887	51°34·8′	0°52·1′W	T	175
Pheasants Nest	Mil Key	SP8651	52°9·3′	0°44·2′W	X	152
Pheasey	Wals	SP0695	52°33·4′	1°54·3′W	T	139
Pheelie	S Ayr	NX2798	55°15·0′	4°42·9′W	X	76
Pheiginn Bothy	Pth & Kin	NN7351	56°38·3′	4°3·8′W	X	42,51,52
Phelp's Fm	Glos	SO8838	52°2·7′	2°10·1′W	FM	150
Phenzhopehaugh	Scot Bord	NT3112	55°24·1′	3°4·9′W	X	79
Phenzhopehaugh Burn	Scot Bord	NT3012	55°24·1′	3°5·9′W	W	79
Phenzhopehaugh Hill	Scot Bord	NT3112	55°24·1′	3°4·9′W	H	79
Phenzhope Rig	Scot Bord	NT3111	55°23·5′	3°4·9′W	H	79
Pheonix Green	Hants	SU7555	51°17·6′	0°55·1′W	T	175,186
Phepson	Worcs	SO9459	52°14·0′	2°4·9′W	T	150
Phesdo	Aberd	NO6775	56°52·2′	2°32·0′W	X	45
Philadelphia	Derby	SK4167	53°12·1′	1°22·8′W	X	120
Philadelphia	Sund	NZ3352	54°51·9′	1°28·7′W	T	88
Philaxdale	Moray	NJ1667	57°41·4′	3°24·1′W	X	28
Philbeach Fm	Pemb	SM8007	51°43·4′	5°10·7′W	FM	157
Phildraw	I of M	SC2871	54°6·6′	4°37·5′W	X	95
Philgown	D & G	NX3649	54°48·8′	4°32·7′W	X	83
Philham	Devon	SS2522	50°58·5′	4°29·2′W	T	190
Philham	Devon	SS7214	50°54·9′	3°48·9′W	X	180

Philhay Fm	N Som	ST4165	51°23·1′	2°50·5′W	FM	171,172,182
Philhope	Scot Bord	NT3809	55°22·5′	2°58·3′W	X	79
Philip and Mary	D & G	NX3245	54°46·6′	4°36·3′W	X	82
Philip Burn	Scot Bord	NT7163	55°51·8′	2°27·4′W	W	67
Philip Burn	Scot Bord	NT7163	55°51·8′	2°27·4′W	W	67
Philiphaugh	Scot Bord	NT4427	55°32·3′	2°52·8′W	T	73
Philiphaugh Fm	Scot Bord	NT4528	55°32·8′	2°51·9′W	FM	73
Philip Hope	Scot Bord	NT8215	55°26·0′	2°16·6′W	W	80
Philip Law	Scot Bord	NT7210	55°23·2′	2°26·1′W	H	80
Philipps House	Wilts	SU0031	51°4·9′	1°59·6′W	X	184
Philip Reed Moss	Durham	NY8122	54°35·8′	2°17·2′W	X	91,92
Philip's Farm Ho	Oxon	SU2598	51°41·0′	1°37·9′W	X	163
Philipshill	S Lanak	NS6055	55°46·3′	4°13·5′W	X	64
Philipshill Wood	Bucks	TQ0094	51°38·4′	0°32·9′W	F	166,176
Philips Knowe	Scot Bord	NT6256	55°48·0′	2°35·9′W	X	67,74
Philips Main	Highld	ND2971	58°37·5′	3°12·9′W	X	7,12
Philips Park	Bury	SD7904	53°32·2′	2°18·6′W	X	109
Philipstown	Aberd	NJ8226	57°19·7′	2°17·5′W	X	38
Philla Cairn	Aberd	NO7871	56°50·1′	2°21·2′W	A	45
Phillack	Corn	SW5638	50°11·7′	5°24·8′W	T	203
Phillant Fm	Glos	SO9128	51°57·3′	2°7·5′W	FM	150,163
Philleigh	Corn	SW8739	50°13·0′	4°58·8′W	T	204
Phillestone Fm	Swan	SS4393	51°37·1′	4°15·7′W	FM	159
Philley Brook	Staffs	SO8188	52°29·6′	2°16·4′W	W	138
Philliols Fm	Dorset	SY8691	50°43·3′	2°11·5′W	FM	194
Philliols Heath	Dorset	SY8692	50°43·9′	2°11·5′W	X	194
Phillippines, The	Kent	TQ4752	51°15·1′	0°6·8′E	X	188
Phillips	Corn	SS2004	50°48·7′	4°32·9′W	X	190
Phillip's Cross	Northum	NT7406	55°21·1′	2°24·2′W	X	80
Phillip's Fm	Lancs	SD6436	53°49·4′	2°32·4′W	FM	102,103
Phillips's Point	Corn	SS1904	50°48·7′	4°33·8′W	X	190
Phillip's Town	Caer	SO1403	51°43·4′	3°14·3′W	T	171
Phillishayes Fm	Devon	ST2108	50°52·2′	3°7·0′W	FM	192,193
Phillis Wood	W Susx	SU8215	50°55·9′	0°49·6′W	F	197
Philliswood Down	W Susx	SU8117	50°57·0′	0°50·4′W	X	197
Phillow's Fm	Essex	TL7507	51°44·3′	0°32·5′E	FM	167
Philogar Hill	Scot Bord	NT7617	55°27·0′	2°22·3′W	H	80
Philo Gorse	Ches	SJ5962	53°9·5′	2°36·4′W	F	117
Philorth Ho	Aberd	NK0064	57°40·2′	1°59·5′W	X	30
Philpie	Angus	NO3049	56°37·9′	3°8·0′W	X	53
Philpin	N Yks	SD7477	54°11·5′	2°23·5′W	X	98
Philpot End	Essex	TL6118	51°50·5′	0°20·6′E	T	167
Philpots	W Susx	TQ3532	51°4·5′	0°4·0′W	X	187
Philpots Court	Glos	ST5696	51°39·9′	2°37·8′W	X	162
Philpotts	Essex	TL5615	51°48·9′	0°16·2′E	X	167
Philpotts Fm	Somer	ST2821	50°59·3′	3°1·2′W	FM	193
Philpstoun	W Loth	NT0476	55°58·3′	3°31·9′W	T	65
Philpstoun Ho	W Loth	NT0677	55°58·9′	3°30·0′W	A	65
Phingask Shore	Aberd	NJ9767	57°41·8′	2°2·6′W	X	30
Phippin Parks	E Yorks	SE6519	53°40·0′	1°0·6′W	X	111
Phocle Green	Heref	SO6226	51°56·1′	2°32·8′W	T	162
Phoebe's Point	Corn	SX0349	50°18·7′	4°45·6′W	X	204
Phoenice Fm	Surrey	TQ1452	51°15·6′	0°21·6′W	FM	187
Phoenix House Fm	N Yks	SE9580	54°12·7′	0°32·2′W	FM	101
Phoenix Row	Durham	NZ1629	54°39·6′	1°44·7′W	T	92
Phoineas Hill	Highld	NH5342	57°26·9′	4°26·5′W	H	26
Phoineas Ho	Highld	NH5242	57°26·9′	4°27·5′W	X	26
Phones	Highld	NN7094	57°1·4′	4°8·0′W	X	35
Phones	Moray	NJ1940	57°26·8′	3°20·5′W	X	28
Phopachy	Highld	NH6046	57°29·2′	4°19·7′W	X	26
Phorp	Moray	NJ0552	57°33·2′	3°34·8′W	X	27
Phurt	I of M	NX4602	54°23·7′	4°21·9′W	X	95
Phyllis Park	D & G	NY1371	55°1·8′	3°21·2′W	X	85
Phynis	Lancs	SD7154	53°59·1′	2°26·1′W	X	103
Phynsons Hayes Fm	Shrops	SJ7344	52°59·8′	2°23·7′W	FM	118
Phypers Fm	Cambs	TL4064	52°15·6′	0°3·5′E	FM	154
Physgill Ho	D & G	NX4236	54°41·9′	4°26·7′W	X	83
Physgill Lodge	D & G	NX4337	54°42·5′	4°25·8′W	X	83
Physichall	Cumbr	NY7245	54°48·2′	2°25·7′W	X	86,87
Physic Well	Oxon	SP4404	51°44·2′	1°21·4′W	W	164
Piall Br	Devon	SX5960	50°25·6′	3°58·7′W	X	202
Piall River	Devon	SX5959	50°25·1′	3°58·7′W	W	202
Pia Troon	Northum	NY8156	54°54·1′	2°17·4′W	X	86,87
Pibble	D & G	NX5160	54°55·0′	4°19·1′W	X	83
Pibble Hill	D & G	NX5360	54°55·0′	4°17·2′W	H	83
Pibsbury	Somer	ST4426	51°2·1′	2°47·5′W	T	193
Pibwrlwyd	Carm	SN4118	51°50·5′	4°18·1′W	T	159
Pibyah Rock	Corn	SW8937	50°12·0′	4°57·0′W	X	204
Pica	Cumbr	NY0222	54°35·3′	3°30·6′W	T	89
Picardy Stone (Symbol Stone)	Aberd	NJ6130	57°21·8′	2°38·4′W	A	29,37
Picardy Stone (Symbol Stone)	Aberd	NJ6130	57°21·8′	2°38·4′W	X	29,37
Piccadilly	Roth	SK4598	53°28·8′	1°18·9′W	T	111
Piccadilly	Warw	SP2298	52°35·0′	1°40·1′W	T	139
Piccadilly Corner	Norf	TM2786	52°25·7′	1°20·7′E	T	156
Piccadilly Fm	Glos	SO9823	51°54·6′	2°1·4′W	FM	163
Piccadilly Sta	Man	SJ8497	53°28·4′	2°14·1′W	X	109
Piccard's Fm	Surrey	SU9848	51°13·6′	0°35·4′W	FM	186
Piccotts End	Herts	TL0509	51°46·4′	0°28·3′W	T	166
Piccotts Fm	Essex	TL7025	51°54·1′	0°28·7′E	FM	167
Pickards Fm	Worcs	SO7681	52°25·8′	2°20·8′W	FM	138
Pickard's Plantn	Lincs	TF1389	53°23·4′	0°17·6′W	F	113,121
Pickburn	Donc	SE5107	53°33·7′	1°13·4′W	T	111
Pickdick Fm	E Susx	TQ8418	50°56·1′	0°37·5′E	FM	199
Picked Copse	Wilts	SU2531	51°4·9′	1°38·2′W	F	184
Picked Hill	Wilts	SU1261	51°21·1′	1°49·3′W	H	173
Pickedstones	Somer	SS8037	51°7·4′	3°42·5′W	X	181
Picken End	Worcs	SO8142	52°4·8′	2°16·2′W	T	150
Pickenham Hall	Norf	TF8504	52°36·4′	0°44·3′E	X	144
Pickerells	Essex	TL5708	51°45·1′	0°16·9′E	X	167
Pickeridge Fm	Somer	ST2318	50°57·6′	3°5·4′W	FM	193
Pickeridge Fm	W Susx	TQ3530	51°3·4′	0°4·0′W	FM	187
Pickeridge Hill	Somer	ST2319	50°58·2′	3°5·4′W	X	193
Pickeridge, The	Bucks	SU9885	51°33·5′	0°34·8′W	X	175,176
Pickerill Holme	Norf	TG4910	52°38·1′	1°41·2′E	W	134
Pickering	Cumbr	SD6985	54°15·8′	2°28·1′W	X	98
Pickering	N Yks	SE7984	54°15·0′	0°46·8′W	T	100
Pickering Beck	N Yks	SE7982	54°13·9′	0°46·9′W	W	100

Pickering Beck	N Yks	SE8190	54°18·2′	0°44·9′W	W	94,100
Pickering Grange Fm	Leic	SK4210	52°41·4′	1°22·3′W	FM	129
Pickering Low Carr	N Yks	SE8080	54°12·8′	0°46·0′W	X	100
Pickering Low Carr Fm	N Yks	SE7979	54°12·3′	0°46·9′W	FM	100
Pickering Nook	Durham	NZ1755	54°53·6′	1°43·7′W	T	88
Pickering Park	K upon H	TA0527	53°44·0′	0°24·1′W	X	107
Pickerings Pasture	Halton	SJ4883	53°20·7′	2°46·5′W	X	108
Pickering Tor	Derby	SK1453	53°4·7′	1°47·1′W	X	119
Pickering Wood	N Yks	SE5243	53°53·1′	1°12·1′W	F	105
Picker's Ditch	Essex	TM1518	51°49·4′	1°7·6′E	W	168,169
Picker's Ditch	Essex	TM1917	51°48·7′	1°11·0′E	W	168,169
Pickersett	N Yks	SD8596	54°21·8′	2°13·4′W	X	98
Pickers Hill Fm	Bri & Hov	TQ3803	50°48·8′	0°2·1′W	FM	198
Pickerston	Aberd	NJ9562	57°39·1′	2°4·6′W	X	30
Pickerstone Ridge	N Yks	SD9994	54°20·7′	2°0·5′W	X	98
Pickerton	Angus	NO5652	56°39·7′	2°42·6′W	T	54
Picket	V of Glam	SS9373	51°27·0′	3°32·0′W	X	170
Picket Corner	Hants	SU2216	50°56·8′	1°40·8′W	X	184
Picket Hill	Hants	SU1805	50°50·9′	1°44·3′W	T	195
Picketlaw	E Renf	NS4652	55°44·5′	4°26·7′W	X	64
Picketlaw Fm	C of Glas	NS5956	55°46·9′	4°14·5′W	FM	64
Picketlaw Resr	E Renf	NS5651	55°44·1′	4°17·2′W	W	64
Picket Piece	Hants	SU3946	51°12·9′	1°26·1′W	T	185
Picket Plain	Hants	SU1905	50°50·9′	1°43·4′W	X	195
Picket Post	Hants	SU1906	50°51·4′	1°43·4′W	X	195
Picket Post Gate	Wilts	ST8444	51°11·9′	2°13·4′W	X	183
Picket Rock	I Scilly	SV8413	49°56·3′	6°19·4′W	X	203
Pickets Hill Fm	Hants	SU8238	51°8·4′	0°49·3′W	FM	186
Picketston	V of Glam	ST0069	51°24·9′	3°25·9′W	X	170
Pickett Fm	Dorset	ST4705	50°50·8′	2°44·8′W	FM	193
Pickett How	Cumbr	NY0009	54°28·2′	3°32·2′W	X	89
Pickett Howe	Cumbr	NY1522	54°35·4′	3°18·5′W	X	89
Picketts	Surrey	TQ2945	51°11·6′	0°8·8′W	X	187
Pickett's Lock Centre	Enf	TQ3694	51°37·9′	0°1·7′W	X	166,177
Picket Twenty Fm	Hants	SU3845	51°12·4′	1°27·0′W	FM	185
Picketty Cotts	W Susx	TQ1018	50°57·3′	0°25·6′W	X	198
Picket Wood	Wilts	ST8754	51°17·3′	2°10·8′W	F	183
Pickford	Cov	SP2781	52°25·8′	1°35·8′W	T	140
Pickford Brook	Cov	SP2782	52°26·4′	1°35·8′W	W	140
Pickford Fm	Cov	SP2881	52°25·8′	1°34·9′W	FM	140
Pickford Green	Cov	SP2781	52°25·8′	1°35·8′W	T	140
Pickford Hill	Hants	SU2646	51°13·0′	1°37·3′W	H	184
Pickham Fm	E Susx	TQ8614	50°54·0′	0°39·1′E	FM	199
Pick Hill	E Susx	TQ5615	50°55·0′	0°13·5′E	X	199
Pick Hill	Kent	TQ8831	51°3·1′	0°41·3′E	X	189
Pickhill	N Yks	SE3483	54°14·7′	1°28·3′W	T	99
Pick Hill Br	Lincs	TF3989	53°23·0′	0°5·8′E	X	113,122
Pick Hill Fm	Essex	TL4001	51°41·6′	0°1·9′E	FM	167
Pickhill Hall	Wrex	SJ4047	53°1·3′	2°53·3′W	X	117
Pickhill Meadows	Wrex	SJ3946	53°0·7′	2°54·1′W	X	117
Pickhill Old Hall	Wrex	SJ3846	53°0·7′	2°55·0′W	X	117
Pickhurst	Surrey	SU9634	51°6·1′	0°37·3′W	X	186
Pickhurst	W Susx	TQ0421	50°59·0′	0°30·7′W	X	197
Pickie Moss	Scot Bord	NT5944	55°41·5′	2°38·7′W	W	73,74
Picking Gill	N Yks	SE2366	54°5·6′	1°38·5′W	X	99
Picklecombe Point	Corn	SX4551	50°20·5′	4°10·3′W	X	201
Pickle Fen	Cambs	TL3883	52°25·9′	0°2·2′E	X	142,143
Pickle Fm	Cumbr	SD5779	54°12·5′	2°39·1′W	FM	97
Picklenash	Glos	SO7126	51°56·1′	2°24·9′W	T	162
Picklescott	Shrops	SO4399	52°35·4′	2°50·1′W	T	137
Picklescott Hill	Shrops	SO4299	52°35·4′	2°51·0′W	X	137
Pickles Hill	Brad	SE0238	53°50·1′	1°57·8′W	T	104
Pickletillem	Fife	NO4324	56°24·5′	2°55·0′W	X	54,59
Pickle Wood	Donc	SK6798	53°28·7′	0°59·0′W	F	111
Pickle Wood	Pemb	SN0514	51°47·7′	4°49·3′W	F	158
Pickley Green	Wigan	SD6502	53°31·1′	2°31·3′W	T	109
Pick Mere	Ches	SJ6877	53°17·6′	2°28·4′W	W	118
Pickmere	Ches	SJ6977	53°17·6′	2°27·5′W	T	118
Pickmore Wood	Cambs	TL6558	52°12·0′	0°25·3′E	F	154
Pickney	Somer	ST1929	51°3·5′	3°9·0′W	T	181,193
Pickney Bush Fm	Kent	TR0629	51°1·6′	0°56·7′E	FM	189
Pick Pale	E Susx	TQ5128	51°2·1′	0°9·6′E	X	188,199
Pickpit Hill	Wilts	SU2450	51°15·2′	1°39·0′W	H	184
Picksharp Ho	N Yks	SE8364	54°4·2′	0°43·5′W	X	100
Picksharp Wood	N Yks	SE8365	54°4·7′	0°43·5′W	F	100
Pickstock	Wrekin	SJ7223	52°48·5′	2°24·5′W	T	127
Pickston	Pth & Kin	NN9928	56°26·3′	3°37·8′W	X	52,53,58
Pickstonhill	Pth & Kin	NO1325	56°24·8′	3°24·2′W	X	53,58
Pickthall Ground	Cumbr	SD2090	54°18·2′	3°13·3′W	X	96
Pickthorn Fm	Shrops	SO6684	52°27·4′	2°29·6′W	FM	138
Picktree	Durham	NZ2853	54°52·5′	1°33·4′W	X	88
Pickup Bank	Black w Dar	SD7222	53°41·9′	2°25·0′W	T	103
Pickwell	Devon	SS4540	51°8·5′	4°12·6′W	X	180
Pickwell	Leic	SK7811	52°41·3′	0°50·3′W	T	129
Pickwell	W Susx	TQ2723	50°59·8′	0°11·0′W	X	198
Pickwell Down	Devon	SS4641	51°9·1′	4°11·7′W	H	180
Pickwell Fm	W Susx	TQ2823	50°59·8′	0°10·2′W	FM	198
Pickwick	Wilts	ST8670	51°26·0′	2°11·7′W	T	173
Pickwood Scar	Cald	SE0722	53°41·9′	1°53·2′W	T	104
Pickworth	Lincs	TF0433	52°53·3′	0°26·8′W	T	130
Pickworth	Rut	SK9913	52°42·6′	0°31·7′W	T	130
Pickworth Great Wood	Rut	SK9814	52°43·1′	0°32·5′W	F	130
Pickworth Lodge	Lincs	TF0432	52°52·8′	0°26·9′W	X	130
Pickworth's Plot	Lincs	SK9068	53°12·3′	0°38·7′W	F	121
Pictfield	Pth & Kin	NO2146	56°36·2′	3°16·8′W	X	53
Picthall	Cumbr	SD2888	54°17·2′	3°5·9′W	X	96,97
Pictillum	Aberd	NJ6200	57°5·6′	2°37·2′W	X	37
Pictillum	Aberd	NJ7416	57°14·3′	2°25·4′W	X	38
Pictillum	Pth & Kin	NO2546	56°36·3′	3°12·9′W	X	53
Picton	Ches	SJ4371	53°14·2′	2°50·8′W	T	117
Picton	Flint	SJ1282	53°19·9′	3°18·9′W	T	116
Picton	N Yks	NZ4107	54°27·6′	1°21·6′W	T	93
Picton Castle	Pemb	SN0013	51°47·0′	4°53·6′W	A	157,158
Picton Fm	Norf	TM1893	52°29·7′	1°13·1′E	FM	134
Picton Gorse	Ches	SJ4369	53°13·1′	2°50·8′W	X	117
Picton Grange	N Yks	NZ4106	54°27·1′	1°21·6′W	X	93
Picton Home Fm	Pemb	SN0014	51°47·6′	4°53·6′W	FM	157,158
Picton Manor Fm	N Yks	NZ4108	54°28·2′	1°21·6′W	FM	93
Picton Park	Pemb	SN0113	51°47·1′	4°52·7′W	X	157,158

Picton Point	Pemb	SN0011	51°46·0′	4°53·5′W	X	157,158
Picton Stell	N Yks	NZ4206	54°27·1′	1°20·7′W	W	93
Pictor Hall	Derby	SK0872	53°14·9′	1°52·4′W	X	119
Pictou	Orkney	HY5217	59°2·5′	2°49·7′W	X	6
Pict's Cross	Heref	SO5626	51°56·1′	2°38·0′W	X	162
Pict's Hill	Somer	ST4327	51°2·6′	2°48·4′W	T	193
Pictshill Ho	Beds	SP9652	52°9·7′	0°35·4′W	X	153
Picts Ness	Shetld	HU2963	60°21·3′	1°28·0′W	X	3
Pidcock Fm	Cambs	TL3192	52°30·8′	0°3·8′W	FM	142
Piddinghoe	E Susx	TQ4302	50°48·2′	0°2·2′E	T	198
Piddington	Bucks	SU8094	51°38·6′	0°50·2′W	T	175
Piddington	Northnts	SP8054	52°10·9′	0°49·4′W	T	152
Piddington	Oxon	SP6417	51°51·1′	1°3·9′W	T	164,165
Piddington Cow Leys	Oxon	SP6319	51°52·2′	1°4·7′W	X	164,165
Piddington Lodge	Northnts	SP8152	52°9·9′	0°48·5′W	X	152
Piddle Brook	Worcs	SO9648	52°8·1′	2°3·1′W	W	150
Piddledown Common	Devon	SX7289	50°41·4′	3°48·4′W	X	191
Piddlehinton	Dorset	SY7197	50°46·5′	2°24·3′W	T	194
Piddles Wood	Dorset	ST7912	50°54·7′	2°17·5′W	F	194
Piddletrenthide	Dorset	SY7099	50°47·6′	2°25·2′W	T	194
Piddle Wood	Somer	ST2419	50°58·2′	3°4·6′W	F	193
Pidford	I of W	SZ5084	50°39·4′	1°17·2′W	X	196
Pidgemore Fm	Glos	SO7907	51°45·9′	2°17·9′W	FM	162
Pidgeon Cott	Kent	TQ9957	51°16·9′	0°51·6′E	X	178
Pidgeon Green	Warw	SP2260	52°14·5′	1°40·3′W	X	151
Pidham Fm	Hants	SU6922	50°59·8′	1°0·6′W	FM	197
Pidley	Cambs	TL3377	52°22·7′	0°2·4′W	T	142
Pidley Fen	Cambs	TL3480	52°24·3′	0°1·4′W	X	142
Pidley Parks	Cambs	TL3477	52°22·7′	0°1·5′W	X	142
Pidnell Fm	Oxon	SU2898	51°41·0′	1°35·3′W	FM	163
Pidney	Dorset	ST7408	50°52·5′	2°21·8′W	T	194
Pidsley	Devon	SS8105	50°50·2′	3°41·0′W	X	191
Piece	Corn	SW6739	50°12·5′	5°15·6′W	T	203
Piece Fm	Derby	SK0285	53°22·0′	1°57·8′W	FM	110
Pie Corner	Heref	SO6461	52°15·0′	2°31·2′W	X	138,149
Pie Cross	N Yks	SD8153	53°58·6′	2°17·0′W	X	103
Pied Bridge Fm	Norf	TM2588	52°26·8′	1°19·1′E	FM	156
Pied Ho	Powys	SO1898	52°34·7′	3°12·2′W	X	136
Piedmont	Glos	SO8907	51°45·9′	2°9·2′W	X	163
Pie Gill	N Yks	SE1367	54°6·2′	1°47·7′W	X	99
Piel Bar	Cumbr	SD2361	54°2·6′	3°10·1′W	W	96
Piel Castle	Cumbr	SD2363	54°3·7′	3°10·2′W	A	96
Piel Channel	Cumbr	SD2364	54°4·2′	3°10·2′W	W	96
Piel Harbour	Cumbr	SD2363	54°3·7′	3°10·2′W	W	96
Piel Island	Cumbr	SD2363	54°3·7′	3°10·2′W	X	96
Pielmuir	D & G	NY0487	55°10·3′	3°30·2′W	X	78
Piend	Devon	SS8306	50°50·7′	3°39·3′W	X	191
Pierbanks Burn	D & G	NY0377	55°4·9′	3°30·7′W	W	84
Pierbanks Fm	D & G	NY0377	55°4·9′	3°30·7′W	FM	84
Pier Burn	Scot Bord	NT7109	55°22·7′	2°27·0′W	W	80
Pierce Barn	Kent	TQ6836	51°6·1′	0°24·4′E	X	188
Piercebridge	Darl	NZ2015	54°32·0′	1°41·0′W	T	93
Piercebridge Grange	Darl	NZ2016	54°32·6′	1°41·0′W	X	93
Piercefield Cliffs	Monm	ST5295	51°39·3′	2°41·2′W	X	162
Piercefield Park	Monm	ST5295	51°39·3′	2°41·2′W	X	162
Pierce How Beck	Cumbr	NY3101	54°24·2′	3°3·4′W	W	90
Pier Cellars	Corn	SX4449	50°19·5′	4°11·1′W	X	201
Pierce's Fm	W Berks	SU6766	51°23·6′	1°1·8′W	FM	175
Pierce Williams	Essex	TL5515	51°49·0′	0°15·3′E	X	167
Piercil End	Sol	SP2076	52°23·1′	1°42·0′W	X	139
Piercing Hill	Essex	TQ4499	51°40·5′	0°5·4′E	T	167,177
Pier of Stursy	Orkney	HY6229	59°9·0′	2°39·4′W	X	5
Pierowall	Orkney	HY4348	59°19·1′	2°59·6′W	T	5
Pierrepont Fm	Norf	TF5723	52°47·1′	0°20·1′E	FM	131
Pierrepont Sch	Surrey	SU8542	51°10·5′	0°46·7′W	X	186
Piers Gill	Cumbr	NY2108	54°27·9′	3°12·7′W	W	89,90
Piersknowe Plantn	Scot Bord	NT7247	55°43·2′	2°26·3′W	F	74
Pies Fm	Hants	SU6834	51°6·3′	1°1·3′W	FM	185,186
Piethorn	N Yks	SE5992	54°19·5′	1°5·2′W	X	100
Piethorne Resr	Roch	SD9612	53°36·5′	2°3·2′W	W	109
Pifelhead Wood	N Yks	SE8495	54°20·9′	0°42·0′W	F	94,100
Piff's Elm	Glos	SO9025	51°55·6′	2°8·3′W	T	163
Pifirrane	Fife	NT0686	56°3·7′	3°30·1′W	A	65
Pig Brook	Warw	SP2539	52°3·2′	1°37·7′W	W	151
Pig Bush	Hants	SU3604	50°50·3′	1°28·9′W	F	196
Pigden Cottage	Surrey	TQ1250	51°14·5′	0°23·3′W	X	187
Pigden Cottage	Surrey	TQ1350	51°14·5′	0°22·5′W	X	187
Pigditch Rhyne	Somer	ST3533	51°5·8′	2°55·3′W	W	182
Pigdon	Northum	NZ1588	55°11·4′	1°45·4′W	T	81
Pigdown	Kent	TQ4743	51°10·3′	0°6·6′E	X	188
Pigeon Coo Fm	I of W	SZ4090	50°42·7′	1°25·6′W	FM	196
Pigeon Hall Fm	Suff	TM0348	52°5·8′	0°58·2′E	FM	155
Pigeon Hill	Highld	ND2740	58°20·8′	3°14·4′W	H	11,12
Pigeon Ho Fm	Flint	SJ3059	53°7·7′	3°2·4′W	FM	117
Pigeon Hoo	Kent	TQ9033	51°4·1′	0°43·1′E	X	189
Pigeon House Bay	N Som	ST4274	51°28·0′	2°49·7′W	W	171,172
Pigeon House Fm	Bucks	SU8888	51°35·3′	0°43·4′W	FM	175
Pigeon House Fm	Dorset	ST8020	50°59·0′	2°16·7′W	FM	183
Pigeon House Fm	Hants	SU3350	51°15·1′	1°31·2′W	FM	185
Pigeon House Fm	Hants	SU6407	50°51·8′	1°5·0′W	FM	196
Pigeon House Fm	Heref	SO5841	52°4·2′	2°36·4′W	FM	149
Pigeon House Fm	N Som	ST4962	51°21·5′	2°43·6′W	FM	172,182
Pigeonhouse Fm	Staffs	SO8284	52°27·5′	2°15·5′W	FM	138
Pigeon House Fm	Worcs	SO6163	52°16·1′	2°33·9′W	FM	138,149
Pigeon House Fm	Worcs	SO8131	51°58·9′	2°16·2′W	FM	150
Pigeon Lock	Oxon	SP4819	51°52·3′	1°17·8′W	X	164
Pigeon Ogo	Corn	SW6714	49°59·1′	5°14·7′W	W	203
Pigeon Point	V of Glam	SS9667	51°23·8′	3°29·3′W	X	170
Pigeons' Fm	Peterb	TF3004	52°37·3′	0°4·4′W	FM	142
Pigeon's Fm	W Berks	SU4965	51°23·1′	1°17·4′W	FM	174
Pigeon's Rough	Shrops	SJ5019	52°46·2′	2°44·1′W	F	126
Piggar	Orkney	HY3404	58°55·4′	3°8·3′W	X	6,7
Piggot's Wood	Bucks	SU8598	51°40·7′	0°45·8′W	F	165
Piggott's Cross	Kent	TQ4749	51°13·5′	0°6·7′E	X	188
Piggotts Fm	Essex	TQ4697	51°39·4′	0°7·0′E	FM	167,177
Piggott's Fm	Herts	TL4223	51°53·5′	0°4·2′E	FM	167
Piggotts Hill	Ches	SJ8272	53°14·9′	2°15·8′W	X	118
Pigg's Grave	Norf	TG0233	52°51·6′	1°0·4′E	X	133
Pig Hill	Devon	SS7544	51°11·1′	3°46·9′W	X	180
Pighole Point	Devon	SX8556	50°23·8′	3°36·7′W	X	202
Pightle Fm	Essex	TL4540	52°2·6′	0°7·3′E	FM	154
Pightles, The	Suff	TM3969	52°16·3′	1°30·6′E	X	156
Pightley	Somer	ST2235	51°6·8′	3°6·5′W	T	182
Pignal Inclosure	Hants	SU3104	50°50·3′	1°33·2′W	F	196
Pig Oak	Dorset	SU0203	50°49·8′	1°57·9′W	T	195
Pigot Ho	Lancs	SD5836	53°49·4′	2°37·9′W	X	102
Pigrey's Wood	Norf	TG2932	52°50·4′	1°24·4′E	F	133
Pig's Bay	Sou-on-Sea	TQ9585	51°32·0′	0°49·1′E	W	178
Pigsfoot Fm	E Susx	TQ5324	50°59·9′	0°11·2′E	FM	199
Pig's Nose	Devon	SX7636	50°12·9′	3°43·9′W	X	202
Pigs Pond Plantn	Norf	TF8727	52°48·7′	0°46·9′E	F	132
Pig Stone	Pemb	SM7109	51°44·2′	5°18·6′W	X	157
Pigstone Bay	Pemb	SM7109	51°44·2′	5°18·6′W	W	157
Pig Street	Heref	SO3647	52°7·3′	2°55·7′W	X	148,149
Pigsty Copse	Wilts	ST9570	51°26·0′	2°3·9′W	F	173
Pigstye Green	Essex	TL6005	51°43·5′	0°19·4′E	T	167
Pigsty Hill	Hants	SZ2099	50°47·6′	1°42·6′W	X	195
Pigtail Corner	Kent	TQ9672	51°25·0′	0°49·5′E	X	178
Pig Tor	Derby	SK0872	53°14·9′	1°52·4′W	X	119
Pig Water	Cambs	TL1992	52°31·0′	0°14·4′W	W	142
Pigwell	Kent	TR0320	50°56·8′	0°53·8′E	X	189
Pig y Baw	Pemb	SN0140	52°1·6′	4°53·7′W	X	145,157
Pigyn Esgob	Conwy	SH7651	53°2·8′	3°50·6′W	X	115
Pigyn Shon-Nicholas	Carm	SN6635	52°0·1′	3°56·7′W	H	146
Pike	Cumbr	NY2821	54°35·0′	3°6·4′W	X	89,90
Pike	Cumbr	NY3031	54°40·4′	3°4·7′W	X	90
Pike	Cumbr	NY4678	55°5·9′	2°50·3′W	X	86
Pikeawassa	Cumbr	NY4318	54°33·5′	2°52·5′W	X	90
Pike Barn	W Susx	TQ1621	50°58·8′	0°20·5′W	X	198
Pikeber	N Yks	SD8056	54°0·2′	2°17·9′W	X	103
Pike Burn	Northum	NY6379	55°6·5′	2°34·4′W	W	86
Pike Corner	Wilts	SU0393	51°38·4′	1°57·0′W	X	163,173
Piked Acre Wood	Lancs	SD7743	53°53·2′	2°20·6′W	F	103
Pikedaw Hill	N Yks	SD8863	54°4·0′	2°10·6′W	X	98
Pike de Bield Moss	Cumbr	NY2306	54°26·9′	3°10·8′W	X	89,90
Piked Howe	Cumbr	SD4798	54°22·7′	2°48·5′W	X	97
Piked Howes	Cumbr	NY4404	54°25·9′	2°51·4′W	X	90
Pike Drain	Lincs	SK9266	53°11·2′	0°37·0′W	W	121
Pike End	Cald	SE0217	53°39·3′	1°57·8′W	T	110
Pike Fell	D & G	NY4193	55°13·9′	2°55·2′W	H	79
Pike Fell	Scot Bord	NT5306	55°21·0′	2°44·0′W	H	79
Pikefish	Kent	TQ6947	51°12·1′	0°25·5′E	X	188
Pikehall	Derby	SK1959	53°7·9′	1°42·6′W	T	119
Pike Hall Fm	Warw	SP4564	52°16·6′	1°20·0′W	FM	151
Pike Hill	Lancs	SD8632	53°47·3′	2°12·3′W	T	103
Pike Hill	N Yks	NZ8800	54°23·5′	0°38·3′W	X	94
Pike Hill	N Yks	SD8793	54°20·2′	2°11·6′W	X	98
Pike Hill	Scot Bord	NT3505	55°20·3′	3°1·1′W	H	79
Pike Hill Moss	N Yks	NZ7701	54°24·2′	0°48·4′W	H	94
Pike Ho	Derby	SK1651	53°3·6′	1°45·3′W	X	119
Pike Ho	Northum	NZ0799	55°17·4′	1°53·0′W	X	81
Pike How	Cumbr	NY4108	54°28·1′	2°54·2′W	X	90
Pike Howe	N Yks	NZ6508	54°28·0′	0°59·4′W	A	94
Pike Howe	N Yks	NZ6809	54°28·5′	0°56·6′W	A	94
Pike Howe	N Yks	SE6996	54°21·5′	0°55·9′W	A	94,100
Pike Knowe	D & G	NY2485	55°9·5′	3°11·1′W	H	79
Pike Law	Cald	SE0417	53°39·2′	1°56·0′W	T	110
Pike Law	Durham	NY9031	54°40·7′	2°8·9′W	X	91,92
Pikeley Rigg	Northum	NY8851	54°51·5′	2°10·8′W	X	87
Pike Low	Ches	SJ9776	53°17·1′	2°2·3′W	X	118
Pike Low	Derby	SK1889	53°24·1′	1°43·3′W	A	110
Pike Lowe	Lancs	SD6222	53°41·8′	2°34·1′W	H	102,103
Pike Lowe	Lancs	SD7323	53°42·4′	2°24·1′W	X	103
Pike Lowe	Sheff	SK2097	53°28·4′	1°41·5′W	X	110
Pike Lowe Stones	Sheff	SK2197	53°28·4′	1°40·6′W	X	110
Pikelow Fm	Ches	SJ8569	53°13·3′	2°13·1′W	FM	118
Pikeman Hill	Cumbr	NY7238	54°44·4′	2°25·7′W	X	91
Pikenaze Fm	Derby	SE0900	53°30·0′	1°51·4′W	FM	110
Pikenaze Moor	Derby	SE1100	53°30·0′	1°49·6′W	X	110
Pike Nook Fm	Ches	SJ5745	53°16·4′	2°41·0′W	FM	117
Pike of Blisco	Cumbr	NY2704	54°25·8′	3°7·1′W	H	89,90
Pike of Carrs	Cumbr	NY3010	54°29·1′	3°4·4′W	H	90
Pike of Stickle	Cumbr	NY2707	54°27·4′	3°7·1′W	X	89,90
Pike Rigg	Northum	NY7354	54°53·0′	2°24·8′W	X	86,87
Pikes Edge	Cumbr	SD7787	54°16·9′	2°20·8′W	X	98
Pikes End Fm	Shrops	SJ4431	52°52·7′	2°49·5′W	FM	126
Pikes End Moss	Shrops	SJ4431	52°52·7′	2°49·5′W	F	126
Pike's Fm	Dorset	SY9493	50°44·4′	2°4·7′W	FM	195
Pike's Fm	Mil Key	SP8143	52°5·0′	0°48·7′W	FM	152
Pikes Fm	Surrey	TQ3946	51°12·0′	0°0·2′W	FM	187
Pikeshaw Wood	N Yks	SE3955	53°59·6′	1°23·9′W	F	104
Pikeshill	Hants	SU2908	50°52·5′	1°34·9′W	T	196
Pikes Hole Fm	S Tyne	NZ3261	54°56·8′	1°29·6′W	FM	88
Pike Side	Cumbr	SD1893	54°19·8′	3°15·2′W	X	96
Pike Side	Lancs	SD7259	54°1·8′	2°25·2′W	X	103
Pikes, The	D & G	NY4493	55°13·9′	2°52·4′W	X	79
Pike Stone	Durham	NZ0525	54°37·5′	1°54·9′W	X	92
Pikestone Brow	Durham	NY9429	54°39·6′	2°5·2′W	X	91,92
Pikestone Hill	D & G	NY1991	55°12·6′	3°15·9′W	H	79
Pikestone Rig	Scot Bord	NT2417	55°26·7′	3°11·7′W	H	79
Pike Stones Bed	Cumbr	SD2266	54°5·3′	3°11·1′W	X	96
Pikeston Fell	Durham	NZ0432	54°41·2′	1°55·9′W	X	92
Pikestye	Heref	SO5348	52°7·9′	2°40·8′W	T	149
Pikethaw Hill	D & G	NY3697	55°16·0′	3°0·0′W	H	79
Pike, The	Derby	SK0895	53°27·3′	1°52·4′W	X	110
Pike, The	D & G	NY2697	55°15·9′	3°9·4′W	H	79
Pike, The	Scot Bord	NT2908	55°21·9′	3°6·8′W	H	79
Pike, The	Scot Bord	NT4904	55°19·9′	2°47·8′W	H	79
Pike, The	S Lanak	NT0652	55°45·4′	3°29·4′W	X	65,72
Pikethorn Wood	Lancs	SD5166	54°5·5′	2°44·5′W	F	97
Piketillam	Aberd	NJ8230	57°21·9′	2°17·5′W	X	29,30
Piketillum	Aberd	NJ9732	57°23·0′	2°2·5′W	X	30
Pikey Hill	Moray	NJ2151	57°32·8′	3°18·7′W	H	28
Pikins	Powys	SN9498	52°34·4′	3°33·5′W	X	136
Pilbach	Cered	SN5459	52°12·8′	4°7·8′W	X	146
Pilchard Cove	Devon	SX8446	50°18·4′	3°37·4′W	W	202
Pilch Fm	Bucks	SP7431	51°58·6′	0°55·0′W	FM	152,165
Pilcox Hall	Essex	TM1325	51°53·2′	1°6·1′E	X	168,169
Pile Fm	Wilts	ST9361	51°21·1′	2°5·6′W	FM	173
Pile Lighthouse	Fife	NO4629	56°27·3′	2°52·1′W	X	54,59
Piles Coppice	Warw	SP3876	52°23·1′	1°26·1′W	F	140
Piles Hill	Devon	SX6560	50°25·7′	3°53·7′W	X	202
Piles Mill	Somer	SS9046	51°12·4′	3°34·1′W	X	181
Pileywell Fm	Devon	SS9714	50°55·2′	3°27·5′W	FM	181
Pilford	Dorset	SU0301	50°48·7′	1°57·1′W	T	195
Pilford Br	Lincs	TF0388	53°23·0′	0°26·7′W	X	112,121
Pilfrey Br	N Lincs	SE8009	53°34·5′	0°47·1′W	X	112
Pilgrim Cott	Shrops	SO5593	52°32·2′	2°39·4′W	X	137,138
Pilgrim Hall	E Susx	TQ5017	50°56·2′	0°8·5′E	X	199
Pilgrim Ho	Kent	TQ4456	51°17·3′	0°4·3′E	X	187
Pilgrim Oak	Notts	SK5554	53°5·1′	1°10·3′W	X	120
Pilgrims	W Berks	SU6668	51°24·7′	1°2·7′W	X	175
Pilgrims Croft	Hants	SU2527	51°2·7′	1°38·2′W	X	184
Pilgrim's Fm	Hants	SU5146	51°12·9′	1°15·8′W	FM	185
Pilgrims Fm	Surrey	TQ4155	51°16·8′	0°1·7′E	FM	187
Pilgrims Hall	Essex	TQ5796	51°38·7′	0°16·5′E	X	167,177
Pilgrims Hatch	Essex	TQ5895	51°38·1′	0°17·4′E	T	167,177
Pilgrim Shed	Suff	TL9476	52°21·1′	0°51·3′E	X	144
Pilgrims Park	I of W	SZ4593	50°44·3′	1°21·4′W	X	196
Pilgrims' Rest	Carm	SN3013	51°47·6′	4°27·5′W	X	159
Pilgrim's Walk	Norf	TL7790	52°29·0′	0°36·8′E	A	144
Pilgrims' Way	Kent	TQ6561	51°19·7′	0°22·5′E	X	177,178,188
Pilgrims' Way	Surrey	SU8847	51°13·2′	0°44·0′W	X	186
Pilgrims' Way	Surrey	TQ2451	51°14·9′	0°13·0′W	A	187
Pilgrims' Way (Trackway)	Kent	TQ6561	51°19·7′	0°22·5′E	A	177,178,188
Pilgrims' Way (Trackway)	Kent	TR0943	51°9·1′	0°59·7′E	A	179,189
Pilgrims' Way (Trackway)	Surrey	SU8847	51°13·2′	0°44·0′W	A	186
Pilgrove Fm	Glos	SO9124	51°55·1′	2°7·5′W	FM	163
Pilham	Lincs	SK8693	53°25·8′	0°41·9′W	T	112
Pilhatchie Burn	D & G	NX1575	55°2·4′	4°53·3′W	W	76
Pilhough	Derby	SK2564	53°10·6′	1°37·1′W	T	119
Pili Palas (Butterfly Palace)	I of Angl	SH5473	53°14·3′	4°10·9′W	X	114,115
Pilkham Hills	Fife	NT1889	56°5·5′	3°18·6′W	X	65,66
Pill	N Som	ST5275	51°28·6′	2°41·1′W	T	172
Pill	Pemb	SM9105	51°42·5′	5°1·1′W	T	157,158
Pilland	Devon	SS5435	51°6·0′	4°4·7′W	X	180
Pillar	Cumbr	NY1712	54°30·0′	3°16·5′W	H	89,90
Pillar Bank	Arg & Bt	NS3475	55°56·6′	4°39·0′W	X	63
Pillard's Corner	Cambs	TL3995	52°32·3′	0°3·4′E	X	142,143
Pillar Rock	Cumbr	NY1712	54°30·0′	3°16·5′W	X	89,90
Pillar Rock Point	N Ayr	NS0629	55°31·2′	5°4·0′W	X	69
Pillars	Scot Bord	NT1956	55°47·7′	3°17·1′W	X	65,66,72
Pillars Lodge	Wilts	ST9969	51°25·4′	2°0·5′W	X	173
Pillars of Hercules	Fife	NO2408	56°15·8′	3°13·2′W	X	59
Pillaton	Corn	SX3664	50°27·4′	4°18·3′W	T	201
Pillaton	Staffs	SJ9413	52°43·1′	2°4·9′W	T	127
Pillatonmill	Corn	SX3663	50°26·9′	4°18·2′W	X	201
Pillaton Old Hall	Staffs	SJ9412	52°42·6′	2°4·9′W	A	127
Pill Br	Somer	ST5023	51°0·5′	2°42·4′W	A	183
Pill Brook	Monm	SO4401	51°42·5′	2°48·2′W	W	171
Pilldu	Card	ST2480	51°31·1′	3°5·3′W	X	171
Pillerton Hersey	Warw	SP3048	52°8·0′	1°33·3′W	T	151
Pillerton Priors	Warw	SP2947	52°7·5′	1°34·2′W	T	151
Pilleth	Powys	SO2568	52°18·5′	3°5·6′W	T	137,148
Pilley	Barns	SE3300	53°30·0′	1°29·7′W	T	110,111
Pilley	Glos	SO9519	51°52·4′	2°4·0′W	T	163
Pilley	Hants	SZ3398	50°47·1′	1°31·5′W	T	196
Pilley Bailey	Hants	SZ3398	50°47·1′	1°31·5′W	T	196
Pilleygreen Lodges	W Susx	SU9011	50°53·7′	0°42·8′W	X	197
Pill Fm	Corn	SW8338	50°12·4′	5°2·1′W	FM	204
Pill Fm	Devon	SS5531	51°3·8′	4°3·8′W	FM	180
Pill Grove	N Som	ST5471	51°26·4′	2°39·3′W	F	172
Pillgwenlly	Newp	ST3187	51°34·9′	2°59·4′W	T	171
Pillham Fm	Somer	ST4546	51°12·9′	2°46·9′W	FM	182
Pillhead	Devon	SS4726	51°1·0′	4°10·5′W	X	180
Pillhead Gout	S Glos	ST5992	51°37·8′	2°35·2′W	X	162,172
Pill Heath Fm	Hants	SU3553	51°16·7′	1°29·5′W	FM	185
Pill Hill	Hants	SU4259	51°19·9′	1°23·4′W	X	174
Pillhill Brook	Hants	SU3244	51°11·9′	1°32·1′W	W	185
Pill Ho	Glos	ST5695	51°39·4′	2°37·8′W	X	162
Pillhouse Rocks	Glos	ST5695	51°39·4′	2°37·8′W	X	162
Pilling	Lancs	SD4048	53°55·7′	2°54·4′W	T	102
Pilling Fm South	Beds	TL0040	52°3·2′	0°32·1′W	FM	153
Pilling Hall	Lancs	SD4149	53°56·3′	2°53·5′W	X	102
Pilling Lane	Lancs	SD3749	53°56·2′	2°57·2′W	T	102
Pilling Marsh	Lancs	SD4149	53°56·3′	2°53·5′W	W	102
Pilling Moss	Lancs	SD4146	53°54·7′	2°53·5′W	X	102
Pilling Sands	Lancs	SD3851	53°57·3′	2°56·3′W	X	102
Pilling's Lock	Leic	SK5618	52°45·6′	1°9·8′W	X	129
Pilling Water	Lancs	SD4346	53°54·7′	2°51·6′W	W	102
Pilliven	Devon	SS8215	50°55·6′	3°40·4′W	X	181
Pill Moor	Somer	ST5442	51°10·8′	2°39·1′W	X	182,183
Pillmore Hill	S Lanak	NS9127	55°31·7′	3°43·2′W	H	71,72
Pillmoss Fm	Warr	SJ6081	53°19·7′	2°35·6′W	FM	109
Pillmouth	Devon	SS4624	50°59·9′	4°11·3′W	T	180,190
Pillocksgreen	Shrops	SO4288	52°29·4′	2°50·9′W	X	137
Pillodrie Ho	Aberd	NJ6923	57°18·1′	2°30·4′W	X	38
Pillow Burn	D & G	NX3787	55°9·3′	4°33·1′W	W	77
Pillowell	Glos	SO6206	51°45·3′	2°32·6′W	T	162
Pillow Mounds	E Susx	TQ4032	51°4·4′	0°0·3′E	A	187
Pillow Mounds	Gwyn	SH4045	52°59·0′	4°22·6′W	A	115,123
Pillow Mounds	Powys	SO1358	52°13·0′	3°16·0′W	A	148
Pillow Mounds	Shrops	SO3098	52°34·8′	3°1·6′W	A	137
Pillows Green	Glos	SO7929	51°57·8′	2°17·7′W	T	150
Pillow, The	Fife	NT6699	56°11·2′	2°32·4′W	X	59
Pillow Wood	Lincs	TF0721	52°46·8′	0°24·4′W	F	130
Pill Rigg Fm	N Yks	SE4093	54°20·1′	1°22·7′W	FM	99
Pill River	Somer	ST0240	51°9·3′	3°23·7′W	W	181
Pills, The	Oxon	SP2304	51°44·3′	1°39·6′W	X	163
Pill, The	Monm	ST4987	51°35·0′	2°43·8′W	X	172
Pillwell	Dorset	ST7819	50°58·5′	2°18·4′W	T	183
Pillwood Fm	E Yorks	TA0434	53°47·8′	0°24·8′W	FM	107
Pilly Hall	N Yks	NZ5708	54°28·1′	1°6·9′W	X	93
Pilmawr	Carm	SN2227	51°55·0′	4°34·9′W	X	145,158
Pilmoor	N Yks	SE4672	54°8·7′	1°17·3′W	X	100
Pilmoor Cottages	N Yks	SE4672	54°8·7′	1°17·3′W	X	100
Pilmoor Fm	N Yks	TA0878	54°11·4′	0°20·3′W	FM	101
Pilmoor Grange	N Yks	SE4672	54°8·7′	1°17·3′W	X	100
Pilmoor Hall	N Yks	SE4572	54°8·8′	1°18·2′W	X	99

Pilmore	Pth & Kin	NO3229	56°27.2'	3°5.7'W	X	53,59
Pilmore Gate Heath	Hants	SU2708	50°52.5'	1°36.6'W	X	195
Pilmour Cott	Fife	NO4917	56°20.8'	2°49.1'W	X	59
Pilmuir	Aberd	NO7092	57°1.3'	2°29.2'W	X	38,45
Pilmuir	D & G	NY1379	55°6.1'	3°21.4'W	X	85
Pilmuir	E Renf	NS5154	55°45.6'	4°22.0'W	X	64
Pilmuir	Fife	NO3903	56°13.2'	2°58.6'W	X	59
Pilmuir	Moray	NJ0258	57°36.3'	3°37.9'W	T	27
Pilmuir	Scot Bord	NT4811	55°23.7'	2°48.8'W	T	79
Pilmuir	Scot Bord	NT5049	55°44.2'	2°47.3'W	X	73
Pilmuir	Scot Bord	NT9067	55°54.0'	2°9.2'W	X	67
Pilmuir Burn	E Loth	NT5983	56°2.5'	2°39.0'W	W	67
Pilmuir Common	D & G	NY1178	55°5.6'	3°23.2'W	X	85
Pilmuir House	E Loth	NT4869	55°54.9'	2°49.5'W	A	66
Pilmuir Rig	Scot Bord	NT4810	55°23.1'	2°48.8'W	X	79
Pilning	S Glos	ST5585	51°34.0'	2°38.6'W	T	172
Pilning Fm	S Glos	ST5785	51°34.0'	2°36.8'W	FM	172
Pilning Sta	S Glos	ST5684	51°33.4'	2°37.7'W	X	172
Pilnyark Burn	S Ayr	NX3792	55°12.0'	4°33.2'W	W	77
Pilot Hill	Hants	SU3960	51°20.5'	1°26.0'W	H	174
Pilot, The	S Ayr	NS3200	55°16.2'	4°38.2'W	H	76
Pilot, The (PH)	Kent	TR0918	50°55.6'	0°58.8'E	X	189
Pilrig	C of Edin	NT2675	55°58.0'	3°10.7'W	T	66
Pilroath	Carm	SN3713	51°47.8'	4°21.4'W	X	159
Pilsbury	Derby	SK1163	53°10.1'	1°49.7'W	X	119
Pilsbury Castle Hills	Derby	SK1163	53°10.1'	1°49.7'W	X	119
Pilsbury Castle Hills (Motte & Baileys)	Staffs	SK1163	53°10.1'	1°49.7'W	A	119
Pilsbury Lodge	Derby	SK1263	53°10.1'	1°48.8'W	X	119
Pilsdon	Dorset	SY4199	50°47.5'	2°49.8'W	T	193
Pilsdon Barn	Dorset	ST4100	50°48.0'	2°49.9'W	X	193
Pilsdon Manor	Dorset	SY4199	50°47.5'	2°49.8'W	A	193
Pilsdon Pen	Dorset	ST4001	50°48.6'	2°50.7'W	X	193
Pilsey Island	W Susx	SU7700	50°47.9'	0°54.1'W	X	197
Pilsey Sand	W Susx	SU7600	50°47.9'	0°54.9'W	X	197
Pilsgate	Peterb	TF0605	52°38.2'	0°25.6'W	T	142
Pilsley	Derby	SK2471	53°14.4'	1°38.0'W	T	119
Pilsley	Derby	SK4262	53°9.4'	1°21.9'W	T	120
Pilsley Green	Derby	SK4261	53°8.9'	1°21.9'W	T	120
Pilson Green	Norf	TG3713	52°40.0'	1°30.7'E	T	133,134
Pilstone	Monm	SO5305	51°44.7'	2°40.5'W	X	162
Pilstones Wood	Staffs	SJ8533	52°53.9'	2°13.0'W	F	127
Pilstye Fm	W Susx	TQ3028	51°2.4'	0°8.4'W	FM	187,198
Piltanton Burn	D & G	NX1156	54°52.0'	4°56.3'W	W	82
Piltdown	E Susx	TQ4422	50°59.0'	0°3.5'E	T	198
Piltochie	Aberd	NJ9635	57°24.6'	2°3.5'W	X	30
Pilton	C of Edin	NT2376	55°58.5'	3°13.6'W	T	66
Pilton	Devon	SS5534	51°5.5'	4°3.9'W	T	180
Pilton	Northnts	TL0284	52°26.9'	0°29.5'W	T	141
Pilton	Rut	SK9102	52°36.7'	0°39.0'W	T	141
Pilton	Somer	ST5940	51°9.7'	2°34.8'W	T	182,183
Pilton	Swan	SS4387	51°33.8'	4°15.5'W	X	159
Pilton Green	Swan	SS4487	51°33.9'	4°14.7'W	T	159
Pilton Lodge	Northnts	TL0085	52°27.5'	0°31.3'W	X	141
Pilton Park	Somer	ST5839	51°9.2'	2°35.6'W	X	182,183
Pilton Wood	Somer	ST5841	51°10.2'	2°35.7'W	F	182,183
Pil Tor	Devon	SX7375	50°33.9'	3°47.2'W	H	191
Piltown	Somer	ST5538	51°8.6'	2°38.2'W	T	182,183
Pilwhirn Burn	D & G	NX1974	55°1.9'	4°49.5'W	W	76
Pimbo	Lancs	SD4904	53°32.1'	2°45.8'W	X	108
Pimbo(Industrial Estate)	Lancs	SD4904	53°32.1'	2°45.8'W	X	108
Pim Hill	Shrops	SJ4821	52°47.3'	2°45.9'W	H	126
Pimhole	Bury	SD8110	53°35.4'	2°16.8'W	T	109
Pimley Manor	Shrops	SJ5214	52°43.5'	2°42.2'W	X	126
Pimlico	C of West	TQ2978	51°29.4'	0°8.1'W	T	176
Pimlico	Herts	TL0905	51°44.2'	0°24.9'W	T	166
Pimlico	Lancs	SD7443	53°53.2'	2°23.3'W	T	103
Pimlico	Northnts	SP6140	52°3.5'	1°6.2'W	X	152
Pimlico Fm	Lincs	TA1107	53°33.1'	0°19.1'W	FM	113
Pimlico Fm	Oxon	SP5531	51°58.7'	1°11.6'W	FM	152
Pimlico Ho	Lincs	TF3448	53°1.0'	0°0.3'E	X	131
Pimlico Sand	Glos	SO7112	51°48.6'	2°24.8'W	X	162
Pimm Fm	Oxon	SP4204	51°44.2'	1°23.1'W	FM	164
Pimperne	Dorset	ST5708	50°52.4'	2°36.3'W	T	194
Pimperne	Dorset	ST9009	50°53.1'	2°8.1'W	T	195
Pimperne Down	Dorset	ST8910	50°53.6'	2°9.0'W	X	195
Pimperne Long Barrow	Dorset	ST9110	50°53.6'	2°7.3'W	A	195
Pimperne Wood	Dorset	ST9111	50°54.1'	2°7.3'W	F	195
Pimphurst	Kent	TQ9242	51°8.9'	0°45.1'E	X	189
Pimp's Court	Kent	TQ7552	51°14.6'	0°30.8'E	X	188
Pinbain Burn	S Ayr	NX1491	55°11.0'	4°54.9'W	W	76
Pinbain Hill	S Ayr	NX1492	55°11.5'	4°54.9'W	H	76
Pinbreck Hill	S Ayr	NX3290	55°10.8'	4°37.9'W	H	76
Pinbreck Hill	S Ayr	NX3493	55°12.5'	4°36.1'W	H	76
Pinbury Park	Glos	SO9504	51°44.3'	2°4.0'W	A	163
Pincey Brook	Essex	TL5415	51°49.0'	0°14.5'E	W	167
Pinchaford	Devon	SX7676	50°34.5'	3°44.7'W	X	191
Pinchbeck	Lincs	TF2325	52°48.7'	0°10.1'W	T	131
Pinchbeck Common	Lincs	TF1921	52°46.6'	0°13.7'W	X	130
Pinchbeck Common	Lincs	TF2021	52°46.6'	0°12.9'W	X	131
Pinchbeck Marsh	Lincs	TF2627	52°49.8'	0°7.4'W	X	131
Pinchbeck North Fen	Lincs	TF1727	52°49.9'	0°15.4'W	X	130
Pinchbeck South Fen	Lincs	TF1922	52°47.2'	0°13.7'W	X	130
Pinchbeck South Fen	Lincs	TF2022	52°47.2'	0°12.8'W	X	131
Pinchbecks Yard	Lincs	TF5157	53°5.6'	0°15.7'E	X	122
Pinchbeck West	Lincs	TF1925	52°48.8'	0°13.7'W	T	130
Pinchbeck West	Lincs	TF2024	52°48.2'	0°12.8'W	T	131
Pinchdyke	Shetld	HU3664	60°21.8'	1°20.3'W	X	2,3
Pincheon Green	Donc	SE6517	53°39.0'	1°0.6'W	T	111
Pinch Hall	E Yorks	SE7944	53°53.4'	0°47.5'W	X	105,106
Pinchinthorpe Hall	Red & Cl	NZ5714	54°31.3'	1°6.7'W	X	93
Pinchinthorpe Ho	Red & Cl	NZ5814	54°31.3'	1°5.8'W	X	93
Pinchley Wood	Glos	SO9916	51°50.8'	2°0.5'W	F	163
Pinchmill Islands	Beds	SP9958	52°12.9'	0°32.7'W	X	153
Pinchom's Hill	Derby	SK3647	53°1.4'	1°27.4'W	X	119,128
Pinchpools	Essex	TL4927	51°55.5'	0°10.4'E	X	167
Pinch Timber Fm	Essex	TL4504	51°43.2'	0°6.3'E	FM	167
Pinckney Green	Wilts	ST8064	51°22.7'	2°16.9'W	T	173
Pinclanty	S Ayr	NX2391	55°11.2'	4°46.4'W	X	76
Pinclanty Loch	S Ayr	NX2490	55°10.6'	4°45.4'W	W	76

Pincock	Lancs	SD5517	53°39.1'	2°40.4'W	T	108
Pincots Fm	S Glos	ST7287	51°35.1'	2°23.9'W	FM	172
Pincott Fm	Glos	SO8814	51°49.7'	2°10.1'W	FM	162
Pincushion	Sund	NZ4252	54°51.9'	1°20.3'W	X	88
Pin Dale	Derby	SK1582	53°20.3'	1°46.1'W	X	110
Pinden	Kent	TQ5969	51°24.1'	0°17.5'E	X	177
Pinderachy	Angus	NO4565	56°46.7'	2°53.6'W	H	44
Pinderhill Fm	E Yorks	TA1352	53°57.3'	0°16.3'W	FM	107
Pinder's Rock	Derby	SK2255	53°5.7'	1°39.9'W	X	119
Pinder Stile	N Yks	SK9868	54°6.7'	2°1.4'W	X	98
Pind Hill	Cumbr	NY8617	54°33.1'	2°12.6'W	X	91,92
Pind Howes	N Yks	NZ7004	54°25.8'	0°54.8'W	A	94
Pindon End	Mil Key	SP7847	52°7.2'	0°51.2'W	X	152
Pindonnan Craigs	S Ayr	NX2787	55°9.1'	4°42.5'W	X	76
Pineapple, The	Falk	NS8888	56°4.6'	3°47.5'W	X	65
Pinegrove	Angus	NO5552	56°39.7'	2°43.6'W	X	54
Pineham	Kent	TR3145	51°9.7'	1°18.6'E	T	179
Pineham	Mil Key	SP8841	52°3.9'	0°42.6'W	T	152
Pineham Fm	Mil Key	SP8244	52°5.5'	0°47.8'W	FM	152
Pine Have	Corn	SW9981	50°35.9'	4°50.0'W	W	200
Pine Hill	Beds	TL0938	52°2.0'	0°24.3'W	X	153
Pinehill Fm	Herts	TL3627	51°55.7'	0°0.9'W	FM	166
Pinehurst	Swin	SU1587	51°35.1'	1°46.6'W	T	173
Pinehurst Fm	E Susx	TQ5326	51°1.0'	0°11.3'E	FM	188,199
Pine Lake	Lancs	SD5172	54°8.7'	2°44.6'W	W	97
Pine Lodge Fm	Dorset	SY7291	50°43.3'	2°23.4'W	FM	194
Pines Dene	Devon	SS4940	51°8.6'	4°9.1'W	X	180
Pines Garden, The	Kent	TR3644	51°9.0'	1°22.9'E	X	179
Pines, The	Lincs	SK8929	52°51.3'	0°40.3'W	X	130
Pines, The	Shrops	SO3287	52°28.8'	2°59.7'W	X	137
Pines, The	Suff	TM3579	52°21.7'	1°27.5'E	X	156
Pine Tree Stud	Leic	SP7598	52°34.7'	0°53.2'W	X	141
Pinetum	Glos	SO7719	51°52.4'	2°19.7'W	X	162
Pinewood	Lancs	SD7447	53°55.4'	2°23.3'W	X	103
Pinewood Film Studios	Bucks	TQ0184	51°33.0'	0°32.2'W	X	176
Pinewood Fm	E Yorks	SE7745	53°54.0'	0°49.3'W	FM	105,106
Pinewood (Sch)	Oxon	SU2386	51°34.6'	1°39.7'W	X	174
Piney Sleight	Somer	ST4854	51°17.2'	2°44.4'W	X	182
Piney Sleight Fm	Somer	ST4755	51°17.7'	2°45.2'W	FM	172,182
Pinfarthings	Glos	SO8500	51°42.1'	2°12.6'W	T	162
Pinfold	Lancs	SD3811	53°35.8'	2°55.8'W	T	108
Pinfold	Lancs	SD6336	53°49.4'	2°33.3'W	X	102,103
Pinfold Fm	Shrops	SJ4732	52°53.2'	2°46.9'W	FM	126
Pinfold Hill	Barns	SE2902	53°31.1'	1°33.3'W	T	110
Pinfold Lees Hill	Leic	SK7819	52°46.0'	0°50.2'W	X	129
Pinfoldpond	Beds	SP9332	51°59.0'	0°38.4'W	T	165
Pinfold Stud	Ches	SJ7977	53°17.6'	2°18.5'W	X	118
Pinfold, The	Wrex	SJ5040	52°57.5'	2°44.3'W	X	117
Pinford	Dorset	ST6617	50°57.3'	2°28.7'W	X	183
Pinford End	Suff	TL8459	52°12.1'	0°42.0'E	T	155
Pinged	Carm	SN4203	51°42.5'	4°16.8'W	T	159
Pingerrach Burn	S Ayr	NX2795	55°13.4'	4°42.8'W	W	76
Pingewood	W Berks	SU6969	51°25.2'	1°0.1'W	T	175
Pingle	D & G	NY3178	55°5.7'	3°4.4'W	X	85
Pingle Br	Norf	TF5202	52°35.9'	0°15.1'E	X	143
Pingle Lodge Fm	Norf	TF5301	52°35.3'	0°15.9'E	FM	143
Pingles Place	E Susx	TQ5101	50°47.6'	0°8.9'E	X	199
Pinglestone Fm	Hants	SU5833	51°5.8'	1°9.9'W	FM	185
Pingley Dyke	Notts	SK7454	53°4.9'	0°53.3'W	W	120
Pingley Fm	Lincs	TA0106	53°32.7'	0°28.1'W	FM	112
Pin Green	Herts	TL2425	51°54.8'	0°11.4'W	T	166
Pingry Fm	Glos	SO5709	51°46.9'	2°37.0'W	FM	162
Pinhaw	N Yks	SD9447	53°55.4'	2°5.1'W	X	103
Pinhay	Devon	SY3191	50°43.1'	2°58.3'W	X	193
Pinhay Bay	Devon	SY3290	50°42.6'	2°57.4'W	W	193
Pinhey's Cross	Devon	SX7846	50°18.3'	3°42.4'W	X	202
Pin Hill	Lincs	SK8399	53°29.1'	0°44.5'W	X	112
Pin Hill Fm	Devon	SY1495	50°45.1'	3°12.8'W	FM	192,193
Pinhills Fm	Wilts	ST9869	51°25.4'	2°1.3'W	FM	173
Pinhill's Fm	Worcs	SP0158	52°13.4'	1°58.7'W	FM	150
Pin Hill Wood	Devon	SY1395	50°45.1'	3°13.6'W	F	192,193
Pinhoe	Devon	SX9694	50°44.4'	3°28.1'W	T	192
Pinhoe Hall	Suff	TL7348	52°6.4'	0°32.0'E	X	155
Pin Hole	Derby	SK5374	53°15.9'	1°11.9'W	A	120
Pinhoulland	Shetld	HU2549	60°13.7'	1°32.4'W	X	3
Pin Howe	N Yks	SE5099	54°23.3'	1°13.4'W	A	100
Pinkerton Hill	E Loth	NT6974	55°57.7'	2°29.4'W	X	67
Pinkery Fm	Somer	SS7241	51°9.5'	3°49.4'W	FM	180
Pinkett's Booth	Cov	SP2781	52°25.8'	1°35.8'W	T	140
Pink Green	Worcs	SP0869	52°19.4'	1°52.6'W	T	139
Pinkhill Fm	Oxon	SP4307	51°45.8'	1°22.2'W	FM	164
Pinkhorn Fm	Kent	TQ8245	51°10.7'	0°36.6'E	FM	188
Pinkhurst	W Susx	TQ1330	51°3.7'	0°22.9'W	X	187
Pinkhurst Fm	Surrey	TQ1136	51°7.0'	0°24.5'W	FM	187
Pinkie Braes	E Loth	NT3672	55°56.5'	3°1.0'W	T	66
Pinkie Ho	E Loth	NT3472	55°56.4'	3°3.0'W	A	66
Pinkney	Wilts	ST8686	51°34.6'	2°11.7'W	T	173
Pinkney Carr Fm	N Yks	NZ2312	54°30.4'	1°38.3'W	FM	93
Pinkney Court	Wilts	ST8687	51°35.1'	2°11.7'W	X	173
Pinkney Fm	Wilts	ST9358	51°19.5'	2°5.6'W	FM	173
Pinkney Park	Wilts	ST8686	51°34.6'	2°11.7'W	X	173
Pinkneys Green	Win & Maid	SU8582	51°32.1'	0°46.1'W	T	175
Pinksey Bottom	Cumbr	NY6903	54°25.5'	2°28.2'W	X	91
Pinks Fm	Kent	TQ9656	51°16.4'	0°49.0'E	FM	178
Pinksmoor	Somer	ST1019	50°58.0'	3°16.5'W	T	181,193
Pinkson Creek	Corn	SW9472	50°30.9'	4°54.0'W	W	200
Pinkstone Rig	S Lanak	NS8023	55°29.4'	3°53.5'W	H	71,72
Pinkwell	Glos	SP0511	51°48.1'	1°55.3'W	X	163
Pink Wood	Somer	ST7037	51°8.1'	2°25.3'W	F	183
Pinkworthy	Devon	SS2800	50°46.7'	4°26.0'W	X	190
Pinkworthy	Somer	SS7241	51°9.5'	3°49.4'W	X	180
Pinkworthy Fm	Devon	SS8920	50°58.4'	3°34.5'W	FM	181
Pinkworthy Pond	Somer	SS7242	51°10.0'	3°49.5'W	W	180
Pinlands Fm	W Susx	TQ1818	50°57.2'	0°18.8'W	FM	198
Pinley	Cov	SP3577	52°23.6'	1°28.7'W	T	140
Pinley Abbey Fm	Warw	SP2165	52°17.2'	1°41.1'W	FM	151
Pinley Green	Warw	SP2066	52°17.7'	1°42.0'W	T	151
Pinmacher	S Ayr	NX1993	55°12.1'	4°50.2'W	X	76
Pinmarsh Fm	Oxon	SU4290	51°36.7'	1°23.2'W	FM	164,174
Pinmerry	S Ayr	NS3411	55°22.2'	4°36.7'W	X	70

Pinmerry	S Ayr	NX2494	55°12.8'	4°45.6'W	X	76
Pin Mill	Suff	TM2037	51°59.5'	1°12.7'E	X	169
Pinminnoch	D & G	NX0254	54°50.8'	5°4.6'W	X	82
Pinminnoch	D & G	NX0255	54°51.3'	5°4.7'W	X	82
Pinminnoch	S Ayr	NX1893	55°12.1'	4°51.2'W	X	76
Pinminnoch Burn	D & G	NX0356	54°51.9'	5°3.8'W	W	82
Pinmoor Fm	Devon	SX7588	50°40.9'	3°45.8'W	FM	191
Pinmore	S Ayr	NX2091	55°11.1'	4°49.2'W	T	76
Pinmore Mains	S Ayr	NX2190	55°10.6'	4°48.2'W	X	76
Pinmullan Burn	S Ayr	NX3294	55°13.0'	4°38.0'W	W	76
Pinn	Devon	SY1086	50°40.2'	3°16.0'W	X	192
Pinnacle	Devon	SX4193	50°43.1'	4°14.8'W	X	190
Pinnacle	Scot Bord	NT5825	55°31.3'	2°39.5'W	X	73,74
Pinnacle	S Lanak	NT0024	55°30.2'	3°34.6'W	H	72
Pinnacle Bield	Cumbr	NY2409	54°28.5'	3°9.9'W	X	89,90
Pinnacle Hill	Herts	TL1626	51°55.5'	0°18.4'W	X	166
Pinnacle Hill	Somer	ST2040	51°9.5'	3°8.3'W	H	182
Pinnacles	Essex	TL4209	51°45.9'	0°3.9'E	T	167
Pinnacles, The	Dorset	SZ0582	50°38.5'	1°55.4'W	X	195
Pinnacles,The	Orkney	ND3097	58°51.6'	3°12.3'W	X	6,7
Pinnacle, The	Kirk	SE2118	53°39.7'	1°40.5'W	X	110
Pinnacle Wood	D & G	NY0484	55°8.7'	3°29.9'W	F	78
Pinn Beacon Plantn	Devon	SY1087	50°40.8'	3°16.1'W	F	192
Pinn Court Fm	Devon	SX9794	50°44.4'	3°27.2'W	FM	192
Pinnelhill Wood	Fife	NT1684	56°2.7'	3°20.5'W	F	65,66
Pinnells End Fm	Glos	SO7601	51°42.7'	2°20.5'W	FM	162
Pinnels	Pth & Kin	NO1803	56°13.0'	3°18.9'W	X	58
Pinner	Harrow	TQ1189	51°35.6'	0°23.5'W	T	176
Pinner Green	Bucks	SP9900	51°41.6'	0°33.7'W	X	165
Pinner Green	Harrow	TQ1190	51°36.1'	0°23.4'W	T	176
Pinner Park Fm	Harrow	TQ1390	51°36.1'	0°21.7'W	FM	176
Pinners Fm	Kent	TR2553	51°14.1'	1°13.8'E	FM	179
Pinnerwood Ho	Harrow	TQ1191	51°36.6'	0°23.4'W	X	176
Pinnerwood Park	Harrow	TQ1190	51°36.1'	0°23.4'W	T	176
Pinneywood Fm	Devon	ST3100	50°48.0'	2°58.4'W	FM	193
Pinn Fm	Kent	TR0535	51°4.9'	0°56.0'E	FM	179,189
Pinnick Wood	Hants	SU1907	50°52.0'	1°43.4'W	F	195
Pinnock Fm	Glos	SP0728	51°57.3'	1°53.5'W	FM	150,163
Pinnocks Fm	Suff	TL9577	52°21.6'	0°52.2'E	FM	144
Pinnockshill	Corn	SX1974	50°32.5'	4°32.9'W	X	201
Pinnock, The	Kent	TQ9144	51°10.0'	0°44.3'E	X	189
Pinnock Village	Glos	SP0728	51°57.3'	1°53.5'W	A	150,163
Pinns Fm	Hants	SU2920	50°59.0'	1°34.8'W	FM	185
Pin's Green	Worcs	SO8049	52°8.6'	2°17.1'W	T	150
Pins Knoll	Dorset	SY5390	50°42.7'	2°39.6'W	X	194
Pinsla Park	Corn	SX1266	50°28.1'	4°38.6'W	X	200
Pinsley Brook	Heref	SO4261	52°14.9'	2°50.6'W	W	137,148,149
Pinsley Green	Ches	SJ5846	53°0.8'	2°37.2'W	T	117
Pinsley Wood	Oxon	SP4213	51°49.1'	1°23.0'W	F	164
Pinslow Fm	Devon	SX3490	50°41.4'	4°20.6'W	FM	190
Pin Stane	S Lanak	NS9410	55°22.6'	3°39.9'W	H	71,78
Pin Stane	S Lanak	NT0116	55°25.9'	3°33.4'W	H	78
Pinstones	Shrops	SO4886	52°28.4'	2°45.5'W	T	137,138
Pinswell	Glos	SP0312	51°48.6'	1°57.0'W	X	163
Pinswell Plantation	Glos	SO9815	51°50.3'	2°1.3'W	F	163
Pinup Reach	Medway	TQ8070	51°24.2'	0°35.7'E	W	178
Pinvalley	S Ayr	NX3395	55°13.5'	4°37.1'W	X	76
Pinverains	S Ayr	NX3398	55°15.1'	4°37.2'W	X	76
Pinverains	S Ayr	NX4199	55°15.8'	4°29.7'W	H	77
Pinvin	Worcs	SO9548	52°8.1'	2°4.0'W	T	150
Pinwall	Leic	SK3000	52°36.1'	1°33.0'W	T	140
Pinwherran Burn	D & G	NX1073	55°1.2'	4°57.9'W	W	76
Pinwherrie	D & G	NX1362	54°55.3'	4°54.7'W	X	82
Pinwherry	S Ayr	NX1986	55°8.4'	4°50.0'W	T	76
Pinwherry Hill	S Ayr	NX1885	55°7.8'	4°50.9'W	X	76
Pinxton	Derby	SK4554	53°5.1'	1°19.3'W	T	120
Piot Crag	Cumbr	NY4510	54°29.2'	2°50.5'W	X	90
Pipe and Lyde	Heref	SO5044	52°5.8'	2°43.4'W	T	149
Pipe Gate	Shrops	SJ7340	52°57.6'	2°23.7'W	T	118
Pipe Grange	Staffs	SK0908	52°40.4'	1°51.6'W	X	128
Pipe Hall	Staffs	SK0909	52°41.0'	1°51.6'W	X	128
Pipehill	Staffs	SK0908	52°40.4'	1°51.6'W	T	128
Pipehouse	Bath & NE Somer	ST7759	51°20.0'	2°19.4'W	T	172
Pipehouse Fm	Ches	SJ5349	53°2.4'	2°41.7'W	FM	117
Pipeland	Fife	NO5015	56°19.7'	2°48.1'W	X	59
Pipe Place	Staffs	SK0807	52°39.9'	1°52.5'W	X	139
Piperclose Ho	Northum	NZ0065	54°59.0'	1°59.6'W	X	87
Pipercroft	D & G	NX7771	55°1.4'	3°55.0'W	X	84
Piperdam Plantn	Angus	NO3035	56°30.4'	3°7.8'W	F	53
Piperdeanrigg	Cumbr	NY4676	55°4.8'	2°50.3'W	X	86
Piper Fm	Leic	SK4722	52°47.8'	1°17.8'W	FM	129
Piperhall	Arg & Bt	NS0958	55°46.9'	5°2.3'W	X	63
Piperhill	Highld	NH8650	57°31.8'	3°53.8'W	T	27
Piper Hill	N Yks	SE2098	54°22.9'	1°41.1'W	X	99
Piper Hill Plantn	N Yks	SE6075	54°10.3'	1°4.4'W	F	100
Piper Hole	Cumbr	NY7203	54°25.5'	2°25.5'W	X	91
Piper Hole Fm	Leic	SK7626	52°49.8'	0°51.9'W	FM	129
Pipe Ridware	Staffs	SK0917	52°45.3'	1°51.6'W	T	128
Piper Lane Lodge	Notts	SK6073	53°15.3'	1°5.6'W	X	120
Piperpool	Fife	NS9793	56°7.4'	3°39.0'W	X	58
Pipers	Herts	TL1613	51°48.4'	0°18.7'W	X	166
Piper's Ash	Ches	SJ4367	53°12.1'	2°50.8'W	T	117
Piper's Burn	Highld	NN5798	57°3.3'	4°21.0'W	W	35
Pipers Copse	Hants	SU2713	50°55.2'	1°36.6'W	F	195
Piper's Copse	W Susx	SU9729	51°3.4'	0°36.6'W	F	186,197
Pipers Corner (Sch)	Bucks	SU8697	51°40.1'	0°45.0'W	X	165
Piper's End	Worcs	SO8434	52°0.5'	2°13.6'W	T	150
Pipers Fm	Herts	TQ0692	51°37.2'	0°27.7'W	FM	176
Piper's Fm	W Susx	SU8419	50°58.1'	0°47.8'W	FM	197
Piper's Hall Fm	Suff	TL8457	52°11.1'	0°41.9'E	FM	155
Piper Shaws	Northum	NY9499	55°17.4'	2°5.2'W	X	80
Piper's Hill	Hants	SU3044	51°11.9'	1°33.8'W	X	185
Piper's Hill	Herts	TL0210	51°47.0'	0°30.9'W	X	166
Piper's Hill	Worcs	SO9665	52°17.2'	2°3.1'W	T	150
Piper's Hill Fm	Warw	SP3756	52°12.3'	1°27.1'W	FM	151
Piper's Hole	I Scilly	SV8816	49°58.0'	6°20.7'W	X	203
Piper's Knowe	Scot Bord	NT3533	55°35.4'	3°1.4'W	X	73
Piper's Knowe	Scot Bord	NT4115	55°25.8'	2°55.5'W	X	79
Pipers Pool	Corn	SX2684	50°38.0'	4°27.3'W	T	201

Pipers, The	Corn	SW4324	50°3·9'	5°35·1'W	X	203
Pipers, The (Standing Stones)	Corn	SW4324	50°3·9'	5°35·1'W	A	203
Piperstile	Cumbr	NY5050	54°50·8'	2°46·3'W	X	86
Piperstones Hill	Pth & Kin	NN9911	56°17·1'	3°37·4'W	X	58
Pipers Vale	Suff	TM1741	52°1·7'	1°10·2'E	X	169
Pipers Wait	Hants	SU2416	50°56·8'	1°39·1'W	X	184
Piper's Wood	Surrey	TQ3749	51°13·6'	0°1·9'W	F	187
Piperton	Angus	NO5963	56°45·7'	2°39·8'W	X	44
Piper Wood	Leic	SK4721	52°47·3'	1°17·8'W	F	129
Pipe Strine	Wrekin	SJ6918	52°45·8'	2°27·2'W	W	127
Pipewell	Northnts	SP8385	52°27·6'	0°46·3'W	T	141
Pipewell Gate	E Susx	TQ9017	50°55·5'	0°42·6'E	A	189
Pipewell Upper Lodge	Northnts	SP8285	52°27·6'	0°47·2'W	X	141
Pipewell Wood	Northnts	SP8286	52°28·2'	0°47·2'W	F	141
Pipley Bottom	S Glos	ST7069	51°25·4'	2°25·5'W	X	172
Pippacott	Devon	SS5237	51°7·0'	4°6·5'W	T	180
Pippingford Park	E Susx	TQ4430	51°3·3'	0°3·7'E	X	187
Pippin Park	Suff	TL7257	52°11·3'	0°31·4'E	X	154
Pippins	Kent	TQ6342	51°9·5'	0°20·3'E	X	188
Pippin's Hill	Heref	SO6950	52°9·1'	2°26·8'W	X	149
Pippin Street	Lancs	SD5924	53°42·9'	2°36·9'W	T	102
Pipplepen Fm	Somer	ST4707	50°51·8'	2°44·8'W	FM	193
Pipps Ford	Suff	TM1053	52°8·3'	1°4·5'E	X	155
Pipps Hill	Essex	TQ6989	51°34·7'	0°26·7'E	T	177,178
Pipps Hill	Essex	TQ7090	51°35·2'	0°27·6'E	X	178
Pipsden	Kent	TQ7730	51°2·7'	0°31·9'E	T	188
Pipsford Fm	Dorset	ST5100	50°48·1'	2°41·3'W	FM	194
Pipshayne	Devon	SS9722	50°59·5'	3°27·7'W	X	181
Pipton	Powys	SO1638	52°2·3'	3°13·1'W	X	161
Pipworth Fm	W Berks	SU5479	51°30·7'	1°12·9'W	FM	174
Pirbright	Surrey	SU9455	51°17·4'	0°38·7'W	T	175,186
Pirbright Camp	Surrey	SU9256	51°18·0'	0°40·4'W	T	175,186
Pirbright Common	Surrey	SU9254	51°16·9'	0°40·4'W	X	186
Pirbright Common	Surrey	SU9258	51°19·0'	0°40·4'W	X	175,186
Pirbright Lodge	Surrey	SU9355	51°17·4'	0°39·6'W	X	175,186
Pire Hill	Staffs	SJ8931	52°52·8'	2°9·4'W	H	127
Pirehill Grange	Staffs	SJ8930	52°52·3'	2°9·4'W	X	127
Pirehill Ho	Staffs	SJ9030	52°52·3'	2°8·5'W	X	127
Pirleyhill	S Ayr	NS2203	55°17·6'	4°47·8'W	X	76
Pirnaton	Scot Bord	NT4249	55°44·1'	2°55·0'W	X	73
Pirn Craig	Scot Bord	NT3437	55°37·6'	3°2·5'W	H	73
Pirnhill	Pth & Kin	NN8716	56°19·6'	3°49·2'W	X	58
Pirn Ho	Scot Bord	NT4447	55°43·0'	2°53·0'W	X	73
Pirnie	Scot Bord	NT6428	55°32·9'	2°33·8'W	X	74
Pirniehall	Stir	NS4786	56°2·8'	4°26·9'W	X	57
Pirnie Rig	D & G	NT1109	55°22·3'	3°23·8'W	X	78
Pirnmill	N Ayr	NR8744	55°38·5'	5°23·3'W	T	62,69
Pirntaton Burn	Scot Bord	NT4248	55°43·6'	2°55·0'W	W	73
Pirriesmill	Aberd	NJ5340	57°27·1'	2°46·5'W	X	29
Pirryshiel Sike	Scot Bord	NY5098	55°16·7'	2°46·8'W	W	79
Pirton	Herts	TL1431	51°58·2'	0°20·0'W	T	166
Pirton	Worcs	SO8847	52°7·5'	2°10·1'W	T	150
Pirton Court	Worcs	SO8746	52°7·0'	2°11·0'W	A	150
Pirton Cross	Herts	TL1629	51°57·1'	0°18·3'W	X	166
Pirton Hall	Beds	TL1232	51°58·7'	0°21·8'W	X	166
Pirzwell	Devon	ST0709	50°52·6'	3°18·9'W	X	192
Pisgah	Cered	SN4151	52°8·3'	4°19·0'W	X	146
Pisgah	Cered	SN6777	52°22·7'	3°56·8'W	T	135
Pisgah	Pemb	SN0506	51°43·4'	4°49·0'W	X	158
Pisgah	Pemb	SN1028	51°55·3'	4°45·4'W	X	145,158
Pisgah	S Ayr	NS4028	55°31·4'	4°31·6'W	X	70
Pisgah	Stir	NN7900	56°10·9'	3°56·5'W	T	57
Pisgah Hill	Scot Bord	NT4516	55°26·3'	2°51·7'W	H	79
Pishill	Oxon	SU7289	51°35·9'	0°57·2'W	T	175
Pishill Bank	Oxon	SU7190	51°36·5'	0°58·1'W	T	175
Pishill Bottom	Oxon	SU7090	51°36·5'	0°59·0'W	X	175
Pishiobury Park	Herts	TL4813	51°48·0'	0°9·2'E	X	167
Pishmack Burn	D & G	NX9896	55°15·1'	3°35·8'W	W	78
Pishwanton Wood	E Loth	NT5365	55°52·8'	2°44·6'W	F	66
Piskies Cove	Corn	SW5527	50°5·8'	5°25·2'W	W	203
Pismire Hill	Sheff	SK3791	53°25·1'	1°26·2'W	T	110,111
Pisser Clough	Cald	SD9433	53°47·8'	2°5·1'W	X	103
Pistern Hill	Derby	SK3420	52°46·8'	1°29·4'W	X	128
Pisternhill Fm	Derby	SK3519	52°46·3'	1°28·5'W	FM	128
Pistle Down	Dorset	SU0910	50°53·6'	1°51·9'W	F	195
Pistol Castle	I of M	SC3371	54°6·7'	4°32·9'W	X	95
Pistol Fm	Stock	SK0090	53°24·6'	1°59·6'W	FM	110
Pistyll	Carm	SN4415	51°49·0'	4°15·4'W	X	159
Pistyll	Carm	SN6217	51°50·3'	3°59·8'W	X	159
Pistyll	Denb	SJ0774	53°15·5'	3°23·2'W	X	116
Pistyll	Denb	SJ0970	53°13·4'	3°21·4'W	X	116
Pistyll	Gwyn	SH3242	52°57·2'	4°29·6'W	T	123
Pistyll	Powys	SO0177	52°23·2'	3°26·9'W	X	136,147
Pistyll	Powys	SO1538	52°2·3'	3°14·0'W	X	161
Pistyll Cain	Gwyn	SH7327	52°49·8'	3°52·7'W	W	124
Pistyll Cim	Gwyn	SH3224	52°47·5'	4°29·1'W	W	123
Pistyll-Dewi	Carm	SN5419	51°51·3'	4°6·8'W	X	159
Pistyll Eynon	Cered	SN6248	52°7·0'	4°0·5'W	X	146
Pistyll Fm	Flint	SJ2460	53°8·1'	3°7·8'W	FM	117
Pistyll-goleu	Rho Cyn Taf	ST0396	51°39·5'	3°23·8'W	X	170
Pistyllgwion	Carm	SN3922	51°52·6'	4°19·9'W	X	145
Pistyllgwion	Carm	SN3922	51°52·6'	4°19·9'W	X	145,159
Pistyllgwyn	Carm	SN4124	51°53·8'	4°18·3'W	X	159
Pistyll Gwyn	Carm	SN5342	52°3·7'	4°8·3'W	X	146
Pistyll-gwyn	Carm	SN6131	51°57·8'	4°1·0'W	X	146
Pistyllgwyn	Carm	SN6227	51°55·7'	4°0·0'W	X	146
Pistyllgwyn	Carm	SN6237	52°1·1'	4°0·3'W	X	146
Pistyll Gwyn	Gwyn	SH8436	52°54·8'	3°43·1'W	W	124,125
Pistyll Gwyn	Gwyn	SH8819	52°45·7'	3°39·2'W	W	124,125
Pistyllgwyn	Powys	SN8849	52°7·9'	3°37·8'W	X	147
Pistyll-gwyn	Powys	SO0261	52°14·5'	3°25·7'W	X	147
Pistyll Ho Fm	Wrex	SJ3655	53°5·5'	2°56·9'W	FM	117
Pistyllmarch	Carm	SN5827	51°55·6'	4°3·5'W	X	146
Pistyll Meigan	Pemb	SN1737	52°0·3'	4°39·6'W	X	145
Pistyll Rhaeadr	Powys	SJ0729	52°51·3'	3°22·5'W	W	125
Pistyll-south	Carm	SN5929	51°56·7'	4°2·7'W	X	146
Pistyll Uchaf	Carm	SN5831	51°57·8'	4°3·6'W	X	146
Pistyll y Graig Ddu	Powys	SJ0918	52°45·4'	3°20·5'W	W	125
Pistyll y Gyfyng	Powys	SJ0224	52°48·5'	3°26·8'W	W	125
Pistyll y Llyn	Cered	SN7594	52°32·0'	3°50·2'W	W	135
Pit	Monm	SO3709	51°46·8'	2°54·4'W	T	161
Pitagowan	Pth & Kin	NN8165	56°45·9'	3°56·4'W	X	43
Pitairlie	Angus	NO5036	56°31·1'	2°48·3'W	X	54
Pitairlie	Moray	NJ2465	57°40·4'	3°16·0'W	X	28
Pitairlie Burn	Angus	NO5136	56°31·1'	2°47·3'W	W	54
Pitairlie Moor Plantation	Angus	NO4937	56°31·6'	2°49·3'W	F	54
Pitbeadlie	Aberd	NO7165	56°46·8'	2°28·0'W	X	45
Pitbee	Aberd	NJ7125	57°19·1'	2°28·4'W	X	38
Pitbirn	Aberd	NK0653	57°34·3'	1°53·5'W	X	30
Pitbladdo	Fife	NO3617	56°20·7'	3°1·7'W	X	59
Pitblae	Aberd	NJ9865	57°40·7'	2°1·6'W	T	30
Pitblain	Aberd	NJ7528	57°20·8'	2°24·5'W	X	38
Pitbrook	Glos	SO6801	51°42·6'	2°27·4'W	X	162
Pitcairlie Fm	Fife	NO2314	56°19·0'	3°14·2'W	FM	58
Pitcairlie Hill	Pth & Kin	NO2116	56°20·0'	3°16·2'W	H	58
Pitcairn	Fife	NO2603	56°13·1'	3°11·2'W	X	59
Pitcairn	Fife	NT1995	56°8·7'	3°17·8'W	X	58
Pitcairn	Pth & Kin	NN8850	56°38·0'	3°49·1'W	X	52
Pitcairngreen	Pth & Kin	NO0627	56°25·8'	3°31·0'W	T	52,53,58
Pitcairn Ho	Fife	NO2702	56°12·6'	3°10·2'W	A	59
Pitcairnie Loch	Pth & Kin	NO0219	56°21·4'	3°34·7'W	W	58
Pitcairns	Pth & Kin	NO0214	56°18·8'	3°34·6'W	X	58
Pitcalnie	Highld	NH8072	57°43·6'	4°0·4'W	T	21
Pitcalzean Ho	Highld	NH8070	57°42·5'	4°0·4'W	X	21
Pitcandlich	Aberd	NJ4314	57°13·1'	2°56·2'W	X	37
Pitcaple	Aberd	NJ7225	57°19·1'	2°27·4'W	T	38
Pitcaple Castle	Aberd	NJ7226	57°19·7'	2°27·4'W	A	38
Pitcarles	Aberd	NO8075	56°52·2'	2°19·2'W	X	45
Pitcarmick	Pth & Kin	NO0856	56°41·5'	3°29·7'W	X	52,53
Pitcarmick Burn	Pth & Kin	NO0656	56°41·4'	3°31·6'W	W	52,53
Pitcarmick Loch	Pth & Kin	NO0556	56°41·4'	3°32·6'W	W	52,53
Pitcarry	Aberd	NO8374	56°51·7'	2°16·3'W	X	45
Pitcastle	Pth & Kin	NN9053	56°39·6'	3°47·2'W	X	52
Pitcastle	Pth & Kin	NN9755	56°40·8'	3°40·4'W	X	52,53
Pitcastle Lochs	Pth & Kin	NN8855	56°40·7'	3°49·2'W	W	52
Pitchaish	Moray	NJ1743	57°28·4'	3°22·6'W	X	28
Pitchbury Ramparts	Essex	TL9629	51°55·7'	0°51·4'E	A	168
Pitchcombe	Glos	SO8508	51°46·5'	2°12·7'W	T	162
Pitchcott	Bucks	SP7720	51°52·6'	0°52·5'W	T	165
Pitchcott Hill	Bucks	SP7720	51°52·6'	0°52·5'W	H	165
Pitchcroft	Wrekin	SJ7317	52°45·2'	2°23·6'W	X	127
Pitchell Fm	Worcs	SP1445	52°6·4'	1°47·3'W	FM	151
Pitcher Ho	Durham	NY9518	54°33·7'	2°4·2'W	X	91,92
Pitcher Oak Wood	Worcs	SP0267	52°18·3'	1°57·8'W	F	150
Pitcher's Green	Suff	TL9158	52°11·5'	0°48·1'E	T	155
Pitcher's Hill	Dorset	SY5095	50°45·4'	2°42·1'W	X	194
Pitches Mount	Suff	TL9642	52°2·7'	0°51·9'E	A	155
Pitchford	Shrops	SJ5303	52°37·6'	2°41·3'W	T	126
Pitchford Hall	Shrops	SJ5204	52°38·1'	2°42·2'W	A	126
Pitchford Park	Shrops	SJ5104	52°38·1'	2°43·0'W	X	126
Pitch Green	Bucks	SP7703	51°43·5'	0°52·7'W	T	165
Pitch Hill	Powys	SO2169	52°19·0'	3°9·1'W	H	137,148
Pitch Hill	Surrey	TQ0842	51°10·2'	0°26·9'W	H	187
Pitchill	Warw	SP0551	52°9·7'	1°55·2'W	X	150
Pitching Piece Barn	Wilts	ST8332	51°5·5'	2°14·2'W	X	183
Pitcholds	Shrops	SO3292	52°31·5'	2°59·7'W	X	137
Pitchorn Fm	Hants	SU5160	51°20·4'	1°15·7'W	FM	174
Pitch Place	Surrey	SU8939	51°8·8'	0°43·3'W	T	186
Pitch Place	Surrey	SU9752	51°15·8'	0°36·2'W	T	186
Pitchroy	Moray	NJ1738	57°25·7'	3°22·5'W	X	28
Pitchroy Kennels	Moray	NJ1738	57°25·7'	3°22·5'W	X	28
Pitcoag	Pth & Kin	NO2021	56°22·7'	3°17·3'W	X	53,58
Pitcombe	Dorset	SY5889	50°42·2'	2°35·3'W	X	194
Pitcombe	Somer	ST6733	51°6·0'	2°27·9'W	T	183
Pitcon	N Ayr	NS2950	55°43·1'	4°42·9'W	X	63
Pitcon Burn	N Ayr	NS2854	55°45·2'	4°44·0'W	W	63
Pitcon Mains	N Ayr	NS2951	55°43·6'	4°42·9'W	X	63
Pitconochie	Fife	NT0586	56°3·7'	3°31·1'W	X	65
Pitcorthie	Fife	NT1186	56°3·8'	3°25·3'W	X	65
Pitcorthie Ho	Fife	NO4804	56°13·8'	2°49·9'W	X	59
Pitcot	Somer	ST6549	51°14·6'	2°29·7'W	T	183
Pitcot	V of Glam	SS8974	51°27·5'	3°35·5'W	T	170
Pitcoudie	Fife	NO2702	56°12·6'	3°10·2'W	X	59
Pitcow	Aberd	NJ8423	57°18·1'	2°15·5'W	X	38
Pitcowdens	Aberd	NO7994	57°2·5'	2°20·3'W	X	38,45
Pitcox	E Loth	NT6475	55°58·3'	2°34·2'W	X	67
Pitcraigie	Moray	NJ2551	57°32·8'	3°14·7'W	X	28
Pitcrocknie	Pth & Kin	NO2548	56°37·3'	3°12·9'W	X	53
Pitcruvie	Fife	NO4104	56°13·7'	2°56·7'W	X	59
Pitcullen	Aberd	NJ6402	57°6·7'	2°35·2'W	X	37
Pitcullo	Fife	NO4119	56°21·8'	2°56·9'W	X	59
Pitcundrum	Angus	NO5639	56°32·7'	2°42·5'W	X	54
Pitcur	Pth & Kin	NO2537	56°31·4'	3°12·7'W	X	53
Pitcur Wood	Pth & Kin	NO2636	56°30·9'	3°11·7'W	F	53
Pitdelphin Fm	Aberd	NO6591	57°0·8'	2°34·1'W	FM	38,45
Pitdinnie	Fife	NT0487	56°4·2'	3°32·1'W	X	65
Pitdoulzie	Aberd	NJ7344	57°29·4'	2°26·6'W	X	29
Pit Down	W Berks	SU3383	51°32·9'	1°31·1'W	X	174
Pitdrichie	Aberd	NO7982	56°56·0'	2°20·3'W	X	45
Pitellachie	Aberd	NJ4206	57°8·7'	2°57·1'W	X	37
Pitempton	C of Dun	NO3834	56°29·9'	3°0·0'W	T	54
Pitermo	Angus	NO3036	56°30·9'	3°7·8'W	X	53
Pitewan	Angus	NO2557	56°42·2'	3°13·0'W	X	53
Pitfancy	Aberd	NJ5943	57°28·8'	2°40·6'W	X	29
Pitfar	Pth & Kin	NT0096	56°9·0'	3°36·1'W	X	58
Pitfichie	Aberd	NJ6716	57°14·3'	2°32·3'W	X	38
Pitfichie Castle	Aberd	NJ6716	57°14·3'	2°32·3'W	A	38
Pitfichie Forest	Aberd	NJ6416	57°14·3'	2°35·3'W	F	37
Pitfichie Forest	Aberd	NJ6516	57°14·3'	2°34·3'W	F	38
Pitfichie Hill	Aberd	NJ6617	57°14·8'	2°33·3'W	H	38
Pitfield Fm	Darl	NZ3519	54°34·1'	1°27·1'W	FM	93
Pitfield Fm	Devon	SY0695	50°45·1'	3°19·6'W	FM	192
Pitfield Fm	Heref	SO3857	52°12·7'	2°54·0'W	FM	148,149
Pitfield Fm	Lancs	SD3938	53°50·3'	2°55·2'W	FM	102
Pitfield Ho	Durham	NZ3245	54°48·2'	1°29·7'W	X	88
Pit Fm	Ches	SJ8266	53°11·7'	2°15·8'W	FM	118
Pit Fm	Cumbr	SD3878	54°11·9'	2°56·6'W	FM	96,97
Pit Fm	Derby	SK4151	53°3·5'	1°22·9'W	FM	120
Pit Fm	Warw	SP2554	52°11·3'	1°37·7'W	FM	151
Pitfold Fm	Dorset	SY4891	50°43·2'	2°43·8'W	FM	193
Pitfoskie	Aberd	NJ9147	57°31·0'	2°8·6'W	X	30
Pitfour Castle	Pth & Kin	NO1920	56°22·2'	3°18·2'W	X	53,58
Pitfour Lake	Aberd	NJ9748	57°31·6'	2°2·5'W	W	30
Pitgair	Aberd	NJ7659	57°37·5'	2°23·6'W	X	29
Pitgair	Aberd	NJ7660	57°38·0'	2°23·7'W	X	29
Pitgarvie	Aberd	NO6669	56°48·9'	2°33·0'W	X	45
Pitgarvie Wood	Aberd	NO6670	56°49·5'	2°33·0'W	F	45
Pitgaveny	Aberd	NJ8124	57°18·6'	2°18·5'W	X	38
Pitgaveny Ho	Moray	NJ2465	57°40·4'	3°16·0'W	X	28
Pitgersie	Aberd	NJ9823	57°18·1'	2°1·5'W	X	38
Pitglassie	Highld	NH5457	57°35·0'	4°26·1'W	X	26
Pitglassie	Moray	NJ3338	57°25·9'	3°6·5'W	X	28
Pitgober	Clackm	NS9798	56°10·1'	3°39·1'W	X	58
Pitgorno	Fife	NO1910	56°16·8'	3°18·1'W	X	58
Pitgrudy	Highld	NH7991	57°53·8'	4°2·0'W	T	21
Pithayes Fm	Devon	SY0496	50°45·6'	3°21·3'W	FM	192
Pithayne Fm	Devon	ST1114	50°55·4'	3°15·6'W	FM	181,193
Pithayne Fms	Devon	ST2409	50°52·8'	3°4·4'W	FM	192,193
Pithill	Hants	SU6613	50°55·0'	1°3·3'W	X	196
Pit Hill	Somer	ST3836	51°7·4'	2°52·8'W	H	182
Pithill Fm	Devon	SX5360	50°25·5'	4°3·8'W	FM	201
Pithill Fm	Devon	SX6357	50°24·0'	3°55·3'W	FM	202
Pithill Fm	Hants	SU6513	50°55·0'	1°4·1'W	FM	196
Pit Ho	Northum	NY8976	55°4·9'	2°9·9'W	X	87
Pit Ho	Northum	NY9385	55°9·8'	2°6·2'W	X	80
Pithogarty	Highld	NH8082	57°49·0'	4°0·7'W	X	21
Pithouse Crags	Northum	NY6791	55°13·0'	2°30·7'W	X	80
Pithouse Fell	Northum	NY9953	54°52·6'	2°0·5'W	H	87
Pithouse Fm	Dorset	SZ1398	50°47·1'	1°48·6'W	FM	195
Pithouse Fm	Oxon	SU6877	51°29·5'	1°0·8'W	FM	175
Pithouse Plantn	Durham	NZ2139	54°45·0'	1°40·0'W	F	93
Pit Houses	Northum	NY8191	55°13·0'	2°17·5'W	X	80
Pitiful Hill Plantn	Notts	SK5973	53°15·3'	1°6·5'W	F	120
Pitillock	Pth & Kin	NO1409	56°16·2'	3°22·9'W	X	58
Pitkeathly Mains	Pth & Kin	NO1116	56°19·9'	3°25·9'W	X	58
Pitkeathly Wells Fm	Pth & Kin	NO1117	56°20·5'	3°25·9'W	FM	58
Pitkennedy	Angus	NO5454	56°40·8'	2°44·6'W	X	54
Pitkerrald	Highld	NH5029	57°19·9'	4°29·0'W	X	26,35
Pitkerrie	Highld	NH8679	57°47·4'	3°54·6'W	X	21
Pitkerro Ho	C of Dun	NO4533	56°29·4'	2°53·1'W	X	54
Pitkevy	Fife	NO2403	56°13·1'	3°13·1'W	X	59
Pitkierie	Fife	NO5505	56°14·4'	2°43·1'W	X	59
Pitkierie Cott	Fife	NO5506	56°14·9'	2°43·1'W	X	59
Pitkindie	Pth & Kin	NO2431	56°28·2'	3°13·6'W	X	53
Pitkinnie	Fife	NT2189	56°5·5'	3°15·7'W	X	66
Pitkinny	Fife	NT1996	56°9·2'	3°17·8'W	X	58
Pitlair	Fife	NO3112	56°18·0'	3°6·5'W	X	59
Pitland Fm	Devon	SX4777	50°34·6'	4°9·3'W	FM	191,201
Pitland Hills	Northum	NY8879	55°6·6'	2°10·9'W	X	87
Pitlandie	Pth & Kin	NN9324	56°24·0'	3°43·6'W	X	52,58
Pitlandie	Pth & Kin	NO0730	56°27·4'	3°30·1'W	X	52,53
Pitland Rhyne	Somer	ST3153	51°16·6'	2°59·0'W	W	182
Pitlands Fm	Surrey	SU8938	51°8·3'	0°43·3'W	FM	186
Pitlands Fm	Win & Maid	SU8378	51°29·9'	0°47·9'W	FM	175
Pitlands Fm	W Susx	SU7912	50°54·4'	0°52·2'W	FM	197
Pitleigh	Somer	SS9337	51°7·6'	3°31·4'W	X	181
Pitleoch	Pth & Kin	NN9641	56°33·2'	3°41·1'W	X	52,53
Pitleoch Burn	Pth & Kin	NN9642	56°33·8'	3°41·1'W	W	52,53
Pitlessie	Fife	NO3309	56°16·4'	3°4·5'W	T	59
Pitlessie Mill	Fife	NO3310	56°16·9'	3°4·5'W	X	59
Pitlethie	Fife	NO4522	56°23·5'	2°53·0'W	X	54,59
Pitley Fm	Essex	TL6632	51°57·9'	0°25·4'E	FM	167
Pitline	Aberd	NJ4306	57°8·7'	2°56·1'W	X	37
Pitliver Ho	Fife	NT0685	56°3·2'	3°30·1'W	X	65
Pitlivie	Angus	NO5538	56°32·2'	2°43·5'W	X	54
Pitlivie Wood	Angus	NO5439	56°32·7'	2°44·4'W	F	54
Pitlochie	Fife	NO1809	56°16·2'	3°19·0'W	X	58
Pitlochie	Fife	NT2397	56°9·8'	3°14·0'W	X	58
Pitlochry	Pth & Kin	NN9458	56°42·4'	3°43·4'W	T	52,53
Pitlour	Fife	NO2011	56°17·3'	3°17·1'W	X	58
Pitlour Hill	Fife	NO2112	56°17·9'	3°16·1'W	H	58
Pitlowie	Pth & Kin	NO2023	56°23·8'	3°17·3'W	X	53,58
Pitlundie	Highld	NH6750	57°31·5'	4°12·8'W	X	26
Pitmachie	Aberd	NJ6728	57°20·7'	2°32·4'W	X	38
Pitmackie	Pth & Kin	NN8140	56°32·5'	3°55·7'W	X	52
Pitmaduthy	Highld	NH7776	57°45·7'	4°3·6'W	T	21
Pitmain Fm	Highld	NH7400	57°4·7'	4°4·3'W	FM	35
Pitmain Lodge	Highld	NH7402	57°5·8'	4°4·3'W	X	35
Pitman's Corner	Suff	TM1466	52°15·3'	1°8·5'E	X	156
Pitmeadow	Pth & Kin	NO0212	56°17·7'	3°34·6'W	X	58
Pitmedden	Aberd	NJ6303	57°7·2'	2°36·2'W	X	37
Pitmedden	Aberd	NJ8927	57°20·3'	2°10·5'W	T	38
Pitmedden	Fife	NO2214	56°19·0'	3°15·2'W	X	58
Pitmedden Forest	Fife	NO2114	56°19·0'	3°16·2'W	F	58
Pitmedden Forest	Pth & Kin	NO2014	56°19·0'	3°17·2'W	F	58
Pitmedden Ho	Aberd	NJ8828	57°20·8'	2°11·5'W	X	38
Pitmedden Ho	C of Aber	NJ8614	57°13·2'	2°13·5'W	X	38
Pitmenzies	Fife	NO2113	56°18·4'	3°16·2'W	X	58
Pitmiddle Wood	Pth & Kin	NO2230	56°27·6'	3°15·5'W	F	53
Pitmikie	Angus	NO6051	56°39·2'	2°38·7'W	X	54
Pitmillan	Aberd	NJ9724	57°18·7'	2°2·5'W	X	38
Pitmilly Ho	Fife	NO5713	56°18·7'	2°41·3'W	X	59
Pitminster	Somer	ST2219	50°58·1'	3°6·3'W	T	193
Pitmorehill Spinney	Northnts	SP7273	52°21·3'	0°56·2'W	F	141
Pitmudie	Angus	NO2756	56°41·7'	3°11·1'W	X	53
Pitmudie Fm	Angus	NO5467	56°47·8'	2°44·7'W	FM	44
Pitmuies	Angus	NO5649	56°38·1'	2°42·6'W	T	54
Pitmuies Mill Farm	Angus	NO5849	56°38·1'	2°40·6'W	FM	54
Pitmuiesmoor	Angus	NO5851	56°39·2'	2°40·7'W	X	54
Pitmullen Ho	Fife	NO5414	56°19·2'	2°44·2'W	X	59
Pitmunie	Aberd	NJ6615	57°13·7'	2°33·3'W	T	38
Pitmurchie Ho	Aberd	NJ6002	57°6·7'	2°39·2'W	X	37
Pitmurthly	Pth & Kin	NO0828	56°26·4'	3°29·1'W	X	52,53,58
Pitnacalder	Aberd	NJ8763	57°39·7'	2°12·6'W	X	30
Pitnacree	Pth & Kin	NN9253	56°39·6'	3°45·3'W	X	52
Pitnamoon	Aberd	NO6874	56°51·6'	2°31·0'W	X	45
Pitnappie	Angus	NO3139	56°32·5'	3°6·9'W	X	53
Pitney	Somer	ST4528	51°3·2'	2°46·7'W	T	193
Pitney Fm	Devon	ST1003	50°49·4'	3°16·3'W	FM	192,193

Pitney Ho	Somer	ST4428	51°3·2'	2°47·6'W	X	193
Pitney Steart Br	Somer	ST4530	51°4·2'	2°46·7'W	X	182
Pitney Wood	Somer	ST4429	51°3·2'	2°47·6'W	F	193
Pitpear Fm	Somer	ST1330	51°4·0'	3°14·1'W	FM	181
Pitpointie	Angus	NO3537	56°31·5'	3°2·9'W	T	54
Pitprone	Aberd	NJ4913	57°12·6'	2°50·2'W	X	37
Pitreadie Fm	Aberd	NO6991	57°0·8'	2°30·2'W	FM	38,45
Pitreavie	Fife	NT1184	56°2·7'	3°25·3'W	X	65
Pitrennie Mill	Aberd	NO7277	56°53·3'	2°27·1'W	X	45
Pitreuchie	Angus	NO4649	56°38·0'	2°52·4'W	T	54
Pitreuchie Fm	Angus	NO4649	56°38·0'	2°52·4'W	FM	54
Pitreuchie Fm	Angus	NO4749	56°38·0'	2°51·4'W	FM	54
Pitroddie Fm	Pth & Kin	NO2125	56°24·9'	3°16·4'W	FM	53,58
Pitscaff	Aberd	NJ9823	57°18·1'	2°1·5'W	X	38
Pitscandly Hill	Angus	NO4953	56°40·2'	2°49·5'W	H	54
Pitscottie	Fife	NO4113	56°18·6'	2°56·8'W	T	59
Pitscow	Aberd	NK0051	57°33·2'	1°59·5'W	X	30
Pitscurry	Aberd	NJ7226	57°19·7'	2°27·4'W	X	38
Pitsea	Essex	TQ7388	51°34·1'	0°30·2'E	T	178
Pitsea Hall Country Park	Essex	TQ7386	51°33·0'	0°30·1'E	X	178
Pitseahall Fleet	Essex	TQ7486	51°33·0'	0°31·0'E	W	178
Pitsea Marsh	Essex	TQ7387	51°33·5'	0°30·1'E	X	178
Pitses	Oldham	SD9403	53°31·7'	2°5·0'W	T	109
Pits Fm	Hants	SU5229	51°3·7'	1°15·1'W	FM	185
Pits Fm	Northnts	SP6745	52°6·2'	1°0·9'W	FM	152
Pitsford	Northnts	SP7568	52°18·5'	0°53·6'W	T	152
Pitsford Hill	Somer	ST1030	51°4·0'	3°16·7'W	T	181
Pitsford Water	Northnts	SP7669	52°19·1'	0°52·7'W	W	152
Pitsham Fm	W Susx	SU8719	50°58·1'	0°45·3'W	FM	197
Pitshill	W Susx	SU9422	50°59·6'	0°39·2'W	X	197
Pitskelly	Aberd	NO7778	56°53·8'	2°22·2'W	X	45
Pitskelly	Angus	NO5435	56°30·5'	2°44·4'W	X	54
Pitsligo Castle	Aberd	NJ9366	57°41·3'	2°6·6'W	A	30
Pitsmoor	Sheff	SK3689	53°24·0'	1°27·1'W	T	110,111
Pitson Fm	Devon	SY0988	50°41·3'	3°16·9'W	FM	192
Pits Plantn	E Yorks	TA1066	54°4·9'	0°18·7'W	F	101
Pits Point	Norf	TG0045	52°58·1'	0°59·1'E	X	133
Pits, The	Cambs	TL6473	52°20·1'	0°24·8'E	X	154
Pits, The	Oxon	SP6032	51°59·2'	1°7·2'W	F	152,165
Pitstock Fm	Kent	TQ9160	51°18·6'	0°44·8'E	FM	178
Pitstone	Bucks	SP9414	51°49·2'	0°37·8'W	T	165
Pitstone Common	Bucks	SP9713	51°48·7'	0°35·2'W	F	165
Pitstone Green	Bucks	SP9415	51°49·8'	0°37·8'W	T	165
Pitstone Hill	Bucks	SP9514	51°49·2'	0°36·9'W	T	165
Pitsundry	Pth & Kin	NO0534	56°29·6'	3°32·1'W	X	52,53
Pitsworthy Fm	Somer	SS8340	51°9·1'	3°40·0'W	FM	181
Pitt	Devon	SS2525	51°0·1'	4°29·3'W	X	190
Pitt	Devon	SS8310	50°52·9'	3°39·4'W	X	191
Pitt	Devon	SS9215	50°55·7'	3°31·8'W	X	181
Pitt	Devon	SS9716	50°56·3'	3°27·6'W	X	181
Pitt	Devon	ST0316	50°56·4'	3°22·5'W	X	181
Pitt	Hants	SU4528	51°3·2'	1°21·1'W	T	185
Pitt	Swan	SS4987	51°33·9'	4°10·3'W	X	159
Pittachar	Pth & Kin	NN8720	56°21·8'	3°49·3'W	X	52,58
Pittachope	Fife	NO3121	56°22·8'	3°6·6'W	X	53,59
Pittaford	Devon	SX8046	50°18·3'	3°40·7'W	X	202
Pittarrow	Aberd	NO7275	56°52·2'	2°27·1'W	X	45
Pittarthie Castle	Fife	NO5209	56°16·5'	2°46·1'W	A	59
Pittarthie Fm	Fife	NO5108	56°16·0'	2°47·0'W	FM	59
Pitt Bridge	Somer	SS9441	51°9·7'	3°30·6'W	X	181
Pitt Court	Glos	ST7596	51°40·0'	2°21·3'W	T	162
Pitt Cross	Devon	SS4309	50°51·8'	4°13·5'W	X	190
Pitt Dene Fm	Cambs	TL3064	52°15·8'	0°5·3'W	FM	153
Pitt Down	Hants	SU4228	51°3·2'	1°23·7'W	X	185
Pitteadie Ho	Fife	NT2589	56°5·5'	3°11·9'W	X	66
Pittencleroch	Pth & Kin	NN8922	56°22·9'	3°47·4'W	X	52,58
Pittencrieff	Fife	NO3715	56°19·6'	3°0·7'W	X	59
Pittencrief Park	Fife	NT0887	56°4·3'	3°28·2'W	X	65
Pittenderich	Aberd	NJ4907	57°9·3'	2°50·1'W	H	37
Pittendreich	Moray	NJ1961	57°38·2'	3°20·9'W	X	28
Pittendreich	Pth & Kin	NO1604	56°13·5'	3°20·8'W	X	58
Pittendriech	Angus	NO5761	56°44·6'	2°41·7'W	X	44
Pittendrum	Aberd	NJ9567	57°41·8'	2°4·6'W	X	30
Pittendynie	Pth & Kin	NO0529	56°26·9'	3°32·0'W	X	52,53,58
Pittengardner	Aberd	NO7476	56°52·7'	2°25·1'W	X	45
Pittenkerrie	Aberd	NO6598	57°4·6'	2°34·2'W	X	38,45
Pittensair	Moray	NJ2860	57°37·7'	3°11·9'W	X	28
Pittensorn	Pth & Kin	NO0839	56°32·3'	3°29·3'W	X	52,53
Pittentaggart	Aberd	NJ4306	57°8·7'	2°56·1'W	X	37
Pittentian	Pth & Kin	NN8720	56°21·8'	3°49·3'W	X	52,58
Pittenweem	Fife	NO5402	56°12·8'	2°44·1'W	T	59
Pittern Hill	Warw	SP3251	52°9·6'	1°31·5'W	X	151
Pitter's Fm	Wilts	ST9568	51°24·9'	2°3·9'W	FM	173
Pittescombe	Devon	SX4578	50°35·1'	4°11·0'W	X	201
Pitteuchar	Fife	NT2899	56°10·9'	3°9·2'W	T	59
Pitt Fm	Bath & NE Somer	ST5554	51°17·2'	2°38·3'W	FM	182,183
Pitt Fm	Corn	SX3373	50°32·2'	4°21·0'W	FM	201
Pitt Fm	Devon	SS5734	51°5·5'	4°2·1'W	FM	180
Pitt Fm	Devon	SS7322	50°59·2'	3°48·2'W	FM	180
Pitt Fm	Devon	SS7529	51°3·0'	3°46·6'W	FM	180
Pitt Fm	Devon	SS8100	50°47·5'	3°40·9'W	FM	191
Pitt Fm	Devon	SS9005	50°50·3'	3°33·4'W	FM	192
Pitt Fm	Devon	SS9304	50°49·8'	3°30·8'W	FM	192
Pitt Fm	Devon	ST0412	50°54·2'	3°21·5'W	FM	181
Pitt Fm	Devon	ST1014	50°55·3'	3°16·4'W	FM	181,193
Pitt Fm	Devon	SX7650	50°20·4'	3°44·2'W	FM	202
Pitt Fm	Devon	SX8792	50°43·2'	3°35·7'W	FM	192
Pitt Fm	Devon	SX9379	50°36·3'	3°30·3'W	FM	192
Pitt Fm	Devon	SY0083	50°38·5'	3°24·5'W	FM	192
Pitt Fm	Devon	SY0896	50°45·6'	3°17·9'W	FM	192
Pitt Fm	Dorset	SY3895	50°45·3'	2°52·4'W	FM	193
Pitt Fm	Hants	SU3726	51°2·2'	1°28·0'W	FM	185
Pitt Fm	Somer	SS8446	51°12·3'	3°39·2'W	FM	181
Pitt Fm	Somer	ST4012	50°54·5'	2°50·8'W	FM	193
Pitt Fm	Surrey	SU8341	51°10·0'	0°48·4'W	FM	186
Pitt Hall Fm	Hants	SU5656	51°18·3'	1°11·4'W	FM	174
Pitt Ho	Devon	SX8578	50°35·7'	3°37·1'W	X	191
Pitt House Fm	Dorset	ST7423	51°0·6'	2°21·9'W	FM	183
Pittiely Burn	Pth & Kin	NN8748	56°36·9'	3°50·0'W	W	52
Pittillock	Fife	NO2705	56°14·2'	3°10·2'W	X	59
Pittington	Durham	NZ3244	54°47·6'	1°29·7'W	T	88
Pittle Mere	Derby	SK1378	53°18·2'	1°47·9'W	X	119
Pittlesheugh	Scot Bord	NT7543	55°41·0'	2°23·4'W	X	74
Pittleworth Fm	Hants	SU3229	51°3·8'	1°32·2'W	FM	185
Pittnetrail	Highld	NC7202	57°59·6'	4°9·4'W	T	16
Pitton	Devon	SX7278	50°35·5'	3°48·1'W	X	191
Pitton	Devon	SX7494	50°44·2'	3°46·8'W	X	191
Pitton	Swan	SS4287	51°33·8'	4°16·4'W	T	159
Pitton	Wilts	SU2131	51°4·9'	1°41·6'W	T	184
Pitton Cross	Swan	SS4387	51°33·8'	4°15·5'W	X	159
Pitton Lodge	Wilts	SU2030	51°4·4'	1°42·5'W	X	184
Pittoothies	Aberd	NJ6215	57°13·7'	2°37·3'W	X	37
Pittormie	Fife	NO4118	56°21·3'	2°56·8'W	X	59
Pitt Place	I of W	SZ4183	50°38·9'	1°24·8'W	X	196
Pitt's Column	Staffs	SJ9628	52°51·2'	2°3·2'W	X	127
Pitts Deep	Hants	SZ3795	50°45·4'	1°28·1'W	X	196
Pittsdown	Corn	SW9546	50°16·9'	4°52·3'W	X	204
Pitts Fm	Ches	SJ4546	53°0·8'	2°48·8'W	FM	117
Pitt's Fm	Dorset	ST6908	50°52·5'	2°26·1'W	FM	194
Pitts Fm	Lincs	TF1353	53°4·0'	0°18·4'W	FM	121
Pitts Fm	Somer	ST5946	51°12·9'	2°34·8'W	FM	182,183
Pitts Fm	Wilts	ST8528	51°3·3'	2°12·5'W	FM	183
Pittsgate Fm	Kent	TQ6837	51°6·7'	0°24·4'E	FM	188
Pitt's Head	Gwyn	SH5751	53°2·5'	4°7·6'W	X	115
Pitts Hill	C of Stoke	SJ8652	53°4·1'	2°12·1'W	T	118
Pittsland Fm	Wilts	SU0384	51°33·5'	1°57·0'W	FM	173
Pitt's Mill	Glos	SO7828	51°57·2'	2°18·8'W	X	150
Pitts, The	Wilts	SU0726	51°2·2'	1°53·6'W	T	184
Pittswood	Kent	TQ6149	51°13·3'	0°18·7'E	T	188
Pitts Wood Inclosure	Hants	SU1914	50°55·7'	1°43·4'W	F	195
Pittsworthy	Devon	SX5192	50°42·7'	4°6·3'W	X	191
Pittulie	Aberd	NJ9567	57°41·8'	2°4·6'W	T	30
Pittulie Castle	Aberd	NJ9467	57°41·8'	2°5·6'W	A	30
Pittuncarty	Pth & Kin	NO1911	56°17·3'	3°18·1'W	X	58
Pittville	Glos	SO9523	51°54·6'	2°4·0'W	T	163
Pitty Beck	Brad	SE1033	53°47·8'	1°50·5'W	W	104
Pittyvaich	Moray	NJ3238	57°25·9'	3°7·5'W	X	28
Pitwell Fm	Northnts	SP5054	52°11·2'	1°15·7'W	FM	151
Pitwellt Pond	Merth Tyd	SO0709	51°46·6'	3°20·5'W	W	160
Pit Wood	Kent	TR2152	51°13·7'	1°10·3'E	F	179
Pitworthy	Devon	SS2804	50°48·8'	4°26·1'W	X	190
Pityme	Corn	SW9476	50°33·1'	4°54·1'W	T	200
Pity Me	Durham	NZ2645	54°48·2'	1°35·3'W	T	88
Pity Me	Northum	NY9176	55°4·9'	2°8·0'W	X	87
Pity Me	Northum	NZ1186	55°10·3'	1°49·2'W	X	81
Pityoulish	Highld	NH9214	57°12·5'	3°46·8'W	X	36
Pivington Mill	Kent	TQ9246	51°11·1'	0°45·2'E	X	189
Pixey Green	Suff	TM2475	52°19·9'	1°17·7'E	X	156
Pixford Fm	Somer	ST1530	51°4·0'	3°12·4'W	FM	181
Pixham	Surrey	TQ1750	51°14·5'	0°19·0'W	T	187
Pixham	Worcs	SO8448	52°8·0'	2°13·6'W	T	150
Pixham Fm	Worcs	SO8348	52°8·0'	2°14·5'W	FM	150
Pixhill	Heref	SO6958	52°13·4'	2°26·8'W	X	149
Pixie's Hall	Corn	SW7230	50°7·8'	5°11·0'W	X	204
Pixie's Hall (Fogou)	Corn	SW7230	50°7·8'	5°11·0'W	A	204
Pixley	Heref	SO6638	52°2·6'	2°29·3'W	T	149
Pixley	Shrops	SJ6825	52°49·5'	2°28·1'W	T	127
Pixley Hill	Durham	NZ1931	54°40·7'	1°41·9'W	X	92
Pixton	Devon	SS5807	50°50·9'	4°0·7'W	X	191
Pixton Hill	Somer	SS9226	51°1·6'	3°32·0'W	H	181
Pixton Park	Somer	SS9227	51°2·2'	3°32·0'W	X	181
Pixy Copse	Somer	SS9326	51°1·6'	3°31·2'W	F	181
Pizien Well	Kent	TQ6753	51°15·3'	0°24·0'E	T	188
Pizwell Fm	Devon	SX6678	50°35·4'	3°53·2'W	FM	191
Place	Devon	SX7671	50°31·8'	3°44·6'W	X	202
Place	N Ayr	NS3054	55°45·2'	4°42·1'W	X	63
Place Barton	Corn	SW8531	50°8·6'	5°0·2'W	X	204
Place Fell	Cumbr	NY4016	54°32·4'	2°55·2'W	H	90
Place Fm	Aberd	NJ8921	57°17·0'	2°10·5'W	FM	38
Place Fm	Devon	SX9087	50°40·6'	3°33·0'W	FM	192
Place Fm	Essex	TQ5898	51°39·7'	0°17·5'E	FM	167,177
Place Fm	Kent	TQ8143	51°9·7'	0°35·7'E	FM	188
Place Fm	Suff	TL8570	52°18·0'	0°43·2'E	FM	144,155
Place Fm	Suff	TM1278	52°21·8'	1°7·2'E	FM	144
Place Fm	Surrey	TQ1437	51°7·5'	0°21·9'W	FM	187
Place Fm	Surrey	TQ3252	51°15·3'	0°6·1'W	FM	187
Place Fm	Wilts	ST9529	51°3·9'	2°3·9'W	A	184
Place Hill	Scot Bord	NT8020	55°28·7'	2°18·6'W	H	74
Place Ho	Corn	SW8532	50°9·2'	5°0·2'W	X	204
Place Ho	Northnts	SP8460	52°14·1'	0°45·8'W	X	152
Place House Fm	Lancs	SD5932	53°47·2'	2°38·1'W	FM	102
Placemill Fm	Aberd	NJ6243	57°28·8'	2°37·6'W	FM	29
Place Moor	Devon	SX7552	50°21·5'	3°45·1'W	X	202
Place Newton	N Yks	SE8872	54°8·4'	0°38·8'W	X	101
Place of Goval	Aberd	NJ8715	57°13·8'	2°12·5'W	X	38
Place of Tilliefoure	Aberd	NJ6519	57°15·9'	2°34·4'W	X	38
Place, The	Suff	TM0969	52°17·0'	1°4·2'E	X	155
Place Wood	Hants	SU6309	50°52·9'	1°5·9'W	F	196
Plackett's Hole	Kent	TQ8659	51°18·2'	0°40·5'E	X	178
Pladda	Arg & Bt	NR5468	55°50·8'	5°55·4'W	X	61
Pladda	Cumbr	NY4272	55°2·6'	2°54·0'W	X	85
Pladda	N Ayr	NS0219	55°25·8'	5°7·3'W	X	69
Pladda Island	Arg & Bt	NM8337	56°28·8'	5°31·0'W	X	49
Plague Stone	Staffs	SJ9855	53°5·8'	2°1·4'W	A	118
Plahageo	N Eil	NB1241	58°16·1'	6°54·2'W	X	13
Plaice Hills Fm	Donc	SE6417	53°39·0'	1°1·5'W	FM	111
Plaide Mhòr	Arg & Bt	NR3492	56°3·1'	6°15·9'W	X	61
Plaids	Highld	NH7882	57°48·9'	4°2·7'W	X	21
Plaidy	Aberd	NJ7254	57°34·8'	2°27·6'W	T	29
Plaidy	Corn	SX2653	50°21·3'	4°26·4'W	T	201
Plain-an-Gwarry	Corn	SW5331	50°7·9'	5°27·0'W	T	203
Plain-an-Gwarry	Corn	SW6942	50°14·2'	5°14·0'W	T	203
Plain Dealings	Pemb	SN0518	51°49·8'	4°49·4'W	T	158
Plaindell	Hants	SU6831	51°4·7'	1°1·4'W	X	185,186
Plainfield	Northum	NT9803	55°19·5'	2°1·5'W	X	81
Plain Fm	Hants	SU6831	51°4·7'	1°1·4'W	FM	185,186
Plain Fm	Kent	TQ7541	51°8·7'	0°30·5'E	FM	188
Plain Fm	Wilts	SU0586	51°34·6'	1°55·3'W	FM	173
Plain Heath	Hants	SZ2198	50°47·1'	1°41·7'W	X	195
Plain of Fidge	Orkney	HY7141	59°15·5'	2°30·0'W	X	5
Plains	Fife	NO2510	56°16·8'	3°12·2'W	X	59
Plains	N Lanak	NS7966	55°52·6'	3°55·6'W	T	64
Plains	Pth & Kin	NO0910	56°16·7'	3°27·7'W	X	58
Plains Farm.	Sund	NZ3754	54°53·0'	1°25·0'W	FM	88
Plainsfield	Devon	SS9012	50°54·1'	3°33·5'W	X	181
Plainsfield	Somer	ST1936	51°7·3'	3°9·1'W	T	181
Plains Fm	Essex	TM0031	51°56·7'	0°55·0'E	FM	168
Plains Fm	Essex	TM0228	51°55·1'	0°56·6'E	FM	168
Plains Fm	N Yks	SE8575	54°10·1'	0°41·5'W	FM	100
Plains Fm, The	Suff	TL9953	52°8·6'	0°54·9'E	FM	155
Plains House Fm	N Lincs	SE7309	53°34·6'	0°53·4'W	FM	112
Plainsides Fm	N Yks	NZ8807	54°27·3'	0°38·1'W	FM	94
Plain Spot	Notts	SK4650	53°3·0'	1°18·4'W	T	120
Plainsteads	Derby	SK0291	53°25·2'	1°57·8'W	X	110
Plains, The	Cambs	TL5488	52°28·3'	0°16·4'E	X	143
Plains, The	Suff	TL8670	52°18·0'	0°44·1'E	F	144,155
Plain Street	Corn	SW9778	50°34·2'	4°51·6'W	T	200
Plain, The	Cald	SD9434	53°48·4'	2°5·1'W	X	103
Plain, The	Kent	TQ7443	51°9·8'	0°29·7'E	X	188
Plain Tree Fm	N Yks	TA0098	54°22·3'	0°27·2'W	FM	101
Plainville Fm	York	SE5759	54°1·7'	1°7·4'W	FM	105
Plain Woods Fm	Northnts	SP7451	52°9·4'	0°54·7'W	FM	152
Plaish	Shrops	SO5296	52°33·8'	2°42·1'W	T	137,138
Plaishbridge Fm	Somer	ST7526	51°2·2'	2°21·0'W	FM	183
Plaish Fm	Somer	ST3749	51°14·4'	2°53·8'W	FM	182
Plaish Park	Shrops	SO5296	52°33·8'	2°42·1'W	X	137,138
Plaistow	Brom	TQ4070	51°24·9'	0°1·2'E	T	177
Plaistow	Derby	SK3456	53°6·2'	1°29·1'W	X	119
Plaistow	Heref	SO6939	52°3·1'	2°26·7'W	X	149
Plaistow	Newham	TQ4082	51°31·4'	0°1·5'E	T	177
Plaistow	Pth & Kin	NO2425	56°24·9'	3°13·5'W	X	53,59
Plaistow	W Susx	TQ0030	51°3·9'	0°34·0'W	T	186
Plaistow Barton	Devon	SS5738	51°7·6'	4°2·2'W	X	180
Plaistow Green	Derby	SK3455	53°5·7'	1°29·1'W	X	119
Plaistow Green	Essex	TL8028	51°55·5'	0°37·5'E	T	168
Plaistow Mill	Devon	SS5637	51°7·1'	4°3·1'W	X	180
Plaistow Place	W Susx	TQ0031	51°4·4'	0°34·0'W	X	186
Plaitford	Hants	SU2719	50°58·4'	1°36·5'W	T	184
Plaitford Common	Hants	SU2718	50°57·9'	1°36·5'W	X	184
Plaitford Green	Hants	SU2821	50°59·5'	1°35·7'W	T	184
Plan	N Ayr	NS3057	55°46·8'	4°42·2'W	X	63
Plan Burn	D & G	NX7571	55°1·3'	3°56·9'W	W	84
Plane Hall Fm	Essex	TM0219	51°50·2'	0°56·3'E	FM	168
Planetarium	C of West	TQ2882	51°31·6'	0°8·9'W	X	176
Planet Fm	Norf	TG1403	52°35·2'	1°10·0'E	FM	144
Plane Tree	Lancs	SD5640	53°51·5'	2°39·7'W	X	102
Plane Tree Fm	N Yks	SE3487	54°16·9'	1°28·2'W	FM	99
Plane Tree Fm	N Yks	SE5194	54°20·6'	1°12·5'W	FM	100
Plane Tree Fm	N Yks	SE9998	54°22·3'	0°28·1'W	FM	94,101
Plane Tree Ho	N Yks	SE4676	54°10·9'	1°17·3'W	X	100
Planetrees	Northum	NY9369	55°1·2'	2°6·1'W	X	87
Plankey Mill	Northum	NY7962	54°57·4'	2°19·2'W	X	86,87
Plank Lane	Wigan	SD6300	53°30·0'	2°33·1'W	T	109
Plann	N Ayr	NS2653	55°44·6'	4°45·9'W	X	63
Plans of Thornton	Angus	NO4046	56°36·4'	2°58·2'W	X	54
Plantain Loch	D & G	NX8360	54°55·4'	3°49·1'W	W	84
Plantation Bridge	Cumbr	SD4896	54°21·7'	2°47·6'W	T	97
Plantation Fm	Cambs	TL2694	52°32·0'	0°8·1'W	FM	142
Plantation Fm	Cambs	TL3291	52°30·3'	0°2·9'W	FM	142
Plantation Fm	Cambs	TL4690	52°29·5'	0°9·4'E	FM	143
Plantation Fm	Cambs	TL5274	52°20·8'	0°14·3'E	FM	143
Plantation Fm	Cambs	TL6484	52°26·0'	0°25·1'E	FM	143
Plantation Fm	Hants	SU5457	51°18·8'	1°13·1'W	FM	174
Plantation Fm	Lancs	SD6642	53°52·6'	2°30·6'W	FM	103
Plantation Fm	Norf	TL9997	52°32·3'	0°56·5'E	FM	144
Plantation Fm	Northum	NU0934	55°36·2'	1°51·0'W	FM	75
Plantation Fm	Red & Cl	NZ6217	54°32·9'	1°2·1'W	FM	94
Plantation Fm	York	SE5957	54°0·6'	1°5·6'W	FM	105
Plantationfoot	D & G	NY1194	55°14·2'	3°23·5'W	T	78
Plantation Hill	Hants	SU5457	51°18·8'	1°13·1'W	X	174
Plantation Ho	Cambs	TL5990	52°29·3'	0°20·9'E	X	143
Plantation Ho	Northum	NU0414	55°25·4'	1°55·8'W	X	81
Plantation Ho	N Yks	NZ3205	54°26·6'	1°30·0'W	X	93
Plantation Ho	N Yks	SE5977	54°11·4'	1°5·3'W	X	100
Plantation Ho	N Yks	SE6738	53°50·3'	0°58·5'W	X	105,106
Plantation Ho	Staffs	SK0141	52°58·2'	1°58·7'W	X	119,128
Plantation of Hillhead	Aberd	NO7976	56°52·8'	2°20·2'W	F	45
Plantation of Hillockhead	Moray	NJ1251	57°32·7'	3°27·8'W	F	28
Plantation Stud	Suff	TL6366	52°16·3'	0°23·7'E	X	154
Plantation, The	Dorset	ST8504	50°50·4'	2°12·4'W	F	194
Plantation, The	Heref	SO6039	52°3·1'	2°34·6'W	F	149
Plantation, The	Suff	TL7359	52°12·3'	0°32·3'E	F	155
Plantation, The	Wilts	SU2670	51°25·9'	1°37·2'W	F	174
Plantema Fm	N Yks	NZ3803	54°25·5'	1°24·4'W	FM	93
Plant Fm	Hants	SU6709	50°52·8'	1°2·5'W	FM	196
Plant-glas	Powys	SJ1812	52°42·2'	3°12·4'W	X	125
Plan, The	Arg & Bt	NS0953	55°44·2'	5°2·1'W	X	63
Plant Ho	Ches	SJ9078	53°18·2'	2°8·6'W	X	118
Plantilly	Renf	NS3357	55°46·9'	4°39·3'W	X	63
Planting End	D & G	NX1258	54°53·1'	4°55·4'W	X	82
Plantingside	Aberd	NO6169	56°48·9'	2°37·9'W	X	45
Plants Brook	Birm	SP1393	52°32·3'	1°48·1'W	W	139
Planwydd	Gwyn	SH3944	52°58·4'	4°23·5'W	X	123
Plardiwick	Staffs	SJ8120	52°46·9'	2°16·5'W	T	127
Plâs	Carm	SN1727	51°54·9'	4°39·3'W	X	145,158
Plâs	Carm	SN3410	51°46·1'	4°24·0'W	X	159
Plâs	Carm	SN4827	51°55·5'	4°12·2'W	X	146
Plas	Cered	SN6265	52°16·2'	4°1·0'W	X	135
Plas	Gwyn	SH4658	53°6·1'	4°17·6'W	X	115,123
Plâs	I of Angl	SH2675	53°14·9'	4°36·1'W	X	114
Plas	Powys	SJ1229	52°51·3'	3°18·0'W	X	125
Plas Adda	Denb	SJ0443	52°58·8'	3°25·4'W	X	125
Plas Aney	Flint	SJ2263	53°9·7'	3°9·6'W	X	117
Plas Ashpool	Denb	SJ1067	53°11·8'	3°20·4'W	A	116
Plasau	Conwy	SH9845	52°59·8'	3°30·8'W	X	116
Plasau	Denb	SJ0648	53°1·5'	3°23·7'W	X	116
Plasau	Gwyn	SH8917	52°44·6'	3°38·3'W	X	124,125
Plasau	Shrops	SJ3520	52°46·7'	2°57·4'W	T	126
Plasauduon	Powys	SO0095	52°32·9'	3°28·1'W	X	136

Plas-bach	Carm	SN3725	51°54·2′	4°21·8′W	X	145
Plas-bâch	Carm	SN6218	51°50·9′	3°59·8′W	X	159
Plasbach	Cered	SN6458	52°12·4′	3°59·0′W	X	146
Plas-bach	Gwyn	SH1121	52°45·5′	4°47·7′W	X	123
Plas-bach	I of Angl	SH3868	53°11·3′	4°25·1′W	X	114
Plas Bach	I of Angl	SH4072	53°13·5′	4°23·4′W	X	114,115
Plas Bach	Powys	SJ2016	52°44·4′	3°10·7′W	X	126
Plasbach Fm	Carm	SN4615	51°49·0′	4°13·7′W	FM	159
Plâs Bela	Conwy	SH9369	53°12·7′	3°35·7′W	X	116
Plas Bellin	Flint	SJ2669	53°13·0′	3°6·1′W	X	117
Plâs-Bennett	Denb	SJ1064	53°10·2′	3°20·4′W	X	116
Plas Berw	I of Angl	SH4671	53°13·1′	4°18·0′W	X	114,115
Plâs Berwyn	Denb	SJ1843	52°58·9′	3°12·9′W	T	125
Plas Bodaden	Gwyn	SH4858	53°6·1′	4°15·8′W	X	115,123
Plas Bodafon	I of Angl	SH4785	53°20·6′	4°17·5′W	X	114
Plas Bodferin	Gwyn	SH1831	52°51·0′	4°41·8′W	X	123
Plas Boduan	Gwyn	SH3237	52°54·5′	4°29·5′W	X	123
Plas Bostock	Wrex	SJ3752	53°3·9′	2°56·0′W	X	117
Plâs Brondanw	Gwyn	SH6142	52°57·7′	4°3·8′W	X	124
Plas Buckley	Wrex	SJ2949	53°2·3′	3°3·1′W	X	117
Plâs Bychan	Conwy	SH9068	53°12·1′	3°38·4′W	X	116
Plâs Cadnant	I of Angl	SH5573	53°14·3′	4°10·0′W	X	114,115
Plas canol	Gwyn	SH5918	52°44·7′	4°4·9′W	X	124
Plas Captain	Denb	SJ0363	53°9·6′	3°26·6′W	X	116
Plas Captain	Flint	SJ1177	53°17·2′	3°19·7′W	X	116
Plas Capten	Gwyn	SH7134	52°53·5′	3°54·6′W	X	124
Plas Cefn Gwyn	Cered	SN6886	52°27·6′	3°56·2′W	X	135
Plas Celyn	Powys	SO2139	52°2·9′	3°8·7′W	X	161
Plas Cemlyn	I of Angl	SH3392	53°24·2′	4°30·3′W	X	114
Plas Cerrig	Flint	SJ1274	53°15·6′	3°18·7′W	X	116
Plas cerrig	Shrops	SJ2721	52°47·1′	3°4·5′W	X	126
Plâs Chambres	Denb	SJ0468	53°12·3′	3°25·8′W	X	116
Plas-Cilcennin	Cered	SN5360	52°13·4′	4°8·7′W	X	146
Plas Cilybebyll	Nth Pt Talb	SN7404	51°43·5′	3°49·1′W	X	170
Plas Clough	Denb	SJ0567	53°11·7′	3°24·9′W	X	116
Plas-coch	Conwy	SH9968	53°12·2′	3°30·3′W	X	116
Plas-coch	Denb	SJ0275	53°16·0′	3°27·8′W	X	116
Plas-coch	Denb	SJ0371	53°13·9′	3°26·8′W	X	116
Plas Coch	Denb	SJ0772	53°14·5′	3°23·2′W	X	116
Plas Coch	Denb	SJ1162	53°9·1′	3°19·4′W	X	116
Plas Côch	Flint	SJ1772	53°14·6′	3°14·2′W	X	116
Plas Coch	I of Angl	SH5168	53°11·5′	4°13·4′W	A	114,115
Plas coch	Powys	SJ1010	52°41·1′	3°19·5′W	X	125
Plas Coch	Wrex	SJ3251	53°3·4′	3°0·5′W	T	117
Plas Coch Fm	Denb	SJ0475	53°16·0′	3°26·0′W	FM	116
Plas-Coedana	I of Angl	SH4282	53°18·9′	4°21·9′W	X	114,115
Plascow	D & G	NX8863	54°57·2′	3°44·5′W	X	84
Plascow Rig	D & G	NX8863	54°57·2′	3°44·5′W	X	84
Plas-criafol	Powys	SH1131	52°52·4′	3°18·9′W	X	125
Plas-crogen	Wrex	SJ2535	52°54·7′	3°6·5′W	X	126
Plas-crwn	Pemb	SN1416	51°48·9′	4°41·5′W	X	158
Plas Curig	Conwy	SH7257	53°5·9′	3°54·3′W	X	115
Plas Cwmcynfelin	Cered	SN6083	52°25·9′	4°3·2′W	X	135
Plas Cwtta	Conwy	SH9769	53°12·7′	3°32·1′W	X	116
Plas Cymyran	I of Angl	SH2975	53°14·9′	4°33·4′W	X	114
Plas Derwen	Monm	SO3013	51°48·9′	3°0·5′W	X	161
Plas Devon	Wrex	SJ3954	53°5·0′	2°54·2′W	X	117
Plas Dinam	Powys	SO0289	52°29·6′	3°26·2′W	T	136
Plas-Dolanog	Powys	SJ0513	52°42·6′	3°24·0′W	X	125
Plas Dolben	Denb	SJ1363	53°9·7′	3°17·7′W	X	116
Plas Dol-y-moch	Gwyn	SH6841	52°57·3′	3°57·5′W	X	124
Plas Drain	Conwy	SH8165	53°10·4′	3°46·4′W	X	116
Plâs-drain	Wrex	SJ2647	53°1·2′	3°5·8′W	X	117
Plas Drâw	Denb	SJ1362	53°9·1′	3°17·7′W	X	116
Plas Du	Gwyn	SH4140	52°56·3′	4°21·6′W	X	123
Plas-Du	Powys	SJ1025	52°49·1′	3°19·7′W	X	125
Plas Efenechtyd	Denb	SJ1055	53°5·3′	3°20·2′W	X	116
Plas Einion	Denb	SJ1354	53°4·8′	3°17·5′W	X	116
Plas Einws	Denb	SJ1159	53°7·5′	3°19·4′W	X	116
Plas Esgair	Powys	SH8801	52°36·0′	3°38·8′W	X	135,136
Plas Fm	Carm	SN5206	51°44·2′	4°8·2′W	FM	159
Plas Fm	Gwyn	SH4661	53°7·7′	4°17·7′W	FM	114,115
Plasgeler	Carm	SN3739	52°1·8′	4°22·2′W	X	145
Plas Glan-yr-Afon	Gwyn	SH5059	53°6·7′	4°14·1′W	A	115
Plas Glasgwm	Conwy	SH7750	53°2·2′	3°49·7′W	X	115
Plas Glyn-y-weddw	Gwyn	SH3231	52°51·3′	4°29·3′W	X	123
Plas Gogerddan	Cered	SN6383	52°25·9′	4°0·5′W	T	135
Plas Goronwy	I of Angl	SH5179	53°17·5′	4°13·7′W	X	114,115
Plas-Goulbourn	Wrex	SJ3342	52°58·5′	2°59·5′W	X	117
Plasgwyn	Carm	SN4014	51°48·3′	4°18·9′W	X	159
Plâs Gwyn	Denb	SJ1260	53°8·0′	3°18·5′W	X	116
Plas Gwyn	Flint	SJ1470	53°13·4′	3°16·9′W	X	116
Plas Gwyn	I of Angl	SH5278	53°16·9′	4°12·8′W	A	114,115
Plas-gwyn	Powys	SJ2122	52°47·6′	3°9·9′W	X	126
Plas Gwynant	Gwyn	SH6350	53°2·0′	4°2·2′W	X	115
Plas-gwyn Mountain	Wrex	SJ2652	53°3·9′	3°5·9′W	X	117
Plas Gwyrfai	Gwyn	SH5357	53°5·6′	4°11·3′W	X	115
Plâs-Harri	Conwy	SH9670	53°13·3′	3°33·1′W	X	116
Plâs Heaton	Denb	SJ0369	53°12·8′	3°26·7′W	A	116
Plas Heaton Fm	Denb	SJ0469	53°12·8′	3°25·9′W	FM	116
Plas Hendre	Cered	SN6082	52°25·3′	4°3·1′W	X	135
Plas Hendre	Gwyn	SH4036	52°54·1′	4°22·3′W	X	123
Plas Hendre	Gwyn	SH5244	52°58·6′	4°11·9′W	X	124
Plashes Fm	Herts	TL3720	51°51·9′	0°0·2′W	FM	166
Plashes Fm	Staffs	SJ9417	52°45·3′	2°4·9′W	FM	127
Plashes Wood	Herts	TL3820	51°51·9′	0°0·7′E	F	166
Plashet	Newham	TQ4184	51°32·5′	0°2·4′E	T	177
Plashett	Carm	SN2709	51°45·4′	4°30·0′W	T	158
Plashett Park	E Susx	TQ4616	50°55·7′	0°5·0′E	X	198
Plashett Park Fm	E Susx	TQ4514	50°54·7′	0°4·1′E	FM	198
Plashetts	Northum	NY6790	55°12·4′	2°30·7′W	X	80
Plashetts	Northum	NY9681	55°7·6′	2°3·3′W	X	81
Plashetts Burn	Northum	NY6691	55°13·0′	2°31·6′W	W	80
Plashett Wood	E Susx	TQ4615	50°55·2′	0°5·0′E	F	198
Plas Heulog	Conwy	SH6974	53°15·1′	3°57·4′W	X	115
Plash Fm	Cambs	TF3905	52°37·7′	0°3·6′E	FM	142,143
Plash Fm	Heref	SO3628	51°57·0′	2°55·5′W	FM	149,161
Plash Fm	Suff	TM1769	52°16·8′	1°11·3′E	FM	156
Plashford Fm	Corn	SX2457	50°23·4′	4°28·2′W	FM	201
Plash Rhyne	Somer	ST3751	51°15·5′	2°53·8′W	W	182
Plash, The	W Susx	SU9225	51°1·2′	0°40·9′W	F	186,197
Plash Wood	Hants	SU6932	51°5·2′	1°0·5′W	F	186
Plashwood	Suff	TM0162	52°13·4′	0°57·0′E	X	155
Plas Iago	I of Angl	SH2776	53°15·4′	4°35·2′W	X	114
Plas Ifa	Denb	SJ2442	52°58·4′	3°7·5′W	X	117
Plâs Iolyn	Conwy	SH8850	53°2·4′	3°39·8′W	X	116
Plasiolyn	Powys	SJ0904	52°37·8′	3°20·3′W	T	136
Plas Isa	Conwy	SH8175	53°15·8′	3°46·6′W	X	116
Plasisa	Conwy	SH8970	53°13·2′	3°39·3′W	X	116
Plasisaf	Conwy	SH9567	53°11·6′	3°33·9′W	X	116
Plas Isaf	Denb	SJ0542	52°58·3′	3°24·5′W	X	125
Plas Isaf	Denb	SJ1263	53°9·7′	3°18·6′W	X	116
Plas Isaf	Denb	SJ1642	52°58·4′	3°14·7′W	X	125
Plas-isaf	Flint	SJ2171	53°14·1′	3°10·6′W	X	117
Plasisaf	Gwyn	SH5456	53°5·1′	4°10·4′W	X	115
Plas Isaf	Gwyn	SH9837	52°55·5′	3°30·6′W	X	125
Plas Isa Fm	Wrex	SJ2744	52°59·5′	3°4·9′W	FM	117
Plas Is Llan	Denb	SJ0577	53°17·1′	3°25·1′W	X	116
Plas Issa Fm	Wrex	SJ3649	53°2·3′	2°56·9′W	FM	117
Plas Ivor	Monm	SO4018	51°51·7′	2°51·9′W	X	161
Plasketlands	Cumbr	NY1046	54°48·3′	3°23·6′W	X	85
Plas Kinmel	Conwy	SH9876	53°16·5′	3°31·4′W	X	116
Plas Lawrence	Pemb	SN1343	52°3·5′	4°43·3′W	X	145
Plâs-Llanarmon	Denb	SJ1855	53°5·4′	3°13·1′W	X	116
Plas Llanddyfnan	I of Angl	SH4878	53°16·9′	4°16·4′W	X	114,115
Plas Llandecwyn	Gwyn	SH6337	52°55·0′	4°1·9′W	X	124
Plas Llandegfan	I of Angl	SH5675	53°15·4′	4°9·1′W	X	114,115
Plas Llandyfrydog	I of Angl	SH4385	53°20·6′	4°21·1′W	X	114
Plas Llanfaelog	I of Angl	SH3373	53°13·9′	4°29·7′W	X	114
Plas Llanfair	I of Angl	SH5371	53°13·2′	4°11·7′W	X	114,115
Plas Llanfihangel	I of Angl	SH4583	53°19·5′	4°19·2′W	X	114,115
Plas Llangaffo	I of Angl	SH4469	53°12·0′	4°19·7′W	X	114,115
Plas Llangwyfan	I of Angl	SH3369	53°11·8′	4°29·6′W	X	114
Plas Llanychan	Denb	SJ1161	53°8·6′	3°19·4′W	X	116
Plas Llanynys	Denb	SJ1062	53°9·1′	3°20·3′W	X	116
Plas Llecha	Monm	ST3793	51°38·2′	2°54·2′W	X	171
Plâs-Llechylched	I of Angl	SH3476	53°15·5′	4°28·9′W	X	114
Plas-Lleucu	Wrex	SJ1937	52°55·7′	3°11·9′W	X	125
Plas Llewelyn	Conwy	SH8774	53°15·3′	3°41·2′W	X	116
Plas Lligwy	I of Angl	SH4985	53°20·7′	4°15·7′W	X	114
Plas-llwyd	Cered	SN4541	52°3·0′	4°15·2′W	X	146
Plas Llwyd	Conwy	SH9978	53°17·6′	3°30·5′W	X	116
Plas Llwyngwern	Gwyn	SH7504	52°37·4′	3°50·4′W	X	135
Plas Llwynonn	I of Angl	SH5169	53°12·1′	4°13·4′W	X	114,115
Plas Llysyn	Powys	SN9597	52°33·9′	3°32·5′W	X	136
Plas-lolyn	Powys	SJ1917	52°44·9′	3°11·6′W	X	125
Plâs Machen	Newp	ST2387	51°34·8′	3°6·3′W	X	171
Plas Madoc	Conwy	SH7963	53°9·3′	3°48·2′W	X	115
Plas Madoc	Wrex	SJ2843	52°59·0′	3°3·9′W	X	117
Plâs-Madog	Conwy	SH9065	53°10·5′	3°38·3′W	X	116
Plas Madog	Gwyn	SH8833	52°53·2′	3°39·5′W	X	124,125
Plas-Maen	Flint	SJ3056	53°6·0′	3°2·3′W	X	117
Plas Maenan	Conwy	SH7866	53°10·9′	3°49·1′W	X	115
Plas Maes-y-groes	Gwyn	SH6070	53°12·8′	4°5·4′W	X	115
Plas-major	Flint	SJ2662	53°9·2′	3°6·0′W	X	117
Plas-Mattw	Conwy	SH8864	53°9·9′	3°40·1′W	X	116
Plas-mawr	Flint	SJ1077	53°17·2′	3°20·6′W	X	116
Plâs-meifod	Denb	SJ0268	53°12·2′	3°27·6′W	X	116
Plas Meilw	I of Angl	SH2280	53°17·5′	4°39·8′W	X	114
Plas Menai (National Outdoor Pursuit Centre)	Gwyn	SH5066	53°10·4′	4°14·3′W	X	114,115
Plas Meredydd	Powys	SO1897	52°34·1′	3°12·2′W	T	136
Plas Milfre	Caer	SO1401	51°42·3′	3°14·3′W	X	171
Plas-Morgan	Gwyn	SH8827	52°50·0′	3°39·4′W	X	124,125
Plas Mostyn Mawr	Flint	SJ2852	53°3·9′	3°4·1′W	X	117
Plas Mynach	Gwyn	SH6016	52°43·7′	4°4·0′W	X	124
Plas Nantglyn	Denb	SJ0061	53°8·5′	3°29·3′W	X	116
Plas Nantyr	Wrex	SJ1537	52°55·7′	3°15·5′W	X	125
Plasnewydd	Carm	SN4432	51°58·1′	4°15·9′W	X	146
Plas-newydd	Carm	SN5808	51°45·4′	4°3·1′W	X	159
Plasnewydd	Carm	SN5930	51°57·3′	4°2·7′W	X	146
Plasnewydd	Carm	SN6732	51°58·5′	3°55·8′W	X	146
Plas-newydd	Carm	SN7336	52°0·7′	3°50·6′W	X	146,160
Plas-newydd	Cered	SN1645	52°4·6′	4°40·7′W	X	145
Plasnewydd	Cered	SN3441	52°2·8′	4°24·9′W	X	145
Plâs-newydd	Conwy	SH9076	53°16·4′	3°38·6′W	X	116
Plas Newydd	Conwy	SH9271	53°13·7′	3°36·7′W	X	116
Plas Newydd	Conwy	SH9466	53°11·1′	3°34·8′W	X	116
Plas newydd	Denb	SJ0072	53°14·4′	3°29·5′W	A	116
Plas Newydd	Denb	SJ0569	53°12·8′	3°25·0′W	X	116
Plas-newydd	Denb	SJ0752	53°3·7′	3°22·9′W	X	116
Plasnewydd	Denb	SJ1340	52°57·3′	3°17·3′W	X	125
Plasnewydd	Denb	SJ1356	53°5·9′	3°17·6′W	X	116
Plas Newydd	Denb	SJ2241	52°57·9′	3°9·3′W	X	117
Plas-newydd	Flint	SJ1574	53°15·6′	3°16·0′W	X	116
Plas-newydd	Flint	SJ1665	53°10·8′	3°15·0′W	X	116
Plas Newydd	Flint	SJ2269	53°13·0′	3°9·7′W	X	117
Plasnewydd	Gwyn	SH2029	52°50·0′	4°39·9′W	X	123
Plasnewydd	Gwyn	SH4554	53°3·9′	4°18·4′W	X	115,123
Plas Newydd	I of Angl	SH5269	53°12·1′	4°12·5′W	A	114,115
Plas Newydd	I of Angl	SH6181	53°18·7′	4°4·8′W	X	114,115
Plasnewydd	Powys	SJ0409	52°40·5′	3°24·8′W	X	125
Plasnewydd	Powys	SN9796	52°33·4′	3°30·8′W	T	136
Plasnewydd Fm	Denb	SJ0581	53°19·3′	3°25·2′W	FM	116
Plas Newydd Fm	Flint	SJ2860	53°8·2′	3°4·2′W	FM	117
Plas Oerddwr	Gwyn	SH5945	52°59·3′	4°5·6′W	X	115
Plas Offa	Wrex	SJ2840	52°57·4′	3°3·9′W	X	117
Plas-onn	Conwy	SH8965	53°10·5′	3°39·2′W	X	116
Plas Onn	Conwy	SH9147	53°0·8′	3°37·1′W	X	116
Plas-onn	Conwy	SH9276	53°16·4′	3°36·8′W	X	116
Plâs-onn	Wrex	SJ2335	52°54·7′	3°8·3′W	X	126
Plas Panton	Conwy	SH9662	53°8·9′	3°32·9′W	X	116
Plasparcau	Carm	SN2527	51°55·2′	4°32·3′W	X	145,158
Plasparcau	Carm	SN2818	51°50·3′	4°29·4′W	X	158
Plasparcau	Carm	SN2827	51°55·1′	4°29·7′W	X	145,158
Plas-paun	Carm	SN2923	51°53·0′	4°28·7′W	X	145,159
Plas Penisarnant	Gwyn	SH6365	53°10·1′	4°2·6′W	X	115
Plas Penmynydd	I of Angl	SH4975	53°15·3′	4°15·4′W	X	114,115
Plas Penrhyn	I of Angl	SH4563	53°8·7′	4°18·7′W	X	114,115
Plas Perthi	Denb	SJ0954	53°4·8′	3°21·1′W	X	116
Plas Pigot	Conwy	SH9564	53°10·0′	3°33·8′W	X	116
Plas Porthamel	I of Angl	SH5067	53°11·0′	4°14·3′W	FM	114,115
Plas Rhiwaedog	Gwyn	SH9434	52°53·8′	3°34·1′W	A	125
Plas-rhiw-Saeson	Powys	SH9005	52°38·1′	3°37·1′W	X	125
Plassey	Wrex	SJ4342	52°58·6′	2°50·5′W	X	117
Plassey, The	Wrex	SJ3545	53°0·1′	2°57·7′W	X	117
Plâs Siors	Denb	SJ1064	53°10·2′	3°20·4′W	X	116
Plas Talgarth (Hotel)	Gwyn	SN6999	52°34·6′	3°55·6′W	X	135
Plas Talhenbont	Gwyn	SH4639	52°55·8′	4°17·1′W	X	123
Plâs Tan-y-Bwlch (Study Centre)	Gwyn	SH6540	52°56·7′	4°0·1′W	X	124
Plas Teg	Flint	SJ2859	53°7·6′	3°4·2′W	A	117
Plaster Down	Devon	SX5172	50°32·0′	4°5·8′W	X	191,201
Plaster Pitts	N Yks	SE7461	54°2·6′	0°51·8′W	X	100
Plaster Pitts Fm	N Yks	SE3175	54°10·4′	1°31·1′W	FM	99
Plaster's Green	Bath & NE Somer	ST5360	51°20·5′	2°40·1′W	T	172,182
Plas-Thelwal	I of Angl	SH5281	53°18·6′	4°12·9′W	X	114,115
Plas-Thomas	Shrops	SJ3439	52°56·9′	2°58·5′W	X	126
Plas Tirion	Conwy	SH7574	53°15·1′	3°52·0′W	X	115
Plas Tirion	Gwyn	SH5262	53°8·3′	4°12·3′W	X	114,115
Plas-Tower-Bridge	Denb	SJ1359	53°7·5′	3°17·6′W	X	116
Plastow Green	Hants	SU5361	51°21·0′	1°13·9′W	T	174
Plastre Court	Kent	TQ8828	51°1·5′	0°41·2′E	X	189,199
Plas Trefarthen	I of Angl	SH4866	53°10·4′	4°16·0′W	X	114,115
Plas Tregeiriog	Wrex	SJ1733	52°53·5′	3°13·6′W	X	125
Plas Troedyraur	Cered	SN2946	52°5·4′	4°29·4′W	X	145
Plas Ucha	Conwy	SH8163	53°9·3′	3°46·4′W	X	116
Plas Ucha	Conwy	SH8175	53°15·8′	3°46·6′W	X	116
Plas Uchaf	Carm	SN6109	51°46·0′	4°0·5′W	X	159
Plas Uchaf	Conwy	SH8549	53°1·8′	3°42·5′W	X	116
Plas Uchaf	Conwy	SH8775	53°15·8′	3°41·2′W	X	116
Plâs-uchaf	Conwy	SH9671	53°13·8′	3°33·1′W	X	116
Plâs-uchaf	Flint	SJ1379	53°18·3′	3°17·9′W	A	116
Plas Uchaf	I of Angl	SH3186	53°20·9′	4°31·9′W	X	114
Plasuchaf	I of Angl	SH4789	53°22·8′	4°17·6′W	X	114
Plas-uchaf	Powys	SJ1724	52°48·7′	3°13·5′W	X	125
Plas-uchaf	Wrex	SJ2745	53°0·1′	3°4·9′W	X	117
Plâs-uchaf Resr	Conwy	SH9671	53°13·8′	3°33·1′W	W	116
Plaswarren	Powys	SO1945	52°6·1′	3°10·6′W	X	148
Plas Warren Hall	Shrops	SJ3338	52°56·4′	2°59·4′W	X	126
Plas-Whitchurch	Pemb	SN1536	51°59·7′	4°41·3′W	X	145
Plâs Wilkin	Flint	SJ1966	53°11·3′	3°12·3′W	X	116
Plas Wynne	Wrex	SJ2137	52°55·7′	3°10·1′W	X	126
Plas-y-bedw	Carm	SN1324	51°53·2′	4°42·7′W	X	145,158
Plas-y-Beili	Carm	SN1523	51°52·7′	4°40·9′W	X	145,158
Plas-y-berllan	Pemb	SN2242	52°3·1′	4°35·4′W	X	145
Plas-y-brain	Flint	SJ2459	53°7·6′	3°7·7′W	X	117
Plas y Brenin	Conwy	SH7157	53°5·9′	3°55·2′W	X	115
Plas-y-Bridell	Pemb	SN1742	52°3·0′	4°39·7′W	X	145
Plas-y-bryn	Gwyn	SH4859	53°6·6′	4°15·8′W	X	115,123
Plas-y-bryn	Powys	SO1192	52°31·4′	3°18·3′W	X	136
Plas-y-Bryniau	Cered	SN5661	52°13·9′	4°6·1′W	X	146
Plasycerdin	Carm	SN2320	51°51·3′	4°33·8′W	X	145,158
Plâs-y-Coed	Gwyn	SH5456	53°5·1′	4°10·4′W	X	115
Plas-y-coed	Torf	SO2600	51°41·9′	3°3·9′W	X	171
Plas-y-Court	Shrops	SJ3112	52°42·3′	3°0·9′W	X	126
Plas-y-darren	Powys	SN9212	51°48·0′	3°33·6′W	X	160
Plas y drain	Powys	SJ0103	52°37·2′	3°27·3′W	X	136
Plas-y-gaer	Powys	SO0324	51°54·6′	3°24·2′W	X	160
Plas y Glyn	I of Angl	SH2984	53°19·8′	4°33·7′W	X	114
Plas-y-gors	Powys	SN9216	51°50·2′	3°33·7′W	X	160
Plas-y-gwer	Carm	SN2815	51°48·7′	4°29·3′W	X	158
Plas y Gwynfryn	Cered	SN6491	52°30·2′	3°59·8′W	X	135
Plasymeibion	Pemb	SN1227	51°54·8′	4°43·6′W	X	145,158
Plas-ym-Mhowys	Flint	SJ2559	53°7·6′	3°6·8′W	X	117
Plas-y-mynydd	Flint	SJ2371	53°14·1′	3°8·8′W	X	117
Plas-y-nant	Denb	SJ1657	53°6·5′	3°14·9′W	X	116
Plas-y-nant	Gwyn	SH5556	53°5·1′	4°9·5′W	X	115
Plas-yn-Betws	Conwy	SH9073	53°14·8′	3°38·5′W	X	116
Plas-yn-Blaenau	Conwy	SH8664	53°9·9′	3°41·9′W	X	116
Plas-yn-Cefn	Denb	SJ0171	53°13·9′	3°28·6′W	X	116
Plas yn Coed	Wrex	SJ3841	52°58·0′	2°55·0′W	X	117
Plas-yn-cornel	Conwy	SH9366	53°11·1′	3°35·7′W	X	116
Plas yn Cwm	Denb	SJ0675	53°16·1′	3°24·2′W	X	116
Plas-yn-Dinam	Denb	SJ0135	52°54·4′	3°27·9′W	X	125
Plas yn Dinas	Powys	SJ2118	52°45·5′	3°9·8′W	A	126
Plas Yn Eglwyseg	Denb	SJ2146	53°0·6′	3°10·2′W	X	117
Plas-yn-fron	Wrex	SJ2748	53°1·7′	3°4·9′W	X	117
Plasyngheidio	Gwyn	SH2938	52°55·0′	4°32·2′W	X	123
Plasynghraen	Powys	SJ0209	52°40·4′	3°26·6′W	X	125
Plâs-yn-glyn	Powys	SJ1227	52°50·2′	3°18·0′W	X	125
Plâs-yn-Grove	Shrops	SJ3837	52°55·9′	2°54·9′W	X	126
Plas-yn-pentre	Denb	SJ2641	52°57·9′	3°5·7′W	A	117
Plâs-yn-rhal	Denb	SJ1458	53°7·0′	3°16·7′W	X	116
Plas yn Rhiw	Gwyn	SH2328	52°49·5′	4°37·2′W	X	123
Plâs-yn-rhôs	Conwy	SH8253	53°3·9′	3°45·3′W	X	116
Plâs-yn-rhôs	Denb	SJ1261	53°8·6′	3°18·5′W	X	116
Plas-yn-rhos	Denb	SJ1647	53°1·1′	3°14·7′W	X	116
Plas-yn-Trofarth	Conwy	SH8569	53°12·6′	3°42·9′W	X	116
Plas-yn-Wern	Wrex	SJ2843	52°59·0′	3°3·9′W	X	117
Plas yn Yale	Denb	SJ1749	53°2·2′	3°13·9′W	F	116
Plas-yn-y-coed	Shrops	SJ3340	52°57·4′	2°59·4′W	X	117
Plas Yolyn	Shrops	SJ3437	52°55·8′	2°58·5′W	X	126
Plas-y-parciau	Carm	SN3222	51°52·5′	4°26·0′W	X	145,159
Plas-yr-Esgob	Denb	SJ1061	53°8·6′	3°20·3′W	X	116
Plasyrhafod	Carm	SN3032	51°57·9′	4°28·1′W	X	145
Plas-yw	Flint	SJ1567	53°11·8′	3°15·9′W	X	116
Plas-y-Ward	Denb	SJ1160	53°8·0′	3°19·4′W	X	116
Plas-y-wenallt	Carm	SN4209	51°45·7′	4°17·0′W	X	159
Plat	Cumbr	NY8810	54°29·4′	2°10·7′W	X	91,92
Plat	Staffs	SJ9648	53°2·0′	2°3·2′W	X	118
Platchaig	Highld	NH4945	57°28·5′	4°30·6′W	X	26
Platnix Fm	E Susx	TQ8016	50°55·1′	0°34·0′E	FM	199
Plât Rèidh	Highld	NC3447	58°23·1′	4°49·9′W	X	9
Platt	Corn	SX0949	50°18·8′	4°40·6′W	X	200,204
Platt	Cumbr	SD7284	54°15·3′	2°25·4′W	X	98
Platt	Kent	TQ6257	51°17·6′	0°19·8′E	T	188
Platt Bridge	Wigan	SD6002	53°31·0′	2°35·8′W	T	109

Platt Brook	Shrops	SJ6122	52°47·9'	2°34·3'W	W	127
Platt Fm	Flint	SJ3060	53°8·2'	3°2·4'W	FM	117
Platt Lane	Shrops	SJ5136	52°55·4'	2°43·3'W	T	126
Plattmill	Shrops	SJ4022	52°47·8'	2°53·0'W	X	126
Platts	Cumbr	NY7316	54°32·6'	2°24·6'W	X	91
Platt's Br	Lincs	TF2625	52°48·7'	0°7·4'W	X	131
Platts Common	Barns	SE3601	53°30·5'	1°27·0'W	T	110,111
Platt's Fm	E Susx	TQ6823	50°59·1'	0°24·0'E	FM	199
Platts Fm	Lincs	SK8745	52°59·9'	0°41·8'W	FM	130
Platts Fm	Sheff	SK2590	53°24·6'	1°37·0'W	FM	110
Platt's Heath	Kent	TQ8750	51°13·3'	0°41·1'E	T	189
Platt, The	E Susx	TQ5834	51°5·2'	0°15·8'E	X	188
Platt, The	Shrops	SJ5534	52°54·3'	2°39·7'W	X	126
Platt Wood Fm	Ches	SJ9583	53°20·9'	2°4·1'W	FM	109
Platwoods Fm	E Yorks	TA0235	53°48·3'	0°26·7'W	FM	106,107
Plaw Field	Norf	TF5001	52°35·4'	0°13·3'E	X	143
Plawhatch Hall	E Susx	TQ3932	51°4·5'	0°0·6'W	X	187
Plawsworth	Durham	NZ2647	54°49·3'	1°35·3'W	T	88
Plaw Wood	E Susx	TQ3933	51°5·0'	0°0·5'W	F	187
Plaxdale Green Fm	Kent	TQ5961	51°19·8'	0°17·3'E	FM	177,188
Plaxtol	Kent	TQ6053	51°15·4'	0°18·0'E	T	188
Plaxton's Br	E Yorks	TA0636	53°48·8'	0°23·0'W	X	107
Playden	E Susx	TQ9121	50°57·6'	0°43·6'E	T	189
Playford	Suff	TM2147	52°4·9'	1°13·9'E	T	169
Playford Hall	Suff	TM2147	52°4·9'	1°13·9'E	A	169
Playford Heath	Suff	TM2146	52°4·3'	1°13·9'E	X	169
Play Hatch	Oxon	SU7476	51°28·9'	0°55·7'W	T	175
Play Hill	Surrey	SU9054	51°16·9'	0°42·2'W	X	186
Playing Place	Corn	SW8141	50°13·9'	5°3·9'W	T	204
Playknowe Plantn	Scot Bord	NT5125	55°31·2'	2°46·1'W	F	73
Playlands	Aberd	NJ4337	57°25·4'	2°56·5'W	X	28
Playley Green	Glos	SO7631	51°58·9'	2°20·6'W	T	150
Playter's Hall	Norf	TF6706	52°37·8'	0°28·5'E	X	143
Playters Old Fm	Suff	TM4487	52°25·8'	1°35·8'E	FM	156
Pleacairn	D & G	NY1273	55°2·9'	3°22·2'W	X	85
Pleahillock	Pth & Kin	NO1641	56°33·5'	3°21·6'W	X	53
Pleak House Fm	Dorset	ST7614	50°55·7'	2°20·1'W	FM	194
Plea Knowe	D & G	NY2296	55°15·4'	3°13·2'W	H	79
Pleaknowe	Scot Bord	NT5206	55°21·0'	2°45·0'W	X	79
Plealey	Shrops	SJ4206	52°39·2'	2°51·0'W	T	126
Plealey Villa	Shrops	SJ4306	52°39·2'	2°50·2'W	X	126
Pleamore Cross	Somer	ST1218	50°57·5'	3°14·8'W	T	181,193
Pleamoss Hill	D & G	NY2688	55°11·1'	3°9·3'W	H	79
Plea Muir	N Lanak	NS6980	56°0·0'	4°5·6'W	X	64
Plean	Stir	NS8387	56°3·9'	3°52·3'W	T	57,65
Pleanbank	Stir	NS8287	56°3·9'	3°53·3'W	X	57,65
Plean Ho	Stir	NS8286	56°3·4'	3°53·3'W	X	57,65
Pleanmill	Stir	NS8586	56°3·4'	3°50·4'W	X	65
Plea Rig	D & G	NX7075	55°3·4'	4°1·7'W	X	77,84
Pleasance	D & G	NX9772	55°2·2'	3°36·3'W	X	84
Pleasance	Fife	NO2312	56°17·9'	3°14·2'W	X	58
Pleasance	Fife	NT1289	56°5·4'	3°24·4'W	X	65
Pleasance	Pth & Kin	NO2239	56°32·4'	3°15·7'W	X	53
Pleasance Fm	Warw	SP2672	52°21·0'	1°36·7'W	FM	140
Pleasance, The	Warw	SP2672	52°21·0'	1°36·7'W	A	140
Pleasantfield	S Ayr	NS3516	55°24·9'	4°36·0'W	X	70
Pleasant Fm	Kent	TQ7850	51°13·5'	0°33·3'E	FM	188
Pleasants	Fife	NT1785	56°3·3'	3°19·5'W	X	65,66
Pleasants	Scot Bord	NT6919	55°28·1'	2°29·0'W	X	80
Pleasant Valley	Pemb	SN1406	51°43·6'	4°41·2'W	T	158
Pleasant View	Lancs	SD4923	53°42·3'	2°45·9'W	X	102
Pleasant View Fm	Lancs	SD7819	53°40·3'	2°19·6'W	FM	109
Pleasant View Fm	V of Glam	SS9671	51°25·9'	3°29·4'W	FM	170
Pleasant Wood	E Yorks	TA0657	54°0·1'	0°22·5'W	X	107
Pleasington	Black w Dar	SD6426	53°44·0'	2°32·3'W	T	102,103
Pleasley	Derby	SK5064	53°10·5'	1°14·7'W	T	120
Pleasleyhill	Notts	SK5063	53°9·9'	1°14·7'W	T	120
Pleasley Park	Derby	SK5165	53°11·0'	1°13·8'W	F	120
Pleasleypark Fm	Derby	SK5166	53°11·6'	1°13·8'W	FM	120
Pleasley Vale	Derby	SK5165	53°11·0'	1°13·8'W	X	120
Pleasure Ho	Kent	TQ8249	51°12·9'	0°36·8'E	X	188
Pleasurewood Hills	Suff	TM5496	52°30·4'	1°45·0'E	X	134
Pleck	Dorset	ST7010	50°53·6'	2°25·2'W	T	194
Pleck	Dorset	ST7717	50°57·4'	2°19·3'W	T	183
Pleck	Wals	SO9997	52°34·5'	2°0·5'W	T	139
Pleckgate	Black w Dar	SD6730	53°46·2'	2°29·6'W	T	103
Pleck or Little Ansty	Dorset	ST7604	50°50·3'	2°20·1'W	T	194
Pleck, The	Heref	SO4918	51°51·7'	2°44·0'W	X	162
Pleck, The	Staffs	SJ8142	52°58·7'	2°16·6'W	X	118
Pledgdon Green	Essex	TL5626	51°54·9'	0°16·5'E	T	167
Pledgdon Hall	Essex	TL5527	51°55·4'	0°15·6'E	X	167
Pledrog	Cered	SN4149	52°7·2'	4°19·0'W	X	146
Pledwick	Wakf	SE3316	53°38·6'	1°29·6'W	T	110,111
Pleming	Corn	SW4931	50°7·8'	5°30·4'W	X	203
Plemstall	Ches	SJ4570	53°13·7'	2°49·0'W	T	117
Plenderleith	Scot Bord	NT7311	55°23·8'	2°25·1'W	X	80
Plendernethy Hill	Scot Bord	NT7556	55°48·1'	2°23·5'W	X	67,74
Plenmeller	Northum	NY7163	54°57·9'	2°26·8'W	T	86,87
Plenmeller Common	Northum	NY7261	54°56·8'	2°25·8'W	H	86,87
Plenploth	Scot Bord	NT4348	55°43·6'	2°54·0'W	X	73
Plenty Ho	Dorset	SY4095	50°45·3'	2°50·7'W	X	193
Pleremore	Worcs	SO8872	52°21·0'	2°10·2'W	X	139
Pleshey	Essex	TL6614	51°48·2'	0°24·9'E	T	167
Plesheybury	Essex	TL6514	51°48·2'	0°24·0'E	X	167
Pleshey Grange	Essex	TL6514	51°48·2'	0°24·0'E	X	167
Plessey Hall Fm	Northum	NZ2279	55°6·5'	1°38·9'W	FM	88
Plessey North Moor Fm	Northum	NZ2376	55°4·9'	1°38·0'W	FM	88
Plessey South Moor Fm	Northum	NZ2375	55°4·4'	1°38·0'W	FM	88
Plessey Woods Country Park	Northum	NZ2479	55°6·5'	1°37·0'W	X	88
Plessey Woods Country Park	Northum	NZ2480	55°7·1'	1°37·0'W	X	81
Plestowes Ho	Warw	SP2960	52°14·5'	1°34·1'W	X	151
Plewlands	Moray	NJ1769	57°42·5'	3°23·1'W	X	28
Plewlands	S Ayr	NS4230	55°32·5'	4°29·8'W	X	70
Plex	Shrops	SJ5119	52°46·2'	2°43·2'W	X	126
Plex Fm	Derby	SK0373	53°15·5'	1°56·9'W	FM	119
Plex Fm	Shrops	SJ5018	52°45·7'	2°44·1'W	FM	126
Plex Moss	Lancs	SD3410	53°35·2'	2°59·4'W	X	108
Pley Moss	E Ayr	NS5641	55°38·7'	4°16·9'W	X	71
Pleystowe Fm	Surrey	TQ1739	51°8·5'	0°19·3'W	FM	187
Pliadan Dubha	Arg & Bt	NR4259	55°45·6'	6°6·3'W	X	60
Plocach	Arg & Bt	NR6813	55°21·6'	5°39·2'W	X	68
Plocaig	Highld	NM4569	56°44·8'	6°9·8'W	X	47
Plocan	Highld	ND0959	58°30·8'	3°33·2'W	X	11,12
Ploc an Rubha	Highld	NG8583	57°47·4'	5°36·6'W	H	19
Ploc an t-Slagain	Highld	NG8393	57°52·7'	5°39·1'W	X	19
Plock of Kyle	Highld	NG7527	57°17·0'	5°43·5'W	X	33
Plocks Fm	Lancs	SD4520	53°40·7'	2°49·5'W	FM	102
Plockton	Highld	NG8033	57°20·3'	5°38·9'W	T	24
Plockton Aerodrome	Highld	NG7933	57°20·3'	5°39·9'W	X	24
Plock Wood	Heref	SO4852	52°10·1'	2°45·2'W	F	148,149
Plockwoods Bank Wood	N Yks	SE6182	54°14·0'	1°3·4'W	F	100
Plocrapol	N Eil	NG1793	57°50·5'	6°45·7'W	T	14
Plodda Falls	Highld	NH2723	57°16·2'	4°51·7'W	W	25
Ploddy Ho	Glos	SO7222	51°54·0'	2°24·0'W	X	162
Plodhill	Aberd	NJ9316	57°14·3'	2°6·5'W	X	38
Plodhill Wood	Aberd	NJ9231	57°22·4'	2°7·5'W	F	30
Plodmire Wood	N Yks	SE2197	54°22·3'	1°40·2'W	F	99
Plod Sgeirean	Arg & Bt	NR4549	55°40·3'	6°2·9'W	W	60
Plomers Hall	Kent	TQ6545	51°11·0'	0°22·0'E	X	188
Plomers Firs Fm	Northnts	SP5635	52°0·9'	1°10·6'W	FM	152
Plompton Hall	N Yks	SE3554	53°59·1'	1°27·6'W	X	104
Plompton High Grange	N Yks	SE3653	53°58·5'	1°26·7'W	X	104
Plompton Square	N Yks	SE3553	53°58·6'	1°27·6'W	X	104
Plora Burn	Scot Bord	NT3635	55°36·5'	3°0·5'W	W	73
Plora Craig	Scot Bord	NT3535	55°36·5'	3°1·5'W	X	73
Plora Rig	Scot Bord	NT3435	55°36·5'	3°2·4'W	H	73
Plotcock	E Ayr	NS4722	55°28·3'	4°24·8'W	X	70
Plot Dairy Fm	Somer	ST4824	51°1·0'	2°44·1'W	FM	193
Plot Fm	Notts	SK8772	53°14·5'	0°41·4'W	FM	121
Plot Gate	Somer	ST5432	51°5·4'	2°39·0'W	T	182,183
Plot Street	Somer	ST5536	51°7·5'	2°38·2'W	T	182,183
Plough Barn	Oxon	SU2792	51°37·8'	1°36·2'W	X	163,174
Plough Fell	Cumbr	SD1691	54°18·7'	3°17·1'W	X	96
Plough Fm	Hants	SU3550	51°15·1'	1°29·5'W	FM	185
Plough Hill	Warw	SP3292	52°31·7'	1°31·3'W	T	140
Plough Inn	Northum	NZ1069	55°1·2'	1°50·2'W	X	88
Ploughland	S Ayr	NS3636	55°35·7'	4°35·7'W	X	70
Ploughlands	Cumbr	NY2856	54°53·9'	3°6·9'W	X	85
Ploughlands	Cumbr	NY7513	54°30·9'	2°22·7'W	X	91
Ploughlands	Scot Bord	NT6230	55°34·0'	2°35·7'W	X	74
Ploughlands	Scot Bord	NT6926	55°31·9'	2°29·0'W	X	74
Ploughlands	Scot Bord	NT7543	55°41·0'	2°23·4'W	X	74
Ploughley Hill	Oxon	SP5231	51°58·7'	1°14·2'W	X	151
Ploughman Wood	Notts	SK6446	53°0·7'	1°2·4'W	F	129
Ploverfield	Highld	NH6149	57°30·9'	4°18·8'W	X	26
Plover Hall	Durham	NZ0012	54°30·4'	1°59·6'W	X	92
Plover Hill	Highld	ND2659	58°31·0'	3°15·7'W	X	11,12
Plover Hill	Northum	NY9262	54°57·4'	2°7·1'W	X	87
Plover Hill	N Yks	SD8475	54°10·5'	2°14·3'W	H	98
Plover Hill Fm	N Yks	SE2472	54°8·8'	1°37·5'W	FM	99
Ploveriggs	Cumbr	NY5916	54°32·5'	2°37·6'W	X	91
Plovermuir	Angus	NO3752	56°39·6'	3°1·2'W	X	54
Plover Plantn	Scot Bord	NT4212	55°24·2'	2°54·5'W	F	79
Plovers	Kent	TQ6839	51°7·8'	0°24·5'E	X	188
Plover Scar	Lancs	SD4254	53°59·0'	2°52·7'W	X	102
Plovers' Gap	Highld	NC8224	58°11·6'	4°0·0'W	X	17
Ploverwards	Moray	NJ5055	57°35·2'	2°49·7'W	X	29
Plowden	Shrops	SO3887	52°28·9'	2°54·4'W	T	137
Plowden Hall	Shrops	SO3786	52°28·3'	2°55·3'W	X	137
Plowden Woods	Shrops	SO3886	52°28·3'	2°54·4'W	F	137
Plowlands Fm	E Yorks	TA3321	53°40·3'	0°1·2'E	FM	107,113
Plowley Brook	Ches	SJ4356	53°6·1'	2°50·7'W	W	117
Ploxgreen	Shrops	SJ3603	52°37·5'	2°56·3'W	T	126
Plucach	Pth & Kin	NN5962	56°44·0'	4°17·8'W	X	42
Plucka Hill	Cumbr	NY8515	54°32·0'	2°13·5'W	X	91,92
Pluckerston	Angus	NO3751	56°39·1'	3°1·2'W	X	54
Pluckham	N Yks	SE8557	54°0·4'	0°41·8'W	X	106
Pluckham Plantn	N Yks	SE8458	54°0·9'	0°42·7'W	F	106
Pluckley	Kent	TQ9245	51°10·5'	0°45·2'E	T	189
Pluckley Sta	Kent	TQ9243	51°9·5'	0°45·1'E	X	189
Pluckley Thorne	Kent	TQ9144	51°10·0'	0°44·3'E	T	189
Pluck Point	Arg & Bt	NR7931	55°31·6'	5°29·7'W	X	68,69
Plucks Gutter	Kent	TR2663	51°19·5'	1°15·0'E	T	179
Pluck the Crow Point	Fife	NO4127	56°26·1'	2°57·0'W	X	54,59
Pluc Mór	Highld	NH7020	57°15·4'	4°8·8'W	H	35
Pludd	Devon	SS4946	51°11·8'	4°9·3'W	X	180
Plud Fm	Somer	ST1842	51°10·5'	3°10·0'W	FM	181
Plumber Manor	Dorset	ST7711	50°54·1'	2°19·2'W	X	194
Plumberow Mount	Essex	TQ8393	51°36·6'	0°39·0'E	X	178
Plumb Island	I Scilly	SV9117	49°58·6'	6°18·2'W	X	203
Plumbland	Cumbr	NY1538	54°44·0'	3°18·8'W	T	89
Plumbland Mill	Cumbr	NY1540	54°45·1'	3°18·8'W	X	85
Plumbley	Sheff	SK4180	53°19·2'	1°22·7'W	T	111,120
Plumb's Fm	W Berks	SU4165	51°23·2'	1°24·3'W	FM	174
Plumbs, The	E Yorks	TA3417	53°38·2'	0°2·0'E	X	113
Plumdon	D & G	NY2065	54°58·6'	3°14·6'W	X	85
Plumford	Kent	TR0058	51°17·4'	0°52·5'E	T	178
Plumgarth	Cumbr	NY1200	54°23·5'	3°20·9'W	X	89
Plumgarths	Cumbr	SD4994	54°20·6'	2°46·7'W	X	97
Plumian Fm	Cambs	TL5950	52°7·8'	0°19·8'E	FM	154
Plumley	Ches	SJ7175	53°16·5'	2°25·7'W	T	118
Plumley Fm	Hants	SU1209	50°53·1'	1°49·4'W	FM	195
Plumley Moor	Ches	SJ7374	53°16·0'	2°23·9'W	X	118
Plumley Wood	Dorset	ST6915	50°56·2'	2°26·1'W	F	183
Plumley Wood	Dorset	SU1109	50°53·1'	1°50·2'W	F	195
Plummer's Fm	Herts	TL2219	51°51·6'	0°13·3'W	FM	166
Plummers Hill Fm	Lincs	SK9228	52°50·7'	0°37·6'W	FM	130
Plummers Plain	W Susx	TQ2128	51°2·5'	0°16·0'W	X	187,198
Plumpe Fm	Cumbr	NY3368	55°0·4'	3°2·4'W	FM	85
Plump Hill	Glos	SO6617	51°51·3'	2°29·2'W	T	162
Plump Ho	N Yks	SE2187	54°16·9'	1°40·2'W	X	99
Plump Ho	N Yks	SE4466	54°5·5'	1°19·2'W	X	99
Plumpton	Cumbr	NY4937	54°43·8'	2°47·1'W	T	90
Plumpton	E Susx	TQ3613	50°54·3'	0°3·6'W	T	198
Plumpton	Northnts	SP5948	52°7·9'	1°7·9'W	T	152
Plumpton Bight	Cumbr	SD3178	54°11·8'	3°3·0'W	W	96,97
Plumpton Cottage Fm	Cumbr	SD3180	54°12·9'	3°3·1'W	FM	96,97
Plumpton End	Northnts	SP7245	52°6·2'	0°56·5'W	T	152
Plumpton Fm	Kent	TR0542	51°8·7'	0°56·2'E	FM	179,189
Plumpton Foot	Cumbr	NY4839	54°44·8'	2°48·0'W	T	90
Plumpton Green	E Susx	TQ3616	50°55·9'	0°3·5'W	T	198
Plumpton Hall	Cumbr	NY4935	54°42·7'	2°47·1'W	X	90
Plumpton Hall	Cumbr	SD3178	54°11·8'	3°3·0'W	X	96,97
Plumpton Hall	N Yks	SE2969	54°7·2'	1°33·0'W	X	99
Plumpton Head	Cumbr	NY5035	54°42·7'	2°46·1'W	X	90
Plumpton Old Hall	Cumbr	NY4936	54°43·2'	2°47·1'W	X	90
Plumpton Place	E Susx	TQ3613	50°54·3'	0°3·6'W	A	198
Plumpton Plain	E Susx	TQ3612	50°53·7'	0°3·6'W	X	198
Plumpton Rocks	N Yks	SE3553	53°58·6'	1°27·6'W	X	104
Plumpton's Fm	Essex	TM0719	51°50·1'	1°0·7'E	FM	168,169
Plumpton Sta	E Susx	TQ3616	50°55·9'	0°3·5'W	X	198
Plumpton Wood	Northnts	SP6049	52°8·4'	1°7·0'W	F	152
Plumpudding Island	Kent	TR2669	51°22·7'	1°15·3'E	X	179
Plumridge Fm	Enf	TQ2799	51°40·8'	0°9·4'W	FM	166,176
Plumridge Hill	Enf	TQ2799	51°40·8'	0°9·4'W	X	166,176
Plumstead	Gren	TQ4478	51°29·2'	0°4·8'E	T	177
Plumstead	Norf	TG1334	52°51·9'	1°10·3'E	T	133
Plumstead Common	Gren	TQ4577	51°28·6'	0°5·7'E	T	177
Plumstead Green	Norf	TG1234	52°51·9'	1°9·4'E	T	133
Plumstead Green	Norf	TG3011	52°39·1'	1°24·4'E	X	133,134
Plumstone Fm	Kent	TR3066	51°21·0'	1°18·6'E	FM	179
Plumstone Mountain	Pemb	SM9123	51°52·2'	5°1·8'W	H	157,158
Plumton Hall	Suff	TL8158	52°11·7'	0°39·3'E	X	155
Plumton Wood	Suff	TL8157	52°11·1'	0°39·3'E	F	155
Plumtree	Notts	SK6132	52°53·2'	1°5·2'W	T	129
Plum Tree Fm	Ches	SJ8367	53°12·2'	2°14·9'W	FM	118
Plum Tree Fm	Kent	TQ8261	51°19·4'	0°37·1'E	FM	178,188
Plumtree Fm	Notts	SK6392	53°25·5'	1°2·7'W	FM	111
Plum Tree Fm	N Yks	NZ6805	54°26·4'	0°56·7'W	FM	94
Plum Tree Fm	Red & Cl	NZ6714	54°31·3'	0°57·5'W	FM	94
Plum Tree Fm	Staffs	SJ7647	53°1·4'	2°21·1'W	FM	118
Plum Tree Fm	Wrex	SJ3852	53°3·9'	2°55·1'W	FM	117
Plumtree Green	Kent	TQ8245	51°10·7'	0°36·6'E	T	188
Plum Tree Ho	N Yks	NZ7817	54°32·8'	0°47·2'W	X	94
Plumtree Moor Plantn	N Yks	SE2898	54°22·8'	1°33·7'W	F	99
Plumtree Park	Notts	SK6131	52°52·6'	1°5·2'W	T	129
Plumtree Wolds	Notts	SK6332	52°53·1'	1°3·4'W	X	129
Plunder Heath	Northum	NY8565	54°59·0'	2°13·6'W	X	87
Plungar	Leic	SK7633	52°53·6'	0°51·8'W	T	129
Plungar Wood	Leic	SK7832	52°53·0'	0°50·0'W	F	129
Plunton Burn	D & G	NX6050	54°49·8'	4°10·3'W	W	83
Plunton Castle	D & G	NX6050	54°49·8'	4°10·3'W	A	83
Plunton Hill	D & G	NX6051	54°50·3'	4°10·4'W	H	83
Plunton Mains	D & G	NX6150	54°49·8'	4°9·4'W	X	83
Plurenden Manor	Kent	TQ9237	51°6·2'	0°44·9'E	X	189
Plurenden Wood	Kent	TQ9338	51°6·7'	0°45·8'E	F	189
Pluscarden	Moray	NJ1456	57°35·4'	3°25·9'W	X	28
Pluscarden Priory	Moray	NJ1457	57°36·0'	3°25·9'W	A	28
Plush	Dorset	ST7102	50°49·2'	2°24·3'W	T	194
Plusha	Corn	SX2580	50°35·8'	4°28·0'W	T	201
Plushabridge	Corn	SX3072	50°31·6'	4°23·5'W	T	201
Plushayes	Devon	SS9818	50°57·4'	3°26·8'W	X	181
Plush Hill	Dorset	ST7101	50°48·7'	2°24·3'W	X	194
Plush Hill	Shrops	SO4596	52°33·8'	2°48·3'W	X	137,138
Plusterwine	Glos	ST5999	51°41·5'	2°35·2'W	T	162
Plwmp	Cered	SN3652	52°8·8'	4°23·4'W	T	145
Plyer's Hill	Somer	ST2813	50°55·0'	3°1·1'W	X	193
Plyford Fm	Devon	SY1494	50°44·6'	3°12·8'W	FM	192,193
Plym Br	C of Plym	SX5258	50°24·4'	4°4·6'W	X	201
Plym Hall	Shrops	SO6985	52°28·0'	2°27·0'W	X	138
Plym Head	Devon	SX6268	50°30·0'	3°56·4'W	W	202
Plymog	Denb	SJ1859	53°7·6'	3°13·1'W	X	116
Plymouth	C of Plym	SX4756	50°23·3'	4°8·8'W	T	201
Plymouth Breakwater	C of Plym	SX4750	50°20·0'	4°8·6'W	X	201
Plympton	C of Plym	SX5356	50°23·4'	4°3·7'W	T	201
Plym Steps	Devon	SX6067	50°29·4'	3°58·0'W	X	202
Plymstock	C of Plym	SX5153	50°21·7'	4°5·3'W	T	201
Plymswood Fm	Corn	SX2298	50°45·5'	4°31·0'W	FM	190
Plymtree	Devon	ST0502	50°48·8'	3°20·5'W	T	192
Plymuir	E Renf	NS4357	55°47·1'	4°29·8'W	X	64
Plym Valley Rly	C of Plym	SX5257	50°23·9'	4°4·6'W	X	201
Plynlimon or Pumlumon Fawr	Cered	SN7886	52°27·7'	3°47·3'W	H	135
Poachers Corner	Leic	SK4417	52°45·2'	1°20·5'W	X	129
Poaka Beck	Cumbr	SD2376	54°10·7'	3°10·4'W	W	96
Poaka Beck Resr	Cumbr	SD2478	54°11·8'	3°9·5'W	W	96
Pobgreen	Oldham	SE0106	53°33·3'	1°58·7'W	T	110
Pobies Geo	Shetld	HU3363	60°21·2'	1°23·6'W	X	2,3
Pobie Skeo	Shetld	HU1656	60°17·5'	1°42·1'W	X	3
Pobie Sukka	Shetld	HU3080	60°30·4'	1°26·7'W	X	1,3
Pòca Buidhe	Highld	NG8964	57°37·3'	5°31·5'W	X	19,24
Pocan Smoo	Highld	NC4267	58°34·0'	4°42·5'W	X	9
Pochin Houses	Blae Gw	SO1604	51°43·9'	3°12·6'W	T	171
Pochriegavin Burn	D & G	NS5403	55°18·2'	4°17·6'W	W	77
Pockendon Field	Herts	TL4023	51°53·5'	0°2·5'E	X	167
Pockerley Buildings	Ghead	NZ2354	54°53·1'	1°38·1'W	X	88
Pocket Gate Fm	Leic	SK5215	52°44·0'	1°13·4'W	FM	129
Pocket Nook	Wigan	SJ6497	53°28·4'	2°32·1'W	T	109
Pockford Fm	Surrey	SU9836	51°7·1'	0°35·6'W	FM	186
Pockinan Burn	E Ayr	NS5042	55°39·2'	4°22·6'W	W	70
Pockleaf	D & G	NT2104	55°19·7'	3°14·3'W	X	79
Pockley	N Yks	SE6385	54°15·6'	1°1·6'W	T	94,100
Pockley Grange	N Yks	SE6289	54°17·8'	1°2·4'W	X	94,100
Pockley Moor	N Yks	SE6193	54°20·0'	1°3·3'W	X	94,100
Pockley Rigg Plantn	N Yks	SE6388	54°17·3'	1°1·5'W	F	94,100
Pocklington	E Yorks	SE8049	53°56·1'	0°46·5'W	T	106
Pocklington Beck	E Yorks	SE8050	53°56·6'	0°46·5'W	W	106
Pocklington Canal	E Yorks	SE7544	53°53·4'	0°51·1'W	W	105,106
Pocklington Common	E Yorks	SE8047	53°55·0'	0°46·5'W	X	106
Pocklington Grange	E Yorks	SE8046	53°54·5'	0°46·5'W	X	106
Pocklington Wood	E Yorks	SE8150	53°56·6'	0°45·5'W	F	106
Pockmuir Burn	S Lanak	NS7633	55°34·7'	3°57·6'W	W	71
Pocknave	S Ayr	NS4531	55°33·1'	4°27·0'W	X	70
Pock Stones Moor	N Yks	SE1160	54°2·3'	1°49·5'W	X	99
Pockthorpe	Norf	TF8127	52°48·8'	0°41·6'E	T	132
Pockthorpe	Norf	TG0324	52°46·7'	1°1·0'E	T	133

Pockthorpe	Norf	TG0718	52°43·4'	1°4·3'E	T	133
Pockthorpe	Norf	TL9196	52°31·9'	0°49·4'E	T	144
Pockthorpe	Norf	TM4096	52°30·8'	1°32·6'E	X	134
Pockthorpe Hall	E Yorks	TA0463	54°3·4'	0°24·3'W	X	101
Pockthorpe Village	E Yorks	TA0363	54°3·4'	0°25·2'W	A	101
Poclose	Corn	SW9650	50°19·1'	4°51·6'W	X	200,204
Pococksgate Fm	E Susx	TQ5833	51°4·7'	0°15·7'E	FM	188
Pocombe Br	Devon	SX8991	50°42·7'	3°34·0'W	X	192
Pode Hole	Lincs	TF2122	52°47·2'	0°11·9'W	T	131
Pode Hole Fm	Peterb	TF2603	52°36·8'	0°7·9'W	FM	142
Poden	Worcs	SP1243	52°5·3'	1°49·1'W	X	150
Podgehole	Durham	NZ0929	54°39·6'	1°51·2'W	X	92
Podgwell Cott	Glos	SO8411	51°48·1'	2°13·5'W	X	162
Podimore	Somer	ST5424	51°1·0'	2°39·0'W	T	183
Podington	Beds	SP9462	52°15·1'	0°37·0'W	T	153
Podkin Fm	Kent	TQ8738	51°6·9'	0°40·7'E	FM	189
Podlie Craig	E Loth	NT5985	56°3·6'	2°39·1'W	X	67
Podlinge	Kent	TR1146	51°10·7'	1°1·5'E	X	179,189
Podmoor	Worcs	SO8672	52°21·0'	2°11·9'W	T	139
Podmore	Norf	TF9512	52°40·5'	0°53·5'E	T	132
Podmore	Staffs	SJ7835	52°55·0'	2°19·2'W	T	127
Podowrin Burn	S Lanak	NS7829	55°32·6'	3°55·6'W	W	71
Podrach	Aberd	NJ8428	57°20·8'	2°15·5'W	X	38
Pods Brook	Essex	TL7224	51°53·5'	0°30·4'E	W	167
Podsmead	Glos	SO8215	51°50·2'	2°15·3'W	T	162
Pods Wood	Essex	TL9017	51°49·4'	0°45·8'E	F	168
Poethfoel	Conwy	SH8161	53°8·2'	3°46·3'W	X	116
Poetsbreck Fm	Norf	TG1113	52°40·6'	1°7·7'E	FM	133
Poets Corner	D & G	NX8598	55°16·0'	3°48·2'W	X	78
Poets' Path No 1	Glos	SO7031	51°58·8'	2°25·8'W	X	149
Poet's Path No 1	Glos	SO7431	51°58·8'	2°22·3'W	X	150
Poets' Path No 2	Glos	SO6933	51°59·9'	2°26·7'W	X	149
Poffley End	Oxon	SP3512	51°48·6'	1°29·1'W	T	164
Pogbie	E Loth	NT4660	55°50·1'	2°51·3'W	X	66
Pogiven Burn	E Ayr	NS5742	55°39·3'	4°15·9'W	W	71
Pogmoor	Barns	SE3206	53°33·2'	1°30·6'W	T	110,111
Po House	Cumbr	SD1482	54°13·8'	3°18·7'W	X	96
Poil, The	Shetld	HU5487	60°34·0'	1°0·4'W	X	1,2
Point	Corn	SW8138	50°12·3'	5°3·8'W	X	204
Point	Devon	SX4887	50°40·0'	4°8·7'W	X	191
Point	Highld	NC8011	58°4·6'	4°1·6'W	X	17
Point Clear	Essex	TM0914	51°47·4'	1°2·2'E	T	168,169
Point Copse	Bucks	SP6740	52°3·5'	1°1·0'W	F	152
Pointer Fm	Lancs	SD3747	53°55·2'	2°57·1'W	FM	102
Pointer Ho	Lancs	SD3939	53°50·9'	2°55·2'W	X	102
Pointer Ho	Lancs	SD5438	53°50·4'	2°41·5'W	X	102
Pointers Fm	Essex	TL9012	51°46·7'	0°45·7'E	FM	168
Point Fm	Arg & Bt	NR9964	55°49·9'	5°12·1'W	FM	62
Point Fm	E Susx	TQ5919	50°56·5'	0°46·9'E	FM	189
Point Fm	Notts	SK7892	53°25·4'	0°49·2'W	FM	112
Point Fm	Pemb	SM8105	51°42·3'	5°9·8'W	FM	157
Point Fm	Powys	SO0993	52°31·9'	3°20·1'W	FM	136
Pointfoot Hill	D & G	NX7088	55°10·4'	4°2·0'W	H	77
Point Ho	Arg & Bt	NR6948	55°40·5'	5°40·0'W	X	62
Point Ho Fm	Flint	SJ3766	53°11·1'	2°56·2'W	FM	117
Pointhorne	Staffs	SK0739	52°57·1'	1°53·3'W	X	128
Pointhouse	Arg & Bt	NR9290	56°3·7'	5°20·0'W	X	55
Point Lynas (Trwyn Eilian)	I of Angl	SH4793	53°24·9'	4°17·7'W	X	114
Point o' Bard	Aberd	NO8168	56°48·4'	2°18·2'W	X	45
Point of Ardnamurchan	Highld	NM4167	56°43·6'	6°13·6'W	X	47
Point of Avelshay	Orkney	HY4428	59°8·4'	2°58·2'W	X	5,6
Point of Ayr	Flint	SJ1285	53°21·5'	3°18·9'W	X	116
Point of Ayre	I of M	NX4605	54°25·3'	4°22·0'W	X	95
Point of Ayre	Orkney	HY5903	58°55·0'	2°42·2'W	X	6
Point of Ayres	Shetld	HU3457	60°18·0'	1°22·6'W	X	2,3
Point of Backaquoy	Orkney	HY3915	59°1·3'	3°3·3'W	X	6
Point of Baits	Orkney	HY4308	58°57·6'	2°59·0'W	X	6,7
Point of Bizber	Orkney	HY5402	58°54·4'	2°47·4'W	X	6,7
Point of Blo-geo	Shetld	HU4012	59°53·7'	1°16·6'W	X	4
Point of Buckquoy	Orkney	HY2428	59°8·2'	3°19·2'W	X	6
Point of Bugarth	Shetld	HU4393	60°37·4'	1°12·4'W	X	1,2
Point of Burkwell	Shetld	HU5899	60°40·5'	0°55·8'W	X	1
Point of Burrian	Orkney	HY7651	59°20·9'	2°24·8'W	X	5
Point of Cairndoon	D & G	NX3738	54°42·9'	4°31·4'W	X	83
Point of Cauldhame	Orkney	HY5633	59°11·2'	2°45·7'W	X	5,6
Point of Cletts	Orkney	ND3096	58°51·2'	3°12·2'W	X	6,7
Point of Comely	Orkney	HY6430	59°9·6'	2°37·3'W	X	5
Point of Comfort Scar	Cumbr	SD2667	54°5·9'	3°7·5'W	X	96,97
Point of Coppister	Shetld	HP5704	60°43·2'	0°56·8'W	X	1
Point of Corse	Orkney	HY3828	59°8·3'	3°4·5'W	X	6
Point of Cott	Orkney	HY4647	59°18·6'	2°56·4'W	X	5
Point of Craig-gate	Orkney	ND2097	58°51·4'	3°22·7'W	X	7
Point of Creeso	Orkney	HY7547	59°18·8'	2°25·9'W	X	5
Point of Crook	Orkney	HY4830	59°9·5'	2°54·1'W	X	5,6
Point of Cumley	Orkney	HY6527	59°8·0'	2°36·2'W	X	5
Point of Dishan	Orkney	HY4716	59°1·9'	2°54·9'W	X	6
Point of Feorwick	Shetld	HU5173	60°26·5'	1°3·9'W	X	2,3
Point of Fethaland	Shetld	HU3795	60°38·5'	1°18·9'W	X	1,2
Point of Freyageo	Orkney	HY6521	59°4·7'	2°36·2'W	X	5
Point of Furrigeo	Orkney	HY4945	59°17·6'	2°53·2'W	X	5
Point of Geldibist	Orkney	HY5039	59°14·3'	2°52·1'W	X	5
Point of Greenbanks	Orkney	HY5010	58°58·7'	2°51·7'W	X	6
Point of Grimsetter	Orkney	HY4808	58°57·6'	2°53·8'W	X	6,7
Point of Grimsetter	Shetld	HP5401	60°41·6'	1°0·2'W	X	1
Point of Gruid	Shetld	HU5361	60°20·0'	1°1·9'W	X	2,3
Point of Guide	Shetld	HU3629	60°2·9'	1°20·7'W	X	4
Point of Hackness	Orkney	ND3391	58°48·3'	3°9·1'W	X	7
Point of Hallbreck	Orkney	HY4326	59°7·3'	2°59·3'W	X	5,6
Point of Hamna-ayre	Shetld	HU3361	60°20·2'	1°23·6'W	X	2,3
Point of Hellia	Orkney	HY3726	59°7·2'	3°5·5'W	X	6
Point of Hellia	Orkney	HY4525	59°6·8'	2°57·1'W	X	5,6
Point of Heogatoug	Shetld	HU5540	60°8·7'	1°0·1'W	X	4
Point of Hisber	Orkney	HY3427	59°7·8'	3°8·7'W	X	6
Point of Hovie	Shetld	HU5439	60°8·2'	1°1·2'W	X	4
Point of Howana Geo	Orkney	HY2220	59°3·9'	3°21·1'W	X	6
Point of Howesti	Orkney	HY2405	58°55·8'	3°18·7'W	X	6,7
Point of Huro	Orkney	HY4938	59°13·8'	2°53·1'W	X	5
Point of Knap	Arg & Bt	NR6972	55°53·4'	5°41·2'W	X	61,62
Point of Lag	D & G	NX3639	54°43·4'	4°32·4'W	X	83
Point of Lenay	Orkney	HY6625	59°6·9'	2°35·1'W	X	5
Point of Lune	Lancs	SD3555	53°59·5'	2°59·1'W	X	102
Point of Lyregeo	Orkney	HY2114	59°0·6'	3°22·0'W	X	6
Point of Mulla	Shetld	HU3963	60°21·2'	1°17·1'W	X	2,3
Point of Nesbister	Shetld	HU3944	60°11·0'	1°17·3'W	X	4
Point of Ness	Highld	ND2071	58°37·4'	3°22·2'W	X	7,12
Point of Ness	Shetld	HU5394	60°37·8'	1°1·4'W	X	1,2
Point of Neven	Orkney	HY4939	59°14·3'	2°53·1'W	X	5
Point of Nevin	Orkney	HY6942	59°16·1'	2°32·1'W	X	5
Point of Nichol's Croo	Orkney	HY4225	59°6·7'	3°0·3'W	X	5,6
Point of Od	Orkney	HY5404	58°55·5'	2°47·5'W	X	6,7
Point of Oxan	Orkney	HY2406	58°56·3'	3°18·7'W	X	6,7
Point of Peterkirk	Orkney	HY4940	59°14·9'	2°53·2'W	X	5
Point of Pitten	Orkney	HY4732	59°10·6'	2°55·1'W	X	5,6
Point of Pundsgeo	Shetld	HU5541	60°9·3'	1°0·1'W	X	4
Point of Pundsta	Shetld	HU4428	60°2·3'	1°12·1'W	X	4
Point of Quida-stack	Shetld	HU2783	60°32·0'	1°30·0'W	X	3
Point of Ridden	Orkney	HY4732	59°10·6'	2°55·1'W	X	5,6
Point of Rugg	Shetld	HU4322	59°59·1'	1°13·3'W	X	4
Point of Sandybank	Orkney	HY5331	59°10·1'	2°48·8'W	X	5,6
Point of Sangwish	Orkney	HY5119	59°3·6'	2°50·8'W	X	6
Point of Scaraber	Orkney	HY5335	59°12·2'	2°48·9'W	X	5,6
Point of Scotland	Shetld	HU4643	60°10·4'	1°9·8'W	X	4
Point of Sheetsbrough	Shetld	HU4479	60°29·8'	1°11·4'W	X	2,3
Point of Sinsoss	Orkney	HY7856	59°23·6'	2°22·8'W	X	5
Point of Skae	Orkney	HY3828	59°8·3'	3°4·5'W	X	6
Point of Sleat	Highld	NM5699	57°1·3'	6°0·8'W	X	32,39
Point of Sletta	Shetld	HU3359	60°19·1'	1°23·7'W	X	2,3
Point of Snusan	Orkney	HY2427	59°7·7'	3°19·2'W	X	6
Point of Stakka	Shetld	HU3628	60°2·4'	1°20·7'W	X	4
Point of Steedie	Orkney	HY4630	59°9·5'	2°56·2'W	X	5,6
Point of Stiva	Shetld	HU4778	60°29·2'	1°8·2'W	X	2,3
Point of Stoer	Highld	NC0235	58°15·8'	5°22·0'W	X	15
Point of Tangpool	Shetld	HU4011	59°53·2'	1°16·6'W	X	4
Point of the Alter	Shetld	HU3633	60°5·1'	1°20·7'W	X	4
Point of the Graand	Orkney	HY4726	59°7·3'	2°55·1'W	X	5,6
Point of the Gunnald	Shetld	HU5491	60°36·2'	1°0·3'W	X	1,2
Point of the Hus	Shetld	HU1948	60°13·2'	1°38·9'W	X	3
Point of the Liddle	Orkney	HY5207	58°57·1'	2°49·6'W	X	6,7
Point of the Pool	Orkney	ND3590	58°47·8'	3°7·0'W	X	7
Point of the Pund	Shetld	HU3838	60°7·8'	1°18·5'W	X	4
Point of the Sluther	Shetld	HU3633	60°5·1'	1°20·7'W	X	4
Point of the Styes	Orkney	HY6542	59°16·1'	2°36·4'W	X	5
Point of the Ward	Orkney	ND3298	58°52·1'	3°10·3'W	X	6,7
Point of the Wart	Orkney	HY4526	59°7·3'	2°57·2'W	X	5,6
Point of Tobar	Orkney	HY5337	59°13·3'	2°48·9'W	X	5
Point of Touthey	Orkney	HY7037	59°13·4'	2°31·0'W	X	5
Point of Tuberry	Orkney	ND3399	58°52·7'	3°9·2'W	X	6,7
Point of Vastray	Orkney	HY3925	59°6·7'	3°3·4'W	X	6
Point of Veniver	Orkney	HY5221	59°4·7'	2°49·8'W	X	5,6
Point of Whitehill	Shetld	HU5382	60°31·4'	1°1·6'W	X	1,2,3
Pointon	Lincs	TF1131	52°52·1'	0°20·7'W	T	130
Pointon Cottage Fm	Lincs	TF0931	52°52·2'	0°22·4'W	FM	130
Pointon Fen	Lincs	TF1431	52°52·1'	0°18·0'W	X	130
Point o'the Scurroes	Orkney	HY4643	59°16·5'	2°56·4'W	X	5
Pointsfield	Aberd	NJ5754	57°34·7'	2°42·7'W	X	29
Point Spaniard	Corn	SW4625	50°4·5'	5°32·6'W	X	203
Point St John	Pemb	SM7125	51°52·8'	5°19·3'W	X	157
Point, The	Orkney	ND3195	58°50·5'	3°11·3'W	X	7
Pointz Castle	Pemb	SM8323	51°52·0'	5°8·7'W	X	157
Poise Brook	Stock	SJ9288	53°23·6'	2°6·8'W	W	109
Poityn	Powys	SN9246	52°6·3'	3°34·2'W	X	147
Pokehill	Kent	TQ5437	51°6·9'	0°12·4'E	X	188
Poke Holes	Lincs	TF2588	53°22·7'	0°6·8'W	X	113,122
Pokelly	E Ayr	NS4445	55°40·7'	4°28·4'W	X	64
Pokelly Hall	E Ayr	NS4545	55°40·7'	4°27·5'W	X	64
Pokelly Hill	E Ayr	NS4645	55°40·7'	4°26·5'W	X	64
Poker's Leys	Derby	SK3522	52°47·9'	1°28·4'W	F	128
Poker's Pool	Dorset	SY3391	50°43·1'	2°56·6'W	W	193
Pokesdown	Bourne	SZ1292	50°43·9'	1°49·4'W	T	195
Poke's Hole	Lincs	TF2985	53°21·0'	0°3·3'W	X	122
Pokeskine Sike	D & G	NY2880	55°6·8'	3°7·3'W	W	79
Polanach	Arg & Bt	NM9350	56°36·0'	5°21·9'W	X	49
Poland Fm	Hants	SU7452	51°16·0'	0°56·0'W	FM	186
Poland Mill	Hants	SU7453	51°16·5'	0°56·0'W	X	186
Polanduich	Arg & Bt	NM8915	56°17·1'	5°24·1'W	X	55
Polapit Tamar	Corn	SX3389	50°40·8'	4°21·5'W	X	190
Polbae	D & G	NX2872	55°1·0'	4°41·0'W	X	76
Polbae Burn	D & G	NX2772	55°1·0'	4°41·9'W	W	76
Polbain	Highld	NB9910	58°2·3'	5°23·8'W	T	15
Polbaith	E Ayr	NS4839	55°37·5'	4°24·4'W	X	70
Polbaith Burn	E Ayr	NS5140	55°38·1'	4°21·6'W	W	70
Polbarrow	Corn	SW7113	49°58·6'	5°11·3'W	X	203
Polbathic	Corn	SX3456	50°23·1'	4°19·7'W	T	201
Polbeth Burn	E Ayr	NS6331	55°33·5'	4°9·9'W	W	71
Polbeth	W Loth	NT0264	55°51·3'	3°33·5'W	T	65
Polborder	Corn	SX3864	50°27·4'	4°16·6'W	T	201
Polbream Cove	Corn	SW7011	49°57·5'	5°12·0'W	W	203
Polbream Point	Corn	SW7215	49°59·7'	5°10·5'W	X	204
Polbroc Burn	D & G	NS7009	55°21·7'	4°2·6'W	W	71,77
Polbrock	Corn	SX0169	50°29·5'	4°48·0'W	T	200
Polcalk	Pth & Kin	NO2346	56°36·2'	3°14·8'W	X	53
Polcardoch	S Ayr	NX1184	55°7·1'	4°57·4'W	X	76
Polchar, The	Highld	NH8909	57°9·8'	3°49·7'W	X	35,36
Polchiffer Burn	D & G	NX5899	55°16·1'	4°13·7'W	W	77
Pol Cornick	Corn	SW6615	49°59·6'	5°15·5'W	W	203
Polcoverack Fm	Corn	SW7718	50°1·5'	5°6·4'W	FM	204
Polcreach	Highld	NJ1436	57°24·6'	3°25·4'W	X	28
Polcrebo Downs	Corn	SW6433	50°9·2'	5°17·9'W	X	203
Polcreek	Corn	SW9138	50°12·5'	4°55·4'W	X	204
Polcries	Corn	SW8019	50°2·1'	5°4·0'W	X	204
Poldar Moss	Stir	NS6598	56°9·6'	4°10·0'W	X	57
Poldean	D & G	NT1000	55°17·4'	3°24·6'W	X	78
Polden Hills	Somer	ST4435	51°6·9'	2°47·6'W	H	182
Poldew	Corn	SX0960	50°24·8'	4°40·9'W	X	200
Poldhu	Corn	SX2179	50°35·2'	4°31·3'W	X	201
Poldhu Cove	Corn	SW6619	50°1·7'	5°15·7'W	W	203
Poldhu Point	Corn	SW6619	50°1·7'	5°15·7'W	X	203
Poldhurst Fm	Kent	TR1158	51°17·1'	1°1·9'E	FM	179
Poldice Valley	Corn	SW7542	50°14·3'	5°9·0'W	X	204
Poldivan Lake	D & G	NX9594	55°14·0'	3°38·6'W	W	78
Poldive Burn	E Ayr	NS7219	55°27·1'	4°1·0'W	W	71
Poldorais	Highld	NG4771	57°39·7'	6°14·1'W	W	23
Poldores Burn	D & G	NX6196	55°14·6'	4°10·8'W	W	77
Poldowrian	Corn	SW7416	50°0·3'	5°8·9'W	X	204
Poldrissick	Corn	SX3859	50°24·7'	4°16·4'W	X	201
Poldue Downs	Corn	SX1381	50°36·2'	4°38·2'W	X	200
Poldullie Br	Aberd	NJ3412	57°11·9'	3°5·1'W	X	37
Polean Fm	Corn	SX2053	50°21·2'	4°31·4'W	FM	201
Pole Bank	Shrops	SO4194	52°32·7'	2°51·8'W	H	137
Polebrook	Northnts	TL0687	52°28·5'	0°26·0'W	T	142
Polebrook Fm	Kent	TQ4745	51°11·3'	0°6·6'E	FM	188
Polebrook Lodge	Northnts	TL0986	52°27·9'	0°23·3'W	X	142
Pole Burn	Stir	NN7509	56°15·7'	4°0·6'W	W	57
Polecat Corner	Hants	SU6750	51°14·9'	1°2·0'W	X	185,186
Polecat End	Oxon	SP6008	51°46·3'	1°7·4'W	F	164,165
Polecats	W Susx	SU9019	50°58·0'	0°42·7'W	X	197
Pole Cott	Shrops	SO4193	52°32·1'	2°51·8'W	X	137
Pole Elm	Worcs	SO8349	52°8·6'	2°14·5'W	T	150
Polefields	Kent	TQ4541	51°9·2'	0°4·8'E	X	188
Pole Fm	Arg & Bt	NN1904	56°11·9'	4°54·6'W	FM	56
Polegate	E Susx	TQ5804	50°49·1'	0°15·0'E	T	199
Polehanger Fm	Beds	TL1337	52°1·4'	0°20·8'W	FM	153
Polehays	Devon	SX4799	50°46·5'	4°9·8'W	X	191
Pole Hill	Highld	NC6441	58°20·5'	4°18·9'W	H	10
Pole Hill	Pth & Kin	NO1926	56°25·4'	3°18·3'W	H	53,58
Pole Hill	Suff	TM2344	52°3·2'	1°15·6'E	X	169
Pole Hill	Wal F	TQ3895	51°38·4'	0°0·1'E	X	166,177
Pole Hill (Tumulus)	Suff	TM2344	52°3·2'	1°15·6'E	A	169
Pole Hole Fm	Herts	TL4512	51°47·5'	0°6·5'E	FM	167
Polemere	Shrops	SJ4109	52°40·8'	2°52·0'W	X	126
Pole Moor	Kirk	SE0615	53°38·1'	1°54·1'W	T	110
Pole of Itlaw,The	Aberd	NJ6756	57°35·8'	2°32·7'W	T	29
Poles	Herts	TL3516	51°49·8'	0°2·1'W	X	166
Poles	Highld	NH7892	57°54·3'	4°3·1'W	T	21
Polesburn	Aberd	NJ8537	57°25·6'	2°14·5'W	X	30
Poles Coppice	Shrops	SJ3904	52°38·1'	2°53·7'W	F	126
Polesden Lacey	Surrey	TQ1352	51°15·6'	0°22·4'W	T	187
Polesdon Ho	Wilts	SU3164	51°22·7'	1°32·9'W	X	174
Poleshill	Somer	ST0823	51°0·2'	3°18·3'W	T	181
Pole's Hole	Wilts	ST8454	51°17·3'	2°13·4'W	T	183
Poles, The	Shrops	SO4674	52°21·9'	2°47·2'W	X	137,138,148
Pole's Wood	Essex	TQ5799	51°40·3'	0°16·6'E	F	167,177
Polesworth	Warw	SK2602	52°37·1'	1°36·6'W	T	140
Pole, The	Ches	SJ6578	53°18·1'	2°31·1'W	X	118
Pole, The	Pemb	SR8897	51°38·2'	5°3·4'W	X	158
Poletrees Fm	Bucks	SP6516	51°50·6'	1°3·0'W	FM	164,165
Pole Wood	Heref	SO4246	52°6·8'	2°50·4'W	F	148,149
Poley's Br	Corn	SX0874	50°32·3'	4°42·2'W	X	200
Polfalden	Highld	NH7952	57°32·8'	4°0·8'W	X	27
Polga Burn	E Ayr	NS5707	55°20·4'	4°14·9'W	W	71,77
Polgassick Fm	Corn	SX0859	50°24·2'	4°41·7'W	FM	200
Polgear	Corn	SW6836	50°11·0'	5°14·6'W	T	203
Polgeel Wood	Corn	SX0169	50°29·5'	4°48·0'W	F	200
Polgerran Wood	Corn	SW8540	50°13·5'	5°0·5'W	F	204
Polgigga	Corn	SW3723	50°3·2'	5°40·1'W	T	203
Polglase	Corn	SW6821	50°2·9'	5°14·1'W	X	203
Polglase	Corn	SW7028	50°6·7'	5°12·7'W	X	203
Polglass	Highld	NC0307	58°0·8'	5°19·6'W	T	15
Polglaze	Corn	SW9649	50°18·6'	4°51·5'W	X	204
Polglaze	Corn	SX0248	50°18·2'	4°46·5'W	X	204
Polglaze	Corn	SX0574	50°32·2'	4°44·7'W	X	200
Polgoda Downs	Corn	SW7952	50°19·8'	5°5·9'W	X	200,204
Polgooth	Corn	SW9950	50°19·2'	4°49·0'W	T	200,204
Polgover	Corn	SX2758	50°24·0'	4°25·7'W	X	201
Polgown	D & G	NS7103	55°18·5'	4°1·5'W	X	77
Polgrain	Corn	SW9542	50°14·8'	4°52·2'W	X	204
Polgrain	Corn	SW9565	50°27·2'	4°52·9'W	X	200
Polgreen	Corn	SW8258	50°23·1'	5°3·6'W	X	200
Polgreen	Corn	SW8666	50°27·5'	5°0·5'W	X	200
Polgwidden Cove	Corn	SW7627	50°6·3'	5°7·6'W	W	204
Polhampton Fm	Hants	SU5250	51°15·0'	1°14·9'W	FM	185
Polhampton Lodge Stud	Hants	SU5154	51°17·2'	1°15·7'W	X	185
Polharmon	Corn	SX0856	50°22·6'	4°41·6'W	X	200
Polharrow Bridge	D & G	NX6084	55°8·1'	4°11·3'W	X	77
Polharrow Burn	D & G	NX5486	55°9·1'	4°17·0'W	W	77
Polharrow Burn	D & G	NX5885	55°8·6'	4°13·2'W	W	77
Polhawn Cove	Corn	SX4149	50°19·4'	4°13·6'W	W	201
Polhay Burn	D & G	NX5993	55°12·9'	4°12·5'W	W	77
Polhendra	Corn	SW8536	50°11·3'	5°0·4'W	X	204
Polhigh Burn	E Ayr	NS6608	55°21·1'	4°6·4'W	W	71,77
Polhill Arms (PH)	Kent	TQ5060	51°19·4'	0°9·6'E	X	177,188
Polhilsa	Corn	SX3472	50°31·7'	4°20·2'W	X	201
Polhollick	Aberd	NO3496	57°3·3'	3°4·8'W	X	37,44
Polholm Rig	D & G	NS7716	55°25·6'	3°56·2'W	H	71,78
Polhormon Fm	Corn	SW6719	50°1·8'	5°14·8'W	FM	203
Polhote Burn	D & G	NS6811	55°22·8'	4°4·6'W	W	71
Poliffenie Burn	D & G	NX6396	55°14·6'	4°8·9'W	W	77
Polin	Highld	NC1959	58°29·2'	5°5·8'W	X	9
Poling	W Susx	TQ0404	50°49·8'	0°31·0'W	T	197
Poling Corner	W Susx	TQ0405	50°50·3'	0°31·0'W	T	197
Polish Home	Gwyn	SH3334	52°52·9'	4°28·5'W	X	123
Polka Cott	Northum	NT8434	55°36·2'	2°14·8'W	X	74
Polkanoggo	Corn	SW7522	50°3·6'	5°8·3'W	X	204
Polkebock Burn	E Ayr	NS6530	55°33·0'	4°8·0'W	W	71
Polkelly	S Lanak	NT0054	55°46·4'	3°35·2'W	X	65,72
Polkemmet Country Park	W Loth	NS9265	55°52·2'	3°43·1'W	X	65
Polkemmet Moor	W Loth	NS9162	55°50·6'	3°44·0'W	F	65
Polkerris	Corn	SX0952	50°20·5'	4°40·7'W	T	200,204
Polkerth	Corn	SW7321	50°3·0'	5°9·9'W	X	204
Polkirt Beach	Corn	SX0144	50°16·0'	4°47·2'W	X	204
Polla	Highld	NC3854	58°26·9'	4°46·1'W	X	9
Poll Achadh Luachrach	Highld	NM6156	56°38·4'	5°53·4'W	W	49
Pollachapuill	Highld	NC1033	58°15·0'	5°13·8'W	X	15
Pollachar	N Eil	NF7414	57°6·3'	7°22·6'W	X	31
Poll a' Charnain	N Eil	NB4326	58°9·2'	6°21·6'W	W	8
Pollach Burn	E Ayr	NS6409	55°21·6'	4°8·3'W	W	71,77
Poll a' Cheò	Arg & Bt	NR5062	55°47·5'	5°58·9'W	W	61
Poll a'Chleirich	Highld	NC4851	58°25·5'	4°35·7'W	X	9
Poll a' Chreoig	Arg & Bt	NR4648	55°39·8'	6°1·9'W	W	60
Poll a Chrosain	Arg & Bt	NM0747	56°31·7'	6°45·5'W	W	46

Polladras	Corn	SW6130	50°7·6′	5°20·3′W	T	203
Poll a' Fearchadh	N Eil	NF7719	57°9·2′	7°20·1′W	W	31
Pollagach Burn	Aberd	NO4093	57°1·7′	2°58·9′W	W	37,44
Pollagharrie	Highld	NH6784	57°49·8′	4°13·9′W	X	21
Poll a' Mhuineil	Highld	NG8406	57°5·9′	5°33·5′W	W	33
Pollamounter	Corn	SW8456	50°22·1′	5°1·9′W	X	200
Pollan	Highld	NC0726	58°11·1′	5°16·5′W	X	15
Pollan Breac	Arg & Bt	NR7950	55°41·8′	5°30·6′W	W	62,69
Pollan Buidhe	Highld	NH0846	57°28·1′	5°11·6′W	X	25
Pollan Buidhe	Highld	NH1922	57°15·4′	4°59·6′W	X	25
Poll an Daimh	Highld	NM8173	56°48·1′	5°34·8′W	W	40
Poll an Dhoire Fheàrna	Arg & Bt	NR4276	55°54·7′	6°7·3′W	W	60,61
Poll an Dubhaidh	Arg & Bt	NR2169	55°50·3′	6°26·9′W	W	60
Poll an Eòin Mór	Highld	NG8994	57°53·4′	5°33·1′W	W	19
Pollan na Muice	Highld	NH0273	57°42·5′	5°18·9′W	X	19
Poll an Oir	N Eil	NF9280	57°42·5′	7°9·8′W	W	18
Poll an Staimh	Highld	NG3764	57°35·6′	6°23·6′W	W	23
Pollard Fm	Corn	SW6827	50°6·1′	5°14·3′W	FM	203
Pollardine Fm	Shrops	SJ3900	52°35·9′	2°53·6′W	FM	126
Pollards Cross	Essex	TL6437	52°0·7′	0°23·8′E	X	154
Pollard's Fm	Corn	SW9152	50°20·1′	4°55·8′W	FM	200,204
Pollardshill Fm	W Susx	TQ1624	51°0·4′	0°20·4′W	FM	198
Pollardsland Wood	E Susx	TQ4227	51°1·7′	0°1·9′E	F	187,198
Pollards Moor	Hants	SU3014	50°55·7′	1°34·0′W	X	196
Pollards Park Ho	Bucks	SU9995	51°38·9′	0°33·7′W	X	165,176
Pollard Street	Norf	TG3332	52°50·3′	1°28·0′E	T	133
Pollards Wood	Bucks	SU9995	51°38·9′	0°33·7′W	F	165,176
Pollard Wood	E Susx	TQ4436	51°6·5′	0°3·8′E	F	187
Poll Arinnis	Highld	NM6544	56°32·0′	5°48·9′W	X	49
Poll Athach	Arg & Bt	NM4054	56°36·6′	6°13·8′W	W	47
Polla Thorr	N Eil	NA9922	58°5·3′	7°6·0′W	X	13
Pollaughan	Corn	SW8736	50°11·4′	4°58·7′W	X	204
Pollawyn Fm	Corn	SW8860	50°24·3′	4°58·6′W	FM	200
Poll Bàn	Arg & Bt	NM4200	56°7·6′	6°8·7′W	W	61
Poll Bhàt	Aberd	NO0695	57°2·5′	3°32·5′W	W	36,43
Poll Buidhe	Highld	NC2457	58°28·2′	5°0·6′W	H	9
Poll Carn	Pemb	SM9524	51°52·9′	4°58·3′W	X	157,158
Pollcrayvie Burn	E Ayr	NX4597	55°14·8′	4°25·9′W	W	77
Poll Creadha	Highld	NG7041	57°24·3′	5°49·3′W	W	24
Poll Domhain Chraigeam	N Eil	NB1743	58°17·3′	6°49·3′W	W	8,13
Polldubh	Highld	NN1468	56°46·2′	5°2·2′W	X	41
Poll Duchaill	Highld	NM4588	56°55·1′	6°10·9′W	X	39
Poll Eistean	N Eil	NB5364	58°29·9′	6°13·9′W	W	8
Poll Gainmhich	N Eil	NB1342	58°16·6′	6°53·3′W	W	13
Poll Gorm	Arg & Bt	NM7311	56°14·5′	5°39·4′W	W	55
Poll Gorm	Arg & Bt	NR3789	56°1·6′	6°12·8′W	W	61
Poll Gorm	Arg & Bt	NR4257	55°44·5′	6°6·2′W	X	60
Poll Gorm	N Eil	NG1796	57°52·1′	6°45·9′W	W	14
Poll-gormack	Highld	NN3896	57°1·9′	4°39·7′W	X	34
Poll-gormack Hill	Highld	NN3997	57°2·4′	4°38·8′W	H	34
Pollgowan Burn	S Ayr	NX2578	55°4·2′	4°44·0′W	W	76
Pollhill	Kent	TQ8652	51°14·4′	0°40·3′E	T	189
Poll Hill	Wirral	SJ2682	53°20·0′	3°6·3′W	T	108
Pollick	E Ayr	NS4354	55°45·5′	4°29·7′W	X	64
Pollie	Highld	NC7515	58°6·6′	4°6·8′W	X	16
Pollie Hill	Highld	NC7517	58°7·7′	4°6·9′W	H	16
Pollingarrow	Corn	SX0276	50°33·3′	4°47·3′W	X	200
Pollingfold	Surrey	TQ0936	51°7·0′	0°26·2′W	X	187
Pollington	E Yorks	SE6119	53°40·1′	1°4·2′W	T	111
Pollington Br	E Yorks	SE6119	53°40·1′	1°4·2′W	X	111
Pollington Grange	E Yorks	SE6118	53°39·5′	1°4·2′W	X	111
Pollinnick	Corn	SX3179	50°35·4′	4°22·9′W	X	201
Polliwilline	Arg & Bt	NR7310	55°20·2′	5°34·3′W	X	68
Polliwilline Bay	Arg & Bt	NR7409	55°19·6′	5°33·3′W	W	68
Poll Loisgann	Highld	NC0616	58°5·7′	5°17·0′W	W	15
Poll Luachrain	Highld	NM5957	56°38·8′	5°55·4′W	X	47
Poll na Cùile	Highld	NC0935	58°16·0′	5°14·9′W	W	15
Poll na Gile	Arg & Bt	NM7707	56°12·5′	5°35·3′W	W	55
Poll na h-Ealaidh	Highld	NG3759	57°32·9′	6°23·3′W	W	23
Poll nam Partan	Highld	NM4984	56°53·0′	6°6·8′W	W	39
Poll nan Corran	Arg & Bt	NM7108	56°12·8′	5°41·1′W	W	55
Poll na Sgeire Ruaidhe	Arg & Bt	NM4435	56°26·5′	6°8·8′W	X	47,48
Poll Noddy	Heref	SO5843	52°5·3′	2°36·4′W	X	149
Pollo	Highld	NH7471	57°42·9′	4°6·4′W	X	21
Polloch	Highld	NM7968	56°45·3′	5°36·5′W	T	40
Pollochro	Stir	NN3311	56°16·0′	4°41·4′W	X	50,56
Pollok	C of Glas	NS5362	55°50·0′	4°20·4′W	T	64
Pollok Country Park	C of Glas	NS5562	55°50·0′	4°18·5′W	X	64
Pollok Ho	C of Glas	NS5461	55°49·5′	4°19·4′W	X	64
Pollokshaws	C of Glas	NS5561	55°49·5′	4°18·4′W	T	64
Pollokshields	C of Glas	NS5763	55°50·6′	4°16·6′W	T	64
Pollosgan	Highld	NG1649	57°26·8′	6°43·6′W	T	23
Pollowick	Highld	NJ0830	57°21·3′	3°31·3′W	X	27,36
Pollroy	Highld	ND0733	58°18·6′	3°34·7′W	X	11,17
Poll Shibachd	N Eil	NA9726	58°7·4′	7°8·3′W	W	13
Pollswells	Aberd	NJ8423	57°18·1′	2°15·5′W	X	38
Poll Tax	Pemb	SN0327	51°54·6′	4°51·5′W	X	145,157,158
Poll Thothatom	N Eil	HW8132	59°7·4′	5°49·1′W	W	8
Pollums House Fm	N Yks	SE4729	53°45·6′	1°16·8′W	FM	105
Polly Bay	Highld	NC0614	58°4·6′	5°16·9′W	W	15
Pollyfield	Kent	TQ7960	51°18·9′	0°34·5′E	X	178,188
Polly Gutter	Cumbr	NY8909	54°28·8′	2°9·8′W	W	91,92
Pollyhaugh Fm	Kent	TQ5465	51°22·0′	0°13·1′E	FM	177
Polly Lochs	Highld	NC0913	58°4·2′	5°13·8′W	W	15
Pollymoor Fm	Staffs	SJ7920	52°46·9′	2°18·3′W	FM	127
Polly More	Highld	NC0717	58°6·3′	5°16·1′W	X	15
Polly Moss	Cumbr	NY8808	54°28·3′	2°10·7′W	X	91,92
Polmaddie	D & G	NX5988	55°10·2′	4°12·4′W	X	77
Polmaddie Burn	S Ayr	NX3289	55°10·3′	4°37·8′W	W	76
Polmaddie Hill	S Ayr	NX3291	55°11·3′	4°37·9′W	H	76
Polmaddy	D & G	NX5887	55°9·7′	4°13·3′W	X	77
Polmaddy Burn	D & G	NX5489	55°10·7′	4°17·1′W	W	77
Polmaddy Gairy	D & G	NX5087	55°9·5′	4°20·8′W	X	77
Polmadie	C of Glas	NS5962	55°50·1′	4°14·6′W	T	64
Polmaily	Highld	NH4730	57°20·4′	4°32·1′W	T	26
Polmark	Corn	SW8874	50°31·9′	4°59·1′W	X	200
Polmarlach Burn	D & G	NS6711	55°22·8′	4°5·5′W	W	71
Polmarth	Corn	SW7036	50°11·0′	5°12·9′W	T	203
Polmartin Fm	Corn	SX1759	50°24·4′	4°34·1′W	FM	201
Polmassick	Corn	SW9745	50°16·4′	4°50·6′W	T	204

Polmear	Corn	SX0853	50°21·0′	4°41·6′W	T	200,204
Polmenna	Corn	SW8639	50°13·0′	4°59·6′W	X	204
Polmenna	Corn	SW9542	50°14·8′	4°52·2′W	X	204
Polmenna	Corn	SX1866	50°28·2′	4°33·5′W	X	201
Polmesk	Corn	SW8639	50°13·0′	4°59·6′W	X	204
Polmeur Burn	D & G	NS7011	55°22·8′	4°2·7′W	W	71
Polmont	Falk	NS9378	55°59·2′	3°42·5′W	T	65
Polmonthill	Falk	NS9479	55°59·8′	3°41·5′W	X	65
Polmont Station	Falk	NS9378	55°59·2′	3°42·5′W	X	65
Polmood	Angus	NO5852	56°39·7′	2°40·7′W	X	54
Polmood	Scot Bord	NT1127	55°32·0′	3°24·2′W	X	72
Polmood Burn	Scot Bord	NT1326	55°31·5′	3°22·3′W	W	72
Polmood Craig	Scot Bord	NT1524	55°30·4′	3°20·3′W	H	72
Polmood Hill	Scot Bord	NT1227	55°32·0′	3°23·2′W	H	72
Polmoodie	D & G	NT1612	55°23·9′	3°19·2′W	X	79
Polmorla	Corn	SW9871	50°30·5′	4°50·6′W	T	200
Polmullach Burn	D & G	NS7002	55°18·0′	4°2·4′W	W	77
Polnaberoch	Arg & Bt	NS3587	56°3·1′	4°38·5′W	X	56
Polnagrie Hill	D & G	NS6709	55°21·7′	4°5·5′W	X	71,77
Polnare Cove	Corn	SW8024	50°4·8′	5°4·1′W	W	204
Polnaskie Br	E Ayr	NS5100	55°16·6′	4°20·3′W	X	77
Polnaskie Burn	E Ayr	NS5201	55°17·1′	4°19·4′W	W	77
Polnessan	E Ayr	NS4111	55°22·3′	4°30·1′W	T	70
Polnessan Burn	E Ayr	NS4311	55°22·3′	4°28·2′W	W	70
Polneul	D & G	NS7012	55°23·3′	4°2·7′W	X	71
Polneul Burn	D & G	NS6911	55°22·8′	4°3·6′W	W	71
Polnicol	Highld	NH7573	57°44·0′	4°5·5′W	X	21
Polnish	Highld	NM7483	56°53·3′	5°42·2′W	T	40
Polnoon	E Renf	NS5851	55°44·2′	4°15·3′W	X	64
Polopit	Northnts	TL0279	52°24·2′	0°29·6′W	T	141
Polostoc Zawn	Corn	SW3621	50°2·1′	5°40·8′W	W	203
Polpenwith	Corn	SW7327	50°6·2′	5°10·1′W	T	204
Polpeor	Corn	SW5136	50°10·5′	5°28·9′W	T	203
Polpeor Cove	Corn	SW7011	49°57·5′	5°12·0′W	W	203
Polperro	Corn	SX2050	50°19·6′	4°31·4′W	T	201
Polperrow	Corn	SW8547	50°17·3′	5°0·7′W	X	204
Polpever	Corn	SX2355	50°22·3′	4°29·0′W	X	201
Polpidnick Fm	Corn	SW7622	50°3·6′	5°7·4′W	FM	204
Polpiece	Corn	SX1559	50°24·3′	4°35·8′W	X	201
Polpry Cove	Corn	SW3529	50°6·4′	5°42·0′W	W	203
Polquhairn	E Ayr	NS4716	55°25·1′	4°24·6′W	X	70
Polquhanity	D & G	NX5989	55°10·8′	4°12·4′W	X	77
Polquhap	E Ayr	NS5816	55°25·3′	4°14·2′W	X	71
Polquheys	E Ayr	NS6215	55°24·8′	4°10·4′W	X	71
Polreath	I Scilly	SV9515	49°57·7′	6°14·8′W	X	203
Polridmouth	Corn	SX1050	50°19·4′	4°39·8′W	W	200,204
Polrobin Burn	D & G	NX4994	55°13·3′	4°22·0′W	W	77
Polruan	Corn	SX1250	50°19·4′	4°38·1′W	T	200
Polrunny Fm	Corn	SX1089	50°40·4′	4°41·0′W	FM	190,200
Polscoe	Corn	SX1160	50°24·8′	4°39·2′W	X	200
Polser Brook	Notts	SK6237	52°55·8′	1°4·3′W	W	129
Polshagg Burn	D & G	NX6095	55°14·0′	4°11·7′W	W	77
Polshag Hill	D & G	NS7009	55°21·7′	4°2·6′W	X	71,77
Polsham	Somer	ST5142	51°10·7′	2°41·7′W	T	182,183
Polshea	Corn	SX0677	50°33·9′	4°44·0′W	X	200
Polshill	E Ayr	NS6513	55°23·8′	4°7·5′W	X	71
Polshot Manor	Surrey	SU9044	51°11·5′	0°42·3′W	X	186
Polskeoch	D & G	NS6802	55°17·9′	4°4·3′W	X	77
Polskeoch Burn	D & G	NS6902	55°17·9′	4°3·4′W	W	77
Polskeoch Rig	D & G	NS6703	55°18·4′	4°5·3′W	X	77
Polsloe	Devon	SX9393	50°43·8′	3°30·6′W	T	192
Polstacher Burn	D & G	NS6709	55°21·7′	4°5·5′W	W	71,77
Polstead	Suff	TL9938	52°0·5′	0°54·4′E	T	155
Polstead Heath	Suff	TL9940	52°1·6′	0°54·4′E	T	155
Polsted Manor	Surrey	SU9647	51°13·1′	0°37·1′W	X	186
Polston	Aberd	NO8697	57°4·1′	2°13·4′W	X	38,45
Polston Burn	D & G	NX7282	55°7·2′	4°0·0′W	W	77
Polston Parks	Devon	SX6951	50°20·9′	3°50·1′W	X	202
Polstreath	Corn	SX0145	50°16·5′	4°47·2′W	X	204
Polstrong	Corn	SW6239	50°12·4′	5°19·8′W	X	203
Polsue Burn	D & G	NX5796	55°14·5′	4°14·5′W	W	77
Polsue Manor Fm	Corn	SW8546	50°16·7′	5°0·7′W	FM	204
Polsue Manor Hotel	Corn	SW8839	50°13·0′	4°57·9′W	X	204
Poltallan Burn	D & G	NS6807	55°20·6′	4°4·5′W	W	71,77
Poltalloch	Arg & Bt	NR8196	56°6·7′	5°30·9′W	T	55
Poltesco	Corn	SW7215	49°59·7′	5°10·5′W	T	204
Poltesco Valley	Corn	SW7116	50°0·2′	5°11·4′W	X	203
Polt Fraochain	Highld	NG9775	57°43·4′	5°24·1′W	H	19
Polthooks Fm	W Susx	SU8205	50°50·5′	0°49·7′W	FM	197
Poltie Burn	D & G	NX6297	55°15·1′	4°9·8′W	W	77
Poltimore	Devon	SX9697	50°46·0′	3°28·1′W	T	192
Poltimore Arms (PH)	Devon	SS7235	51°6·2′	3°49·3′W	X	180
Poltimore Fm	Devon	SY1797	50°46·2′	3°10·2′W	FM	192,193
Poltimore Fm	Somer	ST3013	50°55·0′	2°59·4′W	FM	193
Poltimore Ho	Devon	SX9696	50°45·5′	3°28·1′W	X	192
Polton	Midlo	NT2964	55°52·1′	3°7·6′W	T	66
Polton Ho	Midlo	NT2965	55°52·6′	3°7·7′W	X	66
Polton Wood	Scot Bord	NT5643	55°41·0′	2°41·6′W	F	73
Poltrewgey	Corn	SX0378	50°34·3′	4°46·6′W	X	200
Poltrewgey Fm	Corn	SX0179	50°34·8′	4°48·3′W	FM	200
Polurrian Cove	Corn	SW6618	50°1·2′	5°15·6′W	W	203
Polvaddoch Burn	D & G	NS6702	55°17·9′	4°5·3′W	W	77
Polvaird Burn	D & G	NS6804	55°19·0′	4°4·4′W	W	77
Polvaird Loch	D & G	NS6904	55°19·0′	4°3·4′W	W	77
Polvean Cross	Corn	SX2358	50°24·0′	4°29·1′W	X	201
Polvean Wood	Corn	SX2458	50°24·0′	4°28·2′W	F	201
Polveithan Fm	Corn	SX1553	50°21·1′	4°35·7′W	FM	201
Polventon	Corn	SX1966	50°28·2′	4°32·7′W	X	201
Polventon or Mother Ivey's Bay	Corn	SW8676	50°32·9′	5°0·9′W	W	200
Polwarth	Scot Bord	NT7450	55°44·8′	2°24·4′W	T	67,74
Polwarth Moss	Scot Bord	NT7151	55°45·3′	2°27·3′W	X	67,74
Polwarth Rhodes	Scot Bord	NT7550	55°44·8′	2°23·5′W	X	67,74
Polwhannan Hill	E Ayr	NS7021	55°28·2′	4°3·0′W	H	71
Polwhat Burn	D & G	NS5803	55°18·3′	4°13·8′W	W	77
Polwhat Rig	D & G	NS6002	55°17·8′	4°11·9′W	H	77
Polwhele	Corn	SW8347	50°17·2′	5°2·4′W	X	204
Polwheveral	Corn	SW7328	50°6·8′	5°10·1′W	T	204
Polwhilly	D & G	NX4460	54°54·9′	4°25·6′W	X	83
Polwin Manor Fm	Corn	SW6923	50°4·0′	5°13·3′W	FM	203

Polyphant	Corn	SX2682	50°36·9′	4°27·2′W	T	201
Polzeath	Corn	SW9378	50°34·1′	4°55·0′W	T	200
Pomathorn	Midlo	NT2459	55°49·4′	3°12·3′W	X	66,73
Pomefield Burn	E Ayr	NS6034	55°35·0′	4°12·8′W	W	71
Pomeroy	Derby	SK1167	53°12·2′	1°49·7′W	T	119
Pomeroy	Devon	SY1398	50°46·7′	3°13·7′W	X	192,193
Pomeroy Fm	Wilts	ST8156	51°18·4′	2°16·0′W	FM	173
Pomeroy Wood	Wilts	ST8056	51°18·4′	2°16·8′W	F	173
Pomery	Corn	SW9246	50°16·9′	4°54·8′W	X	204
Pomfret Castle	Oxon	SP3630	51°58·3′	1°28·2′W	X	151
Pomice Fm	Dorset	SY4497	50°46·4′	2°47·3′W	FM	193
Pomona Fm	Heref	SO5642	52°4·7′	2°38·1′W	FM	149
Pomparles Br	Somer	ST4837	51°8·0′	2°44·2′W	X	182
Pomphlett	C of Plym	SX5153	50°21·7′	4°5·3′W	T	201
Ponchydown	Devon	ST0908	50°52·1′	3°17·2′W	X	192
Ponciau	Wrex	SJ2946	53°0·6′	3°3·1′W	T	117
Pond Bay	Hants	SU6563	51°22·0′	1°3·6′W	A	186
Pond Bay	Northnts	SP8285	52°27·6′	0°47·2′W	A	141
Pond Bay	Notts	SK6232	52°53·1′	1°4·3′W	A	129
Pond Bay	Powys	SN8729	51°57·1′	3°38·3′W	A	160
Pond Bays	Shrops	SO5194	52°32·7′	2°43·0′W	A	137,138
Pondcast Fm	I of W	SZ5690	50°42·6′	1°12·0′W	FM	196
Pond Close	Somer	ST1228	51°2·9′	3°14·9′W	T	181,193
Pondclose Fm	Dorset	ST5509	50°53·0′	2°38·0′W	FM	194
Pond Close Wood	N Lincs	TA1012	53°35·8′	0°19·9′W	F	113
Pond Croft	Aberd	NJ6219	57°15·9′	2°37·3′W	X	37
Pond Dale	N Yks	NZ1507	54°27·7′	1°45·7′W	X	92
Ponde	Powys	SO1037	52°1·7′	3°18·3′W	T	161
Ponden Clough	Brad	SD9836	53°49·5′	2°1·4′W	X	103
Ponden Resr	Brad	SD9937	53°50·0′	2°0·5′W	W	103
Ponderosa	Gwyn	SH6617	52°44·3′	3°58·7′W	X	124
Pondersbridge	Cambs	TL2692	52°30·9′	0°8·2′W	T	142
Ponders End	Enf	TQ3595	51°38·5′	0°2·5′W	T	166,177
Pondfield Villa	Durham	NZ1047	54°49·3′	1°50·2′W	X	88
Pond Fm	Dorset	ST6306	50°51·4′	2°31·2′W	FM	194
Pond Fm	Essex	TL9529	51°55·7′	0°50·6′E	FM	168
Pond Fm	Essex	TM1624	51°52·6′	1°8·7′E	FM	168,169
Pond Fm	Glos	ST8889	51°36·2′	2°10·0′W	FM	162,173
Pond Fm	Herts	TL1127	51°56·1′	0°22·7′W	FM	166
Pond Fm	Kent	TQ8240	51°8·0′	0°36·5′E	FM	188
Pond Fm	Kent	TQ8358	51°17·7′	0°37·9′E	FM	178,188
Pond Fm	Lincs	TA0804	53°31·5′	0°21·8′W	FM	112
Pond Fm	Lincs	TF2434	52°53·6′	0°9·0′W	FM	131
Pond Fm	Norf	TF7732	52°51·6′	0°38·2′E	FM	132
Pond Fm	Norf	TG2632	52°50·5′	1°21·8′E	FM	133
Pond Fm	N Yks	NZ9201	54°24·0′	0°34·5′W	FM	94
Pond Fm	Somer	ST7351	51°15·7′	2°22·8′W	FM	183
Pond Fm	Suff	TL8937	52°0·2′	0°45·6′E	FM	155
Pond Fm	Suff	TM4797	52°31·1′	1°38·9′E	FM	134
Pond Fm	Suff	TM4889	52°26·8′	1°39·4′E	FM	156
Pond Fm	Suff	TM5287	52°25·6′	1°42·8′E	FM	156
Pond Fm	Surrey	TQ3744	51°11·0′	0°2·0′W	FM	187
Pond Fm	Wilts	ST9988	51°35·7′	2°0·5′W	FM	173
Pond Glandwgan	Cered	SN7075	52°21·7′	3°54·2′W	W	135,147
Pond Hall	Essex	TM1529	51°55·3′	1°8·0′E	X	168,169
Pond Hall	Suff	TM1138	52°0·2′	1°4·8′E	X	155,169
Pond Hall Fm	Essex	TM2231	51°56·2′	1°14·2′E	FM	169
Pond Hall Fm	Suff	TM0541	52°2·0′	0°59·7′E	FM	155
Pond Hall Fm	Suff	TM1336	51°59·1′	1°6·5′E	FM	169
Pond Hall Fm	Suff	TM1841	52°1·7′	1°11·1′E	FM	169
Pond Head	Surrey	TQ1139	51°8·6′	0°24·4′W	X	187
Pond Head Fm	N Yks	SE5674	54°9·8′	1°8·1′W	FM	100
Pondhead Inclosure	Hants	SU3007	50°51·9′	1°34·0′W	F	196
Pond Head Wood	N Lincs	SE9706	53°32·7′	0°31·8′W	F	112
Pond Hill	Surrey	SU9449	51°14·2′	0°38·8′W	X	186
Pond Hills	Norf	TG1035	52°52·5′	1°7·6′E	X	133
Pond Ho	Essex	TL9932	51°57·3′	0°54·2′E	X	168
Pond Ho	Essex	TM1917	51°48·7′	1°11·0′E	X	168,169
Pondicherry	Northum	NU0401	55°18·4′	1°55·8′W	X	81
Pond Llwernog	Cered	SN7281	52°25·0′	3°52·5′W	W	135
Pond Lodge	Wilts	SU0087	51°35·1′	1°59·6′W	X	173
Pond of Drummond	Pth & Kin	NN8518	56°20·7′	3°51·2′W	W	58
Pond Ooze	Suff	TM1740	52°1·2′	1°10·2′E	X	169
Pond Park	Bucks	SP9502	51°42·7′	0°37·1′W	T	165
Pondpark Fm	Essex	TL6919	51°50·9′	0°27·6′E	FM	167
Pond Rhosrydd	Cered	SN7075	52°21·7′	3°54·2′W	W	135,147
Ponds Bay	E Susx	TQ3930	51°3·4′	0°0·6′W	A	187
Ponds Brow	I Scilly	SV8306	49°52·5′	6°24·4′W	X	203
Ponds Fm	Suff	TM0339	52°1·0′	0°57·9′E	FM	155
Ponds Fm	Surrey	TQ0646	51°12·4′	0°28·6′W	FM	187
Pondside Fm	Hants	SU6219	50°58·3′	1°6·6′W	FM	185
Pond Street	Essex	TL4537	52°1·0′	0°7·2′E	T	154
Pondtail	Hants	SU8254	51°17·0′	0°49·1′W	T	186
Pondtail Copse	W Susx	SU9923	51°0·1′	0°35·0′W	F	197
Pondtail Fm	Surrey	TQ1949	51°13·9′	0°17·3′W	FM	187
Pondtail Fm	W Susx	TQ1622	50°59·4′	0°20·4′W	FM	198
Pondwell	I of W	SZ6191	50°43·2′	1°7·8′W	T	196
Pond Wood	Derby	SK4056	53°6·2′	1°23·7′W	F	120
Pond Wood	Kent	TQ9036	51°5·7′	0°43·2′E	F	189
Pond Wood	N Yks	SE4679	54°12·5′	1°17·3′W	F	100
Pond Wood	Somer	ST0635	51°6·6′	3°20·2′W	F	181
Pondwood Fm	Win & Maid	SU8575	51°28·3′	0°46·2′W	FM	175
Ponesk Burn	E Ayr	NS7229	55°32·5′	4°1·3′W	W	71
Ponesk Burn	E Ayr	NS7331	55°33·6′	4°0·4′W	W	71
Ponfeigh Burn	S Lanak	NS8835	55°36·0′	3°46·2′W	W	71,72
Poniel	S Lanak	NS8434	55°35·4′	3°50·0′W	X	71,72
Poniel Hill	S Lanak	NS8333	55°34·9′	3°50·9′W	H	71,72
Poniel Water	S Lanak	NS8334	55°35·4′	3°51·0′W	W	71,72
Poniou	Corn	SW4438	50°11·4′	5°34·8′W	T	203
Poniou	Corn	SW4931	50°7·8′	5°30·4′W	X	203
Ponjeravah	Corn	SW7329	50°7·3′	5°10·2′W	T	204
Ponsanooth	Corn	SW7537	50°11·7′	5°8·8′W	T	204
Ponsbourne Park	Herts	TL3005	51°43·9′	0°6·7′W	X	166
Ponsbourne Tunnel	Herts	TL3105	51°43·9′	0°5·8′W	X	166
Ponsford	Devon	ST0007	50°51·5′	3°24·9′W	T	192
Ponsil	Shetld	HU5891	60°36·2′	0°55·9′W	X	1,2
Ponsonby	Cumbr	NY0505	54°26·1′	3°27·5′W	T	89
Ponsonby Fell	Cumbr	NY0807	54°27·3′	3°24·7′W	H	89
Ponsonby Old Hall	Cumbr	NY0505	54°26·1′	3°27·5′W	X	89
Ponsongath	Corn	SW7517	50°0·9′	5°8·1′W	T	204

Ponsworthy	Devon	SX7073	50°32·8′	3°49·7′W	T	191
Pont	Corn	SX1452	50°20·5′	4°36·5′W	T	200
Pont Aber	Carm	SN7322	51°53·2′	3°50·3′W	X	160
Pont Aber-Geirw	Gwyn	SH7629	52°50·9′	3°50·1′W	X	124
Pont Aberglaslyn	Gwyn	SH5946	52°59·8′	4°5·7′W	X	115
Pontac Fm	Red & Cl	NZ6221	54°35·1′	1°2·0′W	FM	94
Pont-Allt-y-cafan	Cered	SN3839	52°1·8′	4°21·3′W	X	145
Pontalun	V of Glam	SS8976	51°28·6′	3°35·5′W	X	170
Pontamman	Carm	SN6412	51°47·6′	3°57·9′W	T	159
Pontantwn	Carm	SN4413	51°47·9′	4°15·4′W	T	159
Pont ar Daf	Powys	SN9819	51°51·9′	3°28·5′W	X	160
Pontardawe	Nth Pt Talb	SN7204	51°43·4′	3°50·8′W	T	170
Pontarddulais	Swan	SN5903	51°42·7′	4°2·1′W	T	159
Pont ar Eden	Gwyn	SH7224	52°48·1′	3°53·5′W	X	124
Pont ar Elan	Powys	SN9071	52°19·8′	3°36·5′W	X	136,147
Pontargamddwr	Cered	SN6664	52°15·7′	3°57·4′W	X	146
Pont ar Gonwy	Conwy	SH7744	52°59·0′	3°49·5′W	X	124
Pont-ar-gothi	Carm	SN5021	51°52·3′	4°10·3′W	T	159
Pont ar Hydfer	Powys	SN8627	51°56·0′	3°39·1′W	T	160
Pont ar Ithon	Powys	SO0157	52°12·4′	3°26·5′W	X	147
Pont-ar-llechau	Carm	SN7224	51°54·2′	3°51·2′W	T	160
Pontarsais	Carm	SN4428	51°56·0′	4°15·8′W	T	146
Pont-ar-Yscir	Powys	SO0030	51°57·8′	3°26·9′W	X	160
Pontblyddyn	Flint	SJ2760	53°8·2′	3°5·1′W	T	117
Pontbren	Carm	SN7322	51°53·2′	3°50·3′W	X	160
Pontbren Araeth	Carm	SN6523	51°53·6′	3°57·3′W	T	159
Pontbrengarreg	Powys	SO0424	51°54·6′	3°23·3′W	X	160
Pontbren Llwyd	Rho Cyn Taf	SN9408	51°45·9′	3°31·8′W	X	160
Pont Britannia	Gwyn	SH5471	53°13·2′	4°10·8′W	X	114,115
Pont Briwet	Gwyn	SH6138	52°55·5′	4°3·7′W	X	124
Pont Buarth-glas	Gwyn	SH8216	52°44·0′	3°44·5′W	X	124,125
Pont Burn	Durham	NZ1454	54°53·1′	1°46·5′W	W	88
Pont Cae'r-gors	Gwyn	SH5750	53°1·9′	4°7·5′W	X	115
Pont Caletwyr	Conwy	SH8549	53°1·8′	3°42·5′W	X	116
Pontcanna	Card	ST1677	51°29·4′	3°12·2′W	T	171
Pont Cerrig	Gwyn	SH6326	52°49·1′	4°1·6′W	X	124
Pont Cilan	Denb	SJ0237	52°55·5′	3°27·1′W	X	125
Pont Clydach	Carm	SN7419	51°51·6′	3°49·4′W	X	160
Pontcowin	Carm	SN3319	51°50·9′	4°25·1′W	X	159
Pont Creuddyn	Cered	SN5552	52°9·1′	4°6·8′W	X	146
Pont Croesor	Gwyn	SH5941	52°57·1′	4°5·5′W	X	124
Pont Crug	I of Angl	SH5069	53°12·1′	4°14·3′W	X	114,115
Pont Crugnant	Powys	SN8895	52°32·7′	3°38·7′W	X	135,136
Pont Cwm Pydew	Gwyn	SJ0031	52°52·3′	3°28·7′W	X	125
Pont Cyfyng	Conwy	SH7357	53°6·0′	3°53·4′W	X	115
Pont Cynon	Powys	SJ0120	52°46·4′	3°27·7′W	X	125
Pont Cynon	Rho Cyn Taf	ST0895	51°39·0′	3°19·4′W	X	170
Pont Cysyllte	Denb	SJ2742	52°58·5′	3°4·8′W	T	117
Pont Dafydd	Denb	SJ0474	53°15·5′	3°25·9′W	A	116
Pont-ddu	Carm	SN3014	51°48·2′	4°27·6′W	X	159
Pont-Dic	I of Angl	SH4868	53°11·5′	4°16·1′W	X	114,115
Pont Dôl Dwymyn	Powys	SH8204	52°37·5′	3°44·2′W	X	135,136
Pont Dolgarrog	Conwy	SH7766	53°10·9′	3°50·0′W	X	115
Pont Dôl-gefeiliau	Gwyn	SH7226	52°49·2′	3°53·6′W	X	124
Pontdolgoch	Powys	SO0093	52°31·8′	3°28·1′W	T	136
Pont Dolydd Prysor	Gwyn	SH7436	52°54·6′	3°52·0′W	X	124
Pontefract	Wakf	SE4521	53°41·2′	1°18·7′W	T	105
Pontefract Park	Wakf	SE4422	53°41·8′	1°19·6′W	X	105
Pont Eidda	Conwy	SH8350	53°2·3′	3°44·3′W	X	116
Pont-Einjon	Flint	SJ2568	53°12·5′	3°7·0′W	X	117
Pont Einon	Cered	SN6761	52°14·1′	3°56·5′W	X	146
Ponteland	Northum	NZ1673	55°3·3′	1°44·5′W	T	88
Ponter's Ball	Somer	ST5337	51°8·1′	2°39·9′W	A	182,183
Ponterwyd	Cered	SN7480	52°24·5′	3°50·7′W	T	135
Pontesbury	Shrops	SJ3906	52°39·1′	2°53·7′W	T	126
Pontesbury Hill	Shrops	SJ3905	52°38·6′	2°53·7′W	T	126
Pontesford	Shrops	SJ4106	52°39·2′	2°51·9′W	T	126
Pontesford Hill	Shrops	SJ4004	52°38·1′	2°52·8′W	H	126
Pont Eunant	Powys	SH9622	52°47·4′	3°32·1′W	X	125
Pont-Fadog	Gwyn	SH6022	52°46·9′	4°4·1′W	X	124
Pontfadog	Wrex	SJ2338	52°56·3′	3°8·3′W	T	126
Pont-faen	Cered	SN6049	52°7·5′	4°2·3′W	X	146
Pont Faen	Gwyn	SH4659	53°6·6′	4°17·6′W	X	115,123
Pontfaen	Pemb	SN0234	51°58·4′	4°52·6′W	T	145,157
Pontfaen	Pemb	SN1636	51°59·8′	4°40·4′W	X	145
Pont-faen	Powys	SN9934	52°0·0′	3°27·9′W	T	160
Pont-Faen	Shrops	SJ2736	52°55·2′	3°4·7′W	T	126
Pontfaen Brook	Pemb	SN0233	51°57·9′	4°52·5′W	W	145,157
Pont fawr	Conwy	SH7961	53°8·2′	3°48·1′W	A	115,116
Pont Fronwydd	Gwyn	SH8324	52°48·3′	3°43·7′W	X	124,125
Pont Gallon Burn	Northum	NY7269	55°1·1′	2°25·8′W	W	86,87
Pontgarreg	Carm	SN2737	52°0·5′	4°30·8′W	X	145
Pontgarreg	Cered	SN3354	52°9·8′	4°26·1′W	T	145
Pontgarreg	Pemb	SN1441	52°2·4′	4°42·3′W	X	145
Pont Gethin	Conwy	SH7753	53°3·9′	3°49·7′W	X	115
Pont Gihirych	Powys	SN8821	51°52·8′	3°37·2′W	X	160
Pont Glanrhyd	Cered	SN6351	52°8·7′	3°59·7′W	X	146
Pont Glan-Tanat Uchaf	Powys	SJ1324	52°48·6′	3°17·0′W	X	125
Pont Glan-y-wern	Denb	SJ0965	53°10·7′	3°21·3′W	X	116
Pont Gogoyan	Cered	SN6454	52°10·3′	3°58·9′W	X	146
Pont Gwaithyrhaearn	Caer	SO1604	51°43·9′	3°12·6′W	X	171
Pontgwilym	Powys	SO0430	51°57·9′	3°23·4′W	X	160
Pont Gwladys	Carm	SN6221	51°52·5′	3°59·9′W	X	159
Pont Gyfyng	Gwyn	SH5245	52°59·2′	4°11·9′W	X	115
Pontgynon	Pemb	SN1236	51°59·7′	4°43·9′W	X	145
Pont Helygog	Gwyn	SH7919	52°45·5′	3°47·2′W	X	124
Ponthen	Shrops	SJ3317	52°45·0′	2°59·2′W	T	126
Pont-Henri	Carm	SN4709	51°45·8′	4°12·6′W	T	159
Ponthir	Newp	ST3292	51°37·6′	2°58·6′W	T	171
Ponthirwaun	Cered	SN2645	52°4·8′	4°32·0′W	T	145
Pont Hwfa	I of Angl	SH2382	53°18·6′	4°39·0′W	T	114
Pontiago	Pemb	SM9238	52°0·3′	5°1·4′W	T	157
Pont-iets or Pontyates	Carm	SN4608	51°45·2′	4°13·5′W	T	159
Pontispool Fm	Somer	ST1725	51°1·3′	3°10·6′W	FM	181,193
Pontithel	Powys	SO1636	52°1·2′	3°13·1′W	T	161
Pontllanfraith	Caer	ST1896	51°39·6′	3°10·7′W	T	171
Pont Llanio	Cered	SN6556	52°11·4′	3°58·1′W	X	146
Pont Llanrhaiadr	Gwyn	SH7920	52°46·1′	3°47·2′W	X	124
Pontlliw	Swan	SN6101	51°41·7′	4°0·3′W	T	159
Pont Llogel	Powys	SJ0315	52°43·7′	3°25·8′W	T	125
Pont Llwyn-hîr	Gwyn	SH8834	52°53·8′	3°39·5′W	X	124,125
Pont Llyfnant	Cered	SN7097	52°33·6′	3°54·7′W	X	135
Pont Llyfnant	Powys	SN7079	52°23·9′	3°54·2′W	X	
Pontllyfni	Gwyn	SH4352	53°2·8′	4°20·1′W	T	115,123
Pontlottyn	Caer	SO1106	51°45·0′	3°17·0′W	T	161
Pont-marchog	Cered	SN5051	52°8·5′	4°11·1′W	X	146
Pont Marteg	Powys	SN9571	52°19·9′	3°32·1′W	X	136,147
Pont Melin-fâch	Powys	SN9010	51°46·9′	3°35·3′W	X	160
Pont Moelfre	Conwy	SH9547	53°0·8′	3°33·5′W	X	116
Pont Morlais	Carm	SN5307	51°44·8′	4°7·4′W	X	159
Pont Mwnwgl-y-llyn	Gwyn	SH9235	52°54·3′	3°35·9′W	X	125
Pont Mynach	I of Angl	SH4566	53°10·4′	4°18·7′W	X	114,115
Pont Nant-y-lladron	Gwyn	SH7839	52°56·3′	3°48·5′W	X	124
Pontneddfechan	Powys	SN9007	51°45·3′	3°35·2′W	T	160
Pont-newydd	Carm	SN4407	51°44·6′	4°15·2′W	T	159
Pont Newydd	Carm	SN7323	51°53·7′	3°50·4′W	X	160
Pont Newydd	Carm	SN7538	52°1·8′	3°48·9′W	X	146,160
Pont-newydd	Flint	SJ1865	53°10·8′	3°13·2′W	T	116
Pont Newydd	Powys	SN8828	51°56·6′	3°37·4′W	X	160
Pontnewydd	Torf	ST2996	51°39·7′	3°1·2′W	T	171
Pontnewynydd	Torf	SO2701	51°42·4′	3°3·0′W	T	171
Ponton Heath	Lincs	SK8930	52°51·8′	0°40·3′W	X	130
Ponton Heath Fm	Lincs	SK9029	52°51·3′	0°39·4′W	FM	130
Ponton Park Wood	Lincs	SK9431	52°52·3′	0°35·8′W	F	130
Pontooth	Orkney	HY2817	59°2·3′	3°14·8′W	X	6
Pontop Hall	Durham	NZ1453	54°52·5′	1°46·5′W	A	88
Pontop Pike	Durham	NZ1452	54°52·0′	1°46·5′W	X	88
Pont Pandy-Llwydiarth	Powys	SJ0516	52°44·2′	3°24·0′W	X	125
Pont Parc-y-dai	Carm	SN5313	51°48·0′	4°7·5′W	X	159
Pont Pen-y-benglog	Gwyn	SH6460	53°7·4′	4°1·5′W	X	115
Pont Pill	Corn	SX1351	50°20·0′	4°37·3′W	W	200
Pontrhyd	Cered	SN4359	52°12·7′	4°17·5′W	X	146
Pont Rhyd-ddwl	Gwyn	SH7921	52°46·6′	3°47·2′W	X	124
Pont Rhyd-felin	Carm	SN7346	52°6·1′	3°50·9′W	X	146,147
Pontrhydfendigaid	Cered	SN7366	52°16·9′	3°51·3′W	T	135,147
Pont Rhydgaled	Powys	SN8382	52°25·7′	3°42·9′W	T	135,136
Pont Rhyd-goch	Conwy	SH6760	53°7·5′	3°58·9′W	X	115
Pont Rhyd-goch	Gwyn	SH2530	52°50·6′	4°35·5′W	X	123
Pont Rhydlechog	Conwy	SH8963	53°9·4′	3°39·2′W	X	116
Pont Rhyd-llo	Gwyn	SH1928	52°49·4′	4°40·8′W	X	123
Pont Rhyd-sarn	Gwyn	SH8528	52°50·5′	3°42·0′W	X	124,125
Pont Rhyd-y-berry	Powys	SN9736	52°1·0′	3°29·7′W	T	160
Pontrhydyceirt	Pemb	SN2142	52°3·1′	4°36·2′W	X	145
Pont Rhyd-y-cnau	Powys	SN9111	51°47·5′	3°34·4′W	X	160
Pont Rhyd-y-cyff	Brig	SS8789	51°35·5′	3°37·5′W	T	170
Pont Rhyd-y-fen	Gwyn	SH8239	52°56·4′	3°45·0′W	X	124,125
Pontrhydyfen	Nth Pt Talb	SS7994	51°38·1′	3°44·5′W	T	170
Pont-rhyd-y-groes	Cered	SN7372	52°20·1′	3°51·4′W	T	135,147
Pont Rhyd-y-gwair	Gwyn	SH7920	52°46·1′	3°47·2′W	X	124
Pontrhydyrun	Torf	ST2997	51°40·3′	3°1·2′W	T	171
Pont-Rhys-Powell	Monm	SO3022	51°53·8′	3°0·6′W	X	161
Pont-Rhythallt	Gwyn	SH5463	53°8·9′	4°10·6′W	T	114,115
Pont Ricket	Carm	SN3321	51°52·0′	4°25·1′W	X	145,159
Pontrilas	Heref	SO3927	51°56·5′	2°52·9′W	T	161
Pontrobert	Powys	SJ1012	52°42·1′	3°19·5′W	T	125
Pont Rufeinig Sta	Conwy	SH7151	53°2·7′	3°55·1′W	X	115
Pontruffydd Fm	Denb	SJ0769	53°12·8′	3°23·2′W	FM	116
Pontruffydd Hall Fm	Denb	SJ0869	53°12·9′	3°22·3′W	FM	116
Pont-rug	Gwyn	SH5163	53°8·8′	4°13·3′W	T	114,115
Pontsaeson	Cered	SN5463	52°15·0′	4°7·9′W	X	146
Pont-Scethin	Gwyn	SH6323	52°47·5′	4°1·5′W	X	124
Ponts Fm	E Susx	TQ6424	50°59·7′	0°20·6′E	FM	199
Ponts Green	E Susx	TQ6715	50°54·8′	0°22·9′E	T	199
Pont-shân	Pemb	SN0916	51°48·8′	4°45·9′W	X	158
Pontshill	Heref	SO6321	51°53·4′	2°31·9′W	T	162
Pont-siân	Cered	SN4346	52°5·6′	4°17·1′W	T	146
Pont Siôn Norton	Rho Cyn Taf	ST0891	51°36·9′	3°19·3′W	T	170
Ponts Mill	Corn	SX0756	50°22·6′	4°42·5′W	X	200
Pont Spwdwr	Carm	SN4305	51°43·5′	4°16·0′W	A	159
Pontsticill	Merth Tyd	SO0511	51°47·6′	3°22·3′W	T	160
Pontsticill Reservoir	Merth Tyd	SO0512	51°48·2′	3°22·3′W	W	160
Pont-swil	Denb	SJ1145	52°59·9′	3°19·2′W	X	116
Pont Sylltu	Conwy	SH8866	53°11·0′	3°40·2′W	X	116
Pont Tal-y-bont	Gwyn	SH6841	52°57·3′	3°57·5′W	X	124
Pont Trephilip	Powys	SO1234	52°0·1′	3°16·5′W	X	161
Pont Twrch	Powys	SH9811	52°41·5′	3°30·2′W	X	125
Pontus	Kent	TR0252	51°14·1′	0°54·0′E	X	189
Pontvaen	Heref	SO2344	52°5·6′	3°7·0′W	X	148,161
Pontvane Fm	Powys	SO2050	52°8·8′	3°9·8′W	FM	148
Pont-Walby	Nth Pt Talb	SN8906	51°44·7′	3°36·1′W	T	160
Pont Waun-fach	Powys	SO1826	51°55·8′	3°11·2′W	X	161
Pont Wedwst	Pemb	SN2835	51°59·5′	4°29·9′W	X	145
Pontwgan	Conwy	SH7670	53°13·0′	3°51·0′W	X	115
Pontyates or Pont-iets	Carm	SN4608	51°45·2′	4°13·5′W	T	159
Pontybat Fm	Powys	SO1134	52°0·1′	3°17·4′W	FM	161
Pontyberem	Carm	SN5011	51°46·9′	4°10·1′W	T	159
Pont-y-blew	Wrex	SJ3138	52°56·3′	3°1·2′W	T	126
Pontybodkin	Flint	SJ2759	53°7·6′	3°5·1′W	X	117
Pont y Brenig	Denb	SH9657	53°6·2′	3°32·8′W	X	116
Pont-y-bryn-hurt	Powys	SO1920	51°52·6′	3°10·2′W	X	161
Pont y Cambwll	Denb	SJ0770	53°13·4′	3°23·2′W	X	116
Pont-y-Ceunant	Gwyn	SH9435	52°54·4′	3°34·2′W	X	125
Pont-y-Cim	Gwyn	SH4452	53°2·8′	4°19·2′W	A	115,123
Pont y Clogwyn	Conwy	SH9356	53°5·7′	3°35·5′W	X	116
Pontyclun	Rho Cyn Taf	ST0381	51°31·4′	3°23·5′W	T	170
Pont-y-Coblyn	Conwy	SH7151	53°2·7′	3°55·1′W	X	115
Pont-y-Cribyn	Gwyn	SH3536	52°54·0′	4°26·8′W	X	123
Pontycymer	Brig	SS9091	51°36·7′	3°34·9′W	T	170
Pont y Ddôl	Denb	SH9872	53°14·4′	3°31·3′W	X	116
Pont y Felin	Gwyn	SH4843	52°58·0′	4°15·4′W	X	123
Pont-y-Fenni	Carm	SN2317	51°49·7′	4°33·7′W	X	158
Pont-y-Gafel	Pemb	SN1929	51°56·0′	4°37·6′W	X	145,158
Pont y Gain	Gwyn	SH7532	52°52·5′	3°51·0′W	X	124
Pont y Garreg-fechan	Gwyn	SH3634	52°53·0′	4°25·8′W	X	123
Pont y Garreg-newydd	Conwy	SH8964	53°9·9′	3°39·2′W	X	116
Pont y Garth	Gwyn	SH6307	52°38·9′	4°1·1′W	X	124
Pontyglasier	Pemb	SN1436	51°59·7′	4°42·2′W	T	145
Pont y Glyn-diffwys	Conwy	SH9844	52°59·3′	3°30·8′W	X	125
Pont y Grible	Gwyn	SH7030	52°51·4′	3°55·4′W	X	124
Pont y Gromlech	Gwyn	SH6256	53°5·2′	4°3·2′W	X	115
Pontygwaith	Rho Cyn Taf	ST0094	51°38·4′	3°26·3′W	T	170
Pont y Gydrhos	Gwyn	SH3942	52°57·3′	4°23·4′W	X	123
Pont y Lafar	Gwyn	SH8932	52°52·7′	3°38·6′W	X	124,125
Pont y Llyn-dû	Gwyn	SH7330	52°51·4′	3°52·8′W	X	124
Pont y Meddyg	Pemb	SM9938	52°0·5′	4°55·3′W	X	157
Pont-y-Meibion	Wrex	SJ1935	52°54·6′	3°11·9′W	X	125
Pontymister	Caer	ST2490	51°36·5′	3°5·5′W	T	171
Pontymoel	Torf	SO2900	51°41·9′	3°1·3′W	T	171
Pont y Nant	Conwy	SH9364	53°10·0′	3°35·6′W	X	116
Pont y Pandy	Gwyn	SH7042	52°57·8′	3°55·7′W	X	124
Pont-y-pant	Conwy	SH7553	53°3·8′	3°51·5′W	T	115
Pont y Pennant	Gwyn	SH9020	52°46·2′	3°37·4′W	X	125
Pont-y-pentre	Powys	SJ2119	52°46·0′	3°9·9′W	X	126
Pontyperchill	Powys	SO1295	52°33·0′	3°17·5′W	X	136
Ponty Pinna Fm	Heref	SO3735	52°0·8′	2°54·7′W	FM	149,161
Ponty Pinna Fm	Heref	SO3735	52°0·8′	2°54·7′W	X	149
Pont-y-Plas	Gwyn	SH5245	52°59·2′	4°11·9′W	X	115
Pontypool & Blaenavon Rly	Torf	SO2309	51°46·7′	3°6·6′W	X	161
Pontypool or Pont-y-pŵl	Torf	SO2800	51°41·9′	3°2·1′W	T	171
Pontypridd	Pemb	SN0433	51°57·9′	4°50·8′W	X	145,157
Pontypridd	Rho Cyn Taf	ST0789	51°35·8′	3°20·2′W	T	170
Pont-y-pŵl or Pontypool	Torf	SO2800	51°41·9′	3°2·1′W	T	171
Pont yr Afon-Gam	Gwyn	SH7441	52°57·3′	3°52·1′W	W	124
Pont-yr-Aled	Conwy	SH9570	53°13·2′	3°34·0′W	X	116
Pont yr Alwen	Conwy	SH9652	53°3·6′	3°32·7′W	X	116
Pont-yr-Eilun	Pemb	SM7021	51°50·7′	5°20·0′W	X	157
Pont-yr-hafod	Pemb	SM9026	51°53·8′	5°2·7′W	T	157,158
Pont yr Haiarn	Pemb	SN1428	51°55·4′	4°41·9′W	X	145,158
Pont y Rhuddfa	Conwy	SH9753	53°4·1′	3°31·8′W	X	116
Pont-y-rhyl	Brig	SS9089	51°35·6′	3°34·9′W	T	170
Pont Ysgadan	Powys	SJ0717	52°44·8′	3°22·3′W	X	125
Pontysgawrhyd	Powys	SJ1915	52°43·8′	3°11·6′W	X	125
Pont-Ystrad	Denb	SJ0564	53°10·1′	3°24·9′W	T	116
Pont Ystumanner	Gwyn	SH6607	52°38·9′	3°58·4′W	X	124
Pontystyllod	Denb	SJ1953	53°4·3′	3°12·1′W	X	116
Pont-y-wal	Powys	SO1335	52°0·6′	3°15·7′W	T	161
Pontywaun	Caer	ST2292	51°37·5′	3°7·2′W	T	171
Poodle Gorse	Oxon	SP6225	51°55·4′	1°5·5′W	X	164,165
Pookandraw	Highld	NH6859	57°36·4′	4°12·1′W	X	26
Pookhill Barn	E Susx	TQ4907	50°50·8′	0°7·4′E	X	199
Pooks Fm	W Susx	TQ2220	50°58·2′	0°15·4′W	FM	198
Pooksgreen	Hants	SU3710	50°53·5′	1°28·0′W	T	196
Pool	Corn	SW6741	50°13·6′	5°15·6′W	T	203
Pool	I Scilly	SV8714	49°56·9′	6°21·4′W	T	203
Pool	Leeds	SE2445	53°54·3′	1°37·7′W	T	104
Pool	Orkney	HY5804	58°55·5′	2°43·3′W	X	6
Pool	Orkney	ND4793	58°49·5′	2°54·6′W	X	7
Pool	S Lanak	NS9853	55°45·8′	3°37·1′W	X	65,72
Pool	Staffs	SK0962	53°9·5′	1°51·5′W	X	119
Pool Anthony	Devon	SS9712	50°54·1′	3°27·5′W	X	181
Pool Bank	Ches	SJ4967	53°12·1′	2°45·4′W	X	117
Pool Bank	Ches	SJ5061	53°8·9′	2°44·5′W	X	117
Poolbank	Ches	SJ6948	53°1·9′	2°27·3′W	X	118
Pool Bank	Ches	SJ8963	53°10·1′	2°9·5′W	X	118
Pool Bank	Cumbr	SD4387	54°16·8′	2°52·1′W	X	97
Pool Bank	Leeds	SE2344	53°53·7′	1°38·6′W	X	104
Pool Bay	Orkney	HY6137	59°13·3′	2°40·5′W	W	5
Pool Beck	N Yks	SE4757	54°0·7′	1°16·6′W	W	105
Pool Br	Leeds	SE2445	53°54·3′	1°37·7′W	X	104
Pool Bridge Fm	N Yks	SE4856	54°0·1′	1°15·6′W	FM	105
Pool Bridge Fm	Somer	ST4047	51°13·4′	2°51·2′W	FM	182
Pool Bridge Fm	York	SE6446	53°54·6′	1°1·1′W	FM	105,106
Poolbrook	Worcs	SO7944	52°5·9′	2°18·0′W	T	150
Pool Crofts	Highld	NG8580	57°45·8′	5°36·4′W	T	19
Pool Cross	Devon	SX5189	50°41·1′	4°6·2′W	X	191
Pool Decoy	Lincs	TF4457	53°5·7′	0°9·4′E	F	122
Poole	Angus	NO6251	56°39·2′	2°36·7′W	X	54
Poole	Devon	SS8121	50°58·8′	3°41·3′W	X	181
Poole	Devon	SX3488	50°40·3′	4°20·6′W	X	190
Poole	Devon	SX8145	50°17·8′	3°39·9′W	X	202
Poole	Devon	SX8266	50°29·2′	3°39·4′W	X	202
Poole	N Yks	SE4927	53°44·5′	1°15·0′W	T	105
Poole	Poole	SZ0191	50°43·3′	1°58·8′W	T	195
Poole	Somer	ST1421	50°59·2′	3°13·1′W	T	181,193
Poole Bank Fm	Ches	SJ6455	53°5·7′	2°31·9′W	FM	118
Poole Bay	Bourne	SZ0987	50°41·2′	1°52·0′W	W	195
Poole Fm	Devon	SS4744	51°10·7′	4°11·0′W	FM	180
Poole Fm	Devon	SS9101	50°48·1′	3°32·4′W	FM	192
Poole Fm	Devon	SS9324	51°0·6′	3°31·1′W	FM	181
Poole Fm	Devon	SX5847	50°18·6′	3°59·3′W	FM	202
Poole Fms	Devon	SX7749	50°19·9′	3°43·3′W	FM	202
Poole Hall	Ches	SJ6455	53°5·7′	2°31·9′W	X	118
Poole Harbour	Dorset	SZ0088	50°41·7′	1°59·6′W	W	195
Poole Head	Poole	SZ0588	50°41·7′	1°55·4′W	X	195
Poolehill	Ches	SJ6354	53°5·2′	2°32·7′W	X	118
Poole House Fm	Ches	SJ6355	53°5·7′	2°32·7′W	FM	118
Poole Keynes	Glos	SU0095	51°39·5′	1°59·6′W	T	163
Pool End	Ches	SJ9176	53°17·1′	2°7·7′W	X	118
Pool End	Lincs	SE9905	53°32·2′	0°30·0′W	X	112
Poolend	Staffs	SJ9658	53°7·4′	2°3·2′W	T	118
Poolend Fm	Heref	SO6439	52°3·1′	2°31·1′W	FM	149
Poole Old Hall	Ches	SJ6455	53°5·7′	2°31·9′W	X	118
Poole Park	Dorset	SZ0291	50°43·3′	1°57·9′W	X	195
Poole Place	W Susx	SU9900	50°47·7′	0°35·3′W	X	197
Poole's Cavern	Derby	SK0472	53°14·9′	1°56·0′W	A	119
Poole's Fm	Suff	TM0659	52°11·7′	1°1·2′E	FM	155
Pooles Lodge Fm	Leic	SK7821	52°47·1′	0°50·2′W	FM	129
Poolestown	Dorset	ST7316	50°56·8′	2°22·7′W	T	183
Poolewe	Highld	NG8580	57°45·8′	5°36·4′W	T	19
Pooley Bridge	Cumbr	NY4724	54°36·8′	2°48·8′W	T	90
Pooley Hall	Warw	SK2502	52°37·1′	1°37·4′W	A	140
Pooley Street	Norf	TM0581	52°23·5′	1°1·2′E	T	144
Poolfield Court Fm	Glos	SO5601	51°42·6′	2°37·8′W	FM	162
Poolfields	Warw	SP3253	52°10·7′	1°31·5′W	X	151
Pool Fm	Ches	SJ5052	53°4·0′	2°44·4′W	FM	117
Pool Fm	Ches	SJ5455	53°5·7′	2°40·8′W	FM	117
Pool Fm	Glos	SO7002	51°43·2′	2°25·7′W	FM	162
Pool Fm	Glos	SO8111	51°48·1′	2°16·1′W	FM	162
Pool Fm	Heref	SO3626	51°56·0′	2°55·5′W	FM	161

Pool Fm	Heref	SO6948	52°8·0′	2°26·8′W	FM	149
Pool Fm	N Som	ST4064	51°22·5′	2°51·3′W	FM	172,182
Pool Fm	Oxon	SP6227	51°56·5′	1°5·5′W	FM	164,165
Pool Fm	Powys	SO1658	52°13·1′	3°13·4′W	FM	148
Pool Fm	S Glos	ST6983	51°32·9′	2°26·4′W	FM	172
Pool Fm	Somer	SS8744	51°11·3′	3°36·6′W	FM	181
Pool Fm	Somer	ST0422	50°59·6′	3°21·7′W	FM	181
Pool Fm	Somer	ST5353	51°16·7′	2°40·0′W	FM	182,183
Pool Fm	Staffs	SJ9503	52°37·7′	2°4·0′W	FM	127,139
Pool Fm	Staffs	SJ9763	53°10·1′	2°2·3′W	FM	118
Pool Fm	Warw	SP2086	52°28·5′	1°41·9′W	FM	139
Poolfold	Staffs	SJ8959	53°7·9′	2°9·5′W	T	118
Pool Foot	Cumbr	SD3284	54°15·1′	3°2·2′W	X	96,97
Pool Green Fm	Staffs	SK2022	52°47·9′	1°41·8′W	FM	128
Pool Hall	Heref	SO6653	52°10·7′	2°29·4′W	X	149
Pool Hall	Powys	SO0842	52°4·4′	3°20·1′W	X	147,160
Pool Hall	Shrops	SJ7341	52°58·2′	2°23·7′W	X	118
Pool Hall	Shrops	SO7683	52°26·9′	2°20·8′W	X	138
Poolhall	Staffs	SK0055	53°5·8′	1°59·6′W	X	119
Pool Hall	Staffs	SO8597	52°34·5′	2°12·9′W	X	139
Poolham Hall	Lincs	TF2067	53°11·4′	0°11·8′W	X	122
Poolharry	Aberd	NK0237	57°25·7′	1°57·5′W	X	30
Poolhead	Ches	SJ6263	53°10·0′	2°33·7′W	X	118
Pool Head	Heref	SO5550	52°9·0′	2°39·1′W	T	149
Pool Head	Newp	ST4088	51°35·5′	2°51·6′W	X	171,172
Poolhead	Shrops	SJ4932	52°53·2′	2°45·1′W	T	126
Pool Hey	Lancs	SD3615	53°37·9′	2°57·7′W	T	108
Pool Hill	Glos	SO6717	51°51·3′	2°28·4′W	H	162
Poolhill	Glos	SO7329	51°57·8′	2°23·2′W	T	150
Pool Hill	Powys	SO1775	52°22·2′	3°12·8′W	H	136,148
Pool Ho	Glos	SP0808	51°46·5′	1°52·6′W	X	163
Pool Ho	Shrops	SJ5822	52°47·9′	2°37·0′W	X	126
Pool Ho	Shrops	SJ6403	52°37·7′	2°31·5′W	X	127
Pool Ho	Shrops	SJ6640	52°57·6′	2°30·0′W	X	118
Pool Ho	Shrops	SO5975	52°22·5′	2°35·7′W	X	137,138
Pool Ho	Worcs	SO7968	52°18·8′	2°18·1′W	X	138
Pool Ho	Worcs	SO8441	52°4·3′	2°13·6′W	X	150
Pool House Fm	Ches	SJ9484	53°21·4′	2°5·0′W	FM	109
Poolhouse Fm	Shrops	SO7882	52°26·4′	2°19·0′W	FM	138
Poolhouse Fm	Staffs	SO8288	52°29·6′	2°15·5′W	FM	138
Pool House Fm	Worcs	SO5965	52°17·1′	2°35·7′W	FM	137,138,149
Poolhouse Fm	Worcs	SO7267	52°18·3′	2°24·2′W	FM	138,149
Poolhoy	Highld	ND1960	58°31·5′	3°23·0′W	X	11,12
Poolmill	Heref	SO5824	51°55·0′	2°36·2′W	T	162
Poolmill Cross	Devon	SX8082	50°37·8′	3°41·4′W	X	191
Pool Mill Fm	Devon	SX5748	50°19·1′	4°0·1′W	FM	202
Pool of Cletts	Orkney	ND4690	58°47·9′	2°55·6′W	W	7
Pool of Muckhart	Clackm	NO0000	56°11·2′	3°36·2′W	T	58
Pool of Virkie	Shetld	HU3911	59°53·2′	1°17·7′W	W	4
Poolpardon	Heref	SO2645	52°6·1′	3°4·4′W	X	148
Pool Park	Wrex	SJ2550	53°2·8′	3°6·7′W	X	117
Pool Park Fm	Denb	SJ0955	53°5·3′	3°21·1′W	FM	116
Pool Quay	Powys	SJ2511	52°41·7′	3°6·2′W	T	126
Pool Redding	Powys	SO2058	52°13·1′	3°9·9′W	X	148
Pool River	Brom	TQ3670	51°25·0′	0°2·3′W	W	177
Pool Roag	Highld	NG2744	57°24·5′	6°32·3′W	W	23
Pools Brook	Derby	SK4373	53°15·4′	1°20·9′W	W	120
Poolsbrook	Derby	SK4473	53°15·4′	1°20·0′W	T	120
Pool Scar	Cumbr	SD2691	54°18·8′	3°7·8′W	X	96,97
Pools Fm	Shrops	SO4879	52°24·6′	2°45·5′W	FM	137,138,148
Pools Head	Derby	SK2540	52°57·6′	1°37·3′W	X	119,128
Poolside	Moray	NJ4047	57°30·8′	2°59·6′W	X	28
Poolside	Moray	NJ5249	57°32·0′	2°47·6′W	X	29
Pools of Dee	Aberd	NH9700	57°5·0′	3°41·5′W	W	36
Pools Platt Fm	Ches	SJ6580	53°19·2′	2°31·1′W	FM	109
Poolspringe	Heref	SO5029	51°57·7′	2°43·3′W	X	149
Pool Spring Fm	N Yks	SE4757	54°0·7′	1°16·6′W	FM	105
Pools, The	Heref	SO4373	52°21·4′	2°49·8′W	X	137,148
Pools, The or Valley Bottom	Cambs	TL5077	52°22·5′	0°12·6′E	X	143
Poolstock	Wigan	SD5704	53°32·1′	2°38·5′W	T	108
Pool, The	Orkney	ND3590	58°47·8′	3°7·0′W	W	7
Pool, The	Shetld	HU4281	60°30·9′	1°13·6′W	W	1,2,3
Pool, The	Staffs	SJ8505	52°38·8′	2°12·9′W	X	127,139
Poolthorne Fm	N Lincs	TA0303	53°31·0′	0°26·4′W	FM	112
Pooltown	Highld	NH8153	57°33·4′	3°58·9′W	X	27
Pooltown	Somer	SS9837	51°7·6′	3°27·1′W	T	181
Pool Tree	Durham	NZ0828	54°39·1′	1°52·1′W	X	92
Pooly Fm	Norf	TL7596	52°32·3′	0°35·2′E	FM	143
Poor Common	Dorset	SY9795	50°45·5′	2°2·2′W	X	195
Poor Park	Essex	TL7132	51°57·8′	0°29·7′E	F	167
Poor Piece	Donc	SE6804	53°31·9′	0°58·0′W	X	111
Poors	Kent	TQ9570	51°24·0′	0°48·6′E	X	178
Poors Common	Hants	SZ2098	50°47·1′	1°42·6′W	X	195
Poor's Fen Fm	Cambs	TL5769	52°18·0′	0°18·6′E	FM	154
Poor's Field	Hill	TQ0889	51°35·6′	0°26·1′W	X	176
Poors Fm	Hants	SU6853	51°16·6′	1°1·1′W	FM	185,186
Poors Fm	Oxon	SU6486	51°34·4′	1°4·2′W	FM	175
Poors' Furze	W Berks	SU3579	51°30·8′	1°29·3′W	F	174
Poors Land	Cambs	TL2786	52°27·7′	0°7·4′W	X	142
Poor's Land	Herts	TL4022	51°53·0′	0°2·4′E	X	167
Poors Wood	Warw	SP2473	52°21·5′	1°38·5′W	F	139
Poorton Hill	Dorset	SY5297	50°46·5′	2°40·5′W	X	194
Poortown	I of M	SC2683	54°13·0′	4°39·7′W	X	95
Poor Wood	E Yorks	SE8250	53°56·6′	0°44·6′W	F	106
Pootings	Kent	TQ4549	51°13·5′	0°5·0′E	T	188
Pooty Pools	Essex	TL6206	51°44·0′	0°21·2′E	X	167
Popefield Fm	Herts	TL2007	51°45·2′	0°15·3′W	FM	166
Pope Hill	Pemb	SM9312	51°46·3′	4°59·6′W	T	157,158
Popeley Fields	Kirk	SE2125	53°43·5′	1°40·5′W	X	104
Popenhoe Ho	Norf	TF5008	52°39·2′	0°13·5′E	X	143
Pope's Fm	Herts	TL2507	51°45·1′	0°11·0′W	FM	166
Pope's Fm	Lancs	SD6537	53°49·9′	2°31·5′W	FM	102,103
Popes Green Fm	Suff	TM0039	52°1·0′	0°55·3′E	FM	155
Pope's Hall	Essex	TL8927	51°54·8′	0°45·3′E	X	168
Pope's Hall	Kent	TQ8949	51°12·8′	0°42·8′E	X	189
Pope's Hill	Glos	SO6814	51°49·7′	2°27·5′W	T	162
Pope's Hill	Northum	NY7389	55°11·9′	2°25·0′W	H	80
Pope's Ho	Worcs	SO8663	52°16·1′	2°11·9′W	X	150
Popesmill	Corn	SX2763	50°26·7′	4°25·8′W	X	201
Pope's Seat	Glos	SO9902	51°43·2′	2°0·5′W	X	163
Pope Street Fm	Kent	TR0751	51°13·5′	0°58·3′E	FM	179,189
Popeswood	Bracкn	SU8469	51°25·1′	0°47·1′W	T	175
Pope's Wood	Glos	SO8712	51°48·6′	2°10·9′W	F	162
Pope's Wood	W Berks	SU4474	51°28·0′	1°21·6′W	F	174
Popeswood Fm	E Susx	TQ5123	50°59·4′	0°9·5′E	FM	199
Pop Hall Fm	Lancs	SD4635	53°48·8′	2°48·8′W	FM	102
Popham	Devon	SS7032	51°4·6′	3°51·0′W	T	180
Popham	Hants	SU5543	51°11·2′	1°12·4′W	T	185
Popham Beacons	Hants	SU5243	51°11·3′	1°15·0′W	X	185
Popham Beacons (Tumuli)	Hants	SU5243	51°11·3′	1°15·0′W	A	185
Popham Court Fm	Hants	SU5543	51°11·2′	1°12·4′W	FM	185
Popham Cross	Devon	SS7032	51°4·6′	3°51·0′W	X	180
Popham's Eau	Norf	TF5000	52°34·9′	0°13·2′E	A	143
Pop Hill	V of Glam	ST1570	51°25·6′	3°13·0′W	X	171
Pophley's Wood	Bucks	SU7796	51°39·7′	0°52·8′W	F	165
Poplar	Essex	TL6316	51°49·4′	0°22·3′E	X	167
Poplar	T Ham	TQ3780	51°30·4′	0°1·2′W	T	177
Poplar 2000 Service Area	Ches	SJ6684	53°21·3′	2°30·2′W	X	109
Poplar Bank Fm	Lincs	TF0569	53°12·7′	0°25·3′W	FM	121
Poplar Cottage Fm	Shrops	SO6694	52°32·8′	2°29·7′W	FM	138
Poplar Fm	Bucks	SU9182	51°32·0′	0°40·9′W	FM	175
Poplar Fm	Cambs	TF3704	52°37·2′	0°1·8′E	FM	142,143
Poplar Fm	Cambs	TL4063	52°15·1′	0°3·5′E	FM	154
Poplar Fm	Cambs	TL4495	52°32·3′	0°7·8′E	FM	142,143
Poplar Fm	Ches	SJ6360	53°8·4′	2°32·8′W	FM	118
Poplar Fm	C of Bris	ST5379	51°30·7′	2°40·2′W	FM	172
Poplar Fm	Derby	SK4644	52°59·7′	1°18·5′W	FM	129
Poplar Fm	Essex	TL6527	51°55·2′	0°24·4′E	FM	167
Poplar Fm	E Yorks	TA0335	53°48·3′	0°25·7′W	FM	107
Poplar Fm	E Yorks	TA3028	53°44·2′	0°1·3′W	FM	107
Poplar Fm	Glos	SO7320	51°52·9′	2°23·1′W	FM	162
Poplar Fm	Kent	TR0228	51°1·2′	0°53·2′E	FM	189
Poplar Fm	Leic	SK4711	52°41·9′	1°17·9′W	FM	129
Poplar Fm	Lincs	SK9431	52°52·3′	0°35·8′W	FM	130
Poplar Fm	Lincs	TA3600	53°29·0′	0°3·4′E	FM	113
Poplar Fm	Lincs	TF1051	53°2·9′	0°21·1′W	FM	121
Poplar Fm	Lincs	TF1140	52°57·0′	0°20·5′W	FM	130
Poplar Fm	Lincs	TF1529	52°51·0′	0°17·1′W	FM	130
Poplar Fm	Lincs	TF1743	52°58·5′	0°15·0′W	FM	130
Poplar Fm	Lincs	TF1868	53°12·0′	0°13·6′W	FM	122
Poplar Fm	Lincs	TF2083	53°20·1′	0°11·5′W	FM	122
Poplar Fm	Lincs	TF2119	52°45·5′	0°12·0′W	FM	131
Poplar Fm	Lincs	TF2770	53°12·9′	0°5·5′W	FM	122
Poplar Fm	Lincs	TF4983	53°19·6′	0°16·1′E	FM	122
Poplar Fm	Lincs	TF5060	53°7·2′	0°14·9′E	FM	122
Poplar Fm	Lincs	TF5072	53°13·7′	0°15·2′E	FM	122
Poplar Fm	Lincs	TF5177	53°16·3′	0°16·3′E	FM	122
Poplar Fm	N Lincs	SE8114	53°37·2′	0°46·1′W	FM	112
Poplar Fm	Norf	TF9612	52°40·4′	0°54·4′E	FM	132
Poplar Fm	Norf	TL5197	52°33·2′	0°14·0′E	FM	143
Poplar Fm	Norf	TM0493	52°30·0′	1°0·7′E	FM	144
Poplar Fm	Norf	TM3398	52°32·0′	1°26·5′E	FM	134
Poplar Fm	Notts	SK7251	53°3·3′	0°55·1′W	FM	120
Poplar Fm	N Som	ST4462	51°21·5′	2°47·9′W	FM	172,182
Poplar Fm	N Yks	SE8677	54°11·1′	0°40·5′W	FM	101
Poplar Fm	Red & Cl	NZ5817	54°32·9′	1°5·8′W	FM	93
Poplar Fm	S Glos	ST7287	51°35·1′	2°23·9′W	FM	172
Poplar Fm	Somer	ST3554	51°17·1′	2°55·5′W	FM	182
Poplar Fm	Somer	ST6535	51°7·0′	2°29·6′W	FM	183
Poplar Fm	Staffs	SK0921	52°47·4′	1°51·6′W	FM	128
Poplar Fm	Suff	TL6680	52°23·8′	0°26·8′E	FM	143
Poplar Fm	Suff	TL6778	52°22·7′	0°27·6′E	FM	143
Poplar Fm	Suff	TL9366	52°15·7′	0°50·1′E	FM	155
Poplar Fm	Suff	TL9735	51°58·9′	0°52·5′E	FM	155
Poplar Fm	Suff	TM0059	52°11·8′	0°56·0′E	FM	155
Poplar Fm	Suff	TM0156	52°10·2′	0°56·8′E	FM	155
Poplar Fm	Suff	TM0767	52°16·0′	1°2·4′E	FM	155
Poplar Fm	Suff	TM0862	52°13·2′	1°3·1′E	FM	155
Poplar Fm	Suff	TM0966	52°15·4′	1°4·1′E	FM	155
Poplar Fm	Suff	TM1243	52°2·9′	1°5·9′E	FM	155,169
Poplar Fm	Suff	TM1557	52°10·4′	1°9·1′E	FM	156
Poplar Fm	Suff	TM1678	52°21·7′	1°10·7′E	FM	144,156
Poplar Fm	Suff	TM1755	52°9·3′	1°10·7′E	FM	156
Poplar Fm	Suff	TM1953	52°8·1′	1°12·4′E	FM	156
Poplar Fm	Suff	TM2169	52°16·7′	1°14·8′E	FM	156
Poplar Fm	Suff	TM2267	52°15·6′	1°15·6′E	FM	156
Poplar Fm	Suff	TM2563	52°13·4′	1°18·1′E	FM	156
Poplar Fm	Suff	TM3065	52°14·3′	1°22·5′E	FM	156
Poplar Fm	Suff	TM3140	52°0·8′	1°22·4′E	FM	169
Poplar Fm	Suff	TM3258	52°10·5′	1°24·0′E	FM	156
Poplar Fm	Suff	TM3278	52°21·3′	1°24·8′E	FM	156
Poplar Fm	Suff	TM3445	52°3·5′	1°25·2′E	FM	169
Poplar Fm	Suff	TM3772	52°17·9′	1°29·0′E	FM	156
Poplar Fm	Suff	TM4355	52°8·6′	1°33·5′E	FM	156
Poplar Fm	Suff	TM4471	52°17·2′	1°35·1′E	FM	156
Poplar Fm	Suff	TM5097	52°31·0′	1°41·5′E	FM	134
Poplar Fm	Warw	SP1974	52°22·1′	1°42·9′W	FM	139
Poplar Grove	Lincs	TF1667	53°11·5′	0°15·4′W	X	121
Poplar Grove	Lincs	TF4297	53°27·3′	0°8·7′E	T	113
Poplar Grove Fm	Ches	SJ5070	53°13·7′	2°44·5′W	FM	117
Poplar Grove Fm	Essex	TL8509	51°45·2′	0°41·2′E	FM	168
Poplar Grove Fm	Lancs	SD4644	53°53·6′	2°48·9′W	FM	102
Poplar Grove Fm	N Lincs	SE8304	53°31·8′	0°44·5′W	FM	112
Poplar Hall	Cambs	TL4861	52°13·9′	0°10·4′E	X	154
Poplarhall	Ches	SJ4073	53°15·3′	2°53·6′W	X	117
Poplar Hall	Essex	TM1829	51°55·2′	1°10·6′E	X	168,169
Poplar Hall	Kent	TQ9725	50°59·7′	0°48·8′E	X	189
Poplar Hall	Kent	TQ9963	51°20·1′	0°51·8′E	X	178
Poplar Hall	Suff	TM0446	52°4·7′	0°59·0′E	X	155
Poplar Hall	Suff	TM1661	52°12·5′	1°10·1′E	X	156
Poplar Hall Fm	Ches	SJ4860	53°8·3′	2°46·2′W	FM	117
Poplar Hill	N Yks	SE4074	54°9·9′	1°22·8′W	X	99
Poplar Ho	Kent	TR0130	51°2·3′	0°52·4′E	X	189
Poplar Ho	Lincs	TF4120	52°45·8′	0°5·8′E	X	131
Poplar House Fm	Cambs	TF3500	52°35·1′	0°0·0′W	FM	142
Poplar Lodge Fm	Lincs	TF5180	53°18·0′	0°16·4′E	FM	122
Poplar Lodge FM	Northnts	SP9273	52°21·1′	0°38·6′W	FM	141
Poplars	Herts	TL2623	51°53·7′	0°9·7′W	T	166
Poplars	Kent	TQ7042	51°9·3′	0°26·3′E	X	188
Poplars Barn	W Susx	SU9202	50°48·8′	0°41·3′W	X	197
Poplars Fm	Cambs	TF3803	52°36·7′	0°2·7′E	FM	142,143
Poplars Fm	Ches	SJ6448	53°1·9′	2°31·8′W	FM	118
Poplars Fm	Essex	TL5715	51°48·9′	0°17·1′E	FM	167
Poplars Fm	Essex	TL9403	51°41·8′	0°48·8′E	FM	168
Poplars Fm	E Yorks	SE6619	53°40·0′	0°59·7′W	FM	111
Poplars Fm	Leic	SP4198	52°34·9′	1°23·3′W	FM	140
Poplar's Fm	Leic	SP5782	52°26·2′	1°9·3′W	FM	140
Poplars Fm	Lincs	TF0868	53°12·1′	0°22·6′W	FM	121
Poplars Fm	Lincs	TF2349	53°1·7′	0°9·5′W	FM	131
Poplars Fm	Lincs	TF3357	53°5·8′	0°0·4′W	FM	122
Poplars Fm	Lincs	TF3729	52°50·7′	0°2·5′E	FM	131
Poplars Fm	N Lincs	SE7510	53°35·1′	0°51·6′W	FM	112
Poplars Fm	Norf	TG3020	52°43·9′	1°24·8′E	FM	133,134
Poplars Fm	Norf	TM2283	52°24·2′	1°16·2′E	FM	156
Poplars Fm	Northnts	SP9161	52°14·6′	0°39·6′W	FM	152
Poplars Fm	Northnts	SP9374	52°21·6′	0°37·7′W	FM	141
Poplars Fm	N Yks	SE3759	54°1·8′	1°25·7′W	FM	104
Poplars Fm	N Yks	SE5438	53°50·4′	1°10·3′W	FM	105
Poplars Fm	Oxon	SP3946	52°6·9′	1°25·4′W	FM	151
Poplars' Fm	Peterb	TF3201	52°35·7′	0°2·7′W	FM	142
Poplars Fm	Staffs	SK2211	52°42·0′	1°40·1′W	FM	128
Poplars Fm	Suff	TM3371	52°17·5′	1°25·4′E	FM	156
Poplars Fm	Thurr	TQ6382	51°31·0′	0°21·4′E	FM	177
Poplars Fm	Warw	SP2497	52°34·5′	1°38·4′W	FM	139
Poplars Fm	Worcs	SO9844	52°5·9′	2°1·4′W	FM	150
Poplars Fm	Worcs	SP0670	52°19·9′	1°54·3′W	FM	139
Poplars, The	Essex	TL4840	52°2·5′	0°9·9′E	X	154
Poplars, The	E Yorks	TA2623	53°41·5′	0°5·1′W	X	107,113
Poplars, The	Lincs	TF0582	53°19·7′	0°25·0′W	X	121
Poplars, The	Lincs	TF1087	53°22·3′	0°20·4′W	X	113,121
Poplars, The	Lincs	TF1367	53°11·5′	0°18·1′W	X	121
Poplars, The	Lincs	TF1672	53°14·2′	0°15·3′W	X	121
Poplars, The	Lincs	TF2193	53°25·4′	0°10·3′W	X	113
Poplars, The	Lincs	TF2518	52°44·9′	0°8·5′W	X	131
Poplars, The	Lincs	TF3458	53°6·4′	0°0·5′E	X	122
Poplars, The	Lincs	TF4088	53°22·4′	0°6·7′E	X	113,122
Poplars, The	Lincs	TF4195	53°26·2′	0°7·8′E	X	113
Poplars, The	Northnts	SP9078	52°23·8′	0°40·2′W	X	141
Poplars, The	N Yks	SE3087	54°16·9′	1°31·9′W	X	99
Poplars, The	N Yks	SE5462	54°3·3′	1°10·1′W	X	100
Poplars, The	Warw	SK2406	52°39·3′	1°38·3′W	X	139
Poplartree Br	Cambs	TL3196	52°33·0′	0°3·7′W	X	142
Poplar Tree Fm	Cambs	TF3608	52°39·4′	0°1·0′E	FM	142
Poplartree Fm	Cambs	TF4013	52°42·0′	0°4·7′E	FM	131,142,143
Poplartree Fm	Cambs	TF4514	52°42·5′	0°9·2′E	FM	131
Poplar Tree Fm	Cambs	TL3283	52°26·0′	0°3·1′W	FM	142
Poplartree Fm	Lincs	TF1939	52°56·3′	0°13·3′W	FM	130
Poplar Tree Fm	Lincs	TF3360	53°7·5′	0°0·3′W	FM	122
Poplar Tree Fm	Norf	TF5220	52°45·6′	0°15·6′E	FM	131
Popley	Hants	SU6454	51°17·1′	1°4·5′W	T	185
Popley Fields Ho	Hants	SU6354	51°17·1′	1°5·4′W	X	185
Popley's Gull	Cambs	TL3000	52°35·2′	0°4·5′W	X	142
Poplin Dub	Cumbr	NY4331	54°40·5′	2°52·6′W	X	90
Poppets Hill	Oxon	SU6799	51°41·4′	1°1·4′W	H	164,165
Poppets Hill Fm	Oxon	SU6699	51°41·4′	1°2·3′W	FM	164,165
Poppinghole Fm	E Susx	TQ7521	50°57·9′	0°29·9′E	FM	199
Popping Stone	Cumbr	NY6368	55°0·6′	2°34·3′W	X	86
Poppington Fm	Kent	TR0357	51°16·8′	0°55·0′E	FM	178,179
Poppin Ho	Essex	TL5308	51°45·2′	0°13·4′E	X	167
Poppit Sands	Pemb	SN1548	52°6·2′	4°41·7′W	X	145
Popples	Suff	TL9552	52°8·1′	0°51·4′E	A	155
Popple's Br	Devon	SX5954	50°22·4′	3°58·6′W	X	202
Poppletrees	Stir	NS8690	56°5·6′	3°49·5′W	X	58
Poppy Fm	Cumbr	SD5398	54°22·8′	2°43·0′W	FM	97
Poppy Hill Fm	Beds	TL1838	52°1·9′	0°16·4′W	FM	153
Poppy Hills	Brackn	SU8663	51°21·8′	0°45·5′W	X	175,186
Poppylot Fm	Norf	TL6692	52°30·3′	0°27·2′E	FM	143
Poppylot Fm	Norf	TM1095	52°31·0′	1°6·1′E	FM	144
Poppylots Fm	Norf	TF5306	52°38·0′	0°16·1′E	FM	143
Popton Point	Pemb	SM8903	51°41·4′	5°2·8′W	X	157,158
Porchbrook	Worcs	SO7270	52°19·9′	2°24·3′W	X	138
Porch Cott	Cumbr	NY6916	54°32·5′	2°28·3′W	X	91
Porchester	Notts	SK5942	52°58·6′	1°6·9′W	T	129
Porchester's Post	Somer	SS8233	51°5·3′	3°40·7′W	X	181
Porchfield	I of W	SZ4491	50°43·2′	1°22·2′W	T	196
Porch Fm	Heref	SO6324	51°55·0′	2°31·9′W	FM	162
Pordenack Point	Corn	SW3424	50°3·6′	5°42·6′W	X	203
Porin	Highld	NH3155	57°33·5′	4°49·0′W	X	26
Poringland	Norf	TG2602	52°34·4′	1°20·5′E	T	134
Porisken	E Ayr	NS4344	55°40·1′	4°29·3′W	X	70
Porkellis	Corn	SW6933	50°9·4′	5°13·7′W	T	203
Porkellis Moor	Corn	SW6832	50°8·8′	5°14·5′W	X	203
Porlock	Somer	SS8846	51°12·4′	3°35·8′W	T	181
Porlock Bay	Somer	SS8748	51°13·4′	3°36·7′W	W	181
Porlock Beach	Somer	SS8647	51°12·9′	3°37·5′W	X	181
Porlock Common	Somer	SS8445	51°11·8′	3°39·2′W	H	181
Porlockford	Somer	SS8647	51°12·9′	3°37·5′W	T	181
Porlock Hill	Somer	SS8746	51°12·4′	3°36·7′W	X	181
Porlock Weir	Somer	SS8647	51°12·9′	3°37·5′W	T	181
Porloe	Corn	SW8135	50°10·7′	5°3·7′W	X	204
Porridge Cairn	Scot Bord	NT1522	55°29·3′	3°20·3′W	H	72
Porridge Hall	Essex	TL6428	51°55·8′	0°23·5′E	X	167
Porridge Pot	Essex	TL7612	51°47·0′	0°33·5′E	X	167
Porsham	Devon	SX4862	50°26·5′	4°8·1′W	X	201
Port	Devon	SS7725	51°0·9′	3°44·8′W	X	180
Portabello Fm	Warw	SP2339	52°3·2′	1°39·5′W	FM	151
Port a' Bhàta	Arg & Bt	NM4238	56°28·1′	6°10·9′W	W	47,48
Port a' Bhàta	Arg & Bt	NR4095	56°4·9′	6°10·3′W	W	61
Portabhata	Highld	NM5757	56°38·8′	5°57·4′W	X	47
Port a' Bhàta	Highld	NM6872	56°47·2′	5°47·5′W	W	40
Port a' Bhàthaich	Highld	NM6183	56°52·9′	5°54·9′W	W	40
Port a'Bheachan	Arg & Bt	NM8102	56°9·9′	5°31·2′W	W	55
Port a' Bhearnaig	Arg & Bt	NM8431	56°25·6′	5°29·7′W	W	49
Port a' Bheòil Mhóir	Arg & Bt	NM5924	56°21·1′	5°53·6′W	W	48
Port a' Bhorrain	Arg & Bt	NR6536	55°33·9′	5°43·2′W	W	68
Port a' Bhuailtein	Arg & Bt	NR4197	56°6·0′	6°9·5′W	W	61
Port a'Bhuailteir	Arg & Bt	NR6881	55°58·2′	5°42·6′W	W	55,61
Port à Bhuitin	Arg & Bt	NR8638	56°29·4′	5°28·1′W	W	49
Porta Buidhe	N Ayr	NS0220	55°26·3′	5°7·4′W	W	69

Port a' Chaisteil	Arg & Bt	NM8026	56°22·8'	5°33·4'W	W	49
Port a'Chaisteil	Highld	NM8246	56°33·6'	5°32·4'W	W	49
Port a' Chait	Highld	NH9487	57°51·9'	3°46·7'W	W	21
Port a Chamais	Highld	NM5461	56°40·8'	6°0·5'W	W	47
Port a Chaoil	N Eil	NB2037	58°14·2'	6°45·8'W	W	8,13
Port a' Chaomhain	Arg & Bt	NM4424	56°20·6'	6°8·1'W	W	48
Port a' Chapuill	Arg & Bt	NR3890	56°2·1'	6°11·9'W	W	61
Port a' Chinn	Highld	NC7865	58°33·6'	4°5·3'W	W	10
Port a' Chlaidh	Arg & Bt	NM4538	56°28·2'	6°8·0'W	W	47,48
Portachoillan	Arg & Bt	NR7557	55°45·5'	5°34·7'W	X	62
Port a' Chotain	Arg & Bt	NR3978	55°55·7'	6°10·3'W	W	60,61
Port a'Chroinn	Arg & Bt	NM8026	56°22·8'	5°33·4'W	W	49
Port a'Chruidhe	Arg & Bt	NR9258	55°46·5'	5°18·6'W	W	62
Port a' Chùil	Highld	NG5900	57°2·0'	5°57·9'W	W	32,39
Port a' Churaidh	Arg & Bt	NR7064	55°49·1'	5°39·9'W	W	61,62
Portachur Point	N Ayr	NS1553	55°44·4'	4°56·4'W	X	63
Portacree	D & G	NX1143	54°45·0'	4°55·8'W	W	82
Port Adhar Steòrnabhaigh (Stornoway Aerodrome)	N Eil	NB4533	58°13·0'	6°20·0'W	X	8
Port Afon-fechan	Gwyn	SH8828	52°50·5'	3°39·4'W	X	124,125
Port a' Gharaidh	Arg & Bt	NR6347	55°39·8'	5°45·7'W	W	62
Port a' Ghàraidh	Highld	NG7917	57°11·7'	5°39·0'W	W	33
Port a' Gharbh Uillt	Highld	NM5970	56°45·8'	5°56·2'W	W	39,47
Port a' Gharbh Uillt	Highld	NM6070	56°45·8'	5°55·2'W	W	40
Port a' Ghearrain	Highld	NM9458	56°40·4'	5°21·3'W	W	49
Port a'Ghillie Ghlais	N Ayr	NS0020	55°26·2'	5°9·3'W	W	69
Port a' Ghleannain	Highld	NC0833	58°14·9'	5°15·8'W	W	15
Port a' Ghlinne	Arg & Bt	NM6621	56°19·7'	5°46·7'W	W	49
Port a' Ghoirtein Bhig	Arg & Bt	NM2624	56°20·0'	6°25·5'W	W	48
Portal	Ches	SJ5663	53°10·0'	2°39·1'W	X	117
Port Alasdair	N Eil	NB5560	58°27·8'	6°11·6'W	W	8
Port Alasdair Ruaidh	Arg & Bt	NR8452	55°43·1'	5°25·9'W	W	62,69
Porta Leacach	N Ayr	NS0421	55°26·9'	5°5·5'W	W	69
Port Allen	D & G	NX4741	54°44·7'	4°22·2'W	W	83
Port Allen	Pth & Kin	NO2521	56°22·8'	3°12·4'W	X	53,59
Port Allt a' Mhuilinn	Highld	NC8168	58°35·3'	4°2·3'W	W	10
Port Alltan na Bradhan	Highld	NC0426	58°11·0'	5°19·6'W	W	15
Port Alsaig	Arg & Bt	NR3147	55°38·8'	6°16·1'W	W	60
Portamaggie	D & G	NW9856	54°51·7'	5°8·4'W	W	82
Port a' Mhadaidh	Arg & Bt	NR9269	55°52·4'	5°19·1'W	W	62
Port a' Mhadaidh	N Eil	NF8432	57°16·4'	7°14·1'W	W	22
Port a' Mhiadair	Arg & Bt	NR8350	55°42·0'	5°26·8'W	W	62,69
Port a' Mhinisteir	Arg & Bt	NM6626	56°22·4'	5°46·9'W	W	49
Port a'Mhuilinn	Arg & Bt	NM7516	56°17·2'	5°37·7'W	W	55
Port a' Mhurain	Arg & Bt	NM1251	56°34·0'	6°40·9'W	W	46
Port an Aird Fhada	Arg & Bt	NM4524	56°20·6'	6°7·2'W	W	48
Port an Aiseig	N Eil	NG2095	57°51·7'	6°42·8'W	X	14
Port An Amaill	Highld	NG7492	57°51·9'	5°48·1'W	W	19
Port an Aoinidh Uir	Arg & Bt	NR5774	55°54·1'	5°52·8'W	W	61
Port an Aomaidh	Arg & Bt	NR6972	55°53·4'	5°41·2'W	W	61,62
Portandea	S Ayr	NX0475	55°2·1'	5°3·6'W	X	76
Port an Deora	Arg & Bt	NR7996	56°6·6'	5°32·8'W	W	55
Port an Dòbhrain	Arg & Bt	NN0434	56°27·7'	5°10·4'W	W	50
Port an Doichgil	Highld	NM6477	56°49·7'	5°51·6'W	W	40
Port an Doire Dharaich	Arg & Bt	NR5976	55°55·3'	5°51·0'W	W	61
Port an Dreadhain	Arg & Bt	NM8241	56°30·9'	5°32·2'W	W	49
Port an Droighinn	Arg & Bt	NM7000	56°8·5'	5°41·7'W	W	55,61
Port an Droighionn	Highld	NM5570	56°45·7'	6°0·1'W	X	39,47
Port an Dùin	Arg & Bt	NR6350	55°41·4'	5°45·8'W	W	62
Port an Duine	Arg & Bt	NM8838	56°29·4'	5°26·2'W	W	49
Port an Duine Mhairbh	Arg & Bt	NM2624	56°20·0'	6°25·5'W	W	48
Port an Dùnain	Arg & Bt	NR8672	55°53·9'	5°24·9'W	W	62
Port an Eag-uillt	Arg & Bt	NM6906	56°11·7'	5°43·0'W	W	55
Port an Eas	Arg & Bt	NR2840	55°34·9'	6°18·5'W	W	60
Port an Eas	Arg & Bt	NR3342	55°36·2'	6°13·9'W	W	60
Port an Eilean Mhóir	Highld	NM5471	56°46·2'	6°1·1'W	W	39,47
Port an Eilein	Arg & Bt	NS0176	55°56·4'	5°10·7'W	X	63
Port-an-eilein	Highld	ND0559	58°30·8'	3°37·4'W	X	11,12
Port an-eorna	Highld	NG7731	57°19·2'	5°41·8'W	T	24
Port an Fhasgaidh	Arg & Bt	NM3235	56°26·1'	6°20·4'W	W	46,47,48
Port an Fheadairigaig	Highld	NC6663	58°32·3'	4°17·6'W	W	10
Port an Fhearainn	Highld	NG6159	57°33·7'	5°59·3'W	W	24
Port an Fhir-bhréige	Arg & Bt	NM2621	56°18·4'	6°25·4'W	W	48
Portankill	D & G	NX1432	54°39·2'	4°52·6'W	W	82
Port an Ladhair	Arg & Bt	NR1952	55°41·1'	6°27·8'W	W	60
Port an Lagaidh	Highld	NG8157	57°33·3'	5°39·2'W	W	24
Port an Lionaidh	Arg & Bt	NR7699	56°8·1'	5°35·9'W	W	55
Port an Lochain	Arg & Bt	NS2189	56°3·9'	4°52·1'W	W	56
Port an Lodain	N Eil	NF7009	57°3·5'	7°26·2'W	W	31
Port an Luig Mhóir	Highld	NG5212	57°8·2'	6°5·5'W	W	32
Port Ann	Arg & Bt	NR9086	56°1·5'	5°21·8'W	T	55
Port Ann	Arg & Bt	NR9086	56°1·5'	5°21·8'W	W	55
Port an Obain	Arg & Bt	NR3994	56°4·3'	6°11·2'W	W	61
Port an Obain	Arg & Bt	NR4099	56°7·0'	6°10·5'W	W	61
Port an Righ	Highld	NH8573	57°44·2'	3°55·4'W	W	21
Port an Ròin	Arg & Bt	NM3836	56°26·9'	6°14·6'W	W	47,48
Port an Ròin	Arg & Bt	NM4335	56°26·5'	6°9·7'W	W	47,48
Port an Sgadain	Arg & Bt	NR7084	55°59·9'	5°40·9'W	W	55,61
Port an Sgiathain	Arg & Bt	NR6547	55°39·8'	5°43·8'W	W	62
Port an Sgriodain	Highld	NM6374	56°48·1'	5°52·5'W	W	40
Port an Tairbh	Highld	NC0524	58°10·0'	5°18·4'W	W	15
Port an Tairbh	Highld	NG7911	57°8·5'	5°38·7'W	W	33
Port an Teampuill	Highld	NG6154	57°31·1'	5°59·0'W	W	24
Port an Tighe Mhóir	Arg & Bt	NR3998	56°6·5'	6°11·4'W	W	61
Port an Tiobairt	Arg & Bt	NR7099	56°8·0'	5°41·6'W	W	55,61
Port an Tobair	Arg & Bt	NR2855	55°43·0'	6°19·4'W	W	60
Port an Tobire	Arg & Bt	NM5645	56°32·3'	5°57·7'W	W	47,48
Port an t-Sailainn	Arg & Bt	NR6972	55°53·4'	5°41·2'W	W	61,62
Port an t-Salainn	Arg & Bt	NM4939	56°28·8'	6°4·1'W	W	47,48
Port an t-Salainn	Arg & Bt	NM7708	56°13·0'	5°35·4'W	W	55
Port an t-Sasunnaich	Arg & Bt	NM7430	56°24·8'	5°39·4'W	W	49
Port an t-Slaoichain	Arg & Bt	NM3918	56°17·2'	6°12·6'W	W	48
Port an t-Sluic	Arg & Bt	NM6542	56°30·9'	5°48·8'W	W	49
Port an t-Sluichd	Highld	NM6981	56°52·0'	5°47·0'W	W	40
Port an t-Sruthain	Arg & Bt	NM3844	56°31·2'	6°15·1'W	W	47,48
Port an t-Sruthain	Arg & Bt	NR3878	55°55·7'	6°11·2'W	W	60,61
Port an t-Strathain	Highld	NC6463	58°32·3'	4°19·7'W	W	10
Port an t-Struthain	Arg & Bt	NM8126	56°22·8'	5°32·4'W	W	49
Port an Uillt Ruaidh	Highld	NC8367	58°34·8'	4°0·3'W	W	10
Port an Uisge	Arg & Bt	NR2254	55°42·2'	6°25·1'W	W	60
Port Appin	Arg & Bt	NM9045	56°33·3'	5°24·6'W	T	49
Port Araraibhne	Arg & Bt	NR4298	56°6·6'	6°8·5'W	W	61
Port Arnoil	N Eil	NB2949	58°21·0'	6°37·5'W	W	8
Port Asabuis	Arg & Bt	NR3141	55°35·6'	6°15·7'W	W	60
Portash	Wilts	ST9631	51°4·9'	2°3·0'W	T	184
Port Askaig	Arg & Bt	NR4369	55°51·0'	6°5·9'W	T	60,61
Port Aslaig	Highld	NG7717	57°11·6'	5°41·0'W	W	33
Portavaddie	D & G	NW9855	54°51·2'	5°8·4'W	W	82
Portavadie	Arg & Bt	NR9369	55°52·4'	5°18·1'W	T	62
Portayew	D & G	NX0350	54°48·6'	5°3·5'W	W	82
Portayew Burn	D & G	NX0450	54°48·6'	5°2·6'W	W	82
Port Balure	Arg & Bt	NM8137	56°28·7'	5°32·9'W	W	49
Port Bàn	Arg & Bt	NM0947	56°31·8'	6°43·5'W	W	46
Port Bàn	Arg & Bt	NR2067	55°49·2'	6°27·8'W	W	60
Port Bàn	Arg & Bt	NR3797	56°5·9'	6°13·3'W	W	61
Port Bàn	Arg & Bt	NR6451	55°42·0'	5°44·9'W	W	62
Port Bàn	Arg & Bt	NR6973	55°53·9'	5°41·3'W	W	61,62
Port Bàn	Arg & Bt	NR7065	55°49·7'	5°39·9'W	W	61,62
Port Bàn	Highld	NM5170	56°45·6'	6°4·0'W	W	39,47
Port Bàn	Highld	NM6471	56°46·5'	5°51·3'W	W	40
Port Bàn	Highld	NM6488	56°55·7'	5°52·3'W	W	40
Port Bàn Mhic-a-phi	Arg & Bt	NR6995	56°5·8'	5°42·4'W	W	55,61
Port Bannatyne	Arg & Bt	NS0867	55°51·7'	5°3·6'W	T	63
Port Bàta na Luinge	Arg & Bt	NM4141	56°29·7'	6°12·0'W	W	47,48
Port Beag	Highld	NG3237	57°20·9'	6°26·9'W	W	23,32
Port Beag	N Eil	NB5446	58°20·3'	6°11·7'W	W	8
Port Bealach nan Gall	Arg & Bt	NR7185	56°0·5'	5°40·0'W	W	55
Port Beg	D & G	NW9563	54°55·4'	5°11·5'W	W	82
Port Beul-mhóir	Arg & Bt	NM2522	56°18·9'	6°26·4'W	W	48
Port Bharrapol	Arg & Bt	NL9342	56°28·5'	6°58·7'W	W	46
Port Bheathain	Arg & Bt	NM4018	56°17·3'	6°11·6'W	W	48
Port Brae	Fife	NT2891	56°6·6'	3°9·0'W	T	59
Port Bridge	Devon	SX8557	50°24·3'	3°36·7'W	T	202
Port Buckie	Highld	NH9387	57°51·8'	3°47·7'W	W	21
Port Bun a' Ghlinne	N Eil	NB5244	58°19·1'	6°13·6'W	W	8
Port Bun Aibhne	Arg & Bt	NR2068	55°49·7'	6°27·8'W	W	60
Port Burg	Arg & Bt	NM3845	56°31·7'	6°15·2'W	W	47,48
Portbury	N Som	ST4975	51°28·5'	2°43·7'W	T	172
Portbury Ho	N Som	ST4069	51°25·2'	2°51·4'W	X	171,172,182
Portbury Wharf	N Som	ST4876	51°29·1'	2°44·5'W	X	171,172
Port Cam	Highld	NG7631	57°19·1'	5°42·8'W	W	24
Port Caol	Arg & Bt	NM7805	56°11·4'	5°34·2'W	W	55
Port Caol	Arg & Bt	NR2053	55°41·6'	6°26·9'W	W	60
Port Carlisle	Cumbr	NY2462	54°57·1'	3°10·8'W	T	85
Port Carraig Sgàirn	Arg & Bt	NR2271	55°51·4'	6°26·1'W	W	60
Port Castle Bay	D & G	NX4235	54°41·4'	4°26·7'W	W	83
Port Ceann a' Gharraidh	Arg & Bt	NR4298	56°6·6'	6°8·5'W	W	61
Port Ceann da Aoineadh	Arg & Bt	NM6122	56°20·1'	5°51·6'W	W	49
Port Chaligaig	Highld	NC1859	58°29·1'	5°6·8'W	W	9
Port Challtuinn	Arg & Bt	NM8039	56°29·8'	5°34·0'W	W	49
Port Chamuill	Highld	NC4360	58°30·3'	4°41·2'W	W	9
Port Charlotte	Arg & Bt	NR2558	55°44·5'	6°22·5'W	T	60
Portchester	Hants	SU6105	50°50·7'	1°7·6'W	T	196
Portchester Castle	Hants	SU6204	50°50·2'	1°6·8'W	A	196
Portchester Castle (Roman Fort)	Hants	SU6204	50°50·2'	1°6·8'W	R	196
Port Chicheamaig	Arg & Bt	NM3736	56°26·8'	6°15·6'W	W	47,48
Port Chill Bhraonain	Arg & Bt	NM4458	56°38·9'	6°10·1'W	W	47
Port Chlacha Dubha	Arg & Bt	NM2725	56°20·6'	6°24·6'W	W	48
Port Chlach nan Tonn	Highld	NM6559	56°40·1'	5°49·7'W	W	49
Port Chreadhain	Highld	NM4080	56°50·6'	6°15·4'W	W	39
Port Chreag Fada	Arg & Bt	NR2355	55°42·8'	6°24·2'W	W	60
Port Chubaird	Arg & Bt	NR3342	55°36·2'	6°13·9'W	W	60
Portchullin	Highld	NG8434	57°21·0'	5°35·0'W	X	24
Port Chunn Nèill	Arg & Bt	NM0850	56°33·3'	6°44·7'W	W	46
Port Cill Maluaig	Arg & Bt	NR7270	55°52·4'	5°38·2'W	W	62
Portclair	Highld	NH4113	57°11·1'	4°37·4'W	X	34
Portclair Burn	Highld	NH4014	57°11·6'	4°38·4'W	W	34
Portclair Forest	Highld	NH3914	57°11·6'	4°39·4'W	X	34
Port Clarence	Stock on T	NZ4921	54°35·2'	1°14·1'W	T	93
Portclew	Pemb	SS0198	51°39·0'	4°52·2'W	X	158
Port Corbert	Arg & Bt	NR6528	55°29·6'	5°42·8'W	W	68
Port Cornaa	I of M	SC4787	54°15·6'	4°20·5'W	W	95
Port Cròm	Arg & Bt	NR6529	55°30·2'	5°42·8'W	W	68
Port Dearg	N Ayr	NS0320	55°26·3'	5°6·4'W	W	69
Port Dinorwic or Y Felinheli	Gwyn	SH5267	53°11·0'	4°12·5'W	T	114,115
Port Doir'a' Chrorain	Arg & Bt	NR5876	55°55·2'	5°52·0'W	W	61
Port Domhnuill Chruinn	Arg & Bt	NR3676	55°54·5'	6°13·0'W	W	60,61
Port Donain	Arg & Bt	NM7329	56°24·2'	5°40·3'W	W	49
Port Donnel	D & G	NX8453	54°51·8'	3°48·0'W	W	84
Port Dornach	Arg & Bt	NS0853	55°44·2'	5°3·1'W	W	63
Portdown Bay	D & G	NX0933	54°39·6'	4°57·3'W	W	82
Port Driseach	Arg & Bt	NR9873	55°54·7'	5°13·5'W	X	62
Port Dubh	Arg & Bt	NM7926	56°22·7'	5°34·3'W	W	49
Port Dundas	C of Glas	NS5966	55°52·3'	4°14·8'W	T	64
Port Duntulm	Highld	NG4074	57°41·1'	6°21·3'W	W	23
Porteath	Corn	SW9679	50°34·7'	4°52·5'W	T	200
Port-e-chee	I of M	SC3677	54°10·0'	4°30·3'W	X	95
Port Edgar	C of Edin	NT1178	55°59·5'	3°25·2'W	T	65
Porte Fm	Devon	SS6342	51°9·9'	3°57·2'W	FM	180
Port Eisgein	N Eil	NG0383	57°44·6'	6°59·0'W	X	18
Port Eliot Ho	Corn	SX3657	50°23·6'	4°18·1'W	A	201
Port Ellen	Arg & Bt	NR3645	55°37·9'	6°11·2'W	T	60
Port Ellister	Arg & Bt	NR1852	55°41·0'	6°28·8'W	W	60
Port Elphinstone	Aberd	NJ7720	57°16·5'	2°22·4'W	T	38
Portels Fm	Leic	SK7108	52°40·1'	0°56·6'W	FM	141
Portencalzie	D & G	NX0271	54°59·9'	5°5·3'W	X	76,82
Portencorkrie	D & G	NX0835	54°40·7'	4°58·3'W	W	82
Portencross	N Ayr	NS1748	55°41·7'	4°54·3'W	T	63
Portend	Stir	NN5701	56°11·1'	4°17·8'W	X	57
Porter Clough	Sheff	SK2884	53°21·4'	1°34·3'W	X	110
Porterfield	Renf	NS4966	55°52·1'	4°24·3'W	T	64
Porterhall	S Lanak	NS7936	55°36·4'	3°54·8'W	X	71
Port Erin	I of M	SC1969	54°5·4'	4°45·6'W	T	95
Port Erin Bay	I of M	SC1969	54°5·4'	4°45·6'W	W	95
Porter Oaks	Notts	SK5775	53°16·4'	1°8·3'W	F	120
Port Erradale	Highld	NG7381	57°45·9'	5°48·5'W	W	19
Port Erroll	Aberd	NK0936	57°25·1'	1°50·6'W	T	30
Porters	Essex	TL6016	51°49·4'	0°19·7'E	X	167
Porter's End	Herts	TL1617	51°50·6'	0°18·6'W	T	166
Porters Fen Corner	Norf	TF5909	52°39·6'	0°21·5'E	X	143
Porter's Fm	Essex	TL8319	51°50·6'	0°39·8'E	FM	168
Porters Fm	Hants	SU2715	50°56·3'	1°36·6'W	FM	184
Porter's Fm	Lincs	SK9622	52°47·5'	0°34·2'W	FM	130
Porters Fm	Lincs	TF2015	52°43·4'	0°13·0'W	FM	131
Porter's Fm	Staffs	SJ9259	53°7·9'	2°6·8'W	FM	118
Porters Fm	Suff	TM0371	52°18·2'	0°59·1'E	FM	144,155
Porter's Fm	Suff	TM5180	52°21·9'	1°41·6'E	FM	156
Porter's Hall	Essex	TL6723	51°53·1'	0°26·0'E	A	167
Portersheath Fm	Ches	SJ4363	53°9·9'	2°50·8'W	FM	117
Porter's Hill	Ches	SJ5848	53°1·9'	2°37·2'W	X	117
Porter's Hill	Staffs	SK0821	52°47·4'	1°52·5'W	X	128
Porter's Hill Fm	Worcs	SO8660	52°14·5'	2°11·9'W	FM	150
Porterside	W Loth	NT0176	55°58·3'	3°34·7'W	X	65
Porter's Lodge Fm	Lincs	SK9519	52°45·8'	0°35·1'W	FM	130
Porter's Sluice	Lincs	TF4199	53°28·4'	0°7·9'E	X	113
Porterstown	Aberd	NJ5564	57°40·1'	2°44·8'W	X	29
Porterstown	D & G	NX8791	55°12·3'	3°46·1'W	X	78
Porterswood Fm	Northnts	SP6945	52°6·2'	0°59·2'W	FM	152
Porter, The or Little Don River	Sheff	SK1899	53°29·5'	1°43·3'W	W	110
Portesham	Dorset	SY6085	50°40·0'	2°33·6'W	T	194
Portesham Fm	Dorset	SY6186	50°40·6'	2°32·7'W	FM	194
Portesham Hill	Dorset	SY6086	50°40·6'	2°33·6'W	X	194
Portessie	Moray	NJ4466	57°41·1'	2°55·9'W	T	28
Port e Vullen	I of M	SC4792	54°18·3'	4°20·7'W	T	95
Port-Eynon	Swan	SS4685	51°32·8'	4°12·9'W	T	159
Port-Eynon Bay	Swan	SS4884	51°32·3'	4°11·1'W	W	159
Port-Eynon Point	Swan	SS4784	51°32·3'	4°12·0'W	X	159
Port Fada	Arg & Bt	NL9848	56°31·9'	6°54·3'W	W	46
Port Fada	Arg & Bt	NR8554	55°44·2'	5°25·0'W	W	62
Port Faoileann a' Chlachanaich	Arg & Bt	NM3616	56°16·0'	6°15·4'W	W	48
Portfield	Arg & Bt	NM7126	56°22·5'	5°42·1'W	X	49
Portfield	Lancs	SD7435	53°48·9'	2°23·3'W	X	103
Portfield	Somer	ST4026	51°2·0'	2°51·0'W	T	193
Portfield	W Susx	SU8705	50°50·5'	0°45·5'W	T	197
Portfield Gate	Pemb	SM9215	51°47·9'	5°0·6'W	T	157,158
Portfields	Staffs	SK0623	52°48·5'	1°54·3'W	X	128
Port Fm	Kent	TR2262	51°19·0'	1°11·5'E	FM	179
Port Fm	Wilts	SU1393	51°38·4'	1°48·3'W	FM	163,173
Portford Fm	Ches	SJ7172	53°14·9'	2°25·7'W	FM	118
Port Fròige	Arg & Bt	NR1755	55°42·6'	6°29·9'W	W	60
Port Garbh	Highld	NM4165	56°42·6'	6°13·5'W	X	47
Port Gart an Fhithrich	Arg & Bt	NM3325	56°20·8'	6°18·8'W	W	48
Portgate	Devon	SX4185	50°38·8'	4°14·6'W	X	201
Portgate	Northum	NY8455	54°53·6'	2°14·5'W	X	86,87
Port Gate	Northum	NY9868	55°0·6'	2°1·4'W	X	87
Portgate	Northum	NY9868	55°0·6'	2°1·4'W	X	87
Port Gaverne	Corn	SX0080	50°35·4'	4°49·2'W	T	200
Port Gavillan	D & G	NW9670	54°59·2'	5°10·9'W	W	76,82
Port Geiraha	N Eil	NB5350	58°22·4'	6°13·0'W	W	8
Port Ghabhar	Arg & Bt	NR9268	55°51·9'	5°19·0'W	W	62
Port Gill	D & G	NX0743	54°44·9'	4°59·5'W	W	82
Portgiskey	Corn	SX0146	50°17·1'	4°47·2'W	X	204
Port Glas	Arg & Bt	NS0166	55°51·0'	5°10·3'W	W	63
Port Glasgow	Inverc	NS3274	55°56·0'	4°40·9'W	T	63
Port Gleann na Gaoidh	Arg & Bt	NR2153	55°41·7'	6°26·0'W	W	60
Port Gobhlaig	Highld	NG4375	57°41·7'	6°18·3'W	W	23
Port Goirtean Iar	Arg & Bt	NM2621	56°18·4'	6°25·4'W	W	48
Portgordon	Moray	NJ3964	57°40·0'	3°0·9'W	T	28
Portgower	Highld	ND0013	58°5·9'	3°41·3'W	T	17
Port Grenaugh	I of M	SC3170	54°6·1'	4°34·7'W	W	95
Port Griogaspail	N Eil	NB2214	58°2·0'	6°42·1'W	W	13,14
Port Groudle	I of M	SC4278	54°10·7'	4°24·8'W	W	95
Porth	Corn	SW8362	50°25·3'	5°2·9'W	T	200
Porth	Denb	SJ0459	53°7·4'	3°25·7'W	X	116
Porth	Powys	SO0673	52°21·1'	3°22·4'W	X	136,147
Porth	Rho Cyn Taf	ST0291	51°36·8'	3°24·5'W	T	170
Porthaethwy or Menai Bridge	I of Angl	SH5572	53°13·8'	4°9·9'W	T	114,115
Porthallack	Corn	SW7826	50°5·8'	5°5·9'W	X	204
Porthallow	Corn	SX2251	50°20·2'	4°29·7'W	T	201
Porth Ham	Glos	SO8119	51°52·4'	2°16·2'W	X	162
Port Haunn	Arg & Bt	NM3347	56°32·6'	6°20·2'W	W	47,48
Port Haven	Fife	NT1884	56°2·8'	3°18·5'W	W	65,66
Porth Bach	Gwyn	SH3226	52°48·6'	4°29·2'W	W	123
Porthbean Beach	Corn	SW8836	50°11·4'	4°57·8'W	X	204
Porthbear Beach	Corn	SW8631	50°8·7'	4°59·3'W	X	204
Porth Cadlan	Gwyn	SH2026	52°48·3'	4°39·8'W	W	123
Porth-cadwaladr	I of Angl	SH3666	53°10·2'	4°26·8'W	W	114
Porthcasseg	Monm	ST5298	51°41·0'	2°41·3'W	X	162
Porthcawl	Brig	SS8277	51°29·0'	3°41·6'W	T	170
Porthcawl Point	Brig	SS8176	51°28·5'	3°42·4'W	X	170
Porth Ceiriad	Gwyn	SH3124	52°47·5'	4°30·0'W	W	123
Porth China	I of Angl	SH3368	53°11·2'	4°29·6'W	W	114
Porth Clais	Pemb	SM7423	51°51·8'	5°16·6'W	W	157
Porth clais	Pemb	SM7424	51°52·4'	5°16·6'W	X	157
Porth Cloch	Gwyn	SH1625	52°47·7'	4°43·3'W	W	123
Porthcollum	Corn	SW5533	50°9·0'	5°25·4'W	X	203
Porth Colmon	Gwyn	SH1934	52°52·6'	4°41·0'W	T	123
Porth Colmon	Gwyn	SH1934	52°52·6'	4°41·0'W	W	123
Porth Conger	I Scilly	SV8808	49°53·7'	6°20·3'W	W	203
Porthcothan	Corn	SW8572	50°30·7'	5°1·6'W	T	200
Porthcothan Bay	Corn	SW8572	50°30·7'	5°1·6'W	W	200
Porth Cressa	I Scilly	SV9009	49°54·3'	6°18·7'W	W	203
Porthcurnick Beach	Corn	SW8735	50°10·8'	4°58·6'W	X	204
Porth Curno	Corn	SW3822	50°2·7'	5°39·2'W	W	203
Porthcurno	Corn	SW3822	50°2·7'	5°39·2'W	T	203
Porth Cwyfan	I of Angl	SH3368	53°11·2'	4°29·6'W	W	114
Porth Cynfor or Hell's Mouth	I of Angl	SH3995	53°25·9'	4°25·0'W	W	114
Porth Dafarch	I of Angl	SH2379	53°17·0'	4°38·9'W	W	114
Porth-Dafen	Carm	SN5403	51°42·6'	4°6·4'W	X	159
Porth Diana	I of Angl	SH2578	53°16·5'	4°37·1'W	W	114
Porth Dinllaen	Gwyn	SH2741	52°56·6'	4°34·1'W	X	123
Porth Dinllaen	Gwyn	SH2841	52°56·6'	4°33·2'W	W	123
Porth Dinllaen Fm	Gwyn	SH2739	52°55·5'	4°34·0'W	FM	123
Porth Dwfn	Pemb	SM8032	51°56·8'	5°11·7'W	W	157

Porth Egr	Pemb	SM8032	51°56·8′	5°11·7′W	W	157
Portheiddy	Pemb	SM8031	51°56·3′	5°11·6′W	T	157
Porth Eilian	I of Angl	SH4793	53°24·9′	4°17·7′W	W	114
Port Henderson	Highld	NG7573	57°41·7′	5°46·1′W	T	19
Portheras Cove	Corn	SW3835	50°9·7′	5°39·7′W	W	203
Portheras Fm	Corn	SW3835	50°9·7′	5°39·7′W	FM	203
Porth Felen	Gwyn	SH1424	52°47·1′	4°45·1′W	W	123
Porth Ferin	Gwyn	SH1732	52°51·5′	4°42·7′W	W	123
Porth Ffynnon	Pemb	SM8032	51°56·8′	5°11·7′W	W	157
Porth Fm	Corn	SW8632	50°9·2′	4°59·4′W	FM	204
Porthgain	Pemb	SM8132	51°56·8′	5°10·8′W	T	157
Porth-gain	Pemb	SM8132	51°56·8′	5°10·8′W	W	157
Porth Glastwr	Pemb	SM8634	51°58·0′	5°6·5′W	W	157
Porthglaze Cove	Corn	SW4438	50°11·4′	5°34·8′W	W	203
Porthguarnon	Corn	SW4122	50°2·7′	5°36·7′W	W	203
Porthgwarra	Corn	SW3721	50°2·1′	5°40·0′W	T	203
Porthgwidden	Corn	SW8237	50°11·8′	5°2·9′W	X	204
Porth Gwylan	Gwyn	SH2136	52°53·7′	4°39·3′W	W	123
Porth-gwyn	Pemb	SM7428	51°54·5′	5°16·8′W	W	157
Porthgwyn	Powys	SO0632	51°59·0′	3°21·7′W	X	160
Porthhallow	Corn	SW7923	50°4·2′	5°4·9′W	T	204
Porth Hellick Point	I Scilly	SV9210	49°54·9′	6°17·1′W	X	203
Porth Helygen	I of Angl	SH4990	53°23·4′	4°15·8′W	W	114
Porth Iago	Gwyn	SH1631	52°51·0′	4°43·6′W	W	123
Port Hill	Leic	SP5897	52°34·3′	1°8·2′W	X	140
Port Hill	Leic	SP7893	52°32·0′	0°50·6′W	X	141
Port Hill	Oxon	SU6887	51°34·9′	1°0·7′W	T	175
Port Hill	Scot Bord	NT1719	55°27·7′	3°18·3′W	X	79
Porthill	Shrops	SJ4712	52°42·4′	2°46·7′W	T	126
Porthill	Staffs	SJ8548	53°2·0′	2°13·0′W	T	118
Port Hill Fm	Leic	SP5094	52°32·7′	1°15·4′W	FM	140
Porthilly	Corn	SW9375	50°32·5′	4°54·9′W	T	200
Porthilly Cove	Corn	SW9375	50°32·5′	4°54·9′W	W	200
Porth Joke	Corn	SW7760	50°24·1′	5°7·9′W	W	200
Porth Kea	Corn	SW8242	50°14·5′	5°3·1′W	T	204
Porthkerris Point	Corn	SW8023	50°4·2′	5°4·1′W	X	204
Porthkerry	V of Glam	ST0866	51°23·4′	3°18·9′W	T	170
Porthkerry Country Park	V of Glam	ST0967	51°23·9′	3°18·1′W	X	171
Porthkerry Country Park	V of Glam	ST0967	51°23·9′	3°18·1′W	X	171
Porth Kidney Sands	Corn	SW5438	50°11·7′	5°26·4′W	X	203
Porth Ledden	Corn	SW3532	50°8·0′	5°42·1′W	X	203
Porthleven	Corn	SW6225	50°4·9′	5°19·2′W	T	203
Porthleven Sands	Corn	SW6324	50°4·4′	5°18·4′W	X	203
Porth Llanllawen	Gwyn	SH1426	52°48·2′	4°45·2′W	W	123
Porth Llanlleiana	I of Angl	SH3895	53°25·9′	4°25·9′W	W	114
Porthllechog or Bull Bay	I of Angl	SH4294	53°25·4′	4°22·3′W	T	114
Porth Llechog or Bull Bay	I of Angl	SH4393	53°24·9′	4°21·3′W	W	114
Porth Lleuog	Pemb	SM7327	51°54·0′	5°17·6′W	W	157
Porthllisky	Pemb	SM7323	51°51·8′	5°17·4′W	X	157
Porth Loe	Corn	SW3621	50°2·1′	5°40·8′W	W	203
Porthloo	I Scilly	SV9011	49°55·4′	6°18·8′W	T	203
Porthluney Cove	Corn	SW9741	50°14·3′	4°50·4′W	W	204
Porthlysgi Bay	Pemb	SM7223	51°51·8′	5°18·3′W	W	157
Porthmadog	Gwyn	SH5638	52°55·5′	4°8·1′W	T	124
Porth Maenmelyn	Pemb	SM8839	52°0·8′	5°5·0′W	W	157
Porth-mawr	Cered	SN5267	52°17·1′	4°9·8′W	X	135
Porth-mawr	Pemb	SM7327	51°54·0′	5°17·6′W	W	157
Porth Mawr	Powys	SO2118	51°51·5′	3°8·4′W	A	161
Porth Mear	Corn	SW8471	50°30·2′	5°2·4′W	W	200
Porthmelgan	Pemb	SM7227	51°53·9′	5°18·5′W	W	157
Porthmellin Head	Corn	SW8632	50°9·2′	4°59·4′W	X	204
Porthmeor	Corn	SW4337	50°10·9′	5°35·6′W	T	203
Porthmeor Beach	Corn	SW5140	50°12·7′	5°29·0′W	X	203
Porthmeor Cove	Corn	SW4237	50°10·8′	5°36·5′W	W	203
Porthmeor Point	Corn	SW4237	50°10·8′	5°36·5′W	X	203
Porth Meudwy	Gwyn	SH1625	52°47·7′	4°43·3′W	W	123
Porthminster Point	Corn	SW5239	50°12·2′	5°28·2′W	X	203
Porthmissen	Corn	SW8976	50°33·0′	4°58·3′W	X	200
Porthmissen Bridge	Corn	SW8976	50°33·0′	4°58·3′W	X	200
Porthmoina Cove	Corn	SW4136	50°10·3′	5°37·3′W	W	203
Porth Morran	I Scilly	SV9217	49°58·7′	6°17·4′W	W	203
Porthmynawyd	Pemb	SM8222	51°51·5′	5°9·6′W	W	157
Porth Namarch	I of Angl	SH2283	53°19·1′	4°39·9′W	W	114
Porth Nanven	Corn	SW3530	50°6·9′	5°42·0′W	X	203
Porth Navas	Corn	SW7527	50°6·3′	5°8·4′W	T	204
Porth Nefyn	Gwyn	SH2940	52°56·1′	4°32·3′W	W	123
Porth Neigwl or Hell's Mouth	Gwyn	SH2626	52°48·5′	4°34·5′W	W	123
Porth Nobla	I of Angl	SH3271	53°12·8′	4°30·6′W	W	114
Porth Oer	Gwyn	SH1630	52°50·4′	4°43·5′W	W	123
Porthole Fm	W Susx	SZ8495	50°45·1′	0°48·2′W	FM	197
Porthollan	Corn	SW9541	50°14·2′	4°52·1′W	T	204
Port Holme	Cambs	TL2370	52°19·1′	0°11·3′W	X	153
Porthorion	Gwyn	SH1528	52°49·3′	4°44·3′W	W	123
Porthoustock	Corn	SW8021	50°3·1′	5°4·0′W	T	204
Porth Penrhyn	Gwyn	SH5972	53°13·8′	4°6·3′W	X	114,115
Porth Penrhyn-mawr	I of Angl	SH2883	53°19·2′	4°34·5′W	W	114
Porth Resr	Corn	SW8662	50°25·4′	5°0·4′W	W	200
Porth Ruffydd	I of Angl	SH2179	53°16·9′	4°40·7′W	W	114
Porthselau	Pemb	SM7226	51°53·4′	5°18·4′W	W	157
Porth Simdde	Gwyn	SH1626	52°48·3′	4°43·4′W	W	123
Porth Solfach	Gwyn	SH1121	52°45·5′	4°47·7′W	W	123
Porthstinian	Pemb	SM7224	51°52·3′	5°18·3′W	W	157
Porth Swtan or Church Bay	I of Angl	SH2989	53°22·5′	4°33·8′W	W	114
Porthsychan	Pemb	SM9040	52°1·4′	5°3·3′W	W	157
Porthtaffod	Pemb	SM7123	51°51·8′	5°19·2′W	W	157
Porth Tocyn	Gwyn	SH3126	52°48·5′	4°30·0′W	X	123
Porthtowan	Corn	SW6947	50°16·9′	5°14·2′W	T	203
Porth Towan	Corn	SW6948	50°17·4′	5°14·2′W	W	203
Porthtowan	Corn	SX0248	50°18·2′	4°46·5′W	X	204
Porth Towyn	Gwyn	SH2337	52°54·3′	4°37·5′W	W	123
Porth Trecastell	I of Angl	SH3370	53°12·3′	4°29·6′W	W	114
Porth Trefadog	I of Angl	SH2886	53°20·8′	4°34·6′W	W	114
Porth Tre-wen	Pemb	SM7730	51°55·7′	5°14·2′W	W	157
Porth Trwyn	I of Angl	SH2987	53°21·4′	4°33·8′W	W	114
Porth Twyn-mawr	I of Angl	SH3665	53°9·7′	4°26·8′W	W	114
Porth Tŷ-mawr	Gwyn	SH1833	52°52·1′	4°41·8′W	W	123
Porth Tywyn-mawr	I of Angl	SH2885	53°20·3′	4°34·6′W	W	114
Porthvaynor	Monm	SO4400	51°42·0′	2°48·2′W	X	171

Porth Wen	I of Angl	SH4094	53°25·4′	4°24·1′W	W	114
Porth Wen Bâch	Gwyn	SH1833	52°52·1′	4°41·8′W	W	123
Porthwgan	Wrex	SJ3746	53°0·7′	2°55·9′W	X	117
Porth Widlin	Gwyn	SH1832	52°51·5′	4°41·8′W	W	123
Porth y Bribys	I of Angl	SH2991	53°23·5′	4°33·9′W	W	114
Porth Ychain	Gwyn	SH2036	52°53·7′	4°40·2′W	W	123
Porth y Dyfn	I of Angl	SH2992	53°24·1′	4°33·9′W	W	114
Porth-y-felin	I of Angl	SH2483	53°19·1′	4°38·1′W	T	114
Porth-y-gaelod	Monm	SO4715	51°50·1′	2°45·8′W	X	161
Porth-y-garan	I of Angl	SH2577	53°15·9′	4°37·0′W	W	114
Porthygwichiaid	I of Angl	SH4891	53°23·9′	4°16·8′W	W	114
Porth-y-morddwr	Powys	SO1336	52°1·2′	3°15·7′W	X	161
Porth y Nant	Gwyn	SH3444	52°58·3′	4°27·9′W	W	123
Porth y Nant (National Language Centre)	Gwyn	SH3444	52°58·3′	4°27·9′W	X	123
Porth y Pistyll	Gwyn	SH1624	52°47·2′	4°43·3′W	W	123
Porth-y-pistyll	I of Angl	SH3493	53°24·7′	4°29·4′W	W	114
Porth-y-post	I of Angl	SH2479	53°17·0′	4°38·0′W	W	114
Porth yr Aber	I of Angl	SH4990	53°23·4′	4°15·8′W	W	114
Porth y Rhaw	Pemb	SM7824	51°52·5′	5°13·1′W	W	157
Porthyrhyd	Carm	SN5115	51°49·1′	4°9·3′W	T	159
Porthyrhyd	Carm	SN7137	52°1·2′	3°52·4′W	T	146,160
Porth yr Ogof	Powys	SN9212	51°48·0′	3°33·6′W	X	160
Porthyrychen	I of Angl	SH4693	53°24·9′	4°18·6′W	W	114
Porth Ysgaden	Gwyn	SH2137	52°54·3′	4°39·3′W	W	123
Porthysgaden	Gwyn	SH2237	52°54·3′	4°38·4′W	X	123
Porth Ysglaig	Gwyn	SH2237	52°54·3′	4°38·4′W	W	123
Porth Ysgo	Gwyn	SH2026	52°48·3′	4°39·8′W	W	123
Porth-y-waen	Shrops	SJ2623	52°48·2′	3°5·5′W	T	126
Porth y Wrâch	Gwyn	SH1630	52°50·4′	4°43·5′W	W	123
Porthzennor Cove	Corn	SW4539	50°12·0′	5°34·0′W	W	203
Portico	St Hel	SJ4893	53°26·1′	2°46·6′W	T	108
Port Imeraval	Arg & Bt	NR3545	55°37·8′	6°12·2′W	W	60
Portincaple	Arg & Bt	NS2393	56°6·1′	4°50·3′W	T	56
Portingbury Hills	Essex	TL5320	51°51·7′	0°13·7′E	A	167
Portington	Devon	SX4276	50°34·1′	4°13·5′W	T	201
Portington	E Yorks	SE7830	53°45·9′	0°48·6′W	X	105,106
Portington Grange	E Yorks	SE7931	53°46·4′	0°47·7′W	X	105,106
Portinnisherrich	Arg & Bt	NM9711	56°15·1′	5°16·2′W	T	55
Portinscale	Cumbr	NY2523	54°36·0′	3°9·2′W	T	89,90
Port Iol-bheathain	Arg & Bt	NM7125	56°22·0′	5°42·0′W	W	49
Port Isaac	Corn	SW9980	50°35·3′	4°50·0′W	T	200
Port Isaac Bay	Corn	SX0181	50°35·9′	4°48·3′W	W	200
Portis Fm	Pemb	SN1223	51°52·7′	4°43·5′W	FM	145,158
Portishead	N Som	ST4676	51°29·1′	2°46·3′W	T	171,172
Portishead Down	N Som	ST4575	51°28·5′	2°47·1′W	X	171,172
Portis-pant	Pemb	SN1129	51°55·9′	4°44·6′W	X	145,158
Port Jack	I of M	SC3977	54°10·1′	4°27·6′W	W	95
Port Kale	D & G	NW9855	54°51·2′	5°8·4′W	W	82
Port Kemin	D & G	NX1231	54°38·6′	4°54·4′W	W	82
Portkil	Arg & Bt	NS2580	55°59·1′	4°47·9′W	T	63
Portkil Bay	Arg & Bt	NS2580	55°59·1′	4°47·9′W	W	63
Port Kilbride	Highld	NG3766	57°36·7′	6°23·8′W	W	23
Port Kilcheran	Arg & Bt	NM8238	56°29·3′	5°32·0′W	W	49
Port Kilchoan	Highld	NM5071	56°46·1′	6°5·0′W	W	39,47
Portkil Point	Arg & Bt	NS2580	55°59·1′	4°47·9′W	X	63
Portknockie	Moray	NJ4868	57°42·2′	2°51·9′W	T	28,29
Portknowle	Stock on T	NZ3811	54°29·8′	1°24·4′W	X	93
Port Lag Losguinn	Arg & Bt	NR5792	56°3·8′	5°53·8′W	W	61
Port Laing	Fife	NT1381	56°1·1′	3°23·3′W	W	65
Port Laire	Highld	NG7957	57°33·2′	5°41·2′W	W	24
Port Lamont	Arg & Bt	NS0970	55°53·4′	5°2·8′W	X	63
Portland	Somer	ST4736	51°7·5′	2°45·1′W	T	182
Portland Castle	Dorset	SY6874	50°34·2′	2°26·7′W	A	194
Portland Grange Fm	Derby	SK3261	53°8·9′	1°30·9′W	FM	119
Portland Harbour	Dorset	SY6876	50°35·2′	2°26·7′W	X	194
Portland Ho	W Berks	SU5964	51°22·5′	1°8·7′W	X	174
Portlands Nab	Glos	SO6910	51°47·5′	2°26·6′W	X	162
Portlane Br	Devon	SS3706	50°50·1′	4°18·5′W	X	190
Port Langamull	Arg & Bt	NM3754	56°36·5′	6°16·7′W	W	47
Port Lathaich	Arg & Bt	NM8226	56°22·8′	5°31·4′W	W	49
Port Leathan	Arg & Bt	NR9176	55°56·2′	5°20·3′W	W	62
Port Leathan	Arg & Bt	NR9267	55°51·3′	5°19·0′W	W	62
Portledge Hotel	Devon	SS3924	50°59·8′	4°17·3′W	X	190
Port Leen	D & G	NW9972	55°0·4′	5°8·2′W	W	76,82
Port Leithne	Arg & Bt	NS1052	55°43·7′	5°1·1′W	W	63,69
Portlemouth Barton	Devon	SX7039	50°14·4′	3°49·0′W	X	202
Portlemouth Down	Devon	SX7437	50°13·4′	3°45·6′W	X	202
Portlethen	Aberd	NO9396	57°3·6′	2°6·5′W	T	38,45
Portlethen Village	Aberd	NO9396	57°3·6′	2°6·5′W	T	38,45
Portlevorchy	Highld	NC2251	58°24·9′	5°2·4′W	X	9
Port Lewaigue	I of M	SC4693	54°18·8′	4°21·6′W	W	95
Portley Moor	Heref	SO5061	52°14·9′	2°43·5′W	X	137,138,149
Port Liath	Arg & Bt	NR6975	55°55·0′	5°41·4′W	W	61,62
Portling	D & G	NX8854	54°52·3′	3°44·3′W	X	84
Portling Bay	D & G	NX8853	54°51·8′	3°44·3′W	W	84
Port Lion	Pemb	SM9808	51°44·3′	4°55·2′W	T	157,158
Port Lobh	Arg & Bt	NR3592	56°3·1′	6°14·9′W	W	61
Port Lochan	D & G	NX0743	54°44·9′	4°59·5′W	W	82
Portloe	Corn	SW9339	50°13·1′	4°53·7′W	T	204
Port Logan	D & G	NX0940	54°43·4′	4°57·5′W	T	82
Port Logan or Port Nessock Bay	D & G	NX0940	54°43·4′	4°57·5′W	W	82
Port Longaig	Highld	NM7795	56°59·8′	5°39·8′W	W	33,40
Portlooe	Corn	SX2452	50°20·7′	4°28·0′W	T	201
Port Luinge	Highld	NG7832	57°19·7′	5°40·8′W	W	24
Port Lunna	Arg & Bt	NR7686	56°1·1′	5°35·2′W	W	55
Port Lympne	Kent	TR1034	51°4·2′	1°0·2′E	X	179,189
Portmacdonell	Highld	NH3201	57°4·4′	4°45·8′W	X	34
Portmahomack	Highld	NH9184	57°50·2′	3°49·7′W	T	21
Portman Fm	Somer	ST1829	51°3·5′	3°9·8′W	FM	181,193
Portman's Fm	Suff	TM0238	52°0·4′	0°57·0′E	FM	155
Portmark	D & G	NX4994	55°13·3′	4°22·0′W	X	77
Port Marquis	I of Angl	SH4369	53°11·9′	4°20·6′W	X	114,115
Port Mary	Arg & Bt	NM7413	56°15·6′	5°38·5′W	W	55
Port Mary	D & G	NX7545	54°47·3′	3°56·2′W	W	84
Port Mary Ho	D & G	NX7545	54°47·3′	3°56·2′W	X	84
Port McGean	D & G	NX4948	54°48·5′	4°20·5′W	X	83
Port Mead	Swan	SS6396	51°39·0′	3°58·4′W	T	159
Port Meadow	Oxon	SP4908	51°46·3′	1°17·0′W	X	164

Port Mean	Arg & Bt	NR6406	55°17·7′	5°42·6′W	W	68
Portmeirion	Gwyn	SH5837	52°54·9′	4°6·3′W	T	124
Portmellon	Corn	SX0143	50°15·4′	4°47·1′W	T	204
Port Mhic Bheathain	Arg & Bt	NR7065	55°49·7′	5°39·9′W	W	61,62
Port Mhicheal	Arg & Bt	NR7181	55°58·3′	5°39·8′W	W	55
Port Mhic Isaaic	Arg & Bt	NM7906	56°12·0′	5°33·3′W	W	55
Port Mhoirich	Arg & Bt	NR7169	55°51·8′	5°39·2′W	W	62
Port Mholair	N Eil	NB5636	58°15·0′	6°9·0′W	T	8
Port Mhòr Bhràgair	N Eil	NB2849	58°21·0′	6°38·5′W	W	8
Port Mhuilinn	Highld	NM6485	56°54·0′	5°52·1′W	W	40
Port Mias-sgeire	Arg & Bt	NR1653	55°41·5′	6°30·7′W	W	60
Port Min	Highld	NM4166	56°43·1′	6°13·5′W	W	47
Port Mine	Arg & Bt	NM1254	56°35·6′	6°41·1′W	W	46
Portmoak	Pth & Kin	NO1700	56°11·4′	3°19·8′W	X	58
Portmoak Moss	Pth & Kin	NO1701	56°11·9′	3°19·8′W	F	58
Port Moluag	Arg & Bt	NM8743	56°32·1′	5°27·4′W	W	49
Port Mona	D & G	NX1032	54°39·1′	4°56·3′W	W	82
Port Mona Heughs	D & G	NX1032	54°39·1′	4°56·3′W	X	82
Port Mooar	I of M	SC4890	54°17·2′	4°19·7′W	W	95
Port Mór	Arg & Bt	NL9343	56°29·0′	6°58·8′W	W	46
Port Mór	Arg & Bt	NM2922	56°19·0′	6°22·5′W	W	48
Port Mór	Arg & Bt	NM3617	56°16·6′	6°15·4′W	W	48
Port Mór	Arg & Bt	NM4323	56°20·0′	6°9·0′W	W	48
Port Mór	Arg & Bt	NM7615	56°16·7′	5°36·7′W	W	55
Port Mór	Arg & Bt	NM8531	56°25·6′	5°28·7′W	W	49
Port Mór	Arg & Bt	NN0435	56°28·2′	5°10·5′W	W	50
Port Mór	Arg & Bt	NR2755	55°42·9′	6°20·4′W	W	60
Port Mór	Arg & Bt	NR3594	56°4·2′	6°15·0′W	W	61
Port Mór	Arg & Bt	NR4367	55°49·9′	6°5·8′W	W	60,61
Port Mór	Arg & Bt	NR4750	55°40·9′	6°1·0′W	W	60
Port Mór	Arg & Bt	NR6654	55°43·6′	5°43·2′W	W	62
Port Mór	Arg & Bt	NR7161	55°47·5′	5°38·7′W	W	62
Port Mór	Highld	NC7765	58°33·6′	4°6·4′W	W	10
Port Mór	Highld	NC9565	58°33·9′	3°47·8′W	W	11
Port Mór	Highld	NH9287	57°51·8′	3°48·8′W	W	21
Port Mór	Highld	NM4278	56°49·6′	6°13·3′W	W	39
Port Mór	Highld	NM4279	56°50·1′	6°13·3′W	T	39
Port Mór	Highld	NM5552	56°36·0′	5°59·0′W	W	47
Port Mór	N Ayr	NR9321	55°26·6′	5°15·9′W	W	68,69
Port Mór	N Ayr	NS0425	55°29·0′	5°5·7′W	W	69
Port Mora	D & G	NW9955	54°51·2′	5°7·5′W	W	82
Portmore	Hants	SZ3397	50°46·5′	1°31·5′W	T	196
Portmore Fm	Devon	SS5831	51°3·9′	4°1·2′W	FM	180
Portmore Ho	Scot Bord	NT2548	55°43·4′	3°11·2′W	X	73
Portmore Loch	Scot Bord	NT2549	55°44·0′	3°11·2′W	W	73
Port Mór na Carraig	Arg & Bt	NR2255	55°42·8′	6°25·1′W	W	60
Port Mulgrave	N Yks	NZ7917	54°32·8′	0°46·3′W	T	94
Port Murray	S Ayr	NS2007	55°19·7′	4°49·8′W	W	70,76
Port na Bà	Arg & Bt	NM3954	56°36·6′	6°14·8′W	W	47
Port na Birlinne	Arg & Bt	NM5026	56°21·9′	6°2·4′W	W	48
Port na Birlinne	Arg & Bt	NR5265	55°49·1′	5°57·1′W	W	61
Port na Cagain	Highld	NG2358	57°31·9′	6°37·2′W	W	23
Port na Caillich	Arg & Bt	NM3554	56°36·4′	6°18·7′W	W	47
Port-na-Caraneon	Highld	NM4298	57°0·3′	6°14·5′W	X	39
Port na Cille	Arg & Bt	NR4750	55°40·9′	6°1·0′W	W	60
Port na Cille	Arg & Bt	NR6444	55°38·2′	5°44·6′W	W	62
Portnacloich	Highld	NG7630	57°18·6′	5°42·7′W	X	24
Portnacloich Point	Highld	NG7529	57°18·0′	5°43·6′W	X	33
Port na Clòidheig	Arg & Bt	NM4725	56°21·2′	6°5·3′W	W	48
Port na Copa	N Eil	NF7275	57°39·0′	7°29·5′W	W	18
Port-na-Craig	Pth & Kin	NN9357	56°41·8′	3°44·4′W	X	52
Port na Criche	Arg & Bt	NM4243	56°30·8′	6°11·2′W	W	47,48
Port na Cro	Arg & Bt	NM7609	56°13·5′	5°36·4′W	W	55
Port na Croise	Arg & Bt	NM4226	56°21·6′	6°10·2′W	W	48
Port na Croise	Arg & Bt	NR6529	55°30·2′	5°42·8′W	W	68
Port na Croisg	Highld	NM5861	56°41·0′	5°56·6′W	W	47
Portnacroish	Arg & Bt	NM9247	56°34·4′	5°22·7′W	T	49
Port na Cuilce	Arg & Bt	NM4100	56°7·6′	6°9·6′W	W	61
Port na Cùile	Arg & Bt	NR8139	55°36·0′	5°28·1′W	W	68,69
Port na Cullaidh	Highld	NG5113	57°8·7′	6°6·5′W	W	32
Port na Curaich	Arg & Bt	NM2621	56°18·4′	6°25·4′W	W	48
Port na Cuthaig	Arg & Bt	NR7931	55°31·6′	5°29·7′W	W	68,69
Port na Diollaide	Arg & Bt	NR2271	55°51·4′	6°26·1′W	W	60
Portnadler Bay	Corn	SX2451	50°20·2′	4°28·0′W	W	201
Port na Faoilinn Bàine	Arg & Bt	NM2820	56°17·9′	6°23·4′W	W	48
Port na Feannaiche	N Ayr	NR9122	55°27·1′	5°17·9′W	W	68,69
Port na Fhiurain	Arg & Bt	NR5875	55°54·7′	5°51·9′W	W	61
Port na Gaillinn	Arg & Bt	NR7061	55°47·5′	5°39·7′W	W	62
Port na Gallin	N Ayr	NS0523	55°28·0′	5°4·7′W	W	69
Port na Gulaidh	Arg & Bt	NM4241	56°29·7′	6°11·1′W	W	47,48
Port na h-Aibhne	N Eil	NB1326	58°8·1′	6°52·1′W	W	13
Port na h-Aille	Arg & Bt	NS0458	55°46·8′	5°7·1′W	W	63
Port na h-Atha	Arg & Bt	NR3688	56°1·0′	6°13·7′W	W	61
Portnahaven	Arg & Bt	NR1652	55°41·0′	6°30·7′W	T	60
Port na h-Eathar	Arg & Bt	NM2053	56°35·3′	6°33·2′W	W	46,47
Port na h-Olainn	Arg & Bt	NR5913	55°21·4′	5°47·7′W	W	68
Port na h-Uaille	Highld	NC6465	58°33·4′	4°19·8′W	W	10
Port na h-Uamha	Highld	NG7613	57°9·5′	5°41·8′W	W	33
Port na h-Uamha	Highld	NM7362	56°41·9′	5°42·0′W	W	40
Port na Làthaich	Highld	NM6372	56°47·0′	5°52·3′W	W	40
Port na Lich	Stir	NN4011	56°16·1′	4°34·6′W	W	56
Portnalong	Highld	NG3434	57°19·4′	6°24·7′W	T	32
Port na Long	Highld	NG5900	57°2·0′	5°57·9′W	W	32,39
Portnaluchaig	Highld	NM6589	56°56·2′	5°51·3′W	T	40
Port-na-Luing	Arg & Bt	NM1552	56°34·7′	6°38·0′W	X	46
Port na Luinge	Arg & Bt	NM4426	56°21·7′	6°8·2′W	W	48
Port na Luinge	Arg & Bt	NR3341	55°35·6′	6°13·8′W	W	60
Port na Luinge	Arg & Bt	NR3488	56°0·9′	6°15·6′W	W	61
Port nam Balach	N Ayr	NS0241	55°37·6′	5°8·3′W	W	69
Port nam Bothaig	N Eil	NB5446	58°20·3′	6°11·7′W	W	8
Port nam Buitsichean	Arg & Bt	NM5645	56°32·3′	5°57·7′W	W	47,48
Port nam Faochag	Arg & Bt	NM3736	56°26·8′	6°15·6′W	W	47,48
Port nam Faochag	Arg & Bt	NR6549	55°40·9′	5°43·9′W	W	62
Port nam Fliuchan	Arg & Bt	NR3897	56°5·9′	6°12·3′W	W	61
Port nam Freumh	Highld	NM5553	56°36·6′	5°59·1′W	W	47
Port nam Furm	Arg & Bt	NM7000	56°8·5′	5°41·7′W	W	55,61
Port na Mine	Arg & Bt	NN0232	56°26·6′	5°12·3′W	X	50
Port na Mine	Arg & Bt	NN0333	56°27·1′	5°11·4′W	W	50
Port nam Marbh	Arg & Bt	NM7327	56°23·1′	5°40·2′W	W	49
Port nam Marbh	Arg & Bt	NR6527	55°29·1′	5°42·7′W	W	68

Port nam Meirleach	Arg & Bt	NM7125	56°22·0′	5°42·0′W	W	49
Port nam Meirleach	Arg & Bt	NR6080	55°57·4′	5°50·3′W	W	61
Port nam Muileach	Arg & Bt	NR9964	55°49·9′	5°12·1′W	W	62
Port nam Murrach	Highld	NM6183	56°52·9′	5°54·9′W	W	40
Port na Mòine	Arg & Bt	NM8001	56°9·3′	5°32·1′W	W	55
Port na Morachd	Arg & Bt	NM7713	56°15·7′	5°35·6′W	W	55
Port nam Partan	Arg & Bt	NM3452	56°35·3′	6°19·5′W	W	47
Port na Muic	Highld	ND2133	58°17·0′	3°20·4′W	W	11
Port na Muice Duibhe	Arg & Bt	NM6924	56°21·4′	5°43·9′W	W	49
Port nan Athlaich	Arg & Bt	NR7599	56°8·1′	5°36·8′W	W	55
Port nan Clachan	Arg & Bt	NR6531	55°31·2′	5°42·9′W	W	68
Port nan Clach Cruinn	Arg & Bt	NR7084	55°59·9′	5°40·3′W	W	55,61
Port nan Clàdan	Arg & Bt	NR5263	55°48·1′	5°57·0′W	W	61
Portnancon	Highld	NC4260	58°30·2′	4°42·2′W	X	9
Port nan Crullach	Arg & Bt	NM7226	56°22·5′	5°41·1′W	W	49
Port nan Cuilc	Arg & Bt	NM8327	56°23·4′	5°30·5′W	W	49
Port nan Droigheann	Arg & Bt	NM4419	56°17·9′	6°7·8′W	W	48
Port nan Gall	Highld	NM6560	56°40·6′	5°49·7′W	W	40
Port nan Gallan	Arg & Bt	NM8240	56°30·4′	5°32·1′W	W	49
Port nan Gallan	Arg & Bt	NR2841	55°35·5′	6°18·6′W	W	60
Port nan Gamhna	Arg & Bt	NR8351	55°42·5′	5°26·8′W	W	62,69
Port nan Giuran	N Eil	NB5537	58°15·5′	6°11·1′W	T	8
Port nan Laogh	Arg & Bt	NR6792	56°4·1′	5°44·2′W	W	55,61
Port nan Leadaig	Arg & Bt	NM8240	56°30·4′	5°32·1′W	W	49
Port nan Lìghura	Arg & Bt	NM4042	56°30·2′	6°13·1′W	W	47,48
Port nan Long	N Eil	NF8978	57°41·3′	7°12·7′W	W	18
Port nan Ròn	Arg & Bt	NM3118	56°17·0′	6°20·3′W	W	48
Port nan Sliseag	Arg & Bt	NM7203	56°10·2′	5°39·9′W	W	55
Port nan Spainteach	Highld	NM5063	56°41·8′	6°4·6′W	W	47
Port na Pollaig	Highld	NM6477	56°49·7′	5°51·6′W	W	40
Port na Saille	Arg & Bt	NM7127	56°23·0′	5°42·1′W	W	49
Port na Seralaic	Arg & Bt	NR6344	55°38·2′	5°45·5′W	W	62
Port na Sgìeata	Arg & Bt	NR6080	55°57·4′	5°50·3′W	W	61
Port na Tairbeirt	Arg & Bt	NM7429	56°24·2′	5°39·3′W	W	49
Port na Tràigh-linne	Arg & Bt	NM8225	56°22·3′	5°31·4′W	W	49
Portnaughan Bay	D & G	NW9669	54°58·7′	5°10·8′W	W	82
Portnauld Ho	Renf	NS4968	55°53·1′	4°24·4′W	X	64
Portnellan	Stir	NN4012	56°16·7′	4°34·6′W	X	56
Portnellan	Stir	NN4125	56°23·7′	4°34·1′W	X	51
Portnellan	Stir	NN5806	56°13·8′	4°17·0′W	X	57
Portnellan Fm	W Dunb	NS4086	56°2·7′	4°33·7′W	FM	56
Port Nessock or Port Logan Bay	D & G	NX0940	54°43·4′	4°57·5′W	W	82
Port Nis	N Eil	NB5363	58°29·4′	6°13·8′W	T	8
Portobello	C of Edin	NT3073	55°57·0′	3°6·8′W	T	66
Portobello	D & G	NW9666	54°57·1′	5°10·7′W	W	82
Portobello	E Loth	NT4073	55°57·0′	2°57·2′W	X	66
Portobello	Ghead	NZ2855	54°53·6′	1°33·4′W	T	88
Portobello	I of Angl	SH4889	53°22·8′	4°16·7′W	X	114
Portobello	Northum	NY7064	54°58·4′	2°27·7′W	X	86,87
Portobello	N Yks	NZ2706	54°27·2′	1°34·6′W	X	93
Portobello	N Yks	SE7768	54°6·4′	0°48·9′W	X	100
Portobello	Wakf	SE3318	53°39·7′	1°29·6′W	T	110,111
Portobello	Wolv	SO9598	52°35·0′	2°4·0′W	T	139
Portobello Fm	Beds	TL0532	51°58·8′	0°27·9′W	FM	166
Portobello Fm	Beds	TL2047	52°6·7′	0°14·5′W	FM	153
Portobello Fm	Oxon	SU7294	51°38·6′	0°57·2′W	FM	175
Portocks End	Worcs	SO8346	52°7·0′	2°14·5′W	X	150
Port Odhar	Highld	NC3570	58°35·5′	4°49·9′W	W	9
Port of Brims	Highld	ND0471	58°37·2′	3°38·7′W	W	12
Port of Counan	D & G	NX4136	54°41·9′	4°27·6′W	W	83
Port of Leith	C of Edin	NT2677	55°59·1′	3°10·7′W	X	66
Port of Menteith	Stir	NN5801	56°11·1′	4°16·8′W	T	57
Port of Spittal Bay	D & G	NX0152	54°49·7′	5°5·5′W	W	82
Port of Tarbet	Highld	NC1648	58°23·2′	5°8·4′W	W	9
Port Ohirnie	Arg & Bt	NM6320	56°19·0′	5°49·5′W	W	49
Port Olmsa	Arg & Bt	NR4196	56°5·5′	6°9·4′W	W	61
Porton	Wilts	SU1936	51°7·6′	1°43·3′W	T	184
Porton Down	Wilts	SU2135	51°7·1′	1°41·6′W	X	184
Porton Grounds	Newp	ST4183	51°32·8′	2°50·7′W	X	171,172
Porton Ho	Newp	ST3882	51°32·2′	2°53·2′W	X	171
Portormin	Highld	ND1629	58°14·8′	3°25·4′W	T	11,17
Port o' Warren	D & G	NX8753	54°51·8′	3°45·2′W	X	84
Port o' Warren Bay	D & G	NX8753	54°51·8′	3°45·2′W	W	84
Portpatrick	D & G	NW9954	54°50·7′	5°7·4′W	T	82
Port Phàdruig	Arg & Bt	NM7928	56°23·8′	5°34·4′W	W	49
Port Phadruig	Highld	NM5959	56°39·9′	5°55·5′W	W	47
Port Pheadair	N Eil	NF8445	57°23·4′	7°15·1′W	W	22
Port Quin	Corn	SW9780	50°35·3′	4°52·6′W	T	200
Port Quin Bay	Corn	SW9580	50°35·3′	4°53·4′W	W	200
Portrack	Stock on T	NZ4619	54°34·1′	1°16·9′W	T	93
Portrack Ho	D & G	NX9382	55°7·5′	3°40·3′W	X	78
Port Ramsay	Arg & Bt	NM8845	56°33·2′	5°26·5′W	T	49
Port Raoin Mhóir	Arg & Bt	NR8143	55°38·1′	5°28·3′W	W	62,69
Portreath	Corn	SW6545	50°15·7′	5°17·5′W	T	203
Portree	D & G	NX0053	54°50·2′	5°6·4′W	X	82
Portree	Highld	NG4843	57°24·7′	6°11·3′W	T	23
Portree Forest	Highld	NG4741	57°23·6′	6°12·2′W	F	23
Port Regis (Sch)	Dorset	ST8424	51°1·1′	2°13·3′W	X	183
Portreuddyn Castle	Gwyn	SH5840	52°56·6′	4°6·4′W	X	124
Port Righ	Arg & Bt	NR8137	55°34·9′	5°28·0′W	W	68,69
Port Ronnald	S Ayr	NS3130	55°32·3′	4°40·3′W	X	70
Port Ruadh	Arg & Bt	NM0849	56°32·8′	6°44·6′W	W	46
Port Ruadh	Arg & Bt	NM8137	56°28·7′	5°32·9′W	W	49
Port Ruadh	N Eil	NF6461	57°31·1′	7°36·3′W	W	22
Portrye	N Ayr	NS1758	55°47·1′	4°54·7′W	X	63
Portscatho	Corn	SW8735	50°10·8′	4°58·6′W	T	204
Port Scolpaig	N Eil	NF7068	57°35·1′	7°30·9′W	W	18
Ports Down	C of Port	SU6406	50°51·2′	1°5·1′W	X	196
Portsea	C of Port	SU6300	50°48·0′	1°6·0′W	T	196
Portsea Island	C of Port	SU6501	50°48·5′	1°4·3′W	T	196
Port Selma	Arg & Bt	NM9038	56°29·5′	5°24·2′W	X	49
Port Sgibinis	Arg & Bt	NR4099	56°7·0′	6°10·5′W	W	61
Portskerra	Highld	NC8765	58°33·8′	3°56·2′W	T	10
Portskewett	Monm	ST4988	51°35·5′	2°43·8′W	T	162,172
Portslade-By-Sea	W Susx	TQ2505	50°50·1′	0°13·1′W	T	198
Portslade Village	Bri & Hov	TQ2506	50°50·6′	0°13·1′W	T	198
Portslogan	D & G	NW9858	54°52·8′	5°8·5′W	T	82
Portsmouth	Cald	SD8926	53°44·1′	2°9·6′W	T	103
Portsmouth	C of Port	SU6501	50°48·5′	1°4·3′W	T	196

Portsmouth Arms Sta	Devon	SS6319	50°57·5′	3°56·7′W	X	180
Portsmouth Harbour	C of Port	SU6202	50°49·1′	1°6·8′W	W	196
Port Snoig	Arg & Bt	NL9638	56°26·4′	6°55·5′W	W	46
Port Soderick	I of M	SC3472	54°7·3′	4°32·0′W	W	95
Port Soderick Glen	I of M	SC3472	54°7·3′	4°32·0′W	X	95
Port Soldrick	I of M	SC3069	54°5·6′	4°35·6′W	W	95
Portsonachan	Arg & Bt	NN0520	56°20·2′	5°8·8′W	T	50,56
Portsoy	Aberd	NJ5866	57°41·2′	2°41·8′W	T	29
Port St Mary	I of M	SC2067	54°4·3′	4°44·6′W	T	95
Port St Mary Bay	I of M	SC2167	54°4·3′	4°43·7′W	W	95
Port Stoth	N Eil	NB5265	58°30·4′	6°15·0′W	W	8
Portstown	Aberd	NJ7723	57°18·1′	2°22·4′W	X	38
Port Sunlight	Wirral	SJ3384	53°21·2′	3°0·0′W	T	108
Port Sutton Bridge	Lincs	TF4822	52°46·7′	0°12·1′E	T	131
Portswood	C of Soton	SU4314	50°55·7′	1°22·9′W	T	196
Port Talbot	Nth Pt Talb	SS7589	51°35·4′	3°47·9′W	T	170
Porttannachy	Moray	NJ3864	57°40·0′	3°1·9′W	T	28
Port Tennant	Swan	SS6893	51°37·5′	3°54·0′W	T	159
Port Thairbeirt Dheas	Highld	NM6673	56°47·6′	5°49·5′W	W	40
Port, The	D & G	NX8260	54°55·5′	3°50·1′W	X	84
Port Tigh Ghilleasbuig	Highld	NM8676	56°49·8′	5°30·0′W	W	40
Portuairk	Highld	NM4368	56°44·2′	6°11·7′W	T	47
Port Uamh Beathaig	Arg & Bt	NM4332	56°24·9′	6°9·6′W	W	48
Port Uamh Bride	Arg & Bt	NM4029	56°23·2′	6°12·3′W	W	48
Port Uamh na Gaibhre	Arg & Bt	NM3824	56°20·4′	6°13·9′W	W	48
Port Uamh nan Calman	Arg & Bt	NR5876	55°55·2′	5°52·0′W	W	61
Portuguese Fireplace	Hants	SU2607	50°51·9′	1°37·4′W	X	195
Port Uilleim	Highld	NH9185	57°50·7′	3°49·7′W	W	21
Port Uisken	Arg & Bt	NM3918	56°17·2′	6°12·6′W	W	48
Port Vad	S Ayr	NX0986	55°8·1′	4°59·4′W	W	76
Portvasgo	Highld	NC5864	58°32·7′	4°25·9′W	T	10
Port Vasgo	Highld	NC5865	58°33·3′	4°25·9′W	W	10
Port Wallberry	I of M	SC3774	54°8·4′	4°29·3′W	X	95
Portway	Dorset	SY8085	50°40·1′	2°16·6′W	T	194
Portway	Heref	SO3844	52°5·7′	2°53·9′W	X	148,149,161
Portway	Heref	SO4845	52°6·3′	2°45·2′W	T	148,149
Portway	Heref	SO4867	52°18·2′	2°45·4′W	X	137,138,148
Portway	Heref	SO4935	52°0·9′	2°44·2′W	T	149
Portway	Heref	SO5563	52°16·0′	2°39·2′W	X	137,138,149
Port Way	Oxon	SU6286	51°34·4′	1°5·9′W	X	175
Portway	Powys	SO1948	52°7·7′	3°10·6′W	X	148
Portway	Sand	SO9788	52°29·6′	2°2·3′W	T	139
Portway	Shrops	SO4092	52°31·6′	2°52·7′W	A	137
Portway	Somer	ST4126	51°2·1′	2°50·1′W	T	193
Portway	Somer	ST4836	51°7·5′	2°44·2′W	T	182
Portway	Staffs	SK2109	52°40·9′	1°41·0′W	X	128
Portway	Worcs	SO7733	51°59·9′	2°19·7′W	T	150
Portway	Worcs	SP0872	52°21·0′	1°52·6′W	T	139
Portway Fm	Bucks	SP6725	51°55·4′	1°1·1′W	FM	164,165
Portway Fm	Hants	SU2541	51°10·3′	1°38·2′W	FM	184
Portway Fm	Oxon	SP5129	51°57·7′	1°15·1′W	FM	164
Portway Fm	Somer	ST5822	51°0·0′	2°35·5′W	FM	183
Portway Fm	Somer	ST6838	51°8·7′	2°27·1′W	FM	183
Portway Heave	Suff	TL7478	52°22·6′	0°33·8′E	X	143
Portway Hill	Suff	TL7378	52°22·6′	0°32·9′E	X	143
Portway (Roman Road)	Hants	SU3848	51°14·0′	1°27·0′W	R	185
Portway (Roman Road)	Hants	SU5456	51°18·3′	1°13·1′W	R	174
Portway (Roman Road)	Hants	SU6160	51°20·4′	1°7·1′W	R	175
Portway (Roman Road)	Wilts	SU2138	51°8·7′	1°41·6′W	R	184
Portways	Oxon	SU7193	51°38·1′	0°58·1′W	X	175
Portways Fm	W Susx	TQ2526	51°1·4′	0°12·7′W	FM	187,198
Port Wemyss	Arg & Bt	NR1651	55°40·4′	6°30·6′W	T	60
Port Whapple	D & G	NX3440	54°43·9′	4°34·3′W	W	82
Port Whapple	D & G	NX4947	54°48·0′	4°20·5′W	X	83
Port William	Corn	SX0486	50°38·7′	4°46·0′W	W	200
Port William	D & G	NX3343	54°45·5′	4°35·3′W	T	82
Portwood	Stock	SJ9090	53°24·6′	2°8·6′W	T	109
Portwood Fm	Norf	TM0397	52°32·2′	1°0·0′E	FM	144
Portworthy	Devon	SX5560	50°25·6′	4°2·1′W	X	202
Portwrinkle	Corn	SX3553	50°21·5′	4°18·8′W	T	201
Portyerrock	D & G	NX4738	54°43·1′	4°22·1′W	X	83
Portyerrock Bay	D & G	NX4738	54°43·1′	4°22·1′W	W	83
Porty Ford Fm	Northnts	SP6678	52°24·0′	1°1·4′W	FM	141
Posbury	Devon	SX8097	50°45·8′	3°41·7′W	A	191
Posbury	Devon	SX8197	50°45·9′	3°40·9′W	X	191
Posbury Clump	Devon	SX8197	50°45·9′	3°40·9′W	F	191
Posenhall	Shrops	SJ6501	52°36·6′	2°30·6′W	T	127
Posher Fm	Warw	SP3661	52°15·0′	1°28·0′W	FM	151
Posingford Fm	E Susx	TQ4734	51°5·4′	0°6·3′E	FM	188
Posingford Wood	E Susx	TQ4733	51°4·9′	0°6·3′E	F	188
Poslingford	Suff	TL7648	52°6·4′	0°34·6′E	T	155
Poslingford Ho	Suff	TL7750	52°7·4′	0°35·5′E	X	155
Posnet	Aberd	NJ8517	57°14·9′	2°14·5′W	X	38
Possil Loch	C of Glas	NS5870	55°54·4′	4°15·9′W	W	64
Possil Park	C of Glas	NS5868	55°53·3′	4°15·8′W	T	64
Possingworth Manor Ho	E Susx	TQ5320	50°57·8′	0°11·1′E	A	199
Possingworth Park	E Susx	TQ5420	50°57·8′	0°12·0′E	X	199
Posso	Scot Bord	NT2033	55°35·3′	3°15·7′W	T	73
Posso Craig	Scot Bord	NT1931	55°34·2′	3°16·6′W	H	72
Post-bach	Cered	SN3952	52°8·8′	4°20·8′W	X	145
Postbridge	Devon	SX6579	50°35·9′	3°54·1′W	T	191
Postcombe	Oxon	SU7099	51°41·4′	0°58·8′W	T	165
Post Cross	Devon	ST0507	50°51·5′	3°20·6′W	X	192
Post Down	W Berks	SU3282	51°32·4′	1°31·9′W	X	174
Postdown Fm	W Berks	SU3282	51°32·4′	1°31·9′W	FM	174
Postensplain	Shrops	SO7479	52°24·7′	2°22·5′W	X	138
Posterne Hill	Wilts	SU1968	51°24·9′	1°43·2′W	X	173
Postern Fm	Derby	SK3046	53°0·9′	1°32·8′W	FM	119,128
Posterngate Fm	Surrey	TQ3649	51°13·7′	0°2·7′W	FM	187
Postern Lodge Fm	Derby	SK3146	53°0·9′	1°31·9′W	FM	119,128
Postern Park	Kent	TQ6146	51°11·7′	0°18·6′E	X	188
Postern, The	Kent	TQ6046	51°11·7′	0°17·8′E	X	188
Postford Ho	Surrey	TQ0347	51°13·0′	0°31·1′W	X	186
Postgate Fm	N Yks	NZ7604	54°25·8′	0°49·3′W	FM	94
Post Green	Dorset	SY9593	50°44·4′	2°3·9′W	T	195
Post Gwyn	Powys	SJ0429	52°51·2′	3°25·1′W	H	125
Post Hill	Leeds	SE2433	53°47·8′	1°37·7′W	X	104
Postlake Fm	Devon	SX9880	50°41·2′	3°25·4′W	FM	192
Postland Ho	Lincs	TF2912	52°41·6′	0°5·1′W	X	131,142
Postlebury Wood	Somer	ST7442	51°10·8′	2°21·9′W	F	183

Postling	Kent	TR1438	51°6·3′	1°3·8′E	T	179,189
Postling Green	Kent	TR0735	51°4·8′	0°57·7′E	X	179,189
Postling Wents	Kent	TR1437	51°5·8′	1°3·8′E	X	179,189
Postling Wood	Kent	TR1440	51°7·4′	1°3·9′E	F	179,189
Postlip	Glos	SP0027	51°56·7′	1°59·6′W	T	163
Postlip Hall	Glos	SO9926	51°56·2′	2°0·5′W	A	163
Postlip Ho	Glos	SP0127	51°56·7′	1°58·7′W	X	163
Postlip Warren	Glos	SP0026	51°56·2′	1°59·6′W	F	163
Postmill	N Lincs	TA0208	53°33·8′	0°27·2′W	X	112
Post Mill Fm	Cambs	TL3890	52°29·7′	0°2·4′E	FM	142,143
Post Office Knowe	D & G	NT3006	55°20·8′	3°5·8′W	X	79
Poston Coppice	Shrops	SO5581	52°25·7′	2°39·3′W	F	137,138
Poston Court Fm	Heref	SO3537	52°1·9′	2°56·5′W	FM	149,161
Poston Ho	Heref	SO3637	52°1·9′	2°55·6′W	X	149,161
Postridge Fm	Somer	ST2336	51°7·3′	3°5·6′W	FM	182
Post Rocks	Arg & Bt	NR4079	55°56·3′	6°9·4′W	X	60,61
Postwick	Norf	TG2907	52°37·0′	1°23·4′E	T	134
Postwick Marsh	Norf	TG2906	52°36·4′	1°23·3′E	X	134
Posty	Pemb	SN0723	51°52·6′	4°47·8′W	X	145,158
Posty-Isaf	Carm	SN3321	51°52·0′	4°25·1′W	X	145,159
Posty-Uchaf	Carm	SN3322	51°52·5′	4°25·2′W	X	145,159
Poswick	Heref	SO7057	52°12·9′	2°25·9′W	X	149
Poswick Fm	Heref	SO6663	52°16·1′	2°29·5′W	FM	138,149
Potarch	Aberd	NO6097	57°4·0′	2°39·1′W	X	37,45
Potash	Suff	TM1137	51°59·7′	1°4·8′E	T	155,169
Potash Fm	Bucks	SP7835	52°0·7′	0°51·4′W	FM	152
Potash Fm	Cambs	TL3873	52°20·5′	0°1·9′E	FM	154
Potash Fm	Essex	TL4829	51°56·6′	0°9·6′E	FM	167
Potash Fm	Essex	TL8224	51°53·3′	0°39·1′E	FM	168
Potash Fm	Norf	TM0889	52°27·8′	1°4·1′E	FM	144
Potash Fm	Suff	TL9754	52°9·2′	0°53·2′E	FM	155
Potash Fm	Suff	TL9871	52°18·3′	0°54·7′E	FM	144,155
Potash Fm	Suff	TM0368	52°16·6′	0°58·9′E	FM	155
Potash Fm	Suff	TM0571	52°18·2′	1°0·8′E	FM	144,155
Potash Fm	Suff	TM0873	52°19·2′	1°3·5′E	FM	144,155
Potash Fm	Suff	TM1457	52°10·4′	1°8·2′E	FM	156
Potash Fm	Suff	TM1637	51°59·6′	1°9·2′E	FM	169
Potash Fm	Suff	TM1664	52°14·1′	1°10·2′E	FM	156
Potash Fm	Suff	TM2153	52°8·1′	1°14·2′E	FM	156
Potash Fm	Warw	SP4759	52°13·9′	1°18·3′W	FM	151
Potash Wood	Essex	TQ8490	51°35·0′	0°39·7′E	F	178
Potato Barn	Glos	SP0807	51°45·9′	1°52·7′W	X	163
Potato Town	Oxon	SP3830	51°58·3′	1°26·4′W	X	151
Potbridge	Hants	SU7453	51°16·5′	0°56·0′W	T	186
Pot Bridge Fm	N Yks	SE2654	53°59·1′	1°35·8′W	FM	104
Pot Brinks Moor	Lancs	SD9336	53°49·5′	2°6·0′W	X	103
Pot Burn	D & G	NT1013	55°24·4′	3°24·9′W	W	78
Potburn	Scot Bord	NT1808	55°21·8′	3°17·2′W	X	79
Pot Common	Surrey	SU9042	51°10·4′	0°42·4′W	T	186
Pot Common	W Susx	TQ3138	51°7·8′	0°7·3′W	X	187
Potcote	Northnts	SP6552	52°10·0′	1°2·6′W	X	152
Potcote Fm	Northnts	SP6651	52°9·4′	1°1·7′W	FM	152
Potem's Cross	Devon	SS5722	50°59·0′	4°1·9′W	X	180
Potford Br	Warw	SK2603	52°37·7′	1°36·6′W	X	140
Potford Fm	Wrekin	SJ6321	52°47·4′	2°32·5′W	FM	127
Potford's Dam Fm	Warw	SP4672	52°20·9′	1°19·1′W	FM	140
Potgate Fm	N Yks	SE2775	54°10·4′	1°34·8′W	FM	99
Potgill Holme	Cumbr	SD7091	54°19·1′	2°27·3′W	X	98
Pot Haw Fm	N Yks	SD8954	53°59·2′	2°9·6′W	FM	103
Potheridge Gate	Devon	SS5114	50°54·6′	4°6·8′W	X	180
Pot Hill	D & G	NT1701	55°18·0′	3°18·0′W	H	79
Pothill	Pth & Kin	NN9611	56°17·1′	3°40·4′W	X	58
Pothole Burn	D & G	NX9291	55°12·3′	3°41·4′W	W	78
Potholm	D & G	NY3587	55°10·6′	3°0·8′W	X	79
Potholm Hill	D & G	NY3687	55°10·6′	2°59·9′W	H	79
Pothouse	D & G	NX9292	55°12·9′	3°41·4′W	X	78
Potkiln Fm	Kent	TQ8939	51°7·4′	0°42·4′E	FM	189
Potland	Essex	TM1925	51°53·1′	1°11·3′E	X	168,169
Potland Burn	Northum	NZ2589	55°11·9′	1°36·0′W	W	81
Potland Fm	Northum	NZ2690	55°12·5′	1°35·1′W	FM	81
Potlands	Cumbr	NY6705	54°26·6′	2°30·1′W	X	91
Pot Law	Scot Bord	NT1809	55°22·3′	3°17·2′W	H	79
Pot Law	Scot Bord	NT4748	55°43·6′	2°50·2′W	H	73
Pot Loch	Scot Bord	NT3718	55°27·4′	2°59·3′W	W	79
Potloch Burn	Scot Bord	NT3317	55°26·8′	3°3·1′W	W	79
Potlocks Fm	Derby	SK2935	52°54·9′	1°33·7′W	FM	128
Pot Lords	Ches	SJ9569	53°13·3′	2°4·1′W	X	118
Potluck Ho	Derby	SK1378	53°18·2′	1°47·9′W	X	119
Potman's Heath	Kent	TQ8728	51°1·5′	0°40·4′E	T	189,199
Potmans Place	E Susx	TQ7211	50°52·6′	0°27·1′E	X	199
Pot of Ae	D & G	NX9999	55°16·7′	3°35·0′W	T	78
Potrail Water	S Lanak	NS9309	55°22·1′	3°40·9′W	W	71,78
Potrenick Burn	S Lanak	NS9110	55°22·6′	3°42·8′W	W	71,78
Potrigg	Cumbr	NY5912	54°30·3′	2°37·6′W	X	91
Pot Scar	N Yks	SD7967	54°6·2′	2°18·9′W	X	98
Potsclose	Scot Bord	NT7833	55°35·7′	2°20·5′W	X	74
Potsgrove	Beds	SP9529	51°57·3′	0°36·7′W	T	165
Potslaw	Cumbr	NY6376	55°4·9′	2°34·3′W	X	86
Pots of Ashness	Cumbr	NY1409	54°28·4′	3°19·2′W	X	89
Potstown	D & G	NY2276	55°4·6′	3°12·9′W	X	85
Pottal Valley	Staffs	SJ9614	52°43·7′	2°3·2′W	X	127
Potten End	Herts	TL0108	51°45·9′	0°31·8′W	T	166
Potten Fm	Kent	TQ9139	51°7·3′	0°44·2′E	FM	189
Potten Street	Kent	TR2567	51°21·7′	1°14·3′E	T	179
Potter Brompton	N Yks	SE9777	54°11·0′	0°30·4′W	T	101
Potter Brompton Wold	N Yks	SE9875	54°9·9′	0°29·5′W	X	101
Potter Burn	Northum	NY9653	54°52·6′	2°3·3′W	W	87
Potterells	Herts	TL2304	51°43·5′	0°12·8′W	X	166
Potter Fell	Cumbr	SD5099	54°23·3′	2°45·8′W	X	97
Potter Ford Ho	Lancs	SD7136	53°49·4′	2°26·0′W	X	103
Pottergate Fm	Lincs	SK9856	53°5·8′	0°31·8′W	FM	121
Pottergate Street	Norf	TM1591	52°28·6′	1°10·4′E	T	144
Potter Grange	E Yorks	SE7223	53°42·1′	0°54·1′W	X	105,106,112
Potterhanworth	Lincs	TF0566	53°11·1′	0°25·3′W	T	121
Potterhanworth Booths	Lincs	TF0767	53°11·6′	0°23·5′W	T	121
Potterhanworth Fen	Lincs	TF0967	53°11·6′	0°21·7′W	X	121
Potterhanworth Heath	Lincs	TF0365	53°10·6′	0°27·1′W	X	121
Potterhanworth Wood	Lincs	TF0766	53°11·1′	0°23·5′W	F	121
Potter Heigham	Norf	TG4119	52°43·1′	1°34·5′E	T	134
Potter Hill	Leic	SK7321	52°47·1′	0°54·7′W	T	129

Potter Hill	Notts	SK8561	53°8·6'	0°43·3'W	X	121
Potter Hill	Sheff	SK3397	53°28·4'	1°29·8'W	T	110,111
Potter Hill Fm	Leic	SK7322	52°47·7'	0°54·6'W	FM	129
Potter Hill Fm	N Yks	SE6273	54°9·2'	1°2·6'W	FM	100
Potterhill Fm	S Ayr	NS3921	55°27·6'	4°32·4'W	FM	70
Potter Ho	Durham	NZ2545	54°48·2'	1°36·2'W	X	88
Potter Ho	N Yks	SE5991	54°18·9'	1°5·2'W	X	100
Potteric Carr	Donc	SK5899	53°29·3'	1°7·1'W	X	111
Potteries Fm	Kent	TQ9039	51°7·3'	0°43·3'E	FM	189
Potteries, The	C of Stoke	SJ8846	53°0·9'	2°10·3'W	T	118
Potterland	D & G	NX8055	54°52·8'	3°51·8'W	X	84
Potterland Hill	D & G	NX7955	54°52·8'	3°52·7'W	H	84
Potterland Lane	D & G	NX8055	54°52·8'	3°51·8'W	W	84
Potterland Plantns	D & G	NX7956	54°53·3'	3°52·8'W	F	84
Potter Lane Ho	N Yks	SE1772	54°8·9'	1°44·0'W	X	99
Potterne	Wilts	ST9958	51°19·5'	2°0·5'W	T	173
Potterne Field	Wilts	SU0058	51°19·5'	1°59·6'W	X	173
Potternell Fm	Ches	SJ6480	53°19·2'	2°32·0'W	FM	109
Potterne Park Fm	Wilts	SU0057	51°19·0'	1°59·6'W	FM	173
Potterne Wick	Wilts	SU0057	51°19·0'	1°59·6'W	T	173
Potterne Wood	Wilts	SU0158	51°19·5'	1°58·8'W	F	173
Potternewton	Leeds	SE3036	53°49·4'	1°32·2'W	T	104
Potter Point	Suff	TM2138	52°0·0'	1°13·6'E	X	169
Potter's	Corn	SW7432	50°8·9'	5°9·4'W	X	204
Potters Bar	Herts	TL2501	51°41·9'	0°11·1'W	T	166
Potter's Br	Suff	TM5079	52°21·3'	1°40·7'E	X	156
Potters Brook	Lancs	SD4852	53°57·9'	2°47·1'W	T	102
Potters Close	N Yks	SE3894	54°20·6'	1°24·5'W	X	99
Potters Corner	Kent	TQ9944	51°9·9'	0°51·2'E	T	189
Potter's Cross	Durham	NZ0926	54°38·0'	1°51·2'W	X	92
Potter's Cross	Somer	ST0228	51°2·8'	3°23·5'W	X	181
Potter's Cross	Staffs	SO8484	52°27·5'	2°13·7'W	X	138
Potters Crouch	Herts	TL1105	51°44·2'	0°23·2'W	T	166
Potterscrouch Plantations	Herts	TL1005	51°44·2'	0°24·0'W	F	166
Potter's End	Beds	SP9832	51°58·9'	0°34·0'W	X	165
Potter's Fm	Essex	TQ7798	51°39·4'	0°33·9'E	FM	167
Potter's Fm	Kent	TQ7632	51°3·8'	0°31·1'E	FM	188
Potter's Fm	Oxon	SU6589	51°36·0'	1°3·3'W	FM	175
Potter's Fm	Suff	TM0574	52°19·8'	1°0·9'E	FM	144
Potter's Fm	Suff	TM1653	52°8·2'	1°9·8'E	FM	156
Potter's Fm	Suff	TM4465	52°14·0'	1°34·8'E	FM	156
Potter's Forstal	Kent	TQ8846	51°11·2'	0°41·8'E	T	189
Potter's Green	Cov	SP3782	52°26·3'	1°26·9'W	T	140
Potter's Green	E Susx	TQ5023	50°59·4'	0°8·6'E	T	199
Potter's Green	Herts	TL3520	51°52·0'	0°2·0'W	X	166
Pottersheath	Herts	TL2318	51°51·0'	0°12·5'W	T	166
Potter's Hill	Devon	SS4543	51°10·2'	4°12·6'W	H	180
Potter's Hill	Lincs	SK9718	52°45·3'	0°33·4'W	X	130
Potters Hill	N Som	ST5166	51°23·7'	2°41·9'W	T	172,182
Potter's Hill	Oxon	SP3014	51°49·7'	1°33·5'W	X	164
Potter Sike	Cumbr	NY8608	54°28·3'	2°12·5'W	W	91,92
Potterslade	Pemb	SN0618	51°49·9'	4°48·5'W	X	158
Potter's Lodge	E Yorks	TA0657	54°0·1'	0°22·5'W	X	107
Potters Marston	Leic	SP4996	52°33·8'	1°16·2'W	T	140
Potters Somersal	Derby	SK1436	52°55·5'	1°47·1'W	T	128
Potterspury	Northnts	SP7543	52°5·0'	0°53·9'W	T	152
Potterspury Ho	Northnts	SP7642	52°4·5'	0°53·1'W	X	152
Potterspury Lodge School	Northnts	SP7444	52°5·6'	0°54·8'W	X	152
Potter's Reach	Suff	TM2038	52°0·0'	1°12·7'E	W	169
Potterston	E Ayr	NS3815	55°24·4'	4°33·1'W	X	70
Potter Street	Essex	TL4708	51°45·3'	0°8·2'E	T	167
Potter's Wood	Derby	SK2714	52°43·6'	1°35·6'W	F	128
Potter Tarn	Cumbr	SD4998	54°22·7'	2°46·7'W	W	97
Potterton	Aberd	NJ9415	57°13·8'	2°5·5'W	T	38
Potterton	Leeds	SE4038	53°50·4'	1°23·1'W	T	105
Potterton Br	Leeds	SE4038	53°50·4'	1°23·1'W	X	105
Potterton Burn	Aberd	NJ9317	57°14·9'	2°6·5'W	W	38
Potterton Ho	Aberd	NJ9415	57°13·8'	2°5·5'W	X	38
Pottery	Cumbr	NY5526	54°37·9'	2°41·4'W	X	90
Pottery Field	Leeds	SE3032	53°47·2'	1°32·3'W	T	104
Pottery Ho	Cumbr	NY2162	54°57·0'	3°13·6'W	X	85
Pott Hall	Ches	SJ9479	53°18·7'	2°5·0'W	X	118
Pott Hall	N Yks	SE1578	54°12·1'	1°45·8'W	X	99
Pot, The	Highld	NH7871	57°43·0'	4°2·4'W	W	21
Potthorpe	Norf	TF9422	52°45·9'	0°52·9'E	T	132
Pott House Fm	Tames	SJ9796	53°27·9'	2°2·3'W	FM	109
Pottie	Arg & Bt	NM3221	56°18·6'	6°19·6'W	X	48
Pottie	Arg & Bt	NM3222	56°19·1'	6°19·6'W	X	48
Pottiehill	Pth & Kin	NO1513	56°18·4'	3°22·0'W	X	58
Potting	N Yks	SD9598	54°22·9'	2°4·2'W	X	98
Pottington	Devon	SS5533	51°4·9'	4°3·8'W	T	180
Pottishaw	W Loth	NS9665	55°52·3'	3°39·3'W	X	65
Pottles Fm	Devon	SX9287	50°40·6'	3°31·3'W	FM	192
Pott Moor	N Yks	SE1276	54°11·0'	1°48·5'W	X	99
Potto	N Yks	NZ4703	54°25·5'	1°16·1'W	T	93
Potto Beck	N Yks	NZ4703	54°25·5'	1°16·1'W	W	93
Potto Carr	N Yks	NZ4502	54°24·9'	1°18·0'W	X	93
Potto Grange	N Yks	NZ4604	54°26·0'	1°17·0'W	X	93
Potto Hall (Hotel)	N Yks	NZ4603	54°25·5'	1°17·0'W	X	93
Potto Hill	N Yks	NZ4803	54°25·5'	1°15·2'W	X	93
Potton	Beds	TL2249	52°7·8'	0°12·7'W	T	153
Potton Creek	Essex	TQ9490	51°34·7'	0°48·4'E	W	178
Potton Hall	Suff	TM4571	52°17·2'	1°35·9'E	X	156
Potton Island	Essex	TQ9591	51°35·3'	0°49·3'E	X	178
Potton Point	Essex	TQ9692	51°35·8'	0°50·2'E	X	178
Potton Wood	Beds	TL2550	52°8·3'	0°10·0'W	F	153
Potto Slack	N Yks	NZ4604	54°26·0'	1°17·0'W	W	93
Pottre	Cered	SN3757	52°11·5'	4°22·7'W	X	145
Pott Row	Norf	TF7021	52°45·8'	0°31·6'E	T	132
Pottrow Woods	Norf	TF6921	52°45·8'	0°30·7'E	F	132
Potts	Cumbr	NY7009	54°28·8'	2°27·4'W	X	91
Potts Beck	N Yks	SD9074	54°9·9'	2°8·8'W	W	98
Potts Corner	Lancs	SD4157	54°0·6'	2°53·6'W	X	102
Potts Durtress	Northum	NY8797	55°16·3'	2°11·8'W	X	80
Pott's Fm	Kent	TQ8734	51°4·7'	0°40·6'E	FM	189
Pott's Fm	Suff	TM0041	52°2·1'	0°55·4'E	FM	155
Potts Gill	Cumbr	NY3137	54°43·6'	3°3·9'W	X	90
Potts Green	Essex	TL9022	51°52·1'	0°46·0'E	X	168
Pottshayes Fm	Devon	ST0002	50°48·8'	3°24·8'W	FM	192
Pott's Hill	Herts	TL3236	52°0·6'	0°4·2'W	X	153

Pott Shrigley	Ches	SJ9479	53°18·7'	2°5·0'W	T	118
Potts Moor	N Yks	SD8975	54°10·5'	2°9·7'W	X	98
Potts of Rayne	Aberd	NJ6831	57°22·4'	2°31·5'W	X	29
Potts Wood	Lancs	SD5462	54°3·4'	2°41·7'W	F	97
Pott Yeats	Lancs	SD5462	54°3·4'	2°41·7'W	X	97
Potty Leadnar	Angus	NO4171	56°49·9'	2°57·6'W	X	44
Potwell	Hants	SU6507	50°51·8'	1°4·2'W	X	196
Potwell Fm	Dorset	ST4404	50°50·2'	2°47·3'W	FM	193
Potwells	Herts	TL2103	51°43·0'	0°14·5'W	X	166
Pouchen End	Herts	TL0206	51°44·8'	0°31·0'W	T	166
Pouches Hall	Essex	TL7231	51°57·3'	0°30·6'E	X	167
Poughill	Corn	SS2207	50°50·3'	4°31·3'W	T	190
Poughill	Devon	SS8508	50°51·8'	3°37·7'W	T	191
Poughley	W Berks	SU3473	51°27·5'	1°30·2'W	X	174
Poughley Fm	W Berks	SU4175	51°28·6'	1°24·2'W	FM	174
Poughnhill	Shrops	SO5373	52°21·4'	2°41·0'W	X	137,138
Poukburn	Aberd	NJ9165	57°40·7'	2°8·6'W	X	30
Pouk Hill	Wals	SO9999	52°35·6'	2°0·5'W	X	139
Poulary	Highld	NH1301	57°4·0'	5°4·6'W	X	34
Poulhurst Fm	Kent	TQ6942	51°9·4'	0°25·4'E	FM	188
Poulner	Hants	SU1605	50°50·9'	1°46·0'W	T	195
Poulouriscaig	Highld	NC7665	58°33·6'	4°7·4'W	X	10
Poulshot	Wilts	ST9659	51°20·0'	2°3·1'W	T	173
Poulshot Lodge Fm	Wilts	ST9760	51°20·6'	2°2·2'W	FM	173
Poulston	Devon	SX7754	50°22·6'	3°43·4'W	X	202
Poulstone Court	Heref	SO5628	51°57·2'	2°38·0'W	X	149
Poult Ho, The	Kent	TQ6149	51°13·3'	0°18·7'E	X	188
Poultmoor Fm	Glos	SP0805	51°44·9'	1°52·7'W	FM	163
Poultney Grange	Leic	SP5984	52°27·3'	1°7·5'W	X	140
Poultney Wood	Leic	SK4912	52°42·4'	1°16·1'W	F	129
Poulton	Ches	SJ3958	53°7·2'	2°54·3'W	T	117
Poulton	Glos	SP1001	51°42·7'	1°50·9'W	T	163
Poulton	Shrops	SJ3805	52°38·6'	2°54·6'W	X	126
Poulton	Wirral	SJ3090	53°24·4'	3°2·8'W	T	108
Poulton	Wirral	SJ3382	53°20·1'	3°0·0'W	T	108
Poulton Court	Glos	SO6906	51°45·3'	2°26·6'W	A	162
Poulton Downs	Wilts	SU2071	51°26·5'	1°42·3'W	X	174
Poulton Fields	Glos	SP1002	51°43·2'	1°50·9'W	X	163
Poulton Fm	Kent	TR2641	51°7·6'	1°14·2'E	FM	179
Poulton Fm	Kent	TR2857	51°16·2'	1°16·5'E	FM	179
Poulton Grange	Glos	SP1003	51°43·8'	1°50·9'W	X	163
Poulton Hall	Wirral	SJ3381	53°19·5'	2°59·9'W	X	108
Poultonhall Fm	Ches	SJ3959	53°7·7'	2°54·3'W	FM	117
Poulton Hill Fm	Glos	SU0998	51°41·1'	1°51·8'W	FM	163
Poulton-Le-Fylde	Lancs	SD3439	53°50·8'	2°59·8'W	T	102
Poulton Priory	Glos	SU0999	51°41·6'	1°51·8'W	X	163
Poultons Fm	Warw	SP3247	52°7·5'	1°31·6'W	FM	151
Poultriebuie Burn	D & G	NX5798	55°15·6'	4°14·6'W	W	77
Poultrybuie Hill	D & G	NX4973	55°2·0'	4°21·3'W	H	77
Poulza	Corn	SX2095	50°43·8'	4°32·7'W	X	190
Pounce Hall	Essex	TL5638	52°1·3'	0°16·8'E	X	154
Pounce Hill Fm	Warw	SP3462	52°15·5'	1°29·7'W	FM	151
Pouncers	Devon	SS7311	50°53·3'	3°48·0'W	X	191
Pounceys	Devon	SS8522	50°59·4'	3°37·9'W	X	181
Pound	Devon	SX5068	50°29·8'	4°6·5'W	X	201
Pound	Somer	ST4415	50°56·1'	2°47·4'W	T	193
Pounda	Corn	SX3363	50°26·8'	4°20·8'W	X	201
Pound Bank	Worcs	SO7373	52°21·5'	2°23·4'W	T	138
Pound Bank	Worcs	SO7945	52°6·4'	2°18·0'W	T	150
Pound Bottom	Hants	SU2117	50°57·4'	1°41·7'W	X	184
Poundbury	Dorset	SY6891	50°43·3'	2°26·8'W	A	194
Poundbury Fm	Dorset	SY6790	50°42·8'	2°27·7'W	FM	194
Pound Common	W Susx	SU8725	51°1·3'	0°45·2'W	X	186,197
Pound Copse	Somer	ST7640	51°9·8'	2°20·2'W	F	183
Pound Copse	Wilts	ST9136	51°7·6'	2°7·3'W	F	184
Pound Corner	Suff	TM2654	52°8·5'	1°18·6'E	X	156
Pound Cross	Devon	SX4863	50°27·1'	4°8·1'W	X	201
Pound Farmhouse	Essex	TL7123	51°53·0'	0°29·5'E	X	167
Poundffald	Swan	SS5694	51°37·8'	4°4·4'W	T	159
Poundfield	E Susx	TQ5330	51°3·2'	0°11·4'E	T	188
Pound Fm	Bucks	SU7792	51°37·5'	0°52·9'W	FM	175
Pound Fm	Cumbr	SD4795	54°21·1'	2°48·5'W	FM	97
Pound Fm	Devon	ST0615	50°55·8'	3°19·9'W	FM	181
Pound Fm	Devon	ST1805	50°50·6'	3°9·5'W	FM	192,193
Pound Fm	Dorset	SY6698	50°47·1'	2°28·6'W	FM	194
Pound Fm	Essex	TM0632	51°57·1'	1°0·3'E	FM	168
Pound Fm	E Susx	TQ8514	50°54·0'	0°38·2'E	FM	199
Pound Fm	Glos	SO7013	51°49·1'	2°25·7'W	FM	162
Pound Fm	Glos	SO8313	51°49·2'	2°14·4'W	FM	162
Pound Fm	Heref	SO2548	52°7·8'	3°5·3'W	FM	148
Pound Fm	Heref	SO2854	52°11·0'	3°2·8'W	FM	148
Pound Fm	Heref	SO5459	52°13·9'	2°40·0'W	FM	149
Pound Fm	Heref	SO5535	52°0·9'	2°38·9'W	FM	149
Pound Fm	Heref	SO5662	52°15·5'	2°38·3'W	FM	137,138,149
Pound Fm	Herts	TL1731	51°58·1'	0°17·4'W	FM	166
Pound Fm	Kent	TR2142	51°8·3'	1°9·9'E	FM	179,189
Pound Fm	Norf	TG0314	52°41·4'	1°0·6'E	FM	133
Pound Fm	Oxon	SP6119	51°52·2'	1°6·4'W	FM	164,165
Pound Fm	Suff	TL9545	52°4·4'	0°51·1'E	FM	155
Pound Fm	Suff	TM0076	52°21·0'	0°56·6'E	FM	144
Pound Fm	Suff	TM0236	51°59·4'	0°56·9'E	FM	155
Pound Fm	Suff	TM3262	52°12·7'	1°24·2'E	FM	156
Pound Fm	Surrey	SU9149	51°14·2'	0°41·4'W	FM	186
Pound Fm	Wilts	ST9572	51°27·1'	2°3·9'W	FM	173
Pound Fm	W Susx	SU8624	51°0·8'	0°46·1'W	FM	197
Pound Fm	W Susx	TQ1421	50°58·9'	0°22·2'W	FM	198
Pound Fms	Dorset	SY3397	50°46·4'	2°56·6'W	FM	193
Poundford	E Susx	TQ5524	50°59·9'	0°12·9'E	T	199
Poundgate	E Susx	TQ4928	51°2·1'	0°7·9'E	T	188,199
Poundgate	Kent	TQ6562	51°20·2'	0°22·5'E	X	177,178,188
Pound Gate Fm	Shrops	SO1782	52°26·0'	3°12·9'W	FM	136
Pound Green	E Susx	TQ5023	50°59·4'	0°8·6'E	T	199
Pound Green	Hants	SU5759	51°19·9'	1°10·5'W	T	174
Pound Green	I of W	SZ3386	50°40·6'	1°31·6'W	T	196
Pound Green	Suff	TL7153	52°9·2'	0°30·4'E	T	154
Poundgreen	Wok	SU6967	51°24·1'	1°0·1'W	T	175
Pound Green	Worcs	SO7578	52°24·2'	2°21·7'W	T	138
Pound Green Common	Worcs	SO7578	52°24·2'	2°21·7'W	X	138
Pound Hill	Norf	TM2582	52°23·6'	1°18·8'E	X	156
Pound Hill	Oxon	SP4819	51°52·3'	1°17·8'W	X	164

Pound Hill	W Susx	TQ2937	51°7·3'	0°9·0'W	T	187
Poundhill Heath	Hants	SU2804	50°50·3'	1°35·8'W	X	195
Poundhill Inclosure	Hants	SU2704	50°50·3'	1°36·6'W	F	195
Pound Ho	Heref	SO4765	52°17·1'	2°46·2'W	X	137,138,148
Pound Ho	Powys	SJ2907	52°39·6'	3°2·6'W	X	126
Poundhouse	Devon	SX8649	50°20·0'	3°35·7'W	X	202
Pound House Fm	Devon	SY3599	50°47·4'	2°54·9'W	FM	193
Pound House Fm	S Glos	ST6692	51°37·8'	2°29·1'W	FM	162,172
Pound House, The	Kent	TR0940	51°7·5'	0°59·6'E	X	179,189
Poundisford Lodge	Somer	ST2220	50°58·7'	3°6·3'W	A	193
Poundisford Park	Somer	ST2220	50°58·7'	3°6·3'W	A	193
Poundland	D & G	NX7889	55°11·1'	3°54·5'W	X	78
Poundland	D & G	NX8583	55°7·9'	3°47·8'W	X	78
Poundland	S Ayr	NS2902	55°17·2'	4°41·1'W	X	76
Poundland	S Ayr	NX1787	55°8·9'	4°51·9'W	T	76
Poundland Ho	S Ayr	NX1787	55°8·9'	4°51·9'W	X	76
Poundland Moor	D & G	NX7273	55°2·4'	3°59·8'W	X	77,84
Pound Living	Devon	SX9789	50°41·7'	3°27·1'W	X	192
Poundon	Bucks	SP6425	51°55·4'	1°3·8'W	T	164,165
Poundon Hill	Bucks	SP6325	51°55·4'	1°4·6'W	X	164,165
Poundsbridge	Kent	TQ5341	51°9·1'	0°11·7'E	T	188
Pounds Conce	Corn	SX1271	50°30·8'	4°38·7'W	X	200
Pound's Fm	W Berks	SU3779	51°30·8'	1°27·6'W	FM	174
Poundsford Fm	E Susx	TQ6322	50°58·7'	0°19·7'E	FM	199
Poundsgate	Devon	SX7072	50°32·2'	3°49·7'W	T	191
Pounds Hill	Devon	SS8301	50°48·0'	3°39·2'W	X	191
Poundstock	Corn	SX2099	50°46·0'	4°32·8'W	T	190
Pound Street	Hants	SU4561	51°21·0'	1°20·8'W	T	174
Pound, The	Corn	SW6713	49°58·5'	5°14·6'W	W	203
Pound, The	E Susx	TV6097	50°45·3'	0°16·5'E	W	199
Pound, The	Glos	SO7031	51°58·8'	2°25·8'W	T	149
Pound, The	Powys	SO1374	52°21·7'	3°16·3'W	X	136,148
Pound Wood	Bucks	SU7893	51°38·1'	0°52·0'W	F	175
Pound Wood	Essex	TQ8288	51°33·9'	0°38·0'E	F	178
Pound Wood	Kent	TQ9536	51°5·6'	0°47·5'E	F	189
Pounsley	E Susx	TQ5221	50°58·3'	0°10·3'E	T	199
Pountney Hall	Suff	TM0873	52°19·2'	1°3·5'E	X	144,155
Pountwell	Glos	SP1018	51°51·9'	1°50·9'W	X	163
Pouterlany	Scot Bord	NT7753	55°46·4'	2°21·6'W	X	67,74
Pout Knowe	Scot Bord	NY4294	55°14·5'	2°54·3'W	X	79
Pouton	D & G	NX4645	54°46·8'	4°23·3'W	X	83
Poverest	Brom	TQ4668	51°23·8'	0°6·3'E	T	177
Poverty	Shetld	HU5285	60°33·0'	1°2·6'W	X	1,2,3
Poverty Bottom	E Susx	TQ4602	50°48·2'	0°4·7'E	X	198
Poverty Hill	N Yks	NZ7208	54°28·0'	0°52·9'W	X	94
Povey Cross	Surrey	TQ2642	51°10·0'	0°11·5'W	T	187
Povey Fm	Derby	SK3880	53°19·2'	1°25·4'W	FM	110,111
Povey's Fm	Hants	SU5758	51°19·3'	1°10·5'W	FM	174
Povington Barrow	Dorset	SY8782	50°38·5'	2°10·6'W	A	194
Povington Heath	Dorset	SY8783	50°39·0'	2°10·7'W	X	194
Povington Hill	Dorset	SY8881	50°37·9'	2°9·8'W	H	194
Pow	Cumbr	NY3151	54°51·2'	3°4·1'W	X	85
Pow	Orkney	HY2519	59°3·4'	3°18·0'W	X	6
Pow Bank	Cumbr	NY2542	54°46·3'	3°9·5'W	X	85
Pow Bank	Cumbr	NY3849	54°50·2'	2°57·5'W	X	85
Pow Beck	Cumbr	NX9712	54°29·8'	3°35·0'W	W	89
Pow Beck	Cumbr	NY2424	54°36·6'	3°10·2'W	W	89,90
Pow Beck	Cumbr	NY3949	54°50·2'	2°56·6'W	W	85
Powblack	Stir	NS6696	56°8·5'	4°9·0'W	X	57
Powbridge	Stir	NS8787	56°4·0'	3°48·5'W	X	65
Powbrone Burn	S Lanak	NS6834	55°35·2'	4°5·2'W	W	71
Powburgh Beck	Cumbr	NY3258	54°55·0'	3°3·2'W	W	85
Pow Burn	Angus	NO6456	56°41·9'	2°34·8'W	W	54
Pow Burn	Falk	NS8886	56°3·5'	3°47·5'W	W	65
Powburn	Northum	NU0616	55°26·5'	1°53·9'W	T	81
Pow Burn	Pth & Kin	NO0402	56°12·3'	3°32·4'W	W	58
Pow Burn	Pth & Kin	NT0597	56°9·6'	3°31·3'W	W	58
Pow Burn	S Ayr	NS3727	55°30·8'	4°34·5'W	W	70
Pow Burn	Stir	NS6391	56°5·8'	4°11·7'W	W	57
Powdanna Burn	D & G	NT2002	55°18·6'	3°15·2'W	W	79
Powder Blue Fm	Peterb	TF2405	52°37·9'	0°9·7'W	FM	142
Powderham	Devon	SX9684	50°39·0'	3°27·9'W	T	192
Powderham Castle	Devon	SX9683	50°38·5'	3°27·9'W	A	192
Powderham Castle	Hants	SU8046	51°12·7'	0°50·9'W	A	186
Powdermill Reservoir	E Susx	TQ8019	50°56·8'	0°34·1'E	W	199
Powder Mills	Devon	SX6276	50°34·3'	3°56·6'W	FM	191
Powder Mills	Kent	TQ5647	51°12·3'	0°14·4'E	T	188
Powder Mills Hotel	E Susx	TQ7414	50°54·2'	0°28·9'E	X	199
Powderwells	Pth & Kin	NO2446	56°36·2'	3°13·8'W	X	53
Powdrake	Stir	NS8686	56°3·5'	3°49·4'W	X	65
Powdykes	Orkney	HY4343	59°16·4'	2°59·5'W	X	5
Powell's Fm	Hants	SU2819	50°58·4'	1°35·7'W	FM	184
Powells Fm	Hants	SU6540	51°9·6'	1°3·8'W	FM	185,186
Powell's Pool	Birm	SP1095	52°33·4'	1°50·7'W	W	139
Power's Fm	Essex	TL7212	51°47·0'	0°30·0'E	FM	167
Powers Fm	Worcs	SO8363	52°16·1'	2°14·6'W	FM	138,150
Powers Hall End	Essex	TL8015	51°48·5'	0°37·1'E	T	168
Powerstock	Dorset	SY5196	50°45·9'	2°41·3'W	T	194
Powerstock Common	Dorset	SY5496	50°45·9'	2°38·8'W	F	194
Powflats	W Loth	NT0771	55°55·6'	3°28·9'W	X	65
Pow Fm	Fife	NT0397	56°9·6'	3°33·3'W	FM	58
Powfoot	D & G	NY1465	54°58·6'	3°20·2'W	T	85
Powfoot Scar	D & G	NY1464	54°58·0'	3°20·2'W	X	85
Powfoulis Manor Hotel	Falk	NS9185	56°3·0'	3°44·6'W	X	65
Powgavie	Pth & Kin	NO2825	56°25·0'	3°9·6'W	X	53,59
Pow Gill	Cumbr	NY2542	54°46·3'	3°9·5'W	W	85
Powgree Burn	N Ayr	NS3452	55°44·2'	4°38·2'W	W	63
Pow Green	Heref	SO7144	52°5·9'	2°25·0'W	T	149
Powguild	Fife	NT2092	56°7·1'	3°16·8'W	X	58
Powhaffet	D & G	NY2080	55°6·7'	3°14·8'W	X	79
Pow Heads	Cumbr	NY2540	54°45·2'	3°9·5'W	X	85
Powhill	Cumbr	NY2355	54°53·3'	3°11·6'W	T	85
Pow Hill Country Park	Durham	NZ0151	54°51·5'	1°58·6'W	X	87
Powhillon	D & G	NY0667	54°59·6'	3°27·7'W	X	85
Powick	Worcs	SO8351	52°9·7'	2°14·5'W	T	150
Powick Bridge	Worcs	SO8352	52°10·2'	2°14·5'W	A	150
Powick Hams	Worcs	SO8352	52°10·2'	2°14·5'W	X	150
Powie Burn	Fife	NO4926	56°25·7'	2°49·2'W	W	54,59
Powillimoun	D & G	NX9856	54°53·5'	3°35·0'W	X	84
Powis	Angus	NO6656	56°41·9'	2°32·9'W	X	54

Powis Castle	Powys	SJ2106	52°39·0′	3°9·7′W	A	126
Powis Ho	Cumbr	NY6524	54°36·8′	2°32·1′W	X	91
Powis Ho	Stir	NS8295	56°8·2′	3°53·5′W	X	57
Powisholm	Scot Bord	NY5089	55°11·8′	2°46·7′W	X	79
Powis Mains	Stir	NS8195	56°8·2′	3°54·5′W	X	57
Powkelly Burn	E Ayr	NS5306	55°19·8′	4°18·6′W	W	70,77
Powkesmoor Coppice	Shrops	SO5988	52°29·5′	2°35·8′W	F	137,138
Powkesmoor Fm	Shrops	SO5988	52°29·5′	2°35·8′W	FM	137,138
Powlair	Aberd	NO6291	57°0·8′	2°37·1′W	X	45
Powler's Piece	Devon	SS3718	50°56·5′	4°18·8′W	T	190
Powlesland	Devon	SX6896	50°45·2′	3°51·9′W	X	191
Powley's Hill	Cumbr	NY5013	54°30·8′	2°45·9′W	X	90
Pow Maughan	Cumbr	NY4651	54°51·3′	2°50·0′W	W	86
Powmeadow Burn	S Lanak	NS6032	55°34·0′	4°12·8′W	W	71
Powmill	Angus	NO6355	56°41·4′	2°35·8′W	X	54
Powmill	Pth & Kin	NN8919	56°21·3′	3°47·3′W	X	58
Powmill	Pth & Kin	NT0298	56°10·1′	3°34·3′W	T	58
Powmill Fm	Pth & Kin	NT0298	56°10·1′	3°34·3′W	FM	58
Powmillon Burn	S Lanak	NS6946	55°41·6′	4°4·6′W	W	64
Powmouth	Angus	NO6557	56°42·5′	2°33·9′W	X	54
Powmuck Burn	D & G	NT1904	55°19·7′	3°16·2′W	W	79
Powmyre	Angus	NO3650	56°38·5′	3°2·2′W	X	54
Pownall House Fm	Ches	SJ8178	53°18·2′	2°16·7′W	FM	118
Pownall Park	Ches	SJ8381	53°19·8′	2°14·9′W	T	109
Powneed	Moray	NJ3925	57°18·9′	3°0·3′W	X	37
Powntley Copse	Hants	SU7044	51°11·7′	0°59·5′W	T	186
Powside	Pth & Kin	NO0524	56°24·2′	3°31·9′W	X	52,53,58
Powside	Stir	NS8686	56°3·5′	3°49·4′W	X	65
Powskein Burn	Scot Bord	NT0714	55°24·9′	3°27·7′W	W	78
Powskein Dod	Scot Bord	NT0318	55°27·0′	3°31·6′W	H	78
Powsoddie	Angus	NO5755	56°41·3′	2°41·7′W	X	54
Powterneth Beck	Cumbr	NY5259	54°55·7′	2°44·5′W	W	86
Pow,The	Orkney	HY2205	58°55·8′	3°20·8′W	W	6,7
Pow, The	Orkney	HY6721	59°4·7′	2°34·1′W	X	5
Pow, The	Shetld	HU4963	60°21·1′	1°6·2′W	X	2,3
Pow Water	D & G	NY1169	55°0·7′	3°23·1′W	W	85
Pow Water	Pth & Kin	NN9622	56°23·0′	3°40·6′W	W	52,53,58
Poxwell Manor	Dorset	SY7483	50°39·0′	2°21·7′W	A	194
Poyerston	Pemb	SN0202	51°41·2′	4°51·5′W	X	157,158
Poyle	Bucks	TQ0376	51°28·6′	0°30·6′W	T	176
Poyle Fm	Surrey	SU8949	51°14·2′	0°43·1′W	FM	186
Poyll Vaaish	I of M	SC2467	54°4·4′	4°41·0′W	W	95
Poyllvaaish	I of M	SC2467	54°4·4′	4°41·0′W	X	95
Poynatts Fm	Bucks	SU7790	51°36·4′	0°52·9′W	FM	175
Poynders End	Herts	TL1824	51°54·4′	0°16·7′W	X	166
Poyning	Powys	SO1368	52°18·4′	3°16·2′W	X	136,148
Poynings	W Susx	TQ2612	50°53·8′	0°12·1′W	T	198
Poynings Grange Fm	W Susx	TQ2513	50°54·4′	0°12·9′W	FM	198
Poynters	Surrey	TQ0958	51°18·9′	0°25·8′W	X	187
Poyntington	Somer	ST6520	50°58·9′	2°29·5′W	T	183
Poyntington Down	Dorset	ST6421	50°59·5′	2°30·4′W	X	183
Poyntington Hill	Somer	ST6520	50°58·9′	2°29·5′W	H	183
Poynton	Ches	SJ9283	53°20·9′	2°6·8′W	T	109
Poynton	Wrekin	SJ5717	52°45·2′	2°37·8′W	T	126
Poynton Brook	Ches	SJ9283	53°20·3′	2°6·8′W	W	109
Poyntoncross Ho	Derby	SK1677	53°17·6′	1°45·2′W	X	119
Poynton Grange	Wrekin	SJ5618	52°45·7′	2°38·7′W	X	126
Poynton Green	Wrekin	SJ5618	52°45·7′	2°38·7′W	T	126
Poynton Lake	Ches	SJ9284	53°21·4′	2°6·8′W	W	109
Poynton Springs	Wrekin	SJ5517	52°45·2′	2°39·6′W	F	126
Poyntzfield	Highld	NH7164	57°39·1′	4°9·2′W	X	21,27
Poyntzfield Mills	Highld	NH7063	57°38·6′	4°10·2′W	X	21,27
Poyston	Pemb	SM9619	51°50·2′	4°57·3′W	T	157,158
Poyston Cross	Pemb	SM9719	51°50·2′	4°56·4′W	T	157,158
Poyston West	Pemb	SM9619	51°50·2′	4°57·3′W	X	157,158
Poystreet Green	Suff	TL9858	52°11·3′	0°54·2′E	T	155
Praa Sands	Corn	SW5827	50°5·9′	5°22·7′W	X	203
Praa Sands	Corn	SW5828	50°6·4′	5°22·7′W	T	203
Prabost	Highld	NG4249	57°27·7′	6°17·7′W	T	23
Praddoe Coppice	Shrops	SJ4621	52°47·3′	2°47·6′W	F	126
Pradoe	Shrops	SJ3524	52°48·8′	2°57·5′W	X	126
Prae Wood	Herts	TL1206	51°44·7′	0°22·3′W	F	166
Praie Grounds	Lincs	TF1451	53°2·9′	0°17·6′W	X	121
Prail Castle	Angus	NO6946	56°36·5′	2°29·9′W	X	54
Prail Castle (Fort)	Angus	NO6946	56°36·5′	2°29·9′W	A	54
Prathouse	Fife	NT1487	56°4·3′	3°22·5′W	X	65
Pratis	Fife	NO3806	56°14·8′	2°59·6′W	X	59
Pratling Street	Kent	TQ7459	51°18·4′	0°30·2′E	T	178,188
Pratthall	Derby	SK3273	53°15·4′	1°30·8′W	X	119
Prattle Wood	Oxon	SP5412	51°48·5′	1°12·6′W	F	164
Pratt's Bottom	Brom	TQ4762	51°20·5′	0°7·0′E	T	177,188
Pratt's Fm	Essex	TL7111	51°46·5′	0°29·1′E	FM	167
Pratt's Grove	Brom	TQ4761	51°20·0′	0°7·0′E	F	177,188
Prattshaugh	Aberd	NJ9059	57°37·5′	2°9·6′W	X	30
Prattshayes Fm	Devon	SY0280	50°36·9′	3°22·7′W	FM	192
Pratt's Hill	Devon	SY2292	50°43·6′	3°5·9′W	X	192,193
Praunsley	Devon	SS7630	51°3·6′	3°45·8′W	X	180
Prawle Point	Devon	SX7735	50°12·4′	3°43·0′W	X	202
Prawles Fm	E Susx	TQ7823	50°59·0′	0°32·5′E	FM	199
Prayway Head	Somer	SS7640	51°9·0′	3°46·0′W	X	180
Praze	Corn	SW6327	50°6·0′	5°18·5′W	X	203
Praze	Corn	SX1170	50°30·2′	4°39·5′W	X	200
Praze-an-Beeble	Corn	SW6335	50°10·3′	5°18·8′W	T	203
Preaching Stone	D & G	NX8590	55°11·7′	3°48·0′W	X	78
Preas a' Chamraig	Highld	NC7129	58°14·1′	4°11·3′W	H	16
Preas Dubh	Highld	NH6332	57°21·7′	4°16·2′W	X	26
Preas Mór	Highld	NC3560	58°30·1′	4°49·4′W	H	9
Preas nan Sgiathanach	Highld	NC6809	58°3·3′	4°13·7′W	X	16
Preas Whin	Aberd	NJ3805	57°8·2′	3°1·0′W	X	37
Preceptory	W Loth	NS9672	55°56·0′	3°39·4′W	A	65
Precipice Walk	Gwyn	SH7321	52°46·5′	3°52·6′W	X	124
Predannack Airfield	Corn	SW6816	50°0·2′	5°13·9′W	X	203
Predannack Head	Corn	SW6616	50°0·1′	5°15·6′W	X	203
Predannack Manor Fm	Corn	SW6616	50°0·1′	5°15·6′W	FM	203
Predannack Wollas	Corn	SW6616	50°0·1′	5°15·6′W	X	203
Preen Manor	Shrops	SO5498	52°34·9′	2°40·3′W	X	137,138
Prees	Shrops	SJ5533	52°53·8′	2°39·7′W	T	126
Preesall	Lancs	SD3647	53°55·2′	2°58·1′W	T	102
Preesall Moss Side	Lancs	SD3746	53°54·6′	2°57·1′W	X	102
Preesall Park	Lancs	SD3746	53°54·6′	2°57·1′W	T	102

Presall Sands	Lancs	SD3550	53°56·8′	2°59·0′W	X	102
Prees Branch	Shrops	SJ4934	52°54·3′	2°45·1′W	X	126
Preese Hall	Lancs	SD3736	53°49·2′	2°57·0′W	X	102
Prees Green	Shrops	SJ5631	52°52·7′	2°38·8′W	T	126
Preesgweene	Shrops	SJ2935	52°54·7′	3°2·9′W	T	126
Prees Heath	Shrops	SJ5537	52°56·0′	2°39·8′W	T	126
Preeshenlle	Shrops	SJ3034	52°54·2′	3°2·0′W	T	126
Prees Higher Heath	Shrops	SJ5635	52°54·9′	2°38·8′W	T	126
Prees Lower Heath	Shrops	SJ5732	52°53·3′	2°37·9′W	T	126
Prees Sta	Shrops	SJ5333	52°53·8′	2°41·5′W	X	126
Prees Wood	Shrops	SJ5633	52°53·8′	2°38·8′W	T	126
Pré Hotel	Herts	TL1208	51°45·8′	0°22·2′W	X	166
Prenbrigog	Flint	SJ2664	53°10·3′	3°6·0′W	T	117
Pren Croes	Powys	SJ0113	52°42·6′	3°27·5′W	X	125
Prendergast	Pemb	SM8024	51°52·5′	5°11·4′W	T	157
Prendergast	Pemb	SM9516	51°48·5′	4°58·0′W	T	157,158
Prenderguest	Scot Bord	NT9159	55°49·7′	2°8·2′W	T	67,74,75
Prendwick	Northum	NU0012	55°24·4′	1°59·6′W	X	81
Pren-gwyn	Cered	SN4244	52°4·6′	4°17·9′W	T	146
Prenteg	Gwyn	SH5841	52°57·1′	4°6·4′W	T	124
Prentice Hall Fm	Essex	TL9410	51°45·5′	0°49·1′E	FM	168
Prenton	Wirral	SJ3086	53°22·2′	3°2·7′W	T	108
Presaddfed	I of Angl	SH3580	53°17·7′	4°28·1′W	X	114
Presbury	Devon	SS6219	50°57·5′	3°57·5′W	X	180
Prescalton	Moray	NJ2142	57°27·9′	3°18·6′W	X	28
Prescoed	Monm	ST3499	51°41·4′	2°56·9′W	X	171
Prescombe	Devon	SX5184	50°38·4′	4°6·1′W	X	191,201
Prescombe Down	Wilts	ST9825	51°1·7′	2°1·3′W	X	184
Prescombe Fm	Wilts	ST9924	51°1·2′	2°0·5′W	FM	184
Prescot	Know	SJ4692	53°25·6′	2°48·4′W	T	108
Prescote Manor	Oxon	SP4746	52°6·9′	1°18·4′W	X	151
Prescote Manor Fm	Oxon	SP4747	52°7·4′	1°18·4′W	FM	151
Prescott	Devon	SS9413	50°54·6′	3°30·1′W	X	181
Prescott	Devon	ST0814	50°55·3′	3°18·2′W	T	181
Prescott	Glos	SO9829	51°57·8′	2°1·4′W	T	150,163
Prescott	Shrops	SJ4221	52°47·2′	2°51·2′W	T	126
Prescott	Shrops	SO6681	52°25·8′	2°29·6′W	T	138
Prescott Br	Lancs	SD4613	53°36·9′	2°48·6′W	X	108
Prescott Ho	Glos	SO9829	51°57·8′	2°1·4′W	X	150,163
Prescott's Fm	Lancs	SD4808	53°34·2′	2°46·7′W	FM	108
Presdales	Herts	TL3613	51°48·2′	0°1·3′W	T	166
Preserve Plantn	E Yorks	SE7957	54°0·4′	0°47·3′W	F	105,106
Presford Fm	I of W	SZ4682	50°38·4′	1°20·6′W	FM	196
Preshal Beg	Highld	NG3227	57°15·6′	6°26·2′W	H	32
Preshal More	Highld	NG3329	57°16·7′	6°25·3′W	H	32
Preshaw	Hants	SU5622	50°59·9′	1°11·7′W	X	185
Preshaw Down	Hants	SU5822	50°59·9′	1°10·0′W	X	185
Preshaw Ho	Hants	SU5723	51°0·4′	1°10·9′W	X	185
Preshome	Moray	NJ4161	57°38·4′	2°58·8′W	T	28
Preshute Down	Wilts	SU1374	51°28·1′	1°48·4′W	X	173
Preshute Ho	Wilts	SU1768	51°24·9′	1°44·9′W	X	173
Presley	Moray	NJ0150	57°32·0′	3°38·7′W	X	27
Presnerb	Angus	NO1866	56°47·0′	3°20·1′W	T	43
Press	Derby	SK3665	53°11·1′	1°27·3′W	T	119
Press	Highld	NH8026	57°18·8′	3°59·1′W	X	35
Press Castle	Scot Bord	NT8765	55°52·9′	2°12·0′W	X	67
Pressen	Northum	NT8335	55°36·7′	2°15·8′W	T	74
Pressen Burn	Northum	NT8234	55°36·2′	2°16·7′W	W	74
Pressendye	Aberd	NJ4908	57°9·9′	2°50·1′W	H	37
Pressenhill	Northum	NT8234	55°36·2′	2°16·7′W	X	74
Pressen Hill	Northum	NT8336	55°37·3′	2°15·8′W	X	74
Pressland	Devon	SS5502	50°48·2′	4°3·1′W	X	191
Press Mains	Scot Bord	NT8765	55°52·9′	2°12·0′W	X	67
Pressmennan	E Loth	NT6273	55°57·2′	2°36·1′W	X	67
Pressmennan Wood	E Loth	NT6373	55°57·2′	2°35·1′W	F	67
Pressmore Fm	Bucks	SP9604	51°43·8′	0°36·2′W	FM	165
Pressock	Angus	NO5649	56°38·1′	2°42·6′W	X	54
Press Resrs	Derby	SK3565	53°11·1′	1°28·2′W	W	119
Press Ridge Warren	E Susx	TQ4131	51°3·9′	0°1·1′E	F	187
Prestatyn	Denb	SJ0682	53°19·8′	3°24·3′W	T	116
Prestberries Fm	Glos	SO7826	51°56·2′	2°18·8′W	FM	162
Prestbury	Ches	SJ9077	53°17·6′	2°8·6′W	T	118
Prestbury	Glos	SO9723	51°54·6′	2°2·2′W	T	163
Prestbury Fm	Glos	SO7320	51°52·9′	2°23·1′W	FM	162
Prestbury Park	Glos	SO9524	51°55·1′	2°4·0′W	X	163
Prested Hall	Essex	TL8819	51°50·5′	0°44·1′E	X	168
Presteigne or Llanandras	Powys	SO3164	52°16·4′	3°0·3′W	T	137,148
Presthope	Shrops	SO5897	52°34·4′	2°36·8′W	T	137,138
Prestleigh	Somer	ST6340	51°9·7′	2°31·4′W	T	183
Prestley Hill	Rut	SP8897	52°34·1′	0°41·7′W	H	141
Prestolee	Bolton	SD7505	53°32·7′	2°22·2′W	T	109
Preston	Brent	TQ1887	51°34·4′	0°17·4′W	T	176
Preston	Bri & Hov	TQ3006	50°50·6′	0°8·8′W	T	198
Preston	Devon	SS8504	50°49·7′	3°37·6′W	X	191
Preston	Devon	SX6353	50°21·9′	3°55·2′W	X	202
Preston	Devon	SX7143	50°16·6′	3°48·3′W	X	202
Preston	Devon	SX7451	50°21·0′	3°45·9′W	X	202
Preston	Devon	SX7590	50°42·0′	3°45·8′W	X	191
Preston	Devon	SX8574	50°33·5′	3°37·0′W	T	191
Preston	Dorset	SY7083	50°39·0′	2°25·1′W	T	194
Preston	E Loth	NT3974	55°57·6′	2°58·2′W	T	66
Preston	E Loth	NT5977	55°59·3′	2°39·0′W	T	67
Preston	E Yorks	TA1830	53°45·4′	0°12·2′W	T	107
Preston	Glos	SO6734	52°0·4′	2°28·5′W	T	149
Preston	Glos	SP0400	51°42·2′	1°56·1′W	T	163
Preston	Herts	TL1724	51°54·4′	0°17·6′W	T	166
Preston	Kent	TR0260	51°18·4′	0°54·3′E	T	178
Preston	Kent	TR2561	51°18·4′	1°14·1′E	T	179
Preston	Lancs	SD5329	53°45·6′	2°42·4′W	T	102
Preston	Northum	NU1825	55°31·4′	1°42·5′W	X	75
Preston	N Tyne	NZ3469	55°1·1′	1°27·7′W	T	88
Preston	Rut	SK8702	52°36·8′	0°42·5′W	T	141
Preston	Scot Bord	NT7957	55°48·6′	2°19·7′W	T	67,74
Preston	Shrops	SJ5211	52°41·9′	2°42·2′W	T	126
Preston	Somer	ST1035	51°6·7′	3°16·8′W	X	181
Preston	Torbay	SX8861	50°26·5′	3°34·3′W	T	202
Preston	Wilts	SU0378	51°30·3′	1°57·0′W	T	173
Preston	Wilts	SU2773	51°27·6′	1°36·3′W	T	174
Preston Bagot	Warw	SP1765	52°17·2′	1°45·5′W	T	151
Preston Bissett	Bucks	SP6529	51°57·6′	1°2·8′W	T	164,165

Preston Bowyer	Somer	ST1326	51°1·8′	3°14·1′W	T	181,193
Preston Brockhurst	Shrops	SJ5324	52°48·9′	2°41·4′W	T	126
Preston Brook	Halton	SJ5680	53°19·1′	2°39·2′W	T	108
Preston Brook	Heref	SO6634	52°0·4′	2°29·3′W	W	149
Prestonbury Castle	Devon	SX7490	50°42·0′	3°46·7′W	X	191
Preston Candover	Hants	SU6041	51°10·1′	1°8·1′W	T	185
Preston Capes	Northnts	SP5754	52°11·1′	1°9·6′W	T	152
Preston Carrs	Durham	NZ3125	54°37·4′	1°30·8′W	X	93
Preston Combe	Devon	SX7452	50°21·5′	3°45·9′W	X	202
Preston Coppice	Shrops	SJ4920	52°46·8′	2°45·0′W	F	126
Preston Court	E Susx	TQ4507	50°50·9′	0°4·0′E	X	198
Preston Court	Kent	TR2460	51°17·9′	1°13·2′E	X	179
Preston Cross	Glos	SO6735	52°1·0′	2°28·5′W	X	149
Preston Crowmarsh	Oxon	SU6190	51°36·6′	1°6·8′W	T	164,175
Preston Deanery	Northnts	SP7855	52°11·5′	0°51·1′W	T	152
Preston Down	Hants	SU6241	51°10·1′	1°6·4′W	X	185
Prestonfield	C of Edin	NT2771	55°55·8′	3°9·7′W	T	66
Prestonfield	D & G	NY2068	55°0·3′	3°14·6′W	X	85
Preston Field	E Yorks	TA1732	53°46·5′	0°13·1′W	X	107
Preston Fields	Warw	SP1766	52°17·7′	1°44·6′W	T	151
Preston Fields Fm	Northnts	SP5554	52°11·1′	1°11·3′W	FM	152
Preston Fm	Devon	ST2107	50°51·7′	3°7·0′W	FM	192,193
Preston Fm	Devon	SX5748	50°19·1′	4°0·1′W	FM	202
Preston Fm	Dorset	ST9304	50°50·4′	2°5·6′W	FM	195
Preston Fm	Kent	TQ5262	51°20·4′	0°11·3′E	FM	177,188
Preston Fm	W Susx	SU8511	50°53·8′	0°47·1′W	FM	197
Preston Grange	Hants	SU6040	51°9·6′	1°8·1′W	X	185
Preston Grange	N Tyne	NZ3470	55°1·6′	1°27·7′W	T	88
Preston Green	Warw	SP1665	52°17·2′	1°45·5′W	T	151
Preston Gubbals	Shrops	SJ4919	52°46·2′	2°45·0′W	T	126
Preston Hall	Ches	SJ4846	53°0·8′	2°46·1′W	X	117
Preston Hall	D & G	NY2168	55°0·3′	3°13·7′W	X	85
Preston Hall	E Susx	TQ7309	50°51·5′	0°27·9′E	X	199
Prestonhall	Fife	NO3915	56°19·7′	2°58·7′W	X	59
Preston Hall	Midlo	NT3965	55°52·7′	2°58·1′W	X	66
Preston Hall	Shrops	SJ5324	52°48·9′	2°41·4′W	A	126
Preston Hall	Stock on T	NZ4215	54°32·0′	1°20·6′W	X	93
Preston Haugh	Scot Bord	NT7757	55°48·6′	2°21·6′W	X	67,74
Preston Hill	Dorset	ST8713	50°55·2′	2°10·7′W	X	194
Preston Hill	Northum	NT9223	55°30·3′	2°7·2′W	H	74,75
Preston Hill	Staffs	SJ9014	52°43·7′	2°8·5′W	X	127
Prestonhill Fm	Herts	TL1724	51°54·4′	0°17·6′W	FM	166
Preston Hill Fm	Warw	SP1663	52°16·1′	1°45·5′W	FM	151
Preston Ho	Devon	SS6243	51°10·4′	3°58·1′W	X	180
Preston Ho	Dorset	ST8613	50°55·2′	2°11·6′W	X	194
Preston Ho	E Susx	TQ4607	50°50·9′	0°4·8′E	X	198
Preston Ho	Hants	SU6042	51°10·7′	1°8·1′W	X	185
Preston Ho	N Yks	SE3359	54°1·8′	1°29·4′W	X	104
Preston Ho	W Loth	NS9975	55°57·7′	3°36·6′W	X	65
Preston Island	Fife	NT0085	56°3·1′	3°35·9′W	X	65
Preston Law	Scot Bord	NT2535	55°36·4′	3°11·0′W	H	73
Prestonlea Coppice	Shrops	SJ5423	52°48·4′	2°40·5′W	F	126
Preston-le-Skerne	Durham	NZ3024	54°36·9′	1°31·7′W	T	93
Preston Lodge	Durham	NZ3122	54°35·8′	1°30·8′W	X	93
Preston Lodge	Leic	SK8006	52°39·0′	0°48·6′W	X	141
Preston Lodge Fm	Northnts	SP7956	52°12·0′	0°50·2′W	FM	152
Preston Mains	E Loth	NT5978	55°59·8′	2°39·0′W	X	67
Preston Mains	Midlo	NT4065	55°52·7′	2°57·1′W	X	66
Preston Market Cross	E Loth	NT3974	55°57·6′	2°58·2′W	X	66
Preston Marsh	Heref	SO5646	52°6·9′	2°38·2′W	T	149
Preston Merse	D & G	NX9555	54°53·0′	3°37·8′W	X	84
Prestonmill	D & G	NX9657	54°54·1′	3°36·9′W	T	84
Prestonmill Burn	D & G	NX9757	54°54·1′	3°36·0′W	W	84
Preston Montford	Shrops	SJ4314	52°43·5′	2°50·2′W	T	126
Preston Moor	Devon	SX5699	50°46·6′	4°2·2′W	X	191
Preston Moor	N Yks	SE0694	54°20·7′	1°54·0′W	X	99
Preston Moor	Wrekin	SJ6715	52°44·1′	2°28·9′W	X	127
Preston Oak Hills	Hants	SU6343	51°11·2′	1°5·5′W	F	185
Preston on Stour	Warw	SP2049	52°8·6′	1°42·1′W	T	151
Preston-on-Tees	Stock on T	NZ4315	54°31·9′	1°19·7′W	T	93
Preston on the Hill	Halton	SJ5780	53°19·2′	2°38·3′W	T	108
Preston on Wye	Heref	SO3842	52°4·6′	2°53·9′W	T	148,149,161
Prestonpans	E Loth	NT3874	55°57·6′	2°59·1′W	T	66
Preston Park Sta	Bri & Hov	TQ2906	50°50·6′	0°9·7′W	X	198
Preston Pasture	N Yks	SE0691	54°19·1′	1°54·0′W	X	99
Preston Pastures	Warw	SP2048	52°8·0′	1°42·1′W	X	151
Preston Patrick Hall	Cumbr	SD5483	54°14·7′	2°41·9′W	X	97
Preston Plantn	Scot Bord	NT7859	55°49·7′	2°20·6′W	F	67,74
Preston Plucknett	Somer	ST5316	50°56·7′	2°39·8′W	T	183
Prestons	Devon	SX7599	50°46·9′	3°46·0′W	X	191
Prestons	Kent	TQ5956	51°17·1′	0°17·2′E	X	188
Preston Scar	N Yks	SE0691	54°19·1′	1°54·0′W	X	99
Preston Springs	Shrops	SJ5326	52°50·0′	2°41·5′W	F	126
Preston St Mary	Suff	TL9450	52°7·1′	0°50·4′E	T	155
Preston-under-Scar	N Yks	SE0791	54°19·1′	1°53·1′W	T	99
Preston upon the Weald Moors	Wrekin	SJ6815	52°44·1′	2°28·0′W	T	127
Preston Vale	Staffs	SJ9014	52°43·7′	2°8·5′W	X	127
Preston Wood	Dorset	ST8713	50°55·2′	2°10·7′W	F	194
Preston Wynne	Heref	SO5546	52°6·9′	2°39·0′W	T	149
Prestop Park Fm	Leic	SK3317	52°45·2′	1°30·3′W	FM	128
Prestow Wood	N Som	ST4763	51°22·1′	2°45·3′W	F	172,182
Prestrie	D & G	NX4637	54°42·5′	4°23·0′W	X	83
Prestrie Plantn	D & G	NX4638	54°43·1′	4°23·0′W	F	83
Prestwich	Bury	SD8103	53°31·6′	2°16·8′W	T	109
Prestwick	Northum	NZ1872	55°2·8′	1°42·7′W	T	88
Prestwick	S Ayr	NS3425	55°29·7′	4°37·2′W	T	70
Prestwick Burn	Northum	NY8880	55°7·1′	2°10·9′W	W	80
Prestwick Carr	N upon Ty	NZ1973	55°3·3′	1°41·7′W	X	88
Prestwick Hall	Northum	NZ1872	55°2·8′	1°42·7′W	X	88
Prestwick International Airport	S Ayr	NS3626	55°30·3′	4°35·4′W	X	70
Prestwick Mill Fm	Northum	NZ1773	55°3·3′	1°43·6′W	FM	88
Prestwick Pit Hos	Northum	NZ1871	55°2·2′	1°42·7′W	X	88
Prestwick Whins	Northum	NZ1872	55°2·8′	1°42·7′W	X	88
Prestwold	Leic	SK5721	52°47·2′	1°8·9′W	T	129
Prestwood	Bucks	SP8700	51°41·7′	0°44·1′W	T	165
Prestwood	Staffs	SK1042	52°58·8′	1°50·7′W	T	119,128
Prestwood	Staffs	SO8686	52°28·5′	2°12·0′W	T	139
Pretoria Fm	Cambs	TL1990	52°29·9′	0°14·4′W	FM	142

Pretty Corner	Norf	TG1541	52°55·6′	1°12·3′E	X	133
Pretty Wood	N Yks	SE7369	54°6·9′	0°52·6′W	F	100
Pretwood Hill	Somer	ST3613	50°55·0′	2°54·2′W	H	193
Prewley Fm	Devon	SX5491	50°42·3′	4°3·7′W	FM	191
Prewley Moor	Devon	SX5490	50°41·7′	4°3·7′W	X	191
Prey Heath	Surrey	SU9955	51°17·4′	0°34·4′W	T	175,186
Pricaston	Pemb	SR9196	51°37·7′	5°0·8′W	X	158
Price's Cave	Staffs	SK0049	53°2·5′	1°59·6′W	X	119
Price's Fm	E Susx	TQ5214	50°54·5′	0°10·1′E	FM	199
Price's Fm	Kent	TQ5346	51°11·8′	0°11·8′E	FM	188
Price Town	Brig	SS9392	51°37·2′	3°32·3′W	T	170
Prickeny Burn	E Ayr	NS5505	55°19·3′	4°16·7′W	W	71,77
Prickeny Hill	E Ayr	NS5405	55°19·3′	4°17·6′W	H	70,77
Prickets Hatch	E Susx	TQ4426	51°1·1′	0°3·6′E	X	187,198
Pricketts Hall	Essex	TL8832	51°57·5′	0°44·6′E	X	168
Pricklegate	Kent	TQ7734	51°4·9′	0°32·0′E	X	188
Prickley Fm	Worcs	SO7562	52°15·6′	2°21·6′W	FM	138,150
Prickley Green Fm	Worcs	SO7661	52°15·0′	2°20·7′W	FM	138,150
Prickmoor Wood	Wilts	ST9465	51°23·3′	2°4·8′W	F	173
Prickwillow	Cambs	TL5982	52°25·0′	0°20·7′E	T	143
Priddacombe	Corn	SX1576	50°33·5′	4°36·3′W	X	201
Priddacombe Downs	Corn	SX1677	50°34·1′	4°35·5′W	X	201
Priddbwll	Conwy	SH9363	53°9·4′	3°35·6′W	X	116
Priddbwll	Powys	SJ1926	52°49·8′	3°11·7′W	X	125
Priddellau	Powys	SN8567	52°17·6′	3°40·8′W	X	135,136,147
Pridden	Corn	SW4126	50°4·9′	5°36·9′W	X	203
Priddle's Hill	Somer	ST6432	51°5·4′	2°30·5′W	X	183
Priddleton	Heref	SO5457	52°12·8′	2°40·0′W	X	149
Priddock Wood	Derby	SK2086	53°22·5′	1°41·6′W	F	110
Priddy	Somer	ST5251	51°15·6′	2°40·9′W	T	182,183
Priddy Bank Fm	Lancs	SD7835	53°48·9′	2°19·6′W	FM	103
Priddy Circles	Somer	ST5352	51°16·1′	2°40·0′W	A	182,183
Priddy Hill Fm	Somer	ST5152	51°16·1′	2°41·8′W	FM	182,183
Priddy Mineries (Nature Reserve)	Somer	ST5451	51°15·6′	2°39·2′W	X	182,183
Priddy Nine Barrows	Somer	ST5351	51°15·6′	2°40·0′W	A	182,183
Priddy Road Fm	Somer	ST5649	51°14·5′	2°37·4′W	FM	182,183
Prideaux	Corn	SX0555	50°22·0′	4°44·1′W	X	200
Prideaux Place	Corn	SW9175	50°32·5′	4°56·6′W	X	200
Pride Park	C of Derb	SK3735	52°54·9′	1°26·6′W	T	128
Pridhamsleigh	Devon	SX7467	50°29·6′	3°46·2′W	X	202
Pridhamsleigh Cavern	Devon	SX7467	50°29·6′	3°46·2′W	X	202
Priding	Glos	SO7410	51°47·5′	2°22·2′W	X	162
Priesfield	Angus	NO6748	56°37·6′	2°31·8′W	X	54
Priestacott	Devon	SS4206	50°50·2′	4°14·3′W	T	190
Priestacott	Devon	SS4617	50°56·2′	4°11·1′W	X	180,190
Priestacott	Devon	SX6194	50°44·0′	3°57·8′W	X	191
Priestacott Moor	Devon	SS5021	50°58·4′	4°7·8′W	X	180
Priestaford Ho	Devon	SX7468	50°30·1′	3°46·2′W	X	202
Priest Barn Fm	N Yks	SE5779	54°12·5′	1°7·1′W	FM	100
Priest Barrow	Bath & NE Somer	ST6760	51°20·5′	2°28·0′W	X	172
Priest Bridge	Worcs	SO9859	52°14·0′	2°1·4′W	X	150
Priestburn	Durham	NY9448	54°49·9′	2°5·2′W	X	87
Priestcliffe	Derby	SK1372	53°14·9′	1°47·9′W	T	119
Priestcliffe Ditch	Derby	SK1371	53°14·4′	1°47·9′W	T	119
Priestcliffe Lees	Derby	SK1473	53°15·5′	1°47·0′W	F	119
Priestcombe Fm	Devon	SS8001	50°48·0′	3°41·8′W	FM	191
Priest Craig	D & G	NT1413	55°24·5′	3°21·1′W	X	78
Priestcroft	Cumbr	NY2042	54°46·2′	3°14·2′W	X	85
Priestcrofts	Red & Cl	NZ6617	54°32·9′	0°58·4′W	X	94
Priestdean Burn	Northum	NU1726	55°31·9′	1°43·4′W	W	75
Priest Down	Bath & NE Somer	ST6264	51°22·7′	2°32·4′W	T	172
Priestdykes	D & G	NY1081	55°7·2′	3°24·2′W	X	78
Priestfield	Fife	NO3409	56°16·4′	3°3·5′W	X	59
Priestfield	Wolv	SO9397	52°34·5′	2°5·8′W	T	139
Priestfield	Worcs	SO8244	52°5·9′	2°15·4′W	T	150
Priestfields Fm	Essex	TL7838	52°0·9′	0°36·0′E	FM	155
Priest Gill	N Yks	NZ1306	54°27·2′	1°47·5′W	W	92
Priestgill	S Lanak	NS6942	55°39·5′	4°4·5′W	X	71
Priestgill Head	D & G	NT1301	55°18·0′	3°21·8′W	H	78
Priestgill Rig	S Lanak	NS9525	55°30·7′	3°39·3′W	H	72
Priest Grove	Oxon	SP3016	51°50·7′	1°33·5′W	F	164
Priesthaugh	Scot Bord	NT4604	55°19·9′	2°50·6′W	X	79
Priesthaugh Burn	Scot Bord	NT4603	55°19·3′	2°50·6′W	W	79
Priesthaugh-hill	Scot Bord	NT4602	55°18·8′	2°50·6′W	X	79
Priesthawes	E Susx	TQ6005	50°49·6′	0°16·7′E	X	199
Priesthaywood Fm	Northnts	SP6343	52°5·1′	1°4·4′W	FM	152
Priesthead	D & G	NY0681	55°7·1′	3°28·0′W	X	78
Priesthill	C of Glas	NS5260	55°48·9′	4°21·3′W	T	64
Priesthill	Cumbr	NY3460	54°56·1′	3°1·4′W	X	85
Priesthill	E Ayr	NS7131	55°33·6′	4°2·3′W	X	71
Priesthill	Highld	NH7372	57°43·5′	4°7·5′W	X	21
Priest Hill	Lancs	SD6039	53°51·0′	2°36·1′W	X	102,103
Priest Hill	Leeds	SE3949	53°56·4′	1°23·9′W	X	104
Priest Hill	Leic	SK7602	52°36·9′	0°52·2′W	X	141
Priest Hill	Scot Bord	NY5088	55°11·3′	2°46·7′W	H	79
Priest Hill	Somer	ST4435	51°6·9′	2°47·6′W	H	182
Priest Hill	Surrey	TQ2261	51°20·3′	0°14·5′W	X	176,187
Priesthill Burn	Scot Bord	NY5188	55°11·3′	2°45·7′W	W	79
Priesthill Height	E Ayr	NS7332	55°34·2′	4°0·4′W	H	71
Priestholm	D & G	NY2366	54°59·2′	3°11·8′W	X	85
Priest Holme Br	N Yks	SD9153	53°58·6′	2°7·8′W	X	103
Priestholm or Puffin Island or Ynys Seiriol	I of Angl	SH6582	53°19·3′	4°1·2′W	X	114,115
Priesthope	Scot Bord	NT3539	55°38·7′	3°1·5′W	X	73
Priesthope Burn	Scot Bord	NT0917	55°26·6′	3°25·9′W	W	78
Priesthope Hill	Scot Bord	NT3539	55°38·7′	3°1·5′W	H	73
Priesthorpe	Leeds	SE2035	53°48·9′	1°41·4′W	T	104
Priesthoulland	Shetld	HU2179	60°29·9′	1°36·6′W	X	3
Priest House	W Susx	TQ3632	51°4·5′	0°3·1′W	X	187
Priest Hutton	Lancs	SD5373	54°9·3′	2°42·8′W	T	97
Priest Island	Highld	NB9202	57°57·8′	5°30·5′W	X	15
Priest Knowe	Pth & Kin	NO0110	56°16·6′	3°35·5′W	X	58
Priestland	Ches	SJ5558	53°7·3′	2°39·9′W	X	117
Priestland	E Ayr	NS5737	55°36·6′	4°15·8′W	X	71
Priestlands	D & G	NX9674	55°3·2′	3°37·3′W	X	84
Priest Law	E Loth	NT5162	55°51·2′	2°46·5′W	X	66
Priestlaw	E Loth	NT6463	55°51·8′	2°34·1′W	X	67
Priestlaw Hill	E Loth	NT6562	55°51·2′	2°33·1′W	H	67
Priestley Fm	Beds	TL0133	51°59·4′	0°31·3′W	FM	166
Priestley Green	Cald	SE1326	53°44·1′	1°47·8′W	T	104
Priestley Plantation	Beds	TL0133	51°59·4′	0°31·3′W	F	166
Priestley Wood	Suff	TM0852	52°7·9′	1°2·7′E	F	155
Priestly Ho	Lincs	TF2133	52°53·1′	0°11·7′W	X	131
Prieston	Angus	NO3938	56°32·1′	2°59·1′W	X	54
Prieston	Scot Bord	NT5228	55°32·9′	2°45·2′W	T	73
Priestpool	S Glos	ST5988	51°35·6′	2°35·1′W	X	162,172
Priest Pot	Cumbr	SD3597	54°22·1′	2°59·6′W	W	96,97
Priest's Cove	Corn	SW3531	50°7·4′	5°42·1′W	W	203
Priest's Crag	Cumbr	NY4223	54°36·2′	2°53·4′W	X	90
Priests Fm	Peterb	TF2906	52°38·4′	0°5·2′W	FM	142
Priest's Ho	Somer	ST4325	51°1·5′	2°48·4′W	A	193
Priestside	D & G	NY1066	54°59·1′	3°24·0′W	T	85
Priestside Bank	D & G	NY1064	54°58·0′	3°23·9′W	X	85
Priestside Flow	D & G	NY1266	54°59·1′	3°22·1′W	F	85
Priestside Fm	Inverc	NS3371	55°54·4′	4°39·9′W	FM	63
Priest Sike	Scot Bord	NT3211	55°23·5′	3°4·0′W	W	79
Priest Skear	Lancs	SD4568	54°6·5′	2°50·1′W	X	97
Priest's Knowe	Northum	NZ0494	55°14·7′	1°55·8′W	X	81
Priest's Nose	Pemb	SS0597	51°38·5′	4°48·7′W	X	158
Priest's Pool	Highld	NG7704	57°4·6′	5°40·3′W	W	33
Priest's Pool	S Lanak	NS8619	55°27·3′	3°47·7′W	X	71,78
Priest's Tarn	N Yks	SE0269	54°7·3′	1°57·7′W	W	98
Priest's Water	Aberd	NJ4834	57°23·9′	2°51·5′W	W	28,29
Priest's Way	Derby	SK0970	53°13·9′	1°51·5′W	X	119
Priest's Way	Dorset	SY9977	50°35·8′	2°0·5′W	X	195
Priests Wood	Aberd	NJ5921	57°16·9′	2°40·3′W	F	37
Priestthorpe	Brad	SE1139	53°51·1′	1°49·6′W	T	104
Priestwells	Aberd	NJ6126	57°19·6′	2°38·4′W	X	37
Priest Weston	Shrops	SO2997	52°34·2′	3°2·5′W	T	137
Priestwood	Brackn	SU8669	51°25·0′	0°45·4′W	T	175
Priestwood	Essex	TQ9992	51°35·7′	0°52·8′E	X	178
Priest Wood	Herts	TL3015	51°49·3′	0°6·4′W	F	166
Priestwood	Kent	TQ6564	51°21·3′	0°22·6′E	T	177,178,188
Priest Wood	S Glos	ST6890	51°36·7′	2°27·3′W	F	162,172
Priestwood Fm	Derby	SK2940	52°57·6′	1°33·7′W	FM	119,128
Priestwood Green	Kent	TQ6564	51°21·3′	0°22·6′E	T	177,178,188
Prill, The	Shrops	SJ3719	52°46·1′	2°55·6′W	X	126
Prime Coppices	Dorset	SY3897	50°46·4′	2°52·4′W	F	193
Primethorpe	Leic	SP5293	52°32·2′	1°13·6′W	T	140
Primley Ho	Torbay	SX8760	50°26·0′	3°35·1′W	X	202
Primmore Corner	Somer	ST3029	51°3·6′	2°59·5′W	X	193
Primrose	Fife	NO5512	56°18·2′	2°43·2′W	X	59
Primrose	Fife	NT1084	56°2·7′	3°26·2′W	X	65
Primrose	S Tyne	NZ3263	54°57·9′	1°29·6′W	T	88
Primrosebank	Ches	SJ9266	53°11·7′	2°6·8′W	X	118
Primrose Bank	Cumbr	NY6131	54°40·6′	2°35·9′W	X	91
Primrose Bank	Northum	NU0943	55°41·1′	1°51·0′W	X	75
Primrose Barn	Warw	SP3143	52°5·3′	1°32·5′W	X	151
Primrose Corner	Norf	TG3213	52°40·1′	1°26·3′E	T	133,134
Primrose Fm	Cambs	TF4306	52°38·2′	0°7·2′E	FM	142,143
Primrose Fm	Darl	NZ2223	54°36·3′	1°39·1′W	FM	93
Primrose Fm	Lincs	SK8885	53°21·5′	0°40·3′W	FM	112,121
Primrose Fm	Lincs	TF3821	52°46·4′	0°3·1′E	FM	131
Primrose Fm	Lincs	TF5060	53°7·2′	0°14·9′E	FM	122
Primrose Fm	Norf	TG0725	52°47·2′	1°4·6′E	FM	133
Primrose Fm	Norf	TM0995	52°31·0′	1°5·2′E	FM	144
Primrose Fm	Norf	TM1089	52°27·7′	1°5·9′E	FM	144
Primrose Fm	Notts	SK7465	53°10·9′	0°53·2′W	FM	120
Primrose Fm	N Yks	SE6654	53°58·9′	0°59·2′W	FM	105,106
Primrose Fm	N Yks	SE6769	54°7·0′	0°58·1′W	FM	100
Primrose Fm	York	SE6344	53°53·5′	1°2·1′W	FM	105,106
Primrose Green	Norf	TG0616	52°42·4′	1°3·4′E	T	133
Primrose Hall	Ches	SJ7466	53°11·7′	2°22·9′W	X	118
Primrose Hall	Essex	TM1830	51°55·8′	1°10·7′E	X	168,169
Primrose Hall Fm	Cambs	TL5098	52°33·8′	0°13·2′E	FM	143
Primrosehill	Aberd	NO6468	56°48·4′	2°34·9′W	X	45
Primrose Hill	Bath & NE Somer	ST7366	51°23·8′	2°22·9′W	T	172
Primrose Hill	Cambs	TL5088	52°28·4′	0°12·9′E	X	143
Primrose Hill	Camden	TQ2884	51°32·6′	0°8·9′W	T	176
Primrose Hill	Ches	SJ5368	53°12·7′	2°41·8′W	X	117
Primrosehill	Ches	SJ5662	53°9·5′	2°31·0′W	X	118
Primrose Hill	Ches	SJ6784	53°21·4′	2°29·3′W	X	109
Primrose Hill	Dudley	SO9487	52°29·1′	2°4·9′W	T	139
Primrose Hill	Essex	TM1831	51°56·3′	1°10·7′E	X	168,169
Primrose Hill	E Yorks	SE7252	53°57·8′	0°53·7′W	X	105,106
Primrose Hill	E Yorks	SE7858	54°1·0′	0°48·2′W	X	105,106
Primrose Hill	E Yorks	TA2533	53°46·9′	0°5·8′W	X	107
Primrose Hill	Glos	SO6303	51°43·7′	2°31·8′W	X	162
Primrose Hill	Heref	SO7058	52°13·4′	2°26·0′W	X	149
Primrose Hill	Lancs	SD3809	53°34·7′	2°55·8′W	T	108
Primrose Hill	Lincs	TA1510	53°34·7′	0°15·4′W	X	113
Primrose Hill	Lincs	TF1376	53°16·4′	0°17·9′W	X	121
Primrose Hill	Notts	SK6363	53°9·9′	1°3·1′W	X	120
Primrose Hill	N Yks	SD9350	53°57·0′	2°6·0′W	X	103
Primrose Hill	N Yks	SE4686	54°16·3′	1°17·2′W	X	100
Primrose Hill	N Yks	SE5170	54°7·6′	1°12·8′W	X	100
Primrose Hill	N Yks	SE5537	53°49·8′	1°9·4′W	X	105
Primrose Hill	N Yks	SE6128	53°44·9′	1°4·1′W	X	105
Primrose Hill	N Yks	SE7268	54°6·4′	0°53·5′W	X	100
Primrose Hill	Oxon	SU6195	51°39·3′	1°6·7′W	X	164,165
Primrosehill	Scot Bord	NT7857	55°48·6′	2°20·6′W	X	67,74
Primrose Hill	Suff	TM1553	52°8·2′	1°8·9′E	X	156
Primrose Hill	Warw	SP0956	52°12·4′	1°51·7′W	X	150
Primrosehill Fm	Bucks	SP6732	51°59·2′	1°1·1′W	FM	152,165
Primrose Hill Fm	Cambs	TL5689	52°28·8′	0°18·2′E	FM	143
Primrose Hill Fm	Derby	SK4047	53°1·4′	1°23·8′W	FM	129
Primrose Hill Fm	Durham	NZ1517	54°33·1′	1°45·7′W	FM	92
Primrose Hill Fm	Essex	TL8713	51°47·3′	0°43·1′E	FM	168
Primrose Hill Fm	E Yorks	TA1729	53°44·9′	0°13·1′W	FM	107
Primrose Hill Fm	Lancs	SD4544	53°53·6′	2°49·8′W	FM	102
Primrose Hill Fm	Lincs	TF2851	53°2·7′	0°5·0′W	FM	122
Primrose Hill Fm	Norf	TM1785	52°25·4′	1°11·9′E	FM	156
Primrose Hill Fm	Northnts	SP6442	52°4·6′	1°3·6′W	FM	152
Primrose Hill Fm	N Yks	SE7156	53°59·9′	0°54·6′W	FM	105,106
Primrose Hill Fm	Suff	TL7064	52°15·1′	0°29·8′E	FM	154
Primrose Hill Fm	York	SE6449	53°56·2′	1°1·1′W	FM	105,106
Primrosehill Wood	Ches	SJ5467	53°12·1′	2°40·9′W	F	117
Primrose Ho	N Yks	NZ8011	54°29·5′	0°45·5′W	X	94
Primrose Valley	N Yks	TA1178	54°11·4′	0°17·5′W	T	101
Primside Fm	Scot Bord	NT8026	55°31·9′	2°18·6′W	FM	74
Primsidemill	Scot Bord	NT8126	55°31·9′	2°17·6′W	X	74
Primsland	Worcs	SO9061	52°15·1′	2°8·4′W	T	150
Prince Albert's Cairn	Aberd	NO2593	57°1·6′	3°13·7′W	X	37,44
Prince Albert's Plantn	Norf	TL8594	52°31·0′	0°44·0′E	F	144
Prince Charles's Cave	Highld	NG5112	57°8·1′	6°6·5′W	X	32
Prince Charles's Cave	Highld	NG5148	57°27·5′	6°8·6′W	X	23,24
Prince Charles's Point	Highld	NG3766	57°36·7′	6°23·8′W	X	23
Prince Charles's Well	Highld	NG3956	57°31·4′	6°21·1′W	X	23
Prince Charlie's Cave	Highld	NH1315	57°11·5′	5°5·2′W	X	34
Prince Charlie's Cave	Highld	NM6984	56°53·7′	5°47·1′W	X	40
Prince Charlie's Cave	Highld	NM7984	56°53·9′	5°37·3′W	X	40
Prince Charlie's Cave	Highld	NN4968	56°47·0′	4°27·8′W	X	42
Prince Edward's Rock	Arg & Bt	NR7203	55°16·4′	5°34·9′W	X	68
Prince Hall Hotel	Devon	SX6274	50°33·2′	3°56·5′W	X	191
Prince Hill	Ches	SJ7144	52°59·8′	2°25·5′W	T	118
Princeland	Pth & Kin	NO2140	56°33·0′	3°16·7′W	T	53
Princelett	I of W	SZ5582	50°38·3′	1°12·9′W	X	196
Prince Royd	Kirk	SE1218	53°39·7′	1°48·7′W	T	110
Prince Rupert's Fm	Northnts	SP6880	52°25·1′	0°59·6′W	FM	141
Prince's Cairn, The	Highld	NM7284	56°53·7′	5°44·2′W	X	40
Prince's Common	Corn	SW9267	50°28·2′	4°55·5′W	X	200
Prince's Coverts	Surrey	TQ1560	51°19·9′	0°20·6′W	F	176,187
Princes End	Sand	SO9593	52°32·3′	2°4·0′W	T	139
Princes Gate	Essex	TQ5596	51°38·7′	0°14·8′E	X	167,177
Princes Gate	Pemb	SN1312	51°46·8′	4°42·3′W	T	158
Prince's Golf Links	Kent	TR3560	51°17·7′	1°22·6′E	X	179
Prince's Halfyards	Essex	TL6822	51°52·5′	0°26·8′E	X	167
Prince's Ho	Know	SJ4790	53°24·5′	2°47·4′W	X	108
Prince's Marsh	Hants	SU7726	51°1·9′	0°53·7′W	T	186,197
Prince's Oak	Powys	SJ3414	52°43·4′	2°58·2′W	X	126
Princes Park	Liv	SJ3688	53°23·3′	2°57·3′W	T	108
Princes Park	Liv	SJ3688	53°23·3′	2°57·3′W	T	108
Prince's Place	Dorset	ST5709	50°53·0′	2°36·3′W	X	194
Princes Risborough	Bucks	SP8003	51°43·4′	0°50·1′W	T	165
Princess Alice's Cairn	Aberd	NO2493	57°1·6′	3°14·7′W	H	36,44
Princess Beatrice's Cairn	Aberd	NO2693	57°1·6′	3°12·7′W	X	37,44
Princess Cairn	Highld	NH7597	57°57·0′	4°6·2′W	X	21
Princess Christian's Hospital	Kent	TQ5750	51°13·9′	0°15·3′E	X	188
Princess Helena's Cairn	Aberd	NO2593	57°1·6′	3°13·7′W	X	37,44
Princess Royal's Cairn	Aberd	NO2392	57°1·0′	3°15·6′W	X	44
Princess Stone	Highld	NH9342	57°27·6′	3°46·6′W	A	27
Prince's Stone, The	Aberd	NO2289	56°59·4′	3°16·6′W	X	44
Prince's Wood	Dorset	ST6506	50°51·4′	2°29·5′W	F	194
Princethorpe	Warw	SP4070	52°19·8′	1°24·4′W	T	140
Princetown	Caer	SO1109	51°46·6′	3°17·0′W	T	161
Princetown	Devon	SX5873	50°32·6′	3°59·9′W	T	191
Pringle Ho	Cumbr	NY4136	54°43·2′	2°54·5′W	X	90
Pringles Green	Scot Bord	NT3744	55°41·4′	2°59·7′W	X	73
Pringleton Ho	D & G	NX6348	54°48·7′	4°7·5′W	X	83
Prinkle Fm	E Susx	TQ6514	50°54·3′	0°21·2′E	FM	199
Prinknash Park	Glos	SO8713	51°49·2′	2°10·9′W	A	162
Prinsted	W Susx	SU7605	50°50·6′	0°54·8′W	T	197
Prinsted Point	W Susx	SU7604	50°50·1′	0°54·9′W	X	197
Printonan	Scot Bord	NT7947	55°43·2′	2°19·6′W	X	74
Printstile	Kent	TQ5543	51°10·1′	0°13·4′E	T	188
Print Wood	Warw	SP3864	52°16·6′	1°26·2′W	F	151
Priomh-lochs	Highld	NM3698	57°0·1′	6°20·4′W	W	39
Prion	Denb	SJ0562	53°9·0′	3°24·8′W	T	116
Prion Isa	Denb	SJ0462	53°9·0′	3°25·7′W	X	116
Prion-uchaf	Denb	SJ0462	53°9·0′	3°25·7′W	X	116
Prior Hall	Cumbr	NY2239	54°44·6′	3°12·3′W	X	89,90
Prior Hall	Northum	NZ0385	55°9·8′	1°56·7′W	X	81
Prior Ho	Northum	NT9850	55°44·9′	2°1·5′W	X	75
Prior Ho	Northum	NY8165	54°59·0′	2°17·4′W	X	86,87
Prior House	Cumbr	NY4568	55°0·5′	2°51·2′W	X	86
Priorland	Pth & Kin	NO1820	56°22·2′	3°19·2′W	X	53,58
Priorletham	Fife	NO4912	56°18·1′	2°49·0′W	X	59
Priorling	Cumbr	NY0506	54°26·7′	3°27·5′W	X	89
Prior Moor	N Yks	TA0175	54°9·9′	0°26·8′W	X	101
Prior Muir	Fife	NO5213	56°18·7′	2°46·1′W	X	59
Prior Park	Cumbr	SD1490	54°18·2′	3°18·9′W	X	96
Prior Park	Northum	NT9951	55°45·4′	2°0·5′W	T	75
Priorpot Br	N Yks	SE8071	54°8·0′	0°46·1′W	X	100
Prior Rakes	N Yks	SD8965	54°5·1′	2°9·7′W	X	98
Prior Rigg	Cumbr	NY3555	54°53·4′	3°0·4′W	X	85
Prior Rigg	Cumbr	NY4668	55°0·5′	2°50·2′W	T	86
Prior Rigg	Cumbr	NY4866	54°59·4′	2°48·3′W	X	86
Priors	Essex	TL6909	51°45·5′	0°27·3′E	X	167
Prior Scales	Cumbr	NY0507	54°27·2′	3°27·5′W	X	89
Prior's Close	Durham	NZ3048	54°49·8′	1°31·6′W	X	88
Prior's Coppice	Rut	SK8305	52°38·4′	0°46·0′W	F	141
Prior's Court	Heref	SO5839	52°3·1′	2°36·4′W	X	149
Prior's Court	Heref	SO6637	52°2·1′	2°29·3′W	X	149
Prior's Court	Heref	SO6941	52°4·2′	2°26·7′W	X	149
Priors Court	Worcs	SO8133	51°59·9′	2°16·2′W	X	150
Prior's Court Fm	Somer	ST8052	51°16·2′	2°16·8′W	FM	183
Priorscourt Fm	W Berks	SU4973	51°27·5′	1°17·3′W	FM	174
Prior's Court (Sch)	W Berks	SU4873	51°27·5′	1°18·2′W	X	174
Priorsdale	Cumbr	NY7841	54°46·1′	2°20·1′W	X	86,87
Prior's Down	Dorset	ST7418	50°57·9′	2°21·8′W	F	183
Prior's Fen	Peterb	TF2600	52°35·2′	0°8·0′W	X	142
Priors Field Fm	Cambs	TL3673	52°20·5′	0°0·2′E	FM	154
Prior's Fm	Hants	SU4052	51°16·2′	1°25·2′W	FM	185
Priors Fm	Hill	TQ1184	51°32·9′	0°23·6′W	FM	176
Priors Fm	Peterb	TF2402	52°36·3′	0°9·7′W	FM	142
Prior's Frome	Heref	SO5739	52°3·1′	2°37·2′W	T	149
Priors Gate	Northum	NZ1099	55°17·3′	1°50·1′W	X	81
Prior's Hall	Essex	TL6130	51°56·9′	0°21·0′E	X	167
Priors Halton	Shrops	SO4975	52°22·5′	2°44·6′W	T	137,138,148
Priors Hardwick	Warw	SP4755	52°11·7′	1°18·3′W	T	151
Prior's Hill	Somer	ST5648	51°14·0′	2°37·4′W	H	182,183
Priors Holt	Shrops	SO4189	52°30·0′	2°51·7′W	X	137
Priors Holt Hill	Shrops	SO4190	52°30·5′	2°51·8′W	X	137
Prior's Lands Fm	Norf	TF6409	52°39·5′	0°25·9′E	FM	143

Priors Lea Fm	Warw	SP3247	52°7·5′	1°31·6′W	FM	151
Priorsleas Fm	W Susx	TQ0506	50°50·9′	0°30·1′W	FM	197
Priors Leaze	W Susx	SU7806	50°51·1′	0°53·1′W	X	197
Priorslee	Wrekin	SJ7110	52°41·5′	2°25·3′W	T	127
Prior's Lodge	Glos	SO5904	51°44·2′	2°35·2′W	X	162
Priorslynn	D & G	NY3975	55°4·2′	2°56·9′W	X	85
Priors Marston	Warw	SP4957	52°12·8′	1°16·6′W	T	151
Priors Mesne	Glos	SO5904	51°44·2′	2°35·2′W	X	162
Prior's Norton	Glos	SO8624	51°55·1′	2°11·8′W	T	162
Priors Park	Glos	SO8931	51°58·9′	2°9·2′W	T	150
Prior's Park Fm	Notts	SK7069	53°13·0′	0°56·7′W	FM	120
Prior's Park Fm	Somer	ST2116	50°56·5′	3°7·7′W	FM	193
Prior's Park Wood	Somer	ST2217	50°57·1′	3°6·2′W	F	193
Prior's Reach	Monm	ST5397	51°40·4′	2°40·4′W	W	162
Prior's Wood	Essex	TL5330	51°57·1′	0°14·0′E	F	167
Prior's Wood	Herts	TL1817	51°50·6′	0°16·8′W	F	166
Prior's Wood	N Som	ST4974	51°28·0′	2°43·7′W	F	172
Priors Wood	Oxon	SU6988	51°35·4′	0°59·8′W	F	175
Priorswood	Somer	ST2326	51°1·9′	3°5·5′W	T	193
Prior's Wood	Surrey	SU9446	51°12·6′	0°38·9′W	F	186
Prior's Wood Hall	Lancs	SD5009	53°34·8′	2°44·9′W	A	108
Prior Thorns	Northum	NY9664	54°58·5′	2°3·3′W	X	87
Priorton Barton	Devon	SS8304	50°49·7′	3°39·3′W	X	191
Priorwell	Fife	NO3523	56°23·9′	3°2·7′W	X	54,59
Priorwood	Cumbr	NY3655	54°53·4′	2°59·4′W	X	85
Priory	Cumbr	NY4947	54°49·2′	2°47·2′W	X	86
Priory	Monm	SO2827	51°56·4′	3°2·5′W	A	161
Priory	Pemb	SM9007	51°43·6′	5°2·1′W	T	157,158
Priory Bay	I of W	SZ6390	50°42·6′	1°6·1′W	W	196
Priory Bay	Pemb	SS1397	51°38·7′	4°41·8′W	W	158
Priory Cottage	Shrops	SO4095	52°33·2′	2°52·7′W	X	137
Priory Farmhouse	Norf	TF8817	52°43·3′	0°47·4′E	A	132
Priory Fm	Beds	SP9456	52°11·9′	0°37·1′W	FM	153
Priory Fm	Beds	SP9552	52°9·7′	0°36·3′W	FM	153
Priory Fm	Bucks	SP7432	51°59·1′	0°54·9′W	FM	152,165
Priory Fm	Cambs	TL1167	52°17·6′	0°21·9′W	FM	153
Priory Fm	Cambs	TL3372	52°20·0′	0°2·5′W	FM	154
Priory Fm	Cambs	TL5669	52°18·0′	0°17·7′E	FM	154
Priory Fm	Essex	TM1730	51°55·8′	1°9·8′E	FM	168,169
Priory Fm	E Yorks	SE7118	53°39·5′	0°55·1′W	FM	112
Priory Fm	Glos	SP0900	51°42·2′	1°51·8′W	FM	163
Priory Fm	Hants	SU4748	51°14·0′	1°19·2′W	FM	185
Priory Fm	Hants	SU6058	51°19·3′	1°7·9′W	FM	175
Priory Fm	Hants	SU6852	51°16·0′	1°1·1′W	FM	185,186
Priory Fm	Heref	SO2544	52°5·6′	3°5·3′W	FM	148,161
Priory Fm	Kent	TQ9627	51°0·8′	0°48·0′E	FM	189
Priory Fm	Lancs	SD5769	54°7·1′	2°39·1′W	FM	97
Priory Fm	Leic	SK6314	52°43·4′	1°3·6′W	FM	129
Priory Fm	Leic	SK6820	52°46·6′	0°59·1′W	FM	129
Priory Fm	Leic	SP8295	52°33·0′	0°47·0′W	FM	141
Priory Fm	Lincs	SK8487	53°22·6′	0°43·8′W	FM	112,121
Priory Fm	Lincs	SK9994	53°26·2′	0°30·2′W	FM	112
Priory Fm	Lincs	TF1994	53°26·0′	0°12·1′W	FM	113
Priory Fm	Lincs	TF4878	53°16·9′	0°13·6′E	FM	122
Priory Fm	Monm	SO5114	51°49·6′	2°42·3′W	FM	162
Priory Fm	Monm	ST4396	51°39·8′	2°49·1′W	FM	171
Priory Fm	NE Lincs	TF2299	53°28·6′	0°9·3′W	FM	113
Priory Fm	Norf	TF4813	52°41·9′	0°11·8′E	FM	131,143
Priory Fm	Norf	TF6412	52°41·1′	0°26·0′E	FM	132,143
Priory Fm	Norf	TF8501	52°34·7′	0°44·2′E	FM	144
Priory Fm	Norf	TM2893	52°29·5′	1°21·9′E	FM	134
Priory Fm	Norf	TM4195	52°30·2′	1°33·5′E	A	134
Priory Fm	Oxon	SP3328	51°57·2′	1°30·8′W	FM	164
Priory Fm	Staffs	SJ8716	52°44·7′	2°11·2′W	FM	127
Priory Fm	Staffs	SK0920	52°46·9′	1°51·6′W	FM	128
Priory Fm	Suff	TL9350	52°7·1′	0°49·5′E	FM	155
Priory Fm	Suff	TM1371	52°18·0′	1°7·8′E	FM	144,156
Priory Fm	Suff	TM4170	52°16·7′	1°32·4′E	FM	156
Priory Fm	Suff	TM5089	52°26·7′	1°41·1′E	FM	156
Priory Fm	Warw	SP4958	52°13·3′	1°16·6′W	FM	151
Priory Fm	Wilts	ST7940	51°9·8′	2°17·6′W	FM	183
Priory Fm	Wilts	ST8977	51°29·7′	2°9·1′W	FM	173
Priory Fm	Worcs	SP0557	52°12·9′	1°55·2′W	FM	150
Priory Fm	W Susx	TQ0006	50°50·9′	0°34·4′W	FM	197
Priory Green	Suff	TL9343	52°3·3′	0°49·3′E	T	155
Priory Heath	Suff	TM1942	52°2·2′	1°12·0′E	T	169
Prioryhill	D & G	NY4076	55°4·7′	2°56·0′W	X	85
Priory Hill	Kent	TR0369	51°23·2′	0°55·5′E	X	178,179
Priory Ho	Bucks	SP6429	51°57·6′	1°3·7′W	X	164,165
Priory Ho	Cambs	TF4414	52°42·5′	0°8·3′E	X	131
Priory Home Fm, The	Kent	TR0435	51°4·9′	0°55·1′E	FM	179,189
Priory House	Essex	TL9930	51°56·2′	0°54·1′E	X	168
Priory Mill	Oxon	SP3329	51°57·7′	1°30·8′W	X	164
Priory Piece Fm	Worcs	SP0257	52°12·9′	1°57·8′W	FM	150
Priory Sta	Kent	TR3141	51°7·5′	1°18·5′E	X	179
Priory, The	Devon	SX8669	50°30·8′	3°36·1′W	X	202
Priory, The	Essex	TL7910	51°45·8′	0°36·0′E	X	167
Priory, The	Essex	TL8628	51°55·4′	0°42·7′E	X	168
Priory, The	Glos	SO6909	51°47·0′	2°26·6′W	X	162
Priory, The	Glos	ST9192	51°37·8′	2°7·4′W	X	163,173
Priory, The	Herts	TL1828	51°56·5′	0°16·6′W	A	166
Priory, The	I of W	SZ6390	50°42·6′	1°6·1′W	X	196
Priory, The	Kent	TQ5348	51°12·9′	0°11·8′E	X	188
Priory, The	Kent	TQ6735	51°5·6′	0°23·5′E	X	188
Priory, The	Kent	TQ7453	51°15·2′	0°30·0′E	X	188
Priory, The	Kent	TR0435	51°4·9′	0°55·1′E	X	179,189
Priory, The	Lincs	TF3884	53°20·3′	0°4·8′E	X	122
Priory, The	Northnts	SP7943	52°5·0′	0°50·4′W	X	152
Priory, The	Somer	ST1429	51°3·5′	3°13·2′W	X	181,193
Priory, The	Suff	TL9149	52°6·6′	0°47·8′E	X	155
Priory, The	Suff	TM1178	52°21·8′	1°6·3′E	X	144
Priory, The	Suff	TM2361	52°12·3′	1°16·2′E	X	156
Priory, The	Suff	TM4059	52°10·8′	1°31·0′E	X	156
Priory, The	Surrey	TQ1654	51°16·6′	0°19·8′W	X	187
Priory, The	Surrey	TQ3752	51°15·3′	0°1·8′W	X	187
Priory, The	Traf	SJ7585	53°21·9′	2°22·1′W	X	109
Priory, The	Wan	TQ2175	51°27·9′	0°15·1′W	X	176
Priory, The	Warw	SP4175	52°22·5′	1°23·5′W	X	140
Priory, The	W Berks	SU4668	51°24·8′	1°19·9′W	X	174
Priory, The	W Berks	SU7064	51°22·5′	0°59·3′W	X	175,186
Priory, The	Worcs	SP1446	52°7·0′	1°47·3′W	A	151
Priory, The	W Susx	TQ1911	50°53·4′	0°18·1′W	X	198
Priory Wood	Heref	SO2545	52°6·1′	3°5·3′W	T	148
Priory Wood	Kent	TR0335	51°4·9′	0°54·3′E	F	179,189
Priory Wood	Newp	ST3690	51°36·5′	2°55·1′W	F	171
Prisk	Powys	SO2016	51°50·5′	3°9·3′W	X	161
Prisk	V of Glam	ST0176	51°28·7′	3°25·1′W	T	170
Priske	Corn	SW6720	50°2·3′	5°14·9′W	X	203
Prisk Fm	Pemb	SN0927	51°54·8′	4°46·2′W	FM	145,158
Prisk Fm	Swan	SS5192	51°36·7′	4°8·7′W	FM	159
Priskilly	Pemb	SM9129	51°55·5′	5°2·0′W	X	157,158
Priskilly Forest	Pemb	SM9130	51°56·0′	5°2·0′W	X	157
Prison Band	Cumbr	NY2700	54°23·7′	3°7·0′W	X	89,90
Prison Copse	Glos	SP1015	51°50·2′	1°50·9′W	F	163
Prison Crag	Cumbr	NY4213	54°30·8′	2°53·3′W	X	90
Prison Leat	Devon	SX5776	50°34·2′	4°0·8′W	W	191
Prison, The	Highld	NG4568	57°38·1′	6°15·9′W	H	23
Prissen's Tor	Swan	SS4293	51°37·1′	4°16·5′W	X	159
Prissick Fm	Midd	NZ5116	54°32·4′	1°12·3′W	FM	93
Pristacott	Devon	SS5426	51°1·1′	4°4·5′W	T	180
Priston	Bath & NE Somer	ST6960	51°20·5′	2°26·3′W	T	172
Priston Mill	Bath & NE Somer	ST6961	51°21·1′	2°26·3′W	X	172
Priston New Fm	Bath & NE Somer	ST6761	51°21·1′	2°28·0′W	FM	172
Pristow Green	Norf	TM1389	52°27·7′	1°8·5′E	T	144,156
Pritchard's Hill	Powys	SJ3114	52°43·4′	3°0·9′W	X	126
Pritch Fm	Ches	SJ6247	53°1·4′	2°33·6′W	FM	118
Prittlewell	Sou-on-Sea	TQ8787	51°33·3′	0°42·2′E	T	178
Privet Copse	Hants	SU4058	51°19·4′	1°25·2′W	F	174
Privett	Hants	SU6726	51°2·0′	1°2·3′W	T	185,186
Privett	Hants	SZ5999	50°47·5′	1°9·4′W	T	196
Privett Copse	Hants	SU5956	51°18·2′	1°8·8′W	F	174
Privett Fm	Wilts	SU2023	51°0·6′	1°42·5′W	FM	184
Prixford	Devon	SS5436	51°6·5′	4°4·8′W	T	180
Prizeley	Shrops	SO6974	52°22·0′	2°26·9′W	X	138
Prizet	Cumbr	SD5089	54°17·9′	2°45·7′W	X	97
Proaig	Arg & Bt	NR4557	55°44·6′	6°3·3′W	X	60
Probus	Corn	SW8947	50°17·4′	4°57·4′W	T	204
Proby Fm	Cambs	TL0993	52°31·7′	0°23·2′W	FM	142
Procter High Mark	N Yks	SD9367	54°6·2′	2°6·0′W	H	98
Proctor's Fm	Lancs	SD6953	53°58·6′	2°27·9′W	FM	103
Proctors Stead	Northum	NU2420	55°28·6′	1°36·8′W	X	75
Prod Hills	N Yks	SE5297	54°22·2′	1°11·6′W	X	100
Profits Fm	Surrey	TQ2145	51°11·7′	0°15·7′W	FM	187
Progo	Corn	SW3530	50°6·9′	5°42·0′W	X	203
Proncy	Highld	NH7792	57°54·3′	4°4·1′W	X	21
Proncy Castle	Highld	NH7792	57°54·3′	4°4·1′W	A	21
Proncycroy	Highld	NH7791	57°53·8′	4°4·0′W	X	21
Prony	Aberd	NO3497	57°3·8′	3°4·8′W	X	37,44
Prora	E Loth	NT5279	56°0·3′	2°45·7′W	X	66
Proscribe Burn	E Ayr	NS6723	55°29·2′	4°5·9′W	W	71
Prosen Br	Angus	NO3958	56°42·8′	2°59·3′W	X	54
Prosenhaugh	Angus	NO3759	56°43·4′	3°1·3′W	X	54
Prosen Water	Angus	NO3067	56°47·6′	3°8·3′W	W	44
Prospect	Cumbr	NY1140	54°45·1′	3°22·5′W	T	85
Prospect Corner	Devon	SS5228	51°2·2′	4°6·3′W	X	180
Prospect Fm	Derby	SK4244	52°59·7′	1°22·0′W	FM	129
Prospect Fm	Hants	SU3041	51°10·3′	1°33·9′W	FM	185
Prospect Fm	Lancs	SD4030	53°46·0′	2°54·2′W	FM	102
Prospect Fm	Lancs	SD8644	53°53·8′	2°12·4′W	FM	103
Prospect Fm	Lincs	TF0890	53°24·0′	0°22·1′W	FM	112
Prospect Fm	N Lincs	TA0608	53°33·7′	0°23·6′W	FM	112
Prospect Fm	N Yks	NZ5408	54°28·1′	1°9·6′W	FM	93
Prospect Fm	N Yks	SE5270	54°7·6′	1°11·8′W	FM	100
Prospect Fm	N Yks	SE5364	54°4·4′	1°11·0′W	FM	100
Prospect Fm	Oxon	SU4985	51°33·9′	1°17·2′W	FM	174
Prospect Fm	Sheff	SK2892	53°25·7′	1°34·3′W	FM	110
Prospect Fm	Suff	TM0048	52°5·9′	0°55·6′E	FM	155
Prospect Fm	Suff	TM2656	52°9·6′	1°18·7′E	FM	156
Prospect Fm	Warr	SJ6791	53°25·1′	2°29·4′W	FM	109
Prospect Fm	Warw	SP2667	52°18·3′	1°36·7′W	FM	151
Prospect Fm	York	SE5452	53°57·9′	1°10·2′W	FM	105
Prospecthill	Aberd	NJ6215	57°13·7′	2°37·3′W	X	37
Prospect Hill	E Yorks	TA2530	53°45·3′	0°5·8′W	X	107
Prospect Hill	Fife	NO3118	56°21·2′	3°6·6′W	H	59
Prospect Hill	Northum	NY9962	54°57·4′	2°0·5′W	X	87
Prospect Hill	N Yks	SE2296	54°21·8′	1°39·3′W	X	99
Prospect Hill	Oxon	SP7102	51°43·0′	0°57·9′W	X	165
Prospect Hill	Staffs	SJ8123	52°48·5′	2°16·5′W	H	127
Prospect Hill	Win & Maid	SU8282	51°32·1′	0°47·9′W	X	175
Prospect Hill Fm	Notts	SK7190	53°24·4′	0°55·5′W	FM	112
Prospect Ho	Brad	SE1141	53°52·1′	1°49·5′W	X	104
Prospect Ho	Cumbr	NY1533	54°41·3′	3°18·7′W	X	89
Prospect Ho	E Yorks	SE8036	53°49·1′	0°46·7′W	X	106
Prospect Ho	E Yorks	TA1243	53°52·5′	0°17·4′W	X	107
Prospect Ho	Lancs	SD6021	53°41·3′	2°35·9′W	X	102,103
Prospect Ho	Lincs	SK9393	53°25·8′	0°35·6′W	X	112
Prospect Ho	N Yks	NZ3805	54°26·6′	1°24·4′W	X	93
Prospect Ho	N Yks	NZ7405	54°26·3′	0°51·1′W	X	94
Prospect Ho	N Yks	SE2163	54°4·0′	1°40·3′W	X	99
Prospect Ho	N Yks	SE2554	53°59·1′	1°36·7′W	X	104
Prospect Ho	N Yks	SE3893	54°20·1′	1°24·5′W	X	99
Prospect House Fm	Cambs	TL3497	52°33·5′	0°1·0′W	FM	142
Prospecthouse Fm	N Yks	SE2150	53°57·0′	1°40·4′W	FM	104
Prospect House Fm	N Yks	SE6670	54°7·5′	0°59·0′W	FM	100
Prospect House Fm	N Yks	SE8080	54°12·8′	0°46·0′W	FM	100
Prospect House Fm	N Yks	SE9990	54°18·0′	0°28·3′W	FM	94,101
Prospect House Fm	N Yks	SE9999	54°22·9′	0°28·1′W	FM	94,101
Prospect House Fm	Suff	TM2371	52°17·7′	1°16·6′E	FM	156
Prospect Park	Read	SU6872	51°26·8′	1°0·9′W	X	175
Prospect Place	Denb	SJ2443	52°59·0′	3°7·5′W	X	117
Prospect Place	Norf	TG3201	52°33·7′	1°25·8′E	X	134
Prospect Stile	Bath & NE Somer	ST5856	51°18·3′	2°35·8′W	X	172,182
Prospect Stile	Bath & NE Somer	ST7168	51°24·9′	2°24·6′W	X	172
Prospect Village	Staffs	SK0311	52°42·0′	1°56·9′W	T	128
Prosperity Fm	Lincs	TF4081	53°18·7′	0°6·5′E	FM	122
Prosperous Home Fm	W Berks	SU3265	51°23·2′	1°32·0′W	FM	174
Prospidnick	Corn	SW6431	50°8·2′	5°17·8′W	T	203
Prospidnick Hill	Corn	SW6531	50°8·2′	5°17·0′W	X	203
Protston	Aberd	NJ8164	57°40·2′	2°18·6′W	X	29,30
Protstonhill	Aberd	NJ8164	57°40·2′	2°18·6′W	X	29,30
Proudfoot	Highld	ND3850	58°26·3′	3°3·2′W	X	12
Proud Giltar	Pemb	SS1098	51°39·2′	4°44·4′W	X	158
Prouts Park Fm	Pemb	SN1004	51°42·4′	4°44·6′W	FM	158
Provan Hall	C of Glas	NS6666	55°52·4′	4°8·1′W	A	64
Provanmill	C of Glas	NS6367	55°52·9′	4°11·0′W	T	64
Provanston	Stir	NS6088	56°4·1′	4°14·5′W	X	57
Provence	E Yorks	SE8928	53°44·7′	0°38·6′W	X	106
Provender	Kent	TQ9760	51°18·5′	0°50·0′E	A	178
Providence	Corn	SW9461	50°25·0′	4°53·6′W	X	200
Providence Bay	Cumbr	NX9721	54°34·7′	3°35·2′W	W	89
Providence Fm	Ches	SJ7077	53°17·6′	2°26·6′W	FM	118
Providence Fm	E Yorks	SE8827	53°44·2′	0°39·5′W	FM	106
Providence Fm	N Yks	SE5267	54°6·0′	1°11·9′W	FM	100
Providence Green	N Yks	SE4456	54°0·1′	1°19·3′W	X	105
Providence Green	York	SE6453	53°58·4′	1°1·0′W	X	105,106
Providence Heath	N Yks	SE9897	54°21·8′	0°29·1′W	X	94,101
Providence Hill Fm	N Yks	SE3976	54°10·9′	1°23·7′W	FM	99
Providence Hill Fm	N Yks	SE5074	54°9·8′	1°13·6′W	FM	100
Providence Ho	Lincs	TF2555	53°4·9′	0°7·6′W	X	122
Providence Ho	Lincs	TF2914	52°42·7′	0°5·0′W	X	131
Providence Ho	York	SE6146	53°54·6′	1°3·9′W	X	105
Providence Place	Devon	SX6789	50°41·4′	3°52·6′W	X	191
Provost Lodge	Northnts	TL0090	52°30·2′	0°31·2′W	X	141
Provost Mains	Pth & Kin	NO1816	56°20·0′	3°19·1′W	X	58
Prowse	Devon	SS8405	50°50·2′	3°38·5′W	T	191
Prowses	Devon	SS9206	50°50·8′	3°31·7′W	X	192
Prowse's Luscombe	Devon	SX7956	50°23·7′	3°41·8′W	X	202
Prows Fm	Essex	TL5614	51°48·4′	0°16·2′E	FM	167
Prudhamstone Ho	Northum	NY8868	55°0·6′	2°10·8′W	X	87
Prudhoe	Northum	NZ0962	54°57·4′	1°51·1′W	T	88
Prudhoe Castle	Northum	NZ0963	54°57·9′	1°51·1′W	A	88
Prussia Cove	Corn	SW5527	50°5·8′	5°25·2′W	T	203
Prustacott Fm	Corn	SS2505	50°49·3′	4°28·7′W	FM	190
Pruston Barton	Devon	SX8150	50°20·5′	3°40·0′W	X	202
Pry	Northum	NY9857	54°54·7′	2°1·4′W	X	87
Pryan	Cered	SN3742	52°3·4′	4°22·3′W	X	145
Prydale Ho	Durham	NY9342	54°46·6′	2°6·1′W	X	87
Pry End Drain	N Yks	SE7881	54°13·4′	0°47·8′W	W	100
Pryfield	Northum	NY8347	54°49·3′	2°15·5′W	X	86,87
Pry Fm	Wilts	SU1088	51°35·7′	1°50·9′W	FM	173
Pry Hill	Northum	NY8351	54°51·5′	2°15·5′W	X	86,87
Pry Hill	N Yks	NY8601	54°24·5′	2°12·5′W	X	91,92
Pry Ho	N Yks	SD8591	54°19·1′	2°13·4′W	X	98
Prynela Wood	Wrex	SJ3040	52°57·4′	3°2·1′W	F	117
Pry Rigg	Durham	NZ0212	54°30·4′	1°57·7′W	X	92
Pry Rigg Fm	N Yks	SE5980	54°13·0′	1°5·3′W	FM	100
Pry-Rigg Plantn	N Yks	SE5880	54°13·0′	1°6·2′W	F	100
Prysan	I of Angl	SH4880	53°18·0′	4°16·4′W	X	114,115
Prysau	Flint	SJ1673	53°15·1′	3°15·1′W	X	116
Prysg	Cered	SN6655	52°10·9′	3°57·2′W	X	146
Prysg	Powys	SO1482	52°26·0′	3°15·5′W	W	136
Prysgau	Gwyn	SH5707	52°38·8′	4°6·4′W	X	124
Prysgduon	Powys	SO0178	52°23·7′	3°26·9′W	X	136,147
Prysg-lwyd	Gwyn	SH8020	52°46·1′	3°46·3′W	X	124,125
Prysgol	Gwyn	SH5161	53°7·8′	4°13·2′W	A	114,115
Prys Ho	N Yks	NZ0602	54°25·0′	1°54·0′W	X	92
Prysiau-fâch	Powys	SN9148	52°7·4′	3°35·1′W	X	147
Prysiau-fawr	Powys	SN9148	52°7·4′	3°35·1′W	X	147
Prysiorwerth	I of Angl	SH4072	53°13·5′	4°23·4′W	X	114,115
Prys-mawr	Gwyn	SH8630	52°51·6′	3°41·2′W	X	124,125
Prys-owain Fawr	I of Angl	SH3982	53°18·9′	4°24·6′W	X	114
Pryston	Devon	SS4618	50°56·7′	4°11·2′W	X	180,190
Ptarmigan	Stir	NN3502	56°11·2′	4°39·1′W	H	56
Ptarmigan Lodge	Arg & Bt	NN3500	56°10·1′	4°39·0′W	X	56
Ptarmigan Restaurant	Highld	NJ0004	57°7·2′	3°38·6′W	X	36
Puball Burn	Arg & Bt	NR7126	55°28·7′	5°37·0′W	W	68
Pubil	Pth & Kin	NN4642	56°32·9′	4°29·9′W	X	51
Publow	Bath & NE Somer	ST6264	51°22·7′	2°32·4′W	T	172
Publow Hill	Bath & NE Somer	ST6265	51°23·2′	2°32·4′W	X	172
Publow Leigh	Bath & NE Somer	ST6263	51°22·1′	2°32·4′W	X	172
Puckaster Cove	I of W	SZ5175	50°34·6′	1°16·4′W	W	196
Puckeridge	Herts	TL3823	51°53·5′	0°0·7′E	T	166
Pucketty Fm	Oxon	SU3198	51°41·0′	1°32·7′W	FM	164
Puckham Fm	Glos	SP0022	51°54·0′	1°59·6′W	FM	163
Puckham Woods	Glos	SP0022	51°54·0′	1°59·6′W	F	163
Puck Ho	I of W	SZ5691	50°43·2′	1°12·0′W	X	196
Puckington	Somer	ST3718	50°57·7′	2°53·4′W	T	193
Puckland	Devon	SS2808	50°51·0′	4°26·2′W	X	190
Pucklechurch	S Glos	ST6976	51°29·2′	2°26·4′W	T	172
Pucknall	Hants	SU3824	51°1·1′	1°27·1′W	T	185
Puckpits Inclosure	Hants	SU2509	50°53·0′	1°38·3′W	F	195
Puckpool Point	I of W	SZ6192	50°43·7′	1°7·8′W	X	196
Puckrup	Glos	SO8836	52°1·6′	2°10·1′W	T	150
Pucks Croft	W Susx	TQ2036	51°6·9′	0°16·7′W	X	187
Puck's Glen	Arg & Bt	NS1584	56°1·1′	4°57·6′W	X	56
Puckshipton Ho	Wilts	SU0957	51°19·0′	1°51·9′W	X	173
Puckshole	Glos	SO8305	51°44·8′	2°14·4′W	T	162
Puckstone	Dorset	SZ0283	50°39·0′	1°57·9′W	X	195
Puddcombe Cove	Devon	SX9150	50°20·6′	3°31·5′W	W	202
Puddaven	Devon	SX7861	50°26·4′	3°42·7′W	T	202
Puddephats Fm	Herts	TL0613	51°48·6′	0°27·4′W	FM	166
Puddicombe Ho	Devon	SX7291	50°42·5′	3°48·4′W	X	191
Puddi Moor	Somer	ST5324	51°1·0′	2°39·8′W	X	183
Pudding Burn	Northum	NT8407	55°21·7′	2°14·7′W	W	80
Puddingcake	Kent	TQ8632	51°3·7′	0°39·7′E	X	189
Pudding Hill	Win & Maid	SU8181	51°31·6′	0°49·6′W	X	175
Puddinglake	Ches	SJ7269	53°13·3′	2°24·8′W	T	118
Pudding Law	Scot Bord	NT8417	55°27·0′	2°14·7′W	H	80
Pudding Norton Hall	Norf	TF9228	52°49·1′	0°51·4′E	X	132
Puddingpie Hill	Derby	SK3171	53°14·3′	1°31·7′W	H	119
Pudding Pie Hill	N Yks	SE4381	54°13·6′	1°20·0′W	X	99
Pudding Pie Hill (Tumulus)	N Yks	SE4381	54°13·6′	1°20·0′W	A	99

Pudding Pie Nook	Lancs	SD5435	53°48·8'	2°41·5'W	T	102
Pudding Pie Sand	N Lincs	SE9324	53°42·5'	0°35·0'W	X	106,112
Pudding Poke Fm	Durham	NZ4233	54°41·7'	1°20·5'W	FM	93
Puddingthorn Moor	Durham	NY8442	54°46·6'	2°14·5'W	X	86,87
Puddington	Ches	SJ3273	53°15·2'	3°0·7'W	T	117
Puddington	Devon	SS8310	50°52·9'	3°39·4'W	T	191
Puddington Bottom	Devon	SS8309	50°52·4'	3°39·4'W	X	191
Puddle	Corn	SX0758	50°23·6'	4°42·6'W	T	200
Puddlebridge	Somer	ST3214	50°55·5'	2°57·7'W	T	193
Puddlebrook	Glos	SO6418	51°51·8'	2°31·0'W	X	162
Puddledock	E Susx	TQ6610	50°52·2'	0°21·9'E	X	199
Puddle Dock	Hav	TQ5987	51°33·8'	0°18·0'E	X	177
Puddledock	Kent	TQ4650	51°14·1'	0°5·9'E	T	188
Puddledock	Kent	TQ5170	51°24·8'	0°10·7'E	T	177
Puddledock	Norf	TM0592	52°29·5'	1°1·6'E	T	144
Puddleford Fm	Worcs	SO6867	52°18·2'	2°27·8'W	FM	138,149
Puddle House Fm	Lancs	SD3537	53°49·8'	2°58·8'W	FM	102
Puddle, The	I of M	SC1564	54°2·6'	4°49·1'W	W	95
Puddletown	Dorset	SY7594	50°44·9'	2°20·9'W	T	194
Puddletown Down	Dorset	SY7597	50°46·6'	2°20·9'W	X	194
Puddletown Forest	Dorset	SY7392	50°43·9'	2°22·6'W	F	194
Puddletown Heath	Dorset	SY7392	50°43·9'	2°22·6'W	X	194
Puddleworth	Glos	SO7605	51°44·8'	2°20·5'W	X	162
Puddock	Kent	TQ9625	50°59·7'	0°48·0'E	X	189
Puddock Br	Cambs	TL3587	52°28·1'	0°0·4'W	X	142
Pudds Cross	Herts	TL0002	51°42·7'	0°32·8'W	X	166
Pudford Fm	Worcs	SO7461	52°15·0'	2°22·5'W	FM	138,150
Pudleigh	Somer	ST3110	50°53·4'	2°58·5'W	T	193
Pudleston	Heref	SO5659	52°13·9'	2°38·3'W	T	149
Pudleston Court	Heref	SO5559	52°13·9'	2°39·1'W	X	149
Pudlicote Ho	Oxon	SP3120	51°52·9'	1°32·6'W	X	164
Pudmore Pond	Surrey	SU9041	51°9·9'	0°42·4'W	W	186
Pudnell House Fm	Wilts	ST9556	51°18·4'	2°3·9'W	FM	173
Pudneys Fm	Essex	TL7126	51°54·6'	0°29·6'E	FM	167
Pudsey	Cald	SD9026	53°44·1'	2°8·7'W	T	103
Pudsey	Leeds	SE2233	53°47·8'	1°39·5'W	T	104
Pudsey Hall	Essex	TQ8895	51°37·6'	0°43·4'E	X	168
Pudsham	Devon	SX7174	50°33·3'	3°48·9'W	X	191
Pudsham Down	Devon	SX7374	50°33·4'	3°47·2'W	H	191
Pudson Fm	Devon	SX5795	50°44·5'	4°1·2'W	FM	191
Puesdown Inn	Glos	SP0717	51°51·3'	1°53·5'W	X	163
Puff	Lincs	TF4235	52°53·9'	0°7·1'E	X	131
Puffiland Fm	Corn	SX2356	50°22·9'	4°29·0'W	FM	201
Puffin Island	I Scilly	SV8813	49°56·4'	6°20·6'W	X	203
Puffin Island or Priestholm or Ynys Seiriol	I of Angl	SH6582	53°19·3'	4°1·2'W	X	114,115
Pugeston	Angus	NO6859	56°43·6'	2°30·9'W	X	54
Pugham Fm	Devon	ST0515	50°55·8'	3°20·7'W	FM	181
Pugneys Country Park	Wakf	SE3217	53°39·2'	1°30·5'W	X	110,111
Pug's Hole Fm	Hants	SU2728	51°3·3'	1°36·5'W	FM	184
Pugsley	Devon	SS6423	50°59·7'	3°55·9'W	X	180
Puill Chriadha	N Eil	NB3710	58°0·3'	6°26·6'W	W	14
Puist Coire Ardair	Highld	NN4387	56°57·1'	4°34·4'W	H	34,42
Puist Coire Ardair	Highld	NN4387	56°57·1'	4°34·4'W	H	34,42
Puiteachan	Highld	NN0984	56°54·7'	5°7·8'W	X	41
Pularyan	D & G	NX1468	54°58·6'	4°54·0'W	X	82
Pularyan Burn	D & G	NX1367	54°58·0'	4°54·9'W	W	82
Pulbae Burn	D & G	NX4572	55°1·4'	4°25·1'W	W	77
Pulborough	W Susx	TQ0518	50°57·3'	0°29·9'W	T	197
Pulborough and Petworth Cycle Route	W Susx	TQ0116	50°56·3'	0°33·4'W	X	197
Pulcagrie Burn	D & G	NX5478	55°4·8'	4°16·8'W	W	77
Pulcree	D & G	NX5858	54°54·0'	4°12·4'W	X	83
Pulcree Burn	D & G	NX5957	54°53·5'	4°11·5'W	W	83
Puldagon	Highld	ND3248	58°25·2'	3°9·4'W	X	12
Puldite Skerry	Orkney	HY4318	59°3·0'	2°59·1'W	X	6
Puldrite	Orkney	HY4118	59°3·0'	3°1·2'W	X	6
Pule Hill	Cald	SE0927	53°44·6'	1°51·4'W	T	104
Pule Hill	Kirk	SE0310	53°35·4'	1°56·9'W	H	110
Pule Hill Hall	Barns	SE2801	53°30·5'	1°34·3'W	X	110
Puleston	Wrekin	SJ7322	52°47·9'	2°23·6'W	T	127
Puleston Common	Wrekin	SJ7323	52°48·5'	2°23·6'W	F	127
Puleston Hill	Wrekin	SJ7322	52°47·9'	2°23·6'W	H	127
Pulford	Ches	SJ3758	53°7·2'	2°56·1'W	T	117
Pulford Approach	Ches	SJ4059	53°7·7'	2°53·4'W	X	117
Pulford Brook	Wrex	SJ3659	53°7·7'	2°57·0'W	W	117
Pulganny Burn	D & G	NX2675	55°2·6'	4°43·0'W	W	76
Pulham	Dorset	ST7008	50°52·5'	2°25·2'W	T	194
Pulham Fm	Devon	SS7729	51°3·1'	3°44·9'W	FM	180
Pulham Gorse	Dorset	ST7109	50°53·0'	2°24·4'W	F	194
Pulham Market	Norf	TM1986	52°25·9'	1°13·7'E	T	156
Pulham River	Somer	SS9433	51°5·4'	3°30·4'W	W	181
Pulham St Mary	Norf	TM2085	52°25·3'	1°14·5'E	T	156
Pulharrow Burn	D & G	NX4179	55°5·1'	4°29·0'W	W	77
Pulhayes Fm	Devon	SY0784	50°39·1'	3°18·6'W	FM	192
Pulhowan Burn	D & G	NX3972	55°1·2'	4°30·7'W	W	77
Pulinkum Fm	D & G	NX1232	54°39·1'	4°54·4'W	FM	82
Pulkitto	Orkney	HY3823	59°5·6'	3°4·4'W	X	6
Pullabrook Fm	Devon	SX7979	50°36·1'	3°42·2'W	FM	191
Pulla Cross	Corn	SW7539	50°12·7'	5°8·9'W	X	204
Pullan	Orkney	HY3109	58°58·0'	3°11·5'W	X	6,7
Pullar Cuy	Angus	NO4786	56°58·0'	2°51·8'W	H	44
Pullaugh Burn	D & G	NX5473	55°2·1'	4°16·6'W	W	77
Pullens Fm	Kent	TQ6838	51°7·2'	0°24·4'E	FM	188
Pullens Green	S Glos	ST6192	51°37·8'	2°33·4'W	T	162,172
Pulley	Shrops	SJ4809	52°40·8'	2°45·7'W	T	126
Pull Garth Wood	Cumbr	NY3602	54°24·8'	2°58·8'W	F	90
Pullington	Kent	TQ8132	51°3·7'	0°35·4'E	T	188
Pullower Burn	S Ayr	NX2376	55°3·1'	4°45·8'W	W	76
Pulloxhill	Beds	TL0633	51°59·3'	0°27·0'W	T	166
Pull Woods	Cumbr	NY3601	54°24·3'	2°58·7'W	F	90
Pull Wyke	Cumbr	NY3602	54°24·8'	2°58·8'W	W	90
Pulmulloch Burn	D & G	NS6800	55°16·8'	4°4·3'W	W	77
Pulnagashel Burn	D & G	NX3880	55°5·5'	4°31·9'W	W	77
Pulnee Burn	D & G	NX4573	55°1·9'	4°25·1'W	W	77
Pulniskie Burn	D & G	NX3975	55°2·9'	4°30·8'W	W	77
Pulpit Hill	Arg & Bt	NM8529	56°24·5'	5°28·6'W	T	49
Pulpit Hill	Bucks	SP8305	51°44·5'	0°47·5'W	H	165
Pulpit Hill	Oxon	SU3587	51°35·1'	1°29·3'W	X	174
Pulpit Hill (Fort)	Bucks	SP8305	51°44·5'	0°47·5'W	A	165
Pulpit Law	Scot Bord	NT5855	55°47·4'	2°39·8'W	X	67,73,74
Pulpit Rock	Arg & Bt	NN3213	56°17·0'	4°42·4'W	X	50,56
Pulpit Rock	Dorset	SY6768	50°30·9'	2°27·5'W	X	194
Pulpit, The	E Loth	NT6087	56°4·7'	2°38·1'W	X	67
Pulpry	Corn	SW8536	50°11·3'	5°0·4'W	X	204
Pulran Burn	D & G	NX5375	55°3·1'	4°17·6'W	W	77
Pulreoch Burn	S Ayr	NX3898	55°15·2'	4°32·5'W	W	77
Pulrose	I of M	SC3675	54°8·9'	4°30·3'W	T	95
Pulrossie	Highld	NH7288	57°52·1'	4°9·0'W	X	21
Pulsack Manor	Corn	SW5839	50°12·3'	5°23·1'W	X	203
Pulse Skerry	Orkney	HY2308	58°57·4'	3°19·8'W	X	6,7
Pulsford	Devon	SX8068	50°30·2'	3°41·2'W	T	202
Pulsfordware	Devon	SS8311	50°53·4'	3°39·4'W	X	191
Pulshays	Devon	ST1504	50°50·0'	3°12·0'W	X	192,193
Pulskaig Burn	D & G	NX4686	55°8·9'	4°24·6'W	W	77
Pulsworthy Fm	Devon	SS7829	51°3·1'	3°44·1'W	FM	180
Pultadie	D & G	NX1870	54°59·7'	4°50·3'W	X	76
Pultarson Burn	D & G	NX6175	55°3·3'	4°10·1'W	W	77
Pultayan Burn	D & G	NX2868	54°58·9'	4°40·8'W	W	82
Pulter's Fm	Herts	TL2339	52°2·4'	0°12·0'W	FM	153
Pultheley	Shrops	SO3294	52°32·6'	2°59·8'W	X	137
Pulverbatch	Shrops	SJ4202	52°37·0'	2°51·0'W	T	126
Pulvertoft Hall Fm	Lincs	TF4021	52°46·3'	0°4·9'E	FM	131
Pulwhat Burn	D & G	NX4761	54°55·5'	4°22·8'W	W	83
Pulwhirrin Burn	D & G	NX6049	54°49·2'	4°10·3'W	W	83
Pulwhite	Aberd	NJ6532	57°22·9'	2°34·5'W	X	29
Pulworthy	Devon	SS5104	50°49·2'	4°6·5'W	X	191
Pulworthy	Devon	SS8127	51°2·0'	3°41·4'W	X	181
Pulworthy Brook	Devon	SS4803	50°48·6'	4°9·1'W	W	191
Pulworthy Brook	Devon	SS5103	50°48·7'	4°6·5'W	W	191
Pumkin Hall	Essex	TL5609	51°45·7'	0°16·0'E	X	167
Pumlumon Cwmbiga	Powys	SN8389	52°29·4'	3°43·0'W	H	135,136
Pumlumon Fach	Cered	SN7887	52°28·3'	3°47·4'W	H	135
Pumlumon Fawr or Plynlimon	Cered	SN7886	52°27·7'	3°47·3'W	H	135
Pumney Fm	Oxon	SU5397	51°40·4'	1°13·6'W	FM	164
Pump Br	E Yorks	TA0142	53°52·1'	0°27·4'W	X	106,107
Pumpfield Fm	Hants	SU3809	50°53·0'	1°27·2'W	FM	196
Pump Fm	Ches	SJ8158	53°7·4'	2°16·6'W	FM	118
Pump Fm	Essex	TQ5990	51°35·4'	0°18·1'E	FM	177
Pump Fm	Medway	TQ8067	51°22·6'	0°35·6'E	FM	178
Pumpherston	W Loth	NT0669	55°54·6'	3°29·8'W	T	65
Pumpherston Fm	W Loth	NT0768	55°54·0'	3°28·8'W	FM	65
Pump Hill	Kent	TQ9870	51°23·9'	0°51·2'E	X	178
Pump Ho	Powys	SJ2113	52°42·8'	3°9·8'W	X	126
Pump House Fm	Ches	SJ7368	53°12·7'	2°23·9'W	FM	118
Pumphouse Fm	Worcs	SO9563	52°16·1'	2°4·0'W	FM	150
Pumpkin Hill	Bucks	SU9484	51°33·1'	0°38·3'W	X	175
Pumplaburn	D & G	NY1196	55°15·3'	3°23·6'W	X	78
Pumro Fell	D & G	NY0192	55°13·0'	3°32·9'W	X	78
Pumryd	Gwyn	SH8719	52°45·7'	3°40·1'W	H	124,125
Pumsaint	Carm	SN6540	52°2·8'	3°57·7'W	T	146
Pumwern	Gwyn	SN7299	52°34·7'	3°52·9'W	X	135
Punchard	N Yks	NY9705	54°26·7'	2°2·4'W	X	92
Punchard Moor	N Yks	NY9503	54°25·6'	2°4·2'W	X	91,92
Punch Bowl	D & G	NX4165	54°57·5'	4°28·6'W	X	83
Punch Bowl	Herts	TL1110	51°46·9'	0°23·1'W	X	166
Punchbowl	Monm	SO2811	51°47·8'	3°2·3'W	X	161
Punchbowl	W Susx	SU9809	50°52·6'	0°36·0'W	X	197
Punch Bowl, The	Aberd	NO1191	57°0·4'	3°27·5'W	X	43
Punchbowl, The	Somer	SS8834	51°5·9'	3°35·6'W	X	181
Puncherton	Northum	NT9309	55°22·7'	2°6·2'W	X	80
Puncherton Hill	Northum	NT9209	55°22·7'	2°7·1'W	H	80
Puncheston	Pemb	SN0029	51°55·7'	4°54·1'W	T	145,157,158
Puncheston Common	Pemb	SN0030	51°56·2'	4°54·2'W	X	145,157
Punch Fm	Cambs	TL4664	52°15·5'	0°8·8'E	FM	154
Punch Fm	Norf	TF8916	52°42·7'	0°48·3'E	FM	132
Punch's Cross	Herts	TL1530	51°57·6'	0°19·2'W	X	166
Punch Well Brae	D & G	NX4175	55°2·9'	4°28·9'W	X	77
Puncknowle	Dorset	SY5388	50°41·6'	2°39·5'W	T	194
Pund	Shetld	HU3843	60°10·4'	1°18·4'W	X	4
Pund	Shetld	HU4023	59°59·7'	1°16·5'W	X	4
Pund	Shetld	HU4063	60°21·2'	1°16·0'W	X	2,3
Pund	Shetld	HU4323	59°59·6'	1°13·3'W	X	4
Pund	Shetld	HU4769	60°24·4'	1°8·3'W	X	2,3
Pund	Shetld	HZ2071	59°31·7'	1°38·3'W	X	4
Pundbank	Shetld	HU4763	60°21·2'	1°8·4'W	X	2,3
Pundeavon Burn	N Ayr	NS3056	55°46·3'	4°42·2'W	W	63
Pundeavon Resr	N Ayr	NS2957	55°46·8'	4°43·2'W	W	63
Pundershaw	Northum	NY7780	55°7·1'	2°21·2'W	X	80
Pundershaw	Northum	NY7880	55°7·1'	2°20·3'W	X	80
Pundershaw Burn	Northum	NY7779	55°6·5'	2°21·2'W	W	86,87
Pund Geo	Shetld	HU1655	60°17·0'	1°42·1'W	X	3
Pund Head	Shetld	HU1655	60°17·0'	1°42·1'W	X	3
Pundlercroft	Aberd	NJ8948	57°31·6'	2°10·6'W	X	30
Pund of Grevasand	Shetld	HU2776	60°28·3'	1°30·0'W	X	3
Pund of Grutin	Shetld	HU4068	60°23·9'	1°15·9'W	X	2,3
Pund of Mangaster	Shetld	HU3270	60°25·0'	1°24·6'W	X	3
Punds	Shetld	HT9637	60°7·3'	2°3·8'W	X	4
Punds	Shetld	HU1857	60°18·1'	1°40·0'W	X	3
Punds	Shetld	HU3556	60°17·5'	1°21·5'W	X	2,3
Punds	Shetld	HU3673	60°26·6'	1°20·2'W	X	2,3
Pundsar	Shetld	HU3635	60°6·1'	1°20·7'W	X	4
Punds Geo	Shetld	HP5606	60°44·3'	0°57·9'W	X	1
Punds Geo	Shetld	HU4489	60°35·2'	1°11·3'W	X	1,2
Punds Geo	Shetld	HU4539	60°8·2'	1°10·9'W	X	4
Punds Lochs	Shetld	HU3071	60°25·6'	1°26·8'W	W	3
Punds Ness	Shetld	HU4222	59°59·1'	1°14·3'W	X	4
Punds Stack	Shetld	HU4537	60°7·2'	1°10·9'W	X	4
Punds, The	Shetld	HP6411	60°46·9'	0°49·0'W	X	1
Punds, The	Shetld	HU3412	59°53·8'	1°23·0'W	X	4
Punds Water	Shetld	HU2481	60°31·0'	1°33·3'W	W	3
Punds Water	Shetld	HU2482	60°31·5'	1°33·3'W	W	3
Punds Water	Shetld	HU3271	60°25·6'	1°24·6'W	W	3
Punds Water	Shetld	HU3275	60°27·7'	1°24·6'W	W	3
Pund Voe	Shetld	HU3838	60°7·8'	1°18·5'W	W	4
Punnetts Fm	Kent	TQ9772	51°25·0'	0°50·4'E	FM	178
Punnett's Town	E Susx	TQ6220	50°57·6'	0°18·8'E	T	199
Punsholt Fm	Hants	SU6527	51°2·5'	1°4·0'W	FM	185,186
Punt Gwynedd	Gwyn	SH2727	52°49·0'	4°33·6'W	X	123
Pupers Hill	Devon	SX6767	50°29·5'	3°52·1'W	X	202
Purbeck Hills	Dorset	SY9181	50°37·9'	2°7·3'W	H	195
Purbrook	Hants	SU6707	50°51·7'	1°2·5'W	T	196
Pur Brook	Staffs	SK1021	52°47·4'	1°50·7'W	W	128
Purchase Fm	Kent	TQ9741	51°8·3'	0°49·4'E	FM	189
Purclewan Mill	E Ayr	NS3715	55°24·4'	4°34·0'W	X	70
Purcombe Fm	Devon	SX7968	50°30·2'	3°42·0'W	FM	202
Purcombe Fm	Dorset	SY4196	50°45·9'	2°49·8'W	FM	193
Purcombe Fm	Dorset	SY4199	50°47·5'	2°49·8'W	FM	193
Purdies Fm	Hants	SU7658	51°19·2'	0°54·2'W	FM	175,186
Purdis Fm	Suff	TM2142	52°2·2'	1°13·7'E	FM	169
Purdomstone	D & G	NY2176	55°4·6'	3°13·8'W	X	85
Purdomstone Reservoir	D & G	NY2177	55°5·1'	3°13·8'W	W	85
Pur Down	C of Bris	ST6176	51°29·1'	2°33·3'W	X	172
Purewell	Dorset	SZ1692	50°43·9'	1°46·0'W	T	195
Purfleet	Kent	TQ5577	51°28·5'	0°14·3'E	T	177
Purgatory	Oxon	SP4523	51°54·5'	1°20·4'W	X	164
Purgatory Burn or Mulniegarroch	D & G	NX2168	54°58·7'	4°47·4'W	W	82
Purgavie	Angus	NO2955	56°41·1'	3°9·1'W	X	53
Purin	Fife	NO2606	56°14·7'	3°11·2'W	X	59
Purin Hill	Fife	NO2506	56°14·7'	3°12·2'W	X	59
Puriton	Somer	ST3241	51°10·1'	2°58·0'W	T	182
Puriton Level	Somer	ST3242	51°10·6'	2°58·0'W	X	182
Purleigh	Essex	TL8302	51°41·4'	0°39·3'E	T	168
Purleigh Barns	Essex	TQ8699	51°39·8'	0°41·8'E	X	168
Purleigh Wash Fm	Essex	TL8502	51°41·4'	0°41·0'E	FM	168
Purley	Croy	TQ3161	51°20·2'	0°6·8'W	T	176,177,187
Purley Covert	Glos	ST9295	51°39·5'	2°6·5'W	X	163
Purley Downs	Croy	TQ3261	51°20·2'	0°5·9'W	X	176,177,187
Purley Fm	Essex	TL8524	51°53·3'	0°41·7'E	FM	168
Purley Fm	W Berks	SU4177	51°29·7'	1°24·2'W	FM	174
Purley Fm	Wilts	SU0585	51°34·1'	1°55·3'W	FM	173
Purley Hall	W Berks	SU6475	51°28·5'	1°4·3'W	X	175
Purley on Thames	W Berks	SU6675	51°28·4'	1°2·6'W	T	175
Purley Park	Warw	SP3096	52°33·9'	1°33·0'W	X	140
Purlieu	Hants	SZ1899	50°47·6'	1°44·3'W	X	195
Purlieu, The	Glos	SO6505	51°44·8'	2°30·0'W	X	162
Purlogue	Shrops	SO2876	52°22·9'	3°3·1'W	T	137,148
Purlon Fm	V of Glam	SS9669	51°24·9'	3°29·3'W	FM	170
Purlpit	Wilts	ST8765	51°23·3'	2°10·8'W	T	173
Purls Bridge	Cambs	TL4787	52°27·9'	0°10·2'E	T	143
Purlshill	Essex	TL7933	51°58·2'	0°36·8'E	X	167
Purn	N Som	ST3357	51°18·7'	2°57·3'W	T	182
Purples Hill	Glos	SO5910	51°47·5'	2°35·3'W	X	162
Purps Fm	Devon	SX5462	50°26·6'	4°3·0'W	FM	201
Purrant's Fm	Cambs	TL3687	52°28·1'	0°0·5'E	FM	142
Purroch	E Ayr	NS4635	55°35·3'	4°26·2'W	X	70
Purse Caundle	Dorset	ST6917	50°57·3'	2°26·1'W	T	183
Purser's	Hants	SU6427	51°2·6'	1°4·8'W	X	185
Pursers Fm	Surrey	TQ0845	51°11·9'	0°26·9'W	FM	187
Purser's Hills	Northnts	SP7076	52°22·9'	0°57·9'W	X	141
Purser, The	Shrops	SJ4348	53°1·8'	2°50·6'W	X	117
Purshull Green	Worcs	SO9071	52°20·5'	2°8·4'W	X	139
Purshull Hall	Worcs	SO9070	52°19·9'	2°8·4'W	X	139
Pursley Fm	Herts	TL1900	51°41·4'	0°16·3'W	FM	166
Purslow	Shrops	SO3680	52°25·1'	2°56·1'W	T	137
Purslow Wood	Shrops	SO3580	52°25·1'	2°56·9'W	F	137
Purston Jaglin	Wakf	SE4319	53°40·2'	1°20·5'W	T	111
Purtaquoy	Orkney	HY5215	59°1·4'	2°49·7'W	X	6
Purtington	Somer	ST3909	50°52·9'	2°51·6'W	T	193
Purton	Glos	SO6704	51°44·3'	2°28·3'W	T	162
Purton	Glos	SO6904	51°44·3'	2°26·5'W	T	162
Purton	W Berks	SU4877	51°29·6'	1°18·1'W	X	174
Purton	Wilts	SU0987	51°35·1'	1°51·8'W	T	173
Purton Common	Wilts	SU0888	51°35·7'	1°52·7'W	T	173
Purton Green	Suff	TL7853	52°9·0'	0°36·5'E	X	155
Purton Green Fm	Suff	TL7853	52°9·0'	0°36·5'E	FM	155
Purton Ho	Wilts	SU0987	51°35·1'	1°51·8'W	X	173
Purton Stoke	Wilts	SU0990	51°36·8'	1°51·8'W	T	163,173
Purves Hall	Scot Bord	NT7644	55°41·6'	2°22·5'W	X	74
Purveyor's Fm	W Susx	TQ1224	51°0·5'	0°23·8'W	FM	198
Purvishaugh	Scot Bord	NT5939	55°38·8'	2°38·7'W	X	73,74
Purvishaugh	Scot Bord	NT6039	55°38·8'	2°37·7'W	X	74
Purwell	Herts	TL2029	51°57·0'	0°14·8'W	T	166
Purwell Fm	Oxon	SP4411	51°48·0'	1°21·3'W	FM	164
Pury End	Northnts	SP7045	52°6·2'	0°58·3'W	T	152
Pury Hill	Northnts	SP7346	52°6·7'	0°55·6'W	X	152
Pusehill	Devon	SS4228	51°2·0'	4°14·8'W	X	180
Pusey	Oxon	SU3596	51°39·9'	1°29·2'W	T	164
Puseydale Fm	Ches	SJ6851	53°3·6'	2°28·2'W	FM	118
Pusey Furze	Oxon	SU3598	51°41·0'	1°29·2'W	X	164
Pusey Ho	Oxon	SU3596	51°39·9'	1°29·2'W	X	164
Pusey Lodge Fm	Oxon	SU3796	51°39·9'	1°27·5'W	FM	164
Pusgill Ho	Cumbr	NY6925	54°37·4'	2°28·4'W	X	91
Pusk	Fife	NO4320	56°22·4'	2°54·9'W	X	54,59
Puslinch	Devon	SX5650	50°20·2'	4°1·0'W	A	202
Pussi Geos	Shetld	HP6507	60°44·7'	0°48·0'W	X	1
Pusto Hill Fm	Notts	SK6990	53°24·4'	0°57·3'W	FM	111
Putechan Lodge Hotel	Arg & Bt	NR6531	55°31·2'	5°42·9'W	X	68
Puthall Fm	Wilts	SU2368	51°24·9'	1°39·8'W	FM	174
Putham	Somer	SS9338	51°8·1'	3°31·4'W	X	181
Puthill	Somer	ST3707	50°51·8'	2°53·3'W	X	193
Putlake Fm	Dorset	SZ0078	50°36·3'	1°59·6'W	FM	195
Putland's Fm	E Susx	TQ4627	51°1·7'	0°5·3'E	FM	188,198
Putley	Heref	SO6437	52°2·1'	2°31·1'W	T	149
Putley Common	Heref	SO6338	52°2·6'	2°32·0'W	T	149
Putley Court	Heref	SO6437	52°2·1'	2°31·1'W	X	149
Putley Green	Heref	SO6537	52°2·1'	2°30·2'W	T	149
Putloe	Glos	SO7809	51°47·0'	2°18·7'W	T	162
Putlowes	Bucks	SP7815	51°49·9'	0°51·7'W	X	165
Putnell Fm	Somer	ST2541	51°10·0'	3°4·0'W	FM	182
Putney	Wan	TQ2375	51°27·9'	0°13·4'W	T	176
Putney Br	Wan	TQ2475	51°27·8'	0°12·5'W	X	176
Putney Heath	Wan	TQ2373	51°26·8'	0°13·4'W	T	176
Putney Hill Fm	Cambs	TL5981	52°24·5'	0°20·7'E	FM	143
Putney Maol	Angus	NO4967	56°47·8'	2°49·6'W	H	44
Putney Vale	Wan	TQ2272	51°26·3'	0°14·3'W	T	176
Putnoe	Beds	TL0651	52°9·1'	0°26·6'W	T	153

Putsborough	Devon	SS4440	51°8·5'	4°13·4'W	T	180
Putsborough Sand	Devon	SS4441	51°9·1'	4°13·5'W	X	180
Putshole	Devon	SS4414	50°54·5'	4°12·8'W	X	180,190
Putshole Fm	Devon	SS2319	50°56·8'	4°30·8'W	FM	190
Putson	Heref	SO5138	52°2·5'	2°42·5'W	T	149
Puttenden Manor	Surrey	TQ4045	51°11·4'	0°0·6'E	X	187
Puttenden Manor Fm	Kent	TQ6152	51°14·9'	0°18·8'E	FM	188
Puttenham	Herts	SP8814	51°49·3'	0°43·0'W	T	165
Puttenham	Surrey	SU9347	51°13·1'	0°39·7'W	T	186
Puttenham Common	Surrey	SU9146	51°12·6'	0°41·4'W	X	186
Puttenham Heath	Surrey	SU9447	51°13·1'	0°38·9'W	X	186
Puttenham Place Fm	Bucks	SU9193	51°37·9'	0°40·7'W	FM	175
Putteridge Bury	Herts	TL1124	51°54·4'	0°22·8'W	X	166
Puttock End	Essex	TL8040	52°2·0'	0°37·8'E	T	155
Puttocks	Essex	TL6219	51°51·0'	0°21·5'E	X	167
Puttock's End	Essex	TL5619	51°51·1'	0°16·3'E	T	167
Puttock's End	Herts	TL4131	51°57·8'	0°3·5'E	X	167
Puttockshill	Suff	TL9069	52°17·4'	0°47·6'E	X	155
Putton	Dorset	SY6580	50°37·4'	2°29·3'W	T	194
Putton Mill	Scot Bord	NT7951	55°45·4'	2°19·6'W	X	67,74
Putts Corner	Devon	SY1496	50°45·7'	3°12·8'W	X	192,193
Putt's Fm	Devon	SY1193	50°44·0'	3°15·3'W	FM	192,193
Putt Wood	Kent	TQ9759	51°18·0'	0°50·0'E	F	178
Putwell Hill	Derby	SK1771	53°14·4'	1°44·3'W	X	119
Puxey	Dorset	ST7612	50°54·7'	2°20·1'W	T	194
Puxley	Northnts	SP7541	52°4·0'	0°54·0'W	T	152
Puxton	N Som	ST4063	51°22·0'	2°51·3'W	T	172,182
Puxton Moor	N Som	ST4162	51°21·5'	2°50·5'W	X	172,182
Puzzle Wood	Glos	SO5709	51°46·9'	2°37·0'W	X	162
Pwll	Carm	SN4801	51°41·5'	4°11·6'W	T	159
Pwll	Carm	SN4829	51°56·6'	4°12·3'W	X	146
Pwll	Monm	ST4399	51°41·4'	2°49·1'W	X	171
Pwll	Powys	SJ1904	52°37·9'	3°11·4'W	T	136
Pwll	Shrops	SJ3119	52°46·1'	3°1·0'W	X	126
Pwllacca	Powys	SN9632	51°58·8'	3°30·5'W	X	160
Pwllacca	Powys	SN9956	52°11·8'	3°28·3'W	X	147
Pwllan	Powys	SN9031	51°58·2'	3°35·7'W	X	160
Pwllan	Powys	SO0287	52°28·6'	3°26·2'W	X	136
Pwllan	Powys	SO1098	52°34·6'	3°19·3'W	X	136
Pwll Arian	Pemb	SM8840	52°1·3'	5°5·0'W	W	157
Pwllbo	Powys	SN8550	52°8·4'	3°40·4'W	X	147
Pwll Brwyn	Powys	SJ0022	52°47·4'	3°28·6'W	H	125
Pwll Byfre	Powys	SN8716	51°50·1'	3°38·0'W	X	160
Pwll-caerog	Pemb	SM7830	51°55·7'	5°13·4'W	X	157
Pwllcalled	Denb	SJ1154	53°4·8'	3°19·3'W	X	116
Pwll Cam	Powys	SN9741	52°3·7'	3°29·8'W	W	147,160
Pwllcenawon	Cered	SN6380	52°24·3'	4°0·4'W	X	135
Pwllclai	Cered	SN6270	52°18·9'	4°1·1'W	X	135
Pwll-clai	Cered	SN6380	52°24·3'	4°0·4'W	X	135
Pwll Clai	Conwy	SH8169	53°12·5'	3°46·5'W	X	116
Pwll-clai	Flint	SJ1873	53°15·1'	3°13·3'W	T	116
Pwll Coch	Pemb	SN0643	52°3·3'	4°49·4'W	W	145
Pwll Coch Fm	Card	ST2382	51°32·1'	3°6·2'W	FM	171
Pwll Coch Isaf	I of Angl	SH4387	53°21·6'	4°21·2'W	X	114
Pwllcoch Uchaf	I of Angl	SH4287	53°21·6'	4°22·1'W	X	114
Pwllcoediog Fm	Powys	SN8416	51°50·1'	3°40·6'W	FM	160
Pwllcornel	Cered	SN3742	52°3·4'	4°22·3'W	X	145
Pwll Court Fm	Powys	SO1419	51°52·0'	3°14·6'W	FM	161
Pwllcrochan	Pemb	SM8836	51°59·2'	5°4·9'W	W	157
Pwllcrochan	Pemb	SM9202	51°40·9'	5°0·1'W	T	157,158
Pwllcymbyd	Carm	SN5637	52°1·0'	4°5·5'W	X	146
Pwlldawnau	Pemb	SM8736	51°59·1'	5°5·7'W	W	157
Pwlldefaid	Gwyn	SH1526	52°48·2'	4°44·3'W	X	123
Pwll Deri	Pemb	SM8938	52°0·3'	5°4·1'W	W	157
Pwll-du	Conwy	SH7466	53°10·8'	3°52·7'W	X	115
Pwll-du	Monm	SO2411	51°47·8'	3°5·7'W	X	161
Pwll-du	Powys	SO0244	52°5·4'	3°25·4'W	W	147,160
Pwlldu Bay	Swan	SS5787	51°34·1'	4°3·4'W	W	159
Pwlldu Head	Swan	SS5786	51°33·5'	4°3·4'W	X	159
Pwlldyfarch	Carm	SN3525	51°54·2'	4°23·5'W	X	145
Pwllffein	Cered	SN4246	52°5·6'	4°18·0'W	X	146
Pwll Fm	Flint	SJ2358	53°7·1'	3°8·6'W	FM	117
Pwllglas	Cered	SN3151	52°8·1'	4°27·8'W	X	145
Pwllglas	Cered	SN6055	52°10·8'	4°2·5'W	X	146
Pwll-glâs	Cered	SN6386	52°27·5'	4°0·6'W	X	135
Pwll-glâs	Denb	SJ1154	53°4·8'	3°19·3'W	T	116
Pwll Glas	Pemb	SN0141	52°2·1'	4°53·7'W	W	145,157
Pwll-glas	Pemb	SN1833	51°58·2'	4°38·6'W	X	145
Pwllglas	Powys	SH7802	52°36·4'	3°47·7'W	X	135
Pwllglas	Powys	SN9789	52°29·6'	3°30·6'W	X	136
Pwllgloyw	Powys	SO0333	51°59·5'	3°24·4'W	T	160
Pwllgoed	Gwyn	SH2435	52°53·2'	4°36·6'W	X	123
Pwllgwaelod	Pemb	SN0039	52°1·0'	4°54·5'W	W	145,157
Pwllgwyn	Powys	SO0548	52°7·6'	3°22·9'W	X	147
Pwll Gwy-rhoc	Powys	SO1815	51°49·9'	3°11·0'W	W	161
Pwllhalog	Denb	SJ0877	53°17·2'	3°22·4'W	X	116
Pwllheli	Gwyn	SH3735	52°53·5'	4°25·0'W	T	123
Pwll-helyg	Rho Cyn Taf	ST0595	51°39·0'	3°22·0'W	X	170
Pwll Hir	Pemb	SM9539	52°0·9'	4°58·9'W	W	157
Pwlliago	Powys	SJ0325	52°49·1'	3°26·0'W	X	125
Pwll-isaf	Powys	SN8428	51°56·5'	3°40·9'W	X	160
Pwlliwrch	Powys	SH8301	52°35·9'	3°43·2'W	X	135,136
Pwll Llong	Pemb	SM8433	51°57·5'	5°8·2'W	W	157
Pwll Mair	Monm	SO3521	51°53·3'	2°56·1'W	X	161
Pwll March	Pemb	SM8422	51°51·5'	5°7·8'W	W	157
Pwll Mawdy	Monm	SO2610	51°47·3'	3°4·0'W	X	161
Pwll-Mawr	Card	ST2278	51°30·0'	3°7·0'W	T	171
Pwll-melyn	Flint	SJ1871	53°14·0'	3°13·3'W	T	116
Pwll-melyn	Powys	SH9104	52°37·6'	3°36·2'W	X	136
Pwllmeyric	Monm	ST5192	51°37·7'	2°42·1'W	T	162,172
Pwll Olfa	Pemb	SM8333	51°57·4'	5°9·1'W	W	157
Pwllpeiran	Cered	SN7774	52°21·3'	3°48·0'W	X	135,147
Pwll-Pen	Newp	ST3587	51°34·9'	2°55·9'W	X	171
Pwllperran	Powys	SO1243	52°4·9'	3°16·7'W	X	148,161
Pwllpillo	I of Angl	SH2777	53°16·0'	4°35·2'W	X	114
Pwll Preban	I of Angl	SH2776	53°15·4'	4°35·2'W	X	114
Pwllpridd	Cered	SN6469	52°18·4'	3°59·3'W	X	135
Pwllstrodur	Pemb	SM8633	51°57·5'	5°6·5'W	W	157
Pwll Swnd	Carm	SN7618	51°51·0'	3°47·6'W	W	160
Pwll Tew	Powys	SO1277	52°23·3'	3°17·2'W	X	136,148
Pwll Tra	Torf	ST2594	51°38·6'	3°4·6'W	X	171
Pwll-trap	Carm	SN2616	51°49·2'	4°31·1'W	T	158
Pwll Trewern	Powys	SJ2710	52°41·2'	3°4·4'W	W	126
Pwllwatkin Fm	Nth Pt Talb	SN6908	51°45·6'	3°53·5'W	FM	160
Pwll Whiting	Pemb	SM8433	51°57·5'	5°8·2'W	W	157
Pwll Wmffre	Pemb	SM8932	51°57·0'	5°3·8'W	W	157
Pwllybilwg	Cered	SN5046	52°5·8'	4°11·0'W	X	146
Pwll-y-cibau	Conwy	SH9473	53°14·9'	3°34·9'W	X	116
Pwll-y-cwm	Monm	SO4614	51°49·6'	2°46·6'W	X	161
Pwll-y-cwrw	Powys	SO0935	52°0·6'	3°19·2'W	X	161
Pwll-y-darren	V of Glam	ST0275	51°28·2'	3°24·3'W	X	170
Pwll-y-froga	Swan	SS5991	51°36·3'	4°1·8'W	X	159
Pwll-y-garn	Brig	SS9093	51°37·7'	3°35·0'W	X	170
Pwll-y-gâth	Conwy	SH7652	53°3·3'	3°50·6'W	X	115
Pwll-y-gele	Gwyn	SH7621	52°46·6'	3°49·9'W	X	124
Pwll-y-glaw	Nth Pt Talb	SS7993	51°37·6'	3°44·5'W	T	170
Pwllygrafel	Carm	SN3117	51°49·8'	4°26·8'W	X	159
Pwllygranant	Pemb	SN1247	52°5·6'	4°44·3'W	W	145
Pwll-y-llwnch	Monm	ST3896	51°39·8'	2°53·4'W	X	171
Pwll-y-march	Carm	SN2826	51°54·6'	4°29·6'W	X	145,158
Pwllypant	Caer	ST1588	51°35·3'	3°13·2'W	T	171
Pwllyrheirn	Cered	SN3243	52°3·8'	4°26·7'W	X	145
Pwll-y-rhôs	Flint	SJ1563	53°9·7'	3°15·9'W	W	116
Pwll-yr-hwyaid	I of Angl	SH4466	53°10·3'	4°19·6'W	X	114,115
Pwll-y-rhyd	Powys	SN9013	51°48·5'	3°35·3'W	X	160
Pwllywheel	Cered	SN3554	52°9·8'	4°24·4'W	X	145
Pwll-y-wrach	Powys	SO1732	51°59·1'	3°12·1'W	X	161
Pwllywrach	V of Glam	SS9575	51°28·1'	3°30·3'W	X	170
Pwynt	Powys	SJ1219	52°45·9'	3°17·9'W	X	125
Pyat Hill	Scot Bord	NT3738	55°38·1'	2°59·6'W	H	73
Pyatknowe Fm	Scot Bord	NT0536	55°36·8'	3°30·1'W	FM	72
Pyat's Barn	Staffs	SJ9161	53°9·0'	2°7·7'W	X	118
Pyatshaw	Scot Bord	NT5848	55°43·7'	2°39·7'W	X	73,74
Pyatshaw Knowe	Scot Bord	NT6358	55°49·1'	2°35·0'W	X	67,74
Pyatshaws Rig	D & G	NY2184	55°8·9'	3°13·9'W	H	79
Pyatts Fm	Bucks	SU8192	51°37·5'	0°49·4'W	FM	175
Pydew	I of Angl	SH4275	53°15·2'	4°21·7'W	X	114,115
Pydew Fm	Denb	SJ0481	53°19·3'	3°26·1'W	FM	116
Pyeash	Ches	SJ9166	53°11·7'	2°7·7'W	X	118
Pyebirch Manor	Staffs	SJ8428	52°51·2'	2°13·9'W	X	127
Pye Bridge	Derby	SK4352	53°4·0'	1°21·1'W	T	120
Pye Brook	Shrops	SO5183	52°26·8'	2°42·9'W	W	137,138
Pyeclough Fm	Staffs	SK0464	53°10·6'	1°56·0'W	FM	119
Pyecombe	W Susx	TQ2912	50°53·8'	0°9·5'W	T	198
Pye Corner	Devon	SX9198	50°46·5'	3°32·4'W	T	192
Pye Corner	Kent	TQ8548	51°12·3'	0°39·3'E	T	189
Pye Corner	Newp	ST2887	51°34·9'	3°2·0'W	T	171
Pye Corner	Newp	ST3485	51°33·8'	2°56·7'W	T	171
Pye Corner	Powys	SO2171	52°20·1'	3°9·2'W	X	137,148
Pye Corner	S Glos	ST6479	51°30·8'	2°30·7'W	T	172
Pye Corner	Somer	ST5114	50°55·6'	2°41·4'W	X	194
Pyefield Ho	N Yks	SE1960	54°2·4'	1°42·2'W	X	99
Pyefinch Wood	Monm	SO5116	51°50·7'	2°42·3'W	F	162
Pyefleet Channel	Essex	TM0416	51°48·5'	0°58·0'E	W	168
Pyegreave	Derby	SK0477	53°17·6'	1°56·0'W	X	119
Pyegreave Fm	Ches	SJ9372	53°14·9'	2°5·9'W	FM	118
Pye Green	Staffs	SJ9914	52°43·7'	2°0·5'W	T	127
Pye Hill	Notts	SK4452	53°4·0'	1°20·2'W	T	120
Pye Hill	Somer	ST6138	51°8·6'	2°33·1'W	X	183
Pye Howe	Cumbr	NY3006	54°26·9'	3°4·4'W	X	90
Pyeing Fm	Cumbr	NY4737	54°43·8'	2°49·0'W	FM	90
Pye Rigg Howe	N Yks	NZ9600	54°23·4'	0°30·9'W	A	94
Pye Sand	Essex	TM2426	51°53·5'	1°15·7'E	X	169
Pye's Bridge Fm	Cumbr	SD5079	54°12·5'	2°45·6'W	FM	97
Pyes Fm	Essex	TL6418	51°50·4'	0°23·2'E	FM	167
Pye's Fm	E Susx	TQ7613	50°53·6'	0°30·5'E	FM	199
Pye's Fm	Lincs	TF4099	53°28·4'	0°7·0'E	FM	113
Pyes Hall Fm	Suff	TM4982	52°23·0'	1°39·9'E	FM	156
Pyestock Hill	Hants	SU8353	51°16·4'	0°48·2'W	X	186
Pyestock Wood	Hants	SU8353	51°16·4'	0°48·2'W	F	186
Pyeston	Fife	NO3104	56°13·7'	3°6·3'W	X	59
Pyethorns	N Yks	SD7856	54°0·2'	2°19·7'W	X	103
Pyewell	Devon	SS5028	51°2·1'	4°8·0'W	X	180
Pyewipe	NE Lincs	TA2411	53°35·1'	0°7·2'W	T	113
Pyewipe Fm	Lincs	TF3180	53°18·3'	0°1·6'W	FM	122
Pyewipe Fm	Lincs	TF4385	53°20·8'	0°9·3'E	FM	122
Pyewipe Fm	NE Lincs	TA2208	53°33·5'	0°9·1'W	FM	113
Pyewipe Fm	N Lincs	SK9898	53°28·4'	0°31·0'W	FM	112
Pyewipe Hall Fm	Lincs	SK8496	53°27·5'	0°43·7'W	FM	112
Pyewipe Ho	N Lincs	SK9798	53°28·4'	0°31·9'W	X	112
Pyewipe House Fm	N Lincs	SK9797	53°27·9'	0°31·9'W	FM	112
Pyg Track	Gwyn	SH6255	53°4·7'	4°3·2'W	X	115
Pykards Hall	Suff	TL8055	52°10·1'	0°38·3'E	X	155
Pyke	Moray	NJ3931	57°22·2'	3°0·4'W	X	37
Pykestone Hill	Scot Bord	NT1633	55°35·3'	3°19·5'W	H	72
Pykestone Hill	Scot Bord	NT1731	55°34·2'	3°18·5'W	H	72
Pykestone Knowe	Scot Bord	NT1723	55°29·9'	3°18·4'W	H	72
Pyke, The	Aberd	NJ6228	57°20·7'	2°37·4'W	X	37
Pykitthorn Rig	D & G	NY1391	55°12·6'	3°21·6'W	X	78
Pylafoot	Scot Bord	NT7332	55°35·1'	2°25·3'W	X	74
Pyle	Brig	SS8282	51°31·7'	3°41·7'W	T	170
Pyle	I of W	SZ4779	50°36·8'	1°19·8'W	T	196
Pyle	Swan	SS5888	51°34·6'	4°2·6'W	T	159
Pyle Fm	Hants	SU7112	50°54·4'	0°59·0'W	FM	197
Pyle Fm	Somer	ST2710	50°53·3'	3°1·9'W	FM	193
Pyle Fm	Somer	ST7444	51°11·9'	2°21·9'W	FM	183
Pyle Gate Fm	Kent	TQ4641	51°9·2'	0°5·7'E	FM	188
Pylehill	Hants	SU4919	50°58·3'	1°17·7'W	T	185
Pyle Hill	Surrey	SU9955	51°17·4'	0°34·4'W	T	175,186
Pyleigh	Somer	ST1230	51°4·0'	3°15·0'W	T	181
Pylemoor	Devon	SS9217	50°56·8'	3°31·9'W	X	181
Pylewell Ho	Hants	SZ3595	50°45·4'	1°29·8'W	X	196
Pylewell Lake	Hants	SZ3494	50°44·9'	1°30·7'W	W	196
Pylewell Point	Hants	SZ3594	50°44·9'	1°29·8'W	X	196
Pyllau	Cered	SN6375	52°21·6'	4°0·3'W	X	135
Pyllau Clai	Denb	SJ0758	53°6·9'	3°23·0'W	X	116
Pyllau Clais	Powys	SN9674	52°21·5'	3°31·2'W	X	136,147
Pyllau-cochion	Carm	SN6529	51°56·8'	3°57·5'W	X	146
Pyllau-crynion	Carm	SN5944	52°4·8'	4°3·1'W	F	146
Pyllau Mawn	Powys	SN8778	52°23·5'	3°39·2'W	X	135,136,147
Pyllau'r-bryn	Cered	SN4545	52°5·1'	4°15·3'W	X	146
Pylle	Somer	ST6038	51°8·6'	2°33·9'W	T	183
Pylons Fm	E Susx	TQ6407	50°50·6'	0°20·2'E	FM	199
Pym Chair	Derby	SK0886	53°22·5'	1°52·4'W	X	110
Pymme's Brook	Barnet	TQ2893	51°37·5'	0°8·7'W	W	176
Pymoor (Pymore)	Cambs	TL4986	52°27·3'	0°12·0'E	T	143
Pymore	Dorset	SY4694	50°44·8'	2°45·5'W	T	193
Pymore (Pymoor)	Cambs	TL4986	52°27·3'	0°12·0'E	T	143
Pympne Manor	Kent	TQ8234	51°4·8'	0°36·3'E	X	188
Pynannot	S Ayr	NX2995	55°13·4'	4°40·9'W	X	76
Pyncombe Fm	Somer	ST0626	51°1·8'	3°20·0'W	FM	181
Pyne Fm	Devon	SS8010	50°52·9'	3°42·0'W	FM	191
Pynes	Devon	SX9196	50°45·4'	3°32·3'W	A	192
Pynes	Devon	SX9496	50°45·5'	3°29·8'W	X	192
Pyne's Hill	Devon	SX9491	50°42·8'	3°29·7'W	H	192
Pynkney Hall	Norf	TF8528	52°49·3'	0°45·1'E	X	132
Pyon Hill	Heref	SO4549	52°8·4'	2°47·8'W	H	148,149
Pyotdykes	Angus	NO3434	56°29·9'	3°3·9'W	X	54
Pyothall	W Loth	NT0772	55°56·2'	3°28·9'W	X	65
Pyott's Hill	Hants	SU6654	51°17·1'	1°2·8'W	X	185,186
Pype Hayes	Birm	SP1292	52°31·8'	1°49·0'W	T	139
Pyper's Hill Fm	Cambs	TL5684	52°26·1'	0°18·1'E	FM	143
Pyramid, The	Devon	SS1345	51°10·7'	4°40·1'W	X	180
Pyramid, The	N Yks	SE7169	54°7·0'	0°54·4'W	X	100
Pyramid, The	N Yks	SE7369	54°6·9'	0°52·6'W	X	100
Pyrford	Surrey	TQ0359	51°19·5'	0°30·9'W	T	186
Pyrford Common	Surrey	TQ0359	51°19·5'	0°30·9'W	F	186
Pyrford Court	Surrey	TQ0358	51°18·9'	0°30·9'W	X	186
Pyrford Green	Surrey	TQ0458	51°18·9'	0°30·1'W	T	186
Pyrford Lock	Surrey	TQ0559	51°19·5'	0°29·2'W	X	187
Pyrford Village	Surrey	TQ0458	51°18·9'	0°30·1'W	T	186
Pyrgad	Powys	SO1015	51°49·8'	3°18·0'W	X	161
Pyrland	Somer	ST2326	51°1·9'	3°5·5'W	T	193
Pyrland Hall	Somer	ST2227	51°2·5'	3°6·4'W	X	193
Pyrton	Oxon	SU6895	51°39·2'	1°0·6'W	T	164,165
Pyrton Heath Ho	Oxon	SU6796	51°39·8'	1°1·5'W	X	164,165
Pyrton Hill	Oxon	SU7094	51°38·7'	0°58·9'W	X	175
Pyrton Manor	Oxon	SU6895	51°39·2'	1°0·6'W	A	164,165
Pysgodlyn	Monm	SO2615	51°50·0'	3°4·0'W	X	161
Pytchley	Northnts	SP8574	52°21·7'	0°44·7'W	T	141
Pytchley Grange	Northnts	SP8573	52°21·1'	0°44·7'W	X	141
Pytchley Lodge	Northnts	SP8373	52°21·2'	0°46·5'W	X	141
Pytchley Lodge	Northnts	SP8775	52°22·2'	0°42·9'W	X	141
Pythingdean	W Susx	TQ0320	50°58·4'	0°31·6'W	X	197
Pyt Ho	W Berks	SU5775	51°28·5'	1°10·4'W	X	174
Pythouse	Wilts	ST9028	51°3·3'	2°8·2'W	X	184
Pytindu	Powys	SO0431	51°58·4'	3°23·5'W	X	160
Pytinglas	Powys	SO0331	51°58·4'	3°24·3'W	X	160
Pytingwyn	Powys	SO0431	51°58·4'	3°23·5'W	X	160
Pytte	Devon	SX9889	50°41·7'	3°26·3'W	X	192
Pytt Fm	Somer	ST0521	50°59·1'	3°20·8'W	FM	181
Pyworthy	Devon	SS3102	50°47·8'	4°23·5'W	T	190

Q

Quabbs	Shrops	SO2080	52°25·0'	3°10·2'W	T	137
Quab Hill	Oxon	SU4689	51°36·1'	1°19·8'W	X	174
Quabrook	E Susx	TQ4434	51°5·5'	0°3·8'E	T	187
Quadrant	Corn	SW6911	49°57·5'	5°12·9'W	X	203
Quadring	Lincs	TF2233	52°53·1'	0°10·8'W	T	131
Quadring Eaudike	Lincs	TF2433	52°53·0'	0°9·0'W	T	131
Quadring High Fen	Lincs	TF1932	52°52·6'	0°13·5'W	X	130
Quadring High Fen	Lincs	TF2032	52°52·6'	0°12·6'W	X	131
Quadring Low Fen	Lincs	TF1833	52°53·1'	0°14·4'W	X	130
Qua Fen Common	Cambs	TL5974	52°20·7'	0°20·5'E	X	143
Quagg Fm	Hants	SU6110	50°53·4'	1°7·6'W	FM	196
Quagrigg Moss	Cumbr	NY2004	54°25·8'	3°13·6'W	X	89,90
Quags Corner	W Susx	SU8621	50°59·1'	0°46·1'W	T	197
Quag, The	Norf	TG0943	52°56·8'	1°7·1'E	X	133
Quahead	D & G	NX8563	54°57·2'	3°47·3'W	X	84
Quaikin	Shrops	SJ4530	52°52·1'	2°48·6'W	X	126
Quainton	Bucks	SP7420	51°52·6'	0°55·1'W	T	165
Quainton Hill	Bucks	SP7521	51°53·2'	0°54·2'W	H	165
Quair Water	Scot Bord	NT3133	55°35·4'	3°5·3'W	W	73
Quaish Fm	Somer	ST5541	51°10·2'	2°38·2'W	FM	182,183
Quaker Fm	Cambs	TL5287	52°27·8'	0°14·6'E	FM	143
Quaker Fm	Norf	TG2314	52°40·9'	1°18·4'E	FM	133,134
Quaker's Fm	E Yorks	SE8330	53°45·8'	0°44·0'W	FM	106
Quaker's Fm	Norf	TG1620	52°44·3'	1°12·4'E	FM	133
Quaker's Fm	Suff	TL9362	52°13·6'	0°50·0'E	FM	155
Quakers Grove Fm	N Yks	NZ5309	54°28·7'	1°10·5'W	FM	93
Quakers,The	Heref	SO2936	52°1·3'	3°1·7'W	X	161
Quaker's Yard	Merth Tyd	ST0996	51°39·6'	3°18·5'W	T	171
Quaker's Yard Sta	Merth Tyd	ST0896	51°39·6'	3°19·4'W	X	170
Quaking Ho	Somer	ST1026	51°1·8'	3°16·6'W	X	181,193
Quaking Houses	Durham	NZ1850	54°50·9'	1°42·8'W	T	88
Quaking Pot	N Yks	SD7374	54°9·9'	2°24·4'W	X	98
Quality Corner	Cumbr	NX9819	54°33·6'	3°34·2'W	T	89
Quam	Shetld	HU4588	60°34·6'	1°10·2'W	X	1,2
Quanea Hill	Cambs	TL5779	52°23·4'	0°18·8'E	X	143
Quantans Hill	D & G	NX5894	55°13·4'	4°13·5'W	X	77
Quanterness	Orkney	HY4112	58°59·7'	3°1·1'W	X	6
Quanter Ness	Orkney	HY4113	59°0·3'	3°1·1'W	X	6
Quanterness Skerry	Orkney	HY4214	59°0·8'	3°0·1'W	X	6
Quantock Combe	Somer	ST1737	51°7·8'	3°10·8'W	F	181

Quantock Fm	Somer	ST1536	51°7·3′	3°12·5′W	FM	181
Quantock Fm	Somer	ST2529	51°3·6′	3°3·8′W	FM	193
Quantock Hills	Somer	ST2034	51°6·2′	3°8·2′W	H	182
Quantock Moor Fm	Somer	ST1139	51°8·8′	3°16·0′W	FM	181
Quantock's Head	Somer	ST1244	51°11·5′	3°15·2′W	X	181
Quaquoy	Orkney	HY2325	59°6·6′	3°20·2′W	X	6
Quaremead	Essex	TL5127	51°55·5′	0°12·2′E	X	167
Quarhouse	Glos	SO8702	51°43·2′	2°10·9′W	T	162
Quarles Fm	Norf	TF8838	52°54·6′	0°48·2′E	FM	132
Quarleston	Dorset	ST8505	50°50·9′	2°12·4′W	X	194
Quarleston Fm	Dorset	ST8303	50°49·8′	2°14·1′W	FM	194
Quarley	Hants	SU2743	51°11·4′	1°36·4′W	T	184
Quarley Down Fm	Hants	SU2441	51°10·3′	1°39·0′W	FM	184
Quarley Hill	Hants	SU2642	51°10·8′	1°37·3′W	H	184
Quarley Manor Fm	Hants	SU2742	51°10·8′	1°36·4′W	FM	184
Quarmby	Kirk	SE1117	53°39·2′	1°49·6′W	T	110
Quarme Hill	Somer	SS9336	51°7·0′	3°31·3′W	X	181
Quarndon	Derby	SK3341	52°58·2′	1°30·1′W	T	119,128
Quarndon Common	Derby	SK3341	52°58·2′	1°30·1′W	T	119,128
Quarndon Hill	Derby	SK3341	52°58·2′	1°30·1′W	X	119,128
Quarr	Dorset	ST7626	51°2·2′	2°20·2′W	X	183
Quarr Abbey	I of W	SZ5692	50°43·7′	1°12·0′W	A	196
Quarr Abbey	I of W	SZ5692	50°43·7′	1°12·0′W	X	196
Quarrel Burn Resr	Midlo	NT1858	55°48·8′	3°18·1′W	W	65,66,72
Quarrel Hill	S Ayr	NS2503	55°17·7′	4°44·9′W	X	76
Quarrelly	Heref	SO3431	51°58·7′	2°57·3′W	X	149,161
Quarrels Green	Heref	SO4031	51°58·7′	2°52·0′W	X	149,161
Quarrelton	Renf	NS4262	55°49·8′	4°30·9′W	T	64
Quarrelwood	D & G	NX9684	55°8·6′	3°37·5′W	X	78
Quarrendon	Bucks	SP8015	51°49·9′	0°49·9′W	T	165
Quarrendon Fm	Bucks	SU9695	51°39·0′	0°36·3′W	FM	165,176
Quarrendon House Fm	Bucks	SP7915	51°49·9′	0°50·8′W	FM	165
Quarr Hill	Dorset	SY8486	50°40·6′	2°13·2′W	H	194
Quarr Hill	I of W	SZ5692	50°43·7′	1°12·0′W	T	196
Quarriers Village	Inverc	NS3666	55°51·8′	4°36·8′W	T	63
Quarries Cross	Suff	TM0261	52°12·8′	0°57·8′E	X	155
Quarries, The	I of W	SZ3886	50°40·6′	1°27·3′W	X	196
Quarries, The	Kent	TQ7751	51°14·1′	0°32·5′E	X	188
Quarries, The	Rut	SK9815	52°43·7′	0°32·5′W	X	130
Quarrington	Lincs	TF0544	52°59·2′	0°25·7′W	T	130
Quarrington Fm	Kent	TR0541	51°8·1′	0°56·2′E	FM	179,189
Quarrington Hill	Durham	NZ3337	54°43·9′	1°28·8′W	T	93
Quarrington Hill	Lincs	TF0545	52°59·8′	0°25·7′W	X	130
Quarry	Aberd	NJ7146	57°30·5′	2°28·6′W	X	29
Quarrybank	Ches	SJ5465	53°11·0′	2°40·9′W	T	117
Quarry Bank	Dudley	SO9386	52°28·6′	2°5·8′W	T	139
Quarry Bank Ho	Ches	SJ5466	53°11·6′	2°40·9′W	X	117
Quarry Bank Mill	Ches	SJ8382	53°20·3′	2°14·9′W	X	109
Quarry Banks	Notts	SK5352	53°4·0′	1°12·1′W	F	120
Quarrybeck Ho	Cumbr	NY5462	54°57·3′	2°42·7′W	X	86
Quarry Bends	I of M	SC3694	54°19·2′	4°30·9′W	X	95
Quarry Bottom	Wilts	ST9219	50°58·5′	2°6·5′W	X	184
Quarrybrae	C of Aber	NJ8310	57°11·1′	2°16·4′W	X	38
Quarrybrae of Auchedly	Aberd	NJ9033	57°23·5′	2°9·5′W	X	30
Quarry Croft	Aberd	NJ6220	57°16·4′	2°37·4′W	X	37
Quarryfield	Aberd	NJ4517	57°14·7′	2°54·2′W	X	37
Quarryfield	Highld	NH6352	57°32·5′	4°16·9′W	X	26
Quarry Fm	C of Aber	NJ9010	57°11·1′	2°9·5′W	FM	38
Quarry Fm	Devon	SX6694	50°44·0′	3°53·6′W	FM	191
Quarry Fm	Devon	SX7869	50°30·7′	3°42·9′W	FM	202
Quarry Fm	E Susx	TQ7724	50°59·5′	0°31·7′E	FM	199
Quarry Fm	Lincs	SK9840	52°57·1′	0°32·1′W	FM	130
Quarry Fm	Rut	SK9503	52°37·2′	0°35·4′W	FM	141
Quarry Fm	S Lanak	NS6650	55°43·7′	4°7·6′W	FM	64
Quarry Fm	Somer	ST7019	50°58·4′	2°25·3′W	FM	183
Quarry Fm	Stock on T	NZ4315	54°31·9′	1°19·7′W	FM	93
Quarry Fm	Surrey	TQ3553	51°15·8′	0°3·5′W	FM	187
Quarry Fm	Warw	SP2070	52°19·9′	1°42·0′W	FM	139
Quarryford	E Loth	NT5565	55°52·8′	2°42·7′W	X	66
Quarry Gill	Cumbr	NY2854	54°52·8′	3°6·9′W	X	85
Quarry Grange	Durham	NZ0518	54°33·7′	1°54·9′W	X	92
Quarryhall	Mil Key	SP8545	52°6·0′	0°45·1′W	X	152
Quarryhall Fm	Mil Key	SP8646	52°6·6′	0°44·3′W	FM	152
Quarry Hangers	Surrey	TQ3253	51°15·9′	0°6·1′W	X	187
Quarryhead	Aberd	NJ8139	57°26·7′	2°18·5′W	X	29,30
Quarryhead	Aberd	NJ9065	57°40·7′	2°9·6′W	X	30
Quarry Head	Aberd	NJ9066	57°41·3′	2°9·6′W	X	30
Quarryhead	Aberd	NJ9860	57°38·1′	2°1·5′W	X	30
Quarryhead	Aberd	NJ9942	57°28·4′	2°0·5′W	X	30
Quarryhead	Falk	NS8976	55°58·1′	3°46·3′W	X	65
Quarryhead	Moray	NJ4148	57°31·4′	2°58·6′W	X	28
Quarry Heath	Staffs	SJ9413	52°43·1′	2°4·9′W	T	127
Quarry Hill	Aberd	NJ4631	57°22·2′	2°53·4′W	H	29,37
Quarry Hill	Aberd	NJ4825	57°19·0′	2°51·3′W	H	37
Quarryhill	Aberd	NJ6251	57°33·1′	2°37·6′W	X	29
Quarryhill	Aberd	NJ7548	57°31·5′	2°24·6′W	X	29
Quarryhill	Aberd	NK0460	57°38·1′	1°55·5′W	X	30
Quarryhill	Angus	NO4556	56°41·8′	2°53·4′W	X	54
Quarry Hill	Cumbr	NY0427	54°38·0′	3°28·8′W	X	89
Quarry Hill	Dorset	SY4393	50°44·3′	2°48·1′W	H	193
Quarry Hill	Durham	NZ2138	54°44·4′	1°40·0′W	X	93
Quarry Hill	E Ayr	NS5744	55°40·4′	4°16·0′W	X	71
Quarryhill	Highld	NH7481	57°48·3′	4°6·8′W	X	21
Quarry Hill	Midd	NZ5412	54°30·3′	1°9·5′W	X	93
Quarry Hill	N Yks	NZ1906	54°27·2′	1°42·0′W	H	92
Quarry Hill	N Yks	SD9648	53°55·9′	2°3·2′W	X	103
Quarry Hill	N Yks	SE1784	54°15·3′	1°43·9′W	X	99
Quarry Hill	Scot Bord	NT1536	55°36·9′	3°20·5′W	H	72
Quarry Hill	Staffs	SK2301	52°36·6′	1°39·2′W	T	139
Quarry Hill	Surrey	TQ2651	51°14·9′	0°11·3′W	H	187
Quarry Hill	Worcs	SO6867	52°18·2′	2°27·8′W	H	138,149
Quarry Hill Fm	Cumbr	NY2241	54°45·7′	3°12·3′W	FM	85
Quarry Hill Fm	Glos	SP1005	51°44·9′	1°50·9′W	FM	163
Quarry Hill Ho	Cumbr	NY2241	54°45·7′	3°12·3′W	X	85
Quarry Ho	Durham	NZ1821	54°35·3′	1°42·9′W	X	92
Quarry Ho	Northum	NU1024	55°30·8′	1°50·1′W	X	75
Quarry Ho	Northum	NY6857	54°54·6′	2°29·5′W	X	86,87
Quarry Ho	Northum	NY7956	54°54·1′	2°19·2′W	X	86,87
Quarry Ho	Northum	NY9679	55°6·6′	2°3·3′W	X	87
Quarry Ho	Northum	NZ1486	55°10·3′	1°46·4′W	X	81

Quarry Ho	N Yks	NZ1306	54°27·2′	1°47·5′W	X	92
Quarry Ho	N Yks	SE1979	54°12·6′	1°42·1′W	X	99
Quarry Ho	N Yks	SE2066	54°5·6′	1°41·2′W	X	99
Quarry Ho	N Yks	SE3287	54°16·9′	1°30·1′W	X	99
Quarry Ho	Red & Cl	NZ5612	54°30·3′	1°7·7′W	X	93
Quarry Ho	Somer	ST2117	50°57·1′	3°7·1′W	X	193
Quarryhouse	Orkney	HY5333	59°11·1′	2°48·9′W	X	5,6
Quarryhouse Fm	Durham	NZ0120	54°34·8′	1°58·6′W	FM	92
Quarry House Fm	Lancs	SD5664	54°4·4′	2°39·9′W	FM	97
Quarry House Fm	N Yks	SE1649	53°56·5′	1°45·0′W	FM	104
Quarry House Fm	N Yks	SE2678	54°12·1′	1°35·7′W	FM	99
Quarryhouse Moor	Northum	NU1024	55°30·8′	1°50·1′W	X	75
Quarry Knowe	Scot Bord	NT4119	55°27·9′	2°55·6′W	H	79
Quarry Lodge	N Yks	SE0683	54°14·8′	1°54·1′W	X	99
Quarrymill	Pth & Kin	NO1125	56°24·8′	3°26·1′W	T	53,58
Quarry Moor	N Yks	SE3069	54°7·2′	1°32·0′W	X	99
Quarry Park	D & G	NY2172	55°2·4′	3°13·7′W	X	85
Quarrypit Fm	Worcs	SP0056	52°12·4′	1°59·6′W	FM	150
Quarry Plantn	Northum	NU0430	55°34·1′	1°55·8′W	F	75
Quarry Point	Pemb	SM7204	51°41·5′	5°17·6′W	X	157
Quarryside	Highld	ND1868	58°35·8′	3°24·2′W	X	11,12
Quarrystone Fm	Somer	ST2916	50°56·6′	3°0·3′W	FM	193
Quarry, The	N Yks	SD7993	54°20·2′	2°19·0′W	X	98
Quarry, The	Staffs	SJ7950	53°3·1′	2°18·4′W	X	118
Quarry Wood	Kent	TQ7151	51°14·2′	0°27·4′E	F	188
Quarry Wood	Moray	NJ1863	57°39·2′	3°22·0′W	F	28
Quarrywood	Moray	NJ1864	57°39·8′	3°22·0′W	T	28
Quarry Wood	Win & Maid	SU8685	51°33·7′	0°45·2′W	F	175
Quarry Woods	Shrops	SJ3608	52°40·2′	2°56·4′W	F	126
Quarsdale	Shetld	HU3451	60°14·8′	1°22·7′W	X	3
Quartains	Aberd	NJ7701	57°6·2′	2°22·3′W	X	38
Quartains Moss	Aberd	NJ7701	57°6·2′	2°22·3′W	F	38
Quartalehouse	Aberd	NJ9746	57°30·5′	2°2·5′W	X	30
Quarter	N Ayr	NS1962	55°49·3′	4°52·9′W	X	63
Quarter	S Lanak	NS7251	55°44·4′	4°1·9′W	T	64
Quarter	S Lanak	NS7351	55°44·4′	4°0·9′W	X	64
Quarterbank	Pth & Kin	NN9221	56°22·4′	3°44·5′W	T	52,58
Quarter Barrow	Somer	SS8247	51°12·8′	3°41·0′W	A	181
Quarter Br	I of M	SC3676	54°9·5′	4°30·3′W	X	95
Quarter Burn	Durham	NZ0026	54°38·0′	1°59·6′W	W	92
Quarter Fell	D & G	NX1969	54°59·2′	4°49·3′W	H	82
Quarter Fm	D & G	NX1868	54°58·7′	4°50·2′W	FM	82
Quarter Fm	W Loth	NT0071	55°55·6′	3°35·6′W	FM	65
Quarter Hill	Scot Bord	NT0922	55°29·3′	3°26·0′W	H	72
Quarter Ho	Falk	NS8184	56°2·3′	3°54·2′W	X	57,65
Quarter Ho	Scot Bord	NT1033	55°35·2′	3°25·2′W	X	72
Quarterland	D & G	NX5861	54°55·7′	4°12·5′W	X	83
Quarters Fm	Derby	SK1779	53°18·7′	1°44·3′W	FM	119
Quarters Spit	Essex	TM0011	51°45·9′	0°54·3′E	X	168
Quarterway Ho	Cambs	TL5275	52°21·3′	0°14·3′E	X	143
Quarter Wood	Scot Bord	NT0933	55°35·2′	3°26·2′W	F	72
Quartley Fm	Devon	SS9825	51°1·2′	3°26·9′W	FM	181
Quarts Fm	Somer	ST1417	50°57·0′	3°13·1′W	FM	181,193
Quassawall Loch	Shetld	HU2755	60°17·0′	1°30·2′W	W	3
Quatford	Shrops	SO7390	52°30·7′	2°22·5′W	T	138
Quatford Castle	Shrops	SO7391	52°31·2′	2°22·5′W	X	138
Quatford Wood Ho	Shrops	SO7491	52°31·2′	2°22·6′W	X	138
Quatquoy	Orkney	HY3715	59°1·3′	3°5·4′W	T	6
Quatre Bras	Dorset	SY6493	50°44·4′	2°30·2′W	X	194
Quatt	Shrops	SO7588	52°29·6′	2°21·7′W	T	138
Quatt Fm	Shrops	SO7687	52°29·1′	2°20·8′W	FM	138
Quave Brae	Scot Bord	NT2218	55°27·2′	3°13·6′W	X	79
Quaveburn Cott	Scot Bord	NT2218	55°27·2′	3°13·6′W	X	79
Quay Reach	Essex	TQ9892	51°35·7′	0°51·9′E	W	178
Quay, The	Devon	SS4730	51°3·2′	4°10·6′W	X	180
Quay, The	Essex	TQ9893	51°36·3′	0°52·0′E	X	178
Queach Fm	Suff	TL9169	52°17·4′	0°48·4′E	FM	155
Quear of Eastafea	Orkney	HY4433	59°11·1′	2°58·3′W	X	5,6
Queastybirch Hall Fm	Warr	SJ6081	53°19·7′	2°35·6′W	FM	109
Quebb	Heref	SO3051	52°9·4′	3°1·0′W	X	148
Quebec	Durham	NZ1843	54°47·1′	1°42·8′W	T	88
Quebec	W Susx	SU7221	50°59·2′	0°53·8′W	T	197
Quebec Fm	Leic	SK6017	52°45·1′	1°6·3′W	FM	129
Quebec Fm	Norf	TG1522	52°45·4′	1°11·6′E	FM	133
Quebec Fm	Wilts	ST9543	51°11·4′	2°3·9′W	FM	184
Quebec Hall	Norf	TF9814	52°41·5′	0°56·2′E	X	132
Quedgeley	Glos	SO8114	51°49·7′	2°16·1′W	T	162
Quedley	E Susx	TQ7030	51°2·9′	0°25·9′E	X	188
Queech Fm	Suff	TM1333	51°57·5′	1°6·4′E	FM	168,169
Queefiglamo	Orkney	HY3423	59°5·6′	3°8·6′W	X	6
Queel Burn	Aberd	NO4099	57°4·9′	2°58·9′W	W	37,44
Queena	Orkney	HY2616	59°1·7′	3°16·9′W	X	6
Queena	Orkney	HY2727	59°7·7′	3°16·0′W	X	6
Queen Adelaide	Cambs	TL5681	52°24·5′	0°18·0′E	T	143
Queena Howe	Orkney	HY4249	59°19·7′	3°0·7′W	X	5
Queena Howe (Broch)	Orkney	HY4249	59°19·7′	3°0·7′W	A	5
Queen Alexandra Dock	Card	ST1973	51°27·2′	3°9·6′W	X	171
Queenamidda	Orkney	HY3720	59°4·0′	3°5·4′W	X	6
Queenamoan	Orkney	HY2720	59°3·9′	3°15·9′W	X	6
Queenamuckle	Orkney	HY4121	59°4·6′	3°1·3′W	X	5,6
Queen Anne's Gate	Win & Maid	SU9674	51°27·6′	0°36·7′W	X	175,176
Queen Anne's Ride	Win & Maid	SU9572	51°26·6′	0°37·6′W	X	175,176
Queen Bess Rock	Corn	SW8469	50°29·1′	5°2·3′W	X	200
Queenborough	Devon	SS9606	50°50·9′	3°28·3′W	X	192
Queenborough	Kent	TQ9172	51°25·1′	0°45·2′E	T	178
Queenborough Spit	Kent	TQ8973	51°25·7′	0°43·5′E	X	178
Queen Bower Hunting Lodge	Hants	SU2804	50°50·3′	1°35·8′W	A	195
Queenbury	Herts	TL3635	52°0·0′	0°0·7′W	X	154
Queen Camel	Somer	ST5924	51°1·1′	2°34·7′W	T	183
Queen Charlton	Bath & NE Somer	ST6367	51°24·3′	2°31·5′W	T	172
Queen Dart	Devon	SS8316	50°56·1′	3°39·5′W	T	181
Queen Dike	N Yks	SE8161	54°2·6′	0°45·4′W	A	100
Queen Down Warren	Kent	TQ8262	51°19·9′	0°37·2′E	X	178,188
Queen Eleanor's Bower	Shrops	SJ5313	52°43·0′	2°41·3′W	A	126
Queen Eleanor's Cross	Northnts	SP7558	52°13·1′	0°53·7′W	A	152
Queen Elizabeth 11 Country Park	Northum	NZ2888	55°11·4′	1°33·2′W	X	81

Queen Elizabeth Country Park	Hants	SU7219	50°58·2′	0°58·1′W	X	197
Queen Elizabeth Forest	Hants	SU7218	50°57·6′	0°58·1′W	F	197
Queen Elizabeth II Bridge	Kent	TQ5776	51°27·9′	0°16·0′E	X	177
Queen Elizabeth II Reservoir	Surrey	TQ1167	51°23·7′	0°23·9′W	W	176
Queen Elizabeth Plantn	Suff	TL7874	52°20·3′	0°37·2′E	F	144
Queen Elizabeth's Hunting Lodge	Wal F	TQ3995	51°38·4′	0°0·9′E	A	166,177
Queener Point	Corn	SX4148	50°18·9′	4°13·6′W	X	201
Queenfield	Wilts	ST9166	51°23·8′	2°7·4′W	X	173
Queen Geos	Shetld	HU2774	60°27·2′	1°30·1′W	X	3
Queenhill	Worcs	SO8536	52°1·6′	2°12·7′W	T	150
Queen Holme	Cambs	TL4272	52°19·9′	0°5·4′E	X	154
Queenholme Bloodstock Stables	Cambs	TL4271	52°19·4′	0°5·4′E	X	154
Queen Hoo Hall	Herts	TL2716	51°49·9′	0°9·0′W	A	166
Queenlaines Fm	Swin	SU1990	51°36·7′	1°43·1′W	FM	163,173
Queen Manor Fm	Wilts	SU1731	51°4·9′	1°45·1′W	FM	184
Queen Margaret's Cove	Northum	NU2521	55°29·2′	1°35·8′W	W	75
Queen Mary Reservoir	Surrey	TQ0769	51°24·8′	0°27·3′W	W	176
Queen Mary's Ave	Suff	TL8176	52°21·4′	0°39·9′E	X	144
Queen Mary's Bower	Derby	SK2570	53°13·8′	1°37·1′W	A	119
Queen Mary's Dubb	N Yks	SE3074	54°9·9′	1°32·0′W	W	99
Queen Mary's Hospital	Sutton	TQ2762	51°20·8′	0°10·2′W	X	176,187
Queen Mary's Mount	E Loth	NT3769	55°54·9′	3°0·0′W	X	66
Queen Mother Reservoir, The	Win & Maid	TQ0076	51°28·7′	0°33·2′W	W	176
Queen Oak	Wilts	ST7730	51°4·4′	2°19·3′W	T	183
Queen Oak	Wilts	SU2265	51°23·2′	1°40·6′W	X	174
Queen Pool	Oxon	SP4316	51°50·7′	1°22·2′W	W	164
Queen's Bank Fm	Lincs	TF2714	52°42·8′	0°6·8′W	FM	131
Queen's Barrow	Wilts	ST9636	51°7·6′	2°3·0′W	A	184
Queensberry	D & G	NX9899	55°16·7′	3°35·9′W	H	78
Queen's Bower	I of W	SZ5784	50°39·4′	1°11·2′W	T	196
Queen's Br	Lincs	TF4492	53°24·5′	0°10·4′E	X	113
Queensbridge	Wrex	SJ3740	52°57·5′	2°55·9′W	X	117
Queen's Building	Hill	TQ0775	51°28·1′	0°27·2′W	X	176
Queensbury	Brad	SE0930	53°46·2′	1°51·4′W	T	104
Queensbury	Harrow	TQ1889	51°35·5′	0°17·4′W	T	176
Queen's Cairn	Highld	NH4672	57°42·9′	4°34·6′W	H	20
Queenscairn	Scot Bord	NT7139	55°38·9′	2°27·2′W	X	74
Queen's Cave	Northum	NY9061	54°56·9′	2°8·9′W	X	87
Queen's Copse	Dorset	SU0306	50°51·4′	1°57·1′W	F	195
Queen's Corner	W Susx	SU8525	51°1·3′	0°46·9′W	T	186,197
Queens Cott	Rich	TQ1776	51°28·5′	0°18·5′W	A	176
Queens Court Fm	Kent	TR0060	51°18·5′	0°52·6′E	X	178
Queens Court Fm	Wilts	SU0479	51°30·8′	1°56·2′W	FM	173
Queen's Crags	Northum	NY7970	55°1·7′	2°19·3′W	X	86,87
Queenseat Hill	E Renf	NS5249	55°43·0′	4°20·9′W	X	64
Queen's Eyot	Win & Maid	SU9178	51°29·8′	0°41·0′W	X	175
Queen's Fen	Cambs	TL5164	52°15·4′	0°13·1′E	X	154
Queensferry	C of Edin	NT1278	55°59·5′	3°24·2′W	T	65
Queensferry	Flint	SJ3168	53°12·5′	3°1·6′W	T	117
Queens Fm	Cambs	TL5164	52°15·4′	0°13·1′E	FM	154
Queens Fm	Cambs	TL5257	52°11·6′	0°13·8′E	FM	154
Queen's Fm	Kent	TQ6973	51°26·1′	0°26·3′E	FM	177,178
Queen's Forest, The	Highld	NH9610	57°10·4′	3°42·7′W	F	36
Queen's Ground	Norf	TL6893	52°30·8′	0°28·9′E	X	143
Queenshaugh	Stir	NS8094	56°7·7′	3°55·4′W	X	57
Queen's Head	Shrops	SJ3426	52°49·9′	2°58·4′W	T	126
Queen's Hill	Aberd	NJ5200	57°5·6′	2°47·1′W	H	37
Queenshill	D & G	NX6959	54°54·8′	4°2·2′W	X	83,84
Queen's Ho	Scot Bord	NT7234	55°36·2′	2°26·2′W	X	74
Queenside Hill	Renf	NS2963	55°50·1′	4°43·4′W	H	63
Queenside Loch	Renf	NS2964	55°50·6′	4°43·4′W	W	63
Queenside Muir	Renf	NS2864	55°50·6′	4°44·4′W	X	63
Queen's Inclosure, The	Hants	SU6910	50°53·3′	1°0·8′W	F	197
Queen's Letch	Northum	NY9361	54°56·9′	2°6·1′W	X	87
Queenslie	C of Glas	NS6665	55°51·8′	4°8·0′W	T	64
Queen's Low	Staffs	SJ9623	52°48·5′	2°3·2′W	A	127
Queen's Mere	Wok	SU8165	51°22·9′	0°49·8′W	W	175
Queen's Mire	Scot Bord	NY4799	55°17·2′	2°49·6′W	H	79
Queen's Oak	Suff	TM3474	52°19·1′	1°26·4′E	A	156
Queens Oak Fm	Northnts	SP7444	52°5·6′	0°54·8′W	FM	152
Queen's Parade	Hants	SU8652	51°15·8′	0°45·7′W	X	186
Queen's Park	Beds	TL0349	52°8·0′	0°29·3′W	T	153
Queen's Park	Black w Dar	SD6927	53°44·6′	2°27·8′W	T	103
Queens Park	Bolton	SD7009	53°34·8′	2°26·8′W	X	109
Queen's Park	Bourne	SZ1193	50°44·4′	1°50·3′W	X	195
Queen's Park	Ches	SJ4165	53°11·0′	2°52·6′W	T	117
Queen's Park	C of Glas	NS5862	55°50·1′	4°15·6′W	X	64
Queen's Park	Essex	TQ6796	51°38·5′	0°25·2′E	T	167,177
Queen's Park	Northnts	SP7562	52°15·3′	0°53·7′W	T	152
Queens Park	Shrops	SJ3825	52°49·4′	2°54·8′W	X	126
Queen's Plantn	N Yks	SE7988	54°17·1′	0°46·8′W	F	94,100
Queen's Rig	D & G	NX6065	54°57·9′	4°10·8′W	X	83
Queen's Sconce	Notts	SK7952	53°3·8′	0°48·9′W	A	120,121
Queen's Sedge Moor	Somer	ST5241	51°10·2′	2°40·8′W	X	182,183
Queenstonbank	E Loth	NT5082	56°2·0′	2°47·7′W	X	66
Queen Stone	Heref	SO5618	51°51·8′	2°37·9′W	A	162
Queenstown	Blackp	SD3237	53°49·7′	3°1·6′W	T	102
Queen Street	Kent	TQ6845	51°11·0′	0°24·6′E	T	188
Queen St Sta	C of Glas	NS5965	55°51·7′	4°14·7′W	X	64
Queen's View	Pth & Kin	NN8659	56°42·8′	3°51·3′W	X	43,52
Queen's View	Stir	NS5080	55°59·6′	4°23·9′W	X	64
Queensville	Staffs	SJ9322	52°48·0′	2°5·8′W	T	127
Queensway	Fife	NO2701	56°12·0′	3°10·2′W	T	59
Queen's Well	Angus	NO4182	56°55·8′	2°57·7′W	W	44
Queen's Wood	Glos	SO9825	51°55·6′	2°1·4′W	F	163
Queen's Wood	Hargy	TQ2888	51°34·8′	0°8·8′W	F	176
Queen's Wood	Heref	SO6727	51°56·7′	2°28·4′W	F	162
Queenswood	Herts	TL2603	51°42·9′	0°10·2′W	X	166
Queen's Wood Country Park	Heref	SO5051	52°9·5′	2°43·5′W	X	149
Queen Victoria School	Stir	NN7902	56°12·0′	3°56·6′W	X	57
Queen Wood	Oxon	SU7192	51°37·6′	0°58·1′W	F	175
Queenwood	Surrey	TQ0163	51°21·7′	0°32·6′W	X	176,186
Queenwood	Wilts	ST9670	51°26·0′	2°3·1′W	X	173

Queenwood Fm	Hants	SU3030	51°4·3′	1°33·9′W	FM	185
Queenzieburn	N Lanak	NS6977	55°58·3′	4°5·5′W	T	64
Queest Moor	Heref	SO3052	52°9·9′	3°1·0′W	X	148
Queina Waters	Shetld	HU3484	60°32·6′	1°22·3′W	W	1,2,3
Quell Fm	W Susx	TQ0315	50°55·7′	0°31·7′W	FM	197
Quemerford	Wilts	SU0069	51°25·4′	1°59·6′W	T	173
Quenby Hall	Leic	SK7006	52°39·1′	0°57·5′W	A	141
Quenchwell	Corn	SW7941	50°13·9′	5°5·6′W	X	204
Quendale	Shetld	HU3713	59°54·3′	1°19·8′W	T	4
Quendon	Essex	TL5130	51°57·1′	0°12·2′E	T	167
Quendon Park	Essex	TL5131	51°57·6′	0°12·3′E	A	167
Quendon Wood	Essex	TL5129	51°56·6′	0°12·2′E	F	167
Queniborough	Leic	SK6412	52°42·3′	1°2·8′W	T	129
Queniborough Brook	Leic	SK6711	52°41·8′	1°0·1′W	W	129
Queniborough Hall	Leic	SK6512	52°42·3′	1°1·9′W	X	129
Quenington	Glos	SP1404	51°44·3′	1°47·4′W	T	163
Quentance Fm	Devon	SY0382	50°38·0′	3°21·9′W	FM	192
Quern Geos	Orkney	HY5839	59°14·4′	2°43·7′W	X	5
Quernmore	Lancs	SD5159	54°1·7′	2°44·5′W	T	102
Quernmore	Lancs	SD5160	54°2·3′	2°44·5′W	T	97
Quernmore Park Hall	Lancs	SD5162	54°3·3′	2°44·5′W	A	97
Quernmore Park Hall	Lancs	SD5162	54°3·3′	2°44·5′W	X	97
Queslett	Birm	SP0694	52°32·9′	1°54·3′W	T	139
Quethiock	Corn	SX3164	50°27·3′	4°22·5′W	T	201
Quex Park	Kent	TR3168	51°22·1′	1°19·5′E	X	179
Quey Firth	Shetld	HU3682	60°31·5′	1°20·1′W	W	1,2,3
Queyin Ness	Shetld	HU6671	60°25·3′	0°47·6′W	X	2
Queyon	Shetld	HU5285	60°33·0′	1°2·6′W	X	1,2,3
Quey, The	Shetld	HU2777	60°28·8′	1°30·0′W	X	3
Quhamm	Shetld	HU4168	60°23·9′	1°14·9′W	T	2,3
Quharity Burn	Angus	NO2857	56°42·2′	3°10·1′W	W	53
Quharity Burn	Angus	NO2862	56°44·9′	3°10·2′W	W	44
Quholm	Orkney	HY2412	58°59·6′	3°18·9′W	T	6
Quholm	Orkney	HY5221	59°4·7′	2°49·8′W	X	5,6
Quholmslie	Orkney	HY2512	58°59·6′	3°17·8′W	X	6
Quhytewoollen	D & G	NY1582	55°7·8′	3°19·8′W	X	79
Quick	Tames	SD9703	53°31·7′	2°2·3′W	T	109
Quickbeam Hill	Devon	SX6564	50°27·9′	3°53·8′W	X	202
Quickbourne	E Susx	TQ8325	50°59·9′	0°36·9′E	X	188,199
Quick Br	Devon	SX5960	50°25·6′	3°58·7′W	X	202
Quick Burn	Durham	NZ0943	54°47·2′	1°51·2′W	W	88
Quickburn Grange	Durham	NZ0843	54°47·2′	1°52·1′W	X	88
Quickbury Fm	Essex	TL4914	51°48·5′	0°10·1′E	FM	167
Quickcleugh Burn	Northum	NY8847	54°49·3′	2°10·8′W	W	87
Quickcleugh Moss	Northum	NY8846	54°48·8′	2°10·8′W	X	87
Quick Edge	Tames	SD9603	53°31·7′	2°3·2′W	T	109
Quickening Cote	Northum	NT8806	55°21·1′	2°10·9′W	X	80
Quickening Outer Cleugh	Northum	NT9017	55°27·1′	2°9·1′W	X	80
Quickningair Hill	D & G	NT2707	55°21·3′	3°8·7′W	H	79
Quick's Green	W Berks	SU5876	51°29·0′	1°9·5′W	T	174
Quickswood	Herts	TL2732	51°58·5′	0°8·7′W	X	166
Quida	Shetld	HP6202	60°42·0′	0°51·4′W	X	1
Quida Ness	Shetld	HU1761	60°20·2′	1°41·0′W	X	3
Quidan Ness	Shetld	HU5073	60°26·5′	1°5·0′W	X	2,3
Quiddies Mill	Aberd	NJ7602	57°6·8′	2°23·3′W	X	38
Quidenham	Norf	TM0287	52°26·8′	0°58·8′E	T	144
Quidenham Park	Norf	TM0387	52°26·8′	0°59·6′E	X	144
Quidhampton	Hants	SU5150	51°15·0′	1°15·8′W	T	185
Quidhampton	Wilts	SU1130	51°4·4′	1°50·2′W	T	184
Quidhampton Wood	Swin	SU1179	51°30·8′	1°50·1′W	F	173
Quidin, The	Shetld	HP4805	60°43·8′	1°6·7′W	X	1
Quidney Fm	Norf	TF9106	52°37·3′	0°49·7′E	FM	144
Quien Hill	Arg & Bt	NS0559	55°47·4′	5°6·2′W	H	63
Quiensetter	Shetld	HU3560	60°19·6′	1°21·5′W	X	2,3
Quies	Corn	SW8376	50°32·8′	5°3·4′W	X	200
Quilichan	Highld	NH8537	57°24·8′	3°54·4′W	X	27
Quilkieston	E Ayr	NS4523	55°28·8′	4°26·7′W	X	70
Quilkoe	Angus	NO4453	56°40·2′	2°54·4′W	X	54
Quill Fm	Suff	TM3155	52°8·9′	1°23·0′E	FM	156
Quill Hall Fm	Bucks	SU9798	51°40·6′	0°35·4′W	FM	165,176
Quillichan Burn	Aberd	NJ3014	57°12·9′	3°9·1′W	W	37
Quilquox	Aberd	NJ9038	57°26·2′	2°9·5′W	T	30
Quilsa Shun	Shetld	HU3555	60°16·9′	1°21·5′W	W	3
Quilsa Taing	Shetld	HU5063	60°21·1′	1°5·1′W	X	2,3
Quilse	Shetld	HU1856	60°17·5′	1°40·0′W	X	3
Quilse	Shetld	HU3864	60°21·8′	1°18·2′W	X	2,3
Quilse of Hoganeap	Shetld	HU6188	60°34·5′	0°52·7′W	X	1,2
Quilse, The	Shetld	HU2548	60°13·2′	1°32·4′W	X	3
Quilse, The	Shetld	HU2875	60°27·7′	1°29·0′W	X	3
Quilters' Fm	Essex	TL7800	51°40·5′	0°34·9′E	FM	167
Quilt Hill	Scot Bord	NT1027	55°32·0′	3°25·1′W	H	72
Quilt Ness	Shetld	HU2964	60°21·8′	1°28·0′W	X	3
Quilts	Pth & Kin	NO0211	56°17·1′	3°34·5′W	X	58
Quilva Taing	Shetld	HU1757	60°18·1′	1°41·0′W	X	3
Quina	Orkney	HY3412	58°59·7′	3°8·4′W	X	6
Quina	Orkney	HY3715	59°1·3′	3°5·4′W	X	6
Quina Brook	Shrops	SJ5233	52°53·8′	2°42·4′W	T	126
Quinag	Highld	NC2028	58°12·5′	5°3·3′W	H	15
Quinbury End	Northnts	SP6250	52°8·9′	1°5·2′W	T	152
Quinbury Fm	Herts	TL3926	51°55·1′	0°1·7′E	FM	166
Quince	Devon	SS7722	50°59·3′	3°44·8′W	X	180
Quince's Corner	Essex	TL9713	51°47·1′	0°51·8′E	X	168
Quindry	Orkney	ND4392	58°49·0′	2°58·7′W	X	7
Quine's Hill	I of M	SC3473	54°7·8′	4°32·0′W	T	95
Qui Ness	Shetld	HP6203	60°42·6′	0°51·3′W	X	1
Quinhill	Arg & Bt	NR7656	55°45·0′	5°33·7′W	X	62
Quinish	Arg & Bt	NM4254	56°36·7′	6°11·8′W	X	47
Quinish	N Eil	NF8786	57°45·5′	7°15·3′W	X	18
Quinish Ho	Arg & Bt	NM4154	56°36·6′	6°12·8′W	X	47
Quinish Point	Arg & Bt	NM4057	56°38·2′	6°14·0′W	X	47
Quinloch	Stir	NS5181	56°0·2′	4°22·9′W	X	64
Quinloch Muir	Stir	NS5181	56°0·2′	4°22·9′W	X	64
Quinmoor Fm	Glos	SP2127	51°56·7′	1°41·3′W	FM	163
Quinni	Orkney	HY2523	59°5·5′	3°18·1′W	X	6
Quinni Geo	Shetld	HU4120	59°58·0′	1°15·4′W	X	4
Quinni Loch	Shetld	HU4459	60°19·0′	1°11·7′W	W	2,3
Quinni Moan	Orkney	HY3524	59°6·1′	3°7·6′W	X	6
Quinny Brook	Shrops	SO4486	52°28·4′	2°49·1′W	W	137
Quinta, The	Ches	SJ2837	53°12·2′	2°17·6′W	X	118
Quintfall	Highld	ND3061	58°32·2′	3°11·7′W	X	11,12

Quintin Bottom	E Yorks	TA0762	54°2·8′	0°21·5′W	X	101
Quintin Knowe	E Ayr	NS6507	55°20·6′	4°7·3′W	X	71,77
Quintinshill Br	D & G	NY3269	55°0·9′	3°3·4′W	X	85
Quintin's Man	Devon	SX6283	50°38·1′	3°56·7′W	X	191
Quinton	Dudley	SO9884	52°27·5′	2°1·4′W	T	139
Quinton	Northnts	SP7754	52°11·0′	0°52·0′W	T	152
Quinton	Worcs	SO5761	52°15·0′	2°37·4′W	X	137,138,149
Quinton Green	Northnts	SP7853	52°10·4′	0°51·2′W	X	152
Quinton Hill Fm	Essex	TQ3899	51°40·6′	0°0·2′E	FM	166,177
Quinton Ho	Warw	SP1747	52°7·5′	1°44·7′W	X	151
Quinton Lodge	Rut	SK9413	52°42·6′	0°36·1′W	X	130
Quinton's Orchard	Staffs	SK0818	52°45·8′	1°52·5′W	X	128
Quintrell Downs	Corn	SW8460	50°24·2′	5°2·0′W	T	200
Quinville House	Beds	TL0636	52°1·0′	0°26·9′W	X	153
Quiraing	Highld	NG4569	57°38·6′	6°15·9′W	H	23
Quiraing Lo	Highld	NG4868	57°38·2′	6°12·9′W	X	23
Quires Green	Essex	TL6107	51°44·5′	0°20·3′E	X	167
Quirt	I of Angl	SH4564	53°9·3′	4°18·7′W	X	114,115
Quithe	Aberd	NO7884	56°57·1′	2°21·2′W	X	45
Quithelhead	Aberd	NO7493	57°1·9′	2°25·2′W	X	38,45
Quither	Devon	SX4481	50°36·7′	4°11·9′W	X	201
Quither Common	Devon	SX4480	50°36·2′	4°11·9′W	X	201
Quittlehead	Aberd	NJ5604	57°7·7′	2°43·2′W	X	37
Quivilsda Moss	Shetld	HU5299	60°40·5′	1°2·4′W	X	1
Quixhill	Staffs	SK1041	52°58·2′	1°50·7′W	T	119,128
Quixwood	Scot Bord	NT7863	55°51·8′	2°20·7′W	X	67
Quixwood Moor	Scot Bord	NT7764	55°52·4′	2°21·6′W	X	67
Quob Fm	Hants	SU5511	50°54·0′	1°12·7′W	FM	196
Quobwell Fm	Wilts	ST9289	51°36·2′	2°6·5′W	FM	173
Quochag	Arg & Bt	NS0856	55°45·8′	5°3·2′W	X	63
Quoditch	Devon	SX4097	50°45·3′	4°15·7′W	T	190
Quoditch Cross	Devon	SX4198	50°45·8′	4°14·9′W	X	190
Quoditchmoor Plantations	Devon	SX4098	50°45·8′	4°15·7′W	F	190
Quogach	Arg & Bt	NS0562	55°49·0′	5°6·3′W	X	63
Quoich Water	Aberd	NO0995	57°2·5′	3°29·5′W	W	36,43
Quoich Water	Aberd	NO1092	57°0·9′	3°28·4′W	W	43
Quoig	Pth & Kin	NN8122	56°22·8′	3°55·2′W	X	52
Quoigs Ho	Pth & Kin	NN8305	56°13·6′	3°52·8′W	X	57
Quoins	Essex	TL6417	51°49·9′	0°23·2′E	X	167
Quoisley	Ches	SJ5445	53°0·3′	2°40·7′W	T	117
Quoisley Meres	Ches	SJ5445	53°0·3′	2°40·7′W	W	117
Quoit	Corn	SW9262	50°25·5′	4°55·3′W	T	200
Quoit-at-Cross	Devon	SS9218	50°57·3′	3°31·9′W	X	181
Quoit Fm	Corn	SW9261	50°25·0′	4°55·3′W	FM	200
Quornden	Kent	TQ4752	51°15·1′	0°6·8′E	X	188
Quorndon Fm	N Yks	SE4485	54°15·8′	1°19·1′W	FM	99
Quorndon or Quorn	Leic	SK5616	52°44·6′	1°9·8′W	T	129
Quorn Ho	Leic	SK5616	52°44·6′	1°9·8′W	X	129
Quorn Lodge Fm	Leic	SK5517	52°45·1′	1°10·7′W	FM	129
Quorn or Quorndon	Leic	SK5616	52°44·6′	1°9·8′W	T	129
Quoscies	Aberd	NO8895	57°3·0′	2°11·4′W	X	38,45
Quosquo Hall	N Yks	SE6225	53°43·3′	1°3·2′W	X	105
Quothquan	S Lanak	NS9939	55°38·3′	3°35·8′W	T	72
Quothquan Law	S Lanak	NS9838	55°37·7′	3°36·8′W	H	72
Quothquan Law Farm	S Lanak	NS9838	55°37·7′	3°36·8′W	FM	72
Quothquan Lodge	S Lanak	NS9941	55°39·4′	3°35·9′W	X	72
Quothquan Mill	S Lanak	NS9940	55°38·8′	3°35·9′W	X	72
Quoy	Orkney	ND3290	58°47·8′	3°10·1′W	X	7
Quoyawa	Orkney	HY2302	58°54·2′	3°19·7′W	X	6,7
Quoy Ayre	Orkney	HY6738	59°13·9′	2°34·2′W	X	5
Quoy Banks	Orkney	HY6745	59°17·7′	2°34·3′W	X	5
Quoyberstane	Orkney	HY4612	58°59·8′	2°55·9′W	X	6
Quoybirse	Orkney	HY4447	59°18·6′	2°58·5′W	X	5
Quoyblackie	Orkney	HY4022	59°5·1′	3°2·3′W	X	5,6
Quoybrae Fm	Highld	ND2657	58°30·0′	3°15·7′W	FM	11,12
Quoyburray	Orkney	HY5005	58°56·0′	2°51·6′W	X	6,7
Quoyclarks	Orkney	HY3204	58°55·3′	3°10·4′W	X	6,7
Quoydam	Orkney	ND4390	58°47·9′	2°58·7′W	X	7
Quoydandy	Orkney	HY4609	58°58·2′	2°55·9′W	X	6
Quoyer	Orkney	HY3113	59°0·2′	3°11·6′W	X	6
Quoyfree	Orkney	HY4120	59°4·0′	3°1·3′W	X	5,6
Quoy Geo	Orkney	HY3834	59°11·6′	3°4·6′W	X	6
Quoy Geo	Orkney	HY6135	59°12·3′	2°40·5′W	X	5
Quoyhenry	Orkney	HY3820	59°4·0′	3°4·4′W	X	6
Quoyhorsetter	Orkney	ND4592	58°49·0′	2°56·7′W	X	7
Quoy-i-dale	Orkney	HY2303	58°54·7′	3°19·7′W	X	6,7
Quoykea	Orkney	HY5004	58°55·5′	2°51·6′W	X	6,7
Quoylanks	Orkney	HY5604	58°55·5′	2°45·4′W	X	6
Quoylobs	Orkney	HY4604	58°55·5′	2°55·8′W	X	6,7
Quoyloo	Orkney	HY2420	59°3·9′	3°19·0′W	T	6
Quoymorhouse	Orkney	HY5216	59°2·0′	2°49·7′W	X	6
Quoynabreckan	Orkney	HY4551	59°20·8′	2°57·5′W	X	5
Quoynalonga Ness	Orkney	HY3632	59°10·5′	3°6·7′W	X	6
Quoynee	Highld	ND2058	58°30·4′	3°21·9′W	X	11,12
Quoyness	Orkney	HY2502	58°54·2′	3°17·6′W	T	6,7
Quoy Ness	Orkney	HY6236	59°12·8′	2°39·4′W	X	5
Quoyness	Orkney	HY6737	59°13·4′	2°34·2′W	X	5
Quoy Ness	Orkney	ND3794	58°50·0′	3°5·0′W	X	7
Quoyness	Shetld	HU3948	60°13·1′	1°17·3′W	T	3
Quoyness (Chambered Cairn)	Orkney	HY6737	59°13·4′	2°34·2′W	A	5
Quoy of Herston	Orkney	ND4191	58°48·4′	3°0·8′W	X	7
Quoy of Houton	Orkney	HY3103	58°54·8′	3°11·6′W	X	6,7
Quoyorally	Orkney	ND4686	58°45·8′	2°55·5′W	X	7
Quoyostray	Orkney	HY3833	59°11·0′	3°4·6′W	X	6
Quoy Ribs	Orkney	HY4503	58°54·9′	2°56·8′W	X	6,7
Quoys	Orkney	HY2505	58°55·8′	3°17·7′W	X	6,7
Quoys	Orkney	HY3111	58°59·1′	3°11·5′W	X	6
Quoys	Orkney	HY3725	59°6·7′	3°5·5′W	X	6
Quoys	Orkney	HY4446	59°18·1′	2°58·5′W	X	5
Quoys	Orkney	HY4952	59°21·3′	2°53·3′W	X	5
Quoys	Orkney	HY5704	58°55·5′	2°44·3′W	X	6
Quoys	Orkney	ND4584	58°44·7′	2°56·5′W	X	7
Quoys	Shetld	HP6112	60°47·4′	0°52·3′W	T	1
Quoys	Shetld	HU4681	60°30·9′	1°9·2′W	X	1,2,3
Quoys	Shetld	HU4860	60°19·5′	1°7·4′W	T	2,3
Quoys of Catfirth	Shetld	HU4454	60°16·3′	1°11·8′W	T	3
Quoys of Garth	Shetld	HU4074	60°27·1′	1°15·9′W	X	2,3
Quoys of Reiss	Highld	ND3357	58°30·0′	3°8·5′W	X	12

Quy Water	Cambs	TL5261	52°13·8′	0°13·9′E	W	154

R

Raahead	S Lanak	NS6249	55°43·1′	4°11·4′W	X	64
Raans Fm	Bucks	SU9898	51°40·6′	0°34·6′W	FM	165,176
Raasay Forest	Highld	NG5536	57°21·2′	6°3·9′W	F	24,32
Raasay Forest	Highld	NG5745	57°26·1′	6°2·5′W	F	24
Raasay Ho	Highld	NG5436	57°21·1′	6°4·9′W	X	24,32
Raa Wick	Shetld	HU3491	60°36·3′	1°22·2′W	W	1,2
Rabbit Copse	Hants	SU5626	51°2·1′	1°11·7′W	F	185
Rabbit Crag	Northum	NY7092	55°13·5′	2°27·9′W	X	80
Rabbit Ground Plantation	Glos	SP1511	51°48·1′	1°46·6′W	F	163
Rabbit Hill	Northum	NU0437	55°37·8′	1°55·8′W	H	75
Rabbit Hill Fm	E Yorks	SE6821	53°41·1′	0°57·8′W	FM	105,106
Rabbit Hill Fm	N Yks	SE2365	54°5·1′	1°38·5′W	FM	99
Rabbit Islands	Highld	NC6063	58°32·2′	4°23·8′W	X	10
Rabbit's Cross	Kent	TQ7847	51°11·9′	0°33·3′E	T	188
Rabbits Fm	Kent	TQ5769	51°24·1′	0°15·8′E	FM	177
Rabbits Hill	Oxon	SU6490	51°36·5′	1°4·2′W	X	164,175
Rabbit Warren	Gwyn	SH5633	52°52·8′	4°8·0′W	X	124
Rabbit Warren	York	SE6750	53°56·7′	0°58·3′W	F	105,106
Rabbit Wood	Worcs	SO9557	52°12·9′	2°4·0′W	F	150
Rableyheath	Herts	TL2319	51°51·6′	0°12·4′W	T	166
Rabley Park Fm	Herts	TL2001	51°41·9′	0°15·4′W	FM	166
Rabley Wood	Wilts	SU2070	51°26·0′	1°42·3′W	F	174
Rabson Manor	Wilts	SU0974	51°28·1′	1°51·8′W	X	173
Raby	Cumbr	NY1851	54°51·1′	3°16·2′W	T	85
Raby	Wirral	SJ3179	53°18·5′	3°1·7′W	T	117
Raby Beg	I of M	SC2480	54°11·4′	4°41·4′W	X	95
Raby Castle	Durham	NZ1221	54°35·3′	1°48·4′W	A	92
Raby Cote	Cumbr	NY1752	54°51·6′	3°17·2′W	X	85
Raby Cottages	N Yks	NZ3004	54°26·1′	1°31·8′W	X	93
Raby Grange	Cumbr	NY1851	54°51·1′	3°16·2′W	X	85
Raby Hall	Wirral	SJ3380	53°19·0′	2°59·9′W	X	108
Raby Hill Ho	Durham	NZ1222	54°35·8′	1°48·4′W	X	92
Raby Home Fm	Durham	NZ1021	54°35·3′	1°50·3′W	FM	92
Raby House Fm	Wirral	SJ3279	53°18·5′	3°0·8′W	FM	117
Raby Moar	I of M	SC2380	54°11·4′	4°42·4′W	X	95
Raby Moor Ho	Durham	NZ0922	54°35·8′	1°51·2′W	X	92
Raby Park	Durham	NZ1122	54°35·8′	1°49·4′W	X	92
Raby's Fm	Lancs	SD5239	53°50·9′	2°43·4′W	FM	102
Raby Vale	Wirral	SJ3180	53°19·0′	3°1·7′W	X	108
Raccleugh Head	Scot Bord	NT7452	55°45·9′	2°24·4′W	X	67,74
Racecourse	Suff	TM1842	52°2·2′	1°11·1′E	T	169
Racecourse Downs	Corn	SX0969	50°29·6′	4°41·2′W	X	200
Racecourse Fm	Corn	SX0868	50°29·1′	4°42·0′W	FM	200
Racecourse Fm	Dudley	SO8982	52°26·4′	2°9·3′W	FM	139
Racecourse Fm	Leic	SK8126	52°49·8′	0°47·5′W	FM	130
Racecourse Fm	Shrops	SO7093	52°32·3′	2°26·1′W	FM	138
Racecourse Fm	Staffs	SJ8043	52°59·3′	2°17·5′W	FM	118
Racecourse Plantation	Norf	TG2710	52°38·6′	1°21·7′E	F	133,134
Race Course Plantn	Brad	SE0839	53°51·1′	1°52·3′W	F	104
Racedown	Dorset	ST3901	50°48·6′	2°51·6′W	X	193
Racedown	Hants	SU2644	51°11·9′	1°37·3′W	T	184
Race Fm	Corn	SW6340	50°13·0′	5°19·0′W	FM	203
Race Fm	Dorset	SY9594	50°45·3′	2°3·9′W	FM	195
Race Fm	Oxon	SU4097	51°40·5′	1°24·9′W	FM	164
Raceground Hill	Notts	SK5649	53°2·4′	1°9·5′W	X	129
Race Head	Durham	NY8740	54°45·5′	2°11·7′W	X	87
Race Ho	Staffs	SK1063	53°10·1′	1°50·6′W	X	119
Racer Fm	Lincs	TF0515	52°43·6′	0°26·3′W	FM	130
Race, The	Devon	SS1443	51°9·6′	4°39·2′W	W	180
Race Yate	Durham	NY9416	54°32·6′	2°5·1′W	X	91,92
Racham Banks	W Susx	TQ0512	50°54·1′	0°30·0′W	A	197
Racham Hill	W Susx	TQ0512	50°54·1′	0°30·0′W	H	197
Racham Hill (Tumulus)	W Susx	TQ0512	50°54·1′	0°30·0′W	A	197
Rachan Home Fm	Scot Bord	NT1234	55°35·8′	3°23·4′W	FM	72
Rachan Mill	Scot Bord	NT1134	55°35·7′	3°24·3′W	T	72
Rachelfield	Scot Bord	NT6337	55°37·8′	2°34·8′W	X	74
Rachfynydd	Powys	SO0431	51°58·4′	3°23·5′W	X	160
Rà Chreag	Arg & Bt	NN2124	56°22·7′	4°53·5′W	X	50
Rachub	Gwyn	SH6268	53°11·7′	4°3·5′W	T	115
Rack	D & G	NS7112	55°23·4′	4°1·8′W	X	71
Rack End	Oxon	SP4003	51°43·7′	1°24·9′W	T	164
Rackenford	Devon	SS8518	50°57·2′	3°37·9′W	T	181
Rackenford Manor	Devon	SS8419	50°57·8′	3°38·7′W	X	181
Rackenford Moor	Devon	SS8520	50°58·3′	3°37·9′W	X	181
Rackery	Wrex	SJ3357	53°6·6′	2°59·6′W	X	117
Rackery Hall	Wrex	SJ3257	53°6·6′	3°0·5′W	X	117
Rack Fen	Cambs	TL5690	52°29·4′	0°18·3′E	X	143
Rackford Fm	Roth	SK5383	53°20·7′	1°11·8′W	FM	111,120
Rackham	W Susx	TQ0413	50°54·7′	0°30·9′W	T	197
Rack Haugh	Aberd	NJ6956	57°35·8′	2°30·7′W	X	29
Rackheath	Norf	TG2813	52°40·2′	1°22·7′E	T	133,134
Rack Hill	Norf	TF7844	52°58·1′	0°39·4′E	X	132
Rack Hill	Wilts	ST8475	51°28·7′	2°13·4′W	X	173
Rackleigh	Devon	SS7615	50°55·5′	3°45·5′W	X	180
Rackley	Somer	ST3954	51°17·1′	2°52·1′W	T	182
Racks	D & G	NY0374	55°3·3′	3°30·7′W	T	84
Racksgeirean	N Eil	NF9676	57°40·5′	7°5·5′W	X	18
Rackside	Northum	NT9722	55°29·8′	2°2·4′W	H	75
Rack Wick	Orkney	HY2109	58°57·9′	3°21·9′W	W	6,7
Rackwick	Orkney	HY4449	59°19·7′	2°58·6′W	T	5

Rack Wick	Orkney	HY4450	59°20·2′	2°58·6′W	W	5
Rack Wick	Orkney	HY5042	59°16·0′	2°52·1′W	W	5
Rack Wick	Orkney	ND1998	58°52·3′	3°23·8′W	W	7
Rackwick	Orkney	ND2099	58°52·5′	3°22·8′W	T	7
Rackwood Hill	Durham	NZ0930	54°40·1′	1°51·2′W	X	92
Racton Monument	W Susx	SU7709	50°52·7′	0°53·9′W	X	197
Racton Park Fm	W Susx	SU7809	50°52·7′	0°53·1′W	FM	197
Ractonpark Wood	W Susx	SU7708	50°52·2′	0°54·0′W	F	197
RAC Tower	S Glos	ST6183	51°32·9′	2°33·4′W	X	172
Radbourne	Derby	SK2836	52°55·5′	1°34·6′W	T	128
Radbourne Common	Derby	SK2936	52°55·5′	1°33·7′W	X	128
Radbourne Manor Fm	Warw	SP4558	52°13·3′	1°20·1′W	FM	151
Radbroke Hall	Ches	SJ7674	53°16·0′	2°21·2′W	X	118
Radbrook	Lancs	SD7843	53°53·2′	2°19·7′W	X	103
Radbrook Common	Oxon	SP4607	51°45·8′	1°19·6′W	X	164
Radbrook Fm	Warw	SP3086	52°28·5′	1°33·1′W	FM	140
Radbrook Manor	Warw	SP1948	52°8·0′	1°42·9′W	X	151
Radcliffe	Bury	SD7807	53°33·8′	2°19·5′W	T	109
Radcliffe	Northum	NU2602	55°18·9′	1°35·0′W	T	81
Radcliffe Hall	Lancs	SD6142	53°52·6′	2°35·2′W	X	102,103
Radcliffe Moat	Donc	SE5506	53°33·1′	1°9·8′W	A	111
Radcliffe on Trent	Notts	SK6439	52°56·9′	1°2·4′W	T	129
Radclive	Bucks	SP6733	51°59·7′	1°1·1′W	T	152,165
Radclive Diary Fm	Bucks	SP6833	51°59·7′	1°0·2′W	FM	152,165
Radcot	Oxon	SU2899	51°41·6′	1°35·3′W	T	163
Radcot Bridge Fm	Oxon	SU2799	51°41·6′	1°36·2′W	FM	163
Radcot Cut	Oxon	SP2900	51°42·1′	1°32·7′W	W	164
Radcote Fm	Warw	SP2058	52°13·4′	1°42·0′W	FM	151
Radcot Lock	Oxon	SP2900	51°42·1′	1°34·4′W	X	164
Raddery	Highld	NH7159	57°36·4′	4°9·1′W	T	27
Raddington	Somer	ST0225	51°1·2′	3°23·5′W	T	181
Raddle Bank	Heref	SO5664	52°16·6′	2°38·3′W	X	137,138,149
Raddle Fm	Staffs	SK1910	52°41·5′	1°42·7′W	FM	128
Raddle Fm	Staffs	SK2213	52°43·1′	1°40·1′W	FM	128
Raddlepits	Staffs	SK1045	53°0·4′	1°50·7′W	X	119,128
Raddon	Devon	SS9101	50°48·1′	3°32·4′W	T	192
Raddon	Devon	SX4585	50°38·9′	4°11·2′W	X	201
Raddon Court	Devon	SS9002	50°48·7′	3°33·3′W	X	192
Raddon Hills	Devon	SS8903	50°49·2′	3°34·2′W	H	192
Raddy Fm	Devon	SS4830	51°3·2′	4°9·7′W	FM	180
Radel Haven	Aberd	NK0530	57°21·9′	1°54·6′W	W	30
Radernie	Fife	NO4510	56°17·0′	2°52·9′W	X	59
Radernie	Fife	NO4709	56°16·5′	2°50·9′W	T	59
Radfall	Kent	TR1364	51°20·3′	1°3·9′E	T	179
Radfield	Kent	TQ9462	51°19·7′	0°47·5′E	T	178
Radford	Bath & NE Somer	ST6757	51°18·9′	2°28·0′W	T	172
Radford	C of Nott	SK5540	52°57·5′	1°10·5′W	T	129
Radford	Corn	SX3189	50°40·8′	4°23·2′W	X	190
Radford	Cov	SP3280	52°25·3′	1°31·4′W	T	140
Radford	Oxon	SP4023	51°54·5′	1°24·7′W	T	164
Radford	Worcs	SP0055	52°11·8′	1°59·6′W	T	150
Radfordbridge	Oxon	SP4023	51°54·5′	1°24·7′W	T	164
Radford Fm	Worcs	SP0473	52°21·5′	1°56·1′W	FM	139
Radford Hill	Warw	SP3563	52°16·1′	1°28·8′W	X	151
Radford Semele	Warw	SP3464	52°16·6′	1°29·7′W	T	151
Radholme Laund	Lancs	SD6645	53°54·2′	2°30·6′W	X	103
Radigan Fm	Somer	ST3218	50°57·7′	2°57·7′W	FM	193
Radipole	Dorset	SY6681	50°37·9′	2°28·5′W	T	194
Radipole Lake	Dorset	SY6780	50°37·4′	2°27·6′W	W	194
Radish Plantation	Devon	SY1891	50°42·9′	3°9·3′W	F	192,193
Radlet	Somer	ST2038	51°8·4′	3°8·2′W	T	182
Radlet Common	Somer	ST2037	51°7·8′	3°8·2′W	X	182
Radlet Fm	Somer	ST2038	51°8·4′	3°8·2′W	FM	182
Radlett	Herts	TQ1699	51°40·9′	0°18·9′W	T	166,176
Radlett Aerodrome	Herts	TL1503	51°43·1′	0°19·7′W	X	166
Radley	Devon	SS7323	50°59·8′	3°48·2′W	X	180
Radley	Oxon	SU5298	51°40·9′	1°14·5′W	T	164
Radley Bottom Cottages	W Berks	SU3769	51°25·4′	1°27·7′W	X	174
Radley College	Oxon	SU5199	51°41·5′	1°15·3′W	X	164
Radley Fm	W Berks	SU3770	51°25·9′	1°27·7′W	FM	174
Radley Green	Essex	TL6205	51°43·4′	0°21·1′E	T	167
Radley Park	Oxon	SU5199	51°41·5′	1°15·3′W	X	164
Radley's Fm	Suff	TL9535	51°59·0′	0°50·8′E	FM	155
Radleywood	Ches	SJ5556	53°6·2′	2°39·9′W	X	117
Radlith	Shrops	SJ4105	52°38·6′	2°51·9′W	T	126
Radmanthwaite	Notts	SK5163	53°9·9′	1°13·8′W	T	120
Radmoor	Shrops	SJ6224	52°49·0′	2°33·4′W	T	127
Radmore Fm	Northnts	SP6145	52°6·2′	1°6·2′W	FM	152
Radmore Fm	Northnts	SP6455	52°11·6′	1°3·4′W	FM	152
Radmore Green	Ches	SJ5955	53°5·7′	2°36·3′W	T	117
Radmore Wood	Staffs	SK0925	52°49·6′	1°51·6′W	T	128
Radnage	Bucks	SU7897	51°40·2′	0°51·9′W	T	165
Radnage Bottom Fm	Bucks	SU7898	51°40·8′	0°51·9′W	FM	165
Radnage House	Bucks	SU7996	51°39·7′	0°51·1′W	X	165
Radnall Fm	W Berks	SU4773	51°27·5′	1°19·0′W	FM	174
Radnall Wood	Hants	SU1317	50°57·4′	1°48·5′W	F	184
Radnidge	Devon	SS8625	51°1·0′	3°37·1′W	X	181
Radnor	Corn	SW7044	50°15·3′	5°13·2′W	T	203
Radnor Bank Fm	Ches	SJ8364	53°10·6′	2°14·9′W	FM	118
Radnor Br	Ches	SJ8365	53°11·1′	2°14·9′W	X	118
Radnor Forest	Powys	SO1964	52°16·3′	3°10·8′W	X	148
Radnor Forest	Powys	SO2064	52°16·3′	3°10·0′W	F	137,148
Radnor Hall Fm	Ches	SJ8364	53°10·6′	2°14·9′W	FM	118
Radnor Mere	Ches	SJ8475	53°16·5′	2°14·0′W	W	118
Radnor Park	W Dunb	NS4971	55°54·8′	4°24·5′W	T	64
Radnorshire Gate	Powys	SO1485	52°27·6′	3°15·5′W	X	136
Radnor Wood	Shrops	SO3281	52°25·6′	2°59·6′W	F	137
Radsbury	Devon	SS7145	51°11·6′	3°50·4′W	X	180
Radstock	Bath & NE Somer	ST6854	51°17·3′	2°27·1′W	T	183
Radstone	Northnts	SP5840	52°3·6′	1°8·8′W	T	152
Radway	Warw	SP3748	52°8·0′	1°27·2′W	T	151
Radway Green	Ches	SJ7754	53°5·2′	2°20·2′W	T	118
Radwell	Beds	TL0057	52°12·4′	0°31·8′W	T	153
Radwell	Herts	TL2235	52°0·2′	0°13·0′W	T	153
Radwell Grange	Herts	TL2337	52°1·3′	0°12·0′W	X	153
Radwell Hill	Oxon	SP4431	51°58·8′	1°21·2′W	X	151
Radwinter	Essex	TL6037	52°0·7′	0°20·3′E	T	154
Radwinter End	Essex	TL6139	52°1·8′	0°21·2′E	T	154
Radwinter Manor	Essex	TL5937	52°0·7′	0°19·4′E	X	154
Radwood	Staffs	SJ7740	52°57·7′	2°20·1′W	X	118
Radworthy	Devon	SS6942	51°10·0′	3°52·0′W	X	180
Radworthy Down	Devon	SS7432	51°4·6′	3°47·5′W	X	180
Radyr	Card	ST1280	51°31·0′	3°15·7′W	T	171
Radyr Fm	Card	ST1379	51°30·4′	3°14·8′W	FM	171
Raebreck	Highld	NH9619	57°15·3′	3°43·0′W	X	36
Rae Burn	Cumbr	NY4472	55°2·6′	2°52·2′W	W	85
Raeburn	Cumbr	NY4473	55°3·2′	2°52·2′W	X	85
Rae Burn	Cumbr	NY4775	55°4·2′	2°49·4′W	W	86
Rae Burn	D & G	NT2701	55°18·1′	3°8·6′W	W	79
Raeburn	D & G	NY2971	55°2·0′	3°6·2′W	X	85
Rae Burn	D & G	NY3070	55°1·4′	3°5·3′W	W	85
Raeburn Flow	D & G	NY2971	55°2·0′	3°6·2′W	X	85
Raeburnfoot	D & G	NY2599	55°17·0′	3°10·4′W	X	79
Raeburnfoot	D & G	NY3071	55°2·0′	3°5·3′W	X	85
Raeburnhead	D & G	NT2801	55°18·1′	3°7·6′W	X	79
Raeburnhead	D & G	NY2871	55°1·9′	3°7·2′W	X	85
Raeburnside	D & G	NT2600	55°17·6′	3°9·5′W	X	79
Raebush	Aberd	NJ4202	57°6·6′	2°57·0′W	X	37
Raechester	Northum	NY9787	55°10·9′	2°2·4′W	X	81
Raecleuch Rig	D & G	NT0412	55°23·8′	3°30·5′W	X	78
Raecleugh	Scot Bord	NT6051	55°45·3′	2°37·8′W	X	67,74
Raecleugh Fm	D & G	NT0311	55°23·3′	3°31·4′W	FM	78
Raecloch	Aberd	NJ6747	57°31·0′	2°32·6′W	X	29
Raecruick	Fife	NO2509	56°16·3′	3°12·2′W	X	59
Raedykes	Aberd	NO8390	57°0·3′	2°16·3′W	X	38,45
Raefin	Moray	NJ3957	57°36·2′	3°0·8′W	X	28
Rae Gill	D & G	NY4482	55°8·0′	2°52·3′W	W	79
Raegill Bogs	Scot Bord	NY4995	55°15·0′	2°47·7′W	X	79
Raegill Burn	D & G	NY4083	55°8·5′	2°56·0′W	W	79
Raegill Rig	D & G	NY3982	55°8·0′	2°57·0′W	X	79
Raehills	D & G	NY0694	55°14·1′	3°28·3′W	T	78
Raehow End	Cumbr	NY6736	54°43·3′	2°30·3′W	X	91
Raehutcheon	Moray	NJ3839	57°26·5′	3°1·5′W	X	28
Raelands	Highld	NM6568	56°44·9′	5°50·2′W	X	40
Raelees Wood	Scot Bord	NT4632	55°35·0′	2°51·0′W	F	73
Rae Loch	Pth & Kin	NO1544	56°35·1′	3°22·6′W	W	53
Raemoir Hotel	Aberd	NO6999	57°5·1′	2°30·2′W	X	38,45
Raemore	Fife	NO2114	56°19·0′	3°16·2′W	X	58
Raemore	Moray	NJ4959	57°37·3′	2°50·8′W	X	28,29
Raemore Wood	Highld	NC5504	58°0·4′	4°26·8′W	F	16
Raemurrack	Aberd	NJ4444	57°29·2′	2°55·6′W	X	28
Raera	Arg & Bt	NM8320	56°19·6′	5°30·1′W	X	49
Raes Fm	Norf	TF7117	52°43·6′	0°32·3′E	FM	132
Raeshaw	Scot Bord	NT3651	55°45·1′	3°0·7′W	X	66,73
Raeshaw Fell	Northum	NT7912	55°24·3′	2°19·5′W	H	80
Raeside	N Ayr	NS2752	55°44·1′	4°44·9′W	X	63
Raes Knowes	D & G	NY2983	55°8·4′	3°6·4′W	H	79
Rafael Fach	Pemb	SM9435	51°58·8′	4°59·6′W	X	157
Rafael Fach	Pemb	SM9535	51°58·8′	4°58·7′W	H	157
Rafail Fawr	Pemb	SM9536	51°59·3′	4°58·8′W	X	157
Rafborough	Hants	SU8555	51°17·5′	0°46·5′W	T	175,186
Raffin	Highld	NC0132	58°14·2′	5°22·9′W	X	15
Raffin Burn	Highld	ND0836	58°18·4′	3°33·7′W	W	11,17
Raffin Green	Herts	TL2719	51°51·5′	0°8·9′W	X	166
Raffinshaugh	Aberd	NJ7961	57°38·6′	2°20·6′W	X	29,30
Raffin Stud	Wilts	SU3073	51°27·5′	1°33·7′W	X	174
Raffles Burn	D & G	NY0970	55°1·2′	3°25·0′W	W	85
Rafford	Moray	NJ0656	57°35·3′	3°33·9′W	T	27
RAF Hereford	Heref	SO4543	52°5·2′	2°47·8′W	X	148,149,161
RAF Rudloe Manor	Wilts	ST8469	51°25·4′	2°13·4′W	X	173
Raftra Fm	Corn	SW3624	50°3·2′	5°40·1′W	FM	203
Raga	Shetld	HU4792	60°36·8′	1°8·0′W	T	1,2
Rag Copse	Hants	SU3750	51°15·1′	1°27·8′W	F	185
Rag Copse	Wilts	SU2755	51°17·8′	1°36·4′W	F	174
Ragdale	Leic	SK6619	52°46·1′	1°0·9′W	T	129
Ragdale Hall	Leic	SK6519	52°46·1′	1°1·8′W	X	129
Ragdale Wolds Fm	Leic	SK6520	52°46·7′	1°1·8′W	FM	129
Ragdon	Shrops	SO4591	52°31·1′	2°48·2′W	T	137,138
Rageary Burn	Highld	NG3146	57°25·7′	6°28·4′W	W	23
Ragfield	Fife	NO5909	56°16·6′	2°39·3′W	X	59
Raggal	Aberd	NJ6261	57°38·5′	2°37·7′W	X	29
Raggalds	Brad	SE0831	53°46·8′	1°52·3′W	T	104
Raggart, The	I of M	SC2482	54°12·5′	4°41·5′W	X	95
Ragg Copse	Hants	SU6657	51°18·7′	1°2·8′W	F	175,186
Ragged Appleshaw	Hants	SU3148	51°14·1′	1°33·0′W	T	185
Ragged Farm Ho	Kent	TQ9046	51°11·1′	0°43·5′E	X	189
Ragged Gill	S Lanak	NS9825	55°30·7′	3°36·5′W	W	72
Ragged Hall	N Yks	SD7759	54°1·8′	2°20·7′W	X	103
Raggedhedge Covert	Glos	SP0304	51°44·3′	1°57·0′W	F	163
Ragged Island	I Scilly	SV9413	49°56·6′	6°15·6′W	X	203
Raggengill Burn	S Lanak	NS9423	55°29·6′	3°40·2′W	W	71,72
Raggengill Hill	S Lanak	NS9422	55°29·1′	3°40·2′W	H	71,72
Ragget's Wood	W Susx	TQ2723	50°59·8′	0°11·0′W	F	198
Raggetsyke	D & G	NY2376	55°4·6′	3°11·9′W	X	85
Raggiewhate	D & G	NY1782	55°7·8′	3°17·7′W	X	79
Ragg Hill	S Ayr	NS3925	55°29·8′	4°32·5′W	X	70
Raggot Hill	Corn	SX3197	50°45·1′	4°23·4′W	X	190
Raggra	Highld	ND3144	58°23·0′	3°10·3′W	T	11,12
Rag Hill	Surrey	TQ4256	51°17·3′	0°2·6′E	X	187
Raghill Fm	W Berks	SU6164	51°22·5′	1°7·0′W	FM	175
Raginnis	Corn	SW4625	50°4·5′	5°32·6′W	T	203
Raglan	Monm	SO4107	51°45·8′	2°50·9′W	T	161
Raglan Hill	Shrops	SO4592	52°31·6′	2°48·2′W	H	137,138
Raglan Wood	Shrops	SO4592	52°31·6′	2°48·2′W	F	137,138
Ragley Hall	Warw	SP0755	52°11·8′	1°53·5′W	A	150
Raglington Fm	Hants	SU5413	50°55·1′	1°13·5′W	FM	196
Ragman's Castle	Bucks	SU8490	51°36·4′	0°46·8′W	X	175
Ragmarsh Fm	Essex	TM1531	51°56·4′	1°8·1′E	FM	168,169
Ragmere	Norf	TM0690	52°28·4′	1°2·4′E	T	144
Ragnal	W Berks	SU3173	51°27·5′	1°32·8′W	T	174
Ragnall	Notts	SK8073	53°15·1′	0°47·6′W	T	121
Ragnell Bottom	Oxon	SP4043	52°5·3′	1°24·6′W	X	151
Ragnell Fm	Oxon	SU3198	51°41·0′	1°32·7′W	FM	164
Ragpath Side	Durham	NZ1444	54°47·7′	1°46·5′W	X	88
Rag Path Wood	Durham	NZ2042	54°46·6′	1°40·9′W	F	88
Ragstaff Hill	N Yks	SE0469	54°7·3′	1°55·9′W	X	98
Ragstone Lodge	Essex	TQ8991	51°35·4′	0°44·1′E	X	178
Ragwen Point	Carm	SN2207	51°44·2′	4°34·3′W	X	158
Rahane	Arg & Bt	NS2387	56°2·8′	4°50·1′W	T	56
Rahoy	Highld	NM6356	56°38·4′	5°51·5′W	X	49
Raich Fm	Aberd	NJ6243	57°28·8′	2°37·6′W	FM	29
Raiders Road	D & G	NX6073	55°2·2′	4°11·0′W	X	77
Raigbeg	Highld	NH8129	57°20·4′	3°58·2′W	X	35
Raigh na Gualainn	Highld	NN2677	56°51·4′	4°50·8′W	X	41
Raigmore	Highld	NH6845	57°28·9′	4°11·6′W	X	26
Raike Bank Fm	Lancs	SD9146	53°54·8′	2°7·8′W	FM	103
Raikes	Lancs	SD3542	53°52·5′	2°58·9′W	X	102
Raikes Fm	N Yks	NZ5100	54°23·8′	1°12·4′W	FM	93
Raikes Fm	N Yks	SE0361	54°2·9′	1°56·8′W	FM	98
Raikes Fm	Surrey	TQ1046	51°12·4′	0°25·1′W	FM	187
Raikes Head	Brad	SE0347	53°55·4′	1°56·8′W	X	104
Raikes House Fm	Brad	SE0446	53°54·9′	1°55·9′W	FM	104
Raikes, The	N Yks	SE1864	54°4·5′	1°43·1′W	X	99
Raikes, The	Staffs	SK1159	53°7·9′	1°49·7′W	X	119
Raikinish	N Eil	NF7173	57°37·9′	7°30·3′W	X	18
Railground	Shrops	SO2186	52°28·2′	3°9·4′W	X	137
Rail Head	S Glos	ST6978	51°30·2′	2°26·4′W	X	172
Rails	Sheff	SK2987	53°23·0′	1°33·4′W	T	110
Railsbrough	Shetld	HU4652	60°15·2′	1°9·6′W	T	3
Rails Fm	Staffs	SJ9158	53°7·4′	2°7·7′W	FM	118
Rails Fm	Surrey	SU9354	51°16·9′	0°39·6′W	FM	186
Rails, The	E Susx	TQ5002	50°48·1′	0°8·1′E	X	199
Railway Fm	Ches	SJ7258	53°7·3′	2°24·7′W	FM	118
Raimeirigeodha	N Eil	NG2495	57°51·8′	6°38·8′W	X	14
Rainbarrows	Dorset	SY7392	50°43·9′	2°22·6′W	A	194
Rainberg Beag	Arg & Bt	NR5587	56°1·1′	5°55·4′W	X	61
Rainberg Mór	Arg & Bt	NR5687	56°1·1′	5°54·5′W	H	61
Rainborough Park	Roth	SK3999	53°29·4′	1°24·3′W	X	110,111
Rainbow Bottom	Wilts	SU1552	51°16·2′	1°46·7′W	X	184
Rainbow Fm	Oxon	SP3202	51°43·2′	1°31·8′W	FM	164
Rainbow Hall Fm	Herts	TL0716	51°50·2′	0°26·4′W	FM	166
Rainbow Hill	Worcs	SO8556	52°12·4′	2°12·8′W	T	150
Raincliffe Fm	N Yks	TA0088	54°16·9′	0°27·4′W	FM	101
Raincliffe Woods	N Yks	SE9988	54°16·9′	0°28·3′W	F	94,101
Raincliff Ings	N Yks	TA1475	54°9·7′	0°14·8′W	X	101
Raindale Head	N Yks	SE8093	54°19·8′	0°45·8′W	X	94,100
Raineach Mhór	Arg & Bt	NR2959	55°45·2′	6°18·7′W	X	60
Raine Ho	Cumbr	NY3843	54°46·9′	2°57·4′W	X	85
Raines Hall	Cumbr	SD5186	54°16·3′	2°44·7′W	X	97
Rainford	St Hel	SD4701	53°30·4′	2°47·5′W	T	108
Rainford Brook	St Hel	SJ4998	53°28·8′	2°45·7′W	W	108
Rainford Hall	St Hel	SJ5098	53°28·8′	2°44·8′W	X	108
Rainford Junction	St Hel	SD4702	53°31·0′	2°47·5′W	T	108
Rain Gill	Lancs	SD7354	53°59·1′	2°24·3′W	W	103
Rain Hall	Lancs	SD8946	53°54·8′	2°9·6′W	X	103
Rainham	Hav	TQ5282	51°31·2′	0°11·8′E	T	177
Rainham	Medway	TQ8165	51°21·5′	0°36·4′E	T	178
Rainham Creek	Medway	TQ8268	51°23·1′	0°37·3′E	W	178
Rainham Lodge Fm	Hav	TQ5484	51°32·3′	0°13·6′E	FM	177
Rainham Marshes	Hav	TQ5280	51°30·1′	0°11·8′E	X	177
Rain Hill	Herts	TL3135	52°0·1′	0°5·1′W	X	153
Rainhill	St Hel	SJ4991	53°25·0′	2°45·6′W	T	108
Rainhill Stoops	St Hel	SJ5090	53°24·5′	2°44·7′W	T	108
Rainors	Cumbr	NY0903	54°25·1′	3°23·7′W	X	89
Rainow	Ches	SJ9576	53°17·1′	2°4·1′W	T	118
Rainow Hill	Ches	SJ8962	53°9·5′	2°9·5′W	X	118
Rainowlow	Ches	SJ9577	53°17·6′	2°4·1′W	T	118
Rainsbarrow Wood	Cumbr	SD1893	54°19·8′	3°15·2′W	F	96
Rainsber Wood	Lancs	SD7847	53°55·4′	2°19·7′W	F	103
Rainsborough	Northnts	SP5234	52°0·4′	1°14·2′W	A	151
Rainsborrow Crag	Cumbr	NY4406	54°27·0′	2°51·4′W	X	90
Rains Brook	Warw	SP4969	52°19·2′	1°16·5′W	W	151
Rains Brook	Warw	SP5071	52°20·3′	1°15·6′W	W	140
Rainsbrook	Warw	SP5172	52°20·8′	1°14·7′W	X	140
Rainsbutt Fm	N Lincs	SE7715	53°37·8′	0°49·7′W	FM	112
Rainscar	N Yks	SD8471	54°8·3′	2°14·3′W	X	98
Rainscombe Hill Fm	Wilts	SU1765	51°23·3′	1°45·0′W	FM	173
Rainscombe Ho	Wilts	SU1663	51°22·2′	1°45·8′W	X	173
Rains Fm	N Yks	SE8880	54°12·7′	0°38·6′W	FM	101
Rains Grove	I of W	SZ4685	50°40·0′	1°20·6′W	X	196
Rainshaw Fm	N Yks	SE4357	54°0·7′	1°20·2′W	FM	105
Rainshaw Sike	D & G	NY2099	55°17·0′	3°15·1′W	W	79
Rain's Hill	Scot Bord	NY5492	55°13·5′	2°43·0′W	X	79
Rain Shore	Roch	SD8515	53°38·1′	2°13·2′W	T	109
Rain Slack Well	N Yks	SD9872	54°8·9′	2°1·4′W	W	98
Rainsough	Bury	SD8102	53°31·2′	2°16·8′W	T	109
Rain Stang	N Yks	SE0875	54°10·5′	1°52·2′W	H	99
Rainster Rocks	Derby	SK2154	53°5·2′	1°40·8′W	X	119
Rain, The	Pemb	SM8513	51°46·7′	5°6·6′W	X	157
Rainthorpe Hall	Norf	TM2097	52°31·8′	1°15·0′E	A	134
Rainton	D & G	NX5951	54°50·3′	4°11·3′W	X	83
Rainton	N Yks	SE3775	54°10·4′	1°25·6′W	T	99
Rainton Bridge	Sund	NZ3448	54°49·8′	1°27·8′W	T	88
Rainton Gate	Durham	NZ3246	54°48·7′	1°29·7′W	T	88
Raintonpark Wood	Durham	NZ3046	54°48·7′	1°31·6′W	F	88
Rainworth	Notts	SK5958	53°7·2′	1°6·7′W	T	120
Rainworth Lodge	Notts	SK5857	53°6·7′	1°7·6′W	X	120
Rainworth Water	Notts	SK6463	53°9·9′	1°2·2′W	W	120
Rainy Rock	Pemb	SM7607	51°43·3′	5°14·2′W	X	157
Rairaig	Arg & Bt	NM4956	56°38·0′	6°5·1′W	X	47
Ràiream	N Eil	NG2195	57°51·7′	6°41·8′W	X	14
Rairing Sike	Cumbr	NY6571	55°2·2′	2°32·4′W	W	86
Rairnis	N Eil	NF8648	57°25·1′	7°13·4′W	X	22
Raisaburgh	Highld	NG5064	57°36·1′	6°10·6′W	X	23,24
Rais Beck	Cumbr	NY6406	54°27·1′	2°32·9′W	W	91
Raisbeck	Cumbr	NY6407	54°27·7′	2°32·9′W	T	91
Raisbeck	N Yks	SE6067	54°6·0′	1°4·5′W	X	100
Raisbeck Wood	Red & Cl	NZ6218	54°33·4′	1°2·1′W	F	94
Raisdale	N Yks	SE5499	54°23·3′	1°9·7′W	X	100
Raisdale Beck	N Yks	SE5599	54°23·3′	1°8·8′W	W	100
Raise	Cumbr	NY3417	54°32·9′	3°0·8′W	H	90
Raise	Cumbr	NY7146	54°48·7′	2°26·6′W	T	86,87
Raise Beck	Cumbr	NY3211	54°29·6′	3°2·6′W	W	90
Raise Gill	Cumbr	NY2816	54°32·3′	3°6·3′W	W	89,90
Raise Lodge	Cumbr	NY2645	54°47·9′	3°8·6′W	X	85
Raisen's Dyke	Lincs	TF1911	52°41·2′	0°14·0′W	W	130,142
Raisgeir	N Eil	NF5961	57°30·9′	7°41·3′W	X	22

Raisgill	N Yks	SD9078	54°12·1'	2°8·8'W	X	98
Raisgill Hall	Cumbr	NY6305	54°26·6'	2°33·8'W	X	91
Raisin Hall	N Yks	SE2894	54°20·7'	1°33·7'W	X	99
Raismoor	Cumbr	SD6488	54°17·4'	2°32·8'W	X	97
Raisthorpe Manor	N Yks	SE8561	54°2·5'	0°41·7'W	X	100
Raisthwaite	Cumbr	SD2589	54°17·7'	3°8·7'W	X	96
Raistrick Greave	Cald	SD9330	53°46·2'	2°6·0'W	X	103
Rais Wood	N Yks	SD9178	54°12·1'	2°7·9'W	F	98
Rait	Pth & Kin	NO2226	56°25·4'	3°15·4'W	T	53,58
Raitcastle	Highld	NH8852	57°32·9'	3°51·8'W	X	27
Rait Castle	Highld	NH8952	57°32·9'	3°50·8'W	A	27
Raith	Pth & Kin	NN9318	56°20·8'	3°43·4'W	X	58
Raith	S Ayr	NS3926	55°30·3'	4°32·5'W	X	70
Raithburn	E Ayr	NS4746	55°41·3'	4°25·6'W	X	64
Raith Burn	Renf	NS2963	55°50·1'	4°43·4'W	W	63
Raith Burn	S Ayr	NS3827	55°30·9'	4°33·5'W	W	70
Raithby	Lincs	TF3184	53°20·4'	0°1·5'W	T	122
Raithby	Lincs	TF3767	53°11·2'	0°3·4'E	T	122
Raithby Br	Lincs	TF3668	53°11·7'	0°2·6'E	X	122
Raithhill	S Ayr	NS4018	55°26·0'	4°31·3'W	X	70
Raithhill Fm	S Ayr	NS4221	55°27·7'	4°29·5'W	FM	70
Raith Ho	Fife	NT2591	56°6·6'	3°11·9'W	X	59
Raithill	E Ayr	NS4846	55°41·3'	4°24·6'W	X	64
Raithmuir	E Ayr	NS5042	55°39·2'	4°22·6'W	X	70
Raith Park	Fife	NT2592	56°7·1'	3°11·9'W	X	59
Raithwaite	N Yks	NZ8711	54°29·5'	0°39·0'W	X	94
Raitloan	Highld	NH8853	57°33·5'	3°51·9'W	X	27
Raitshill	Aberd	NJ8628	57°20·8'	2°13·5'W	X	38
Raitts Burn	Highld	NH7604	57°6·9'	4°2·4'W	W	35
Raizes, The	S Glos	ST7972	51°27·0'	2°17·7'W	X	172
Raiziehill	N Lanak	NS8667	55°53·2'	3°48·9'W	X	65
Rake	Cumbr	NY2301	54°24·2'	3°10·8'W	X	89,90
Rake	Cumbr	SD2781	54°13·4'	3°6·8'W	X	96,97
Rake	Devon	SX7247	50°18·8'	3°47·5'W	X	202
Rake	Hants	SU8027	51°2·4'	0°51·1'W	T	186,197
Rake Beck	N Yks	NZ0705	54°26·7'	1°53·1'W	W	92
Rake Bottom	Dorset	ST6802	50°49·2'	2°26·9'W	X	194
Rakebottom Fm	Suff	TL7677	52°22·0'	0°35·5'E	FM	143
Rake Common	Hants	SU7826	51°1·9'	0°52·9'W	T	186,197
Rake Crags	Cumbr	NY3111	54°29·6'	3°3·5'W	X	90
Rake Dike	Kirk	SE1005	53°32·7'	1°50·5'W	W	110
Rake End	Cumbr	NY7135	54°42·8'	2°26·6'W	X	91
Rake End	Derby	SK0275	53°16·6'	1°57·8'W	X	119
Rake End	Staffs	SK0718	52°45·8'	1°53·4'W	T	128
Rake Firs	W Susx	SU8128	51°3·0'	0°50·3'W	F	186,197
Rake Fm	Flint	SJ3365	53°10·9'	2°59·7'W	FM	117
Rake Fm	N Yks	NZ7706	54°26·9'	0°48·3'W	FM	94
Rakefoot	Cumbr	NY2822	54°35·5'	3°6·4'W	X	89,90
Rakefoot	Lancs	SD6641	53°52·1'	2°30·6'W	X	103
Rake Hall	Ches	SJ4173	53°15·3'	2°52·7'W	X	117
Rake Head	Cald	SD9825	53°43·5'	2°1·4'W	X	103
Rake Head	Lancs	SD8421	53°41·3'	2°14·1'W	T	103
Rakehead Crag	Cumbr	NY1906	54°26·8'	3°14·5'W	X	89,90
Rake Heath	Suff	TL7677	52°22·0'	0°35·5'E	X	143
Rakeheath Fm	Suff	TL7577	52°22·0'	0°34·6'E	FM	143
Rake Hill	Dorset	ST6901	50°48·7'	2°26·0'W	X	194
Rake Hill	Leeds	SE3837	53°49·9'	1°24·9'W	X	104
Rakehill Fm	Devon	ST2403	50°49·5'	3°4·4'W	FM	192,193
Rake Law	S Lanak	NS8717	55°26·3'	3°46·7'W	H	71,78
Rakepark Lodge	Shrops	SJ5828	52°51·1'	2°37·0'W	X	126
Rakes Dale	Staffs	SK0642	52°58·8'	1°54·2'W	T	119,128
Rakeshole Fm	Kent	TR2044	51°9·4'	1°9·2'E	FM	179,189
Rakes Moss	Derby	SE0500	53°30·0'	1°55·1'W	X	110
Rakes Rocks	Derby	SE0500	53°30·0'	1°55·1'W	X	110
Rakes, The	Lincs	TF2144	52°59·0'	0°11·4'W	X	131
Rakes, The	Staffs	SK1256	53°6·3'	1°48·8'W	X	119
Rakes Wood	Leeds	SE4241	53°52·1'	1°21·3'W	F	105
Rakes Wood	N Yks	SD9477	54°11·6'	2°5·1'W	F	98
Rake, The	Ches	SJ3962	53°9·3'	2°54·3'W	X	117
Rakeway	Staffs	SK0242	52°58·8'	1°57·8'W	T	119,128
Rakewood	Roch	SD9414	53°37·6'	2°5·0'W	T	109
Raking Gill	D & G	NT1915	55°25·6'	3°16·4'W	W	79
Ralegh's Cross Inn	Somer	ST0334	51°6·1'	3°22·7'W	X	181
Raleigh	Devon	SS5634	51°5·5'	4°3·0'W	T	180
Raleigh Ho	Devon	SS5634	51°5·5'	4°3·0'W	X	180
Raleigh Manor	Somer	SS9239	51°8·6'	3°32·3'W	X	181
Ralfland Forest	Cumbr	NY5313	54°30·9'	2°43·1'W	X	90
Ralf Shield	Northum	NZ0189	55°12·0'	1°58·6'W	X	81
Raliabeag	Highld	NN7097	57°3·0'	4°8·1'W	X	35
Ralia Lodge	Highld	NN7197	57°3·0'	4°7·1'W	X	35
Ralingham Hall	Cambs	TL5099	52°34·3'	0°13·2'E	X	143
Ralliss	Cumbr	SD1584	54°14·9'	3°17·8'W	X	96
Rallt	Powys	SN9398	52°34·4'	3°34·3'W	X	136
Rallt	Swan	SS5293	51°37·2'	4°7·9'W	T	159
Rallt Fm	I of Angl	SH3080	53°17·6'	4°32·6'W	FM	114
Rallt Goch	I of Angl	SH3489	53°22·6'	4°29·3'W	X	114
Ralph Crosses	N Yks	NZ6702	54°24·8'	0°57·6'W	A	94
Ralph's Barn	Glos	SP1121	51°53·5'	1°50·0'W	X	163
Ralph's Barrow	Dorset	SZ0898	50°47·1'	1°52·8'W	A	195
Ralph's Cleugh	Northum	NY7598	55°16·8'	2°23·2'W	X	80
Ralph's Cupboard	Corn	SW6445	50°15·7'	5°18·3'W	X	203
Ralstonhill	E Ayr	NS4438	55°36·9'	4°28·2'W	X	70
Ralton Burn	Scot Bord	NY4790	55°12·3'	2°49·5'W	W	79
Raltonside	Scot Bord	NY4889	55°11·8'	2°48·6'W	X	79
Ram	Carm	SN5846	52°5·9'	4°4·0'W	T	146
Ramageton	S Ayr	NS4731	55°33·2'	4°25·1'W	X	70
Ramah	Shetld	HU3577	60°28·8'	1°21·3'W	T	2,3
Ram Alley	Wilts	SU2263	51°22·2'	1°40·6'W	T	174
Ramarageo	N Eil	NB1838	58°14·7'	6°47·9'W	X	8,13
Ramasaig	Highld	NG1644	57°24·1'	6°43·2'W	T	23
Ramasaig Bay	Highld	NG1543	57°23·6'	6°44·2'W	W	23
Ramasaig Cliff	Highld	NG1544	57°24·1'	6°44·2'W	X	23
Ramberry	Orkney	HY4213	59°0·3'	3°0·1'W	X	6
Rame	Corn	SW7234	50°10·0'	5°11·2'W	T	204
Rame	Corn	SX4249	50°19·4'	4°12·8'W	T	201
Rame Head	Corn	SX4148	50°18·9'	4°13·6'W	X	201
Rameldry	Fife	NO3106	56°14·7'	3°6·4'W	X	59
Rameldry	Fife	NO3206	56°14·8'	3°5·4'W	X	59
Rameldry Mill Bank	Fife	NO3106	56°14·7'	3°6·4'W	X	59
Ram Fm	Lincs	TF0162	53°9·0'	0°29·0'W	FM	121

Ram Gill	S Lanak	NT0326	55°31·3'	3°31·8'W	W	72
Ram Hall	Sol	SP2478	52°24·2'	1°38·4'W	A	139
Ram Hill	S Glos	ST6779	51°30·8'	2°28·1'W	T	172
Ramhurst Manor	Kent	TQ5646	51°11·7'	0°14·4'E	X	188
Rami Geo	Orkney	ND4677	58°40·9'	2°55·4'W	X	7
Rami Geo	Orkney	ND4785	58°45·2'	2°54·5'W	X	7
Ram Jam Inn	Rut	SK9415	52°43·7'	0°36·1'W	X	130
Ram Lane	Kent	TQ9646	51°11·0'	0°48·7'E	T	189
Ramley	Hants	SZ2996	50°46·0'	1°34·9'W	X	196
Ramly Geo	Orkney	HY2729	59°8·8'	3°16·1'W	X	6
Ramma Geo	Orkney	HY6925	59°6·9'	2°32·0'W	X	5
Rammamere Fm	Bucks	SP9230	51°57·9'	0°39·3'W	FM	152,165
Rammamere Heath	Bucks	SP9230	51°57·9'	0°39·3'W	X	152,165
Rammerscales	D & G	NY0877	55°5·0'	3°26·0'W	X	85
Rammer Wood	E Loth	NT6371	55°56·1'	2°35·1'W	F	67
Rammey Marsh	Enf	TQ3799	51°40·6'	0°0·7'W	X	166,177
Rammy Geo	Orkney	HY5233	59°11·1'	2°49·9'W	X	5,6
Ramna Beorgs	Shetld	HU3792	60°36·8'	1°18·9'W	X	1,2
Ramna Geo	Orkney	HY3030	59°9·3'	3°13·0'W	X	6
Ramnageo	Shetld	HP6200	60°41·0'	0°51·4'W	T	1
Ramna Geo	Shetld	HU3532	60°4·5'	1°21·8'W	X	4
Ramna Geo	Shetld	HU3725	60°0·8'	1°19·7'W	X	4
Ramna Geo	Shetld	HU4696	60°38·9'	1°9·0'W	X	1
Ramna Geo	Shetld	HU5069	60°24·4'	1°5·0'W	X	2,3
Ramna Geo	Shetld	HU5591	60°36·2'	0°59·2'W	X	1,2
Ramna Geo	Shetld	HU6772	60°25·8'	0°46·5'W	X	2
Ramna Hill	Shetld	HU3778	60°29·3'	1°19·1'W	H	2,3
Ramna Stacks (Nature Reserve)	Shetld	HU3797	60°39·5'	1°18·9'W	X	1
Ramna Taing	Shetld	HU3242	60°9·9'	1°24·9'W	X	4
Ramna Vord	Shetld	HU1855	60°17·0'	1°40·0'W	H	3
Ramnor Inclosure	Hants	SU3104	50°50·3'	1°33·2'W	F	196
Ramornie	Fife	NO3209	56°16·4'	3°5·4'W	T	59
Ramornie Mill	Fife	NO3209	56°16·4'	3°5·4'W	X	59
Rampart Field	Suff	TL7871	52°18·7'	0°37·1'E	X	144,155
Rampart, The	Essex	TL9017	51°49·4'	0°45·8'E	A	168
Ramp Holme	Cumbr	SD3995	54°21·1'	2°55·9'W	X	96,97
Rampisham	Dorset	ST5602	50°49·2'	2°37·1'W	T	194
Rampisham Down	Dorset	ST5401	50°48·6'	2°38·8'W	X	194
Rampisham Hill	Dorset	ST5402	50°49·2'	2°38·8'W	H	194
Rampsbeck Hotel	Cumbr	NY4523	54°36·2'	2°50·7'W	X	90
Rampsgill	Cumbr	NY4315	54°31·9'	2°52·4'W	X	90
Rampsgill Beck	Cumbr	NY4415	54°31·9'	2°51·5'W	W	90
Rampsgill Head	Cumbr	NY4413	54°30·8'	2°51·5'W	X	90
Ramps Hill	Wilts	SU0185	51°34·1'	1°58·7'W	X	173
Ramps Holme	N Yks	SD9198	54°22·9'	2°7·9'W	X	98
Rampshowe	Cumbr	NY5807	54°27·6'	2°38·5'W	X	91
Rampside	Cumbr	SD2466	54°5·3'	3°9·3'W	T	96
Rampside Sands	Cumbr	SD2465	54°4·8'	3°9·3'W	X	96
Rampson	Cumbr	NY8513	54°31·0'	2°13·5'W	X	91,92
Rampton	Cambs	TL4267	52°17·2'	0°5·3'E	T	154
Rampton	Notts	SK7978	53°17·8'	0°48·5'W	T	120,121
Rampyards	Highld	ND2656	58°29·4'	3°15·7'W	X	11,12
Ramrageo	N Eil	NB5462	58°28·9'	6°12·7'W	X	8
Ramridge Cott	Hants	SU3047	51°13·5'	1°33·8'W	X	185
Ramridge Fm	Herts	TL1518	51°51·2'	0°19·4'W	FM	166
Ramridge Ho	Hants	SU3147	51°13·5'	1°33·0'W	X	185
Ramrig	Scot Bord	NT8748	55°43·8'	2°12·0'W	X	74
Ramsaycleuchburn	Scot Bord	NT3402	55°18·7'	3°2·0'W	X	79
Ramsay Ness	Orkney	HY4845	59°17·6'	2°54·3'W	X	5
Ramsay's Monument	Midlo	NT2258	55°48·8'	3°14·2'W	X	66,73
Ramsbottom	Bury	SD7816	53°38·6'	2°19·6'W	T	109
Ramsburn	Moray	NJ5652	57°33·6'	2°43·7'W	T	29
Ramsbury	Wilts	SU2771	51°26·5'	1°36·3'W	T	174
Ramsbury Manor	Wilts	SU2570	51°25·9'	1°38·0'W	A	174
Rams Cleuch	Scot Bord	NT3501	55°18·2'	3°1·0'W	X	79
Ram's Cliff	Wilts	SU0152	51°16·3'	1°58·8'W	X	184
Ramscliffe Fm	Devon	SS5416	50°55·7'	4°4·3'W	FM	180
Rams Clough	Lancs	SD6352	53°58·0'	2°33·4'W	X	102,103
Rams Clough	Lancs	SD6441	53°52·1'	2°32·4'W	X	102,103
Rams Combe	Somer	SS8140	51°9·1'	3°41·7'W	X	181
Rams Combe	Somer	ST1637	51°7·8'	3°11·6'W	X	181
Ramscraigs	Highld	ND1326	58°13·1'	3°28·4'W	T	17
Ramsdale	N Yks	NZ9203	54°25·1'	0°34·5'W	X	94
Rams Dale	Orkney	HY3307	58°57·0'	3°9·4'W	X	6,7
Ramsdale Beck	N Yks	NZ9303	54°25·1'	0°33·6'W	F	94
Ramsdale Fm	Leic	SP4992	52°31·7'	1°16·3'W	FM	140
Ramsdale Ho	Notts	SK5849	53°2·3'	1°7·7'W	X	129
Ramsdean	Hants	SU7022	50°59·8'	0°59·8'W	T	197
Ramsdean Down	Hants	SU7120	50°58·7'	0°58·9'W	X	197
Ramsdell	Hants	SU5857	51°18·8'	1°9·7'W	T	174
Ramsdell Hall	Ches	SJ8458	53°7·4'	2°13·9'W	X	118
Ramsden	Brom	TQ4766	51°22·7'	0°7·1'E	T	177
Ramsden	Kent	TQ9230	51°2·5'	0°44·7'E	X	189
Ramsden	Oxon	SP3515	51°50·2'	1°29·1'W	T	164
Ramsden	Worcs	SO9246	52°7·0'	2°6·6'W	T	150
Ramsden Bellhouse	Essex	TQ7194	51°37·4'	0°28·6'E	T	167,178
Ramsden Clough	Kirk	SE1203	53°31·7'	1°48·7'W	X	110
Ramsden Clough Reservoir	Cald	SD9121	53°41·4'	2°7·8'W	W	103
Ramsden Coppice	Heref	SO5334	52°0·4'	2°40·7'W	F	149
Ramsden Fm	Kent	TQ8132	51°3·7'	0°35·4'E	FM	188
Ramsden Fm	Kent	TQ9238	51°6·8'	0°45·0'E	FM	189
Ramsden Hall School	Essex	TQ6995	51°37·9'	0°26·9'E	X	167,177
Ramsden Head	N Yks	SE7895	54°20·9'	0°47·6'W	X	94,100
Ramsden Heath	Essex	TQ7195	51°37·9'	0°28·6'E	T	167
Ramsden Heath	Oxon	SP3415	51°50·2'	1°30·0'W	X	164
Ramsden Park Fm	Essex	TQ7194	51°37·4'	0°28·6'E	FM	167,178
Ramsden Resr	Kirk	SE1105	53°32·7'	1°49·6'W	W	110
Ramsden Wood	Cald	SD9221	53°41·4'	2°6·9'W	T	103
Ramsdown Cross	Devon	SX4280	50°36·1'	4°13·6'W	X	201
Ramsdown Fm	I of W	SZ4882	50°38·4'	1°18·9'W	FM	196
Ramsey	Cambs	TL2885	52°27·1'	0°6·6'W	T	142
Ramsey	Essex	TM2130	51°55·7'	1°13·3'E	T	169
Ramsey	I of M	SC4594	54°19·3'	4°22·6'W	T	95
Ramsey Bay	I of M	SC4695	54°19·9'	4°21·7'W	W	95
Ramsey Beach	Devon	SS6449	51°13·7'	3°56·5'W	X	180
Ramseycleuch	Scot Bord	NT2714	55°25·1'	3°8·8'W	X	79
Ramsey Fen	Cambs	TL3191	52°30·3'	0°3·8'W	X	142
Ramsey Fm	Devon	ST0620	50°58·5'	3°20·0'W	FM	181
Ramsey Fm	Suff	TM0542	52°2·5'	0°59·8'E	FM	155

Ramsey Forty Foot	Cambs	TL3087	52°28·2'	0°4·8'W	T	142
Ramsey Hall	Essex	TM1829	51°55·2'	1°10·6'E	X	168,169
Ramsey Heights	Cambs	TL2585	52°27·1'	0°9·2'W	X	142
Ramsey Hollow	Cambs	TL3286	52°27·6'	0°3·0'W	X	142
Ramsey Island	Essex	TL9405	51°42·8'	0°48·9'E	X	168
Ramsey Island	Essex	TL9505	51°42·8'	0°49·8'E	T	168
Ramsey Island	Pemb	SM6923	51°51·7'	5°20·9'W	X	157
Ramsey Knowe	Scot Bord	NT2516	55°26·2'	3°10·7'W	H	79
Ramsey Marsh	Essex	TL9305	51°42·9'	0°48·0'E	W	168
Ramsey Mere	Cambs	TL3189	52°29·2'	0°3·8'W	X	142
Ramsey Mereside	Cambs	TL2889	52°29·3'	0°6·5'W	T	142
Ramsey's Burn	Northum	NT8702	55°19·0'	2°11·9'W	W	80
Ramsey Sound	Pemb	SM7124	51°52·3'	5°19·2'W	W	157
Ramsey St Mary's	Cambs	TL2588	52°28·8'	0°9·2'W	T	142
Ramsey Tyrells	Essex	TQ6799	51°40·1'	0°25·3'E	X	167,177
Ramsey Wood	Suff	TM0643	52°3·0'	1°0·7'E	F	155
Ramsgate	Kent	TR3864	51°19·7'	1°25·4'E	T	179
Rams Geo	Orkney	HY4820	59°4·1'	2°53·9'W	X	5,6
Rams Geo	Orkney	HY5420	59°4·1'	2°47·7'W	X	5,6
Rams Geo	Shetld	HU3593	60°37·4'	1°21·1'W	X	1,2
Ramsgill	N Yks	SE1171	54°8·3'	1°49·5'W	T	99
Ramsgill Beck	N Yks	SE0970	54°7·8'	1°51·3'W	W	99
Ramsgill Bents	N Yks	SE1071	54°8·3'	1°50·4'W	X	99
Ramsgill Moor	N Yks	SE0870	54°7·8'	1°52·2'W	X	99
Ramsgreave Hall	Lancs	SD6731	53°46·7'	2°29·6'W	X	103
Ramshaw	Durham	NY9547	54°49·3'	2°4·2'W	T	87
Ramshaw	Durham	NZ1426	54°38·0'	1°46·6'W	T	92
Ramshaw	Northum	NY7160	54°56·3'	2°26·7'W	X	86,87
Ramshaw	N Yks	SD9748	53°55·9'	2°2·3'W	X	103
Ramshaw	Staffs	SK0262	53°9·5'	1°57·8'W	X	119
Ramshaw Fell	Northum	NY7060	54°56·3'	2°27·7'W	H	86,87
Ramshaw Fm	Derby	SK3776	53°17·0'	1°26·3'W	FM	119
Ramshaw Heugh	Durham	NZ1527	54°38·5'	1°45·6'W	X	92
Ramshaw Rig	D & G	NY1697	55°15·9'	3°18·9'W	H	79
Ramshaw Rocks	Staffs	SK0162	53°9·5'	1°58·7'W	X	119
Ramshaw Wood	D & G	NX8258	54°54·4'	3°50·0'W	F	84
Rams Head	Shetld	HU1849	60°13·8'	1°40·0'W	X	3
Rams Head	Shetld	HU2446	60°12·1'	1°33·5'W	X	4
Ram's Head Spinney	Leic	SP7799	52°35·2'	0°51·4'W	F	141
Rams Hill	Kent	TQ7042	51°9·3'	0°26·3'E	X	188
Rams Hill	Oxon	SU3186	51°34·6'	1°32·8'W	X	174
Ram's Hill Fm	Dorset	ST8117	50°57·4'	2°15·8'W	FM	183
Ramsholt	Suff	TM3141	52°1·4'	1°22·4'E	T	169
Ramshope Burn	Northum	NT7304	55°20·0'	2°25·1'W	W	80
Ramshope Fm	Northum	NT7304	55°20·0'	2°25·1'W	FM	80
Ramshope Lodge	Northum	NT7204	55°20·0'	2°26·1'W	X	80
Ramshorn	Staffs	SK0845	53°0·4'	1°52·4'W	T	119,128
Ramshorn Common	Staffs	SK0745	53°0·4'	1°53·3'W	X	119,128
Ramshorn Down	Devon	SX7973	50°32·9'	3°42·1'W	H	191
Ramshorn Fm	Pemb	SN1010	51°45·6'	4°44·8'W	FM	158
Ramshott Lodge	Suff	TM2942	52°2·0'	1°20·7'E	X	169
Ramside Hall (Hotel)	Durham	NZ3144	54°47·6'	1°30·6'W	X	88
Ramsland	Devon	SX6051	50°20·8'	3°57·7'W	X	202
Ramsley	Devon	SX6493	50°43·5'	3°55·2'W	T	191
Ramsley Fm	Norf	TF9621	52°45·3'	0°54·7'E	FM	132
Ramsley Lodge	Derby	SK2875	53°16·5'	1°34·4'W	X	119
Ramsley Moor	Derby	SK0693	53°26·3'	1°54·2'W	X	110
Ramsley Moor	Derby	SK2875	53°16·5'	1°34·4'W	X	119
Ramsley Resr	Derby	SK2874	53°16·0'	1°34·4'W	W	119
Ramslye	Kent	TQ5638	51°7·4'	0°14·1'E	T	188
Rams Ness	Shetld	HU6087	60°34·0'	0°53·8'W	X	1,2
Ramsnest Common	Surrey	SU9433	51°5·5'	0°39·1'W	T	186
Ramsquoy	Orkney	HY3009	58°58·0'	3°12·6'W	X	6,7
Rams-raer	Shetld	HU3631	60°4·0'	1°20·7'W	X	4
Ramstile Fm	Kent	TQ9038	51°6·8'	0°43·3'E	FM	189
Ramstone	Aberd	NJ6717	57°14·8'	2°32·4'W	X	38
Rams Tor	Swan	SS6187	51°34·1'	3°59·9'W	X	159
Ram's Wood	Pemb	SM9920	51°50·8'	4°54·7'W	F	157,158
Ramtor Rock	Devon	SS2119	50°56·8'	4°32·5'W	X	190
Ranachan	Highld	NM7861	56°41·5'	5°37·1'W	X	40
Ranachan Burn	Arg & Bt	NR7024	55°27·6'	5°37·9'W	W	68
Ranachan Hill	Arg & Bt	NR6825	55°28·1'	5°39·8'W	H	68
Ranageig	Pth & Kin	NO1049	56°37·7'	3°27·6'W	X	53
Ranah Stones Fm	Barns	SE2002	53°31·1'	1°41·5'W	X	110
Ranais	N Eil	NB4024	58°8·0'	6°24·5'W	T	14
Ranbeck	Cumbr	NY6532	54°41·2'	2°32·2'W	X	91
Ranbeck	N Yks	SE7257	54°0·5'	0°53·7'W	X	105,106
Ranbury Ring	Glos	SP0900	51°42·2'	1°51·8'W	A	163
Ranby	Lincs	TF2278	53°17·3'	0°9·8'W	T	122
Ranby	Notts	SK6580	53°19·0'	1°1·0'W	T	111,120
Ranby Cottage Fm	Notts	SK6583	53°20·6'	1°1·0'W	FM	111,120
Ranby Hall	Notts	SK6583	53°20·6'	1°1·0'W	X	111,120
Ranby Hill	Lincs	TF2278	53°17·3'	0°9·8'W	X	122
Ranby Ho (Sch)	Notts	SK6581	53°19·6'	1°1·0'W	X	111,120
Rancliffe Wood	Notts	SK5930	52°52·1'	1°7·0'W	F	129
Rand	Lincs	TF1078	53°17·5'	0°20·6'W	T	121
Randale Beck	Cumbr	NY4612	54°30·3'	2°49·6'W	W	90
Randalholme	Cumbr	NY7048	54°49·8'	2°27·6'W	A	86,87
Randalinton	Cumbr	NY4065	54°58·8'	2°55·8'W	X	85
Randall's Fm	E Susx	TQ7916	50°55·2'	0°33·2'E	FM	199
Randall's Fm	Norf	TM1692	52°29·2'	1°11·3'E	FM	144
Randall's Fm	Wok	SU7966	51°23·5'	0°51·5'W	FM	175
Randall's Mill	Norf	TG4126	52°46·9'	1°34·8'E	X	134
Randalls Park	Surrey	TQ1557	51°18·3'	0°20·6'W	X	187
Randall Wood	Kent	TQ6870	51°24·5'	0°25·3'E	F	177,178
Randan Wood	Worcs	SO9272	52°21·0'	2°6·6'W	F	139
Randel Crag	Cumbr	NY2529	54°39·3'	3°9·3'W	X	89,90
Randerside	Cumbr	NY3421	54°35·0'	3°0·9'W	X	90
Randerston	Fife	NO6010	56°17·1'	2°38·3'W	X	59
Rand Grange	N Yks	SE2588	54°17·5'	1°36·5'W	X	99
Rand Hill Plantn	N Yks	SE2486	54°16·4'	1°37·5'W	F	99
Randilow Fm	Ches	SJ7446	53°0·9'	2°22·8'W	FM	118
Randlawfoot	Cumbr	NY4952	54°51·9'	2°47·3'W	X	86
Randlehayes Fm	Devon	SY0391	50°42·9'	3°22·1'W	FM	192
Randolph's	Kent	TQ8537	51°6·4'	0°39·0'E	X	189
Randolph's Copse	W Susx	TQ2714	50°54·9'	0°11·2'W	F	198
Randolph's Fm	W Susx	TQ2715	50°55·5'	0°11·2'W	FM	198
Randolph's Leap	Moray	NH9949	57°31·5'	3°40·7'W	X	27
Random	Shrops	SO6077	52°23·6'	2°34·9'W	X	138
Rands Drain	Norf	TF5309	52°39·7'	0°16·1'E	W	143

Rands Fm	E Yorks	TA2030	53°45·4'	0°10·4'W	FM	107
Rands Fm	Suff	TM0140	52°1·5'	0°56·2'E	FM	155
Rand's Wood	Cambs	TL6250	52°7·7'	0°22·4'E	F	154
Randswood Fm	Cambs	TL6250	52°7·7'	0°22·4'E	FM	154
Randwick	Glos	SO8206	51°45·4'	2°15·3'W	T	162
Rand Wood	Lincs	TF0878	53°17·5'	0°22·4'W	F	121
Randygill Top	Cumbr	NY6800	54°23·9'	2°29·2'W	H	91
Randy Mere	N Yks	NZ8101	54°24·1'	0°44·7'W	W	94
Randy Pike	Cumbr	NY3601	54°24·3'	2°58·7'W	X	90
Ranelagh Fm	Brackn	SU9273	51°27·1'	0°40·2'W	FM	175
Ranelands Fm	N Yks	SE0362	54°3·5'	1°56·8'W	FM	98
Raneleigh Fm	Devon	SX5150	50°20·1'	4°5·2'W	FM	201
Ranfold	W Susx	TQ1229	51°3·2'	0°23·7'W	X	187,198
Ranfurly	Renf	NS3965	55°51·3'	4°33·9'W	T	63
Rangag	Highld	ND1744	58°22·9'	3°24·7'W	X	11,12
Rangas	N Eil	NF9376	57°40·4'	7°8·5'W	X	18
Range Castle	D & G	NY0876	55°4·4'	3°26·0'W	X	85
Range Castle (Fort)	D & G	NY0876	55°4·4'	3°26·0'W	A	85
Rangecastle Hill	D & G	NY1893	55°13·7'	3°16·9'W	H	79
Range Cleuch	Scot Bord	NT1910	55°22·9'	3°16·3'W	X	79
Range Fm	Derby	SK4656	53°6·2'	1°18·4'W	FM	120
Range Fm	Norf	TG1134	52°52·0'	1°8·5'E	FM	133
Rangegill Burn	D & G	NY0777	55°5·0'	3°27·0'W	W	85
Rangely Kip	E Loth	NT6067	55°53·9'	2°37·9'W	H	67
Rangemore	Staffs	SK1823	52°48·5'	1°43·6'W	T	128
Ranger's Lawn	Oxon	SP3319	51°52·3'	1°30·8'W	X	164
Ranger's Lodge	Oxon	SP3319	51°52·3'	1°30·8'W	X	164
Ranger's Lodge	Win & Maid	SU9573	51°27·1'	0°37·6'W	X	175,176
Ranger's Lodge Fm	Wilts	SU1629	51°3·8'	1°45·9'W	FM	184
Ranger, The	Staffs	SK0543	52°59·3'	1°55·1'W	X	119,128
Rangeway Bank Fm	Ches	SJ5171	53°14·3'	2°43·6'W	FM	117
Rangeworthy	S Glos	ST6886	51°34·6'	2°27·3'W	T	172
Ranie Point	Corn	SX0281	50°35·9'	4°47·5'W	X	200
Rankeilour Ho	Fife	NO3311	56°17·5'	3°4·5'W	X	59
Rankeilour Mains	Fife	NO3212	56°18·0'	3°5·5'W	X	59
R Anker	Staffs	SK2205	52°38·8'	1°40·1'W	W	139
Rankins Fm	Kent	TQ7548	51°12·5'	0°30·7'E	FM	188
Rankin's Rocks	Arg & Bt	NM2818	56°16·8'	6°23·2'W	X	48
Rankinston	E Ayr	NS4514	55°24·0'	4°26·4'W	T	70
Rankle Burn	Scot Bord	NT3109	55°22·5'	3°4·9'W	W	79
Ranksborough Gorse	Dorset	ST7210	50°53·6'	2°23·5'W	F	194
Ranksborough Hall	Rut	SK8310	52°41·1'	0°45·9'W	X	130
Ranksborough Hill	Rut	SK8211	52°41·7'	0°46·8'W	H	130
Rank's Green	Essex	TL7518	51°50·2'	0°32·8'E	T	167
Rank, The	Wilts	ST8554	51°17·3'	2°12·5'W	X	183
Rankthorns Plantn	Cumbr	SD4187	54°16·8'	2°54·0'W	F	96,97
Ranley Gill	Cumbr	SD8187	54°16·9'	2°17·1'W	X	98
Ranmoor	Sheff	SK3186	53°22·4'	1°31·6'W	T	110,111
Ranmore Common	Surrey	TQ1450	51°14·5'	0°21·6'W	T	187
Ranmore Common	Surrey	TQ1451	51°15·0'	0°21·6'W	F	187
Ranna	Aberd	NJ4806	57°8·8'	2°51·1'W	X	37
Rannachy	Moray	NJ4464	57°40·0'	2°55·9'W	X	28
Rannagulzion Fm	Pth & Kin	NO1753	56°39·9'	3°20·8'W	FM	53
Rannagulzion Ho	Pth & Kin	NO1751	56°38·9'	3°20·8'W	X	53
Rannas	Moray	NJ4664	57°40·0'	2°53·8'W	X	28,29
Rannelow	Lincs	SE9002	53°30·7'	0°38·2'W	X	112
Rannerdale	Cumbr	NY1618	54°33·3'	3°17·5'W	X	89
Rannerdale Beck	Cumbr	NY1719	54°33·8'	3°16·6'W	W	89,90
Rannerdale Knotts	Cumbr	NY1618	54°33·3'	3°17·5'W	X	89
Ranneys	I Scilly	SV8508	49°53·6'	6°22·8'W	X	203
Ranneys, The	Corn	SX2651	50°20·2'	4°26·3'W	X	201
Rannoch Barracks	Pth & Kin	NN4956	56°40·5'	4°27·4'W	X	42,51
Rannoch Forest	Pth & Kin	NN4553	56°38·9'	4°31·2'W	X	42,51
Rannoch Forest	Pth & Kin	NN4565	56°45·3'	4°31·7'W	X	42
Rannoch Forest	Pth & Kin	NN5754	56°39·6'	4°19·5'W	X	42,51
Rannoch Lodge	Pth & Kin	NN5057	56°41·1'	4°26·5'W	X	42,51
Rannoch Moor	Highld	NN3349	56°36·4'	4°42·8'W	X	50
Rannoch Moor	Highld	NN3552	56°38·1'	4°41·0'W	X	41
Rannoch Moor	Pth & Kin	NN4152	56°38·2'	4°35·1'W	X	42,51
Rannoch River	Highld	NM7246	56°33·3'	5°42·2'W	W	49
Rannoch School	Pth & Kin	NN5956	56°40·7'	4°17·6'W	X	42,51
Rannoch Sta	Pth & Kin	NN4257	56°40·9'	4°34·3'W	X	42,51
Ranny Bay	V of Glam	ST1868	51°24·5'	3°10·4'W	W	171
Ranochan	Highld	NM8282	56°53·0'	5°34·2'W	T	40
Ransa Hill	N Yks	SD8849	53°56·5'	2°10·6'W	H	103
Ranscombe	Devon	ST0026	51°1·7'	3°25·2'W	X	181
Ranscombe	Devon	SX7644	50°17·2'	3°44·1'W	X	202
Ranscombe	Devon	SX8681	50°37·3'	3°36·3'W	X	191
Ranscombe	Medway	TQ7167	51°22·8'	0°27·8'E	X	178
Ranscombe	Somer	SS9443	51°10·8'	3°30·6'W	X	181
Ranscombe Bottom	Wilts	SU0368	51°24·9'	1°57·0'W	X	173
Ranscombe Camp	E Susx	TQ4309	50°52·0'	0°2·3'E	A	198
Ranscombe Fm	E Susx	TQ4308	50°51·5'	0°2·3'E	FM	198
Ranscombe Fm	Hants	SU6333	51°5·8'	1°5·6'W	FM	185
Ransfield	C of Edin	NT1470	55°55·2'	3°22·1'W	X	65
Ranskill	Notts	SK6587	53°22·8'	1°1·0'W	T	111,120
Ranslett Ho	Shrops	SJ5905	52°38·7'	2°36·0'W	X	126
Ransom Hall	Notts	SK5759	53°7·7'	1°8·5'W	X	120
Ranson Moor	Cambs	TL3792	52°30·7'	0°1·5'E	X	142,143
Ransonmoor Fm	Cambs	TL3791	52°30·2'	0°1·5'E	FM	142,143
Ransonmoor Grange	Cambs	TL3993	52°31·3'	0°3·3'E	X	142,143
Ranston	Dorset	ST8612	50°54·7'	2°11·6'W	X	194
Ranston Hill	Dorset	ST8612	50°54·7'	2°11·6'W	X	194
Ranston Hill Bldgs	Dorset	ST8712	50°54·7'	2°10·7'W	X	194
Rantan	Orkney	HY2928	59°8·2'	3°14·0'W	X	6
Ranton	Staffs	SJ8524	52°49·0'	2°13·0'W	T	127
Ranton Abbey	Staffs	SJ8324	52°49·0'	2°14·7'W	X	127
Ranton Green	Staffs	SJ8422	52°48·0'	2°13·8'W	T	127
Ranton Hall	Staffs	SJ8424	52°49·0'	2°13·8'W	X	127
Ranton Ho	Staffs	SJ8523	52°48·5'	2°12·9'W	X	127
Rantree	N Yks	SD7264	54°4·5'	2°25·3'W	X	98
Rantreeburn	Aberd	NJ8558	57°37·0'	2°14·6'W	X	30
Rantree Fold	Lancs	SD6565	54°5·0'	2°31·7'W	X	97
Rantree Gill	N Yks	SD7164	54°4·5'	2°26·2'W	W	98
Ranvilles Fm	Hants	SU3318	50°57·9'	1°31·4'W	FM	185
Ranworth	Norf	TG3514	52°40·6'	1°29·0'E	T	133,134
Ranworth Broad	Norf	TG3515	52°41·1'	1°29·0'E	W	133,134
Ranworth Marshes	Norf	TG3615	52°41·1'	1°29·9'E	W	133,134
Raonacloy	Highld	NC5603	57°59·8'	4°25·7'W	X	16
Raon na Crèadha	N Eil	NB4433	58°13·0'	6°21·1'W	T	8

Raor Lodge	Pth & Kin	NO0147	56°36·5'	3°36·3'W	X	52,53
Rapaire	N Eil	NB1313	58°1·1'	6°51·1'W	H	13,14
Rape Haw	Cumbr	SD2162	54°3·1'	3°12·0'W	X	96
Raperlaw	Scot Bord	NT5523	55°30·2'	2°42·3'W	X	73
Raper Lodge	Derby	SK2165	53°11·1'	1°40·7'W	X	119
Raper's Fm	N Yks	SE8293	54°19·8'	0°43·9'W	FM	94,100
Raphael	Corn	SX1950	50°19·6'	4°32·2'W	X	201
Rapkyns	W Susx	TQ1331	51°4·3'	0°22·8'W	T	187
Rapley Fm	Brackn	SU8965	51°22·9'	0°42·9'W	FM	175
Rapley Lake	Brackn	SU8964	51°22·3'	0°42·9'W	W	175,186
Raploch	Stir	NS7894	56°7·6'	3°57·3'W	T	57
Rapness	Orkney	HY5141	59°15·4'	2°51·1'W	T	5
Rapness Sound	Orkney	HY5139	59°14·4'	2°51·0'W	W	5
Rappach	Highld	NC2401	57°58·1'	4°58·1'W	X	15
Rappach Water	Highld	NH2998	57°56·6'	4°52·9'W	W	20
Rappaig	Highld	NH2999	57°57·1'	4°52·9'W	X	20
Rapplaburn	Aberd	NJ7340	57°27·2'	2°26·5'W	X	29
Rappla Wood	Aberd	NJ7340	57°27·2'	2°26·5'W	F	29
Rapplich	Aberd	NJ5623	57°18·0'	2°43·4'W	X	37
Rapps	Somer	ST3317	50°57·1'	2°56·8'W	T	193
Rapscott	Devon	SS6930	51°3·5'	3°51·8'W	X	180
Rapsgate Park	Glos	SO9910	51°47·6'	2°0·5'W	X	163
Rapson	Devon	SS5717	50°56·3'	4°1·7'W	X	180
Raptor Foundation, The	Cambs	TL3375	52°21·6'	0°2·4'W	X	142
Rarainis	N Eil	NF8554	57°28·3'	7°14·8'W	X	22
R Aran	Powys	SO1366	52°17·4'	3°16·1'W	W	136,148
Rare Breeds Fm	Shrops	SO5790	52°30·6'	2°37·6'W	FM	137,138
Rare Breeds Fm	Wilts	SU2042	51°10·8'	1°42·4'W	FM	184
Rarer Dean	Durham	NZ1342	54°46·6'	1°47·4'W	X	88
Ràrsaidh	Highld	NG8211	57°8·6'	5°35·7'W	X	33
Rascal Moor	E Yorks	SE8236	53°49·1'	0°44·9'W	T	106
Rascals	W Susx	TQ1525	51°1·0'	0°21·2'W	X	187,198
Rascarrel	D & G	NX7948	54°49·0'	3°52·6'W	X	84
Rascarrel Bay	D & G	NX8048	54°49·0'	3°51·6'W	W	84
Rascarrel Moss	D & G	NX8049	54°49·5'	3°51·7'W	X	84
Rash	Cumbr	NY2539	54°44·7'	3°9·5'W	X	89,90
Rash	Cumbr	SD6689	54°18·0'	2°30·9'W	X	98
Rash Boglea	Aberd	NJ8645	57°29·9'	2°13·6'W	X	30
Rash Br	Cumbr	SD6589	54°18·0'	2°31·9'W	X	97
Rashbush Rigg	Cumbr	NY6470	55°1·6'	2°33·4'W	X	86
Rashcrook	Moray	NJ2257	57°36·0'	3°17·8'W	X	28
Rashenlochy	Aberd	NJ7600	57°5·7'	2°23·3'W	X	38
Rashercap	Northum	NU1703	55°19·5'	1°43·5'W	X	81
Rashes Burn	Highld	NC6633	58°16·2'	4°16·6'W	W	16
Rashes Fm	W Susx	TQ3435	51°6·1'	0°4·8'W	FM	187
Rashfield	Arg & Bt	NS1483	56°0·5'	4°58·6'W	X	56
Rashgillpark	D & G	NX9880	55°6·5'	3°35·5'W	X	78
Rashick Knap	Angus	NO7355	56°41·4'	2°26·0'W	X	54
Rashieburn	Aberd	NJ8320	57°16·5'	2°16·5'W	X	38
Rashieburn	Orkney	HY4605	58°56·0'	2°55·8'W	X	6,7
Rashiegrain	Scot Bord	NT3500	55°17·6'	3°1·0'W	X	79
Rashiegrain Height	D & G	NY3697	55°16·0'	3°0·0'W	H	79
Rashiehall	Pth & Kin	NO1730	56°27·5'	3°20·4'W	X	53
Rashiehill	Falk	NS7781	56°0·6'	3°57·9'W	X	64
Rashiehill	Falk	NS8473	55°56·4'	3°51·0'W	X	65
Rashie Hill	Pth & Kin	NO0408	56°15·5'	3°32·5'W	X	58
Rashiehill	Pth & Kin	NO0409	56°16·1'	3°32·6'W	X	58
Rashiehill	Stir	NS6189	56°4·7'	4°13·6'W	X	57
Rashiehill	W Loth	NS9661	55°50·1'	3°39·2'W	X	65
Rashiehill Muir	W Loth	NS9659	55°49·0'	3°39·1'W	X	65,72
Rashiel	D & G	NY3983	55°8·5'	2°57·0'W	X	79
Rashielea	Pth & Kin	NO0533	56°29·0'	3°32·1'W	X	52,53
Rashielee	Renf	NS4670	55°54·2'	4°27·4'W	T	64
Rashiereive	Aberd	NJ9722	57°17·6'	2°2·5'W	X	38
Rashierigg	W Loth	NS9462	55°50·6'	3°41·1'W	X	65
Rashieslack	Aberd	NJ6234	57°23·9'	2°37·5'W	X	29
Rashillhouse	E Ayr	NS3843	55°39·5'	4°34·1'W	X	63,70
Rashleighayes	Devon	SS9308	50°51·9'	3°30·9'W	X	192
Rashleigh Barton	Devon	SS6712	50°53·8'	3°53·1'W	X	180
Rashleigh Fm	Devon	SX6790	50°41·9'	3°52·6'W	FM	191
Rashleiyett	N Ayr	NS3157	55°46·9'	4°41·3'W	X	63
Rashley	N Ayr	NS2345	55°40·2'	4°48·4'W	X	63
Rashmire Wood	Cumbr	NY4835	54°42·7'	2°48·0'W	F	90
Rash, The	N Yks	SE5048	53°55·8'	1°13·9'W	F	105
Rash, The	N Yks	SE5054	53°59·0'	1°13·8'W	F	105
Rashwood	Worcs	SO9165	52°17·2'	2°7·5'W	T	150
Rashy Burn	Aberd	NJ3802	57°6·5'	3°1·0'W	W	37
Rashy Height	D & G	NX9398	55°16·1'	3°40·6'W	X	78
Rashy Hill	Scot Bord	NT3606	55°20·9'	3°0·1'W	H	79
Rashypans	Aberd	NJ8148	57°31·6'	2°18·6'W	X	29,30
Raskelf	N Yks	SE4971	54°8·2'	1°14·6'W	T	100
Raskelf Moor	N Yks	SE4771	54°8·2'	1°16·4'W	X	100
Raslie	Arg & Bt	NR8298	56°7·8'	5°30·0'W	X	55
Rasp Bank	N Yks	NZ1502	54°25·0'	1°45·7'W	X	92
Raspberry Hill	Kent	TQ8968	51°23·0'	0°43·4'E	X	178
Rasp Hill	Cumbr	NY7727	54°38·5'	2°21·0'W	X	91
Rasp Howe	Cumbr	NY4603	54°25·4'	2°49·5'W	X	90
Raspit Hill	Kent	TQ5854	51°16·0'	0°16·3'E	X	188
Rassal	Highld	NG8442	57°25·3'	5°35·4'W	X	24
Rassau	Blae Gw	SO1512	51°48·2'	3°13·6'W	T	161
Rassett Hill	Cumbr	NY7305	54°26·6'	2°24·6'W	H	91
Rassler Wood	Bucks	SU8285	51°33·7'	0°48·6'W	F	175
Rastrick	Cald	SE1321	53°41·4'	1°47·8'W	T	104
Raswell Fm	Somer	ST2131	51°4·6'	3°7·3'W	FM	182
Raswell, The	Surrey	SU9938	51°8·2'	0°34·7'W	X	186
Ratae (Roman Town) (Leicester)	C of Leic	SK5804	52°38·1'	1°8·2'W	R	140
Ratagan	Highld	NG9119	57°13·1'	5°27·2'W	T	33
Ratagan Forest	Highld	NG8920	57°13·6'	5°29·3'W	F	33
Ratagan Forest	Highld	NG9020	57°13·6'	5°28·3'W	F	25,33
Ratby	Leic	SK5105	52°38·7'	1°14·4'W	T	140
Ratby Burroughs	Leic	SK4906	52°39·2'	1°16·1'W	F	140
Ratcher Hill	Notts	SK5759	53°7·7'	1°8·5'W	X	120
Ratchet Hill	Leic	SK4416	52°44·6'	1°20·5'W	X	129
Ratcheugh	Northum	NU2315	55°25·9'	1°37·8'W	X	81
Ratcheugh Crag	Northum	NU2214	55°25·4'	1°38·7'W	X	81
Ratch-hill	Aberd	NJ7717	57°14·8'	2°22·4'W	X	38
Ratchie, The	Shetld	HU3912	59°53·7'	1°17·7'W	X	4
Ratchill	Scot Bord	NT1136	55°36·8'	3°24·3'W	X	72
Ratchwood	Northum	NU1428	55°33·0'	1°46·3'W	X	75

Ratcliff	T Ham	TQ3580	51°30·4'	0°2·9'W	T	177
Ratcliffe Br	Leic	SP3299	52°35·5'	1°31·3'W	X	140
Ratcliffe Br	Warw	SP3198	52°35·0'	1°32·1'W	X	140
Ratcliffe College	Leic	SK6215	52°44·0'	1°4·5'W	X	129
Ratcliffe College (Sch)	Leic	SK6215	52°44·0'	1°4·5'W	X	129
Ratcliffe Culey	Leic	SP3299	52°35·5'	1°31·3'W	T	140
Ratcliffe Grange	Notts	SK5577	53°17·5'	1°10·1'W	X	120
Ratcliffe Ho	Leic	SP3399	52°35·5'	1°30·4'W	X	140
Ratcliffe House Fm	Warr	SJ6694	53°26·7'	2°30·3'W	FM	109
Ratcliffe on Soar	Leic	SK4929	52°51·6'	1°15·9'W	T	129
Ratcliffe on the Wreake	Leic	SK6314	52°43·4'	1°3·6'W	T	129
Ratcliffes	Devon	SX9599	50°47·1'	3°29·0'W	X	192
Ratcliff's Fm	Essex	TM1725	51°53·1'	1°9·6'E	FM	168,169
Ratclyffe	Devon	ST0500	50°47·7'	3°20·5'W	X	192
Rat Combe	Devon	SX6496	50°45·1'	3°55·3'W	X	191
Ratefield Fm	Heref	SO5162	52°15·5'	2°42·7'W	FM	137,138,149
Ratford	Wilts	ST9872	51°27·1'	2°1·3'W	T	173
Ratford Bridge	Pemb	SM8912	51°46·3'	5°3·1'W	X	157,158
Ratfyn	Wilts	SU1642	51°10·9'	1°45·9'W	T	184
Ratfyn Barrow	Wilts	SU1541	51°10·3'	1°46·7'W	A	184
Ratgoed Hall	Gwyn	SH7712	52°41·7'	3°48·8'W	X	124
Rathad a' Gharaidh Dhuibh	Highld	NG4532	57°18·7'	6°13·6'W	X	32
Rathad a' Phentland	N Eil	NB2735	58°13·4'	6°38·5'W	X	8,13
Ratham Mill	W Susx	SU8106	50°51·1'	0°50·6'W	X	197
Rathburne Ho	Scot Bord	NT6857	55°48·6'	2°30·2'W	X	67
Rathe	Pemb	SM9819	51°50·2'	4°55·5'W	X	157,158
Rathen	Aberd	NK0060	57°38·1'	1°59·5'W	T	30
Rather Heath	Cumbr	SD4896	54°21·7'	2°47·6'W	X	97
Rather Standard	N Yks	SE0568	54°6·7'	1°55·0'W	X	98
Ratherton	Devon	SS3401	50°47·3'	4°20·9'W	X	190
Rathfinny Fm	E Susx	TQ4901	50°47·6'	0°7·2'E	FM	199
Rat Hill	Wilts	ST8678	51°30·3'	2°11·7'W	H	173
Rathillet	Fife	NO3620	56°22·3'	3°1·7'W	T	54,59
Rathillet Ho	Fife	NO3520	56°22·3'	3°2·7'W	X	54,59
Rathliesbeag	Highld	NN2185	56°55·6'	4°56·0'W	X	34,41
Rathmell	N Yks	SD8059	54°1·8'	2°17·9'W	T	103
Rathmell Beck	N Yks	SD8059	54°1·8'	2°17·9'W	W	103
Rathmell Common	N Yks	SD7661	54°2·9'	2°21·6'W	X	98
Rathmoss	Cumbr	SD2580	54°12·9'	3°8·6'W	X	96
Ratho	C of Edin	NT1370	55°55·2'	3°23·1'W	T	65
Ratho Byres	C of Edin	NT1471	55°55·7'	3°22·1'W	X	65
Ratho Hall	C of Edin	NT1371	55°55·7'	3°23·1'W	X	65
Ratho Mains	C of Edin	NT1370	55°55·2'	3°23·1'W	X	65
Ratho Station	C of Edin	NT1372	55°56·2'	3°23·1'W	T	65
Rath-soluis	Highld	NG3834	57°19·5'	6°20·7'W	X	32
Rath, The	Pemb	SM9818	51°49·7'	4°55·5'W	A	157,158
Rathvale	Cumbr	SD2580	54°12·9'	3°8·6'W	X	96
Rathven	Moray	NJ4465	57°40·5'	2°55·9'W	T	28
Rat Island	Devon	SS1443	51°9·6'	4°39·2'W	X	180
Rat Island	Essex	TM0517	51°49·1'	0°58·9'E	X	168
Rat Island	Pemb	SM8402	51°40·8'	5°7·1'W	X	157
Ratlake	Hants	SU4123	51°0·5'	1°24·5'W	T	185
Ratley	Warw	SP3847	52°7·4'	1°26·3'W	T	151
Ratlich	Aberd	NO2194	57°2·1'	3°17·6'W	X	36,44
Ratling	Kent	TR2453	51°14·1'	1°12·9'E	T	179,189
Ratling Court	Kent	TR2453	51°14·1'	1°12·9'E	X	179,189
Ratlinghope	Shrops	SO4096	52°33·8'	2°52·7'W	T	137
Ratlinghope Hill	Shrops	SO4097	52°34·3'	2°52·7'W	H	137
Ratlin Side	Scot Bord	NT2119	55°27·8'	3°14·5'W	H	79
Ratsborough Fm	Essex	TQ9598	51°39·0'	0°49·5'E	FM	168
Rats Castle	Kent	TQ6253	51°15·4'	0°19·7'E	X	188
Rats Hill	Oxon	SU3783	51°32·9'	1°27·6'W	X	174
Ratshill Bank	Glos	SO9917	51°51·3'	2°0·5'W	F	163
Ratsloe	Devon	SX9597	50°46·0'	3°29·0'W	T	192
Rattar	Highld	ND2673	58°38·6'	3°16·0'W	X	7,12
Rattar Ho	Highld	ND2573	58°38·6'	3°17·0'W	X	7,12
Rattar Moss	Highld	ND2772	58°38·1'	3°15·0'W	X	7,12
Rattenbury	Corn	SS2302	50°47·7'	4°30·3'W	X	190
Ratten Castle	Cumbr	NY3940	54°45·3'	2°56·4'W	X	85
Ratten Clough	Lancs	SD7938	53°50·5'	2°18·7'W	X	103
Ratten Clough Br	Lancs	SD9339	53°51·1'	2°6·0'W	X	103
Rattenraw	Northum	NY8595	55°15·2'	2°13·7'W	X	80
Ratten Row	Cumbr	NY3240	54°45·3'	3°3·0'W	T	85
Ratten Row	Cumbr	NY3949	54°50·2'	2°56·6'W	T	85
Ratten Row	Lancs	SD4241	53°52·0'	2°52·5'W	T	102
Ratten Row	Norf	TF5113	52°41·8'	0°14·5'E	T	131,143
Rattery	Devon	SX7461	50°26·4'	3°46·1'W	T	202
Rattla Corner	Suff	TM4466	52°14·5'	1°34·8'E	X	156
Rattle	Derby	SK3463	53°10·0'	1°29·1'W	X	119
Rattlebeck	Cumbr	NY3441	54°45·8'	3°1·1'W	X	85
Rattle Brook	Devon	SX5585	50°39·0'	4°2·7'W	W	191
Rattlebrook Hill	Devon	SX5585	50°39·0'	4°2·7'W	H	191
Rattle Hall	Kent	TR0150	51°13·0'	0°53·1'E	X	189
Rattle Hill	Heref	SO6132	51°59·3'	2°33·7'W	X	149
Rattlerow Hill	Suff	TM2375	52°19·9'	1°16·8'E	X	156
Rattlesden	Suff	TL9759	52°11·9'	0°53·4'E	T	155
Rattles, The	Devon	SS1343	51°9·6'	4°40·1'W	W	180
Ratton Syke	N Yks	SD7166	54°5·6'	2°26·2'W	W	98
Rattra	D & G	NX6049	54°49·2'	4°10·3'W	X	83
Rattray	Pth & Kin	NO1845	56°35·6'	3°19·7'W	T	53
Rattray Head	Aberd	NK1158	57°37·0'	1°48·5'W	X	30
Rattray Ho	Aberd	NK0957	57°35·9'	1°50·5'W	X	30
Rattycombe Fm	Devon	SX8781	50°37·3'	3°35·5'W	FM	192
Rauceby Grange	Lincs	TF0147	53°0·9'	0°29·3'W	X	130
Rauceby Sta	Lincs	TF0344	52°59·2'	0°27·5'W	X	130
Raughmere Fm	W Susx	SU8507	50°51·6'	0°47·1'W	FM	197
Raughton	Cumbr	NY3947	54°49·1'	2°56·5'W	T	85
Raughtonhead Hill	Cumbr	NY3746	54°48·5'	2°58·4'W	X	85
Raughton Head	Cumbr	NY3745	54°48·0'	2°58·4'W	T	85
Raunds	Northnts	SP9972	52°20·5'	0°32·4'W	T	141,153
Raunds Grange	Northnts	TL0172	52°20·4'	0°30·6'W	X	141,153
Ravelaw Fm	Scot Bord	NT8550	55°44·8'	2°13·9'W	FM	67,74
Raveley Wood Fm	Cambs	TL2578	52°23·4'	0°9·4'W	FM	142
Ravelrig Hill	C of Edin	NT1466	55°53·0'	3°22·1'W	H	65
Ravelston	C of Edin	NT2274	55°57·4'	3°14·5'W	T	66
Ravelstone	Ches	SJ5172	53°14·8'	2°43·7'W	X	117
Raven Beck	Cumbr	NY5741	54°46·0'	2°39·7'W	W	86
Ravenbridge Mill	Cumbr	NY6042	54°46·5'	2°36·9'W	X	86
Raven Burn	Scot Bord	NT6103	55°19·4'	2°36·4'W	W	80
Raven Crag	Cumbr	NY1904	54°25·7'	3°14·5'W	X	89,90

Raven Crag	Cumbr	NY2411	54°29·6'	3°10·0'W	X	89,90
Raven Crag	Cumbr	NY2806	54°26·9'	3°6·2'W	X	89,90
Raven Crag	Cumbr	NY3018	54°33·4'	3°4·5'W	X	90
Raven Crag	Cumbr	NY3908	54°28·1'	2°56·1'W	H	90
Raven Crag	Cumbr	NY4104	54°25·9'	2°54·2'W	X	90
Raven Crag	Cumbr	NY4111	54°29·7'	2°54·2'W	X	90
Raven Crag	Cumbr	NY4707	54°27·6'	2°48·6'W	X	90
Raven Crag	Cumbr	SD1396	54°21·4'	3°19·9'W	H	96
Ravencragg	Cumbr	NY4521	54°35·1'	2°50·6'W	X	90
Raven Crags	Cumbr	NY3630	54°39·9'	2°59·1'W	X	90
Raven Craig	D & G	NT1413	55°24·5'	3°21·1'W	H	78
Raven Currick Rigg	Northum	NY8657	54°54·7'	2°12·7'W	X	87
Ravendale Top	NE Lincs	TA2300	53°29·2'	0°8·4'W	X	113
Ravendean Burn	Scot Bord	NT1157	55°48·1'	3°24·8'W	W	65,72
Ravenfield	Roth	SK4895	53°27·2'	1°16·2'W	T	111
Ravenfield Common	Roth	SK4994	53°26·7'	1°15·3'W	X	111
Ravenfield Grange	Roth	SK4994	53°26·7'	1°15·3'W	X	111
Ravenfield Park	Roth	SK4895	53°27·2'	1°16·2'W	X	111
Ravengill Dod	S Lanak	NS9119	55°27·4'	3°43·0'W	H	71,78
Ravenglass	Cumbr	SD0896	54°21·3'	3°24·5'W	T	96
Ravenglass and Eskdale Railway	Cumbr	NY1600	54°23·6'	3°17·2'W	X	89
Ravenglass and Eskdale Railway	Cumbr	SD1198	54°22·4'	3°21·8'W	X	96
Raven Hall Hotel	N Yks	NZ9801	54°23·9'	0°29·0'W	X	94
Ravenhead	Ches	SJ5871	53°14·3'	2°37·4'W	X	117
Ravenhead	St Hel	SJ5094	53°26·7'	2°44·8'W	T	108
Raven Hill	Aberd	NJ4332	57°22·8'	2°56·4'W	H	37
Raven Hill	Donc	SE5303	53°31·5'	1°11·6'W	X	111
Raven Hill	Oxon	SP4130	51°58·3'	1°23·8'W	X	151
Raven Hill Fm	E Yorks	TA0366	54°5·0'	0°25·1'W	FM	101
Raven Hill Fm	N Yks	NZ4804	54°26·0'	1°15·2'W	FM	93
Raven Hill Fm	N Yks	NZ8612	54°30·0'	0°39·9'W	FM	94
Raven Hills	Durham	NY9627	54°38·5'	2°3·3'W	X	91,92
Ravenhills Green	Worcs	SO7454	52°11·3'	2°22·4'W	T	150
Raven Ho	Derby	SK3561	53°8·9'	1°28·2'W	X	119
Raven Howe	Cumbr	NY4514	54°31·3'	2°50·6'W	H	90
Raveningham	Norf	TM3996	52°30·8'	1°31·7'E	T	134
Raveningham Covert	Norf	TM3895	52°30·3'	1°30·8'E	F	134
Raven Meols Hills	Sefton	SD2705	53°32·4'	3°5·7'W	X	108
Raven Nest Crags	N Yks	SE0060	54°2·4'	1°59·6'W	X	98
Ravenoaks	Cumbr	NY4422	54°35·7'	2°51·6'W	X	90
Raven Ray	N Yks	SD6975	54°10·4'	2°28·1'W	X	98
Raven Rock	Highld	NH4660	57°36·5'	4°34·2'W	H	20
Raven Rock Fm	Lancs	SD9238	53°50·5'	2°6·9'W	FM	103
Raven Royd	Brad	SE0940	53°51·6'	1°51·4'W	X	104
Raven's Barrow	Cumbr	SD4187	54°16·8'	2°54·0'W	X	96,97
Ravensbay	Arg & Bt	NR8352	55°43·0'	5°26·9'W	X	62,69
Ravensbrook Fm	Wilts	SU0389	51°36·2'	1°57·0'W	FM	173
Ravensburgh Castle	Beds	TL0929	51°57·2'	0°24·4'W	X	166
Ravensburgh Castle (Fort)	Beds	TL0929	51°57·2'	0°24·4'W	A	166
Ravensby Ho	Angus	NO5334	56°30·0'	2°45·4'W	X	54
Ravenscar	N Yks	NZ9801	54°23·9'	0°29·0'W	T	94
Raven Scar	N Yks	SD7275	54°10·4'	2°25·3'W	X	98
Raven Scar	N Yks	SD9778	54°12·1'	2°2·3'W	X	98
Ravenscar Fm	Lancs	SD5463	54°3·9'	2°41·8'W	FM	97
Raven Scars	Lancs	SD5850	53°56·9'	2°38·0'W	X	102
Ravenscar Wood	Stock on T	NZ4410	54°29·2'	1°18·8'W	F	93
Ravenscleugh	D & G	NY1490	55°12·1'	3°20·6'W	X	78
Ravenscleugh	Northum	NY9391	55°13·0'	2°6·2'W	X	80
Ravenscliffe	Brad	SE1935	53°48·9'	1°42·3'W	T	104
Ravenscliffe	C of Stoke	SJ8452	53°4·1'	2°13·9'W	T	118
Ravenscliffe	Derby	SK1950	53°3·1'	1°42·6'W	X	119
Ravens Close	Lancs	SD6270	54°7·7'	2°34·5'W	X	97
Ravens Clough	Derby	SK1294	53°26·8'	1°48·7'W	X	110
Raven's Clough	Lancs	SD8337	53°50·0'	2°15·1'W	X	103
Raven's Clough	Staffs	SJ9263	53°10·1'	2°6·8'W	X	118
Ravens Cove	Devon	SX8236	50°13·0'	3°38·9'W	W	202
Raven's Crag	Northum	NU0436	55°37·3'	1°55·8'W	X	75
Ravenscraig	Aberd	NK0948	57°31·6'	1°50·5'W	X	30
Ravenscraig	Inverc	NS2575	55°56·4'	4°47·7'W	T	63
Raven's Craig Glen	N Ayr	NS2652	55°44·1'	4°45·8'W	X	63
Ravenscraig Steel Works	N Lanak	NS7756	55°47·2'	3°57·3'W	X	64
Ravenscroft	E Ayr	NS4614	55°24·0'	4°25·5'W	X	70
Ravenscroft Hall	Ches	SJ7067	53°12·2'	2°26·5'W	X	118
Ravensdale	I of M	SC3591	54°17·5'	4°31·7'W	X	95
Ravensdale	N Yks	SE5766	54°5·4'	1°7·3'W	X	100
Ravensdale Cottages	Derby	SK1773	53°15·5'	1°44·3'W	X	119
Ravensdale Fm	E Susx	TQ6132	51°4·1'	0°18·3'E	FM	188
Ravensdell Wood	Beds	TL0114	51°49·2'	0°31·7'W	F	166
Ravensden	Beds	TL0754	52°10·7'	0°25·7'W	T	153
Ravensden Ho	Beds	TL0655	52°11·2'	0°26·6'W	X	153
Raven Seat	Durham	NY9732	54°41·2'	2°2·4'W	X	92
Ravenseat	N Yks	NY8603	54°25·6'	2°12·5'W	T	91,92
Ravenseat Moor	N Yks	NY8504	54°26·1'	2°13·5'W	X	91,92
Ravensfield Fm	Essex	TL8832	51°57·5'	0°44·6'E	FM	168
Ravensfleet	Lincs	SK8096	53°27·5'	0°47·3'W	X	112
Raven's Fm	Cambs	TF3906	52°38·3'	0°3·7'E	FM	142,143
Ravens Fm	Essex	TL6122	51°52·6'	0°20·7'E	FM	167
Raven's Fm	Essex	TL8008	51°44·7'	0°36·8'E	FM	168
Raven's Fm	Norf	TF6705	52°37·3'	0°28·4'E	FM	143
Ravensgio	Shetld	HU5191	60°36·2'	1°3·6'W	X	1,2
Raven's Green	Essex	TM1024	51°52·7'	1°3·5'E	T	168,169
Raven's Hall	Cambs	TL6554	52°9·8'	0°25·1'E	X	154
Ravenshall	D & G	NX5252	54°50·7'	4°17·9'W	X	83
Ravenshall	Staffs	SJ7547	53°1·4'	2°22·0'W	T	118
Raven's Hall	Suff	TL9846	52°4·8'	0°53·8'E	X	155
Ravenshall Point	D & G	NX5252	54°50·7'	4°17·9'W	X	83
Ravenshaugh	Northum	NY8276	55°4·9'	2°16·5'W	X	86,87
Ravenshaw	Aberd	NO7571	56°50·0'	2°24·1'W	X	45
Ravenshaw	N Yks	SD7563	54°4·0'	2°22·5'W	X	98
Ravenshaw	N Yks	SD9849	53°56·5'	2°1·4'W	X	103
Ravenshaw	Renf	NS3871	55°54·5'	4°35·1'W	X	63
Ravenshaw Hall	Sol	SP1779	52°24·8'	1°44·6'W	A	139
Ravenshayes	Devon	SS9404	50°49·8'	3°29·9'W	X	192
Ravenshead	Notts	SK5554	53°5·1'	1°10·3'W	T	120
Ravens Heugh	Northum	NZ0198	55°16·8'	1°58·6'W	X	81
Ravensheugh Crags	Northum	NY8374	55°3·9'	2°15·5'W	X	86,87
Ravensheugh Sands	E Loth	NT6281	56°1·5'	2°36·1'W	X	67
Ravenshill	Glos	SO6924	51°55·1'	2°26·7'W	X	162

Ravenshill	Northum	NY6294	55°14·6'	2°35·4'W	X	80
Ravenshill Fm	Worcs	SO9056	52°12·4'	2°8·4'W	FM	150
Ravenshill Moor	Northum	NY6395	55°15·1'	2°34·5'W	H	80
Ravenshill Wood	Worcs	SO7353	52°10·7'	2°23·3'W	F	150
Ravens Holme	Lancs	SD8043	53°53·2'	2°17·8'W	X	103
Ravenshurst	Wilts	SU0388	51°35·7'	1°57·0'W	X	173
Ravenside	Cumbr	NY4249	54°50·2'	2°53·8'W	X	85
Ravenside	Northum	NZ0958	54°55·2'	1°51·1'W	X	88
Ravensike Rigg	Durham	NY8618	54°33·7'	2°12·6'W	X	91,92
Ravens Knowe	Northum	NT7806	55°21·1'	2°20·4'W	H	80
Ravenslie	E Ayr	NS3848	55°42·2'	4°34·2'W	X	63
Raven's Lodge	Cumbr	SD4685	54°15·7'	2°49·3'W	X	97
Ravensmoor	Ches	SJ6250	53°3·0'	2°33·6'W	T	118
Ravensnest	Derby	SK3461	53°8·9'	1°29·1'W	X	119
Raven's Nest	D & G	NY1694	55°14·2'	3°18·8'W	X	79
Ravens Nest	N Yks	SE1563	54°4·0'	1°45·8'W	X	99
Ravens' Nest	Somer	SS7740	51°9·0'	3°45·1'W	X	180
Ravensnest Wood	Monm	ST5099	51°41·5'	2°43·0'W	F	162
Ravensneuk Fm	Midlo	NT2258	55°48·8'	3°14·2'W	FM	66,73
Ravens Park	N Yks	NY9706	54°27·2'	2°2·4'W	X	92
Raven's Peak	N Yks	SE1455	53°59·7'	1°46·8'W	X	104
Raven's Point	I of Angl	SH2477	53°15·9'	4°37·9'W	X	114
Ravensroost Wood	Wilts	SU0288	51°35·7'	1°57·9'W	F	173
Ravensthorpe	Kirk	SE2220	53°40·8'	1°39·6'W	T	104
Ravensthorpe	Northnts	SP6670	52°19·7'	1°1·5'W	T	141
Ravensthorpe	Peterb	TF1600	52°35·0'	0°16·9'W	T	142
Ravensthorpe Manor	N Yks	SE4886	54°16·3'	1°15·4'W	X	100
Ravensthorpe Resr	Northnts	SP6770	52°19·7'	1°0·6'W	W	141
Ravensthorpe Sta	Kirk	SE2219	53°40·3'	1°39·6'W	X	110
Ravenstock Green Fm	Essex	TL5542	52°3·5'	0°16·1'E	FM	154
Ravenstone	Leic	SK4013	52°43·0'	1°24·1'W	T	129
Ravenstone	Mil Key	SP8450	52°8·7'	0°45·9'W	T	152
Ravenstone Castle	D & G	NX4046	54°47·3'	4°28·9'W	A	83
Ravenstonedale	Cumbr	NY7203	54°25·5'	2°25·5'W	T	91
Ravenstonedale Common	Cumbr	NY6801	54°24·5'	2°29·2'W	H	91
Ravenstonedale Moor	Cumbr	NY6806	54°27·1'	2°29·2'W	X	91
Ravenstone (Hotel)	Cumbr	NY2329	54°39·3'	3°11·2'W	X	89,90
Ravenstone Mains	D & G	NX4144	54°46·2'	4°27·9'W	X	83
Ravenstone Mill	Mil Key	SP8548	52°7·7'	0°45·1'W	X	152
Ravenstone Moor	N Yks	SE1064	54°4·6'	1°50·4'W	X	99
Ravenstone Moss	D & G	NX4042	54°45·1'	4°28·7'W	X	83
Ravenstone Road Copse	Northnts	SP8453	52°10·4'	0°45·9'W	F	152
Ravenstone Rocks	Oldham	SE0207	53°33·8'	1°57·8'W	X	110
Raven Stones	N Yks	SE1158	54°1·3'	1°49·5'W	X	104
Raven Stones	N Yks	SE7898	54°22·2'	0°47·5'W	X	94,100
Raven Stones Brow	Oldham	SE0304	53°32·2'	1°56·9'W	X	110
Ravenstor	Derby	SK1673	53°15·5'	1°45·2'W	X	119
Raven's Tor	Devon	SX7681	50°37·2'	3°44·8'W	H	191
Ravens Tor	Staffs	SK1353	53°4·7'	1°48·0'W	X	119
Ravenstown	Cumbr	SD3675	54°10·3'	2°58·4'W	T	96,97
Ravenstruther	S Lanak	NS9245	55°41·4'	3°42·6'W	X	72
Ravenswell Fm	Glos	SP0316	51°50·8'	1°57·0'W	FM	163
Ravenswick	N Yks	SE7087	54°16·7'	0°55·1'W	X	94,100
Ravenswood	Scot Bord	NT5734	55°36·1'	2°40·5'W	X	73,74
Ravenswood	W Susx	TQ3730	51°3·4'	0°2·3'W	X	187
Ravenswood Sch	Devon	SS9118	50°57·3'	3°32·7'W	X	181
Ravenswood Village Settlement	Wok	SU8264	51°22·4'	0°48·9'W	T	175,186
Ravensworth	N Yks	NZ1407	54°27·7'	1°46·6'W	T	92
Ravensworth Castle	Ghead	NZ2359	54°55·8'	1°38·0'W	A	88
Ravensworth Castle	N Yks	NZ1407	54°27·7'	1°46·6'W	A	92
Ravensworth Grange	Ghead	NZ2257	54°54·7'	1°39·0'W	X	88
Ravensworth Lodge	N Yks	NZ1409	54°28·8'	1°46·6'W	X	92
Ravensworth Park Fm	Ghead	NZ2358	54°55·2'	1°38·0'W	FM	88
Raven Thorn	Cumbr	SD7295	54°21·2'	2°25·4'W	X	98
Raventhorpe Fm	N Lincs	SE9308	53°33·9'	0°35·3'W	FM	112
Raventhorpe Village	E Yorks	TA0042	53°52·1'	0°28·3'W	A	106,107
Raventhorpe Village	N Lincs	SE9307	53°33·3'	0°35·4'W	A	112
Raventofts Hall	N Yks	SE2564	54°4·5'	1°36·7'W	X	99
Raventofts Ho	N Yks	SE2565	54°5·1'	1°36·7'W	X	99
Raven Tor	Cumbr	SD2798	54°22·6'	3°7·0'W	X	96,97
Raven Tor	Derby	SK2867	53°12·2'	1°34·4'W	X	119
Raven Winder	Cumbr	SD3574	54°9·7'	2°59·3'W	X	96,97
Raven Wood	E Susx	TQ4330	51°3·3'	0°2·8'E	F	187
Ravie Hill	Orkney	HY2525	59°6·6'	3°18·1'W	H	6
Ravine Head	Hants	SU8452	51°15·9'	0°47·4'W	X	186
Ravock	Durham	NY9514	54°31·5'	2°4·2'W	X	91,92
Ravock Castle	Durham	NY9514	54°31·5'	2°4·2'W	X	91,92
Raw	Northum	NT7602	55°18·9'	2°22·3'W	X	80
Raw	N Yks	NZ9305	54°26·2'	0°33·5'W	T	94
Rawbarrow Camp	Glos	SP1007	51°45·9'	1°50·9'W	A	163
Rawburn	Scot Bord	NT6756	55°48·0'	2°31·1'W	X	67,74
Rawburn Cott	Scot Bord	NT6755	55°47·5'	2°31·1'W	X	67,74
Rawcar	N Yks	SE3099	54°23·4'	1°31·9'W	X	99
Rawcliffe	E Yorks	SE6822	53°41·6'	0°57·8'W	T	105,106
Rawcliffe	York	SE5855	53°59·5'	1°6·5'W	T	105
Rawcliffe Bridge	E Yorks	SE7021	53°41·1'	0°56·0'W	T	105,106,112
Rawcliffe Fm	York	SE5755	53°59·5'	1°7·4'W	FM	105
Rawcliffe Hall	Lancs	SD4141	53°52·0'	2°53·4'W	X	102
Rawcliffe House Fm	N Yks	SE7991	54°18·7'	0°46·7'W	FM	94,100
Rawcliffe Howe	N Yks	SE7991	54°18·7'	0°46·7'W	A	94,100
Rawcliffe Moor	York	SE5856	54°0·0'	1°6·5'W	X	105
Rawcliffe Moors	E Yorks	SE7218	53°39·4'	0°54·2'W	X	112
Rawcliffe Moss	Lancs	SD4145	53°54·1'	2°53·5'W	X	102
Rawcliffe Moss	Lancs	SD4443	53°53·1'	2°50·7'W	X	102
Rawcliffe Pastures	E Yorks	SE7022	53°41·6'	0°56·0'W	X	105,106,112
Rawdales	E Yorks	TA0030	53°45·6'	0°28·6'W	X	106,107
Rawden Hill	Leeds	SE2944	53°53·7'	1°33·1'W	H	104
Rawdon	Leeds	SE2139	53°51·0'	1°40·4'W	T	104
Rawdon Carrs	Leeds	SE2138	53°50·5'	1°40·4'W	T	104
Rawer	D & G	NX0059	54°53·4'	5°6·7'W	X	82
Rawer	Pth & Kin	NN8350	56°37·9'	3°54·0'W	X	52
Rawes	Pth & Kin	NO3028	56°26·6'	3°7·7'W	X	53,59
Rawflat	Scot Bord	NT5824	55°30·7'	2°39·5'W	X	73,74
Raw Fm	Northum	NY9498	55°16·8'	2°5·2'W	FM	80
Raw Fm	S Lanak	NS8637	55°37·0'	3°48·2'W	FM	71,72
Rawfold	Cumbr	SD2089	54°17·7'	3°13·3'W	X	96
Rawfolds	Kirk	SE1924	53°43·0'	1°42·3'W	T	104
Rawfoot	Cumbr	NY5217	54°33·0'	2°44·1'W	X	90
Rawfoot	Northum	NY8684	55°9·3'	2°12·8'W	X	80

Raw Ghyll	Cumbr	SD4599	54°23·3'	2°50·4'W	X	97
Raw Green	Barns	SE2707	53°33·8'	1°35·1'W	T	110
Rawgreen	Northum	NY9256	54°54·2'	2°7·1'W	T	87
Rawhall	Norf	TF9418	52°43·7'	0°52·8'E	X	132
Raw Hall	Norf	TG0130	52°50·0'	0°59·4'E	X	133
Rawhall Wood	Norf	TF9418	52°43·7'	0°52·8'E	F	132
Rawhall Wood	Suff	TL9058	52°11·5'	0°47·2'E	F	155
Raw Head	Ches	SJ5054	53°5·1'	2°44·4'W	X	117
Raw Head	Cumbr	NY3006	54°26·9'	3°4·4'W	X	90
Rawhead	Cumbr	NY5216	54°32·5'	2°44·1'W	X	90
Rawhead Fm	Ches	SJ5154	53°5·1'	2°43·5'W	FM	117
Rawhead Fm	Cumbr	SD5691	54°19·0'	2°40·2'W	FM	97
Raw Hill	Northum	NT7601	55°18·4'	2°22·3'W	H	80
Rawhills Fm	S Lanak	NS8536	55°36·5'	3°49·1'W	FM	71,72
Raw Holdings	W Loth	NT0967	55°53·5'	3°26·9'W	X	65
Rawkins Brook	Derby	SK0499	53°29·5'	1°56·0'W	W	110
Rawland Howe	N Yks	NZ7509	54°28·5'	0°50·1'W	A	94
Rawlesbury Fm	Dorset	ST7604	50°50·3'	2°20·1'W	FM	194
Rawling Ho	Barns	SE2606	53°33·2'	1°36·0'W	X	110
Rawlings Fm	Bucks	SU9693	51°37·9'	0°36·4'W	FM	175,176
Rawlings Fm	Wilts	ST9374	51°28·1'	2°5·7'W	FM	173
Rawlins Fm	Hants	SU6057	51°18·8'	1°8·0'W	FM	175
Rawlinshaw	N Yks	SD7867	54°6·1'	2°19·8'W	X	98
Rawlinson Nab	Cumbr	SD3893	54°20·0'	2°56·8'W	X	96,97
Rawlinson's Intake	Cumbr	SD3790	54°18·4'	2°57·7'W	X	96,97
Rawlsbury Camp	Dorset	ST7605	50°50·9'	2°20·1'W	A	194
Rawmarsh	Roth	SK4396	53°27·8'	1°20·7'W	T	111
Rawney	Cumbr	NY5476	55°4·8'	2°42·8'W	X	86
Rawnsley	Staffs	SK0212	52°42·6'	1°57·8'W	T	128
Rawnsley Hills	Staffs	SK0113	52°43·1'	1°58·7'W	X	128
Rawn's Rocks	Devon	SS5948	51°13·1'	4°0·8'W	X	180
Raw Pike	Cumbr	NY3007	54°27·5'	3°4·4'W	X	90
Rawreth	Essex	TQ7893	51°36·7'	0°34·6'E	T	178
Rawreth Hall	Essex	TQ7992	51°36·1'	0°35·5'E	X	178
Rawreth Shot	Essex	TQ7793	51°36·7'	0°33·8'E	T	178
Rawridding	Cumbr	SD6988	54°17·4'	2°28·2'W	X	98
Raw Ridding	Lancs	SD6069	54°7·2'	2°36·3'W	X	97
Rawridge	Devon	ST2006	50°51·1'	3°7·8'W	T	192,193
Rawridge Fm	Devon	ST2006	50°51·1'	3°7·8'W	FM	192,193
Raws	E Ayr	NS4739	55°37·5'	4°25·4'W	X	70
Raws	Moray	NJ3337	57°25·4'	3°6·5'W	X	28
Raw Side	Northum	NY8584	55°9·3'	2°13·7'W	X	80
Rawson Green	Derby	SK3746	53°0·8'	1°26·5'W	T	119,128
Rawsons	Cumbr	SD4686	54°16·3'	2°49·3'W	X	97
Rawsons Syke	N Yks	SE6894	54°20·5'	0°56·8'W	X	94,100
Rawstone	Devon	SS7426	51°1·4'	3°47·4'W	X	180
Rawstone Moors	Devon	SS7426	51°1·4'	3°47·4'W	X	180
Rawtenstall	Lancs	SD8124	53°43·0'	2°16·9'W	T	103
Rawthey Br	Cumbr	SD7197	54°22·3'	2°26·4'W	X	98
Rawthey Gill	Cumbr	SD7493	54°20·2'	2°23·6'W	W	98
Rawthey Gill Foot	Cumbr	SD7494	54°20·7'	2°23·6'W	X	98
Rawthorpe	Kirk	SE1617	53°39·2'	1°45·1'W	T	110
Rawyards	N Lanak	NS7766	55°52·5'	3°57·5'W	T	64
Raxhayes Fm	Devon	SY1296	50°45·6'	3°14·5'W	FM	192,193
Raxton	Aberd	NJ8732	57°23·0'	2°12·5'W	X	30
Raxton Burn	Aberd	NJ8430	57°21·9'	2°15·5'W	W	29,30
Raxton Wood	Aberd	NJ8733	57°23·5'	2°12·5'W	F	30
Rayback Sike	Durham	NY8420	54°34·7'	2°14·4'W	W	91,92
Rayback Sike Rigg	Durham	NY8321	54°35·3'	2°15·4'W	X	91,92
Ray Bank Nursery	N Yks	SE1261	54°2·9'	1°48·6'W	F	99
Raybarrow Pool	Devon	SX6390	50°41·8'	3°56·0'W	W	191
Ray Br	N Yks	SD9354	53°59·2'	2°6·0'W	X	103
Raybrook Barn	Glos	SP0712	51°48·6'	1°53·5'W	X	163
Ray Burn	Northum	NT9421	55°29·2'	2°5·3'W	W	74,75
Ray Burn	Northum	NY9684	55°9·3'	2°3·3'W	W	81
Rayburn Lake	Northum	NZ1092	55°13·6'	1°50·1'W	W	81
Ray Creek	Essex	TM0913	51°46·8'	1°2·2'E	W	168,169
Raydale	N Yks	SD8983	54°14·8'	2°9·7'W	X	98
Raydale	N Yks	SD9085	54°15·9'	2°8·8'W	X	98
Raydale Beck	N Yks	SD8983	54°14·8'	2°9·7'W	W	98
Raydale Grange	N Yks	SD8984	54°15·3'	2°9·7'W	X	98
Raydale Ho	N Yks	SD9084	54°15·3'	2°8·8'W	X	98
Raydale Side	N Yks	NY9100	54°24·0'	2°7·9'W	X	91,92
Ray Demesne	Northum	NY9685	55°9·8'	2°3·3'W	X	81
Raydon	Suff	TM0538	52°0·4'	0°59·6'E	T	155
Raydon Common	Suff	TL9979	52°22·6'	0°55·8'E	X	144
Raydon Great Wood	Suff	TM0540	52°1·5'	0°59·7'E	F	155
Raydon Hall	Suff	TM4250	52°5·9'	1°32·4'E	X	156
Raydon Hall Fm	Suff	TM0539	52°0·9'	0°59·6'E	FM	155
Rayer's Hill	Glos	SO8730	51°58·3'	2°11·0'W	X	150
Ray Fell	Northum	NY9585	55°9·8'	2°4·3'W	X	81
Ray Fm	Bucks	SP7706	51°45·1'	0°52·7'W	FM	165
Ray Fm	Essex	TM2331	51°56·2'	1°15·0'E	FM	169
Raygarthfield	Cumbr	NY5745	54°48·1'	2°39·7'W	X	86
Raygill	Cumbr	SD7690	54°18·6'	2°21·7'W	X	98
Raygill	Durham	NZ0316	54°32·6'	1°56·8'W	X	92
Raygill	N Yks	SD9445	53°54·3'	2°5·1'W	T	103
Raygill Ho	N Yks	SD6771	54°8·3'	2°29·9'W	X	98
Raygill Ho	N Yks	SD9089	54°18·0'	2°8·8'W	X	98
Raygill Ho	N Yks	SE1170	54°7·8'	1°49·5'W	X	99
Raygill House Moor	N Yks	SE0869	54°7·3'	1°52·2'W	X	99
Raygill House Plantn	N Yks	SE1070	54°7·8'	1°50·4'W	F	99
Raygill House Wig Stones	N Yks	SE0969	54°7·2'	1°51·3'W	X	99
Ray Gill Laithe	N Yks	SD9362	54°3·5'	2°6·0'W	X	98
Raygill Moss	Lancs	SD8049	53°56·4'	2°17·9'W	X	103
Raygill Sike	N Yks	SD9089	54°18·0'	2°8·8'W	W	98
Ray Gut	Essex	TQ8584	51°31·7'	0°40·4'E	W	178
Rayham	Kent	TR0071	51°24·4'	0°52·9'E	X	178
Ray Head	Lancs	SD7852	53°58·1'	2°19·7'W	X	103
Rayheugh	Northum	NU1327	55°32·4'	1°47·2'W	X	75
Rayheugh Moor	Northum	NU1227	55°32·4'	1°48·2'W	X	75
Ray Island	Essex	TM0014	51°47·6'	0°54·4'E	X	168
Raylands	Essex	TL6414	51°48·3'	0°23·1'E	X	167
Raylands Fm	E Susx	TQ5407	50°50·7'	0°11·6'E	FM	199
Raylees	Northum	NY9291	55°13·0'	2°7·1'W	T	80
Raylees Burn	Northum	NY9191	55°13·0'	2°8·1'W	W	80
Raylees Common	Northum	NY9289	55°12·0'	2°7·1'W	X	80
Rayleigh	Essex	TQ8190	51°35·0'	0°37·1'E	T	178
Ray Lodge Fm	Surrey	TQ3744	51°11·0'	0°2·0'W	FM	187
Raymeadow Fm	Glos	SP0334	52°0·5'	1°57·0'W	FM	150

Rayment's Fm	Essex	TL6035	51°59·6'	0°20·2'E	FM	154
Ray Mill	Wilts	ST9269	51°25·4'	2°6·5'W	X	173
Raymonds	Bucks	SP9403	51°43·3'	0°38·0'W	X	165
Raymond's Fm	Somer	ST3333	51°5·8'	2°57·0'W	FM	182
Raymond's Hill	Devon	SY3296	50°45·8'	2°57·5'W	T	193
Rayne	Cumbr	NY6505	54°26·6'	2°32·0'W	X	91
Rayne	Essex	TL7222	51°52·4'	0°30·3'E	T	167
Rayne Hatch Fm	Essex	TL7827	51°55·0'	0°35·7'E	FM	167
Rayne Hatch Wood	Essex	TL7927	51°55·0'	0°36·6'E	F	167
Rayne Lodge	Essex	TL7423	51°52·9'	0°32·1'E	X	167
Rayner's Falgate	Norf	TL9496	52°31·9'	0°52·0'E	X	144
Rayners Lane	Harrow	TQ1287	51°34·5'	0°22·6'W	T	176
Raynes Park	Merton	TQ2368	51°24·1'	0°13·5'W	T	176
Raynham Park	Norf	TF8826	52°48·2'	0°47·7'E	X	132
Rayrigg Hall	Cumbr	SD4098	54°22·7'	2°55·0'W	A	96,97
Ray Sand	Essex	TR0499	51°39·4'	0°57·4'E	X	168
Ray Sand Channel		TM0701	51°40·4'	1°0·0'E	W	168
Rayseat	Cumbr	NY6807	54°27·7'	2°29·2'W	X	91
Rays Fm	Shrops	SO7183	52°26·9'	2°25·2'W	FM	138
Rayside	Cumbr	NY5315	54°31·9'	2°43·2'W	X	90
Rayside Plantn	N Yks	SD7571	54°8·3'	2°22·5'W	F	98
Rayslack Ho	N Yks	SE8970	54°7·3'	0°37·9'W	X	101
Rayson Hall	Cumbr	NY6334	54°42·2'	2°34·0'W	A	91
Raystede Centre for Animal Welfare	E Susx	TQ4814	50°54·6'	0°6·7'E	X	198
Rayton Angle	Notts	SK6180	53°19·0'	1°4·6'W	F	111,120
Rayton Fm	Notts	SK6179	53°18·5'	1°4·7'W	FM	120
Raywell Ho	E Yorks	SE9930	53°45·7'	0°29·5'W	X	106
Raywell Park	E Yorks	SE9830	53°45·7'	0°30·4'W	X	106
Ray Wood	N Yks	SE7270	54°7·5'	0°53·5'W	F	100
Raywood Fm	Kent	TQ9448	51°12·1'	0°47·0'E	FM	189
Razor's Fm	Hants	SU6556	51°18·2'	1°3·7'W	FM	175,186
R Bray	Devon	SS6930	51°3·5'	3°51·8'W	W	180
Rea	Glos	SO8115	51°50·2'	2°16·2'W	X	162
Reabhile Deas	N Eil	NF7664	57°33·3'	7°24·6'W	X	18
Rea Br	Shrops	SO6189	52°30·1'	2°34·1'W	X	138
Rea Brook	Shrops	SJ3404	52°38·0'	2°58·1'W	W	126
Reabrook	Shrops	SJ3604	52°38·0'	2°56·3'W	T	126
Rea Brook	Shrops	SJ4007	52°39·7'	2°52·8'W	W	126
Rea Brook	Shrops	SO6486	52°28·5'	2°31·4'W	W	138
Reach	Cambs	TL5666	52°16·4'	0°17·6'E	T	154
Reach	Devon	SS7727	51°2·0'	3°44·9'W	X	180
Reach Court Fm	Kent	TR3544	51°9·0'	1°22·0'E	FM	179
Reaches Marsh Fm	Lincs	TF2847	53°0·5'	0°5·1'W	FM	131
Reach Lode	Cambs	TL5567	52°17·0'	0°16·7'E	W	154
Rea Cliffe Fm	Staffs	SJ9459	53°7·9'	2°5·0'W	FM	118
Read	Lancs	SD7634	53°48·3'	2°21·5'W	T	103
Reader's Corner	Essex	TL7204	51°42·7'	0°29·8'E	T	167
Read Hall	Lancs	SD7534	53°48·3'	2°22·4'W	X	103
Reading	Read	SU7173	51°27·3'	0°58·3'W	T	175
Readingate Fm	E Yorks	SE7720	53°40·5'	0°49·6'W	FM	105,106
Readingate Fm	E Yorks	SE7720	53°40·5'	0°49·6'W	FM	105,106,112
Reading Green	Suff	TM2074	52°19·4'	1°14·1'E	X	156
Readings	Essex	TL6004	51°42·9'	0°19·4'E	X	167
Readings	Glos	SO6116	51°50·7'	2°33·6'W	T	162
Reading Service Area	W Berks	SU6769	51°25·2'	1°1·8'W	X	175
Reading Sewer	Kent	TQ8829	51°2·0'	0°41·3'E	W	189,199
Reading Street	Kent	TQ9230	51°2·5'	0°44·7'E	T	189
Reading Street	Kent	TR3869	51°22·4'	1°25·6'E	T	179
Readon Farm Ho	Hants	SU7449	51°14·4'	0°56·0'W	X	186
Read Park	Lancs	SD7534	53°48·3'	2°22·4'W	X	103
Read's Cavern	Somer	ST4658	51°19·3'	2°46·1'W	A	172,182
Read's Cross	Norf	TM3797	52°31·4'	1°30·0'E	X	134
Reads Fm	Devon	SX7248	50°19·3'	3°47·5'W	FM	202
Reads Hill Fm	Devon	ST2904	50°50·1'	3°0·1'W	FM	193
Read's Island	N Lincs	SE9622	53°41·4'	0°32·4'W	X	106,112
Readycon Dean Resr	Oldham	SD9812	53°36·5'	2°1·4'W	W	109
Readyfield Fm	Notts	SK7359	53°7·6'	0°54·1'W	FM	120
Readymoney	Corn	SX1151	50°20·0'	4°39·0'W	T	200,204
Ready Token	Glos	SP1004	51°44·3'	1°50·9'W	T	163
Reafirth	Shetld	HU5191	60°36·2'	1°3·6'W	X	1,2
Rea Fm	Shrops	SJ5612	52°42·5'	2°38·7'W	FM	126
Reagam	N Eil	NF8644	57°22·9'	7°13·1'W	X	22
Reagarth Fm	N Yks	SE6284	54°15·1'	1°2·5'W	FM	100
Reagill	Cumbr	NY6017	54°33·0'	2°36·7'W	T	91
Rea Gill	Cumbr	NY8807	54°27·7'	2°10·7'W	W	91,92
Reagill Grange	Cumbr	NY6016	54°32·5'	2°36·7'W	A	91
Reahope Burn	Durham	NY9741	54°46·1'	2°2·4'W	W	87
Reahope Moor	Durham	NY9640	54°45·5'	2°3·3'W	X	87
Reamy Rigg	Cumbr	NY5683	55°8·6'	2°41·0'W	X	80
Reaphay	Somer	ST1720	50°58·6'	3°10·6'W	X	181,193
Reaps	Derby	SK0697	53°28·4'	1°54·2'W	X	110
Reaps	Lancs	SD6630	53°46·2'	2°30·5'W	X	103
Reaps Cross	Cald	SD9430	53°46·2'	2°5·0'W	A	103
Reaps Moor	Staffs	SK0861	53°9·0'	1°52·4'W	X	119
Reaps Moss	Lancs	SD8922	53°41·9'	2°9·6'W	X	103
Rearquhar	Highld	NH7492	57°54·2'	4°7·1'W	T	21
Rearsby	Leic	SK6514	52°43·4'	1°1·9'W	T	129
Rearsby House Fm	Leic	SK6414	52°43·4'	1°2·7'W	FM	129
Rear Wood	Kent	TQ6437	51°6·8'	0°21·0'E	F	188
Reasby	Lincs	TF0679	53°18·1'	0°24·2'W	T	121
Reasby Grange	Lincs	TF0579	53°18·1'	0°25·1'W	X	121
Rease Heath	Ches	SJ6454	53°5·2'	2°31·8'W	T	118
Reaside	Shrops	SO6778	52°24·2'	2°28·7'W	X	138
Reaside Manor Fm	Shrops	SO6774	52°22·0'	2°28·7'W	FM	138
Reason Hill	Kent	TQ7350	51°13·6'	0°29·1'E	X	188
Reaster	Highld	ND2565	58°34·3'	3°16·9'W	X	11,12
Reaster Ho	Highld	ND2664	58°33·7'	3°15·8'W	X	11,12
Reathwaite	Cumbr	NY3044	54°47·4'	3°4·9'W	X	85
Reaulay	Highld	NG7058	57°33·5'	5°50·2'W	X	24
Reaveley	Northum	NU0217	55°27·1'	1°57·7'W	X	81
Reaveley Burn	Northum	NU0217	55°27·1'	1°57·7'W	W	81
Reaveley Greens	Northum	NU0118	55°27·6'	1°58·6'W	X	81
Reaveleyhill	Northum	NU0017	55°27·1'	1°59·6'W	X	81
Reaveley Hill	Northum	NU0018	55°27·6'	1°59·6'W	H	81
Reaverack	Shetld	HU1065	60°22·4'	1°48·6'W	X	3
Reaver Crag	Northum	NY9375	55°4·4'	2°6·1'W	X	87
Reawick	Shetld	HU3244	60°11·0'	1°24·9'W	T	4
Rea Wick	Shetld	HU3344	60°11·0'	1°23·8'W	W	4
Reawick Ho	Shetld	HU3244	60°11·0'	1°24·9'W	X	4

Reawla	Corn	SW6036	50°10·8'	5°21·3'W	T	203
Reay	Highld	NC9564	58°33·4'	3°47·8'W	T	11
Reay Burn	Highld	NC9662	58°32·3'	3°46·7'W	W	11
Reay Forest	Highld	NC2939	58°18·6'	4°54·7'W	X	15
Reay Forest	Highld	NC3040	58°19·2'	4°53·7'W	X	9
Reaygarth	Northum	NY6264	54°58·4'	2°35·2'W	X	86
Rebeg	Highld	NH5642	57°27·0'	4°23·5'W	X	26
Rebel Hill	Northum	NY8459	54°55·8'	2°14·6'W	H	86,87
Rebellion Knoll	Derby	SK1881	53°19·8'	1°43·4'W	X	110
Rechullin	Highld	NG8557	57°33·4'	5°35·2'W	T	24
Reckerby Fm	Lincs	TF3932	52°52·3'	0°4·3'E	FM	131
Reckford Fm	Suff	TM4367	52°15·1'	1°34·0'E	FM	156
Reckoning House Fm	Notts	SK4946	53°0·8'	1°15·8'W	FM	129
Recletich	Moray	NJ2834	57°23·7'	3°11·4'W	X	28
Rectory Fm	Beds	SP9641	52°3·8'	0°35·6'W	FM	153
Rectory Fm	Beds	TL0956	52°11·7'	0°23·9'W	FM	153
Rectory Fm	Beds	TL1135	52°0·4'	0°22·6'W	FM	153
Rectory Fm	Beds	TL1755	52°11·1'	0°16·9'W	FM	153
Rectory Fm	Bucks	SP6325	51°55·4'	1°4·6'W	FM	164,165
Rectory Fm	Bucks	SP7126	51°55·9'	0°57·6'W	FM	165
Rectory Fm	Bucks	SP8018	51°51·5'	0°49·9'W	FM	165
Rectory Fm	Bucks	SP8511	51°47·7'	0°45·7'W	FM	165
Rectory Fm	Bucks	SP8630	51°57·9'	0°44·5'W	FM	152,165
Rectory Fm	Bucks	SP8930	51°57·9'	0°41·9'W	FM	152,165
Rectory Fm	Cambs	TL1193	52°31·6'	0°21·4'W	FM	142
Rectory Fm	Cambs	TL1957	52°12·1'	0°15·1'W	FM	153
Rectory Fm	Cambs	TL1971	52°19·7'	0°14·8'W	FM	153
Rectory Fm	Cambs	TL2779	52°23·9'	0°7·6'W	FM	142
Rectory Fm	Cambs	TL3551	52°8·7'	0°1·2'W	FM	154
Rectory Fm	Cambs	TL3762	52°14·6'	0°0·8'E	FM	154
Rectory Fm	Cambs	TL4140	52°2·7'	0°3·8'E	FM	154
Rectory Fm	Cambs	TL4252	52°9·1'	0°4·9'E	FM	154
Rectory Fm	Cambs	TL4650	52°8·0'	0°8·4'E	FM	154
Rectory Fm	Cambs	TL4665	52°16·1'	0°8·8'E	FM	154
Rectory Fm	Cambs	TL4742	52°3·6'	0°9·1'E	FM	154
Rectory Fm	Cambs	TL5054	52°10·1'	0°12·0'E	FM	154
Rectory Fm	Cambs	TL5751	52°8·3'	0°18·1'E	FM	154
Rectory Fm	Derby	SK4027	52°50·6'	1°24·0'W	FM	129
Rectory Fm	Devon	SX4398	50°45·9'	4°13·2'W	FM	190
Rectory Fm	Enf	TQ3098	51°40·2'	0°6·8'W	FM	166,176,177
Rectory Fm	Essex	TL5142	52°3·6'	0°12·6'E	FM	154
Rectory Fm	Essex	TL8137	52°0·3'	0°38·6'E	FM	155
Rectory Fm	E Yorks	SE7054	53°58·9'	0°55·5'W	FM	105,106
Rectory Fm	E Yorks	TA0047	53°54·8'	0°28·2'W	FM	106,107
Rectory Fm	Glos	SO9005	51°44·9'	2°8·3'W	FM	163
Rectory Fm	Glos	SO9708	51°46·5'	2°2·2'W	FM	163
Rectory Fm	Herts	SP9814	51°49·3'	0°43·0'W	FM	165
Rectory Fm	Herts	TL1431	51°58·2'	0°20·0'W	FM	166
Rectory Fm	Kent	TQ8051	51°14·0'	0°35·1'E	FM	188
Rectory Fm	Lincs	SK8852	53°3·7'	0°40·8'W	FM	121
Rectory Fm	Lincs	SK8937	52°55·6'	0°40·2'W	FM	130
Rectory Fm	Lincs	TF0589	53°23·5'	0°24·9'W	FM	112,121
Rectory Fm	Lincs	TF1110	52°40·8'	0°21·1'W	FM	130,142
Rectory Fm	Lincs	TF1712	52°41·8'	0°15·7'W	FM	130,142
Rectory Fm	Lincs	TF1896	53°27·1'	0°13·0'W	FM	113
Rectory Fm	Lincs	TF1992	53°24·9'	0°12·2'W	FM	113
Rectory Fm	Lincs	TF2848	53°1·1'	0°5·1'W	FM	131
Rectory Fm	Mil Key	SP8438	52°2·3'	0°46·1'W	FM	152
Rectory Fm	Mil Key	SP8748	52°7·6'	0°43·3'W	FM	152
Rectory Fm	Mil Key	SP8949	52°8·2'	0°41·6'W	FM	152
Rectory Fm	Mil Key	SP9144	52°5·4'	0°39·9'W	FM	152
Rectory Fm	Northnts	SP4948	52°7·9'	1°16·7'W	FM	151
Rectory Fm	Northnts	SP5042	52°4·7'	1°15·8'W	FM	151
Rectory Fm	Northnts	SP6985	52°27·7'	0°58·7'W	FM	141
Rectory Fm	Northnts	SP7052	52°9·9'	0°58·2'W	FM	152
Rectory Fm	Northnts	SP7152	52°9·9'	0°57·3'W	FM	152
Rectory Fm	Northnts	SP7454	52°11·0'	0°54·7'W	FM	152
Rectory Fm	Northnts	SP7548	52°7·7'	0°53·9'W	FM	152
Rectory Fm	Northnts	SP7656	52°12·1'	0°52·9'W	FM	152
Rectory Fm	Northnts	SP7842	52°4·5'	0°51·3'W	FM	152
Rectory Fm	Northnts	SP7871	52°20·1'	0°50·9'W	FM	141
Rectory Fm	Northnts	SP8068	52°18·5'	0°49·2'W	FM	152
Rectory Fm	Northnts	SP8272	52°20·6'	0°47·4'W	FM	141
Rectory Fm	Northnts	SP8383	52°26·6'	0°46·3'W	FM	141
Rectory Fm	Northnts	SP8471	52°20·1'	0°45·6'W	FM	141
Rectory Fm	Northnts	SP9575	52°22·1'	0°35·9'W	FM	141
Rectory Fm	Northnts	SP9766	52°17·2'	0°34·3'W	FM	153
Rectory Fm	Northnts	SP9980	52°24·8'	0°32·3'W	FM	141
Rectory Fm	Northnts	TL0886	52°27·9'	0°24·2'W	FM	142
Rectory Fm	Northnts	TL0989	52°29·5'	0°23·3'W	FM	142
Rectory Fm	Northnts	TL1184	52°26·8'	0°21·6'W	FM	142
Rectory Fm	N Yks	SE9175	54°10·0'	0°35·9'W	FM	101
Rectory Fm	Oxon	SP2402	51°43·2'	1°38·8'W	FM	163
Rectory Fm	Oxon	SP3541	52°4·2'	1°29·0'W	FM	151
Rectory Fm	Oxon	SU3598	51°41·0'	1°29·2'W	FM	164
Rectory Fm	Somer	ST7230	51°4·4'	2°23·6'W	FM	183
Rectory Fm	Staffs	SK0323	52°48·5'	1°56·9'W	FM	128
Rectory Fm	Suff	TL6871	52°18·9'	0°28·3'E	FM	154
Rectory Fm	Suff	TL6873	52°20·0'	0°28·3'E	FM	154
Rectory Fm	Suff	TM0652	52°7·9'	1°1·0'E	FM	155
Rectory Fm	Suff	TM2471	52°17·7'	1°17·5'E	FM	156
Rectory Fm	Suff	TM2661	52°12·3'	1°18·9'E	FM	156
Rectory Fm	Warw	SP2533	51°59·9'	1°37·8'W	FM	151
Rectory Fm	Warw	SP2945	52°6·4'	1°34·2'W	FM	151
Rectory Fm	Warw	SP4363	52°16·0'	1°21·8'W	FM	151
Rectory Fm	Wilts	SU1826	51°2·2'	1°44·2'W	FM	184
Rectory Fm	Wok	SU7863	51°21·9'	0°52·4'W	FM	175,186
Rectory Fm	Worcs	SO8335	52°1·0'	2°14·5'W	FM	150
Rectory Fm	Worcs	SO9238	52°2·7'	2°6·6'W	FM	150
Rectory Fm	Worcs	SO9656	52°12·4'	2°3·1'W	FM	150
Rectory Park	Kent	TQ7038	51°7·2'	0°26·1'E	X	188
Rectory, The	Cumbr	NY2852	54°51·7'	3°6·9'W	X	85
Rectory, The	Lincs	TF1310	52°40·8'	0°19·3'W	T	130,142
Rectory Wood	Devon	SX7390	50°42·0'	3°47·5'W	F	191
Reculver	Kent	TR2269	51°22·8'	1°11·8'E	T	179
Red Abbey	Shrops	SJ3714	52°43·4'	2°55·6'W	X	126
Redacre Hall Fm	Ches	SJ9481	53°19·8'	2°5·0'W	FM	109
Red-a-ven Brook	Devon	SX5791	50°42·3'	4°1·1'W	W	191
Redavie	Moray	NJ1356	57°35·4'	3°26·9'W	X	28
Redayre	Shetld	HU3245	60°11·6'	1°24·9'W	X	4

Red Ball	Devon	ST0817	50°56·9'	3°18·2'W	T	181
Red Bank	Cumbr	NY3305	54°26·4'	3°1·6'W	X	90
Red Bank	Cumbr	SD5296	54°21·7'	2°43·9'W	X	97
Redbank	D & G	NX9457	54°54·0'	3°38·8'W	X	84
Red Bank	St Hel	SJ5994	53°26·7'	2°36·6'W	X	108
Red Bank Fm	Lancs	SD4768	54°6·6'	2°48·2'W	FM	97
Red Bank Fm	N Yks	SE1392	54°19·6'	1°47·6'W	FM	99
Redbank Fm	Staffs	SK1321	52°47·4'	1°48·0'W	FM	128
Redbank Hill	D & G	NX9358	54°54·6'	3°39·7'W	H	84
Redbanks	Orkney	HY5210	58°58·7'	2°49·6'W	X	6
Red Barn	Monm	SO4906	51°45·3'	2°43·9'W	X	162
Red Barn	Oxon	SU4488	51°35·6'	1°21·5'W	X	174
Red Barn	Swin	SU1379	51°30·8'	1°48·4'W	X	173
Red Barn Fm	Bucks	SU8290	51°36·4'	0°48·6'W	FM	175
Red Barn Fm	Bucks	SU9593	51°37·9'	0°37·2'W	FM	175,176
Red Barn Fm	Cambs	TL5472	52°19·7'	0°16·0'E	FM	154
Red Barn Fm	Cambs	TL5487	52°27·8'	0°16·4'E	FM	143
Red Barn Fm	E Susx	TQ4714	50°54·6'	0°5·8'E	FM	198
Red Barn Fm	Hants	SU6438	51°8·5'	1°4·7'W	FM	185
Red Barn Fm	Lincs	TF0477	53°17·0'	0°26·0'W	FM	121
Red Barn Fm	Norf	TF7333	52°52·2'	0°34·6'E	FM	132
Red Barn Fm	Norf	TL9699	52°33·4'	0°53·9'E	FM	144
Red Barn Fm	Norf	TM2181	52°23·2'	1°15·3'E	FM	156
Red Barn Fm	Somer	ST7547	51°13·5'	2°21·1'W	FM	183
Red Barn Fm	Suff	TM3471	52°17·5'	1°26·3'E	FM	156
Red Barns	Durham	NZ2339	54°45·0'	1°38·1'W	X	93
Redbarns	Northum	NU1834	55°36·2'	1°42·4'W	X	75
Red Barns Fm	Durham	NZ1931	54°40·7'	1°41·9'W	FM	92
Red Barns Fm	S Tyne	NZ3162	54°57·3'	1°30·5'W	FM	88
Red Barn Wood	N Yks	NZ9007	54°27·3'	0°36·3'W	F	94
Red Beard's Well	Aberd	NO7690	57°0·3'	2°23·3'W	X	38,45
Red Beck	Cald	SE1224	53°43·0'	1°48·7'W	W	104
Red Beck	Cumbr	NY6267	55°0·0'	2°35·2'W	W	86
Red Beck Gill	N Yks	SE1285	54°15·9'	1°48·5'W	W	99
Redberth	Pemb	SM9010	51°45·2'	5°2·2'W	X	157,158
Redberth	Pemb	SN0804	51°42·4'	4°46·3'W	T	158
Redbog	Aberd	NJ9054	57°34·8'	2°9·6'W	X	30
Red Bog	S Lanak	NS7038	55°37·3'	4°3·4'W	X	71
Redbog Fm	Aberd	NK0442	57°28·4'	1°55·5'W	FM	30
Redbog Fm	Moray	NJ2857	57°36·1'	3°11·8'W	FM	28
Redborough	Powys	SO2349	52°8·3'	3°7·1'W	X	148
Redborough Fm	Bucks	SP9122	51°53·6'	0°40·3'W	FM	165
Redborough Fm	Kent	TQ9553	51°14·8'	0°48·0'E	FM	189
Redbourn	Herts	TL1012	51°48·0'	0°23·9'W	T	166
Redbournbury	Herts	TL1210	51°46·9'	0°22·2'W	T	166
Redbourne	N Lincs	SK9799	53°29·0'	0°31·9'W	T	112
Redbourne Grange Fm	N Lincs	SK9697	53°27·9'	0°32·8'W	FM	112
Redbourne Hayes	N Lincs	SE9900	53°29·5'	0°30·1'W	X	112
Red Boy, The	N Eil	NL5685	56°50·0'	7°38·0'W	X	31
Red Br	Lancs	SD4618	53°39·6'	2°48·6'W	X	108
Red Br	Lincs	TF1664	53°9·9'	0°15·5'W	X	121
Red Br	Norf	TL9992	52°29·6'	0°56·3'E	X	144
Red Br	Suff	TM1777	52°21·1'	1°11·6'E	X	156
Redbrae	D & G	NX3855	54°52·1'	4°31·0'W	X	83
Redbrae	Falk	NS8773	55°56·5'	3°48·1'W	X	65
Redbraes	Orkney	HY2908	58°57·5'	3°13·6'W	X	6,7
Redbrick Ho (PH)	Notts	SK5665	53°11·0'	1°9·3'W	X	120
Redbridge	C of Soton	SU3713	50°55·1'	1°28·0'W	T	196
Redbridge	Dorset	SY7888	50°41·7'	2°18·3'W	T	194
Red Bridge	Lancs	SD4775	54°10·3'	2°48·3'W	T	97
Redbridge	Redbr	TQ4288	51°34·6'	0°3·4'E	T	177
Redbridge Fm	E Susx	TQ5028	51°2·1'	0°8·8'E	FM	188,199
Red Bridge Sewer	N Yks	SE7474	54°9·6'	0°51·6'W	W	100
Red Brook	Ches	SJ7574	53°16·0'	2°22·1'W	W	118
Red Brook	Ches	SJ9081	53°19·8'	2°8·6'W	W	109
Red Brook	Derby	SK0788	53°23·6'	1°53·3'W	W	110
Red Brook	Devon	SX6662	50°26·8'	3°52·9'W	W	202
Redbrook	Glos	SO5310	51°47·4'	2°40·5'W	T	162
Redbrook	Hants	SU1513	50°55·2'	1°46·8'W	X	195
Red Brook	Traf	SJ7090	53°24·6'	2°26·7'W	W	109
Redbrook	Wrex	SJ5040	52°57·5'	2°44·3'W	T	117
Redbrook Clough	Kirk	SE0211	53°36·0'	1°57·8'W	X	110
Redbrook Fm	Barns	SE3207	53°33·8'	1°30·6'W	FM	110,111
Redbrook Fm	Ches	SJ9180	53°19·3'	2°7·7'W	FM	109
Redbrook Resr	Kirk	SE0209	53°34·9'	1°57·8'W	W	110
Red Brow	Halton	SJ5781	53°19·7'	2°38·3'W	X	108
Redbrow Plantation	N Yks	SE9490	54°18·1'	0°32·9'W	F	94,101
Redbrow Plantation	N Yks	SE9590	54°18·0'	0°32·0'W	F	94,101
Red Bull	Ches	SJ8355	53°5·8'	2°14·8'W	T	118
Red Bull	Staffs	SJ7035	52°54·9'	2°26·4'W	T	127
Redburn	Aberd	NJ4202	57°6·6'	2°57·0'W	X	37
Redburn	Aberd	NJ8254	57°34·8'	2°17·6'W	X	29,30
Redburn	Aberd	NJ8617	57°14·9'	2°13·5'W	X	38
Redburn	Durham	NY9243	54°47·2'	2°7·0'W	X	87
Red Burn	E Ayr	NS4406	55°19·7'	4°27·1'W	W	70,77
Red Burn	Highld	NG3150	57°27·9'	6°28·7'W	W	23
Red Burn	Highld	NH5205	57°7·0'	4°26·2'W	W	35
Redburn	Highld	NH5767	57°40·5'	4°23·4'W	X	21
Redburn	Highld	NH7283	57°49·4'	4°8·8'W	X	21
Redburn	Highld	NH9447	57°30·3'	3°45·7'W	X	27
Red Burn	Highld	NN5999	57°3·9'	4°19·1'W	W	35
Red Burn	Moray	NJ3057	57°36·1'	3°9·8'W	W	28
Red Burn	N Ayr	NS2468	55°52·6'	4°48·4'W	W	63
Red Burn	N Ayr	NS3340	55°37·8'	4°38·7'W	W	70
Red Burn	N Lanak	NS7775	55°57·4'	3°57·8'W	W	64
Red Burn	Northum	NU1322	55°29·7'	1°47·2'W	W	75
Redburn	Northum	NY7764	54°58·5'	2°21·1'W	T	86,87
Red Burn	Northum	NY8574	55°3·9'	2°13·7'W	W	87
Red Burn	Shetld	HU3821	59°58·6'	1°18·7'W	W	4
Red Burn	Shetld	HU3924	60°0·2'	1°17·5'W	W	4
Redburn Common	Durham	NY9044	54°47·7'	2°8·9'W	X	87
Redburn Edge	Durham	NY8945	54°48·2'	2°9·8'W	X	87
Red Burrow Fm	Leic	SK3613	52°43·0'	1°27·6'W	FM	128
Redbury Fm	Essex	TM0428	51°55·0'	0°58·4'E	FM	168
Red Cairn	Aberd	NO6394	57°2·4'	2°36·1'W	X	37,45
Red Cap	E Yorks	SE7141	53°51·9'	0°54·8'W	X	105,106
Redcap Fm	Lincs	TF2166	53°10·9'	0°11·0'W	FM	122
Redcap Fm	Suff	TM4373	52°18·3'	1°34·3'E	FM	156
Redcaps	Beds	TL0132	51°58·9'	0°31·4'W	X	166
Redcar	Brad	SE0342	53°52·7'	1°56·8'W	X	104

Redcar	N Lincs	TA0002	53°30·5′	0°29·1′W	X	112
Redcar	Red & Cl	NZ6124	54°36·7′	1°2·9′W	T	94
Redcar Ho	Durham	NZ3729	54°39·5′	1°25·2′W	X	93
Redcar Ho	N Yks	SE5876	54°10·8′	1°6·3′W	X	100
Red Carle	Cumbr	NY6630	54°40·1′	2°31·2′W	X	91
Redcar Rocks	Red & Cl	NZ6125	54°37·2′	1°2·9′W	X	94
Redcarr Plantn	N Yks	SE8577	54°11·1′	0°41·4′W	F	100
Redcar Sands	Red & Cl	NZ6125	54°37·2′	1°2·9′W	X	94
Redcar Tarn	Brad	SE0342	53°52·7′	1°56·8′W	W	104
Red Castle	Angus	NO6850	56°38·7′	2°30·9′W	A	54
Redcastle	Angus	NO6850	56°38·7′	2°30·9′W	X	54
Redcastle	D & G	NX8165	54°58·2′	3°51·1′W	X	84
Red Castle	Heref	SO4648	52°7·9′	2°46·9′W	X	148,149
Redcastle	Highld	NH5849	57°30·8′	4°21·8′W	X	26
Red Castle	Shrops	SJ5729	52°51·6′	2°37·9′W	A	126
Red Castle Fm	Suff	TL9069	52°17·4′	0°47·6′E	FM	155
Red Chamber	Swan	SS4286	51°33·3′	4°16·4′W	X	159
Red Cleave	Devon	SS6148	51°13·1′	3°59·0′W	X	180
Redcleuch Edge	Scot Bord	NT3410	55°23·0′	3°2·1′W	H	79
Red Cliff	I of W	SZ6285	50°39·9′	1°7·0′W	X	196
Red Cliff	Pemb	SM7806	51°42·8′	5°12·4′W	X	157
Redcliff Castle	Corn	SW8469	50°29·1′	5°2·3′W	A	200
Redcliff Channel	E Yorks	SE9724	53°42·4′	0°31·4′W	W	106,112
Redcliffe Bay	N Som	ST4475	51°28·5′	2°48·0′W	T	171,172
Redcliffe Fm	Dorset	SY9386	50°40·6′	2°5·6′W	FM	195
Redcliffe Fm	N Yks	TA0783	54°14·1′	0°21·1′W	FM	101
Redcliffe Middle Sand	E Yorks	SE9723	53°41·9′	0°31·4′W	X	106,112
Redcliff Point	Dorset	SY7181	50°37·9′	2°24·2′W	X	194
Redcliff Sand	E Yorks	SE9925	53°43·0′	0°29·6′W	X	106
Redcloak	Aberd	NO8587	56°58·7′	2°14·4′W	X	45
Red Clough	Derby	SK0890	53°24·6′	1°52·4′W	X	110
Redcoats	Herts	TL2026	51°55·4′	0°14·9′W	X	166
Redcoll	E Loth	NT4475	55°58·1′	2°53·4′W	X	66
Red Copse	W Susx	SU9110	50°53·2′	0°42·0′W	F	197
Red Court	Surrey	SU9032	51°5·0′	0°42·5′W	X	186
Red Cove	Arg & Bt	NR6842	55°37·2′	5°40·6′W	X	62
Red Cow Fm	Herts	TL0517	51°50·7′	0°28·1′W	FM	166
Red Crag	Cumbr	NY4515	54°31·9′	2°50·6′W	H	90
Red Craig	Aberd	NJ3114	57°13·0′	3°8·1′W	X	37
Red Craig	Aberd	NJ4526	57°19·5′	2°54·3′W	X	37
Red Craig	Aberd	NO4290	57°0·1′	2°56·8′W	H	44
Red Craig	Aberd	NO4995	57°2·9′	2°50·0′W	H	37,44
Red Craig	Angus	NO2976	56°52·5′	3°9·4′W	X	44
Redcraig	S Ayr	NS4727	55°31·0′	4°25·0′W	X	70
Redcraigs	Aberd	NJ9201	57°6·2′	2°7·5′W	X	38
Redcroft	D & G	NX7170	55°0·7′	4°0·6′W	X	77,84
Red Cross	Devon	SS9602	50°48·7′	3°28·2′W	X	192
Redcross	Worcs	SO8873	52°21·5′	2°10·2′W	T	139
Red Cross Fm	Cambs	TL2393	52°31·5′	0°10·8′W	FM	142
Redcross Fm	Somer	SS9430	51°3·8′	3°30·4′W	FM	181
Redcross Plantn	Norf	TL8993	52°30·4′	0°47·5′E	F	144
Reddafold Water	Devon	SX7878	50°35·6′	3°43·0′W	X	191
Red Daren	Heref	SO2930	51°58·1′	3°1·6′W	X	161
Reddaway	Devon	SX6295	50°44·5′	3°57·0′W	X	191
Red Deer Fm	Devon	SS8923	51°0·0′	3°34·5′W	FM	181
Redden	Angus	NO6055	56°41·4′	2°38·7′W	X	54
Redden	Scot Bord	NT7737	55°37·8′	2°21·5′W	X	74
Redden Burn	Scot Bord	NT7736	55°37·3′	2°21·5′W	W	74
Red Dial	Cumbr	NY2545	54°47·9′	3°9·6′W	T	85
Reddicap Heath	Birm	SP1395	52°33·4′	1°48·1′W	T	139
Red Dike	N Yks	SE8888	54°17·0′	0°38·5′W	X	94,101
Redding	E Ayr	NS4242	55°39·0′	4°30·4′W	X	70
Redding	E Ayr	NS5039	55°37·5′	4°22·5′W	X	70
Redding	Falk	NS9278	55°59·2′	3°43·4′W	T	65
Redding	S Lanak	NS6740	55°38·4′	4°6·3′W	X	71
Redding Hanging	Wilts	ST9037	51°8·2′	2°8·2′W	X	184
Redding Muir	Falk	NS9076	55°58·1′	3°45·3′W	X	65
Reddingmuirhead	Falk	NS9177	55°58·7′	3°44·4′W	T	65
Reddings	D & G	NT0707	55°21·1′	3°27·6′W	X	78
Reddings	Essex	TL9802	51°41·1′	0°52·3′E	X	168
Redding's Fm	Bucks	SP6808	51°46·2′	1°0·5′W	FM	164,165
Reddings Fm	Glos	SO9020	51°52·9′	2°8·3′W	FM	163
Reddings Fm	Monm	ST5399	51°41·5′	2°40·4′W	FM	162
Redding's Inclosure	Monm	SO5413	51°49·1′	2°39·6′W	F	162
Reddings, The	Glos	SO7209	51°47·0′	2°24·0′W	X	162
Reddings, The	Glos	SO9021	51°53·5′	2°8·3′W	T	163
Reddish	Stock	SJ8993	53°26·3′	2°9·5′W	T	109
Reddish	Warr	SJ6988	53°23·5′	2°27·6′W	T	109
Reddish Hall	Warr	SJ6484	53°21·3′	2°32·0′W	X	109
Reddish North Sta	Stock	SJ8994	53°26·8′	2°9·5′W	X	109
Reddish South Sta	Stock	SJ8993	53°26·3′	2°9·5′W	X	109
Redditch	Worcs	SP0467	52°18·3′	1°56·1′W	T	150
Red Ditches Fm	Bucks	SP6640	52°3·5′	1°1·8′W	FM	152
Reddivallen	Corn	SX0988	50°39·9′	4°41·8′W	X	190,200
Reddochbraes	S Lanak	NS7737	55°36·9′	3°56·7′W	X	71
Red Down	Corn	SX2685	50°38·6′	4°27·3′W	X	201
Red Down	Pemb	SN0501	51°40·7′	4°48·8′W	X	158
Red Down	Swin	SU1991	51°37·3′	1°43·1′W	X	163,173
Rede	Suff	TL8055	52°10·1′	0°38·3′E	T	155
Red Earth Fm	Black w Dar	SD7516	53°38·6′	2°22·3′W	FM	109
Red Earth Fm	Staffs	SJ9759	53°7·9′	2°2·3′W	FM	118
Rede Br	Northum	NY8683	55°8·7′	2°12·8′W	X	80
Rede Hall	Suff	TL8057	52°11·1′	0°38·4′E	X	155
Rede Hall	Surrey	TQ3141	51°9·4′	0°7·2′W	X	187
Redeham Hall	Surrey	TQ3241	51°9·4′	0°6·4′W	X	187
Redend Point	Dorset	SZ0382	50°38·5′	1°57·1′W	X	195
Red Ends	Northum	NU2614	55°25·4′	1°34·9′W	X	81
Redenhall	Norf	TM2684	52°24·7′	1°19·8′E	T	156
Redenham	Hants	SU3049	51°14·6′	1°33·8′W	T	185
Redenham Ho	Hants	SU2949	51°14·6′	1°34·7′W	X	185
Redericks Fm	Herts	TL4612	51°47·5′	0°7·4′E	FM	167
Redesdale	Northum	NY8396	55°15·7′	2°15·6′W	X	80
Redesdale Camp	Northum	NY8298	55°16·8′	2°16·6′W	T	80
Redesdale Forest	Northum	NT7501	55°18·4′	2°23·2′W	X	80
Redes Mere	Ches	SJ8471	53°14·4′	2°14·0′W	W	118
Redesmouth	Northum	NY8682	55°8·2′	2°12·7′W	T	80
Redeswire Fray 1575	Scot Bord	NT7007	55°21·6′	2°28·0′W	A	80
Redeswood	Northum	NY8582	55°8·2′	2°13·7′W	X	80
Rede Wood	Suff	TM1550	52°6·6′	1°8·8′E	F	156
Redfants Manor Fm	Essex	TL7129	51°56·2′	0°29·7′E	FM	167
Redfern Manor	Warw	SP2674	52°22·0′	1°36·7′W	X	140
Redfield	Bucks	SP7628	51°56·9′	0°53·3′W	X	165
Redfield	D & G	NX6655	54°52·6′	4°4·9′W	X	83,84
Redfield	Highld	NH6150	57°31·4′	4°18·8′W	X	26
Redfield	Pth & Kin	NO1628	56°26·5′	3°21·3′W	X	53,58
Redfields	Hants	SU8050	51°14·8′	0°50·8′W	X	186
Red Flatt	Cumbr	NY1652	54°51·6′	3°18·1′W	X	85
Red Fm	W Berks	SU4869	51°25·3′	1°18·2′W	FM	174
Redfold	Aberd	NJ4543	57°28·7′	2°54·6′W	X	28,29
Redfold Fm	W Susx	TQ0719	50°57·9′	0°28·2′W	FM	197
Redford	Aberd	NJ5952	57°33·6′	2°40·7′W	X	29
Redford	Aberd	NJ8829	57°21·3′	2°11·5′W	X	38
Redford	Aberd	NO7570	56°49·5′	2°24·1′W	X	45
Redford	Angus	NO4152	56°39·6′	2°57·3′W	X	54
Redford	Angus	NO5644	56°35·4′	2°42·5′W	T	54
Redford	Angus	NO6056	56°41·9′	2°38·7′W	X	54
Redford	Devon	SX7244	50°17·2′	3°47·4′W	X	202
Redford	Dorset	ST6005	50°50·8′	2°33·7′W	T	194
Redford	Durham	NZ0731	54°40·7′	1°53·1′W	X	92
Redford	Falk	NS9574	55°57·1′	3°40·5′W	X	65
Redford	Fife	NT2697	56°9·9′	3°11·1′W	X	59
Redford	Moray	NJ4027	57°20·0′	2°59·3′W	X	37
Redford	Pemb	SN1313	51°47·3′	4°42·3′W	X	158
Redford	Pth & Kin	NN8512	56°17·4′	3°51·0′W	X	58
Redford	Pth & Kin	NO1433	56°29·1′	3°23·3′W	X	53
Redford	Shrops	SO6072	52°20·9′	2°34·8′W	X	138
Redford	W Susx	SU8626	51°1·8′	0°46·0′W	T	186,197
Redford Br	S Lanak	NT0149	55°43·7′	3°34·1′W	X	72
Redfordgreen	Scot Bord	NT3616	55°26·3′	3°0·3′W	X	79
Redford Ho	W Susx	TQ0616	50°56·2′	0°29·1′W	X	197
Redford Water	Somer	ST8045	51°12·5′	2°16·8′W	W	183
Redford Wood	Angus	NO4961	56°44·5′	2°49·6′W	F	44
Red Furlong Fm	Bucks	SP6525	51°55·4′	1°2·9′W	FM	164,165
Red Furlongs	Shrops	SO5482	52°26·3′	2°40·2′W	X	137,138
Red Gables	Leic	SK3210	52°41·4′	1°31·2′W	X	128
Red Gait Head	N Yks	SD7273	54°9·4′	2°25·3′W	X	98
Red Gap	Hartpl	NZ4328	54°39·0′	1°19·6′W	X	93
Red Gap Moor	Hartpl	NZ4329	54°39·5′	1°19·6′W	X	93
Redgate	Corn	SX2268	50°29·3′	4°30·2′W	X	201
Redgate	Cumbr	NY8111	54°29·9′	2°17·2′W	X	91,92
Red Gate	D & G	NX3739	54°43·4′	4°31·2′W	X	83
Redgate	Durham	NZ0838	54°44·5′	1°52·1′W	X	92
Redgate	E Ayr	NS5228	55°31·7′	4°20·2′W	X	70
Redgate	Rut	SP8699	52°35·2′	0°43·4′W	X	141
Redgate	Shrops	SO2179	52°24·4′	3°9·3′W	X	137,148
Redgate	Somer	SS9932	51°4·9′	3°26·1′W	X	181
Red Gate Fm	Beds	TL0556	52°11·8′	0°27·4′W	FM	153
Redgate Fm	Cambs	TF3703	52°36·7′	0°1·8′E	FM	142,143
Redgate Fm	Essex	TL5639	52°1·9′	0°16·8′E	FM	154
Redgate Head	Cumbr	NY4575	55°4·2′	2°51·3′W	X	86
Redgatehead	Cumbr	NY5177	55°5·4′	2°45·6′W	X	86
Redgate Hill	Norf	TF6839	52°55·6′	0°30·4′E	X	132
Redgate Ho	Suff	TM1640	52°1·2′	1°9·3′E	X	169
Redgate Mill Fm	E Susx	TQ5532	51°4·2′	0°13·1′E	FM	188
Redgates	Corn	SX1184	50°37·7′	4°40·0′W	X	200
Red Gates	Heref	SO2848	52°7·8′	3°2·7′W	X	148
Redgates	Norf	TF8811	52°40·1′	0°47·2′E	X	132
Redgate Wood	Notts	SK6759	53°7·7′	0°59·5′W	F	120
Red Geo	Highld	ND1873	58°38·5′	3°24·3′W	X	7,12
Red Geo	Orkney	HY2801	58°53·7′	3°14·5′W	X	6,7
Red Geo	Orkney	ND2097	58°51·4′	3°22·7′W	X	7
Red Geo	Shetld	HU3190	60°35·8′	1°25·5′W	X	1
Red Geo	Shetld	HU3545	60°11·5′	1°21·6′W	X	4
Red Gill	Cumbr	SD8099	54°23·4′	2°18·1′W	W	98
Red Gill	Durham	NY9111	54°29·9′	2°7·9′W	W	91,92
Red Gill	N Eil	NB0112	58°0·1′	7°3·2′W	X	13
Redgill Craig	D & G	NT1312	55°23·9′	3°22·0′W	X	78
Red Gill Moss	Durham	NY8715	54°32·1′	2°11·6′W	X	91,92
Redgleam	Durham	NY7935	54°42·8′	2°19·1′W	X	91
Red Glen	Orkney	HY2201	58°53·6′	3°20·7′W	X	6,7
Red Glen	Orkney	HY2501	58°53·7′	3°17·6′W	X	6,7
Redgorton	Pth & Kin	NO0828	56°26·4′	3°29·1′W	T	52,53,58
Red Gowt	Lincs	TF5369	53°12·0′	0°17·8′E	X	122
Redgrave	Suff	TM0477	52°21·4′	1°0·1′E	T	144
Redgrave Fen	Suff	TM0479	52°22·5′	1°0·2′E	W	144
Redgrave Park Fm	Suff	TM0577	52°21·4′	1°1·0′E	FM	144
Redgreet	Staffs	SJ7930	52°52·3′	2°18·3′W	X	127
Red Grooves Ho	Durham	NY9129	54°39·6′	2°7·9′W	X	91,92
Red Gyll	Cumbr	NY3946	54°48·6′	2°56·5′W	X	85
Red Hall	Ches	SJ5350	53°3·0′	2°41·7′W	X	117
Red Hall	Ches	SJ6653	53°4·6′	2°30·0′W	X	118
Red Hall	Ches	SJ6758	53°7·3′	2°29·2′W	X	118
Red Hall	Cumbr	NY2445	54°47·9′	3°10·5′W	X	85
Redhall	D & G	NY0786	55°9·8′	3°27·2′W	X	78
Redhall	D & G	NY2869	55°0·9′	3°7·1′W	X	85
Redhall	Herts	TQ0697	51°39·9′	0°27·6′W	X	166,176
Red Hall	Leeds	SE3438	53°50·5′	1°28·6′W	X	104
Redhall	Moray	NJ3360	57°37·8′	3°6·9′W	X	28
Red Hall	Norf	TG2413	52°40·3′	1°19·2′E	X	133,134
Redhall	Scot Bord	NT9462	55°51·3′	2°5·3′W	X	67
Red Hall	Shrops	SO5882	52°26·3′	2°36·7′W	X	137,138
Redhall	Stir	NS7294	56°7·6′	4°3·1′W	X	57
Redhall	Stir	NS8191	56°6·1′	3°54·3′W	X	57
Red Hall	Worcs	SO9078	52°24·2′	2°8·4′W	X	139
Redhall Fm	Bucks	SP7828	51°56·9′	0°51·5′W	FM	165
Red Hall Fm	Staffs	SJ7847	53°1·4′	2°19·3′W	FM	118
Red Hall Fm	Stock on T	NZ4410	54°29·2′	1°18·8′W	FM	93
Red Hall Fm	Wrex	SJ3939	52°56·9′	2°54·1′W	FM	126
Red Hall Ho	Aberd	NO7476	56°52·7′	2°25·1′W	X	45
Redhall Moss	D & G	NY0887	55°10·4′	3°26·2′W	X	78
Red Hall Wood	Stock on T	NZ4411	54°29·8′	1°18·8′W	F	93
Redham Mead	Medway	TQ7178	51°28·7′	0°28·1′E	X	178
Red Haven	D & G	NX8151	54°50·6′	3°50·8′W	X	84
Redhayes	Devon	SX9793	50°43·9′	3°27·2′W	X	192
Redhays	Devon	SS6104	50°49·4′	3°58·0′W	X	191
Red Head	Angus	NO7047	56°37·1′	2°28·9′W	X	54
Red Head	Highld	ND3477	58°40·8′	3°7·8′W	X	7,12
Red Head	Orkney	HY5640	59°14·9′	2°45·8′W	X	5
Red Head	Shetld	HU2974	60°27·2′	1°27·9′W	X	3
Redheath	Herts	TQ0697	51°39·9′	0°27·6′W	X	166,176
Red Hemmels	Northum	NZ0060	54°56·3′	1°59·6′W	X	87
Redheugh	Angus	NO4463	56°45·6′	2°54·5′W	X	44
Redheugh	Midlo	NT3362	55°51·0′	3°3·8′W	X	66
Redheugh	N Ayr	NS3155	55°45·8′	4°41·2′W	X	63
Redheugh	Northum	NY7888	55°11·4′	2°20·3′W	X	80
Redheugh	Scot Bord	NY4990	55°12·3′	2°47·7′W	X	79
Redheugh Fm	Scot Bord	NT8270	55°55·6′	2°16·8′W	FM	67
Redheugh Knowe	Northum	NU0830	55°34·1′	1°52·0′W	X	75
Red Hill	Aberd	NJ4333	57°23·3′	2°56·4′W	H	28
Red Hill	Aberd	NJ5832	57°22·8′	2°41·5′W	H	29,37
Red Hill	Aberd	NJ6109	57°10·5′	2°38·2′W	H	37
Redhill	Aberd	NJ6836	57°25·1′	2°31·5′W	X	29
Redhill	Aberd	NJ7704	57°7·8′	2°22·3′W	T	38
Red Hill	Bath & NE Somer	ST6260	51°20·5′	2°32·3′W	X	172
Red Hill	Birm	SP0476	52°23·2′	1°56·1′W	X	139
Red Hill	Bourne	SZ0895	50°45·5′	1°52·8′W	T	195
Redhill	Brig	SS8679	51°30·1′	3°38·2′W	X	170
Red Hill	Bri & Hov	TQ2808	50°51·7′	0°10·5′W	X	198
Red Hill	Bri & Hov	TQ3403	50°48·9′	0°5·5′W	X	198
Red Hill	Derby	SK5377	53°17·5′	1°11·9′W	X	120
Redhill	Devon	SS7608	50°51·7′	3°45·3′W	X	191
Red Hill	Donc	SK5896	53°27·7′	1°7·2′W	X	111
Red Hill	Hants	SU3841	51°10·2′	1°27·0′W	X	185
Red Hill	Hants	SU7210	50°53·3′	0°58·2′W	T	197
Red Hill	Heref	SO5038	52°2·5′	2°43·3′W	T	149
Redhill	Herts	TL3033	51°59·0′	0°6·0′W	T	166
Redhill	Highld	NH7248	57°30·5′	4°7·7′W	X	27
Red Hill	I of Angl	SH5975	53°15·4′	4°6·4′W	X	114,115
Red Hill	Kent	TQ6954	51°15·8′	0°25·7′E	T	188
Red Hill	Leic	SK4930	52°52·2′	1°15·9′W	X	129
Red Hill	Leic	SP5397	52°34·3′	1°12·7′W	T	140
Red Hill	Lincs	SK8283	53°20·5′	0°45·7′W	X	121
Red Hill	Lincs	SK9930	52°51·7′	0°31·4′W	X	130
Red Hill	Lincs	TF2482	53°19·5′	0°7·9′W	X	122
Red Hill	Lincs	TF2680	53°18·3′	0°6·1′W	X	122
Red Hill	Lincs	TF3774	53°15·0′	0°3·6′E	X	122
Redhill	Moray	NJ1661	57°38·1′	3°24·0′W	X	28
Redhill	Moray	NJ5646	57°30·4′	2°43·6′W	X	29
Redhill	Norf	TF9301	52°34·6′	0°51·3′E	X	144
Red Hill	Northnts	SP8876	52°19·5′	0°42·1′W	X	141
Red Hill	Notts	SK5746	53°0·7′	1°8·6′W	T	129
Red Hill	Notts	SK5847	53°1·3′	1°7·7′W	X	129
Redhill	N Som	ST4963	51°22·1′	2°43·6′W	T	172,182
Red Hill	Oxon	SP5807	51°45·8′	1°9·2′W	X	164
Red Hill	Pemb	SM9418	51°49·6′	4°59·0′W	T	157,158
Red Hill	Powys	SO1550	52°8·7′	3°14·1′W	H	148
Red Hill	Roth	SK5083	53°20·7′	1°14·5′W	X	111,120
Red Hill	S Glos	ST5988	51°35·6′	2°35·1′W	X	162,172
Redhill	Shrops	SJ4609	52°40·8′	2°47·5′W	T	126
Redhill	Shrops	SJ7310	52°41·5′	2°23·6′W	T	127
Red Hill	Somer	ST3826	51°2·0′	2°52·7′W	X	193
Red Hill	Somer	ST6050	51°15·1′	2°34·0′W	H	183
Redhill	Staffs	SJ8328	52°51·2′	2°14·7′W	T	127
Redhill	Surrey	TQ2750	51°14·3′	0°10·4′W	T	187
Red Hill	Wakf	SE4425	53°43·4′	1°19·6′W	T	105
Red Hill	Warw	SP0765	52°17·2′	1°53·4′W	T	150
Red Hill	Warw	SP1356	52°12·4′	1°48·2′W	T	151
Red Hill	W Berks	SU4264	51°22·6′	1°23·4′W	X	174
Red Hill	Worcs	SO8653	52°10·7′	2°11·9′W	T	150
Redhill	Wrekin	SJ7111	52°42·0′	2°25·3′W	T	127
Redhill Aerodrome	Surrey	TQ3047	51°12·7′	0°7·9′W	X	187
Redhill Downs	Corn	SX1671	50°30·8′	4°35·3′W	X	201
Redhill Downs	Corn	SX2070	50°30·4′	4°31·9′W	X	201
Red Hill Fm	Cambs	TL4973	52°20·3′	0°11·6′E	FM	154
Redhill Fm	Devon	ST0817	50°56·9′	3°18·2′W	FM	181
Redhill Fm	Glos	SO6103	51°43·7′	2°33·5′W	FM	162
Redhill Fm	Glos	SO7531	51°58·9′	2°21·4′W	FM	150
Red Hill Fm	Glos	SO7624	51°55·1′	2°20·5′W	FM	162
Redhill Fm	Glos	SO8203	51°43·8′	2°15·2′W	FM	162
Redhill Fm	I of W	SZ5480	50°37·3′	1°13·8′W	FM	196
Redhill Fm	Leic	SK4216	52°44·6′	1°22·3′W	FM	129
Red Hill Fm	Leic	SP4794	52°32·7′	1°18·0′W	FM	140
Redhill Fm	Northnts	SP5051	52°9·5′	1°15·7′W	FM	151
Redhill Fm	Shrops	SJ7311	52°42·0′	2°23·6′W	FM	127
Redhill Fm	Staffs	SJ9126	52°50·1′	2°7·6′W	FM	127
Redhill Fm	Warw	SP1455	52°11·8′	1°47·3′W	FM	151
Red Hill Fm	Warw	SP2986	52°28·5′	1°34·0′W	FM	140
Redhill Fm	Worcs	SO9776	52°23·2′	2°2·2′W	FM	139
Redhill Ho	Glos	SO6202	51°43·2′	2°32·6′W	X	162
Redhill House	W Susx	SU9626	51°1·7′	0°37·5′W	X	186,197
Redhill Lodge	Rut	SP9299	52°35·1′	0°38·1′W	X	141
Red Hill of Sneuk	Orkney	ND2396	58°50·9′	3°19·6′W	X	6,7
Red Hills	Cumbr	NY4961	54°56·7′	2°47·3′W	X	86
Redhills	Cumbr	NY5028	54°38·9′	2°46·1′W	T	90
Red Hills	Cumbr	SD1879	54°12·3′	3°15·0′W	X	96
Red Hills	Cumbr	SD4577	54°11·4′	2°50·2′W	X	97
Redhills	Devon	SX9092	50°43·3′	3°33·1′W	T	192
Redhills	D & G	NY0377	55°4·9′	3°30·7′W	X	84
Redhills	Pth & Kin	NN9822	56°23·0′	3°38·7′W	X	52,53,58
Redhills Fm	Beds	TL0230	51°57·8′	0°30·5′W	FM	166
Redhill Wood	Northnts	SP5050	52°9·0′	1°15·8′W	F	151
Redhill Wood	W Berks	SU4264	51°22·6′	1°23·4′W	F	174
Red Ho	Cumbr	NY3553	54°52·3′	3°0·3′W	X	85
Red Ho	Darl	NZ2324	54°36·9′	1°38·2′W	X	93
Red Ho	Derby	SK1667	53°12·2′	1°45·2′W	X	119
Red Ho	Derby	SK1870	53°13·8′	1°43·4′W	X	119
Red Ho	Donc	SE5209	53°34·7′	1°12·5′W	X	111
Red Ho	Donc	SE6706	53°33·0′	0°58·9′W	X	111
Red Ho	Donc	SE7210	53°35·1′	0°54·3′W	X	112
Red Ho	Durham	NZ0622	54°35·8′	1°54·0′W	X	92
Red Ho	Durham	NZ0645	54°48·2′	1°54·0′W	X	87
Red Ho	Essex	TL5409	51°45·7′	0°14·3′E	X	167
Red Ho	Essex	TL7739	52°1·5′	0°35·2′E	X	155
Red Ho	E Susx	TR0020	50°56·9′	0°51·2′E	X	189
Red Ho	Lincs	TF1871	53°13·6′	0°13·5′W	X	122
Red Ho	Lincs	TF2435	52°54·1′	0°9·0′W	X	131
Red Ho	Lincs	TF3919	52°45·3′	0°4·0′E	X	131

Red Ho	Monm	SO3610	51°47·3'	2°55·3'W	X	161
Red Ho	Norf	TG1038	52°54·1'	1°7·8'E	X	133
Red Ho	Norf	TM0888	52°27·2'	1°4·1'E	X	144
Red Ho	Northum	NY8867	55°0·1'	2°10·8'W	X	87
Red Ho	Northum	NY9361	54°56·9'	2°6·1'W	X	87
Red Ho	Northum	NZ0273	55°3·3'	1°57·7'W	X	87
Red Ho	Notts	SK6997	53°28·1'	0°57·2'W	X	111
Red Ho	N Yks	NZ7704	54°25·8'	0°48·4'W	X	94
Red Ho	N Yks	SE1894	54°20·7'	1°43·0'W	X	99
Red Ho	N Yks	SE3081	54°13·7'	1°32·0'W	X	99
Red Ho	N Yks	SE3097	54°22·3'	1°31·9'W	X	99
Red Ho	N Yks	SE5172	54°8·7'	1°12·7'W	X	100
Red Ho	N Yks	SE5257	54°0·6'	1°12·0'W	X	105
Red Ho	N Yks	SE6963	54°3·7'	0°56·3'W	X	100
Red Ho	N Yks	SE8992	54°19·2'	0°37·5'W	X	94,101
Red Ho	Powys	SJ2116	52°44·4'	3°9·8'W	X	126
Red Ho	Powys	SJ2414	52°43·3'	3°7·1'W	X	126
Red Ho	Powys	SJ2502	52°36·9'	3°6·1'W	X	126
Red Ho	Powys	SJ2604	52°38·0'	3°5·2'W	X	126
Red Ho	Powys	SJ2714	52°43·4'	3°4·5'W	X	126
Red Ho	Powys	SN9989	52°29·6'	3°28·9'W	X	136
Red Ho	Powys	SO0086	52°28·0'	3°27·9'W	X	136
Red Ho	Powys	SO0592	52°31·3'	3°23·6'W	X	136
Red Ho	Powys	SO0792	52°31·3'	3°21·8'W	X	136
Red Ho	Powys	SO1094	52°32·4'	3°19·2'W	X	136
Red Ho	Powys	SO1198	52°34·6'	3°18·4'W	X	136
Red Ho	Powys	SO1593	52°31·9'	3°14·8'W	X	136
Red Ho	Pth & Kin	NO1800	56°11·4'	3°18·8'W	X	58
Red Ho	Red & Cl	NZ7015	54°31·8'	0°54·7'W	X	94
Red Ho	Sand	SP0494	52°32·9'	1°56·1'W	X	139
Red Ho	Stock on T	NZ4217	54°33·0'	1°20·6'W	X	93
Red Ho	Suff	TM1048	52°5·7'	1°4·3'E	X	155,169
Red Ho	Suff	TM1343	52°2·9'	1°6·8'E	X	169
Red Ho	Suff	TM2268	52°16·1'	1°15·6'E	X	156
Red Ho	Suff	TM2365	52°14·5'	1°16·4'E	X	156
Red Ho	Suff	TM2662	52°12·8'	1°18·9'E	X	156
Red Ho	Suff	TM2667	52°15·5'	1°19·1'E	X	156
Red Ho	Suff	TM4354	52°8·1'	1°33·5'E	X	156
Red Ho	Suff	TM4557	52°9·6'	1°35·3'E	X	156
Red Ho	Suff	TM4687	52°25·8'	1°37·5'E	X	156
Red Ho	Surrey	TQ2142	51°10·1'	0°15·8'W	X	187
Red Ho	Warw	SP3151	52°9·6'	1°32·4'W	X	151
Red Ho	W Loth	NS9965	55°52·3'	3°36·4'W	X	65
Red Ho	Worcs	SO8135	52°1·0'	2°16·2'W	X	150
Red Ho	W Susx	TQ2422	50°59·3'	0°13·6'W	X	198
Red Ho Fm	Shrops	SO3686	52°28·3'	2°56·1'W	FM	137
Red Holm	Orkney	HY5439	59°14·4'	2°47·9'W	X	5
Redholme	V of Glam	ST0369	51°24·9'	3°23·3'W	X	170
Redhorn Hill	Wilts	SU0555	51°17·9'	1°55·3'W	X	173
Red Ho, The	Lincs	SK9344	52°59·3'	0°36·5'W	X	130
Red Ho, The	Powys	SO1797	52°34·1'	3°13·1'W	X	136
Red Ho, The	Suff	TM2257	52°10·2'	1°15·2'E	X	156
Red Ho, The	Suff	TM2952	52°7·4'	1°21·1'E	X	156
Redhouse	Aberd	NJ5820	57°16·4'	2°41·3'W	X	37
Redhouse	Aberd	NJ8026	57°19·7'	2°19·5'W	X	38
Redhouse	Aberd	NJ9053	57°34·3'	2°9·6'W	X	30
Redhouse	Arg & Bt	NR8261	55°47·8'	5°28·2'W	X	62
Red House	Beds	TL0360	52°13·9'	0°29·1'W	X	153
Redhouse	Corn	SW4426	50°5·0'	5°34·3'W	X	203
Redhouse	D & G	NY2969	55°0·9'	3°6·2'W	X	85
Red House	Durham	NZ2746	54°48·7'	1°34·4'W	X	88
Redhouse	E Loth	NT4677	55°59·2'	2°51·5'W	X	66
Red House	E Yorks	TA3526	53°43·0'	0°3·2'E	X	107
Redhouse	Fife	NT2096	56°9·3'	3°16·8'W	X	58
Redhouse	Suff	TM0971	52°18·1'	1°4·3'E	X	144,155
Red House	Suff	TM3679	52°21·7'	1°28·4'E	X	156
Red House Br	Lincs	TF3919	52°45·3'	0°4·0'E	X	131
Redhouse Burn	Arg & Bt	NR8261	55°47·8'	5°28·2'W	W	62
Red House Community Home	Norf	TG2123	52°45·8'	1°16·9'E	X	133,134
Red House Fm	Bath & NE Somer	ST6256	51°18·3'	2°32·3'W	FM	172
Red House Fm	Bucks	SP6115	51°50·0'	1°6·5'W	FM	164,165
Red House Fm	Cambs	TL3898	52°34·0'	0°2·6'E	FM	142,143
Red House Fm	Cambs	TL5878	52°22·9'	0°19·7'E	FM	143
Red House Fm	Derby	SK1748	53°2·0'	1°44·4'W	FM	119
Red House Fm	Derby	SK3460	53°8·4'	1°29·1'W	FM	119
Redhouse Fm	Essex	TL7434	51°58·9'	0°32·4'E	FM	155
Red House Fm	Essex	TL9830	51°56·2'	0°53·2'E	FM	168
Red House Fm	Essex	TM1126	51°53·8'	1°4·4'E	FM	168,169
Redhouse Fm	Essex	TM1828	51°54·7'	1°10·6'E	FM	168,169
Red House Fm	E Yorks	SE7616	53°38·3'	0°50·6'W	FM	112
Red House Fm	E Yorks	SE9438	53°50·0'	0°33·9'W	FM	106
Redhouse Fm	E Yorks	TA3230	53°45·2'	0°0·5'E	FM	107
Red House Fm	Glos	SO8829	51°57·8'	2°10·1'W	FM	150
Red House Fm	Herts	SP8816	51°50·4'	0°43·0'W	FM	165
Red House Fm	Kent	TR1566	51°21·4'	1°5·7'E	FM	179
Red House Fm	Lincs	SK9294	53°26·3'	0°36·5'W	FM	112
Red House Fm	Lincs	TF0769	53°12·7'	0°23·5'W	FM	121
Red House Fm	Lincs	TF2560	53°7·6'	0°7·5'W	FM	122
Red House Fm	Lincs	TF2629	52°50·9'	0°7·3'W	FM	131
Red House Fm	Lincs	TF3522	52°47·0'	0°0·5'E	FM	131
Red House Fm	Lincs	TF3628	52°50·2'	0°1·5'E	FM	131
Red House Fm	Lincs	TF4228	52°50·1'	0°6·9'E	FM	131
Red House Fm	Lincs	TF4330	52°51·1'	0°7·8'E	FM	131
Red House Fm	Norf	TM1585	52°25·5'	1°10·1'E	FM	144,156
Red House Fm	Norf	TM3494	52°29·8'	1°27·3'E	FM	134
Red House Fm	Northnts	SP5653	52°10·6'	1°10·5'W	FM	152
Red House Fm	N Yks	SE1899	54°23·4'	1°42·9'W	FM	99
Red House Fm	N Yks	SE2873	54°9·4'	1°33·9'W	FM	99
Red House Fm	N Yks	SE3570	54°7·7'	1°27·4'W	FM	99
Red House Fm	N Yks	SE3587	54°16·9'	1°27·3'W	FM	99
Red House Fm	N Yks	SE6998	54°22·6'	0°55·8'W	FM	94,100
Red House Fm	N Yks	TA0097	54°21·8'	0°27·2'W	FM	101
Red House Fm	Oxon	SP4606	51°45·3'	1°19·6'W	FM	164
Red House Fm	Pemb	SN1203	51°41·9'	4°42·8'W	FM	158
Red House Fm	Redbr	TQ4789	51°35·1'	0°7·7'E	FM	177
Red House Fm	Shrops	SO5495	52°33·3'	2°40·3'W	FM	137,138
Red House Fm	Somer	ST6921	50°59·5'	2°26·1'W	FM	183
Redhouse Fm	Suff	TL9145	52°4·4'	0°47·6'E	FM	155
Redhouse Fm	Suff	TL9972	52°18·8'	0°55·6'E	FM	144,155
Redhouse Fm	Suff	TM0366	52°15·5'	0°58·9'E	FM	155
Red House Fm	Suff	TM0888	52°4·7'	1°0·8'E	FM	155
Redhouse Fm	Suff	TM0764	52°14·3'	1°2·3'E	FM	155
Redhouse Fm	Suff	TM0770	52°17·6'	1°2·5'E	FM	144,155
Redhouse Fm	Suff	TM0843	52°3·0'	1°2·4'E	FM	155,169
Red House Fm	Suff	TM0958	52°11·1'	1°3·8'E	FM	155
Redhouse Fm	Suff	TM1040	52°1·3'	1°4·1'E	FM	155,169
Red House Fm	Suff	TM1360	52°12·0'	1°7·4'E	FM	156
Red House Fm	Suff	TM1746	52°4·4'	1°10·4'E	FM	169
Redhouse Fm	Suff	TM1753	52°8·2'	1°10·7'E	FM	156
Red House Fm	Suff	TM1764	52°14·1'	1°11·1'E	FM	156
Red House Fm	Suff	TM1836	51°59·0'	1°10·9'E	FM	169
Red House Fm	Suff	TM1850	52°6·5'	1°11·4'E	FM	156
Red House Fm	Suff	TM2158	52°10·8'	1°14·4'E	FM	156
Redhouse Fm	Suff	TM2169	52°16·7'	1°14·8'E	FM	156
Red House Fm	Suff	TM2236	51°58·9'	1°14·4'E	FM	169
Redhouse Fm	Suff	TM2352	52°7·5'	1°15·9'E	FM	156
Red House Fm	Suff	TM2456	52°9·6'	1°16·9'E	FM	156
Red House Fm	Suff	TM2464	52°13·9'	1°17·2'E	FM	156
Redhouse Fm	Suff	TM2540	52°1·0'	1°17·1'E	FM	169
Red House Fm	Suff	TM2574	52°19·3'	1°18·5'E	FM	156
Red House Fm	Suff	TM2676	52°20·4'	1°19·5'E	FM	156
Red House Fm	Suff	TM2762	52°12·8'	1°19·8'E	FM	156
Red House Fm	Suff	TM2767	52°15·5'	1°20·0'E	FM	156
Red House Fm	Suff	TM3039	52°0·3'	1°21·5'E	FM	169
Red House Fm	Suff	TM3073	52°18·6'	1°22·9'E	FM	156
Redhouse Fm	Suff	TM3169	52°16·5'	1°23·6'E	FM	156
Red House Fm	Suff	TM3278	52°21·3'	1°24·8'E	FM	156
Red House Fm	Suff	TM3352	52°7·3'	1°24·6'E	FM	156
Red House Fm	Suff	TM3361	52°12·1'	1°25·0'E	FM	156
Redhouse Fm	Suff	TM3440	52°0·8'	1°25·0'E	FM	169
Red House Fm	Suff	TM3456	52°9·4'	1°25·7'E	FM	156
Red House Fm	Suff	TM3480	52°22·3'	1°26·7'E	FM	156
Redhouse Fm	Suff	TM4061	52°11·9'	1°31·1'E	FM	156
Redhouse Fm	Suff	TM4063	52°13·0'	1°31·2'E	FM	156
Redhouse Fm	Suff	TM4065	52°14·1'	1°31·3'E	FM	156
Red House Fm	Suff	TM4370	52°16·7'	1°34·1'E	FM	156
Red House Fm	Suff	TM4374	52°18·8'	1°34·3'E	FM	156
Red House Fm	Suff	TM4681	52°22·5'	1°37·3'E	FM	156
Red House Fm	Suff	TM4783	52°23·6'	1°38·2'E	FM	156
Red House Fm	Suff	TM4979	52°21·4'	1°39·8'E	FM	156
Red House Fm	Surrey	SU9042	51°10·4'	0°42·4'W	FM	186
Red House Fm	Warr	SJ5893	53°26·2'	2°37·5'W	FM	108
Redhouse Fm	Warw	SP2892	52°31·7'	1°34·8'W	FM	140
Redhouse Fm	Warw	SP2961	52°15·0'	1°34·1'W	FM	151
Redhouse Fm	Warw	SP3349	52°8·5'	1°30·7'W	FM	151
Redhouse Fm	Warw	SP3466	52°17·7'	1°29·7'W	FM	151
Redhouse Fm	Wilts	SU3250	51°15·1'	1°32·1'W	FM	185
Redhouse Fm	W Susx	TQ2713	50°54·4'	0°11·2'W	FM	198
Red House Fm, The	Monm	SO4710	51°47·4'	2°45·7'W	FM	161
Red House Fm, The	Suff	TM3866	52°14·7'	1°29·6'E	FM	156
Redhouse Moor	Northum	NU0038	55°38·4'	1°59·6'W	X	75
Redhouses	Arg & Bt	NR3563	55°47·5'	6°13·2'W	T	60,61
Red Houses	Durham	NZ1146	54°48·8'	1°49·3'W	X	88
Red Houses	Suff	TM1057	52°10·5'	1°4·7'E	X	155
Redhouse Wood	N Yks	SE5257	54°0·6'	1°12·0'W	F	105
Red Hovel	Northnts	SP7987	52°28·2'	0°49·8'W	X	141
Red How	Cumbr	NY0721	54°34·8'	3°25·9'W	X	89
Redhow	Cumbr	NY1422	54°35·4'	3°19·4'W	X	89
Red How	Cumbr	NY2502	54°24·7'	3°8·9'W	X	89,90
Red Howles	Red & Cl	NZ6223	54°36·1'	1°2·0'W	X	94
Red Hurst	Derby	SK1069	53°13·3'	1°50·6'W	X	119
Redhythe	Aberd	NJ5666	57°41·2'	2°43·8'W	X	29
Redhythe Point	Aberd	NJ5767	57°41·7'	2°42·8'W	X	29
Redinhorne	Glos	SO5615	51°50·1'	2°37·9'W	X	162
Redisham	Suff	TM4084	52°24·3'	1°32·1'E	T	156
Redisham Hall	Suff	TM4085	52°24·8'	1°32·2'E	X	156
Redkirk	D & G	NY3065	54°58·7'	3°5·2'W	X	85
Redkirk Point	D & G	NY3065	54°58·7'	3°5·2'W	X	85
Red Lake	Devon	SX6366	50°28·9'	3°55·5'W	W	202
Red Lake	Somer	ST4631	51°4·8'	2°45·9'W	W	182
Red Lake	Wrekin	SJ6810	52°41·4'	2°28·0'W	T	127
Redlake Fm	Devon	SX7092	50°43·0'	3°50·1'W	FM	191
Redlake Fm	Somer	ST5440	51°9·7'	2°39·1'W	FM	182,183
Red Lakes	Aberd	NK0365	57°40·7'	1°56·5'W	X	30
Redland	C of Bris	ST5875	51°28·6'	2°35·9'W	T	172
Redland	Devon	SS6312	50°53·7'	3°56·5'W	X	180
Redland	Orkney	HY2613	59°0·1'	3°16·8'W	X	6
Redland	Orkney	HY3717	59°2·4'	3°5·4'W	X	6
Redland	Orkney	HY3724	59°6·2'	3°5·5'W	T	6
Redland	V of Glam	ST0773	51°27·1'	3°19·9'W	X	170
Redland End	Bucks	SP8302	51°42·9'	0°47·5'W	T	165
Redland Fm	Corn	SX3068	50°29·5'	4°23·4'W	FM	201
Redland Hill	Orkney	HY2513	59°0·1'	3°17·8'W	H	6
Redlands	Dorset	SY6682	50°38·4'	2°28·5'W	T	194
Redlands	Essex	TL4541	52°3·1'	0°7·3'E	X	154
Redlands	E Susx	TQ7423	50°59·0'	0°29·1'E	X	199
Redlands	Hants	SU8049	51°14·3'	0°50·9'W	X	186
Redlands	Kent	TQ4349	51°13·6'	0°3·3'E	X	187
Redlands	Somer	ST4833	51°5·9'	2°44·2'W	T	182
Redlands	Somer	ST5413	50°55·1'	2°38·9'W	X	194
Redlands	Surrey	TQ1644	51°11·2'	0°20·0'W	X	187
Redlands	Swin	SU1991	51°37·3'	1°43·1'W	T	163,173
Redlands	Warw	SP3356	52°12·3'	1°30·6'W	X	151
Redlands	W Susx	SU8119	50°58·1'	0°50·4'W	X	197
Redlands	W Susx	TQ1120	50°58·3'	0°24·8'W	X	198
Redlands Bank	Cumbr	NY6423	54°36·3'	2°33·0'W	X	91
Redlands Covert	Suff	TM4355	52°8·6'	1°33·5'E	F	156
Redlands Fm	Essex	TM1718	51°49·3'	1°9·3'E	FM	168,169
Redlands Fm	Herts	TL2838	52°1·8'	0°7·7'W	FM	153
Redlands Fm	Northnts	SP9670	52°19·4'	0°35·1'W	FM	141,153
Redlands Fm	Somer	ST4335	51°6·9'	2°48·5'W	FM	182
Redlands Fm	Somer	ST6436	51°7·6'	2°30·5'W	FM	183
Redlands Fm	Surrey	TQ1646	51°12·3'	0°20·0'W	FM	187
Redlands Fm	W Susx	SU9617	50°56·9'	0°37·6'W	FM	197
Redlands Fm	W Susx	SZ7999	50°47·3'	0°52·4'W	FM	197
Redlands, The	Glos	SO7817	51°51·3'	2°18·8'W	X	162
Redlands Wood	Surrey	TQ1645	51°11·8'	0°20·0'W	F	187
Redlane	Somer	ST2012	50°54·4'	3°7·9'W	T	193
Redlane Barn	W Berks	SU4679	51°30·7'	1°19·8'W	X	174
Redlane End	Cumbr	NY4538	54°44·3'	2°50·8'W	X	90
Redlap Cove	Devon	SX8748	50°19·5'	3°34·9'W	W	202
Redlap Ho	Devon	SX8748	50°19·5'	3°34·9'W	X	202
Redlatches	Angus	NO2059	56°43·2'	3°18·0'W	X	53
Red Lay	Heref	SO3445	52°6·2'	2°57·4'W	X	148,149
Red Lea Fm	Black w Dar	SD6422	53°41·8'	2°32·3'W	FM	102,103
Redleas	Aberd	NK0942	57°28·3'	1°50·5'W	X	30
Red Leas Fm	Lincs	TF3890	53°23·6'	0°4·9'E	FM	113
Redliggate	D & G	NX8155	54°52·8'	3°50·9'W	X	84
Redlingfield	Suff	TM1870	52°17·3'	1°12·2'E	T	156
Red Lion	Powys	SO0677	52°23·2'	3°22·5'W	X	136,147
Redlion Brook	Ches	SJ8069	53°13·3'	2°17·6'W	W	118
Redlion Fm	Ches	SJ7352	53°4·1'	2°23·8'W	FM	118
Red Lion Fm	Hartpl	NZ4430	54°40·0'	1°18·6'W	FM	93
Red Lion Fm	Lancs	SD4735	53°48·8'	2°47·9'W	FM	102
Red Lion Hill	Powys	SO0577	52°23·2'	3°23·4'W	H	136,147
Red Lion Ho	Kent	TR1162	51°19·3'	1°2·1'E	X	179
Red Lion Pond	E Susx	TQ4405	50°49·8'	0°3·1'E	W	198
Redlish	N Yks	SE1262	54°3·5'	1°48·6'W	X	99
Redlish Ho	N Yks	SE1361	54°2·9'	1°47·7'W	X	99
Red Lo	Leeds	SE2823	53°42·4'	1°34·1'W	X	104
Red Loch	Aberd	NJ9962	57°39·1'	2°0·5'W	W	30
Red Loch	S Lanak	NS9547	55°42·6'	3°39·8'W	W	72
Red Lodge	Leic	SK6918	52°45·5'	0°58·2'W	X	129
Red Lodge	Northnts	SP8074	52°21·7'	0°49·1'W	X	141
Red Lodge	Northnts	TL0587	52°28·5'	0°26·8'W	X	142
Red Lodge	Suff	TL6970	52°18·4'	0°29·1'E	T	154
Red Lodge	Suff	TM3347	52°4·6'	1°24·4'E	X	169
Red Lodge	Wilts	SU0688	51°35·7'	1°54·4'W	X	173
Red Lodge Fm	Derby	SK4177	53°17·5'	1°22·7'W	FM	120
Red Lodge Fm	Hants	SU2740	51°9·7'	1°36·4'W	FM	184
Red Lodge Fm	Leic	SK7506	52°39·0'	0°53·1'W	FM	141
Redlodge Fm	Norf	TF8205	52°37·0'	0°41·7'E	FM	144
Red Lodge Fm	Northnts	SP9494	52°32·4'	0°36·4'W	FM	141
Red Lumb	Roch	SD8415	53°38·1'	2°14·1'W	T	109
Redlynch	Somer	ST7033	51°6·0'	2°25·3'W	T	183
Redlynch	Wilts	SU2020	50°59·0'	1°42·5'W	T	184
Redlynch Park	Somer	ST7033	51°6·0'	2°25·3'W	X	183
Red Lyons Fm	Essex	TQ8999	51°39·7'	0°44·4'E	FM	168
Redmain	Cumbr	NY1333	54°41·3'	3°20·6'W	T	89
Redmains	E Loth	NT4469	55°54·9'	2°53·3'W	X	66
Red Man	Aberd	NO8988	56°59·2'	2°10·4'W	X	45
Redman Plain	N Yks	SE7293	54°19·9'	0°53·1'W	X	94,100
Redman's Hill	Dorset	SU0707	50°52·0'	1°53·6'W	X	195
Redmarley	Worcs	SO7566	52°17·7'	2°21·6'W	X	138,150
Redmarley D'Abitot	Glos	SO7531	51°58·9'	2°21·4'W	T	150
Redmarshall	Stock on T	NZ3821	54°35·2'	1°24·3'W	T	93
Red Mea	N Yks	SD8198	54°22·9'	2°17·1'W	X	98
Redmile	Leic	SK7935	52°54·6'	0°49·1'W	T	129
Redmire	Cumbr	NY3729	54°39·4'	2°58·2'W	X	90
Red Mire	Lancs	SD6765	54°5·0'	2°29·9'W	W	98
Redmire	Northum	NY7885	55°9·8'	2°20·3'W	X	80
Redmire	N Yks	SD9377	54°11·6'	2°6·0'W	X	98
Redmire	N Yks	SE0491	54°19·1'	1°55·9'W	T	98
Redmire Fm	N Yks	NZ7610	54°29·0'	0°49·2'W	FM	94
Redmire Force	N Yks	SE0490	54°18·6'	1°55·9'W	W	98
Redmire Forest	N Yks	SE0494	54°20·7'	1°55·9'W	X	98
Redmire Moor	N Yks	SE0493	54°20·2'	1°55·9'W	X	98
Redmire Pasture	N Yks	SE0592	54°19·7'	1°55·0'W	X	98
Red Mires	Derby	SK0484	53°21·4'	1°56·0'W	X	110
Redmires	N Yks	SE2269	54°7·2'	1°39·4'W	X	99
Redmire Scar	N Yks	SE0592	54°19·7'	1°55·0'W	X	98
Redmire Scar	N Yks	SE0691	54°19·1'	1°54·0'W	X	99
Redmires Resrs	Sheff	SK2685	53°21·9'	1°36·1'W	W	110
Redmonds Edge	Lancs	SD6517	53°39·1'	2°31·4'W	X	109
Redmoor	Ches	SJ9875	53°16·6'	2°1·4'W	X	118
Red Moor	Corn	SX0761	50°25·3'	4°42·6'W	X	200
Redmoor	Corn	SX0861	50°25·3'	4°41·8'W	T	200
Redmoor Copse	Northnts	SP7442	52°4·5'	0°54·8'W	F	152
Redmoor Fm	Ches	SJ9983	53°20·9'	2°0·5'W	FM	109
Redmoor Fm	Derby	SK4045	53°0·3'	1°23·8'W	FM	129
Redmoor Fm	Dorset	ST7930	51°4·4'	2°17·6'W	FM	183
Redmoor Ho	N Yks	SE6738	53°50·3'	0°58·5'W	X	105,106
Redmoor Plantn	Cambs	TL5583	52°25·6'	0°17·2'E	F	143
Red Moss	Aberd	NJ7017	57°14·8'	2°29·4'W	X	38
Red Moss	Aberd	NJ7401	57°6·2'	2°25·3'W	X	38
Redmoss	Aberd	NJ8231	57°22·4'	2°17·5'W	T	29,30
Redmoss	Aberd	NJ8659	57°37·5'	2°13·6'W	X	30
Red Moss	Aberd	NJ9115	57°13·8'	2°8·5'W	X	38
Red Moss	Aberd	NJ9117	57°14·9'	2°8·5'W	X	38
Red Moss	Aberd	NO8694	57°2·5'	2°13·4'W	X	38,45
Red Moss	Bolton	SD6310	53°35·4'	2°33·1'W	X	109
Red Moss	Highld	ND2263	58°33·2'	3°19·9'W	X	11,12
Red Moss	Highld	ND2839	58°20·3'	3°13·3'W	X	11,12
Redmoss	Scot Bord	NY4584	55°9·1'	2°51·4'W	X	79
Red Moss	S Lanak	NS8726	55°31·1'	3°47·0'W	X	71,72
Redmoss Fm	E Dunb	NS6476	55°57·7'	4°10·3'W	FM	64
Red Moss Hotel	S Lanak	NS8726	55°31·1'	3°47·0'W	X	71,72
Red Moss Loch	S Ayr	NS2612	55°22·5'	4°44·3'W	W	70
Redmyre	Aberd	NO7475	56°52·2'	2°25·1'W	X	45
Redmyre	Aberd	NO8997	57°4·1'	2°10·4'W	X	38,45
Red Myre	Fife	NO2513	56°18·5'	3°12·3'W	W	59
Redmyre	Pth & Kin	NO2833	56°29·3'	3°9·7'W	X	53
Redmyre Loch	Pth & Kin	NO2833	56°29·3'	3°9·7'W	W	53
Redmyres	C of Aber	NJ8808	57°10·0'	2°11·5'W	X	38
Red Nab	Cumbr	SD3899	54°23·2'	2°56·9'W	X	96,97
Red Nab	Lancs	SD4059	54°1·7'	2°54·5'W	X	102
Rednal	Birm	SP0076	52°23·2'	1°59·6'W	T	139
Rednal	Shrops	SJ3628	52°51·0'	2°56·6'W	T	126
Rednal Mill	Shrops	SJ3729	52°51·5'	2°55·7'W	X	126
Redneck Fm	Suff	TL8280	52°23·5'	0°40·9'E	FM	144
Redneck Heath	Suff	TL8181	52°24·0'	0°40·0'E	F	144
Rednend Fm	S Glos	ST5784	51°33·4'	2°36·8'W	FM	172
Redness Point	Cumbr	NX9719	54°33·6'	3°35·1'W	X	89
Redness Point	Cumbr	NY2227	54°38·2'	3°12·1'W	X	89,90
Red Nev	Orkney	HY4145	59°17·5'	3°1·7'W	X	5
Rednock House	Stir	NN5901	56°11·1'	4°15·9'W	X	57
Red Nose	Highld	NH8066	57°40·3'	4°0·3'W	X	21,27

Redoak	Kent	TR1847	51°11·1'	1°7·6'E	X	179,189
Red Oaks Hill	Essex	TL6039	52°1·8'	0°20·3'E	X	154
Redomsford	Devon	SS3015	50°54·8'	4°24·7'W	T	190
Redoubt, The	E Susx	TV6299	50°46·3'	0°18·2'E	X	199
Redpale Fm	E Susx	TQ6516	50°55·4'	0°21·3'E	FM	199
Redpath	Northum	NZ0092	55°13·6'	1°59·6'W	X	81
Redpath	Scot Bord	NT5835	55°36·7'	2°39·6'W	T	73,74
Redpath	Scot Bord	NT6859	55°49·6'	2°30·2'W	X	67,74
Redpath Hill	Scot Bord	NT5936	55°37·2'	2°38·6'W	H	73,74
Redpeth	Northum	NY6863	54°57·9'	2°29·6'W	X	86,87
Red Pike	Cumbr	NY1610	54°29·0'	3°17·4'W	H	89
Red Pike	Cumbr	NY1615	54°31·6'	3°17·5'W	H	89
Red Pits	Norf	TG0928	52°48·8'	1°6·5'E	T	133
Red Point	Highld	NC9365	58°33·9'	3°49·9'W	X	11
Red Point	Highld	NG7268	57°38·9'	5°48·8'W	H	19,24
Redpoint	Highld	NG7369	57°39·5'	5°47·9'W	T	19,24
Redpoint Fm	Highld	NG7368	57°38·9'	5°47·8'W	FM	19,24
Red Pool Spinney	Leic	SP6094	52°32·7'	1°6·5'W	F	140
Red Post	Corn	SS2605	50°49·3'	4°27·8'W	T	190
Red Post	Devon	SX8363	50°27·5'	3°38·5'W	X	202
Red Post	Dorset	ST6319	50°58·4'	2°31·2'W	X	183
Red Post	Dorset	SY8896	50°46·0'	2°9·8'W	X	194
Redpost Cross	Devon	SS6202	50°48·3'	3°57·1'W	X	191
Red Post Cross	Somer	ST5125	51°1·6'	2°41·5'W	X	183
Red Quarr Fm	Somer	ST5651	51°15·6'	2°37·4'W	FM	182,183
Red Rail	Heref	SO5428	51°57·2'	2°39·8'W	T	149
Red Ratcher	Derby	SE0503	53°31·8'	1°55·1'W	X	110
Redree Burn	E Ayr	NS6311	55°22·7'	4°9·3'W	W	71
Red Rice	Hants	SU3341	51°10·3'	1°31·3'W	T	185
Redrice Wood	Corn	SX1465	50°27·6'	4°36·9'W	F	200
Red Rise	Hants	SU2403	50°49·8'	1°39·2'W	F	195
Red River	Corn	SW5134	50°9·5'	5°28·8'W	W	203
Red River	Corn	SW6041	50°13·5'	5°21·5'W	W	203
Redroad Hill	Surrey	SU9060	51°20·1'	0°42·1'W	X	175,186
Red Rock	Highld	ND1836	58°18·6'	3°23·5'W	X	11
Red Rock	N Eil	NF9888	57°47·1'	7°4·4'W	X	18
Red Rock	Scot Bord	NT7971	55°56·1'	2°19·7'W	X	67
Red Rock	Wigan	SD5809	53°34·8'	2°37·7'W	T	108
Red Rocks	Highld	NM5259	56°39·7'	6°2·4'W	X	47
Red Rocks	Wirral	SJ2088	53°23·2'	3°11·8'W	X	108
Redroof Fm	Lincs	TF2846	53°0·0'	0°5·1'W	FM	131
Red Roofs	Angus	NO5552	56°39·7'	2°43·6'W	X	54
Red Roofs	Cambs	TL4777	52°22·5'	0°10·0'E	X	143
Red Rose Fm	Essex	TL6002	51°41·9'	0°19·3'E	FM	167
Red Roses	Carm	SN2011	51°46·4'	4°36·2'W	T	158
Redrot Cove	Devon	SX6639	50°14·4'	3°52·4'W	W	202
Red Row	Northum	NZ2599	55°17·3'	1°36·0'W	T	81
Redruth	Corn	SW6942	50°14·2'	5°14·0'W	T	203
Redscar	Cumbr	SD4592	54°19·5'	2°50·3'W	X	97
Red Scar	D & G	NX7687	55°10·0'	3°56·4'W	X	78
Red Scar	Lancs	SD5832	53°47·2'	2°37·8'W	T	102
Redscar Br	Northum	NT9433	55°35·7'	2°5·3'W	X	74,75
Redscar Burn	Northum	NY7557	54°54·7'	2°23·0'W	W	86,87
Redscarhead	Scot Bord	NT2444	55°41·3'	3°12·1'W	T	73
Redscar Heugh	D & G	NS8118	55°26·7'	3°52·4'W	X	71,78
Redscar Law	Scot Bord	NT3842	55°40·3'	2°58·7'W	H	73
Red Screes	Cumbr	NY3909	54°28·6'	2°56·1'W	X	90
Redshank's Fm	Cambs	TL2193	52°31·5'	0°12·6'W	FM	142
Redshaw	Northum	NY9392	55°13·6'	2°6·2'W	X	80
Redshaw	N Yks	SD8085	54°15·9'	2°18·0'W	X	98
Redshaw	S Lanak	NS8628	55°32·2'	3°48·0'W	X	71,72
Redshaw	Staffs	SJ9661	53°9·0'	2°3·2'W	X	118
Redshaw Burn	S Lanak	NT0313	55°24·3'	3°31·5'W	W	78
Redshaw Gill	N Yks	SE1556	54°0·2'	1°45·9'W	X	104
Redshaw Hall	N Yks	SE1556	54°0·2'	1°45·9'W	X	104
Redshaw Moss	N Yks	SD8084	54°15·3'	2°18·0'W	X	98
Redshead	S Lanak	NS8738	55°37·6'	3°47·2'W	X	71,72
Redshill	E Loth	NT5266	55°53·3'	2°45·6'W	X	66
Redshin Cove	Northum	NU0150	55°44·9'	1°58·6'W	W	75
Red Shoot Wood	Hants	SU1808	50°52·5'	1°44·3'W	F	195
Redside	E Loth	NT5782	56°2·0'	2°41·0'W	X	67
Redside	Midlo	NT3059	55°49·4'	3°6·6'W	X	66,73
Redside Burn	Midlo	NT3159	55°49·4'	3°5·6'W	W	66,73
Red Sike	Cumbr	NY6277	55°5·4'	2°35·3'W	W	86
Redsike	Cumbr	NY6377	55°5·4'	2°34·4'W	X	86
Redsike Head	Scot Bord	NT2026	55°31·5'	3°15·6'W	H	73
Redsmouth Ho	Northum	NY8681	55°7·6'	2°12·7'W	X	80
Red Spa Moor	Lancs	SD9135	53°48·9'	2°7·8'W	X	103
Red Stane	Shetld	HU4227	60°1·8'	1°14·3'W	X	4
Red Stead	Northum	NU2516	55°26·5'	1°35·9'W	X	81
Redstocks	Wilts	ST9362	51°21·7'	2°5·6'W	T	173
Redstone	Devon	SX4593	50°43·2'	4°11·4'W	X	190
Redstone	Moray	NH9954	57°34·1'	3°40·9'W	X	27
Redstone	Pth & Kin	NO1834	56°29·7'	3°19·5'W	X	53
Redstone Bank	Pemb	SN1115	51°48·3'	4°44·1'W	X	158
Redstone Cross	Pemb	SN1016	51°48·9'	4°45·0'W	X	158
Redstone Hill	Aberd	NO6579	56°54·3'	2°34·0'W	X	45
Redstone Hill	Beds	TL1848	52°7·3'	0°16·2'W	X	153
Red Stone Hill	Somer	SS8139	51°8·5'	3°41·7'W	X	181
Redstone Rig	D & G	NX4385	55°8·3'	4°27·4'W	X	77
Redstone Rig	E Loth	NT6063	55°51·8'	2°37·9'W	X	67
Redstone Rock	Worcs	SO8169	52°19·4'	2°16·3'W	X	138
Redstones	Aberd	NJ6206	57°8·9'	2°37·2'W	X	37
Redstones	Aberd	NJ9740	57°27·3'	2°2·5'W	X	30
Red Street	Staffs	SJ8251	53°3·6'	2°15·7'W	T	118
Redsyke	S Lanak	NT0537	55°37·3'	3°30·1'W	X	72
Red Syke Fm	Cumbr	NY3626	54°37·8'	2°59·1'W	FM	90
Red Taingy	Moray	NJ2050	57°32·2'	3°19·7'W	X	28
Red Tarn	Cumbr	NY2603	54°25·3'	3°8·0'W	W	89,90
Red Tarn	Cumbr	NY3415	54°31·8'	3°0·8'W	W	90
Red Tarn Beck	Cumbr	NY3515	54°31·8'	2°59·8'W	W	90
Red Tile Fm	Cambs	TL3384	52°26·5'	0°2·2'W	FM	142
Red Tile Fm	Cambs	TL5464	52°15·4'	0°15·8'E	FM	154
Redtye	Corn	SX0263	50°26·2'	4°46·9'W	T	200
Redvales	Bury	SD8008	53°34·3'	2°17·7'W	T	109
Redwalls	N Ayr	NS3546	55°41·0'	4°37·0'W	X	63
Redward	Essex	TQ9896	51°37·9'	0°52·1'E	X	168
Redway	I of W	SZ5384	50°39·4'	1°14·6'W	X	196
Redwell	Aberd	NJ6410	57°11·0'	2°35·3'W	X	37
Redwell	Angus	NO3950	56°38·5'	2°59·2'W	X	54

Red Well	Northnts	SP8868	52°18·4'	0°42·2'W	A	152
Redwell Fisheries	Lancs	SD5469	54°7·1'	2°41·8'W	X	97
Redwell Hall Fm	Northum	NZ0351	54°51·5'	1°56·8'W	FM	87
Redwell Hills Fm	Durham	NZ1351	54°51·5'	1°47·4'W	FM	88
Redwells	Fife	NO5508	56°16·0'	2°43·1'W	X	59
Redwells	Fife	NT2299	56°10·9'	3°15·0'W	X	58
Redwells Wood	Fife	NO5508	56°16·0'	2°43·1'W	F	59
Red Well, The	Cambs	TL3362	52°14·6'	0°2·7'W	A	154
Redwell Wood	Herts	TL2102	51°42·4'	0°14·5'W	F	166
Redwell Wood Fm	Herts	TL2002	51°42·5'	0°15·4'W	FM	166
Red Wharf Bay	I of Angl	SH5381	53°18·6'	4°12·0'W	T	114,115
Red Wharf Bay or Traeth-coch	I of Angl	SH5480	53°18·1'	4°11·0'W	W	114,115
Redwick	Newp	ST4184	51°33·3'	2°50·7'W	T	171,172
Redwick	S Glos	ST5485	51°34·0'	2°39·4'W	T	172
Redwing	Cumbr	NY7341	54°46·0'	2°24·8'W	X	86,87
Red Wing	Durham	NY8432	54°41·2'	2°14·5'W	X	91,92
Redwings Horse Sanctuary	Norf	TG2517	52°42·5'	1°20·2'E	X	133,134
Redwith	Shrops	SJ2821	52°47·1'	3°3·7'W	X	126
Redwith	Shrops	SJ3024	52°48·8'	3°1·9'W	T	126
Red Wood	Glos	SO7003	51°43·7'	2°25·7'W	F	162
Redwood	Heref	SO5665	52°17·1'	2°38·3'W	X	137,138,149
Red Wood	Kent	TQ6866	51°22·3'	0°25·2'E	F	177,178
Red Wood	Shrops	SO3183	52°26·7'	3°0·5'W	F	137
Redwood Fm	Ches	SJ9369	53°13·3'	2°5·9'W	FM	118
Redwood Fm	N Som	ST5269	51°25·3'	2°41·0'W	FM	172,182
Redwood Lodge	Cambs	TL1770	52°19·2'	0°16·6'W	X	153
Redwoods Fm	Devon	ST0119	50°58·0'	3°24·2'W	FM	181
Redworth	Darl	NZ2423	54°36·3'	1°37·3'W	T	93
Redworth Hall	Darl	NZ2323	54°36·3'	1°38·2'W	X	93
Redwrae	S Ayr	NS4228	55°31·5'	4°29·7'W	X	70
Red Wychend	Heref	SO6247	52°7·4'	2°32·9'W	X	149
Redyeates Cross	Devon	SS8807	50°51·3'	3°35·1'W	X	192
Redyeates Fm	Devon	SS8707	50°51·3'	3°35·9'W	FM	192
Redyett	Stir	NS5387	56°3·5'	4°21·2'W	X	57
Red Yetts	Clackm	NS9692	56°6·8'	3°39·9'W	X	58
Reecastle Crag	Cumbr	NY2717	54°32·8'	3°7·3'W	X	89,90
Reecleuch Hill	D & G	NS8516	55°25·7'	3°48·6'W	X	71,78
Reed	Devon	SX8383	50°38·3'	3°38·9'W	X	191
Reed	Herts	TL3636	52°0·6'	0°0·7'W	T	154
Reed Barn	Lancs	SD6547	53°55·3'	2°31·6'W	X	102,103
Reed Bower	Pth & Kin	NO1301	56°11·9'	3°23·7'W	X	58
Reed Court Fm	Kent	TQ7248	51°12·5'	0°28·1'E	FM	188
Reeded Barn Fm	Cambs	TL5151	52°8·4'	0°12·8'E	FM	154
Reed End	Herts	TL3436	52°0·6'	0°2·5'W	T	154
Reed Fen	Cambs	TL4598	52°33·9'	0°8·8'E	X	143
Reed Fm	Kent	TR1750	51°12·7'	1°6·8'E	FM	179,189
Reed Fm, The	Ches	SJ9879	53°18·7'	2°1·4'W	FM	118
Reedgate Fm	Ches	SJ6582	53°20·3'	2°31·1'W	FM	109
Reed Hall	Herts	TL3635	52°0·0'	0°0·7'W	X	154
Reedham	Lincs	TF2456	53°5·4'	0°8·5'W	T	122
Reedham	Norf	TG4201	52°33·4'	1°34·6'E	T	134
Reedham Ferry	Norf	TG4001	52°33·5'	1°32·8'E	X	134
Reedham Marsh	Norf	TG3619	52°43·3'	1°30·1'E	W	133,134
Reedham Marshes	Norf	TG4503	52°34·4'	1°37·4'E	X	134
Reedham Sta	Croy	TQ3060	51°19·7'	0°7·3'W	X	176,177,187
Reed Hill	Ches	SJ9779	53°18·7'	2°2·3'W	X	118
Reed Hill	Ches	SJ9780	53°19·3'	2°2·3'W	X	109
Reedholme Common	Donc	SE6717	53°39·0'	0°58·8'W	X	111
Reedholme Fm	N Yks	NZ3100	54°23·9'	1°30·9'W	FM	93
Reed House Fm	Ches	SJ6679	53°18·7'	2°30·2'W	FM	118
Reed House Fm	Traf	SJ7289	53°24·1'	2°24·9'W	FM	109
Reedie	Angus	NO3552	56°39·6'	3°3·2'W	X	54
Reedie Hill Fm	Fife	NO2013	56°18·4'	3°17·1'W	FM	58
Reedieleys	Fife	NO2310	56°16·8'	3°14·2'W	X	58
Reeding	Northum	NY9450	54°50·9'	2°5·2'W	X	87
Reedland Marshes	Suff	TM4872	52°17·6'	1°38·6'E	W	156
Reedley	Lancs	SD8435	53°48·9'	2°14·2'W	T	103
Reednees Grange	E Yorks	SE7719	53°39·9'	0°49·7'W	X	112
Reedness	E Yorks	SE7923	53°42·1'	0°47·8'W	T	105,106,112
Reed Point	Lincs	TF2051	53°2·8'	0°12·2'W	T	122
Reed Point	Scot Bord	NT7872	55°56·7'	2°20·7'W	X	67
Reeds Beck	Lincs	TF1764	53°9·8'	0°14·6'W	W	121
Reeds Beck Fm	Lincs	TF2065	53°10·3'	0°11·9'W	FM	122
Reed's Cross	Devon	ST0811	50°53·7'	3°18·1'W	X	192
Reed's Fm	Essex	TL6607	51°44·5'	0°24·7'E	FM	167
Reeds Fm	Kent	TQ6444	51°10·5'	0°21·2'E	FM	188
Reed's Fm	St Hel	SJ4799	53°29·3'	2°47·5'W	FM	108
Reed's Fm	W Susx	SU9103	50°49·4'	0°42·1'W	FM	197
Reed's Fm	W Susx	TQ2517	50°56·6'	0°12·9'W	FM	198
Reedsford	Northum	NT8932	55°35·1'	2°10·0'W	T	74
Reedshaw Moss	N Yks	SD9541	53°52·2'	2°4·1'W	F	103
Reedsholes	Lincs	TF2123	52°47·7'	0°11·9'W	X	131
Reeds Holme	Lancs	SD8024	53°43·0'	2°17·8'W	T	103
Reed Sike	Northum	NY9380	55°7·1'	2°6·2'W	W	80
Reed's Moss	St Hel	SJ4798	53°28·8'	2°47·5'W	X	108
Reeds Rigg	Northum	NY8758	54°55·2'	2°11·7'W	X	87
Reeds, The	N Yks	SE2885	54°15·8'	1°33·8'W	F	99
Reedswood Crag	Northum	NY7597	55°16·2'	2°23·2'W	X	80
Reedweel	D & G	NX8261	54°56·0'	3°50·1'W	X	84
Reedy	Devon	SX8289	50°41·6'	3°39·9'W	T	191
Reedy Cliff	Corn	SW9780	50°35·3'	4°51·7'W	X	200
Reedy Edge	Scot Bord	NY4899	55°17·2'	2°48·7'W	H	79
Reedy Loch	Scot Bord	NT8253	55°46·5'	2°16·8'W	X	67,74
Reef	N Eil	NB1134	58°12·3'	6°54·7'W	T	13
Reef, The	Arg & Bt	NM0044	56°29·8'	6°52·1'W	X	46
Reef, The	Arg & Bt	NM0045	56°30·3'	6°52·1'W	X	46
Reef, The	E Loth	NT7574	55°57·8'	2°23·6'W	X	67
Reehewan	Angus	NO4476	56°52·6'	2°54·7'W	X	44
Ree Hill	D & G	NX7181	55°6·7'	4°0·9'W	X	77
Reeker Pike	Northum	NY6682	55°8·1'	2°31·6'W	X	80
Reekie	Aberd	NJ5315	57°13·7'	2°46·3'W	X	37
Reekie Linn	Angus	NO2553	56°40·0'	3°13·0'W	W	53
Reekimlane	Moray	NJ3625	57°18·9'	3°3·3'W	X	37
Reekitlane	Aberd	NJ5102	57°6·6'	2°48·1'W	X	37
Reeks Wood	W Susx	SU8929	51°3·4'	0°43·4'W	F	186,197
Reeky Knowes	Orkney	HY3826	59°7·2'	3°4·5'W	A	6
Reeley Mires Fm	Ghead	NZ1461	54°56·9'	1°46·5'W	FM	88
Reelig Ho	Highld	NH5543	57°27·5'	4°24·6'W	X	26

Reen Cross	Corn	SW7753	50°20·3'	5°7·7'W	X	200,204
Reenes	Northum	NY8284	55°9·2'	2°16·5'W	X	80
Reenlarig Burn	Moray	NJ0646	57°29·9'	3°33·6'W	W	27
Reen Manor	Corn	SW7654	50°20·8'	5°8·5'W	T	200
Reen Sands	Corn	SW7654	50°20·8'	5°8·5'W	X	200
Reepham	Lincs	TF0373	53°14·9'	0°27·0'W	T	121
Reepham	Norf	TG1023	52°46·0'	1°7·2'E	T	133
Reepham Moor	Lincs	TF0574	53°15·4'	0°25·2'W	X	121
Rees	Corn	SW7952	50°19·8'	5°5·9'W	X	200,204
Reestones	Northum	NZ0675	55°4·4'	1°53·9'W	X	87
Reeth	N Yks	SE0399	54°23·4'	1°56·8'W	T	98
Reeth	W Susx	SU9128	51°2·9'	0°41·7'W	X	186,197
Reeth Bay	I of W	SZ5075	50°34·6'	1°17·2'W	X	196
Reeth High Moor	N Yks	NY9701	54°24·5'	2°2·4'W	X	92
Reeth Low Moor	N Yks	NZ0100	54°24·0'	1°58·7'W	X	92
Reeva	Shetld	HZ2070	59°31·2'	1°38·3'W	X	4
Reeve	Devon	SS6708	50°51·6'	3°53·0'W	X	191
Reeve Castle	Devon	SS7002	50°48·4'	3°50·3'W	X	191
Reeve Hill	S Lanak	NT0022	55°29·1'	3°34·5'W	H	72
Reeve Ho	Corn	SX2496	50°44·5'	4°29·3'W	X	190
Reeve's Coombe	Devon	SX8379	50°36·2'	3°38·8'W	X	191
Reeves Cotts	Herts	TL2403	51°42·9'	0°11·9'W	X	166
Reeves Edge	Lancs	SD6857	54°0·7'	2°28·9'W	X	103
Reeves Gorse	Lincs	SK9349	53°2·0'	0°36·4'W	F	130
Reeves Green	Sol	SP2677	52°23·7'	1°36·7'W	T	140
Reeves Hall	Essex	TM0415	51°48·0'	0°57·9'E	X	168
Reeveshall Marsh	Essex	TM0416	51°48·5'	0°58·0'E	X	168
Reeves Hill	Heref	SO3169	52°19·1'	3°0·3'W	H	137,148
Reeves Plantation	Lincs	SK9950	53°2·5'	0°31·0'W	F	121
Reeves Rest	Surrey	TQ2655	51°17·0'	0°11·2'W	X	187
Reev's Moor	Derby	SK2238	52°56·6'	1°40·0'W	X	128
Refail	Gwyn	SH1729	52°49·9'	4°42·6'W	X	123
Refail	Powys	SJ1900	52°35·7'	3°11·4'W	T	136
Refaithy	Highld	ND3148	58°25·2'	3°10·4'W	X	11,12
Reffley Wood	Norf	TF6521	52°45·9'	0°27·1'E	F	132
Reffolds Copse	Surrey	TQ1943	51°10·7'	0°17·5'W	F	187
Reform Stone	Derby	SK2180	53°19·2'	1°40·7'W	X	110
Refouble	Highld	NH9540	57°26·6'	3°44·5'W	X	27
Refreish	Moray	NJ2223	57°17·7'	3°17·2'W	X	36
Refuge	Orkney	HY3315	59°1·3'	3°9·5'W	X	6
Refuge Fm	E Yorks	TA0770	54°7·1'	0°21·4'W	FM	101
Regaby	I of M	SC4397	54°20·9'	4°24·5'W	T	95
Regaby Beg	I of M	SC4297	54°20·9'	4°25·4'W	X	95
Regal Burn	S Lanak	NS6833	55°34·6'	4°5·2'W	W	71
Regal Hill	S Lanak	NS6933	55°34·6'	4°4·2'W	X	71
Regaule	Moray	NJ0249	57°31·5'	3°37·7'W	X	27
Regency Ho	Devon	ST1312	50°54·3'	3°13·9'W	X	181,193
Regent Ho	N Lincs	TA1024	53°42·3'	0°19·6'W	X	107,113
Regent's Park	C of West	TQ2882	51°31·6'	0°8·9'W	T	176
Regent's Park	C of West	TQ2882	51°31·6'	0°8·9'W	X	176
Regent's Wood	Staffs	SK0314	52°43·7'	1°56·9'W	F	128
Regil	Bath & NE Somer	ST5362	51°21·5'	2°40·1'W	T	172,182
Regilbury Court	Bath & NE Somer	ST5262	51°21·5'	2°41·0'W	X	172,182
Regilbury Park Fm	Bath & NE Somer	ST5362	51°21·5'	2°40·1'W	FM	172,182
Regland Burn	D & G	NX6885	55°8·8'	4°3·8'W	W	77
Regland Loch	D & G	NX6985	55°8·8'	4°2·9'W	W	77
Regoul	Highld	NH8851	57°32·4'	3°51·8'W	X	27
Regvlbivm (Roman Fort)	Kent	TR2369	51°22·8'	1°12·7'E	R	179
Rehaurie	Highld	NH9348	57°30·8'	3°46·7'W	X	27
Rehiran	Highld	NH8346	57°29·6'	3°56·7'W	X	27
Rehoboth Fm	Pemb	SM8531	51°56·4'	5°7·3'W	FM	157
Reibinis	N Eil	NG1892	57°50·0'	6°44·6'W	X	14
Reidchalmai	Highld	NC7203	58°0·1'	4°9·5'W	X	16
Réidh a' Bhuirg	Arg & Bt	NR1864	55°47·5'	6°29·5'W	X	60
Reidh a' Ghuail	Highld	NM7795	56°59·8'	5°39·8'W	X	33,40
Reidhall	Angus	NO5967	56°47·8'	2°39·8'W	X	44
Réidh Breac	Highld	NH0236	57°22·5'	5°17·1'W	X	25
Reidhbreac	Highld	NH6396	57°56·2'	4°18·4'W	X	21
Reidh-dhail	Highld	NM4364	56°42·1'	6°11·5'W	X	47
Réidh Dorch	Moray	NJ1715	57°13·4'	3°22·0'W	H	36
Réidh Eilean	Arg & Bt	NM2426	56°21·0'	6°27·6'W	X	48
Réidh nan Loch	Highld	NG4333	57°19·2'	6°15·7'W	X	32
Reidlin	Highld	NC7302	57°59·6'	4°8·4'W	X	16
Reidside	Aberd	NJ6057	57°36·3'	2°39·7'W	X	29
Reidside Burn	Aberd	NJ6055	57°35·3'	2°39·7'W	W	29
Reidside Moss	Aberd	NJ6056	57°35·8'	2°39·7'W	X	29
Reidstack	Aberd	NJ5762	57°39·0'	2°42·8'W	X	29
Reidston	E Ayr	NS4517	55°25·6'	4°26·5'W	X	70
Reidswell	Aberd	NJ6542	57°28·3'	2°34·6'W	X	29
Reieval	Highld	NG3965	57°36·2'	6°21·7'W	H	23
Reiff	Highld	NB9614	58°4·4'	5°27·1'W	T	15
Reiff Bay	Highld	NB9614	58°4·4'	5°27·1'W	W	15
Reiffer Park	D & G	NX4445	54°46·8'	4°25·1'W	X	83
Reigate	Surrey	TQ2649	51°13·8'	0°11·3'W	T	187
Reigate Heath	Surrey	TQ2350	51°14·4'	0°13·9'W	T	187
Reigate Hill	Surrey	TQ2552	51°15·4'	0°12·1'W	X	187
Reighton	N Yks	TA1375	54°9·7'	0°15·7'W	T	101
Reighton Field	N Yks	TA1274	54°9·2'	0°16·7'W	X	101
Reighton Gap	N Yks	TA1376	54°10·3'	0°15·7'W	X	101
Reighton Sands	N Yks	TA1476	54°10·3'	0°14·8'W	X	101
Reilly Fm	Renf	NS4269	55°53·6'	4°31·2'W	FM	64
Reilth Fm	Shrops	SO2786	52°28·3'	3°4·1'W	FM	137
Reilth Top	Shrops	SO2888	52°29·4'	3°3·2'W	H	137
Reimshill	Aberd	NJ7541	57°27·8'	2°24·5'W	X	29
Reinacharn Lodge	Aberd	NJ4408	57°9·8'	2°55·1'W	X	37
Reinakyllich	Pth & Kin	NN9466	56°46·7'	3°43·6'W	X	43
Reinchall	Aberd	NO8593	57°1·9'	2°14·4'W	X	38,45
Reindeer Ho	Highld	NH9709	57°9·9'	3°41·7'W	X	36
Reinden Wood	Kent	TR2141	51°7·8'	1°9·9'E	F	179,189
Reineabhal	N Eil	NF7525	57°12·3'	7°22·5'W	H	22
Rein Gill	S Lanak	NS9826	55°31·3'	3°36·5'W	W	72
Reinigeadal	N Eil	NB2201	57°55·0'	6°41·2'W	X	14
Reins Fm	N Yks	SE5585	54°15·7'	1°8·9'W	FM	100
Reins Wood	N Yks	SE5685	54°15·7'	1°8·0'W	F	100
Rein, The	N Yks	SE4437	53°49·9'	1°19·5'W	X	105
Rein, The (Earthwork)	N Yks	SE4437	53°49·9'	1°19·5'W	A	105
Rèisa an t-Sruith	Arg & Bt	NR7399	56°8·0'	5°38·8'W	X	55

Rèisa Mhic Phaidean	Arg & Bt	NM7500	56°8·6'	5°36·9'W	X	55
Reisgill	Highld	ND2336	58°18·6'	3°18·4'W	X	11
Reisgill Burn	Highld	ND2337	58°19·2'	3°18·4'W	W	11
Reisk	Angus	NO4055	56°41·2'	2°58·3'W	X	54
Reiskmore	Highld	NH7172	57°43·4'	4°9·5'W	X	21
Reismeave	Highld	NC7865	58°33·6'	4°5·3'W	X	10
Reisque	Aberd	NJ8820	57°16·5'	2°11·5'W	X	38
Reiss	Highld	ND3354	58°28·4'	3°8·4'W	T	12
Reiss Lodge	Highld	ND3354	58°28·4'	3°8·4'W	X	12
Reivesley	Aberd	NJ8228	57°20·8'	2°17·5'W	X	38
Reivoch	Renf	NS3957	55°47·0'	4°33·6'W	X	63
Rejerrah	Corn	SW8056	50°22·0'	5°5·2'W	T	200
Rejerrah Fm	Corn	SW8056	50°22·0'	5°5·2'W	FM	200
Relandsgate	Cumbr	NY6220	54°34·7'	2°34·9'W	X	91
Relaquheim	Aberd	NJ3112	57°11·9'	3°8·1'W	X	37
Relashes	Moray	NJ5550	57°32·5'	2°44·6'W	X	29
Releath	Corn	SW6633	50°9·3'	5°16·2'W	T	203
Relic Hill	D & G	NX9888	55°10·8'	3°35·7'W	H	78
Relief	D & G	NY1977	55°5·1'	3°15·7'W	X	85
Relubbus	Corn	SW5631	50°8·0'	5°24·5'W	T	203
Relugas	Moray	NH9948	57°30·9'	3°40·7'W	T	27
Remembrance Wood	Essex	TM1631	51°56·4'	1°8·9'E	F	168,169
Remenham	Wok	SU7784	51°33·2'	0°53·0'W	T	175
Remenham Court	Wok	SU7683	51°32·7'	0°53·8'W	X	175
Remenham Hill	Wok	SU7882	51°32·1'	0°52·1'W	T	175
Remenham Place	Wok	SU7782	51°32·1'	0°53·0'W	X	175
Remichie	Moray	NJ1054	57°34·3'	3°29·8'W	X	28
Remilton	Fife	NO3413	56°18·5'	3°3·6'W	X	59
Remiltoun	Fife	NT0387	56°4·2'	3°33·0'W	X	65
Remony	Pth & Kin	NN7643	56°34·0'	4°0·6'W	X	51,52
Remore	Highld	NH5642	57°27·0'	4°23·5'W	X	26
Remore	Highld	NH9448	57°30·8'	3°45·7'W	X	27
Remote	Midlo	NT4065	55°52·7'	2°57·1'W	X	66
Remote, The	Ches	SJ3372	53°14·7'	2°59·8'W	X	117
Rempstone	Notts	SK5724	52°48·9'	1°8·9'W	T	129
Rempstone Fm	Dorset	SY9882	50°38·5'	2°1·3'W	FM	195
Rempstone Hall	Dorset	SY9982	50°38·5'	2°0·5'W	X	195
Rempstone Heath	Dorset	SY9884	50°39·6'	2°1·3'W	F	195
Remuil Hill	Arg & Bt	NR6212	55°23·0'	5°44·8'W	H	68
Remusaig	Highld	NC7302	57°59·6'	4°8·4'W	T	16
Renacres Hall (Hospl)	Lancs	SD3612	53°36·3'	2°57·6'W	X	108
Renagour	Stir	NN5001	56°10·9'	4°24·6'W	X	57
Renaten	Moray	NJ2632	57°22·6'	3°13·4'W	X	37
Renby Fm	E Susx	TQ5333	51°4·8'	0°11·4'E	FM	188
Rence Park Fm	Suff	TM2035	51°58·4'	1°12·6'E	FM	169
Rench Fm	S Lanak	NS6338	55°37·2'	4°10·1'W	FM	71
Rendall	Orkney	HY3920	59°4·0'	3°3·3'W	X	6
Rendall	Orkney	HY4850	59°20·3'	2°54·4'W	X	5
Rendcomb	Glos	SP0209	51°47·0'	1°57·9'W	T	163
Rendcomb Buildings	Glos	SP0309	51°47·0'	1°57·0'W	X	163
Rendcomb Park	Glos	SP0110	51°47·6'	1°58·7'W	X	163
Rendham	Suff	TM3564	52°13·7'	1°26·9'E	T	156
Rendham Barnes	Suff	TM3564	52°13·7'	1°26·9'E	X	156
Rendham Hall Fm	Suff	TM3565	52°14·2'	1°26·9'E	FM	156
Rendlesham	Suff	TM3253	52°7·8'	1°23·8'E	T	156
Rendlesham Forest	Suff	TM3349	52°5·6'	1°24·5'E	F	169
Rendlesham Forest	Suff	TM3450	52°6·1'	1°25·4'E	F	156
Rendlesham Hall Fm	Suff	TM3354	52°8·3'	1°24·7'E	FM	156
Rendy Fm	Somer	ST1524	51°0·8'	3°12·3'W	FM	181,193
Renfrew	Renf	NS4966	55°52·1'	4°24·3'W	T	64
Renhold	Beds	TL0852	52°9·6'	0°24·9'W	T	153
Renhurst Fm	E Susx	TQ5830	51°3·1'	0°15·6'E	FM	188
Renish	E Yorks	TA3130	53°45·2'	0°0·4'W	X	107
Renishaw	Derby	SK4477	53°17·5'	1°20·0'W	T	120
Renishaw Park	Derby	SK4378	53°18·1'	1°20·9'W	X	120
Renish Island	N Eil	NG0481	57°43·5'	6°57·9'W	X	18
Renish Point	N Eil	NG0482	57°44·1'	6°57·9'W	X	18
Renmure	Angus	NO6452	56°39·8'	2°34·8'W	X	54
Rennald Burn	D & G	NY2696	55°15·4'	3°9·4'W	W	79
Renney Rocks	Devon	SX4948	50°19·0'	4°6·9'W	X	201
Rennibister	Orkney	HY3912	58°59·7'	3°3·2'W	X	6
Rennies Burn	Northum	NT8011	55°23·8'	2°18·5'W	W	80
Rennieshill	Aberd	NJ8920	57°16·5'	2°10·5'W	X	38
Rennieston	Scot Bord	NT7120	55°28·6'	2°27·1'W	X	74
Rennington	Northum	NU2118	55°27·6'	1°39·6'W	T	81
Renningtonmoor	Northum	NU2017	55°27·0'	1°40·6'W	X	81
Rennison	N Yks	NZ1814	54°31·5'	1°42·9'W	X	92
Rennison's Carr Fm	N Lincs	TA0111	53°35·4'	0°28·0'W	FM	112
Renny Fm	N Yks	NZ4100	54°23·9'	1°21·7'W	FM	93
Rennygill Sike	Durham	NY8519	54°34·2'	2°13·5'W	W	91,92
Rennyhill	Fife	NO5704	56°13·9'	2°41·2'W	X	59
Renny Park Coppice	Cumbr	NY3601	54°24·3'	2°58·7'W	F	90
Rennys Barn	Northum	NY9255	54°53·6'	2°7·1'W	X	87
Renny Slip	Pemb	SM7508	51°43·8'	5°15·1'W	W	157
Renscault Fm	I of M	SC3580	54°11·6'	4°31·3'W	FM	95
Renscombe Fm	Dorset	SY9677	50°35·8'	2°3·0'W	FM	195
Rensey	Devon	SS7209	50°52·2'	3°48·8'W	X	191
Renshaw Wood	Shrops	SJ8306	52°39·3'	2°14·7'W	T	127
Renshent	I of M	SC2977	54°9·9'	4°36·7'W	X	95
Renson	Devon	SX3896	50°44·7'	4°17·4'W	X	190
Renters Fm	Essex	TL9011	51°46·1'	0°45·6'E	FM	168
Renton	W Dunb	NS3878	55°58·3'	4°35·3'W	T	63
Renton Barns	Scot Bord	NT8265	55°52·9'	2°16·8'W	X	67
Renton Hall	E Loth	NT5471	55°56·0'	2°43·7'W	X	66
Renton Ho	Scot Bord	NT8265	55°52·9'	2°16·8'W	X	67
Renwick	Cumbr	NY5943	54°47·1'	2°37·8'W	T	86
Renwick Fell	Cumbr	NY6145	54°48·1'	2°36·0'W	X	86
Reoch Hill	E Ayr	NS5632	55°33·9'	4°16·6'W	X	71
Repentancehill	D & G	NY1571	55°1·8'	3°19·4'W	X	85
Repentance Tower	D & G	NY1572	55°2·4'	3°19·4'W	A	85
Reperry Cross	Corn	SX0463	50°26·3'	4°45·2'W	X	200
Reppoch Knowe	E Ayr	NS5930	55°32·9'	4°13·7'W	X	71
Repps	Norf	TG4117	52°42·0'	1°34·4'E	T	134
Repps Level	Norf	TG4118	52°42·5'	1°34·5'E	X	134
Repton	Derby	SK3026	52°50·1'	1°32·9'W	T	128
Repton Common	Derby	SK3224	52°49·0'	1°31·1'W	X	128
Repton School	Derby	SK3027	52°50·6'	1°32·9'W	A	128
Repton Shrubs	Derby	SK3123	52°48·5'	1°32·0'W	F	128
Reraig	Highld	NG8127	57°17·1'	5°37·6'W	T	33
Reraig Burn	Highld	NG8436	57°22·1'	5°35·1'W	W	24
Reraig Cottage	Highld	NG8336	57°22·0'	5°36·1'W	X	24
Rereach	Highld	NH8547	57°30·2'	3°54·7'W	X	27
Reres Wood	Fife	NO4821	56°23·0'	2°50·1'W	F	54,59
Rerwick	Orkney	HY5311	58°59·3'	2°48·6'W	X	6
Rerwick	Shetld	HU3719	59°57·5'	1°19·8'W	T	4
Rerwick Head	Orkney	HY5411	58°59·3'	2°47·5'W	X	6
Rerwick Point	Orkney	HY5312	58°59·8'	2°48·6'W	X	6
Resaurie	Highld	NH7045	57°28·9'	4°9·6'W	T	27
Rescassa	Corn	SW9842	50°14·8'	4°49·6'W	T	204
Rescobie	Angus	NO5052	56°39·7'	2°48·5'W	T	54
Rescobie Loch	Angus	NO5151	56°39·2'	2°47·5'W	W	54
Rescorla	Corn	SW9848	50°18·1'	4°49·8'W	X	204
Rescorla	Corn	SX0257	50°23·0'	4°46·7'W	T	200
Reservoir Cottage	Cumbr	NY4407	54°27·6'	2°51·4'W	X	90
Reservoir Ho	N Yks	SE1679	54°12·6'	1°44·9'W	X	99
Reservoir Plantn	N Yks	SE1195	54°21·3'	1°49·4'W	F	99
Reservoir Wood	Leic	SK8130	52°51·9'	0°47·4'W	F	130
Reset Plantn	N Lanak	NS7561	55°49·8'	3°59·3'W	F	64
Resipole	Highld	NM7264	56°43·0'	5°43·1'W	X	40
Reskadinnick	Corn	SW6341	50°13·5'	5°19·0'W	T	203
Reskajeage Downs	Corn	SW6343	50°14·6'	5°19·1'W	X	203
Reskivers	Corn	SW9244	50°15·8'	4°54·7'W	X	204
Reslaw Wood	Heref	SO6923	51°54·5'	2°26·6'W	F	162
Resolis	Highld	NH6765	57°39·6'	4°13·3'W	T	21
Resolis Mains	Highld	NH6765	57°39·6'	4°13·3'W	X	21
Resolven	Nth Pt Talb	SN8202	51°42·5'	3°42·1'W	T	170
Resourie	Highld	NM8670	56°46·6'	5°29·7'W	X	40
Resparva	Corn	SW8854	50°21·1'	4°58·4'W	X	200
Resparveth	Corn	SW9050	50°19·0'	4°56·6'W	X	200,204
Resphill Wood	N Yks	SE0852	53°58·1'	1°52·3'W	F	104
Rest	Carm	SN1822	51°52·3'	4°38·2'W	X	145,158
Restalrig	C of Edin	NT2874	55°57·5'	3°8·8'W	T	66
Rest and be thankful	Arg & Bt	NN2307	56°13·6'	4°50·9'W	X	56
Rest Bay	Brig	SS7978	51°29·5'	3°44·2'W	W	170
Rest Dodd	Cumbr	NY4313	54°30·8'	2°52·4'W	H	90
Restenneth	Angus	NO4751	56°39·1'	2°51·4'W	X	54
Rest Hill Fm	Oxon	SP4329	51°57·7'	1°22·1'W	FM	164
Resting Hill	Orkney	HY5536	59°12·8'	2°46·8'W	X	5
Restland	Devon	SX6396	50°45·1'	3°56·1'W	X	191
Restlands	W Susx	TQ3830	51°3·4'	0°1·5'W	X	187
Restna Lochs	Shetld	HU2054	60°16·4'	1°37·8'W	W	3
Restocknach	Moray	NJ2531	57°22·1'	3°14·4'W	X	37
Reston	Cumbr	SD4598	54°22·7'	2°50·4'W	T	97
Reston	Scot Bord	NT8862	55°51·3'	2°11·1'W	T	67
Restonhill	Scot Bord	NT8960	55°50·2'	2°10·1'W	X	67
Restormel	Corn	SX1061	50°25·3'	4°40·1'W	X	200
Rest Park	N Yks	SE5333	53°47·7'	1°11·3'W	X	105
Restronguet Barton	Corn	SW8136	50°11·2'	5°3·7'W	X	204
Restronguet Creek	Corn	SW8138	50°12·3'	5°3·8'W	W	204
Restronguet Passage	Corn	SW8137	50°11·8'	5°3·7'W	T	204
Restronguet Point	Corn	SW8137	50°11·8'	5°3·7'W	X	204
Restrop	Wilts	SU0886	51°34·6'	1°52·7'W	T	173
Rest, The	Brig	SS8078	51°29·5'	3°43·3'W	X	170
Resugga	Corn	SW8550	50°18·9'	5°0·8'W	X	200,204
Resugga	Corn	SW9452	50°20·2'	4°53·3'W	X	200,204
Resugga Castle	Corn	SW9451	50°19·6'	4°53·3'W	A	200,204
Resugga Green	Corn	SX0256	50°22·5'	4°46·7'W	T	200
Resugga Lane-end	Corn	SW9451	50°19·6'	4°53·3'W	X	200,204
Resurrance	Corn	SW8854	50°21·1'	4°58·4'W	X	200
Reswallie	Angus	NO5051	56°39·1'	2°48·5'W	X	54
Retallack	Corn	SW5631	50°8·0'	5°24·5'W	X	203
Retallack	Corn	SW9365	50°27·1'	4°54·6'W	T	200
Retanach	Moray	NJ5649	57°32·0'	2°43·6'W	X	29
Retarrier Ledges	I Scilly	SV8206	49°52·4'	6°25·2'W	X	203
Reterth Fm	Corn	SW9463	50°26·1'	4°53·7'W	FM	200
Retford	Notts	SK7080	53°19·0'	0°56·5'W	T	120
Retford (Gamston) Airport	Notts	SK6976	53°16·8'	0°57·5'W	X	120
Rethie Taing	Orkney	HY6544	59°17·1'	2°36·4'W	X	5
Retire	Corn	SX0064	50°26·7'	4°48·6'W	T	200
Retire Common	Corn	SX0063	50°26·2'	4°48·6'W	X	200
Retorrick Mill	Corn	SW8666	50°27·5'	5°0·5'W	X	200
Retreat Fm	Essex	TL7908	51°44·7'	0°36·0'E	FM	167
Retreat Fm	Suff	TM3285	52°25·0'	1°25·1'E	FM	156
Retreat Ho	Scot Bord	NT7760	55°50·2'	2°21·6'W	X	67
Retreat, The	Corn	SW9163	50°26·0'	4°56·2'W	X	200
Retreat, The (Mus)	Angus	NO5078	56°53·7'	2°48·8'W	X	44
Retta Skerries	Shetld	HU3438	60°7·8'	1°22·8'W	X	4
Rettendon	Essex	TQ7698	51°39·4'	0°33·1'E	T	167
Rettendon Grange Fm	Essex	TQ7896	51°38·3'	0°34·7'E	FM	167
Rettendon Hall	Essex	TQ7796	51°38·3'	0°33·9'E	X	167
Rettendon Lodge	Essex	TQ7896	51°38·3'	0°34·7'E	X	167
Rettendon Place	Essex	TQ7795	51°37·8'	0°33·8'E	X	167
Rett Geo	Shetld	HU6087	60°34·0'	0°53·8'W	X	1,2
Rettie	Aberd	NJ6363	57°39·6'	2°36·7'W	X	29
Rett, The	Shetld	HP6509	60°45·8'	0°47·9'W	X	1
Rett, The	Shetld	HU5490	60°35·7'	1°0·3'W	X	1,2
Rettunter	Shetld	HU3726	60°1·3'	1°19·7'W	X	4
Rettuvie, The	Shetld	HU3784	60°32·5'	1°19·0'W	X	1,2,3
Returno Fm	Pemb	SN0914	51°47·8'	4°45·8'W	FM	158
Retyn Fm	Corn	SW8858	50°23·3'	4°58·6'W	FM	200
Reuchal	S Ayr	NX1784	55°7·3'	4°51·8'W	X	76
Reudle	Arg & Bt	NM3646	56°32·2'	6°17·2'W	X	47,48
Revack Lodge	Highld	NJ0325	57°18·6'	3°36·2'W	X	36
Reva Hill	Leeds	SE1543	53°53·2'	1°45·9'W	X	104
Reva Resr	Leeds	SE1542	53°52·7'	1°45·9'W	W	104
Revedge	Staffs	SK0153	53°4·7'	1°58·7'W	X	119
Revels Fm	Essex	TL6938	52°1·1'	0°28·2'E	FM	154
Revel's Hall	Herts	TL3313	51°48·2'	0°3·9'W	X	166
Revelshay Fm	Dorset	ST4000	50°48·0'	2°50·7'W	FM	193
Revesby	Lincs	TF2961	53°8·1'	0°3·9'W	T	122
Revesby Abbey	Lincs	TF3062	53°8·6'	0°3·0'W	X	122
Revesby Bridge	Lincs	TF3060	53°7·5'	0°3·0'W	T	122
Reveston Ho	W Loth	NS9363	55°51·2'	3°42·1'W	X	65
Reveton	Devon	SX7249	50°19·9'	3°47·5'W	X	202
Revidge	Black w Dar	SD6729	53°45·6'	2°29·6'W	T	103
Revidge	Staffs	SK0759	53°7·9'	1°53·3'W	H	119
Revri Geo	Shetld	HU5382	60°31·4'	1°1·6'W	X	1,2,3
Rew	Devon	SX7138	50°13·9'	3°48·2'W	T	202
Rew	Devon	SX7570	50°31·2'	3°45·4'W	T	202
Rew	Dorset	ST6905	50°50·9'	2°26·0'W	T	194
Rew	Dorset	SY6389	50°42·2'	2°31·1'W	X	194
Rew Down	I of W	SZ5477	50°35·6'	1°13·8'W	X	196
Rewe	Devon	SX8899	50°47·0'	3°34·9'W	X	192
Rewe	Devon	SX9499	50°47·1'	3°29·8'W	T	192
Rewe Fm	Somer	ST1021	50°59·1'	3°16·6'W	FM	181,193
Rewell Hill	W Susx	SU9809	50°52·6'	0°36·0'W	X	197
Rewell Ho	W Susx	SU9908	50°52·0'	0°35·2'W	X	197
Rewell Wood	W Susx	SU9808	50°52·0'	0°36·1'W	F	197
Rew Fm	I of W	SZ5478	50°36·2'	1°13·8'W	FM	196
Rew Hill	Dorset	SY6388	50°41·7'	2°31·0'W	X	194
Rewlach	Staffs	SK0961	53°9·0'	1°51·5'W	X	119
Rew Manor	Dorset	SY6389	50°42·2'	2°31·1'W	X	194
Rewsalls Fm	Essex	TM0313	51°47·0'	0°57·0'E	FM	168
Rew Street	I of W	SZ4794	50°44·8'	1°19·6'W	T	196
Rexon	Devon	SX4188	50°40·4'	4°14·6'W	T	190
Rexon Cross	Devon	SX4188	50°40·4'	4°14·6'W	T	190
Rexter Geo	Shetld	HP5603	60°42·6'	0°57·9'W	X	1
Rexton	Devon	SX4089	50°41·0'	4°15·5'W	X	190
Rexton Fm	Somer	ST1134	51°6·1'	3°15·9'W	FM	181
Rexworthy Fm	Somer	ST2536	51°7·3'	3°3·9'W	FM	182
Rexy Barrow	Somer	SS7741	51°9·5'	3°45·2'W	A	180
Reybridge	Wilts	ST9169	51°25·4'	2°7·4'W	T	173
Rey Cross	Durham	NY9012	54°30·4'	2°8·8'W	A	91,92
Reydon	Suff	TM4978	52°20·8'	1°39·8'E	T	156
Reydon Grange	Suff	TM4778	52°20·9'	1°38·0'E	X	156
Reydon Grove Fm	Suff	TM4879	52°21·4'	1°38·9'E	FM	156
Reydon Hall	Suff	TM4878	52°20·9'	1°38·9'E	X	156
Reydon Marshes	Suff	TM4876	52°19·8'	1°38·8'E	X	156
Reydon Smear	Suff	TM4978	52°20·8'	1°39·8'E	T	156
Reydon Wood	Suff	TM4778	52°20·9'	1°38·0'E	F	156
Reymerston	Norf	TG0206	52°37·1'	0°59·4'E	T	144
Reymerston Hall	Norf	TG0106	52°37·1'	0°58·6'E	X	144
Reynalton	Pemb	SN0908	51°44·5'	4°45·6'W	T	158
Reynard Crag	N Yks	SE2259	54°1·8'	1°39·4'W	X	104
Reynard's Cave	Derby	SK1452	53°4·1'	1°47·1'W	X	119
Reynold's Fm	Ches	SJ7761	53°9·0'	2°20·2'W	FM	118
Reynolds Place	Kent	TQ5667	51°23·1'	0°14·9'E	X	177
Reynoldston	Swan	SS4890	51°35·5'	4°11·3'W	T	159
Reynolds Wood	Herts	TL1921	51°52·7'	0°15·9'W	F	166
Reyson Oasts	E Susx	TQ8319	50°56·7'	0°36·7'E	X	199
Rezare	Corn	SX3677	50°34·4'	4°18·6'W	T	201
Rhadyr	Monm	SO3602	51°43·0'	2°55·2'W	T	171
Rhaeadr-bach	Gwyn	SH6669	53°12·3'	4°0·0'W	W	115
Rhaeadr Cynfal	Gwyn	SH7041	52°57·3'	3°55·7'W	W	124
Rhaeadr Du	Gwyn	SH6638	52°55·6'	3°59·2'W	W	124
Rhaeadr-fawr	Gwyn	SH6670	53°12·9'	4°0·0'W	W	115
Rhaeadr Mawddach	Gwyn	SH7327	52°49·8'	3°52·7'W	W	124
Rhaeadr Ogwen	Gwyn	SH6460	53°7·4'	4°1·5'W	W	115
Rhaeadr y Bedd	Conwy	SH9159	53°7·3'	3°37·3'W	W	116
Rhaeadr y Cwm	Gwyn	SH7341	52°57·3'	3°53·0'W	W	124
Rhagett Hall	Denb	SJ0943	52°58·8'	3°20·9'W	X	125
Rhaiadr Du	Gwyn	SH7224	52°48·1'	3°53·5'W	W	124
Rhandir	Carm	SN6819	51°51·5'	3°54·6'W	X	159
Rhandir	Cered	SN4251	52°8·3'	4°18·1'W	X	146
Rhandir	Conwy	SH8371	53°13·6'	3°44·8'W	T	116
Rhandir	Gwyn	SH3029	52°50·1'	4°31·0'W	X	123
Rhandir	Shrops	SJ2428	52°50·9'	3°7·3'W	X	126
Rhandirmwyn	Carm	SN7843	52°4·6'	3°46·4'W	T	146,147,160
Rhandir Uchaf	Cered	SN6071	52°19·4'	4°2·9'W	X	135
Rhandregynwen Fm	Powys	SJ2819	52°46·1'	3°3·6'W	FM	126
Rhan Hir Fm	Conwy	SH8766	53°11·0'	3°41·1'W	FM	116
Rhanich	Highld	NH7080	57°47·7'	4°10·8'W	X	21
Rhanneg	Denb	SJ0034	52°53·9'	3°28·8'W	H	125
Rhaoine	Highld	NC6405	58°1·1'	4°17·7'W	X	16
Rhaslas Pond	Caer	SO0907	51°45·5'	3°18·7'W	W	161
Rhayader	Powys	SN9768	52°18·3'	3°30·2'W	T	136,147
Rhea Fm	Heref	SO6939	52°3·1'	2°26·7'W	FM	149
Rhean-fawr	Swan	SS5695	51°38·4'	4°4·5'W	X	159
Rheda	Cumbr	NY0216	54°32·0'	3°30·5'W	X	89
Rhedyn	Gwyn	SH2932	52°51·7'	4°32·0'W	X	123
Rhedyn-coch	I of Angl	SH4166	53°10·3'	4°22·3'W	X	114,115
Rhedynog Bellaf	Gwyn	SH4138	52°55·2'	4°21·5'W	X	123
Rhees Green	Norf	TM2092	52°29·1'	1°14·8'E	X	134
Rheeves	Moray	NJ1160	57°37·5'	3°29·0'W	X	28
Rhee Wall	Kent	TR0026	51°0·1'	0°51·4'E	A	189
Rheewall Fm	Kent	TR0126	51°0·1'	0°52·3'E	FM	189
Rhegreanoch	Highld	NC0916	58°5·8'	5°14·0'W	X	15
Rheguile	Highld	NH6985	57°50·4'	4°11·9'W	X	21
Rheidol Falls	Cered	SN7178	52°23·3'	3°53·3'W	W	135,147
Rheilffordd Llyn Tegid or Bala Lake Railway	Gwyn	SH9133	52°53·2'	3°36·8'W	X	125
Rheindown	Highld	NH5247	57°29·6'	4°27·7'W	X	26
Rheindown Wood	Highld	NH5047	57°29·6'	4°29·7'W	F	26
Rheld	Powys	SO2217	51°51·0'	3°7·6'W	X	161
Rhelonie	Highld	NH5597	57°56·6'	4°26·5'W	X	21
Rhelonie Lodge	Highld	NH5793	57°54·5'	4°24·3'W	X	21
Rhemore	Highld	NM5750	56°35·0'	5°57·0'W	X	47
Rhemullen	Highld	ND1531	58°15·8'	3°26·5'W	X	11,17
Rhenab Fm	I of M	SC4688	54°16·1'	4°21·5'W	FM	95
Rhenass Fm	I of M	SC3185	54°14·2'	4°35·2'W	FM	95
Rhencullen	I of M	SC3291	54°17·5'	4°34·5'W	T	95
Rhendhoo	I of M	SC3898	54°21·4'	4°29·2'W	X	95
Rhenetra	Highld	NG4251	57°28·8'	6°17·8'W	T	23
Rhennie Fm	I of M	SC4486	54°15·0'	4°23·3'W	FM	95
Rhenny	I of M	SC3080	54°11·5'	4°35·9'W	X	95
Rhenny Plantation	I of M	SC3079	54°11·0'	4°35·9'W	F	95
Rhenwyllan	I of M	SC2168	54°4·9'	4°43·8'W	X	95
Rheol	Powys	SO0256	52°11·9'	3°25·6'W	X	147
Rheola	Nth Pt Talb	SN8304	51°43·6'	3°41·3'W	X	170
Rheola Brook	Nth Pt Talb	SN8305	51°44·1'	3°41·3'W	W	160
Rhesgoed	Denb	SJ1558	53°7·0'	3°15·8'W	X	116
Rhespass	Shrops	SO2584	52°27·2'	3°5·8'W	X	137
Rhestr Cerrig	Cered	SN8078	52°23·5'	3°45·4'W	X	135,136,147
Rhes-y-Cae	Flint	SJ1870	53°13·5'	3°13·3'W	T	116
Rhevackin	Highld	NH5239	57°25·3'	4°27·4'W	X	26
Rhewey	Powys	SO1557	52°12·5'	3°14·2'W	X	148
Rhewl	Denb	SJ0662	53°9·1'	3°23·9'W	T	116
Rhewl	Denb	SJ1060	53°8·0'	3°20·3'W	T	116
Rhewl	Denb	SJ1844	52°59·5'	3°12·9'W	T	125

Rhewl	Flint	SJ1869	53°12·9'	3°13·3'W	X	116
Rhewl	Monm	ST5093	51°38·3'	2°43·0'W	X	162,172
Rhewl	Powys	SO1161	52°14·6'	3°17·8'W	X	148
Rhewl	Shrops	SJ3034	52°54·2'	3°2·0'W	T	126
Rhewl	Wrex	SJ3639	52°56·9'	2°56·7'W	T	126
Rhewl-fawr	Flint	SJ1281	53°19·4'	3°18·9'W	T	116
Rhewl Fm	Denb	SJ0574	53°15·5'	3°25·0'W	FM	116
Rhewl-Mostyn	Flint	SJ1580	53°18·9'	3°16·1'W	T	116
Rhewl-wen	Denb	SJ1149	53°2·1'	3°19·2'W	X	116
Rhewyncoch	Carm	SN3134	51°59·0'	4°27·3'W	X	145
Rhialgwm	Powys	SJ0521	52°46·9'	3°24·1'W	H	125
Rhian	Highld	NC5616	58°6·8'	4°26·2'W	X	16
Rhianacoil	Highld	ND1845	58°23·4'	3°23·7'W	X	11,12
Rhian Breck	Highld	NC5905	58°1·0'	4°22·7'W	X	16
Rhian Bridge	Highld	NC5616	58°6·8'	4°26·2'W	X	16
Rhian Burn	Highld	NC5854	58°27·3'	4°25·5'W	W	10
Rhiangoll	Powys	SO1825	51°55·3'	3°11·2'W	W	161
Rhiangoll	Powys	SO1930	51°58·0'	3°10·3'W	W	161
Rhibo	Conwy	SH7765	53°10·3'	3°50·0'W	X	115
Rhibreack	Highld	NH6983	57°49·3'	4°11·9'W	X	21
Rhicarn	Highld	NC0825	58°10·6'	5°15·4'W	X	15
Rhiconich	Highld	NC2552	58°25·5'	4°59·3'W	T	9
Rhiconich River	Highld	NC2551	58°25·0'	4°59·3'W	W	9
Rhicullen	Highld	NH6971	57°42·8'	4°11·5'W	T	21
Rhidorroch Forest	Highld	NH2398	57°56·4'	4°58·9'W	X	20
Rhidorroch Ho	Highld	NH1795	57°54·7'	5°4·9'W	X	20
Rhidorroch River	Highld	NH2194	57°54·2'	5°0·8'W	W	20
Rhiedorrach	Pth & Kin	NO1274	56°51·2'	3°26·1'W	X	43
Rhiewport	Powys	SJ1701	52°36·3'	3°13·1'W	X	136
Rhiews	Shrops	SJ6337	52°56·0'	2°32·6'W	T	127
Rhifail	Highld	NC7249	58°24·9'	4°11·0'W	X	10
Rhifail Loch	Highld	NC7142	58°21·1'	4°11·8'W	W	10
Rhigolter	Highld	NC3357	58°28·4'	4°51·3'W	X	9
Rhigos	Rho Cyn Taf	SN9205	51°44·2'	3°33·5'W	T	160
Rhilean Burn	Highld	NH8937	57°24·9'	3°50·4'W	W	27
Rhilochan	Highld	NC7407	58°2·3'	4°7·6'W	T	16
Rhinaclach	Stir	NN6001	56°11·1'	4°14·9'W	X	57
Rhinagoup	Moray	NJ1050	57°32·1'	3°29·7'W	X	28
Rhinamain	Highld	NH6193	57°54·6'	4°20·3'W	X	21
Rhind	Clackm	NS8691	56°6·1'	3°49·5'W	X	58
Rhindbuckie Wood	Aberd	NO7193	57°1·9'	2°28·2'W	F	38,45
Rhind Hill	Fife	NO2503	56°13·1'	3°12·1'W	H	59
Rhindhu	Moray	NJ2421	57°16·7'	3°15·2'W	X	36
Rhinduie Ho	Highld	NH5845	57°28·6'	4°21·6'W	X	26
Rhinefield Ho	Hants	SU2603	50°49·8'	1°37·5'W	X	195
Rhinefield Ornamental Drive	Hants	SU2604	50°50·3'	1°37·5'W	X	195
Rhinefield Sandy's Inclosure	Hants	SU2504	50°50·3'	1°38·3'W	F	195
Rhinns of Islay	Arg & Bt	NR2157	55°43·8'	6°26·2'W	X	60
Rhinns of Kells	D & G	NX5083	55°7·4'	4°20·7'W	H	77
Rhinns Point	Arg & Bt	NR1751	55°40·5'	6°29·7'W	X	60
Rhinog Fach	Gwyn	SH6627	52°49·7'	3°58·9'W	H	124
Rhinog Fawr	Gwyn	SH6528	52°50·2'	3°59·8'W	H	124
Rhins, The	D & G	NX0650	54°48·7'	5°0·7'W	X	82
Rhins, The	D & G	NX0860	54°54·1'	4°59·3'W	X	82
Rhinstock	Aberd	NJ3216	57°14·0'	3°7·1'W	X	37
Rhinturk	Moray	NJ3632	57°22·7'	3°3·4'W	X	37
Rhippinllwyd	Cered	SN2842	52°3·2'	4°30·1'W	T	145
Rhippinllwyd	Cered	SN3050	52°7·6'	4°28·6'W	T	145
Rhiroy	Highld	NH1589	57°51·4'	5°6·6'W	T	20
Rhisalach	Highld	NC2212	58°3·9'	5°0·6'W	X	15
Rhiston	Shrops	SO2595	52°33·1'	3°6·0'W	X	137
Rhitongue	Highld	NC6059	58°30·1'	4°23·7'W	T	10
Rhivaig	Highld	NH7289	57°52·6'	4°9·0'W	X	21
Rhives	Highld	NC8200	57°58·7'	3°59·2'W	X	17
Rhives	Highld	NH6656	57°34·7'	4°14·0'W	X	26
Rhives	Highld	NH7473	57°44·0'	4°6·5'W	T	21
Rhivichie	Highld	NC2354	58°26·6'	5°1·5'W	X	9
Rhiw	Caer	ST2098	51°40·7'	3°9·0'W	X	171
Rhiw	Carm	SN1422	51°52·2'	4°41·7'W	X	145,158
Rhiw	Carm	SN6125	51°54·6'	4°0·9'W	X	146
Rhiw	Conwy	SH7472	53°14·1'	3°52·9'W	X	115
Rhiw	Conwy	SH8158	53°6·6'	3°46·3'W	X	116
Rhiw	Conwy	SH9864	53°10·0'	3°31·1'W	X	116
Rhiw	Gwyn	SH2228	52°49·5'	4°38·1'W	T	123
Rhiw	Powys	SN9236	52°1·0'	3°34·0'W	X	160
Rhiw	Powys	SO1254	52°10·9'	3°16·8'W	X	148
Rhiw	Rho Cyn Taf	ST0086	51°34·1'	3°26·2'W	X	170
Rhiwabon or Ruabon	Wrex	SJ3043	52°59·0'	3°2·2'W	T	117
Rhiwaedog-is-afon	Gwyn	SH9732	52°52·8'	3°31·4'W	X	125
Rhiwaedog-uwch-afon	Gwyn	SH9331	52°52·2'	3°35·0'W	X	125
Rhiwargor	Powys	SH9624	52°48·5'	3°32·2'W	X	125
Rhiwarthen Isaf	Cered	SN6479	52°23·8'	3°59·5'W	X	135
Rhiwbebyll	Denb	SJ1265	53°10·7'	3°18·6'W	T	116
Rhiwbergoch	Powys	SN8630	51°57·6'	3°39·2'W	X	160
Rhiwbina	Card	ST1581	51°31·5'	3°13·1'W	T	171
Rhiwbina Fm	Card	ST1482	51°32·1'	3°14·0'W	FM	171
Rhiwbren Fawr	Cered	SN4757	52°11·6'	4°13·9'W	X	146
Rhiwbrwdwal	Rho Cyn Taf	ST0683	51°32·5'	3°20·9'W	X	170
Rhiwbryfdir	Gwyn	SH6946	53°0·0'	3°56·7'W	T	115
Rhiwceiliog	Brig	SS9784	51°33·0'	3°28·7'W	T	170
Rhiw Cilgwyn	Carm	SN7241	52°3·4'	3°51·6'W	H	146,147,160
Rhiwddolion	Conwy	SH7655	53°4·9'	3°50·7'W	X	115
Rhiw-ddu	Carm	SN7220	51°52·1'	3°51·2'W	X	160
Rhiwderin	Newp	ST2687	51°34·9'	3°3·7'W	T	171
Rhiw Dyfeity Fawr	Powys	SN8793	52°31·6'	3°39·5'W	X	135,136
Rhiwe	Pemb	SN0922	51°52·1'	4°46·1'W	X	145,158
Rhiwen	Gwyn	SH5763	53°8·9'	4°7·9'W	T	114,115
Rhiwen	Powys	SN9792	52°31·2'	3°30·7'W	X	136
Rhiwerfa	Gwyn	SH6506	52°38·3'	3°59·3'W	X	124
Rhiwfallen	Gwyn	SH4656	53°5·0'	4°17·6'W	X	115,123
Rhiwfawr	Nth Pt Talb	SN7410	51°46·7'	3°49·2'W	T	160
Rhiw Fawr	Powys	SJ1017	52°44·8'	3°19·6'W	X	125
Rhiw Fawr	Powys	SN8396	52°33·2'	3°43·1'W	X	135,136
Rhiw Felen	Gwyn	SH7829	52°50·9'	3°48·3'W	X	124
Rhiwfelen	Powys	SH7800	52°35·3'	3°47·7'W	X	135
Rhiwfelin	Rho Cyn Taf	ST0385	51°33·6'	3°23·6'W	X	170
Rhiwfelin Fach	Rho Cyn Taf	ST0485	51°33·6'	3°22·7'W	X	170
Rhiw Fer	Brig	SS9292	51°37·2'	3°33·2'W	X	170
Rhiw-for-fawr	Gwyn	SH5138	52°55·4'	4°12·6'W	X	124
Rhiw Fwnws	Powys	SO1653	52°10·4'	3°13·3'W	X	148
Rhiwgaeron	Gwyn	SH5908	52°39·3'	4°4·7'W	X	124
Rhiwgam	Powys	SN7994	52°32·1'	3°46·6'W	X	135
Rhiw-gam	Powys	SO0880	52°24·9'	3°20·8'W	X	136
Rhiwgan	Powys	SN8898	52°34·3'	3°38·8'W	X	135,136
Rhiw-garn	Rho Cyn Taf	ST0289	51°35·7'	3°24·5'W	X	170
Rhiwgoch	Cered	SN5571	52°19·3'	4°7·3'W	X	135
Rhiw Gôch	Conwy	SH7554	53°4·4'	3°51·6'W	X	115
Rhiw Gôch	Gwyn	SH6169	53°12·2'	4°4·5'W	X	115
Rhiw Goch	I of Angl	SH3782	53°18·8'	4°26·4'W	X	114
Rhiw Goch	Powys	SN7695	52°32·6'	3°49·3'W	X	135
Rhiw Goch	Powys	SN8599	52°34·8'	3°41·4'W	X	135,136
Rhiwgoch	Powys	SN9732	51°58·9'	3°29·6'W	X	160
Rhiw Gôch (Homestead)	Gwyn	SH6169	53°12·2'	4°4·5'W	A	115
Rhiwgriafol	Powys	SN8399	52°34·8'	3°43·2'W	X	135,136
Rhiw Gwgan	Gwyn	SH7310	52°40·6'	3°52·3'W	X	124
Rhiw Gwraidd	Powys	SO0163	52°15·6'	3°26·6'W	H	147
Rhiw Gwredydd	Gwyn	SH6913	52°42·2'	3°55·9'W	X	124
Rhiw hiriaeth	Powys	SJ0705	52°38·3'	3°22·1'W	X	125
Rhiw-hiriaeth Isaf	Powys	SJ0806	52°38·9'	3°21·2'W	X	125
Rhiw-ial Fm	Denb	SJ1856	53°5·9'	3°13·1'W	FM	116
Rhiwiau	Carm	SN7526	51°55·4'	3°48·7'W	H	146,160
Rhiwiau	Conwy	SH9460	53°7·8'	3°34·7'W	X	116
Rhiwiau	Denb	SH9960	53°7·9'	3°30·2'W	X	116
Rhiwiau	Powys	SO0524	51°54·6'	3°22·5'W	X	160
Rhiwiau	Powys	SO0839	52°2·7'	3°20·1'W	X	160
Rhiwiau	Powys	SO1661	52°14·7'	3°13·4'W	X	148
Rhiwiau Isaf	Conwy	SH6773	53°14·5'	3°59·2'W	X	115
Rhiwiau-uchaf	Carm	SN7425	51°54·8'	3°49·5'W	X	146,160
Rhiwinder	Rho Cyn Taf	ST0287	51°34·6'	3°24·5'W	T	170
Rhiwisg	Denb	SJ1558	53°7·0'	3°15·8'W	X	116
Rhiwlas	Carm	SN4503	51°42·5'	4°14·2'W	X	159
Rhiwlas	Cered	SN5360	52°13·4'	4°8·7'W	X	146
Rhiwlas	Cered	SN6187	52°28·0'	4°2·4'W	X	135
Rhiwlas	Cered	SN7570	52°19·1'	3°49·6'W	X	135,147
Rhiwlas	Conwy	SH8068	53°12·0'	3°47·4'W	X	116
Rhiwlas	Denb	SJ0360	53°7·9'	3°26·6'W	X	116
Rhiwlas	Gwyn	SH5765	53°10·0'	4°7·9'W	T	114,115
Rhiwlas	Gwyn	SH9237	52°55·4'	3°36·0'W	X	125
Rhiwlas	I of Angl	SH5378	53°17·0'	4°11·9'W	X	114,115
Rhiwlas	Powys	SJ0518	52°45·3'	3°24·1'W	X	125
Rhiwlas	Powys	SJ1932	52°53·0'	3°11·8'W	T	125
Rhiwlas Fm	Monm	SO3907	51°45·7'	2°52·6'W	FM	161
Rhiwlas Hall	Powys	SN7299	52°34·7'	3°52·9'W	X	135
Rhiwlas Hill	Powys	SN9377	52°23·1'	3°33·9'W	H	136,147
Rhiw Lawr	Powys	SO2166	52°17·4'	3°9·1'W	X	137,148
Rhiwlug	Cered	SN4044	52°4·5'	4°19·7'W	X	146
Rhiwlwyfen	Powys	SN7698	52°34·2'	3°49·4'W	X	135
Rhiw-mallaen	Carm	SN7440	52°2·9'	3°49·9'W	X	146,147,160
Rhiwmoel	I of Angl	SH4288	53°22·2'	4°22·1'W	X	114
Rhiwnachor	Powys	SJ0818	52°45·3'	3°21·4'W	X	125
Rhiwnant	Powys	SN8860	52°13·8'	3°38·0'W	W	147
Rhiwnant	Powys	SN8961	52°14·4'	3°37·1'W	X	147
Rhiwogof	Gwyn	SH7010	52°40·6'	3°55·0'W	X	124
Rhiwonnen	Cered	SN5754	52°10·2'	4°5·1'W	X	146
Rhiw Pool	Powys	SO1866	52°17·3'	3°11·7'W	W	136,148
Rhiwrerfyn	Carm	SN5739	52°2·1'	4°4·7'W	X	146
Rhiw Rhwstyn	Powys	SO0751	52°9·2'	3°21·2'W	X	147
Rhiwsaeson	Rho Cyn Taf	ST0782	51°32·0'	3°20·1'W	X	170
Rhiwsaeth	Powys	SJ0722	52°47·5'	3°22·3'W	X	125
Rhiw-saithbren	Carm	SN5233	51°58·8'	4°8·9'W	X	146
Rhiwson	Cered	SN5046	52°5·8'	4°11·0'W	X	146
Rhiw-tir	Gwyn	SH6045	52°59·3'	4°4·7'W	X	115
Rhiw Tor Cymry	Brig	SS8392	51°37·1'	3°41·0'W	H	170
Rhiw Trumau	Powys	SO1929	51°57·5'	3°10·3'W	X	161
Rhiw Wen	Carm	SN7319	51°51·5'	3°50·3'W	X	160
Rhiw Wen	Powys	SO2235	52°0·7'	3°7·8'W	X	161
Rhiw y Fan	Powys	SO2134	52°0·2'	3°8·7'W	X	161
Rhiw-yr-adar	Carm	SN5923	51°53·5'	4°2·6'W	X	159
Rhiw-yr-uchain	Rho Cyn Taf	ST0491	51°36·8'	3°22·8'W	X	170
Rhiw yr Ysgyfarnog	Powys	SO0119	51°51·9'	3°25·9'W	X	160
Rhoail	Arg & Bt	NM6337	56°28·2'	5°50·4'W	X	49
Rhobell Fawr	Gwyn	SH7825	52°48·8'	3°48·2'W	H	124
Rhobell-y-big	Gwyn	SH7828	52°50·4'	3°48·3'W	H	124
Rhodd's Fm	Suff	TM0746	52°4·6'	1°1·6'E	FM	155,169
Rhode	Somer	ST2734	51°6·3'	3°2·2'W	T	182
Rhode Barton	Dorset	SY3493	50°44·2'	2°55·7'W	X	193
Rhode Common	Kent	TR0656	51°16·2'	0°57·6'E	T	179
Rhode Court	Kent	TR0556	51°16·2'	0°56·7'E	X	179
Rhode Fm	Devon	SS9610	50°53·0'	3°28·3'W	FM	192
Rhode Fm	Devon	SS9804	50°49·8'	3°26·5'W	FM	192
Rhode Fm	Hants	SU7534	51°6·3'	0°55·3'W	FM	186
Rhode Hill	Devon	SY3394	50°44·7'	2°56·6'W	X	193
Rhodes	Bury	SD8405	53°32·7'	2°14·1'W	T	109
Rhodes Fm	Shrops	SO6896	52°33·9'	2°27·9'W	FM	138
Rhodes Hill	Northum	NT9440	55°39·5'	2°5·3'W	H	74,75
Rhodesia	Notts	SK5680	53°19·1'	1°9·2'W	T	111,120
Rhodes Minnis	Kent	TR1543	51°9·0'	1°4·8'E	T	179,189
Rhodeswood Resr	Derby	SK0498	53°29·0'	1°56·0'W	W	110
Rhodiad-y-Brenin	Pemb	SM7627	51°54·0'	5°15·0'W	X	157
Rhod Isaf	Pemb	SM7023	51°51·7'	5°20·0'W	X	157
Rhodmad	Cered	SN5974	52°21·0'	4°3·8'W	X	135
Rhod Uchaf	Pemb	SM7024	51°52·3'	5°20·1'W	W	157
Rhodyate Fm	N Som	ST4058	51°19·3'	2°51·3'W	FM	172,182
Rhoin Fm	Arg & Bt	NR6823	55°27·0'	5°39·7'W	FM	68
Rholben	Monm	SO2816	51°50·5'	3°2·3'W	X	161
Rhome	Powys	SN9534	51°59·9'	3°31·4'W	X	160
Rhonadale	Arg & Bt	NR7838	55°35·4'	5°30·9'W	X	68,69
Rhonadale Burn	Arg & Bt	NR7738	55°35·3'	5°31·9'W	W	68,69
Rhondda	Rho Cyn Taf	SS9796	51°39·4'	3°29·0'W	T	170
Rhondda Fach	Rho Cyn Taf	ST0095	51°38·9'	3°26·3'W	X	170
Rhondda Fawr	Rho Cyn Taf	SS9894	51°38·4'	3°28·1'W	X	170
Rhondda River or Afon Rhondda Fawr	Rho Cyn Taf	SS9398	51°40·5'	3°32·5'W	W	170
Rhone Hill	D & G	NX7367	54°59·1'	3°58·7'W	H	83,84
Rhonehouse or Kelton Hill	D & G	NX7459	54°54·8'	3°57·5'W	T	83,84
Rhongyr-isaf	Powys	SN8414	51°49·0'	3°40·6'W	X	160
Rhongyr-uchaf	Powys	SN8415	51°49·5'	3°40·6'W	X	160
Rhon Hill	Bucks	SP6324	51°54·9'	1°4·6'W	X	164,165
Rhonllwyn	Powys	SO1464	52°16·3'	3°15·2'W	X	148
Rhooks	Carm	SN3212	51°47·1'	4°25·8'W	X	159
Rhoon Fm	Norf	TF5621	52°46·1'	0°19·1'E	FM	131
Rhoose	V of Glam	ST0666	51°23·4'	3°20·7'W	T	170
Rhoose Point	V of Glam	ST0665	51°22·8'	3°20·7'W	X	170
Rhôs	Carm	SN3835	51°59·6'	4°21·2'W	T	145
Rhôs	Carm	SN4703	51°42·5'	4°12·5'W	X	159
Rhôs	Carm	SN6536	52°0·6'	3°57·6'W	X	146
Rhôs	Denb	SJ1261	53°8·6'	3°18·5'W	T	116
Rhos	Flint	SJ1174	53°15·6'	3°19·6'W	X	116
Rhôs	I of Angl	SH5578	53°17·0'	4°10·1'W	X	114,115
Rhos	Nth Pt Talb	SN7303	51°42·9'	3°49·9'W	T	170
Rhos	Powys	SJ0300	52°35·6'	3°25·5'W	X	136
Rhos	Powys	SJ0514	52°43·2'	3°24·0'W	X	125
Rhos	Powys	SJ1232	52°52·9'	3°18·1'W	H	125
Rhos	Powys	SJ2717	52°45·0'	3°4·5'W	T	126
Rhos	Powys	SO0779	52°24·3'	3°21·6'W	X	136,147
Rhos	Powys	SO1256	52°12·0'	3°16·9'W	X	148
Rhos	Powys	SO1351	52°9·3'	3°15·9'W	X	148
Rhos	Shrops	SJ2735	52°54·7'	3°4·7'W	X	126
Rhosaflo	Powys	SJ0606	52°38·9'	3°23·0'W	X	125
Rhosaman	Carm	SN7314	51°48·9'	3°50·2'W	T	160
Rhosbadrig	I of Angl	SH3572	53°13·4'	4°27·9'W	X	114
Rhosbeddau	I of Angl	SH3575	53°15·0'	4°28·0'W	X	114
Rhosbeirio	I of Angl	SH3991	53°23·7'	4°24·9'W	X	114
Rhos-berse	Wrex	SJ2850	53°2·8'	3°4·0'W	X	117
Rhosbothan	I of Angl	SH5171	53°13·2'	4°13·5'W	X	114,115
Rhôs Botwnnog	Gwyn	SH2632	52°51·7'	4°34·7'W	X	123
Rhos Bryn-llwyn	Conwy	SH9360	53°7·8'	3°35·6'W	X	116
Rhôs-cae'r-ceiliog	Conwy	SJ0046	53°0·4'	3°29·0'W	X	116
Rhoscefnhir	I of Angl	SH5276	53°15·9'	4°12·7'W	T	114,115
Rhoscellan	Cered	SN5985	52°26·9'	4°4·1'W	X	135
Rhos Cilcennin	Cered	SN5262	52°14·4'	4°9·7'W	X	146
Rhoscolyn	I of Angl	SH2675	53°14·9'	4°36·1'W	T	114
Rhoscolyn Beacon	I of Angl	SH2674	53°14·3'	4°36·0'W	X	114
Rhoscolyn Head	I of Angl	SH2575	53°14·8'	4°37·0'W	X	114
Rhos Common	Nth Pt Talb	SN7907	51°45·2'	3°44·8'W	X	160
Rhôs Common	Powys	SJ2818	52°45·5'	3°3·6'W	T	126
Rhoscrowther	Pemb	SM9002	51°40·9'	5°1·9'W	T	157,158
Rhos-crug	Powys	SO1774	52°21·7'	3°12·7'W	H	136,148
Rhoscrugebolion	Carm	SN2631	51°57·3'	4°31·5'W	X	145
Rhoscryman	I of Angl	SH2990	53°23·0'	4°33·9'W	X	114
Rhos Dawel	Gwyn	SH9538	52°56·0'	3°33·3'W	X	125
Rhos-ddû	Gwyn	SH2535	52°53·3'	4°35·7'W	T	123
Rhosddu	Pemb	SN2133	51°58·2'	4°36·0'W	X	145
Rhos-ddu	Wrex	SJ3351	53°3·4'	2°59·6'W	T	117
Rhosddu Fm	Powys	SJ2017	52°44·9'	3°10·7'W	FM	126
Rhos Dirion	Powys	SO2133	51°59·6'	3°8·6'W	X	161
Rhos Dringarth	Powys	SN9521	51°52·9'	3°31·1'W	X	160
Rhôs-Drynog	Powys	SH8300	52°35·4'	3°43·2'W	X	135,136
Rhosdylluan	Gwyn	SH8628	52°50·5'	3°41·2'W	T	124,125
Rhosesmor	Flint	SJ2168	53°12·4'	3°10·6'W	T	117
Rhosfach	Carm	SN1425	51°53·8'	4°41·8'W	X	145,158
Rhos-fâch	Carm	SN5609	51°45·9'	4°4·8'W	X	159
Rhosfach	Pemb	SN1128	51°55·3'	4°44·5'W	T	145,158
Rhos fach	Pemb	SN1330	51°56·5'	4°42·8'W	X	145
Rhosfach	Powys	SH9700	52°35·5'	3°30·8'W	X	136
Rhos Fach	Powys	SO1833	51°59·6'	3°11·3'W	X	161
Rhosfach	Shrops	SJ2631	52°52·5'	3°5·6'W	X	126
Rhosfallog	Powys	SO1274	52°21·7'	3°17·1'W	X	136,148
Rhosfarced	Pemb	SN1136	51°59·7'	4°44·8'W	X	145
Rhos-farch	Gwyn	SH6901	52°35·7'	3°55·6'W	X	135
Rhosfawr	Cered	SN2647	52°5·9'	4°32·0'W	X	145
Rhos Fawr	Cered	SN7474	52°21·2'	3°50·6'W	X	135,147
Rhos-fawr	Gwyn	SH3839	52°55·7'	4°24·2'W	T	123
Rhos Fawr	Pemb	SN0227	51°54·6'	4°52·3'W	X	145,157,158
Rhosfawr	Powys	SJ0921	52°47·0'	3°20·6'W	X	125
Rhosfawr	Powys	SJ1306	52°38·9'	3°16·8'W	X	125
Rhosfawr	Powys	SJ1314	52°43·2'	3°16·9'W	X	125
Rhosfawr	Powys	SN9988	52°29·1'	3°28·8'W	X	136
Rhos Fawr	Powys	SO1934	52°0·2'	3°10·4'W	X	161
Rhôs-fawr	Swan	SN6503	51°42·8'	3°56·9'W	X	159
Rhos Fawr Hill	Powys	SJ1204	52°37·8'	3°17·6'W	H	136
Rhosferig	Powys	SO0152	52°9·7'	3°26·4'W	X	147
Rhos Fiddle	Shrops	SO2085	52°27·7'	3°10·3'W	X	137
Rhos Fign	Cered	SN8171	52°19·7'	3°44·4'W	X	135,136,147
Rhos Fm	Conwy	SH8362	53°8·8'	3°44·6'W	FM	116
Rhos Fm	Powys	SJ2314	52°43·3'	3°8·0'W	FM	126
Rhos Fm, The	Shrops	SO1881	52°25·5'	3°12·0'W	FM	136
Rhosforlo	Powys	SN9851	52°9·1'	3°29·1'W	X	147
Rhosgadfan	Gwyn	SH5057	53°5·6'	4°14·0'W	T	115
Rhos Garn Whilgarn	Cered	SN4551	52°8·4'	4°15·5'W	H	146
Rhosgeler	Carm	SN3835	51°59·6'	4°21·2'W	X	145
Rhos Gelli-gron	Cered	SN7263	52°15·3'	3°52·1'W	X	146,147
Rhosgoch	Carm	SN2012	51°46·9'	4°36·2'W	X	158
Rhosgôch	Carm	SN6342	52°3·8'	3°59·5'W	X	146
Rhosgoch	Cered	SN4453	52°9·4'	4°16·4'W	X	146
Rhos-goch	Cered	SN5863	52°15·1'	4°4·4'W	X	146
Rhosgoch	Cered	SN6173	52°20·5'	4°2·0'W	X	135
Rhosgoch	Cered	SN6582	52°25·4'	3°58·7'W	X	135
Rhos Goch	Gwyn	SH2633	52°52·2'	4°34·7'W	X	123
Rhosgoch	I of Angl	SH4089	53°22·7'	4°23·9'W	T	114
Rhos-goch	Powys	SJ2806	52°39·1'	3°3·5'W	X	126
Rhosgoch	Powys	SN9877	52°23·1'	3°29·5'W	X	136,147
Rhosgoch	Powys	SO1847	52°7·2'	3°11·5'W	T	148
Rhos Goch Common	Powys	SO1948	52°7·7'	3°10·6'W	X	148
Rhosgoch-fach	Cered	SN4454	52°10·0'	4°16·5'W	X	146
Rhosgranog	Pemb	SM8627	51°54·3'	5°6·3'W	X	157
Rhos-grug	Powys	SO1772	52°20·6'	3°12·7'W	X	136,148
Rhos-gwawr	Rho Cyn Taf	SN9900	51°41·6'	3°27·3'W	X	170
Rhosgyll	Gwyn	SH4540	52°56·3'	4°18·0'W	T	123
Rhos Haminiog	Cered	SN5464	52°15·5'	4°8·0'W	T	146
Rhoshay	Powys	SO1878	52°23·9'	3°11·9'W	W	136,148
Rhoshelyg	Carm	SN5313	51°48·0'	4°7·5'W	X	159
Rhoshelyg	I of Angl	SH4972	53°13·7'	4°15·3'W	X	114,115
Rhoshenfryn	Powys	SO0868	52°18·4'	3°20·6'W	X	136,147
Rhos-hill	Pemb	SN1940	52°2·0'	4°37·9'W	X	145
Rhos-hill	Pemb	SN2332	51°57·7'	4°34·2'W	X	145
Rhos Hill	Powys	SO2669	52°19·1'	3°4·7'W	X	137,148
Rhos Hir	Powys	SO1777	52°23·3'	3°12·8'W	X	136,148

Rhoshirwaun	Gwyn	SH1929	52°49·9'	4°40·8'W	T	123
Rhos-Isa	Conwy	SH9064	53°10·0'	3°38·3'W	X	116
Rhôs Isaf	Denb	SJ1853	53°4·3'	3°13·0'W	X	116
Rhos-isaf	Flint	SJ2756	53°6·0'	3°5·0'W	X	117
Rhos Isaf	Gwyn	SH4857	53°5·6'	4°15·8'W	T	115,123
Rhos Isaf	I of Angl	SH5778	53°17·0'	4°8·3'W	X	114,115
Rhos Isaf	Pemb	SN0037	52°0·0'	4°54·4'W	X	145,157
Rhos Ithel	Flint	SJ2260	53°8·1'	3°9·6'W	X	117
Rhoslan	Gwyn	SH4840	52°56·4'	4°15·3'W	T	123
Rhoslanog	Pemb	SM8532	51°56·9'	5°7·3'W	X	157
Rhos-las	Gwyn	SH4950	53°1·8'	4°14·7'W	X	115,123
Rhoslefain	Gwyn	SH5705	52°37·7'	4°6·4'W	T	124
Rhosllanerchrugog	Wrex	SJ2946	53°0·6'	3°3·1'W	T	117
Rhôs Lligwy	I of Angl	SH4886	53°21·2'	4°16·6'W	T	114
Rhos-llyn	Cered	SN2147	52°5·8'	4°36·4'W	X	145
Rhos-lwyd	Cered	SN5866	52°16·7'	4°4·5'W	X	135
Rhoslydan	Denb	SJ1649	53°2·1'	3°14·8'W	X	116
Rhosmaen	Carm	SN6323	51°53·6'	3°59·1'W	T	159
Rhos-maen	Cered	SN5864	52°15·6'	4°4·4'W	X	146
Rhosmaen	Pemb	SN0741	52°2·3'	4°48·4'W	X	145
Rhosmaen	Pemb	SN1336	51°59·7'	4°43·0'W	X	145
Rhosmeheryn	Powys	SN8971	52°19·8'	3°37·3'W	X	135,136,147
Rhosmeirch	I of Angl	SH4677	53°16·3'	4°18·2'W	T	114,115
Rhosmor	I of Angl	SH3371	53°12·8'	4°29·7'W	X	114
Rhôs-mynach	I of Angl	SH4891	53°23·9'	4°16·8'W	X	114
Rhôs Nantperfedd	Cered	SN7875	52°21·8'	3°47·1'W	X	135,147
Rhosneigr	I of Angl	SH3173	53°13·9'	4°31·5'W	T	114
Rhosneigr Sta	I of Angl	SH3273	53°13·9'	4°30·6'W	X	114
Rhosneigwl	Gwyn	SH2529	52°50·1'	4°35·5'W	X	123
Rhosnesni	Wrex	SJ3450	53°2·8'	2°58·7'W	T	117
Rhos Newydd	I of Angl	SH5878	53°17·0'	4°7·4'W	X	114,115
Rhôs-on-Sea	Conwy	SH8381	53°19·0'	3°45·0'W	T	116
Rhôs or Colwyn Bay	Conwy	SH8679	53°18·0'	3°42·2'W	W	116
Rhos Owen	I of Angl	SH5376	53°15·9'	4°11·8'W	X	114,115
Rhos Peiran	Cered	SN7876	52°22·3'	3°47·1'W	X	135,147
Rhos Pen Bwa	Powys	SJ1114	52°43·2'	3°18·7'W	X	125
Rhos-Pengwern	Denb	SJ1939	52°56·8'	3°11·9'W	X	125
Rhôs Point	Conwy	SH8481	53°19·0'	3°44·1'W	X	116
Rhospwllygawnen	Carm	SN2929	51°56·2'	4°28·9'W	X	145
Rhosrhydd	Cered	SN7075	52°21·7'	3°54·2'W	X	135,147
Rhosrobin	Wrex	SJ3252	53°3·9'	3°0·5'W	T	117
Rhos Saith-maen	Powys	SN9460	52°13·9'	3°32·7'W	X	147
Rhossili	Swan	SS4188	51°34·3'	4°17·3'W	T	159
Rhossili Bay	Swan	SS3990	51°35·4'	4°19·1'W	W	159
Rhossili Down	Swan	SS4290	51°35·4'	4°16·5'W	X	159
Rhosson	Pemb	SM7225	51°52·9'	5°18·4'W	T	157
Rhos-swydd	Powys	SO1264	52°16·3'	3°17·0'W	X	148
Rhos, The	Pemb	SN0014	51°47·6'	4°53·6'W	T	157,158
Rhostono	Powys	SO0262	52°15·1'	3°25·7'W	X	147
Rhostrehwfa	I of Angl	SH4474	53°14·7'	4°19·9'W	T	114,115
Rhostryfan	Gwyn	SH4957	53°5·6'	4°14·9'W	T	115,123
Rhostwarch	Pemb	SN1235	51°59·1'	4°43·9'W	X	145
Rhostyllen	Wrex	SJ3148	53°1·7'	3°1·3'W	T	117
Rhos Uchaf Hall	Flint	SJ2656	53°6·0'	3°5·9'W	X	117
Rhos Waun-lloi	Cered	SN7571	52°19·6'	3°49·7'W	X	135,147
Rhôs-wen	Caer	SO1700	51°41·8'	3°11·7'W	X	171
Rhos Wen	Carm	SN5238	52°1·5'	4°9·0'W	X	146
Rhos-wen	Cered	SN2548	52°6·4'	4°32·9'W	X	145
Rhoswen	Gwyn	SH6941	52°57·3'	3°56·6'W	X	124
Rhoswiel	Shrops	SJ2936	52°55·2'	3°3·0'W	T	126
Rhos-y-beddau	Powys	SN9961	52°14·5'	3°28·4'W	X	147
Rhosybedw	Carm	SN6344	52°4·9'	3°59·6'W	X	146
Rhosybol	I of Angl	SH4288	53°22·2'	4°22·1'W	T	114
Rhos-y-brithdir	Powys	SJ1322	52°47·6'	3°17·0'W	T	125
Rhos-y-brwyner	Flint	SJ2961	53°8·7'	3°3·3'W	X	117
Rhos-y-Bryn	Pemb	SN1033	51°58·0'	4°45·6'W	X	145
Rhosycaerau	Pemb	SM9137	51°59·8'	5°2·3'W	T	157
Rhosychen	Carm	SN2729	51°56·2'	4°30·6'W	X	145,158
Rhos y Clegyrn	Pemb	SM9135	51°58·7'	5°2·2'W	X	157
Rhos-y-cribed	Pemb	SM7324	51°52·3'	5°17·5'W	X	157
Rhosydd	Gwyn	SH3737	52°54·6'	4°25·0'W	X	123
Rhosydd	I of Angl	SH3278	53°16·6'	4°30·8'W	X	114
Rhosydd	I of Angl	SH4771	53°13·1'	4°17·1'W	X	114,115
Rhosydd	I of Angl	SH5179	53°17·5'	4°13·7'W	X	114,115
Rhos-y-Gad	I of Angl	SH5179	53°17·5'	4°13·7'W	X	114,115
Rhosygadair	Cered	SN2350	52°7·4'	4°34·7'W	X	145
Rhosygadair Fawr	Cered	SN2349	52°6·9'	4°34·7'W	X	145
Rhosygadair Newydd	Cered	SN2449	52°6·9'	4°33·8'W	T	145
Rhosygadfa	Shrops	SJ3234	52°54·2'	3°0·3'W	T	126
Rhosygarreg	Powys	SN8095	52°32·6'	3°45·8'W	X	135,136
Rhos-y-garth	Cered	SN6372	52°20·0'	4°0·2'W	T	135
Rhos y Gell	Cered	SN7375	52°21·7'	3°51·5'W	X	135,147
Rhos y Gelynnen	Powys	SN8963	52°15·5'	3°37·2'W	X	147
Rhosygilwen	Pemb	SN2040	52°2·0'	4°37·1'W	T	145
Rhos-y-gilwern	Powys	SN9550	52°8·5'	3°31·7'W	X	147
Rhos-y-glascoed	Powys	SJ1313	52°42·7'	3°16·9'W	X	125
Rhos-y-gwaliau	Gwyn	SH9434	52°53·8'	3°34·1'W	T	125
Rhos-y-gweision	Powys	SJ0708	52°39·9'	3°22·1'W	X	125
Rhos-y-gwydi	Pemb	SN1024	51°53·2'	4°45·3'W	X	145,158
Rhos-y-llan	Gwyn	SH2337	52°54·3'	4°37·5'W	T	123
Rhos-y-llyn	Pemb	SN2432	51°57·8'	4°33·3'W	X	145
Rhos y Llyn	Powys	SN7592	52°30·9'	3°50·1'W	X	135
Rhos y madoc	Wrex	SJ3142	52°58·5'	3°1·3'W	T	117
Rhos-y-maerdy	Denb	SJ0638	52°56·1'	3°23·5'W	X	125
Rhos-y-mawn	Conwy	SH8566	53°11·0'	3°42·9'W	X	116
Rhosymedre	Wrex	SJ2842	52°58·5'	3°3·9'W	T	117
Rhos-y-meirch	Powys	SO2769	52°19·1'	3°3·9'W	T	137,148
Rhos Ymryson	Cered	SN4650	52°7·9'	4°14·6'W	X	146
Rhosyn-coch	Carm	SN2921	51°51·9'	4°28·6'W	T	145,159
Rhosynwst	Denb	SJ1443	52°58·9'	3°16·5'W	X	125
Rhosyrhiw	Cered	SN7473	52°20·7'	3°50·6'W	X	135,147
Rhôs-yr-yrfa	Caer	ST1398	51°40·7'	3°15·1'W	X	171
Rhos y Silio	Powys	SH8002	52°36·4'	3°45·9'W	X	135,136
Rhosywir	Powys	SN8399	52°34·8'	3°43·2'W	X	135,136
Rhotteridge Fm	Wilts	ST9366	51°23·8'	2°5·6'W	FM	173
Rhowniar Outward Bound	Gwyn	SN6098	52°34·0'	4°3·5'W	X	135
Rhu	Arg & Bt	NR8264	55°49·5'	5°28·4'W	X	62
Rhu	Arg & Bt	NS2684	56°1·3'	4°47·1'W	T	56
Rhual	Flint	SJ2264	53°10·3'	3°9·6'W	A	117
Rhuallt	Denb	SJ0775	53°16·1'	3°23·3'W	T	116
Rhuban	N Eil	NF7812	57°5·4'	7°18·5'W	X	31

Rhubana	Highld	NM6892	56°57·9'	5°48·5'W	X	40
Rhubha na Moch-thra	Highld	NM7943	56°31·9'	5°35·2'W	X	49
Rhubha nan Sasan	Highld	NG8192	57°52·1'	5°41·1'W	X	19
Rhubina Fm	Newp	ST2581	51°31·6'	3°4·5'W	FM	171
Rhubodach	Arg & Bt	NS0273	55°54·8'	5°9·7'W	X	63
Rhuddall Heath	Ches	SJ5562	53°9·4'	2°40·0'W	T	117
Rhuddallt	Carm	SN7947	52°6·7'	3°45·6'W	H	146,147
Rhuddallt	Gwyn	SH6718	52°44·8'	3°57·8'W	X	124
Rhuddgaer	I of Angl	SH4464	53°9·3'	4°19·6'W	X	114,115
Rhuddlan	Cered	SN4943	52°4·1'	4°11·8'W	X	146
Rhuddlan	Denb	SJ0278	53°17·6'	3°27·8'W	T	116
Rhuddwr Brook	Powys	SO1684	52°27·1'	3°13·8'W	W	136
Rhude	Devon	SS3006	50°50·0'	4°24·5'W	X	190
Rhude Cross	Corn	SS2608	50°51·0'	4°27·9'W	X	190
Rhudle	Arg & Bt	NR8494	56°5·7'	5°27·9'W	X	55
Rhudle Mill	Arg & Bt	NR8495	56°6·2'	5°28·0'W	X	55
Rhue	Highld	NH1097	57°55·6'	5°12·0'W	T	19
Rhue Ho	Highld	NM6184	56°53·4'	5°55·0'W	X	40
Rhulan	Powys	SN9336	52°1·0'	3°33·2'W	X	160
Rhulen	Powys	SO1349	52°8·2'	3°15·9'W	X	148
Rhulen Hill	Powys	SO1348	52°7·6'	3°15·9'W	H	148
Rhumach	Highld	NM6385	56°54·0'	5°53·1'W	X	40
Rhunahaorine	Arg & Bt	NR7048	55°40·5'	5°39·0'W	X	62
Rhunahaorine Point	Arg & Bt	NR6948	55°40·5'	5°40·0'W	X	62
Rhu-na-haven	Aberd	NO5197	57°3·9'	2°48·0'W	X	37,44
Rhu Nòa	Highld	NH0064	57°37·6'	5°20·5'W	X	19
Rhu Point	Arg & Bt	NR8263	55°48·9'	5°28·3'W	X	62
Rhuroin	Highld	NG7954	57°31·6'	5°41·0'W	X	24
Rhuthun or Ruthin	Denb	SJ1258	53°7·0'	3°18·5'W	T	116
Rhuvaal	Arg & Bt	NR4279	55°56·3'	6°7·5'W	X	60,61
Rhuveag	Stir	NN4819	56°20·6'	4°27·1'W	X	57
Rhuvid	Powys	SO1481	52°25·5'	3°15·5'W	X	136
Rhuvid Bank	Powys	SO1481	52°25·5'	3°15·5'W	X	136
Rhuvoult	Highld	NC2454	58°26·6'	5°0·5'W	T	9
Rhu Wood	Arg & Bt	NS3593	56°6·3'	4°38·7'W	F	56
Rhwngddwyafon	Gwyn	SH5345	52°59·2'	4°11·0'W	X	115
Rhwng-y-ddwy-afon	Denb	SJ0458	53°6·9'	3°25·7'W	X	116
Rhwngddwyborth	Gwyn	SH1731	52°51·0'	4°42·7'W	X	123
Rhyblid	Carm	SN7828	51°56·5'	3°46·1'W	X	146,160
Rhych Point	Brig	SS8276	51°28·5'	3°41·6'W	X	170
Rhŷd	Cered	SN2543	52°3·7'	4°32·8'W	T	145
Rhyd	Gwyn	SH6341	52°57·2'	4°2·0'W	T	124
Rhyd	Powys	SH9700	52°35·5'	3°30·8'W	X	136
Rhyd-afallen	Pemb	SN0823	51°52·6'	4°47·0'W	X	145,158
Rhydairy	Shrops	SJ2925	52°49·3'	3°2·8'W	X	126
Rhydale	Carm	SN5012	51°47·4'	4°10·1'W	X	159
Rhydargaeau	Carm	SN4326	51°54·9'	4°16·6'W	T	146
Rhydau	Gwyn	SH5665	53°10·0'	4°8·8'W	X	114,115
Rhydcaernarfon	Carm	SN2429	51°56·1'	4°33·2'W	X	145,158
Rhydcoch Fm	Cered	SN3646	52°5·5'	4°23·2'W	FM	145
Rhydcriw	Gwyn	SH6310	52°40·5'	4°1·2'W	X	124
Rhydcymerau	Carm	SN5738	52°1·6'	4°4·7'W	T	146
Rhydd	Worcs	SO8345	52°6·4'	2°14·5'W	T	150
Rhydd Covert	Worcs	SO8075	52°22·6'	2°17·2'W	F	138
Rhydd-ddu	Cered	SN4849	52°7·3'	4°12·8'W	X	146
Rhyd Ddu	Carm	SN7143	52°4·5'	3°52·5'W	X	146,147,160
Rhyd-Ddu	Gwyn	SH5652	53°3·0'	4°8·5'W	T	115
Rhyd-ddu	Pemb	SN1836	51°59·8'	4°38·7'W	X	145
Rhyd-Ddu Path	Gwyn	SH5852	53°3·0'	4°6·7'W	X	115
Rhyddgoed-fawr	Carm	SN3239	52°1·7'	4°26·5'W	X	145
Rhydd Green	Worcs	SO8345	52°6·4'	2°14·5'W	T	150
Rhydding	Nth Pt Talb	SS7598	51°40·3'	3°48·1'W	T	170
Rhyd-dolwen	Gwyn	SH9244	52°59·2'	3°36·1'W	X	125
Rhyddwr	Powys	SO1786	52°28·2'	3°12·9'W	X	136
Rhyd-dwrial	Denb	SJ1358	53°7·0'	3°17·6'W	X	116
Rhydeidion	Conwy	SH9265	53°10·5'	3°36·5'W	X	116
Rhydeinon	Cered	SN4254	52°9·9'	4°18·2'W	X	146
Rhyderwen	Cered	SN3853	52°9·3'	4°21·7'W	X	145
Rhyd-esgyn	Powys	SJ2714	52°43·4'	3°4·5'W	X	126
Rhyd-fawr	Powys	SO1926	51°55·8'	3°10·3'W	X	161
Rhydfechan	Cered	SN4054	52°9·9'	4°20·0'W	X	146
Rhydfelin	Powys	SO0255	52°11·3'	3°25·6'W	X	147
Rhyd Fm	Denb	SJ0580	53°18·7'	3°25·1'W	FM	116
Rhydfudr	Cered	SN5967	52°17·2'	4°3·6'W	X	135
Rhyd-fudr	Cered	SN6567	52°17·3'	3°58·4'W	X	135
Rhyd Galed	Carm	SN7141	52°3·4'	3°52·5'W	X	146,147,160
Rhydgaled	Cered	SN5664	52°15·6'	4°6·2'W	X	146
Rhydgaled	Conwy	SH9964	53°10·1'	3°30·2'W	T	116
Rhyd Galed	Denb	SJ0057	53°6·3'	3°29·2'W	X	116
Rhyd-galed	Gwyn	SH7102	52°36·3'	3°53·9'W	X	135
Rhydgaled	Pemb	SN1443	52°3·5'	4°42·4'W	X	145
Rhyd-goch	Carm	SN2428	51°55·6'	4°33·2'W	X	145,158
Rhydgwillim	Powys	SO0348	52°7·5'	3°24·6'W	X	147
Rhydhalog	Rho Cyn Taf	ST0279	51°30·3'	3°24·3'W	X	170
Rhydhir	Carm	SN3132	51°57·9'	4°27·2'W	X	145
Rhydhir	Powys	SO1574	52°21·7'	3°14·5'W	X	136,148
Rhyd-hir Brook	Powys	SN9969	52°18·8'	3°28·5'W	W	136,147
Rhydicar Fm	Heref	SO4824	51°55·0'	2°45·0'W	FM	161
Rhyd-Ifan	Conwy	SH8176	53°16·3'	3°46·7'W	X	116
Rhydins	Carm	SN8139	52°2·4'	3°43·7'W	X	160
Rhyd-isa	Denb	SJ1954	53°4·9'	3°12·2'W	X	116
Rhydlafr Fm	Card	ST1179	51°30·4'	3°16·6'W	FM	171
Rhydlanfair	Conwy	SH8252	53°3·4'	3°45·2'W	X	116
Rhydlas	Cered	SN5567	52°17·2'	4°7·2'W	X	135
Rhydleos	Powys	SJ2030	52°51·9'	3°10·9'W	X	126
Rhydlewis	Cered	SN3447	52°6·0'	4°25·0'W	T	145
Rhydlios	Gwyn	SH1830	52°50·5'	4°41·7'W	T	123
Rhyd-lydan	Carm	SN6241	52°3·3'	4°0·4'W	X	146
Rhydlydan	Cered	SN4352	52°8·9'	4°17·3'W	X	146
Rhydlydan	Conwy	SH8950	53°2·4'	3°38·9'W	T	116
Rhydlydan	Powys	SO0593	52°31·8'	3°23·6'W	T	136
Rhyd-lydan	Powys	SO1645	52°6·1'	3°13·2'W	X	148
Rhyd-meirionydd	Cered	SN6086	52°27·5'	4°3·2'W	X	135
Rhydmoelddu	Powys	SO0976	52°22·7'	3°19·8'W	X	136,147
Rhydness	Powys	SO1341	52°3·9'	3°15·8'W	X	148,161
Rhydoldog Fm	Powys	SN9467	52°17·7'	3°32·9'W	FM	136,147
Rhydolfordd	Powys	SO2358	52°13·1'	3°7·2'W	X	148
Rhydolion	Gwyn	SH2827	52°49·0'	4°32·7'W	X	123
Rhydonnen	Denb	SJ1163	53°9·6'	3°19·5'W	X	116
Rhydonnen-isaf	Denb	SJ1742	52°58·4'	3°13·8'W	X	125

Rhydorddwy Fawr	Denb	SJ0381	53°19·3'	3°27·0'W	X	116
Rhydowen	Carm	SN1928	51°55·5'	4°37·6'W	T	145,158
Rhyd-Owen	Carm	SN5544	52°4·8'	4°6·6'W	X	146
Rhydowen	Cered	SN4445	52°5·1'	4°16·2'W	T	146
Rhyd-Owen-isaf	Powys	SN8928	51°56·6'	3°36·5'W	X	160
Rhyd-Rhys-Harry	Carm	SN2429	51°56·1'	4°33·2'W	X	145,158
Rhyd-Rosser	Cered	SN5667	52°17·2'	4°6·3'W	T	135
Rhyd-Sais	Cered	SN4450	52°7·8'	4°16·4'W	X	146
Rhydspence	Heref	SO2447	52°7·2'	3°6·2'W	T	148
Rhydtalog	Flint	SJ2354	53°4·9'	3°8·6'W	T	117
Rhyd-uchaf	Gwyn	SH9037	52°55·4'	3°37·8'W	T	125
Rhydw	Carm	SN4415	51°49·0'	4°15·4'W	X	159
Rhydwen	Carm	SN1421	51°51·6'	4°41·7'W	X	145,158
Rhyd-wen	Cered	SN4150	52°7·8'	4°19·0'W	X	146
Rhyd-wen	Denb	SJ0381	53°19·3'	3°27·0'W	X	116
Rhydwen	Gwyn	SH7116	52°43·8'	3°54·2'W	X	124
Rhyd-wen	Gwyn	SH9229	52°51·1'	3°35·8'W	X	125
Rhydwen	Pemb	SN1834	51°58·7'	4°38·6'W	X	145
Rhyd-wen	Powys	SN8323	51°53·8'	3°41·6'W	X	160
Rhydwhyman	Powys	SO2198	52°34·7'	3°9·6'W	X	137
Rhydwydd	Carm	SN7639	52°2·4'	3°48·1'W	X	146,160
Rhydwyn	I of Angl	SH3188	53°22·0'	4°32·0'W	T	114
Rhydybannau	Cered	SN5251	52°8·5'	4°9·4'W	X	146
Rhyd-y-Beillen	Cered	SN4054	52°9·9'	4°20·0'W	X	146
Rhydybengan	Gwyn	SH2529	52°50·1'	4°35·5'W	X	123
Rhyd-y-bod	Gwyn	SH8927	52°50·0'	3°38·5'W	X	124,125
Rhyd-y Bont	I of Angl	SH2777	53°16·0'	4°35·2'W	X	114
Rhyd-y-bont	Powys	SO1831	51°58·5'	3°11·2'W	X	161
Rhyd-y-Brown	Pemb	SN0621	51°51·5'	4°48·6'W	T	145,158
Rhyd-y-ceir Brook	Powys	SN9864	52°16·1'	3°29·3'W	W	147
Rhyd-y-ceirw	Denb	SJ2256	53°6·0'	3°9·5'W	X	117
Rhyd-y-clafdy	Gwyn	SH3234	52°52·9'	4°29·4'W	T	123
Rhydyclwydau Brook	Powys	SO0078	52°23·7'	3°27·8'W	W	136,147
Rhyd-y-Creuau	Conwy	SH8057	53°6·0'	3°47·1'W	X	116
Rhyd-y-criw	Gwyn	SH5805	52°37·7'	4°5·5'W	X	124
Rhydycroesau	Shrops	SJ2430	52°52·0'	3°7·3'W	T	126
Rhydycul	Powys	SJ1025	52°49·1'	3°19·7'W	X	125
Rhyd-y-cwm	Shrops	SO1781	52°25·5'	3°12·8'W	T	136
Rhyd-y-cwrt	Cered	SN4952	52°9·0'	4°12·0'W	X	146
Rhyd-y-cyffn	Wrex	SJ4041	52°58·0'	2°53·2'W	X	117
Rhydycynydd	Cered	SN4744	52°4·6'	4°13·6'W	X	146
Rhydyddauddwr Fm	Denb	SJ0376	53°16·6'	3°26·9'W	FM	116
Rhyd-y-defaid	Gwyn	SH9038	52°55·9'	3°37·8'W	X	125
Rhydydefaid	I of Angl	SH3778	53°16·7'	4°26·3'W	X	114
Rhyd-y-delyn Fawr	I of Angl	SH5275	53°15·3'	4°12·7'W	X	114,115
Rhydydorth	Cered	SN5266	52°16·6'	4°9·8'W	X	135
Rhyd-y-fedw	Monm	ST4795	51°39·3'	2°45·6'W	X	171
Rhydyfelin	Carm	SN2837	52°0·5'	4°30·0'W	T	145
Rhydyfelin	Cered	SN5979	52°23·7'	4°3·9'W	T	135
Rhyd-y-felin	Powys	SJ0325	52°49·1'	3°26·0'W	X	125
Rhydyfelin	Powys	SO0893	52°31·9'	3°21·0'W	T	136
Rhydyfelin	Rho Cyn Taf	ST0988	51°35·2'	3°18·4'W	T	171
Rhydyferwig	Cered	SN3858	52°12·0'	4°21·8'W	X	145
Rhyd-y-ffynnon Fm	Carm	SN6018	51°50·8'	4°1·6'W	FM	159
Rhydyfirian	Cered	SN6078	52°23·2'	4°2·9'W	X	135
Rhydyfodrwydd	Cered	SN4745	52°5·2'	4°13·6'W	X	146
Rhyd-y-foel	Conwy	SH9176	53°16·4'	3°37·7'W	T	116
Rhydyfran	Carm	SN2211	51°46·4'	4°34·4'W	X	158
Rhyd-y-fran	Carm	SN6347	52°6·5'	3°59·6'W	X	146
Rhydyfran	Cered	SN5152	52°9·0'	4°10·3'W	X	146
Rhyd-y-fro	Nth Pt Talb	SN7105	51°44·0'	3°51·7'W	T	160
Rhydyfydr	Cered	SN5252	52°9·0'	4°9·4'W	X	146
Rhydygaled	Powys	SJ1427	52°50·3'	3°16·2'W	X	125
Rhyd-y-garreg-ddu	Carm	SN3226	51°54·7'	4°26·2'W	X	145
Rhyd-y-gath	Pemb	SN2131	51°57·2'	4°35·9'W	X	145
Rhydygele	Pemb	SM8524	51°52·6'	5°7·0'W	T	157
Rhyd y Gethin	Denb	SJ0233	52°53·4'	3°27·0'W	X	125
Rhydyglafes	Denb	SJ0439	52°56·6'	3°25·3'W	X	125
Rhydyglyn	Carm	SN6035	52°0·0'	4°2·0'W	X	146
Rhyd-y-gof-isaf	Cered	SN5552	52°9·1'	4°6·8'W	X	146
Rhyd-y-goleu	Flint	SJ2365	53°10·8'	3°8·7'W	X	117
Rhyd-y-groes	Gwyn	SH5866	53°10·6'	4°7·1'W	X	114,115
Rhyd-y-groes	I of Angl	SH3992	53°24·3'	4°24·9'W	X	114
Rhyd-y-groes	Powys	SJ2400	52°35·8'	3°6·9'W	X	126
Rhydygwiail	Powys	SH8205	52°38·0'	3°44·2'W	X	124,125
Rhyd-y-gwin	Swan	SN6703	51°42·8'	3°55·1'W	T	159
Rhyd-y-gwystl	Gwyn	SH4039	52°55·7'	4°22·4'W	T	123
Rhyd-y-llechau	Powys	SJ0717	52°44·8'	3°22·3'W	X	125
Rhyd-y-maen	Monm	SO4202	51°43·1'	2°50·0'W	X	171
Rhydymaen	Pemb	SN1140	52°1·8'	4°44·9'W	X	145
Rhydymain	Gwyn	SH8022	52°47·2'	3°46·4'W	T	124,125
Rhydymarchog	Carm	SN3824	51°53·7'	4°20·9'W	X	145,159
Rhyd-y-meirch	Monm	SO3107	51°45·7'	2°59·6'W	T	161
Rhyd-y-meirch	Powys	SJ9206	52°38·7'	3°35·4'W	X	125
Rhyd-y-meudwy	Denb	SJ1251	53°3·2'	3°18·4'W	T	116
Rhydymoch	Carm	SN1323	51°52·7'	4°42·6'W	X	145,158
Rhydymwyn	Flint	SJ2066	53°11·3'	3°11·4'W	T	117
Rhyd-y-pandy	Swan	SN6601	51°41·7'	3°55·9'W	X	159
Rhyd-y-parc	Carm	SN2127	51°55·0'	4°35·8'W	X	145,158
Rhydypennau	Cered	SN6285	52°27·0'	4°1·4'W	X	135
Rhyd-yr-arian	I of Angl	SH4873	53°14·2'	4°16·2'W	X	114,115
Rhyd-yr-Eidion Fawr	Conwy	SH9264	53°10·0'	3°36·5'W	X	116
Rhyd-yr-eirin	Conwy	SH9368	53°12·1'	3°35·7'W	X	116
Rhyd Yr Ewig	Conwy	SH9343	52°58·7'	3°35·2'W	X	125
Rhydyrhaiarn	Cered	SN4351	52°8·3'	4°17·3'W	X	146
Rhyd-yr-haw	Carm	SN4323	51°53·2'	4°16·5'W	X	159
Rhyd-yr-onnen	Gwyn	SH6102	52°36·1'	4°2·8'W	T	135
Rhydyronnen	Powys	SN8786	52°27·9'	3°39·4'W	X	135,136
Rhydyrychen	Conwy	SH8648	53°1·3'	3°41·6'W	X	116
Rhyd-y-sarn	Gwyn	SH6942	52°57·8'	3°56·6'W	T	124
Rhydyware	Powys	SO1996	52°33·6'	3°11·3'W	X	136
Rhydywernen	Gwyn	SH9740	52°57·1'	3°31·6'W	X	125
Rhydywrach	Carm	SN1619	51°50·6'	4°39·9'W	T	158
Rhyl	Denb	SJ0181	53°19·2'	3°28·8'W	T	116
Rhyllech	Gwyn	SH3435	52°53·5'	4°27·7'W	X	123
Rhyll Manor	Devon	SS8627	51°2·1'	3°37·2'W	X	181
Rhyllon	Denb	SJ0475	53°16·0'	3°26·0'W	X	116
Rhymer's Glen	Scot Bord	NT5232	55°35·0'	2°45·3'W	F	73
Rhymney	Powys	SO0468	52°18·3'	3°24·1'W	X	136,147
Rhymney Hill	Caer	SO1208	51°46·1'	3°16·1'W	H	161

Rhymney / Rhymni	Caer	SO1107	51°45·5′	3°17·0′W	T	161
Rhymney River (Afon Rhymni)	Caer	SO1107	51°45·5′	3°17·0′W	W	161
Rhymney River or Afon Rhymni	Caer	ST1589	51°35·8′	3°13·2′W	W	171
Rhymney Valley	Caer	ST1592	51°37·5′	3°13·3′W	X	171
Rhymney Valley Ridgeway Footpath	Caer	SO1007	51°45·5′	3°17·8′W	X	161
Rhymney Valley Ridgeway Footpath	Caer	ST1693	51°38·0′	3°12·4′W	X	171
Rhymney Valley Ridgeway Footpath	Rho Cyn Taf	ST1287	51°34·7′	3°15·8′W	X	171
Rhymni / Rhymney	Caer	SO1107	51°45·5′	3°17·0′W	T	161
Rhyn	Shrops	SJ3037	52°55·8′	3°2·1′W	T	126
Rhynabaich	Aberd	NO3096	57°3·2′	3°8·8′W	X	37,44
Rhynafiach	Moray	NJ2242	57°28·0′	3°17·6′W	X	28
Rhynagarrie	Moray	NJ2342	57°28·0′	3°16·6′W	X	28
Rhynd	Fife	NO4623	56°24·0′	2°52·0′W	X	54,59
Rhynd	Fife	NT0491	56°6·4′	3°32·2′W	X	58
Rhynd	Pth & Kin	NO1520	56°22·1′	3°22·1′W	T	53,58
Rhyndaston-fawr	Pemb	SM8924	51°52·7′	5°3·5′W	X	157,158
Rhyndaston Mountain	Pemb	SM8822	51°51·6′	5°4·3′W	H	157
Rhyne	I of M	SC3480	54°11·6′	4°32·3′W	X	95
Rhynemoor Fm	Somer	ST3455	51°17·7′	2°56·4′W	FM	182
Rhyne Park Fm	Essex	TL8836	51°59·7′	0°44·7′E	FM	155
Rhynie	Aberd	NJ4927	57°20·1′	2°50·4′W	T	37
Rhynie	Highld	NH8479	57°47·6′	3°56·4′W	X	21
Rhyscog	Powys	SO0948	52°7·6′	3°19·4′W	X	147
Rhyse	Heref	SO3557	52°12·7′	2°56·7′W	X	148,149
Rhysgog	Powys	SJ1518	52°45·4′	3°15·2′W	X	125
Rhysgog	Powys	SN9454	52°10·7′	3°32·6′W	X	147
Rhysgog-isaf	Cered	SN6754	52°10·3′	3°56·3′W	X	146
Rhysgwyllt	Pemb	SM9330	51°56·0′	5°0·3′W	X	157
Rhysnant Fm	Powys	SJ2518	52°45·5′	3°6·3′W	FM	126
Rhyswg Fawr	Caer	ST2294	51°38·6′	3°7·2′W	X	171
Riach	Moray	NJ2358	57°36·6′	3°16·9′W	X	28
Rialton Barton	Corn	SW8461	50°24·8′	5°2·0′W	X	200
Riasg Buidhe	Arg & Bt	NR4095	56°4·9′	6°10·3′W	X	61
Riasg Hill	Highld	NC7728	58°13·7′	4°5·2′W	X	17
Ribba Hall	N Yks	SD9683	54°14·8′	2°3·3′W	X	98
Ribbans, The	Shetld	HU4753	60°15·8′	1°8·5′W	H	3
Ribbesford	Worcs	SO7874	52°22·1′	2°19·0′W	T	138
Ribbesford Ho	Worcs	SO7873	52°21·5′	2°19·0′W	X	138
Ribbesford Woods	Worcs	SO7872	52°21·0′	2°19·0′W	F	138
Ribble Bank Fm	Lancs	SD4325	53°43·3′	2°51·4′W	FM	102
Ribble Head	N Yks	SD7779	54°12·6′	2°20·7′W	T	98
Ribblehead Sta	N Yks	SD7678	54°12·1′	2°21·7′W	X	98
Ribblehead Viaduct	N Yks	SD7579	54°12·6′	2°22·6′W	X	98
Ribblesdale	N Yks	SD8157	54°0·8′	2°17·0′W	X	103
Ribbleton	Lancs	SD5630	53°46·1′	2°39·6′W	T	102
Ribble View Fm	Lancs	SD4223	53°42·3′	2°52·3′W	FM	102
Ribble View Fm	Lancs	SD6134	53°48·3′	2°35·1′W	FM	102,103
Ribble Way	Lancs	SD5830	53°46·1′	2°37·8′W	X	102
Ribble Way	Lancs	SD7544	53°53·7′	2°22·4′W	X	103
Ribble Way	N Yks	SD7878	54°12·1′	2°19·8′W	X	98
Ribbonfield	Fife	NO5908	56°16·0′	2°39·3′W	X	59
Ribby	Lancs	SD4031	53°46·6′	2°54·2′W	T	102
Ribby Fm	Corn	SX1457	50°23·2′	4°36·6′W	FM	200
Ribchester	Lancs	SD6435	53°48·8′	2°32·4′W	T	102,103
Ribchester Br	Lancs	SD6635	53°48·9′	2°30·6′W	X	103
Riber	Derby	SK3059	53°7·9′	1°32·7′W	T	119
Riber Castle Wildlife Park	Derby	SK3059	53°7·9′	1°32·7′W	X	119
Riber Hill	Derby	SK3058	53°7·3′	1°32·7′W	X	119
Ribigill	Highld	NC5854	58°27·3′	4°25·5′W	X	10
Ribston Big Wood	N Yks	SE4054	53°59·1′	1°23·0′W	F	105
Ribston Hall	N Yks	SE3953	53°58·5′	1°23·9′W	A	104
Ribston Lodge	N Yks	SE3954	53°59·1′	1°23·9′W	X	104
Ribton Hall	Cumbr	NY0430	54°39·6′	3°28·9′W	X	89
Ribton Ho	Cumbr	NY0530	54°39·6′	3°27·9′W	X	89
Riby	Lincs	TA1807	53°33·0′	0°12·7′W	T	113
Riby Cross Roads	Lincs	TA1808	53°33·6′	0°12·7′W	X	113
Riby Gap	Lincs	TA1809	53°34·1′	0°12·7′W	X	113
Riby Grange	Lincs	TA1707	53°33·0′	0°13·6′W	X	113
Riby Grove Fm	Lincs	TA1706	53°32·5′	0°13·6′W	FM	113
Riccal Dale	N Yks	SE6287	54°16·7′	1°2·4′W	X	94,100
Riccal Ho	N Yks	SE6780	54°12·9′	0°58·0′W	X	100
Riccall	N Yks	SE6237	53°49·8′	1°3·1′W	T	105
Riccall Common	N Yks	SE6436	53°49·2′	1°1·3′W	X	105,106
Riccall Grange	N Yks	SE6337	53°49·8′	1°2·2′W	X	105,106
Riccal Moor	N Yks	SE6581	54°13·5′	0°59·8′W	X	100
Riccalton	Scot Bord	NT7311	55°23·8′	2°25·1′W	X	80
Riccards Fm	E Susx	TQ7618	50°56·3′	0°30·7′E	FM	199
Riccart Cleuch	S Lanak	NS9111	55°23·1′	3°42·8′W	X	71,78
Riccart Law Rig	S Lanak	NS9111	55°23·1′	3°42·8′W	X	71,78
Riccarton	E Ayr	NS4236	55°35·8′	4°30·0′W	T	70
Riccarton	S Lanak	NS7453	55°45·5′	4°0·0′W	X	64
Riccarton	W Loth	NT0175	55°57·7′	3°34·7′W	X	65
Riccarton Burn	Scot Bord	NY5496	55°15·6′	2°43·0′W	W	79
Riccarton Burn	W Loth	NT0174	55°57·2′	3°34·7′W	W	65
Riccarton Fm	Scot Bord	NY5495	55°15·1′	2°43·0′W	FM	79
Riccarton Hills	W Loth	NT0173	55°56·6′	3°34·7′W	H	65
Riccarton Junction	Scot Bord	NY5497	55°16·2′	2°43·0′W	X	79
Riccarton Mains	C of Edin	NT1869	55°54·7′	3°18·3′W	X	65,66
Rice Bridge	W Susx	TQ2621	50°58·7′	0°11·9′W	X	198
Ricebridge Fm	Surrey	TQ2248	51°13·3′	0°14·8′W	FM	187
Rice Fm	Somer	ST4740	51°9·6′	2°45·1′W	FM	182
Rice Head	Cumbr	NY7343	54°47·1′	2°24·8′W	X	86,87
Rice Hill Fm	N Yks	SE6762	54°3·2′	0°58·2′W	FM	100
Rice Wood	Peterb	TF1104	52°37·6′	0°21·2′W	F	142
Richardcairn	D & G	NX7950	54°50·1′	3°52·6′W	X	84
Richards Castle	Heref	SO4870	52°19·8′	2°45·4′W	A	137,138,148
Richards Castle	Heref	SO4969	52°19·2′	2°44·5′W	T	137,138,148
Richardson Village	Wilts	SU0974	51°28·1′	1°51·8′W	A	173
Richardton	E Ayr	NS5636	55°36·0′	4°16·7′W	X	71
Richarkarie	Aberd	NJ3001	57°5·9′	3°8·9′W	X	37
Richborough Cas	Kent	TR3260	51°17·7′	1°20·1′E	X	179
Richborough Fm	Kent	TR3160	51°17·8′	1°19·2′E	FM	179
Richborough Port	Kent	TR3361	51°18·2′	1°21·0′E	T	179
Riches Fm	Suff	TL8357	52°11·1′	0°41·0′E	FM	155
Richings Park	Bucks	TQ0379	51°30·3′	0°30·6′W	T	176

Richland Fm	Heref	SO5650	52°9·0′	2°38·2′W	FM	149
Richmond	Aberd	NK1045	57°30·0′	1°49·5′W	X	30
Richmond	N Yks	NZ1701	54°24·5′	1°43·9′W	T	92
Richmond	Rich	TQ1874	51°27·4′	0°17·7′W	T	176
Richmond	Sheff	SK4085	53°21·9′	1°23·5′W	T	111,120
Richmond Fm	Notts	SK5951	53°3·4′	1°6·8′W	FM	120
Richmond Fm	N Yks	SE4177	54°11·5′	1°21·9′W	FM	99
Richmond Fm	Suff	TM4149	52°5·4′	1°31·5′E	FM	169
Richmond Fm	W Susx	TQ1326	51°1·6′	0°22·9′W	FM	187,198
Richmond Hall	Cambs	TF4111	52°40·9′	0°5·6′E	X	131,142,143
Richmond Hill	Donc	SE5503	53°31·5′	1°9·8′W	X	111
Richmond Hill	I of M	SC3474	54°8·4′	4°32·1′W	X	95
Richmond Hill	Leeds	SE3133	53°47·8′	1°31·3′W	T	104
Richmond Hill	Northum	NZ0870	55°1·7′	1°52·1′W	X	88
Richmond Hill	N Yks	SE2965	54°5·0′	1°33·0′W	X	99
Richmond Hill	Oxon	SU5899	51°41·4′	1°9·3′W	X	164
Richmond Hill	Rich	TQ1874	51°27·4′	0°17·7′W	X	176
Richmond Houses	Lancs	SD6042	53°52·6′	2°36·1′W	X	102,103
Richmond Lodge	Bucks	SP8228	51°56·9′	0°48·0′W	X	165
Richmond Out Moor	N Yks	NZ1302	54°25·0′	1°47·6′W	X	92
Richmond Park	Rich	TQ2072	51°26·3′	0°16·0′W	X	176
Richmond Plains	Cumbr	NY3740	54°45·3′	2°58·3′W	X	85
Richmonds Fm	Essex	TL4306	51°44·3′	0°4·7′E	FM	167
Richmond's Green	Essex	TL6229	51°56·4′	0°21·8′E	T	167
Richmond's in the Wood	Essex	TL5830	51°57·0′	0°18·3′E	X	167
Richorn Plantn	D & G	NX8359	54°55·0′	3°49·1′W	F	84
Rich's Holford	Somer	ST1433	51°5·6′	3°13·3′W	T	181
Rickard's Down	Devon	SS4227	51°1·5′	4°14·8′W	T	180
Rickarton	Aberd	NO8189	56°59·8′	2°18·3′W	T	45
Rickarton Ho	Aberd	NO8388	56°59·2′	2°16·3′W	X	45
Rickerby	Cumbr	NY4156	54°54·0′	2°54·8′W	T	85
Rickerby Ho	Cumbr	NY2952	54°51·7′	3°5·9′W	X	85
Rickerscote	Staffs	SJ9220	52°46·9′	2°6·7′W	T	127
Rickeston	Pemb	SM8709	51°44·6′	5°4·7′W	X	157
Rickeston Hall	Pemb	SM8425	51°53·1′	5°7·9′W	X	157
Rickets Head	Pemb	SM8518	51°49·4′	5°6·8′W	X	157
Rickettswood Fm	Surrey	TQ2343	51°10·6′	0°14·0′W	FM	187
Ricketwood Fm	Notts	SK6550	53°2·8′	1°1·4′W	FM	120
Rickford	N Som	ST4859	51°19·9′	2°44·4′W	T	172,182
Rickham	Devon	SX7537	50°13·4′	3°44·8′W	X	202
Rickham Common	Devon	SX7337	50°13·4′	3°46·4′W	X	202
Rickinghall	Suff	TM0475	52°20·3′	1°0·1′E	T	144
Rickland Fm	Suff	TL9434	51°58·5′	0°49·9′E	FM	155
Ricklees Fm	Ghead	NZ1460	54°56·3′	1°46·5′W	FM	88
Rickle Pits	E Yorks	TA0354	53°58·5′	0°25·4′W	X	107
Rickleton	Sund	NZ2853	54°52·5′	1°33·4′W	T	88
Rickling	Essex	TL4931	51°57·7′	0°10·5′E	T	167
Rickling Green	Essex	TL5029	51°56·6′	0°11·3′E	T	167
Rickling Hall	Essex	TL4930	51°57·1′	0°10·5′E	A	167
Rickman's Hill	Bucks	SU9784	51°33·0′	0°35·7′W	H	175,176
Rickmansworth	Herts	TQ0494	51°38·3′	0°29·4′W	T	166,176
Ricknall Grange	Durham	NZ3024	54°36·9′	1°31·7′W	X	93
Rickney	E Susx	TQ6206	50°50·1′	0°18·4′E	T	199
Rickneys	Herts	TL3215	51°49·3′	0°4·7′W	X	166
Rickstead Fm	Leic	SK7900	52°35·8′	0°49·6′W	FM	141
Ricksy Ball	Somer	SS7338	51°7·9′	3°48·5′W	X	180
Ricochet Hill	Surrey	SU9052	51°15·8′	0°42·2′W	X	186
Ri Cruin	Arg & Bt	NR8297	56°7·2′	5°30·0′W	X	55
Ridby Court Fm	Heref	SO4631	51°58·7′	2°46·8′W	FM	149,161
Riddell	Scot Bord	NT5124	55°30·7′	2°46·1′W	T	73
Riddel Law	Scot Bord	NT5356	55°48·0′	2°44·5′W	H	66,73
Riddlestone Fm	Devon	SS6405	50°50·0′	3°55·5′W	FM	191
Riddiford	Devon	SS6110	50°52·6′	3°58·2′W	X	191
Riddindyke	D & G	NY1365	54°58·6′	3°21·1′W	X	85
Ridding Fm	Ches	SJ7059	53°7·9′	2°26·5′W	FM	118
Ridding Ho	Cumbr	NY7805	54°26·6′	2°19·9′W	X	91
Ridding Ho	Derby	SK2475	53°16·5′	1°38·0′W	X	119
Ridding Lane	N Yks	SD6868	54°6·7′	2°29·0′W	X	98
Riddingleys Top	Cumbr	NY4922	54°35·7′	2°46·9′W	X	90
Riddings	Cumbr	SD6296	54°21·7′	2°34·7′W	X	97
Riddings	Derby	SK1739	52°57·1′	1°44·4′W	X	128
Riddings	Derby	SK2250	53°3·0′	1°39·9′W	X	119
Riddings	Derby	SK4252	53°4·1′	1°22·0′W	T	120
Riddings	D & G	NX9097	55°15·5′	3°43·4′W	X	78
Riddings	N Yks	SE0299	54°23·4′	1°57·7′W	X	98
Riddings	N Yks	SE0755	53°59·7′	1°53·2′W	X	104
Riddings	Shrops	SO1986	52°28·2′	3°11·1′W	X	136
Riddings	Staffs	SK0939	52°57·1′	1°51·6′W	X	128
Riddings Bank	D & G	NS7800	55°17·0′	3°54·8′W	X	78
Riddings Fm	Cumbr	NY4075	55°4·2′	2°55·9′W	FM	85
Riddings Fm	Donc	SE6016	53°38·5′	1°5·1′W	FM	111
Riddings Fm	Hants	SU5462	51°21·5′	1°13·1′W	FM	174
Riddings Gate	Shrops	SO6478	52°24·2′	2°31·4′W	X	138
Riddingsgill Wood	N Yks	SE1269	54°7·2′	1°48·6′W	F	99
Riddingshill	Cumbr	NY4074	55°3·7′	2°55·9′W	X	85
Riddingshill	D & G	NX9177	55°4·8′	3°42·0′W	X	84
Riddings Hill Fm	Notts	SK6455	53°5·5′	1°2·3′W	FM	120
Riddings Ho	Derby	SK4352	53°4·0′	1°21·1′W	X	120
Ridding Side Fm	Cumbr	SD3185	54°15·6′	3°3·1′W	FM	96,97
Riddings Park	Derby	SK1950	53°3·1′	1°42·6′W	X	119
Riddings Rigg	N Yks	NZ0100	54°24·0′	1°58·7′W	X	92
Riddings, The	Cumbr	NY3125	54°37·2′	3°3·5′W	X	90
Riddings, The	N Yks	SD8259	54°1·8′	2°16·1′W	X	103
Ridding, The	N Yks	SD6370	54°7·7′	2°33·6′W	X	97
Riddingwood	D & G	NX9784	55°8·6′	3°36·5′W	X	78
Riddingwood Ho	D & G	NX9883	55°8·1′	3°35·6′W	X	78
Riddle	Devon	SS6238	51°7·7′	3°57·9′W	X	180
Riddlebank	D & G	NX9266	54°58·9′	3°40·8′W	X	84
Riddlecombe	Devon	SS6113	50°54·2′	3°58·2′W	T	180
Riddlehamhope	Northum	NY9149	54°50·4′	2°8·0′W	X	87
Riddlehamhope Fell	Northum	NY8949	54°50·4′	2°9·9′W	X	87
Riddlehead	Aberd	NJ7031	57°22·4′	2°29·5′W	X	29
Riddle Hill	Oxon	SU5484	51°33·4′	1°12·9′W	X	174
Riddlesay	Cumbr	NY7609	54°28·8′	2°21·8′W	X	91
Riddlesden	Brad	SE0742	53°52·7′	1°53·2′W	T	104
Riddlesden Fm	Leic	SP5486	52°28·4′	1°11·9′W	FM	140
Riddlesdown	Croy	TQ3260	51°19·7′	0°5·9′W	F	176,177,187
Riddles Wood	Essex	TM1218	51°49·4′	1°5·0′E	F	168,169
Riddlesworth Hall School	Norf	TL9681	52°23·9′	0°53·3′E	X	144
Riddlesworth Stud	Norf	TL9581	52°23·8′	0°52·4′E	X	144

Riddle, The	Heref	SO4762	52°15·5′	2°46·2′W	T	137,138,148
Riddletonhill	Scot Bord	NT6230	55°34·0′	2°35·7′W	X	74
Riddoch-hill	W Loth	NS9765	55°52·3′	3°38·3′W	X	65
Riddon Ridge	Devon	SX6676	50°34·3′	3°53·2′W	H	191
Riddox, The	Heref	SO3852	52°10·0′	2°54·0′W	X	148,149
Riddrie	C of Glas	NS6366	55°52·3′	4°10·9′W	T	64
Ridd's Fm	Lincs	SK9325	52°49·1′	0°36·8′W	FM	130
Riddy Wood	Cambs	TL2181	52°25·0′	0°12·8′W	F	142
Rider Lane Fm	N Yks	SE7363	54°3·7′	0°52·7′W	FM	100
Riders Rig	D & G	NX4788	55°10·0′	4°23·7′W	X	77
Rider's Rings	Devon	SX6764	50°27·9′	3°52·1′W	A	202
Rides Fm	Kent	TR0170	51°23·8′	0°53·8′E	FM	178
Ride, The	Staffs	SJ9604	52°38·3′	2°3·1′W	X	127,139
Ridgacre	Birm	SP0084	52°27·5′	1°59·6′W	T	139
Ridgaling Fm	Lancs	SD8439	53°51·1′	2°14·2′W	FM	103
Ridge	Bath & NE Somer	ST5556	51°18·3′	2°38·3′W	T	172,182
Ridge	Corn	SX2477	50°34·2′	4°28·8′W	H	201
Ridge	Devon	SS9009	50°52·4′	3°33·4′W	X	192
Ridge	Devon	ST2906	50°51·2′	3°0·1′W	T	193
Ridge	Dorset	ST7310	50°53·6′	2°22·7′W	X	194
Ridge	Dorset	SY9386	50°40·6′	2°5·6′W	T	195
Ridge	Hants	SU3418	50°57·9′	1°30·6′W	T	185
Ridge	Herts	TL2100	51°41·4′	0°14·6′W	T	166
Ridge	Lancs	SD4862	54°3·3′	2°47·2′W	T	97
Ridge	Lancs	SD8540	53°51·6′	2°13·3′W	X	103
Ridge	Pemb	SM9430	51°56·1′	4°59·4′W	X	157
Ridge	Shrops	SO3595	52°33·2′	2°57·1′W	X	137
Ridge	Wilts	ST9531	51°4·9′	2°3·9′W	T	184
Ridgebarn Fm	Bucks	SP7411	51°47·8′	0°55·2′W	FM	165
Ridgebourne	Heref	SO2856	52°12·1′	3°2·8′W	X	148
Ridge Cliff	Dorset	SY4291	50°43·2′	2°48·9′W	X	193
Ridgeclose Fm	Derby	SK0878	53°18·2′	1°52·4′W	FM	119
Ridgecombe	Devon	SX4084	50°38·3′	4°15·4′W	X	201
Ridge Common	Hants	SU7324	51°0·9′	0°57·2′W	T	197
Ridge Coppice	Dorset	ST5302	50°49·2′	2°39·7′W	F	194
Ridge Copse	Hants	SU5310	50°53·5′	1°14·4′W	F	196
Ridge Copse	I of W	SZ4892	50°43·8′	1°18·8′W	F	196
Ridge Copse	Somer	ST7841	51°10·3′	2°18·5′W	F	183
Ridge Court	Devon	ST2201	50°48·4′	3°6·0′W	X	192,193
Ridge End	Northum	NY7285	55°9·8′	2°25·9′W	X	80
Ridge End	Staffs	SK0962	53°9·5′	1°51·5′W	X	119
Ridge-End	Stock	SJ9686	53°22·5′	2°3·2′W	X	109
Ridge End Burn	Northum	NY6696	55°15·7′	2°31·7′W	W	80
Ridge End Burn	Northum	NY7097	55°16·2′	2°27·9′W	W	80
Ridge End Ho	N Yks	SE0661	54°2·9′	1°54·1′W	X	99
Ridge Fm	Ches	SJ7073	53°15·4′	2°26·6′W	FM	118
Ridge Fm	Dorset	ST4605	50°50·8′	2°45·6′W	FM	193
Ridge Fm	Dorset	SY3597	50°46·4′	2°54·9′W	FM	193
Ridge Fm	Hants	SU5310	50°53·5′	1°14·4′W	FM	196
Ridge Fm	Hants	SU7124	51°0·9′	0°58·9′W	FM	197
Ridge Fm	Kent	TQ5163	51°21·0′	0°10·5′E	FM	177,188
Ridge Fm	Somer	ST0725	51°1·2′	3°19·2′W	FM	181
Ridge Fm	Somer	ST0919	50°58·0′	3°17·4′W	FM	181
Ridge Fm	Staffs	SK0862	53°9·5′	1°52·4′W	FM	119
Ridge Fm	Surrey	TQ1135	51°6·4′	0°24·5′W	FM	187
Ridge Fm	Surrey	TQ1837	51°7·4′	0°18·4′W	FM	187
Ridge Fm	Wilts	ST9533	51°6·0′	2°3·9′W	FM	184
Ridge Fm	Wok	SU7964	51°22·4′	0°51·5′W	FM	175,186
Ridge Fm, The	Shrops	SO2898	52°34·7′	3°3·4′W	FM	137
Ridge Fold	Stock	SJ9686	53°22·5′	2°3·2′W	X	109
Ridge Gate	Devon	SS6641	51°9·4′	3°54·6′W	X	180
Ridgegate Resr	Ches	SJ9571	53°14·4′	2°4·1′W	W	118
Ridge Green	Surrey	TQ3048	51°13·2′	0°7·9′W	T	187
Ridge Hall	Derby	SK0578	53°18·2′	1°55·1′W	X	119
Ridge Hall	N Yks	NZ7617	54°32·8′	0°49·1′W	X	94
Ridge Hall Fm	Ches	SJ9470	53°13·9′	2°5·0′W	FM	118
Ridgehill	Ches	SJ9370	53°13·9′	2°5·9′W	X	118
Ridge Hill	Devon	ST3006	50°51·2′	2°59·3′W	X	193
Ridge Hill	Dorset	ST6805	50°50·9′	2°26·9′W	X	194
Ridge Hill	Dorset	SY6598	50°47·1′	2°29·4′W	H	194
Ridge Hill	Heref	SO5035	52°0·9′	2°43·3′W	X	149
Ridge Hill	Heref	SO6233	51°59·9′	2°32·8′W	X	149
Ridgehill	Herts	TL2002	51°42·5′	0°15·4′W	X	166
Ridge Hill	Tames	SJ9699	53°29·5′	2°3·2′W	T	109
Ridge Hill	Wilts	ST9532	51°5·5′	2°3·9′W	X	184
Ridgehill Fm	Ches	SJ5464	53°10·5′	2°40·9′W	FM	117
Ridge Hill Manor	W Susx	TQ3735	51°6·1′	0°2·2′W	X	187
Ridge Hill Wood	Staffs	SO8787	52°29·1′	2°11·1′W	F	139
Ridge Ho	N Yks	SE6696	54°21·6′	0°58·6′W	X	94,100
Ridge House Fm	N Yks	SE1460	54°2·4′	1°46·8′W	FM	99
Ridgeland Fm	E Susx	TQ4119	50°57·4′	0°0·8′E	FM	198
Ridge Lane	Warw	SP2994	52°32·8′	1°33·9′W	T	140
Ridgemarsh	Bucks	TQ0194	51°38·4′	0°32·0′W	T	166,176
Ridgemoor Fm	Hants	SU4659	51°19·9′	1°20·0′W	FM	174
Ridgend Fm	Worcs	SO7761	52°15·0′	2°19·8′W	FM	138,150
Ridge Nether Moor	Derby	SK1594	53°26·8′	1°46·0′W	X	110
Ridge Row	Kent	TR2042	51°8·3′	1°9·1′E	T	179,189
Ridge Sand, The	Glos	SO6703	51°43·7′	2°28·3′W	X	162
Ridges Copse	Hants	SU3849	51°14·6′	1°26·9′W	F	185
Ridge, The	Derby	SK1195	53°27·3′	1°49·7′W	X	110
Ridge, The	Devon	SX9883	50°38·5′	3°27·5′W	X	192
Ridge, The	E Susx	TQ4532	51°4·4′	0°4·6′E	X	188
Ridge, The	E Susx	TQ5136	51°6·4′	0°9·8′E	X	188
Ridge, The	Glos	ST7896	51°40·0′	2°18·7′W	X	162
Ridge, The	Leeds	SE4138	53°50·4′	1°22·2′W	A	105
Ridge, The	W Susx	SU8731	51°4·5′	0°45·1′W	X	186
Ridge Top	Derby	SK0386	53°22·5′	1°56·9′W	X	110
Ridge Top Fm	N Yks	SE1753	53°58·6′	1°44·0′W	FM	104
Ridgewalk Moor	Derby	SK1395	53°27·3′	1°47·8′W	X	110
Ridgeway	Bucks	SP8305	51°44·5′	0°47·5′W	X	165
Ridgeway	C of Bris	ST6275	51°28·6′	2°32·4′W	T	172
Ridgeway	Derby	SK3551	53°3·5′	1°28·3′W	T	119
Ridgeway	Derby	SK4081	53°19·7′	1°23·6′W	T	111,120
Ridgeway	Devon	SY2393	50°44·1′	3°5·1′W	X	192,193
Ridge Way	Dorset	SY7194	50°44·9′	2°24·3′W	X	194
Ridgeway	Heref	SO5059	52°13·9′	2°43·5′W	X	149
Ridgeway	Heref	SO7438	52°2·6′	2°22·4′W	X	150
Ridgeway	Kent	TR0740	51°7·5′	0°57·9′E	T	179,189
Ridgeway	Newp	ST2988	51°35·4′	3°1·1′W	T	171

Ridgeway	Oxon	SU3684	51°33·5'	1°28·5'W	X	174
Ridgeway	Oxon	SU6687	51°34·9'	1°2·5'W	X	175
Ridgeway	Oxon	SU6891	51°37·1'	1°0·7'W	X	164,175
Ridgeway	Oxon	SU6892	51°37·6'	1°0·7'W	X	164,175
Ridgeway	Pemb	SN0515	51°48·2'	4°49·3'W	X	158
Ridgeway	Pemb	SN1305	51°43·0'	4°42·0'W	T	158
Ridgeway	Somer	ST7445	51°12·5'	2°21·9'W	T	183
Ridgeway	Staffs	SJ8953	53°4·7'	2°9·4'W	T	118
Ridgeway	Wilts	SU1168	51°24·9'	1°50·1'W	X	173
Ridge Way	Wilts	SU1271	51°26·5'	1°49·3'W	X	173
Ridgeway Cross	Heref	SO7147	52°7·5'	2°25·0'W	T	149
Ridgeway Down	Oxon	SU4384	51°33·4'	1°22·4'W	X	174
Ridgeway Fm	Devon	ST1202	50°48·9'	3°14·6'W	FM	192,193
Ridgeway Fm	Devon	ST2000	50°47·9'	3°7·7'W	FM	192,193
Ridgeway Fm	E Susx	TQ6730	51°2·9'	0°23·3'E	FM	188
Ridgeway Fm	Hants	SU4952	51°16·1'	1°17·5'W	FM	185
Ridgeway Fm	Heref	SO7048	52°8·0'	2°25·9'W	FM	149
Ridgeway Fm	Kent	TR1865	51°20·8'	1°8·2'E	FM	179
Ridgeway Fm	Leic	SK6612	52°42·3'	1°1·0'W	FM	129
Ridgeway Fm	Surrey	SU8938	51°8·3'	0°43·3'W	FM	186
Ridgeway Fm	Swin	SU2582	51°32·4'	1°38·0'W	FM	174
Ridgeway Fm	Wilts	ST9880	51°31·4'	2°1·3'W	FM	173
Ridgeway Fm	Worcs	SO8150	52°9·1'	2°16·3'W	FM	150
Ridgeway Fm, The	Warw	SP5273	52°21·4'	1°13·8'W	FM	140
Ridgeway Hill	Dorset	SY6785	50°40·1'	2°27·6'W	X	194
Ridgeway Hill	Dorset	SY9281	50°37·9'	2°6·4'W	X	195
Ridgeway Moor	Derby	SK4081	53°19·7'	1°23·6'W	T	111,120
Ridgeway, The	Pemb	SN0600	51°40·2'	4°47·9'W	X	158
Ridgeway, The	Warw	SP0560	52°14·5'	1°55·2'W	X	150
Ridgeway Walk (Ffordd y Bryniau)	Card	ST1083	51°32·6'	3°17·5'W	X	171
Ridgewell	Essex	TL7340	52°2·1'	0°31·7'E	T	155
Ridgewell	Oxon	SU6891	51°37·1'	1°0·7'W	X	164,175
Ridge Wharf	Dorset	SY9387	50°41·2'	2°5·6'W	X	195
Ridgewood	E Susx	TQ4719	50°57·3'	0°6·0'E	T	198
Ridge Wood	Kent	TQ6462	51°20·2'	0°21·7'E	F	177,188
Ridgewood Fm	E Susx	TQ4719	50°57·3'	0°6·0'E	FM	198
Ridgewood Hill	Devon	ST1513	50°54·8'	3°12·2'W	X	181,193
Ridgewood Ho	E Susx	TQ4719	50°57·3'	0°6·0'E	X	198
Ridgewood Stud	Surrey	TQ2445	51°11·7'	0°13·1'W	X	187
Ridgmont	Beds	SP9736	52°1·1'	0°34·8'W	T	153
Ridgmont	E Yorks	TA2428	53°44·3'	0°6·8'W	X	107
Ridgmont Sta	Beds	SP9637	52°1·6'	0°35·6'W	X	153
Ridgnalls	Essex	TL9832	51°57·3'	0°53·3'E	X	168
Ridgwardine	Shrops	SJ6838	52°56·5'	2°28·2'W	X	127
Ridgway	Shrops	SO3986	52°28·4'	2°53·5'W	T	137
Ridgway	Surrey	TQ0459	51°19·5'	0°30·1'W	T	186
Ridgway Hill	Shrops	SO3986	52°28·4'	2°53·5'W	X	137
Ridgway Ho	Surrey	SU8145	51°12·1'	0°50·0'W	X	186
Ridgy Pool	Lancs	SD4245	53°54·1'	2°52·6'W	W	102
Ridham Dock	Kent	TQ9268	51°22·9'	0°45·9'E	X	178
Ridhe Eilein	Arg & Bt	NR6248	55°40·3'	5°46·7'W	X	62
Riding Court Fm	Win & Maid	SU9977	51°29·2'	0°34·1'W	FM	175,176
Riding Cross	Devon	SS6425	51°0·7'	3°55·9'W	X	180
Riding Fm	Ghead	NZ2455	54°53·6'	1°37·1'W	FM	88
Riding Gate	Somer	ST7329	51°3·8'	2°22·7'W	T	183
Ridinghill	Aberd	NK0255	57°35·4'	1°57·5'W	X	30
Riding Hill	Scot Bord	NT1640	55°39·0'	3°19·7'W	H	72
Riding Hill	Shetld	HU3868	60°23·9'	1°18·1'W	H	2,3
Riding Hills	Northum	NZ0062	54°57·4'	1°59·6'W	X	87
Riding House Fm	Derby	SK1584	53°21·4'	1°46·1'W	FM	110
Riding Lane	Kent	TQ5651	51°14·4'	0°14·5'E	X	188
Riding Mill	Northum	NZ0161	54°56·9'	1°58·6'W	T	87
Ridings Beck	E Yorks	SE8252	53°57·7'	0°44·6'W	W	106
Riding Stack	Shetld	HU3063	60°21·3'	1°26·9'W	X	3
Ridings, The	Glos	ST7695	51°39·4'	2°20·4'W	X	162
Riding, The	Northum	NY8284	55°9·2'	2°16·5'W	X	80
Riding Wood Resr	Kirk	SE1105	53°32·7'	1°49·6'W	W	110
Ridlees Burn	Northum	NT8506	55°21·1'	2°13·8'W	W	80
Ridlees Cairn	Northum	NT8404	55°20·0'	2°14·7'W	X	80
Ridleeshope	Northum	NT8206	55°21·1'	2°16·6'W	X	80
Ridlers	Somer	SS8726	51°1·6'	3°36·3'W	X	181
Ridley	Kent	TQ6163	51°20·8'	0°19·1'E	T	177,188
Ridley	Northum	NY7963	54°57·9'	2°19·3'W	T	86,87
Ridley Bank Fm	Ches	SJ5653	53°4·6'	2°39·0'W	FM	117
Ridley Common	Northum	NY7661	54°56·8'	2°22·1'W	X	86,87
Ridley Crag	Northum	NY8499	55°17·3'	2°14·7'W	H	80
Ridley Fm	Ches	SJ5453	53°4·6'	2°40·8'W	FM	117
Ridley Green Fm	Ches	SJ5554	53°5·1'	2°39·9'W	FM	117
Ridley Hall	Essex	TL7515	51°48·6'	0°32·7'E	X	167
Ridley Halls	Northum	NY9757	54°54·7'	2°2·4'W	X	87
Ridley Hill Fm	Ches	SJ5555	53°5·7'	2°39·9'W	FM	117
Ridley Mill	Northum	NZ0560	54°56·3'	1°54·9'W	X	87
Ridley Plain	Hants	SU2006	50°51·4'	1°42·6'W	X	195
Ridley Shiel	Northum	NY7892	55°13·6'	2°20·3'W	X	80
Ridley Stokoe	Northum	NY7485	55°9·8'	2°24·1'W	T	80
Ridley Wood	Hants	SU2006	50°51·4'	1°42·6'W	F	195
Ridleywood	Wrex	SJ4051	53°3·4'	2°53·3'W	T	117
Ridley Wood Fm	Wrex	SJ3951	53°3·4'	2°54·2'W	FM	117
Ridlington	Norf	TG3430	52°49·2'	1°28·8'E	T	133
Ridlington	Rut	SK8402	52°36·8'	0°45·2'W	T	141
Ridlington Fm	W Susx	SU9517	50°56·9'	0°38·5'W	FM	197
Ridlington Street	Norf	TG3430	52°49·2'	1°28·8'E	T	133
Ridsdale	Northum	NY9084	55°9·3'	2°9·0'W	T	80
Rid's Hill	Bucks	SP6614	51°49·5'	1°2·1'W	H	164,165
Ridway Fms	Heref	SO4428	51°57·1'	2°48·5'W	FM	149,161
Riechip	Pth & Kin	NO0647	56°36·6'	3°31·4'W	X	52,53
Rie Meikle	Pth & Kin	NO0752	56°39·3'	3°30·6'W	H	52,53
Riemore	Pth & Kin	NO0549	56°37·7'	3°32·5'W	X	52,53
Riemore Hill	Pth & Kin	NO0550	56°38·2'	3°32·5'W	H	52,53
Riemore Lodge	Pth & Kin	NO0449	56°37·6'	3°33·4'W	X	52,53
Rienachait	Highld	NC0430	58°13·2'	5°19·8'W	T	15
Rientraid	Highld	NC1933	58°15·2'	5°4·6'W	X	15
Riera Geo	Highld	ND3543	58°22·5'	3°6·2'W	X	12
Riereach Burn	Highld	NH8445	57°29·1'	3°55·6'W	W	27
Rievaulx	N Yks	SE5785	54°15·7'	1°7·1'W	T	100
Rievaulx Moor	N Yks	SE5889	54°17·8'	1°6·1'W	X	100
Rievaulx Terrace	N Yks	SE5884	54°15·1'	1°6·2'W	X	100
Rieve Hill	E Renf	NS5450	55°43·5'	4°19·0'W	X	64
River Sike	Scot Bord	NY5091	55°12·9'	2°46·7'W	W	79
Rievie Hill	Orkney	ND2397	58°51·5'	3°19·6'W	X	6,7
Rifagan Minish	N Eil	NF9170	57°37·1'	7°10·1'W	X	18
Rifern	Highld	NM7888	56°56·1'	5°38·5'W	X	40
Riff	Orkney	HY4118	59°3·0'	3°1·2'W	X	6
Riffa Beck	N Yks	SE2546	53°54·8'	1°36·7'W	W	104
Riffa Fm	N Yks	SE2446	53°54·8'	1°37·7'W	FM	104
Riffag Mhór	N Eil	NF9063	57°33·3'	7°10·5'W	X	18
Riffa Manor	N Yks	SE2546	53°54·8'	1°36·7'W	X	104
Riffa Wood	N Yks	SE2546	53°54·8'	1°36·7'W	F	104
Riffhams	Essex	TL7706	51°43·7'	0°34·2'E	X	167
Riffin	Aberd	NJ7542	57°28·3'	2°24·6'W	X	29
Riff of Lythe	Orkney	HY4132	59°10·5'	3°1·4'W	X	5,6
Riff of Wasbister	Orkney	HY4033	59°11·0'	3°2·5'W	X	5,6
Riff, The	Orkney	ND5198	58°52·3'	2°50·5'W	X	6,7
Rifle Green	Torf	SO2509	51°46·7'	3°4·8'W	T	161
Rift Fm	Northum	NZ1165	54°59·0'	1°49·3'W	FM	88
Rift Fm, The	Durham	NZ3145	54°48·2'	1°30·6'W	FM	88
Rift House	Hartpl	NZ4930	54°40·0'	1°14·0'W	T	93
Rifton	Devon	SS8917	50°56·7'	3°34·4'W	X	181
Rifton Moor	Devon	SS8917	50°56·7'	3°34·4'W	X	181
Rigangower	W Dunb	NS4375	55°56·8'	4°30·4'W	X	64
Rigbister	Orkney	ND4776	58°40·4'	2°54·4'W	X	7
Rigbolt Ho	Lincs	TF1928	52°50·4'	0°13·6'W	X	130
Rig Burn	D & G	NS7111	55°22·8'	4°1·7'W	W	71
Rig Burn	D & G	NY3290	55°12·2'	3°3·7'W	W	79
Rigby House Fm	Lancs	SD5912	53°36·4'	2°36·8'W	FM	108
Rigery Fm	Herts	TL3620	51°51·9'	0°1·1'W	FM	166
Rigfoot	D & G	NX8671	55°1·5'	3°46·6'W	X	84
Rigfoot	D & G	NY1670	55°1·3'	3°18·4'W	X	85
Rigfoot	D & G	NY2966	54°59·3'	3°6·1'W	X	85
Rigfoot	D & G	NY3793	55°13·9'	2°59·0'W	X	79
Rigfoot	E Renf	NS4055	55°46·0'	4°32·6'W	X	64
Rigfoot	Scot Bord	NT7259	55°49·7'	2°26·4'W	X	67,74
Rigfoot	S Lanak	NS6646	55°41·6'	4°7·5'W	X	64
Rigfoot Moss	S Lanak	NS6747	55°42·1'	4°6·6'W	X	64
Rigg	D & G	NY2966	54°59·3'	3°6·1'W	T	85
Rigg	Durham	NY9222	54°35·8'	2°7·0'W	X	91,92
Rigg	Highld	NG5156	57°31·8'	6°9·1'W	X	23,24
Rigg	Lancs	SD5742	53°52·6'	2°38·8'W	X	102
Rigga Dale	Shetld	HP4903	60°42·7'	1°5·6'W	X	1
Riggalls Fm	Lincs	TF2951	53°2·7'	0°4·1'W	FM	122
Rigg Beck	Cumbr	NY2120	54°34·4'	3°12·9'W	W	89,90
Rigg Beck	Cumbr	NY8006	54°27·2'	2°18·1'W	W	91,92
Rigg Burn	Highld	NG5055	57°31·2'	6°10·1'W	W	23,24
Riggcroft	Cumbr	NY4375	55°4·2'	2°53·1'W	X	85
Rigg End	Cumbr	NY6805	54°26·6'	2°29·2'W	X	91
Rigg End	Cumbr	NY6838	54°44·4'	2°29·4'W	X	91
Rigg End	Cumbr	SD7285	54°15·8'	2°25·4'W	X	98
Riggend	N Lanak	NS7670	55°54·7'	3°58·6'W	T	64
Rigg End Fm	N Yks	SE7593	54°19·9'	0°50·4'W	FM	94,100
Rigg Fm	D & G	NS7112	55°23·4'	4°1·8'W	FM	71
Rigg Fm	N Yks	NZ9106	54°26·7'	0°35·4'W	FM	94
Riggfoot	D & G	NX9779	55°5·9'	3°36·4'W	X	84
Riggfoot	D & G	NY0883	55°8·2'	3°26·2'W	X	78
Riggfoot	E Ayr	NS5813	55°23·7'	4°14·1'W	X	71
Riggfoot Ho	Cumbr	NY4667	54°59·9'	2°50·6'W	X	86
Rigg Hall	N Yks	NZ9105	54°26·2'	0°35·4'W	X	94
Rigg Hall	N Yks	TA0098	54°22·3'	0°27·2'W	X	101
Rigghead	Cumbr	NY3425	54°37·2'	3°0·9'W	X	90
Rigghead	D & G	NX8876	55°4·2'	3°44·8'W	X	84
Rigghead	D & G	NY0375	55°3·9'	3°30·7'W	X	84
Rigghead	E Ayr	NS4932	55°33·8'	4°23·2'W	X	70
Rigghead	N Lanak	NS7669	55°54·1'	3°58·6'W	X	64
Rigghead Fm	E Ayr	NS5714	55°24·2'	4°15·1'W	FM	71
Riggheads	D & G	NY0784	55°8·7'	3°27·1'W	X	78
Riggheads	D & G	NY2868	55°0·3'	3°7·1'W	X	85
Riggheads Fm	D & G	NY0895	55°14·7'	3°26·4'W	FM	78
Rigghill	E Ayr	NS4645	55°40·7'	4°26·5'W	X	64
Rigg Hill	E Ayr	NS5609	55°21·5'	4°15·9'W	X	71,77
Rigghill Burn	N Ayr	NS2267	55°52·1'	4°50·2'W	W	63
Rigg Ho	Cumbr	NY0523	54°35·8'	3°27·8'W	X	89
Rigg Ho	N Yks	SD8491	54°19·1'	2°14·3'W	X	98
Rigg Ho	N Yks	SE3065	54°5·0'	1°32·1'W	X	99
Riggindale	Cumbr	NY4512	54°30·3'	2°50·5'W	X	90
Riggindale Beck	Cumbr	NY4511	54°29·7'	2°50·5'W	W	90
Riggindale Crag	Cumbr	NY4411	54°29·7'	2°51·5'W	X	90
Rigging Gill	Cumbr	NY0728	54°38·6'	3°26·0'W	X	89
Rigging Hill	N Ayr	NS2358	55°47·2'	4°48·9'W	H	63
Rigging Sike	Scot Bord	NY4691	55°12·9'	2°50·5'W	W	79
Riggin's Hill	D & G	NX6753	54°51·5'	4°3·9'W	H	83,84
Riggins, The	Aberd	NJ4846	57°30·3'	2°51·6'W	X	28,29
Riggles Fm	Devon	ST1809	50°52·7'	3°9·6'W	FM	192,193
Riggles, The	Powys	SO1865	52°16·9'	3°11·7'W	X	136,148
Rigg Mill Beck	N Yks	NZ9007	54°27·3'	0°36·3'W	W	94
Rigg Mill Wood	N Yks	NZ9007	54°27·3'	0°36·3'W	F	94
Riggmoor	D & G	NY2866	54°59·3'	3°7·1'W	X	85
Rigg Moor	N Yks	SE3262	54°3·4'	1°30·3'W	X	99
Rigg of England	Lancs	SD8238	53°50·5'	2°16·0'W	X	103
Riggonhead	E Loth	NT4174	55°57·6'	2°56·3'W	X	66
Rigg or Cruggleton Bay	D & G	NX4744	54°46·3'	4°22·3'W	W	83
Rigg Plantn	E Yorks	SE9436	53°48·9'	0°33·9'W	F	106
Rigg Plantn	N Yks	SE1694	54°20·7'	1°44·8'W	F	99
Rigg Plantn	N Yks	SE8261	54°2·5'	0°44·4'W	F	100
Riggs	Cumbr	NY1830	54°39·8'	3°15·9'W	X	89,90
Riggs	Fife	NO2807	56°15·3'	3°9·3'W	X	59
Riggs Beck	N Yks	SD9683	54°14·8'	2°3·3'W	W	98
Rigg Screes	Cumbr	NY2120	54°34·4'	3°12·9'W	H	89,90
Riggs Fm	N Yks	SE8277	54°11·2'	0°44·2'W	FM	100
Riggs Fm	N Yks	SE8558	54°0·9'	0°41·7'W	FM	106
Riggs Head Fm	N Yks	TA0087	54°16·4'	0°27·4'W	FM	101
Riggshield	Cumbr	NY4763	54°57·8'	2°49·2'W	X	86
Riggshill Fm	Kent	TQ9452	51°14·3'	0°47·1'E	FM	189
Riggs Ho	N Yks	SD9988	54°17·5'	2°0·5'W	X	98
Riggs Ho	N Yks	SE1465	54°5·1'	1°46·7'W	X	99
Riggs Moor	N Yks	SE0373	54°9·4'	1°56·8'W	X	98
Riggs, The	Brad	SE1141	53°52·1'	1°49·5'W	X	104
Riggs, The	Cumbr	NY4921	54°35·1'	2°46·9'W	H	90
Riggs, The	Cumbr	SD3188	54°17·2'	3°3·2'W	H	96,97
Riggs, The	Cumbr	SD7998	54°22·9'	2°19·0'W	X	98
Riggs, The	N Yks	NZ9107	54°27·3'	0°35·4'W	X	94
Riggs, The	N Yks	SE7975	54°10·1'	0°47·0'W	X	100
Riggs, The	Scot Bord	NT3334	55°36·0'	3°3·4'W	T	73
Rigg, The	Cumbr	NY4711	54°29·7'	2°48·7'W	X	90
Rigg, The	D & G	NY3291	55°12·8'	3°3·7'W	X	79
Rigg, The	Durham	NZ0016	54°32·6'	1°59·6'W	X	92
Rigg, The	Durham	NZ0111	54°29·9'	1°58·7'W	X	92
Rigg, The	E Ayr	NS5621	55°28·0'	4°16·2'W	X	71
Rigg, The	Northum	NY6483	55°8·7'	2°33·5'W	H	80
Rigg, The	Shetld	HU1652	60°15·4'	1°42·2'W	X	3
Riggwood	Cumbr	NY2134	54°41·9'	3°13·1'W	X	89,90
Rigg Wood	Cumbr	SD3092	54°19·4'	3°4·2'W	F	96,97
Righead	Fife	NS9788	56°4·7'	3°38·9'W	X	65
Rig Head	Scot Bord	NT1924	55°30·4'	3°16·5'W	X	72
Righead	S Lanak	NS8338	55°37·5'	3°51·1'W	X	71,72
Righead Plantn	E Ayr	NS4047	55°41·7'	4°32·3'W	F	64
Righe Dubh Loch Portain	N Eil	NF9271	57°37·7'	7°9·1'W	X	18
Righe nam Ban	N Eil	NF9674	57°39·5'	7°5·4'W	X	18
Rig Hill	E Ayr	NS5309	55°21·4'	4°18·7'W	X	70,77
Righi, The	Ches	SJ4757	53°6·7'	2°47·1'W	X	117
Rightadown	Devon	SS4203	50°48·5'	4°14·2'W	X	190
Righton's Grave	Somer	ST3838	51°8·5'	2°52·8'W	X	182
Rigifa'	Highld	ND3072	58°38·1'	3°11·9'W	X	7,12
Rigifa Fm	C of Aber	NJ9400	57°5·7'	2°5·5'W	FM	38
Riglaw	E Renf	NS4055	55°46·0'	4°32·6'W	X	64
Rigmaden Fm	Cumbr	SD6185	54°15·8'	2°35·5'W	FM	97
Rigmaden Park	Cumbr	SD6184	54°15·3'	2°35·5'W	X	97
Rigmuir	S Lanak	NS6652	55°44·8'	4°7·7'W	X	64
Rignall Fm	Bucks	SP8802	51°42·8'	0°43·2'W	FM	165
Rignell Fm	Oxon	SP4232	51°59·3'	1°22·9'W	FM	151
Rignell Hall	Oxon	SP4232	51°59·3'	1°22·9'W	X	151
Rig of Airie	D & G	NX6077	55°4·3'	4°11·1'W	X	77
Rig of Burnfoot	D & G	NX5965	54°57·8'	4°11·7'W	X	83
Rig of Clenrie	D & G	NX5382	55°6·9'	4°17·9'W	X	77
Rig of Craig Gilbert	D & G	NX5874	55°2·7'	4°12·9'W	X	77
Rig of Crow Nest	D & G	NX4781	55°6·2'	4°23·5'W	X	77
Rig of Drumbuie	D & G	NX5781	55°6·4'	4°14·1'W	H	77
Rig of Drumruck	D & G	NX5764	54°57·3'	4°13·6'W	X	83
Rig of Drumwhar	D & G	NX5374	55°2·6'	4°17·6'W	X	77
Rig of Kirkennan	D & G	NX3784	55°7·7'	4°33·0'W	X	77
Rig of Kirriereoch	D & G	NX3787	55°9·3'	4°33·1'W	X	77
Rig of Larg Fell	D & G	NX3774	55°2·3'	4°32·6'W	X	77
Rig of Loch Enoch	D & G	NX4383	55°7·2'	4°27·3'W	H	77
Rig of Millmore	D & G	NX4388	55°9·9'	4°27·5'W	X	77
Rig of Munshalloch	D & G	NX4486	55°8·9'	4°26·4'W	X	77
Rig of Stroan	D & G	NX3980	55°5·6'	4°30·9'W	X	77
Rig of the Gloon	D & G	NX4284	55°7·8'	4°28·3'W	X	77
Rig of the Jarkness	D & G	NX4481	55°6·2'	4°26·3'W	X	77
Rig of the Shalloch	S Ayr	NX3891	55°11·5'	4°32·3'W	X	77
Rig Plantation	D & G	NS8402	55°18·2'	3°49·2'W	F	78
Rigs Burn	Scot Bord	NT0723	55°29·8'	3°27·9'W	W	72
Rigsby	Lincs	TF4375	53°15·4'	0°9·0'E	T	122
Rigsby Wood (Nature Reserve)	Lincs	TF4276	53°15·9'	0°8·2'E	X	122
Rigside	S Lanak	NS8835	55°36·0'	3°46·2'W	T	71,72
Rig, The	D & G	NY3581	55°7·4'	3°0·7'W	X	79
Rig, The	Pth & Kin	NN9607	56°14·9'	3°40·3'W	X	58
Rig, The	Scot Bord	NT0921	55°28·7'	3°26·0'W	H	72
Rig, The	S Lanak	NT0214	55°24·9'	3°32·5'W	H	78
Rigton Carr Fm	Leeds	SE3543	53°53·2'	1°27·6'W	FM	104
Rigton Grange	Leeds	SE3543	53°53·2'	1°27·6'W	X	104
Rigton High Moor	N Yks	SE2650	53°57·0'	1°35·8'W	X	104
Rigton Hill	Leeds	SE3744	53°53·7'	1°25·8'W	X	104
Rigton Lodge	N Yks	SE2849	53°56·4'	1°34·0'W	X	104
Rikkyo Sch	W Susx	TQ0533	51°5·4'	0°29·7'W	X	187
Riley Bank	Ches	SJ5174	53°15·9'	2°43·7'W	X	117
Riley Graves	Derby	SK2276	53°17·1'	1°39·8'W	A	119
Riley Green	Lancs	SD6225	53°43·4'	2°34·1'W	T	102,103
Rileyhill	Staffs	SK1115	52°44·2'	1°49·8'W	T	128
Riley Ho	Devon	SX8480	50°36·7'	3°38·0'W	X	191
Rillage Point	Devon	SS5448	51°13·0'	4°5·0'W	X	180
Rilla Mill	Corn	SX2973	50°32·1'	4°24·4'W	T	201
Rillaton	Corn	SX2973	50°32·1'	4°24·4'W	T	201
Rill Fm	Corn	SX3568	50°29·6'	4°19·2'W	FM	201
Rill Fm	Devon	SX7564	50°28·0'	3°45·3'W	FM	202
Rill Fm	Devon	SY0292	50°43·4'	3°22·9'W	FM	192
Rill Fm	Devon	SY1194	50°44·6'	3°15·3'W	FM	192,193
Rillington	N Yks	SE8574	54°9·5'	0°41·5'W	T	100
Rillington Low Moor	N Yks	SE8376	54°10·6'	0°43·3'W	X	100
Rillington Manor	N Yks	SE8574	54°9·5'	0°41·5'W	X	100
Rill Ledges	Corn	SW6713	49°58·5'	5°14·6'W	X	203
Rill, The	Corn	SW6713	49°58·5'	5°14·6'W	X	203
Rilshaw	Ches	SJ6665	53°11·1'	2°30·1'W	X	118
Rimac	Lincs	TF4691	53°24·0'	0°12·2'E	T	113
Rimbleton	Fife	NO2600	56°11·5'	3°11·1'W	T	59
Rimey Law	Durham	NY9244	54°47·7'	2°7·0'W	X	87
Rimington	Lancs	SD8045	53°54·3'	2°17·9'W	T	103
Rimington Moor	Lancs	SD8343	53°53·2'	2°15·1'W	X	103
Rimpston	Devon	SX7746	50°18·3'	3°43·3'W	X	202
Rimpton	Somer	ST6021	50°59·5'	2°33·8'W	T	183
Rimsdale	Highld	NC7340	58°20·1'	4°9·7'W	X	10
Rimsdale Burn	Highld	NC7339	58°19·5'	4°9·6'W	W	16
Rimsdale Burn	Highld	NC7441	58°20·6'	4°8·7'W	W	10
Rimsdale Hill	Highld	NC7540	58°20·1'	4°7·6'W	H	10
Rimside Moor	Northum	NU0906	55°21·1'	1°51·1'W	X	81
Rimsmoor Pond	Dorset	SY8192	50°43·9'	2°15·8'W	W	194
Rimswell	E Yorks	TA3128	53°43·6'	0°0·4'W	T	107
Rimswell Lodge	E Yorks	TA3127	53°43·6'	0°0·4'W	X	107
Rimswell Valley	E Yorks	TA3228	53°44·1'	0°0·5'E	T	107
Rinalloch	Aberd	NJ6408	57°9·9'	2°35·3'W	X	37
Rinaston	Pemb	SM9825	51°53·5'	4°55·7'W	X	157,158
Rinavoan	Aberd	NJ4215	57°13·6'	2°57·2'W	X	37
Rinders Fm	Lincs	TF4153	53°3·6'	0°6·6'E	FM	122
Rindleford	Shrops	SO7395	52°33·4'	2°23·5'W	T	138
Rineten	Aberd	NJ2700	57°5·4'	3°11·8'W	X	37
Ring	Orkney	HY4248	59°19·1'	3°0·7'W	X	5
Ring	W Dunb	NS4081	56°0·0'	4°33·5'W	X	64
Ringan	D & G	NX4845	54°46·9'	4°21·4'W	X	83
Ring and Kirkland	D & G	NX3360	54°54·7'	4°35·9'W	X	82
Ringanwhey	D & G	NX7565	54°58·1'	3°56·7'W	X	84

Ringasta	Shetld	HU3714	59°54·8′	1°19·8′W	T	4
Ringate Fm	Norf	TF8437	52°54·2′	0°44·6′E	FM	132
Ringbane	D & G	NX6573	55°2·2′	4°6·3′W	X	77,84
Ringbeck	N Yks	SE2174	54°9·9′	1°40·3′W	X	99
Ring Burn	D & G	NX2172	55°0·9′	4°47·6′W	W	76
Ring Chesters	Northum	NT8628	55°33·0′	2°12·9′W	A	74
Ringcombe	Devon	SS8328	51°2·6′	3°39·8′W	X	181
Ringdale Manor	Oxon	SU2892	51°37·8′	1°35·3′W	X	163,174
Ring Dam	Lincs	SK9933	52°53·4′	0°31·3′W	W	130
Ringden Fm	E Susx	TQ7130	51°2·9′	0°26·8′E	FM	188
Ringdoo Point	D & G	NX1755	54°51·6′	4°50·7′W	X	82
Ringdoo Point	D & G	NX5451	54°50·2′	4°16·0′W	X	83
Ringdoo Point	D & G	NX6045	54°47·1′	4°10·2′W	X	83
Ring Down	Somer	ST1816	50°56·5′	3°9·6′W	X	181,193
Ringdown Common	Somer	ST1816	50°56·5′	3°9·6′W	X	181,193
Ringehay	Staffs	SJ9952	53°4·2′	2°0·5′W	X	118
Ringers	Essex	TL5333	51°58·7′	0°14·1′E	X	167
Ringers Barn Fm	Suff	TL9280	52°23·3′	0°49·7′E	FM	144
Ringer's Fm	Essex	TL7613	51°47·5′	0°33·5′E	FM	167
Ring Fm	Cambs	TL4077	52°22·6′	0°3·8′E	FM	142,143
Ring Fm	Fife	NO3609	56°16·4′	3°1·6′W	FM	59
Ringford	D & G	NX6857	54°53·7′	4°3·1′W	T	83,84
Ringford Fm	Corn	SX1392	50°42·1′	4°38·5′W	FM	190
Ring Gate	Cumbr	NY5256	54°54·0′	2°44·5′W	X	86
Ringham Low	Derby	SK1666	53°11·7′	1°45·2′W	A	119
Ringham Low	Derby	SK1761	53°9·0′	1°44·3′W	A	119
Ring Haw	Northnts	TL0597	52°33·9′	0°26·7′W	F	142
Ringhay Wood	N Yks	SE4535	53°48·8′	1°18·6′W	F	105
Ringheel	D & G	NX3348	54°48·2′	4°35·5′W	X	82
Ring Hill	Essex	TL5138	52°1·4′	0°12·4′E	X	154
Ring Hill	Glos	SO8209	51°47·0′	2°15·3′W	X	162
Ring Hill	S Lanak	NS9915	55°25·4′	3°35·3′W	H	78
Ring Hill (Fort)	Essex	TL5138	52°1·4′	0°12·4′E	A	154
Ringhurst Fm	S Glos	ST6384	51°33·5′	2°31·6′W	FM	172
Ringie Geo	Orkney	HY5336	59°12·7′	2°48·9′W	X	5
Ringill	Highld	NG5617	57°11·0′	6°1·8′W	X	32
Ringing Hill	Lancs	SD5144	53°53·6′	2°44·3′W	X	102
Ringing Hill	Leic	SK4518	52°45·7′	1°19·6′W	T	129
Ringing Keld Gutter	Cumbr	SD7192	54°19·6′	2°26·3′W	W	98
Ringinglow	Sheff	SK2883	53°20·8′	1°34·4′W	T	110
Ringing Roger	Derby	SK1287	53°23·0′	1°48·8′W	X	110
Ringing Stone	Arg & Bt	NM0248	56°32·0′	6°50·4′W	X	46
Ringland	Newp	ST3588	51°35·5′	2°55·9′W	T	171
Ringland	Norf	TG1314	52°41·1′	1°9·5′E	T	133
Ringland Hills	Norf	TG1312	52°40·1′	1°9·4′E	X	133
Ringlands Plantn	E Yorks	SE8852	53°57·6′	0°39·1′W	F	106
Ringlands Plantn	E Yorks	TA0270	54°7·2′	0°25·9′W	F	101
Ringles Cross	E Susx	TQ4722	50°58·9′	0°6·0′E	T	198
Ringlestone	Kent	TQ7557	51°17·3′	0°31·0′E	T	178,188
Ringlestone	Kent	TQ8755	51°16·0′	0°41·2′E	T	178
Ringleton Manor	Kent	TR2957	51°16·2′	1°17·4′E	X	179
Ringley	Bolton	SD7605	53°32·7′	2°21·3′W	T	109
Ringmer	E Susx	TQ4412	50°53·6′	0°3·2′E	T	198
Ringmoor	Dorset	ST8008	50°52·5′	2°16·7′W	X	194
Ring Moor	Lincs	TF1554	53°4·5′	0°16·6′W	X	121
Ringmoor Cottage	Devon	SX5566	50°28·8′	4°2·2′W	X	202
Ringmoor Down	Devon	SX5666	50°28·8′	4°1·4′W	X	202
Ringmoor (Settlement & Field System)	Dorset	ST8008	50°52·5′	2°16·7′W	A	194
Ringmore	Devon	SX6545	50°17·6′	3°53·3′W	T	202
Ring Moss	D & G	NX3367	54°58·4′	4°36·1′W	X	82
Ring o' Bells	Lancs	SD4510	53°35·3′	2°49·4′W	T	108
Ring 'O' Bells Fm	S Glos	ST7276	51°29·2′	2°23·8′W	FM	172
Ring of Bookan	Orkney	HY2814	59°0·7′	3°14·7′W	A	6
Ring of Brogar	Orkney	HY2913	59°0·2′	3°13·7′W	A	6
Ring of Castlehill	Highld	ND2861	58°32·1′	3°13·7′W	A	11,12
Ringour	D & G	NX6672	55°1·7′	4°5·4′W	X	77,84
Ring Pit Fm	Salf	SJ6994	53°26·8′	2°27·6′W	FM	109
Ringsbury Camp	Wilts	SU0786	51°34·6′	1°53·5′W	A	173
Ringsdon Clump	Devon	SX9483	50°38·5′	3°29·6′W	F	192
Ring's End	Cambs	TF3902	52°36·1′	0°3·6′E	T	142,143
Ringses	Northum	NU1018	55°27·6′	1°50·1′W	X	81
Ringses, The	Northum	NU0132	55°35·1′	1°58·6′W	A	75
Ringsfield	Suff	TM4088	52°26·5′	1°32·3′E	T	156
Ringsfield Corner	Suff	TM4087	52°25·9′	1°32·2′E	T	156
Ringsfield Hall	Suff	TM3987	52°25·9′	1°31·4′E	X	156
Ringshall	Herts	SP9814	51°49·2′	0°34·3′W	T	165
Ringshall	Suff	TM0452	52°7·9′	0°59·2′E	T	155
Ringshall Coppice	Bucks	SP9715	51°49·7′	0°35·1′W	F	165
Ringshall Grange	Suff	TM0452	52°7·9′	0°59·2′E	X	155
Ringshall Ho	Suff	TM0550	52°6·8′	1°0·0′E	X	155
Ringshall Stocks	Suff	TM0551	52°7·4′	1°0·1′E	T	155
Rings Hill	Dorset	SY8680	50°37·4′	2°11·5′W	X	194
Rings Hill Fm	Medway	TQ7165	51°21·7′	0°27·8′E	FM	178
Ringshill Place	Kent	TQ7264	51°21·2′	0°28·6′E	X	178,188
Ringslade	Devon	SX8472	50°32·4′	3°37·8′W	X	191
Ringstead	Norf	TF7040	52°56·1′	0°32·2′E	T	132
Ringstead	Northnts	SP9875	52°22·1′	0°33·2′W	T	141
Ringstead Bay	Dorset	SY7581	50°37·9′	2°20·8′W	W	194
Ringstead Common	Norf	TF7240	52°56·0′	0°34·0′E	X	132
Ringstead Downs	Norf	TF6939	52°55·5′	0°31·3′E	X	132
Ringstead Grange	Northnts	SP9774	52°21·6′	0°34·1′W	X	141
Ringstead Village	Dorset	SY7481	50°37·9′	2°21·7′W	A	194
Rings, The	Dorset	SY9581	50°38·0′	2°3·9′W	A	195
Rings, The	Scot Bord	NT0932	55°34·6′	3°26·2′W	X	72
Rings, The	Stock on T	NZ4215	54°32·0′	1°20·6′W	X	93
Rings, The	Wilts	SU0048	51°14·1′	1°59·6′W	F	184
Rings, The (Fort and Settlement)	Scot Bord	NT0932	55°34·6′	3°26·2′W	A	72
Ringstone Edge Moor	Cald	SE0418	53°39·7′	1°56·0′W	X	110
Ringstone Edge Resr	Cald	SE0418	53°39·7′	1°56·0′W	W	110
Ringstone Hill	Barns	SE4210	53°35·3′	1°21·5′W	X	111
Ring Stone Hill	Lancs	SD8936	53°49·5′	2°9·6′W	X	103
Ringstones	Lancs	SD6665	54°5·0′	2°30·8′W	X	98
Ringstones Fm	Derby	SK0089	53°24·1′	1°59·6′W	FM	110
Rings Wharley Fm	Beds	SP9443	52°4·9′	0°37·3′W	FM	153
Ringtail Fm	Mil Key	SP9444	52°5·4′	0°37·3′W	FM	153
Ringtail Green	Essex	TL6716	51°49·3′	0°25·8′E	T	167
Ring, The	D & G	NX8397	55°15·5′	3°50·0′W	X	78
Ring, The	Glos	SO9826	51°56·2′	2°1·4′W	X	163

Ring, The	Shrops	SJ3904	52°38·1′	2°53·7′W	A	126
Ring, The (Settlement)	Glos	SO9826	51°56·2′	2°1·4′W	A	163
Ringvinachan	D & G	NX1146	54°46·7′	4°55·9′W	X	82
Ringway	N Yks	SE2952	53°58·0′	1°33·1′W	X	104
Ringwell Hill	Somer	ST4617	50°57·2′	2°45·7′W	X	193
Ringwood	E Susx	TV5798	50°45·8′	0°14·0′E	X	199
Ringwood	Hants	SU1505	50°50·9′	1°46·8′W	T	195
Ringwood	Pth & Kin	NO0440	56°32·8′	3°33·2′W	X	52,53
Ringwood Bar	Essex	TQ9695	51°37·4′	0°50·3′E	X	168
Ringwood Fm	Oxon	SP3212	51°48·6′	1°31·8′W	FM	164
Ringwood Forest	Hants	SU1108	50°52·5′	1°50·2′W	F	195
Ringwould	Kent	TR3548	51°11·2′	1°22·2′E	T	179
Rinibar	Orkney	ND4193	58°49·5′	3°0·8′W	X	7
Rink Hill	Scot Bord	NT4732	55°35·0′	2°50·0′W	H	73
Rink, The	Scot Bord	NT4832	55°35·0′	2°49·1′W	T	73
Rinmore	Aberd	NJ4117	57°14·7′	2°58·2′W	X	37
Rinn a' Chrubain	N Ayr	NR9023	55°27·6′	5°18·9′W	X	68,69
Rinnagailloch	Aberd	NJ4011	57°11·4′	2°59·1′W	X	37
Rinnans	Stir	NS5489	56°4·6′	4°20·3′W	X	57
Rinn Chircnis	Arg & Bt	NL9339	56°26·9′	6°58·5′W	X	46
Rinn Druim Tallig	N Eil	NB3150	58°21·6′	6°35·5′W	X	8
Rinni Gill	Orkney	ND2299	58°52·5′	3°20·7′W	X	6,7
Rinnigill	Orkney	ND3193	58°49·4′	3°11·2′W	T	7
Rinnion Hills	Cumbr	NY5669	55°1·1′	2°40·9′W	X	86
Rinn Mollerap	N Eil	NB3150	58°21·6′	6°35·5′W	X	8
Rinn nan Gruban	N Eil	NB3049	58°21·0′	6°36·4′W	X	8
Rinn Thorbhais	Arg & Bt	NL9339	56°26·9′	6°58·5′W	X	46
Rinour	Moray	NJ1740	57°26·8′	3°22·5′W	X	28
Rinsey	Corn	SW5927	50°5·9′	5°21·8′W	T	203
Rinsey Croft	Corn	SW6028	50°6·5′	5°21·0′W	T	203
Rinsey Head	Corn	SW5826	50°5·3′	5°22·6′W	X	203
Rintoul	Pth & Kin	NO0705	56°14·0′	3°29·6′W	X	58
Rinuden	Highld	NH5537	57°24·3′	4°24·3′W	X	26
Rinzoorach Burn	Stir	NN3801	56°10·7′	4°36·1′W	W	56
Riosaidh	N Eil	NB3923	58°7·4′	6°25·5′W	X	14
Riosgaidh	N Eil	NF7928	57°14·1′	7°18·8′W	X	22
Ripack Stack	Shetld	HU3411	59°53·2′	1°23·1′W	X	4
Ripe	E Susx	TQ5110	50°52·4′	0°9·2′E	T	199
Ripe Hill	Aberd	NO2491	57°0·5′	3°14·6′W	H	44
Riphay Barton	Somer	SS9224	51°0·6′	3°32·0′W	X	181
Ripletts	Shrops	SO5879	52°24·7′	2°36·7′W	X	137,138
Ripley	Derby	SK4050	53°3·0′	1°23·8′W	T	120
Ripley	Hants	SZ1698	50°47·1′	1°46·0′W	T	195
Ripley	N Yks	SE2860	54°2·4′	1°33·9′W	T	99
Ripley	Surrey	TQ0556	51°17·8′	0°29·2′W	T	187
Ripley Grange	Essex	TQ4498	51°40·0′	0°5·3′E	X	167,177
Ripley Green	Surrey	TQ0557	51°18·4′	0°29·2′W	X	187
Ripley Park	N Yks	SE2760	54°2·4′	1°34·8′W	X	99
Ripley's Fm	N Yks	SE9994	54°20·2′	0°28·2′W	FM	94,101
Ripley Wood	Hants	SU1600	50°48·2′	1°46·0′W	F	195
Riplingham	E Yorks	SE9631	53°46·2′	0°32·2′W	T	106
Riplingham Grange	E Yorks	SE9633	53°47·3′	0°32·2′W	X	106
Riplingham Ho	E Yorks	SE9632	53°46·8′	0°32·2′W	X	106
Riplingham Village	E Yorks	SE9532	53°46·8′	0°33·1′W	A	106
Riplington	Hants	SU6623	51°0·4′	1°3·2′W	X	185
Riplington	Northum	NZ1182	55°8·2′	1°49·2′W	X	81
Ripney Hill Fm	Kent	TQ9473	51°25·6′	0°47·8′E	FM	178
Ripon	N Yks	SE3171	54°8·3′	1°31·1′W	T	99
Ripon Canal	N Yks	SE3269	54°7·2′	1°30·2′W	W	99
Ripon Hall Fm	Lancs	SD4842	53°52·5′	2°47·0′W	FM	102
Ripon Parks	N Yks	SE3074	54°9·9′	1°32·0′W	X	99
Rippachie	Aberd	NJ4111	57°11·4′	2°58·1′W	X	37
Rippack Stack	Shetld	HT9636	60°6·8′	2°3·8′W	X	4
Rippack, The	Shetld	HZ2170	59°31·2′	1°37·2′W	H	4
Rippator or Rival Tor	Devon	SX6488	50°40·8′	3°55·1′W	X	191
Ripper's Cross	Kent	TQ9543	51°9·4′	0°47·7′E	T	189
Ripperston Fm	Pemb	SM8111	51°45·5′	5°10·0′W	FM	157
Rippingale	Lincs	TF0928	52°50·5′	0°22·5′W	T	130
Rippingdale Fen	Lincs	TF1427	52°49·9′	0°18·1′W	X	130
Ripple	Kent	TR3449	51°11·8′	1°21·4′E	T	179
Ripple	Worcs	SO8737	52°2·1′	2°11·0′W	T	150
Ripple Court	Kent	TQ9745	51°10·4′	0°49·5′E	X	189
Ripple Court	Kent	TR3448	51°11·2′	1°21·3′E	X	179
Ripple Fm	Kent	TR0649	51°12·4′	0°57·3′E	FM	179,189
Ripple Fm	Kent	TR3549	51°11·7′	1°22·2′E	FM	179
Ripple Stone	Shetld	HU6290	60°35·6′	0°51·6′W	A	1,2
Ripplewood	Heref	SO6560	52°14·5′	2°30·4′W	X	138,149
Rippon Burn	Durham	NZ1146	54°48·8′	1°49·3′W	W	88
Ripponden	Cald	SE0319	53°40·3′	1°56·9′W	T	110
Rippon Hall	Norf	TG2122	52°45·2′	1°16·9′E	X	133,134
Rippon Tor	Devon	SX7475	50°33·9′	3°46·4′W	H	191
Ripsley Ho	W Susx	SU8229	51°3·5′	0°49·4′W	X	186,197
Ripton Ho	Durham	NZ0823	54°36·4′	1°52·1′W	X	92
Rireavach	Highld	NH0295	57°54·3′	5°20·0′W	T	19
Rires	Fife	NO4604	56°13·8′	2°51·8′W	X	59
Risabus	Arg & Bt	NR3143	55°36·6′	6°15·9′W	T	60
Risaw	N Yks	SE3067	54°6·1′	1°32·1′W	X	99
Risbury	Heref	SO5455	52°11·7′	2°40·0′W	A	149
Risbury	Heref	SO5555	52°11·7′	2°39·1′W	T	149
Risby	E Yorks	TA0034	53°47·8′	0°28·5′W	T	106,107
Risby	Lincs	TF1491	53°24·4′	0°16·7′W	T	113
Risby	Suff	TL7966	52°16·0′	0°37·8′E	T	155
Risby Moor	Lincs	TF1290	53°23·9′	0°18·5′W	X	113
Risby Park	E Yorks	TA0035	53°48·3′	0°28·5′W	X	106,107
Risby Park Fm	E Yorks	SE9935	53°48·3′	0°29·4′W	FM	106
Risby Poor's Heath	Suff	TL7767	52°16·6′	0°36·1′E	X	155
Risby Poor's Heath	Suff	TL7868	52°17·1′	0°37·0′E	X	155
Risby's Fm	Essex	TM1221	51°51·1′	1°5·1′E	FM	168,169
Risby Village	E Yorks	TA0034	53°47·8′	0°28·5′W	A	106,107
Risby Warren	N Lincs	SE9313	53°36·6′	0°35·2′W	X	112
Risby Warren Fm	N Lincs	SE9314	53°37·1′	0°35·2′W	FM	112
Risca	Caer	ST2490	51°36·5′	3°5·5′W	T	171
Riscombe	Somer	SS8339	51°8·5′	3°40·0′W	X	181
Risdale Fm	Lincs	TF4256	53°5·2′	0°7·6′E	FM	122
Risden	Kent	TQ7729	51°2·2′	0°31·9′E	X	188,199
Risdon	Devon	SX4993	50°43·3′	4°8·0′W	X	191
Risdon	Devon	SX5799	50°46·6′	4°1·3′W	X	191
Rise	Cumbr	NY7244	54°47·7′	2°25·7′W	X	86,87
Rise	E Yorks	TA1542	53°51·9′	0°14·7′W	T	107
Rise Barn	E Susx	TQ4208	50°51·5′	0°1·4′E	X	198

Riseborough Hagg	N Yks	SE7583	54°14·5′	0°50·5′W	X	100
Riseborough Hall	N Yks	SE7582	54°13·9′	0°50·5′W	X	100
Rise Carr	Darl	NZ2816	54°32·6′	1°33·6′W	T	93
Risedale Beck	N Yks	SE1596	54°21·8′	1°45·7′W	W	99
Riseden	E Susx	TQ6130	51°3·0′	0°18·2′E	X	188
Riseden	Kent	TQ7035	51°5·6′	0°26·1′E	T	188
Rise End	Derby	SK2755	53°5·7′	1°35·4′W	T	119
Rise Fm	E Susx	TQ4108	50°51·5′	0°0·6′E	FM	198
Rise Fm	N Yks	SE7481	54°13·4′	0°51·5′W	FM	100
Risegate	Lincs	TF2029	52°50·9′	0°12·7′W	T	131
Risegate Eau	Lincs	TF2531	52°51·9′	0°8·2′W	W	131
Risegate Outfall	Lincs	TF3031	52°51·9′	0°3·7′W	W	131
Rise Grange	E Yorks	TA1442	53°51·9′	0°15·6′W	X	107
Risegreen	Northum	NY8644	54°47·7′	2°12·6′W	X	87
Rise Hall	E Yorks	TA1542	53°51·9′	0°14·7′W	X	107
Rise Hall	Suff	TM1448	52°5·6′	1°7·8′E	X	169
Rise Hill	Cumbr	SD7388	54°17·5′	2°24·5′W	H	98
Rise Hill	Notts	SK4954	53°5·1′	1°15·7′W	X	120
Riseholme	Lincs	SK9875	53°16·0′	0°31·4′W	T	121
Riseholme Gorse	Lincs	SK9876	53°16·5′	0°31·4′W	F	121
Riseholme Village	Lincs	SK9875	53°16·0′	0°31·4′W	A	121
Risehow	Cumbr	NY0234	54°41·7′	3°30·8′W	T	89
Risehow Fm	Cumbr	NY0235	54°42·3′	3°30·8′W	FM	89
Riseley	Beds	TL0462	52°15·0′	0°28·2′W	T	153
Riseley	N Yks	SE3064	54°4·5′	1°32·1′W	X	99
Riseley	Wok	SU7263	51°21·9′	0°57·6′W	T	175,186
Riseley Fm	Wok	SU7363	51°21·9′	0°56·7′W	FM	175,186
Riseley Lodge Fm	Beds	TL0462	52°15·0′	0°28·2′W	FM	153
Riseley Mill	Hants	SU7362	51°21·4′	0°56·7′W	X	175,186
Rise Park	C of Nott	SK5546	53°0·7′	1°10·4′W	T	129
Rise Park	Hav	TQ5191	51°36·1′	0°11·2′E	T	177
Rise Plot	Lincs	SK9634	52°53·9′	0°34·0′W	X	130
Rise Rocks Fm	Leic	SK4612	52°42·5′	1°18·7′W	FM	129
Rise Wood	E Yorks	TA1441	53°51·4′	0°15·6′W	F	107
Risey Burn	Northum	NY9384	55°9·3′	2°6·2′W	W	80
Risga	Highld	NM6060	56°40·5′	5°54·6′W	X	40
Rishangles	Suff	TM1668	52°16·3′	1°10·4′E	T	156
Rishangles Lodge	Suff	TM1568	52°16·3′	1°9·5′E	X	156
Rishton	Lancs	SD7230	53°46·2′	2°25·1′W	T	103
Rishton Resr	Lancs	SD7129	53°45·6′	2°26·0′W	W	103
Rishworth	Cald	SE0318	53°39·7′	1°56·9′W	T	110
Rishworth Drain	Cald	SD9716	53°38·7′	2°2·3′W	W	109
Rishworth Moor	Cald	SD9917	53°39·2′	2°0·5′W	X	109
Rishworth Moor	Cald	SE0017	53°39·2′	1°59·6′W	X	110
Rising Bridge	Lancs	SD7825	53°43·5′	2°19·6′W	T	103
Risingbridge	Worcs	SO9170	52°19·9′	2°7·5′W	X	139
Risingbrook	Staffs	SJ9221	52°47·4′	2°6·7′W	T	127
Risingclaw Burn	S Lanak	NT0320	55°28·1′	3°31·6′W	W	72
Risingclaw Heights	S Lanak	NT0320	55°28·1′	3°31·6′W	H	72
Rising Clough	Derby	SK2188	53°23·5′	1°40·6′W	X	110
Risinghurst	Oxon	SP5507	51°45·8′	1°11·8′W	T	164
Risings, The	Northnts	SP7754	52°11·0′	0°52·0′W	X	152
Rising Sun	Corn	SX3970	50°30·7′	4°15·9′W	T	201
Rising Sun	N Yks	SE5371	54°8·2′	1°10·9′W	X	100
Rising Sun Fm	Derby	SK1577	53°17·6′	1°46·1′W	FM	119
Rising Sun Fm	N Tyne	NZ3068	55°0·6′	1°31·4′W	FM	88
Rising Sun Fm	N Yks	SE4665	54°5·0′	1°17·4′W	FM	100
Risk	D & G	NX4468	54°59·2′	4°25·9′W	X	83
Risk	D & G	NX7160	54°55·3′	4°0·3′W	X	83,84
Risk	Renf	NS3759	55°48·1′	4°35·6′W	X	63
Riska Island	Highld	NM6672	56°47·1′	5°49·4′W	X	40
Riskamain	Highld	ND1737	58°19·1′	3°24·5′W	X	11
Riskaness	Shetld	HU2348	60°13·2′	1°34·6′W	X	3
Riskend	N Lanak	NS7378	55°58·9′	4°1·7′W	X	64
Riskinhope	Scot Bord	NT2318	55°27·2′	3°12·6′W	X	79
Riskinhope Burn	Scot Bord	NT2318	55°27·2′	3°12·6′W	W	79
Riskinhope Hope	Scot Bord	NT2418	55°27·3′	3°11·7′W	X	79
Riskinhope Hope	Scot Bord	NT2518	55°27·3′	3°10·7′W	X	79
Risley	Derby	SK4635	52°54·9′	1°18·5′W	T	129
Risley	Warr	SJ6592	53°25·7′	2°31·2′W	T	109
Risley Lodge Fm	Derby	SK4536	52°55·4′	1°19·4′W	FM	129
Risley Moss Nature Park	Warr	SJ6691	53°25·1′	2°30·3′W	X	109
Rislip Fm	Bucks	SP8827	51°56·3′	0°42·8′W	FM	165
Rispain	D & G	NX4339	54°43·5′	4°25·9′W	X	83
Rispa Pike	Cumbr	NY6301	54°24·4′	2°33·8′W	X	91
Risp Hill	D & G	NY2280	55°6·7′	3°12·9′W	H	79
Risp Howe	Cumbr	NY8611	54°29·9′	2°12·5′W	X	91,92
Rispie Hill	D & G	NY1199	55°16·9′	3°23·6′W	H	78
Risplith	N Yks	SE2468	54°6·7′	1°37·6′W	T	99
Rispond	Highld	NC4565	58°33·0′	4°39·3′W	X	9
Rispond Bay	Highld	NC4565	58°33·0′	4°39·3′W	W	9
Risquehouse	Aberd	NJ5233	57°23·4′	2°47·5′W	X	29
Rissick	Corn	SW3926	50°4·8′	5°38·5′W	X	203
Ristbrow	N Yks	SE5488	54°17·3′	1°9·8′W	X	100
Riste Fm	Leic	SK4522	52°47·9′	1°19·6′W	FM	129
Ristie	Shetld	HT9541	60°9·5′	2°4·9′W	X	4
Riston Grange	E Yorks	TA1143	53°52·5′	0°18·3′W	X	107
Riston Whins Ho	E Yorks	TA1443	53°52·5′	0°15·5′W	X	107
Ritec,The	Pemb	SN0901	51°40·8′	4°45·4′W	W	158
Rit Ness	Shetld	HU3362	60°20·7′	1°23·6′W	X	2,3
Ritson	Devon	SX7852	50°21·6′	3°42·5′W	X	202
Ritta Taing	Shetld	HU4450	60°14·2′	1°11·8′W	X	3
Ritten Hamar	Shetld	HP6416	60°49·6′	0°48·9′W	X	1
Ritto Hill	Northum	NT9516	55°26·5′	2°4·3′W	H	81
Ritton	Northum	NZ0893	55°14·1′	1°52·0′W	X	81
Ritton Castle	Shrops	SO3497	52°34·2′	2°58·0′W	A	137
Ritton White Ho	Northum	NZ0594	55°14·7′	1°54·9′W	X	81
Ritty Cleuch	Scot Bord	NT2819	55°27·8′	3°7·9′W	X	79
Ritty Rig	Scot Bord	NT2528	55°32·7′	3°10·9′W	X	73
Ritty Rig	Scot Bord	NT2927	55°32·1′	3°7·1′W	H	73
Riva	Shetld	HU2974	60°27·2′	1°27·9′W	X	3
Rivacre Valley Country Park	Ches	SJ3777	53°17·4′	2°56·3′W	X	117
Riva Hill Fm	N Yks	SE2164	54°4·5′	1°40·3′W	FM	99
Rival Lodge	W Susx	SU7822	50°59·8′	0°52·9′W	X	197
Rivar	Wilts	SU3161	51°21·1′	1°32·9′W	T	174
Rivar Down	Wilts	SU3061	51°21·1′	1°33·8′W	X	174
Rivar Hill	Wilts	SU3161	51°21·1′	1°32·9′W	X	174
Riva Taing	Shetld	HU2380	60°30·4′	1°34·4′W	X	3
Rivaton	Devon	SS4514	50°54·5′	4°11·9′W	X	180,190

Rivefold	Aberd	NJ6436	57°25·0′	2°35·5′W	X	29
Rivehill	Aberd	NJ9458	57°37·0′	2°5·6′W	X	30
Rivehill	C of Aber	NJ8309	57°10·5′	2°16·4′W	X	38
Rive Hill	E Ayr	NS5742	55°39·3′	4°15·9′W	X	71
Rivelin Dams	Sheff	SK2786	53°22·4′	1°35·2′W	W	110
Rivelin Mill Br	Sheff	SK2887	53°23·0′	1°34·3′W	X	110
Rivelin Rocks	Sheff	SK2787	53°23·0′	1°35·2′W	X	110
Riven Burn	Shetld	HP5000	60°41·1′	1°4·6′W	W	1
Rivenhall	Essex	TL8217	51°49·5′	0°38·9′E	T	168
Rivenhall End	Essex	TL8316	51°49·0′	0°39·7′E	T	168
Rivenhall Pl	Essex	TL8119	51°50·6′	0°38·1′E	A	168
Riven Hill	Shetld	HU4461	60°20·1′	1°11·7′W	H	2,3
Riven Loch	N Lanak	NS8362	55°50·5′	3°51·7′W	X	65
Riven Noust	Shetld	HU5073	60°26·5′	1°5·0′W	X	2,3
River	Kent	TR2943	51°8·6′	1°16·8′E	T	179
River	W Susx	SU9322	50°59·6′	0°40·1′W	T	197
River Abel	Powys	SJ1318	52°45·4′	3°16·9′W	W	125
River Add	Arg & Bt	NR9195	56°6·4′	5°21·2′W	W	55
River Adur	W Susx	TQ1817	50°56·6′	0°18·8′W	W	198
River Aer	Pemb	SM9834	51°58·3′	4°56·1′W	W	157
River Affric	Highld	NH0719	57°13·5′	5°11·4′W	W	33
River Affric	Highld	NH0920	57°14·1′	5°9·4′W	W	25,33
River Affric	Highld	NH3028	57°18·9′	4°48·9′W	W	26
River Ailort	Highld	NM7782	56°52·8′	5°39·2′W	W	40
River Aire	Brad	SE1938	53°50·5′	1°42·3′W	W	104
River Aire	E Yorks	SE6722	53°41·6′	0°58·7′W	W	105,106
River Aire	N Yks	SD9058	54°1·3′	2°8·7′W	W	103
River Aire	N Yks	SD9552	53°58·1′	2°4·2′W	W	103
River Aire	N Yks	SE5124	53°42·8′	1°13·2′W	W	105
River Alde	Suff	TM3166	52°14·8′	1°23·4′E	W	156
River Alde	Suff	TM4553	52°7·5′	1°35·2′E	W	156
River Alham	Somer	ST6638	51°8·6′	2°28·8′W	W	183
River Aline	Highld	NM6948	56°34·3′	5°45·2′W	W	49
River Allen	Corn	SW8245	50°16·1′	5°3·2′W	W	204
River Allen	Corn	SX0476	50°33·3′	4°45·6′W	W	200
River Allen	Dorset	ST9906	50°51·4′	2°0·5′W	W	195
River Allen	Northum	NY7961	54°56·8′	2°19·2′W	W	86,87
River Almond	Pth & Kin	NN7533	56°28·6′	4°1·3′W	W	51,52
River Almond	Pth & Kin	NO0029	56°26·8′	3°36·9′W	W	52,53,58
River Almond	W Loth	NT0166	55°52·9′	3°34·5′W	W	65
River Aln	Northum	NU0111	55°23·8′	1°58·6′W	W	81
River Aln	Northum	NU1113	55°24·9′	1°49·1′W	W	81
River Alne	Warw	SP1158	52°13·4′	1°49·9′W	W	150
River Alne	Warw	SP1564	52°16·7′	1°46·4′W	W	151
River Alport	Derby	SK1292	53°25·7′	1°48·8′W	W	110
River Alre	Hants	SU5732	51°5·3′	1°10·8′W	W	185
River Alt	Liv	SJ4194	53°26·6′	2°52·9′W	W	108
River Alt	Sefton	SD3403	53°31·4′	2°59·3′W	W	108
River Alun	Pemb	SM7526	51°53·5′	5°15·8′W	W	157
River Alver	Hants	SZ5899	50°47·5′	1°10·2′W	W	196
River Alwin	Northum	NT9206	55°21·1′	2°7·1′W	W	80
River Alyn or Afon Alun	Denb	SJ1859	53°7·6′	3°13·1′W	W	116
River Alyn or Afon Alun	Flint	SJ2958	53°7·1′	3°3·2′W	W	117
River Amber	Derby	SK3462	53°9·5′	1°29·1′W	W	119
River Amble	Corn	SW9974	50°32·1′	4°49·8′W	W	200
River Ancholme	Lincs	TF0289	53°23·5′	0°27·6′W	W	112,121
River Anker	Warw	SP3495	52°33·3′	1°29·5′W	W	140
River Annan	D & G	NY1096	55°15·3′	3°24·5′W	W	78
River Annan	D & G	NY1969	55°0·8′	3°15·6′W	W	85
River Annas	Cumbr	SD0887	54°16·5′	3°24·4′W	W	96
River Ant	Norf	TG3620	52°43·8′	1°30·1′E	W	133,134
River Anton	Hants	SU3543	51°11·3′	1°29·6′W	W	185
River Applecross	Highld	NG7347	57°27·7′	5°46·6′W	W	24
River Aran	Powys	SO1571	52°20·1′	3°14·5′W	W	136,148
River Aray	Arg & Bt	NN0814	56°17·0′	5°5·7′W	W	50,56
River Ardle	Pth & Kin	NO0761	56°44·1′	3°30·8′W	W	43
River Arkaig	Highld	NN1788	56°57·1′	5°0·1′W	W	34,41
River Arnisdale	Highld	NG8609	57°7·6′	5°31·7′W	W	33
River Arrow	Heref	SO3560	52°14·3′	2°56·7′W	W	137,148,149
River Arrow	Heref	SO4458	52°13·3′	2°48·8′W	W	148,149
River Arrow	Powys	SO1853	52°10·4′	3°11·6′W	X	148
River Arrow	Powys	SO2451	52°9·4′	3°6·3′W	W	148
River Arrow	Warw	SP0859	52°14·0′	1°52·6′W	W	150
River Arrow	Worcs	SP0370	52°19·9′	1°57·0′W	W	139
River Arun	W Susx	TQ0214	50°55·2′	0°32·5′W	W	197
River Arun	W Susx	TQ1232	51°4·8′	0°23·7′W	W	187
River Ash	Herts	TL4116	51°49·7′	0°3·2′E	W	167
River Ash	Surrey	TQ0868	51°24·3′	0°26·4′W	W	176
River Ashburn	Devon	SX7571	50°31·8′	3°45·4′W	W	202
River Ashop	Derby	SK1289	53°24·1′	1°48·8′W	W	110
River Asland or Douglas	Lancs	SD4524	53°42·8′	2°49·6′W	W	102
River Attadale	Highld	NG9337	57°22·8′	5°26·2′W	W	25
River Auchalick	Arg & Bt	NR9275	55°55·6′	5°19·3′W	W	62
River Averon or Alness River	Highld	NH6273	57°43·8′	4°18·6′W	W	21
River Avich	Arg & Bt	NM9614	56°16·7′	5°17·3′W	W	55
River Avill	Somer	SS9743	51°10·9′	3°28·0′W	W	181
River Avon	Bath & NE Somer	ST6768	51°24·8′	2°28·1′W	W	172
River Avon	Devon	SX7351	50°20·9′	3°46·7′W	W	202
River Avon	Hants	SU1301	50°48·7′	1°48·5′W	W	195
River Avon	Moray	NJ1612	57°11·7′	3°23·0′W	W	36
River Avon	Moray	NJ1834	57°23·6′	3°21·4′W	W	28
River Avon	Warw	SP2659	52°13·9′	1°36·8′W	W	151
River Avon	Warw	SP4476	52°23·0′	1°20·8′W	W	140
River Avon	Wilts	ST9577	51°29·7′	2°3·9′W	W	173
River Avon	Wilts	SU1256	51°18·4′	1°49·3′W	W	173
River Avon	Wilts	SU1331	51°4·9′	1°48·5′W	W	184
River Avon	Wilts	SU1559	51°20·0′	1°46·7′W	W	173
River Avon	W Loth	NS9473	55°56·6′	3°41·4′W	W	65
River Avon	Worcs	SO9746	52°7·0′	2°2·2′W	W	150
River Awe	Arg & Bt	NN0230	56°25·5′	5°12·2′W	W	50
River Axe	Dorset	ST3303	50°49·6′	2°56·7′W	W	193
River Axe	Somer	ST3954	51°17·1′	2°52·1′W	W	182
River Ayr	E Ayr	NS4524	55°29·4′	4°26·8′W	W	70
River Ayr	E Ayr	NS6426	55°30·8′	4°8·8′W	W	71
River Ba	Arg & Bt	NM5440	56°29·5′	5°59·3′W	W	47,48
River Bà	Highld	NN2648	56°35·8′	4°49·6′W	W	50
River Bain	Lincs	TF2480	53°18·4′	0°7·9′W	W	122
River Bain	N Yks	SD9288	54°17·5′	2°7·0′W	W	98
River Balder	Durham	NY8917	54°33·1′	2°9·8′W	W	91,92
River Balder	Durham	NY9920	54°34·8′	2°0·5′W	W	92
River Balvag	Stir	NN5619	56°20·7′	4°19·4′W	W	57
River Bank	Cambs	TL5368	52°17·6′	0°15·0′E	T	154
Riverbank	Orkney	HY6441	59°15·5′	2°37·4′W	X	5
River Banwell	N Som	ST3565	51°23·1′	2°55·7′W	W	171,182
River Barle	Somer	SS7339	51°8·4′	3°48·5′W	W	180
River Barle	Somer	SS7937	51°7·4′	3°43·4′W	W	180
River Barle	Somer	SS8533	51°5·3′	3°38·1′W	W	181
River Barrisdale	Highld	NG9003	57°4·5′	5°27·4′W	W	33
River Batherm	Devon	SS9723	51°0·1′	3°27·7′W	W	181
River Beal	Roch	SD9311	53°36·0′	2°5·9′W	W	109
River Beane	Herts	TL2723	51°53·7′	0°8·9′W	W	166
River Beauly	Highld	NH4844	57°27·9′	4°31·6′W	W	26
River Bedalder or Warleggan River	Corn	SX1471	50°30·8′	4°37·0′W	W	200
River Bela	Cumbr	SD5079	54°12·5′	2°45·6′W	W	97
River Belah	Cumbr	NY7912	54°30·4′	2°19·0′W	W	91
River Belah	Cumbr	NY8310	54°29·3′	2°15·3′W	W	91,92
River Bellart	Arg & Bt	NM4548	56°33·5′	6°8·6′W	W	47,48
River Beult	Kent	TQ7747	51°11·9′	0°32·4′E	W	188
River Beult	Kent	TQ8543	51°9·6′	0°39·1′E	W	189
River Bewl	Kent	TQ6935	51°5·6′	0°25·2′E	W	188
River Biss	Wilts	ST8656	51°18·4′	2°11·7′W	W	173
River Blackwater	Essex	TL7824	51°53·4′	0°35·6′E	W	167
River Blackwater	Essex	TL8313	51°47·4′	0°39·6′E	W	168
River Blackwater	Hants	SU2820	50°59·0′	1°35·7′W	W	184
River Blackwater	Hants	SU3218	50°57·9′	1°32·3′W	W	185
River Bladnoch	D & G	NX3070	55°0·0′	4°39·0′W	W	76
River Bladnoch	D & G	NX3368	54°59·0′	4°36·2′W	W	82
River Bladnoch	D & G	NX3854	54°51·5′	4°31·0′W	W	83
River Bleng	Cumbr	NY0906	54°26·7′	3°23·8′W	W	89
River Blithe	Staffs	SJ9838	52°56·6′	2°1·4′W	W	127
River Blithe	Staffs	SK0232	52°53·4′	1°57·8′W	W	128
River Blyth	Northum	NZ2379	55°6·5′	1°37·9′W	W	88
River Blyth	Northum	NZ2781	55°7·6′	1°34·2′W	W	81
River Blyth	Suff	TM4376	52°19·9′	1°34·4′E	W	156
River Blythe	Sol	SP1978	52°24·2′	1°42·8′W	W	139
River Bogie	Aberd	NJ5236	57°25·0′	2°47·5′W	W	29
River Bollin	Ches	SJ7386	53°22·5′	2°23·9′W	W	109
River Bollin	Ches	SJ9371	53°14·4′	2°5·9′W	W	118
River Borgie	Highld	NC6657	58°29·1′	4°17·4′W	W	10
River Bottom Wood	Kent	TR2842	51°8·1′	1°15·9′E	F	179
River Bourn	Essex	TL5843	52°4·0′	0°18·7′E	W	154
River Bourne	Kent	TQ6548	51°12·7′	0°22·1′E	W	188
River Bourne	W Berks	SU6071	51°26·3′	1°7·8′W	W	175
River Bourne	Wilts	SU2139	51°9·2′	1°41·6′W	W	184
River Bourne	Wilts	SU2258	51°19·5′	1°40·7′W	W	174
River Bovey	Devon	SX7483	50°38·2′	3°46·5′W	W	191
River Box	Suff	TL9243	52°3·3′	0°48·4′E	W	155
River Boyd	S Glos	ST6972	51°27·0′	2°26·4′W	W	172
River Braan	Pth & Kin	NN9639	56°32·1′	3°41·0′W	W	52,53
River Bradford	Derby	SK2063	53°10·1′	1°41·6′W	W	119
River Brain	Essex	TL7719	51°50·7′	0°34·6′E	W	167
River Bran	Highld	NH1758	57°34·8′	5°3·2′W	W	25
River Bran	Highld	NH2160	57°35·9′	4°59·3′W	W	20
River Brant	Lincs	SK9047	53°1·0′	0°39·1′W	W	130
River Brant	Lincs	SK9459	53°7·4′	0°35·3′W	W	121
River Brathay	Cumbr	NY2902	54°24·8′	3°5·2′W	W	89
River Brathay	Cumbr	NY3503	54°25·3′	2°59·7′W	W	90
River Breamish	Northum	NT9416	55°26·5′	2°5·3′W	W	80
River Breamish	Northum	NU0621	55°29·2′	1°53·9′W	W	75
River Breamish	Northum	NU0719	55°28·1′	1°52·9′W	W	81
River Brede	E Susx	TQ8417	50°55·6′	0°37·5′E	W	199
River Brede	E Susx	TQ8517	50°55·6′	0°38·3′E	W	189,199
River Brent	Ealing	TQ1682	51°31·7′	0°19·3′W	W	176
River Brett	Suff	TM0144	52°3·7′	0°56·3′E	W	155
River Bride	Dorset	SY5289	50°42·2′	2°40·4′W	W	194
River Bridge	Somer	ST3844	51°11·7′	2°52·9′W	X	182
River Brin	Highld	NH6627	57°19·1′	4°13·0′W	W	26,35
River Brit	Dorset	SY4795	50°45·4′	2°44·7′W	W	193
River Brittle	Highld	NG4023	57°13·7′	6°18·0′W	W	32
River Brock	Lancs	SD5040	53°51·5′	2°45·2′W	W	102
River Brogaig	Highld	NG4667	57°37·6′	6°14·8′W	W	23
River Broom	Highld	NH1981	57°47·2′	5°2·2′W	W	20
River Brora	Highld	NC6613	58°5·4′	4°15·9′W	W	16
River Brora	Highld	NC8704	58°0·9′	3°54·3′W	W	17
River Browney	Durham	NZ1245	54°48·2′	1°48·4′W	W	88
River Browney	Durham	NZ2444	54°47·7′	1°37·2′W	W	88
River Brue	Somer	ST3744	51°11·7′	2°53·7′W	W	182
River Brue	Somer	ST4839	51°9·1′	2°44·2′W	W	182
River Brue	Somer	ST5532	51°5·4′	2°38·2′W	W	182,183
River Brue	Somer	ST6434	51°6·5′	2°30·5′W	W	183
River Brun	Lancs	SD8731	53°46·8′	2°11·4′W	W	103
River Bulbourne	Herts	SP9609	51°46·5′	0°36·1′W	W	165
River Bure	Norf	TG3815	52°41·0′	1°31·7′E	W	133,134
River Burn	Devon	SX4978	50°35·2′	4°7·6′W	W	191,201
River Burn	Norf	TF8538	52°54·7′	0°45·5′E	W	132
River Burn	N Yks	SE1780	54°13·2′	1°43·9′W	W	99
River Caen	Devon	SS5140	51°8·6′	4°7·4′W	W	180
River Calder	Cald	SE1522	53°41·9′	1°46·0′W	W	104
River Calder	Cumbr	NY0607	54°27·2′	3°26·6′W	W	89
River Calder	Highld	NN6698	57°3·5′	4°12·1′W	W	35
River Calder	Lancs	SD5244	53°53·6′	2°43·4′W	W	102
River Calder	Lancs	SD8234	53°48·4′	2°16·0′W	W	103
River Calder	Leeds	SE4126	53°44·0′	1°22·3′W	W	105
River Calder	Renf	NS3262	55°49·6′	4°40·5′W	W	63
River Calder	Wakf	SE3118	53°39·7′	1°31·4′W	W	110,111
River Caldew	Cumbr	NY2829	54°39·3′	3°6·5′W	W	89,90
River Caldew	Cumbr	NY3332	54°41·0′	3°1·9′W	W	90
River Caldew	Cumbr	NY3851	54°51·2′	2°57·5′W	W	85
River Cale	Somer	ST7126	51°2·2′	2°24·4′W	W	183
River Callop	Highld	NM9177	56°50·5′	5°25·1′W	W	40
River Cam	Cambs	TL4963	52°14·9′	0°11·4′E	W	154
River Cam	Glos	SO7503	51°43·7′	2°21·3′W	W	162
River Cam	Somer	ST6025	51°1·6′	2°33·8′W	W	183
River Camel	Corn	SX0267	50°28·4′	4°47·1′W	W	200
River Cam or Granta	Essex	TL5141	52°3·0′	0°12·5′E	W	154
River Cam or Granta	Essex	TL5430	51°57·1′	0°14·9′E	W	167
River Cam or Rhee	Cambs	TL2745	52°5·6′	0°8·4′W	W	153
River Cam or Rhee	Cambs	TL3647	52°6·5′	0°0·4′W	W	154
River Can	Essex	TL6311	51°46·7′	0°22·2′E	W	167
River Canaird	Highld	NC1702	57°58·4′	5°5·2′W	W	15
River Cannich	Highld	NH2732	57°21·0′	4°52·1′W	W	25
River Cannich	Highld	NH3232	57°21·1′	4°47·1′W	W	26
River Carey	Devon	SX3585	50°38·7′	4°19·7′W	W	201
River Carey	Devon	SX4197	50°45·3′	4°14·9′W	W	190
River Carnach	Highld	NM8898	57°1·7′	5°29·1′W	W	33,40
River Carron	Falk	NS9182	56°1·4′	3°44·5′W	W	65
River Carron	Highld	NH0549	57°29·6′	5°14·8′W	W	25
River Carron	Highld	NH4589	57°52·1′	4°36·3′W	W	20
River Carron	Highld	NH5490	57°52·8′	4°27·3′W	W	21
River Carron	Stir	NS6684	56°2·1′	4°8·6′W	W	57,64
River Cary	Somer	ST4630	51°4·2′	2°45·9′W	W	182
River Cary	Somer	ST4829	51°3·7′	2°44·1′W	W	193
River Cary	Somer	ST5830	51°4·3′	2°35·6′W	W	182,183
River Cassley	Highld	NC3521	58°9·1′	4°47·8′W	W	15
River Cassley	Highld	NC4111	58°3·8′	4°41·2′W	W	16
River Cegidog	Flint	SJ2656	53°6·0′	3°5·9′W	W	117
River Ceiriog	Wrex	SJ1533	52°53·5′	3°15·4′W	W	125
River Ceiriog or Afon Ceiriog	Wrex	SJ2438	52°56·3′	3°7·4′W	W	126
River Cerne	Dorset	SY6699	50°47·6′	2°28·6′W	W	194
River Char	Dorset	SY3894	50°44·8′	2°52·3′W	W	193
River Chater	Rut	SK9003	52°37·3′	0°39·8′W	W	141
River Chelmer	Essex	TL7608	51°44·8′	0°33·4′E	W	167
River Chelmer	Essex	TL8108	51°44·7′	0°37·7′E	W	168
River Chelt	Glos	SO8825	51°55·6′	2°10·1′W	W	162
River Chelt	Glos	SO9819	51°52·4′	2°1·3′W	W	163
River Cherwell	Northnts	SP4739	52°3·1′	1°18·5′W	W	151
River Cherwell	Northnts	SP5249	52°8·4′	1°14·0′W	W	151
River Cherwell	Oxon	SP4822	51°53·9′	1°17·7′W	W	164
River Chess	Herts	TQ0496	51°39·4′	0°29·4′W	W	166,176
River Chet	Norf	TM3799	52°32·5′	1°30·1′E	W	134
River Chew	Bath & NE Somer	ST5762	51°21·6′	2°36·7′W	W	172,182
River Chew	Bath & NE Somer	ST6565	51°23·2′	2°29·8′W	W	172
River Chilt	W Susx	TQ0617	50°56·8′	0°29·1′W	W	197
River Chracaig	Highld	NG4844	57°25·3′	6°11·4′W	W	23
River Churn	Glos	SO9813	51°49·2′	2°1·3′W	W	163
River Churn	Glos	SP0102	51°43·2′	1°58·7′W	W	163
River Churnet	Staffs	SJ9656	53°6·3′	2°3·2′W	W	118
River Churnet	Staffs	SK0060	53°8·5′	1°59·6′W	W	119
River Churnet	Staffs	SK0544	52°59·8′	1°55·1′W	W	119,128
River Clachaig	Arg & Bt	NM5635	56°26·9′	5°57·1′W	W	47,48
River Claw	Devon	SX3498	50°45·7′	4°20·8′W	W	190
River Cluanie	Highld	NH0611	57°9·2′	5°12·0′W	W	33
River Clun	Heref	SO3975	52°22·4′	2°53·4′W	W	137,148
River Clun	Shrops	SO2881	52°25·6′	3°3·1′W	W	137
River Clwyd or Afon Clwyd	Denb	SJ0967	53°11·8′	3°21·3′W	W	116
River Clydach	Monm	SO2212	51°48·3′	3°7·5′W	W	161
River Clydach	Nth Pt Talb	SN7402	51°42·4′	3°49·0′W	W	170
River Clyde	C of Glas	NS5964	55°51·2′	4°14·7′W	W	64
River Clyde	Renf	NS3774	55°56·1′	4°36·1′W	W	63
River Clyde	S Lanak	NS8050	55°44·0′	3°54·2′W	W	65,72
River Clyde	S Lanak	NS9324	55°30·1′	3°41·2′W	W	71,72
River Clyst	Devon	SX9998	50°46·6′	3°25·6′W	W	192
River Clywedog	Wrex	SJ3848	53°1·8′	2°55·1′W	W	117
River Cober	Corn	SW6730	50°7·7′	5°15·2′W	W	203
River Cocker	Cumbr	NY1426	54°37·6′	3°19·5′W	W	89
River Cocker	Lancs	SD4651	53°57·4′	2°49·0′W	W	102
River Coe	Highld	NN1556	56°39·8′	5°0·7′W	W	41
River Coiltie	Highld	NH4626	57°18·2′	4°32·9′W	W	26
River Cole	Oxon	SU2294	51°38·9′	1°40·5′W	W	163,174
River Cole	Sol	SP0976	52°23·2′	1°51·7′W	W	139
River Cole	Swin	SU2086	51°34·6′	1°42·3′W	W	174
River Coln	Glos	SP1305	51°44·8′	1°48·3′W	W	163
River Colne	Bucks	TQ0389	51°35·7′	0°30·4′W	W	176
River Colne	Essex	TL7736	51°59·9′	0°35·1′E	W	155
River Colne	Essex	TL9327	51°54·7′	0°48·8′E	W	168
River Colne	Herts	TQ1299	51°40·9′	0°22·4′W	W	166,176
River Colne	Hill	TQ0475	51°28·1′	0°29·8′W	W	176
River Colne	Kirk	SE0914	53°37·6′	1°51·4′W	W	110
River Coly	Devon	SY2294	50°44·7′	3°6·0′W	W	192,193
River Common	W Susx	SU9423	51°0·1′	0°39·2′W	X	197
River Conder	Lancs	SD4856	54°0·1′	2°47·2′W	W	102
River Conon	Highld	NG4063	57°35·2′	6°20·6′W	W	23
River Conon	Highld	NH4255	57°33·7′	4°38·0′W	W	26
River Cononish	Stir	NN3128	56°25·1′	4°43·9′W	W	50
River Coquet	Northum	NT8707	55°21·7′	2°11·9′W	W	80
River Coquet	Northum	NT9601	55°18·4′	2°3·4′W	W	81
River Coquet	Northum	NU2203	55°19·5′	1°38·8′W	W	81
River Corve	Shrops	SO4978	52°24·1′	2°44·6′W	W	137,138,148
River Coulin	Highld	NH0254	57°32·2′	5°18·0′W	W	25
River Coupall	Highld	NN2155	56°39·4′	4°54·8′W	W	41
River Cover	N Yks	SE0582	54°14·3′	1°55·0′W	W	98
River Cover	N Yks	SE0784	54°15·3′	1°53·1′W	W	99
River Crake	Cumbr	SD2987	54°16·7′	3°5·0′W	W	96,97
River Crane	Dorset	SU0807	50°52·0′	1°52·8′W	W	195
River Crane	Houns	TQ1175	51°28·0′	0°23·7′W	W	176
River Cree	D & G	NX3377	55°3·8′	4°36·5′W	W	76
River Cree	D & G	NX3575	55°2·8′	4°34·5′W	W	77
River Cree	D & G	NX4263	54°56·5′	4°27·6′W	W	83
River Cree	S Ayr	NX3081	55°5·9′	4°39·4′W	W	76
River Creedy	Devon	SS8402	50°48·6′	3°38·4′W	W	191
River Creran	Arg & Bt	NN0348	56°35·2′	5°12·0′W	W	50
River Creran	Arg & Bt	NN0751	56°36·9′	5°8·3′W	W	41
River Crimple or Crimple Beck	N Yks	SE3552	53°58·0′	1°27·6′W	W	104
River Croal	Bolton	SD7406	53°33·2′	2°23·1′W	W	109
River Croco	Ches	SJ7566	53°11·7′	2°22·0′W	W	118
River Croe	Highld	NG9819	57°13·3′	5°20·3′W	W	33
River Crouch	Essex	TQ6792	51°36·3′	0°25·1′E	W	177,178
River Crouch	Essex	TQ7193	51°36·8′	0°28·6′E	W	178
River Crouch	Essex	TR0095	51°37·3′	0°53·8′E	W	168
River Culm	Devon	ST0410	50°53·1′	3°21·5′W	W	192
River Culm	Devon	ST1714	50°55·4′	3°10·5′W	W	181,193
River Culm	Devon	SX9498	50°46·5′	3°29·8′W	W	192
River Culvery	Devon	SX8297	50°45·9′	3°40·0′W	W	191

River Cur	Arg & Bt	NN1101	56°10·1′	5°2·2′W	W	56
River Dalch	Devon	SS7610	50°52·8′	3°45·4′W	W	191
River Dalch	Devon	SS8213	50°54·5′	3°40·3′W	W	181
Riverdale	Heref	SO3832	51°59·2′	2°53·8′W	X	149,161
River Dane	Ches	SJ6672	53°14·9′	2°30·2′W	W	118
River Dane	Ches	SJ8066	53°11·7′	2°17·6′W	W	118
River Dane	Ches	SK0067	53°12·2′	1°59·6′W	W	119
River Darent	Kent	TQ5257	51°17·7′	0°11·2′E	W	188
River Darent	Kent	TQ5466	51°22·6′	0°13·2′E	W	177
River Dart	Devon	SS9208	50°51·9′	3°31·7′W	W	192
River Dart	Devon	SX6972	50°32·2′	3°50·5′W	W	191
River Dart	Devon	SX7070	50°31·2′	3°49·7′W	W	202
River Dart	Devon	SX7272	50°32·3′	3°48·0′W	W	191
River Dart	Devon	SX7663	50°27·5′	3°44·4′W	W	202
River Dart Country Park	Devon	SX7370	50°31·2′	3°47·1′W	X	202
River Darwen	Black w Dar	SD6824	53°42·9′	2°28·7′W	W	103
River Darwen	Lancs	SD6228	53°45·1′	2°34·2′W	W	102,103
River Dean	Ches	SJ8881	53°19·8′	2°10·4′W	W	109
River Dean	Ches	SJ9178	53°18·2′	2°7·7′W	W	118
River Dearne	Barns	SE3209	53°34·8′	1°30·6′W	W	110,111
River Dearne	Donc	SE4602	53°31·0′	1°18·0′W	W	111
River Deben	Suff	TM2943	52°2·5′	1°20·8′E	W	169
River Deben	Suff	TM2957	52°10·0′	1°21·3′E	W	156
River Dee	Aberd	NJ8600	57°5·7′	2°13·4′W	W	38
River Dee	Aberd	NN9894	57°1·8′	3°40·4′W	W	36,43
River Dee	Aberd	NO1290	56°59·8′	3°26·5′W	W	43
River Dee	Aberd	NO4998	57°4·5′	2°50·0′W	W	37,44
River Dee	Aberd	NO7396	57°3·5′	2°26·3′W	W	38,45
River Dee	Cumbr	SD6590	54°18·5′	2°31·9′W	W	97
River Dee	Cumbr	SD7286	54°16·4′	2°25·4′W	W	98
River Dee	D & G	NX7157	54°53·7′	4°0·3′W	W	83,84
River Dee	Flint	SJ2180	53°18·9′	3°10·7′W	W	108
River Dee or Afon Dyfrdwy	Ches	SJ4159	53°7·7′	2°52·5′W	W	117
River Dee or Afon Dyfrdwy	Denb	SJ0339	52°56·6′	3°26·2′W	W	125
River Dee or Afon Dyfrdwy	Flint	SJ1683	53°20·5′	3°15·3′W	W	116
River Dee or Black Water of Dee	D & G	NX5574	55°2·6′	4°15·7′W	W	77
River Dee or Black Water of Dee	D & G	NX6569	55°0·1′	4°6·2′W	W	83,84
River Dee or Loch Ken	D & G	NX7168	54°59·6′	4°0·6′W	W	83,84
River Deer	Devon	SS3200	50°46·8′	4°22·6′W	W	190
River Deerness	Durham	NZ1840	54°45·5′	1°42·8′W	W	88
River Delph	Norf	TL5293	52°31·0′	0°14·8′E	W	143
Riverdene	N Yks	SE7675	54°10·1′	0°49·7′W	X	100
River Dene	Warw	SP2851	52°9·6′	1°35·0′W	W	151
River Derwent	C of Derb	SK3834	52°54·4′	1°25·7′W	W	128
River Derwent	Cumbr	NY1933	54°41·4′	3°15·0′W	W	89,90
River Derwent	Derby	SK1596	53°27·9′	1°46·0′W	W	110
River Derwent	Derby	SK2860	53°8·4′	1°34·5′W	W	119
River Derwent	Derby	SK4332	52°53·3′	1°21·3′W	W	129
River Derwent	Durham	NZ0450	54°50·9′	1°55·8′W	W	87
River Derwent	Ghead	NZ1758	54°55·2′	1°43·7′W	W	88
River Derwent	N Yks	SE7770	54°7·4′	0°48·9′W	W	100
River Derwent	N Yks	SE8478	54°11·7′	0°42·3′W	W	100
River Derwent	N Yks	SE9490	54°18·1′	0°32·9′W	W	94,101
River Derwent	N Yks	SE9879	54°12·1′	0°29·4′W	W	101
River Derwent	York	SE6945	53°54·0′	0°56·6′W	W	105,106
River Dessarry	Highld	NM9492	56°58·7′	5°22·9′W	W	33,40
River Dever	Hants	SU4739	51°9·1′	1°19·3′W	W	185
River Deveron	Aberd	NJ4439	57°26·5′	2°55·5′W	W	28
River Deveron	Aberd	NJ6447	57°31·0′	2°35·6′W	W	29
River Deveron	Moray	NJ4034	57°23·8′	2°59·4′W	W	28
River Devon	Clackm	NS9797	56°9·5′	3°39·1′W	W	58
River Devon	Leic	SK7940	52°57·3′	0°49·0′W	W	129
River Devon	Leic	SK8039	52°56·8′	0°48·2′W	W	130
River Devon	Notts	SK7847	53°1·1′	0°49·8′W	W	129
River Devon	Notts	SK7851	53°3·3′	0°49·8′W	W	120,121
River Devon	Pth & Kin	NO0201	56°11·7′	3°34·3′W	W	58
River Dhoo	I of M	SC3278	54°10·5′	4°34·0′W	W	95
River Dibb	N Yks	SE0563	54°4·0′	1°55·0′W	W	98
River Dikler	Glos	SP1723	51°54·6′	1°44·8′W	W	163
River Ding	Somer	ST2914	50°55·5′	3°0·2′W	W	193
River Dionard	Highld	NC3254	58°26·8′	4°52·2′W	W	9
River Divelish	Dorset	ST7711	50°54·1′	2°19·2′W	W	194
River Divie	Moray	NJ0443	57°28·3′	3°35·6′W	W	27
River Dochart	Stir	NN5028	56°25·5′	4°25·5′W	W	51
River Doe	Highld	NH2013	57°10·6′	4°58·2′W	W	34
River Doe	N Yks	SD7175	54°10·4′	2°26·9′W	W	98
River Doe Lea	Derby	SK4568	53°12·7′	1°19·2′W	W	120
River Don	Aberd	NJ2309	57°10·2′	3°15·9′W	W	36
River Don	Aberd	NJ5017	57°14·7′	2°49·3′W	W	37
River Don	Aberd	NJ8115	57°13·8′	2°18·4′W	W	38
River Don	Lancs	SD8634	53°48·4′	2°12·3′W	W	103
River Don	Roth	SK4697	53°28·3′	1°18·0′W	W	111
River Don	Sheff	SK2996	53°27·8′	1°33·4′W	W	110
River Don	Sund	NZ3259	54°55·7′	1°29·6′W	W	88
River Doon	E Ayr	NS4506	55°19·7′	4°26·2′W	W	70,77
River Doon	S Ayr	NS3313	55°23·2′	4°37·8′W	W	70
River Dore	Heref	SO3241	52°4·0′	2°59·1′W	W	148,161
River Dore	Heref	SO3831	51°58·7′	2°53·8′W	W	149,161
River Dorn	Oxon	SP4521	51°53·4′	1°20·4′W	W	164
River Douchary	Highld	NH2589	57°51·6′	4°56·5′W	W	20
River Douglas	Lancs	SD5109	53°34·8′	2°44·0′W	W	108
River Douglas or Asland	Lancs	SD4524	53°42·8′	2°49·6′W	W	102
River Dove	Barns	SE3904	53°32·1′	1°24·3′W	W	110,111
River Dove	N Yks	SE6891	54°18·8′	0°56·9′W	W	94,100
River Dove	N Yks	SE7180	54°12·9′	0°54·3′W	W	100
River Dove	Staffs	SK1258	53°7·4′	1°48·8′W	W	119
River Dove	Staffs	SK1531	52°52·8′	1°46·2′W	W	128
River Dove	Suff	TM1574	52°19·5′	1°9·7′E	W	144,156
River Dove	Suff	TM1574	52°19·5′	1°9·7′E	W	144,156
River Dovey or Afon Dyfi	Gwyn	SH8511	52°41·3′	3°41·7′W	W	124,125
River Dovey or Afon Dyfi	Gwyn	SN7099	52°34·6′	3°54·7′W	W	135
River Dovey or Afon Dyfi	Powys	SH8104	52°37·5′	3°45·1′W	W	135,136
River Drolsay	Arg & Bt	NR3365	55°48·5′	6°15·2′W	W	60,61
River Drone	Derby	SK3775	53°16·5′	1°26·3′W	W	119
River Druie	Highld	NH9010	57°10·3′	3°48·7′W	W	36
River Drynoch	Highld	NG4330	57°17·6′	6°15·5′W	W	32
River Duckow	Ches	SJ6440	52°57·6′	2°31·8′W	W	118
River Duckow	Shrops	SJ6434	52°54·4′	2°31·7′W	W	127
River Duddon	Cumbr	NY2501	54°24·2′	3°8·9′W	W	89,90
River Duddon	Cumbr	SD2093	54°19·8′	3°13·4′W	W	96
River Dudwell	E Susx	TQ6924	50°59·7′	0°24·9′E	W	199
River Dulas	Conwy	SH9075	53°15·9′	3°38·5′W	W	116
River Dulas	Powys	SO0465	52°16·7′	3°24·0′W	W	136,147
River Dulnain	Highld	NH8015	57°12·9′	3°58·8′W	W	35
River Dulnain	Highld	NH9724	57°18·0′	3°42·1′W	W	36
River Dun	Hants	SU3126	51°2·2′	1°33·1′W	W	185
River Dun Navigation	Donc	SE6108	53°34·1′	1°4·3′W	W	111
River Dunsop	Lancs	SD6552	53°58·0′	2°31·6′W	W	102,103
River Duntz	Devon	SS4319	50°57·2′	4°13·7′W	W	180,190
River Duror	Highld	NN0153	56°37·9′	5°14·2′W	W	41
River Dyke	Highld	NC8547	58°24·0′	3°57·6′W	W	10
River E	Highld	NH5414	57°11·9′	4°24·5′W	X	35
River Eachaig	Arg & Bt	NS1484	56°1·0′	4°58·6′W	W	56
River Eamont	Cumbr	NY4827	54°38·4′	2°47·9′W	W	90
River Eamont	Cumbr	NY5529	54°39·5′	2°41·4′W	W	90
River Eamont	Cumbr	NY5730	54°40·0′	2°39·6′W	W	91
River Earn	Pth & Kin	NN7223	56°23·2′	4°3·9′W	W	51,52
River Earn	Pth & Kin	NN7521	56°22·1′	4°1·0′W	W	51,52,57
River Earn	Pth & Kin	NO0117	56°20·4′	3°35·6′W	W	58
River East Allen	Northum	NY8353	54°52·5′	2°15·5′W	W	86,87
River East Onny	Shrops	SO3996	52°33·7′	2°53·6′W	W	137
River Eau	Lincs	SK8999	53°29·0′	0°39·1′W	W	112
River Ebble	Wilts	SU1326	51°2·2′	1°48·5′W	W	184
River Ecclesbourne	Derby	SK3244	52°59·8′	1°31·0′W	W	119,128
River Eden	Cumbr	NY3758	54°55·0′	2°58·5′W	W	85
River Eden	Cumbr	NY5049	54°50·2′	2°46·3′W	W	86
River Eden	Cumbr	NY5534	54°42·2′	2°41·5′W	W	90
River Eden	Cumbr	NY6818	54°33·6′	2°29·3′W	W	91
River Eden	Cumbr	SD7798	54°22·9′	2°20·8′W	W	98
River Eden	Fife	NO1808	56°15·7′	3°19·0′W	W	58
River Eden	Fife	NO3713	56°18·6′	3°0·7′W	W	59
River Eden	Fife	NO4920	56°22·4′	2°49·1′W	W	54,59
River Eden	Kent	TQ5045	51°11·3′	0°9·2′E	W	188
River Eden	Surrey	TQ4046	51°12·0′	0°0·6′E	W	187
River Edw	Powys	SO1251	52°9·3′	3°16·8′W	W	148
River Eea	Cumbr	SD3778	54°11·9′	2°57·6′W	W	96,97
River Egel	Nth Pt Talb	SN7107	51°45·1′	3°51·7′W	W	160
River Ehen	Cumbr	NY0112	54°29·9′	3°31·3′W	W	89
River Eidart	Aberd	NN9191	57°0·1′	3°47·2′W	W	43
River Eidart	Highld	NN9192	57°0·6′	3°47·2′W	W	43
River Einig	Highld	NH3598	57°56·7′	4°46·8′W	W	20
River Elchaig	Highld	NG9727	57°17·6′	5°21·7′W	W	25,33
River Ellen	Cumbr	NY0637	54°43·4′	3°27·1′W	W	89
River Ellen	Cumbr	NY1641	54°45·7′	3°17·9′W	W	85
River Ellen	Cumbr	NY2437	54°43·6′	3°10·4′W	W	89,90
River Elwy	Conwy	SH9471	53°13·8′	3°34·9′W	W	116
River Ember	Surrey	TQ1466	51°23·1′	0°21·3′W	W	176
River Ems	Hants	SU7507	50°51·7′	0°55·7′W	W	197
River Enborne	W Berks	SU4563	51°22·1′	1°20·8′W	W	174
River Ennig	Powys	SO1632	51°59·0′	3°13·0′W	W	161
River Enrick	Highld	NH4430	57°20·3′	4°35·1′W	W	26
River Erewash	Derby	SK4837	52°55·9′	1°16·7′W	W	129
River Erewash	Notts	SK4754	53°5·1′	1°17·5′W	W	120
River Ericht	Pth & Kin	NN5061	56°43·2′	4°26·6′W	W	42
River Ericht	Pth & Kin	NO1551	56°38·8′	3°22·7′W	W	53
River Ericht	Pth & Kin	NO2044	56°35·1′	3°17·7′W	W	53
River Erme	Devon	SX6358	50°24·6′	3°55·3′W	W	202
River Erradale	Highld	NG7570	57°40·1′	5°45·9′W	W	19
River Esk	Cumbr	NY2102	54°24·7′	3°12·6′W	W	89,90
River Esk	Cumbr	SD1297	54°21·9′	3°20·8′W	W	96
River Esk	D & G	NY3487	55°10·6′	3°1·8′W	W	79
River Esk	D & G	NY3873	55°3·1′	2°57·8′W	W	85
River Esk	E Loth	NT3471	55°55·9′	3°2·9′W	W	66
River Esk	N Yks	NZ7307	54°27·4′	0°52·0′W	W	94
River Esk	N Yks	NZ8708	54°27·8′	0°39·0′W	W	94
River Eskin	Highld	NH6210	57°9·9′	4°16·5′W	W	35
River Esragan	Arg & Bt	NM9937	56°29·2′	5°15·4′W	W	49
River Etherow	Derby	SJ9892	53°25·7′	2°1·4′W	W	109
River Etherow	Derby	SK1299	53°29·5′	1°48·7′W	W	110
River Etive	Highld	NN1447	56°34·9′	5°1·3′W	W	50
River Etive	Highld	NN2252	56°37·8′	4°53·7′W	W	41
River Euchar	Arg & Bt	NM8419	56°19·1′	5°29·1′W	W	55
River Euchar	Arg & Bt	NM8420	56°19·6′	5°29·2′W	W	49
River Evelix	Highld	NH7392	57°54·2′	4°8·1′W	W	21
River Evenlode	Glos	SP2128	51°57·2′	1°41·3′W	W	163
River Evenlode	Oxon	SP2522	51°54·0′	1°37·8′W	W	163
River Evenlode	Oxon	SP3320	51°52·9′	1°30·8′W	W	164
River Evenlode	Warw	SP2066	52°17·7′	1°42·0′W	W	151
River Ewe	Highld	NG8679	57°45·2′	5°35·3′W	W	19
River Exe	Devon	SS9300	50°47·6′	3°30·7′W	W	192
River Exe	Somer	SS7741	51°9·5′	3°45·2′W	W	180
River Exe	Somer	SS9330	51°3·8′	3°31·2′W	W	181
River Eye	Glos	SP1622	51°54·0′	1°45·7′W	W	163
River Eye	Leic	SK7818	52°45·5′	0°50·2′W	W	129
River Eye	Leic	SK8523	52°48·1′	0°43·9′W	W	130
River Fal	Corn	SW9349	50°18·5′	4°54·1′W	W	204
River Fal	Corn	SW9352	50°20·1′	4°54·2′W	W	200,204
River Falloch	Stir	NN3320	56°20·8′	4°41·7′W	W	50,56
River Falloch	Stir	NN3521	56°21·4′	4°39·8′W	W	50,56
River Farg	Pth & Kin	NO1210	56°16·7′	3°24·8′W	W	58
River Farg	Pth & Kin	NO1412	56°17·8′	3°22·9′W	W	58
River Farigaig	Highld	NH5626	57°18·4′	4°23·0′W	W	26,35
River Farrar	Highld	NH2438	57°24·2′	4°55·3′W	W	25
River Farrar	Highld	NH3539	57°25·0′	4°44·4′W	W	26
River Fechlin	Highld	NH4914	57°11·8′	4°29·5′W	W	34
River Fechlin	Highld	NH5013	57°11·3′	4°28·5′W	W	35
River Feshie	Highld	NH8503	57°6·5′	3°53·5′W	W	35,36
River Feshie	Highld	NN8492	57°0·5′	3°54·2′W	W	35,43
River Feshie	Highld	NN8886	56°57·4′	3°50·0′W	W	43
River Fiag	Highld	NC4524	58°10·9′	4°37·7′W	W	16
River Fiddich	Moray	NJ3130	57°21·6′	3°8·4′W	W	37
River Fiddich	Moray	NJ3339	57°26·4′	3°6·5′W	W	28
River Fiddich	Moray	NJ3426	57°24·8′	3°5·5′W	W	28
River Fillan	Stir	NN3726	56°24·1′	4°38·0′W	W	50
River Findhorn	Highld	NH7016	57°13·2′	4°8·7′W	W	35
River Findhorn	Highld	NH9444	57°28·7′	3°45·6′W	W	27
River Finnan	Highld	NM9183	56°53·7′	5°25·4′W	W	40
River Fleet	Highld	NC6504	58°0·5′	4°16·6′W	W	16
River Fleet	Highld	NH7599	57°58·0′	4°6·3′W	W	21
River Flit	Beds	TL0937	52°1·5′	0°24·3′W	W	153
River Fm	Cambs	TL4456	52°11·2′	0°6·8′E	FM	154
River Fm	Lincs	SK9060	53°8·0′	0°38·9′W	FM	121
River Fm	Norf	TG1018	52°43·4′	1°7·0′E	FM	133
River Fm	Norf	TG3129	52°48·8′	1°26·1′E	FM	133,134
River Font	Northum	NZ1487	55°10·9′	1°46·4′W	W	81
Riverford	Highld	NH5454	57°33·4′	4°26·0′W	X	26
Riverford Br	Devon	SX7763	50°27·5′	3°43·6′W	X	202
River Forsa	Arg & Bt	NM6138	56°28·7′	5°52·4′W	W	49
River Forth	Falk	NS9088	56°4·6′	3°45·6′W	W	65
River Forth	Stir	NS6396	56°8·5′	4°11·9′W	W	57
River Forth	Stir	NS8691	56°6·1′	3°49·5′W	W	58
River Foss	N Yks	SE6165	54°4·9′	1°3·6′W	W	100
River Foss	York	SE6156	54°0·0′	1°3·7′W	W	105
River Foulness	E Yorks	SE7939	53°50·7′	0°47·5′W	W	105,106
River Fowey	Corn	SX1254	50°21·6′	4°38·2′W	W	200
River Fowey	Corn	SX2172	50°31·5′	4°31·1′W	W	201
River Foyers	Highld	NH4918	57°13·9′	4°29·6′W	W	34
River Foyers	Highld	NH4920	57°15·0′	4°29·7′W	W	26
River Freshney	NE Lincs	TA2409	53°34·0′	0°7·2′W	W	113
River Frome	Dorset	SY7190	50°42·8′	2°24·3′W	W	194
River Frome	Dorset	SY9387	50°41·2′	2°5·6′W	W	195
River Frome	Glos	SO7706	51°45·4′	2°19·6′W	W	162
River Frome	Glos	SO9303	51°43·8′	2°5·7′W	W	163
River Frome	S Glos	ST6783	51°32·9′	2°28·2′W	W	172
River Frome	Somer	ST7745	51°12·5′	2°19·4′W	W	183
River Frome	Somer	ST8057	51°18·9′	2°16·8′W	W	173
River Fyne	Arg & Bt	NN2216	56°18·4′	4°52·2′W	W	50,56
River Fynn	Suff	TM2047	52°4·9′	1°13·1′E	W	169
River Gade	Herts	TL0701	51°42·1′	0°26·7′W	W	166
River Gairn	Aberd	NJ1801	57°5·8′	3°20·7′W	W	36
River Gairn	Aberd	NJ2701	57°5·9′	3°11·8′W	W	37
River Gallain	Arg & Bt	NM8518	56°18·6′	5°28·1′W	W	55
River Gannel	Corn	SW8259	50°23·7′	5°3·7′W	W	200
River Garnock	N Ayr	NS2939	55°37·1′	4°42·5′W	W	70
River Garnock	N Ayr	NS2947	55°41·4′	4°42·8′W	W	63
River Garnock	N Ayr	NS2959	55°47·9′	4°43·2′W	W	63
River Garry	Highld	NH1500	57°3·5′	5°2·6′W	W	34
River Garry	Pth & Kin	NN7369	56°48·0′	4°4·3′W	W	42
River Garry	Pth & Kin	NN8165	56°45·9′	3°56·4′W	W	43
River Gaunless	Durham	NZ1425	54°37·4′	1°46·6′W	W	92
River Gaur	Pth & Kin	NN4856	56°40·5′	4°28·4′W	W	42,51
River Gele (Afon Gele)	Conwy	SH9678	53°17·6′	3°33·2′W	W	116
River Gelt	Cumbr	NY5059	54°55·6′	2°46·4′W	W	86
River Giedd	Powys	SN7913	51°48·4′	3°44·9′W	W	160
River Gilpin	Cumbr	SD4786	54°16·3′	2°48·4′W	W	97
River Gipping	Suff	TM0560	52°12·2′	1°0·4′E	W	155
River Gipping	Suff	TM1344	52°3·4′	1°6·8′E	W	169
River Glass	Highld	NH3634	57°22·3′	4°43·2′W	W	26
River Glass	Highld	NH5866	57°40·0′	4°22·4′W	W	21
River Glass	I of M	SC3582	54°12·7′	4°31·4′W	W	95
River Glass	I of M	SC3679	54°11·1′	4°30·4′W	W	95
River Glaven	Norf	TG0441	52°55·9′	1°2·5′E	W	133
River Glem	Suff	TL8448	52°6·2′	0°41·6′E	W	155
River Glen	Lincs	TF1317	52°44·6′	0°19·2′W	W	130
River Glen	Lincs	TF2427	52°49·8′	0°9·2′W	W	131
River Glen	Northum	NT9330	55°34·1′	2°6·2′W	W	74,75
River Glenderamackin	Cumbr	NY3325	54°37·2′	3°1·8′W	W	90
River Glenderamackin	Cumbr	NY3428	54°38·8′	3°0·9′W	W	90
River Glennan	Highld	NG9127	57°17·4′	5°27·6′W	W	25,33
River Gloy	Highld	NN2487	56°56·7′	4°53·2′W	W	34,41
River Glyme	Oxon	SP3525	51°55·6′	1°29·1′W	W	164
River Glyme	Oxon	SP4220	51°52·9′	1°23·0′W	W	164
River Glywedog	Wrex	SJ2949	53°2·3′	3°3·1′W	W	117
River Goil	Arg & Bt	NN1903	56°11·4′	4°54·6′W	W	56
River Gour	Highld	NM9364	56°43·6′	5°22·6′W	W	40
River Gowan	Cumbr	SD4598	54°22·7′	2°50·4′W	W	97
River Gowy	Ches	SJ4669	53°13·2′	2°48·1′W	W	117
River Gowy	Ches	SJ5260	53°8·3′	2°42·6′W	W	117
River Gowy	Ches	SJ5457	53°6·7′	2°40·8′W	W	117
River Goyt	Derby	SK0172	53°14·9′	1°58·7′W	W	119
River Goyt	Derby	SK0178	53°18·2′	1°58·7′W	W	119
River Goyt	Stock	SJ9589	53°24·1′	2°4·1′W	W	109
River Granta	Cambs	TL4851	52°8·5′	0°10·2′E	W	154
River Granta or Cam	Essex	TL5141	52°3·0′	0°12·5′E	W	154
River Granta or Cam	Essex	TL5430	51°57·1′	0°14·9′E	W	167
River Gray	Bexley	TQ4771	51°25·4′	0°7·3′E	W	177
River Great Ouse	Beds	TL1251	52°9·0′	0°21·4′W	W	153
River Great Ouse	Cambs	TL3974	52°21·0′	0°2·9′E	W	142,143
River Great Ouse	Cambs	TL4571	52°19·3′	0°8·1′E	W	154
River Great Ouse	Mil Key	SP7941	52°3·9′	0°50·5′W	W	152
River Great Ouse	Norf	TF6120	52°45·4′	0°23·6′E	W	132
River Great Ouse	Norf	TL6092	52°30·4′	0°21·9′E	W	143
Rivergreen Mill	Northum	NZ1384	55°9·3′	1°47·3′W	X	81
River Greet	Notts	SK7055	53°5·5′	0°56·9′W	W	120
River Greta	Cumbr	NY2723	54°36·1′	3°7·4′W	W	89,90
River Greta	Durham	NY9311	54°29·9′	2°6·1′W	W	91,92
River Greta	Lancs	SD6372	54°8·8′	2°33·6′W	W	97
River Greta	N Yks	SD6671	54°8·3′	2°30·8′W	W	98
River Grizedale	Lancs	SD5656	54°0·1′	2°39·9′W	W	102
River Grudie	Highld	NG9566	57°38·5′	5°25·6′W	W	19
River Grudie	Highld	NH2864	57°38·3′	4°52·4′W	W	20
River Gryfe	Renf	NS3766	55°51·8′	4°35·8′W	W	63
River Gryfe	Renf	NS4366	55°52·0′	4°30·1′W	W	64
River Gwash	Lincs	TF0408	52°39·8′	0°27·3′W	W	141
River Gwash	Rut	SK9708	52°39·9′	0°33·5′W	W	141
River Gwash	Rut	TF0310	52°40·9′	0°28·2′W	W	130
River Gwenfro	Wrex	SJ3051	53°3·3′	3°2·3′W	W	117
River Haddeo	Somer	SS9529	51°3·3′	3°29·5′W	W	181
River Haffes	Powys	SN8317	51°50·6′	3°41·5′W	W	160
Riverhall	E Susx	TQ6033	51°4·7′	0°17·4′E	X	188
River Hall	Herts	TL0715	51°49·6′	0°26·4′W	X	166
River Hall	Kent	TQ8638	51°6·9′	0°39·8′E	X	189
River Halladale	N Eil	NB0309	57°58·5′	7°1·0′W	W	13
River Hamble	Hants	SU5010	50°53·5′	1°17·0′W	W	196
River Hamps	Staffs	SK0652	53°4·2′	1°54·2′W	W	119
River Hart	Hants	SU7757	51°18·6′	0°53·3′W	W	175,186
River Haultin	Highld	NG4451	57°28·9′	6°15·8′W	W	23

River Hayle	Corn	SW5832	50°8·6'	5°22·9'W	W	203
Riverhead	Kent	TQ5156	51°17·2'	0°10·3'E	T	188
River Head	N Lincs	SE9900	53°29·5'	0°30·1'W	X	112
River Head Fm	E Yorks	SE8539	53°50·7'	0°42·1'W	FM	106
Riverhead Fm	N Yks	SE9396	54°21·3'	0°33·7'W	FM	94,101
River Heddon	Devon	SS6547	51°12·6'	3°55·6'W	W	180
River Helmsdale	Highld	NC9119	58°9·1'	3°50·6'W	W	17
River Hems	Devon	SX7865	50°28·6'	3°42·8'W	W	202
River Hertford	N Yks	TA0780	54°12·5'	0°21·1'W	W	101
River Hill	Kent	TQ5352	51°15·0'	0°11·9'E	X	188
Riverhill	King	TQ2065	51°22·5'	0°16·2'W	X	176
Riverhill	W Susx	TQ0021	50°59·0'	0°34·1'W	X	197
River Hill Fm	Hants	SU7841	51°10·0'	0°52·7'W	FM	186
Riverhill Fm	Northum	NY9073	55°3·3'	2°9·0'W	FM	87
Riverhill Ho	Kent	TQ5452	51°15·0'	0°12·8'E	X	188
River Hindburn	Lancs	SD6465	54°5·0'	2°32·6'W	W	97
River Hinnisdal	Highld	NG4158	57°32·5'	6°19·2'W	W	23
River Hipper	Derby	SK3570	53°13·8'	1°28·1'W	W	119
River Hiz	Beds	TL1834	51°59·7'	0°16·5'W	W	153
River Hiz	Herts	TL1832	51°58·7'	0°16·5'W	W	166
River Hodder	Lancs	SD6546	53°54·8'	2°31·6'W	W	102,103
River Hodder	Lancs	SD6860	54°2·3'	2°28·9'W	W	98
River Hodder	Lancs	SD6942	53°52·6'	2°27·9'W	W	103
River Hodder	Lancs	SD6949	53°56·4'	2°27·9'W	W	103
River Hodder	Lancs	SD7058	54°1·3'	2°27·1'W	W	103
River Holme	Kirk	SE1312	53°36·5'	1°47·8'W	W	110
River Hooke	Dorset	SY5499	50°47·6'	2°38·8'W	W	194
River Hope	Highld	NC4760	58°30·3'	4°37·1'W	W	9
River Horneval	Highld	NG2747	57°26·1'	6°32·5'W	W	23
River House Fm	Somer	ST3844	51°11·7'	2°52·9'W	FM	182
River Hull	E Yorks	TA0545	53°53·7'	0°23·7'W	W	107
River Humber	E Yorks	SE9523	53°41·9'	0°33·2'W	W	106,112
River Humber	NE Lincs	TA2415	53°37·2'	0°7·1'W	W	113
River Humber	N Lincs	TA1326	53°43·3'	0°16·8'W	W	107
River Hurich	Highld	NM8469	56°46·0'	5°31·6'W	W	40
River Idle	Notts	SK6693	53°26·0'	1°0·0'W	W	111
River Idle	Notts	SK7186	53°22·2'	0°55·6'W	W	112,120
River Idle	Notts	SK7396	53°27·6'	0°53·6'W	W	112
River Inny	Corn	SX3577	50°34·4'	4°19·4'W	W	201
River Inver	Highld	NC1223	58°9·6'	5°11·3'W	W	15
River Irk	Man	SD8402	53°31·1'	2°14·1'W	W	109
River Irt	Cumbr	NY1002	54°24·6'	3°22·8'W	W	89
River Irt	Cumbr	SD0798	54°22·4'	3°25·5'W	W	96
River Irthing	Cumbr	NY6065	54°58·9'	2°37·1'W	W	86
River Irthing	Cumbr	NY6875	55°4·4'	2°29·6'W	W	86,87
River Irvine	E Ayr	NS4236	55°35·8'	4°30·0'W	W	70
River Irvine	E Ayr	NS6137	55°36·7'	4°12·0'W	W	71
River Irwell	Bury	SD7913	53°37·0'	2°18·6'W	W	109
River Isbourne	Glos	SP0227	51°56·7'	1°57·9'W	W	163
River Isbourne	Glos	SP0337	52°2·1'	1°57·0'W	W	150
River Ise	Northnts	SP8582	52°26·0'	0°44·6'W	W	141
River Isis or Thames	Oxon	SP4610	51°47·4'	1°19·6'W	W	164
River Isis or Thames	Wilts	SU0693	51°38·4'	1°54·4'W	W	163,173
River Isla	Angus	NO1873	56°50·7'	3°20·2'W	W	43
River Isla	Angus	NO2160	56°43·8'	3°17·0'W	W	44
River Isla	Moray	NJ4045	57°29·7'	2°59·6'W	W	28
River Isla	Moray	NJ5149	57°32·0'	2°48·6'W	W	29
River Isla	Pth & Kin	NO2443	56°34·6'	3°13·8'W	W	53
River Isle	Somer	ST3822	50°59·9'	2°52·6'W	W	193
River Itchen	C of Soton	SU4312	50°54·6'	1°22·9'W	W	196
River Itchen	Hants	SU4723	51°0·5'	1°19·4'W	W	185
River Itchen	Warw	SP4061	52°15·0'	1°24·4'W	W	151
River Ithon	Powys	SO0663	52°15·7'	3°22·2'W	W	147
River Ithon	Powys	SO0875	52°22·2'	3°20·7'W	W	136,147
River Ithon	Powys	SO1162	52°15·2'	3°17·8'W	W	148
River Ive	Cumbr	NY4143	54°47·0'	2°54·6'W	W	85
River Ivel	Beds	TL1846	52°6·2'	0°16·2'W	W	153
River Ivel Navigation	Beds	TL1539	52°2·5'	0°19·0'W	W	153
River Iwerne	Dorset	ST8610	50°53·6'	2°11·6'W	W	194
River Jordan	Dorset	SY7082	50°38·4'	2°25·1'W	W	194
River Keekle	Cumbr	NY0120	54°34·2'	3°31·5'W	W	89
River Keer	Lancs	SD5573	54°9·3'	2°40·9'W	W	97
River Kelvin	E Dunb	NS6674	55°56·7'	4°8·3'W	W	64
River Kemp	Shrops	SO3681	52°25·6'	2°56·1'W	W	137
River Kenn	Devon	SX9484	50°39·0'	3°29·6'W	W	192
River Kenn	N Som	ST4269	51°25·3'	2°49·7'W	W	171,172,182
River Kennal	Corn	SW7637	50°11·7'	5°7·9'W	W	204
River Kennet	W Berks	SU3967	51°24·3'	1°26·0'W	W	174
River Kennet	W Berks	SU6167	51°24·2'	1°7·0'W	W	175
River Kennet	Wilts	SU1568	51°24·9'	1°46·7'W	W	173
River Kennett	Cambs	TL7068	52°17·3'	0°30·0'E	W	154
River Kensey	Corn	SX2686	50°39·1'	4°27·3'W	W	201
River Kent	Cumbr	NY4506	54°27·2'	2°50·5'W	W	90
River Kent	Cumbr	SD5190	54°18·4'	2°44·8'W	W	97
River Kenwyn	Corn	SW7946	50°16·6'	5°5·7'W	W	204
River Kerry	Highld	NG8272	57°41·4'	5°39·0'W	W	19
River Key	Wilts	SU0788	51°35·7'	1°53·5'W	W	173
River Kiachnish	Highld	NN0968	56°46·1'	5°7·1'W	W	41
River Killin	Highld	NH5208	57°8·6'	4°26·3'W	W	35
River Kinder	Derby	SK0688	53°23·6'	1°54·2'W	W	110
River Kingie	Highld	NM9996	57°0·9'	5°18·2'W	W	33,40
River Kingie	Highld	NN0297	57°1·6'	5°15·3'W	W	33
River Kinglass	Arg & Bt	NN1436	56°29·0'	5°0·8'W	W	50
River Kirkaig	Highld	NC0918	58°6·9'	5°14·1'W	W	15
River Kishorn	Highld	NG8343	57°25·3'	5°36·4'W	W	24
River Knaik	Pth & Kin	NN8112	56°17·4'	3°54·9'W	W	57
River Kyle	N Yks	SE4865	54°5·0'	1°15·6'W	W	100
River Kym	Cambs	TL1066	52°17·1'	0°22·8'W	W	153
River Lael	Highld	NH2284	57°48·9'	4°59·3'W	W	20
River Laggan	Arg & Bt	NR3356	55°43·7'	6°14·7'W	W	60
River Lair	Highld	NG9949	57°29·5'	5°20·8'W	W	25
River Lambourn	W Berks	SU4172	51°27·0'	1°24·2'W	W	174
River Laneshaw	Lancs	SD9340	53°51·6'	2°6·0'W	W	103
River Larig	Stir	NN4217	56°19·2'	4°32·9'W	W	56
River Larig	Stir	NN4518	56°20·0'	4°30·0'W	W	57
River Lark	Cambs	TL6182	52°25·0'	0°22·4'E	W	143
River Lark	Suff	TL6674	52°20·6'	0°26·6'E	W	143
River Lark	Suff	TL7273	52°19·9'	0°31·9'E	W	154
River Lark	Suff	TL7871	52°18·7'	0°37·1'E	W	144,155
River Laroch	Highld	NN0755	56°39·1'	5°8·4'W	W	41
River Lathkill	Derby	SK1966	53°11·7'	1°42·5'W	W	119
River Lavant	W Susx	SU8508	50°52·1'	0°47·1'W	W	197
River Laver	N Yks	SE2273	54°9·4'	1°39·4'W	W	99
River Leach	Glos	SP1310	51°47·5'	1°48·3'W	W	163
River Leach	Glos	SP2102	51°43·2'	1°41·4'W	W	163
River Leadon	Glos	SO7529	51°57·8'	2°21·4'W	W	150
River Leadon	Glos	SO7821	51°53·5'	2°18·8'W	W	162
River Leadon	Heref	SO6940	52°3·7'	2°26·7'W	W	149
River Leam	Northnts	SP5260	52°14·4'	1°13·9'W	W	151
River Leam	Warw	SP3768	52°18·8'	1°27·0'W	W	151
River Lea or Lee	Essex	TL3704	51°43·3'	0°0·6'W	W	166
River Lea or Lee	Hack	TQ3487	51°34·2'	0°3·6'W	W	176,177
River Lea or Lee	Herts	TL2013	51°48·4'	0°15·2'W	W	166
River Lea or Lee	Wal F	TQ3692	51°36·8'	0°1·7'W	W	177
River Leasgeary	Highld	NG4744	57°25·2'	6°12·4'W	W	23
River Lednock	Pth & Kin	NN6930	56°26·9'	4°7·1'W	W	51
River Lednock	Pth & Kin	NN7625	56°24·3'	4°0·1'W	W	51,52
River Leen	C of Nott	SK5443	52°59·1'	1°11·3'W	W	129
River Leen	Notts	SK5451	53°3·4'	1°11·3'W	W	120
River Lee or Lea	Hack	TQ3487	51°34·2'	0°3·6'W	W	176,177
River Lee or Lea	Herts	TL2013	51°48·4'	0°15·2'W	W	166
River Lee or Lea	Wal F	TQ3692	51°36·8'	0°1·7'W	W	177
River Leith	Cumbr	NY5524	54°36·8'	2°41·4'W	W	90
River Leith	Cumbr	NY5824	54°36·8'	2°38·6'W	W	91
River Lemon	Devon	SX7972	50°32·4'	3°42·1'W	W	191
River Len	Kent	TQ8054	51°15·6'	0°35·2'E	W	188
River Leòig	Arg & Bt	NR2367	55°49·3'	6°24·9'W	W	60
River Lerryn	Corn	SX1457	50°23·2'	4°36·6'W	W	200
River Leven	Cumbr	SD3483	54°14·6'	3°0·3'W	W	96,97
River Leven	Fife	NO2000	56°11·4'	3°16·9'W	W	58
River Leven	Fife	NO3100	56°11·5'	3°6·3'W	W	59
River Leven	Highld	NN2160	56°42·1'	4°55·0'W	W	41
River Leven	N Yks	NZ5006	54°27·1'	1°13·3'W	W	93
River Leven	N Yks	NZ6009	54°28·6'	1°4·0'W	W	94
River Leven	W Dunb	NS3977	55°57·8'	4°34·3'W	W	63
River Lew	Devon	SS5200	50°47·1'	4°5·6'W	W	191
River Lew	Devon	SX5189	50°41·1'	4°6·2'W	W	191
River Lickle	Cumbr	SD2189	54°17·7'	3°12·4'W	W	96
River Lickle	Cumbr	SD2393	54°19·9'	3°10·6'W	W	96
River Liever	Arg & Bt	NM9008	56°13·4'	5°22·8'W	W	55
River Lim	Dorset	SY3393	50°44·2'	2°56·6'W	W	193
River Limden	E Susx	TQ7027	51°1·3'	0°25·8'E	W	188,199
River Line	E Susx	TQ7518	50°56·3'	0°29·8'E	W	199
River Ling	Highld	NG9835	57°21·9'	5°21·1'W	W	25
River Linnet	Suff	TL8263	52°14·3'	0°40·3'E	W	155
River Liver	Arg & Bt	NN0835	56°28·3'	5°6·6'W	W	50
River Livet	Moray	NJ2027	57°19·9'	3°19·3'W	W	36
River Livet	Moray	NJ2523	57°17·7'	3°14·2'W	W	37
River Liza	Cumbr	NY1613	54°30·6'	3°17·4'W	W	89
River Loanan	Highld	NC2418	58°7·2'	4°58·8'W	W	15
River Lochay	Stir	NN4836	56°29·8'	4°27·7'W	W	51
River Lochy	Arg & Bt	NN2529	56°25·5'	4°49·8'W	W	50
River Lochy	Highld	NN1480	56°52·7'	5°2·7'W	W	34,41
River Lodden	Dorset	ST8227	51°2·8'	2°15·0'W	W	183
River Loddon	Hants	SU6754	51°17·1'	1°2·0'W	W	185,186
River Loddon	Hants	SU6857	51°18·7'	1°1·1'W	W	175,186
River Loddon	Wok	SU7569	51°25·1'	0°54·9'W	W	175
River Lodon	Heref	SO6149	52°8·5'	2°33·8'W	W	149
River Lossie	Moray	NJ2059	57°37·1'	3°19·9'W	W	28
River Lostock	Lancs	SD5019	53°40·1'	2°45·0'W	W	108
River Lostock	Lancs	SD5525	53°43·4'	2°40·5'W	W	102
River Loud	Lancs	SD6341	53°52·1'	2°33·3'W	W	102,103
River Loughor (Afon Llwchwr)	Carm	SN6108	51°45·4'	4°0·4'W	W	159
River Lovat or River Ouzel	Mil Key	SP8840	52°3·3'	0°42·6'W	W	152
River Loveny or St Neot River	Corn	SX1868	50°29·2'	4°33·6'W	W	201
River Lowman	Devon	SS9813	50°54·7'	3°26·7'W	W	181
River Lowman	Devon	ST0017	50°56·9'	3°25·0'W	W	181
River Lowther	Cumbr	NY5124	54°36·8'	2°45·1'W	W	90
River Lowther	Cumbr	NY5612	54°30·3'	2°40·3'W	W	90
River Loxford	Highld	NC2545	58°21·8'	4°59·0'W	W	9
River Loxley	Sheff	SK3189	53°24·1'	1°31·6'W	W	110,111
River Loy	Highld	NN1084	56°54·8'	5°6·8'W	W	34,41
River Loyne	Highld	NH0805	57°6·0'	5°9·7'W	W	33
River Loyne	Highld	NH2108	57°7·9'	4°57·0'W	W	34
River Lugg	Heref	SO5153	52°10·6'	2°42·6'W	W	149
River Lugg	Powys	SO2567	52°18·0'	3°5·6'W	W	137,148
River Luineag	Highld	NH9209	57°9·8'	3°46·7'W	W	36
River Lumburn	Devon	SX4573	50°32·4'	4°10·9'W	W	201
River Lundy	Highld	NN1577	56°51·1'	5°1·6'W	W	41
River Lune	Cumbr	NY6205	54°26·6'	2°34·7'W	W	91
River Lune	Cumbr	SD6182	54°14·2'	2°35·5'W	W	97
River Lune	Durham	NY8820	54°34·7'	2°10·7'W	W	91,92
River Lune	Lancs	SD4254	53°59·0'	2°52·7'W	W	102
River Lyd	Devon	SX4583	50°37·8'	4°11·1'W	W	201
River Lydden	Dorset	ST7414	50°55·7'	2°21·8'W	W	194
River Lydden	Dorset	ST7515	50°56·3'	2°21·0'W	W	183
River Lymn	Lincs	TF3868	53°11·7'	0°4·4'E	W	122
River Lyne	Cumbr	NY4065	54°58·8'	2°55·8'W	W	85
River Lyne	Cumbr	NY4972	55°2·6'	2°47·5'W	W	86
River Lyne	Northum	NZ2492	55°13·5'	1°36·9'W	W	81
River Lynher	Corn	SX3269	50°30·0'	4°21·8'W	W	201
River Lyon	Pth & Kin	NN6047	56°35·9'	4°16·4'W	W	51
River Lyvennet	Cumbr	NY6122	54°35·7'	2°35·8'W	W	91
River Mallie	Highld	NN0787	56°56·3'	5°9·9'W	W	41
River Manifold	Staffs	SK0958	53°7·4'	1°51·5'W	W	119
River Marden	Wilts	ST9473	51°27·6'	2°4·8'W	W	173
River Mardle	Devon	SX6967	50°29·5'	3°50·4'W	W	202
River Marron	Cumbr	NY0624	54°36·4'	3°26·9'W	W	89
River Mashie	Highld	NN5788	56°57·9'	4°20·7'W	W	42
River Massan	Arg & Bt	NS1087	56°2·6'	5°2·6'W	W	56
River Maun	Notts	SK6668	53°12·5'	1°0·3'W	W	120
River Mease	Derby	SK2712	52°42·5'	1°35·6'W	W	128
River Meavy	Devon	SX5265	50°28·2'	4°4·8'W	W	201
River Meden	Notts	SK5769	53°13·1'	1°8·4'W	W	120
River Medina	I of W	SZ5087	50°41·1'	1°17·1'W	W	196
River Medway	Kent	TQ6447	51°12·1'	0°21·2'E	W	188
River Medway	Medway	TQ8873	51°25·7'	0°42·7'E	W	178
River Meese	Wrekin	SJ6922	52°47·9'	2°27·2'W	W	127
River Meig	Highld	NH1648	57°29·4'	5°3·7'W	W	25
River Meig	Highld	NH3354	57°33·0'	4°47·0'W	W	26
River Mel	Cambs	TL3747	52°6·5'	0°0·4'E	W	154
River Menalhyl	Corn	SW8964	50°26·5'	4°57·9'W	W	200
River Meoble	Highld	NM7987	56°55·6'	5°37·4'W	W	40
River Meon	Hants	SU5508	50°52·4'	1°12·7'W	W	196
River Meon	Hants	SU6017	50°57·2'	1°8·4'W	W	185
River Mere	Devon	SS7223	50°53·5'	4°9·3'W	W	180
River Mere	Devon	SS5111	50°53·0'	4°6·7'W	W	191
River Mersey	Liv	SJ4581	53°19·6'	2°49·1'W	W	108
River Mersey	Traf	SJ7693	53°26·2'	2°21·3'W	W	109
River Mimram	Herts	TL2116	51°50·0'	0°14·2'W	W	166
River Mint	Cumbr	SD5596	54°21·7'	2°41·1'W	W	97
River Misbourne	Bucks	SU9992	51°37·3'	0°33·8'W	W	175,176
River Mite	Cumbr	NY1502	54°24·6'	3°18·2'W	W	89
River Mite	Cumbr	SD1098	54°22·4'	3°22·7'W	W	96
River Moidart	Highld	NM7574	56°48·4'	5°40·7'W	W	40
River Mole	Devon	SS7223	50°59·8'	3°49·1'W	W	180
River Mole	Surrey	TQ1163	51°21·5'	0°24·0'W	W	176,187
River Mole	Surrey	TQ1654	51°16·6'	0°19·8'W	W	187
River Monnow	Heref	SO3033	51°59·7'	3°0·8'W	W	161
River Monnow	Heref	SO3423	51°54·3'	2°57·2'W	W	161
River Morda	Shrops	SJ2628	52°50·9'	3°5·5'W	W	126
River Morda	Shrops	SJ3123	52°48·3'	3°1·0'W	W	126
River Moriston	Highld	NH3414	57°11·5'	4°44·4'W	W	34
River Mudale	Highld	NC5435	58°17·0'	4°28·9'W	W	16
River Mude	Dorset	SZ1893	50°44·4'	1°44·3'W	W	195
River Muick	Aberd	NO3288	56°59·0'	3°6·7'W	W	44
River Nadder	Wilts	ST9124	51°1·2'	2°7·3'W	W	184
River Nadder	Wilts	SU0631	51°4·9'	1°54·5'W	W	184
River Nairn	Highld	NH6226	57°18·5'	4°17·0'W	W	26,35
River Nairn	Highld	NH7947	57°30·1'	4°0·7'W	W	27
River Nant	Arg & Bt	NN0128	56°24·4'	5°13·1'W	W	50
River Nar	Norf	TF7513	52°41·4'	0°35·8'E	W	132,143
River Naver	Highld	NC7251	58°26·0'	4°11·1'W	W	10
River Neath / Afon Nedd	Nth Pt Talb	SS7798	51°40·3'	3°46·3'W	W	160,170
River Neb	I of M	SC2983	54°13·1'	4°36·9'W	W	95
River Neet	Corn	SS2509	50°51·5'	4°28·8'W	W	190
River Nell or Feochan Mhór	Arg & Bt	NM8825	56°22·4'	5°25·5'W	W	49
River Nene	Cambs	TF3200	52°35·1'	0°2·7'W	W	142
River Nene	Cambs	TL2498	52°34·2'	0°9·8'W	W	142
River Nene	Lincs	TF4719	52°45·1'	0°11·1'E	W	131
River Nene	Northnts	SP6959	52°13·7'	0°59·0'W	W	152
River Nene	Northnts	SP9569	52°18·9'	0°36·0'W	W	153
River Nene	Northnts	SP9979	52°24·2'	0°32·3'W	W	141
River Nene	Northnts	TL0586	52°27·9'	0°26·9'W	W	142
River Nene (old course)	Cambs	TL3291	52°30·3'	0°2·9'W	W	142
River Nent	Cumbr	NY7446	54°48·7'	2°23·8'W	W	86,87
River Ness	Highld	NH6441	57°26·6'	4°15·5'W	W	26
River Nethan	S Lanak	NS7634	55°35·3'	3°57·6'W	W	71
River Nethan	S Lanak	NS8044	55°40·7'	3°54·1'W	W	71,72
River Nethy	Highld	NJ0213	57°12·1'	3°36·9'W	W	36
River Nevis	Highld	NN1371	56°47·8'	5°3·3'W	W	41
River Nidd	N Yks	SE0175	54°10·5'	1°58·7'W	W	98
River Nidd	N Yks	SE1172	54°8·9'	1°49·5'W	W	99
River Nidd	N Yks	SE3258	54°1·3'	1°30·3'W	W	104
River Nidd	N Yks	SE4654	53°59·0'	1°17·5'W	W	105
River Nith	D & G	NS7113	55°23·9'	4°1·8'W	W	71
River Nith	D & G	NX8890	55°11·7'	3°45·1'W	W	78
River Nith	D & G	NX9969	55°0·6'	3°34·3'W	W	84
River Nith	E Ayr	NS5308	55°20·9'	4°18·7'W	W	70,77
River Noe	Arg & Bt	NN0733	56°27·2'	5°7·5'W	W	50
River Noe	Derby	SK1982	53°20·3'	1°42·5'W	W	110
River North	Brad	SE0137	53°50·0'	1°58·7'W	W	104
River North Esk	Angus	NO5377	56°53·2'	2°45·8'W	W	44
River North Esk	Angus	NO6466	56°47·3'	2°34·9'W	W	45
River North Esk	Midlo	NT2158	55°48·8'	3°15·2'W	W	73
River North Esk	Midlo	NT3167	55°53·7'	3°5·8'W	W	66
River North Tyne	Northum	NY7585	55°9·8'	2°23·1'W	W	80
River North Tyne	Northum	NY9270	55°1·7'	2°7·1'W	W	87
River Oakment	Devon	SS5901	50°47·7'	3°59·7'W	W	191
River Ock	Oxon	SU3593	51°38·3'	1°29·3'W	W	164,174
River Og	Wilts	SU1973	51°27·6'	1°43·2'W	W	173
River Oich	Highld	NH3406	57°7·2'	4°44·1'W	W	34
River Onny	Shrops	SO3987	52°28·9'	2°53·5'W	W	137
River Orchy	Arg & Bt	NN2431	56°26·6'	4°50·9'W	W	50
River Ore	Fife	NT2195	56°8·7'	3°15·8'W	W	58
River Ore	Fife	NT3097	56°9·9'	3°7·2'W	W	59
River Ore	Suff	TM4046	52°3·8'	1°30·5'E	W	169
River Orrin	Highld	NH2045	57°27·8'	4°59·6'W	W	25
River Orrin	Highld	NH4150	57°31·0'	4°38·8'W	W	26
River Orwell	Suff	TM2039	52°0·6'	1°12·7'E	W	169
River Ose	Highld	NG3442	57°23·7'	6°25·2'W	W	23
River Ossian	Highld	NN4171	56°48·5'	4°35·8'W	W	42
River Otter	Devon	ST1601	50°48·4'	3°11·1'W	W	192,193
River Otter	Devon	SY0886	50°40·2'	3°17·7'W	W	192
River Ottery	Corn	SX2489	50°40·7'	4°29·1'W	W	190
River Oude	Arg & Bt	NM8415	56°17·0'	5°28·9'W	W	55
River Oughton	Herts	TL1730	51°57·6'	0°17·4'W	W	166
River Ouse	E Susx	TQ4123	50°59·6'	0°0·9'E	W	198
River Ouse	N Yks	SE4860	54°2·3'	1°15·6'W	W	100
River Ouse	N Yks	SE7126	53°43·8'	0°55·0'W	W	105,106
River Ouse	York	SE5945	53°54·1'	1°5·7'W	W	105
River Ouzel	Beds	SP9421	51°53·0'	0°37·7'W	W	165
River Ouzel or River Lovat	Mil Key	SP8840	52°3·3'	0°42·6'W	W	152
River Oykel	Highld	NC3207	58°1·5'	4°50·2'W	W	15
River Oykel	Highld	NC3900	57°57·9'	4°42·8'W	W	16
River Pang	W Berks	SU5371	51°26·4'	1°13·9'W	W	174
River Pang	W Berks	SU6173	51°27·4'	1°6·9'W	W	175
River Pant	Essex	TL6036	52°0·2'	0°20·3'E	W	154
River Pant	Essex	TL7327	51°55·1'	0°31·3'E	W	167
River Park Fm	W Susx	SU9424	51°0·7'	0°39·2'W	FM	197
River Parrett	Somer	ST2942	51°10·6'	3°0·6'W	W	182
River Parrett	Somer	ST4320	50°58·8'	2°48·3'W	W	193
River Pattack	Highld	NN5585	56°56·3'	4°22·5'W	W	42
River Pean	Highld	NM9490	56°57·6'	5°22·8'W	W	33,40
River Peffery	Highld	NH5259	57°36·1'	4°28·1'W	W	26
River Penk	Staffs	SJ9011	52°42·0'	2°8·5'W	W	127
River Perry	Shrops	SJ3232	52°53·1'	3°0·2'W	W	126

River Perry	Shrops	SJ3926	52°49·9'	2°53·9'W	W	126
River Perry	Shrops	SJ4220	52°46·7'	2°51·2'W	W	126
River Petteril	Cumbr	NY4352	54°51·8'	2°52·9'W	W	85
River Petteril	Cumbr	NY4642	54°46·4'	2°49·9'W	W	86
River Petteril	Cumbr	NY4937	54°43·8'	2°47·1'W	W	90
River Piddle or Trent	Dorset	SY8093	50°44·4'	2°16·6'W	W	194
River Piddle or Trent	Dorset	SY9087	50°41·2'	2°8·1'W	W	195
River Pinn	Hill	TQ0787	51°34·5'	0°27·0'W	W	176
River Plym	C of Plym	SX5055	50°22·8'	4°6·2'W	W	201
River Plym	Devon	SX5765	50°28·3'	4°0·5'W	W	202
River Polloch	Highld	NM7868	56°45·3'	5°37·4'W	W	40
River Polly	Highld	NC0713	58°4·1'	5°15·9'W	W	15
River Pont	Northum	NZ0069	55°1·2'	1°59·6'W	W	87
River Pont	Northum	NZ1674	55°3·9'	1°44·5'W	W	88
River Pool	Cumbr	SD4690	54°18·4'	2°49·4'W	W	97
River Poulter	Derby	SK5269	53°13·2'	1°12·9'W	W	120
River Poulter	Notts	SK6774	53°15·8'	0°59·3'W	W	120
River Purwell	Herts	TL1930	51°57·6'	0°15·7'W	W	166
River Quaich	Pth & Kin	NN8040	56°32·5'	3°56·6'W	W	52
River Quarme	Somer	SS9137	51°7·6'	3°33·1'W	W	181
River Quin	Herts	TL3927	51°55·7'	0°1·7'E	W	166
River Quoich	Highld	NH0107	57°6·9'	5°16·7'W	W	33
River Rase	Lincs	TF0488	53°23·0'	0°25·8'W	W	112,121
River Rase	Lincs	TF1389	53°23·4'	0°17·6'W	W	113,121
River Rawthey	Cumbr	SD6591	54°19·0'	2°31·9'W	W	97
River Rawthey	Cumbr	SD7495	54°21·2'	2°23·6'W	W	98
River Ray	Oxon	SP5817	51°51·1'	1°9·1'W	W	164
River Ray	Wilts	SU1190	51°36·8'	1°50·1'W	W	163,173
River Rea	Birm	SP0683	52°26·9'	1°54·3'W	W	139
River Rea	Shrops	SO6773	52°21·5'	2°28·7'W	W	138
River Rede	Northum	NT7005	55°20·5'	2°27·9'W	W	80
River Rede	Northum	NY8892	55°13·6'	2°10·9'W	W	80
River Redlake	Shrops	SO3275	52°22·4'	2°59·5'W	W	137,148
River Rha	Highld	NG4065	57°36·3'	6°20·7'W	W	23
River Rhee	Herts	TL2541	52°3·4'	0°10·2'W	W	153
River Rhee or Cam	Cambs	TL2745	52°5·6'	0°8·4'W	W	153
River Rhee or Cam	Cambs	TL3647	52°6·5'	0°0·4'W	W	154
River Rhiw	Powys	SJ1202	52°36·8'	3°17·6'W	W	136
River Rib	Herts	TL3920	51°51·9'	0°1·5'E	W	166
River Ribble	Lancs	SD5228	53°45·0'	2°43·3'W	W	102
River Ribble	Lancs	SD7644	53°53·7'	2°21·5'W	W	103
River Ribble	N Yks	SD7974	54°9·9'	2°18·9'W	W	98
River Riccal	N Yks	SE6285	54°15·7'	1°2·5'W	W	94,100
River Riccal	N Yks	SE6979	54°12·4'	0°56·1'W	W	100
River Rivelin	Sheff	SK3187	53°23·0'	1°31·6'W	W	110,111
River Roach	Essex	TQ9692	51°35·8'	0°50·2'E	W	178
River Roch	Roch	SD8311	53°36·0'	2°15·0'W	W	109
River Roden	Shrops	SJ4828	52°51·1'	2°45·9'W	W	126
River Roden	Shrops	SJ5624	52°48·9'	2°38·8'W	W	126
River Roding	Essex	TL5814	51°48·4'	0°17·9'E	W	167
River Roding	Essex	TQ4395	51°38·4'	0°4·4'E	W	167,177
River Roeburn	Lancs	SD6161	54°2·9'	2°35·3'W	W	97
River Rom	Hav	TQ4990	51°35·6'	0°9·5'E	W	177
River Romesdal	Highld	NG4354	57°30·5'	6°17·0'W	W	23
River Rothay	Cumbr	NY3308	54°28·0'	3°1·6'W	W	90
River Rother	Derby	SK3967	53°12·2'	1°24·6'W	W	119
River Rother	E Susx	TQ7026	51°0·7'	0°25·8'E	W	188,199
River Rother	E Susx	TQ9225	50°59·8'	0°44·6'E	W	189
River Rother	Roth	SK4583	53°20·8'	1°19·0'W	W	111,120
River Rothrr	W Susx	SU9420	50°58·5'	0°39·3'W	W	197
River Roy	Highld	NN3085	56°55·8'	4°47·2'W	W	34,41
River Roy	Highld	NN3792	56°59·7'	4°40·5'W	W	34
River Ruel	Arg & Bt	NR9983	56°0·1'	5°13·0'W	W	55
River Runie	Highld	NC1402	57°58·4'	5°8·2'W	W	15
River Ryburn	Cald	SE0419	53°40·3'	1°56·0'W	W	110
River Ryburn	Cald	SE0422	53°41·9'	1°56·0'W	W	104
River Rye	N Yks	SE6779	54°12·4'	0°57·9'W	W	100
River Ryton	Notts	SK6482	53°20·1'	1°1·9'W	W	111,120
River Salwarpe	Worcs	SO8863	52°16·1'	2°10·2'W	W	150
River Sand	Highld	NG7679	57°45·0'	5°45·4'W	W	19
River Sark	D & G	NY3276	55°4·7'	3°3·5'W	W	85
River Scaddle	Highld	NM9568	56°45·8'	5°20·8'W	W	40
Rivers' Corner	Dorset	ST7712	50°54·7'	2°19·2'W	T	194
Riversdale	I of M	SC4395	54°19·8'	4°24·5'W	X	95
Riversdown Ho	Hants	SU6024	51°1·0'	1°8·3'W	X	185
River Seaton	Corn	SX3056	50°23·0'	4°23·1'W	W	201
River Sem	Wilts	ST9127	51°2·8'	2°7·3'W	W	184
River Sence	Leic	SK3604	52°38·2'	1°27·7'W	W	140
River Sence	Leic	SK6802	52°36·9'	0°59·3'W	W	141
River Sence	Leic	SP5698	52°34·8'	1°10·0'W	W	140
River Sence	Leic	SP6598	52°34·8'	1°2·0'W	W	141
River Seph	N Yks	SE5692	54°19·5'	1°7·9'W	W	100
River Sett	Derby	SK0585	53°22·0'	1°55·1'W	W	110
River Seven	N Yks	SE7381	54°13·4'	0°52·4'W	W	100
River Seven	N Yks	SE7491	54°18·8'	0°51·3'W	W	94,100
River Severn	Glos	SO7311	51°48·1'	2°23·1'W	W	162
River Severn	Powys	SO1493	52°31·9'	3°15·7'W	W	136
River Severn	Shrops	SJ4014	52°43·5'	2°52·9'W	W	126
River Severn	Shrops	SJ6603	52°37·7'	2°29·7'W	W	127
River Severn	Shrops	SO7777	52°23·7'	2°19·9'W	W	138
River Severn	Worcs	SO8449	52°8·6'	2°13·6'W	W	150
River's Fm	Somer	ST1127	51°2·4'	3°15·8'W	FM	181,193
River's Fm	W Susx	TQ3327	51°1·8'	0°5·8'W	FM	187,198
River Sgitheach	Highld	NH5765	57°39·4'	4°23·3'W	W	21
Rivers Hall	Essex	TM0033	51°57·8'	0°55·1'E	X	168
Rivers Hall	Suff	TM2745	52°3·6'	1°19·1'E	X	169
River Sheaf	Sheff	SK3281	53°19·7'	1°30·8'W	W	110,111
River Sheil	Highld	NM6669	56°45·5'	5°49·2'W	W	40
River Sheppey	Somer	ST5444	51°11·8'	2°39·1'W	W	182,183
River Sherbourne	Cov	SP3081	52°25·8'	1°33·1'W	W	140
River Sherway	Kent	TQ8544	51°10·1'	0°39·2'E	W	189
River Shiel	Highld	NH0013	57°10·1'	5°18·0'W	W	33
River Shin	Highld	NC5702	57°59·3'	4°24·7'W	W	16
River Shin	Highld	NH5798	57°57·2'	4°24·5'W	W	21
River Shira	Arg & Bt	NN1314	56°17·2'	5°0·8'W	W	50,56
River Sid	Devon	SY1492	50°43·5'	3°12·7'W	W	192,193
Riverside	Card	ST1776	51°28·8'	3°11·3'W	T	171
Riverside	Devon	SX4358	50°24·3'	4°12·2'W	T	201
Riverside	Stir	NS8094	56°7·7'	3°55·4'W	T	57
Riverside	Worcs	SP0468	52°18·8'	1°56·1'W	T	139

Riverside Country Park	Medway	TQ8068	51°23·2'	0°35·6'E	X	178
Riverside Docklands	Lancs	SD5129	53°45·5'	2°44·2'W	T	102
Riverside Doveleys	Staffs	SK1141	52°58·2'	1°49·8'W	X	119,128
Riverside Fm	N Som	ST3968	51°24·7'	2°52·2'W	FM	171,182
Riverside Fm	Suff	TL9850	52°7·0'	0°53·9'E	FM	155
Riverside Park	Swin	SU2199	51°41·6'	1°41·4'W	X	163
River Simene	Dorset	SY4594	50°44·8'	2°46·4'W	W	193
River Skerne	Durham	NZ3026	54°37·9'	1°31·7'W	W	93
River Skinsdale	Highld	NC7523	58°11·0'	4°7·1'W	W	16
River Skinsdale	Highld	NC7621	58°9·9'	4°6·0'W	W	17
River Skirfare	N Yks	SD8875	54°10·5'	2°10·6'W	W	98
River Skirfare	N Yks	SD9669	54°7·3'	2°3·3'W	W	98
River Slea	Hants	SU8038	51°8·4'	0°51·0'W	W	186
River Slea	Lincs	TF0847	53°0·8'	0°23·0'W	W	130
Riverslea Fm	Lincs	TF2361	53°8·1'	0°9·3'W	FM	122
River Sligachan	Highld	NG4927	57°16·1'	6°9·3'W	W	32
Riversmead	Devon	SS5935	51°6·1'	4°0·4'W	X	180
Riversmead Fm	Glos	SO8015	51°50·2'	2°17·0'W	FM	162
Riversmeet Ho	Devon	SX9787	50°40·6'	3°27·1'W	X	192
River Smite	Notts	SK7540	52°57·4'	0°52·6'W	W	129
River Snail	Cambs	TL6368	52°17·4'	0°23·8'E	W	154
River Snizort	Highld	NG4145	57°25·6'	6°18·4'W	W	23
River Soar	Leic	SK5519	52°46·2'	1°10·7'W	W	129
River Soar	Leic	SP5599	52°35·4'	1°10·9'W	W	140
River Solva	Pemb	SM8327	51°54·2'	5°8·9'W	W	157
River Somer	Bath & NE Somer	ST6754	51°17·3'	2°28·0'W	W	183
River Sorn	Arg & Bt	NR3664	55°48·1'	6°12·3'W	W	60,61
River South Esk	Angus	NO3372	56°50·3'	3°5·4'W	W	44
River South Esk	Angus	NO5458	56°42·9'	2°44·6'W	W	54
River South Esk	Midlo	NT2948	55°43·5'	3°7·4'W	W	73
River South Esk	Midlo	NT3366	55°53·2'	3°3·8'W	W	66
River South Tyne	Cumbr	NY7538	54°44·4'	2°22·9'W	W	91
River South Tyne	Northum	NY6962	54°57·3'	2°28·6'W	W	86,87
River Sow	Staffs	SJ9322	52°48·0'	2°5·8'W	W	127
River Sowe	Warw	SP3575	52°22·5'	1°28·8'W	W	140
River Spean	Highld	NN2680	56°53·0'	4°50·9'W	W	34,41
River Spean	Highld	NN4383	56°55·0'	4°34·3'W	W	34,42
River Spey	Highld	NH7801	57°5·3'	4°0·3'W	W	35
River Spey	Highld	NH9620	57°15·8'	3°43·0'W	W	36
River Spey	Highld	NJ0830	57°21·3'	3°31·3'W	W	27,36
River Spey	Highld	NN4595	57°1·5'	4°32·8'W	W	34
River Spey	Moray	NJ3151	57°32·9'	3°8·7'W	W	28
River Sprint	Cumbr	NY4904	54°26·0'	2°46·8'W	W	90
River Sprint	Cumbr	SD5297	54°22·2'	2°43·9'W	W	97
River Stiffkey	Norf	TF9336	52°53·4'	0°52·5'E	W	132
River Stinchar	S Ayr	NX2089	55°10·0'	4°49·1'W	W	76
River Stinchar	S Ayr	NX3896	55°14·2'	4°32·4'W	W	77
River Stor	W Susx	TQ0616	50°56·2'	0°29·1'W	W	197
River Stort	Essex	TL4829	51°56·6'	0°9·6'E	W	167
River Stort (Navigation)	Essex	TL3909	51°46·0'	0°1·3'E	W	166
River Stour	Dorset	ST7821	50°59·5'	2°18·4'W	W	183
River Stour	Dorset	ST8014	50°55·7'	2°16·7'W	W	194
River Stour	Dorset	SY9699	50°47·7'	2°3·0'W	W	195
River Stour	Dudley	SO9584	52°27·5'	2°4·0'W	W	139
River Stour	Essex	TL8839	52°1·3'	0°44·8'E	W	155
River Stour	Essex	TL9433	51°57·9'	0°49·8'E	W	168
River Stour	Essex	TM1932	51°56·8'	1°11·6'E	W	168,169
River Stour	Kent	TR3162	51°18·8'	1°19·3'E	W	179
River Stour	Suff	TL6653	52°9·2'	0°26·0'E	W	154
River Stour	Warw	SP2546	52°6·9'	1°37·7'W	W	151
River Stour	Worcs	SO8273	52°21·5'	2°15·5'W	W	138
River Strae	Arg & Bt	NN1631	56°26·4'	4°58·6'W	W	50
River Strathy	Highld	NC8155	58°28·3'	4°1·9'W	W	10
River Strine	Wrekin	SJ6518	52°45·7'	2°30·7'W	W	127
River Swale	N Yks	NY8801	54°24·5'	2°10·7'W	W	91,92
River Swale	N Yks	NZ1301	54°24·5'	1°47·6'W	W	92
River Swale	N Yks	NZ1900	54°24·0'	1°42·0'W	W	92
River Swale	N Yks	SD9797	54°22·4'	2°2·4'W	W	98
River Swale	N Yks	SE3683	54°14·7'	1°26·4'W	W	99
River Swarbourn	Staffs	SK1417	52°45·3'	1°47·2'W	W	128
River Swere	Oxon	SP4133	51°59·9'	1°23·8'W	W	151
River Swift	Hants	SU3753	51°16·7'	1°27·8'W	W	185
River Swift	Leic	SP5382	52°26·2'	1°12·8'W	W	140
River Swift	Leic	SP5784	52°27·3'	1°9·3'W	W	140
River Swilgate	Glos	SO9028	51°57·3'	2°8·3'W	W	150,163
River Swincombe	Devon	SX6372	50°32·1'	3°55·6'W	W	191
River's Wood	W Susx	TQ3327	51°1·8'	0°5·8'W	F	187,198
River Synderford	Dorset	ST3802	50°49·1'	2°52·4'W	W	193
River Taf (Afon Taf)	Carm	SN3209	51°45·5'	4°25·7'W	W	159
River Taff	Merth Tyd	SO0701	51°42·2'	3°20·4'W	W	170
River Taff or Afon Taf	Card	ST1380	51°31·0'	3°14·8'W	W	171
River Tale	Devon	SY0898	50°46·7'	3°17·9'W	W	192
River Talisker	Highld	NG3330	57°17·2'	6°25·4'W	W	32
River Talladale	Highld	NG9168	57°39·5'	5°29·7'W	W	19
River Tamar	Devon	SX2999	50°46·2'	4°25·1'W	W	190
River Tamar	Devon	SX4266	50°28·6'	4°13·2'W	W	201
River Tame	Birm	SP1590	52°30·7'	1°46·3'W	W	139
River Tame	N Yks	NZ5210	54°29·2'	1°11·4'W	W	93
River Tame	Staffs	SK1812	52°42·6'	1°43·6'W	W	128
River Tame	Tames	SJ9293	53°26·3'	2°6·8'W	W	109
River Taodail	Highld	NG9541	57°25·1'	5°24·4'W	W	25
River Tarbert	Highld	NM9259	56°40·9'	5°23·3'W	W	49
River Tarff	Highld	NH3901	57°4·6'	4°38·9'W	W	34
River Tas	Norf	TM2198	52°32·3'	1°15·9'E	W	134
River Tavy	Devon	SX4772	50°31·9'	4°9·2'W	W	191,201
River Taw	Devon	SS6024	51°0·1'	3°59·3'W	W	180
River Taw	Devon	SX6598	50°46·2'	3°54·5'W	W	191
River Tawd	Lancs	SD4709	53°34·7'	2°47·6'W	W	108
River Tawe	Swan	SS6798	51°40·1'	3°55·0'W	W	159
River Tawe or Afon Tawe	Nth Pt Talb	SN7102	51°42·4'	3°51·6'W	W	170
River Tay	Pth & Kin	NN7947	56°36·2'	3°57·8'W	W	51,52
River Tay	Pth & Kin	NO0441	56°33·3'	3°33·3'W	W	52,53
River Tay	Pth & Kin	NO1138	56°31·8'	3°26·4'W	W	53
River Tay	Pth & Kin	NO1422	56°23·2'	3°23·1'W	W	53,58
River Team	Durham	NZ2455	54°53·6'	1°37·1'W	W	88
River Tean	Staffs	SK0238	52°56·6'	1°57·8'W	W	128
River Tees	Cumbr	NY7434	54°42·3'	2°23·8'W	W	91
River Tees	Darl	NZ3511	54°29·8'	1°27·2'W	W	93
River Tees	Durham	NZ0317	54°33·1'	1°56·8'W	W	92

River Teign	Devon	SX8288	50°41·0'	3°39·8'W	W	191
River Teign	Devon	SX9072	50°32·5'	3°32·8'W	W	192,202
River Teirw	Wrex	SJ1836	52°55·2'	3°12·8'W	W	125
River Teise	Kent	TQ6946	51°11·5'	0°25·5'E	W	188
River Teise	Kent	TQ7240	51°8·2'	0°27·9'E	W	188
River Teith	Stir	NN6803	56°12·3'	4°7·2'W	W	57
River Teme	Powys	SO1780	52°24·9'	3°12·8'W	W	136
River Teme	Powys	SO3072	52°20·7'	3°1·3'W	W	137,148
River Teme	Shrops	SO4876	52°23·0'	2°45·4'W	W	137,138,148
River Teme	Worcs	SO6068	52°18·8'	2°34·8'W	W	138
River Teme	Worcs	SO8252	52°10·2'	2°15·4'W	W	150
River Ter	Essex	TL7117	51°49·8'	0°29·3'E	W	167
River Ter	Essex	TL7812	51°46·9'	0°35·2'E	W	167
River Tern	Shrops	SJ5812	52°42·5'	2°36·9'W	W	126
River Tern	Shrops	SJ6327	52°50·6'	2°32·6'W	W	127
River Terrig	Flint	SJ2356	53°6·0'	3°8·6'W	W	117
River Terrig	Flint	SJ2460	53°8·1'	3°7·8'W	W	117
River Test	Hants	SU3433	51°5·9'	1°30·5'W	W	185
River Test	Hants	SU3911	50°54·1'	1°26·3'W	W	196
River Teviot	Scot Bord	NT3904	55°19·8'	2°57·3'W	W	79
River Teviot	Scot Bord	NT5719	55°28·0'	2°40·4'W	W	80
River Teviot	Scot Bord	NT5920	55°28·6'	2°38·5'W	W	73,74
River Teviot	Scot Bord	NT6825	55°31·3'	2°30·0'W	W	74
River Thame	Oxon	SP6605	51°44·6'	1°2·2'W	W	164,165
River Thames	Bucks	SU7983	51°32·7'	0°51·3'W	W	175
River Thames	King	TQ1767	51°23·6'	0°18·7'W	W	176
River Thames	Oxon	SU5984	51°33·3'	1°8·5'W	W	174
River Thames	Thurr	TQ5577	51°28·5'	0°14·3'E	W	177
River Thames	Thurr	TQ7581	51°30·3'	0°31·7'E	W	178
River Thames or Isis	Oxon	SP4610	51°47·4'	1°19·6'W	W	164
River Thames or Isis	Wilts	SU0693	51°38·4'	1°54·4'W	W	163,173
River Thaw	V of Glam	SS9878	51°29·7'	3°27·8'W	W	170
River Thaw	V of Glam	ST0270	51°25·5'	3°24·2'W	W	170
River Thet	Norf	TL9584	52°25·4'	0°52·5'E	W	144
River Thrushel	Devon	SX4388	50°40·5'	4°12·9'W	W	190
River Thrushel	Devon	SX5292	50°42·8'	4°5·4'W	W	191
River Thurne	Norf	TG4218	52°42·6'	1°35·4'E	W	134
River Thurso	Highld	ND1154	58°28·2'	3°31·1'W	W	11,12
River Tiddy	Corn	SX3262	50°26·3'	4°21·6'W	W	201
River Tiffey	Norf	TG0903	52°35·3'	1°5·5'E	W	144
River Til	Beds	TL0368	52°18·3'	0°29·0'W	W	153
River Till	Lincs	SK8886	53°22·0'	0°40·2'W	W	112,121
River Till	Lincs	SK9078	53°17·7'	0°38·6'W	W	121
River Till	Northum	NU0030	55°34·1'	1°59·6'W	W	75
River Till	Wilts	SU0740	51°9·8'	1°53·6'W	W	184
River Tillingham	E Susx	TQ8719	50°56·6'	0°40·5'E	W	189,199
River Tilt	Pth & Kin	NN9676	56°52·1'	3°41·9'W	W	43
River Tirry	Highld	NC5417	58°7·3'	4°28·3'W	W	16
River Todale	N Eil	NB1029	58°9·5'	6°55·4'W	W	13
Riverton	Devon	SS6330	51°3·4'	3°56·9'W	T	180
River Tone	Somer	ST1121	50°59·1'	3°15·7'W	W	181,193
River Tone	Somer	ST3227	51°2·5'	2°57·8'W	W	193
River Tora	Highld	NG4047	57°26·6'	6°19·5'W	W	23
River Torne	Donc	SE6502	53°30·9'	1°0·8'W	W	111
River Torne	N Lincs	SE7104	53°31·9'	0°55·3'W	W	112
River Torne	N Lincs	SE7608	53°34·0'	0°50·7'W	W	112
River Torne or Goole Dike	Donc	SK6095	53°27·1'	1°5·4'W	W	111
River Torridge	Devon	SS4110	50°52·3'	4°15·2'W	W	190
River Torridge	Devon	SS4526	51°1·0'	4°12·2'W	W	180,190
River Torridge	Devon	SS5206	50°50·3'	4°5·7'W	W	191
River Torridge	Devon	SS5314	50°54·6'	4°5·1'W	W	180
River Torridon	Highld	NG9255	57°32·5'	5°28·1'W	W	25
River Toscaig	Highld	NG7337	57°22·3'	5°46·1'W	W	24
River Tove	Northnts	SP6547	52°7·3'	1°2·6'W	W	152
River Tove	Northnts	SP7746	52°6·6'	0°52·1'W	W	152
River Towy (Afon Tywi)	Carm	SN3611	51°46·7'	4°22·2'W	W	159
River Towy (Afon Tywi)	Carm	SN4420	51°51·6'	4°15·5'W	W	159
River Traligill	Highld	NC2720	58°8·4'	4°55·9'W	W	15
River Treig	Highld	NN3578	56°52·1'	4°42·0'W	W	41
River Trent	C of Nott	SK5435	52°54·8'	1°11·4'W	W	129
River Trent	N Lincs	SE8302	53°30·7'	0°44·5'W	W	112
River Trent	Notts	SK7754	53°4·9'	0°50·6'W	W	120
River Trent	Notts	SK8170	53°13·5'	0°46·8'W	W	121
River Trent	Staffs	SJ9231	52°52·8'	2°6·7'W	W	127
River Trent	Staffs	SK2119	52°46·3'	1°40·9'W	W	128
River Trent or Piddle	Dorset	SY8093	50°44·4'	2°16·6'W	W	194
River Trent or Piddle	Dorset	SY9087	50°41·2'	2°8·1'W	W	195
River Tromie	Highld	NN7689	56°58·8'	4°2·0'W	W	42
River Tromie	Highld	NN7695	57°2·0'	4°2·1'W	W	35
River Troney	Devon	SX7597	50°45·8'	3°46·0'W	W	191
River Trothy	Monm	SO4014	51°49·5'	2°51·8'W	W	161
River Trothy	Monm	SO5111	51°48·0'	2°42·2'W	W	162
River Truim	Highld	NN6688	56°58·1'	4°11·8'W	W	42
River Truim	Highld	NN6894	57°1·4'	4°10·0'W	W	35
River Tud	Norf	TG0812	52°40·2'	1°5·0'E	W	133
River Tummel	Pth & Kin	NN7459	56°42·6'	4°3·0'W	W	42,51,52
River Tummel	Pth & Kin	NN8960	56°43·4'	3°48·4'W	W	43
River Tummel	Pth & Kin	NN9555	56°40·8'	3°42·4'W	W	52,53
River Turret	Highld	NN3393	57°0·1'	4°44·5'W	W	34
River Tutt	N Yks	SE3764	54°4·5'	1°25·7'W	W	99
River Tweed	Northum	NT9651	55°45·4'	2°3·4'W	W	74,75
River Tweed	Scot Bord	NT1435	55°36·3'	3°21·5'W	W	72
River Tweed	Scot Bord	NT4136	55°37·1'	2°55·8'W	W	73
River Tweed	Scot Bord	NT7738	55°38·4'	2°21·5'W	W	74
River Tweed	Scot Bord	NT9351	55°45·4'	2°6·3'W	W	67,74,75
River Tweed	Scot Bord	NT9351	55°45·4'	2°6·3'W	W	67,74,75
River Twiss	N Yks	SD6974	54°9·9'	2°28·1'W	W	98
River Tyne	E Loth	NT5071	55°56·0'	2°47·6'W	W	66
River Tyne	E Loth	NT6178	55°59·9'	2°37·1'W	W	67
River Tyne	Ghead	NZ1565	54°59·0'	1°45·5'W	W	88
River Tyne	Northum	NY9564	54°58·5'	2°4·3'W	W	87
River Uck	E Susx	TQ4520	50°57·9'	0°4·3'E	W	198
River Ugie	Aberd	NK0749	57°32·1'	1°52·5'W	W	30
River Umber	Devon	SS5945	51°11·4'	4°0·7'W	W	180
River Unk	Shrops	SO2886	52°28·3'	3°3·2'W	W	137
River Ure	Arg & Bt	NN0647	56°34·8'	5°9·1'W	W	50
River Ure	N Yks	SD7996	54°21·8'	2°19·0'W	W	98
River Ure	N Yks	SD9390	54°18·6'	2°6·0'W	W	98
River Ure	N Yks	SE2677	54°11·5'	1°35·7'W	W	99
River Ure	N Yks	SE4661	54°2·8'	1°17·4'W	W	100

River Urie	Aberd	NJ6434	57°24·0′	2°35·5′W	W	29
River Urie	Aberd	NJ7523	57°18·1′	2°24·4′W	W	38
River Usk	Monm	SO3403	51°43·5′	2°56·9′W	W	171
River Usk	Powys	SO2018	51°51·5′	3°9·3′W	W	161
River Usk (Afon Wysg)	Monm	SO2714	51°49·4′	3°3·2′W	W	161
River Usk (Afon Wysg)	Powys	SN9329	51°57·2′	3°33·0′W	W	160
River Vagastie	Highld	NC5532	58°15·4′	4°27·8′W	W	16
River Valency	Corn	SX1291	50°41·5′	4°39·3′W	W	190
River Ver	Herts	TL1208	51°45·8′	0°22·2′W	W	166
Riverview Park	Kent	TQ6671	51°25·0′	0°23·6′E	T	177,178
River Vyrnwy	Powys	SJ3118	52°45·6′	3°0·9′W	W	126
River Vyrnwy or Afon Efyrnwy	Powys	SJ0314	52°43·1′	3°25·8′W	W	125
River Waldon	Devon	SS3810	50°52·2′	4°17·8′W	W	190
River Walkham	Devon	SX4870	50°30·8′	4°8·3′W	W	201
River Walkham	Devon	SX5576	50°34·2′	4°2·5′W	W	191
River Wallabrook	Devon	SX4877	50°34·6′	4°8·4′W	W	191,201
River Wampool	Cumbr	NY2453	54°52·2′	3°10·6′W	W	85
River Wandle	Merton	TQ2572	51°26·2′	0°11·7′W	W	176
River Wansbeck	Northum	NZ1485	55°9·8′	1°46·4′W	W	81
River Wantsum	Kent	TR2367	51°21·7′	1°12·6′E	W	179
River Waring	Lincs	TF2671	53°13·5′	0°6·3′W	W	122
River Wash	Devon	SX7954	50°22·6′	3°41·7′W	W	202
River Washburn	N Yks	SE1260	54°2·4′	1°48·6′W	W	99
River Washburn	N Yks	SE1359	54°1·9′	1°47·7′W	W	104
River Washburn	N Yks	SE2050	53°57·0′	1°41·3′W	W	104
River Waveney	Norf	TM2381	52°23·1′	1°17·0′E	W	156
River Waveney	Suff	TM0579	52°22·5′	1°1·1′E	W	144
River Waveney	Suff	TM4591	52°27·9′	1°36·8′E	W	134
River Waver	Cumbr	NY1751	54°51·1′	3°17·1′W	W	85
River Waycock	V of Glam	ST0868	51°24·5′	3°19·0′W	W	170
River Wear	Durham	NY9438	54°44·5′	2°5·2′W	W	91,92
River Wear	Durham	NZ2436	54°43·3′	1°37·2′W	W	93
River Wear	Durham	NZ2851	54°51·4′	1°33·4′W	W	88
River Weaver	Ches	SJ5551	53°3·5′	2°39·9′W	W	117
River Weaver	Ches	SJ5576	53°17·0′	2°40·1′W	W	117
River Weaver	Ches	SJ6246	53°0·8′	2°33·6′W	W	118
River Weaver	Ches	SJ6657	53°6·8′	2°30·1′W	W	118
River Weaver	Devon	ST0203	50°49·3′	3°23·1′W	W	192
River Webburn	Devon	SX7172	50°32·2′	3°48·8′W	W	191
River Welland	Lincs	TF2625	52°48·7′	0°7·4′W	W	131
River Welland	Northnts	SP8893	52°31·9′	0°41·8′W	W	141
River Welland	Peterb	TF1707	52°39·1′	0°15·8′W	W	142
River Wenning	Lancs	SD6169	54°7·2′	2°35·4′W	W	97
River Wenning	N Yks	SD7367	54°6·1′	2°24·4′W	W	98
River Wensum	Norf	TF9229	52°49·7′	0°51·4′E	W	132
River Wensum	Norf	TG1217	52°42·8′	1°8·7′E	W	133
River Went	N Yks	SE5017	53°39·1′	1°14·2′W	W	111
River West Allen	Northum	NY7851	54°51·4′	2°20·1′W	W	86,87
River Westend	Derby	SK1494	53°26·8′	1°46·9′W	W	110
River West Onny	Shrops	SO3494	52°32·6′	2°58·0′W	W	137
River Wey	Dorset	SY6681	50°37·9′	2°28·5′W	W	194
River Wey	Surrey	SU9444	51°11·5′	0°38·9′W	W	186
River Wey	Surrey	TQ0658	51°18·9′	0°28·3′W	W	187
River Wey	Surrey	TQ0663	51°21·6′	0°28·3′W	W	176,187
River Wey Navigation	Surrey	TQ0562	51°21·1′	0°29·1′W	W	176,187
River Wey Navington	Surrey	TQ0154	51°16·8′	0°32·7′W	W	186
River Wharfe	Leeds	SE1945	53°54·3′	1°42·2′W	W	104
River Wharfe	N Yks	SD9475	54°10·5′	2°5·1′W	W	98
River Wharfe	N Yks	SE4843	53°53·1′	1°15·8′W	W	105
River Wheeler or Afon Chwiler	Denb	SJ1070	53°13·4′	3°20·5′W	W	116
River Wheelock	Ches	SJ7160	53°8·4′	2°25·6′W	W	118
River Whipling	Notts	SK7437	52°55·8′	0°53·5′W	W	129
River Whitewater	Hants	SU7461	51°20·8′	0°55·9′W	W	175,186
River Wid	Essex	TL6801	51°41·2′	0°26·2′E	W	167
River Wid	Essex	TQ6098	51°39·7′	0°19·2′E	W	167,177
River Windrush	Glos	SP1023	51°54·6′	1°50·9′W	W	163
River Windrush	Oxon	SP2213	51°49·1′	1°40·5′W	W	163
River Windrush	Oxon	SP3806	51°45·3′	1°26·6′W	W	164
River Winniford	Dorset	SY4194	50°44·8′	2°49·8′W	W	193
River Winster	Cumbr	SD4285	54°15·7′	2°53·0′W	W	96,97
River Winterborne	Dorset	SY8498	50°47·1′	2°13·2′W	W	194
River Wiske	N Yks	NZ3201	54°24·4′	1°30·0′W	W	93
River Wiske	N Yks	NZ3603	54°25·5′	1°26·3′W	W	93
River Wiske	N Yks	SE3786	54°16·3′	1°25·5′W	W	99
River Wissey	Norf	TL6498	52°33·5′	0°25·6′E	W	143
River Wissey	Norf	TL7299	52°33·9′	0°32·7′E	W	143
River Wissey	Norf	TL8396	52°32·1′	0°42·3′E	W	144
River Witham	Lincs	SK9231	52°52·3′	0°37·6′W	W	130
River Witham	Lincs	TF0471	53°13·8′	0°26·1′W	W	121
River Witham	Lincs	TF2153	53°3·9′	0°11·2′W	W	122
River Witham	Lincs	TF2847	53°0·5′	0°5·1′W	W	131
River Wolf	Devon	ST1303	50°49·4′	3°13·7′W	W	192,193
River Wolf	Devon	SX4188	50°40·4′	4°14·6′W	W	190
River Wolf	Devon	SX4594	50°43·7′	4°11·4′W	W	190
River Worfe	Shrops	SJ7501	52°36·6′	2°21·8′W	W	127
River Worfe	Shrops	SO7594	52°32·8′	2°21·7′W	W	138
River Wreake	Leic	SK6415	52°44·0′	1°2·7′W	W	129
River Wye	Bucks	SU8991	51°36·9′	0°42·5′W	W	175
River Wye	Derby	SK1770	53°13·8′	1°44·3′W	W	119
River Wye	Heref	SO2746	52°6·7′	3°3·6′W	W	148
River Wye	Heref	SO4241	52°4·1′	2°50·4′W	W	148,149,161
River Wye	Heref	SO5517	51°51·2′	2°38·8′W	W	162
River Wye	Heref	SO5536	52°1·5′	2°39·0′W	W	149
River Wye	Monm	ST5492	51°37·7′	2°39·5′W	W	162,172
River Wye	Powys	SN8482	52°25·7′	3°42·0′W	W	135,136
River Wye	Powys	SN9174	52°21·4′	3°35·6′W	W	136,147
River Wye	Powys	SO0053	52°10·2′	3°27·3′W	W	147
River Wye	Powys	SO0746	52°6·5′	3°21·1′W	W	147
River Wye	Powys	SO0844	52°5·4′	3°20·2′W	W	147,160
River Wye / Afon Gwy	Powys	SO1438	52°2·3′	3°14·8′W	W	148,160,161
River Wylye	Wilts	ST8537	51°8·2′	2°12·5′W	W	183
River Wylye	Wilts	SU0038	51°8·7′	1°59·6′W	W	184
River Wyre	Lancs	SD4842	53°52·5′	2°47·0′W	W	102
River Yar	I of W	SZ3587	50°41·1′	1°29·9′W	W	196
River Yar	I of W	SZ5485	50°40·0′	1°13·8′W	W	196
River Yar	I of W	SZ6186	50°40·5′	1°7·8′W	W	196
River Yare	Norf	TG1008	52°38·0′	1°6·6′E	W	144
River Yare	Norf	TG3603	52°34·6′	1°29·4′E	W	134

River Yarrow	Lancs	SD5217	53°39·1′	2°43·2′W	W	108
River Yarrow	Lancs	SD6416	53°38·6′	2°32·3′W	W	109
River Yarty	Devon	ST2507	50°51·7′	3°3·6′W	W	192,193
River Yealm	Devon	SX5449	50°19·6′	4°2·7′W	W	201
River Yealm	Devon	SX6057	50°24·0′	3°57·8′W	W	202
River Yeo	Bath & NE Somer	ST5358	51°19·4′	2°40·1′W	W	172,182
River Yeo	Devon	SS3721	50°58·2′	4°18·9′W	W	190
River Yeo	Devon	SS4322	50°58·8′	4°13·8′W	W	180,190
River Yeo	Devon	SS5734	51°5·5′	4°2·1′W	W	180
River Yeo	Devon	SS7306	50°50·6′	3°47·9′W	W	191
River Yeo	Devon	SS7626	51°1·4′	3°45·7′W	W	180
River Yeo	Devon	SS8326	51°1·5′	3°39·7′W	W	181
River Yeo	Devon	SX8399	50°47·0′	3°39·2′W	W	191
River Yeo	Dorset	ST5913	50°55·1′	2°34·6′W	W	194
River Yeo	N Som	ST4264	51°22·6′	2°49·6′W	W	172,182
River Yeo	Somer	ST5621	50°59·4′	2°37·2′W	W	183
River Yeo (Ivel)	Somer	ST4723	51°0·5′	2°44·9′W	W	193
River Yox	Suff	TM3770	52°16·8′	1°28·9′E	W	156
River Ythan	Aberd	NJ7039	57°26·7′	2°29·5′W	W	29
River Ythan	Aberd	NJ7836	57°25·1′	2°21·5′W	W	29,30
River Ythan	Aberd	NJ9033	57°23·5′	2°9·5′W	W	30
River Ythan	Aberd	NK0026	57°19·7′	1°59·5′W	W	38
Rivestone	Aberd	NJ5545	57°29·8′	2°44·6′W	X	29
Rivetts Fm	Essex	TL4606	51°44·2′	0°7·3′E	FM	167
Rivey Hill	Cambs	TL5648	52°6·7′	0°17·1′E	X	154
Rivington	Lancs	SD6214	53°37·5′	2°34·1′W	T	109
Rivington Country Park	Lancs	SD6214	53°37·5′	2°34·1′W	X	109
Rivington Hall Barn	Lancs	SD6314	53°37·5′	2°33·2′W	A	109
Rivington Lodge	D & G	NX7358	54°54·3′	3°58·4′W	X	83,84
Rivington Moor	Lancs	SD6414	53°37·5′	2°32·2′W	X	109
Rivington Pike	Lancs	SD6413	53°37·0′	2°32·2′W	X	109
Rivington Reservoirs	Lancs	SD6213	53°37·0′	2°34·1′W	W	109
Rivington Service Area	Bolton	SD6211	53°35·9′	2°34·0′W	X	109
Rivling	Cumbr	SD7586	54°16·4′	2°22·6′W	X	98
Rivock	Brad	SE0844	53°53·8′	1°52·3′W	X	104
Rivock Edge	Brad	SE0744	53°53·8′	1°53·2′W	H	104
Rivock Oven	Brad	SE0744	53°53·8′	1°53·2′W	F	104
Rivoulich	Highld	NH5233	57°22·1′	4°27·2′W	X	26
Rivox	D & G	NT0305	55°20·0′	3°31·3′W	X	78
Rivox Burn	D & G	NT0205	55°20·0′	3°32·3′W	W	78
Rivox Fell	D & G	NT0005	55°20·0′	3°34·2′W	H	78
Rivox Moor	D & G	NT0305	55°20·0′	3°31·3′W	H	78
Rivra	Highld	NH6790	57°53·0′	4°14·1′W	X	21
Riv, The	Orkney	HY6847	59°18·8′	2°33·2′W	X	5
Rivulet Ho	Lincs	TF5162	53°8·3′	0°15·9′E	X	122
Rivvalee	Shetld	HP4805	60°43·8′	1°6·7′W	X	1
Rix	Devon	SS9514	50°55·2′	3°29·2′W	X	181
Rixdale Fm	Devon	SX9477	50°35·2′	3°29·5′W	FM	192
Rix Fm	Norf	TF8615	52°42·3′	0°45·6′E	FM	132
Rixhill	Devon	SX4772	50°31·9′	4°9·2′W	X	191,201
Rixlade	Devon	SS4126	51°0·9′	4°15·6′W	X	180,190
Rixlade	Devon	SX9395	50°44·9′	3°30·6′W	X	192
Rixon	Dorset	ST7914	50°55·7′	2°17·5′W	T	194
Rixown	Durham	NZ4334	54°42·2′	1°19·5′W	X	93
Rixton	Warr	SJ6890	53°24·6′	2°28·5′W	T	109
Rixton Moss	Warr	SJ6690	53°24·6′	2°30·3′W	X	109
Rixton New Hall	Warr	SJ6989	53°24·1′	2°27·6′W	X	109
Rixton Old Hall	Warr	SJ6889	53°24·1′	2°28·5′W	X	109
RNAS Yeovilton	Somer	ST5523	51°0·5′	2°38·1′W	X	183
R Neath	Nth Pt Talb	SN8907	51°45·3′	3°36·1′W	W	160
Roach	Devon	SS9604	50°49·8′	3°28·2′W	X	192
Roach Bridge	Lancs	SD5928	53°45·0′	2°36·9′W	T	102
Roachburn Fm	Cumbr	NY6160	54°56·2′	2°36·1′W	FM	86
Roach End	Staffs	SJ9964	53°10·6′	2°0·5′W	X	118
Roaches	Tames	SD9803	53°31·7′	2°1·4′W	T	109
Roaches Ho, The	Staffs	SK0161	53°9·0′	1°58·7′W	X	119
Roaches, The	Staffs	SK0063	53°10·1′	1°59·6′W	X	119
Roach Fm	Devon	ST0201	50°48·3′	3°23·1′W	FM	192
Roach Grange Fm	Leeds	SE4131	53°46·7′	1°22·3′W	FM	105
Roach House Fm	Derby	SK3166	53°11·6′	1°31·8′W	FM	119
Roachill	Devon	SS8422	50°59·4′	3°38·8′W	T	181
Roach Side Fm	Staffs	SJ9962	53°9·5′	2°0·5′W	FM	118
Roach Wood	Wilts	SU0473	51°27·6′	1°56·2′W	F	173
Roadburn	Aberd	NJ5144	57°29·3′	2°48·6′W	X	29
Road Castle	Somer	SS8637	51°7·5′	3°37·4′W	A	181
Roade	Northnts	SP7551	52°9·4′	0°53·8′W	T	152
Roade Cutting	Northnts	SP7552	52°9·9′	0°53·8′W	X	152
Roadend	E Susx	TQ8818	50°56·1′	0°40·9′E	X	189,199
Roadend	S Ayr	NS4125	55°29·8′	4°30·6′W	X	70
Roadend Cottage	Cumbr	NY5046	54°48·6′	2°46·3′W	X	86
Road Fm	Beds	TL0341	52°3·7′	0°29·5′W	FM	153
Road Fm	Bucks	SP8802	51°42·8′	0°43·2′W	FM	165
Road Fm	Devon	SX7497	50°45·8′	3°46·8′W	FM	191
Road Fm	Essex	TL6333	51°58·5′	0°22·8′E	FM	167
Road Fm	Glos	SO7911	51°48·1′	2°17·9′W	FM	162
Road Fm	Heref	SO3324	51°54·9′	2°58·1′W	FM	161
Road Fm	Suff	TM4083	52°23·8′	1°32·1′E	FM	156
Roadfoot	D & G	NX4363	54°56·5′	4°26·6′W	X	83
Roadford Lake (reservoir)	Devon	SX4291	50°42·1′	4°13·9′W	W	190
Road Green	Devon	SY2494	50°44·7′	3°4·3′W	T	192,193
Road Green	Norf	TM2693	52°29·5′	1°20·2′E	T	134
Roadhead	Cumbr	NY5174	55°3·7′	2°45·6′W	T	86
Roadhead	N Lanak	NS8764	55°51·6′	3°47·9′W	X	65
Roadhead Fm	S Lanak	NS9939	55°38·3′	3°35·8′W	FM	72
Roadhead Fm	Stir	NS8187	56°3·9′	3°54·2′W	FM	57,65
Road Hill	Somer	SS8536	51°6·9′	3°38·2′W	H	181
Roadinghead	E Ayr	NS5721	55°28·0′	4°15·3′W	X	71
Road Lane Fm	Dorset	ST7613	50°55·2′	2°20·1′W	FM	194
Roadmeetings	S Lanak	NS8649	55°43·5′	3°48·5′W	T	72
Roadnook Fm	Derby	SK3758	53°7·3′	1°26·4′W	FM	119
Road Pitt Fm	Devon	SY2195	50°45·2′	3°6·8′W	FM	192,193
Roads Fm	Glos	SO5705	51°44·8′	2°37·0′W	FM	162
Roads Fm	Lincs	TF3538	52°55·6′	0°0·9′E	FM	131
Roadside	Aberd	NJ5520	57°16·4′	2°44·3′W	X	37
Roadside	Aberd	NJ6217	57°14·8′	2°37·3′W	X	37
Roadside	Aberd	NJ6906	57°8·9′	2°30·3′W	X	38
Roadside	Aberd	NJ7948	57°31·6′	2°20·6′W	X	29,30
Roadside	Aberd	NJ9765	57°40·7′	2°2·6′W	X	30
Roadside	D & G	NX9763	54°57·3′	3°36·1′W	X	84

Roadside	E Ayr	NS5717	55°25·8′	4°15·2′W	X	71
Roadside	Highld	ND1560	58°31·5′	3°27·1′W	T	11,12
Roadside	Shetld	HU2952	60°15·3′	1°28·1′W	X	3
Roadside Cott	Aberd	NO7989	56°59·8′	2°20·3′W	X	45
Roadside Fm	Cambs	TL3288	52°28·7′	0°3·0′W	FM	142
Road Side Fm	Ches	SJ7674	53°16·0′	2°21·2′W	FM	118
Roadside Fm	Ches	SJ8275	53°16·5′	2°15·8′W	FM	118
Roadside of Catterline	Aberd	NO8678	56°53·8′	2°13·3′W	T	45
Roadside of Croftbain	Moray	NJ2125	57°18·8′	3°18·2′W	X	36
Roadside of Kinneff	Aberd	NO8476	56°52·8′	2°15·3′W	T	45
Roadside of Law	Aberd	NJ5626	57°19·6′	2°43·4′W	X	37
Roadside Woods	Scot Bord	NT7865	55°52·9′	2°20·7′W	F	67
Road Street House	Ches	SJ5463	53°10·0′	2°40·9′W	X	117
Road, The	I Scilly	SV8912	49°55·9′	6°19·7′W	W	203
Roadwater	Somer	ST0338	51°8·2′	3°22·8′W	T	181
Roadway	Devon	SS4742	51°9·6′	4°10·9′W	X	180
Road Weedon	Northnts	SP6359	52°13·8′	1°4·3′W	T	152
Road Wood	Notts	SK8573	53°15·1′	0°43·2′W	F	121
Roag	Highld	NG2743	57°24·0′	6°32·2′W	T	23
Roagh	N Eil	NB0000	57°53·6′	7°3·3′W	W	18
Roag Island	Highld	NG2742	57°23·5′	6°32·2′W	X	23
Roa Island	Cumbr	SD2364	54°4·2′	3°10·2′W	T	96
Roake Fm	Hants	SU3131	51°4·9′	1°33·1′W	FM	185
Roakham Bottom	Wilts	ST9836	51°7·6′	2°1·3′W	X	184
Roall Manor Fm	N Yks	SE5624	53°42·8′	1°8·7′W	FM	105
Roamwood Green Fm	Suff	TM1564	52°14·2′	1°9·3′E	FM	156
Roan	Cumbr	NY4576	55°4·8′	2°51·3′W	X	86
Roan	Scot Bord	NY4889	55°11·8′	2°48·6′W	X	79
Roanaby	Orkney	HY5905	58°56·1′	2°42·3′W	W	6
Roanes, The	Lincs	TF2254	53°4·4′	0°10·3′W	X	122
Roan Fell	D & G	NY4593	55°13·9′	2°51·5′W	H	79
Roan Fell Flow	Scot Bord	NY4591	55°12·9′	2°51·4′W	X	79
Roan Fm	Cumbr	NY4974	55°3·7′	2°47·5′W	FM	86
Roan Head	Orkney	ND3796	58°51·1′	3°5·0′W	X	6,7
Roanhead Fm	Cumbr	SD2075	54°10·1′	3°13·1′W	FM	96
Roanheads	Aberd	NK1346	57°30·5′	1°46·5′W	T	30
Roanlands	Cumbr	SD1885	54°15·5′	3°15·1′W	X	96
Roans	Cumbr	NY6218	54°33·6′	2°34·8′W	X	91
Roansgreen	Cumbr	NY5082	55°8·0′	2°46·6′W	X	79
Roanstrees	Cumbr	NY5178	55°5·9′	2°45·6′W	X	86
Roan, The	Orkney	HY6729	59°9·1′	2°34·1′W	X	5
Roan, The	Scot Bord	NT5543	55°41·0′	2°42·5′W	X	73
Roareim	N Eil	NA6946	58°16·9′	7°38·4′W	X	13
Roar Hill	Aberd	NJ3902	57°6·6′	3°0·0′W	H	37
Roaring Middle		TF5437	52°54·7′	0°17·8′E	X	131
Roas Bank	Medway	TQ8878	51°28·4′	0°42·8′E	X	178
Roast Green	Essex	TL4632	51°58·3′	0°7·9′E	T	167
Roaston	S Ayr	NS3509	55°21·1′	4°35·7′W	X	70,77
Roath	Card	ST1977	51°29·4′	3°9·6′W	T	171
Roath Dock	Card	ST2074	51°27·8′	3°8·7′W	X	171
Roath Park	Card	ST1879	51°30·5′	3°10·5′W	T	171
Robberhill	Ches	SJ5148	53°1·9′	2°43·4′W	X	117
Robber's Bridge	Somer	SS8246	51°12·3′	3°41·0′W	X	181
Robbers' Stone	Wilts	SU0051	51°15·7′	1°59·6′W	X	184
Robbers Waterfall, The or Eas nam Meirleach	Highld	NN1444	56°33·3′	5°1·1′W	W	50
Robbie's Rigg	Cumbr	NY5584	55°9·1′	2°41·9′W	X	80
Robbiewhat	D & G	NY0971	55°1·8′	3°25·0′W	X	85
Robb's Fm	Suff	TL7948	52°6·3′	0°37·2′E	FM	155
Robeanne House Fm	E Yorks	SE8642	53°52·3′	0°41·1′W	FM	106
Roberby Fm	Cumbr	NY5936	54°43·3′	2°37·8′W	FM	91
Roberby Water	Cumbr	NY5936	54°43·3′	2°37·8′W	W	91
Robert Hall	Lancs	SD6369	54°7·2′	2°33·5′W	A	97
Roberthill	D & G	NY1179	55°6·1′	3°23·3′W	X	85
Robert Irvine's Skerries	Shetld	HU4482	60°31·4′	1°11·4′W	X	1,2,3
Robert Irvine's Skerry	Shetld	HU3193	60°37·4′	1°25·5′W	X	1
Robertland	D & G	NX9982	55°7·6′	3°34·6′W	X	78
Robertland	E Ayr	NS4447	55°41·7′	4°28·5′W	X	64
Robert Law	S Lanak	NS8831	55°33·8′	3°46·1′W	H	71,72
Robert Ness	Arg & Bt	NS2781	55°59·7′	4°46·0′W	X	63
Roberton	Aberd	NJ6756	57°35·8′	2°32·7′W	X	29
Roberton	D & G	NX5948	54°48·7′	4°11·2′W	X	83
Roberton	Scot Bord	NT4214	55°25·2′	2°54·5′W	T	79
Roberton	S Lanak	NS9428	55°32·3′	3°40·3′W	T	71,72
Roberton Burn	S Lanak	NS9130	55°33·3′	3°43·2′W	W	71,72
Roberton Law	S Lanak	NS9129	55°32·8′	3°43·2′W	H	71,72
Roberton Mains	S Lanak	NT0947	55°42·7′	3°26·5′W	X	72
Roberts Berry Fm	Wilts	ST8780	51°31·4′	2°10·9′W	FM	173
Robertsbridge	E Susx	TQ7323	50°59·0′	0°28·3′E	T	199
Roberts' Crooie	Shetld	HU4034	60°5·6′	1°16·4′W	X	4
Robertsend	Worcs	SO8334	52°0·5′	2°14·5′W	X	150
Robert's Fm	Bucks	TQ0192	51°37·3′	0°32·1′W	FM	176
Roberts Fm	Kent	TQ8640	51°8·0′	0°39·9′E	FM	189
Robertson Park	Renf	NS4560	55°48·8′	4°28·0′W	X	64
Robert's Seat	N Yks	NY8704	54°26·1′	2°11·6′W	X	91,92
Robertstown	Moray	NJ2344	57°29·0′	3°16·6′W	T	28
Robertstown	Rho Cyn Taf	SO0003	51°43·2′	3°26·5′W	T	170
Roberts Wall Fm	Pemb	SN1000	51°40·2′	4°44·5′W	FM	158
Robert Tait's Hill	Shetld	HU2653	60°15·9′	1°31·3′W	H	3
Roberttown	Kirk	SE1922	53°41·9′	1°42·3′W	T	104
Robeston Back	Pemb	SN0715	51°48·3′	4°47·6′W	T	158
Robeston Cross	Pemb	SM8809	51°44·6′	5°3·9′W	X	157
Robeston Wathen	Pemb	SN0815	51°48·3′	4°46·7′W	T	158
Robeston West	Pemb	SM8809	51°44·6′	5°3·9′W	T	157
Robey Fields Fm	Derby	SK4146	53°0·8′	1°22·9′W	FM	129
Robgill Mains	D & G	NY2471	55°1·9′	3°10·9′W	X	85
Robgill Tower	D & G	NY2471	55°1·9′	3°10·9′W	X	85
Rob Hall	Suff	TM0570	52°17·6′	1°0·8′E	X	144,155
Rob Hall Fm	Rut	TF0110	52°40·9′	0°30·0′W	FM	130
Robhurst	Kent	TQ9134	51°4·6′	0°44·0′E	T	189
Robie Geo	Orkney	ND2393	58°49·3′	3°19·5′W	X	7
Robie's Geo	Shetld	HU4424	60°0·2′	1°12·2′W	X	4
Robies Gorse Fm	Leic	SK3704	52°38·2′	1°26·8′W	FM	140
Robie's Haven	Aberd	NK1137	57°25·6′	1°48·6′W	W	30
Robie's Knowe	Orkney	HY3626	59°7·2′	3°6·6′W	A	6
Robiesland	S Lanak	NS8941	55°39·2′	3°45·4′W	X	71,72
Robie's Noust	Shetld	HU1761	60°20·2′	1°41·0′W	X	3
Robie's Point	Shetld	HU3537	60°7·2′	1°21·7′W	X	4
Robieston	Aberd	NJ5242	57°28·2′	2°47·6′W	X	29
Robin-a-Tiptoe Hill	Leic	SK7704	52°37·9′	0°51·3′W	H	141

Robin Cross Hill	N Yks	SE0695	54°21·3′	1°54·0′W	X	99
Robin Friend	Norf	TG1443	52°56·7′	1°11·5′E	X	133
Robin Hill	Staffs	SJ9057	53°6·8′	2°8·6′W	T	118
Robin Ho	Sund	NZ3346	54°48·7′	1°28·8′W	X	88
Robin Hood	Cumbr	NY2232	54°40·9′	3°12·2′W	X	89,90
Robin Hood	Cumbr	NY5206	54°27·1′	2°44·0′W	H	90
Robin Hood	Derby	SK2772	53°14·9′	1°35·3′W	T	119
Robin Hood	Lancs	SD5211	53°35·8′	2°43·1′W	T	108
Robin Hood	Leeds	SE3227	53°44·5′	1°30·5′W	T	104
Robin Hood	Peterb	TL1398	52°34·3′	0°19·6′W	A	142
Robinhood End	Essex	TL7036	52°0·0′	0°29·0′E	T	154
Robin Hood Fm	Notts	SK5849	53°2·3′	1°7·7′W	FM	129
Robin Hood Fm	N Yks	NZ2200	54°23·9′	1°39·2′W	FM	93
Robin Hood Hill	Notts	SK6353	53°4·5′	1°3·2′W	X	120
Robin Hood Hill (Settlement)	Notts	SK6353	53°4·5′	1°3·2′W	A	120
Robin Hood's Arbour	Win & Maid	SU8580	51°31·0′	0°46·1′W	X	175
Robin Hood's Arbour (Earthwork)	Win & Maid	SU8580	51°31·0′	0°46·1′W	A	175
Robin Hood's Ball	Wilts	SU1046	51°13·0′	1°51·0′W	A	184
Robin Hood's Bay	N Yks	NZ9504	54°25·6′	0°31·7′W	W	94
Robin Hood's Bay	N Yks	NZ9505	54°26·1′	0°31·7′W	T	94
Robin Hood's Bog	Northum	NU0826	55°31·9′	1°52·0′W	X	75
Robin Hood's Bower	Wilts	ST8742	51°10·9′	2°10·8′W	A	183
Robin Hood's Butts	N Yks	NZ7111	54°29·6′	0°53·8′W	X	94
Robin Hood's Butts	N Yks	NZ9601	54°24·0′	0°30·9′W	X	94
Robin Hoods Butts	Shrops	SO4396	52°33·8′	2°50·1′W	X	137
Robin Hood's Butts	Somer	ST2214	50°55·4′	3°6·2′W	X	193
Robin Hood's Butts	Somer	ST2312	50°54·4′	3°5·3′W	X	193
Robin Hoods Butts (Tumuli)	Shrops	SO4396	52°33·8′	2°50·1′W	A	137
Robin Hood's Butts (Tumuli)	Somer	ST2214	50°55·4′	3°6·2′W	A	193
Robin Hood's Butts (Tumuli)	Somer	ST2312	50°54·4′	3°5·3′W	A	193
Robin Hood's Butts (Tumulus)	N Yks	NZ7111	54°29·6′	0°53·8′W	A	94
Robin Hood's Butts (Tumulus)	N Yks	NZ9601	54°24·0′	0°30·9′W	A	94
Robin Hood's Cave	Derby	SK2483	53°20·8′	1°38·0′W	X	110
Robin Hood's Cave	Notts	SK5154	53°5·1′	1°13·9′W	X	120
Robin Hood's Cave	Notts	SK6670	53°13·6′	1°0·3′W	X	120
Robin Hood's Cross	Derby	SK1880	53°19·2′	1°43·4′W	X	110
Robin Hood's Grave	Cald	SE1721	53°41·4′	1°44·1′W	A	104
Robin Hood's Grave	Cumbr	NY6110	54°29·3′	2°35·7′W	X	91
Robin Hood's Hills	Notts	SK5154	53°5·1′	1°13·9′W	X	120
Robin Hood's Howl	N Yks	SE6886	54°16·1′	0°56·9′W	X	94,100
Robin Hood's Picking Rods	Derby	SK0091	53°25·2′	1°59·6′W	A	110
Robin Hood's Stoop	Derby	SK2180	53°19·2′	1°40·7′W	X	110
Robin Hood's Stride	Derby	SK2262	53°9·5′	1°39·9′W	X	119
Robin Hood's Well	Derby	SK2679	53°18·7′	1°36·2′W	W	119
Robin Hood's Well	Donc	SE5111	53°35·8′	1°13·4′W	X	111
Robin Hood's Well	Notts	SK4949	53°2·4′	1°15·7′W	W	129
Robin Hood's Well	N Yks	SD8678	54°12·1′	2°12·5′W	X	98
Robin Hood's Well	N Yks	SD9765	54°5·1′	2°2·3′W	W	98
Robin Hood's Well	N Yks	SE0586	54°16·4′	1°55·0′W	W	98
Robin Hood Way	Notts	SK5043	52°59·2′	1°14·9′W	X	129
Robin Hood Way	Notts	SK6265	53°10·9′	1°3·9′W	X	120
Robin How	Somer	SS9042	51°10·2′	3°34·0′W	A	181
Robin Park	Wigan	SD5605	53°32·6′	2°39·4′W	X	108
Robinrock Flothers	Northum	NY7471	55°2·2′	2°24·0′W	X	86,87
Robins	W Susx	SU8425	51°1·3′	0°47·8′W	T	186,197
Robins Acre	Essex	TL5209	51°45·8′	0°12·6′E	X	167
Robins Bank	Powys	SN9788	52°29·1′	3°30·6′W	X	136
Robin's Bottom Plantn	N Yks	TA0080	54°12·6′	0°27·6′W	F	101
Robin's Brook	Essex	TL8424	51°53·0′	0°40·8′E	W	168
Robin's Castle	Durham	NZ0627	54°38·5′	1°54·0′W	X	92
Robinscroft	Heref	SO6936	52°1·5′	2°26·7′W	X	149
Robin's Dam	Pth & Kin	NO0439	56°32·3′	3°33·2′W	W	52,53
Robins Fm	Surrey	SU9733	51°5·5′	0°36·5′W	FM	186
Robins Folly Fm	Beds	TL0657	52°12·3′	0°26·5′W	FM	153
Robinsland	Scot Bord	NT1551	55°44·9′	3°20·8′W	X	65,72
Robinson	Cumbr	NY2016	54°32·2′	3°13·8′W	H	89,90
Robinson Crags	Cumbr	NY2017	54°32·8′	3°13·8′W	X	89,90
Robinson Haggs	N Yks	NZ8511	54°29·5′	0°40·8′W	X	94
Robinson Ho	Cumbr	NY4739	54°44·8′	2°49·0′W	X	90
Robinson Lodge	N Yks	SE5366	54°5·5′	1°11·0′W	X	100
Robinson's Cairn	Cumbr	NY1712	54°30·0′	3°16·5′W	X	89,90
Robinson's Corner	Ches	SJ6754	53°5·2′	2°29·2′W	X	118
Robinson's End	Warw	SP3291	52°31·2′	1°31·3′W	T	140
Robinson's Moss	Derby	SK0499	53°29·5′	1°56·0′W	X	110
Robinson's Tent	N Yks	SD7264	54°4·5′	2°25·3′W	X	98
Robin's Rock	Corn	SX0350	50°19·3′	4°45·7′W	X	200,204
Robin's Rocks	Corn	SW4238	50°11·4′	5°36·5′W	X	203
Robins Ward	S Ayr	NX1579	55°4·5′	4°53·4′W	X	76
Robin's Wood	Kent	TQ7634	51°4·9′	0°31·2′E	F	188
Robins Wood Hill	Glos	SO8415	51°50·2′	2°13·5′W	H	162
Robin Tup's Plantn	E Loth	NT6070	55°55·5′	2°38·0′W	F	67
Robin Upright's Hill	Somer	ST1538	51°8·3′	3°12·5′W	X	181
Robin Wood	Derby	SK3525	52°49·5′	1°28·4′W	F	128
Robin Wood	Northnts	SP5237	52°2·0′	1°14·1′W	F	151
Robin Wood's Rock	Northum	NU2327	55°32·4′	1°37·7′W	X	75
Robjohns Fm	Essex	TL6831	51°57·4′	0°27·1′E	FM	167
Roblaw Hall	Cumbr	NY2853	54°52·2′	3°6·9′W	X	85
Robleston Hall	Pemb	SM9121	51°51·2′	5°1·7′W	X	157,158
Robley Belt	Hants	SU5054	51°17·2′	1°16·6′W	F	185
Robolls Hill	Arg & Bt	NR3966	55°49·3′	6°9·6′W	H	60,61
Roborough	Devon	SS5635	51°6·0′	4°3·0′W	X	180
Roborough	Devon	SS5717	50°56·3′	4°1·7′W	T	180
Roborough	Devon	SX5062	50°26·6′	4°6·4′W	T	201
Roborough Castle	Devon	SS7345	51°11·6′	3°48·7′W	X	180
Roborough Down	Devon	SX5167	50°29·3′	4°5·7′W	X	201
Roborough Ho	Devon	SX5063	50°27·1′	4°6·4′W	X	201
Rob Rash	Cumbr	NY3304	54°25·9′	3°1·6′W	X	90
Rob Ridding	Cumbr	NY8112	54°30·4′	2°17·2′W	X	91,92
Robridding	Derby	SK3264	53°10·6′	1°30·9′W	X	119
Rob Roy's Cave	Stir	NN3310	56°15·4′	4°41·3′W	X	50,56
Rob Roy's House	Arg & Bt	NN1516	56°18·3′	4°59·0′W	X	50,56
Rob Roy's Prison	Stir	NN3302	56°11·1′	4°41·0′W	X	56
Robroyston	C of Glas	NS6366	55°52·3′	4°10·9′W	T	64
Rob's Bog	S Lanak	NS9625	55°30·7′	3°38·4′W	X	72
Rob's Craig	D & G	NX7043	54°46·2′	4°0·8′W	X	83,84
Robsheugh Burn	Northum	NZ0874	55°3·9′	1°52·1′W	W	88
Robsheugh Fm	Northum	NZ0974	55°3·9′	1°51·1′W	FM	88
Rob's Hill	Aberd	NO8184	56°57·1′	2°18·3′W	X	45
Rob's Hill	S Lanak	NS8130	55°33·2′	3°52·8′W	X	71,72
Robson Ho	N Yks	SD9796	54°21·8′	2°2·4′W	X	98
Robson's Spring	N Yks	SE6281	54°13·5′	1°2·5′W	F	100
Rob's Pikes	Northum	NY6899	55°17·3′	2°29·8′W	X	80
Rob's Reed	Angus	NO4952	56°39·7′	2°49·5′W	X	54
Rob's Reed (Dun)	Angus	NO4952	56°39·7′	2°49·5′W	A	54
Robstone	S Ayr	NX2199	55°15·4′	4°48·6′W	X	76
Robury Ring	Shrops	SO3993	52°32·1′	2°53·6′W	A	137
Roby	Know	SJ4390	53°24·5′	2°51·0′W	T	108
Roby Mill	Lancs	SD5107	53°33·7′	2°44·0′W	T	108
Roby's Fm	Lancs	SD4303	53°31·5′	2°51·2′W	FM	108
Roc Dearg	Arg & Bt	NN0300	56°9·4′	5°9·9′W	X	55
Rocester	Staffs	SK1039	52°57·1′	1°50·7′W	T	128
Roch	Pemb	SM8721	51°51·1′	5°5·2′W	T	157
Rochallie	Pth & Kin	NO1551	56°38·8′	3°22·7′W	X	53
Rochard Dike	N Yks	SE1061	54°2·9′	1°50·4′W	W	99
Roch Br	Pemb	SM8722	51°51·6′	5°5·2′W	X	157
Rochdale	Roch	SD8913	53°37·0′	2°9·6′W	T	109
Rochdale Canal	Cald	SD9524	53°43·0′	2°4·1′W	W	103
Rochdale Canal	Cald	SE0026	53°44·1′	1°59·6′W	W	104
Rochdale Canal	Roch	SD9419	53°40·3′	2°5·0′W	W	109
Roche	Corn	SW9860	50°24·5′	4°50·2′W	T	200
Roche Abbey	Roth	SK5489	53°23·9′	1°10·9′W	A	111,120
Roche Castle	Carm	SN2910	51°46·0′	4°28·3′W	A	159
Roche Court	Hants	SU5808	50°52·3′	1°10·2′W	X	196
Roche Court	Wilts	SU2534	51°6·5′	1°38·2′W	X	184
Roche Court Down	Wilts	SU2535	51°7·1′	1°38·2′W	X	184
Roche Grange	Staffs	SJ9963	53°10·1′	2°0·5′W	T	118
Rochehead Fm	Shrops	SO6475	52°22·5′	2°31·3′W	FM	138
Roche Rock	Corn	SW9959	50°24·0′	4°49·3′W	X	200
Roches Moutonnees	Highld	NJ0025	57°18·5′	3°39·1′W	X	36
Roche Sta	Corn	SW9861	50°25·1′	4°50·2′W	X	200
Rochester	Medway	TQ7268	51°23·3′	0°28·7′E	T	178
Rochester	Northum	NY8398	55°16·8′	2°15·6′W	T	80
Rochester Airport	Medway	TQ7464	51°21·1′	0°30·3′E	X	178,188
Rochester Fm	Essex	TL7216	51°49·2′	0°30·1′E	FM	167
Rochetts	Essex	TQ5694	51°37·6′	0°15·6′E	X	167,177
Rochford	Essex	TQ8790	51°34·9′	0°42·3′E	T	178
Rochford	Worcs	SO6268	52°18·8′	2°33·0′W	T	138
Rochford Mount	Worcs	SO6366	52°17·7′	2°32·2′W	X	138,149
Rochford Tower	Lincs	TF3544	52°58·8′	0°1·1′E	A	131
Roch Gate	Pemb	SM8720	51°50·5′	5°5·1′W	T	157
Rochsoles	N Lanak	NS7567	55°53·1′	3°59·5′W	X	64
Rochuln	Moray	NJ0747	57°30·5′	3°32·7′W	X	27
Rock	Caer	ST1798	51°40·7′	3°11·6′W	T	171
Rock	Corn	SW9476	50°33·1′	4°54·1′W	T	200
Rock	Devon	ST2702	50°49·0′	3°1·8′W	T	193
Rock	Devon	SX7896	50°45·3′	3°43·4′W	X	191
Rock	I of W	SZ4283	50°38·9′	1°24·0′W	X	196
Rock	Northum	NU2020	55°28·7′	1°40·6′W	T	75
Rock	Nth Pt Talb	SS7993	51°37·6′	3°44·5′W	T	170
Rock	Pemb	SS0599	51°39·6′	4°48·8′W	X	158
Rock	Somer	ST3222	50°59·8′	2°57·8′W	T	193
Rock	Worcs	SO7371	52°20·4′	2°23·4′W	T	138
Rock	W Susx	TQ1213	50°54·6′	0°24·0′W	T	198
Rock and Spindle, The	Fife	NO5415	56°19·8′	2°44·2′W	X	59
Rock Basin	Derby	SK2178	53°18·2′	1°40·7′W	X	119
Rockbeare	Devon	SY0294	50°44·5′	3°23·0′W	T	192
Rockbeare Hill	Devon	SY0694	50°44·5′	3°19·6′W	X	192
Rockbeare Ho	Devon	SY0394	50°44·5′	3°22·1′W	X	192
Rockbourne	Hants	SU1118	50°57·9′	1°50·2′W	T	184
Rockbourne Down	Hants	SU1021	50°59·5′	1°51·1′W	X	184
Rock Br	Powys	SO2965	52°17·0′	3°2·1′W	X	137,148
Rock Castle	N Yks	NZ1806	54°27·2′	1°42·9′W	X	92
Rock Castle	N Yks	SE1191	54°19·1′	1°49·4′W	X	99
Rockcliffe	Cumbr	NY3561	54°56·6′	3°0·5′W	T	85
Rockcliffe	D & G	NX8453	54°51·8′	3°48·0′W	T	84
Rockcliffe	Glos	SP1524	51°55·1′	1°46·5′W	X	163
Rockcliffe	Lancs	SD8722	53°41·9′	2°11·4′W	T	103
Rockcliffe Cross	Cumbr	NY3462	54°57·1′	3°1·4′W	T	85
Rockcliffe Fm	Red & Cl	NZ7419	54°33·9′	0°50·9′W	FM	94
Rockcliffe Marsh	Cumbr	NY3263	54°57·7′	3°3·3′W	W	85
Rockcliffe Moss	Cumbr	NY3762	54°57·2′	2°58·6′W	F	85
Rock Coppice	Worcs	SO7673	52°21·5′	2°20·7′W	F	138
Rock Cottage	Shrops	SJ6632	52°53·3′	2°29·9′W	X	127
Rock Dingle	Powys	SO2067	52°18·0′	3°10·0′W	X	137,148
Rockells Fm	Essex	TL4636	52°0·4′	0°8·0′E	FM	154
Rockend	Aberd	NK0226	57°19·7′	1°57·6′W	X	38
Rock End	Staffs	SJ8956	53°6·3′	2°9·5′W	T	118
Rocken End	I of W	SZ4975	50°34·6′	1°18·1′W	X	196
Rockenhayne	Devon	SY1990	50°42·5′	3°8·4′W	X	192,193
Rockerhayne	Devon	SY2196	50°45·7′	3°6·8′W	X	192,193
Rockers, The	Northum	NZ3183	55°8·7′	1°30·4′W	X	81
Rock Ferry	Wirral	SJ3286	53°22·2′	3°0·9′W	T	108
Rockfield	Arg & Bt	NR8655	55°44·7′	5°24·1′W	X	62
Rockfield	Highld	NH9282	57°49·1′	3°48·6′W	T	21
Rockfield	Monm	SO4814	51°49·6′	2°44·9′W	T	161
Rockfield Fm	Monm	SO4615	51°50·1′	2°46·6′W	FM	161
Rockfield Ho	Derby	SK1469	53°13·3′	1°47·0′W	X	119
Rockfield Ho	Highld	NH9082	57°49·1′	3°50·6′W	X	21
Rockfield Mills	Highld	NH9082	57°49·1′	3°50·6′W	X	21
Rockfield Park	Monm	SO4815	51°50·1′	2°44·9′W	X	161
Rock Fm	Ches	SJ5366	53°11·6′	2°41·8′W	FM	117
Rock Fm	Denb	SJ2145	53°0·0′	3°10·2′W	FM	117
Rock Fm	Derby	SK2161	53°9·0′	1°40·8′W	FM	119
Rock Fm	Glos	SO6820	51°52·9′	2°27·5′W	FM	162
Rock Fm	Heref	SO6455	52°11·8′	2°31·2′W	FM	149
Rock Fm	I of M	SC3180	54°11·5′	4°35·0′W	FM	95
Rock Fm	Kent	TQ6852	51°14·8′	0°24·8′E	FM	188
Rock Fm	Kent	TQ7940	51°8·1′	0°33·9′E	FM	188
Rock Fm	Leic	SK4815	52°44·1′	1°16·9′W	FM	129
Rock Fm	Pemb	SM8921	51°51·1′	5°3·4′W	FM	157,158
Rock Fm	Pemb	SN1008	51°44·6′	4°44·7′W	FM	158
Rock Fm	Shrops	SJ3239	52°56·9′	3°0·3′W	FM	126
Rock Fm	Shrops	SO5275	52°22·5′	2°41·9′W	FM	137,138
Rock Fm	Somer	ST1634	51°6·2′	3°11·6′W	FM	181
Rock Fm	Warw	SP3573	52°21·5′	1°28·8′W	FM	140
Rockford	Devon	SS7547	51°12·7′	3°47·0′W	T	180
Rockford	Hants	SU1508	50°52·5′	1°46·8′W	T	195
Rockford Common	Hants	SU1708	50°52·5′	1°45·1′W	X	195
Rockgreen	Shrops	SO5275	52°22·5′	2°41·9′W	T	137,138
Rockhallhead	D & G	NY0576	55°4·4′	3°28·8′W	X	85
Rockhallhead Hill	D & G	NY0676	55°4·4′	3°27·9′W	H	85
Rockhall Hotel	D & G	NY0575	55°3·9′	3°28·8′W	X	85
Rockhall Mains	D & G	NY0475	55°3·9′	3°29·8′W	X	84
Rockhall Moor	D & G	NY0676	55°4·4′	3°27·9′W	X	85
Rockham Bay	Devon	SS4546	51°11·8′	4°12·7′W	W	180
Rockhampton	S Glos	ST6593	51°38·3′	2°30·0′W	T	162,172
Rockhampton Rhine	S Glos	ST6494	51°38·9′	2°30·8′W	W	162,172
Rockhead	Corn	SX0784	50°37·7′	4°43·4′W	T	200
Rock Head Fm	N Yks	NZ7604	54°25·8′	0°49·3′W	FM	94
Rock Head Fm	N Yks	NZ8411	54°29·5′	0°41·8′W	FM	94
Rock Hill	Shrops	SO2879	52°24·5′	3°3·1′W	H	137,148
Rockhill	Shrops	SO2879	52°24·5′	3°3·1′W	T	137,148
Rockhillflat	D & G	NY1487	55°10·4′	3°20·6′W	X	78
Rockhill Fm	Arg & Bt	NN0721	56°20·8′	5°6·9′W	FM	50,56
Rockhill Fm	Dorset	ST7115	50°56·3′	2°24·4′W	FM	183
Rockhill Fm	Shrops	SO5672	52°20·9′	2°38·4′W	FM	137,138
Rockhills	Essex	TL5905	51°43·5′	0°18·5′E	X	167
Rock Hills	Hants	SU2302	50°49·3′	1°40·0′W	X	195
Rock Ho	Devon	ST0113	50°54·7′	3°24·1′W	X	181
Rock Ho	Northum	NY7560	54°56·3′	2°23·0′W	X	86,87
Rock Ho	N Yks	SE7594	54°20·4′	0°50·4′W	X	94,100
Rock Ho	Powys	SJ2704	52°38·0′	3°4·3′W	X	126
Rock Ho	Staffs	SJ7637	52°56·0′	2°21·0′W	X	127
Rock Ho	Torbay	SX9267	50°29·8′	3°31·0′W	X	202
Rockhole Hill	Red & Cl	NZ7519	54°33·9′	0°50·0′W	X	94
Rockhope Burn	Durham	NY9539	54°45·0′	2°4·2′W	W	91,92
Rockhouse Bank	E Susx	TQ6705	50°49·4′	0°22·7′E	X	199
Rock House Fm	N Yks	SE9289	54°17·5′	0°34·8′W	FM	94,101
Rockhouse Fm	Somer	ST2233	51°5·7′	3°6·4′W	FM	182
Rockhurst Fm	Derby	SK2158	53°7·4′	1°40·8′W	FM	119
Rocking Hall	N Yks	SE1157	54°0·8′	1°49·5′W	X	104
Rockingham	Northnts	SP8691	52°30·8′	0°43·6′W	T	141
Rockingham Forest	Northnts	SP9490	52°30·2′	0°36·5′W	X	141
Rockingham Park	Northnts	SP8690	52°30·3′	0°43·6′W	X	141
Rockingham's Fm	Essex	TL9216	51°48·8′	0°47·5′E	FM	168
Rocking Moor	N Yks	SE1057	54°0·8′	1°50·4′W	X	104
Rocking Stone	Cald	SE0330	53°46·2′	1°56·9′W	X	104
Rocking Stone	D & G	NX4069	54°59·6′	4°29·6′W	X	83
Rocking Stone	D & G	NX5976	55°3·8′	4°12·0′W	X	77
Rocking Stone	N Ayr	NS3855	55°45·9′	4°34·5′W	X	63
Rocking Stone	N Yks	SE0858	54°1·3′	1°52·3′W	X	104
Rocking Stone	N Yks	SE1157	54°0·8′	1°49·5′W	X	104
Rocking Stone	N Yks	SE1556	54°0·2′	1°45·9′W	X	104
Rocking Stone	S Ayr	NX4292	55°12·1′	4°28·5′W	X	77
Rocking Stones	Sheff	SK1797	53°28·4′	1°44·2′W	X	110
Rockland All Saints	Norf	TL9996	52°31·8′	0°56·4′E	T	144
Rockland Broad	Norf	TG3305	52°35·8′	1°26·8′E	W	134
Rockland Manor	Norf	TL9898	52°32·9′	0°55·6′E	X	144
Rocklands	Cered	SN1949	52°6·8′	4°38·2′W	X	145
Rocklands Fm	E Susx	TQ6610	50°52·2′	0°21·9′E	FM	199
Rocklands Fm	Heref	SO5718	51°51·8′	2°37·1′W	FM	162
Rockland St Mary	Norf	TG3104	52°35·3′	1°25·0′E	T	134
Rockland St Peter	Norf	TL9997	52°32·3′	0°56·5′E	T	144
Rocklane Fm	Bucks	SP8825	51°55·2′	0°42·8′W	FM	165
Rockley	Notts	SK7174	53°15·7′	0°55·7′W	T	120
Rockley	Shrops	SO2594	52°32·6′	3°6·0′W	A	137
Rockley	Wilts	SU1671	51°26·5′	1°45·8′W	T	173
Rockley Abbey Fm	Barns	SE3301	53°30·5′	1°29·7′W	FM	110,111
Rockley Down	Wilts	SU1473	51°27·6′	1°47·5′W	X	173
Rockley Fm	Devon	SS7038	51°7·8′	3°51·1′W	FM	180
Rockley Ford	Somer	ST7254	51°17·3′	2°23·7′W	T	183
Rockley Sands	Poole	SY9791	50°43·3′	2°2·2′W	X	195
Rockleys Fm	Essex	TL9010	51°45·6′	0°45·6′E	FM	168
Rock Lodge Fm	Derby	SK1371	53°14·4′	1°47·9′W	FM	119
Rock Lough Hos	Northum	NU1819	55°28·1′	1°42·5′W	X	81
Rock McGibbon	D & G	NX0863	54°55·7′	4°59·4′W	X	82
Rock Midstead	Northum	NU1820	55°28·7′	1°42·5′W	X	75
Rock Mill	Devon	ST2702	50°49·0′	3°1·8′W	X	193
Rock Mill	Northum	NU2021	55°29·2′	1°40·6′W	X	75
Rockmoor Down	Hants	SU3459	51°20·0′	1°30·3′W	X	174
Rockmoor Fm	Worcs	SO7271	52°20·4′	2°24·3′W	FM	138
Rock Moor Ho	Northum	NU1820	55°28·7′	1°42·5′W	X	75
Rockmount	I of M	SC2783	54°13·1′	4°38·8′W	X	95
Rock Nab	Northum	NU1720	55°28·7′	1°43·4′W	X	75
Rocknell Fm	Devon	ST0516	50°56·4′	3°20·7′W	FM	181
Rockness	Glos	ST8498	51°41·1′	2°13·5′W	T	162
Rock Nose	Devon	SS4129	51°2·5′	4°15·7′W	X	180
Rock of Providence	D & G	NX4434	54°40·9′	4°24·8′W	X	83
Rock of Woolbury	Shrops	SO3179	52°24·5′	3°0·5′W	X	137,148
Rockram Wood	Hants	SU2913	50°55·2′	1°34·9′W	F	196
Rockrobin	E Susx	TQ6232	51°4·1′	0°19·1′E	T	188
Rocks	Somer	SS9124	51°0·5′	3°32·8′W	X	181
Rocksavage	Halton	SJ5180	53°19·1′	2°43·7′W	T	108
Rocksea Fm	Corn	SX0273	50°31·6′	4°47·2′W	FM	200
Rocks Fm	Ches	SJ9883	53°20·9′	2°1·4′W	FM	109
Rocks Fm	E Susx	TQ8017	50°55·7′	0°34·1′E	FM	199
Rockshaw Ho	Surrey	TQ3153	51°15·9′	0°6·9′W	X	187
Rockside	Arg & Bt	NR2263	55°47·1′	6°25·6′W	X	60
Rocksley	Mil Key	SP8338	52°2·3′	0°47·0′W	X	152
Rocks of Balmedie	Aberd	NJ9518	57°15·4′	2°4·5′W	X	38
Rocks of Smeargeo	Orkney	HY7141	59°15·5′	2°30·0′W	X	5
Rock South Fm	Northum	NU1918	55°27·6′	1°41·5′W	FM	81
Rocks Park	E Susx	TQ4621	50°58·4′	0°5·2′E	T	198
Rockstead Fm	Hants	SU1217	50°57·4′	1°49·4′W	FM	184
Rocks, The	S Glos	ST7970	51°26·0′	2°17·7′W	X	172
Rockstone Manor Fm	Suff	TM3576	52°20·1′	1°27·4′E	FM	156
Rockstowes	Glos	ST7797	51°40·5′	2°19·6′W	T	162
Rock, The	C of Aber	NJ8314	57°13·2′	2°16·4′W	X	38
Rock, The	Devon	SX4571	50°31·3′	4°10·8′W	X	201
Rock, The	Heref	SO5363	52°16·0′	2°40·9′W	X	137,138,149
Rock, The	Shrops	SO3596	52°33·7′	2°57·1′W	X	137
Rockvale	D & G	NX6345	54°47·1′	4°7·4′W	X	83

Rock View	N Yks	SE1965	54°5·1′	1°42·2′W	X	99
Rockville	Arg & Bt	NS2390	56°4·5′	4°50·2′W	X	56
Rockville	E Loth	NT5581	56°1·4′	2°42·9′W	X	66
Rockwell End	Bucks	SU7988	51°35·3′	0°51·2′W	T	175
Rockwell Green	Somer	ST1220	50°58·6′	3°14·8′W	T	181,193
Rockwells Fm	Somer	ST6838	51°8·7′	2°27·1′W	FM	183
Rockwood Park	W Susx	TQ3836	51°6·6′	0°1·3′W	X	187
Rocky Covert	Scot Bord	NT7224	55°30·8′	2°26·2′W	F	74
Rockyden	Aberd	NJ7230	57°21·8′	2°27·5′W	X	29
Rocky Hill	I Scilly	SV9111	49°55·4′	6°18·0′W	T	203
Rockylane Fm	Oxon	SU7183	51°32·7′	0°58·2′W	FM	175
Rockylls Hall	Suff	TL9960	52°12·4′	0°55·1′E	X	155
Rocky Plain	N Yks	SE4697	54°22·2′	1°17·1′W	X	100
Rocky Valley	Corn	SX0789	50°40·4′	4°43·5′W	X	190,200
Rocombe Bottom	Devon	SY3294	50°44·7′	2°57·4′W	X	193
Rocott Lodge	Leic	SK8111	52°41·7′	0°47·7′W	X	130
Roda Geo	Shetld	HU3167	60°23·4′	1°25·8′W	X	3
Rodbaston	Staffs	SJ9211	52°42·0′	2°6·7′W	T	127
Rodborough	Glos	SO8404	51°44·3′	2°13·5′W	T	162
Rodborough Common	Glos	SO8503	51°43·8′	2°12·6′W	X	162
Rodborough Hill	Surrey	SU9341	51°9·9′	0°39·8′W	X	186
Rodbourne	Swin	SU1486	51°34·6′	1°47·5′W	T	173
Rodbourne	Wilts	ST9383	51°33·0′	2°5·7′W	T	173
Rodbourne Bottom	Wilts	ST9382	51°32·4′	2°5·7′W	T	173
Rodbourne Rail Fm	Wilts	ST9384	51°33·5′	2°5·7′W	FM	173
Rodbridge Corner	Suff	TL8543	52°3·5′	0°42·3′E	T	155
Rodbridge Ho	Suff	TL8643	52°3·5′	0°43·2′E	X	155
Rodd	Heref	SO3262	52°15·4′	2°59·4′W	T	137,148
Roddam	Northum	NU0220	55°28·7′	1°57·7′W	T	75
Roddam and Green	Northum	NU2338	55°38·3′	1°37·6′W	X	75
Roddam Burn	Northum	NT9918	55°27·6′	2°0·5′W	W	81
Roddam Burn	Northum	NU0320	55°28·7′	1°56·7′W	W	75
Roddam Rigg	Northum	NU0219	55°28·1′	1°57·7′W	X	81
Rodden	Dorset	SY6184	50°39·5′	2°32·7′W	T	194
Rodden Barn Fm	Dorset	SY6184	50°39·5′	2°32·7′W	FM	194
Rodden Brook	Somer	ST8047	51°13·5′	2°16·8′W	W	183
Roddenbury Hill	Somer	ST7943	51°11·4′	2°17·6′W	H	183
Rodden Down Fm	Somer	ST7947	51°13·5′	2°17·7′W	FM	183
Rodden Fm	Somer	ST7946	51°13·0′	2°17·7′W	FM	183
Rodden House	Dorset	SY6184	50°39·5′	2°32·7′W	A	194
Roddenloft	E Ayr	NS4824	55°29·4′	4°23·9′W	X	70
Rodden Manor	Somer	ST7947	51°13·5′	2°17·7′W	A	183
Rodden Ridge	Dorset	SY6183	50°39·0′	2°32·7′W	X	194
Rodd Hurst	Heref	SO3262	52°15·4′	2°59·4′W	T	137,148
Roddige	Staffs	SK1713	52°43·1′	1°44·5′W	X	128
Roddinghill	N Ayr	NS3642	55°38·9′	4°35·9′W	X	63,70
Roddinglaw	C of Edin	NT1671	55°55·7′	3°20·2′W	X	65,66
Roddlesworth	Lancs	SD6521	53°41·3′	2°31·4′W	X	102,103
Roddlesworth Resrs	Lancs	SD6522	53°41·8′	2°31·4′W	W	102,103
Rodds Barn	Heref	SO3154	52°11·0′	3°0·2′W	X	148
Rodd's Bridge	Corn	SS2104	50°48·7′	4°32·1′W	X	190
Rodd, The	Heref	SO3262	52°15·4′	2°59·4′W	A	137,148
Roddymoor	Durham	NZ1536	54°43·4′	1°45·6′W	T	92
Rode	Somer	ST8053	51°16·8′	2°16·8′W	T	183
Rode Br	Somer	ST8054	51°17·3′	2°16·8′W	A	183
Rode Common	Somer	ST8154	51°17·3′	2°16·0′W	X	183
Rodegreen	Ches	SJ8867	53°12·2′	2°10·4′W	X	118
Rode Hall	Ches	SJ8157	53°6·8′	2°16·6′W	X	118
Rode Hall Fm	Ches	SJ8866	53°11·7′	2°10·4′W	FM	118
Rode Heath	Ches	SJ8057	53°6·8′	2°17·5′W	T	118
Rodeheath	Ches	SJ8766	53°11·7′	2°11·3′W	T	118
Rode Hill	Somer	ST8054	51°17·3′	2°16·8′W	T	183
Rodel	N Eil	NG0483	57°44·6′	6°58·0′W	T	18
Rodelpark	N Eil	NG0583	57°44·6′	6°57·0′W	X	18
Rode Mill	Ches	SJ8257	53°6·8′	2°15·7′W	X	118
Rode Moors	Devon	SS9804	50°49·8′	3°26·5′W	X	192
Roden	Wrekin	SJ5716	52°44·6′	2°37·8′W	T	126
Roden Downs	W Berks	SU5382	51°32·3′	1°13·8′W	X	174
Rodenhurst Hall	Wrekin	SJ5815	52°44·1′	2°36·9′W	X	126
Roden's Hall	Wrex	SJ4048	53°1·8′	2°53·3′W	X	117
Rode Pool	Ches	SJ8157	53°6·8′	2°16·6′W	W	118
Rodford	S Glos	ST6981	51°31·9′	2°26·4′W	T	172
Rodge Brook	I of W	SZ4590	50°42·7′	1°21·4′W	W	196
Rodge Hill	Worcs	SO7462	52°15·6′	2°22·5′W	X	138,150
Rodge Hill Fm	Worcs	SO7462	52°15·6′	2°22·5′W	FM	138,150
Rodgeley Lodge	Staffs	SJ8629	52°51·7′	2°12·1′W	X	127
Rodgerhead	Stir	NS7988	56°4·4′	3°56·2′W	X	57
Rodger Law	S Lanak	NS9405	55°19·9′	3°39·8′W	H	71,78
Rodger Law	S Lanak	NS9818	55°27·0′	3°36·3′W	H	78
Rodger's Fm	E Susx	TQ8214	50°54·0′	0°35·7′E	FM	199
Rodgers, The	E Loth	NT6184	56°3·1′	2°37·1′W	X	67
Rodgers Wood	Bucks	SU9696	51°39·5′	0°36·3′W	F	165,176
Rodger Trod	N Yks	TA0196	54°21·2′	0°26·3′W	X	101
Rodgrove	Somer	ST7424	51°1·1′	2°21·9′W	T	183
Rodham Fm	Cambs	TL4598	52°33·9′	0°8·8′E	FM	143
Rodhill Gate	Lancs	SD7647	53°55·4′	2°21·5′W	X	103
Rodhuish	Somer	ST0139	51°8·7′	3°24·5′W	T	181
Rodhuish Common	Somer	SS9939	51°8·7′	3°26·3′W	X	181
Rodie Cleuch	Scot Bord	NT2121	55°28·8′	3°14·6′W	X	73
Rodinbain	E Ayr	NS3714	55°23·8′	4°34·0′W	X	70
Rodinghead Ho	E Ayr	NS4831	55°33·2′	4°24·1′W	X	70
Rodings, The	Essex	TL5814	51°48·4′	0°17·9′E	X	167
Rodington	Wrekin	SJ5814	52°43·6′	2°36·9′W	T	126
Rodington Heath	Wrekin	SJ5714	52°43·6′	2°37·8′W	T	126
Roding Valley Sta	Redbr	TQ4192	51°36·8′	0°2·6′E	X	177
Rodknoll Fm	Derby	SK3069	53°13·3′	1°32·6′W	FM	119
Rodlease Ho	Hants	SZ3298	50°47·1′	1°32·4′W	X	196
Rodley	Glos	SO7411	51°48·1′	2°22·2′W	T	162
Rodley	Leeds	SE2236	53°49·4′	1°39·5′W	T	104
Rodmarton	Glos	ST9497	51°40·5′	2°4·8′W	T	163
Rodmarton Manor	Glos	ST9497	51°40·5′	2°4·8′W	X	163
Rodmead Fm	Wilts	ST8136	51°7·6′	2°15·9′W	FM	183
Rodmead Hill	Wilts	ST8236	51°7·6′	2°15·0′W	H	183
Rodmell	E Susx	TQ4105	50°49·9′	0°0·5′E	T	198
Rodmer Clough	Cald	SD9529	53°45·7′	2°4·1′W	T	103
Rodmersham	Kent	TQ9261	51°19·2′	0°45·7′E	T	178
Rodmersham Green	Kent	TQ9161	51°19·2′	0°44·9′E	T	178
Rod Moor	Sheff	SK2688	53°23·5′	1°36·1′W	X	110
Rodmore Fm	Glos	SO5803	51°43·7′	2°36·1′W	FM	162
Rodmore Fm	Somer	ST6537	51°8·1′	2°29·6′W	FM	183
Rodney Fm	Bath & NE Somer	ST7969	51°25·4′	2°17·7′W	FM	172
Rodney Ho	Oxon	SP5821	51°53·3′	1°9·0′W	X	164
Rodney Sch	Notts	SK6858	53°7·1′	0°58·6′W	X	120
Rodney's Pillar	Powys	SJ2914	52°43·4′	3°2·7′W	X	126
Rodney's Stone	Moray	NH9857	57°35·8′	3°41·9′W	A	27
Rodney Stoke	Somer	ST4850	51°15·0′	2°44·3′W	T	182
Rodone Hotel	Scot Bord	NT2321	55°28·9′	3°12·7′W	X	73
Rodridge Fm	Durham	NZ4135	54°42·7′	1°21·4′W	FM	93
Rodridge Hall	Durham	NZ4136	54°43·3′	1°21·4′W	X	93
Rodsall Manor	Surrey	SU9245	51°12·0′	0°40·6′W	X	186
Rodshill	Aberd	NJ7739	57°26·7′	2°22·5′W	X	29,30
Rodsley	Derby	SK2040	52°57·7′	1°41·7′W	T	119,128
Rodsleywood	Derby	SK1941	52°58·2′	1°42·6′W	X	119,128
Rod's Pot	Somer	ST4758	51°19·4′	2°45·2′W	X	172,182
Rods, The	Suff	TM3948	52°4·9′	1°29·7′E	F	169
Rodsworthy	Devon	SS7822	50°59·3′	3°43·9′W	X	180
Rodway	Somer	ST2540	51°9·5′	3°4·0′W	T	182
Rodway	Wrekin	SJ6618	52°45·8′	2°29·8′W	T	127
Rodway Fm	Somer	ST2540	51°9·5′	3°4·0′W	FM	182
Rodway Fms	Devon	ST2403	50°49·5′	3°4·4′W	FM	192,193
Rodway Hill	Glos	SO7820	51°52·9′	2°18·8′W	X	162
Rodway Hill	S Glos	ST6675	51°28·6′	2°29·0′W	X	172
Rodway Manor	Wrekin	SJ6618	52°45·8′	2°29·8′W	X	127
Rodwell	Dorset	SY6778	50°36·3′	2°27·6′W	T	194
Rodwell Fm	Surrey	TQ0362	51°21·1′	0°30·9′W	FM	176,186
Rodwell Fm	Wilts	SU0374	51°28·1′	1°57·0′W	FM	173
Roe	N Eil	NF7576	57°39·7′	7°26·6′W	X	18
Roebank Burn	N Ayr	NS3555	55°45·9′	4°37·4′W	W	63
Roe Barrow	Devon	SS6944	51°11·1′	3°52·1′W	A	180
Roe Beck	Cumbr	NY3941	54°45·9′	2°56·5′W	W	85
Roe Beck	N Yks	NY9505	54°26·7′	2°4·2′W	W	91,92
Roe Beck Head	N Yks	NY9404	54°26·1′	2°5·1′W	X	91,92
Roeberry	Orkney	ND4293	58°49·5′	2°59·8′W	X	7
Roeberry Taing	Orkney	ND4293	58°49·5′	2°59·8′W	X	7
Roe Br	Lancs	SD4840	53°51·5′	2°47·0′W	X	102
Roebuck Fm	Ches	SJ7380	53°19·2′	2°23·9′W	FM	109
Roebuck Fm	Somer	ST1336	51°7·2′	3°14·2′W	FM	181
Roebuck Fm	Suff	TM0952	52°7·8′	1°3·6′E	FM	155
Roebuck Gate Fm	Somer	ST1335	51°6·7′	3°14·2′W	FM	181
Roebuck Low	Oldham	SD9607	53°33·8′	2°3·2′W	T	109
Roebuck Wood	W Berks	SU5073	51°27·5′	1°16·4′W	F	174
Roe Carr	N Lincs	SE7305	53°32·4′	0°53·5′W	X	112
Roe Clett	Shetld	HU3978	60°29·3′	1°16·9′W	X	2,3
Roecliffe	N Yks	SE3765	54°5·0′	1°25·6′W	T	99
Roecliffe Fm	Leic	SK3714	52°43·6′	1°26·7′W	FM	128
Roecliffe Grange	N Yks	SE3666	54°5·6′	1°26·6′W	X	99
Roecliffe Manor	Leic	SK5312	52°42·4′	1°12·5′W	X	129
Roecliffe Moor	N Yks	SE3664	54°4·5′	1°26·6′W	X	99
Roe Cross	Tames	SJ9896	53°27·9′	2°1·4′W	T	109
Roedale	Bri & Hov	TQ3107	50°51·1′	0°8·0′W	X	198
Roedean	Bri & Hov	TQ3403	50°48·9′	0°5·5′W	T	198
Roe Downs	Hants	SU6636	51°7·4′	1°3·0′W	X	185,186
Roe End	Herts	TL0415	51°49·7′	0°29·1′W	T	166
Roe Fm	Lancs	SD4741	53°52·0′	2°47·9′W	FM	102
Roe Green	Herts	TL2208	51°45·7′	0°13·5′W	T	166
Roe Green	Herts	TL3133	51°59·0′	0°5·1′W	T	166
Roe Green	Salf	SD7501	53°30·5′	2°22·2′W	T	109
Roehampton	Wan	TQ2274	51°27·3′	0°14·2′W	T	176
Roehampton Gate	Rich	TQ2174	51°27·3′	0°15·1′W	X	176
Roehead	Cumbr	NY4723	54°36·2′	2°48·8′W	X	90
Roeheath	E Susx	TQ3919	50°57·4′	0°0·9′W	X	198
Roehill	Cumbr	NY3944	54°47·5′	2°56·5′W	X	85
Roehill	Moray	NJ4555	57°35·2′	2°54·7′W	X	28,29
Roe Ho	Cumbr	NY4038	54°44·3′	2°55·5′W	X	90
Roe Ho	Northum	NZ0360	54°56·3′	1°56·8′W	X	87
Roehoe Stud	Notts	SK6529	52°51·5′	1°1·7′W	X	129
Roehoe Wood	Notts	SK6429	52°51·5′	1°2·6′W	F	129
Roe Inclosure	Hants	SU1908	50°52·5′	1°43·4′W	F	195
Roe Lane Fm	Notts	SK7092	53°25·4′	0°56·4′W	FM	112
Roe Lee	Black w Dar	SD6830	53°46·2′	2°28·7′W	T	103
Roel Fm	Glos	SP0724	51°55·1′	1°53·5′W	FM	163
Roel Gate	Glos	SP0524	51°55·1′	1°55·2′W	X	163
Roel Hill Fm	Glos	SP0524	51°55·1′	1°55·2′W	FM	163
Roemead Fm	Somer	ST6147	51°13·5′	2°33·1′W	FM	183
Roe Ness	Orkney	HY4631	59°10·0′	2°56·2′W	X	5,6
Roe Ness	Shetld	HU3242	60°9·9′	1°24·9′W	X	4
Roeness	Shetld	HU3243	60°10·5′	1°24·9′W	X	4
Roe Park	Ches	SJ8558	53°7·4′	2°13·0′W	F	118
Roepark Fm	Ches	SJ8658	53°7·4′	2°12·1′W	FM	118
Roer Water	Shetld	HU3386	60°33·6′	1°23·4′W	W	1,2,3
Roesound	Shetld	HU3245	60°11·6′	1°24·9′W	X	4
Roe Sound	Shetld	HU3366	60°22·9′	1°23·6′W	W	2,3
Roesound	Shetld	HU3465	60°22·3′	1°22·5′W	X	2,3
Roestock	Herts	TL2105	51°44·1′	0°14·5′W	T	166
Roe, The	Denb	SJ0374	53°15·5′	3°26·8′W	T	116
Roewath	Cumbr	NY3844	54°47·5′	2°57·4′W	X	85
Roe Wood	Herts	TL3134	51°59·6′	0°5·1′W	F	153
Roe Wood	Notts	SK6958	53°7·1′	0°57·7′W	F	120
Roewood Fm	Notts	SK7058	53°7·1′	0°56·8′W	FM	120
Ro-fawr	Carm	SN5720	51°51·9′	4°4·2′W	X	159
Roffey	Essex	TL6218	51°50·5′	0°21·5′E	X	167
Roffey	W Susx	TQ1932	51°4·7′	0°17·7′W	T	187
Roffey Hall	Essex	TL4909	51°45·8′	0°9·9′E	X	167
Roffey Hurst	W Susx	TQ2032	51°4·7′	0°16·8′W	X	187
Rofford Hall	Oxon	SU6298	51°40·9′	1°5·8′W	X	164,165
Roga Field	Shetld	HU3283	60°32·0′	1°24·5′W	X	1,3
Rogan's Seat	N Yks	NY9103	54°25·6′	2°7·9′W	H	91,92
Rogart	Highld	NC7303	58°0·1′	4°8·5′W	T	16
Rogart Sta	Highld	NC7201	57°59·1′	4°9·4′W	X	16
Rogate	W Susx	SU8023	51°0·3′	0°51·2′W	T	197
Rogate Common	W Susx	SU7925	51°1·4′	0°52·0′W	F	186,197
Rogate Lodge	W Susx	SU8024	51°0·8′	0°51·2′W	X	197
Roger Ground	Cumbr	SD3597	54°22·1′	2°59·6′W	T	96,97
Roger Head	Cumbr	NY6622	54°35·8′	2°31·2′W	X	91
Rogerhill	S Lanak	NS7843	55°40·2′	3°55·9′W	X	71
Roger Howe	Cumbr	NY6103	54°25·5′	2°35·6′W	X	91
Rogerlay	Carm	SN4108	51°45·1′	4°17·8′W	X	159
Rogerley Hall	Durham	NZ0137	54°43·9′	1°58·6′W	X	92
Rogerley Hill	Durham	NZ1753	54°52·5′	1°43·7′W	X	88
Roger Moor	Lancs	SD9143	53°53·2′	2°7·8′W	X	103
Rogermoor Fm	Durham	NZ0222	54°35·8′	1°57·7′W	FM	92
Roger Ridding Fm	Cumbr	SD3489	54°17·8′	3°0·4′W	FM	96,97
Roger Sand	Lincs	TF4741	52°57·0′	0°11·7′E	X	131
Rogersceugh	Cumbr	NY2159	54°55·4′	3°13·5′W	X	85
Rogerseat	Aberd	NJ7136	57°25·1′	2°28·5′W	X	29
Rogers End	Essex	TL5842	52°3·5′	0°18·7′E	X	154
Roger's Fm	Suff	TL9341	52°2·3′	0°49·2′E	FM	155
Roger's Fm	W Susx	TQ1207	50°51·3′	0°24·1′W	FM	198
Roger's Hill Fm	Dorset	SY8195	50°45·5′	2°15·8′W	FM	194
Rogershook	Pemb	SN0517	51°49·3′	4°49·4′W	X	158
Rogerstone	Newp	ST2787	51°34·9′	3°2·8′W	T	171
Rogerstone Grange	Monm	ST5096	51°39·9′	2°43·0′W	F	162
Rogers' Tower	Corn	SW4834	50°9·4′	5°31·3′W	X	203
Rogers Wood	E Susx	TQ8525	50°59·9′	0°38·6′E	F	189,199
Roger's Wood	Kent	TQ8237	51°6·4′	0°36·4′E	F	188
Rogerthorpe Manor	Wakf	SE4615	53°38·0′	1°17·8′W	X	111
Rogerton	S Lanak	NS6256	55°46·9′	4°11·6′W	T	64
Rogeston	Pemb	SM8816	51°48·4′	5°4·1′W	X	157
Roghaiseal Beag	N Eil	NB3342	58°17·4′	6°32·9′W	X	8,13
Roghaiseal Mòr	N Eil	NB3341	58°16·9′	6°32·8′W	H	8,13
Rogheadh	Highld	NG2160	57°32·9′	6°39·4′W	X	23
Rogie	Highld	NH4459	57°35·9′	4°36·2′W	X	26
Rogie Falls	Highld	NH4458	57°35·4′	4°36·1′W	W	26
Rogiehill	Aberd	NJ8008	57°10·0′	2°19·4′W	X	38
Rogiet	Monm	ST4687	51°35·0′	2°46·4′W	T	171,172
Rogiet Moor	Monm	ST4687	51°35·0′	2°46·4′W	X	171,172
Rogues Alley	Cambs	TF3605	52°37·8′	0°1·0′E	X	142
Rohallion Castle	Pth & Kin	NO0340	56°32·8′	3°34·2′W	A	52,53
Rohallion Lodge	Pth & Kin	NO0438	56°31·7′	3°33·2′W	X	52,53
Roileag	N Ayr	NR8840	55°36·7′	5°21·5′W	X	62,69
Roineabhal	N Eil	NG0486	57°46·2′	6°58·2′W	H	18
Ròinebhal	N Eil	NB2321	58°5·7′	6°41·6′W	H	13,14
Roineval	Highld	NG4135	57°20·2′	6°17·8′W	H	32
Roinn a' Bhogha Shàmhaich	Highld	NG7002	57°3·4′	5°47·1′W	X	33
Roinn a' Bhuic	N Eil	NB4057	58°25·7′	6°26·8′W	X	8
Roinn an Fhaing Mhóir	Highld	NG7260	57°34·6′	5°48·3′W	X	24
Roinn a' Roidh	N Eil	NB5065	58°30·4′	6°17·0′W	X	8
Roinn Clùmhach	Arg & Bt	NS1152	55°43·7′	5°0·2′W	X	63,69
Roinnean a' Chamais	Highld	NC0230	58°13·1′	5°21·8′W	X	15
Roinn na Beinne	Highld	NG7302	57°3·5′	5°44·2′W	H	33
Rois-Bheinn	Highld	NM7577	56°50·1′	5°40·9′W	H	40
Ròisinis	N Eil	NF8653	57°27·8′	7°13·8′W	X	22
Roisinish Bay	N Eil	NF8763	57°33·2′	7°13·5′W	W	18
Roisnis an Ear	N Eil	NB5034	58°13·7′	6°15·0′W	X	8
Roisnis an Iar	N Eil	NB5033	58°13·2′	6°15·0′W	X	8
Roke	Oxon	SU6293	51°38·2′	1°5·9′W	T	164,175
Rokeby Close	Durham	NZ1111	54°29·9′	1°49·4′W	X	92
Rokeby Grange	Durham	NZ0714	54°31·5′	1°53·1′W	X	92
Rokeby Park	Durham	NZ0813	54°31·0′	1°52·2′W	X	92
Rokefield	Surrey	TQ1349	51°14·0′	0°22·5′W	X	187
Roke Fm	Dorset	SY8395	50°45·5′	2°14·1′W	FM	194
Roke Fm	Hants	SU5418	50°57·8′	1°13·5′W	FM	185
Roke Fm	Hants	SU7649	51°14·3′	0°54·3′W	FM	186
Rokeles Hall	Norf	TF9301	52°34·6′	0°51·3′E	X	144
Roke Manor	Hants	SU3322	51°0·0′	1°31·4′W	X	185
Roke Manor Fm	Hants	SU3322	51°0·0′	1°31·4′W	FM	185
Rokemarsh	Oxon	SU6292	51°37·6′	1°5·9′W	T	164,175
Roker	Sund	NZ4059	54°55·7′	1°22·1′W	T	88
Roker Rocks	Sund	NZ4159	54°55·7′	1°21·2′W	X	88
Rokers	W Susx	TQ1312	50°54·0′	0°23·2′W	X	198
Rolf's Fm	E Susx	TQ6127	51°1·4′	0°18·1′E	FM	188,199
Rolf's Wood	Dorset	ST8813	50°55·2′	2°9·9′W	F	194
Roliphant's Fm	Devon	SS9914	50°55·2′	3°25·8′W	FM	181
Rollesby	Norf	TG4515	52°40·9′	1°37·9′E	T	134
Rollesby Broad	Norf	TG4614	52°40·3′	1°38·7′E	W	134
Rolleston	Devon	SS5627	51°1·7′	4°2·8′W	X	180
Rolleston	Leic	SK7300	52°35·8′	0°54·9′W	T	141
Rolleston	Notts	SK7452	53°3·8′	0°53·3′W	T	120
Rollestone	Devon	SX9295	50°44·9′	3°31·5′W	X	192
Rollestone	Sheff	SK3684	53°21·3′	1°27·1′W	T	110,111
Rollestone	Wilts	SU0743	51°11·4′	1°53·6′W	T	184
Rollestone Camp	Wilts	SU0944	51°11·9′	1°51·9′W	T	184
Rolleston Lodge Fm	Leic	SK7201	52°36·4′	0°55·8′W	FM	141
Rolleston on Dove	Staffs	SK2327	52°50·6′	1°39·1′W	T	128
Rolleston Park	Staffs	SK2126	52°50·1′	1°40·9′W	X	128
Rolleston Wood	Leic	SP7499	52°35·3′	0°54·1′W	F	141
Rolley Low	Derby	SK1873	53°15·5′	1°43·4′W	A	119
Rollick Stones	Derby	SK0898	53°29·0′	1°52·4′W	X	110
Rolling Br	N Yks	SE5044	53°53·6′	1°13·9′W	X	105
Rolling Gate Crags	N Yks	SE0060	54°2·4′	1°59·6′W	X	98
Rollington Fm	Dorset	SY9682	50°38·5′	2°3·0′W	FM	195
Rollinson Haggs	Cumbr	NY8205	54°26·7′	2°16·2′W	X	91,92
Rollright Heath Fm	Oxon	SP3431	51°58·8′	1°29·9′W	FM	151
Rollright Stones	Warw	SP2931	51°58·8′	1°34·3′W	A	151
Rolls Fm	Essex	TL5007	51°44·7′	0°10·8′E	FM	167
Roll's Fm	Essex	TL7514	51°48·1′	0°32·7′E	FM	167
Rolls Fm	Essex	TL9408	51°44·4′	0°49·0′E	FM	168
Rollshayes Fm	Devon	ST1704	50°50·0′	3°10·3′W	FM	192,193
Roll's Lode	Cambs	TL5779	52°23·4′	0°18·8′E	W	143
Rolls Mill	Dorset	ST7713	50°55·2′	2°19·2′W	T	194
Rolls Park	Essex	TQ4494	51°37·8′	0°5·2′E	X	167,177
Rollstone	Devon	SS4123	50°59·3′	4°15·5′W	X	180,190
Rollstone Fm	Hants	SU4302	50°49·2′	1°23·0′W	FM	196
Rollswood Fm	Warw	SP1256	52°12·4′	1°49·1′W	FM	150
Rolly	Shrops	SJ3222	52°47·7′	3°0·1′W	X	126
Rolphs Farmhouse	Essex	TL8020	51°51·2′	0°37·2′E	X	168
Rolphs Fm	Essex	TL7012	51°47·1′	0°28·3′E	FM	167
Rolphy Green	Essex	TL6715	51°48·7′	0°25·8′E	X	167
Rolster Br	Devon	SX7756	50°23·7′	3°43·5′W	X	202
Rolston	E Yorks	TA2145	53°53·5′	0°9·1′W	T	107
Rolstone	N Som	ST3962	51°21·5′	2°52·2′W	T	182
Rolstone Barton	Devon	SS7905	50°50·1′	3°42·7′W	X	191
Rolston Sands	E Yorks	TA2145	53°53·5′	0°9·1′W	X	107
Rolston Seats	E Yorks	TA1945	53°53·5′	0°10·9′W	X	107
Rolts Wood	Cambs	TL2682	52°25·5′	0°8·4′W	F	142
Rolva, The	Powys	SO2790	52°30·4′	3°4·1′W	X	137
Rolvenden	Kent	TQ8431	51°3·2′	0°37·9′E	T	188

Rolvenden Layne	Kent	TQ8530	51°2·6′	0°38·7′E	T	189
Rolvenden Sta	Kent	TQ8632	51°3·7′	0°39·7′E	X	189
Ro Lwyd	Conwy	SH7650	53°2·2′	3°50·6′W	X	115
Romach Hill	Moray	NJ0650	57°32·1′	3°33·7′W	H	27
Romach Loch	Moray	NJ0652	57°33·2′	3°33·8′W	W	27
Romaldkirk	Durham	NY9922	54°35·8′	2°0·5′W	T	92
Romaldkirk Moor	Durham	NY9621	54°35·3′	2°3·3′W	X	91,92
Roman Bank	Notts	SK6488	53°23·3′	1°1·9′W	X	120
Roman Bank	Shrops	SO5191	52°31·1′	2°42·9′W	X	137,138
Roman Bank (Earthwork)	Notts	SK6488	53°23·3′	1°1·9′W	A	111,120
Romanby	N Yks	SE3693	54°20·1′	1°26·4′W	T	99
Roman Camp Cottages	W Loth	NT0770	55°55·1′	3°28·8′W	X	65
Romancamp Gate	Moray	NJ3661	57°38·3′	3°3·9′W	X	28
Roman Camp, The	Norf	TG1841	52°55·6′	1°15·0′E	X	133
Roman Castle	N Yks	SE3484	54°15·3′	1°28·3′W	X	99
Roman Fell	Cumbr	NY7520	54°34·7′	2°22·8′W	H	91
Roman Galley (PH)	Kent	TR2267	51°21·7′	1°11·7′E	X	179
Roman Hill	Aberd	NJ4118	57°15·2′	2°58·2′W	H	37
Roman Hill	Suff	TM5493	52°28·8′	1°44·8′E	T	134
Roman Hill Fm	Essex	TM0021	51°51·3′	0°54·7′E	FM	168
Roman Hill Ho	Essex	TM0021	51°51·3′	0°54·7′E	X	168
Roman Hole	Lincs	TF1596	53°27·1′	0°15·7′W	X	113
Romannobridge	Scot Bord	NT1648	55°43·3′	3°19·8′W	T	72
Romanno House Fm	Scot Bord	NT1648	55°43·3′	3°19·8′W	FM	72
Roman Park	Pth & Kin	NO0120	56°22·0′	3°35·7′W	X	52,53,58
Roman Ridge	Leeds	SE4229	53°45·6′	1°21·4′W	X	105
Roman Ridge (Dyke)	Roth	SK4296	53°27·8′	1°21·6′W	A	111
Roman Ridge (Roman Road)	Leeds	SE4229	53°45·6′	1°21·4′W	R	105
Roman Ridge (Roman Road)	Wakf	SE4915	53°38·0′	1°15·1′W	R	111
Roman River	Essex	TM0120	51°50·8′	0°55·5′E	W	168
Roman Road Dairy	Dorset	SY5991	50°43·3′	2°34·5′W	X	194
Romans Castle	Pemb	SM8910	51°45·2′	5°3·0′W	A	157,158
Romansleigh	Devon	SS7220	50°58·1′	3°49·0′W	T	180
Roman Steps	Gwyn	SH6530	52°51·3′	3°59·9′W	X	124
Romanway	Cumbr	NY4937	54°43·8′	2°47·1′W	X	90
Roman Woods	W Susx	TQ1133	51°5·4′	0°24·5′W	F	187
Rombalds Moor	Brad	SE0845	53°54·3′	1°52·3′W	X	104
Romden Castle	Kent	TQ8942	51°9·0′	0°42·5′E	X	189
Romden Wood	Kent	TQ8941	51°8·4′	0°42·5′E	F	189
Rome	Angus	NO5266	56°47·2′	2°46·7′W	X	44
Rome	N Yks	SD7962	54°3·5′	2°18·8′W	X	98
Rome Fm	Notts	SK8470	53°13·5′	0°44·1′W	FM	121
Rome Hill	S Lanak	NS9724	55°30·2′	3°37·4′W	H	72
Romeley Hall Fm	Derby	SK4774	53°15·9′	1°17·3′W	FM	120
Romers Common	Worcs	SO5962	52°15·5′	2°35·6′W	X	137,138,149
Romer's Wood	Worcs	SO6063	52°16·1′	2°34·8′W	F	138,149
Romer Wood	Bucks	SP7123	51°54·3′	0°57·7′W	F	165
Romesbeach	D & G	NX8674	55°3·1′	3°46·6′W	X	84
Romesdal	Highld	NG4053	57°29·8′	6°19·9′W	T	23
Romford	Dorset	SU0709	50°53·1′	1°53·6′W	T	195
Romford	Hav	TQ5289	51°35·0′	0°12·0′E	T	177
Romford	Kent	TQ6441	51°8·9′	0°21·1′E	T	188
Romiley	Stock	SJ9490	53°24·6′	2°5·0′W	T	109
Romney, Hythe and Dymchurch Railway	Kent	TR0827	51°0·5′	0°58·3′E	X	189
Romney Lock	Win & Maid	SU9777	51°29·2′	0°35·8′W	X	175,176
Romney Marsh	Kent	TR0529	51°1·6′	0°55·8′E	X	189
Romney Salts	Kent	TR0623	50°58·4′	0°56·6′E	X	189
Romney Sands	Kent	TR0823	50°58·3′	0°58·2′E	X	189
Romney Street	Kent	TQ5461	51°19·9′	0°13·0′E	X	177,188
Rompa	Shetld	HU4023	59°59·7′	1°16·5′W	X	4
Romp Hall	Beds	TL0457	52°12·3′	0°28·3′W	X	153
Romping Downs	Surrey	SU9153	51°16·4′	0°41·3′W	X	186
Romsey	Hants	SU3521	50°59·5′	1°29·7′W	T	185
Romsey Oak Fm	Wilts	ST8155	51°17·9′	2°16·0′W	FM	173
Romsey Town	Cambs	TL4758	52°12·3′	0°9·5′E	T	154
Roms Greave	Cald	SE0032	53°47·3′	1°59·6′W	X	104
Romshed Fm	Kent	TQ5551	51°14·5′	0°13·6′E	FM	188
Romsley	Shrops	SO7882	52°26·4′	2°19·0′W	T	138
Romsley	Worcs	SO9679	52°24·8′	2°3·1′W	T	139
Romsley Hill	Worcs	SO9678	52°24·2′	2°3·1′W	T	139
Ronachan	Arg & Bt	NR7454	55°43·9′	5°35·5′W	X	62
Ronachan Bay	Arg & Bt	NR7455	55°44·4′	5°35·6′W	W	62
Ronachan Ho	Arg & Bt	NR7455	55°44·4′	5°35·6′W	X	62
Ronachan Point	Arg & Bt	NR7455	55°44·4′	5°35·6′W	X	62
Ronague	I of M	SC2472	54°7·1′	4°41·2′W	X	95
Rònaigh	N Eil	NF8955	57°29·0′	7°10·9′W	X	22
Rònaigh Beag	N Eil	NF8957	57°30·0′	7°11·1′W	X	22
Ronaldsvoe	Orkney	ND4393	58°49·5′	2°58·7′W	T	7
Ronald's Well	Highld	NC6133	58°16·1′	4°21·7′W	W	16
Rona or Rònaidh	N Eil	HW8132	59°7·4′	5°49·1′W	X	8
Ronas Hill	Shetld	HU3083	60°32·0′	1°26·7′W	H	1,3
Ronas Voe	Shetld	HU2881	60°31·0′	1°28·9′W	W	3
Rona, The	Shetld	HU3260	60°19·6′	1°24·7′W	W	3
Roncombe Fm	Devon	SY1694	50°44·6′	3°11·1′W	FM	192,193
Roncombe Gate	Devon	SY1694	50°44·6′	3°11·1′W	X	192,193
Rondlay	Wrekin	SJ7007	52°39·8′	2°26·2′W	T	127
Rondle Wood	W Susx	SU8225	51°1·3′	0°49·5′W	F	186,197
Rones, The	Moray	NJ3724	57°18·4′	3°2·3′W	X	37
Roneval	N Eil	NF8114	57°6·6′	7°15·7′W	H	31
Ron Hill	Shrops	SO6776	52°23·1′	2°28·7′W	X	138
Ronish	N Eil	NF8011	57°5·0′	7°16·5′W	X	31
Ronksley Hall Fm	Sheff	SK2787	53°23·0′	1°35·2′W	FM	110
Ronksley Moor	Derby	SK1595	53°27·3′	1°46·0′W	X	110
Ronkswood	Worcs	SO8654	52°11·3′	2°11·9′W	T	150
Ronnachmore	Arg & Bt	NR3058	55°44·7′	6°17·7′W	X	60
Ron, The	Aberd	NK1157	57°36·4′	1°48·5′W	X	30
Roobies Fm	Somer	ST2140	51°9·5′	3°7·4′W	FM	182
Rood Ashton	Wilts	ST8855	51°17·9′	2°9·9′W	X	173
Roodee	Ches	SJ4065	53°11·0′	2°53·5′W	X	117
Rood End	Sand	SP0088	52°29·6′	1°59·6′W	T	139
Rooden Resr	Roch	SD9711	53°36·0′	2°2·3′W	W	109
Roodge	Devon	SS5526	51°1·1′	4°3·7′W	X	180
Roodland	S Ayr	NS3819	55°26·5′	4°33·2′W	X	70
Roodlands Fm	Kent	TQ4748	51°13·0′	0°6·7′E	FM	188
Roodrans, The	Shetld	HU2784	60°32·7′	1°30·0′W	X	3
Roods	Durham	NZ0313	54°31·0′	1°56·8′W	X	92

Roog	Shetld	HU3452	60°15·3′	1°22·6′W	X	3
Rooier Head	Shetld	HU5762	60°20·5′	0°57·5′W	X	2
Rooin	Shetld	HU6392	60°36·7′	0°50·5′W	X	1,2
Rook	Devon	SX6060	50°25·6′	3°57·9′W	X	202
Rookabear	Devon	SS5230	51°3·3′	4°6·3′W	X	180
Rook Barugh	N Yks	SE7282	54°14·0′	0°53·7′W	X	100
Rookbeare Fm	Devon	SS8507	50°51·3′	3°37·6′W	FM	191
Rookby	Cumbr	NY8010	54°29·3′	2°18·1′W	T	91,92
Rookby Scarth	Cumbr	NY8009	54°28·8′	2°18·1′W	X	91,92
Rookcross Fm	W Susx	TQ1620	50°58·3′	0°20·5′W	FM	198
Rookdale	N Yks	SE9171	54°7·8′	0°36·0′W	X	101
Rooke Fm	Corn	SW9976	50°33·2′	4°49·9′W	FM	200
Rookelands	Kent	TR0630	51°2·2′	0°56·7′E	X	189
Rooken	Northum	NY8096	55°15·7′	2°18·5′W	X	80
Rook End	Essex	TL5532	51°58·1′	0°15·8′E	T	167
Rooken Edge	Northum	NY7896	55°15·7′	2°20·3′W	H	80
Rooker Hill	N Yks	SE3969	54°7·2′	1°23·8′W	X	99
Rookery	Heref	SO4176	52°23·0′	2°51·6′W	F	137,148
Rookery	Warw	SP1866	52°17·7′	1°43·8′W	X	151
Rookery Dairy	Dorset	ST5403	50°49·7′	2°38·8′W	X	194
Rookery Fm	Bath & NE Somer	ST5158	51°19·4′	2°41·8′W	FM	172,182
Rookery Fm	Bucks	SP6818	51°51·6′	1°0·4′W	FM	164,165
Rookery Fm	Bucks	SP7126	51°55·9′	0°57·6′W	FM	165
Rookery Fm	Cambs	TL4604	52°37·1′	0°9·8′E	FM	143
Rookery Fm	Cambs	TL3480	52°24·3′	0°1·4′W	FM	142
Rookery Fm	Cambs	TL3699	52°34·5′	0°0·8′E	FM	142
Rookery Fm	Cambs	TL4692	52°30·6′	0°9·5′E	FM	143
Rookery Fm	Ches	SJ5071	53°14·3′	2°44·5′W	FM	117
Rookery Fm	Ches	SJ5760	53°8·4′	2°38·2′W	FM	117
Rookery Fm	Ches	SJ6242	52°58·7′	2°33·6′W	FM	118
Rookery Fm	Devon	ST2108	50°52·2′	3°7·0′W	FM	192,193
Rookery Fm	Dorset	ST6207	50°51·9′	2°32·0′W	FM	194
Rookery Fm	Dorset	ST9416	50°56·8′	2°4·7′W	FM	184
Rookery Fm	Essex	TL9529	51°55·7′	0°50·6′E	FM	168
Rookery Fm	Essex	TQ8498	51°39·3′	0°40·0′E	FM	168
Rookery Fm	Hants	SU7737	51°7·9′	0°53·6′W	FM	186
Rookery Fm	Kent	TR2560	51°17·9′	1°14·1′E	FM	179
Rookery Fm	Lincs	TA1803	53°30·9′	0°12·8′W	FM	113
Rookery Fm	Lincs	TF1683	53°20·1′	0°15·1′W	FM	121
Rookery Fm	Lincs	TF3283	53°19·9′	0°0·7′W	FM	122
Rookery Fm	Lincs	TF3599	53°28·5′	0°2·5′E	FM	113
Rookery Fm	Lincs	TF4668	53°11·6′	0°11·5′E	FM	122
Rookery Fm	Lincs	TF5262	53°8·2′	0°16·7′E	FM	122
Rookery Fm	Norf	TF5900	52°34·7′	0°21·2′E	FM	143
Rookery Fm	Norf	TF6918	52°44·2′	0°30·6′E	FM	132
Rookery Fm	Norf	TG0307	52°37·6′	1°0·4′E	FM	144
Rookery Fm	Norf	TG0730	52°49·9′	1°4·8′E	FM	133
Rookery Fm	Norf	TG1339	52°54·6′	1°10·5′E	FM	133
Rookery Fm	Norf	TG2831	52°49·9′	1°23·5′E	FM	133
Rookery Fm	Norf	TG3103	52°34·8′	1°25·0′E	FM	134
Rookery Fm	Norf	TG3532	52°50·3′	1°29·8′E	FM	133
Rookery Fm	Norf	TG4020	52°43·7′	1°33·7′E	FM	134
Rookery Fm	Norf	TM0097	52°32·5′	0°57·4′E	FM	144
Rookery Fm	Norf	TM0797	52°32·1′	1°3·5′E	FM	144
Rookery Fm	Norf	TM1187	52°26·6′	1°6·7′E	FM	144
Rookery Fm	Norf	TM1589	52°27·6′	1°10·3′E	FM	144,156
Rookery Fm	Norf	TM1887	52°26·5′	1°12·9′E	FM	156
Rookery Fm	Norf	TM2692	52°29·0′	1°20·1′E	FM	134
Rookery Fm	Norf	TM3189	52°27·2′	1°24·4′E	FM	156
Rookery Fm	Northnts	SP7450	52°8·8′	0°54·7′W	FM	152
Rookery Fm	Northnts	SP7954	52°10·9′	0°50·3′W	FM	152
Rookery Fm	N Som	ST4161	51°20·9′	2°50·4′W	FM	172,182
Rookery Fm	S Glos	ST5784	51°33·4′	2°36·8′W	FM	172
Rookery Fm	S Glos	ST7175	51°28·6′	2°24·7′W	FM	172
Rookery Fm	Shrops	SJ7704	52°38·2′	2°20·0′W	FM	127
Rookery Fm	Shrops	SO7890	52°30·7′	2°19·1′W	FM	138
Rookery Fm	Somer	ST5751	51°15·6′	2°36·6′W	FM	182,183
Rookery Fm	Staffs	SK1402	52°37·2′	1°47·2′W	FM	139
Rookery Fm	Suff	TL7457	52°11·3′	0°33·1′E	FM	155
Rookery Fm	Suff	TL8947	52°5·6′	0°45·9′E	FM	155
Rookery Fm	Suff	TL8954	52°9·3′	0°46·2′E	FM	155
Rookery Fm	Suff	TL9356	52°10·3′	0°49·9′E	FM	155
Rookery Fm	Suff	TL9560	52°12·4′	0°51·6′E	FM	155
Rookery Fm	Suff	TM0447	52°5·2′	0°59·1′E	FM	155
Rookery Fm	Suff	TM0570	52°17·6′	1°0·8′E	FM	144,155
Rookery Fm	Suff	TM0835	51°58·7′	1°2·1′E	FM	155,169
Rookery Fm	Suff	TM0849	52°6·2′	1°2·6′E	FM	155,169
Rookery Fm	Suff	TM0862	52°13·2′	1°3·1′E	FM	155
Rookery Fm	Suff	TM0940	52°1·4′	1°3·2′E	FM	155,169
Rookery Fm	Suff	TM1058	52°11·0′	1°4·7′E	FM	155
Rookery Fm	Suff	TM2052	52°7·6′	1°13·2′E	FM	156
Rookery Fm	Suff	TM2175	52°19·9′	1°15·0′E	FM	156
Rookery Fm	Suff	TM2760	52°11·7′	1°19·7′E	FM	156
Rookery Fm	Suff	TM2875	52°19·8′	1°21·2′E	FM	156
Rookery Fm	Suff	TM2961	52°23·0′	1°22·3′E	FM	156
Rookery Fm	Suff	TM3063	52°13·3′	1°22·4′E	FM	156
Rookery Fm	Suff	TM3071	52°17·6′	1°22·8′E	FM	156
Rookery Fm	Suff	TM3074	52°19·2′	1°22·9′E	FM	156
Rookery Fm	Suff	TM3280	52°22·4′	1°24·9′E	FM	156
Rookery Fm	Suff	TM3283	52°24·0′	1°25·0′E	FM	156
Rookery Fm	Suff	TM3565	52°14·2′	1°26·9′E	FM	156
Rookery Fm	Suff	TM3665	52°14·2′	1°27·8′E	FM	156
Rookery Fm	Suff	TM3783	52°23·8′	1°29·4′E	FM	156
Rookery Fm	Suff	TM3967	52°15·2′	1°30·5′E	FM	156
Rookery Fm	Suff	TM4058	52°10·3′	1°31·0′E	FM	156
Rookery Fm	Suff	TM4081	52°22·7′	1°32·0′E	FM	156
Rookery Fm	Surrey	TQ3144	51°11·0′	0°7·1′W	FM	187
Rookery Fm	W Berks	SU4971	51°26·4′	1°17·3′W	FM	174
Rookery Fm	Wilts	ST9791	51°37·3′	2°2·2′W	FM	163,173
Rookery Fm	W Susx	SZ8697	50°46·2′	0°46·4′W	FM	197
Rookery Fm	W Susx	SZ8999	50°47·2′	0°43·9′W	FM	197
Rookery Fm, The	Suff	TM2260	52°11·8′	1°15·3′E	FM	156
Rookery Hall	Ches	SJ6556	53°6·2′	2°31·0′W	X	118
Rookery Hall	Warw	SP4374	52°22·0′	1°21·7′W	X	140
Rookery Hill	E Susx	TQ4600	50°47·1′	0°4·7′E	X	198
Rookery Ho	N Yks	SE5570	54°7·6′	1°9·1′W	X	100
Rookery Park	Suff	TM3968	52°15·7′	1°30·5′E	X	156
Rookery Pool	Ches	SJ6370	53°13·8′	2°32·8′W	W	118
Rookery, The	Brom	TQ4362	51°20·6′	0°3·6′E	X	177,187

Rookery, The	Ches	SJ6243	52°59·2′	2°33·6′W	X	118
Rookery, The	Essex	TL8441	52°2·4′	0°41·4′E	X	155
Rookery, The	Glos	SO6616	51°50·7′	2°29·2′W	X	162
Rookery, The	Herts	TL2305	51°44·0′	0°12·7′W	X	166
Rookery, The	Kent	TR2757	51°16·2′	1°15·7′E	X	179
Rookery, The	Leic	SP5879	52°24·6′	1°8·4′W	F	140
Rookery The	N Yks	SD9683	54°14·8′	2°3·3′W	X	98
Rookery, The	Rut	SK9907	52°39·3′	0°31·8′W	X	141
Rookery, The	Shrops	SJ4632	52°53·2′	2°47·8′W	X	126
Rookery, The	Shrops	SO6874	52°22·0′	2°27·8′W	X	138
Rookery, The	Suff	TM0071	52°18·3′	0°56·4′E	X	144,155
Rookery, The	Suff	TM0977	52°21·3′	1°4·5′E	X	144
Rookery, The	Suff	TM1869	52°16·8′	1°12·2′E	X	156
Rookery, The	Suff	TM3158	52°10·5′	1°23·1′E	X	156
Rookery, The	Suff	TM5086	52°25·1′	1°41·0′E	X	156
Rookery, The	Surrey	TQ1348	51°13·4′	0°22·5′W	X	187
Rookery Top	Lincs	TF1598	53°28·2′	0°15·6′W	X	113
Rookery Wood	Ches	SJ7254	53°5·2′	2°24·7′W	F	118
Rookesbury Park School	Hants	SU5811	50°54·0′	1°10·1′W	X	196
Rookfield Ho	Lincs	TF1236	52°54·8′	0°19·7′W	X	130
Rook Fm	Surrey	TQ3155	51°17·0′	0°6·9′W	FM	187
Rook Hall	Essex	TL6834	51°59·0′	0°27·2′E	X	154
Rook Hall	Essex	TL8808	51°44·6′	0°43·8′E	X	168
Rook Hall	Suff	TM1372	52°18·5′	1°7·9′E	X	144,156
Rookham	Somer	ST5448	51°14·0′	2°39·1′W	X	182,183
Rookhay Fm	Wilts	SU0123	51°0·6′	1°58·8′W	FM	184
Rookhills Fm	Derby	SK2635	52°54·9′	1°36·4′W	FM	128
Rook Hope	Durham	NY9342	54°46·6′	2°6·1′W	X	87
Rookhope	Durham	NY9342	54°46·6′	2°6·1′W	T	87
Rookhope Burn	Durham	NY9142	54°46·6′	2°8·0′W	W	87
Rookhope Chimney	Durham	NY9143	54°47·2′	2°8·0′W	X	87
Rookhope Head	Durham	NY8744	54°47·7′	2°11·7′W	X	87
Rooking	Cumbr	NY4015	54°31·9′	2°55·2′W	T	90
Rookin House Fm	Cumbr	NY3825	54°37·2′	2°57·2′W	FM	90
Rookland	Northum	NT9407	55°21·7′	2°5·2′W	X	80
Rooklands Fm	W Susx	TQ1619	50°57·8′	0°20·5′W	FM	198
Rook Law	E Loth	NT6367	55°53·9′	2°35·1′W	X	67
Rookley	I of W	SZ5083	50°38·9′	1°17·2′W	T	196
Rookley Green	I of W	SZ5083	50°38·9′	1°17·2′W	T	196
Rookley Manor	Hants	SU3932	51°5·4′	1°26·2′W	X	185
Rookling Law	Northum	NT8406	55°21·1′	2°14·7′W	X	80
Rooks Bridge	Somer	ST3652	51°16·0′	2°54·7′W	T	182
Rooks Castle Fm	Somer	ST2532	51°5·2′	3°3·9′W	FM	182
Rooksey Green	Suff	TL9251	52°7·7′	0°48·7′E	T	155
Rooks Fm	Devon	SS5525	51°0·6′	4°3·6′W	FM	180
Rooksgrove Fm	Hants	SU5923	51°0·4′	1°9·2′W	FM	185
Rooks Hill	Kent	TQ5653	51°15·5′	0°14·5′E	T	188
Rook's Ho	Somer	ST2412	50°54·4′	3°4·5′W	X	193
Rooksmoor	Glos	SO8403	51°43·8′	2°13·5′W	T	162
Rooksmoor Copse	Dorset	ST7311	50°54·1′	2°22·7′W	F	194
Rook's Nest	Herts	TL2426	51°55·4′	0°11·4′W	X	166
Rook's Nest	Somer	ST0833	51°5·6′	3°18·4′W	T	181
Rooksnest	W Berks	SU3275	51°28·6′	1°32·0′W	X	174
Rooks Nest Fm	Surrey	TQ3652	51°15·3′	0°2·7′W	FM	187
Rook Street	Wilts	ST8131	51°4·9′	2°15·9′W	T	183
Rook Tor	Devon	SX6061	50°26·2′	3°57·9′W	X	202
Rooktree Fm	Beds	SP9439	52°2·7′	0°37·4′W	FM	153
Rookwith	N Yks	SE2086	54°16·4′	1°41·2′W	T	99
Rookwith Grange	N Yks	SE2186	54°16·4′	1°40·2′W	X	99
Rook Wood	Bucks	SP9000	51°41·7′	0°41·5′W	F	165
Rookwood	W Susx	SZ7899	50°47·3′	0°53·2′W	T	197
Rookwood Fm	Hants	SU6513	50°55·0′	1°4·1′W	FM	196
Rookwood Hall	Essex	TL5611	51°46·8′	0°16·1′E	X	167
Rookwoods	Essex	TL7734	51°58·8′	0°35·0′E	X	155
Rookwoods	Glos	SO9205	51°44·9′	2°6·6′W	X	163
Rookyard Fm	Suff	TM0563	52°13·8′	1°0·5′E	FM	155
Rookyards	Suff	TM3882	52°23·3′	1°30·3′E	X	156
Rooley Hill	Cald	SE0322	53°41·9′	1°56·9′W	X	104
Rooley Moor	Roch	SD8518	53°39·7′	2°13·2′W	X	109
Roome Fm	Dorset	ST7911	50°54·1′	2°17·5′W	FM	194
Roome Rocks	Fife	NO6207	56°15·5′	2°36·4′W	X	59
Room Hill	Somer	SS8536	51°6·9′	3°38·2′W	H	181
Rooms Fm	Shrops	SJ6739	52°57·1′	2°29·1′W	FM	127
Roonans, The	Shetld	HU3279	60°29·9′	1°24·5′W	X	3
Roonans, The	Shetld	HU3378	60°29·3′	1°23·5′W	H	2,3
Roonies, The	Shetld	HU3185	60°33·1′	1°25·6′W	X	3
Roonies, The	Shetld	HU4652	60°15·2′	1°9·6′W	X	3
Roonions	Shetld	HU3257	60°18·0′	1°24·8′W	H	3
Roo Point	Orkney	HY4006	58°56·5′	3°2·1′W	X	6,7
Roos	E Yorks	TA2930	53°45·3′	0°2·2′W	T	107
Roos Drain	E Yorks	TA2828	53°44·2′	0°3·2′W	W	107
Roose	Corn	SX1790	50°41·1′	4°35·1′W	X	190
Roose	Cumbr	SD2269	54°6·9′	3°11·2′W	T	96
Roosebeck	Cumbr	SD2567	54°5·9′	3°8·4′W	T	96
Roosebeck Ho	Cumbr	SD2668	54°6·4′	3°7·5′W	X	96,97
Roosebeck Sands	Cumbr	SD2667	54°5·9′	3°7·5′W	X	96,97
Roosecote	Cumbr	SD2268	54°6·4′	3°11·2′W	T	96
Roosecote Sands	Cumbr	SD2167	54°5·8′	3°12·1′W	X	96
Rooseferry Fm	Pemb	SM9906	51°43·2′	4°54·2′W	FM	157,158
Roos Hall	Suff	TM4189	52°27·0′	1°33·2′E	A	156
Roos Hall	Suff	TM4190	52°27·5′	1°33·3′E	A	134,156
Roos Loch	Orkney	HY6544	59°17·1′	2°36·4′W	W	5
Roost End	Essex	TL7043	52°3·8′	0°29·2′E	T	154
Roos, The	Essex	TL5436	52°0·3′	0°15·0′E	X	154
Roost Hill	Staffs	SK0053	53°4·7′	1°59·6′W	X	119
Roosthitchen	Somer	SS7240	51°8·9′	3°49·4′W	X	180
Roos Tor	Devon	SX5476	50°34·2′	4°3·3′W	X	191,201
Roost, The	Orkney	HY4855	59°23·0′	2°54·4′W	W	5
Roos Wick	Orkney	HY6545	59°17·7′	2°36·4′W	W	5
Root	Lancs	SD6649	53°56·4′	2°30·7′W	X	103
Rooten	Aberd	NO8289	56°59·8′	2°17·3′W	X	45
Rootfield	Highld	NH5552	57°32·4′	4°24·9′W	T	26
Rootham's Green	Beds	TL1057	52°12·2′	0°23·0′W	T	153
Roother's Fm	Essex	TL5731	51°57·5′	0°17·5′E	FM	167
Roothill	Surrey	TQ1947	51°12·8′	0°17·4′W	X	187
Rooting Manor	Kent	TQ9445	51°10·5′	0°46·9′E	X	189
Rooting Street	Kent	TQ9545	51°10·5′	0°47·8′E	T	189
Rootpark	S Lanak	NS9554	55°46·3′	3°40·0′W	T	65,72
Root Stacks	Shetld	HP6114	60°48·5′	0°52·2′W	X	1
Rope Barn	Durham	NY9649	54°50·4′	2°3·3′W	X	87

Rope Fm	Dorset	ST8029	51°3·8'	2°16·7'W	FM	183
Ropegreen Br	Ches	SJ6952	53°4·1'	2°27·4'W	X	118
Rope Hall	Ches	SJ6852	53°4·1'	2°28·2'W	X	118
Ropehaven	Corn	SX0348	50°18·2'	4°45·6'W	X	204
Rope Lake Head	Dorset	SY9277	50°35·8'	2°6·4'W	X	195
Ropelaw Burn	S Lanak	NT0325	55°30·8'	3°31·7'W	W	72
Ropelawshiel	Scot Bord	NT3110	55°23·0'	3°4·9'W	X	79
Ropelaw Sike	Scot Bord	NT3010	55°23·0'	3°5·9'W	W	79
Rope Moor Cotts	Durham	NZ2727	54°38·5'	1°34·5'W	X	93
Roper Castle or Round Table	Cumbr	NY8811	54°29·9'	2°10·7'W	X	91,92
Roper Castle or Round Table (Roman Signal Station)	Cumbr	NY8811	54°29·9'	2°10·7'W	R	91,92
Roper Fm	Norf	TG0831	52°50·4'	1°5·7'E	FM	133
Roper Hill	Lincs	TF3783	53°19·8'	0°3·8'E	X	122
Roper's Fm	Essex	TL6605	51°43·4'	0°24·6'E	FM	167
Roper's Fm	Essex	TQ9290	51°34·8'	0°46·7'E	FM	178
Ropers Fm	Worcs	SP0542	52°4·8'	1°55·2'W	FM	150
Ropershill	Leic	SK3920	52°46·8'	1°24·9'W	X	128
Ropley	Hants	SU6431	51°4·7'	1°4·8'W	T	185
Ropley Dean	Hants	SU6231	51°4·7'	1°6·5'W	T	185
Ropley Lodge	Hants	SU6232	51°5·3'	1°6·5'W	X	185
Ropley Soke	Hants	SU6533	51°5·8'	1°3·9'W	T	185,186
Roppa Wood	N Yks	SE5891	54°18·9'	1°6·1'W	F	100
Ropsley Heath	Lincs	SK9935	52°54·4'	0°31·3'W	X	130
Ropsley	Lincs	SK9934	52°53·9'	0°31·3'W	T	130
Ropsley Rise Wood	Lincs	SK9634	52°53·9'	0°34·0'W	F	130
Roquharold	Aberd	NJ7519	57°15·9'	2°24·4'W	X	38
Rora	Aberd	NK0550	57°32·7'	1°54·5'W	T	30
Rora Head	Orkney	ND1799	58°52·5'	3°25·9'W	X	7
Rora Ho	Devon	SX8074	50°33·4'	3°41·3'W	X	191
Rora Moss	Aberd	NK0451	57°33·2'	1°55·5'W	X	30
Rorandle	Aberd	NJ6518	57°15·3'	2°34·4'W	X	38
Rora Wood	Devon	SX8074	50°33·4'	3°41·3'W	F	191
Rorie	D & G	NX9986	55°9·7'	3°34·7'W	X	78
Roromore	Pth & Kin	NN6346	56°35·4'	4°13·4'W	X	51
Roroyere	Pth & Kin	NN6147	56°35·9'	4°15·4'W	X	51
Rorrington	Shrops	SJ3000	52°35·8'	3°1·6'W	T	126
Rorrington Hill	Shrops	SJ3100	52°35·8'	3°0·7'W	X	126
Rorrington Lodge	Shrops	SJ2900	52°35·8'	3°2·5'W	X	126
Rosa	Denb	SJ0563	53°9·6'	3°24·8'W	X	116
Rosaigh	N Eil	NG2095	57°51·7'	6°42·8'W	X	14
Rosal	Highld	NC6841	58°20·5'	4°14·8'W	X	10
Rosalie Fm	Ches	SJ6459	53°7·9'	2°31·9'W	FM	118
Rosalie Fm	Suff	TL6954	52°9·7'	0°28·7'E	FM	154
Rosall Fm	Bucks	SP6922	51°53·8'	0°59·4'W	FM	165
Ros a' Mheallain	Highld	NG3740	57°22·7'	6°22·1'W	H	23
Rosamondford Ho	Devon	SY0291	50°42·9'	3°22·9'W	X	192
Rosamond's Bower	Northnts	SP5138	52°2·5'	1°15·0'W	F	151
Rosamul	N Eil	NF7863	57°32·8'	7°22·5'W	X	18
Rosarie	Moray	NJ3849	57°31·9'	3°1·7'W	X	28
Rosary Fm	Norf	TF5611	52°40·7'	0°18·9'E	FM	131,143
Roscarrs	N Yks	SE6431	53°46·5'	1°1·3'W	X	105,106
Roscassa	Corn	SW8437	50°11·9'	5°1·2'W	X	204
Ros Castle	Northum	NU0825	55°31·4'	1°52·0'W	X	75
Roscobie	Fife	NT0892	56°7·0'	3°28·3'W	X	58
Roscobie Hills	Fife	NT0892	56°7·0'	3°28·3'W	H	58
Roscobie Muir	Fife	NT0994	56°8·1'	3°27·4'W	X	58
Roscobie Resr	Fife	NT0993	56°7·5'	3°27·4'W	W	58
Roscroggan	Corn	SW6442	50°14·1'	5°18·2'W	T	203
Roscrowgey	Corn	SW7420	50°2·5'	5°9·0'W	X	204
Roscullion Fm	Corn	SW9072	50°30·8'	4°57·4'W	FM	200
Rosdail	Highld	NG8513	57°9·7'	5°32·9'W	X	33
Rose	Corn	SW7754	50°20·9'	5°7·7'W	T	200
Rose	Corn	SX1176	50°33·4'	4°39·7'W	X	200
Rose Acre	Bucks	SP9402	51°42·8'	0°38·0'W	X	165
Rose Acre	Herts	TL0904	51°43·7'	0°24·9'W	X	166
Roseacre	Kent	TQ7955	51°16·2'	0°34·4'E	T	178,188
Roseacre	Lancs	SD4336	53°49·3'	2°51·5'W	T	102
Rose-an-Grouse	Corn	SW5335	50°10·1'	5°27·2'W	T	203
Rose Ash	Devon	SS7821	50°58·8'	3°43·9'W	T	180
Rosebank	Angus	NO6142	56°34·4'	2°37·6'W	X	54
Rosebank	C of Edin	NT1867	55°53·6'	3°18·2'W	X	65,66
Rose Bank	Cumbr	NY3646	54°48·5'	2°59·3'W	X	85
Rosebank	Devon	SS4811	50°52·9'	4°9·3'W	X	191
Rosebank	D & G	NX8776	55°4·2'	3°45·8'W	X	84
Rosebank	D & G	NX9873	55°2·7'	3°35·4'W	X	84
Rosebank	D & G	NY1681	55°7·2'	3°18·6'W	X	79
Rosebank	E Dunb	NS6773	55°56·2'	4°7·3'W	T	64
Rosebank	Fife	NO3200	56°11·5'	3°5·3'W	X	59
Rosebank	Fife	NO4503	56°13·2'	2°52·8'W	X	59
Rosebank	Highld	NH6771	57°42·8'	4°13·5'W	X	21
Rosebank	Moray	NJ4761	57°38·4'	2°52·8'W	X	28,29
Rosebank	Orkney	HY2622	59°5·0'	3°17·0'W	X	6
Rosebank	Orkney	HY3315	59°1·3'	3°9·5'W	X	6
Rosebank	Orkney	HY6329	59°9·0'	2°38·3'W	X	5
Rosebank	Pth & Kin	NO2538	56°31·9'	3°12·7'W	X	53
Rosebank	Scot Bord	NT7334	55°36·2'	2°25·3'W	X	74
Rosebank	S Lanak	NS8049	55°43·4'	3°54·2'W	T	72
Rosebank	W Loth	NT0365	55°52·4'	3°32·6'W	X	65
Rosebank Fm	Aberd	NJ9326	57°19·7'	2°6·5'W	FM	38
Rosebank Fm	Heref	SO4865	52°17·1'	2°45·3'W	FM	137,138,148
Rosebank Fm	Salf	SJ7093	53°26·2'	2°26·7'W	FM	109
Rose Bank Fm	Staffs	SJ9451	53°3·6'	2°5·0'W	FM	118
Rosebank Mains	Fife	NT0789	56°5·3'	3°29·2'W	X	65
Rosebank Plantation	Highld	NH2361	57°36·5'	4°57·3'W	F	20
Roseberry Common	Red & Cl	NZ5712	54°30·2'	1°6·8'W	X	93
Roseberry Fm	N Yks	SE5767	54°6·0'	1°7·3'W	FM	100
Roseberry Topping	Red & Cl	NZ5712	54°30·2'	1°6·8'W	H	93
Rosebery	Midlo	NT3057	55°48·3'	3°6·6'W	T	66,73
Rosebery Resr	Midlo	NT3056	55°47·8'	3°6·6'W	W	66,73
Rose Br	Cumbr	NY3745	54°48·0'	2°58·4'W	X	85
Rosebrae	Aberd	NJ7946	57°30·5'	2°20·6'W	X	29,30
Rosebrae	Moray	NJ1764	57°39·8'	3°23·0'W	X	28
Rosebrae	Moray	NJ2458	57°36·6'	3°15·9'W	X	28
Rosebrough	Northum	NU1326	55°31·9'	1°47·2'W	X	75
Rosebrough Moor	Northum	NU1225	55°31·4'	1°48·2'W	X	75
Rosebud Fm	Somer	ST4644	51°11·8'	2°46·0'W	FM	182
Rose Burn	E Ayr	NS5519	55°26·9'	4°17·1'W	W	71
Roseburn Ho	C of Edin	NT2273	55°56·9'	3°14·5'W	A	66
Roseburrain	D & G	NY1687	55°10·5'	3°18·7'W	X	79
Roseburrain (Settlement)	D & G	NY1687	55°10·5'	3°18·7'W	A	79
Rosebush	Pemb	SN0729	51°55·8'	4°48·0'W	T	145,158
Rosebush Reservoir	Pemb	SN0629	51°55·8'	4°48·9'W	W	145,158
Rosecare	Corn	SX1695	50°43·8'	4°36·1'W	T	190
Rosecare Villa Fm	Corn	SX1794	50°43·2'	4°35·2'W	FM	190
Rosecarrock	Corn	SW9880	50°35·3'	4°50·9'W	A	200
Rose Castle	Cumbr	NY3746	54°48·5'	2°58·4'W	A	85
Rose Castle	Cumbr	SD3399	54°23·2'	3°1·5'W	X	96,97
Rosecliston Park	Corn	SW8159	50°23·6'	5°4·5'W	X	200
Rose Clough	Derby	SK1299	53°29·5'	1°48·7'W	X	110
Rose Cott	Ches	SJ4455	53°5·6'	2°49·8'W	X	117
Rose Cott	Cumbr	NY7313	54°30·9'	2°24·6'W	X	91
Rose Cott	Durham	NZ0419	54°34·2'	1°55·9'W	X	92
Rose Cott	N Lincs	SE9508	53°33·8'	0°33·5'W	X	112
Rose Cott	Stir	NN5824	56°23·5'	4°17·6'W	X	51
Rose Cottage	Cumbr	NY0802	54°24·6'	3°24·6'W	X	89
Rose Cottage	N Yks	SE4542	53°52·6'	1°18·5'W	X	105
Rose Cottage	N Yks	SE5080	54°13·0'	1°13·6'W	X	100
Rose Cottage Fm	Lincs	TF1969	53°12·5'	0°12·7'W	FM	122
Rose Cottage Fm	N Yks	SE6672	54°8·6'	0°59·0'W	FM	100
Rose Cottage Fm	Pemb	SM8909	51°44·6'	5°3·0'W	FM	157,158
Rose Cottage Fm	Somer	ST4426	51°2·1'	2°47·5'W	FM	193
Rose Cottage Fm	Surrey	TQ2344	51°11·1'	0°14·0'W	FM	187
Rose Court Fm	Cambs	TL1986	52°27·8'	0°14·5'W	FM	142
Rose Court Fm	Medway	TQ8876	51°27·3'	0°42·8'E	FM	178
Rosecraddoc Manor	Corn	SX2667	50°28·9'	4°26·8'W	X	201
Rose Craig	Pth & Kin	NN9536	56°30·5'	3°41·9'W	H	52,53
Rosecraig	Pth & Kin	NN9637	56°31·1'	3°41·0'W	X	52,53
Rosecraigie	Orkney	HY4718	59°3·0'	2°54·9'W	X	6
Rose Croft	Red & Cl	NZ7117	54°32·8'	0°53·7'W	X	94
Rosecroft Fm	N Yks	SE5760	54°2·2'	1°7·4'W	FM	100
Rosedale	Corn	SX3357	50°23·6'	4°20·6'W	X	201
Rosedale	Heref	SO5661	52°15·0'	2°38·3'W	X	137,138,149
Rosedale	Herts	TL3403	51°42·8'	0°3·2'W	T	166
Rosedale	Norf	TF5009	52°39·7'	0°13·5'E	X	143
Rosedale Abbey	N Yks	SE7295	54°21·0'	0°53·1'W	T	94,100
Rosedale Fm	Dorset	SU0204	50°50·4'	1°57·9'W	FM	195
Rosedale Fm	Essex	TQ8999	51°39·7'	0°44·4'E	FM	168
Rosedale Fm	Lincs	TF3211	52°41·1'	0°2·4'W	FM	131,142
Rosedale Fm	N Yks	TA1176	54°10·3'	0°17·6'W	FM	101
Rosedale Head	N Yks	NZ6701	54°24·2'	0°57·6'W	H	94
Rosedale Intake	N Yks	NZ7109	54°28·5'	0°53·8'W	X	94
Rosedale Moor	N Yks	SE7299	54°23·1'	0°53·1'W	X	94,100
Roseden	Northum	NU0321	55°29·2'	1°56·7'W	X	75
Roseden Edge	Northum	NU0221	55°29·2'	1°57·7'W	X	75
Rosedene Fm	Norf	TL6895	52°31·8'	0°29·0'E	FM	143
Rosedinnick	Corn	SW9165	50°27·1'	4°56·3'W	T	200
Rosedown	Devon	SS2724	50°59·6'	4°27·5'W	T	190
Rose Down	Pemb	SN1110	51°45·6'	4°43·9'W	X	158
Rosefarm	Highld	NH7665	57°39·7'	4°4·2'W	X	21,27
Rosefield	D & G	NY2166	54°59·2'	3°13·6'W	X	85
Rosefield	Highld	NH8552	57°32·9'	3°54·8'W	X	27
Rosefield	Pth & Kin	NO1731	56°28·1'	3°20·4'W	X	53
Rose Fm	Aberd	NJ8044	57°29·4'	2°19·6'W	FM	29,30
Rose Fm	Brad	SE1445	53°54·3'	1°46·8'W	FM	104
Rose Fm	Devon	ST2402	50°49·0'	3°4·3'W	FM	192,193
Rose Fm	Essex	TM0929	51°55·4'	1°2·8'E	FM	168,169
Rose Fm	Kent	TQ9144	51°10·0'	0°44·3'E	FM	189
Rose Fm	Leic	SP5896	52°33·8'	1°8·3'W	FM	140
Rose Fm	Lincs	SK8759	53°7·5'	0°41·6'W	FM	121
Rose Fm	Lincs	TF3586	53°21·5'	0°2·1'E	FM	113,122
Rose Fm	Norf	TF9203	52°35·7'	0°50·5'E	FM	144
Rose Fm	Norf	TM0796	52°31·6'	1°3·5'E	FM	144
Rose Fm	Norf	TM4193	52°29·1'	1°33·4'E	FM	134
Rose Fm	N Yks	SE5036	53°49·3'	1°14·0'W	FM	105
Rose Fm	Oxon	SU6876	51°29·0'	1°0·9'W	FM	175
Rose Fm	Peterb	TF2605	52°37·9'	0°7·9'W	FM	142
Rose Fm	Somer	ST3752	51°16·1'	2°53·8'W	FM	182
Rose Fm	Suff	TM2664	52°13·9'	1°19·0'E	FM	156
Rose Fm	Suff	TM2974	52°19·2'	1°22·0'E	FM	156
Roseghyll Mill	Cumbr	NY0837	54°43·4'	3°25·3'W	X	89
Rosegill	Highld	ND2471	58°37·5'	3°18·0'W	X	7,12
Rose Green	Essex	TL9028	51°55·3'	0°46·2'E	T	168
Rose Green	Suff	TL9337	52°0·1'	0°49·1'E	T	155
Rose Green	Suff	TL9744	52°3·8'	0°52·8'E	T	155
Rose Green	W Susx	SZ9099	50°47·2'	0°40·3'W	T	197
Rose-Ground Fm	Ches	SJ5651	53°3·5'	2°39·0'W	FM	117
Rose Grove	Lancs	SD8132	53°47·3'	2°16·9'W	T	103
Rose Grove	Shrops	SO1785	52°27·6'	3°12·9'W	X	136
Rosehall	Aberd	NJ6829	57°21·3'	2°31·5'W	X	38
Rosehall	Aberd	NJ8916	57°14·3'	2°10·5'W	X	38
Rosehall	D & G	NX9873	55°2·7'	3°35·4'W	X	84
Rosehall	D & G	NY0782	55°7·7'	3°27·1'W	X	78
Rosehall	Highld	NC4701	57°58·6'	4°34·8'W	X	16
Rosehall	N Lanak	NS7363	55°50·9'	4°1·3'W	T	64
Rosehall	N Lanak	NS8659	55°48·9'	3°48·7'W	X	65,72
Rose Hall	Norf	TF4816	52°43·5'	0°11·9'E	X	131
Rosehall	Stir	NN7004	56°12·9'	4°5·3'W	X	57
Rose Hall Fm	Essex	TQ5398	51°39·8'	0°13·1'E	FM	167,177
Rose Hall Fm	Herts	TL0200	51°41·6'	0°31·1'W	FM	166
Rosehall Fm	Warw	SP1055	52°11·8'	1°50·8'W	FM	150
Rosehaugh	Moray	NJ1664	57°39·7'	3°24·0'W	X	28
Rosehaugh Mains	Highld	NH6855	57°34·2'	4°12·0'W	X	26
Rosehearty	Aberd	NJ9367	57°41·8'	2°6·6'W	T	30
Rosehill	Aberd	NO5499	57°5·0'	2°45·1'W	X	37,44
Rosehill	Angus	NO6055	56°41·4'	2°38·7'W	X	54
Rosehill	Angus	NO6746	56°36·5'	2°31·8'W	X	54
Rosehill	Arg & Bt	NR6637	55°34·5'	5°42·3'W	X	68
Rosehill	Black w Dar	SD7021	53°41·3'	2°26·8'W	T	103
Rosehill	Bolton	SD7108	53°34·3'	2°25·9'W	T	109
Rose Hill	Bucks	SU9284	51°33·1'	0°40·0'W	T	175
Rosehill	C of Aber	NJ9108	57°10·0'	2°8·5'W	T	38
Rose Hill	C of Derb	SK3535	52°54·5'	1°28·4'W	T	128
Rosehill	Corn	SW4530	50°7·2'	5°33·7'W	X	203
Rosehill	Corn	SW7854	50°20·9'	5°6·9'W	T	200
Rosehill	Corn	SX0364	50°26·8'	4°46·1'W	T	200
Rosehill	Cumbr	NX9920	54°34·2'	3°33·3'W	X	89
Rose Hill	Cumbr	NY4356	54°54·0'	2°52·9'W	X	85
Rosehill	Devon	SS4410	50°52·3'	4°12·7'W	X	190
Rosehill	Devon	SS5211	50°53·0'	4°5·9'W	X	191
Rosehill	D & G	NX8892	55°12·8'	3°45·2'W	X	78
Rosehill	D & G	NX9581	55°7·0'	3°38·3'W	X	78
Rose Hill	Durham	NY9338	54°44·5'	2°6·1'W	X	91,92
Rose Hill	E Susx	TQ4516	50°55·7'	0°4·2'E	T	198
Rose Hill	E Yorks	TA1826	53°43·3'	0°12·3'W	X	107
Rosehill	Glos	SO6833	51°59·9'	2°27·6'W	X	149
Rose Hill	Highld	NH7479	57°47·2'	4°6·7'W	X	21
Rosehill	Highld	NH7580	57°47·8'	4°5·7'W	X	21
Rosehill	Kent	TQ9128	51°1·4'	0°43·8'E	X	189
Rose Hill	Lancs	SD8331	53°46·7'	2°15·1'W	T	103
Rosehill	Midlo	NT2154	55°46·6'	3°15·1'W	X	66,73
Rosehill	Moray	NJ1656	57°35·4'	3°23·8'W	X	28
Rosehill	N Tyne	NZ3166	54°59·5'	1°30·5'W	T	88
Rose Hill	N Yks	NZ3510	54°29·3'	1°27·2'W	X	93
Rosehill	Orkney	HY2511	58°59·0'	3°17·8'W	X	6
Rose Hill	Oxon	SP5303	51°43·6'	1°13·6'W	T	164
Rosehill	Pemb	SM8915	51°47·9'	5°3·2'W	T	157,158
Rose Hill	Pemb	SM9309	51°44·7'	4°59·5'W	X	157,158
Rosehill	Pemb	SN0214	51°47·6'	4°51·9'W	X	157,158
Rosehill	Shrops	SJ4715	52°44·0'	2°46·7'W	X	126
Rosehill	Shrops	SJ6630	52°52·2'	2°29·9'W	T	127
Rosehill	S Lanak	NS8540	55°38·7'	3°49·2'W	X	71,72
Rose Hill	Somer	ST2331	51°4·6'	3°5·6'W	X	182
Rosehill	Stir	NS8586	56°3·4'	3°50·4'W	X	65
Rose Hill	Stock on T	NZ4211	54°29·8'	1°20·7'W	X	93
Rose Hill	Suff	TM1843	52°2·8'	1°11·2'E	T	169
Rose Hill	Surrey	TQ1649	51°13·9'	0°19·9'W	T	187
Rose Hill	Sutton	TQ2666	51°23·0'	0°11·0'W	T	176
Rosehill	Traf	SJ7686	53°22·5'	2°21·2'W	T	109
Rosehill	Win & Maid	SU8082	51°32·1'	0°50·4'W	X	175
Rosehill	Wrex	SJ3542	52°58·5'	2°57·7'W	X	117
Rosehill Fm	Beds	TL1333	51°59·3'	0°20·9'W	FM	166
Rosehill Fm	Bucks	SP6428	51°57·0'	1°3·7'W	FM	164,165
Rose Hill Fm	Bucks	SP6925	51°55·4'	0°59·4'W	FM	165
Rose Hill Fm	Norf	TL6398	52°33·6'	0°24·7'E	FM	143
Rose Hill Fm	Sefton	SD3704	53°32·0'	2°56·6'W	FM	108
Rose Hill Ho	Suff	TM3760	52°11·5'	1°28·5'E	X	156
Rose Hill (Sch)	Glos	ST7690	51°36·7'	2°20·4'W	X	162,172
Roseisle	Moray	NJ1467	57°41·3'	3°26·1'W	X	28
Rosekinghall	Angus	NO4943	56°34·8'	2°49·4'W	X	54
Roseland	Corn	SX2763	50°26·7'	4°25·8'W	T	201
Roseland Cross	Devon	SS3613	50°53·8'	4°19·6'W	X	190
Roseland Fm	Derby	SK5067	53°12·1'	1°14·7'W	FM	120
Roselands	E Susx	TQ6200	50°46·8'	0°18·3'E	T	199
Roseland Wood	Derby	SK4967	53°12·1'	1°15·6'W	F	120
Roselane Fm	Mil Key	SP7948	52°7·7'	0°50·4'W	FM	152
Rose Lawn Coppice	Poole	SZ0097	50°46·6'	1°59·6'W	F	195
Roselyon	Corn	SX1661	50°25·4'	4°35·1'W	X	201
Rose Mains	Midlo	NT4065	55°52·7'	2°57·1'W	X	66
Rosemanowas	Corn	SW7335	50°10·5'	5°10·4'W	X	204
Rosemarket	Pemb	SM9508	51°44·2'	4°57·8'W	T	157,158
Rosemarkie	Highld	NH7357	57°35·4'	4°7·0'W	T	27
Rosemarkie Bay	Highld	NH7457	57°35·4'	4°6·0'W	W	27
Rosemary Farmhouse	Kent	TQ6932	51°4·0'	0°25·1'E	X	188
Rosemary Fm	Essex	TL7936	51°59·8'	0°36·8'E	FM	155
Rosemary Hill	Pemb	SM9423	51°52·3'	4°59·2'W	X	157,158
Rosemary Lane	Devon	ST1514	50°55·4'	3°12·2'W	T	181,193
Rosemaund	Heref	SO5647	52°7·4'	2°38·2'W	X	149
Rosemay	Midlo	NT2255	55°47·2'	3°14·2'W	X	66,73
Rosemelling	Corn	SX0457	50°23·1'	4°45·1'W	T	200
Rosemergy	Corn	SW4136	50°10·3'	5°37·3'W	T	203
Rosemerryn Fm	Corn	SW7830	50°7·9'	5°6·0'W	FM	204
Rosemire	Orkney	HY2621	59°4·4'	3°17·0'W	X	6
Rosemodress	Corn	SW4423	50°3·4'	5°34·2'W	X	203
Rosemoor	Devon	SS5018	50°56·8'	4°7·7'W	X	180
Rose Moor	Devon	SS8415	50°55·6'	3°38·7'W	X	181
Rosemoor	Pemb	SM8710	51°45·1'	5°4·8'W	X	157
Rosemorder	Corn	SW7522	50°3·6'	5°8·3'W	X	204
Rosemore	Heref	SO7157	52°12·9'	2°25·1'W	X	149
Rosemorran	Corn	SW4732	50°8·3'	5°32·1'W	X	203
Rosemount	Angus	NO6961	56°44·6'	2°30·0'W	X	45
Rosemount	C of Aber	NJ9306	57°8·9'	2°6·5'W	T	38
Rose Mount	N Yks	SE9669	54°6·7'	0°31·5'W	X	101
Rosemount	Pth & Kin	NO1630	56°27·5'	3°21·3'W	X	53
Rosemount	Pth & Kin	NO1943	56°34·6'	3°18·7'W	T	53
Rosemount	Pth & Kin	NO2043	56°34·6'	3°17·7'W	X	53
Rosemount	S Ayr	NS3729	55°31·9'	4°34·5'W	X	70
Rosemount Ho	Highld	NH7879	57°47·3'	4°2·7'W	X	21
Rosemullion	Corn	SW7827	50°6·3'	5°5·9'W	X	204
Rosemullion Head	Corn	SW7927	50°6·4'	5°5·1'W	X	204
Rosenannon	Corn	SW9566	50°27·7'	4°52·9'W	T	200
Rosenannon Downs	Corn	SW9567	50°28·3'	4°53·0'W	H	200
Rosen Cliff	Corn	SW9237	50°12·0'	4°54·5'W	X	204
Rose Ness	Orkney	ND5298	58°52·3'	2°49·5'W	X	6,7
Rosenewton	Moray	NJ1564	57°39·7'	3°25·0'W	X	28
Roseney Fm	Corn	SX0560	50°24·7'	4°44·3'W	FM	200
Rosen Green	Pemb	SM9813	51°47·0'	4°55·3'W	X	157,158
Rosenithon	Corn	SW8021	50°3·1'	5°4·0'W	T	204
Rosepool	Pemb	SM8611	51°45·7'	5°5·7'W	X	157
Roserrans	Corn	SW9262	50°25·5'	4°55·3'W	X	200
Roserrow	Corn	SW9478	50°34·2'	4°54·2'W	X	200
Roser's Cross	E Susx	TQ5520	50°57·7'	0°12·8'E	T	199
Rosery Fm	Suff	TM2448	52°5·3'	1°16·6'E	FM	169
Rosery, The	Suff	TM1261	52°12·6'	1°6·6'E	X	155
Roses Bower	Northum	NY7976	55°4·9'	2°19·3'W	X	86,87
Rose's Bower	Northum	NY9971	55°2·3'	2°0·5'W	X	87
Roseseat	Aberd	NJ7331	57°22·4'	2°26·5'W	X	29
Roses Fm	Ches	SJ7077	53°17·6'	2°26·6'W	FM	118
Roses Fm	Corn	SW6735	50°10·4'	5°15·4'W	FM	203
Roses Fm	Essex	TQ6090	51°35·4'	0°19·0'E	FM	177
Rose's Fm	Kent	TQ7532	51°3·9'	0°30·2'E	FM	188
Roses Fm	Notts	SK7130	52°52·0'	0°56·3'W	FM	129
Roses Fm	Somer	ST2714	50°55·5'	3°1·9'W	FM	193
Rosesuggan	Corn	SW8962	50°25·4'	4°57·9'W	X	200
Rose Tree Fm	N Yks	SE2049	53°56·4'	1°41·3'W	FM	104
Rosetta	D & G	NT0504	55°19·5'	3°29·4'W	X	78

Rosetta	Scot Bord	NT2441	55°39·6′	3°12·0′W	X	73
Rose Vale	Corn	SW4426	50°5·0′	5°34·3′W	X	203
Rosevalley	Aberd	NJ8716	57°14·3′	2°12·5′W	X	38
Rose Valley	Pemb	SN0000	51°40·0′	4°53·1′W	T	158
Rosevalley Ho	Highld	NH8048	57°30·6′	3°59·7′W	X	27
Rosevallon	Corn	SW9343	50°15·3′	4°53·9′W	X	204
Roseveath Fm	Corn	SX0261	50°25·2′	4°46·9′W	FM	200
Rosevean	Corn	SX0258	50°23·5′	4°46·8′W	T	200
Rosevean	I Scilly	SV8405	49°51·9′	6°23·5′W	X	203
Rosevear	Corn	SW6924	50°4·5′	5°13·3′W	T	203
Rosevear	I Scilly	SV8305	49°51·9′	6°24·3′W	X	203
Rosevidney	Corn	SW5333	50°9·0′	5°27·1′W	X	203
Rose View	Midlo	NT2356	55°47·7′	3°13·3′W	X	66,73
Rose Villa	Cambs	TF4214	52°42·5′	0°6·5′E	X	131
Roseville	Dudley	SO9393	52°32·3′	2°5·8′W	T	139
Rosevine	Corn	SW8736	50°11·4′	4°58·7′W	T	204
Rosewall Hill	Corn	SW4939	50°12·1′	5°30·7′W	H	203
Rosewarne	Corn	SW6136	50°10·8′	5°20·5′W	T	203
Rosewarne	Corn	SW6440	50°13·0′	5°18·1′W	T	203
Rosewarrick	Corn	SX0163	50°26·2′	4°47·8′W	X	200
Rosewastis	Corn	SW9161	50°24·9′	4°56·1′W	X	200
Roseweek	Corn	SX0150	50°19·2′	4°47·4′W	X	200,204
Rosewell	Angus	NO4051	56°39·1′	2°58·3′W	X	54
Rosewell	Midlo	NT2862	55°51·0′	3°8·6′W	T	66
Rose Wood	Somer	ST4255	51°17·7′	2°49·5′W	F	172,182
Roseworth	Stock on T	NZ4221	54°35·2′	1°20·6′W	T	93
Roseworthy	Corn	SW6139	50°12·4′	5°20·6′W	T	203
Roseworthy	Corn	SW7947	50°17·1′	5°5·8′W	T	204
Roseworthy Barton	Corn	SW6139	50°12·4′	5°20·6′W	T	203
Rosewyn	Corn	SW8954	50°21·1′	4°57·6′W	X	200
Rosey Copse	Oxon	SU3292	51°37·8′	1°31·9′W	F	164,174
Rosgill	Arg & Bt	NM0948	56°32·3′	6°43·6′W	X	46
Rosgill	Cumbr	NY5316	54°32·5′	2°43·2′W	T	90
Rosgill Hall Wood	Cumbr	NY5416	54°32·5′	2°42·2′W	F	90
Rosgill Moor	Cumbr	NY5215	54°31·9′	2°44·1′W	X	90
Rosherville	Kent	TQ6374	51°26·7′	0°21·1′E	T	177
Ros Hill Wood	Northum	NU0925	55°31·4′	1°51·0′W	F	75
Ros Ho	S Lanak	NS7355	55°46·6′	4°1·0′W	X	64
Roshven	Highld	NM7078	56°50·5′	5°45·8′W	T	40
Roshven Fm	Highld	NM7178	56°50·5′	5°44·8′W	FM	40
Rosier Fm	W Susx	TQ0925	51°1·1′	0°26·4′W	FM	187,198
Rosikie Point	N Eil	NF8788	57°46·6′	7°15·5′W	X	18
Rosinish	N Eil	NF8012	57°5·5′	7°16·6′W	X	31
Rosinish	N Eil	NL6187	56°51·3′	7°33·3′W	X	31
Roskear	Corn	SW9673	50°31·5′	4°52·3′W	X	200
Roskear Croft	Corn	SW6541	50°13·6′	5°17·3′W	T	203
Rosken	Corn	SW8972	50°30·8′	4°58·2′W	X	200
Röskestal	Corn	SW3722	50°2·6′	5°40·0′W	X	203
Roskhill	Highld	NG2745	57°25·1′	6°32·4′W	T	23
Roskhill River	Highld	NG2846	57°25·6′	6°31·4′W	W	23
Roskief	Corn	SW8250	50°18·8′	5°3·4′W	X	200,204
Roskill	N Yks	SE2484	54°15·3′	1°37·5′W	X	99
Roskill Ho	Highld	NH6654	57°33·6′	4°13·9′W	X	26
Röskilly	Corn	SW4727	50°5·6′	5°31·9′W	X	203
Roskilly	Corn	SW7520	50°2·5′	5°8·2′W	X	204
Roskorwell	Corn	SW7923	50°4·2′	5°4·9′W	T	204
Roskrow	Corn	SW7635	50°10·6′	5°7·9′W	X	204
Roskruge Barton	Corn	SW7723	50°4·2′	5°6·6′W	X	204
Roskruge Beacon	Corn	SW7723	50°4·2′	5°6·6′W	A	204
Roskruge Beacon	Corn	SW7723	50°4·2′	5°6·6′W	X	204
Roskymer Barton	Corn	SW6924	50°4·5′	5°13·3′W	X	203
Rosley	Cumbr	NY3245	54°48·0′	3°3·0′W	T	85
Rosleyrigg	Cumbr	NY3146	54°48·5′	3°4·0′W	X	85
Roslin	I of W	SZ4982	50°38·4′	1°18·0′W	X	196
Roslin	Midlo	NT2763	55°51·5′	3°9·5′W	T	66
Roslin Glen	Midlo	NT2662	55°51·0′	3°10·5′W	X	66
Rosliston	Derby	SK2416	52°44·7′	1°38·3′W	T	128
Rosneath	Arg & Bt	NS2583	56°0·7′	4°48·0′W	T	56
Rosneath Bay	Arg & Bt	NS2682	56°0·2′	4°47·0′W	W	56
Rosneath Home Fm	Arg & Bt	NS2681	55°59·7′	4°47·0′W	FM	63
Rosneath Point	Arg & Bt	NS2780	55°59·2′	4°46·0′W	X	63
Rôspannel	Corn	SW3926	50°4·8′	5°38·5′W	X	203
Rôspletha	Corn	SW3822	50°2·7′	5°39·2′W	X	203
Ross	D & G	NX6444	54°46·6′	4°6·4′W	T	83
Ross	Highld	NH2564	57°38·2′	4°55·4′W	X	20
Ross	Northum	NU1337	55°37·8′	1°47·2′W	T	75
Ross	Pth & Kin	NN7621	56°22·2′	4°0·0′W	X	51,52,57
Ross	Pth & Kin	NN9922	56°23·0′	3°37·7′W	X	52,53,58
Ross	Pth & Kin	NO2122	56°23·3′	3°16·3′W	X	53,58
Ross	Scot Bord	NT9660	55°50·2′	2°3·4′W	T	67
Rossa Fm	Lincs	TF4981	53°18·5′	0°14·6′E	FM	122
Rossal	Highld	NC6803	58°0·1′	4°13·5′W	X	16
Rossal Farm	Arg & Bt	NM5427	56°22·5′	5°58·6′W	FM	48
Rossall Grange	Shrops	SJ4615	52°44·0′	2°47·6′W	X	126
Rossall Point	Lancs	SD3147	53°55·1′	3°2·6′W	X	102
Rossall School	Lancs	SD3144	53°53·5′	3°2·6′W	X	102
Rossal Wood	Highld	NC4504	58°0·2′	4°36·9′W	F	16
Ross Back Sands	Northum	NU1437	55°37·8′	1°46·2′W	X	75
Rossbank	Arg & Bt	NS3584	56°1·5′	4°38·4′W	X	56
Ross Bay	D & G	NX6444	54°46·6′	4°6·4′W	W	83
Ross Bay	D & G	NX6544	54°46·6′	4°5·5′W	W	83,84
Ross Castle	Cumbr	NY3863	54°57·7′	2°57·7′W	X	85
Rossdhu Ho	Arg & Bt	NS3689	56°4·2′	4°37·6′W	X	56
Rossellewood Fm	Notts	SK6451	53°3·4′	1°2·3′W	FM	120
Rossendale Valley	Lancs	SD8522	53°41·9′	2°13·2′W	X	103
Rossendale Way	Lancs	SD8327	53°44·6′	2°15·1′W	X	103
Rossett	Cumbr	NY2906	54°26·9′	3°5·3′W	X	89,90
Rossett	Wrex	SJ3657	53°6·6′	2°57·0′W	T	117
Rossett Crag	Cumbr	NY2507	54°27·4′	3°9·0′W	X	89,90
Rossett Gill	Cumbr	NY2507	54°27·4′	3°9·0′W	W	89,90
Rossett Green	N Yks	SE3052	53°58·0′	1°32·1′W	T	104
Rossett Pike	Cumbr	NY2407	54°27·4′	3°9·9′W	H	89,90
Ross Green	Worcs	SO7661	52°15·0′	2°20·7′W	T	138,150
Rosshall	Renf	NS5063	55°50·5′	4°23·3′W	X	64
Rosshayne Fm	Devon	ST2306	50°51·1′	3°5·3′W	FM	192,193
Ross Hill	D & G	NX6470	55°0·6′	4°7·2′W	X	77
Rosside	Cumbr	SD2778	54°11·8′	3°6·7′W	X	96,97
Rossie	Fife	NO2512	56°17·9′	3°12·3′W	X	59
Rossie	Pth & Kin	NN9913	56°18·2′	3°37·5′W	X	58
Rossiebank	Pth & Kin	NN9913	56°18·2′	3°37·5′W	X	58

Rossie Drain	Fife	NO2810	56°16·9′	3°9·3′W	W	59
Rossie Hill	Pth & Kin	NO2731	56°28·2′	3°10·6′W	H	53
Rossie Ho	Fife	NO2612	56°17·9′	3°11·3′W	X	59
Rossie Ho	Pth & Kin	NO0818	56°21·0′	3°28·9′W	X	58
Rossie Island or Inchbraoch	Angus	NO7056	56°41·9′	2°28·9′W	T	54
Rossie Law	Pth & Kin	NN9912	56°17·6′	3°37·5′W	X	58
Rossie Mills	Angus	NO6956	56°41·9′	2°29·9′W	X	54
Rossie Moor	Angus	NO6554	56°40·8′	2°33·8′W	X	54
Rossie Ochill	Pth & Kin	NO0812	56°17·7′	3°28·7′W	X	58
Rossie Priory	Pth & Kin	NO2830	56°27·7′	3°9·7′W	X	53
Rossie School	Angus	NO6653	56°40·3′	2°32·8′W	X	54
Rossie's Loch	Shetld	HT9739	60°8·4′	2°2·7′W	W	4
Rossington	Donc	SK6298	53°28·7′	1°3·5′W	T	111
Rossington Br	Donc	SK6299	53°29·3′	1°3·5′W	X	111
Rossington Grange Fm	Donc	SK6097	53°28·2′	1°5·4′W	FM	111
Rossington Hall School	Donc	SK6396	53°27·6′	1°2·7′W	X	111
Rosskeen	Highld	NH6869	57°41·8′	4°12·4′W	X	21
Rossland	Renf	NS4470	55°54·1′	4°29·3′W	T	64
Rossley Manor	Glos	SO9919	51°52·4′	2°0·5′W	X	163
Ross Links	Northum	NU1337	55°37·8′	1°47·2′W	X	75
Ross Low	Northum	NU1435	55°36·8′	1°46·2′W	W	75
Rosslynlee Hospl	Midlo	NT2660	55°49·9′	3°10·4′W	X	66
Ross Mains	D & G	NY0688	55°10·9′	3°28·1′W	X	78
Ross Moor	E Yorks	SE7343	53°52·9′	0°53·0′W	X	105,106
Rossmoor Grange	E Yorks	SE7245	53°54·0′	0°53·8′W	X	105,106
Rossmoor Lodge	E Yorks	SE7244	53°53·5′	0°53·9′W	X	105,106
Rossmore	Poole	SZ0593	50°44·4′	1°55·4′W	T	195
Rossmyre	Orkney	HY3812	58°59·7′	3°4·3′W	X	6
Ross of Mull	Arg & Bt	NM3821	56°18·8′	6°13·8′W	X	48
Ross-on-Wye	Heref	SO6024	51°55·0′	2°34·5′W	T	162
Ross Park	Arg & Bt	NS3587	56°3·1′	4°38·5′W	X	56
Ross Point	Fife	NT2285	56°3·3′	3°14·7′W	X	66
Ross Point	Northum	NU1339	55°38·9′	1°47·2′W	X	75
Ross Point	Scot Bord	NT9660	55°50·2′	2°3·4′W	X	67
Ross Point	Stir	NS3695	56°7·4′	4°37·9′W	X	56
Ross Priory	W Dunb	NS4187	56°3·2′	4°32·8′W	X	56
Ross Roads	D & G	NX6643	54°46·1′	4°4·6′W	W	83,84
Ross Rock	Highld	NM6059	56°39·9′	5°54·6′W	X	49
Ross's Camp	Cumbr	SD1298	54°22·4′	3°20·9′W	X	96
Ross's Plantn	W Loth	NT1074	55°57·3′	3°26·0′W	F	65
Ross, The	N Ayr	NR9628	55°30·4′	5°13·4′W	X	68,69
Ross, The	N Ayr	NS0030	55°31·6′	5°9·7′W	H	69
Ross, The	N Ayr	NS0030	55°31·6′	5°9·7′W	X	69
Rossway	Herts	SP9507	51°45·4′	0°37·0′W	X	165
Rossway Home Fm	Herts	SP9507	51°45·4′	0°37·0′W	FM	165
Ross Wood	Pth & Kin	NN7521	56°22·1′	4°1·0′W	F	51,52,57
Ross Wood	Stir	NS3795	56°7·5′	4°36·9′W	F	56
Rosteague	Corn	SW8733	50°9·8′	4°58·6′W	X	204
Roster	Highld	ND2540	58°20·8′	3°16·4′W	T	11,12
Rostherne	Ches	SJ7483	53°20·8′	2°23·0′W	T	109
Rostherne Mere	Ches	SJ7484	53°21·4′	2°23·0′W	W	109
Rostholme	Donc	SE5606	53°33·1′	1°8·9′W	T	111
Rosthwaite	Cumbr	NY2514	54°31·2′	3°9·1′W	T	89,90
Rosthwaite	Cumbr	SD2490	54°18·2′	3°9·7′W	T	96
Rosthwaite Fell	Cumbr	NY2512	54°30·1′	3°9·1′W	X	89,90
Rosthwaite Fm	Cumbr	SD4093	54°20·0′	2°54·9′W	FM	96,97
Rostigan	Corn	SW9764	50°26·7′	4°51·2′W	X	200
Roston	Derby	SK1341	52°58·2′	1°48·0′W	T	119,128
Roston Common	Derby	SK1441	52°58·2′	1°47·1′W	X	119,128
Rostowrack Downs	Corn	SW9556	50°22·3′	4°52·6′W	X	200
Rosudgeon	Corn	SW5529	50°6·9′	5°25·3′W	T	203
Rosudgeon Common	Corn	SW5529	50°6·9′	5°25·3′W	X	203
Rosuick	Corn	SW7420	50°2·5′	5°9·0′W	X	204
Rosullah	Aberd	NJ8032	57°22·9′	2°19·5′W	X	29,30
Rosy Burn	Aberd	NJ6655	57°35·3′	2°33·7′W	W	29
Rosyburn	Aberd	NJ6655	57°35·3′	2°33·7′W	X	29
Rosy Hill	N Yks	NZ2300	54°23·9′	1°38·3′W	X	93
Rosyth	Fife	NT1083	56°2·1′	3°26·2′W	T	65
Rosyth Castle	Fife	NT1182	56°1·6′	3°25·2′W	A	65
Rosyth Church	Fife	NT0882	56°1·6′	3°28·1′W	A	65
Rotchell	D & G	NY1274	55°3·4′	3°22·2′W	X	85
Rotchfords	Essex	TL9330	51°56·3′	0°48·9′E	T	168
Rotcombe	Bath & NE Somer	ST6458	51°19·4′	2°30·6′W	T	172
Rothamsted	Herts	TL1213	51°48·5′	0°22·1′W	A	166
Rothamsted Experimental Station	Herts	TL1213	51°48·5′	0°22·1′W	X	166
Rothbury	Northum	NU0501	55°18·4′	1°54·8′W	T	81
Rothbury Forest	Northum	NZ0599	55°17·4′	1°54·8′W	X	81
Rothen	Aberd	NJ6058	57°36·9′	2°39·7′W	X	29
Rothens	Aberd	NJ6817	57°14·8′	2°31·4′W	X	38
Rotherbridge	W Susx	SU9620	50°58·5′	0°37·6′W	T	197
Rotherby	Leic	SK6716	52°44·5′	1°0·0′W	T	129
Rotherby Lodge	Leic	SK6816	52°44·5′	0°59·2′W	X	129
Rotherfield	E Susx	TQ5529	51°2·6′	0°13·1′E	T	188,199
Rotherfield Farmhouse	E Susx	TQ4022	50°59·0′	0°0·1′E	X	198
Rotherfield Greys	Oxon	SU7282	51°32·2′	0°57·3′W	T	175
Rotherfield Hall	E Susx	TQ5428	51°2·1′	0°12·2′E	X	188,199
Rotherfield Park	Hants	SU6932	51°5·2′	1°0·5′W	X	186
Rotherfield Peppard	Oxon	SU7181	51°31·6′	0°58·2′W	T	175
Rotherham	Roth	SK4392	53°25·6′	1°20·8′W	T	111
Rotherham's Oak Fm	Sol	SP1373	52°21·5′	1°48·1′W	FM	139
Rotherhill Ho	W Susx	SU8522	50°59·7′	0°46·9′W	X	197
Rotherhithe	Sthwk	TQ3579	51°29·9′	0°2·9′W	T	177
Rotherhope Cleugh	Cumbr	NY7042	54°46·6′	2°27·6′W	X	86,87
Rotherhope Fell	Cumbr	NY7141	54°46·0′	2°26·6′W	X	86,87
Rotherhope Fell	Cumbr	NY7239	54°45·0′	2°25·7′W	H	91
Rotherhope Tower	Cumbr	NY7143	54°47·1′	2°26·6′W	X	86,87
Rotherhurst	E Susx	TQ5528	51°2·0′	0°13·0′E	X	188,199
Rother Levels	E Susx	TQ9125	50°59·8′	0°43·7′E	X	189
Rotherley Bottom	Wilts	ST9519	50°58·5′	2°3·9′W	X	184
Rotherley Down	Wilts	ST9519	50°58·5′	2°3·9′W	X	184
Rothern Br	Devon	SS4719	50°57·2′	4°10·3′W	A	180
Rothers Sker	Swan	SS6186	51°33·6′	3°59·9′W	X	159
Rothersthorpe	Northnts	SP7156	52°12·1′	0°57·3′W	T	152
Rothersyke Fm	Cumbr	NY0008	54°27·7′	3°32·1′W	FM	89
Rother Valley Country Park	Roth	SK4582	53°20·2′	1°19·0′W	X	111,120
Rother Valley Cycle Route, The	W Susx	SU9024	51°0·7′	0°42·6′W	X	197

Rotherwas	Heref	SO5338	52°2·5′	2°40·7′W	T	149
Rotherwick	Hants	SU7156	51°18·2′	0°58·5′W	T	175,186
Rotherwood	Leic	SK3515	52°44·1′	1°28·5′W	X	128
Rotheryhaugh	Northum	NY6771	55°2·2′	2°30·6′W	X	86,87
Rothes	Moray	NJ2749	57°31·8′	3°12·7′W	T	28
Rothesay	Arg & Bt	NS0864	55°50·1′	5°3·5′W	T	63
Rothesay Bay	Arg & Bt	NS0865	55°50·7′	5°3·6′W	W	63
Rothesbank	S Lanak	NS8545	55°41·3′	3°49·3′W	X	72
Rothiebrisbane	Aberd	NJ7437	57°25·6′	2°25·5′W	X	29
Rothiemay Crossroads	Moray	NJ5449	57°32·0′	2°45·6′W	X	29
Rothiemoon	Highld	NH9920	57°15·8′	3°40·0′W	X	36
Rothiemurchus	Highld	NH9308	57°9·3′	3°45·7′W	X	36
Rothiemurchus Lodge	Highld	NH9506	57°8·2′	3°43·6′W	X	36
Rothienorman	Aberd	NJ7235	57°24·5′	2°27·5′W	T	29
Rothiesholm	Orkney	HY6223	59°5·8′	2°39·3′W	T	5
Rothiesholm Head	Orkney	HY6021	59°4·7′	2°41·4′W	X	5,6
Rothie Vale	Aberd	NJ7337	57°25·6′	2°26·5′W	X	29
Rothill	Northum	NU0612	55°24·4′	1°53·9′W	X	81
Rothill Fm	N Yks	SE6640	53°51·4′	0°59·4′W	FM	105,106
Rothills	Moray	NJ1767	57°41·4′	3°23·1′W	X	28
Rothley	Leic	SK5812	52°42·4′	1°8·1′W	T	129
Rothley	Northum	NZ0487	55°10·9′	1°55·8′W	X	81
Rothley Brook	Leic	SK5509	52°40·8′	1°10·8′W	W	140
Rothley Brook	Leic	SK5712	52°42·4′	1°9·0′W	W	129
Rothley Crags	Northum	NZ0488	55°11·4′	1°55·8′W	H	81
Rothley Cross Roads	Northum	NZ0489	55°12·0′	1°55·8′W	X	81
Rothley Grange	Leic	SK5713	52°42·9′	1°9·0′W	X	129
Rothley Hall	Northum	NZ0589	55°12·0′	1°54·9′W	X	81
Rothley Lakes	Northum	NZ0490	55°12·5′	1°55·8′W	W	81
Rothley Lodge	Leic	SK5914	52°43·5′	1°7·2′W	X	129
Rothley Lodge	Northum	NZ0487	55°10·9′	1°55·8′W	X	81
Rothley Park Fm	Northum	NZ0488	55°11·4′	1°55·8′W	FM	81
Rothley Plain	Leic	SK5613	52°42·9′	1°9·9′W	T	129
Rothley Shield East	Northum	NZ0490	55°12·5′	1°55·8′W	X	81
Rothley Sta	Leic	SK5612	52°42·4′	1°9·9′W	X	129
Rothley West Shield	Northum	NZ0390	55°12·5′	1°56·7′W	X	81
Rothmackenzie	Aberd	NJ5758	57°36·9′	2°42·7′W	X	29
Rothney	Aberd	NJ6327	57°20·2′	2°36·4′W	T	37
Rothnick	Aberd	NO8795	57°3·0′	2°12·4′W	X	38,45
Rothwell	Leeds	SE3428	53°45·1′	1°28·6′W	T	104
Rothwell	Lincs	TF1599	53°28·7′	0°15·6′W	T	113
Rothwell	Northnts	SP8181	52°25·5′	0°48·1′W	T	141
Rothwell Grange Fm	Lincs	TF1399	53°28·8′	0°17·4′W	FM	113
Rothwell Grange Fm	Northnts	SP8380	52°24·9′	0°46·4′W	FM	141
Rothwell Haigh	Leeds	SE3428	53°45·1′	1°28·6′W	T	104
Rothwell Lodge	Northnts	SP8280	52°24·9′	0°47·3′W	X	141
Rothwell Stackgarth	Lincs	TA1400	53°29·3′	0°16·5′W	X	113
Rothwell Top Fm	Lincs	TF1397	53°27·7′	0°17·5′W	FM	113
Rotmell Fm	Pth & Kin	NO0047	56°36·5′	3°37·3′W	FM	52,53
Rotmell Loch	Pth & Kin	NO0247	56°36·5′	3°35·3′W	W	52,53
Rotmell Wood	Pth & Kin	NO0146	56°36·0′	3°36·3′W	F	52,53
Rotsea	E Yorks	TA0651	53°56·9′	0°22·7′W	T	107
Rotsea Carr Fm	E Yorks	TA0751	53°56·9′	0°21·8′W	FM	107
Rotsea Drain	E Yorks	TA0651	53°56·9′	0°22·7′W	W	107
Rottal	Angus	NO3669	56°48·7′	3°2·4′W	T	44
Rottal Lodge	Angus	NO3769	56°48·8′	3°1·5′W	X	44
Rottearns	Pth & Kin	NN8407	56°14·7′	3°51·9′W	X	58
Rotten Bottom	D & G	NT1414	55°25·0′	3°21·1′W	X	78
Rotten Burn	S Lanak	NS6752	55°44·8′	4°6·7′W	W	64
Rottenburn Br	N Ayr	NS2468	55°52·6′	4°48·4′W	X	63
Rottenbutts Wood	Cumbr	SD6689	54°18·0′	2°30·9′W	F	98
Rotten Calder	S Lanak	NS6554	55°45·9′	4°8·7′W	W	64
Rotten Edge	N Yks	SD7857	54°0·8′	2°19·7′W	X	103
Rotten End	Essex	TL7229	51°56·2′	0°30·5′E	T	167
Rotten End	Suff	TM3567	52°15·3′	1°27·0′E	X	156
Rotten Green	Hants	SU7955	51°17·5′	0°51·6′W	T	175,186
Rotten Gutter	Orkney	ND3494	58°50·0′	3°8·1′W	X	7
Rotten Hill	Lancs	SD5557	54°0·7′	2°40·8′W	X	102
Rotten Park	N Yks	SE0056	54°0·2′	1°59·6′W	X	104
Rottenraw Burn	Angus	NO5840	56°33·3′	2°40·5′W	W	54
Rottenreoch	Pth & Kin	NN8420	56°21·7′	3°52·2′W	X	52,58
Rottenreoch (Long Cairn)	Pth & Kin	NN8420	56°21·7′	3°52·2′W	A	52,58
Rotten Rigg	Durham	NY9125	54°37·4′	2°7·9′W	X	91,92
Rotten Row	Bucks	SU7986	51°34·3′	0°51·2′W	T	175
Rottenrow	E Ayr	NS4819	55°26·7′	4°23·8′W	X	70
Rotten Row	Norf	TG0812	52°40·2′	1°5·0′E	X	133
Rottenrow	S Ayr	NS4730	55°32·6′	4°25·1′W	X	70
Rotten Row	Sol	SP1875	52°22·6′	1°43·7′W	T	139
Rotten Row	W Berks	SU5871	51°26·3′	1°9·5′W	T	174
Rotten Row Fm	Shrops	SO7378	52°24·2′	2°23·4′W	FM	138
Rottenstocks	Falk	NS8676	55°58·1′	3°49·1′W	X	65
Rottenyard	E Ayr	NS6115	55°24·8′	4°11·3′W	X	71
Rottingdean	Bri & Hov	TQ3702	50°48·3′	0°3·0′W	T	198
Rottington	Cumbr	NX9613	54°30·3′	3°35·9′W	T	89
Rottington Cottages	Cumbr	NX9612	54°29·8′	3°35·9′W	X	89
Rotton Park	Birm	SP0487	52°29·1′	1°56·1′W	T	139
Roucan	D & G	NY0277	55°4·9′	3°31·7′W	X	84
Rouch	Staffs	SJ9346	53°0·9′	2°5·9′W	X	118
Rouchester Fm	Northum	NY8977	55°5·5′	2°9·9′W	FM	87
Roud	I of W	SZ5180	50°37·3′	1°16·4′W	T	196
Roudham Hall	Norf	TL9587	52°27·0′	0°52·6′E	X	144
Roudham Heath	Norf	TL9387	52°27·0′	0°50·8′E	F	144
Roudsea Wood	Cumbr	SD3382	54°14·0′	3°1·3′W	F	96,97
Rouen Bay	Aberd	NO8675	56°52·2′	2°13·3′W	W	45
Rougemont	N Yks	SE2946	53°54·8′	1°33·1′W	A	104
Rougham	Norf	TF8320	52°45·0′	0°43·1′E	T	132
Rougham	Suff	TL9161	52°13·1′	0°48·2′E	T	155
Rougham Corner	Norf	TL7892	52°30·0′	0°37·7′E	F	144
Rougham Green	Suff	TL9061	52°13·1′	0°47·3′E	T	155
Rougham Park	Suff	TL9064	52°14·7′	0°47·4′E	F	155
Rougham Place	Suff	TL9263	52°14·1′	0°49·1′E	X	155
Roughay Fm	Hants	SU5221	50°59·4′	1°15·2′W	FM	185
Roughazie	S Lanak	NS6238	55°37·2′	4°11·1′W	X	71
Rough Bank	Aberd	NJ4810	57°10·9′	2°51·2′W	X	37
Rough Bank	Aberd	NO6080	56°54·8′	2°39·0′W	H	45
Rough Bank	Derby	SK1090	53°24·6′	1°50·6′W	X	110
Rough Bank	Roch	SD9412	53°36·5′	2°5·0′W	T	109
Roughbank Height	D & G	NY3593	55°13·9′	3°0·9′W	H	79
Rough Beech	Surrey	TQ3242	51°9·9′	0°6·3′W	X	187
Roughbirchworth	Barns	SE2601	53°30·5′	1°36·1′W	T	110

Roughborough Fm	N Yks	SE7670	54°7·5′	0°49·8′W	FM	100
Rough Breck	Notts	SK5973	53°15·3′	1°6·5′W	F	120
Rough Burn	Aberd	NO5489	56°59·7′	2°45·0′W	W	44
Rough Burn	D & G	NT0300	55°17·3′	3°31·2′W	W	78
Rough Burn	E Ayr	NS4709	55°21·3′	4°24·4′W	W	70,77
Roughburn	Highld	NN3781	56°53·8′	4°40·1′W	X	34,41
Rough Burn	N Ayr	NS2861	55°49·0′	4°44·3′W	W	63
Rough Castle	Falk	NS8479	55°59·7′	3°51·1′W	X	65
Rough Castle (Roman Fort)	Falk	NS8479	55°59·7′	3°51·1′W	R	65
Rough Castles	Northum	NU0907	55°21·7′	1°51·1′W	X	81
Rough Chase	Worcs	SO7937	52°2·1′	2°18·0′W	X	150
Roughcleuch Burn	D & G	NY0380	55°6·5′	3°30·8′W	W	78
Roughcleugh Burn	Fife	NT0094	56°8·0′	3°36·1′W	W	58
Rough Cleugh Burn	Scot Bord	NT7164	55°52·3′	2°27·4′W	W	67
Rough Close	Cumbr	NY2736	54°43·1′	3°7·6′W	X	89,90
Rough Close	N Yks	SD8568	54°6·7′	2°13·4′W	X	98
Rough Close	Powys	SO2561	52°14·8′	3°5·5′W	X	137,148
Rough Close	Sol	SP2678	52°24·2′	1°36·7′W	F	140
Rough Close	Staffs	SJ9239	52°57·1′	2°6·7′W	T	127
Rough Common	Kent	TR1259	51°17·7′	1°2·8′E	T	179
Roughcote	Staffs	SJ9444	52°59·8′	2°5·0′W	T	118
Rough Crag	Cumbr	NY3110	54°29·1′	3°3·5′W	X	90
Rough Crag	Cumbr	NY4511	54°29·7′	2°50·5′W	X	90
Rough Crag	Cumbr	SD1697	54°21·9′	3°17·2′W	H	96
Rough Crags	Cumbr	NY2802	54°24·7′	3°6·1′W	X	89,90
Rough Craig	Angus	NO3573	56°50·9′	3°3·5′W	X	44
Rough Craig	Angus	NO4068	56°48·2′	2°58·5′W	H	44
Rough Craigs	D & G	NT1715	55°25·6′	3°18·3′W	X	79
Roughdiamond	E Ayr	NS6137	55°36·7′	4°12·0′W	X	71
Roughdiamond	S Lanak	NS6137	55°36·7′	4°12·0′W	X	71
Roughdike	N Lanak	NS8461	55°50·0′	3°50·7′W	X	65
Rough Down	Wilts	ST9749	51°14·6′	2°2·2′W	X	184
Rough Down	Wilts	SU1770	51°26·0′	1°44·9′W	X	173
Roughdown Common	Herts	TL0405	51°44·3′	0°29·2′W	F	166
Roughdyke Fm	E Ayr	NS4930	55°32·7′	4°23·2′W	FM	70
Rough Edge	Cumbr	NY4010	54°29·2′	2°55·1′W	X	90
Roughethill	Cumbr	NY5453	54°52·4′	2°42·6′W	X	86
Rough Firth	D & G	NX8353	54°51·4′	3°48·9′W	W	84
Rough Flow Moss	S Lanak	NS8020	55°27·8′	3°53·4′W	H	71,72
Rough Fm	Warw	SP2250	52°9·1′	1°40·3′W	FM	151
Rough Gill	Scot Bord	NY4489	55°11·8′	2°52·4′W	W	79
Rough Gill Brows	Cumbr	SD7583	54°14·8′	2°22·6′W	X	98
Rough Grain	Scot Bord	NT2717	55°26·7′	3°8·8′W	W	79
Rough Grey Bottom	Devon	ST1507	50°51·6′	3°12·1′W	X	192,193
Rough Grounds	Derby	SK1538	52°56·6′	1°46·2′W	X	128
Roughhaugh	Aberd	NJ6607	57°9·4′	2°33·3′W	X	38
Rough Haugh	Highld	NC7248	58°24·4′	4°11·0′W	T	10
Rough Haw	N Yks	SD9655	53°59·7′	2°3·2′W	H	103
Rough Hay	Staffs	SK2023	52°48·5′	1°41·8′W	T	128
Rough Hays	Staffs	SK1628	52°51·2′	1°45·3′W	X	128
Rough-hey	Ches	SJ9168	53°12·8′	2°7·7′W	X	118
Rough Hill	Cumbr	NY4919	54°34·1′	2°46·9′W	X	90
Rough Hill	D & G	NX8073	55°2·5′	3°52·2′W	X	84
Rough Hill	E Ayr	NS5445	55°40·8′	4°18·9′W	X	64
Rough Hill	E Ayr	NS5942	55°39·3′	4°14·0′W	X	71
Rough Hill	E Yorks	TA2236	53°48·6′	0°8·4′W	H	107
Rough Hill	Heref	SO5237	52°2·0′	2°41·6′W	X	149
Rough Hill	N Ayr	NS2658	55°47·3′	4°46·1′W	X	63
Rough Hill	Notts	SK5628	52°51·0′	1°9·7′W	X	129
Rough Hill	Oxon	SP3541	52°4·2′	1°29·0′W	X	151
Rough Hill	Roch	SD9120	53°40·8′	2°7·8′W	H	103
Rough Hill	Warw	SP0352	52°10·2′	1°57·0′W	X	150
Rough Hill	Warw	SP2548	52°8·0′	1°37·7′W	X	151
Rough Hill	Wilts	SU1373	51°27·6′	1°48·4′W	X	173
Rough Hill Burn	E Ayr	NS5545	55°40·9′	4°17·9′W	W	64
Rough Hill Fm	Oxon	SP3541	52°4·2′	1°29·0′W	FM	151
Roughhill Moss	E Ayr	NS6218	55°26·4′	4°10·5′W	X	71
Rough Hills	Warw	SP1459	52°14·0′	1°47·3′W	X	151
Rough Hills Fm	N Yks	SE6869	54°7·0′	0°57·2′W	FM	100
Rough Hill Wood	Heref	SO5232	51°59·3′	2°41·5′W	F	149
Rough Hill Wood	Heref	SO7548	52°8·0′	2°21·5′W	F	150
Rough Hill Wood	Notts	SK6576	53°16·9′	1°1·1′W	F	120
Rough Hill Wood	Warw	SP0564	52°16·7′	1°55·2′W	F	150
Rough Holden	Brad	SE0645	53°54·3′	1°54·1′W	X	104
Rough Hole Point	Devon	SX8752	50°21·7′	3°34·9′W	X	202
Rough Holme	Cumbr	SD3998	54°22·7′	2°55·9′W	X	96,97
Roughhill	Ches	SJ3862	53°9·3′	2°55·2′W	X	117
Roughilly Wood	Aberd	NJ5963	57°39·6′	2°40·8′W	F	29
Rough Island	D & G	NX7684	55°8·3′	3°56·3′W	A	78
Rough Island	D & G	NX8453	54°51·8′	3°48·0′W	X	84
Rough Knowe	Scot Bord	NT3625	55°31·1′	3°0·4′W	H	73
Rough Knowe	S Lanak	NS8831	55°33·8′	3°46·1′W	X	71,72
Roughlands	Falk	NS8883	56°1·9′	3°47·4′W	X	65
Roughlands Fm	Corn	SX1776	50°33·5′	4°34·6′W	FM	201
Roughlea Burn	S Ayr	NX2686	55°8·2′	4°43·4′W	W	76
Rough Leaze Fm	Wilts	SU0068	51°24·9′	1°59·6′W	FM	173
Roughlee	Lancs	SD8440	53°51·6′	2°14·2′W	T	103
Roughlee	Scot Bord	NT6511	55°23·8′	2°32·7′W	X	80
Roughlees Fm	Northum	NZ0593	55°14·1′	1°54·9′W	FM	81
Roughley	Birm	SP1299	52°35·6′	1°49·0′W	T	139
Roughley	Scot Bord	NY5295	55°15·1′	2°44·9′W	X	79
Roughley Burn	Scot Bord	NY5196	55°15·6′	2°45·8′W	W	79
Roughley Corner	N Yks	SE2891	54°19·1′	1°33·8′W	X	99
Roughley Sike	Scot Bord	NY5295	55°15·1′	2°44·9′W	W	79
Rough Loch	D & G	NX3149	54°48·7′	4°37·4′W	X	82
Rough Mire	Cumbr	NY2326	54°37·6′	3°11·1′W	X	89,90
Rough Moor	Lancs	SD5446	53°54·7′	2°41·6′W	X	102
Roughmoor	Somer	ST2025	51°1·4′	3°8·1′W	T	193
Roughmoor	Swin	SU1186	51°34·6′	1°50·1′W	T	173
Roughmoor Grounds	Northnts	SP6464	52°16·5′	1°3·3′W	X	152
Rough Moss	Scot Bord	NT3348	55°43·5′	3°3·6′W	H	73
Rough Moss	S Lanak	NS7037	55°36·8′	4°3·4′W	X	71
Rough Naze	D & G	NS7104	55°19·0′	4°1·5′W	H	77
Rough of Stain	Highld	ND3460	58°31·7′	3°7·5′W	X	12
Rougholme	Cumbr	SD1095	54°20·8′	3°22·7′W	X	96
Roughpark	Aberd	NJ3412	57°11·9′	3°5·1′W	T	37
Rough Park	Leic	SK3918	52°45·7′	1°24·9′W	F	128
Rough Park	Roth	SK5590	53°24·5′	1°9·9′W	F	111
Rough Park	Staffs	SK1119	52°46·3′	1°49·8′W	X	128
Rough Park	Wrekin	SJ6704	52°38·2′	2°28·9′W	X	127

Rough Park Plantn	Fife	NT2395	56°8·7′	3°13·9′W	F	58
Rough Piece	Notts	SK5682	53°20·2′	1°9·1′W	F	111,120
Rough Pike	Northum	NY6286	55°10·3′	2°35·4′W	H	80
Rough Pitty Side	Derby	SK2752	53°4·1′	1°35·4′W	F	119
Roughridge Hill	Wilts	SU0565	51°23·3′	1°55·3′W	X	173
Rough Rigg	Durham	NY8234	54°42·3′	2°16·3′W	X	91,92
Roughrigg	N Lanak	NS8270	55°54·8′	3°52·8′W	T	65
Roughrigg Reservoir	N Lanak	NS8064	55°51·5′	3°54·6′W	W	65
Rough Scar	D & G	NY1063	54°57·5′	3°23·9′W	X	85
Rough Shoulder	D & G	NS6903	55°18·5′	4°3·4′W	X	77
Roughside	Cumbr	NY7845	54°48·2′	2°20·1′W	X	86,87
Rough Side	Derby	SK2174	53°16·0′	1°40·7′W	X	119
Roughside	E Ayr	NS6215	55°24·8′	4°10·4′W	X	71
Roughside	Northum	NY7483	55°8·7′	2°24·0′W	X	80
Roughside Moor	Northum	NY7383	55°8·7′	2°25·0′W	X	80
Roughside Wood	Scot Bord	NT7360	55°50·2′	2°25·4′W	F	67,74
Roughsike	Cumbr	NY5275	55°4·3′	2°44·7′W	T	86
Rough Sike	Cumbr	NY6773	55°3·3′	2°30·6′W	W	86,87
Rough Sike	Cumbr	NY7532	54°41·2′	2°22·8′W	W	91
Roughs, The	Kent	TR1334	51°4·2′	1°2·8′E	X	179,189
Roughs, The	Surrey	TQ0349	51°14·1′	0°31·1′W	X	186
Roughstones	Pth & Kin	NO0946	56°36·1′	3°28·5′W	X	52,53
Rough Strand	D & G	NX5688	55°10·2′	4°15·2′W	W	77
Roughtalley's Wood	Essex	TL4803	51°42·6′	0°8·9′E	F	167
Roughten Gill	Cumbr	NY2927	54°38·2′	3°5·6′W	W	89,90
Roughten Gill	Cumbr	NY3027	54°38·2′	3°4·7′W	W	90
Roughters	E Susx	TQ8615	50°54·5′	0°39·1′E	X	189,199
Rough, The	Derby	SK2115	52°44·2′	1°40·9′W	F	128
Rough, The	Staffs	SK2222	52°47·9′	1°40·0′W	X	128
Rough, The	Worcs	SP1048	52°8·0′	1°50·8′W	X	150
Roughton	Lincs	TF2464	53°9·8′	0°8·3′W	T	122
Roughton	Monm	ST3394	51°38·7′	2°57·7′W	X	171
Roughton	Norf	TG2137	52°53·3′	1°17·5′E	T	133
Roughton	Shrops	SO7594	52°32·8′	2°21·7′W	T	138
Roughton Gill	Cumbr	NY2935	54°42·5′	3°5·7′W	W	89,90
Roughton Heath	Norf	TG2238	52°53·8′	1°18·4′E	X	133
Roughton Moor	Lincs	TF2063	53°9·3′	0°11·9′W	X	122
Roughton Moor	Lincs	TF2164	53°9·8′	0°11·0′W	T	122
Roughton Road Sta	Norf	TG2140	52°54·9′	1°17·6′E	X	133
Rough Tor	Corn	SX1480	50°35·6′	4°37·3′W	H	200
Rough Tor	Devon	SX6079	50°35·9′	3°58·3′W	H	191
Roughtor Fm	Corn	SX1382	50°36·7′	4°38·2′W	FM	200
Roughtor Marsh	Corn	SX1581	50°36·2′	4°36·5′W	W	201
Roughtor Moors	Corn	SX1480	50°35·6′	4°37·3′W	X	200
Rough Twr	Essex	TM3927	51°53·6′	1°28·8′E	X	169
Rough Walks	Suff	TM5079	52°21·3′	1°40·7′E	X	156
Roughway	Kent	TQ6252	51°14·9′	0°19·7′E	T	188
Rough Wood	Lincs	SK8474	53°15·6′	0°44·0′W	F	121
Roughwood	N Ayr	NS3452	55°44·2′	4°38·2′W	X	63
Rough Wood	Notts	SK6354	53°5·0′	1°3·2′W	F	120
Roughwood Fm	Ches	SJ7858	53°7·4′	2°19·3′W	FM	118
Roughwood Hill Fm	Ches	SJ7857	53°6·8′	2°19·3′W	FM	118
Roughwood Park	Bucks	TQ0095	51°38·9′	0°32·9′W	X	166,176
Rouken Glen Park	E Renf	NS5458	55°47·9′	4°19·3′W	X	64
Roulston Scar	N Yks	SE5181	54°13·6′	1°12·6′W	X	100
Rounce's Coverts	Norf	TG1639	52°54·5′	1°13·1′E	F	133
Rouncil Fm	Warw	SP2769	52°19·3′	1°35·8′W	FM	151
Roundabout	Glos	ST8997	51°40·5′	2°9·2′W	F	163
Roundabout Fm	Norf	TG0629	52°49·4′	1°3·9′E	FM	133
Roundabout Hill	Oxon	SU4387	51°35·0′	1°22·4′W	X	174
Roundabout Spinney	Leic	SK4900	52°36·0′	1°16·2′W	F	140
Roundabout, The	S Glos	ST6085	51°34·0′	2°34·2′W	X	172
Roundabout, The	Staffs	SJ7823	52°48·5′	2°19·2′W	X	127
Roundabury	Corn	SX2870	50°30·5′	4°25·2′W	A	201
Roundadee	Orkney	HY2214	59°0·6′	3°21·0′W	X	6
Roundal, The	Clackm	NS9097	56°9·4′	3°45·8′W	X	58
Roundash	Devon	SS7512	50°53·9′	3°46·3′W	X	180
Roundaway Fm	Hants	SU3250	51°15·1′	1°32·1′W	FM	185
Roundball Covert	Devon	SY1598	50°46·8′	3°12·0′W	F	192,193
Roundball Hill	Devon	SY1599	50°47·3′	3°12·0′W	X	192,193
Round Bank	Powys	SO2188	52°29·3′	3°9·4′W	X	137
Round Bank	Shrops	SO2487	52°28·8′	3°6·7′W	X	137
Round Barn	Essex	TM0101	51°40·5′	0°54·8′E	X	168
Round Barrow	Dorset	SY8391	50°43·3′	2°14·1′W	A	194
Round Bottom	Wilts	SU2117	50°57·4′	1°41·7′W	H	184
Roundbridge Fm	Surrey	TQ0257	51°18·4′	0°31·8′W	FM	186
Roundbury	Corn	SX2566	50°28·3′	4°27·6′W	A	201
Roundbury	Corn	SX3172	50°31·6′	4°22·7′W	A	201
Round Bush	D & G	NY2367	54°59·7′	3°11·8′W	X	85
Roundbush	Essex	TL8501	51°40·9′	0°41·0′E	T	168
Roundbush	Glos	SO7729	51°57·8′	2°19·7′W	X	150
Round Bush	Herts	TQ1498	51°40·4′	0°20·7′W	T	166,176
Roundbush Fm	Essex	TL9218	51°49·9′	0°47·6′E	FM	168
Roundbush Green	Essex	TL5914	51°48·3′	0°18·8′E	T	167
Roundbush Rocks	V of Glam	ST1869	51°25·1′	3°10·4′W	X	171
Round Castle	Oxon	SP4513	51°49·1′	1°20·4′W	A	164
Round Chimneys Fm	Dorset	ST6809	50°53·0′	2°26·9′W	FM	194
Round Close	Cumbr	NX9918	54°33·1′	3°33·3′W	X	89
Round Close Fm	Red & Cl	NZ6314	54°31·3′	1°1·2′W	FM	94
Roundclose Hill	Cumbr	NY1328	54°38·6′	3°20·5′W	X	89
Round Clump	Hants	SU1122	51°0·1′	1°50·2′W	F	184
Round Coppice Fm	Bucks	TQ0384	51°33·0′	0°30·5′W	FM	176
Round Course	Cambs	TL5961	52°13·7′	0°20·1′E	X	154
Round Covert	Norf	TF8011	52°40·2′	0°40·1′E	F	132
Round Covert Fm	Norf	TL7993	52°30·6′	0°38·7′E	FM	144
Round Craigs	D & G	NX6493	55°13·0′	4°7·8′W	X	77
Round Dikes	Brad	SE0550	53°57·0′	1°55·0′W	A	104
Round Down	Dorset	SZ0277	50°35·8′	1°57·9′W	X	195
Round Down	Wilts	SU1955	51°17·9′	1°43·3′W	H	173
Round Down	W Susx	SU7717	50°57·1′	0°53·8′W	X	197
Round Down	W Susx	SU7918	50°57·6′	0°52·1′W	X	197
Roundell's Allotment	N Yks	SE1459	54°1·9′	1°46·8′W	X	104
Round Elm	Glos	SO8705	51°44·8′	2°10·9′W	X	162
Rounden Wood	E Susx	TQ6721	50°58·1′	0°23·1′E	F	199
Round Fell	D & G	NX5372	55°1·5′	4°17·6′W	H	77
Roundfell	D & G	NX8960	54°55·6′	3°43·5′W	X	84
Round Fell	D & G	NX8961	54°56·1′	3°43·5′W	H	84
Roundgreen	Barns	SE3303	53°31·6′	1°29·7′W	X	110,111
Round Green	Kent	TQ7539	51°7·6′	0°30·4′E	X	188
Round Green	Luton	TL0922	51°53·4′	0°24·6′W	T	166

Round Grove	Norf	TM3194	52°29·9′	1°24·6′E	F	134
Roundham	Somer	ST4209	50°52·9′	2°49·1′W	T	193
Roundham Head	Torbay	SX8960	50°26·0′	3°33·4′W	X	202
Roundhaugh	Aberd	NJ7723	57°18·1′	2°22·4′W	X	38
Roundhay	Leeds	SE3337	53°49·9′	1°29·5′W	T	104
Roundhayes Fm	Corn	SX1594	50°43·2′	4°36·9′W	FM	190
Roundhay Fm	Northnts	SP8856	52°11·9′	0°42·3′W	FM	152
Roundhay Park	Leeds	SE3338	53°50·5′	1°29·5′W	X	104
Roundhill	Aberd	NJ8253	57°34·3′	2°17·6′W	X	29,30
Round Hill	Angus	NO4274	56°51·5′	2°56·6′W	X	44
Round Hill	Angus	NO4676	56°52·6′	2°52·7′W	X	44
Round Hill	Barns	SK1499	53°29·5′	1°46·9′W	X	110
Round Hill	Bath & NE Somer	ST6060	51°20·5′	2°34·1′W	X	172
Round Hill	Bath & NE Somer	ST6955	51°17·8′	2°26·3′W	X	172,183
Round Hill	Bri & Hov	TQ2708	50°51·7′	0°11·3′W	X	198
Round Hill	Cald	SE1320	53°40·8′	1°47·8′W	X	104
Roundhill	Cumbr	NY1448	54°49·4′	3°19·9′W	X	85
Roundhill	Cumbr	NY3342	54°46·4′	3°2·1′W	X	85
Round Hill	Cumbr	NY7436	54°43·3′	2°23·8′W	H	91
Round Hill	Cumbr	NY8616	54°32·6′	2°12·6′W	X	91,92
Round Hill	Derby	SE0604	53°32·2′	1°54·2′W	X	110
Round Hill	Derby	SE1200	53°30·0′	1°48·7′W	X	110
Round Hill	Derby	SK1097	53°28·4′	1°50·6′W	X	110
Round Hill	Derby	SK1396	53°27·9′	1°47·8′W	X	110
Round Hill	Derby	SK3328	52°51·1′	1°30·2′W	X	128
Round Hill	Devon	SS8030	51°3·6′	3°42·4′W	H	181
Round Hill	Devon	SS9106	50°50·8′	3°32·5′W	H	192
Round Hill	Essex	TQ7986	51°32·9′	0°35·3′E	X	178
Round Hill	Fife	NO3822	56°23·4′	2°59·8′W	H	54,59
Round Hill	Glos	SO7218	51°51·8′	2°24·0′W	X	162
Round Hill	Glos	SP0427	51°56·7′	1°56·1′W	H	163
Round Hill	Hants	SU2614	50°55·7′	1°37·4′W	X	195
Round Hill	Hants	SU3301	50°48·7′	1°31·5′W	X	196
Round Hill	Hants	SU8033	51°5·7′	0°51·1′W	X	186
Round Hill	Highld	NC6234	58°16·6′	4°20·7′W	H	16
Round Hill	Highld	NC6639	58°19·4′	4°16·8′W	H	16
Round Hill	Kent	TQ5462	51°20·4′	0°13·1′E	X	177,188
Round Hill	Moray	NJ2835	57°24·2′	3°11·4′W	X	28
Round Hill	Moray	NJ3022	57°17·3′	3°9·2′W	H	37
Round Hill	Moray	NJ3427	57°20·0′	3°5·3′W	H	37
Round Hill	Norf	TM4492	52°28·5′	1°36·0′E	X	134
Round Hill	Northum	NY7477	55°5·5′	2°24·0′W	X	86,87
Round Hill	Northum	NY7552	54°52·0′	2°22·9′W	X	86,87
Round Hill	Northum	NY8054	54°53·1′	2°18·3′W	X	86,87
Round Hill	Notts	SK5157	53°6·7′	1°13·9′W	X	120
Round Hill	Notts	SK6345	53°0·2′	1°3·3′W	X	129
Round Hill	N Yks	NZ5901	54°24·3′	1°5·0′W	H	93
Round Hill	N Yks	SD8179	54°12·6′	2°17·1′W	X	98
Round Hill	N Yks	SE1050	53°57·0′	1°50·4′W	X	104
Round Hill	N Yks	SE1253	53°58·6′	1°48·6′W	H	104
Round Hill	N Yks	SE1476	54°11·0′	1°46·7′W	X	99
Round Hill	N Yks	SE2647	53°55·4′	1°35·8′W	X	104
Round Hill	N Yks	SE4549	53°56·3′	1°18·5′W	X	105
Round Hill	N Yks	SE5493	54°20·0′	1°9·8′W	X	100
Round Hill	Oldham	SE0209	53°34·9′	1°57·8′W	X	110
Round Hill	Orkney	HY2203	58°54·7′	3°20·8′W	H	6,7
Round Hill	Oxon	SP3839	52°3·1′	1°26·4′W	X	151
Round Hill	Oxon	SP3931	51°58·8′	1°25·5′W	X	151
Round Hill	Oxon	SP4908	51°46·3′	1°17·0′W	A	164
Round Hill	Oxon	SU3684	51°33·5′	1°28·5′W	X	174
Round Hill	Oxon	SU4187	51°35·1′	1°24·1′W	A	174
Round Hill	Oxon	SU6697	51°40·3′	1°2·3′W	X	164,165
Round Hill	Oxon	SU7485	51°33·8′	0°55·6′W	X	175
Round Hill	Sheff	SK2093	53°26·2′	1°41·5′W	X	110
Round Hill	Shrops	SO3499	52°35·3′	2°58·1′W	X	137
Round Hill	Shrops	SO4292	52°31·6′	2°50·9′W	H	137
Round Hill	Shrops	SO6797	52°34·4′	2°28·8′W	X	138
Roundhill	S Lanak	NS6540	55°38·3′	4°8·3′W	X	71
Round Hill	Somer	ST1836	51°7·3′	3°9·9′W	X	181
Round Hill	Somer	ST7131	51°4·9′	2°24·5′W	X	183
Round Hill	Staffs	SK0119	52°46·4′	1°58·7′W	X	128
Roundhill	Staffs	SK0265	53°11·2′	1°57·8′W	X	119
Round Hill	Staffs	SO8783	52°26·9′	2°11·1′W	X	139
Round Hill	Stock on T	NZ4312	54°30·3′	1°19·7′W	A	93
Round Hill	Suff	TM4457	52°9·7′	1°34·5′E	X	156
Round Hill	Torbay	SX8962	50°27·1′	3°33·4′W	X	202
Round Hill	Warw	SP1062	52°15·6′	1°50·8′W	H	150
Round Hill	Warw	SP1461	52°15·1′	1°47·3′W	X	151
Round Hill	Warw	SP3149	52°8·5′	1°32·4′W	A	151
Round Hill	Warw	SP3337	52°2·1′	1°30·7′W	X	151
Round Hill	Warw	SP4057	52°12·8′	1°24·5′W	X	151
Round Hill	Wilts	ST9126	51°2·2′	2°7·3′W	X	184
Round Hill	Wilts	SU3057	51°18·9′	1°33·8′W	X	174
Round Hill	Worcs	SO7066	52°17·7′	2°26·0′W	X	138,149
Round Hill	Worcs	SO7353	52°10·7′	2°23·3′W	X	150
Round Hill	Worcs	SO8954	52°11·3′	2°9·3′W	X	150
Round Hill Downs	Wilts	SU2175	51°28·6′	1°41·5′W	X	174
Roundhill Fm	Bucks	SP7309	51°46·7′	0°56·1′W	FM	165
Roundhill Fm	Bucks	SP7833	51°59·6′	0°51·4′W	FM	152,165
Roundhill Fm	Bucks	SP8107	51°45·6′	0°49·2′W	FM	165
Roundhill Fm	Cumbr	NY3805	54°26·4′	2°56·9′W	FM	90
Roundhill Fm	Darl	NZ3011	54°29·8′	1°31·8′W	FM	93
Roundhill Fm	Glos	SP1222	51°54·0′	1°49·1′W	FM	163
Roundhill Fm	Hants	SU1318	50°57·9′	1°48·5′W	FM	184
Roundhill Fm	N Yks	SE1265	54°5·1′	1°48·6′W	FM	99
Round Hill Fm	N Yks	SE2393	54°20·2′	1°38·4′W	FM	99
Roundhill Fm	Oxon	SP5530	51°58·2′	1°11·6′W	FM	152
Roundhill Fm	Swin	SU2094	51°38·9′	1°42·3′W	FM	163,174
Roundhill Fm	Warw	SP2840	52°3·7′	1°35·1′W	FM	151
Round Hill Fm	Wilts	ST8140	51°9·8′	2°15·9′W	FM	183
Roundhill Grange	Somer	ST7131	51°4·9′	2°24·5′W	X	183
Roundhill Moss	Derby	SE0602	53°31·1′	1°54·2′W	X	110
Roundhillock	Aberd	NK0053	57°34·3′	1°59·5′W	X	30
Roundhillock	Aberd	NK0849	57°32·1′	1°51·5′W	X	30
Round Hill of Mark	Angus	NO3382	56°55·7′	3°5·6′W	X	44
Round Hill Plantns	Dorset	SY5895	50°45·4′	2°35·3′W	F	194
Roundhill Plump	N Yks	SE2392	54°19·6′	1°38·4′W	F	99
Roundhill Resr	N Yks	SE1477	54°11·6′	1°46·7′W	W	99

Round Hills	Lincs	SK9930	52°51·7′	0°31·4′W	X	130
Round Hills	Norf	TG4701	52°33·3′	1°39·0′E	X	134
Round Hills	N Yks	SE1967	54°6·2′	1°42·1′W	X	99
Round Hills (Earthwork)	Lincs	SK9930	52°51·7′	0°31·4′W	A	130
Round Hill (Settlement)	Somer	ST1836	51°7·3′	3°9·9′W	A	181
Round Hill Spinney	Leic	SK7703	52°37·4′	0°51·3′W	F	141
Round Hill (Tumulus)	Derby	SK3328	52°51·1′	1°30·2′W	A	128
Round Hill (Tumulus)	N Yks	SE1050	53°57·0′	1°50·4′W	A	104
Roundhill Wood	Oxon	SU5497	51°40·4′	1°12·8′W	F	164
Roundhill Wood	Warw	SP2952	52°10·2′	1°34·2′W	F	151
Roundhill Wood	Worcs	SO9858	52°13·4′	2°1·4′W	F	150
Round Ho	Ches	SJ7368	53°12·7′	2°23·9′W	X	118
Round Ho	Glos	SU2098	51°41·1′	1°42·2′W	X	163
Round Ho	Herts	TL3615	51°49·3′	0°1·2′W	X	166
Round Ho	Lincs	TF3645	52°59·3′	0°2·0′E	X	131
Round Ho	Norf	TG3802	52°34·0′	1°31·1′E	X	134
Round Ho	Northnts	SP9374	52°21·6′	0°37·7′W	X	141
Round Ho	Shrops	SJ6800	52°36·0′	2°27·9′W	X	127
Round Ho	Suff	TL8160	52°12·7′	0°39·4′E	X	155
Round Hole	Corn	SW8576	50°32·9′	5°1·7′W	X	200
Round Hole	Corn	SW8976	50°33·0′	4°58·3′W	X	200
Round Holm	Shetld	HP5605	60°43·7′	0°57·9′W	X	1
Round Holt	Notts	SK6390	53°24·4′	1°2·7′W	F	111
Roundhome	Aberd	NJ6139	57°26·6′	2°38·5′W	X	29
Round Ho The	Somer	SS9835	51°6·5′	3°27·0′W	X	181
Round Ho, The	W Berks	SU5165	51°23·1′	1°15·6′W	X	174
Roundhouse	Cumbr	NY3332	54°41·0′	3°1·9′W	X	90
Round House Fm	Birm	SP1396	52°33·9′	1°48·1′W	FM	139
Roundhouse Fm	Bucks	SU7587	51°34·8′	0°54·7′W	FM	175
Roundhouse, The	Arg & Bt	NM1554	56°35·7′	6°38·1′W	X	46
Round How	Cumbr	NY2108	54°27·9′	3°12·7′W	X	89,90
Round How	Cumbr	NY3920	54°34·5′	2°56·2′W	H	90
Round How	Cumbr	NY4016	54°32·4′	2°55·2′W	X	90
Roundhurst Common	W Susx	SU9330	51°3·9′	0°40·0′W	X	186
Roundhurst Fms	W Susx	SU9230	51°3·9′	0°40·8′W	FM	186
Round Island	D & G	NX3052	54°50·3′	4°38·4′W	X	82
Round Island	Dorset	SY9887	50°41·2′	2°1·3′W	X	195
Round Island	I Scilly	SV9017	49°58·6′	6°19·1′W	X	203
Round Knoll	Dorset	SY4995	50°45·4′	2°43·0′W	H	193,194
Round Knott	Cumbr	NY3333	54°41·5′	3°1·9′W	H	90
Round Knowl	Staffs	SK0562	53°9·5′	1°55·1′W	X	119
Round Law	Northum	NY7295	55°15·2′	2°26·0′W	H	80
Roundlaw	Pth & Kin	NN9619	56°21·4′	3°40·5′W	X	58
Round Law	Pth & Kin	NO2333	56°29·2′	3°14·6′W	X	53
Round Lighnot	Aberd	NJ7929	57°21·3′	2°20·5′W	X	38
Round Loaf	Lancs	SD6318	53°39·7′	2°33·2′W	X	109
Round Loch of Glenhead	D & G	NX4580	55°5·7′	4°25·3′W	W	77
Round Loch of the Dungeon	D & G	NX4684	55°7·8′	4°24·5′W	W	77
Round Maple	Suff	TL9543	52°3·3′	0°51·1′E	T	155
Round Meadows	Northum	NY8259	54°55·8′	2°16·4′W	X	86,87
Round Meadows	Staffs	SJ9548	53°2·0′	2°4·1′W	X	118
Round Oak	Dudley	SO9287	52°29·1′	2°6·7′W	T	139
Round Oak	Shrops	SO3984	52°27·3′	2°53·5′W	T	137
Round Oak Hill	Heref	SO4446	52°6·8′	2°48·7′W	H	148,149
Round Oak, The	Shrops	SO5869	52°19·3′	2°36·6′W	X	137,138
Round Plantn	D & G	NX1158	54°53·1′	4°56·4′W	F	82
Round Point	Shetld	HU5137	60°7·1′	1°4·4′W	X	4
Round Rigg	Cumbr	NY6370	55°1·6′	2°34·3′W	X	86
Round Robin Fm	Swin	SU2291	51°37·3′	1°40·5′W	FM	163,174
Round Roblets	Essex	TL6313	51°47·7′	0°22·2′E	X	167
Roundseats Fm	Sheff	SK2981	53°19·7′	1°33·5′W	FM	110
Round's Green	Sand	SO9889	52°30·2′	2°1·4′W	T	139
Roundshaw	Sutton	TQ3063	51°21·3′	0°7·6′W	T	176,177,187
Roundshaw Fm	E Ayr	NS5624	55°29·6′	4°16·3′W	FM	71
Roundshill Fm	Warw	SP2670	52°19·9′	1°36·7′W	FM	140
Roundshill Park Wood	Kent	TQ8137	51°6·4′	0°35·5′E	F	188
Rounds of Tivla	Shetld	HP6110	60°46·4′	0°52·3′W	X	1
Rounds of Tivla (cairns)	Shetld	HP6110	60°46·4′	0°52·3′W	A	1
Round Spinney	Northnts	SP7965	52°16·9′	0°50·1′W	T	152
Roundstone Fm	W Susx	TQ0803	50°49·2′	0°27·6′W	FM	197
Roundstonefoot	D & G	NT1408	55°21·8′	3°21·0′W	X	78
Roundstonefoot Burn	D & G	NT1309	55°22·3′	3°21·9′W	W	78
Round Street	Kent	TQ6568	51°23·4′	0°22·7′E	T	177,178
Roundstreet Common	W Susx	TQ0528	51°2·7′	0°29·7′W	T	187,197
Roundswell	Devon	SS5431	51°3·8′	4°4·6′W	T	180
Round Table	I of M	SC2475	54°8·7′	4°41·3′W	X	95
Round Table or Roper Castle	Cumbr	NY8811	54°29·9′	2°10·7′W	X	91,92
Round Table or Roper Castle (Roman Signal Station)	Cumbr	NY8811	54°29·9′	2°10·7′W	R	91,92
Round, The	Orkney	HY5006	58°56·6′	2°51·6′W	X	6,7
Roundthorn	Cumbr	NY5331	54°40·6′	2°43·3′W	X	90
Roundthorn	Man	SJ8088	53°23·5′	2°17·6′W	T	109
Roundthorn	Shrops	SO5578	52°24·1′	2°39·3′W	X	137,138
Roundthwaite	Cumbr	NY6003	54°25·5′	2°36·6′W	T	91
Roundthwaite Beck	Cumbr	NY5903	54°25·5′	2°37·5′W	W	91
Roundthwaite Common	Cumbr	NY5902	54°25·0′	2°37·5′W	X	91
Roundton	Powys	SO2995	52°33·1′	3°2·4′W	H	137
Roundton (Fort)	Powys	SO2995	52°33·1′	3°2·4′W	A	137
Round Top	Northum	NY7176	55°4·9′	2°26·8′W	X	86,87
Round Towers	Blae Gw	SO1810	51°47·2′	3°10·9′W	X	161
Roundtown	Hants	SU6649	51°14·4′	1°2·9′W	X	185,186
Roundtree Fm	Surrey	TQ0854	51°16·7′	0°26·7′W	FM	187
Roundway	Wilts	SU0163	51°22·2′	1°58·7′W	T	173
Roundway Down	Wilts	SU0165	51°23·3′	1°58·7′W	A	173
Roundway Hill	Wilts	SU0264	51°22·7′	1°57·9′W	H	173
Roundway Ho	Wilts	SU0062	51°21·7′	1°59·6′W	X	173
Round Wood	Bucks	SP6531	51°58·7′	1°2·8′W	F	152,165
Round Wood	Leeds	SE1936	53°49·4′	1°42·3′W	F	104
Round Wood	Suff	TM1956	52°9·7′	1°12·5′E	F	156
Round Wood	Wilts	ST8452	51°16·2′	2°13·4′W	F	183
Roundwood Fm	Hants	SU5045	51°12·4′	1°16·7′W	FM	185
Roundwood Hill	Norf	TG1939	52°54·5′	1°15·8′E	X	133
Roundwyck Ho	W Susx	SU9829	51°3·3′	0°35·7′W	X	186,197
Roundy Burn	Angus	NO3950	56°38·5′	2°59·2′W	W	54
Roundyhill	Angus	NO3750	56°38·5′	3°1·2′W	T	54
Roundylane Fm	Ches	SJ9280	53°19·3′	2°6·8′W	FM	109
Rountengil	N Yks	SD9981	54°13·7′	2°0·5′W	X	98
Rounumuck Hill	Moray	NJ3425	57°18·9′	3°5·3′W	H	37
Rousay	Orkney	HY4030	59°9·4′	3°2·5′W	X	5,6
Rousay Sound	Orkney	HY4529	59°8·9′	2°57·2′W	W	5,6
Rousdon	Devon	SY2991	50°43·1′	3°0·0′W	T	193
Rouse Fm	Brom	TQ4064	51°21·7′	0°1·0′E	FM	177,187
Rouses Fm	Essex	TM1415	51°47·8′	1°6·6′E	FM	168,169
Rousham	Oxon	SP4724	51°55·0′	1°18·6′W	T	164
Rousham Copse	Oxon	SP4623	51°54·5′	1°19·5′W	F	164
Rousham Gap	Oxon	SP4622	51°53·9′	1°19·5′W	X	164
Rousham Park	Oxon	SP4724	51°55·0′	1°18·6′W	X	164
Rousker	Shetld	HU6189	60°35·1′	0°52·7′W	X	1,2
Rousland	Falk	NS9779	55°59·8′	3°38·6′W	X	65
Rous Lench	Worcs	SP0153	52°10·8′	1°58·7′W	T	150
Rous's Covert	Staffs	SJ7801	52°36·6′	2°19·1′W	F	127
Routdane Burn	N Ayr	NS2657	55°46·8′	4°46·0′W	W	63
Routdaneburn	N Ayr	NS2755	55°45·7′	4°45·0′W	X	63
Routenbeck	Cumbr	NY1930	54°39·8′	3°14·9′W	X	89,90
Routenburn	N Ayr	NS1961	55°48·8′	4°52·9′W	X	63
Routen Fm	Cumbr	NY1016	54°32·1′	3°23·0′W	FM	89
Router	Devon	SX4183	50°37·7′	4°14·5′W	X	201
Rout Fm	W Susx	TQ2525	51°0·9′	0°12·7′W	FM	187,198
Routh	E Yorks	TA0942	53°52·0′	0°20·1′W	T	107
Routh Carrs	E Yorks	TA0841	53°51·5′	0°21·1′W	X	107
Routh Carrs	E Yorks	TA0944	53°53·1′	0°20·1′W	X	107
Routh Lodge	E Yorks	SE8044	53°53·4′	0°46·5′W	X	106
Routin Br	D & G	NX8879	55°5·8′	3°44·9′W	X	84
Routin Cleuch	D & G	NY0877	55°5·0′	3°26·0′W	X	85
Routing Burn	Scot Bord	NY4693	55°13·9′	2°50·5′W	W	79
Routing Gill	Cumbr	NY4025	54°37·2′	2°55·3′W	X	90
Routin Gill	N Yks	SD9196	54°21·8′	2°7·9′W	W	98
Routin Lynn	Northum	NT9736	55°37·3′	2°2·4′W	X	75
Routledge Burn	Cumbr	NY5182	55°8·0′	2°45·7′W	W	79
Routon Syke	Cumbr	NY0319	54°33·7′	3°29·6′W	X	89
Routrundle	Devon	SX5571	50°31·5′	4°2·4′W	X	202
Rout's Green	Bucks	SU7898	51°40·8′	0°51·9′W	T	165
Routster	N Yks	SD7663	54°4·0′	2°21·6′W	X	98
Routs Wood, The	Newp	ST3888	51°35·5′	2°53·3′W	F	171
Rove Gill	Durham	NY9513	54°31·0′	2°4·2′W	W	91,92
Rovegill	Durham	NY9613	54°31·0′	2°3·3′W	X	91,92
Roveries	Shrops	SO3292	52°31·5′	2°59·7′W	X	137
Roves Fm	Swin	SU2088	51°35·7′	1°42·3′W	FM	174
Rovie Fm	Highld	NC7102	57°59·6′	4°10·5′W	FM	16
Rovie Lodge	Highld	NC7103	58°0·1′	4°10·5′W	X	16
Row	Corn	SX0976	50°33·4′	4°41·4′W	T	200
Row	Cumbr	NY0113	54°30·4′	3°31·3′W	X	89
Row	Cumbr	NY4874	55°3·7′	2°48·4′W	X	86
Row	Cumbr	NY6234	54°42·2′	2°35·0′W	T	91
Row	Cumbr	SD1194	54°20·3′	3°21·7′W	X	96
Row	Cumbr	SD4589	54°17·9′	2°50·3′W	T	97
Row	Stir	NS7499	56°10·3′	4°1·3′W	X	57
Rowacks	Aberd	NJ8900	57°5·7′	2°10·4′W	X	38
Rowallan	E Ayr	NS4342	55°39·0′	4°29·3′W	X	70
Rowama	Orkney	HY3517	59°2·4′	3°7·5′W	X	6
Rowan Bank	Aberd	NJ4705	57°8·2′	2°52·1′W	X	37
Rowan Bauds	Moray	NJ5451	57°33·1′	2°45·7′W	X	29
Rowanburn	D & G	NY4077	55°5·3′	2°56·0′W	T	85
Rowanburnfoot	D & G	NY4175	55°4·2′	2°55·0′W	X	85
Rowanburnhead	D & G	NY4077	55°5·3′	2°56·0′W	X	85
Rowanbush	Aberd	NJ6410	57°11·0′	2°35·3′W	X	37
Rowanfield	Glos	SO9222	51°54·0′	2°6·6′W	T	163
Rowanfield Cott	Arg & Bt	NR8296	56°6·7′	5°29·9′W	X	55
Rowanhill	Aberd	NJ7752	57°33·7′	2°22·6′W	X	29,30
Rowanhill	Aberd	NK0253	57°34·3′	1°57·5′W	X	30
Rowanhill	S Ayr	NS3834	55°34·6′	4°33·8′W	X	70
Rowan Island	D & G	NX2952	54°50·3′	4°39·3′W	X	82
Rowanlea	Scot Bord	NT6543	55°41·0′	2°33·0′W	X	74
Rowanmyle Ho	S Ayr	NS4327	55°30·9′	4°28·8′W	X	70
Rowanside Burn	N Ayr	NS2345	55°40·2′	4°48·4′W	W	63
Rowanside Hills	N Ayr	NS2346	55°40·8′	4°48·5′W	X	63
Rowanston	S Ayr	NS3105	55°18·9′	4°39·4′W	X	70,76
Rowantree	Aberd	NJ6163	57°39·6′	2°38·8′W	X	29
Rowantree	Aberd	NJ6453	57°34·2′	2°35·7′W	X	29
Rowantree	Aberd	NJ6824	57°18·6′	2°31·4′W	X	38
Rowantree	Cumbr	SD7793	54°20·2′	2°20·8′W	X	98
Rowantree Beck	Durham	NY8919	54°34·2′	2°9·8′W	W	91,92
Rowantree Burn	E Ayr	NS5733	55°34·4′	4°15·7′W	W	71
Rowantree Cove	D & G	NY4092	55°13·4′	2°56·2′W	X	79
Rowantree Crag	Cumbr	NY5212	54°30·3′	2°44·1′W	X	90
Rowantree Crags	N Yks	SE1562	54°3·5′	1°45·8′W	X	99
Rowantree Craig	E Ayr	NS4701	55°17·0′	4°24·1′W	X	77
Rowantree Craig	Pth & Kin	NN9707	56°14·9′	3°39·3′W	X	58
Rowantree Force	Cumbr	SD1493	54°19·8′	3°18·9′W	W	96
Rowantree Gill	N Yks	SE1166	54°5·6′	1°49·5′W	W	99
Rowantree Grains	Cumbr	SD6695	54°21·2′	2°31·0′W	X	98
Rowantree Grains	S Lanak	NT0414	55°24·9′	3°30·6′W	W	78
Rowan Tree Hill	Cumbr	SD3992	54°19·4′	2°55·9′W	X	96,97
Rowan Tree Hill	Highld	NC6433	58°16·1′	4°18·6′W	H	16
Rowantree Hill	N Ayr	NS2362	55°49·4′	4°49·1′W	H	63
Rowantree Hill	S Ayr	NX3391	55°11·4′	4°37·0′W	H	76
Rowantree Hill	Scot Bord	NT3602	55°18·7′	3°0·1′W	H	79
Rowantree How	Cumbr	SD1595	54°20·9′	3°18·0′W	X	96
Rowantree Knowe	Scot Bord	NT4703	55°19·3′	2°49·7′W	H	79
Rowantree Law	Scot Bord	NT4649	55°44·1′	2°51·2′W	H	73
Rowantree Mea	N Yks	SD8599	54°23·4′	2°13·4′W	X	98
Rowantree Park	N Yks	SE0192	54°19·7′	1°58·7′W	X	98
Rowantree Scar	N Yks	SE0292	54°19·7′	1°57·7′W	X	98
Rowan Tree Yards	N Yks	SE1161	54°2·9′	1°49·5′W	X	99
Rowardennan	Stir	NS3699	56°9·6′	4°38·0′W	T	56
Rowardennan Forest	Stir	NS3995	56°7·5′	4°35·0′W	F	56
Rowardennan Lodge	Stir	NS3599	56°9·6′	4°39·0′W	X	56
Rowarth	Derby	SK0189	53°24·1′	1°58·7′W	T	110
Row Ash	Hants	SU5413	50°55·1′	1°13·5′W	T	196
Rowater	Aberd	NJ5555	57°35·2′	2°44·7′W	X	29
Rowbarns	Surrey	TQ1052	51°15·6′	0°25·0′W	X	187
Rowbarrow	Hants	SU3504	50°50·3′	1°29·8′W	X	196
Rowbarrows	Somer	SS8741	51°9·7′	3°36·6′W	A	181
Rowbarton	Somer	ST2225	51°1·4′	3°6·3′W	T	193
Rowbatch	Powys	SO2657	52°12·6′	3°4·6′W	X	148
Row Beam	Orkney	ND5298	58°52·3′	2°49·5′W	X	6,7
Rowberrow	Somer	ST4558	51°19·3′	2°47·0′W	T	172,182
Rowberrow Warren	Somer	ST4657	51°18·8′	2°46·1′W	F	172,182
Rowberry Court	Heref	SO5549	52°8·5′	2°39·1′W	X	149
Rowberry Ho	Wilts	ST9222	51°0·1′	2°6·5′W	X	184
Rowborough	Warw	SP2339	52°3·2′	1°39·5′W	X	151
Rowborough Down	I of W	SZ4584	50°39·5′	1°21·4′W	X	196
Rowborough Fm	I of W	SZ4684	50°39·5′	1°20·6′W	FM	196
Rowborough Fm	I of W	SZ6088	50°41·5′	1°8·6′W	FM	196
Rowborough Fm	Swin	SU2087	51°35·1′	1°42·3′W	FM	174
Rowbridge	I of W	SZ4486	50°40·5′	1°22·3′W	X	196
Rowbrook	Devon	SX6872	50°32·2′	3°51·4′W	X	191
Row Brook	Shrops	SJ5102	52°37·1′	2°43·0′W	W	126
Row Brow	Cumbr	NY0836	54°42·9′	3°25·3′W	T	89
Row Brow Fm	N Yks	TA0088	54°16·9′	0°27·4′W	FM	101
Rowbrow Wood	N Yks	TA0088	54°16·9′	0°27·4′W	F	101
Rowburrow Wood	Heref	SO7445	52°6·4′	2°22·4′W	F	150
Rowbury Fm	Hants	SU3540	51°9·7′	1°29·6′W	FM	185
Rowbury Fm	W Berks	SU4375	51°28·6′	1°22·5′W	FM	174
Rowchester Ho	Scot Bord	NT7343	55°41·0′	2°25·3′W	X	74
Rowchoish	Stir	NN3304	56°12·2′	4°41·1′W	X	56
Rowcliffe Fm	Devon	SS7321	50°58·7′	3°48·2′W	FM	180
Rowdale Ho	Derby	SK2070	53°13·8′	1°41·6′W	X	119
Rowdale Ho	Shrops	SO7693	52°32·3′	2°20·8′W	X	138
Rowde	Wilts	ST9762	51°21·7′	2°2·2′W	T	173
Rowdean Hill	Wilts	ST9337	51°8·2′	2°5·6′W	X	184
Rowdeford School	Wilts	ST9763	51°22·2′	2°2·2′W	X	173
Rowde Hill Fm	Wilts	ST9562	51°21·7′	2°3·9′W	FM	173
Rowdell	W Susx	TQ1112	50°54·0′	0°24·9′W	X	198
Rowden	Devon	SX4187	50°39·9′	4°14·6′W	X	190
Rowden	Devon	SX4496	50°44·8′	4°12·3′W	X	190
Rowden	Devon	SX4781	50°36·8′	4°9·4′W	X	191,201
Rowden	Devon	SX5547	50°18·5′	4°1·8′W	X	202
Rowden	Devon	SX6498	50°46·2′	3°55·3′W	T	191
Rowden	Devon	SX8054	50°22·7′	3°40·9′W	X	202
Rowden	N Yks	SE2557	54°0·7′	1°36·7′W	T	104
Rowden Abbey	Heref	SO6356	52°12·3′	2°32·1′W	X	149
Rowden Fm	Bucks	SP9121	51°53·0′	0°40·3′W	FM	165
Rowden Fm	Devon	SS4412	50°53·4′	4°12·7′W	FM	180,190
Rowden Fm	Devon	SS8016	50°56·1′	3°42·1′W	FM	181
Rowden Fm	Dorset	SY5590	50°42·7′	2°37·9′W	FM	194
Rowden Fm	Wilts	ST9172	51°27·0′	2°7·4′W	FM	173
Rowden Hill	Dorset	ST6500	50°48·1′	2°29·4′W	H	194
Rowden Hill	Wilts	ST9172	51°27·0′	2°7·4′W	X	173
Rowden Ho	Heref	SO6356	52°12·3′	2°32·1′W	X	149
Rowden House Fm	Leic	SP3696	52°33·9′	1°27·7′W	FM	140
Rowden Mill Fm	Shrops	ST7113	50°55·2′	2°24·4′W	FM	194
Rowden Moor	Devon	SX6499	50°46·7′	3°55·4′W	X	191
Rowden Paddocks	Heref	SO6456	52°12·3′	2°31·2′W	X	149
Rowden's Cleeve	Wilts	SU1454	51°17·3′	1°47·6′W	F	184
Rowdens Fm	Somer	ST2037	51°7·8′	3°8·2′W	FM	182
Rowden's Fm	Wilts	SU2724	51°1·1′	1°36·5′W	FM	184
Rowdon Fm	Somer	ST0838	51°8·3′	3°18·5′W	FM	181
Rowdon Rock	Devon	SX8186	50°39·9′	3°40·7′W	X	191
Row Down	Hants	SU4302	50°49·2′	1°23·0′W	X	196
Row Down	W Berks	SU3079	51°30·8′	1°33·7′W	X	174
Rowdown Fm	W Berks	SU4478	51°30·2′	1°21·6′W	FM	174
Rowe Ditch	Heref	SO3759	52°13·8′	2°54·9′W	A	148,149
Rowe Ditch	Heref	SO3760	52°14·3′	2°55·0′W	A	137,148,149
Rowe Fm	Lincs	SK8242	52°58·4′	0°46·3′W	FM	130
Rowe Fm	Shrops	SJ5002	52°37·0′	2°43·9′W	FM	126
Rowe Fm	Worcs	SO8062	52°15·6′	2°17·2′W	FM	138,150
Rowe Head	Cumbr	SD2677	54°11·3′	3°7·6′W	T	96,97
Rowel Brook	Oxon	SP4614	51°49·6′	1°19·6′W	W	164
Rowell	Cumbr	SD5182	54°14·1′	2°44·7′W	X	97
Rowell Fm	Suff	TM0465	52°14·9′	0°59·7′E	FM	155
Rowell Leyes	Northnts	SP6767	52°18·1′	1°0·6′W	X	152
Rowells Fm	Cambs	TL3485	52°27·0′	0°1·3′W	FM	142
Rowell's Fm	Cambs	TL3584	52°26·5′	0°0·4′W	FM	142
Roweltown	Cumbr	NY4971	55°2·1′	2°47·5′W	X	86
Rowen	Conwy	SH7571	53°13·5′	3°51·9′W	T	115
Ro Wen	Gwyn	SH6013	52°42·0′	4°3·9′W	X	124
Rowen	Orkney	HY5430	59°9·5′	2°47·8′W	X	5,6
Row End	Cumbr	NY3023	54°36·1′	3°4·6′W	X	90
Row End	Cumbr	NY7415	54°32·0′	2°23·7′W	X	91
Row End	Cumbr	NY7510	54°29·3′	2°22·7′W	X	91
Row End	Cumbr	SD5386	54°16·4′	2°42·9′W	X	97
Rowens	Highld	ND2347	58°24·5′	3°18·6′W	X	11,12
Rowens Burn	Highld	ND2348	58°25·1′	3°18·6′W	X	11,12
Rowe Place Fm	Kent	TQ7260	51°19·0′	0°28·5′E	FM	178,188
Rower Hill	Devon	ST2305	50°50·6′	3°5·2′W	H	192,193
Rowe's Fm	Essex	TL6108	51°45·1′	0°20·3′E	FM	167
Rowe's Fm	Lincs	TF1038	52°55·9′	0°21·4′W	FM	130
Rowes Fm	Somer	ST0231	51°4·4′	3°23·5′W	FM	181
Rowe's Fm	Wok	SU7364	51°22·5′	0°56·7′W	FM	175,186
Rowetts Fm	Kent	TQ9871	51°24·4′	0°51·2′E	FM	178
Rowe Wood	Bucks	SU7685	51°33·8′	0°53·8′W	F	175
Rowfant	W Susx	TQ3237	51°7·2′	0°6·4′W	X	187
Rowfields Hall Fm	Derby	SK1949	53°2·5′	1°42·6′W	FM	119
Row Fm	Cumbr	NY0703	54°25·1′	3°25·6′W	FM	89
Row Fm	Cumbr	SD1093	54°19·7′	3°22·6′W	FM	96
Row Fm	E Yorks	TA3420	53°39·8′	0°2·1′E	FM	107,113
Row Fm	N Yks	TA0187	54°16·4′	0°26·5′W	FM	101
Row Fms	Cumbr	SD5782	54°14·2′	2°39·2′W	FM	97
Row Fms	Somer	ST7653	51°16·8′	2°20·3′W	FM	183
Rowfold Grange	W Susx	TQ1025	51°1·1′	0°25·5′W	X	187,198
Row Foot	Cumbr	NY0112	54°29·9′	3°31·3′W	X	89
Row Foot	Cumbr	NY7202	54°25·0′	2°25·5′W	X	91
Rowfoot	Northum	NY6860	54°56·3′	2°29·5′W	T	86,87
Rowford	Somer	ST2327	51°2·5′	3°5·5′W	T	193
Rowgardenswood	Surrey	TQ2443	51°10·6′	0°13·2′W	X	187
Rowgate	N Yks	SE8671	54°7·9′	0°40·6′W	X	101
Rowgate Hill	Lincs	TF2978	53°17·2′	0°3·5′W	X	122
Rowgill Burn	Cumbr	NY6741	54°46·0′	2°30·4′W	W	86,87
Row Green	Essex	TL7420	51°51·3′	0°32·0′E	T	167
Row Hall	Cumbr	NY0836	54°42·9′	3°25·3′W	X	89
Rowhay Wood	Hants	SU5221	50°59·4′	1°15·2′W	F	185
Row Head	Orkney	HY2218	59°2·8′	3°21·1′W	X	6
Row Heath	Essex	TM1519	51°49·9′	1°7·6′E	T	168,169
Row Heath	Norf	TG1741	52°55·6′	1°14·1′E	X	133
Rowhedge	Essex	TM0221	51°51·3′	0°56·4′E	T	168

Rowhedge Fm	Suff	TL8649	52°6·7'	0°43·4'E	FM	155
Row Hill	Dorset	ST6303	50°49·8'	2°31·1'W	X	194
Row Hill	Staffs	SK1729	52°51·7'	1°44·4'W	X	128
Rowhill	Surrey	TQ0363	51°21·6'	0°30·8'W	T	176,186
Rowhook	W Susx	TQ1234	51°5·9'	0°23·6'W	T	187
Rowhook Manor	W Susx	TQ1334	51°5·9'	0°22·8'W	X	187
Rowhope	Northum	NT8512	55°24·4'	2°13·8'W	X	80
Rowhope Burn	Northum	NT8413	55°24·9'	2°14·7'W	W	80
Rowhope Burn	Northum	NT9615	55°26·0'	2°3·4'W	W	81
Rowhope Burn	Scot Bord	NT8522	55°29·7'	2°13·8'W	W	74
Rowhowe Ho	N Yks	SE9585	54°15·3'	0°32·1'W	X	94,101
Row Howes	N Yks	SE9485	54°15·4'	0°33·0'W	A	94,101
Rowington	Warw	SP2069	52°19·4'	1°42·0'W	T	139,151
Rowington Green	Warw	SP2069	52°19·4'	1°42·0'W	T	139,151
Rowland	Derby	SK2172	53°14·9'	1°40·7'W	T	119
Rowland	Orkney	HY4601	58°53·8'	2°55·7'W	X	6,7
Rowland Cote	Derby	SK1386	53°22·5'	1°47·9'W	X	110
Rowland Hall	E Yorks	SE7230	53°45·9'	0°54·0'W	X	105,106
Rowland Hill	E Yorks	SE7751	53°57·2'	0°49·2'W	X	105,106
Rowland Hill	N Lincs	TA0820	53°40·2'	0°21·5'W	X	107,112
Rowland Plantation	N Lincs	SE9511	53°35·5'	0°33·5'W	F	112
Rowland's Castle	Hants	SU7310	50°53·3'	0°57·3'W	T	197
Rowlands Fm	I of W	SZ5688	50°41·6'	1°12·0'W	FM	196
Rowland's Fm	Somer	ST3416	50°56·4'	2°56·0'W	A	193
Rowlands Gill	Ghead	NZ1658	54°55·2'	1°44·6'W	T	88
Rowland's Green	Heref	SO6836	52°1·5'	2°27·6'W	T	149
Rowlands Wood	I of W	SZ5689	50°42·1'	1°12·0'W	F	196
Rowland Wood	E Susx	TQ5115	50°55·1'	0°9·3'E	F	199
Rowledge	Surrey	SU8243	51°11·0'	0°49·2'W	T	186
Rowlee Fm	Derby	SK1589	53°24·1'	1°46·1'W	FM	110
Rowlee Pasture	Derby	SK1590	53°24·6'	1°46·1'W	X	110
Rowler	Northnts	SP5434	52°0·3'	1°12·4'W	X	152
Rowles Fm	Oxon	SP5316	51°50·6'	1°13·4'W	FM	164
Rowlestone	Heref	SO3727	51°56·5'	2°54·6'W	T	161
Rowley	Devon	SS7219	50°57·6'	3°49·0'W	X	180
Rowley	Durham	NZ0848	54°49·9'	1°52·1'W	X	88
Rowley	E Susx	TQ6731	51°3·5'	0°23·4'E	X	188
Rowley	Powys	SO2864	52°16·4'	3°2·9'W	X	137,148
Rowley	Shrops	SJ3006	52°39·1'	3°1·7'W	T	126
Rowleybank Fm	Ches	SJ7082	53°20·3'	2°26·6'W	FM	109
Rowley Barton	Devon	SS6543	51°10·5'	3°55·5'W	X	180
Rowley Beck	Durham	NZ0426	54°38·0'	1°55·9'W	W	92
Rowley Brook	Powys	SJ2907	52°39·6'	3°2·6'W	W	126
Rowley Brook	Shrops	SO6775	52°22·6'	2°28·7'W	W	138
Rowley Burn	Durham	NZ1842	54°46·6'	1°42·8'W	W	88
Rowley Burn	Northum	NY9056	54°54·2'	2°8·9'W	W	87
Rowley Coppice	Shrops	SO7697	52°34·5'	2°20·8'W	F	138
Rowley Corner	Norf	TF8202	52°35·3'	0°41·6'E	X	144
Rowley Down	Devon	SS6643	51°10·5'	3°54·6'W	H	180
Rowley Fm	Bucks	TQ0082	51°31·9'	0°33·1'W	FM	176
Rowley Fm	Ches	SJ5565	53°11·1'	2°40·0'W	FM	117
Rowley Fm	Durham	NZ1742	54°46·6'	1°43·7'W	FM	88
Rowley Fm	Heref	SO5259	52°13·9'	2°41·8'W	FM	149
Rowley Fm	Norf	TF8301	52°34·8'	0°42·5'E	FM	144
Rowley Fm	Shrops	SO5999	52°35·5'	2°35·9'W	FM	137,138
Rowley Fm	Shrops	SO7696	52°33·9'	2°20·8'W	FM	138
Rowley Fm	Somer	ST5134	51°6·4'	2°41·6'W	FM	182,183
Rowley Fm	Worcs	SO8063	52°16·1'	2°17·2'W	FM	138,150
Rowley Fm	W Susx	TQ2739	51°8·4'	0°10·7'W	FM	187
Rowley Fms	Staffs	SK1121	52°47·4'	1°49·8'W	FM	128
Rowley Gate	Staffs	SJ9556	53°6·3'	2°4·1'W	X	118
Rowley Green	Barnet	TQ2196	51°39·2'	0°14·7'W	T	166,176
Rowley Hall	Ches	SJ7968	53°12·8'	2°18·5'W	X	118
Rowley Hall	Lancs	SD8633	53°47·8'	2°12·3'W	X	103
Rowley Head	Northum	NY9056	54°54·2'	2°8·9'W	X	87
Rowleyhill	Ches	SJ4353	53°4·5'	2°50·6'W	X	117
Rowley Hill	Kirk	SE1914	53°37·6'	1°42·4'W	T	110
Rowley Hill	Shrops	SJ2906	52°39·1'	3°2·6'W	H	126
Rowley Hill	Staffs	SJ9011	52°42·0'	2°8·5'W	X	127
Rowley Hill Fm	Essex	TL5340	52°2·5'	0°14·2'E	FM	154
Rowley Ho	Bath & NE Somer	ST7360	51°20·5'	2°22·9'W	X	172
Rowley Lodge	Durham	NZ0526	54°38·0'	1°54·9'W	X	92
Rowley Manor (Hotel)	E Yorks	SE9732	53°46·8'	0°31·3'W	X	106
Rowley Mile Course	Suff	TL6162	52°14·2'	0°21·9'E	X	154
Rowley Park	Staffs	SJ9122	52°48·0'	2°7·6'W	T	127
Rowley Regis	Sand	SO9687	52°29·1'	2°3·1'W	T	139
Rowley Regis Sta	Dudley	SO9886	52°28·6'	2°1·4'W	X	139
Rowley's Green	Cov	SP3483	52°26·9'	1°29·6'W	T	140
Rowley's Hill	Cambs	TL4249	52°7·5'	0°4·9'E	X	154
Rowley Wood	Bucks	SU9983	51°32·5'	0°34·0'W	F	175,176
Rowley Wood	Northnts	SP7850	52°8·8'	0°51·2'W	F	152
Rowling	Kent	TR2754	51°14·6'	1°15·5'E	T	179
Rowling End	Cumbr	NY2220	54°34·4'	3°12·0'W	X	89,90
Rowling Ho	Kent	TR2754	51°14·6'	1°15·5'E	X	179
Rowling House	Kent	TR2654	51°14·6'	1°14·7'E	X	179
Rowlings	E Yorks	TA1843	53°52·4'	0°11·9'W	X	107
Rowling Street	Kent	TR0236	51°5·5'	0°53·5'E	X	189
Rowls, The	Shrops	SO3099	52°35·3'	3°1·6'W	X	137
Rowly	Surrey	TQ0440	51°9·2'	0°30·4'W	T	186
Rowly Fm	Surrey	TQ0340	51°9·2'	0°31·2'W	FM	186
Rowlyn	Conwy	SH7567	53°11·4'	3°51·8'W	X	115
Rowmire Beck	N Yks	SE8266	54°5·2'	0°44·4'W	W	100
Rowmore	Arg & Bt	NS2489	56°3·9'	4°49·2'W	X	56
Rownal	Shrops	SO2398	52°34·7'	3°7·8'W	X	137
Rownall	Staffs	SJ9549	53°2·5'	2°4·1'W	T	118
Rownall Fm	Staffs	SJ9550	53°3·1'	2°4·1'W	FM	118
Rownall Hall	Staffs	SJ9549	53°2·5'	2°4·1'W	X	118
Rowner	Hants	SU5801	50°48·6'	1°10·2'W	T	196
Rowner Fm	W Susx	TQ0726	51°1·6'	0°28·1'W	FM	187,197
Rownest Wood	Hants	SU5542	51°10·7'	1°12·4'W	F	185
Rowneybury	Herts	TL4713	51°48·0'	0°8·3'E	X	167
Rowney Fm	Herts	TL4613	51°48·0'	0°7·4'E	FM	167
Rowney Fm	Staffs	SJ7335	52°54·9'	2°23·7'W	FM	127
Rowney Fm	Suff	TL8556	52°10·5'	0°42·7'E	FM	155
Rowney Green	Worcs	SP0471	52°20·5'	1°56·1'W	T	139
Rowney Priory	Herts	TL3420	51°52·0'	0°2·8'W	X	166
Rowney's Fm	Essex	TL9030	51°56·4'	0°46·2'E	FM	168
Rowney Warren Wood	Beds	TL1140	52°3·1'	0°22·5'W	F	153
Rowney Wood	Essex	TL5733	51°58·6'	0°17·6'E	F	167
Rownham Fm	S Glos	ST7776	51°29·2'	2°19·5'W	FM	172
Rownhams	Hants	SU3817	50°57·3'	1°27·2'W	T	185
Rownhams Service Area	Hants	SU3817	50°57·3'	1°27·2'W	X	185
Rownton Brook	Lancs	SD5359	54°1·7'	2°42·6'W	W	102
Rowntree Fm	Durham	NZ1128	54°39·1'	1°49·3'W	FM	92
Row-of-trees	Ches	SJ8279	53°18·7'	2°15·8'W	T	118
Rowrah	Cumbr	NY0518	54°33·1'	3°27·7'W	T	89
Row Ridding	Cumbr	SD2489	54°17·7'	3°9·6'W	X	96
Rowridge	Devon	SS9911	50°53·6'	3°25·8'W	X	192
Rowse	Corn	SX3764	50°27·4'	4°17·4'W	X	201
Rowse's Fm	Essex	TL9614	51°47·6'	0°50·9'E	FM	168
Rows Fm	Devon	SS9422	50°59·5'	3°30·2'W	FM	181
Rows Fm	Essex	TL9517	51°49·3'	0°50·2'E	FM	168
Row's Fm	Somer	ST2231	51°4·6'	3°6·4'W	FM	182
Rowsham	Bucks	SP8418	51°51·5'	0°46·4'W	T	165
Rowsham Br	Bucks	SP8417	51°50·9'	0°46·4'W	X	165
Rowside	Northum	NY7859	54°55·8'	2°20·2'W	X	86,87
Rowsley	Derby	SK2566	53°11·7'	1°37·1'W	T	119
Rowsley Wood	Derby	SK2666	53°11·7'	1°36·2'W	F	119
Rowstock	Oxon	SU4789	51°36·1'	1°18·9'W	T	174
Rowston	Lincs	TF0856	53°5·6'	0°22·8'W	T	121
Rowston	Pemb	SR9997	51°38·4'	4°53·9'W	X	158
Rowston Field Fm	Lincs	TF1056	53°5·6'	0°21·0'W	FM	121
Rowston Grange	Lincs	TF1055	53°5·1'	0°21·1'W	X	121
Rowston Top	Lincs	TF0556	53°5·7'	0°25·5'W	X	121
Row's Wood	Warr	SJ5983	53°20·8'	2°36·5'W	F	108
Row Taing	Orkney	ND3795	58°50·5'	3°5·0'W	X	7
Rowten Pot	N Yks	SD6978	54°12·1'	2°28·1'W	X	98
Rowter Fm	Derby	SK1382	53°20·3'	1°47·9'W	FM	110
Row, The	Bucks	SP6815	51°50·0'	1°0·4'W	X	164,165
Row, The	Cumbr	NY5577	55°5·4'	2°41·9'W	X	86
Row, The	N Yks	SE6592	54°19·4'	0°59·6'W	X	94,100
Row, The	Shrops	SO3087	52°28·8'	3°1·4'W	X	137
Rowthorne	Derby	SK4764	53°10·5'	1°17·4'W	T	120
Rowting Burn	Cumbr	NY6738	54°44·4'	2°30·3'W	W	91
Rowton	Ches	SJ4464	53°10·5'	2°49·9'W	T	117
Rowton	Shrops	SJ3612	52°42·4'	2°56·4'W	T	126
Rowton	Shrops	SO4080	52°25·1'	2°52·5'W	X	137
Rowton	Wrekin	SJ6119	52°46·3'	2°34·3'W	T	127
Rowton Beck	Durham	NY9025	54°37·4'	2°8·9'W	W	91,92
Rowton Brook Fell	Lancs	SD5459	54°1·7'	2°41·7'W	X	102
Rowton Castle	Shrops	SJ3712	52°42·4'	2°55·5'W	X	126
Rowton Fm	E Yorks	TA1340	53°50·9'	0°16·5'W	FM	107
Rowton Grange Fm	Shrops	SJ3711	52°41·8'	2°55·5'W	FM	126
Rowton Ho	Shrops	SJ6901	52°36·6'	2°27·1'W	X	127
Rowton Moor	Ches	SJ4464	53°10·5'	2°49·9'W	T	117
Rowton's Well	Birm	SP0996	52°33·9'	1°51·6'W	W	139
Rowton Villas	E Yorks	TA1339	53°50·3'	0°16·5'W	X	107
Rowtor	Devon	SX5991	50°42·3'	3°59·4'W	H	191
Row Town	Surrey	TQ0463	51°21·6'	0°30·0'W	T	176,186
Row Wood	Essex	TL5515	51°49·0'	0°15·3'E	F	167
Row Wood	Herts	TL2916	51°49·9'	0°7·3'W	F	166
Row Wood	Lincs	TF0726	52°49·5'	0°24·3'W	F	130
Roxburgh	Scot Bord	NT6930	55°34·0'	2°29·1'W	T	74
Roxburgh Barns	Scot Bord	NT7032	55°35·1'	2°28·1'W	X	74
Roxburgh Mains	Scot Bord	NT6829	55°33·5'	2°30·0'W	T	74
Roxburgh Mill	Scot Bord	NT7031	55°34·6'	2°28·1'W	X	74
Roxburgh Moor	Scot Bord	NT6729	55°33·5'	2°31·0'W	X	74
Roxburgh Newtown	Scot Bord	NT6731	55°34·5'	2°31·0'W	X	74
Roxby	N Lincs	SE9216	53°38·2'	0°36·1'W	T	112
Roxby	N Yks	NZ7616	54°32·3'	0°49·1'W	T	94
Roxby Beck	N Yks	NZ7516	54°32·3'	0°50·0'W	W	94
Roxby Carrs	N Lincs	SE9517	53°38·7'	0°33·4'W	X	112
Roxby High Moor	N Yks	NZ7511	54°29·6'	0°50·1'W	X	94
Roxby Ho	N Yks	SE3282	54°14·2'	1°30·1'W	X	99
Roxby Low Moor	N Yks	NZ7613	54°30·6'	0°49·1'W	X	94
Roxby Old Moor	N Yks	NZ7511	54°29·6'	0°50·1'W	X	94
Roxby Woods	N Yks	NZ7516	54°32·3'	0°50·0'W	F	94
Roxeth	Harrow	TQ1486	51°33·9'	0°20·9'W	T	176
Roxford	Herts	TL3010	51°46·6'	0°6·5'W	X	166
Roxham Fm	Norf	TL6399	52°34·1'	0°24·7'E	FM	143
Rox Hill Clump	Wilts	SU1238	51°8·7'	1°49·3'W	F	184
Roxhill Manor Fm	Beds	SP9743	52°4·8'	0°34·7'W	FM	153
Roxholm Grange	Lincs	TF0651	53°3·0'	0°24·7'W	X	121
Roxholm Hall	Lincs	TF0550	53°2·5'	0°25·6'W	X	121
Roxley Court	Herts	TL2229	51°57·0'	0°13·1'W	X	166
Roxton	Beds	TL1554	52°10·6'	0°18·7'W	T	153
Roxton Fm	NE Lincs	TA1612	53°35·7'	0°14·4'W	FM	113
Roxton Ho	Beds	TL1554	52°10·6'	0°18·7'W	X	153
Roxton Wood	Lincs	TA1611	53°35·2'	0°14·4'W	F	113
Roxwell	Essex	TL6408	51°45·0'	0°22·9'E	T	167
Roxwell Brook	Essex	TL6307	51°44·5'	0°22·1'E	W	167
Roy	Orkney	ND5299	58°52·8'	2°49·5'W	X	6,7
Royal Aircraft Estab	Hants	SU8654	51°16·9'	0°45·6'W	X	186
Royal Albert Dock	Newham	TQ4280	51°30·3'	0°3·2'E	X	177
Royal Albert Hall	Ken & Ch	TQ2679	51°30·0'	0°10·7'W	X	176
Royal Border Br	Northum	NT9953	55°46·5'	2°0·5'W	X	75
Royal Botanic Gardens	Rich	TQ1876	51°28·5'	0°17·7'W	X	176
Royal British Legion Village	Kent	TQ7257	51°17·4'	0°28·4'E	T	178,188
Royal Cinque Ports Golf Links	Kent	TR3655	51°14·9'	1°23·3'E	X	179
Royal Common	Surrey	SU9242	51°10·4'	0°40·6'W	F	186
Royal Content Fm	Worcs	SO9374	52°22·1'	2°5·8'W	FM	139
Royal Cott	Stir	NN4209	56°15·1'	4°32·6'W	X	56
Royal Cottage (PH)	Staffs	SK0263	53°10·1'	1°57·8'W	X	119
Royal Crescent	Bath & NE Somer	ST7465	51°23·2'	2°22·0'W	X	172
Royal Drift, The	Glos	SO6904	51°44·3'	2°26·5'W	X	162
Royal Forest	Highld	NN2053	56°38·3'	4°55·7'W	X	41
Royal Gardens	Win & Maid	SU9775	51°28·2'	0°35·8'W	X	175,176
Royal Highland Showground	C of Edin	NT1373	55°56·8'	3°23·1'W	X	65
Royal Hill	Devon	SX6172	50°32·1'	3°57·3'W	H	191
Royal Hill	Norf	TG1314	52°41·1'	1°9·5'E	X	133
Royal Holloway College	Surrey	SU9970	51°25·4'	0°34·2'W	X	175,176
Royal Horticultural Society's Gardens	Surrey	TQ0658	51°18·9'	0°28·3'W	X	187
Royal Hospital	Ken & Ch	TQ2878	51°29·4'	0°9·0'W	X	176
Royal Hospital School	Suff	TM1635	51°58·5'	1°9·1'E	X	169
Royal Hostel	Surrey	SU9143	51°11·0'	0°41·5'W	X	186
Royal Hunting Lodge Fm	N Yks	SE5462	54°3·3'	1°10·1'W	FM	100
Royal Leamington Spa	Warw	SP3165	52°17·2'	1°32·3'W	T	151
Royal Liver Bldg	Liv	SJ3390	53°24·4'	3°0·1'W	X	108
Royal Lodge	Win & Maid	SU9672	51°26·6'	0°36·7'W	X	175,176
Royal Mausoleum	Win & Maid	SU9775	51°28·2'	0°35·8'W	X	175,176
Royal Military Academy	Brackn	SU8560	51°20·2'	0°46·4'W	X	175,186
Royal Military Canal	Kent	TQ9630	51°2·4'	0°48·1'E	W	189
Royal Military Canal	Kent	TR1034	51°4·2'	1°0·2'E	W	179,189
Royal Military College of Science	Oxon	SU2589	51°36·2'	1°37·9'W	X	174
Royal Military Road	E Susx	TQ9118	50°56·0'	0°43·5'E	X	189
Royal Military Road	Kent	TR0734	51°4·3'	0°57·7'E	X	179,189
Royal Norfolk Showground	Norf	TG1410	52°39·0'	1°10·2'E	X	133
Royal Oak	Durham	NZ2023	54°36·4'	1°41·0'W	T	93
Royal Oak	Lancs	SD4103	53°31·5'	2°53·0'W	T	108
Royal Oak	N Yks	TA1078	54°11·4'	0°18·4'W	T	101
Royal Oak	Shrops	SJ8308	52°40·4'	2°14·7'W	A	127
Royal Oak Industrial Estate	Northnts	SP5563	52°16·0'	1°11·2'W	X	152
Royal Oak Point	Kent	TQ9673	51°25·5'	0°49·6'E	X	178
Royal Pavilion	Bri & Hov	TQ3104	50°49·5'	0°8·0'W	X	198
Royal Pavilion	Hants	SU8450	51°14·8'	0°47·4'W	X	186
Royal Pier	Hants	SU4110	50°53·5'	1°24·6'W	X	196
Royal Portbury Dock,The	N Som	ST5077	51°29·6'	2°42·8'W	X	172
Royal Quays	N Tyne	NZ3566	54°59·5'	1°26·8'W	X	88
Royal School	Win & Maid	SU9671	51°26·0'	0°36·7'W	X	175,176
Royal's Green	Ches	SJ6242	52°58·7'	2°33·6'W	T	118
Royal Shakespeare Theatre	Warw	SP2054	52°11·3'	1°42·0'W	X	151
Royal Sovereign		TV7194	50°43·4'	0°25·8'E	X	199
Royal St George's Golf Links	Kent	TR3558	51°16·6'	1°22·6'E	X	179
Royals, The	Ches	SJ6046	53°0·8'	2°35·4'W	X	118
Royalswood Fm	Ches	SJ6045	53°0·3'	2°35·4'W	FM	118
Royalton	Corn	SW9561	50°25·0'	4°52·8'W	X	200
Royal Tunbridge Wells	Kent	TQ5839	51°7·9'	0°15·9'E	T	188
Royalty Cott	Ches	SJ4255	53°5·6'	2°51·6'W	X	117
Royalty Fm	Lincs	TF4059	53°6·8'	0°5·9'E	FM	122
Royalty Fm	Northum	NT9347	55°43·2'	2°6·3'W	FM	74,75
Royalty Fm East	Lincs	TF4159	53°6·8'	0°6·8'E	FM	122
Royalty, The	Lincs	TF2855	53°4·8'	0°4·9'W	X	122
Royal Veterinary College	Herts	TL2303	51°43·0'	0°12·8'W	X	166
Royal Victoria Country Park	Hants	SU4507	50°51·9'	1°21·2'W	X	196
Royal Victoria Dock	Newham	TQ4080	51°30·3'	0°1·4'E	X	177
Royal Welsh Showground	Powys	SO0451	52°9·2'	3°23·8'W	X	147
Roybridge	Highld	NN2781	56°53·5'	4°50·0'W	T	34,41
Roych Clough	Derby	SK0883	53°20·9'	1°52·4'W	X	110
Roych, The	Derby	SK0784	53°21·4'	1°53·3'W	X	110
Roych Tor	Derby	SK0883	53°20·9'	1°52·4'W	X	110
Royd	Barns	SE2103	53°31·6'	1°40·6'W	T	110
Royd Edge	Kirk	SE0909	53°34·9'	1°51·4'W	X	110
Royden Park	Wirral	SJ2486	53°22·2'	3°8·1'W	X	108
Royd Ho	Brad	SE0335	53°48·9'	1°56·9'W	X	104
Royd Ho	N Yks	SD9945	53°54·3'	2°0·5'W	X	103
Roydhouse	Kirk	SE2112	53°36·5'	1°40·5'W	T	110
Royd Moor	Barns	SE2204	53°32·2'	1°39·7'W	T	110
Royd Moor	Wakf	SE4413	53°36·9'	1°19·7'W	T	111
Royd Moor Resr	Barns	SE2204	53°32·2'	1°39·7'W	W	110
Roydon	Essex	TL4010	51°46·5'	0°2·2'E	T	167
Roydon	Norf	TF7022	52°46·4'	0°31·6'E	T	132
Roydon	Norf	TM0980	52°22·9'	1°4·7'E	T	144
Roydon Common	Norf	TF6822	52°46·4'	0°29·8'E	F	132
Roydon Fen	Norf	TM1079	52°22·3'	1°5·5'E	W	144
Roydon Hall	Essex	TM1930	51°55·7'	1°11·5'E	X	168,169
Roydon Hall	Kent	TQ6651	51°14·3'	0°23·1'E	A	188
Roydon Hall	Suff	TM0858	52°11·1'	1°3·0'E	X	155
Roydon Hall Fm	Derby	SK4329	52°51·6'	1°21·3'W	FM	129
Roydon Hamlet	Essex	TL4107	51°44·9'	0°2·9'E	T	167
Roydon Lea	Essex	TL4210	51°46·5'	0°3·9'E	X	167
Roydon Manor	Hants	SU3100	50°48·2'	1°33·2'W	X	196
Royds Farm	Roth	SE3900	53°30·0'	1°24·3'W	FM	110,111
Royds Green	Leeds	SE3526	53°44·0'	1°27·8'W	T	104
Royds Hall	Brad	SE1428	53°45·1'	1°46·8'W	X	104
Royhall	Aberd	NJ6716	57°14·3'	2°32·3'W	X	38
Royl Dale	Shetld	HU3828	60°2·4'	1°18·6'W	X	4
Royle	Lancs	SD8234	53°48·4'	2°16·0'W	X	103
Royledge	Staffs	SK0459	53°7·9'	1°56·0'W	X	119
Royle Fm	Derby	SK2519	52°46·3'	1°37·4'W	FM	128
Royle Reddings	Glos	SO5802	51°43·1'	2°36·1'W	X	162
Royl Field	Shetld	HU3928	60°2·4'	1°17·5'W	H	4
Royl Tongue	Shetld	HU3828	60°2·4'	1°18·6'W	X	4
Roy's Folly	Pth & Kin	NO1301	56°11·9'	3°23·7'W	X	58
Roy's Hill	Moray	NJ1440	57°26·8'	3°25·5'W	H	28
Roy's Hill	Moray	NJ2735	57°24·2'	3°12·4'W	X	28
Royston	Aberd	NJ8448	57°31·6'	2°15·6'W	X	29,30
Royston	Barns	SE3511	53°35·9'	1°27·9'W	T	110,111
Royston	C of Glas	NS6066	55°52·3'	4°13·8'W	T	64
Royston	D & G	NX6652	54°50·9'	4°4·8'W	X	83,84
Royston	Herts	TL3541	52°3·3'	0°1·5'W	T	154
Royston	Wrex	SJ3745	53°0·2'	2°55·9'W	X	117
Roystone Grange	Derby	SK2056	53°6·3'	1°41·7'W	X	119
Royston Ho	Somer	ST2112	50°54·4'	3°7·0'W	X	193
Royston Manor	Notts	SK7288	53°23·3'	0°54·6'W	X	112,120
Royston Manor	Notts	SK7288	53°23·3'	0°54·6'W	X	112,120
Royston Water	Somer	ST2213	50°54·9'	3°6·2'W	T	193
Royton	Oldham	SD9107	53°33·8'	2°7·7'W	T	109
Rozelle	S Ayr	NS3318	55°25·9'	4°37·9'W	X	70
R Pitt	Somer	ST6930	51°4·3'	2°26·2'W	W	183
R Rawthey	Cumbr	SD6894	54°20·7'	2°29·1'W	W	98
R Tain	Highld	NH7980	57°47·9'	4°1·7'W	W	21
R Tawe	Powys	SN8413	51°48·5'	3°40·6'W	W	160
R Tawe	Powys	SN8418	51°51·2'	3°40·7'W	W	160
Ruabhal	N Eil	NF7840	57°20·5'	7°20·7'W	H	22
Ruabhal	N Eil	NF8253	57°27·6'	7°17·7'W	H	22
Ruabon Mountain	Wrex	SJ2446	53°0·6'	3°7·6'W	H	117
Ruabon or Rhiwabon	Wrex	SJ3043	52°59·0'	3°2·2'W	T	117
Ruadh Chleit	N Eil	NB2908	57°59·0'	6°34·6'W	H	13,14
Ruadh Loch	Highld	NC0013	58°3·9'	5°23·0'W	W	15

Ruadh Mheall	Stir	NN6731	56°27·4'	4°9·0'W	H	51
Ruadh-phort	N Eil	NF7605	57°1·6'	7°20·0'W	W	31
Ruadh Sgeir	Arg & Bt	NM3014	56°14·8'	6°21·1'W	X	48
Ruadh Sgeir	Arg & Bt	NR7292	56°4·2'	5°39·4'W	X	55
Ruadh Stac	Highld	NG5123	57°14·1'	6°7·1'W	H	32
Ruadh-stac Beag	Highld	NG9761	57°35·9'	5°23·4'W	H	19
Ruadh Stac Beag	Highld	NH0277	57°44·6'	5°19·1'W	H	19
Ruadh Stac Beag	Highld	NG9247	57°28·2'	5°27·7'W	X	25
Ruadh-stac Mór	Highld	NG9561	57°35·8'	5°25·4'W	H	19
Ruadh Stac Mór	Highld	NH0175	57°43·5'	5°20·0'W	H	19
Ruaig	Arg & Bt	NM0647	56°31·6'	6°46·4'W	T	46
Ruaival	N Eil	NF0998	57°48·3'	8°34·6'W	X	18
Ruallan	Highld	NH8245	57°29·1'	3°57·6'W	X	27
Ruanaich	Arg & Bt	NM2723	56°19·5'	6°24·5'W	X	48
Ruan High Lanes	Corn	SW9039	50°13·1'	4°56·3'W	T	204
Ruan Lanihorne	Corn	SW8941	50°14·1'	4°57·2'W	T	204
Ruan Major	Corn	SW7016	50°0·2'	5°12·2'W	T	203
Ruan Minor	Corn	SW7215	49°59·7'	5°10·5'W	T	204
Ruan Pool	Corn	SW6915	49°59·7'	5°13·0'W	W	203
Ruan River	Corn	SW8941	50°14·1'	4°57·2'W	W	204
Ruantallain	Arg & Bt	NR5083	55°58·8'	6°0·0'W	X	61
Ruarach	Highld	NG9521	57°14·3'	5°23·4'W	X	25,33
Ruardean	Glos	SO6117	51°51·3'	2°33·6'W	T	162
Ruardean Hill	Glos	SO6317	51°51·3'	2°31·8'W	T	162
Ruardean Walk	Glos	SO6315	51°50·2'	2°31·8'W	F	162
Ruardean Woodside	Glos	SO6216	51°50·7'	2°32·7'W	T	162
Rubbery Fm	Somer	ST5730	51°4·3'	2°36·4'W	FM	182,183
Rubbing Ho	N Yks	NZ1001	54°24·5'	1°50·3'W	X	92
Rubbingstob Hill	Northum	NY8978	55°6·0'	2°9·9'W	X	87
Rubble Hills	Devon	SS6328	51°2·3'	3°56·9'W	X	180
Rubbytown	Devon	SX4374	50°32·9'	4°12·6'W	X	201
Ruberry	Orkney	ND3096	58°51·0'	3°12·3'W	X	6,7
Ruberry Hill	Norf	TG0343	52°57·0'	1°1·7'E	X	133
Rubers Law	Scot Bord	NT5815	55°25·9'	2°39·4'W	H	80
Rubery	Birm	SO9977	52°23·7'	2°0·5'W	T	139
Rubha à Bhàthaich Bhàin	Arg & Bt	NN1609	56°14·5'	4°57·7'W	X	56
Rubha a' Bhuic	Arg & Bt	NR4652	55°42·0'	6°2·1'W	X	60
Rubha a' Chaiginn	Highld	NM8551	56°36·4'	5°29·7'W	X	49
Rubha a' Chairn	Highld	NC0015	58°5·0'	5°23·1'W	X	15
Rubha a' Chàirn	N Eil	NB3410	58°0·2'	6°29·7'W	X	13,14
Rubha a' Chaisteil	Highld	NG7712	57°8·9'	5°40·7'W	X	33
Rubha a' Chamais Bhàin	Highld	NG7816	57°11·1'	5°40·0'W	X	33
Rubha a'Chamais Bhain	Highld	NM8347	56°34·1'	5°31·5'W	X	49
Rubha a' Choit	Highld	NM5571	56°46·2'	6°0·1'W	X	39,47
Rubha a' Chuinnlein	Arg & Bt	NR3644	55°37·3'	6°11·2'W	X	60
Rubha a'Ghraineig	Arg & Bt	NM1555	56°36·3'	6°38·2'W	X	46
Rubha Aird a' Mhuile	N Eil	NF7029	57°14·2'	7°27·8'W	X	22
Rubha Aird an Iasgaich	Highld	NM4962	56°41·2'	6°5·5'W	X	47
Rubha Aird an Tuirc	Highld	NH1787	57°50·4'	5°4·5'W	X	20
Rubha Aird Beithe	Highld	NM6160	56°40·5'	5°53·6'W	X	40
Rubha Aird Beithe	Highld	NM7063	56°42·4'	5°45·0'W	X	40
Rubha Aird Druimnich	Highld	NM5772	56°46·8'	5°58·2'W	X	39,47
Rubha Aird Druimnich	Highld	NM5960	56°40·4'	5°55·6'W	X	47
Rubha Aird Earnaich	Highld	NM7062	56°41·8'	5°45·0'W	X	40
Rubha Aird na Machrach	N Eil	NF7446	57°23·5'	7°25·2'W	X	22
Rubha Aird nan Eisirein	Arg & Bt	NM5339	56°29·0'	6°0·3'W	X	47,48
Rubha Aird Shlignich	Highld	NM5660	56°40·3'	5°58·5'W	X	47
Rubha Airigh Bheirg	N Ayr	NR8847	55°40·5'	5°21·9'W	X	62,69
Rubha Airigh Dhughaill	N Ayr	NR8738	55°35·6'	5°22·4'W	X	68,69
Rubha Airinis	N Eil	NB4330	58°11·3'	6°21·9'W	X	8
Rubha Alasdair Ruaidh	Highld	NG8235	57°21·5'	5°37·0'W	X	24
Rubha Alltan Pheadair	N Eil	NB4225	58°8·6'	6°22·6'W	X	14
Rubha Allt na Slabhruidh	Highld	NM8272	56°47·6'	5°33·7'W	X	40
Rubha a' Mhaide	N Eil	NB3707	57°58·7'	6°26·4'W	X	14
Rubha a' Mhill	Arg & Bt	NR4273	55°53·1'	6°7·1'W	X	60,61
Rubha a'Mhòthair	Highld	NM7541	56°30·7'	5°39·0'W	X	49
Rubh'a a' Mhullaich Bhàin	Arg & Bt	NR4752	55°42·0'	6°1·2'W	X	60
Rubha an Aird Dheirg	Highld	NM5455	56°37·6'	6°0·2'W	X	47
Rubha an Aisig	Highld	NM5959	56°39·9'	5°55·5'W	X	47
Rubha an Aisig Mhóir	Highld	NM6259	56°40·0'	5°52·6'W	X	49
Rubha an Amair	Arg & Bt	NS0361	55°48·4'	5°8·2'W	X	63
Rubha an Daimh	Highld	NM7461	56°41·4'	5°41·0'W	X	40
Rubha an Daraich	Highld	NG7809	57°7·4'	5°39·6'W	X	33
Rubha an Dobhrain	Arg & Bt	NR4094	56°4·3'	6°10·2'W	X	61
Rubha an Doire Chuilinn	Highld	NC2025	58°10·9'	5°3·2'W	X	15
Rubha an Dùin Bhàin	Highld	NM4470	56°45·3'	6°10·8'W	X	39,47
Rubha an Dùine	N Eil	NF9771	57°37·9'	7°4·1'W	X	18
Rubha an Eilein Mhóir	Highld	NM5861	56°40·9'	5°56·6'W	X	47
Rubha an Eireannaich	Highld	NM8475	56°49·2'	5°31·9'W	X	40
Rubha an Fhasaidh	Highld	NM4387	56°54·4'	6°12·8'W	X	39
Rubha an Iasgaich	Highld	NM4883	56°52·5'	6°7·7'W	X	39
Rubha an Inbhire	Highld	NG5441	57°23·8'	6°5·2'W	X	24
Rubha an Ridire	Highld	NM7340	56°30·1'	5°40·9'W	X	49
Rubha an Rìgh	Arg & Bt	NR7062	55°48·1'	5°39·8'W	X	61,62
Rubha an Trilleachain	N Eil	NB2145	58°16·2'	6°45·3'W	X	8
Rubha an t-Sàile	Arg & Bt	NR2959	55°45·2'	6°18·7'W	X	60
Rubha an t-Sasunnaich	Highld	NM7042	56°31·1'	5°43·9'W	X	49
Rubha an t-Seileir	N Eil	NB5655	58°25·2'	6°10·2'W	X	8
Rubha an t-Siùmpain	N Eil	NB5737	58°15·5'	6°8·1'W	X	8
Rubha' an t-Suibhein	Arg & Bt	NM3645	56°31·6'	6°17·1'W	X	47,48
Rubha an Tuir	Highld	NC8965	58°33·8'	3°54·0'W	H	10
Rubha an Uisge	N Eil	NF1199	57°48·9'	8°32·7'W	X	18
Rubha Aoineadh an Reithe	Arg & Bt	NR4475	55°54·3'	6°5·3'W	X	60,61
Rubha Aosail Sligneach	Highld	NG6027	57°16·5'	5°58·4'W	X	32
Rubha a' Phuirt Leathainn	Highld	NM6070	56°45·8'	5°56·3'W	X	40
Rubha Ard	Arg & Bt	NM1860	56°39·1'	6°35·6'W	X	46
Rubha Ard Ealasaid	Arg & Bt	NM5645	56°32·3'	5°57·7'W	X	47,48
Rubha Ard Ghlaisen	Highld	NG6151	57°29·4'	5°58·8'W	X	24
Rubha' Ard na Bà	Highld	NG8584	57°47·9'	5°36·6'W	X	19
Rubha Ardnish	Highld	NG6824	57°15·1'	5°50·3'W	X	32
Rubha Ard Sgànalish	Arg & Bt	NM4143	56°30·7'	6°12·2'W	X	47,48
Rubha Ard Slisneach	Highld	NG7409	57°7·2'	5°43·5'W	X	33
Rubha Ard Treisnis	Highld	NG7626	57°16·4'	5°42·5'W	X	33
Rubha Arspaig	N Eil	NB2035	58°10·8'	6°45·6'W	X	8,13
Rubha Bàgh Clann Nèill	Highld	NG4515	57°9·6'	6°12·6'W	X	32
Rubha Bàgh nan Capull	Arg & Bt	NR3789	56°1·6'	6°12·8'W	X	61
Rubha Baile na h-Airde	Arg & Bt	NM4435	56°26·5'	6°8·8'W	X	47,48
Rubha Bàn	Arg & Bt	NM2154	56°36·0'	6°32·3'W	X	46,47
Rubha Bàn	Arg & Bt	NM8645	56°33·2'	5°28·5'W	X	49
Rubha Bàn	Arg & Bt	NM9733	56°27·0'	5°17·2'W	X	49
Rubha Ban	Arg & Bt	NN3301	56°10·6'	4°41·0'W	X	56
Rubha Ban	Arg & Bt	NN3313	56°17·1'	4°41·4'W	X	50,56
Rubha Ban	Arg & Bt	NR3162	55°46·8'	6°17·0'W	X	60,61
Rubha Bàn	Arg & Bt	NR3789	56°1·6'	6°12·8'W	X	61
Rubha Bàn	Arg & Bt	NR9974	55°55·3'	5°12·6'W	X	62
Rubha Bàn	Highld	NG3435	57°19·9'	6°24·7'W	X	32
Rubha Bàn	Highld	NG4969	57°38·7'	6°11·9'W	X	23
Rubha Bàn	Highld	NG5017	57°10·8'	6°7·7'W	X	32
Rubha Bàn	Highld	NG7379	57°44·9'	5°48·4'W	X	19
Rubha Bàn	Highld	NH4215	57°12·2'	4°36·5'W	X	34
Rubha Bàn	Highld	NM1595	56°57·8'	6°40·9'W	X	39
Rubha Bàn	Highld	NM6892	56°57·9'	5°48·5'W	X	40
Rubha Bàn	N Ayr	NR8745	55°39·4'	5°22·7'W	X	62,69
Rubha Bàn	N Eil	NF7812	57°5·4'	7°18·5'W	X	31
Rubha Bàn Mór	Pth & Kin	NN5268	56°47·1'	4°24·9'W	X	42
Rubha Bàn na Leideig	Arg & Bt	NM7332	56°25·8'	5°40·4'W	X	49
Rubha Bàrr na h-Earba	Arg & Bt	NM9515	56°17·3'	5°18·3'W	X	55
Rubha Bàrr nan Gobag	Arg & Bt	NR4474	55°53·7'	6°5·3'W	X	60,61
Rubha Basadearn	N Eil	NF8010	57°4·4'	7°16·4'W	X	31
Rubha Beag	Arg & Bt	NR9179	55°57·8'	5°20·5'W	X	62
Rubha Beag	Highld	NG8997	57°55·0'	5°33·3'W	X	19
Rubha Beag	Highld	NH0998	57°56·1'	5°13·1'W	X	19
Rubha Beul à Chaolais	Arg & Bt	NM2921	56°18·5'	6°22·5'W	X	48
Rubh'a' Bhacain	Arg & Bt	NR7096	56°6·3'	5°41·5'W	X	55,61
Rubh' a' Bhacain	Highld	NC0522	58°8·9'	5°18·3'W	X	15
Rubha Bhachlaig	Arg & Bt	NR4274	55°53·7'	6°7·2'W	X	60,61
Rubha Bhadan	Arg & Bt	NR8769	55°52·3'	5°23·8'W	X	62
Rubh' a' Bhaid Bheithe	Highld	NN0259	56°41·1'	5°13·5'W	X	41
Rubh' a' Bhàigh Uaine	N Eil	NB4229	58°10·7'	6°22·8'W	X	8
Rubh' a Bhaile	Arg & Bt	NM2763	56°41·0'	6°27·0'W	X	46,47
Rubh'a' Bhaile-dhoire	Arg & Bt	NR5893	56°4·4'	5°52·9'W	X	61
Rubh' a' Bhaile Fo Thuath	N Eil	NF9087	57°46·2'	7°12·4'W	X	18
Rubh' a' Bhaillein	Arg & Bt	NR5280	55°57·2'	5°57·9'W	X	61
Rubh' a' Bhàin Mhóir	N Eil	NA9722	58°5·3'	7°8·0'W	X	13
Rubh' a' Bhàird	N Eil	NB3101	57°55·3'	6°32·1'W	X	14
Rubha Bhalamuis Bhig	N Eil	NB2801	57°55·2'	6°35·1'W	X	14
Rubha Bharr	Arg & Bt	NN0739	56°30·5'	5°7·7'W	X	50
Rubh' a' Bharra Ghainmheachain	Arg & Bt	NM6122	56°20·1'	5°51·6'W	X	49
Rubh'a'Bharr Ruaidh	Arg & Bt	NR7559	55°46·6'	5°34·8'W	X	62
Rubha Bheanachain	Highld	NG4475	57°41·8'	6°17·3'W	X	23
Rubh' a' Bhearnaig	Arg & Bt	NM8431	56°25·6'	5°29·7'W	X	49
Rubha Bheithe	Highld	NM6259	56°40·0'	5°52·6'W	X	49
Rubha Bhilidh	N Eil	NF8632	57°16·5'	7°12·2'W	X	22
Rubh' a' Bhinnein	Arg & Bt	NM2263	56°40·8'	6°31·9'W	X	46,47
Rubh' a' Bhiogair	N Eil	NB3451	58°22·3'	6°32·5'W	X	8
Rubha Bhlanisgaidh	N Eil	NB3755	58°24·5'	6°29·7'W	X	8
Rubha Bhocaig	N Eil	NG1891	57°49·4'	6°44·5'W	X	14
Rubh' a' Bhogha Mhóir	Arg & Bt	NM3737	56°27·4'	6°15·7'W	X	47,48
Rubha Bhogha-sgeir	N Eil	NB0008	57°57·9'	7°3·9'W	X	13
Rubha Bhoisnis	N Eil	NF8880	57°42·4'	7°13·8'W	X	18
Rubha Bholsa	Arg & Bt	NR3778	55°55·6'	6°12·2'W	X	60,61
Rubha Bholuim	N Eil	NF8328	57°14·2'	7°14·8'W	X	22
Rubha Bhoraraic	Arg & Bt	NR4265	55°48·8'	6°6·7'W	X	60,61
Rubha Bhrà	Highld	NC8766	58°34·3'	3°56·1'W	X	10
Rubha Bhreatanich	Arg & Bt	NR7180	55°57·8'	5°39·7'W	X	55,61
Rubha Bhreidein	Highld	NG3656	57°31·3'	6°24·1'W	X	23
Rubha Bhrengadal	N Eil	NA1504	57°51·8'	8°29·2'W	X	18
Rubha Bhride	Arg & Bt	NR5570	55°51·9'	5°54·5'W	X	61
Rubha Bhrisdeadh-ramh	Arg & Bt	NM3639	56°28·4'	6°16·8'W	X	47,48
Rubha Bhriste	N Eil	NA1506	57°52·9'	8°29·4'W	X	18
Rubh' a' Bhrocaire	Highld	NC0617	58°6·2'	5°17·1'W	X	15
Rubha Bhrolluim	N Eil	NB3202	57°55·9'	6°31·2'W	X	14
Rubh'a Bhuachaille	Highld	NC2065	58°32·4'	5°5·1'W	X	9
Rubha Bhuailt	N Eil	NF7918	57°8·7'	7°18·0'W	X	31
Rubha Bhuailte	Highld	NM6863	56°42·3'	5°47·0'W	X	40
Rubha Bhuic	N Eil	NB0108	57°57·9'	7°2·9'W	X	13
Rubha Biorach	Arg & Bt	NR4556	55°44·1'	6°3·3'W	X	60
Rubha Boraige Móire	Arg & Bt	NL9447	56°31·2'	6°58·1'W	X	46
Rubha Brataig	N Eil	NB0638	58°14·2'	7°0·1'W	X	13
Rubha Breac	Arg & Bt	NM3724	56°20·4'	6°14·9'W	X	48
Rubha Breac	Arg & Bt	NM7513	56°15·6'	5°37·5'W	X	55
Rubha Breac	Arg & Bt	NR3389	56°1·4'	6°16·7'W	X	61
Rubha Breac	N Eil	NF8954	57°28·4'	7°10·8'W	X	22
Rubha Breacaichte	Highld	NG5951	57°29·4'	6°0·8'W	X	24
Rubha Briodog	N Eil	NB2401	57°55·0'	6°39·2'W	X	14
Rubha Buaile Linnis	N Eil	NA9923	58°5·9'	7°6·1'W	X	13
Rubha Buidhe	Arg & Bt	NM5226	56°21·9'	6°0·5'W	X	48
Rubha Buidhe	Arg & Bt	NM7313	56°15·6'	5°39·5'W	X	55
Rubha Buidhe	Arg & Bt	NR2757	55°44·0'	6°20·5'W	X	60
Rubha Buidhe	Arg & Bt	NR4654	55°43·0'	6°2·2'W	X	60
Rubha Buidhe	Highld	NG5136	57°21·1'	6°7·9'W	X	23,24,32
Rubha Buidhe	Highld	NG7811	57°8·4'	5°39·7'W	X	33
Rubha Buidhe	Highld	NG7925	57°16·0'	5°39·5'W	X	33
Rubha Buidhe	Highld	NH1292	57°52·9'	5°9·8'W	X	19
Rubha Buidhe	N Eil	NB2009	57°59·2'	6°43·8'W	X	13,14
Rubha Buidhe	N Eil	NB3710	58°0·3'	6°26·6'W	X	14
Rubha Buidhe Mhic Iomhair	Arg & Bt	NR4298	56°6·6'	6°8·5'W	X	61
Rubha Cadail	Highld	NH0997	57°55·6'	5°13·1'W	X	19
Rubha Camas a' Mhaoraich	Highld	NH0896	57°55·0'	5°14·0'W	X	19
Rubha Camas an t-Salainn	Highld	NG7609	57°7·3'	5°41·6'W	X	33
Rubha Camas na Cailinn	Highld	NG8408	57°7·0'	5°33·6'W	X	33
Rubha Camas nam Meanbh-chuileag	Arg & Bt	NR6689	56°2·5'	5°45·0'W	X	55,61
Rubha Camas Pliasgaig	Highld	NG3903	57°2·9'	6°17·8'W	X	32,39
Rubha Cam nan Gall	N Eil	NF8847	57°24·6'	7°11·3'W	X	22
Rubha Caol	Arg & Bt	NR3486	55°59·8'	6°15·5'W	X	61
Rubha Caol	Arg & Bt	NR7490	56°3·3'	5°37·3'W	X	55
Rubha Caol	Highld	NG7613	57°9·5'	5°41·8'W	X	33
Rubha Caol	N Eil	NB2447	58°19·8'	6°42·4'W	X	8
Rubha Caol	N Eil	NF8279	57°41·6'	7°19·8'W	X	18
Rubha Caolard	Arg & Bt	NR8783	55°59·8'	5°24·5'W	X	55
Rubha Caolas Liùrsaigh	N Eil	NF8540	57°20·8'	7°13·8'W	X	22
Rubha Caolas Mhic Iain Duibh	N Eil	NF8654	57°28·3'	7°13·8'W	X	22
Rubha Caradal	Highld	NG5605	57°4·5'	6°1·1'W	X	32,39
Rubha Càrnach	N Eil	NB0116	58°2·2'	7°3·5'W	X	13
Rubha Carrach	Highld	NM4670	56°45·4'	6°8·9'W	X	39,47
Rubha Carraig-chrom	N Eil	NF7408	57°3·1'	7°22·2'W	X	31
Rubha Carraig nan Darrach	Arg & Bt	NR4197	56°6·0'	6°9·5'W	X	61
Rubha Carr-innis	Highld	NG2705	57°3·6'	6°29·7'W	X	39
Rubha Chabharstaidh	N Eil	NB3620	58°5·7'	6°28·3'W	X	14
Rubh' Achadh a' Chùirn	Highld	NG6624	57°15·1'	5°52·3'W	X	32
Rubh' a' Chaiginn Lionta	Arg & Bt	NR5590	56°2·7'	5°55·6'W	X	61
Rubh'a' Chairn Bhàin	Arg & Bt	NR6653	55°43·1'	5°43·1'W	X	62
Rùbh' a' Chairn Bhig	Arg & Bt	NM9534	56°27·5'	5°19·2'W	X	49
Rubh' a' Chàirn Lèith	Highld	NG3670	57°38·8'	6°25·0'W	X	23
Rubh' a' Chairn Mhóir	Highld	NM6778	56°50·4'	5°48·8'W	X	40
Rubh' a'Chamais	Arg & Bt	NR5978	55°56·3'	5°51·1'W	X	61
Rubh' a' Chamais Ruaidh	Highld	NG7459	57°34·1'	5°46·3'W	X	24
Rubhachan Eoghainn	Arg & Bt	NR5180	55°57·2'	5°58·9'W	X	61
Rubh' a' Chaoil	Arg & Bt	NM3346	56°32·1'	6°20·1'W	X	47,48
Rubha Chaolais	Highld	NM6980	56°51·5'	5°46·9'W	X	40
Rubh' a' Chaolais	N Eil	NF7501	56°59·4'	7°20·6'W	X	31
Rubha Charnain	N Eil	NF9987	57°46·6'	7°3·3'W	X	18
Rubh' a' Charnain	N Eil	NL6086	56°50·7'	7°34·2'W	X	31
Rubha Chàrnain	N Eil	NL6896	56°56·4'	7°27·1'W	X	31
Rubh' a' Charnain Mhóir	N Eil	NF9079	57°41·9'	7°11·8'W	X	18
Rubha Charn nan Cearc	Highld	NG5503	57°3·4'	6°2·0'W	X	32,39
Rubha Cheanna Mhuir	Highld	NN1091	56°58·5'	5°7·1'W	X	34
Rubh' a' Cheathraimh Ghairbh	Highld	NC1852	58°25·4'	5°6·5'W	X	9
Rubh' a' Chinn Mhóir	Highld	NG5932	57°19·2'	5°59·7'W	X	24,32
Rubh' a' Chlachain	N Eil	NF8668	57°35·8'	7°14·9'W	X	18
Rubha Chlachan	Arg & Bt	NR6105	55°17·1'	5°45·4'W	X	68
Rubh' a' Chladaich	Arg & Bt	NR4362	55°47·2'	6°5·5'W	X	60,61
Rubh' a' Chlàdain	Arg & Bt	NR3342	55°36·2'	6°13·9'W	X	60
Rubha Chlaidh	N Eil	NF7711	57°4·9'	7°19·4'W	X	31
Rubh' a' Chlaidheimh	Arg & Bt	NM3425	56°20·8'	6°17·9'W	X	48
Rubh'a' Chlèirich	Arg & Bt	NR5365	55°49·2'	5°56·1'W	X	61
Rubh' a' Chlèirich	N Eil	NB3120	58°5·5'	6°33·4'W	X	13,14
Rubha Chliuthairt	N Eil	NG1589	57°48·3'	6°47·4'W	X	14
Rubh' a' Choin	Highld	NC0314	58°4·5'	5°20·0'W	X	15
Rubh' a' Choin	Highld	NG8390	57°51·1'	5°39·0'W	X	19
Rubh' a' Chonnaidh	Highld	NG5832	57°19·1'	6°0·7'W	X	24,32
Rubh' a' Chorrain	N Eil	NF9083	57°44·0'	7°12·1'W	X	18
Rubha Chràiginis	Arg & Bt	NL9245	56°30·0'	6°59·9'W	X	46
Rubh' a' Chrois-aoinidh	Arg & Bt	NR5080	55°57·1'	5°59·8'W	X	61
Rubh' a' Chroisein	Highld	NM4278	56°49·6'	6°13·3'W	X	39
Rubh' a' Chromain	Arg & Bt	NM5220	56°18·7'	6°0·2'W	X	48
Rubha Chuaig	Highld	NG6959	57°34·0'	5°51·3'W	X	24
Rubha Chuidhtinis	N Eil	NB5634	58°13·9'	6°8·9'W	X	8
Rubha Chuidhtinis	N Eil	NG1086	57°46·5'	6°52·2'W	X	14
Rubh'a'Chuil	Arg & Bt	NM7106	56°11·8'	5°41·0'W	X	55
Rubha Chùil-tairbh	Highld	NG6360	57°34·3'	5°57·4'W	X	24
Rubh' a' Chùirn	Arg & Bt	NR3844	55°37·4'	6°9·3'W	X	60
Rubha Chulinish	Arg & Bt	NM3942	56°30·1'	6°14·0'W	X	47,48
Rubh'a' Chumhainn Bhig	Arg & Bt	NR5782	55°58·4'	5°53·2'W	X	61
Rubha Cill Maluaig	Arg & Bt	NR7169	55°51·8'	5°39·2'W	X	62
Rubha Clach an Tràghaidh	Arg & Bt	NR8966	55°50·7'	5°21·8'W	X	62
Rubha Clach Chuilein	Arg & Bt	NM3441	56°29·4'	6°18·8'W	X	47,48
Rubha Cladh Eòin	Arg & Bt	NR7686	56°1·1'	5°35·2'W	X	55
Rubha Coigeach	Highld	NB9818	58°6·6'	5°25·2'W	X	15
Rubha Crago	N Eil	NG2397	57°52·9'	6°39·9'W	X	14
Rubha Creadha	N Eil	NB1202	57°55·1'	6°51·4'W	X	14
Rubha Creagan Dubha	N Ayr	NR9352	55°43·3'	5°17·3'W	X	62,69
Rubha Creag Mhic Fhionnlaidh	N Eil	NF9054	57°28·5'	7°9·9'W	X	22
Rubha Crion	Highld	NG5948	57°27·8'	6°0·6'W	X	24
Rubha Croinn	Arg & Bt	NM7838	56°29·2'	5°35·9'W	X	49
Rubha Cruaidhlinn	Highld	NG5618	57°11·5'	6°1·9'W	X	32
Rubha Cruinn	Highld	NG3030	57°17·1'	6°28·4'W	X	32
Rubha Cruitiridh	Arg & Bt	NR7160	55°47·0'	5°38·7'W	X	62
Rubha Cùil	Arg & Bt	NM7308	56°12·9'	5°39·2'W	X	55
Rubha Cuilinn	Arg & Bt	NM9105	56°11·8'	5°21·7'W	X	55
Rubha Cumhann	Highld	NM7069	56°45·6'	5°45·3'W	X	40
Rubha Dà Chuain	Highld	NM6591	56°57·3'	5°51·4'W	X	40
Rubha Daraich	Highld	NM7268	56°45·1'	5°43·3'W	X	40
Rubha dà Uisge	Arg & Bt	NM7935	56°27·6'	5°34·8'W	X	49
Rubha Dearg	Arg & Bt	NM9542	56°31·8'	5°19·6'W	X	49
Rubha Dearg	Highld	NM6544	56°32·0'	5°48·9'W	X	49
Rubha Dearg	Highld	NN0266	56°44·9'	5°13·8'W	X	41
Rubha Dearg	Highld	NN0975	56°49·9'	5°7·4'W	X	41
Rubha Dearg-uillt	Arg & Bt	NR8246	55°39·8'	5°27·5'W	X	62,69
Rubha Deas	N Eil	NB5635	58°14·4'	6°9·0'W	X	8
Rubha Doire Làrach	Highld	NN0941	56°31·6'	5°5·9'W	X	50
Rubha Doire na Boceinein	Highld	NG6232	57°19·3'	5°56·7'W	X	24,32
Rubha Domhain	N Eil	NL5783	56°49·0'	7°36·9'W	X	31
Rubha Dubh	Arg & Bt	NM0948	56°32·3'	6°43·6'W	X	46
Rubha Dubh	Arg & Bt	NM4023	56°19·9'	6°11·9'W	X	48
Rubha Dubh	Arg & Bt	NM5621	56°19·4'	5°56·3'W	X	48
Rubha Dubh	Arg & Bt	NN3301	56°10·6'	4°41·0'W	X	56
Rubha Dubh	Arg & Bt	NR2660	55°45·6'	6°21·6'W	X	60
Rubha Dubh	Arg & Bt	NR2742	55°36·0'	6°19·6'W	X	60
Rubha Dubh	Arg & Bt	NR3991	56°2·7'	6°11·0'W	X	61
Rubha Dubh	Arg & Bt	NR3993	56°3·8'	6°11·1'W	X	61
Rubha Dubh	Arg & Bt	NR6546	55°39·3'	5°43·7'W	X	62
Rubha Dubh	Arg & Bt	NR9872	55°54·2'	5°13·4'W	X	62
Rubha Dubh	Highld	NC0006	58°0·2'	5°22·6'W	X	15
Rubha Dubh	Highld	NG2362	57°34·1'	6°37·5'W	X	23
Rubha Dubh	Highld	NG3953	57°29·8'	6°20·9'W	X	23
Rubha Dubh	Highld	NG4313	57°8·4'	6°14·4'W	X	32
Rubha Dubh	Highld	NG4512	57°8·0'	6°12·4'W	X	32
Rubha Dubh	Highld	NG6303	57°3·7'	5°54·1'W	X	32
Rubha Dubh	Highld	NM5761	56°40·9'	5°57·6'W	X	47
Rubha Dubh	N Eil	NF8113	57°6·1'	7°15·7'W	X	31
Rubha Dubh	N Eil	NG1699	57°53·7'	6°47·1'W	X	14
Rubha Dubh a' Bhàta	Highld	NM8294	56°59·4'	5°34·9'W	X	33,40
Rubha Dubh a' Ghrianain	Highld	NG3031	57°17·7'	6°28·4'W	X	32
Rubha Dubh an Ròin	N Eil	NF8646	57°24·0'	7°13·2'W	X	22
Rubha Dubh Ard	Highld	NC0403	57°58·7'	5°18·4'W	X	15
Rubha Dubh Ard	Highld	NG6214	57°9·6'	5°55·7'W	X	32
Rubha Dubh nam Fiadh	Highld	NH0501	57°3·8'	5°12·5'W	X	33
Rubha Dubh nan Cuileann	Arg & Bt	NM8103	56°10·4'	5°31·2'W	X	55
Rubha Dubh Sheisiader	N Eil	NB5532	58°12·8'	6°9·8'W	X	8
Rubha Dubh Tighary	N Eil	NF7072	57°37·3'	7°31·2'W	X	18

Rubha Dubh Uisge	Highld	NN0177	56°50·8′	5°15·3′W	X	41
Rubha Duilich	Highld	NC0114	58°4·5′	5°22·0′W	X	15
Rubha Dùin Bhàin	Arg & Bt	NR5914	55°21·9′	5°47·8′W	X	68
Rubha Dùnan	Highld	NC0106	58°0·2′	5°21·6′W	X	15
Rubha Dùn Iasgain	Arg & Bt	NM3639	56°28·4′	6°16·8′W	X	47,48
Rubha Eacleit	N Eil	NB1843	58°17·4′	6°48·3′W	X	8
Rubha Eilagadale	Highld	NM5771	56°46·3′	5°58·2′W	X	39,47
Rubha Eilean Anabaich	N Eil	NB2105	57°57·1′	6°42·5′W	X	13,14
Rubha Eilean Mhàrtain	Arg & Bt	NR3992	56°3·2′	6°11·1′W	X	61
Rubha Eistein	N Eil	NB1910	57°59·7′	6°44·9′W	X	13,14
Rubha Eredine	Arg & Bt	NM9609	56°14·0′	5°17·0′W	X	55
Rubha Fada	N Eil	NF7104	57°0·8′	7°24·8′W	X	31
Rubha Fásachd	Arg & Bt	NM1652	56°34·7′	6°37·0′W	X	46
Rubh' a Fhreastaig	Arg & Bt	NM7928	56°23·8′	5°34·4′W	X	49
Rubha Fhuar a'Chos	Stir	NS3696	56°8·0′	4°37·9′W	X	56
Rubha Fianuis	N Eil	NB1838	58°14·7′	6°47·9′W	X	8,13
Rubha Fiart	Arg & Bt	NM7835	56°27·6′	5°35·7′W	X	49
Rubha Fiola	Arg & Bt	NM7110	56°13·9′	5°41·2′W	X	55
Rubha Fion-àird	Arg & Bt	NM8637	56°28·9′	5°28·1′W	X	49
Rubha fo Deas	N Eil	NF8539	57°20·2′	7°13·7′W	X	22
Rubha Gainmheine	Arg & Bt	NM9915	56°17·4′	5°14·4′W	X	55
Rubha Gainmhich	Arg & Bt	NM5737	56°28·0′	5°56·3′W	X	47,48
Rubha Gar	Highld	ND0659	58°30·8′	3°36·3′W	X	11,12
Rubha Garbh	Arg & Bt	NM9341	56°31·2′	5°21·5′W	X	49
Rubha Garbh	Arg & Bt	NM9342	56°31·7′	5°21·5′W	X	49
Rubha Garbh	Arg & Bt	NR4196	56°5·5′	6°9·4′W	X	61
Rubha Garbh	Arg & Bt	NR7576	55°55·7′	5°35·7′W	X	62
Rubha Garbh	Arg & Bt	NS1492	56°5·3′	4°58·9′W	X	56
Rubha Garbh	Highld	NG2836	57°20·3′	6°30·8′W	X	23
Rubha Garbh	Highld	NG5332	57°19·0′	6°5·7′W	X	24,32
Rubha Garbh	Highld	NM7090	56°56·9′	5°46·5′W	X	33,40
Rubha Garbh	N Eil	NB0119	58°3·8′	7°3·7′W	X	13
Rubha Garbhaig	Highld	NG4968	57°38·2′	6°11·9′W	X	23
Rubha Garbh-àird	Arg & Bt	NM8736	56°28·3′	5°27·1′W	X	49
Rubha Garbh Airde	Arg & Bt	NM7620	56°19·4′	5°36·9′W	X	49,55
Rubha Garbh-ard	Arg & Bt	NR7895	56°6·0′	5°33·7′W	X	55
Rubha Garbhard	N Ayr	NR8926	55°29·2′	5°19·9′W	X	68,69
Rubh' a' Geodha	Arg & Bt	NR4399	56°7·1′	6°7·6′W	X	61
Rubha Geodha na Cloinne	N Eil	NB1839	58°15·2′	6°48·0′W	X	8,13
Rubha Geodha nam Mult	Arg & Bt	NR1965	55°48·1′	6°28·6′W	X	60
Rubha Ghaisinis	N Eil	NF8244	57°22·8′	7°17·0′W	T	22
Rubha Ghall	Arg & Bt	NN2943	56°33·1′	4°46·5′W	X	50
Rubha Gharsan	N Eil	NB2648	58°20·4′	6°40·4′W	X	8
Rubha Ghead a' Leighe	Highld	NM6477	56°49·7′	5°51·6′W	X	40
Rubh' a' Ghearrain	Arg & Bt	NM4536	56°27·1′	6°7·9′W	X	47,48
Rubh' a' Gheodha Bhuidhe	Highld	NG4817	57°10·7′	6°9·7′W	X	32
Rubha Ghill	N Eil	NF1199	57°48·9′	8°32·7′W	X	18
Rubh' a' Ghiubhais	Highld	NG8256	57°32·8′	5°38·1′W	X	24
Rubh' a' Ghlaisich	Arg & Bt	NM5549	56°34·4′	5°58·9′W	X	47,48
Rubha Ghlamraidh	Arg & Bt	NR1758	55°44·2′	6°30·1′W	X	60
Rubha Gholl Shùil	N Eil	NB3711	58°0·9′	6°26·7′W	X	14
Rubha Ghralish	N Eil	NL5679	56°46·8′	7°37·5′W	X	31
Rubh'a' Ghrùdaidh	Highld	NC3663	58°31·7′	4°48·5′W	X	9
Rubh'a Ghuail	Arg & Bt	NR2265	55°48·2′	6°25·7′W	X	60
Rubh' a' Ghuirmein	Arg & Bt	NM7335	56°27·4′	5°40·6′W	X	49
Rubha Gisgil	Highld	NC1640	58°18·9′	5°8·0′W	H	9
Rubha Giubhais	Highld	NN0292	56°58·9′	5°15·0′W	X	33
Rubha Glas	Arg & Bt	NR3148	55°39·3′	6°16·2′W	X	60
Rubha Glas	Arg & Bt	NR3645	55°37·9′	6°11·2′W	X	60
Rubha Glas	Arg & Bt	NR9973	55°54·7′	5°12·5′W	X	62
Rubha Glas	Highld	NG7558	57°33·6′	5°45·2′W	X	24
Rubha Glas	N Ayr	NR8847	55°40·5′	5°21·9′W	X	62,69
Rubha Glas	N Eil	NB0216	58°2·2′	7°2·5′W	X	13
Rubha Glas	N Eil	NB1833	58°12·0′	6°47·5′W	X	8,13
Rubha Glas	N Eil	NF8474	57°39·0′	7°17·4′W	X	18
Rubha Glas	N Eil	NL6597	56°56·8′	7°30·2′W	X	31
Rubha Gorm	Arg & Bt	NM5547	56°33·3′	5°58·8′W	X	47,48
Rubha Greannach	N Eil	NF7623	57°11·3′	7°21·4′W	X	22
Rubha Greotach	N Eil	NL5887	56°51·2′	7°36·2′W	X	31
Rubha Grianain	Arg & Bt	NR9163	55°49·2′	5°19·7′W	X	62
Rubha Groulin	Highld	NM4671	56°45·9′	6°8·9′W	X	39,47
Rubha Guail	Highld	NG7315	57°10·4′	5°44·9′W	X	33
Rubha Hanais	Arg & Bt	NL9345	56°30·1′	6°58·9′W	X	46
Rubha Hestabhal	N Eil	NB1740	58°15·7′	6°49·1′W	X	8,13
Rubha-hinni-gya	N Eil	NB0203	57°55·3′	7°1·5′W	X	13,18
Rubha Hogh	Arg & Bt	NM1759	56°38·5′	6°36·5′W	X	46
Rubha Hunish	Highld	NG4076	57°42·2′	6°21·4′W	X	23
Rubh' Ailltinis	N Eil	NB3608	57°59·2′	6°27·5′W	X	14
Rubha Iosal	N Eil	NB4216	58°3·7′	6°22·0′W	X	14
Rubh' Aird a' Chaoil	Arg & Bt	NM7030	56°24·6′	5°43·3′W	X	49
Rubh' Aird Alanais	Arg & Bt	NR3593	56°3·6′	6°15·0′W	X	61
Rubh Aird a' Mhadaidh	Highld	NC2942	58°20·3′	4°54·8′W	X	9
Rubh' Aird an Anail	Highld	NG8876	57°43·7′	5°33·2′W	X	19
Rubh' Aird an Daraich	Arg & Bt	NM3522	56°19·2′	6°16·7′W	X	48
Rubh' Aird an Droighinn	Arg & Bt	NN0233	56°27·1′	5°12·3′W	X	50
Rubh' Aird an Fheidh	Highld	NM6375	56°48·6′	5°52·5′W	X	40
Rubh' Aird an t- Sionnaich	Highld	NC1443	58°20·4′	5°10·2′W	X	9
Rubh' Aird Cumnaich	Highld	NM7090	56°56·9′	5°46·5′W	X	33,40
Rubh' Aird Eirnish	Arg & Bt	NM8039	56°29·8′	5°34·0′W	X	49
Rubh' Aird Ghainimh	Arg & Bt	NM8946	56°33·8′	5°25·6′W	X	49
Rubh' Aird Ghamhsgail	Highld	NM6983	56°53·1′	5°47·1′W	X	40
Rubh' Aird Luing	Arg & Bt	NM7405	56°11·3′	5°38·1′W	X	55
Rubh' Aird Lungadain	Arg & Bt	NM6223	56°20·6′	5°50·6′W	X	49
Rubh' Aird-mhicheil	N Eil	NF7233	57°16·5′	7°26·1′W	X	22
Rubh' Aird Mhóir	Highld	NM6883	56°53·1′	5°48·0′W	X	40
Rubh' Aird na Murrach	Highld	NM8293	56°58·9′	5°34·8′W	X	33,40
Rubh' Aird nan Carnan	Arg & Bt	NM5227	56°22·5′	6°0·5′W	X	48
Rubh' Aird na Sgitheich	Arg & Bt	NR4779	55°56·5′	6°2·7′W	X	60,61
Rubh' Aird Phlacaig	Arg & Bt	NN0435	56°28·2′	5°10·5′W	X	50
Rubh Aird Rainich	Arg & Bt	NN0838	56°30·0′	5°6·7′W	X	50
Rubha Lagain Aillidh	Arg & Bt	NM7519	56°18·9′	5°37·8′W	X	55
Rubha Lagganroaig	Arg & Bt	NR9164	55°49·7′	5°19·8′W	X	62
Rubha Laileum	N Eil	NF8027	57°13·6′	7°17·7′W	X	22
Rubha Laimhrige	Arg & Bt	NR5366	55°49·7′	5°56·2′W	X	61
Rubha Lamanais	Arg & Bt	NR2068	55°49·7′	6°27·8′W	X	60
Rubha Lamasaigh	N Eil	NF8432	57°16·4′	7°14·1′W	X	22
Rubha Langanes	Highld	NG2306	57°4·0′	6°33·7′W	X	39
Rubha Lang-aoinidh	Arg & Bt	NR4880	55°57·1′	6°1·8′W	X	60,61
Rubha Leacach	N Eil	NA9721	58°4·7′	7°7·9′W	X	13
Rubha Leac an Fheòir	Arg & Bt	NR2745	55°37·6′	6°19·8′W	X	60

Rubha Leac nan Laogh	Arg & Bt	NR2642	55°35·9′	6°20·6′W	X	60
Rubha Leathan	Arg & Bt	NR9260	55°47·6′	5°18·6′W	X	62
Rubha Leathan	Highld	NM7368	56°45·2′	5°42·3′W	X	40
Rubha Leathan	N Eil	NB0102	57°54·7′	7°2·5′W	X	18
Rubha Leathann	Arg & Bt	NR7062	55°48·1′	5°39·8′W	X	61,62
Rubha Leathann	Arg & Bt	NR7077	55°56·1′	5°40·5′W	X	61,62
Rubha Leathann	N Eil	NB3654	58°24·0′	6°30·6′W	X	8
Rubha Leth Thorcaill	Arg & Bt	NM6642	56°31·0′	5°47·8′W	X	49
Rubha Leumair	Highld	NC0426	58°11·0′	5°19·6′W	X	15
Rubha Liasain	N Eil	NF8749	57°25·7′	7°12·5′W	X	22
Rubha Liath	Arg & Bt	NM0846	56°31·2′	6°44·4′W	X	46
Rubha Liath	Arg & Bt	NR4755	55°43·6′	6°1·3′W	X	60
Rubha Liath	Arg & Bt	NR5381	55°57·8′	5°57·0′W	X	61
Rubha Liath	N Eil	NF8009	57°3·9′	7°16·3′W	X	31
Rubha Liath	N Eil	NL5481	56°47·8′	7°39·6′W	X	31
Rubha Linsiadair	N Eil	NB2032	58°11·5′	6°45·4′W	X	8,13
Rubha Loisgte	N Eil	NB0019	58°3·8′	7°4·8′W	X	13
Rubha Luidhneis	Arg & Bt	NR2968	55°50·0′	6°19·2′W	X	60
Rubha Luinngeanach	Highld	NM6270	56°45·9′	5°53·2′W	X	40
Rubha MacShannuich	Arg & Bt	NR7007	55°18·5′	5°37·0′W	X	68
Rubha Maol	Highld	NG2455	57°30·3′	6°36·0′W	X	23
Rubha Maol na Mine	Arg & Bt	NM3440	56°28·9′	6°18·8′W	X	47,48
Rubha Màs a' Chnuic	N Eil	NF9794	57°50·2′	7°5·9′W	X	18
Rubha ma-thuath	N Eil	NF8146	57°23·8′	7°18·2′W	X	22
Rubha Meadhonach	Highld	NM9655	56°38·8′	5°19·2′W	X	49
Rubha Meadhonach	N Eil	NB5638	58°16·0′	6°9·2′W	X	8
Rubha Meallain Bhuidhe	Highld	NH1199	57°56·7′	5°11·1′W	X	19
Rubha Meall na Hoe	N Eil	NF8217	57°8·3′	7°15·0′W	X	31
Rubha Meall nan Caorach	N Eil	NF7908	57°3·3′	7°17·2′W	X	31
Rubha Meall nan Gamhna	Arg & Bt	NM3836	56°26·9′	6°14·6′W	X	47,48
Rubh' a' Mhadaidh-ruaidh	Highld	NB9810	58°2·3′	5°24·8′W	X	15
Rubha Mhaide	N Eil	NF8480	57°42·2′	7°17·9′W	X	18
Rubh'a' Mhàil	Arg & Bt	NR4279	55°56·3′	6°7·5′W	X	60,61
Rubha Mhàirtein	Arg & Bt	NM7124	56°21·4′	5°42·0′W	X	49
Rubha Mhanais	N Eil	NF7173	57°37·9′	7°30·3′W	X	18
Rubha Mhànais	N Eil	NF9280	57°42·5′	7°9·8′W	X	18
Rubh' a' Mharaiche	Arg & Bt	NR5812	55°20·8′	5°48·6′W	X	68
Rubha Mhealaboist	N Eil	NB4633	58°13·0′	6°19·0′W	X	8
Rubha Mhein	Arg & Bt	NR7860	55°47·2′	5°32·0′W	X	62
Rubha Mhic	Arg & Bt	NR7359	55°46·5′	5°36·7′W	X	62
Rubha Mhic-aoidh	Arg & Bt	NM3125	56°20·7′	6°20·8′W	X	48
Rubha Mhic Chaisein	Arg & Bt	NM8804	56°11·1′	5°24·5′W	X	55
Rubha Mhic Gille-mhìcheil	N Eil	NF9363	57°33·4′	7°7·5′W	X	18
Rubha Mhìcheil	N Eil	NF7301	56°59·3′	7°22·6′W	X	31
Rubha Mhic-'ille-mhaoil	Arg & Bt	NR6194	56°5·0′	5°50·0′W	X	61
Rubha Mhic Mharcuis	Arg & Bt	NM7317	56°17·7′	5°39·7′W	X	55
Rubh' a' Mhìle	Highld	NM5062	56°41·2′	6°4·5′W	X	47
Rubh a' Mhill Bhain	Highld	NC2055	58°27·0′	5°4·6′W	X	9
Rubh' a' Mhill Dheirg	Highld	NC0228	58°12·0′	5°21·7′W	X	15
Rubh' a' Mhill Mhóir	Arg & Bt	NM3741	56°29·5′	6°15·9′W	X	47,48
Rubh'a' Mhinidhe Beag	Arg & Bt	NR8578	55°57·1′	5°26·2′W	X	62
Rubh' a' Mhorbhuile	N Eil	NL6894	56°55·4′	7°27·0′W	X	31
Rubh'a'Mhucard	Highld	NC1637	58°17·3′	5°7·8′W	X	15
Rubh' a' Mhuilt	Highld	NC4762	58°31·4′	4°37·2′W	X	9
Rubha Mhuirich	N Eil	NF0898	57°48·2′	8°35·6′W	X	18
Rubha Mór	Arg & Bt	NM2464	56°41·4′	6°30·0′W	X	46,47
Rubha Mór	Arg & Bt	NM4839	56°28·8′	6°5·1′W	X	47,48
Rubha Mór	Arg & Bt	NM5744	56°31·8′	5°56·6′W	X	47,48
Rubha Mór	Arg & Bt	NM6711	56°14·3′	5°45·2′W	X	55
Rubha Mór	Arg & Bt	NM8942	56°31·6′	5°25·4′W	X	49
Rubha Mór	Arg & Bt	NM9141	56°31·1′	5°23·4′W	X	49
Rubha Mór	Arg & Bt	NN1710	56°15·1′	4°56·8′W	X	50,56
Rubha Mór	Arg & Bt	NR2366	55°48·7′	6°24·9′W	X	60
Rubha Mór	Arg & Bt	NR2948	55°39·3′	6°18·1′W	X	60
Rubha Mór	Arg & Bt	NR4095	56°4·9′	6°10·3′W	X	61
Rubha Mór	Arg & Bt	NS3499	56°9·5′	4°39·9′W	X	56
Rubha Mór	Highld	NB9814	58°4·4′	5°25·0′W	X	15
Rubha Mór	Highld	NC7634	58°16·9′	4°6·4′W	X	17
Rubha Mór	Highld	NG7614	57°10·0′	5°41·8′W	X	33
Rubha Mór	Highld	NG8034	57°20·9′	5°38·9′W	X	24
Rubha Mor	Highld	NG8696	57°54·4′	5°36·3′W	X	19
Rubha Mór	Highld	NM9655	56°38·8′	5°19·2′W	X	49
Rubha Mór	N Eil	NB0637	58°13·7′	7°0·0′W	H	13
Rubha Mór	N Eil	NF7266	57°34·2′	7°28·7′W	X	18
Rubha Mór	N Eil	NF8113	57°6·1′	7°15·7′W	X	31
Rubha Mór	N Eil	NF9367	57°35·6′	7°7·8′W	X	18
Rubha Mór	N Eil	NL6997	56°57·0′	7°26·2′W	X	31
Rubha Mór Corrachra	Arg & Bt	NR9868	55°52·0′	5°13·3′W	X	62
Rubha Mór Kames	Arg & Bt	NR9770	55°53·1′	5°14·3′W	X	62
Rubha Mór Nighean Eoin	Arg & Bt	NR4098	56°6·5′	6°10·5′W	X	61
Rubha na Beirghe	N Eil	NB2347	58°19·7′	6°43·4′W	X	8
Rubha na Beithe	Arg & Bt	NS2096	56°7·6′	4°53·3′W	X	56
Rubha na Bò Maoile	Arg & Bt	NL9548	56°31·8′	6°57·2′W	X	46
Rubha na Brataich	N Eil	NF8329	57°14·8′	7°14·9′W	X	22
Rubha na Brèige	Highld	NC0519	58°7·3′	5°18·2′W	X	15
Rubha na Buaile	N Eil	NG1795	57°51·6′	6°45·8′W	X	14
Rubha na Bùth	N Eil	NF8954	57°28·4′	7°10·8′W	X	22
Rubha na Caillich	Arg & Bt	NR5366	55°49·7′	5°56·2′W	X	61
Rubha na Caillich	Arg & Bt	NR7168	55°51·3′	5°39·1′W	X	62
Rubha na Caillich	Highld	NG8024	57°15·5′	5°38·4′W	X	33
Rubha na Caillich	Highld	NM6271	56°46·4′	5°53·3′W	X	40
Rubha na Caillich	N Eil	NB3554	58°23·9′	6°31·7′W	X	8
Rubha na Carraig-géire	Arg & Bt	NM2621	56°18·4′	6°25·4′W	X	48
Rubh'an Achaidh Mhóir	Highld	NM6692	56°57·9′	5°50·5′W	X	40
Rubhan a' chall	Highld	NM4562	56°41·1′	6°9·4′W	X	47
Rubha na Cille	Arg & Bt	NM7028	56°23·6′	5°43·2′W	X	49
Rubha na Cille	Arg & Bt	NR6879	55°57·1′	5°42·5′W	X	61,62
Rubha na Cloiche	Highld	NC8666	58°34·3′	3°57·1′W	X	10
Rubha na Cloiche	Highld	NG5633	57°19·6′	6°2·8′W	X	24,32
Rubha na Cloiche	Highld	NM8160	56°41·1′	5°34·1′W	X	40
Rubha na Cloiche-muilinn	Arg & Bt	NR5366	55°49·7′	5°56·2′W	X	61
Rubha na Cloich' Uaine	Highld	NG5954	57°31·0′	6°1·0′W	X	24
Rubha na Codha	Arg & Bt	NM6420	56°19·1′	5°48·5′W	X	49
Rubha na Coille Bige	Arg & Bt	NR4197	56°6·0′	6°9·5′W	X	61
Rubha na Crannaig	Highld	NM4984	56°53·0′	6°6·8′W	X	39
Rubha na Craoibhe	Highld	NM7540	56°30·2′	5°38·9′W	X	49
Rubha na Creadha	N Eil	NA9812	57°59·9′	7°6·2′W	X	13
Rubha na Creige	Arg & Bt	NN0334	56°27·7′	5°11·4′W	X	50
Rubha na Creige Móire	Highld	NG4017	57°10·5′	6°17·6′W	X	32
Rubha na Creige Mòire	N Eil	NB4217	58°4·3′	6°22·0′W	X	14

Rubha na Creige Móire	N Eil	NF8320	57°9·9′	7°14·2′W	X	31
Rubha na Croite	Arg & Bt	NM4939	56°28·8′	6°4·1′W	X	47,48
Rubha na Cruibe	N Eil	NF8219	57°9·4′	7°15·1′W	X	31
Rubha na Cùilidh	Arg & Bt	NR6972	55°53·4′	5°41·2′W	X	61,62
Rubha na Diollaide	Arg & Bt	NM3838	56°27·9′	6°14·8′W	X	47,48
Rubha na Faing	Arg & Bt	NM7029	56°24·1′	5°43·2′W	X	49
Rubha Na Faing	Arg & Bt	NR1553	55°41·5′	6°31·7′W	X	60
Rubha na Faing	N Eil	NG2398	57°53·4′	6°40·0′W	X	14
Rubha na Faing Móire	Highld	NM6477	56°49·7′	5°51·6′W	X	40
Rubha na Faoileige	Arg & Bt	NR1757	55°43·7′	6°30·0′W	X	60
Rubha na Faoilinn	Arg & Bt	NM5921	56°19·5′	5°53·4′W	X	48,49
Rubha na Faoilinn	Arg & Bt	NM7227	56°23·1′	5°41·2′W	X	49
Rubha na Fearn	Highld	NG7261	57°35·2′	5°48·4′W	X	24
Rubha na Fearna	Highld	NG7060	57°34·6′	5°50·4′W	X	24
Rubha na Feòla	Highld	NG8455	57°32·3′	5°36·1′W	X	24
Rubha na Feundain	Arg & Bt	NM7826	56°22·7′	5°35·3′W	X	49
Rubha na Fidhle	Arg & Bt	NM9307	56°12·9′	5°19·9′W	X	55
Rubha na Gainmhich	Arg & Bt	NR4346	55°38·6′	6°4·6′W	X	60
Rubha na Gairbhe	Highld	NG2253	57°29·2′	6°37·9′W	X	23
Rubha na Gaoith	Arg & Bt	NM8137	56°28·7′	5°32·9′W	X	49
Rubhan a' Ghille Dhuibh	Highld	NC0305	57°59·7′	5°19·5′W	X	15
Rubha na Gibhte	N Eil	NF8225	57°12·6′	7°15·6′W	X	22
Rubha na Greine	N Eil	NB5633	58°13·4′	6°8·8′W	X	8
Rubha na Guailne	Highld	NG6845	57°26·4′	5°51·5′W	X	24
Rubha na h-Acairseid	Arg & Bt	NR4962	55°47·4′	5°59·8′W	X	60,61
Rubha na h-Acairseid	Highld	NM5972	56°46·9′	5°56·3′W	X	39,47
Rubha na h-Acairseid	N Eil	NF7301	56°59·3′	7°22·6′W	X	31
Rubha na h-Aibhne Duibhe	N Eil	NF9277	57°40·9′	7°9·6′W	X	18
Rubha na h-Airde	Arg & Bt	NM3841	56°29·6′	6°15·0′W	X	47,48
Rubha na h-Airde	Arg & Bt	NR7083	55°59·3′	5°40·8′W	X	55,61
Rubha na h-Airde	Highld	NG7859	57°34·3′	5°42·3′W	X	24
Rubha na h-Airde	Highld	NM7669	56°45·8′	5°39·5′W	X	40
Rubha na h-Airde	N Eil	NB1638	58°14·6′	6°49·9′W	X	13
Rubha na h- Airde	N Eil	NB2145	58°18·6′	6°45·3′W	X	8
Rubha na h-Airde Bàine	Arg & Bt	NR8654	55°44·2′	5°24·1′W	X	62
Rubha na h-Airde Beithe	Highld	NG7716	57°11·1′	5°41·0′W	X	33
Rubha na h'Airde Droighniche	Arg & Bt	NR7388	56°2·1′	5°38·2′W	X	55
Rubha na h-Airde Glaise	Arg & Bt	NM6024	56°21·1′	5°52·6′W	X	49
Rubha na h-Airde Glaise	Highld	NG5145	57°25·9′	6°8·4′W	X	23,24
Rubha na h-Airde Glaise	Highld	NG7326	57°16·4′	5°45·5′W	X	33
Rubha na h-Airde Glaise	Highld	NG8056	57°32·7′	5°40·1′W	X	24
Rubha na h-Airde Luachraich	Highld	NM6245	56°32·5′	5°51·8′W	X	49
Rubha na h-Airde Mòire	Arg & Bt	NR1960	55°45·4′	6°28·3′W	X	60
Rubha na h-Airde Mòire	Arg & Bt	NR1963	55°47·0′	6°28·5′W	X	60
Rubha na h-Airde Uinnsinn	Highld	NM8752	56°36·9′	5°27·8′W	X	49
Rubha na h-Airigh Bàine	Highld	NG5117	57°10·8′	6°6·8′W	X	32
Rubha na h-Aiseig	Highld	NG4476	57°42·3′	6°17·4′W	X	23
Rubha na h-Aoir	N Eil	NF9569	57°36·7′	7°6·0′W	X	18
Rubha na h' Eaglaise	Highld	NM6258	56°39·5′	5°52·6′W	X	49
Rubha na h-Eala	Highld	NM6968	56°45·0′	5°46·3′W	X	40
Rubha na h-Earba	Arg & Bt	NR8365	55°50·0′	5°27·5′W	X	62
Rubha na h-Earba	Highld	NM9155	56°38·7′	5°24·1′W	X	49
Rubha na h-Earraid	Highld	NH0198	57°55·9′	5°21·2′W	X	19
Rubha na h-Easgainne	Highld	NG5311	57°7·7′	6°4·4′W	X	32
Rubha na h-Eighich	N Eil	NF7927	57°13·5′	7°18·7′W	X	22
Rubha na h-Eigin	Highld	NG6852	57°30·2′	5°51·9′W	X	24
Rubha na h-Ivlain	N Eil	NF8978	57°41·3′	7°12·7′W	X	18
Rubha na Hoe	N Eil	NF8375	57°39·5′	7°18·5′W	X	18
Rubha na h-Ordaig	N Eil	NF8414	57°6·8′	7°12·8′W	X	31
Rubha na h-Uamh	N Eil	NF7603	57°0·5′	7°19·8′W	X	31
Rubha na h-Uamha	Arg & Bt	NM4027	56°22·1′	6°12·2′W	X	48
Rubha na h-Uamha	Highld	NG3437	57°21·0′	6°24·9′W	X	23,32
Rubha na h-Uamha	Highld	NG7234	57°20·6′	5°46·9′W	X	24
Rubha na h-Uamha	N Eil	NB2302	57°55·5′	6°40·3′W	X	14
Rubha na h-Uamha-sàile	Arg & Bt	NR6094	56°5·0′	5°51·0′W	X	61
Rubh' an Aird Dhuirche	Highld	NG5729	57°17·5′	6°1·5′W	X	32
Rubh'an Aird Fhada	Arg & Bt	NM8111	56°14·7′	5°31·6′W	X	55
Rubha ná Leac	Highld	NG6038	57°22·4′	5°59·1′W	X	24,32
Rubha na Leacaig	Highld	NC2056	58°27·6′	5°4·7′W	X	9
Rubha na Lèim	Highld	NM8246	56°33·6′	5°32·4′W	X	49
Rubha na Leip	Arg & Bt	NM5155	56°37·5′	6°3·1′W	X	47
Rubha na Leitreach	Arg & Bt	NM6343	56°31·4′	5°50·8′W	X	49
Rubha na Lice	Arg & Bt	NM8029	56°24·4′	5°33·5′W	X	49
Rubha na Lice	Arg & Bt	NR5807	55°18·1′	5°48·3′W	X	68
Rubha na Lice Buidhe	Arg & Bt	NM4200	56°7·6′	6°8·7′W	X	61
Rubha na Lice Uaine or Greenstone Point	Highld	NG8598	57°55·4′	5°37·4′W	X	19
Rubha na Lic Móire	Arg & Bt	NM9207	56°12·9′	5°20·8′W	X	55
Rubh' an Alt-toir	Highld	NC1826	58°11·4′	5°5·3′W	X	15
Rubha na Lugain	Arg & Bt	NR7360	55°47·1′	5°36·8′W	X	62
Rubha na Magach	Highld	NN4685	56°56·1′	4°31·4′W	X	34,42
Rubha na Maoile	Highld	NC1434	58°15·6′	5°9·7′W	X	15
Rubha nam Bàrr	Arg & Bt	NR7491	56°3·8′	5°37·4′W	X	55
Rubha nam Bòth	Highld	NG2355	57°30·3′	6°37·0′W	X	23
Rubha nam Bràithrean	Arg & Bt	NM4318	56°17·4′	6°8·7′W	X	48
Rubha nam Brathairean	Highld	NG5262	57°35·1′	6°8·5′W	X	23,24
Rubha nam Brisgein	N Eil	NF8857	57°30·0′	7°12·1′W	X	22
Rubha nam Bùth	Arg & Bt	NM5843	56°31·3′	5°55·6′W	X	47,48
Rubha na Mèine	N Eil	NF7828	57°14·0′	7°19·8′W	X	22
Rubha na Mèise Bàine	Arg & Bt	NR3341	55°35·6′	6°13·8′W	X	60
Rubha nam Fàd	Highld	NC0722	58°9·0′	5°16·3′W	X	15
Rubha nam Faoileag	N Eil	NB1233	58°11·8′	6°53·6′W	X	13
Rubha nam Faoileann	Arg & Bt	NM6704	56°10·6′	5°44·8′W	X	55
Rubha nam Faoileann	Arg & Bt	NM7316	56°17·2′	5°39·6′W	X	55
Rubha nam Faoileann	Arg & Bt	NM9043	56°32·2′	5°24·5′W	X	49
Rubha nam Fasaichean	Highld	NM7290	56°57·0′	5°44·5′W	X	33,40
Rubha nam Feannag	Arg & Bt	NR7062	55°48·1′	5°39·8′W	X	61,62
Rubha nam Feannag	Highld	NM5651	56°35·5′	5°58·0′W	X	47
Rubha nam Fear	Arg & Bt	NM6320	56°19·0′	5°49·5′W	X	49
Rubha nam Fias	Highld	NC1735	58°16·2′	5°6·7′W	X	15
Rubha nam Frangach	Arg & Bt	NN0704	56°11·6′	5°6·2′W	X	56
Rubha nam Maol Móra	Arg & Bt	NM3316	56°15·9′	6°18·3′W	X	48
Rubha nam Maraich	Arg & Bt	NR6977	55°56·1′	5°41·5′W	X	61,62
Rubha nam Meirleach	Highld	NM3691	56°56·4′	6°20·0′W	X	39
Rubha nam Mòine	Highld	NM9957	56°40·0′	5°16·4′W	X	49
Rubha na Mòine	Arg & Bt	NM5037	56°27·8′	6°3·1′W	X	47,48
Rubha na Mòine	Arg & Bt	NM7614	56°16·2′	5°36·6′W	X	55
Rubha na Moine	Arg & Bt	NR7895	56°6·0′	5°33·7′W	X	55

Rubha na Mòine	Highld	NC0514	58°4·6'	5°17·9'W	X	15
Rubha na Moine	Highld	NG3804	57°3·4'	6°18·8'W	X	32,39
Rubha na Mòine	Highld	NG7459	57°34·1'	5°46·3'W	X	24
Rubha na Mòine	Highld	NG9693	57°53·1'	5°26·0'W	X	19
Rubha na Mòine	N Eil	NB1301	57°54·6'	6°50·3'W	X	14
Rubha na Mòine	N Eil	NB1334	58°12·3'	6°52·7'W	X	13
Rubha na Mòine	N Eil	NB3210	58°0·2'	6°31·7'W	X	13,14
Rubha na Mòine	N Eil	NB4636	58°14·6'	6°19·2'W	X	8
Rubha na Mòine	N Eil	NF9998	57°52·5'	7°4·2'W	X	18
Rubha na Mòine	N Eil	NG1794	57°51·0'	6°45·7'W	X	14
Rubha na Moine	Stir	NN3912	56°16·6'	4°35·6'W	X	50,56
Rubha nam Plèac	N Eil	NF9467	57°35·6'	7°6·8'W	X	18
Rubha na Muireart	N Eil	NF7704	57°1·1'	7°18·9'W	X	31
Rubha na Muir-làin	Arg & Bt	NR4448	55°39·7'	6°3·8'W	X	60
Rubha nan Aighean	Highld	NM6962	56°41·8'	5°45·9'W	X	40
Rubha nan Caorach	Arg & Bt	NR6977	55°56·1'	5°41·5'W	X	61,62
Rubha nan Caorach	Arg & Bt	NR9064	55°49·7'	5°20·7'W	X	62
Rubha nan Caorach	N Eil	NB4830	58°11·5'	6°16·8'W	X	8
Rubha nan Caorach	N Eil	NF7275	57°39·0'	7°29·5'W	X	18
Rubha nan Caorach	N Eil	NF9157	57°30·1'	7°9·1'W	X	22
Rubha nan Carn	Arg & Bt	NM9634	56°27·5'	5°18·2'W	X	49
Rubha nan Carn	Pth & Kin	NN3653	56°38·7'	4°40·0'W	X	41
Rubha nan Cearc	Arg & Bt	NM3125	56°20·7'	6°20·8'W	X	48
Rubha nan Clach	Highld	NG3033	57°18·7'	6°28·6'W	X	32
Rubha nan Clach Dearga	Highld	NM6475	56°48·7'	5°51·5'W	X	40
Rubha nan Còsan	Highld	NC0734	58°15·4'	5°16·9'W	X	15
Rubha nan Crann	Arg & Bt	NR6181	55°58·1'	5°49·4'W	X	61
Rubha nan Cudaigean	Highld	NG3854	57°30·3'	6°22·0'W	X	23
Rubha nan Cudaigean	N Eil	NB3810	58°0·4'	6°25·6'W	X	14
Rubha nan Cudaigean	N Eil	NF8581	57°42·8'	7°16·9'W	X	18
Rubha nan Cùl Gheodhachan	Highld	NC1964	58°31·9'	5°6·1'W	X	9
Rubha nan Earachan	Arg & Bt	NR4363	55°47·8'	6°5·6'W	X	60,61
Rubha nan Eoin	Arg & Bt	NS2192	56°5·5'	4°52·2'W	X	56
Rubha nan Eun	Arg & Bt	NN0017	56°18·5'	5°13·5'W	X	50,55
Rubha nan Eun	N Eil	NF7307	57°2·5'	7°23·1'W	X	31
Rubha nan Gall	Arg & Bt	NM4141	56°29·7'	6°12·0'W	X	47,48
Rubha nan Gall	Arg & Bt	NM5057	56°38·5'	6°4·2'W	X	47
Rubha nan Gall	N Eil	NF9163	57°33·4'	7°9·5'W	X	18
Rubha nan Gall	N Eil	NF9371	57°37·7'	7°8·1'W	X	18
Rubha nan Gall Mór	Arg & Bt	NM7431	56°25·3'	5°39·4'W	X	49
Rubha nan Gearranan	N Eil	NB1844	58°17·9'	6°48·3'W	X	8
Rubha nan Giogan	N Eil	NF7864	57°33·3'	7°22·6'W	X	18
Rubha nan Goirteanan	Arg & Bt	NM4030	56°23·7'	6°12·4'W	X	48
Rubha nan Leacag	Arg & Bt	NR7358	55°46·0'	5°36·7'W	X	62
Rubha nan Leacan	Arg & Bt	NR3139	55°34·5'	6°15·6'W	X	60
Rubha nan Oirean	Arg & Bt	NM3551	56°34·8'	6°18·5'W	X	47
Rubha nan Ròn	Arg & Bt	NM7716	56°17·3'	5°35·8'W	X	55
Rubha nan Ròn	N Eil	NF8159	57°30·8'	7°19·2'W	X	22
Rubha nan Sailthean	Arg & Bt	NM7227	56°23·1'	5°41·2'W	X	49
Rubha nan Scarlan	Arg & Bt	NR6006	55°17·6'	5°46·4'W	X	68
Rubha nan Sgarbh	Arg & Bt	NR7934	55°33·2'	5°29·8'W	X	68,69
Rubha nan Sgarbh	Highld	NG6054	57°31·0'	6°0·0'W	X	24
Rubha nan Sgarbh	Highld	NH7087	57°51·5'	4°11·0'W	X	21
Rubha nan Sgarbh	N Eil	NB2006	57°57·6'	6°43·6'W	X	13,14
Rubha nan Sgarbh	N Eil	NB4929	58°11·0'	6°15·7'W	X	8
Rubha nan Sgarbh	N Eil	NF9787	57°46·5'	7°5·3'W	X	18
Rubha nan Sgarbh	N Eil	NG0299	57°53·1'	7°1·2'W	X	18
Rubha nan Sìdhean	N Eil	NB1233	58°11·8'	6°53·6'W	X	13
Rubha nan Sòrnagan	Highld	NM8854	56°38·1'	5°27·0'W	X	49
Rubha nan Torranan	Arg & Bt	NM4441	56°29·7'	6°9·1'W	X	47,48
Rubha nan Totag	N Eil	NB0303	57°55·3'	7°0·5'W	X	13,18
Rubha nan Trì Chlach	Highld	NM4988	56°55·2'	6°7·0'W	X	39
Rubha nan Uan	Arg & Bt	NM1657	56°37·4'	6°37·4'W	X	46
Rubha nan Uan	N Eil	NB0216	58°2·2'	7°2·5'W	X	13
Rubh' an Aoil	Arg & Bt	NM7610	56°14·0'	5°36·4'W	X	55
Rubh' an Aonain Luachraich	Arg & Bt	NR4656	55°44·1'	6°2·3'W	X	60
Rubha na Pairce	Highld	NM3691	56°56·4'	6°20·0'W	X	39
Rubha na Peileig	Arg & Bt	NR9665	55°50·4'	5°15·0'W	X	62
Rubha na Rainich	N Eil	NF9263	57°33·5'	7°8·5'W	X	18
Rubha na Reing	Arg & Bt	NM3325	56°20·8'	6°18·8'W	X	48
Rubha na Rodagrich	N Eil	NF8953	57°27·9'	7°10·8'W	X	22
Rubha na Roinne	Highld	NG4200	57°1·4'	6°14·6'W	X	32,39
Rubha na Sealbhaig	Arg & Bt	NM4758	56°39·0'	6°7·2'W	X	47
Rubha na Seann Charraige	Arg & Bt	NM0545	56°30·5'	6°47·3'W	X	46
Rubha na Sgàth Mòire	Highld	NG6261	57°34·8'	5°58·4'W	X	24
Rubha na Sgianadin	Highld	NG6226	57°16·0'	5°56·4'W	X	32
Rubha na Spreidhe	Highld	NH1635	57°22·4'	5°3·1'W	X	25
Rubha na Sròine	Arg & Bt	NM3642	56°30·0'	6°17·0'W	X	47,48
Rubha na Sròine	Arg & Bt	NM7237	56°28·5'	5°41·7'W	X	49
Rubha na Sròine	Highld	NM7960	56°41·0'	5°36·1'W	X	40
Rubha na Stiùre	N Eil	NB1639	58°15·0'	6°50·0'W	X	13
Rubha na Strianaich	N Eil	NB5229	58°11·1'	6°12·7'W	X	8
Rubha na Suileag	Highld	NC1520	58°8·1'	5°8·1'W	X	15
Rubha na Totaig	N Eil	NF9178	57°41·4'	7°10·7'W	X	18
Rubha na Tragha	Highld	NG4276	57°42·3'	6°19·4'W	X	23
Rubha na Traighe	Arg & Bt	NR7599	56°8·1'	5°36·8'W	X	55
Rubha na Tràighe Bàine	Arg & Bt	NM3838	56°27·9'	6°14·8'W	X	47,48
Rubha na Tràighe-maoraich	Arg & Bt	NM3524	56°20·3'	6°16·8'W	X	48
Rubha na Tràille	Arg & Bt	NR5162	55°47·5'	5°57·9'W	X	61
Rubha na Tuth	Arg & Bt	NR7375	55°55·1'	5°37·5'W	X	62
Rubh' an Dòbhrain	Arg & Bt	NM5140	56°29·4'	6°2·3'W	X	47,48
Rubh' an Dobhrain	Highld	NC1539	58°18·3'	5°9·0'W	X	15
Rubh' an Droma	N Eil	NL5783	56°49·0'	7°36·9'W	X	31
Rubh' an Droma Bhàin	Highld	NG6227	57°16·6'	5°56·4'W	X	32
Rubh' an Duilisg	N Eil	NB0506	57°57·0'	6°58·7'W	X	13,14
Rubh'an Dùin	Arg & Bt	NR2558	55°44·5'	6°22·5'W	X	60
Rubh' an Dùin Bhàin	Highld	NM5454	56°37·1'	6°0·1'W	X	47
Rubh' an Duine	Arg & Bt	NR5062	55°47·5'	5°58·9'W	X	61
Rubh' an Dùnain	Arg & Bt	NR3590	56°2·0'	6°14·8'W	X	61
Rubh' an Dùnain	Highld	NC0434	58°15·3'	5°20·0'W	X	15
Rubh' an Dùnain	Highld	NG3816	57°9·9'	6°19·6'W	X	32
Rubh' an Dùnain	Highld	NM7460	56°40·9'	5°40·9'W	X	40
Rubh' an Dùnain	N Eil	NB2448	58°20·3'	6°42·5'W	X	8
Rubha Nead a' Gheòidh	Arg & Bt	NM0946	56°31·2'	6°43·5'W	X	46
Rubha Neidalt	N Eil	NB2448	58°20·3'	6°42·5'W	X	8
Rubh' an Eireannaich	Highld	NG6424	57°15·0'	5°54·3'W	X	32
Rubh' an Eoin	Arg & Bt	NN0118	56°19·0'	5°12·6'W	X	50,55
Rubh' an Eòrna	N Eil	NG2494	57°51·3'	6°38·7'W	X	14
Rubh' an Eun	Arg & Bt	NS1152	55°43·7'	5°0·2'W	X	63,69
Rubh' an Fhaing	Arg & Bt	NM0148	56°32·0'	6°51·4'W	X	46
Rubh' an Fhaing	N Eil	NF8475	57°39·5'	7°17·5'W	X	18
Rubh'an Fheurain	Arg & Bt	NM8226	56°22·8'	5°31·4'W	X	49
Rubh' an Fhir Lèithe	Highld	NC1863	58°31·3'	5°7·0'W	X	9
Rubh' an Goirtein	Highld	NG2252	57°28·6'	6°37·8'W	X	23
Rubh' an Iasgaich	Arg & Bt	NM5254	56°37·0'	6°2·1'W	X	47
Rubh' an Iasgaich	Highld	NG5502	57°2·9'	6°1·9'W	X	32,39
Rubha Nic Eamoin	Highld	NG2404	57°2·9'	6°32·6'W	X	39
Rubh an Ime	N Eil	NB1337	58°14·0'	6°52·9'W	X	13
Rubh an Ionair	N Eil	NF8037	57°18·9'	7°18·5'W	X	22
Rubh' an Laorin	Arg & Bt	NM4157	56°38·3'	6°13·0'W	X	47
Rubh'an Leanachais	Arg & Bt	NR5670	55°51·9'	5°53·6'W	X	61
Rubh'an Lèim	Arg & Bt	NR5772	55°53·0'	5°52·7'W	X	61
Rubh an Lionaidh	Arg & Bt	NR7598	56°7·6'	5°36·8'W	X	55
Rubh' an Lochain	Highld	NG6132	57°19·2'	5°57·7'W	X	24,32
Rubh' an Losaid	N Eil	NG0086	57°46·1'	7°2·3'W	X	18
Rubha No	Arg & Bt	NN1408	56°14·0'	4°59·6'W	X	56
Rubh' an Oib	Arg & Bt	NR7587	56°1·6'	5°36·2'W	X	55
Rubh' an Olan	Highld	NH1788	57°50·9'	5°4·5'W	X	20
Rubh' an Righ	Arg & Bt	NM5255	56°37·5'	6°2·1'W	X	47
Rubh' an Roin	Arg & Bt	NM8312	56°15·3'	5°29·8'W	X	55
Rubh' an Sgòir Mhóir	Arg & Bt	NM0545	56°30·5'	6°47·3'W	X	46
Rubh'an Stearnail	Arg & Bt	NR6651	55°42·0'	5°43·0'W	X	62
Rubh' an Tacair	Arg & Bt	NR7382	55°58·9'	5°37·9'W	X	55
Rubh an Tairbh	N Eil	NF9057	57°30·1'	7°10·1'W	X	22
Rubh an' Tangaird	Highld	NM4783	56°52·4'	6°8·7'W	X	39
Rubh' an Taroin	N Eil	NA9929	58°9·1'	7°6·5'W	X	13
Rubh' an Teampuill	N Eil	NF9791	57°48·6'	7°5·7'W	X	18
Rubh' an Tighe	N Eil	NB0014	58°1·1'	7°4·4'W	X	13
Rubh'an Tighe Loisgte	Arg & Bt	NM8212	56°15·3'	5°30·7'W	X	55
Rubh' an Tòrra Mhóir	Highld	NG5232	57°18·9'	6°6·7'W	X	24,32
Rubh' an Tòrr Bhig	Highld	NG6327	57°16·6'	5°55·4'W	X	32
Rubh' an Tòrr Mhóir	Highld	NG6328	57°17·1'	5°55·5'W	X	32
Rubh' an Tòthain	N Eil	NA9910	57°58·9'	7°5·1'W	X	13
Rubh' an Truisealaich	Arg & Bt	NR7096	56°6·3'	5°41·5'W	X	55,61
Rubh' an Trusaidh	Highld	NG6227	57°16·6'	5°56·4'W	X	32
Rubh' an t-Sabhail	Highld	NM7759	56°40·4'	5°38·0'W	X	49
Rubh' an t-Sagairt	N Eil	NF8857	57°30·0'	7°12·1'W	X	22
Rubh' an t-Sàilein	Arg & Bt	NR5082	55°58·2'	6°0·0'W	X	61
Rubh' an t-Sailleir	Highld	NG4376	57°42·3'	6°18·4'W	X	23
Rubh' an t-Salinn	Arg & Bt	NR4364	55°48·3'	6°5·6'W	X	60,61
Rubh' an t-Seana Bhalla	N Eil	NF7404	57°1·0'	7°21·9'W	X	31
Rubh' an t-Seana-chaisteil	N Eil	NF9087	57°46·2'	7°12·4'W	X	18
Rubh' an t-Sean Chaisteil	Arg & Bt	NM1961	56°39·6'	6°34·7'W	X	46
Rubh' an t-Sean-Chaisteil	Arg & Bt	NM5549	56°34·4'	5°58·9'W	X	47,48
Rubh' an t-Sean Eich	N Eil	NB4932	58°12·6'	6°15·9'W	X	8
Rubh' an t-Sìl	N Eil	NB5331	58°12·2'	6°11·8'W	X	8
Rubh' an t-Sionnaich	Highld	NM6661	56°41·2'	5°48·8'W	X	40
Rubh' ant-Sìth	N Eil	NL5780	56°47·4'	7°36·6'W	X	31
Rubh' an t- Socaich Ghlais	Highld	NC2368	58°34·1'	5°2·1'W	X	9
Rubh' an t-Soithich	N Eil	NF9684	57°44·8'	7°6·1'W	X	18
Rubh' an Tuirc	N Eil	NF9784	57°44·9'	7°5·1'W	X	18
Rubh' an Uillt Dharaich	Highld	NG5432	57°19·0'	6°4·7'W	X	24,32
Rubh' Aoineadh Mhéinis	Arg & Bt	NM6521	56°19·6'	5°47·6'W	X	49
Rubha Aonghais	Highld	NG4412	57°7·9'	6°13·4'W	X	32
Rubha Phlocrapoil	N Eil	NG1893	57°50·5'	6°44·7'W	X	14
Rubha Phòil	Highld	NG6403	57°3·7'	5°53·1'W	X	32
Rubha Phollaidh	Highld	NC0614	58°4·6'	5°16·9'W	H	15
Rubh' a' Phuirt Allaidh	Arg & Bt	NR6249	55°40·8'	5°46·7'W	X	62
Rubh' a' Phuirt Bhàin	Arg & Bt	NR2559	55°45·0'	6°22·5'W	X	60
Rubh' a' Phuirt Bhig	Arg & Bt	NM0746	56°31·1'	6°45·4'W	X	46
Rubh' a' Phuirt Mhóir	Arg & Bt	NR2457	55°43·9'	6°23·4'W	X	60
Rubha Port an t-Seilich	Arg & Bt	NR4367	55°49·9'	6°5·8'W	X	60,61
Rubha Port Bhiosd	Arg & Bt	NL9648	56°31·8'	6°56·2'W	X	46
Rubha Port na Caranean	Highld	NM4298	57°0·3'	6°14·5'W	X	39
Rubha Port Scolpaig	N Eil	NF6968	57°35·1'	7°31·9'W	X	18
Rubha Preasach	Arg & Bt	NR9071	55°53·4'	5°21·1'W	X	62
Rubha Raerinis	N Eil	NB4324	58°8·1'	6°21·5'W	X	14
Rubha Ramadail	N Eil	NB4831	58°12·0'	6°16·9'W	X	8
Rubha Raonuill	Highld	NM7399	57°1·8'	5°44·0'W	X	33,40
Rubha Raouill	N Eil	NF7166	57°34·1'	7°29·7'W	X	18
Rubh' Ardalanish	Arg & Bt	NM3516	56°16·0'	6°16·4'W	X	48
Rubh' Ard an Duine	Arg & Bt	NM8330	56°25·0'	5°30·6'W	X	49
Rubh' Ard Bhaideanach	Highld	NC4156	58°28·1'	4°43·1'W	X	9
Rubh' Ard-na-goine	Highld	NB9908	58°1·2'	5°23·7'W	X	15
Rubha Reamhar	Highld	NM6695	56°59·5'	5°50·7'W	X	40
Rubha Reamhar	N Eil	NG0684	57°45·2'	6°56·1'W	X	18
Rubha Reamhar	N Eil	NG0897	57°52·3'	6°55·0'W	X	14,18
Rubha Redegich	Arg & Bt	NM8230	56°25·0'	5°31·6'W	X	49
Rubha Reidh	Highld	NG7391	57°51·3'	5°49·1'W	X	19
Rubha Reireag	Highld	NG5730	57°18·0'	6°1·6'W	X	24,32
Rubha Riabhach	Arg & Bt	NM6928	56°23·5'	5°44·1'W	X	49
Rubha Riabhach	Arg & Bt	NM9242	56°31·7'	5°22·5'W	X	49
Rubha Riabhach	Arg & Bt	NM9407	56°12·9'	5°18·9'W	X	55
Rubha Riabhach	Arg & Bt	NR7962	55°48·3'	5°31·2'W	X	62
Rubha Riabhach	Arg & Bt	NR8349	55°41·4'	5°26·7'W	X	62,69
Rubha Riabhag	Arg & Bt	NR6880	55°57·7'	5°42·6'W	X	55,61
Rubha Riadhain	Highld	NG3861	57°34·1'	6°22·4'W	X	23
Rubha Righinn	Arg & Bt	NM7002	56°9·6'	5°41·8'W	X	55
Rubh' Arisaig	Highld	NM6184	56°53·4'	5°55·0'W	X	40
Rubh' Armli	Highld	NC3955	58°27·5'	4°45·1'W	X	9
Rubh' Arnal	N Eil	NF7365	57°33·7'	7°27·7'W	X	18
Rubha Rodha	Highld	NC0523	58°9·4'	5°18·4'W	X	15
Rubha Roinich	N Eil	NF7727	57°13·4'	7°20·7'W	X	22
Rubha Roiseal	N Eil	NF8734	57°17·6'	7°11·3'W	X	22
Rubha Roiseil	N Eil	NF8536	57°18·6'	7°13·5'W	X	22
Rubha Rollanish	N Eil	NB1236	58°13·4'	6°53·8'W	X	13
Rubha Romagi	N Eil	NG0396	57°51·6'	7°0·0'W	X	18
Rubha Ròsal	N Eil	NB1540	58°15·5'	6°51·1'W	X	13
Rubha Ruadh	Arg & Bt	NR2846	55°38·1'	6°18·9'W	X	60
Rubha Ruadh	Highld	NC1651	58°24·8'	5°8·5'W	X	9
Rubha Ruadh	Highld	NC4562	58°31·4'	4°39·2'W	X	9
Rubha Ruadh	Highld	NM5262	56°41·3'	6°2·5'W	X	47
Rubha Ruadh	Highld	NM5772	56°46·8'	5°58·2'W	X	39,47
Rubha Ruadh	Highld	NM9661	56°42·0'	5°19·5'W	X	40
Rubha Ruadh	N Eil	NA9812	57°59·9'	7°6·2'W	X	13
Rubha Ruadh	N Eil	NA9816	58°2·1'	7°6·5'W	X	13
Rubha Ruadh	N Eil	NG0099	57°53·0'	7°3·2'W	X	18
Rubha Ruadha	Highld	NG8208	57°6·9'	5°35·6'W	X	33
Rubha Salach	Arg & Bt	NM7609	56°13·5'	5°36·4'W	X	55
Rubha Salach	N Ayr	NS0241	55°37·6'	5°8·3'W	X	69
Rubha Saltaig	Arg & Bt	NM0148	56°32·0'	6°51·4'W	X	46
Rubha Saonach	Stir	NN4109	56°15·1'	4°33·5'W	X	56
Rubha Sasunnaich	Arg & Bt	NM7218	56°18·2'	5°40·7'W	X	55
Rubh' Asbhig	N Eil	NB5532	58°12·8'	6°9·8'W	X	8
Rubh' a' Scarp	N Eil	NB1134	58°12·3'	6°54·7'W	X	13
Rubha Seanach	Arg & Bt	NM8025	56°22·2'	5°33·3'W	X	49
Rubha Sgeirigin	N Eil	NF9998	57°52·5'	7°4·2'W	X	18
Rubha Sgeir na Muir-làin	Arg & Bt	NR7062	55°48·1'	5°39·8'W	X	61,62
Rubha Sgeir nan Sgarbh	N Eil	NG0294	57°50·4'	7°0·8'W	X	18
Rubha Sgor-innis	Arg & Bt	NM2763	56°41·0'	6°27·0'W	X	46,47
Rubha Sgorr an t-Snidhe	Highld	NM3493	56°57·4'	6°22·1'W	X	39
Rubha Sgorr nam Bàn-naomha	Highld	NG2204	57°2·9'	6°34·6'W	X	39
Rubha Sgùta	N Eil	NG0683	57°44·7'	6°56·0'W	X	18
Rubha Shanndabhaig	N Eil	NF8342	57°21·7'	7°15·9'W	X	22
Rubha Sheader	N Eil	NL6292	56°54·0'	7°32·7'W	X	31
Rubha Sheallacro	N Eil	NF8735	57°18·2'	7°11·4'W	X	22
Rubha Sheileasdail	N Eil	NF8430	57°15·3'	7°14·0'W	X	22
Rubha Sheotharaid	N Eil	NB1135	58°12·8'	6°54·8'W	X	13
Rubha Shilldinis	N Eil	NB4530	58°11·4'	6°19·9'W	X	8
Rubha Sloc an Eòrna	Highld	NG5708	57°6·2'	6°0·3'W	X	32,39
Rubha Stillaig	Arg & Bt	NR9267	55°51·3'	5°19·0'W	X	62
Rubha Stoer	Highld	NC0232	58°14·2'	5°21·9'W	X	15
Rubha Strombrat	N Eil	NF8143	57°22·2'	7°18·0'W	X	22
Rubha Suainphort	Highld	NM6661	56°41·2'	5°48·8'W	X	40
Rubha Sùghar	Highld	NG5153	57°30·2'	6°8·9'W	X	23,24
Rubha Suisnish	Highld	NG5815	57°10·0'	5°59·7'W	X	32
Rubha Teithil	Arg & Bt	NM9642	56°31·8'	5°18·6'W	X	49
Rubha Thamasleit	N Eil	NF7938	57°19·4'	7°19·6'W	X	22
Rubha Thearna Sgurr	Highld	NG3619	57°11·4'	6°21·7'W	X	32
Rubha Thòl	N Eil	NB1741	58°16·3'	6°49·1'W	X	8,13
Rubha Thormaid	Highld	NC5468	58°34·8'	4°30·2'W	X	10
Rubha Thornais	N Eil	NF7547	57°24·1'	7°24·2'W	X	22
Rubha Thuilm	N Eil	NB4430	58°11·3'	6°20·9'W	X	8
Rubha Thurnabhaigh	N Eil	NB4326	58°9·2'	6°21·6'W	X	8
Rubha Thùrnaig	Highld	NG8684	57°47·9'	5°35·6'W	X	19
Rubha Tolaig Beag	N Eil	NB2346	58°19·2'	6°43·4'W	X	8
Rubha Tolmach	Arg & Bt	NM8329	56°24·5'	5°30·6'W	X	49
Rubha Tràigh an Dùin	Arg & Bt	NM0443	56°29·4'	6°48·1'W	X	46
Rubha Tràigh Gheal	Arg & Bt	NM6823	56°20·8'	5°44·8'W	X	49
Rubha Uamh an Tuill	Arg & Bt	NR5162	55°47·5'	5°57·9'W	X	61
Rubha Vallarip	N Eil	NG0582	57°44·1'	6°56·9'W	X	18
Rubha Voreven	Highld	NG4075	57°41·6'	6°21·3'W	X	23
Rubhay	Devon	SX8094	50°44·2'	3°41·7'W	X	191
Rubh Cuil-cheanna	Highld	NN0161	56°42·2'	5°14·6'W	X	41
Rubh' Dhubhard	Highld	NC1333	58°15·0'	5°10·7'W	X	15
Rubh' Dubh	N Eil	NB5229	58°11·1'	6°12·7'W	X	8
Rubh' Eilean an t-Santachaidh	Arg & Bt	NM3425	56°20·8'	6°17·9'W	X	48
Rubh' Iain Ic Ailein	Arg & Bt	NM6827	56°23·0'	5°45·0'W	X	49
Rubh' Leam na Làraich	Highld	NM3979	56°50·0'	6°16·3'W	X	39
Rubh na Banntraich	N Eil	NB5431	58°12·2'	6°10·8'W	X	8
Rubh na Gaoith	N Eil	NB4738	58°15·7'	6°18·3'W	X	8
Rubh na h- Airde Bige	Highld	NC2049	58°23·8'	5°4·3'W	X	9
Rubh' na h-Innse Moire	Highld	NH8385	57°50·6'	3°57·8'W	X	21
Rubh nam Bàirneach	N Eil	NB5531	58°12·3'	6°9·7'W	X	8
Rubh' nam Bùthan	Arg & Bt	NM3622	56°19·3'	6°15·7'W	X	48
Rubh na Staing	Arg & Bt	NM0737	56°26·4'	5°7·6'W	X	50
Rubh' Uisinis	N Eil	NB3503	57°56·5'	6°28·2'W	X	14
Rubha an Aird	Arg & Bt	NM3855	56°37·1'	6°15·8'W	X	47
Ru Borneskeitaig	Highld	NG3771	57°39·4'	6°24·1'W	X	23
Ruborough Camp	Somer	ST2233	51°5·7'	3°6·4'W	A	182
Ruchazie	C of Glas	NS6566	55°52·4'	4°9·0'W	T	64
Ruchill	C of Glas	NS5768	55°53·3'	4°16·7'W	T	64
Ruchill	N Lanak	NS7578	55°59·0'	3°59·8'W	X	64
Ruchilside	Pth & Kin	NN7620	56°21·6'	4°0·0'W	X	51,52,57
Ruchlaw	E Loth	NT6174	55°57·7'	2°37·0'W	X	67
Ruchlaw Mains	E Loth	NT6174	55°57·7'	2°37·0'W	X	67
Ruchlaw West Mains	E Loth	NT6172	55°56·6'	2°37·0'W	X	67
Ru Chorachan	Highld	NG3761	57°34·0'	6°23·4'W	X	23
Ruckcroft	Cumbr	NY5344	54°47·6'	2°43·4'W	T	86
Ruckhall	Heref	SO4439	52°3·0'	2°48·6'W	X	149,161
Ruckinge	Kent	TR0233	51°3·9'	0°53·4'E	T	189
Ruckland	Lincs	TF3378	53°17·2'	0°0·1'E	T	122
Rucklers Lane	Herts	TL0604	51°43·7'	0°27·5'W	T	166
Ruckley	Shrops	SJ5300	52°36·0'	2°41·2'W	T	126
Ruckley Grange	Shrops	SJ7706	52°39·3'	2°20·0'W	X	127
Ruckleywood Fm	Shrops	SJ7805	52°38·8'	2°19·1'W	FM	127
Ruckmans Fm	Surrey	TQ1336	51°7·0'	0°22·7'W	FM	187
Rudbaxton	Pemb	SM9620	51°50·7'	4°57·3'W	T	157,158
Rudbaxton Water	Pemb	SM9621	51°51·3'	4°57·3'W	W	157,158
Rudby	N Yks	NZ4706	54°27·1'	1°16·1'W	T	93
Rudchester	Northum	NZ1167	55°0·1'	1°49·3'W	X	88
Rudda Fm	N Yks	SE8999	54°22·9'	0°29·0'W	FM	94,101
Rudda Howe	N Yks	SE9799	54°22·9'	0°30·0'W	A	94,101
Ruddenleys	Scot Bord	NT2051	55°45·0'	3°16·0'W	X	66,73
Ruddens	E Yorks	TA1641	53°51·4'	0°13·8'W	X	107
Rudder Rock	N Som	ST2260	51°20·3'	3°6·8'W	X	182
Rudd Hall	N Yks	SE2494	54°20·7'	1°37·4'W	X	99
Rudd Hall Fm	N Yks	SE2494	54°20·7'	1°37·4'W	FM	99
Rudd Hills Fm	Cumbr	NY7712	54°30·4'	2°20·9'W	FM	91
Rudding Dower	N Yks	SE3353	53°58·6'	1°29·4'W	X	104
Rudding Park	N Yks	SE3352	53°58·0'	1°29·4'W	X	104
Ruddings	N Yks	SE4689	54°17·9'	1°17·2'W	X	100
Ruddings Fm	N Yks	SE4152	53°58·0'	1°22·1'W	FM	105
Ruddings Fm, The	Notts	SK7769	53°13·0'	0°50·4'W	FM	120
Ruddings Wood	E Yorks	SE7340	53°51·3'	0°53·0'W	F	105,106
Ruddington	Notts	SK5733	52°53·7'	1°8·8'W	T	129
Ruddington Fields Fm	Notts	SK5632	52°53·2'	1°9·7'W	FM	129
Ruddington Grange	Notts	SK5734	52°54·3'	1°8·7'W	X	129
Ruddington Moor	Notts	SK5531	52°52·7'	1°10·6'W	X	129
Ruddingwood	Notts	SK7670	53°13·5'	0°51·3'W	X	120
Ruddins	York	SE5455	53°59·5'	1°10·2'W	X	105
Ruddle	Glos	SO6811	51°48·0'	2°27·5'W	T	162
Ruddle Mill, The	Donc	SK5394	53°26·6'	1°11·7'W	X	111
Ruddlemoor	Corn	SX0055	50°21·9'	4°48·4'W	T	200

Ruddlemoor Fm	Wilts	ST9030	51°4·4′	2°8·2′W	FM	184
Ruddons Point	Fife	NO4500	56°11·6′	2°52·7′W	X	59
Ruddy Ball	Devon	SS7150	51°14·3′	3°50·5′W	X	180
Ruddy Carr	Durham	NZ0733	54°41·8′	1°53·1′W	X	92
Rudfarlington Fm	N Yks	SE3454	53°59·1′	1°28·5′W	FM	104
Rudford	Glos	SO7721	51°53·5′	2°19·7′W	T	162
Rudfyn Manor	Warw	SP2573	52°21·5′	1°37·6′W	X	140
Rudgate	Leeds	SE4547	53°55·3′	1°18·5′W	X	105
Rudgate (Roman Road)	Leeds	SE4547	53°55·3′	1°18·5′W	R	105
Rudge	Devon	SS7407	50°51·2′	3°47·0′W	X	191
Rudge	Devon	SX7880	50°36·7′	3°43·1′W	X	191
Rudge	Shrops	SO8197	52°34·5′	2°16·4′W	T	138
Rudge	Somer	ST8251	51°15·7′	2°15·1′W	T	183
Rudge	Wilts	SU2769	51°25·4′	1°36·3′W	X	174
Rudge Coppice	Wilts	SU2769	51°25·4′	1°36·3′W	F	174
Rudge Farm Ho	Wilts	SU2868	51°24·9′	1°35·5′W	X	174
Rudge Fm	Devon	SX8597	50°45·9′	3°37·5′W	FM	191
Rudge Fm	Dorset	SY5290	50°42·7′	2°40·4′W	FM	194
Rudge Fm	Heref	SO5935	52°1·0′	2°35·5′W	FM	149
Rudge Hall	Shrops	SO8197	52°34·5′	2°16·4′W	X	138
Rudge Heath	Shrops	SO7995	52°33·4′	2°18·2′W	T	138
Rudge Rew	Devon	SS7407	50°51·2′	3°47·0′W	X	191
Rudge, The	Heref	SO6420	51°52·9′	2°31·0′W	X	162
Rudge, The	Staffs	SJ7634	52°54·4′	2°21·0′W	X	127
Rudgeway	S Glos	ST6286	51°34·5′	2°32·5′W	T	172
Rudgeway Fm	Glos	SO9028	51°57·3′	2°8·3′W	FM	150,163
Rudgeway Fm	Glos	SO9030	51°58·3′	2°8·3′W	FM	150
Rudgwick	W Susx	TQ0833	51°5·4′	0°27·1′W	T	187
Rudgwick Grange	W Susx	TQ0731	51°4·3′	0°28·0′W	X	187
Rudha Dubh	N Eil	NF8556	57°29·3′	7°15·0′W	X	22
Rudha Garbh	Arg & Bt	NM9342	56°31·7′	5°21·5′W	X	49
Rudhall	Heref	SO6225	51°55·6′	2°32·8′W	T	162
Rudhall Brook	Heref	SO6325	51°55·6′	2°31·9′W	W	162
Rudhall Ho	Heref	SO6225	51°55·6′	2°32·8′W	A	162
Rudham Grange	Norf	TF8225	52°47·7′	0°42·4′E	X	132
Rudheath	Ches	SJ6773	53°15·4′	2°29·3′W	T	118
Rudheath Lodge	Ches	SJ7469	53°13·3′	2°23·0′W	X	118
Rudheath Woods	Ches	SJ7470	53°13·8′	2°23·0′W	T	118
Rud Hill	Sheff	SK2684	53°21·4′	1°36·2′W	X	110
Rudimoor Fms	Heref	SO4257	52°12·7′	2°50·5′W	FM	148,149
Rudland Beck	N Yks	SE6994	54°20·5′	0°55·9′W	W	94,100
Rudland Fm	N Yks	SE6493	54°20·0′	1°0·5′W	FM	94,100
Rudland Ho	N Yks	SE6593	54°19·9′	0°59·6′W	X	94,100
Rudland Rigg	N Yks	SE6594	54°20·5′	0°59·6′W	H	94,100
Rudland Slack	N Yks	SE6494	54°20·5′	1°0·5′W	X	94,100
Rudley Green	Essex	TL8303	51°42·0′	0°39·3′E	T	168
Rudley Mill	Hants	SU6212	50°54·5′	1°6·7′W	X	196
Rudloe	Wilts	ST8470	51°26·0′	2°13·4′W	T	173
Rudram's Gap	Norf	TG3533	52°50·8′	1°29·8′E	X	133
Rudry	Caer	ST1986	51°34·3′	3°9·7′W	T	171
Rudsey Fm	Notts	SK7051	53°3·3′	0°56·9′W	FM	120
Rudston	E Yorks	TA0967	54°5·5′	0°19·6′W	T	101
Rudston Beacon	E Yorks	TA0965	54°4·4′	0°19·6′W	A	101
Rudstone Walk	E Yorks	SE9134	53°47·9′	0°36·7′W	X	106
Rudston Grange	E Yorks	TA0668	54°6·1′	0°22·3′W	X	101
Rudway Barton	Devon	SS9401	50°48·2′	3°29·9′W	X	192
Rudwick Hall	Herts	TL1419	51°51·7′	0°20·3′W	X	166
Rudyard	Staffs	SJ9458	53°7·4′	2°5·0′W	T	118
Rudyard Hall	Staffs	SJ9659	53°7·9′	2°3·2′W	X	118
Rudyard Manor	Staffs	SJ9559	53°7·9′	2°4·1′W	X	118
Rudyard Reservoir	Staffs	SJ9459	53°7·9′	2°5·0′W	W	118
Rue	D & G	NX9181	55°6·9′	3°42·1′W	X	78
Rue	Orkney	HY6644	59°17·1′	2°35·3′W	X	5
Rue Barn Fm	Staffs	SJ8027	52°50·6′	2°17·4′W	FM	127
Ruecastle	Scot Bord	NT6120	55°28·6′	2°36·6′W	X	74
Ruecok	Shetld	HP6614	60°48·5′	0°46·7′W	X	1
Ruecrofts	Cumbr	SD6392	54°19·6′	2°33·7′W	X	97
Rue Fm	Dorset	ST6815	50°56·2′	2°26·9′W	FM	183
Rue Gill	D & G	NT1600	55°17·5′	3°18·9′W	W	79
Ruegill Hill	D & G	NT1501	55°18·0′	3°19·9′W	H	79
Rue Hill	Staffs	SK0947	53°1·5′	1°51·5′W	X	119,128
Ruel	Cered	SN6185	52°27·0′	4°2·3′W	X	135
Ruelake Pit	Devon	SX6388	50°40·8′	3°56·0′W	W	191
Ruelow Wood	Staffs	SK0147	53°1·5′	1°58·7′W	F	119,128
Ruemach Hill	Highld	NM6384	56°53·5′	5°53·0′W	H	40
Rue Moss Hall	Ches	SJ7961	53°9·0′	2°18·4′W	X	118
Rue Point	I of M	NX4003	54°24·1′	4°27·5′W	X	95
Rues Fm	N Yks	SE1753	53°58·6′	1°44·0′W	FM	104
Rue's Fm	Suff	TM3137	51°59·2′	1°22·3′E	FM	169
Ruet	Surrey	TQ0935	51°6·5′	0°26·2′W	X	187
Ruewood	Shrops	SJ4927	52°50·5′	2°45·0′W	T	126
Ru-fear-Vatersay	N Eil	NL6897	56°57·0′	7°27·2′W	X	31
Ruffa Ho	N Yks	SE8183	54°14·4′	0°45·0′W	X	100
Ruffets	Monm	ST5089	51°36·1′	2°42·9′W	X	162,172
Ruffett Wood	Surrey	TQ2558	51°18·7′	0°12·0′W	F	187
Ruff Fm	Lancs	SD4307	53°33·6′	2°51·2′W	FM	108
Ruffins Copse	I of W	SZ4794	50°44·8′	1°19·6′W	F	196
Ruffin's Hill	Kent	TR0735	51°4·8′	0°57·7′E	X	179,189
Ruffin's Ho	Suff	TL8058	52°11·7′	0°38·4′E	X	155
Ruffinswick Fm	Oxon	SU2688	51°35·6′	1°37·1′W	FM	174
Ruff Loch	Shetld	HU3631	60°4·0′	1°20·7′W	W	4
Rufford	Lancs	SD4515	53°38·0′	2°49·5′W	T	108
Rufford Country Park	Notts	SK6465	53°10·9′	1°2·1′W	X	120
Rufford Fm	Derby	SK3270	53°13·8′	1°30·8′W	FM	119
Rufford Forest Fm	Notts	SK6158	53°7·2′	1°4·9′W	FM	120
Rufford Hills Fm	Notts	SK6565	53°10·9′	1°1·2′W	FM	120
Rufford Old Hall	Lancs	SD4616	53°38·5′	2°48·6′W	A	108
Rufford Stud Fm	Notts	SK6462	53°9·3′	1°2·2′W	FM	120
Rufforth	York	SE5251	53°57·4′	1°12·0′W	T	105
Rufforth Grange	York	SE5350	53°56·8′	1°11·1′W	X	105
Rufforth Hall	York	SE5152	53°57·9′	1°12·9′W	X	105
Ruffs	Notts	SK5248	53°1·8′	1°13·1′W	T	129
Ruffs Cottages	W Susx	SU9003	50°49·4′	0°42·9′W	X	197
Ruffside	Durham	NY9951	54°51·5′	2°0·5′W	X	87
Ruffside Hall	Durham	NY9951	54°51·5′	2°0·5′W	X	87
Ruffside Moor	Durham	NY9850	54°50·9′	2°1·4′W	X	87
Rufus Castle	Dorset	SY6971	50°32·5′	2°25·9′W	A	194
Rufus Stone	Hants	SU2712	50°54·6′	1°36·6′W	A	195
Rûg	Denb	SJ0544	52°59·3′	3°24·5′W	X	125
Rugby	Warw	SP5075	52°22·5′	1°15·5′W	T	140

Rugby Radio Station	Warw	SP5574	52°21·9′	1°11·1′W	X	140
Rugden	Heref	SO6131	51°58·8′	2°33·7′W	X	149
Rugden	Kent	TQ8827	51°0·9′	0°41·2′E	X	189,199
Rugeley	Staffs	SK0418	52°45·8′	1°56·0′W	T	128
Rugg	Shetld	HU4472	60°26·0′	1°11·5′W	X	2,3
Ruggadon	Devon	SX8581	50°37·3′	3°37·2′W	X	191
Ruggaton Fm	Devon	SS5545	51°11·4′	4°4·1′W	FM	180
Rugged Knowes	E Loth	NT5684	56°3·1′	2°41·9′W	X	67
Ruggen	Shetld	HU4638	60°7·7′	1°9·8′W	X	4
Ruggin	Somer	ST1818	50°57·6′	3°9·7′W	T	181,193
Rugglesmere	Lancs	SD7043	53°53·2′	2°27·0′W	X	103
Ruggleypitt	Devon	SS8326	51°1·5′	3°39·7′W	X	181
Rugg's Fm	Somer	SS9831	51°4·4′	3°27·0′W	FM	181
Rugg's Hall	Norf	TG2530	52°49·5′	1°20·8′E	X	133
Rughouse	Devon	SX8390	50°42·1′	3°39·0′W	X	191
Ruglands	Somer	SS9832	51°4·9′	3°27·0′W	X	181
Ruglen	S Ayr	NS2904	55°18·3′	4°41·2′W	T	76
Rugley	Northum	NU1610	55°23·3′	1°44·4′W	T	81
Rugley Walls	Northum	NZ0286	55°10·3′	1°57·7′W	X	81
Rugley Wood	Northum	NU1710	55°23·3′	1°43·5′W	F	81
Rugmoor Fm	Bath & NE Somer	ST5259	51°19·9′	2°41·0′W	FM	172,182
Rugog	Gwyn	SH7309	52°40·1′	3°52·3′W	X	124
Rugpits	Shrops	SO5970	52°19·8′	2°35·7′W	X	137,138
Rugroad	Devon	SX7096	50°45·2′	3°50·2′W	X	191
Rugwood Fm	Essex	TR0092	51°35·7′	0°53·7′E	FM	178
Rugwood Head	Essex	TR0190	51°34·6′	0°54·4′E	X	178
Ruhba Leacach	N Eil	NB0107	57°57·4′	7°2·8′W	X	13
Ruhumman	Pth & Kin	NN9634	56°29·5′	3°40·9′W	H	52,53
Ruichlachrie	Pth & Kin	NN8170	56°48·6′	3°56·5′W	X	43
Ruidear	N Eil	NB0915	58°2·0′	6°55·3′W	H	13,14
Ruidh' Dorcha	Highld	NG8976	57°43·7′	5°32·2′W	X	19
Ruidinish	N Eil	NF8464	57°33·6′	7°16·6′W	X	18
Ru Idrigill	Highld	NG3763	57°35·1′	6°23·6′W	X	23
Ruieantaoir	Highld	NH5697	57°56·6′	4°25·5′W	X	21
Ruievard	Highld	NH5776	57°45·3′	4°23·7′W	X	21
Ruifour	Highld	NH5237	57°24·2′	4°27·3′W	X	26
Ruigh a' Chnoic Bhig	Highld	NC3032	58°14·9′	4°53·3′W	H	15
Ruigh' a' Chnoic Mhóir	Highld	NC3230	58°13·9′	4°51·2′W	H	15
Ruigh-aiteachain	Highld	NN8493	57°1·1′	3°54·2′W	X	35,43
Ruigh an Lagain	Highld	NN3561	56°43·0′	4°41·3′W	X	41
Ruigh Chnoc	Highld	NC2120	58°8·2′	5°2·0′W	X	15
Ruighe Breac	Highld	NM8685	56°54·7′	5°30·5′W	X	40
Ruighe Chail	Pth & Kin	NN7572	56°49·6′	4°2·4′W	X	42
Ruighe Chnoc	Highld	NC2812	58°4·1′	4°54·5′W	H	15
Ruighe Coire nan Easaichean	Highld	NN0496	57°1·1′	5°13·3′W	X	33
Ruighe Ghlas	Pth & Kin	NN5163	56°44·4′	4°25·7′W	X	42
Ruighe Mór	Highld	NM8248	56°34·7′	5°32·5′W	X	49
Ruighe na Beinne	Highld	NN1990	56°58·2′	4°58·2′W	H	34
Ruighe na Corpaich	Highld	NG8716	57°11·4′	5°31·0′W	X	33
Ruighe nan Leum	Highld	NN8889	56°59·0′	3°50·1′W	X	43
Ruighe nan Saorach	Pth & Kin	NN6764	56°45·2′	4°10·1′W	X	42
Ruigh Liath	N Eil	NF9267	57°35·5′	7°8·8′W	X	18
Ruigh Mheallain	Highld	NH0387	57°50·0′	5°18·6′W	H	19
Ruigh nan Clach	Aberd	NO0087	56°58·1′	3°38·2′W	X	43
Ruigh Raonuill	Highld	NN4376	56°51·2′	4°34·0′W	H	42
Ruigh Speanan	Moray	NJ1807	57°9·1′	3°20·9′W	H	36
Ruilick	Highld	NH5146	57°29·0′	4°28·7′W	T	26
Ruinsford Fm	Heref	SO2934	52°0·2′	3°1·7′W	FM	161
Ruinsival	Highld	NM3594	56°57·9′	6°21·1′W	H	39
Ruins Plantn	Notts	SK6390	53°24·4′	1°2·7′W	F	111
Ruir Holm	Shetld	HU5995	60°38·3′	0°54·8′W	X	1,2
Ruisaurie	Highld	NH5046	57°29·0′	4°29·7′W	T	26
Ruisgarry	N Eil	NF9282	57°43·6′	7°10·0′W	T	18
Ruishton	Somer	ST2624	51°0·9′	3°2·9′W	T	193
Ruishton Ho	Somer	ST2624	51°0·9′	3°2·9′W	X	193
Ruislip	Hill	TQ0887	51°34·5′	0°26·1′W	T	176
Ruislip Common	Hill	TQ0889	51°35·6′	0°26·1′W	T	176
Ruislip Gardens	Hill	TQ0986	51°34·0′	0°25·2′W	T	176
Ruislip Lido	Hill	TQ0889	51°35·6′	0°26·1′W	W	176
Ruislip Manor	Hill	TQ1086	51°34·0′	0°24·4′W	T	176
Ruiteachan Eòrna	Arg & Bt	NR4097	56°6·0′	6°10·4′W	X	61
Ruith Chnoc	Highld	NC1902	57°58·5′	5°3·2′W	H	15
Ruith-chnoc	Highld	NC3101	57°58·2′	4°51·0′W	H	15
Ruith Mhuilinn	Pth & Kin	NN8151	56°38·4′	3°56·0′W	W	52
Ruiton	Dudley	SO9192	52°31·8′	2°7·6′W	T	139
Rule Cross	Corn	SS2315	50°54·7′	4°30·7′W	X	190
Ruleholme Bridge	Cumbr	NY4960	54°56·2′	2°47·3′W	X	86
Ruleos	N Eil	NF7000	56°58·7′	7°25·5′W	X	31
Rulesgill	Shetld	HP5002	60°42·1′	1°4·5′W	X	1
Rulesmains Fm	Scot Bord	NT7954	55°47·0′	2°19·7′W	FM	67,74
Rules Ness	Shetld	HU5342	60°9·8′	1°2·2′W	X	4
Rule, The	I of M	SC3795	54°19·7′	4°30·0′W	X	95
Ruletownhead	Scot Bord	NT6112	55°24·3′	2°36·5′W	X	80
Rule Water	Scot Bord	NT6016	55°26·4′	2°37·5′W	W	80
Rulkies Hill	Shetld	HU4492	60°36·8′	1°11·3′W	X	1,2
Rull	Devon	SS7712	50°53·9′	3°44·6′W	X	180
Rull	Devon	SS9018	50°57·3′	3°33·6′W	X	181
Rull	Devon	ST0901	50°48·3′	3°17·1′W	X	192
Rullecheddan	Arg & Bt	NS0766	55°51·2′	5°4·6′W	X	63
Rull Fm	Devon	ST0108	50°52·0′	3°24·0′W	FM	192
Rull Fm	Devon	ST2302	50°49·0′	3°5·2′W	FM	192,193
Rull Fm	Devon	SY0498	50°46·7′	3°21·3′W	FM	192
Rull Fm	Somer	ST2413	50°54·9′	3°4·5′W	FM	193
Rull Green Fm	Devon	ST0911	50°53·7′	3°17·3′W	FM	192
Rull Ho	Devon	ST1011	50°53·7′	3°16·4′W	X	192,193
Rullie	Falk	NS7884	56°2·3′	3°57·0′W	X	57,64
Rullion Green	Midlo	NT2262	55°50·9′	3°14·3′W	X	66
Ruloe	Ches	SJ5872	53°14·8′	2°37·4′W	T	117
Rumachroy	Highld	NH9144	57°28·7′	3°48·6′W	X	27
Rumble	Shetld	HU6060	60°19·4′	0°54·3′W	X	2
Rumblers Fm	Herts	TL0309	51°46·4′	0°30·0′W	FM	166
Rumble, The	Shetld	HU4876	60°28·2′	1°7·1′W	X	2,3
Rumbleton	Scot Bord	NT6845	55°42·1′	2°30·1′W	X	74
Rumbletonlaw	Scot Bord	NT6745	55°42·1′	2°31·1′W	X	74
Rumbletonrig	Scot Bord	NT6746	55°42·6′	2°31·1′W	X	74
Rumble Wick	Shetld	HU5539	60°8·2′	1°0·1′W	W	4
Rumbleyond	Aberd	NO8190	57°0·3′	2°18·3′W	X	38,45
Rumblie Burn	Aberd	NJ5409	57°10·4′	2°45·2′W	W	37

Rumbling Br	Pth & Kin	NN9941	56°33·3′	3°38·1′W	X	52,53
Rumbling Br	Pth & Kin	NT0199	56°10·7′	3°35·2′W	X	58
Rumbling Bridge	Pth & Kin	NT0199	56°10·7′	3°35·2′W	T	58
Rumbling Burn	S Ayr	NS3630	55°32·4′	4°35·5′W	W	70
Rumbling Hole	Lancs	SD6779	54°12·6′	2°29·9′W	X	98
Rumbling Kern	Northum	NU2617	55°27·0′	1°34·9′W	X	81
Rumblings	Shetld	HP6019	60°51·2′	0°53·2′W	X	1
Rumbling Street	Derby	SK3275	53°16·5′	1°30·8′W	X	119
Rumbold's Fm	Essex	TL7406	51°43·8′	0°31·6′E	FM	167
Rumbolds Fm	Oxon	SU6494	51°38·7′	1°4·1′W	FM	164,175
Rumbolds Fm	W Susx	TQ0030	51°3·9′	0°34·0′W	FM	186
Rumbow Cottages	Worcs	SO9479	52°24·8′	2°4·9′W	T	139
Rumburgh	Suff	TM3481	52°22·8′	1°26·7′E	T	156
Rumburgh Fm	Suff	TM3682	52°23·3′	1°28·5′E	FM	156
Rumburghplace Fm	Suff	TM3580	52°22·3′	1°27·5′E	FM	156
Rumbush	Sol	SP1075	52°22·6′	1°50·8′W	T	139
Rumby Hill	Durham	NZ1734	54°42·3′	1°43·7′W	X	92
Rumdewan	Fife	NO3007	56°15·3′	3°7·3′W	X	59
Ru Meanish	Highld	NG4074	57°41·1′	6°21·3′W	X	23
Ru Melvick	N Eil	NF8312	57°5·6′	7°13·6′W	H	31
Rumerhedge Wood	Oxon	SU6781	51°31·7′	1°1·7′W	F	175
Rumer Hill	Staffs	SJ9809	52°41·0′	2°1·4′W	T	127
Rumer Hill	Warw	SP1550	52°9·1′	1°46·4′W	X	151
Rumer Hill Fm	Warw	SP1550	52°9·1′	1°46·4′W	FM	151
Rumford	Corn	SW8970	50°29·7′	4°58·1′W	T	200
Rumford	Falk	NS9377	55°58·7′	3°42·4′W	T	65
Rumford Hill	Staffs	SO8587	52°29·1′	2°12·9′W	X	139
Rumgally House	Fife	NO4014	56°19·1′	2°57·8′W	A	59
Rumgally Mains	Fife	NO4014	56°19·1′	2°57·8′W	X	59
Rumleigh	Devon	SX4468	50°29·7′	4°11·6′W	X	201
Rumley Point	Orkney	ND4894	58°50·1′	2°53·6′W	X	7
Rumley Wood	Essex	TL7023	51°53·0′	0°28·6′E	F	167
Rummer's Fm	Cambs	TF4205	52°37·7′	0°6·3′E	FM	142,143
Rummond	Fife	NO4716	56°20·3′	2°51·0′W	X	59
Rumness	Angus	NO6945	56°36·0′	2°29·8′W	X	54
Rumney	Card	ST2179	51°30·5′	3°7·9′W	T	171
Rumney Great Wharf	Card	ST2478	51°30·0′	3°5·3′W	X	171
Rumples Hill	D & G	NX7071	55°1·2′	4°1·6′W	X	77,84
Rumps Point	Corn	SW9381	50°35·8′	4°55·1′W	X	200
Rump, The	Shetld	HU5540	60°8·7′	1°0·1′W	X	4
Rumsam	Devon	SS5631	51°3·9′	4°2·9′W	T	180
Rumsdale Plantn	N Yks	SE6988	54°17·2′	0°56·0′W	F	94,100
Rumsdale Water	Highld	NC9840	58°20·5′	3°44·1′W	W	11
Rumsey Ho	Wilts	ST9770	51°26·0′	2°2·2′W	X	173
Rumsted Court	Kent	TQ8359	51°18·3′	0°37·9′E	X	178,188
Rumster	Highld	ND2137	58°19·1′	3°20·4′W	X	11
Rumster Forest	Highld	ND2038	58°19·7′	3°21·5′W	F	11
Rumwell	Somer	ST1923	51°0·3′	3°8·9′W	T	181,193
Rumwell Park	Somer	ST1923	51°0·3′	3°8·9′W	X	181,193
Rumwood Court	Kent	TQ7952	51°14·6′	0°34·3′E	X	188
Rumworth Lodge Resr	Bolton	SD6707	53°33·8′	2°29·5′W	W	109
Runa	Orkney	HY2626	59°7·1′	3°17·1′W	X	6
Runacraig	Stir	NN5714	56°18·1′	4°18·2′W	X	57
Runas	Orkney	HY3117	59°2·3′	3°11·7′W	X	6
Runcigill	Orkney	ND2198	58°52·0′	3°21·7′W	X	6,7
Run Common	Surrey	TQ0341	51°9·8′	0°31·2′W	X	186
Runcorn	Halton	SJ5281	53°19·7′	2°42·8′W	T	108
Runcorn Gap	Halton	SJ5083	53°20·7′	2°44·7′W	X	108
Runcorn Hill	Halton	SJ5081	53°19·7′	2°44·6′W	X	108
Runcorn-Widnes Bridge	Halton	SJ5083	53°20·7′	2°44·7′W	X	108
Runcton	W Susx	SU8802	50°48·9′	0°44·7′W	T	197
Runcton Bottom	Norf	TF6408	52°38·9′	0°25·9′E	X	143
Runcton Fm	Suff	TM1245	52°4·0′	1°6·0′E	FM	155,169
Runcton Holme	Norf	TF6109	52°39·5′	0°23·2′E	T	143
Rundell Dyke	Notts	SK7553	53°4·4′	0°52·4′W	W	120
Rundells	Essex	TL4706	51°44·2′	0°8·1′E	X	167
Rundle Beck	Leic	SK7533	52°53·6′	0°52·7′W	W	129
Rundlesshill	Glos	SO7620	51°52·9′	2°20·5′W	X	162
Rundlestone	Devon	SX5775	50°33·7′	4°0·8′W	X	191
Runfold	Surrey	SU8747	51°13·2′	0°44·9′W	T	186
Runfold Manor	Surrey	SU8747	51°13·2′	0°44·9′W	X	186
Rungay's Br	Norf	TF5508	52°39·1′	0°17·9′E	X	143
Runhall	Norf	TG0507	52°37·5′	1°2·1′E	T	144
Runham	Norf	TG4611	52°38·7′	1°38·6′E	T	134
Runham	Norf	TG5108	52°36·9′	1°42·9′E	T	134
Runham Fm	Kent	TQ8751	51°13·9′	0°41·1′E	FM	189
Run Hill	Shetld	HU4340	60°8·8′	1°13·0′W	H	4
Runie, The	Shetld	HU2557	60°18·0′	1°32·4′W	X	3
Runival	Highld	NG9106	57°6·1′	5°26·6′W	X	33
Runivraid	Highld	NH3432	57°21·2′	4°45·1′W	X	26
Runkin's Corner	Essex	TM0029	51°55·6′	0°54·9′E	X	168
Runk, The	Shetld	HU2577	60°28·8′	1°32·2′W	X	3
Runland Fm	Devon	SS3018	50°56·4′	4°24·8′W	FM	190
Runmerry	Moray	NJ1161	57°38·1′	3°29·0′W	X	28
Runn	Shetld	HU3822	59°59·1′	1°18·6′W	X	4
Runna Clett	Orkney	HY6645	59°17·7′	2°35·3′W	X	5
Runnage Fm	Devon	SX6679	50°36·0′	3°53·2′W	FM	191
Runnaguman	Pth & Kin	NO1856	56°41·6′	3°19·9′W	H	53
Runnapitten	Orkney	HY4852	59°21·3′	2°54·4′W	X	5
Runnarto	Orkney	HY1700	58°53·0′	3°25·9′W	X	7
Runnell, The	E Yorks	TA3624	53°41·9′	0°4·0′E	X	107,113
Runnel Stone	Corn	SW3620	50°1·5′	5°40·8′W	X	203
Runner Foot	Northum	NY6366	54°59·5′	2°34·3′W	X	86
Runners Burn	Northum	NT8206	55°21·1′	2°16·6′W	W	80
Runn Hill	Shetld	HU4557	60°17·9′	1°10·7′W	H	2,3
Runningburn	Scot Bord	NT7138	55°38·3′	2°27·2′W	X	74
Running Hill Head	Oldham	SE0106	53°33·3′	1°58·7′W	T	110
Runnington	Somer	ST1121	50°59·1′	3°15·7′W	T	181,193
Running Waters	Durham	NZ3240	54°45·5′	1°29·7′W	T	88
Runningwell	Essex	TQ7596	51°38·4′	0°32·1′E	X	167
Runnon Moor	Devon	SS5204	50°49·2′	4°5·7′W	X	191
Runn, The	Shetld	HU3822	59°59·1′	1°18·6′W	H	4
Runnygurnal	Aberd	NJ9223	57°18·1′	2°7·5′W	X	38
Runnymead	Surrey	TQ0072	51°26·5′	0°33·3′W	A	176
Runnymead Park	Surrey	TQ0071	51°26·0′	0°33·3′W	X	176
Runnymede Ho	Surrey	SU9973	51°27·1′	0°34·1′W	X	175,176
Runscar Scar	N Yks	SD7679	54°12·6′	2°21·7′W	X	98
Runsell Grange	Kent	TQ9241	51°8·4′	0°45·1′E	X	189
Runsell Green	Essex	TL7905	51°43·1′	0°35·9′E	T	167
Runsford Hole	W Berks	SU5982	51°32·3′	1°8·6′W	W	174

Runshaw Hall	Lancs	SD5420	53°40·7'	2°41·4'W	X	102
Runshaw Moor	Lancs	SD5319	53°40·2'	2°42·3'W	T	108
Runston Chapel	Monm	ST4991	51°37·2'	2°43·8'W	A	162,172
Runston Village	Monm	ST4991	51°37·2'	2°43·8'W	A	162,172
Runswick Bay	N Yks	NZ8016	54°32·2'	0°45·4'W	T	94
Runswick Bay	N Yks	NZ8116	54°32·2'	0°44·5'W	W	94
Runswick Sands	N Yks	NZ8115	54°31·7'	0°44·5'W	X	94
Runtaleave	Angus	NO2868	56°48·1'	3°10·3'W	X	44
Runthall	Orkney	HY6229	59°9·0'	2°39·4'W	X	5
Run, The	I of W	SZ6587	50°41·0'	1°4·4'W	W	196
Run, The	Norf	TF9146	52°58·9'	0°51·1'E	W	132
Runt's Wood	Bucks	SP7223	51°54·3'	0°56·8'W	F	165
Runwayskiln	Pemb	SM7707	51°43·3'	5°13·3'W	X	157
Runwell	Essex	TQ7494	51°37·3'	0°31·2'E	T	167,178
Runwell Hall Fm	Essex	TQ7596	51°38·4'	0°32·1'E	FM	167
Runwick Ho	Surrey	SU8245	51°12·1'	0°49·2'W	X	186
Ruperra Castle	Caer	ST2186	51°34·3'	3°8·0'W	A	171
Ruppera Home Fm	Caer	ST2286	51°34·3'	3°7·1'W	FM	171
Ruragh	Angus	NO4271	56°49·9'	2°56·6'W	H	44
Rurhella	Shetld	HP6417	60°50·1'	0°48·9'W	X	1
Rurra Geo	Shetld	HP6611	60°46·9'	0°46·8'W	X	1
Ruscar	Shetld	HT9740	60°8·9'	2°2·7'W	X	4
Ruscoe	N Yks	SE0874	54°9·9'	1°52·2'W	X	99
Ruscombe	Glos	SO8307	51°45·9'	2°14·4'W	T	162
Ruscombe	Wok	SU7976	51°28·9'	0°51·3'W	T	175
Ruscote	Oxon	SP4441	52°4·2'	1°21·1'W	T	151
Ru-scu	N Eil	NB0206	57°56·9'	7°1·7'W	X	13
Rusey Beach	Corn	SX1294	50°43·2'	4°39·4'W	X	190
Rusey Cliff	Corn	SX1293	50°42·6'	4°39·4'W	X	190
Rusg a' Bhiora	Pth & Kin	NN5755	56°40·2'	4°19·6'W	X	42,51
Rusgay	N Eil	NF9474	57°39·4'	7°7·4'W	X	18
Rush	Aberd	NJ7954	57°34·8'	2°20·6'W	X	29,30
Rushaclousit	Orkney	HY5430	59°9·5'	2°47·8'W	X	5,6
Rushacre Fm	Pemb	SN1015	51°48·3'	4°45·0'W	FM	158
Rusha Fm	W Loth	NS9960	55°49·6'	3°36·3'W	FM	65
Rushall	Heref	SO6434	52°0·4'	2°31·1'W	T	149
Rushall	Norf	TM1982	52°23·8'	1°13·5'E	T	156
Rushall	Wals	SK0301	52°36·6'	1°56·9'W	T	139
Rushall	Wilts	SU1255	51°17·9'	1°49·3'W	T	173
Rushall Canal	Wals	SK0401	52°36·6'	1°56·1'W	W	139
Rushall Down	Wilts	SU0749	51°14·6'	1°53·6'W	X	184
Rushall Down	Wilts	SU1053	51°16·8'	1°51·0'W	X	184
Rushall Fm	W Berks	SU5872	51°26·9'	1°9·5'W	FM	174
Rushall Hall	Wals	SP0299	52°35·6'	1°57·8'W	X	139
Rushall Hill	Wilts	SU1154	51°17·3'	1°50·1'W	X	184
Rushall Manor Fm	W Berks	SU5872	51°26·9'	1°9·5'W	FM	174
Rushaw	E Ayr	NS4941	55°38·6'	4°23·5'W	X	70
Rush Barrow	Devon	SS3717	50°56·0'	4°18·8'W	A	190
Rushbed Gutter	Lancs	SD5959	54°1·8'	2°37·1'W	W	102
Rushbeds Wood	Bucks	SP6615	51°50·0'	1°2·1'W	F	164,165
Rushbottom Wood	Suff	TL8256	52°10·6'	0°40·1'E	F	155
Rushbourne Manor	Kent	TR1963	51°19·7'	1°9·0'E	X	179
Rushbrooke	Suff	TL8961	52°13·1'	0°46·4'E	T	155
Rushbrooke Fm	Suff	TL9451	52°7·6'	0°50·5'E	FM	155
Rushbrook Fm	Kent	TQ9244	51°10·0'	0°45·2'E	FM	189
Rushbrook Fm	Warw	SP0971	52°20·5'	1°51·7'W	FM	139
Rushbury	Shrops	SO5191	52°31·1'	2°42·9'W	T	137,138
Rushbury Ho	Glos	SO9928	51°57·3'	2°0·5'W	X	150,163
Rushcombe Bottom	Dorset	SY9997	50°46·6'	2°0·5'W	T	195
Rushcott Fm	Devon	SS5228	51°2·2'	4°6·3'W	FM	180
Rush Court	Oxon	SU6091	51°37·1'	1°7·6'W	X	164,175
Rush Covert	Norf	TL7595	52°31·7'	0°35·2'E	F	143
Rushden	Herts	TL3031	51°58·0'	0°6·1'W	T	166
Rushden	Northnts	SP9566	52°17·3'	0°36·0'W	T	153
Rushdens Fm	W Berks	SU5571	51°26·3'	1°12·1'W	FM	174
Rushdown Fm	W Berks	SU5876	51°29·0'	1°9·5'W	FM	174
Rushen Abbey	I of M	SC2770	54°6·1'	4°38·3'W	A	95
Rushend	Northum	NY7886	55°10·3'	2°20·3'W	X	80
Rushenden	Kent	TQ9071	51°24·6'	0°44·3'E	T	178
Rusher's Cross	E Susx	TQ6028	51°2·0'	0°17·3'E	T	188,199
Rushes Fm	Leeds	SE2541	53°52·1'	1°36·8'W	FM	104
Rushett	Kent	TQ4349	51°13·6'	0°3·3'E	X	187
Rushett	Kent	TQ9659	51°18·0'	0°49·1'E	X	178
Rushett Common	Surrey	TQ0242	51°10·3'	0°32·1'W	X	186
Rushett Fm	King	TQ1760	51°19·8'	0°18·8'W	FM	176,187
Rushetts	Surrey	TQ1840	51°9·1'	0°18·4'W	X	187
Rushey Fields Fm	Leic	SK5414	52°43·5'	1°11·6'W	FM	129
Rushey Fm	Cambs	TL1363	52°15·4'	0°20·3'W	FM	153
Rushey Hill	Northum	NY7170	55°1·7'	2°26·8'W	X	86,87
Rushey Law	Northum	NY9078	55°6·0'	2°9·0'W	X	87
Rushey Lock	Oxon	SP3200	51°42·1'	1°31·8'W	X	164
Rushey Mead	C of Leic	SK6007	52°39·7'	1°6·4'W	T	140
Rushfield	Kent	TR0733	51°3·8'	0°57·6'E	X	179,189
Rushfield	Pth & Kin	NT1199	56°10·8'	3°25·6'W	X	58
Rushfield Ho	Leic	SK7303	52°37·4'	0°54·9'W	X	141
Rush Fm	N Yks	SE3487	54°16·9'	1°28·2'W	FM	99
Rush Fm	York	SE6245	53°54·1'	1°3·0'W	FM	105
Rushford	Devon	SX4476	50°34·0'	4°11·8'W	T	201
Rushford	Norf	TL9281	52°23·8'	0°49·7'E	T	144
Rushford	Warw	SP0551	52°9·7'	1°55·2'W	X	150
Rushford Barton	Devon	SX7089	50°41·4'	3°50·0'W	X	191
Rushford Fm	Surrey	TQ3944	51°10·9'	0°0·3'W	FM	187
Rushford Heath	Suff	TL9381	52°23·8'	0°50·6'E	X	144
Rushford Mill Fm	Devon	SX7088	50°40·9'	3°50·0'W	FM	191
Rushfordroad Belts	Suff	TL9079	52°22·8'	0°47·9'E	F	144
Rushford Wood	Devon	SX7089	50°41·4'	3°50·0'W	F	191
Rush Green	Bark & Dag	TQ5087	51°33·9'	0°10·2'E	T	177
Rush Green	Bucks	TQ0285	51°33·5'	0°31·3'W	X	176
Rush Green	Essex	TM1615	51°47·7'	1°8·3'E	T	168,169
Rush Green	Herts	TL2023	51°53·8'	0°15·0'W	T	166
Rush Green	Herts	TL3325	51°54·7'	0°3·6'W	X	166
Rush Green	Herts	TL3512	51°47·6'	0°2·1'W	T	166
Rush Green	Herts	TL3918	51°50·8'	0°1·5'E	X	166
Rush Green	Norf	TG0706	52°37·0'	1°3·9'E	T	144
Rushgreen	Warr	SJ6987	53°23·0'	2°27·6'W	T	109
Rush-head	Aberd	NJ8146	57°30·5'	2°18·6'W	X	29,30
Rush Hill	Bath & NE Somer	ST7362	51°21·6'	2°22·9'W	T	172
Rush Hill	Norf	TG4221	52°44·2'	1°35·5'E	W	134
Rush Hill	N Yks	SE7559	54°1·5'	0°50·9'W	X	105,106
Rush Hill	Somer	ST6255	51°17·8'	2°32·3'W	X	172
Rush Ho	N Yks	SE3979	54°12·6'	1°23·7'W	X	99
Rush Ho	N Yks	SE4487	54°16·8'	1°19·0'W	X	99
Rushings	Beds	SP9328	51°56·8'	0°38·4'W	X	165
Rushington	Hants	SU3512	50°54·6'	1°29·7'W	T	196
Rush Isles	Brad	SD9937	53°50·0'	2°0·5'W	X	103
Rushlade	Devon	SX7572	50°32·3'	3°45·5'W	X	191
Rushlade	Staffs	SJ9536	52°55·5'	2°4·1'W	X	127
Rushlake Green	E Susx	TQ6218	50°56·5'	0°18·7'E	T	199
Rushland Cross	Cumbr	SD3488	54°17·2'	3°0·4'W	T	96,97
Rushland Valley	Cumbr	SD3487	54°16·7'	3°0·4'W	X	96,97
Rushley	Staffs	SK1251	53°3·6'	1°48·9'W	X	119
Rushley Fm	Notts	SK5458	53°7·2'	1°11·2'W	FM	120
Rushley Fm	Somer	ST5320	50°58·9'	2°39·8'W	FM	183
Rushley Green	Essex	TL7836	51°59·9'	0°36·0'E	T	155
Rushley Island	Essex	TQ9688	51°33·6'	0°50·1'E	X	178
Rushley Lodge	Derby	SK3164	53°10·6'	1°31·8'W	X	119
Rushlye Down	E Susx	TQ6137	51°6·8'	0°18·4'E	X	188
Rushlye Fm	E Susx	TQ6136	51°6·3'	0°18·4'E	FM	188
Rushmead Fm	Wilts	ST8164	51°22·7'	2°16·0'W	FM	173
Rush Meadow	Norf	TF9713	52°41·0'	0°55·3'E	X	132
Rushmere	Beds	SP9127	51°56·3'	0°40·2'W	T	165
Rushmere	Suff	TM4987	52°25·7'	1°40·2'E	T	156
Rushmere Fm	Kent	TQ9752	51°14·2'	0°49·7'E	FM	189
Rushmere Heath	Suff	TM2044	52°3·3'	1°12·9'E	X	169
Rushmere Lodge Fm	Suff	TM4259	52°10·8'	1°32·8'E	FM	156
Rushmere St Andrew	Suff	TM1945	52°3·8'	1°12·1'E	T	169
Rushmere Street	Suff	TM2046	52°4·3'	1°13·0'E	T	169
Rushmire	Cumbr	NY3923	54°36·2'	2°56·2'W	X	90
Rushmoor	Carm	SN3116	51°49·3'	4°26·7'W	X	159
Rushmoor	Surrey	SU8740	51°9·4'	0°45·0'W	T	186
Rushmoor	Wrekin	SJ6113	52°43·0'	2°34·2'W	T	127
Rushmoor Arena	Hants	SU8551	51°15·3'	0°46·5'W	X	186
Rushmoor Bottom	Hants	SU8551	51°15·3'	0°46·5'W	X	186
Rushmore	Hants	SU6514	50°55·5'	1°4·1'W	T	196
Rushmore Down	Hants	SU3454	51°17·3'	1°30·4'W	X	185
Rushmore Fm	Dorset	SU0812	50°54·7'	1°52·8'W	FM	195
Rushmore Hill	Brom	TQ4761	51°20·0'	0°7·0'E	T	177,188
Rushmore Park	Wilts	ST9517	50°57·4'	2°3·9'W	X	184
Rushock	Heref	SO3058	52°13·2'	3°1·1'W	T	148
Rushock	Worcs	SO8871	52°20·5'	2°10·2'W	T	139
Rushock Hill	Heref	SO2959	52°13·7'	3°2·0'W	H	148
Rusholme	Man	SJ8695	53°27·3'	2°12·2'W	T	109
Rusholme	S Glos	ST5890	51°36·7'	2°36·0'W	X	162,172
Rusholme Grange	N Yks	SE7026	53°43·8'	0°55·9'W	X	105,106
Rusholme Hall	N Yks	SE6926	53°43·8'	0°56·8'W	X	105,106
Rushop Hall	Derby	SK0982	53°20·3'	1°51·5'W	X	110
Rushpit Wood	Rut	SK8909	52°40·6'	0°40·6'W	F	141
Rush Plantn	E Yorks	SE7955	53°59·3'	0°47·3'W	F	105,106
Rush Plantn	N Yks	SE4872	54°8·7'	1°15·5'W	F	100
Rushpole Wood	Hants	SU3009	50°53·0'	1°34·0'W	F	196
Rushpool Fm	Notts	SK5562	53°9·4'	1°10·2'W	FM	120
Rushpool Hall Hotel	Red & Cl	NZ6620	54°34·5'	0°58·3'W	X	94
Rush, The	N Yks	SE7361	54°2·6'	0°52·7'W	X	100
Rushton	Ches	SJ5864	53°10·5'	2°37·3'W	T	117
Rushton	Dorset	SY8786	50°40·6'	2°10·7'W	T	194
Rushton	Northnts	SP8482	52°26·0'	0°45·5'W	T	141
Rushton	N Yks	SE9583	54°14·3'	0°32·1'W	T	101
Rushton	Shrops	SJ6008	52°40·3'	2°35·1'W	T	127
Rushton Bank	Staffs	SJ9362	53°9·5'	2°5·9'W	X	118
Rushton Beck	N Yks	SE9581	54°13·2'	0°32·2'W	W	101
Rushton Cott	Shrops	SJ6107	52°39·8'	2°34·2'W	X	127
Rushton Grange	Northnts	SP8283	52°26·6'	0°47·2'W	X	141
Rushtonhall	Staffs	SJ9261	53°9·0'	2°6·8'W	X	118
Rushton Hill	Dorset	ST9607	50°52·0'	2°3·0'W	X	195
Rushton's Fm	Wok	SU8270	51°25·6'	0°48·8'W	FM	175
Rushton Spencer	Staffs	SJ9462	53°9·5'	2°5·0'W	T	118
Rushup Edge	Derby	SK1183	53°20·9'	1°49·7'W	X	110
Rush Wall	Newp	ST4086	51°34·4'	2°51·6'W	X	171,172
Rushwick	Worcs	SO8153	52°10·7'	2°16·3'W	T	150
Rushwood Fm	N Yks	SE2699	54°23·4'	1°35·6'W	FM	99
Rushwood Hall	N Yks	SE2978	54°12·1'	1°32·9'W	X	99
Rushybank	Devon	SX3594	50°43·6'	4°19·9'W	X	190
Rushy Clough	Cald	SD9434	53°48·4'	2°5·1'W	X	103
Rushy Common	Oxon	SP3807	51°45·9'	1°26·6'W	X	164
Rushy Cups	Shetld	HU3414	59°54·8'	1°23·0'W	X	4
Rushyford	Durham	NZ2828	54°39·0'	1°33·5'W	T	93
Rushyford Beck	Durham	NZ2928	54°39·0'	1°32·6'W	W	93
Rushyford Gate	Corn	SX2276	50°33·6'	4°30·4'W	X	201
Rushy Green	E Susx	TQ4512	50°53·6'	0°4·1'E	T	198
Rushy Hill	Lancs	SD8916	53°38·7'	2°9·6'W	H	109
Rushyhill	N Lanak	NS6370	55°54·5'	4°11·1'W	X	64
Rushy Knowe	Northum	NY6588	55°11·4'	2°32·6'W	H	80
Rushy Knowe	Northum	NY6781	55°7·6'	2°30·6'W	H	80
Rushy Knowe	Northum	NY9299	55°17·4'	2°7·1'W	H	80
Rushy Knowe	Scot Bord	NY6198	55°16·7'	2°36·4'W	X	80
Rushy Leasowes	Shrops	SJ3618	52°45·6'	2°56·5'W	X	126
Rushymead	Bucks	SU9595	51°39·0'	0°37·2'W	X	165,176
Rushy Moor	Donc	SE5612	53°36·3'	1°8·8'W	X	111
Rushy Moor	N Yks	NY9508	54°28·3'	2°4·2'W	X	91,92
Rushy Rig	D & G	NX9489	55°11·3'	3°39·5'W	X	78
Rushy Rig	Scot Bord	NT5902	55°18·9'	2°38·3'W	H	80
Rushy Rigg	Northum	NY7075	55°4·4'	2°27·8'W	X	86,87
Rushy Wood Fm	Somer	ST4611	50°54·0'	2°45·7'W	FM	193
Ruska Kame	Shetld	HP6318	60°50·7'	0°49·9'W	X	1
Ruskey Wood	N Yks	SE2279	54°12·6'	1°39·3'W	F	99
Rusk Holm	Orkney	HY5135	59°12·2'	2°51·0'W	X	5,6
Ruskich	Pth & Kin	NN6447	56°36·0'	4°12·5'W	X	51
Ruskich Wood	Highld	NH4822	57°16·1'	4°30·8'W	F	26
Ruskie	Stir	NN6200	56°10·6'	4°12·9'W	T	57
Ruskington	Lincs	TF0850	53°2·4'	0°22·9'W	T	121
Ruskington Fen	Lincs	TF1252	53°3·4'	0°19·3'W	X	121
Rusko	D & G	NX5858	54°54·0'	4°12·4'W	X	83
Rusko Castle	D & G	NX5860	54°55·1'	4°12·5'W	A	83
Rusland	Cumbr	SD3389	54°17·8'	3°1·3'W	T	96,97
Rusland	Orkney	HY5040	59°14·9'	2°52·1'W	X	5
Rusland Heights	Cumbr	SD3588	54°17·3'	2°59·5'W	X	96,97
Rusland Pool	Cumbr	SD3487	54°16·7'	3°0·4'W	W	96,97
Rusling End	Herts	TL2021	51°52·7'	0°15·0'W	T	166
Rus Mickle	Cumbr	SD4587	54°16·8'	2°50·3'W	X	97
Rusna Stacks	Shetld	HU2046	60°12·1'	1°37·9'W	X	3,4
Rus Ness	Orkney	HY4426	59°7·3'	2°58·2'W	X	5,6
Rusness	Orkney	HY7344	59°17·2'	2°27·9'W	X	5
Rusper	W Susx	TQ2037	51°7·4'	0°16·7'W	T	187
Rusper Court Ho	W Susx	TQ2136	51°6·9'	0°15·9'W	X	187
Ruspidge	Glos	SO6512	51°48·6'	2°30·1'W	T	162
Russa Dale	Orkney	HY3309	58°58·0'	3°9·4'W	X	6,7
Russamyre	Orkney	HY3306	58°56·4'	3°9·4'W	X	6,7
Russa Ness	Shetld	HU3647	60°12·6'	1°20·5'W	X	3
Russaness Hill	Shetld	HU3749	60°13·7'	1°19·4'W	H	3
Russa Taing	Orkney	HY4047	59°18·6'	3°2·7'W	X	5
Russel	Highld	NG8140	57°24·1'	5°38·3'W	X	24
Russel Burn	Highld	NG8140	57°24·1'	5°38·3'W	W	24
Russell Fm	Bucks	SP8704	51°43·9'	0°44·0'W	FM	165
Russell Fm	Suff	TL6883	52°25·4'	0°28·6'E	FM	143
Russell Green	Essex	TL7413	51°47·5'	0°31·8'E	X	167
Russell Hall Fm	N Yks	NZ9108	54°27·8'	0°35·3'W	FM	94
Russell Hill	Croy	TQ3061	51°20·2'	0°7·6'W	T	176,177,187
Russell Hill Fm	Monm	SO3704	51°44·1'	2°54·3'W	FM	171
Russell Ho	Lancs	SD3646	53°54·6'	2°58·0'W	X	102
Russell Lodge	Norf	TM0789	52°27·8'	1°3·2'E	X	144
Russell Mains	Fife	NO3512	56°18·0'	3°2·6'W	X	59
Russellplace Fm	Surrey	SU9451	51°15·3'	0°38·8'W	FM	186
Russells	Lancs	SD6268	54°6·6'	2°34·5'W	X	97
Russell's Cairn	Northum	NT8515	55°26·0'	2°13·8'W	A	80
Russell's End	Glos	SO7433	51°59·9'	2°22·3'W	X	150
Russell's Fm	Essex	TL7930	51°56·6'	0°36·7'E	FM	167
Russell's Fm	Hants	SU6214	50°55·6'	1°6·7'W	FM	196
Russell's Fm	Lincs	TF2959	53°7·0'	0°3·9'W	FM	122
Russell's Green	E Susx	TQ7011	50°52·6'	0°25·4'E	T	199
Russell's Hall	Dudley	SO9289	52°30·2'	2°6·7'W	T	139
Russell's Hill	Suff	TM0564	52°14·4'	1°0·6'E	F	155
Russell's Hill (Moat)	Suff	TM0564	52°14·4'	1°0·6'E	A	155
Russell's Inclosure	Glos	SO6110	51°47·5'	2°33·5'W	F	162
Russell's Lake	C of Port	SU6802	50°49·0'	1°1·7'W	W	196
Russell's Water	Oxon	SU7089	51°36·0'	0°59·0'W	T	175
Russell's Water Common	Oxon	SU7189	51°36·0'	0°58·1'W	X	175
Russell's Wood	N Yks	SE7496	54°21·5'	0°51·3'W	F	94,100
Russel's Green	Suff	TM2572	52°18·2'	1°18·4'E	T	156
Russ Hill	Surrey	TQ2340	51°9·0'	0°14·1'W	T	187
Russia Hall	Ches	SJ4758	53°7·2'	2°47·1'W	X	117
Russland	Orkney	HY3017	59°2·3'	3°12·7'W	T	6
Russland	Orkney	HY6822	59°5·3'	2°33·0'W	X	5
Russley Downs	Swin	SU2680	51°31·3'	1°37·1'W	X	174
Russley Park	Swin	SU2680	51°31·3'	1°37·1'W	X	174
Russ Ness	Orkney	HY6940	59°15·0'	2°32·1'W	X	5
Russness Bay	Orkney	HY4522	59°5·1'	2°57·1'W	W	5,6
Russon Burn	D & G	NX5563	54°56·7'	4°15·4'W	W	83
Ru Stafnish	Arg & Bt	NR7713	55°21·9'	5°30·7'W	X	68,69
Rusten's Manor	Norf	TM1298	52°32·5'	1°8·0'E	X	144
Rusthall	Kent	TQ5639	51°8·0'	0°14·2'E	T	188
Rusthall Fm	Kent	TQ5638	51°7·4'	0°14·1'E	FM	188
Rusthall Ho	Kent	TQ5539	51°8·0'	0°13·3'E	X	188
Rustic House Fm	Leic	SK8019	52°46·0'	0°48·5'W	FM	130
Rustic Lodge	Pth & Kin	NN7645	56°35·1'	4°0·7'W	X	51,52
Rustifhead Slack	N Yks	SE8590	54°18·2'	0°41·2'W	W	94,100
Rustin Fm	N Som	ST5162	51°21·5'	2°41·8'W	FM	172,182
Rustington	W Susx	TQ0502	50°48·7'	0°30·2'W	T	197
Ruston	Devon	SS7612	50°53·9'	3°45·4'W	X	180
Ruston Carr Plantation	N Yks	SE9680	54°12·6'	0°31·3'W	F	101
Ruston Cliff Wood	N Yks	SE9886	54°15·9'	0°29·3'W	F	94,101
Ruston Parva	E Yorks	TA0661	54°2·3'	0°22·5'W	T	101
Ruswarp	N Yks	NZ8809	54°28·4'	0°38·1'W	T	94
Ruswick Manor	N Yks	SE1989	54°18·0'	1°42·1'W	X	99
Ruthall	Shrops	SO5989	52°30·1'	2°35·8'W	T	137,138
Ruther	Highld	ND2557	58°29·9'	3°16·7'W	X	11,12
Rutherend	S Lanak	NS6649	55°43·2'	4°7·6'W	X	64
Rutherford	Durham	NZ0311	54°29·9'	1°56·8'W	X	92
Rutherford	Scot Bord	NT1654	55°46·6'	3°19·9'W	X	65,66,72
Rutherford	Scot Bord	NT6430	55°34·0'	2°33·8'W	X	74
Rutherford Burnside	Scot Bord	NT6630	55°34·0'	2°31·9'W	X	74
Rutherford Laboratory	Oxon	SU4786	51°34·5'	1°18·9'W	X	174
Rutherford Lodge	Scot Bord	NT6531	55°34·5'	2°32·9'W	X	74
Rutherford Mains	Scot Bord	NT6430	55°34·0'	2°33·8'W	X	74
Rutherford Mains	Scot Bord	NT6530	55°34·0'	2°32·9'W	X	74
Rutherford's Cairn	Scot Bord	NT6155	55°47·5'	2°36·9'W	X	67,74
Rutherglen	C of Glas	NS5862	55°50·1'	4°15·6'W	T	64
Ruthernbridge	Corn	SX0166	50°27·8'	4°47·9'W	X	200
Ruthers of Howe	Highld	ND3063	58°33·2'	3°11·7'W	X	11,12
Ruthin	V of Glam	SS9779	51°30·3'	3°28·7'W	T	170
Ruthin Castle	Denb	SJ1257	53°6·4'	3°18·5'W	A	116
Ruthin or Rhuthun	Denb	SJ1258	53°7·0'	3°18·5'W	T	116
Ruthland Fm	Heref	SO3528	51°57·0'	2°56·4'W	FM	149,161
Ruthrie	Moray	NJ2641	57°27·5'	3°13·5'W	X	28
Ruthrieston	C of Aber	NJ9204	57°7·9'	2°7·5'W	T	38
Ruthven	Aberd	NJ5046	57°30·3'	2°49·6'W	T	29
Ruthven	Angus	NO2848	56°37·4'	3°10·0'W	T	53
Ruthven	Highld	NH6026	57°18·5'	4°19·0'W	X	26,35
Ruthven	Highld	NH8133	57°22·6'	3°58·3'W	T	27
Ruthven	Highld	NN7699	57°4·2'	4°2·3'W	X	35
Ruthven	Moray	NJ1521	57°16·6'	3°24·1'W	X	36
Ruthven	Scot Bord	NT8244	55°41·6'	2°16·7'W	X	74
Ruthven Barracks	Highld	NN7699	57°4·2'	4°2·3'W	X	35
Ruthvenfield Ho	Pth & Kin	NO0825	56°24·8'	3°29·0'W	X	52,53,58
Ruthven Ho	Angus	NO3047	56°36·8'	3°8·0'W	X	53
Ruthven Ho	Pth & Kin	NO0825	56°24·8'	3°29·0'W	X	52,53,58
Ruthven Water	Pth & Kin	NN9410	56°16·5'	3°42·3'W	W	58
Ruthvoes	Corn	SW9260	50°24·4'	4°55·3'W	T	200
Ruthwaite	Cumbr	NY2336	54°43·0'	3°11·3'W	T	89,90
Ruthwaite Lodge	Cumbr	NY3513	54°30·7'	2°59·8'W	X	90
Ruthwell	D & G	NY0967	54°59·6'	3°24·9'W	T	85
Rutland Farm Park	Rut	SK8608	52°40·0'	0°43·3'W	X	141
Rutland Fm	Cambs	TL4790	52°29·5'	0°10·3'E	FM	143
Rutland Railway Museum	Rut	SK8813	52°42·7'	0°41·4'W	X	130
Rutlands	Essex	TL7119	51°50·8'	0°29·4'E	X	167
Rutlands Fm	Cambs	TF4201	52°35·5'	0°6·2'E	FM	142,143
Rutland Stud	Cambs	TL6758	52°11·9'	0°27·0'E	X	154
Rutland Water	Rut	SK9106	52°38·9'	0°38·9'W	W	141
Rutleigh Ball Fm	Devon	SS5101	50°47·6'	4°6·5'W	FM	191
Rutmoor Beck	N Yks	SE7896	54°21·5'	0°47·6'W	W	94,100

Ruttels	Essex	TL4533	51°58·8'	0°7·1'E	X	167
Rutter Force	Cumbr	NY6815	54°32·0'	2°29·2'W	W	91
Rutter's Fm	Beds	TL0456	52°11·8'	0°28·3'W	FM	153
Rutters Fm	Suff	TM1147	52°5·1'	1°5·2'E	FM	155,169
Ruttersleigh Common	Somer	ST2616	50°56·6'	3°2·8'W	F	193
Rutter's Plantn	N Yks	SE5774	54°9·8'	1°7·2'W	F	100
Ruttingham Fm	E Susx	TQ4424	51°0·1'	0°3·5'E	FM	198
Ruttle Wood	Highld	NH4743	57°27·4'	4°32·6'W	F	26
Rutton Fm	Devon	SY0499	50°47·2'	3°21·3'W	FM	192
Ruttonside Burn	D & G	NT0307	55°21·1'	3°31·4'W	W	78
Ruubha Shamhnan Insir	Highld	NG3704	57°3·4'	6°19·8'W	X	32,39
Ruvrapund	Shetld	HU6492	60°36·6'	0°49·4'W	X	1,2
Ruxford Barton	Devon	SS8102	50°48·6'	3°41·0'W	X	191
Ruxhill	Devon	SS4309	50°51·8'	4°13·5'W	X	190
Ruxley	Brom	TQ4870	51°24·8'	0°8·1'E	T	177
Ruxmoor	Corn	SS2214	50°54·1'	4°31·5'W	X	190
Ruxox Fm	Beds	TL0435	52°0·5'	0°28·7'W	FM	153
Ruxton	Heref	SO5529	51°57·7'	2°38·9'W	T	149
Ruxton Green	Heref	SO5419	51°52·3'	2°39·7'W	T	162
Ruyhedlar	Shetld	HT9740	60°8·9'	2°2·7'W	X	4
Ruyton Castle	Shrops	SJ3922	52°47·8'	2°53·9'W	A	126
Ruyton Manor	Shrops	SJ3722	52°47·8'	2°55·7'W	X	126
Ruyton-XI-Towns	Shrops	SJ3922	52°47·8'	2°53·9'W	T	126
Ruzza	Corn	SX0760	50°24·7'	4°42·6'W	X	200
Rvtvpiae (Richborough Cas) (Roman Fort)	Kent	TR3260	51°17·7'	1°20·1'E	R	179
Rwyth Fm	Carm	SN4821	51°52·3'	4°12·1'W	FM	159
Ryal	Northum	NZ0174	55°3·9'	1°58·6'W	T	87
Ryal	W Loth	NT0771	55°55·6'	3°28·9'W	X	65
Ryal East Fm	Northum	NZ0174	55°3·9'	1°58·6'W	FM	87
Ryal Fold	Black w Dar	SD6621	53°41·3'	2°30·5'W	X	103
Ryall	Dorset	SY4094	50°44·8'	2°50·6'W	T	193
Ryall	Worcs	SO8640	52°3·7'	2°11·9'W	T	150
Ryall Bottom	Dorset	SY4195	50°45·3'	2°49·8'W	X	193
Ryall Fm	Devon	SS2915	50°54·8'	4°25·6'W	FM	190
Ryall Fm	Durham	NZ3629	54°39·5'	1°26·1'W	FM	93
Ryall Heath Fm	Rut	TF0113	52°42·5'	0°29·9'W	FM	130
Ryall's Court	Worcs	SO8541	52°4·3'	2°12·7'W	X	150
Ryalls Fm	Dorset	ST7515	50°56·3'	2°21·0'W	FM	183
Ryal South Fm	Northum	NZ0174	55°3·9'	1°58·6'W	FM	87
Ryarsh	Kent	TQ6759	51°18·6'	0°24·2'E	T	178,188
Ryarsh Wood	Kent	TQ6560	51°19·1'	0°22·5'E	F	177,178,188
Ryat Fm	E Renf	NS5257	55°47·3'	4°21·2'W	FM	64
Ryat Linn Resr	E Renf	NS5257	55°47·3'	4°21·2'W	W	64
Ryburn Resr	Cald	SE0218	53°39·8'	1°57·8'W	W	110
Rybury	Wilts	SU0863	51°22·2'	1°52·7'W	A	173
Rychorrach	Highld	NH9934	57°23·4'	3°40·4'W	X	27
Rychraggan	Highld	NH4630	57°20·3'	4°33·1'W	T	26
Rychraggan Burn	Highld	NH9528	57°20·1'	3°44·2'W	W	36
Rycote	Oxon	SP6604	51°44·1'	1°2·3'W	X	164,165
Rycote Lake	Oxon	SP6704	51°44·1'	1°1·4'W	W	164,165
Rycotelane Fm	Oxon	SP6603	51°43·5'	1°2·3'W	FM	164,165
Rydal	Cumbr	NY3606	54°27·0'	2°58·8'W	T	90
Rydal Beck	Cumbr	NY3608	54°28·0'	2°58·8'W	W	90
Rydale Lodge (Hotel)	N Yks	SE6479	54°12·4'	1°0·7'W	X	100
Rydal Fell	Cumbr	NY3509	54°28·6'	2°59·8'W	H	90
Rydal Head	Cumbr	NY3611	54°29·7'	2°58·9'W	X	90
Rydal Mount	Cumbr	NY3606	54°27·0'	2°58·8'W	A	90
Rydal Water	Cumbr	NY3506	54°27·0'	2°59·7'W	W	90
Rydding's Fm	Lancs	SD6940	53°51·6'	2°27·9'W	FM	103
Ryde	I of W	SZ5992	50°43·7'	1°9·5'W	T	196
Ryde East Sands	I of W	SZ6092	50°43·7'	1°8·6'W	X	196
Ryde Fm	Surrey	TQ0655	51°17·3'	0°28·4'W	FM	187
Ryde Ho	I of W	SZ5892	50°43·7'	1°10·3'W	X	196
Ryden Fm	Worcs	SP0245	52°6·4'	1°57·9'W	FM	150
Ryden Mains	N Lanak	NS7468	55°53·6'	4°0·5'W	X	64
Rydens	Surrey	TQ1165	51°22·6'	0°23·9'W	T	176
Ryde Roads	I of W	SZ5893	50°44·3'	1°10·3'W	W	196
Ryder's Hill	Devon	SX6569	50°30·5'	3°53·9'W	H	202
Ryder's Rocks	Devon	SX6764	50°27·9'	3°52·1'W	X	202
Rydeshill	Surrey	SU9751	51°15·2'	0°36·2'W	T	186
Rydiness Fm	Somer	ST2915	50°56·0'	3°0·2'W	FM	193
Rydinghurst	Surrey	TQ0339	51°8·7'	0°31·3'W	X	186
Rydon	Devon	SS3304	50°48·9'	4°21·9'W	X	190
Rydon	Devon	SX8482	50°37·8'	3°38·0'W	X	191
Rydon	Devon	SX8773	50°33·0'	3°35·3'W	T	192
Rydon	Somer	ST2829	51°3·6'	3°1·3'W	X	193
Rydon Fm	Devon	SX9987	50°40·7'	3°25·4'W	FM	192
Rydon Fm	Somer	ST0942	51°10·4'	3°17·7'W	FM	181
Rydon Fm	Somer	ST2829	51°3·6'	3°1·3'W	FM	193
Rydon Hill	Devon	SX8368	50°30·2'	3°38·6'W	X	202
Rydon Ho	Devon	ST0700	50°47·8'	3°18·8'W	X	192
Rye	E Susx	TQ9120	50°57·1'	0°43·6'E	T	189
Ryebank	Ches	SJ5747	53°1·4'	2°38·1'W	X	117
Ryebank	Shrops	SJ5131	52°52·7'	2°43·3'W	T	126
Ryebank Rife	W Susx	SU9801	50°48·2'	0°36·2'W	W	197
Rye Bay	E Susx	TQ9617	50°55·4'	0°47·7'E	W	189
Ryebrook	Staffs	SK0753	53°4·7'	1°53·3'W	X	119
Ryecastle	D & G	NY1188	55°10·9'	3°23·4'W	X	78
Ryecastle Burn	D & G	NY1188	55°10·9'	3°23·4'W	W	78
Ryece Hall	Suff	TL9554	52°9·2'	0°51·4'E	X	155
Ryeclose	Dorset	SY7687	50°41·2'	2°20·0'W	X	194
Ryeclose	Northum	NY7586	55°10·3'	2°23·1'W	X	80
Rye Close	Northum	NY8450	54°50·9'	2°14·5'W	X	86,87
Ryeclose Fm	Cumbr	NY4859	54°55·6'	2°48·3'W	FM	86
Rye Close Fm	Durham	NZ3023	54°36·3'	1°31·7'W	FM	93
Rye Clough	Lancs	SD7250	53°57·0'	2°25·2'W	X	103
Rye Common	Hants	SU7750	51°14·9'	0°53·4'W	T	186
Rye Court	Worcs	SO7735	52°1·0'	2°19·7'W	X	150
Rye Court Fm	Glos	SO8530	51°58·3'	2°12·7'W	FM	150
Ryecroft	Brad	SE0738	53°50·5'	1°53·2'W	T	104
Ryecroft	Roth	SK4496	53°27·8'	1°19·8'W	T	111
Ryecroft	Shrops	SJ2803	52°37·4'	3°3·4'W	X	126
Ryecroft	Staffs	SK0558	53°7·4'	1°55·1'W	X	119
Ryecroft Fm	Brad	SE2030	53°46·2'	1°41·4'W	FM	104
Ryecroft Fm	Ches	SJ7584	53°21·4'	2°22·1'W	FM	109
Ryecroft Fm	Leic	SK5619	52°46·2'	1°9·8'W	FM	129
Ryecroft Gate	Staffs	SJ9361	53°9·0'	2°5·9'W	T	118
Rye Dale	N Yks	SE5982	54°14·1'	1°5·3'W	X	100
Rye Dale	N Yks	SE6979	54°12·4'	0°56·1'W	X	100
Ryedale Burn	Scot Bord	NY4890	55°12·3'	2°48·6'W	W	79
Rye End	Herts	TL1918	51°51·1'	0°15·9'W	X	166
Ryefield	Aberd	NJ5953	57°34·2'	2°40·7'W	X	29
Ryefield	Highld	NH6152	57°32·5'	4°18·9'W	X	26
Ryefield	W Susx	SU7722	50°59·8'	0°53·8'W	X	197
Ryefield Fm	Herts	TL2116	51°50·0'	0°14·2'W	FM	166
Ryefield Ho	N Ayr	NS2850	55°43·0'	4°43·9'W	X	63
Ryeflat	S Lanak	NS9447	55°42·5'	3°40·8'W	X	72
Ryeflat Moss	S Lanak	NS9548	55°43·1'	3°39·9'W	X	72
Rye Fm	Beds	SP9621	51°53·0'	0°35·9'W	FM	165
Rye Fm	N Yks	SE5195	54°21·1'	1°12·5'W	FM	100
Rye Fm	Oxon	SU5096	51°39·9'	1°16·2'W	FM	164
Rye Fm	Warw	SP1794	52°32·9'	1°44·6'W	FM	139
Rye Fm	W Susx	TQ2015	50°55·5'	0°17·2'W	FM	198
Ryeford	Glos	SO8104	51°44·3'	2°16·1'W	T	162
Ryeford	Heref	SO6422	51°54·0'	2°31·0'W	X	162
Rye Foreign	E Susx	TQ9022	50°58·2'	0°42·8'E	T	189
Ryegate Fm	Herts	TL3910	51°46·5'	0°1·3'E	FM	166
Ryegrain Rig	D & G	NS6703	55°18·4'	4°5·3'W	X	77
Rye Green Fm	E Susx	TQ6623	50°59·2'	0°22·3'E	FM	199
Rye Harbour	E Susx	TQ9319	50°56·5'	0°45·2'E	T	189
Ryehill	Aberd	NJ6625	57°19·1'	2°33·4'W	T	38
Ryehill	Aberd	NK0857	57°36·4'	1°51·5'W	X	30
Ryehill	Angus	NO3642	56°34·2'	3°2·0'W	X	54
Ryehill	Cumbr	NY3741	54°45·8'	2°58·3'W	X	85
Rye-hill	Cumbr	NY4465	54°58·8'	2°52·1'W	X	85
Ryehill	D & G	NS7908	55°21·3'	3°54·1'W	X	71,78
Ryehill	D & G	NY1465	54°58·6'	3°20·2'W	X	85
Rye Hill	Dorset	SU0410	50°53·6'	1°56·2'W	X	195
Rye Hill	Essex	TL4506	51°44·3'	0°6·4'E	X	167
Ryehill	E Yorks	TA2225	53°42·7'	0°8·7'W	T	107,113
Ryehill	I of M	SC4197	54°20·9'	4°26·4'W	X	95
Ryehill	Northum	NU0201	55°18·4'	1°57·7'W	X	81
Rye Hill	Northum	NY8971	55°2·3'	2°9·9'W	X	87
Rye Hill	Northum	NY9558	54°55·2'	2°4·3'W	X	87
Rye Hill	N Yks	NZ5711	54°29·7'	1°6·8'W	X	93
Rye Hill	Oxon	SP4035	52°1·0'	1°24·6'W	X	151
Ryehill	Pth & Kin	NO2243	56°34·6'	3°15·7'W	X	53
Ryehill Burn	D & G	NY2498	55°16·5'	3°11·3'W	W	79
Ryehill Fm	Midd	NZ5213	54°30·8'	1°11·4'W	FM	93
Rye Hill Fm	N Lincs	TA1214	53°36·9'	0°18·0'W	FM	113
Rye Hill Fm	Northnts	SP5548	52°7·9'	1°11·4'W	FM	152
Rye Hill Fm	Oxon	SP3437	52°2·1'	1°29·9'W	FM	151
Rye Hill Fm	Wilts	ST8440	51°9·8'	2°13·3'W	FM	183
Ryehill Lodge	Northnts	SP6066	52°17·6'	1°6·8'W	X	152
Ryehill Manor	E Yorks	TA2226	53°43·2'	0°8·7'W	X	107
Rye Hill Plantations	Lincs	TA1314	53°36·9'	0°17·1'W	F	113
Ryehills	D & G	NY3478	55°5·8'	3°1·6'W	X	85
Rye Hills Fm	N Yks	SE7072	54°8·6'	0°55·3'W	FM	100
Rye Hills Fm	Warw	SP2892	52°31·7'	1°34·8'W	FM	140
Ryeholmes Br	Northnts	SP8863	52°15·7'	0°42·2'W	X	152
Rye House Fm	N Yks	SE6382	54°14·0'	1°1·6'W	FM	100
Rye House Sta	Herts	TL3809	51°46·0'	0°0·4'E	X	166
Ryeish Green	Wok	SU7267	51°24·1'	0°57·5'W	T	175
Ryeland	S Lanak	NS6539	55°37·8'	4°8·2'W	X	71
Ryeland Hill	E Yorks	SE9230	53°45·7'	0°35·8'W	X	106
Ryelands	Heref	SO4858	52°13·3'	2°45·3'W	T	148,149
Ryelands Fm	Worcs	SO8670	52°19·9'	2°11·9'W	FM	139
Ryelands Fm	W Susx	TQ3228	51°2·4'	0°6·6'W	FM	187,198
Ryelandside	S Lanak	NS6439	55°37·8'	4°9·2'W	X	71
Ryelaw Fm	Fife	NO2200	56°11·4'	3°15·0'W	FM	58
Ryeleahead	Scot Bord	NY4581	55°7·5'	2°51·3'W	X	79
Rye Loaf Hill	N Yks	SD8663	54°4·0'	2°12·4'W	H	98
Ryeman	Corn	SW4930	50°7·3'	5°30·3'W	X	203
Rye Marsh Fm	E Susx	TQ9018	50°56·0'	0°42·6'E	FM	189
Ryemeadows	Heref	SO6534	52°0·4'	2°30·2'W	X	149
Rye Meads	Herts	TL3810	51°46·5'	0°0·4'E	X	166
Rye Mouth	N Yks	SE8275	54°10·1'	0°44·2'W	X	100
Rye Muir	D & G	NY0480	55°6·6'	3°29·9'W	X	78
Ryemuir	D & G	NY0480	55°6·6'	3°29·9'W	X	78
Ryemuir Burn	D & G	NY0581	55°7·1'	3°28·9'W	W	78
Rye Park	Devon	SS6439	51°8·3'	3°56·3'W	X	180
Rye Park	Herts	TL3709	51°46·0'	0°0·5'W	T	166
Ryeriggs	Moray	NJ4056	57°35·7'	2°59·8'W	X	28
Ryeriggs Croft	Moray	NJ4056	57°35·7'	2°59·8'W	X	28
Rye Rocks	Pemb	SM7309	51°44·3'	5°16·9'W	X	157
Ryer's Down	Swan	SS4592	51°36·6'	4°13·9'W	X	159
Ryes	D & G	NX9159	54°55·1'	3°41·6'W	X	84
Rye's Fm	Suff	TM1656	52°9·8'	1°9·9'E	FM	156
Ryes Hill	D & G	NX9062	54°56·7'	3°42·6'W	X	84
Ryes, The	Essex	TL8638	52°0·8'	0°43·0'E	X	155
Rye Street	Worcs	SO7835	52°1·0'	2°18·8'W	T	150
Ryestreet Common	Medway	TQ7477	51°28·1'	0°30·7'E	X	178
Rye Street Fm	Medway	TQ7476	51°27·6'	0°30·7'E	FM	178
Rye, The	Surrey	TQ1658	51°18·8'	0°19·7'W	W	187
Rye Topping Fm	N Yks	SE9480	54°12·7'	0°33·1'W	FM	101
Rye Water	N Ayr	NS2752	55°44·1'	4°44·9'W	W	63
Ryewater Fm	Dorset	ST6610	50°53·5'	2°28·6'W	FM	194
Ryeworth	Glos	SO9621	51°53·5'	2°3·1'W	T	163
Ryfield	Highld	NH5656	57°34·5'	4°24·0'W	X	26
Ryhall	Rut	TF0310	52°40·9'	0°28·2'W	T	130
Ryhill	Wakf	SE3814	53°37·5'	1°25·1'W	T	110,111
Ryhope	Sund	NZ4052	54°51·9'	1°22·2'W	T	88
Ryhope Colliery	Sund	NZ4053	54°52·5'	1°22·2'W	T	88
Ryknild Street (Roman Road)	Derby	SK2930	52°52·2'	1°33·7'W	R	128
Ryknild Street (Roman Road)	Derby	SK3943	52°59·2'	1°24·7'W	R	119,128
Ryknild Street Roman Road	Glos	SP1331	51°58·9'	1°48·2'W	R	151
Ryknild Street (Roman Road)	Glos	SP1525	51°55·6'	1°46·5'W	R	163
Ryknild Street (Roman Road)	Staffs	SK0902	52°37·2'	1°51·6'W	R	139
Ryknild Street (Roman Road)	Warw	SP0859	52°14·0'	1°52·6'W	R	150
Ryknild Street (Roman Road)	Worcs	SP0573	52°21·5'	1°55·2'W	R	139
Rylah	Derby	SK4667	53°12·1'	1°18·3'W	T	120
Ryland	Aberd	NJ6658	57°36·9'	2°33·7'W	X	29
Ryland Lodge	Stir	NN7902	56°12·0'	3°56·6'W	X	57
Rylands	Cumbr	NY3340	54°45·3'	3°2·0'W	X	85
Rylands	E Susx	TQ3615	50°55·3'	0°3·5'W	X	198
Rylands	Notts	SK5335	52°54·8'	1°12·3'W	T	129
Rylands Fm	Essex	TL6942	52°3·3'	0°28·3'E	FM	154
Ryle Mill	Northum	NU0311	55°23·8'	1°56·7'W	X	81
Ryley	Shrops	SO6072	52°20·9'	2°34·8'W	X	138
Ryley's Fm	Wilts	ST8679	51°30·8'	2°11·7'W	FM	173
Ryleys, The	Ches	SJ8378	53°18·2'	2°14·9'W	X	118
Rylstone	N Yks	SD9658	54°1·3'	2°3·2'W	T	103
Rylstone Fell	N Yks	SD9957	54°0·8'	2°0·5'W	X	103
Rymans	W Susx	SU8403	50°49·5'	0°48·1'W	A	197
Ryme Intrinseca	Dorset	ST5810	50°53·5'	2°35·4'W	T	194
Rymer Barn	Suff	TL8774	52°20·2'	0°45·1'E	X	144
Rymer Ho	N Yks	SE4682	54°14·1'	1°17·2'W	X	100
Rymer Ho	Suff	TL8675	52°20·7'	0°44·2'E	X	144
Rymes Place Fm	Glos	SO7524	51°55·1'	2°21·4'W	FM	162
Rynehill Fm	Oxon	SP2722	51°54·0'	1°36·1'W	FM	163
Rynettin	Highld	NJ0114	57°12·6'	3°37·9'W	X	36
Ryngmer Park	E Susx	TQ4312	50°53·6'	0°2·4'E	X	198
Ryntaing	Aberd	NJ3320	57°16·2'	3°6·2'W	X	37
Rynuan	Highld	NH9915	57°13·1'	3°39·9'W	X	36
Ryon Hill Ho	Warw	SP2257	52°12·9'	1°40·3'W	X	151
Rysa Bay	Orkney	ND3096	58°51·0'	3°12·3'W	W	6,7
Rysa Little	Orkney	ND3197	58°51·6'	3°11·3'W	X	6,7
Rysa Lodge	Orkney	ND3096	58°51·0'	3°12·3'W	X	6,7
Rysa Sound	Orkney	ND3097	58°51·6'	3°12·3'W	W	6,7
Rysaurie	Highld	NH9226	57°19·0'	3°47·1'W	X	36
Ryscar Fm	Lancs	SD3340	53°51·4'	3°0·7'W	FM	102
Ryslaw	Scot Bord	NT7948	55°43·7'	2°19·6'W	X	74
Rysome Garth	E Yorks	TA3622	53°40·8'	0°4·0'E	X	107,113
Ryston Hall	Norf	TF6201	52°35·2'	0°23·9'E	X	143
Rytha	Corn	SX3256	50°23·0'	4°21·4'W	X	201
Rytham Gate	E Yorks	SE7842	53°52·3'	0°48·4'W	X	105,106
Ryther	N Yks	SE5539	53°50·9'	1°9·4'W	T	105
Ryther Grange	N Yks	SE5537	53°49·8'	1°9·4'W	X	105
Rythorpe Grange Fm	York	SE6354	53°58·9'	1°1·9'W	FM	105,106
Ryton	Ghead	NZ1564	54°58·5'	1°45·5'W	T	88
Ryton	Glos	SO7231	51°58·8'	2°24·1'W	T	149
Ryton	Glos	SO7332	51°59·4'	2°23·2'W	T	150
Ryton	N Yks	SE7975	54°10·1'	0°47·0'W	T	100
Ryton	Shrops	SJ7602	52°37·2'	2°20·9'W	T	127
Ryton	Warw	SP3986	52°28·5'	1°25·1'W	T	140
Ryton Br	Warw	SP3675	52°22·5'	1°27·9'W	X	140
Ryton End	Sol	SP2179	52°24·8'	1°41·1'W	X	139
Ryton Gdns	Warw	SP4074	52°22·0'	1°24·4'W	X	140
Ryton Grange	Ghead	NZ1464	54°58·5'	1°46·5'W	X	88
Ryton Grange	N Yks	SE7675	54°10·1'	0°49·7'W	X	100
Ryton Grove	Shrops	SJ4903	52°37·6'	2°44·8'W	X	126
Ryton Heath Fm	Warw	SP3972	52°20·9'	1°25·2'W	FM	140
Ryton Lodge	Warw	SP3773	52°21·5'	1°27·0'W	X	140
Ryton-on-Dunsmore	Warw	SP3874	52°22·0'	1°26·1'W	T	140
Ryton Pool	Warw	SP3772	52°20·9'	1°27·0'W	W	140
Ryton Wood	Warw	SP3772	52°20·9'	1°27·0'W	F	140
Ryton Woodside	Ghead	NZ1462	54°57·4'	1°46·5'W	T	88
Ryvoan Bothy	Highld	NJ0011	57°11·0'	3°38·8'W	X	36

S

Saasaig	Highld	NG6608	57°6·5'	5°51·4'W	T	32
Saaversteen	Shetld	HZ2174	59°33·3'	1°37·2'W	X	4
Sabden	Lancs	SD7737	53°50·0'	2°20·6'W	T	103
Sabden Brook	Lancs	SD7535	53°48·9'	2°22·4'W	W	103
Sabden Fold	Lancs	SD8038	53°50·5'	2°17·8'W	X	103
Sabden Hall	Lancs	SD8138	53°50·5'	2°16·9'W	X	103
Saberstone	Shetld	HU3781	60°30·9'	1°19·1'W	X	1,2,3
Sàbhal Beag	Highld	NC3742	58°20·4'	4°46·6'W	H	9
Sàbhal Mór	Highld	NC3544	58°21·5'	4°48·7'W	H	9
Sabine's Green	Essex	TQ5496	51°38·7'	0°13·9'E	T	167,177
Sabiston	Orkney	HY2921	59°4·5'	3°13·8'W	T	6
Sachel Court	Surrey	TQ0334	51°6·0'	0°31·3'W	X	186
Sacheveral Fm	Derby	SK2259	53°7·9'	1°39·9'W	FM	119
Sackers Green	Suff	TL9039	52°1·2'	0°46·5'E	T	155
Sacketts Hill Fm	Kent	TR3668	51°21·9'	1°23·8'E	FM	179
Sack Hill	Wilts	ST8946	51°13·0'	2°9·1'W	X	184
Sacksfield Fm	Glos	SO7629	51°57·8'	2°20·6'W	FM	150
Sackville Fm	E Susx	TQ6211	50°52·8'	0°18·6'E	FM	199
Sackville Ho	Highld	ND2561	58°32·1'	3°16·8'W	X	11,12
Sackville Lodge	Beds	TL0463	52°15·6'	0°28·2'W	X	153
Sacombe	Herts	TL3319	51°51·5'	0°3·7'W	T	166
Sacombebury Fm	Herts	TL3318	51°50·9'	0°3·7'W	FM	166
Sacombe Green	Herts	TL3419	51°51·4'	0°2·9'W	T	166
Sacombe Hill Fm	Herts	TL3219	51°51·5'	0°4·6'W	FM	166
Sacombe Ho	Herts	TL3418	51°50·9'	0°2·9'W	X	166
Sacombs Ash	Herts	TL4517	51°50·2'	0°6·7'E	X	167
Sacquoy Head	Orkney	HY3835	59°12·1'	3°4·6'W	X	6
Sacrewell Farm and Country Centre	Peterb	TF0700	52°35·5'	0°24·8'W	X	142
Sacrewell Lodge Fm	Peterb	TF0700	52°35·5'	0°24·8'W	FM	142
Sacriston	Durham	NZ2447	54°49·3'	1°37·2'W	T	88
Sacriston Wood	Durham	NZ2348	54°49·8'	1°38·1'W	F	88
Sadberge	Darl	NZ3417	54°33·1'	1°28·0'W	T	93
Sadberge Hall	Darl	NZ3415	54°32·0'	1°28·1'W	X	93
Sadborow	Dorset	ST3702	50°49·1'	2°53·3'W	X	193
Sadbury Hill	Northum	NY8276	55°4·9'	2°16·5'W	X	86,87
Saddell	Arg & Bt	NR7832	55°31·6'	5°30·7'W	T	68,69
Saddell Bay	Arg & Bt	NR7931	55°31·6'	5°29·7'W	W	68,69
Saddell Glen	Arg & Bt	NR7733	55°32·6'	5°31·7'W	X	68,69
Saddell Ho	Arg & Bt	NR7931	55°31·6'	5°29·7'W	X	68,69

Saddell Water	Arg & Bt	NR7733	55°32·6'	5°31·7'W	W	68,69
Saddington	Leic	SP6591	52°31·0'	1°2·1'W	T	141
Saddington Lodge Fm	Leic	SP6491	52°31·0'	1°3·0'W	FM	140
Saddington Resr	Leic	SP6691	52°31·0'	1°1·2'W	W	141
Saddleback Hill	Surrey	SU8862	51°21·2'	0°43·8'W	X	175,186
Saddleback or Blencathra	Cumbr	NY3227	54°38·3'	3°2·8'W	H	90
Saddlebank	Pth & Kin	NO0131	56°27·9'	3°36·0'W	X	52,53
Saddle Bow	Durham	NY9323	54°36·4'	2°6·1'W	X	91,92
Saddle Bow	Norf	TF6015	52°42·8'	0°22·5'E	T	132
Saddlebow Hill	Heref	SO4527	51°56·6'	2°47·6'W	X	161
Saddle Crags	Cumbr	NY5208	54°28·2'	2°44·0'W	H	90
Saddle Craigs	D & G	NT1213	55°24·4'	3°23·0'W	X	78
Saddle End	Lancs	SD6145	53°54·2'	2°35·2'W	X	102,103
Saddle Fell	Lancs	SD6147	53°55·3'	2°35·2'W	X	102,103
Saddle Gate	Somer	SS7143	51°10·5'	3°50·3'W	H	180
Saddle Head	Pemb	SR9592	51°35·6'	4°57·2'W	X	158
Saddle Hill	Aberd	NJ5734	57°23·9'	2°42·5'W	H	29
Saddle Hill	Aberd	NO8391	57°0·8'	2°16·3'W	H	38,45
Saddle Hill	Clackm	NN9500	56°11·1'	3°41·1'W	X	58
Saddle Hill	E Loth	NT6968	55°54·5'	2°29·3'W	X	67
Saddle Hill	Highld	NH7843	57°27·9'	4°1·6'W	H	27
Saddle Hill	Lancs	SD6957	54°0·7'	2°28·0'W	X	103
Saddle Hill	Shrops	SO4178	52°24·0'	2°51·6'W	X	137,148
Saddle Lake Fm	Shrops	SJ5924	52°49·0'	2°36·1'W	FM	126
Saddle of Swarister	Shetld	HU5284	60°32·4'	1°2·6'W	X	1,2,3
Saddle Point	Pemb	SR9893	51°36·2'	4°54·6'W	X	158
Saddle Rock	Corn	SW9662	50°25·6'	4°52·0'W	X	200
Saddlers	Lancs	SD8138	53°50·5'	2°16·9'W	X	103
Saddler's Knott	Cumbr	NY1018	54°33·2'	3°23·1'W	X	89
Saddlers Knowe	Northum	NT8109	55°22·7'	2°17·6'W	H	80
Saddlesall	Staffs	SK1117	52°45·3'	1°49·8'W	X	128
Saddlescombe	W Susx	TQ2711	50°53·3'	0°11·3'W	T	198
Saddle Street	Dorset	ST3803	50°49·6'	2°52·4'W	T	193
Saddle, The	Arg & Bt	NS2296	56°7·7'	4°51·4'W	H	56
Saddle, The	Cumbr	NY1615	54°31·6'	3°17·5'W	X	89
Saddle, The	Highld	NG9313	57°9·9'	5°25·0'W	H	33
Saddle, The	Moray	NJ0103	57°6·7'	3°37·6'W	X	36
Saddle, The	N Ayr	NR9843	55°38·6'	5°12·2'W	X	62,69
Saddle Tor	Devon	SX7576	50°34·5'	3°45·5'W	H	191
Saddlewood Manor	Glos	ST8189	51°36·2'	2°16·1'W	A	162,173
Saddleworth	Oldham	SD9805	53°32·7'	2°1·4'W	X	109
Saddleworth Moor	Oldham	SE0305	53°32·7'	1°56·9'W	X	110
Saddle Yoke	D & G	NT1412	55°23·9'	3°21·0'W	H	78
Sadgill	Cumbr	NY4805	54°26·5'	2°47·7'W	T	90
Sadgill Wood	Cumbr	NY4805	54°26·5'	2°47·7'W	F	90
Sadland Fm	Lincs	TF2146	53°0·1'	0°11·4'W	FM	131
Sadler Ho	N Yks	SE8499	54°23·0'	0°42·0'W	X	94,100
Sadlers	W Berks	SU3564	51°22·7'	1°29·4'W	X	174
Sadlers Fm	Essex	TL5541	52°3·0'	0°16·0'E	FM	154
Sadlers Fm	Glos	SO9711	51°48·1'	2°2·2'W	FM	163
Sadlers Hall Fm	Essex	TQ7688	51°34·0'	0°32·8'E	FM	178
Sadney Fm	Lincs	TA0201	53°30·0'	0°27·3'W	FM	112
Sae Breck	Shetld	HU2178	60°29·4'	1°36·6'W	X	3
Saed Geo	Orkney	HY2223	59°5·5'	3°21·2'W	X	6
Saefti Hill	Shetld	HU3490	60°35·8'	1°22·3'W	H	1,2
Saethon	Gwyn	SH2932	52°51·7'	4°32·0'W	X	123
Saeva Ness	Orkney	HY4815	59°1·4'	2°53·9'W	X	6
Sae Water	Shetld	HU4262	60°20·7'	1°13·8'W	W	2,3
Sae Waters	Shetld	HU3188	60°34·7'	1°25·6'W	W	1
Safefield Ho	Cambs	TL1978	52°23·5'	0°14·7'W	X	142
Safford's Fm	Suff	TM2679	52°22·0'	1°19·6'E	FM	156
Saffron Gardens	Thurr	TQ6682	51°31·0'	0°23·9'E	X	177,178
Saffron Green	Herts	TQ2197	51°39·8'	0°14·6'W	X	166,176
Saffron's Cross	Heref	SO5451	52°9·6'	2°40·0'W	T	149
Saffron Walden	Essex	TL5438	52°1·4'	0°15·1'E	T	154
Sagar Fold	Lancs	SD7040	53°51·6'	2°27·0'W	X	103
Sagebury Fm	Worcs	SO9366	52°17·8'	2°5·8'W	FM	150
Sage's Fm	N Som	ST5161	51°21·0'	2°41·8'W	FM	172,182
Sageston	Pemb	SN0503	51°41·8'	4°48·9'W	T	158
Sageston Mountain	Pemb	SN0603	51°41·8'	4°48·0'W	X	158
Saghay Beg	N Eil	NF9986	57°46·0'	7°3·3'W	X	18
Saghay More	N Eil	NF9986	57°46·0'	7°3·3'W	X	18
Saham Grove	Norf	TF9206	52°37·3'	0°50·6'E	X	144
Saham Hall	Norf	TF8801	52°34·7'	0°46·9'E	X	144
Saham Hills	Norf	TF9003	52°35·7'	0°48·7'E	T	144
Saham Park	Norf	TF9204	52°36·2'	0°50·5'E	F	144
Saham Toney	Norf	TF8902	52°35·2'	0°47·8'E	T	144
Saideal na Ceapaich	Highld	NM6586	56°54·6'	5°51·2'W	W	40
Saidlas Burn	Shetld	HU4779	60°29·8'	1°8·2'W	W	2,3
Saighdean Odhara	Arg & Bt	NM6031	56°24·9'	5°53·0'W	X	49
Saighton	Ches	SJ4462	53°9·4'	2°49·8'W	T	117
Saighton Hall Fm	Ches	SJ4362	53°9·4'	2°50·7'W	FM	117
Saighton Lane Fm	Ches	SJ4463	53°9·9'	2°49·9'W	FM	117
Sail	Cumbr	NY1920	54°34·4'	3°14·8'W	X	89,90
Sail à Bhuiridh	Highld	NM9068	56°45·6'	5°25·7'W	X	40
Sàil a' Charnain	N Eil	NG2297	57°52·8'	6°40·9'W	X	14
Sàil a' Choilich	N Eil	NG0891	57°49·1'	6°54·6'W	X	14,18
Sail an Ias	Highld	NC4240	58°19·5'	4°41·4'W	X	9
Sail an Im	N Ayr	NR9646	55°40·1'	5°14·2'W	X	62,69
Sail an Ruathair	Highld	NC3314	58°5·3'	4°49·5'W	H	15
Sail an Tuim Bhàin	Highld	NH1761	57°36·4'	5°3·3'W	X	20
Sail Beck	Cumbr	NY1818	54°33·3'	3°15·7'W	W	89,90
Sail Bheag	Highld	NH0190	57°51·6'	5°20·8'W	H	19
Sail Chalmadale	N Ayr	NR9140	55°36·8'	5°18·7'W	X	62,69
Sail Chaorainn	Highld	NH1315	57°11·5'	5°5·2'W	H	34
Sail Chlachach	Pth & Kin	NN4764	56°44·8'	4°29·7'W	X	42
Sail Choineas	Highld	NC4145	58°22·1'	4°42·6'W	X	9
Sail Chruaidh	Highld	NH0289	57°51·1'	5°19·7'W	X	19
Sail Chruaidh	Highld	NH0793	57°53·3'	5°14·9'W	X	19
Sail Dhubh	Stir	NN3934	56°28·5'	4°36·4'W	X	50
Sàileag	Highld	NH0114	57°10·7'	5°17·1'W	X	33
Sàilean an Eorna	Highld	NM7063	56°42·4'	5°45·0'W	W	40
Sàilean Ardalum	Arg & Bt	NM4240	56°29·1'	6°11·0'W	W	47,48
Sàilean Dubh	Highld	NM6271	56°46·4'	5°53·3'W	W	40
Sàilean Dubh	Highld	NM7468	56°45·2'	5°41·4'W	W	40
Sàilean Mór	Arg & Bt	NM3741	56°29·5'	6°15·9'W	W	47,48
Sàilean Mór	Arg & Bt	NR7591	56°3·8'	5°36·4'W	W	55
Sàilean MÒR	Highld	NM5859	56°39·9'	5°56·5'W	W	47
Sàilean na h-Airde	Arg & Bt	NR7083	55°59·3'	5°40·8'W	W	55,61
Sàilean na h-Earba	Arg & Bt	NR7390	56°3·2'	5°38·3'W	W	55
Sàilean nan Cuileag	Highld	NM6963	56°42·4'	5°46·0'W	W	40
Sàilean nan Each	Arg & Bt	NM6930	56°24·6'	5°44·2'W	W	49
Sail Eilid a' Mhoraire	Highld	NC3542	58°20·4'	4°48·6'W	X	9
Sailfoot	D & G	NT1407	55°21·2'	3°21·0'W	X	78
Sailfoot Burn	D & G	NT1407	55°21·2'	3°21·0'W	W	78
Sailfoot Law	D & G	NT1507	55°21·2'	3°20·0'W	H	79
Sailfoot Linn	D & G	NT1508	55°21·8'	3°20·0'W	W	79
Sàil Garbh	Highld	NC4134	58°16·2'	4°42·2'W	H	16
Sàil Gharbh	Highld	NC2129	58°13·1'	5°2·4'W	H	15
Sàil Gorm	Highld	NC1930	58°13·6'	5°4·5'W	H	15
Sail Hills	Cumbr	NY1213	54°30·5'	3°21·1'W	X	89
Sailhouse Bay	Orkney	HY2807	58°56·9'	3°14·6'W	W	6,7
Sàil Liath	Highld	NH0782	57°47·4'	5°14·3'W	H	19
Sàil Mhór	Highld	NC2946	58°22·4'	4°55·0'W	X	9
Sàil Mhór	Highld	NG9360	57°35·2'	5°27·3'W	H	19
Sàil Mhór	Highld	NH0388	57°50·6'	5°18·7'W	H	19
Sail na Cloiche Moire	Highld	NG7452	57°30·4'	5°45·9'W	X	24
Sàil nan Aighean	Highld	NC4240	58°19·5'	4°41·4'W	X	9
Sàil na Slataich	Highld	NC3130	58°13·8'	4°52·2'W	H	15
Sailors' Grave	N Yks	TA0292	54°19·0'	0°25·5'W	X	101
Sailor's Home	Lincs	TF4449	53°1·4'	0°9·2'E	X	131
Sàil Rac	Highld	NC3440	58°19·3'	4°49·6'W	X	9
Sàil Riabhach	Highld	NH0340	57°24·7'	5°16·3'W	H	25
Sàil Romascaig	Highld	NC4848	58°23·9'	4°35·6'W	X	9
Sails	N Yks	SD8096	54°21·8'	2°18·0'W	X	98
Sails Beck	E Yorks	SE7449	53°56·1'	0°52·0'W	W	105,106
Sailsbury Hill	Shrops	SJ6732	52°53·3'	2°29·0'W	X	127
Sainfoin Close	Oxon	SP6501	51°42·5'	1°3·2'W	X	164,165
Sainham Fm	I of W	SZ5281	50°37·8'	1°15·5'W	FM	196
Sainsfoins	Cambs	TL4550	52°8·0'	0°7·5'E	X	154
Sains Hall	Essex	TL8609	51°45·2'	0°42·1'E	X	168
Saintbridge	Glos	SO8516	51°50·8'	2°12·7'W	T	162
Saintbury	Glos	SP1139	52°3·2'	1°50·0'W	T	150
Saintbury Grounds	Glos	SP1041	52°4·3'	1°50·9'W	X	150
Saintbury Hill	Glos	SP1238	52°2·7'	1°49·1'W	X	150
Saint Foin	Scot Bord	NT7839	55°38·9'	2°20·6'W	X	74
Saint Hill	Devon	ST0908	50°52·1'	3°17·2'W	T	192
Sainthill	Glos	SO7518	51°51·8'	2°21·4'W	X	162
Saint Hill	W Susx	TQ3835	51°6·1'	0°1·3'W	X	187
Saint Hill Fm	Devon	SX7387	50°40·4'	3°47·5'W	FM	191
Saint Leonards	S Lanak	NS6554	55°45·9'	4°8·7'W	T	64
Saintlow Inclosure	Glos	SO6310	51°47·5'	2°31·8'W	F	162
Saintoft Grange	N Yks	SE7989	54°17·7'	0°46·8'W	X	94,100
Saintofts Plantn	E Yorks	SE8653	53°58·2'	0°40·9'W	F	106
Saint's Hill	Kent	TQ5241	51°9·1'	0°10·8'E	T	188
Saint Sunday's Beck	Cumbr	SD5488	54°17·4'	2°42·0'W	W	97
Saints Way	Corn	SX0264	50°26·8'	4°47·0'W	X	200
'S Airdhe Beinn	Arg & Bt	NM4753	56°36·3'	6°6·9'W	H	47
Saite Fm	Somer	ST6938	51°8·7'	2°26·2'W	FM	183
Saithbont	Gwyn	SH2729	52°50·1'	4°33·7'W	X	123
Saith ffynnon	Flint	SJ1577	53°17·2'	3°16·1'W	T	116
Saith Maen	Powys	SN8315	51°49·5'	3°41·5'W	A	160
Saith Maen	Powys	SN8614	51°49·0'	3°38·8'W	X	160
Saith-maen	Powys	SN9460	52°13·9'	3°32·7'W	A	147
Saito	Shetld	HP5915	60°49·1'	0°54·4'W	X	1
Sakeham Fm	W Susx	TQ2219	50°57·7'	0°15·4'W	FM	198
Salachail	Arg & Bt	NN0551	56°36·9'	5°10·2'W	X	41
Salachan	Highld	NN0051	56°36·8'	5°15·1'W	X	41
Salachan Burn	Highld	NM9852	56°37·2'	5°17·1'W	W	49
Salachan Burn	Highld	NN0151	56°36·8'	5°14·1'W	W	41
Salachan Glen	Highld	NM9852	56°37·2'	5°17·1'W	X	49
Salachary	Arg & Bt	NM8404	56°11·0'	5°28·4'W	X	55
Salacher	Highld	NG6851	57°29·7'	5°51·8'W	X	24
Salachie	Highld	NH4887	57°51·5'	4°33·2'W	X	20
Salachie Burn	Highld	NH5086	57°50·6'	4°31·1'W	W	20
Salachill	Pth & Kin	NN9542	56°33·8'	3°42·1'W	X	52,53
Salachran	Arg & Bt	NM3823	56°19·9'	6°13·5'W	X	48
Salachy	Highld	NC3307	58°1·5'	4°49·2'W	X	15
Salamanca Beck	E Yorks	SE7958	54°1·0'	0°47·2'W	W	105,106
Salbri Fm	I of Angl	SH3788	53°22·1'	4°26·6'W	FM	114
Salcey Forest	Northnts	SP8051	52°9·3'	0°49·4'W	F	152
Salcey Green	Mil Key	SP8049	52°8·2'	0°49·5'W	X	152
Salcey Lawn	Northnts	SP8051	52°9·3'	0°49·4'W	X	152
Salcombe	Devon	SX7339	50°14·5'	3°46·5'W	T	202
Salcombe Hill	Devon	SY1488	50°41·4'	3°12·7'W	X	192
Salcombe Hill Cliff	Devon	SY1387	50°40·8'	3°13·5'W	X	192
Salcombe Mouth	Devon	SY1487	50°40·8'	3°12·7'W	X	192
Salcombe Regis	Devon	SY1488	50°41·4'	3°12·7'W	T	192
Salcote Hall	Essex	TL8707	51°44·1'	0°42·9'E	X	168
Salcott Channel	Essex	TL9813	51°47·1'	0°52·6'E	W	168
Salcott Creek	Essex	TL9513	51°47·1'	0°50·0'E	W	168
Salcott-cum-Virley	Essex	TL9413	51°47·1'	0°49·2'E	T	168
Salden	Bucks	SP8229	51°57·4'	0°48·0'W	T	165
Salden Wood	Bucks	SP8231	51°58·5'	0°48·0'W	F	152,165
Saldons Fm	Worcs	SO9558	52°13·4'	2°4·0'W	FM	150
Sale	Traf	SJ7891	53°25·2'	2°19·5'W	T	109
Saleby	Lincs	TF4578	53°17·0'	0°10·9'E	T	122
Saleby Manor	Lincs	TF4578	53°17·0'	0°10·9'E	X	122
Saleby Woodhouse	Lincs	TF4477	53°16·5'	0°10·0'E	X	122
Sale Fell	Cumbr	NY1929	54°39·2'	3°14·9'W	H	89,90
Sale Fm	Powys	SJ2710	52°41·2'	3°4·4'W	FM	126
Sale Fm, The	Staffs	SK1514	52°43·6'	1°46·3'W	FM	128
Sale Green	Worcs	SO9357	52°12·9'	2°5·8'W	T	150
Sale How	Cumbr	NY2728	54°38·8'	3°7·5'W	H	89,90
Salehow Beck	Cumbr	NY2828	54°38·8'	3°6·5'W	W	89,90
Salehurst	E Susx	TQ4939	51°8·1'	0°8·2'E	X	188
Salehurst	E Susx	TQ7424	50°59·6'	0°29·2'E	T	199
Salem	Carm	SN6226	51°55·2'	4°0·0'W	T	146
Salem	Cered	SN6684	52°26·5'	3°57·9'W	T	135
Salem	Corn	SW7444	50°15·4'	5°9·9'W	T	204
Sale Moss	Scot Bord	NT6952	55°45·9'	2°29·2'W	X	67,74
Salen	Arg & Bt	NM5743	56°31·2'	5°56·6'W	T	47,48
Salen	Highld	NM6864	56°42·9'	5°47·0'W	T	40
Salen Bay	Arg & Bt	NM5743	56°31·2'	5°56·6'W	W	47,48
Salen Bay	Highld	NM6864	56°42·9'	5°47·0'W	W	40
Salendine Nook	Kirk	SE1017	53°39·2'	1°50·5'W	T	110
Salen Forest	Arg & Bt	NM5047	56°33·2'	6°3·6'W	F	47,48
Salenside	Scot Bord	NT4620	55°28·5'	2°50·8'W	T	73
Sales Bank Wood	Cumbr	SD3086	54°16·1'	3°4·1'W	F	96,97
Salesbury	Lancs	SD6732	53°47·2'	2°29·6'W	T	103
Salesbury Hall	Lancs	SD6735	53°48·9'	2°29·7'W	X	103
Salesfrith Fm	Essex	TL7702	51°41·6'	0°34·1'E	FM	167
Sales Point	Essex	TM0308	51°44·3'	0°56·8'E	X	168
Sales Point	Essex	TM0309	51°44·8'	0°56·8'E	X	168
Saletarn Knotts	Cumbr	NY4405	54°26·5'	2°51·4'W	X	90
Sale Water Park	Traf	SJ8092	53°25·7'	2°17·7'W	X	109
Saleway	Worcs	SO9259	52°14·0'	2°6·6'W	T	150
Saleway Fm	Worcs	SO9259	52°14·0'	2°6·6'W	FM	150
Salford	Beds	SP9339	52°2·7'	0°38·2'W	T	153
Salford	Oxon	SP2828	51°57·2'	1°35·2'W	T	163
Salford	Salf	SJ8098	53°28·9'	2°17·7'W	T	109
Salford Bridge	Warw	SP0851	52°9·7'	1°52·6'W	X	150
Salford Coppice	Worcs	SP0451	52°9·7'	1°56·1'W	F	150
Salford Court Fm	Worcs	SO7062	52°15·6'	2°26·0'W	FM	138,149
Salford Fm	Warw	SP0652	52°10·2'	1°54·3'W	FM	150
Salford Ford	Beds	SP9338	52°2·2'	0°38·3'W	T	153
Salford Hall	Warw	SP0649	52°8·6'	1°54·3'W	A	150
Salford Lodge	Warw	SP0450	52°9·1'	1°56·1'W	X	150
Salford Priors	Warw	SP0751	52°9·7'	1°53·5'W	T	150
Salford Quays	Salf	SJ8097	53°28·4'	2°17·7'W	X	109
Salfords	Surrey	TQ2846	51°12·2'	0°9·7'W	T	187
Salgate Fm	Norf	TF5715	52°42·8'	0°19·9'E	FM	131
Salhouse	Norf	TG3014	52°40·7'	1°24·6'E	T	133,134
Salhouse Broad	Norf	TG3115	52°41·2'	1°25·5'E	W	133,134
Salhouse Hall	Norf	TG3014	52°40·7'	1°24·6'E	X	133,134
Saligo	Arg & Bt	NR2166	55°48·7'	6°26·8'W	X	60
Saligo Bay	Arg & Bt	NR2066	55°48·6'	6°27·7'W	W	60
Saligo River	Arg & Bt	NR2166	55°48·7'	6°26·8'W	W	60
Salinae (Droitwich)	Worcs	SO8963	52°16·1'	2°9·3'W	R	150
Saline	Fife	NT0292	56°6·9'	3°34·1'W	T	58
Saline Burn	Fife	NT0193	56°7·4'	3°35·1'W	W	58
Saline Hill	Fife	NT0393	56°7·4'	3°33·2'W	H	58
Saline Shaw Fm	Fife	NS9993	56°7·4'	3°37·0'W	FM	58
Saling Grove	Essex	TL7025	51°54·1'	0°28·7'E	X	167
Saling Hall Garden	Essex	TL7025	51°54·1'	0°28·7'E	X	167
Salisbury	Wilts	SU1430	51°4·4'	1°47·6'W	T	184
Salisbury Bank	Flint	SJ1883	53°20·5'	3°13·5'W	X	116
Salisbury Clumps	Wilts	SU1539	51°9·2'	1°46·7'W	F	184
Salisbury Crags	C of Edin	NT2673	55°56·9'	3°10·7'W	X	66
Salisbury Fm	Lancs	SD5934	53°48·3'	2°36·9'W	FM	102
Salisbury Fm	Monm	ST4288	51°35·5'	2°49·8'W	FM	171,172
Salisbury Hall	Herts	TL1902	51°42·5'	0°16·3'W	A	166
Salisbury Middle	Flint	SJ1881	53°19·4'	3°13·5'W	X	116
Salisbury Plain	Wilts	SU0645	51°12·5'	1°54·5'W	X	184
Salisbury Trench	Hants	SU2514	50°55·7'	1°38·3'W	X	195
Salkeld Br	Dorset	ST7712	50°54·7'	2°19·2'W	X	194
Salkeld Cross	Cumbr	NY1636	54°43·0'	3°17·8'W	X	89
Salkeld Dykes	Cumbr	NY5436	54°43·3'	2°42·4'W	T	90
Sallachail	Highld	NN0662	56°42·8'	5°9·7'W	X	41
Sallachan	Highld	NM9762	56°42·6'	5°18·5'W	X	40
Sallachan Point	Highld	NM9961	56°42·1'	5°16·5'W	X	40
Sallachry	Arg & Bt	NN0712	56°15·9'	5°6·5'W	X	50,56
Sallachy	Highld	NC5408	58°2·5'	4°27·9'W	X	16
Sallachy	Highld	NG9130	57°19·0'	5°27·8'W	T	25
Sallan Port	Arg & Bt	NS0460	55°47·9'	5°7·2'W	W	63
Salla Ruidear	N Eil	NB1016	58°2·6'	6°54·4'W	X	13,14
Salle	Norf	TG1025	52°47·1'	1°7·3'E	T	133
Salle Moor Hall	Norf	TG0924	52°46·6'	1°6·3'E	A	133
Salle Park	Norf	TG1124	52°46·6'	1°8·1'E	X	133
Sallets Green	Essex	TL6318	51°50·4'	0°22·4'E	X	167
Sallies, The	Heref	SO3550	52°8·9'	2°56·6'W	X	148,149
Sallings Common	Worcs	SO6061	52°15·0'	2°34·8'W	X	138,149
Sallochan	S Ayr	NX1284	55°7·1'	4°56·5'W	X	76
Sallochy	Stir	NS3895	56°7·5'	4°35·9'W	X	56
Sallow Copse	Bucks	SP9713	51°48·7'	0°35·2'W	F	165
Sallows	Cumbr	NY4304	54°25·9'	2°52·3'W	H	90
Sallowvallets Inclosure	Glos	SO6013	51°49·1'	2°34·4'W	F	162
Sallow Walk Covert	Suff	TM4774	52°18·7'	1°37·8'E	F	156
Sally Grain	Durham	NY8039	54°45·0'	2°18·2'W	W	91,92
Sally Hill	Cumbr	NY0504	54°25·6'	3°27·4'W	X	89
Sally's Grove	Suff	TM2959	52°11·1'	1°21·4'E	F	156
Sallywood Fm	Glos	ST8298	51°41·1'	2°15·2'W	FM	162
Salmans	Kent	TQ5143	51°10·2'	0°10·0'E	T	188
Salmestone Grange	Kent	TR3569	51°22·5'	1°23·0'E	A	179
Salmonby	Lincs	TF3273	53°14·5'	0°0·9'W	T	122
Salmond's Muir	Angus	NO5737	56°31·6'	2°41·5'W	X	54
Salmon Field	Northum	NY9156	54°54·2'	2°8·0'W	X	87
Salmongill Craig	D & G	NT1712	55°23·9'	3°18·2'W	X	79
Salmon Hall	Cumbr	NY0129	54°39·0'	3°31·6'W	X	89
Salmon Hall	N Yks	SE3876	54°10·9'	1°24·6'W	X	99
Salmon Ho	N Yks	SE2783	54°14·8'	1°34·7'W	X	99
Salmonhutch	Devon	SX8298	50°46·4'	3°40·0'W	T	191
Salmon Point Scar	Carm	SN3507	51°44·5'	4°23·0'W	X	159
Salmon Pool	S Glos	ST5385	51°34·0'	2°40·3'W	W	172
Salmonsbridge Fm	W Susx	SU9423	51°0·1'	0°39·2'W	FM	197
Salmonsbury	Glos	SP1721	51°53·5'	1°44·8'W	A	163
Salmon's Fm	Cambs	TL4677	52°22·5'	0°9·1'E	FM	143
Salmon's Fm	Essex	TQ6592	51°36·4'	0°23·4'E	FM	177,178
Salmonswell Fm	Northum	NY9466	54°59·6'	2°5·2'W	FM	87
Salome Fm	Cambs	TL1378	52°23·5'	0°20·0'W	FM	142
Salome Lodge	Cambs	TL1277	52°23·0'	0°20·9'W	X	142
Salome Wood	Cambs	TL1277	52°23·0'	0°20·9'W	F	142
Salperton	Glos	SP0720	51°52·9'	1°53·5'W	T	163
Salperton Park	Glos	SP0719	51°52·4'	1°53·5'W	T	163
Salph End	Beds	TL0752	52°9·6'	0°25·7'W	T	153
Salsburgh	N Lanak	NS8262	55°50·5'	3°52·6'W	T	65
Salt	Staffs	SJ9527	52°50·7'	2°4·1'W	T	127
Salta	Cumbr	NY0845	54°47·7'	3°25·4'W	T	85
Saltaire	Brad	SE1337	53°50·0'	1°47·7'W	T	104
Salta Moss	Cumbr	NY0845	54°47·7'	3°25·4'W	X	85
Saltash	Corn	SX4160	50°25·3'	4°13·9'W	X	201
Saltash	Corn	SX4258	50°24·3'	4°13·0'W	T	201
Salta Skerry	Shetld	HP6506	60°44·2'	0°48·0'W	X	1
Saltavik Bay	N Eil	NF7714	57°6·5'	7°19·7'W	W	31
Salt Ayre	Lancs	SD4562	54°3·3'	2°50·0'W	X	97
Saltayre	Shetld	HU4651	60°14·7'	1°9·7'W	X	3
Saltbarn Fm	E Susx	TQ9222	50°58·1'	0°44·5'E	FM	189
Salt Beck	E Yorks	SE7753	53°58·3'	0°49·2'W	W	105,106
Saltbeck	Leic	SK8134	52°54·1'	0°47·3'W	F	130
Saltbox	Oxon	SU5184	51°33·4'	1°15·5'W	X	174

Saltbox Fm	Lincs	TF0842	52°58·1'	0°23·1'W	FM	130
Salt Box Fm	Lincs	TF4395	53°26·2'	0°9·6'E	FM	113
Salt Br	Powys	SO2299	52°35·2'	3°8·7'W	X	137
Saltbrook Meadow Fm	Staffs	SK1629	52°51·7'	1°45·3'W	FM	128
Saltburn	Highld	NH7269	57°41·8'	4°8·4'W	T	21,27
Saltburn-By-The-Sea	Red & Cl	NZ6621	54°35·0'	0°58·3'W	T	94
Saltburn Grange	Red & Cl	NZ6720	54°34·5'	0°57·4'W	X	94
Saltburn Sands	Red & Cl	NZ6621	54°35·0'	0°58·3'W	X	94
Saltburn Scar	Red & Cl	NZ6721	54°35·0'	0°57·4'W	X	94
Saltby	Leic	SK8526	52°49·7'	0°43·9'W	T	130
Saltby Heath Fm	Leic	SK8726	52°49·7'	0°42·1'W	FM	130
Saltby Lodge	Leic	SK8427	52°50·3'	0°44·8'W	X	130
Saltby Pasture	Leic	SK8325	52°49·2'	0°45·7'W	X	130
Salt Cellar	Derby	SK1989	53°24·1'	1°42·4'W	X	110
Salt Coates	Cumbr	NY1853	54°52·2'	3°16·2'W	T	85
Saltcoats	Cumbr	SD0796	54°21·3'	3°25·4'W	T	96
Saltcoats	E Loth	NT4882	56°1·9'	2°49·6'W	T	66
Saltcoats	Essex	TQ8197	51°38·8'	0°37·4'E	X	168
Saltcoats	N Ayr	NS2441	55°38·1'	4°47·3'W	T	70
Saltcotes	Lancs	SD3728	53°44·9'	2°56·9'W	T	102
Saltcot Hills	D & G	NY0565	54°58·5'	3°28·6'W	X	85
Saltdean	Bri & Hov	TQ3802	50°48·3'	0°2·1'W	T	198
Salt End	E Yorks	TA1628	53°44·4'	0°14·1'W	T	107
Salt End Jetties	E Yorks	TA1527	53°43·8'	0°15·0'W	X	107
Salterbeck	Cumbr	NX9926	54°37·4'	3°33·4'W	T	89
Salter Carr Fm	Darl	NZ3517	54°33·1'	1°27·1'W	FM	93
Salter Fell	Lancs	SD6459	54°1·8'	2°32·6'W	X	102,103
Salterfen Rocks	Sund	NZ4154	54°53·0'	1°21·2'W	X	88
Salterford Fm	Notts	SK6052	53°3·9'	1°5·9'W	FM	120
Salterforth	Lancs	SD8845	53°54·3'	2°10·5'W	T	103
Saltergate	N Yks	SE8594	54°20·3'	0°41·1'W	X	94,100
Saltergate Beck	N Yks	SE2756	54°0·2'	1°34·9'W	W	104
Saltergate Hill	N Yks	SE2657	54°0·7'	1°35·8'W	X	104
Saltergate Moor	N Yks	SE8595	54°20·8'	0°41·1'W	X	94,100
Saltergill	N Yks	NZ4010	54°29·3'	1°22·5'W	X	93
Saltergill Beck	Stock on T	NZ4110	54°29·3'	1°21·6'W	W	93
Salter Grain	D & G	NY4094	55°14·4'	2°56·2'W	W	79
Salter Hall	Cumbr	NY0516	54°32·1'	3°27·7'W	X	89
Salterhill	Moray	NJ2067	57°41·4'	3°20·1'W	X	28
Salterhill Fm	Falk	NS8571	55°55·4'	3°50·0'W	FM	65
Salter Houses	Stock on T	NZ4227	54°38·4'	1°20·5'W	X	93
Salterland	C of Glas	NS5160	55°48·9'	4°22·2'W	X	64
Salterley Grange	Glos	SO9417	51°51·3'	2°4·8'W	X	163
Saltern Cove	Torbay	SX8958	50°24·9'	3°33·4'W	W	202
Salterns	Devon	SS4626	51°1·0'	4°11·4'W	X	180,190
Salternshill	Hants	SZ4099	50°47·6'	1°25·6'W	X	196
Salternshill Copse	Hants	SZ4199	50°47·6'	1°24·7'W	F	196
Salterns, The	Hants	SZ3293	50°44·3'	1°32·4'W	X	196
Salter's Bank	Lancs	SD3028	53°44·9'	3°3·3'W	X	102
Salter's Brook	Bath & NE Somer	ST6161	51°21·0'	2°33·2'W	W	172
Salters Brook	Ches	SJ4968	53°12·6'	2°45·4'W	W	117
Salter's Brook	Derby	SE1300	53°30·0'	1°47·8'W	W	110
Salter's Brook Br	Derby	SE1300	53°30·0'	1°47·8'W	X	110
Salters Burn	Midlo	NT4262	55°51·1'	2°55·1'W	W	66
Saltersford Brook	Leic	SK3113	52°43·1'	1°32·1'W	W	128
Saltersford Fm	Ches	SJ7768	53°12·8'	2°20·3'W	FM	118
Saltersford Hall	Ches	SJ9876	53°17·1'	2°1·4'W	X	118
Saltersford Hall Fm	Ches	SJ7767	53°12·2'	2°20·3'W	FM	118
Salter's Gate	Durham	NZ0742	54°46·6'	1°53·0'W	X	88
Salters Green Fm	E Susx	TQ5627	51°1·5'	0°13·9'E	FM	188,199
Salters Heath	Hants	SU6157	51°18·8'	1°7·1'W	T	175
Salters Heath	E Susx	TQ5054	51°16·1'	0°9·4'E	X	188
Salter's Hill	Glos	SP0428	51°57·3'	1°56·1'W	X	150,163
Salter's Hill	Leic	SK7411	52°41·7'	0°53·9'W	X	129
Saltershill	Shrops	SJ6428	52°51·1'	2°31·7'W	T	127
Salter's Hill Fm	Leic	SK7412	52°42·3'	0°53·9'W	FM	129
Salter Sitch	Derby	SK2878	53°18·1'	1°34·4'W	X	119
Salters Lode	Norf	TF5801	52°35·3'	0°20·3'E	T	143
Salter's or Chetwynd Br	Staffs	SK1813	52°43·1'	1°43·6'W	X	128
Salter's Road	Northum	NT9015	55°26·0'	2°9·0'W	X	80
Salter's Road	Northum	NT9712	55°24·4'	2°2·4'W	X	81
Salter Street	Sol	SP1274	52°22·1'	1°49·0'W	T	139
Salterswall	Ches	SJ6267	53°12·2'	2°33·7'W	T	118
Salter's Well Fm	Warw	SP2531	51°58·8'	1°37·8'W	FM	151
Salterswell Ho	Ches	SJ5563	53°10·0'	2°40·0'W	X	117
Salter Syke	Lancs	SD9141	53°52·2'	2°7·8'W	X	103
Salterton	Wilts	SU1235	51°7·1'	1°49·3'W	T	184
Salterton Down	Wilts	SU1435	51°7·1'	1°47·6'W	X	184
Salterton Fm	Wilts	SU1235	51°7·1'	1°49·3'W	FM	184
Salterwath	Cumbr	NY5809	54°28·7'	2°38·5'W	X	91
Salter Wood	Cumbr	NY5806	54°37·9'	2°38·6'W	F	91
Saltess	Orkney	HY7644	59°17·2'	2°24·8'W	X	5
Saltfleet	Lincs	TF4593	53°25·1'	0°11·3'E	T	113
Salt Fleet	Medway	TQ7678	51°28·6'	0°32·5'E	W	178
Saltfleetby All Saints	Lincs	TF4590	53°23·4'	0°11·2'E	T	113
Saltfleetby Grange	Lincs	TF4488	53°22·4'	0°10·3'E	X	113,122
Saltfleetby St Clement	Lincs	TF4591	53°24·0'	0°11·3'E	T	113
Saltfleetby St Peter	Lincs	TF4389	53°22·9'	0°9·4'E	T	113,122
Saltfleetby-Theddlethorpe Dunes	Lincs	TF4791	53°24·0'	0°13·1'E	X	113
Saltfleet Haven	Lincs	TF4693	53°25·0'	0°12·2'E	W	113
Saltford	Bath & NE Somer	ST6867	51°24·3'	2°27·2'W	T	172
Salt Grass	Hants	SZ3091	50°43·3'	1°34·1'W	X	196
Salt Greens Plantn	E Loth	NT6279	56°0·4'	2°36·1'W	F	67
Saltham Ho	W Susx	SU8801	50°48·3'	0°44·7'W	X	197
Salthaugh Grange	E Yorks	TA2321	53°40·5'	0°7·9'W	X	107,113
Salthaugh Sands	E Yorks	TA2320	53°40·0'	0°7·9'W	X	107,113
Salt Heath	Staffs	SJ9527	52°50·7'	2°4·1'W	X	127
Salt Hill	Hants	SU6720	50°58·8'	1°2·3'W	X	185
Salt Hill	Slough	SU9680	51°30·9'	0°36·6'W	T	175,176
Salthill Ho	W Susx	SU8306	50°51·1'	0°48·9'W	X	197
Salt Ho	Carm	SN2909	51°45·5'	4°28·3'W	X	159
Saltholme	Stock on T	NZ4923	54°36·2'	1°14·1'W	X	93
Saltholme	Stock on T	NZ5023	54°36·2'	1°13·1'W	X	93
Salthouse	Corn	SS2002	50°47·6'	4°32·9'W	X	190
Salthouse	Cumbr	SD1780	54°12·8'	3°15·9'W	X	96
Salthouse	Cumbr	SD2069	54°6·9'	3°13·0'W	T	96

Salthouse	Norf	TG0743	52°56·9'	1°5·3'E	T	133
Salthouse Bay	N Som	ST3971	51°26·3'	2°52·3'W	W	171,172
Salthouse Fm	Staffs	SJ9446	53°0·9'	2°5·0'W	FM	118
Salthouse Head	Aberd	NK1344	57°29·4'	1°46·5'W	X	30
Salthouse Heath	Norf	TG0742	52°56·4'	1°5·2'E	X	133
Salthouse Pill	Swan	SS5295	51°38·3'	4°7·9'W	W	159
Salthouse Point	Arg & Bt	NS0178	55°57·5'	5°10·8'W	X	63
Salthouse Point	Swan	SS5295	51°38·3'	4°7·9'W	X	159
Salt House, The	Swan	SS4684	51°32·3'	4°12·8'W	A	159
Salthrop Fm	Swin	SU1279	51°30·8'	1°49·2'W	FM	173
Salthrop Ho	Swin	SU1180	51°31·4'	1°50·1'W	X	173
Saltings	Essex	TQ9294	51°36·9'	0°46·8'E	X	168,178
Saltinish	N Eil	NF7008	57°3·0'	7°26·1'W	X	31
Saltire Wood	Aberd	NO6170	56°49·4'	2°37·9'W	F	45
Salt Island	I of Angl	SH2583	53°19·1'	4°37·2'W	X	114
Saltkiln	N Yks	SE3989	54°17·9'	1°23·6'W	X	99
Saltley	Birm	SP0987	52°29·1'	1°51·6'W	T	139
Saltmarsh	Newp	ST3582	51°32·2'	2°55·8'W	T	171
Saltmarshe	E Yorks	SE7824	53°42·6'	0°48·7'W	T	105,106,112
Saltmarshe Castle	Heref	SO6757	52°12·9'	2°28·6'W	X	149
Saltmarshe Grange	E Yorks	SE7828	53°44·8'	0°48·6'W	X	105,106
Saltmarshe Sta	E Yorks	SE7825	53°43·2'	0°48·7'W	X	105,106
Salt Marsh Fm	N Lincs	TA1124	53°42·3'	0°18·7'W	FM	107,113
Saltmarsh Grange	E Yorks	SE8730	53°45·8'	0°40·4'W	X	106
Saltmill Creek	Corn	SX4259	50°24·8'	4°13·1'W	W	201
Saltmoor Fm	Somer	ST3431	51°4·7'	2°56·1'W	FM	182
Saltmore Fm	Herts	TL2239	52°2·4'	0°12·9'W	FM	153
Salt Ness	Orkney	HY4719	59°3·5'	2°55·0'W	X	6
Salt Ness	Orkney	ND2789	58°47·2'	3°15·3'W	X	7
Saltness	Orkney	ND2790	58°47·7'	3°15·3'W	T	7
Saltness	Shetld	HU2448	60°13·2'	1°33·5'W	X	3
Salt Ness	Shetld	HU3450	60°14·2'	1°22·7'W	X	3
Saltness	Shetld	HU3566	60°22·9'	1°21·4'W	X	2,3
Salt Ness	Shetld	HU4880	60°30·3'	1°7·1'W	X	1,2,3
Saltness	Shetld	HU5362	60°20·6'	1°1·9'W	X	2,3
Saltney	Flint	SJ3764	53°10·4'	2°56·1'W	T	117
Saltom Bay	Cumbr	NX9515	54°31·4'	3°36·9'W	W	89
Salton	N Yks	SE7180	54°12·9'	0°54·3'W	T	100
Salton Grange	N Yks	SE7281	54°13·4'	0°53·3'W	X	100
Salton Lodge	N Yks	SE7181	54°13·4'	0°54·2'W	X	100
Saltoun Forest	E Loth	NT4666	55°53·3'	2°51·4'W	F	66
Saltoun Hall	E Loth	NT4668	55°54·4'	2°51·4'W	X	66
Saltoun Home Fm	E Loth	NT4668	55°54·4'	2°51·4'W	FM	66
Salt Pan	Orkney	HY4106	58°56·5'	3°1·0'W	X	6,7
Salt Pan Bay	D & G	NW9667	54°57·6'	5°10·8'W	W	82
Saltpan Point	Arg & Bt	NR2858	55°44·6'	6°19·6'W	X	60
Saltpan Reach	Kent	TQ8673	51°25·7'	0°40·9'E	W	178
Saltpan Rocks	D & G	NX8954	54°52·4'	3°43·4'W	X	84
Saltpan Rocks	Northum	NU0249	55°44·3'	1°57·7'W	X	75
Salt Pans	D & G	NX0746	54°46·6'	4°59·6'W	X	82
Salt Pans Bay	D & G	NW9661	54°54·4'	5°10·5'W	W	82
Saltpetre House	Hants	SU3209	50°53·0'	1°32·3'W	A	196
Salt Pie	Brad	SE1033	53°47·8'	1°50·5'W	X	104
Saltpill Duck Pond	Devon	SS5033	51°4·8'	4°8·1'W	W	180
Salt Pye Fm	N Yks	SD9345	53°54·3'	2°6·0'W	FM	103
Saltram Ho	C of Plym	SX5255	50°22·8'	4°4·5'W	X	201
Saltrens	Devon	SS4521	50°58·3'	4°12·1'W	T	180,190
Saltridge Hill	Glos	SO8811	51°48·1'	2°10·0'W	H	162
Salt Scar	Red & Cl	NZ6126	54°37·8'	1°2·9'W	X	94
Salts Hole	Wilts	SU0890	51°36·8'	1°52·7'W	W	163,173
Salt Skerry	Highld	ND3969	58°36·5'	3°2·5'W	X	12
Salt's Mill	Brad	SE1438	53°50·5'	1°46·8'W	X	104
Salts, The	Norf	TF4815	52°43·0'	0°11·9'E	X	131
Salt Way	Glos	SP1011	51°48·1'	1°50·9'W	A	163
Salt Way	Worcs	SO9362	52°15·6'	2°5·8'W	A	150
Salt Way	Worcs	SO9942	52°4·8'	2°0·5'W	X	150
Saltway Fm	Glos	SP1010	51°47·5'	1°50·9'W	FM	163
Saltwell	Ghead	NZ2561	54°56·8'	1°36·2'W	T	88
Salt Well	Lincs	SK8539	52°56·7'	0°43·7'W	W	130
Saltwick	Northum	NZ1779	55°6·6'	1°43·6'W	X	88
Saltwick	Northum	NZ1780	55°7·1'	1°43·6'W	T	81
Salt Wick	Shetld	HU5386	60°33·5'	1°1·5'W	W	1,2,3
Salt Wick	Shetld	HU5489	60°35·1'	1°0·4'W	W	1,2
Saltwick Bay	N Yks	NZ9110	54°28·9'	0°35·3'W	W	94
Saltwick Nab	N Yks	NZ9111	54°29·4'	0°35·3'W	X	94
Saltwood	Kent	TR1535	51°4·7'	1°4·6'E	T	179,189
Saltwood, The	Devon	SX9372	50°32·5'	3°30·2'W	X	192,202
Salum	Arg & Bt	NM0648	56°32·2'	6°46·5'W	T	46
Salum Bay	Arg & Bt	NM0648	56°32·2'	6°46·5'W	W	46
Salutation Fm	N Yks	NZ3502	54°25·0'	1°27·2'W	FM	93
Sal-vaich	Highld	ND0326	58°13·0'	3°38·6'W	H	17
Salvington	W Susx	TQ1305	50°50·2'	0°23·3'W	T	198
Salwarpe	Worcs	SO8761	52°15·1'	2°11·0'W	T	150
Salwayash	Dorset	SY4596	50°45·9'	2°46·4'W	T	193
Salwick Hall	Lancs	SD4632	53°47·1'	2°48·8'W	X	102
Salwick Sta	Lancs	SD4632	53°47·1'	2°48·8'W	X	102
Samadalan	Highld	NG7305	57°5·1'	5°44·3'W	X	33
Samalaman Ho	Highld	NM6577	56°49·8'	5°50·7'W	X	40
Samalaman Island	Highld	NM6678	56°50·3'	5°49·7'W	X	40
Samalan Island	Arg & Bt	NM4536	56°27·1'	6°7·9'W	X	47,48
Samber Hill	I of W	SZ4581	50°37·8'	1°21·4'W	X	196
Sambourne	Warw	SP0561	52°15·1'	1°55·2'W	T	150
Sambourne	Wilts	ST8644	51°11·9'	2°11·6'W	T	183
Sambourne Oak Fm	Warw	SP0563	52°16·1'	1°55·2'W	FM	150
Sambourne Warren Fm	Warw	SP0461	52°15·1'	1°56·1'W	FM	150
Sambre Beck	Lincs	TF1073	53°14·8'	0°20·7'W	W	121
Sambrook	Wrekin	SJ7124	52°49·0'	2°25·4'W	T	127
Samgarth Beck	Cumbr	SD1294	54°20·3'	3°20·8'W	W	96
Samhla	N Eil	NF7962	57°32·3'	7°21·4'W	T	22
Samhnan Insir	Highld	NG3704	57°3·4'	6°19·8'W	X	32,39
Sam Ho	N Yks	SE4769	54°7·1'	1°16·4'W	X	100
Samieston	Scot Bord	NT7221	55°29·2'	2°26·2'W	X	74
Samlesbury	Lancs	SD5930	53°46·1'	2°36·9'W	T	102
Samlesbury Aerodrome	Lancs	SD6231	53°46·7'	2°34·2'W	X	102,103
Samlesbury Bottoms	Lancs	SD6128	53°45·1'	2°35·1'W	T	102,103
Samlesbury Hall	Lancs	SD6230	53°46·1'	2°34·2'W	A	102,103
Sampford Arundel	Somer	ST1018	50°57·5'	3°16·5'W	T	181,193
Sampford Brett	Somer	ST0840	51°9·3'	3°18·5'W	T	181
Sampford Chapple	Devon	SS6201	50°47·8'	3°57·1'W	T	191
Sampford Courtenay	Devon	SS6301	50°47·8'	3°56·3'W	T	191

Sampford Moor	Somer	ST1117	50°57·0'	3°15·6'W	T	181,193
Sampford Moors	Devon	SX6399	50°46·7'	3°56·2'W	X	191
Sampford Peverell	Devon	ST0314	50°55·3'	3°22·4'W	T	181
Sampford Point	Devon	ST1116	50°56·4'	3°15·6'W	X	181,193
Sampford Spiney	Devon	SX5372	50°32·0'	4°4·1'W	T	191,201
Samphire Bed	Lincs	TF4496	53°26·7'	0°10·5'E	X	113
Samphire Hoe Country Park	Kent	TR2938	51°6·0'	1°16·6'E	X	179
Samphire Island	Corn	SW6344	50°15·1'	5°19·1'W	X	203
Samphire Rock	Corn	SX1295	50°43·7'	4°39·5'W	X	190
Samphrey	Shetld	HU4676	60°28·2'	1°9·3'W	X	2,3
Sample's Fm	E Yorks	SE9735	53°48·4'	0°31·2'W	FM	106
Sampool	Cumbr	SD4884	54°15·2'	2°47·5'W	X	97
Sampool Br	Cumbr	SD4785	54°15·7'	2°48·4'W	X	97
Sampson	Pemb	SR9696	51°37·8'	4°56·5'W	X	158
Sampson Barton	Devon	SS6821	50°58·6'	3°52·4'W	X	180
Sampsons	Essex	TL9904	51°42·2'	0°53·2'E	X	168
Sampson's Bratfull	Cumbr	NY0908	54°27·8'	3°23·8'W	X	89
Sampson's Bratfull (Long Cairn)	Cumbr	NY0908	54°27·8'	3°23·8'W	A	89
Sampson's Creek	Essex	TL9914	51°47·6'	0°53·5'E	W	168
Sampson's Fm	Essex	TL9915	51°48·1'	0°53·6'E	FM	168
Sampsons Hall	Suff	TL9943	52°3·2'	0°54·5'E	X	155
Samsiston	D & G	NS6913	55°23·9'	4°3·7'W	X	71
Samson	I Scilly	SV8712	49°55·8'	6°21·3'W	X	203
Samson Court	Newp	ST3783	51°32·8'	2°54·1'W	X	171
Samson Flats	I Scilly	SV8812	49°55·8'	6°20·4'W	X	203
Samson Hill	I Scilly	SV8714	49°56·9'	6°21·4'W	H	203
Samson House	N Yks	SE4286	54°16·3'	1°20·9'W	X	99
Samson's Bay	Devon	SS5448	51°13·0'	4°5·0'W	W	180
Samson's Jack	Swan	SS4792	51°36·6'	4°12·2'W	X	159
Samson's Jack (Standing Stone)	Swan	SS4792	51°36·6'	4°12·2'W	A	159
Samsonslane	Orkney	HY6525	59°6·9'	2°36·2'W	X	5
Samson's Stone	Stir	NN6007	56°14·4'	4°15·1'W	X	57
Samuel Closes Fm	N Lincs	SE7506	53°33·0'	0°51·7'W	FM	112
Samuel's Corner	Essex	TQ9587	51°33·1'	0°49·2'E	T	178
Samuel's Geo	Highld	ND3864	58°33·8'	3°3·5'W	X	12
Samuelston	E Loth	NT4870	55°55·5'	2°49·5'W	T	66
Samuelston Loanhead	E Loth	NT4771	55°56·0'	2°50·5'W	X	66
Samuelston South Mains	E Loth	NT4869	55°54·9'	2°49·5'W	X	66
Samways Fm	Wilts	ST9723	51°0·6'	2°2·2'W	FM	184
Sam Wood	N Yks	SE4769	54°7·1'	1°16·4'W	F	100
Sanachan	Highld	NG8340	57°24·2'	5°36·3'W	T	24
Sanaigmore	Arg & Bt	NR2370	55°50·9'	6°25·1'W	X	60
Sanaigmore Bay	Arg & Bt	NR2371	55°51·4'	6°25·2'W	W	60
Sanblister	Shetld	HU3810	59°52·7'	1°18·8'W	X	4
Sancreed	Corn	SW4129	50°6·5'	5°37·0'W	T	203
Sancroft Manor	Suff	TM2772	52°18·2'	1°20·2'E	X	156
Sancton	E Yorks	SE9039	53°50·6'	0°37·5'W	T	106
Sancton Grange	E Yorks	SE8939	53°50·6'	0°38·4'W	X	106
Sancton Hill	E Yorks	SE9139	53°50·6'	0°36·6'W	X	106
Sancton Wold	E Yorks	SE9140	53°51·1'	0°36·6'W	X	106
Sanctuary	Devon	SS8802	50°48·6'	3°35·0'W	X	192
Sanctuary	Swan	SS4887	51°33·9'	4°11·2'W	X	159
Sanctuary, The	Wilts	SU1167	51°24·3'	1°50·1'W	A	173
Sand	Devon	SY1492	50°43·5'	3°12·7'W	A	192,193
Sand	Highld	NG6848	57°28·0'	5°51·7'W	X	24
Sand	Highld	NG9091	57°51·8'	5°31·9'W	T	19
Sand	Shetld	HU3447	60°12·6'	1°22·7'W	T	3
Sand	Somer	ST4346	51°12·9'	2°48·6'W	T	182
Sandaber	N Yks	SD7567	54°6·1'	2°22·5'W	X	98
Sand Acre Cotts	Lincs	TF1933	52°53·1'	0°13·5'W	X	130
Sandaig	Arg & Bt	NL9343	56°29·0'	6°58·8'W	T	46
Sandaig	Highld	NG7101	57°2·9'	5°46·1'W	X	33
Sandaig	Highld	NG7714	57°10·0'	5°40·8'W	X	33
Sandaig Bay	Highld	NG7101	57°2·9'	5°46·1'W	W	33
Sandaig Burn	Highld	NG7202	57°3·4'	5°45·1'W	W	33
Sandaig Islands	Highld	NG7614	57°10·0'	5°41·8'W	X	33
Sanda Island	Arg & Bt	NR7204	55°16·9'	5°35·0'W	X	68
Sandal	Wakf	SE3318	53°39·7'	1°29·6'W	T	110,111
Sandal Castle	Wakf	SE3318	53°39·7'	1°29·6'W	A	110,111
Sandale	Cumbr	NY2440	54°45·2'	3°10·4'W	T	85
Sandal Fm	N Yks	SE1034	53°48·4'	1°50·5'W	FM	104
Sandal Holme Fm	Lancs	SD6743	53°53·2'	2°29·7'W	FM	103
Sanda Little	Shetld	HU3442	60°9·9'	1°22·7'W	X	4
Sandall Beat Wood	Donc	SE6103	53°31·4'	1°4·4'W	F	111
Sandall Grange	Donc	SE6307	53°33·6'	1°2·5'W	X	111
Sandall Grove	Donc	SE6107	53°33·6'	1°4·3'W	F	111
Sandal Magna	Wakf	SE3418	53°39·7'	1°28·7'W	T	110,111
Sanda Roads	Arg & Bt	NR7205	55°17·4'	5°35·0'W	W	68
Sanda Stack	Shetld	HT9438	60°7·9'	2°6·0'W	X	4
Sanda Stour	Shetld	HU3441	60°9·4'	1°22·8'W	X	4
Sandavore	Highld	NM4784	56°53·0'	6°8·7'W	T	39
Sanday	Highld	NG2704	57°3·0'	6°29·7'W	X	39
Sanday	Orkney	HY6640	59°15·0'	2°35·3'W	X	5
Sanday Sound	Orkney	HY6634	59°11·7'	2°35·2'W	W	5
Sandbach	Ches	SJ7560	53°8·4'	2°22·0'W	T	118
Sandbach Fm	Ches	SJ8672	53°14·9'	2°12·2'W	FM	118
Sandbach Heath	Ches	SJ7660	53°8·4'	2°21·1'W	T	118
Sandbach Service Area	Ches	SJ7760	53°8·4'	2°20·2'W	X	118
Sandbach Sta	Ches	SJ7361	53°9·0'	2°23·8'W	X	118
Sandback	Orkney	HY6744	59°17·1'	2°34·3'W	X	5
Sandbank	Arg & Bt	NS1680	55°58·9'	4°56·5'W	T	63
Sand Bank	Lancs	SD5837	53°49·9'	2°37·9'W	X	102
Sand Banks	Kent	TR0362	51°19·5'	0°55·2'E	X	178,179
Sandbanks	Poole	SZ0487	50°41·2'	1°56·2'W	T	195
Sand Bay	N Som	ST3264	51°22·5'	2°58·2'W	W	182
Sand Bay	S Glos	ST5185	51°33·9'	2°42·0'W	W	172
Sandbay Fm	N Som	ST3365	51°23·0'	2°57·4'W	FM	171,182
Sandbeach	Essex	TM0205	51°42·7'	0°55·8'E	X	168
Sand Beck	Lincs	SK9051	53°3·2'	0°39·0'W	W	121
Sand Beck	N Yks	SE1499	54°23·4'	1°46·6'W	W	99
Sandbeck Fm	Lincs	SK8495	53°26·9'	0°43·7'W	FM	112
Sandbeck Hall	Roth	SK5690	53°24·5'	1°9·0'W	X	111
Sandbeck Ho	Leeds	SE4149	53°56·4'	1°22·1'W	X	105
Sandbeck Lodge	Roth	SK5591	53°25·0'	1°9·9'W	X	111
Sandbed	Cumbr	NY3769	55°0·9'	2°58·7'W	X	85
Sandbed	Cumbr	SD7299	54°23·4'	2°25·5'W	X	98
Sandbed	D & G	NX9483	55°8·1'	3°39·3'W	X	78

Sandbed	D & G	NY1284	55°8·8′	3°22·4′W	X	78
Sandbeds	Cumbr	NY0321	54°34·7′	3°29·6′W	X	89
Sand Beds	Cumbr	SD5997	54°22·3′	2°37·4′W	X	97
Sandbeds	Lancs	SD5668	54°6·6′	2°40·0′W	H	97
Sandbeds Fm	N Lincs	SK7699	53°29·2′	0°50·9′W	FM	112
Sand Beds Head Pike	N Yks	SD7279	54°12·6′	2°25·3′W	X	98
Sandborough	Staffs	SK1119	52°46·3′	1°49·8′W	T	128
Sandbraes	Lincs	TA1101	53°29·9′	0°19·2′W	T	113
Sandbraes	N Ayr	NS0427	55°30·1′	5°5·8′W	X	69
Sandburn Ho	York	SE6659	54°1·6′	0°59·1′W	X	105,106
Sandburn Wood	York	SE6758	54°1·1′	0°58·2′W	F	105,106
Sand Cliffs	Norf	TG5115	52°40·7′	1°43·2′E	X	134
Sandcombe Fm	Devon	SY1593	50°44·1′	3°11·9′W	FM	192,193
Sand Cotts	N Yks	SE9176	54°10·5′	0°35·9′W	X	101
Sandcroma	Orkney	HY2222	59°4·9′	3°21·2′W	X	6
Sand Dale	N Yks	SE8785	54°15·4′	0°39·4′W	X	94,101
Sandebus Fm	Lincs	SK8683	53°20·4′	0°42·1′W	FM	121
Sand Edge	Durham	NZ0840	54°45·5′	1°52·1′W	X	88
Sandeel Beds	Northum	NU1141	55°40·0′	1°49·1′W	X	75
Sandend	Aberd	NJ5566	57°41·2′	2°44·8′W	T	29
Sandend Bay	Aberd	NJ5666	57°41·2′	2°43·8′W	W	29
Sanden Ho	Cumbr	NY1751	54°51·1′	3°17·1′W	X	85
Sanders	Devon	SX8648	50°19·5′	3°35·7′W	X	202
Sanders Close	Northum	NY6453	54°52·5′	2°30·4′W	X	86,87
Sander's Covert	Northnts	SP7167	52°18·0′	0°57·1′W	F	152
Sandersdean	E Loth	NT5371	55°56·0′	2°44·7′W	X	66
Sander's Green	Herts	TL3324	51°54·1′	0°3·6′W	X	166
Sanders Loch	Highld	ND1874	58°39·0′	3°24·3′W	W	7,12
Sanders Loch	Highld	ND2175	58°39·6′	3°21·2′W	W	7,12
Sanderson's Brook	Ches	SJ7264	53°10·6′	2°24·7′W	W	118
Sanderstead	Croy	TQ3361	51°20·2′	0°5·0′W	T	176,177,187
Sand Farm	N Som	ST3364	51°22·5′	2°57·4′W	FM	182
Sandfield	D & G	NX7563	54°57·0′	3°56·7′W	X	84
Sandfield	Shetld	HP6113	60°48·0′	0°52·2′W	X	1
Sand Field	Shetld	HU3148	60°13·2′	1°25·9′W	H	3
Sandfield Cott	Lancs	SD3949	53°56·3′	2°55·3′W	X	102
Sandfield Fm	Devon	ST0809	50°52·6′	3°18·1′W	FM	192
Sandfield Fm	N Yks	SE5359	54°1·7′	1°11·0′W	FM	105
Sandfield Fm	Suff	TM0075	52°20·4′	0°56·6′E	FM	144
Sandfield Fm	Worcs	SP0039	52°3·2′	1°59·6′W	FM	150
Sandfield Ho	Ches	SJ7577	53°17·6′	2°22·1′W	X	118
Sandfield Ho	N Yks	NZ8711	54°29·5′	0°39·0′W	X	94
Sandfield Ho	Wilts	ST9959	51°20·0′	2°0·5′W	X	173
Sandfields	Nth Pt Talb	SS7490	51°35·9′	3°48·8′W	T	170
Sandfields	Staffs	SK1108	52°40·4′	1°49·8′W	T	128
Sandfields Fm	Oxon	SP3229	51°57·7′	1°31·7′W	FM	164
Sandfields Fm	Warw	SP1653	52°10·7′	1°45·6′W	FM	151
Sand Fiold	Orkney	HY2419	59°3·3′	3°19·0′W	X	6
Sandford	Cumbr	NY7216	54°32·6′	2°25·5′W	T	91
Sandford	Devon	SS8202	50°48·6′	3°40·1′W	T	191
Sandford	Dorset	SY9289	50°42·3′	2°6·4′W	T	195
Sandford	Hants	SU1601	50°48·7′	1°46·0′W	T	195
Sandford	I of W	SZ5481	50°37·8′	1°13·8′W	T	196
Sandford	Leeds	SE2535	53°48·9′	1°36·8′W	T	104
Sandford	N Som	ST4259	51°19·9′	2°49·6′W	T	172,182
Sandford	Shrops	SJ3423	52°48·3′	2°58·3′W	T	126
Sandford	Shrops	SJ5834	52°54·3′	2°37·1′W	T	126
Sandford	Shrops	SO7892	52°31·8′	2°19·1′W	X	138
Sandford	S Lanak	NS7143	55°40·1′	4°2·6′W	T	71
Sandford	Worcs	SO8545	52°6·4′	2°12·7′W	T	150
Sandford Ash	Devon	SS7704	50°49·6′	3°44·4′W	X	191
Sandford Barton	Devon	SS6801	50°47·8′	3°52·0′W	X	191
Sandford Batch	N Som	ST4158	51°19·3′	2°50·4′W	T	172,182
Sandford Bay	Aberd	NK1243	57°28·9′	1°47·5′W	W	30
Sandford Beck	N Yks	SD7662	54°3·4′	2°21·6′W	W	98
Sandford Br	Ches	SJ6147	53°1·4′	2°34·5′W	X	118
Sandfordbrake Fm	Oxon	SP5501	51°42·5′	1°11·8′W	FM	164
Sandford Brook	Oxon	SU4697	51°40·4′	1°19·7′W	FM	164
Sandford Brow	N Yks	SD7762	54°3·5′	2°20·7′W	X	98
Sandford Fm	Heref	SO6426	51°56·1′	2°31·0′W	FM	162
Sandford Fm	Somer	ST2737	51°7·9′	3°2·2′W	FM	182
Sandford Fm	Wok	SU7873	51°27·3′	0°52·3′W	FM	175
Sandford Hall	Shrops	SJ3323	52°48·3′	2°59·2′W	X	126
Sand Ford Head	Fife	NO4619	56°21·9′	2°52·0′W	X	59
Sandfordhill	Aberd	NK1141	57°27·8′	1°48·5′W	T	30
Sandford Hill	C of Stoke	SJ9144	52°59·8′	2°7·6′W	T	118
Sandford Hill	N Som	ST4259	51°19·9′	2°49·6′W	T	172,182
Sandford Ho	Dorset	SY9390	50°42·8′	2°5·6′W	X	195
Sandford Ho	N Yks	NZ1800	54°24·0′	1°42·9′W	X	92
Sandford Ho	Shrops	SJ5237	52°55·9′	2°42·4′W	X	126
Sandford Lodge	Aberd	NK1243	57°28·9′	1°47·5′W	X	30
Sandford Mill	Wok	SU7873	51°27·3′	0°52·3′W	X	175
Sandford-on-Thames	Oxon	SP5301	51°42·5′	1°13·6′W	T	164
Sandford Orcas	Dorset	ST6220	50°58·9′	2°32·1′W	T	183
Sandford Park	Oxon	SP4126	51°56·1′	1°23·8′W	X	164
Sandford Pool	Oxon	SP5201	51°42·6′	1°14·5′W	W	164
Sandford's Fm	Essex	TL8011	51°46·3′	0°36·9′E	FM	168
Sandford's Knoll	Glos	SO7901	51°42·7′	2°17·8′W	X	162
Sandford St Martin	Oxon	SP4226	51°56·1′	1°23·0′W	T	164
Sandford Woods	Hants	SU5459	51°19·9′	1°13·1′W	F	174
Sand Gap	Cumbr	SD2085	54°15·5′	3°13·3′W	X	96
Sand Gate	Cumbr	SD3575	54°10·2′	2°59·3′W	T	96,97
Sandgate	Kent	TR2035	51°4·5′	1°8·8′E	T	179,189
Sand Gate Marsh	Cumbr	SD3576	54°10·8′	2°59·3′W	W	96,97
Sandgates	Surrey	TQ0365	51°22·7′	0°30·8′W	X	176
Sand Geo	Orkney	HY2223	59°5·5′	3°21·2′W	X	6
Sand Geo	Orkney	HY4820	59°4·1′	2°53·9′W	X	5,6
Sand Geos	Orkney	HY4525	59°6·8′	2°57·1′W	X	5,6
Sandgeo Taing	Orkney	HY6101	58°53·9′	2°40·1′W	X	6
Sandgreen	D & G	NX5752	54°50·8′	4°13·2′W	T	83
Sand Ground	Cumbr	SD3499	54°23·2′	3°0·6′W	X	96,97
Sand Haile Flats	Lincs	TF4596	53°26·7′	0°11·4′E	X	113
Sandhall	Cumbr	SD3077	54°11·3′	3°3·9′W	X	96,97
Sand Hall	E Yorks	SE7623	53°42·1′	0°50·5′W	X	105,106,112
Sandhall Fm	E Susx	TQ6810	50°52·1′	0°23·6′E	FM	199
Sandhall Fm	E Yorks	SE7523	53°42·1′	0°51·4′W	FM	105,106,112
Sand Hall Fm	N Lincs	SE7511	53°35·6′	0°51·6′W	FM	112
Sandhall Fm	N Lincs	SE9318	53°39·2′	0°35·2′W	FM	112
Sandhaven	Aberd	NJ9667	57°41·8′	2°3·6′W	T	30
Sandhaven	Arg & Bt	NS1581	55°59·4′	4°57·5′W	X	63

Sand Haw	N Yks	SE0366	54°5·6′	1°56·8′W	X	98
Sandhayes	Wilts	ST8346	51°13·0′	2°14·2′W	X	183
Sandhead	D & G	NX0950	54°48·8′	4°57·9′W	T	82
Sandhead Bay	D & G	NX0949	54°48·2′	4°57·9′W	W	82
Sandhill	Barns	SE4306	53°33·2′	1°20·6′W	T	111
Sandhill	Bucks	SP7326	51°55·9′	0°55·9′W	T	165
Sandhill	Cambs	TL5786	52°27·2′	0°19·0′E	T	143
Sand Hill	Cumbr	NY1821	54°34·9′	3°15·7′W	H	89,90
Sand Hill	Cumbr	NY2328	54°38·7′	3°11·2′W	X	89,90
Sandhill	Cumbr	NY7145	54°48·2′	2°26·6′W	X	86,87
Sand Hill	Moray	NJ3821	57°16·8′	3°1·2′W	H	37
Sand Hill	N Eil	NF9382	57°43·6′	7°9·0′W	H	18
Sand Hill	N Lincs	SE8018	53°39·4′	0°47·0′W	X	112
Sand Hill	N Lincs	SE8407	53°33·4′	0°43·5′W	X	112
Sand Hill	N Yks	NZ6610	54°29·1′	0°58·5′W	X	94
Sand Hill	N Yks	SE2087	54°16·9′	1°41·1′W	X	99
Sand Hill	N Yks	SE2789	54°18·0′	1°34·7′W	X	99
Sandhill	Orkney	HY5633	59°11·2′	2°45·7′W	X	5,6
Sand Hill	Powys	SN8915	51°49·6′	3°36·3′W	X	160
Sandhill	Roth	SK4497	53°28·3′	1°19·8′W	X	111
Sandhill	S Ayr	NS3428	55°31·3′	4°37·3′W	X	70
Sandhill	S Ayr	NS4117	55°25·5′	4°30·3′W	X	70
Sandhill	Shetld	HU3065	60°22·3′	1°26·9′W	X	3
Sandhill Fm	Donc	SE7211	53°35·6′	0°54·3′W	FM	112
Sandhill Fm	E Susx	TQ5328	51°2·1′	0°11·3′E	FM	188,199
Sandhill Fm	E Susx	TQ5433	51°4·8′	0°12·3′E	FM	188
Sand Hill Fm	E Yorks	SE7936	53°49·1′	0°47·6′W	FM	105,106
Sand Hill Fm	E Yorks	SE8332	53°46·9′	0°44·0′W	FM	106
Sandhill Fm	Lincs	TF4364	53°9·5′	0°8·7′E	FM	122
Sandhill Fm	N Lincs	SE7504	53°31·9′	0°51·7′W	FM	112
Sandhill Fm	N Yks	SE5274	54°9·8′	1°11·8′W	FM	100
Sandhill Fm	Oxon	SU2289	51°36·2′	1°40·5′W	FM	174
Sandhill Fm	Somer	ST0240	51°9·3′	3°23·7′W	FM	181
Sandhill Fm	W Susx	TQ3536	51°6·7′	0°3·9′W	FM	187
Sandhill Ho	N Yks	SE4580	54°13·1′	1°18·2′W	X	99
Sandhill Ho	W Susx	SU8022	50°59·7′	0°51·2′W	X	197
Sandhill Park	Somer	ST1529	51°3·5′	3°12·4′W	X	181,193
Sandhills	Bourne	SZ1891	50°43·3′	1°44·3′W	X	195
Sandhills	D & G	NY2065	54°58·6′	3°14·6′W	X	85
Sandhills	Dorset	ST5800	50°48·1′	2°35·4′W	T	194
Sandhills	Dorset	ST6810	50°53·5′	2°26·9′W	T	194
Sandhills	Kent	TR3654	51°14·4′	1°23·3′E	X	179
Sandhills	Leeds	SE3739	53°51·0′	1°25·8′W	T	104
Sandhills	Liv	SJ3393	53°26·0′	3°0·1′W	T	108
Sand Hills	N Lincs	SE9903	53°31·1′	0°30·0′W	X	112
Sandhills	Oxon	SP5607	51°45·8′	1°10·9′W	T	164
Sandhills	Surrey	SU9337	51°7·7′	0°39·9′W	T	186
Sandhills	Surrey	TQ3249	51°13·7′	0°6·2′W	X	187
Sandhills	W Susx	TQ1227	51°2·1′	0°23·8′W	X	187,198
Sandhills Fm	Derby	SK1539	52°57·1′	1°46·2′W	FM	128
Sandhills Fm	E Susx	TQ6416	50°55·4′	0°20·4′E	FM	199
Sandhills Fm	I of W	SZ4690	50°42·7′	1°20·5′W	FM	196
Sand Hills Fm	Stock on T	NZ4308	54°28·2′	1°19·8′W	FM	93
Sandhills Fm	Surrey	TQ3249	51°13·7′	0°6·2′W	FM	187
Sandhills Stonce	Notts	SK7853	53°4·3′	0°49·7′W	A	120
Sandhoe	Northum	NY9766	54°59·6′	2°2·4′W	T	87
Sandhole	Aberd	NJ9659	57°37·5′	2°3·6′W	X	30
Sandhole	Aberd	NJ9951	57°33·2′	2°0·5′W	X	30
Sandhole	Arg & Bt	NS0199	56°8·8′	5°11·8′W	T	55
Sand Hole	E Yorks	SE8137	53°49·6′	0°45·7′W	T	106
Sandhole	Kent	TQ6960	51°19·1′	0°25·9′E	X	177,178,188
Sandhole Cliff	Devon	SS2220	50°57·4′	4°31·7′W	X	190
Sandhole Fm	Ches	SJ8566	53°11·7′	2°13·1′W	FM	118
Sandholes	Ches	SJ5043	52°59·2′	2°44·3′W	X	117
Sandholes	Kent	TQ5045	51°11·3′	0°9·2′E	X	188
Sand Holes	Notts	SK5752	53°4·0′	1°8·6′W	F	120
Sandholes Fm	Ches	SJ9181	53°19·8′	2°7·7′W	FM	109
Sand Holm	Orkney	HY2914	59°0·7′	3°13·7′W	X	6
Sandholm	Scot Bord	NY4989	55°11·8′	2°47·6′W	X	79
Sandholme	E Yorks	SE8230	53°45·8′	0°44·9′W	T	106
Sandholme	Lincs	TF3337	52°55·1′	0°0·9′W	T	131
Sandholme	N Yks	SE3382	54°14·2′	1°29·2′W	X	99
Sandholme	N Yks	SE4186	54°16·3′	1°21·8′W	X	99
Sandholme Fm	E Yorks	TA0944	53°53·1′	0°20·1′W	FM	107
Sandholme Grange	E Yorks	SE8330	53°45·8′	0°44·0′W	X	106
Sandholme Landing	E Yorks	SE8531	53°46·3′	0°42·2′W	X	106
Sandholme Lodge	E Yorks	SE8331	53°46·4′	0°44·0′W	X	106
Sandholme Mill	Lancs	SD5143	53°53·1′	2°44·3′W	X	102
Sandholmes	N Yks	SE4375	54°10·4′	1°20·1′W	X	99
Sandhouse	I of M	SC2682	54°12·5′	4°39·7′W	X	95
Sand House Fm	N Lincs	SE8018	53°39·4′	0°47·0′W	FM	112
Sand House Fm	N Lincs	SE8604	53°31·8′	0°41·7′W	FM	112
Sandhouse Fm	N Lincs	SE9512	53°36·0′	0°33·5′W	FM	112
Sandhurst	Brackn	SU8361	51°20·7′	0°48·1′W	T	175,186
Sandhurst	Glos	SO8223	51°54·6′	2°15·3′W	T	162
Sandhurst	Kent	TQ7928	51°1·6′	0°33·5′E	T	188,199
Sandhurst Cross	Kent	TQ7827	51°1·1′	0°32·7′E	T	188,199
Sandhurst Fm	Derby	SK2153	53°4·7′	1°40·8′W	FM	119
Sandhurst Fm	Kent	TQ6438	51°7·3′	0°21·0′E	FM	188
Sandhurst Hill	Glos	SO8324	51°55·1′	2°14·4′W	H	162
Sandhurst Lodge	Brackn	SU8263	51°21·8′	0°48·9′W	X	175,186
Sand Hutton	N Yks	SE3882	54°14·2′	1°24·6′W	T	99
Sand Hutton	N Yks	SE6958	54°1·0′	0°56·4′W	T	105,106
Sand Hutton Common	N Yks	SE6757	54°0·5′	0°58·2′W	X	105,106
Sandiacre	Derby	SK4736	52°55·4′	1°17·6′W	T	129
Sandick	Devon	SS6232	51°4·5′	3°57·8′W	X	180
Sandick Cross	Devon	SS6331	51°4·0′	3°56·9′W	X	180
Sandieston	Renf	NS3561	55°49·1′	4°37·6′W	X	63
Sandiford Lodge	Ches	SJ5766	53°11·6′	2°38·2′W	X	117
Sandilandgate	S Lanak	NS8249	55°43·5′	3°52·3′W	X	72
Sandilands	Lincs	TF5280	53°17·9′	0°17·3′E	T	122
Sandilands	S Lanak	NS8938	55°37·6′	3°45·3′W	T	71,72
Sandilands Fm	Ches	SJ6682	53°20·3′	2°30·2′W	FM	109
Sandilands Fm	S Lanak	NS8837	55°37·1′	3°46·3′W	FM	71,72
Sandi Sand	Orkney	HY5403	58°55·0′	2°47·4′W	X	6,7
Sandiway	Ches	SJ6071	53°14·3′	2°35·6′W	T	118
Sandiway Fm	Ches	SJ6378	53°18·1′	2°32·9′W	FM	118
Sandiway Ho	Ches	SJ6271	53°14·3′	2°33·8′W	X	118
Sandiway Lodge	Ches	SJ6070	53°13·8′	2°35·5′W	X	118
Sandlands	Cumbr	NY1651	54°51·1′	3°18·1′W	X	85

Sandlands Fm	Leic	SK6818	52°45·6′	0°59·1′W	FM	129
Sandlands House Fm	N Yks	SE7778	54°11·8′	0°48·8′W	FM	100
Sandlebridge Fm	Ches	SJ8077	53°17·6′	2°17·6′W	FM	118
Sandle Dairy Fm	Hants	SU1315	50°56·3′	1°48·5′W	FM	184
Sandleford Place	W Berks	SU4764	51°22·6′	1°19·1′W	X	174
Sandleheath	Hants	SU1214	50°55·7′	1°49·4′W	T	195
Sandleheath	Hants	SU1215	50°56·3′	1°49·4′W	T	184
Sandleigh	Lincs	TF3761	53°7·9′	0°3·3′E	X	122
Sandle Manor	Hants	SU1314	50°55·7′	1°48·5′W	X	195
Sandley Stud	Dorset	ST7724	51°1·1′	2°19·3′W	X	183
Sandlin Fms	Worcs	SO7651	52°9·6′	2°20·7′W	FM	150
Sandling	Kent	TQ7558	51°17·9′	0°31·0′E	T	178,188
Sandling Park	Kent	TR1436	51°5·2′	1°3·7′E	X	179,189
Sandling Sta	Kent	TR1436	51°5·2′	1°3·7′E	X	179,189
Sand Loch	Aberd	NK0328	57°20·8′	1°56·6′W	W	38
Sandloch Hill	S Ayr	NX0574	55°1·6′	5°2·6′W	H	76
Sand Lodge	Shetld	HU4324	60°0·2′	1°13·2′W	X	4
Sandlow Green	Ches	SJ7866	53°11·7′	2°19·4′W	T	118
Sandmill Burn	D & G	NX0951	54°49·3′	4°58·0′W	W	82
Sandmill Fm	D & G	NX0861	54°54·7′	4°59·3′W	FM	82
Sandmoor Fm	Donc	SE7013	53°36·8′	0°56·1′W	FM	112
Sand Moors or South Moors	Donc	SE7113	53°36·8′	0°55·2′W	X	112
Sandness	Shetld	HU1857	60°18·1′	1°40·0′W	T	3
Sandness Hill	Shetld	HU1955	60°17·0′	1°38·9′W	H	3
Sand Nook Fm	Lincs	TF1869	53°12·5′	0°13·6′W	FM	122
Sand of Hayes	Shetld	HU3810	59°52·7′	1°18·8′W	X	4
Sand of Rothiesholm	Orkney	HY6324	59°6·3′	2°38·3′W	X	5
Sand of Sand	Shetld	HU5892	60°36·7′	0°55·9′W	X	1,2
Sand of the Crook	Orkney	HY6621	59°4·7′	2°35·1′W	X	5
Sand of Wright	Orkney	ND4293	58°49·5′	2°59·8′W	X	7
Sandon	Essex	TL7404	51°42·7′	0°31·5′E	T	167
Sandon	Herts	TL3234	51°59·6′	0°4·2′W	T	153
Sandon	Staffs	SJ9429	52°51·7′	2°4·9′W	T	127
Sandonbank	Staffs	SJ9428	52°51·2′	2°4·9′W	T	127
Sandon Bridge	Essex	TL7505	51°43·2′	0°32·4′E	X	167
Sandon Hall Fm	Essex	TL7403	51°42·1′	0°31·5′E	FM	167
Sandon Park	Staffs	SJ9529	52°51·7′	2°4·1′W	X	127
Sandons	Essex	TL5941	52°2·9′	0°19·5′E	X	154
Sandon Wood	Staffs	SJ9629	52°51·7′	2°3·2′W	F	127
Sandon Wood Fm	Staffs	SJ9630	52°52·3′	2°3·2′W	FM	127
Sandown	I of W	SZ5984	50°39·4′	1°9·5′W	T	196
Sandown Bay	I of W	SZ6083	50°38·8′	1°8·7′W	W	196
Sandown Castle	Kent	TR3754	51°14·4′	1°24·1′E	A	179
Sandown Park	Kent	TQ6040	51°8·4′	0°17·6′E	T	188
Sandown Park	Surrey	TQ1365	51°22·6′	0°22·2′W	X	176
Sandpit	Dorset	ST4204	50°50·2′	2°49·0′W	T	193
Sandpit Copse	Northnts	SP7950	52°8·8′	0°50·3′W	F	152
Sandpit Cotts	Leic	SP5097	52°34·3′	1°15·3′W	X	140
Sandpit Fm	Ches	SJ8367	53°12·2′	2°14·9′W	FM	118
Sandpit Fm	Leic	SK7226	52°49·8′	0°55·5′W	FM	129
Sandpit Fm	Norf	TM1592	52°29·2′	1°10·4′E	FM	144
Sandpit Fm	Suff	TM3265	52°14·3′	1°24·3′E	FM	156
Sandpit Fm	Warw	SP4167	52°18·2′	1°23·5′W	FM	151
Sandpit Gate	Brackn	SU9571	51°26·0′	0°37·6′W	X	175,176
Sandpit Green	Herts	SP9906	51°44·9′	0°33·6′W	X	165
Sandpit Hill	Devon	ST2209	50°52·7′	3°6·1′W	X	192,193
Sandpit Hill	Donc	SE6301	53°30·4′	1°2·6′W	X	111
Sandpit Hill	Essex	TQ8086	51°32·9′	0°36·2′E	X	178
Sandpit Hill	Norf	TL9786	52°26·4′	0°54·3′E	X	144
Sandpit Hill Fm	Bucks	SP6433	51°59·7′	1°3·7′W	FM	152,165
Sandpit Hollow	Notts	SK6933	52°53·6′	0°58·1′W	X	129
Sandpit Plantn	Norf	TL9394	52°30·8′	0°51·1′E	F	144
Sandpits	Glos	SO8329	51°57·8′	2°14·5′W	T	150
Sandpits	Glos	ST7499	51°41·6′	2°22·2′W	X	162
Sandpits Fm	Suff	TL9971	52°18·3′	0°55·5′E	FM	144,155
Sandpits Fm	Wilts	ST8968	51°24·9′	2°9·1′W	FM	173
Sandpit Wood	Kent	TQ8535	51°5·3′	0°38·9′E	F	189
Sandplace	Corn	SX2556	50°22·9′	4°27·3′W	T	201
Sand Point	N Som	ST3165	51°23·0′	2°59·1′W	X	171,182
Sandpot	Cumbr	NY7702	54°25·0′	2°20·8′W	X	91
Sandquoy	Orkney	HY5633	59°11·2′	2°45·7′W	X	5,6
Sandquoy	Orkney	HY7445	59°17·7′	2°26·9′W	X	5
Sandraw	Cumbr	NY1844	54°47·3′	3°16·1′W	X	85
Sandray	N Eil	NL6491	56°53·6′	7°30·7′W	X	31
Sand Rhyne	N Som	ST3365	51°23·0′	2°57·4′W	W	171,182
Sandridge	Devon	SX8656	50°23·8′	3°35·9′W	X	202
Sandridge	Herts	TL1710	51°46·8′	0°17·8′W	T	166
Sandridgebury	Herts	TL1610	51°46·8′	0°18·7′W	X	166
Sandridge Fm	Wilts	ST9464	51°22·7′	2°4·8′W	FM	173
Sandridge Park	Wilts	ST9364	51°22·7′	2°5·6′W	X	173
Sandriggs	Cumbr	NY7411	54°29·9′	2°23·7′W	X	91
Sandriggs Fm	Cumbr	NY5621	54°35·2′	2°40·4′W	FM	90
Sandringham	Norf	TF6928	52°49·6′	0°30·9′E	T	132
Sandringham Country Park	Norf	TF6727	52°49·1′	0°29·1′E	X	132
Sandringham Ho	Norf	TF6928	52°49·6′	0°30·9′E	X	132
Sandrocks	W Susx	TQ3222	50°59·2′	0°6·8′W	X	198
Sandroyd School	Wilts	ST9518	50°57·9′	2°3·9′W	X	184
Sandrum	D & G	NX9097	55°15·5′	3°43·4′W	X	78
Sands	Bucks	SU8393	51°38·0′	0°47·7′W	T	175
Sands Bottom	Lancs	SD5149	53°56·3′	2°44·4′W	X	102
Sandscale Haws (Nature Reserve)	Cumbr	SD1875	54°10·1′	3°14·9′W	X	96
Sandsclose	Cumbr	NY0119	54°33·6′	3°31·4′W	X	89
Sands Court	S Glos	ST7478	51°30·3′	2°22·1′W	X	172
Sandsdale	Orkney	ND3189	58°47·2′	3°11·1′W	X	7
Sands End	Ham & Ful	TQ2676	51°28·4′	0°10·8′W	T	176
Sandsend	N Yks	NZ8612	54°30·0′	0°39·9′W	T	94
Sandsend	Orkney	HY5119	59°3·6′	2°50·8′W	X	6
Sandsend	Orkney	HY5332	59°10·6′	2°48·9′W	X	5,6
Sandsend Ness	N Yks	NZ8613	54°30·5′	0°39·9′W	X	94
Sandsend Wyke	N Yks	NZ8712	54°30·0′	0°39·0′W	W	94
Sandsfield Fm	E Yorks	TA1346	53°54·1′	0°16·4′W	FM	107
Sands Fm	Durham	NZ3328	54°39·0′	1°28·9′W	FM	93
Sands Fm	E Yorks	TA2320	53°40·0′	0°7·9′W	FM	107,113
Sand's Fm	Northnts	SP6753	52°10·5′	1°0·8′W	FM	152
Sands Fm	Oxon	SU3092	51°37·8′	1°33·6′W	FM	164,174
Sands Fm	S Glos	ST7375	51°28·6′	2°22·9′W	FM	172
Sands Fm	Wilts	SU0171	51°26·5′	1°58·7′W	FM	173
Sands Fm	W Susx	TQ1518	50°57·2′	0°21·4′W	FM	198

Sands Fm	W Susx	TQ1534	51°5·9′	0°21·1′W	FM	187
Sandsfoot Castle	Dorset	SY6777	50°35·7′	2°27·6′W	A	194
Sands Geo	Orkney	ND2688	58°46·7′	3°16·3′W	X	7
Sands Hall	Durham	NZ3428	54°39·0′	1°28·0′W	X	93
Sands Ho	E Yorks	TA1968	54°5·9′	0°10·4′W	X	101
Sands Ho	E Yorks	TA2221	53°40·5′	0°8·8′W	X	107,113
Sand Side	Cumbr	SD2282	54°13·9′	3°11·4′W	T	96
Sandside	Cumbr	SD3077	54°11·3′	3°3·9′W	T	96,97
Sandside	Cumbr	SD4880	54°13·0′	2°47·4′W	T	97
Sand Side	D & G	NX6849	54°49·4′	4°2·9′W	T	83,84
Sand Side	Lancs	SD4350	53°56·8′	2°51·7′W	T	102
Sandside	Orkney	HY5907	58°57·2′	2°42·3′W	X	6
Sandside Bay	Highld	NC9665	58°33·9′	3°46·8′W	W	11
Sandside Bay	Orkney	HY5906	58°56·6′	2°42·3′W	W	6
Sandside Burn	Highld	NC9660	58°31·2′	3°46·7′W	W	11
Sandside Head	Highld	NC9566	58°34·4′	3°47·8′W	X	11
Sandside Ho	Highld	NC9565	58°33·9′	3°47·8′W	X	11
Sand Sike	Durham	NY8330	54°40·1′	2°15·4′W	W	91,92
Sand Skerry	Shetld	HU5274	60°27·1′	1°2·8′W	X	2,3
Sands of Breckon	Shetld	HP5205	60°43·7′	1°2·3′W	X	1
Sands of Cumlewick	Shetld	HU4222	59°59·1′	1°14·3′W	X	4
Sands of Doomy	Orkney	HY5534	59°11·7′	2°46·8′W	X	5,6
Sands of Evie	Orkney	HY3726	59°7·2′	3°5·5′W	X	6
Sands of Mussetter	Orkney	HY5433	59°11·1′	2°47·8′W	X	5,6
Sands of Nigg	Highld	NH7771	57°43·0′	4°3·4′W	X	21
Sands of Odie	Orkney	HY6229	59°9·0′	2°39·4′W	X	5
Sands of Woo	Orkney	HY5140	59°14·9′	2°51·1′W	X	5
Sandsound	Shetld	HU3548	60°13·2′	1°21·6′W	T	3
Sandsound Voe	Shetld	HU3548	60°13·2′	1°21·6′W	W	3
Sands Taing	Orkney	ND3694	58°50·0′	3°6·0′W	X	7
Sandstell Pt	Northum	NU0052	55°45·9′	1°59·6′W	X	75
Sands, The	Oxon	SP6201	51°42·5′	1°5·8′W	X	164,165
Sands, The	Shrops	SJ7504	52°38·2′	2°21·8′W	X	127
Sands, The	Swan	SS4885	51°32·8′	4°11·1′W	X	159
Sandstone Trail	Ches	SJ5051	53°3·5′	2°44·4′W	X	117
Sandstone Trail	Ches	SJ5462	53°9·4′	2°40·9′W	X	117
Sands Water	Orkney	ND2493	58°49·3′	3°18·5′W	W	7
Sands Wood	E Yorks	TA1267	54°5·4′	0°16·8′W	F	101
Sands Wood	N Yks	SE8774	54°9·5′	0°39·6′W	F	101
Sand Tarn	Cumbr	SD7598	54°22·9′	2°22·7′W	W	98
Sandtoft	N Lincs	SE7408	53°34·0′	0°52·5′W	T	112
Sandtop Bay	Pemb	SS1296	51°38·1′	4°42·6′W	W	158
Sanduck	Devon	SX7683	50°38·2′	3°44·8′W	X	191
Sand Vatn	Shetld	HU5137	60°7·1′	1°4·4′W	W	4
Sand Villa	Lancs	SD4350	53°56·8′	2°51·7′W	X	102
Sandvis Geo	Shetld	HU4117	59°56·4′	1°15·5′W	X	4
Sand Voe	Shetld	HU3446	60°12·1′	1°22·7′W	W	4
Sandvoe	Shetld	HU3591	60°36·3′	1°21·1′W	T	1,2
Sand Voe	Shetld	HU3691	60°36·3′	1°20·0′W	W	1,2
Sand Water	Shetld	HP5103	60°42·7′	1°3·4′W	W	1
Sand Water	Shetld	HU2582	60°31·5′	1°32·2′W	W	3
Sand Water	Shetld	HU2644	60°11·0′	1°31·4′W	W	4
Sand Water	Shetld	HU2953	60°15·9′	1°28·1′W	W	3
Sand Water	Shetld	HU3147	60°12·6′	1°25·9′W	W	3
Sand Water	Shetld	HU4154	60°16·4′	1°15·0′W	W	3
Sand Water	Shetld	HU4274	60°27·1′	1°13·7′W	W	2,3
Sand Water	Shetld	HU4366	60°22·8′	1°12·7′W	W	2,3
Sand Water	Shetld	HU4690	60°35·7′	1°9·1′W	W	1,2
Sand Water	Shetld	HU5298	60°40·0′	1°2·4′W	W	1
Sandwater Hill	Shetld	HP5103	60°42·7′	1°3·4′W	H	1
Sandwater Hill	Shetld	HU5398	60°40·0′	1°1·3′W	H	1
Sandwath	Cumbr	NY3047	54°49·0′	3°4·9′W	X	85
Sandwath	Cumbr	NY7004	54°26·1′	2°27·3′W	X	91
Sandwath Ho	N Yks	NZ1711	54°29·9′	1°43·8′W	X	92
Sandway	Kent	TQ8851	51°13·9′	0°42·0′E	T	189
Sandwell	Sand	SP0289	52°30·2′	1°57·8′W	T	139
Sandwell Old Manor	Devon	SX7559	50°25·3′	3°45·2′W	X	202
Sandwell Valley Country Park	Sand	SP0292	52°31·8′	1°57·8′W	X	139
Sandwich	Kent	TR3358	51°16·6′	1°20·8′E	T	179
Sandwich Bay	Kent	TR3759	51°17·1′	1°24·3′E	W	179
Sandwich Bay Estate	Kent	TR3657	51°16·0′	1°23·4′E	T	179
Sandwich Flats	Kent	TR3560	51°17·7′	1°22·6′E	X	179
Sandwich Stud	Cambs	TL6862	52°14·1′	0°28·0′E	X	154
Sandwick	Cumbr	NY4219	54°34·0′	2°53·4′W	X	90
Sandwick	Orkney	HY2519	59°3·4′	3°18·0′W	X	6
Sandwick	Orkney	ND4388	58°46·8′	2°58·7′W	X	7
Sand Wick	Orkney	ND4389	58°47·4′	2°58·7′W	W	7
Sandwick	Shetld	HP6102	60°42·1′	0°52·5′W	X	1
Sand Wick	Shetld	HP6202	60°42·0′	0°51·4′W	W	1
Sand Wick	Shetld	HU2777	60°28·8′	1°30·0′W	W	3
Sandwick	Shetld	HU2877	60°28·8′	1°28·9′W	X	3
Sand Wick	Shetld	HU3633	60°5·1′	1°20·7′W	W	4
Sandwick	Shetld	HU3924	60°0·2′	1°17·5′W	X	4
Sand Wick	Shetld	HU4323	59°59·6′	1°13·3′W	W	4
Sandwick	Shetld	HU4323	59°59·6′	1°13·3′W	T	4
Sandwick	Shetld	HU4568	60°23·9′	1°10·5′W	X	2,3
Sand Wick	Shetld	HU4668	60°23·9′	1°9·4′W	W	2,3
Sand Wick	Shetld	HU4744	60°10·9′	1°8·7′W	W	4
Sand Wick	Shetld	HU5361	60°20·0′	1°1·9′W	W	2,3
Sandwick	Shetld	HU5461	60°20·0′	1°0·8′W	T	2
Sand Wick	Shetld	HU5496	60°38·9′	1°0·2′W	W	1
Sandwick Ho	Orkney	ND4389	58°47·4′	2°58·7′W	X	7
Sandwith	Cumbr	NX9614	54°30·9′	3°36·0′W	T	89
Sandwith Moor	N Yks	SE2152	53°58·1′	1°40·4′W	X	104
Sandwith Newtown	Cumbr	NX9614	54°30·9′	3°36·0′W	T	89
Sandwith Wham	N Yks	SE1774	54°9·9′	1°44·0′W	W	99
Sand Wood	Cambs	TL2353	52°9·9′	0°11·7′W	F	153
Sandwood	Highld	NC2264	58°31·9′	5°3·0′W	X	9
Sandwood Bay	Highld	NC2266	58°33·0′	5°3·1′W	W	9
Sandwood Ho	E Yorks	SE7632	53°47·0′	0°50·4′W	X	105,106
Sandwood Loch	Highld	NC2264	58°31·9′	5°3·0′W	W	9
Sandy	Beds	TL1649	52°7·9′	0°17·9′W	T	153
Sandy	Carm	SN4900	51°40·9′	4°10·7′W	T	159
Sandy Balls	Hants	SU1614	50°55·7′	1°46·0′W	X	195
Sandy Bank	Lincs	TF2655	53°4·9′	0°6·7′W	T	122
Sandybank	Orkney	HY5431	59°10·1′	2°47·8′W	X	5,6
Sandybank	Orkney	HY6426	59°7·4′	2°37·2′W	X	5
Sandy Bank	Shrops	SJ5136	52°55·4′	2°43·3′W	X	126
Sandy Barrow	Dorset	SY7289	50°42·2′	2°23·4′W	A	194
Sandy Bay	Brig	SS8276	51°28·5′	3°41·6′W	W	170
Sandy Bay	Devon	SY0379	50°36·4′	3°21·9′W	W	192
Sandy Bay	Pemb	SS1297	51°38·7′	4°42·6′W	W	158
Sandy Beck	N Yks	SD9755	53°59·7′	2°2·3′W	X	103
Sandy Bottom	Norf	TL9787	52°26·9′	0°54·3′E	X	144
Sandybraes	Northum	NZ0379	55°6·6′	1°56·8′W	X	87
Sandybrook Hall	Derby	SK1748	53°2·0′	1°44·4′W	X	119
Sandybrow	Ches	SJ5767	53°12·1′	2°38·2′W	X	117
Sandy Brow	Cumbr	NY3047	54°49·0′	3°4·9′W	X	85
Sandy Brow	Know	SJ4497	53°28·2′	2°50·2′W	X	108
Sandy Burn	S Lanak	NS9143	55°40·4′	3°43·6′W	W	71,72
Sandy Carrs	Durham	NZ3942	54°46·5′	1°23·2′W	T	88
Sandy Cove	Corn	SX0949	50°18·8′	4°40·6′W	W	200,204
Sandy Crags	Northum	NY9797	55°16·3′	2°2·4′W	X	81
Sandycroft	Flint	SJ3366	53°11·5′	2°59·8′W	T	117
Sandy Cross	E Susx	TQ5820	50°57·7′	0°15·4′E	T	199
Sandy Cross	Heref	SO6756	52°12·3′	2°28·6′W	X	149
Sandy Cross	Surrey	SU8847	51°13·2′	0°44·0′W	T	186
Sandyden Ho	E Susx	TQ5831	51°3·6′	0°15·7′E	X	188
Sandy Dike	N Yks	SE0969	54°7·2′	1°51·3′W	W	99
Sandy Down	Hants	SZ3199	50°47·6′	1°33·2′W	T	196
Sandydown Fm	Hants	SU3835	51°7·0′	1°27·0′W	FM	185
Sandy Downs	Angus	NO5531	56°28·4′	2°43·4′W	X	54
Sandy Edge	Scot Bord	NT5201	55°18·3′	2°44·9′W	X	79
Sandy End Fm	Norf	TF5204	52°37·0′	0°15·1′E	FM	143
Sandy Fm	Wilts	ST8385	51°34·1′	2°14·3′W	FM	173
Sandyford	Angus	NO4154	56°40·7′	2°57·3′W	X	54
Sandyford	C of Stoke	SJ8552	53°4·1′	2°13·0′W	T	118
Sandy Ford	Derby	SK3251	53°3·6′	1°30·9′W	X	119
Sandy Ford	Devon	SX5787	50°40·1′	4°1·0′W	X	191
Sandyford	D & G	NY2093	55°13·7′	3°15·0′W	X	79
Sandyford	Durham	NY9647	54°49·3′	2°3·3′W	X	87
Sandyford	N Lanak	NS7961	55°49·9′	3°55·5′W	X	64
Sandyford	Northum	NZ0781	55°7·6′	1°53·0′W	X	81
Sandyford	S Ayr	NS3825	55°29·8′	4°33·4′W	X	70
Sandyford Burn	Northum	NU1127	55°32·4′	1°49·1′W	W	75
Sandyford Cottage	Northum	NZ0258	54°55·2′	1°57·7′W	X	87
Sandyford Fm	Staffs	SJ8536	52°55·5′	2°13·0′W	FM	127
Sandyford Moor	Northum	NU0926	55°31·9′	1°51·0′W	X	75
Sandyford Rigg	Northum	NY7162	54°57·4′	2°26·7′W	X	86,87
Sandyfords Fm	Northum	NT9238	55°38·4′	2°7·2′W	FM	74,75
Sandyford Sike	Northum	NY7551	54°51·4′	2°22·9′W	W	86,87
Sandy Furze	Notts	SK7690	53°24·3′	0°51·0′W	X	112
Sandygap Fm	Cumbr	SD5377	54°11·4′	2°42·8′W	FM	97
Sandygate	Devon	SX8674	50°33·5′	3°36·2′W	T	191
Sandy Gate	Devon	SX9691	50°42·8′	3°28·0′W	T	192
Sandygate	I of M	SC3797	54°20·8′	4°30·0′W	T	95
Sandy Gate	N Yks	SE0271	54°8·3′	1°57·7′W	X	98
Sandygate	Sheff	SK3186	53°22·4′	1°31·6′W	T	110,111
Sandygate Fm	Lincs	TF3816	52°43·7′	0°3·0′E	FM	131
Sandy Geo	Orkney	HY5322	59°5·2′	2°48·7′W	X	5,6
Sandy Geo	Orkney	HY6628	59°8·5′	2°35·2′W	X	5
Sandy Geo	Orkney	ND1799	58°52·5′	3°25·9′W	X	7
Sandyhall	Orkney	HY3919	59°3·5′	3°3·3′W	X	6
Sandyhaugh	D & G	NY3792	55°13·3′	2°59·0′W	X	79
Sandy Haven	Pemb	SM8507	51°43·5′	5°6·4′W	T	157
Sandyhaven Pill	Pemb	SM8507	51°43·5′	5°6·4′W	W	157
Sandy Heath	Beds	TL1949	52°7·8′	0°15·3′W	X	153
Sandy Heys	Derby	SK0789	53°24·1′	1°53·3′W	X	110
Sandy Hill	Aberd	NO5985	56°57·5′	2°40·0′W	X	44
Sandyhill	Cumbr	SD4797	54°22·2′	2°48·5′W	X	97
Sandyhill	Fife	NO5912	56°18·2′	2°39·3′W	X	59
Sandy Hill	Norf	TG2927	52°47·7′	1°24·2′E	X	133,134
Sandy Hill	N Yks	SD8290	54°18·6′	2°16·2′W	X	98
Sandy Hill	N Yks	SE4877	54°11·4′	1°15·4′W	X	100
Sandy Hill	Orkney	ND4487	58°46·3′	2°57·6′W	H	7
Sandy Hill	Scot Bord	NT1043	55°40·6′	3°25·4′W	H	72
Sandyhill	Shrops	SJ4036	52°55·3′	2°53·1′W	X	126
Sandy Hill	Suff	TM1352	52°7·7′	1°7·1′E	X	156
Sandy Hill	Suff	TM4890	52°27·3′	1°39·4′E	X	134
Sandyhill Burn	Moray	NJ2949	57°31·3′	3°10·7′W	W	28
Sandy Hill Fm	Glos	SP1615	51°50·2′	1°45·7′W	FM	163
Sandy Hill Fm	Northnts	SP7979	52°24·4′	0°49·9′W	FM	141
Sandyhillock	Aberd	NJ7304	57°7·8′	2°26·3′W	X	38
Sandy Hillock	Angus	NO2680	56°54·6′	3°12·5′W	H	44
Sandyhillock	Moray	NJ2545	57°29·6′	3°14·6′W	X	28
Sandyhills	Aberd	NJ6763	57°39·6′	2°32·7′W	X	29
Sandyhills	D & G	NX8855	54°52·9′	3°44·3′W	X	84
Sandyhills Bay	D & G	NX8955	54°52·9′	3°43·4′W	W	84
Sandy Hirst	E Loth	NT6379	56°0·4′	2°35·2′W	X	67
Sandy Ho	Northum	NT9332	55°35·1′	2°6·2′W	X	74,75
Sandy Hole Pass	Devon	SX6281	50°37·0′	3°56·7′W	X	191
Sandyholm	S Lanak	NS8148	55°42·9′	3°53·2′W	X	72
Sandy Knowe	D & G	NS7110	55°22·3′	4°1·7′W	X	71
Sandyknowe	Scot Bord	NT4054	55°46·8′	2°57·0′W	X	66,73
Sandyknowe	Scot Bord	NT6434	55°36·1′	2°33·8′W	X	74
Sandylake	Corn	SX1260	50°24·8′	4°38·4′W	T	200
Sandylands	Lancs	SD4263	54°3·8′	2°52·8′W	T	96,97
Sandylands	Northum	NU0304	55°20·1′	1°56·7′W	X	81
Sandylands	Somer	ST1222	50°59·7′	3°14·9′W	T	181,193
Sandy Lane	Brad	SE1035	53°48·9′	1°50·5′W	T	104
Sandy Lane	E Yorks	TA0863	54°3·3′	0°20·6′W	X	101
Sandylane	Stock	SJ9891	53°25·2′	2°1·4′W	X	109
Sandylane	Swan	SS5588	51°34·6′	4°5·2′W	T	159
Sandy Lane	Wilts	ST9667	51°24·4′	2°3·1′W	T	173
Sandy Lane	Wrex	SJ4040	52°57·5′	2°53·2′W	T	117
Sandylane Covert	Suff	TM4576	52°19·9′	1°36·2′E	F	156
Sandylane Fm	Ches	SJ8564	53°10·6′	2°13·1′W	FM	118
Sandy Lane Fm	Devon	SS4636	51°6·4′	4°11·6′W	FM	180
Sandy Lane Fm	Flint	SJ3360	53°8·2′	2°59·7′W	FM	117
Sandylane Fm	Oxon	SP6404	51°44·1′	1°4·0′W	FM	164,165
Sandy Lane Fm	St Hel	SJ5588	53°23·5′	2°40·2′W	FM	108
Sandy Lane Fm	Suff	TM4670	52°16·6′	1°36·8′E	FM	156
Sandy Lane Fm	Thurr	TQ5580	51°30·1′	0°14·4′E	FM	177
Sandylane Plantation	Beds	SP9635	52°0·5′	0°35·7′W	F	153
Sandy Lees Fm	Stock on T	NZ3918	54°33·6′	1°23·4′W	FM	93
Sandy Leys Fm	Staffs	SJ9431	52°52·8′	2°4·9′W	FM	127
Sandy Loch	Aberd	NO2286	56°57·8′	3°16·5′W	W	44
Sandy Loch	Orkney	HY2103	58°54·7′	3°21·8′W	W	6,7
Sandy Loch Reservoir	Shetld	HU4440	60°8·8′	1°12·0′W	W	4
Sandy Lochs	Shetld	HU3277	60°28·8′	1°24·6′W	W	3
Sandy Lochs	Shetld	HU3387	60°34·2′	1°23·4′W	W	1,2
Sandymere	Devon	SS4330	51°3·1′	4°14·0′W	W	180
Sandymoor Cross	Devon	SX3898	50°45·8′	4°17·4′W	X	190
Sandymount Covert	Suff	TM4872	52°17·6′	1°38·6′E	F	156
Sandy Mouth	Corn	SS2009	50°51·4′	4°33·1′W	W	190
Sandypark	Devon	SS6832	51°4·6′	3°52·7′W	X	180
Sandy Park	Devon	SX7189	50°41·4′	3°49·2′W	X	191
Sandy Park	Devon	SX9691	50°42·8′	3°28·0′W	X	192
Sandypits Fm	Essex	TL7615	51°48·6′	0°33·6′E	FM	167
Sandy Point	Essex	TM0914	51°47·4′	1°2·2′E	X	168,169
Sandy Point	Essex	TM2218	51°49·2′	1°13·7′E	X	169
Sandyrigs Wood	Fife	NO5002	56°12·7′	2°47·9′W	F	59
Sandy's Belt	Norf	TF7426	52°48·4′	0°35·3′E	F	132
Sandys Fm	Devon	ST2107	50°51·7′	3°7·0′W	FM	192,193
Sandy's Gears	Northum	NY6996	55°15·7′	2°28·8′W	X	80
Sandy's Hill	Dorset	SU0510	50°53·6′	1°55·3′W	X	195
Sandysike	Cumbr	NY3965	54°58·8′	2°56·8′W	X	85
Sandysike	Cumbr	NY5164	54°58·3′	2°45·5′W	X	86
Sandy Sike	Northum	NY7777	55°5·5′	2°21·2′W	W	86,87
Sandy Sike	N Yks	SD8188	54°17·5′	2°17·1′W	W	98
Sandysike Rigg	Northum	NY8288	55°11·4′	2°16·5′W	H	80
Sandy Sikes Gill	N Yks	SE0473	54°9·4′	1°55·9′W	W	98
Sandy's Letch	N Tyne	NZ2474	55°3·8′	1°37·0′W	W	88
Sandy's Mill	E Loth	NT5575	55°58·2′	2°42·8′W	X	66
Sandystones	Scot Bord	NT5926	55°31·8′	2°38·5′W	X	73,74
Sandy Voe	Shetld	HU3537	60°7·2′	1°21·7′W	W	4
Sandy Warren	Beds	TL1848	52°7·3′	0°16·2′W	F	153
Sandy Water	Shetld	HU3086	60°33·7′	1°26·7′W	W	1,3
Sandy Water	Shetld	HU4998	60°40·0′	1°5·7′W	W	1
Sandy Way	Devon	SX6669	50°30·6′	3°53·0′W	X	202
Sandyway	Heref	SO4925	51°55·5′	2°44·1′W	X	162
Sandy Way	I of W	SZ4582	50°38·4′	1°21·4′W	T	196
Sandyway	Somer	SS7933	51°5·3′	3°43·3′W	X	180
Sandyway	Staffs	SK1008	52°40·4′	1°50·7′W	X	128
Sandyway	Worcs	SO8759	52°14·0′	2°11·0′W	X	150
Sandyway Cross	Devon	SS7933	51°5·3′	3°43·3′W	X	180
Sandyway Heads	Northum	NZ0474	55°3·9′	1°55·8′W	X	87
Sandyway Wood	Corn	SX0758	50°23·6′	4°42·6′W	F	200
Sandywell Park	Glos	SP0120	51°52·9′	1°58·7′W	X	163
Sandy Wood	Essex	TL7515	51°48·6′	0°32·7′E	F	167
Sane Copse	Northnts	SP8554	52°10·9′	0°45·0′W	F	152
Sanfitt	Brad	SE0550	53°57·0′	1°55·0′W	X	104
Sangar	Orkney	HY5041	59°15·4′	2°52·1′W	X	5
San Geo	Shetld	HU5390	60°35·7′	1°1·4′W	X	1,2
Sango Bay	Highld	NC4167	58°34·0′	4°43·5′W	W	9
Sangobeg	Highld	NC4266	58°33·5′	4°42·5′W	T	9
Sango Island	Corn	SX4253	50°21·6′	4°12·9′W	X	201
Sangomore	Highld	NC4067	58°34·0′	4°44·6′W	T	9
Sanguishayes Fm	Devon	ST0403	50°49·4′	3°21·4′W	FM	192
Sanham Fm	Leic	SK7215	52°43·9′	0°55·6′W	FM	129
Sanham Green	W Berks	SU3366	51°23·8′	1°31·1′W	T	174
Saniger Fm	Glos	SO6701	51°42·6′	2°28·3′W	FM	162
Saniger Sands	Glos	SO6500	51°42·1′	2°30·0′W	X	162
Sankence Lodge	Norf	TG1725	52°47·0′	1°13·5′E	X	133,134
Sankey Bridges	Warr	SJ5887	53°22·9′	2°37·5′W	T	108
Sankey Brook	Warr	SJ5991	53°25·1′	2°36·6′W	W	108
Sankey Valley Park	St Hel	SJ5397	53°28·3′	2°42·1′W	X	108
Sankey Valley Park	St Hel	SJ5595	53°27·2′	2°40·3′W	X	108
Sankey Valley Park	Warr	SJ5888	53°23·5′	2°37·5′W	X	108
Sankyns Green	Worcs	SO7964	52°16·7′	2°18·1′W	T	138,150
Sanna	Highld	NM4469	56°44·8′	6°10·8′W	T	47
Sanna Bay	Highld	NM4369	56°44·8′	6°11·8′W	W	47
Sannacott Fm	Devon	SS7528	51°2·5′	3°46·6′W	FM	180
Sannaig	Arg & Bt	NR5164	55°48·6′	5°58·0′W	X	61
Sanna Point	Highld	NM4370	56°45·3′	6°11·8′W	X	39,47
Sanndabhaig	N Eil	NB4432	58°12·4′	6°21·0′W	T	8
Sanndabhaig	N Eil	NF8243	57°22·2′	7°17·0′W	T	22
Sannet Hall Fm	N Yks	SD8368	54°6·7′	2°15·2′W	FM	98
Sannox	N Ayr	NS0145	55°39·7′	5°9·4′W	T	63,69
Sannox Bay	N Ayr	NS0145	55°39·7′	5°9·4′W	W	63,69
Sanquhar	D & G	NS7809	55°21·8′	3°55·1′W	T	71,78
Sanquhar Castle	D & G	NS7809	55°21·8′	3°55·1′W	A	71,78
Sanquhar Mains	Moray	NJ0456	57°35·3′	3°35·9′W	X	27
Sansaw	Shrops	SJ5023	52°48·4′	2°44·1′W	X	126
Sansaw Heath	Shrops	SJ5122	52°47·8′	2°43·2′W	T	126
Sans Fm	Wilts	ST9324	51°1·2′	2°5·6′W	FM	184
Sansome Fm	Worcs	SO7938	52°2·6′	2°18·0′W	FM	150
Sansom's Plantn	Suff	TL8872	52°19·1′	0°45·9′E	F	144,155
Sansom Wood	Notts	SK5851	53°3·4′	1°7·7′W	F	120
Sansom Wood Fm	Notts	SK5951	53°3·4′	1°6·8′W	FM	120
Sanson Seal	Northum	NT9654	55°47·0′	2°3·4′W	X	74,75
Santa Pod Raceway	Beds	SP9560	52°14·0′	0°36·1′W	X	153
Santery Hill Wood	Worcs	SO9173	52°21·5′	2°7·5′W	F	139
Santingley Grange	Wakf	SE3816	53°38·6′	1°25·1′W	X	110,111
Santley	Shrops	SJ3400	52°35·9′	2°58·1′W	X	126
Santon	Cumbr	NY1001	54°24·0′	3°22·8′W	T	89
Santon	I of M	SC3273	54°7·8′	4°33·9′W	X	95
Santon	N Lincs	SE9212	53°36·0′	0°36·2′W	T	112
Santon Barn	Beds	SP9156	52°11·9′	0°39·7′W	X	152
Santon Bridge	Cumbr	NY1101	54°24·1′	3°21·8′W	T	89
Santon Burn	I of M	SC3074	54°8·3′	4°35·7′W	W	95
Santon Downham	Suff	TL8187	52°27·3′	0°40·2′E	T	144
Santon Fm	Kent	TR2661	51°18·4′	1°14·9′E	FM	179
Santon Head	I of M	SC3370	54°6·2′	4°32·8′W	X	95
Santon Ho	Norf	TL8287	52°27·3′	0°41·1′E	X	144
Santon Ho	Surrey	TQ2348	51°13·3′	0°13·9′W	X	187
Santon Warren	Norf	TL8288	52°27·8′	0°41·1′E	F	144
Santon Wood	N Lincs	SE9310	53°34·9′	0°35·3′W	F	112
Santoo Head	Orkney	ND2096	58°50·9′	3°22·7′W	X	7
Sanvey Castle	Leic	SK7805	52°38·5′	0°50·4′W	A	141
Saorphin	Arg & Bt	NM3920	56°18·3′	6°12·7′W	X	48
Sapcote	Leic	SP4893	52°32·2′	1°17·1′W	T	140
Sapey Bridge	Heref	SO7255	52°11·8′	2°24·2′W	T	149
Sapey Brook	Heref	SO7057	52°12·9′	2°25·9′W	W	149
Sapey Common	Heref	SO7064	52°16·6′	2°26·0′W	T	138,149
Saphock	Aberd	NJ7629	57°21·3′	2°23·5′W	X	38
Sapiston	Suff	TL9175	52°20·6′	0°48·6′E	T	144
Sapley	Cambs	TL2473	52°20·7′	0°10·4′W	T	153
Sapley Farm Ho	Hants	SU5148	51°14·0′	1°15·8′W	X	185

Sapley Park Fm	Cambs	TL2474	52°21·2′	0°10·4′W	FM	142
Saplings	Aberd	NJ4918	57°15·2′	2°50·3′W	X	37
Saplings of Logie	Aberd	NJ4818	57°15·2′	2°51·3′W	X	37
Saplings, The	Shrops	SO4991	52°31·1′	2°44·7′W	X	137,138
Saplins Wood	Shrops	SJ6205	52°38·7′	2°33·3′W	F	127
Sappers Fm	Essex	TQ7591	51°35·7′	0°32·0′E	FM	178
Sapperton	Derby	SK1834	52°54·4′	1°43·5′W	T	128
Sapperton	Glos	SO9403	51°43·8′	2°4·8′W	T	163
Sapperton	Lincs	TF0133	52°53·3′	0°29·5′W	T	130
Sapperton Manor Fm	E Susx	TQ5919	50°57·1′	0°16·2′E	FM	199
Sappington Court	Kent	TR1152	51°13·9′	1°1·7′E	X	179,189
Sappy Moss	Cumbr	SD6985	54°15·8′	2°28·1′W	X	98
Saracens	Kent	TQ9344	51°10·0′	0°46·0′E	X	189
Saracen's Head	Lincs	TF3427	52°49·7′	0°0·3′W	T	131
Sarah's Cottage	I of M	SC2984	54°13·6′	4°37·0′W	X	95
Sarah's Wood	Leic	SK3115	52°44·1′	1°32·0′W	F	128
Saratt Bottom	Herts	TQ0398	51°40·5′	0°30·2′W	X	166,176
Sarclet	Highld	ND3443	58°22·5′	3°7·2′W	T	12
Sarclet Head	Highld	ND3543	58°22·5′	3°6·2′W	X	12
Sardesons Fm	Lincs	TF1044	52°59·2′	0°21·3′W	FM	130
Sardis	Carm	SN5806	51°44·3′	4°3·0′W	T	159
Sardis	Pemb	SN1306	51°43·5′	4°42·1′W	T	158
Saredon Hall Fm	Staffs	SJ9508	52°40·4′	2°4·0′W	FM	127
Saredon Hill	Staffs	SJ9407	52°39·9′	2°4·9′W	H	127,139
Sares Wood	Dorset	SY7992	50°43·9′	2°17·5′W	F	194
Sarffle	Wrex	SJ1433	52°53·5′	3°16·3′W	X	125
Sargeantlaw	Renf	NS4559	55°48·2′	4°27·9′W	X	64
Sargill Beck	N Yks	SD8892	54°19·7′	2°10·7′W	W	98
Sargill Parks	N Yks	SD9192	54°19·7′	2°7·9′W	X	98
Sarisbury	Hants	SU5008	50°52·4′	1°17·0′W	T	196
Sarkfoot Point	Cumbr	NY3365	54°58·8′	3°2·4′W	X	85
Sarkhall	Cumbr	NY3471	55°2·0′	3°1·5′W	X	85
Sarkshields	D & G	NY2774	55°3·6′	3°8·1′W	X	85
Sarkside	D & G	NY3070	55°1·4′	3°5·3′W	X	85
Sarn	Brig	SS9083	51°32·3′	3°34·8′W	T	170
Sarn	Conwy	SH8674	53°15·3′	3°42·1′W	X	116
Sarn	Flint	SJ1179	53°18·3′	3°19·7′W	T	116
Sarn	Powys	SN9597	52°33·9′	3°32·5′W	X	136
Sarn	Powys	SO2090	52°30·4′	3°10·3′W	T	137
Sarn	Shrops	SJ3135	52°54·7′	3°1·2′W	X	126
Sarnau	Carm	SN2932	51°57·9′	4°29·0′W	X	145
Sarnau	Carm	SN3318	51°50·4′	4°25·1′W	X	159
Sarnau	Carm	SN4324	51°53·8′	4°16·5′W	X	159
Sarnau	Carm	SN7829	51°57·0′	3°46·1′W	X	146,160
Sarnau	Cered	SN3150	52°7·6′	4°27·7′W	T	145
Sarnau	Denb	SJ0852	53°3·7′	3°22·0′W	X	116
Sarnau	Gwyn	SH9739	52°56·6′	3°31·6′W	T	125
Sarnau	Powys	SJ2315	52°43·9′	3°8·0′W	T	126
Sarnau	Powys	SO0232	51°58·9′	3°25·2′W	T	160
Sarnau Fawr	Cered	SN6577	52°22·7′	3°58·6′W	X	135
Sarnau Fm	Carm	SN3120	51°51·4′	4°26·9′W	FM	145,159
Sarn-bâch	Gwyn	SH3026	52°48·5′	4°30·9′W	T	123
Sarnbigog	Powys	SN9198	52°34·4′	3°36·1′W	X	136
Sarn Br	Powys	SJ2212	52°42·2′	3°8·9′W	X	126
Sarn Br	Wrex	SJ4344	52°59·7′	2°50·6′W	X	117
Sarnden	Kent	TQ7932	51°3·8′	0°33·7′E	X	188
Sarnesfield	Heref	SO3750	52°8·9′	2°54·9′W	T	148,149
Sarnesfield Coppice	Heref	SO3752	52°10·0′	2°54·9′W	F	148,149
Sarness Fm	Kent	TR1149	51°12·3′	1°1·6′E	FM	179,189
Sarnfadog	I of Angl	SH4281	53°18·4′	4°21·9′W	X	114,115
Sarn Galed	Flint	SJ2267	53°11·9′	3°9·7′W	X	117
Sarngoch	Carm	SN2321	51°51·8′	4°33·9′W	X	145,158
Sarn Gynfelyn	Cered	SN5885	52°26·9′	4°5·0′W	X	135
Sarn Helen	Conwy	SH7654	53°4·4′	3°50·7′W	X	115
Sarn Helen	Gwyn	SH7232	52°52·5′	3°53·7′W	X	124
Sarn Helen	Gwyn	SH7241	52°57·3′	3°53·9′W	X	124
Sarn Helen	Powys	SN8711	51°47·4′	3°37·9′W	X	160
Sarn Helen	Powys	SN9626	51°55·6′	3°30·4′W	X	160
Sarn Helen	Powys	SN9754	52°10·7′	3°30·0′W	X	147
Sarn Helen (Roman Road)	Carm	SN6442	52°3·8′	3°58·6′W	R	146
Sarn Helen (Roman Road)	Cered	SN6449	52°7·6′	3°58·8′W	R	146
Sarn Helen (Roman Road)	Cered	SN6459	52°13·0′	3°59·1′W	R	146
Sarn Helen (Roman Road)	Cered	SN6466	52°16·8′	3°59·2′W	A	135
Sarn Helen (Roman Road)	Gwyn	SH7232	52°52·5′	3°53·7′W	R	124
Sarn Helen (Roman Road)	Gwyn	SH7241	52°57·3′	3°53·9′W	R	124
Sarn Helen (Roman Road)	Nth Pt Talb	SN8003	51°43·0′	3°43·8′W	R	170
Sarn Helen (Roman Road)	Powys	SN8711	51°47·4′	3°37·9′W	R	160
Sarn Helen (Roman Road)	Powys	SN9626	51°55·6′	3°30·4′W	R	160
Sarn Hill Wood	Worcs	SO8533	52°0·0′	2°12·7′W	F	150
Sarn Hir	Gwyn	SH5827	52°49·6′	4°6·1′W	X	124
Sarnlas	Carm	SN1718	51°50·1′	4°39·0′W	X	158
Sarn Meyllteyrn	Gwyn	SH2332	52°51·6′	4°37·4′W	T	123
Sarn Park Service Area	Brig	SS9082	51°32·5′	3°34·8′W	X	170
Sarn-y-bryn-caled	Powys	SJ2105	52°38·5′	3°9·7′W	X	126
Sarn-y-geifr	Carm	SN7940	52°3·0′	3°45·5′W	X	146,147,160
Saron	Carm	SN3737	52°0·7′	4°22·1′W	T	145
Saron	Carm	SN6012	51°47·6′	4°1·4′W	T	159
Saron	Denb	SJ0260	53°7·9′	3°27·5′W	T	116
Saron	Gwyn	SH4658	53°6·1′	4°17·6′W	T	115,123
Saron	Gwyn	SH5265	53°9·9′	4°12·4′W	T	114,115
Sarratt	Herts	TQ0499	51°41·0′	0°29·3′W	T	166,176
Sarratt Bottom	Herts	TQ0398	51°40·5′	0°30·2′W	T	
Sarratt Mill Ho	Herts	TQ0398	51°40·5′	0°30·2′W	X	166,176
Sarre	Kent	TR2564	51°20·1′	1°14·2′E	T	179
Sarre Penn	Kent	TR2364	51°20·1′	1°12·5′E	W	179
Sarre Wall	Kent	TR2464	51°20·1′	1°13·3′E	A	179
Sars Brook	Oxon	SP2722	51°54·0′	1°36·1′W	W	163
Sarscow Fm	Lancs	SD5018	53°39·6′	2°45·0′W	FM	108
Sarsden	Oxon	SP2823	51°54·5′	1°35·2′W	T	163
Sarsden Glebe Fm	Oxon	SP2923	51°54·5′	1°34·3′W	FM	164
Sarsden Halt	Oxon	SP2724	51°55·1′	1°36·1′W	T	163
Sarsden Ho	Oxon	SP2822	51°54·0′	1°35·2′W	X	163
Sarsden Lodge	Oxon	SP2721	51°53·4′	1°36·1′W	X	163
Sarsen Stones or Grey Wethers	Wilts	SU1371	51°26·5′	1°48·4′W	X	173
Sarsgrove Fm	Oxon	SP3024	51°55·1′	1°33·4′W	FM	164
Sarsgrove Wood	Oxon	SP3024	51°55·1′	1°33·4′W	F	164
Sarsgrum	Highld	NC3764	58°32·3′	4°47·5′W	X	9
Sarson Wood	Hants	SU3042	51°10·8′	1°33·9′W	F	185
Sarstay	N Eil	NF9775	57°40·0′	7°4·4′W	X	18

Sartfell	I of M	SC3387	54°15·3′	4°33·4′W	H	95
Sartfield	I of M	SC3599	54°21·8′	4°32·0′W	T	95
Sartfield Fm	I of M	SC3187	54°15·2′	4°35·2′W	FM	95
Sart Fm	Devon	ST2800	50°47·9′	3°0·9′W	FM	193
Sarthwaite	Cumbr	SD6992	54°19·6′	2°28·2′W	X	98
Sascombe Vineyard	Cambs	TL6955	52°10·3′	0°28·7′E	X	154
Sascott	Shrops	SJ4211	52°41·9′	2°51·1′W	T	126
Saswick Ho	Lancs	SD4237	53°49·8′	2°52·5′W	X	102
Satchells	Scot Bord	NT5021	55°29·1′	2°47·0′W	X	73
Satellite Earth Station	Corn	SW7221	50°3·0′	5°10·7′W	X	204
Satellite Earth Station	Heref	SO4237	52°1·9′	2°50·3′W	X	149,161
Satinstown Fm	E Susx	TQ5921	50°58·2′	0°16·3′E	FM	199
Satley	Durham	NZ1143	54°47·2′	1°49·3′W	T	88
Satmar	Kent	TR2539	51°6·6′	1°13·3′E	T	179
Satnall Hills	Staffs	SJ9820	52°46·9′	2°1·4′W	H	127
Satran	Highld	NG4030	57°17·5′	6°18·5′W	T	32
Satron	N Yks	SD9397	54°22·4′	2°6·0′W	T	98
Satron Hangers	N Yks	SD9497	54°22·4′	2°5·1′W	X	98
Satron High Walls	N Yks	SD9496	54°21·8′	2°5·1′W	X	98
Satron Moor	N Yks	SD9395	54°21·3′	2°6·0′W	X	98
Satron Side	N Yks	SD9497	54°22·4′	2°5·1′W	X	98
Satter Hill	Aberd	NJ5922	57°17·5′	2°40·4′W	H	37
Satterleigh	Devon	SS6622	50°59·1′	3°54·2′W	T	180
Satterthwaite	Cumbr	SD3392	54°19·4′	3°1·4′W	T	96,97
Satur	D & G	NY2275	55°4·1′	3°12·9′W	X	85
Satura Crag	Cumbr	NY4213	54°30·8′	2°53·3′W	X	90
Saturday Br	Lincs	TF3520	52°45·9′	0°0·5′E	X	131
Saturland	C of Glas	NS5160	55°48·9′	4°22·2′W	X	64
Satwell	Oxon	SU7083	51°32·7′	0°59·0′W	T	175
Satyrhills	Aberd	NJ9957	57°36·4′	2°0·5′W	X	30
Saucebridge	Northnts	SP7857	52°12·6′	0°51·1′W	X	152
Saucelands Fm	W Susx	TQ1121	50°58·9′	0°24·7′W	FM	198
Sauchans	Stir	NN7000	56°10·8′	4°5·2′W	X	57
Sauchanwood Hill	Pth & Kin	NN8703	56°12·6′	3°48·9′W	H	58
Sauchar Point	Fife	NT4999	56°11·1′	2°48·9′W	X	59
Sauchen	Aberd	NJ6911	57°11·6′	2°30·3′W	T	38
Sauchenbush	Aberd	NJ6001	57°6·2′	2°39·2′W	X	37
Sauchenbush	Aberd	NJ7206	57°8·9′	2°27·3′W	X	38
Sauchenbush	Aberd	NJ7560	57°38·0′	2°24·7′W	X	29
Sauchenbush	Moray	NJ2751	57°32·9′	3°12·7′W	X	28
Sauchenford Smallholdings	Stir	NS8288	56°4·5′	3°53·3′W	X	57,65
Sauchenhillock	Aberd	NJ8627	57°20·3′	2°13·5′W	X	38
Sauchenloan	Aberd	NJ6735	57°24·5′	2°32·5′W	X	29
Sauchenloan	Aberd	NJ7625	57°19·2′	2°23·5′W	X	38
Sauchenshaw	Aberd	NO8595	57°3·0′	2°14·4′W	X	38,45
Sauchentree	Aberd	NJ8436	57°25·1′	2°15·5′W	X	29,30
Sauchentree	Aberd	NJ8963	57°39·7′	2°10·6′W	X	30
Saucher	Pth & Kin	NO1933	56°29·2′	3°18·5′W	T	53
Sauchet Water	E Loth	NT6173	55°57·2′	2°37·0′W	W	67
Sauchie	Clackm	NS8994	56°7·8′	3°46·7′W	T	58
Sauchie	Pth & Kin	NO0719	56°21·5′	3°29·9′W	X	58
Sauchieburn	Aberd	NO6669	56°48·9′	2°33·0′W	X	45
Sauchieburn Ho	Stir	NS7789	56°4·9′	3°58·1′W	X	57
Sauchie Home Fm	Stir	NS7788	56°4·4′	3°58·1′W	FM	57
Sauchie Law	Scot Bord	NT2910	55°23·0′	3°6·8′W	H	79
Sauchinford Burn	Stir	NS8586	56°3·4′	3°50·4′W	W	65
Sauchope	Fife	NO6208	56°16·0′	2°36·4′W	X	59
Sauchrie	S Ayr	NS3014	55°23·7′	4°40·6′W	X	70
Sauchrie Burn	S Ayr	NS2815	55°24·2′	4°42·6′W	W	70
Saudi Field	Shetld	HU4791	60°36·2′	1°8·0′W	H	1,2
Sauf Hall	Darl	NZ3719	54°34·1′	1°25·2′W	X	93
Saughall	Ches	SJ3670	53°13·6′	2°57·1′W	T	117
Saughall Massie	Wirral	SJ2588	53°23·3′	3°7·3′W	T	108
Saugh Burn	D & G	NX4387	55°9·4′	4°27·4′W	W	77
Saugh Burn	D & G	NX4784	55°7·9′	4°23·6′W	W	77
Saughen Braes	W Dunb	NS4678	55°58·5′	4°27·6′W	X	64
Saugh Hill	D & G	NY2499	55°17·0′	3°11·4′W	H	79
Saugh Hill	S Ayr	NX2097	55°14·3′	4°49·4′W	H	76
Saugh Hill Plantn	D & G	NY2594	55°14·3′	3°10·3′W	F	79
Saugh Ho	Northum	NZ0385	55°9·8′	1°56·7′W	X	81
Saugh Ho	Northum	NZ0879	55°6·6′	1°52·0′W	X	88
Saughieside Hill	Northum	NT8624	55°30·8′	2°12·9′W	H	74
Saughland	Midlo	NT4161	55°50·6′	2°56·1′W	X	66
Saughy Law	Scot Bord	NT3845	55°41·9′	2°58·8′W	X	73
Saughmont	Angus	NO5340	56°33·2′	2°45·4′W	X	54
Saughs	C of Glas	NS6468	55°53·4′	4°10·0′W	X	64
Saughs	Cumbr	NY5179	55°6·4′	2°45·7′W	X	86
Saughs	Moray	NJ4762	57°38·9′	2°52·8′W	X	28,29
Saugh Sikes	Durham	NZ0139	54°45·0′	1°58·6′W	W	92
Saughton	C of Edin	NT2071	55°55·8′	3°16·4′W	T	66
Saughtree	Scot Bord	NY5696	55°15·6′	2°41·1′W	T	80
Saughtree Fell	Scot Bord	NY5698	55°16·7′	2°41·1′W	H	80
Saughtreegate	Cumbr	NY5351	54°51·3′	2°43·5′W	X	86
Saughtree Grain	Scot Bord	NY5699	55°17·2′	2°41·1′W	X	80
Saughtrees	Cumbr	NY5178	55°5·9′	2°45·6′W	X	86
Saughtrees	D & G	NY1294	55°14·2′	3°22·6′W	X	78
Saughwells	Moray	NJ3855	57°35·1′	3°1·8′W	X	28
Saughy Crag	Northum	NT7703	55°19·5′	2°21·3′W	X	80
Saughy Hill	Northum	NT8910	55°23·3′	2°10·0′W	H	80
Saughy Rigg	Northum	NY7368	55°0·6′	2°24·9′W	X	86,87
Saughy Sike	Northum	NY7474	55°3·8′	2°24·0′W	W	86,87
Saul	Glos	SO7409	51°47·0′	2°22·2′W	T	162
Saul Lodge	Glos	SO7408	51°46·4′	2°22·2′W	X	162
Saulmore	Arg & Bt	NM8933	56°26·8′	5°25·0′W	X	49
Saul's Fm	Devon	SS6712	50°53·8′	3°53·1′W	FM	180
Saul Warth	Glos	SO7408	51°46·4′	2°22·2′W	X	162
Sauncy Wood	Herts	TL1515	51°49·5′	0°19·5′W	F	166
Saundby	Notts	SK7888	53°23·2′	0°49·2′W	T	112,120,121
Saundby Park	Notts	SK7788	53°23·2′	0°50·1′W	F	112,120
Saundby Park Fm	Notts	SK7688	53°23·2′	0°51·0′W	FM	112,120
Saundercroft Fm	Devon	SY0197	50°46·1′	3°23·9′W	FM	192
Saunders Fm	Dorset	ST7405	50°50·9′	2°21·8′W	FM	194
Saundersfoot	Pemb	SN1304	51°42·5′	4°42·0′W	T	158
Saundersfoot Bay	Pemb	SN1404	51°42·5′	4°41·1′W	W	158
Saunders Ho	Durham	NZ0811	54°29·9′	1°52·2′W	X	92
Saunderton	Bucks	SP7901	51°42·4′	0°51·0′W	T	165
Saunderton Lee	Bucks	SU8099	51°41·3′	0°50·2′W	T	165
Saunderton Sta	Bucks	SU8198	51°40·7′	0°49·3′W	X	165
Saunich	Pth & Kin	NN6463	56°44·6′	4°13·0′W	X	42

Saunton	Devon	SS4537	51°6·9′	4°12·5′W	T	180
Saunton Down	Devon	SS4338	51°7·4′	4°14·2′W	X	180
Saunton Sands	Devon	SS4435	51°5·8′	4°13·3′W	X	180
Sauol-Less	Orkney	HY5050	59°20·3′	2°52·2′W	X	5
Sausthorpe	Lincs	TF3869	53°12·2′	0°4·4′E	T	122
Savage's Fm	Wilts	SU1831	51°4·9′	1°44·2′W	FM	184
Savage's Wood	S Glos	ST6282	51°32·4′	2°32·5′W	F	172
Savage Wood	Suff	TM4884	52°24·1′	1°39·2′E	F	156
Saval	Highld	NC5808	58°2·6′	4°23·9′W	T	16
Savalbeg	Highld	NC5907	58°2·1′	4°22·8′W	X	16
Savary	Highld	NM6346	56°33·0′	5°50·9′W	X	49
Savary Bay	Highld	NM6345	56°32·5′	5°50·9′W	W	49
Savary Glen	Highld	NM6447	56°33·6′	5°50·0′W	X	49
Savary River	Highld	NM6447	56°33·6′	5°50·0′W	W	49
Sava Skerry	Shetld	HU5360	60°19·5′	1°1·9′W	X	2,3
Savath	Corn	SX0261	50°25·2′	4°46·9′W	X	200
Savay Fm	Bucks	TQ0487	51°34·6′	0°29·6′W	FM	176
Savecroft Fm	Bucks	SP9404	51°43·8′	0°37·9′W	FM	165
Savee Fm	Oxon	SP4045	52°6·3′	1°24·6′W	FM	151
Savenick	Orkney	ND5299	58°52·8′	2°49·5′W	X	6,7
Saveock	Corn	SW7545	50°16·0′	5°9·1′W	T	204
Saverley Green	Staffs	SJ9638	52°56·6′	2°3·2′W	T	127
Savernake Forest	Wilts	SU2266	51°23·8′	1°40·6′W	F	174
Savernake Lodge	Wilts	SU2366	51°23·8′	1°39·8′W	X	174
Saverock	Orkney	HY4212	58°59·7′	3°0·1′W	X	6
Savers Field	Shetld	HU3925	60°0·7′	1°17·5′W	X	4
Savick Brook	Lancs	SD4830	53°46·1′	2°46·9′W	W	102
Savick Brook	Lancs	SD5835	53°48·8′	2°37·9′W	W	102
Savile Park	Cald	SE0823	53°42·4′	1°52·3′W	T	104
Savile Town	Kirk	SE2420	53°40·8′	1°37·8′W	T	104
Saville	Orkney	HY6844	59°17·1′	2°33·2′W	X	5
Saville Green	Lancs	SD8832	53°47·3′	2°10·5′W	X	103
Saville's Pool	Warw	SP4452	52°10·1′	1°21·0′W	W	151
Savil Less	Orkney	HY5053	59°21·9′	2°52·3′W	X	5
Savill Gardens, The	Surrey	SU9770	51°25·5′	0°35·9′W	X	175,176
Savin Royd Wood	Wakf	SE3013	53°37·0′	1°32·4′W	F	110,111
Savio Ho	Ches	SJ9477	53°17·6′	2°5·0′W	X	118
Saviskaill	Orkney	HY4033	59°11·0′	3°2·5′W	X	5,6
Saviskaill Bay	Orkney	HY4233	59°11·1′	3°0·4′W	W	5,6
Saviskaill Head	Orkney	HY4034	59°11·6′	3°2·5′W	X	5,6
Savoch	Aberd	NK0458	57°37·0′	1°55·5′W	X	30
Savock	Aberd	NJ9523	57°18·1′	2°4·5′W	X	38
Savourys	Devon	SS6913	50°54·3′	3°51·4′W	X	180
Sawbridge	Warw	SP5065	52°17·1′	1°15·6′W	T	151
Sawbridge Hall	Cumbr	NY7112	54°30·4′	2°26·5′W	X	91
Sawbridgeworth	Herts	TL4815	51°49·1′	0°9·2′E	T	167
Sawbury Hill	Heref	SO6255	52°11·8′	2°33·0′W	X	149
Sawcliffe Fm	N Lincs	SE9114	53°37·1′	0°37·0′W	FM	112
Sawcliffe Village	Wakf	SE4114	53°37·5′	1°22·4′W	A	111
Sawcombe Fm	Glos	ST7994	51°38·9′	2°17·8′W	FM	162,172
Sawddle fechan	Carm	SN7620	51°52·1′	3°47·7′W	W	160
Sawdern	Pemb	SM8903	51°41·4′	5°2·8′W	X	157,158
Sawdern Point	Pemb	SM8803	51°41·4′	5°3·6′W	X	157,158
Sawdon	N Yks	SE9484	54°14·8′	0°33·0′W	T	101
Sawdon	N Yks	SE9485	54°15·4′	0°33·0′W	X	94,101
Sawdon Beck	N Yks	SE9584	54°14·8′	0°32·1′W	W	101
Sawdon Dale	N Yks	SE9484	54°14·8′	0°33·0′W	X	101
Sawdon Heights	N Yks	SE9285	54°15·4′	0°34·8′W	X	94,101
Sawerston	E Ayr	NS5129	55°32·2′	4°21·2′W	X	70
Sawgate Fm	Leic	SK7917	52°44·9′	0°49·4′W	FM	129
Sawkill Fm	N Yks	SE7569	54°6·9′	0°50·7′W	FM	100
Sawley	Derby	SK4731	52°52·7′	1°17·7′W	T	129
Sawley	Lancs	SD7746	53°54·8′	2°20·6′W	T	103
Sawley	N Yks	SE2467	54°6·1′	1°37·6′W	T	99
Sawley Cut	Leic	SK4730	52°52·2′	1°17·7′W	W	129
Sawley Grange	Lancs	SD7946	53°54·8′	2°18·8′W	X	103
Sawley Hall	N Yks	SE2566	54°5·6′	1°36·6′W	X	99
Sawley Lodge	Lancs	SD7747	53°55·4′	2°20·6′W	X	103
Sawley Moor	N Yks	SE2367	54°6·1′	1°38·5′W	X	99
Sawley Moor Fm	N Yks	SE2367	54°6·1′	1°38·5′W	FM	99
Sawmill Cottage	Cumbr	NY4501	54°24·3′	2°50·4′W	X	90
Sawmill Cottages	Cumbr	NY5727	54°38·4′	2°39·6′W	X	91
Sawmill Croft	Aberd	NJ6850	57°32·6′	2°31·6′W	X	29
Sawmill Wood	Durham	NZ1246	54°48·8′	1°48·4′W	F	88
Sawn Moor	Roth	SK4988	53°23·4′	1°15·4′W	X	111,120
Sawny Bean's Cave	S Ayr	NX0987	55°8·7′	4°59·4′W	X	76
Sawood	Brad	SE0434	53°48·4′	1°55·9′W	T	104
Sawpit Wood	Bucks	SP6740	52°3·5′	1°1·0′W	F	152
Sawrey Ground	Cumbr	SD3399	54°23·2′	3°1·5′W	X	96,97
Sawston	Cambs	TL4849	52°7·4′	0°10·1′E	T	154
Sawston Hall	Cambs	TL4849	52°7·4′	0°10·1′E	A	154
Sawtrees Fm	Herts	TL3817	51°50·3′	0°0·6′E	FM	166
Sawtrees Wood	Herts	TL3818	51°50·8′	0°0·6′E	F	166
Sawtry	Cambs	TL1683	52°26·2′	0°17·2′W	T	142
Sawtry Fen	Cambs	TL1883	52°26·2′	0°15·4′W	X	142
Sawtry Roughs	Cambs	TL1882	52°25·6′	0°15·5′W	X	142
Saw Wood	Leeds	SE3839	53°51·0′	1°24·9′W	F	104
Saw Wood Ho	Leeds	SE3738	53°50·5′	1°25·8′W	X	104
Sawyer's	Suff	TL9037	52°0·2′	0°46·5′E	X	155
Sawyer's Fm	Essex	TL6007	51°44·6′	0°19·4′E	FM	167
Sawyer's Hall	Essex	TQ5994	51°37·6′	0°18·2′E	X	167,177
Sawyer's Hill	Somer	ST1620	50°58·6′	3°11·4′W	T	181,193
Sawyers Hill	Wilts	SU0290	51°36·8′	1°57·9′W	T	163,173
Saxa's Kettle	Shetld	HP6515	60°49·0′	0°47·8′W	X	1
Saxa Vord	Shetld	HP6316	60°49·6′	0°50·0′W	H	1
Saxa-Vord	Shetld	HP6413	60°48·0′	0°48·9′W	X	1
Saxby	Leic	SK8220	52°46·5′	0°46·7′W	T	130
Saxby	Lincs	TF0086	53°21·9′	0°29·4′W	T	112,121
Saxby	W Susx	SU9603	50°49·3′	0°37·8′W	T	197
Saxby All Saints	N Lincs	SE9916	53°38·1′	0°29·7′W	T	112
Saxby All Saints Br	N Lincs	SE9716	53°38·1′	0°31·6′W	X	112
Saxby All Saints Carrs	N Lincs	SE9715	53°37·6′	0°31·6′W	X	112
Saxby Cliff	Lincs	SK9785	53°21·4′	0°32·1′W	X	112,121
Saxby Lowlands Fm	Lincs	TF0286	53°21·9′	0°27·6′W	FM	112,121
Saxbys	Kent	TQ4741	51°9·2′	0°6·5′E	X	188
Saxby Wolds	N Lincs	TA0017	53°38·6′	0°28·8′W	X	112
Saxelbye	Leic	SK7020	52°46·6′	0°58·2′W	T	129
Saxelbye Park	Leic	SK6920	52°46·6′	0°58·2′W	X	129
Saxelbye Road Fm	Leic	SK7019	52°46·1′	0°57·3′W	FM	129
Saxelby Pastures	Leic	SK6922	52°47·7′	0°58·2′W	X	129

Saxham Business Park	Suff	TL8065	52°15·4'	0°38·6'E	X	155
Saxham Street	Suff	TM0861	52°12·7'	1°3·1'E	T	155
Saxilby	Lincs	SK8975	53°16·1'	0°39·5'W	T	121
Saxilby Moor	Lincs	SK8874	53°15·6'	0°40·4'W	X	121
Saxilby Sykes	Lincs	SK8777	53°17·2'	0°41·3'W	X	121
Saxley Fm	Hants	SU3240	51°9·7'	1°32·2'W	FM	185
Saxlingham	Norf	TG0239	52°54·9'	1°0·7'E	T	133
Saxlingham Green	Norf	TM2496	52°31·2'	1°18·5'E	T	134
Saxlingham Nethergate	Norf	TM2297	52°31·8'	1°16·8'E	T	134
Saxlingham Thorpe	Norf	TM2197	52°31·8'	1°15·9'E	X	134
Saxmundham	Suff	TM3863	52°13·0'	1°29·5'E	T	156
Saxonbury	E Susx	TQ5732	51°4·2'	0°14·8'E	A	188
Saxonbury Fm	E Susx	TQ5832	51°4·2'	0°15·7'E	FM	188
Saxonbury Hill	E Susx	TQ5733	51°4·7'	0°14·9'E	H	188
Saxon Court	E Susx	TQ5123	50°59·4'	0°9·5'E	X	199
Saxondale	Notts	SK6839	52°56·9'	0°58·9'W	T	129
Saxon Down	E Susx	TQ4410	50°52·5'	0°3·2'E	X	198
Saxon Fm	Cambs	TL5976	52°21·8'	0°20·5'E	FM	143
Saxon Hall	Cambs	TL6760	52°13·0'	0°27·1'E	X	154
Saxon Howe	Pth & Kin	NO0035	56°30·0'	3°37·0'W	X	52,53
Saxon Shore Way	Kent	TQ6874	51°26·6'	0°25·4'E	X	177,178
Saxon Shore Way	Kent	TQ9429	51°1·9'	0°46·4'E	X	189
Saxon Shore Way	Kent	TR3656	51°15·5'	1°23·3'E	X	179
Saxon Shore Way	Medway	TQ7176	51°27·7'	0°28·1'E	X	178
Saxon Shore Way	Medway	TQ7876	51°27·5'	0°34·1'E	X	178
Saxon's Lode	Worcs	SO8638	52°2·6'	2°11·9'W	X	150
Saxon's Lowe	Staffs	SJ8736	52°55·5'	2°11·2'W	A	127
Saxon Street	Cambs	TL6759	52°12·5'	0°27·0'E	T	154
Saxstead Bottom	Suff	TM2665	52°14·4'	1°19·0'E	X	156
Saxstead Lodge	Suff	TM2664	52°13·9'	1°19·0'E	X	156
Saxtead	Suff	TM2665	52°14·4'	1°19·0'E	T	156
Saxtead Green	Suff	TM2564	52°13·9'	1°18·1'E	T	156
Saxtead Little Green	Suff	TM2565	52°14·5'	1°18·1'E	T	156
Saxted Bottom	Suff	TM3047	52°4·6'	1°21·8'E	X	169
Saxthorpe	Norf	TG1130	52°49·8'	1°8·3'E	T	133
Saxton	N Yks	SE4736	53°49·3'	1°16·7'W	T	105
Saxton Grange	N Yks	SE4838	53°50·4'	1°15·8'W	X	105
Saxton's Fm	W Susx	TQ1927	51°2·0'	0°17·8'W	FM	187,198
Saxton's Lings	Notts	SK6738	52°56·3'	0°59·8'W	X	129
Saxworthy	Devon	SS3717	50°56·0'	4°18·8'W	X	190
Saybridge Lodge	Essex	TL6103	51°42·4'	0°20·2'E	X	167
Sayerland Ho	E Susx	TQ5806	50°50·1'	0°15·0'E	X	199
Sayers Common	W Susx	TQ2618	50°57·1'	0°12·0'W	T	198
Sayers Croft	Surrey	TQ0840	51°9·2'	0°27·0'W	X	187
Sayes Court	Kent	TR0266	51°21·6'	0°54·5'E	X	178
Sayes Park Fm	Herts	TL4513	51°48·0'	0°6·6'E	FM	167
Sayles Fm	Cumbr	SD3086	54°16·1'	3°4·1'W	FM	96,97
Saynden Fm	Kent	TQ7642	51°9·2'	0°31·4'E	FM	188
Say's Copse	Northnts	SP7243	52°5·1'	0°56·6'W	F	152
Says Court Fm	S Glos	ST6981	51°31·9'	2°26·4'W	FM	172
Saywell Fm	Kent	TQ8757	51°17·1'	0°41·3'E	FM	178
Saywood	Notts	SK7264	53°10·3'	0°55·0'W	X	120
S Burn of Gremista	Shetld	HU4542	60°9·9'	1°10·9'W	W	4
Scaalie Point	Shetld	HU3628	60°2·4'	1°20·7'W	X	4
Scabbacombe Head	Devon	SX9251	50°21·2'	3°30·7'W	X	202
Scabbacombe Sands	Devon	SX9151	50°21·2'	3°31·6'W	X	202
Scabba Wood	Donc	SE5201	53°30·4'	1°12·5'W	F	111
Scabbed Craigs	D & G	NX5285	55°8·5'	4°18·9'W	X	77
Scabcleuch	Scot Bord	NT2414	55°25·1'	3°11·6'W	X	79
Scabcleuch Burn	Scot Bord	NT2415	55°25·6'	3°11·6'W	W	79
Scabcleuch Hill	Scot Bord	NT2314	55°25·1'	3°12·6'W	H	79
Scab Craigs	D & G	NX4183	55°7·2'	4°29·2'W	X	77
Scabgill	S Lanak	NS9449	55°43·6'	3°40·8'W	X	72
Scabra Head	Orkney	HY3631	59°9·9'	3°6·7'W	X	6
Scackleton	N Yks	SE6472	54°8·6'	1°0·8'W	T	100
Scackleton Grange	N Yks	SE6372	54°8·6'	1°1·7'W	X	100
Scackleton Low Moor	N Yks	SE6471	54°8·1'	1°0·8'W	X	100
Scackleton Moor	N Yks	SE6572	54°8·6'	0°59·9'W	F	100
Scadabhagh	N Eil	NG1792	57°49·9'	6°45·6'W	T	14
Scadbury Park	Brom	TQ4570	51°24·9'	0°5·5'E	X	177
Scaddow Rig	Scot Bord	NT3630	55°33·8'	3°0·5'W	X	73
Scaddows, The	Derby	SK3322	52°47·9'	1°30·2'W	X	128
Scadghill Fm	Corn	SS2210	50°52·0'	4°31·4'W	FM	190
Scad Head	Orkney	HY2800	58°53·1'	3°14·5'W	X	6,7
Scad Hill	Aberd	NJ4222	57°17·4'	2°57·3'W	H	37
Scad Hill	Pth & Kin	NN9302	56°12·2'	3°43·0'W	H	58
Scad Law	Northum	NY7596	55°15·7'	2°23·2'W	X	80
Sca Fell	Cumbr	NY2006	54°26·8'	3°13·6'W	X	89,90
Scafell	Powys	SO0891	52°30·8'	3°20·9'W	X	136
Scafell Pike	Cumbr	NY2107	54°27·4'	3°12·7'W	H	89,90
Scaffacre Fm	Leic	SK4422	52°47·9'	1°20·4'W	FM	129
Scaffold Hill Fm	N Tyne	NZ3069	55°1·1'	1°31·4'W	FM	88
Scaftworth	Notts	SK6691	53°24·9'	1°0·0'W	T	111
Scaftworth Grange	Notts	SK6692	53°25·5'	1°0·0'W	X	111
Scagglethorpe	N Yks	SE8372	54°8·5'	0°43·3'W	T	100
Scagglethorpe Grange	N Yks	SE8273	54°9·0'	0°44·3'W	X	100
Scagglethorpe Moor	N Yks	SE5355	53°59·5'	1°11·1'W	X	105
Scaife Ho	Durham	NZ1020	54°34·8'	1°50·3'W	X	92
Scair Tacks	Orkney	HY6844	59°17·1'	2°33·2'W	X	5
Scaitcliffe	Lancs	SD7528	53°45·1'	2°22·3'W	T	103
Scalabhal	N Eil	NB1419	58°4·3'	6°50·6'W	H	13,14
Scalabhal Beag	N Eil	NB1618	58°3·9'	6°48·5'W	H	13,14
Scalabhal Mula	N Eil	NB1420	58°4·9'	6°50·6'W	H	13,14
Scalabhal Shanndaig	N Eil	NB1518	58°3·8'	6°49·5'W	H	13,14
Scaladal Burn	Highld	NG1840	57°22·1'	6°41·0'W	W	23
Scalan	Moray	NJ2419	57°15·6'	3°15·1'W	X	36
Scalands Fm	E Susx	TQ7222	50°58·5'	0°27·4'E	FM	199
Scalands Wood	E Susx	TQ7122	50°58·5'	0°26·5'E	F	199
Scalasaig	Arg & Bt	NR3994	56°4·3'	6°11·2'W	T	61
Scalby	E Yorks	SE8329	53°45·3'	0°44·1'W	T	106
Scalby	N Yks	TA0190	54°18·0'	0°26·5'W	T	101
Scalby Hayes	N Yks	SE9991	54°18·5'	0°28·3'W	X	94,101
Scalby Lodge	N Yks	TA0291	54°18·5'	0°25·5'W	X	101
Scalby Mills	N Yks	TA0390	54°18·0'	0°24·6'W	X	101
Scalby Nabs	N Yks	SE9990	54°18·0'	0°28·3'W	X	94,101
Scalby Ness Rocks	N Yks	TA0391	54°18·5'	0°24·6'W	X	101
Scald Bank	Lancs	SD9243	53°53·2'	2°6·9'W	X	103
Scald End	Beds	TL0457	52°12·3'	0°28·3'W	T	153
Scaldersitch	Staffs	SK1159	53°7·9'	1°49·7'W	X	119
Scalderskew	Cumbr	NY0807	54°27·3'	3°24·7'W	X	89
Scalderskew Wood	Cumbr	NY0808	54°27·8'	3°24·7'W	F	89
Scald Hill	Northum	NT9221	55°29·2'	2°7·2'W	H	74,75
Scaldhill	Northum	NT9327	55°32·4'	2°6·2'W	X	74,75
Scald Hill	Oxon	SU6393	51°38·2'	1°5·0'W	X	164,175
Scaldhurst Fm	Essex	TQ8794	51°37·0'	0°42·5'E	FM	168,178
Scalding	Powys	SO1342	52°4·4'	3°15·8'W	X	148,161
Scald Law	Midlo	NT1961	55°50·4'	3°17·2'W	H	65,66
Scald Law	Northum	NY9488	55°11·4'	2°5·2'W	X	80
Scald Pike	Northum	NY6387	55°10·8'	2°34·4'W	X	80
Scaldwell	Northnts	SP7672	52°20·7'	0°52·7'W	T	141
Scaldwell Spinney	Northnts	SP7673	52°21·2'	0°52·6'W	F	141
Scale	Cumbr	SD7693	54°20·2'	2°21·7'W	X	98
Scale	Lancs	SD6265	54°5·0'	2°34·4'W	X	97
Scalebank	Cumbr	NY7144	54°47·7'	2°26·6'W	X	86,87
Scalebarrow Knott	Cumbr	NY5115	54°31·9'	2°45·0'W	H	90
Scale Beck	Cumbr	NY0905	54°26·2'	3°23·8'W	W	89
Scale Beck	Cumbr	NY1517	54°32·7'	3°18·4'W	W	89
Scale Beck	Cumbr	NY6614	54°31·5'	2°31·1'W	W	91
Scale Beck	Cumbr	NY6714	54°31·5'	2°30·2'W	X	91
Scaleber	Lancs	SD6373	54°9·3'	2°33·6'W	X	97
Scaleber	N Yks	SD9253	53°58·6'	2°6·9'W	X	103
Scaleber Beck	N Yks	SD8361	54°2·9'	2°15·2'W	W	98
Scaleber Fm	N Yks	SD6371	54°8·3'	2°33·6'W	FM	97
Scaleber Force	N Yks	SD8462	54°3·5'	2°14·2'W	W	98
Scaleber Park Hospl	Brad	SE1545	53°54·3'	1°45·9'W	X	104
Scaleby	Cumbr	NY4463	54°57·8'	2°52·1'W	T	85
Scaleby Castle	Cumbr	NY4462	54°57·2'	2°52·0'W	X	85
Scalebyhill	Cumbr	NY4463	54°57·8'	2°52·1'W	T	85
Scaleby Moss	Cumbr	NY4363	54°57·8'	2°53·0'W	F	85
Scaleclose Force	Cumbr	NY2414	54°31·2'	3°10·0'W	W	89,90
Scale Cross	N Yks	NZ6708	54°28·0'	0°57·6'W	X	94
Scale Fm	N Yks	SD8075	54°10·5'	2°18·0'W	FM	98
Scale Foot	N Yks	NZ6708	54°28·0'	0°57·6'W	X	94
Scale Force	Cumbr	NY1517	54°32·7'	3°18·4'W	W	89
Scalegate	Cumbr	NY4820	54°34·6'	2°47·8'W	X	90
Scalegill	Cumbr	NY1935	54°42·5'	3°15·0'W	X	89,90
Scalegill	Cumbr	NY5805	54°26·6'	2°38·4'W	X	91
Scale Gill Foot Moss	Cumbr	SD7684	54°15·3'	2°21·7'W	X	98
Scalegill Hall	Cumbr	NX9914	54°30·9'	3°33·2'W	X	89
Scalegill Wood	Cumbr	NY1843	54°46·8'	3°16·1'W	F	85
Scale Green	Cumbr	SD3292	54°19·4'	3°2·3'W	F	96,97
Scale Hall	Lancs	SD4662	54°3·3'	2°49·1'W	T	97
Scale Hill	Cumbr	NY1521	54°34·9'	3°18·5'W	X	89
Scalehill	Cumbr	NY5438	54°44·3'	2°42·4'W	X	90
Scalehill	D & G	NY1579	55°6·1'	3°19·5'W	X	85
Scale Ho	Cumbr	NY5845	54°48·1'	2°38·8'W	X	86
Scale Ho	N Yks	SD9756	54°0·2'	2°2·3'W	X	103
Scale House Barn	Lancs	SD5866	54°5·5'	2°38·1'W	X	97
Scalehow Beck	Cumbr	NY4118	54°33·5'	2°54·3'W	W	90
Scalehowe Wood	Cumbr	NY7123	54°36·3'	2°26·5'W	F	91
Scale Knott	Cumbr	NY1517	54°32·7'	3°18·4'W	X	89
Scale Knotts	Cumbr	NY4505	54°26·5'	2°50·5'W	X	90
Scalelands	Cumbr	NY0315	54°31·5'	3°29·5'W	X	89
Scale Mire	N Yks	SD7270	54°7·8'	2°25·3'W	X	98
Scale Nab	E Yorks	TA2073	54°8·6'	0°9·4'W	X	101
Scale Rigg	Cumbr	NY5743	54°47·1'	2°39·7'W	X	86
Scales	Cumbr	NY1616	54°32·2'	3°17·5'W	X	89
Scales	Cumbr	NY1625	54°37·0'	3°17·6'W	X	89
Scales	Cumbr	NY3426	54°37·7'	3°0·9'W	T	90
Scales	Cumbr	NY3733	54°41·5'	2°58·2'W	X	90
Scales	Cumbr	NY4505	54°26·5'	2°50·5'W	X	90
Scales	Cumbr	NY5742	54°46·5'	2°39·7'W	T	86
Scales	Cumbr	SD2772	54°8·6'	3°6·6'W	T	96,97
Scales	Cumbr	SD7487	54°16·9'	2°23·5'W	X	98
Scales Br	Wilts	SU1355	51°17·9'	1°48·4'W	X	173
Scalesbrook Wood	Suff	TM4079	52°21·6'	1°31·9'E	F	156
Scalesceugh	Cumbr	NY4449	54°50·2'	2°51·9'W	X	85
Scales Cross	Northum	NZ0356	54°54·2'	1°56·8'W	X	87
Scales Demesne	Cumbr	NY1846	54°48·4'	3°16·1'W	X	85
Scales Farm	Cumbr	NY4239	54°44·8'	2°53·6'W	FM	90
Scales Fell	Cumbr	NY3327	54°38·3'	3°1·9'W	X	90
Scales Fm	Cumbr	NY0929	54°39·1'	3°24·2'W	FM	89
Scales Fm	Cumbr	NY4820	54°34·6'	2°47·8'W	FM	90
Scales Gill	N Yks	SE1549	53°56·1'	1°45·9'W	X	104
Scales Hall	Cumbr	NY4240	54°45·3'	2°53·7'W	X	85
Scales House Fm	N Yks	SE1649	53°56·5'	1°45·0'W	FM	104
Scalesmoor	Cumbr	NY0821	54°34·8'	3°25·0'W	X	89
Scales Moor	Cumbr	NY5743	54°47·1'	2°39·7'W	H	86
Scales Moor	N Yks	SD7177	54°11·5'	2°26·3'W	X	98
Scales Park	Cumbr	SD2771	54°8·0'	3°6·6'W	X	96,97
Scales Park	Herts	TL4133	51°58·9'	0°3·6'E	F	167
Scales Tarn	Cumbr	NY3228	54°38·8'	3°2·8'W	W	90
Scalestones Point	Lancs	SD4565	54°4·9'	2°50·0'W	X	97
Scalewood	D & G	NY2075	55°4·0'	3°14·7'W	X	85
Scalford	Leic	SK7624	52°48·7'	0°51·9'W	T	129
Scalford Hall	Leic	SK7423	52°48·2'	0°53·7'W	X	129
Scalibar Fm	N Yks	SE3754	53°59·1'	1°25·7'W	FM	104
Scaling	N Yks	NZ7413	54°30·7'	0°51·0'W	T	94
Scaling Dam	Red & Cl	NZ7412	54°30·1'	0°51·0'W	X	94
Scaling Dam Res	N Yks	NZ7412	54°30·1'	0°51·0'W	W	94
Scalla Field	Shetld	HU3615	59°55·4'	1°20·9'W	X	4
Scalla Field	Shetld	HU3857	60°18·0'	1°18·3'W	H	2,3
Scallafield Scord	Shetld	HU3857	60°18·0'	1°18·3'W	X	2,3
Scalla Moor	N Yks	SE7663	54°3·7'	0°49·9'W	X	100
Scalla Moor Fm	N Yks	SE8184	54°15·0'	0°45·0'W	FM	100
Scallasaig	Highld	NG8619	57°13·0'	5°32·2'W	X	33
Scallastle	Arg & Bt	NM6938	56°28·9'	5°44·7'W	X	49
Scallastle Bay	Arg & Bt	NM6939	56°29·4'	5°44·7'W	W	49
Scallastle River	Arg & Bt	NM6937	56°28·4'	5°44·6'W	W	49
Scalley Fm	Northnts	SP9873	52°21·0'	0°33·3'W	FM	141,153
Scalloch Burn	S Ayr	NX2887	55°9·1'	4°41·5'W	W	76
Scallow	Cumbr	NY0719	54°33·7'	3°25·9'W	X	89
Scalloway	Shetld	HU4039	60°8·3'	1°16·3'W	T	4
Scallow Beck	Cumbr	NY0719	54°33·7'	3°25·9'W	W	89
Scallow Grove	N Lincs	SE9003	53°31·2'	0°38·1'W	X	112
Scallows Hall	Lincs	TF2494	53°25·9'	0°7·6'W	X	113
Scalm Park Fm	N Yks	SE5632	53°47·1'	1°8·6'W	FM	105
Scalpaidh	Highld	NG7827	57°17·0'	5°40·6'W	X	33
Scalpay	Highld	NG6031	57°18·7'	5°58·7'W	X	24,32
Scalpay Ho	Highld	NG6328	57°17·1'	5°55·5'W	X	32
Scalpay or Scalpaigh	N Eil	NG2295	57°51·7'	6°40·8'W	X	14
Scalp Rock	Highld	NG2963	57°34·8'	6°31·6'W	X	23
Scalpsie	Arg & Bt	NS0558	55°46·8'	5°6·1'W	X	63
Scalpsie Bay	Arg & Bt	NS0557	55°46·3'	5°6·1'W	W	63
Scalp, The	Lincs	TF3838	52°55·5'	0°3·6'E	X	131
Scalp, The	Moray	NJ3636	57°24·9'	3°3·5'W	H	28
Scaly Moss	Cumbr	NY0613	54°30·5'	3°26·7'W	X	89
Scamadale	Highld	NM7090	56°56·9'	5°46·5'W	X	33,40
Scamblesby	Lincs	TF2778	53°17·3'	0°5·3'W	T	122
Scamblesby Grove	Lincs	TF2977	53°16·7'	0°3·5'W	X	122
Scamblesby Thorpe	Lincs	TF2979	53°17·8'	0°3·5'W	X	122
Scamford	Pemb	SM9119	51°50·1'	5°1·6'W	X	157,158
Scamland	E Yorks	SE7643	53°52·9'	0°50·2'W	T	105,106
Scammadale	Arg & Bt	NM8820	56°19·8'	5°25·3'W	X	49
Scammi Dale	Shetld	HU1856	60°17·5'	1°40·0'W	X	3
Scammonden	Kirk	SE0415	53°38·1'	1°56·0'W	X	110
Scammonden Water	Kirk	SE0515	53°38·1'	1°55·1'W	W	110
Scamnell Fm	Staffs	SJ8629	52°51·7'	2°12·1'W	FM	127
Scamodale	Highld	NM8373	56°48·1'	5°32·8'W	T	40
Scamperdale	Kent	TQ4348	51°13·0'	0°3·2'E	X	187
Scampston	N Yks	SE8675	54°10·1'	0°40·5'W	T	101
Scampston Beck	N Yks	SE8676	54°10·6'	0°40·5'W	W	101
Scampston Grange	N Yks	SE8578	54°11·7'	0°41·4'W	X	100
Scampston Mill Fm	N Yks	SE8674	54°9·5'	0°40·6'W	FM	101
Scampston Park	N Yks	SE8675	54°10·1'	0°40·5'W	X	101
Scampton	Lincs	SK9479	53°18·2'	0°35·0'W	T	121
Scampton Gorse	Lincs	SK9379	53°18·2'	0°35·9'W	F	121
Scampton Ho	Lincs	SK9479	53°18·2'	0°35·0'W	X	121
Scamridge	N Yks	SE8986	54°16·0'	0°37·6'W	X	94,101
Scamridge Dikes	N Yks	SE8985	54°15·4'	0°37·6'W	A	94,101
Scamridge Fm	N Yks	SE8985	54°15·4'	0°37·6'W	FM	94,101
Scanabhal	N Eil	NB0924	58°6·8'	6°56·0'W	H	13,14
Scanbeck Howle	Red & Cl	NZ6323	54°36·1'	1°1·1'W	X	94
Scandal Beck	Cumbr	NY7207	54°27·7'	2°25·5'W	W	91
Scandal Beck	Cumbr	NY7500	54°23·9'	2°22·7'W	W	91
Scandale Beck	Cumbr	NY3707	54°27·5'	2°57·9'W	W	90
Scandale Fell	Cumbr	NY3808	54°28·1'	2°57·0'W	X	90
Scandale Head	Cumbr	NY3809	54°28·6'	2°57·0'W	X	90
Scandale Pass	Cumbr	NY3809	54°28·6'	2°57·0'W	X	90
Scaniport	Highld	NH6239	57°25·5'	4°17·4'W	X	26
Scanistle	Arg & Bt	NR4067	55°49·8'	6°8·7'W	X	60,61
Scantips	Shetld	HU3413	59°54·3'	1°23·0'W	H	4
Scapa Bay	Orkney	HY4307	58°57·1'	2°59·0'W	W	6,7
Scapa Flow	Orkney	HY3800	58°53·2'	3°4·1'W	W	6,7
Scapegoat Hill	Kirk	SE0816	53°38·7'	1°52·3'W	T	110
Scar	Orkney	HY6745	59°17·7'	2°34·3'W	X	5
Scaraben	Highld	ND0626	58°13·0'	3°35·5'W	H	17
Scaracleit	N Eil	NF8846	57°24·1'	7°11·2'W	X	22
Scarah Mill	N Yks	SE2761	54°2·9'	1°34·8'W	X	99
Scarah Moor	N Yks	SE2762	54°3·4'	1°34·8'W	X	99
Scaraileòd	N Eil	NF8452	57°27·2'	7°15·7'W	X	22
Scara Ruadh	N Eil	NG0588	57°47·3'	6°57·4'W	X	14,18
Scarasdale Point	N Eil	NF8889	57°47·2'	7°14·5'W	X	18
Scarastabeg	N Eil	NG0092	57°49·3'	7°2·7'W	T	18
Scarastavore	N Eil	NG0092	57°49·3'	7°2·7'W	T	18
Scara Taing	Orkney	HY3633	59°11·0'	3°6·7'W	X	6
Scara Taing	Orkney	HY4024	59°6·2'	3°2·4'W	X	5,6
Scaravay	N Eil	NG0177	57°41·3'	7°0·6'W	X	18
Scarba	Arg & Bt	NM7004	56°10·6'	5°41·9'W	X	55
Scarbank	D & G	NX8693	55°13·3'	3°47·1'W	X	78
Scarbarrow Hill	Cumbr	SD2469	54°6·9'	3°9·3'W	H	96
Scarberry Hill	Cumbr	NY6743	54°47·1'	2°30·4'W	H	86,87
Scarborough	Kent	TQ7262	51°20·1'	0°28·5'E	X	178,188
Scarborough	N Yks	TA0388	54°16·9'	0°24·7'W	T	101
Scarborough Fm	Glos	SP1131	51°58·9'	1°50·0'W	FM	150
Scarborough Hill	Norf	TG2928	52°48·3'	1°24·3'E	X	133,134
Scarborough House Fm	N Yks	SE3583	54°14·7'	1°27·4'W	FM	99
Scarboro Wood	Norf	TF8740	52°55·7'	0°47·3'E	F	132
Scarbrae	D & G	NX8681	55°6·9'	3°46·8'W	X	78
Scar Brow	Cumbr	SD6081	54°13·6'	2°36·4'W	X	97
Scarce Law	Scot Bord	NT5147	55°43·1'	2°46·4'W	H	73
Scarce Rig	Scot Bord	NT2553	55°46·1'	3°11·3'W	X	66,73
Scarcewater	Corn	SW9154	50°21·2'	4°55·9'W	T	200
Scarcliffe	Derby	SK4968	53°12·6'	1°15·6'W	T	120
Scarcliffe Fm	N Yks	SD9847	53°55·4'	2°1·4'W	FM	103
Scarcliffe Grange	Derby	SK5070	53°13·7'	1°14·7'W	X	120
Scarcliffe Park	Derby	SK5170	53°13·7'	1°13·8'W	F	120
Scar Close	Lancs	SD4872	54°8·7'	2°47·3'W	X	97
Scar Close	N Yks	SD7577	54°11·5'	2°22·6'W	X	98
Scarcote Fm	N Yks	NZ1301	54°24·5'	1°47·6'W	FM	92
Scar Crag	Cumbr	NY1920	54°34·4'	3°14·8'W	X	89,90
Scar Crags	Cumbr	NY2120	54°34·4'	3°12·9'W	X	89,90
Scarcroft	Leeds	SE3541	53°52·1'	1°27·6'W	T	104
Scarcroft Hill	Leeds	SE3741	53°52·1'	1°25·8'W	X	104
Scard	I of M	SC2273	54°7·6'	4°43·0'W	X	95
Scardale	Cumbr	NY7521	54°35·3'	2°22·8'W	X	91
Scardale Plantn	N Yks	SE9072	54°8·4'	0°36·9'W	F	101
Scardroy	Highld	NH2151	57°31·1'	4°59·3'W	X	25
Scardroy Burn	Highld	NH1952	57°31·6'	5°0·9'W	W	25
Scardroy Lodge	Highld	NH2151	57°31·1'	4°58·9'W	X	25
Scare Gun	Orkney	HY5111	58°59·3'	2°50·7'W	X	6
Scare Hill	Aberd	NJ6819	57°15·9'	2°31·4'W	H	38
Scare Hill	Aberd	NO7283	56°56·5'	2°27·2'W	X	45
Scare Hill	Bri & Hov	TQ2910	50°52·7'	0°9·6'W	X	198
Scareleys	Aberd	NJ9147	57°31·0'	2°8·6'W	X	30
Scar End	Durham	NY8830	54°40·1'	2°10·7'W	X	91,92
Scar End Point	Cumbr	SD2163	54°3·7'	3°12·0'W	X	96
Scares	D & G	NX2633	54°40·0'	4°41·5'W	X	82
Scare, The	Cumbr	NY4865	54°58·9'	2°48·3'W	X	86
Scare Wood	Aberd	NJ6612	57°12·1'	2°33·3'W	F	38
Scarey Tor	Devon	SX6092	50°42·9'	3°58·6'W	H	191
Scarfa Skerry	Shetld	HU4739	60°8·2'	1°8·7'W	X	4
Scarfataing	Shetld	HU3363	60°21·2'	1°23·6'W	X	2,3
Scarfa Taing	Shetld	HU6099	60°40·4'	0°53·6'W	X	1
Scarf Caves	Highld	NG5042	57°24·2'	6°9·3'W	X	23,24
Scarff	Shetld	HU2480	60°30·4'	1°33·3'W	X	3
Scarffbanks	Moray	NJ2366	57°40·9'	3°17·0'W	X	28
Scarfhall Point	Orkney	HY4448	59°19·1'	2°58·5'W	X	5
Scarfhill Howe	N Yks	SE8194	54°20·3'	0°44·8'W	A	94,100
Scarfi Taing	Shetld	HU3511	59°53·2'	1°22·0'W	X	4

Scarfi Taing	Shetld	HU3516	59°55·9'	1°21·9'W	X	4
Scarfi Taing	Shetld	HU3621	59°58·6'	1°20·8'W	X	4
Scarfi Taing	Shetld	HU3729	60°2·9'	1°19·6'W	X	4
Scarfi Taing	Shetld	HU4014	59°54·8'	1°16·6'W	X	4
Scarfi Taing	Shetld	HU4744	60°10·9'	1°8·7'W	X	4
Scar Fm	Ches	SJ4648	53°1·8'	2°47·9'W	FM	117
Scar Fm	Glos	SO7530	51°58·3'	2°21·4'W	FM	150
Scar Fm	Heref	SO6136	52°1·5'	2°33·7'W	FM	149
Scar Fm	Heref	SO6752	52°10·2'	2°28·6'W	FM	149
Scar Folds	N Yks	SE0284	54°15·3'	1°57·7'W	X	98
Scar Foot	Cumbr	NY5037	54°43·8'	2°46·2'W	X	90
Scar Foot	Cumbr	SD4892	54°19·5'	2°47·6'W	X	97
Scarf Point	Orkney	HY5306	58°56·6'	2°48·5'W	X	6,7
Scarf Rig	Scot Bord	NT3431	55°34·3'	3°2·4'W	H	73
Scarfskerry	Highld	ND2674	58°39·1'	3°16·0'W	T	7,12
Scarf Skerry	Orkney	HY5901	58°53·9'	2°42·2'W	X	6
Scarf Skerry	Orkney	ND4093	58°49·5'	3°1·9'W	X	7
Scarf Skerry	Shetld	HU2377	60°28·8'	1°34·4'W	X	3
Scarfskerry Point	Highld	ND2574	58°39·1'	3°17·1'W	X	7,12
Scarf Stane	Shetld	HU3583	60°32·0'	1°21·2'W	X	1,2,3
Scarf Taing	Orkney	ND4992	58°49·0'	2°52·5'W	X	7
Scarf Taing	Shetld	HU4334	60°5·6'	1°13·1'W	X	4
Scarf Water	Shetld	HU2843	60°10·5'	1°29·2'W	W	4
Scargill	Durham	NZ0510	54°29·4'	1°54·9'W	T	92
Scargill Castle	Durham	NZ0510	54°29·4'	1°54·9'W	A	92
Scargill Fm	Lancs	SD5067	54°6·0'	2°45·5'W	FM	97
Scargill High Moor	Durham	NY9909	54°28·8'	2°0·5'W	X	92
Scargill Ho	N Yks	SD9771	54°8·3'	2°2·3'W	X	98
Scargill Low Moor	Durham	NZ0111	54°29·9'	1°58·7'W	X	92
Scargill Pasture	N Yks	SE2353	53°58·6'	1°38·5'W	X	104
Scargill Resr	N Yks	SE2353	53°58·6'	1°38·5'W	W	104
Scargreen	Cumbr	NY0605	54°26·2'	3°26·5'W	X	89
Scar Head	Cumbr	SD2894	54°20·4'	3°6·0'W	T	96,97
Scar Hill	Aberd	NJ4801	57°6·1'	2°51·0'W	H	37
Scar Hill	Aberd	NJ4811	57°11·5'	2°51·2'W	H	37
Scar Hill	D & G	NX5660	54°55·1'	4°14·4'W	H	83
Scar Hill	Moray	NJ2453	57°33·9'	3°15·8'W	X	28
Scarhill	Pth & Kin	NO1312	56°17·8'	3°23·9'W	X	58
Scar Hill	Scot Bord	NT3222	55°29·5'	3°4·1'W	H	73
Scar Hill	S Lanak	NS7422	55°28·8'	3°59·2'W	X	71
Scar Ho	N Yks	NZ0003	54°25·6'	1°59·6'W	X	92
Scar Ho	N Yks	SD9278	54°12·1'	2°6·9'W	X	98
Scar Ho	N Yks	SE0677	54°11·6'	1°54·1'W	X	99
Scar Hos	N Yks	SD8998	54°22·9'	2°9·7'W	X	98
Scar House Reservoir	N Yks	SE0576	54°11·0'	1°55·0'W	W	98
Scarinish	Arg & Bt	NM0444	56°30·0'	6°48·2'W	T	46
Scarisbrick	Lancs	SD3713	53°36·8'	2°56·7'W	T	108
Scarisbrick Hall (Sch)	Lancs	SD3912	53°36·3'	2°54·9'W	X	108
Scarisdale Point	Arg & Bt	NM5137	56°27·8'	6°2·1'W	X	47,48
Scarisdale River	Arg & Bt	NM5237	56°27·9'	6°1·1'W	W	47,48
Scarisdale Rocks	Arg & Bt	NM5238	56°28·4'	6°1·2'W	X	47,48
Scarisdale Wood	Arg & Bt	NM5238	56°28·4'	6°1·2'W	F	47,48
Scar Island	D & G	NX3053	54°50·8'	4°38·4'W	X	82
Scarista	N Eil	NG0193	57°49·9'	7°1·8'W	X	18
Scar Jockey	Northum	NU1441	55°40·0'	1°46·2'W	X	75
Scar Lathing	Cumbr	NY2204	54°25·8'	3°11·7'W	X	89,90
Scarlaw	Scot Bord	NT6556	55°48·0'	2°33·1'W	X	67,74
Scar Law	Scot Bord	NT6557	55°48·6'	2°33·1'W	X	67,74
Scarlet's Fm	Essex	TL9628	51°55·2'	0°51·4'E	FM	168
Scarlett	I of M	SC2566	54°3·9'	4°40·0'W	X	95
Scarlett Hall	Northum	NZ0484	55°9·3'	1°55·8'W	X	81
Scarlett Point	I of M	SC2566	54°3·9'	4°40·0'W	X	95
Scarletts	Kent	TQ4440	51°8·7'	0°3·9'E	X	187
Scarlett's Fm	Hants	SU5361	51°21·0'	1°13·9'W	FM	174
Scarlett's Fm	Wok	SU8177	51°29·4'	0°49·6'W	FM	175
Scarlet Wood	N Yks	SE6578	54°11·9'	0°59·8'W	F	100
Scarmclate	Highld	ND1959	58°31·0'	3°23·0'W	X	11,12
Scarnber Laithe	N Yks	SD9458	54°1·3'	2°5·1'W	X	103
Scarnber Wood	N Yks	SD9357	54°0·8'	2°6·0'W	F	103
Scarne	Corn	SX3383	50°37·6'	4°21·3'W	X	201
Scarness	Cumbr	NY2230	54°39·8'	3°12·1'W	T	89,90
Scarning	Norf	TF9512	52°40·5'	0°53·5'E	T	132
Scarning Dale	Norf	TF9412	52°40·5'	0°52·6'E	X	132
Scarning Fen Nature Reserve	Norf	TF9812	52°40·4'	0°56·1'E	X	132
Scarnor Point	Corn	SW9781	50°35·8'	4°51·7'W	X	200
Scar Nose	Moray	NJ4968	57°42·2'	2°50·9'W	X	28,29
Scarp	N Eil	NA9715	58°1·5'	7°7·5'W	X	13
Scarp Hill	Surrey	SU9053	51°16·4'	0°42·2'W	X	186
Scarpigar	Orkney	HY5010	58°58·7'	2°51·7'W	X	6
Scar Point	D & G	NY0066	54°59·0'	3°33·3'W	X	84
Scar Quilse	Shetld	HU4260	60°19·6'	1°13·9'W	X	2,3
Scarra	Orkney	HY2214	59°0·6'	3°21·0'W	X	6
Scarrabine Fm	Corn	SW9879	50°34·8'	4°50·8'W	FM	200
Scarrabus	Arg & Bt	NR3465	55°48·6'	6°14·3'W	X	60,61
Scarrataing	Orkney	HY2617	59°2·3'	3°16·9'W	X	6
Scarra Taing	Orkney	HY5038	59°13·8'	2°52·1'W	X	5
Scarr Hill	Brad	SE1834	53°48·4'	1°43·2'W	X	104
Scarrigarth	Orkney	HY6338	59°13·9'	2°38·4'W	X	5
Scarrington	Notts	SK7341	52°57·9'	0°54·4'W	T	129
Scarrington Ho	Notts	SK7442	52°58·4'	0°53·5'W	X	129
Scarrish Wood	N Yks	SE7272	54°8·6'	0°53·5'W	F	100
Scarrow Beck	Norf	TG1831	52°50·2'	1°14·6'E	W	133
Scarrowhill	Cumbr	NY5150	54°50·8'	2°45·4'W	X	86
Scarrow Hill	Cumbr	NY5661	54°56·8'	2°40·8'W	X	86
Scarrowmanwick	Cumbr	NY5847	54°49·2'	2°38·8'W	X	86
Scarrowmanwick Fell	Cumbr	NY6047	54°49·2'	2°36·9'W	X	86
Scarrows	Cumbr	NY5439	54°44·9'	2°42·5'W	X	90
Scarr, The	Glos	SO7228	51°57·2'	2°24·1'W	T	149
Scarsa	Orkney	HY1800	58°53·0'	3°24·9'W	X	7
Scarset Rigg	Durham	NY9023	54°36·4'	2°8·9'W	X	91,92
Scars Fm	N Som	ST4962	51°21·5'	2°43·6'W	FM	172,182
Scarside	Cumbr	NY5318	54°33·6'	2°43·2'W	X	90
Scarside	Cumbr	NY6308	54°28·2'	2°33·8'W	X	91
Scar Side	Cumbr	NY6309	54°28·7'	2°33·8'W	X	91
Scar Side Ho	N Yks	SE0263	54°4·0'	1°57·7'W	X	98
Scarsike Head	Durham	NY9141	54°46·1'	2°8·0'W	X	87
Scar Sikes	Cumbr	NY6804	54°26·1'	2°29·2'W	X	91
Scarsoch Bheag	Aberd	NN9385	56°56·9'	3°45·1'W	H	43
Scar Spring Wood	N Yks	SE0997	54°22·3'	1°51·3'W	F	99
Scars, The	Northum	NZ2993	55°14·1'	1°32·2'W	X	81
Scars, The	S Glos	ST5287	51°35·0'	2°41·2'W	X	172
Scart	Renf	NS3767	55°52·4'	4°35·9'W	X	63
Scartan Bay	Orkney	ND4678	58°41·4'	2°55·4'W	W	7
Scartan Point	Orkney	ND4778	58°41·5'	2°54·4'W	X	7
Scarth Bight	Cumbr	SD1873	54°9·0'	3°14·9'W	W	96
Scarth Channel	Cumbr	SD1773	54°9·0'	3°15·8'W	W	96
Scar, The	D & G	NX0467	54°57·8'	5°3·3'W	X	82
Scar, The	Heref	SO3544	52°5·7'	2°56·5'W	X	148,149,161
Scar, The	N Yks	NZ9011	54°29·4'	0°36·2'W	X	94
Scar, The	N Yks	SE5976	54°10·8'	1°5·3'W	F	100
Scarth Gap Pass	Cumbr	NY1813	54°30·6'	3°15·6'W	X	89,90
Scarth Hill	Lancs	SD4206	53°33·1'	2°52·1'W	T	108
Scarthingmoor Fm	Notts	SK7668	53°12·5'	0°51·3'W	FM	120
Scarthingmoor House Fm	Notts	SK7668	53°12·5'	0°51·3'W	FM	120
Scarthingwell	N Yks	SE4937	53°49·9'	1°14·9'W	T	105
Scarth Lees	N Yks	NZ4601	54°24·4'	1°17·1'W	X	93
Scarth Nick	N Yks	NZ4700	54°23·8'	1°16·1'W	X	93
Scarth Nick Fm	N Yks	NZ4701	54°24·4'	1°16·1'W	FM	93
Scartho	NE Lincs	TA2606	53°32·4'	0°5·5'W	T	113
Scartho Wood	NE Lincs	TA2405	53°31·9'	0°7·3'W	F	113
Scarth Wood Fm	N Yks	NZ4600	54°23·8'	1°17·1'W	FM	93
Scarth Wood Moor	N Yks	SE4699	54°23·3'	1°17·1'W	X	100
Scart Island	Pth & Kin	NO1302	56°12·4'	3°23·7'W	X	58
Scarton Point	Highld	ND3576	58°40·3'	3°6·8'W	X	7,12
Scar Top	Brad	SD9937	53°50·0'	2°0·5'W	X	103
Scar Top	Cumbr	NY6229	54°39·5'	2°34·9'W	X	91
Scar Top	N Yks	SD7479	54°12·6'	2°23·5'W	X	98
Scar Top	N Yks	SD9489	54°18·0'	2°5·1'W	X	98
Scar Top	N Yks	SD9589	54°18·0'	2°4·2'W	X	98
Scar Top	N Yks	SD9684	54°15·3'	2°3·3'W	X	98
Scar Top Ho	N Yks	SE0263	54°4·0'	1°57·7'W	X	98
Scart Rock		NS2144	55°39·6'	4°50·3'W	X	63,70
Scart Rock		NS2729	55°31·7'	4°44·0'W	X	70
Scart Rock	E Loth	NT6779	56°0·4'	2°31·3'W	X	67
Scart Rocks	Arg & Bt	NR7305	55°17·5'	5°34·1'W	X	68
Scarty Head	D & G	NX0448	54°47·6'	5°2·5'W	X	82
Scarvar Ayre	Shetld	HU4270	60°25·0'	1°13·7'W	X	2,3
Scarva Taing	Orkney	HY3614	59°0·8'	3°6·4'W	X	6
Scarva Taing	Orkney	HY5708	58°57·7'	2°44·4'W	X	6
Scarva Taing	Shetld	HU3569	60°24·5'	1°21·4'W	X	2,3
Scarvie Clett	Orkney	HY5315	59°1·4'	2°48·6'W	X	6
Scarvister	Shetld	HU3042	60°9·9'	1°27·1'W	T	4
Scarvi Taing	Shetld	HU1759	60°19·2'	1°41·0'W	X	3
Scar Water	D & G	NS7304	55°19·1'	3°59·6'W	W	77
Scar Water	D & G	NX8097	55°15·4'	3°52·9'W	W	78
Scarwell	Orkney	HY2320	59°3·9'	3°20·1'W	T	6
Scarwell Wood	N Yks	SE9887	54°16·4'	0°29·3'W	F	94,101
Scar Wood	N Yks	NZ8100	54°23·6'	0°44·7'W	F	94
Scar Wood	N Yks	SE6276	54°10·8'	1°2·6'W	F	100
Scar Wood	N Yks	SE9497	54°21·8'	0°32·8'W	F	94,101
Scary Hill	Oxon	SU3284	51°33·5'	1°31·9'W	X	174
Scat Ness	Shetld	HU3809	59°52·1'	1°18·8'W	X	4
Scatness	Shetld	HU3810	59°52·7'	1°18·8'W	T	4
Scatraig	Highld	NH7137	57°24·6'	4°8·4'W	X	27
Scatsta	Shetld	HU3972	60°26·1'	1°17·0'W	T	2,3
Scatsta Ness	Shetld	HU3873	60°26·6'	1°18·1'W	X	2,3
Scatterbrook Fm	Essex	TQ8899	51°39·7'	0°43·5'E	FM	168
Scatterdells Wood	Herts	TL0402	51°42·7'	0°29·3'W	F	166
Scatterford Fm	Glos	SO5608	51°46·4'	2°37·9'W	FM	162
Scatterty	Aberd	NJ5656	57°35·8'	2°43·7'W	X	29
Scatterty	Aberd	NJ6957	57°36·4'	2°30·7'W	X	29
Scattlands	Shetld	HU4588	60°34·6'	1°10·2'W	X	1,2
Scatwell Fm	Highld	NH3956	57°34·2'	4°41·1'W	FM	26
Scatwell Ho	Highld	NH3955	57°33·7'	4°41·0'W	X	26
Scat Wick	Orkney	ND3592	58°48·9'	3°7·0'W	W	7
Scaud	Northum	NT9514	55°25·4'	2°4·3'W	X	81
Scaud Hill	Durham	NY8036	54°43·4'	2°18·2'W	H	91,92
Scaun	Orkney	HY4452	59°21·3'	2°58·6'W	X	5
Scaup	Northum	NY6697	55°16·2'	2°31·7'W	X	80
Scaup Burn	Northum	NY6599	55°17·3'	2°32·6'W	W	80
Scaup Pikes	Northum	NY6598	55°16·7'	2°32·6'W	H	80
Scaurbank	Cumbr	NY3869	55°1·0'	2°57·8'W	X	85
Scaur Fm	D & G	NX8575	55°3·6'	3°47·6'W	FM	84
Scaur Head	N Yks	SD8688	54°17·5'	2°12·5'W	X	98
Scaurhead	S Ayr	NX2282	55°6·3'	4°47·0'W	X	76
Scaur Hill	S Lanak	NS8830	55°33·3'	3°46·1'W	H	71,72
Scaur Law	D & G	NX7399	55°16·4'	3°59·5'W	X	77
Scaur or Kippford	D & G	NX8354	54°52·3'	3°49·0'W	T	84
Scaur, The	Wrekin	SJ7320	52°46·9'	2°23·6'W	H	127
Scaut Hill	Moray	NJ3331	57°22·1'	3°6·4'W	H	37
Scaut Hill	Moray	NJ3342	57°28·1'	3°6·6'W	H	28
Scaut Hill	S Lanak	NS9634	55°35·6'	3°38·6'W	H	72
Scavaig River	Highld	NG4819	57°11·8'	6°9·8'W	W	32
Scaval	Orkney	HY6022	59°5·2'	2°41·4'W	X	5,6
Scaw	Cumbr	NY0025	54°36·9'	3°32·5'W	X	89
Scaw	Cumbr	NY1215	54°31·6'	3°21·2'W	X	89
Scawby	N Lincs	SE9605	53°32·2'	0°32·7'W	T	112
Scawby Brook	N Lincs	SE9806	53°32·7'	0°30·8'W	W	112
Scawby Brook Fm	N Lincs	SE9806	53°32·7'	0°30·8'W	FM	112
Scawby Grange	N Lincs	SE9504	53°31·7'	0°33·6'W	X	112
Scawby Grove	N Lincs	SE9605	53°32·2'	0°32·7'W	X	112
Scawby Hall	N Lincs	SE9605	53°32·2'	0°32·7'W	A	112
Scawby Park	N Lincs	SE9706	53°32·7'	0°31·8'W	X	112
Scawcett Fm	N Lincs	SE7505	53°32·4'	0°51·7'W	FM	112
Scawd Bank	D & G	NY4393	55°13·9'	2°53·3'W	H	79
Scaw'd Fell	D & G	NT1402	55°18·5'	3°20·9'W	H	78
Scaw'd Law	D & G	NS9203	55°18·8'	3°41·7'W	H	78
Scawd Law	Scot Bord	NT1633	55°35·3'	3°19·5'W	H	72
Scawd Law	Scot Bord	NT3523	55°30·0'	3°1·3'W	H	73
Scawd Law	Scot Bord	NT3640	55°39·2'	3°0·6'W	H	73
Scaw'd Law	Scot Bord	NT4901	55°18·3'	2°47·8'W	H	79
Scaw'd Law	Scot Bord	NT6505	55°20·5'	2°32·7'W	X	80
Scaw'd Law	Scot Bord	NT7511	55°23·8'	2°23·3'W	X	80
Scawdmans Hill	S Lanak	NT0531	55°34·1'	3°30·0'W	H	72
Scawgill Br	Cumbr	NY1725	54°37·0'	3°16·7'W	X	89,90
Scawling Wood	N Yks	SE5280	54°13·0'	1°11·7'W	F	100
Scawns	Corn	SX2262	50°26·1'	4°30·0'W	X	201
Scaws	Cumbr	NY5230	54°40·0'	2°44·2'W	X	90
Scawsby	Donc	SE5404	53°32·0'	1°10·7'W	T	111
Scawsby Hall	Donc	SE5305	53°32·6'	1°11·6'W	X	111
Scawthorpe	Donc	SE5505	53°32·6'	1°9·8'W	T	111
Scawthwaite Close	Cumbr	NY2435	54°42·5'	3°10·4'W	X	89,90
Scawton	N Yks	SE5483	54°14·6'	1°9·9'W	T	100
Scawton Moor	N Yks	SE5682	54°14·1'	1°8·0'W	X	100
Scawton Moor Ho	N Yks	SE5383	54°14·6'	1°10·8'W	X	100
Scawton Park	N Yks	SE5484	54°15·2'	1°9·9'W	X	100
Scaw Well	Cumbr	NY1216	54°32·1'	3°21·2'W	X	89
Scayne's Hill	W Susx	TQ3623	50°59·6'	0°3·3'W	T	198
Sceibion Bach	Denb	SJ0759	53°7·4'	3°23·0'W	X	116
Scencliffe Grange	N Yks	SE5279	54°12·5'	1°11·7'W	X	100
Scethrog	Powys	SO1025	51°55·2'	3°18·1'W	T	161
Sceugh	Cumbr	NY4443	54°47·0'	2°51·8'W	X	85
Sceugh Dyke	Cumbr	NY4540	54°45·4'	2°50·9'W	X	86
Sceugh Fm	Cumbr	NY5429	54°39·5'	2°42·4'W	FM	90
Sceugh Head	Cumbr	NY4442	54°46·4'	2°51·8'W	X	85
Sceugh Hill Fm	Cumbr	NY4442	54°46·4'	2°51·8'W	FM	85
Sceughmire	Cumbr	NY3553	54°52·3'	3°0·3'W	X	85
Sceugh Mire	Cumbr	NY4443	54°47·0'	2°51·8'W	X	85
Scews	Orkney	ND3095	58°50·5'	3°12·3'W	X	7
Schache	Powys	SO0057	52°12·4'	3°27·4'W	X	147
Schaw	E Ayr	NS4420	55°27·2'	4°27·6'W	X	70
Schaw Park	Clackm	NS9094	56°7·8'	3°45·7'W	X	58
Schiehallion	Pth & Kin	NN7154	56°39·9'	4°5·8'W	H	42,51,52
Schil,The	Scot Bord	NT8622	55°29·7'	2°12·9'W	H	74
Scholaby	I of M	SC2270	54°6·0'	4°42·9'W	X	95
Schola Europaea	Oxon	SU5195	51°39·3'	1°15·4'W	X	164
Scholar Green	Ches	SJ8357	53°6·8'	2°14·8'W	T	118
Scholebrook Fm	Brad	SE2131	53°46·7'	1°40·5'W	FM	104
Scholecroft Fm	Leeds	SE2426	53°44·0'	1°37·8'W	FM	104
Schole Hill	Barns	SE2302	53°31·1'	1°38·8'W	X	110
Scholemoor	Brad	SE1332	53°47·3'	1°47·7'W	T	104
Scholes	Brad	SE0137	53°50·0'	1°58·7'W	T	104
Scholes	Kirk	SE1607	53°33·8'	1°45·1'W	T	110
Scholes	Kirk	SE1625	53°43·5'	1°45·0'W	T	104
Scholes	Leeds	SE3737	53°49·9'	1°25·9'W	T	104
Scholes	Roth	SK3995	53°27·3'	1°24·4'W	T	110,111
Scholes	Wigan	SD5805	53°32·6'	2°37·6'W	T	108
Scholes Coppice	Roth	SK3995	53°27·3'	1°24·4'W	F	110,111
Scholes Fm	Leic	SK6621	52°47·2'	1°0·9'W	FM	129
Scholes Height	Lancs	SD7519	53°40·3'	2°22·3'W	H	109
Scholes Park	Leeds	SE3736	53°49·4'	1°25·9'W	X	104
Scholey Hill	Leeds	SE3725	53°43·4'	1°25·9'W	T	104
Scholl	Highld	ND3854	58°28·5'	3°3·3'W	X	12
School Aycliffe	Durham	NZ2523	54°36·3'	1°36·4'W	T	93
School Barn Fm	Essex	TL8145	52°4·7'	0°38·9'E	FM	155
Schoolbrae	Orkney	HY6426	59°7·4'	2°37·2'W	X	5
School Clough	Staffs	SK0763	53°10·1'	1°53·3'W	X	119
School Ellis	Cumbr	SD1783	54°14·4'	3°16·0'W	X	96
School Fm	Cambs	TL3796	52°32·9'	0°1·6'E	FM	142,143
School Fm	Cambs	TL5070	52°18·7'	0°12·4'E	FM	154
School Fm	Ches	SJ7960	53°8·4'	2°18·4'W	FM	118
School Fm	Essex	TL8234	51°58·7'	0°39·4'E	FM	155
School Fm	Glos	SO7812	51°48·6'	2°18·8'W	FM	162
School Fm	Kent	TQ7164	51°21·2'	0°27·7'E	FM	178,188
School Fm	Kent	TQ7833	51°4·3'	0°32·8'E	FM	188
School Fm	Leic	SK7902	52°36·8'	0°49·6'W	FM	141
School Fm	Lincs	TF4873	53°14·2'	0°13·5'E	FM	122
School Fm	Suff	TL9046	52°5·0'	0°46·8'E	FM	155
School Green	Brad	SE1133	53°47·8'	1°49·6'W	T	104
School Green	Ches	SJ6464	53°10·6'	2°31·9'W	T	118
School Green	Essex	TL7331	51°57·3'	0°31·5'E	T	167
School Green	I of W	SZ3386	50°40·6'	1°31·6'W	T	196
Schoolgreen	Wok	SU7367	51°24·1'	0°56·6'W	T	175
Schoolhill	Aberd	NJ5611	57°11·5'	2°43·2'W	X	37
Schoolhill	Aberd	NJ7602	57°6·8'	2°23·3'W	X	38
Schoolhill	Aberd	NO9098	57°4·6'	2°9·4'W	X	38,45
School Hill	Lancs	SD6268	54°6·6'	2°34·5'W	X	97
School Ho	I of M	SC4494	54°19·3'	4°23·5'W	X	95
School Ho	Northum	NZ0154	54°53·1'	1°58·6'W	X	87
School House	Dorset	ST3602	50°49·1'	2°54·1'W	T	193
Schoolhouse	Orkney	HY5606	58°56·6'	2°45·4'W	X	6
School House Fm	Kent	TQ7241	51°8·8'	0°27·9'E	FM	188
School House Fm	N Yks	NZ4004	54°26·0'	1°22·6'W	FM	93
Schoolhouse Fm	Suff	TL9866	52°15·6'	0°54·5'E	FM	155
School House Fm	W Susx	SU9527	51°2·3'	0°38·3'W	FM	186,197
Schoolhouse, The	N Ayr	NR8935	55°34·0'	5°20·4'W	X	68,69
School Knott	Cumbr	SD4297	54°22·2'	2°53·1'W	H	96,97
School Lane	Lancs	SD5626	53°44·0'	2°39·6'W	X	102
Schoolmaster Pasture	N Yks	NZ0503	54°25·6'	1°55·0'W	X	92
Schoolton	Shetld	HU4864	60°21·7'	1°7·3'W	X	2,3
School Wood	Heref	SO4365	52°17·1'	2°49·7'W	F	137,148,149
Schooner Point	Highld	NM3098	56°59·9'	6°26·3'W	X	39
Schoose	Cumbr	NY0127	54°38·0'	3°31·6'W	X	89
Schusan	Orkney	ND4490	58°47·9'	2°57·7'W	X	7
Sciberscross	Highld	NC7710	58°4·0'	4°4·6'W	X	17
Scilly Bank	Cumbr	NX9919	54°33·6'	3°33·3'W	T	89
Scilly Isles, The	Surrey	TQ1565	51°22·6'	0°20·5'W	X	176
Scilly Rock	I Scilly	SV8615	49°57·4'	6°22·3'W	X	203
Scissett	Kirk	SE2410	53°35·4'	1°37·8'W	T	110
Sclanor Hill	E Ayr	NS7430	55°33·1'	3°59·4'W	X	71
Sclaten	Shetld	HP6412	60°47·4'	0°49·0'W	X	1
Sclattiebrae	Aberd	NJ8308	57°10·0'	2°16·4'W	X	38
Scleddau	Pemb	SM9434	51°58·2'	4°59·6'W	T	157
Sclenteuch	S Ayr	NS3905	55°19·0'	4°31·8'W	X	70,77
Sclenteuch Moor	S Ayr	NS3807	55°20·1'	4°32·8'W	X	70,77
Sclenteuch Moor Plantation	S Ayr	NS3806	55°19·5'	4°32·8'W	F	70,77
Sclerder Abbey	Corn	SX2252	50°20·7'	4°29·7'W	X	201
Scoardale Fm	E Yorks	SE8455	53°59·3'	0°42·7'W	FM	106
Scoat Fell	Cumbr	NY1511	54°29·5'	3°18·3'W	X	89
Scoat Tarn	Cumbr	NY1510	54°28·9'	3°18·3'W	W	89
Scobbiscombe	Devon	SX6246	50°18·1'	3°55·9'W	X	202
Scobchester	Devon	SX5196	50°44·9'	4°6·3'W	X	191
Scobchester Down	Devon	SX5296	50°44·9'	4°5·5'W	H	191
Scob Hill	Devon	SS7546	51°12·2'	3°47·0'W	H	180
Scobitor	Devon	SX7274	50°33·3'	3°48·0'W	X	191
Scoble	Devon	SX7539	50°14·5'	3°44·8'W	X	202
Scobull	Arg & Bt	NM4627	56°22·3'	6°6·4'W	X	48
Scobull Point	Arg & Bt	NM4626	56°21·7'	6°6·3'W	X	48

Scock Ness	Orkney	HY4532	59°10·5'	2°57·2'W	X	5,6
Scockness	Orkney	HY4532	59°10·5'	2°57·2'W	X	5,6
Scocles Fm	Kent	TQ9571	51°24·5'	0°48·6'E	FM	178
Scocus	E Susx	TQ5523	50°59·4'	0°12·9'E	X	199
Scocus Wood	E Susx	TQ5422	50°58·8'	0°12·0'E	F	199
Scodaig	Arg & Bt	NR7896	56°6·6'	5°33·8'W	X	55
Scofton	Notts	SK6280	53°19·0'	1°3·7'W	T	111,120
Scofton Wood	Notts	SK6280	53°19·0'	1°3·7'W	F	111,120
Scogarth	Cumbr	NY3426	54°37·7'	3°0·9'W	X	90
Scogging's Fm	Suff	TM2871	52°17·6'	1°21·0'E	FM	156
Scogglethorpe Ings	N Yks	SE8274	54°9·6'	0°44·2'W	X	100
Scole	Norf	TM1579	52°22·2'	1°9·9'E	T	144,156
Scole Common	Norf	TM1480	52°22·8'	1°9·1'E	T	144,156
Scole Lodge	Norf	TM1579	52°22·2'	1°9·9'E	X	144,156
Scoles Farmhouse	Dorset	SY9679	50°36·9'	2°3·0'W	A	195
Scoles Gate	Suff	TL8054	52°9·5'	0°38·3'E	X	155
Scolla	Shetld	HP6300	60°41·0'	0°50·3'W	X	1
Scolla Wick	Shetld	HP6300	60°41·0'	0°50·3'W	W	1
Scollit Side	N Yks	NY9206	54°27·2'	2°7·0'W	X	91,92
Scollock	Pemb	SN0024	51°53·0'	4°54·0'W	X	145,157,158
Scollock Bill	Pemb	SN0024	51°53·0'	4°54·0'W	X	145,157,158
Scollops Fm	Kent	TQ4950	51°14·0'	0°8·4'E	FM	188
Scolly's Cross	Aberd	NO6587	56°58·6'	2°34·1'W	X	45
Scolpaig	N Eil	NF7275	57°39·0'	7°29·5'W	X	18
Scolpaig Bay	N Eil	NF7275	57°39·0'	7°29·5'W	W	18
Scolt Head Island (Nature Reserve)	Norf	TF8146	52°59·1'	0°42·2'E	X	132
Scolton Manor Country Park	Pemb	SM9821	51°51·3'	4°55·6'W	X	157,158
Scolty	Aberd	NO6793	57°1·9'	2°32·2'W	H	38,45
Scolty Ho	Aberd	NO6893	57°1·9'	2°31·2'W	X	38,45
Scomuir	Orkney	HY4704	58°55·5'	2°54·7'W	X	6,7
Sconce Point	I of W	SZ3389	50°42·2'	1°31·6'W	X	196
Scone Palace	Pth & Kin	NO1126	56°25·3'	3°26·1'W	X	53,58
Scone Park	Pth & Kin	NO1126	56°25·3'	3°26·1'W	X	53,58
Scones Lethendy	Pth & Kin	NO1228	56°26·4'	3°25·2'W	X	53,58
Scone Wood	Pth & Kin	NO1226	56°25·3'	3°25·2'W	F	53,58
Sconser	Highld	NG5131	57°18·4'	6°7·6'W	T	24,32
Sconser Lodge Hotel	Highld	NG5332	57°19·0'	6°5·7'W	X	24,32
Scooks Farm Ho	Kent	TQ9857	51°16·9'	0°50·7'E	X	178
Scoolary	Highld	ND2968	58°35·9'	3°12·8'W	X	11,12
Scoonie	Fife	NO3801	56°12·1'	2°59·5'W	T	59
Scoonieburn	Pth & Kin	NO1221	56°22·6'	3°25·1'W	T	53,58
Scooniehill	Fife	NO5114	56°19·2'	2°47·1'W	X	59
Scoop Hill	D & G	NY1695	55°14·8'	3°18·8'W	H	79
Scoor	Arg & Bt	NM4119	56°17·8'	6°10·7'W	X	48
Scoot More	Moray	NJ1739	57°26·3'	3°22·5'W	X	28
Scopa Wick	Shetld	HU1861	60°20·2'	1°39·9'W	W	3
Scope Beck	Cumbr	NY2118	54°33·3'	3°12·9'W	W	89,90
Scope End	Cumbr	NY2218	54°33·3'	3°11·9'W	X	89,90
Scopwick	Lincs	TF0758	53°6·7'	0°23·7'W	T	121
Scopwick Heath	Lincs	TF0558	53°6·8'	0°25·5'W	X	121
Scopwick Ho	Lincs	TF0658	53°6·8'	0°24·6'W	X	121
Scopwick Lodge Fm	Lincs	TF0458	53°6·8'	0°26·4'W	FM	121
Scopwick Low Field Fm	Lincs	TF0859	53°7·3'	0°22·8'W	FM	121
Scorabhig	N Eil	NG2495	57°51·8'	6°38·8'W	W	14
Scoraclett	N Eil	NG2299	57°53·9'	6°41·1'W	H	14
Scora Dale	Shetld	HU5173	60°26·5'	1°3·9'W	X	2,3
Scora Field	Shetld	HU2580	60°30·4'	1°32·2'W	X	3
Scoraig	Highld	NH0096	57°54·8'	5°22·1'W	T	19
Scora Water	Shetld	HU3371	60°25·6'	1°23·5'W	W	2,3
Scor Berg	Shetld	HU3829	60°2·9'	1°18·6'W	X	4
Scorbern Plantn	N Yks	SE7787	54°16·6'	0°48·6'W	F	94,100
Scorborough	E Yorks	TA0145	53°53·7'	0°27·4'W	T	106,107
Scorborough Beck	E Yorks	TA0145	53°53·7'	0°27·4'W	W	106,107
Scorbro Rush Plantn	E Yorks	SE8445	53°53·9'	0°42·9'W	F	106
Scord	Shetld	HU3355	60°16·9'	1°23·7'W	X	3
Scord	Shetld	HU3810	59°52·7'	1°18·8'W	X	4
Scordaback	Shetld	HP5103	60°42·7'	1°3·4'W	H	1
Scordar	Shetld	HU3797	60°39·5'	1°18·9'W	X	1
Scord of Brouster	Shetld	HU2551	60°14·8'	1°32·4'W	A	3
Scord of Grunnigeo	Shetld	HU5990	60°35·6'	0°54·9'W	X	1,2
Scord of Sandvoe	Shetld	HU3489	60°35·2'	1°22·3'W	X	1,2
Scord of Sound	Shetld	HU3750	60°14·2'	1°19·4'W	X	3
Scord of Wadbister	Shetld	HU4449	60°13·6'	1°11·8'W	X	3
Scords Wood	Kent	TQ4752	51°15·1'	0°6·8'E	F	188
Scord, The	Shetld	HU4981	60°30·8'	1°6·0'W	X	1,2,3
Score	Devon	SS5145	51°11·3'	4°7·5'W	X	180
Score	Highld	NH9745	57°29·3'	3°42·6'W	X	27
Score Bank	Halton	SJ4780	53°19·1'	2°47·3'W	X	108
Scoreby Farmhouse	York	SE6955	53°59·4'	0°56·4'W	X	105,106
Scoreby Grange	York	SE6854	53°58·9'	0°57·4'W	X	105,106
Scoreby Lodge	York	SE6851	53°57·3'	0°57·4'W	X	105,106
Scoreby Manor Ho	York	SE6952	53°57·8'	0°56·5'W	X	105,106
Scoreby Wood	York	SE7052	53°57·8'	0°55·6'W	F	105,106
Score Head	Scot Bord	NT8818	55°27·6'	2°11·0'W	X	80
Score Head	Shetld	HU5145	60°11·4'	1°4·3'W	X	4
Score Hill	Shetld	HU5144	60°10·9'	1°4·3'W	H	4
Score Holm	Shetld	HU5165	60°22·2'	1°4·0'W	X	2,3
Score Horan or Beinn an Sguirr	Highld	NG2859	57°32·6'	6°32·3'W	X	23
Score Minni	Shetld	HU5145	60°11·4'	1°4·3'W	X	4
Scorguie Ho	Highld	NH6446	57°29·3'	4°15·7'W	X	26
Scorhill Circle	Devon	SX6587	50°40·3'	3°54·3'W	A	191
Scorhill Tor	Devon	SX6587	50°40·3'	3°54·3'W	X	191
Scorlinch Fm	Devon	ST0300	50°47·7'	3°22·2'W	FM	192
Scor na Caillich	N Eil	NF9465	57°34·5'	7°6·7'W	W	18
Scorra Dale	Orkney	HY3205	58°55·9'	3°10·4'W	X	6,7
Scorriclet	Highld	ND2450	58°26·2'	3°17·6'W	X	11,12
Scorrieholm	S Lanak	NS7837	55°36·9'	3°55·8'W	X	71
Scorrier	Corn	SW7244	50°15·4'	5°11·5'W	T	204
Scorrier Ho	Corn	SW7243	50°14·8'	5°11·5'W	X	204
Scorrie, The	Angus	NO2775	56°51·9'	3°11·4'W	X	44
Scorriton	Devon	SX7068	50°30·1'	3°49·6'W	T	202
Scorriton Down	Devon	SX6868	50°30·1'	3°51·3'W	X	202
Scors Burn	Moray	NJ3222	57°17·3'	3°7·2'W	W	37
Scorsham Fm	Corn	SS2505	50°49·3'	4°28·7'W	FM	190
Scors of Blackwater	Moray	NJ3223	57°17·8'	3°7·2'W	X	37
Scorton	Lancs	SD5048	53°55·8'	2°45·3'W	T	102

Scorton	N Yks	NZ2500	54°23·9'	1°36·5'W	T	93
Scorton Beck	N Yks	NZ2500	54°23·9'	1°36·5'W	W	93
Scorton Grange	N Yks	NZ2600	54°23·9'	1°35·6'W	X	93
Scorton Road Fm	N Yks	NZ2702	54°25·0'	1°34·6'W	FM	93
Sco Ruston	Norf	TG2821	52°44·5'	1°23·1'E	T	133,134
Scoska Moor	N Yks	SD8972	54°8·9'	2°9·7'W	X	98
Scoska Wood	N Yks	SD9172	54°8·9'	2°7·9'W	F	98
Scosthrop	N Yks	SD9059	54°1·9'	2°8·7'W	X	103
Scosthrop High Moor	N Yks	SD8662	54°3·5'	2°12·4'W	X	98
Scosthrop Moor	N Yks	SD8761	54°2·9'	2°11·5'W	X	98
Scotbheinn	N Eil	NF8656	57°29·4'	7°14·0'W	T	22
Scotby	Cumbr	NY4454	54°52·9'	2°51·9'W	T	85
Scotby Ghyll	Cumbr	NY4554	54°52·9'	2°51·0'W	X	86
Scotby Ho	Cumbr	NY4355	54°53·4'	2°52·9'W	X	85
Scotby Holmes	Cumbr	NY4357	54°54·5'	2°52·9'W	X	85
Scotby Shield	Cumbr	NY4554	54°52·9'	2°51·0'W	X	86
Scotch Corner	N Yks	NZ2105	54°26·6'	1°40·1'W	X	93
Scotch Corner	N Yks	SE5281	54°13·6'	1°11·7'W	X	100
Scotchcoultard	Northum	NY7170	55°1·7'	2°26·8'W	X	86,87
Scotchcoultard Waste	Northum	NY7071	55°2·2'	2°27·7'W	X	86,87
Scotchells Brook	I of W	SZ5884	50°39·4'	1°10·4'W	W	196
Scotchergill	Cumbr	SD7187	54°16·9'	2°26·3'W	X	98
Scotchers Fm	Surrey	TQ0061	51°20·6'	0°33·5'W	FM	176,186
Scotches	Derby	SK3448	53°1·9'	1°29·2'W	T	119
Scotch Green	Lancs	SD5440	53°51·5'	2°41·5'W	X	102
Scotch Green Fm	Suff	TL7250	52°7·5'	0°31·2'E	FM	154
Scotch Halls	Northum	NY8454	54°53·1'	2°14·5'W	X	86,87
Scotch Hill	Moray	NJ3555	57°35·1'	3°4·8'W	X	28
Scotch Hill	Staffs	SK1622	52°48·0'	1°45·4'W	X	128
Scotch Isle Fm	Durham	NZ0936	54°43·4'	1°51·2'W	FM	92
Scotch Kershope	Scot Bord	NY5285	55°9·7'	2°44·8'W	X	79
Scotch Knowe	Scot Bord	NY5588	55°11·3'	2°42·0'W	X	80
Scotch Peter's Resr	Blae Gw	SO1508	51°46·1'	3°13·5'W	W	161
Scotch Pine (PH)	Carm	SN6410	51°46·6'	3°57·8'W	X	159
Scotch Wood	W Berks	SU4269	51°25·3'	1°23·4'W	F	174
Scotforth	Lancs	SD4859	54°1·7'	2°47·2'W	T	102
Scotgate	Kirk	SE1211	53°36·0'	1°48·7'W	T	110
Scotgrove Wood	Lincs	TF1370	53°13·1'	0°18·0'W	F	121
Scot Hall	Cumbr	NY0802	54°24·6'	3°24·6'W	X	89
Scot Hay	Staffs	SJ8047	53°1·4'	2°17·5'W	T	118
Scothern	Lincs	TF0377	53°17·0'	0°26·9'W	T	121
Scothern Grange	Lincs	TF0578	53°17·5'	0°25·1'W	X	121
Scoth Fm	Lincs	TF0722	52°47·3'	0°24·4'W	FM	130
Scotland	Devon	SS2803	50°48·3'	4°26·1'W	X	190
Scotland	Devon	SS8007	50°51·2'	3°41·9'W	X	191
Scotland	Dorset	SY9684	50°39·6'	2°3·0'W	X	195
Scotland	Leic	SK3822	52°47·9'	1°25·8'W	T	128
Scotland	Leic	SP6898	52°34·8'	0°59·4'W	T	141
Scotland	Lincs	TF0030	52°51·7'	0°30·5'W	T	130
Scotland	W Berks	SU5669	51°25·3'	1°11·3'W	T	174
Scotland Bank	Heref	SO3043	52°5·1'	3°0·9'W	X	148,161
Scotland Corner	Corn	SW9468	50°28·8'	4°53·8'W	X	200
Scotland Corner (Tumuli)	Corn	SW9468	50°28·8'	4°53·8'W	A	200
Scotland Cottage	Hants	SU1120	50°59·0'	1°50·2'W	X	184
Scotland End	Oxon	SP3433	51°59·9'	1°29·9'W	T	151
Scotland Fens	Suff	TM3547	52°4·5'	1°26·2'E	X	169
Scotland Fm	Cambs	TL3660	52°13·5'	0°0·1'W	FM	154
Scotland Fm	Corn	SW8054	50°20·9'	5°5·2'W	FM	200
Scotland Fm	Derby	SK4336	52°55·4'	1°21·2'W	FM	129
Scotland Fm	Devon	SX3791	50°42·0'	4°18·1'W	FM	190
Scotland Fm	Hants	SU7353	51°16·5'	0°56·8'W	FM	186
Scotland Fm	Hants	SU7529	51°3·6'	0°55·4'W	FM	186,197
Scotland Fm	Lincs	SK8965	53°10·7'	0°39·7'W	FM	121
Scotland Fm	Lincs	TF4072	53°13·8'	0°6·3'E	FM	122
Scotland Fm	Lincs	TF4072	53°13·8'	0°6·3'E	FM	122
Scotland Fm	Notts	SK5127	52°50·5'	1°14·2'W	FM	129
Scotland Fm	Notts	SK6074	53°15·8'	1°5·6'W	FM	120
Scotland Fm	N Yks	SE5294	54°20·6'	1°11·6'W	FM	100
Scotland Fm	Somer	ST8151	51°15·7'	2°16·0'W	FM	183
Scotland Gate	D & G	NY3474	55°3·6'	3°1·6'W	X	85
Scotland Gate	Northum	NZ2584	55°9·2'	1°36·0'W	T	81
Scotland Hill Fm	Cered	SN2444	52°4·2'	4°33·7'W	FM	145
Scotland Hill Fm	Notts	SK5926	52°49·9'	1°7·0'W	FM	129
Scotland Nursery	Derby	SK3359	53°7·9'	1°30·0'W	X	119
Scotlands	Wolv	SJ9301	52°36·6'	2°5·8'W	T	127,139
Scotlands Fm	S Glos	ST6495	51°39·4'	2°31·0'W	FM	162
Scotland's Haven	Highld	ND3174	58°39·2'	3°10·9'W	W	7,12
Scotland Street	Suff	TL9936	51°59·4'	0°54·3'E	T	155
Scotlandwell	Pth & Kin	NO1801	56°11·9'	3°18·9'W	T	58
Scotland Wood	Northnts	SP7378	52°23·9'	0°55·2'W	F	141
Scotland Wood	N Yks	SE5240	53°51·5'	1°12·1'W	F	105
Scotland Wood Fm	Northnts	SP7377	52°23·4'	0°55·2'W	FM	141
Scot Lane End	Bolton	SD6209	53°34·8'	2°34·0'W	T	109
Scotman's Flash	Wigan	SD5703	53°31·6'	2°38·5'W	W	108
Scotman's Sled		TF5330	52°51·0'	0°16·7'E	W	131
Scotmill	Arg & Bt	NR7956	55°45·1'	5°30·9'W	X	62
Scotney Castle	Kent	TQ6835	51°5·6'	0°24·3'E	X	188
Scotney Court	Kent	TR0119	50°56·3'	0°52·0'E	X	189
Scotney Fm	N Lincs	SE9516	53°38·1'	0°33·4'W	FM	112
Scotneys	Essex	TL7537	52°0·5'	0°33·4'E	X	155
Scotnish	Arg & Bt	NR7588	56°2·2'	5°36·3'W	X	55
Scotnish Fm	Arg & Bt	NR7588	56°2·2'	5°36·3'W	FM	55
Scotsborough Ho	Pemb	SN1101	51°40·8'	4°43·9'W	A	158
Scotsbrig	D & G	NY2176	55°4·6'	3°13·8'W	X	85
Scotsburn	Highld	NH7275	57°45·1'	4°8·6'W	X	21
Scotsburn	Moray	NJ0860	57°37·5'	3°32·0'W	X	27
Scotsburn	Moray	NJ2760	57°37·7'	3°12·9'W	X	28
Scots Burn	S Lanak	NS7834	55°35·3'	3°55·7'W	W	71
Scotsburn Ho	Highld	NH7276	57°45·6'	4°8·6'W	X	21
Scotsburn Wood	Highld	NH7176	57°45·6'	4°9·6'W	F	21
Scotscalder Sta	Highld	ND0955	58°28·7'	3°33·2'W	X	11,12
Scotscraig	Fife	NO4428	56°26·7'	2°54·1'W	X	54,59
Scots' Dike	Cumbr	NY3573	55°3·1'	3°0·6'W	A	85
Scotsdike	Cumbr	NY3873	55°3·1'	2°57·8'W	X	85
Scots Dike	N Yks	NZ1802	54°25·0'	1°42·9'W	A	92
Scotsfield	D & G	NY2369	55°0·8'	3°11·8'W	X	85
Scots Float	E Susx	TQ9322	50°58·1'	0°45·3'E	X	189
Scot's Fm	Oxon	SU6683	51°32·8'	1°2·5'W	FM	175
Scotsford Fm	E Susx	TQ6024	50°59·8'	0°17·2'E	FM	199
Scots' Gap	Northum	NZ0486	55°10·3'	1°55·8'W	T	81

Scotsgrove Ho	Bucks	SP7107	51°45·7'	0°57·9'W	X	165
Scotshall	Fife	NO5305	56°14·4'	2°45·1'W	X	59
Scotsham	Devon	SS8310	50°52·9'	3°39·4'W	X	191
Scotshill	Moray	NJ3553	57°34·0'	3°4·7'W	X	28
Scot's Ho	S Tyne	NZ3260	54°56·3'	1°29·6'W	X	88
Scots Hole	Heref	SO5239	52°3·1'	2°41·6'W	A	149
Scotsland Fm	Surrey	TQ0040	51°9·3'	0°33·8'W	FM	186
Scotsman's Knowe	Northum	NT9018	55°27·6'	2°9·1'W	X	80
Scotsmill	Aberd	NJ5618	57°15·3'	2°43·3'W	X	37
Scotsmill	Aberd	NJ6065	57°40·6'	2°39·8'W	X	29
Scotsmill	Aberd	NJ8213	57°12·7'	2°17·4'W	X	38
Scotsmill	Scot Bord	NT2739	55°38·6'	3°9·2'W	X	73
Scot's Poor	Wilts	SU2856	51°18·4'	1°35·5'W	X	174
Scotstarvit	Fife	NO3611	56°17·5'	3°1·6'W	X	59
Scotstarvit Tower	Fife	NO3711	56°17·5'	3°0·6'W	A	59
Scotston	Aberd	NJ6231	57°22·3'	2°37·5'W	X	29,37
Scotston	Aberd	NJ6852	57°33·7'	2°31·6'W	X	29
Scotston	Aberd	NJ8638	57°26·2'	2°13·5'W	X	30
Scotston	Aberd	NJ9837	57°25·7'	2°1·5'W	X	30
Scotston	Aberd	NO7373	56°51·1'	2°26·1'W	T	45
Scotston	Angus	NO3339	56°32·6'	3°4·9'W	X	53
Scotston	Angus	NO6357	56°42·5'	2°35·8'W	X	54
Scotston	Pth & Kin	NN9042	56°33·7'	3°46·9'W	X	52
Scotston	Scot Bord	NT7652	55°45·9'	2°22·5'W	X	67,74
Scotston Hill	Angus	NO3440	56°33·1'	3°4·0'W	H	54
Scotston Hill	Arg & Bt	NR9090	56°3·7'	5°21·9'W	H	55
Scotstonhill	Moray	NJ2662	57°38·8'	3°13·9'W	X	28
Scotston of Kirkside	Aberd	NO7363	56°45·7'	2°26·0'W	X	45
Scotston of Usan	Angus	NO7154	56°40·9'	2°28·0'W	X	54
Scotstonrig	Scot Bord	NT1345	55°41·7'	3°22·6'W	X	72
Scotstoun	C of Glas	NS5268	55°53·2'	4°21·5'W	T	64
Scotstoun	Scot Bord	NT1445	55°41·7'	3°21·7'W	X	72
Scotstoun Bank	Scot Bord	NT1444	55°41·2'	3°21·6'W	X	72
Scotstown	Aberd	NJ6864	57°40·1'	2°31·7'W	X	29
Scotstown	Aberd	NJ7606	57°8·9'	2°23·3'W	X	38
Scotstown	Aberd	NK1052	57°33·7'	1°49·5'W	X	30
Scotstown	Cumbr	NY5374	55°3·7'	2°43·7'W	X	86
Scotstown	Highld	NM8163	56°42·7'	5°34·2'W	T	40
Scotstown Head	Aberd	NK1251	57°33·2'	1°47·5'W	X	30
Scotsventure	Fife	NO5509	56°16·5'	2°43·2'W	X	59
Scotswood	N upon Ty	NZ2064	54°58·5'	1°40·8'W	T	88
Scotswood	Win & Maid	SU9466	51°23·3'	0°38·6'W	T	175
Scottackleys	Moray	NJ1250	57°32·2'	3°27·7'W	X	28
Scottag	Highld	ND2557	58°29·9'	3°16·7'W	X	11,12
Scottarie Burn	Highld	NC8008	58°3·0'	4°1·5'W	W	17
Scottas	Highld	NG7400	57°2·4'	5°43·1'W	T	33
Scottas Burn	Highld	NG7401	57°2·9'	5°43·1'W	W	33
Scotter	Lincs	SE8800	53°29·6'	0°40·0'W	T	112
Scotterfield Ho	Lincs	SE9001	53°30·1'	0°38·2'W	X	112
Scotterthorpe	Lincs	SE8702	53°30·7'	0°40·9'W	T	112
Scotterwood Fm	Lincs	SE8600	53°29·6'	0°41·8'W	FM	112
Scott Hill Wood	N Yks	NZ7906	54°26·8'	0°46·5'W	F	94
Scott Ho	Lancs	SD7040	53°51·6'	2°27·0'W	X	103
Scott Ho Fm	N Yks	SD9944	53°53·8'	2°0·5'W	FM	103
Scottie's Fm	Essex	TL8920	51°51·0'	0°45·0'E	FM	168
Scottiestone	Aberd	NJ6609	57°10·5'	2°33·3'W	X	38
Scottish Industrial Railway Centre	E Ayr	NS4707	55°20·2'	4°24·3'W	X	70,77
Scott Laithe	Lancs	SD7948	53°55·9'	2°18·8'W	X	103
Scottle Holm	Shetld	HU4744	60°10·9'	1°8·7'W	X	4
Scottlethoprpe Lodge	Lincs	TF0519	52°45·7'	0°26·2'W	X	130
Scottlethorpe	Lincs	TF0521	52°46·8'	0°26·2'W	X	130
Scottlethorpe Grange	Lincs	TF0419	52°45·7'	0°27·1'W	X	130
Scotto	Orkney	HY4943	59°16·5'	2°53·2'W	X	5
Scotton	Lincs	SK8899	53°29·1'	0°40·0'W	T	112
Scotton	N Yks	SE1896	54°21·8'	1°43·0'W	T	99
Scotton	N Yks	SE3259	54°1·8'	1°30·3'W	T	104
Scotton Beck	N Yks	SE1795	54°21·3'	1°43·9'W	W	99
Scotton Common	Lincs	SK8599	53°29·1'	0°42·7'W	X	112
Scotton Hall	N Yks	SE1896	54°21·8'	1°43·0'W	X	99
Scottow	Norf	TG2823	52°45·6'	1°23·2'E	T	133,134
Scott's Br	Norf	TF5104	52°37·0'	0°14·2'E	X	143
Scottsdale	Somer	ST1517	50°57·0'	3°12·2'W	X	181,193
Scotts Dod	S Lanak	NT0222	55°29·2'	3°32·6'W	H	72
Scotts Fm	Essex	TL5407	51°44·7'	0°14·2'E	FM	167
Scotts Fm	Essex	TL8202	51°41·5'	0°38·4'E	FM	168
Scott's Fm	Essex	TQ9399	51°39·6'	0°47·8'E	FM	168
Scott's Fm	Wilts	SU0068	51°24·9'	1°59·6'W	FM	173
Scott's Hall	Essex	TQ8993	51°36·5'	0°44·2'E	X	178
Scott's Hall	Suff	TM4667	52°15·0'	1°36·6'E	X	156
Scottshall Coverts	Suff	TM4667	52°15·0'	1°36·6'E	F	156
Scott's Lodge	Kent	TQ4557	51°17·8'	0°5·2'E	X	188
Scotts Mill	Wilts	ST9573	51°27·6'	2°3·9'W	X	173
Scottsquar Hill	Glos	SO8408	51°46·5'	2°13·5'W	X	162
Scott's View	Scot Bord	NT5934	55°36·1'	2°38·6'W	X	73,74
Scotts Walls	Fife	NT1687	56°4·4'	3°20·5'W	X	65,66
Scott's Wood	Notts	SK7291	53°24·9'	0°54·6'W	F	112
Scott Willoughby	Lincs	TF0537	52°55·4'	0°25·9'W	T	130
Scotwater Br	Lincs	SK8958	53°6·9'	0°39·8'W	X	121
Scoughall	E Loth	NT6183	56°2·6'	2°37·1'W	X	67
Scoughall Rocks	E Loth	NT6183	56°2·6'	2°37·1'W	X	67
Scoulag	Arg & Bt	NS1059	55°47·5'	5°1·4'W	X	63
Scoulag Point	Arg & Bt	NS1160	55°48·0'	5°0·5'W	X	63
Scoul Eilean	Arg & Bt	NM7611	56°14·6'	5°36·5'W	X	55
Scouller	Arg & Bt	NR3762	55°47·0'	6°11·3'W	X	60,61
Scoulters	Orkney	HY6722	59°5·3'	2°34·1'W	X	5
Scoulton	Norf	TF9800	52°33·9'	0°55·7'E	T	144
Scoulton Hall	Norf	TL9799	52°33·4'	0°54·8'E	X	144
Scoulton Heath	Norf	TF9801	52°34·5'	0°55·7'E	F	144
Scoulton Mere	Norf	TF9801	52°34·5'	0°55·7'E	W	144
Scounslow Green	Staffs	SK0929	52°51·7'	1°51·6'W	T	128
Scoup	N Ayr	NS3551	55°43·7'	4°37·2'W	X	63
Scoured Pig	Scot Bord	NT5851	55°45·3'	2°39·7'W	X	67,73,74
Scourfield	Pemb	SN0119	51°50·3'	4°52·9'W	X	157,158
Scourie	Highld	NC1544	58°21·0'	5°9·2'W	T	9
Scourie Bay	Highld	NC1445	58°21·5'	5°10·3'W	W	9
Scourie More	Highld	NC1444	58°21·0'	5°10·2'W	X	9
Scousburgh	Shetld	HU3717	59°56·4'	1°19·8'W	T	4
Scouse Fm	Devon	SY3498	50°46·9'	2°55·8'W	FM	193
Scoutber Crag	N Yks	SD7760	54°2·4'	2°20·7'W	X	98

Scoutber End	N Yks	SD7760	54°2·4'	2°20·7'W	X	98
Scoutbog	Aberd	NJ8126	57°19·7'	2°18·5'W	X	38
Scout Dike	Barns	SE2304	53°32·2'	1°38·8'W	T	110
Scout Dike Resr	Barns	SE2305	53°32·7'	1°38·8'W	W	110
Scout Fm	Herts	TL1012	51°48·0'	0°23·9'W	FM	166
Scout Fm	Tames	SD9701	53°30·6'	2°2·3'W	FM	109
Scout Green	Cumbr	NY5907	54°27·7'	2°37·5'W	T	91
Scouthal	Highld	ND2353	58°27·8'	3°18·7'W	X	11,12
Southead	Oldham	SD9605	53°32·7'	2°3·2'W	T	109
Scout Head	Stir	NS7393	56°7·0'	4°2·1'W	H	57
Scout Hill	Cumbr	SD5682	54°14·2'	2°40·1'W	H	97
Scout Moor	Lancs	SD8219	53°40·3'	2°15·9'W	X	109
Scout Pt	Scot Bord	NT9563	55°51·9'	2°4·4'W	X	67
Scout Scar	Cumbr	SD4891	54°19·0'	2°47·5'W	X	97
Scoutts Fm	S Ayr	NS4126	55°30·4'	4°30·6'W	FM	70
Scoval	Highld	NG1851	57°28·0'	6°41·7'W	X	23
Scoveston	Pemb	SM9306	51°43·1'	4°59·4'W	X	157,158
Scoveston Fort	Pemb	SM9406	51°43·1'	4°58·6'W	X	157,158
Scow	Cumbr	SD7285	54°15·8'	2°25·4'W	X	98
Scow	Cumbr	SD7785	54°15·9'	2°20·8'W	X	98
Scow Hall	N Yks	SE2052	53°58·1'	1°41·3'W	X	104
Scowles	Glos	SO5610	51°47·5'	2°37·9'W	T	162
Scowles, The	Glos	SO6004	51°44·2'	2°34·4'W	X	162
Scows	Orkney	HY3609	58°58·1'	3°6·3'W	X	6,7
Scraada	Shetld	HU2179	60°29·9'	1°36·6'W	X	3
Scrabster	Highld	NC5954	58°27·4'	4°24·5'W	X	10
Scrabster	Highld	ND0970	58°36·8'	3°33·5'W	T	12
Scrabster Hill	Highld	ND0769	58°36·2'	3°35·5'W	X	11,12
Scrabster Ho	Highld	ND0969	58°36·2'	3°33·5'W	X	12
Scrabster Loch	Highld	ND0870	58°36·8'	3°34·5'W	W	12
Scraeback	Shetld	HU3855	60°16·9'	1°18·3'W	X	3
Scrae Field	Shetld	HU4136	60°6·7'	1°15·3'W	H	4
Scraesburgh	Scot Bord	NT6718	55°27·5'	2°30·9'W	T	80
Scraesburgh Fell	Scot Bord	NT7812	55°24·3'	2°20·4'W	X	80
Scraesburgh Hope	Scot Bord	NT7812	55°24·3'	2°20·4'W	X	80
Scraesdon Fort	Corn	SX3954	50°22·1'	4°15·5'W	A	201
Scrafield	Lincs	TF3068	53°11·8'	0°2·8'W	T	122
Scragged Oak	Kent	TQ8061	51°19·4'	0°35·4'E	T	178,188
Scragley Hill	Surrey	SU9154	51°17·6'	0°41·3'W	X	186
Scrag Oak	E Susx	TQ6329	51°2·5'	0°19·9'E	X	188,199
Scrag Oak	E Susx	TQ8615	50°54·5'	0°39·1'E	X	189,199
Scraib Wood	Moray	NJ5450	57°32·5'	2°45·6'W	F	29
Scrainwood	Northum	NT9909	55°22·7'	2°0·5'W	T	81
Scraith Burn	Durham	NY8038	54°44·4'	2°18·2'W	W	91,92
Scrane End	Lincs	TF3841	52°57·1'	0°3·7'E	T	131
Scrape Burn	Scot Bord	NT1533	55°35·2'	3°20·5'W	X	72
Scrape Burn	Scot Bord	NT1734	55°35·8'	3°18·6'W	W	72
Scrape, The	Scot Bord	NT1732	55°34·7'	3°18·6'W	H	72
Scrapsgate	Kent	TQ9474	51°26·1'	0°47·9'E	T	178
Scraptoft	C of Leic	SK6405	52°38·6'	1°2·8'W	T	140
Scraptoft Hill Fm	Leic	SK6605	52°38·6'	1°1·1'W	FM	141
Scraptoft Lodge Fm	Leic	SK6506	52°39·1'	1°1·9'W	FM	141
Scrapton	Somer	ST2910	50°53·3'	3°0·2'W	T	193
Scratby	Norf	TG5015	52°40·7'	1°42·3'E	T	134
Scratby Hall	Norf	TG5015	52°40·7'	1°42·3'E	X	134
Scratch Alley	N Yks	NZ8315	54°31·6'	0°42·6'W	X	94
Scratchbury	Wilts	ST9144	51°11·9'	2°7·3'W	A	184
Scratchbury Hill	Wilts	ST9144	51°11·9'	2°7·3'W	H	184
Scratchell's Bay	I of W	SZ2984	50°39·5'	1°35·0'W	W	196
Scratchings Fm	W Susx	SU9828	51°2·8'	0°35·7'W	FM	186,197
Scratchmere Scar	Cumbr	NY5137	54°43·8'	2°45·2'W	X	90
Scratchwood	Barnet	TQ2094	51°38·1'	0°15·6'W	X	166,176
Scratchwood Service Area	Barnet	TQ2094	51°38·1'	0°15·6'W	X	166,176
Scrathy Holes	Scot Bord	NT6303	55°19·4'	2°34·6'W	X	80
Scraulac	Aberd	NJ3105	57°8·1'	3°7·9'W	H	37
Scravels	Essex	TL6910	51°46·0'	0°27·3'E	X	167
Scrawsdon Fm	Corn	SX3170	50°30·6'	4°22·6'W	FM	201
Scrayingham	N Yks	SE7360	54°2·1'	0°52·7'W	T	100
Scrayingham Grange	N Yks	SE7560	54°2·1'	0°50·9'W	X	100
Screadan	Highld	ND1324	58°12·0'	3°28·3'W	X	17
Scredda	Corn	SX0154	50°21·4'	4°47·5'W	T	200
Scredington	Lincs	TF0940	52°57·0'	0°22·3'W	T	130
Screedy	Somer	ST0925	51°1·3'	3°17·5'W	T	181
Screel	D & G	NX8053	54°51·7'	3°51·8'W	X	84
Screel Hill	D & G	NX7755	54°52·7'	3°54·6'W	H	84
Screens Wood	W Susx	TQ0008	50°52·0'	0°34·3'W	F	197
Screes, The	Cumbr	NY1504	54°25·7'	3°18·2'W	X	89
Screes, The	Cumbr	NY6834	54°42·2'	2°29·4'W	X	91
Scremby	Lincs	TF4467	53°11·0'	0°9·7'E	T	122
Scremerston	Northum	NU0049	55°44·3'	1°59·6'W	T	75
Scremerston Hill	Northum	NU0047	55°43·2'	1°59·6'W	X	75
Scremerston Town Fm	Northum	NU0147	55°43·2'	1°58·6'W	FM	75
Screveton	Notts	SK7343	52°59·0'	0°54·4'W	T	129
Scribheal an Ear	N Eil	NB4648	58°21·1'	6°20·0'W	X	8
Scrible Downs	Corn	SX1477	50°34·0'	4°37·2'W	H	200
Scriddles Fm	Lancs	SD7547	53°55·4'	2°22·4'W	FM	103
Scrifearnach	N Eil	NF7977	57°40·4'	7°22·6'W	X	18
Scrimpo	Orkney	HY4532	59°10·5'	2°57·2'W	X	5,6
Scrinadle	Arg & Bt	NR5077	55°55·5'	5°59·7'W	H	61
Scrip Low	Staffs	SK1246	53°0·9'	1°48·9'W	A	119,128
Scrip's Fm	Essex	TL8420	51°51·1'	0°40·7'E	FM	168
Scripton	Durham	NZ2338	54°44·4'	1°38·1'W	X	93
Scrithabhal	N Eil	NB4854	58°24·4'	6°18·4'W	H	8
Scrithwaite Fm	Cumbr	SD2191	54°18·8'	3°12·4'W	FM	96
Scrivan	N Ayr	NR9328	55°30·4'	5°16·2'W	X	68,69
Scrivelsby	Lincs	TF2666	53°10·8'	0°6·5'W	T	122
Scrivelsby Court	Lincs	TF2666	53°10·8'	0°6·5'W	A	122
Scrivelsby Grange	Lincs	TF2665	53°10·3'	0°6·5'W	X	122
Scriven	N Yks	SE3458	54°1·3'	1°28·4'W	T	104
Scriventon	Kent	TQ5542	51°9·6'	0°13·4'E	X	188
Scrog Bank	Cumbr	NY6822	54°35·8'	2°29·3'W	X	91
Scrogbank Rig	Scot Bord	NT3837	55°37·6'	2°58·6'W	X	73
Scroggerfield	Angus	NO4147	56°36·9'	2°57·2'W	X	54
Scrogg Fm	N Yks	SE1689	54°18·0'	1°44·8'W	FM	99
Scrogg Fm	N Yks	SE1892	54°19·6'	1°43·0'W	FM	99
Scroggie Hall	D & G	NX6779	55°5·5'	4°4·6'W	X	77,84
Scroggiehill Fm	D & G	NX8064	54°57·6'	3°52·0'W	FM	84
Scroggs	D & G	NY1681	55°7·2'	3°18·6'W	X	79
Scroggs	Durham	NZ0322	54°35·8'	1°56·8'W	X	92
Scroggs Fm	Cumbr	SD4699	54°23·3'	2°49·5'W	FM	97

Scroghill	Aberd	NJ9646	57°30·5'	2°3·5'W	X	30
Scrog Hill	Northum	NU2521	55°29·2'	1°35·8'W	H	75
Scrogs of Drumruck	D & G	NX5762	54°56·2'	4°13·5'W	X	83
Scrogs Wood	N Yks	SE6957	54°0·5'	0°56·4'W	F	105,106
Scrogton	S Lanak	NS8230	55°33·2'	3°51·8'W	X	71,72
Scrogtonhead	S Lanak	NS8230	55°33·2'	3°51·8'W	X	71,72
Scrombeck Fm	N Yks	SE5020	53°40·7'	1°14·2'W	FM	105
Scronkey	Lancs	SD4147	53°55·2'	2°53·5'W	T	102
Scroo	Shetld	HU4029	60°2·9'	1°16·4'W	H	4
Scrooby	Notts	SK6590	53°24·4'	1°0·9'W	T	111
Scrooby Top Ho	Notts	SK6588	53°23·3'	1°0·9'W	X	111,120
Scroof	Scot Bord	NT4043	55°40·9'	2°56·8'W	X	73
Scroof Hill	Scot Bord	NT4043	55°40·9'	2°56·8'W	H	73
Scrope Fm	Wilts	SU2669	51°25·4'	1°37·2'W	FM	174
Scrope's Wood	Wilts	SU2668	51°24·9'	1°37·2'W	F	174
Scropton	Derby	SK1930	52°52·3'	1°42·7'W	T	128
Scrot Mòr	N Eil	NF6360	57°30·5'	7°37·2'W	X	22
Scrubbett's Fm	Glos	ST8093	51°38·4'	2°16·9'W	FM	162,173
Scrubb Fm	Hants	SU5930	51°4·2'	1°9·1'W	FM	185
Scrubbity Barrows	Dorset	ST9717	50°57·4'	2°2·2'W	A	184
Scrubditch	Glos	SP0007	51°45·9'	1°59·6'W	A	163
Scrub Hill	Essex	TQ6091	51°35·9'	0°19·0'E	X	177
Scrub Hill	Lincs	TF2355	53°4·9'	0°9·4'W	T	122
Scrub Holt Fm	NE Lincs	TA2104	53°31·4'	0°10·1'W	FM	113
Scrubs	Bucks	SP8505	51°44·5'	0°45·7'W	X	165
Scrubs Fm	Oxon	SP2507	51°45·9'	1°37·9'W	FM	163
Scrubs, The	Essex	TQ8490	51°35·0'	0°39·7'E	F	178
Scrubs, The	Glos	SO8908	51°46·5'	2°9·2'W	X	163
Scrubs, The	Wilts	SU2056	51°18·4'	1°42·4'W	X	174
Scruel Barton	Devon	SY2093	50°44·1'	3°7·6'W	X	192,193
Scruit	Orkney	HY3028	59°8·3'	3°12·9'W	X	6
Scruschloch	Angus	NO2357	56°42·2'	3°15·0'W	X	53
Scruton	N Yks	SE3092	54°19·6'	1°31·9'W	T	99
Scruton Grange	N Yks	SE2992	54°19·6'	1°32·8'W	X	99
Scrwgan	Powys	SJ1823	52°48·1'	3°12·6'W	T	125
Scuan	Orkney	HY3312	58°59·7'	3°9·5'W	X	6
Scuarhead	Scot Bord	NT4227	55°32·2'	2°54·7'W	X	73
Scuddaborg	Highld	NG3764	57°35·6'	6°23·6'W	X	23
Scudills Wick	Shetld	HU4756	60°17·4'	1°8·5'W	W	2,3
Scuffings	E Susx	TQ4316	50°55·8'	0°2·5'E	X	198
Scugdale Beck	N Yks	NZ5000	54°23·8'	1°13·4'W	W	93
Scugdale Beck	N Yks	SE5199	54°23·3'	1°12·5'W	W	100
Scugdale Fm	Red & Cl	NZ5816	54°32·4'	1°5·8'W	FM	93
Scugdale Hall	N Yks	NZ5100	54°23·8'	1°12·4'W	X	93
Scuggate	Cumbr	NY4474	55°3·7'	2°52·2'W	T	85
Scugger Ho	Cumbr	NY4052	54°51·8'	2°55·7'W	X	85
Scugg Fm	Cumbr	NY4474	55°3·7'	2°52·2'W	FM	85
Scug Wood	Moray	NJ3742	57°28·1'	3°2·6'W	F	28
Sculcoates	K upon H	TA0930	53°45·5'	0°20·4'W	T	107
Scullridge	Lincs	TF4947	53°0·2'	0°13·6'E	X	131
Scullsgate Ho	Kent	TQ7932	51°3·8'	0°33·7'E	X	188
Sculpin's Fm	Essex	TL7133	51°58·4'	0°29·8'E	FM	167
Sculptor's Cave	Moray	NJ1770	57°43·0'	3°23·1'W	A	28
Sculthorpe	Norf	TF8931	52°50·8'	0°48·8'E	T	132
Sculthorpe Airfield	Norf	TF8631	52°50·9'	0°46·1'E	X	132
Sculthorpe Fen	Norf	TF9030	52°50·3'	0°49·7'E	X	132
Sculthorpe Moor	Norf	TF9030	52°50·3'	0°49·7'E	X	132
Scult, The	Shetld	HU4775	60°27·6'	1°8·2'W	X	2,3
Scunthorpe	N Lincs	SE8910	53°35·0'	0°38·9'W	T	112
Scupholme	Lincs	TF4091	53°24·1'	0°6·8'E	X	113
Scur Beck	Durham	NZ0017	54°33·1'	1°59·6'W	W	92
Scurdargue	Aberd	NJ4828	57°20·6'	2°51·4'W	X	37
Scurdie	Shetld	HU2545	60°11·6'	1°32·5'W	X	4
Scurdie Ness	Angus	NO7356	56°42·0'	2°26·0'W	X	54
Scurf Carr Plantns	N Yks	SE9681	54°13·2'	0°31·2'W	F	101
Scurf Dike	E Yorks	TA0550	53°56·4'	0°23·6'W	W	107
Scurf Dyke Fm	E Yorks	TA0450	53°56·4'	0°24·5'W	FM	107
Scurff Hall	N Yks	SE6826	53°43·8'	0°57·7'W	X	105,106
Scurgill	Cumbr	NY0109	54°28·3'	3°31·2'W	X	89
Scurlage	Swan	SS4687	51°33·9'	4°12·9'W	T	159
Scurragh Ho	N Yks	NZ2103	54°25·6'	1°40·2'W	X	93
Scurran Burn	S Ayr	NX1581	55°5·6'	4°53·5'W	W	76
Scurran of Lochterlandoch	Moray	NJ2535	57°24·2'	3°14·4'W	X	28
Scurran of Morinsh	Moray	NJ2435	57°24·2'	3°15·4'W	X	28
Scurran of Well	Moray	NJ2436	57°24·7'	3°15·4'W	X	28
Scurran, The	Pth & Kin	NN8929	56°26·7'	3°47·6'W	X	52,58
Scurrival Point	N Eil	NF6909	57°3·4'	7°27·2'W	X	31
Scuta	Shetld	HU6194	60°37·7'	0°52·6'W	X	1,2
Scuthamer Knob	Oxon	SU4584	51°33·4'	1°20·7'W	A	174
Scuthi Head	Orkney	HY6340	59°15·0'	2°38·4'W	X	5
Scuthvie Bay	Orkney	HY7744	59°17·2'	2°23·7'W	W	5
Scutta Voe	Shetld	HU2749	60°13·7'	1°30·3'W	W	3
Scuttishill Fm	Devon	SX8191	50°42·6'	3°40·7'W	FM	191
Scuts Fm	Hants	SU7455	51°17·6'	0°55·9'W	FM	175,186
Sea	Somer	ST3413	50°55·0'	2°56·0'W	T	193
Seabank Cott	Arg & Bt	NS3377	55°57·7'	4°40·1'W	X	63
Sea Bank Fm	Lincs	TF4789	53°22·9'	0°13·0'E	FM	113,122
Sea Bank Fm	Lincs	TF5379	53°17·4'	0°18·1'E	FM	122
Seabank Villa	Arg & Bt	NM4828	56°22·9'	6°4·5'W	X	48
Sea Barn Fm	Dorset	SY6280	50°37·3'	2°31·9'W	FM	194
Seabeach Ho	W Susx	SU9209	50°52·6'	0°41·2'W	X	197
Seabegs Wood	Falk	NS8179	55°59·6'	3°54·0'W	F	65
Seabhal	N Eil	NB5149	58°21·8'	6°15·0'W	H	8
Seabhal	N Eil	NF7627	57°13·4'	7°21·7'W	H	22
Seaborough	Dorset	ST4206	50°51·3'	2°49·1'W	T	193
Seaborough Court	Dorset	ST4205	50°50·7'	2°49·0'W	X	193
Seaborough Hill	Somer	ST4206	50°51·3'	2°49·1'W	H	193
Seabridge	Staffs	SJ8343	52°59·3'	2°14·8'W	T	118
Seabrook	Kent	TR1834	51°4·1'	1°7·1'E	T	179,189
Seaburn	Sund	NZ4059	54°55·7'	1°22·1'W	T	88
Seacliff	E Loth	NT6084	56°3·1'	2°38·1'W	X	67
Seacombe	Wirral	SJ3290	53°24·4'	3°1·0'W	T	108
Seacombe Cliff	Dorset	SY9876	50°35·3'	2°1·3'W	X	195
Seacourt Stream	Oxon	SP4807	51°45·8'	1°17·9'W	W	164
Seacox Heath	E Susx	TQ7330	51°2·8'	0°28·5'E	T	188
Sea Craig	Fife	NO4228	56°26·7'	2°56·0'W	X	54,59
Seacroft	Leeds	SE3536	53°49·4'	1°27·7'W	T	104
Seacroft	Lincs	TF5660	53°7·1'	0°20·3'E	T	122
Sea Croft	Scot Bord	NT4810	55°23·1'	2°48·8'W	W	79
Sea Cut	N Yks	SE9989	54°17·5'	0°28·3'W	W	94,101

Sea Cut	N Yks	TA0089	54°17·4'	0°27·4'W	W	101
Seadyke	Lincs	TF3236	52°54·5'	0°1·8'W	T	131
Sea Dyke End	Cumbr	NY1354	54°52·6'	3°20·9'W	X	85
Seafar	N Lanak	NS7574	55°56·8'	3°59·7'W	T	64
Seafield	Angus	NO6745	56°36·0'	2°31·8'W	X	54
Seafield	Arg & Bt	NR3159	55°45·2'	6°16·8'W	X	60
Seafield	C of Aber	NJ9104	57°7·9'	2°8·5'W	T	38
Seafield	D & G	NY2064	54°58·1'	3°14·6'W	X	85
Seafield	Falk	NS8678	55°59·1'	3°49·2'W	X	65
Seafield	Highld	NG8340	57°24·2'	5°36·3'W	X	24
Seafield	Highld	NH6946	57°29·4'	4°10·7'W	X	26
Seafield	Highld	NH9183	57°49·7'	3°49·7'W	X	21
Seafield	Midlo	NT2564	55°52·1'	3°11·5'W	T	66
Seafield	Moray	NJ0261	57°38·0'	3°38·0'W	X	27
Seafield	Orkney	HY4107	58°57·0'	3°1·0'W	X	6,7
Seafield	S Ayr	NS3220	55°27·0'	4°38·9'W	T	70
Seafield	Shetld	HU5192	60°36·8'	1°3·6'W	X	1,2
Seafield	W Loth	NT0066	55°52·9'	3°35·5'W	T	65
Seafield Bay	Suff	TM1233	51°57·5'	1°5·5'E	W	168,169
Seafield Fm	Arg & Bt	NR7787	56°1·7'	5°34·3'W	FM	55
Seafield Fm	Moray	NJ5166	57°41·1'	2°48·8'W	FM	29
Seafield Ho	Fife	NT2788	56°5·0'	3°9·9'W	X	66
Seafield Mains	Fife	NO4717	56°20·8'	2°51·0'W	X	59
Seafield Tower	Fife	NT2788	56°5·0'	3°9·9'W	A	66
Sea Fm	Lincs	TF3999	53°28·4'	0°6·1'E	FM	113
Seaford	E Susx	TV4899	50°46·5'	0°6·3'E	T	198
Seaford Bay	E Susx	TV4798	50°46·0'	0°5·5'E	W	198
Seaford College	W Susx	SU9416	50°56·4'	0°39·3'W	X	197
Seaford Grange	Worcs	SO9550	52°9·1'	2°4·0'W	X	150
Seaford Head	E Susx	TV4997	50°45·4'	0°7·1'E	X	199
Seaforth	Sefton	SJ3297	53°28·2'	3°1·1'W	T	108
Sea Geo	Orkney	HY2602	58°54·2'	3°16·6'W	X	6,7
Sea Geo	Orkney	ND4995	58°50·6'	2°52·5'W	X	7
Seager Hill	Heref	SO6138	52°2·6'	2°33·7'W	H	149
Seagrave	Leic	SK6117	52°45·1'	1°5·4'W	T	129
Seagrave Grange	Leic	SK6018	52°45·6'	1°6·2'W	X	129
Seagrave's Fm	Bucks	SU9393	51°37·9'	0°39·0'W	FM	175
Seagrave Wolds	Leic	SK6319	52°46·1'	1°3·6'W	X	129
Seagreens	Aberd	NO7765	56°46·8'	2°22·1'W	X	45
Seagrove Bay	I of W	SZ6391	50°43·1'	1°6·1'W	W	196
Seagry Heath	Wilts	ST9581	51°31·9'	2°3·9'W	T	173
Seagry Ho	Wilts	ST9480	51°31·4'	2°4·8'W	X	173
Seagry Wood	Wilts	ST9481	51°31·9'	2°4·8'W	F	173
Seaham	Durham	NZ4149	54°50·3'	1°21·3'W	T	88
Seaham Grange	Durham	NZ4051	54°51·4'	1°22·2'W	X	88
Seaham Hall	Durham	NZ4250	54°50·8'	1°20·3'W	X	88
Seaheugh Burn	D & G	NY0767	54°59·6'	3°26·8'W	W	85
Seahill Fm	Ches	SJ3569	53°13·1'	2°58·0'W	FM	117
Sea Ho	Northum	NU0249	55°44·3'	1°57·7'W	X	75
Seahouses	Northum	NU2132	55°35·1'	1°39·6'W	T	75
Sea Houses	Northum	NU2617	55°27·0'	1°34·9'W	X	81
Seal	Kent	TQ5456	51°17·2'	0°12·9'E	T	188
Sealand	Flint	SJ3568	53°12·5'	2°58·0'W	T	117
Sealand Manor	Flint	SJ3368	53°12·5'	2°59·8'W	X	117
Sealand Nursery	Flint	SJ3567	53°12·0'	2°58·0'W	X	117
Sealand Reen	Newp	ST2982	51°32·2'	3°1·0'W	W	171
Sealands	V of Glam	SS9072	51°26·4'	3°34·6'W	X	170
Seal Brook	Derby	SK2612	52°42·5'	1°36·5'W	W	128
Seal Carr	Fife	NT2882	56°1·8'	3°8·9'W	X	66
Seal Chart	Kent	TQ5655	51°16·6'	0°14·6'E	F	188
Seal Cott	Arg & Bt	NR3688	56°1·0'	6°13·7'W	X	61
Seale	Surrey	SU8947	51°13·1'	0°43·1'W	T	186
Seal Edge	Derby	SK1088	53°23·6'	1°50·6'W	X	110
Seale Hayne (College)	Devon	SX8273	50°32·9'	3°39·6'W	X	191
Seal Fields Fm	Derby	SK2611	52°42·0'	1°36·5'W	FM	128
Seal Flats	Derby	SK1189	53°24·1'	1°49·7'W	X	110
Sealford Fm	Cumbr	SD5779	54°12·5'	2°39·1'W	FM	97
Seal Houses	N Yks	NY9804	54°26·1'	2°1·4'W	X	92
Seal Houses Moor	N Yks	NY9905	54°26·7'	2°0·5'W	X	92
Seal Howe	Cumbr	NY5912	54°30·3'	2°37·6'W	H	91
Seali Burn	Shetld	HU3574	60°27·2'	1°21·3'W	W	2,3
Sea Life Centre	C of Port	SZ6398	50°46·9'	1°6·0'W	X	196
Sea Lion Cove Sta	I of M	SC4278	54°10·7'	4°24·8'W	X	95
Sealky Head	Highld	ND3852	58°27·4'	3°3·3'W	X	12
Seal Pastures	Derby	SK2913	52°43·1'	1°33·8'W	X	128
Seal Rock		NS3129	55°31·8'	4°40·2'W	X	70
Seal Rock	Arg & Bt	NR7625	55°28·3'	5°32·2'W	X	68,69
Seal Rock	Highld	NG3755	57°30·8'	6°23·0'W	X	23
Seal Rock	I Scilly	SV8514	49°56·8'	6°23·1'W	X	203
Seal Sand		TF5633	52°52·5'	0°19·5'E	X	131
Seal Sands	Stock on T	NZ5225	54°37·3'	1°11·3'W	X	93
Seals Hole	Corn	SX1092	50°42·0'	4°41·1'W	W	190
Seal Skears	Northum	NZ3092	55°13·5'	1°31·3'W	X	81
Seal Skerry	Orkney	HY4320	59°4·1'	2°59·2'W	X	5,6
Seal Skerry	Orkney	HY5331	59°10·1'	2°48·8'W	X	5,6
Seal Skerry	Orkney	HY7856	59°23·6'	2°22·8'W	X	5
Sealskerry Bay	Orkney	HY5331	59°10·1'	2°48·8'W	W	5,6
Seals' Rock	Devon	SS1348	51°12·3'	4°40·2'W	X	180
Seal Stones	Derby	SK1188	53°23·6'	1°49·7'W	X	110
Sealyham	Pemb	SM9627	51°54·5'	4°57·6'W	X	157,158
Seamab Hill	Clackm	NN9901	56°11·7'	3°37·2'W	H	58
Seamark	Fife	NT1597	56°9·7'	3°21·7'W	X	58
Sea Mark Fm	Lancs	SD5534	53°48·3'	2°40·6'W	FM	102
Seamaw Loch	Pth & Kin	NO2231	56°28·1'	3°15·5'W	W	53
Seamer	N Yks	NZ4910	54°29·2'	1°14·2'W	T	93
Seamer	N Yks	TA0183	54°14·2'	0°26·6'W	T	101
Seamer Beacon	N Yks	TA0087	54°16·4'	0°27·4'W	A	101
Seamer Carr	N Yks	TA0281	54°13·1'	0°25·8'W	X	101
Seamer Carr Fm	N Yks	TA0181	54°13·1'	0°26·6'W	FM	101
Seamer Carr Ho	N Yks	TA0382	54°13·6'	0°24·8'W	X	101
Seamer Carrs	N Yks	NZ4809	54°28·7'	1°15·1'W	X	93
Sea Mere	Norf	TG0301	52°34·4'	1°0·1'E	W	144
Sea Mere Fm	Norf	TG0301	52°34·4'	1°0·1'E	FM	144
Seamer Grange Fm	N Yks	NZ4810	54°29·2'	1°15·1'W	FM	93
Seamer Great Wood	N Yks	SE6380	54°13·0'	1°1·6'W	F	100
Seamer Hill	N Yks	NZ5009	54°28·7'	1°13·3'W	X	93
Seamer Ings	N Yks	TA0081	54°13·1'	0°27·6'W	X	101
Seamer Moor	N Yks	NZ4908	54°28·1'	1°14·2'W	X	93
Seamer Moor Fm	N Yks	NZ4908	54°28·1'	1°14·2'W	FM	93
Seamer Sta	N Yks	TA0383	54°14·2'	0°24·8'W	X	101

Seamew Crag	Cumbr	NY3602	54°24·8′	2°58·8′W	X	90
Sea Mill	Cumbr	SD2769	54°6·9′	3°6·6′W	T	96,97
Seamill	N Ayr	NS2047	55°41·2′	4°51·4′W	T	63
Sea Mills	C of Bris	ST5576	51°29·1′	2°38·5′W	T	172
Sea Mills	Corn	SW9273	50°31·4′	4°55·7′W	T	200
Sea Moor Fm	Brad	SE0548	53°55·9′	1°55·0′W	FM	104
Seamore Tarn	Cumbr	NY7327	54°38·5′	2°24·7′W	W	91
Seana Bhaile	N Eil	NF8658	57°30·5′	7°14·1′W	X	22
Seanachaisteal	Highld	NC4069	58°35·0′	4°44·7′W	X	9
Seana Chaisteal	N Eil	NF9087	57°46·2′	7°12·4′W	X	18
Seanachaisteal (Dun)	Highld	NC4069	58°35·0′	4°44·7′W	A	9
Seana Chamas	Highld	NG7384	57°47·6′	5°48·7′W	W	19
Seana Chreag	Highld	NG9494	57°53·5′	5°28·1′W	X	19
Seana Ghabhail	Highld	NN2567	56°46·0′	4°51·3′W	X	41
Sean Airigh	Highld	NC9458	58°30·1′	3°48·7′W	H	11
Sean Airigh Pharlain	Arg & Bt	NR7663	55°48·8′	5°34·1′W	X	62
Seana Mheallan	Highld	NG9355	57°32·5′	5°27·1′W	X	25
Seana Phort	N Eil	NF6462	57°31·7′	7°36·4′W	W	22
Seanarmhail	Arg & Bt	NN0248	56°35·2′	5°13·0′W	X	50
Seana Sgeir	Highld	NC1759	58°29·1′	5°7·9′W	X	9
Sean Bhaile	Arg & Bt	NM3617	56°16·6′	6°15·4′W	X	48
Sean Chlaigionn	Arg & Bt	NR4172	55°52·6′	6°8·0′W	X	60,61
Sean-choille or Genechal, The	Aberd	NO2993	57°1·6′	3°9·7′W	X	37,44
Sean-chreag	Highld	NG8231	57°19·3′	5°36·8′W	X	24
Sean Dùn	Arg & Bt	NM8439	56°29·9′	5°30·1′W	A	49
Sean Ghleann	Arg & Bt	NR7561	55°47·7′	5°34·9′W	X	62
Sean-mhàm	Arg & Bt	NM4544	56°31·4′	6°8·3′W	X	47,48
Sean Mheall	Highld	NN2494	57°0·5′	4°53·4′W	H	34
Seanna Bhraigh	Highld	NH2887	57°50·6′	4°53·4′W	H	20
Seann Chaisteal	N Eil	NG4398	57°54·1′	6°19·8′W	X	14
Seann Chruach	Highld	NM7680	56°51·7′	5°40·0′W	H	40
Seannlac	Highld	NM6776	56°49·3′	5°48·6′W	X	40
Seann Tom	N Eil	NB5359	58°27·2′	6°13·6′W	X	8
Seanor Fm	Derby	SK4164	53°10·5′	1°22·8′W	FM	120
Sean-talamh Mór	Arg & Bt	NR3465	55°48·6′	6°14·3′W	X	60,61
Sea Palling	Norf	TG4226	52°46·9′	1°35·7′E	T	134
Sea Park	Moray	NJ0661	57°38·0′	3°34·0′W	X	27
Sea Pool	Highld	NM6570	56°46·0′	5°50·3′W	W	40
Searby	Lincs	TA0705	53°32·1′	0°22·7′W	T	112
Searby Top	Lincs	TA0807	53°33·1′	0°21·8′W	X	112
Searches Fm	Herts	TL1103	51°43·1′	0°23·2′W	FM	166
Searchfield Fm	Hants	SU1719	50°58·4′	1°45·1′W	FM	184
Search Fm	Wilts	ST7934	51°6·5′	2°17·6′W	FM	183
Sea Reach	Medway	TQ7681	51°30·3′	0°32·6′E	W	178
Sea Reach	Newp	ST3282	51°32·2′	2°58·4′W	W	171
Searigg	D & G	NY1071	55°1·8′	3°24·1′W	X	85
Searigg Cottage	D & G	NY1071	55°1·8′	3°24·1′W	X	85
Searles	E Susx	TQ4225	51°0·6′	0°1·8′E	X	187,198
Searles Fm	W Berks	SU6870	51°25·7′	1°0·9′W	FM	175
Searles Hall	Essex	TL4800	51°41·0′	0°8·8′E	X	167
Searson's Fm	Suff	TM2735	51°58·2′	1°18·7′E	FM	169
Seasalter	Kent	TR0965	51°21·0′	1°0·5′E	T	179
Seasalter Level	Kent	TR0864	51°20·4′	0°59·6′E	X	179
Seascale	Cumbr	NY0301	54°24·0′	3°29·2′W	T	89
Seascale Hall	Cumbr	NY0302	54°24·5′	3°29·3′W	A	89
Seas End Hall	Lincs	TF3127	52°49·7′	0°2·9′W	X	131
Seaside	D & G	NX8051	54°50·6′	3°51·7′W	X	84
Seaside	Pth & Kin	NO2824	56°24·4′	3°9·6′W	T	53,59
Season Point	Devon	SX5247	50°18·5′	4°4·3′W	X	201
Sea Spray	Dorset	SY9977	50°35·8′	2°0·5′W	X	195
Seat	Cumbr	NY1813	54°30·6′	3°15·6′W	X	89,90
Seat	Cumbr	NY2840	54°45·2′	3°6·7′W	X	85
Seata Fm	N Yks	SD9988	54°17·5′	2°0·5′W	FM	98
Sea Taing	Orkney	ND4895	58°50·6′	2°53·6′W	X	7
Seatallan	Cumbr	NY1308	54°27·8′	3°20·1′W	H	89
Seater	Highld	ND2460	58°31·6′	3°17·8′W	X	11,12
Seater	Highld	ND3572	58°38·1′	3°6·7′W	X	7,12
Seater	Orkney	HY7243	59°16·6′	2°29·0′W	X	5
Seat Fm	Cumbr	NY4622	54°35·7′	2°49·7′W	FM	90
Seat Hall	N Yks	SD6570	54°7·7′	2°31·7′W	X	97
Seathaugh	Pth & Kin	NN8710	56°16·4′	3°49·0′W	X	58
Seat Hill	Cumbr	NY6517	54°33·1′	2°32·0′W	X	91
Seat Hill	S Lanak	NT0351	55°44·8′	3°32·3′W	H	65,72
Seat Hill	Somer	ST7038	51°8·7′	2°25·3′W	H	183
Seat Hill Fm	Cumbr	NY4863	54°57·8′	2°48·3′W	FM	86
Seat Ho	N Yks	SD9257	54°0·8′	2°6·9′W	X	103
Seathope	Scot Bord	NT3740	55°39·2′	2°59·6′W	X	73
Seathope Law	Scot Bord	NT3840	55°39·2′	2°58·7′W	H	73
Seathorne	Lincs	TF5765	53°9·8′	0°21·3′E	T	122
Seathorpe Rig	Scot Bord	NT3742	55°40·3′	2°59·7′W	H	73
Seat How	Cumbr	NY2125	54°37·1′	3°13·0′W	X	89,90
Seat How	N Yks	SE1297	54°22·3′	1°48·5′W	H	99
Seathwaite	Cumbr	NY2312	54°30·1′	3°10·9′W	T	89,90
Seathwaite	Cumbr	NY3804	54°25·9′	2°56·9′W	X	90
Seathwaite	Cumbr	SD2296	54°21·5′	3°11·6′W	T	96
Seathwaite Fell	Cumbr	NY2210	54°29·0′	3°11·8′W	H	89,90
Seathwaite Fells	Cumbr	SD2597	54°22·0′	3°8·8′W	X	96
Seathwaite Tarn	Cumbr	SD2598	54°22·6′	3°8·9′W	W	96
Seatle	Cumbr	SD3783	54°14·6′	2°57·6′W	T	96,97
Seatle Plantn	Cumbr	SD3783	54°14·6′	2°57·6′W	F	96,97
Seat of Mandrup	Shetld	HU3624	60°0·2′	1°20·8′W	X	4
Seatoller	Cumbr	NY2413	54°30·6′	3°10·0′W	T	89,90
Seatoller Fell	Cumbr	NY2213	54°30·6′	3°11·9′W	X	89,90
Seaton	C of Aber	NJ9408	57°10·0′	2°5·5′W	T	38
Seaton	Corn	SX3054	50°21·9′	4°23·0′W	T	201
Seaton	Cumbr	NY0130	54°39·6′	3°31·7′W	T	89
Seaton	Devon	SY2490	50°42·5′	3°4·2′W	T	192,193
Seaton	Durham	NZ3949	54°50·3′	1°23·1′W	T	88
Seaton	E Yorks	TA1646	53°54·1′	0°13·7′W	T	107
Seaton	Kent	TR2258	51°16·9′	1°11·4′E	T	179
Seaton	Northum	NZ3276	55°4·9′	1°29·5′W	T	88
Seaton	Rut	SP9098	52°34·6′	0°39·9′W	T	141
Seaton Bank Top	Durham	NZ3949	54°50·3′	1°23·1′W	X	88
Seaton Bay	Devon	SY2489	50°42·0′	3°4·2′W	W	192
Seaton Beach	Corn	SX3054	50°21·9′	4°23·0′W	X	201
Seaton Burn	N Tyne	NZ2374	55°3·8′	1°38·0′W	T	88
Seaton Burn	N Tyne	NZ2572	55°2·8′	1°36·1′W	W	88
Seaton Burn Hall	N Tyne	NZ2473	55°3·3′	1°37·0′W	X	88
Seaton Carew	Hartpl	NZ5229	54°39·4′	1°11·2′W	T	93
Seaton Delaval	Northum	NZ3075	55°4·4′	1°31·4′W	T	88
Seaton & District Electric Tramway	Devon	SY2591	50°43·1′	3°3·4′W	X	192,193
Seaton Down	Devon	SY2391	50°43·0′	3°5·1′W	X	192,193
Seaton Down (Earthwork)	Devon	SY2391	50°43·0′	3°5·1′W	A	192,193
Seaton Down Hill	Devon	SY2391	50°43·0′	3°5·1′W	X	192,193
Seaton Grange	E Yorks	TA1647	53°54·6′	0°13·6′W	X	107
Seaton Grange	Rut	SP8998	52°34·6′	0°40·8′W	X	141
Seaton Hall	Cumbr	SD1089	54°17·6′	3°22·5′W	A	96
Seaton Hall	N Yks	NZ7817	54°32·8′	0°47·2′W	X	94
Seaton Ho	Angus	NO6542	56°34·4′	2°33·7′W	X	54
Seaton Ho	Northum	NU2612	55°24·3′	1°34·9′W	X	81
Seaton Hold	E Yorks	TA1648	53°55·1′	0°13·6′W	X	107
Seaton Hole	Devon	SY2389	50°42·0′	3°5·0′W	W	192
Seaton Junction	Devon	SY2496	50°45·8′	3°4·3′W	X	192,193
Seaton Moor Ho	Durham	NZ3849	54°50·3′	1°24·1′W	X	88
Seaton New Hall	E Yorks	SE7839	53°50·7′	0°48·5′W	X	105,106
Seaton Old Hall	E Yorks	SE7739	53°50·7′	0°49·4′W	X	105,106
Seaton Park	C of Aber	NJ9409	57°10·6′	2°5·5′W	X	38
Seaton Point	Northum	NU2612	55°24·3′	1°34·9′W	X	81
Seaton Red House Fm	Northum	NZ3177	55°5·4′	1°30·4′W	FM	88
Seaton Ross	E Yorks	SE7841	53°51·8′	0°48·4′W	T	105,106
Seaton Sands	Hartpl	NZ5329	54°39·4′	1°10·3′W	X	93
Seaton Sea Rocks	Northum	NZ3380	55°7·0′	1°28·5′W	X	81
Seaton Sluice	Northum	NZ3376	55°4·9′	1°28·6′W	T	88
Seaton Terrace	Northum	NZ3175	55°4·4′	1°30·4′W	X	88
Seatown	Aberd	NJ5966	57°41·2′	2°40·8′W	X	29
Seatown	Aberd	NK1057	57°36·4′	1°49·5′W	X	30
Seatown	Dorset	SY4291	50°43·2′	2°48·9′W	T	193
Seatown	Moray	NJ2370	57°43·1′	3°17·1′W	T	28
Seatown	Moray	NJ4265	57°40·5′	2°57·9′W	T	28
Seatown	Moray	NJ5067	57°41·7′	2°49·9′W	X	29
Seat Robert	Cumbr	NY5211	54°29·8′	2°44·0′W	H	90
Seats	Aberd	NJ6212	57°12·1′	2°37·3′W	X	37
Seats	Cumbr	NY8413	54°31·0′	2°14·4′W	X	91,92
Seat Sandal	Cumbr	NY3411	54°29·7′	3°0·7′W	H	90
Seatsides	Northum	NY7566	54°59·5′	2°23·0′W	X	86,87
Seatter	Orkney	HY2613	59°0·1′	3°16·8′W	X	6
Seatter	Orkney	HY4611	58°59·2′	2°55·9′W	X	6
Seatter	Orkney	HY5607	58°57·1′	2°45·4′W	X	6
Seat, The	Cumbr	SD1697	54°21·9′	3°17·2′W	H	96
Seat, The	Pth & Kin	NN9506	56°14·4′	3°41·2′W	X	58
Seat, The	S Lanak	NS9925	55°30·8′	3°35·5′W	H	72
Seaty Hill	N Yks	SD9065	54°5·1′	2°8·8′W	X	98
Seaty Hill (Tumulus)	N Yks	SD9065	54°5·1′	2°8·8′W	A	98
Seaureaugh Moor	Corn	SW7337	50°11·6′	5°10·5′W	T	204
Seave Green	N Yks	NZ5600	54°23·8′	1°7·8′W	T	93
Seaves Fm	N Yks	SE5871	54°8·1′	1°6·3′W	FM	100
Seaview	Highld	NH8091	57°53·8′	4°1·0′W	X	21
Seaview	I of W	SZ6291	50°43·1′	1°6·9′W	T	196
Seaview	Northum	NU0050	55°44·9′	1°59·6′W	X	75
Sea View Fm	Devon	SY0985	50°39·7′	3°16·9′W	FM	192
Sea View Fm	Lincs	TF4692	53°24·5′	0°12·2′E	FM	113
Seaville	Cumbr	NY1653	54°52·1′	3°18·1′W	T	85
Seaville Cote	Cumbr	NY1554	54°52·7′	3°19·1′W	X	85
Seavington St Mary	Somer	ST3914	50°55·6′	2°51·7′W	T	193
Seavington St Michael	Somer	ST4015	50°56·1′	2°50·9′W	T	193
Seavy Carr Wood	N Yks	SE4841	53°52·0′	1°15·8′W	F	105
Seavy Pond	N Yks	SE8393	54°19·8′	0°43·0′W	W	94,100
Seavy Rigg	Cumbr	NY8118	54°33·7′	2°17·2′W	X	91,92
Seavy Sike	Cumbr	NY7734	54°42·3′	2°21·0′W	W	91
Seavy Sike	Durham	NZ0010	54°29·4′	1°59·6′W	W	92
Seavy Slack	N Yks	SE7992	54°19·3′	0°46·7′W	X	94,100
Seawall Fm	N Som	ST3868	51°24·7′	2°53·1′W	FM	171,182
Seaward	D & G	NX6649	54°49·3′	4°4·7′W	X	83,84
Seawardstone	Devon	SX7851	50°21·0′	3°42·5′W	X	202
Seawell Grounds	Northnts	SP6252	52°10·0′	1°5·2′W	X	152
Seawell Wood	Northnts	SP6252	52°10·0′	1°5·2′W	F	152
Seawick	Essex	TM1213	51°46·8′	1°4·8′E	T	168,169
Sea Wood	Cumbr	SD2973	54°9·1′	3°4·8′W	F	96,97
Seawood Fm	Cumbr	SD2973	54°9·1′	3°4·8′W	FM	96,97
Sebastopol	Norf	TG0634	52°52·1′	1°4·0′E	X	133
Sebastopol	Scot Bord	NT5854	55°46·9′	2°39·7′W	X	67,73,74
Sebastopol	Torf	ST2898	51°40·8′	3°2·1′W	T	171
Sebay	Orkney	HY5205	58°56·0′	2°49·6′W	X	6,7
Sebay Skerries	Orkney	HY5205	58°56·0′	2°49·6′W	X	6,7
Sebergham	Cumbr	NY3541	54°45·8′	3°0·2′W	T	85
Sebergham Castle Fm	Cumbr	NY3243	54°46·9′	3°3·0′W	FM	85
Sebonig	Gwyn	SH5920	52°45·8′	4°5·0′W	X	124
Seccombe	Devon	SX7949	50°19·9′	3°41·6′W	X	202
Seccombe Fm	Devon	SX4393	50°43·2′	4°13·1′W	FM	190
Seckerleigh	Devon	SS9709	50°52·5′	3°27·5′W	X	192
Seckford Hall	Suff	TM2548	52°5·3′	1°17·5′E	A	169
Seckington	Devon	SS5820	50°58·0′	4°1·0′W	X	180
Seckington	Warw	SK2607	52°39·8′	1°36·5′W	T	140
Seckington Cross	Devon	SS6208	50°51·5′	3°57·3′W	X	191
Seckington Fm	Devon	SS2921	50°58·0′	4°25·7′W	FM	190
Seckington Water	Devon	SS2820	50°57·5′	4°26·6′W	W	190
Seckley Wood	Worcs	SO7678	52°24·2′	2°20·8′W	F	138
Second Coast	Highld	NG9290	57°51·3′	5°29·9′W	T	19
Second Drove	Cambs	TL5386	52°27·3′	0°15·5′E	T	143
Second Holme Fm	Lincs	TF3199	53°28·5′	0°1·2′W	FM	113
Second Inchna Burn	Stir	NS8599	56°10·4′	3°50·7′W	W	58
Second Wood	Bucks	SU9496	51°39·5′	0°38·1′W	F	165
Sec Tor	Devon	SY3198	50°46·9′	2°58·3′W	X	193
Sector	Devon	SY3198	50°46·9′	2°58·3′W	T	193
Sedan Fm	Corn	SX1489	50°40·5′	4°37·6′W	FM	190,200
Sedbergh	Cumbr	SD6592	54°19·6′	2°31·9′W	T	97
Sedborough	Devon	SS3621	50°58·1′	4°19·8′W	X	190
Sedbury	Glos	ST5493	51°38·3′	2°39·5′W	T	162,172
Sedbury Cliffs	Glos	ST5593	51°38·3′	2°38·6′W	X	162,172
Sedbury East Fm	N Yks	NZ2004	54°26·1′	1°41·1′W	FM	93
Sedbury Hall	N Yks	NZ1905	54°26·6′	1°42·0′W	X	92
Sedbury Home Fm	N Yks	NZ2005	54°26·6′	1°41·1′W	FM	93
Sedbury Park	Glos	ST5593	51°38·3′	2°38·6′W	X	162,172
Sedbury Park	N Yks	NZ2005	54°26·6′	1°41·1′W	X	93
Sedbusk	N Yks	SD8891	54°19·1′	2°10·6′W	T	98
Sedbusk High Pasture	N Yks	SD8891	54°19·1′	2°10·6′W	X	98
Seddington	Beds	TL1747	52°6·8′	0°17·1′W	T	153
Sedgeberrow	Worcs	SP0238	52°2·7′	1°57·9′W	T	150
Sedgeborough	Somer	ST0532	51°5·0′	3°21·0′W	X	181
Sedgebrook	Lincs	SK8537	52°55·7′	0°43·7′W	T	130
Sedgebrook Lodge	Northnts	SP7366	52°17·5′	0°55·4′W	X	152
Sedgebrook Lodge Fm	Northnts	SP7466	52°17·5′	0°54·5′W	FM	152
Sedge Copse	Lincs	TF0790	53°24·0′	0°23·0′W	F	112
Sedgecroft	Devon	ST3300	50°48·0′	2°56·7′W	X	193
Sedgedrove Fm	Norf	TL5796	52°32·6′	0°19·3′E	FM	143
Sedge Fen	Cambs	TL5674	52°20·7′	0°17·8′E	X	143
Sedge Fen	Norf	TG3216	52°41·7′	1°26·4′E	W	133,134
Sedge Fen	Suff	TL6684	52°26·0′	0°26·9′E	X	143
Sedge Fen Fm	Norf	TL6292	52°30·3′	0°23·6′E	FM	143
Sedgefield	Durham	NZ3528	54°39·0′	1°27·0′W	T	93
Sedgeford	Norf	TF7136	52°53·9′	0°32·9′E	T	132
Sedgehill	Wilts	ST8628	51°3·3′	2°11·6′W	T	183
Sedgehill Manor	Wilts	ST8527	51°2·8′	2°12·5′W	X	183
Sedgemere	Sol	SP2275	52°22·6′	1°40·2′W	T	139
Sedgemoor 1685	Somer	ST3535	51°6·9′	2°55·3′W	A	182
Sedgemoor Hill	Somer	ST4330	51°4·2′	2°48·4′W	H	182
Sedgemoor Old Rhyne	Somer	ST3325	51°1·5′	2°56·9′W	W	193
Sedgemoor Service Area	Somer	ST3552	51°16·0′	2°55·5′W	X	182
Sedges Fm	Bucks	SP8900	51°41·7′	0°42·3′W	FM	165
Sedgeworth Fm	N Lincs	SE9418	53°39·2′	0°34·2′W	FM	112
Sedgfield Ho	N Yks	SE3391	54°19·1′	1°29·1′W	X	99
Sedgley	Dudley	SO9194	52°32·9′	2°7·6′W	T	139
Sedgley Park	Bury	SD8202	53°31·1′	2°15·9′W	T	109
Sedgwick	Cumbr	SD5187	54°16·8′	2°44·7′W	T	97
Sedgwick Castle	W Susx	TQ1827	51°2·0′	0°18·6′W	A	187,198
Sedgwick Ho	Cumbr	SD5187	54°16·8′	2°44·7′W	X	97
Sedgwick Home Fm	W Susx	TQ1827	51°2·0′	0°18·6′W	FM	187,198
Sedgwick Park	W Susx	TQ1826	51°1·5′	0°18·7′W	X	187,198
Sedgwicks	Lancs	SD7755	53°59·7′	2°20·6′W	X	103
Sedlescombe	E Susx	TQ7818	50°56·3′	0°32·4′E	T	199
Sedling Burn	Durham	NY8641	54°46·1′	2°12·6′W	W	87
Sedling Fell	Durham	NY8642	54°46·6′	2°12·6′W	X	87
Sedlow Wood	E Susx	TQ3414	50°54·8′	0°5·2′W	F	198
Sedrup	Bucks	SP7911	51°47·8′	0°50·9′W	T	165
Sedsall	Derby	SK1137	52°56·1′	1°49·8′W	X	128
Seechem Fm	Worcs	SP0572	52°21·0′	1°55·2′W	FM	139
Seed	Kent	TQ9456	51°16·4′	0°47·3′E	T	178
Seedalls	Lancs	SD6846	53°54·8′	2°28·8′W	X	103
Seedalls	Lancs	SD7246	53°54·8′	2°25·2′W	X	103
Seed Fm	Heref	SO7047	52°7·5′	2°25·9′W	FM	149
Seed Green	Lancs	SD7248	53°49·9′	2°32·4′W	X	102,103
Seed Hill	Cumbr	NY1001	54°24·0′	3°22·8′W	X	89
Seed Lee	Lancs	SD5824	53°42·9′	2°37·8′W	T	102
Seedley	Salf	SJ8099	53°29·5′	2°17·7′W	T	109
Seed Rigg	Northum	NY6568	55°0·6′	2°32·4′W	X	86
Seefar	Pth & Kin	NO0947	56°36·6′	3°28·5′W	X	52,53
Seeley Brook	Worcs	SO9760	52°14·5′	2°2·2′W	W	150
Seeley Fm	Kent	TR0641	51°8·1′	0°57·1′E	FM	179,189
See Morris Hill	D & G	NX9078	55°5·3′	3°43·0′W	H	84
Seend	Wilts	ST9461	51°21·1′	2°4·8′W	T	173
Seend Bridge Fm	Wilts	ST9459	51°20·0′	2°4·8′W	FM	173
Seend Cleeve	Wilts	ST9360	51°20·6′	2°5·6′W	T	173
Seend Head	Wilts	ST9260	51°20·6′	2°6·5′W	T	173
Seenes Law	Scot Bord	NT5559	55°49·6′	2°42·7′W	H	66,73
Seer Green	Bucks	SU9691	51°36·8′	0°36·4′W	T	175,176
Seeside	D & G	NX9076	55°4·2′	3°42·9′W	X	84
Seeswood Pool	Warw	SP3290	52°30·7′	1°31·3′W	W	140
Seething	Norf	TM3197	52°31·5′	1°24·7′E	T	134
Seething Old Hall	Norf	TM3198	52°32·1′	1°24·8′E	X	134
Seething Wells	King	TQ1767	51°23·6′	0°18·7′W	T	176
Sef Dale	Shetld	HU3512	59°53·8′	1°22·0′W	X	4
Sefster	Shetld	HU3050	60°14·3′	1°27·0′W	T	3
Sefta Point	Shetld	HU5666	60°22·7′	0°58·6′W	X	2
Sefter Fm	W Susx	SZ8999	50°47·2′	0°43·9′W	FM	197
Sefton	Sefton	SD3501	53°30·3′	2°58·4′W	T	108
Sefton Park	Liv	SJ3787	53°22·8′	2°56·4′W	T	108
Sefton Park	Liv	SJ3787	53°22·8′	2°56·4′W	X	108
Segal	Orkney	HY2002	58°54·1′	3°22·8′W	X	7
Segenhoe Manor	Beds	SP9835	52°0·5′	0°33·9′W	A	153
Segensworth	Hants	SU5208	50°52·4′	1°15·3′W	T	196
Seggarsdean	E Loth	NT5357	55°57·1′	2°44·7′W	X	66
Seggat	Aberd	NJ7341	57°27·8′	2°26·5′W	X	29
Seggy Bight	Shetld	HU2959	60°19·1′	1°28·0′W	W	3
Seggie	Fife	NO4419	56°21·9′	2°53·9′W	X	59
Seggie Bank	Pth & Kin	NO0906	56°14·5′	3°27·7′W	X	58
Seggie Burn	Shetld	HU4364	60°21·7′	1°12·7′W	W	2,3
Seggiecrook	Aberd	NJ5926	57°19·6′	2°40·4′W	X	37
Seggiecrook	Moray	NJ5252	57°33·6′	2°47·7′W	X	29
Seggieden	Aberd	NJ5427	57°20·1′	2°45·4′W	X	37
Seggieden	Angus	NO4644	56°35·3′	2°52·3′W	X	54
Seggieden	Pth & Kin	NO1621	56°22·7′	3°21·2′W	X	53,58
Seggiehill	Fife	NO4319	56°21·8′	2°54·9′W	X	59
Seggimoor Beck	Lincs	TF0191	53°24·6′	0°28·4′W	W	112
Seghill	Northum	NZ2874	55°3·8′	1°33·3′W	T	88
Seghill Hall	Northum	NZ2874	55°3·8′	1°33·3′W	X	88
Segil	Shetld	HU4697	60°39·5′	1°9·0′W	X	1
Segmore Fm	Suff	TM3469	52°16·4′	1°26·2′E	FM	156
Segontivm (Roman Fort)	Gwyn	SH4862	53°8·3′	4°15·9′W	R	114,115
Segrwyd	Denb	SJ0263	53°9·6′	3°27·5′W	X	116
Segrwyd	Denb	SJ0464	53°10·1′	3°25·8′W	X	116
Segrwyd	Pemb	SM8332	51°56·9′	5°9·1′W	X	157
Segrwyd Ucha	Denb	SJ0363	53°9·6′	3°26·6′W	X	116
Segsbury Down	Oxon	SU3883	51°32·9′	1°26·7′W	X	174
Seifton	Shrops	SO4883	52°26·8′	2°45·5′W	T	137,138
Seighford	Staffs	SJ8824	52°49·0′	2°10·3′W	T	127
Seil	Arg & Bt	NM7617	56°17·8′	5°36·8′W	X	55
Seilag	Highld	NM8172	56°47·5′	5°34·7′W	X	40
Seilastotar	N Eil	NB5460	58°27·8′	6°12·6′W	X	8
Seildeim	N Eil	NB1540	58°15·6′	6°51·1′W	X	13
Seileach Mór	Highld	NH4153	57°32·6′	4°38·9′W	X	26
Seilebost	N Eil	NG0696	57°51·7′	6°57·0′W	T	14,18
Seilg Geo	N Eil	NF1097	57°47·8′	8°33·5′W	X	18
Seilibridh	N Eil	NB1318	58°3·8′	6°51·5′W	H	13,14
Seil Sound	Arg & Bt	NM7715	56°16·8′	5°35·7′W	W	55
Seion	Gwyn	SH5467	53°11·1′	4°10·7′W	T	114,115
Seisdon	Staffs	SO8494	52°32·9′	2°13·8′W	T	138
Seisiadar	N Eil	NB5434	58°13·8′	6°10·9′W	T	8
Seismological Station	D & G	NT2405	55°20·2′	3°11·5′W	X	79

Seive Dale	N Yks	SE8688	54°17·1'	0°40·3'W	X	94,101
Selaby Basses	Durham	NZ1517	54°33·1'	1°45·7'W	X	92
Selaby Fm	Durham	NZ1518	54°33·7'	1°45·7'W	FM	92
Selaby Hall	Durham	NZ1518	54°33·7'	1°45·7'W	X	92
Selah	Cumbr	NY6142	54°46·5'	2°36·0'W	X	86
Selah	Devon	ST2805	50°50·6'	3°1·0'W	X	193
Selattyn	Shrops	SJ2633	52°53·6'	3°5·6'W	T	126
Selattyn Hill	Shrops	SJ2534	52°54·1'	3°6·5'W	X	126
Sel Ayre	Shetld	HU1754	60°16·5'	1°41·1'W	X	3
Selber	N Yks	SD6573	54°9·3'	2°31·7'W	X	97
Selbie	Aberd	NJ8022	57°17·5'	2°19·5'W	X	38
Selbiehill	Aberd	NJ8023	57°18·1'	2°19·5'W	X	38
Selborne	Hants	SU7433	51°5·7'	0°56·2'W	T	186
Selborne Common	Hants	SU7333	51°5·7'	0°57·1'W	X	186
Selborne Hanger	Hants	SU7333	51°5·7'	0°57·1'W	F	186
Selbourne Priory	Hants	SU7534	51°6·3'	0°55·3'W	A	186
Sel Burn	Scot Bord	NT7156	55°48·0'	2°27·3'W	W	67,74
Selby	N Yks	SE6132	53°47·1'	1°4·0'W	T	105
Selby Canal	N Yks	SE5828	53°44·9'	1°6·8'W	W	105
Selby Dam	N Yks	SE5931	53°46·6'	1°5·9'W	W	105
Selby Fm	Kent	TR1033	51°3·7'	1°0·2'E	FM	179,189
Selby Fork	N Yks	SE4630	53°46·1'	1°17·7'W	X	105
Selby Ho	Cumbr	NY1853	54°52·2'	3°16·2'W	X	85
Selby Ho	Northum	NZ1389	55°12·0'	1°47·3'W	X	81
Selby's Cove	Northum	NZ0297	55°16·3'	1°57·7'W	X	81
Selby's Fm	Kent	TQ5647	51°12·3'	0°14·4'E	FM	188
Selby's Hill	Northum	NT8336	55°37·3'	2°15·8'W	X	74
Selby's Stead	Northum	NU1807	55°21·6'	1°42·5'W	X	81
Selbystown	Cumbr	NY4972	55°2·6'	2°47·5'W	X	86
Selchie Geo	Shetld	HU3621	59°58·6'	1°20·8'W	X	4
Selcoth	D & G	NT1307	55°21·2'	3°21·9'W	X	78
Selcoth Burn	D & G	NT1406	55°20·7'	3°20·9'W	W	78
Selcoth Burn	D & G	NT1506	55°20·7'	3°20·0'W	W	79
Selden	W Susx	TQ0805	50°50·3'	0°27·6'W	X	197
Selden Fm	W Susx	TQ0706	50°50·8'	0°28·4'W	FM	197
Seldom Seen	Cumbr	NY3718	54°33·4'	2°58·0'W	X	90
Seldom Seen	Cumbr	NY7641	54°46·0'	2°22·0'W	X	86,87
Seldom Seen	Northum	NY8167	55°0·1'	2°17·4'W	X	86,87
Seldom Seen Fm	Leic	SK6221	52°47·2'	1°4·4'W	FM	129
Seldom Seen Fm	Leic	SK7204	52°38·0'	0°55·8'W	FM	141
Seldon Fm	Devon	SS5704	50°49·3'	4°1·4'W	FM	191
Sele Bottom	Cumbr	SD1691	54°18·7'	3°17·1'W	X	96
Seleggan Fm	Corn	SW6940	50°13·1'	5°13·9'W	FM	203
Selehurst	W Susx	TQ2126	51°1·5'	0°16·1'W	X	187,198
Seler	Denb	SJ1264	53°10·2'	3°18·6'W	X	116
Self Grain	S Lanak	NS6934	55°35·2'	4°4·3'W	W	71
Self Hills	N Yks	SE7562	54°3·1'	0°50·8'W	X	100
Selgar's Mill	Devon	ST0511	50°53·7'	3°20·7'W	X	192
Selgrove	Kent	TR0158	51°17·4'	0°53·4'E	T	178
Selham	W Susx	SU9320	50°58·5'	0°40·1'W	T	197
Selham Common	W Susx	SU9219	50°58·0'	0°41·0'W	X	197
Selham Ho	W Susx	SU9319	50°58·0'	0°40·1'W	X	197
Selhurst	Croy	TQ3267	51°23·4'	0°5·8'W	T	176,177
Selhurst Common	Surrey	TQ0140	51°9·2'	0°33·0'W	X	186
Selhurst Park	W Susx	SU9211	50°53·7'	0°41·1'W	X	197
Selhurst Park Fm	W Susx	SU9210	50°53·2'	0°41·1'W	FM	197
Selie Ness	Shetld	HU3460	60°19·6'	1°22·6'W	X	2,3
Seli Geo	Shetld	HU3545	60°11·5'	1°21·6'W	X	4
Seli Geo	Shetld	HU5059	60°19·0'	1°5·2'W	X	2,3
Seli Geo	Shetld	HU5138	60°7·7'	1°4·4'W	X	4
Seli Stack	Shetld	HU2546	60°12·1'	1°32·4'W	X	4
Seli Voe	Shetld	HU2848	60°13·2'	1°29·2'W	W	3
Selker	Cumbr	SD0788	54°17·0'	3°25·3'W	X	96
Selker Bay	Cumbr	SD0788	54°17·0'	3°25·3'W	W	96
Selkirk	Scot Bord	NT4728	55°32·8'	2°50·0'W	T	73
Selkirk Common	Scot Bord	NT4827	55°32·3'	2°49·0'W	X	73
Selki Skerry	Orkney	ND3883	58°44·1'	3°3·8'W	X	7
Sella	Cumbr	SD1992	54°19·3'	3°14·3'W	X	96
Sellack	Heref	SO5627	51°56·6'	2°38·0'W	T	162
Sellack Boat	Heref	SO5628	51°57·2'	2°38·0'W	T	149
Sellack Marsh	Heref	SO5727	51°56·6'	2°37·1'W	X	162
Sellafield Sta	Cumbr	NY0203	54°25·0'	3°30·2'W	X	89
Sellafirth	Shetld	HU5297	60°39·4'	1°2·4'W	T	1
Sellake	Devon	ST0014	50°55·2'	3°25·0'W	X	181
Sellan	Corn	SW4230	50°7·1'	5°36·2'W	T	203
Selland's Fm	Essex	TL6137	52°0·7'	0°21·2'E	FM	154
Sella Ness	Shetld	HU3973	60°26·6'	1°17·0'W	X	2,3
Sella Park Ho	Cumbr	NY0305	54°26·1'	3°29·3'W	X	89
Sellars Fm	Lincs	TF2248	53°1·2'	0°10·5'W	FM	131
Sell Burn	Northum	NY8073	55°3·3'	2°18·4'W	W	86,87
Sellerley Fm	Lancs	SD4754	53°59·0'	2°48·1'W	FM	102
Sellet Hall	Cumbr	SD5185	54°15·7'	2°44·7'W	X	97
Sellet Hall	Lancs	SD6077	54°11·5'	2°36·4'W	A	97
Sellet Lodge	Cumbr	SD5286	54°16·3'	2°43·8'W	X	97
Sellet Mill	Lancs	SD6077	54°11·5'	2°36·4'W	X	97
Selley Bridge Fm	N Yks	SE8378	54°11·7'	0°43·2'W	FM	100
Selley Hall	Shrops	SO2676	52°22·9'	3°4·8'W	X	137,148
Sell Gill Holes	N Yks	SD8174	54°9·7'	2°17·0'W	X	98
Sellibister	Orkney	HY7243	59°16·6'	2°29·0'W	X	5
Sellick	Devon	SX3399	50°46·2'	4°21·7'W	X	190
Sellick's Green	Somer	ST2119	50°58·1'	3°7·1'W	T	193
Sellindge	Kent	TR1038	51°6·4'	1°0·4'E	T	179,189
Selling	Kent	TR0456	51°16·2'	0°55·9'E	T	178,179
Sellinge Fm	Kent	TR0829	51°1·6'	0°58·4'E	FM	189
Selling Sta	Kent	TR0557	51°16·7'	0°56·8'E	X	179
Sell Moor	Scot Bord	NT4744	55°41·4'	2°50·1'W	H	73
Sells Green	Wilts	ST9562	51°21·7'	2°3·9'W	T	173
Selly Geo	Highld	ND3866	58°34·9'	3°3·5'W	X	12
Selly Hill	N Yks	NZ8609	54°28·4'	0°40·0'W	T	94
Selly Manor	Birm	SP0481	52°25·9'	1°56·1'W	X	139
Selly Oak	Birm	SP0382	52°26·4'	1°57·0'W	T	139
Selly Park	Birm	SP0582	52°26·4'	1°55·2'W	T	139
Selmeston	E Susx	TQ5107	50°50·8'	0°9·1'E	T	199
Selm Muir Wood	W Loth	NT0864	55°51·9'	3°27·8'W	F	65
Selms	W Loth	NT0866	55°53·0'	3°27·8'W	X	65
Selsdon	Croy	TQ3562	51°20·7'	0°3·3'W	T	177,187
Selsdon Wood	Croy	TQ3661	51°20·1'	0°2·5'W	F	177,187
Selset Reservoir	Durham	NY9121	54°35·3'	2°7·9'W	W	91,92
Selsey	W Susx	SZ8593	50°44·0'	0°47·3'W	T	197
Selsey Bill	W Susx	SZ8592	50°43·5'	0°47·4'W	X	197

Selsfield Common	W Susx	TQ3434	51°5·6'	0°4·8'W	X	187
Selsfield Ho	W Susx	TQ3434	51°5·6'	0°4·8'W	X	187
Selside	Cumbr	SD5399	54°23·3'	2°43·0'W	T	97
Selside	N Yks	SD7875	54°10·5'	2°19·8'W	T	98
Selside Brow	Cumbr	NY4809	54°28·7'	2°47·7'W	X	90
Selside End	Cumbr	NY4912	54°30·3'	2°46·8'W	H	90
Selside Hall	Cumbr	SD5399	54°23·3'	2°43·0'W	X	97
Selside Moss	N Yks	SD7877	54°11·5'	2°19·8'W	X	98
Selside Pike	Cumbr	NY4911	54°29·8'	2°46·8'W	H	90
Selside Shaw	N Yks	SD7876	54°11·0'	2°19·8'W	X	98
Selsley	Glos	SO8303	51°43·8'	2°14·4'W	T	162
Selsley Common	Glos	SO8303	51°43·8'	2°14·4'W	X	162
Selsmire	Cumbr	NY6007	54°27·7'	2°36·6'W	X	91
Selsmore	Hants	SZ7399	50°47·4'	0°57·5'W	X	197
Selson	Kent	TR3055	51°15·1'	1°18·2'E	T	179
Selsted	Kent	TR2144	51°9·4'	1°10·0'E	T	179,189
Selston	Notts	SK4653	53°4·6'	1°18·4'W	T	120
Selston Common	Notts	SK4752	53°4·0'	1°17·5'W	T	120
Selston Green	Notts	SK4553	53°4·6'	1°19·3'W	T	120
Selston Hall	Notts	SK4654	53°5·1'	1°18·4'W	X	120
Selvedge	Pemb	SN0020	51°50·8'	4°53·8'W	X	145,157,158
Selvie	Angus	NO2747	56°36·8'	3°10·9'W	X	53
Selvieland	Renf	NS4467	55°52·5'	4°29·2'W	X	64
Selvinge Fm	Somer	ST3717	50°57·2'	2°53·4'W	FM	193
Selwick	Orkney	HY2305	58°55·8'	3°19·8'W	X	6,7
Selwicks Bay	E Yorks	TA2570	54°6·9'	0°4·8'W	W	101
Selworthy	Somer	SS9146	51°12·4'	3°33·2'W	T	181
Selworthy Beacon	Somer	SS9148	51°13·5'	3°33·3'W	H	181
Selworthy Sand	Somer	SS9049	51°14·0'	3°34·2'W	X	181
Selwyns Wood	E Susx	TQ5520	50°57·7'	0°12·8'E	F	199
Sembletree Knowe	D & G	NY1595	55°14·8'	3°19·8'W	X	79
Semblister	Shetld	HU3350	60°14·2'	1°23·7'W	T	3
Semeil	Aberd	NJ3811	57°11·4'	3°1·1'W	X	37
Semer	Suff	TL9946	52°4·8'	0°54·7'E	T	155
Semerdale Hall	N Yks	SD9288	54°17·5'	2°7·0'W	X	98
Semere Green	Norf	TM1884	52°24·9'	1°12·7'E	X	156
Semer Gate Fm	Suff	TL9945	52°4·3'	0°54·6'E	FM	155
Semer Lodge	Suff	TM0045	52°4·3'	0°55·5'E	X	155
Semersdon Fm	Corn	SX3096	50°44·6'	4°24·2'W	FM	190
Semer Water	N Yks	SD9187	54°17·0'	2°7·9'W	W	98
Sem Hill	Wilts	ST8826	51°2·2'	2°9·9'W	T	183
Semington	Wilts	ST8960	51°20·6'	2°9·1'W	T	173
Semington Br	Wilts	ST8961	51°21·1'	2°9·1'W	X	173
Semington Brook	Wilts	ST9060	51°20·6'	2°8·2'W	W	173
Semley	Wilts	ST8926	51°2·2'	2°9·0'W	T	184
Semley Common	Wilts	ST8727	51°2·8'	2°10·7'W	X	183
Semley Hill	Wilts	ST8825	51°1·7'	2°9·9'W	X	183
Semple Ho	Hants	SU3318	50°57·9'	1°31·4'W	X	185
Sempringham	Lincs	TF1133	52°53·2'	0°20·6'W	T	130
Sempringham House Fm	Lincs	TF1232	52°52·7'	0°19·7'W	FM	130
Sempstead	E Susx	TQ8023	50°58·9'	0°34·3'E	X	199
Sempstead Wood	E Susx	TQ8024	50°59·5'	0°34·3'E	F	199
Send	Surrey	TQ0255	51°17·3'	0°31·8'W	T	186
Send Grove	Surrey	TQ0154	51°16·8'	0°32·7'W	T	186
Sendholme	Surrey	TQ0154	51°16·8'	0°32·7'W	X	186
Sendhurst Grange	Surrey	TQ0254	51°16·8'	0°31·9'W	X	186
Send Marsh	Surrey	TQ0355	51°17·3'	0°31·0'W	T	186
Sene Fm	Kent	TR1735	51°4·6'	1°6·3'E	FM	179,189
Senghenydd	Caer	ST1190	51°36·3'	3°16·7'W	T	171
Senghenydd Dyke	Caer	ST1192	51°37·4'	3°16·8'W	A	171
Senna Green Fm	Ches	SJ6378	53°18·1'	2°32·9'W	FM	118
Senna Lane Fm	Ches	SJ6378	53°18·1'	2°32·9'W	FM	118
Sennen	Corn	SW3525	50°4·2'	5°41·8'W	T	203
Sennen Cove	Corn	SW3526	50°4·7'	5°41·9'W	T	203
Sennicotts	W Susx	SU8307	50°51·6'	0°48·9'W	X	197
Sennington Village	Glos	SP0221	51°53·5'	1°57·9'W	A	163
Sennotts	W Susx	TQ3923	50°59·6'	0°0·8'W	X	198
Sennowe Hall	Norf	TF9825	52°47·4'	0°56·6'E	X	132
Sennybridge	Powys	SN9228	51°56·6'	3°33·9'W	T	160
Sennybridge Training Area	Powys	SN9239	52°2·6'	3°34·1'W	X	160
Sentence Castle	Pemb	SN1111	51°46·2'	4°44·0'W	A	158
Sentry Edge	Cald	SE0526	53°44·1'	1°55·0'W	X	104
Sentrys	Devon	SS8010	50°52·9'	3°42·0'W	X	191
Senwick Bay	D & G	NX6547	54°48·2'	4°5·6'W	W	83,84
Senwick Church	D & G	NX6546	54°47·7'	4°5·6'W	A	83,84
Senwick Ho (Hotel)	D & G	NX6446	54°47·7'	4°6·5'W	X	83
Senwick Wood	D & G	NX6547	54°48·2'	4°5·6'W	F	83,84
Seolait Mhic Neacail	N Eil	NF9676	57°40·5'	7°5·5'W	W	18
Sepham Fm	Kent	TQ5160	51°19·4'	0°10·4'E	FM	177,188
Seppings Hill	D & G	NY3995	55°15·0'	2°57·1'W	H	79
Sepscott Fm	Devon	SS5936	51°6·6'	4°0·5'W	FM	180
Septa Field	Shetld	HU2782	60°31·5'	1°30·0'W	X	3
Sequer's Br	Devon	SX6351	50°20·8'	3°55·2'W	X	202
Sergeant Knowe	D & G	NY2094	55°14·3'	3°15·1'W	X	79
Sergeant Man	Cumbr	NY2808	54°28·0'	3°6·2'W	X	89,90
Sergeant's Crag	Cumbr	NY2711	54°29·6'	3°7·2'W	H	89,90
Sergehill	Herts	TL1004	51°43·7'	0°24·0'W	X	166
Serlby	Notts	SK6389	53°23·9'	1°2·7'W	T	111,120
Serpentine, The	C of West	TQ2780	51°30·5'	0°9·8'W	W	176
Serpent, The	Shrops	SO5372	52°20·9'	2°41·0'W	X	137,138
Serridge Green	Glos	SO6214	51°49·6'	2°32·7'W	F	162
Serridge Ho	S Glos	ST6779	51°30·8'	2°28·1'W	X	172
Serridge Inclosure	Glos	SO6213	51°49·1'	2°32·7'W	F	162
Serrigar	Orkney	ND4387	58°46·3'	2°58·7'W	X	7
Serrington	Wilts	SU0636	51°7·6'	1°54·5'W	T	184
Serstone Fm	Devon	SS7202	50°48·4'	3°48·6'W	FM	191
Servis Fm	Devon	SS4719	50°57·2'	4°10·3'W	FM	180
Sescut Fm	Oxon	SP5210	51°47·4'	1°14·4'W	FM	164
Sessacott	Devon	SS3516	50°55·4'	4°20·5'W	X	190
Sessay	N Yks	SE4575	54°10·4'	1°18·2'W	T	99
Sessay Park	N Yks	SE4574	54°9·8'	1°18·2'W	X	99
Sessay Wood	N Yks	SE4773	54°9·3'	1°16·4'W	F	100
Sessingham Fm	E Susx	TQ5308	50°51·3'	0°10·8'E	FM	199
Sessionfield	S Ayr	NS3818	55°26·0'	4°33·2'W	X	70
Session Heath	Suff	TL7984	52°25·7'	0°38·4'E	F	144
Sessland	Devon	SX6797	50°45·7'	3°52·8'W	X	191
Sessnie Croft	Aberd	NJ8737	57°25·6'	2°12·5'W	X	30
Setchel Fen	Cambs	TL4771	52°19·3'	0°9·8'E	X	154
Setchey	Norf	TF6313	52°41·6'	0°25·1'E	T	132,143
Setcops	Lincs	TA0502	53°30·5'	0°24·6'W	X	112

Setley	Hants	SU3000	50°48·2'	1°34·1'W	T	196
Setley Common	Hants	SZ3099	50°47·6'	1°34·1'W	X	196
Setley Plain	Hants	SU2900	50°48·2'	1°34·9'W	X	196
Setmurthy Common	Cumbr	NY1631	54°40·3'	3°17·7'W	F	89
Seton	E Loth	NT4174	55°57·6'	2°56·3'W	T	66
Setonhill	E Loth	NT4676	55°58·7'	2°51·5'W	X	66
Seton Ho	E Loth	NT4175	55°58·1'	2°56·3'W	X	66
Seton Lodge	Stir	NS7593	56°7·1'	4°0·2'W	X	57
Seton Mains	E Loth	NT4275	55°58·1'	2°55·3'W	T	66
Seton Sands	E Loth	NT4276	55°58·7'	2°55·3'W	X	66
Setons Halt	Norf	TF9339	52°55·1'	0°52·7'E	X	132
Seton West Mains	E Loth	NT4074	55°57·6'	2°57·2'W	X	66
Setta Barrow	Devon	SS7238	51°7·9'	3°49·4'W	A	180
Setter	Orkney	HY3415	59°1·3'	3°8·5'W	X	6
Setter	Orkney	HY6238	59°13·9'	2°39·5'W	X	5
Setter	Orkney	ND3389	58°47·3'	3°9·1'W	X	7
Setter	Shetld	HU2050	60°14·3'	1°37·8'W	X	3
Setter	Shetld	HU2948	60°13·2'	1°28·1'W	X	3
Setter	Shetld	HU3736	60°6·7'	1°19·6'W	X	4
Setter	Shetld	HU3792	60°36·8'	1°18·9'W	X	1,2
Setter	Shetld	HU3962	60°20·7'	1°17·1'W	X	2,3
Setter	Shetld	HU4325	60°0·7'	1°13·2'W	X	4
Setter	Shetld	HU4337	60°7·2'	1°13·1'W	X	4
Setter	Shetld	HU4581	60°30·9'	1°10·3'W	T	1,2,3
Setter	Shetld	HU4991	60°36·2'	1°5·8'W	X	1,2
Setter	Shetld	HU5141	60°9·3'	1°4·4'W	X	4
Setter	Shetld	HU6291	60°36·1'	0°51·6'W	X	1,2
Setterah Park	Cumbr	NY5121	54°35·2'	2°45·1'W	X	90
Setter Hill	Shetld	HU4043	60°10·4'	1°16·2'W	H	4
Setter Hill	Shetld	HU5463	60°21·1'	1°0·8'W	H	2
Setter Holm	Shetld	HU4870	60°24·9'	1°7·2'W	X	2,3
Setter House	Shetld	HU3954	60°16·4'	1°17·2'W	X	3
Settersquoy	Orkney	HY3009	58°58·0'	3°12·6'W	X	6,7
Setthorns	D & G	NY2680	55°6·8'	3°9·2'W	X	79
Setthorns Cottage	Hants	SU2600	50°48·2'	1°37·5'W	X	195
Set Thorns Inclosure	Hants	SZ2699	50°47·6'	1°37·5'W	F	195
Settie	Stir	NS6394	56°7·4'	4°11·8'W	X	57
Settings Fm	Rut	SK9302	52°36·7'	0°37·2'W	FM	141
Settiscarth	Orkney	HY3618	59°2·9'	3°6·4'W	T	6
Settlands, The	Pemb	SM8513	51°46·7'	5°6·6'W	W	157
Settle	N Yks	SD8163	54°4·0'	2°17·0'W	T	98
Settlebeck Gill	Cumbr	SD6693	54°20·1'	2°31·0'W	W	98
Settle Hill	Bath & NE Somer	ST6164	51°22·7'	2°33·2'W	H	172
Settle Scar	N Yks	SD8564	54°4·5'	2°13·3'W	X	98
Settling Nose	Pemb	SM8515	51°47·8'	5°6·7'W	X	157
Settlingstones	Northum	NY8468	55°0·6'	2°14·6'W	X	86,87
Settlingstones Burn	Northum	NY8469	55°1·2'	2°14·6'W	W	86,87
Settrington	N Yks	SE8370	54°7·4'	0°43·4'W	T	100
Settrington Beacon	N Yks	SE8670	54°7·4'	0°40·6'W	A	101
Settrington Beck	N Yks	SE8271	54°7·9'	0°44·3'W	W	100
Settrington Grange	N Yks	SE8369	54°6·8'	0°43·4'W	X	100
Settrington Ho	N Yks	SE8470	54°7·4'	0°42·5'W	X	100
Settrington Wood	N Yks	SE8569	54°6·8'	0°41·6'W	F	100
Setts Fm	Glos	SP0411	51°48·1'	1°56·1'W	FM	163
Sett Valley Trail	Derby	SK0186	53°22·5'	1°58·7'W	X	110
Seumas Cleite	N Eil	NB4023	58°7·4'	6°24·5'W	X	14
Seven Acre Covert	Mil Key	SP9048	52°7·6'	0°40·7'W	F	152
Seven Acre Fm	Essex	TL8001	51°41·0'	0°36·6'E	FM	168
Seven Acre Hill	Oxon	SU3486	51°34·5'	1°30·2'W	X	174
Seven Acre Plantn	Norf	TL8698	52°33·1'	0°45·0'E	F	144
Seven Acres	Cumbr	SD3778	54°11·9'	2°57·5'W	X	96,97
Sevenacres Mains	N Ayr	NS3344	55°39·9'	4°38·9'W	X	63,70
Seven Acre Wood	Ches	SJ5978	53°18·1'	2°36·5'W	F	117
Seven Acre Wood	Rut	SK8103	52°37·4'	0°47·8'W	F	141
Seven Ash	Devon	SS6044	51°10·9'	3°59·8'W	X	180
Seven Ash	Somer	ST1533	51°5·6'	3°12·4'W	T	181
Seven Barrows	Dorset	SY9188	50°41·7'	2°7·3'W	A	195
Seven Barrows	Hants	SU4655	51°17·8'	1°20·0'W	A	174,185
Seven Barrows	W Berks	SU3282	51°32·4'	1°31·9'W	A	174
Seven Barrows	Wilts	SU2148	51°14·1'	1°41·6'W	A	184
Sevenbarrows Ho	W Berks	SU3282	51°32·4'	1°31·9'W	X	174
Seven Brethren	D & G	NY2182	55°7·8'	3°13·9'W	X	79
Seven Brethren (Stone Circle)	D & G	NY2182	55°7·8'	3°13·9'W	A	79
Seven Bridges Fm	Wilts	SU1292	51°37·8'	1°49·2'W	FM	163,173
Seven Elms	Warw	SP2758	52°13·4'	1°35·9'W	X	151
Sevenford Ho	N Yks	SE7295	54°21·0'	0°53·1'W	X	94,100
Sevenhampton	Glos	SP0321	51°53·5'	1°57·0'W	T	163
Sevenhampton	Swin	SU2090	51°36·7'	1°42·3'W	T	163,174
Sevenhampton Place	Swin	SU2189	51°36·2'	1°41·4'W	X	174
Seven Hills	Durham	NY9610	54°29·4'	2°3·3'W	X	91,92
Seven Hills	Norf	TL9081	52°23·9'	0°48·0'E	X	144
Seven Hills	Suff	TL8673	52°19·6'	0°44·2'E	X	144,155
Seven Hills	Suff	TM2241	52°1·6'	1°14·6'E	X	169
Seven Hills	Worcs	SO7975	52°22·6'	2°18·1'W	X	138
Seven Hills Ho	Suff	TL8674	52°20·2'	0°44·2'E	X	144
Seven Hills (Tumuli)	Norf	TL9081	52°23·9'	0°48·0'E	A	144
Seven Hills (Tumuli)	Suff	TL8673	52°19·6'	0°44·2'E	A	144,155
Seven Kings	Redbr	TQ4587	51°34·0'	0°5·9'E	T	177
Seven Kings Water	Redbr	TQ4690	51°35·6'	0°6·9'E	W	177
Seven Lords Lands	Devon	SX7476	50°34·4'	3°46·4'W	X	191
Seven Mile Ho	Norf	TG0344	52°57·5'	1°1·7'E	X	134
Seven Mile Ho	Norf	TG4501	52°33·3'	1°37·3'E	X	134
Seven Mile House Fm	N upon Ty	NZ2275	55°4·4'	1°38·9'W	FM	88
Seven Mile Plantation	S Glos	ST7884	51°33·5'	2°18·7'W	F	172
Seven Mile Wood	Notts	SK5650	53°2·9'	1°9·5'W	F	120
Sevenoaks	Kent	TQ5255	51°16·7'	0°11·2'E	T	188
Sevenoaks Common	Kent	TQ5252	51°15·0'	0°11·1'E	T	188
Seven Oaks Fm	Leic	SP6298	52°34·8'	1°4·7'W	FM	140
Seven Oaks Fm	N Yks	SE7183	54°14·5'	0°54·2'W	FM	100
Seven Oaks Fm	Powys	SJ3315	52°44·0'	2°59·1'W	FM	126
Sevenoaks Weald	Kent	TQ5250	51°14·0'	0°11·0'E	T	188
Seven Rock Point	Devon	SY3290	50°42·6'	2°57·4'W	X	193
Sevenscore	Kent	TR3364	51°19·9'	1°21·1'E	X	179
Seven Sisters	E Susx	TV5396	50°44·8'	0°10·5'E	X	199
Seven Sisters	Nth Pt Talb	SN8208	51°45·7'	3°42·2'W	T	160
Seven Sisters	Shrops	SJ3936	52°55·3'	2°54·0'W	X	126
Seven Sisters Country Park	E Susx	TV5298	50°45·9'	0°9·7'E	X	199

Seven Sisters Fm	Ches	SJ7575	53°16·5'	2°22·1'W	FM	118
Seven Sisters' Rocks	Heref	SO5415	51°50·1'	2°39·7'W	X	162
Seven Sisters, The (Springs)	Moray	NJ1044	57°28·9'	3°29·6'W	W	28
Seven Spouts Fm	Derby	SK3425	52°49·5'	1°29·3'W	FM	128
Seven Springs	Ches	SJ9884	53°21·4'	2°1·4'W	X	109
Seven Springs	Glos	SO9617	51°51·3'	2°3·1'W	T	163
Seven Star Green	Essex	TL9325	51°53·6'	0°48·7'E	T	168
Sevenstones	Corn	SX3871	50°31·2'	4°16·7'W	X	201
Seven Stones Cross	Devon	SX6549	50°19·8'	3°53·4'W	X	202
Seven Wells	Glos	SP1134	52°0·5'	1°50·0'W	X	150
Seven Wells	Powys	SO0684	52°27·0'	3°22·6'W	X	136
Seven Wells Down	Somer	ST6421	50°59·5'	2°30·4'W	H	183
Seven Wells Wood	Somer	ST1737	51°7·8'	3°10·8'W	F	181
Several	D & G	NX1236	54°41·3'	4°54·6'W	X	82
Several Burn	D & G	NX0867	54°57·9'	4°59·5'W	W	82
Several Down	W Berks	SU5082	51°32·3'	1°16·4'W	X	174
Severalls Fm	Oxon	SU5991	51°37·1'	1°8·5'W	FM	164,174
Severalls Fm	Suff	TM2565	52°14·5'	1°18·1'E	FM	156
Several Moor	D & G	NX0868	54°58·4'	4°59·6'W	X	82
Several Rig	Scot Bord	NT5357	55°48·5'	2°44·6'W	X	66,73
Severals	Cambs	TL4184	52°26·4'	0°4·9'E	X	142,143
Severals	W Susx	SU8621	50°59·1'	0°46·1'W	F	197
Severals Belt	N Yks	SE9574	54°9·4'	0°32·3'W	X	101
Severals Fm	Donc	SE7009	53°34·6'	0°56·2'W	FM	112
Severals Fm	Essex	TL4934	51°59·3'	0°10·6'E	FM	154
Severals Fm	Suff	TL9138	52°0·7'	0°47·4'E	FM	155
Severals, The	Suff	TL8472	52°19·1'	0°42·4'E	F	144,155
Several, The	D & G	NX2156	54°52·3'	4°47·0'W	X	82
Severcombe Fm	Bath & NE Somer	ST7160	51°20·5'	2°24·6'W	FM	172
Severidges Fm	Somer	ST0524	51°0·7'	3°20·9'W	FM	181
Severie	Stir	NN7008	56°15·1'	4°5·4'W	X	57
Severie Cottage	Stir	NN7008	56°15·1'	4°5·4'W	X	57
Severn Bank	Worcs	SO8543	52°5·3'	2°12·7'W	X	150
Severnbank Ho	Worcs	SO8063	52°16·1'	2°17·2'W	X	138,150
Severn Beach	S Glos	ST5484	51°33·4'	2°39·4'W	T	172
Severn End	Worcs	SO8442	52°4·8'	2°13·6'W	X	150
Severn Hall	Shrops	SO7296	52°33·9'	2°24·4'W	X	138
Severn Ham	Glos	SO8832	51°59·4'	2°10·1'W	X	150
Severn Ho	Powys	SJ2815	52°43·9'	3°3·6'W	X	126
Severn House Fm	Glos	ST6498	51°41·0'	2°30·9'W	FM	162
Severn Lodge	Shrops	SO7581	52°25·8'	2°21·7'W	X	138
Severn Road Bridge	Glos	ST5590	51°36·7'	2°38·6'W	X	162,172
Severn Spar Fm	Suff	TM2657	52°10·1'	1°18·7'E	FM	156
Severn Stoke	Worcs	SO8544	52°5·9'	2°12·7'W	T	150
Severn Tunnel Junc	Monm	ST4687	51°35·0'	2°46·4'W	X	171,172
Severn Valley Country Park	Shrops	SO7583	52°26·9'	2°21·7'W	X	138
Severn Valley Railway	Worcs	SO7580	52°25·3'	2°21·7'W	X	138
Severn View Fm	Glos	SO5703	51°43·7'	2°37·0'W	FM	162
Severn View Service Area	S Glos	ST5789	51°36·1'	2°36·9'W	X	162,172
Severn Way	Glos	SO8831	51°58·9'	2°10·1'W	X	150
Sevick End	Beds	TL0954	52°10·6'	0°24·0'W	T	153
Sevington	Kent	TR0340	51°7·6'	0°54·5'E	T	179,189
Sevington	Wilts	ST8678	51°30·3'	2°11·7'W	X	173
Sevington Fm	Hants	SU5729	51°3·7'	1°10·8'W	FM	185
Sevington Fm	Heref	SO6849	52°8·5'	2°27·7'W	FM	149
Sewalds Hall Fm	Essex	TL4907	51°44·7'	0°9·9'E	FM	167
Sewards End	Essex	TL5638	52°1·3'	0°16·8'E	T	154
Seward's Fm	Cambs	TL3783	52°25·9'	0°1·3'E	FM	142,143
Sewards Fm	Devon	ST0604	50°49·9'	3°19·7'W	FM	192
Seward's Hall	Essex	TL6722	51°52·5'	0°26·0'E	X	167
Sewardstone	Essex	TQ3897	51°39·5'	0°0·1'E	T	166,177
Sewardstonebury	Essex	TQ3995	51°38·4'	0°0·9'E	T	166,177
Sewborwens	Cumbr	NY4930	54°40·0'	2°47·0'W	X	90
Sewell	Beds	SP9922	51°53·5'	0°33·3'W	T	165
Sewell Houses	Cumbr	NY4544	54°47·5'	2°50·9'W	X	86
Sewells Fm	Essex	TL8313	51°47·4'	0°39·6'E	FM	168
Sewell's Fm	E Susx	TQ4116	50°55·8'	0°0·8'E	FM	198
Sewerby	E Yorks	TA1968	54°5·9'	0°10·4'W	T	101
Sewerby Cott	E Yorks	TA1868	54°5·9'	0°11·3'W	X	101
Sewerby Fields	E Yorks	TA1968	54°5·9'	0°10·4'W	X	101
Sewerby Hall	E Yorks	TA2069	54°6·4'	0°9·5'W	X	101
Sewerby Rocks	E Yorks	TA2068	54°5·9'	0°9·5'W	X	101
Sewing Shields	Northum	NY8170	55°1·7'	2°17·4'W	X	86,87
Sewingshields Crags	Northum	NY7970	55°1·7'	2°19·3'W	X	86,87
Seworgan	Corn	SW7031	50°8·3'	5°12·8'W	T	203
Sewstern	Leic	SK8821	52°47·0'	0°41·3'W	T	130
Sewstern Grange	Leic	SK8720	52°46·5'	0°42·2'W	X	130
Sexhow	N Yks	NZ4706	54°27·1'	1°16·1'W	T	93
Sexhow Grange	N Yks	NZ4805	54°26·5'	1°15·2'W	X	93
Sexton	Devon	SX6352	50°21·4'	3°55·2'W	X	202
Sexton's Cross	Devon	SX8687	50°40·5'	3°36·4'W	X	191
Sexton's Moat	Norf	TM1095	52°31·0'	1°6·1'E	A	144
Sexton Wood	Norf	TM2991	52°28·4'	1°22·7'E	F	134
Sexton Wood Fm	Norf	TM2991	52°28·4'	1°22·7'E	FM	134
Seymour Court	Bucks	SU8388	51°35·3'	0°47·7'W	X	175
Seymour Drain	Notts	SK8281	53°19·4'	0°45·7'W	W	121
Seymour Hall Fm	Suff	TL8855	52°9·9'	0°45·3'E	FM	155
Seymour Ho	Cumbr	NY1946	54°48·4'	3°15·2'W	X	85
Seymour's Court	Somer	ST8152	51°16·2'	2°16·0'W	A	183
Seymour Villas	Devon	SS4644	51°10·7'	4°11·8'W	X	180
Sezincote	Glos	SP1730	51°58·3'	1°44·8'W	T	151
Sezincote Warren	Glos	SP1431	51°58·9'	1°47·4'W	X	151
Sgaigein	Arg & Bt	NM3837	56°27·4'	6°14·7'W	X	47,48
Sgairail	Arg & Bt	NR3675	55°54·0'	6°11·5'W	X	60,61
Sgairneach Mhór	Pth & Kin	NN5974	56°50·4'	4°18·2'W	H	42
Sgairneach Mor	Stir	NN2820	56°20·7'	4°46·5'W	X	50,56
Sgaladal	N Eil	NB0221	58°4·9'	7°2·9'W	H	13
Sgaorishal	Highld	NG3501	57°1·7'	6°21·6'W	H	32,39
Sgaoth Aird	N Eil	NB1603	57°55·8'	6°47·4'W	H	13,14
Sgaoth Iosal	N Eil	NB1504	57°56·3'	6°48·5'W	H	13,14
Sgaps Geo	Highld	ND2936	58°18·7'	3°12·2'W	X	11
Sgaraman nam Fiadh	Highld	NH6106	57°7·7'	4°17·3'W	H	35
Sgarbach	Highld	ND3763	58°33·3'	3°4·5'W	X	12
Sgarbhag	Highld	NC0532	58°14·3'	5°18·8'W	X	15
Sgarbhag	Highld	NC1340	58°18·8'	5°11·1'W	X	9
Sgarbh Beag	Arg & Bt	NR4178	55°55·8'	6°8·4'W	X	60,61

Sgarbh Breac	Arg & Bt	NR4076	55°54·7'	6°9·2'W	H	60,61
Sgarbh Choinneach	N Eil	NB0411	57°59·6'	7°0·1'W	X	13
Sgarbh Dubh	Arg & Bt	NR3775	55°54·0'	6°12·0'W	H	60,61
Sgarbh Sgeir	N Eil	NB3809	57°59·8'	6°25·6'W	X	14
Sgarbh Sgeir	N Eil	NB4460	58°27·5'	6°22·9'W	X	8
Sgarbhstac	N Eil	NA1504	57°51·8'	8°29·2'W	X	18
Sgat Beag	Arg & Bt	NR9466	55°50·9'	5°17·0'W	X	62
Sgath a' Bhannaich	Highld	NG6259	57°33·8'	5°58·3'W	H	24
Sgat Mór	Arg & Bt	NR9366	55°50·8'	5°18·0'W	X	62
Sgavoch Rock	S Ayr	NX0781	55°5·4'	5°1·0'W	X	76
Sgeir a' Bhathaidh	N Eil	NB3100	57°54·8'	6°32·0'W	X	14
Sgeir a' Bhuallt	N Eil	NG0398	57°52·6'	7°0·1'W	X	18
Sgeir a' Bhuic	Highld	NC4763	58°32·0'	4°37·2'W	X	9
Sgeir a' Bhuic	Highld	NG8389	57°50·5'	5°38·9'W	X	19
Sgeir a' Caolas	Arg & Bt	NR6647	55°39·9'	5°42·8'W	X	62
Sgeir a'Caolas	Arg & Bt	NR6747	55°39·9'	5°41·9'W	X	62
Sgeir a' Chadh	Highld	NC2250	58°24·4'	5°2·3'W	X	9
Sgeir a' Chàil	N Eil	NF9679	57°42·1'	7°5·7'W	X	18
Sgeir a' Chàise	N Eil	NB0705	57°56·5'	6°56·6'W	X	13,14
Sgeir a' Chaisteil	Arg & Bt	NM2742	56°29·7'	6°25·7'W	X	46,47,48
Sgeir a' Chaolais	Highld	NM6270	56°45·9'	5°53·2'W	X	40
Sgeir a' Chapuill	Highld	NG3064	57°35·4'	6°30·6'W	X	23
Sgeir a' Charraigein	Arg & Bt	NM4538	56°28·2'	6°8·0'W	X	47,48
Sgeir a' Cheòthain	N Eil	NF7756	57°29·0'	7°23·0'W	X	22
Sgeir a' Chlachain	Arg & Bt	NR4345	55°38·1'	6°4·6'W	X	60
Sgeir a' Chlaidheimh	Highld	NC1337	58°17·2'	5°10·9'W	X	15
Sgeir a' Chlaidheimh Beag	Arg & Bt	NM4232	56°24·8'	6°10·5'W	X	48
Sgeir a' Chlaidheimh Mór	Arg & Bt	NM4232	56°24·8'	6°10·5'W	X	48
Sgeir a' Chléirich	Arg & Bt	NM7712	56°15·2'	5°35·6'W	X	55
Sgeir a' Chlogaid	N Eil	NL6593	56°54·7'	7°29·8'W	X	31
Sgeir a' Choin	N Eil	NF8443	57°22·3'	7°15·0'W	X	22
Sgeir a' Chotain	N Eil	NF7566	57°34·3'	7°25·7'W	X	18
Sgeir a' Chuain	Highld	NG2158	57°31·8'	6°39·2'W	X	23
Sgeir a' Chuain	Highld	NG2940	57°22·5'	6°30·0'W	X	23
Sgeir a' Chuain	Highld	NG3065	57°35·9'	6°30·7'W	X	23
Sgeir á Chuain	N Eil	NF9877	57°41·1'	7°3·6'W	X	18
Sgeir a' Ghaill	Highld	NM7397	57°0·8'	5°43·9'W	X	33,40
Sgeir á Ghair	Highld	NG7261	57°35·2'	5°48·4'W	X	24
Sgeir a'Gheoidh	Arg & Bt	NM7011	56°14·4'	5°42·3'W	X	55
Sgeir a' Gheòidh	Arg & Bt	NM7926	56°22·7'	5°34·3'W	X	49
Sgeir a'Mhaim-ard	Highld	NM4193	56°57·6'	6°15·2'W	X	39
Sgeir a' Mhill	N Eil	NF8312	57°5·6'	7°13·6'W	X	31
Sgeir a' Mhurain	N Eil	NB1441	58°16·1'	6°52·2'W	X	13
Sgeir an Aon Iomairt	Highld	NB9605	57°59·5'	5°26·6'W	X	15
Sgeir an Araig	Highld	NG8389	57°50·5'	5°38·9'W	X	19
Sgeir an Daimh	Highld	NG2498	57°53·4'	6°39·0'W	X	14
Sgeiran Dubh	Arg & Bt	NR1552	55°40·9'	6°31·6'W	X	60
Sgeir an Dùin	Highld	NG3555	57°30·7'	6°25·0'W	X	23
Sgeir an Durdain	Highld	NM6372	56°47·0'	5°52·3'W	X	40
Sgeir an Eididh	Highld	NM6171	56°46·4'	5°54·3'W	X	40
Sgeir an Eirionnaich	Arg & Bt	NM2843	56°30·3'	6°24·8'W	X	46,47,48
Sgeir an Eitich	Arg & Bt	NM8532	56°26·1'	5°28·8'W	X	49
Sgeir an Fhéidh	Arg & Bt	NM2520	56°17·8'	6°26·3'W	X	48
Sgeir an Fhéidh	Arg & Bt	NR5083	55°58·8'	6°0·0'W	X	61
Sgeir an Fhéidh	N Eil	NF7813	57°6·0'	7°18·6'W	X	31
Sgeir an Fhéidh	N Eil	NF8321	57°10·5'	7°14·3'W	X	31
Sgeir an Fheòir	Arg & Bt	NM2843	56°30·3'	6°24·8'W	X	46,47,48
Sgeir an Fheòir	Highld	NG8136	57°22·0'	5°38·1'W	X	24
Sgeir an Fheòir	Highld	NM6286	56°54·5'	5°54·1'W	X	40
Sgeir an Fhiodh	Arg & Bt	NR7067	55°50·7'	5°40·0'W	X	61,62
Sgeir an Leum Mhóir	N Eil	NG1993	57°50·6'	6°43·7'W	X	14
Sgeir an Oir	Arg & Bt	NM2520	56°17·8'	6°26·3'W	X	48
Sgeir an Oir	Highld	NC6164	58°32·8'	4°22·8'W	X	10
Sgeir an Ròin	Arg & Bt	NR6845	55°38·8'	5°40·8'W	X	62
Sgeir an Roin	Highld	NG6724	57°15·1'	5°51·3'W	X	32
Sgeir an Rubha Mhóir	N Eil	NF7266	57°34·2'	7°28·7'W	X	18
Sgeir an Tairbh	Arg & Bt	NL9648	56°31·8'	6°56·2'W	X	46
Sgeir an t-Sabhail	Highld	NG8824	57°15·7'	5°30·5'W	X	33
Sgeir an t-Sàilein	Arg & Bt	NM8341	56°30·9'	5°31·2'W	X	49
Sgeir an t-Seangain	Highld	NM7162	56°41·9'	5°44·0'W	X	40
Sgeir an t-Sruith	Highld	NG6215	57°10·1'	5°55·8'W	X	32
Sgeir a' Phuirt	Highld	NG2804	57°3·1'	6°28·7'W	X	39
Sgeir a' Sgadain	N Eil	NB3102	57°55·8'	6°32·2'W	X	14
Sgeir Beul na h-Uamhaidh	Arg & Bt	NM7397	56°18·8'	5°39·8'W	X	55
Sgeir Bhàn	N Eil	NB2648	58°20·4'	6°40·4'W	X	8
Sgeir Bharrach	Arg & Bt	NM0449	56°32·6'	6°48·5'W	X	46
Sgeir Bheag	Arg & Bt	NR6650	55°41·5'	5°43·0'W	X	62
Sgeir Bheag	Highld	NG3039	57°21·9'	6°29·0'W	X	23,32
Sgeir Bheag	Highld	NG3424	57°14·0'	6°24·0'W	X	32
Sgeir Bheathaig	Arg & Bt	NR8553	55°43·6'	5°25·0'W	X	62
Sgeir Bhiorach	Arg & Bt	NR3290	56°1·9'	6°17·7'W	X	61
Sgeir Bhioramuill	Arg & Bt	NM4438	56°28·1'	6°8·9'W	X	47,48
Sgeir Bhuidha	Highld	NG7732	57°19·7'	5°41·8'W	X	24
Sgeir Bhuidhe	Arg & Bt	NM5220	56°18·7'	6°0·2'W	X	48
Sgeir Bhuidhe	Arg & Bt	NM7312	56°15·0'	5°39·4'W	X	55
Sgeir Bhuidhe	Arg & Bt	NM7720	56°19·5'	5°36·0'W	X	49,55
Sgeir Bhuidhe	Arg & Bt	NR8143	55°38·1'	5°28·3'W	X	62,69
Sgeir Bhuidhe	Arg & Bt	NR8351	55°42·5'	5°26·8'W	X	62,69
Sgeir Bhuidhe	Arg & Bt	NR9259	55°47·0'	5°18·6'W	X	62
Sgeir Bhuidhe	Highld	NG6937	57°22·2'	5°50·1'W	X	24,32
Sgeir Bhuidhe	Highld	NG8035	57°21·4'	5°39·0'W	X	24
Sgeir Bhuidhe	Highld	NG8133	57°20·4'	5°37·9'W	X	24
Sgeir Bhuidhe	Highld	NM5857	56°38·8'	5°56·4'W	X	47
Sgeir Biodaig	Highld	NG5708	57°6·2'	6°0·3'W	X	32,39
Sgeir Blàr nan Each	Arg & Bt	NM2438	56°27·5'	6°28·4'W	X	46,47,48
Sgeir Blàth-shuileach	Arg & Bt	NR6651	55°42·0'	5°43·0'W	X	62
Sgeir Bruachaig	Arg & Bt	NN0806	56°12·7'	5°5·3'W	X	56
Sgeir Bun an Locha	Arg & Bt	NR6976	55°55·6'	5°41·4'W	X	61,62
Sgeir Caillich	Arg & Bt	NM9142	56°31·7'	5°23·4'W	X	49
Sgeir Chàise	N Eil	NF7818	57°8·7'	7°19·0'W	X	31
Sgeir Chaol	Arg & Bt	NR6842	55°37·2'	5°40·6'W	X	62
Sgeir Charach	N Eil	NB1935	58°13·1'	6°46·7'W	X	8,13
Sgeir Charrach	Highld	NM5873	56°47·4'	5°57·3'W	X	39,47
Sgeir Chnapach	Highld	NG5438	57°22·2'	6°5·0'W	X	24,32
Sgeir Chorrach Mhór	Arg & Bt	NM0846	56°31·2'	6°44·4'W	X	46
Sgeir Chreagach	Highld	NG9038	57°23·3'	5°29·2'W	X	25
Sgeir Chreagag	Arg & Bt	NM7709	56°13·5'	5°35·4'W	X	55
Sgeir Chrisnain	N Eil	NL5480	56°47·2'	7°39·6'W	X	31
Sgeir Chruaidh	N Eil	NF9980	57°42·8'	7°2·8'W	X	18
Sgeir Cnoc Easgann	N Eil	NG1087	57°47·0'	6°52·3'W	X	14

Sgeir Coillt	N Eil	NB4862	58°28·7'	6°18·9'W	X	8
Sgeir Criaraidh	Arg & Bt	NM7510	56°14·0'	5°37·4'W	X	55
Sgeir Cùl an Rubha	Arg & Bt	NR6078	55°56·4'	5°50·2'W	X	61,62
Sgeir Dhearg	Arg & Bt	NM4054	56°36·6'	6°13·8'W	X	47
Sgeir Dhearg	Highld	NG6333	57°19·8'	5°55·8'W	X	24,32
Sgeir Dhearg	N Eil	NB1443	58°17·2'	6°52·3'W	X	13
Sgeir Dhoirbh	Arg & Bt	NM2811	56°13·1'	6°22·8'W	X	48
Sgeir Dhomhnail Chaim	N Eil	NF9984	57°44·9'	7°3·1'W	X	18
Sgeir Dhomhnuill	N Eil	NA1000	57°49·4'	8°33·8'W	X	18
Sgeir Dhonn	Arg & Bt	NM8230	56°25·0'	5°31·6'W	X	49
Sgeir Dhonncha	Arg & Bt	NR6877	55°56·1'	5°42·4'W	X	61,62
Sgeir Dhreumasdail	N Eil	NF7438	57°19·2'	7°24·5'W	X	22
Sgeir Dhubh	Arg & Bt	NM3838	56°27·9'	6°14·8'W	X	47,48
Sgeir Dhubh	Arg & Bt	NM8103	56°10·4'	5°31·2'W	X	55
Sgeir Dhubh	Arg & Bt	NM8122	56°20·6'	5°32·2'W	X	49
Sgeir Dhubh	Highld	NG5232	57°18·9'	6°6·7'W	X	24,32
Sgeir Dhubh	Highld	NG5236	57°21·1'	6°6·9'W	X	23,24,32
Sgeir Dhubh	Highld	NG5262	57°35·1'	6°8·5'W	X	23,24
Sgeir Dhubh	Highld	NG7459	57°34·1'	5°46·3'W	X	24
Sgeir-dhubh an Aomaidh	Arg & Bt	NR6972	55°53·4'	5°41·2'W	X	61,62
Sgeir Dhubh Bheag	Arg & Bt	NM3937	56°27·4'	6°13·7'W	X	47,48
Sgeir Dhubh Mhór	N Eil	NB1236	58°13·4'	6°53·8'W	X	13
Sgeir Dorcha	Highld	NG4918	57°11·3'	6°8·8'W	X	32
Sgeir Dubh	Highld	NG6925	57°15·7'	5°49·4'W	X	32
Sgeir Dubh	N Eil	NF9685	57°45·4'	7°6·2'W	X	18
Sgeir Dubhail	Arg & Bt	NM4241	56°29·7'	6°11·1'W	X	47,48
Sgeir Dubh Mór	N Eil	NF7577	57°40·2'	7°26·6'W	X	18
Sgeir Dùghall	Highld	NG7760	57°34·8'	5°43·3'W	X	19,24
Sgeirean a' Bhàigh	N Eil	NG4198	57°54·0'	6°21·8'W	X	14
Sgeirean a'Mhaoil	Arg & Bt	NM7104	56°10·7'	5°40·9'W	X	55
Sgeirean an Arbhair	N Eil	NB4024	58°8·0'	6°24·5'W	X	14
Sgeirean an Ròin	Arg & Bt	NM0546	56°31·1'	6°47·3'W	X	46
Sgeirean an Uisge Ghlais	Highld	NG7530	57°18·6'	5°43·7'W	X	24
Sgeirean Beaga	Arg & Bt	NM3955	56°37·1'	6°14·8'W	X	47
Sgeirean Buidhe	Arg & Bt	NR2840	55°34·9'	6°18·5'W	X	60
Sgeirean Buidhe	Arg & Bt	NR5267	55°50·2'	5°57·2'W	X	61
Sgeirean Buidhe	Highld	NG8053	57°31·1'	5°40·0'W	X	24
Sgeirean Buidhe	Highld	NM6485	56°54·0'	5°52·1'W	X	40
Sgeirean Buidhe Bhorlum	Highld	NG6160	57°34·3'	5°59·4'W	X	24
Sgeirean Buidhe Ghil	Arg & Bt	NR2744	55°37·0'	6°19·7'W	X	60
Sgeirean Dhubha Fhiadhach	Highld	NM6375	56°48·6'	5°52·5'W	X	40
Sgeirean Dubha	Arg & Bt	NM6409	56°12·9'	5°48·0'W	X	55
Sgeirean Dubha	Arg & Bt	NM8126	56°22·8'	5°32·4'W	X	49
Sgeirean Fada	Arg & Bt	NR3489	56°1·5'	6°15·7'W	X	61
Sgeirean Fiaclach	N Eil	NL6794	56°55·3'	7°28·0'W	X	31
Sgeirean Glasa	Highld	NB9602	57°57·9'	5°26·5'W	X	15
Sgeirean Glasa	Highld	NC1549	58°23·7'	5°9·4'W	X	9
Sgeirean Glasa	Highld	NM7499	57°1·9'	5°43·0'W	X	33,40
Sgeirean Gobhlach	Highld	NM6489	56°56·2'	5°52·3'W	X	40
Sgeirean Leathann	Arg & Bt	NR2875	55°53·7'	6°20·6'W	X	60
Sgeirean Mór	Arg & Bt	NM2841	56°29·2'	6°24·7'W	X	46,47,48
Sgeirean Mór	Arg & Bt	NM4024	56°20·5'	6°12·0'W	X	48
Sgeirean Móra	Highld	NG7954	57°31·6'	5°41·0'W	X	24
Sgeirean Móra	Highld	NM3691	56°56·4'	6°20·0'W	X	39
Sgeirean na Giusaich	Arg & Bt	NM2842	56°29·7'	6°24·7'W	X	46,47,48
Sgeirean nan Cuiseag	Arg & Bt	NM1551	56°34·1'	6°37·9'W	X	46
Sgeirean nan Torran	Highld	NM9356	56°39·3'	5°22·2'W	X	49
Sgeirean Ràrsaidh	Highld	NG8211	57°8·6'	5°35·7'W	X	33
Sgeirean Shallachain	Highld	NM9762	56°42·6'	5°18·5'W	X	40
Sgeirean Tarsuinn	Highld	NG6432	57°19·3'	5°54·7'W	X	24,32
Sgeirean Tiddaborra	N Eil	NB1834	58°12·5'	6°47·6'W	X	8,13
Sgeirean Tràghaidh	Arg & Bt	NR1965	55°48·1'	6°28·6'W	X	60
Sgeireig a' Bhogadain	Arg & Bt	NM3516	56°16·0'	6°16·4'W	X	48
Sgeir Eoghainn	N Eil	NA9825	58°6·9'	7°7·2'W	X	13
Sgeir Eskernish	Highld	NM4484	56°52·9'	6°11·7'W	X	39
Sgeir Fhada	Arg & Bt	NR3544	55°37·3'	6°12·1'W	X	60
Sgeir Fhada	Highld	NG5708	57°6·2'	6°0·3'W	X	32,39
Sgeir Fhada	Highld	NG9139	57°23·9'	5°28·2'W	X	25
Sgeir Fhada	Highld	NM4079	56°50·0'	6°15·3'W	X	39
Sgeir Fhada	Highld	NM5561	56°40·9'	5°59·6'W	X	47
Sgeir Fhadabhig	N Eil	NF9882	57°43·8'	7°4·0'W	X	18
Sgeir Fharspaig	Arg & Bt	NM1451	56°34·1'	6°38·9'W	X	46
Sgeir Fhearchair	Highld	NG7025	57°15·7'	5°48·4'W	X	33
Sgeir Fhiacail	Arg & Bt	NR6654	55°43·6'	5°43·2'W	X	62
Sgeir Fiaclach Beag	N Eil	NL7399	56°58·3'	7°22·5'W	X	31
Sgeir Fiaclach Mór	N Eil	NL7399	56°58·3'	7°22·5'W	X	31
Sgeir Fiavig Tarras	N Eil	NB0235	58°12·4'	7°3·9'W	X	13
Sgeir Gallan	N Eil	NB0439	58°14·7'	7°2·2'W	X	13
Sgeir Ghainmheach	Highld	NM6386	56°54·5'	5°53·1'W	X	40
Sgeir Ghlas	Arg & Bt	NM6243	56°31·4'	5°51·7'W	X	49
Sgeir Ghlas	Highld	NG7366	57°37·9'	5°47·7'W	X	19,24
Sgeir Ghlas	Highld	NG7657	57°33·1'	5°44·2'W	X	24
Sgeir Ghlas	Highld	NM6979	56°51·0'	5°46·8'W	X	40
Sgeir Ghlas	N Eil	NB0030	58°9·7'	7°5·6'W	X	13
Sgeir Ghlas	N Eil	NB3210	58°5·5'	6°32·4'W	X	13,14
Sgeir Ghlas	N Eil	NG1896	57°52·1'	6°44·9'W	X	14
Sgeir Ghlas Bheag	N Eil	NA9825	58°6·9'	7°7·2'W	X	13
Sgeir Ghlas na Roinne	N Eil	NA9820	58°4·2'	7°6·9'W	X	13
Sgeir Ghobhlach	Arg & Bt	NM2712	56°13·6'	6°23·8'W	X	48
Sgeir Ghobhlach	Highld	NM4370	56°45·3'	6°11·8'W	X	39,47
Sgeir Ghobhlach	N Eil	NG1893	57°50·5'	6°44·7'W	X	14
Sgeir Ghoblach	Highld	NG7041	57°24·3'	5°49·3'W	X	24
Sgeir Ghobhlach	N Eil	NA9824	58°6·4'	7°7·2'W	X	13
Sgeir Gigalum	Arg & Bt	NR6546	55°39·3'	5°43·7'W	X	62
Sgeir Gobhlach	Highld	NG6625	57°15·6'	5°52·4'W	X	32
Sgeir Gormul	Highld	NG6315	57°10·1'	5°54·8'W	X	32
Sgeir In-ao	N Eil	NG2991	57°49·9'	6°33·4'W	X	14
Sgeir Iosal	Highld	NC1750	58°24·3'	5°7·4'W	T	9
Sgeirislum	N Eil	NF7303	57°0·4'	7°22·8'W	X	31
Sgeir Lag Choan	Arg & Bt	NN0233	56°27·1'	5°12·3'W	X	50
Sgeir Laith	Arg & Bt	NM7821	56°20·0'	5°35·0'W	X	49
Sgeir Lang	Highld	NG3670	57°38·8'	6°25·0'W	X	23
Sgeir Leathan	Arg & Bt	NM0946	56°31·2'	6°43·5'W	X	46
Sgeir Leathan	Arg & Bt	NM4024	56°20·5'	6°12·0'W	X	48
Sgeir Leathan	Arg & Bt	NM4436	56°27·1'	6°8·8'W	X	47,48
Sgeir Leathan	Arg & Bt	NM7226	56°22·5'	5°41·3'W	X	49
Sgeir Leathan	Highld	NC4366	58°33·5'	4°41·4'W	X	9
Sgeir Leathan	Highld	NG8408	57°7·0'	5°33·6'W	X	33
Sgeir Leathann	Arg & Bt	NM4100	56°7·6'	6°9·6'W	X	61

Sgeir Leathann	Arg & Bt	NR3290	56°1·9'	6°17·7'W	X	61
Sgeir Leathann	Arg & Bt	NR3686	55°59·9'	6°13·6'W	X	61
Sgeir Leathann	Arg & Bt	NR8771	55°53·4'	5°23·9'W	X	62
Sgeir Leathann	N Eil	NB5041	58°17·5'	6°15·5'W	X	8
Sgeir Leehinish	N Eil	NL6590	56°53·1'	7°29·6'W	X	31
Sgeir Leomadal	N Eil	NF9894	57°50·3'	7°4·9'W	X	18
Sgeir Leth a' Chuain	Arg & Bt	NM6410	56°13·7'	5°48·0'W	X	55
Sgeir Leum	N Eil	NB3611	58°0·8'	6°27·7'W	X	14
Sgeir Liath	Arg & Bt	NM8739	56°30·0'	5°27·2'W	X	49
Sgeir Liath	Arg & Bt	NR4754	55°43·1'	6°1·3'W	X	60
Sgeir Liath	N Eil	NA9823	58°5·8'	7°7·1'W	X	13
Sgeir Liath	N Eil	NB0001	57°54·1'	7°3·4'W	X	18
Sgeir Liath	N Eil	NB0133	58°11·3'	7°4·8'W	X	13
Sgeir Liath	N Eil	NF6503	57°0·1'	7°30·6'W	X	31
Sgeir Liath	N Eil	NF7068	57°35·1'	7°30·9'W	X	18
Sgeir Liath	N Eil	NG0093	57°49·8'	7°2·8'W	X	18
Sgeir Liath	N Eil	NL6497	56°56·8'	7°31·1'W	X	31
Sgeir Linis	N Eil	NB4226	58°9·1'	6°22·6'W	X	8
Sgeir Mac Righ Lochlainn	N Eil	NA0500	57°49·2'	8°38·9'W	X	18
Sgeir Màire	Arg & Bt	NR7062	55°48·1'	5°39·8'W	X	61,62
Sgeir Maldaig	Arg & Bt	NM5139	56°28·9'	6°2·2'W	X	47,48
Sgeir Maol Mhoraidh	Highld	NG8092	57°52·1'	5°42·1'W	X	19
Sgeir Maol Mhoraidh Shuas	Highld	NG8192	57°52·1'	5°41·1'W	X	19
Sgeir Mhali	Highld	NM7461	56°41·4'	5°41·0'W	X	40
Sgeir Mhaola Cinn	Arg & Bt	NR8772	55°53·9'	5°24·0'W	X	62
Sgeir Mhic Chomhain	Arg & Bt	NM7039	56°29·5'	5°43·7'W	X	49
Sgeir Mhic Coma	N Eil	NG0086	57°46·1'	7°2·3'W	X	18
Sgeir Mhic Eachain	Highld	NG6202	57°3·1'	5°55·0'W	X	32
Sgeir Mhic Iamain	N Eil	NF8542	57°21·8'	7°13·9'W	X	22
Sgeir Mhogalach	Arg & Bt	NM7010	56°13·9'	5°42·2'W	X	55
Sgeir Mhòr	Arg & Bt	NL9648	56°31·8'	6°56·2'W	X	46
Sgeir Mhòr	Arg & Bt	NM3956	56°37·6'	6°14·9'W	X	47
Sgeir Mhòr	Arg & Bt	NM4825	56°21·3'	6°4·3'W	X	48
Sgeir Mhòr	Arg & Bt	NM4827	56°22·4'	6°4·4'W	X	48
Sgeir Mhòr	Arg & Bt	NM5227	56°22·5'	6°0·5'W	X	48
Sgeir Mhòr	Arg & Bt	NM6542	56°30·9'	5°48·8'W	X	49
Sgeir Mhòr	Arg & Bt	NR6650	55°41·5'	5°43·0'W	X	62
Sgeir Mhòr	Arg & Bt	NR6739	55°35·6'	5°41·4'W	X	68
Sgeir Mhòr	Highld	NC0619	58°7·3'	5°17·2'W	X	15
Sgeir Mhòr	Highld	NG3040	57°22·5'	6°29·0'W	X	23
Sgeir Mhòr	Highld	NG3915	57°9·4'	6°18·5'W	X	32
Sgeir Mhòr	Highld	NG4943	57°24·7'	6°10·3'W	X	23
Sgeir Mhòr	Highld	NG5708	57°6·2'	6°0·3'W	X	32,39
Sgeir Mhòr	Highld	NG5719	57°12·1'	6°0·9'W	X	32
Sgeir Mhòr	Highld	NM5651	56°35·5'	5°58·0'W	X	47
Sgeir Mhòr	Highld	NM6693	56°58·4'	5°50·6'W	X	40
Sgeir Mhòr	N Eil	NB2750	58°21·5'	6°39·6'W	X	8
Sgeir Mhòr	N Eil	NF7104	57°0·8'	7°24·8'W	X	31
Sgeir Mhòr	N Eil	NG0499	57°53·2'	6°59·2'W	X	18
Sgeir Mhòr	N Eil	NL5779	56°46·8'	7°36·6'W	X	31
Sgeir Mhòr a' Bhrein-phuirt	Arg & Bt	NR5084	55°59·3'	6°0·1'W	X	61
Sgeir Mhòr Bhalamuis	N Eil	NB2900	57°54·7'	6°34·1'W	X	14
Sgeir Mhòr Shilldinis	N Eil	NB4631	58°11·9'	6°18·9'W	X	8
Sgeir Mianais	N Eil	NG4196	57°53·0'	6°21·7'W	X	14
Sgeir Moil Duinn	N Eil	NA9416	58°1·9'	7°10·6'W	X	13
Sgeir Mol Srupair	N Eil	NB4219	58°5·4'	6°22·2'W	X	14
Sgeir na Caillich	Arg & Bt	NM2917	56°16·3'	6°22·2'W	X	48
Sgeir na Caillich	Arg & Bt	NM8012	56°15·2'	5°32·7'W	X	55
Sgeir na Caillich	Highld	NG8024	57°15·5'	5°38·4'W	X	33
Sgeir na Caorach	Highld	NG2256	57°30·8'	6°38·1'W	X	23
Sgeir na Cille	Arg & Bt	NM3945	56°31·7'	6°14·2'W	X	47,48
Sgeir na Cusha	Arg & Bt	NM7210	56°13·9'	5°40·3'W	X	55
Sgeir na Dubhaidh	Arg & Bt	NR8771	55°53·4'	5°23·9'W	X	62
Sgeir na Eireann	Highld	NG4872	57°40·3'	6°13·1'W	X	23
Sgeir na Fàinne	Arg & Bt	NM0549	56°32·7'	6°47·5'W	X	46
Sgeir na Faoilinn	Arg & Bt	NM4130	56°23·7'	6°11·4'W	X	48
Sgeir na Faoilinn	Arg & Bt	NM6827	56°23·0'	5°45·0'W	X	49
Sgeir na Galla	N Eil	NB1141	58°16·0'	6°55·2'W	X	13
Sgeir na h-Aireig	Arg & Bt	NM7414	56°16·1'	5°38·6'W	X	55
Sgeir na h-Aon Chaorach	N Eil	NB1137	58°13·9'	6°54·9'W	X	13
Sgeir na h-Aon Chaorach	N Eil	NB1441	58°16·1'	6°52·2'W	X	13
Sgeir na h-Aon Chaorach	N Eil	NB1740	58°15·7'	6°49·1'W	X	8,13
Sgeir na h-Eigheach	N Eil	NB2800	57°54·7'	6°35·1'W	X	14
Sgeir na h-Iolaire	Arg & Bt	NM2843	56°30·3'	6°24·8'W	X	46,47,48
Sgeir na Laimhrige Mòire	Arg & Bt	NM4436	56°27·1'	6°8·8'W	X	47,48
Sgeir na Lùib	Arg & Bt	NR7758	55°46·1'	5°32·9'W	X	62
Sgeir na Luing	Arg & Bt	NR8956	55°45·3'	5°21·3'W	X	62
Sgeir na Maoile	Arg & Bt	NR7497	56°7·0'	5°37·7'W	X	55
Sgeir nam Ban	Arg & Bt	NR4649	55°40·3'	6°1·9'W	X	60
Sgeir nam Biast	Highld	NG2356	57°30·8'	6°37·1'W	X	23
Sgeir nam Faochag	Arg & Bt	NM5126	56°21·9'	6°1·5'W	X	48
Sgeir nam Faoileann	Arg & Bt	NM7415	56°16·7'	5°38·6'W	X	55
Sgeir nam Faoileann	Arg & Bt	NM7501	56°9·2'	5°36·9'W	X	55
Sgeir nam Fiadh	Highld	NG6113	57°9·0'	5°56·6'W	X	32
Sgeir nam Figheadair	Arg & Bt	NM7405	56°11·3'	5°38·1'W	X	55
Sgeir nam Maol	Highld	NG3981	57°44·8'	6°22·7'W	X	23
Sgeir nam Marag	Arg & Bt	NM6510	56°13·7'	5°47·0'W	X	55
Sgeir nam Meann	Highld	NM6169	56°45·3'	5°54·1'W	X	40
Sgeir nam Mult	Highld	NB9603	57°58·4'	5°26·5'W	X	15
Sgeir na Muice	N Eil	NG0382	57°44·0'	6°58·9'W	X	18
Sgeir na Muice	N Eil	NL6795	56°55·8'	7°28·0'W	X	31
Sgeir nan Caorach	N Eil	NG1897	57°52·7'	6°44·9'W	X	14
Sgeir nan Cliabh	N Eil	NB1935	58°13·1'	6°46·7'W	X	8,13
Sgeir nan Each	N Eil	NB3720	58°5·7'	6°27·3'W	X	14
Sgeir nan Eathar Bàna	Highld	NG4474	57°41·2'	6°17·2'W	X	23
Sgeir nan Eilid	Highld	NM7084	56°53·7'	5°46·1'W	X	40
Sgeir nan Eun	Highld	NG6153	57°30·5'	5°58·9'W	X	24
Sgeir nan Eun	Highld	NM5163	56°41·8'	6°3·6'W	X	47
Sgeir nan Gabhar	Arg & Bt	NM6805	56°11·1'	5°43·9'W	X	55
Sgeir nan Gabhar	Arg & Bt	NM7111	56°14·4'	5°41·3'W	X	55
Sgeir nan Gael	Arg & Bt	NM7735	56°27·5'	5°36·7'W	X	49
Sgeir nan Gall	Highld	NC0835	58°16·0'	5°15·9'W	X	15
Sgeir nan Garbhanach	Arg & Bt	NM1250	56°33·5'	6°40·8'W	X	46
Sgeir nan Gealag	Highld	NG8310	57°8·0'	5°34·7'W	X	33
Sgeir nan Gillean	Highld	NM9054	56°38·1'	5°25·0'W	X	49
Sgeir nan Gobhar	Arg & Bt	NM7039	56°29·5'	5°43·7'W	X	49
Sgeir na Nighinn	Arg & Bt	NR2974	55°53·4'	6°19·6'W	X	60
Sgeir nan Leac	Arg & Bt	NM4438	56°28·1'	6°8·9'W	X	47,48

Sgeir nan Ròn	Arg & Bt	NM4242	56°30·2'	6°11·1'W	X	47,48
Sgeir nan Ruideag	Highld	NG3574	57°40·9'	6°26·3'W	X	23
Sgeir nan Saoidhean	N Eil	NB1141	58°16·0'	6°55·2'W	X	13
Sgeir nan Sgarbh	Arg & Bt	NR2874	55°53·2'	6°20·6'W	X	60
Sgeir nan Sgarbh	Arg & Bt	NR7067	55°50·7'	5°40·0'W	X	61,62
Sgeir nan Sgarbh	Highld	NG2106	57°3·9'	6°35·7'W	X	39
Sgeir nan Sgarbh	Highld	NG4075	57°41·6'	6°21·3'W	X	23
Sgeir nan Sgarbh	N Eil	NB3000	57°54·7'	6°33·0'W	X	14
Sgeir nan Sgarbh	N Eil	NF1199	57°48·9'	8°32·7'W	X	18
Sgeir nan Sian	Arg & Bt	NR4663	55°47·9'	6°2·7'W	X	60,61
Sgeir nan Sligean	Arg & Bt	NR3150	55°40·4'	6°16·3'W	X	60
Sgeir nan Tom	Arg & Bt	NM8847	56°34·3'	5°26·6'W	X	49
Sgeir nan Uan	Arg & Bt	NM8543	56°32·1'	5°29·3'W	X	49
Sgeir nan Uibhein	N Eil	NL5785	56°50·0'	7°37·0'W	X	31
Sgeir na Parlamaid	N Eil	NF9676	57°40·5'	7°5·5'W	X	18
Sgeir na Ruideag	N Eil	NG4398	57°54·1'	6°19·8'W	X	14
Sgeir na Skeineadh	Arg & Bt	NM3738	56°27·9'	6°15·7'W	X	47,48
Sgeir na Snàthaid	N Eil	NF7166	57°34·1'	7°29·7'W	X	18
Sgeir na Tràghad	Highld	NC0327	58°11·5'	5°20·6'W	X	15
Sgeir na Trian	Highld	NG7364	57°36·8'	5°47·6'W	X	24
Sgeir Nèill	Highld	NM6260	56°40·5'	5°52·7'W	X	40
Sgeir Noddimull	N Eil	NL6391	56°53·5'	7°31·6'W	X	31
Sgeir Nuadh	Arg & Bt	NR6750	55°41·5'	5°42·0'W	X	62
Sgeir Orival	N Eil	NF7377	57°40·1'	7°28·6'W	X	18
Sgeir Philip	Highld	NM6486	56°54·6'	5°52·1'W	X	40
Sgeir Phlocach	Arg & Bt	NR3644	55°37·3'	6°11·2'W	X	60
Sgeir Phlocach	Arg & Bt	NR5263	55°48·1'	5°57·0'W	X	61
Sgeir Poll nan Corran	Arg & Bt	NM7107	56°12·3'	5°41·1'W	X	55
Sgeir Port a' Ghuail	Arg & Bt	NR8769	55°52·3'	5°23·8'W	X	62
Sgeir Ramasgaig	Highld	NG6607	57°5·9'	5°51·3'W	X	32
Sgeir Rebrie	N Eil	NB1339	58°15·0'	6°53·1'W	X	13
Sgeir Revan	Highld	NB9705	57°59·5'	5°25·6'W	X	15
Sgeir Righinn	N Eil	NA7245	58°16·5'	7°35·3'W	X	13
Sgeir Robin	N Eil	NB1639	58°15·1'	6°50·0'W	X	13
Sgeir Ruadh	Arg & Bt	NM2722	56°19·0'	6°24·5'W	X	48
Sgeir Ruadh	Arg & Bt	NM4341	56°29·7'	6°10·1'W	X	47,48
Sgeir Ruadh	Arg & Bt	NM7336	56°27·9'	5°40·7'W	X	49
Sgeir Ruadh	Highld	NC1651	58°24·8'	5°8·5'W	X	9
Sgeir Ruadh	Highld	NC8866	58°34·3'	3°55·1'W	X	10
Sgeir Ruadh	N Eil	NF7072	57°37·3'	7°31·2'W	X	18
Sgeir Rubha	Arg & Bt	NR7374	55°54·6'	5°37·5'W	X	62
Sgeir Sgaothaig	Highld	NM4385	56°53·4'	6°12·7'W	X	39
Sgeir Sgianailt	N Eil	NB2036	58°13·7'	6°45·7'W	X	8,13
Sgeir Sgòrach	Arg & Bt	NM4638	56°28·2'	6°7·0'W	X	47,48
Sgeir Sgoraig	Arg & Bt	NM8136	56°28·2'	5°32·9'W	X	49
Sgeir Shalach	Highld	NG7036	57°21·6'	5°49·0'W	X	24
Sgeir Shealg	Arg & Bt	NL9148	56°31·6'	7°1·1'W	X	46
Sgeir Shuas	Highld	NG6261	57°34·8'	5°58·4'W	X	24
Sgeir Sine	N Eil	NF9778	57°41·6'	7°4·7'W	X	18
Sgeir Stapaig	Highld	NG6127	57°16·5'	5°57·4'W	X	32
Sgeir Tanais	N Eil	NB4219	58°5·4'	6°22·2'W	X	14
Sgeir Tarcall	N Eil	NB0801	57°54·4'	6°55·3'W	X	14,18
Sgeir Thal	N Eil	NB2401	57°55·0'	6°39·2'W	X	14
Sgeir Thindealan	N Eil	NB1833	58°12·0'	6°47·5'W	X	8,13
Sgeir Thraid	Highld	NG6233	57°19·8'	5°56·8'W	X	24,32
Sgeir Toman	N Eil	NA7245	58°16·5'	7°35·3'W	X	13
Sgeir Tràighe	Arg & Bt	NR4576	55°54·8'	6°4·4'W	X	60,61
Sgeir Uilleim	Arg & Bt	NM0946	56°31·2'	6°43·5'W	X	46
Sgeir Urgha	N Eil	NG1898	57°53·2'	6°45·0'W	X	14
Sgeir Vuran	N Eil	NF9684	57°44·8'	7°6·1'W	X	18
Sgeiteadh	Highld	NG3522	57°13·0'	6°22·9'W	X	32
Sgeotasaigh	N Eil	NG1897	57°52·7'	6°44·9'W	H	14
Sgeotraval	N Eil	NB1024	58°6·9'	6°55·0'W	H	13,14
Sgeun	N Eil	NB0313	58°0·7'	7°1·3'W	H	13
Sgianait	Arg & Bt	NS0675	55°56·0'	5°5·9'W	X	63
Sgian Dubh	Stir	NN5816	56°19·2'	4°17·3'W	H	57
Sgiath a' Chàise	Stir	NN6314	56°18·2'	4°12·4'W	H	57
Sgiath an Dobhrain	N Ayr	NR9834	55°33·7'	5°11·8'W	X	69
Sgiath Bhàn	Highld	NG8218	57°12·3'	5°36·1'W	H	33
Sgiath Bheinn	Highld	NG6413	57°9·1'	5°53·7'W	H	32
Sgiath-bheinn an Uird	Highld	NG6211	57°8·0'	5°55·5'W	H	32
Sgiath-bheinn Chrossavaig	Highld	NG6111	57°7·9'	5°56·5'W	H	32
Sgiath-bheinn Tokavaig	Pth & Kin	NN4639	56°31·3'	4°29·8'W	X	51
Sgiath Bhuidhe	Stir	NN4638	56°30·8'	4°29·7'W	H	51
Sgiath Bhuidhe	Stir	NN4631	56°27·0'	4°29·5'W	H	51
Sgiath Chrom	Stir	NN4631	56°27·0'	4°29·5'W	H	51
Sgiath Chùil	Pth & Kin	NN4640	56°31·9'	4°29·8'W	X	51
Sgiath Ghlas	Arg & Bt	NN1730	56°25·9'	4°57·6'W	X	50
Sgiath Ghorm	Arg & Bt	NM5644	56°31·7'	5°57·6'W	X	47,48
Sgiath Mhòr	Arg & Bt	NM5644	56°31·7'	5°57·6'W	X	47,48
Sgiath Ruadh	Arg & Bt	NM6521	56°19·6'	5°47·6'W	X	49
Sgicheanan	N Eil	NB3834	58°13·3'	6°27·2'W	X	8
Sgidegro	Arg & Bt	NR8163	55°48·9'	5°29·3'W	X	62
Sgier à Choire	Arg & Bt	NR6598	56°7·3'	5°46·4'W	X	55,61
Sgier Mhòr	N Eil	NB5461	58°28·3'	6°12·7'W	T	8
Sgiogarstaigh	Powys	SO0840	52°3·3'	3°20·1'W	W	147,160
Sgithwen Brook	Powys	SO0940	52°3·3'	3°19·2'W	W	147,161
Sgithwen Brook	Highld	NH4992	57°53·8'	4°32·4'W	X	20
Sgodachail	Highld	NG2261	57°33·5'	6°38·4'W	T	23
Sgoir Beag	Arg & Bt	NR9162	55°48·6'	5°19·7'W	X	62
Sgolaig	N Eil	NB3605	57°57·6'	6°27·3'W	H	14
Sgonnan	Highld	NC3013	58°4·7'	4°52·5'W	H	15
Sgonnan Mòr	Highld	NC5749	58°24·6'	4°26·4'W	H	10
Sgor a' Bhatain	Highld	NH4577	57°45·6'	4°35·8'W	H	20
Sgor a' Chaorainn	Highld	NG6513	57°9·1'	5°52·7'W	H	32
Sgòrach Breac	Highld	NC5648	58°24·1'	4°27·4'W	H	10
Sgor a Chleirich	Arg & Bt	NS0984	56°0·9'	5°3·4'W	H	56
Sgòrach Mòr	Highld	NH9000	57°4·9'	3°48·4'W	H	36
Sgòran Dubh Beag	Highld	NH9000	57°4·9'	3°48·4'W	H	36
Sgòran Dubh Mòr	Aberd	NO3093	57°1·6'	3°8·7'W	H	37,44
Sgor an h-Iolaire						
Sgor an Lochain Uaine or The Angel's Peak	Aberd	NN9597	57°3·4'	3°43·4'W	H	36,43
Sgòr Bhothain	Highld	NN7685	56°56·6'	4°1·8'W	H	42
Sgòr Cainnteach	Arg & Bt	NR6950	55°41·6'	5°40·1'W	X	62
Sgòr Chaonasaid	Highld	NC5749	58°24·6'	4°26·4'W	H	10
Sgòr Choinnich	Highld	NN4468	56°46·9'	4°32·8'W	H	42
Sgòr Choinnich	Highld	NN7484	56°56·1'	4°3·8'W	H	42
Sgòr Dubh	Aberd	NO0392	57°0·8'	3°35·4'W	H	43
Sgòr Eilde Beag	Highld	NN2165	56°44·8'	4°55·2'W	X	41
Sgòr Gaibhre	Pth & Kin	NN4467	56°46·4'	4°32·7'W	H	42

Sgor Gaoith	Highld	NN9098	57°3·9'	3°48·4'W	H	36,43
Sgòr Gaoithe	Highld	NH4218	57°13·8'	4°36·6'W	H	34
Sgòr Gaoithe	Highld	NJ0536	57°24·5'	3°34·4'W	H	27
Sgòr Gaoithe	Highld	NJ0721	57°16·5'	3°32·1'W	H	36
Sgor Gorm	Aberd	NJ2713	57°12·4'	3°12·0'W	H	37
Sgòr Iutharn	Highld	NN4974	56°50·2'	4°28·1'W	H	42
Sgòr Mòr	Aberd	NO0091	57°0·2'	3°38·3'W	H	43
Sgòr Mòr	Aberd	NO1182	56°55·5'	3°27·3'W	H	43
Sgornach Ruadh	Arg & Bt	NR0609	56°14·3'	5°7·4'W	X	56
Sgor na h-Ulaidh	Highld	NN1151	56°37·0'	5°4·4'W	H	41
Sgòr na Ruadhraich	Highld	NH3135	57°22·7'	4°48·2'W	H	26
Sgorr a' Chadail	Highld	NG8957	57°33·5'	5°31·2'W	H	24
Sgorrach Nuadh	Stir	NN5725	56°24·0'	4°18·6'W	X	51
Sgorr a' Choise	Highld	NN0855	56°39·1'	5°7·5'W	H	41
Sgorr a Mham-lic	Arg & Bt	NM9638	56°29·7'	5°18·4'W	X	49
Sgorr an Fhàraidh	Highld	NM4889	56°55·7'	6°8·0'W	X	39
Sgorr an Fhuarain	Highld	NN1864	56°44·2'	4°58·1'W	X	41
Sgorr an Iubhair	Highld	NN1665	56°44·7'	5°0·1'W	X	41
Sgorr an Tarmachain	Highld	NM8371	56°47·1'	5°32·7'W	X	40
Sgorr Bhogachain	Arg & Bt	NR3951	55°41·2'	6°8·7'W	X	60
Sgorr Chalum	Highld	NN1268	56°46·2'	5°4·1'W	H	41
Sgorr Craobh a' Chaorainn	Highld	NM8975	56°49·4'	5°27·0'W	H	40
Sgorr Deas	Highld	NC1006	58°0·4'	5°12·5'W	H	15
Sgorr Dhearg	Highld	NN0555	56°39·0'	5°10·4'W	H	41
Sgorr Dhonuill	Highld	NN0455	56°39·0'	5°11·4'W	H	41
Sgorr Gaoithe	Highld	NH4831	57°20·9'	4°31·1'W	X	26
Sgorr Mhòr	Arg & Bt	NM9224	56°22·0'	5°21·6'W	H	49
Sgorr Mhòr	Arg & Bt	NR6797	56°6·8'	5°44·4'W	H	55,61
Sgorr Mhòr	Highld	NM3099	57°0·5'	6°26·4'W	X	39
Sgorr Mòr	Highld	NM3791	56°56·4'	6°19·0'W	X	39
Sgorr na Ciche or Pap of Glencoe	Highld	NN1259	56°41·4'	5°3·7'W	H	41
Sgorr na Diollaid	Highld	NH2836	57°23·2'	4°51·2'W	H	25
Sgorr nam Faoileann	Arg & Bt	NR4360	55°46·2'	6°5·4'W	H	60
Sgorr nam Fiannaidh	Highld	NN1358	56°40·8'	5°2·7'W	H	41
Sgorr nan Cearc	Highld	NM8977	56°50·5'	5°27·1'W	H	40
Sgorr nan Lochan Uaine	Highld	NG9653	57°31·5'	5°24·0'W	H	25
Sgorr Reidh	Highld	NM3198	57°0·0'	6°25·3'W	X	39
Sgorr Ruadh	Highld	NG9550	57°29·9'	5°24·8'W	H	25
Sgorr Sgaileach	Highld	NM4891	56°56·8'	6°8·2'W	X	39
Sgòrr Tuath	Highld	NC1007	58°1·0'	5°12·5'W	H	15
Sgorshuil	Arg & Bt	NR8035	55°33·8'	5°28·9'W	X	68,69
Sgoth	N Eil	NF8331	57°15·8'	7°15·1'W	X	22
Sgreadan	Arg & Bt	NR3795	56°4·8'	6°13·2'W	T	61
Sgreadan Hill	Arg & Bt	NR7429	55°30·4'	5°34·3'W	H	68
Sgribhis-bheinn	Highld	NC3171	58°35·9'	4°54·0'W	H	9
Sgriob na Caillich	Arg & Bt	NR4776	55°54·9'	6°2·5'W	X	60,61
Sgriob ruadh	Arg & Bt	NM4955	56°37·4'	6°5·1'W	X	47
Sgrithir	N Eil	NB1232	58°11·2'	6°53·6'W	H	13
Sguide an Leanna	Arg & Bt	NR3491	56°2·5'	6°15·8'W	W	61
Sguiler	N Ayr	NR9929	55°31·1'	5°10·6'W	X	69
Sguinean nan Creagan Briste	N Eil	NB5553	58°24·1'	6°11·1'W	X	8
Sgùlain Chreagach	Arg & Bt	NM4554	56°36·8'	6°8·9'W	X	47
Sgùlan Beag	Arg & Bt	NM6131	56°24·9'	5°52·0'W	X	49
Sgùlan Breac	Arg & Bt	NM4554	56°36·8'	6°8·9'W	X	47
Sgùlan Dubh	Arg & Bt	NM4455	56°37·3'	6°9·9'W	X	47
Sgùlan Mòr	Arg & Bt	NM6132	56°25·4'	5°52·1'W	H	49
Sgùman Còinntich	Highld	NG9730	57°19·2'	5°21·8'W	H	25
Sgùman Mòr	Highld	NH8118	57°14·5'	3°57·9'W	H	35
Sgurr a' Bhac Chaolais	Highld	NG9511	57°8·9'	5°22·9'W	H	33
Sgurr a' Bhàgh	Highld	NG2455	57°30·3'	6°36·0'W	X	23
Sgurr a' Bhàsteir	Highld	NG4625	57°15·0'	6°12·2'W	H	32
Sgurr a' Bhealaich Dheirg	Highld	NH0314	57°10·7'	5°15·1'W	H	33
Sgurr a' Bhraonain	Highld	NG9019	57°13·1'	5°28·2'W	H	33
Sgurr a' Bhuic	Highld	NM8350	56°35·8'	5°31·6'W	H	49
Sgurr a' Bhuic	Highld	NM8765	56°43·9'	5°28·5'W	X	40
Sgurr a' Bhuic	Highld	NN2070	56°47·5'	4°56·4'W	H	41
Sgurr a' Chadha Dheirg	Highld	NH1869	57°40·7'	5°2·7'W	H	20
Sgurr a' Chàise	Highld	NG5702	57°3·0'	5°59·9'W	H	32,39
Sgurr a' Chaorachain	Highld	NG7941	57°24·6'	5°40·3'W	H	24
Sgurr a' Chaorachain	Highld	NH0844	57°27·0'	5°11·5'W	H	25
Sgurr a' Chaorainn	Highld	NM8966	56°44·5'	5°26·6'W	H	40
Sgurrachd Ire	Highld	NH3459	57°35·7'	4°46·2'W	H	26
Sgurr a' Chlaidheimh	Highld	NG9503	57°4·6'	5°22·5'W	H	33
Sgurr a' Choinnich	Arg & Bt	NS1595	56°7·0'	4°58·1'W	H	56
Sgurr a' Choire-bheithe	Highld	NG8901	57°3·4'	5°28·3'W	H	33
Sgurr a Choire Bhig	Highld	NG4619	57°11·7'	6°11·8'W	X	32
Sgurr a' Choire Ghairbh	Highld	NG9920	57°13·9'	5°19·4'W	H	25,33
Sgurr a' Choire Ghlais	Highld	NH2543	57°26·9'	4°54·5'W	H	25
Sgurr a' Choire-rainich	Highld	NH2457	57°34·4'	4°56·1'W	H	25
Sgurr a' Choire Riabhaich	Highld	NM9087	56°55·9'	5°26·6'W	X	40
Sgurr a' Chuilinn	Highld	NG9812	57°9·5'	5°20·0'W	H	33
Sgurr a' Ghaorachain	Highld	NG7941	57°24·6'	5°40·3'W	H	24
Sgurr a' Gharaidh	Highld	NG8844	57°26·5'	5°31·5'W	H	24
Sgurr a' Gharg Gharaidh	Highld	NG9115	57°11·0'	5°27·0'W	H	33
Sgurr a' Gharraidh	Highld	NH0349	57°29·6'	5°16·8'W	X	25
Sgurr a' Ghlaisein	Highld	NH3646	57°28·7'	4°43·7'W	H	26
Sgurr a' Ghlas Leathaid	Highld	NH2456	57°33·9'	4°56·1'W	H	25
Sgurr a' Ghreadaidh	Highld	NG4423	57°13·8'	6°14·1'W	H	32
Sgurr a' Ghrianain	Highld	NM7488	56°56·0'	5°42·4'W	H	40
Sgurr Airigh na Beinne	Highld	NG9200	57°2·9'	5°25·3'W	H	33
Sgurr Alasdair	Highld	NG4520	57°12·3'	6°12·9'W	H	32
Sgurr a' Mhadaidh Ruaidh	Highld	NG4758	57°32·7'	6°13·2'W	X	23
Sgurr a' Mhadaidh-ruaidh	Highld	NM7896	57°0·4'	5°38·9'W	H	33,40
Sgurr a' Mhadaidh	Highld	NG4423	57°13·8'	6°14·1'W	H	32
Sgurr a' Mhàim	Highld	NN1666	56°45·2'	5°0·1'W	H	41
Sgurr a' Mhalaidh	Highld	NG4656	57°31·6'	6°14·1'W	X	23
Sgurr a' Mhaoraich	Highld	NG9806	57°6·3'	5°19·7'W	H	33
Sgurr a' Mheadhoin	Highld	NM7476	56°49·5'	5°41·8'W	H	40
Sgurr a' Mhuidhe	Highld	NM8582	56°53·0'	5°31·3'W	X	40
Sgurr a' Mhuilinn	Highld	NG9848	57°28·9'	5°21·7'W	X	25
Sgurr a' Mhuilinn	Highld	NH2655	57°33·4'	4°54·0'W	H	25
Sgurr an Airgid	Highld	NG9422	57°14·8'	5°24·4'W	H	25,33
Sgurr an Albanaich	Highld	NM6888	56°55·8'	5°48·3'W	H	40
Sgurran Dearg	Pth & Kin	NN5963	56°44·5'	4°17·9'W	H	42
Sgurr an Doire Leathain	Highld	NH0109	57°8·0'	5°16·8'W	H	33
Sgurr an Dùin	N Eil	NF8173	57°38·3'	7°20·3'W	H	18
Sgurr an Duine	Highld	NG3521	57°12·5'	6°22·8'W	X	32
Sgurr an Easain	Highld	NM8270	56°46·5'	5°33·6'W	X	40

Sgurr an Easain Dhuibh	Highld	NG5702	57°3·0′	5°59·9′W	H	32,39
Sgurr an Eilein Ghiubhais	Highld	NM7297	57°0·7′	5°44·9′W	H	33,40
Sgurr an Fheadain	Highld	NG4524	57°14·4′	6°13·1′W	H	32
Sgùrr an Fhidhleir	Highld	NC0905	57°59·9′	5°13·4′W	H	15
Sgurr an Fhithich	Highld	NN3491	56°59·1′	4°43·5′W	X	34
Sgurr an Fhuarail	Highld	NH0513	57°10·2′	5°13·1′W	H	33
Sgurr an Fhuarain	Highld	NM9897	57°1·5′	5°19·2′W	H	33,40
Sgurr an Fhuarain Duibh	Highld	NM9085	56°54·8′	5°26·5′W	H	40
Sgurr an Iubhair	Highld	NM8578	56°50·9′	5°31·1′W	X	40
Sgurr an Iubhair	Highld	NN0072	56°48·1′	5°16·1′W	H	41
Sgurr an Lochain	Highld	NH0010	57°8·5′	5°17·9′W	H	33
Sgurran Ruadha	N Eil	NG1392	57°49·8′	6°49·6′W	X	14
Sgurran Seilich	Highld	NG5700	57°1·9′	5°59·8′W	H	32,39
Sgurr an Teintein	Highld	NM6374	56°48·1′	5°52·5′W	H	40
Sgurr an t-Saighdeir	Highld	NN4781	56°54·0′	4°30·3′W	X	34,42
Sgurr an t-Sasunnaich	Highld	NM6788	56°55·7′	5°49·3′W	X	40
Sgurr an t-Searraich	Highld	NG9519	57°13·2′	5°23·3′W	H	33
Sgurr an Tuill Bhàin	Highld	NH0168	57°39·7′	5°19·7′W	H	19
Sgurr an Uillt Tharsuinn	Highld	NG9223	57°15·3′	5°26·4′W	H	25,33
Sgurr an Ursainn	Highld	NM8786	56°55·2′	5°29·5′W	X	40
Sgurr an Utha	Highld	NM8883	56°53·7′	5°28·4′W	H	40
Sgurr Aoide	Highld	NG9024	57°15·8′	5°28·5′W	H	25,33
Sgurr a' Phollain	Highld	NH3644	57°27·7′	4°43·6′W	H	26
Sgurr Ban	Highld	NG9760	57°35·3′	5°23·3′W	H	19
Sgurr Bàn	Highld	NH0574	57°43·1′	5°16·0′W	H	19
Sgurr Beag	Highld	NG3324	57°14·0′	6°25·0′W	X	32
Sgurr Beag	Highld	NG4724	57°14·5′	6°11·1′W	H	32
Sgurr Beag	Highld	NG8029	57°18·2′	5°38·7′W	X	33
Sgurr Beag	Highld	NG9910	57°8·5′	5°18·9′W	H	33
Sgurr Beag	Highld	NM9597	57°1·4′	5°22·2′W	H	33,40
Sgurr Bhuidhe	Highld	NM7294	56°59·1′	5°44·7′W	H	33,40
Sgurr Breac	Highld	NG5907	57°5·7′	5°58·3′W	H	32,39
Sgurr Breac	Highld	NG5909	57°6·8′	5°58·4′W	X	32,39
Sgurr Breac	Highld	NH1571	57°41·7′	5°5·8′W	H	20
Sgurr Breac	Highld	NM8492	56°58·4′	5°32·8′W	H	33,40
Sgurr Brittle	Highld	NG3920	57°12·1′	6°18·8′W	X	32
Sgurr Buidhe	Highld	NG3325	57°14·5′	6°25·1′W	X	32
Sgurr Chòinich	Highld	NN1294	57°0·2′	5°5·3′W	H	34
Sgurr Choinnich	Highld	NH0744	57°27·0′	5°12·5′W	H	25
Sgurr Chòinnich Beag	Highld	NN2271	56°48·1′	4°54·5′W	H	41
Sgurr Chòinnich Mór	Highld	NN2271	56°48·1′	4°54·5′W	H	41
Sgurr Coir' an Lochain	Highld	NG4521	57°12·8′	6°12·9′W	H	32
Sgurr Coire Choinnichean	Highld	NG7901	57°3·1′	5°38·2′W	H	33
Sgurr Coire na Feinne	Highld	NH0209	57°8·0′	5°15·9′W	H	33
Sgurr Coire nan Eirichealach	Highld	NG9906	57°6·3′	5°18·7′W	H	33
Sgurr Coire nan Eun	Highld	NH1946	57°28·4′	5°0·6′W	H	25
Sgurr Coire nan Gobhar	Highld	NM8097	57°1·0′	5°37·0′W	H	33,40
Sgurr Còs na Breachd-laoidh	Highld	NM9494	56°59·7′	5°23·0′W	H	33,40
Sgurr Creag an Eich	Highld	NH0583	57°47·9′	5°16·4′W	H	19
Sgurr Dearg	Arg & Bt	NM6634	56°26·7′	5°47·4′W	H	49
Sgurr Dearg	Highld	NG4421	57°12·8′	6°13·9′W	H	32
Sgurr Dearg	Highld	NG8713	57°9·8′	5°30·9′W	X	33
Sgurr Dhomhnuill	Highld	NM8867	56°45·0′	5°27·6′W	H	40
Sgurr Dhomhnuill Beag	Highld	NM7475	56°49·0′	5°41·7′W	H	40
Sgurr Dhomhnuill Mór	Highld	NM7475	56°49·0′	5°41·7′W	H	40
Sgurr Dubh	Highld	NG9405	57°5·7′	5°23·6′W	H	33
Sgurr Dubh	Highld	NG9755	57°32·6′	5°23·1′W	H	25
Sgurr Dubh	Highld	NG9872	57°41·8′	5°22·9′W	H	19
Sgurr Dubh	Highld	NH0167	57°39·2′	5°19·6′W	H	19
Sgurr Dubh	Highld	NH0672	57°42·0′	5°14·9′W	H	19
Sgurr Dubh Beag	Highld	NG4620	57°12·3′	6°11·9′W	H	32
Sgurr Dubh Mór	Highld	NG4520	57°12·3′	6°12·9′W	H	32
Sgurr Eilde Mór	Highld	NN2365	56°44·8′	4°53·2′W	H	41
Sgurr Eireagoraidh	Highld	NM7196	57°0·2′	5°45·8′W	X	33,40
Sgurr Fhuaran	Highld	NG9716	57°11·7′	5°21·1′W	H	33
Sgurr Fhuar-thuill	Highld	NH2343	57°26·8′	4°56·5′W	H	25
Sgurr Finnisg-aig	Highld	NN1876	56°50·7′	4°58·6′W	H	41
Sgurr Fiona	Highld	NH0683	57°47·9′	5°15·4′W	H	19
Sgurr Gaorsaic	Highld	NH0321	57°14·5′	5°15·4′W	H	25,33
Sgurr Geal	Pth & Kin	NO0466	56°46·8′	3°33·8′W	H	43
Sgurr Ghiubhsachain	Highld	NM8775	56°49·3′	5°29·0′W	H	40
Sgurr Gorm	Highld	NM7674	56°48·5′	5°39·7′W	X	40
Sgurr Hain	Highld	NG5020	57°12·4′	6°7·9′W	H	32
Sgurr Innse	Highld	NN2974	56°49·8′	4°47·7′W	H	41
Sgurr Lagain	Highld	NM6986	56°54·7′	5°47·2′W	X	40
Sgurr Leac nan Each	Highld	NG9113	57°9·9′	5°26·9′W	H	33
Sgurr Liath	Highld	NM6989	56°56·3′	5°47·4′W	X	40
Sgurr Marcasaidh	Highld	NH3559	57°35·7′	4°45·2′W	H	26
Sgurr Mhairi	Highld	NG5130	57°17·8′	6°7·5′W	X	24,32
Sgurr Mhic Bharraich	Highld	NG9117	57°12·0′	5°27·1′W	H	33
Sgurr Mhic Choinnich	Highld	NG4421	57°12·8′	6°13·9′W	H	32
Sgurr Mhór	Arg & Bt	NM5521	56°19·3′	5°57·3′W	X	48
Sgurr Mhór	Highld	NG8661	57°35·6′	5°34·4′W	H	19,24
Sgurr Mhurlagain	Highld	NN0194	56°59·9′	5°16·1′W	H	33
Sgurr Mór	Arg & Bt	NM9239	56°30·1′	5°22·3′W	H	49
Sgurr Mór	Highld	NG3031	57°17·7′	6°28·4′W	X	32
Sgurr Mór	Highld	NG3424	57°14·0′	6°24·0′W	X	32
Sgurr Mór	Highld	NG4370	57°39·1′	6°18·0′W	H	23
Sgurr Mór	Highld	NG8228	57°17·7′	5°36·6′W	H	33
Sgurr Mór	Highld	NG8707	57°6·5′	5°30·6′W	H	33
Sgurr Mór	Highld	NH2071	57°41·8′	5°0·8′W	H	20
Sgurr Mór	Highld	NM8292	56°58·3′	5°34·8′W	H	33,40
Sgurr Mór	Highld	NM9698	57°1·9′	5°21·3′W	H	33,40
Sgurr na ba Glaise	Highld	NM7777	56°50·1′	5°38·9′W	H	40
Sgurr na Banachdich	Highld	NG4422	57°13·3′	6°14·0′W	H	32
Sgurr na Bana Mhoraire	Highld	NG8752	57°30·8′	5°32·9′W	H	24
Sgurr na Bà Ruaidhe	Highld	NM8592	56°58·4′	5°31·8′W	X	33,40
Sgurr na Bhairnich	Highld	NG4624	57°14·4′	6°12·1′W	H	32
Sgurr na Boinaid	Highld	NM8678	56°50·9′	5°30·1′W	X	40
Sgurr na Cairbe	Highld	NH3046	57°28·6′	4°49·7′W	H	26
Sgurr na Carnach	Highld	NG9715	57°11·1′	5°21·1′W	H	33
Sgurr na Ciche	Highld	NM9096	57°0·7′	5°27·1′W	H	33,40
Sgurr na Ciste Duibhe	Highld	NG9814	57°10·6′	5°20·1′W	H	33
Sgurr na Cloiche	Highld	NG9631	57°19·7′	5°22·9′W	H	25
Sgurr na Coinnich	Highld	NG7622	57°14·3′	5°42·3′W	H	33
Sgurr na Conbhaire	Highld	NH0843	57°26·5′	5°11·5′W	H	25
Sgurr na Creige	Highld	NG9314	57°10·5′	5°25·0′W	H	33
Sgurr na Fearstaig	Highld	NH2243	57°26·8′	4°57·5′W	H	25

Sgurr na Feartaig	Highld	NH0444	57°26·9′	5°15·5′W	X	25
Sgurr na Gaoith	Highld	NM6986	56°54·7′	5°47·2′W	X	40
Sgurr na Garblaich	Highld	NM7288	56°55·9′	5°44·4′W	X	40
Sgurr na Gréine	Highld	NM6550	56°35·2′	5°49·2′W	X	49
Sgurr na Gréine	Highld	NM8170	56°46·5′	5°34·6′W	X	40
Sgurr na h-Aide	Highld	NG7708	57°6·8′	5°40·5′W	X	33
Sgurr na h-Aide	Highld	NM8893	56°59·0′	5°28·9′W	H	33,40
Sgurr na h-Eanchainne	Highld	NM9965	56°44·3′	5°16·7′W	H	40
Sgurr na h-Eige	Highld	NH0527	57°17·8′	5°13·7′W	H	25,33
Sgurr na h-Inghinn	Highld	NM8867	56°45·0′	5°27·6′W	H	40
Sgurr na h-Iolaire	Highld	NG6109	57°6·9′	5°56·4′W	H	32
Sgurr na h-Uamha	Highld	NG4724	57°14·5′	6°11·1′W	H	32
Sgurr na Làire	Highld	NM8965	56°44·0′	5°26·5′W	H	40
Sgurr na Laire Brice	Highld	NG8912	57°9·3′	5°28·9′W	H	33
Sgurr na Laocainn	Highld	NG9877	57°44·5′	5°23·2′W	X	19
Sgurr na Lapaich	Highld	NH1524	57°16·4′	5°3·7′W	H	25
Sgurr na Lapaich	Highld	NH1635	57°22·4′	5°3·1′W	H	25
Sgurr nam Boc	Highld	NG3520	57°11·9′	6°22·8′W	X	32
Sgurr nam Caorach	Highld	NM7189	56°56·4′	5°45·4′W	X	40
Sgurr nam Feadan	Highld	NM8097	57°1·0′	5°37·0′W	H	33,40
Sgurr nam Fhir Duibhe	Highld	NG9860	57°35·4′	5°22·3′W	H	19
Sgurr nam Fiadh	Highld	NG3226	57°15·0′	6°26·1′W	X	32
Sgurr nam Meann	Highld	NM4367	56°43·7′	6°11·6′W	H	47
Sgurr nam Meirleach	Highld	NM8693	56°59·0′	5°30·9′W	H	33,40
Sgurr na Mòraich	Highld	NG9619	57°13·2′	5°22·3′W	H	33
Sgurr na Muice	Highld	NH2241	57°25·7′	4°57·4′W	H	25
Sgurr nan Caorach	Highld	NG5802	57°3·0′	5°59·0′W	H	32,39
Sgurr nan Ceannaichean	Highld	NH0848	57°29·2′	5°11·7′W	H	25
Sgurr nan Cearcall	Highld	NG4116	57°10·0′	6°16·6′W	X	32
Sgurr nan Ceathreamhnan	Highld	NH0522	57°15·1′	5°13·5′W	H	25,33
Sgurr nan Clachan Géala	Highld	NH1634	57°21·8′	5°3·1′W	H	25
Sgurr nan Clach Geala	Highld	NH1871	57°41·8′	5°2·8′W	H	20
Sgurr nan Cnamh	Highld	NM8864	56°43·4′	5°27·5′W	H	40
Sgurr nan Coireachan	Highld	NM9088	56°56·4′	5°26·7′W	H	40
Sgurr nan Coireachan	Highld	NM9395	57°0·2′	5°24·1′W	H	33,40
Sgurr nan Conbhairean	Highld	NH1213	57°10·4′	5°6·1′W	H	34
Sgurr nan Conobhan	Highld	NG7640	57°24·0′	5°43·2′W	H	24
Sgurr nan Each	Highld	NG5322	57°13·6′	6°5·1′W	X	32
Sgurr nan Each	Highld	NH1869	57°40·7′	5°2·7′W	H	20
Sgurr nan Eag	Highld	NG4519	57°11·7′	6°12·8′W	H	32
Sgurr nan Eugallt	Highld	NG9304	57°5·1′	5°24·5′W	H	33
Sgurr nan Gall	Highld	NG6052	57°29·9′	5°59·9′W	X	24
Sgurr nan Gillean	Highld	NG4725	57°15·0′	6°11·2′W	H	32
Sgurr nan Gillean	Highld	NM3793	56°57·5′	6°19·1′W	H	39
Sgurr nan Gobhar	Highld	NG4222	57°13·2′	6°16·0′W	H	32
Sgurr nan Gobhar	Highld	NG7806	57°5·7′	5°39·4′W	H	33
Sgurr nan Saighead	Highld	NG9717	57°12·2′	5°21·2′W	H	33
Sgurr nan Spainteach	Highld	NG9914	57°10·6′	5°19·1′W	H	33
Sgurr nan Uan	Highld	NG3234	57°19·3′	6°26·7′W	X	32
Sgurr na Paite	Highld	NM8281	56°52·4′	5°34·2′W	H	40
Sgurr na Plaide	Highld	NM8485	56°54·6′	5°32·4′W	H	40
Sgurr na Ruaidhe	Highld	NH2842	57°26·4′	4°51·5′W	H	25
Sgurr na Sgine	Highld	NG9411	57°8·9′	5°23·9′W	H	33
Sgurr na Stri	Highld	NG5019	57°11·9′	6°7·9′W	H	32
Sgurr Nighean Mhic Choinich	Highld	NM7487	56°55·4′	5°42·4′W	H	40
Sgùrr Onrachdain	Highld	NG3856	57°31·4′	6°22·1′W	X	23
Sgurr Ruadh	Highld	NH0485	57°49·0′	5°17·5′W	H	19
Sgurr Scaladail	N Eil	NB1608	57°58·5′	6°47·7′W	X	13,14
Sgurr Sgèithe	Highld	NM8598	57°1·6′	5°32·1′W	H	33,40
Sgurr Sgiath Airigh	Highld	NG9205	57°5·6′	5°25·5′W	H	33
Sgurr Sgumain	Highld	NG4420	57°12·2′	6°13·9′W	H	32
Sgurr Shalachain	Highld	NM8153	56°37·3′	5°33·7′W	H	49
Sgurr Thionail	Highld	NG9808	57°7·4′	5°19·8′W	H	33
Sgurr Thuilm	Highld	NG4324	57°14·3′	6°15·1′W	H	32
Sgurr Thuilm	Highld	NM9387	56°55·9′	5°23·7′W	H	40
Sgurr Toll Lochain	Highld	NH2348	57°29·5′	4°56·7′W	X	25
Sgwylfa Wood	Powys	SO0694	52°32·4′	3°22·8′W	F	136
Shaabers Head	Shetld	HU2759	60°19·1′	1°30·2′W	X	3
Shabbington	Bucks	SP6607	51°45·7′	1°2·2′W	T	164,165
Shabbington Wood	Bucks	SP6210	51°47·3′	1°5·7′W	F	164,165
Shab Hill	Glos	SO9315	51°50·2′	2°5·7′W	T	163
Shackerdale Fm	Notts	SK7244	52°59·5′	0°55·2′W	FM	129
Shackerland Hall Fm	Suff	TL9968	52°16·7′	0°55·4′E	FM	155
Shackerley	Shrops	SJ8106	52°39·3′	2°16·5′W	T	127
Shackerstone	Leic	SK3706	52°39·3′	1°26·8′W	T	140
Shackerstone Fields Fm	Leic	SK3507	52°39·8′	1°28·5′W	FM	140
Shacker, The	Notts	SK7343	52°59·0′	0°54·4′W	W	129
Shackla Bank	Cumbr	SD6191	54°19·0′	2°35·6′W	X	97
Shacklecross	Derby	SK4234	52°54·3′	1°22·1′W	T	129
Shacklefield Ho	N Yks	SE4760	54°2·3′	1°16·5′W	X	100
Shackleford Heath	Surrey	SU9344	51°11·5′	0°39·8′W	X	186
Shacklehill	S Ayr	NS4125	55°29·8′	4°30·6′W	X	70
Shacklesborough	Durham	NY9017	54°33·1′	2°8·9′W	X	91,92
Shackleton	Cald	SD9829	53°45·7′	2°1·4′W	T	103
Shackleton Moor	Cald	SD9832	53°47·3′	2°1·4′W	X	103
Shacklewell	Hack	TQ3385	51°33·1′	0°4·5′W	T	176,177
Shacklewell Lodge	Rut	SK9607	52°39·4′	0°34·4′W	X	141
Shacklford	Surrey	SU9345	51°12·0′	0°39·7′W	T	186
Shaddelows Fm	Suff	TL9734	51°58·4′	0°52·5′E	FM	155
Shade	Cald	SD9323	53°42·4′	2°6·0′W	T	103
Shade Common	Cambs	TL5874	52°20·7′	0°19·6′E	X	143
Shadehouse Fm	Dorset	ST8021	50°59·5′	2°16·7′W	FM	183
Shaden Moor	Devon	SX5463	50°27·2′	4°3·0′W	X	201
Shade Oak	Shrops	SJ4127	52°50·5′	2°52·2′W	X	126
Shade, The	Kent	TQ8869	51°23·6′	0°42·5′E	W	178
Shade, The	Leic	SP4690	52°30·6′	1°19·8′W	X	140
Shadfen	Northum	NZ2285	55°9·8′	1°38·9′W	X	81
Shadfen Park	Northum	NZ2285	55°9·8′	1°38·9′W	X	81
Shadforth	Durham	NZ3440	54°45·5′	1°27·9′W	T	88
Shadingfield	Suff	TM4384	52°24·2′	1°34·8′E	T	156
Shadowbarn Fm	Suff	TM3386	52°25·6′	1°26·0′E	FM	156
Shadowbush Fm	Suff	TL7750	52°7·4′	0°35·5′E	FM	155
Shadow Hill	Norf	TM2485	52°25·2′	1°18·1′E	X	156
Shadoxhurst	Kent	TQ9738	51°6·7′	0°49·3′E	T	189
Shadrack	Devon	SX8363	50°27·5′	3°38·5′W	X	202
Shadsworth	Black w Dar	SD7027	53°44·6′	2°26·9′W	T	103
Shadwell	Glos	ST7897	51°40·5′	2°18·7′W	T	162
Shadwell	Leeds	SE3439	53°51·0′	1°28·6′W	T	104

Shadwell	Norf	TL9383	52°24·9′	0°50·7′E	T	144
Shadwell	T Ham	TQ3580	51°30·4′	0°2·9′W	T	177
Shadwell Hall	Shrops	SO2785	52°27·7′	3°4·1′W	X	137
Shadwell Park	Norf	TL9282	52°24·4′	0°49·8′E	X	144
Shaffalong	Staffs	SJ9652	53°4·2′	2°3·2′W	T	118
Shafford Fm	Herts	TL1209	51°46·3′	0°22·2′W	FM	166
Shaftenhoe End	Herts	TL4037	52°1·1′	0°2·8′E	T	154
Shaftesbury	Dorset	ST8622	51°0·1′	2°11·6′W	T	183
Shaftholme	Donc	SE5708	53°34·2′	1°7·9′W	X	111
Shaftland Cross	Worcs	SO9357	52°12·9′	2°5·8′W	X	150
Shaftoe Crags	Northum	NZ0582	55°8·2′	1°54·9′W	H	81
Shaftoe Grange	Northum	NZ0481	55°7·6′	1°55·8′W	X	81
Shaftoe Moor	Northum	NZ0482	55°8·2′	1°55·8′W	X	81
Shafton	Barns	SE3911	53°35·9′	1°24·2′W	T	110,111
Shafton Two Gates	Barns	SE3910	53°35·3′	1°24·2′W	T	110,111
Shaftsboro Fm	Devon	SS4845	51°11·3′	4°10·1′W	FM	180
Shaftwell Sike	Durham	NY9933	54°41·8′	2°0·5′W	W	92
Shaft Wood	Lincs	TF0683	53°20·2′	0°24·1′W	F	121
Shaggart	Aberd	NJ7110	57°11·1′	2°28·3′W	X	38
Shaggie Burn	Pth & Kin	NN8826	56°25·0′	3°48·5′W	W	52,58
Shaggs	Dorset	SY8583	50°39·0′	2°12·3′W	T	194
Shag Point	Devon	SS4847	51°12·4′	4°10·2′W	X	180
Shag Rock	Corn	SW7454	50°20·8′	5°10·2′W	X	204
Shag Rock	Corn	SW9439	50°13·1′	4°52·9′W	X	204
Shag Rock	Corn	SX1750	50°19·5′	4°33·9′W	X	201
Shag Rock	Devon	SX7536	50°12·9′	3°44·7′W	X	202
Shag Rock	Devon	SX9674	50°33·6′	3°27·7′W	X	192
Shag Rock	Pemb	SM7308	51°43·7′	5°16·8′W	X	157
Shag Stone	Devon	SX4848	50°19·0′	4°7·7′W	X	201
Shaiba	N Yks	SE1598	54°22·9′	1°45·7′W	X	99
Shail	N Eil	NG0785	57°45·8′	6°55·2′W	X	18
Shakeford	Shrops	SJ6728	52°51·1′	2°29·0′W	T	127
Shaken Bridge Fm	N Yks	SE5588	54°17·3′	1°8·9′W	FM	100
Shakenhurst	Worcs	SO6772	52°20·9′	2°28·7′W	X	138
Shakenhurst Fm	Worcs	SO6773	52°21·5′	2°28·7′W	FM	138
Shakenoak Fm	Oxon	SP3714	51°49·6′	1°27·4′W	FM	164
Shakerley	Wigan	SD6903	53°31·6′	2°27·6′W	T	109
Shakerley Mere	Ches	SJ7371	53°14·4′	2°23·9′W	W	118
Shakers' Furze	Norf	TL9195	52°31·4′	0°49·3′E	F	144
Shaker's Road	Suff	TL7765	52°15·5′	0°36·0′E	X	155
Shakers Wood	Norf	TL8096	52°32·2′	0°39·6′E	F	144
Shakesfield	Glos	SO6931	51°58·8′	2°26·7′W	T	149
Shakespeare Cliff	Kent	TR3039	51°6·5′	1°17·5′E	X	179
Shakespeare Fm	Bucks	SP6720	51°52·7′	1°1·2′W	A	164,165
Shakestones	Essex	TL6805	51°43·3′	0°26·3′E	X	167
Shaking Moss	Cumbr	SD7989	54°18·0′	2°18·9′W	X	98
Shaky Br	Powys	SO0861	52°14·6′	3°20·5′W	X	147
Shalbourne	Wilts	SU3163	51°22·1′	1°32·9′W	T	174
Shalcombe	I of W	SZ3985	50°40·0′	1°26·5′W	T	196
Shalden	Hants	SU6941	51°10·1′	1°0·4′W	T	186
Shalden Green	Hants	SU6943	51°11·2′	1°0·4′W	T	186
Shalden Park Fm	Hants	SU7043	51°11·1′	0°59·5′W	FM	186
Shalden Park Wood	Hants	SU7042	51°10·6′	0°59·5′W	F	186
Shalder's Ayre	Shetld	HU3839	60°8·3′	1°18·5′W	X	4
Shalder Sound	Shetld	HU2280	60°30·5′	1°35·5′W	W	3
Shaldon	Devon	SX9372	50°32·5′	3°30·2′W	T	192,202
Shales More	Essex	TQ5098	51°39·9′	0°10·5′E	F	167,177
Shalfleet	I of W	SZ4189	50°42·2′	1°24·8′W	T	196
Shalford	Essex	TL7229	51°56·2′	0°30·5′E	T	167
Shalford	Somer	ST7130	51°4·3′	2°24·5′W	T	183
Shalford	Surrey	TQ0046	51°12·5′	0°33·7′W	T	186
Shalford Common	Surrey	TQ0146	51°12·5′	0°32·9′W	X	186
Shalford Fm	W Berks	SU5664	51°22·6′	1°11·3′W	FM	174
Shalford Green	Essex	TL7127	51°55·1′	0°29·6′E	T	167
Shallam Dike	Norf	TG4116	52°41·5′	1°34·4′E	W	134
Shallcross Hall Fm	Derby	SK0179	53°18·7′	1°58·7′W	FM	119
Shallgreen	Angus	NO4063	56°45·5′	2°58·4′W	X	44
Shalloch	Aberd	NJ8057	57°36·4′	2°19·6′W	X	29,30
Shalloch	D & G	NX8378	55°5·2′	3°49·6′W	X	84
Shalloch	Moray	NJ3552	57°33·5′	3°4·7′W	X	28
Shalloch	S Ayr	NS4316	55°25·0′	4°28·4′W	X	70
Shalloch	S Ayr	NX3892	55°12·0′	4°32·3′W	H	77
Shalloch Burn	D & G	NS5601	55°17·2′	4°15·6′W	W	77
Shalloch Burn	D & G	NX8278	55°5·2′	3°50·5′W	W	84
Shalloch Burn	S Ayr	NS4303	55°18·0′	4°28·0′W	W	77
Shalloch Burn	S Ayr	NX3790	55°10·9′	4°33·2′W	W	77
Shalloch Craig Face	S Ayr	NX3790	55°10·9′	4°33·2′W	X	77
Shalloch Mill	S Ayr	NX1795	55°13·2′	4°52·2′W	X	76
Shalloch on Minnoch	S Ayr	NX3689	55°10·3′	4°34·1′W	X	77
Shalloch on Minnoch	S Ayr	NX3990	55°10·9′	4°31·3′W	H	77
Shallochpark Fm	S Ayr	NX1896	55°13·7′	4°51·3′W	FM	76
Shalloch Well	S Ayr	NX2786	55°8·5′	4°42·4′W	X	76
Shallochwreck Burn	S Ayr	NX0677	55°3·2′	5°1·8′W	W	76
Shallowford	Devon	SS6828	51°2·4′	3°52·6′W	T	180
Shallowford	Devon	SS7144	51°11·1′	3°50·4′W	X	180
Shallowford	Devon	SX6975	50°33·8′	3°50·6′W	X	191
Shallowford	Staffs	SJ8729	52°51·7′	2°11·2′W	T	127
Shallow Grange	Derby	SK0970	53°13·9′	1°51·5′W	X	119
Shallowplough	Aberd	NJ9133	57°23·5′	2°8·5′W	X	30
Shallows, The	Hants	SU1617	50°57·4′	1°45·9′W	W	184
Shallow Water Common	Corn	SX1476	50°33·5′	4°37·2′W	X	200
Shalmsford Street	Kent	TR0954	51°15·0′	1°0·1′E	T	179,189
Shalmstry	Highld	ND1364	58°33·6′	3°29·2′W	X	11,12
Shalstone	Bucks	SP6436	52°1·4′	1°3·6′W	T	152
Shalstone Grounds Fm	Bucks	SP6336	52°1·4′	1°4·5′W	FM	152
Shalter	Orkney	HY3931	59°9·9′	3°3·5′W	X	6
Shalunt	Arg & Bt	NS0471	55°53·8′	5°7·7′W	X	63
Shalunt Cott	Arg & Bt	NS0570	55°53·3′	5°6·6′W	X	63
Shambellie Grange	D & G	NX9666	54°58·9′	3°37·1′W	X	84
Shambellie Ho	D & G	NX9566	54°58·9′	3°38·0′W	X	84
Shambellie Wood	D & G	NX9566	54°58·9′	3°38·0′W	F	84
Shambleton Hill	Fife	NO3723	56°24·0′	3°0·8′W	X	54,59
Sham Castle	Bath & NE Somer	ST7764	51°22·7′	2°19·4′W	X	172
Shamland	Devon	SS4226	51°0·9′	4°14·8′W	A	180,190
Shamley Green	Surrey	TQ0243	51°10·9′	0°32·0′W	T	186
Shammer Ho	Norf	TF8237	52°54·4′	0°42·8′E	X	132
Shanacles	W Dunb	NS4084	56°1·6′	4°33·6′W	X	56,64
Shancastle	D & G	NX8190	55°11·7′	3°51·7′W	X	78
Shancastle Doon	D & G	NX8190	55°11·7′	3°51·7′W	H	78

Shandford	Angus	NO4962	56°45·1'	2°49·6'W	X	44
Shandford Hill	Angus	NO4863	56°45·6'	2°50·6'W	X	44
Shandon	Arg & Bt	NS2586	56°2·4'	4°48·1'W	T	56
Shandon	Stir	NS4789	56°4·4'	4°27·0'W	X	57
Shandscross	Aberd	NJ7351	57°33·2'	2°26·6'W	X	29
Shandston	Moray	NJ3651	57°32·9'	3°3·7'W	X	28
Shandwick	Highld	NH8575	57°45·3'	3°55·5'W	T	21
Shandwick Bay	Highld	NH8675	57°45·3'	3°54·5'W	W	21
Shandwick Ho	Highld	NH7875	57°45·2'	4°2·5'W	X	21
Shandwick Inn	Highld	NH7775	57°45·1'	4°3·5'W	X	21
Shandwick Mains	Highld	NH7974	57°44·6'	4°1·5'W	X	21
Shandy Hall	N Yks	SE5377	54°11·4'	1°10·8'W	A	100
Shangton	Leic	SP7196	52°33·7'	0°56·8'W	T	141
Shangton Grange	Leic	SP7297	52°34·2'	0°55·9'W	X	141
Shangton Holt	Leic	SP7197	52°34·2'	0°56·7'W	F	141
Shank	Angus	NO4066	56°47·2'	2°58·5'W	X	44
Shank	D & G	NX8285	55°9·0'	3°50·7'W	X	78
Shank Br	Midlo	NT3361	55°50·5'	3°3·8'W	X	66
Shankbridge End	Cumbr	NY4670	55°1·5'	2°50·3'W	X	86
Shank Burn	N Lanak	NS7570	55°54·7'	3°59·5'W	W	64
Shank Burn	Northum	NT9513	55°24·9'	2°4·3'W	W	81
Shank Burn	Northum	NT9614	55°25·4'	2°3·4'W	W	81
Shank Covert	Scot Bord	NT7530	55°34·0'	2°23·4'W	F	74
Shank End	Cumbr	NY6876	55°4·9'	2°29·6'W	X	86,87
Shankend	D & G	NY6549	55°13·2'	3°18·8'W	X	79
Shankend Fm	Scot Bord	NT5206	55°21·0'	2°45·0'W	FM	79
Shankend Hill	Scot Bord	NT5204	55°19·9'	2°45·0'W	H	79
Shankendshiel	Scot Bord	NT5304	55°19·9'	2°44·0'W	X	79
Shankfieldhead	Cumbr	NY4871	55°2·1'	2°48·4'W	X	86
Shankfoot	D & G	NX8567	54°59·3'	3°47·4'W	X	84
Shankfoot	Northum	NY7463	54°57·9'	2°23·9'W	X	86,87
Shankfoot	Scot Bord	NT4707	55°21·5'	2°49·7'W	X	79
Shankhead	Northum	NY7861	54°56·8'	2°20·2'W	X	86,87
Shankhead	Stir	NS7485	56°2·7'	4°0·9'W	X	57
Shank Hill	Angus	NO4067	56°47·7'	2°58·5'W	X	44
Shankhill	Cumbr	NY4771	55°2·1'	2°49·3'W	X	86
Shank Houp	S Lanak	NT0128	55°32·4'	3°33·7'W	W	72
Shankhouse	Northum	NZ2778	55°6·0'	1°34·2'W	X	88
Shanklin	I of W	SZ5881	50°37·8'	1°10·4'W	T	196
Shanklin Chine	I of W	SZ5881	50°37·8'	1°10·4'W	X	196
Shanklin Down	I of W	SZ5680	50°37·2'	1°12·1'W	H	196
Shank of Barry	Aberd	NJ5553	57°34·2'	2°44·7'W	X	29
Shank of Cardowan	Aberd	NO6278	56°53·8'	2°37·0'W	X	45
Shank of Cochlie	Angus	NO4476	56°52·6'	2°54·7'W	X	44
Shank of Donald Young	Angus	NO4273	56°50·9'	2°56·6'W	X	44
Shank of Driesh	Angus	NO2772	56°50·3'	3°11·3'W	X	44
Shank of Drumfollow	Angus	NO2574	56°51·3'	3°13·3'W	X	44
Shank of Drumwhallo	Angus	NO2573	56°50·8'	3°13·3'W	X	44
Shank of Flobbit	Angus	NO4774	56°51·5'	2°51·7'W	X	44
Shank of Inchgrundle	Angus	NO4078	56°53·6'	2°58·6'W	X	44
Shank of Lairs	Angus	NO3682	56°55·8'	3°2·6'W	X	44
Shank of Mondair	Angus	NO5780	56°54·8'	2°41·9'W	X	44
Shank of Omachie	Angus	NO4837	56°31·6'	2°50·3'W	X	54
Shank of Peats	Angus	NO4370	56°49·3'	2°55·6'W	X	44
Shanks Ho	Somer	ST7526	51°2·2'	2°21·0'W	X	183
Shanks, The	Northum	NY6679	55°6·5'	2°31·5'W	X	86
Shankston	E Ayr	NS4011	55°22·3'	4°31·1'W	X	70
Shankston Loch	S Ayr	NS3911	55°22·3'	4°32·0'W	W	70
Shank, The	D & G	NT2504	55°19·7'	3°10·5'W	X	79
Shannaburn	Aberd	NJ8801	57°6·2'	2°11·4'W	X	38
Shannacher	Pth & Kin	NN9223	56°23·5'	3°44·5'W	X	52,58
Shannally	Angus	NO2953	56°40·1'	3°9·1'W	X	53
Shannas	Aberd	NJ9943	57°28·9'	2°0·5'W	X	30
Shannel	Aberd	NO6095	57°2·9'	2°39·1'W	X	37,45
Shannelton	Aberd	NJ6258	57°36·9'	2°37·7'W	X	29
Shannick Point	Corn	SW9137	50°12·0'	4°55·3'W	X	204
Shannobank	Scot Bord	NT7562	55°51·3'	2°23·5'W	X	67
Shannoch	Aberd	NJ5416	57°14·2'	2°45·3'W	X	37
Shannoch	Pth & Kin	NO0031	56°27·9'	3°36·9'W	X	52,53
Shannochie	N Ayr	NR9721	55°26·7'	5°12·1'W	T	69
Shannochill	Stir	NS5499	56°9·9'	4°20·6'W	T	57
Shannockhill	Clackm	NS9295	56°8·4'	3°43·8'W	X	58
Shannocks	Aberd	NJ7151	57°33·1'	2°28·6'W	X	29
Shanny Rig	Scot Bord	NT4137	55°37·6'	2°55·8'W	X	73
Shanquhar	Aberd	NJ5435	57°24·4'	2°45·5'W	X	29
Shanraw	Stir	NN8003	56°12·5'	3°55·6'W	X	57
Shanry	Pth & Kin	NO2026	56°25·6'	3°17·4'W	X	53,58
Shanter	S Ayr	NS2107	55°19·7'	4°48·9'W	X	70,76
Shanterhill	Aberd	NJ9043	57°28·9'	2°9·5'W	X	30
Shantock Hall	Herts	TL0002	51°42·7'	0°32·8'W	X	166
Shantron	Arg & Bt	NS3488	56°3·6'	4°39·5'W	X	56
Shantron Hill	Arg & Bt	NS3387	56°3·1'	4°40·5'W	X	56
Shantron Muir	Arg & Bt	NS3387	56°3·1'	4°40·5'W	X	56
Shantullich	Highld	NH6353	57°33·0'	4°16·9'W	X	26
Shanwell	Fife	NO4726	56°25·6'	2°51·1'W	X	54,59
Shanwell	Pth & Kin	NO0804	56°13·4'	3°28·6'W	X	58
Shanzie	Pth & Kin	NO2750	56°38·4'	3°11·0'W	X	53
Shap	Cumbr	NY5615	54°31·9'	2°40·4'W	T	90
Shapbeck Gate	Cumbr	NY5518	54°33·6'	2°41·3'W	X	90
Shap Blue Quarry	Cumbr	NY5610	54°29·3'	2°40·3'W	X	90
Shapcombe Fm	Devon	ST1504	50°50·0'	3°12·0'W	FM	192,193
Shapcott Barton	Devon	SS8423	50°59·9'	3°38·8'W	X	181
Shap Fells	Cumbr	NY5408	54°28·2'	2°42·2'W	X	90
Shapinsay	Orkney	HY5017	59°2·5'	2°51·8'W	X	6
Shapinsay Sound	Orkney	HY5113	59°0·3'	2°50·7'W	W	6
Shapley	Devon	SX6884	50°38·7'	3°51·6'W	X	191
Shapley	Devon	SX7182	50°37·6'	3°49·1'W	X	191
Shapley Common	Devon	SX6982	50°37·6'	3°50·8'W	X	191
Shapley Heath	Hants	SU7554	51°17·0'	0°55·1'W	X	186
Shapley Tor	Devon	SX7082	50°37·6'	3°49·9'W	H	191
Shap Lodge	Cumbr	NY5610	54°29·3'	2°40·3'W	X	90
Shaplow Dale	Derby	SK1452	53°4·1'	1°47·1'W	X	119
Shap Pink Quarry	Cumbr	NY5508	54°28·2'	2°41·2'W	X	90
Shapridge	Glos	SO6716	51°50·7'	2°28·4'W	T	162
Shap Summit	Cumbr	NY5711	54°29·8'	2°39·4'W	X	91
Shap Summit	Cumbr	NY5812	54°30·3'	2°38·5'W	H	91
Shap Thorn	Cumbr	NY5711	54°29·8'	2°39·4'W	H	91
Shaptor Rock	Devon	SX8080	50°36·7'	3°41·4'W	X	191
Shap Wells Hotel	Cumbr	NY5709	54°28·7'	2°39·4'W	X	91
Shapwick	Dorset	ST9301	50°48·7'	2°5·6'W	T	195
Shapwick	Somer	ST4138	51°8·5'	2°50·2'W	T	182
Shapwick Grange Fm	Devon	SY3192	50°43·6'	2°58·3'W	FM	193
Shapwick Heath	Somer	ST4340	51°9·6'	2°48·5'W	X	182
Shapwick Hill	Devon	SY3093	50°44·2'	2°59·1'W	H	193
Shapwick Ho (Hotel)	Somer	ST4138	51°8·5'	2°50·2'W	X	182
Sharcombe Park	Somer	ST5745	51°12·4'	2°36·5'W	X	182,183
Sharcott	Somer	SS8539	51°8·6'	3°38·3'W	X	181
Sharcott	Wilts	SU1459	51°20·0'	1°47·6'W	T	173
Shardale	N Yks	SE8972	54°8·4'	0°37·0'W	X	101
Shard Br	Lancs	SD3641	53°51·9'	2°58·0'W	X	102
Shardeloes	Bucks	SU9397	51°40·1'	0°38·9'W	X	165
Shardeloes Fm	Bucks	SU9497	51°40·1'	0°38·1'W	FM	165
Shardelow's Fm	Cambs	TL6245	52°5·0'	0°22·3'E	FM	154
Shard End	Birm	SP1588	52°29·6'	1°46·3'W	T	139
Shardlow	Derby	SK4330	52°52·2'	1°21·3'W	T	129
Shardlowe's Fm	Essex	TL7830	51°56·6'	0°35·8'E	FM	167
Shardlowe's Wood	Essex	TL7831	51°57·2'	0°35·8'E	F	167
Share Ditch	Swin	SU1593	51°38·4'	1°46·6'W	W	163,173
Share Fm	Kent	TQ7139	51°7·7'	0°27·0'E	FM	188
Share Marsh	Suff	TM4991	52°27·8'	1°40·3'E	X	134
Shareshill	Staffs	SJ9406	52°39·3'	2°4·9'W	T	127,139
Sharfleet Creek	Kent	TQ8571	51°24·7'	0°40·0'E	W	178
Sharfleet Creek	Kent	TQ9467	51°22·4'	0°47·6'E	W	178
Sharford Bridge	Dorset	SY9684	50°39·6'	2°3·0'W	A	195
Shargerwells	Aberd	NJ6549	57°32·0'	2°34·6'W	X	29
Sharkham Point	Torbay	SX9354	50°22·8'	3°29·9'W	X	202
Shark's Fin	Corn	SW3226	50°4·7'	5°44·4'W	X	203
Shark's Fin	Corn	SW8121	50°3·2'	5°3·2'W	X	204
Sharland Fm	Devon	SS7505	50°50·1'	3°46·1'W	FM	191
Sharlands	E Susx	TQ5321	50°58·3'	0°11·1'E	X	199
Sharlston	Wakf	SE3918	53°39·7'	1°24·2'W	T	110,111
Sharlston Common	Wakf	SE3819	53°40·2'	1°25·1'W	T	110,111
Sharmans Cross	Sol	SP1379	52°24·8'	1°48·1'W	T	139
Sharman's Hill	Northnts	SP5457	52°12·7'	1°12·2'W	H	152
Sharmer Fm	Warw	SP3562	52°15·5'	1°28·8'W	FM	151
Sharnal Street	Medway	TQ7974	51°26·4'	0°34·9'E	T	178
Sharnberry Flat	Durham	NZ0230	54°40·1'	1°57·7'W	X	92
Sharnbrook	Beds	SP9959	52°13·4'	0°32·6'W	T	153
Sharnbrook Summit	Beds	SP9762	52°15·1'	0°34·3'W	X	153
Sharnden	E Susx	TQ6028	51°2·0'	0°17·3'E	X	188,199
Sharnden Old Manor Fm	E Susx	TQ6027	51°1·4'	0°17·3'E	FM	188,199
Sharney Brook	Oxon	SP3000	51°42·1'	1°33·6'W	W	164
Sharneyford	Lancs	SD8824	53°43·0'	2°10·5'W	T	103
Sharney Sike	Northum	NY9976	55°5·0'	2°0·5'W	W	87
Sharnford	Leic	SP4891	52°31·1'	1°17·2'W	T	140
Sharnford Fields	Leic	SP4790	52°30·6'	1°18·0'W	X	140
Sharnford Lodge Fm	Leic	SP4890	52°30·6'	1°17·2'W	FM	140
Sharnhill Green	Dorset	ST7005	50°50·9'	2°25·2'W	T	194
Sharoe Brook	Lancs	SD5233	53°47·7'	2°43·3'W	W	102
Sharoe Green	Lancs	SD5333	53°47·7'	2°42·4'W	T	102
Sharow	N Yks	SE3271	54°8·3'	1°30·2'W	T	99
Sharpcliffe Hall	Staffs	SK0152	53°4·2'	1°58·7'W	X	119
Sharp Craig	D & G	NX7498	55°15·9'	3°58·5'W	X	77
Sharp Edge	Cumbr	NY3228	54°38·8'	3°2·8'W	X	90
Sharpenhoe	Beds	TL0630	51°57·7'	0°27·0'W	T	166
Sharpenhurst Fm	W Susx	TQ1327	51°2·1'	0°22·9'W	FM	187,198
Sharpenton Hill	Somer	ST3936	51°7·4'	2°51·9'W	H	182
Sharpers Head	Devon	SX7835	50°12·4'	3°42·2'W	X	202
Sharper's Head	Northum	NU0054	55°47·0'	1°59·6'W	X	75
Sharperton	Northum	NT9503	55°19·5'	2°4·3'W	T	81
Sharperton Edge	Northum	NT9704	55°20·1'	2°2·4'W	X	81
Sharpes Fm	Essex	TL5828	51°55·9'	0°18·3'E	FM	167
Sharpes Fm	Hants	SU3625	51°1·6'	1°28·8'W	FM	185
Sharpham Barton	Devon	SX8158	50°24·8'	3°40·1'W	X	202
Sharpham Ho	Devon	SX8257	50°24·3'	3°39·3'W	X	202
Sharpham Park	Somer	ST4637	51°8·0'	2°45·9'W	X	182
Sharp Haw	N Yks	SD9555	53°59·7'	2°4·2'W	H	103
Sharphill	N Ayr	NS2543	55°39·2'	4°46·5'W	X	63,70
Sharp Hill Fm	N Yks	SE1187	54°17·0'	1°49·4'W	FM	99
Sharphill Wood	Notts	SK5834	52°54·3'	1°7·9'W	F	129
Sharpitor	Devon	SX5570	50°30·9'	4°2·3'W	X	202
Sharpitor	Devon	SX7237	50°13·4'	3°47·3'W	X	202
Sharpitor	Devon	SX7781	50°37·2'	3°43·9'W	X	191
Sharp Knott	Cumbr	NY1020	54°34·3'	3°23·1'W	H	89
Sharplaw	Scot Bord	NT6521	55°29·1'	2°32·8'W	X	74
Sharplaw	Scot Bord	NT7719	55°28·1'	2°21·4'W	X	80
Sharples	Bolton	SD7011	53°35·9'	2°26·8'W	T	109
Sharples Hall	Lancs	SD4547	53°55·2'	2°49·8'W	X	102
Sharples Higher End	Black w Dar	SD6616	53°38·6'	2°30·4'W	X	109
Sharpley	Northum	NY8772	55°2·8'	2°11·8'W	X	87
Sharpley Hall Fm	Durham	NZ3850	54°50·8'	1°24·1'W	FM	88
Sharpley Heath	Staffs	SJ9635	52°55·0'	2°3·2'W	T	127
Sharpley Hill	Notts	SK5527	52°50·5'	1°10·6'W	X	129
Sharplow Fm	Derby	SK1652	53°4·1'	1°45·3'W	FM	119
Sharpnage Wood	Heref	SO6036	52°1·5'	2°34·6'W	F	149
Sharpness	Glos	SO6702	51°43·2'	2°28·3'W	T	162
Sharp Ness	Kent	TQ8572	51°25·2'	0°40·0'E	X	178
Sharpness Head	Essex	TQ9888	51°33·6'	0°51·8'E	X	178
Sharpness Point	N Tyne	NZ3769	55°1·1'	1°24·9'W	X	88
Sharps Bottom	Derby	SK3320	52°46·8'	1°30·2'W	X	128
Sharp's Br	Lincs	TF2424	52°48·2'	0°9·2'W	X	131
Sharpsbridge	E Susx	TQ4320	50°57·9'	0°2·6'E	T	198
Sharp's Corner	E Susx	TQ5717	50°56·1'	0°14·5'E	T	199
Sharp's Covert	Leic	SK3504	52°38·2'	1°28·6'W	F	140
Sharps Fm	E Susx	TQ4320	50°57·9'	0°2·6'E	FM	198
Sharps Fm	Somer	ST0725	51°1·2'	3°19·2'W	FM	181
Sharpshaw Fm	Somer	ST7545	51°12·5'	2°21·1'W	FM	183
Sharp's Hill	Bucks	SP6819	51°52·2'	1°0·3'W	X	164,165
Sharp's Hill	Notts	SK6476	53°16·9'	1°2·0'W	F	120
Sharp's Place	Kent	TQ5148	51°12·9'	0°10·1'E	X	188
Sharpstone	Bath & NE Somer	ST7859	51°20·0'	2°18·6'W	T	172
Sharpstone Hill	Shrops	SJ4909	52°40·8'	2°44·9'W	X	126
Sharpstones	Shrops	SO5094	52°32·7'	2°43·8'W	X	137,138
Sharp Street	Norf	TG3820	52°43·7'	1°31·9'E	T	133,134
Sharpthorne	W Susx	TQ3732	51°4·5'	0°2·3'W	T	187
Sharptor	Corn	SX2573	50°32·1'	4°27·8'W	T	201
Sharp Tor	Corn	SX2673	50°32·1'	4°26·9'W	X	201
Sharp Tor	Devon	SX5584	50°38·5'	4°2·7'W	X	191
Sharp Tor	Devon	SX6461	50°26·2'	3°54·5'W	X	202
Sharp Tor	Devon	SX6872	50°32·2'	3°51·4'W	H	191
Sharp Tor	Devon	SX7289	50°41·4'	3°48·4'W	X	191
Sharp Tor	Devon	SX7336	50°12·9'	3°46·4'W	X	202
Sharpway Gate	Worcs	SO9565	52°17·2'	2°4·0'W	T	150
Sharrag Grounds	Leic	SP5785	52°27·8'	1°9·3'W	X	140
Sharrington	Norf	TG0336	52°53·2'	1°1·4'E	T	133
Sharrow	Sheff	SK3485	53°21·9'	1°28·9'W	T	110,111
Sharrow Bay	Cumbr	NY4521	54°35·1'	2°50·6'W	W	90
Sharrow Cottages	Cumbr	NY4521	54°35·1'	2°50·6'W	X	90
Sharrow Hall	Derby	SK2336	52°55·5'	1°39·1'W	X	128
Sharrow Point	Corn	SX3952	50°21·0'	4°15·4'W	X	201
Sharsted Court	Kent	TQ9558	51°17·5'	0°48·2'E	X	178
Sharsted Fm	Medway	TQ7763	51°20·5'	0°32·9'E	FM	178,188
Sharston	Man	SJ8388	53°23·6'	2°14·9'W	T	109
Shatcombe Fm	Dorset	ST4902	50°49·2'	2°43·1'W	FM	193,194
Shatcombe Fm	Dorset	SY5695	50°45·4'	2°37·0'W	FM	194
Shatterford	Worcs	SO7981	52°25·8'	2°18·1'W	T	138
Shatterling	Kent	TR2658	51°16·8'	1°14·8'E	T	179
Shatton	Derby	SK1982	53°20·3'	1°42·5'W	T	110
Shatton Edge	Derby	SK1981	53°19·8'	1°42·5'W	X	110
Shatton Hall	Cumbr	NY1428	54°38·6'	3°19·5'W	X	89
Shatton Lodge	Cumbr	NY1428	54°38·6'	3°19·5'W	X	89
Shatton Moor	Derby	SK1881	53°19·8'	1°43·4'W	X	110
Shatwell Fm	Somer	ST6530	51°4·3'	2°29·6'W	FM	183
Shaugh Fm	Devon	ST1703	50°49·5'	3°10·3'W	FM	192,193
Shaugh Moor	Devon	SX5663	50°27·2'	4°1·3'W	X	202
Shaugh Prior	Devon	SX5463	50°27·2'	4°3·0'W	T	201
Shavards Fm	Hants	SU6120	50°58·8'	1°7·5'W	FM	185
Shave Cross	Dorset	SY4198	50°46·9'	2°49·8'W	X	193
Shave Fm	Somer	ST3314	50°55·5'	2°56·8'W	FM	193
Shave Fm	Somer	ST7235	51°7·0'	2°23·6'W	FM	183
Shave Green Inclosure	Hants	SU2812	50°54·6'	1°35·7'W	F	195
Shave Hill	Dorset	ST7525	51°1·7'	2°21·0'W	X	183
Shave Hill	Somer	ST4307	50°51·8'	2°48·2'W	X	193
Shavercombe Head	Devon	SX6065	50°28·3'	3°58·0'W	W	202
Shavercombe Tor	Devon	SX5966	50°28·8'	3°58·9'W	X	202
Shavers End	Worcs	SO7768	52°18·8'	2°19·8'W	X	138
Shaves Fm	W Susx	TQ2514	50°54·9'	0°12·9'W	FM	198
Shaves Wood	W Susx	TQ2514	50°54·9'	0°12·9'W	F	198
Shave Wood	Hants	SU2912	50°54·6'	1°34·9'W	F	196
Shavington	Ches	SJ6951	53°3·6'	2°27·3'W	T	118
Shavington Green Fm	Ches	SJ7051	53°3·6'	2°26·5'W	FM	118
Shavington Ho	Ches	SJ7052	53°4·1'	2°26·5'W	X	118
Shavington Park	Shrops	SJ6339	52°57·1'	2°32·6'W	X	127
Shavington Wood Fm	Shrops	SJ6139	52°57·1'	2°34·4'W	FM	127
Shaw	Brad	SE0235	53°48·9'	1°57·8'W	T	104
Shaw	Cumbr	NX9914	54°30·9'	3°33·2'W	X	89
Shaw	D & G	NY1680	55°6·7'	3°18·6'W	X	79
Shaw	D & G	NY3083	55°8·4'	3°5·5'W	X	79
Shaw	E Ayr	NS4242	55°39·0'	4°30·2'W	X	70
Shaw	Northum	NZ2199	55°17·3'	1°39·7'W	X	81
Shaw	Oldham	SD9308	53°34·4'	2°5·9'W	T	109
Shaw	Swin	SU1185	51°34·1'	1°50·1'W	T	173
Shaw	W Berks	SU4868	51°24·8'	1°18·2'W	T	174
Shaw	Wilts	ST8865	51°23·3'	2°10·0'W	T	173
Shaw Bank	Cumbr	NY3021	54°35·0'	3°4·6'W	X	90
Shawbank	Shrops	SO4683	52°26·8'	2°47·3'W	T	137,138
Shaw Beck	N Yks	NZ0602	54°25·0'	1°54·0'W	W	92
Shawbirch	Wrekin	SJ6413	52°43·0'	2°31·6'W	T	127
Shaw Bottom	Staffs	SK0163	53°10·1'	1°58·7'W	X	119
Shawbrae Moor Plantn	D & G	NY1874	55°3·5'	3°16·6'W	F	85
Shawbraes	Scot Bord	NT8662	55°51·3'	2°13·0'W	X	67
Shawbriggs Fm	N Lincs	TA0920	53°40·1'	0°20·6'W	FM	107,112
Shawbroom	Shrops	SJ7328	52°51·2'	2°23·7'W	X	127
Shaw Brow	Cumbr	NY5661	54°56·8'	2°40·8'W	X	86
Shawburn	Scot Bord	NT5326	55°31·8'	2°44·2'W	X	73
Shaw Burn	Scot Bord	NT6709	55°22·7'	2°30·8'W	W	80
Shawbury	Shrops	SJ5521	52°47·3'	2°39·6'W	T	126
Shawbury Airfield	Shrops	SJ5422	52°47·9'	2°40·5'W	X	126
Shawbury Heath	Shrops	SJ5420	52°46·8'	2°40·5'W	F	126
Shawbury Park	Shrops	SJ5519	52°46·2'	2°39·6'W	X	126
Shawbury Wood	Warw	SP2588	52°29·6'	1°37·5'W	F	140
Shawclough	Roch	SD8814	53°37·6'	2°10·5'W	T	109
Shaw Common	Glos	SO6927	51°56·7'	2°26·7'W	T	162
Shaw Cote	N Yks	SD9191	54°19·1'	2°7·9'W	X	98
Shawcroft Fm	Ches	SJ7872	53°14·9'	2°19·4'W	FM	118
Shawcroft Hall Fm	Ches	SJ7872	53°14·9'	2°19·4'W	FM	118
Shawcross	Ches	SJ8675	53°16·5'	2°12·2'W	X	118
Shaw Cross	Kirk	SE2622	53°41·9'	1°36·0'W	X	104
Shaw Dene Ho	W Berks	SU4770	51°25·9'	1°19·0'W	X	174
Shawdon Burn	Northum	NU0914	55°25·4'	1°51·0'W	W	81
Shawdon Hall	Northum	NU0914	55°25·4'	1°51·0'W	T	81
Shawdon Hill	Northum	NU0813	55°24·9'	1°52·0'W	X	81
Shawdon Wood-House	Northum	NU0815	55°26·0'	1°52·0'W	X	81
Shawe Hall	Staffs	SK0046	53°0·9'	1°59·6'W	X	119,128
Shawell	Leic	SP5480	52°25·2'	1°12·0'W	T	140
Shawell Grange	Leic	SP5479	52°24·6'	1°12·0'W	X	140
Shawell Lodge Fm	Leic	SP5581	52°25·7'	1°11·1'W	FM	140
Shawell Wood	Leic	SP5581	52°25·7'	1°11·1'W	F	140
Shawend	N Lanak	NS7377	55°58·4'	4°1·7'W	X	64
Shawfair	Midlo	NT3170	55°55·3'	3°5·8'W	X	66
Shaw Fell	D & G	NX6974	55°2·8'	4°2·6'W	H	77,84
Shawfield	D & G	NY0076	55°4·4'	3°33·5'W	X	84
Shawfield	Northum	NY6264	54°58·4'	2°35·2'W	X	86
Shawfield	Roch	SD8714	53°37·6'	2°11·4'W	T	109
Shawfield	Staffs	SK0661	53°9·0'	1°54·2'W	T	119
Shaw Field Head	N Yks	SE0957	54°0·8'	1°51·3'W	X	104
Shawfield Head	N Yks	SE2551	53°57·5'	1°36·7'W	T	104
Shaw Fm	N Yks	NZ0005	54°26·7'	1°59·6'W	FM	92
Shaw Fm	Shrops	SJ7207	52°39·8'	2°24·4'W	FM	127
Shaw Fm	Staffs	SK0131	52°52·8'	1°58·7'W	FM	128
Shaw Fm	W Berks	SU4769	51°25·3'	1°19·1'W	FM	174
Shaw Fm	Wilts	SU0380	51°31·4'	1°57·0'W	FM	173
Shaw Fm	Win & Maid	SU9775	51°28·2'	0°35·8'W	FM	175,176
Shaw Fm, The	Northum	NU1400	55°17·9'	1°46·3'W	FM	81
Shawford	Hants	SU4624	51°1·0'	1°20·3'W	T	185
Shawford	Somer	ST7953	51°16·8'	2°17·7'W	T	183
Shawford Ho	Hants	SU4724	51°1·0'	1°19·4'W	X	185
Shawforth	Lancs	SD8920	53°40·8'	2°9·6'W	T	103

Shaw Gate	Lancs	SD9241	53°52·2'	2°6·9'W	X	103
Shaw Green	Herts	TL2932	51°58·5'	0°6·9'W	T	166
Shaw Green	Lancs	SD5218	53°39·6'	2°43·2'W	T	108
Shaw Green	N Yks	SE2652	53°58·0'	1°35·8'W	T	104
Shaw Green Fm	Ches	SJ7583	53°20·8'	2°22·1'W	FM	109
Shaw Hall	N Yks	SE1752	53°58·1'	1°44·0'W	X	104
Shawhall Fm	Staffs	SJ9105	52°38·8'	2°7·6'W	FM	127,139
Shaw Head	Cumbr	NY4672	55°2·6'	2°50·3'W	X	86
Shawhead	Cumbr	NY5276	55°4·8'	2°44·7'W	X	86
Shawhead	D & G	NX8775	55°3·7'	3°45·7'W	T	84
Shawhead	D & G	NY1377	55°5·0'	3°21·3'W	X	85
Shawhead	D & G	NY2269	55°0·8'	3°12·8'W	X	85
Shawhead	N Lanak	NS7363	55°50·9'	4°1·3'W	T	64
Shawhead	Northum	NY6951	54°51·4'	2°28·5'W	X	86,87
Shawhead	Northum	NY7564	54°58·4'	2°23·0'W	X	86,87
Shawhead	S Lanak	NS7244	55°40·6'	4°1·7'W	X	71
Shawhead	S Lanak	NS7821	55°28·3'	3°55·4'W	X	71
Shaw Head Fm	Lancs	SD9242	53°52·7'	2°6·9'W	FM	103
Shawhead Plantn	D & G	NY1377	55°5·0'	3°21·3'W	F	85
Shaw Heath	Ches	SJ7679	53°18·7'	2°21·2'W	T	118
Shaw Heath	Stock	SJ8989	53°24·1'	2°9·5'W	T	109
Shaw Hill	Cumbr	NY2154	54°52·7'	3°13·5'W	X	85
Shaw Hill	D & G	NX5971	55°1·1'	4°11·9'W	H	77
Shawhill	D & G	NX7646	54°47·9'	3°55·3'W	X	84
Shawhill	D & G	NY1980	55°6·7'	3°15·8'W	X	79
Shawhill	D & G	NY2065	54°58·6'	3°14·6'W	X	85
Shaw Hill	D & G	NY3083	55°8·4'	3°5·5'W	H	79
Shaw Hill	D & G	NY3088	55°11·1'	3°5·5'W	H	79
Shawhill	E Ayr	NS4537	55°36·4'	4°27·2'W	X	70
Shaw Hill	Highld	NH9748	57°30·9'	3°42·7'W	X	27
Shaw Hill	Lancs	SD5720	53°40·7'	2°38·6'W	X	102
Shaw Hill	Scot Bord	NT1145	55°41·7'	3°24·5'W	H	72
Shawhill	S Lanak	NS9340	55°38·8'	3°41·6'W	X	71,72
Shaw Hill	S Lanak	NT0334	55°35·7'	3°31·9'W	H	72
Shaw Hill	Wilts	SU2452	51°16·2'	1°39·0'W	X	184
Shawhill Fm	S Ayr	NS3726	55°30·3'	4°34·4'W	FM	70
Shaw Ho	Ches	SJ5464	53°10·5'	2°40·9'W	X	117
Shaw Ho	Cumbr	NY2154	54°52·7'	3°13·5'W	X	85
Shaw Ho	Cumbr	NY4857	54°54·5'	2°48·2'W	X	86
Shaw Ho	Cumbr	NY5925	54°37·4'	2°37·7'W	X	91
Shaw Ho	Derby	SK3724	52°49·0'	1°26·7'W	X	128
Shaw Ho	Northum	NZ0364	54°58·5'	1°56·8'W	X	87
Shaw Ho	N Yks	SD7876	54°11·0'	2°19·8'W	X	98
Shaw Ho	Wilts	ST8965	51°23·3'	2°9·1'W	X	173
Shaw Ho	Wilts	SU1365	51°23·3'	1°48·4'W	X	173
Shaw Knowe	E Ayr	NS6727	55°31·4'	4°6·0'W	X	71
Shawl	Heref	SO3359	52°13·7'	2°58·5'W	X	148,149
Shaw Lands	Barns	SE3306	53°33·2'	1°29·7'W	T	110,111
Shawlands	C of Glas	NS5661	55°49·5'	4°17·5'W	T	64
Shawlands	Surrey	TQ3642	51°9·9'	0°2·9'W	X	187
Shawlands Fm	Hants	SU4325	51°1·6'	1°22·8'W	FM	185
Shaw Lane Fm	Derby	SK1437	52°56·1'	1°47·1'W	FM	128
Shawls Fm	Heref	SO3033	51°59·7'	3°0·8'W	FM	161
Shaw Mills	N Yks	SE2562	54°3·4'	1°36·7'W	T	99
Shawmire	Cumbr	NY7202	54°25·0'	2°25·5'W	X	91
Shaw Moor	Derby	SK0491	53°25·2'	1°56·0'W	X	110
Shaw Moor	N Yks	NZ0503	54°25·6'	1°55·0'W	X	92
Shaw Moor	Tames	SJ9897	53°28·4'	2°1·4'W	X	109
Shaw Moor Fm	N Yks	SE6583	54°14·6'	0°59·7'W	FM	100
Shaw Moss	Cumbr	SD1985	54°15·5'	3°14·2'W	X	96
Shawmount	Scot Bord	NT4829	55°33·4'	2°49·0'W	X	73
Shaw of Dryfe	D & G	NY1591	55°12·6'	3°19·7'W	X	79
Shaw of Touch	Stir	NS7494	56°7·6'	4°1·2'W	X	57
Shaw Paddock	N Yks	SD7895	54°21·2'	2°19·9'W	X	98
Shaw Park	E Susx	TQ3618	50°56·9'	0°3·4'W	X	198
Shawpark	Highld	NH6556	57°34·7'	4°15·0'W	X	26
Shawpark	Scot Bord	NT4729	55°33·4'	2°50·0'W	X	73
Shawpits Fm	E Susx	TQ5812	50°53·4'	0°15·2'E	FM	199
Shaw Ridge	N Yks	SE6396	54°21·6'	1°1·4'W	H	94,100
Shawrig	D & G	NY2770	55°1·4'	3°8·1'W	X	85
Shaw Rig	D & G	NY2793	55°13·8'	3°8·4'W	H	79
Shawrigg Hill	Cumbr	SD5984	54°15·2'	2°37·3'W	H	97
Shaws	Derby	SK2249	53°2·5'	1°39·9'W	X	119
Shaws	D & G	NX9487	55°10·2'	3°39·4'W	X	78
Shaws	Lancs	SD3947	53°55·2'	2°55·3'W	X	102
Shaws	Northum	NY7863	54°57·9'	2°20·2'W	X	86,87
Shaws	N Yks	SD7994	54°20·7'	2°19·0'W	X	98
Shaws	Scot Bord	NT4829	55°33·4'	2°49·0'W	X	73
Shaws	Scot Bord	NY5194	55°14·6'	2°45·8'W	X	79
Shaws	S Lanak	NS7749	55°43·4'	3°57·1'W	X	64
Shaws	S Lanak	NS9140	55°38·7'	3°43·5'W	X	71,72
Shawsburn	S Lanak	NS7750	55°43·9'	3°57·1'W	T	64
Shaw's Corner	Herts	TL1916	51°50·0'	0°16·0'W	X	166
Shaw's Fm	Derby	SK1853	53°4·7'	1°43·5'W	FM	119
Shaw's Fm	Essex	TM0227	51°54·5'	0°56·6'E	FM	168
Shaw's Fm	Essex	TQ7997	51°38·8'	0°35·6'E	FM	167
Shaw's Fm	Lancs	SD3715	53°37·9'	2°56·8'W	FM	108
Shaws Fm	N Yks	SE2080	54°13·2'	1°41·2'W	FM	99
Shaw's Hill	D & G	NX9486	55°9·7'	3°39·4'W	H	78
Shaw's Hill	D & G	NY0181	55°7·1'	3°32·7'W	H	78
Shaw's Hill	Scot Bord	NT3721	55°29·0'	2°59·4'W	H	73
Shawsholm	D & G	NX8891	55°12·3'	3°45·2'W	X	78
Shaw Side	Cumbr	NY7842	54°46·6'	2°20·1'W	X	86,87
Shaw Side	N Yks	NZ0006	54°27·2'	1°59·6'W	X	92
Shaw Side	Oldham	SD9308	53°34·4'	2°5·9'W	T	109
Shawsknowe	S Ayr	NS3303	55°17·8'	4°37·4'W	X	76
Shaws Mid Hill	Scot Bord	NT3820	55°28·4'	2°58·4'W	H	73
Shawsmill	Fife	NT2293	56°7·7'	3°14·8'W	X	58
Shaw's Moor	N Yks	SE5282	54°14·1'	1°11·7'W	X	100
Shawsmuir	D & G	NX8892	55°12·8'	3°45·2'W	X	78
Shaw's Park Fm	Notts	SK5424	52°48·9'	1°11·5'W	FM	129
Shaws, The	Northum	NY8383	55°8·7'	2°15·6'W	X	80
Shawstown	Cumbr	NY4674	55°3·7'	2°50·3'W	X	86
Shaws Under Loch	Scot Bord	NT3919	55°27·9'	2°57·5'W	W	79
Shaws Upper Loch	Scot Bord	NT3818	55°27·4'	2°58·4'W	W	79
Shawswell	Glos	SP0211	51°48·1'	1°57·9'W	X	163
Shaw, The	D & G	NX9099	55°16·6'	3°43·5'W	X	78
Shawton	S Lanak	NS6848	55°42·7'	4°5·6'W	T	64
Shawtonhill	S Lanak	NS6749	55°43·2'	4°6·6'W	T	64
Shawtop	Staffs	SK0063	53°10·1'	1°59·6'W	X	119
Shaw Village	Wilts	SU1365	51°23·3'	1°48·4'W	A	173
Shaw Walls Fm	Staffs	SK0549	53°2·5'	1°55·1'W	FM	119
Shawwell Ho	Northum	NY9866	54°59·6'	2°1·4'W	X	87
Shaw Wood	Derby	SK1185	53°21·9'	1°49·7'W	X	110
Shaw Wood	Donc	SE6105	53°32·5'	1°4·4'W	F	111
Shaw Wood	N Yks	SE6971	54°8·1'	0°56·2'W	F	100
Shawwood	S Ayr	NS4126	55°30·4'	4°30·6'W	X	70
Shaw Wood Fm	Derby	SK3854	53°5·1'	1°25·6'W	FM	119
Shayes, The	Shrops	SJ4728	52°51·1'	2°46·8'W	X	126
Shay Fm	Lancs	SD5936	53°49·4'	2°37·0'W	FM	102
Shay Gate	Brad	SE1035	53°48·9'	1°50·5'W	T	104
Shay Grange Fm	Brad	SE1336	53°49·4'	1°47·7'W	FM	104
Shay Ho	Lancs	SD7054	53°59·1'	2°27·0'W	X	103
Shay House Fm	Brad	SE1034	53°48·4'	1°50·5'W	FM	104
Shay Lane	Lancs	SD8834	53°48·4'	2°10·5'W	X	103
Shay Lodge	Derby	SK0372	53°14·9'	1°56·9'W	X	119
Shays	Lancs	SD7553	53°58·6'	2°22·5'W	X	103
Shay, The	Cald	SE0731	53°46·8'	1°53·2'W	X	104
Sheader	Highld	NG4063	57°35·2'	6°20·6'W	X	23
Sheader Rocks	N Eil	NL6291	56°53·5'	7°32·6'W	X	31
Sheaffyknowe	S Lanak	NS9247	55°42·5'	3°42·7'W	X	72
Sheafhayne Manor	Devon	ST2509	50°52·8'	3°3·6'W	A	192,193
Sheala Hill	Cumbr	NY5177	55°5·4'	2°45·6'W	X	86
Shealinghill	D & G	NX9073	55°2·6'	3°42·9'W	X	84
Sheals	Moray	NJ3940	57°27·0'	3°0·5'W	X	28
Shealwalls	Pth & Kin	NO2452	56°39·5'	3°13·9'W	X	53
Sheanachie	Arg & Bt	NR7512	55°21·3'	5°32·5'W	X	68
Sheanawally Point	N Ayr	NS1552	55°43·8'	4°56·3'W	X	63,69
Shean Burn	Moray	NJ1650	57°32·2'	3°23·7'W	W	28
Sheandow	Moray	NJ2731	57°22·1'	3°12·4'W	X	37
Sheandow	Moray	NJ2739	57°26·4'	3°12·5'W	X	28
Sheans	N Ayr	NR9933	55°33·2'	5°10·8'W	X	69
Sheanspark	Moray	NJ3645	57°29·7'	3°3·6'W	X	28
Shear	Shrops	SO6073	52°21·5'	2°34·8'W	X	138
Shear Burn	W Loth	NT0658	55°48·6'	3°29·6'W	W	65,72
Sheardale	Clackm	NS9596	56°9·0'	3°41·0'W	X	58
Shear Down Fm	Hants	SU5653	51°16·6'	1°11·4'W	FM	185
Sheardrum	Fife	NT0394	56°8·0'	3°33·2'W	X	58
Sheareston	Pth & Kin	NN9218	56°20·8'	3°44·4'W	X	58
Shearing Place	Essex	TL7944	52°4·2'	0°37·1'E	X	155
Shearlangstone	Devon	SX6449	50°19·7'	3°54·3'W	X	202
Shearleat	Highld	NH8641	57°27·0'	3°53·5'W	X	27
Shearman's Wath Br	Lincs	TF2471	53°13·5'	0°8·1'W	X	122
Shearnfold Wood	Kent	TQ7034	51°5·0'	0°26·0'E	F	188
Shearplace Hill	Dorset	SY6498	50°47·1'	2°30·3'W	X	194
Shearsby	Leic	SP6290	52°30·5'	1°4·8'W	T	140
Shearstock Fm	Dorset	ST8224	51°1·1'	2°15·0'W	FM	183
Shearston	Somer	ST2830	51°4·1'	3°1·3'W	T	182
Shearstone	Devon	SX8152	50°21·6'	3°40·0'W	X	202
Shear Water	Wilts	ST8442	51°10·9'	2°13·3'W	W	183
Shearwood Copse	Wilts	SU2120	50°59·0'	1°41·7'W	F	184
Sheat Manor	I of W	SZ4984	50°38·5'	1°18·0'W	X	196
Sheaval	N Eil	NB1130	58°10·1'	6°54·4'W	H	13
Sheaves Fm	Shrops	SO5396	52°33·8'	2°41·2'W	FM	137,138
Shebbear	Devon	SS4309	50°51·8'	4°13·5'W	T	190
Shebdon	Staffs	SJ7625	52°49·6'	2°21·0'W	T	127
Shebdon Fm	Staffs	SJ7626	52°50·1'	2°21·0'W	FM	127
Shebeg	I of M	SC2773	54°7·7'	4°38·4'W	X	95
Shebirswhilse	Shetld	HU5989	60°35·1'	0°54·9'W	X	1,2
Shebster	Highld	ND0163	58°32·9'	3°41·6'W	T	11,12
Sheddens	E Renf	NS5757	55°47·4'	4°16·4'W	T	64
Sheddock	D & G	NX4739	54°43·6'	4°22·1'W	X	83
Sheddocksley	C of Aber	NJ8907	57°9·5'	2°10·5'W	T	38
Shedfield	Hants	SU5613	50°55·1'	1°11·8'W	T	196
Shedfield Grange	Hants	SU5513	50°55·1'	1°12·7'W	X	196
Shedfield Ho	Hants	SU5513	50°55·1'	1°12·7'W	X	196
Shedog Fm	N Ayr	NR9130	55°31·4'	5°18·2'W	FM	68,69
Shedrick Hill	Dorset	ST3804	50°50·2'	2°52·4'W	X	193
Sheds Fm	Notts	SK7680	53°18·9'	0°51·1'W	FM	120
Shedyard Fm	Derby	SK0184	53°21·4'	1°58·7'W	FM	110
Sheel Law	Northum	NY8285	55°9·8'	2°16·5'W	X	80
Sheelynn	Fife	NO3604	56°13·7'	3°1·5'W	X	59
Sheen	Staffs	SK1161	53°9·0'	1°49·7'W	T	119
Sheen Hill	Staffs	SK1062	53°9·5'	1°50·6'W	H	119
Sheen Hill	Worcs	SP1045	52°6·4'	1°50·8'W	X	150
Sheenhill Fm	Worcs	SP1045	52°6·4'	1°50·8'W	FM	150
Sheens of Breitoe	Shetld	HU4133	60°5·0'	1°15·3'W	H	4
Sheeoch Linn	Aberd	NO7490	57°0·3'	2°25·2'W	W	38,45
Sheep of Ardtalnaig	Pth & Kin	NN7236	56°30·2'	4°4·3'W	X	51,52
Sheepbanks	Northum	NT9504	55°20·0'	2°4·3'W	X	81
Sheepbell Fm	Surrey	TQ1357	51°18·3'	0°22·3'W	FM	187
Sheepbone Buttress	Cumbr	NY1814	54°31·1'	3°15·6'W	X	89,90
Sheepbridge	Derby	SK3774	53°15·9'	1°26·3'W	T	119
Sheepbridge Court Fm	Wok	SU7265	51°23·0'	0°57·5'W	FM	175
Sheepclose Fm	N Yks	SE6765	54°4·8'	0°58·1'W	FM	100
Sheepcoates Fm	Essex	TL8710	51°45·7'	0°43·0'E	FM	168
Sheepcombe Fm	S Glos	ST6186	51°34·5'	2°33·4'W	FM	172
Sheepcot	Glos	ST5498	51°41·0'	2°39·5'W	X	162
Sheepcote	Heref	SO5640	52°3·6'	2°38·1'W	X	149
Sheepcote Close	N Yks	SE3695	54°21·2'	1°26·3'W	X	99
Sheepcote Fm	Brom	TQ4868	51°23·7'	0°8·0'E	FM	177
Sheepcote Fm	Bucks	SU9287	51°34·7'	0°39·9'W	FM	175
Sheepcote Fm	Heref	SO2546	52°6·7'	3°5·3'W	FM	148
Sheepcote Fm	Leeds	SE3542	53°52·6'	1°27·6'W	FM	104
Sheepcote Fm	Oxon	SU6287	51°34·9'	1°5·9'W	FM	175
Sheepcote Fm	Worcs	SO8445	52°6·4'	2°13·6'W	FM	150
Sheepcote Hall	Suff	TM0658	52°11·1'	1°1·2'E	X	155
Sheepcote Hill	Lincs	TA0401	53°30·0'	0°25·5'W	X	112
Sheep Cote Hill	Lincs	TF2573	53°14·6'	0°7·2'W	X	122
Sheepcotes	Essex	TL7308	51°44·9'	0°30·8'E	X	167
Sheepcotes	Essex	TL9500	51°40·1'	0°49·6'E	X	168
Sheepcotes Fm	Essex	TL7113	51°47·6'	0°29·2'E	FM	167
Sheepcotes Fm	Essex	TL8120	51°51·2'	0°38·1'E	FM	168
Sheepcotes Fm	Essex	TQ8294	51°37·1'	0°38·1'E	FM	168,178
Sheepcote Valley	Bri & Hov	TQ3404	50°49·4'	0°5·5'W	X	198
Sheepcot Fm	Essex	TL8738	52°0·8'	0°43·9'E	FM	155
Sheepcot Fm	Oxon	SU5484	51°33·4'	1°12·9'W	FM	174
Sheepcot Hill	Bucks	SP7714	51°49·4'	0°52·6'W	X	165
Sheepcourt Fm	Kent	TR1247	51°11·2'	1°2·4'E	FM	179,189
Sheepcroft Fm	Oxon	SU3492	51°37·8'	1°30·1'W	FM	164,174
Sheep Down	Dorset	SY6088	50°41·6'	2°33·6'W	X	194
Sheep Down	W Berks	SU4684	51°33·4'	1°19·8'W	X	174
Sheep Down	W Berks	SU4982	51°32·3'	1°17·2'W	X	174
Sheepdrove	W Berks	SU3379	51°30·8'	1°31·1'W	T	174
Sheepdrove Fm	W Berks	SU3482	51°32·4'	1°30·2'W	FM	174
Sheepfields	Cumbr	NY0307	54°27·2'	3°29·3'W	X	89
Sheep Fold	Lancs	SD6132	53°47·2'	2°35·1'W	X	102,103
Sheepfold, The	Devon	SX6480	50°36·5'	3°54·9'W	X	191
Sheepfoot Grange	N Yks	SE8177	54°11·2'	0°45·1'W	X	100
Sheepgrove Fm	Hants	SU6562	51°21·4'	1°3·6'W	FM	175,186
Sheepham	Devon	SX6552	50°21·4'	3°53·5'W	X	202
Sheephatch	Surrey	SU8744	51°11·5'	0°44·9'W	X	186
Sheepheight	Orkney	HY4949	59°19·7'	2°53·3'W	X	5
Sheep Hill	Durham	NZ1757	54°54·7'	1°43·7'W	T	88
Sheep Hill	N Ayr	NS2554	55°45·1'	4°46·9'W	X	63
Sheephill Fm	Sheff	SK2983	53°20·8'	1°33·5'W	FM	110
Sheep Hills	Derby	SK2548	53°2·0'	1°37·2'W	X	119
Sheephills Fm	N Yks	SE4074	54°9·9'	1°22·8'W	FM	99
Sheephouse	Barns	SE2400	53°30·0'	1°37·9'W	X	110
Sheephouse	Dorset	ST9807	50°52·0'	2°1·3'W	X	195
Sheephouse	Glos	SO8508	51°46·5'	2°12·7'W	X	162
Sheephouse	Powys	SO2141	52°3·9'	3°8·8'W	X	148,161
Sheephouse Copse	Hants	SU7545	51°12·2'	0°55·2'W	F	186
Sheep House Fm	Glos	SP1011	51°48·1'	1°50·9'W	FM	163
Sheephouse Fm	Glos	SP2006	51°45·4'	1°42·2'W	FM	163
Sheephouse Fm	Glos	ST7797	51°40·5'	2°19·6'W	FM	162
Sheephouse Fm	Oxon	SU3996	51°39·9'	1°25·8'W	FM	164
Sheephouse Fm	Oxon	SU4387	51°35·0'	1°22·4'W	FM	174
Sheephouse Fm	Oxon	SU5684	51°33·4'	1°11·1'W	FM	174
Sheephouse Fm	Oxon	SU7681	51°31·6'	0°53·9'W	FM	175
Sheephouse Fm	S Glos	ST6684	51°33·5'	2°29·0'W	FM	172
Sheephouse Fm	Somer	ST7035	51°7·0'	2°25·3'W	FM	183
Sheephouse Fm	Staffs	SJ9854	53°5·2'	2°1·4'W	FM	118
Sheephouse Fm	Wilts	ST8931	51°4·9'	2°9·0'W	FM	184
Sheephouse Fm	Win & Maid	SU8983	51°32·6'	0°42·6'W	FM	175
Sheephouse Wood	Barns	SK2499	53°29·5'	1°37·9'W	F	110
Sheephouse Wood	Bucks	SP7023	51°54·3'	0°58·6'W	F	165
Sheepie	Shetld	HT9541	60°9·5'	2°4·9'W	X	4
Sheep Island	Arg & Bt	NR7305	55°17·5'	5°34·1'W	X	68
Sheep Island	Cumbr	SD2163	54°3·7'	3°12·0'W	X	96
Sheep Island	Pemb	SM8401	51°40·2'	5°7·0'W	X	157
Sheepknowes	D & G	NY1883	55°8·3'	3°16·8'W	X	79
Sheep Lair Hill	Durham	NY8719	54°34·2'	2°11·6'W	H	91,92
Sheeplands Fm	E Susx	TQ5008	50°51·3'	0°8·3'E	FM	199
Sheeplands Fm	Wok	SU7877	51°29·4'	0°52·2'W	FM	175
Sheeplane	Beds	SP9330	51°57·9'	0°38·4'W	T	165
Sheeplea House Fm	Derby	SK3465	53°11·1'	1°29·1'W	FM	119
Sheepleas, The	Surrey	TQ0851	51°15·1'	0°26·8'W	X	187
Sheepless Hill	Wilts	SU3560	51°20·5'	1°29·5'W	X	174
Sheep Leys Fm	Warw	SP1850	52°9·1'	1°43·8'W	FM	151
Sheep Park	Aberd	NJ6050	57°32·6'	2°39·6'W	X	29
Sheep Park	D & G	NX3951	54°49·9'	4°30·0'W	X	83
Sheeppark	Highld	NH6966	57°40·2'	4°11·3'W	X	21
Sheeppath Glen	E Loth	NT6970	55°55·6'	2°29·3'W	X	67
Sheeppen Br	Wilts	SU1095	51°39·5'	1°50·9'W	X	163
Sheep Pond	Hants	SU6019	50°58·3'	1°8·3'W	X	185
Sheep Pund	Shetld	HU3624	60°0·2'	1°20·8'W	X	4
Sheepridge	Bucks	SU8889	51°35·8'	0°43·4'W	T	175
Sheepridge	Kirk	SE1519	53°40·3'	1°46·0'W	T	110
Sheepright Geo	Orkney	HY4943	59°16·5'	2°53·2'W	X	5
Sheep Rock	Corn	SW6646	50°16·3'	5°16·7'W	X	203
Sheep Rock	Shetld	HZ2271	59°31·7'	1°36·2'W	X	4
Sheepsbyre	Devon	SS7215	50°55·5'	3°48·9'W	X	180
Sheepscar	Leeds	SE3134	53°48·3'	1°31·3'W	T	104
Sheepscombe	Glos	SO8910	51°47·5'	2°9·2'W	T	163
Sheep Skerry	Orkney	HY3628	59°8·3'	3°6·6'W	X	6
Sheep Skerry	Orkney	HY4727	59°7·9'	2°55·1'W	X	5,6
Sheep Skerry	Orkney	ND2688	58°46·7'	3°16·3'W	X	7
Sheepskin Hall	Lincs	TF1511	52°41·3'	0°17·5'W	X	130,142
Sheepskin Plantn	Suff	TL7572	52°19·3'	0°34·5'E	F	155
Sheepstead Fm	Oxon	SU4597	51°40·4'	1°20·6'W	FM	164
Sheepstead Folly	Oxon	SU4598	51°41·0'	1°20·6'W	X	164
Sheepstor	Devon	SX5567	50°29·3'	4°2·3'W	T	202
Sheeps Tor	Devon	SX5668	50°29·9'	4°1·4'W	H	202
Sheepthorns Spinney	Leic	SP7095	52°33·1'	0°57·7'W	F	141
Sheeptick End	Beds	SP9839	52°2·7'	0°33·9'W	X	153
Sheepwalk	Heref	SO3059	52°13·7'	3°1·1'W	X	148
Sheep Walk	N Yks	SE7073	54°9·1'	0°55·3'W	X	100
Sheepwalk	Staffs	SK0259	53°7·9'	1°57·8'W	X	119
Sheepwalk Fm	Cambs	TL1194	52°32·2'	0°21·4'W	FM	142
Sheepwalk Fm	Norf	TM3793	52°29·2'	1°29·9'E	FM	134
Sheepwalk Fm	York	SE6444	53°53·5'	1°1·2'W	FM	105,106
Sheepwalk Plantn	N Yks	SE9687	54°16·4'	0°31·1'W	F	94,101
Sheepwalks Fm	Durham	NZ1046	54°48·8'	1°50·2'W	FM	88
Sheepwalks, The	Staffs	SO8185	52°28·0'	2°16·4'W	X	138
Sheepwalk, The	E Yorks	TA0966	54°4·9'	0°19·6'W	X	101
Sheepwash	Devon	SS4806	50°50·3'	4°9·1'W	T	191
Sheepwash	Devon	SS7927	51°2·0'	3°43·2'W	X	180
Sheepwash	Northum	NZ2585	55°9·8'	1°36·0'W	T	81
Sheep Wash	N Yks	SD7860	54°2·4'	2°19·7'W	X	98
Sheepwash Bank	Derby	SK2384	53°21·4'	1°38·9'W	X	110
Sheepwash Brook	Notts	SK5625	52°49·4'	1°9·7'W	W	129
Sheepwash Fm	Hants	SU6509	50°52·8'	1°4·2'W	FM	196
Sheepwash Fm	I of W	SZ5280	50°37·3'	1°15·5'W	FM	196
Sheepwash Grange	Lincs	TF0070	53°13·3'	0°29·7'W	X	121
Sheepway	N Som	ST4976	51°29·1'	2°43·7'W	T	172
Sheep Well	Wilts	ST9827	51°2·8'	2°1·3'W	X	184
Sheepy Magna	Leic	SK3201	52°36·6'	1°31·2'W	T	140
Sheepy Parva	Leic	SK3301	52°36·6'	1°30·4'W	T	140
Sheepy Wood	Leic	SK3204	52°38·2'	1°31·2'W	F	140
Sheerhatch Wood	Beds	TL1347	52°6·8'	0°20·6'W	F	153
Sheering	Essex	TL5013	51°48·0'	0°10·9'E	T	167
Sheering Hall	Essex	TL4913	51°48·0'	0°10·1'E	X	167
Sheering Hall	Essex	TL5722	51°52·7'	0°17·3'E	X	167
Sheering Hall	Essex	TL7326	51°54·6'	0°31·3'E	X	167
Sheerland	Kent	TQ9345	51°10·5'	0°46·1'E	X	189
Sheerness	Kent	TQ9175	51°26·7'	0°45·3'E	T	178
Sheernest	Cumbr	SD5278	54°12·0'	2°43·7'W	X	97
Sheers Barton	Corn	SX3482	50°37·1'	4°20·4'W	X	201
Sheer's Copse	Oxon	SP3919	51°52·3'	1°25·6'W	F	164

Sheerwater	Kent	TR2660	51°17·9′	1°14·9′E	X	179
Sheerwater	Surrey	TQ0260	51°20·0′	0°31·8′W	T	176,186
Sheet	Hants	SU7524	51°0·9′	0°55·5′W	T	197
Sheet	Shrops	SO5374	52°22·0′	2°41·0′W	T	137,138
Sheetaberg	Shetld	HP6407	60°44·7′	0°49·1′W	X	1
Sheethanger Common	Herts	TL0305	51°44·3′	0°30·1′W	X	166
Sheet Hedges Wood	Leic	SK5208	52°40·3′	1°13·5′W	F	140
Sheet Hill	Kent	TQ6054	51°16·0′	0°18·0′E	X	188
Sheetloch Burn	S Lanak	NS6733	55°34·6′	4°6·1′W	W	71
Sheetloch Burn	S Lanak	NS6733	55°34·6′	4°6·1′W	W	71
Sheets Heath	Surrey	SU9457	51°18·5′	0°38·7′W	T	175,186
Shee Water	Pth & Kin	NO1367	56°47·4′	3°25·0′W	W	43
Sheffield	Corn	SW4526	50°5·0′	5°33·5′W	T	203
Sheffield	Sheff	SK3587	53°23·0′	1°28·0′W	T	110,111
Sheffield Bottom	W Berks	SU6469	51°25·2′	1°4·4′W	T	175
Sheffield Br	E Susx	TQ4023	50°59·6′	0°0·1′E	X	198
Sheffield Fm	N Lincs	SE9016	53°38·2′	0°37·9′W	FM	112
Sheffield Forest	E Susx	TQ4226	51°1·2′	0°1·9′E	F	187,198
Sheffield Green	E Susx	TQ4124	51°0·1′	0°1·0′E	T	198
Sheffield Green	E Susx	TQ4125	51°0·6′	0°1·0′E	T	187,198
Sheffield Ho	Lincs	TF0656	53°5·7′	0°24·6′W	X	121
Sheffield Moor	N Yks	NZ7812	54°30·1′	0°47·3′W	X	94
Sheffield Park	E Susx	TQ4124	51°0·1′	0°1·0′E	A	198
Sheffield Park	Sheff	SK3686	53°22·4′	1°27·1′W	T	110,111
Sheffield Park Fm	E Susx	TQ4124	51°0·1′	0°1·0′E	FM	198
Sheffield Park Sta	E Susx	TQ4023	50°59·6′	0°0·1′E	X	198
Sheffield Pike	Cumbr	NY3618	54°33·4′	2°59·0′W	H	90
Sheffield's Hill	N Lincs	SE9015	53°37·7′	0°37·9′W	X	112
Shefford	Beds	TL1439	52°2·5′	0°19·9′W	T	153
Shefford Park Fm	W Berks	SU3773	51°27·5′	1°27·7′W	FM	174
Shefford Woodlands	W Berks	SU3673	51°27·5′	1°28·5′W	T	174
Shegear Fm	Heref	SO3436	52°1·3′	2°57·3′W	FM	149,161
Sheigra	Highld	NC1860	58°29·7′	5°6·9′W	T	9
Sheilavig	N Eil	NB0030	58°9·7′	7°5·6′W	X	13
Sheilavig Skerry	N Eil	NB0234	58°11·9′	7°3·9′W	X	13
Sheil Burn	D & G	NS8211	55°23·0′	3°51·3′W	W	71,78
Sheil Burn	D & G	NX4378	55°4·6′	4°27·1′W	W	77
Sheildfield	Northum	NY8380	55°7·1′	2°15·6′W	X	80
Sheildhill	D & G	NX7270	55°0·7′	3°59·7′W	X	77,84
Sheildmuir	N Lanak	NS7755	55°46·6′	3°57·2′W	T	64
Sheilds	E Dunb	NS6578	55°58·8′	4°9·4′W	X	64
Sheilds	S Lanak	NS6151	55°44·2′	4°12·4′W	X	64
Sheilds Cott	E Dunb	NS6577	55°58·3′	4°9·3′W	X	64
Sheil Hill	D & G	NX3181	55°5·9′	4°38·5′W	X	76
Sheil Hill	D & G	NX3582	55°6·6′	4°34·8′W	H	77
Sheilhill	Pth & Kin	NN8511	56°16·9′	3°51·0′W	X	58
Sheil Hill	S Lanak	NS7728	55°32·1′	3°56·5′W	X	71
Sheiling Burn	Arg & Bt	NS3092	56°5·7′	4°43·5′W	W	56
Sheiling Rig	D & G	NS8513	55°24·1′	3°48·5′W	X	71,78
Sheillahill	D & G	NX7454	54°52·1′	3°57·4′W	X	83,84
Sheils, The	Aberd	NO7472	56°50·6′	2°25·1′W	X	45
Sheilwalls	Stir	NS7484	56°2·2′	4°0·9′W	X	57,64
Sheinton	Shrops	SJ6103	52°37·6′	2°34·2′W	T	127
Sheinton Common	Shrops	SJ6103	52°37·6′	2°34·2′W	X	127
Sheinwood	Shrops	SJ6102	52°37·1′	2°34·2′W	X	127
Sheirdrim Hill	Arg & Bt	NR7958	55°46·1′	5°31·0′W	H	62
Shelborn Br	Essex	TL8023	51°52·8′	0°37·3′E	X	168
Shelderton	Shrops	SO4077	52°23·5′	2°52·5′W	T	137,148
Shelderton Hill	Heref	SO4177	52°23·5′	2°51·6′W	H	137,148
Shelderton Rock	Shrops	SO4177	52°23·5′	2°51·6′W	X	137,148
Sheldon	Aberd	NJ8224	57°18·6′	2°17·5′W	X	38
Sheldon	Birm	SP1584	52°27·5′	1°46·4′W	T	139
Sheldon	Derby	SK1768	53°12·8′	1°44·3′W	T	119
Sheldon	Devon	ST1208	50°52·1′	3°14·7′W	T	192,193
Sheldon Centre	Devon	SX8387	50°40·5′	3°39·0′W	X	191
Sheldon Fm	Staffs	SK0655	53°5·8′	1°54·2′W	FM	119
Sheldon Grange	Devon	ST1209	50°52·7′	3°14·7′W	X	192,193
Sheldon Hall	Birm	SP1687	52°29·1′	1°45·5′W	A	139
Sheldon Hill	Devon	ST1109	50°52·7′	3°15·5′W	X	192,193
Sheldon Manor	Wilts	ST8874	51°28·1′	2°10·0′W	A	173
Sheldons Fm	Hants	SU7159	51°19·8′	0°58·5′W	FM	175,186
Sheldrake Pool	Northum	NU1342	55°40·5′	1°47·2′W	W	75
Sheldwich	Kent	TR0156	51°16·3′	0°53·3′E	T	178
Sheldwich Lees	Kent	TR0156	51°16·3′	0°53·3′E	T	178
Shelf	Brig	SS9380	51°30·8′	3°32·1′W	T	170
Shelf	Cald	SE1228	53°45·1′	1°48·7′W	T	104
Shelfanger	Norf	TM1083	52°24·5′	1°5·7′E	T	144
Shelfanger Hall	Norf	TM1083	52°24·5′	1°5·7′E	X	144
Shelf Benches	Derby	SK0794	53°26·8′	1°53·3′W	X	110
Shelf Brook	Derby	SK0694	53°26·8′	1°54·2′W	W	110
Shelf Fm	Devon	ST1706	50°51·1′	3°10·4′W	FM	192,193
Shelfield	Wals	SK0302	52°37·2′	1°56·9′W	T	139
Shelfield	Warw	SP1262	52°15·6′	1°49·1′W	T	150
Shelfield Fm	Lancs	SD8837	53°50·0′	2°10·5′W	FM	103
Shelfield Green	Warw	SP1261	52°15·1′	1°49·1′W	T	150
Shelfleys	Northnts	SP7357	52°12·6′	0°55·5′W	T	152
Shelf Moor	Derby	SK0894	53°26·8′	1°52·4′W	X	110
Shelf Moss	Derby	SK0895	53°27·3′	1°52·4′W	X	110
Shelford	Notts	SK6642	52°58·5′	1°0·6′W	T	129
Shelford	Warw	SP4288	52°29·5′	1°22·5′W	T	140
Shelford Creek	Essex	TQ9890	51°34·7′	0°51·9′E	W	178
Shelford Fm	Kent	TR1660	51°18·1′	1°6·3′E	FM	179
Shelford Fm	Warw	SP4289	52°30·1′	1°22·5′W	FM	140
Shelford Head	Essex	TQ9989	51°34·1′	0°52·7′E	X	178
Shelford Lodge Fm	Notts	SK6540	52°57·4′	1°1·5′W	FM	129
Shelford Manor	Notts	SK6743	52°59·0′	0°59·7′W	X	129
Shell	Worcs	SO9559	52°14·0′	2°4·0′W	T	150
Shellachan	Arg & Bt	NM8720	56°19·7′	5°26·3′W	X	49
Shellachan	Arg & Bt	NN0326	56°23·4′	5°11·0′W	X	50
Shellacres	Northum	NT8943	55°41·1′	2°10·1′W	X	74
Shellag Point	I of M	SC4699	54°22·0′	4°21·8′W	X	95
Shelland	Suff	TM0060	52°12·3′	0°56·0′E	T	155
Shelland Hall	Suff	TL9959	52°11·8′	0°55·1′E	X	155
Shelland Wood	Suff	TM0061	52°12·9′	0°56·1′E	F	155
Shell Bay	Dorset	SZ0386	50°40·6′	1°57·1′W	W	195
Shell Bay	Fife	NO4600	56°11·6′	2°51·8′W	W	59
Shell Beach	Highld	NG6727	57°16·7′	5°51·5′W	X	32
Shell Br	Lincs	TF3416	52°43·7′	0°0·5′W	X	131
Shellbraes	Northum	NZ0071	55°2·3′	1°59·6′W	X	87
Shell Brook	Ches	SJ9464	53°10·6′	2°5·0′W	W	118

Shellbrook	Leic	SK3316	52°44·7′	1°30·3′W	T	128
Shell Brook	Shrops	SJ3639	52°56·9′	2°56·7′W	W	126
Shellbrook Hill	Shrops	SJ3540	52°57·4′	2°57·7′W	X	117
Shell Cottage	Worcs	SO9559	52°14·0′	2°4·0′W	A	150
Shelley	Essex	TL5505	51°43·6′	0°15·1′E	T	167
Shelley	Kirk	SE2011	53°36·0′	1°41·5′W	T	110
Shelley	Suff	TM0338	52°0·4′	0°57·9′E	T	155
Shelley Common	Hants	SU3118	50°57·9′	1°33·1′W	X	185
Shelley Fm	Hants	SU3217	50°57·3′	1°32·3′W	FM	185
Shelley Fm	W Susx	TQ2432	51°4·7′	0°13·4′W	FM	187
Shelley Plain	W Susx	TQ2431	51°4·1′	0°13·4′W	X	187
Shelley Priory Fm	Suff	TM0038	52°0·5′	0°55·2′E	FM	155
Shelleys	Kent	TQ4659	51°18·9′	0°6·1′E	X	188
Shelleys	W Susx	TQ1813	50°54·5′	0°18·9′W	X	198
Shelley's Folly	E Susx	TQ4014	50°54·7′	0°0·1′W	X	198
Shelley Woodhouse	Kirk	SE2110	53°35·4′	1°40·6′W	T	110
Shellfield	Arg & Bt	NS0079	55°58·0′	5°11·8′W	X	63
Shell Fm	Cambs	TL6081	52°24·4′	0°21·5′E	FM	143
Shell Green	Halton	SJ5387	53°22·9′	2°42·0′W	T	108
Shell Haven	Thurr	TQ7481	51°30·3′	0°30·8′E	W	178
Shellhaven Point	Thurr	TQ7682	51°30·8′	0°32·6′E	X	178
Shell Hill	Orkney	ND2897	58°51·5′	3°14·4′W	H	6,7
Shelligan Burn	Pth & Kin	NN9429	56°26·7′	3°42·7′W	W	52,53,58
Shellingford	Oxon	SU3193	51°38·3′	1°32·7′W	T	164,174
Shell Island	Gwyn	SH5526	52°49·0′	4°8·7′W	X	124
Shellmorehill Fm	Ches	SJ8170	53°13·8′	2°16·7′W	FM	118
Shell Ness	Kent	TR0567	51°22·1′	0°57·1′E	X	178,179
Shell Ness	Kent	TR3562	51°18·7′	1°22·7′E	X	179
Shelloch	Pth & Kin	NN8963	56°45·0′	3°48·5′W	X	43
Shelloch Burn	Stir	NS6589	56°4·7′	4°9·7′W	W	57
Shellow Bowells	Essex	TL6007	51°44·6′	0°19·4′E	T	167
Shellow Cross Fm	Essex	TL6108	51°45·1′	0°20·3′E	FM	167
Shellow Fm	Ches	SJ8868	53°12·8′	2°10·4′W	FM	118
Shellow Hall	Essex	TL6007	51°44·6′	0°19·4′E	X	167
Shellow Wood	Ches	SJ8868	53°12·8′	2°10·4′W	F	118
Shell's Fm	Somer	ST4017	50°57·2′	2°50·9′W	FM	193
Shell Top	Devon	SX5963	50°27·2′	3°58·8′W	X	202
Shellwood Cross	Surrey	TQ2145	51°11·7′	0°15·7′W	T	187
Shellwood Manor	Surrey	TQ2045	51°11·7′	0°16·6′W	X	187
Shell Woods	Corn	SX0872	50°31·2′	4°42·1′W	F	200
Shelly	Northum	NZ1189	55°12·0′	1°49·2′W	X	81
Shelly Bars	Cumbr	SD2362	54°3·1′	3°10·2′W	X	96
Shelly Point	Fife	NO4719	56°21·9′	2°51·0′W	X	59
Shelmore Ho	Staffs	SJ7921	52°47·4′	2°18·3′W	X	127
Shelmore Wood	Staffs	SJ8021	52°47·4′	2°17·4′W	F	127
Shelsley Beauchamp	Worcs	SO7363	52°16·1′	2°23·3′W	T	138,150
Shelsley Walsh	Worcs	SO7262	52°15·6′	2°24·2′W	T	138,149
Shelspit Farms	Bucks	SP7533	51°59·7′	0°54·1′W	FM	152,165
Shelstone Tor	Devon	SX5589	50°41·2′	4°2·8′W	X	191
Shelswell	Oxon	SP6030	51°58·1′	1°7·2′W	X	152,165
Shelswell Park	Oxon	SP6030	51°58·1′	1°7·2′W	X	152,165
Shelswell Plantation	Oxon	SP5931	51°58·7′	1°8·1′W	F	152
Shelter Crags	Cumbr	NY2505	54°26·3′	3°9·0′W	X	89,90
Shelterfield	Angus	NO5740	56°33·3′	2°41·5′W	X	54
Shelterhall	Clackm	NS9898	56°10·1′	3°38·1′W	X	58
Shelterhouse Corner	Suff	TL8277	52°21·9′	0°40·8′E	X	144
Shelt Hill	Notts	SK6448	53°1·8′	1°2·3′W	X	129
Shelthorpe	Leic	SK5317	52°45·1′	1°12·5′W	T	129
Shelton	Beds	TL0368	52°18·3′	0°29·0′W	T	153
Shelton	C of Stoke	SJ8746	53°0·9′	2°11·2′W	T	118
Shelton	Norf	TM2290	52°28·0′	1°16·5′E	T	134
Shelton	Notts	SK7844	52°59·5′	0°49·9′W	T	129
Shelton	Shrops	SJ4613	52°43·0′	2°47·6′W	T	126
Shelton Common	Norf	TM2490	52°27·9′	1°18·3′E	X	134
Shelton Gorse	Beds	TL0268	52°18·3′	0°29·8′W	F	153
Shelton Grange Fm	Beds	TL0369	52°18·8′	0°28·9′W	FM	153
Shelton Green	Norf	TM2390	52°28·0′	1°17·4′E	X	134
Shelton Lock	C of Derb	SK3731	52°52·7′	1°26·6′W	T	128
Shelton Lodge Fm	Notts	SK7743	52°59·0′	0°50·8′W	FM	129
Shelton under Harley	Staffs	SJ8139	52°57·1′	2°16·6′W	T	127
Sheltwood Fm	Worcs	SO9867	52°18·3′	2°1·4′W	FM	150
Shelve	Shrops	SO3398	52°34·8′	2°58·9′W	T	137
Shelve Hill	Shrops	SO3298	52°34·8′	2°59·8′W	X	137
Shelvin	Devon	ST1604	50°50·0′	3°11·2′W	T	192,193
Shelvin Fm	Kent	TR2247	51°11·0′	1°11·0′E	FM	179,189
Shelvingford	Kent	TR2165	51°20·7′	1°10·8′E	T	179
Shelvock	Shrops	SJ3724	52°48·8′	2°55·7′W	X	126
Shelwick	Heref	SO5243	52°5·2′	2°41·6′W	T	149
Shelwick Green	Heref	SO5243	52°5·2′	2°41·6′W	T	149
Shemmings Fm	Essex	TL9220	51°51·0′	0°47·7′E	FM	168
Shemore	Arg & Bt	NS3488	56°3·6′	4°39·5′W	X	56
Shempston	Moray	NJ1868	57°41·9′	3°22·1′W	X	28
Shemrigghead	D & G	NY0991	55°12·5′	3°25·4′W	X	78
Shenachie	Highld	NH8234	57°23·1′	3°57·3′W	X	27
Shenavail	Pth & Kin	NN8350	56°37·9′	3°54·0′W	X	52
Shenavall	Highld	NH0681	57°46·9′	5°15·3′W	X	19
Shenavallie	Arg & Bt	NM8840	56°30·5′	5°26·3′W	X	49
Shenberrow Hill	Glos	SP0733	52°0·0′	1°53·5′W	H	150
Shendale Hill	Shetld	HU1955	60°17·0′	1°38·9′W	H	3
Shendish	Herts	TL0504	51°43·7′	0°28·4′W	X	166
Shenfield	Essex	TQ6195	51°38·1′	0°20·0′E	T	167,177
Shenfield Common	Essex	TQ6093	51°37·0′	0°19·1′E	X	177
Shenington	Oxon	SP3742	52°4·7′	1°27·2′W	T	151
Shenlarich	Pth & Kin	NN6941	56°32·8′	4°7·4′W	X	51
Shenley	Herts	TL1900	51°41·4′	0°16·3′W	T	166
Shenley Brook End	Mil Key	SP8335	52°0·7′	0°47·0′W	T	152
Shenleybury	Herts	TL1801	51°41·9′	0°17·2′W	T	166
Shenley Church End	Mil Key	SP8336	52°1·2′	0°47·0′W	T	152
Shenley Dens Fm	Mil Key	SP8036	52°1·2′	0°49·7′W	FM	152
Shenley Fields	Birm	SP0281	52°25·9′	1°57·8′W	T	139
Shenley Fm	Kent	TQ8542	51°9·1′	0°39·1′E	FM	189
Shenley Fm	Northnts	SP5774	52°21·9′	1°9·4′W	FM	140
Shenley Hall	Herts	TL1900	51°41·4′	0°16·3′W	X	166
Shenley Hill Fm	Mil Key	SP8137	52°1·8′	0°48·8′W	FM	152
Shenley Lodge	Herts	TL2002	51°42·5′	0°15·4′W	X	166
Shenley Lodge	Mil Key	SP8436	52°1·2′	0°46·2′W	T	152
Shenley Wood	Mil Key	SP8236	52°1·2′	0°47·9′W	T	152
Shenlow Hill	Oxon	SP3542	52°4·7′	1°29·0′W	H	151
Shenmore	Heref	SO3938	52°2·5′	2°53·0′W	T	149,161
Shennach Farm	Highld	NJ1130	57°21·4′	3°28·3′W	FM	36

Shennanton	D & G	NX3463	54°56·3′	4°35·1′W	X	82
Shennanton Ho	D & G	NX3464	54°56·8′	4°35·1′W	X	82
Shennar Howe	Orkney	HY2816	59°1·8′	3°14·8′W	A	6
Shennas	D & G	NX1272	55°0·7′	4°56·0′W	X	76
Shennington	Warw	SP2450	52°9·1′	1°38·6′W	X	151
Shennock	D & G	NX3166	54°57·9′	4°38·0′W	W	82
Shenrick	D & G	NX8372	55°2·0′	3°49·4′W	X	84
Shenstone	Cumbr	SD5089	54°17·9′	2°45·7′W	X	97
Shenstone	Staffs	SK1004	52°38·3′	1°50·7′W	T	139
Shenstone	Worcs	SO8673	52°21·5′	2°11·9′W	T	139
Shenstone Court	Staffs	SK1003	52°37·7′	1°50·7′W	X	139
Shenstone Lodge School	Staffs	SK1103	52°37·7′	1°49·8′W	X	139
Shenstone Park	Staffs	SK1203	52°37·7′	1°49·0′W	X	139
Shenstone Woodend	Staffs	SK1102	52°37·2′	1°49·8′W	T	139
Shenton	Leic	SK3800	52°36·0′	1°25·9′W	T	140
Shentulloch Knowe	S Ayr	NX2784	55°7·5′	4°42·4′W	X	76
Shenval	Aberd	NJ3001	57°5·9′	3°8·9′W	X	37
Shenval	Highld	NH4029	57°19·7′	4°39·0′W	X	26
Shenval	Moray	NJ1730	57°21·4′	3°22·3′W	X	36
Shenval	Moray	NJ2129	57°20·9′	3°18·3′W	T	36
Shenval	Moray	NJ2638	57°25·8′	3°13·5′W	X	28
Shenval	Moray	NJ3630	57°21·6′	3°3·4′W	X	37
Shenval	Pth & Kin	NO0033	56°29·0′	3°37·0′W	X	52,53
Shenvalla	I of M	SC2481	54°11·9′	4°41·5′W	X	95
Shenvalley	I of M	SC1867	54°4·3′	4°46·5′W	X	95
Shenvalley	I of M	SC2975	54°8·8′	4°36·7′W	X	95
Shenvault	Moray	NJ0443	57°28·3′	3°35·6′W	X	27
Shenwall	Aberd	NJ4244	57°29·2′	2°57·6′W	X	28
Shepards Close	Kent	TR2054	51°14·8′	1°9·5′E	X	179,189
Shepeau Stow	Lincs	TF3012	52°41·6′	0°4·2′W	T	131,142
Sheperdine Sands	Glos	ST5997	51°40·5′	2°35·2′W	X	162
Sheperds Fm	Lincs	TF2050	53°2·3′	0°12·2′W	FM	122
Sheperdshaugh	Aberd	NO7676	56°52·7′	2°23·2′W	X	45
Sheperd's Ho	N Yks	NZ6307	54°27·5′	1°1·3′W	X	94
Sheperd's Well	Powys	SO1864	52°16·3′	3°11·7′W	X	148
Shephall	Herts	TL2523	51°53·7′	0°10·6′W	T	166
Shepheard's Hurst	Surrey	TQ3146	51°12·1′	0°7·1′W	X	187
Shepherd Hall	Cumbr	NY0633	54°41·2′	3°27·1′W	X	89
Shepherd Hill	N Yks	NZ4701	54°24·4′	1°16·1′W	X	93
Shepherd Hill	Wakf	SE2820	53°40·8′	1°34·2′W	T	104
Shepherdlands	Fife	NT0090	56°5·8′	3°36·0′W	X	58
Shepherd's Bottom	Dorset	ST9017	50°57·4′	2°8·2′W	X	184
Shepherd's Burn	Northum	NY7382	55°8·1′	2°25·0′W	W	80
Shepherd's Bush	Ham & Ful	TQ2280	51°30·6′	0°14·1′W	T	176
Shepherd's Chine	I of W	SZ4479	50°36·8′	1°22·3′W	X	196
Shepherdscleuch	Scot Bord	NT2617	55°26·7′	3°9·8′W	X	79
Shepherd's Close	N Yks	NZ5902	54°24·8′	1°5·0′W	X	93
Shepherd's Corner Fm	Dorset	ST8307	50°52·0′	2°14·1′W	FM	194
Shepherd's Cottage	Cumbr	NY7121	54°35·2′	2°26·5′W	X	91
Shepherds Cottage	Northum	NU2228	55°33·0′	1°38·6′W	X	75
Shepherds Croft	Pth & Kin	NT0797	56°9·7′	3°29·4′W	X	58
Shepherd's Dene	Northum	NZ0061	54°56·9′	1°59·6′W	X	87
Shepherds Down	Hants	SU5819	50°58·3′	1°10·0′W	X	185
Shepherds' Fen	Suff	TL6885	52°26·5′	0°28·7′E	X	143
Shepherd's Flat Fm	Derby	SK2077	53°17·6′	1°41·6′W	FM	119
Shepherds Fm	Corn	SW8154	50°20·9′	5°4·3′W	FM	200
Shepherds Fm	Devon	SX9990	50°42·3′	3°25·4′W	FM	192
Shepherd's Fm	Lancs	SD3931	53°46·6′	2°55·1′W	FM	102
Shepherd's Fm	Lancs	SD4551	53°57·4′	2°49·9′W	FM	102
Shepherd's Fm	Lincs	TF1277	53°16·9′	0°18·8′W	FM	121
Shepherds Fm	Lincs	TF2826	52°49·2′	0°5·6′W	FM	131
Shepherd's Fm	Suff	TM3554	52°8·3′	1°26·5′E	FM	156
Shepherd's Fm	W Susx	TQ3338	51°7·8′	0°5·6′W	FM	187
Shepherd's Furze Fm	Bucks	SP6825	51°55·4′	1°0·3′W	FM	164,165
Shepherd's Gate	Norf	TF5518	52°44·5′	0°18·2′E	T	131
Shepherd's Green	Oxon	SU7183	51°32·7′	0°58·2′W	T	175
Shepherd's Grove	Suff	TL9772	52°18·9′	0°53·8′E	X	144,155
Shepherd's Hall	N Yks	NZ0804	54°26·1′	1°52·2′W	X	92
Shepherdshield	Northum	NY7674	55°3·8′	2°22·1′W	F	86,87
Shepherd Shield	Northum	NY7775	55°4·4′	2°21·2′W	X	86,87
Shepherd's Hill	Cumbr	NY5142	54°46·5′	2°45·3′W	H	86
Shepherd's Hill	E Susx	TQ5122	50°58·9′	0°9·5′E	X	199
Shepherds Hill	Kent	TR0355	51°15·7′	0°55·0′E	X	178,179
Shepherd's Hill	Norf	TF8637	52°54·1′	0°46·3′E	X	132
Shepherds Hill	N Yks	SE8184	54°15·0′	0°45·0′W	X	100
Shepherd's Hill	Surrey	SU9032	51°5·0′	0°42·5′W	T	186
Shepherds Hill Ho	Hill	TQ0690	51°36·2′	0°27·8′W	X	176
Shepherdshill Wood	Corn	SX0049	50°18·7′	4°48·2′W	F	204
Shepherds Ho	Northum	NU0031	55°34·6′	1°59·6′W	X	75
Shepherds Ho	Red & Cl	NZ6820	54°34·5′	0°56·5′W	X	94
Shepherds Houses	Ches	SJ5175	53°16·4′	2°43·7′W	X	117
Shepherdskirk Bungalow	Northum	NU0438	55°38·4′	1°55·8′W	X	75
Shepherdskirk Hill	Northum	NU0438	55°38·4′	1°55·8′W	H	75
Shepherd's Lane Fm	Notts	SK4661	53°8·9′	1°18·3′W	FM	120
Shepherds Law	Northum	NU0816	55°26·5′	1°52·0′W	H	81
Shepherd's Lodge	Durham	NZ0721	54°35·3′	1°53·1′W	X	92
Shepherds Lodge	Notts	SK6472	53°14·7′	1°2·0′W	X	120
Shepherds Lodge	N Yks	NY9705	54°26·7′	2°2·4′W	X	92
Shepherd's Lodge	N Yks	SE2263	54°4·0′	1°39·4′W	X	99
Shepherd's Patch	Glos	SO7204	51°44·3′	2°23·9′W	T	162
Shepherd's Ph	Notts	SK6337	52°55·8′	1°3·4′W	X	129
Shepherds Pit	Oxon	SP5608	51°46·3′	1°10·9′W	X	164
Shepherd's Plantn	Norf	TL8897	52°32·5′	0°46·7′E	F	144
Shepherd's Point	Arg & Bt	NS1988	56°3·3′	4°54·0′W	X	56
Shepherd's Port	Norf	TF6533	52°52·4′	0°27·5′E	T	132
Shepherd's Seat	Angus	NO5055	56°41·3′	2°48·5′W	X	54
Shepherds' Shore	Wilts	SU0466	51°23·8′	1°56·2′W	X	173
Shepherds' Taing	Shetld	HU1659	60°19·2′	1°42·1′W	X	3
Shepherds Trail	I of W	SZ4881	50°37·8′	1°18·9′W	X	196
Shepherd's Tump	Powys	SO1565	52°16·8′	3°14·4′W	H	136,148
Shepherdswell or						
Sibertswold	Kent	TR2547	51°10·9′	1°13·6′E	T	179
Shepherdswhim	Powys	SO2990	52°30·4′	3°2·4′W	T	137
Sheplegh Court	Devon	SX8049	50°20·0′	3°40·8′W	X	202
Shepley	Kirk	SE1909	53°34·9′	1°42·4′W	T	110
Sheppard's Stone	Notts	SK5556	53°6·1′	1°10·3′W	X	120
Sheppardstown	Highld	ND2039	58°20·2′	3°21·5′W	X	11,12
Sheppard's Wood	Suff	TM4684	52°24·1′	1°37·4′E	F	156
Sheppenhall Hall	Ches	SJ6145	53°0·3′	2°34·5′W	X	118
Shepperdine	S Glos	ST6195	51°39·4′	2°33·4′W	T	162

Shepperton	Surrey	TQ0767	51°23·7'	0°27·3'W	T	176
Shepperton Green	Surrey	TQ0767	51°23·7'	0°27·3'W	T	176
Shepreth	Cambs	TL3947	52°6·5'	0°2·2'E	T	154
Shepshed	Leic	SK4719	52°46·2'	1°17·8'W	T	129
Shepton Beauchamp	Somer	ST4017	50°57·2'	2°50·9'W	T	193
Shepton Br	Hants	SU3704	50°50·3'	1°28·1'W	X	196
Shepton Ho	Somer	ST4016	50°56·7'	2°50·9'W	X	193
Shepton Mallet	Somer	ST6143	51°11·3'	2°33·1'W	T	183
Shepton Montague	Somer	ST6731	51°4·9'	2°27·9'W	T	183
Shepway	Kent	TQ7753	51°15·1'	0°32·6'E	T	188
Shepway Cross	Kent	TR1234	51°4·2'	1°2·0'E	X	179,189
Sheraton	Durham	NZ4435	54°42·7'	1°18·6'W	T	93
Sheraton Grange Fm	Durham	NZ4333	54°41·7'	1°19·5'W	FM	93
Sheraton Hill	Durham	NZ4435	54°42·7'	1°18·6'W	X	93
Sheraton W Grange	Durham	NZ4333	54°41·7'	1°19·5'W	X	93
Sherberton	Devon	SX6473	50°32·7'	3°54·8'W	T	191
Sherberton Common	Devon	SX6973	50°32·8'	3°50·6'W	X	191
Sherborne	Dorset	ST6316	50°56·8'	2°31·2'W	T	183
Sherborne	Glos	SP1714	51°49·7'	1°44·8'W	T	163
Sherborne	Somer	ST5855	51°17·8'	2°35·8'W	T	172,182
Sherborne Brook	Glos	SP1615	51°50·2'	1°45·7'W	W	163
Sherborne Castle	Dorset	ST6416	50°56·8'	2°30·4'W	A	183
Sherborne Causeway	Dorset	ST8323	51°0·6'	2°14·2'W	X	183
Sherborne Common	Glos	SP1815	51°50·2'	1°43·9'W	X	163
Sherborne Lake	Dorset	ST6516	50°56·8'	2°29·5'W	W	183
Sherborne Park	Glos	SP1614	51°49·7'	1°45·7'W	X	163
Sherborne Rocks	Devon	SY2287	50°40·9'	3°5·9'W	X	192
Sherborne St John	Hants	SU6255	51°17·7'	1°6·3'W	T	175,185
Sherbourne	Shrops	SO6074	52°22·0'	2°34·9'W	X	138
Sherbourne	Warw	SP2662	52°15·6'	1°36·7'W	T	151
Sherbourne Brook	Warw	SP2461	52°15·0'	1°38·5'W	W	151
Sherbourne Fm	Surrey	TQ0648	51°13·5'	0°28·5'W	FM	187
Sherbourne Hill	Warw	SP2461	52°15·0'	1°38·5'W	X	151
Sherbourne Street	Suff	TL9541	52°2·2'	0°51·0'E	T	155
Sherbourne Valley	E Susx	TQ8223	50°58·9'	0°36·0'E	X	199
Sherbrooke Thorns	N Yks	SE7682	54°13·9'	0°49·6'W	F	100
Sherbrook Valley	Staffs	SJ9818	52°45·8'	2°1·4'W	X	127
Sherburn	Durham	NZ3142	54°46·6'	1°30·7'W	T	88
Sherburn	N Yks	SE9577	54°11·0'	0°32·2'W	T	101
Sherburn Brow	N Yks	SE9575	54°10·0'	0°32·3'W	X	101
Sherburn Carr	N Yks	SE9577	54°11·0'	0°32·2'W	X	101
Sherburn Common Fm	N Yks	SE5034	53°48·2'	1°14·0'W	FM	105
Sherburn Cut	N Yks	SE9578	54°11·6'	0°32·2'W	W	101
Sherburn Grange	Durham	NZ3042	54°46·6'	1°31·6'W	T	88
Sherburn Hill	Durham	NZ3342	54°46·6'	1°28·8'W	T	88
Sherburn in Elmet	N Yks	SE4933	53°47·7'	1°15·0'W	T	105
Sherburn Ings	N Yks	SE9678	54°11·6'	0°31·3'W	X	101
Sherburn Lodge	N Yks	SE5034	53°48·2'	1°14·0'W	X	105
Sherburn Lodge	N Yks	SE9476	54°10·5'	0°33·2'W	X	101
Sherburn Tower Fm	Ghead	NZ1559	54°55·8'	1°45·5'W	FM	88
Sherburn Whins	N Yks	SE9672	54°8·3'	0°31·4'W	X	101
Sherburn Wold	N Yks	SE9674	54°9·4'	0°31·4'W	X	101
Sherburn Wold Fm	N Yks	SE9574	54°9·4'	0°32·3'W	FM	101
Sherdley Park	St Hel	SJ5193	53°26·1'	2°43·8'W	X	108
Sherdon Fm	Somer	SS7934	51°5·8'	3°43·3'W	FM	180
Sherdon Water	Somer	SS7834	51°5·8'	3°44·2'W	W	180
Sherdon Water	Somer	SS8035	51°6·3'	3°42·5'W	W	181
Shere	Surrey	TQ0747	51°13·0'	0°27·7'W	T	187
Shereburgh	Scot Bord	NT8226	55°31·9'	2°16·7'W	H	74
Shereford	Norf	TF8829	52°49·8'	0°47·8'E	T	132
Sherenden Fm	Kent	TQ6246	51°11·6'	0°19·5'E	FM	188
Sherfield Court	Hants	SU6756	51°18·2'	1°1·9'W	X	175,186
Sherfield English	Hants	SU2922	51°0·0'	1°34·8'W	T	185
Sherfield Hall	Hants	SU6656	51°18·2'	1°2·8'W	X	175,186
Sherfield on Loddon	Hants	SU6757	51°18·7'	1°1·9'W	T	175,186
Sherfin	Lancs	SD7825	53°43·5'	2°19·6'W	T	103
Sherford	Devon	SX7744	50°17·2'	3°43·2'W	T	202
Sherford	Dorset	SY9193	50°44·4'	2°7·3'W	T	195
Sherford	Somer	ST2223	51°0·3'	3°6·3'W	T	193
Sherford Br	Dorset	SY9192	50°43·9'	2°7·3'W	X	195
Sherford Down	Devon	SX7644	50°17·2'	3°44·1'W	X	202
Sherford River	Dorset	SY9492	50°43·9'	2°4·7'W	W	195
Sherholt Lodge	Staffs	SK1620	52°46·9'	1°45·4'W	X	128
Shericles Fm	Leic	SK4602	52°37·1'	1°18·8'W	FM	140
Sheriffcleuch Burn	S Lanak	NS7920	55°27·8'	3°54·4'W	W	71
Sheriffcleugh	S Lanak	NS8021	55°28·3'	3°53·5'W	X	71,72
Sheriff Fm	Brad	SE1239	53°51·1'	1°48·6'W	FM	104
Sheriff Fms	W Susx	TQ3629	51°2·9'	0°3·2'W	FM	187,198
Sheriffhales Common	Shrops	SJ7712	52°42·5'	2°20·0'W	X	127
Sheriff Hall	E Loth	NT5681	56°1·4'	2°41·9'W	X	67
Sheriffhall	Midlo	NT3167	55°53·7'	3°5·8'W	X	66
Sheriffhall Mains	Midlo	NT3268	55°54·3'	3°4·8'W	X	66
Sheriff Hill	Ghead	NZ2660	54°56·3'	1°35·2'W	T	88
Sheriff Hutton	N Yks	SE6566	54°5·4'	1°0·0'W	T	100
Sheriff Hutton Carr	N Yks	SE6667	54°5·9'	0°59·0'W	X	100
Sherifflatts	S Lanak	NS9737	55°37·2'	3°37·7'W	X	72
Sheriffmuir	Moray	NJ3052	57°33·4'	3°9·7'W	X	28
Sheriff Muir	Stir	NN8202	56°12·0'	3°53·7'W	X	57
Sheriff Park	Cumbr	NY5521	54°35·2'	2°41·4'W	X	90
Sheriff's Common	N Ayr	NS1656	55°46·0'	4°55·5'W	X	63
Sheriffs Court	Kent	TR2964	51°20·0'	1°17·6'E	X	179
Sheriffseat	Aberd	NJ6257	57°36·3'	2°37·7'W	X	29
Sheriff's Fm	Lincs	TF2958	53°6·4'	0°4·0'W	FM	122
Sheriffside	E Loth	NT5567	55°53·9'	2°42·7'W	X	66
Sheriff's Lench	Worcs	SP0149	52°8·6'	1°58·7'W	T	150
Sheriff's Lench Fm	Worcs	SP0248	52°8·1'	1°57·9'W	FM	150
Sheriff's Port	N Ayr	NS1555	55°45·4'	4°56·5'W	W	63
Sheriffs Stone	Northum	NY9047	54°49·3'	2°8·9'W	X	87
Sheriffston	Moray	NJ2561	57°38·2'	3°14·9'W	X	28
Sheriffyards Ho	Clackm	NS9294	56°7·8'	3°43·8'W	X	58
Sherill	Devon	SX3879	50°35·5'	4°17·0'W	X	201
Sheringham	Norf	TG1543	52°56·7'	1°12·4'E	T	133
Sheringham Hall	Norf	TG1342	52°56·2'	1°10·6'E	X	133
Sheringham Park	Norf	TG1341	52°55·7'	1°10·5'E	X	133
Sherington	Mil Key	SP8846	52°6·5'	0°42·5'W	T	152
Sherington Br	Mil Key	SP8845	52°6·0'	0°42·5'W	X	152
Sheringwood	Norf	TG1641	52°55·6'	1°13·2'E	T	133
Sherman Bridge	E Susx	TQ5305	50°49·7'	0°10·7'E	X	199
Shermanbury	W Susx	TQ2019	50°57·7'	0°17·1'W	T	198
Shermanbury Grange	W Susx	TQ2019	50°57·7'	0°17·1'W	X	198
Shermanbury Place	W Susx	TQ2118	50°57·1'	0°16·3'W	X	198
Shermans Fm	Devon	SY1297	50°46·2'	3°14·5'W	FM	192,193
Shernal Green	Worcs	SO9161	52°15·1'	2°7·5'W	T	150
Shernborne	Norf	TF7132	52°51·7'	0°32·8'E	T	132
Shernborne Hall	Norf	TF7032	52°51·7'	0°31·9'E	A	132
Shernden Fm	Kent	TQ4443	51°10·3'	0°4·0'E	FM	187
Shernden Wood	Kent	TQ4442	51°9·8'	0°4·0'E	F	187
Shernfold Park	E Susx	TQ5934	51°5·2'	0°16·6'E	X	188
Shernick	Corn	SS2704	50°48·8'	4°27·0'W	X	190
Sherrabeg	Highld	NN5693	57°0·6'	4°21·8'W	X	35
Sherracombe	Devon	SS7135	51°6·2'	3°50·2'W	X	180
Sherra Law	Scot Bord	NT2944	55°41·3'	3°7·3'W	H	73
Sherramore	Highld	NN5593	57°0·6'	4°22·8'W	X	35
Sherramore Forest	Highld	NN4997	57°2·6'	4°28·9'W	X	34
Sherramore Forest	Highld	NN5397	57°2·7'	4°24·9'W	X	35
Sherrard's Green	Worcs	SO7946	52°7·0'	2°18·0'W	T	150
Sherrardspark	Herts	TL2313	51°48·4'	0°12·6'W	T	166
Sherraside Rig	Scot Bord	NT1525	55°30·9'	3°20·3'W	H	72
Sherratt's Wood	Staffs	SJ9834	52°54·4'	2°1·4'W	F	127
Sherrell Fm	Devon	SX6257	50°24·0'	3°56·1'W	FM	202
Sherrerdspark Wood	Herts	TL2313	51°48·4'	0°12·6'W	F	166
Sherricliffe Fm	Leic	SK7930	52°51·9'	0°49·2'W	FM	129
Sherriff Faulds	S Lanak	NS6952	55°44·9'	4°4·8'W	X	64
Sherriffhales	Shrops	SJ7512	52°42·5'	2°21·8'W	T	127
Sherriffhales Manor	Shrops	SJ7512	52°42·5'	2°21·8'W	X	127
Sherriff Hutton Ings	N Yks	SE6567	54°5·9'	0°59·9'W	X	100
Sherrifford Cott	S Lanak	NS9340	55°38·8'	3°41·6'W	X	71,72
Sherriff's Fm	Heref	SO3458	52°13·2'	2°57·6'W	FM	148,149
Sherriffton	Pth & Kin	NO1027	56°25·9'	3°27·1'W	X	53,58
Sherriff Wood	Derby	SK2378	53°18·1'	1°38·9'W	F	119
Sherrington	Wilts	ST9639	51°9·2'	2°3·0'W	T	184
Sherrington Down	Wilts	ST9437	51°8·2'	2°4·8'W	X	184
Sherrington Manor	E Susx	TQ5007	50°50·8'	0°8·2'E	X	199
Sherrow-Booth	Ches	SJ9578	53°18·2'	2°4·1'W	X	118
Sherrycombe	Devon	SS6048	51°13·1'	3°59·9'W	X	180
Sherry Geo	Orkney	HY6034	59°11·7'	2°41·5'W	X	5,6
Sherry Gill	Cumbr	NY5309	54°28·7'	2°43·1'W	W	90
Sherston	Wilts	ST8585	51°34·1'	2°12·6'W	T	173
Shervage Wood	Somer	ST1640	51°9·4'	3°11·7'W	F	181
Sherwell	Devon	SX6774	50°33·3'	3°52·3'W	X	191
Sherwell Fm	Corn	SX3871	50°31·2'	4°16·7'W	FM	201
Sherwin's Fm	Essex	TL9515	51°48·2'	0°50·1'E	FM	168
Sherwood	C of Nott	SK5743	52°59·1'	1°8·7'W	T	129
Sherwood	Devon	SX8596	50°45·4'	3°37·4'W	X	191
Sherwood Bank	Shrops	SJ5324	52°48·9'	2°41·4'W	X	126
Sherwood Cottages	Midlo	NT3164	55°52·1'	3°5·7'W	X	66
Sherwood Fm	Devon	SY0999	50°47·2'	3°17·1'W	FM	192
Sherwood Forest	Notts	SK6062	53°9·3'	1°5·8'W	F	120
Sherwood Forest Country Park	Notts	SK6167	53°12·0'	1°4·8'W	X	120
Sherwood Green	Devon	SS5520	50°57·9'	4°3·5'W	T	180
Sherwood Ho	N Yks	SD8168	54°6·7'	2°17·0'W	X	98
Sherwood Lodge	Notts	SK5750	53°2·9'	1°8·6'W	X	120
Sherwood Park	Kent	TQ6040	51°8·4'	0°17·6'E	T	188
Sherwood Pines Forest Park	Notts	SK6162	53°9·3'	1°4·9'W	F	120
Sherwood Rough	W Susx	SU9909	50°52·5'	0°35·2'W	F	197
Sherwoods	Hants	SU7457	51°18·7'	0°55·9'W	X	175,186
Shesgnan	Highld	NN4395	57°1·4'	4°34·7'W	X	34
Shesgnan Burn	Highld	NN4295	57°1·4'	4°35·7'W	W	34
Shetfields	Shrops	SO6075	52°22·5'	2°34·9'W	X	138
Shethin	Aberd	NJ8832	57°23·0'	2°11·5'W	X	30
Shetland Islands	Shetld	HU4167	60°23·4'	1°14·9'W	X	2,3
Shettleston	C of Glas	NS6463	55°50·7'	4°9·9'W	T	64
Shetton Fm	Heref	SO4444	52°5·7'	2°52·2'W	FM	148,149,161
Sheuchan	D & G	NX1161	54°54·7'	4°56·5'W	X	82
Sheuchan Craig	D & G	NX4274	55°2·4'	4°27·9'W	X	77
Sheuchan Hill	D & G	NX1262	54°55·3'	4°55·6'W	F	82
Shevado	Aberd	NJ9049	57°32·1'	2°9·6'W	X	30
Shevington	Wigan	SD5408	53°34·2'	2°41·3'W	T	108
Shevington Moor	Wigan	SD5410	53°35·3'	2°41·3'W	T	108
Shevington Vale	Wigan	SD5309	53°34·8'	2°42·2'W	T	108
Sheviock	Corn	SX3755	50°22·6'	4°17·2'W	T	201
Sheviock Wood	Corn	SX3756	50°23·1'	4°17·2'W	F	201
Shevock,The	Aberd	NJ5830	57°21·8'	2°41·4'W	W	29,37
Shewalton	N Ayr	NS3336	55°35·6'	4°37·8'W	T	70
Shewalton Moss	N Ayr	NS3435	55°35·1'	4°37·6'W	X	70
Shewel Wood	Glos	SO9810	51°47·6'	2°1·3'W	F	163
Shewglie	Highld	NH4129	57°19·7'	4°38·0'W	X	26
Shewglie Wood	Highld	NH4128	57°19·2'	4°38·0'W	F	26
Shewhill Barn	Glos	SP1118	51°51·9'	1°50·0'W	X	163
Shewington	Midlo	NT2860	55°49·9'	3°8·5'W	X	66
Shewte	Devon	SX7979	50°36·1'	3°42·2'W	X	191
Sheylors Fm	Wilts	ST8067	51°24·3'	2°16·9'W	FM	173
Shiaba	Arg & Bt	NM4319	56°17·9'	6°8·8'W	X	48
Shian	Arg & Bt	NM2623	56°19·5'	6°25·5'W	X	48
Shian	Arg & Bt	NR5387	56°1·0'	5°57·4'W	X	61
Shian	Stir	NS5589	56°4·6'	4°19·3'W	X	57
Shianbank	Pth & Kin	NO1527	56°25·9'	3°22·3'W	X	53,58
Shian Bay	Arg & Bt	NR5287	56°1·0'	5°58·3'W	W	61
Shian Burn	Pth & Kin	NN8440	56°32·5'	3°52·7'W	W	52
Shian Hillock	Highld	NH9149	57°31·3'	3°48·7'W	A	27
Shian Island	Arg & Bt	NR5288	56°1·5'	5°58·4'W	X	61
Shian of Tulisk	Moray	NJ1545	57°29·5'	3°24·6'W	X	28
Shian River	Arg & Bt	NR5486	56°0·5'	5°56·3'W	W	61
Shiant Islands or Na h-Eileanan Mòra	N Eil	NG4297	57°53·5'	6°20·7'W	X	14
Shiaram Mór	N Eil	NB1036	58°13·3'	6°55·9'W	X	13
Shibden Dale	Cald	SE1027	53°44·6'	1°50·5'W	X	104
Shibden Hall	Cald	SE1025	53°43·5'	1°50·5'W	A	104
Shibden Head	Brad	SE0929	53°45·7'	1°51·4'W	T	104
Shibden Hill	Scot Bord	NT7319	55°28·1'	2°25·2'W	H	80
Shibhinis	N Eil	NF6261	57°31·0'	7°38·3'W	X	22
Shide	I of W	SZ5088	50°41·6'	1°17·1'W	T	196
Shidlaw	Northum	NT8038	55°38·4'	2°18·6'W	X	74
Shiel	Aberd	NJ2712	57°11·8'	3°12·0'W	X	37
Shiel	Aberd	NJ5510	57°11·0'	2°44·2'W	X	37
Shiel	Aberd	NJ6344	57°29·3'	2°36·6'W	X	29
Shiel	D & G	NX6179	55°5·4'	4°10·3'W	X	77
Shiel	D & G	NY2891	55°12·7'	3°7·5'W	X	79
Shiel	E Ayr	NS5625	55°30·1'	4°16·4'W	X	71
Shiel	Moray	NJ5351	57°33·1'	2°46·7'W	X	29
Shielbog	Aberd	NJ8322	57°17·6'	2°16·5'W	X	38
Shielbrae	Stir	NS7490	56°5·4'	4°1·1'W	X	57
Shielbrae	Stir	NS7589	56°4·9'	4°0·1'W	X	57
Shiel Bridge	Highld	NG9318	57°12·6'	5°25·2'W	T	33
Shiel Bridge	Highld	NM6768	56°45·0'	5°48·2'W	X	40
Shielburn	Aberd	NJ6745	57°29·9'	2°32·6'W	X	29
Shiel Burn	D & G	NX4373	55°1·9'	4°27·0'W	W	77
Shiel Burn	D & G	NX6698	55°15·7'	4°6·1'W	W	77
Shiel Burn	D & G	NY2893	55°13·8'	3°7·5'W	W	79
Shielburn	Moray	NJ4661	57°38·4'	2°53·8'W	X	28,29
Shiel Burn	Moray	NJ5251	57°33·1'	2°47·7'W	W	29
Shiel Burn	Scot Bord	NT3746	55°42·5'	2°59·7'W	W	73
Shiel Burn	S Lanak	NS8032	55°34·3'	3°53·8'W	W	71,72
Shiel Burn	S Lanak	NS9627	55°31·8'	3°38·4'W	W	72
Shiel Burn	S Lanak	NS9907	55°21·1'	3°35·1'W	W	78
Shiel Burn	Stir	NN3922	56°22·0'	4°35·9'W	W	50
Shiel Cleuch	S Lanak	NS9503	55°18·8'	3°38·8'W	X	78
Shielcleugh Edge	Northum	NT9217	55°27·1'	2°7·2'W	H	80
Shield	Cumbr	NY3058	54°55·0'	3°5·1'W	X	85
Shieldaig	Highld	NG8072	57°41·3'	5°41·0'W	T	19
Shieldaig	Highld	NG8153	57°31·1'	5°39·0'W	T	24
Shieldaig Forest	Highld	NG8565	57°37·7'	5°35·6'W	X	19,24
Shieldaig Island	Highld	NG8154	57°31·7'	5°39·0'W	X	24
Shieldbank	Fife	NT0193	56°7·4'	3°35·1'W	X	58
Shield Burn	D & G	NX7387	55°9·9'	3°59·2'W	W	77
Shield Burn	E Ayr	NS4712	55°22·9'	4°24·5'W	W	70
Shieldburn	S Lanak	NS6150	55°43·7'	4°12·4'W	X	64
Shield Burn	S Lanak	NS8923	55°29·5'	3°45·0'W	W	71,72
Shield Fm	Durham	NZ0449	54°50·4'	1°55·8'W	FM	87
Shield Green	Northum	NY9260	54°56·3'	2°7·1'W	X	87
Shield Green	Northum	NZ1992	55°13·6'	1°41·6'W	X	81
Shieldgreen	Scot Bord	NT2743	55°40·8'	3°9·2'W	X	73
Shieldhall	C of Glas	NS5365	55°51·6'	4°20·5'W	T	64
Shield Hall	Northum	NY9558	54°55·2'	2°4·3'W	X	87
Shield Head	Cumbr	NY4652	54°51·8'	2°50·1'W	X	86
Shieldhill	Cumbr	NY7442	54°46·6'	2°23·8'W	X	86,87
Shieldhill	D & G	NX9189	55°11·2'	3°42·3'W	X	78
Shieldhill	D & G	NY0385	55°9·2'	3°30·9'W	X	78
Shieldhill	E Renf	NS5149	55°42·9'	4°21·9'W	X	64
Shieldhill	Falk	NS8876	55°58·1'	3°47·2'W	X	65
Shieldhill	Falk	NS8976	55°58·1'	3°46·3'W	T	65
Shieldhill	S Lanak	NT0040	55°38·9'	3°34·9'W	T	72
Shield Hilltop	Cumbr	NY7442	54°46·6'	2°23·8'W	X	86,87
Shieldholm	S Lanak	NS8021	55°28·3'	3°53·5'W	X	71,72
Shield Knowe	D & G	NX9692	55°12·9'	3°37·6'W	H	78
Shield Mains	E Ayr	NS4319	55°26·6'	4°28·5'W	X	70
Shiel Dod	S Lanak	NS9403	55°18·8'	3°39·8'W	X	78
Shield on the Wall	Northum	NY7266	54°59·5'	2°25·8'W	X	86,87
Shield on the Wall	Northum	NY8270	55°1·7'	2°16·5'W	X	86,87
Shieldridge	Northum	NY8045	54°48·2'	2°18·2'W	X	86,87
Shield Rig	D & G	NX5481	55°6·4'	4°16·9'W	X	77
Shield Row	Durham	NZ2053	54°52·5'	1°40·9'W	T	88
Shieldrum Fm	Pth & Kin	NO1455	56°41·0'	3°23·8'W	FM	53
Shields	Aberd	NO8996	57°3·6'	2°10·4'W	X	38,45
Shields	N Lanak	NS8468	55°53·7'	3°50·9'W	X	65
Shields	Renf	NS3760	55°48·6'	4°35·6'W	X	63
Shields	S Ayr	NS3725	55°29·8'	4°34·4'W	X	70
Shields	S Lanak	NS8936	55°36·6'	3°45·3'W	X	71,72
Shields Burn	S Lanak	NS8937	55°37·1'	3°45·3'W	W	71,72
Shields Rig	S Lanak	NT0353	55°45·9'	3°32·3'W	X	65,72
Shields, The	Somer	ST5127	51°2·6'	2°41·6'W	F	183
Shields, The	Northum	NY9883	55°8·7'	2°1·5'W	X	81
Shield Tor	Devon	SS5246	51°11·9'	4°6·7'W	X	180
Shield Water	Cumbr	NY6840	54°45·5'	2°29·4'W	W	86,87
Shiel Dykes	Northum	NU1506	55°21·1'	1°45·4'W	X	81
Shieldykes Hill	D & G	NX7292	55°12·6'	4°0·3'W	X	77
Shielfield	Scot Bord	NT5151	55°45·2'	2°46·4'W	X	66,73
Shielfield Wood	Scot Bord	NT6037	55°37·7'	2°37·7'W	F	74
Shielfoot	Highld	NM6670	56°46·0'	5°49·3'W	T	40
Shielgreen	Cumbr	NY4368	55°0·4'	2°53·0'W	X	85
Shiel Head	D & G	NX8377	55°4·7'	3°49·5'W	X	84
Shielhill	Aberd	NK0752	57°33·7'	1°52·5'W	X	30
Shielhill	Angus	NO4236	56°31·0'	2°56·1'W	X	54
Shielhill	Angus	NO4257	56°42·3'	2°56·4'W	X	54
Shielhill	C of Aber	NJ9312	57°12·2'	2°6·5'W	X	38
Shiel Hill	D & G	NS7604	55°19·3'	3°56·8'W	H	78
Shiel Hill	D & G	NS7816	55°25·6'	3°55·2'W	X	71,78
Shiel Hill	D & G	NT0107	55°21·1'	3°33·3'W	X	78
Shiel Hill	D & G	NX2871	55°0·5'	4°41·0'W	X	76
Shiel Hill	D & G	NX1558	54°53·9'	4°19·0'W	X	83
Shiel Hill	D & G	NX6079	55°5·4'	4°11·2'W	X	77
Shiel Hill	D & G	NX6289	55°10·8'	4°9·6'W	X	77
Shiel Hill	D & G	NX8554	54°52·3'	3°47·1'W	H	84
Shiel Hill	D & G	NY2694	55°14·3'	3°9·4'W	H	79
Shielhill	Inverc	NS2472	55°54·8'	4°48·5'W	X	63
Shielhill	Northum	NZ0282	55°8·2'	1°57·7'W	X	81
Shielhill	Pth & Kin	NO1133	56°29·1'	3°26·3'W	X	53
Shiel Hill	S Ayr	NX1981	55°5·7'	4°49·8'W	X	76
Shiel Hill	S Ayr	NX4194	55°13·1'	4°29·5'W	H	77
Shielhill Br	Angus	NO4258	56°42·9'	2°56·4'W	X	54
Shielhope	Northum	NU0828	55°33·0'	1°52·0'W	X	75
Shielhope Burn	Scot Bord	NT1921	55°28·8'	3°16·5'W	W	72
Shielhope Head or Water Head	Scot Bord	NT1925	55°31·0'	3°16·5'W	H	72
Shielhope Hill	Scot Bord	NT2019	55°27·8'	3°15·5'W	X	79
Shielingmoss	D & G	NY4377	55°5·3'	2°53·1'W	X	85
Shieling of Saughs	Angus	NO3975	56°52·0'	2°59·6'W	X	44
Shieling, The	Highld	NH8914	57°12·5'	3°49·8'W	X	35,36
Shielin of Mark	Angus	NO3382	56°55·7'	3°5·6'W	X	44
Shiel Knowe	Scot Bord	NY5496	55°15·6'	2°43·0'W	X	79
Shielknowes	Falk	NS8272	55°55·9'	3°52·9'W	X	65
Shiel Loch	D & G	NS7303	55°18·5'	3°59·6'W	W	77
Shiellow Crags	Northum	NU0537	55°37·8'	1°54·8'W	X	75
Shiellow Wood	Northum	NU0537	55°37·8'	1°54·8'W	F	75
Shiells	Fife	NO2809	56°16·3'	3°9·3'W	X	59
Shiel Moss	D & G	NY2795	55°14·9'	3°8·5'W	X	79
Shiel Muir	Moray	NJ4761	57°38·4'	2°52·8'W	X	28,29
Shieloans	S Lanak	NS6236	55°36·1'	4°11·0'W	X	71

Shiel of Castlemaddie (Bothy)	D & G	NX5390	55°11·2′	4°18·1′W	X	77
Shiel of Glentanar	Aberd	NO4089	56°59·6′	2°58·8′W	X	44
Shielparks	Moray	NJ5451	57°33·1′	2°45·7′W	X	29
Shiel Rig	D & G	NT0105	55°20·0′	3°33·2′W	X	78
Shiel Rig	D & G	NX5964	54°57·3′	4°11·7′W	X	83
Shiel Rig	D & G	NY2794	55°14·3′	3°8·5′W	X	79
Shiel Rig	D & G	NY2798	55°16·5′	3°8·5′W	H	79
Shiel Rig	E Ayr	NS6617	55°26·0′	4°6·6′W	X	71
Shiel Rig	E Ayr	NX4694	55°13·2′	4°24·8′W	X	77
Shiels	Aberd	NJ9319	57°16·0′	2°6·5′W	X	38
Shiels	Aberd	NO7573	56°51·1′	2°24·1′W	X	45
Shiels	Falk	NS8584	56°2·4′	3°50·3′W	X	65
Shielshaugh	Scot Bord	NT4126	55°31·7′	2°55·6′W	X	73
Shiels Ho	Aberd	NJ9319	57°16·0′	2°6·5′W	X	38
Shielsknowe	Scot Bord	NT7111	55°23·8′	2°27·0′W	X	80
Shielstockbraes	Scot Bord	NT7523	55°30·3′	2°23·3′W	X	74
Shielswood	Scot Bord	NT4519	55°28·0′	2°51·8′W	X	79
Shielswood Loch	Scot Bord	NT4519	55°28·0′	2°51·8′W	W	79
Shielton	Highld	ND2050	58°26·1′	3°21·7′W	X	11,12
Shien Hill	Pth & Kin	NO1726	56°25·4′	3°20·3′W	X	53,58
Shierglas	Pth & Kin	NN8864	56°45·5′	3°49·5′W	T	43
Shifford	Oxon	SP3701	51°42·6′	1°27·5′W	X	164
Shifford Lock	Oxon	SP3701	51°42·6′	1°27·5′W	X	164
Shifford's Grange Fm	Staffs	SJ6935	52°54·9′	2°27·3′W	FM	127
Shifna-hir	Flint	SJ2266	53°11·4′	3°9·6′W	X	117
Shifnal	Shrops	SJ7407	52°39·8′	2°22·7′W	T	127
Shiggerland Loch	D & G	NX3183	55°7·0′	4°38·6′W	W	76
Shilbottle	Northum	NU1908	55°22·2′	1°41·6′W	T	81
Shilbottle Grange	Northum	NU2008	55°22·2′	1°40·6′W	T	81
Shilcott Wood	Oxon	SP3721	51°53·4′	1°27·3′W	F	164
Shildon	Durham	NZ2326	54°38·0′	1°38·2′W	T	93
Shildon	Northum	NY9651	54°51·5′	2°3·3′W	X	87
Shildon	Northum	NZ0268	55°0·6′	1°57·7′W	X	87
Shildonhill	Northum	NZ0366	54°59·6′	1°56·8′W	X	87
Shillahill	D & G	NY1080	55°6·6′	3°24·2′W	X	78
Shillakers Fm	Lincs	TF1617	52°44·5′	0°16·5′W	FM	130
Shilla Mill	Corn	SW9378	50°34·1′	4°55·0′W	X	200
Shillamill	Devon	SX4671	50°31·3′	4°10·0′W	X	201
Shillamill Lakes	Corn	SX1757	50°23·3′	4°34·1′W	W	201
Shilland Fm	Devon	SS3110	50°52·1′	4°23·7′W	FM	190
Shillay	N Eil	NF8891	57°48·3′	7°14·7′W	X	18
Shill Brook	Oxon	SP2706	51°45·4′	1°36·1′W	W	163
Shillett Wood	Somer	SS8545	51°11·8′	3°38·4′W	F	181
Shilley Green Fm	Herts	TL2023	51°53·8′	0°15·0′W	FM	166
Shilley Pool	Devon	SX6591	50°42·4′	3°54·3′W	W	191
Shillford	E Renf	NS4456	55°46·6′	4°28·8′W	T	64
Shill Hill	Glos	SP0116	51°50·8′	1°58·7′W	X	163
Shillhope Law	Northum	NT8709	55°22·7′	2°11·9′W	H	80
Shilling Cleuch	S Lanak	NS9618	55°26·9′	3°38·2′W	X	78
Shillingford	Devon	SS9823	51°0·1′	3°26·8′W	T	181
Shillingford	Oxon	SU5992	51°37·7′	1°8·5′W	T	164,174
Shillingford Abbot	Devon	SX9088	50°41·1′	3°33·0′W	T	192
Shillingford St George	Devon	SX9087	50°40·6′	3°33·0′W	T	192
Shillingham Manor	Corn	SX4057	50°23·7′	4°14·7′W	X	201
Shillinghill	Pth & Kin	NN7917	56°20·1′	3°57·0′W	X	57
Shillingland	D & G	NX7391	55°12·1′	3°59·3′W	X	77
Shillingland	D & G	NX7784	55°8·4′	3°55·3′W	X	78
Shillingland Hill	D & G	NX7392	55°12·6′	3°59·3′W	H	77
Shillingland Moor	D & G	NX7885	55°8·9′	3°54·4′W	X	78
Shillinglee Home Fm	W Susx	SU9632	51°5·0′	0°37·4′W	FM	186
Shillinglee Park	W Susx	SU9632	51°5·0′	0°37·4′W	A	186
Shillingridge Wood	Bucks	SU8288	51°35·3′	0°48·6′W	F	175
Shillingstone	Dorset	ST8211	50°54·1′	2°15·0′W	T	194
Shillingstone Hill	Dorset	ST8309	50°53·0′	2°14·1′W	X	194
Shillingstone Ho	Dorset	ST8210	50°53·6′	2°15·0′W	X	194
Shillington	Beds	TL1234	51°59·8′	0°21·7′W	T	153
Shillington Bury	Beds	TL1235	52°0·4′	0°21·7′W	X	153
Shillington Manor	Beds	TL1232	51°58·7′	0°21·8′W	X	166
Shilling Wood	Pth & Kin	NN7622	56°22·7′	4°0·0′W	F	51,52
Shillingworth	Renf	NS3864	55°50·8′	4°34·8′W	X	63
Shillmoor	Northum	NT8807	55°21·7′	2°10·9′W	T	80
Shill Moor	Northum	NT9415	55°26·0′	2°5·3′W	H	80
Shillochan	Highld	NH9323	57°17·4′	3°46·1′W	X	36
Shillofad	Aberd	NO7288	56°59·2′	2°27·2′W	H	45
Shillowhead Fm	S Lanak	NS9530	55°33·4′	3°39·4′W	FM	72
Shiloh	D & G	NY0591	55°12·5′	3°29·1′W	X	78
Shiloh Hall Fm	Stock	SK0089	53°24·1′	1°59·6′W	FM	110
Shilston Barton	Devon	SX6753	50°21·9′	3°51·8′W	X	202
Shilston Br	Devon	SX6753	50°21·9′	3°51·8′W	X	202
Shilstone	Devon	SS6000	50°47·2′	3°58·8′W	X	191
Shilstone	Devon	SS6524	51°0·2′	3°55·1′W	X	180
Shilstone	Devon	SS7646	51°12·2′	3°46·1′W	X	180
Shilstone	Devon	SX7090	50°41·9′	3°50·1′W	X	191
Shilstone Fm	Devon	SS6026	51°1·2′	3°59·4′W	FM	180
Shilstone Hill	Devon	SS7645	51°11·7′	3°46·1′W	X	180
Shilstone Tor	Devon	SX6590	50°41·9′	3°54·3′W	X	191
Shilton	Oxon	SP2608	51°46·4′	1°37·0′W	T	163
Shilton	Warw	SP4084	52°27·4′	1°24·3′W	T	140
Shilton Downs Fm	Oxon	SP2509	51°47·0′	1°37·9′W	FM	163
Shilton Fields Fm	Warw	SP4185	52°27·9′	1°23·4′W	FM	140
Shilton Lodge Fm	Warw	SP4285	52°27·9′	1°22·5′W	FM	140
Shilvinghampton	Dorset	SY6284	50°39·5′	2°31·9′W	X	194
Shilvington	Northum	NZ1581	55°7·6′	1°45·5′W	T	81
Shilvington Br	Northum	NZ1479	55°6·6′	1°46·4′W	X	88
Shilvington Burn	Northum	NZ1680	55°7·1′	1°44·5′W	W	81
Shimmings	W Susx	SU9821	50°59·0′	0°35·8′W	X	197
Shimpling	Norf	TM1583	52°24·4′	1°10·1′E	T	144,156
Shimpling	Suff	TL8651	52°7·8′	0°43·4′E	T	155
Shimpling Park Fm	Suff	TL8752	52°8·3′	0°44·4′E	FM	155
Shimpling Place	Norf	TM1583	52°24·4′	1°10·1′E	X	144,156
Shimpling Street	Suff	TL8752	52°8·3′	0°44·4′E	T	155
Shimplingthorne	Suff	TL8751	52°7·8′	0°44·3′E	X	155
Shinafoot	Pth & Kin	NN9613	56°18·1′	3°40·4′W	X	58
Shinagag	Pth & Kin	NN9567	56°47·2′	3°42·7′W	X	43
Shinborough	Essex	TL7430	51°56·7′	0°32·3′E	X	167
Shincliffe	Durham	NZ2940	54°45·5′	1°32·5′W	T	88
Shindry Fm	N Yks	SE1893	54°20·2′	1°43·0′W	FM	99
Shiney Row	Sund	NZ3252	54°51·9′	1°29·7′W	T	88
Shin Falls	Highld	NH5799	57°57·7′	4°24·5′W	W	21
Shinfield	Wok	SU7368	51°24·6′	0°56·6′W	T	175
Shinfield Court	Wok	SU7168	51°24·6′	0°58·4′W	X	175
Shinfield Grange	Wok	SU7468	51°24·6′	0°55·8′W	X	175
Shin Forest	Highld	NH5699	57°57·7′	4°25·6′W	F	21
Shinfur	Angus	NO4982	56°55·8′	2°49·8′W	X	44
Shingay	Cambs	TL3046	52°6·1′	0°5·7′W	T	153
Shingham	Norf	TF7605	52°37·1′	0°36·4′E	T	143
Shingle Barn	Kent	TQ7051	51°14·2′	0°26·5′E	X	188
Shinglebarn Wood	Surrey	TQ4246	51°12·0′	0°2·3′E	F	187
Shingle Fm	Suff	TM3562	52°12·6′	1°26·8′E	FM	156
Shingle Hall	Herts	TL4617	51°50·2′	0°7·5′E	X	167
Shingle Hall	Suff	TM4083	52°23·8′	1°32·1′E	X	156
Shingle Hall or Olives	Essex	TL6220	51°51·5′	0°21·5′E	X	167
Shinglehead Point	Essex	TL9910	51°45·4′	0°53·4′E	X	168
Shingle Ho	Suff	TM3084	52°24·6′	1°23·3′E	X	156
Shingle Street	Suff	TM3642	52°1·8′	1°26·8′E	T	169
Shingleton Fm	Kent	TR2852	51°13·5′	1°16·3′E	FM	179
Shingly Hill	Orkney	HY4328	59°8·4′	2°59·3′W	X	5,6
Shining Cliff Woods	Derby	SK3352	53°4·1′	1°30·0′W	F	119
Shining Clough	Derby	SK0998	53°29·0′	1°51·5′W	X	110
Shining Ford	Staffs	SK0663	53°10·1′	1°54·2′W	X	119
Shiningford Fm	Derby	SK2452	53°4·1′	1°38·1′W	FM	119
Shiningpool Moss	Scot Bord	NT7052	55°45·9′	2°28·3′W	X	67,74
Shining Tor	Ches	SJ9973	53°15·5′	2°0·5′W	H	118
Shining Tor	Derby	SK1454	53°5·2′	1°47·1′W	X	119
Shinmount	D & G	NX5584	55°8·0′	4°16·0′W	H	77
Shinnelhead	D & G	NX7299	55°16·4′	4°0·5′W	X	77
Shinnel Water	D & G	NS7100	55°16·9′	4°1·4′W	W	77
Shinnel Water	D & G	NX7993	55°13·2′	3°53·7′W	W	78
Shinner's Bridge	Devon	SX7862	50°26·9′	3°42·7′W	T	202
Shinnery	Highld	ND0756	58°29·2′	3°35·2′W	X	11,12
Shinness	Highld	NC5413	58°5·2′	4°28·1′W	X	16
Shinness Lodge	Highld	NC5314	58°5·7′	4°29·2′W	X	16
Shinni Mire	Shetld	HU3479	60°29·9′	1°22·4′W	X	2,3
Shinning Clough Moss	Derby	SK0997	53°28·4′	1°51·5′W	X	110
Shinniwers Dale	Shetld	HU4987	60°34·1′	1°5·9′W	X	1,2
Shinriggie	D & G	NX0966	54°57·4′	4°58·6′W	A	82
Shin, The	D & G	NY2888	55°11·1′	3°7·4′W	X	79
Shinvall	Highld	ND1644	58°22·8′	3°25·7′W	X	11,12
Shiny Brook	Kirk	SE0607	53°33·8′	1°54·2′W	W	110
Shipbourne	Kent	TQ5952	51°14·9′	0°17·1′E	T	188
Shipbourne Fm	W Susx	TQ0423	51°0·0′	0°30·7′W	FM	197
Shipbriggs	Pth & Kin	NO2324	56°24·4′	3°14·4′W	X	53,58
Shipbrookhill	Ches	SJ6771	53°14·3′	2°29·3′W	X	118
Ship Burial	Suff	TM2848	52°5·2′	1°20·1′E	A	169
Shipdham	Norf	TF9507	52°37·8′	0°53·3′E	T	144
Shipham	Somer	ST4457	51°18·8′	2°47·8′W	T	172,182
Shiphay	Torbay	SX8965	50°28·7′	3°33·5′W	T	202
Ship Hill	Surrey	SU9665	51°22·8′	0°36·8′W	X	175,176
Shiphorns	Scot Bord	NT2449	55°44·0′	3°12·2′W	X	73
Shiplake	Oxon	SU7678	51°30·0′	0°53·9′W	T	175
Shiplake Bottom	Oxon	SU7080	51°31·1′	0°59·1′W	T	175
Shiplake Hill	Oxon	SU7180	51°31·1′	0°58·2′W	X	175
Shiplake Ho	Oxon	SU7678	51°30·0′	0°53·9′W	X	175
Shiplake Row	Oxon	SU7578	51°30·0′	0°54·8′W	T	175
Shiplake Sta	Oxon	SU7779	51°30·5′	0°53·0′W	X	175
Shiplate	N Som	ST3556	51°18·2′	2°55·6′W	T	182
Shiplate Manor Fm	N Som	ST3556	51°18·2′	2°55·6′W	FM	182
Shiplate Slait	N Som	ST3657	51°18·7′	2°54·7′W	X	182
Shiplaw	Scot Bord	NT2349	55°44·0′	3°13·1′W	T	73
Shiplaw Burn	Scot Bord	NT2248	55°43·4′	3°14·1′W	W	73
Shiplett House Fm	N Som	ST3655	51°17·7′	2°54·7′W	FM	182
Shipley	Brad	SE1437	53°50·0′	1°46·8′W	T	104
Shipley	Derby	SK4445	53°0·3′	1°20·3′W	T	129
Shipley	Northum	NU1416	55°26·5′	1°46·3′W	X	81
Shipley	Shrops	SO8095	52°33·4′	2°17·3′W	T	138
Shipley	W Susx	TQ1421	50°58·9′	0°22·2′W	T	198
Shipley Bottom	Swin	SU2278	51°30·3′	1°40·6′W	X	174
Shipley Br	Devon	SX6862	50°26·8′	3°51·2′W	X	202
Shipley Bridge	Surrey	TQ3040	51°8·9′	0°8·1′W	T	187
Shipley Burn	Northum	NU1518	55°27·6′	1°45·3′W	W	81
Shipley Common	Derby	SK4543	52°59·2′	1°19·4′W	T	129
Shipley Country Park	Derby	SK4344	52°59·7′	1°21·2′W	X	129
Shipley Gate	Notts	NT4645	55°42·0′	2°51·1′W	T	129
Shipley Glen	Brad	SE1338	53°50·5′	1°47·7′W	F	104
Shipley High Moor	Brad	SE1136	53°49·5′	1°49·6′W	X	104
Shipley Hill	Leic	SK6213	52°42·9′	1°4·5′W	X	129
Shipley Hill	Northum	NU1419	55°28·1′	1°46·3′W	X	81
Shipley Hills	Kent	TQ6366	51°22·4′	0°20·9′E	X	177
Shipley Lane	Northum	NU1418	55°27·6′	1°46·3′W	X	81
Shipley Moat	Durham	NZ1133	54°41·8′	1°49·3′W	A	92
Shipleymoor	Northum	NU1317	55°27·0′	1°47·2′W	X	81
Shipley Moss	Durham	NZ1034	54°42·3′	1°50·3′W	X	92
Shipley Shiels	Northum	NY7789	55°11·9′	2°21·3′W	X	80
Shipley Smallburns	Northum	NU1418	55°27·6′	1°46·3′W	X	81
Shipley Tor	Devon	SX6863	50°27·4′	3°51·2′W	X	202
Shipley Wood	Northum	NU1517	55°27·0′	1°45·3′W	F	81
Shipload Bay	Devon	SS4227	51°1·2′	4°30·2′W	W	190
Shipman Head	I Scilly	SV8716	49°58·0′	6°21·5′W	X	203
Shipman Knotts	Cumbr	NY4706	54°27·0′	2°48·6′W	H	90
Shipmeadow	Suff	TM3889	52°27·0′	1°30·6′E	T	156
Shipmeadow	Suff	TM3890	52°27·6′	1°30·6′E	T	134
Shipmeadow Common	Suff	TM3788	52°26·5′	1°29·6′E	X	156
Shippards Chine	I of W	SZ3784	50°39·5′	1°28·2′W	X	196
Shippea Hill Fm	Cambs	TL6183	52°25·5′	0°22·5′E	FM	143
Shippea Hill Sta	Cambs	TL6484	52°26·0′	0°25·1′E	X	143
Shippen	Devon	SX6740	50°14·9′	3°51·6′W	X	202
Shippersea Bay	Durham	NZ4445	54°48·1′	1°18·5′W	W	88
Shipping	Pemb	SN1108	51°44·6′	4°43·9′W	T	158
Shipping Fm	Pemb	SM9506	51°43·2′	4°57·7′W	FM	157,158
Shippon	Oxon	SU4898	51°41·0′	1°17·9′W	T	164
Shiprods	W Susx	TQ2118	50°57·1′	0°16·3′W	X	198
Shiprods Fm	W Susx	TQ1128	51°2·7′	0°24·6′W	FM	187,198
Ship Stack	Shetld	HP6613	60°47·9′	0°46·7′W	X	1
Shipstal Point	Dorset	SY9888	50°41·7′	2°1·3′W	X	195
Shipston-on-Stour	Warw	SP2540	52°3·7′	1°37·7′W	T	151
Shipton	Bucks	SP7727	51°56·4′	0°52·4′W	T	165
Shipton	Glos	SP0318	51°51·9′	1°57·0′W	T	163
Shipton	N Yks	SE5558	54°1·1′	1°9·2′W	T	105
Shipton	Shrops	SO5691	52°31·1′	2°38·5′W	T	137,138
Shipton Barrow	Oxon	SP2615	51°50·2′	1°37·0′W	A	163
Shipton Bellinger	Hants	SU2345	51°12·5′	1°39·9′W	T	184
Shipton Court	Oxon	SP2717	51°51·3′	1°36·1′W	A	163
Shipton Dale	E Yorks	SE9050	53°56·5′	0°37·3′W	X	106
Shipton Gorge	Dorset	SY4991	50°43·2′	2°43·0′W	T	193,194
Shipton Grange	E Yorks	SE8441	53°51·7′	0°42·9′W	X	106
Shipton Grange	N Yks	SE5459	54°1·7′	1°10·1′W	X	105
Shipton Green	W Susx	SZ8099	50°47·3′	0°51·5′W	T	197
Shipton Hill	Dorset	SY5092	50°43·8′	2°42·1′W	H	194
Shipton Hill (Fort)	Dorset	SY5092	50°43·8′	2°42·1′W	A	194
Shipton Ho	Oxon	SP4716	51°50·7′	1°18·7′W	X	164
Shipton Lee	Bucks	SP7321	51°53·2′	0°56·0′W	X	165
Shipton Moor	N Yks	SE5459	54°1·7′	1°10·1′W	X	105
Shipton Moyne	Glos	ST8989	51°36·2′	2°9·1′W	T	173
Shipton Oliffe	Glos	SP0318	51°51·9′	1°57·0′W	T	163
Shipton-on-Cherwell	Oxon	SP4816	51°50·7′	1°17·8′W	T	164
Shipton Slade Fm	Oxon	SP4617	51°51·2′	1°19·5′W	FM	164
Shipton Solers	Glos	SP0318	51°51·9′	1°57·0′W	T	163
Shipton Sta	Oxon	SP2818	51°51·8′	1°35·2′W	X	163
Shiptonthorpe	E Yorks	SE8543	53°52·8′	0°42·0′W	T	106
Shipton under Wychwood	Oxon	SP2717	51°51·3′	1°36·1′W	T	163
Shipton Wood	Glos	ST9091	51°37·3′	2°8·3′W	F	163,173
Shiral	Carm	SN2639	52°1·6′	4°31·8′W	X	145
Shirburn	Oxon	SU6995	51°39·2′	0°59·8′W	T	165
Shirburn Castle	Oxon	SU6996	51°39·7′	0°59·7′W	X	165
Shirburn Hill	Oxon	SU7195	51°39·2′	0°58·0′W	X	165
Shirburn Lodge	Oxon	SU7194	51°38·6′	0°58·0′W	X	175
Shirburn Wood	Oxon	SU7194	51°38·6′	0°58·0′W	F	175
Shircombe	Somer	SS9331	51°4·3′	3°31·3′W	X	181
Shircombe Fm	Somer	SS8430	51°3·7′	3°38·9′W	FM	181
Shirdfold Fm	Ches	SJ9082	53°20·3′	2°8·6′W	FM	109
Shirdley Hill	Lancs	SD3512	53°36·3′	2°58·5′W	T	108
Shire	Cumbr	NY6135	54°42·8′	2°35·9′W	X	91
Shire Br	Notts	SK8248	53°1·6′	0°46·2′W	X	130
Shirebrook	Derby	SK5267	53°12·1′	1°12·9′W	T	120
Shire Brook	Sheff	SK4184	53°21·3′	1°22·6′W	W	111,120
Shirecliffe	Sheff	SK3490	53°24·6′	1°28·9′W	T	110,111
Shire Combe	Swan	SS5487	51°34·0′	4°6·0′W	X	159
Shire Ditch	Worcs	SO7640	52°3·7′	2°20·6′W	A	150
Shire Dyke	Notts	SK8148	53°1·6′	0°47·1′W	W	130
Shire Dyke	Notts	SK8451	53°3·2′	0°44·4′W	W	121
Shire End Ho	Pth & Kin	NO0909	56°16·1′	3°27·7′W	X	58
Shire Gate	Oxon	SP2104	51°44·3′	1°41·4′W	X	163
Shiregreen	Sheff	SK3692	53°25·7′	1°27·1′W	T	110,111
Shiregrove Br	Shrops	SO2499	52°35·3′	3°6·9′W	X	137
Shirehall	Shrops	SJ5012	52°42·4′	2°44·0′W	X	126
Shirehall	Suff	TL8563	52°14·3′	0°43·0′E	X	155
Shire Hall	Wok	SU7269	51°25·2′	0°57·5′W	X	175
Shirehall Moor	Corn	SX1058	50°23·7′	4°40·0′W	X	200
Shirehampton	C of Bris	ST5377	51°29·6′	2°40·2′W	T	172
Shirehampton Park	C of Bris	ST5477	51°29·6′	2°39·4′W	X	172
Shire Hill	Derby	SK0594	53°26·8′	1°55·1′W	H	110
Shire Hill Fm	Essex	TL5537	52°0·8′	0°15·9′E	FM	154
Shirehill Fm	S Glos	ST7876	51°29·2′	2°18·6′W	FM	172
Shire Hill Lodge	Northnts	TL0093	52°31·8′	0°31·1′W	X	141
Shire Horse Fm	N Yks	TA0098	54°22·3′	0°27·2′W	FM	101
Shirelane Fm	Herts	SP9307	51°45·5′	0°38·8′W	FM	165
Shiremoor	N Tyne	NZ3171	55°2·2′	1°30·5′W	T	88
Shirenewton	Monm	ST4793	51°38·2′	2°45·6′W	T	171,172
Shire Oak	Wals	SK0504	52°38·3′	1°55·2′W	T	139
Shireoaks	Derby	SK0783	53°20·9′	1°53·3′W	T	110
Shireoaks	Notts	SK5580	53°19·1′	1°10·1′W	T	111,120
Shire Oaks	N Yks	SE4845	53°54·2′	1°15·8′W	F	105
Shire Oaks Fm	N Yks	SE5066	54°5·5′	1°13·7′W	FM	100
Shireoaks Hill Fm	Notts	SK5471	53°14·2′	1°11·0′W	FM	120
Shire Rack	Dorset	ST9718	50°57·9′	2°2·2′W	X	184
Shireshead	Lancs	SD5051	53°57·4′	2°45·3′W	X	102
Shires Mill	Fife	NT0087	56°4·2′	3°35·9′W	T	65
Shires, The	N Yks	SE5267	54°6·0′	1°11·9′W	X	100
Shire Wood	Lincs	TF2861	53°8·1′	0°4·8′W	F	122
Shirewood Fm	Lincs	TF2962	53°8·6′	0°3·9′W	FM	122
Shirkley Hall	Staffs	SJ9259	53°7·9′	2°6·8′W	X	118
Shirkoak	Kent	TQ9436	51°5·6′	0°46·6′E	T	189
Shirland	Derby	SK3958	53°7·3′	1°24·6′W	T	119
Shirland Lodge	Derby	SK4057	53°6·8′	1°23·7′W	X	120
Shirlaw Pike	Northum	NU1003	55°19·5′	1°50·1′W	H	81
Shirlett	Shrops	SO6697	52°34·4′	2°29·7′W	T	138
Shirlett Common	Shrops	SO6598	52°35·0′	2°30·6′W	X	138
Shirlett High Park	Shrops	SO6698	52°35·0′	2°29·7′W	F	138
Shirley	C of Soton	SU4013	50°55·1′	1°25·5′W	T	196
Shirley	Croy	TQ3566	51°22·8′	0°3·2′W	T	177
Shirley	Derby	SK2141	52°58·2′	1°40·8′W	T	119,128
Shirley	Hants	SZ1798	50°47·1′	1°45·1′W	T	195
Shirley	Sol	SP1279	52°24·8′	1°49·0′W	T	139
Shirley	Staffs	SK0448	53°2·0′	1°56·0′W	X	119
Shirley Br	Derby	SK2143	52°59·3′	1°40·8′W	X	119,128
Shirley Brook	Derby	SK2141	52°58·2′	1°40·8′W	W	119,128
Shirley Common	Derby	SK2142	52°58·7′	1°40·8′W	X	119,128
Shirley Common	Hants	SZ1899	50°47·6′	1°44·3′W	X	195
Shirley Fm	Heref	SO3865	52°17·0′	2°54·1′W	FM	137,148,149
Shirley Fm	Kent	TQ9332	51°3·5′	0°45·6′E	FM	189
Shirley Heath	Sol	SP1177	52°23·7′	1°49·9′W	T	139
Shirley holms	Hants	SZ3098	50°47·1′	1°34·1′W	T	196
Shirley Lodge Fm	Derby	SK2041	52°58·2′	1°41·7′W	FM	119,128
Shirley Moor	Kent	TQ9332	51°3·5′	0°45·6′E	X	189
Shirley Oldpark Fm	Derby	SK1941	52°58·2′	1°42·6′W	FM	119,128
Shirley Park	Derby	SK2042	52°58·7′	1°41·7′W	X	119,128
Shirley Sta	Sol	SP1078	52°24·2′	1°50·8′W	X	139
Shirley Warren	C of Soton	SU3914	50°55·7′	1°26·3′W	T	196
Shirleywich	Staffs	SJ9825	52°49·6′	2°1·4′W	X	127
Shirley Wood	Donc	SE5611	53°35·8′	1°8·8′W	F	111
Shirl Heath	Heref	SO4359	52°13·8′	2°49·7′W	T	148,149
Shirlowe	Wrekin	SJ6016	52°44·6′	2°35·2′W	X	127
Shirmers	D & G	NX6574	55°2·8′	4°6·4′W	X	77,84
Shirmers Burn	D & G	NX6676	55°3·9′	4°5·5′W	W	77,84
Shirmers Moss	D & G	NX6575	55°3·3′	4°6·4′W	X	77,84
Shirne Hill	Warw	SP4353	52°10·6′	1°21·9′W	X	151
Shirralds	Moray	NJ5065	57°40·6′	2°49·8′W	X	29
Shirralds Wood	Moray	NJ5064	57°40·0′	2°49·8′W	F	29
Shirrall Fm	Staffs	SP1699	52°35·6′	1°45·4′W	FM	139

Shirrel	N Lanak	NS7361	55°49·8'	4°1·2'W	X	64
Shirrel Burn	N Lanak	NS7361	55°49·8'	4°1·2'W	W	64
Shirrell Heath	Hants	SU5714	50°55·6'	1°11·0'W	T	196
Shirrenden	Kent	TQ6940	51°8·3'	0°25·3'E	X	188
Shirva Fm	E Dunb	NS6975	55°57·3'	4°5·4'W	FM	64
Shirwell	Devon	SS5937	51°7·1'	4°0·5'W	T	180
Shiskine	N Ayr	NR9129	55°30·9'	5°18·2'W	T	68,69
Shi-Tennaji (School)	Suff	TL7170	52°18·3'	0°30·9'E	X	154
Shitlington Common	Northum	NY8081	55°7·6'	2°18·4'W	H	80
Shitlington Crags	Northum	NY8380	55°7·1'	2°15·6'W	X	80
Shitlington Hall	Northum	NY8280	55°7·1'	2°16·5'W	X	80
Shittleheugh	Northum	NY8694	55°14·6'	2°12·8'W	X	80
Shittlehope	Durham	NZ0038	54°44·5'	1°59·6'W	X	92
Shivery Knott	Cumbr	NY2815	54°31·8'	3°6·3'W	X	89,90
Shlatach Ho	Highld	NM8980	56°52·1'	5°27·3'W	X	40
Shoalgate Cross	Devon	SX6397	50°45·6'	3°56·2'W	X	191
Shoal Hill	Staffs	SJ9711	52°42·0'	2°2·3'W	H	127
Shoal Neck	I Scilly	SV8607	49°53·1'	6°21·9'W	W	203
Shoals Bank	Heref	SO3949	52°8·4'	2°53·1'W	X	148,149
Shoalstone Point	Torbay	SX9456	50°23·9'	3°29·1'W	X	202
Shobdon	Heref	SO3961	52°14·9'	2°53·2'W	T	137,148,149
Shobdon Marsh	Heref	SO4160	52°14·3'	2°51·4'W	X	137,148,149
Shobley	Hants	SU1806	50°51·4'	1°44·3'W	T	195
Shobnall	Staffs	SK2323	52°48·5'	1°39·1'W	T	128
Shobrooke	Devon	SS8600	50°47·5'	3°36·7'W	T	191
Shobrooke Fm	Devon	SS7504	50°49·6'	3°46·1'W	FM	191
Shobrooke Lake	Devon	SS8701	50°48·1'	3°35·8'W	W	192
Shobrooke Mill Fm	Devon	SS8600	50°47·5'	3°36·7'W	FM	191
Shobrooke Park	Devon	SS8501	50°48·1'	3°37·5'W	X	191
Shobrook Lake	Devon	SS8602	50°48·6'	3°36·7'W	W	191
Shoby	Leic	SK6820	52°46·6'	0°59·1'W	T	129
Shoby Lodge Fm	Leic	SK6819	52°46·1'	0°59·1'W	FM	129
Shoby Scholes	Leic	SK6720	52°46·6'	1°0·0'W	X	129
Shochie Burn	Pth & Kin	NO0231	56°27·9'	3°35·0'W	W	52,53
Shochie Burn	Pth & Kin	NO0729	56°26·9'	3°30·1'W	W	52,53,58
Shockendon	W Berks	SU5474	51°28·0'	1°13·0'W	X	174
Shockerwick Ho	Bath & NE Somer	ST8068	51°24·9'	2°16·9'W	X	173
Shocklach	Ches	SJ4349	53°2·4'	2°50·6'W	T	117
Shocklach Green	Ches	SJ4349	53°2·4'	2°50·6'W	T	117
Shocklach Hall	Ches	SJ4348	53°1·8'	2°50·6'W	X	117
Shodshill Mill	S Lanak	NS9448	55°43·1'	3°40·8'W	X	72
Shodshill Moss	S Lanak	NS9348	55°43·1'	3°41·8'W	X	72
Shoebury Common	Sou-on-Sea	TQ9184	51°31·6'	0°45·6'E	X	178
Shoebury Ness	Sou-on-Sea	TQ9383	51°31·0'	0°47·3'E	X	178
Shoeburyness	Sou-on-Sea	TQ9384	51°31·5'	0°47·3'E	T	178
Shoelands	Surrey	SU9147	51°13·1'	0°41·4'W	X	186
Shoelodge Reef	Devon	SX8237	50°13·5'	3°38·9'W	X	202
Shoemaker's Hill	Donc	SE5916	53°38·5'	1°6·0'W	X	111
Shoestanes	Scot Bord	NT3954	55°46·8'	2°57·9'W	X	66,73
Shoestanes Burn	Scot Bord	NT3954	55°46·8'	2°57·9'W	W	66,73
Shogmoor	Bucks	SU7989	51°35·9'	0°51·2'W	X	175
Sholach	Pth & Kin	NO1343	56°34·5'	3°24·5'W	X	53
Sholden	Kent	TR3552	51°13·3'	1°22·3'E	T	179
Sholden Downs	Kent	TR3552	51°13·3'	1°22·3'E	X	179
Sholebroke Lodge	Northnts	SP6944	52°5·6'	0°59·2'W	X	152
Sholford Fm	Somer	ST0229	51°3·4'	3°23·5'W	FM	181
Sholing	C of Soton	SU4511	50°54·0'	1°21·2'W	T	196
Sholing Common	C of Soton	SU4512	50°54·6'	1°21·2'W	T	196
Sholma Wick	Shetld	HU1662	60°20·8'	1°42·1'W	W	3
Sholtoquoy	Orkney	HY5321	59°4·7'	2°48·7'W	X	5,6
Sholver	Oldham	SD9507	53°33·8'	2°4·1'W	T	109
Shomere Pool	Shrops	SJ5007	52°39·7'	2°44·0'W	W	126
Shona Beag	Highld	NM6673	56°47·6'	5°49·5'W	X	40
Shonehouse Fm	Ches	SJ5355	53°5·7'	2°41·7'W	FM	117
Shonest Fm	I of M	SC4182	54°12·8'	4°25·9'W	FM	95
Shonks Brook	Essex	TL4907	51°44·7'	0°9·9'E	W	167
Shonk's Moat	Herts	TL4430	51°57·2'	0°6·1'E	A	167
Shon-Sheffrey's Resr	Blae Gw	SO1211	51°47·7'	3°16·2'W	W	161
Shoostran	Shetld	HU3041	60°9·4'	1°27·1'W	H	4
Shootash	Hants	SU3222	51°0·0'	1°32·3'W	T	185
Shooters Clough	Derby	SK0074	53°16·0'	1°59·6'W	X	119
Shooters Clough	Lancs	SD6558	54°1·3'	2°31·6'W	X	102,103
Shooters Hill	Glos	SP0304	51°44·3'	1°57·0'W	X	163
Shooters Hill	Gren	TQ4376	51°28·1'	0°3·9'E	T	177
Shooter's Hill	Northnts	SP9574	52°21·6'	0°35·9'W	X	141
Shooter's Hill	Shrops	SJ5025	52°49·5'	2°44·1'W	X	126
Shooter's Hill	Warw	SP4150	52°9·0'	1°23·6'W	X	151
Shooter's Hollow	Cambs	TL1767	52°17·5'	0°16·7'W	X	153
Shooter's Knoll	Shrops	SO4290	52°30·5'	2°50·9'W	X	137
Shooters Lea Fm	Derby	SK3164	53°10·6'	1°31·8'W	FM	119
Shooters Nab	Kirk	SE0610	53°35·4'	1°54·1'W	X	110
Shooters Pile	Lancs	SD5558	54°1·2'	2°40·8'W	X	102
Shootersway	Herts	SP9707	51°45·4'	0°35·3'W	T	165
Shootersway Fm	Herts	SP9608	51°46·0'	0°36·1'W	FM	165
Shootfield	Kent	TQ4757	51°17·8'	0°6·9'E	X	188
Shoot Hill	Shrops	SJ4112	52°42·4'	2°52·0'W	T	126
Shooting Butts Fm	Staffs	SK0217	52°45·3'	1°57·8'W	FM	128
Shooting House Hill	Cumbr	SD2681	54°13·4'	3°7·7'W	H	96,97
Shooting House Rigg	N Yks	NZ9002	54°24·6'	0°36·4'W	X	94
Shootlands	Surrey	TQ1345	51°11·8'	0°22·6'W	X	187
Shootrough	Shrops	SO4996	52°33·8'	2°44·7'W	X	137,138
Shoots, The	S Glos	ST5186	51°34·5'	2°42·0'W	X	172
Shoot Wood	Hants	SU2303	50°49·8'	1°40·0'W	X	195
Shop	Corn	SS2214	50°54·1'	4°31·5'W	T	190
Shop	Corn	SW8873	50°31·3'	4°59·1'W	T	200
Shop	Devon	SS3911	50°52·8'	4°16·9'W	T	190
Shop Corner	Suff	TM2034	51°57·9'	1°12·6'E	T	169
Shope Tree Scar	Cumbr	SD1672	54°8·5'	3°16·7'W	X	96
Shop Fm	I of Angl	SH3181	53°18·2'	4°31·8'W	FM	114
Shop Fm	Suff	TM2255	52°9·1'	1°15·1'E	FM	156
Shopford	Cumbr	NY5674	55°3·8'	2°40·9'W	T	86
Shopham Br	W Susx	SU9818	50°57·4'	0°35·9'W	X	197
Shophouse Fm	Surrey	TQ0644	51°11·3'	0°28·6'W	FM	187
Shopland Hall	Essex	TQ8988	51°33·8'	0°44·0'E	X	178
Shopmoss Knowe	Cumbr	NY5974	55°3·8'	2°38·1'W	X	86
Shopnoller	Somer	ST1632	51°5·1'	3°11·6'W	H	181
Shopp Hill	W Susx	SU9328	51°2·9'	0°40·0'W	T	186,197
Shopwyke	W Susx	SU8805	50°50·5'	0°44·6'W	T	197
Shop-yr-onwy	Gwyn	SH9237	52°55·4'	3°36·0'W	X	125

Shoraclett	Orkney	HY5608	58°57·7'	2°45·4'W	X	6
Shoraidh	N Eil	NF8060	57°31·3'	7°20·3'W	X	22
Shorda Hellier	Shetld	HP6116	60°49·6'	0°52·2'W	X	1
Shordley Hall	Flint	SJ3258	53°7·1'	3°0·6'W	X	117
Shordley Manor	Flint	SJ3159	53°7·7'	3°1·5'W	X	117
Shore	Cald	SD9126	53°44·1'	2°7·8'W	T	103
Shore	Highld	NG8680	57°45·8'	5°35·4'W	X	19
Shore	Roch	SD9216	53°38·7'	2°6·8'W	T	109
Shore Bottom	Devon	ST2303	50°49·5'	3°5·2'W	T	192,193
Shoreditch	Hack	TQ3282	51°31·5'	0°5·4'W	T	176,177
Shoreditch	Somer	ST2422	50°59·8'	3°4·6'W	T	193
Shore Fm	Essex	TM1732	51°56·9'	1°9·9'E	FM	168,169
Shoregill	Cumbr	NY7701	54°24·5'	2°20·8'W	T	91
Shore Hall	Essex	TL6736	52°0·1'	0°26·4'E	X	154
Shore Hall	Roch	SD9217	53°39·2'	2°6·9'W	X	109
Shoreham	E Susx	TQ7823	50°59·0'	0°32·5'E	X	199
Shoreham	Kent	TQ5161	51°19·9'	0°10·4'E	T	177,188
Shoreham Beach	W Susx	TQ2204	50°49·6'	0°15·7'W	T	198
Shoreham-By-Sea	W Susx	TQ2203	50°49·0'	0°15·7'W	T	198
Shore Hill	Shetld	HP5702	60°42·1'	0°56·8'W	H	1
Shorelands	Highld	ND3653	58°27·9'	3°5·3'W	X	12
Shore Mill	Highld	NH7565	57°39·7'	4°5·2'W	X	21,27
Shore Moor	Roch	SD9219	53°40·3'	2°6·9'W	X	109
Shore Plantn	D & G	NX6745	54°47·2'	4°4·7'W	F	83,84
Shoresdean	Northum	NT9546	55°42·7'	2°4·3'W	T	74,75
Shores Green	Oxon	SP3709	51°46·9'	1°27·4'W	T	164
Shoreside	Shetld	HU2847	60°12·6'	1°29·2'W	X	3
Shores, The	Shrops	SJ3117	52°45·0'	3°0·9'W	X	126
Shoreston Hall	Northum	NU2032	55°35·1'	1°40·5'W	X	75
Shoreswood	Northum	NT9346	55°42·7'	2°6·2'W	X	74,75
Shoreswood Hall	Northum	NT9546	55°42·7'	2°4·3'W	X	74,75
Shore, The	Fife	NO2318	56°21·1'	3°14·3'W	X	58
Shoreton	Highld	NH6162	57°37·9'	4°19·2'W	X	21
Shore Top Fm	Bury	SD7606	53°33·2'	2°21·3'W	FM	109
Shoretown	Highld	NH5959	57°36·2'	4°21·1'W	X	26
Shorkley Hill	N Yks	SD9063	54°4·0'	2°8·8'W	X	98
Shorland	Devon	SS6741	51°9·4'	3°53·7'W	X	180
Shorley	Hants	SU5726	51°2·1'	1°10·7'W	T	185
Shorley Copse	Hants	SU5827	51°2·6'	1°10·0'W	F	185
Shorn Cliff	Glos	ST5499	51°41·5'	2°39·5'W	X	162
Shorncliffe Camp	Kent	TR1935	51°4·6'	1°8·0'E	T	179,189
Shorncote	Glos	SU0296	51°40·0'	1°57·9'W	T	163
Shorndown Equine Clinic	Bucks	SP8127	51°56·4'	0°48·9'W	X	165
Shorne	Kent	TQ6971	51°25·0'	0°26·2'E	T	177,178
Shorne Marshes	Kent	TQ6974	51°26·6'	0°26·3'E	X	177,178
Shorne Ridgeway	Kent	TQ6970	51°24·5'	0°26·2'E	T	177,178
Shorne Wood (Country Park)	Kent	TQ6770	51°24·5'	0°24·5'E	F	177,178
Shorn Hill	Dorset	SY6387	50°41·1'	2°31·0'W	X	194
Shorn Hill	Hants	SU3315	50°56·2'	1°31·4'W	X	196
Shornhill	Leic	SK3407	52°39·8'	1°29·4'W	X	140
Shornhill Fm	Glos	SP0016	51°50·8'	1°59·6'W	FM	163
Shorston Fm	Corn	SS2617	50°55·8'	4°28·2'W	FM	190
Shortacombe	Devon	SS5841	51°9·3'	4°1·4'W	X	180
Shortacombe	Devon	SS7634	51°5·8'	3°45·9'W	X	180
Shortacombe	Devon	SX5286	50°39·5'	4°5·3'W	T	191,201
Shortacombe	Devon	SX7796	50°45·3'	3°44·2'W	X	191
Shortacres	Scot Bord	NT6724	55°30·8'	2°30·9'W	X	74
Shortacross	Corn	SX2957	50°23·5'	4°24·0'W	T	201
Shortbridge	E Susx	TQ4521	50°58·4'	0°4·3'E	T	198
Shortburn Fm	Devon	SX4178	50°35·0'	4°14·4'W	FM	201
Shortcleuch Water	S Lanak	NS9015	55°25·2'	3°43·8'W	W	71,78
Shortcombe Fm	Bath & NE Somer	ST5555	51°17·8'	2°38·3'W	FM	172,182
Short Cross	Dorset	ST5903	50°49·7'	2°34·5'W	X	194
Short Cross	Dudley	SO9684	52°27·5'	2°3·1'W	T	139
Short Cross	Powys	SJ2605	52°38·5'	3°5·2'W	X	126
Shortdale Fm	Cumbr	NY4058	54°55·0'	2°55·7'W	FM	85
Short Dam Level	Norf	TM4892	52°28·4'	1°39·5'E	X	134
Short Ditch	Powys	SO1874	52°21·7'	3°11·9'W	A	136,148
Short Drop Cave	Lancs	SD6778	54°12·0'	2°29·9'W	X	98
Shorteath Common	Hants	SU7736	51°7·3'	0°53·6'W	F	186
Short Edge	Derby	SK0578	53°18·2'	1°55·1'W	X	119
Shortengrove	Wilts	SU0633	51°6·0'	1°54·5'W	X	184
Shorter Cross	Devon	SX7359	50°25·3'	3°46·9'W	X	202
Short Ferry	Lincs	TF0971	53°13·7'	0°21·6'W	X	121
Shortfield Common	Surrey	SU8442	51°10·5'	0°47·5'W	T	186
Shortfields	Staffs	SJ7750	53°3·0'	2°20·2'W	X	118
Shortflatt	Northum	NZ0880	55°7·1'	1°52·0'W	X	81
Shortflatt Tower	Northum	NZ0781	55°7·6'	1°53·0'W	A	81
Shortgate	E Susx	TQ4915	50°55·1'	0°7·6'E	T	199
Short Gill	Cumbr	SD6784	54°15·3'	2°30·0'W	W	98
Short Green	Norf	TM0986	52°26·1'	1°4·9'E	T	144
Shortgrove	Essex	TL5235	51°59·8'	0°13·2'E	X	154
Shortgrove	Heref	SO5166	52°17·6'	2°42·7'W	X	137,138,149
Shortgrove Wood	Northnts	SP6041	52°4·1'	1°7·1'W	F	152
Short Guen	Shetld	HU6568	60°23·7'	0°48·7'W	X	2
Shorthampton	Oxon	SP3220	51°52·9'	1°31·7'W	T	164
Short Hazels	Derby	SK3319	52°46·3'	1°30·2'W	X	128
Short Heath	Birm	SP0992	52°31·8'	1°51·6'W	T	139
Short Heath	Derby	SK3014	52°43·6'	1°32·9'W	T	128
Shortheath	Hants	SU7736	51°7·3'	0°53·6'W	T	186
Shortheath	Surrey	SU8344	51°11·6'	0°48·3'W	T	186
Short Heath	Wals	SJ9700	52°36·1'	2°2·3'W	T	127,139
Shorthill	Shrops	SJ4208	52°40·2'	2°51·1'W	T	126
Shorthill Hagg	E Yorks	TA0138	53°49·9'	0°27·5'W	X	106,107
Shorthope	Scot Bord	NT2212	55°24·0'	3°13·5'W	X	79
Shortie Geo	Orkney	ND4286	58°45·7'	2°59·7'W	X	7
Short Island	Corn	SX0790	50°40·9'	4°43·5'W	X	190
Short Knowes	Northum	NY9478	55°6·0'	2°5·2'W	X	87
Shortland Copse	W Susx	SU9932	51°5·0'	0°34·8'W	F	186
Shortland Fm	Somer	ST5219	50°58·3'	2°40·6'W	FM	183
Shortlands	Brom	TQ3968	51°23·9'	0°0·3'E	T	177
Shortlands Plantn	E Yorks	SE8955	53°59·2'	0°38·1'W	F	106
Short Lane	E Yorks	TA1870	54°7·0'	0°11·3'W	X	101
Short Lane Fm	Norf	TF9640	52°55·5'	0°55·4'E	FM	132
Shortlanesend	Corn	SW8047	50°17·2'	5°4·9'W	T	204
Shortlees	E Ayr	NS4235	55°35·2'	4°30·0'W	T	70
Shortlick Hill	N Yks	SE1676	54°11·0'	1°44·9'W	X	99
Shortmoor	Devon	ST2204	50°50·1'	3°6·1'W	T	192,193

Shortmoor	Dorset	ST4801	50°48·6'	2°43·9'W	T	193
Short Moor	Northum	NY8975	55°4·4'	2°9·9'W	X	87
Short Moss Hags	N Yks	SD8397	54°22·3'	2°15·3'W	X	98
Shorton	Torbay	SX8862	50°27·1'	3°34·3'W	T	202
Short Reach	Medway	TQ7770	51°24·3'	0°33·1'E	W	178
Short Reach	Suff	TM4455	52°8·6'	1°34·4'E	W	156
Shortridge	Devon	SS6322	50°59·1'	3°56·7'W	X	180
Shortridge	Devon	SX7496	50°45·2'	3°46·8'W	X	191
Shortridge Fm	Devon	SS5424	51°0·0'	4°4·5'W	FM	180
Shortridge Fm	E Susx	TQ6927	51°1·3'	0°25·0'E	FM	188,199
Shortridge Hall	Northum	NU2407	55°21·6'	1°36·9'W	X	81
Shortrig	D & G	NY1674	55°3·5'	3°18·5'W	X	85
Shortrig	Falk	NS8373	55°56·4'	3°52·0'W	X	65
Shortroods	Renf	NS4765	55°51·5'	4°26·2'W	T	64
Short's Corner	Lincs	TF3152	53°3·2'	0°2·3'W	X	122
Short's Fm	Essex	TL6011	51°46·7'	0°19·6'E	FM	167
Shorts Fm	Kent	TQ8535	51°5·3'	0°38·9'E	FM	189
Short's Fm	Suff	TM1468	52°16·3'	1°8·6'E	FM	156
Shorts Green Fm	Dorset	ST8425	51°1·7'	2°13·3'W	FM	183
Shortstanding	Glos	SO5713	51°49·1'	2°37·0'W	T	162
Short Stile	Cumbr	NY4411	54°29·7'	2°51·5'W	X	90
Shortstown	Beds	TL0746	52°6·3'	0°25·9'W	T	153
Short Street	Wilts	ST8348	51°14·1'	2°14·2'W	T	183
Shortten Hall	N Yks	SE7677	54°11·2'	0°49·7'W	X	100
Short Trees	Norf	TF6824	52°47·5'	0°29·9'E	X	132
Shortwaite	N Yks	NZ7808	54°27·9'	0°47·4'W	X	94
Shortwood	Glos	ST8499	51°41·6'	2°13·5'W	T	162
Shortwood	Heref	SO5950	52°9·0'	2°35·6'W	X	149
Short Wood	Lincs	TF0977	53°17·0'	0°21·5'W	F	121
Short Wood	Northnts	SP7776	52°22·8'	0°51·7'W	F	141
Short Wood	Northnts	TL0191	52°30·7'	0°30·3'W	F	141
Short Wood	Northum	NZ0562	54°57·4'	1°54·9'W	F	87
Shortwood	S Glos	ST6775	51°28·6'	2°28·1'W	T	172
Short Wood	Shrops	SO3784	52°27·3'	2°55·2'W	F	137
Short Wood	Wrekin	SJ6509	52°40·9'	2°30·7'W	F	127
Shortwood Common	Devon	SY0583	50°38·6'	3°20·2'W	X	192
Shortwood Cottages	Staffs	SJ7936	52°55·5'	2°18·3'W	X	127
Shortwoodend	D & G	NT1307	55°21·2'	3°21·9'W	X	78
Shortwood Fm	Northnts	TL0496	52°33·3'	0°27·6'W	FM	141
Shortwood Fm	Notts	SK4941	52°58·1'	1°15·8'W	FM	129
Shortwood Fm	Notts	SK6965	53°10·9'	0°57·6'W	FM	120
Shortwood Fm	Somer	ST5146	51°12·9'	2°41·7'W	FM	182,183
Shortwood Fm	Staffs	SJ7936	52°55·5'	2°18·3'W	FM	127
Shortwood Fm	Worcs	SP0169	52°19·4'	1°58·7'W	FM	139
Shortwood Ho	Bath & NE Somer	ST5955	51°17·8'	2°34·9'W	X	172,182
Shortwood Ho	Northnts	SP7775	52°22·3'	0°51·7'W	X	141
Shortwood Lodge	S Glos	ST6876	51°29·2'	2°27·3'W	X	172
Shortwoods	Staffs	SK0037	52°56·1'	1°59·6'W	X	128
Shorwell	I of W	SZ4582	50°38·4'	1°21·4'W	T	196
Shoscombe	Bath & NE Somer	ST7156	51°18·4'	2°24·6'W	T	172
Shoscombe Vale	Bath & NE Somer	ST7156	51°18·4'	2°24·6'W	T	172
Shotatton	Shrops	SJ3622	52°47·7'	2°56·5'W	T	126
Shote Fm	Shrops	SO6376	52°23·1'	2°32·2'W	FM	138
Shotesham	Norf	TM2599	52°33·2'	1°19·5'E	T	134
Shotesham Park	Norf	TM2298	52°32·3'	1°16·8'E	X	134
Shot Fm	Essex	TQ7793	51°36·7'	0°33·8'E	FM	178
Shotford Hall	Norf	TM2582	52°23·6'	1°18·8'E	X	156
Shotford Heath	Suff	TM2481	52°23·1'	1°17·9'E	X	156
Shotgate	Essex	TQ7692	51°36·2'	0°32·9'E	T	178
Shothaugh	Northum	NZ1699	55°17·3'	1°44·5'W	X	81
Shotheids	Scot Bord	NT7119	55°28·1'	2°27·1'W	X	80
Shothole	Dorset	ST8506	50°51·4'	2°12·4'W	X	194
Shot Lathe	N Yks	NY8901	54°24·5'	2°9·7'W	X	91,92
Shotley	Northnts	SP9297	52°34·0'	0°38·2'W	T	141
Shotley	Suff	TM2335	51°58·3'	1°15·2'E	T	169
Shotley Bridge	Durham	NZ0852	54°52·0'	1°52·1'W	T	88
Shotleyfell Plantn	Northum	NZ0452	54°52·0'	1°55·8'W	F	87
Shotleyfield	Northum	NZ0653	54°52·5'	1°54·0'W	T	87
Shotley Gate	Suff	TM2433	51°57·2'	1°16·0'E	T	169
Shotley Grove	Durham	NZ0852	54°52·0'	1°52·1'W	X	88
Shotley Hall	Northum	NZ0852	54°52·0'	1°52·1'W	X	88
Shotley Hall	Suff	TM2336	51°58·9'	1°15·2'E	X	169
Shotley Marshes	Suff	TM2435	51°58·3'	1°16·1'E	X	169
Shotley Park	Durham	NZ0953	54°52·5'	1°51·2'W	X	88
Shotley Point	Suff	TM2534	51°57·8'	1°16·9'E	X	169
Shotlinn	S Lanak	NS7048	55°42·7'	4°3·7'W	X	64
Shot Moss	Cumbr	NY8219	54°34·2'	2°16·3'W	X	91,92
Shotover Hill	Oxon	SP5606	51°45·2'	1°10·9'W	H	164
Shotover Ho	Oxon	SP5806	51°45·2'	1°9·2'W	A	164
Shotover Plain	Oxon	SP5606	51°45·2'	1°10·9'W	X	164
Shotridge Wood	Oxon	SU7293	51°38·1'	0°57·2'W	F	175
Shot Rock	Northum	NZ4444	54°47·6'	1°18·5'W	X	88
Shotten	Shrops	SJ3413	52°42·9'	2°58·2'W	X	126
Shottenden	Kent	TR0454	51°15·1'	0°55·8'E	T	179,189
Shottenden Manor	Kent	TQ9946	51°10·9'	0°51·2'E	X	189
Shottermill	Surrey	SU8832	51°5·1'	0°44·2'W	T	186
Shotters Fm	Hants	SU7132	51°5·2'	0°58·8'W	FM	186
Shottery	Warw	SP1854	52°11·3'	1°43·8'W	T	151
Shottesbrooke Fm	Win & Maid	SU8478	51°29·9'	0°47·0'W	FM	175
Shottesbrooke Park	Win & Maid	SU8377	51°29·4'	0°47·9'W	X	175
Shotteswell	Warw	SP4245	52°6·3'	1°22·8'W	T	151
Shottisham	Suff	TM3144	52°3·0'	1°22·5'E	T	169
Shottisham Creek	Suff	TM3043	52°2·5'	1°21·6'E	W	169
Shottisham Hall	Suff	TM3143	52°2·5'	1°22·5'E	X	169
Shottle	Derby	SK3149	53°2·5'	1°31·9'W	T	119
Shottlegate	Derby	SK3247	53°1·4'	1°31·0'W	T	119,128
Shottle Hall	Derby	SK3047	53°1·4'	1°32·8'W	X	119,128
Shotton	Durham	NZ3625	54°37·4'	1°26·1'W	T	93
Shotton	Durham	NZ4139	54°44·9'	1°21·4'W	T	93
Shotton	Flint	SJ3068	53°12·5'	3°2·5'W	T	117
Shotton	Northum	NT8430	55°33·1'	2°14·8'W	X	74
Shotton	Northum	NZ2278	55°6·0'	1°38·9'W	T	88
Shotton Beck	Durham	NZ3625	54°37·4'	1°26·1'W	W	93
Shotton Colliery	Durham	NZ3940	54°45·4'	1°23·2'W	T	88
Shotton Grange	Northum	NZ2276	55°4·9'	1°38·9'W	X	88
Shotton Hall	Shrops	SJ4921	52°47·3'	2°45·3'W	X	126
Shotton Hill	Northum	NT8429	55°33·5'	2°14·8'W	H	74

Shotton Hill	N Yks	SE6598	54°22·6′	0°59·5′W	X	94,100
Shotton Moor	Durham	NZ1023	54°36·4′	1°50·3′W	X	92
Shotton Village	Durham	NZ3625	54°37·4′	1°26·1′W	A	93
Shotts	D & G	NX9091	55°12·3′	3°43·3′W	X	78
Shotts	N Ayr	NS3650	55°43·2′	4°36·2′W	X	63
Shotts	N Lanak	NS8760	55°49·5′	3°47·8′W	T	65
Shotts Burn	N Lanak	NS8062	55°50·4′	3°54·5′W	W	65
Shottsburn	N Lanak	NS8463	55°51·0′	3°50·7′W	X	65
Shotwick	Ches	SJ3371	53°14·2′	2°59·8′W	T	117
Shotwick Dale	Ches	SJ3472	53°14·7′	2°58·9′W	X	117
Shotwick Ho	Ches	SJ3570	53°13·6′	2°58·0′W	X	117
Shotwicklodge Fm	Ches	SJ3571	53°14·2′	2°58·0′W	FM	117
Shotwood Hill	Staffs	SK2228	52°51·2′	1°40·0′W	X	128
Shoughlaige-e-Caine	I of M	SC3187	54°15·3′	4°35·2′W	X	95
Shougle	Moray	NJ0855	57°34·8′	3°31·9′W	X	27
Shougle	Moray	NJ2155	57°35·0′	3°18·8′W	X	28
Shoulder	Moray	NJ2036	57°24·7′	3°19·4′W	X	28
Shoulder Hall	Essex	TQ6597	51°39·1′	0°23·5′E	X	167,177
Shoulder of Corlae	D & G	NX6796	55°14·7′	4°5·1′W	X	77
Shoulder of Lune	Lancs	SD3955	53°59·5′	2°55·4′W	X	102
Shoulder, The	Scot Bord	NY3599	55°17·1′	3°1·0′W	X	79
Shouldham	Norf	TF6708	52°38·9′	0°28·5′E	T	143
Shouldham Thorpe	Norf	TF6608	52°38·9′	0°27·6′E	T	143
Shouldham Warren	Norf	TF6710	52°39·9′	0°28·6′E	F	132,143
Shoulsbarrow Common	Devon	SS7039	51°8·4′	3°51·1′W	H	180
Shoulsbarrow Fm	Devon	SS6940	51°8·9′	3°52·0′W	FM	180
Shoulsbury Castle	Devon	SS7039	51°8·4′	3°51·1′W	A	180
Shoulthwaite Fm	Cumbr	NY2920	54°34·5′	3°5·5′W	FM	89,90
Shoulthwaite Gill	Cumbr	NY2919	54°33·9′	3°5·5′W	W	89,90
Shoulton	Worcs	SO8158	52°13·4′	2°16·3′W	T	150
Shout Scar	N Yks	SD7078	54°12·1′	2°27·2′W	X	98
Shovelboard	Renf	NS3869	55°53·5′	4°35·0′W	X	63
Shovel Down	Devon	SX6585	50°39·2′	3°54·2′W	H	191
Shovel Ho	Somer	ST2832	51°5·2′	3°1·3′W	X	182
Shovelstrode Fm	E Susx	TQ4237	51°7·1′	0°2·1′E	FM	187
Shovelstrode Manor	E Susx	TQ4238	51°7·6′	0°2·1′E	X	187
Shover's Green	E Susx	TQ6530	51°3·0′	0°21·6′E	T	188
Showborough Ho	Glos	SO9038	52°2·7′	2°8·4′W	X	150
Showbottom Belt	Glos	SP1612	51°48·6′	1°45·7′W	F	163
Show Burn	Cumbr	NY5372	55°2·7′	2°43·7′W	W	86
Showell Fm	Oxon	SP3529	51°57·7′	1°29·0′W	FM	164
Showell Fm	Wilts	ST9070	51°26·0′	2°8·2′W	FM	173
Showell Grange	Wrekin	SJ7224	52°49·0′	2°24·5′W	X	127
Showell Mill	Wrekin	SJ7124	52°49·0′	2°25·4′W	X	127
Showells	W Berks	SU4172	51°27·0′	1°24·2′W	X	174
Showells Fm	Oxon	SP3413	51°49·1′	1°30·0′W	FM	164
Showery Tor	Corn	SX1481	50°36·2′	4°37·3′W	X	200
Showle Court	Heref	SO6143	52°5·3′	2°33·8′W	X	149
Showley Fold	Lancs	SD6632	53°47·2′	2°30·6′W	X	103
Showley Hall	Lancs	SD6533	53°47·8′	2°31·5′W	X	102,103
Showside	Cumbr	NY7741	54°46·1′	2°21·0′W	X	86,87
Showsley Grounds	Northnts	SP7150	52°8·9′	0°57·3′W	X	152
Show, The	Cumbr	NY5371	55°2·1′	2°43·7′W	X	86
Shoyswell Manor	E Susx	TQ6927	51°1·3′	0°25·0′E	X	188,199
Shraleybrook	Staffs	SJ7849	53°2·5′	2°19·3′W	T	118
Shraley Ho	Staffs	SJ7749	53°2·5′	2°20·2′W	X	118
Shravedell Heath	Suff	TL7977	52°21·9′	0°38·1′E	X	144
Shrawardine	Shrops	SJ3915	52°44·0′	2°53·8′W	T	126
Shrawardine Castle	Shrops	SJ3916	52°44·5′	2°53·8′W	X	126
Shrawardine Castle	Shrops	SJ4015	52°44·0′	2°52·9′W	A	126
Shrawardine Pool	Shrops	SJ3916	52°44·5′	2°53·8′W	W	126
Shrawley	Worcs	SO8064	52°16·7′	2°17·2′W	T	138,150
Shrawley Wood	Worcs	SO8066	52°17·7′	2°17·2′W	F	138,150
Shrawley Wood Ho	Worcs	SO8065	52°17·2′	2°17·2′W	X	138,150
Shray Hill	Wrekin	SJ6519	52°46·3′	2°30·7′W	X	127
Shredicote Fm	Staffs	SJ8716	52°44·7′	2°11·2′W	FM	127
Shredicote Hall Fm	Staffs	SJ8716	52°44·7′	2°11·2′W	FM	127
Shreding Green	Bucks	TQ0281	51°31·3′	0°31·4′W	T	176
Shreen Water	Dorset	ST8129	51°3·8′	2°15·9′W	W	183
Shrewbridge Ho	Ches	SJ6450	53°3·0′	2°31·8′W	X	118
Shrewley	Warw	SP2167	52°18·3′	1°41·1′W	T	151
Shrewsbury	Shrops	SJ4912	52°42·4′	2°44·9′W	T	126
Shrewsbury Castle	Shrops	SJ4912	52°42·4′	2°44·9′W	A	126
Shrewton	Wilts	SU0643	51°11·4′	1°54·5′W	T	184
Shrewton Folly	Wilts	SU0948	51°14·1′	1°51·9′W	X	184
Shrewton Ho	Wilts	SU0744	51°11·9′	1°53·6′W	X	184
Shrewton Lodge	Wilts	SU0845	51°12·5′	1°52·7′W	X	184
Shride Fm	Somer	ST3832	51°5·3′	2°52·7′W	FM	182
Shrigley Hall Hotel	Ches	SJ9479	53°18·7′	2°5·0′W	X	118
Shrigley Park	Ches	SJ9479	53°18·7′	2°5·0′W	X	118
Shrigley Park Fm	Ches	SJ9480	53°19·3′	2°5·0′W	FM	109
Shrill Down	W Berks	SU4980	51°31·2′	1°17·2′W	X	174
Shrine Fm	Kent	TR1437	51°5·8′	1°3·8′E	FM	179,189
Shrine's Wood	Bucks	SP6941	52°4·0′	0°59·2′W	F	152
Shripney	W Susx	SU9302	50°48·8′	0°40·4′W	T	197
Shripney Manor	W Susx	SU9302	50°48·8′	0°40·4′W	A	197
Shrivenham	Oxon	SU2489	51°36·2′	1°38·8′W	T	174
Shrobb Lodge Fm	Northnts	SP7741	52°4·0′	0°52·2′W	FM	152
Shroner Hill Fm	Hants	SU5135	51°7·0′	1°15·9′W	FM	185
Shroner Wood	Hants	SU5135	51°7·0′	1°15·9′W	F	185
Shropham	Norf	TL9893	52°30·2′	0°55·4′E	T	144
Shropham Fen	Norf	TL9993	52°30·1′	0°56·3′E	X	144
Shropham Hall	Norf	TL9693	52°30·2′	0°53·7′E	X	144
Shropshire Fm	Shrops	SO7682	52°26·4′	2°20·8′W	FM	138
Shropshire Union Canal	Ches	SJ4365	53°11·0′	2°50·8′W	W	117
Shropshire Union Canal	Ches	SJ6447	53°1·4′	2°31·8′W	W	118
Shropshire Union Canal	Powys	SJ2511	52°41·7′	3°6·2′W	W	126
Shropshire Union Canal	Powys	SO1493	52°31·9′	3°15·7′W	W	136
Shropshire Union Canal	Shrops	SJ3325	52°49·3′	2°59·3′W	W	126
Shropshire Union Canal	Staffs	SJ8021	52°47·4′	2°17·4′W	W	127
Shropshire Union Canal (Llagollen Branch)	Ches	SJ5646	53°0·8′	2°38·9′W	W	117
Shropshire Union Canal (Llangollen Branch)	Denb	SJ2242	52°58·4′	3°9·3′W	W	117
Shropshire Union Canal Middlewich Branch	Ches	SJ6458	53°7·3′	2°31·9′W	W	118
Shropshire Way	Shrops	SJ5122	52°47·8′	2°43·2′W	X	126
Shropshire Way	Shrops	SO4779	52°24·6′	2°46·4′W	X	137,148
Shroton Lines	Dorset	ST8413	50°55·2′	2°13·3′W	X	194
Shroton or Iwerne Courtney	Dorset	ST8512	50°54·7′	2°12·4′W	T	194
Shrove Furlong Fm	Bucks	SP7506	51°45·1′	0°54·4′W	FM	165
Shrover	Hants	SU6712	50°54·4′	1°2·4′W	X	196
Shrubberies, The	Leic	SK3408	52°40·4′	1°29·4′W	X	128,140
Shrubbery Fm	Beds	TL0756	52°11·7′	0°25·7′W	FM	153
Shrubbery Fm	E Yorks	TA2621	53°40·5′	0°5·1′W	FM	107,113
Shrubbery Fm	Norf	TM1090	52°28·3′	1°5·9′E	FM	144
Shrubbery Fm	Suff	TM0369	52°17·1′	0°59·0′E	FM	155
Shrubbery Fm	Suff	TM2156	52°9·7′	1°14·3′E	FM	156
Shrubbery Fm	Suff	TM2656	52°9·6′	1°18·7′E	FM	156
Shrubbery Fm	Suff	TM3355	52°8·9′	1°24·7′E	FM	156
Shrubbery Fm	Wals	SP0699	52°35·6′	1°54·3′W	FM	139
Shrubbery, The	Lincs	TF1813	52°42·3′	0°14·8′W	X	130,142
Shrubbery, The	Norf	TF7009	52°39·4′	0°31·2′E	F	143
Shrubbery, The	Norf	TM1685	52°25·4′	1°11·0′E	F	144,156
Shrubbery, The	Suff	TM0577	52°21·4′	1°1·0′E	F	144
Shrubb Fm	E Susx	TQ6825	51°0·2′	0°24·1′E	FM	188,199
Shrubbs	Essex	TL5114	51°48·5′	0°11·8′E	X	167
Shrubbs Fm	Surrey	SU9662	51°21·2′	0°36·9′W	FM	175,176,186
Shrub End	Essex	TL9723	51°52·5′	0°52·1′E	T	168
Shrub Fm	Norf	TG1132	52°50·9′	1°8·4′E	FM	133
Shrub Fm	Suff	TL8854	52°9·4′	0°45·3′E	FM	155
Shrub Fm	Wilts	ST8376	51°29·2′	2°14·3′W	FM	173
Shrub Hill	Kent	TR1364	51°20·3′	1°3·9′E	X	179
Shrubhill	Stir	NN7400	56°10·8′	4°1·4′W	X	57
Shrubhill Fm	Norf	TL6688	52°28·1′	0°27·0′E	FM	143
Shrub Hill Sta	Worcs	SO8555	52°11·8′	2°12·8′W	X	150
Shrubland Ho	Cambs	TL5979	52°23·4′	0°20·6′E	X	143
Shrubland Park	Suff	TM1252	52°7·8′	1°6·2′E	X	155
Shrublands	Norf	TM0592	52°29·5′	1°1·6′E	X	144
Shrublands	W Susx	SU9218	50°57·5′	0°41·0′W	X	197
Shrublands Fm	Suff	TM3267	52°15·4′	1°24·4′E	FM	156
Shrublands, The	Norf	TM4792	52°28·4′	1°38·6′E	X	134
Shrub's Fm	Essex	TL8935	51°59·1′	0°45·5′E	FM	155
Shrubs Hill	Surrey	SU9667	51°23·9′	0°36·8′W	T	175,176
Shrubs Wood	Bucks	SP6924	51°54·8′	0°59·4′W	F	165
Shrubs Wood	Bucks	TQ0093	51°37·8′	0°32·9′W	F	176
Shrutherhill	S Lanak	NS7649	55°43·4′	3°58·0′W	T	64
Shuart	Kent	TR2667	51°21·6′	1°15·2′E	X	179
Shuckburgh Fm	Northnts	SP6778	52°24·0′	1°0·5′W	FM	141
Shuckburgh Park	Warw	SP4961	52°14·9′	1°16·5′W	X	151
Shuckers Fm	W Susx	TQ1824	51°0·4′	0°18·7′W	FM	198
Shucknall	Heref	SO5842	52°4·7′	2°36·4′W	T	149
Shucknall Hill	Heref	SO5943	52°5·3′	2°35·5′W	H	149
Shuckstone Fields Fm	Derby	SK3457	53°6·8′	1°29·1′W	FM	119
Shuckton Manor Ho	Derby	SK2643	52°59·3′	1°36·4′W	X	119,128
Shuduins	Shetld	HU2052	60°15·4′	1°37·8′W	X	3
Shudy Camps	Cambs	TL6144	52°4·5′	0°21·4′E	T	154
Shudy Camps Park	Cambs	TL6244	52°4·5′	0°22·2′E	X	154
Shufflesheeps	W Susx	SU8429	51°3·5′	0°47·7′W	X	186,197
Shugborough	Staffs	SJ9922	52°48·0′	2°0·5′W	A	127
Shugborough Park	Staffs	SJ9922	52°48·0′	2°0·5′W	X	127
Shukes Bank	Heref	SO4048	52°7·9′	2°52·2′W	X	148,149
Shulbrede Priory	W Susx	SU8729	51°3·5′	0°45·1′W	A	186,197
Shulishadermor	Highld	NG4743	57°24·7′	6°12·3′W	T	23
Shulista	Highld	NG4274	57°41·2′	6°19·3′W	T	23
Shull	Durham	NZ0833	54°41·8′	1°52·1′W	X	92
Shuma Court	N Ayr	NS1966	55°51·5′	4°53·1′W	X	63
Shumla Stane	Shetld	HU2354	60°16·4′	1°34·6′W	X	3
Shuna	Arg & Bt	NM7608	56°13·0′	5°36·3′W	X	55
Shuna Cott	Arg & Bt	NM7507	56°12·4′	5°37·2′W	X	55
Shuna Ho	Arg & Bt	NM7709	56°13·5′	5°35·4′W	X	55
Shuna Island	Arg & Bt	NM9149	56°35·4′	5°23·8′W	X	49
Shuna Little	Shetld	HU3154	60°16·4′	1°25·9′W	W	3
Shunan, The	Orkney	HY3019	59°3·4′	3°12·7′W	W	6
Shuna Point	Arg & Bt	NM7606	56°11·9′	5°36·2′W	X	55
Shuna Sound	Arg & Bt	NM7508	56°12·9′	5°37·3′W	W	55
Shùn Bheinn	Arg & Bt	NR4074	55°53·6′	6°9·1′W	X	60,61
Shundraw	Cumbr	NY3023	54°36·1′	3°4·6′W	X	90
Shunesley	Shrops	SO6779	52°24·7′	2°28·7′W	X	138
Shunner Howe	N Yks	SE7399	54°23·1′	0°52·1′W	A	94,100
Shunnies	Aberd	NJ6120	57°16·4′	2°38·3′W	X	37
Shun, The	Shetld	HU2981	60°31·0′	1°27·8′W	W	1,3
Shurdington	Glos	SO9218	51°51·9′	2°6·6′W	T	163
Shurdington Hill	Glos	SO9217	51°51·3′	2°6·6′W	X	163
Shure Taings	Shetld	HP6514	60°48·5′	0°47·8′W	X	1
Shurland	Kent	TQ9971	51°24·4′	0°52·1′E	A	178
Shurlock Row	Win & Maid	SU8374	51°27·8′	0°47·9′W	T	175
Shurnock	Worcs	SP0260	52°14·5′	1°57·8′W	T	150
Shurnock Court	Worcs	SP0260	52°14·5′	1°57·8′W	A	150
Shurrery	Highld	ND0357	58°29·7′	3°39·4′W	X	11,12
Shurrery Lodge	Highld	ND0356	58°29·2′	3°39·3′W	X	11,12
Shurton	Somer	ST2044	51°11·6′	3°8·3′W	T	182
Shushions Manor	Staffs	SJ8414	52°43·6′	2°13·8′W	X	127
Shustoke	Warw	SP2290	52°30·7′	1°40·1′W	T	139
Shustoke Resrs	Warw	SP2291	52°31·2′	1°40·1′W	W	139
Shute	Devon	SS8900	50°47·6′	3°34·1′W	T	192
Shute	Devon	SX4081	50°36·6′	4°15·3′W	X	201
Shute	Devon	SY2597	50°46·3′	3°3·4′W	T	192,193
Shute Cross	Devon	SX6858	50°24·7′	3°51·1′W	X	202
Shute End	Wilts	SU1728	51°3·3′	1°45·1′W	T	184
Shute Fm	Devon	SS9720	50°58·4′	3°27·6′W	FM	181
Shute Fm	Wilts	ST8441	51°10·3′	2°13·3′W	FM	183
Shute Fms	Somer	ST0229	51°3·4′	3°23·5′W	FM	181
Shute Hill	Devon	SY2598	50°46·8′	3°3·4′W	H	192,193
Shute Hill	Somer	ST0325	51°1·2′	3°22·6′W	H	181
Shute Ho	Devon	SY2596	50°45·8′	3°3·4′W	X	192,193
Shutelake	Devon	ST0204	50°49·9′	3°23·1′W	X	192
Shutelake Fm	Devon	SS9707	50°51·4′	3°27·4′W	FM	192
Shuteley Fm	Devon	SS5819	50°57·4′	4°0·9′W	FM	180
Shutes Fm	Devon	ST1208	50°52·1′	3°14·7′W	FM	192,193
Shute Shelve Hill	Somer	ST4255	51°17·7′	2°49·5′W	H	172,182
Shutford	Oxon	SP3840	52°3·7′	1°26·3′W	T	151
Shutford Grounds Fm	Oxon	SP3740	52°3·7′	1°27·2′W	FM	151
Shut Heath	Staffs	SJ8621	52°47·4′	2°12·1′W	T	127
Shuthonger	Glos	SO8835	52°1·0′	2°10·1′W	T	150
Shuthonger Common	Glos	SO8835	52°1·0′	2°10·1′W	X	150
Shutlanehead	Staffs	SJ8242	52°58·7′	2°15·7′W	X	118
Shutlanger	Northnts	SP7249	52°8·3′	0°56·5′W	T	152
Shutlanger Grove Fm	Northnts	SP7248	52°7·8′	0°56·5′W	FM	152
Shutley	Shrops	SO6779	52°24·7′	2°28·7′W	X	138
Shutlingsloe Fm	Ches	SJ9869	53°13·3′	2°1·4′W	FM	118
Shutta	Corn	SX2553	50°21·3′	4°27·2′W	T	201
Shutta	Corn	SX3673	50°32·3′	4°18·5′W	X	201
Shuttaford	Devon	SX7169	50°30·6′	3°48·8′W	X	202
Shuttamoor	Devon	SX8282	50°37·8′	3°39·7′W	X	191
Shutterdown Spinney	Northnts	SP7176	52°22·9′	0°57·0′W	F	141
Shutterflat	N Ayr	NS3954	55°45·4′	4°33·5′W	X	63
Shuttern Brook	Devon	SX8696	50°45·4′	3°36·6′W	W	191
Shuttern Brook	Devon	SX8797	50°45·9′	3°35·8′W	W	192
Shutteroaks	Somer	ST4311	50°54·0′	2°48·3′W	X	193
Shutter Shaw Fm	Staffs	SJ9257	53°6·8′	2°6·8′W	FM	118
Shutterton	Devon	SX9679	50°36·3′	3°27·8′W	X	192
Shutterton Br	Devon	SX9678	50°35·8′	3°27·8′W	X	192
Shutt Green	Staffs	SJ8709	52°41·0′	2°11·1′W	T	127
Shutt Ho	N Yks	SE2763	54°4·0′	1°34·8′W	X	99
Shuttington	Warw	SK2505	52°38·8′	1°37·4′W	T	140
Shuttington Br	Warw	SK2405	52°38·8′	1°38·3′W	X	139
Shuttington Fields Fm	Warw	SK2605	52°38·8′	1°36·5′W	FM	140
Shuttle Rake	Derby	SK1579	53°18·7′	1°46·1′W	X	119
Shuttlesfield	Kent	TR1841	51°7·8′	1°7·3′E	T	179,189
Shuttleton Fm	Devon	ST1211	50°53·7′	3°14·7′W	FM	192,193
Shuttlewood	Derby	SK4672	53°14·8′	1°18·2′W	T	120
Shuttlewood Common	Derby	SK4773	53°15·4′	1°17·3′W	X	120
Shuttlewood's Fm	Leic	SK6120	52°46·7′	1°5·3′W	FM	129
Shuttleworth	Bury	SD8017	53°39·2′	2°17·7′W	T	109
Shuttleworth Agricultural College	Beds	TL1444	52°5·2′	0°19·8′W	X	153
Shuttleworth Hall	Lancs	SD7832	53°47·3′	2°19·6′W	A	103
Shuttleworth Hall	Lancs	SD8248	53°55·9′	2°16·0′W	X	103
Shuttleworth Pasture	Lancs	SD9035	53°48·9′	2°8·7′W	X	103
Shutt Nook	N Yks	SE2657	54°0·7′	1°35·8′W	X	104
Shuttocks Hill	Heref	SO5065	52°17·1′	2°43·6′W	H	137,138,149
Shutton	Heref	SO6525	51°55·6′	2°30·1′W	T	162
Shutt's Copse	Hants	SU6326	51°2·0′	1°5·7′W	F	185
Shutwell	Warw	SP5056	52°12·2′	1°15·7′W	X	151
Shwt	Brig	SS8986	51°34·0′	3°35·7′W	T	170
Siabost	N Eil	NB2646	58°19·3′	6°40·3′W	T	8
Siabost bho Dheas	N Eil	NB2546	58°19·3′	6°41·3′W	T	8
Siabost bho Thuath	N Eil	NB2647	58°19·8′	6°40·4′W	T	8
Siadar	N Eil	NB3854	58°24·0′	6°28·6′W	T	8
Siadar Iarach	N Eil	NB3954	58°24·1′	6°27·6′W	T	8
Siadar Uarach	N Eil	NB3854	58°24·0′	6°28·6′W	T	8
Sialabhig Mòr	N Eil	NB5143	58°18·6′	6°14·6′W	W	8
Siambar-wen	Conwy	SH8059	53°7·1′	3°47·2′W	X	116
Siamber Wen	Denb	SJ0340	52°57·2′	3°26·2′W	X	125
Siamber Wen	Denb	SJ0679	53°18·2′	3°24·2′W	A	116
Siamber Wen	Flint	SJ1767	53°11·9′	3°14·1′W	X	116
Siambr-gerrig	Wrex	SJ1933	52°53·5′	3°11·8′W	X	125
Siambr Trawsfynydd	Powys	SN7992	52°31·0′	3°46·6′W	X	135
Siambr-wen	Denb	SJ0647	53°1·0′	3°23·7′W	X	116
Siambr-wen	Powys	SJ0723	52°48·0′	3°22·4′W	X	125
Siam Hall	Suff	TL9340	52°1·7′	0°49·2′E	X	155
Siaram Bosta	N Eil	NB1340	58°15·6′	6°53·1′W	X	13
Sibbaldbie	D & G	NY1487	55°10·4′	3°20·6′W	T	78
Sibbaldbieside	D & G	NY1387	55°10·4′	3°21·5′W	X	78
Sibberings Fm	Bolton	SD6110	53°35·4′	2°34·9′W	FM	109
Sibberscote Manor	Shrops	SJ4207	52°39·7′	2°51·1′W	X	126
Sibbersfield Hall	Ches	SJ4255	53°5·6′	2°51·6′W	X	117
Sibbertoft	Northnts	SP6882	52°26·1′	0°59·6′W	T	141
Sibberton Lodge	Peterb	TL0699	52°34·9′	0°25·7′W	X	142
Sibbies Geo	Orkney	HY5239	59°14·4′	2°50·0′W	X	5
Sibdon Carwood	Shrops	SO4183	52°26·7′	2°51·7′W	T	137
Sibdon Castle Fm	Shrops	SO4183	52°26·7′	2°51·7′W	FM	137
Sibdown Fm	I of W	SZ4984	50°39·4′	1°18·0′W	FM	196
Sibertswold or Shepherdswell	Kent	TR2547	51°10·9′	1°13·6′E	T	179
Sibford Ferris	Oxon	SP3537	52°2·1′	1°29·0′W	T	151
Sibford Gower	Oxon	SP3537	52°2·1′	1°29·0′W	T	151
Sibford Grounds Fm	Oxon	SP3636	52°1·5′	1°28·1′W	FM	151
Sibford Heath Fm	Oxon	SP3439	52°3·1′	1°29·9′W	FM	151
Sible Hedingham	Essex	TL7734	51°58·8′	0°35·0′E	T	155
Siblet's Wood	Bucks	SU9889	51°35·7′	0°34·7′W	F	175,176
Sibleys	Essex	TL5629	51°56·5′	0°16·6′E	X	167
Sibley's Green	Essex	TL6128	51°55·9′	0°20·9′E	T	167
Siblyback	Corn	SX2372	50°31·5′	4°29·5′W	X	201
Siblyback Lake (resr)	Corn	SX2370	50°30·4′	4°29·4′W	W	201
Siblyback Moor	Corn	SX2374	50°32·6′	4°29·5′W	X	201
Sibmister	Highld	ND1666	58°34·7′	3°26·2′W	X	11,12
Sibsey	Lincs	TF3550	53°2·0′	0°1·2′E	T	122
Sibsey Fen Side	Lincs	TF3452	53°3·1′	0°0·4′E	T	122
Sibson	Cambs	TL0997	52°33·8′	0°23·1′W	T	142
Sibson	Leic	SK3500	52°36·0′	1°28·6′W	T	140
Sibson Aerodrome	Cambs	TL0996	52°33·3′	0°23·1′W	X	142
Sibson Mill	Leic	SK3402	52°37·1′	1°29·5′W	X	140
Sibson Wolds	Leic	SK3603	52°37·6′	1°27·7′W	F	140
Sibster	Highld	ND1459	58°30·9′	3°28·1′W	X	11,12
Sibster	Highld	ND3252	58°27·3′	3°9·4′W	X	12
Sibsterburn	Highld	ND1458	58°30·4′	3°28·1′W	X	11,12
Sibthorpe	Notts	SK7645	53°0·1′	0°51·6′W	T	129
Sibthorpe Place	Notts	SK7273	53°15·2′	0°54·8′W	T	120
Sibton	Suff	TM3669	52°16·3′	1°28·0′E	T	156
Sibton Abbey	Suff	TM3569	52°16·4′	1°27·1′E	X	156
Sibton Green	Suff	TM3771	52°17·4′	1°28·9′E	X	156
Sibton Park	Suff	TM3770	52°16·8′	1°28·9′E	X	156
Sibton Park (School)	Kent	TR1541	51°7·9′	1°4·8′E	X	179,189
Sibton Wood	Kent	TR1442	51°8·5′	1°4·0′E	F	179,189
Siccar Point	Scot Bord	NT8171	55°56·2′	2°17·8′W	X	67
Sicey Fm	E Yorks	TA0836	53°48·8′	0°21·2′W	FM	107
Sicily Oak Fm	Ches	SJ5452	53°4·0′	2°40·8′W	FM	117
Sickergill	Cumbr	NY5942	54°46·5′	2°37·8′W	X	86
Sickers Fell	Cumbr	SD6793	54°20·1′	2°30·0′W	X	98
Sicklebit Wood	N Yks	SE5639	53°50·9′	1°8·5′W	F	105
Sicklebrook Fm	Derby	SK3779	53°18·6′	1°26·3′W	FM	119
Sickle Croft	Donc	SE5910	53°35·2′	1°6·1′W	X	111
Sicklesmere	Suff	TL8760	52°12·6′	0°44·6′E	T	155
Sicklinghall	N Yks	SE3648	53°55·9′	1°26·7′W	T	104
Sicklinghall Ho	N Yks	SE3647	53°55·3′	1°26·7′W	X	104
Sid	Devon	SY1388	50°41·3′	3°13·5′W	T	192

Sid Abbey	Devon	SY1388	50°41·3'	3°13·5'W	X	192
Sidborough	Devon	SS9014	50°55·1'	3°33·5'W	X	181
Sidbrook	Somer	ST2527	51°2·5'	3°3·8'W	T	193
Sidbury	Devon	SY1391	50°43·0'	3°13·6'W	T	192,193
Sidbury	Shrops	SO6885	52°28·0'	2°27·9'W	T	138
Sidbury	Wilts	SU2150	51°15·2'	1°41·6'W	A	184
Sidbury Castle	Devon	SY1291	50°43·0'	3°14·4'W	X	192,193
Sidbury Castle (Fort)	Devon	SY1291	50°43·0'	3°14·4'W	A	192,193
Sidbury Dingle	Shrops	SO6786	52°28·5'	2°28·8'W	X	138
Sidbury Hill	Wilts	SU2150	51°15·2'	1°41·6'W	H	184
Sidcliffe	Devon	SY1388	50°41·3'	3°13·5'W	X	192
Sidcot	N Som	ST4257	51°18·8'	2°49·5'W	T	172,182
Sidcup	Bexley	TQ4672	51°25·9'	0°6·4'E	T	177
Siddal	Cald	SE1023	53°42·4'	1°50·5'W	T	104
Siddick	Cumbr	NY0031	54°40·1'	3°32·6'W	T	89
Siddington	Ches	SJ8471	53°14·4'	2°14·0'W	T	118
Siddington	Glos	SU0399	51°41·6'	1°57·0'W	T	163
Siddington Fm	Heref	SO6935	52°1·0'	2°26·7'W	FM	149
Siddington Heath	Ches	SJ8370	53°13·8'	2°14·9'W	T	118
Siddington Ho	Glos	SP0400	51°42·2'	1°56·1'W	X	163
Siddle Grange	N Yks	NZ4201	54°24·4'	1°20·8'W	X	93
Siddle Ho	N Yks	SE5230	53°46·1'	1°12·3'W	X	105
Siddows Hall	Lancs	SD7240	53°51·6'	2°25·1'W	X	103
Side	Cumbr	NY0609	54°28·3'	3°26·6'W	X	89
Side	S Lanak	NS8636	55°36·5'	3°48·1'W	X	71,72
Side	Stir	NN8204	56°13·1'	3°53·7'W	X	57
Sideabhal	N Eil	NB2717	58°3·7'	6°37·3'W	H	13,14
Side Bank Wood	N Yks	SE1198	54°22·9'	1°49·4'W	F	99
Sidebottom Fold	Tames	SJ9798	53°29·0'	2°2·3'W	X	109
Side Burn	D & G	NY0179	55°6·0'	3°32·7'W	W	84
Side Downs	Devon	ST0000	50°47·7'	3°24·8'W	X	192
Side Edge	N Yks	NY8603	54°25·6'	2°12·5'W	X	91,92
Side End	Cumbr	NY0608	54°27·8'	3°26·6'W	H	89
Side End Fm	Ches	SJ9879	53°18·7'	2°1·4'W	FM	118
Side Fell	Cumbr	NY5973	55°3·2'	2°38·1'W	X	86
Side Fm	Lincs	SK9185	53°21·5'	0°37·5'W	FM	112,121
Side Fm	Oxon	SP3214	51°49·7'	1°31·7'W	FM	164
Sidegarth	Lancs	SD5468	54°6·6'	2°41·8'W	X	97
Sidegate Fm	Norf	TG5100	52°32·6'	1°42·5'E	FM	134
Sideham	Devon	SS5427	51°1·7'	4°4·5'W	X	180
Sidehead	N Ayr	NS3748	55°42·1'	4°35·2'W	X	63
Sidehead	S Ayr	NS4532	55°33·7'	4°27·0'W	X	70
Side Hill	S Lanak	NS6837	55°36·8'	4°5·3'W	H	71
Sidehill	S Lanak	NS7043	55°40·0'	4°3·6'W	X	71
Sidehill Stud	Cambs	TL6662	52°14·1'	0°26·3'E	X	154
Side Ho	Cumbr	NY2906	54°26·9'	3°5·3'W	X	89,90
Side Ho	Cumbr	SD3187	54°16·7'	3°3·2'W	X	96,97
Side Ho	Cumbr	SD4898	54°22·7'	2°47·6'W	X	97
Side Ho	Northum	NY6754	54°53·0'	2°30·4'W	X	86,87
Side Hollows Fm	Leic	SK3211	52°42·0'	1°31·2'W	FM	128
Side Moor	Devon	SS8222	50°59·4'	3°40·5'W	X	181
Sidemoor	Worcs	SO9571	52°20·5'	2°4·0'W	T	139
Side Netley	Shrops	SJ4601	52°36·5'	2°47·4'W	X	126
Sidenhales Fm	Sol	SP1374	52°22·1'	1°48·1'W	FM	139
Side of the Moor	Bolton	SD7412	53°36·5'	2°23·2'W	T	109
Side Pike	Cumbr	NY2905	54°26·4'	3°5·3'W	H	89,90
Sidestrand	Norf	TG2639	52°54·3'	1°22·1'E	T	133
Side, The	Cumbr	NY1113	54°30·5'	3°22·1'W	X	89
Sideway	C of Stoke	SJ8743	52°59·3'	2°11·2'W	T	118
Sideway Bank	Cumbr	NY6318	54°33·6'	2°33·9'W	X	91
Side Well	N Yks	SD9685	54°15·9'	2°3·3'W	X	98
Sidewood	S Lanak	NS9652	55°45·3'	3°39·0'W	X	65,72
Sidford	Devon	SY1390	50°42·4'	3°13·5'W	T	192,193
Sidhean Achadh nan Eun	Highld	NC6311	58°4·3'	4°18·9'W	H	16
Sidhean Achadh nan Gamhna	Highld	NM6848	56°34·3'	5°46·2'W	X	49
Sidhean a' Chatha	Stir	NN3516	56°18·7'	4°39·6'W	H	50,56
Sidhean a' Choin Bhàin	Highld	NH5980	57°47·5'	4°21·8'W	X	21
Sidhean Allt Mhic-artair	Arg & Bt	NM5022	56°19·7'	6°2·2'W	X	48
Sidhean a' Mhill	Highld	NG7862	57°35·9'	5°42·5'W	H	19,24
Sidhean an Airgid	N Eil	NB2513	58°1·5'	6°39·0'W	H	13,14
Sidhean an Aoinidh Bhig or Little Bonnet of Lorn	Highld	NM6750	56°35·3'	5°47·2'W	X	49
Sidheanan Gorm	N Eil	NB3617	58°4·1'	6°28·1'W	H	14
Sidhean an Radhairc	Highld	NH5194	57°54·9'	4°30·4'W	H	20
Sidhean Beag	Arg & Bt	NR9598	56°8·1'	5°17·5'W	H	55
Sidhean Bealaidh	Pth & Kin	NO0081	56°54·8'	3°38·1'W	H	43
Sidhean Bhuirgh	N Eil	NF7649	57°25·2'	7°23·4'W	X	22
Sidhean Bitheasdail	N Eil	NB1000	57°54·0'	6°53·2'W	X	14
Sidhean Corr	Arg & Bt	NR7673	55°54·1'	5°34·6'W	X	62
Sidhean Dubh	Arg & Bt	NM6927	56°23·0'	5°44·1'W	X	49
Sidhean Dubh	Highld	NH5204	57°6·5'	4°26·2'W	X	35
Sidhean Dubh	Highld	NN3349	56°36·4'	4°42·8'W	X	50
Sidhean Dubh Mór	Highld	NC5118	58°7·8'	4°31·3'W	X	16
Sidhean Dubh na Cloiche Bàine	Highld	NH5001	57°4·8'	4°28·0'W	H	35
Sidhean Fuar	Highld	ND2641	58°21·3'	3°15·4'W	X	11,12
Sidhean Liath	Highld	NH5003	57°5·9'	4°28·1'W	X	35
Sidhean Mór	Highld	NC0134	58°15·3'	5°23·0'W	H	15
Sidhean Mór	Highld	ND1843	58°22·3'	3°23·6'W	X	11,12
Sidhean Mór	Highld	NG8171	57°40·8'	5°39·9'W	H	19
Sidhean Mór	Highld	NG8374	57°42·5'	5°38·1'W	H	19
Sidhean Mór	Highld	NH5995	57°55·6'	4°22·4'W	H	21
Sidhean Mór	Highld	NH6396	57°56·2'	4°18·4'W	H	21
Sidhean Mór	Highld	NM4667	56°43·8'	6°8·7'W	X	47
Sidhean Mór	Highld	NM7286	56°54·8'	5°44·3'W	H	40
Sidhean Mór	Highld	NM8783	56°53·6'	5°29·4'W	X	40
Sidhean Mór	N Eil	NB0307	57°57·5'	7°0·8'W	H	13
Sidhean Mór	N Eil	NB3833	58°12·7'	6°27·2'W	X	8
Sidhean na Mannoch	Moray	NJ1945	57°29·5'	3°20·6'W	X	28
Sidhean na Mòine	Highld	NG7587	57°49·2'	5°46·9'W	X	19
Sidhean nan Cearc	Highld	NH3568	57°40·6'	4°45·6'W	H	20
Sidhean nan Creagan Gorm	N Eil	NB4340	58°16·7'	6°22·5'W	X	8
Sidhean nan Ealachan	Highld	NC0834	58°15·4'	5°15·9'W	H	15
Sidhean na Raplaich	Highld	NM6351	56°35·7'	5°51·2'W	H	49
Sidhean na Sròine	Highld	NH1977	57°45·0'	5°2·0'W	H	20
Sidhean Raireag	Highld	NH3491	57°52·9'	4°47·5'W	H	20
Sidhean Riabhach	Arg & Bt	NM3324	56°20·2'	6°18·8'W	X	48
Sidhean Riabhach	Arg & Bt	NM8129	56°24·4'	5°32·5'W	X	49
Sidhean Ruigh na Beinn	Highld	NC6307	58°2·1'	4°18·7'W	H	16
Sidhean Sluaigh	Arg & Bt	NS0797	56°7·9'	5°5·9'W	H	56
Sidhean Tuath	N Eil	NF7270	57°36·3'	7°29·1'W	X	18
Sidhein Mór	Arg & Bt	NR9669	55°52·5'	5°15·2'W	X	62
Sidh Mór	Arg & Bt	NM9100	56°9·1'	5°21·5'W	H	55
Sidh Mor	Arg & Bt	NM9103	56°10·7'	5°21·6'W	H	55
Sidh Trom'aidh	Pth & Kin	NN3943	56°33·3'	4°36·7'W	H	50
Sidinish	N Eil	NF8763	57°33·2'	7°13·5'W	T	18
Sidlaw Hills	Angus	NO2736	56°30·9'	3°10·7'W	H	53
Sidlesham	W Susx	SZ8598	50°46·7'	0°47·3'W	T	197
Sidlesham Common	W Susx	SU8500	50°47·8'	0°47·2'W	T	197
Sidley	E Susx	TQ7409	50°51·5'	0°28·7'E	T	199
Sidley Wood	Hants	SU4055	51°17·8'	1°25·2'W	F	174,185
Sidlow	Surrey	TQ2546	51°12·2'	0°12·3'W	T	187
Sidmouth	Devon	SY1287	50°40·8'	3°14·4'W	T	192
Sidnal Fm	Shrops	SO2696	52°33·6'	3°5·1'W	FM	137
Sidnall	Heref	SO5951	52°9·6'	2°35·6'W	X	149
Sidnall Fm	Shrops	SO6490	52°30·6'	2°31·4'W	FM	138
Sidney Ho	Wrekin	SJ6616	52°44·7'	2°29·8'W	X	127
Sidney Plantation	Wrekin	SJ6517	52°45·2'	2°30·7'W	F	127
Sidney Wood	Surrey	TQ0134	51°6·0'	0°33·1'W	F	186
Sidnye Fm	W Susx	TQ2927	51°1·9'	0°9·2'W	FM	187,198
Sidonia	Heref	SO5827	51°56·6'	2°36·3'W	X	162
Sidown Hill	Hants	SU4457	51°18·9'	1°21·7'W	H	174
Sidway	Staffs	SJ7639	52°57·1'	2°21·0'W	T	127
Sidway Mill Fm	Staffs	SJ7639	52°57·1'	2°21·0'W	FM	127
Sidwood	Northum	NY7688	55°11·4'	2°22·2'W	X	80
Sidwood	Northum	NY7789	55°11·9'	2°21·3'W	X	80
Siefton Batch	Shrops	SO4784	52°27·3'	2°46·4'W	X	137,138
Siege Cross Fm	W Berks	SU5367	51°24·2'	1°13·9'W	FM	174
Siegework	Derby	SK1752	53°4·1'	1°44·4'W	A	119
Sigdon	Devon	SX7446	50°18·3'	3°45·8'W	X	202
Sigford	Devon	SX7773	50°32·9'	3°43·8'W	T	191
Siggar Ness	Shetld	HU3411	59°53·2'	1°23·1'W	X	4
Sigglesthorne	E Yorks	TA1545	53°53·5'	0°14·6'W	T	107
Sigglesthorne Grange	E Yorks	TA1644	53°53·0'	0°13·7'W	X	107
Sight Hill	Arg & Bt	NS0172	55°54·3'	5°10·6'W	H	63
Sighthill	C of Edin	NT1971	55°55·8'	3°17·3'W	T	65,66
Sighthill	C of Glas	NS6066	55°52·3'	4°13·8'W	T	64
Sight Rock	N Eil	NF9975	57°40·1'	7°2·4'W	X	18
Sighty Crag	Cumbr	NY6080	55°7·0'	2°37·2'W	H	80
Sigingstone	V of Glam	SS9771	51°26·0'	3°28·5'W	T	170
Siglan Fm	I of Angl	SH5372	53°13·7'	4°11·7'W	FM	114,115
Sigla Water	Shetld	HU5293	60°37·3'	1°2·5'W	W	1,2
Siglen	Conwy	SH7464	53°9·7'	3°52·7'W	X	115
Siglen Uchaf	Denb	SJ1365	53°10·3'	3°17·7'W	X	116
Signal Bank	Shrops	SJ4601	52°36·5'	2°47·4'W	X	126
Signal Ho	I of W	SZ4790	50°42·7'	1°19·7'W	X	196
Signal Rock	Highld	NN1256	56°39·7'	5°3·6'W	H	41
Signet	Oxon	SP2410	51°47·5'	1°38·7'W	T	163
Signet Hill	Oxon	SP2311	51°48·1'	1°39·6'W	X	163
Signpost Corner	I of M	SC3878	54°10·6'	4°28·5'W	X	95
Sigston Castle	N Yks	SE4195	54°21·2'	1°21·7'W	X	99
Sigston Grange	N Yks	SE4394	54°20·6'	1°19·9'W	X	99
Sigston Wood	N Yks	SE4293	54°20·1'	1°20·8'W	F	99
Sigsworth Crags	N Yks	SE1469	54°7·2'	1°46·7'W	X	99
Sigsworth Moor	N Yks	SE1470	54°7·8'	1°46·7'W	X	99
Sigtoft Fm	Lincs	TF4452	53°3·0'	0°9·3'E	FM	122
Sigwells	Somer	ST6423	51°0·5'	2°30·4'W	T	183
Sike Beck	N Yks	SE4750	53°56·9'	1°16·6'W	W	105
Sikehead Dam	Durham	NY9546	54°48·8'	2°4·2'W	W	87
Sike Ho	Cumbr	NX9912	54°29·8'	3°33·2'W	X	89
Sike Moor	N Yks	SD8078	54°12·1'	2°18·0'W	X	98
Sikes Beck	N Yks	SE3382	54°14·2'	1°29·2'W	W	99
Sikes Fm	E Yorks	SE7933	53°47·5'	0°47·6'W	FM	105,106
Sikeside	Cumbr	NY4466	54°59·4'	2°52·1'W	X	85
Sike Whinns	Cumbr	NX9923	54°35·8'	3°33·4'W	X	89
Silbury Hill	Wilts	SU1068	51°24·9'	1°51·0'W	A	173
Silchester	Hants	SU6262	51°21·5'	1°6·2'W	T	175
Silchester Common	Hants	SU6262	51°21·5'	1°6·2'W	X	175
Silchester Fm	Hants	SU6261	51°20·9'	1°6·2'W	FM	175
Silchester Hall	Hants	SU6362	51°21·4'	1°5·3'W	X	175
Silcoates Sch	Wakf	SE3122	53°41·9'	1°31·4'W	X	104
Silcock's Fm	Norf	TG3528	52°48·1'	1°29·6'E	FM	133,134
Silcock's Wood	Kent	TQ9532	51°3·5'	0°47·4'E	F	189
Silcombe Cross	Devon	SS7524	51°0·3'	3°46·5'W	X	180
Silcombe Fm	Somer	SS8348	51°13·4'	3°40·1'W	FM	181
Silda Wick	Shetld	HU6189	60°35·1'	0°52·7'W	W	1,2
Sildinis	N Eil	NB2819	58°4·6'	6°36·4'W	T	13,14
Sildries	Shetld	HU5140	60°8·7'	1°4·4'W	X	4
Sileby	Leic	SK6015	52°44·0'	1°6·3'W	T	129
Silecroft	Cumbr	SD1381	54°13·3'	3°19·6'W	T	96
Silena Fm	Corn	SW4023	50°3·3'	5°39·6'W	FM	203
Silent Pool	Surrey	TQ0648	51°13·5'	0°28·5'W	W	187
Silfield	Norf	TM1299	52°33·1'	1°8·0'E	T	144
Silford	Devon	SS4328	51°2·0'	4°14·0'W	T	180
Silford Copse	Hants	SU5312	50°54·5'	1°14·4'W	F	196
Silian	Cered	SN5751	52°8·6'	4°5·0'W	T	146
Silkenworthy Knap	Devon	SS6344	51°11·0'	3°57·2'W	H	180
Silkhay Fms	Dorset	SY4698	50°47·0'	2°45·6'W	FM	193
Silk Hill	Wilts	SU1846	51°13·0'	1°44·1'W	H	184
Silkhouse	Devon	SX7091	50°42·5'	3°50·1'W	X	191
Silkin Way	Wrekin	SJ6713	52°43·1'	2°28·9'W	X	127
Silklands	Devon	SS4116	50°55·5'	4°15·4'W	X	180,190
Silkmead Fm	Herts	TL3931	51°57·8'	0°1·8'E	FM	166
Silks Fm	Kent	TR0645	51°10·2'	0°57·2'E	FM	179,189
Silkstead	Hants	SU4424	51°1·1'	1°22·0'W	T	185
Silkstone	Barns	SE2805	53°32·7'	1°34·2'W	T	110
Silkstone Common	Barns	SE2904	53°32·2'	1°33·3'W	T	110
Silkstone Fall	Barns	SE2905	53°32·7'	1°33·3'W	X	110
Silk Stream	Barnet	TQ2090	51°36·0'	0°15·6'W	W	176
Silk Willoughby	Lincs	TF0542	52°58·1'	0°25·8'W	T	130
Silk Wood	Glos	ST8489	51°36·2'	2°13·5'W	F	162,173
Silkwood Top	Devon	SS7037	51°7·3'	3°51·1'W	H	180
Sillathwaite	Cumbr	NY0512	54°29·9'	3°27·6'W	X	89
Sillaton	Corn	SX3963	50°26·9'	4°15·7'W	X	201
Sillerhole	Fife	NO3802	56°12·6'	2°59·5'W	T	59
Sillerton	Aberd	NJ7342	57°28·3'	2°26·6'W	X	29
Sillery Sands	Devon	SS7449	51°13·8'	3°47·9'W	X	180
Sill Field	Cumbr	SD5585	54°15·8'	2°41·0'W	X	97
Sillick Moor	Devon	SS3300	50°46·8'	4°21·8'W	X	190
Silligrove	Shrops	SO7177	52°23·7'	2°25·2'W	X	138
Silloans	Northum	NT8200	55°17·9'	2°16·6'W	X	80
Sillo Craig	Angus	NO7355	56°41·4'	2°26·0'W	X	54
Silloth	Cumbr	NY1153	54°52·1'	3°22·8'W	T	85
Silloth Bay	Cumbr	NY1054	54°52·6'	3°23·7'W	W	85
Sills	Northum	NT8200	55°17·9'	2°16·6'W	X	80
Sills Burn	Northum	NT8201	55°18·4'	2°16·6'W	W	80
Sill's Fm	Lancs	SD4913	53°36·9'	2°45·8'W	FM	108
Sillycoats	Aberd	NO7265	56°46·8'	2°27·0'W	X	45
Silly Dale	Derby	SK1876	53°17·1'	1°43·4'W	X	119
Sillyearn	Moray	NJ5254	57°34·7'	2°47·7'W	X	29
Sillyearn Hill	Moray	NJ5153	57°34·1'	2°48·7'W	H	29
Sillyearn Wood	Moray	NJ5152	57°33·6'	2°48·7'W	F	29
Sillyflatt	Aberd	NO8271	56°50·1'	2°17·2'W	X	45
Sillyhall	Cumbr	NY7243	54°47·1'	2°25·7'W	X	86,87
Sillyhole	E Ayr	NS4706	55°19·7'	4°24·3'W	X	70,77
Sillywinny Wood	Pth & Kin	NO0613	56°18·3'	3°30·7'W	F	58
Sillywrea	Northum	NY8061	54°56·8'	2°18·3'W	X	86,87
Siloam Fm	Medway	TQ8164	51°21·0'	0°36·3'E	FM	178,188
Silo Fm	Notts	SK5149	53°2·4'	1°14·0'W	FM	129
Siloh	Carm	SN7337	52°1·3'	3°50·7'W	T	146,160
Silpho	N Yks	SE9692	54°19·1'	0°31·0'W	T	94,101
Silpho Brow Fm	N Yks	SE9893	54°19·6'	0°29·2'W	FM	94,101
Silsden	Brad	SE0446	53°54·9'	1°55·9'W	T	104
Silsden Br	Brad	SE0345	53°54·3'	1°56·8'W	X	104
Silsden Moor	Brad	SE0449	53°56·5'	1°55·9'W	X	104
Silsden Resr	Brad	SE0447	53°55·4'	1°55·9'W	W	104
Silsoe	Beds	TL0735	52°0·4'	0°26·1'W	T	153
Silsworth Lodge	Northnts	SP6171	52°20·3'	1°5·9'W	X	140
Silt Fen Fm	Norf	TL5999	52°34·2'	0°21·2'E	FM	143
Silton	Dorset	ST7829	51°3·8'	2°18·5'W	T	183
Silton Grange	N Yks	SE4491	54°19·0'	1°19·0'W	X	99
Siluria	Powys	SO2258	52°13·1'	3°8·1'W	X	148
Silva Dale	Shetld	HP5809	60°45·9'	0°55·6'W	X	1
Silverband	Cumbr	NY6727	54°38·5'	2°30·3'W	X	91
Silverband Mine	Cumbr	NY7031	54°40·6'	2°27·5'W	X	91
Silverband Shop	Durham	NY8327	54°38·5'	2°15·4'W	X	91,92
Silverbank	Aberd	NO7196	57°3·5'	2°28·2'W	T	38,45
Silver Barrow	Wilts	SU0447	51°13·6'	1°56·2'W	A	184
Silverbarton	Fife	NT2286	56°3·9'	3°14·7'W	X	66
Silver Bay	I of Angl	SH2975	53°14·9'	4°33·4'W	W	114
Silverbeck	Surrey	SU8539	51°8·9'	0°46·7'W	X	186
Silver Birch	Cumbr	SD4086	54°16·2'	2°54·9'W	X	96,97
Silverbridge Lake	Devon	SX5652	50°21·3'	4°1·1'W	W	202
Silverburn	Fife	NO3902	56°12·7'	2°58·6'W	X	59
Silver Burn	I of M	SC2769	54°5·5'	4°38·3'W	W	95
Silverburn	Midlo	NT2060	55°49·9'	3°16·2'W	T	66
Silverburn Fm	I of M	SC2771	54°6·6'	4°38·4'W	FM	95
Silver Carn	I Scilly	SV8306	49°52·5'	6°24·4'W	X	203
Silver Carrs	Northum	NU2902	55°18·9'	1°32·2'W	X	81
Silver Cove	Cumbr	NY1311	54°29·5'	3°20·2'W	X	89
Silvercove Beck	Cumbr	NY1312	54°30·0'	3°20·2'W	W	89
Silver Crag	Cumbr	NY3918	54°33·5'	2°56·2'W	X	90
Silver Craigs	Arg & Bt	NR8984	55°59·5'	5°22·6'W	H	55
Silverdale	E Susx	TQ7325	51°0·1'	0°28·3'E	X	188,199
Silverdale	I of M	SC2770	54°6·1'	4°38·3'W	X	95
Silverdale	Lancs	SD4675	54°10·3'	2°49·2'W	T	97
Silverdale	N Yks	SD8370	54°7·8'	2°15·2'W	X	98
Silverdale	Staffs	SJ8146	53°0·9'	2°16·6'W	T	118
Silverdale Barn	N Yks	SD8369	54°7·2'	2°15·2'W	X	98
Silverdale Glen	I of M	SC2771	54°6·6'	4°38·4'W	X	95
Silverdale Green	Lancs	SD4674	54°9·8'	2°49·2'W	T	97
Silverdale Moss	Lancs	SD4777	54°11·4'	2°48·3'W	X	97
Silverdale Sta	Lancs	SD4775	54°10·3'	2°48·3'W	X	97
Silverden	Kent	TQ7828	51°1·6'	0°32·7'E	X	188,199
Silver Down	Wilts	SU2856	51°18·4'	1°35·5'W	X	174
Silver End	Dudley	SO9186	52°28·5'	2°7·6'W	T	139
Silver End	Essex	TL7641	52°2·6'	0°34·4'E	X	155
Silver End	Essex	TL8019	51°50·7'	0°37·2'E	T	168
Silver Flowe	D & G	NX4782	55°6·8'	4°23·5'W	X	77
Silverford	Aberd	NJ4324	57°18·4'	2°56·3'W	X	37
Silver Fox Fm	N Yks	SE5181	54°13·6'	1°12·6'W	FM	100
Silvergate	Norf	TG1727	52°48·0'	1°13·6'E	T	133,134
Silver Glen	Clackm	NS8997	56°9·4'	3°46·8'W	X	58
Silver Green	Norf	TM2593	52°29·5'	1°19·3'E	T	134
Silverhall	Orkney	HY6739	59°14·4'	2°34·2'W	X	5
Silver Hill	Cumbr	NY2522	54°35·5'	3°9·2'W	X	89,90
Silver Hill	D & G	NX7045	54°47·2'	4°0·9'W	H	83,84
Silver Hill	E Susx	TQ7325	51°0·1'	0°28·3'E	T	188,199
Silverhill	E Susx	TQ8010	50°51·9'	0°33·9'E	T	199
Silver Hill	Highld	NM5961	56°41·0'	5°55·6'W	X	47
Silver Hill	Lincs	TA1603	53°30·9'	0°14·6'W	X	113
Silverhill	Northum	NZ1073	55°3·3'	1°50·2'W	X	88
Silver Hill	N Yks	NY9300	54°24·0'	2°6·0'W	X	91,92
Silverhill	N Yks	NZ0908	54°28·3'	1°51·2'W	X	92
Silver Hill	N Yks	SE1566	54°5·6'	1°45·8'W	X	99
Silver Hill	Staffs	SK1719	52°46·3'	1°44·5'W	X	128
Silver Hill Fm	Corn	SW7231	50°8·4'	5°11·1'W	FM	204
Silverhill Fm	Derby	SK2037	52°56·0'	1°41·7'W	FM	128
Silverhill Fm	Derby	SK2936	52°55·5'	1°33·7'W	FM	128
Silverhill Fm	Notts	SK4661	53°8·9'	1°18·3'W	FM	120
Silver Hill Fm	N Yks	SE1996	54°21·8'	1°42·0'W	FM	99
Silverhillock	Angus	NO4847	56°37·0'	2°50·4'W	X	54
Silverhillocks	Aberd	NJ7363	57°39·6'	2°26·7'W	X	29
Silverhill Park	E Susx	TQ8011	50°52·4'	0°33·9'E	T	199
Silverhills	Moray	NJ2067	57°41·4'	3°20·1'W	X	28
Silverhill Wood	Cumbr	NY3670	55°1·5'	2°59·6'W	F	85
Silver Holme	Cumbr	SD3790	54°18·4'	2°57·7'W	X	96,97
Silverholme	Lancs	SD5728	53°45·0'	2°38·7'W	X	102
Silver How	Cumbr	NY0501	54°24·0'	3°27·4'W	X	89
Silver How	Cumbr	NY3206	54°26·9'	3°2·5'W	H	90
Silver How	Cumbr	SD1998	54°22·5'	3°14·4'W	X	96
Silvericks Fm	E Susx	TQ6617	50°55·9'	0°22·1'E	FM	199
Silver Knap	Somer	ST6624	51°1·1'	2°28·7'W	T	183
Silverknowes	C of Edin	NT2076	55°58·5'	3°16·5'W	T	66
Silverlace Green	Suff	TM3260	52°11·6'	1°24·1'E	X	156
Silverlake Fm	Dorset	ST6115	50°56·2'	2°32·9'W	FM	183
Silverlands	Devon	SX8578	50°35·7'	3°37·1'W	X	191
Silverlands	E Susx	TQ5333	51°4·8'	0°11·4'E	X	188

Silverlands	Surrey	TQ0165	51°22·7'	0°32·5'W	X	176
Silverlea	Aberd	NJ8444	57°29·4'	2°15·6'W	X	29,30
Silverleys	Aberd	NJ5726	57°19·6'	2°42·4'W	X	37
Silverley's Green	Suff	TM2975	52°19·7'	1°22·1'E	X	156
Silver Mere	Surrey	TQ0860	51°20·0'	0°26·6'W	W	176,187
Silvermoor	Northum	NU2015	55°26·0'	1°40·6'W	X	81
Silvermoss	Aberd	NJ8333	57°23·5'	2°16·5'W	X	29,30
Silvermuir	S Lanak	NS9145	55°41·4'	3°43·6'W	T	72
Silver Point	Cumbr	NY3918	54°33·5'	2°56·2'W	X	90
Silverrig Fm	S Lanak	NS6848	55°42·7'	4°5·6'W	FM	64
Silver Rig Loch	D & G	NX3773	55°1·7'	4°32·6'W	W	77
Silver Rock	Highld	NH7999	57°58·1'	4°2·3'W	X	21
Silver Sand		TF6442	52°57·2'	0°26·9'E	X	132
Silversands Bay	Fife	NT2085	56°3·3'	3°16·6'W	W	66
Silverside	Northum	NU0105	55°20·6'	1°58·6'W	X	81
Silver Side	Pth & Kin	NO0541	56°33·3'	3°32·3'W	F	52,53
Silversike	Cumbr	NY4769	55°1·0'	2°49·3'W	X	86
Silverstone	Northnts	SP6644	52°5·7'	1°1·8'W	T	152
Silverstone Fields Fm	Northnts	SP6745	52°6·2'	1°0·9'W	FM	152
Silverstone Fm	Norf	TF9523	52°46·4'	0°53·9'E	FM	132
Silver Strand	Stir	NN4908	56°14·7'	4°25·8'W	X	57
Silver Street	Glos	SO7801	51°42·7'	2°18·7'W	T	162
Silver Street	Kent	TQ8760	51°18·7'	0°41·4'E	T	178
Silver Street	Somer	ST1721	50°59·2'	3°10·6'W	T	181,193
Silver Street	Somer	ST5432	51°5·4'	2°39·0'W	T	182,183
Silver Street	Worcs	SP0775	52°22·6'	1°53·4'W	T	139
Silver Street Fm	Suff	TL6447	52°6·0'	0°24·1'E	FM	154
Silverstreet Wood	Wilts	ST9466	51°23·8'	2°4·8'W	F	173
Silverstripe	Aberd	NJ6751	57°33·1'	2°32·6'W	X	29
Silverton	Devon	SS9502	50°48·7'	3°29·0'W	T	192
Silverton	Pth & Kin	NN8209	56°15·8'	3°53·9'W	X	57
Silverton	W Dunb	NS4075	55°56·7'	4°33·3'W	T	64
Silverton Hill	Northum	NT9308	55°22·2'	2°6·2'W	H	80
Silvertonhill	S Lanak	NS7254	55°46·0'	4°2·0'W	T	64
Silver Top	Cumbr	NY5860	54°56·2'	2°38·9'W	X	86
Silvertown	Newham	TQ4179	51°29·8'	0°2·3'E	T	177
Silver Valley	Corn	SW7647	50°17·1'	5°8·3'W	X	204
Silver Valley	Corn	SX3870	50°30·7'	4°16·7'W	X	201
Silver Well	Ches	SJ5676	53°17·0'	2°39·2'W	W	117
Silverwell	Corn	SW7448	50°17·6'	5°10·0'W	T	204
Silverwell Fm	Corn	SW7448	50°17·6'	5°10·0'W	FM	204
Silverwells	Aberd	NJ7246	57°30·5'	2°27·6'W	X	29
Silverwells	Angus	NO6442	56°34·4'	2°34·7'W	X	54
Silverwells	Pth & Kin	NO1037	56°31·2'	3°27·3'W	X	53
Silverwells	Scot Bord	NT8866	55°53·5'	2°11·1'W	X	67
Silverwood	E Ayr	NS4538	55°36·9'	4°27·2'W	X	70
Silverwood Fm	Cambs	TF4516	52°43·6'	0°9·2'E	FM	131
Silverybield Crag	Cumbr	NY2104	54°25·8'	3°12·6'W	X	89,90
Silvie	Angus	NO2748	56°37·3'	3°10·9'W	X	53
Silvington	Shrops	SO6279	52°24·7'	2°33·1'W	T	138
Silvington Common	Shrops	SO6279	52°24·7'	2°33·1'W	X	138
Sil Wick	Shetld	HU2941	60°9·4'	1°28·2'W	W	4
Silwick	Shetld	HU2942	60°10·0'	1°28·2'W	T	4
Silwood Park	Win & Maid	SU9468	51°24·4'	0°38·5'W	X	175
Silworthy	Devon	SS3414	50°54·3'	4°21·3'W	X	190
Silworthy Cross	Devon	SS3315	50°54·9'	4°22·2'W	X	190
Simber Hill	Bucks	SP7420	51°52·6'	0°55·1'W	X	165
Simbriss Fm	Somer	ST6247	51°13·5'	2°32·3'W	FM	183
Simfield	N Yks	SE2571	54°8·3'	1°36·6'W	X	99
Simfields	Staffs	SJ9246	53°0·9'	2°6·7'W	X	118
Sim Hill	Barns	SE2901	53°30·5'	1°33·4'W	T	110
Simister	Bury	SD8305	53°32·7'	2°15·0'W	T	109
Simli Field	Shetld	HU1951	60°14·8'	1°38·9'W	H	3
Simm Bottom	N Yks	SE0358	54°1·3'	1°56·8'W	X	104
Simmerson Hill	Cumbr	NY5755	54°53·5'	2°39·8'W	H	86
Simmondley	Derby	SK0193	53°26·3'	1°58·7'W	T	110
Simmonds Green	Ches	SJ4849	53°2·4'	2°46·1'W	X	117
Simmond's Hall Fm	Glos	SO8912	51°48·6'	2°9·2'W	FM	163
Simmond's Hill	Ches	SJ5172	53°14·8'	2°43·7'W	X	117
Simmon House Fm	Lincs	TF3753	53°3·6'	0°3·1'E	FM	122
Simm's Cross	Halton	SJ5185	53°21·8'	2°43·8'W	T	108
Simms Fm	Oxon	SP5321	51°53·3'	1°13·4'W	FM	164
Simm's Lane End	St Hel	SD5400	53°29·9'	2°41·2'W	T	108
Simms Stud Fm	Hants	SU6463	51°22·0'	1°4·4'W	FM	175
Simmy Nook	Lancs	SD6236	53°49·4'	2°34·2'W	X	102,103
Simonburn	Northum	NY8773	55°3·1'	2°11·8'W	T	87
Simonburn Common	Northum	NY8473	55°3·3'	2°14·6'W	X	86,87
Simonds Fm	Norf	TM1487	52°26·6'	1°9·3'E	FM	144,156
Simon Fell	N Yks	SD7574	54°9·9'	2°22·6'W	H	98
Simonfield	Derby	SK4142	52°58·7'	1°23·0'W	X	129
Simon Howe	N Yks	SE8398	54°22·5'	0°42·9'W	A	94,100
Simon Howe Rigg	N Yks	SE8297	54°22·0'	0°43·9'W	X	94,100
Simon Kell	Cumbr	NY0610	54°28·8'	3°26·6'W	X	89
Simonsbath	Somer	SS7739	51°8·5'	3°45·1'W	T	180
Simon's Br	Man	SJ8390	53°24·6'	2°14·9'W	X	109
Simon's Burn	E Ayr	NS4134	55°34·7'	4°30·9'W	W	70
Simonsburrow	Devon	ST1416	50°56·5'	3°13·1'W	T	181,193
Simon's Castle	Powys	SO2893	52°32·0'	3°3·3'W	X	137
Simon's Castle (Motte & Bailey)	Powys	SO2893	52°32·0'	3°3·3'W	A	137
Simonside	Northum	NZ0298	55°16·8'	1°57·7'W	H	81
Simonside	S Tyne	NZ3463	54°57·9'	1°27·7'W	T	88
Simonside Hills	Northum	NZ0298	55°16·8'	1°57·7'W	H	81
Simon's Knowe	S Lanak	NS9913	55°24·3'	3°35·3'W	H	78
Simon's Seat	Cumbr	SD6699	54°23·4'	2°31·0'W	X	98
Simon's Seat	N Yks	SE0759	54°1·9'	1°53·2'W	X	104
Simon's Stone	Corn	SX1673	50°31·9'	4°35·4'W	X	201
Simonstone	Lancs	SD7634	53°48·3'	2°21·5'W	T	103
Simonstone	Lancs	SD7734	53°48·4'	2°20·5'W	T	103
Simonstone	N Yks	SD8791	54°19·1'	2°11·6'W	T	98
Simonstone Fm	Brig	SS9281	51°31·3'	3°33·0'W	FM	170
Simonstone Hall	Lancs	SD7734	53°48·4'	2°20·5'W	X	103
Simonswood	Ches	SJ8570	53°13·9'	2°13·1'W	X	118
Simonswood Hall	Lancs	SD4101	53°30·4'	2°53·0'W	A	108
Simonswood Moss	Lancs	SJ4499	53°29·3'	2°50·2'W	X	108
Simpkins	Essex	TL6326	51°54·7'	0°22·6'E	X	167
Simpkin's Covert	Staffs	SJ8223	52°48·5'	2°15·6'W	X	127
Simpleside Hill	Pth & Kin	NN9910	56°16·6'	3°37·4'W	X	58
Simprim	Angus	NO3046	56°36·3'	3°8·0'W	X	53
Simprim	Scot Bord	NT8545	55°42·1'	2°13·9'W	X	74

Simprim Burn	Scot Bord	NT8444	55°41·6'	2°14·8'W	W	74
Simprim Mains	Scot Bord	NT8545	55°42·1'	2°13·9'W	X	74
Simpson	Devon	SS3604	50°49·0'	4°19·3'W	X	190
Simpson	Devon	SX7456	50°23·7'	3°46·0'W	X	202
Simpson	Mil Key	SP8835	52°0·6'	0°42·7'W	T	152
Simpson	Pemb	SM8818	51°49·5'	5°4·2'W	T	157
Simpson Cross	Pemb	SM8919	51°50·0'	5°3·4'W	T	157,158
Simpson Green	Brad	SE1838	53°50·5'	1°43·2'W	T	104
Simpson Ground	Cumbr	SD3986	54°16·2'	2°55·8'W	X	96,97
Simpson Ground Resr	Cumbr	SD3986	54°16·2'	2°55·8'W	W	96,97
Simpson Hill	Pemb	SM8818	51°49·5'	5°4·2'W	X	157
Simpsonland	S Lanak	NS7152	55°44·9'	4°2·9'W	X	64
Simpson's Pot	N Yks	SD6977	54°11·5'	2°28·1'W	X	98
Sim's Hill	Pth & Kin	NN9907	56°14·9'	3°37·4'W	H	58
Sims' Hill	S Glos	ST6277	51°29·7'	2°32·5'W	X	172
Sim's Hill	S Lanak	NS8619	55°27·3'	3°47·7'W	X	71,78
Sim's Knowe	Scot Bord	NT5607	55°21·6'	2°41·2'W	X	80
Sina	Corn	SX1466	50°28·1'	4°36·9'W	X	200
Sinah Common	Hants	SZ6999	50°47·4'	1°0·9'W	X	197
Sinah Lake	Hants	SU6900	50°48·0'	1°0·9'W	W	197
Sinai Park	Staffs	SK2223	52°48·5'	1°40·0'W	X	128
Sinc Giedd	Powys	SN8117	51°50·6'	3°43·3'W	H	160
Sincks, The	Norf	TF6509	52°39·4'	0°26·8'E	F	143
Sinclair Hills	Aberd	NJ9862	57°39·1'	2°1·5'W	H	30
Sinclair's Bay	Highld	ND3656	58°29·5'	3°5·4'W	W	12
Sinclair's Hill	Scot Bord	NT8150	55°44·8'	2°17·7'W	T	67,74
Sinclair's Stove	Shetld	HU3626	60°1·3'	1°20·8'W	X	4
Sinclairston	E Ayr	NS4716	55°25·1'	4°24·6'W	T	70
Sinclairtown	Fife	NT2993	56°7·7'	3°8·1'W	T	59
Sincombe Fm	Oxon	SU3585	51°34·0'	1°29·3'W	FM	174
Sindallthorpe Ho	Cambs	TL6083	52°25·5'	0°21·6'E	X	143
Sinderby	N Yks	SE3481	54°13·7'	1°28·3'W	T	99
Sindercombe	Devon	SS7827	51°2·0'	3°44·0'W	X	180
Sinderhope	Northum	NY8451	54°51·5'	2°14·5'W	T	86,87
Sinderhope Carrs	Northum	NY8651	54°51·5'	2°12·7'W	X	87
Sinderhope Gate	Northum	NY8552	54°52·0'	2°13·6'W	X	87
Sinderland Brook	Traf	SJ7690	53°24·6'	2°21·3'W	W	109
Sinderland Green	Traf	SJ7390	53°24·6'	2°24·0'W	T	109
Sindle's Fm	W Susx	SU7609	50°52·8'	0°54·8'W	FM	197
Sindlesham	Wok	SU7769	51°25·1'	0°53·2'W	T	175
Sindlesham Mill	Wok	SU7670	51°25·7'	0°54·0'W	X	175
Sinen Gill	Cumbr	NY2927	54°38·2'	3°5·6'W	W	89,90
Sinen Gill	Cumbr	NY3028	54°38·8'	3°4·7'W	W	90
Siney Sitch	Derby	SK1980	53°19·2'	1°42·5'W	W	110
Siney Tarn	Cumbr	NY1601	54°24·1'	3°17·2'W	W	89
Sinfin	C of Derb	SK3431	52°52·8'	1°29·3'W	T	128
Sinfin Moor	C of Derb	SK3531	52°52·8'	1°28·4'W	T	128
Singdean	Scot Bord	NT5801	55°18·3'	2°39·3'W	X	80
Singdean Burn	Scot Bord	NT5702	55°18·9'	2°40·2'W	W	80
Singe Wood	Oxon	SP3414	51°49·6'	1°30·0'W	F	164
Singingside Burn	Scot Bord	NT8118	55°27·6'	2°17·6'W	W	80
Singla Field	Shetld	HU4997	60°39·5'	1°5·7'W	X	1
Single Barrow	Devon	SX7079	50°36·0'	3°49·8'W	A	191
Singleborough	Bucks	SP7632	51°59·1'	0°53·2'W	T	152,165
Singlecote Fm	Peterb	TF2606	52°38·5'	0°7·9'W	FM	142
Singledge	Hants	SU5304	50°50·2'	1°14·5'W	X	196
Singledge	Kent	TR2845	51°9·7'	1°16·1'E	X	179
Single Hill	Somer	ST7256	51°18·4'	2°23·7'W	T	172
Singlesole Fm	Peterb	TF2507	52°39·0'	0°8·7'W	FM	142
Singleton	Kent	TQ9841	51°8·3'	0°50·2'E	X	189
Singleton	Lancs	SD3838	53°50·3'	2°56·1'W	T	102
Singleton	W Susx	SU8713	50°54·8'	0°45·4'W	T	197
Singleton Forest	W Susx	SU8815	50°55·9'	0°44·5'W	F	197
Singleton Hall (Sch)	Lancs	SD3739	53°50·9'	2°57·0'W	X	102
Singleton Ho	Lancs	SD6435	53°48·8'	2°32·4'W	X	102,103
Singleton Park	Cumbr	SD5491	54°19·0'	2°42·0'W	X	97
Singleton Park	Devon	SS9601	50°48·2'	3°28·2'W	X	192
Singleton's Fm	Lancs	SD4837	53°49·8'	2°47·0'W	FM	102
Singleton's Fm	Lancs	SD5023	53°42·3'	2°45·0'W	FM	102
Singlewell	Kent	TQ6570	51°24·5'	0°22·7'E	T	177,178
Singlie	Scot Bord	NT3621	55°29·0'	3°0·3'W	X	73
Singlie Burn	Scot Bord	NT3522	55°29·5'	3°1·3'W	W	73
Singlie Hill	Scot Bord	NT3521	55°29·0'	3°1·3'W	H	73
Singliehill End	Scot Bord	NT3621	55°29·0'	3°0·3'W	X	73
Singmoor	Northum	NT9509	55°22·7'	2°4·3'W	X	81
Singret	Wrex	SJ3455	53°5·5'	2°58·7'W	T	117
Sinians of Cutclaws	Orkney	HY3631	59°9·9'	3°6·7'W	X	6
Sinigeo	Highld	ND2174	58°39·1'	3°21·2'W	X	7,12
Sinilie	Orkney	ND4285	58°45·2'	2°59·7'W	X	7
Sink	Stir	NS8288	56°4·5'	3°53·3'W	X	57,65
Sink Beck	Cumbr	NY6929	54°39·6'	2°28·4'W	W	91
Sinkfall	Cumbr	SD2173	54°9·1'	3°12·2'W	X	96
Sink Fm	Suff	TM3051	52°6·8'	1°22·0'E	FM	156
Sink Fm	Suff	TM3558	52°10·4'	1°26·6'E	FM	156
Sink Fm	Worcs	SO8244	52°5·9'	2°15·4'W	FM	150
Sink Green	Heref	SO5437	52°2·0'	2°39·8'W	X	149
Sink Ho	Durham	NZ1521	54°35·3'	1°45·7'W	X	92
Sinkhurst Green	Kent	TQ8142	51°9·1'	0°35·7'E	T	188
Sinkinson House Fm	N Yks	SE7158	54°1·0'	0°54·6'W	FM	105,106
Sink Moss	Ches	SJ6783	53°20·8'	2°29·3'W	X	109
Sinks Covert	N Lincs	TA1215	53°37·4'	0°18·0'W	F	113
Sinnaboth	Aberd	NJ4612	57°12·0'	2°53·2'W	X	37
Sinnahard	Aberd	NJ4813	57°12·5'	2°51·2'W	X	37
Sinna Skerry	Shetld	HU4773	60°26·5'	1°8·3'W	X	2,3
Sinna Stack	Shetld	HP5810	60°46·4'	0°55·6'W	X	1
Sinna Water	Shetld	HU3673	60°26·6'	1°23·5'W	W	2,3
Sinney Fields	Warw	SP4090	52°30·6'	1°24·2'W	X	140
Sinniberg	Shetld	HU6087	60°34·0'	0°53·8'W	X	1,2
Sinnington	N Yks	SE7485	54°15·6'	0°51·4'W	T	94,100
Sinnington Common	N Yks	SE7285	54°15·6'	0°53·3'W	X	94,100
Sinnington Common Fm	N Yks	SE7184	54°15·0'	0°54·2'W	FM	100
Sinnington Lodge	N Yks	SE7484	54°15·0'	0°51·4'W	X	100
Sinnington Manor	N Yks	SE7285	54°15·6'	0°53·3'W	X	94,100
Sinnow Wood	Donc	SK6392	53°25·5'	1°2·7'W	F	
Sinns Barton	Corn	SW6944	50°15·3'	5°14·1'W	X	203
Sinntean	N Eil	NB5065	58°30·4'	6°17·0'W	X	8
Sinodun Hills	Oxon	SU5692	51°37·7'	1°11·1'W	H	164,174
Sinodun Hills (Fort)	Oxon	SU5692	51°37·7'	1°11·1'W	A	164,174
Sinope	Leic	SK4015	52°44·1'	1°24·1'W	X	129
Sinsharnie	Aberd	NJ4843	57°28·7'	2°51·6'W	X	28,29

Sinton	Worcs	SO8463	52°16·1'	2°13·7'W	T	138,150
Sinton Green	Worcs	SO8160	52°14·5'	2°16·3'W	T	138,150
Sinton's End Fm	Heref	SO6849	52°8·5'	2°27·7'W	FM	149
Siolaigh	N Eil	NF5962	57°31·4'	7°41·4'W	X	22
Siolaigh Mòr	N Eil	NF8438	57°19·6'	7°14·6'W	X	22
Sion Hill	Bath & NE Somer	ST7466	51°23·8'	2°22·0'W	T	172
Sion Hill Fm	Bucks	SP7425	51°55·3'	0°55·0'W	FM	165
Sion Hill Fm	N Yks	SE4068	54°6·6'	1°22·9'W	FM	99
Sion Hill Hall	N Yks	SE3784	54°15·3'	1°25·5'W	X	99
Sion Hill Ho	Worcs	SO8378	52°24·2'	2°14·6'W	X	138
Sion Ho	Worcs	SO8976	52°23·2'	2°9·3'W	X	139
Sionside	Northum	NU0933	55°35·7'	1°51·0'W	X	75
Siôp Fach	Powys	SO0836	52°1·1'	3°20·0'W	X	160
Sior Loch	Arg & Bt	NM9623	56°21·6'	5°17·7'W	W	49
Siorrabhaig	N Eil	NB3754	58°24·0'	6°29·6'W	W	8
Sipson	Hill	TQ0778	51°29·7'	0°27·1'W	T	176
Sipton Burn	Northum	NY8550	54°50·9'	2°13·6'W	W	87
Sipton Shield	Northum	NY8450	54°50·9'	2°14·5'W	X	86,87
Sir Archibald's Plantation	Stir	NS5586	56°3·0'	4°19·2'W	F	57
Sir Edward's Lake	Northum	NZ0379	55°6·6'	1°56·8'W	W	87
Sirelands	Cumbr	NY5254	54°53·0'	2°44·5'W	X	86
Sirhowy	Blae Gw	SO1410	51°47·2'	3°14·4'W	T	161
Sirhowy River	Blae Gw	SO1408	51°46·1'	3°14·4'W	W	161
Sirhowy River	Caer	ST1891	51°36·9'	3°10·7'W	W	171
Sirhowy River	Caer	ST1990	51°36·4'	3°9·8'W	W	171
Sirhowy Valley	Blae Gw	SO1605	51°44·5'	3°12·6'W	X	161
Sirhowy Valley	Caer	ST1792	51°37·5'	3°11·6'W	X	171
Sirhowy Valley Country Park	Caer	ST1891	51°36·9'	3°10·7'W	X	171
Sirior Bach	Conwy	SH9374	53°15·4'	3°35·8'W	X	116
Sirior Goch Fm	Conwy	SH9273	53°14·8'	3°36·7'W	FM	116
Sir John's Castle	Highld	ND2473	58°38·6'	3°18·1'W	X	7,12
Sir John's Hill	Carm	SN2909	51°45·5'	4°28·3'W	H	159
Sir Rowland Winn's Drain	N Lincs	SE9614	53°37·1'	0°32·5'W	W	112
Sir Tatton Sykes's Monument	E Yorks	SE9561	54°2·4'	0°32·5'W	X	101
Sir Watkin's Tower	Denb	SJ2149	53°2·2'	3°10·3'W	X	117
Sirwick Taing	Shetld	HU3242	60°9·9'	1°24·9'W	X	4
Sir William Hill	Derby	SK2177	53°17·6'	1°40·7'W	H	119
Siseley Fm	Kent	TQ7431	51°3·3'	0°29·4'E	FM	188
Sisland	Norf	TM3498	52°32·0'	1°27·4'E	T	134
Siss Cross	N Yks	NZ7010	54°29·1'	0°54·7'W	X	94
Sisservernes Fm	Herts	TL2217	51°50·5'	0°13·3'W	FM	166
Sissinghurst	Kent	TQ7937	51°6·5'	0°33·8'E	T	188
Sissinghurst Castle	Kent	TQ8038	51°7·0'	0°34·7'E	A	188
Sissons Fm	Peterb	TF1707	52°39·1'	0°15·8'W	FM	142
Sisterhood Fm	Devon	SY2999	50°47·4'	3°0·1'W	FM	193
Sisterpath	Scot Bord	NT7548	55°43·7'	2°23·4'W	X	74
Sisterpath Waulkmill	Scot Bord	NT7548	55°43·7'	2°23·4'W	X	74
Sisters Fm	Glos	SU0697	51°40·5'	1°54·4'W	FM	163
Sisters, The	Corn	SX0689	50°40·3'	4°44·4'W	X	200
Sisters, The	E Loth	NT5585	56°3·6'	2°42·9'W	X	66
Sisters, The	Glos	SP0305	51°44·9'	1°57·0'W	F	163
Siston	S Glos	ST6875	51°28·6'	2°27·3'W	T	172
Siston Common	S Glos	ST6674	51°28·1'	2°29·0'W	T	172
Siston Court	S Glos	ST6875	51°28·6'	2°27·3'W	A	172
Sitch	Derby	SK0291	53°25·2'	1°57·8'W	X	110
Sitch Fm	Derby	SK2551	53°3·6'	1°37·2'W	FM	119
Sitch Ho	Derby	SK0079	53°18·7'	1°59·6'W	X	119
Sitcott	Devon	SX3690	50°41·4'	4°18·9'W	X	190
Siteley	Shrops	SJ3609	52°40·7'	2°56·4'W	X	126
Site of Dowalton Loch	D & G	NX4046	54°47·3'	4°28·9'W	X	83
Sithean a' Choire Odhair	Highld	NG7623	57°14·8'	5°42·3'W	X	33
Sithean Airigh Mhurchaidh	N Eil	NB4544	58°18·9'	6°20·8'W	X	8
Sitheanan Dubha	Highld	NG8489	57°50·6'	5°37·9'W	H	19
Sithean Beag	Highld	NG5808	57°6·2'	5°59·3'W	X	32,39
Sithean Beinn a' Mhorrain	Highld	NG3649	57°27·5'	6°23·7'W	H	23
Sithean Bhealaich Chumhainn	Highld	NG5046	57°26·4'	6°9·5'W	H	23,24
Sithean Corr-meille	Highld	ND0839	58°20·1'	3°33·8'W	X	11,12,17
Sithean Dubh	Highld	ND0458	58°30·2'	3°38·4'W	X	11,12
Sithean Dubh	Highld	ND1527	58°13·7'	3°26·4'W	X	17
Sithean Feuraich	Highld	NC3353	58°26·3'	4°51·2'W	X	9
Sithean Freiceadain	Highld	NC6322	58°10·2'	4°19·3'W	X	16
Sithean Glac an Ime	Highld	NG6030	57°18·1'	5°58·6'W	X	24,32
Sithean Mór	Highld	NC1348	58°23·1'	5°11·4'W	H	9
Sithean Mór	Highld	NC3562	58°31·2'	4°49·5'W	H	9
Sithean Mór	Highld	NG5907	57°5·7'	5°58·3'W	H	32,39
Sithean Mór	Highld	NG5947	57°27·2'	6°0·6'W	H	24
Sithean na Gearra	Highld	ND0837	58°19·0'	3°33·7'W	H	11,17
Sithean na Gearrsaich	Highld	NC6054	58°27·4'	4°23·5'W	H	10
Sithean na h-Iolaireich	Highld	NC2570	58°35·2'	5°0·2'W	H	9
Sith MOR	Arg & Bt	NS3096	56°7·8'	4°43·7'W	X	56
Sith Mór	Highld	NH7117	57°13·8'	4°7·8'W	H	35
Sithney	Corn	SW6328	50°6·5'	5°18·5'W	T	203
Sithney Common	Corn	SW6428	50°6·5'	5°17·7'W	T	203
Sithney Green	Corn	SW6429	50°7·1'	5°17·7'W	T	203
Sitmelane	Pth & Kin	NO1723	56°23·8'	3°20·2'W	X	53,58
Sittaford Tor	Devon	SX6383	50°38·1'	3°55·9'W	H	191
Sitterlow Fm	Derby	SK1953	53°4·7'	1°42·6'W	FM	119
Sitterton	Dorset	SY8494	50°45·0'	2°13·2'W	T	194
Sittingbourne	Kent	TQ9063	51°20·3'	0°44·1'E	T	178
Sittingbourne & Kemsley Light Rly	Kent	TQ9164	51°20·8'	0°45·0'E	X	178
Sittinghillock	Aberd	NJ4847	57°30·9'	2°51·6'W	X	28,29
Sittinglow	Derby	SK0779	53°18·7'	1°53·3'W	X	119
Sittles	Staffs	SK1712	52°42·6'	1°44·5'W	X	128
Sittyton	Aberd	NJ8520	57°16·5'	2°14·5'W	T	38
Sitwell Grange	Derby	SK4361	53°8·9'	1°21·0'W	X	120
Siusaigh	N Eil	NF8246	57°23·9'	7°17·2'W	X	22
Siwards How	York	SE6250	53°56·8'	1°2·9'W	A	105
Sixacre Fm	Devon	SS7048	51°13·2'	3°51·3'W	FM	180
Six Acre Plantn	Cambs	TL6089	52°28·8'	0°21·8'E	F	143
Six Ashes	Shrops	SO6877	52°23·6'	2°27·8'W	X	138
Six Ashes	Shrops	SO7988	52°29·6'	2°18·2'W	T	138
Six Ash Fm	Oxon	SP3434	52°0·4'	1°29·9'W	FM	151
Six Bells	Blae Gw	SO2203	51°43·5'	3°7·4'W	T	171
Six Brothers Field	Surrey	TQ3154	51°16·4'	0°6·9'W	X	187
Six Dikes	N Yks	SE9087	54°16·5'	0°36·7'W	A	94,101

Six Hills	Leic	SK6420	52°46·7′	1°2·7′W	T	129
Sixhills	Lincs	TF1787	53°22·2′	0°14·1′W	T	113,121
Sixhills Walk Fm	Lincs	TF1987	53°22·2′	0°12·3′W	FM	113,122
Six Hundreds Fm	Lincs	TF2045	52°59·6′	0°12·3′W	FM	131
Six Lanes End	Kirk	SE2314	53°37·6′	1°38·7′W	X	110
Sixmile	Kent	TR1344	51°9·6′	1°3·2′E	T	179,189
Six Mile Bottom	Cambs	TL5757	52°11·6′	0°18·2′E	X	154
Six-Mile Bridge	N upon Ty	NZ2373	55°3·3′	1°38·0′W	X	88
Sixpence	S Ayr	NX2085	55°7·9′	4°49·0′W	X	76
Sixpenny Handley	Dorset	ST9917	50°57·4′	2°0·5′W	T	184
Sixpenny Hill Plantn	E Yorks	TA2271	54°7·5′	0°7·6′W	F	101
Six Roads End	Staffs	SK1527	52°50·7′	1°46·2′W	X	128
Sixscore Fm	Lincs	TF1614	52°42·9′	0°16·6′W	FM	130
Sixteen Acre Plantn	Donc	SE5609	53°34·7′	1°8·8′W	F	111
Sixteen Foot Drain	Cambs	TL4694	52°31·7′	0°9·5′E	W	143
Six Tunnels Fm	Herts	TL0413	51°48·6′	0°29·1′W	FM	166
Sixty Acre Moor	Devon	SX4697	50°45·4′	4°10·6′W	X	190
Sixty Acres Fm	Corn	SW8153	50°20·4′	5°4·3′W	FM	200,204
Six Wells Bottom	Wilts	ST7634	51°6·5′	2°20·2′W	X	183
Sizergh Castle	Cumbr	SD4987	54°16·8′	2°46·6′W	A	97
Sizewell	Suff	TM4761	52°11·7′	1°37·3′E	T	156
Sizewell Belts	Suff	TM4663	52°12·8′	1°36·5′E	X	156
Skaag	Shetld	HU4321	59°58·6′	1°13·3′W	X	4
Skaaga	Shetld	HU1655	60°17·0′	1°42·1′W	X	3
Skaari	N Eil	NF9885	57°45·4′	7°4·2′W	X	18
Skaigh	Devon	SX6293	50°43·5′	3°56·9′W	T	191
Skaigh Warren	Devon	SX6393	50°43·5′	3°56·1′W	X	191
Skaig Loch	S Ayr	NX3285	55°8·1′	4°37·7′W	W	76
Skail	Highld	NC7146	58°23·3′	4°11·9′W	X	10
Skail Burn	Highld	NC7048	58°24·3′	4°13·0′W	W	10
Skaildaquoy Point	Orkney	HY4700	58°53·3′	2°54·7′W	X	6,7
Skaill	Highld	ND2435	58°18·1′	3°17·3′W	X	11
Skaill	Orkney	HY3510	58°58·6′	3°7·4′W	X	6
Skaill	Orkney	HY3918	59°2·9′	3°3·3′W	X	6
Skaill	Orkney	HY4552	59°21·3′	2°57·6′W	X	5
Skaill	Orkney	HY4630	59°9·5′	2°56·2′W	X	5,6
Skaill	Orkney	HY4802	58°54·4′	2°53·7′W	X	6,7
Skaill	Orkney	HY5632	59°10·6′	2°45·7′W	X	5,6
Skaill	Orkney	HY5806	58°56·6′	2°43·3′W	T	6
Skaill	Orkney	HY6940	59°15·0′	2°32·1′W	X	5
Skaill Ho	Orkney	HY2318	59°2·8′	3°20·0′W	A	6
Skaill Home Fm	Orkney	HY2318	59°2·8′	3°20·0′W	FM	6
Skaill Skerries	Orkney	HY5906	58°56·6′	2°42·3′W	X	6
Skairfield	D & G	NY0979	55°6·1′	3°25·1′W	X	85
Skairs, The	Aberd	NJ6901	57°6·2′	2°30·2′W	X	38
Skaith	D & G	NX3766	54°58·0′	4°32·3′W	X	83
Skaith	Orkney	HY3706	58°56·5′	3°5·2′W	W	6,7
Skaithmuir	Scot Bord	NT8443	55°41·1′	2°14·8′W	X	74
Skaith, The	Northum	NU2323	55°30·3′	1°37·7′W	X	75
Skallary	N Eil	NL6999	56°58·1′	7°26·4′W	T	31
Skants	Corn	SX2558	50°24·0′	4°27·4′W	X	201
Skara Brae	Orkney	HY2218	59°2·8′	3°21·1′W	A	6
Skares	Aberd	NJ6334	57°24·0′	2°36·5′W	X	29
Skares	E Ayr	NS5217	55°25·7′	4°19·9′W	T	70
Skares, The	Aberd	NK0833	57°23·5′	1°51·6′W	X	30
Skarpi Geo	Shetld	HU6692	60°36·6′	0°47·2′W	X	1,2
Skate	D & G	NX3548	54°48·2′	4°33·6′W	X	83
Skatebrae	Aberd	NJ6938	57°26·1′	2°30·5′W	X	29
Skatelan Skerry	Orkney	HY2709	58°58·0′	3°15·7′W	X	6,7
Skate Point	N Ayr	NS1658	55°47·1′	4°55·6′W	X	63
Skate Point	N Eil	NL5480	56°47·2′	7°39·6′W	X	31
Skatequoy	Orkney	HY3934	59°11·6′	3°3·6′W	X	6
Skateraw	E Loth	NT7375	55°58·3′	2°25·5′W	X	67
Skateraw Harbour	E Loth	NT7375	55°58·3′	2°25·5′W	X	67
Skate Road	Northum	NU1537	55°37·8′	1°45·3′W	W	75
Skate's Fm	Hants	SU6060	51°20·4′	1°7·9′W	FM	175
Skate Stack	Shetld	HP5711	60°46·9′	0°56·7′W	X	1
Skate, The	Shetld	HU5263	60°21·1′	1°3·0′W	X	2,3
Skatie Shore	Aberd	NO8987	56°58·7′	2°10·4′W	X	45
Skaw	Shetld	HP6616	60°49·5′	0°46·7′W	X	1
Skaw	Shetld	HU5966	60°22·7′	0°55·3′W	T	2
Skaw Banks	Shetld	HP6715	60°49·0′	0°45·6′W	X	1
Skaw Taing	Shetld	HU3978	60°29·3′	1°16·9′W	X	2,3
Skaw Taing	Shetld	HU6067	60°23·2′	0°54·2′W	X	2
Skaw Voe	Shetld	HU5866	60°22·7′	0°56·4′W	W	2
Skaylock Hill	Durham	NZ0344	54°47·7′	1°56·8′W	X	87
Skea	Orkney	HY2930	59°9·3′	3°14·0′W	X	6
Skea	Orkney	HY5804	58°55·5′	2°43·3′W	X	6
Skea	Shetld	HU3785	60°33·1′	1°19·0′W	X	1,2,3
Skeabost	Highld	NG4247	57°26·7′	6°17·5′W	X	23
Skeabost Ho (Hotel)	Highld	NG4148	57°27·2′	6°18·6′W	X	23
Skeabrae	Orkney	HY2720	59°3·9′	3°15·9′W	T	6
Skeaf Ho	N Yks	SE2572	54°8·8′	1°36·6′W	X	99
Skea Hill	Orkney	HY4244	59°17·0′	3°0·6′W	H	5
Skealtraval	N Eil	NF8570	57°36·9′	7°16·1′W	H	18
Skea Skerries	Orkney	HY4440	59°14·8′	2°58·4′W	X	5
Skeath House Fm	Staffs	SJ9327	52°50·7′	2°5·8′W	FM	127
Skedsbush	E Loth	NT5165	55°52·8′	2°46·6′W	X	66
Skeeby	N Yks	NZ1902	54°25·0′	1°42·0′W	T	92
Skeeby Beck	N Yks	NZ2001	54°24·5′	1°41·1′W	W	93
Skeeby Grange	N Yks	NZ2003	54°25·6′	1°41·1′W	X	93
Skeeby Plantn	N Yks	NZ2103	54°25·6′	1°40·2′W	F	93
Skeels	Cumbr	NY5722	54°35·7′	2°39·5′W	X	91
Skeete	Kent	TR1341	51°7·9′	1°3·1′E	T	179,189
Skeet Hill	Kent	TQ5065	51°22·1′	0°9·7′E	X	177
Skeetings Fm	E Yorks	TA0359	54°1·2′	0°25·3′W	FM	107
Skeet's Green	Suff	TM1352	52°7·7′	1°7·1′E	X	156
Skeet's Hill	Norf	TG2300	52°33·4′	1°17·8′E	X	134
Skeffington	Leic	SK7402	52°36·9′	0°54·0′W	T	141
Skeffington Gap Fm	Leic	SK7502	52°36·9′	0°53·1′W	FM	141
Skeffington Lodge Fm	Leic	SK7502	52°36·9′	0°53·1′W	FM	141
Skeffington Vale	Leic	SK7401	52°36·3′	0°54·0′W	X	141
Skeffington Wood	Leic	SK7503	52°37·4′	0°53·1′W	F	141
Skeffling	E Yorks	TA3719	53°39·2′	0°4·8′E	T	113
Skeffling Clays	E Yorks	TA3617	53°38·1′	0°3·8′E	X	113
Skegby	Notts	SK4961	53°8·9′	1°15·6′W	T	120
Skegby	Notts	SK7870	53°13·5′	0°49·5′W	T	120,121
Skegdale Beck	N Yks	NZ0503	54°25·6′	1°55·0′W	W	92
Skeggie	Shetld	HP6413	60°48·0′	0°48·9′W	T	1
Skeggles Water	Cumbr	NY4703	54°25·4′	2°48·6′W	W	90
Skegness	Lincs	TF5663	53°8·7′	0°20·4′E	T	122
Skegness (Ingoldmells) Aerodrome	Lincs	TF5667	53°10·9′	0°20·5′E	X	122
Skeibhill	Aberd	NJ6352	57°33·7′	2°36·6′W	X	29
Skeirrip	I of M	SC4584	54°13·9′	4°22·3′W	X	95
Skeith Stone	Fife	NO5704	56°13·9′	2°41·2′W	A	59
Skelabosdale	Highld	NC9721	58°10·2′	3°44·6′W	X	17
Skelberry	Shetld	HU3686	60°33·6′	1°20·1′W	T	1,2,3
Skelberry	Shetld	HU3916	59°55·9′	1°17·6′W	T	4
Skelberry	Shetld	HU4763	60°21·2′	1°8·4′W	X	2,3
Skelbist	Orkney	HY4422	59°5·1′	2°58·1′W	X	5,6
Skelbister	Orkney	HY3609	58°58·1′	3°6·3′W	X	6,7
Skelbo	Highld	NH7995	57°55·9′	4°2·1′W	T	21
Skelbo Muir	Highld	NH7893	57°54·8′	4°3·1′W	T	21
Skelbo Street	Highld	NH7994	57°55·4′	4°2·1′W	X	21
Skelbo Wood	Highld	NH7894	57°55·4′	4°3·1′W	F	21
Skelbrae	Orkney	HY6743	59°16·6′	2°34·3′W	X	5
Skelbrooke	Donc	SE5012	53°36·4′	1°14·2′W	T	111
Skelcies	Cumbr	NY7711	54°29·9′	2°20·9′W	X	91
Skeld	Shetld	HT9741	60°9·5′	2°2·7′W	X	4
Skelda Ho	N Yks	SD8851	53°57·5′	2°10·6′W	X	103
Skelda Ness	Shetld	HU3040	60°8·9′	1°27·1′W	X	4
Skelda Voe	Shetld	HU3144	60°11·0′	1°26·0′W	W	4
Skelday	Orkney	HY3123	59°5·6′	3°11·8′W	X	6
Skelday Hill	Orkney	HY3224	59°6·1′	3°10·7′W	H	6
Skelder Ho	Dorset	ST8303	50°49·8′	2°14·1′W	X	194
Skelder Plantn	N Yks	NZ8409	54°28·4′	0°41·8′W	F	94
Skelderskeugh Fm	N Yks	NZ6610	54°29·1′	0°58·5′W	FM	94
Skelderskew Moor	N Yks	NZ6511	54°29·7′	0°59·4′W	X	94
Skelder Taing	Shetld	HU4769	60°24·4′	1°8·3′W	X	2,3
Skeld Gate	N Yks	SD9458	54°1·3′	2°5·1′W	X	103
Skelding Moor	N Yks	SE2070	54°7·8′	1°41·2′W	X	99
Skeld of Gue	Orkney	HY7553	59°22·0′	2°25·9′W	X	5
Skeldon Ho	S Ayr	NS3713	55°23·3′	4°34·0′W	X	70
Skeldon Mains	S Ayr	NS3713	55°23·3′	4°34·0′W	X	70
Skeldon Mills	E Ayr	NS3814	55°23·8′	4°33·1′W	X	70
Skeldon Moor	Cumbr	SD2673	54°9·1′	3°7·6′W	X	96,97
Skeldyke	Lincs	TF3337	52°55·1′	0°0·9′W	T	131
Skeleton Hovel	Bri & Hov	TQ2609	50°52·2′	0°12·2′W	X	198
Skelfhill	Scot Bord	NT4504	55°19·9′	2°51·6′W	T	79
Skelfhill Burn	Scot Bord	NT4503	55°19·3′	2°51·6′W	W	79
Skelfhill Fell	Scot Bord	NT4501	55°18·3′	2°51·6′W	H	79
Skelfhillhope	Scot Bord	NT4402	55°18·8′	2°52·5′W	X	79
Skelfhill Pen	Scot Bord	NT4403	55°19·3′	2°52·5′W	H	79
Skelfrey Park	E Yorks	SE8642	53°52·3′	0°41·1′W	X	106
Skelghyll Wood	Cumbr	NY3803	54°25·4′	2°56·9′W	F	90
Skelgill	Cumbr	NY2420	54°34·4′	3°10·1′W	X	89,90
Skella Dale	Shetld	HU3767	60°23·4′	1°19·2′W	X	2,3
Skellands	N Yks	SD8960	54°2·4′	2°9·7′W	X	98
Skellarie Rock	D & G	NX4551	54°50·0′	4°24·4′W	X	83
Skellater Ho	Aberd	NJ3110	57°10·8′	3°8·0′W	X	37
Skell Bank Wood	N Yks	SE2668	54°6·7′	1°35·7′W	F	99
Skell Beck	N Yks	SE1769	54°7·2′	1°44·0′W	W	99
Skell Dikes	N Yks	SE9987	54°16·4′	0°28·4′W	A	94,101
Skell Gill	N Yks	SD9291	54°19·1′	2°7·0′W	X	98
Skell Gill	N Yks	SE1968	54°6·7′	1°42·1′W	X	99
Skell Gill	N Yks	SE2069	54°7·2′	1°41·2′W	X	99
Skell Gill Wood	N Yks	SE2069	54°7·2′	1°41·2′W	F	99
Skell Grain	N Yks	SE1769	54°7·2′	1°44·0′W	X	99
Skellicks Beck	N Yks	SD9886	54°16·4′	2°1·4′W	W	98
Skellies The	Aberd	NK1058	57°37·0′	1°49·5′W	X	30
Skelling	Cumbr	NY6233	54°41·7′	2°35·0′W	X	91
Skelling Moor	Cumbr	NY6243	54°47·1′	2°35·0′W	X	86
Skellingthorpe	Lincs	SK9271	53°13·9′	0°36·9′W	T	121
Skellingthorpe Moor	Lincs	SK9270	53°13·4′	0°36·9′W	X	121
Skellion	Cumbr	NY5257	54°54·6′	2°44·5′W	X	86
Skellister	Shetld	HU4654	60°16·3′	1°9·6′W	T	3
Skellorn Green	Ches	SJ9281	53°19·8′	2°6·8′W	T	109
Skellow	Donc	SE5310	53°35·3′	1°11·5′W	T	111
Skells Lodge	Cumbr	SD2473	54°9·1′	3°9·4′W	X	96
Skelly	Angus	NO5177	56°53·2′	2°47·8′W	X	44
Skellyhill	S Lanak	NS7837	55°36·9′	3°55·8′W	X	71
Skellyis, The	Aberd	NK1243	57°28·9′	1°47·5′W	W	30
Skelly Neb	Cumbr	NY4320	54°34·6′	2°52·5′W	X	90
Skellyton	S Lanak	NS7851	55°44·5′	3°56·2′W	X	64
Skelmanthorpe	Kirk	SE2310	53°35·5′	1°38·7′W	T	110
Skelmersdale	Lancs	SD4806	53°33·1′	2°46·7′W	T	108
Skelmonae	Aberd	NJ8839	57°26·7′	2°11·5′W	X	30
Skelmorlie	N Ayr	NS1967	55°52·0′	4°53·1′W	T	63
Skelmorlie Castle	N Ayr	NS1965	55°50·9′	4°53·0′W	A	63
Skelmorlie Mains	N Ayr	NS1966	55°51·5′	4°53·1′W	X	63
Skelmorlie Water	N Ayr	NS2065	55°50·9′	4°52·1′W	W	63
Skelmuir	Aberd	NJ9842	57°28·4′	2°1·5′W	X	30
Skelmuir Hill	Aberd	NJ9841	57°27·8′	2°1·5′W	H	30
Skelpick	Highld	NC7255	58°28·1′	4°11·2′W	T	10
Skelpick Burn	Highld	NC7355	58°28·2′	4°10·2′W	W	10
Skelpie	Fife	NO3608	56°15·9′	3°1·6′W	X	59
Skelsceugh	Cumbr	NY0418	54°33·1′	3°28·6′W	X	89
Skelshaw	Lancs	SD7250	53°57·0′	2°25·2′W	X	103
Skelshaw Brook	Lancs	SD7250	53°57·0′	2°25·2′W	W	103
Skelsmergh Hall Fm	Cumbr	SD5395	54°21·1′	2°43·0′W	FM	97
Skelsmergh Tarn	Cumbr	SD5396	54°21·7′	2°43·0′W	W	97
Skelston Burn	D & G	NX8285	55°9·0′	3°50·7′W	W	78
Skelston Moor	D & G	NX8086	55°9·5′	3°52·6′W	X	78
Skelterton Hill	N Yks	SD9860	54°2·4′	2°1·4′W	H	98
Skelton	Cumbr	NY4335	54°42·7′	2°52·7′W	T	90
Skelton	E Yorks	SE7625	53°43·2′	0°50·5′W	T	105,106
Skelton	N Yks	NZ0900	54°24·0′	1°51·3′W	X	92
Skelton	Red & Cl	NZ6518	54°33·4′	0°59·3′W	T	94
Skelton	York	SE5756	54°0·1′	1°7·4′W	T	105
Skelton Banks Fm	N Yks	SE7690	54°18·2′	0°49·5′W	FM	94,100
Skelton Beck	Red & Cl	NZ6519	54°34·0′	0°59·3′W	W	94
Skelton Castle	Red & Cl	NZ6519	54°34·0′	0°59·3′W	X	94
Skelton Common	E Yorks	SE7729	53°45·3′	0°49·5′W	X	105,106
Skelton Cote Fm	N Yks	SE1294	54°20·7′	1°48·5′W	FM	99
Skelton Grange	E Yorks	SE8729	53°45·2′	0°40·4′W	X	106
Skelton Green	Red & Cl	NZ6518	54°33·4′	0°59·3′W	X	94
Skelton House Fm	Lincs	TF0176	53°16·5′	0°28·7′W	FM	121
Skelton Moor	N Yks	NZ0701	54°24·5′	1°53·1′W	X	92
Skelton Moor	York	SE5857	54°0·6′	1°6·5′W	X	105
Skelton on Ure	N Yks	SE3668	54°6·6′	1°26·5′W	T	99
Skelton Pasture	Cumbr	NY4238	54°44·3′	2°53·6′W	X	90
Skelton Pike	Cumbr	NY5483	55°8·6′	2°42·9′W	X	79
Skeltons Bank	Shrops	SO2585	52°27·7′	3°5·8′W	X	137
Skelton Tower	N Yks	SE8292	54°19·3′	0°43·9′W	X	94,100
Skelton Wath Fm	N Yks	SE8579	54°12·2′	0°41·4′W	FM	100
Skelton Windmill	N Yks	SE3769	54°7·2′	1°25·6′W	X	99
Skelton Wood End	Cumbr	NY4038	54°44·3′	2°55·5′W	X	90
Skelwick	Orkney	HY4844	59°17·0′	2°54·3′W	T	5
Skel Wick	Orkney	HY4945	59°17·6′	2°53·2′W	W	5
Skelwith Bridge	Cumbr	NY3403	54°25·3′	3°0·6′W	T	90
Skelwith Fold	Cumbr	NY3502	54°24·8′	2°59·7′W	X	90
Skelwith Force	Cumbr	NY3403	54°25·3′	3°0·6′W	W	90
Skelwith Pool	Cumbr	SD3481	54°13·5′	3°0·3′W	W	96,97
Skenchill	Heref	SO4818	51°51·7′	2°44·9′W	X	161
Skendleby	Lincs	TF4369	53°12·2′	0°8·9′E	T	122
Skendleby Holme Fm	Lincs	TF4268	53°11·6′	0°7·9′E	FM	122
Skendleby Psalter	Lincs	TF4371	53°13·2′	0°8·9′E	T	122
Skene Ho	Aberd	NJ7609	57°10·5′	2°23·4′W	X	38
Skene Moss	Aberd	NJ7510	57°11·1′	2°24·4′W	F	38
Skeney Skar	Northum	NU2337	55°37·8′	1°37·6′W	X	75
Skenfrith	Monm	SO4520	51°52·8′	2°47·5′W	T	161
Skenfrith Castle	Monm	SO4520	51°52·8′	2°47·5′W	A	161
Skennist	Orkney	HY4952	59°21·3′	2°53·3′W	X	5
Skenstoft	Orkney	HY5119	59°3·6′	2°50·8′W	X	6
Skeoch	D & G	NX8677	55°4·7′	3°46·7′W	X	84
Skeoch	S Ayr	NS4729	55°32·1′	4°25·0′W	X	70
Skeoch	S Lanak	NS6348	55°42·6′	4°10·4′W	X	64
Skeoch	Stir	NS8191	56°6·1′	3°54·3′W	X	57
Skeoch Hill	D & G	NX8678	55°5·3′	3°46·7′W	H	84
Skeoch Wood	Arg & Bt	NS0865	55°50·7′	5°3·6′W	F	63
Skeog	D & G	NX4539	54°43·6′	4°24·0′W	X	83
Skeo Head	Shetld	HU3080	60°30·4′	1°26·7′W	X	1,3
Skeo Ness	Shetld	HU4769	60°24·4′	1°8·3′W	X	2,3
Skeo of Gossaford	Shetld	HU3466	60°22·9′	1°22·5′W	X	2,3
Skeo Taing	Shetld	HP6408	60°45·3′	0°49·0′W	X	1
Skeo Taing	Shetld	HU4663	60°21·2′	1°9·5′W	X	2,3
Skeo, The	Shetld	HU4434	60°5·6′	1°12·0′W	X	4
Sker Court	Brig	SS8079	51°30·1′	3°43·3′W	X	170
Sker Ho	Brig	SS7979	51°30·1′	3°44·2′W	X	170
Skerinish	Highld	NG4151	57°28·8′	6°18·8′W	X	23
Skerinish Quay	Highld	NG4052	57°29·3′	6°19·9′W	X	23
Skern	Devon	SS4530	51°3·1′	4°12·3′W	X	180
Skerne	E Yorks	TA0455	53°59·1′	0°24·4′W	T	107
Skerne Beck	E Yorks	TA0453	53°58·0′	0°24·5′W	W	107
Skerne Grange	E Yorks	TA0455	53°59·1′	0°24·4′W	X	107
Skerne Hill	E Yorks	TA0356	53°59·6′	0°25·3′W	X	107
Skerne Leys	E Yorks	TA0256	53°59·6′	0°26·2′W	X	106,107
Skerne Park	Darl	NZ2812	54°30·4′	1°33·6′W	T	93
Skernieland	E Ayr	NS4643	55°39·6′	4°26·4′W	X	70
Skerningham	Darl	NZ3018	54°33·6′	1°31·7′W	X	93
Skernish	Arg & Bt	NR6737	55°34·5′	5°41·3′W	X	68
Skeroblin Cruach	Arg & Bt	NR7027	55°29·2′	5°38·0′W	H	68
Skeroblingarry	Arg & Bt	NR7026	55°28·7′	5°38·0′W	X	68
Skeroblin Hill	Arg & Bt	NR6927	55°29·2′	5°38·9′W	H	68
Skeroblin Loch	Arg & Bt	NR7026	55°28·7′	5°38·0′W	W	68
Skeroblinraid	Arg & Bt	NR7025	55°28·1′	5°37·9′W	X	68
Skerp	Orkney	ND2989	58°47·2′	3°13·2′W	X	7
Skerpie	Orkney	ND4895	58°50·6′	2°53·6′W	X	7
Sker Point	Brig	SS7879	51°30·0′	3°45·1′W	X	170
Skerraton	Devon	SX7064	50°27·9′	3°49·5′W	X	202
Skerraton Down	Devon	SX7065	50°28·5′	3°49·5′W	X	202
Skerray	Highld	NC6663	58°32·3′	4°17·6′W	T	10
Skerray Bay	Highld	NC6663	58°32·3′	4°17·6′W	W	10
Skerricha	Highld	NC2350	58°24·4′	5°1·3′W	X	9
Skerrie	Moray	NJ1169	57°42·4′	3°29·1′W	X	28
Skerries of Clestrain	Orkney	HY2806	58°56·4′	3°14·6′W	X	6,7
Skerries of Coubister	Orkney	HY3814	59°0·8′	3°4·3′W	X	6
Skerries of Easter Paill	Shetld	HU1947	60°12·7′	1°38·9′W	X	3
Skerries of Fugliness	Shetld	HU3191	60°36·3′	1°25·5′W	X	1
Skerries of Kellister	Shetld	HP5403	60°42·7′	1°0·1′W	X	1
Skerries of Lakequoy	Orkney	HY5208	58°57·7′	2°49·6′W	X	6,7
Skerries of Skaigram	Orkney	ND4683	58°44·1′	2°55·5′W	X	7
Skerries, The or Ynysoedd y Moelrhoniaid	I of Angl	SH2694	53°25·1′	4°36·7′W	X	114
Skerrington	E Ayr	NS5718	55°26·4′	4°15·2′W	X	71
Skerrington Mains	E Ayr	NS4637	55°36·4′	4°26·2′W	X	70
Skerrisdale Moar	I of M	SC2987	54°15·3′	4°37·1′W	X	95
Skerrols	Arg & Bt	NR3563	55°47·5′	6°13·2′W	X	60,61
Skerry Fell Fad	Arg & Bt	NR6318	55°24·2′	5°44·2′W	X	68
Skerryford	Pemb	SM9214	51°47·4′	5°0·6′W	T	157,158
Skerry Grange	N Yks	SE3748	53°55·8′	1°25·8′W	X	104
Skerry Hill	N Yks	NZ9305	54°26·2′	0°33·5′W	X	94
Skerry Mór	Highld	ND2835	58°18·1′	3°13·2′W	X	11
Skerry of Cletts	Orkney	HY2506	58°56·3′	3°17·7′W	X	6,7
Skerry of Eshaness	Shetld	HU2076	60°28·3′	1°37·7′W	X	3
Skerry of Lambaness	Shetld	HU1662	60°20·8′	1°42·1′W	X	3
Skerry of Lunning	Shetld	HU5066	60°22·8′	1°5·1′W	X	2,3
Skerry of Ness	Orkney	HY2507	58°56·9′	3°17·7′W	X	6,7
Skerry of Okraquoy	Shetld	HU4431	60°3·9′	1°12·1′W	X	4
Skerry of Scord	Shetld	HU3932	60°4·5′	1°17·5′W	X	4
Skerry of Stools	Shetld	HU2258	60°18·6′	1°35·6′W	X	3
Skerry of Vasa	Orkney	HY4618	59°3·0′	2°56·0′W	X	6
Skerry of Wastbist	Orkney	HY4841	59°15·4′	2°54·2′W	X	5
Skerry of Work	Orkney	HY4813	59°0·3′	2°53·8′W	X	6
Skerry of Yinstay	Orkney	HY5111	58°59·3′	2°50·7′W	X	6
Skerry, The	Aberd	NK1443	57°28·9′	1°45·5′W	X	30
Skerry, The	Shetld	HU3639	60°8·3′	1°20·6′W	X	4
Skerry, The	Shetld	HZ1969	59°30·7′	1°39·4′W	X	4
Skerry Wick	Shetld	HU5384	60°32·4′	1°1·5′W	X	1,2,3
Skersan	Shetld	HU3719	59°57·5′	1°19·8′W	X	4
Skers Fm	Hants	SU2613	50°55·2′	1°37·4′W	FM	195
Skersund Skerry	Shetld	HU4638	60°7·7′	1°9·8′W	X	4
Skerth Drain	Lincs	TF2244	52°59·0′	0°10·6′W	W	131
Skerton	Lancs	SD4763	54°3·9′	2°48·2′W	T	97
Skervie Skerry	Shetld	HU3838	60°7·8′	1°18·5′W	X	4
Skervuile Lighthouse	Arg & Bt	NR6071	55°52·6′	5°49·8′W	X	61,62
Skesquoy	Orkney	HY3025	59°6·6′	3°12·9′W	X	6
Sketchley	Leic	SP4292	52°31·7′	1°22·5′W	T	140
Sketchley Brook	Warw	SP3992	52°31·7′	1°25·1′W	W	140

Sketchley Hill	Leic	SP4393	52°32·2'	1°21·6'W	X	140
Sketewan	Pth & Kin	NN9352	56°39·1'	3°44·3'W	X	52
Skethaquoy	Orkney	HY4248	59°19·1'	3°0·7'W	X	5
Skettegill	Cumbr	SD5286	54°16·3'	2°43·8'W	X	97
Sketty	Swan	SS6292	51°36·8'	3°59·2'W	T	159
Sketty Hall	Swan	SS6292	51°36·8'	3°59·2'W	X	159
Skeugh Fm	N Yks	SE5967	54°6·0'	1°5·4'W	FM	100
Skeugh Head	N Yks	SD8899	54°23·4'	2°10·7'W	X	98
Skeun	N Eil	NB1427	58°8·6'	6°51·2'W	H	13
Skeviot Fm	Monm	ST4189	51°36·0'	2°50·7'W	FM	171,172
Skew Br	Powys	SO0898	52°34·6'	3°21·1'W	X	136
Skewbridge	D & G	NY0771	55°1·7'	3°26·9'W	X	85
Skewen	Nth Pt Talb	SS7297	51°39·7'	3°50·7'W	T	170
Skewes	Corn	SW6333	50°9·2'	5°18·7'W	X	203
Skewes	Corn	SW9665	50°27·2'	4°52·1'W	T	200
Skewfe Fm	N Yks	SE3367	54°6·1'	1°29·3'W	FM	99
Skew Green	N Yks	SE5077	54°11·4'	1°13·6'W	X	100
Skewjack Fm	Corn	SW3624	50°3·7'	5°41·0'W	FM	203
Skewkirk Hall	N Yks	SE4754	53°59·0'	1°16·6'W	X	105
Skews	Cumbr	NY5018	54°33·5'	2°46·0'W	X	90
Skewsby	N Yks	SE6271	54°8·1'	1°2·6'W	T	100
Skeynes Park	Kent	TQ4346	51°11·9'	0°3·2'E	X	187
Skeys Wood	Worcs	SO7777	52°23·7'	2°19·9'W	F	138
Skeyton	Norf	TG2425	52°46·8'	1°19·7'E	T	133,134
Skeyton Corner	Norf	TG2527	52°47·8'	1°20·7'E	T	133,134
Skeyton Lodge	Norf	TG2424	52°46·2'	1°19·7'E	X	133,134
Skiag	Highld	NC7403	58°0·2'	4°7·5'W	H	16
Skiag	Pth & Kin	NN7040	56°32·3'	4°6·4'W	X	51,52
Skiag Bridge	Highld	NC2324	58°10·4'	5°0·1'W	X	15
Skiall	Highld	ND0267	58°35·1'	3°40·7'W	X	11,12
Skiary	Highld	NG9207	57°6·7'	5°25·6'W	X	33
Skibbereen	Durham	NZ2733	54°41·7'	1°34·4'W	X	93
Skibbowick	Orkney	HY5210	58°58·7'	2°49·6'W	X	6
Skibeden	N Yks	SE0152	53°58·1'	1°58·7'W	X	104
Skiberhoull	Shetld	HU5462	60°20·6'	1°0·8'W	X	2
Skibinish	N Eil	NF8275	57°39·4'	7°19·5'W	X	18
Skibo Castle	Highld	NH7389	57°52·6'	4°8·0'W	X	21
Skichen Muir	Angus	NO5241	56°33·8'	2°46·4'W	X	54
Skidbrooke	Lincs	TF4492	53°24·5'	0°10·4'E	T	113
Skidbrooke North End	Lincs	TF4494	53°25·6'	0°10·4'E	T	113
Skidby	E Yorks	TA0133	53°47·2'	0°27·6'W	T	106,107
Skidby Ings Fm	E Yorks	TA0735	53°48·3'	0°22·1'W	FM	107
Skidby Mill	E Yorks	TA0233	53°47·2'	0°26·7'W	X	106,107
Skiddaw	Cumbr	NY2629	54°39·3'	3°8·4'W	H	89,90
Skiddaw	Stir	NS6289	56°4·7'	4°12·6'W	X	57
Skiddaw Forest	Cumbr	NY2729	54°39·3'	3°7·5'W	X	89,90
Skiddaw Ho	Cumbr	NY2829	54°39·3'	3°6·5'W	X	89,90
Skiddy	Orkney	HY3921	59°4·6'	3°2·4'W	X	6
Skidge	Orkney	HY2426	59°7·1'	3°19·2'W	X	6
Skid Hill Fm	Brom	TQ4059	51°19·0'	0°0·9'E	FM	187
Skierda Water	Shetld	HU3077	60°28·8'	1°26·8'W	W	3
Skiff Fm	E Yorks	SE8236	53°49·1'	0°44·9'W	FM	106
Skiff Wood	Renf	NS4059	55°48·1'	4°32·7'W	F	64
Skigersta River	N Eil	NB5461	58°28·3'	6°12·7'W	W	8
Skighaugh	Essex	TM1626	51°53·6'	1°8·8'E	X	168,169
Skilgate	Somer	SS9827	51°2·2'	3°26·9'W	T	181
Skilgate Wood	Somer	SS9726	51°1·7'	3°27·7'W	F	181
Skiling Mill	Scot Bord	NT0638	55°37·8'	3°29·1'W	X	72
Skilling	Dorset	SY4692	50°43·7'	2°45·5'W	T	193
Skillington	Lincs	SK8925	52°49·1'	0°40·4'W	T	130
Skilly	Corn	SW4727	50°5·6'	5°31·9'W	X	203
Skillymarno	Aberd	NJ9552	57°33·7'	2°4·6'W	X	30
Skilmafilly	Aberd	NJ9039	57°26·7'	2°9·5'W	X	30
Skimblescott	Shrops	SO5892	52°31·7'	2°36·9'W	X	137,138
Skimmer Hills	E Loth	NT4766	55°53·3'	2°50·4'W	X	66
Skinburness	Cumbr	NY1255	54°53·2'	3°21·9'W	T	85
Skinburnessbank	Cumbr	NY1255	54°53·2'	3°21·9'W	X	85
Skinburness Marsh	Cumbr	NY1455	54°53·2'	3°20·0'W	W	85
Skinfast Haven	Fife	NO5703	56°13·3'	2°41·2'W	X	59
Skinflats	Falk	NS9083	56°1·9'	3°45·5'W	T	65
Skinford	D & G	NX8483	55°7·9'	3°48·7'W	X	78
Skinham Point	Corn	SX4360	50°25·4'	4°12·2'W	X	201
Skinhoga	Shetld	HU2257	60°18·1'	1°35·6'W	X	3
Skinidin	Highld	NG2247	57°26·0'	6°37·5'W	T	23
Skinnand	Lincs	SK9457	53°6·3'	0°35·3'W	X	121
Skinnard Village	Lincs	SK9457	53°6·3'	0°35·3'W	A	121
Skinner Ground Fm	N Yks	SD9351	53°57·5'	2°6·0'W	FM	103
Skinner Pastures	Cumbr	SD3487	54°16·7'	3°0·4'W	F	96,97
Skinner's Bottom	Corn	SW7246	50°16·4'	5°11·6'W	T	204
Skinner's Fm	Devon	ST0409	50°52·6'	3°21·5'W	FM	192
Skinners Fm	Dorset	ST7506	50°51·4'	2°20·9'W	FM	194
Skinners Fm	Dorset	ST7707	50°52·0'	2°19·2'W	FM	194
Skinners Fm	Essex	TQ4898	51°39·9'	0°8·8'E	FM	167,177
Skinner's Fm	E Susx	TQ6031	51°3·6'	0°17·4'E	FM	188
Skinners Fm	I of W	SZ4793	50°44·3'	1°19·7'W	FM	196
Skinners Fm	Kent	TQ4546	51°11·9'	0°4·9'E	FM	188
Skinners Green	W Berks	SU4465	51°23·2'	1°21·7'W	T	174
Skinner's Mill Fm	Glos	SO8609	51°47·0'	2°11·8'W	FM	162
Skinnerton	Highld	NH8682	57°49·0'	3°54·7'W	T	21
Skinnet	Highld	NC5861	58°31·1'	4°25·8'W	T	10
Skinnet	Highld	ND1261	58°32·0'	3°30·2'W	X	11,12
Skinningrove	Red & Cl	NZ7119	54°33·9'	0°53·7'W	T	94
Skinscoe	I of M	SC4584	54°13·9'	4°22·3'W	X	95
Skiordar	Shetld	HT9640	60°8·9'	2°3·8'W	X	4
Skiords	Shetld	HU3156	60°17·5'	1°25·9'W	H	3
Skipadock	Shetld	HU3468	60°23·9'	1°22·5'W	X	2,3
Skip Br	N Yks	SE4855	53°59·6'	1°15·7'W	X	105
Skip Bridge	Darl	NZ3111	54°29·8'	1°30·9'W	X	93
Skipi Geo	Orkney	HY2428	59°8·2'	3°19·2'W	X	6
Skipisdale	N Eil	NL5581	56°47·8'	7°38·7'W	X	31
Skiplam	N Yks	SE6587	54°16·7'	0°59·7'W	X	94,100
Skiplam Moor	N Yks	SE6391	54°18·9'	1°1·5'W	X	94,100
Skiplam Wood	N Yks	SE6686	54°16·2'	0°58·8'W	F	94,100
Skiplam Wood	N Yks	SE6688	54°17·2'	0°58·8'W	F	94,100
Skipmyre	D & G	NY0481	55°7·1'	3°29·9'W	X	78
Skipness	Arg & Bt	NR9057	55°45·9'	5°20·4'W	T	62
Skipness Bay	Arg & Bt	NR9057	55°45·9'	5°20·4'W	W	62
Skipness Ho	Arg & Bt	NR9057	55°45·9'	5°20·4'W	X	62
Skipness Point	Arg & Bt	NR9157	55°45·9'	5°19·5'W	X	62
Skipness River	Arg & Bt	NR8958	55°46·4'	5°21·4'W	W	62

Skipper's Bridge	D & G	NY3783	55°8·5'	2°58·9'W	X	79
Skipper's Fm	Suff	TL8858	52°11·5'	0°45·4'E	FM	155
Skippers Hall Fm	Cambs	TL6349	52°7·1'	0°23·2'E	FM	154
Skippers Hill	E Susx	TQ5525	51°0·4'	0°13·0'E	X	188,199
Skipper's Island	Essex	TM2124	51°52·5'	1°13·0'E	X	169
Skippie Geo	Highld	ND3968	58°36·0'	3°2·5'W	X	12
Skipping Block	Norf	TG0705	52°36·4'	1°3·8'E	X	144
Skippool	Lancs	SD3540	53°51·4'	2°58·9'W	T	102
Skippool Br	Lancs	SD3540	53°51·4'	2°58·9'W	X	102
Skiprigg	Cumbr	NY3845	54°48·0'	2°57·4'W	T	85
Skipsea	E Yorks	TA1655	53°58·9'	0°13·4'W	T	107
Skipsea Brough	E Yorks	TA1654	53°58·4'	0°13·5'W	T	107
Skipsea Grange	E Yorks	TA1753	53°57·8'	0°12·6'W	X	107
Skipsea Sands	E Yorks	TA1854	53°58·4'	0°11·6'W	X	107
Skipster Hagg Fm	N Yks	SE7286	54°16·1'	0°53·2'W	FM	94,100
Skipster Hagg Wood	N Yks	SE7386	54°16·1'	0°52·3'W	F	94,100
Skipta Skerry	Shetld	HU5890	60°35·6'	0°56·0'W	X	1,2
Skipton	N Yks	SD9851	53°57·5'	2°1·4'W	T	103
Skipton Grange	N Yks	SE3780	54°13·1'	1°25·5'W	X	99
Skipton Hall	N Yks	SE4983	54°14·7'	1°14·5'W	T	100
Skipton Moor	N Yks	SE0150	53°57·0'	1°58·7'W	X	104
Skipton-on-Swale	N Yks	SE3679	54°12·6'	1°26·5'W	T	99
Skipton Pits	N Yks	SE0150	53°57·0'	1°58·7'W	X	104
Skipwith	N Yks	SE6638	53°50·3'	0°59·4'W	T	105,106
Skipwith Common	N Yks	SE6537	53°49·8'	1°0·3'W	X	105,106
Skipwith Holmes	N Yks	SE6438	53°50·3'	1°1·2'W	X	105,106
Skirbeck	Lincs	TF3343	52°58·3'	0°0·8'W	T	131
Skir Beck	N Yks	SD8159	54°1·8'	2°17·0'W	X	103
Skirbeck Fm	Lincs	TF1981	53°19·0'	0°12·4'W	FM	122
Skirbeck Fm	Lincs	TF3254	53°4·2'	0°1·4'W	FM	122
Skirbeck Quarter	Lincs	TF3242	52°57·8'	0°1·7'W	T	131
Skirden	Lancs	SD7851	53°57·5'	2°19·7'W	X	103
Skirden Hall	Lancs	SD7655	53°59·7'	2°21·5'W	X	103
Skird Hill	Orkney	ND2591	58°48·3'	3°17·4'W	X	7
Skirethorns	N Yks	SD9864	54°4·6'	2°1·4'W	T	98
Skirfare Br	N Yks	SD9769	54°7·3'	2°2·3'W	X	98
Skirfolds	Aberd	NJ5855	57°35·2'	2°41·7'W	X	29
Skirgens Fm	Worcs	SO9762	52°15·6'	2°2·2'W	FM	150
Skir Hill	Devon	SX6570	50°31·1'	3°53·9'W	X	202
Skiridan	Highld	NG3425	57°14·6'	6°24·1'W	X	32
Skirlaugh	E Yorks	TA1439	53°50·3'	0°15·6'W	T	107
Skirlaugh Grange	E Yorks	TA1438	53°49·8'	0°15·7'W	X	107
Skirling	Scot Bord	NT0739	55°38·4'	3°28·2'W	T	72
Skirling Craigs	Scot Bord	NT0839	55°38·4'	3°27·3'W	X	72
Skirling Mains	Scot Bord	NT0738	55°37·9'	3°28·2'W	X	72
Skirl Naked	Northum	NT9725	55°31·4'	2°2·4'W	X	75
Skirmett	Bucks	SU7790	51°36·4'	0°52·9'W	T	175
Skirmore Ho	Lincs	TF4554	53°4·0'	0°10·3'E	X	122
Skirnawilse	Shetld	HT9537	60°7·3'	2°4·9'W	X	4
Skirpen Beck	E Yorks	SE7457	54°0·5'	0°51·8'W	W	105,106
Skirpenbeck	E Yorks	SE7457	54°0·5'	0°51·8'W	T	105,106
Skirrid Fm	Monm	SO3317	51°51·1'	2°58·0'W	FM	161
Skirsgill	Cumbr	NY5028	54°38·9'	2°46·1'W	X	90
Skirsgill Hill	Cumbr	NY4923	54°36·2'	2°46·9'W	X	90
Skirt Island	I Scilly	SV9013	49°56·4'	6°18·9'W	X	203
Skirts of Foudland	Aberd	NJ6032	57°22·9'	2°39·5'W	X	29,37
Skirts, The	Norf	TG0544	52°57·5'	1°3·5'E	X	133
Skirvil Taing	Orkney	HY5120	59°4·1'	2°50·8'W	X	5,6
Skirwith	Cumbr	NY6132	54°41·1'	2°35·9'W	T	91
Skirwith Abbey	Cumbr	NY6132	54°41·1'	2°35·9'W	X	91
Skirwith Beck	Cumbr	NY6232	54°41·1'	2°34·9'W	W	91
Skirwith Cave	N Yks	SD7073	54°9·4'	2°27·1'W	X	98
Skirwith Fell	Cumbr	NY6935	54°42·8'	2°28·4'W	X	91
Skirwith High Moor	Cumbr	NY6232	54°41·1'	2°34·9'W	X	91
Skirwith Low Moor	Cumbr	NY5933	54°41·7'	2°37·7'W	X	91
Skirza	Highld	ND3868	58°36·0'	3°3·5'W	T	12
Skirza Head	Highld	ND3968	58°36·0'	3°2·5'W	X	12
Ski Slope PH	Lancs	SD7738	53°50·5'	2°20·6'W	X	103
Skitby	Cumbr	NY4465	54°58·8'	2°52·1'W	T	85
Skitham	Lancs	SD4243	53°53·0'	2°52·5'W	T	102
Skitsack	Shetld	HP5709	60°45·9'	0°56·7'W	X	1
Skitter Beck	N Lincs	TA1216	53°37·9'	0°18·0'W	W	113
Skitter Ness	N Lincs	TA1325	53°42·8'	0°16·9'W	X	107,113
Skittle Green	Bucks	SP7702	51°42·9'	0°52·7'W	T	165
Skiurds, The	Shetld	HU3178	60°29·3'	1°25·7'W	H	3
Skivo	W Loth	NT0563	55°51·3'	3°30·6'W	X	65
Skletta Bay	Shetld	HU4968	60°23·8'	1°6·2'W	W	2,3
Skogar	Orkney	HY2623	59°5·5'	3°17·0'W	X	6
Skokholm Island	Pemb	SM7305	51°42·1'	5°16·7'W	X	157
Skomer Head	Pemb	SM7108	51°43·7'	5°18·6'W	X	157
Skomer Island	Pemb	SM7209	51°44·2'	5°17·8'W	X	157
Skorn	Orkney	HY2423	59°5·5'	3°19·1'W	X	6
Skoun	N Eil	NG0399	57°53·2'	7°0·2'W	X	18
Skreens Park	Essex	TL6207	51°44·5'	0°21·2'E	X	167
Skreens Park Fm	Essex	TL6208	51°45·1'	0°21·2'E	FM	167
Skriag	Highld	NG2648	57°26·6'	6°33·6'W	X	23
Skriaig	Highld	NG4440	57°23·0'	6°15·1'W	H	23
Skrikes Fm	N Yks	SE1564	54°4·5'	1°45·8'W	FM	99
Skrinkle Haven	Pemb	SS0897	51°38·6'	4°46·1'W	W	158
Skroo	Shetld	HZ2274	59°33·3'	1°36·2'W	X	4
Skrowa Skerry	Orkney	HY2110	58°58·5'	3°22·0'W	X	6
Skuda	Shetld	HP5105	60°43·8'	1°3·4'W	X	1
Skuda Sound	Shetld	HU6099	60°40·4'	0°53·6'W	W	1
Skuiley	Angus	NO4077	56°53·1'	2°58·6'W	X	44
Skulamus	Highld	NG6622	57°14·0'	5°52·2'W	T	32
Skula Water	Shetld	HU2652	60°15·4'	1°31·3'W	W	3
Skulia Geo	Shetld	HU5692	60°36·7'	0°58·1'W	X	1,2
Skuligarth	Shetld	HU2049	60°13·8'	1°37·8'W	X	3
Skullomie	Highld	NC6160	58°30·6'	4°22·7'W	T	10
Skult	Shetld	HU3565	60°22·3'	1°21·4'W	X	2,3
Skult, The	Shetld	HU3443	60°10·5'	1°22·7'W	X	4
Skurdie Geo	Shetld	HU5284	60°32·4'	1°2·6'W	X	1,2,3
Skutes Water	Shetld	HU6291	60°36·1'	0°51·6'W	W	1,2
Sky-Barn Fm	Lincs	SK9164	53°10·2'	0°37·9'W	FM	121
Skyber Fm	Pemb	SM9629	51°55·6'	4°57·6'W	FM	157,158
Skyborry Green	Shrops	SO2674	52°21·8'	3°4·8'W	T	137,148
Skybrae	Aberd	NJ6706	57°8·9'	2°32·3'W	X	38
Skyburriowe Fm	Corn	SW6922	50°3·4'	5°13·3'W	FM	203
Skye Bridge	Highld	NG7426	57°16·4'	5°44·5'W	X	33
Skye Green	Essex	TL8722	51°52·1'	0°43·4'E	T	168

Skyehead	Cumbr	NY4872	55°2·6'	2°48·4'W	X	86
Skye of Curr	Highld	NH9924	57°18·0'	3°40·1'W	T	36
Skyer Beck	Durham	NY8627	54°38·5'	2°12·6'W	W	91,92
Skyer's Fm	Hants	SU5857	51°18·8'	1°9·7'W	FM	174
Skyer's Wood	Hants	SU5856	51°18·2'	1°9·7'W	F	174
Sky Fea	Orkney	HY2694	58°49·9'	3°16·4'W	X	7
Skyfog	Pemb	SM8027	51°54·1'	5°11·5'W	T	157
Skygarth Fm	Cumbr	NY6126	54°37·9'	2°35·8'W	FM	91
Sky Hill	I of M	SC4393	54°18·8'	4°24·4'W	H	95
Skyline Loch	Highld	ND0147	58°24·3'	3°41·2'W	W	11,12
Skymore Hill	Pth & Kin	NO0210	56°16·6'	3°34·5'W	H	58
Skynlais	Powys	SO1539	52°2·8'	3°14·0'W	X	161
Skyrakes	N Yks	SD9654	53°59·2'	2°3·2'W	X	103
Skyrakes Fm	N Yks	SD9754	53°59·2'	2°2·3'W	FM	103
Skyre Burn	D & G	NX5459	54°54·5'	4°16·2'W	W	83
Skyreburn	D & G	NX5755	54°52·4'	4°13·3'W	T	83
Skyreburn Bay	D & G	NX5754	54°51·9'	4°13·3'W	W	83
Skyreholme	N Yks	SE0660	54°2·4'	1°54·1'W	T	99
Skythorn Hill	Pth & Kin	NN9201	56°11·6'	3°44·0'W	X	58
Slab	Hants	SU7835	51°6·8'	0°52·8'W	X	186
Slab House Inn (PH)	Somer	ST5948	51°14·0'	2°34·8'W	X	182,183
Slachristock Burn	N Lanak	NS7182	56°1·1'	4°3·7'W	W	57,64
Slack	Aberd	NJ5106	57°8·8'	2°48·1'W	X	37
Slack	Aberd	NJ5731	57°22·3'	2°42·4'W	X	29,37
Slack	Cald	SD9728	53°45·1'	2°2·3'W	T	103
Slack	Clackm	NS9591	56°6·3'	3°40·9'W	X	58
Slack	Cumbr	NY2948	54°49·6'	3°5·9'W	X	85
Slack	Cumbr	NY5545	54°48·1'	2°41·6'W	X	86
Slack	Cumbr	SD7185	54°15·8'	2°26·3'W	X	98
Slack	Derby	SK3362	53°9·5'	1°30·0'W	T	119
Slack	Kirk	SE0817	53°39·2'	1°52·3'W	T	110
Slack	Lancs	SD8552	53°58·1'	2°13·3'W	X	103
Slack	Lancs	SD9239	53°51·1'	2°6·9'W	X	103
Slack	Moray	NJ1837	57°25·2'	3°21·5'W	X	28
Slack	Orkney	HY2104	58°55·2'	3°21·8'W	X	6,7
Slackadale	Aberd	NJ7454	57°34·8'	2°25·6'W	X	29
Slackbraes Wood	Cumbr	NY3970	55°1·5'	2°56·8'W	F	85
Slackbuie	Highld	NH6741	57°26·7'	4°12·5'W	X	26
Slackbuie	Moray	NJ3453	57°34·0'	3°5·7'W	X	28
Slack Burn	Aberd	NJ6418	57°15·3'	2°35·3'W	W	37
Slack Burn	Aberd	NO6679	56°54·3'	2°33·0'W	W	45
Slack Burn	D & G	NX7558	54°54·3'	3°56·6'W	W	84
Slackcote	Oldham	SD9709	53°34·9'	2°2·3'W	T	109
Slackdale	Aberd	NJ5460	57°37·9'	2°45·8'W	X	29
Slack Den	Aberd	NO6679	56°54·3'	2°33·0'W	X	45
Slackdhu	Stir	NS5581	56°0·3'	4°19·1'W	X	64
Slack Edge	Derby	SK0192	53°25·7'	1°58·7'W	X	110
Slacke Hall	Derby	SK0781	53°19·8'	1°53·3'W	X	110
Slackend	Aberd	NJ6436	57°25·0'	2°35·5'W	X	29
Slackend	Moray	NJ1051	57°32·7'	3°29·8'W	X	28
Slackend	Moray	NJ3963	57°39·4'	3°0·9'W	X	28
Slackend	W Loth	NS9772	55°56·1'	3°38·5'W	X	65
Slackhall	Derby	SK0781	53°19·8'	1°53·3'W	T	110
Slack Head	Cumbr	SD4978	54°12·0'	2°46·5'W	T	97
Slackhead	Moray	NJ4062	57°38·9'	2°59·9'W	T	28
Slack Heugh	D & G	NX6443	54°46·1'	4°6·4'W	X	83
Slack Ho	Durham	NY8538	54°44·5'	2°13·6'W	X	91,92
Slackholme End	Lincs	TF5370	53°12·5'	0°17·9'E	T	122
Slack House Fm	Lancs	SD4206	53°33·1'	2°52·1'W	FM	108
Slack Laithe	Lancs	SD9137	53°50·0'	2°7·8'W	X	103
Slack Lane Fm	Brad	SE0239	53°51·1'	1°57·8'W	FM	104
Slack of Myrack	Moray	NJ1848	57°31·1'	3°21·7'W	X	28
Slack of Scotston	Aberd	NJ6752	57°33·7'	2°32·6'W	X	29
Slack Pool	Aberd	NO6177	56°53·2'	2°38·0'W	W	45
Slacks	D & G	NX8773	55°2·6'	3°45·7'W	X	84
Slacks	D & G	NY0583	55°8·2'	3°29·0'W	X	78
Slacks	E Ayr	NS5737	55°36·6'	4°15·8'W	X	71
Slacks Fm	Roth	SK4990	53°24·5'	1°15·4'W	FM	111
Slackshaw Burn	E Ayr	NS6824	55°29·8'	4°4·9'W	W	71
Slacks of Cairnbanno	Aberd	NJ8546	57°30·5'	2°14·6'W	X	30
Slacks of Glencarvie	Aberd	NJ3405	57°8·1'	3°5·0'W	X	37
Slacks of Pitreadie	Aberd	NO6889	56°59·7'	2°31·1'W	X	45
Slack's Rigg	Cumbr	NY7736	54°43·4'	2°21·0'W	H	91
Slacks, The	W Dunb	NS4675	55°56·9'	4°27·5'W	H	64
Slacks Wood	N Yks	NZ5812	54°30·2'	1°5·8'W	F	93
Slack,The	Cumbr	SD4179	54°12·4'	2°53·9'W	X	96,97
Slack, The	Durham	NZ1125	54°37·4'	1°49·4'W	T	92
Slack, The	N Yks	SE9669	54°6·7'	0°31·5'W	X	101
Slack Wood	Aberd	NJ6418	57°15·3'	2°35·3'W	F	37
Slackwood Fm	Lancs	SD4774	54°9·8'	2°48·3'W	A	97
Slad	Glos	SO8707	51°45·9'	2°10·9'W	T	162
Sladbrook	Glos	SO7728	51°57·2'	2°19·7'W	T	150
Sladbury's Old Ho	Essex	TM1917	51°48·7'	1°11·0'E	X	168,169
Sladdacott	Corn	SX2295	50°43·9'	4°31·0'W	X	190
Slade	Angus	NO5544	56°35·4'	2°43·5'W	X	54
Slade	Devon	SS3108	50°51·0'	4°23·7'W	X	190
Slade	Devon	SS6701	50°47·8'	3°52·9'W	X	191
Slade	Devon	SS7605	50°50·1'	3°45·3'W	X	191
Slade	Devon	SS8326	51°1·5'	3°39·7'W	X	181
Slade	Devon	ST1108	50°52·1'	3°15·5'W	T	192,193
Slade	Devon	SX5958	50°24·5'	3°58·7'W	A	202
Slade	Devon	SX7347	50°18·8'	3°46·6'W	X	202
Slade	Devon	SY2097	50°46·3'	3°7·7'W	X	192,193
Slade	Hants	SZ3298	50°47·1'	1°32·4'W	X	196
Slade	Kent	TQ9354	51°15·4'	0°46·4'E	T	189
Slade	Pemb	SM8922	51°51·6'	5°3·5'W	X	157,158
Slade	Pemb	SM9416	51°48·5'	4°58·9'W	T	157,158
Slade	Pemb	SN0230	51°56·2'	4°52·4'W	X	145,157
Slade	Pemb	SS0798	51°39·1'	4°47·0'W	X	158
Slade	Shrops	SJ5628	52°51·1'	2°38·8'W	X	126
Slade	Somer	SS8730	51°3·7'	3°36·4'W	X	181
Slade	Somer	SS9440	51°9·2'	3°30·6'W	X	181
Slade	Swan	SS4886	51°33·4'	4°11·2'W	X	159
Slade	V of Glam	SS8873	51°26·9'	3°36·3'W	X	170
Slade Barn Fm	Glos	SP0621	51°53·5'	1°54·4'W	FM	163
Slade Barn Fm	Glos	SP0728	51°57·3'	1°53·5'W	FM	150,163
Slade Bottom	Glos	SO5605	51°44·8'	2°37·8'W	F	162
Slade Bottom	Suff	TL7267	52°16·7'	0°31·7'E	X	154
Slade Bottom Fm	Hants	SU4152	51°16·2'	1°24·3'W	FM	185
Slade Brook	Northnts	SP8079	52°24·4'	0°49·0'W	W	141

Slade Cross	Devon	SX7981	50°37·2′	3°42·3′W	X	191
Slade End	Oxon	SU5890	51°36·6′	1°9·4′W	T	164,174
Slade Fm	Bucks	SU9688	51°35·2′	0°36·5′W	FM	175,176
Slade Fm	Cambs	TL6067	52°16·9′	0°21·1′E	FM	154
Slade Fm	Devon	SS3222	50°58·6′	4°23·2′W	FM	190
Slade Fm	Devon	SS6733	51°5·1′	3°53·6′W	FM	180
Slade Fm	Devon	SS9117	50°56·8′	3°32·7′W	FM	181
Slade Fm	Devon	ST1308	50°52·1′	3°13·8′W	FM	192,193
Slade Fm	Devon	SX7445	50°17·7′	3°45·8′W	FM	202
Slade Fm	Devon	SY1095	50°45·1′	3°16·2′W	FM	192,193
Slade Fm	Hants	SU7130	51°4·1′	0°58·8′W	FM	186
Slade Fm	Leic	SK4825	52°49·5′	1°16·9′W	FM	129
Slade Fm	Northnts	SP7867	52°18·0′	0°51·0′W	FM	152
Slade Fm	Oxon	SP2625	51°55·6′	1°36·9′W	FM	163
Slade Fm	Oxon	SP5022	51°53·9′	1°16·0′W	FM	164
Slade Fm	Powys	SO0927	51°56·3′	3°19·0′W	FM	161
Slade Fm	Surrey	TQ0856	51°17·8′	0°26·7′W	FM	187
Slade Fm	Warw	SP2730	51°58·3′	1°36·0′W	FM	151
Slade Fm	W Susx	SU7924	51°0·8′	0°52·0′W	FM	197
Slade Fm, The	Northnts	SP5833	51°59·8′	1°8·9′W	FM	152
Slade Gate	W Berks	SU5874	51°27·9′	1°9·5′W	X	174
Slade Green	Bexley	TQ5276	51°28·0′	0°11·7′E	T	177
Slade Heath	Staffs	SJ9206	52°39·3′	2°6·7′W	T	127,139
Slade Hills	Norf	TG1313	52°40·6′	1°9·5′E	X	133
Slade Ho	Lincs	TF3235	52°54·0′	0°1·8′W	X	131
Slade Ho	N Yks	SE1658	54°1·3′	1°44·9′W	X	104
Slade Ho	Staffs	SK1051	53°3·6′	1°50·6′W	X	119
Slade Hollow	Derby	SK2339	52°57·1′	1°39·1′W	X	128
Slade Hollow	Staffs	SK1246	53°0·9′	1°48·9′W	X	119,128
Slade Hooton	Roth	SK5289	53°24·0′	1°12·7′W	T	111,120
Sladelands	W Susx	TQ0026	51°1·7′	0°34·1′W	X	186,197
Sladen Green	Hants	SU4154	51°17·2′	1°24·3′W	T	185
Slade Resrs	Devon	SS5045	51°11·3′	4°8·4′W	W	180
Slades	N Yks	SD9279	54°12·6′	2°6·9′W	X	98
Slades	Shrops	SJ3826	52°49·9′	2°54·8′W	X	126
Sladesbridge	Corn	SX0171	50°30·5′	4°48·0′W	T	200
Slades Covert	Suff	TL8872	52°19·1′	0°45·9′E	F	144,155
Slades Fm	Cambs	TL5465	52°15·9′	0°15·8′E	FM	154
Slades Fm	Essex	TL5709	51°45·7′	0°16·9′E	FM	167
Slades Fm	Herts	TL1697	51°39·8′	0°19·0′W	FM	166,176
Slades Green	Worcs	SO8534	52°0·5′	2°12·7′W	T	150
Slade Sike	Northum	NY8280	55°7·1′	2°16·5′W	W	80
Slades, The	Oxon	SP7301	51°42·4′	0°56·2′W	X	165
Slades, The	Somer	ST1735	51°6·7′	3°10·8′W	X	181
Slades, The	Suff	TM2176	52°20·5′	1°15·1′E	F	156
Slade, The	Hants	SU7126	51°2·0′	0°58·9′W	X	186,197
Slade Wood	Monm	ST4589	51°36·1′	2°47·3′W	F	171,172
Slade Wood	Worcs	SP0253	52°10·8′	1°57·8′W	F	150
Slad Fm	Mil Key	SP8631	51°58·5′	0°44·5′W	FM	152,165
Slad Fm	Pemb	SM9119	51°50·1′	5°1·6′W	FM	157,158
Sladnor Park Ho	Torbay	SX9268	50°30·3′	3°31·0′W	X	202
Slads Fm	Glos	ST8992	51°37·8′	2°9·1′W	FM	163,173
Slaethornrig	S Ayr	NX4291	55°11·5′	4°28·5′W	X	77
Slafarquhar	N Lanak	NS7383	56°1·6′	4°1·8′W	X	57,64
Slagachorrie	Highld	NH9051	57°32·4′	3°49·8′W	X	27
Slaggan	Highld	NG8494	57°53·3′	5°38·2′W	X	19
Slaggan Bay	Highld	NG8394	57°53·2′	5°39·2′W	W	19
Slaggiburn	Cumbr	NY7142	54°46·6′	2°26·6′W	X	86,87
Slaggyford	Northum	NY6752	54°51·9′	2°30·4′W	T	86,87
Slag Hill	Northum	NY8446	54°48·8′	2°14·5′W	X	86,87
Slag Hills	Derby	SK3459	53°7·9′	1°29·1′W	X	119
Slagnaw	D & G	NX7458	54°54·3′	3°57·5′W	X	83,84
Slaidburn	Lancs	SD7152	53°58·0′	2°26·1′W	T	103
Slaid Hill	Leeds	SE3340	53°51·6′	1°29·5′W	X	104
Slaidhill	Scot Bord	NT4209	55°22·5′	2°54·5′W	X	79
Slai na Gour	Aberd	NO4495	57°2·8′	2°54·9′W	H	37,44
Slainges, The	Aberd	NO8676	56°52·8′	2°13·3′W	X	45
Slains Castle	Aberd	NK0529	57°21·3′	1°54·6′W	A	38
Slains Castle	Aberd	NK1036	57°25·1′	1°49·6′W	X	30
Slainsfield	Northum	NT9439	55°38·9′	2°5·3′W	X	74,75
Slains Lodge	Aberd	NK0936	57°25·1′	1°50·6′W	X	30
Slains Park	Aberd	NO8575	56°52·2′	2°14·3′W	X	45
Slaite Coire	Highld	NM8288	56°56·2′	5°34·5′W	X	40
Slaithwaite	Kirk	SE0813	53°37·0′	1°52·3′W	T	110
Slaithwaite Moor	Kirk	SE0414	53°37·6′	1°56·0′W	X	110
Slakes Fm	Cumbr	NY6627	54°38·5′	2°31·2′W	FM	91
Slaley	Derby	SK2757	53°6·8′	1°35·4′W	T	119
Slaley	Northum	NY9757	54°54·7′	2°2·4′W	T	87
Slaley Forest	Northum	NY9555	54°53·6′	2°4·3′W	F	87
Slamannan	Falk	NS8573	55°56·4′	3°50·0′W	T	65
Slamptonhill	Aberd	NJ9542	57°28·4′	2°4·5′W	X	30
Slaney Place	Kent	TQ7944	51°10·3′	0°34·0′E	X	188
Slanger Burn	N Ayr	NS2462	55°49·4′	4°48·1′W	W	63
Slantycombe Fm	Devon	ST0119	50°58·0′	3°24·2′W	FM	181
Slap	Hants	SU2002	50°49·3′	1°42·6′W	X	195
Slape Cross	Somer	ST3238	51°8·5′	2°57·9′W	T	182
Slape Gill	N Yks	SE0077	54°11·6′	1°59·6′W	W	98
Slape Manor	Dorset	SY4798	50°47·0′	2°44·7′W	A	193
Slape Moor	Somer	ST1027	51°2·4′	3°16·6′W	X	181,193
Slaper Leys	E Yorks	TA0254	53°58·6′	0°26·3′W	X	106,107
Slape Scar	Cumbr	SD3897	54°22·1′	2°56·8′W	X	96,97
Slapestone Edge	Cumbr	NY3008	54°28·0′	3°4·4′W	X	90
Slapestones	Cumbr	NY8613	54°31·0′	2°12·6′W	X	91,92
Slapestone Wath	N Yks	SE0289	54°18·0′	1°57·7′W	X	98
Slapewath	Red & Cl	NZ6415	54°31·8′	1°0·2′W	T	94
Slape Wath Moor	N Yks	SE5998	54°22·7′	1°5·1′W	X	100
Slaphouse	S Ayr	NS3319	55°26·4′	4°38·0′W	X	70
Slapton	Bucks	SP9320	51°52·5′	0°38·5′W	T	165
Slapton	Devon	SX8245	50°17·8′	3°39·0′W	T	202
Slapton	Northnts	SP6446	52°6·7′	1°3·5′W	T	152
Slaptonhill Fm	Northnts	SP6347	52°7·3′	1°4·4′W	FM	152
Slapton Ley	Devon	SX8243	50°16·7′	3°39·0′W	W	202
Slapton Manor	Northnts	SP6346	52°6·8′	1°4·4′W	X	152
Slapton Sands	Devon	SX8244	50°17·3′	3°39·0′W	X	202
Slat Bheinn	Highld	NG5319	57°12·0′	6°4·9′W	X	32
Slat Bheinn	Highld	NG9002	57°3·9′	5°27·4′W	H	33
Slatch Fm	Herof	SO7143	52°5·3′	2°25·0′W	FM	149
Slatebarn Fm	Cambs	TL2992	52°30·9′	0°5·5′W	FM	142
Slate Brae	S Lanak	NT0221	55°28·6′	3°32·6′W	H	72
Slate Cleuch	Scot Bord	NT2529	55°33·2′	3°10·9′W	X	73
Slate Delfs Hill	Cald	SE0021	53°41·4′	1°59·6′W	X	104
Slated Fm	N Yks	SD7565	54°5·1′	2°22·5′W	FM	98
Slated House Fm	Lincs	TF4156	53°5·2′	0°6·7′E	FM	122
Slatefield	Angus	NO4549	56°38·0′	2°53·3′W	X	54
Slate Fm	Norf	TF5802	52°35·8′	0°20·4′E	FM	143
Slateford	C of Edin	NT2270	55°55·3′	3°14·4′W	T	66
Slateford	E Loth	NT5369	55°55·0′	2°44·7′W	X	66
Slateford	Renf	NS4272	55°55·2′	4°31·3′W	X	64
Slateford	S Ayr	NS3012	55°22·6′	4°40·6′W	X	70
Slateford Burn	Pth & Kin	NO0810	56°16·7′	3°28·7′W	W	58
Slate Hall Fm	Cambs	TL3963	52°15·1′	0°2·6′E	FM	154
Slate Hall Fm	Herts	TL3434	51°59·5′	0°2·5′W	FM	154
Slatehaugh	Moray	NJ0653	57°33·7′	3°33·8′W	X	27
Slate Haugh	Moray	NJ4662	57°38·9′	2°53·8′W	X	28,29
Slate Hill	Cumbr	NY7943	54°47·1′	2°19·2′W	X	86,87
Slate Hill	Cumbr	SD4283	54°14·6′	2°53·0′W	X	96,97
Slate Hill	Northum	NZ0877	55°5·5′	1°52·1′W	X	88
Slatehill Fm	Pemb	SM8107	51°43·4′	5°9·9′W	FM	157
Slate Hills Fm	Leic	SK3202	52°37·1′	1°31·2′W	FM	140
Slate Ho	Lincs	TF2637	52°55·2′	0°7·1′W	X	131
Slate Ho	N Lincs	SE9005	53°32·3′	0°38·1′W	X	112
Slate Ho	N Lincs	SE9701	53°30·0′	0°31·8′W	X	112
Slate Ho	Powys	SO1484	52°27·1′	3°15·5′W	X	136
Slate Ho	Staffs	SK0354	53°5·2′	1°56·9′W	X	119
Slatehole	E Ayr	NS4923	55°28·9′	4°22·9′W	X	70
Slatehouse	D & G	NX8387	55°10·1′	3°49·8′W	X	78
Slate House Fm	Lincs	SK9942	52°58·2′	0°31·1′W	FM	130
Slate House Fm	Lincs	TF0354	53°4·6′	0°27·3′W	FM	121
Slate House Fm	Lincs	TF2856	53°5·4′	0°4·9′W	FM	122
Slate House Fm	Lincs	TF3150	53°2·1′	0°2·4′W	FM	122
Slate House Fm	Staffs	SK1062	53°9·5′	1°50·6′W	FM	119
Slatehouse Fm	W Susx	TQ2426	51°1·4′	0°13·5′W	FM	187,198
Slatehouse Hill	D & G	NX8287	55°10·0′	3°50·7′W	H	78
Slate Ledge	Durham	NZ0126	54°38·0′	1°58·6′W	X	92
Slateley Hall Fm	Warw	SP2298	52°35·0′	1°40·1′W	FM	139
Slatemill Bridge	Pemb	SM8209	51°44·5′	5°9·1′W	X	157
Slatenber	N Yks	SD7172	54°8·8′	2°26·2′W	X	98
Slatepit Dale	Derby	SK3468	53°12·7′	1°29·0′W	T	119
Slatepit Moor	Tames	SD9900	53°30·0′	2°0·5′W	X	109
Slatepit Moss	N Yks	SE8504	54°26·1′	2°13·5′W	H	91,92
Slate Pit Moss	Oldham	SE0403	53°31·7′	1°56·0′W	X	110
Slatepits Copse	Oxon	SP3216	51°50·7′	1°31·7′W	F	164
Slate Quarry Moss	Cumbr	NY8418	54°33·7′	2°14·4′W	X	91,92
Slatequarry Wood	Cumbr	NY5532	54°41·1′	2°41·5′W	F	90
Slater Barn	N Yks	SD9574	54°10·0′	2°4·2′W	X	98
Slaterfield	Northum	NY8674	55°3·9′	2°12·7′W	X	87
Slaterich	Arg & Bt	NM8129	56°24·4′	5°32·5′W	X	49
Slate Rigg Fm	N Yks	SE2861	54°2·9′	1°33·9′W	FM	99
Slate Row	D & G	NX8053	54°51·7′	3°51·8′W	X	84
Slater's Lodge	Northnts	SP9767	52°17·8′	0°34·3′W	X	153
Slates	Inverc	NS3469	55°53·4′	4°38·8′W	X	63
Slates Fm	Lincs	SK9789	53°23·6′	0°32·1′W	FM	112,121
Slates Fm	Lincs	TF3185	53°21·0′	0°1·5′W	FM	122
Slates Fm	Lincs	TF4485	53°20·8′	0°10·2′E	FM	122
Slates Hill	Durham	NY9316	54°32·6′	2°6·1′W	X	91,92
Slate Sikes	Cumbr	NY8517	54°33·1′	2°13·5′W	X	91,92
Slates, The	Lincs	TF2589	53°23·2′	0°6·8′W	X	113,122
Slates, The	Lincs	TF2993	53°25·3′	0°3·1′W	X	113
Slate, The	Arg & Bt	NR6316	55°23·1′	5°44·1′W	H	68
Slatich	Pth & Kin	NN6347	56°36·0′	4°13·4′W	X	51
Slatrach Bay	Arg & Bt	NM8129	56°24·4′	5°32·5′W	W	49
Slattadale	Highld	NG8871	57°41·0′	5°32·9′W	X	19
Slattadale Forest	Highld	NG8871	57°41·0′	5°32·9′W	F	19
Slattenslade	Devon	SS6748	51°13·2′	3°53·9′W	X	180
Slatters Fm	Bucks	SP6212	51°48·4′	1°5·6′W	FM	164,165
Slattocks	Roch	SD8808	53°34·3′	2°10·5′W	T	109
Slaty Crag	Cumbr	NY5879	55°6·5′	2°39·1′W	X	86
Slaty Ford	Durham	NZ0541	54°46·1′	1°54·9′W	X	87
Slaty Ford	Northum	NY7687	55°10·9′	2°22·2′W	X	80
Slaty Law	N Ayr	NS2661	55°48·9′	4°46·2′W	H	63
Slatywaird	Aberd	NO8680	56°54·9′	2°13·3′W	X	45
Slaugham	W Susx	TQ2528	51°2·5′	0°12·6′W	T	187,198
Slaugham Common	W Susx	TQ2428	51°2·5′	0°13·5′W	X	187,198
Slaugham Manor	W Susx	TQ2527	51°2·0′	0°12·6′W	X	187,198
Slaugham Place	W Susx	TQ2527	51°2·0′	0°12·6′W	A	187,198
Slaughden	Suff	TM4655	52°8·5′	1°36·1′E	X	156
Slaughs	Angus	NO3746	56°36·4′	3°1·1′W	X	54
Slaughterbridge	Corn	SX1085	50°38·3′	4°40·8′W	T	200
Slaughterbridge Fm	W Susx	TQ1223	51°0·0′	0°23·8′W	FM	198
Slaughter Fm	Glos	SP1521	51°53·5′	1°46·5′W	FM	163
Slaughterford	Wilts	ST8473	51°27·6′	2°13·4′W	T	173
Slaughtergate Fm	Dorset	ST7926	51°2·2′	2°17·6′W	FM	183
Slaughter Hill	Ches	SJ7355	53°5·7′	2°23·8′W	T	118
Slaughterhouse Point	Kent	TQ8769	51°23·6′	0°41·7′E	X	178
Slaughter's Wood	Luton	TL1123	51°53·9′	0°22·8′W	F	166
Slaughter, The	Glos	SO5514	51°49·6′	2°38·8′W	X	162
Slawston	Leic	SP7794	52°32·5′	0°51·5′W	T	141
Slawston Hill	Leic	SP7894	52°32·5′	0°50·6′W	H	141
Slay Barn	Oxon	SP5903	51°43·6′	1°8·4′W	X	164
Slay Barrow	Wilts	SU0851	51°15·7′	1°52·7′W	A	184
Slay Down	Wilts	SU0950	51°15·2′	1°51·9′W	X	184
Slayersdale Fm	E Yorks	TA0161	54°2·3′	0°27·0′W	FM	101
Slayhills Marsh	Kent	TQ8670	51°24·1′	0°40·8′E	W	178
Slayley Fm	Derby	SK4776	53°17·0′	1°17·3′W	FM	120
Slay Pits	Donc	SE6709	53°34·6′	0°58·9′W	T	111
Slay, The	Wilts	SU3056	51°18·4′	1°33·8′W	X	174
Sleach Water	Highld	ND0344	58°22·7′	3°39·0′W	W	11,12
Sleadale	Highld	NG3228	57°16·1′	6°26·3′W	X	32
Sleadale Burn	Highld	NG3229	57°16·6′	6°26·3′W	W	32
Sleadon Rocks	Devon	SX8136	50°13·0′	3°39·7′W	X	202
Sleaford	Hants	SU8038	51°8·4′	0°51·0′W	T	186
Sleaford	Lincs	TF0645	52°59·7′	0°24·8′W	T	130
Sleagill	Cumbr	NY5919	54°34·1′	2°37·6′W	T	91
Sleagill Head	Cumbr	NY5919	54°34·1′	2°37·6′W	X	91
Slealandsburn	Cumbr	NY4170	55°1·5′	2°54·9′W	X	85
Slean End	Lancs	SD5047	53°55·2′	2°45·3′W	X	102
Sleap	Shrops	SJ4826	52°50·0′	2°45·9′W	T	126
Sleap	Wrekin	SJ6317	52°45·2′	2°32·5′W	X	127
Sleap Brook	Shrops	SJ4927	52°50·5′	2°45·0′W	W	126
Sleapford	Wrekin	SJ6315	52°44·1′	2°32·5′W	T	127
Sleap Moor	Wrekin	SJ6416	52°44·7′	2°31·6′W	X	127
Sleapshyde	Herts	TL2006	51°44·6′	0°15·3′W	T	166
Sleastary	Highld	NH6496	57°56·2′	4°17·4′W	X	21
Sleastonhow	Cumbr	NY6524	54°36·8′	2°32·1′W	X	91
Sleathwaite	Cumbr	NY1200	54°23·5′	3°20·9′W	X	89
Sleau Meayll	I of M	SC3982	54°12·8′	4°27·7′W	H	95
Slebech	Pemb	SN0215	51°48·2′	4°51·9′W	X	157,158
Slebech Park	Pemb	SN0214	51°47·6′	4°51·9′W	X	157,158
Sled	Angus	NO6945	56°36·0′	2°29·8′W	X	54
Sledale Pasture	N Yks	SD8499	54°23·4′	2°14·4′W	X	98
Sledbank	Cumbr	SD1282	54°13·8′	3°20·6′W	X	96
Sledbrook Hill	Barns	SE1903	53°31·6′	1°42·4′W	X	110
Sleddale	N Yks	SD8586	54°16·4′	2°13·4′W	X	98
Sleddale	Red & Cl	NZ6112	54°30·2′	1°3·1′W	X	94
Sleddale Beck	Cumbr	NY5109	54°28·7′	2°45·0′W	W	90
Sleddale Beck	N Yks	NZ6309	54°28·6′	1°1·2′W	W	94
Sleddale Fell	Cumbr	NY4806	54°27·1′	2°47·7′W	X	90
Sleddale Forest	Cumbr	NY4802	54°24·9′	2°47·7′W	X	90
Sleddale Grange	Cumbr	NY5411	54°29·8′	2°42·2′W	X	90
Sleddale Hall	Cumbr	NY5411	54°29·8′	2°42·2′W	X	90
Sleddale Pasture	N Yks	SD8587	54°16·9′	2°13·4′W	X	98
Sleddale Pike	Cumbr	NY5309	54°28·7′	2°43·1′W	H	90
Slede Ooze	Medway	TQ8271	51°24·7′	0°37·4′E	X	178
Sledge Green	Worcs	SO8134	52°0·5′	2°16·2′W	T	150
Sledge Meadows	Durham	NY9347	54°49·3′	2°6·1′W	X	87
Sled Hill	E Loth	NT5770	55°55·5′	2°40·8′W	H	67
Sledmere	E Yorks	SE9364	54°4·0′	0°34·3′W	T	101
Sledmere Castle	E Yorks	SE9464	54°4·0′	0°33·4′W	X	101
Sledmere Field Fm	E Yorks	SE9260	54°1·9′	0°35·3′W	FM	101
Sledmere Grange	E Yorks	SE9662	54°2·9′	0°31·6′W	X	101
Sledmere Ho	E Yorks	SE9364	54°4·0′	0°34·3′W	X	101
Sledwich Cotts	Durham	NZ0915	54°32·1′	1°51·2′W	X	92
Sledwich Hall	Durham	NZ0915	54°32·1′	1°51·2′W	X	92
Sleeches	E Susx	TQ5026	51°1·1′	0°8·7′E	X	188,199
Sleeches Cross	E Susx	TQ5834	51°5·2′	0°15·8′E	T	188
Sleech Wood	Dorset	SY3393	50°44·2′	2°56·6′W	F	193
Sleek Burn	Northum	NZ2883	55°8·7′	1°33·2′W	W	81
Sleekers Fm	Devon	SX5390	50°41·7′	4°4·5′W	FM	191
Sleek of Tarty	Aberd	NJ9927	57°20·3′	2°0·5′W	X	38
Sleek Stone	Pemb	SM8514	51°47·2′	5°6·7′W	X	157
Sleep Brook	Dorset	SU1111	50°54·1′	1°50·2′W	W	195
Sleepers Hill	Hants	SU4629	51°3·7′	1°20·2′W	T	185
Sleepieshill Wood	Moray	NJ2961	57°38·3′	3°10·9′W	F	28
Sleepy Hollow Farm Park	Glos	SP1635	52°1·0′	1°45·6′W	X	151
Sleepy Lowe	Cald	SE0329	53°45·7′	1°56·9′W	X	104
Sleepytown	Aberd	NJ6027	57°20·2′	2°39·4′W	X	37
Sleet Beck	Cumbr	NY4977	55°5·3′	2°47·5′W	W	86
Sleetbeck	Cumbr	NY5076	55°4·8′	2°46·6′W	T	86
Sleetburn Fm	Durham	NY9218	54°33·7′	2°7·0′W	FM	91,92
Sleet Fell	Cumbr	NY4218	54°33·5′	2°53·4′W	H	90
Sleet How	Cumbr	NY2022	54°35·5′	3°13·9′W	X	89,90
Sleet Moor	Derby	SK4053	53°4·6′	1°23·8′W	T	120
Sleet Moor	N Yks	SE0468	54°6·7′	1°55·9′W	X	98
Sleet Moss	Orkney	HY3225	59°6·7′	3°10·8′W	X	6
Sleeves Wood	E Susx	TQ5322	50°58·8′	0°11·2′E	F	199
Slegaby	I of M	SC3980	54°11·7′	4°27·7′W	X	95
Slegden	Scot Bord	NT7347	55°43·2′	2°25·4′W	X	74
Sleibhte-coire	Arg & Bt	NM5531	56°24·7′	5°57·9′W	X	48
Sleicham	N Eil	NF9984	57°44·9′	7°3·1′W	X	18
Slèidmeall	Arg & Bt	NR2772	55°52·1′	6°21·4′W	X	60
Sleight	Dorset	SY9898	50°47·1′	2°1·3′W	T	195
Sleight Bldgs	Dorset	SY8081	50°37·9′	2°16·6′W	X	194
Sleight Edge	Durham	NY9022	54°35·8′	2°8·9′W	X	91,92
Sleight Fm	Bath & NE Somer	ST6058	51°19·4′	2°34·1′W	FM	172
Sleight Fm	Somer	ST7853	51°16·8′	2°18·5′W	FM	183
Sleight Fm	Wilts	SU0159	51°20·0′	1°58·8′W	FM	173
Sleightholme	Cumbr	NY1953	54°52·2′	3°15·3′W	X	85
Sleightholme	Durham	NY9510	54°29·4′	2°4·2′W	X	91,92
Sleightholme Beck	Durham	NY9510	54°29·4′	2°4·2′W	W	91,92
Sleightholme Dale	N Yks	SE6589	54°17·8′	0°59·7′W	X	94,100
Sleightholme Fm	N Yks	SE7876	54°10·7′	0°47·9′W	FM	100
Sleightholme Moor	Durham	NY9208	54°28·3′	2°7·0′W	X	92
Sleights	E Yorks	SE8524	53°42·6′	0°42·3′W	X	106,112
Sleights	N Yks	NZ8607	54°27·3′	0°40·0′W	T	94
Sleight's Fm	E Yorks	TA0548	53°55·3′	0°23·7′W	FM	107
Sleights Fm	E Yorks	TA0759	54°1·2′	0°21·6′W	FM	107
Sleights Fm	N Yks	SE7375	54°10·2′	0°52·5′W	FM	100
Sleights Fm	N Yks	SE8476	54°10·6′	0°42·4′W	FM	100
Sleights Ho	N Yks	SE6591	54°18·9′	0°59·6′W	X	94,100
Sleights Moor	N Yks	NZ8504	54°25·7′	0°41·0′W	X	94
Sleight's Wood	Lincs	SK9526	52°49·6′	0°35·0′W	F	130
Sleights Wood	Suff	TL9672	52°18·9′	0°52·9′E	F	144,155
Sleight, The	Bath & NE Somer	ST6559	51°20·0′	2°29·8′W	H	172
Sleigh Wood	Derby	SK3566	53°11·6′	1°28·2′W	F	119
Slei Gill	N Yks	NZ0203	54°25·6′	1°57·7′W	W	92
Sleitaval	N Eil	NF8174	57°38·8′	7°20·4′W	X	18
Sleiteabhal	N Eil	NG0591	57°48·9′	6°57·6′W	H	14,18
Slèiteachal Mhòr	N Eil	NB2118	58°4·1′	6°43·4′W	H	13,14
Sleiteil Rocks	Highld	NC6263	58°32·3′	4°21·8′W	X	10
Sleivemore	Arg & Bt	NR4062	55°47·1′	6°8·4′W	X	60,61
Sleivevin	Arg & Bt	NR3357	55°44·2′	6°14·8′W	X	60
Slences	Oldham	SD9410	53°35·4′	2°5·0′W	X	109
Sleningford Grange	N Yks	SE2877	54°11·5′	1°33·8′W	X	99
Sleningford Mill	N Yks	SE2878	54°12·1′	1°33·8′W	X	99
Sleningford Park	N Yks	SE2777	54°11·5′	1°34·8′W	X	99
Slepe	Dorset	SY9293	50°44·4′	2°6·4′W	T	195
Slepe Fm	Dorset	SY9585	50°40·1′	2°3·9′W	FM	195
Slepe Heath	Dorset	SY9485	50°40·1′	2°4·7′W	X	195
Sletchcott	Devon	SS6821	50°58·6′	3°52·4′W	X	180
Sletell	Highld	NC6363	58°32·3′	4°20·7′W	X	10
Slethat	D & G	NY0870	55°1·2′	3°25·9′W	X	85
Sletill Burn	Highld	NC9446	58°23·6′	3°48·3′W	W	11
Sletill Hill	Highld	NC9246	58°23·6′	3°50·4′W	H	11
Slettnish	N Eil	NA9716	58°2·0′	7°7·6′W	X	13
Slett of the Heel	Orkney	HY1904	58°55·2′	3°23·9′W	X	7
Sleughwhite	Moray	NJ0549	57°31·5′	3°34·7′W	X	27
Sleves Holm	Norf	TL7096	52°32·3′	0°30·8′E	X	143
Slewcairn	D & G	NX9261	54°56·2′	3°40·7′W	X	84

Slewdrum Forest	Aberd	NO6295	57°2·9′	2°37·1′W	F	37,45
Slew Wood	Devon	SX4189	50°41·0′	4°14·7′W	X	190
Sliabh a' Bhiorain	Arg & Bt	NR5912	55°20·8′	5°47·6′W	H	68
Sliabhach	Highld	NH2743	57°26·9′	4°52·5′W	X	25
Sliabh Aird na Sgitheich	Arg & Bt	NR4878	55°56·0′	6°1·6′W	X	60,61
Sliabh Allt an Tairbh	Arg & Bt	NR5489	56°2·1′	5°56·5′W	X	61
Sliabh a' Mheallaidh	Arg & Bt	NR4350	55°40·8′	6°4·9′W	X	60
Sliabh an Ruighe Dhuibh	Highld	NH3423	57°16·3′	4°44·7′W	H	26
Sliabh Aom	Arg & Bt	NR4172	55°52·6′	6°8·0′W	X	60,61
Sliabh Bainneach	Moray	NJ0741	57°27·2′	3°32·5′W	H	27
Sliabh Bàn	Highld	NN6496	57°2·4′	4°14·0′W	X	35
Sliabh Bhirgeadain	Arg & Bt	NR3970	55°51·4′	6°9·8′W	X	60,61
Sliabh Bhrothain	Arg & Bt	NR2169	55°50·3′	6°26·9′W	X	60
Sliabhclachd	Highld	NJ0720	57°15·9′	3°32·1′W	X	36
Sliabh Fada	N Ayr	NR9226	55°29·3′	5°17·1′W	X	68,69
Sliabh Fada	Pth & Kin	NN7952	56°38·9′	3°58·0′W	H	42,51,52
Sliabh Gaoil	Arg & Bt	NR8173	55°54·3′	5°29·8′W	X	62
Sliabh Loraich	Highld	NN3879	56°52·7′	4°39·1′W	X	41
Sliabh Meadhonach	Highld	NG2104	57°2·8′	6°35·6′W	H	39
Sliabh Meurain	N Ayr	NR9523	55°27·7′	5°14·1′W	X	68,69
Sliabh Mòr	Arg & Bt	NR2268	55°49·8′	6°25·9′W	H	60
Sliabh na Creige Airde	Highld	NG8699	57°2·8′	5°30·6′W	X	39
Sliabh na h-Airde	N Eil	NF7854	57°28·0′	7°21·8′W	T	22
Sliabh nam Feur Lochan	Arg & Bt	NR3367	55°49·6′	6°15·4′W	X	60,61
Sliabh nan Coiseachan	Arg & Bt	NR3166	55°49·0′	6°17·2′W	X	60,61
Sliabh nan Dearc	Arg & Bt	NR9059	55°47·0′	5°20·5′W	X	62
Sliabh Riabhach	Arg & Bt	NR3793	56°3·7′	6°13·1′W	X	61
Sliaghnagairn	Moray	NJ1733	57°23·1′	3°22·4′W	X	28
Slibrigh	N Eil	NB4838	58°15·8′	6°17·3′W	X	8
Slickconerie	D & G	NX1570	54°59·7′	4°53·1′W	H	76
Slickly	Highld	ND2966	58°34·8′	3°12·8′W	T	11,12
Sliddens Moss	Derby	SE0703	53°31·7′	1°53·3′W	X	110
Sliddery	N Ayr	NR9323	55°27·7′	5°16·0′W	T	68,69
Slidderybrae	Aberd	NO6096	57°3·5′	2°39·1′W	X	37,45
Sliddery Point	D & G	NX4844	54°46·3′	4°21·4′W	X	83
Sliddery Water	N Ayr	NR9526	55°29·3′	5°14·3′W	W	68,69
Slidderywater Foot	N Ayr	NR9321	55°26·6′	5°15·9′W	X	68,69
Slideslow	Worcs	SO9770	52°19·9′	2°2·2′W	T	139
Sliding Hill	Dorset	ST4000	50°48·0′	2°50·7′W	X	193
Sliding Hill	Oxon	SU6691	51°37·1′	1°2·4′W	X	164,175
Slidy Hill	Monm	ST4890	51°36·6′	2°44·7′W	X	171,172
Slieau Chiarn	I of M	SC3176	54°9·4′	4°34·9′W	H	95
Slieau Curn	I of M	SC3490	54°17·0′	4°32·6′W	H	95
Slieau Dhoo	I of M	SC3589	54°16·5′	4°31·6′W	H	95
Slieau Freoaghane	I of M	SC3488	54°15·9′	4°32·5′W	H	95
Slieau Lewaigue	I of M	SC4592	54°18·3′	4°22·5′W	H	95
Slieau Lhean	I of M	SC4287	54°15·5′	4°25·1′W	H	95
Slieau Maggle	I of M	SC3486	54°14·8′	4°32·5′W	H	95
Slieau Managh	I of M	SC3990	54°17·1′	4°28·0′W	H	95
Slieau Mooar Plantn	I of M	SC2376	54°9·2′	4°42·2′W	F	95
Slieau Ouyr	I of M	SC4387	54°15·5′	4°24·2′W	H	95
Slieau Plantation	I of M	SC2373	54°7·6′	4°42·1′W	F	95
Slieau Ree	I of M	SC3782	54°12·7′	4°29·6′W	H	95
Slieau Ruy	I of M	SC3282	54°12·6′	4°34·2′W	H	95
Slieau Ruy	I of M	SC4387	54°15·5′	4°24·2′W	H	95
Slieau Whallian	I of M	SC2680	54°11·4′	4°39·6′W	H	95
Slieauwhallian	I of M	SC2780	54°11·4′	4°38·7′W	X	95
Slieau Whallian Plantn	I of M	SC2781	54°12·0′	4°38·7′W	F	95
Sliegeag	N Eil	NB3250	58°21·7′	6°34·5′W	X	8
Sliemore	Highld	NJ0320	57°15·9′	3°36·0′W	X	36
Slieu Curn Plantation	I of M	SC3490	54°17·0′	4°32·6′W	F	95
Slifehurst	W Susx	TQ0027	51°2·2′	0°34·0′W	X	186,197
Sligachan Hotel	Highld	NG4829	57°17·2′	6°10·5′W	X	32
Sligatu	Shetld	HU4782	60°31·4′	1°8·1′W	X	1,2,3
Sligeanach (Shielings)	Arg & Bt	NN2137	56°29·7′	4°54·0′W	X	50
Sligga Skerry	Shetld	HU4380	60°30·3′	1°12·5′W	X	1,2,3
Slighhouses	Scot Bord	NT8259	55°49·7′	2°16·8′W	X	67,74
Slight Side	Cumbr	NY2005	54°26·3′	3°13·6′W	X	89,90
Sligneach	Arg & Bt	NM2823	56°19·5′	6°23·5′W	X	48
Sligneach Beag	Highld	NM5560	56°40·3′	5°59·5′W	X	47
Sligneach Mór	Highld	NM5660	56°40·3′	5°58·5′W	X	47
Sligo	Highld	NH6751	57°32·0′	4°12·8′W	X	26
Sligrachan	Arg & Bt	NS1690	56°4·3′	4°56·9′W	X	56
Sligrachan Hill	Arg & Bt	NS1590	56°4·3′	4°57·9′W	H	56
Slimbridge	Glos	SO7303	51°43·7′	2°23·1′W	T	162
Slimeford	Corn	SX4369	50°30·2′	4°15·2′W	X	201
Slime Road	Glos	ST5592	51°37·7′	2°38·6′W	W	162,172
Slimeroad Sand	S Glos	ST5692	51°37·7′	2°37·8′W	X	162,172
Slimmingford Rig	S Lanak	NS7922	55°28·9′	3°54·4′W	X	71
Slinches	Kent	TR0727	51°0·5′	0°57·4′E	X	189
Slindon	Staffs	SJ8232	52°53·7′	2°15·6′W	T	127
Slindon	W Susx	SU9608	50°52·0′	0°37·8′W	T	197
Slindon Common	W Susx	SU9607	50°51·5′	0°37·8′W	X	197
Slindon Park	W Susx	SU9508	50°52·0′	0°38·6′W	X	197
Slines Oak	Surrey	TQ3757	51°18·0′	0°1·7′W	X	187
Slinfold	W Susx	TQ1131	51°4·3′	0°24·5′W	T	187
Slinfold Lodge	W Susx	TQ1030	51°3·8′	0°25·4′W	X	187
Slinford Manor	W Susx	TQ1129	51°3·2′	0°24·6′W	X	187,198
Sling	Glos	SO5807	51°45·8′	2°36·1′W	T	162
Sling	Gwyn	SH6067	53°11·1′	4°5·3′W	X	115
Sling	I of Angl	SH5877	53°16·5′	4°7·4′W	X	114,115
Sling Common	Worcs	SO9477	52°23·7′	2°4·9′W	X	139
Slingley Hill	Durham	NZ3848	54°49·8′	1°24·1′W	X	88
Slingsby	N Yks	SE6975	54°10·2′	0°56·2′W	T	100
Slingsby Banks Wood	N Yks	SE6973	54°9·1′	0°56·2′W	F	100
Slingsby Carr	N Yks	SE7176	54°10·7′	0°54·3′W	X	100
Slingsby Carr Cut	N Yks	SE7276	54°10·7′	0°53·4′W	W	100
Slingsby Heights	N Yks	SE6973	54°9·1′	0°56·2′W	X	100
Slinke Dean	Corn	SW4624	50°3·9′	5°32·6′W	X	203
Slioch	Aberd	NJ5638	57°26·1′	2°43·5′W	X	29
Slioch	Highld	NH0068	57°39·7′	5°20·7′W	H	19
Slios Garbh	Highld	NG8888	57°50·1′	5°33·8′W	X	19
Slios Garbh	Highld	NM8384	56°54·1′	5°33·4′W	X	40
Slip End	Beds	TL0818	51°51·2′	0°25·5′W	T	166
Slip End	Herts	TL2836	52°0·7′	0°7·7′W	T	153
Slipe, The	Beds	SP9156	52°11·9′	0°39·7′W	F	152
Slip Ho	Cumbr	NY8312	54°30·4′	2°15·3′W	X	91,92
Slip Inn Bridge	Midd	NZ5016	54°32·4′	1°13·2′W	X	93
Slip Mill	Kent	TQ7531	51°3·3′	0°30·2′E	X	188
Slipper Chapel	Norf	TF9235	52°52·9′	0°51·6′E	X	132

Slipperfield Loch	Scot Bord	NT1350	55°44·4′	3°22·7′W	W	65,72
Slipperfield Mount	Scot Bord	NT1151	55°44·9′	3°24·6′W	H	65,72
Slipperhill	Corn	SX2878	50°34·8′	4°25·4′W	X	201
Slipper Low Fm	Derby	SK2156	53°6·3′	1°40·8′W	FM	119
Slipper Stones	Devon	SX5688	50°40·7′	4°1·9′W	X	191
Slippery Crags	Northum	NT8804	55°20·0′	2°10·9′W	X	80
Slippery Ford	Brad	SE0040	53°51·6′	1°59·6′W	T	104
Slippery Gowt Fm	Lincs	TF3441	52°57·2′	0°0·1′E	FM	131
Slippery Point	Devon	SX6838	50°13·9′	3°50·7′W	X	202
Slippery Stones	Derby	SK1695	53°27·3′	1°45·1′W	X	110
Slipstone Crags	N Yks	SE1382	54°14·3′	1°47·6′W	X	99
Slipton	Northnts	SP9579	52°24·3′	0°35·8′W	T	141
Slipton Lodge	Northnts	SP9581	52°25·4′	0°35·8′W	X	141
Slisneach	Highld	NG7508	57°6·7′	5°42·5′W	X	33
Slitch Ridge	Cumbr	SD2464	54°4·2′	3°9·3′W	X	96
Slit Foot	Durham	NY8342	54°46·6′	2°15·4′W	X	86,87
Slithers, The	Shetld	HU3611	59°53·2′	1°20·9′W	X	4
Slithers, The	Shetld	HU4008	59°51·6′	1°16·7′W	X	4
Slitrig Water	Scot Bord	NT5007	55°21·5′	2°46·9′W	W	79
Slitting Mill	Staffs	SK0217	52°45·3′	1°57·8′W	T	128
Slittingmill Fm	Derby	SK4376	53°17·0′	1°20·9′W	FM	120
Sliving Sike	N Yks	SE8699	54°23·0′	0°40·1′W	W	94,101
Sloaga Brune	Shetld	HU4127	60°1·8′	1°15·4′W	X	4
Sloc a'Bhrighide	Arg & Bt	NM8036	56°28·3′	5°33·9′W	W	49
Sloca-dubha	N Eil	NG0382	57°44·0′	6°58·9′W	W	18
Sloc a' Ghallubhaich	Highld	NG2506	57°4·0′	6°31·8′W	W	39
Sloc a' Mhadaidh	Highld	NG3642	57°23·8′	6°23·2′W	X	23
Sloc a' Mhaide	N Eil	NF8011	57°5·0′	7°16·5′W	W	31
Sloc a'Mhuilinn	Arg & Bt	NM8443	56°32·0′	5°30·3′W	W	49
Sloc an Eich Dhuinn	Arg & Bt	NM7418	56°18·3′	5°38·8′W	X	55
Sloc an Eitheir	Arg & Bt	NM8442	56°31·5′	5°30·3′W	W	49
Slocan Léim	Arg & Bt	NR6345	55°38·7′	5°45·6′W	X	62
Sloc an Neteogh	Arg & Bt	NM3645	56°31·6′	6°17·1′W	W	47,48
Sloc an Tairbh	N Eil	NF7200	56°58·7′	7°23·5′W	W	31
Sloc an t-Siomain	Arg & Bt	NM7417	56°17·8′	5°38·7′W	W	55
Sloc Brodach	Arg & Bt	NR4774	55°53·8′	6°2·4′W	X	60,61
Sloc Caol	N Eil	NF8112	57°5·6′	7°15·6′W	W	31
Sloc Dubh	N Eil	NF8028	57°14·1′	7°17·8′W	W	22
Sloc Dubh na Thabhann	N Eil	NF8127	57°13·6′	7°16·7′W	W	22
Sloc Eòghainn	Arg & Bt	NM6338	56°28·7′	5°50·5′W	X	49
Sloc Glamarigeo	N Eil	NL5986	56°50·7′	7°35·2′W	W	31
Sloc Grisivick	N Eil	NL6293	56°54·6′	7°32·8′W	W	31
Sloch	Highld	NM6981	56°52·0′	5°47·0′W	X	40
Slochd	Arg & Bt	NM4627	56°22·3′	6°6·4′W	X	48
Slochd	Highld	NH8424	57°17·8′	3°55·0′W	X	35
Slochd a' Mhuilt	Arg & Bt	NM4218	56°17·3′	6°9·7′W	X	48
Slochd Bay	Arg & Bt	NM4526	56°21·7′	6°7·3′W	W	48
Slochd Beag	Highld	NH8490	56°59·5′	3°54·1′W	X	35,43
Slochd Burn	Moray	NJ2518	57°15·1′	3°14·1′W	W	37
Slochd Dubh	Highld	NG4016	57°9·9′	6°17·6′W	X	32
Slochd Maol Doiridh	Arg & Bt	NR2947	55°38·7′	6°18·0′W	X	60
Slochd Mór	Highld	NG2653	57°29·3′	6°33·9′W	X	23
Slochd Mór	Highld	NH8325	57°18·3′	3°56·1′W	X	35
Slochd MÓR	Moray	NJ1202	57°6·3′	3°26·7′W	H	36
Slochd na Feòla	Arg & Bt	NM4522	56°19·6′	6°7·0′W	X	48
Slochd nan Speach	Arg & Bt	NN0635	56°28·3′	5°8·5′W	X	50
Slochd Summit	Highld	NH8325	57°18·3′	3°56·1′W	X	35
Slochd Uigshader	Highld	NG3749	57°27·6′	6°22·7′W	X	23
Sloc Heisegeo	N Eil	NL5481	56°47·8′	7°39·6′W	W	31
Slochnacraig	Pth & Kin	NO1268	56°48·0′	3°26·0′W	T	43
Slocka	Shetld	HU2883	60°32·0′	1°28·9′W	X	3
Slockavullin	Arg & Bt	NR8297	56°7·2′	5°30·0′W	T	55
Slockenray	S Ayr	NX1491	55°11·0′	4°54·9′W	X	76
Slocker Hole	Somer	ST6647	51°13·5′	2°28·8′W	X	183
Slockmill	D & G	NX0934	54°40·1′	4°57·3′W	X	82
Slock, The	E Ayr	NX4589	55°10·5′	4°25·6′W	X	77
Sloc Mnài Mhic-a-Mhir	Arg & Bt	NM8342	56°31·5′	5°31·2′W	W	49
Sloc Mór	Arg & Bt	NM1556	56°36·8′	6°38·3′W	W	46
Sloc na Dubhaich	Highld	NM4178	56°49·5′	6°14·3′W	W	39
Sloc na Gamhna	Arg & Bt	NM2661	56°39·9′	6°27·9′W	W	46,47
Sloc nam Fearna	Arg & Bt	NR8673	55°54·4′	5°25·0′W	X	62
Sloc nan Con	Arg & Bt	NM4332	56°24·9′	6°9·6′W	W	48
Sloc nan Sgarbh	Arg & Bt	NM7418	56°18·3′	5°38·8′W	W	55
Sloc nan Uan	Arg & Bt	NM7418	56°18·3′	5°38·8′W	X	55
Sloc na Sealbhaig	N Eil	NL5579	56°46·7′	7°38·5′W	W	31
Slocombeslade	Devon	SS7747	51°12·8′	3°45·3′W	X	180
Sloc Roe	N Eil	NF7276	57°39·5′	7°29·6′W	X	18
Sloc Ruadh	N Eil	NF7809	57°3·8′	7°18·3′W	W	31
Sloc Ruaridh	N Ayr	NS0127	55°30·0′	5°8·5′W	X	69
Slodahill	D & G	NY1683	55°8·3′	3°18·6′W	X	79
Sloda Hill	D & G	NY1684	55°8·8′	3°18·7′W	H	79
Slodbrook Fm	Dorset	ST7929	51°3·8′	2°17·6′W	FM	183
Sloden Inclosure	Hants	SU2113	50°55·2′	1°41·7′W	F	195
Sloe Fm	Suff	TM0354	52°9·0′	0°58·4′E	FM	155
Sloehabbert	D & G	NX4050	54°49·4′	4°29·0′W	X	83
Sloe Ho	Essex	TL8031	51°57·8′	0°37·6′E	X	168
Sloemans Fm	Enf	TL3200	51°41·2′	0°5·0′W	FM	166
Sloethorn Park	N Yks	NZ6507	54°27·5′	0°59·4′W	X	94
Sloe Wood	N Yks	SE3077	54°11·5′	1°32·0′W	F	99
Slogan	Moray	NJ3841	57°27·6′	3°1·5′W	X	28
Slogarie Fm	D & G	NX6567	54°59·0′	4°6·2′W	FM	83,84
Slogarie Hill	D & G	NX6367	54°59·0′	4°8·0′W	H	83
Sloggan Craggan	Pth & Kin	NN9534	56°29·4′	3°41·9′W	H	52,53
Sloley	Norf	TG2924	52°46·1′	1°24·1′E	T	133,134
Sloley Barton	Devon	SS5737	51°7·1′	4°2·4′W	X	180
Sloley Hall	Norf	TG2923	52°45·6′	1°24·0′E	X	133,134
Sloley Stone	Devon	SS7139	51°8·4′	3°50·3′W	X	180
Slomcombe	Devon	SX7386	50°39·8′	3°47·4′W	T	191
Slongaber	D & G	NX8079	55°5·7′	3°52·4′W	X	84
Slongaber Hill	D & G	NX8080	55°6·2′	3°52·4′W	X	78
Slonk Hill Fm	W Susx	TQ2206	50°50·7′	0°15·6′W	FM	198
Sloo	Devon	SS3723	50°59·2′	4°19·0′W	X	190
Sloothby	Lincs	TF4970	53°12·6′	0°14·3′E	T	122
Sloothby Ings	Lincs	TF5069	53°12·0′	0°15·2′E	X	122
Sloperton Fm	Wilts	ST9565	51°23·3′	2°3·9′W	FM	173
Sloroch's Wood	Moray	NJ3556	57°35·6′	3°4·8′W	F	28
Slosh	Cumbr	NY6819	54°34·1′	2°29·3′W	X	91
Sloswicks Fm	Notts	SK5675	53°16·4′	1°9·2′W	FM	120
Sloswicks Springs	Notts	SK5675	53°16·4′	1°9·2′W	F	120
Slot Burn	E Ayr	NS6731	55°33·5′	4°6·1′W	W	71

Slouch Hill	Aberd	NJ4832	57°22·8′	2°51·4′W	H	29,37
Slouch Moss	S Lanak	NS6234	55°35·1′	4°10·9′W	X	71
Slouchnamorroch Bay	D & G	NX0939	54°42·8′	4°57·5′W	W	82
Slouchnawen Bay	D & G	NW9563	54°55·4′	5°11·5′W	W	82
Slough	Devon	SS7424	51°0·3′	3°47·4′W	X	180
Slough	Monm	SO4101	51°42·5′	2°50·8′W	X	171
Slough	Powys	SO3063	52°15·9′	3°1·1′W	T	137,148
Slough	Slough	SU9979	51°30·3′	0°34·0′W	T	175,176
Slough Bottom Fm	Bucks	SU8197	51°40·2′	0°49·3′W	FM	165
Slough Court	Somer	ST3427	51°2·5′	2°56·1′W	A	193
Slough Dyke	Notts	SK8159	53°7·6′	0°47·0′W	W	121
Slough Fm	Devon	ST0211	50°53·6′	3°23·2′W	FM	192
Slough Fm	Dorset	ST5603	50°49·7′	2°37·1′W	FM	194
Slough Fm	Essex	TL5632	51°58·1′	0°16·7′E	FM	167
Slough Fm	Essex	TM0427	51°54·5′	0°58·3′E	FM	168
Slough Fm	Monm	ST4790	51°36·6′	2°45·5′W	FM	171,172
Slough Fm	Suff	TL8946	52°5·0′	0°45·9′E	FM	155
Slough Fm	Suff	TL9048	52°6·1′	0°46·9′E	FM	155
Slough Fm	Suff	TM0166	52°15·5′	0°57·1′E	FM	155
Slough Fm	Suff	TM3983	52°23·8′	1°31·2′E	FM	156
Slough Glebe Fm	Bucks	SU8098	51°40·7′	0°50·2′W	FM	165
Slough Green	Somer	ST2720	50°58·7′	3°2·0′W	T	193
Slough Green	W Susx	TQ2826	51°1·4′	0°10·1′W	T	187,198
Slough Hall	Suff	TL9344	52°3·9′	0°49·3′E	X	155
Slough Hill	Bucks	SU8097	51°40·2′	0°50·2′W	H	165
Slough Hill	D & G	NS8417	55°26·2′	3°49·6′W	H	71,78
Slough Hill	Suff	TL8652	52°8·3′	0°43·5′E	T	155
Slough Ho	Essex	TL8003	51°42·0′	0°36·7′E	A	168
Slough Ho	Thurr	TQ6286	51°33·2′	0°20·6′E	X	177
Slough House Fm	Essex	TL8709	51°45·1′	0°43·0′E	FM	168
Slough House Fm	Essex	TM0922	51°51·7′	1°2·5′E	FM	168,169
Slough House Fm	Essex	TQ7299	51°40·0′	0°29·6′E	FM	167
Slough Place	W Susx	TQ2826	51°1·4′	0°10·1′W	X	187,198
Slough, The	Cumbr	SD5595	54°21·2′	2°41·1′W	X	97
Slough, The	Norf	TL8982	52°24·4′	0°47·1′E	X	144
Slough Trading Estate	SLOUGH	SU9581	51°31·4′	0°37·4′W	X	175,176
Slouthy	Pemb	SM9926	51°54·0′	4°54·9′W	X	157,158
Slowley Fm	Somer	SS9938	51°8·2′	3°26·2′W	FM	181
Slowley Green Fm	Warw	SP2689	52°30·1′	1°36·6′W	FM	140
Slowley Hall	Warw	SP2688	52°29·6′	1°36·6′W	X	140
Slowley Wood	Somer	SS9938	51°8·2′	3°26·2′W	F	181
Slown's Cairn	E Ayr	NS5103	55°18·2′	4°20·4′W	X	77
Slowwe Ho	Glos	SO7111	51°48·0′	2°24·8′W	X	162
Sloyne, The	Wirral	SJ3387	53°22·8′	3°0·0′W	W	108
Sluain Burn	Arg & Bt	NS0898	56°8·4′	5°5·0′W	W	56
Sludge Hall	Leic	SK7105	52°38·5′	0°56·6′W	X	141
Slue	Corn	SX3095	50°44·0′	4°24·2′W	X	190
Slufters Inclosure	Hants	SU2210	50°53·6′	1°40·8′W	F	195
Slugach	Highld	NG9056	57°33·0′	5°30·1′W	X	25
Slugach	N Eil	NF7815	57°7·0′	7°18·8′W	X	31
Slugaid a' Chruachain	Arg & Bt	NM4421	56°19·0′	6°7·9′W	X	48
Slugaide Glas	Arg & Bt	NR2846	55°38·1′	6°18·9′W	W	60
Slugan	N Eil	NF7663	57°32·7′	7°24·5′W	X	18
Slugan Dubh	Arg & Bt	NM2921	56°18·5′	6°22·5′W	W	48
Slugan Liath	Highld	NH6723	57°17·0′	4°11·9′W	X	26,35
Sluggan	Highld	NH8721	57°16·2′	3°52·0′W	T	35,36
Sluggan Br	Highld	NH8622	57°16·7′	3°53·0′W	X	35,36
Sluggangranish	Highld	NH8914	57°12·5′	3°49·8′W	X	35,36
Sluggans	Highld	NG4744	57°25·2′	6°12·4′W	T	23
Slug of Auchrannie	Angus	NO2752	56°39·5′	3°11·0′W	X	53
Slug Road	Aberd	NO7395	57°3·0′	2°26·2′W	X	38,45
Slug Road	Aberd	NO8089	56°59·8′	2°19·3′W	X	45
Sluice Common	Norf	TF6001	52°35·2′	0°22·1′E	X	143
Sluice Fm	Lancs	SD3917	53°39·0′	2°55·0′W	FM	108
Sluice Fm	Lincs	TF3431	52°51·8′	0°0·2′W	FM	131
Sluice Fm	Newp	ST2579	51°30·5′	3°4·5′W	FM	171
Sluice Fm	Suff	TM2841	52°1·5′	1°19·8′E	FM	169
Sluice, The	Lancs	SD4116	53°38·5′	2°53·1′W	W	108
Sluice, The	Suff	TM4766	52°14·4′	1°37·5′E	X	156
Sluice Wood	Norf	TF7303	52°36·1′	0°33·7′E	F	143
Sluidubh	Pth & Kin	NN9526	56°25·1′	3°41·7′W	X	52,53,58
Sluie Hill	Aberd	NO6297	57°4·0′	2°37·1′W	H	37,45
Sluie Ho	Aberd	NO6296	57°3·5′	2°37·1′W	X	37,45
Sluie Woods	Aberd	NO6197	57°4·0′	2°38·1′W	F	37,45
Slumbay Harbour	Highld	NG8938	57°23·3′	5°30·2′W	W	24
Slungie Hill	Pth & Kin	NO0507	56°15·0′	3°31·5′W	H	58
Slunkrainy	D & G	NX0547	54°47·1′	5°1·5′W	X	82
Slutswell	Glos	SO9812	51°48·6′	2°1·3′W	X	163
Sluvad Fm	Torf	ST3199	51°41·4′	2°59·5′W	FM	171
Sluxton	Swan	SS4289	51°34·9′	4°16·4′W	X	159
Slwch Fm	Powys	SO0628	51°56·8′	3°21·7′W	FM	160
Slwch Tump	Powys	SO0528	51°56·8′	3°22·5′W	X	160
Slwch Tump (Fort)	Powys	SO0528	51°56·8′	3°22·5′W	A	160
Slyborough Hill	Leic	SK7126	52°49·8′	0°56·4′W	X	129
Sly Corner	Kent	TQ9632	51°3·5′	0°48·2′E	T	189
Slyddon	Corn	SX2689	50°40·7′	4°27·4′W	X	190
Slydie	Aberd	NJ6709	57°10·5′	2°32·3′W	X	38
Slyer's Fm	Cambs	TL3680	52°24·3′	0°0·4′E	FM	142
Slyes Fm	E Susx	TQ6007	50°50·6′	0°16·8′E	FM	199
Slyfield	Surrey	SU9952	51°15·7′	0°34·5′W	T	186
Slyfield Ho	Surrey	TQ1357	51°18·3′	0°22·3′W	A	187
Sly Hill	Orkney	HY6222	59°5·3′	2°39·3′W	X	5
Slymaback	Stir	NN7610	56°16·2′	3°59·7′W	X	57
Slymansdale	Staffs	SJ7840	52°57·7′	2°19·2′W	X	118
Slymlakes Fm	Devon	SY2896	50°45·8′	3°0·9′W	FM	193
Slyne	Lancs	SD4765	54°4·9′	2°48·2′W	T	97
Slyne Hall Heights	Lancs	SD4766	54°5·5′	2°48·2′W	X	97
Slype Fm	Northnts	SP8959	52°13·6′	0°41·4′W	FM	152
Sly's Barn	Norf	TF8336	52°53·6′	0°43·6′E	X	132
Slys Fm	Hants	SU6327	51°2·6′	1°5·7′W	FM	185
Slythehurst	Surrey	TQ0839	51°8·6′	0°27·0′W	X	187
Smacam Down	Dorset	SY6599	50°47·6′	2°29·4′W	X	194
Smaden Head	N Yks	SE2168	54°6·7′	1°40·3′W	X	99
Sma' Glen	Pth & Kin	NN9029	56°26·7′	3°46·6′W	X	52,58
Smail Burn	Scot Bord	NT2917	55°26·8′	3°6·9′W	W	79
Smailes	N Yks	NZ9406	54°26·7′	0°32·6′W	X	94
Smailholm	Scot Bord	NT6436	55°37·2′	2°33·9′W	T	74
Smailholm Mains	Scot Bord	NT6535	55°36·7′	2°32·9′W	X	74
Smailholm Tower	Scot Bord	NT6334	55°36·1′	2°34·8′W	A	74
Smailsburn	Durham	NY9341	54°46·1′	2°6·1′W	X	87

Smailsburn Common	Durham	NY9342	54°46·6′	2°6·1′W	X	87
Smaithwaite	Cumbr	NY3119	54°33·9′	3°3·6′W	X	90
Smaithwaite Fm	Cumbr	NY0819	54°33·7′	3°24·9′W	FM	89
Smalden Ho	Lancs	SD7549	53°56·4′	2°22·4′W	X	103
Smalehope Burn	Northum	NT9314	55°25·4′	2°6·2′W	W	80
Smales	Northum	NY7184	55°9·2′	2°26·9′W	X	80
Smales Burn	Northum	NY7183	55°8·7′	2°26·9′W	W	80
Smales Leap	Northum	NY7184	55°9·2′	2°26·9′W	X	80
Smalesmouth	Northum	NY7284	55°9·2′	2°25·9′W	X	80
Smalesmouth	Northum	NY7385	55°9·8′	2°25·0′W	X	80
Smallacombe	Devon	SS8129	51°3·1′	3°41·5′W	X	181
Smallacombe	Devon	SX3786	50°39·3′	4°18·0′W	X	201
Smallacombe	Somer	SS7339	51°8·4′	3°48·5′W	X	180
Smalla Combe	Somer	SS8447	51°12·9′	3°39·3′W	F	181
Smallacombe Fm	Devon	SX9276	50°34·7′	3°31·1′W	FM	192
Smallacombe Moors	Devon	SS8524	51°0·5′	3°38·0′W	X	181
Smallacombe Rocks	Devon	SX7578	50°35·5′	3°45·6′W	X	191
Smallacoombe Downs	Corn	SX2275	50°33·1′	4°30·4′W	X	201
Small Acres Fm	Hants	SU7750	51°14·9′	0°53·4′W	FM	186
Smallands Hall Fm	Essex	TL8210	51°45·8′	0°38·6′E	FM	168
Smalla Waters	Shetld	HU2654	60°16·4′	1°31·3′W	W	3
Smallbank	Aberd	NO6866	56°47·3′	2°31·0′W	X	45
Small Banks	Brad	SE0748	53°55·9′	1°53·2′W	X	104
Smallberry Hill	E Susx	TQ5224	50°59·9′	0°10·4′E	X	199
Smallbridge	Kent	TQ7038	51°7·2′	0°26·1′E	X	188
Smallbridge	Roch	SD9115	53°38·1′	2°7·8′W	T	109
Smallbridge Fm	Dorset	SU0711	50°54·1′	1°53·6′W	FM	195
Smallbridge Fm	Suff	TL9156	52°10·4′	0°48·0′E	FM	155
Smallbridge Hall	Suff	TL9233	51°58·0′	0°48·1′E	A	168
Small Brook	Ches	SJ7562	53°9·5′	2°22·0′W	W	118
Small Brook	Devon	SS3006	50°50·0′	4°24·5′W	W	190
Small Brook	Devon	SX6290	50°41·8′	3°56·9′W	W	191
Smallbrook	Devon	SX8698	50°46·5′	3°36·6′W	T	191
Smallbrook	Glos	SO5900	51°42·1′	2°35·2′W	T	162
Smallbrook	Surrey	SU8939	51°8·8′	0°43·3′W	X	186
Small Brook	Warw	SP2046	52°7·0′	1°42·1′W	W	151
Smallbrook Fm	I of W	SZ5990	50°42·6′	1°9·5′W	FM	196
Smallbrook Plains	Devon	SX6865	50°28·4′	3°51·2′W	X	202
Smallburgh	Norf	TG3324	52°46·0′	1°27·6′E	T	133,134
Smallburgh Hall	Norf	TG3223	52°45·5′	1°26·7′E	X	133,134
Smallburn	Aberd	NJ4644	57°29·2′	2°53·6′W	X	28,29
Smallburn	Aberd	NJ5224	57°18·5′	2°47·3′W	X	37
Smallburn	Aberd	NK0140	57°27·3′	1°58·5′W	X	30
Smallburn	Angus	NO5243	56°34·8′	2°46·4′W	X	54
Smallburn	E Ayr	NS6826	55°30·9′	4°5·0′W	T	71
Smallburn	Moray	NJ2857	57°32·3′	3°13·7′W	X	28
Small Burn	Northum	NY6563	54°57·9′	2°32·4′W	W	86
Small Burn	Northum	NY7073	55°3·3′	2°27·7′W	W	86,87
Small Burn	Northum	NY9480	55°7·1′	2°5·2′W	W	80
Small Burn	Northum	NY9775	55°4·4′	2°2·4′W	W	87
Small Burn	Northum	NZ1473	55°3·3′	1°46·4′W	W	88
Smallburn	Northum	NZ1574	55°3·9′	1°45·5′W	X	88
Smallburn	Northum	NZ1592	55°13·6′	1°45·4′W	X	81
Smallburn Hill	Aberd	NK0140	57°27·3′	1°58·5′W	H	30
Smallburn Resr	N Ayr	NS3056	55°46·3′	4°42·2′W	W	63
Smallburns	Northum	NY7947	54°49·3′	2°19·2′W	X	86,87
Smallburns Moor	Northum	NY7946	54°48·8′	2°19·2′W	X	86,87
Small Cleugh	Northum	NY6655	54°53·6′	2°31·4′W	X	86
Small Clough	Derby	SK0696	53°27·9′	1°54·2′W	X	110
Small Clough	Derby	SK1284	53°21·4′	1°48·8′W	X	110
Smalldale	Derby	SK0977	53°17·6′	1°51·5′W	T	119
Smalldale	Derby	SK1681	53°19·8′	1°45·2′W	T	110
Small Dean Fm	Bucks	SU8298	51°40·7′	0°48·4′W	FM	165
Smalldene	Northum	NU1402	55°19·0′	1°46·3′W	X	81
Smalldene Fm	Bucks	SP8606	51°45·0′	0°44·9′W	FM	165
Small Dole	W Susx	TQ2112	50°53·9′	0°16·4′W	T	198
Smalldon Fm	Devon	SS6229	51°2·9′	3°57·7′W	FM	180
Small Down	Hants	SU6720	50°58·8′	1°2·3′W	X	185
Small Down Fm	Somer	ST6640	51°9·7′	2°28·8′W	FM	183
Small Down Knoll	Somer	ST6640	51°9·7′	2°28·8′W	H	183
Small Downs, The		TR3855	51°14·9′	1°25·0′E	W	179
Small End	Lincs	TF4455	53°4·6′	0°9·4′E	T	122
Smalley	Derby	SK4044	52°59·7′	1°23·8′W	T	129
Smalley Common	Derby	SK4142	52°58·7′	1°23·0′W	T	129
Smalley Fold	Lancs	SD6332	53°47·2′	2°33·3′W	X	102,103
Smalley Green	Derby	SK4043	52°59·2′	1°23·8′W	T	129
Smalley Hall	Derby	SK4043	52°59·2′	1°23·8′W	X	129
Smallfield	Sheff	SK2494	53°26·8′	1°37·9′W	X	110
Smallfield	Surrey	TQ3143	51°10·5′	0°7·2′W	T	187
Smallfield Place	Surrey	TQ3243	51°10·5′	0°6·3′W	A	187
Smallford	Herts	TL1907	51°45·2′	0°16·2′W	T	166
Smallford Fm	Herts	TL1806	51°44·6′	0°17·1′W	FM	166
Smallford Trail	Herts	TL2007	51°45·2′	0°15·3′W	X	166
Small Gill	N Yks	SD7957	54°0·8′	2°18·8′W	X	103
Smallham Fm	W Susx	TQ1823	50°59·9′	0°18·7′W	FM	198
Smallhanger	Devon	SX5759	50°25·0′	4°0·4′W	X	202
Small Heath	Birm	SP1085	52°28·0′	1°50·8′W	T	139
Smallhedge Fm	Donc	SE6315	53°37·9′	1°2·4′W	FM	111
Small Hill Barton	Corn	SX1794	50°43·2′	4°35·2′W	X	190
Small Ho	N Yks	SD9452	53°58·1′	2°5·1′W	X	103
Smallholm	D & G	NY0977	55°5·0′	3°25·1′W	T	85
Smallholmbank	D & G	NY0976	55°4·5′	3°25·1′W	X	85
Smallholms	D & G	NY2973	55°3·0′	3°6·3′W	X	85
Smallhope Burn	Northum	NY7395	55°15·2′	2°25·1′W	W	80
Smallhope Rigg	Northum	NY7196	55°15·7′	2°26·9′W	X	80
Smallhurst	Ches	SJ9469	53°13·3′	2°5·0′W	X	118
Small Hythe	Kent	TQ8930	51°2·5′	0°42·2′E	T	189
Smallicombe Fm	Devon	SY2097	50°46·3′	3°7·7′W	FM	192,193
Smallie	Shetld	HT9538	60°7·9′	2°4·9′W	X	4
Small Isles	Arg & Bt	NR5468	55°50·8′	5°55·4′W	X	61
Smallmarsh	Devon	SS6022	50°59·1′	3°59·3′W	T	180
Small Mead Fm	Read	SU7069	51°25·2′	0°59·2′W	FM	175
Smallmoor	I of W	SZ4681	50°37·8′	1°20·6′W	X	196
Small Mount	Highld	NC9928	58°14·0′	3°42·7′W	H	17
Small Mouth	Dorset	SY6676	50°35·2′	2°28·4′W	W	194
Small Muir	D & G	NX3949	54°48·9′	4°29·9′W	X	83
Small Ord Point	Pemb	SS1496	51°38·2′	4°40·9′W	X	158
Smallrice	Staffs	SJ9531	52°52·8′	2°4·1′W	T	127
Smallridge	Devon	ST3000	50°48·0′	2°59·2′W	T	193
Smallridge Fm	Devon	SX7888	50°41·0′	3°43·2′W	FM	191
Smallrigg	D & G	NY0780	55°6·6′	3°27·0′W	X	78
Small River Lea or Lee	Herts	TL3602	51°42·2′	0°1·5′W	W	166
Small River Lee or Lea	Herts	TL3602	51°42·2′	0°1·5′W	W	166
Small Shaw	Cald	SD9930	53°46·2′	2°0·5′W	X	103
Smallshaw	Tames	SD9400	53°30·0′	2°5·0′W	T	109
Smallshaw Fm	Staffs	SK0465	53°11·2′	1°56·0′W	FM	119
Small Shaw Height	Lancs	SD8525	53°43·5′	2°13·2′W	X	103
Smallshoes	Essex	TL6412	51°47·2′	0°23·1′E	X	167
Smalls, The	Pemb	SM4608	51°43·0′	5°40·3′W	X	157
Smallstone Beck	Cumbr	SD1898	54°22·5′	3°15·3′W	W	96
Smallstones Fm	Oxon	SP3118	51°51·8′	1°32·6′W	FM	164
Smallstones Point	Devon	SY0984	50°39·1′	3°16·9′W	X	192
Smallthorne	C of Stoke	SJ8850	53°3·1′	2°10·3′W	T	118
Smallthwaite Ho	Cumbr	NY4339	54°44·8′	2°52·7′W	X	90
Small Water	Cumbr	NY4510	54°29·2′	2°50·5′W	W	90
Small Waters	Shetld	HP5802	60°42·1′	0°55·8′W	W	1
Small Way	Somer	ST6430	51°4·3′	2°30·4′W	T	183
Smallways Br	N Yks	NZ1011	54°29·9′	1°50·3′W	X	92
Smallwood	Ches	SJ8060	53°8·4′	2°17·5′W	T	118
Smallwood	Worcs	SP0467	52°18·3′	1°56·1′W	T	150
Smallwood Green	Suff	TL9359	52°11·9′	0°49·9′E	T	155
Smallwood Hey	Lancs	SD3948	53°55·7′	2°55·3′W	T	102
Smallwood Manor	Staffs	SK1029	52°51·7′	1°50·7′W	X	128
Smallworth	Norf	TM0080	52°23·1′	0°56·7′E	T	144
Smallworthy	Devon	SX5498	50°46·0′	4°3·8′W	X	191
Smalmstown	Cumbr	NY3668	55°0·4′	2°59·6′W	X	85
Sma Lochs	Shetld	HU2252	60°15·4′	1°35·7′W	W	3
Smannell	Hants	SU3848	51°14·0′	1°27·0′W	T	185
Smaque Fm	N Lincs	SE7409	53°34·6′	0°52·5′W	FM	112
Smarber	N Yks	SD9797	54°22·4′	2°2·4′W	X	98
Smardale	Cumbr	NY7308	54°28·2′	2°24·6′W	T	91
Smardale Br	Cumbr	NY7205	54°26·6′	2°25·5′W	X	91
Smardale Fell	Cumbr	NY7306	54°27·2′	2°24·6′W	H	91
Smardale Mill	Cumbr	NY7409	54°28·8′	2°23·7′W	X	91
Smarden	Kent	TQ8842	51°9·0′	0°41·7′E	T	189
Smarden Bell	Kent	TQ8642	51°9·0′	0°40·0′E	T	189
Smart Gill	Durham	NZ0215	54°32·1′	1°57·7′W	X	92
Smarthill	Cumbr	NY1548	54°49·4′	3°19·0′W	X	85
Smart's Buildings	Staffs	SK0215	52°44·2′	1°57·8′W	X	128
Smart's Cairn	Aberd	NO6977	56°53·3′	2°30·1′W	A	45
Smart's Heath	Surrey	SU9855	51°17·4′	0°35·3′W	X	175,186
Smart's Hill	Herts	TL3320	51°52·0′	0°3·7′W	X	166
Smart's Hill	Kent	TQ5241	51°9·1′	0°10·8′E	T	188
Smartwick	Beds	TL0856	52°11·7′	0°24·8′W	X	153
Smasha Hill	Scot Bord	NT4416	55°26·3′	2°52·7′W	H	79
Smatcher, The	Powys	SO2159	52°13·7′	3°9·0′W	H	148
Smaull	Arg & Bt	NR2168	55°49·7′	6°26·9′W	X	60
Smawith Dike	York	SE5352	53°57·9′	1°11·1′W	W	105
Smaws Fm	N Yks	SE4743	53°53·1′	1°16·7′W	FM	105
Smaws Quarry	N Yks	SE4642	53°52·6′	1°17·6′W	X	105
Smaws Quarry	N Yks	SE4643	53°53·1′	1°17·6′W	X	105
Smay Down	Wilts	SU3159	51°20·0′	1°32·9′W	X	174
Smeafield	Northum	NU0937	55°37·8′	1°51·0′W	X	75
Smeale Fm	I of M	NX4102	54°23·6′	4°26·5′W	FM	95
Smean	Highld	ND0327	58°13·5′	3°38·6′W	H	17
Smearber Fm	N Yks	SD9349	53°56·5′	2°6·0′W	FM	103
Smeardon Down	Devon	SX5278	50°35·2′	4°5·1′W	X	191,201
Smear Fm	Suff	TM5078	52°20·8′	1°40·6′E	FM	156
Smearholme	N Yks	SE3186	54°16·4′	1°31·0′W	X	99
Smearinish	N Eil	NG0087	57°46·6′	7°2·3′W	X	18
Smearsett Scar	N Yks	SD8067	54°6·2′	2°17·9′W	X	98
Smeathalls Fm	N Yks	SE5125	53°43·4′	1°13·2′W	FM	105
Smeatharpe	Devon	ST1910	50°53·3′	3°8·7′W	T	192,193
Smeathe's Plantation	Wilts	SU1774	51°28·1′	1°44·9′W	F	173
Smeathe's Ridge	Wilts	SU1775	51°28·7′	1°44·9′W	X	173
Smeath Hill	Inverc	NS3166	55°51·7′	4°41·6′W	X	63
Smeathorns	Red & Cl	NZ6713	54°30·7′	0°57·5′W	X	94
Smeaton	Corn	SX3863	50°26·9′	4°16·5′W	X	201
Smeaton	Corn	SX3967	50°29·1′	4°15·8′W	X	201
Smeaton	E Loth	NT3569	55°54·8′	3°2·0′W	X	66
Smeaton	Fife	NT2893	56°7·7′	3°9·1′W	T	59
Smeaton Hall	Ches	SJ5847	53°1·4′	2°37·2′W	X	117
Smeaton Ho	E Loth	NT5978	55°59·8′	2°39·0′W	X	67
Smeaton Shaw	E Loth	NT3668	55°54·3′	3°1·0′W	X	66
Smeaton's Tower	C of Plym	SX4753	50°21·7′	4°8·7′W	X	201
Smeatonwood Fm	Ches	SJ5946	53°0·8′	2°36·3′W	FM	117
Smedheugh	Scot Bord	NT4927	55°32·3′	2°48·1′W	X	73
Smedley Sytch	Staffs	SK0662	53°9·5′	1°54·2′W	X	119
Smedmore Hill	Dorset	SY9279	50°36·9′	2°6·4′W	X	195
Smedmore Ho	Dorset	SY9278	50°36·3′	2°6·4′W	X	195
Smeeds Fm	Kent	TR1139	51°6·9′	1°1·3′E	FM	179,189
Smeekley Wood	Derby	SK2976	53°17·0′	1°33·5′W	F	119
Smeer Hall	Lancs	SD6265	54°5·0′	2°34·4′W	X	97
Smeesley	Shrops	SO6587	52°29·0′	2°30·5′W	X	138
Smeeth	Kent	TR0739	51°7·0′	0°57·9′E	T	179,189
Smeeth	Suff	TL7181	52°24·2′	0°31·2′E	X	143
Smeetham Hall	Essex	TL8441	52°2·4′	0°41·4′E	X	155
Smeeth Fm	Norf	TF7307	52°38·2′	0°33·8′E	FM	143
Smeeth House Fm	Norf	TF5208	52°39·1′	0°15·2′E	FM	143
Smeeth Lode	Norf	TF5712	52°41·2′	0°19·8′E	W	131,143
Smeeth, The	Norf	TF5210	52°40·2′	0°15·3′E	T	131,143
Smeeth Wood	Norf	TG1402	52°34·6′	1°9·9′E	F	144
Smeeton Gorse	Leic	SP6790	52°30·5′	1°0·4′W	X	141
Smeeton Hill	Leic	SP6791	52°31·0′	1°0·4′W	H	141
Smeeton Westerby	Leic	SP6792	52°31·5′	1°0·3′W	T	141
Smeid, The	Shetld	HP4905	60°43·8′	1°5·6′W	X	1
Smelthwaites	Lancs	SD7149	53°56·4′	2°26·1′W	X	103
Smelter	N Yks	SD9682	54°14·3′	2°3·3′W	X	98
Smelthouses	N Yks	SE1964	54°4·5′	1°42·2′W	T	99
Smelting Hill	Derby	SK2080	53°19·2′	1°41·6′W	X	110
Smelting Syke	Northum	NY9359	54°55·8′	2°6·1′W	X	87
Smelt Mill Beck	N Yks	NZ1505	54°26·7′	1°45·7′W	W	92
Smemington	Devon	SS5528	51°2·2′	4°3·7′W	X	180
Smenham	Glos	SP2123	51°54·5′	1°41·3′W	X	163
Smerby Rocks	Arg & Bt	NR7523	55°27·2′	5°33·1′W	X	68,69
Smerclate	N Eil	NF7415	57°6·9′	7°22·7′W	T	31
Smerla Water	Shetld	HU3860	60°19·6′	1°18·2′W	W	2,3
Smerlie	Highld	ND2337	58°19·2′	3°18·4′W	X	11
Smerquoy	Orkney	HY4011	58°58·5′	3°2·2′W	X	6
Smerral	Highld	ND1733	58°16·9′	3°24·5′W	X	11
Smerral	Highld	ND2362	58°32·6′	3°18·9′W	X	11,12
Smerrill Grange	Derby	SK1961	53°9·0′	1°42·5′W	X	119
Smerrill Moor	Derby	SK1860	53°8·4′	1°43·4′W	X	119
Smerrills Fm	Derby	SK2834	52°54·4′	1°34·6′W	FM	128
Smerrill Village	Derby	SK2061	53°9·0′	1°41·7′W	A	119
Smestow	Staffs	SO8591	52°31·2′	2°12·9′W	T	139
Smestow Brook	Staffs	SO8593	52°32·3′	2°12·9′W	W	139
Smestow Gate	Staffs	SO8492	52°31·8′	2°13·8′W	X	138
Smethcote Fm	Shrops	SJ5610	52°41·4′	2°38·7′W	FM	126
Smethcote Manor	Shrops	SJ5020	52°46·8′	2°44·1′W	X	126
Smethcott	Shrops	SO4599	52°35·4′	2°48·3′W	T	137,138
Smethcott Common	Shrops	SJ4400	52°35·9′	2°49·2′W	X	126
Smethcott Dingle	Shrops	SJ4500	52°35·9′	2°48·3′W	F	126
Smetherd Fm	Dorset	ST7410	50°53·6′	2°21·8′W	FM	194
Smethwick	Sand	SP0287	52°29·1′	1°57·8′W	T	139
Smethwick Green	Ches	SJ8063	53°10·1′	2°17·5′W	T	118
Smewins Fm	Win & Maid	SU8476	51°28·8′	0°47·0′W	FM	175
Smezzel	Kent	TR2243	51°8·8′	1°10·8′E	X	179,189
Smidda Tonga	Shetld	HU4979	60°29·8′	1°6·0′W	X	2,3
Smiddy	Orkney	ND4793	58°49·5′	2°54·6′W	X	7
Smiddyboyne	Aberd	NJ6063	57°39·6′	2°39·8′W	X	29
Smiddyburn	Aberd	NJ7332	57°22·9′	2°26·5′W	X	29
Smiddyburn	Aberd	NJ9420	57°16·5′	2°5·5′W	X	38
Smiddyhill	Aberd	NJ4306	57°8·7′	2°56·1′W	X	37
Smiddyhill	Aberd	NJ5717	57°14·8′	2°42·3′W	X	37
Smiddyhill	Aberd	NJ8527	57°20·3′	2°14·5′W	X	38
Smiddyhill	Aberd	NJ9755	57°35·4′	2°2·6′W	X	30
Smiddyhill	Aberd	NK0131	57°22·4′	1°58·5′W	X	30
Smiddyhill	Aberd	NK0847	57°31·0′	1°51·5′W	X	30
Smiddyhill	Aberd	NO7470	56°49·5′	2°25·1′W	X	45
Smiddy Hill	Angus	NO5143	56°34·8′	2°47·4′W	X	54
Smiddy Hill	Angus	NO6165	56°46·8′	2°37·8′W	X	45
Smiddyhill	Scot Bord	NT6961	55°50·7′	2°29·3′W	X	67
Smiddyhowe	Aberd	NJ6932	57°22·9′	2°30·5′W	X	29
Smiddyquoy	Highld	ND2160	58°31·5′	3°20·9′W	X	11,12
Smiddyquoy	Orkney	HY5009	58°58·2′	2°51·7′W	X	6,7
Smiddyseat	Aberd	NJ9461	57°38·6′	2°5·6′W	X	30
Smiddy Shaw Reservoir	Durham	NZ0446	54°48·8′	1°55·8′W	W	87
Smiddy-Well Rigg	Northum	NY8089	55°11·9′	2°18·4′W	X	80
Smid Hope Burn	Scot Bord	NT0416	55°26·0′	3°30·6′W	W	78
Smigel Burn	Highld	NC9156	58°29·0′	3°51·7′W	W	10
Smigel Burn	Highld	NC9257	58°29·5′	3°50·7′W	W	11
Smilley Wood	Suff	TM2658	52°10·7′	1°18·7′E	F	156
Sminhay Fms	Dorset	SY3899	50°47·5′	2°52·4′W	FM	193
Sminhays Corner	Somer	ST0134	51°6·0′	3°24·5′W	X	181
Smirack	Moray	NJ4063	57°39·4′	2°59·9′W	X	28
Smirisary	Highld	NM6477	56°49·7′	5°51·6′W	T	40
Smirlee Field	Shetld	HU3751	60°14·8′	1°19·4′W	X	3
Smirlees Dale	Shetld	HP5913	60°48·0′	0°54·5′W	X	1
Smirle Wood	D & G	NX4335	54°41·4′	4°25·7′W	F	83
Smirna Dale	Shetld	HU3274	60°27·2′	1°24·6′W	X	3
Smirisary Hill	Highld	NM6475	56°48·7′	5°51·5′W	H	40
Smisby	Derby	SK3419	52°46·3′	1°29·4′W	T	128
Smite Brook	Warw	SP4380	52°25·2′	1°21·7′W	W	140
Smite Fms	Worcs	SO8858	52°13·4′	2°10·1′W	FM	150
Smite Hill	Worcs	SO8958	52°13·4′	2°9·3′W	T	150
Smite Hill Fm	Notts	SK7236	52°55·2′	0°55·3′W	FM	129
Smitha	Devon	SS6919	50°57·6′	3°51·5′W	X	180
Smithaleigh	Devon	SX5855	50°22·9′	3°59·5′W	T	202
Smitham Hill	Bath & NE Somer	ST5554	51°17·2′	2°38·3′W	H	182,183
Smitham Station	Croy	TQ3059	51°19·1′	0°7·7′W	X	187
Smithbrook	W Susx	SU9223	51°0·2′	0°40·9′W	T	197
Smith End Green	Worcs	SO7752	52°10·2′	2°19·8′W	T	150
Smithen Down	Wilts	SU1135	51°7·1′	1°50·2′W	X	184
Smithers Cross	Glos	SO6116	51°50·7′	2°33·6′W	X	162
Smither's Fm	Essex	TQ8888	51°33·8′	0°43·1′E	FM	178
Smither's Pit	Devon	SY2498	50°46·8′	3°4·3′W	X	192,193
Smithey Fen	Cambs	TL4570	52°18·8′	0°8·0′E	X	154
Smithey Fen Fm	Cambs	TL4471	52°19·3′	0°7·2′E	FM	154
Smithfield	Angus	NO4838	56°32·1′	2°50·3′W	X	54
Smithfield	Cumbr	NY4465	54°58·8′	2°52·1′W	T	85
Smithfield	Cumbr	NY7512	54°30·4′	2°22·7′W	X	91
Smithfield	Fife	NO3307	56°15·3′	3°4·4′W	X	59
Smithfield	S Ayr	NS4327	55°30·9′	4°28·8′W	X	70
Smithfield	Scot Bord	NT2740	55°39·1′	3°9·2′W	X	73
Smithfield Fm	Lincs	TA0601	53°29·9′	0°23·7′W	FM	112
Smithfield Fm	Powys	SO0254	52°10·8′	3°25·6′W	FM	147
Smith Green	Lancs	SD4954	53°59·0′	2°46·2′W	T	102
Smith Hall Fm	Derby	SK2645	53°0·3′	1°36·3′W	FM	119,128
Smith Hill	Devon	SX6375	50°33·8′	3°55·7′W	X	191
Smith House Fm	Stock on T	NZ3917	54°33·0′	1°23·4′W	FM	93
Smithies	Barns	SE3508	53°34·3′	1°27·9′W	T	110,111
Smithies Fm	Suff	TL8857	52°11·0′	0°45·4′E	FM	155
Smithies, The	Shrops	SO6797	52°34·4′	2°28·8′W	T	138
Smithill's Hall	Bolton	SD7011	53°35·9′	2°26·8′W	A	109
Smithills Moor	Bolton	SD6613	53°37·0′	2°30·4′W	X	109
Smithincott	Devon	ST0611	50°53·7′	3°19·8′W	T	192
Smithland Hill	D & G	NX8655	54°52·9′	3°46·2′W	H	84
Smithley	Barns	SE3803	53°31·6′	1°25·2′W	T	110,111
Smithmoor Common	Worcs	SO8741	52°4·3′	2°11·0′W	X	150
Smiths Arms Inn	Dorset	SY6697	50°46·5′	2°28·6′W	X	194
Smith's Barn	Glos	SP1217	51°51·3′	1°49·2′W	X	163
Smith's Br	Lincs	TF2214	52°42·8′	0°11·2′W	X	131
Smith's Combe	Somer	ST1342	51°10·5′	3°14·3′W	X	181
Smith's Covert	Glos	SP0605	51°44·9′	1°54·4′W	F	163
Smith's End	Herts	TL4037	52°1·1′	0°2·8′E	T	154
Smith's Fm	Kent	TQ9631	51°2·9′	0°48·2′E	FM	189
Smith's Fm	Norf	TL5694	52°31·5′	0°18·4′E	FM	143
Smith's Fm	Somer	ST3423	51°0·4′	2°56·1′W	FM	193
Smith's Gorse	Derby	SK3322	52°47·9′	1°30·2′W	F	128
Smith's Green	Ches	SJ7553	53°4·7′	2°22·0′W	T	118
Smiths Green	Ches	SJ8170	53°13·8′	2°16·7′W	T	118
Smith's Green	Essex	TL5721	51°52·2′	0°17·2′E	T	167
Smith's Green	Essex	TL6640	52°2·2′	0°25·6′E	T	154
Smith's Green Fm	Essex	TL5632	51°58·1′	0°16·7′E	FM	167
Smiths Hamar	Shetld	HU2454	60°16·4′	1°33·5′W	H	3
Smith's Hill Fm	Oxon	SU3784	51°33·5′	1°27·6′W	FM	174
Smithsland	Devon	SS4705	50°49·7′	4°10·0′W	X	191

Smith's Lawn	Win & Maid	SU9770	51°25·5'	0°35·9'W	X	175,176
Smithson's Fm	Lancs	SD3848	53°55·7'	2°56·2'W	FM	102
Smith Sound	I Scilly	SV8608	49°53·6'	6°22·0'W	W	203
Smith's Shield	Northum	NY7566	54°59·5'	2°23·0'W	X	86,87
Smithsteads	Cumbr	NY4672	55°2·6'	2°50·3'W	X	86
Smithston	Aberd	NJ5129	57°21·2'	2°48·4'W	X	37
Smithston	E Ayr	NS4112	55°22·8'	4°30·1'W	X	70
Smithston Burn	E Ayr	NS4312	55°22·9'	4°28·3'W	W	70
Smithstone Fm	N Lanak	NS7275	55°57·3'	4°2·6'W	FM	64
Smithstone Ho	N Ayr	NS2944	55°39·8'	4°42·7'W	X	63,70
Smithstown	Highld	NG7977	57°44·0'	5°42·3'W	T	19
Smithstown	Highld	NH7954	57°33·9'	4°0·9'W	X	27
Smithstown	Moray	NJ3336	57°24·8'	3°6·5'W	X	28
Smithstown	Moray	NJ4867	57°41·7'	2°51·9'W	X	28,29
Smithton	Highld	NH7145	57°28·9'	4°8·6'W	T	27
Smithwick Fm	Wilts	ST9662	51°21·7'	2°3·1'W	FM	173
Smithwood Common	Surrey	TQ0541	51°9·7'	0°29·5'W	X	187
Smithwood Green	Suff	TL9052	52°8·2'	0°47·0'E	T	155
Smithy	D & G	NX8593	55°13·3'	3°48·0'W	X	78
Smithy Beck	Cumbr	NY1215	54°31·6'	3°21·2'W	W	89
Smithy Bridge	Roch	SD9315	53°38·1'	2°5·9'W	T	109
Smithy Briggs	E Yorks	TA2036	53°48·6'	0°10·2'W	X	107
Smithy Brook	Kirk	SE2517	53°39·2'	1°36·9'W	W	110
Smithy Burn	Angus	NO4573	56°51·0'	2°53·7'W	W	44
Smithy Burn	Durham	NY9633	54°41·8'	2°3·3'W	W	91,92
Smithy Clough	Derby	SK1099	53°29·5'	1°50·5'W	X	110
Smithycroft	Aberd	NJ7924	57°18·6'	2°20·5'W	X	38
Smithy Fell	Cumbr	NY1323	54°35·9'	3°20·4'W	X	89
Smithy Fm	N Yks	SE4294	54°20·6'	1°20·8'W	FM	99
Smithy Fold	Lancs	SD8143	53°53·2'	2°16·9'W	X	103
Smithyford	Aberd	NJ3617	57°14·6'	3°3·2'W	X	37
Smithy Gate	Flint	SJ1775	53°16·2'	3°14·3'W	T	116
Smithy Green	Ches	SJ7474	53°16·0'	2°23·0'W	T	118
Smithy Green	Cumbr	SD3082	54°14·0'	3°4·0'W	X	96,97
Smithygreen	Fife	NO3705	56°14·3'	3°0·5'W	X	59
Smithy Green	Stock	SJ8785	53°21·9'	2°11·3'W	T	109
Smithyhall	Pth & Kin	NO2437	56°31·4'	3°13·7'W	X	53
Smithyhill	Aberd	NK0237	57°25·7'	1°57·5'W	X	30
Smithyhill	Aberd	NK0753	57°34·3'	1°52·5'W	X	30
Smithy Hill	D & G	NX0262	54°55·1'	5°4·9'W	X	82
Smithy Hill	Fife	NT3499	56°11·0'	3°3·4'W	T	59
Smithyhillock	Aberd	NK0057	57°36·4'	1°59·5'W	X	30
Smithy Ho	Cumbr	SD6579	54°12·6'	2°31·8'W	X	97
Smithy Ho	Lancs	SD5828	53°45·0'	2°37·8'W	X	102
Smithy Holme	N Yks	NY8701	54°24·5'	2°11·6'W	X	91,92
Smithy House	Angus	NO2740	56°33·0'	3°10·8'W	X	53
Smithy House Fm	N Yks	NZ3305	54°26·6'	1°29·0'W	FM	93
Smithy Houses	Derby	SK3847	53°1·4'	1°25·6'W	T	119,128
Smithy Lane Ends	Lancs	SD4012	53°36·3'	2°54·0'W	T	108
Smithy Lane Fm	Stock	SJ9990	53°24·6'	2°0·5'W	FM	109
Smithy Marsh	Notts	SK8166	53°11·3'	0°46·9'W	X	121
Smithy Moor	Derby	SK3861	53°8·9'	1°25·5'W	X	119
Smithy Moor Fm	Staffs	SK1345	53°0·4'	1°48·0'W	FM	119,128
Smithyquoy	Orkney	HY4746	59°18·1'	2°55·4'W	X	5
Smithy Sound	Orkney	HY4731	59°10·0'	2°55·1'W	W	5,6
Smithyton	Angus	NO5547	56°37·0'	2°43·5'W	X	54
Smithy Wood	Lancs	SD6369	54°7·2'	2°33·5'W	F	97
Smittaldy	Orkney	HY4545	59°17·5'	2°57·4'W	X	5
Smittergill Burn	Cumbr	NY6739	54°44·9'	2°30·3'W	W	91
Smittergill Head	Cumbr	NY6739	54°44·9'	2°30·3'W	X	91
Smittons	D & G	NX6391	55°11·9'	4°8·7'W	X	77
Smock Alley	W Susx	TQ0916	50°56·2'	0°26·5'W	T	198
Smockham Fm	Kent	TQ5740	51°8·5'	0°15·1'E	FM	188
Smockington	Leic	SP4589	52°30·1'	1°19·8'W	T	140
Smocombe Ho	Somer	ST2234	51°6·2'	3°6·5'W	X	182
Smo Dales	Shetld	HU2977	60°28·8'	1°27·1'W	X	3
Smoile Fm	Leic	SK3919	52°46·3'	1°24·9'W	FM	128
Smokedown Fm	Oxon	SU2998	51°41·0'	1°34·4'W	FM	164
Smokeham Fm	Somer	ST1534	51°6·1'	3°12·5'W	FM	181
Smoke House Fm	W Susx	TQ1321	50°58·9'	0°23·0'W	FM	198
Smokejack Fm	Surrey	TQ1137	51°7·5'	0°24·4'W	FM	187
Smoker Brook	Ches	SJ7176	53°17·1'	2°25·7'W	W	118
Smoker Hill Fm	Ches	SJ7076	53°17·0'	2°26·6'W	FM	118
Smoker's Hole	Norf	TG0339	52°54·8'	1°1·6'E	X	133
Smokershole	Norf	TL8791	52°29·3'	0°45·7'E	X	144
Smokes Wood	Kent	TQ8457	51°17·2'	0°38·7'E	F	178,188
Smokey Fm	Worcs	SO9943	52°5·4'	2°0·5'W	FM	150
Smoky Ho	Suff	TM4052	52°7·1'	1°30·6'E	X	156
Smoky Ho	W Susx	SU9219	50°58·0'	0°41·0'W	X	197
Smoky Row	Bucks	SP8106	51°45·0'	0°49·2'W	T	165
Smoo	Highld	NC4166	58°33·4'	4°43·5'W	X	9
Smoogarth	Orkney	HY3615	59°1·3'	3°6·4'W	X	6
Smoogro	Orkney	HY3605	58°55·9'	3°6·2'W	X	6,7
Smoogro Skerry	Orkney	HY3605	58°55·9'	3°6·2'W	X	6,7
Smoo Lodge	Highld	NC4167	58°34·0'	4°43·5'W	X	9
Smooth Lea Fm	Stock	SJ9989	53°24·1'	2°0·5'W	FM	109
Smo Taing	Shetld	HU4327	60°1·8'	1°13·2'W	X	4
Smoulden Fm	N Yks	SE0248	53°55·9'	1°57·8'W	FM	104
Smout House Fm	N Yks	SE6297	54°22·1'	1°2·3'W	FM	94,100
Smuaisebhal	N Eil	NB2030	58°10·5'	6°45·3'W	H	8,13
Smuggler's Burn	Stir	NN7409	56°15·7'	4°1·6'W	W	57
Smuggler's Cave	N Tyne	NZ3671	55°2·2'	1°25·8'W	X	88
Smuggler's Lane	Dorset	ST8711	50°54·1'	2°10·7'W	X	194
Smuggy's Pike	Cumbr	NY6180	55°7·0'	2°36·5'W	X	80
Smugley Fm	Kent	TQ7236	51°6·1'	0°27·8'E	FM	188
Smug Oak	Herts	TL1302	51°42·5'	0°21·5'W	T	166
Smuraig	N Ayr	NR9923	55°27·8'	5°10·3'W	X	69
Smylett Hall	E Yorks	SE7851	53°57·2'	0°48·3'W	X	105,106
Smyllum Park	S Lanak	NS8943	55°40·3'	3°45·5'W	X	71,72
Smynacott	Devon	SS8310	50°52·9'	3°39·4'W	X	191
Smyrna	Pth & Kin	NO1853	56°40·0'	3°19·8'W	X	53
Smyrton	S Ayr	NX1080	55°4·9'	4°58·2'W	X	76
Smyrton Hill	S Ayr	NX1179	55°4·4'	4°57·2'W	H	76
Smythacott	Devon	SS4318	50°56·6'	4°13·7'W	X	180,190
Smytham Manor	Devon	SS4816	50°55·6'	4°9·4'W	X	180
Smythapark	Devon	SS6238	51°7·7'	3°57·9'W	X	180
Smythemoor	Shrops	SJ6333	52°53·8'	2°32·6'W	X	127
Smythen	Devon	SS6410	50°52·6'	3°55·6'W	X	191
Smythen Cross	Devon	SS5643	51°10·4'	4°3·2'W	X	180
Smythen Fm	Devon	SS5544	51°10·8'	4°4·1'W	FM	180
Smythes Fm	Devon	ST1612	50°54·3'	3°11·3'W	FM	181,193
Smythe's Green	Essex	TL9218	51°49·9'	0°47·6'E	T	168
Snab	Cumbr	NY3031	54°40·4'	3°4·7'W	X	90
Snab	D & G	NY2776	55°4·6'	3°8·2'W	X	85
Snaba Hill	Orkney	HY3514	59°0·8'	3°7·4'W	X	6
Snabb	E Ayr	NS4904	55°18·7'	4°22·3'W	X	77
Snabdaugh	Northum	NY7884	55°9·2'	2°20·3'W	X	80
Snabdaugh Moor	Northum	NY7783	55°8·7'	2°21·2'W	X	80
Snabe	S Lanak	NS6439	55°37·8'	4°9·2'W	X	71
Snaberlee Rig	Scot Bord	NY5091	55°12·9'	2°46·7'W	X	79
Snab Green Fm	Lancs	SD5773	54°9·3'	2°39·1'W	FM	97
Snabhead	Falk	NS9275	55°57·6'	3°43·4'W	X	65
Snab Hill	D & G	NX5682	55°6·9'	4°15·0'W	H	77
Snableazes	Northum	NU2214	55°25·4'	1°38·7'W	X	81
Snab of Moy	Moray	NH9860	57°37·4'	3°42·0'W	X	27
Snab Point	C of Edin	NT1877	55°59·0'	3°18·4'W	X	65,66
Snab Point	Cumbr	SD2063	54°3·7'	3°12·9'W	X	96
Snab Point	Northum	NZ3092	55°13·5'	1°31·3'W	X	81
Sna Broch	Shetld	HU5793	60°37·2'	0°57·0'W	A	1,2
Snabrough	Shetld	HP5602	60°42·1'	0°57·9'W	H	1
Snab Sands	Cumbr	SD2064	54°4·2'	3°12·9'W	X	96
Snabs, The	Pth & Kin	NO2930	56°27·7'	3°8·7'W	X	53
Snab, The	Lancs	SD5668	54°6·6'	2°40·0'W	X	97
Snade	D & G	NX8485	55°9·0'	3°48·8'W	X	78
Snademill	D & G	NX8487	55°10·1'	3°48·8'W	X	78
Snadon	Aberd	NO7265	56°46·8'	2°27·0'W	X	45
Snaefell	I of M	SC3988	54°16·0'	4°27·9'W	H	95
Snaefell Mountain Railway	I of M	SC4186	54°15·0'	4°26·0'W	X	95
Snagaras	N Eil	NF7502	56°59·9'	7°20·7'W	X	31
Snag Fm	Somer	ST7228	51°3·3'	2°23·6'W	FM	183
Snagg Fm	Somer	ST6335	51°7·0'	2°31·3'W	FM	183
Snaggs Fm	Wilts	ST8629	51°3·8'	2°11·6'W	FM	183
Snagshall	E Susx	TQ7824	50°59·5'	0°32·6'E	T	199
Snaid Burn	Stir	NN3411	56°16·0'	4°40·4'W	W	50,56
Snaigow Fm	Pth & Kin	NO0743	56°34·4'	3°30·4'W	FM	52,53
Snaigow Ho	Pth & Kin	NO0842	56°33·9'	3°29·4'W	X	52,53
Snailbeach	Shrops	SJ3702	52°37·0'	2°55·4'W	T	126
Snail-creep Hanging	Wilts	ST9436	51°7·6'	2°4·8'W	X	184
Snail Down	Wilts	SU2152	51°16·2'	1°41·5'W	X	184
Snail's Bottom	Somer	ST6751	51°15·7'	2°28·0'W	X	183
Snailsden	Barns	SE1403	53°31·6'	1°46·9'W	X	110
Snailsden Resr	Barns	SE1303	53°31·7'	1°47·8'W	W	110
Snails Hill	Somer	ST4613	50°55·1'	2°45·7'W	T	193
Snails Pit Fm	Norf	TF8107	52°38·1'	0°40·9'E	FM	144
Snailswell	Herts	TL1732	51°58·7'	0°17·4'W	T	166
Snailswood Fm	Kent	TQ9738	51°6·7'	0°49·3'E	FM	189
Snailwell	Cambs	TL6467	52°16·8'	0°24·6'E	T	154
Snailwell Stud	Cambs	TL6467	52°16·8'	0°24·6'E	X	154
Snainton	N Yks	SE9282	54°13·8'	0°34·9'W	T	101
Snainton Dike	N Yks	SE9089	54°17·6'	0°36·6'W	A	94,101
Snainton Ings Ho	N Yks	SE9279	54°12·1'	0°35·0'W	X	101
Snaip	S Lanak	NT0333	55°35·1'	3°31·6'W	X	72
Snaip Hill	S Lanak	NT0232	55°34·6'	3°32·8'W	H	72
Snaisgill	Durham	NY9527	54°38·5'	2°4·2'W	T	91,92
Snaith	E Yorks	SE6422	53°41·7'	1°1·4'W	T	105,106
Snaith & Cowick Moors	E Yorks	SE7118	53°39·5'	0°55·1'W	X	112
Snaiton Ings	N Yks	SE9280	54°12·7'	0°34·9'W	X	101
Snaizeholme	N Yks	SD8386	54°16·4'	2°15·2'W	X	98
Snaizeholme Beck	N Yks	SD8386	54°16·4'	2°15·2'W	W	98
Snaizeholme Fell	N Yks	SD8185	54°15·9'	2°17·1'W	X	98
Snaizeholme Pasture	N Yks	SD8388	54°17·5'	2°15·3'W	X	98
Snaizwold Fell	Cumbr	SD7488	54°17·5'	2°23·5'W	X	98
Snake Hall	E Yorks	SE8733	53°47·4'	0°40·3'W	X	106
Snake Hall	Lincs	TF3017	52°44·3'	0°4·1'W	X	131
Snake Hall Plantn	E Yorks	SE8634	53°47·9'	0°41·2'W	F	106
Snakemoor	Hants	SU5016	50°56·7'	1°16·9'W	X	185
Snake Pass	Derby	SK0892	53°25·7'	1°52·4'W	X	110
Snake Path	Derby	SK0790	53°24·6'	1°53·3'W	X	110
Snake Plantn	N Lincs	SE8606	53°32·9'	0°41·7'W	F	112
Snakes Wood	Suff	TM0137	51°59·9'	0°56·1'E	F	155
Snake Wood	Norf	TL8190	52°28·9'	0°40·3'E	F	144
Snap	Shetld	HU3242	60°9·9'	1°24·9'W	X	4
Snapa Water	Shetld	HU2974	60°27·2'	1°27·9'W	W	3
Snape	Devon	SS6120	50°58·0'	3°58·4'W	X	180
Snape	Northum	NY8963	54°57·9'	2°9·9'W	X	87
Snape	N Yks	SE2684	54°15·3'	1°35·6'W	T	99
Snape	Suff	TM3959	52°10·9'	1°30·2'E	T	156
Snape Bank Fm	Ches	SJ7451	53°3·6'	2°22·9'W	FM	118
Snape Brook	Ches	SJ8372	53°14·9'	2°14·9'W	W	118
Snape Fm	Ches	SJ7451	53°3·6'	2°22·9'W	FM	118
Snape Fm	E Susx	TQ6229	51°2·5'	0°19·0'E	FM	188,199
Snape Fm	W Susx	TQ0522	50°59·5'	0°29·8'W	FM	197
Snape Gate	Durham	NY9637	54°43·9'	2°3·3'W	X	91,92
Snape Green	Lancs	SD3714	53°37·4'	2°56·7'W	T	108
Snapehall	Staffs	SJ7941	52°58·2'	2°18·4'W	X	118
Snape Hill	Barns	SE4104	53°32·1'	1°22·5'W	T	111
Snape Hill	Derby	SK3579	53°18·6'	1°28·1'W	T	119
Snape Hill	Lincs	TF4577	53°16·4'	0°10·9'E	X	122
Snape Hill	Suff	TM0274	52°19·8'	0°58·3'E	X	144
Snape Ho	E Susx	TQ6230	51°3·0'	0°19·1'E	X	188
Snape Ho	N Yks	SD7756	54°0·2'	2°20·6'W	X	103
Snape Lawns	N Yks	SE2583	54°14·8'	1°36·6'W	X	99
Snape Lodge Fm	N Yks	SE2482	54°14·2'	1°37·5'W	FM	99
Snape Mires	N Yks	SE2885	54°15·8'	1°33·8'W	X	99
Snape Park	N Yks	SE2583	54°14·8'	1°36·6'W	X	99
Snaper Ho	N Yks	SE5991	54°18·9'	1°5·2'W	X	100
Snapes Fm	Derby	SK2640	52°57·6'	1°36·4'W	FM	119,128
Snape's Fm	Suff	TL7460	52°12·9'	0°33·2'E	FM	155
Snapes Manor	Devon	SX7439	50°14·5'	3°45·6'W	X	202
Snapes Wood	Northnts	SP9582	52°25·9'	0°35·8'W	F	141
Snapes Wood	N Yks	SE6886	54°16·1'	0°56·9'W	F	94,100
Snape Warren	Suff	TM4057	52°9·8'	1°31·0'E	X	156
Snape Watering	Suff	TM3860	52°11·4'	1°29·3'E	X	156
Snape Wood	E Susx	TQ6330	51°3·0'	0°19·9'E	F	188
Snape Wood Fm	Lancs	SD4847	53°55·2'	2°47·1'W	FM	102
Snap Fm	Wilts	SU2176	51°29·2'	1°41·5'W	FM	174
Snap Hill	E Susx	TQ5400	50°47·0'	0°11·5'E	X	199
Snaple Point	Swan	SS6086	51°33·6'	4°0·8'W	X	159
Snapper	Devon	SS5934	51°5·5'	4°0·4'W	T	180
Snapper, The	Shetld	HU6587	60°33·9'	0°48·4'W	X	1,2
Snap Village	Wilts	SU2276	51°29·2'	1°40·6'W	A	174
Snap Wood	Hants	SU7632	51°5·2'	0°54·5'W	F	186
Snarehill Fm	Norf	TL8881	52°23·9'	0°46·2'E	FM	144
Snarehill Hall	Norf	TL8983	52°25·0'	0°47·2'E	X	144
Snarehill Wood	Norf	TL9082	52°24·4'	0°48·0'E	F	144
Snaresbrook	Wal F	TQ3989	51°35·2'	0°0·8'E	T	177
Snarestone	Leic	SK3409	52°40·9'	1°29·4'W	T	128,140
Snarestone Lodge	Leic	SK3409	52°40·9'	1°29·4'W	X	128,140
Snar Fm	S Lanak	NS8620	55°27·9'	3°47·8'W	FM	71,72
Snarford	Lincs	TF0582	53°19·7'	0°25·0'W	T	121
Snarford Br	Lincs	TF0481	53°19·2'	0°25·9'W	X	121
Snargate	Kent	TQ9828	51°1·3'	0°49·8'E	T	189
Snargate Fm	N Yks	SE6071	54°8·1'	1°4·5'W	FM	100
Snargate Hill	N Yks	SE6072	54°8·7'	1°4·5'W	X	100
Snargate Wood	N Yks	SE6172	54°8·7'	1°3·6'W	F	100
Snarhead	S Lanak	NS8616	55°25·7'	3°47·7'W	X	71,78
Snarhead Hill	D & G	NS8615	55°25·2'	3°47·6'W	H	71,78
Snarker Pike	Cumbr	NY3807	54°27·5'	2°57·0'W	H	90
Snarkhurst Wood	Kent	TQ8255	51°16·1'	0°36·9'E	F	178,188
Snar Law	S Lanak	NS8517	55°26·3'	3°48·6'W	X	71,78
Snarlton Fm	Wilts	ST8157	51°18·9'	2°16·0'W	FM	173
Snarlton Fm	Wilts	ST9263	51°22·2'	2°6·5'W	FM	173
Snarraness	Shetld	HU2356	60°17·5'	1°34·5'W	X	3
Snarra Ness	Shetld	HU2357	60°18·1'	1°34·5'W	X	3
Snarra Voe	Shetld	HP5602	60°42·1'	0°57·9'W	W	1
Snarravoe	Shetld	HP5602	60°42·1'	0°57·9'W	X	1
Snar Water	S Lanak	NS8519	55°27·3'	3°48·7'W	W	71,78
Snar Water	S Lanak	NS8620	55°27·9'	3°47·8'W	W	71,72
Snary Beck	Cumbr	NY0822	54°35·3'	3°25·0'W	W	89
Snash Ness	Orkney	HY7755	59°23·1'	2°23·8'W	X	5
Snatchangers Fm	Hants	SU7449	51°14·4'	0°56·0'W	FM	186
Snatch Ho	Bath & NE Somer	ST5358	51°19·4'	2°40·1'W	X	172,182
Snatchwood	Torf	SO2602	51°42·9'	3°3·9'W	T	171
Snave	Kent	TR0129	51°1·7'	0°52·4'E	T	189
Snawdon	E Loth	NT5867	55°53·9'	2°39·9'W	X	67
Snawdon	Scot Bord	NT5648	55°43·7'	2°41·6'W	X	73
Snawdon Burn	Scot Bord	NT5648	55°43·7'	2°41·6'W	W	73
Snawdon Wood	E Loth	NT5966	55°53·4'	2°38·9'W	F	67
Snaxland	Devon	SS2925	51°0·2'	4°25·9'W	X	190
Sneachdach Slinnean	Highld	NH6202	57°5·6'	4°16·2'W	X	35
Sneachill	Worcs	SO9053	52°10·7'	2°8·4'W	T	150
Snead	Powys	SO3192	52°31·5'	3°0·6'W	T	137
Snead Common	Worcs	SO7269	52°19·3'	2°24·3'W	T	138
Snead Fms	Worcs	SO7369	52°19·3'	2°23·4'W	FM	138
Sneads Green	Worcs	SO8667	52°18·3'	2°11·9'W	T	150
Snear Hill	Northum	NT9624	55°30·8'	2°3·4'W	H	74,75
Snear Hill	N Yks	SD8655	53°59·7'	2°12·4'W	X	103
Sneath Common	Norf	TM1589	52°27·6'	1°10·3'E	T	144,156
Sneating Hall	Essex	TM2022	51°51·4'	1°12·1'E	X	169
Sneaton	N Yks	NZ8907	54°27·3'	0°37·2'W	T	94
Sneaton High Moor	N Yks	NZ8801	54°24·1'	0°38·2'W	X	94
Sneaton Low Moor	N Yks	NZ8903	54°25·1'	0°37·3'W	X	94
Sneatonthorpe	N Yks	NZ9006	54°26·7'	0°36·3'W	T	94
Sneckan,The	Shetld	HU5252	60°15·2'	1°3·1'W	X	3
Sneck, The	Orkney	HY4953	59°21·9'	2°53·3'W	X	5
Sneck Yate Bank	N Yks	SE5087	54°16·8'	1°13·5'W	X	100
Sneckyeat	Cumbr	NY1227	54°38·1'	3°21·4'W	X	89
Sneckyeat Fm	Cumbr	NX9916	54°32·0'	3°33·2'W	FM	89
Sneddon Law	E Ayr	NS5241	55°38·7'	4°20·7'W	X	70
Snedshill	Wrekin	SJ7009	52°40·9'	2°26·2'W	T	127
Sned Wood	Heref	SO4066	52°17·6'	2°52·4'W	F	137,148,149
Sneedham's Green	Glos	SO8414	51°49·7'	2°13·5'W	X	162
Sneep	Scot Bord	NT6538	55°38·3'	2°32·9'W	X	74
Sneep Covert	Scot Bord	NT6538	55°38·3'	2°32·9'W	F	74
Sneep, The	Northum	NY7988	55°11·4'	2°19·4'W	X	80
Sneer Hill	Northum	NT9011	55°23·8'	2°9·0'W	H	80
Snehaval Mór	N Eil	NB0417	58°2·9'	7°0·6'W	H	13
Sneinton	C of Nott	SK5839	52°57·0'	1°7·8'W	T	129
Snelda Hill	Shetld	HU3761	60°20·1'	1°19·3'W	H	2,3
Snelland	Lincs	TF0780	53°18·6'	0°23·2'W	T	121
Snelling Fm	Dorset	SY8189	50°42·3'	2°15·8'W	FM	194
Snellings	Cumbr	NX9908	54°27·7'	3°33·1'W	X	89
Snell's Fm	Wilts	SU0181	51°31·9'	1°58·7'W	FM	173
Snell's Nook	Leic	SK5018	52°45·7'	1°15·1'W	X	129
Snelsetter	Orkney	ND3288	58°46·7'	3°10·1'W	X	7
Snelsmore Common	W Berks	SU4570	51°25·9'	1°20·8'W	F	174
Snelsmore East Common	W Berks	SU4771	51°26·4'	1°19·0'W	F	174
Snelsmore Fm	W Berks	SU4772	51°26·9'	1°19·0'W	FM	174
Snelsmore House	W Berks	SU4670	51°25·9'	1°19·9'W	X	174
Snelson	Mil Key	SP9354	52°10·8'	0°38·0'W	X	153
Snelson Ho	Ches	SJ8074	53°16·0'	2°17·6'W	X	118
Snelston	Derby	SK1543	52°59·3'	1°46·2'W	T	119,128
Snelston Common	Derby	SK1541	52°58·2'	1°46·2'W	X	119,128
Snelston Firs	Derby	SK1542	52°58·7'	1°46·2'W	X	119,128
Snetterton	Norf	TL9991	52°29·1'	0°56·3'E	T	144
Snetterton Heath	Norf	TM0189	52°27·9'	0°57·9'E	X	144
Snettisham	Norf	TF6834	52°52·9'	0°30·2'E	T	132
Snettisham Ho	Norf	TF6933	52°52·3'	0°31·1'E	X	132
Snettisham Scalp	Norf	TF6433	52°52·4'	0°26·6'E	X	132
Sneuan	Shetld	HU3054	60°16·4'	1°27·0'W	X	3
Sneuga	Shetld	HP5712	60°47·5'	0°56·7'W	H	1
Sneugans	Shetld	HU2052	60°15·4'	1°37·8'W	X	3
Sneugans	Shetld	HU5563	60°21·1'	0°59·7'W	X	2
Sneugie	Shetld	HU3862	60°20·7'	1°18·2'W	H	2,3
Sneug, The	Shetld	HT9439	60°8·4'	2°6·0'W	H	4
Sneuie, The	Shetld	HU3481	60°30·9'	1°22·3'W	H	1,2,3
Sneuk	Orkney	HY4747	59°18·6'	2°55·4'W	X	5
Sneuk Head	Orkney	ND2095	58°50·4'	3°22·7'W	X	7
Sneu of Ellister	Shetld	HU3922	59°59·1'	1°17·6'W	X	4
Snever Dale	N Yks	SE8688	54°17·1'	0°40·3'W	X	94,101
Snever Wood	N Yks	SE5380	54°13·0'	1°10·8'W	F	100
Snevlabreck	Shetld	HU5499	60°40·5'	1°0·2'W	X	1
Sneyd Fm	Staffs	SJ9702	52°37·2'	2°2·3'W	FM	127,139
Sneyd Green	C of Stoke	SJ8849	53°2·5'	2°10·3'W	T	118
Sneyd Park	C of Bris	ST5575	51°28·6'	2°38·5'W	T	172
Snibe Hill	D & G	NX4681	55°6·2'	4°24·4'W	H	77
Snibston	Leic	SK4113	52°43·0'	1°23·2'W	T	129
Snickert Knees	S Lanak	NS9925	55°30·8'	3°35·5'W	H	72
Sniddle Holes	Lancs	SD6252	53°58·0'	2°34·3'W	X	102,103

Snig's End	Glos	SO7928	51°57·2'	2°17·9'W	T	150
Snilesworth Lodge	N Yks	SE5095	54°21·1'	1°13·4'W	X	100
Snilesworth Moor	N Yks	SE5296	54°21·7'	1°11·6'W	X	100
Snipe Dales	Lincs	TF3368	53°11·8'	0°0·1'W	X	122
Snipefield	Aberd	NJ6631	57°22·3'	2°33·5'W	X	29
Snipe Fm	Suff	TM2253	52°8·1'	1°15·0'E	FM	156
Snipe Hall Fm	Lancs	SD4712	53°36·4'	2°47·6'W	FM	108
Snipehill Br	Glos	ST5594	51°38·8'	2°38·6'W	X	162,172
Snipe Ho	Darl	NZ2812	54°30·4'	1°33·6'W	X	93
Snipe Ho	Northum	NU1508	55°22·2'	1°45·4'W	X	81
Snipe Loch	E Ayr	NS3817	55°25·5'	4°33·2'W	W	70
Snipe Moor	Dorset	SY7591	50°43·3'	2°20·9'W	X	194
Snipe Pt	Northum	NU1244	55°41·6'	1°48·1'W	X	75
Sniperley Hall	Durham	NZ2544	54°47·7'	1°36·2'W	X	88
Snipes Dene Wood	Ghead	NZ1859	54°55·8'	1°42·7'W	F	88
Snipeshill	Kent	TQ9263	51°20·2'	0°45·8'E	T	178
Snippigar	Orkney	HY5504	58°55·5'	2°46·4'W	X	6
Snip Wood	Mil Key	SP9253	52°10·3'	0°38·9'W	F	152
Sniseabhal	N Eil	NF7534	57°17·1'	7°23·2'W	T	22
Snitter	Northum	NU0203	55°19·5'	1°57·7'W	T	81
Snitterby	Lincs	SK9894	53°26·3'	0°31·1'W	T	112
Snitterby Carr	Lincs	TF0195	53°26·8'	0°28·3'W	X	112
Snitterby Cliff Fm	Lincs	SK9694	53°26·3'	0°32·9'W	FM	112
Snitterby Sandhays	Lincs	SK9994	53°26·2'	0°30·2'W	X	112
Snitterfield	Warw	SP2159	52°14·0'	1°41·2'W	T	151
Snitter Mill	Northum	NU0302	55°19·0'	1°56·7'W	X	81
Snitterton	Derby	SK2760	53°8·4'	1°35·4'W	T	119
Snitter Windyside	Northum	NU0104	55°20·1'	1°58·6'W	X	81
Snittlegarth	Cumbr	NY2137	54°43·6'	3°13·2'W	X	89,90
Snittlegate	Kirk	SE1504	53°32·2'	1°46·0'W	X	110
Snitton	Shrops	SO5575	52°22·5'	2°39·3'W	T	137,138
Snittongate	Shrops	SO5675	52°22·5'	2°38·4'W	T	137,138
Snoad Fm	Kent	TQ9455	51°15·9'	0°47·2'E	FM	178
Snoadhill Fm	Kent	TQ9342	51°8·9'	0°46·0'E	FM	189
Snoadstreet	Kent	TQ9952	51°14·2'	0°51·4'E	X	189
Snoad Wood	Kent	TQ7641	51°8·7'	0°31·4'E	F	188
Snob Cott	Aberd	NO8088	56°59·2'	2°19·3'W	X	45
Snobden Hill Wood	Heref	SO3964	52°16·5'	2°53·2'W	F	137,148,149
Snodbury	Durham	NY8342	54°46·6'	2°15·4'W	X	86,87
Snod Coppice	Shrops	SJ3812	52°42·4'	2°54·7'W	F	126
Snoddington Down Fm	Hants	SU2545	51°12·5'	1°38·1'W	FM	184
Snoddington Manor	Hants	SU2344	51°11·9'	1°39·9'W	X	184
Snodehill Fm	Kent	TR2046	51°10·5'	1°9·2'E	FM	179,189
Snodhill	Heref	SO3140	52°3·5'	3°0·0'W	T	148,161
Snod Hill	N Yks	SE8697	54°21·9'	0°40·2'W	H	94,101
Snodhill Castle	Heref	SO3240	52°3·5'	2°59·1'W	A	148,161
Snodhill Park	Heref	SO3139	52°2·9'	3°0·0'W	X	161
Snodland	Kent	TQ7061	51°19·6'	0°26·8'E	T	178,188
Snodribie	N Eil	NB0125	58°7·0'	7°4·2'W	H	13
Snods Edge	Northum	NZ0652	54°52·0'	1°54·0'W	T	87
Snodwell Fm	Devon	ST2104	50°50·0'	3°6·9'W	FM	192,193
Snodworth	Lancs	SD7032	53°47·3'	2°26·9'W	X	103
Snook Bank	Northum	NU1305	55°20·6'	1°47·3'W	X	81
Snook or North Point	Northum	NU2231	55°34·6'	1°38·6'W	X	75
Snook Point	Northum	NU0943	55°41·1'	1°51·0'W	X	75
Snook Point	Northum	NU2426	55°31·9'	1°36·8'W	X	75
Snooks Fm	Hants	SZ3396	50°46·0'	1°31·5'W	FM	196
Snook, The	Northum	NU0943	55°41·1'	1°51·0'W	X	75
Snoots Common	Cambs	TL4973	52°20·3'	0°11·6'E	X	154
Snope Burn	Northum	NY6954	54°53·0'	2°28·6'W	W	86,87
Snope Common	Northum	NY7054	54°53·0'	2°27·6'W	X	86,87
Snoreham Hall	Essex	TQ8899	51°39·7'	0°43·5'E	X	168
Snorscomb	Northnts	SP5956	52°12·2'	1°7·8'W	X	152
Snorscomb Mill	Northnts	SP5956	52°12·2'	1°7·8'W	X	152
Snotterton Hall	Durham	NZ1019	54°34·2'	1°50·3'W	X	92
Snout Corner	Cambs	TL4961	52°13·8'	0°11·3'E	X	154
Snouthead	Scot Bord	NT3327	55°32·2'	3°3·3'W	X	73
Snout Hill	Scot Bord	NT1223	55°29·8'	3°23·1'W	H	72
Snouts	Cumbr	NY5176	55°4·8'	2°45·6'W	X	86
Snow Ball	Devon	SS5240	51°8·6'	4°6·6'W	H	180
Snowball Fm	Bucks	SP6335	52°0·8'	1°4·5'W	FM	152
Snowball Fm	Bucks	SU9384	51°33·1'	0°39·1'W	FM	175
Snowball Plantn	N Yks	SE6657	54°0·5'	0°59·2'W	F	105,106
Snowbuil	Shetld	HU3173	60°26·6'	1°25·7'W	X	3
Snow Close Fm	N Yks	SE3072	54°8·8'	1°32·0'W	FM	99
Snowclose Plantn	E Yorks	TA0046	53°54·3'	0°28·3'W	F	106,107
Snowden Carr	N Yks	SE1750	53°57·0'	1°44·0'W	X	104
Snowden Close	Cumbr	NY6068	55°0·5'	2°37·1'W	X	86
Snowden Crags	N Yks	SE1751	53°57·5'	1°44·0'W	X	104
Snowdenham Ho	Surrey	TQ0044	51°11·4'	0°33·7'W	X	186
Snowden Hill	Barns	SE2600	53°30·0'	1°36·1'W	T	110
Snowden's Br	Corn	SX2355	50°22·3'	4°29·0'W	X	201
Snowdon	Devon	SX6668	50°30·0'	3°53·0'W	X	202
Snowdon Fm	Shrops	SJ7701	52°36·6'	2°20·0'W	FM	127
Snowdon Hill	Somer	ST3009	50°52·8'	2°59·3'W	X	193
Snowdon Mountain Railway	Gwyn	SH5957	53°5·7'	4°5·9'W	X	115
Snowdon or Yr Wyddfa	Gwyn	SH6054	53°4·1'	4°5·0'W	H	115
Snowdon Ranger Path	Gwyn	SH5855	53°4·6'	4°6·8'W	X	115
Snowdown	Kent	TR2451	51°13·1'	1°12·9'E	T	179,189
Snow End	Herts	TL4032	51°58·4'	0°2·7'E	T	167
Snower Hill	Surrey	TQ2149	51°13·9'	0°15·6'W	X	187
Snow Falls	N Yks	SD7074	54°9·9'	2°27·2'W	W	98
Snowfield Fm	N Yks	SE4966	54°5·5'	1°14·6'W	FM	100
Snowfields	Powys	SO1789	52°29·8'	3°13·0'W	X	136
Snowford Br	Warw	SP3966	52°17·7'	1°25·3'W	X	151
Snowford Grange	Warw	SP3866	52°17·7'	1°26·2'W	X	151
Snowford Hill	Warw	SP4064	52°16·6'	1°24·4'W	X	151
Snowford Lodge	Warw	SP3865	52°17·1'	1°26·2'W	X	151
Snow Gate	Highld	NN6382	56°54·8'	4°14·6'W	X	42
Snow Gill	S Lanak	NT0326	55°31·3'	3°31·8'W	W	72
Snowgill Hill	S Lanak	NT0227	55°31·9'	3°32·7'W	H	72
Snow Hall	Durham	NZ1816	54°32·6'	1°42·9'W	X	92
Snow Hall	Northum	NY7986	55°10·3'	2°19·4'W	X	80
Snow Hall	Red & Cl	NZ5613	54°30·8'	1°7·7'W	X	93
Snow Hill	Ches	SJ6452	53°4·1'	2°31·8'W	T	118
Snowhill	Cumbr	NY2738	54°44·2'	3°7·6'W	X	89,90
Snow Hill	Wakf	SE3222	53°41·8'	1°30·5'W	T	104
Snow Hill	Win & Maid	SU9672	51°26·6'	0°36·7'W	X	175,176
Snow Hill Fm	Brad	SE0350	53°57·0'	1°56·8'W	FM	104
Snowhill Fm	Bucks	SP9705	51°44·3'	0°35·3'W	FM	165
Snowhope Close	Durham	NY9536	54°43·4'	2°4·2'W	X	91,92
Snowhope Hill	Durham	NY9434	54°42·3'	2°5·1'W	X	91,92
Snowhope Moor	Durham	NY9435	54°42·8'	2°5·2'W	X	91,92
Snow Lea	Kirk	SE0917	53°39·2'	1°51·4'W	T	110
Snowre Hall	Norf	TL6299	52°34·1'	0°23·8'E	A	143
Snow's Down	Dorset	ST9107	50°52·0'	2°7·3'W	X	195
Snows Fm	Essex	TL5612	51°47·3'	0°16·1'E	FM	167
Snow's Hall	Suff	TM3570	52°16·9'	1°27·1'E	X	156
Snowshill	Glos	SP0933	52°0·0'	1°51·7'W	T	150
Snowshill Hill	Glos	SP1232	51°59·4'	1°49·1'W	X	150
Snowstorm Gorse	Glos	SP1801	51°42·7'	1°44·0'W	F	163
Snow Street	Norf	TM0981	52°23·4'	1°4·7'E	T	144
Snowswick Fm	Oxon	SU2295	51°39·4'	1°40·5'W	FM	163
Snoxhall Fm	Surrey	TQ0637	51°7·6'	0°28·7'W	FM	187
Snuasimul	N Eil	NL6695	56°55·8'	7°29·0'W	X	31
Snubsnape Fm	Lancs	SD5220	53°40·7'	2°43·2'W	FM	102
Snub, The	Aberd	NK0028	57°20·8'	1°59·5'W	X	38
Snub, The	Angus	NO3375	56°52·0'	3°5·5'W	X	44
Snuckle, The	Shetld	HU4248	60°13·1'	1°14·0'W	X	3
Snuff Hill	Worcs	SO9474	52°22·1'	2°4·9'W	X	139
Snugborough	I of M	SC3577	54°10·0'	4°31·2'W	X	95
Snurridge	Devon	SS7028	51°2·4'	3°50·9'W	X	180
Snydale	Wakf	SE4020	53°40·7'	1°23·3'W	T	105
Snydale Hall	Wakf	SE4021	53°41·3'	1°23·2'W	X	105
Snydles Fm	Devon	SS6619	50°57·5'	3°54·1'W	FM	180
Snypes	E Renf	NS4855	55°46·1'	4°24·9'W	X	64
Snypes Dam	E Renf	NS4855	55°46·1'	4°24·9'W	W	64
Soa	Arg & Bt	NM0746	56°31·1'	6°45·4'W	X	46
Soa	Arg & Bt	NM1551	56°34·1'	6°37·9'W	X	46
Soaidh Beag	N Eil	NB0505	57°56·5'	6°58·6'W	X	13,14
Soaidh Mòr	N Eil	NB0605	57°56·5'	6°57·6'W	X	13,14
Soa Island	Arg & Bt	NM2419	56°17·2'	6°27·2'W	X	48
Soake	Hants	SU6611	50°53·9'	1°3·3'W	T	196
Soakham Downs	Kent	TR0349	51°12·5'	0°54·8'E	X	179,189
Soakham Fm	Kent	TR0448	51°11·9'	0°55·6'E	FM	179,189
Soal Fm	Hants	SU7224	51°0·9'	0°58·0'W	FM	197
Soame Br	E Renf	NS5142	55°42·4'	4°21·8'W	X	64
Soames Fm	Hants	SU6530	51°4·2'	1°3·9'W	FM	185,186
Soa Point	Arg & Bt	NM0645	56°30·6'	6°46·3'W	X	46
Soap Rock	Corn	SW6714	49°59·1'	5°14·7'W	X	203
Soar	Card	ST0983	51°32·6'	3°18·3'W	X	171
Soar	Carm	SN2840	52°2·1'	4°30·1'W	X	145
Soar	Carm	SN6228	51°56·2'	4°0·1'W	X	146
Soar	Denb	SJ0060	53°7·9'	3°29·3'W	X	116
Soar	Devon	SX7037	50°13·4'	3°49·0'W	T	202
Soar	Gwyn	SH6135	52°53·9'	4°3·6'W	T	124
Soar	I of Angl	SH3872	53°13·5'	4°25·2'W	T	114
Soar	Powys	SN9732	51°58·9'	3°29·6'W	T	160
Soar Brook	Leic	SP4791	52°31·1'	1°18·0'W	W	140
Soar Hill	Pemb	SN0139	52°1·1'	4°53·6'W	X	145,157
Soarley Beeches	Hants	SU2206	50°51·4'	1°40·9'W	X	195
Soar Mill Cove	Devon	SX6937	50°13·3'	3°49·8'W	W	202
Soars Lodge Fm	Leic	SP5994	52°32·7'	1°7·4'W	FM	140
Soar y Mynydd	Cered	SN7853	52°9·9'	3°46·6'W	X	146,147
Soay	N Eil	NA0601	57°49·7'	8°38·0'W	X	18
Soay Harbour	Highld	NG4415	57°9·5'	6°13·6'W	W	32
Soay Sound	Highld	NG4416	57°10·1'	6°13·6'W	W	32
Soay Stac	N Eil	NA0701	57°49·8'	8°36·9'W	X	18
Sober Hall	Stock on T	NZ4412	54°30·3'	1°18·8'W	X	93
Sober Hill	E Yorks	SE8037	53°49·6'	0°46·7'W	X	106
Sober Hill	E Yorks	SE8326	53°43·7'	0°44·1'W	X	106
Sober Hill	E Yorks	SE9238	53°50·0'	0°35·7'W	X	106
Soberlie Hill	Shetld	HT9540	60°8·9'	2°4·9'W	X	4
Soberton	Hants	SU6116	50°56·6'	1°7·5'W	T	185
Soberton Heath	Hants	SU6014	50°55·6'	1°8·4'W	T	196
Soberton Towers	Hants	SU6116	50°56·6'	1°7·5'W	X	185
Sòbhail	N Eil	NB3425	58°8·3'	6°30·7'W	H	13,14
Sòbhal Mòr	N Eil	NB3819	58°5·2'	6°26·2'W	H	14
Sobul	Shetld	HP6004	60°43·1'	0°53·5'W	H	1
Socach	Arg & Bt	NR8899	56°8·5'	5°24·3'W	X	55
Socach a' Mhàim	Arg & Bt	NM6133	56°26·0'	5°52·2'W	X	49
Socach Burn	Aberd	NJ4610	57°10·9'	2°51·1'W	W	37
Socach Burn	Arg & Bt	NR8899	56°8·5'	5°23·3'W	W	55
Socach Hill	Highld	NC8806	58°2·0'	3°53·3'W	X	17
Socach Mòr	Aberd	NO1180	56°54·4'	3°27·2'W	X	43
Socach, The	Aberd	NJ2714	57°12·9'	3°12·1'W	H	37
Socach, The	Aberd	NJ3207	57°9·2'	3°7·0'W	H	37
Socach, The	Aberd	NJ3219	57°15·7'	3°7·2'W	H	37
Socach, The	Aberd	NJ4810	57°10·9'	2°51·2'W	H	37
Socach Uachdarach	Arg & Bt	NN1403	56°11·3'	4°59·4'W	X	56
Soccach	Moray	NJ1248	57°31·1'	3°27·7'W	X	28
Social Cottage	I of M	SC4283	54°13·4'	4°25·0'W	X	95
Society	W Loth	NT0979	56°0·0'	3°27·1'W	X	65
Sockbridge	Cumbr	NY5026	54°37·8'	2°46·1'W	T	90
Sockbridge Mill	Cumbr	NY4927	54°38·4'	2°47·0'W	X	90
Sockburn	Darl	NZ2620	54°34·7'	1°35·4'W	X	93
Sockburn	Darl	NZ3407	54°27·7'	1°28·1'W	T	93
Sock Dennis Fm	Somer	ST5121	50°59·4'	2°41·5'W	FM	183
Sockenber	Cumbr	NY6321	54°35·2'	2°33·9'W	X	91
Sockenholes Fm	W Susx	SU9620	50°58·5'	0°37·6'W	FM	197
Sockety	Dorset	ST4806	50°51·3'	2°43·9'W	T	193
Sockety Fm	Somer	ST4413	50°55·1'	2°47·4'W	FM	193
Sock Fm	Somer	ST5119	50°58·3'	2°41·5'W	FM	183
Sock Hill	Devon	SS9910	50°53·1'	3°25·8'W	X	192
Sockhill Fm	Somer	ST5618	50°57·8'	2°37·2'W	FM	183
Socknersh Manor	E Susx	TQ6923	50°59·4'	0°24·9'E	X	199
Sodam Mill	S Glos	ST6990	51°36·7'	2°26·5'W	X	162,172
Sodbury Common	S Glos	ST7383	51°32·9'	2°23·0'W	X	172
Sodgley	Heref	SO4462	52°15·4'	2°48·8'W	X	137,148,149
Sodington Hall	Worcs	SO6971	52°20·4'	2°26·9'W	X	138
Sodom	Denb	SJ0971	53°13·9'	3°21·4'W	T	116
Sodom	Shetld	HU5462	60°20·6'	1°0·8'W	X	2
Sodom	Wilts	SU0081	51°31·9'	1°59·6'W	T	173
Sodston Ho	Pemb	SN1016	51°48·9'	4°45·0'W	X	158
Sodylt	Shrops	SJ3440	52°57·4'	2°58·5'W	X	117
Sodylt Bank	Shrops	SJ3439	52°56·9'	2°58·5'W	T	126
Soflen	Conwy	SH8257	53°6·1'	3°45·3'W	A	116
Softlaw East Mains	Scot Bord	NT7531	55°34·6'	2°23·4'W	X	74
Softley	Durham	NZ0926	54°38·0'	1°51·2'W	X	92
Softley	Northum	NY6755	54°53·6'	2°30·4'W	X	86,87
Sogg's Ho	E Susx	TQ7923	50°58·9'	0°33·4'E	X	199
Soham	Cambs	TL5973	52°20·1'	0°20·4'E	T	154
Soham Cotes	Cambs	TL5775	52°21·3'	0°18·7'E	T	143
Soham Fen	Cambs	TL6074	52°20·7'	0°21·3'E	X	143
Soham Lode	Cambs	TL5774	52°20·7'	0°18·7'E	W	143
Soham Lode	Cambs	TL6172	52°19·6'	0°22·2'E	W	154
Soham Mere	Cambs	TL5773	52°20·2'	0°18·7'E	X	154
Soham Town Corner	Suff	TM2364	52°14·0'	1°16·3'E	X	156
Soho	Carm	SN4903	51°42·6'	4°10·7'W	X	159
Soho	C of West	TQ2981	51°31·0'	0°8·1'W	T	176
Soho	Sand	SP0389	52°30·2'	1°56·9'W	T	139
Soho	Somer	ST6948	51°14·1'	2°26·3'W	T	183
Soigné Fm	Norf	TF7717	52°43·5'	0°37·7'E	FM	132
Soigné Wood	Norf	TF7617	52°43·5'	0°36·8'E	F	132
Soil Hill	Cald	SE0731	53°46·8'	1°53·2'W	H	104
Soillerie	Highld	NH8101	57°5·3'	3°57·4'W	X	35
Soilsham	Highld	NH8028	57°19·9'	3°59·1'W	X	35
Soilwell	Glos	SO6405	51°44·8'	2°30·9'W	X	162
Soilzarie	Pth & Kin	NO1359	56°43·1'	3°24·8'W	X	53
Solam	Arg & Bt	NR4148	55°39·6'	6°6·6'W	X	60
Solberge Hall	N Yks	SE3589	54°18·0'	1°27·3'W	X	99
Solberg Village	N Yks	SE3589	54°18·0'	1°27·3'W	A	99
Solbury	Pemb	SM8912	51°46·3'	5°3·1'W	X	157,158
Soldiers' Hill	Cambs	TL4968	52°17·6'	0°11·5'E	X	154
Soldier's Hill	Devon	SY1488	50°41·4'	3°12·7'W	X	192
Soldier's Leap, The	Pth & Kin	NN9162	56°44·5'	3°46·5'W	X	43
Soldier's Lump	Derby	SE0804	53°32·2'	1°52·3'W	X	110
Soldiers' Point	I of Angl	SH2383	53°19·1'	4°39·0'W	X	114
Soldier's Ring	Hants	SU0817	50°57·4'	1°52·8'W	A	184
Soldier's Ring	Surrey	SU8846	51°12·6'	0°44·0'W	A	186
Soldon	Devon	SS3210	50°52·1'	4°22·9'W	X	190
Soldon Cross	Devon	SS3210	50°52·1'	4°22·9'W	T	190
Soldridge	Hants	SU6534	51°6·3'	1°3·9'W	T	185,186
Sole Bay	Suff	TM5176	52°19·7'	1°41·4'E	W	156
Sole Beck	N Yks	SE1879	54°12·6'	1°43·0'W	W	99
Sole Burn	D & G	NX0165	54°56·7'	5°6·0'W	W	82
Soleburn	D & G	NX0364	54°56·2'	5°4·1'W	X	82
Sole Common	W Berks	SU4070	51°25·9'	1°25·1'W	F	174
Sole End Fm	Warw	SP3287	52°29·0'	1°31·3'W	FM	140
Sole Fm	W Berks	SU4171	51°26·4'	1°24·2'W	FM	174
Sole Geo	Orkney	HY3129	59°8·8'	3°11·9'W	X	6
Sole Hill Fm	Hants	SU2822	51°0·0'	1°35·7'W	FM	184
Solelands Fm	W Susx	TQ1020	50°58·4'	0°25·6'W	FM	198
Solent Court	Hants	SZ5005	50°50·8'	1°17·0'W	X	196
Solent, The		SZ5098	50°47·0'	1°17·1'W	W	196
Solent Way	Hants	SU5202	50°49·1'	1°15·3'W	X	196
Solent Way	Hants	SU7305	50°50·6'	0°57·4'W	X	197
Sole's Fm	Kent	TR2550	51°12·5'	1°13·7'E	FM	179
Soles Hill	Staffs	SK0952	53°4·1'	1°51·5'W	H	119
Sole Street	Kent	TQ6567	51°22·9'	0°22·7'E	T	177,178
Sole Street	Kent	TR0949	51°12·3'	0°59·9'E	T	179,189
Sole Street Ho	Kent	TR0258	51°17·3'	0°54·2'E	X	178
Solfach	Gwyn	SH1524	52°47·2'	4°44·2'W	X	123
Solihull	Sol	SP1579	52°24·8'	1°46·4'W	T	139
Solihull Lodge	Sol	SP0978	52°24·2'	1°51·7'W	T	139
Soliken	Aberd	NJ4211	57°11·4'	2°57·1'W	H	37
Solinger Fm	Bucks	SP8303	51°43·4'	0°47·5'W	FM	165
Solitote	Highld	NG4274	57°41·2'	6°19·3'W	T	23
Solland	Devon	SS6101	50°47·8'	3°58·0'W	X	191
Sollas	N Eil	NF8174	57°38·8'	7°20·4'W	T	18
Sollers Dilwyn	Heref	SO4255	52°11·7'	2°50·5'W	T	148,149
Sollers Hope	Heref	SO6133	51°59·9'	2°33·7'W	T	149
Sollom	Lancs	SD4518	53°39·6'	2°49·5'W	T	108
Solmain	Cumbr	NY5267	55°0·0'	2°44·6'W	X	86
Solomon's Court	Glos	SO9003	51°43·8'	2°8·3'W	A	163
Solomons Fm	Medway	TQ7874	51°26·4'	0°34·1'E	FM	178
Solomon's Temple	Derby	SK0571	53°14·4'	1°55·1'W	X	119
Solomon's Tump	Glos	SO7319	51°52·4'	2°23·1'W	X	162
Solomons Court	Surrey	TQ2658	51°18·7'	0°11·1'W	X	187
Solon Beag	N Eil	NL5784	56°49·5'	7°37·0'W	T	31
Solon Mòr	N Eil	NL5784	56°49·5'	7°37·0'W	X	31
Solsgirth	E Dunb	NS6774	55°56·7'	4°7·3'W	X	64
Solsgirth	Pth & Kin	NS9895	56°8·5'	3°38·0'W	X	58
Solton Manor Fm	Kent	TR3345	51°9·6'	1°20·3'E	FM	179
Solus Craggie	Highld	ND0018	58°8·6'	3°41·5'W	X	17
Solva	Pemb	SM8024	51°52·5'	5°11·4'W	T	157
Solwaybank	D & G	NY3077	55°5·2'	3°5·4'W	X	85
Solway Firth		NX9839	54°44·4'	3°34·6'W	W	89
Solway Firth		NX9848	54°49·2'	3°34·8'W	W	84
Solway Fishery	D & G	NX9366	54°58·9'	3°39·9'W	X	84
Solway Moss	Cumbr	NY3469	55°0·9'	3°1·5'W	X	85
Somerby	Highld	NH5257	57°35·0'	4°28·1'W	X	26
Somerby	Leic	SK7710	52°41·2'	0°51·2'W	T	129
Somerby	Lincs	SK8589	53°23·7'	0°42·9'W	X	112,121
Somerby	Lincs	TA0606	53°32·6'	0°23·6'W	T	112
Somerby Lodge	Leic	SK7910	52°41·1'	0°49·5'W	X	129
Somerby Low Fm	Lincs	TA0505	53°32·1'	0°24·5'W	FM	112
Somerby Top	Lincs	TA0707	53°33·2'	0°22·7'W	X	112
Somercotes	Derby	SK4253	53°4·6'	1°22·0'W	T	120
Somercotes Haven	Lincs	TA4000	53°28·9'	0°7·0'E	W	113
Somerdale	Bath & NE Somer	ST6569	51°25·4'	2°29·8'W	T	172
Somerden	Kent	TQ5046	51°11·8'	0°9·2'E	X	188
Somerden Green	Kent	TQ5045	51°11·3'	0°9·2'E	X	188
Somerdon Ho	E Yorks	TA1630	53°45·4'	0°14·0'W	X	107
Somerfield Ct	Kent	TR1037	51°5·8'	1°0·4'E	X	179,189
Somerford	Ches	SJ8065	53°11·1'	2°17·6'W	T	118
Somerford	Dorset	SZ1793	50°44·4'	1°45·2'W	T	195
Somerford	Staffs	SJ9008	52°40·4'	2°9·4'W	T	127
Somerford Booths Hall	Ches	SJ8365	53°11·1'	2°14·9'W	X	118
Somerford Br	Wilts	ST9783	51°33·0'	2°2·2'W	X	173
Somerford Common	Wilts	SU0286	51°34·6'	1°57·9'W	F	173
Somerford Fm	Ches	SJ8263	53°10·1'	2°15·7'W	FM	118
Somerford Fm	Wilts	SU0086	51°34·6'	1°59·6'W	FM	173
Somerford Hall	Staffs	SJ9008	52°40·4'	2°8·5'W	X	127
Somerford Hall Fm	Ches	SJ8165	53°11·1'	2°16·7'W	FM	118
Somerford Keynes	Glos	SU0195	51°39·5'	1°58·7'W	T	163
Somerford Park Fm	Ches	SJ8164	53°10·6'	2°16·7'W	FM	118
Somerford Wood	Staffs	SJ9007	52°39·9'	2°8·5'W	F	127,139

Somerhill	Kent	TQ6045	51°11·1′	0°17·8′E	A	188
Someries	Luton	TL1120	51°52·3′	0°22·9′W	X	166
Someries Castle	Beds	TL1120	51°52·3′	0°22·9′W	A	166
Someries Stud	Cambs	TL6462	52°14·1′	0°24·5′E	X	154
Somerleaze	Somer	ST5145	51°12·4′	2°41·7′W	X	182,183
Somerley	Hants	SU1307	50°52·0′	1°48·5′W	X	195
Somerley	W Susx	SZ8198	50°46·8′	0°50·7′W	T	197
Somerley Park	Hants	SU1308	50°52·5′	1°48·5′W	X	195
Somerleyton	Suff	TM4897	52°31·1′	1°39·7′E	T	134
Somerleyton Marshes	Suff	TM4896	52°30·5′	1°39·7′E	X	134
Somerleyton Park	Suff	TM4997	52°31·1′	1°40·6′E	X	134
Somerleyton Sta	Suff	TM4796	52°30·6′	1°38·8′E	X	134
Somers	Devon	SS5525	51°0·6′	4°3·6′W	X	180
Somersal Herbert	Derby	SK1335	52°55·0′	1°48·0′W	T	128
Somersal Ho	Derby	SK1435	52°55·0′	1°47·1′W	X	128
Somersall Hall	Derby	SK3570	53°13·8′	1°28·1′W	X	119
Somersbury Wood	Surrey	TQ1037	51°7·5′	0°25·3′W	F	187
Somersby	Lincs	TF3472	53°13·9′	0°0·9′E	T	122
Somerset and North Devon Coast Path	Somer	SS8847	51°12·9′	3°35·8′W	X	181
Somerset Court	Somer	ST3449	51°14·4′	2°56·3′W	X	182
Somerset Fm	Surrey	SU9243	51°11·0′	0°40·6′W	FM	186
Somerset Fm	V of Glam	SS9469	51°24·8′	3°31·1′W	FM	170
Somerset Fm	N Yks	NZ4400	54°23·9′	1°18·9′W	X	93
Somerset Hospl	Wilts	SU3068	51°24·8′	1°33·7′W	X	174
Somersham	Cambs	TL3678	52°23·2′	0°0·3′E	T	142
Somersham	Suff	TM0848	52°5·7′	1°2·6′E	T	155,169
Somersham Fore Fen	Cambs	TL3779	52°23·7′	0°1·2′E	X	142,143
Somersham High North Fen	Cambs	TL3681	52°24·8′	0°0·4′E	X	142
Somersham Park	Cambs	TL3577	52°22·7′	0°0·6′W	X	142
Somers, The	Warw	SP2282	52°26·4′	1°40·2′W	X	139
Somers Town	Camden	TQ2982	51°31·6′	0°8·0′W	T	176
Somers Town	C of Port	SZ6499	50°47·4′	1°5·1′W	T	196
Somerton	Newp	ST3387	51°34·9′	2°57·6′W	T	171
Somerton	Oxon	SP4928	51°57·1′	1°16·8′W	T	164
Somerton	Somer	ST4828	51°3·2′	2°44·1′W	T	193
Somerton	Suff	TL8153	52°9·0′	0°39·1′E	T	155
Somerton Castle	Lincs	SK9558	53°6·9′	0°34·4′W	A	121
Somerton Door	Somer	ST4730	51°4·2′	2°45·0′W	X	182
Somerton Fm	I of W	SZ4994	50°44·8′	1°17·9′W	FM	196
Somerton Hall	Suff	TL8152	52°8·4′	0°39·1′E	X	155
Somerton Hill	Somer	ST4628	51°3·2′	2°45·8′W	T	193
Somerton Holmes	Norf	TG4621	52°44·1′	1°39·0′E	X	134
Somerton Moor	Somer	ST4531	51°4·8′	2°46·7′W	X	182
Somerton Randle	Somer	ST5028	51°3·2′	2°42·4′W	X	183
Somerwood	Shrops	SJ5614	52°43·6′	2°38·7′W	T	126
Sompting	W Susx	TQ1704	50°49·6′	0°19·9′W	T	198
Sompting Abbotts	W Susx	TQ1605	50°50·2′	0°20·8′W	T	198
Sonachan Hotel	Highld	NM4566	56°43·2′	6°9·6′W	X	47
Sonachan House	Arg & Bt	NN0320	56°20·1′	5°10·8′W	X	50
Sonach Croft	Aberd	NJ8731	57°22·4′	2°12·5′W	X	30
Songar Grange	Warw	SP1961	52°15·0′	1°42·9′W	X	151
Sonning	Wok	SU7575	51°28·4′	0°54·8′W	T	175
Sonning Common	Oxon	SU7080	51°31·1′	0°59·1′W	T	175
Sonning Eye	Oxon	SU7576	51°28·9′	0°54·8′W	T	175
Sonso Ness	Shetld	HU2958	60°18·6′	1°28·0′W	X	3
Sontley	Wrex	SJ3346	53°0·7′	2°59·5′W	T	117
Sontley Lodge Fm	Wrex	SJ3247	53°1·2′	3°0·4′W	FM	117
Sook Hill	Northum	NY7367	55°0·1′	2°24·9′W	X	86,87
Sookholme	Notts	SK5466	53°11·5′	1°11·1′W	T	120
Sookholme Bath	Notts	SK5466	53°11·5′	1°11·1′W	W	120
Soolbank	Cumbr	SD6692	54°19·6′	2°30·9′W	X	144
Soolmis Vird	Shetld	HU3173	60°26·6′	1°25·7′W	H	3
Soolmisvird Water	Shetld	HU3172	60°26·1′	1°25·7′W	W	3
Soonhope	Scot Bord	NT5254	55°46·9′	2°45·5′W	X	66,73
Soonhope Burn	Scot Bord	NT2641	55°39·7′	3°10·1′W	W	73
Soonhope Burn	Scot Bord	NT5356	55°48·0′	2°44·5′W	W	66,73
Soot Burn	Northum	NY8180	55°7·1′	2°17·4′W	W	80
Sooth Clett	Orkney	ND3883	58°44·1′	3°3·8′W	X	7
Sootywells	Aberd	NO7573	56°51·1′	2°24·1′W	X	45
Sopers Fm	W Susx	TQ1616	50°56·1′	0°20·6′W	FM	198
Sopley	Hants	SZ1597	50°46·6′	1°46·9′W	T	195
Sopley Common	Dorset	SZ1397	50°46·6′	1°48·6′W	X	195
Sopley Park	Hants	SZ1696	50°46·0′	1°46·0′W	X	195
Soppit Farm	Northum	NY9293	55°14·1′	2°7·1′W	FM	80
Sopwell	Herts	TL1505	51°44·1′	0°19·7′W	T	166
Sopworth	Wilts	ST8286	51°34·6′	2°15·2′W	T	173
Soray	N Eil	NA7245	58°16·5′	7°35·3′W	X	13
Sorbie	D & G	NX4346	54°47·3′	4°26·1′W	T	83
Sorbie	D & G	NY3690	55°12·3′	2°59·9′W	X	79
Sorbie	Fife	NO5308	56°16·0′	2°45·1′W	X	59
Sorbie	N Ayr	NS2444	55°39·7′	4°47·4′W	X	63,70
Sorbie Fm	D & G	NX4547	54°47·9′	4°24·2′W	FM	83
Sorbies	Cumbr	NY5076	55°4·8′	2°46·6′W	X	86
Sorbietrees	Scot Bord	NY4884	55°9·1′	2°48·5′W	X	79
Sôr Brook	Monm	ST3494	51°38·7′	2°56·8′W	W	171
Sor Brook	Oxon	SP4437	52°2·0′	1°21·1′W	W	151
Sordale	Highld	ND1461	58°32·0′	3°28·1′W	X	11,12
Sordale Hill	Highld	ND1561	58°32·0′	3°27·1′W	H	11,12
Sorgwm	Powys	SO1627	51°56·3′	3°12·9′W	X	161
Soriby Bay	Arg & Bt	NM4240	56°29·1′	6°11·0′W	W	47,48
Sorisdale	Arg & Bt	NM2763	56°41·0′	6°27·0′W	T	46,47
Sorisdale Bay	Arg & Bt	NM2762	56°40·5′	6°27·0′W	W	46,47
Sorley	Devon	SX7246	50°18·2′	3°47·5′W	T	202
Sorn	E Ayr	NS5526	55°30·6′	4°17·3′W	T	71
Sornach a' Ghearrain	Arg & Bt	NM4526	56°21·7′	6°7·3′W	X	48
Sornagan	Highld	NM5857	56°38·8′	5°56·4′W	X	47
Sornbeg	E Ayr	NS5035	55°35·4′	4°22·4′W	X	70
Sorn Cas	E Ayr	NS5426	55°30·6′	4°18·3′W	A	70
Sorne	Arg & Bt	NM4456	56°37·8′	6°10·0′W	X	47
Sorne Point	Arg & Bt	NM4257	56°38·3′	6°12·0′W	X	47
Sornfallow	S Lanak	NS9233	55°35·0′	3°42·4′W	X	71,72
Sornhill	E Ayr	NS5034	55°34·9′	4°22·3′W	A	70
Sornhill	E Ayr	NS5134	55°34·9′	4°21·4′W	T	70
Sorn Mains	E Ayr	NS5428	55°31·7′	4°18·3′W	X	70
Soroba	Arg & Bt	NM8004	56°10·9′	5°32·3′W	T	55
Soroba	Arg & Bt	NM8628	56°24·0′	5°27·6′W	T	49
Soroba Hill	Arg & Bt	NM7905	56°11·4′	5°33·3′W	H	55
Sorobaidh Bay	Arg & Bt	NL9942	56°28·7′	6°52·9′W	W	46
Soroba Lodge	Arg & Bt	NM8527	56°23·4′	5°28·6′W	X	49
Sorrelsykes Park	N Yks	SE0288	54°17·5′	1°57·7′W	X	98
Sorrow Beck	N Yks	SE4691	54°19·0′	1°17·2′W	W	100
Sorrowful Hill	N Yks	NZ1510	54°29·4′	1°45·7′W	X	92
Sorrowlessfield Mains	Scot Bord	NT5636	55°37·2′	2°41·5′W	X	73
Sorrowstones	Cumbr	NY0902	54°24·6′	3°23·7′W	X	89
Sorrysike Moor	D & G	NY1374	55°3·4′	3°21·3′W	F	85
Sortat	Highld	ND2863	58°33·2′	3°13·8′W	T	11,12
Sort Hills	Lincs	SK8582	53°19·9′	0°43·0′W	X	121
Sorton	Orkney	HY3515	59°1·3′	3°7·4′W	X	6
Sortridge	Devon	SX5071	50°31·4′	4°6·6′W	X	201
Sosgill	Cumbr	NY1023	54°35·9′	3°23·2′W	X	89
Sotby	Lincs	TF2078	53°17·4′	0°11·6′W	T	122
Sotby House Fm	Lincs	TF1978	53°17·4′	0°12·5′W	FM	122
Sotby Wood	Lincs	TF1877	53°16·8′	0°13·4′W	F	122
Sotersta	Shetld	HU2644	60°11·0′	1°31·4′W	X	4
Sothall	Sheff	SK4482	53°20·2′	1°19·9′W	T	111,120
Sotheron's Plantn	E Yorks	SE8035	53°48·5′	0°46·7′W	F	106
Sothers Brecks	Shetld	HP6016	60°49·6′	0°53·3′W	X	1
Sothers Daal	Shetld	HU2151	60°14·8′	1°36·7′W	X	3
Sothers Field	Shetld	HP6315	60°49·0′	0°50·0′W	H	1
Sothers Stack	Shetld	HP6016	60°49·6′	0°53·3′W	X	1
Sotherton	Suff	TM4479	52°21·5′	1°35·4′E	X	156
Sotherton Corner	Suff	TM4378	52°21·0′	1°34·5′E	X	156
Sotherton Hall	Suff	TM4278	52°21·0′	1°33·6′E	X	156
Sotland	Shetld	HP6113	60°48·0′	0°52·2′W	X	1
Sots Hole	Lincs	TF1264	53°9·9′	0°19·1′W	T	121
Sot's Hole	Lincs	TF4131	52°51·7′	0°6·1′E	X	131
Sotterley	Suff	TM4584	52°24·2′	1°36·5′E	T	156
Sotterley Common	Suff	TM4784	52°24·1′	1°38·3′E	X	156
Sotterley Park	Suff	TM4585	52°24·7′	1°36·6′E	X	156
Sotterley Wood	Suff	TM4685	52°24·7′	1°37·4′E	F	156
Sotwell Hill	Oxon	SU5990	51°36·6′	1°8·5′W	X	164,174
Soudley	Shrops	SJ7228	52°51·2′	2°24·5′W	T	127
Soudley	Shrops	SO4791	52°31·1′	2°46·5′W	T	137,138
Soudley Park	Shrops	SJ7227	52°50·6′	2°24·5′W	X	127
Soughan's Fm	Ches	SJ4447	53°1·3′	2°49·7′W	FM	117
Sough Hill	N Yks	NZ1614	54°31·5′	1°44·7′W	X	92
Soughley	Barns	SE1802	53°31·1′	1°43·3′W	T	110
Sough Sike	Cumbr	NY6178	55°5·9′	2°36·2′W	W	86
Soughton Fm	Flint	SJ2367	53°11·9′	3°8·8′W	FM	117
Soughton Hall	Flint	SJ2467	53°11·9′	3°7·9′W	A	117
Soughton Ho	Flint	SJ2566	53°11·4′	3°6·9′W	X	117
Soughton or Sychdyn	Flint	SJ2466	53°11·4′	3°7·8′W	T	117
Sough Top	Derby	SK1370	53°13·9′	1°47·9′W	H	119
Souland Gate	Cumbr	NY4625	54°37·3′	2°49·8′W	X	90
Soulbury	Bucks	SP8827	51°56·3′	0°42·8′W	T	165
Soulby	Cumbr	NY4625	54°37·3′	2°49·8′W	T	90
Soulby	Cumbr	NY7411	54°29·9′	2°23·7′W	T	91
Soulby Fell	Cumbr	NY4524	54°36·7′	2°50·7′W	H	90
Soulby Fell Fm	Cumbr	NY4525	54°37·3′	2°50·7′W	FM	90
Soulby Grange	Cumbr	NY7311	54°29·9′	2°24·6′W	X	91
Souldern	Oxon	SP5231	51°58·7′	1°14·2′W	T	151
Souldern Grounds	Oxon	SP5030	51°58·2′	1°15·9′W	X	151
Souldern Mill	Oxon	SP5131	51°58·7′	1°15·1′W	X	151
Souldow	Moray	NJ1446	57°30·0′	3°25·6′W	X	28
Souldrop	Beds	SP9861	52°14·5′	0°33·5′W	T	153
Soulgill Beck	Durham	NY8819	54°34·2′	2°10·7′W	W	91,92
Soulgill Edge	Durham	NY8819	54°34·2′	2°10·7′W	X	91,92
Soulgill Grain	Durham	NY8518	54°33·7′	2°13·5′W	W	91,92
Soulseat Burn	D & G	NX1057	54°52·6′	4°57·3′W	W	82
Soulseat Loch	D & G	NX1058	54°53·1′	4°57·3′W	W	82
Soulsgrave Fm	N Yks	NZ9004	54°25·6′	0°36·3′W	FM	94
Soulsgrave Slack	N Yks	NZ9004	54°25·6′	0°36·3′W	W	94
Soulton Brook	Shrops	SJ5430	52°52·2′	2°40·6′W	W	126
Soulton Hall	Shrops	SJ5430	52°52·2′	2°40·6′W	A	126
Sound	Ches	SJ6248	53°1·9′	2°33·6′W	T	118
Sound	Orkney	HY4631	59°10·0′	2°56·2′W	X	5,6
Sound	Shetld	HU3850	60°14·2′	1°18·3′W	T	3
Sound	Shetld	HU4583	60°32·0′	1°10·3′W	T	1,2,3
Sound	Shetld	HU4640	60°8·8′	1°9·8′W	T	4
Soundborough	Glos	SP0521	51°53·5′	1°55·2′W	X	163
Sound Bottom	Wilts	SU2271	51°26·5′	1°40·6′W	X	174
Sound Copse	Wilts	SU2271	51°26·5′	1°40·6′W	F	174
Sound Gruney	Shetld	HU5896	60°38·9′	0°55·9′W	X	1
Sound Hall	Ches	SJ6148	53°1·9′	2°34·5′W	X	118
Sound Heath	Ches	SJ6147	53°1·4′	2°34·5′W	T	118
Sounding Burn	E Loth	NT5769	55°55·0′	2°40·8′W	W	67
Soundmoor	Moray	NJ3652	57°33·5′	3°3·7′W	X	28
Sound Moor	Moray	NJ3653	57°34·0′	3°3·7′W	X	28
Soundness Fm	Oxon	SU7087	51°34·9′	0°59·0′W	FM	175
Soundness Ho	Oxon	SU7187	51°34·9′	0°58·1′W	X	175
Sound Oak	Ches	SJ6149	53°2·5′	2°34·5′W	X	118
Sound of Arisaig	Highld	NM6580	56°51·4′	5°50·8′W	W	40
Sound of Barra	N Eil	NF7509	57°3·7′	7°21·3′W	W	31
Sound of Berneray	N Eil	NF9079	57°41·9′	7°11·8′W	W	18
Sound of Berneray	N Eil	NL5581	56°47·8′	7°38·7′W	W	31
Sound of Brough	Shetld	HU4778	60°29·2′	1°8·2′W	W	2,3
Sound of Bute	Arg & Bt	NS0255	55°45·1′	5°8·9′W	W	63
Sound of Canna	Highld	NG3002	57°2·1′	6°26·6′W	W	32,39
Sound of Eigg	Highld	NM4382	56°51·8′	6°12·5′W	W	39
Sound of Eriskay	N Eil	NF7913	57°6·0′	7°17·6′W	W	31
Sound of Faray	Orkney	HY5437	59°13·3′	2°47·9′W	W	5
Sound of Fiaray	N Eil	NF6909	57°3·4′	7°27·2′W	W	31
Sound of Fuday	N Eil	NF7107	57°2·5′	7°25·0′W	W	31
Sound of Gigha	Arg & Bt	NR6749	55°41·0′	5°42·0′W	W	62
Sound of Handa	Highld	NC1547	58°22·6′	5°9·3′W	W	9
Sound of Harris	N Eil	NF9681	57°43·2′	7°5·9′W	W	18
Sound of Havra	Shetld	HU3742	60°9·9′	1°19·5′W	W	4
Sound of Hellisay	N Eil	NF7503	57°0·5′	7°20·8′W	W	31
Sound of Houbansetter	Shetld	HU3460	60°19·6′	1°22·6′W	W	2,3
Sound of Hoxa	Orkney	ND3993	58°49·5′	3°2·9′W	W	7
Sound of Hoy	Shetld	HU3744	60°11·0′	1°19·5′W	W	4
Sound of Insh	Arg & Bt	NM7418	56°18·3′	5°38·8′W	W	55
Sound of Iona	Arg & Bt	NM2923	56°19·6′	6°22·6′W	W	48
Sound of Islay	Arg & Bt	NR4371	55°52·1′	6°6·0′W	W	60,61
Sound of Jura	Arg & Bt	NR6683	55°59·2′	5°44·7′W	W	55,61
Sound of Kerrera	Arg & Bt	NM8227	56°23·4′	5°31·5′W	W	49
Sound of Longataing	Orkney	HY4531	59°10·0′	2°57·2′W	W	5,6
Sound of Luing	Arg & Bt	NM7209	56°13·4′	5°40·2′W	W	55
Sound of Mingulay	N Eil	NL5885	56°50·1′	7°36·1′W	W	31
Sound of Monach	N Eil	NF7063	57°32·5′	7°30·5′W	W	18
Sound of Monach (Caolas Mhonach)		NF7062	57°31·9′	7°30·4′W	W	22
Sound of Mull		NM5549	56°34·4′	5°58·9′W	W	47,48
Sound of Mull	Arg & Bt	NM6940	56°30·0′	5°44·8′W	W	49
Sound of Orfasay	Shetld	HU4978	60°29·2′	1°6·0′W	W	2,3
Sound of Orosay	N Eil	NF7006	57°1·9′	7°25·9′W	W	31
Sound of Pabbay	N Eil	NL6288	56°51·9′	7°32·4′W	W	31
Sound of Papa	Shetld	HU1758	60°18·6′	1°41·0′W	W	3
Sound of Pladda	N Ayr	NS0320	55°26·3′	5°6·4′W	W	69
Sound of Raasay	Highld	NG5554	57°30·9′	6°5·0′W	W	24
Sound of Rhum	Highld	NM4290	56°56·0′	6°14·0′W	W	39
Sound of Sanda	Arg & Bt	NR7106	55°17·9′	5°36·0′W	X	68
Sound of Sandray	N Eil	NL6393	56°54·6′	7°31·8′W	W	31
Sound of Shiant or Caolas nan Eilean	N Eil	NB3701	57°55·5′	6°26·0′W	W	14
Sound of Shillay	N Eil	NF8890	57°47·7′	7°14·6′W	W	18
Sound of Shuna	Arg & Bt	NM9249	56°35·5′	5°22·8′W	W	49
Sound of Sleat	Highld	NG6703	57°3·8′	5°50·1′W	W	32
Sound of Sleat	Highld	NG7209	57°7·2′	5°45·5′W	W	33
Sound of Stack	N Eil	NF7908	57°3·3′	7°17·2′W	W	31
Sound of Stromay	N Eil	NF9888	57°47·1′	7°4·4′W	W	18
Sound of Taransay	N Eil	NG0499	57°53·2′	6°59·2′W	W	18
Sound of the Green Holms	Orkney	HY5226	59°7·4′	2°49·8′W	W	5,6
Sound of Ulva	Arg & Bt	NM4439	56°28·7′	6°9·0′W	W	47,48
Sound of Vatersay	N Eil	NL6297	56°56·7′	7°33·1′W	W	31
Sound Plantation	Norf	TG4320	52°43·6′	1°36·3′E	F	134
Sound, The	C of Plym	SX4752	50°21·1′	4°8·7′W	W	201
Sound, The	D & G	NX6543	54°46·1′	4°5·5′W	W	83,84
Soundwell	S Glos	ST6575	51°28·6′	2°29·8′W	T	172
Sourbank	Moray	NJ0756	57°35·3′	3°32·9′W	X	27
Sour Beck	N Yks	SE2097	54°22·3′	1°41·1′W	W	99
Sourbutts Fm	Ches	SJ9266	53°11·7′	2°6·8′W	FM	118
Sourby	N Yks	SE1653	53°58·6′	1°44·9′W	X	104
Source of Afon Tywi	Cered	SN8063	52°15·4′	3°45·1′W	W	147
Source of Little Ouse River	Suff	TM0378	52°22·0′	0°59·3′E	W	144
Source of Loughor	Carm	SN6617	51°50·4′	3°56·3′W	W	159
Source of River Carron	E Dunb	NS6381	56°0·4′	4°11·4′W	W	64
Source of River Ithon	Powys	SO1084	52°27·0′	3°19·1′W	W	136
Source of River Lea or Lee	Luton	TL0624	51°54·5′	0°27·1′W	W	166
Source of River Lugg	Powys	SO1774	52°21·7′	3°12·7′W	W	136,148
Source of River Severn	Powys	SN8289	52°29·4′	3°43·9′W	W	135,136
Source of River Teme	Powys	SO1284	52°27·1′	3°17·3′W	W	136
Source of River Tweed or Tweed's Well	Scot Bord	NT0514	55°24·9′	3°29·6′W	W	78
Source of River Waveney	Suff	TM0478	52°21·9′	1°0·2′E	W	144
Source of River Wye	Powys	SN8087	52°28·3′	3°45·6′W	W	135,136
Source of Tawe	Powys	SN8321	51°52·8′	3°41·6′W	W	160
Source of the Afton	E Ayr	NS6401	55°17·3′	4°8·1′W	W	77
Source of the Leven	N Yks	NZ6107	54°27·5′	1°3·1′W	W	94
Source of The Mule	Powys	SO1085	52°27·6′	3°19·1′W	W	136
Source of the Nith	E Ayr	NS5506	55°19·9′	4°16·7′W	W	71,77
Source of the River Dart	Devon	SS8816	50°56·2′	3°35·3′W	W	181
Source of the River Fowey	Corn	SX1780	50°35·7′	4°34·8′W	W	201
Source of the River Itchen	Hants	SU5827	51°2·6′	1°10·0′W	W	185
Source of the River Test	Hants	SU5349	51°14·5′	1°14·1′W	W	185
Source of the River Thames	Glos	ST9899	51°41·6′	2°1·3′W	W	163
Source of Usk	Carm	SN8123	51°53·8′	3°43·4′W	W	160
Sourdenhead	Moray	NJ2852	57°33·4′	3°11·7′W	X	28
Sourfoot Fell	Cumbr	NY1323	54°35·9′	3°20·4′W	X	89
Sourhall	Cald	SD9124	53°43·0′	2°7·8′W	X	103
Sour Hill	D & G	NX6753	54°51·5′	4°3·9′W	H	83,84
Sourhope	Scot Bord	NT8420	55°28·7′	2°14·8′W	T	74
Sourhope Burn	Scot Bord	NT8521	55°29·2′	2°13·8′W	W	74
Sour Howes	Cumbr	NY4203	54°25·4′	2°53·2′W	H	90
Sourin	Orkney	HY4331	59°10·0′	2°59·3′W	T	5,6
Sour Leys Fm	N Yks	SE5788	54°17·3′	1°7·0′W	FM	100
Sourlie	N Ayr	NS3441	55°38·3′	4°37·8′W	T	70
Sourlies	Highld	NM8695	57°0·1′	5°31·0′W	X	33,40
Sour Milk Gill	Cumbr	NY1615	54°31·6′	3°17·5′W	W	89
Sour Milk Gill	Cumbr	NY2212	54°30·1′	3°11·8′W	W	89,90
Sour Milk Gill	Cumbr	NY3108	54°28·0′	3°3·5′W	W	90
Sour Milk Hills	N Yks	SE5494	54°20·6′	1°9·7′W	X	100
Sourmire Moor	N Yks	SE1178	54°12·1′	1°49·5′W	X	99
Sour Nook	Cumbr	NY3740	54°45·3′	2°58·3′W	T	85
Sour Nook	N Yks	SE1099	54°23·4′	1°50·3′W	X	99
Soursike Fm	N Yks	NZ3505	54°26·6′	1°27·2′W	FM	93
Sourton	Devon	SX5390	50°41·7′	4°4·5′W	T	191
Sourton Down	Devon	SX5491	50°42·3′	4°3·7′W	X	191
Sourton Tors	Devon	SX5489	50°41·2′	4°3·6′W	H	191
Soussons Down	Devon	SX6779	50°36·0′	3°52·4′W	H	191
Soussons Fm	Devon	SX6879	50°36·0′	3°51·5′W	FM	191
Souter	Scot Bord	NT8670	55°55·6′	2°13·0′W	X	67
Souterford	Aberd	NJ7822	57°17·5′	2°21·4′W	X	38
Soutergate	Cumbr	SD2281	54°13·4′	3°11·4′W	X	96
Souter Head	C of Aber	NJ9601	57°6·3′	2°3·5′W	X	38
Souterhill	Aberd	NJ8208	57°10·0′	2°17·4′W	X	38
Souter Johnnie's Cottage	S Ayr	NS2407	55°19·8′	4°46·0′W	X	70,76
Souter Lighthouse	S Tyne	NZ4064	54°58·4′	1°22·1′W	X	88
Soutermoor	Cumbr	NY4871	55°2·1′	2°48·4′W	X	86
Souter Point	S Tyne	NZ4162	54°57·3′	1°21·2′W	X	88
Souterrain	Fife	NO5000	56°11·7′	2°47·9′W	X	59
Souterrain	N Eil	NB5163	58°29·3′	6°15·9′W	A	8
Souterrain	Shetld	HU5139	60°8·2′	1°4·4′W	A	4
Souterrains	Orkney	ND2373	58°38·5′	3°19·1′W	X	7
Souter's Croft Wood	D & G	NX4855	54°52·3′	4°21·7′W	F	83
Souter's Grave	D & G	NX9490	55°11·8′	3°39·5′W	X	78
Souterstead	Cumbr	SD2793	54°19·9′	3°6·9′W	X	96,97
Souterton	Aberd	NJ5945	57°29·9′	2°40·6′W	X	29
South Acre	Norf	TF8114	52°41·8′	0°41·1′E	T	132
South Acre Fm	E Yorks	SE7342	53°52·4′	0°53·0′W	FM	105,106
South Acton	Ealing	TQ1979	51°30·1′	0°16·7′W	T	176
South Acton	Northum	NU1801	55°18·4′	1°42·6′W	X	81
South Airfield Fm	Notts	SK8155	53°5·4′	0°47·0′W	FM	121
South Airmyn Grange	E Yorks	SE7322	53°41·6′	0°53·3′W	X	105,106,112
South Aittit	Orkney	HY4219	59°3·5′	3°0·2′W	X	6
South Alkham	Kent	TR2441	51°7·7′	1°12·5′E	T	179,189
Southall	Ealing	TQ1280	51°30·7′	0°22·8′W	T	176

South Allans	Aberd	NJ9114	57°13·3′	2°8·5′W	X	38
South Allenford Fm	Hants	SU0817	50°57·4′	1°52·8′W	FM	184
South Aller	Devon	SS6927	51°1·9′	3°51·7′W	X	180
South Allerton	S Lanak	NS5951	55°44·2′	4°14·3′W	X	64
Southall Fm	Worcs	SO8665	52°17·2′	2°11·9′W	FM	150
Southall Ho	Shrops	SO7278	52°24·2′	2°24·3′W	X	138
South Allington	Devon	SX7938	50°14·0′	3°41·4′W	T	202
South Alloa	Falk	NS8791	56°6·2′	3°48·6′W	T	58
Southam	Cumbr	NX9912	54°29·8′	3°33·2′W	T	89
Southam	E Susx	TQ3818	50°56·9′	0°1·7′W	X	198
Southam	Glos	SO9725	51°55·6′	2°2·2′W	T	163
Southam	Warw	SP4162	52°15·5′	1°23·6′W	T	151
South Ambersham	W Susx	SU9120	50°58·6′	0°41·8′W	T	197
Southam de la Bere	Glos	SO9725	51°55·6′	2°2·2′W	A	163
Southam Fields	Warw	SP4361	52°15·0′	1°21·8′W	X	151
Southam Holt	Warw	SP4360	52°14·4′	1°21·8′W	X	151
Southampton	C of Soton	SU4213	50°55·1′	1°23·8′W	T	196
Southampton Common	C of Soton	SU4114	50°55·7′	1°24·6′W	X	196
Southampton (Eastleigh) Airport	Hants	SU4517	50°57·3′	1°21·2′W	X	185
Southampton Fm	I of M	SC3473	54°7·8′	4°32·0′W	FM	95
Southampton Water	Hants	SU4606	50°51·3′	1°20·4′W	W	196
South Andet	Aberd	NJ8334	57°24·0′	2°16·5′W	X	29,30
Southannan	N Ayr	NS2053	55°44·5′	4°51·6′W	X	63
Southannan Mains	N Ayr	NS2153	55°44·5′	4°50·7′W	X	63
Southannan Sands	N Ayr	NS1953	55°44·5′	4°52·6′W	X	63
South Anston	Roth	SK5183	53°20·7′	1°13·6′W	T	111,120
South Arcan	Highld	NH4952	57°32·2′	4°30·9′W	X	26
South Ardachy	Highld	NH2100	57°3·6′	4°56·7′W	X	34
South Arditte	Pth & Kin	NO0128	56°26·3′	3°35·9′W	X	52,53,58
South Ardo	Angus	NO6262	56°45·1′	2°36·8′W	X	45
South Ardoyne	Aberd	NJ6427	57°20·2′	2°35·4′W	X	37
South Ardwell	D & G	NX0744	54°45·5′	4°59·5′W	X	82
South Artrochie	Aberd	NK0030	57°21·9′	1°59·5′W	X	30
South Ascot	Win & Maid	SU9267	51°23·9′	0°40·3′W	T	175
South Ascrib	Highld	NG3063	57°34·8′	6°30·6′W	X	23
South Ashford	Kent	TR0041	51°8·2′	0°51·9′E	T	189
South Ash Manor	Kent	TQ5963	51°20·9′	0°17·4′E	A	177,188
South Auchenbrain	E Ayr	NS5230	55°32·7′	4°20·3′W	X	70
South Auchenmade	N Ayr	NS3348	55°42·1′	4°39·0′W	X	63
South Auchinclech	Aberd	NJ8208	57°10·0′	2°17·4′W	X	38
South Auchmachar	Aberd	NJ9549	57°32·1′	2°4·6′W	X	30
South Auchmachor	Aberd	NJ9549	57°32·1′	2°4·6′W	X	30
South Auchnavaird	Aberd	NJ9439	57°26·7′	2°5·5′W	X	30
South Auchray	Angus	NO3634	56°29·9′	3°1·9′W	X	54
South Auchronie	Aberd	NJ8109	57°10·5′	2°18·4′W	X	38
Southay	Somer	ST2708	50°52·2′	3°1·9′W	X	193
Southay	Somer	ST4319	50°58·3′	2°48·3′W	T	193
South Ayre	Shetld	HU4471	60°25·5′	1°11·6′W	X	2,3
South Aywick	Shetld	HU5386	60°33·5′	1°1·5′W	T	1,2,3
South Backhill	Aberd	NJ7839	57°26·7′	2°21·5′W	X	29,30
South Baddesley	Hants	SZ3596	50°46·0′	1°29·8′W	T	196
South Baldutho	Fife	NO5006	56°14·9′	2°48·0′W	X	59
South Balfern	D & G	NX4450	54°49·5′	4°25·3′W	X	83
South Balkeith	Highld	NH7981	57°48·4′	4°1·7′W	X	21
South Ballachulish	Highld	NN0459	56°41·2′	5°11·6′W	T	41
South Ballaird	S Ayr	NX1187	55°8·7′	4°57·5′W	X	76
South Ballo	Pth & Kin	NO2634	56°29·8′	3°11·7′W	X	53
South Balloch	S Ayr	NX3295	55°13·5′	4°38·1′W	X	76
South Balluderon	Angus	NO3738	56°32·0′	3°1·0′W	X	54
South Balmakelly	Aberd	NO6967	56°47·9′	2°30·0′W	X	45
South Balmoor	Aberd	NK1046	57°30·5′	1°49·5′W	X	30
South Balnoon	Aberd	NJ6343	57°28·8′	2°36·6′W	X	29
South Balquhindachy	Aberd	NJ8541	57°27·8′	2°14·5′W	X	30
Southbank	Aberd	NJ7908	57°10·0′	2°20·4′W	X	38
South Bank	Gwyn	SH5534	52°53·3′	4°8·9′W	X	124
South Bank	Gwyn	SH6014	52°42·6′	4°3·9′W	X	124
Southbank	N Ayr	NR9921	55°26·8′	5°10·3′W	X	69
South Bank	Red & Cl	NZ5320	54°34·6′	1°10·4′W	T	93
South Bank	York	SE5950	53°56·8′	1°5·6′W	T	105
South Bankend	S Lanak	NS7833	55°34·8′	3°55·7′W	X	71
South Bankhead	Falk	NS8973	55°56·5′	3°46·2′W	X	65
South Bank Wood	Midlo	NT2259	55°49·3′	3°14·3′W	F	66,73
Southbar	Renf	NS4569	55°53·6′	4°28·3′W	X	64
South Barff fm	Lincs	TA0400	53°29·4′	0°25·5′W	FM	112
South Barham	Kent	TR1948	51°11·6′	1°8·5′E	X	179,189
South Barn	Dorset	SZ0078	50°36·3′	1°59·6′W	X	195
South Barn Fm	Lincs	SK9653	53°4·2′	0°33·6′W	FM	121
South Barnkirk	D & G	NX3965	54°57·5′	4°30·4′W	X	83
South Barns	Aberd	NO6968	56°48·4′	2°30·0′W	X	45
South Barns	Pth & Kin	NO0735	56°30·1′	3°30·2′W	X	52,53
South Barr	N Ayr	NS3651	55°43·7′	4°36·3′W	X	63
South Barrow	Somer	ST6027	51°2·7′	2°33·9′W	T	183
South Barrule	I of M	SC2575	54°8·7′	4°40·3′W	H	95
South Barrule Plantation	I of M	SC2776	54°9·3′	4°38·5′W	F	95
South Barsalloch	D & G	NX3541	54°44·5′	4°33·4′W	X	83
South Barton	Devon	SX5450	50°20·1′	4°2·7′W	X	201
South Bay	Arg & Bt	NR8671	55°53·3′	5°24·9′W	W	62
South Bay	N Ayr	NS2341	55°38·1′	4°48·3′W	W	70
South Bay	N Yks	TA0487	54°16·3′	0°23·8′W	W	101
South Bay	Orkney	HY6001	58°53·9′	2°41·2′W	W	6
South Bay	Orkney	HY7551	59°20·9′	2°25·9′W	W	5
South Bay	S Ayr	NS3130	55°32·3′	4°40·3′W	W	70
South Bay of Eswick	Shetld	HU4853	60°15·8′	1°7·5′W	W	3
South Beach	Norf	TG5304	52°34·7′	1°44·5′E	X	134
South Beach	Northum	NZ3279	55°6·5′	1°29·5′W	T	88
South Beachmore	Arg & Bt	NR6841	55°36·7′	5°40·6′W	X	62
South Beach or Marian-y-de	Gwyn	SH3734	52°53·0′	4°24·9′W	T	123
South Beck	Lincs	TF0737	52°55·4′	0°24·1′W	W	130
South Beddington	Sutton	TQ2963	51°21·3′	0°8·4′W	T	176,187
South Beer	Corn	SX3091	50°41·9′	4°24·1′W	X	190
South Beer	Devon	SX3598	50°45·7′	4°20·0′W	X	190
South Beer Fm	Devon	SX7094	50°44·1′	3°50·2′W	FM	191
South Bellsdyke	Falk	NS9084	56°2·4′	3°45·5′W	X	65
South Bellyeoman	Fife	NT1088	56°4·8′	3°26·3′W	X	65
South Belton	E Loth	NT6576	55°58·8′	2°33·2′W	X	67
Southbelt Plantn	E Yorks	SE9948	53°55·4′	0°29·1′W	F	106
South Benelip	Shetld	HU6669	60°24·2′	0°47·6′W	X	2
South Benfleet	Essex	TQ7786	51°32·9′	0°33·6′E	T	178

South Bentley Inclosure	Hants	SU2312	50°54·7′	1°40·0′W	F	195
South Bents	Sund	NZ4060	54°56·2′	1°22·1′W	T	88
South Bersted	W Susx	SU9300	50°47·8′	0°40·4′W	T	197
South Biggart	N Ayr	NS4053	55°44·9′	4°32·5′W	X	64
South Bight of Rovahead	Shetld	HU4745	60°11·5′	1°8·7′W	W	4
South Binness Island	Hants	SU6903	50°49·6′	1°0·8′W	X	197
South Bishop or Em-sger	Pemb	SM6522	51°51·1′	5°24·3′W	X	157
South Bishops Den	Kent	TR0857	51°16·7′	0°59·3′E	F	179
South Blachrie	Aberd	NJ7843	57°28·9′	2°21·6′W	X	29,30
South Blackbog	Aberd	NJ7932	57°22·9′	2°20·5′W	X	29,30
South Black Burn	N Ayr	NS2465	55°51·0′	4°48·3′W	W	63
South Black Hill	Midlo	NT1960	55°49·8′	3°17·2′W	H	65,66
South Blackwater	Aberd	NK0953	57°34·3′	1°50·5′W	X	30
South Blainslie	Scot Bord	NT5443	55°41·0′	2°43·5′W	T	73
South Bockhampton	Dorset	SZ1795	50°45·5′	1°45·2′W	T	195
South Bodiechell	Aberd	NJ7843	57°28·9′	2°21·6′W	X	29,30
South Bogbain	Moray	NJ3951	57°33·0′	3°0·7′W	X	28
South Boggiehead	Aberd	NJ6655	57°35·3′	2°33·7′W	X	29
Southbogs	Aberd	NJ6022	57°17·5′	2°39·4′W	X	37
South Boisdale	N Eil	NF7417	57°8·0′	7°22·9′W	T	31
South Border	N Ayr	NS3652	55°44·3′	4°36·3′W	X	63
South Boreland	D & G	NX1757	54°52·7′	4°50·7′W	X	82
Southborough	Brom	TQ4267	51°23·3′	0°2·8′E	T	177
Southborough	Kent	TQ5842	51°9·5′	0°16·0′E	T	188
Southborough	King	TQ1866	51°23·1′	0°17·9′W	T	176
Southbourne	Bourne	SZ1491	50°43·3′	1°47·7′W	T	195
Southbourne	W Susx	SU7605	50°50·6′	0°54·8′W	T	197
South Bowhill Fm	Fife	NO4508	56°15·9′	2°52·8′W	FM	59
South Bowood	Dorset	SY4498	50°47·0′	2°47·3′W	T	193
South Brachmont	Aberd	NO8194	57°2·5′	2°18·3′W	T	38,45
South Brackenridge	S Lanak	NS7638	55°37·4′	3°57·7′W	X	71
South Bradieston	Aberd	NO7368	56°48·4′	2°26·1′W	X	45
South Bradon Fm	Somer	ST3618	50°57·7′	2°54·3′W	FM	193
South Braeside of Ludquharn	Aberd	NK0343	57°28·9′	1°56·5′W	X	30
South Bramwith	Donc	SE6211	53°35·8′	1°3·4′W	T	111
South Branchal	Inverc	NS3466	55°51·8′	4°38·7′W	X	63
South Brandon Fm	Durham	NZ2038	54°44·4′	1°40·9′W	FM	93
South Bray	Devon	SS6624	51°0·2′	3°54·2′W	X	180
South Breck	Orkney	HY3916	59°1·9′	3°3·3′W	X	6
South Breckbie	Orkney	HY2426	59°7·1′	3°19·2′W	X	6
South Breckenholme	N Yks	SE8359	54°1·5′	0°43·6′W	X	106
South Brent	Devon	SX6960	50°25·7′	3°50·3′W	T	202
South Brewham	Somer	ST7236	51°7·6′	2°23·6′W	T	183
South Brideswell	Aberd	NJ5110	57°11·0′	2°48·2′W	X	37
South Briggs	Aberd	NJ6651	57°33·1′	2°33·6′W	X	29
South Bromley	T Ham	TQ3881	51°30·9′	0°0·3′W	T	177
South Brook	Beds	TL1355	52°11·1′	0°20·4′W	W	153
Southbrook	Devon	SX8179	50°36·2′	3°40·5′W	X	191
Southbrook	Devon	SX9780	50°36·9′	3°27·0′W	X	192
Southbrook	Devon	SY0296	50°45·6′	3°23·0′W	X	192
Southbrook	Wilts	ST8131	51°4·9′	2°15·9′W	T	183
South Brooks	Kent	TR0218	50°55·8′	0°52·9′E	X	189
South Broomage	Falk	NS8681	56°0·8′	3°49·3′W	T	65
South Broomford	Northum	NU1925	55°31·4′	1°41·5′W	X	75
South Broomhill	Aberd	NJ6046	57°30·4′	2°39·6′W	X	29
South Broomhill	Northum	NZ2599	55°17·3′	1°36·0′W	T	81
South Brownhill	Aberd	NJ6451	57°33·1′	2°35·6′W	X	29
South Brownhill	S Lanak	NS6542	55°39·4′	4°8·3′W	X	71
South Buchanty	Pth & Kin	NN9327	56°25·6′	3°43·6′W	X	52,58
South Buckland Fms	Dorset	SY6581	50°37·9′	2°29·3′W	FM	194
South Burdon	Darl	NZ3315	54°32·0′	1°29·0′W	X	93
Southburgh	Norf	TG0004	52°36·0′	0°57·6′E	T	144
South Burlingham	Norf	TG3707	52°36·8′	1°30·5′E	T	134
Southburn	D & G	NY1881	55°7·2′	3°16·7′W	X	79
South Burn	Durham	NZ2549	54°50·4′	1°36·2′W	W	88
Southburn	E Yorks	SE9954	53°58·6′	0°29·0′W	T	106
South Burn	N Ayr	NS2653	55°44·6′	4°45·9′W	W	63
South Burn	Orkney	ND2299	58°52·5′	3°20·7′W	W	6,7
South Burn	Shetld	HU2846	60°12·1′	1°29·2′W	W	4
Southburn Beck	E Yorks	SE9854	53°58·6′	0°29·9′W	W	106
South Burn of Burrafirth	Shetld	HU3656	60°17·5′	1°20·4′W	W	2,3
South Burn of Lumbister	Shetld	HU4895	60°38·4′	1°6·8′W	W	1,2
South Burn of Murrion	Shetld	HU2579	60°29·9′	1°32·2′W	W	3
South Burnside	Aberd	NJ9036	57°25·1′	2°9·5′W	X	30
South Burnt Hill	N Ayr	NS2565	55°51·0′	4°47·3′W	X	63
South Burrow Cott	Devon	SS4633	51°4·8′	4°11·5′W	X	180
Southbury Fm	Glos	SO9913	51°49·2′	2°0·5′W	FM	163
South Cadbury	Somer	ST6325	51°1·6′	2°31·3′W	T	183
South Cadeby Village	Lincs	TF2487	53°22·2′	0°7·8′W	A	113,122
South Cairn	D & G	NW9769	54°58·7′	5°9·9′W	X	82
South Calder Water	N Lanak	NS7657	55°47·7′	3°58·2′W	W	64
South Calder Water	N Lanak	NS8658	55°48·4′	3°48·7′W	W	65,72
South Califf	Shetld	HU4445	60°11·5′	1°11·9′W	X	4
South Callange	Fife	NO4211	56°17·5′	2°55·8′W	X	59
South Camaloun	Aberd	NJ7539	57°26·7′	2°24·5′W	X	29
South Camphill	N Ayr	NS2754	55°45·2′	4°45·0′W	X	63
South Cape	I of M	SC4383	54°13·4′	4°24·1′W	X	95
South Cara	Orkney	ND4792	58°49·0′	2°54·6′W	X	7
South Carlton	Lincs	SK9576	53°16·6′	0°34·1′W	T	121
South Carlton	Notts	SK5983	53°20·7′	1°6·4′W	T	111,120
South Carne	Corn	SX2081	50°36·3′	4°32·3′W	T	201
South Carolina	N Yks	SE5067	54°6·0′	1°13·7′W	X	100
South Carr	Lincs	SE8300	53°29·6′	0°44·5′W	X	112
South Carr Fm	N Lincs	SK7296	53°27·6′	0°54·5′W	FM	112
South Carr Fm	Notts	SK5572	53°14·8′	1°10·1′W	FM	120
South Carse	D & G	NX9959	54°55·2′	3°34·1′W	X	84
South Carthat	D & G	NY0576	55°4·4′	3°28·8′W	X	85
South Cartington	Northum	NU0303	55°19·5′	1°56·7′W	X	81
South Cassingray	Fife	NO4807	56°15·4′	2°49·9′W	X	59
South Castlehill	D & G	NX9274	55°3·2′	3°41·0′W	X	84
South Cathkin Fm	S Lanak	NS6257	55°47·5′	4°11·6′W	FM	64
South Cave	E Yorks	SE9231	53°46·3′	0°35·8′W	T	106
South Cerney	Glos	SU0497	51°40·5′	1°56·1′W	T	163
South Chailey	E Susx	TQ3917	50°56·4′	0°0·9′W	T	198
South Channel		TR3272	51°24·2′	1°20·5′E	W	179
South Channel	Cumbr	SD2964	54°4·3′	3°4·7′W	W	96,97
South Channel	Essex	TL9810	51°45·4′	0°52·5′E	W	168
South Channel	Highld	NM6286	56°54·5′	5°54·1′W	W	40
South Channel	Highld	NM6572	56°47·1′	5°50·4′W	W	40

South Channel	N Lincs	SE9621	53°40·8′	0°32·4′W	W	106,112
South Chard	Somer	ST3205	50°50·7′	2°57·6′W	T	193
South Charford Fm	Hants	SU1618	50°57·9′	1°45·9′W	FM	184
South Charlton	Northum	NU1620	55°28·7′	1°44·4′W	T	75
South Charlton Bog	Northum	NU1719	55°28·1′	1°43·4′W	X	81
South Charlton Fm	Northum	NU1619	55°28·1′	1°44·4′W	FM	81
South Cheek or Old Peak	N Yks	NZ9802	54°24·5′	0°29·0′W	X	94
South Cheriton	Somer	ST6924	51°1·1′	2°26·1′W	T	183
South Cheshire Way	Ches	SJ7453	53°4·7′	2°22·9′W	X	118
South Cheshire Way	Shrops	SJ5343	52°59·2′	2°41·6′W	X	117
South Church	Durham	NZ2128	54°39·0′	1°40·0′W	T	93
Southchurch	Sou-on-Sea	TQ9085	51°32·1′	0°44·8′E	T	178
South Clarewood	Northum	NZ0268	55°0·6′	1°57·7′W	X	87
South Cleatlam	Durham	NZ1218	54°33·7′	1°48·4′W	X	92
South Clettraval	N Eil	NF7471	57°36·9′	7°27·1′W	H	18
South Cliff	E Yorks	TA2146	53°54·0′	0°9·1′W	X	107
South Cliff	Kent	TR3967	51°21·3′	1°26·4′E	X	179
South Cliffe	E Yorks	SE8736	53°49·0′	0°40·3′W	T	106
South Cliffe Common	E Yorks	SE8635	53°48·5′	0°41·2′W	X	106
South Cliff Fm	N Lincs	TA0022	53°41·3′	0°28·7′W	FM	106,107,112
South Clifton	Notts	SK8270	53°13·5′	0°45·9′W	T	121
South Clough	Oldham	SE0307	53°33·8′	1°56·9′W	X	110
South Clunes	Highld	NH5541	57°26·4′	4°24·5′W	T	26
South Clutag	D & G	NX3752	54°50·4′	4°31·9′W	X	83
South Coast Cycle Route	W Susx	SU8900	50°47·8′	0°43·8′W	X	197
South Coast Cycle Route	W Susx	TQ1602	50°48·6′	0°20·8′W	X	197,198
South Cobbinshaw	W Loth	NT0157	55°48·0′	3°34·3′W	X	65,72
South Cockerham	Devon	SS7028	51°2·4′	3°50·9′W	X	180
South Cockerington	Lincs	TF3788	53°22·5′	0°4·0′E	T	113,122
South Cockerington Grange	Lincs	TF4290	53°23·5′	0°8·5′E	X	113
South Cocknage Fm	Staffs	SJ9140	52°57·7′	2°7·6′W	FM	118
South Cockspow	Stir	NS8391	56°6·1′	3°52·4′W	X	57
South Coldoch	Stir	NS7097	56°9·1′	4°5·1′W	X	57
South Coldstream	Aberd	NJ7800	57°5·7′	2°21·3′W	X	38
South Collafirth	Shetld	HU3482	60°31·5′	1°22·3′W	X	1,2,3
South Colleonard	Aberd	NJ6662	57°39·1′	2°33·7′W	X	29
South Collielaw	Aberd	NK1043	57°28·9′	1°49·5′W	X	30
Southcombe	Devon	SS4412	50°53·4′	4°12·7′W	X	180,190
Southcombe	Devon	SX7176	50°34·4′	3°48·9′W	X	191
Southcombe Fm	Devon	SS3503	50°48·4′	4°20·1′W	FM	190
Southcombe Fm	Devon	SX3976	50°33·9′	4°16·0′W	FM	201
Southcombe Hill	Devon	SX7593	50°43·6′	3°45·9′W	H	191
South Common	Devon	SS6944	51°11·1′	3°52·1′W	X	180
South Common	Devon	ST3001	50°48·5′	2°59·2′W	T	193
South Common	E Susx	TQ3817	50°56·4′	0°1·8′W	X	198
South Common	Lincs	SK9769	53°12·8′	0°32·4′W	X	121
South Common	Scot Bord	NT4827	55°32·3′	2°49·0′W	X	73
South Common	Somer	SS8044	51°11·2′	3°42·6′W	X	181
South Cookney	Aberd	NO8692	57°1·4′	2°13·4′W	T	38,45
South Coombe	Corn	SX3673	50°32·3′	4°18·5′W	X	201
South Coombe	Devon	SS7800	50°47·4′	3°43·5′W	X	191
South Coombe	Devon	SS8114	50°55·0′	3°41·2′W	X	181
South Coombe	Devon	SS8815	50°55·7′	3°35·2′W	X	181
Southcoombe	Devon	SS9505	50°50·3′	3°29·1′W	X	192
Southcoombe	Oxon	SP3327	51°56·7′	1°30·8′W	T	164
South Coombeshead	Corn	SX3572	50°31·7′	4°19·3′W	X	201
South Coos	Shetld	HP6715	60°49·0′	0°45·6′W	X	1
South Corbelly	D & G	NX9862	54°56·8′	3°35·1′W	X	84
South Cornelly	Brig	SS8180	51°30·6′	3°42·5′W	T	170
South Corriegills	N Ayr	NS0334	55°33·8′	5°7·0′W	T	69
South Corrielaw	D & G	NY1783	55°8·3′	3°17·7′W	T	79
South Corry	Highld	NM8352	56°36·8′	5°31·7′W	X	49
South Corse	Shetld	HU4543	60°10·4′	1°10·8′W	X	4
South Corston	Pth & Kin	NO2337	56°31·4′	3°14·6′W	X	53
South Cote	N Yks	SE2378	54°12·1′	1°38·4′W	X	99
Southcote	Read	SU6871	51°26·3′	1°0·9′W	T	175
South Cote	Scot Bord	NT7921	55°29·2′	2°19·5′W	X	74
Southcote Fm	Devon	ST2001	50°48·4′	3°7·7′W	FM	192,193
Southcote Mill	Read	SU6971	51°26·3′	1°0·0′W	X	175
Southcott	Corn	SX1995	50°43·8′	4°33·5′W	T	190
Southcott	Devon	SS4416	50°55·6′	4°12·8′W	T	180,190
Southcott	Devon	SS4627	51°1·5′	4°11·4′W	X	180
Southcott	Devon	SS6117	50°56·4′	3°58·3′W	X	180
Southcott	Devon	SS6306	50°50·5′	3°56·4′W	X	191
Southcott	Devon	SS7011	50°53·3′	3°50·5′W	X	191
Southcott	Devon	SS7505	50°50·1′	3°46·1′W	X	191
Southcott	Devon	SX5495	50°44·4′	4°3·8′W	X	191
Southcott	Devon	SX7580	50°36·6′	3°45·6′W	X	191
Southcott	Wilts	SU1759	51°20·0′	1°45·0′W	T	173
Southcott Barton	Devon	SS4822	50°58·9′	4°9·5′W	X	180
Southcott Fm	Devon	SS3502	50°47·9′	4°20·1′W	FM	190
Southcott Fm	Devon	SS6438	51°7·7′	3°56·2′W	FM	180
Southcott Fm	Devon	ST1107	50°51·6′	3°15·5′W	FM	192,193
Southcourt	Bucks	SP8112	51°48·3′	0°49·1′W	T	165
South Couston	W Loth	NS9570	55°55·0′	3°40·4′W	X	65
South Cove	Suff	TM4980	52°21·9′	1°39·9′E	T	156
South Cowshaw	D & G	NY0284	55°8·7′	3°31·8′W	X	78
South Crag	Cumbr	NY2510	54°29·0′	3°9·0′W	X	89,90
South Craig	Angus	NO2373	56°50·8′	3°15·3′W	X	44
Southcraig	E Ayr	NS4340	55°38·0′	4°29·2′W	X	70
South Craig	S Ayr	NS4215	55°24·5′	4°29·3′W	X	70
South Craighead	Aberd	NJ9939	57°26·7′	2°0·5′W	X	30
South Craigieford	Aberd	NJ9727	57°20·3′	2°2·5′W	X	38
South Craleckan	Arg & Bt	NN0200	56°9·4′	5°10·8′W	X	55
South Cranna	Aberd	NJ6452	57°33·7′	2°35·6′W	X	29
South Creagan	Arg & Bt	NM9743	56°32·4′	5°17·7′W	X	49
South Creake	Norf	TF8635	52°53·0′	0°46·3′E	T	132
Southcrest	Worcs	SP0366	52°17·8′	1°57·0′W	T	150
South Crichie	Aberd	NJ7834	57°24·0′	2°21·5′W	X	29,30
South Crooks	Renf	NS4368	55°53·0′	4°30·2′W	X	64
South Crosland	Kirk	SE1112	53°36·5′	1°49·6′W	T	110
South Cross	Devon	SY2794	50°44·7′	3°1·7′W	X	193
South Croxton	Leic	SK6810	52°41·2′	0°59·2′W	T	129
South Croydon	Croy	TQ3263	51°21·3′	0°5·9′W	T	176,177,187
South Cubbington Wood	Warw	SP3568	52°18·8′	1°28·8′W	F	151
South Cuil	Highld	NG3963	57°35·2′	6°21·6′W	T	23
South Culsh	Aberd	NJ8847	57°31·0′	2°11·6′W	X	30
South Cult	Fife	NT0295	56°8·5′	3°34·2′W	X	58

South Cumberhead	S Lanak	NS7734	55°35·3'	3°56·7'W	X	71
South Cushnie	Aberd	NJ7961	57°38·6'	2°20·6'W	X	29,30
South Dairy Mountain	Pemb	SN0116	51°48·7'	4°52·8'W	X	157,158
South Dale	N Yks	TA0875	54°9·8'	0°20·3'W	X	101
Southdale	Shetld	HU6091	60°36·1'	0°38·8'W	X	1,2
Southdale Fm	N Lincs	SE8920	53°40·4'	0°38·8'W	FM	106,112
South Dalton	E Yorks	SE9645	53°53·8'	0°31·9'W	T	106
South Dalton Wold	E Yorks	SE9444	53°53·3'	0°33·8'W	X	106
South Damhead	C of Aber	NJ9202	57°6·8'	2°7·5'W	X	38
South Darenth	Kent	TQ5669	51°24·1'	0°15·0'E	T	177
South Dean	Brad	SD9935	53°48·9'	2°0·5'W	X	103
Southdean	Scot Bord	NT6309	55°22·7'	2°34·6'W	T	80
Southdean Burn	Scot Bord	NT4304	55°19·9'	2°53·5'W	W	79
South Dean Fm	Devon	SS6448	51°13·1'	3°56·5'W	FM	180
Southdean Fm	W Susx	SU9421	50°59·1'	0°39·3'W	FM	197
Southdean Lodge	Scot Bord	NT6408	55°22·1'	2°33·6'W	X	80
Southdean Mill	Scot Bord	NT6310	55°23·2'	2°33·6'W	X	80
Southdean Rig	Scot Bord	NT4305	55°20·4'	2°53·5'W	H	79
Southdeanrig	Scot Bord	NT6408	55°22·1'	2°33·6'W	X	80
South Deep	Dorset	SZ0186	50°40·6'	1°58·8'W	W	195
South Deep	Kent	TQ9765	51°21·2'	0°50·2'E	W	178
South Deep	Pth & Kin	NO2218	56°21·1'	3°15·3'W	W	58
South Den	Angus	NO4845	56°35·9'	2°50·4'W	X	54
Southdene	Know	SJ4197	53°28·2'	2°52·9'W	T	108
South Denes	Norf	TG5304	52°34·7'	1°44·5'E	T	134
South Denhill	Aberd	NJ7935	57°24·6'	2°20·5'W	X	29,30
South Dennetys	Aberd	NO7086	56°58·1'	2°29·2'W	X	45
South Devon Coast Path	Devon	SX5348	50°19·1'	4°3·5'W	X	201
South Devon Rly	Devon	SX7664	50°28·0'	3°44·5'W	X	202
South Dike	Lincs	TF3991	53°24·1'	0°5·9'E	W	113
South Dike	Lincs	TF4292	53°24·6'	0°8·6'E	W	113
South Dinnicoombe	Corn	SX2196	50°44·4'	4°31·8'W	X	190
South Dissington	Northum	NZ1270	55°1·7'	1°48·3'W	X	88
South District	Norf	TL5298	52°33·7'	0°15·0'E	X	143
South Docken Bush	N Yks	SE3161	54°2·9'	1°31·2'W	X	99
South Dog	E Loth	NT5186	56°4·1'	2°46·8'W	X	66
South Doll	Stir	NS8787	56°4·0'	3°48·5'W	X	65
South Dornaford	Devon	SS5900	50°47·2'	3°59·6'W	X	191
Southdown	Bath & NE Somer	ST7363	51°22·2'	2°22·9'W	T	172
Southdown	Corn	SX4352	50°21·1'	4°12·0'W	T	201
Southdown	Devon	SS5323	50°59·5'	4°5·3'W	X	180
Southdown	Devon	SS6004	50°49·4'	3°58·9'W	X	191
Southdown	Devon	SS6215	50°55·3'	3°57·4'W	X	180
South Down	Devon	SS6646	51°12·1'	3°54·7'W	X	180
South Down	Devon	SX5591	50°42·3'	4°2·8'W	H	191
Southdown	Devon	SX6841	50°15·5'	3°50·7'W	X	202
South Down	Dorset	ST8006	50°51·4'	2°16·7'W	X	194
South Down	Hants	SU4624	51°1·0'	1°20·3'W	T	185
South Down	Hants	SU5438	51°8·6'	1°13·3'W	X	185
South Down	Somer	ST2012	50°54·4'	3°7·9'W	T	193
South Down	Wilts	ST8435	51°7·1'	2°13·3'W	X	183
South Down	Wilts	ST9821	50°59·5'	2°1·3'W	X	184
Southdown Cliff	Devon	SX9253	50°22·3'	3°30·7'W	X	202
South Down Common	Devon	SY2288	50°41·4'	3°5·9'W	X	192
Southdown Fm	Devon	SX6938	50°13·9'	3°49·8'W	FM	202
Southdown Fm	Devon	SX9153	50°22·3'	3°31·6'W	FM	202
South Down Fm	Dorset	SY7582	50°38·5'	2°20·8'W	FM	194
Southdown Fm	Glos	SP0622	51°54·0'	1°54·4'W	FM	163
Southdown Fm	Oxon	SU2591	51°37·3'	1°37·9'W	FM	163,174
Southdown Fm	Wilts	SU1024	51°1·1'	1°51·1'W	FM	184
Southdown Fms	Devon	ST0714	50°55·3'	3°19·0'W	FM	181
South Downs	Bri & Hov	TQ3109	50°52·2'	0°7·9'W	H	198
South Downs	Devon	SX7661	50°26·4'	3°44·4'W	X	202
South Downs	Devon	SX8556	50°23·8'	3°36·7'W	X	202
Southdowns	Hants	SU5934	51°6·4'	1°9·0'W	X	185
Southdowns	Kent	TQ5769	51°24·1'	0°15·8'E	X	177
South Downs	W Susx	SU8913	50°54·8'	0°43·7'W	H	197
South Down Sleight	Wilts	ST9247	51°13·6'	2°6·5'W	X	184
South Downs Way	E Susx	TV5397	50°45·4'	0°10·5'E	X	199
South Downs Way	W Susx	SU8616	50°56·4'	0°46·2'W	X	197
South Downs Way	W Susx	TQ3012	50°53·8'	0°8·7'W	X	198
South Draffan	S Lanak	NS7945	55°41·3'	3°55·0'W	X	64
South Drain	Somer	ST3842	51°10·7'	2°52·8'W	W	182
South Dron	Fife	NO4217	56°20·8'	2°55·9'W	X	59
South Dronley	Angus	NO3435	56°30·4'	3°3·9'W	X	54
South Drove Drain	Lincs	TF1812	52°41·8'	0°14·8'W	W	130,142
South Drove Drain	Lincs	TF2316	52°43·9'	0°10·3'W	W	131
South Druimachro Fm	Arg & Bt	NR6447	55°39·8'	5°44·7'W	FM	62
South Drum	Falk	NS8377	55°58·6'	3°52·1'W	X	65
South Drumboy	E Ayr	NS4948	55°42·4'	4°23·8'W	X	64
South Drumloch	S Lanak	NS6750	55°43·8'	4°6·6'W	X	64
South Duffield	N Yks	SE6833	53°47·6'	0°57·6'W	T	105,106
South Dumbuils	Pth & Kin	NO0916	56°19·9'	3°27·9'W	X	58
South Dumpston	Aberd	NK0249	57°32·1'	1°57·7'W	X	30
South Dunn	Highld	ND1955	58°28·8'	3°22·9'W	X	11,12
South Duryard	Devon	SX8996	50°45·4'	3°34·0'W	X	192
South Dyke	N Yks	SE4437	53°49·9'	1°19·5'W	A	105
South Dyke Fm	N Yks	SE1292	54°19·6'	1°48·5'W	FM	99
South Earlswood	Surrey	TQ2747	51°12·7'	0°10·5'W	T	187
Southease	E Susx	TQ4205	50°49·8'	0°1·4'E	T	198
Southease Hill	E Susx	TQ4103	50°48·8'	0°0·5'E	X	198
South East Fm	Northum	NU1908	55°22·2'	1°41·6'W	FM	81
South East Fm	Northum	NZ1273	55°3·3'	1°48·3'W	FM	88
South East Fullarton	Pth & Kin	NO3044	56°35·2'	3°7·9'W	X	53
South East Point	Cumbr	SD2361	54°2·6'	3°10·1'W	X	96
South Eau Fm	Lincs	TF2608	52°39·5'	0°7·8'W	FM	142
South Egliston	Dorset	SY8979	50°36·9'	2°8·9'W	X	195
South Elkington	Lincs	TF2988	53°22·6'	0°3·2'W	T	113,122
South Elmham Hall	Suff	TM3083	52°24·0'	1°23·3'E	X	156
South Elmsall	Wakf	SE4711	53°35·8'	1°17·0'W	T	111
South Elphinstone	E Loth	NT3970	55°55·4'	2°58·1'W	T	66
South Emlett	Devon	SS8007	50°51·2'	3°41·9'W	X	191
Southenay Fm	Kent	TR0939	51°6·9'	0°59·6'E	FM	179,189
Southend	Aberd	NJ7148	57°31·5'	2°28·6'W	X	29
Southend	Arg & Bt	NR6908	55°19·0'	5°38·0'W	T	68
South End	Beds	TL0448	52°7·5'	0°28·5'W	T	153
South End	Bucks	SP8525	51°55·3'	0°45·4'W	T	165
South End	Bucks	SP9519	51°51·9'	0°36·8'W	X	165
Southend	Bucks	SU7589	51°35·9'	0°54·6'W	T	175

South End	Cumbr	SD2063	54°3·7'	3°12·9'W	T	96
South End	E Yorks	TA1940	53°50·8'	0°11·1'W	T	107
South End	E Yorks	TA3918	53°38·6'	0°6·6'E	X	113
Southend	Glos	ST7495	51°39·4'	2°22·2'W	T	162
South End	Hants	SU1015	50°56·3'	1°51·1'W	T	184
Southend	Hants	SU6113	50°55·0'	1°7·5'W	X	196
South End	Heref	SO7344	52°5·9'	2°23·3'W	X	150
South-end	Herts	TL4316	51°49·7'	0°4·9'E	X	167
South End	Leic	SK5814	52°43·5'	1°8·1'W	X	129
Southend	Lew	TQ3871	51°25·5'	0°0·5'W	T	177
South End	N Lincs	TA1120	53°40·1'	0°18·8'W	T	107,113
South End	Norf	TL9990	52°28·5'	0°56·2'E	T	144
South End	N Yks	SE5717	53°39·0'	1°7·8'W	X	111
Southend	Oxon	SP5801	51°42·5'	1°9·2'W	T	164
Southend	W Berks	SU4278	51°30·2'	1°23·3'W	T	174
Southend	W Berks	SU5970	51°25·8'	1°8·7'W	T	174
Southend	Wilts	SU1973	51°27·6'	1°43·2'W	X	173
Southend Airport	Essex	TQ8789	51°34·4'	0°42·3'E	X	178
Southend Flat	Sou-on-Sea	TQ8984	51°31·6'	0°43·9'E	X	178
Southend Fm	Glos	SO7224	51°55·1'	2°24·0'W	FM	162
Southend Fm	Glos	SO8929	51°57·8'	2°9·2'W	FM	150,163
Southend Fm	Hants	SU6760	51°20·3'	1°1·9'W	FM	175,186
Southend Fm	Herts	TL1009	51°46·4'	0°23·9'W	FM	166
Southend Fm	Herts	TL3117	51°50·4'	0°5·5'W	FM	166
South End Fm	N Yks	SE4387	54°16·9'	1°20·0'W	FM	99
South End Fm	Suff	TM4185	52°24·8'	1°33·0'E	FM	156
Southend Fm	Worcs	SO8439	52°3·2'	2°13·6'W	FM	150
Southend Fm	W Susx	SU8400	50°47·8'	0°48·1'W	FM	197
South End Haws	Cumbr	SD2261	54°2·6'	3°11·1'W	X	96
Southend Hill	Bucks	SP9116	51°50·3'	0°40·4'W	H	165
Southend-on-Sea	Sou-on-Sea	TQ8786	51°32·7'	0°42·2'E	T	178
Southend Pier	Sou-on-Sea	TQ8884	51°31·6'	0°43·0'E	X	178
South Engine Drain	N Lincs	SE7302	53°30·8'	0°53·5'W	W	112
South Engine Drain	N Lincs	SE7608	53°34·0'	0°50·7'W	W	112
Southerby Ho	N Yks	SE3677	54°11·5'	1°26·5'W	X	99
Southerfell	Cumbr	NY3527	54°38·3'	3°0·0'W	X	90
Souther Fell	Cumbr	NY3528	54°38·8'	3°0·0'W	H	90
Southerfield	Cumbr	NY1648	54°49·4'	3°18·0'W	X	85
Southerfield Hall	Cumbr	NY1649	54°50·0'	3°18·0'W	X	85
Southerfield Ho	Cumbr	NY1548	54°49·4'	3°19·0'W	X	85
Southerham Old Barns	E Susx	TQ4209	50°52·0'	0°1·5'E	X	198
Souther Hill	Shetld	HU3966	60°22·8'	1°17·1'W	H	2,3
Southerhouse	Shetld	HU3717	59°56·4'	1°19·8'W	X	4
Southerhouse	Shetld	HU3734	60°5·6'	1°19·6'W	X	4
Souther House	Shetld	HU4066	60°22·8'	1°16·0'W	X	2,3
Southerly	Devon	SX5288	50°40·6'	4°5·3'W	T	191
Southerly Down	Devon	SX5387	50°40·1'	4°4·4'W	H	191
Southerly Nick	Scot Bord	NT4038	55°38·2'	2°56·8'W	H	73
Southerly Park Fm	Warw	SP1354	52°11·3'	1°48·2'W	FM	151
Southerly Ridge	D & G	NY0899	55°16·8'	3°26·5'W	X	78
Southern 100 Course	I of M	SC2569	54°5·5'	4°40·1'W	X	95
Southernby	Cumbr	NY3639	54°44·8'	2°59·2'W	T	90
Southern Cross	W Susx	TQ2505	50°50·1'	0°13·1'W	T	198
Southerndale	Cumbr	NY2429	54°39·3'	3°10·3'W	X	89,90
Southernden	Kent	TQ8646	51°11·2'	0°40·1'E	X	189
Southerndown	V of Glam	SS8873	51°26·9'	3°36·3'W	T	170
Southerness	D & G	NX9754	54°52·5'	3°35·9'W	T	84
Southerness Point	D & G	NX9754	54°52·5'	3°35·9'W	X	84
Southern Green	Herts	TL3131	51°57·9'	0°5·2'W	T	166
Southernknowe	Northum	NT8824	55°30·8'	2°11·0'W	X	74
Southern Law	Durham	NZ3636	54°43·3'	1°26·0'W	X	93
Southern Law	E Loth	NT6362	55°51·2'	2°35·0'W	X	67
Southern Upland Way	D & G	NX5481	55°6·4'	4°16·9'W	X	77
Southern Upland Way	Inverc	NS2872	55°54·9'	4°44·7'W	X	63
Southern Upland Way	Scot Bord	NT2212	55°24·0'	3°13·5'W	X	79
Southern Upland Way	Scot Bord	NT3031	55°34·3'	3°6·2'W	X	73
Southern Upland Way	Scot Bord	NT6355	55°47·5'	2°35·0'W	X	67,74
Southern Wood	Devon	SS7848	51°13·3'	3°44·4'W	F	180
Southerquoy	Orkney	HY2317	59°2·3'	3°20·0'W	T	6
South Erradale	Highld	NG7471	57°40·6'	5°47·0'W	T	19
Souther Scales	N Yks	SD7476	54°11·0'	2°23·5'W	X	98
Souther Scales Fell	N Yks	SD7576	54°11·0'	2°22·6'W	X	98
Southerton	Devon	SY0790	50°42·4'	3°18·6'W	T	192
Southerton	Fife	NT2690	56°6·1'	3°10·9'W	X	59
Souther Wood	Northnts	SP9783	52°26·4'	0°34·0'W	F	141
Southery	Norf	TL6294	52°31·4'	0°23·7'E	T	143
Southery Fens	Norf	TL6093	52°30·9'	0°21·9'E	X	143
South Essie	Aberd	NK0852	57°33·7'	1°51·5'W	X	30
South Esworthy Fm	Devon	SS8721	50°58·9'	3°36·2'W	FM	181
South Ewster	N Lincs	SE8302	53°30·7'	0°44·5'W	X	112
Southey	Devon	SS6300	50°47·2'	3°56·2'W	X	191
Southey Barton	Devon	ST0913	50°54·8'	3°17·3'W	X	181
Southey Creek	Essex	TL8805	51°43·0'	0°43·7'E	W	168
Southey Fm	Somer	ST3620	50°58·8'	2°54·3'W	FM	193
Southey Green	Essex	TL7732	51°57·7'	0°35·0'E	T	167
Southey Hill	Scot Bord	NT1829	55°33·1'	3°17·6'W	H	72
Southey Moor	Somer	ST1911	50°53·8'	3°8·7'W	X	192,193
Southey Wood	Peterb	TF1002	52°36·5'	0°22·1'W	F	142
South Faddonhill	Aberd	NJ8342	57°28·3'	2°16·5'W	X	29,30
South Falaknowe	Scot Bord	NT8666	55°53·5'	2°13·0'W	X	67
South Falfield	Fife	NO4507	56°15·4'	2°52·8'W	X	59
South Fallaws	Angus	NO3636	56°31·0'	3°2·0'W	X	54
South Fambridge	Essex	TQ8595	51°37·6'	0°40·8'E	T	168
South Farden Croft	Aberd	NJ9626	57°19·7'	2°3·5'W	X	38
South Farnborough	Hants	SU8754	51°16·9'	0°44·8'W	T	186
South Fawley	W Berks	SU3980	51°31·3'	1°25·9'W	T	174
South Fea	Orkney	HY3409	58°58·1'	3°8·4'W	X	6,7
South Fearns	Highld	NG5835	57°20·7'	6°0·9'W	X	24,32
South Fen	Cambs	TL4277	52°22·6'	0°5·6'E	X	142,143
South Fen	Norf	TG3426	52°47·1'	1°28·6'E	X	133,134
South Fens	Northum	NZ0574	55°3·9'	1°54·9'W	X	87
South Feorline	N Ayr	NR9028	55°30·3'	5°19·1'W	T	68,69
South Fergushill	N Ayr	NS3243	55°39·3'	4°39·8'W	X	63,70
South Ferriby	N Lincs	SE9820	53°40·3'	0°30·6'W	T	106,112
South Ferriby Cliff	N Lincs	SE9922	53°41·3'	0°29·6'W	X	106,112
Southfield	Aberd	NJ8544	57°29·4'	2°14·6'W	X	30
Southfield	Cumbr	NY5618	54°33·6'	2°40·4'W	X	90
Southfield	Cumbr	NY6918	54°33·6'	2°28·3'W	X	91
Southfield	Cumbr	SD1280	54°12·7'	3°20·5'W	X	96
Southfield	D & G	NY0267	54°59·5'	3°31·5'W	X	84

Southfield	D & G	NY1378	55°5·6'	3°21·4'W	X	85
South Field	E Yorks	SE9060	54°1·9'	0°37·1'W	X	101
South Field	E Yorks	SE9351	53°57·0'	0°34·6'W	X	106
South Field	E Yorks	TA0225	53°42·9'	0°26·9'W	T	106,107
South Field	E Yorks	TA2432	53°46·4'	0°6·7'W	X	107
Southfield	Falk	NS8472	55°55·9'	3°51·0'W	X	65
Southfield	Falk	NS8985	56°3·0'	3°46·5'W	X	65
Southfield	Fife	NO4321	56°22·9'	2°54·9'W	X	54,59
Southfield	Heref	SO4957	52°12·8'	2°44·4'W	X	148,149
Southfield	Kent	TQ9148	51°12·2'	0°44·4'E	X	189
Southfield	Lancs	SD8737	53°50·0'	2°11·4'W	X	103
Southfield	Midlo	NT3767	55°53·8'	3°0·0'W	X	66
Southfield	Northum	NZ2675	55°4·4'	1°35·1'W	T	88
South Field	Notts	SK7365	53°10·9'	0°54·1'W	X	120
South Field	N Yks	SD8949	53°56·5'	2°9·6'W	X	103
Southfield	N Yks	SE6982	54°14·0'	0°56·1'W	X	100
Southfield	Orkney	ND4895	58°50·6'	2°53·6'W	X	7
Southfield	Pemb	SN0423	51°52·5'	4°50·5'W	X	145,157,158
Southfield	Pth & Kin	NO1507	56°15·1'	3°21·9'W	X	58
Southfield	Pth & Kin	NO2530	56°27·6'	3°12·6'W	X	53
Southfield	Scot Bord	NT4708	55°22·0'	2°49·7'W	X	79
Southfield	Stir	NS6896	56°8·6'	4°7·0'W	X	57
South Field	Win & Maid	SU9578	51°29·8'	0°37·5'W	T	175,176
Southfield Cott	S Lanak	NS7944	55°40·7'	3°55·0'W	X	71
South Field Down	Dorset	SY6296	50°46·0'	2°31·9'W	X	194
South Field Drain	N Lincs	SE8104	53°31·8'	0°46·3'W	W	112
Southfield Fm	Durham	NZ1355	54°53·6'	1°47·4'W	FM	88
Southfield Fm	Durham	NZ3526	54°37·9'	1°27·0'W	FM	93
Southfield Fm	Durham	NZ4338	54°44·4'	1°19·5'W	FM	93
Southfield Fm	E Loth	NT4474	55°57·6'	2°53·4'W	FM	66
Southfield Fm	E Yorks	TA1051	53°56·8'	0°19·0'W	FM	107
Southfield Fm	E Yorks	TA1353	53°57·9'	0°16·2'W	FM	107
Southfield Fm	E Yorks	TA3821	53°40·3'	0°5·8'E	FM	107,113
Southfield Fm	Glos	SO7812	51°48·6'	2°18·8'W	FM	162
Southfield Fm	Hants	SU4747	51°13·4'	1°19·2'W	FM	185
Southfield Fm	Hants	SU7036	51°7·4'	0°59·6'W	FM	186
Southfield Fm	Lincs	TF3195	53°26·4'	0°1·3'W	FM	113
Southfield Fm	Lincs	TF3666	53°10·7'	0°2·5'E	FM	122
Southfield Fm	N Lincs	TA0909	53°34·2'	0°20·8'W	FM	112
Southfield Fm	Northnts	SP8875	52°22·2'	0°42·0'W	FM	141
Southfield Fm	Northum	NU2030	55°34·0'	1°40·5'W	FM	75
Southfield Fm	Notts	SK7661	53°8·7'	0°51·4'W	FM	120
Southfield Fm	N Yks	SE3673	54°9·3'	1°26·5'W	FM	99
Southfield FM	N Yks	TA1073	54°8·7'	0°18·5'W	FM	
Southfield Fm	S Lanak	NS7944	55°40·7'	3°55·0'W	FM	71
Southfield Fm	Somer	ST7755	51°17·9'	2°19·4'W	FM	172
Southfield Fm	Somer	ST7847	51°13·5'	2°18·5'W	FM	183
Southfield Fm	Suff	TL6163	52°14·7'	0°21·9'E	FM	154
Southfield Fm	Warw	SP2141	52°4·3'	1°41·2'W	FM	151
South Fieldhead	S Lanak	NS6542	55°39·4'	4°8·3'W	X	71
South Field Hill	Dorset	SY6297	50°46·5'	2°32·0'W	X	194
Southfield Ho	E Yorks	TA1754	53°58·4'	0°12·6'W	X	107
Southfield Ho	Lincs	TF3385	53°20·9'	0°0·3'E	X	122
Southfield Ho	Somer	ST7346	51°13·0'	2°22·8'W	X	183
Southfield Lodge	Rut	SP8798	52°34·6'	0°42·6'W	X	141
Southfield Manor	Glos	SO9519	51°52·4'	2°4·0'W	X	163
Southfield Reservoir	E Yorks	SE6519	53°40·0'	1°0·6'W	W	111
Southfields	Essex	TQ6689	51°34·7'	0°24·1'E	X	177,178
Southfields	E Yorks	TA2431	53°45·9'	0°6·7'W	X	107
Southfields	Northnts	SP6348	52°7·8'	1°4·4'W	X	152
Southfields	Thurr	TQ6681	51°30·4'	0°23·9'E	T	177,178
Southfields	Wan	TQ2573	51°26·8'	0°11·7'W	T	176
Southfields Fm	Beds	TL0857	52°12·3'	0°24·8'W	FM	153
Southfields Fm	Herts	TL3330	51°57·4'	0°3·5'W	FM	166
Southfields Fm	Lincs	TA3302	53°30·1'	0°0·7'E	FM	113
Southfields Fm	Lincs	TF3137	52°55·1'	0°2·7'W	FM	131
Southfields Fm	N Yks	NZ2204	54°26·1'	1°39·2'W	FM	93
Southfields Fm	Oxon	SP3942	52°4·7'	1°25·5'W	FM	151
Southfields Fm	Warw	SP2087	52°29·1'	1°41·9'W	FM	139
Southfield Villa	Pemb	SN0322	51°52·0'	4°51·3'W	X	145,157,158
South Filla Runnie	Shetld	HU4161	60°20·1'	1°14·9'W	H	2,3
South Flanders	Stir	NS6296	56°8·5'	4°12·8'W	X	57
South Flat Howe	N Yks	NZ6600	54°23·7'	0°58·6'W	A	94
South Flats	Durham	NZ0313	54°31·0'	1°56·8'W	X	92
South Flats	Norf	TG4906	52°35·9'	1°41·0'E	X	134
Southfleet	Kent	TQ6171	51°25·1'	0°19·3'E	T	177
South Flobbets	Aberd	NJ7934	57°24·0'	2°20·5'W	T	29,30
South Floin Geo	Shetld	HU4595	60°38·4'	1°10·1'W	X	1,2
South Fm	Cambs	TL3046	52°6·1'	0°5·7'W	FM	153
South Fm	Devon	ST1109	50°52·7'	3°15·5'W	FM	192,193
South Fm	Devon	SY0782	50°38·1'	3°18·5'W	FM	192
South Fm	Dorset	ST9001	50°48·7'	2°8·1'W	FM	195
South Fm	E Yorks	SE6721	53°41·1'	0°58·7'W	FM	105,106
South Fm	E Yorks	SE8735	53°48·5'	0°40·3'W	FM	106
South Fm	E Yorks	TA2517	53°38·3'	0°6·1'W	FM	113
South Fm	Glos	SP1702	51°43·2'	1°44·8'W	FM	163
South Fm	Hants	SU6820	50°58·8'	1°1·5'W	FM	185
South Fm	Lincs	SK9061	53°8·5'	0°38·9'W	FM	121
South Fm	Lincs	TF2782	53°19·4'	0°5·2'W	FM	122
South Fm	Lincs	TF4293	53°25·1'	0°8·6'E	FM	113
South Fm	NE Lincs	TF2496	53°27·0'	0°7·6'W	FM	113
South Fm	Norf	TM0190	52°28·5'	0°58·0'E	FM	144
South Fm	Northum	NY8778	55°6·0'	2°11·8'W	FM	87
South Fm	Northum	NZ2197	55°16·2'	1°39·7'W	FM	81
South Fm	N Som	ST4062	51°21·5'	2°51·3'W	FM	172,182
South Fm	N Yks	SE2264	54°4·5'	1°39·4'W	FM	99
South Fm	N Yks	SE5969	54°7·0'	1°5·4'W	FM	100
South Fm	N Yks	SE6677	54°11·3'	0°58·9'W	FM	100
South Fm	Oxon	SP3702	51°43·2'	1°27·5'W	FM	164
South Fm	Oxon	SU3489	51°36·2'	1°30·2'W	FM	174
South Fm	Peterb	TF3003	52°36·8'	0°4·4'W	FM	142
South Fm	Swin	SU1977	51°29·7'	1°43·2'W	FM	173
South Fm	Warw	SP3388	52°29·6'	1°30·4'W	FM	140
South Fm	Wilts	ST9525	51°1·7'	2°3·9'W	FM	184
South Fm	Wilts	SU1394	51°38·9'	1°48·3'W	FM	163,173
South Fm	York	SE6951	53°57·3'	0°56·5'W	FM	105,106
South Fms	Bucks	SP7219	51°52·1'	0°56·9'W	FM	165
South Fms	Wilts	SU0760	51°20·6'	1°53·6'W	FM	173
South Fod	Fife	NT1287	56°4·3'	3°24·4'W	X	65
South Folds	Aberd	NJ9616	57°14·3'	2°3·5'W	X	38

South Footie	Aberd	NJ6101	57°6·2'	2°38·2'W	X	37
Southford	I of W	SZ5178	50°36·2'	1°16·4'W	T	196
South Foreland	Kent	TR3543	51°8·5'	1°22·0'E	X	179
South Forest	Brackn	SU9470	51°25·5'	0°38·5'W	F	175
South Forest	Notts	SK6264	53°10·4'	1°3·9'W	X	120
South Fornet	Aberd	NJ7810	57°11·1'	2°21·4'W	X	38
South Forr	Pth & Kin	NN8619	56°21·2'	3°50·2'W	X	58
South Forty Foot Drain	Lincs	TF1629	52°51·0'	0°16·2'W	W	130
South Forty Foot Drain	Lincs	TF2543	52°58·4'	0°7·9'W	W	131
South Foul Sike	Durham	NY8743	54°47·2'	2°11·7'W	W	87
South Fowlis	Aberd	NJ5510	57°11·0'	2°44·2'W	X	37
South Friarton	Pth & Kin	NO1429	56°27·0'	3°23·3'W	X	53,58
South Frith	Kent	TQ5844	51°10·6'	0°16·0'E	X	188
South Gare Breakwater	Red & Cl	NZ5527	54°38·3'	1°8·4'W	X	93
South Garphar	S Ayr	NX1182	55°6·0'	4°57·3'W	X	76
South Garvan	Highld	NM9877	56°50·7'	5°18·3'W	T	40
South Garvan River	Highld	NM9775	56°49·6'	5°19·2'W	W	40
South Gask	Pth & Kin	NO2336	56°30·8'	3°14·6'W	X	53
Southgate	Cered	SN5979	52°23·7'	4°3·9'W	T	135
Southgate	Enf	TQ3094	51°38·0'	0°6·9'W	T	166,176,177
Southgate	Halton	SJ5381	53°19·7'	2°41·9'W	T	108
Southgate	Norf	TF8634	52°52·5'	0°46·2'E	T	132
Southgate	Norf	TG1424	52°46·5'	1°10·8'E	T	133
Southgate	Swan	SS5588	51°34·6'	4°5·2'W	T	159
Southgate	W Susx	TQ2636	51°6·8'	0°11·6'W	T	187
Southgate Br	Suff	TL8663	52°14·2'	0°43·8'E	X	155
South Gavel	Shetld	HZ2271	59°31·7'	1°36·2'W	X	4
South Gellan	Aberd	NJ4902	57°6·6'	2°50·1'W	X	37
South Geo	Orkney	HY6637	59°13·4'	2°35·3'W	X	5
South Geo	Orkney	HY6715	59°1·5'	2°34·0'W	X	5
South Geo of Brettabister	Shetld	HU4857	60°17·9'	1°7·4'W	X	2,3
South Geo of Brough	Shetld	HP5712	60°47·5'	0°56·7'W	X	1
South Gibcracks	Essex	TL7702	51°41·6'	0°34·1'E	X	167
South Gill	Shetld	HU2382	60°31·5'	1°34·4'W	W	3
South Gill Beck	N Yks	SE1870	54°7·8'	1°43·1'W	W	99
South Glassmount	Fife	NT2487	56°4·4'	3°12·8'W	X	66
South Glen	D & G	NX8255	54°52·8'	3°49·9'W	X	84
South Glendale	N Eil	NF7914	57°6·6'	7°17·7'W	T	31
South Glenton	Aberd	NO8288	56°59·2'	2°17·3'W	X	45
South Gluss	Shetld	HU3477	60°28·8'	1°22·4'W	T	2,3
South Godstone	Surrey	TQ3648	51°13·1'	0°2·8'W	T	187
South Goldstone or Oxscar	Northum	NU2137	55°37·8'	1°39·6'W	X	75
South Goringlee Fm	W Susx	TQ1020	50°58·4'	0°25·6'W	FM	198
South Gorley	Hants	SU1610	50°53·6'	1°46·0'W	T	195
South Gormack	Pth & Kin	NO1545	56°35·6'	3°22·6'W	X	53
South Gosforth	N upon Ty	NZ2467	55°0·1'	1°37·1'W	T	88
South Grain	Angus	NO4176	56°52·6'	2°57·6'W	W	44
South Grain	D & G	NT2902	55°18·7'	3°6·7'W	W	79
South Grain	E Loth	NT6165	55°52·8'	2°37·0'W	W	67
South Grain	Scot Bord	NT2118	55°27·2'	3°14·5'W	W	79
South Grain	Scot Bord	NT3933	55°35·5'	2°57·6'W	W	73
South Grain Beck	Durham	NZ0331	54°40·7'	1°56·8'W	W	92
South Grain Pike	D & G	NT2901	55°18·1'	3°6·7'W	H	79
South Grain Rig	D & G	NT2902	55°18·7'	3°6·7'W	H	79
South Grain Tarn	N Yks	SD9281	54°13·7'	2°6·9'W	W	98
South Grange	Durham	NZ2938	54°44·4'	1°32·5'W	X	93
Southgrange	E Ayr	NS4351	55°43·9'	4°29·6'W	X	64
South Grange	E Yorks	SE7239	53°50·8'	0°53·9'W	X	105,106
South Grange	E Yorks	SE8754	53°58·7'	0°40·0'W	X	106
South Grange	Suff	TM3668	52°15·8'	1°27·9'E	X	156
South Grange Fm	E Yorks	SE9350	53°56·5'	0°34·6'W	FM	106
South Green	Essex	TM0319	51°50·2'	0°57·2'E	T	168
South Green	Essex	TQ6893	51°36·9'	0°26·0'E	T	177,178
South Green	Kent	TQ8460	51°18·8'	0°38·8'E	T	178,188
South Green	Norf	TF5419	52°45·0'	0°17·3'E	T	131
South Green	Norf	TG0510	52°39·2'	1°2·3'E	T	133
South Green	Norf	TM2183	52°24·2'	1°15·3'E	X	156
South Green	Suff	TM1775	52°20·0'	1°11·5'E	T	156
South Greenbrae	Aberd	NJ9243	57°28·9'	2°7·5'W	X	30
South Greenholm	Scot Bord	NY4990	55°12·3'	2°47·7'W	X	79
South Greenslade Fm	Somer	SS9630	51°3·8'	3°28·7'W	FM	181
Southground Point	Corn	SX1050	50°19·4'	4°39·8'W	X	200,204
Southgrove Copse	Wilts	SU2359	51°20·0'	1°39·8'W	F	174
Southgrove Fm	Wilts	SU2258	51°19·5'	1°40·7'W	FM	174
South Gulham Fm	Lincs	TF0493	53°25·6'	0°25·7'W	FM	112
South Gut	Pemb	SM5909	51°43·9'	5°29·0'W	X	157
South Gyle	C of Edin	NT1872	55°56·3'	3°18·3'W	T	65,66
South Gyran	Orkney	HY2415	59°1·2'	3°18·9'W	X	6
South-haa	Shetld	HU3688	60°34·7'	1°20·1'W	T	1,2
South Hackney	Hack	TQ3584	51°32·6'	0°2·8'W	T	177
South Haddo	Aberd	NJ7538	57°26·2'	2°24·5'W	X	29
South Haddon	Somer	SS9527	51°2·2'	3°29·5'W	X	181
South Hale Fm	Surrey	TQ3047	51°12·7'	0°7·9'W	FM	187
South Hall	Essex	TM2230	51°55·7'	1°14·1'E	X	169
South Hall	Essex	TQ9392	51°35·8'	0°47·6'E	X	178
South Hall	E Yorks	TA0251	53°56·9'	0°26·3'W	X	106,107
South Hall	Northum	NZ0474	55°3·9'	1°55·8'W	X	87
South Hall Fm	Arg & Bt	NS0672	55°54·4'	5°5·8'W	FM	63
South Hall Fm	Hav	TQ5381	51°30·7'	0°12·7'E	FM	177
South Ham	Hants	SU6151	51°15·5'	1°7·2'W	T	185
South Ham	Shetld	HU2965	60°22·3'	1°27·9'W	X	3
South Ham	Shetld	HU4939	60°8·2'	1°6·6'W	X	4
South Hampstead	Camden	TQ2684	51°32·7'	0°10·6'W	T	176
South Hanningfield	Essex	TQ7497	51°38·9'	0°31·3'E	T	167
South Happas	Angus	NO4440	56°33·2'	2°54·2'W	X	54
South Harbour	Shetld	HZ2069	59°30·7'	1°38·3'W	W	4
South Harefield	Hill	TQ0589	51°35·6'	0°28·7'W	T	176
South Harris	N Eil	NG1093	57°50·2'	6°52·7'W	X	14
South Harris Forest	N Eil	NG1098	57°52·9'	6°53·1'W	X	14
South Harris Forest or Coille Ceann a Deas na Hearadh	N Eil	NG0898	57°52·8'	6°55·1'W	X	14,18
South Harris or Ceann a Deas na Hearadh	N Eil	NG0693	57°50·1'	6°56·7'W	X	14,18
South Harrow	Harrow	TQ1386	51°33·9'	0°21·8'W	T	176
South Harting	W Susx	SU7819	50°58·1'	0°53·0'W	T	197
South Hart Law	Scot Bord	NT5557	55°48·5'	2°42·6'W	X	66,73
South Harton	Devon	SX7682	50°37·7'	3°44·8'W	X	191
South Harva	Shetld	HU3626	60°1·3'	1°20·8'W	X	4

South Hatfield	Herts	TL2206	51°44·6'	0°13·6'W	T	166
South Haven	Pemb	SM7308	51°43·7'	5°16·8'W	W	157
South Haven	Shetld	HZ2272	59°32·3'	1°36·2'W	W	4
South Haven Point	Dorset	SZ0386	50°40·6'	1°57·1'W	X	195
South Hawkhillock	Aberd	NK0038	57°26·2'	1°59·5'W	X	30
South Hawkshaw Rig	Scot Bord	NT2626	55°31·6'	3°9·9'W	H	73
South Hay	Hants	SU7739	51°8·9'	0°53·6'W	X	186
South Hay Fm	Aberd	NK0733	57°23·5'	1°52·6'W	FM	30
South Hayling	Hants	SZ7299	50°47·4'	0°58·3'W	T	197
South Hayne	Devon	SS7725	51°0·9'	3°44·8'W	X	180
South Hayne Fm	Devon	SS9922	50°59·5'	3°26·0'W	FM	181
South Hazelrigg	Northum	NU0532	55°35·1'	1°54·8'W	X	75
South Head	Cumbr	NX9512	54°29·8'	3°36·9'W	X	89
South Head	Derby	SK0584	53°21·4'	1°55·1'W	H	110
South Head	Highld	ND3749	58°25·8'	3°4·3'W	X	12
South Head	Shetld	HP6607	60°44·7'	0°46·9'W	X	1
South Head	Shetld	HU2382	60°31·5'	1°34·4'W	X	3
South Head	Shetld	HU3881	60°30·9'	1°18·0'W	X	1,2,3
South Head	Shetld	HU6397	60°39·3'	0°50·4'W	X	1
South Head Fm	Derby	SK0685	53°22·0'	1°54·2'W	FM	110
South Head of Caldersgeo	Shetld	HU2078	60°29·4'	1°37·7'W	X	3
South Head of Colsay	Shetld	HU3518	59°57·0'	1°21·9'W	X	4
South Healand	Devon	SS5117	50°56·2'	4°6·9'W	X	180
South Heale	Devon	SS5620	50°57·9'	4°2·7'W	X	180
South Healey	Northum	NZ0891	55°13·0'	1°52·0'W	X	81
South Heath	Bucks	SP9101	51°42·3'	0°40·6'W	T	165
South Heath	Dorset	SY8689	50°42·0'	2°11·5'W	X	194
South Heath	Essex	TM1119	51°50·0'	1°4·1'E	T	168,169
South Height	Scot Bord	NT3934	55°36·0'	2°57·7'W	H	73
South Heighton	E Susx	TQ4502	50°48·2'	0°3·9'E	T	198
South Hele	Devon	ST0222	50°59·6'	3°23·4'W	X	181
South Hellia	Shetld	HU3784	60°32·5'	1°19·0'W	X	1,2,3
South-heog	Shetld	HU3481	60°30·9'	1°22·3'W	X	1,2,3
South Hessary Tor	Devon	SX5972	50°32·1'	3°59·0'W	H	191
South Hetton	Durham	NZ3745	54°48·2'	1°25·0'W	T	88
South Hidden Fm	W Berks	SU3674	51°28·1'	1°28·5'W	FM	174
South Hiendley	Wakf	SE3912	53°36·4'	1°24·2'W	T	110,111
South Hill	Angus	NO6763	56°45·7'	2°31·9'W	X	45
South Hill	Corn	SX3272	50°31·7'	4°21·8'W	T	201
South Hill	Derby	SK3760	53°8·4'	1°26·4'W	X	119
South Hill	Devon	SS4606	50°50·2'	4°10·8'W	X	190
South Hill	Devon	SS4917	50°56·2'	4°8·6'W	X	180
South Hill	Devon	SS5736	51°6·6'	4°2·2'W	X	180
South Hill	Devon	SX4491	50°42·1'	4°12·2'W	X	190
South Hill	Devon	SX8195	50°44·8'	3°40·8'W	X	191
South Hill	E Susx	TV5098	50°46·0'	0°8·0'E	X	199
South Hill	E Susx	TV5498	50°45·9'	0°11·4'E	X	199
South Hill	Glos	SO9415	51°50·2'	2°4·8'W	X	163
South Hill	I Scilly	SV8712	49°55·8'	6°21·3'W	H	203
South Hill	N Som	ST3456	51°18·2'	2°56·4'W	T	182
South Hill	Oxon	SP3531	51°58·8'	1°29·0'W	X	151
South Hill	Pemb	SM8311	51°45·6'	5°8·3'W	T	157
South Hill	Pemb	SM9425	51°53·4'	4°59·2'W	X	157,158
South Hill	Shetld	HU1852	60°15·4'	1°40·0'W	H	3
South Hill	Shetld	HU3650	60°14·2'	1°20·5'W	H	3
South Hill	Somer	SS8435	51°6·4'	3°39·0'W	X	181
South Hill	Somer	SS9031	51°4·3'	3°33·8'W	X	181
South Hill	Somer	ST4727	51°2·6'	2°45·0'W	H	193
South Hill	W Susx	TQ3234	51°5·6'	0°6·5'W	X	187
South Hill Fm	Bri & Hov	TQ2910	50°52·7'	0°9·6'W	FM	198
South Hill Fm	Devon	SS5107	50°50·8'	4°6·6'W	FM	191
South Hill Fm	Devon	SX6798	50°46·2'	3°52·8'W	FM	191
South Hill Fm	Kent	TR0944	51°9·6'	0°59·7'E	FM	179,189
South Hill Fm	Somer	ST2617	50°57·1'	3°2·8'W	FM	193
South Hill Fm	Warw	SP2831	51°58·8'	1°35·1'W	FM	151
South Hill Head	Scot Bord	NT2141	55°39·6'	3°14·9'W	H	73
South Hill of Dripps	S Lanak	NS5854	55°45·8'	4°15·4'W	X	64
South Hill of Lunna	Shetld	HU4767	60°23·3'	1°8·3'W	H	2,3
South Hill Park	Brackn	SU8766	51°23·4'	0°44·6'W	X	175
South Hills	Lincs	SE8600	53°29·6'	0°41·8'W	X	112
South Hills	Pemb	SN0301	51°40·6'	4°50·6'W	X	157,158
South Hillswood Fm	Staffs	SJ9958	53°7·4'	2°0·5'W	FM	118
Southhill Wood	S Lanak	NT1045	55°41·7'	3°25·5'W	F	72
South Hinksey	Oxon	SP5004	51°44·2'	1°16·2'W	T	164
South Ho	Dorset	SY7098	50°47·1'	2°25·2'W	X	194
South Ho	Essex	TL4916	51°49·6'	0°10·1'E	X	167
South Ho	S Ayr	NX3084	55°7·5'	4°39·5'W	X	76
South Hole	Devon	SS2220	50°57·4'	4°31·7'W	T	190
South Hole Fm	Devon	SS4539	51°8·0'	4°12·5'W	FM	180
South Holland Ho	Lincs	TF4219	52°45·2'	0°6·7'E	X	131
South Holland Lodge	Lincs	TF4519	52°45·2'	0°9·3'E	X	131
South Holland Main Drain	Lincs	TF3315	52°43·2'	0°1·4'W	W	131
South Hollymill	Aberd	NJ7155	57°35·3'	2°28·6'W	X	29
Southholm	S Lanak	NS9742	55°39·9'	3°37·8'W	X	72
South Holme	Notts	SK8065	53°10·8'	0°47·8'W	X	121
South Holme	N Yks	SE6977	54°11·3'	0°56·1'W	T	100
South Holme Fm	N Yks	SE3797	54°22·3'	1°25·4'W	FM	99
South Holme Fm	N Yks	SE6877	54°11·3'	0°57·1'W	FM	100
South Holmes Copse	Hants	SU3822	51°0·0'	1°27·1'W	F	185
South Holm of Burravoe	Shetld	HU3789	60°35·2'	1°19·0'W	X	1,2
South Holms	Shetld	HP5710	60°46·4'	0°56·7'W	X	1
South Holmwood	Surrey	TQ1745	51°11·8'	0°19·1'W	T	187
South Holt Fm	W Susx	SU7412	50°54·4'	0°56·5'W	FM	197
Southhook	N Ayr	NS3840	55°37·9'	4°34·0'W	X	70
South Hook Point	Pemb	SM8605	51°42·4'	5°5·5'W	X	157
South Hornchurch	Hav	TQ5183	51°31·8'	0°11·0'E	T	177
South Horrington	Somer	ST5746	51°12·9'	2°36·6'W	X	182
South Hourat	N Ayr	NS2853	55°44·6'	4°44·0'W	X	63
South House	N Yks	SD7874	54°9·9'	2°19·8'W	X	98
South House Fm	Essex	TL8605	51°43·0'	0°42·0'E	FM	168
South House Fm	Essex	TM0218	51°49·7'	0°56·3'E	FM	168
Southhouse Fm	Essex	TM1928	51°54·7'	1°11·4'E	FM	168,169
South House Fm	Norf	TG4213	52°39·9'	1°35·1'E	FM	134
South House Fm	N Yks	SE6196	54°21·6'	1°3·3'W	FM	94,100
South House Fm	W Susx	TQ0923	51°0·0'	0°26·4'W	FM	198
South House Moor	N Yks	SD7676	54°11·0'	2°21·6'W	X	98
South Huish	Devon	SX6941	50°15·5'	3°49·9'W	T	202
South Hurst Fm	Warw	SP2875	52°22·6'	1°34·9'W	FM	140
South Hyde Fm	Heref	SO7344	52°5·9'	2°23·3'W	FM	150
South Hykeham	Lincs	SK9364	53°10·1'	0°36·1'W	T	121

South Hylton	Sund	NZ3556	54°54·1'	1°26·8'W	T	88
Southill	Beds	TL1542	52°4·1'	0°18·9'W	T	153
Southill	Devon	SX6787	50°40·3'	3°52·6'W	X	191
Southill	Dorset	SY6680	50°37·4'	2°28·5'W	T	194
Southill Barton	Devon	ST0610	50°53·1'	3°19·8'W	X	192
Southill Fm	Notts	SK7271	53°14·1'	0°54·9'W	FM	120
Southill Fm	Somer	ST6742	51°10·8'	2°27·9'W	FM	183
Southill Fm	W Loth	NS9964	55°51·8'	3°36·4'W	FM	65
Southill Hall	Durham	NZ2747	54°49·3'	1°34·4'W	X	88
Southill Ho	Somer	ST6742	51°10·8'	2°27·9'W	X	183
Southill Park	Beds	TL1441	52°3·6'	0°19·8'W	X	153
Southills Fm	Devon	SX8254	50°22·7'	3°39·2'W	FM	202
South Inch	Aberd	NK0662	57°39·1'	1°53·5'W	X	30
South Inch	N Ayr	NS2045	55°40·2'	4°51·3'W	X	63
South Inch	Pth & Kin	NO1122	56°23·2'	3°26·0'W	X	53,58
South Ings	Lincs	SE8301	53°30·2'	0°44·5'W	X	112
South Ings	York	SE5943	53°53·0'	1°5·7'W	X	105
Southing's Fm	Herts	TL0313	51°48·6'	0°30·0'W	FM	166
South Ings Fm	N Yks	SE6984	54°15·1'	0°56·0'W	FM	100
Southington	Hants	SU5049	51°14·5'	1°16·6'W	T	185
Southington Fm	Heref	SO6853	52°10·7'	2°27·7'W	FM	149
South Isle	Shetld	HU4623	59°59·6'	1°10·0'W	X	4
South Isle of Gletness	Shetld	HU4750	60°14·2'	1°8·6'W	X	3
South Itlaw	Aberd	NJ6658	57°36·9'	2°33·7'W	X	29
South Jetty	Lancs	SD3959	54°1·6'	2°55·5'W	X	102
South Keithney	Aberd	NJ7218	57°15·4'	2°27·4'W	X	38
South Kelsey	Lincs	TF0498	53°28·3'	0°25·6'W	T	112
South Kelsey Carrs	Lincs	TF0297	53°27·8'	0°27·4'W	X	112
South Kensington	Ken & Ch	TQ2678	51°29·4'	0°10·7'W	T	176
South Kenton Sta	Brent	TQ1787	51°34·4'	0°18·3'W	X	176
South Kersie	Falk	NS8790	56°5·6'	3°48·5'W	X	58
South Kessock	Highld	NH6546	57°29·3'	4°14·7'W	T	26
South Kilbride Fm	E Ayr	NS3946	55°41·1'	4°33·2'W	FM	63
South Kilburn Parks	N Yks	SE5078	54°12·0'	1°13·6'W	X	100
South Kilduff	Pth & Kin	NO0600	56°11·3'	3°30·4'W	X	58
South Killingholme	N Lincs	TA1416	53°37·9'	0°16·1'W	T	113
South Killingholme Haven	N Lincs	TA1817	53°38·4'	0°12·5'W	W	113
South Kills Wick	Shetld	HU4009	59°52·1'	1°16·7'W	X	4
South Killyquharn	Aberd	NJ8861	57°38·6'	2°11·6'W	X	30
South Kilrusken	N Ayr	NS2050	55°42·9'	4°51·5'W	X	63
South Kilvington	N Yks	SE4284	54°15·2'	1°20·9'W	T	99
South Kilworth	Leic	SP6081	52°25·7'	1°6·7'W	T	140
South Kilworth Lodge	Leic	SP5982	52°26·2'	1°7·5'W	X	140
South Kinaldy	Fife	NO5109	56°16·5'	2°47·0'W	X	59
South Kingennie	Angus	NO4735	56°30·5'	2°51·2'W	T	54
South Kingsfield	E Yorks	TA1462	54°2·7'	0°15·1'W	X	101
South Kinkell	Pth & Kin	NN9416	56°19·7'	3°42·4'W	X	58
South Kinloch	Aberd	NK0949	57°32·1'	1°50·5'W	X	30
South Kirkby	Wakf	SE4410	53°35·3'	1°19·7'W	T	111
South Kirklane	Stir	NS7196	56°8·6'	4°4·1'W	X	57
South Kirkton	Aberd	NJ7305	57°8·4'	2°26·3'W	T	38
South Kirkton	Aberd	NK1050	57°32·7'	1°49·5'W	X	30
South Kirktonmoor	E Renf	NS5551	55°44·1'	4°18·1'W	X	64
South Kiscadale	N Ayr	NS0425	55°29·0'	5°5·7'W	T	69
South Knaven	Aberd	NJ8942	57°28·3'	2°10·5'W	X	30
South Knighton	C of Leic	SK6001	52°36·4'	1°6·4'W	T	140
South Knighton	Devon	SX8172	50°32·4'	3°40·4'W	T	191
South Knowe of Bodwell	Shetld	HU4149	60°13·7'	1°15·1'W	X	3
South Kyme	Lincs	TF1749	53°1·8'	0°14·9'W	T	130
South Kyme Fen	Lincs	TF1748	53°1·2'	0°14·9'W	X	130
South Ladie	Shetld	HU4488	60°34·7'	1°11·3'W	X	1,2
Southladie Voe	Shetld	HU4487	60°34·1'	1°11·3'W	W	1,2
South Lagalgarve	Arg & Bt	NR6529	55°30·2'	5°42·8'W	X	68
South Laggan	Highld	NN2996	57°1·7'	4°48·6'W	X	34
South Laggan Forest	Highld	NN2493	56°59·9'	4°53·4'W	F	34
South Laggan Forest	Highld	NN2894	57°0·6'	4°49·5'W	F	34
South Lake	Wok	SU7572	51°26·8'	0°54·9'W	W	175
Southlake Moor	Somer	ST3630	51°4·2'	2°54·4'W	X	182
South Lambeth	Lam	TQ3076	51°28·3'	0°7·3'W	T	176,177
South Lambhill	Cumbr	NY4272	55°2·6'	2°54·0'W	X	85
South Lambieletham	Fife	NO5012	56°18·1'	2°48·0'W	X	59
South Lancing	W Susx	TQ1804	50°49·6'	0°19·1'W	T	198
Southland	Pemb	SM9609	51°44·8'	4°56·9'W	X	157,158
South Landing	E Yorks	TA2369	54°6·4'	0°6·7'W	X	101
Southlands	Dorset	SY6777	50°35·7'	2°27·6'W	T	194
Southlands	E Yorks	TA0662	54°2·8'	0°22·4'W	X	101
Southlands	Surrey	TQ3850	51°14·2'	0°1·0'W	X	187
Southlands Fm	Devon	ST1507	50°51·6'	3°12·1'W	FM	192,193
Southlands Fm	Essex	TL7502	51°41·6'	0°32·3'E	FM	167
Southlands Fm	Essex	TQ7694	51°37·3'	0°32·9'E	FM	167,178
Southlands Fm	W Susx	TQ0917	50°56·8'	0°26·5'W	FM	198
South Lane	Barns	SE2606	53°33·2'	1°36·0'W	T	110
South Lane	Devon	SS3412	50°53·3'	4°21·2'W	X	190
South Lane Fm	Red & Cl	NZ6913	54°30·7'	0°55·6'W	FM	94
South Lane Fm	St Hel	SJ5388	53°23·4'	2°42·0'W	FM	108
South Langston	Devon	SX6448	50°19·2'	3°54·3'W	X	202
South Lanridge	N Lanak	NS8061	55°49·9'	3°54·5'W	X	65
South Lasts	C of Aber	NJ8303	57°7·3'	2°16·4'W	X	38
South Latch	Pth & Kin	NO2532	56°28·7'	3°12·6'W	X	53
South Law	Aberd	NJ8758	57°37·0'	2°12·6'W	X	30
South Lawn	Oxon	SP2814	51°49·7'	1°35·2'W	X	163
South Laws	Scot Bord	NT8349	55°44·3'	2°15·8'W	X	74
South Layton	Durham	NZ3826	54°37·9'	1°24·3'W	X	93
South Leaze	Swin	SU1282	51°32·4'	1°49·2'W	X	173
South Leaze Fm	Glos	SU0197	51°40·5'	1°58·7'W	FM	163
South Leckaway	Angus	NO4348	56°37·5'	2°55·3'W	X	54
South Ledaig	Arg & Bt	NM9035	56°27·9'	5°24·1'W	X	49
South Lee	N Eil	NF9165	57°34·4'	7°9·7'W	H	18
Southlee	Shetld	HU3454	60°16·4'	1°22·6'W	X	3
Southlee	Shetld	HU4371	60°25·5'	1°12·6'W	X	2,3
Southlee	Shetld	HU4866	60°22·8'	1°7·3'W	X	2,3
South Lees	Kent	TQ9570	51°24·0'	0°48·6'E	X	178
South Lees	Shetld	HU3076	60°28·3'	1°26·8'W	X	3
Southlees Marshes	Kent	TQ9470	51°24·0'	0°47·7'E	X	178
South Leigh	Devon	SS7128	51°2·4'	3°50·0'W	X	180
Southleigh	Devon	SY2093	50°44·1'	3°7·6'W	T	192,193
South Leigh	Oxon	SP3908	51°46·4'	1°25·7'W	T	164
Southleigh Fm	Hants	SU7307	50°51·7'	0°57·4'W	FM	197
South Leigh Fm	Wilts	ST8741	51°10·3'	2°10·8'W	FM	183
Southleigh Forest	Hants	SU7308	50°52·2'	0°57·4'W	F	197

Southleigh Hills	Devon	SY2092	50°43·6′	3°7·6′W	X	192,193
Southleigh Park	Hants	SU7307	50°51·7′	0°57·4′W	X	197
Southleigh Wood	Wilts	ST8742	51°10·9′	2°10·8′W	F	183
South Lendon	Devon	SX8392	50°43·2′	3°39·1′W	X	191
South Lethans	Fife	NT0694	56°8·0′	3°30·3′W	X	58
South Leverton	Notts	SK7880	53°18·9′	0°49·3′W	T	120,121
South Ley	Devon	SS6144	51°10·9′	3°58·9′W	X	180
Southley Fm	Ches	SJ5759	53°7·8′	2°38·2′W	FM	117
Southley Fm	Hants	SU5146	51°12·9′	1°15·8′W	FM	185
South Liddel	Orkney	ND4683	58°44·1′	2°55·5′W	X	7
South Linden	Northum	NZ1595	55°15·2′	1°45·4′W	X	81
South Lingy Moor	N Yks	NZ2503	54°25·6′	1°36·5′W	X	93
South Links	Orkney	ND4896	58°51·2′	2°53·6′W	X	6,7
South Linn	C of Aber	NJ8202	57°6·8′	2°17·4′W	X	38
South Linton	Northum	NZ2591	55°13·0′	1°36·0′W	X	81
South Lissens	N Ayr	NS3247	55°41·5′	4°39·9′W	X	63
South Little Tack	Aberd	NJ9142	57°28·3′	2°8·5′W	X	30
South Littleton	Worcs	SP0746	52°7·0′	1°53·5′W	T	150
South Littleton of Rattray	Pth & Kin	NO1945	56°35·7′	3°18·7′W	X	53
South Lochboisdale	N Eil	NF7717	57°8·1′	7°19·9′W	T	31
South Lochend	Shetld	HU3723	59°59·7′	1°19·7′W	X	4
South Loch Stofast	Shetld	HU5071	60°25·5′	1°5·0′W	W	2,3
South Lodge	Leic	SP5381	52°25·7′	1°12·8′W	X	140
South Lodge	Lincs	SK9520	52°46·4′	0°35·1′W	X	130
South Lodge	Lincs	TF0432	52°52·8′	0°26·9′W	X	130
South Lodge	Northnts	SP7768	52°18·5′	0°51·8′W	X	152
South Lodge	Northnts	SP8363	52°15·8′	0°46·6′W	X	152
South Lodge	Notts	SK5675	53°16·4′	1°9·2′W	X	120
South Lodge	Notts	SK6272	53°14·7′	1°3·8′W	X	120
South Lodge	Notts	SK6427	52°50·4′	1°2·6′W	X	129
South Lodge Fm	Lincs	SK9834	52°53·9′	0°32·2′W	FM	130
South Lodge Fm	Northnts	TL0682	52°25·8′	0°26·1′W	FM	142
South Lodge Fm	Rut	SK8106	52°39·0′	0°47·8′W	FM	141
South Loftus	Red & Cl	NZ7217	54°32·8′	0°52·8′W	X	94
South Logan	E Ayr	NS5524	55°29·6′	4°17·3′W	X	71
South Logiebrae	W Loth	NS9471	55°55·5′	3°41·3′W	X	65
South Loirston	C of Aber	NJ9401	57°6·3′	2°5·5′W	X	38
South Lopham	Norf	TM0481	52°23·6′	1°0·3′E	T	144
South Lord's Land	Cumbr	SD6986	54°16·4′	2°28·1′W	X	98
South Lothian	Aberd	NK0455	57°35·4′	1°55·5′W	X	30
South Lough Ho	Northum	NZ0671	55°2·3′	1°53·9′W	X	87
South Low	Northum	NU0342	55°40·5′	1°56·7′W	W	75
South Low	Northum	NU0643	55°41·1′	1°53·8′W	W	75
South Lowfield Fm	N Yks	SE2994	54°20·7′	1°32·8′W	FM	99
South Luffenham	Rut	SK9401	52°36·2′	0°36·3′W	T	141
South Luffenham Heath	Rut	SK9502	52°36·7′	0°35·4′W	X	141
South Lyham	Northum	NU0730	55°34·1′	1°52·9′W	X	75
South Lynch	Hants	SU4127	51°2·7′	1°24·5′W	X	185
Southlynch Plantn	Hants	SU4227	51°2·7′	1°23·7′W	F	185
South Mains	Aberd	NJ6540	57°27·2′	2°34·5′W	X	29
South Mains	Aberd	NJ6633	57°23·4′	2°33·5′W	X	29
South Mains	Aberd	NJ7655	57°35·3′	2°23·6′W	X	29
South Mains	Aberd	NK0033	57°23·5′	1°59·5′W	X	30
South Mains	Angus	NO4547	56°37·0′	2°53·3′W	X	54
South Mains	D & G	NS7808	55°21·3′	3°55·0′W	X	71,78
South Mains	Renf	NS4266	55°51·9′	4°31·1′W	X	64
South Mains	S Ayr	NS2708	55°20·4′	4°43·2′W	X	70,76
South Mains	S Ayr	NS3617	55°25·4′	4°35·1′W	X	70
South Mains	Scot Bord	NT0837	55°37·3′	3°27·2′W	X	72
South Mains	Scot Bord	NT1654	55°46·6′	3°19·9′W	X	65,66,72
South Mains	Stir	NS8590	56°5·6′	3°50·5′W	X	58
South Mains	W Loth	NT0172	55°56·1′	3°34·6′W	X	65
South Mains of Ardiffery	Aberd	NK0535	57°24·6′	1°54·5′W	X	30
South Mains of Auchmaliddie	Aberd	NJ8844	57°29·4′	2°11·6′W	X	30
South Mains of Cononsyth	Angus	NO5746	56°36·5′	2°41·6′W	X	54
South Malling	E Susx	TQ4111	50°53·1′	0°0·7′E	T	198
Southmarsh	Somer	ST7330	51°4·4′	2°22·7′W	T	183
South Marston	Swin	SU1988	51°35·7′	1°43·2′W	T	173
Southmead	C of Bris	ST5878	51°30·2′	2°35·9′W	T	172
South Mead Fm	Somer	ST5123	51°0·5′	2°41·5′W	FM	183
Southmead Fm	Somer	ST5429	51°3·7′	2°39·0′W	FM	183
South Medrox	N Lanak	NS7270	55°54·6′	4°2·4′W	X	64
South Medwin	S Lanak	NT0547	55°42·7′	3°30·3′W	W	72
South Melville	Midlo	NT3166	55°53·2′	3°5·7′W	X	66
South Merstham	Surrey	TQ2952	51°15·4′	0°8·7′W	T	187
South Middleton	Northum	NT9923	55°30·3′	2°0·5′W	T	75
South Middleton Village	Northum	NZ0584	55°9·3′	1°54·9′W	A	81
South Mid Field	Shetld	HU3752	60°15·3′	1°19·4′W	H	3
South Mid Frew	Stir	NS6797	56°9·1′	4°8·0′W	X	57
South Midtown	Aberd	NK0438	57°26·2′	1°55·5′W	X	30
South Milford	N Yks	SE4931	53°46·6′	1°15·0′W	T	105
South Mill	Devon	ST2402	50°49·0′	3°4·3′W	X	192,193
South Millbrex	Aberd	NJ8243	57°28·9′	2°17·6′W	X	29,30
Southmill Fm	Norf	TF8828	52°49·2′	0°47·8′E	FM	132
South Milmain	D & G	NX0852	54°49·8′	4°58·9′W	X	82
South Milton	Devon	SX6942	50°16·0′	3°49·9′W	T	202
South Mimms	Herts	TL2201	51°41·9′	0°13·7′W	T	166
South Mimms Service Area	Herts	TL2200	51°41·4′	0°13·7′W	X	166
South Minnes	Aberd	NJ9522	57°17·6′	2°4·5′W	X	38
Southminster	Essex	TQ9599	51°39·6′	0°49·6′E	T	168
South Moile	D & G	NX0971	55°0·1′	4°58·8′W	X	76
South Molton	Devon	SS7125	51°0·8′	3°50·0′W	T	180
South Monecht	Aberd	NJ7405	57°8·4′	2°25·3′W	X	38
South Moon Ridings	S Glos	ST7488	51°35·6′	2°22·1′W	F	162,172
South Moor	Devon	SS5224	51°0·0′	4°6·2′W	X	180
South Moor	Devon	SX5297	50°45·5′	4°5·5′W	X	191
South Moor	Durham	NZ1851	54°51·5′	1°42·8′W	T	88
South Moor	Lincs	TF1097	53°27·7′	0°20·2′W	X	113
South Moor	Northum	NU1906	55°21·1′	1°41·6′W	X	81
Southmoor	Oxon	SU3998	51°41·0′	1°25·8′W	T	164
South Moor	Somer	ST3434	51°6·3′	2°56·2′W	X	182
South Moor	Somer	ST4123	51°0·4′	2°50·1′W	X	193
South Moor	Somer	ST5037	51°8·0′	2°42·5′W	X	182,183
Southmoor Fm	Devon	SS6806	50°50·5′	3°52·1′W	FM	191
South Moor Fm	Durham	NZ3426	54°37·9′	1°28·0′W	FM	93
South Moor Fm	N Yks	SE9090	54°18·1′	0°36·6′W	FM	94,101
South Moorhouse	E Renf	NS5251	55°44·0′	4°21·0′W	X	64
South Moors or Sand Moors	Donc	SE7113	53°36·8′	0°55·2′W	X	112
South Morar	Highld	NM7687	56°55·5′	5°40·4′W	X	40
South Moreton	Oxon	SU5688	51°35·5′	1°11·1′W	T	174
South Mouth	Shetld	HU6871	60°25·3′	0°45·4′W	W	2
South Muasdale	Arg & Bt	NR6738	55°35·1′	5°41·4′W	X	68
Southmuir	Angus	NO3753	56°40·1′	3°1·2′W	T	54
South Muirton	Aberd	NO6567	56°47·8′	2°33·9′W	X	45
South Mundham	W Susx	SU8700	50°47·8′	0°45·5′W	T	197
South Munstead Fm	Surrey	SU9840	51°9·3′	0°35·5′W	FM	186
South Murnich	Highld	NH5319	57°14·5′	4°25·7′W	X	35
South Muskham	Notts	SK7957	53°6·5′	0°48·8′W	T	120,121
South Nab	N Yks	SE0856	54°0·2′	1°52·3′W	X	104
South Ness	Fife	NT6698	56°10·1′	2°32·4′W	X	59
South Ness	Orkney	ND3091	58°48·3′	3°12·2′W	X	7
South Ness	Shetld	HT9636	60°6·8′	2°3·8′W	X	4
South Ness	Shetld	HU3469	60°24·5′	1°22·5′W	X	2,3
Southness	Shetld	HU3469	60°24·5′	1°22·5′W	X	2,3
South Ness	Shetld	HU4840	60°8·8′	1°7·6′W	X	4
South Nesting	Shetld	HU4554	60°16·3′	1°10·7′W	X	3
South Nesting Bay	Shetld	HU4956	60°17·4′	1°6·3′W	W	2,3
South Nethercott	Devon	SX6894	50°44·1′	3°51·9′W	X	191
Southnett Fm	Worcs	SO6770	52°19·9′	2°28·7′W	FM	138
South Nettlehirst	N Ayr	NS3749	55°42·7′	4°35·2′W	X	63
South Nevi	Orkney	HY6000	58°53·4′	2°41·2′W	X	6
South Newbald	E Yorks	SE9135	53°48·4′	0°36·7′W	T	106
South Newbarns	Cumbr	SD2169	54°6·9′	3°12·1′W	T	96
South Newington	Oxon	SP4033	51°59·9′	1°24·6′W	T	151
South Newsham	Northum	NZ3078	55°6·0′	1°31·4′W	T	88
South Newton	Inverc	NS3367	55°52·3′	4°39·7′W	X	63
South Newton	Wilts	SU0834	51°6·5′	1°52·8′W	T	184
South Nittanshead	Aberd	NJ8653	57°34·3′	2°13·6′W	X	30
South Normanton	Derby	SK4456	53°6·2′	1°20·2′W	T	120
South Norwood	Croy	TQ3368	51°24·0′	0°4·9′W	T	176,177
South Norwood Country Park	Croy	TQ3568	51°23·9′	0°3·2′W	X	177
South Nutfield	Surrey	TQ3049	51°13·7′	0°7·9′W	T	187
South Oakley Inclosure	Hants	SU2205	50°50·9′	1°40·9′W	F	195
South Oaze	Kent	TR0565	51°21·0′	0°57·0′E	X	179
South Ockendon	Thurr	TQ5881	51°30·6′	0°17·0′E	T	177
South Ockendon Hall	Thurr	TQ6083	51°31·6′	0°18·8′E	X	177
Southoe	Cambs	TL1864	52°15·9′	0°15·9′W	T	153
Southolt	Suff	TM1968	52°16·2′	1°13·0′E	T	156
Southolt Hall	Suff	TM2070	52°17·3′	1°13·9′E	X	156
Southope Burn	Northum	NT8305	55°20·6′	2°15·7′W	W	80
South Ord	Northum	NT9850	55°44·9′	2°1·5′W	X	75
South or Little Haw	N Yks	SE0878	54°12·1′	1°52·2′W	X	99
South or Meikle Port of Spittal	D & G	NX0351	54°49·2′	5°3·6′W	X	82
South Ormsby	Lincs	TF3775	53°15·5′	0°3·6′E	T	122
Southorpe	E Yorks	TA1946	53°54·0′	0°10·9′W	X	107
Southorpe	Peterb	TF0803	52°37·1′	0°23·9′W	T	142
Southorpe Fm	Durham	NZ1013	54°31·0′	1°50·3′W	FM	92
Southorpe Fm	Lincs	SK8895	53°26·9′	0°40·1′W	FM	112
Southorpe Grange	E Yorks	TA1945	53°53·5′	0°10·9′W	X	107
Southorpe Village	E Yorks	TA1946	53°54·0′	0°10·9′W	A	107
Southorpe Village	Lincs	SK8995	53°26·9′	0°39·2′W	A	112
South Orrok	Aberd	NJ9619	57°16·0′	2°3·5′W	X	38
South or Sow Street	Staffs	SK0119	52°46·4′	1°58·7′W	X	128
South Ossett	Wakf	SE2819	53°40·2′	1°34·2′W	T	110
South Otterington	N Yks	SE3787	54°16·9′	1°25·5′W	T	99
South Outflow	Orkney	HY5301	58°53·9′	2°48·5′W	X	6,7
South Outmarsh	Norf	TF6123	52°47·1′	0°23·6′E	X	132
Southover	Dorset	SY4889	50°42·1′	2°43·8′W	T	193
Southover	Dorset	SY6294	50°44·9′	2°31·9′W	T	194
Southover	E Susx	TQ4109	50°52·0′	0°0·6′E	T	198
Southover	E Susx	TQ6525	51°0·3′	0°21·5′E	T	188,199
Southover Heath	Dorset	SY7892	50°43·9′	2°18·3′W	X	194
Southover Ho	Dorset	SY7993	50°44·4′	2°17·5′W	X	194
South Owersby	Lincs	TF0693	53°25·6′	0°23·9′W	T	112
South Owersby Ho	Lincs	TF0693	53°25·6′	0°23·9′W	X	112
Southowram	Cald	SE1123	53°42·4′	1°49·6′W	T	104
South Oxhey	Herts	TQ1192	51°37·2′	0°23·4′W	T	176
South Palmerston	E Ayr	NS5019	55°26·8′	4°21·9′W	X	70
South Parade Pier	C of Port	SZ6598	50°46·9′	1°4·3′W	X	196
Southpark	Aberd	NK0056	57°35·9′	1°59·5′W	X	30
South Park	Darl	NZ2813	54°30·9′	1°33·6′W	X	93
Southpark	D & G	NX6245	54°47·1′	4°8·3′W	X	83
South Park	D & G	NX8069	55°0·3′	3°52·1′W	X	84
South Park	Durham	NZ1236	54°43·4′	1°48·4′W	X	92
South Park	E Susx	TQ7626	51°0·6′	0°30·9′E	X	188,199
South Park	E Yorks	TA2229	53°44·8′	0°8·6′W	X	107
South Park	Glos	SO9120	51°52·9′	2°7·5′W	X	163
South Park	Hants	SU2749	51°14·6′	1°36·4′W	X	184
South Park	Kent	TQ5242	51°9·6′	0°10·8′E	X	188
South Park	Lincs	TF0689	53°23·5′	0°24·0′W	X	112,121
South Park	Surrey	TQ2448	51°13·3′	0°13·1′W	T	187
South Park Fm	Suff	TM1856	52°9·8′	1°11·7′E	FM	156
South Park Fm	Surrey	SU9135	51°6·7′	0°41·6′W	FM	186
South Park Fm	Surrey	TQ3448	51°13·2′	0°4·5′W	FM	187
South Park of Bradieston	Aberd	NO7568	56°48·4′	2°24·1′W	X	45
South Parks	Fife	NO2601	56°12·0′	3°11·1′W	T	59
South Parks Fm	N Yks	SE3173	54°9·4′	1°31·1′W	FM	99
Southpark Wood	Devon	SX7369	50°30·7′	3°47·1′W	F	202
Southpark Wood	Kent	TQ8646	51°11·2′	0°40·1′E	F	189
South Park Wood	Scot Bord	NT2340	55°39·1′	3°13·0′W	F	73
South Peeke	Devon	SX3593	50°43·0′	4°19·9′W	X	190
South Pelaw	Durham	NZ2652	54°52·0′	1°35·3′W	T	88
South Perrott	Dorset	ST4706	50°51·3′	2°44·8′W	T	193
South Persie	Pth & Kin	NO1353	56°39·9′	3°24·7′W	X	53
South Petherton	Somer	ST4316	50°56·7′	2°48·3′W	T	193
South Petherwin	Corn	SX3081	50°36·7′	4°23·9′W	T	201
South Pickenham	Norf	TF8504	52°36·4′	0°44·3′E	T	144
South Pier	Blackp	SD3033	53°47·6′	3°3·3′W	X	102
South Pier	S Tyne	NZ3768	55°0·6′	1°24·9′W	X	88
South Pike	Northum	NT9713	55°24·9′	2°2·4′W	X	81
South Pill	Corn	SX4259	50°24·8′	4°13·1′W	T	201
South Plantn	Durham	NZ0844	54°47·7′	1°52·1′W	F	88
South Plantn	N Yks	SE9468	54°6·2′	0°33·3′W	F	101
South Point	Arg & Bt	NR5807	55°18·1′	5°48·3′W	X	68
South Pool	Devon	SX7740	50°15·1′	3°43·1′W	T	202
Southpool Creek	Devon	SX7639	50°14·5′	3°44·0′W	W	202
South Poorton	Dorset	SY5197	50°46·5′	2°41·3′W	T	194
South Port	Arg & Bt	NN0420	56°20·2′	5°9·8′W	X	50,56
Southport	Sefton	SD3417	53°39·0′	2°59·5′W	T	108
Southport Sands	Sefton	SD3219	53°40·0′	3°1·3′W	X	108
South Powrie	C of Dun	NO4234	56°29·9′	2°56·1′W	T	54
South Priorhill	S Lanak	NS7539	55°38·0′	3°58·7′W	X	71
Southpund	Shetld	HU3465	60°22·3′	1°22·5′W	T	2,3
Southpunds	Shetld	HU4020	59°58·0′	1°16·5′W	T	4
South Putechantuy	Arg & Bt	NR6631	55°31·3′	5°42·0′W	X	68
South Quarme Allotment	Somer	SS9436	51°7·0′	3°30·5′W	X	181
South Quarme Fm	Somer	SS9236	51°7·0′	3°32·2′W	FM	181
South Queich	Pth & Kin	NO0204	56°13·4′	3°34·4′W	W	58
South Queich	Pth & Kin	NO0603	56°12·9′	3°30·5′W	W	58
South Quilquox	Aberd	NJ8937	57°25·7′	2°10·5′W	T	30
South Quintinespie	D & G	NX6864	54°57·4′	4°3·3′W	X	83,84
Southra	V of Glam	ST1570	51°25·6′	3°13·0′W	X	171
South Radworthy	Devon	SS7432	51°4·6′	3°47·5′W	T	180
South Raedykes	Aberd	NO8389	56°59·8′	2°16·3′W	X	45
South Ramni Geo	Shetld	HZ2271	59°31·7′	1°36·2′W	X	4
South Rauceby	Lincs	TF0245	52°59·8′	0°28·4′W	T	130
South Rauceby Lodge	Lincs	TF0144	52°59·3′	0°29·3′W	X	130
South Raynham	Norf	TF8724	52°47·1′	0°46·8′E	T	132
South Redbog	Aberd	NJ9854	57°34·8′	2°1·5′W	X	30
South Redbog	Aberd	NK0442	57°28·4′	1°55·5′W	X	30
South Redbriggs	Aberd	NJ7945	57°29·9′	2°20·6′W	X	29,30
South Reddish	Stock	SJ8992	53°25·7′	2°9·5′W	T	109
South Reed	Devon	SX4991	50°42·2′	4°7·9′W	X	191
Southrepps	Norf	TG2536	52°52·7′	1°21·0′E	T	133
Southrepps Common	Norf	TG2634	52°51·6′	1°21·8′E	X	133
Southrepps Hall	Norf	TG2437	52°53·3′	1°20·2′E	A	133
South Reston	Lincs	TF4083	53°19·8′	0°6·5′E	T	122
Southrey	Lincs	TF1366	53°11·0′	0°18·1′W	T	121
Southrey Wood	Lincs	TF1368	53°12·1′	0°18·1′W	F	121
Southridge	Herts	TL2001	51°41·9′	0°15·4′W	X	166
Southridge Fm	W Berks	SU5778	51°30·1′	1°10·3′W	FM	174
South Riding	Northum	NY9495	55°15·2′	2°5·2′W	X	80
Southrigg Fm	N Lanak	NS9266	55°52·8′	3°43·1′W	FM	65
South Rocks	Sund	NZ4157	54°54·6′	1°21·2′W	X	88
South Ronaldsay	Orkney	ND4489	58°47·4′	2°57·7′W	X	7
Southrop	Glos	SP2003	51°43·8′	1°42·2′W	T	163
Southrop	Oxon	SP3532	51°59·4′	1°29·0′W	T	151
Southrope	Hants	SU6744	51°11·7′	1°2·1′W	T	185,186
South Ross	E Yorks	SE7341	53°51·8′	0°53·0′W	X	105,106
South Ruislip	Hill	TQ1185	51°33·4′	0°23·5′W	T	176
South Runcton	Norf	TF6308	52°38·9′	0°25·0′E	T	143
South Rusky Hill	Orkney	HY3409	58°58·1′	3°8·4′W	H	6,7
South Sail	Shetld	HP6608	60°45·2′	0°46·8′W	X	1
South Sandlaw	Aberd	NJ6959	57°37·5′	2°30·7′W	X	29
South Sands	Devon	SX7237	50°13·4′	3°47·3′W	X	202
South Sands	E Yorks	TA1765	54°4·3′	0°12·3′W	X	101
South Sands	Gwyn	SH4259	53°6·5′	4°21·2′W	X	115,123
South Sands	Gwyn	SH4260	53°7·1′	4°21·3′W	X	114,115
South Sands	N Yks	TA0488	54°16·9′	0°23·7′W	X	101
South Sands	S Ayr	NS3230	55°32·3′	4°39·3′W	X	70
South Scarle	Notts	SK8464	53°10·2′	0°44·2′W	T	121
South Scousburgh	Shetld	HU3717	59°56·4′	1°19·8′W	T	4
South Screapadal	Highld	NG5844	57°25·6′	6°1·4′W	X	24
Southsea	C of Port	SZ6499	50°47·4′	1°5·1′W	T	196
Southsea	Wrex	SJ3051	53°3·3′	3°2·3′W	T	117
Southsea Common	C of Port	SZ6498	50°46·9′	1°5·1′W	X	196
South Seatter	Orkney	HY2316	59°1·7′	3°20·0′W	X	6
South Setter	Shetld	HU3954	60°16·4′	1°17·2′W	X	3
South Setter	Shetld	HU4143	60°10·4′	1°15·2′W	X	4
South Shian	Arg & Bt	NM9041	56°31·1′	5°24·4′W	T	49
South Shields	S Tyne	NZ3666	54°59·5′	1°25·8′W	T	88
South Shields Fm	Durham	NZ1241	54°46·1′	1°48·4′W	FM	88
South Ship Channel	Dorset	SY7074	50°34·1′	2°25·0′W	W	194
South Ship Geo	Shetld	HP6204	60°43·1′	0°51·3′W	X	1
South Shore	Blackp	SD3033	53°47·6′	3°3·3′W	T	102
South Shortcleugh	S Lanak	NS9216	55°25·8′	3°42·0′W	X	71,78
South Shuns	Shetld	HU4360	60°19·6′	1°12·8′W	W	2,3
Southside	Aberd	NJ7328	57°20·8′	2°26·5′W	X	38
South Side	Durham	NZ0113	54°31·0′	1°58·7′W	X	92
South Side	Durham	NZ1026	54°38·0′	1°50·3′W	T	92
Southside	Midlo	NT3663	55°51·6′	3°0·9′W	X	66
South Side	Norf	TF9945	52°58·2′	0°58·2′E	X	132
South Side	Norf	TG0045	52°58·1′	0°59·1′E	X	133
Southside	Northum	NU2106	55°21·1′	1°39·7′W	X	81
Southside	Orkney	HY5629	59°9·0′	2°45·7′W	T	5,6
Southside	S Ayr	NS3530	55°32·4′	4°36·5′W	X	70
Southside	Scot Bord	NT0534	55°35·7′	3°30·0′W	X	72
Southside Fm	Hants	SU4343	51°11·3′	1°22·7′W	FM	185
South Side Mount	E Yorks	TA1066	54°4·9′	0°18·7′W	X	101
South Side Mount (Tumulus)	E Yorks	TA1066	54°4·9′	0°18·7′W	A	101
Southside Plantation	N Lincs	TA0311	53°35·4′	0°26·2′W	F	112
Southside Plantn	Scot Bord	NT6754	55°46·9′	2°31·1′W	F	67,74
Southsitch House	Derby	SK2848	53°2·0′	1°34·5′W	A	119
South Skelmanae	Aberd	NJ9058	57°37·0′	2°9·6′W	X	30
South Skerry	Orkney	HY5214	59°0·9′	2°49·7′W	X	6
South Slealands	Cumbr	NY4269	55°1·0′	2°54·0′W	X	85
South Slett	Orkney	ND4388	58°46·8′	2°58·7′W	X	7
South Slipperfield	Scot Bord	NT1351	55°44·9′	3°22·7′W	X	65,72
South Snods	Northum	NZ0651	54°51·5′	1°54·0′W	X	87
South Snuckle	Shetld	HU4134	60°5·6′	1°15·3′W	X	4
South Somercotes	Lincs	TF4193	53°25·1′	0°7·7′E	T	113
South Somercotes Fen Houses	Lincs	TF3993	53°25·2′	0°5·9′E	X	113
South Somercotes Ings	Lincs	TF4192	53°24·6′	0°7·7′E	X	113
South Somerset Cycle Route	Somer	ST4116	50°56·7′	2°50·0′W	X	193
South Sound	Shetld	HU3072	60°26·1′	1°26·8′W	W	3
South Sound	Shetld	HU3269	60°24·5′	1°24·6′W	W	3
South Sound	Shetld	HU5390	60°35·7′	1°1·4′W	W	1,2
South Stack	I of Angl	SH2082	53°18·5′	4°41·7′W	X	114
South Stack (Ynys Lawd)	I of Angl	SH2082	53°18·5′	4°41·7′W	X	114
South Staffs Circular Cycle Way	Staffs	SJ8712	52°42·6′	2°11·1′W	X	127

South Stainley	N Yks	SE3063	54°4·0′	1°32·1′W	T	99
South Stainmore	Cumbr	NY8413	54°31·0′	2°14·4′W	T	91,92
South Stanley	Durham	NZ1952	54°52·0′	1°41·8′W	T	88
South Stany Hill	Shetld	HU4541	60°9·3′	1°10·9′W	H	4
South Steel	Northum	NU2904	55°20·0′	1°32·1′W	X	81
South Stifford	Thurr	TQ5978	51°28·9′	0°17·8′E	T	177
Southstoke	Bath & NE Somer	ST7461	51°21·1′	2°22·0′W	T	172
South Stoke	Oxon	SU5983	51°32·8′	1°8·6′W	T	174
South Stoke	W Susx	TQ0209	50°52·5′	0°32·6′W	T	197
South Stole	Shetld	HU2076	60°28·3′	1°37·7′W	X	3
South Stonehousehill	Aberd	NK0539	57°26·7′	1°54·5′W	X	30
South Stour	Kent	TR0338	51°6·5′	0°54·4′E	T	179,189
South Straiton	Fife	NO4122	56°23·5′	2°56·9′W	T	54,59
South Street	Brom	TQ4357	51°17·9′	0°3·5′E	T	187
South Street	E Susx	TQ3918	50°56·9′	0°0·9′W	T	198
South Street	Kent	TQ6363	51°20·8′	0°20·8′E	T	177,188
South Street	Kent	TQ8361	51°19·3′	0°38·0′E	T	178,188
South Street	Kent	TR0557	51°16·7′	0°56·8′E	T	179
South Street	Kent	TR1265	51°20·9′	1°3·1′E	T	179
South Stroxworthy	Devon	SS3419	50°57·0′	4°21·4′W	X	190
South Studdock	Pemb	SM8502	51°40·8′	5°6·2′W	X	157
South Taing	Orkney	HY6227	59°8·0′	2°39·4′W	X	5
South Taing	Orkney	HY6715	59°1·5′	2°34·0′W	X	5
South Taing	Orkney	HY7752	59°21·5′	2°23·8′W	X	5
South Tararet	Shetld	HU4562	60°20·6′	1°10·6′W	X	2,3
South Tarbet Bay	Highld	NM7991	56°57·7′	5°37·7′W	W	33,40
South Tarbrax	Angus	NO4341	56°33·7′	2°55·2′W	X	54
South Tarbrax	S Lanak	NT0353	55°45·9′	3°32·3′W	X	65,72
South Tavy Head	Devon	SX5981	50°36·9′	3°59·2′W	W	191
South Tawton	Devon	SX6594	50°44·0′	3°54·4′W	T	191
South Tawton Common	Devon	SX6391	50°42·4′	3°56·0′W	X	191
South Techmuiry	Aberd	NJ9559	57°37·5′	2°4·6′W	X	30
South Tehidy	Corn	SW6542	50°14·1′	5°17·4′W	T	203
South Teign River	Devon	SX6785	50°39·2′	3°52·5′W	W	191
South Terminal	W Susx	TQ2841	51°9·5′	0°9·8′W	X	187
South Teuchan	Aberd	NK0838	57°26·2′	1°51·5′W	X	30
South Thoresby	Lincs	TF4076	53°16·0′	0°6·4′E	T	122
South Thornborough Fm	N Yks	SE3892	54°19·6′	1°24·5′W	FM	99
South Thorne	Devon	SS6440	51°8·8′	3°56·3′W	X	180
South Threave	S Ayr	NS2403	55°17·6′	4°45·9′W	X	76
South Tidworth	Wilts	SU2348	51°14·1′	1°39·8′W	T	184
South Tillydaff	Aberd	NJ7106	57°8·9′	2°28·3′W	X	38
South Tillykerrie	Aberd	NJ6212	57°12·1′	2°37·3′W	X	37
South Tinkers Hole Fm	Bucks	SP8522	51°53·6′	0°45·5′W	FM	165
Southton of Blackruthven	Pth & Kin	NO0623	56°23·7′	3°30·9′W	X	52,53,58
South Top	Aberd	NO0997	57°3·6′	3°29·6′W	H	36,43
South Tottenham	Hargy	TQ3388	51°34·7′	0°4·4′W	T	176,177
South Tottington Sands	W Susx	TQ2212	50°53·9′	0°15·5′W	X	198
South Town	Devon	SX9683	50°38·5′	3°27·9′W	T	192
South Town	Hants	SU6536	51°7·4′	1°3·9′W	T	185,186
Southtown	Norf	TG5206	52°35·8′	1°43·7′E	T	134
Southtown	Orkney	ND4895	58°50·6′	2°53·6′W	X	7
Southtown	Shetld	HU3769	60°24·5′	1°19·2′W	X	2,3
Southtown	Somer	ST3216	50°56·6′	2°57·7′W	T	193
Southtown	Somer	ST5538	51°8·6′	2°38·2′W	T	182,183
Southtown of Bandirran	Pth & Kin	NO2030	56°27·6′	3°17·4′W	X	53
Southtown of Melgund	Angus	NO5456	56°41·9′	2°44·6′W	X	54
South Treffgarne	Pemb	SN1612	51°46·8′	4°39·7′W	X	158
South Tulloford	Aberd	NJ7932	57°22·9′	2°20·5′W	X	29,30
South Turnmuir Plantn	D & G	NY1280	55°6·6′	3°22·3′W	F	78
South Twerton	Bath & NE Somer	ST7364	51°22·7′	2°22·9′W	T	172
South Two Mark	D & G	NX0752	54°49·8′	4°59·9′W	X	82
South Tynedale Railway	Cumbr	NY7146	54°48·7′	2°26·6′W	X	86,87
South Ugie Water	Aberd	NJ9548	57°31·6′	2°4·6′W	W	30
South Uist	N Eil	NF7618	57°8·6′	7°21·0′W	X	31
South Uist or Uibhist a Deas	N Eil	NF7933	57°16·8′	7°19·2′W	X	22
South Ulverston	Cumbr	SD3078	54°11·8′	3°4·0′W	T	96,97
South Uplaw	E Renf	NS4454	55°45·5′	4°28·7′W	X	64
South Upper Barrack	Aberd	NJ9041	57°27·8′	2°9·5′W	X	30
South View	Ches	SJ6260	53°8·4′	2°33·7′W	X	118
South View	Hants	SU6352	51°16·0′	1°5·4′W	T	185
South View	Lincs	TF5464	53°9·3′	0°18·6′E	X	122
South View	Northum	NY8048	54°49·8′	2°18·3′W	X	86,87
South View Fm	Lincs	TF0106	52°38·8′	0°30·0′W	FM	141
Southview Fm	Lincs	TF1343	52°58·6′	0°18·6′W	FM	130
South View Fm	Northnts	SP9268	52°18·4′	0°38·6′W	FM	152
South View Fm	N Yks	NZ4001	54°24·4′	1°22·6′W	FM	93
Southview Fm	N Yks	SE8086	54°16·0′	0°45·9′W	FM	94,100
Southville	Devon	SX7443	50°16·6′	3°45·7′W	T	202
Southville	Torf	ST2995	51°39·2′	3°1·2′W	T	171
South Ville	York	SE6258	54°1·1′	1°2·8′W	X	105
South Voe	Shetld	HU3637	60°7·2′	1°20·6′W	W	4
South Voe	Shetld	HU3732	60°4·5′	1°19·6′W	W	4
South Voe of Gletness	Shetld	HU4650	60°14·2′	1°9·7′W	W	3
South Voxter	Shetld	HU3661	60°20·2′	1°20·4′W	X	2,3
South Voxter	Shetld	HU4328	60°2·3′	1°13·2′W	X	4
Southwaite	Cumbr	NY1228	54°38·6′	3°21·4′W	X	89
Southwaite	Cumbr	NY4544	54°47·5′	2°50·9′W	T	86
Southwaite	Cumbr	NY7803	54°25·6′	2°19·9′W	X	91
Southwaite Fm	Cumbr	NY4425	54°37·3′	2°51·6′W	FM	90
Southwaite Hill	Cumbr	NY4545	54°48·1′	2°50·9′W	X	86
Southwaite Service Area	Cumbr	NY4445	54°48·1′	2°51·8′W	X	85
South Wald	Orkney	HY3817	59°2·4′	3°4·3′W	X	6
South Walk Fm	Lincs	TF2184	53°20·6′	0°10·5′W	FM	122
South Walls	Orkney	ND3189	58°47·2′	3°11·1′W	X	7
South Walsham	Norf	TG3613	52°40·0′	1°29·8′E	T	133,134
South Walsham Broad	Norf	TG3614	52°40·6′	1°29·9′E	W	133,134
South Walsham Marshes	Norf	TG4607	52°36·5′	1°38·4′E	X	134
South Wamses	Northum	NU2338	55°38·3′	1°37·6′W	X	75
South Ward	Shetld	HU3264	60°21·8′	1°24·7′W	H	3
South Ward	Shetld	HU3360	60°19·6′	1°23·6′W	H	2,3
South Ward	Shetld	HU3670	60°25·0′	1°20·3′W	H	2,3
Southward Bottom	Lancs	SD8729	53°45·7′	2°11·4′W	X	103
Southward Down	Wilts	SU2674	51°28·1′	1°37·2′W	X	174
Southward Edge	Northum	NZ1193	55°14·1′	1°49·2′W	X	81
South Ward of Reafirth	Shetld	HU5087	60°34·1′	1°4·8′W	X	1,2
South Wards	Shetld	HU2956	60°17·5′	1°28·0′W	H	3
Southward Well Point	I Scilly	SV8812	49°55·8′	6°20·5′W	X	203
Southwark Br	C of Lon	TQ3280	51°30·4′	0°5·5′W	X	176,177
Southwark Park	Sthwk	TQ3579	51°29·9′	0°2·9′W	X	177
South Warnborough	Hants	SU7247	51°13·3′	0°57·7′W	T	186
South Warrackston	Aberd	NJ5520	57°16·4′	2°44·3′W	X	37
South Warren	Suff	TM4458	52°10·2′	1°34·5′E	X	156
South Warren Fm	Surrey	TQ0148	51°13·6′	0°32·8′W	FM	186
South Warren Hill	Dorset	SY4899	50°47·5′	2°43·9′W	X	193
Southwater	W Susx	TQ1526	51°1·5′	0°21·2′W	T	187,198
South Waterland	E Ayr	NS4052	55°44·4′	4°32·5′W	X	64
South Waterland	E Ayr	NS4152	55°44·4′	4°31·5′W	X	64
Southwater Street	W Susx	TQ1527	51°2·1′	0°21·2′W	T	187,198
Southway	C of Plym	SX4860	50°25·4′	4°8·0′W	T	201
Southway	Somer	ST5142	51°10·7′	2°41·7′W	T	182,183
Southway Fm	Devon	SX8692	50°43·2′	3°36·5′W	FM	191
South Weald	Essex	TQ5793	51°37·1′	0°16·5′E	T	177
South Weald Common	Essex	TQ5596	51°38·7′	0°14·8′E	X	167,177
Southweek	Devon	SX4393	50°43·2′	4°13·1′W	X	190
Southweek Wood	Devon	SX4493	50°43·2′	4°12·2′W	F	190
South Weirs	Hants	SU2801	50°48·7′	1°35·8′W	T	195
Southwell	Dorset	SY6870	50°32·0′	2°26·7′W	T	194
Southwell	Notts	SK7053	53°4·4′	0°56·9′W	T	120
Southwell Lane Wood	Suff	TM4583	52°23·6′	1°36·5′E	F	156
South Wells of Rothie	Aberd	NJ7036	57°25·1′	2°29·5′W	X	29
Southwell Trail	Notts	SK6656	53°6·1′	1°0·4′W	X	120
Southwell Trail	Notts	SK6856	53°6·0′	0°58·7′W	X	120
South West Coast Path	Corn	SW3628	50°5·8′	5°41·1′W	X	203
South West Coast Path	Corn	SW7352	50°19·7′	5°11·0′W	X	204
South West Coast Path	Corn	SW8836	50°11·4′	4°57·8′W	X	204
South West Coast Path	Corn	SW9077	50°33·5′	4°57·5′W	X	200
South West Coast Path	Corn	SX1598	50°45·4′	4°37·0′W	X	190
South West Coast Path	Devon	SS2826	51°0·7′	4°26·7′W	X	190
South West Coast Path	Devon	SS5948	51°13·1′	4°0·8′W	X	180
South West Coast Path	Devon	SX8242	50°16·2′	3°39·0′W	X	202
South West Coast Path	Devon	SY0882	50°38·1′	3°17·7′W	X	192
South West Coast Path	Devon	SY3190	50°42·6′	2°58·3′W	X	193
South West Coast Path	Dorset	SY6280	50°37·3′	2°31·9′W	X	194
South Weston	Oxon	SU7098	51°40·8′	0°58·9′W	T	165
South West Point	Devon	SS1343	51°9·6′	4°40·1′W	X	180
South Weydale	Highld	ND1463	58°33·1′	3°28·2′W	X	11,12
South Wheatley	Corn	SX2492	50°42·3′	4°29·2′W	T	190
South Wheatley	Notts	SK7685	53°21·6′	0°51·1′W	T	112,120
South Whimple Fm	Devon	SY0094	50°44·5′	3°24·7′W	FM	192
South Whinfell	Cumbr	NY5726	54°37·9′	2°39·5′W	X	91
South Whitebog	Aberd	NJ8548	57°31·6′	2°14·6′W	X	30
South Whiteness	Shetld	HU3842	60°9·9′	1°18·4′W	X	4
South Whitewell	Aberd	NJ9460	57°38·1′	2°5·6′W	X	30
Southwick	Hants	SU6208	50°52·3′	1°6·7′W	T	196
Southwick	Northnts	TL0192	52°31·2′	0°30·3′W	T	141
South Wick	Orkney	HY5051	59°20·8′	2°52·3′W	W	5
South Wick	Shetld	HU3191	60°36·3′	1°25·5′W	W	1
Southwick	Somer	ST3546	51°12·8′	2°55·5′W	T	182
Southwick	Sund	NZ3758	54°55·2′	1°24·9′W	T	88
Southwick	Wilts	ST8355	51°17·9′	2°14·2′W	T	173
Southwick	W Susx	TQ2405	50°50·1′	0°14·0′W	T	198
Southwick Burn	D & G	NX8960	54°55·6′	3°43·5′W	W	84
Southwick Court	Wilts	ST8455	51°17·9′	2°13·4′W	X	173
Southwick Fm	Glos	SO8830	51°58·3′	2°10·1′W	FM	150
Southwick Fm	Somer	ST3646	51°12·8′	2°54·6′W	FM	182
Southwick Grange	Northnts	TL0392	52°31·2′	0°28·5′W	X	141
Southwick Hill	W Susx	TQ2407	50°51·2′	0°13·9′W	X	198
Southwick Ho	D & G	NX9357	54°54·0′	3°39·7′W	X	84
Southwick Ho	Hants	SU6608	50°52·3′	1°3·3′W	X	196
South Wick of Sound	Shetld	HU4582	60°31·4′	1°10·3′W	W	1,2,3
Southwick Park	Glos	SO8830	51°58·3′	2°10·1′W	X	150
Southwick Water	D & G	NX9055	54°52·9′	3°42·5′W	W	84
Southwick Wood	Northnts	TL0391	52°30·7′	0°28·5′W	F	141
South Widcombe	Bath & NE Somer	ST5856	51°18·3′	2°35·8′W	T	172,182
South Wigston	Leic	SP5998	52°34·8′	1°7·4′W	T	140
South Wilderton	Kent	TQ9956	51°16·3′	0°51·6′E	X	178
South Willesborough	Kent	TR0240	51°7·6′	0°53·6′E	T	189
South Willingham	Lincs	TF1983	53°20·1′	0°12·4′W	T	122
South Wimbledon	Merton	TQ2570	51°25·1′	0°11·7′W	T	176
South Wingate	Durham	NZ4134	54°42·2′	1°21·4′W	T	93
South Wingfield	Derby	SK3755	53°5·7′	1°26·4′W	T	119
South Winterborne	Dorset	SY6988	50°41·7′	2°26·0′W	W	194
South Witham	Lincs	SK9219	52°45·9′	0°37·8′W	T	130
Southwitton	Northum	NZ0687	55°10·9′	1°53·9′W	X	81
South Wold	E Yorks	SE9529	53°45·2′	0°33·1′W	X	106
South Wold	N Yks	SE8770	54°7·3′	0°39·7′W	X	101
Southwold	Suff	TM5076	52°19·7′	1°40·6′E	T	156
Southwold Covert	Suff	TM4676	52°19·8′	1°37·0′E	F	156
Southwold Fm	E Yorks	SE9244	53°53·3′	0°35·6′W	FM	106
Southwold Fm	N Lincs	TA0315	53°37·5′	0°26·1′W	FM	112
South Wolds School	E Yorks	SE9844	53°53·2′	0°30·1′W	X	106
South Womblehill	Aberd	NJ7813	57°12·7′	2°21·4′W	X	38
South Wonford	Devon	SS3808	50°51·2′	4°17·7′W	T	190
South Wongs Fm	Donc	SK5891	53°25·0′	1°7·2′W	FM	111
South Wonston	Hants	SU4635	51°7·0′	1°20·2′W	T	185
South Wonston Fm	Hants	SU4636	51°7·5′	1°20·2′W	FM	185
Southwood	Brom	TQ4457	51°17·9′	0°4·3′E	X	187
Southwood	Derby	SK3521	52°47·4′	1°28·5′W	T	128
South Wood	Derby	SK3620	52°46·8′	1°27·6′W	F	128
Southwood	Devon	SS6120	50°58·0′	3°58·4′W	X	180
South Wood	Devon	SS7431	51°4·1′	3°47·5′W	F	180
Southwood	Devon	SS9309	50°52·5′	3°30·9′W	X	192
Southwood	Devon	SX8447	50°18·9′	3°37·4′W	X	202
South Wood	Devon	SX8688	50°41·1′	3°36·4′W	F	191
South Wood	Essex	TL8610	51°45·7′	0°42·1′E	F	168
South Wood	Hants	SU5848	51°13·9′	1°9·8′W	F	185
Southwood	Hants	SU8455	51°17·5′	0°47·3′W	T	175,186
Southwood	Kent	TQ5348	51°12·9′	0°11·8′E	X	188
South Wood	Lincs	TF0225	52°49·0′	0°28·8′W	F	130
Southwood	Norf	TG3905	52°35·6′	1°32·1′E	T	134
South Wood	Norf	TL9282	52°24·4′	0°49·8′E	F	144
South Wood	Northnts	SP8987	52°28·7′	0°41·0′W	F	141
South Wood	N Yks	SE2261	54°2·9′	1°39·4′W	X	99
South Wood	N Yks	SE6674	54°9·7′	0°58·9′W	F	100
Southwood	Pemb	SM8521	51°51·0′	5°6·9′W	X	157
Southwood	Pth & Kin	NN8920	56°21·8′	3°47·4′W	X	52,58
South Wood	Pth & Kin	NO1639	56°32·4′	3°21·5′W	F	53
Southwood	Shrops	SO6574	52°22·0′	2°30·4′W	X	138
Southwood	Somer	ST5533	51°5·9′	2°38·2′W	T	182,183
Southwood	Worcs	SO7462	52°15·6′	2°22·5′W	T	138,150
Southwood Common	Somer	ST6437	51°8·1′	2°30·5′W	X	183
South Woodend	Falk	NS8078	55°59·1′	3°55·0′W	X	65
South Woodfield Fm	Donc	SE6303	53°31·4′	1°2·6′W	FM	111
South Wood Fm	Devon	ST2004	50°50·0′	3°7·8′W	A	192,193
Southwood Fm	Devon	SX8386	50°40·0′	3°39·0′W	FM	191
Southwood Fm	Devon	SX9375	50°34·1′	3°30·3′W	FM	192
Southwood Fm	Essex	TL6703	51°42·3′	0°25·4′E	FM	167
Southwood Fm	Hants	SU6342	51°10·7′	1°5·5′W	FM	185
Southwood Fm	Hants	SU7040	51°9·5′	0°59·6′W	FM	186
Southwood Fm	Leic	SK3620	52°46·8′	1°27·6′W	FM	128
Southwood Fm	N Yks	NZ2900	54°23·9′	1°32·8′W	FM	93
Southwood Fm	S Glos	ST7289	51°36·2′	2°23·9′W	FM	162,172
Southwood Fm	S Lanak	NS9323	55°29·6′	3°41·2′W	FM	71,72
Southwood Fm	Suff	TM2158	52°10·8′	1°14·4′E	FM	156
Southwood Fm	W Susx	SU8003	50°49·5′	0°51·5′W	FM	197
Southwood Fms	Devon	SY0293	50°43·9′	3°22·9′W	FM	192
South Woodfoot	D & G	NY3172	55°2·5′	3°4·4′W	X	85
South Woodford	Redbr	TQ4090	51°35·7′	0°1·7′E	T	177
South Woodham Ferrers	Essex	TQ8097	51°38·8′	0°36·5′E	T	168
Southwoodhead	D & G	NY2872	55°2·5′	3°7·2′W	X	85
South Woodhill	E Ayr	NS4039	55°37·4′	4°32·0′W	X	70
Southwood Ho	N Yks	SE2981	54°13·7′	1°32·9′W	X	99
South Wood of Lenihuline	Arg & Bt	NS0069	55°52·6′	5°11·4′W	F	63
South Woods	N Yks	SE5084	54°15·2′	1°13·5′W	F	100
Southwoods Hall	N Yks	SE5084	54°15·2′	1°13·5′W	X	100
South Wood's Hill Fm	Lancs	SD4445	53°54·1′	2°50·7′W	FM	102
Southwood Wood	Devon	SX5954	50°22·4′	3°58·6′W	F	202
South Woolley Fm	Devon	SS5938	51°7·7′	4°0·5′W	FM	180
South Wootton	Norf	TF6422	52°46·5′	0°26·3′E	T	132
South Wootton Common	Norf	TF6523	52°47·0′	0°27·2′E	F	132
South Wootton Ho	Somer	ST5135	51°7·0′	2°41·6′W	X	182,183
Southworth Hall Fm	Warr	SJ6293	53°26·2′	2°33·9′W	FM	109
South Wraxall	Wilts	ST8364	51°22·7′	2°14·3′W	T	173
South Yantlet Creek	Medway	TQ8270	51°24·2′	0°37·4′E	W	178
South Yardhope	Northum	NT9200	55°17·9′	2°7·1′W	X	80
South Yardley	Birm	SP1284	52°27·5′	1°49·0′W	T	139
South Yarrows	Highld	ND3043	58°22·5′	3°11·3′W	X	11,12
South Yeo	Devon	SS4022	50°58·7′	4°16·4′W	X	180,190
South Yeo	Devon	SS5100	50°47·1′	4°6·4′W	T	191
South Yeo	Devon	SS8608	50°51·9′	3°36·8′W	X	191
South Ythsie	Aberd	NJ8830	57°21·9′	2°11·5′W	X	30
South Zeal	Devon	SX6593	50°43·5′	3°54·4′W	T	191
Soutra	Angus	NO4461	56°44·5′	2°54·5′W	X	44
Soutra Aisle	Scot Bord	NT4558	55°49·0′	2°52·2′W	A	66,73
Soutra Fm	Midlo	NT4559	55°49·5′	2°52·2′W	FM	66,73
Soutra Hill	Scot Bord	NT4559	55°49·5′	2°52·2′W	H	66,73
Sovell Down	Dorset	ST9810	50°53·6′	2°1·3′W	X	195
Sovereign Harbour	E Susx	TQ6401	50°47·3′	0°20·0′E	X	199
Sow and Pigs	Northum	NZ3381	55°7·6′	1°28·5′W	X	81
Sowanna Fm	Corn	SW6721	50°2·8′	5°14·9′W	FM	203
Sowbath	Shrops	SJ5722	52°47·9′	2°37·9′W	X	126
Sowber Gate	N Yks	SE3588	54°17·4′	1°27·3′W	X	99
Sowber Hill Fm	N Yks	SE2595	54°21·2′	1°36·5′W	FM	99
Sowber Hill Fm	N Yks	SE3589	54°18·0′	1°27·3′W	FM	99
Sowberry Court	Oxon	SU5983	51°32·8′	1°8·6′W	X	174
Sowbrook Fm	Derby	SK4539	52°57·0′	1°19·4′W	FM	129
Sowburnrig	Midlo	NT3456	55°47·8′	3°2·7′W	X	66,73
Sow Dale	Lincs	TF3466	53°10·7′	0°0·7′E	X	122
Sowden	Devon	SX9983	50°38·5′	3°25·3′W	X	192
Sowden Beck	N Yks	SE1384	54°15·3′	1°47·6′W	W	99
Sowden Beck Fm	N Yks	SE1484	54°15·3′	1°46·7′W	FM	99
Sowdens	E Susx	TQ8519	50°56·7′	0°38·4′E	X	189,199
Sow Dike	York	SE6356	54°0·0′	1°1·9′W	W	105,106
Sowdley Wood	Shrops	SO3280	52°25·1′	2°59·6′W	F	137
Sowe Common	Cov	SP3783	52°26·9′	1°26·9′W	X	140
Sowe Fields Fm	Warw	SP3784	52°27·4′	1°26·9′W	FM	140
Sowells Fm	Devon	ST0710	50°53·2′	3°18·9′W	FM	192
Sowe Mouth	Warw	SP3272	52°20·9′	1°31·4′W	W	140
Sowen Dod	D & G	NS8614	55°24·7′	3°47·6′W	H	71,78
Sowens Knowe	D & G	NX9494	55°14·0′	3°39·6′W	H	78
Sowerby	Cald	SE0423	53°42·4′	1°56·0′W	T	104
Sowerby	N Yks	SE4381	54°13·6′	1°20·0′W	T	99
Sowerby Bridge	Cald	SE0623	53°42·4′	1°54·1′W	T	104
Sowerby Cotts	Cumbr	SD1973	54°9·0′	3°14·0′W	X	96
Sowerby Grange	N Yks	SE3992	54°19·6′	1°23·6′W	X	99
Sowerby Grange	N Yks	SE4193	54°20·1′	1°21·7′W	X	99
Sowerby Hall	Cumbr	NY3836	54°43·2′	2°57·3′W	X	90
Sowerby Hall	Cumbr	SD1972	54°8·5′	3°14·0′W	X	96
Sowerby Hall Fm	Lancs	SD4738	53°50·4′	2°47·9′W	FM	102
Sowerby Ho	N Yks	SE4094	54°20·6′	1°22·7′W	X	99
Sowerby Lodge	Cumbr	SD1972	54°8·5′	3°14·0′W	X	96
Sowerby Park	Cumbr	NY7913	54°31·0′	2°19·0′W	X	91
Sowerby Parks	N Yks	SE4378	54°12·0′	1°20·0′W	X	99
Sowerby Parks Fm	N Yks	SE4477	54°11·5′	1°19·1′W	FM	99
Sowerby Row	Cumbr	NY3940	54°45·3′	2°56·4′W	T	85
Sowerby Wood	Cumbr	NY3652	54°51·8′	2°59·4′W	F	85
Sower Carr	Lancs	SD3743	53°53·0′	2°57·1′W	T	102
Sowerhill	Somer	SS8924	51°0·5′	3°34·6′W	X	181
Sower Hill Fm	Oxon	SU3087	51°35·1′	1°33·6′W	FM	174
Sowermire Fm	Cumbr	SD6284	54°15·3′	2°34·6′W	FM	97
Sowermyrr	Cumbr	NY0804	54°25·6′	3°24·7′W	X	89
Sowerthwaite Fm	N Yks	SD7769	54°7·2′	2°20·7′W	FM	98
Sow How	Cumbr	SD3987	54°16·7′	2°55·8′W	X	96,97
Sowley Green	Suff	TL7050	52°7·6′	0°29·4′E	T	154
Sowley Ho	Hants	SZ3796	50°46·0′	1°28·1′W	X	196
Sowley Pond	Hants	SZ3796	50°46·0′	1°28·1′W	W	196
Sow Moor	Surrey	SU9861	51°20·6′	0°35·2′W	X	175,176,186
Sow of Atholl, The	Pth & Kin	NN6274	56°50·5′	4°15·3′W	H	42
Sowood	Cald	SE0718	53°39·7′	1°53·2′W	T	110
Sowood Green	Cald	SE0718	53°39·7′	1°53·2′W	T	110
Sow or South Street	Staffs	SK0119	52°46·4′	1°58·7′W	X	128
Sow's Geo	Highld	ND2176	58°40·1′	3°21·2′W	X	7,12
Sow Skerry	Orkney	HY2704	58°55·3′	3°15·6′W	X	6,7
Sow Skerry	Orkney	HY6001	58°53·9′	2°41·2′W	X	6
Sowter's Fm	W Susx	SU9023	51°0·2′	0°42·6′W	FM	197

Sow, The	Orkney	HY1802	58°54·1'	3°24·9'W	X	7
Sowton	Devon	SX9792	50°43·3'	3°27·2'W	T	192
Sowton	Devon	SY1199	50°47·3'	3°15·4'W	X	192,193
Sowton Barton	Devon	SX8388	50°41·0'	3°39·0'W	T	191
Sowton & Digby Station	Devon	SX9691	50°42·8'	3°28·0'W	X	192
Sowtontown	Devon	SX5176	50°34·1'	4°5·9'W	X	191,201
Sowy River	Somer	ST3927	51°2·6'	2°51·8'W	W	193
Sowy River	Somer	ST3932	51°5·3'	2°51·9'W	X	182
Soyal	Highld	NH5791	57°53·4'	4°24·3'W	T	21
Soyea Island	Highld	NC0421	58°8·3'	5°19·3'W	X	15
Soy Gunna	Arg & Bt	NM1052	56°34·5'	6°42·9'W	X	46
Soyland Moor	Cald	SD9819	53°40·3'	2°1·4'W	X	109
Soyland Town	Cald	SE0320	53°40·8'	1°56·9'W	T	104
Spa Bottom Fm	N Yks	SE3351	53°57·5'	1°29·4'W	FM	104
Spacey Houses	N Yks	SE3151	53°57·5'	1°31·2'W	T	104
Spa Clough Head	Cald	SE0231	53°46·8'	1°57·8'W	X	104
Spa Common	Norf	TG2930	52°49·4'	1°24·3'E	T	133
Spaddock Hall	Lancs	SD5340	53°51·5'	2°42·5'W	X	102
Spadeadam Fm	Cumbr	NY5870	55°1·6'	2°39·0'W	FM	86
Spadeadam Forest	Cumbr	NY6372	55°2·7'	2°34·3'W	F	86
Spade Green	Staffs	SK0809	52°41·0'	1°52·5'W	X	128
Spade Mill Resrs	Lancs	SD6137	53°49·9'	2°35·1'W	W	102,103
Spade Oak Fm	Bucks	SU8887	51°34·7'	0°43·4'W	FM	175
Spa Flat	Brad	SE1143	53°53·2'	1°49·5'W	X	104
Spa Fm	Bucks	SP6713	51°48·9'	1°1·3'W	FM	164,165
Spa Fm	Norf	TG1925	52°46·9'	1°15·3'E	FM	133,134
Spa Fm	Northnts	TL0095	52°32·9'	0°31·1'W	FM	141
Spa Gill Wood	N Yks	SE2568	54°6·7'	1°36·6'W	F	99
Spa Gill Wood	N Yks	SE2569	54°7·2'	1°36·6'W	F	99
Spa Ho	Nth Pt Talb	SN7003	51°42·9'	3°52·5'W	X	170
Spa Ho	N Yks	SE4283	54°14·7'	1°20·9'W	X	99
Spa Ho	Roth	SK4488	53°23·5'	1°19·9'W	X	111,120
Spàinebhig	N Eil	NB5364	58°29·9'	6°13·9'W	W	8
Spain Fm	Devon	SY0092	50°43·4'	3°24·6'W	FM	192
Spain's End Fm	Essex	TL6636	52°0·1'	0°25·5'E	FM	154
Spains Hall	Essex	TL6006	51°44·0'	0°19·4'E	X	167
Spain's Hall	Essex	TL6734	51°59·0'	0°26·3'E	A	154
Spains Wood	Essex	TL6007	51°44·6'	0°19·4'E	F	167
Spalding	Lincs	TF2422	52°47·1'	0°9·3'W	T	131
Spalding Common	Lincs	TF2220	52°46·1'	0°11·1'W	X	131
Spalding Marsh	Lincs	TF2726	52°49·2'	0°6·5'W	X	131
Spalding's Chair Hill	Suff	TL9380	52°23·3'	0°50·4'E	X	144
Spaldington	E Yorks	SE7633	53°47·5'	0°50·4'W	T	105,106
Spaldington Common	E Yorks	SE7732	53°47·0'	0°49·5'W	X	105,106
Spaldington Grange	E Yorks	SE7532	53°47·0'	0°51·3'W	X	105,106
Spaldwick	Cambs	TL1272	52°20·3'	0°21·0'W	T	153
Spalefield	Fife	NO5506	56°14·6'	2°43·1'W	X	59
Spalford	Notts	SK8369	53°12·9'	0°45·0'W	T	121
Spalford Warren (Nature Res)	Notts	SK8368	53°12·4'	0°45·0'W	X	121
Spallander Burn	S Ayr	NS3708	55°20·6'	4°33·8'W	W	70,77
Spa Lodge Fm	Lincs	TF0714	52°43·0'	0°24·6'W	FM	130
Spalsbury Fm	Devon	ST0217	50°56·9'	3°23·3'W	FM	181
Span	Derby	SE0500	53°30·0'	1°55·1'W	X	110
Span Bottom	Devon	SS7235	51°6·2'	3°49·3'W	X	180
Spanby	Lincs	TF0938	52°55·9'	0°22·3'W	T	130
Spancarr	Derby	SK3466	53°11·6'	1°29·1'W	X	119
Span Clough	Derby	SK0692	53°25·7'	1°54·2'W	X	110
Spaney Geo	Orkney	HY6036	59°12·8'	2°41·5'W	X	5
Span Fm	I of W	SZ5479	50°36·7'	1°13·8'W	FM	196
Spango	D & G	NS8218	55°26·8'	3°51·5'W	X	71,78
Spango	Inverc	NS2374	55°55·8'	4°49·6'W	T	63
Spango Br	D & G	NS8217	55°26·2'	3°51·5'W	X	71,78
Spango Hill	D & G	NS8118	55°26·7'	3°52·4'W	H	71,78
Spango Water	D & G	NS7818	55°26·7'	3°55·3'W	W	71,78
Spanham	Durham	NZ0110	54°29·4'	1°58·7'W	X	92
Span Head	Devon	SS7436	51°6·8'	3°47·6'W	W	180
Spanhoe Fm	Northnts	SP9496	52°33·5'	0°36·4'W	FM	141
Spanhoe Wood	Northnts	SP9495	52°32·9'	0°36·4'W	F	141
Spaniard Rocks	Swan	SS4092	51°36·5'	4°18·3'W	X	159
Spaniards Inn	Camden	TQ2687	51°34·3'	0°10·5'W	X	176
Spaniel Fm	N Yks	SE9870	54°7·2'	0°29·6'W	FM	101
Spaniorum Fm	S Glos	ST5681	51°31·8'	2°37·7'W	FM	172
Spaniorum Hill	S Glos	ST5681	51°31·8'	2°37·7'W	H	172
Spanish Green	Hants	SU6958	51°19·2'	1°0·2'W	T	175,186
Spanish Head	I of M	SC1865	54°3·2'	4°46·4'W	H	95
Span Moor	Derby	SK0692	53°25·7'	1°54·2'W	X	110
Spanoak Wood	Beds	TL0667	52°17·7'	0°26·3'W	F	153
Spara Br	Devon	SX8484	50°38·9'	3°38·1'W	A	191
Sparbent	Ches	SK0069	53°13·3'	1°59·6'W	X	119
Spar Cave	Highld	NG5312	57°8·2'	6°4·5'W	X	32
Sparchford	Shrops	SO4983	52°26·8'	2°44·6'W	X	137,138
Spargrove	Somer	ST6738	51°8·7'	2°27·9'W	X	183
Sparham	Norf	TG0719	52°44·0'	1°4·2'E	T	133
Sparham Hall	Norf	TF8711	52°40·1'	0°46·3'E	X	132
Sparham Hall	Norf	TG0718	52°43·4'	1°4·3'E	X	133
Sparhamhill	Norf	TG0818	52°43·4'	1°5·2'E	T	133
Sparham Ho	Norf	TG0720	52°44·5'	1°4·4'E	X	133
Sparham Hole	Norf	TG0519	52°44·0'	1°2·6'E	X	133
Spar Hill	Essex	TL8303	51°42·0'	0°39·3'E	X	168
Spark Bridge	Cumbr	SD3084	54°15·1'	3°4·0'W	T	96,97
Sparkbrook	Birm	SP0884	52°27·5'	1°52·5'W	T	139
Sparkes's Fm	Suff	TM2261	52°12·4'	1°15·4'E	FM	156
Sparket	Cumbr	NY4325	54°37·3'	2°52·5'W	X	90
Sparket Mill	Cumbr	NY4326	54°37·8'	2°52·6'W	X	90
Sparkey Wood	Essex	TL8312	51°46·8'	0°39·6'E	F	168
Sparkford	Somer	ST6026	51°2·2'	2°33·8'W	T	183
Sparkford Hill	Somer	ST6025	51°1·6'	2°33·8'W	X	183
Sparkford Wood	Somer	ST6127	51°2·7'	2°33·0'W	F	183
Spark Hagg	N Yks	SE5834	53°48·2'	1°6·7'W	X	105
Spark Hall	Warr	SJ6282	53°20·3'	2°33·8'W	X	109
Sparkhayne	Devon	SS9721	50°59·0'	3°27·7'W	X	181
Sparkhill	Birm	SP0983	52°26·9'	1°51·7'W	T	139
Sparklane Fm	Ches	SJ7962	53°9·5'	2°18·4'W	FM	118
Sparklow	Derby	SK1265	53°11·2'	1°48·8'W	X	119
Sparks	E Susx	TQ8022	50°58·4'	0°34·2'E	X	199
Sparks Fm	Somer	ST2919	50°58·2'	3°0·3'W	FM	193
Spark's Fm	Suff	TL7278	52°22·6'	0°32·0'E	FM	143
Spark's Hall	Kent	TQ8048	51°12·4'	0°35·0'E	X	188
Sparkwell	Devon	SX5857	50°24·0'	3°59·5'W	T	202
Sparkwell	Devon	SX7865	50°28·6'	3°42·8'W	X	202
Sparl	Shetld	HU3666	60°22·8'	1°20·3'W	X	2,3
Sparnelbank	E Ayr	NS4935	55°35·4'	4°23·3'W	X	70
Sparnock Fm	Corn	SW7842	50°14·4'	5°6·4'W	FM	204
Sparnon	Corn	SW3924	50°3·8'	5°38·5'W	X	203
Sparnon Gate	Corn	SW6843	50°14·7'	5°14·9'W	T	203
Spar Plantn	Scot Bord	NT6008	55°22·1'	2°37·4'W	F	80
Sparretts Fm	Corn	SX2371	50°31·0'	4°29·4'W	FM	201
Sparr Fm	W Susx	TQ0427	51°2·2'	0°30·6'W	FM	186,197
Sparrington Fm	Heref	SO5653	52°10·6'	2°38·2'W	FM	149
Sparrowbush Fm	Dorset	ST8703	50°49·8'	2°10·7'W	FM	194
Sparrowbush Ledge	Devon	SY2689	50°42·0'	3°2·5'W	X	192,193
Sparrowe's Nest	Suff	TM1547	52°5·0'	1°8·7'E	X	169
Sparrow Fm	Wilts	ST8775	51°28·7'	2°10·8'W	FM	173
Sparrow Gorse	Lincs	SK9746	53°0·4'	0°32·9'W	F	130
Sparrow Green	Norf	TF9514	52°41·5'	0°53·5'E	T	132
Sparrowgrove	Ches	SJ7162	53°9·5'	2°25·6'W	X	118
Sparrow Hall	Kent	TQ8446	51°11·2'	0°38·4'E	X	188
Sparrow Hall	N Yks	NZ5000	54°23·8'	1°13·4'W	X	93
Sparrow Hall	N Yks	SE7081	54°13·4'	0°55·2'W	X	100
Sparrow Hall	N Yks	SE8269	54°6·9'	0°44·3'W	X	100
Sparrow Hall	Suff	TL9279	52°22·7'	0°49·7'E	X	144
Sparrow Hall Fm	Cambs	TL4794	52°31·7'	0°10·4'E	FM	143
Sparrow Hall Fm	York	SE6645	53°54·1'	0°59·3'W	FM	105,106
Sparrowhawk Fm	N Yks	SE1666	54°5·6'	1°44·9'W	FM	99
Sparrow Hill	Norf	TG0142	52°56·5'	0°59·9'E	X	133
Sparrow Hill	Norf	TL9097	52°32·5'	0°48·5'E	X	144
Sparrow Hill	Somer	ST4152	51°16·1'	2°50·4'W	T	182
Sparrow Lodge	Northnts	SP7538	52°2·4'	0°54·0'W	X	152
Sparrowpit	Derby	SK0880	53°19·3'	1°52·4'W	T	110
Sparrows End	Essex	TL5236	52°0·3'	0°13·3'E	X	154
Sparrow's Fm	Essex	TL7514	51°48·1'	0°32·7'E	FM	167
Sparrow's Fm	Essex	TM2028	51°54·6'	1°12·3'E	FM	169
Sparrow's Green	E Susx	TQ6332	51°4·1'	0°20·0'E	T	188
Sparrow's Hall	Essex	TL6235	51°59·6'	0°22·0'E	X	154
Sparrowthorn	Glos	SO9712	51°48·6'	2°2·2'W	X	163
Sparrow Wycke	Essex	TL8602	51°41·4'	0°41·9'E	X	168
Sparsholt	Hants	SU4331	51°4·8'	1°22·8'W	T	185
Sparsholt	Oxon	SU3487	51°35·1'	1°30·2'W	T	174
Sparsholt Down	Oxon	SU3384	51°33·5'	1°31·0'W	X	174
Sparsholt Field	Oxon	SU3386	51°34·5'	1°31·0'W	X	174
Sparting Brook	Lancs	SD5338	53°50·4'	2°42·4'W	W	102
Spartleton	E Loth	NT6565	55°52·9'	2°33·1'W	H	67
Spartleton Edge	E Loth	NT6565	55°52·9'	2°33·1'W	H	67
Spartley Burn	Northum	NT9711	55°23·8'	2°2·4'W	W	81
Spartylea	Northum	NY8548	54°49·8'	2°13·6'W	T	87
Spartywell	Northum	NY7851	54°51·4'	2°20·1'W	X	86,87
Spath	Staffs	SK0835	52°55·0'	1°52·5'W	T	128
Spa, The	E Yorks	TA1866	54°4·8'	0°11·4'W	X	101
Spa, The	N Yks	TA0487	54°16·3'	0°23·8'W	X	101
Spa, The	Wrekin	SJ6313	52°43·0'	2°32·5'W	X	127
Spath, The	Derby	SK2235	52°55·0'	1°40·0'W	X	128
Spa Trail	Lincs	TF2366	53°10·8'	0°9·2'W	X	122
Spaunton	N Yks	SE7289	54°17·7'	0°53·2'W	T	94,100
Spaunton Knowl	N Yks	SE7191	54°18·8'	0°54·1'W	X	94,100
Spaunton Lodge	N Yks	SE7092	54°19·4'	0°55·0'W	X	94,100
Spaunton Moor	N Yks	SE7286	54°16·1'	0°53·2'W	X	94,100
Spaunton Moor	N Yks	SE7293	54°19·9'	0°53·1'W	X	94,100
Spa Well	Cumbr	NY5709	54°28·7'	2°39·4'W	W	91
Spa Well	Northum	NY8564	54°58·5'	2°13·6'W	W	87
Spa Well Fm	E Yorks	SE6421	53°41·1'	1°1·4'W	FM	105,106
Spa Wells (Sulphur)	Darl	NZ3410	54°29·3'	1°28·1'W	W	93
Spaxton	Somer	ST2237	51°7·9'	3°6·5'W	T	182
Speakman House	Warr	SJ6797	53°28·4'	2°29·4'W	A	109
Spean Bridge	Highld	NN2281	56°53·4'	4°54·9'W	T	34,41
Spearbed Copse	Hants	SU4001	50°48·7'	1°25·6'W	F	196
Spear Head	Highld	ND0971	58°37·3'	3°33·5'W	X	12
Spear Hill	W Susx	TQ1317	50°56·7'	0°23·1'W	X	198
Spears Hill	Fife	NO4528	56°26·7'	2°53·1'W	H	54,59
Spears Hill	Suff	TM0677	52°21·4'	1°1·9'E	X	144
Spears Hill Fm	Suff	TM0777	52°21·3'	1°2·8'E	FM	144
Spearywell	Hants	SU3127	51°2·7'	1°33·1'W	T	185
Spearywell Wood	Hants	SU3128	51°3·3'	1°33·1'W	F	185
Speccott	Devon	SS5014	50°54·6'	4°7·6'W	X	180
Spechley Park	Worcs	SO8953	52°10·7'	2°9·3'W	X	150
Speckington	Somer	ST5623	51°0·5'	2°37·2'W	T	183
Speck's Fm	Essex	TL8834	51°58·6'	0°44·6'E	FM	155
Spectacle	Angus	NO7048	56°37·6'	2°28·9'W	X	54
Spectacle Wood	Notts	SK6579	53°18·5'	1°1·1'W	F	120
Speddoch	D & G	NX8582	55°7·4'	3°47·8'W	X	78
Speddoch Hill	D & G	NX8381	55°6·8'	3°49·6'W	H	78
Speddochhill	D & G	NX8481	55°6·8'	3°48·7'W	X	78
Speddyd	Denb	SJ1064	53°10·2'	3°20·4'W	X	116
Spedlins	D & G	NY0986	55°9·8'	3°25·3'W	X	78
Spedlin's Flow	D & G	NY0987	55°10·4'	3°25·3'W	X	78
Speech House Hotel	Glos	SO6212	51°48·6'	2°32·7'W	X	162
Speech House Walk	Glos	SO6311	51°48·0'	2°31·8'W	F	162
Speed Gate	Kent	TQ5765	51°22·0'	0°15·7'E	T	177
Speediehill	Pth & Kin	NO0434	56°29·6'	3°33·1'W	X	52,53
Speedsdairy Fm	Beds	TL1038	52°2·0'	0°23·4'W	FM	153
Speed the Plough	Beds	TL0832	51°58·8'	0°25·3'W	X	166
Speedwel Belt	Beds	SP9531	51°58·4'	0°36·6'W	X	165
Speedwell	C of Bris	ST6374	51°28·1'	2°31·6'W	T	172
Speedwell Cavern	Derby	SK1382	53°20·3'	1°47·9'W	X	110
Speedwell Fm	Beds	SP9532	51°58·9'	0°36·6'W	FM	165
Speedwell Fm	Cambs	TF4204	52°37·1'	0°6·3'E	FM	142,143
Speel Bank	Cumbr	SD3581	54°13·5'	2°59·4'W	X	96,97
Speel Bank	Cumbr	SD3680	54°13·0'	2°58·5'W	X	96,97
Speen	Bucks	SU8499	51°41·2'	0°46·7'W	T	165
Speen	W Berks	SU4668	51°24·8'	1°19·9'W	T	174
Speen Fm	Bucks	SU8399	51°41·2'	0°47·6'W	FM	165
Speen Hill	Win & Maid	SU8382	51°32·1'	0°47·8'W	X	175
Speen Ho	W Berks	SU4567	51°24·2'	1°20·8'W	X	174
Speet Gill	Cumbr	NY2847	54°49·0'	3°6·8'W	W	85
Speeton	N Yks	TA1474	54°9·2'	0°14·8'W	T	101
Speeton Cliffs	N Yks	TA1575	54°9·7'	0°13·9'W	X	101
Speeton Field	N Yks	TA1473	54°8·6'	0°14·9'W	X	101
Speeton Grange	N Yks	TA1374	54°9·2'	0°15·8'W	X	101
Speeton Hills	N Yks	TA1475	54°9·7'	0°14·8'W	X	101
Speeton Manor	N Yks	TA1574	54°9·2'	0°13·9'W	X	101
Speeton Moor	N Yks	TA1674	54°9·2'	0°13·0'W	X	101
Speeton Sands	N Yks	TA1575	54°9·7'	0°13·9'W	X	101
Speicein Còinnich	Highld	NC1004	57°59·3'	5°12·4'W	H	15
Speinne Beag	Arg & Bt	NM5248	56°33·8'	6°1·7'W	X	47,48
Speinne Mòr	Arg & Bt	NM4949	56°34·2'	6°4·7'W	H	47,48
Speiran, The	Pth & Kin	NN9537	56°31·1'	3°41·9'W	X	52,53
Speir Gairs	Scot Bord	NT1317	55°26·6'	3°22·1'W	X	78
Speke	Liv	SJ4483	53°20·7'	2°50·1'W	T	108
Speke Hall	Liv	SJ4182	53°20·1'	2°52·8'W	A	108
Spekes Bottom	Medway	TQ7965	51°21·6'	0°34·7'E	X	178
Spekes Cross	Devon	SS6609	50°52·1'	3°53·9'W	X	191
Speke's Hill	Somer	ST3318	50°57·7'	2°56·9'W	X	193
Speke's Mill Mouth	Devon	SS2223	50°59·0'	4°31·8'W	W	190
Spelders Hill	Kent	TR0643	51°9·2'	0°57·1'E	X	179,189
Speldhurst	Kent	TQ5541	51°9·1'	0°13·4'E	T	188
Spella Fm	N Yks	SE5969	54°7·0'	1°5·4'W	FM	100
Spella Ho	Northnts	SP4752	52°10·1'	1°18·4'W	X	151
Spellar Park	N Yks	SE5971	54°8·1'	1°5·4'W	X	100
Spellar Wood	Lincs	SK9243	52°58·8'	0°37·4'W	F	130
Spellbrook	Herts	TL4817	51°50·1'	0°9·3'E	T	167
Spell Close Fm	Stock on T	NZ4310	54°29·3'	1°19·8'W	FM	93
Speller Hill	Notts	SK7541	52°57·9'	0°52·6'W	X	129
Spellers	Herts	TL4113	51°48·1'	0°3·1'E	X	167
Speller, The	Shrops	SO5189	52°30·0'	2°42·9'W	X	137,138
Spell Howe	N Yks	TA0678	54°11·4'	0°22·1'W	A	101
Spell Howe Plantn	N Yks	TA0679	54°12·0'	0°22·1'W	F	101
Spellow Fm	E Yorks	TA0059	54°1·3'	0°28·0'W	FM	106,107
Spellow Fm	Notts	SK6639	52°56·9'	1°0·7'W	FM	129
Spellow Grange	N Yks	SE3763	54°3·9'	1°25·7'W	X	99
Spellow Hill	Notts	SK6640	52°57·4'	1°0·6'W	X	129
Spellow Hill	N Yks	SE3862	54°3·4'	1°24·8'W	X	99
Spellow Hills	Lincs	TF4072	53°13·8'	0°6·3'E	X	122
Spellow Hills (Long Barrow)	Lincs	TF4072	53°13·8'	0°6·3'E	A	122
Spelmonden	Kent	TQ7037	51°6·6'	0°26·4'E	X	188
Spelsbury	Oxon	SP3421	51°53·4'	1°30·0'W	T	164
Spelter	Brig	SS8593	51°37·7'	3°39·3'W	T	170
Spelthorn Wood	Suff	TL8748	52°6·1'	0°44·2'E	F	155
Spen	Kirk	SE1925	53°43·5'	1°42·3'W	T	104
Spen	Lancs	SD8238	53°50·5'	2°16·0'W	X	103
Spen Banks	Ghead	NZ1559	54°55·8'	1°45·5'W	F	88
Spen Brook	Lancs	SD8238	53°50·5'	2°16·0'W	X	103
Spence Combe	Devon	SS7901	50°48·0'	3°42·6'W	X	191
Spence Cross	Devon	ST0901	50°48·3'	3°17·1'W	X	192
Spence Fm	Dorset	SY3596	50°45·8'	2°54·9'W	FM	193
Spence Moor	Lancs	SD7939	53°51·1'	2°18·7'W	X	103
Spencer Beck	Midd	NZ5318	54°33·5'	1°10·4'W	W	93
Spencer Close	N Yks	SE3099	54°23·4'	1°31·9'W	X	99
Spencerfield	Fife	NT1483	56°2·2'	3°22·4'W	X	65
Spencer Lodge	Northnts	SP8474	52°21·7'	0°45·6'W	X	141
Spencers	Essex	TL7539	52°1·5'	0°33·4'E	X	155
Spencer's Fm	Bucks	SP9904	51°43·8'	0°33·6'W	FM	165
Spencers Fm	Essex	TL5107	51°44·7'	0°11·6'E	FM	167
Spencer's Fm	Oxon	SP6802	51°43·0'	1°0·5'W	FM	164,165
Spencersgreen	Bucks	SP9009	51°46·6'	0°41·3'W	X	165
Spencer's Ho	Lancs	SJ4399	53°29·3'	2°51·1'W	X	108
Spencers Wood	Wok	SU7166	51°23·5'	0°58·4'W	T	175
Spenceston	S Ayr	NX2186	55°8·4'	4°48·1'W	X	76
Spency Croft	Cumbr	NY7146	54°48·7'	2°26·6'W	X	86,87
Spendelows Fm	Peterb	TL1692	52°31·0'	0°17·0'W	FM	142
Spendiff	Medway	TQ7574	51°26·5'	0°31·5'E	X	178
Spendlane Fm	Derby	SK1649	53°2·5'	1°45·3'W	FM	119
Spen Fm	Lancs	SD8945	53°54·3'	2°9·6'W	FM	103
Spenford Br	Shrops	SJ4729	52°51·6'	2°46·8'W	X	126
Spengill Head	Cumbr	NY6900	54°23·9'	2°28·2'W	X	91
Spen Green	Ches	SJ8160	53°8·4'	2°16·6'W	T	118
Spen Head Fm	Lancs	SD8945	53°54·3'	2°9·6'W	FM	103
Spen Ho	E Yorks	SE8039	53°50·7'	0°46·6'W	X	106
Spenmoss	Ches	SJ8261	53°9·0'	2°15·7'W	X	118
Spennells	Worcs	SO8474	52°22·1'	2°13·7'W	T	138
Spennithorne	N Yks	SE1389	54°18·0'	1°47·6'W	T	99
Spennithorne Wood	N Yks	SE1488	54°17·5'	1°46·7'W	F	99
Spenny Fm	Kent	TQ7045	51°11·0'	0°26·3'E	FM	188
Spennymoor	Durham	NZ2533	54°41·7'	1°36·3'W	T	93
Spens Fm	Lancs	SD6366	54°5·6'	2°33·5'W	FM	97
Spen Valley Heritage Trail	Kirk	SE1925	53°43·5'	1°42·3'W	X	104
Spernall	Warw	SP0862	52°15·6'	1°52·6'W	T	150
Spernall Park	Warw	SP1062	52°15·6'	1°50·8'W	F	150
Spernic Cove	Corn	SW7516	50°0·3'	5°8·0'W	W	204
Sperris Quoit	Corn	SW4738	50°11·5'	5°32·3'W	A	203
Sperry Barton	Somer	ST0129	51°3·3'	3°24·4'W	X	181
Spestos	Devon	SX7298	50°46·3'	3°48·5'W	X	191
Spetchley	Worcs	SO8953	52°10·7'	2°9·3'W	T	150
Spetisbury	Dorset	ST9102	50°49·3'	2°7·3'W	T	195
Spettisbury Rings	Dorset	ST9101	50°48·7'	2°7·3'W	A	195
Spexhall	Suff	TM3780	52°22·2'	1°29·3'E	T	156
Spexhall Hall	Suff	TM3781	52°22·8'	1°29·3'E	X	156
Spexhall Manor	Suff	TM3879	52°21·7'	1°30·1'E	X	156
Speybank	Highld	NH8406	57°8·1'	3°54·5'W	T	35
Spey Bay	Moray	NJ3564	57°39·9'	3°4·9'W	T	28
Spey Bay	Moray	NJ3767	57°41·6'	3°2·9'W	W	28
Speybridge	Highld	NJ0326	57°19·1'	3°36·2'W	T	36
Spey Bridge	Highld	NN7098	57°3·5'	4°8·2'W	X	35
Spey Dam	Highld	NN5893	57°0·6'	4°19·9'W	X	35
Spey Fm	Moray	NJ3362	57°38·8'	3°6·6'W	FM	28
Spey Ho	E Susx	TQ5824	50°59·8'	0°15·5'E	X	199
Speyside Way	Moray	NJ1828	57°20·4'	3°21·3'W	X	36
Speyside Way	Moray	NJ2946	57°30·2'	3°10·6'W	X	28
Speyslaw	Moray	NJ2866	57°40·9'	3°12·0'W	X	28
Speyview	Moray	NJ2541	57°27·4'	3°14·5'W	X	28
Spiceball Country Park	Oxon	SP4541	52°4·2'	1°20·2'W	X	151
Spice Gill	Cumbr	SD7486	54°16·4'	2°23·5'W	X	98
Spiceland	Devon	ST0813	50°54·8'	3°18·1'W	X	181
Spicer Hill	Barns	SE2004	53°32·2'	1°41·5'W	X	110
Spicer Ho	Barns	SE2005	53°32·7'	1°41·5'W	X	110
Spicer's Fm	W Susx	TQ2928	51°2·4'	0°9·2'W	FM	187,198
Spicery	Devon	SX8394	50°44·3'	3°39·1'W	X	191
Spicey Buildings	Wilts	SU2457	51°18·9'	1°38·9'W	X	174
Spickels	N Yks	SE0187	54°17·0'	1°58·7'W	X	98
Spickets Brook	Essex	TL8710	51°45·7'	0°43·0'E	W	168

Spidean a' Choire Léith	Highld	NG9257	57°33·6'	5°28·2'W	H	25
Spidean Còinich	Highld	NC2027	58°12·0'	5°3·3'W	H	15
Spidean Coir an Laoigh	Highld	NG8950	57°29·7'	5°30·8'W	H	24
Spidean Coire nan Clach	Highld	NG9659	57°34·8'	5°24·3'W	H	25
Spidean Dhomhuill Bhric	Highld	NG9212	57°9·4'	5°25·9'W	H	33
Spidean Mialach	Highld	NH0604	57°5·4'	5°11·7'W	X	33
Spidean nan Clach	Highld	NG9276	57°43·8'	5°29·1'W	H	19
Spider Hall	Suff	TM0438	52°0·4'	0°58·7'E	X	155
Spiers Bank Ho	N Yks	SE7593	54°19·9'	0°50·4'W	X	94,100
Spier's Copse	Hants	SU6355	51°17·7'	1°5·4'W	F	175,185
Spiers Ho	N Yks	SE7591	54°18·8'	0°50·4'W	X	94,100
Spiers Piece Fm	Wilts	ST9156	51°18·4'	2°7·4'W	FM	173
Spierston	E Ayr	NS4621	55°27·8'	4°25·7'W	X	70
Spiggie	Shetld	HU3617	59°56·4'	1°20·9'W	X	4
Spiggot Hill	N Yks	SD8866	54°5·6'	2°10·6'W	X	98
Spigot Ho	Cumbr	SD4394	54°20·5'	2°52·2'W	X	97
Spigot Lodge	N Yks	SE0887	54°17·0'	1°52·2'W	X	99
Spike Hall	Cambs	TL5954	52°9·9'	0°19·9'E	X	154
Spike Ho	Essex	TL6424	51°53·6'	0°23·4'E	X	167
Spike Island	Halton	SJ5184	53°21·3'	2°43·8'W	X	108
Spiker's Hill	N Yks	SE9887	54°16·4'	0°29·3'W	X	94,101
Spilcombe Copse	Devon	ST1900	50°47·9'	3°8·6'W	F	192,193
Spillarsford	Aberd	NK0159	57°37·5'	1°58·5'W	X	30
Spills Hill Fm	Kent	TQ8043	51°10·3'	0°34·9'E	FM	188
Spilmersford Mains	E Loth	NT4569	55°54·9'	2°52·4'W	X	66
Spilsby	Lincs	TF4066	53°10·6'	0°6·1'E	T	122
Spilsill Court	Kent	TQ7943	51°9·7'	0°34·0'E	X	188
Spilsmere Wood	Oxon	SP6130	51°58·1'	1°6·3'W	F	152,165
Spin	N Eil	NF7931	57°15·7'	7°19·0'W	H	22
Spindle Muir	Moray	NJ1565	57°40·3'	3°25·0'W	F	28
Spindlestone	Northum	NU1533	55°35·7'	1°45·3'W	T	75
Spindle, The	Shetld	HU3346	60°12·1'	1°23·8'W	X	4
Spindle Thorn	N Yks	SE7192	54°19·4'	0°54·1'W	X	94,100
Spinfield	Bucks	SU8386	51°34·2'	0°47·8'W	X	175
Spinkhill	Derby	SK4578	53°18·1'	1°19·1'W	T	120
Spinks Gill Wood	Lancs	SD5970	54°7·7'	2°37·2'W	F	97
Spink's Hill	Norf	TM3492	52°28·8'	1°27·2'E	X	134
Spinks Lodge	Suff	TL7982	52°24·6'	0°38·3'E	X	144
Spinneag	Arg & Bt	NM3520	56°18·2'	6°16·6'W	X	48
Spinnel's Fm	Essex	TM1630	51°55·8'	1°8·9'E	FM	168,169
Spinner, The	Shetld	HU2156	60°17·5'	1°36·7'W	H	3
Spinney Abbey	Cambs	TL5571	52°19·1'	0°16·9'E	X	154
Spinney Fm	Leic	SK6315	52°44·0'	1°3·6'W	FM	129
Spinney Fm	Leic	SK7621	52°47·1'	0°52·0'W	FM	129
Spinney Fm	Lincs	TF1522	52°47·2'	0°17·3'W	FM	130
Spinney Fm	Lincs	TF2246	53°0·1'	0°10·5'W	FM	131
Spinney Fm	Northnts	SP7366	52°17·5'	0°55·4'W	FM	152
Spinney Hill	Northnts	SP7763	52°15·8'	0°51·9'W	T	152
Spinney Hills	C of Leic	SK6004	52°38·1'	1°6·4'W	T	140
Spinney Lodge	Mil Key	SP8048	52°7·7'	0°49·5'W	X	152
Spinney, The	Beds	SP9754	52°10·8'	0°34·5'W	X	153
Spinney, The	E Susx	TQ5619	50°57·2'	0°13·7'E	X	199
Spinney, The	Oxon	SP5712	51°48·5'	1°10·0'W	F	164
Spinningdale	Highld	NH6789	57°52·5'	4°14·1'W	T	21
Spinsters Rock	Devon	SX6990	50°41·9'	3°50·9'W	X	191
Spion Kop	Arg & Bt	NR8360	55°47·3'	5°27·2'W	X	62
Spion Kop	Notts	SK5566	53°11·5'	1°10·2'W	T	120
Spion Rocks	Moray	NJ0703	57°6·8'	3°31·7'W	X	36
Spiral Stone, The	I of M	SC4585	54°14·5'	4°22·3'W	A	95
Spiral Wood	Angus	NO5338	56°32·2'	2°45·4'W	F	54
Spire	Lancs	SD6846	53°54·8'	2°28·8'W	X	103
Spire	Somer	SS8832	51°4·8'	3°35·6'W	X	181
Spirean Beag	Highld	NN6696	57°2·4'	4°12·0'W	X	35
Spirebush Hill	E Ayr	NS7233	55°34·7'	4°1·4'W	H	71
Spire Cross	Somer	SS8833	51°5·4'	3°35·6'W	X	181
Spire Ho	Cumbr	NY4631	54°40·5'	2°49·8'W	X	90
Spire Hollins	Derby	SK0378	53°18·2'	1°56·9'W	X	119
Spire's Cross	Devon	SS6400	50°47·3'	3°55·4'W	X	191
Spireslack	E Ayr	NS7429	55°32·6'	3°59·4'W	X	71
Spirls Geo	Shetld	HU3529	60°2·9'	1°21·8'W	X	4
Spirraid an t-Seilich	Highld	NH6604	57°6·7'	4°12·3'W	X	35
Spirrey Fm	D & G	NX0361	54°54·5'	5°4·0'W	FM	82
Spirthill	Wilts	ST9975	51°28·7'	2°0·5'W	T	173
Spital	Aberd	NJ8322	57°17·6'	2°16·5'W	X	38
Spital	Aberd	NJ9842	57°28·4'	2°1·5'W	X	30
Spital	Cumbr	SD5294	54°20·6'	2°43·9'W	X	97
Spital	Cumbr	SD5779	54°12·5'	2°39·1'W	X	97
Spital	Denb	SJ0377	53°17·1'	3°26·9'W	X	116
Spital	Durham	NY9312	54°30·4'	2°6·1'W	X	91,92
Spital	Northum	NZ0766	54°59·6'	1°53·0'W	X	88
Spital	Win & Maid	SU9575	51°28·2'	0°37·5'W	T	175,176
Spital	Wirral	SJ3483	53°20·6'	2°59·1'W	T	108
Spital Beck	N Yks	SE4385	54°15·8'	1°20·0'W	W	99
Spital Beck	N Yks	SE7263	54°3·7'	0°53·6'W	W	100
Spital Br	N Yks	SE7064	54°4·3'	0°55·4'W	X	100
Spitalbrook	Herts	TL3708	51°45·5'	0°0·5'W	T	166
Spital Burn	Aberd	NO6582	56°55·9'	2°34·1'W	W	45
Spital Carrs	Northum	NZ3187	55°10·8'	1°30·4'W	X	81
Spital Cott	Aberd	NO6484	56°57·0'	2°35·1'W	X	45
Spitalcroft Fm	Donc	SK5795	53°27·2'	1°8·1'W	FM	111
Spitalfields	T Ham	TQ3381	51°31·0'	0°4·6'W	T	176,177
Spital Fm	Essex	TL9412	51°46·6'	0°49·1'E	FM	168
Spital Fm	Notts	SK6286	53°22·3'	1°3·7'W	FM	111,120
Spital Fm	Notts	SK6847	53°1·2'	0°58·8'W	FM	129
Spitalford	Northum	NU2321	55°29·2'	1°37·7'W	X	75
Spital Gate	Glos	SP0202	51°43·2'	1°57·9'W	A	163
Spital Grange	Durham	NY9412	54°30·4'	2°5·1'W	X	91,92
Spitalhaugh	Scot Bord	NT1649	55°43·9'	3°19·8'W	X	72
Spitalhill	Derby	SK1845	53°0·4'	1°43·5'W	T	119,128
Spital Hill	Donc	SK6193	53°26·1'	1°4·5'W	T	111
Spital Hill	Northum	NZ1786	55°10·3'	1°43·6'W	X	81
Spital Hill	N Yks	SE4580	54°13·1'	1°18·2'W	X	99
Spital Ho	N Yks	TA0279	54°12·0'	0°25·8'W	X	101
Spital Ho	Scot Bord	NT9253	55°46·5'	2°7·2'W	X	67,74,75
Spital Ho Fm	Northum	NZ3087	55°10·8'	1°31·3'W	FM	81
Spital in the Street	Lincs	SK9690	53°24·1'	0°33·0'W	T	112
Spital Mains	Scot Bord	NT9252	55°45·9'	2°7·2'W	X	67,74,75
Spital Park	Durham	NY9412	54°30·4'	2°5·1'W	X	91,92
Spital Point	Northum	NZ3186	55°10·3'	1°30·4'W	X	81
Spitals	Cumbr	NY6226	54°37·9'	2°34·9'W	X	91
Spitals Cross	Kent	TQ4347	51°12·5'	0°3·2'E	X	187
Spital Shield	Northum	NY8858	54°55·2'	2°10·8'W	X	87
Spitalshield Moor	Northum	NY8658	54°55·2'	2°12·7'W	X	87
Spital Shore	Highld	NH5649	57°30·8'	4°23·8'W	X	26
Spital, The	Northum	NY6863	54°57·9'	2°29·6'W	X	86,87
Spital, The	Northum	NY9265	54°59·0'	2°7·1'W	X	87
Spital Tongues	N upon Ty	NZ2365	54°59·0'	1°38·0'W	T	88
Spital Tower	Scot Bord	NT5817	55°27·0'	2°39·4'W	X	80
Spital Wood	E Susx	TQ8124	50°59·4'	0°35·1'E	F	199
Spital Wood	Notts	SK6848	53°1·7'	0°58·8'W	F	129
Spitbank Fort	C of Port	SZ6397	50°46·4'	1°6·0'W	A	196
Spitchwick Manor	Devon	SX7072	50°32·2'	3°49·7'W	X	191
Spite Hall	Red & Cl	NZ5714	54°31·3'	1°6·7'W	X	93
Spite Inn Fm	Powys	SN8641	52°3·6'	3°39·4'W	FM	147,160
Spite Moor	Pemb	SM8028	51°54·7'	5°11·5'W	X	157
Spitend Marshes	Kent	TQ9767	51°22·3'	0°50·2'E	X	178
Spitend Point	Kent	TQ9866	51°21·7'	0°51·0'E	X	178
Spitewinter	Derby	SK3466	53°11·6'	1°29·1'W	X	119
Spitewinter Fm	Derby	SK3074	53°16·0'	1°32·6'W	FM	119
Spitfire Bottoms	Notts	SK6675	53°16·3'	1°0·2'W	X	120
Spithead		SZ6395	50°45·3'	1°6·0'W	W	196
Spithersquoy	Orkney	HY3526	59°7·2'	3°7·6'W	X	6
Spithope Burn	Northum	NT7604	55°20·0'	2°22·3'W	W	80
Spithopehead	Northum	NT7603	55°19·5'	2°22·3'W	X	80
Spithurst	E Susx	TQ4217	50°56·3'	0°1·7'E	T	198
Spitlar Cross	Devon	SX6695	50°44·6'	3°53·6'W	X	191
Spitlye Wood	E Susx	TQ5728	51°2·0'	0°14·7'E	F	188,199
Spit Point	Corn	SX0752	50°20·4'	4°42·4'W	X	200,204
Spittal	Corn	SX0773	50°31·7'	4°43·0'W	X	200
Spittal	D & G	NX0355	54°51·3'	5°3·7'W	X	82
Spittal	D & G	NX3657	54°53·1'	4°33·0'W	T	83
Spittal	D & G	NX4660	54°54·9'	4°23·7'W	X	83
Spittal	E Ayr	NS4448	55°42·3'	4°28·5'W	X	64
Spittal	E Loth	NT4677	55°59·2'	2°51·5'W	T	66
Spittal	E Yorks	SE7652	53°57·7'	0°50·1'W	T	105,106
Spittal	Fife	NT2194	56°8·2'	3°15·8'W	X	58
Spittal	Highld	ND1654	58°28·2'	3°25·9'W	T	11,12
Spittal	Northum	NU0051	55°45·4'	1°59·6'W	T	75
Spittal	Pemb	SM9723	51°52·4'	4°56·5'W	T	157,158
Spittal	S Lanak	NS6758	55°48·1'	4°6·9'W	X	64
Spittal	S Lanak	NS9845	55°41·5'	3°36·9'W	X	72
Spittal	Stir	NS4786	56°2·8'	4°26·9'W	T	57
Spittal	Stir	NS5186	56°2·9'	4°23·1'W	X	57
Spittal	W Dunb	NS4283	56°1·1'	4°31·6'W	X	56,64
Spittal Ballat	Stir	NS5290	56°5·1'	4°22·3'W	X	57
Spittal Beck	E Yorks	SE7652	53°57·7'	0°50·1'W	W	105,106
Spittal Brook	Pemb	SM9824	51°52·9'	4°55·7'W	W	157,158
Spittalburn	Angus	NO4446	56°36·4'	2°54·3'W	X	54
Spittal Burn	S Lanak	NT0637	55°37·3'	3°29·1'W	W	72
Spittalfield	Pth & Kin	NO1040	56°32·9'	3°27·4'W	T	53
Spittal Fm	Cumbr	NY2649	54°50·1'	3°8·7'W	FM	85
Spittal Fm	Midlo	NT1657	55°48·2'	3°20·0'W	FM	65,66,72
Spittal Fm	S Lanak	NT0638	55°37·8'	3°29·1'W	FM	72
Spittal Hill	Highld	ND1655	58°28·8'	3°26·0'W	H	11,12
Spittal Hill	Midlo	NT1658	55°48·7'	3°20·0'W	H	65,66,72
Spittalhill	S Ayr	NS4033	55°34·1'	4°31·8'W	X	70
Spittalhill	Stir	NS6486	56°3·1'	4°10·6'W	X	57
Spittal Ho	S Lanak	NS7744	55°40·7'	3°56·9'W	X	71
Spittal House Fm	N Yks	SE3792	54°19·6'	1°25·4'W	FM	99
Spittal Ings	Cumbr	NY8811	54°29·9'	2°10·7'W	X	91,92
Spittal Mains	Highld	ND1654	58°28·2'	3°25·9'W	X	11,12
Spittalmoor Forest Fm	Notts	SK6572	53°14·7'	1°1·1'W	FM	120
Spittalmyre	Aberd	NO7166	56°47·3'	2°28·0'W	X	45
Spittal of Glenmuick	Aberd	NO3085	56°57·3'	3°8·6'W	X	44
Spittal of Glenshee	Pth & Kin	NO1069	56°48·5'	3°28·0'W	T	43
Spittal-on-Rule	Scot Bord	NT5819	55°28·0'	2°39·4'W	X	80
Spittalriddinghill	D & G	NY1868	55°0·2'	3°16·5'W	X	85
Spittalrigg	E Loth	NT4773	55°57·1'	2°50·5'W	X	66
Spittalside	S Ayr	NS4227	55°30·9'	4°29·7'W	X	70
Spittal, The	Northum	NY8454	54°53·1'	2°14·5'W	X	86,87
Spittalton	Stir	NS6899	56°10·2'	4°7·1'W	X	57
Spittalwood	Highld	NH5550	57°31·3'	4°24·8'W	X	26
Spitten Fm	Worcs	SP0051	52°9·7'	1°59·6'W	FM	150
Spit, The	Kent	TR0667	51°22·1'	0°58·0'E	X	179
Spit, The	W Susx	SZ8794	50°44·6'	0°45·6'W	X	197
Spittleborough Fm	Wilts	SU0982	51°32·4'	1°51·8'W	FM	173
Spittle Brook	Warw	SP0758	52°13·4'	1°53·5'W	W	150
Spittle Croft	N Yks	SD9073	54°9·4'	2°8·8'W	X	98
Spittle Fm	Devon	SS6817	50°56·5'	3°52·3'W	FM	180
Spittlegate	Lincs	SK9134	52°54·0'	0°38·4'W	T	130
Spittle Ho	Ches	SJ8977	53°17·6'	2°9·5'W	X	118
Spittle Ings Ho	N Yks	SE1356	54°0·2'	1°47·7'W	X	104
Spittles, The	Dorset	SY3492	50°43·7'	2°55·7'W	X	193
Spitzbrook	Kent	TQ7246	51°11·5'	0°28·1'E	X	188
Spixworth	Norf	TG2415	52°41·4'	1°19·3'E	T	133,134
Spixworth Br	Norf	TG2316	52°42·0'	1°18·4'E	X	133,134
Splash Br	Hants	SU2011	50°54·1'	1°42·5'W	X	195
Splash Leys Fm	Warw	SP3949	52°8·5'	1°25·4'W	FM	151
Splatcove Point	Devon	SX7337	50°13·4'	3°46·4'W	X	202
Splatford Fm	Devon	SX9085	50°39·5'	3°33·0'W	FM	192
Splatt	Corn	SW9476	50°33·1'	4°54·1'W	T	200
Splatt	Corn	SX2288	50°40·1'	4°30·8'W	T	190
Splatt	Devon	SS6005	50°49·9'	3°58·9'W	T	191
Splatt	Somer	ST2237	51°7·9'	3°6·5'W	T	182
Splatt Br	Glos	SO7406	51°45·4'	2°22·2'W	X	162
Splattenridden	Corn	SW5336	50°10·6'	5°27·2'W	X	203
Splatt's Barn	Glos	ST7788	51°35·7'	2°19·5'W	X	162,172
Splatts Ho	Wilts	ST9966	51°23·8'	2°0·5'W	X	173
Splatt's Wood	Glos	ST7788	51°35·7'	2°19·5'W	F	162,172
Splayne's Green	E Susx	TQ4324	51°0·1'	0°2·7'E	T	198
Splears	N Eil	NF9577	57°41·0'	7°6·6'W	X	18
Splitwell Cross	Devon	SS8306	50°50·7'	3°39·3'W	X	191
Splott	Card	ST1976	51°28·9'	3°9·6'W	T	171
Splott	V of Glam	SS9475	51°28·1'	3°31·2'W	X	170
Splott Fm	Bath & NE Somer	ST7058	51°19·5'	2°25·4'W	FM	172
Splott Fm	V of Glam	SS9469	51°24·8'	3°31·1'W	FM	170
Splotts Moor	Somer	ST5240	51°9·7'	2°40·8'W	X	182,183
Spoad Hill	Shrops	SO2580	52°25·0'	3°5·8'W	X	137
Spodegreen Fm	Ches	SJ7385	53°21·9'	2°23·9'W	FM	109
Spofforth	N Yks	SE3651	53°57·5'	1°26·7'W	T	104
Spofforth Castle	N Yks	SE3651	53°57·5'	1°26·7'W	A	104
Spofforth Haggs	N Yks	SE3250	53°56·9'	1°30·3'W	X	104
Spofforth Hall	N Yks	SE3650	53°56·9'	1°26·7'W	X	104
Spofforth Moor	N Yks	SE3351	53°57·5'	1°29·4'W	X	104
Spofforth Park	N Yks	SE3549	53°56·4'	1°27·6'W	X	104
Spoilbank Wood	Herts	TQ2699	51°40·8'	0°10·3'W	F	166,176
Spollycombe Copse	Hants	SU7342	51°10·6'	0°57·0'W	F	186
Sponden Ho	Kent	TQ7929	51°2·2'	0°33·6'E	X	188,199
Spondon	C of Derb	SK4035	52°54·9'	1°23·9'W	T	129
Spondon Wood	Derby	SK4137	52°56·0'	1°23·0'W	F	129
Spondon Wood Fm	Derby	SK4137	52°56·0'	1°23·0'W	FM	129
Sponds	Ches	SJ9679	53°18·7'	2°3·2'W	X	118
Sponds Hill	Ches	SJ9780	53°19·3'	2°2·3'W	X	109
Spon End	Cov	SP3279	52°24·7'	1°31·4'W	T	140
Spo Ness	Orkney	HY4846	59°18·1'	2°54·3'W	X	5
Spong Carr	Norf	TG3904	52°35·1'	1°32·1'E	F	134
Sponger Point	Shetld	HU5967	60°23·2'	0°55·3'W	X	2
Spong Fm	Kent	TR1245	51°10·1'	1°2·3'E	FM	179,189
Spong Hill	Norf	TF9819	52°44·2'	0°56·4'E	X	132
Spon Green	Flint	SJ2863	53°9·8'	3°4·2'W	T	117
Sponish	N Eil	NF8864	57°33·8'	7°12·6'W	X	18
Sponish Harbour	N Eil	NF9269	57°36·6'	7°9·0'W	W	18
Sponish House	N Eil	NF9269	57°36·6'	7°9·0'W	X	18
Spood's Fm	E Susx	TQ5422	50°58·8'	0°12·0'E	FM	199
Spoonbed Hill	Glos	SO8612	51°48·6'	2°11·8'W	X	162
Spoon Burn	D & G	NT1510	55°22·9'	3°20·1'W	W	79
Spooner Row	Norf	TM0997	52°32·1'	1°5·3'E	T	144
Spooner's Fm	Cambs	TL6182	52°25·0'	0°22·4'E	FM	143
Spoo Ness	Shetld	HP5607	60°44·8'	0°57·9'W	X	1
Spoon Hall	Cumbr	SD2996	54°21·5'	3°5·1'W	X	96,97
Spoonhill Hall Fm	Shrops	SO6296	52°33·9'	2°33·2'W	FM	138
Spoonhill Wood	Shrops	SO6195	52°33·3'	2°34·1'W	F	138
Spoonley	Shrops	SJ6636	52°55·5'	2°29·9'W	X	127
Spoonley Fm	Glos	SP0425	51°55·6'	1°56·1'W	FM	163
Spoonleygate	Shrops	SO8096	52°33·9'	2°17·3'W	T	138
Spoon's Hall	Essex	TL8433	51°58·1'	0°41·1'E	X	168
Spoose Holm	Shetld	HU3438	60°7·8'	1°22·8'W	X	4
Spoot-hellier	Shetld	HU3040	60°8·9'	1°27·1'W	X	4
Spooyt Vane	I of M	SC3088	54°15·8'	4°36·2'W	W	95
Spord, The	Orkney	HY2221	59°4·4'	3°21·2'W	W	6
Sporhams	Essex	TL7603	51°42·1'	0°33·2'E	X	167
Sporle	Norf	TF8411	52°40·2'	0°43·7'E	T	132
Sporle Wood	Norf	TF8611	52°40·1'	0°45·5'E	F	132
Sportfield	Pth & Kin	NN9727	56°25·7'	3°39·8'W	X	52,53,58
Sportman's Hall	N Yks	SE5491	54°18·9'	1°9·8'W	X	100
Sportsman Fm	Stock	SJ9889	53°24·1'	2°1·4'W	FM	109
Sportsman's Arms (PH)	Conwy	SH9559	53°7·3'	3°33·7'W	X	116
Sportsman's Inn (PH)	Somer	SS7933	51°5·3'	3°43·3'W	X	180
Sportsmans Lodge Fm	Somer	ST6330	51°4·3'	2°31·3'W	FM	183
Sportsman's Rest	N Yks	SE0778	54°12·1'	1°53·1'W	X	99
Spot Acre	Staffs	SJ9437	52°56·1'	2°5·0'W	X	127
Spot Fm	Norf	TF6621	52°45·9'	0°28·0'E	FM	132
Spot Grange	Staffs	SJ9435	52°55·0'	2°4·9'W	X	127
Spoth	D & G	NS7914	55°24·6'	3°54·2'W	X	71,78
Spothfore Burn	D & G	NS7715	55°25·1'	3°56·2'W	W	71,78
Spothfore Burn	D & G	NS7815	55°25·1'	3°55·2'W	W	71,78
Spot House Fm	Kent	TQ9735	51°5·0'	0°49·2'E	FM	189
Spotland Bridge	Roch	SD8813	53°37·0'	2°10·5'W	T	109
Spots Law	D & G	NT1902	55°18·6'	3°16·1'W	X	79
Spotsmains	Scot Bord	NT6636	55°37·2'	2°32·0'W	X	74
Spott	Angus	NO3365	56°46·6'	3°5·3'W	X	44
Spott	E Loth	NT6775	55°58·3'	2°31·3'W	T	67
Spott Burn	E Loth	NT6876	55°58·8'	2°30·3'W	W	67
Spott Dod	E Loth	NT6674	55°57·7'	2°32·2'W	X	67
Spotted Lodge	Lincs	TF1970	53°13·1'	0°12·7'W	X	122
Spottes Burn	D & G	NX8068	54°59·8'	3°52·1'W	W	84
Spottes Hall	D & G	NX8066	54°58·7'	3°52·1'W	X	84
Spott Fm	E Loth	NT6775	55°58·3'	2°31·3'W	FM	67
Spot, The	Staffs	SJ9436	52°55·5'	2°5·0'W	X	127
Spott Ho	E Loth	NT6775	55°58·3'	2°31·3'W	X	67
Spottiswoode	Scot Bord	NT6049	55°44·2'	2°37·8'W	X	74
Spottiswoode Loch	Scot Bord	NT6149	55°44·2'	2°36·8'W	W	74
Spottle Hill Fm	Lincs	TF2191	53°24·3'	0°10·4'W	FM	113
Spott Mill	E Loth	NT6574	55°57·7'	2°33·2'W	X	67
Spott West Mains	E Loth	NT6774	55°57·7'	2°31·3'W	X	67
Spouse's Grove	Suff	TL9336	51°59·6'	0°49·1'E	F	155
Spout	Cumbr	SD6892	54°19·6'	2°29·1'W	X	98
Spout	Derby	SK3051	53°3·6'	1°32·7'W	X	119
Spout Bank	Cumbr	NY5366	54°59·4'	2°43·6'W	X	86
Spout Burn	Arg & Bt	NS1378	55°57·8'	4°59·3'W	W	63
Spout Burn	D & G	NS6500	55°16·8'	4°7·1'W	W	77
Spout Burn	D & G	NX6756	54°53·1'	4°4·0'W	W	83,84
Spout Crag	Cumbr	SD2888	54°17·2'	3°5·9'W	H	96,97
Spout Craig	D & G	NT0813	55°24·4'	3°26·7'W	X	78
Spout Fm	Kent	TQ8153	51°15·1'	0°36·0'E	FM	188
Spout Fm	Shrops	SJ4137	52°55·9'	2°52·3'W	FM	126
Spout Force	Cumbr	NY1826	54°37·6'	3°15·8'W	W	89,90
Spout Geo	Shetld	HU3728	60°2·4'	1°19·7'W	X	4
Spouthead	E Dunb	NS6578	55°58·8'	4°9·4'W	X	64
Spout Ho	Cumbr	SD4491	54°18·9'	2°51·2'W	X	97
Spout Ho	Cumbr	SD5481	54°13·6'	2°41·9'W	X	97
Spout Ho	N Yks	SE1480	54°13·2'	1°46·7'W	X	99
Spout Ho	N Yks	SE2748	53°55·9'	1°34·9'W	X	104
Spout Ho	N Yks	SE5793	54°20·0'	1°7·0'W	X	100
Spout Ho	N Yks	SE6296	54°21·6'	1°2·3'W	X	94,100
Spout Ho	N Yks	SE6499	54°23·2'	1°0·4'W	X	94,100
Spout House Fm	Cumbr	NY1500	54°23·6'	3°18·1'W	FM	89
Spout House Fm	Lancs	SD4009	53°34·7'	2°54·0'W	FM	108
Spout House Hill	Sheff	SK2794	53°26·8'	1°35·2'W	X	110
Spoutloch Burn	S Lanak	NS6633	55°34·6'	4°7·1'W	W	71
Spout of Ballagan	Stir	NS5780	55°59·8'	4°17·1'W	W	64
Spout of Ballochleam	Stir	NS6589	56°4·7'	4°9·7'W	W	57
Spout of the Clints	D & G	NX5066	54°58·2'	4°20·2'W	W	83
Spout Rolla	Pth & Kin	NN7228	56°25·9'	4°4·1'W	W	51,52
Spoutscross	N Lanak	NS8855	55°46·8'	3°46·7'W	X	65,72
Spout,The	Cumbr	SD6499	54°23·4'	2°32·8'W	W	97
Spout Wells	D & G	NX0658	54°53·0'	5°1·0'W	X	82
Spoutwells	Pth & Kin	NO1327	56°25·9'	3°24·2'W	X	53,58
Spoutwells	Pth & Kin	NO1341	56°33·4'	3°24·5'W	X	53

Spout Wood	Powys	SJ1510	52°41·1′	3°15·0′W	F	125
Spout Wood	Shrops	SJ4037	52°55·9′	2°53·2′W	F	126
Spouty Dennans	D & G	NX7645	54°47·3′	3°55·3′W	X	84
Spragg's Wood	Suff	TL9349	52°6·6′	0°49·5′E	F	155
Sprat Beach	Somer	ST2859	51°19·8′	3°1·6′W	X	182
Spratford Stream	Devon	ST0210	50°53·1′	3°23·2′W	W	192
Spratsbourne Fm	Kent	TQ7637	51°6·5′	0°31·2′E	FM	188
Spratsbrook Fm	E Susx	TQ5637	51°6·9′	0°14·1′E	FM	188
Sprat's Down	Hants	SU4601	50°48·6′	1°20·4′W	X	196
Sprat's Hatch Fm	Hants	SU7652	51°16·0′	0°54·2′W	FM	186
Spratt' Green Fm	Norf	TG2025	52°46·9′	1°16·1′E	FM	133,134
Spratton	Northnts	SP7170	52°19·6′	0°57·1′W	T	141
Spratton Br	Northnts	SP7168	52°18·6′	0°57·1′W	X	152
Spratton Grange	Northnts	SP7169	52°19·1′	0°57·1′W	X	152
Spratton Lodge	Northnts	SP7069	52°19·1′	0°58·0′W	X	152
Spratt's Marsh	Essex	TL9830	51°56·2′	0°53·2′E	X	168
Spratt's Street	Suff	TM3350	52°6·2′	1°24·5′E	X	156
Sprattyhall	Fife	NO4704	56°13·8′	2°50·9′W	X	59
Spray Hill	Kent	TQ6735	51°5·6′	0°23·5′E	X	188
Spray House Fm	Derby	SK0389	53°24·1′	1°56·9′W	FM	110
Spray's Fms	E Susx	TQ6918	50°56·4′	0°24·7′E	FM	199
Sprays Hill	Somer	ST3510	50°53·4′	2°55·1′W	X	193
Sprays Wood	E Susx	TQ7111	50°52·6′	0°26·2′E	F	199
Spray's Wood	E Susx	TQ7117	50°55·8′	0°26·4′E	F	199
Spray Wood	W Berks	SU4178	51°30·2′	1°24·2′W	F	174
Spreacombe Manor	Devon	SS4841	51°9·1′	4°10·0′W	X	180
Spreaderhill	Aberd	NK0457	57°36·4′	1°55·5′W	X	30
Spready Oaks	Notts	SK6270	53°13·6′	1°3·9′W	F	120
Spreakley	Surrey	SU8441	51°10·0′	0°47·5′W	T	186
Sprecott	Devon	SS6439	51°8·3′	3°56·3′W	X	180
Sprey Moor	Corn	SX1675	50°33·0′	4°35·5′W	X	201
Sprey Point	Devon	SX9573	50°33·1′	3°28·6′W	X	192
Spreyton	Devon	SX6996	50°45·2′	3°51·0′W	T	191
Spreyton Wood	Devon	SX7196	50°45·2′	3°49·3′W	F	191
Spriddlestone	Devon	SX5351	50°20·7′	4°3·6′W	T	201
Spriddlestone Ho	Devon	SX5251	50°20·7′	4°4·4′W	X	201
Spridlington	Lincs	TF0084	53°20·8′	0°29·5′W	T	121
Spridlington Manor Fm	Lincs	SK9783	53°20·3′	0°32·2′W	FM	121
Spriggs	Essex	TL6005	51°43·5′	0°19·4′E	X	167
Spriggs	Essex	TL6232	51°58·0′	0°21·9′E	X	167
Sprigg's Fm	Essex	TL5840	52°2·4′	0°18·6′E	FM	154
Sprigg's Fm	Essex	TL6102	51°41·8′	0°20·2′E	FM	167
Sprig's Alley	Oxon	SU6798	51°40·8′	0°53·7′W	T	165
Springate	Essex	TL5628	51°55·9′	0°16·5′E	X	167
Springbank	Arg & Bt	NR3361	55°46·4′	6°15·0′W	X	60
Spring Bank	Cumbr	NY2224	54°36·6′	3°12·0′W	T	89,90
Spring Bank	Cumbr	NY4125	54°37·3′	2°54·4′W	X	90
Springbank	D & G	NX0460	54°54·0′	5°3·0′W	X	82
Springbank	Glos	SO9123	51°54·6′	2°7·5′W	T	163
Springbank	Pth & Kin	NN8412	56°17·4′	3°52·0′W	X	58
Springbank	S Ayr	NS3926	55°30·3′	4°32·5′W	X	70
Springbank	S Lanak	NS9142	55°39·8′	3°43·5′W	X	71,72
Springbank Fm	Ches	SJ7562	53°9·5′	2°22·0′W	FM	118
Springbank Fm	Ches	SJ9380	53°19·3′	2°5·9′W	FM	109
Springbank Fm	Leic	SK3810	52°41·4′	1°25·9′W	FM	128
Spring Bank Fm	N Yks	SE3958	54°1·2′	1°23·9′W	FM	104
Springbank Ho	Suff	TL9976	52°21·0′	0°55·7′E	X	144
Spring Bank Wood	N Yks	SE5982	54°14·1′	1°5·3′W	F	100
Spring Bank Wood	N Yks	SE7486	54°16·1′	0°51·4′W	F	94,100
Springboig	C of Glas	NS6564	55°51·3′	4°9·0′W	T	64
Springbok Fm	Surrey	TQ0334	51°6·0′	0°31·3′W	FM	186
Springbottom Fm	Wilts	SU1240	51°9·8′	1°49·3′W	FM	184
Spring Bottom Hill	Dorset	SY7482	50°38·5′	2°21·7′W	H	194
Springbourne	Bourne	SZ1092	50°43·9′	1°51·1′W	T	195
Spring Brook	Warw	SP1072	52°21·0′	1°50·8′W	W	139
Springburn	C of Glas	NS6068	55°53·3′	4°13·9′W	T	64
Springburn	Moray	NJ1859	57°37·1′	3°21·9′W	X	28
Spring Burrow Lodge	Leic	SK4417	52°45·2′	1°20·5′W	X	129
Springcliff Fm	N Lincs	SK9698	53°28·4′	0°32·8′W	FM	112
Spring Close Fm	N Yks	SE3446	53°54·8′	1°28·5′W	FM	104
Spring Coppice	Bucks	SU8392	51°37·5′	0°47·7′W	F	175
Spring Coppice	Powys	SJ1904	52°37·9′	3°11·4′W	F	136
Spring Coppice	Powys	SJ1905	52°38·4′	3°11·4′W	F	125
Spring Coppice	Shrops	SJ4606	52°39·2′	2°47·5′W	F	126
Spring Coppice	Shrops	SJ8007	52°39·9′	2°17·3′W	F	127
Spring Coppice	Shrops	SJ8307	52°39·9′	2°14·7′W	F	127
Spring Coppice	Shrops	SO7099	52°35·5′	2°26·2′W	F	138
Spring Coppice Fm	Bucks	SP8400	51°41·8′	0°46·7′W	FM	165
Springcote	N Yks	SD7276	54°11·0′	2°25·4′W	X	98
Spring Cottage	Leic	SK3016	52°44·7′	1°32·9′W	T	128
Spring Covert	Norf	TL7996	52°32·2′	0°38·8′E	F	144
Spring Crag Wood	Brad	SE0544	53°53·8′	1°55·0′W	F	104
Springdale Fm	E Yorks	TA0738	53°49·9′	0°22·0′W	FM	107
Springdale Fm	E Yorks	TA0868	54°6·0′	0°20·5′W	FM	101
Spring Ditch	Suff	TM5184	52°24·0′	1°41·8′E	W	156
Springelane Hall	Ches	SJ6152	53°4·1′	2°34·5′W	X	118
Spring Elms	Essex	TL7907	51°44·2′	0°35·9′E	X	167
Spring End	N Yks	SD9597	54°22·4′	2°4·2′W	T	98
Springfield	Aberd	NJ7408	57°10·0′	2°25·3′W	X	38
Springfield	Arg & Bt	NS0179	55°58·0′	5°10·9′W	X	63
Springfield	Birm	SP0981	52°25·9′	1°51·7′W	T	139
Springfield	Caer	ST1895	51°39·1′	3°10·7′W	T	171
Springfield	Cumbr	NX9913	54°30·4′	3°33·2′W	X	89
Springfield	Cumbr	NY5443	54°47·0′	2°42·5′W	X	86
Springfield	Darl	NZ2812	54°30·4′	1°33·6′W	X	93
Springfield	Devon	SS9517	50°56·8′	3°29·3′W	X	181
Springfield	D & G	NX7563	54°57·0′	3°56·7′W	X	84
Springfield	D & G	NX8984	55°8·5′	3°44·1′W	X	78
Springfield	D & G	NY3268	55°0·4′	3°3·4′W	T	85
Springfield	E Dunb	NS6474	55°56·6′	4°10·2′W	X	64
Springfield	E Loth	NT7571	55°56·1′	2°23·6′W	X	67
Springfield	Essex	TL7108	51°44·9′	0°29·0′E	T	167
Springfield	E Susx	TQ9121	50°57·6′	0°43·6′E	X	189
Springfield	Fife	NO3411	56°17·5′	3°3·5′W	T	59
Springfield	Heref	SO4961	52°14·9′	2°44·4′W	X	137,138,148
Springfield	Highld	NH6663	57°38·5′	4°14·2′W	T	21
Springfield	Kent	TQ7342	51°9·3′	0°28·8′E	X	188
Springfield	Kent	TR0526	51°0·0′	0°55·7′E	X	189
Springfield	Lincs	TF0987	53°22·4′	0°21·3′W	X	112,121
Springfield	Midlo	NT2256	55°47·7′	3°14·2′W	X	66,73
Springfield	Mil Key	SP8738	52°2·2′	0°43·5′W	T	152
Springfield	Monm	ST4397	51°40·4′	2°49·1′W	X	171
Springfield	Moray	NJ0459	57°36·9′	3°36·0′W	X	27
Springfield	N Lincs	TA0108	53°33·8′	0°28·1′W	X	112
Springfield	Orkney	HY3315	59°1·3′	3°9·5′W	X	6
Springfield	Orkney	HY4428	59°8·4′	2°58·2′W	X	5,6
Springfield	Pth & Kin	NO1935	56°30·3′	3°18·5′W	X	53
Springfield	Sand	SO9688	52°29·6′	2°3·1′W	T	139
Springfield	Shetld	HU3448	60°13·2′	1°22·7′W	X	3
Springfield	Shetld	HU3716	59°55·9′	1°19·8′W	X	4
Springfield	Shetld	HU3955	60°16·9′	1°17·2′W	X	3
Springfield	Shetld	HU4666	60°22·8′	1°9·4′W	X	2,3
Springfield	S Lanak	NT0235	55°36·2′	3°32·9′W	X	72
Springfield	Somer	ST6041	51°10·2′	2°33·9′W	X	183
Springfield	Surrey	TQ1449	51°14·0′	0°21·6′W	X	187
Springfield	Thurr	TQ6281	51°30·5′	0°20·5′E	X	177
Springfield	Wigan	SD5706	53°33·2′	2°38·5′W	T	108
Springfield	W Loth	NS9366	55°52·8′	3°42·2′W	X	65
Springfield	W Loth	NT0178	55°59·3′	3°34·8′W	X	65
Springfield	Wolv	SO9199	52°35·6′	2°7·6′W	T	139
Springfield Barn	Rut	SK9110	52°41·0′	0°38·8′W	X	130
Springfield Cross	Devon	SS5435	51°6·0′	4°4·7′W	X	180
Springfield Fm	Bucks	SP8130	51°58·0′	0°48·9′W	FM	152,165
Springfield Fm	Bucks	SP9002	51°42·8′	0°41·4′W	FM	165
Springfield Fm	Cumbr	NY0727	54°38·0′	3°26·0′W	FM	89
Springfield Fm	Cumbr	NY4450	54°50·8′	2°51·9′W	FM	85
Springfield Fm	Derby	SK5077	53°17·5′	1°14·6′W	FM	120
Springfield Fm	E Yorks	TA1948	53°55·1′	0°10·9′W	FM	107
Springfield Fm	Know	SJ4786	53°22·3′	2°47·4′W	FM	108
Springfield Fm	Leic	SK6619	52°46·1′	1°0·9′W	FM	129
Springfield Fm	Leic	SP4892	52°31·7′	1°17·1′W	FM	140
Springfield Fm	Lincs	TF2082	53°19·5′	0°11·5′W	FM	122
Springfield Fm	N Lincs	SK9297	53°27·9′	0°36·4′W	FM	112
Springfield Fm	Northnts	SP4751	52°9·5′	1°18·4′W	FM	151
Springfield Fm	N Yks	NZ4401	54°24·4′	1°18·9′W	FM	93
Springfield Fm	N Yks	SE2156	54°0·2′	1°40·4′W	FM	104
Springfield Fm	N Yks	SE4689	54°17·9′	1°17·2′W	FM	100
Springfield Fm	N Yks	SE5172	54°8·7′	1°12·7′W	FM	100
Springfield Fm	S Glos	ST7485	51°34·0′	2°22·1′W	FM	172
Springfield Fm	S Lanak	NT0238	55°37·8′	3°33·0′W	FM	72
Springfield Fm	Somer	ST7854	51°17·3′	2°18·5′W	FM	183
Springfield Fm	Warr	SJ6392	53°25·7′	2°33·0′W	FM	109
Springfield Fm	Warw	SP2650	52°9·1′	1°36·8′W	FM	151
Springfield Fm	Warw	SP3140	52°3·7′	1°32·5′W	FM	151
Springfield Fm	W Susx	TQ2231	51°4·1′	0°15·1′W	FM	187
Springfieldhill	D & G	NX8984	55°8·5′	3°44·1′W	FM	78
Springfield Ho	Midlo	NT2964	55°52·1′	3°7·6′W	X	66
Springfield Ho	N Yks	SE3265	54°5·0′	1°30·2′W	X	99
Springfield Ho	N Yks	SE9576	54°10·5′	0°32·3′W	X	101
Springfield Ho	Rut	SK8610	52°41·1′	0°43·3′W	X	130
Springfield Ho	Somer	ST6539	51°9·2′	2°29·6′W	X	183
Springfield Ho	Somer	ST7445	51°12·5′	2°21·9′W	X	183
Springfield Ho	Staffs	SJ8503	52°37·7′	2°12·9′W	X	127,139
Springfield Ho	Wilts	SU0877	51°29·7′	1°52·7′W	X	173
Springfield Hotel	Flint	SJ2072	53°14·6′	3°11·5′W	X	117
Springfield House (Sch)	Sol	SP2076	52°23·1′	1°42·0′W	X	139
Springfield Lyons	Essex	TL7308	51°44·9′	0°30·8′E	X	167
Springfield Reservoir	S Lanak	NS9052	55°45·2′	3°44·7′W	W	65,72
Springfields	C of Stoke	SJ8644	52°59·8′	2°12·1′W	T	118
Springfields	Lincs	TF2624	52°48·2′	0°7·5′W	X	131
Springfields	Staffs	SJ8139	52°57·1′	2°16·6′W	X	127
Springfields	Staffs	SK0735	52°55·0′	1°53·3′W	X	128
Springfield Sch	Leeds	SE2341	53°52·1′	1°38·6′W	X	104
Springfields Fm	Leic	SP5186	52°28·4′	1°14·5′W	FM	140
Springfield Wood	E Loth	NT4861	55°50·6′	2°49·4′W	F	66
Springfield Wood	Fife	NO3312	56°18·0′	3°4·5′W	F	59
Spring Fm	Ches	SJ5967	53°12·2′	2°36·4′W	FM	117
Spring Fm	Ches	SJ6959	53°7·9′	2°27·4′W	FM	118
Spring Fm	Derby	SK3829	52°51·7′	1°25·7′W	FM	128
Spring Fm	Essex	TM1427	51°54·2′	1°7·1′E	FM	168,169
Spring Fm	E Susx	TQ4224	51°0·1′	0°1·8′E	FM	198
Spring Fm	Herts	TL3201	51°41·8′	0°5·0′W	FM	166
Spring Fm	Kent	TQ6544	51°10·5′	0°22·0′E	FM	188
Spring Fm	Kent	TR0128	51°1·2′	0°52·3′E	FM	189
Spring Fm	N Lincs	TA1223	53°41·7′	0°17·8′W	FM	107,113
Spring Fm	Norf	TF9415	52°42·1′	0°52·7′E	FM	132
Spring Fm	Norf	TG1516	52°42·2′	1°11·3′E	FM	133
Spring Fm	Northnts	SP5742	52°4·6′	1°9·7′W	FM	152
Spring Fm	Notts	SK5040	52°57·5′	1°14·9′W	FM	129
Spring Fm	Notts	SK7038	52°56·3′	0°57·1′W	FM	129
Spring Fm	N Yks	SE8572	54°8·4′	0°41·5′W	FM	100
Spring Fm	Oxon	SU6082	51°32·3′	1°7·7′W	FM	175
Spring Fm	Somer	ST5454	51°17·2′	2°39·2′W	FM	182,183
Spring Fm	Somer	ST5823	51°0·5′	2°35·5′W	FM	183
Spring Fm	Suff	TM0079	52°22·6′	0°56·7′E	FM	144
Spring Fm	Suff	TM0771	52°18·1′	1°2·6′E	FM	144,155
Spring Fm	Suff	TM2983	52°24·0′	1°22·4′E	FM	156
Spring Fm	Warw	SP2258	52°13·4′	1°40·3′W	FM	151
Spring Fm	Warw	SP4885	52°27·9′	1°17·2′W	FM	140
Spring Fm	Wilts	ST8921	50°59·5′	2°9·0′W	FM	184
Spring Fm	Worcs	SO9481	52°25·9′	2°4·9′W	FM	139
Spring Fm	W Susx	TQ2231	51°4·1′	0°15·1′W	FM	187
Spring Fms	Warw	SP3755	52°11·8′	1°27·1′W	FM	151
Spring-garden	E Susx	TQ4627	51°1·7′	0°5·3′E	X	188,198
Spring Garden	S Ayr	NS2907	55°19·9′	4°41·3′W	X	70,76
Spring Gardens	Durham	NZ1726	54°38·0′	1°43·8′W	X	92
Spring Gardens	Somer	ST7649	51°14·6′	2°20·2′W	T	183
Spring Gdns	Shrops	SJ5013	52°43·0′	2°44·0′W	T	126
Spring Gill Beck	N Yks	SE1194	54°20·7′	1°49·4′W	W	99
Spring Grange	Leic	SK6508	52°40·2′	1°1·9′W	X	141
Spring Green	Lancs	SD9343	53°53·2′	2°6·0′W	T	103
Spring Grove	Houns	TQ1576	51°28·5′	0°20·3′W	T	176
Spring Grove	Wrex	SJ3851	53°3·4′	2°55·1′W	X	117
Spring Grove Fm	Bucks	SP8029	51°57·5′	0°49·7′W	FM	165
Spring Grove Ho	Somer	ST1024	51°0·7′	3°16·6′W	X	181,193
Spring Hag	Cumbr	SD4898	54°22·7′	2°47·6′W	X	97
Spring Hall	Cambs	TL5659	52°12·7′	0°17·4′E	X	154
Spring Hall	N Yks	SE2475	54°10·5′	1°37·5′W	X	99
Springhall	Pth & Kin	NO1109	56°16·2′	3°25·6′W	X	58
Springhall	Scot Bord	NT7535	55°36·7′	2°23·4′W	X	74
Spring Hall Fm	Brad	SE0833	53°47·8′	1°52·3′W	FM	104
Spring Hall Fm	Cambs	TL4054	52°10·2′	0°3·2′E	FM	154
Spring Hall Fm	Suff	TL8450	52°7·3′	0°41·7′E	FM	155
Springham Fm	E Susx	TQ5913	50°53·9′	0°16·1′E	FM	199
Spring Head	Dorset	ST6805	50°50·9′	2°26·9′W	W	194
Springhead	Dorset	ST8716	50°56·8′	2°10·7′W	X	183
Spring Head	Kent	TQ6172	51°25·7′	0°19·4′E	X	177
Spring Head	Notts	SK8065	53°10·8′	0°47·8′W	W	121
Spring Head	N Yks	SD9745	53°54·3′	2°2·3′W	X	103
Spring Head	N Yks	SE4869	54°7·1′	1°15·5′W	X	100
Springhead	Oldham	SD9504	53°32·2′	2°4·1′W	T	109
Spring Head	Staffs	SK0166	53°11·7′	1°58·7′W	X	119
Spring Head	Suff	TL8460	52°12·7′	0°42·0′E	F	155
Spring Head Fm	Brad	SE0536	53°49·5′	1°55·0′W	FM	104
Spring Head Fm	Lancs	SD7950	53°57·0′	2°18·8′W	FM	103
Springhead Fm	W Susx	TQ0613	50°54·6′	0°29·1′W	FM	197
Springhead Hill	W Susx	TQ0612	50°54·1′	0°29·2′W	H	197
Spring Heads	N Yks	SE7292	54°19·3′	0°53·2′W	X	94,100
Springhill	Aberd	NJ8005	57°8·4′	2°19·4′W	X	38
Springhill	Aberd	NK1042	57°28·3′	1°49·5′W	X	30
Springhill	Cumbr	NY0122	54°35·3′	3°31·5′W	X	89
Springhill	Derby	SK2747	53°1·4′	1°35·4′W	X	119,128
Spring Hill	Derby	SK3344	52°59·8′	1°30·1′W	X	119,128
Spring Hill	Durham	NY9525	54°37·5′	2°4·2′W	X	91,92
Springhill	E Ayr	NS6419	55°27·0′	4°8·6′W	X	71
Springhill	E Renf	NS5057	55°47·2′	4°23·1′W	T	64
Spring Hill	Glos	SO8023	51°54·6′	2°17·1′W	X	162
Spring Hill	Glos	SP0517	51°51·3′	1°55·3′W	X	163
Spring Hill	Glos	SP1234	52°0·5′	1°49·1′W	X	150
Springhill	I of W	SZ5095	50°45·4′	1°17·1′W	T	196
Spring Hill	Lancs	SD7428	53°45·1′	2°23·2′W	T	103
Spring Hill	Leic	SK4415	52°44·1′	1°20·5′W	X	129
Springhill	N Lanak	NS8858	55°48·4′	3°46·8′W	T	65,72
Springhill	Northum	NT9950	55°44·9′	2°0·5′W	X	75
Spring Hill	Northum	NU2031	55°34·6′	1°40·5′W	X	75
Spring Hill	Northum	NZ1985	55°9·8′	1°41·7′W	X	81
Spring Hill	Notts	SK5959	53°7·7′	1°6·7′W	X	120
Spring Hill	Notts	SK6997	53°28·1′	0°57·2′W	X	111
Spring Hill	Notts	SK7445	53°0·1′	0°53·4′W	X	129
Spring Hill	N Yks	NZ9301	54°24·0′	0°33·6′W	X	94
Spring Hill	Oldham	SD9405	53°32·7′	2°5·0′W	T	109
Springhill	Oxon	SP4612	51°48·5′	1°19·6′W	X	164
Springhill	Scot Bord	NT7838	55°38·4′	2°20·5′W	X	74
Springhill	Shrops	SJ5138	52°56·5′	2°43·3′W	X	126
Springhill	S Lanak	NT0043	55°40·5′	3°35·0′W	X	72
Springhill	Staffs	SJ9704	52°38·3′	2°2·3′W	T	127,139
Spring Hill	Staffs	SJ9720	52°46·9′	2°2·3′W	H	127
Springhill	Staffs	SK0605	52°38·8′	1°54·3′W	T	139
Springhill	Warw	SP3152	52°10·2′	1°32·4′W	X	151
Springhill	Warw	SP5173	52°21·4′	1°14·7′W	X	140
Spring Hill	Wilts	SU2770	51°25·9′	1°36·3′W	X	174
Spring Hill	Wolv	SO8895	52°33·4′	2°10·2′W	T	139
Spring Hill	Wrex	SJ2134	52°54·1′	3°10·1′W	X	126
Springhill Covert	Suff	TL8767	52°16·4′	0°44·9′E	F	155
Springhill Fm	Birm	SK1300	52°36·1′	1°48·1′W	FM	139
Springhill Fm	Kent	TQ5240	51°8·6′	0°10·8′E	FM	188
Springhill Fm	Kent	TQ8130	51°2·7′	0°35·3′E	FM	188
Springhill Fm	Northnts	SP7568	52°18·5′	0°53·6′W	FM	152
Springhill Fm	N Yks	SE2553	53°58·6′	1°36·7′W	FM	104
Springhill Fm	Oxon	SP2516	51°50·8′	1°37·8′W	FM	163
Springhill Fm	Oxon	SP2828	51°57·2′	1°35·2′W	FM	163
Springhill Fm	Oxon	SP3708	51°46·4′	1°27·4′W	FM	164
Spring Hill Fm	Oxon	SP4232	51°59·3′	1°22·9′W	FM	151
Springhill Fm	Shrops	SO2580	52°25·0′	3°5·8′W	FM	137
Springhill Fm	S Lanak	NS8330	55°33·2′	3°50·9′W	FM	71,72
Springhill Fm	Warw	SP5173	52°21·4′	1°14·7′W	FM	140
Spring Hill Fm	Worcs	SO9846	52°7·0′	2°1·4′W	FM	150
Springhill (HM Prison)	Bucks	SP6821	51°53·2′	1°0·3′W	X	164,165
Spring Hill School	N Yks	SE3073	54°9·4′	1°32·0′W	X	99
Spring Ho	Cumbr	SD1190	54°18·1′	3°21·6′W	X	96
Spring Ho	Darl	NZ3515	54°32·0′	1°27·1′W	X	93
Spring Ho	Derby	SK3265	53°11·1′	1°30·9′W	X	119
Spring Ho	E Yorks	SE7241	53°51·9′	0°53·9′W	X	105,106
Spring Ho	Northum	NY8446	54°48·8′	2°14·5′W	X	86,87
Spring Ho	Northum	NY9555	54°53·6′	2°4·3′W	X	87
Spring Ho	N Yks	NZ5604	54°25·9′	1°7·8′W	X	93
Spring Ho	N Yks	NZ6300	54°23·7′	1°1·4′W	X	94
Spring Ho	N Yks	SE1366	54°5·6′	1°47·7′W	X	99
Spring Ho	N Yks	SE3090	54°18·5′	1°31·9′W	X	99
Spring Ho	N Yks	SE4479	54°12·5′	1°19·1′W	X	99
Spring Ho	N Yks	SE4968	54°6·6′	1°14·6′W	X	100
Spring Ho	N Yks	SE5564	54°4·4′	1°9·2′W	X	100
Spring Ho	Stock on T	NZ3916	54°32·5′	1°23·4′W	X	93
Spring Ho Fm	Derby	SK1584	53°21·4′	1°46·1′W	FM	110
Springholm	D & G	NX8070	55°0·9′	3°52·2′W	X	84
Spring House	N Yks	SE0064	54°4·6′	1°59·6′W	X	98
Spring House Fm	E Yorks	SE7649	53°56·1′	0°50·1′W	FM	105,106
Spring House Fm	Leic	SK4725	52°49·5′	1°17·7′W	FM	129
Spring House Fm	N Yks	SE2176	54°11·0′	1°40·3′W	FM	99
Spring House Fm	N Yks	SE2262	54°3·5′	1°39·4′W	FM	99
Spring House Fm	N Yks	SE2850	53°57·0′	1°34·0′W	FM	104
Spring House Fm	N Yks	SE4472	54°8·8′	1°19·2′W	FM	99
Spring House Fm	Red & Cl	NZ7219	54°33·9′	0°52·8′W	FM	94
Spring House Fm	York	SE6343	53°53·0′	1°2·1′W	FM	105,106
Springing Greens	Aberd	NO7982	56°56·0′	2°20·3′W	X	45
Spring Keld	Cumbr	NY0804	54°25·6′	3°24·7′W	X	89
Springkell	D & G	NY2575	55°4·1′	3°10·0′W	T	85
Springlands	E Susx	TQ7420	50°57·4′	0°29·0′E	X	199
Springlands	W Susx	TQ2219	50°57·7′	0°15·4′W	X	198
Spring le Howl	N Yks	SE7371	54°8·0′	0°52·5′W	X	100
Springleys	Aberd	NJ7434	57°24·0′	2°25·5′W	X	29
Spring Lodge	N Yks	SE5220	53°40·7′	1°12·4′W	X	105
Spring Mill Resr	Lancs	SD8717	53°39·2′	2°11·4′W	W	109
Spring Park	Brom	TQ3764	51°21·7′	0°1·5′W	X	177,187
Spring Park	Croy	TQ3665	51°22·3′	0°2·4′W	T	177
Spring Park Fm	E Yorks	TA0334	53°47·8′	0°25·8′W	FM	107
Spring Pond Fm	Hants	SU4847	51°13·4′	1°18·4′W	FM	185
Spring Rd Sta	Birm	SP1182	52°26·4′	1°49·9′W	X	139
Springs	E Ayr	NS4322	55°28·3′	4°28·6′W	X	70
Springs	Lancs	SD8044	53°53·8′	2°17·8′W	X	103

Springs	Lancs	SD8646	53°54·8′	2°12·4′W	X	103
Spring's Fm	Notts	SK6656	53°6·1′	1°0·4′W	FM	120
Springs Fm	Notts	SK6998	53°28·7′	0°57·2′W	FM	111
Springs Fm	Notts	SK7464	53°10·3′	0°53·2′W	FM	120
Springs Fm	N Yks	SD9445	53°54·3′	2°5·1′W	FM	103
Springs Fm	S Glos	ST7478	51°30·3′	2°22·1′W	FM	172
Springs Fm	S Glos	ST7674	51°28·1′	2°20·3′W	FM	172
Springs Fm	Shrops	SJ5837	52°56·0′	2°37·1′W	FM	126
Springs Ho	Lancs	SD6143	53°53·1′	2°35·2′W	X	102,103
Springs Hydro	Leic	SK3512	52°42·5′	1°28·5′W	X	128
Spring Side	Lancs	SD7653	53°58·6′	2°21·5′W	X	103
Springside	N Ayr	NS3738	55°36·8′	4°34·8′W	T	70
Springslade Lodge	Staffs	SJ9716	52°44·7′	2°2·3′W	X	127
Springslade Pool	Staffs	SJ9616	52°44·7′	2°3·2′W	W	127
Springs Resr	Black w Dar	SD6914	53°37·5′	2°27·7′W	W	109
Springs, The	Brad	SE1240	53°51·6′	1°48·6′W	X	104
Springs, The	Norf	TG2714	52°40·8′	1°21·9′E	W	133,134
Springs, The	Shrops	SJ2432	52°53·0′	3°7·4′W	X	126
Springs, The	Shrops	SJ4130	52°52·1′	2°52·2′W	X	126
Spring Stones	D & G	NX8452	54°51·2′	3°48·0′W	X	84
Springs Wood	Lancs	SD6478	54°12·0′	2°32·7′W	F	97
Springs Wood	Lancs	SD7748	53°55·9′	2°20·6′W	F	103
Springs Wood	N Yks	SE2249	53°56·4′	1°39·5′W	F	104
Springthorpe	Lincs	SK8789	53°23·7′	0°41·1′W	T	112,121
Springthorpe Grange	Lincs	SK8990	53°24·2′	0°39·3′W	X	112
Spring Vale	Barns	SE2503	53°31·6′	1°37·0′W	T	110
Spring Vale	I of W	SZ6291	50°43·1′	1°6·9′W	X	196
Springvale	Roth	SK4889	53°24·0′	1°16·3′W	X	111,120
Springvale	Suff	TM1243	52°2·9′	1°5·9′E	X	155,169
Spring Valley	I of M	SC3575	54°8·9′	4°31·2′W	T	95
Springwater Fm	Hants	SU7461	51°20·8′	0°55·9′W	FM	175,186
Springwell	Essex	TL5241	52°3·0′	0°13·4′E	T	154
Springwell	Sund	NZ2858	54°55·2′	1°33·4′W	T	88
Springwell	Sund	NZ3655	54°53·6′	1°25·9′W	T	88
Springwell Brook	Lincs	TF0754	53°4·6′	0°23·8′W	W	121
Springwell Cottage Fm	Durham	NZ0941	54°46·1′	1°51·2′W	FM	88
Springwell Field	E Yorks	SE9143	53°52·7′	0°36·5′W	X	106
Springwell Fm	Durham	NZ0843	54°47·2′	1°52·1′W	FM	88
Spring Well Fm	N Yks	SE0951	53°57·5′	1°51·4′W	FM	104
Spring Well Fm	Oxon	SP5421	51°53·3′	1°12·5′W	FM	164
Springwell Ho	Cumbr	NY0938	54°44·0′	3°24·4′W	X	89
Springwell Ho	Northum	NY9157	54°54·7′	2°8·0′W	X	87
Spring Well Ho	N Yks	SE5435	53°48·7′	1°10·4′W	X	105
Springwell House Fm	Hartpl	NZ4728	54°38·9′	1°15·9′W	FM	93
Springwells	Aberd	NJ5862	57°39·0′	2°41·8′W	X	29
Springwells	D & G	NY0891	55°12·5′	3°26·3′W	T	78
Springwells	Scot Bord	NT7643	55°41·0′	2°22·5′W	X	74
Spring Wells	Shetld	HU3384	60°32·6′	1°23·4′W	W	1,2,3
Spring Wood	Brad	SE1940	53°51·6′	1°42·3′W	F	104
Spring Wood	Cumbr	NY6016	54°32·5′	2°36·7′W	F	91
Spring Wood	Durham	NZ2436	54°43·3′	1°37·2′W	F	93
Spring Wood	Essex	TL5239	52°1·9′	0°13·3′E	F	154
Spring Wood	E Yorks	SE8141	53°51·8′	0°45·7′W	F	106
Spring Wood	Leeds	SE2643	53°53·2′	1°35·9′W	F	104
Spring Wood	Leic	SK3822	52°47·9′	1°25·8′W	F	128
Spring Wood	Leic	SK4101	52°36·5′	1°23·3′W	F	140
Spring Wood	Lincs	TF0624	52°48·4′	0°25·2′W	X	130
Spring Wood	N Lincs	SE9511	53°35·5′	0°33·5′W	F	112
Spring Wood	Norf	TM2895	52°30·5′	1°22·0′E	F	134
Spring Wood	Northnts	SP9687	52°28·6′	0°34·8′W	F	141
Spring Wood	Notts	SK4942	52°58·6′	1°15·8′W	F	129
Spring Wood	N Yks	NZ8104	54°25·7′	0°44·7′W	F	94
Spring Wood	N Yks	SE1270	54°7·8′	1°48·6′W	F	99
Spring Wood	N Yks	SE1781	54°13·7′	1°43·9′W	F	99
Spring Wood	N Yks	SE2774	54°9·9′	1°34·8′W	F	99
Spring Wood	N Yks	SE3748	53°55·8′	1°25·8′W	F	104
Spring Wood	N Yks	SE4879	54°12·5′	1°15·4′W	F	100
Spring Wood	N Yks	SE5289	54°17·9′	1°11·6′W	F	100
Spring Wood	N Yks	SE5584	54°15·2′	1°8·9′W	F	100
Spring Wood	N Yks	SE5883	54°14·6′	1°6·2′W	F	100
Spring Wood	N Yks	SE6277	54°11·3′	1°2·6′W	F	100
Spring Wood	N Yks	SE6483	54°14·6′	1°0·7′W	F	100
Spring Wood	N Yks	SE6887	54°16·7′	0°56·9′W	F	94,100
Spring Wood	N Yks	SE7165	54°4·8′	0°54·5′W	F	100
Spring Wood	N Yks	SE7187	54°16·7′	0°54·2′W	F	94,100
Springwood	Scot Bord	NT7133	55°35·6′	2°27·2′W	X	74
Springwood Cott	N Yks	SE9592	54°19·1′	0°31·9′W	X	94,101
Springwood Fm	Ches	SJ7778	53°18·1′	2°20·3′W	FM	118
Springwood Fm	Derby	SK4268	53°12·7′	1°21·9′W	FM	120
Spring Wood Fm	Notts	SK7355	53°5·5′	0°54·2′W	FM	120
Springwood Fm	Notts	SK8673	53°15·1′	0°42·3′W	FM	121
Springwood Lodge	Northnts	SP9787	52°28·6′	0°33·9′W	X	141
Sprink	Staffs	SK1261	53°9·0′	1°48·8′W	X	119
Sprinkle Fm	Pemb	SM9910	51°45·4′	4°54·4′W	FM	157,158
Sprinkle Pill	Pemb	SM9910	51°45·4′	4°54·4′W	W	157,158
Sprinkling Tarn	Cumbr	NY2209	54°28·5′	3°11·8′W	W	89,90
Sprinks Barn Fm	Staffs	SK1821	52°47·4′	1°43·6′W	FM	128
Sprinks Fm	Staffs	SJ9257	53°6·8′	2°6·8′W	FM	118
Sprintgill	Cumbr	SD7299	54°23·4′	2°25·5′W	X	98
Sprint Mill	Cumbr	SD5196	54°21·7′	2°44·8′W	X	97
Sprites, The	Lincs	TF1354	53°4·5′	0°18·4′W	X	121
Sprit Strand	D & G	NX3181	55°5·9′	4°38·5′W	W	76
Sprivers	Kent	TQ6939	51°7·7′	0°25·3′E	X	188
Sproat Ghyll Fm	Cumbr	NY6007	54°27·7′	2°36·6′W	FM	91
Sproatley	E Yorks	TA1934	53°47·6′	0°11·2′W	T	107
Sproatley Drain	E Yorks	TA2033	53°47·0′	0°10·3′W	W	107
Sproatley Grange	E Yorks	TA2033	53°47·0′	0°10·3′W	X	107
Spronkett's	W Susx	TQ2423	50°59·8′	0°13·6′W	X	198
Sproston Green	Ches	SJ7366	53°11·7′	2°23·8′W	T	118
Sproston Hall	Ches	SJ7366	53°11·7′	2°23·8′W	X	118
Sprotbrough	Donc	SE5302	53°31·0′	1°11·6′W	T	111
Sprott's Fm	Suff	TL9839	52°1·1′	0°53·5′E	FM	155
Sprottyneuk	Aberd	NJ8145	57°29·9′	2°18·6′W	X	29,30
Sproughton	Suff	TM1244	52°3·5′	1°5·9′E	T	155,169
Sproughton Manor	Suff	TM1245	52°4·0′	1°6·0′E	X	155,169
Sprouston	Scot Bord	NT7535	55°36·7′	2°23·4′W	T	74
Sproutes	W Susx	TQ1121	50°58·9′	0°24·7′W	X	198
Sprowston	Norf	TG2411	52°39·2′	1°19·1′E	T	133,134
Sproxton	Leic	SK8524	52°48·6′	0°43·9′W	T	130

Sproxton	N Yks	SE6181	54°13·5′	1°3·4′W	T	100
Sproxton Lodge	Leic	SK8825	52°49·2′	0°41·2′W	X	130
Sproxton Moor	N Yks	SE5781	54°13·5′	1°7·1′W	X	100
Sproxton Thorns	Leic	SK8423	52°48·1′	0°44·8′W	F	130
Spruce Gill Beck	N Yks	SE1380	54°13·2′	1°47·6′W	W	99
Spruce Gill Fm	N Yks	SE1889	54°18·0′	1°43·0′W	FM	99
Sprucely	Durham	NZ3431	54°40·6′	1°27·9′W	X	93
Spruce Ride	Glos	SO6211	51°48·0′	2°32·7′W	X	162
Spruisty Grange Fm	N Yks	SE2958	54°1·3′	1°33·0′W	FM	104
Spruisty Hall Fm	N Yks	SE2958	54°1·3′	1°33·0′W	FM	104
Spruisty Hill Fm	N Yks	SE2958	54°1·3′	1°33·0′W	FM	104
Sprunston	Cumbr	NY3948	54°49·6′	2°56·5′W	T	85
Sprydoncote	Devon	SX9899	50°47·1′	3°26·4′W	X	192
Sprydon Plantation	Devon	SX9999	50°47·1′	3°25·6′W	F	192
Sprytown	Devon	SX4185	50°38·8′	4°14·6′W	X	201
Spuir	N Eil	NF8584	57°44·4′	7°17·2′W	X	18
Spunham	Cumbr	SD1683	54°14·4′	3°16·9′W	X	96
Spunham	Cumbr	SD2588	54°17·2′	3°8·7′W	X	96
Spunhill	Shrops	SJ4133	52°53·7′	2°52·2′W	T	126
Spunkie	E Ayr	NS4354	55°45·5′	4°29·7′W	X	64
Spurban Hill	Kent	TQ8827	51°0·9′	0°41·2′E	X	189,199
Spur Hill	Surrey	SU9054	51°16·9′	0°42·2′W	X	186
Spur Island	Pemb	SS1496	51°38·2′	4°40·9′W	X	158
Spurlands End	Bucks	SU8997	51°40·1′	0°42·4′W	T	165
Spurlens Rig	Scot Bord	NT2554	55°46·7′	3°11·3′W	X	66,73
Spurles Fm	Somer	ST6819	50°58·4′	2°27·0′W	FM	183
Spurleybrook Fm	Staffs	SJ8427	52°50·7′	2°13·9′W	FM	127
Spurlswood Beck	Durham	NZ0426	54°38·0′	1°55·9′W	W	92
Spur Ness	Orkney	HY6033	59°11·2′	2°41·5′W	X	5,6
Spurness Sound	Orkney	HY6132	59°10·6′	2°40·5′W	W	5
Spurn Head	E Yorks	TA3910	53°34·3′	0°6·4′E	X	113
Spurn Hill	Pth & Kin	NO0552	56°39·3′	3°32·5′W	H	52,53
Spur of the Isle	Orkney	HY3528	59°8·3′	3°7·7′W	X	6
Spurrell's Cross	Devon	SX6559	50°25·2′	3°53·6′W	A	202
Spurriers	Essex	TL5903	51°42·4′	0°18·5′E	X	167
Spurrigg End	Cumbr	NY8316	54°32·6′	2°15·3′W	X	91,92
Spursholt Ho	Hants	SU3321	50°59·5′	1°31·4′W	X	185
Spurstow	Ches	SJ5556	53°6·2′	2°39·9′W	T	117
Spurstow Hall	Ches	SJ5656	53°6·2′	2°39·0′W	X	117
Spurstow Lower Hall	Ches	SJ5655	53°5·7′	2°39·0′W	X	117
Spurstow Spa	Ches	SJ5754	53°5·1′	2°38·1′W	W	117
Spurtham Fm	Devon	ST1906	50°51·1′	3°8·7′W	FM	192,193
Spur, The	Highld	ND1769	58°36·3′	3°25·2′W	X	12
Spurtree	Shrops	SO6069	52°19·3′	2°34·8′W	T	138
Spurway Barton	Devon	SS8921	50°58·9′	3°34·5′W	X	181
Spurway Mill	Devon	SS8920	50°58·4′	3°34·5′W	X	181
Spurways	Devon	SS9818	50°57·4′	3°26·8′W	X	181
Sput a' Chleibh	Pth & Kin	NN7317	56°20·0′	4°2·8′W	X	57
Spùtan a' Ghobhair	Highld	NH1121	57°14·7′	5°7·5′W	W	25
Sputan Bàn	Highld	NH1322	57°15·3′	5°5·5′W	W	25
Spùt Bàn	Stir	NN3123	56°22·4′	4°43·7′W	W	50
Spùt Dubh	Arg & Bt	NM5154	56°37·0′	6°3·1′W	W	47
Spùt Dubh	Stir	NN3814	56°17·7′	4°36·6′W	W	50,56
Spùt Rolla	Pth & Kin	NN7228	56°25·9′	4°4·1′W	W	51,52
Spycott	Devon	SS6321	50°58·6′	3°56·7′W	X	180
Spye Park Ho	Wilts	ST9567	51°24·4′	2°3·9′W	X	173
Spyhill	Aberd	NO7591	57°0·8′	2°24·2′W	X	38,45
Spy Hill	Brad	SE1242	53°52·7′	1°48·6′W	X	104
Spy Hill	Ches	SJ5271	53°14·3′	2°42·7′W	X	117
Spy Hill	N Yks	SE7564	54°4·2′	0°50·8′W	X	100
Spying Hillock	Angus	NO1973	56°50·7′	3°19·2′W	H	43
Spyknave Hill	N Yks	NZ4709	54°28·7′	1°16·1′W	X	93
Spylaw	Northum	NU0531	55°34·6′	1°54·8′W	X	75
Spy Law	Northum	NU2210	55°23·3′	1°38·7′W	X	81
Spylaw	Northum	NZ0397	55°16·3′	1°56·7′W	X	81
Spylaw	Scot Bord	NT7232	55°35·1′	2°26·2′W	X	74
Spylaw Burn	Northum	NZ0496	55°15·7′	1°55·8′W	W	81
Spylaw Cottage	Scot Bord	NT2152	55°45·5′	3°15·1′W	X	66,73
Spynie	Moray	NJ2265	57°40·3′	3°18·0′W	X	28
Spynie Canal	Moray	NJ2366	57°40·9′	3°17·0′W	W	28
Spy Rigg	Northum	NY6975	55°4·4′	2°28·7′W	X	86,87
Spyway	Dorset	SY5293	50°44·3′	2°40·4′W	T	194
Spyway Barn	Dorset	SY9977	50°35·8′	2°0·5′W	X	195
Squabb Wood	Hants	SU3321	50°59·5′	1°31·4′W	F	185
Squab Hall	Warw	SP3261	52°15·0′	1°31·5′W	X	151
Squallacombe	Somer	SS7238	51°7·9′	3°49·4′W	H	180
Squallham	Norf	TG1533	52°51·3′	1°12·0′E	X	133
Squalls Fm	Wilts	ST9426	51°2·2′	2°4·7′W	FM	184
Square and Compass	Pemb	SM8531	51°56·4′	5°7·3′W	T	157
Square Covert	Norf	TL9284	52°25·4′	0°49·8′E	X	144
Square Covert	Suff	TL7774	52°20·4′	0°36·3′E	F	144
Square Covert	Suff	TM2141	52°1·6′	1°13·7′E	F	169
Square Ho	Durham	NZ1645	54°48·2′	1°44·6′W	X	88
Squarehouse Fm	Ches	SJ5159	53°7·8′	2°43·5′W	FM	117
Square of Sibster	Highld	ND3153	58°27·9′	3°10·5′W	X	11,12
Squares Fm	Flint	SJ2857	53°6·6′	3°4·1′W	FM	117
Square Spinney	Leic	SK6605	52°38·6′	1°1·1′W	F	141
Square, The	Cumbr	NY4665	54°58·9′	2°50·2′W	X	86
Square, The	N Yks	SE8165	54°4·7′	0°45·3′W	X	100
Squeaks Ho	Essex	TL9400	51°40·1′	0°48·7′E	X	168
Squeen	I of M	SC3594	54°19·1′	4°31·8′W	X	95
Squerryes Court	Kent	TQ4453	51°15·7′	0°4·2′E	A	187
Squibs Fm	E Susx	TQ7224	50°59·6′	0°27·5′E	FM	199
Squids Gate Fm	Kent	TQ9849	51°12·6′	0°50·5′E	FM	189
Squilver	Shrops	SO3797	52°34·3′	2°55·4′W	X	137
Squilver Fm	Shrops	SO3297	52°34·2′	2°59·8′W	FM	137
Squire Hall	Shrops	SO3592	52°31·6′	2°57·1′W	X	137
Squire's Br	Lincs	SK9082	53°19·9′	0°38·5′W	X	121
Squires Fm	E Susx	TQ5018	50°56·7′	0°8·5′E	FM	199
Squire's Fm	Surrey	TQ1446	51°12·3′	0°21·7′W	FM	187
Squires Gate	Blackp	SD3132	53°47·0′	3°2·4′W	T	102
Squire's Great Wood	Surrey	TQ1446	51°12·3′	0°21·7′W	F	187
Squire's Hill	Suff	TM4975	52°19·2′	1°39·6′E	X	156
Squirrel Bank	N Yks	SE1985	54°15·9′	1°42·1′W	X	99
Squirrel Fm	Shrops	SO5475	52°22·5′	2°40·1′W	FM	137,138
Squirrel Hall Fm	N Yks	SE9167	54°5·7′	0°36·1′W	FM	101
Squirrel's Corner	Dorset	SU0214	50°55·8′	1°57·9′W	X	195
Squirrel's Hall	Suff	TM0072	52°18·8′	0°56·5′E	X	144,155
Squirrels Hall	Suff	TM0536	51°59·3′	0°59·5′E	X	155
Squirrels, The	E Yorks	SE7549	53°56·1′	0°51·0′W	X	105,106

Squirrel Wood	Donc	SE5411	53°35·8′	1°10·6′W	F	111
Squirrel Wood	Kent	TQ8359	51°18·3′	0°37·9′E	F	178,188
Squitch Ho	Staffs	SK0826	52°50·1′	1°52·5′W	X	128
Sraid Ruadh	Arg & Bt	NL9547	56°31·2′	6°57·1′W	T	46
Srath a' Bhàthaich	Highld	NG8747	57°28·1′	5°32·6′W	X	24
Srath Ach' a' Bhathaich	Highld	NH7095	57°55·8′	4°11·2′W	X	21
Srath a Chomair	Highld	NG8615	57°10·8′	5°32·0′W	X	33
Srath a' Chraisg	Highld	NC5324	58°11·1′	4°29·5′W	X	16
Srath a' Ghlinne	Pth & Kin	NN6717	56°19·9′	4°8·6′W	X	57
Srath an Aoinidh Bhig	Highld	NM6650	56°35·3′	5°48·2′W	X	49
Srathan Buidhe	Highld	NG9474	57°42·8′	5°27·0′W	X	19
Srath an Eilich	Highld	NN6496	57°2·4′	4°14·0′W	X	35
Srath Ascaig	Highld	NG8633	57°20·5′	5°32·9′W	X	24
Srath Bàn	N Eil	NB1119	58°4·2′	6°53·6′W	X	13,14
Srath Beag	Highld	NC3853	58°26·4′	4°46·0′W	X	9
Srath Beag	Highld	NG5722	57°13·7′	6°1·1′W	X	32
Srath Bearnach	Arg & Bt	NM6831	56°25·1′	5°45·3′W	X	49
Srath Beinn Dearg	Highld	NH0180	57°46·2′	5°20·3′W	X	19
Srath Bhata	Arg & Bt	NR4152	55°41·8′	6°6·9′W	X	60
Srath Carnaig	Highld	NH7098	57°57·4′	4°11·3′W	X	21
Srath Chrombuill	Highld	NH1264	57°37·9′	5°8·5′W	X	19
Srath Coille na Feàrna	Highld	NC3750	58°24·7′	4°46·9′W	X	9
Srath Creag nam Fitheach	Arg & Bt	NM4841	56°29·9′	6°5·2′W	X	47,48
Srath Dionard	Highld	NC3453	58°26·3′	4°50·1′W	X	9
Srath Dubh-uisage	Arg & Bt	NN2915	56°18·1′	4°45·4′W	X	50,56
Srath Duilleach	Highld	NH0328	57°18·3′	5°15·8′W	X	25,33
Srath Litean	N Eil	NG0586	57°46·3′	6°57·2′W	X	14,18
Srath Luachrach	Arg & Bt	NR3970	55°51·4′	6°9·8′W	X	60,61
Srath Luib na Seilich	Highld	NC3341	58°19·8′	4°50·6′W	X	9
Srath Lungard	Highld	NG9264	57°37·3′	5°28·5′W	X	19
Srath Maol Chaluim	Highld	NG7347	57°27·7′	5°46·6′W	X	24
Srath Mór	Arg & Bt	NR2668	55°49·9′	6°22·1′W	X	60
Srath Mór	Highld	NG5624	57°14·8′	6°2·2′W	X	32
Srath Mór	Highld	NH5770	57°42·1′	4°23·5′W	X	21
Srath na Crèitheach	Highld	NG5022	57°13·5′	6°8·0′W	X	32
Srath na Frithe	Highld	NC8227	58°13·2′	4°0·1′W	X	17
Srath Nairn	Highld	NH6629	57°20·2′	4°13·1′W	X	26,35
Srath nan Caran	Highld	NC3136	58°17·1′	4°52·5′W	X	15
Srath nan Coileach	Arg & Bt	NR8960	55°47·5′	5°21·5′W	W	62
Srath nan Lòn	Highld	NC2300	57°57·5′	4°59·0′W	X	15
Srath nan Lub	Arg & Bt	NS0691	56°4·6′	5°6·6′W	X	56
Srath Nimhe	Highld	NH2191	57°52·6′	5°0·6′W	X	20
Srath Ossian	Highld	NN4173	56°49·5′	4°35·9′W	X	42
Srath Shuardail	Highld	NM7346	56°33·3′	5°41·2′W	X	49
Srath Tarabhan	Pth & Kin	NN3739	56°31·1′	4°38·5′W	X	50
Srath Uladail	Highld	NM7050	56°35·4′	5°44·3′W	X	49
Sreag Dhubh	Highld	NN1247	56°34·9′	5°3·2′W	X	50
Sreang Glas a' Chuill	Highld	NH6507	57°8·3′	4°13·4′W	H	35
Sreath a' Ghlas-choire	Highld	NH0415	57°11·3′	5°14·2′W	X	33
Sreath an Fhraoch-choire	Highld	NH0315	57°11·3′	5°15·1′W	X	33
Srianach	N Eil	NB4010	58°0·5′	6°23·6′W	H	14
Sriar Water	S Lanak	NS8519	55°27·3′	3°48·7′W	W	71
Sroin Uaidh	Stir	NN3310	56°15·4′	4°41·3′W	X	50,56
Sròmaigh	N Eil	NF8058	57°30·2′	7°20·1′W	X	22
Sròn a' Bhoididh	Pth & Kin	NO0082	56°55·4′	3°38·1′W	H	43
Sron a' Bhreatuinnaich	Highld	NM7968	56°45·3′	5°36·5′W	X	40
Sròn a' Bhuic	Highld	NC1722	58°9·2′	5°6·1′W	H	15
Sròn a' Bhùirich	Highld	NN4297	57°2·5′	4°35·8′W	H	34
Sròn Ach' a' Bhacaidh	Highld	NH6198	57°57·2′	4°20·5′W	H	21
Sròn a' Chàirn Deirg	Highld	NH0099	57°56·4′	5°22·3′W	X	19
Sròn a' Chais	N Eil	NB3405	57°57·6′	6°29·3′W	X	13,14
Sròn a' Champair	N Eil	NB5647	58°20·9′	6°9·7′W	X	8
Sròn a' Chaoineidh	Pth & Kin	NN7636	56°30·2′	4°0·4′W	H	51,52
Sron á Chaorainn	Stir	NN4812	56°16·8′	4°26·9′W	X	57
Sròn a' Chlachain	Stir	NN5532	56°27·7′	4°20·8′W	H	51
Sròn a' Chlaonaidh	Pth & Kin	NN5165	56°45·4′	4°25·8′W	H	42
Sròn a' Chleirich	Pth & Kin	NN7876	56°51·8′	3°59·6′W	H	42
Sròn a Choin	Highld	NM8690	56°57·4′	5°30·7′W	X	33,40
Sròn a' Choire	Highld	NH0685	57°49·0′	5°15·5′W	X	19
Sròn a' Choire Ghairbh	Highld	NN2294	57°0·4′	4°55·4′W	H	34
Sròn a' Choire Odhair-bhig	Highld	NN2058	56°41·0′	4°55·9′W	X	41
Sròn a' Choit	Highld	NG9070	57°40·5′	5°30·8′W	H	19
Sròn à Chorra Bhuilg	Highld	NN9869	56°46·4′	5°17·9′W	X	40
Sròn a' Chrann-lithe	Arg & Bt	NM5638	56°28·5′	5°57·3′W	X	47,48
Sròn a' Chrò	Pth & Kin	NN9073	56°50·4′	3°47·7′W	H	43
Sròn a' Chuilinn	Highld	NH0204	57°5·3′	5°15·6′W	X	33
Sròn a' Chùirn Deirg	Highld	NG8994	57°53·4′	5°33·1′W	X	19
Sron a Ghamhuinn	Pth & Kin	NN8847	56°36·4′	3°49·0′W	X	52
Sròn a' Gharbh Choire Bhig	Highld	NM9161	56°41·9′	5°24·4′W	X	40
Sròn a' Ghearrain	Highld	NN2146	56°34·6′	4°54·4′W	X	50
Sron á Gheill	Highld	NN3494	57°0·7′	4°43·6′W	H	34
Sron a' Gheodha Dhuibh	Highld	NG7792	57°52·0′	5°45·1′W	X	19
Sròn a' Gheodha Dhuibh	Highld	NG9898	57°55·8′	5°24·2′W	X	19
Sròn a' Ghlinne	Arg & Bt	NM6622	56°20·2′	5°46·7′W	X	49
Sròn a' Ghobhainn	N Eil	NB1032	58°11·2′	6°55·6′W	X	13
Sròn a' Ghoire	Highld	NN4587	56°57·2′	4°32·5′W	X	34,42
Sròn a' Ghoirtein	N Eil	NB0111	57°59·5′	7°3·1′W	X	13
Sròn a' Ghrobain	Highld	NG4430	57°17·6′	6°14·5′W	H	32
Sròn Aileach	Pth & Kin	NN6715	56°18·8′	4°8·6′W	X	57
Sròn Albannach	Arg & Bt	NR7349	55°41·1′	5°36·2′W	X	62
Sron Alla Tolan	N Eil	NB5142	58°18·0′	6°14·5′W	X	8
Sròn a' Mhàis	Highld	NG7857	57°33·2′	5°42·2′W	X	24
Sròn a' Mhill	Highld	NG4843	57°24·7′	6°11·3′W	X	23
Sròn a' Mhill Bhuidhe	Pth & Kin	NN4445	56°34·5′	4°31·9′W	X	51
Sròn a' Mhoil	Highld	NG9492	57°52·5′	5°28·0′W	X	19
Sròn a' Mhuilt	Highld	NG7574	57°42·2′	5°46·1′W	X	19
Sròn an Aighe	Highld	NG3746	57°26·0′	6°22·5′W	H	23
Sròn an Aighe	Highld	NG4266	57°36·9′	6°18·7′W	X	23
Sron an Aonaich	Highld	NJ0005	57°7·8′	3°38·7′W	X	36
Sròn an Droma	Arg & Bt	NM7600	56°8·7′	5°35·9′W	X	55
Sròn an Drutain	Highld	NM8390	56°57·3′	5°33·7′W	X	33,40
Sròn an Dubh-aird	Highld	NG8755	57°32·4′	5°33·1′W	X	24
Sròn an Dùin	N Eil	NL5481	56°47·8′	7°39·6′W	X	31
Sròn an Dùn-chàirn	Highld	NG8698	57°55·5′	5°36·4′W	X	19
Sròn an Eirreannach	Highld	NC7538	58°19·0′	4°7·6′W	H	16
Sròn an Fhithich	Highld	NG8253	57°31·1′	5°38·0′W	X	24
Sròn an Fhraoich	Arg & Bt	NL9340	56°27·4′	6°58·6′W	X	46
Sròn an Fhuaraidh	N Eil	NB5546	58°20·3′	6°10·7′W	X	8
Sròn an Fhuarain	Highld	NN4374	56°50·1′	4°34·0′W	X	42

Sròn an Ime	Highld	NM9866	56°44·8'	5°17·8'W	X	40
Sròn an Lagain Ghairbh	Highld	NN3364	56°44·5'	4°43·4'W	X	41
Sron an Laoigh Burn	Arg & Bt	NS3292	56°5·7'	4°41·6'W	W	56
Sron an Lochain	Highld	NN2473	56°49·2'	4°52·6'W	X	41
Sròn an Tairbh	Highld	NG7725	57°15·9'	5°41·4'W	X	33
Sròn an Tigh Mhóir	Highld	NM9695	57°0·3'	5°21·1'W	H	33,40
Sròn an Toistear	N Eil	NB1703	57°55·9'	6°46·4'W	H	13,14
Sròn an t-Saighdeir	Highld	NM3298	57°0·0'	6°24·3'W	H	39
Sròn an t-Seileir	N Eil	NB5656	58°25·7'	6°10·3'W	X	8
Sron an t-Sluichd	Highld	NM9674	56°49·0'	5°20·1'W	X	40
Sròn an Tuirc	Highld	NC5438	58°18·6'	4°29·0'W	H	16
Sròn Aonaich	Stir	NN3700	56°10·1'	4°37·1'W	X	56
Sròn Aonghais	Aberd	NJ3011	57°11·3'	3°9·0'W	H	37
Sròn Ard	N Eil	NB1112	58°0·5'	6°53·1'W	H	13,14
Srón Ard a' Mhullaich	Highld	NG5427	57°16·3'	6°4·4'W	X	32
Sròn Armailte	Stir	NN5207	56°14·2'	4°22·8'W	H	57
Sron Badan nam Meann	Highld	NH1813	57°10·6'	5°0·2'W	X	34
Sròn Bealaidh	Pth & Kin	NN8333	56°28·7'	3°53·5'W	H	52
Sròn Beinne Mheadhoin	Highld	NM9069	56°46·2'	5°25·7'W	X	40
Sròn Bheag	Highld	NM4662	56°41·1'	6°8·4'W	X	47
Sròn Bheag	Pth & Kin	NN5262	56°43·8'	4°24·7'W	H	42
Sròn Bheith	Arg & Bt	NR7486	56°1·1'	5°37·1'W	X	55
Sròn Bheithe	Arg & Bt	NR5079	55°56·6'	5°59·8'W	X	61
Sròn Bhreac	Arg & Bt	NM5422	56°19·9'	5°58·3'W	X	48
Sròn Bhreac	Highld	NN2291	56°58·8'	4°55·3'W	H	34
Sròn Bhreac-liath	Arg & Bt	NN0316	56°18·0'	5°10·6'W	X	50,55
Sròn Bhuic	Aberd	NJ2105	57°8·0'	3°17·9'W	X	36
Sròn Bhùirich	Highld	NN7582	56°55·0'	4°2·7'W	H	42
Sròn Càrsacleit	N Eil	NB1605	57°56·9'	6°47·5'W	H	13,14
Sròn Challaid	Pth & Kin	NN8031	56°27·6'	3°56·4'W	H	52
Sròn Charnach	Pth & Kin	NO0669	56°48·4'	3°31·9'W	H	43
Sròn Chon	Pth & Kin	NN6866	56°46·3'	4°9·1'W	H	42
Sròn Chona Choirein	Pth & Kin	NN4944	56°34·1'	4°27·0'W	H	51
Sròn Chrìon a' Bhacain	Pth & Kin	NO0172	56°50·0'	3°36·9'W	H	43
Sròn Chrom	N Eil	NB3910	58°0·4'	6°24·6'W	X	14
Sròn Clach an Rubha	N Eil	NB5646	58°20·3'	6°9·7'W	X	8
Sròn Coire na h-Iolaire	Highld	NN5170	56°48·1'	4°26·0'W	X	42
Sròn Creag na Ceapaich	Highld	NH0789	57°51·2'	5°14·7'W	X	19
Sròn Criche	Arg & Bt	NS0995	56°6·8'	5°3·9'W	X	56
Sròn Cruaich	Arg & Bt	NS0596	56°7·3'	5°7·8'W	H	56
Sròn Daraich	Arg & Bt	NM5330	56°24·1'	5°59·7'W	X	48
Sròn Daraich	Highld	NG6112	57°8·5'	5°56·6'W	H	32
Srón Dearg	Arg & Bt	NS0976	55°56·6'	5°3·1'W	X	63
Sròn Deirg	Angus	NO2173	56°50·8'	3°17·3'W	X	44
Sròn Dha Mhurchaidh	Pth & Kin	NN6039	56°31·6'	4°16·1'W	H	51
Sròn Doire	Arg & Bt	NR8378	55°57·0'	5°28·1'W	X	62
Sròndoire	Arg & Bt	NR8478	55°57·0'	5°27·1'W	X	62
Sròn Dréineach	Highld	NN5274	56°50·3'	4°25·1'W	X	42
Sròn Dubh	Aberd	NO1587	56°58·2'	3°23·4'W	H	43
Sròn Dubh	Aberd	NO2896	57°3·2'	3°10·8'W	X	37,44
Sròn Dubh	Arg & Bt	NM5928	56°23·2'	5°53·8'W	X	48
Sròn Dubh	Arg & Bt	NR3745	55°37·9'	6°10·3'W	X	60
Sròn Dubh	Arg & Bt	NR9566	55°50·9'	5°16·0'W	X	62
Sròn Dubh	Highld	ND0140	58°20·5'	3°41·0'W	H	11,12
Sròn Dubh	Highld	NG4754	57°30·6'	6°13·0'W	H	23
Sròndubh	Highld	NG8681	57°46·3'	5°35·4'W	X	19
Sròn Dubh	Highld	NH0765	57°38·3'	5°13·5'W	H	19
Sròn Dubh	Highld	NH4628	57°19·3'	4°33·0'W	X	26
Sròn Dubh	Highld	NH4726	57°18·2'	4°31·9'W	H	26
Sròn Dubh	Highld	NM9667	56°45·3'	5°19·8'W	X	40
Sròn Dubh	Pth & Kin	NN9079	56°53·6'	3°47·9'W	H	43
Sròn Dubh an Eilich	Highld	NM7674	56°48·5'	5°39·7'W	X	40
Sròn Eanchainne	Pth & Kin	NN4839	56°31·4'	4°27·8'W	H	51
Sròn Eich	Pth & Kin	NN6145	56°34·8'	4°15·3'W	H	51
Sròn Eilean an Air	Highld	NG7388	57°49·7'	5°48·9'W	X	19
Sròn Eite	N Eil	NB5656	58°25·7'	6°10·3'W	X	8
Sròn Fhuar	N Eil	NF8481	57°42·7'	7°17·9'W	X	18
Sròn Garbh	Arg & Bt	NR5671	55°52·5'	5°53·6'W	X	61
Sròn Garbh	Arg & Bt	NR6017	55°23·6'	5°47·0'W	X	68
Sròn Garbh	Highld	NN0396	57°1·0'	5°14·3'W	X	33
Sròn Garbh	Highld	NN5181	56°54·0'	4°26·3'W	X	42
Sròn Garbh Choire	Highld	NN4490	56°58·8'	4°33·6'W	H	34
Sròn Geodh'an Tairbh	Highld	NG9695	57°54·1'	5°26·1'W	X	19
Sròn Ghaoithe	N Eil	NG0885	57°45·8'	6°54·1'W	X	18
Sròn Ghaothar	Highld	NM7790	56°57·1'	5°39·6'W	X	33,40
Sròn Gharbh	Arg & Bt	NM6325	56°21·7'	5°49·8'W	X	49
Sron Gharbh	Arg & Bt	NN3233	56°27·8'	4°43·2'W	X	50
Sròn Gharbh	Arg & Bt	NR4963	55°48·0'	5°59·9'W	X	60,61
Sròn Gharbh	Highld	NC1512	58°3·8'	5°7·7'W	X	15
Sròn Gharbh	Highld	ND0526	58°13·0'	3°36·6'W	X	17
Sròn Gharbh	Highld	NG4231	57°18·1'	6°16·5'W	X	32
Sròn Gharbh	Highld	NN0867	56°45·6'	5°8·0'W	X	41
Sròn Gharbh	Highld	NN1758	56°40·9'	4°58·8'W	H	41
Sròn Gharbh	Pth & Kin	NN8982	56°55·2'	3°49·0'W	H	43
Sròn Gharbh	Stir	NN3721	56°21·5'	4°37·9'W	H	50,56
Sron Ghobhair	Highld	NC2561	58°30·4'	4°59·7'W	X	9
Sròn Ghorm	Highld	NH3571	57°42·2'	4°45·7'W	H	20
Sròn Godamuil	N Eil	NG1098	57°52·9'	6°53·1'W	X	14
Sròn Gun Aran	Highld	NH4087	57°50·9'	4°41·3'W	H	20
Sròn Gunasdail	N Eil	NB1100	57°54·0'	6°52·2'W	X	14
Sròn Leachd a' Chaorainn	Highld	NN4263	56°44·2'	4°34·5'W	H	42
Sròn Leathad Chleansaid	Highld	NC6118	58°8·0'	4°21·2'W	H	16
Sron Liath	Highld	NH3076	57°44·8'	4°50·9'W	H	20
Sròn Liath	Highld	NM9785	56°55·0'	5°19·6'W	H	40
Sròn Liath	Highld	NN1181	56°53·2'	5°5·7'W	X	34,41
Sròn Liath	N Eil	NB4114	58°2·6'	6°22·9'W	X	14
Sròn Lice na Fearna	Highld	NG9802	57°4·1'	5°19·5'W	X	33
Sròn Lom	Highld	NC3521	58°9·1'	4°47·8'W	X	15
Sròn Mallanach	Arg & Bt	NS2597	56°8·3'	4°48·5'W	H	56
Sròn Meallan a' Ghàmhna	Highld	NG8189	57°50·5'	5°40·9'W	X	19
Sròn Mhadadh	Arg & Bt	NM7600	56°8·7'	5°35·9'W	H	55
Sròn Mhic Gille-mhartainn	Highld	NN6298	57°3·4'	4°16·1'W	X	35
Sròn Mhór	Arg & Bt	NM8802	56°10·1'	5°24·4'W	H	55
Sròn Mhór	Arg & Bt	NM8825	56°22·4'	5°25·5'W	X	49
Sròn Mhór	Arg & Bt	NS0989	56°3·6'	5°3·6'W	X	56
Sròn Mhór	Highld	ND0819	58°9·3'	3°33·3'W	X	17
Sròn Mhór	Highld	NG3130	57°17·1'	6°27·4'W	X	32
Sròn Mhór	Highld	NG8718	57°12·5'	5°31·2'W	X	33
Sròn Mhór	Highld	NM5362	56°41·3'	6°1·6'W	H	47
Sròn Mhór	Highld	NM8191	56°57·8'	5°35·7'W	X	33,40
Sròn Mhór	N Eil	NB1429	58°9·7'	6°51·3'W	H	13
Sròn Mhór	Pth & Kin	NN6526	56°24·7'	4°10·8'W	H	51
Sròn Mhór	Pth & Kin	NN8457	56°41·7'	3°53·2'W	H	52
Sron Mor na h-Uamhaidh	Highld	NN6397	57°2·9'	4°15·0'W	X	35
Sròn na Ban-righ	Highld	NN8788	56°58·4'	3°51·1'W	H	43
Sròn na Breun Leitir	Highld	NH0306	57°6·4'	5°14·7'W	H	33
Sròn-na-Bruic	Arg & Bt	NR9593	56°5·4'	5°17·3'W	X	55
Sròn na Buiteinich	Highld	NN0297	57°1·6'	5°15·3'W	X	33
Sròn na Caillich	Highld	NG7377	57°43·8'	5°48·3'W	X	19
Sròn na Caime	Pth & Kin	NN5561	56°43·4'	4°21·7'W	H	42
Sròn na Carra	Highld	NG7473	57°41·7'	5°47·1'W	X	19
Srón na Ciche	Highld	NG4419	57°11·7'	6°13·8'W	X	32
Sron na Cléite	Highld	NG7389	57°50·2'	5°49·0'W	X	19
Sròn na Cloiche Sgoilte	Highld	NN3872	56°48·9'	4°38·8'W	X	41
Sron na Creige	Highld	NN6398	57°3·4'	4°15·1'W	X	35
Sròn na Creige Fraoich	N Eil	NB5142	58°18·0'	6°14·5'W	X	8
Sròn na Creise	Highld	NN2352	56°37·8'	4°52·7'W	X	41
Sròn na Croiche	Highld	NC4501	57°58·5'	4°36·8'W	H	16
Sròn na Faiceachan	Pth & Kin	NN8176	56°51·9'	3°56·7'W	H	43
Sròn na Fàire Móire	Highld	NG9694	57°53·6'	5°26·0'W	X	19
Sròn na Frianich	Highld	NH0945	57°27·6'	5°10·6'W	X	25
Sron na Frithe	Highld	NH1232	57°20·6'	5°7·0'W	X	25
Sròn na Gaoithe	Aberd	NO1579	56°53·9'	3°23·3'W	H	43
Sròn na Gaoithe	Highld	NH0030	57°19·3'	5°18·8'W	H	25
Sròn na Gaoithe	Highld	NM7066	56°44·0'	5°45·2'W	H	40
Sron na Gaoithe	Highld	NN7594	57°1·5'	4°3·1'W	H	35
Sròn na Garbh-bheinne	Highld	NN3368	56°46·7'	4°43·5'W	X	41
Sron na Gàrbh-bheinne	Highld	NN3575	56°50·5'	4°41·8'W	X	41
Sròn na Garbh Uidhe	Highld	NC3726	58°11·8'	4°45·9'W	H	16
Sròn na Goibhre	Highld	NH1372	57°42·2'	5°7·8'W	X	19
Sròn na h-Airde Bhaine	Highld	NG6939	57°23·2'	5°50·2'W	X	24,32
Sròn na h-Eagaig	Pth & Kin	NN5869	56°47·7'	4°19·0'W	H	42
Sròn na h-Eiteich	Pth & Kin	NN6571	56°48·9'	4°12·2'W	X	42
Sròn na h-Innearach	Pth & Kin	NN9669	56°48·3'	3°41·7'W	H	43
Sron na h-Iolaire	Arg & Bt	NN1841	56°31·8'	4°57·1'W	X	50
Sròn na h-Iolaire	Highld	NM3891	56°56·4'	6°18·0'W	X	39
Sron na h-Iolaire	Highld	NM4989	56°55·7'	6°7·1'W	X	39
Sròn na Lairige	Highld	NH9601	57°5·6'	3°42·5'W	H	36
Sròn na Lice	N Eil	HW6130	59°5·7'	6°9·9'W	X	8
Sròn na Macranaich	Pth & Kin	NN9381	56°54·7'	3°45·0'W	H	43
Sròn na Maoile	Pth & Kin	NN6917	56°19·9'	4°6·7'W	H	57
Sròn nam Bó	Highld	NN2385	56°55·6'	4°54·1'W	X	34,41
Sròn nam Boc	Arg & Bt	NM5220	56°18·7'	6°0·2'W	X	48
Sròn nam Boc	Arg & Bt	NM5738	56°28·5'	5°56·3'W	X	47,48
Sròn nam Boc	Arg & Bt	NM6424	56°21·2'	5°48·8'W	X	49
Sròn nam Boc	Highld	NM7151	56°36·0'	5°43·4'W	H	49
Sròn nam Bràthan	Highld	NM6260	56°40·5'	5°52·7'W	X	40
Sròn nam Broc	Highld	NM8474	56°48·7'	5°31·9'W	X	40
Sròn nam Faiceachan	Pth & Kin	NN6367	56°46·7'	4°14·1'W	X	42
Sròn nam Feannag	Arg & Bt	NN0535	56°28·3'	5°9·5'W	X	50
Sròn nam Fiadh	Aberd	NO1279	56°53·9'	3°26·2'W	X	43
Sron nam Forsair	Highld	NN2448	56°35·7'	4°51·5'W	X	50
Sròn nam Fòrsairean	Stir	NN4425	56°23·8'	4°31·2'W	H	51
Sròn na Mòine	Arg & Bt	NM4347	56°32·9'	6°10·4'W	X	47,48
Sròn na Muic	Highld	NH4115	57°12·2'	4°37·5'W	H	34
Sròn nan Aighean	Highld	NG2951	57°28·4'	6°30·8'W	H	23
Sron nan Cabar	Arg & Bt	NN1643	56°32·8'	4°59·1'W	X	50
Sron nan Colan	Stir	NN3130	56°26·2'	4°44·0'W	H	50
Sròn nan Creagan	Highld	NN4075	56°50·6'	4°36·9'W	X	42
Sròn nan Eun	Stir	NN4035	56°29·1'	4°35·5'W	H	51
Sròn nan Gabhar	Aberd	NO1585	56°57·2'	3°23·4'W	H	43
Sròn nan Gabhar	Highld	NG7774	57°42·3'	5°44·1'W	X	19
Sròn nan Gall	Highld	NN3268	56°46·7'	4°44·5'W	X	41
Sròn nan Giubhas	Highld	NN2446	56°34·6'	4°51·5'W	X	50
Sròn nan Iarnachan	Highld	NC5203	57°59·8'	4°29·8'W	H	16
Sròn nan Laogh	Highld	NH6201	57°5·0'	4°16·2'W	X	35
Sròn nan Oban	Highld	NG8190	57°51·0'	5°41·0'W	X	19
Sròn nan Saobhaidh	Highld	NH4051	57°31·5'	4°39·9'W	X	26
Sròn nan Searrach	Stir	NN6126	56°24·6'	4°14·7'W	H	51
Sròn nan Tarmachan	Highld	NN5183	56°55·1'	4°26·4'W	X	42
Sròn na Ribha	N Eil	NB5446	58°20·3'	6°11·7'W	X	8
Sròn na Saobhaidh	Highld	NM7760	56°41·0'	5°38·0'W	X	40
Sron na Saobhaidh	Pth & Kin	NO0676	56°52·2'	3°32·1'W	H	43
Sròn na Saobhaidhe	Arg & Bt	NM8605	56°11·6'	5°26·5'W	H	55
Sròn na Saobhaidhe	Highld	NH5284	57°49·5'	4°29·1'W	H	20
Sròn na Saobhaidhe	Highld	NN2967	56°46·1'	4°47·4'W	X	41
Sròn na Teiste	Highld	NM4078	56°49·5'	6°15·2'W	X	39
Srón Nead	Highld	NN4191	56°59·2'	4°36·6'W	X	34
Sròn Ocrhulan	Highld	NG2563	57°34·7'	6°35·6'W	X	23
Sròn Odhar	Pth & Kin	NN7414	56°18·4'	4°1·7'W	H	57
Sronphadruig Lodge	Pth & Kin	NN7178	56°52·8'	4°6·6'W	X	42
Sròn Plocach	Arg & Bt	NR9674	55°55·2'	5°15·4'W	X	62
Sròn Port na Moralachd	Arg & Bt	NM8644	56°32·6'	5°28·4'W	X	49
Sròn Raineach	Highld	NM7098	57°1·2'	5°46·9'W	X	33,40
Sròn Ranachan	Highld	NM7761	56°41·5'	5°38·1'W	X	40
Sròn Reithe	Arg & Bt	NN0610	56°14·8'	5°7·4'W	H	50,56
Sròn Riabach	Angus	NO1675	56°51·8'	3°22·2'W	X	43
Sròn Riach	Aberd	NN9997	57°3·4'	3°39·5'W	X	36,43
Sròn ri Gaoith	N Eil	NB0729	58°9·4'	6°58·4'W	H	13
Sròn Romul	N Eil	NA9615	58°1·5'	7°8·5'W	H	13
Sròn Ruadh	Highld	NC6250	58°25·3'	4°21·3'W	H	10
Sron Ruadh	Highld	NM8294	56°59·4'	5°34·9'W	X	33,40
Sròn Ruadh	Highld	NN4673	56°49·6'	4°31·0'W	X	42
Sròn Ruadh	N Eil	NB4636	58°14·6'	6°19·2'W	X	8
Sròn Ruadh	N Eil	NB5041	58°17·5'	6°15·5'W	X	8
Sròn Ruail	Highld	NG2004	57°2·8'	6°36·6'W	X	39
Sron Rubha na Gaoithe	Highld	NC9911	58°4·9'	3°42·3'W	X	17
Sròn Ruighe Clomhaiche	Pth & Kin	NN4959	56°42·2'	4°27·5'W	H	42,51
Sròn Saobhaidhe	Angus	NO1773	56°50·7'	3°21·2'W	H	43
Sròn Scourst	N Eil	NB1009	57°58·8'	6°53·9'W	H	13,14
Sròn Slugain Uaine	Highld	NB9507	58°0·6'	5°27·7'W	X	15
Sròn Smearasmuil	N Eil	NB0908	57°58·2'	6°54·8'W	H	13,14
Sròn Smeur	Pth & Kin	NN4560	56°42·6'	4°31·5'W	H	42
Sròn Smuramaig	N Eil	NB3304	57°57·0'	6°30·3'W	X	13,14
Sròn Teanga a' Chnaip	Highld	NN0171	56°47·5'	5°15·1'W	X	41
Sròn Thoraraidh	Highld	NM8083	56°53·4'	5°36·3'W	X	40
Sròn Thorcasmol	N Eil	NB2608	57°58·9'	6°37·6'W	X	13,14
Sròn Tuath	N Eil	NF8655	57°28·9'	7°13·9'W	X	22
Sròn Uamha	Arg & Bt	NR6105	55°17·1'	5°45·4'W	X	68
Sron Udemul	N Eil	NA9615	58°1·5'	7°8·5'W	H	13
Sròn Udromuil	N Eil	NG0992	57°49·6'	6°53·7'W	X	14
Sròn Ulladail	N Eil	NB0813	58°0·9'	6°56·2'W	H	13,14
Sròn Urraidh	Arg & Bt	NM2943	56°30·3'	6°23·8'W	X	46,47,48
Sron Vourlinn	Highld	NG4571	57°39·7'	6°16·1'W	H	23
Srthean Liath	Highld	NC3326	58°11·7'	4°50·0'W	H	15
Sruth a' Chomhraig	N Eil	NF8546	57°24·0'	7°14·2'W	W	22
Sruthan Allallaidh	Arg & Bt	NR4158	55°45·0'	6°7·2'W	W	60
Sruthan Beag	N Eil	NF7927	57°13·5'	7°18·7'W	W	22
Sruthan na Comaraig	N Eil	NF8258	57°30·3'	7°18·1'W	W	22
Sruthan na Criche	Arg & Bt	NR5778	55°56·3'	5°53·0'W	W	61
Sruthan Rabhairt	Arg & Bt	NR2841	55°35·5'	6°18·6'W	W	60
Sruthan Ruadh	Arg & Bt	NR4059	55°45·5'	6°8·2'W	W	60
Sruth Earshader	N Eil	NB1634	58°12·5'	6°49·6'W	W	13
Sruth Geal	Stir	NN6709	56°15·6'	4°8·4'W	W	57
Sruth Thorna Dhuibhe	N Eil	NB3431	58°11·5'	6°31·1'W	W	8,13
SS Great Britain	C of Bris	ST5772	51°27·0'	2°36·7'W	X	172
Staarvey	I of M	SC2884	54°13·6'	4°37·9'W	X	95
Staba Field	Shetld	HU4236	60°6·7'	1°14·2'W	X	4
Stabaness	Shetld	HU3266	60°22·9'	1°24·7'W	X	3
St Abbs	Scot Bord	NT9167	55°54·0'	2°8·2'W	T	67
St Abb's Haven	Scot Bord	NT9166	55°53·5'	2°8·2'W	X	67
St Abb's Head	Scot Bord	NT9169	55°55·1'	2°8·2'W	X	67
Stabdon Fm	Devon	SS6506	50°50·5'	3°54·7'W	FM	191
Stab Hill	D & G	NX1472	55°0·7'	4°54·1'W	H	76
Stabilee	Renf	NS4068	55°53·0'	4°33·0'W	X	64
Stablebarn Fm	W Susx	TQ0522	50°59·5'	0°29·8'W	FM	197
Stable Barrow	Dorset	SY7999	50°47·6'	2°17·5'W	A	194
Stable Clough	Derby	SE0902	53°31·1'	1°51·4'W	X	110
Stable Clough	Derby	SK0998	53°29·0'	1°51·5'W	X	110
Stable Edge	Durham	NY9228	54°39·1'	2°7·0'W	X	91,92
Stable Fm	Worcs	SO8043	52°5·3'	2°17·1'W	FM	150
Stableford	Shrops	SO7598	52°35·0'	2°21·7'W	T	138
Stableford	Staffs	SJ8138	52°56·6'	2°16·6'W	T	127
Stable Green	Devon	SS6411	50°53·2'	3°55·6'W	X	191
Stable Harvey	Cumbr	SD2891	54°18·8'	3°6·0'W	X	96,97
Stable Harvey Moss	Cumbr	SD2791	54°18·8'	3°6·9'W	X	96,97
Stable Hills	Cumbr	NY2621	54°35·0'	3°8·3'W	X	89,90
Stable Holme	N Yks	SE5696	54°21·6'	1°7·9'W	X	100
Stables Breast	Lancs	SD5852	53°58·0'	2°38·0'W	X	102
Stables Fm	Durham	NZ3147	54°49·3'	1°30·6'W	FM	88
Stab, The	Shetld	HU2885	60°33·1'	1°28·9'W	X	3
Stac a' Bhanain	N Eil	NB2036	58°13·7'	6°45·7'W	X	8,13
Stac a' Bhodaich	Arg & Bt	NM0445	56°30·5'	6°48·2'W	X	46
Stac a' Bhothain	Highld	NG2959	57°32·7'	6°31·3'W	X	23
Stacach	N Ayr	NR9942	55°38·1'	5°11·2'W	X	62,69
Stac à Chagair	Arg & Bt	NR6740	55°36·1'	5°41·5'W	X	62
Stac a' Chaorruin	Highld	NH0174	57°43·0'	5°20·0'W	H	19
Stac a' Chomhraig	N Eil	NB4110	58°0·5'	6°22·6'W	X	14
Stac a' Chùirn	Arg & Bt	NN1918	56°19·4'	4°55·2'W	H	50,56
Stacageo	N Eil	NA9922	58°5·3'	7°6·0'W	X	13
Stacaiseal	N Eil	NB3037	58°14·6'	6°35·6'W	H	8,13
Stac a' Langa	N Eil	NA1000	57°49·4'	8°33·8'W	X	18
Staca Leathann	N Eil	NA9828	58°8·5'	7°7·5'W	X	13
Stac a' Mheadais	Highld	NG3325	57°14·5'	6°25·1'W	X	32
Staca Mhic Cubhaig	N Eil	NB3956	58°25·1'	6°27·7'W	X	8
Staca na Berie	N Eil	NB0235	58°12·4'	7°3·9'W	X	13
Stacanan Neidacliv	N Eil	NB0538	58°14·2'	7°1·1'W	X	13
Stac an Aoineidh	Arg & Bt	NM2522	56°18·9'	6°26·4'W	X	48
Stac an Armin	N Eil	NA1506	57°52·9'	8°29·4'W	X	18
Stacan Dubha	Highld	NM4664	56°42·2'	6°8·5'W	X	47
Stacan Dubha	Moray	NJ0101	57°5·6'	3°37·6'W	X	36
Stac an Fharaidh	Moray	NJ0003	57°6·7'	3°38·6'W	X	36
Stac an Fhir Mhaoil	N Eil	NB4216	58°3·7'	6°22·0'W	X	14
Stacan Gobhlach	Highld	NG4574	57°41·3'	6°16·2'W	X	23
Stac an Tuill	Highld	NG3521	57°12·5'	6°22·8'W	X	32
Stac an Tùill	N Eil	NB1242	58°16·6'	6°54·3'W	X	13
Stac Buidhe	Highld	NG4474	57°41·2'	6°17·2'W	X	23
Stac Buidhe	Highld	NN5293	57°0·5'	4°25·8'W	X	35
Stac Buidhe	Highld	NN6295	57°1·8'	4°16·0'W	X	35
Stac Creag Dhearg	Pth & Kin	NN9273	56°50·4'	3°45·8'W	X	43
Stac Dhomhnuill Chaim	N Eil	NB0031	58°10·2'	7°5·7'W	X	13
Stac Dona	N Eil	NA0601	57°49·7'	8°38·0'W	X	18
Stac Dubh	Highld	NC5865	58°33·3'	4°25·9'W	X	10
Stacey Bank	Sheff	SK2890	53°24·6'	1°34·3'W	T	110
Stacey's Fm	Essex	TL6910	51°46·0'	0°27·3'E	FM	167
Stac Glas Bun an Uisge	Arg & Bt	NM4130	56°23·7'	6°11·4'W	X	48
Stac Gorm	Highld	NH6327	57°19·0'	4°16·0'W	H	26,35
Stac Hills	N Yks	SE8871	54°7·9'	0°38·8'W	X	101
Stacie's Fm	Essex	TM1030	51°56·0'	1°3·7'E	FM	168,169
Stackaberg	Shetld	HU6192	60°36·7'	0°52·6'W	X	1,2
Stackan Longa	Shetld	HU5988	60°34·5'	0°54·9'W	X	1,2
Stack Aros	Highld	NG2760	57°33·1'	6°33·4'W	X	23
Stack Cleugh	Cumbr	NY5874	55°3·8'	2°39·0'W	X	86
Stack Clò Kearvaig	Highld	NC2973	58°36·9'	4°56·2'W	X	9
Stack End	Kirk	SE0212	53°36·5'	1°57·8'W	X	110
Stack Hill	Lincs	TF0144	52°59·3'	0°29·3'W	X	130
Stack Hill	Shetld	HU4566	60°22·8'	1°10·5'W	H	2,3
Stackhill Ho	N Yks	SD9493	54°20·2'	2°5·1'W	X	98
Stack Holm	Durham	NY8821	54°35·3'	2°10·7'W	X	91,92
Stackhoull	Shetld	HP6014	60°48·5'	0°53·3'W	X	1
Stackhouse	N Yks	SD8165	54°5·1'	2°17·0'W	T	98
Stackhouse Cove	Corn	SW5428	50°6·3'	5°26·1'W	W	203
Stackhouse Fm	N Yks	SE5360	54°2·2'	1°11·0'W	FM	100
Stackie Geos	Orkney	HY5728	59°8·5'	2°44·6'W	X	5,6
Stack Islands	N Eil	NF7807	57°2·8'	7°18·2'W	X	31
Stacklawhill	E Ayr	NS3743	55°39·4'	4°35·0'W	X	63,70
Stackley Ho	Leic	SP6699	52°35·3'	1°1·1'W	X	141
Stack Mooar	I of M	SC4892	54°18·3'	4°19·8'W	X	95
Stack O'da Noup	Shetld	HU3516	59°55·9'	1°21·9'W	X	4
Stack of Billyageo	Shetld	HU4421	59°58·6'	1°12·2'W	X	4
Stack of Birrier	Shetld	HU6394	60°37·7'	0°50·4'W	X	1,2
Stack of Glencoul	Highld	NC2928	58°12·7'	4°54·2'W	H	15
Stack of Grunnigeo	Shetld	HU5990	60°35·6'	0°54·9'W	X	1,2
Stack of Kame	Orkney	ND4892	58°49·0'	2°53·5'W	X	7
Stack of Louin	Shetld	HP6615	60°49·0'	0°46·7'W	X	1
Stack of Mid Clyth	Highld	ND2937	58°19·2'	3°12·2'W	X	11
Stack of Okraquoy	Shetld	HU4431	60°3·9'	1°12·1'W	X	4
Stack of Otter Geo	Shetld	HU4011	59°53·2'	1°16·6'W	X	4
Stack of Pulli	Shetld	HU4433	60°5·0'	1°12·1'W	X	4
Stack of Russalore	Shetld	HP6515	60°49·0'	0°47·8'W	X	1

Stack of Sandwick	Shetld	HU3532	60°4·5'	1°21·8'W	X	4
Stack of Skudiburgh	Highld	NG3764	57°35·6'	6°23·6'W	X	23
Stack of Stavgeo	Shetld	HU3786	60°33·6'	1°19·0'W	X	1,2,3
Stack of Sumra	Shetld	HU2683	60°32·1'	1°31·1'W	X	3
Stack of the Brough	Shetld	HU4015	59°55·3'	1°16·6'W	X	4
Stack of the Crubb	Shetld	HU3784	60°32·5'	1°19·0'W	X	1,2,3
Stack of the Horse	Shetld	HU5381	60°30·8'	1°1·6'W	X	1,2,3
Stack of the Rettuvie	Shetld	HU3784	60°32·5'	1°19·0'W	X	1,2,3
Stack of Ulbster	Highld	ND3341	58°21·4'	3°8·2'W	X	12
Stack of Wirrgeo	Shetld	HU6162	60°20·5'	0°53·2'W	X	2
Stackpole	Pemb	SR9896	51°37·8'	4°54·7'W	T	158
Stackpole Elidor or Cheriton	Pemb	SR9897	51°38·4'	4°54·8'W	T	158
Stackpole Head	Pemb	SR9994	51°36·8'	4°53·8'W	X	158
Stackpole Quay	Pemb	SR9995	51°37·3'	4°53·8'W	X	158
Stackpole Warren	Pemb	SR9894	51°36·8'	4°54·7'W	X	158
Stack Rock	Pemb	SM8604	51°41·9'	5°5·4'W	X	157
Stack Rocks	Pemb	SM8113	51°46·6'	5°10·1'W	X	157
Stacks	Falk	NT0380	56°0·4'	3°32·9'W	X	65
Stacksford	Norf	TM0590	52°28·4'	1°1·5'E	T	144
Stacks of Duncansby	Highld	ND3971	58°37·6'	3°2·5'W	X	7,12
Stacks of Houssness	Shetld	HU3728	60°2·4'	1°19·7'W	X	4
Stacks of Poindie	Shetld	HP5713	60°48·0'	0°56·7'W	X	1
Stacks of Scambro	Shetld	HU6792	60°36·6'	0°46·1'W	X	1,2
Stacks of Skroo	Shetld	HZ2074	59°33·3'	1°38·3'W	X	4
Stacks of Stuis	Shetld	HU4697	60°39·5'	1°9·0'W	X	1
Stacks of Vatsland	Shetld	HU4646	60°12·0'	1°9·7'W	X	4
Stacks of Wirrvie	Shetld	HZ2273	59°32·8'	1°36·2'W	X	4
Stacksteads	Lancs	SD8421	53°41·4'	2°14·1'W	T	103
Stacks, The	Highld	ND2374	58°39·1'	3°19·1'W	X	7,12
Stacks, The	Highld	ND2735	58°18·1'	3°14·3'W	X	11
Stacks, The	I of M	SC2173	54°7·6'	4°43·9'W	X	95
Stack, The	I of M	SC1465	54°3·1'	4°50·1'W	X	95
Stack, The	I of M	SC2585	54°14·1'	4°40·7'W	X	95
Stack, The	N Eil	NF7807	57°2·8'	7°18·2'W	X	31
Stack, The	Pemb	SM7405	51°42·1'	5°15·9'W	X	157
Stack Wood	Suff	TL9940	52°1·6'	0°54·4'E	F	155
Stackyard Green	Suff	TL9645	52°4·3'	0°52·0'E	T	155
Stac Lachlainn	Highld	NG4475	57°41·8'	6°17·3'W	X	23
Stac Lee	N Eil	NA1404	57°51·8'	8°30·2'W	X	18
Stac Liath	Arg & Bt	NM2623	56°19·5'	6°25·5'W	X	48
Stac Meall Chuaich	Highld	NN7088	56°58·2'	4°7·9'W	X	42
Stac Mhic Aonghais	Highld	NB9505	57°59·5'	5°27·6'W	X	15
Stac Mhic Mhurchaidh	Arg & Bt	NM2426	56°21·0'	6°27·6'W	X	48
Stac Mòr Gharraboist	N Eil	NB4933	58°13·1'	6°16·0'W	X	8
Stac na Cùoraich Lachduinne	N Eil	NB1742	58°16·8'	6°49·2'W	X	8,13
Stac na Cathaig	Highld	NH6330	57°20·7'	4°16·1'W	H	26
Stac na Faoileig	N Eil	NB3452	58°22·8'	6°32·6'W	X	8
Stac na h-Acain	Highld	NH2836	57°23·2'	4°51·2'W	X	25
Stac na h-Iolair	Pth & Kin	NO0177	56°52·7'	3°37·0'W	H	43
Stac na L-Iolaire	Highld	NJ0108	57°9·4'	3°37·7'W	H	36
Stac Nam Balg	N Eil	NB1143	58°17·1'	6°55·4'W	X	13
Stac nam Bodach	Pth & Kin	NN9770	56°48·9'	3°40·8'W	H	43
Stac nam Faoileann	Highld	NM4093	56°57·6'	6°16·2'W	X	39
Stac na Morain	Arg & Bt	NM7414	56°16·1'	5°38·6'W	X	55
Stac nan Sgarbh	N Eil	NB5143	58°18·6'	6°14·6'W	X	8
Stacombe	Devon	SX7787	50°40·4'	3°44·1'W	X	191
Stac Pollaidh	Highld	NC1010	58°2·6'	5°12·7'W	H	15
Stac Rhos	Powys	SH9727	52°50·1'	3°31·3'W	H	125
Stac Shuardail	N Eil	NB4830	58°11·5'	6°16·8'W	X	8
Stac Suisnish	Highld	NG5816	57°10·5'	5°59·8'W	X	32
Stac Thabhaidh	N Eil	NB4222	58°7·0'	6°22·4'W	X	14
Stadborough Copse	Wilts	ST9494	51°38·9'	2°4·8'W	F	163,173
Stadbury Fm	Devon	SX6845	50°17·6'	3°50·8'W	FM	202
Staddicombe	Devon	SX7269	50°30·6'	3°47·9'W	X	202
Staddiscombe	C of Plym	SX5151	50°20·6'	4°5·3'W	T	201
Staddle Bridge Ho	N Yks	SE4498	54°22·8'	1°18·9'W	X	99
Staddlethorpe	E Yorks	SE8328	53°44·7'	0°44·1'W	T	106
Staddlethorpe	E Yorks	SE8425	53°43·1'	0°43·2'W	X	106
Staddlethorpe Grange	E Yorks	SE8427	53°44·2'	0°43·2'W	X	106
Staddlethorpe Ho	E Yorks	SE8425	53°43·1'	0°43·2'W	X	106
Staddon	Devon	SS2622	50°58·5'	4°28·3'W	T	190
Staddon	Devon	SS3503	50°48·4'	4°20·1'W	T	190
Staddon	Devon	SX4288	50°40·5'	4°13·8'W	X	190
Staddon	Devon	SX6761	50°26·3'	3°52·0'W	X	202
Staddon Fm	Devon	SS6702	50°48·4'	3°52·9'W	FM	191
Staddon Fm	Somer	SS8837	51°7·5'	3°35·6'W	FM	181
Staddon Heights	Devon	SX4951	50°20·6'	4°7·0'W	X	201
Staddon Hill	Somer	SS8737	51°7·5'	3°36·5'W	H	181
Staddon Moor Cross	Devon	SS6702	50°48·4'	3°52·9'W	X	191
Staddon Point	Devon	SX4850	50°20·1'	4°7·8'W	X	201
Staden	Derby	SK0772	53°14·9'	1°53·3'W	T	119
Staden Grange	Derby	SK0771	53°14·4'	1°53·3'W	X	119
Staden Low	Derby	SK0772	53°14·9'	1°53·3'W	X	119
Stadhampton	Oxon	SU6098	51°40·9'	1°7·5'W	T	164,165
Stadhaugh Manor Fm	Suff	TM2973	52°18·7'	1°22·0'E	FM	156
Stadhlaigearraidh	N Eil	NF7638	57°19·3'	7°22·5'W	T	22
Stadium	Suff	TL6577	52°22·2'	0°25·8'E	X	143
Stadmorslow	Staffs	SJ8655	53°5·8'	2°12·1'W	T	118
Stadson Fm	Devon	SS4304	50°49·1'	4°13·4'W	FM	190
St Aelbaiarn's Well	Gwyn	SH3844	52°58·4'	4°24·4'W	A	123
Staerough Hill	Scot Bord	NT8227	55°32·4'	2°16·7'W	H	74
St Aethans	Moray	NJ1268	57°41·9'	3°28·1'W	T	28
Staffa	Arg & Bt	NM3235	56°26·1'	6°20·4'W	X	46,47,48
Staffhurst Wood	Surrey	TQ4148	51°13·1'	0°1·5'E	F	187
Staffield	Cumbr	NY5442	54°46·5'	2°42·5'W	T	86
Staffin	Highld	NG4867	57°37·6'	6°12·8'W	X	23
Staffin Bay	Highld	NG4869	57°38·7'	6°12·9'W	W	23
Staffin Island	Highld	NG4969	57°38·7'	6°11·9'W	X	23
Staffland Fm	Somer	ST2932	51°5·2'	3°0·4'W	FM	182
Stafflar	S Ayr	NS4133	55°34·1'	4°30·9'W	X	70
Staffler	D & G	NY3371	55°2·0'	3°2·5'W	X	85
Stafford	Staffs	SJ9223	52°48·5'	2°6·7'W	T	127
Stafford Barton	Devon	SS5811	50°53·1'	4°0·7'W	X	191
Stafford Barton	Devon	ST1005	50°50·5'	3°16·3'W	X	192,193
Stafford Beer	Devon	SS5905	50°49·9'	3°59·8'W	X	191
Stafford Bridge	Beds	TL0054	52°10·7'	0°31·8'W	X	153
Stafford Brook	Staffs	SK0219	52°46·4'	1°57·8'W	W	128
Stafford Castle	Staffs	SJ9022	52°48·0'	2°8·5'W	X	127
Stafford Common	Swan	SS5997	51°39·5'	4°1·9'W	X	159
Stafford Cross	Devon	SY2191	50°43·0'	3°6·8'W	X	192,193
Stafford Fm	Dorset	SY7288	50°41·7'	2°23·4'W	FM	194
Stafford Ho	Dorset	SY7289	50°42·2'	2°23·4'W	A	194
Stafford Ho	Shrops	SJ6828	52°51·2'	2°28·1'W	X	127
Staffordlake	Surrey	SU9458	51°19·0'	0°38·7'W	X	175,186
Stafford Lodge	Staffs	SJ9524	52°49·0'	2°4·0'W	X	127
Stafford Moor Fishery	Devon	SS5911	50°53·1'	3°59·9'W	X	191
Stafford Park	Wrekin	SJ7108	52°40·4'	2°25·3'W	T	127
Stafford's Corner	Essex	TL9616	51°48·7'	0°51·0'E	T	168
Stafford's Green	Dorset	ST6321	50°59·5'	2°31·2'W	T	183
Staffordshire Moorlands Walks	Staffs	SJ9655	53°5·8'	2°3·2'W	X	118
Staffordshire Moorlands Walks	Staffs	SK0249	53°2·5'	1°57·8'W	X	119
Staffordshire Way	Ches	SJ8658	53°7·4'	2°12·1'W	X	118
Staffordshire Way	Staffs	SJ8612	52°42·6'	2°12·0'W	X	127
Staffordshire Way	Staffs	SJ9850	53°3·1'	2°1·4'W	X	118
Staffordshire Way	Staffs	SK0443	52°59·3'	1°56·0'W	X	119,128
Staffordshire Way	Staffs	SK0643	52°59·3'	1°54·2'W	X	119,128
Staffordshire Way	Staffs	SK0825	52°49·6'	1°52·5'W	X	128
Staffordshire Way	Staffs	SO8391	52°31·2'	2°14·6'W	X	138
Staffordshire & Worcestershire Canal	Staffs	SJ9210	52°41·5'	2°6·7'W	W	127
Staffordshire & Worcestershire Canal	Staffs	SO8688	52°29·6'	2°12·0'W	W	139
Staffordshire & Worcestershire Canal	Worcs	SO8273	52°21·5'	2°15·5'W	W	138
Staff, The	Orkney	HY7555	59°23·1'	2°25·9'W	X	5
Staffurth's Br	Cambs	TL3694	52°31·8'	0°0·7'E	X	142
Stagbatch	Heref	SO4658	52°13·3'	2°47·0'W	T	148,149
Stagbrough Hill	Worcs	SO7872	52°21·0'	2°19·0'W	X	138
Stag Burn	Aberd	NO6482	56°55·9'	2°35·0'W	W	45
Stagbury Hill	Hants	SU2815	50°56·3'	1°35·7'W	X	184
Stagden Cross	Essex	TL6314	51°48·3'	0°22·3'E	T	167
Stagebank	Scot Bord	NT4153	55°46·3'	2°56·0'W	X	66,73
Stagehall	Scot Bord	NT4544	55°41·4'	2°52·1'W	T	73
Stagehall Hill	Scot Bord	NT4444	55°41·4'	2°53·0'W	H	73
Stagenhoe	Herts	TL1822	51°53·3'	0°16·7'W	X	166
Staggarth	N Yks	SD6768	54°6·7'	2°29·9'W	X	98
Stag Gate	Dorset	SY9299	50°47·7'	2°6·4'W	X	195
Stagg Mill	Devon	ST0016	50°56·3'	3°25·0'W	X	181
Stagg's Folly	Dorset	ST6100	50°48·1'	2°32·8'W	X	194
Stag Hall Fm	Herts	TL3324	51°54·1'	0°3·6'W	FM	166
Stag Hill	Surrey	SU9850	51°14·7'	0°35·4'W	X	186
Stag Ho	Darl	NZ2516	54°32·6'	1°36·4'W	X	93
St Agnell's fm	Herts	TL0813	51°48·5'	0°25·6'W	FM	166
St Agnes	Corn	SW7250	50°18·6'	5°11·8'W	T	204
St Agnes	I Scilly	SV8807	49°53·2'	6°20·3'W	X	203
St Agnes	Scot Bord	NT6863	55°51·8'	2°30·2'W	X	67
St Agnes Beacon	Corn	SW7050	50°18·5'	5°13·4'W	X	203
St Agnes Head	Corn	SW6951	50°19·1'	5°14·3'W	X	203
St Agnes Ho	N Yks	SE5291	54°19·0'	1°11·6'W	X	100
Stagpark Fm	W Susx	SU9525	51°1·2'	0°38·3'W	FM	186,197
Stagsden	Beds	SP9849	52°8·1'	0°33·7'W	T	153
Stagsden West End	Beds	SP9747	52°7·0'	0°34·6'W	T	153
Stags End	Herts	TL0612	51°48·0'	0°27·4'W	X	166
Stags Fell	N Yks	SD8993	54°20·2'	2°9·7'W	X	98
Stagshaw Bank	Northum	NY9867	55°0·1'	2°1·4'W	X	87
Stagshaw High Ho	Northum	NY9767	55°0·1'	2°2·4'W	X	87
Stagshaw Ho	Northum	NY9866	54°59·6'	2°1·4'W	X	87
Stag's Head	Devon	SS6727	51°1·9'	3°53·4'W	T	180
Stags Holt	Cambs	TF4300	52°35·0'	0°7·0'E	X	142,143
Stag's Plain	Oxon	SP3217	51°51·3'	1°31·7'W	X	164
Stagstones Fm	Cumbr	NY5331	54°40·6'	2°43·3'W	FM	90
Stagwell	I of W	SZ4692	50°43·8'	1°20·5'W	X	196
Stain	Highld	ND3460	58°31·7'	3°7·5'W	X	12
Stainborough Castle	Barns	SE3103	53°31·6'	1°31·5'W	X	110,111
Stainborough Fold	Barns	SE3102	53°31·1'	1°31·5'W	X	110,111
Stainburn	Cumbr	NY0229	54°39·0'	3°30·7'W	T	89
Stainburn	N Yks	SE2448	53°55·9'	1°37·7'W	T	104
Stainburn Bank	N Yks	SE2348	53°55·9'	1°38·6'W	X	104
Stainburn Hall Fm	Cumbr	NY0229	54°39·0'	3°30·7'W	FM	89
Stainburn Moor	N Yks	SE2451	53°57·5'	1°37·6'W	X	104
Stainby	Lincs	SK9022	52°47·5'	0°39·5'W	T	130
Stainby Lodge	Lincs	SK8923	52°48·1'	0°40·4'W	X	130
Stainby Warren	Lincs	SK9122	52°47·5'	0°38·6'W	F	130
Staincliffe	Kirk	SE2323	53°42·4'	1°38·7'W	T	104
Staincross	Barns	SE3310	53°35·4'	1°29·7'W	T	110,111
Staindale	N Yks	NZ3906	54°27·1'	1°23·5'W	X	93
Staindale	N Yks	NZ5201	54°24·3'	1°11·5'W	X	93
Stain Dale	N Yks	SE8790	54°18·1'	0°39·4'W	X	94,101
Staindale Beck	N Yks	NZ3806	54°27·1'	1°24·4'W	W	93
Staindale Beck	N Yks	SE8689	54°17·6'	0°40·3'W	W	94,101
Staindale Grange	N Yks	NZ3606	54°27·1'	1°26·3'W	X	93
Staindale Hill	N Yks	NZ4007	54°27·7'	1°22·6'W	X	93
Staindale Lodge	N Yks	SE8588	54°17·1'	0°41·2'W	X	94,100
Stainderber	Lancs	SD6473	54°9·3'	2°32·7'W	X	97
Staindrop	Durham	NZ1220	54°34·7'	1°48·4'W	T	92
Stained Hill	Lincs	TF3074	53°15·1'	0°2·7'W	X	122
Stainers Fm	N Yks	SE7680	54°12·8'	0°49·7'W	FM	100
Stainery Clough	Sheff	SK2095	53°27·3'	1°41·5'W	X	110
Staines	Surrey	TQ0471	51°25·9'	0°29·8'W	T	176
Staines Fm	Essex	TL5630	51°57·0'	0°16·6'E	FM	167
Staines Green	Herts	TL2911	51°47·2'	0°7·4'W	T	166
Staines Moor	Surrey	TQ0372	51°26·5'	0°30·7'W	X	176
Staines Reservoirs	Surrey	TQ0573	51°27·0'	0°28·9'W	W	176
Stainfield	Lincs	TF0725	52°48·9'	0°24·3'W	T	130
Stainfield	Lincs	TF1173	53°14·8'	0°19·8'W	T	121
Stainfield Common	Lincs	TF1172	53°14·2'	0°19·8'W	X	121
Stainfield Fen	Lincs	TF0972	53°14·3'	0°21·6'W	X	121
Stainfield Grange	Lincs	TF1073	53°14·8'	0°20·7'W	X	121
Stainfield Wood	Lincs	TF1172	53°14·2'	0°19·8'W	F	121
Stainforth	Donc	SE6411	53°35·7'	1°1·6'W	T	111
Stainforth	N Yks	SD8267	54°6·2'	2°16·1'W	T	98
Stainforth and Keadby Canal	Donc	SE6613	53°36·8'	0°59·7'W	W	111
Stainforth Force	N Yks	SD8167	54°6·2'	2°17·0'W	W	98
Stainforth Gill Head	N Yks	SE1352	53°58·1'	1°47·7'W	X	104
Stainforth & Keadby Canal	Donc	SE7312	53°36·2'	0°53·4'W	W	112
Staingills	Cumbr	NY5931	54°40·6'	2°37·7'W	X	91
Staing Mhór	Arg & Bt	NM8108	56°13·1'	5°31·5'W	W	55
Stain Hill	Lincs	TF4785	53°20·7'	0°12·9'E	X	122
Staining	Lancs	SD3436	53°49·2'	2°59·7'W	T	102
Staining Gill Beck	N Yks	SE0473	54°9·4'	1°55·9'W	W	98
Staining Wood Fm	Lancs	SD3732	53°47·1'	2°57·0'W	FM	102
Stainland	Cald	SE0719	53°40·3'	1°53·2'W	T	110
Stainland	Highld	ND1266	58°34·7'	3°30·3'W	X	11,12
Stainley Hall Fm	N Yks	SE3162	54°3·4'	1°31·2'W	FM	99
Stainley Ho	N Yks	SE3062	54°3·4'	1°32·1'W	X	99
Stainley Mill	N Yks	SE3162	54°3·4'	1°31·2'W	X	99
Stainmore Common	Cumbr	NY8516	54°32·6'	2°13·5'W	X	91,92
Stainmore Forest	Durham	NY9410	54°29·4'	2°5·1'W	X	91,92
Stainrigg	Scot Bord	NT7843	55°41·0'	2°20·6'W	X	74
Stainrigg Mains	Scot Bord	NT7743	55°41·0'	2°21·5'W	X	74
Stainsacre	N Yks	NZ9108	54°27·8'	0°35·3'W	T	94
Stainsborough Hall	Derby	SK2653	53°4·7'	1°36·3'W	X	119
Stainsby	Derby	SK4465	53°11·1'	1°20·1'W	T	120
Stainsby	Lincs	TF3371	53°13·4'	0°0·1'W	T	122
Stainsby Beck	Stock on T	NZ4616	54°32·5'	1°16·9'W	W	93
Stainsby Common	Derby	SK4364	53°10·5'	1°21·0'W	X	120
Stainsby Ho	Derby	SK4044	52°59·7'	1°23·8'W	X	129
Stainsby Pond	Derby	SK4464	53°10·5'	1°20·1'W	W	120
Stainsby Village	Midd	NZ4615	54°31·9'	1°16·9'W	A	93
Stainswick Fm	Oxon	SU2487	51°35·1'	1°38·8'W	FM	174
Stainton	Cumbr	NY3756	54°53·9'	2°58·5'W	T	85
Stainton	Cumbr	NY4828	54°38·9'	2°47·9'W	T	90
Stainton	Cumbr	SD1294	54°20·3'	3°20·8'W	X	96
Stainton	Cumbr	SD5285	54°15·8'	2°43·8'W	T	97
Stainton	Donc	SK5593	53°26·1'	1°9·9'W	T	111
Stainton	Durham	NZ0618	54°33·7'	1°54·0'W	T	92
Stainton	Midd	NZ4814	54°31·4'	1°15·1'W	T	93
Stainton	N Yks	SE1096	54°21·8'	1°50·3'W	T	99
Stainton Beck	Cumbr	SD1394	54°20·3'	3°19·9'W	W	96
Stainton Beck	Cumbr	SD5284	54°15·2'	2°43·8'W	W	97
Stainton Beck	Midd	NZ4714	54°31·4'	1°16·0'W	W	93
Stainton by Langworth	Lincs	TF0677	53°17·0'	0°24·2'W	T	121
Stainton Cotes	N Yks	SD8953	53°58·6'	2°9·6'W	X	103
Stainton Covert	Lincs	TF2281	53°18·9'	0°9·7'W	F	122
Staintondale	N Yks	SE9998	54°22·3'	0°28·1'W	T	94,101
Staintondale Moor	N Yks	SE9799	54°22·9'	0°30·0'W	X	94,101
Stainton Fell	Cumbr	SD1494	54°20·3'	3°18·9'W	X	96
Stainton Gap	Cumbr	SD2983	54°14·5'	3°5·0'W	X	96,97
Stainton Grange	Darl	NZ3321	54°35·2'	1°28·9'W	X	93
Stainton Grange	Midd	NZ4913	54°30·8'	1°14·2'W	X	93
Stainton Ground	Cumbr	SD2192	54°19·3'	3°12·5'W	X	96
Stainton Hall	N Yks	SD8852	53°58·1'	2°10·6'W	X	103
Stainton Hill Ho	Durham	NZ3222	54°35·8'	1°29·9'W	X	93
Stainton House	N Yks	SD8852	53°58·1'	2°10·6'W	X	103
Stainton le Vale	Lincs	TF1794	53°26·0'	0°13·9'W	T	113
Stainton Little Wood	Donc	SK5594	53°26·6'	1°9·9'W	F	111
Stainton Low Wood	N Yks	SE0997	54°22·3'	1°51·3'W	F	99
Stainton Moor	N Yks	SE0895	54°21·3'	1°52·2'W	X	99
Stainton Moor Beck	N Yks	SE1095	54°21·3'	1°50·3'W	W	99
Stainton Pike	Cumbr	SD1594	54°20·3'	3°18·0'W	X	96
Stainton Vale	Midd	NZ4714	54°31·4'	1°16·0'W	X	93
Stainton with Adgarley	Cumbr	SD2472	54°8·5'	3°9·4'W	T	96
Stainton Wood	Lincs	TF0778	53°17·5'	0°23·3'W	F	121
Stainton Woodhouse Fm	Donc	SK5693	53°26·1'	1°9·0'W	FM	111
Stair	Cumbr	NY2321	54°34·9'	3°11·1'W	T	89,90
Stair	S Ayr	NS4323	55°28·8'	4°28·6'W	T	70
Stairaird	E Ayr	NS4625	55°29·9'	4°25·8'W	X	70
Stair Br	Pth & Kin	NO0339	56°32·2'	3°34·2'W	X	52,53
Stairbridge Fm	W Susx	TQ2721	50°58·7'	0°11·1'W	FM	198
Staircase Ho	Leeds	SE2443	53°53·2'	1°37·7'W	X	104
Stairfield	D & G	NX4639	54°43·6'	4°23·1'W	X	83
Stairfoot	Barns	SE3705	53°32·7'	1°26·1'W	T	110,111
Stairfoot	Corn	SW8650	50°18·9'	5°0·0'W	X	200,204
Stairhaven	D & G	NX2053	54°50·6'	4°47·8'W	T	82
Stairhill	E Ayr	NS4624	55°29·4'	4°25·8'W	X	70
Stairhill Fm	Devon	SX8199	50°46·9'	3°40·9'W	FM	191
Stair Ho	E Ayr	NS4423	55°28·8'	4°27·7'W	A	70
Stair Hole	Dorset	SY8279	50°36·9'	2°14·9'W	X	194
Stair Law	Scot Bord	NT2809	55°22·4'	3°7·7'W	H	79
Stairlaw Burn	Scot Bord	NT2809	55°22·4'	3°7·7'W	W	79
Stairlie	N Ayr	NS2149	55°42·3'	4°50·5'W	X	63
Stair Lodge	D & G	NX1766	54°57·6'	4°51·1'W	X	82
Stairs Hill	Brad	SE0034	53°48·4'	1°59·6'W	X	104
Stairs, The	V of Glam	ST1869	51°25·1'	3°10·4'W	X	171
Staithe	Norf	TM4993	52°28·9'	1°40·4'E	X	134
Staithe	Suff	TM3489	52°27·1'	1°27·0'E	X	156
Staithe Fm	Norf	TG3602	52°34·1'	1°29·4'E	FM	134
Staithe Fm	Norf	TG4108	52°37·2'	1°34·0'E	FM	134
Staithes	N Yks	NZ7818	54°33·3'	0°47·2'W	T	94
Staith Ho	Cumbr	NY0742	54°46·1'	3°26·3'W	X	85
Stake Allotments	N Yks	SD9485	54°15·9'	2°5·1'W	X	98
Stake Beck	Cumbr	NY2608	54°28·0'	3°8·1'W	W	89,90
Stake Beck	Cumbr	NY7428	54°39·0'	2°23·8'W	W	91
Stake Clough	Derby	SK0073	53°15·5'	1°59·6'W	X	119
Stake End	Lancs	SD6251	53°57·5'	2°34·3'W	X	102,103
Stake Fell	N Yks	SD9586	54°16·4'	2°4·2'W	X	98
Stake Fm	Ches	SJ9972	53°14·9'	2°0·5'W	FM	118
Stake Fm	Kent	TQ5554	51°16·1'	0°13·7'E	FM	188
Stakeford	Northum	NZ2685	55°9·8'	1°35·1'W	T	81
Stake Ford Cross	Dorset	ST6109	50°53·0'	2°32·9'W	X	194
Stake Gutter	Staffs	SK0263	53°10·1'	1°57·8'W	X	119
Stake Hill	Brad	SE0133	53°47·8'	1°58·7'W	X	104
Stake Hill	D & G	NS8812	55°23·6'	3°45·7'W	H	71,78
Stake Hill	D & G	NY3692	55°13·3'	2°59·9'W	H	79
Stake Hill	Durham	NY9322	54°35·8'	2°6·1'W	X	91,92
Stake Hill	Roch	SD8908	53°34·4'	2°9·6'W	T	109
Stake Ho	Lancs	SD5449	53°56·3'	2°41·6'W	X	102
Stake House Fell	Lancs	SD5549	53°56·4'	2°40·7'W	X	102
Stake Law	Scot Bord	NT2632	55°34·8'	3°10·0'W	H	73
Stake Law	Scot Bord	NT2731	55°34·3'	3°9·0'W	H	73
Stakeley	Cumbr	NY5608	54°28·2'	2°40·3'W	X	90
Stake Lode	Norf	TL6790	52°29·2'	0°28·0'E	W	143
Stake Moss	D & G	NS8712	55°23·6'	3°46·6'W	X	71,78
Stake Moss	N Yks	SD9382	54°14·1'	2°6·0'W	X	98
Stakenbridge	Worcs	SO8879	52°24·8'	2°10·2'W	T	139

Stake Ness	Aberd	NJ6465	57°40·7′	2°35·8′W	X	29
Stake Pass	Cumbr	NY2608	54°28·0′	3°8·1′W	X	89,90
Stake Pool	Lancs	SD4148	53°55·7′	2°53·5′W	X	102
Staker Hill	Derby	SK0670	53°13·9′	1°54·2′W	X	119
Staker's Cross	Somer	ST4007	50°51·8′	2°50·8′W	X	193
Stakers Fm	W Susx	TQ1626	51°1·5′	0°20·4′W	FM	187,198
Stakes	Lancs	SD6443	53°53·2′	2°32·4′W	X	102,103
Stakesby Vale Fm	N Yks	NZ8810	54°28·9′	0°38·1′W	FM	94
Stakes Fm	Hants	SU5319	50°58·3′	1°14·3′W	FM	185
Stake Side	Derby	SK0073	53°15·5′	1°59·6′W	X	119
Stakes Moss	Cumbr	SD4684	54°15·2′	2°49·3′W	X	97
St Albans	Herts	TL1507	51°45·2′	0°19·6′W	T	166
St Albans Fm	Somer	ST3422	50°59·9′	2°56·0′W	FM	193
St Alban's or St Aldhelm's Head	Dorset	SY9675	50°34·7′	2°3·0′W	X	195
Stalbridge	Dorset	ST7317	50°57·3′	2°22·7′W	T	183
Stalbridge Common	Dorset	ST7416	50°56·8′	2°21·8′W	X	183
Stalbridge Park	Dorset	ST7218	50°57·9′	2°23·5′W	X	183
Stalbridge Weston	Dorset	ST7116	50°56·8′	2°24·4′W	T	183
St Aldam's Ash Fm	S Glos	ST7077	51°29·7′	2°25·5′W	FM	172
St Aldhelm's or St Alban's Head	Dorset	SY9675	50°34·7′	2°3·0′W	X	195
Staley Hall (Hotel)	Northum	NY9855	54°53·6′	2°1·4′W	X	87
St Algar's Fm	Somer	ST7841	51°10·3′	2°18·5′W	FM	183
Stalham	Norf	TG3725	52°46·5′	1°31·2′E	T	133,134
Stalham Green	Norf	TG3824	52°45·9′	1°32·1′E	T	133,134
Stalisfield Green	Kent	TQ9552	51°14·3′	0°48·0′E	T	189
Stallachan Dubha	Highld	NM5362	56°41·3′	6°1·6′W	H	47
Stalla Dubh	Highld	NG9542	57°25·6′	5°24·4′W	X	25
Stallance	Kent	TQ8148	51°12·4′	0°35·9′E	X	188
Stallards	Somer	ST1318	50°57·5′	3°13·9′W	X	181,193
Stallashaw Moss	S Lanak	NT0053	55°45·9′	3°35·2′W	X	65,72
Stallbrook Hall	Staffs	SJ8822	52°48·0′	2°10·3′W	X	127
Stallcombe Ho	Devon	SY0389	50°41·8′	3°22·0′W	X	192
Stalldown Barrow	Devon	SX6362	50°26·7′	3°55·4′W	X	202
St Allen	Corn	SW8250	50°18·8′	5°3·4′W	T	200,204
Stallen	Dorset	ST6016	50°56·8′	2°33·8′W	T	183
Stallenge Fm	Somer	ST1527	51°2·4′	3°12·4′W	FM	181,193
Stallenge-Thorne Fm	Devon	ST0220	50°58·5′	3°23·4′W	FM	181
Stall Ho	W Susx	TQ0721	50°58·9′	0°28·2′W	X	197
Stallingborough	NE Lincs	TA2011	53°35·1′	0°10·8′W	T	113
Stallingborough Top	Lincs	TA1611	53°35·2′	0°14·4′W	X	113
Stalling Busk	N Yks	SD9185	54°15·9′	2°7·9′W	T	98
Stalling Busk Pasture	N Yks	SD9285	54°15·9′	2°7·0′W	X	98
Stalling Down	V of Glam	ST0174	51°27·6′	3°25·1′W	X	170
Stallington	Staffs	SJ9439	52°57·1′	2°5·0′W	T	127
Stallington Grange	Staffs	SJ9440	52°57·7′	2°5·0′W	X	118
Stallington Wood	Suff	TL9343	52°3·3′	0°49·3′E	F	155
Stallion Hill	Glos	SO7123	51°54·5′	2°24·9′W	X	162
Stallion's Green	Kent	TQ6250	51°13·8′	0°19·6′E	X	188
Stall Moor	Devon	SX6264	50°27·8′	3°56·3′W	X	202
Stallode	Suff	TL6984	52°25·9′	0°29·6′E	X	143
Stallode Fm	Suff	TL7084	52°25·9′	0°30·4′E	FM	143
Stallode Wash	Suff	TL6884	52°25·9′	0°28·7′E	X	143
Stalloe	Powys	SO2298	52°34·7′	3°8·7′W	X	137
Stallpits Fm	Oxon	SU2289	51°36·2′	1°40·5′W	FM	174
Stall's Fm	Somer	ST7139	51°9·2′	2°24·5′W	FM	183
Stalls Fm	Wilts	ST8043	51°11·4′	2°16·8′W	FM	183
Stalmine	Lancs	SD3745	53°54·1′	2°57·1′W	T	102
Stalmine Moss	Lancs	SD3945	53°54·1′	2°55·3′W	X	102
Stalmine Moss Side	Lancs	SD3745	53°54·1′	2°57·1′W	T	102
Stalybridge	Tames	SJ9698	53°29·0′	2°3·2′W	T	109
Stambermill	Dudley	SO9184	52°27·5′	2°7·5′W	T	139
Stamborough	Somer	ST0236	51°7·1′	3°23·6′W	T	181
Stambourne	Essex	TL7238	52°1·0′	0°30·8′E	T	154
Stambourne Green	Essex	TL7038	52°1·1′	0°29·0′E	T	154
Stamford	Lincs	TF0207	52°39·3′	0°29·1′W	T	141
Stamford	Northum	NU2219	55°28·1′	1°38·7′W	X	81
Stamford Bridge	Ches	SJ4667	53°12·1′	2°48·1′W	T	117
Stamford Bridge	E Yorks	SE7155	53°59·4′	0°54·6′W	T	105,106
Stamford Hall	Warw	SP2849	52°8·5′	1°35·1′W	X	151
Stamfordham	Northum	NZ0771	55°2·3′	1°53·0′W	T	88
Stamford Heath	Ches	SJ4567	53°12·1′	2°49·0′W	X	117
Stamford Hill	Corn	SS2207	50°50·3′	4°31·3′W	X	190
Stamford Hill	Hack	TQ3387	51°34·2′	0°4·5′W	T	176,177
Stamford Ho	Lincs	TF3165	53°10·2′	0°2·0′W	X	122
Stamford Lodge	Peterb	TF1400	52°35·4′	0°18·6′W	X	142
Stamford Mill	Ches	SJ4666	53°11·5′	2°48·1′W	X	117
Stamfords Fm	Essex	TQ8898	51°39·2′	0°43·5′E	FM	168
Stamfrey Fm	N Yks	NZ4103	54°25·5′	1°21·7′W	FM	93
Stammers	W Susx	SU9711	50°53·6′	0°36·9′W	X	197
Stammer's Fm	Essex	TL8109	51°45·2′	0°37·7′E	FM	168
Stammery Hill	Devon	SY3298	50°46·9′	2°57·5′W	X	193
Stampas Fm	Corn	SW7855	50°21·4′	5°6·9′W	FM	200
Stamperland	E Renf	NS5758	55°47·9′	4°16·4′W	T	64
Stamp Hill Fm	Cumbr	NY6526	54°37·9′	2°32·1′W	FM	91
Stampwell Fm	Bucks	SU9789	51°35·7′	0°35·6′W	FM	175,176
Stamshaw	C of Port	SU6402	50°49·1′	1°5·1′W	T	196
Stanage	Derby	SK2178	53°18·2′	1°40·7′W	X	119
Stanage Edge	Derby	SK2384	53°21·4′	1°38·9′W	X	110
Stanage End	Derby	SK2286	53°22·5′	1°39·7′W	X	110
Stanage Ho	Derby	SK2178	53°18·2′	1°40·7′W	X	119
Stanage Park	Powys	SO3371	52°20·2′	2°58·6′W	X	137,148
Stanah	Cumbr	NY3119	54°33·9′	3°3·6′W	X	90
Stanah	Lancs	SD3542	53°52·5′	2°58·9′W	T	102
Stanah Gill	Cumbr	NY3218	54°33·4′	3°2·7′W	W	90
Stanaway Fm	Suff	TM2053	52°8·1′	1°13·3′E	FM	156
Stanborough	Herts	TL2211	51°47·3′	0°13·5′W	T	166
Stanborough Ho	Devon	SX7752	50°21·5′	3°43·4′W	X	202
Stanborough Hundred (Hotel)	Devon	SX7751	50°21·0′	3°43·4′W	X	202
Stanbridge	Beds	SP9624	51°54·6′	0°35·9′W	T	165
Stanbridge	Dorset	SU0003	50°49·8′	1°59·6′W	T	195
Stanbridge Earls	Hants	SU3323	51°0·6′	1°31·4′W	A	185
Stanbridge Fm	Hants	SU7521	50°59·2′	0°55·5′W	FM	197
Stanbridgeford	Beds	SP9623	51°54·1′	0°35·9′W	T	165
Stanbridge Ho	W Susx	TQ2627	51°1·9′	0°11·8′W	X	187,198
Stanbridge Mill Fm	Dorset	SU0108	50°52·5′	1°58·8′W	FM	195
Stanbridge Ranvilles Fm	Hants	SU3222	51°0·0′	1°32·3′W	FM	185

Stan Brook	Essex	TL5929	51°56·4′	0°19·2′E	W	167
Stanbrook	Essex	TL6029	51°56·4′	0°20·1′E	T	167
Stanbrook	Worcs	SO8349	52°8·6′	2°14·5′W	T	150
Stanbrook Fm	Glos	SO7727	51°56·7′	2°19·7′W	FM	162
Stanbury	Brad	SE0037	53°50·0′	1°59·6′W	T	104
Stanbury	Corn	SS2013	50°53·5′	4°33·2′W	A	190
Stanbury	Corn	SS2310	50°52·0′	4°30·5′W	X	190
Stanbury Cross	Devon	SS3404	50°48·9′	4°21·0′W	X	190
Stanbury Moor	Brad	SD9736	53°49·5′	2°2·3′W	X	103
Stanbury Mouth	Corn	SS1913	50°53·5′	4°34·0′W	W	190
Stanbury Park	Wok	SU7166	51°23·5′	0°58·4′W	X	175
Stanbury Point	W Susx	SU7603	50°49·5′	0°54·9′W	X	197
Stanbutch	Shrops	SO4093	52°32·1′	2°52·7′W	X	137
Stanch	Suff	TL7786	52°26·8′	0°36·7′E	X	144
Stanchil's Fm	Suff	TL8168	52°17·0′	0°39·6′E	FM	155
St Anchorite's Rock	Devon	SX5947	50°18·6′	3°58·4′W	X	202
Stancil	Donc	SK6095	53°27·1′	1°5·4′W	X	111
Stancliffe Hall	Derby	SK2664	53°10·6′	1°36·3′W	X	119
Stancombe	Devon	SX7958	50°24·8′	3°41·8′W	X	202
Stancombe	Devon	SX8073	50°32·9′	3°41·3′W	X	191
Stancombe Cross	Devon	SX7745	50°17·8′	3°43·2′W	X	202
Stancombe Down	W Berks	SU3581	51°31·8′	1°29·3′W	X	174
Stancombe Fm	Dorset	SY5492	50°43·8′	2°38·7′W	FM	194
Stancombe Fm	Glos	SO8906	51°45·4′	2°9·2′W	FM	163
Stancombe Fm	Somer	ST0922	50°59·6′	3°17·4′W	FM	181
Stancombe Fm	W Berks	SU3582	51°32·4′	1°29·3′W	FM	174
Stancombe Park	Glos	ST7397	51°40·5′	2°23·0′W	X	162
Stancombe Wood	Glos	SP0328	51°57·3′	1°57·0′W	F	150,163
Stancomb Fm	Hants	SU6435	51°6·9′	1°4·8′W	FM	185
Stand	Bury	SD7905	53°32·7′	2°18·6′W	T	109
Stand	N Lanak	NS7668	55°53·6′	3°58·5′W	T	64
Standalane	E Ayr	NS4042	55°39·0′	4°32·1′W	X	70
Stand Alane	Fife	NT0091	56°6·3′	3°36·0′W	X	58
Standalane	Scot Bord	NT2441	55°39·6′	3°12·0′W	X	73
Standalone	Durham	NZ1940	54°45·5′	1°41·9′W	X	88
Standalone	Durham	NZ2929	54°39·6′	1°32·6′W	X	93
Stand Alone	N Yks	NZ2808	54°28·2′	1°33·7′W	X	93
Standalone Farm Centre	Herts	TL2033	51°59·2′	0°14·8′W	X	166
Standalone Fm	Beds	TL1041	52°3·6′	0°23·3′W	FM	153
Standalone Fm	Beds	TL2348	52°7·2′	0°11·8′W	FM	153
Standal's Fm	Bucks	SP8110	51°47·2′	0°49·1′W	FM	165
Standard	D & G	NX8688	55°10·6′	3°47·0′W	X	78
Standard	N Yks	SD9599	54°23·4′	2°4·2′W	X	98
Standard	N Yks	SE0050	53°57·0′	1°59·6′W	X	104
Standard	N Yks	SE0854	53°59·2′	1°52·3′W	X	104
Standard	Orkney	HY3030	59°9·3′	3°13·0′W	X	6
Standard	S Ayr	NX2681	55°5·8′	4°43·2′W	X	76
Standard	S Ayr	NX3085	55°8·1′	4°39·6′W	X	76
Standard Flat	N Yks	SE0358	54°1·3′	1°56·8′W	X	104
Standard Hill	E Yorks	TA1973	54°8·6′	0°10·3′W	X	101
Standard Hill	Kent	TQ8563	51°20·4′	0°39·8′E	X	178
Standard Hill	Northum	NY8275	55°4·4′	2°16·5′W	X	86,87
Standardhill Fm	Kent	TR1943	51°8·9′	1°8·3′E	FM	179,189
Standard Hill Ho	E Susx	TQ6912	50°53·2′	0°24·6′E	X	199
Standard Knowe	S Ayr	NX1977	55°3·5′	4°49·6′W	H	76
Standard Knowe	Scot Bord	NT7813	55°24·9′	2°20·4′W	H	80
Standard Man	N Yks	NY9504	54°26·1′	2°4·2′W	X	91,92
Standards	Durham	NY8522	54°35·8′	2°13·5′W	X	91,92
Standard Stone	Fife	NS9587	56°4·1′	3°40·8′W	A	65
Standburn	D & G	NY2182	55°7·8′	3°13·9′W	X	79
Standburn	Falk	NS9274	55°57·1′	3°43·3′W	T	65
Stand Crags	Cumbr	NY3810	54°29·1′	2°57·0′W	X	90
Standedge	Oldham	SE0110	53°35·4′	1°58·7′W	X	110
Standeford	Staffs	SJ9107	52°39·9′	2°7·6′W	T	127,139
Standel	Powys	SO0530	51°57·9′	3°22·6′W	X	160
Standen	Kent	TQ8540	51°8·0′	0°39·0′E	T	189
Standen	W Susx	TQ3835	51°6·1′	0°1·3′W	X	187
Stand End	Cumbr	NY4748	54°49·7′	2°49·1′W	X	86
Standen Hall	Lancs	SD7440	53°51·6′	2°23·3′W	T	103
Standen Hey	Lancs	SD7339	53°51·0′	2°24·2′W	X	103
Standen Ho	I of W	SZ5087	50°41·1′	1°17·1′W	X	196
Standen Ho	Wilts	SU3053	51°16·8′	1°33·8′W	X	185
Standen Manor	W Berks	SU3266	51°23·8′	1°32·0′W	X	174
Standen Street	Kent	TQ8030	51°2·7′	0°34·5′E	T	188
Standen Wood	Kent	TQ8031	51°3·2′	0°34·5′E	F	188
Standerlands	Lancs	SD4764	54°4·4′	2°48·2′W	X	97
Standerwick	Somer	ST8150	51°15·2′	2°15·9′W	T	183
Standerwick Court	Somer	ST8151	51°15·7′	2°16·0′W	X	183
Standford	Hants	SU8134	51°6·2′	0°50·2′W	T	186
Standford Bridge	Wrekin	SJ7024	52°49·0′	2°26·3′W	T	127
Standford Hall	Wrekin	SJ7022	52°47·9′	2°26·3′W	X	127
Standhill	Scot Bord	NT5623	55°30·2′	2°41·4′W	X	73
Standhill	W Loth	NS9167	55°53·3′	3°44·1′W	X	65
Standhill Fm	Oxon	SU6499	51°41·4′	1°4·1′W	FM	164,165
Standhill Fm	W Loth	NS8966	55°52·7′	3°46·0′W	FM	65
Standhill Fm	W Loth	NS9667	55°53·4′	3°39·3′W	FM	65
Standhills	Sheff	SK2982	53°20·3′	1°33·5′W	X	110
Standing Burn	S Lanak	NS8929	55°32·8′	3°45·1′W	W	71,72
Standing Crag	Cumbr	NY2913	54°30·7′	3°5·4′W	X	89,90
Standingfauld	Pth & Kin	NN8713	56°18·0′	3°49·1′W	X	58
Standinghall Fm	W Susx	TQ3135	51°6·2′	0°7·3′W	FM	187
Standingstone	Cumbr	NY2549	54°50·1′	3°9·6′W	T	85
Standingstone	D & G	NX6352	54°50·9′	4°7·6′W	X	83
Standingstone	D & G	NX7359	54°54·8′	3°58·4′W	X	83,84
Standingstone	D & G	NX7749	54°49·5′	3°54·5′W	X	84
Standingstone	E Loth	NT5773	55°57·1′	2°40·9′W	X	67
Standingstone	Moray	NJ1364	57°39·7′	3°27·0′W	X	28
Standingstone Clints	Northum	NY7976	55°4·9′	2°19·3′W	X	86,87
Standingstone Edge	D & G	NY2982	55°7·9′	3°6·4′W	X	79
Standing Stone Hill	N Yks	SE2162	54°3·5′	1°40·3′W	X	99
Standingstone Hill	S Lanak	NS7535	55°35·8′	3°58·6′W	X	71
Standingstone Rigg	Cumbr	NY4364	54°58·3′	2°53·0′W	X	85
Standingstone Rigg	Cumbr	NY6471	55°2·2′	2°33·4′W	X	86
Standingstones	Aberd	NO7393	57°1·9′	2°26·2′W	X	38,45
Standingstones	Aberd	NO8497	57°4·1′	2°15·4′W	X	38,45
Standingstones	C of Aber	NJ8612	57°12·2′	2°13·4′W	X	38
Standing Stones	Cumbr	NY0513	54°30·5′	3°27·6′W	X	89
Standing Stones	Cumbr	SD1380	54°12·7′	3°19·6′W	X	96
Standing Stones of Glenterrow	D & G	NX1462	54°55·3′	4°53·7′W	A	82

Standingstones Rigg	N Yks	SE9796	54°21·3′	0°30·0′W	X	94,101
Standing Tarn	Cumbr	SD2474	54°9·6′	3°9·4′W	W	96
Standish	Glos	SO8008	51°46·5′	2°17·0′W	T	162
Standish	Wigan	SD5610	53°35·3′	2°39·5′W	T	108
Standish Cote	Cumbr	SD2479	54°12·3′	3°9·5′W	X	96
Standish Hall	Wigan	SD5509	53°34·8′	2°40·4′W	X	108
Standish Hospital	Glos	SO8106	51°45·4′	2°16·1′W	X	162
Standish Lower Ground	Wigan	SD5507	53°33·7′	2°40·4′W	T	108
Standish Moreton Fm	Glos	SO7908	51°46·5′	2°17·9′W	FM	162
Standish Park Fm	Glos	SO8207	51°45·9′	2°15·3′W	FM	162
Standish Wood	Glos	SO8307	51°45·9′	2°14·4′W	F	162
Stand Knowe	Scot Bord	NT3217	55°26·8′	3°4·1′W	H	79
Standlake	Oxon	SP3903	51°43·7′	1°25·7′W	T	164
Standlake Common	Oxon	SP3901	51°42·6′	1°25·7′W	X	164
Standle Fm	Glos	ST7298	51°41·0′	2°23·9′W	FM	162
Stand Low	Derby	SK1553	53°4·7′	1°46·2′W	A	119
Standlynch Down	Wilts	SU2023	51°0·6′	1°42·5′W	X	184
Standlynch Fm	Wilts	SU1924	51°1·1′	1°43·4′W	FM	184
Standmilane Craig	Stir	NS6791	56°5·9′	4°7·8′W	X	57
Standon	Hants	SU4226	51°2·1′	1°23·7′W	T	185
Standon	Herts	TL3822	51°53·0′	0°0·7′E	T	166
Standon	Staffs	SJ8134	52°54·4′	2°16·5′W	T	127
Standon Fm	Devon	SX5481	50°36·9′	4°3·4′W	FM	191,201
Standon Friars	Herts	TL4022	51°53·0′	0°2·4′E	X	167
Standon Green End	Herts	TL3619	51°51·4′	0°1·1′W	T	166
Standon Hill	Devon	SX5581	50°36·9′	4°2·6′W	H	191
Standon Homestead	Surrey	TQ1338	51°8·0′	0°22·7′W	X	187
Standon Lodge	Herts	TL4020	51°51·9′	0°2·4′E	X	167
Standon Old Hall	Staffs	SJ8035	52°55·0′	2°17·4′W	X	127
Standpretty	Orkney	HY3724	59°6·2′	3°5·5′W	X	6
St Andrews	Fife	NO5116	56°20·3′	2°47·1′W	T	59
St Andrews Bay	Fife	NO5318	56°21·4′	2°45·2′W	W	59
St Andrew's Church	Somer	ST1644	51°11·6′	3°11·7′W	A	181
St Andrew's Fm	Essex	TL8700	51°40·3′	0°42·7′E	FM	168
St Andrew's Glebe Fm	Norf	TF7206	52°37·7′	0°32·9′E	FM	143
St Andrew's Hall	Suff	TM3886	52°25·4′	1°30·4′E	X	156
St Andrew's Hill	Devon	ST0107	50°51·5′	3°24·0′W	X	192
St Andrews' Major	V of Glam	ST1371	51°26·1′	3°14·7′W	T	171
St Andrews Quay	K upon H	TA0726	53°43·4′	0°22·3′W	X	107
St Andrews Rd Sta	C of Bris	ST5179	51°30·7′	2°42·0′W	X	172
St Andrew's School	Arg & Bt	NS2587	56°2·9′	4°48·1′W	X	56
St Andrew's Well	Dorset	SY4793	50°44·3′	2°44·7′W	T	193
St Andrews Wells	Fife	NO4314	56°19·2′	2°54·8′W	X	59
St Andrew's Wood	Devon	ST0605	50°50·4′	3°19·7′W	T	192
Standridge	Lancs	SD7353	53°58·6′	2°24·3′W	X	103
Standridge Hill	Lancs	SD7148	53°55·9′	2°26·1′W	X	103
Standrise Plantn	N Yks	SD9448	53°55·9′	2°5·1′W	F	103
Standrop Burn	Northum	NT9318	55°27·6′	2°6·2′W	W	80
Standrop Rigg	Northum	NT9418	55°27·6′	2°5·3′W	X	80
Standryford	Aberd	NJ8918	57°15·4′	2°10·5′W	X	38
Standtrae Knowe	Scot Bord	NT2214	55°25·1′	3°13·5′W	H	79
Standwell	Northum	NZ0868	55°0·6′	1°52·1′W	X	88
Standwell Fm	Suff	TM1974	52°19·4′	1°13·2′E	FM	156
Stane	N Lanak	NS8859	55°48·9′	3°46·8′W	T	65,72
Stane	Orkney	ND4587	58°46·3′	2°56·6′W	X	7
Stanebent	N Lanak	NS8960	55°49·5′	3°45·9′W	X	65
Stanecastle	N Ayr	NS3339	55°37·2′	4°38·7′W	T	70
Stanedge Grange	Derby	SK1659	53°7·9′	1°45·2′W	X	119
Stanedge Lodge	Derby	SK2484	53°21·4′	1°38·0′W	X	110
Stanedge Pole	Derby	SK2484	53°21·4′	1°38·0′W	X	110
Stanegarth	Cumbr	NY4917	54°33·0′	2°46·9′W	X	90
Stanegate (Roman Road)	Cumbr	NY4760	54°56·2′	2°49·2′W	R	86
Stanegate (Roman Road)	Northum	NY6465	54°58·9′	2°33·3′W	R	86
Stanegate (Roman Road)	Northum	NY8167	55°0·1′	2°17·4′W	R	86,87
Staneley Resr	Renf	NS4661	55°49·3′	4°27·1′W	W	64
Staneloof	Orkney	HY4807	58°57·1′	2°53·7′W	X	6,7
Stane Loro	Shetld	HU3827	60°1·8′	1°18·6′W	X	4
Stanerandy	Orkney	HY2627	59°7·7′	3°17·1′W	X	6
Stanerandy (Standing Stones)	Orkney	HY2627	59°7·7′	3°17·1′W	A	6
Stanes Fm	W Susx	SU7908	50°52·2′	0°52·3′W	FM	197
Staneshaw Rigg	Cumbr	NY7140	54°45·5′	2°26·6′W	X	86,87
Stanes Moor	Shetld	HU3372	60°26·1′	1°23·5′W	X	2,3
Stane Street (Roman Road)	Essex	TL6522	51°52·6′	0°24·2′E	R	167
Stane Street (Roman Road)	Essex	TL8622	51°52·2′	0°42·5′E	R	168
Stane Street (Roman Road)	Herts	TL4223	51°53·5′	0°4·2′E	R	167
Stane Street (Roman Road)	Surrey	TQ1646	51°12·3′	0°20·0′W	R	187
Stane Street (Roman Road)	Surrey	TQ2264	51°21·9′	0°14·5′W	R	176,187
Stane Street (Roman Road)	W Susx	SU9511	50°53·7′	0°38·6′W	R	197
Stane Street (Roman Road)	W Susx	TQ0927	51°2·1′	0°26·3′W	R	187,198
Stanes Water	Shetld	HU3372	60°26·1′	1°23·5′W	W	2,3
Stanevatstoe Hill	Shetld	HU2054	60°16·4′	1°37·8′W	H	3
Stanevatstoe Loch	Shetld	HU2154	60°16·4′	1°36·7′W	W	3
Staneydale Temple	Shetld	HU2850	60°14·3′	1°29·2′W	A	3
Staney Hall Fm	Durham	NZ1639	54°45·0′	1°44·7′W	FM	92
Staney Hill	Orkney	HY3215	59°1·3′	3°10·6′W	X	6
Staney Hill	Scot Bord	NT4405	55°20·4′	2°52·5′W	H	79
Stanfield	C of Stoke	SJ8751	53°3·6′	2°11·2′W	T	118
Stanfield	Norf	TF9320	52°44·8′	0°52·0′E	T	132
Stanfield Hall	Norf	TG1400	52°33·6′	1°9·8′E	X	144
Stanfield Hall Fm	N Yks	SE7883	54°14·4′	0°47·8′W	FM	100
Stanford	Beds	TL1641	52°3·5′	0°18·1′W	T	153
Stanford	Kent	TR1238	51°6·3′	1°2·1′E	T	179,189
Stanford	Norf	TL8594	52°31·0′	0°44·0′E	T	144
Stanford	Shrops	SJ3312	52°42·3′	2°59·1′W	T	126
Stanford Bishop	Heref	SO6851	52°9·6′	2°27·7′W	T	149
Stanford Bridge	Worcs	SO7165	52°17·2′	2°25·1′W	T	138,149
Stanford Bridge Fm	Kent	TQ9242	51°8·9′	0°45·1′E	FM	189
Stanford Brook	Surrey	SU9553	51°16·3′	0°37·9′W	W	186
Stanford Brook	Warw	SP2533	51°59·9′	1°37·8′W	W	151
Stanford Brook	W Susx	TQ2732	51°4·6′	0°10·8′W	W	187
Stanford Bury Fm	Beds	TL1440	52°3·0′	0°19·9′W	FM	153

Stanford Common	Surrey	SU9454	51°16·9'	0°38·7'W	F	186
Stanford Ct	Worcs	SO7065	52°17·2'	2°26·0'W	X	138,149
Stanford Dingley	W Berks	SU5771	51°26·3'	1°10·4'W	T	174
Stanford End	Wok	SU7063	51°21·9'	0°59·3'W	T	175,186
Stanford Hall	Glos	SP1902	51°43·2'	1°43·1'W	X	163
Stanford Hall	Leic	SP5879	52°24·6'	1°8·4'W	A	140
Stanford Hall	Notts	SK5523	52°48·3'	1°10·6'W	X	129
Stanford Hills	Notts	SK5423	52°48·3'	1°11·5'W	T	129
Stanford Hills Fm	Notts	SK5424	52°48·9'	1°11·5'W	FM	129
Stanford House Fm	Oxon	SU3493	51°38·3'	1°30·1'W	FM	164,174
Stanford in the Vale	Oxon	SU3493	51°38·3'	1°30·1'W	T	164,174
Stanford-le-Hope	Thurr	TQ6882	51°30·9'	0°25·7'E	T	177,178
Stanford Mear	Northnts	SP5977	52°23·5'	1°7·6'W	X	140
Stanford on Avon	Northnts	SP5878	52°24·0'	1°8·4'W	T	140
Stanford on Soar	Notts	SK5422	52°47·8'	1°11·5'W	T	129
Stanford on Teme	Worcs	SO7065	52°17·2'	2°26·0'W	T	138,149
Stanford Park Fm	Oxon	SU3593	51°38·3'	1°29·3'W	FM	164,174
Stanford Place	Oxon	SU3095	51°39·4'	1°33·6'W	X	164
Stanford Resr	Northnts	SP6080	52°25·1'	1°6·7'W	W	140
Stanford Rivers	Essex	TL5301	51°41·4'	0°13·2'E	T	167
Stanford Village	Northnts	SP5979	52°24·6'	1°7·6'W	A	140
Stanford Warren	Norf	TL8693	52°30·4'	0°44·8'E	X	144
Stanford Water	Norf	TL8695	52°31·5'	0°44·9'E	W	144
Stanfree	Derby	SK4774	53°15·9'	1°17·3'W	T	120
Stang	Cumbr	NY3517	54°32·9'	2°59·9'W	X	90
Stang	N Yks	NZ0107	54°27·7'	1°58·7'W	X	92
Stangasetter	Orkney	HY6644	59°17·1'	2°35·3'W	X	5
Stangate Creek	Kent	TQ8771	51°24·7'	0°41·7'E	W	178
Stangate Hill	Cambs	TL1879	52°24·0'	0°15·5'W	X	142
Stangate Spit	Kent	TQ8772	51°25·2'	0°41·8'E	X	178
Stangau	Carm	SN7626	51°55·4'	3°47·8'W	X	146,160
Stang Brae	N Yks	SE1871	54°8·3'	1°43·1'W	X	99
Stang End	Cumbr	NY3202	54°24·8'	3°2·4'W	X	90
Stangend Currick	Durham	NY8443	54°47·1'	2°14·5'W	X	86,87
Stangends	Cumbr	NY1103	54°25·1'	3°21·9'W	X	89
Stanger	Cumbr	NY1327	54°38·1'	3°20·4'W	X	89
Stanger	Orkney	HY2526	59°7·1'	3°18·1'W	X	6
Stanger Head	Orkney	HY5142	59°16·0'	2°51·1'W	X	5
Stangerhill	Cumbr	NY2038	54°44·1'	3°14·1'W	X	89,90
Stangerthwaite	Cumbr	SD6289	54°18·0'	2°34·6'W	X	97
Stang Gill	Durham	NZ0208	54°28·3'	1°57·7'W	W	92
Stanggill Barn	N Yks	SD8868	54°6·7'	2°10·6'W	X	98
Stang Howe	N Yks	NZ7613	54°30·6'	0°49·1'W	A	94
Stanghow Moor	Red & Cl	NZ6514	54°31·3'	0°59·3'W	X	94
Stangrah	Cumbr	SD1185	54°15·4'	3°21·6'W	X	96
Stangraidh	N Eil	NB4122	58°6·9'	6°23·4'W	X	14
Stangram	N Eil	NF7775	57°39·2'	7°24·5'W	X	18
Stangrave Hall	Surrey	TQ3451	51°14·8'	0°4·4'W	X	187
Stanground	Peterb	TL2096	52°33·1'	0°13·4'W	T	142
Stangs Fm	Pemb	SN0310	51°45·5'	4°50·9'W	FM	157,158
Stang Side	N Yks	NZ0105	54°26·7'	1°58·7'W	X	92
Stang, The	Durham	NZ0208	54°28·3'	1°57·7'W	F	92
Stanhill	Lancs	SD7227	53°44·6'	2°25·1'W	T	103
Stanhill Court	Surrey	TQ2342	51°10·1'	0°14·1'W	X	187
Stanhill Fm	Kent	TQ5070	51°24·8'	0°9·8'E	FM	177
Stanhoe	Norf	TF8037	52°54·2'	0°41·0'E	T	132
Stanhope	D & G	NY0867	54°59·6'	3°25·9'W	X	85
Stanhope	Durham	NY9939	54°45·0'	2°0·5'W	T	92
Stanhope	Kent	TQ9940	51°7·7'	0°51·0'E	T	189
Stanhope	Scot Bord	NT1229	55°33·1'	3°23·3'W	T	72
Stanhope Burn	Durham	NY9843	54°47·2'	2°1·4'W	W	87
Stanhope Burn	Scot Bord	NT1328	55°32·5'	3°22·3'W	W	72
Stanhope Common	Durham	NY9642	54°46·6'	2°3·3'W	X	87
Stanhope Fm	Notts	SK7678	53°17·8'	0°51·2'W	FM	120
Stanhope Foot	Scot Bord	NT3118	55°27·3'	3°5·0'W	X	79
Stanhope Gate	Durham	NY9525	54°37·5'	2°4·2'W	X	91,92
Stanhope Hope	Scot Bord	NT1328	55°32·5'	3°22·3'W	X	72
Stanhope Law	Scot Bord	NT3218	55°27·3'	3°4·1'W	H	79
Stanhowe	N Yks	SE2998	54°22·8'	1°32·8'W	X	99
Stanion	Northnts	SP9186	52°28·1'	0°39·2'W	T	141
Stanion Lodge	Northnts	SP9286	52°28·1'	0°38·3'W	X	141
Staniston Hill	N Yks	SE2550	53°57·0'	1°36·7'W	X	104
Staniwells	N Lincs	SE9501	53°30·1'	0°33·7'W	X	112
Stank	Cumbr	SD2370	54°7·5'	3°10·3'W	T	96
Stank	D & G	NY0368	55°0·1'	3°30·6'W	X	84
Stank	Leeds	SE3044	53°53·7'	1°32·2'W	X	104
Stank	N Yks	SE0555	53°59·7'	1°55·0'W	X	104
Stank	Stir	NN5710	56°15·9'	4°18·1'W	X	57
Stank End	Cumbr	NY1650	54°50·5'	3°18·1'W	X	85
Stanker Hill Fm	Notts	SK5650	53°2·9'	1°9·5'W	FM	120
Stankeye	Aberd	NO6974	56°51·6'	2°35·0'W	X	45
Stank Glen	Stir	NN5710	56°15·9'	4°18·1'W	X	57
Stank Hall	N Yks	SE4095	54°21·2'	1°22·7'W	X	99
Stank Ho	Leeds	SE4034	53°48·3'	1°23·1'W	X	105
Stank Ho	N Yks	SE0654	53°59·2'	1°54·1'W	X	104
Stank House Fm	Red & Cl	NZ6917	54°32·9'	0°55·6'W	FM	94
Stanklyn	Worcs	SO8574	52°22·1'	2°12·8'W	T	139
Stanks	Leeds	SE3635	53°48·8'	1°26·8'W	T	104
Stanks, The	Worcs	SO8239	52°3·2'	2°15·4'W	X	150
Stank, The	Scot Bord	NT8128	55°33·0'	2°17·6'W	W	74
Stanky Hill	Powys	SO1676	52°22·8'	3°13·6'W	H	136,148
Stanlake Park	Wok	SU8075	51°28·3'	0°50·5'W	X	175
Stanley	Cumbr	NX9814	54°30·9'	3°34·1'W	X	89
Stanley	Darl	NZ2719	54°34·2'	1°34·5'W	X	93
Stanley	Derby	SK4140	52°57·6'	1°23·0'W	T	129
Stanley	Durham	NZ1952	54°52·0'	1°41·8'W	T	88
Stanley	Glos	SO7413	51°49·1'	2°22·2'W	X	162
Stanley	Lancs	SD4707	53°33·7'	2°47·6'W	X	108
Stanley	Lancs	SD6245	53°54·2'	2°34·3'W	X	102,103
Stanley	Notts	SK4562	53°9·4'	1°19·2'W	T	120
Stanley	Pth & Kin	NO1033	56°29·1'	3°27·2'W	T	53
Stanley	Pth & Kin	NO1133	56°29·1'	3°26·3'W	T	53
Stanley	Shrops	SO6884	52°27·4'	2°27·9'W	T	138
Stanley	Shrops	SO7583	52°26·9'	2°21·7'W	T	138
Stanley	Staffs	SJ9352	53°4·2'	2°5·9'W	T	118
Stanley	Wakf	SE3424	53°42·9'	1°28·7'W	T	104
Stanley	Wilts	ST9672	51°27·1'	2°3·1'W	T	173
Stanley Abbey Fm	Wilts	ST9672	51°27·1'	2°3·1'W	FM	173
Stanley Bank Plantation	Cumbr	NY5723	54°36·3'	2°39·5'W	F	91
Stanley Burn	Durham	NZ1850	54°50·9'	1°42·8'W	W	88
Stanley Burn	Ghead	NZ1162	54°57·4'	1°49·3'W	W	88
Stanley Carrs	Norf	TM4392	52°28·5'	1°35·1'E	F	134
Stanley Common	Derby	SK4142	52°58·7'	1°23·0'W	T	129
Stanley Common	W Susx	SU8530	51°4·0'	0°46·8'W	F	186
Stanley Crook	Durham	NZ1638	54°44·4'	1°44·7'W	T	92
Stanley Downton	Glos	SO8004	51°44·3'	2°17·0'W	T	162
Stanley Embankment	I of Angl	SH2880	53°17·6'	4°34·4'W	X	114
Stanley Farm	Pth & Kin	NO1034	56°29·6'	3°27·3'W	FM	53
Stanley Ferry	Wakf	SE3523	53°42·4'	1°27·8'W	T	104
Stanley Fm	Lancs	SD4437	53°49·8'	2°50·6'W	FM	102
Stanley Fm	Lancs	SD4505	53°32·6'	2°49·4'W	FM	108
Stanley Fm	Lancs	SD4739	53°50·9'	2°47·9'W	FM	102
Stanley Fm	Lancs	SD5062	54°3·3'	2°45·4'W	FM	97
Stanley Fm	W Susx	SU8629	51°3·5'	0°46·0'W	FM	186,197
Stanley Force	Cumbr	SD1799	54°23·0'	3°16·3'W	W	96
Stanley Gate	Lancs	SD4305	53°32·6'	2°51·2'W	T	108
Stanley Grange	Derby	SK4240	52°57·6'	1°22·1'W	X	129
Stanley Grange	Lancs	SD4534	53°48·2'	2°49·7'W	X	102
Stanley Grange	Lancs	SD6027	53°44·5'	2°36·0'W	X	102,103
Stanley Grange	N Yks	NZ5311	54°29·7'	1°10·5'W	X	93
Stanley Green	Poole	SZ0192	50°43·9'	1°58·8'W	T	195
Stanley Green	Shrops	SJ5235	52°54·9'	2°42·4'W	T	126
Stanley Green	Stock	SJ8584	53°21·4'	2°13·1'W	T	109
Stanley Hall	Ches	SJ9785	53°22·0'	2°2·3'W	X	109
Stanley Hall	Essex	TL8332	51°57·6'	0°40·2'E	X	168
Stanley Hall	Shrops	SO7195	52°33·4'	2°25·3'W	X	138
Stanley Hall Fm	Cambs	TL3588	52°28·6'	0°0·3'W	FM	142
Stanley Head	Staffs	SJ9351	53°3·6'	2°5·9'W	X	118
Stanley Hill	Heref	SO6744	52°5·8'	2°28·5'W	T	149
Stanley Ho	Glos	SO7017	51°51·3'	2°25·7'W	X	162
Stanley Ho	Lancs	SD6429	53°45·6'	2°32·4'W	A	102,103
Stanley House Fm	Lancs	SD3933	53°47·6'	2°55·1'W	FM	102
Stanley House Fm	N Yks	NZ5310	54°29·2'	1°10·5'W	FM	93
Stanley Lodge	Derby	SK1776	53°17·1'	1°44·3'W	X	119
Stanley Lodge	Lancs	SD4534	53°48·2'	2°49·7'W	X	102
Stanley Moor	Derby	SK0471	53°14·4'	1°56·0'W	X	119
Stanley Moor	Derby	SK1776	53°17·1'	1°44·3'W	X	119
Stanley Moor	Staffs	SJ9251	53°3·6'	2°6·8'W	T	118
Stanley Moor Resr	Derby	SK0471	53°14·4'	1°56·0'W	W	119
Stanley Mount	Glos	SP0029	51°57·8'	1°59·6'W	X	150,163
Stanley Park	Blackp	SD3235	53°48·7'	3°1·6'W	X	102
Stanley Pontlarge	Glos	SO9930	51°58·3'	2°0·5'W	T	150
Stanley Pool	Staffs	SJ9351	53°3·6'	2°5·9'W	W	118
Stanleytown	Rho Cyn Taf	ST0194	51°38·4'	3°25·5'W	T	170
Stanley Wood	Durham	NZ1640	54°45·5'	1°44·7'W	F	88
Stanley Wood	Durham	NZ2051	54°51·4'	1°40·9'W	F	88
Stanley Wood	Glos	SO8002	51°43·2'	2°17·0'W	F	162
Stanley Wood	Glos	SP0029	51°57·8'	1°59·6'W	F	150,163
Stanley Wood	Nth Pt Talb	SS7299	51°40·8'	3°50·7'W	F	170
Stanlo Tump	Powys	SO2263	52°15·8'	3°8·2'W	X	137,148
Stanlow	Ches	SJ4375	53°16·4'	2°50·9'W	T	117
Stanlow	Shrops	SO7999	52°35·5'	2°18·2'W	T	138
Stanlow Banks	Ches	SJ4178	53°18·0'	2°52·7'W	X	117
Stanlow Point	Ches	SJ4277	53°17·5'	2°51·8'W	X	117
Stanmer	Bri & Hov	TQ3309	50°52·1'	0°6·2'W	T	198
Stanmer Down	E Susx	TQ3411	50°53·2'	0°5·3'W	X	198
Stanmer Park	Bri & Hov	TQ3409	50°52·1'	0°5·4'W	X	198
Stan Moor	Somer	ST3529	51°3·6'	2°55·3'W	X	193
Stanmoor Br	Somer	ST3530	51°4·2'	2°55·3'W	X	182
Stanmoor Hall	Cambs	TL4548	52°6·9'	0°7·5'E	X	154
Stanmoor Mead	Somer	ST3528	51°3·1'	2°55·3'W	X	193
Stanmore	Hants	SU4628	51°3·2'	1°20·2'W	T	185
Stanmore	Harrow	TQ1691	51°36·6'	0°19·1'W	T	176
Stanmore	Shrops	SO7492	52°31·8'	2°22·6'W	T	138
Stanmore	W Berks	SU4779	51°30·7'	1°19·0'W	T	174
Stanmore Common	Harrow	TQ1593	51°37·7'	0°19·9'W	F	176
Stanmore Copse	Wilts	SU0775	51°28·7'	1°53·6'W	F	173
Stanmore Fm	Shrops	SO7491	52°31·2'	2°22·6'W	FM	138
Stanmore Hall	Harrow	TQ1693	51°37·7'	0°19·1'W	X	176
Stanmore Hill	Lincs	TF3185	53°21·0'	0°1·5'W	X	122
Stanmore Ho	S Lanak	NS8944	55°40·9'	3°45·5'W	X	71,72
Stannage Fm	Ches	SJ4156	53°6·1'	2°52·5'W	FM	117
Stanner	Powys	SO2658	52°13·2'	3°4·6'W	T	148
Stannergate	C of Dun	NO4330	56°27·8'	2°55·1'W	T	54
Stanner Nab	Ches	SJ5357	53°6·7'	2°41·7'W	H	117
Stanner Rocks	Powys	SO2658	52°13·2'	3°4·6'W	X	148
Stannersburn	Northum	NY7286	55°10·3'	2°25·9'W	T	80
Stanners Hill	Surrey	SU9963	51°21·7'	0°34·3'W	T	175,176,186
Stannershill Fm	Surrey	SU9963	51°21·7'	0°34·3'W	FM	175,176,186
Stannery	Staffs	SK0766	53°11·7'	1°53·3'W	X	119
Stanneryhaugh	Aberd	NO6974	56°51·6'	2°30·1'W	X	45
Stannery Knowe	E Ayr	NS4912	55°23·0'	4°22·6'W	H	70
St Annes	Lancs	SD3128	53°44·9'	3°2·4'W	T	102
St Anne's Park	C of Bris	ST6272	51°27·0'	2°32·4'W	T	172
Stannetts	Essex	TQ9391	51°35·3'	0°47·6'E	X	178
Stanneybrook Fm	Ches	SJ5773	53°15·4'	2°38·3'W	FM	117
Stanney Woods Country Park	Ches	SJ3974	53°15·8'	2°54·5'W	X	117
Stanningfield	Suff	TL8756	52°10·4'	0°45·4'E	T	155
Stanninghall Fm	Norf	TG2517	52°42·5'	1°20·2'E	FM	133,134
Stanning Hill	Corn	SX1675	50°33·0'	4°35·5'W	X	201
Stanningley	Leeds	SE2234	53°48·4'	1°39·5'W	T	104
Stannings	E Yorks	SE9362	54°3·0'	0°34·4'W	X	101
Stannington	Northum	NZ2179	55°6·5'	1°39·8'W	T	88
Stannington	Sheff	SK3088	53°23·5'	1°32·5'W	T	110,111
Stannington Bridge	Northum	NZ2178	55°6·0'	1°39·8'W	X	88
Stannington Children's Hospital	Northum	NZ1882	55°8·2'	1°42·6'W	X	81
Stannington Station	Northum	NZ2181	55°7·6'	1°39·8'W	X	81
Stannington Vale	Northum	NZ2278	55°6·0'	1°38·9'W	X	88
Stannochy	Angus	NO5858	56°43·0'	2°40·7'W	X	54
Stannock	D & G	NX4737	54°42·5'	4°22·1'W	X	83
Stannon	Devon	SX6480	50°36·5'	3°54·9'W	X	191
Stannon Tor	Devon	SX6481	50°37·0'	3°55·0'W	H	191
St Ann's	C of Nott	SK5740	52°57·5'	1°8·7'W	T	129
St Anns	Corn	SX4262	50°26·4'	4°13·1'W	X	201
St Ann's	D & G	NY0793	55°13·6'	3°27·3'W	T	78
St Ann's Chapel	Corn	SX4171	50°31·3'	4°14·2'W	T	201
St Ann's Chapel	Devon	SX6647	50°18·7'	3°52·5'W	T	202
St Ann's Cottage	Angus	NO5659	56°43·5'	2°42·7'W	X	54
St Ann's Head	Pemb	SM8002	51°40·7'	5°10·5'W	X	157
St Ann's Heath	Surrey	TQ0068	51°24·4'	0°33·3'W	X	176
St Ann's Hill	Surrey	TQ0267	51°23·8'	0°31·6'W	H	176
St Ann's Manor	Notts	SK5025	52°49·4'	1°15·1'W	X	129
St Ann's Well	Cumbr	NY3559	54°55·5'	3°0·4'W	W	85
St Ann's Well	Worcs	SO7745	52°6·4'	2°19·8'W	A	150
Stanpit	Dorset	SZ1792	50°43·9'	1°45·2'W	T	195
Stanpit Marsh	Bourne	SZ1691	50°43·3'	1°46·0'W	X	195
Stansa na Fèille	N Eil	NF7631	57°15·6'	7°22·0'W	X	22
Stansa na Fèille	N Eil	NF8053	57°27·5'	7°19·7'W	X	22
Stansbatch	Heref	SO3461	52°14·8'	2°57·6'W	T	137,148,149
Stansfield	Suff	TL7852	52°8·5'	0°36·5'E	T	155
Stansfield Hall	Suff	TL7851	52°7·9'	0°36·4'E	X	155
Stansfield Moor	Cald	SD9228	53°45·1'	2°6·9'W	X	103
Stansgate Abbey Fm	Essex	TL9305	51°42·9'	0°48·0'E	FM	168
Stansheil Hill	Scot Bord	NT7813	55°24·9'	2°20·4'W	H	80
Stanshope	Staffs	SK1254	53°5·2'	1°48·8'W	T	119
Stansley Wood	Staffs	SK0524	52°49·0'	1°55·1'W	F	128
Stansmore Hall	Staffs	SJ9643	52°59·3'	2°3·2'W	X	118
Stansore Point	Hants	SZ4698	50°47·0'	1°20·5'W	X	196
Stanstead	Kent	TQ6062	51°20·3'	0°18·2'E	T	177,188
Stanstead	Suff	TL8449	52°6·7'	0°41·6'E	T	155
Stanstead Abbots	Herts	TL3911	51°47·0'	0°1·3'E	T	166
Stanstead Great Wood	Suff	TL8548	52°6·2'	0°42·5'E	F	155
Stanstead Hall	Essex	TL8228	51°55·5'	0°39·2'E	X	168
Stanstead Hall	Suff	TL9853	52°8·6'	0°54·6'E	X	155
Stanstead Ho	Surrey	TQ3548	51°13·1'	0°3·6'W	X	187
Stanstead Lodge	Herts	TL4111	51°47·0'	0°3·0'E	X	167
Stansted Forest	W Susx	SU7411	50°53·9'	0°56·5'W	F	197
Stansted Hall	Essex	TL5224	51°53·9'	0°12·9'E	X	167
Stansted Ho	Essex	TL5225	51°54·4'	0°13·0'E	X	167
Stansted Ho	W Susx	SU7610	50°53·3'	0°54·8'W	X	197
Stansted Mountfitchet	Essex	TL5124	51°53·9'	0°12·1'E	T	167
Stanstill	Highld	ND2760	58°31·6'	3°14·7'W	X	11,12
Stansty Park	Wrex	SJ3152	53°3·9'	3°1·4'W	X	117
Stanswood Bay	Hants	SU4700	50°48·1'	1°19·6'W	W	196
Stanswood Fm	Hants	SU4600	50°48·1'	1°20·4'W	FM	196
Stanterton	Devon	SS9316	50°56·2'	3°31·0'W	X	181
St Anthony	Corn	SW8532	50°9·2'	5°0·2'W	T	204
St Anthony Head	Corn	SW8431	50°8·6'	5°1·0'W	X	204
St Anthony-in-Meneage	Corn	SW7825	50°5·3'	5°5·8'W	T	204
St Anthony's	Cumbr	SD4982	54°14·1'	2°46·5'W	X	97
St Anthony's	N upon Ty	NZ2863	54°57·9'	1°33·3'W	T	88
St Anthony's Cheshire Home	Staffs	SO8894	52°32·9'	2°10·2'W	X	139
St Anthony's-Lewston School	Dorset	ST6312	50°54·6'	2°31·2'W	X	194
St Anthony's Well	Angus	NO3341	56°33·6'	3°5·0'W	X	53
St Anthony's Well	Carm	SN3409	51°45·5'	4°23·9'W	W	159
Stanthorne Hall	Ches	SJ6866	53°11·6'	2°28·3'W	X	118
Stanthorne Lodge	Ches	SJ6866	53°11·6'	2°28·3'W	X	118
Stanthorne Mill	Ches	SJ6966	53°11·7'	2°27·4'W	X	118
Stanthwaite	Cumbr	NY2536	54°43·1'	3°9·4'W	X	89,90
Stantling Burn	Cumbr	NY6079	55°6·5'	2°37·2'W	W	86
Stantling Craig Reservoir	Scot Bord	NT4239	55°38·7'	2°54·9'W	W	73
Stantling Flow	Cumbr	NY5980	55°7·0'	2°38·1'W	X	80
Stanton	Derby	SK2719	52°46·3'	1°35·6'W	X	128
Stanton	Devon	SX7050	50°20·4'	3°49·2'W	X	202
Stanton	Glos	SP0634	52°0·5'	1°54·4'W	T	150
Stanton	Monm	SO3121	51°53·2'	2°59·8'W	T	161
Stanton	Northum	NZ1389	55°12·0'	1°47·3'W	T	81
Stanton	Shrops	SJ7707	52°39·9'	2°20·0'W	X	127
Stanton	Staffs	SK1246	53°0·9'	1°48·9'W	T	119,128
Stanton	Suff	TL9673	52°19·4'	0°53·0'E	T	144,155
Stanton Br	Wilts	SU0961	51°21·1'	1°51·9'W	X	173
Stantonbury	Mil Key	SP8441	52°3·9'	0°46·1'W	T	152
Stantonbury Hill	Bath & NE Somer	ST6763	51°22·1'	2°28·1'W	H	172
Stantonbury Ho	Bath & NE Somer	ST6764	51°22·7'	2°28·1'W	X	172
Stantonbury Park Fm	Mil Key	SP8442	52°4·4'	0°46·1'W	FM	152
Stanton by Bridge	Derby	SK3627	52°50·6'	1°27·5'W	T	128
Stanton-by-Dale	Derby	SK4638	52°56·5'	1°18·5'W	T	129
Stanton Chare	Suff	TL9574	52°20·0'	0°52·1'E	T	144
Stanton Dairy	Wilts	SU0860	51°20·6'	1°52·7'W	X	173
Stanton Dale Fm	Staffs	SK1048	53°2·0'	1°50·6'W	FM	119
Stanton Drew	Bath & NE Somer	ST5963	51°22·1'	2°35·0'W	T	172,182
Stantonfence	Northum	NZ1388	55°11·4'	1°47·3'W	X	81
Stanton Fields	Glos	SP0635	52°1·0'	1°54·4'W	X	150
Stanton Fitzwarren	Swin	SU1790	51°36·7'	1°44·9'W	T	163,173
Stanton Fm	Cambs	TL4863	52°14·9'	0°10·5'E	FM	154
Stanton Ford	Derby	SK2473	53°15·4'	1°38·0'W	X	119
Stanton Gate	Derby	SK4838	52°56·5'	1°16·7'W	T	129
Stanton Great Wood	Oxon	SP5809	51°46·8'	1°9·2'W	F	164
Stanton Hall	Derby	SK2364	53°10·6'	1°38·9'W	A	119
Stanton Hall	Northum	NZ1389	55°12·0'	1°47·3'W	A	81
Stanton Harcourt	Oxon	SP4105	51°44·8'	1°24·0'W	T	164
Stanton Heath	Shrops	SJ5923	52°48·4'	2°36·1'W	X	126
Stanton Hill	Notts	SK4860	53°8·3'	1°16·5'W	T	120
Stantonhill Fm	Shrops	SJ7607	52°39·9'	2°20·9'W	FM	127
Stanton Ho	Derby	SK2619	52°46·3'	1°36·5'W	X	128
Stanton Ho	Northum	NZ1390	55°12·5'	1°47·3'W	X	81
Stanton in Peak	Derby	SK2464	53°10·6'	1°38·0'W	T	119
Stanton Lacy	Shrops	SO4978	52°24·1'	2°44·6'W	T	137,138,148
Stanton Lees	Derby	SK2563	53°10·0'	1°37·2'W	T	119
Stanton Little Wood	Oxon	SP5811	51°47·9'	1°9·1'W	F	164
Stanton Lodge	Leic	SP5093	52°32·2'	1°15·4'W	X	140
Stanton Lodge Fm	Notts	SK6329	52°51·5'	1°3·5'W	FM	129
Stanton Long	Shrops	SO5790	52°30·6'	2°37·6'W	T	137,138
Stanton Moor Plantation	Derby	SK2463	53°10·1'	1°38·1'W	F	119
Stanton-on-the-Wolds	Notts	SK6330	52°52·1'	1°3·4'W	T	129
Stanton Park	Wilts	ST8979	51°30·8'	2°9·1'W	F	173
Stanton Post Mill	Suff	TL9773	52°19·4'	0°53·8'E	X	144,155
Stanton Post Mill	Suff	TL9773	52°19·4'	0°53·8'E	X	144,155
Stanton Prior	Bath & NE Somer	ST6762	51°21·6'	2°28·0'W	T	172
Stanton's Fm	Essex	TL7619	51°50·7'	0°33·7'E	A	167
Stantons Fm	E Susx	TQ3714	50°54·8'	0°2·7'W	FM	198
Stanton's Fm	Hants	SU5159	51°19·9'	1°15·7'W	FM	174

Stantons Fm	Suff	TL9137	52°0·1'	0°47·4'E	FM	155
Stanton's Hall	Surrey	TQ3644	51°11·0'	0°2·9'W	X	187
Stanton St Bernard	Wilts	SU0962	51°21·7'	1°51·9'W	T	173
Stanton St John	Oxon	SP5709	51°46·8'	1°10·0'W	T	164
Stanton St Quintin	Wilts	ST9079	51°30·8'	2°8·3'W	T	173
Stanton Street	Suff	TL9566	52°15·7'	0°51·8'E	T	155
Stanton under Bardon	Leic	SK4610	52°41·4'	1°18·8'W	T	129
Stanton upon Hine Heath	Shrops	SJ5624	52°48·9'	2°38·8'W	T	126
Stanton Wick	Bath & NE Somer	ST6162	51°21·6'	2°33·2'W	T	172
Stanton Wick Fm	Bath & NE Somer	ST6161	51°21·0'	2°33·2'W	FM	172
Stanton Woodhouse	Derby	SK2564	53°10·6'	1°37·1'W	A	119
Stantor Barton	Torbay	SX8863	50°27·6'	3°34·3'W	X	202
Stantway	Glos	SO7213	51°49·1'	2°24·0'W	T	162
Stanwardine Grange	Shrops	SJ4328	52°51·0'	2°50·4'W	X	126
Stanwardine Hall	Shrops	SJ4227	52°50·5'	2°51·3'W	A	126
Stanwardine in the Fields	Shrops	SJ4124	52°48·9'	2°52·1'W	T	126
Stanwardine in the Wood	Shrops	SJ4227	52°50·5'	2°51·3'W	T	126
Stanwardine Park	Shrops	SJ4024	52°48·9'	2°53·0'W	X	126
Stanway	Essex	TL9524	51°53·0'	0°50·4'E	T	168
Stanway	Glos	SP0632	51°59·4'	1°54·4'W	T	150
Stanway	Shrops	SO5391	52°31·1'	2°41·2'W	X	137,138
Stanway Ash Wood	Glos	SP0832	51°59·4'	1°52·6'W	F	150
Stanway Green	Essex	TL9623	51°52·5'	0°51·2'E	T	168
Stanway Green	Suff	TM2470	52°17·2'	1°17·5'E	T	156
Stanway Grounds	Glos	SP0533	52°0·0'	1°55·2'W	X	150
Stanway House	Glos	SP0632	51°59·4'	1°54·4'W	A	150
Stanway Manor	Shrops	SO5291	52°31·1'	2°42·0'W	X	137,138
Stanways	Essex	TL5516	51°49·5'	0°15·3'E	X	167
Stanwell	Surrey	TQ0573	51°27·0'	0°28·9'W	T	176
Stanwell Moor	Surrey	TQ0474	51°27·6'	0°29·8'W	T	176
Stanwell Place	Surrey	TQ0474	51°27·6'	0°29·8'W	X	176
Stanwell Spring	Northnts	SP8769	52°19·0'	0°43·0'W	W	152
Stanwick	Northnts	SP9771	52°19·9'	0°34·2'W	T	141,153
Stanwick Pastures	Northnts	TL0070	52°19·4'	0°31·6'W	F	141,153
Stanwick-St-John	N Yks	NZ1811	54°29·9'	1°42·9'W	X	92
Stanwix	Cumbr	NY3957	54°54·5'	2°56·7'W	T	85
Stanworth Fm	Lancs	SD6424	53°42·9'	2°32·3'W	FM	102,103
Stanyard	Shrops	SJ3131	52°52·6'	3°1·1'W	X	126
Stanyards	Surrey	TQ0062	51°21·1'	0°33·4'W	X	176,186
Stany Ayre	Orkney	HY6035	59°12·3'	2°41·5'W	X	5,6
Stanycliffe	Roch	SD8807	53°33·8'	2°10·5'W	T	109
Stanydale	Shetld	HU2850	60°14·3'	1°29·2'W	T	3
Stany Fields	Shetld	HU2550	60°14·3'	1°32·4'W	X	3
Stanygill Rig	Scot Bord	NY4486	55°10·2'	2°52·3'W	X	79
Stany Hamars	Orkney	ND2399	58°52·6'	3°19·6'W	X	6,7
Stany Hill	Shetld	HU4594	60°37·9'	1°10·1'W	X	1,2
Stany Hog	Shetld	HU5158	60°18·4'	1°4·1'W	X	2,3
Stany Holm	Shetld	HU6689	60°35·0'	0°47·2'W	X	1,2
Stany Knowe	Orkney	HY2214	59°0·6'	3°21·0'W	X	6
Stanypunds	Shetld	HU2743	60°10·5'	1°30·3'W	X	4
Stany Sneulit	Shetld	HU3087	60°34·2'	1°26·7'W	X	1
Stanzaker Hall Fm	Lancs	SD5041	53°52·0'	2°45·2'W	FM	102
Staoineag (Bothy)	Highld	NN2967	56°46·1'	4°47·4'W	X	41
Staoinebrig	N Eil	NF7433	57°16·5'	7°24·1'W	T	22
Staoisha	Arg & Bt	NR4071	55°52·0'	6°8·9'W	X	60,61
Staoisha Eararach	Arg & Bt	NR3972	55°52·5'	6°9·9'W	X	60,61
Staon Bheinn	Arg & Bt	NR5382	55°58·3'	5°57·1'W	H	61
Stape	N Yks	SE7993	54°19·8'	0°46·7'W	T	94,100
Stapehill	Dorset	SU0500	50°48·2'	1°55·4'W	T	195
Stapeley	Ches	SJ6749	53°2·5'	2°29·1'W	T	118
Stapeley	Shrops	SO3198	52°34·8'	3°0·7'W	X	137
Stapeley Fm	Shrops	SO6392	52°31·7'	2°32·3'W	FM	138
Stapeley Hall	Ches	SJ6750	53°3·0'	2°29·1'W	X	118
Stapeley Hill	Shrops	SO3199	52°35·3'	3°0·7'W	X	137
Stapely Down Fm	Hants	SU7448	51°13·8'	0°56·0'W	FM	186
Stapely Fm	Hants	SU7548	51°13·8'	0°55·2'W	FM	186
Stapenhall Fm	Warw	SP3960	52°14·4'	1°25·3'W	FM	151
Stapenhill	Staffs	SK2521	52°47·4'	1°37·4'W	T	128
Stapenhill Fm	Glos	SP1936	52°1·6'	1°43·0'W	FM	151
Staplake Mount	Devon	SX9782	50°38·0'	3°27·0'W	X	192
Staple	Kent	TR2756	51°15·7'	1°15·6'E	T	179
Staple Ash Cottages	Hants	SU7024	51°0·9'	0°59·7'W	X	197
Staple Ash Fm	W Susx	SU8415	50°55·9'	0°47·9'W	FM	197
Staple Common	Somer	ST2615	50°56·0'	3°2·8'W	F	193
Staple Court Fm	Devon	ST0320	50°58·5'	3°22·5'W	FM	181
Staple Cross	Devon	ST0320	50°58·5'	3°22·5'W	T	181
Staplecross	E Susx	TQ7822	50°58·4'	0°32·5'E	T	199
Staple Cross	Hants	SU6109	50°52·9'	1°7·6'W	X	196
Stapledon Fm	Devon	SS3804	50°49·0'	4°17·6'W	FM	190
Staple-edge Wood	Glos	SO6410	51°47·5'	2°30·9'W	F	162
Staplefield	W Susx	TQ2728	51°2·5'	0°10·9'W	T	187,198
Staplefield Place	W Susx	TQ2728	51°2·5'	0°10·9'W	X	187,198
Staplefields	W Susx	TQ1712	50°54·0'	0°19·8'W	X	198
Staple Fitzpaine	Somer	ST2618	50°57·6'	3°2·8'W	T	193
Staple Fm	Glos	SP0114	51°49·7'	1°58·7'W	FM	163
Staple Fm	Kent	TR1539	51°6·8'	1°4·7'E	FM	179,189
Staple Fm	Somer	ST2618	50°57·6'	3°2·8'W	FM	193
Stapleford	Cambs	TL4751	52°8·5'	0°9·3'E	T	154
Stapleford	Devon	SS5703	50°48·8'	4°1·4'W	X	191
Stapleford	Herts	TL3116	51°49·9'	0°5·5'W	T	166
Stapleford	Leic	SK8118	52°45·4'	0°47·6'W	T	130
Stapleford	Lincs	SK8857	53°6·4'	0°40·7'W	T	121
Stapleford	Notts	SK5037	52°55·9'	1°15·0'W	T	129
Stapleford	Wilts	SU0737	51°8·2'	1°53·6'W	T	184
Stapleford Abbotts	Essex	TQ5095	51°38·3'	0°10·5'E	T	167,177
Stapleford Aerodrome	Essex	TQ4997	51°39·3'	0°9·6'E	X	167,177
Stapleford Castle	Wilts	SU0637	51°8·2'	1°54·5'W	X	184
Stapleford Castle (Ring & Bailey)	Wilts	SU0637	51°8·2'	1°54·5'W	A	184
Stapleford Down	Wilts	SU0937	51°8·2'	1°51·9'W	X	184
Stapleford Fm	Hants	SU5115	50°56·2'	1°16·1'W	FM	196
Stapleford Hall	Ches	SJ4964	53°10·5'	2°45·4'W	X	117
Stapleford Hall Fm	Essex	TQ5095	51°38·3'	0°10·5'E	FM	167,177
Stapleford Hill	Notts	SK4938	52°56·5'	1°15·8'W	X	129
Stapleford House	Lincs	SK8756	53°5·9'	0°41·6'W	X	121
Stapleford Lodge	Leic	SK7917	52°44·9'	0°49·4'W	X	129
Stapleford Mill	Bucks	SP8928	51°56·8'	0°41·9'W	X	165

Stapleford Mill Fm	Ches	SJ4864	53°10·5'	2°46·3'W	FM	117
Stapleford Moor	Lincs	SK8655	53°5·4'	0°42·5'W	X	121
Stapleford Park	Leic	SK8118	52°45·4'	0°47·6'W	X	130
Stapleford's Fm	Essex	TL8633	51°58·1'	0°42·9'E	FM	168
Stapleford Tawney	Essex	TQ5099	51°40·4'	0°10·6'E	T	167,177
Stapleford Wood	Lincs	SK8556	53°5·9'	0°43·4'W	F	121
Staplegate Fm	Northnts	SP6141	52°4·1'	1°6·2'W	FM	152
Staplegate Ho	Lincs	SK8690	53°24·2'	0°42·0'W	X	112
Staplegordon	D & G	NY3588	55°11·2'	3°0·8'W	X	79
Staplegrove	Somer	ST2126	51°1·9'	3°7·2'W	T	193
Staplehay	Somer	ST2121	50°59·2'	3°7·1'W	T	193
Staplehill	Devon	SX8273	50°32·9'	3°39·6'W	X	191
Staple Hill	S Glos	ST6576	51°29·1'	2°29·9'W	T	172
Staple Hill	Somer	ST2316	50°56·5'	3°5·4'W	H	193
Staple Hill	Surrey	SU9764	51°22·2'	0°36·0'W	X	175,176,186
Staple Hill	Worcs	SO9773	52°21·5'	2°2·2'W	T	139
Staple Hill	Worcs	SP1050	52°9·1'	1°50·8'W	X	150
Staple Hill Fm	Somer	ST2515	50°56·0'	3°3·7'W	FM	193
Staple Hill Ho	Warw	SP2955	52°11·8'	1°34·1'W	X	151
Staplehurst	Kent	TQ7843	51°9·7'	0°33·1'E	T	188
Staplehurst Fm	Oxon	SP5218	51°51·7'	1°14·3'W	FM	164
Staplehurst Manor	Kent	TQ7842	51°9·2'	0°33·1'E	X	188
Staple Island	Northum	NU2337	55°37·8'	1°37·6'W	X	75
Staple Lawns	Somer	ST2518	50°57·6'	3°3·7'W	T	193
Stapeley Ho	Ches	SJ6750	53°3·0'	2°29·1'W	X	118
Staple Moss	Durham	NY8523	54°36·4'	2°13·5'W	X	91,92
Staple Oak Fell	Lancs	SD6451	53°57·5'	2°32·5'W	X	102,103
Staple Park Fm	Somer	ST2518	50°57·6'	3°3·7'W	FM	193
Staple Park Wood	Somer	ST2417	50°57·1'	3°4·5'W	F	193
Staple Plantation	Somer	ST1141	51°9·9'	3°16·0'W	F	181
Staplers	I of W	SZ5189	50°42·1'	1°16·3'W	T	196
Staplers Fm	I of W	SZ5288	50°41·6'	1°15·4'W	FM	196
Staples Fm	Herts	TL2719	51°51·5'	0°8·9'W	FM	166
Staples Hill	W Susx	TQ0027	51°2·2'	0°34·0'W	T	186,197
Staple Sound	Northum	NU2336	55°37·3'	1°37·7'W	W	75
Staplestreet	Kent	TR0560	51°18·4'	0°56·9'E	T	179
Stapleton	C of Bris	ST6175	51°28·6'	2°33·3'W	T	172
Stapleton	Corn	SX2495	50°43·9'	4°29·3'W	X	190
Stapleton	Cumbr	NY5071	55°2·1'	2°46·5'W	T	86
Stapleton	Heref	SO3265	52°17·0'	2°59·4'W	T	137,148
Stapleton	Leic	SP4398	52°34·9'	1°21·5'W	T	140
Stapleton	N Yks	NZ2612	54°30·4'	1°35·5'W	T	93
Stapleton	N Yks	SE5119	53°40·1'	1°13·3'W	T	111
Stapleton	Shrops	SJ4604	52°38·1'	2°47·5'W	T	126
Stapleton	Somer	ST4621	50°59·4'	2°45·8'W	T	193
Stapleton Brockey	Leic	SP4399	52°35·5'	1°21·5'W	X	140
Stapleton Fm	Devon	SS4513	50°54·0'	4°11·9'W	FM	180,190
Stapleton Fm	Devon	SS5543	51°10·3'	4°4·1'W	FM	180
Stapleton Fm	Hants	SU0815	50°56·3'	1°52·8'W	FM	184
Stapleton Grange	D & G	NY2268	55°0·3'	3°12·7'W	X	85
Stapleton Grange	N Yks	NZ2611	54°29·9'	1°35·5'W	X	93
Stapleton Hill	Heref	SO3366	52°17·5'	2°58·5'W	X	137,148,149
Stapleton Manor	N Yks	NZ2611	54°29·9'	1°35·5'W	X	93
Stapleton Mead Fm	Somer	ST4422	50°59·9'	2°47·5'W	FM	193
Stapleton Park	N Yks	SE5018	53°39·6'	1°14·2'W	X	111
Stapleton Tower	D & G	NY2368	55°0·3'	3°11·8'W	A	85
Staple Tors	Devon	SX5475	50°33·6'	4°3·3'W	X	191,201
Staplewood Hill	Hants	SU3709	50°53·0'	1°28·1'W	X	196
Stapley	Somer	ST1813	50°54·9'	3°9·6'W	T	181,193
Stapley Cross	Somer	ST1914	50°55·4'	3°8·8'W	X	181,193
Staploe	Beds	TL1460	52°13·8'	0°19·4'W	T	153
Staplow	Heref	SO6941	52°4·2'	2°26·7'W	T	149
Stapnall's Fm	Oxon	SU6280	51°31·2'	1°6·0'W	FM	175
Stapness	Shetld	HU2348	60°13·2'	1°34·6'W	X	3
Star	Fife	NO3103	56°13·1'	3°6·3'W	T	59
Star	I of Angl	SH5072	53°13·7'	4°14·4'W	X	114
Star	I of Angl	SH5172	53°13·7'	4°13·5'W	X	114,115
Star	Pemb	SN2434	51°58·8'	4°33·4'W	T	145
Star	Somer	ST4358	51°19·3'	2°48·7'W	T	172,182
Stara	Orkney	HY2424	59°6·0'	3°19·1'W	X	6
Star and Garter	E Renf	NS5253	55°45·1'	4°21·1'W	X	64
Starapark	Corn	SX1386	50°38·9'	4°38·3'W	X	200
Starbank	Lancs	SD5254	53°59·0'	2°43·5'W	X	102
Star Barton	Devon	SX8895	50°44·9'	3°34·9'W	X	192
Starbeck	N Yks	SE3256	54°0·2'	1°30·3'W	T	104
Starbirns	S Lanak	NS7740	55°38·5'	3°56·8'W	X	71
Starbold Fm	Warw	SP4160	52°14·4'	1°23·6'W	FM	151
Starborough Castle	Surrey	TQ4244	51°10·9'	0°2·3'E	X	187
Starborough Fm	Surrey	TQ4144	51°10·9'	0°1·4'E	FM	187
Starbotton	N Yks	SD9574	54°10·0'	2°4·2'W	T	98
Starbotton Fell	N Yks	SD9677	54°11·6'	2°3·3'W	X	98
Starbotton Out Moor	N Yks	SD9676	54°11·0'	2°3·3'W	X	98
Star Burn	S Lanak	NS9230	55°33·4'	3°42·3'W	W	71,72
Star Carr	N Lincs	SE7401	53°30·3'	0°52·6'W	X	112
Star Carr Fm	N Yks	TA0281	54°13·1'	0°25·7'W	FM	101
Star Castle	I Scilly	SV8910	49°54·8'	6°19·6'W	A	203
Starcleuch Edge	Scot Bord	NT4800	55°17·7'	2°48·7'W	H	79
Star Cliff	Pemb	SS1296	51°38·1'	4°42·6'W	X	158
Starcombe	Devon	SY1594	50°44·6'	3°11·9'W	X	192,193
Star Cottage Stables	N Yks	SE7870	54°7·4'	0°48·0'W	X	100
Starcross	Devon	SX9781	50°37·4'	3°27·0'W	T	192
Stardens	Glos	SO7226	51°56·1'	2°24·0'W	X	162
Stare Bridge	Warw	SP3371	52°20·4'	1°30·5'W	A	140
Stare Dam	Pth & Kin	NO0438	56°31·7'	3°33·2'W	W	52,53
Staredam	Pth & Kin	NO0538	56°31·7'	3°32·2'W	X	52,53
Starehole Bay	Devon	SX7236	50°12·8'	3°47·3'W	W	202
Stareton	Warw	SP3371	52°20·4'	1°30·5'W	T	140
Star Fen	Lincs	TF1545	52°59·6'	0°16·8'W	X	130
Starfitt Fm	N Yks	SE6885	54°15·6'	0°56·9'W	FM	94,100
Star Fm	Glos	ST8996	51°40·0'	2°9·2'W	FM	163
Star Fm	Lincs	TF3552	53°3·1'	0°1·3'E	FM	122
Star Fm	S Glos	ST7973	51°27·6'	2°17·7'W	FM	172
Star & Garter Home	Rich	TQ1873	51°26·8'	0°17·7'W	X	176
Stargate	Ghead	NZ1663	54°57·9'	1°44·7'W	T	88
Stargate Fm	Suff	TL6678	52°22·7'	0°26·7'E	FM	143
Stargill	Cumbr	NY0426	54°37·5'	3°28·8'W	X	89
Stargrove	Hants	SU4161	51°21·0'	1°24·3'W	X	174
Star Hall	Lancs	SD8643	53°53·2'	2°12·4'W	X	103
Star Hill	Monm	SO4702	51°43·1'	2°45·6'W	T	171
Starhill	Moray	NJ4755	57°35·2'	2°52·7'W	X	28,29

Star Hill Plantation	Hants	SU7858	51°19·2'	0°52·5'W	F	175,186
Star Ho	Essex	TL6306	51°44·0'	0°22·0'E	X	167
Star Ho	Kent	TQ4958	51°18·3'	0°8·6'E	X	188
Starhouse Fm	Suff	TM0870	52°17·5'	1°3·4'E	FM	144,155
St Arild's Ho	S Glos	ST6190	51°36·7'	2°33·4'W	X	162,172
Starilie	Orkney	ND4694	58°50·1'	2°55·6'W	X	7
Star Inn Fm	Angus	NO3330	56°27·7'	3°4·8'W	FM	53
Starkeys	Kent	TQ7165	51°21·7'	0°27·8'E	A	178
Starkholmes	Derby	SK3058	53°7·3'	1°32·7'W	T	119
Starkie Ho	Ches	SJ9281	53°19·8'	2°6·8'W	X	109
Starlaw	W Loth	NT0067	55°53·4'	3°35·5'W	X	65
Starling	Bury	SD7710	53°35·4'	2°20·4'W	T	109
Starling Ayre	Orkney	HY5738	59°13·9'	2°44·7'W	X	5
Starling Brook	Lancs	SD6736	53°49·4'	2°29·7'W	W	103
Starling Castle	Cumbr	NY0104	54°25·6'	3°31·1'W	X	89
Starling Dodd	Cumbr	NY1415	54°31·6'	3°19·3'W	H	89
Starling Hill	Orkney	HY3422	59°5·1'	3°8·6'W	X	6
Starlings Castle	Wrex	SJ2436	52°55·2'	3°7·4'W	X	126
Starling's Green	Essex	TL4531	51°57·7'	0°7·0'E	T	167
Starlings' Hill	Norf	TG0734	52°52·0'	1°4·9'E	X	133
Starlock Hay Fen Common	Cambs	TL5173	52°20·3'	0°13·4'E	X	154
Starmoor Wood	Norf	TF9328	52°49·1'	0°52·3'E	F	132
Star Moss	Fife	NO3004	56°13·7'	3°7·3'W	X	59
Starnafin	Aberd	NK0558	57°37·0'	1°54·5'W	X	30
Starnash	E Susx	TQ5510	50°52·3'	0°12·6'E	X	199
Starney Bay	Scot Bord	NT9167	55°54·0'	2°8·2'W	W	67
Starnhill Fm	Notts	SK7238	52°56·3'	0°55·3'W	FM	129
Starn Loch	D & G	NX8598	55°16·0'	3°48·2'W	W	78
Starnmire	Cumbr	NY3540	54°45·3'	3°0·2'W	X	85
St. Arnolds Seat	Angus	NO4363	56°45·6'	2°55·5'W	H	44
Starns Water	Shetld	HU4966	60°22·8'	1°6·2'W	W	2,3
Starnthwaite Ghyll	Cumbr	SD4392	54°19·5'	2°52·2'W	X	97
Starpet Rig	E Ayr	NS7131	55°33·6'	4°2·3'W	H	71
Starr	E Ayr	NX4893	55°12·7'	4°22·9'W	X	77
Starra Fiold	Orkney	HY3523	59°5·6'	3°7·6'W	X	6
Starragro	N Eil	NB3848	58°20·8'	6°28·2'W	W	8
Starraton	Devon	SS8714	50°55·1'	3°36·1'W	X	181
Starrbank Ho	Fife	NO3320	56°22·3'	3°4·6'W	X	53,59
Starr Carr Ho	E Yorks	TA1146	53°54·1'	0°18·2'W	X	107
Starr Fm	N Yks	SE0042	53°52·7'	1°59·6'W	FM	104
Starr Hills	Lancs	SD3130	53°46·0'	3°2·4'W	X	102
Starricks Fm	Lancs	SD5473	54°9·3'	2°41·8'W	FM	97
Starrie Geo	Orkney	HY6134	59°11·7'	2°40·5'W	X	5
Star Rock	Pemb	SR9793	51°36·2'	4°55·5'W	X	158
Starrock Wood	Surrey	TQ2857	51°18·1'	0°9·4'W	F	187
Starr's Green	E Susx	TQ7515	50°54·7'	0°29·8'E	T	199
Starr, The	Fife	NO3420	56°22·3'	3°3·7'W	X	54,59
Starry Geo	Orkney	HY4147	59°18·6'	3°1·7'W	X	5
Starry Geo	Orkney	HY5237	59°13·3'	2°50·0'W	X	5
Starryheugh Fm	D & G	NX9575	55°3·8'	3°38·2'W	FM	84
Starry Hill	Cumbr	NY1555	54°53·2'	3°19·1'W	X	85
Starryshaw Fm	N Lanak	NS8960	55°49·5'	3°45·9'W	FM	65
Stars Coppice	Shrops	SO5090	52°30·6'	2°43·8'W	F	137,138
Starsland Fm	Somer	ST3029	51°3·6'	2°59·5'W	FM	193
Stars of Forneth	Pth & Kin	NO1045	56°35·6'	3°27·5'W	X	53
Star Stile	Essex	TL8231	51°57·1'	0°39·3'E	X	168
Starston	Norf	TM2384	52°24·7'	1°17·1'E	T	156
Starston Hall	Norf	TM2386	52°25·8'	1°17·2'E	X	156
Start	Corn	SW5436	50°10·6'	5°26·4'W	X	203
Start	Devon	SX8044	50°17·3'	3°40·7'W	T	202
Start Bay	Devon	SX8442	50°16·2'	3°37·3'W	W	202
Start Fm	Devon	SX8137	50°13·5'	3°39·7'W	FM	202
Start Fm	Essex	TL5208	51°45·3'	0°12·5'E	FM	167
Startforth	Durham	NZ0416	54°32·6'	1°55·9'W	T	92
Startforth Grange	Durham	NZ0315	54°32·1'	1°56·8'W	X	92
Starth Hill Fm	Cumbr	NY4036	54°43·2'	2°55·5'W	FM	90
Start Hill	Essex	TL5221	51°52·2'	0°12·9'E	T	167
Startifants	Lancs	SD6242	53°52·6'	2°34·3'W	X	102,103
Startley	Wilts	ST9482	51°32·4'	2°4·8'W	T	173
Startoes	Cumbr	NY0220	54°34·2'	3°30·5'W	X	89
Starton	Clackm	NS9592	56°6·8'	3°40·9'W	X	58
Starton Beck	N Yks	SE0160	54°2·4'	1°58·7'W	W	98
Startop's End	Bucks	SP9214	51°49·3'	0°39·5'W	T	165
Start Point	Corn	SX0485	50°38·1'	4°45·9'W	X	200
Start Point	Devon	SX8337	50°13·5'	3°38·0'W	X	202
Start Point	Orkney	HY7843	59°16·6'	2°22·7'W	X	5
Start's Green Fm	Worcs	SO8083	52°26·9'	2°17·3'W	FM	138
Startup	Northum	NZ1678	55°6·0'	1°44·5'W	X	88
Startup Hill	S Lanak	NS9729	55°32·9'	3°37·5'W	H	72
Starvall	Glos	SP1416	51°50·8'	1°47·4'W	X	163
St Arvans	Monm	ST5196	51°39·9'	2°42·1'W	T	162
Starve Acre	Hants	SU8458	51°19·1'	0°47·3'W	X	175,186
Starveall	Bucks	SP7612	51°48·3'	0°53·5'W	X	165
Starveall	S Glos	ST7987	51°35·1'	2°17·8'W	T	172
Starveall	W Berks	SU5480	51°31·2'	1°12·9'W	X	174
Starveall	Wilts	ST9939	51°9·2'	2°0·5'W	X	184
Starveall Fm	Oxon	SU5783	51°32·8'	1°10·3'W	FM	174
Starveall Fm	Swin	SU2682	51°32·4'	1°37·1'W	FM	174
Starveall Fm	W Berks	SU4582	51°32·3'	1°20·7'W	FM	174
Starveall Fm	Wilts	ST8773	51°27·6'	2°10·8'W	FM	173
Starveall Fm	Wilts	SU2961	51°21·1'	1°34·6'W	FM	174
Starvecrow	Kent	TQ5949	51°13·3'	0°17·0'E	T	188
Starvecrow	Shrops	SO5981	52°25·8'	2°35·8'W	X	137,138
Star Wood	E Loth	NT5968	55°54·5'	2°38·9'W	F	67
Star Wood	Glos	SP0514	51°49·7'	1°55·3'W	F	163
Star Wood	Staffs	SK0545	53°0·4'	1°55·1'W	F	119,128
St Asaph or Llanelwy	Denb	SJ0374	53°15·5'	3°26·8'W	T	116
Statenborough	Kent	TR3155	51°15·1'	1°19·0'E	T	179
State Rock	N Eil	NF9875	57°40·1'	7°3·4'W	X	18
Statfold Barn Fm	Staffs	SK2406	52°39·3'	1°38·3'W	FM	139
Statfold Fm	Staffs	SK2307	52°39·9'	1°39·2'W	FM	139
Statfold Hall	Staffs	SK2307	52°39·9'	1°39·2'W	X	139
Statfold St Andrew	Suff	TM3560	52°11·5'	1°26·7'E	T	156
Statham	Warr	SJ6787	53°23·0'	2°29·4'W	T	109
St Athan	V of Glam	ST0167	51°23·8'	3°25·0'W	T	170
Stàthanis	N Eil	NB5266	58°31·0'	6°15·0'W	X	8
Stathe	Somer	ST3728	51°3·1'	2°53·5'W	T	193
Stathe Court	Somer	ST3628	51°3·1'	2°54·4'W	X	193
Stathern	Leic	SK7731	52°52·5'	0°51·0'W	T	129
Stathern Lodge	Leic	SK7532	52°53·0'	0°52·7'W	X	129

Stathern Wood	Leic	SK7831	52°52·5'	0°50·1'W	F	129
Station Fm	E Yorks	SE9359	54°1·4'	0°34·4'W	FM	106
Station Fm	E Yorks	TA0558	54°0·7'	0°23·4'W	FM	107
Station Fm	Leic	SP5392	52°31·6'	1°12·7'W	FM	140
Station Fm	Leic	SP6284	52°27·3'	1°4·9'W	FM	140
Station Fm	Lincs	TF3650	53°2·0'	0°2·1'E	FM	122
Station Fm	N Lincs	SE9703	53°31·1'	0°31·8'W	FM	112
Station Fm	N Lincs	TA1421	53°40·6'	0°16·0'W	FM	107,113
Station Fm	Norf	TG0603	52°35·4'	1°2·9'E	FM	144
Station Fm	Norf	TL5996	52°32·5'	0°21·1'E	FM	143
Station Fm	Northnts	SP8254	52°10·9'	0°47·6'W	FM	152
Station Fm	Notts	SK7435	52°54·7'	0°53·6'W	FM	129
Station Fm	N Yks	NZ3103	54°25·5'	1°30·9'W	FM	93
Station Fm	N Yks	NZ5807	54°27·5'	1°5·9'W	FM	93
Station Fm	N Yks	SE3788	54°17·4'	1°25·5'W	FM	99
Station Fm	N Yks	SE5067	54°6·0'	1°13·7'W	FM	100
Station Hill	Cumbr	NY2549	54°50·1'	3°9·6'W	T	85
Station Town	Durham	NZ4036	54°43·3'	1°22·3'W	T	93
Station Whin	N Yks	SE4082	54°14·2'	1°22·8'W	F	99
Station Yard	Lincs	TF2481	53°18·9'	0°7·9'W	X	122
Statland Common	Norf	TM0298	52°32·8'	0°59·2'E	T	144
Stattic Point	Highld	NG9796	57°54·7'	5°25·1'W	X	19
Statts Ho (ruin)	Devon	SX6282	50°37·5'	3°56·7'W	X	191
St Audrie's Bay	Somer	ST1043	51°11·0'	3°16·9'W	W	181
St Audrie's School	Somer	ST1142	51°10·5'	3°16·0'W	X	181
Staughton Green	Cambs	TL1365	52°16·5'	0°20·2'W	T	153
Staughton Highway	Cambs	TL1364	52°16·0'	0°20·2'W	T	153
Staughton Manor	Cambs	TL1264	52°16·0'	0°21·1'W	X	153
Staughton Moor	Beds	TL1361	52°14·4'	0°20·3'W	T	153
St Augustine Fm	Glos	SP0500	51°42·2'	1°55·3'W	FM	163
St Augustine's Well	Kent	TR3463	51°19·3'	1°21·9'E	A	179
Staunch Fm	Essex	TL9132	51°57·4'	0°47·2'E	FM	168
Staunch Hill Fm	Cambs	TL1074	52°21·4'	0°22·7'W	FM	142
Staunchley Hill	Scot Bord	NT5146	55°42·6'	2°46·4'W	H	73
Staunton	Glos	SO5512	51°48·5'	2°38·8'W	T	162
Staunton	Glos	SO7829	51°57·8'	2°18·8'W	T	150
Staunton Court	Glos	SO7829	51°57·8'	2°18·8'W	X	150
Staunton Grange	Notts	SK7945	53°0·0'	0°49·0'W	X	129
Staunton Green	Heref	SO3661	52°14·8'	2°55·9'W	X	137,148,149
Staunton Hall	Notts	SK8043	52°58·9'	0°48·1'W	A	130
Staunton Harold Hall	Leic	SK3720	52°46·8'	1°26·7'W	A	128
Staunton Harold Resr	Derby	SK3723	52°48·4'	1°26·7'W	W	128
Staunton in the Vale	Notts	SK8043	52°58·9'	0°48·1'W	T	130
Staunton on Arrow	Heref	SO3660	52°14·3'	2°55·8'W	T	137,148,149
Staunton on Wye	Heref	SO3645	52°6·2'	2°55·7'W	T	148,149
Staunton Park	Heref	SO3661	52°14·8'	2°55·9'W	X	137,148,149
Staunton Plantation	Somer	SS9644	51°11·4'	3°28·9'W	F	181
Staupes	N Yks	SE2257	54°0·8'	1°39·4'W	T	104
Staups Moor	Cald	SD9526	53°44·1'	2°4·1'W	X	103
St Austell	Corn	SX0252	50°20·3'	4°46·6'W	T	200,204
St Austell Bay	Corn	SX0650	50°19·3'	4°43·2'W	W	200,204
St Austins	Hants	SZ3197	50°46·5'	1°33·2'W	T	196
St Austin's Priory	Devon	SX6156	50°23·5'	3°57·0'W	X	202
St Austin's Stone	E Yorks	SE9334	53°47·9'	0°34·9'W	X	106
Stauvin	Lancs	SD6164	54°4·5'	2°35·3'W	X	97
Stava Geo	Shetld	HU4538	60°7·7'	1°10·9'W	X	4
Stava Ness	Shetld	HU5060	60°19·5'	1°5·2'W	X	2,3
Stave Hall Fm	Warw	SP4483	52°26·8'	1°20·8'W	FM	140
Staveley	Cumbr	SD4698	54°22·7'	2°49·5'W	T	97
Staveley	Derby	SK4374	53°15·9'	1°20·9'W	T	120
Staveley	N Yks	SE3662	54°3·4'	1°26·6'W	T	99
Staveley Head Fell	Cumbr	NY4701	54°24·3'	2°48·6'W	X	90
Staveley-in-Cartmel	Cumbr	SD3786	54°16·2'	2°57·6'W	T	96,97
Staveley Park	Cumbr	SD4798	54°22·7'	2°48·5'W	X	97
Staveley Wold	E Yorks	SE9150	53°56·5'	0°36·4'W	X	106
Stavers Geo	Shetld	HU6588	60°34·5'	0°48·3'W	X	1,2
Staverton	Devon	SX7964	50°28·0'	3°41·9'W	T	202
Staverton	Glos	SO8923	51°54·6'	2°9·2'W	T	163
Staverton	Northnts	SP5361	52°14·9'	1°13·0'W	T	152
Staverton	Wilts	ST8560	51°20·6'	2°12·5'W	T	173
Staverton Br	Devon	SX7863	50°27·5'	3°42·7'W	A	202
Staverton Bridge	Glos	SO8922	51°54·0'	2°9·2'W	X	163
Staverton Lodge	Northnts	SP5359	52°13·8'	1°13·0'W	X	152
Staverton Park	Suff	TM3550	52°6·1'	1°26·3'E	F	156
Stavordale Priory	Somer	ST7332	51°5·4'	2°22·7'W	A	183
Staward Manor	Northum	NY8160	54°56·3'	2°17·4'W	X	86,87
Staward Peel	Northum	NY7960	54°56·3'	2°19·2'W	A	86,87
Stawberry Hall	Suff	TM0750	52°6·8'	1°1·8'E	X	155
Stawell	Somer	ST3638	51°8·5'	2°54·5'W	T	182
Stawley	Somer	ST0622	50°59·6'	3°20·0'W	T	181
Stawley Wood Fm	Somer	ST0623	51°0·2'	3°20·0'W	FM	181
Staxigoe	Highld	ND3852	58°27·4'	3°3·3'W	T	12
Staxton	N Yks	TA0179	54°12·0'	0°26·7'W	T	101
Staxton Brow	N Yks	TA0178	54°11·5'	0°26·7'W	F	101
Staxton Wold	N Yks	TA0277	54°11·0'	0°25·8'W	X	101
Staye	Orkney	HY5605	58°56·1'	2°45·4'W	X	6
Stay Fm	N Yks	SE4791	54°19·0'	1°16·2'W	FM	100
Staylee	N Lanak	NS7771	55°55·2'	3°57·7'W	X	64
Staylittle	Cered	SN6489	52°29·2'	3°59·8'W	T	135
Staylittle	Powys	SN8892	52°31·1'	3°38·6'W	T	135,136
St Aylotts	Essex	TL5639	52°1·9'	0°16·8'E	A	154
Staynall	Lancs	SD3643	53°53·0'	2°58·0'W	T	102
Stayner Hall	N Yks	SE6231	53°46·5'	1°3·1'W	X	105
Staythorpe	Notts	SK7553	53°4·4'	0°52·4'W	T	120
St Baldred's Boat	E Loth	NT6185	56°3·6'	2°37·1'W	X	67
St Baldred's Cradle	E Loth	NT6381	56°1·5'	2°35·2'W	X	67
St Bathan's Ho	Scot Bord	NT7661	55°50·7'	2°22·6'W	X	67
St Bees	Cumbr	NX9711	54°29·3'	3°35·0'W	T	89
St Bees Head	Cumbr	NX9413	54°30·3'	3°37·8'W	X	89
St Bellarmin's Tor	Corn	SX1370	50°30·2'	4°37·9'W	X	200
St Benet's Abbey	Norf	TG3815	52°41·0'	1°31·7'E	A	133,134
St Bennet's Well	Highld	NH7965	57°39·8'	4°1·2'W	A	21,27
St Bertram's Well	Staffs	SK1351	53°3·6'	1°48·0'W	A	119
St Beuno's	Denb	SJ0874	53°15·5'	3°22·3'W	X	116
St Blane's Church	Arg & Bt	NS0953	55°44·2'	5°2·5'W	A	63
St Blane's Hill	Arg & Bt	NS0952	55°43·7'	5°2·1'W	H	63,69
St Blazey	Corn	SX0654	50°21·5'	4°43·3'W	T	200
St Blazey Gate	Corn	SX0653	50°20·9'	4°43·2'W	T	200,204
St Boniface Down	I of W	SZ5678	50°36·2'	1°12·1'W	X	196
St Boswells	Scot Bord	NT5930	55°34·0'	2°38·6'W	T	73,74
St Botolphs	Pemb	SM8907	51°43·6'	5°2·9'W	X	157,158
St Botolph's Brook	Essex	TL9626	51°54·1'	0°51·3'E	W	168
St Brandan's Stanes	Aberd	NJ6061	57°38·5'	2°39·7'W	A	29
St Brannocks	Devon	SS4837	51°7·0'	4°9·9'W	X	180
St Brelades	Cumbr	NY4354	54°52·9'	2°52·9'W	X	85
St Breock	Corn	SW9771	50°30·5'	4°51·4'W	T	200
St Breock Downs	Corn	SW9668	50°28·8'	4°52·2'W	X	200
St Breock Downs Fm	Corn	SW9868	50°28·9'	4°50·5'W	FM	200
St Breward	Corn	SX0976	50°33·4'	4°41·4'W	T	200
St Briavels	Glos	SO5604	51°44·2'	2°37·8'W	T	162
St Briavels Common	Glos	SO5402	51°43·1'	2°39·6'W	T	162
St Brides	Derby	SK3625	52°49·5'	1°27·5'W	X	128
St Brides	Pemb	SM7910	51°44·9'	5°11·7'W	T	157
St Brides Bay	Pemb	SM7917	51°48·7'	5°12·0'W	W	157
St Bride's Chapel	Stir	NN5809	56°15·4'	4°17·1'W	A	57
St Brides Fm	Hants	SU0720	50°59·0'	1°53·6'W	FM	184
St Brides Haven	Pemb	SM8011	51°45·5'	5°10·9'W	W	157
St Bride's Hill	D & G	NY3182	55°7·9'	3°4·5'W	H	79
St Brides Major	V of Glam	SS8974	51°27·5'	3°35·5'W	T	170
St Bride's Netherwent	Monm	ST4389	51°36·1'	2°49·0'W	X	172
St Bride's Ring	Angus	NO4735	56°30·5'	2°51·2'W	X	54
St Bride's Ring (Dun)	Angus	NO4735	56°30·5'	2°51·2'W	A	54
St Bride's-super-Ely	V of Glam	ST0977	51°29·3'	3°18·3'W	T	171
St Brides Wentlooge	Newp	ST2982	51°32·2'	3°1·0'W	T	171
St Bridget	Moray	NJ1618	57°15·0'	3°23·1'W	X	36
St Brigids Sch	Denb	SJ0667	53°11·8'	3°24·0'W	X	116
St Brydes	Renf	NS3860	55°48·6'	4°34·7'W	X	63
St Budeaux	C of Plym	SX4458	50°24·3'	4°11·3'W	T	201
St Buryan	Corn	SW4025	50°4·3'	5°37·7'W	T	203
St Cadix	Corn	SX1353	50°21·1'	4°37·3'W	X	200
St Cadoc Fm	Corn	SW8875	50°32·4'	4°59·1'W	FM	200
St Cadoc's Point	Corn	SW8775	50°32·4'	5°0·0'W	X	200
St Canna's Chair	Carm	SN1718	51°50·1'	4°39·0'W	A	158
St Cassian's	W Berks	SU3665	51°23·2'	1°28·6'W	X	174
St Catharine's Dub	Aberd	NK0428	57°20·8'	1°55·6'W	X	38
St Catherine	Bath & NE Somer	ST7770	51°25·9'	2°19·5'W	T	172
St Catherines	Arg & Bt	NN1207	56°13·4'	5°1·5'W	T	56
St Catherine's	Cumbr	SD4099	54°23·2'	2°55·0'W	X	96,97
St Catherines	Orkney	HY6325	59°6·9'	2°38·3'W	X	5
St Catherines	York	SE5756	54°0·1'	1°7·4'W	X	105
St Catherine's Bay	Orkney	HY6326	59°7·4'	2°38·3'W	W	5
St Catherine's Chapel	Dorset	ST8002	50°49·3'	2°16·7'W	A	194
St Catherines Chapel	Dorset	SY5784	50°39·5'	2°36·1'W	A	194
St Catherine's Court	Bath & NE Somer	ST7770	51°25·9'	2°19·5'W	A	172
St Catherine's Cross	Norf	TF7537	52°54·3'	0°36·5'E	X	132
St Catherine's Down	I of W	SZ4978	50°36·2'	1°18·1'W	X	196
St Catherines End Ho	Bath & NE Somer	ST7671	51°26·5'	2°20·3'W	X	172
St Catherine's Fm	Lincs	TF4158	53°6·3'	0°6·8'E	FM	122
St Catherines Fm	Worcs	SO9440	52°3·7'	2°4·9'W	FM	150
St Catherine's Hill	Dorset	SZ1495	50°45·5'	1°47·7'W	T	195
St Catherine's Hill	Hants	SU4827	51°2·6'	1°18·5'W	H	185
St Catherine's Hill	I of W	SZ4977	50°35·7'	1°18·1'W	H	196
St Catherine's Island	Pemb	SN1300	51°40·3'	4°41·9'W	X	158
St Catherine's Oratory	I of W	SZ4977	50°35·7'	1°18·1'W	A	196
St Catherine's Point	I of W	SZ4975	50°34·6'	1°18·1'W	X	196
St Catherine's Tor	Devon	SS2224	50°59·6'	4°31·8'W	X	190
St Catherine's Well	Donc	SK5699	53°29·3'	1°8·9'W	W	111
St Catherine's Well	Worcs	SO9540	52°3·7'	2°4·0'W	A	150
St Catherine's Wells	Aberd	NJ8558	57°37·0'	2°14·6'W	X	30
St Chad's Well	Norf	TL9383	52°24·9'	0°50·7'E	A	144
St Cherries	Devon	SX7095	50°44·6'	3°50·2'W	X	191
St Chloe	Glos	SO8401	51°42·7'	2°13·5'W	T	162
St Christopher's Well	Lincs	SK8632	52°52·9'	0°42·9'W	A	130
St Clair's Fm	Hants	SU5721	50°59·4'	1°10·9'W	FM	185
St Clair's Fm	Hants	SU6015	50°56·1'	1°8·4'W	FM	196
St Clears	Carm	SN2716	51°49·2'	4°30·2'W	T	158
St Cleer	Corn	SX2468	50°29·4'	4°28·5'W	T	201
St Cleer's Well	Corn	SX2568	50°29·4'	4°27·7'W	A	201
St Clement	Corn	SW8543	50°15·1'	5°0·6'W	T	204
St Clements Ch	N Eil	NG0483	57°44·6'	6°58·0'W	A	18
St Clement's Isle	Corn	SW4726	50°5·1'	5°31·8'W	X	203
St Clement's or Fiddler's Reach	Thurr	TQ5976	51°27·9'	0°17·7'E	W	177
St Clement's Wells	E Loth	NT3771	55°55·9'	3°0·1'W	X	66
St Clement Woods	Corn	SW8248	50°17·7'	5°3·3'W	F	204
St Clere	Kent	TQ5759	51°18·7'	0°15·6'E	X	188
St Clere's Hall	Essex	TL7605	51°43·2'	0°33·3'E	X	167
St Clere's Hall	Essex	TM1214	51°47·3'	1°4·8'E	A	168,169
St Cleres Hall	Thurr	TQ6781	51°30·4'	0°24·8'E	X	177,178
St Clether	Corn	SX2084	50°37·9'	4°32·3'W	T	201
St Cloud	Aberd	NJ6730	57°21·8'	2°32·5'W	X	29
St Cloud	Worcs	SO8348	52°8·0'	2°14·5'W	X	150
St Colmac	Arg & Bt	NS0467	55°51·6'	5°7·5'W	T	63
St Colmac Burn	Arg & Bt	NS0466	55°51·1'	5°7·4'W	W	63
St Colme Ho	Fife	NT1884	56°2·8'	3°18·5'W	X	65,66
St Colm's Abbey	Fife	NT1882	56°1·7'	3°18·5'W	A	65,66
St Colm's Well	Aberd	NJ6660	57°38·0'	2°33·7'W	A	29
St Colm's Well	Aberd	NO4988	56°59·1'	2°49·9'W	W	44
St Columba's Cave	Arg & Bt	NR7576	55°55·7'	5°35·7'W	X	62
St Columba's Well	D & G	NW9872	55°0·3'	5°9·1'W	A	76,82
St Columb Major	Corn	SW9163	50°26·0'	4°56·2'W	T	200
St Columb Minor	Corn	SW8462	50°25·3'	5°2·1'W	T	200
St Columb Road	Corn	SW9159	50°23·9'	4°56·1'W	T	200
St Combs	Aberd	NK0563	57°39·7'	1°54·5'W	T	30
St Conan's Kirk	Arg & Bt	NN1126	56°23·6'	5°3·3'W	A	50
St Connel's Church	D & G	NS7215	55°25·0'	4°0·9'W	A	71
St Constantines Cells	Cumbr	NY4653	54°52·4'	2°50·1'W	A	86
St Constantine's Church	Corn	SW8674	50°31·8'	5°0·8'W	A	200
St Cross	Hants	SU4727	51°2·7'	1°19·4'W	T	185
St Cross South Elmham	Suff	TM2984	52°24·6'	1°22·4'E	T	156
St Cuthberts	Northum	NT8742	55°40·5'	2°12·0'W	X	74
St Cuthbert's Cave	Northum	NU0536	55°37·3'	1°54·8'W	A	75
St Cuthman's School	W Susx	SU8624	51°0·8'	0°46·1'W	X	197
St Cyres' Hill	Devon	ST1402	50°48·9'	3°12·9'W	X	192,193
St Cyrus	Aberd	NO7464	56°46·3'	2°25·1'W	T	45
St David's	Pth & Kin	NN9420	56°21·9'	3°42·5'W	T	52,53,58
St David's Cairn	Northum	NT9511	55°23·8'	2°4·3'W	H	81
St David's College	Denb	SJ1243	52°58·9'	3°18·2'W	X	125
St Davids Harbour	Fife	NT1482	56°1·6'	3°22·4'W	X	65
St David's Head (Penmaen Dewi)	Pemb	SM7227	51°53·9'	5°18·5'W	X	157
St David's Hospital	Carm	SN3920	51°51·6'	4°19·9'W	X	145,159
St David's Station	Devon	SX9193	50°43·8'	3°32·3'W	X	192
St David's (Tyddewi)	Pemb	SM7525	51°52·9'	5°15·8'W	T	157
St David's Well	Brig	SS8278	51°29·6'	3°41·6'W	A	170
St Day	Corn	SW7342	50°14·3'	5°10·6'W	T	204
St Decumans	Somer	ST0642	51°10·4'	3°20·3'W	T	181
St Deiniol's Ash	Flint	SJ3166	53°11·4'	3°1·6'W	X	117
St Dennis	Corn	SW9557	50°22·9'	4°52·6'W	T	200
St Dennis	Warw	SP2942	52°4·8'	1°34·2'W	X	151
St Denys	C of Soton	SU4313	50°55·1'	1°22·9'W	T	196
St Dials	Torf	ST2894	51°38·6'	3°2·0'W	T	171
St Dial's Fm	Monm	SO5011	51°48·0'	2°43·1'W	FM	162
St Dogmaels	Pemb	SN1645	52°4·6'	4°40·7'W	T	145
St Dogmaels Abbey	Pemb	SN1645	52°4·6'	4°40·7'W	A	145
St Dogwells Fm	Pemb	SM9627	51°54·5'	4°57·6'W	FM	157,158
St Dominick	Corn	SX4067	50°29·1'	4°14·9'W	T	201
St Donats	V of Glam	SS9368	51°24·3'	3°31·9'W	T	170
St Donat's Bay	V of Glam	SS9367	51°23·8'	3°31·9'W	W	170
St Donats Fm	Heref	SO4845	52°6·3'	2°45·2'W	FM	148,149
St Dunstan's Fm	E Susx	TQ6019	50°57·1'	0°17·1'E	FM	199
St Duthus's Chapel	Highld	NH7882	57°48·9'	4°2·7'W	A	21
St Dympna's	Devon	SY2491	50°43·1'	3°4·2'W	T	192,193
Stead	Brad	SE1446	53°54·8'	1°46·8'W	T	104
Steadfield House Fm	N Yks	NZ3006	54°27·2'	1°31·8'W	FM	93
Steadholm Bay	N Ayr	NS1350	55°42·7'	4°58·2'W	W	63,69
Stead of Aithsness	Shetld	HU3259	60°19·1'	1°24·7'W	W	3
Stead of Culswick	Shetld	HU2643	60°10·5'	1°31·4'W	W	4
Steads Burn	Northum	NZ2496	55°15·7'	1°36·9'W	W	81
Steadstone Cott	D & G	NX8358	54°54·4'	3°49·1'W	X	84
Stead Vallets Fm	Shrops	SO4576	52°23·0'	2°48·1'W	FM	137,138,148
Steady Knowe	D & G	NX1472	55°0·7'	4°54·1'W	X	76
Steall	Highld	NN1868	56°46·3'	4°58·2'W	X	41
Steall a' Ghreip	Highld	NG4673	57°40·8'	6°15·2'W	X	23
Steallaire Bàn Loch	Arg & Bt	NN0708	56°13·8'	5°6·4'W	W	56
Steallan Dubh	Highld	NH8713	57°11·9'	3°51·8'W	W	35,36
Steall an Eisg	Highld	NM8154	56°37·9'	5°33·8'W	X	49
Steam Mills	Glos	SO6415	51°50·2'	2°31·0'W	T	162
Stean	N Yks	SE0873	54°9·4'	1°52·2'W	T	99
Steanbow	Somer	ST5739	51°9·2'	2°36·5'W	T	182,183
Steanbow Park Dairy Unit	Somer	ST5839	51°9·2'	2°35·6'W	X	182,183
Steane	Northnts	SP5539	52°3·0'	1°11·5'W	X	152
Steane Grounds Fm	Northnts	SP5438	52°2·5'	1°12·4'W	FM	152
Steane Park	Northnts	SP5538	52°2·5'	1°11·5'W	X	152
Stean Moor	N Yks	SE0671	54°8·3'	1°54·1'W	X	99
Steaquoy	Orkney	HY5116	59°2·0'	2°50·7'W	X	6
Stears	Glos	SO6812	51°48·6'	2°27·5'W	X	162
Stearsby	N Yks	SE6171	54°8·1'	1°3·6'W	T	100
Stearsby Hag	N Yks	SE6271	54°8·1'	1°2·6'W	F	100
Steart	Devon	SS9320	50°58·4'	3°31·1'W	X	181
Steart	Somer	SS9340	51°9·2'	3°31·4'W	X	181
Steart	Somer	ST2745	51°12·2'	3°2·3'W	T	182
Steart	Somer	ST5627	51°2·7'	2°37·3'W	T	183
Stearthill Fm	Bucks	SP8031	51°58·5'	0°49·7'W	FM	152,165
Steart Hill Fm	Somer	ST5726	51°2·1'	2°36·4'W	FM	183
Stebb Hill	Orkney	HY6623	59°5·8'	2°35·1'W	X	5
Stebbing	Essex	TL6624	51°53·6'	0°25·1'E	T	167
Stebbing Brook	Essex	TL6623	51°53·1'	0°25·1'E	W	167
Stebbingford Fm	Essex	TL6722	51°52·5'	0°26·0'E	FM	167
Stebbing Green	Essex	TL6823	51°53·0'	0°26·9'E	T	167
Stebbing Park	Essex	TL6524	51°53·6'	0°24·3'E	X	167
Stebbing's Grove	Norf	TF9805	52°36·6'	0°55·9'E	F	144
Stebbligrind	Shetld	HU3946	60°12·1'	1°17·3'W	X	4
Stebden Hill	N Yks	SE0060	54°2·4'	1°59·6'W	X	98
Stechford	Birm	SP1287	52°29·1'	1°49·0'W	T	139
Stedcombe Ho	Devon	SY2691	50°43·1'	3°2·5'W	A	192,193
Stede Court	Kent	TQ8753	51°15·0'	0°41·2'E	X	189
Stedehill Wood	Kent	TQ8854	51°15·5'	0°42·1'E	F	189
Stede Quarter	Kent	TQ8738	51°6·9'	0°40·7'E	T	189
Stedham	W Susx	SU8622	50°59·7'	0°46·1'W	T	197
Stedham Common	W Susx	SU8521	50°59·2'	0°47·0'W	X	197
St Edith's	Wilts	ST9764	51°22·7'	2°2·2'W	X	173
St Edith's Well	Staffs	SJ8316	52°44·7'	2°14·7'W	A	127
Stedman's Fm	Suff	TL8055	52°10·1'	0°38·3'E	FM	155
Stedment	Shrops	SO3896	52°33·7'	2°54·5'W	X	137
St Edmund's Fm	Suff	TM2670	52°17·1'	1°19·2'E	FM	156
St Edmund's Hill	Essex	TL8936	51°59·6'	0°45·6'E	X	155
St Edmund's Monument	Suff	TM1876	52°20·5'	1°12·4'E	X	156
St Edmund's Point	Norf	TF6742	52°57·2'	0°29·6'E	X	132
St Edward's Well	Glos	SP1924	51°55·1'	1°43·0'W	A	163
Steeds	Stir	NS7697	56°9·2'	3°59·3'W	X	57
Steeds Fm	Oxon	SU2794	51°38·9'	1°36·2'W	FM	163,174
Steel	Northum	NY8982	55°8·2'	2°9·9'W	T	80
Steel	Northum	NY9152	54°52·0'	2°8·0'W	X	87
Steel	Northum	NY9358	54°55·2'	2°6·1'W	T	87
Steelands	Lancs	SD7546	53°54·8'	2°22·4'W	X	103
Steel Bank	Sheff	SK3387	53°23·0'	1°29·8'W	T	110,111
Steel Burn	Scot Bord	NT4035	55°36·5'	2°56·7'W	X	73
Steelcrags Wood	Northum	NY9151	54°51·5'	2°8·0'W	F	87
Steel Croft	Cumbr	SD5498	54°22·8'	2°42·1'W	X	97
Steel Cross	E Susx	TQ5231	51°3·7'	0°10·5'E	T	188
Steele Hill	Corn	SX2498	50°45·5'	4°29·3'W	X	190
Steele Knowe	Scot Bord	NT6508	55°22·1'	2°32·7'W	X	80
Steel End	Cumbr	NY3212	54°30·2'	3°2·6'W	X	90
Steelend	Fife	NT0492	56°6·9'	3°32·2'W	T	58
Steelend	Fife	NT0593	56°7·5'	3°31·3'W	X	58
Steel End	Northum	NU1341	55°40·0'	1°47·2'W	X	75
Steele Road	Scot Bord	NY5293	55°14·0'	2°44·9'W	T	79
Steeleroad-end	Scot Bord	NY5393	55°14·0'	2°43·9'W	T	79
Steeles Fm	Hants	SU4157	51°18·9'	1°24·3'W	FM	174
Steele's Knowe	Pth & Kin	NN9607	56°14·9'	3°40·3'W	H	58
Steele, The	Scot Bord	NT1856	55°47·7'	3°18·0'W	X	65,66,72
Steele, The	Scot Bord	NY5193	55°14·0'	2°45·8'W	X	79
Steeley Burn	Durham	NZ1143	54°47·2'	1°49·3'W	W	88
Steeley Fm	Durham	NZ1143	54°47·2'	1°49·3'W	FM	88
Steel Fell	Cumbr	NY3111	54°29·6'	3°3·5'W	H	90
Steel Fm	Shrops	SJ5436	52°55·4'	2°40·7'W	FM	126

Steelgate	Cumbr	NY4041	54°45·9'	2°55·5'W	X	85
Steel Grange Fm	Shrops	SJ5436	52°55·4'	2°40·7'W	FM	126
Steel Green	Cumbr	SD1678	54°11·7'	3°16·8'W	T	96
Steel Hall	Northum	NY9356	54°54·2'	2°6·1'W	X	87
Steel Heath	Shrops	SJ5436	52°55·4'	2°40·7'W	T	126
Steel House Fm	Staffs	SJ9457	53°6·8'	2°5·0'W	FM	118
Steel House Gill	N Yks	SE0979	54°12·6'	1°51·3'W	W	99
Steel House Moor	N Yks	SE0879	54°12·6'	1°52·2'W	X	99
Steel Knotts	Cumbr	NY4418	54°33·5'	2°51·5'W	H	90
Steel Lane Head	Cald	SE0618	53°39·7'	1°54·1'W	X	110
Steelmoor Plantn	Scot Bord	NT6328	55°32·9'	2°34·8'W	F	74
Steelpark	E Ayr	NS4822	55°28·3'	4°23·9'W	X	70
Steel Rigg	Cumbr	NY4708	54°28·1'	2°48·6'W	X	90
Steel Rigg	Northum	NY7567	55°0·1'	2°23·0'W	X	86,87
Steel Rigg	Northum	NY9979	55°6·6'	2°0·1'W	X	87
Steels	Devon	ST0620	50°58·5'	3°20·0'W	X	181
Steelsbrae	Moray	NJ3061	57°38·3'	3°9·9'W	X	28
Steel's Fm	Essex	TQ7098	51°39·5'	0°27·9'E	FM	167
Steel's Fm	Suff	TM2442	52°2·1'	1°16·4'E	FM	169
Steelstrath	Aberd	NO6368	56°48·4'	2°35·9'W	X	45
Steel, The	E Ayr	NS7125	55°30·4'	4°2·1'W	X	71
Steel, The	Northum	NY7860	54°56·3'	2°20·2'W	X	86,87
Steely Crag	Northum	NT9524	55°30·8'	2°4·3'W	X	74,75
Steen's Bridge	Heref	SO5457	52°12·8'	2°40·0'W	T	149
Steens Cleuch	S Lanak	NS9609	55°22·1'	3°38·0'W	X	78
Steep	Hants	SU7425	51°1·4'	0°56·3'W	T	186,197
Steep Down	W Susx	TQ1607	50°51·3'	0°20·7'W	X	198
Steeperton Tor	Devon	SX6188	50°40·7'	3°57·7'W	H	191
Steep Fm	Hants	SU7425	51°1·4'	0°56·3'W	FM	186,197
Steep Head	Devon	SS7030	51°3·5'	3°50·9'W	H	180
Steephill	I of W	SZ5577	50°35·6'	1°13·0'W	T	196
Steep Hill	Oxon	SP4523	51°54·5'	1°20·4'W	X	164
Steephill Wood	E Susx	TQ8118	50°56·2'	0°35·0'E	F	199
Steep Holm	N Som	ST2260	51°20·3'	3°6·8'W	X	182
Steeping River	Lincs	TF4561	53°7·8'	0°10·4'E	W	122
Steep Lane	Cald	SE0223	53°42·4'	1°57·8'W	T	104
Steeple	Cumbr	NY1511	54°29·5'	3°18·3'W	H	89
Steeple	Dorset	SY9181	50°37·9'	2°7·3'W	T	195
Steeple	Essex	TL9302	51°41·2'	0°47·9'E	T	168
Steeple Ashton	Wilts	ST9056	51°18·4'	2°8·2'W	T	173
Steeple Aston	Oxon	SP4725	51°55·5'	1°18·6'W	T	164
Steeple Barton	Oxon	SP4425	51°55·5'	1°21·2'W	T	164
Steeple Bumpstead	Essex	TL6841	52°2·7'	0°27·4'E	T	154
Steeplechase	Suff	TL7249	52°7·0'	0°31·1'E	X	154
Steeple Claydon	Bucks	SP6926	51°55·9'	0°59·4'W	T	165
Steeple Court	Hants	SU5112	50°54·5'	1°16·1'W	X	196
Steeple Cove	Devon	SX7036	50°12·8'	3°49·0'W	W	202
Steeple Creek	Essex	TL9204	51°42·3'	0°47·1'E	W	168
Steeple Cross	N Yks	SE4990	54°18·4'	1°14·4'W	X	100
Steeple Gidding	Cambs	TL1381	52°25·1'	0°19·9'W	T	142
Steeple Hill	Essex	TL9301	51°40·7'	0°47·9'E	X	168
Steeplehouse Fm	Staffs	SK1351	53°3·6'	1°48·0'W	FM	119
Steeple Langford	Wilts	SU0337	51°8·2'	1°57·0'W	T	184
Steeple Langford Cow Down	Wilts	SU0339	51°9·2'	1°57·0'W	X	184
Steeple Morden	Cambs	TL2842	52°3·9'	0°7·6'W	T	153
Steeple Plantn	Notts	SK6384	53°21·2'	1°2·8'W	F	111,120
Steeple Point	Corn	SS1911	50°52·4'	4°34·0'W	X	190
Steeple Stones	Lancs	SD9538	53°50·5'	2°4·1'W	X	103
Steeple, The	Arg & Bt	NN2000	56°9·8'	4°53·5'W	H	56
Steepleton Ho	Hants	SU3634	51°6·5'	1°28·8'W	X	185
Steepleton Lodge	Northnts	SP6569	52°19·1'	1°2·4'W	X	152
Steeple View Fm	Essex	TQ6790	51°35·3'	0°25·0'E	FM	177,178
Steeple Wick	Essex	TL9404	51°42·3'	0°48·9'E	X	168
Steep Low	Staffs	SK1256	53°6·3'	1°48·8'W	X	119
Steep Marsh	Hants	SU7526	51°1·9'	0°55·4'W	T	186,197
Steep Marsh Fm	Hants	SU7526	51°1·9'	0°55·4'W	FM	186,197
Steepness Hill	Oxon	SP4331	51°58·8'	1°22·0'W	X	151
Steep Park	E Susx	TQ5327	51°1·5'	0°11·3'E	X	188,199
Steep Wood	Lancs	SD8048	53°55·9'	2°17·9'W	F	103
Steepwood Fm	W Susx	TQ0822	50°59·5'	0°27·3'W	FM	197
Steeraway	Wrekin	SJ6509	52°40·9'	2°30·7'W	T	127
Steer Bridge	Ches	SJ5546	53°0·8'	2°39·8'W	X	117
Steerleys Copse	Hants	SU4101	50°48·7'	1°24·7'W	F	196
Steer Point	Devon	SX5449	50°19·6'	4°2·7'W	X	201
Steer Rig	Scot Bord	NT8524	55°30·8'	2°13·8'W	X	74
Steer's Place	Kent	TQ6350	51°13·8'	0°20·5'E	X	188
Steers Pool	Cumbr	SD2591	54°18·8'	3°8·8'W	W	96
Steeths, The	Orkney	HY5240	59°14·9'	2°50·0'W	X	5
Steeton	Brad	SE0344	53°53·8'	1°56·8'W	T	104
Steeton Grange	N Yks	SE5244	53°53·6'	1°12·1'W	X	105
Steeton Hall	N Yks	SE4831	53°46·6'	1°15·9'W	A	105
Steeton Hall	N Yks	SE5344	53°53·6'	1°11·2'W	A	105
Steeton Moor	Brad	SE0242	53°52·7'	1°57·8'W	X	104
Steeton Village	N Yks	SE5343	53°53·1'	1°11·2'W	A	105
Steggall's Wood	Suff	TM1272	52°18·5'	1°7·0'E	F	144,155
Steggies	Shetld	HU3436	60°6·7'	1°22·8'W	X	4
Steilston	D & G	NX9081	55°6·9'	3°43·0'W	X	78
Steilston Ho	D & G	NX8980	55°6·4'	3°44·0'W	X	78
Stein	Highld	NG2656	57°30·9'	6°34·1'W	X	23
Steinacleit	N Eil	NB3954	58°24·1'	6°27·6'W	A	8
Steineval	Highld	NG2437	57°20·7'	6°34·8'W	H	23
Stein Head	D & G	NX4837	54°42·6'	4°21·1'W	X	83
Steinis	N Eil	NB4433	58°13·0'	6°21·1'W	T	8
Steinis	N Eil	NG2098	57°53·3'	6°43·0'W	X	14
Steinisval	N Eil	NB0121	58°4·9'	7°3·9'W	H	13
Steinmanhill	Aberd	NJ7642	57°28·3'	2°23·6'W	X	29
Steinman Hill	Aberd	NJ7643	57°28·9'	2°23·6'W	H	29
Steinstane Burn	D & G	NT1406	55°20·7'	3°20·9'W	W	78
Steisay	N Eil	NF8563	57°33·1'	7°15·5'W	X	22
Stèiseal	N Eil	NB3325	58°8·3'	6°31·7'W	H	13,14
Steiseigh	N Eil	NF8544	57°22·9'	7°14·1'W	X	22
Steisinish	N Eil	NF9882	57°43·8'	7°4·0'W	X	18
Steis Point	Shetld	HU1753	60°15·9'	1°41·1'W	X	3
St Elizabeth's School & Home	Herts	TL4416	51°49·7'	0°5·8'E	X	167
Stella	Ghead	NZ1763	54°57·9'	1°43·6'W	T	88
Stell Burn	D & G	NS7404	55°19·1'	3°58·7'W	W	77
Stell Bush	D & G	NS7700	55°17·0'	3°55·8'W	X	78
Stell Bush Edge	D & G	NT2106	55°20·8'	3°14·3'W	H	79

Stell Green	Northum	NY8072	55°2·8'	2°18·4'W	X	86,87
Stellhead	D & G	NX6593	55°13·0'	4°6·9'W	X	77
Stell Hill	D & G	NT2705	55°20·3'	3°8·6'W	H	79
Stelling Hall	Northum	NZ0565	54°59·0'	1°54·9'W	X	87
Stelling Lodge Fm	Kent	TR1448	51°11·7'	1°4·2'E	FM	179,189
Stelling Minnis	Kent	TR1446	51°10·6'	1°4·1'E	T	179,189
Stell Knowe	D & G	NT2301	55°18·1'	3°12·3'W	H	79
Stell Knowe	Scot Bord	NY5187	55°10·7'	2°45·7'W	H	79
Stellock	D & G	NX3641	54°44·5'	4°32·4'W	X	83
Stell Plantn	Durham	NZ0717	54°33·1'	1°53·1'W	F	92
Stell, The	N Yks	NZ3101	54°24·5'	1°30·9'W	W	93
Stell, The	N Yks	SE3096	54°21·8'	1°31·9'W	W	99
Stell Wood	E Loth	NT5564	55°52·3'	2°42·7'W	F	66
Stelshaw	Cumbr	NY5182	55°8·0'	2°45·7'W	X	79
St Elvan	Corn	SW6427	50°6·0'	5°17·6'W	X	203
Stelvio	Newp	ST2987	51°34·9'	3°1·1'W	T	171
St Elvis Fm	Pemb	SM8124	51°52·5'	5°10·5'W	FM	157
Stember	Pemb	SM8915	51°47·9'	5°3·2'W	X	157,158
Stember	Pemb	SM9720	51°50·7'	4°56·4'W	X	157,158
Stembister	Orkney	HY5402	58°54·4'	2°47·4'W	X	6,7
Stemborough Mill	Leic	SP5391	52°31·1'	1°12·7'W	X	140
Stembridge	Somer	ST4220	50°58·8'	2°49·2'W	T	193
Stembridge	Swan	SS4691	51°36·0'	4°13·0'W	T	159
Stembridge Brook	V of Glam	SS9474	51°27·5'	3°31·2'W	W	170
Stembridge Tower Mill	Somer	ST4330	51°4·2'	2°48·4'W	X	182
Stembridge Tower Mill	Somer	ST4330	51°4·2'	2°48·4'W	X	182
Stem Point	Corn	SW8466	50°27·5'	5°2·2'W	X	200
Stemster	Highld	ND0365	58°34·0'	3°39·6'W	X	11,12
Stemster	Highld	ND1761	58°32·0'	3°25·1'W	X	11,12
Stemster	Highld	ND1844	58°22·9'	3°23·7'W	X	11,12
Stemster	Highld	ND3350	58°26·3'	3°8·4'W	X	12
Stemster	Highld	ND3672	58°38·1'	3°5·7'W	X	7,12
Stemster Hill	Highld	ND0366	58°34·5'	3°39·6'W	H	11,12
Stemster Hill	Highld	ND2041	58°21·3'	3°21·5'W	H	11,12
Stemster Ho	Highld	ND1860	58°31·5'	3°24·0'W	X	11,12
Stenalees	Corn	SX0157	50°23·0'	4°47·6'W	T	200
Stenaquoy	Orkney	HY5631	59°10·1'	2°45·7'W	X	5,6
Stenbury Down	I of W	SZ5379	50°36·7'	1°14·7'W	X	196
Stenbury Manor Fm	I of W	SZ5279	50°36·7'	1°15·5'W	FM	196
Stenbury Trail	I of W	SZ5185	50°40·0'	1°16·3'W	X	196
Stencoose	Corn	SW7145	50°15·9'	5°12·4'W	T	203
St Endellion	Corn	SW9978	50°34·3'	4°49·9'W	T	200
Steng-a-tor	Devon	SX5688	50°40·7'	4°1·9'W	X	191
Steng Cross	Northum	NY9690	55°12·5'	2°3·3'W	A	81
Steng Moss	Northum	NY9691	55°13·0'	2°3·3'W	X	81
Stenhill	Corn	SX2989	50°40·8'	4°24·8'W	X	190
Stenhill	Devon	ST0510	50°53·1'	3°20·7'W	T	192
Stenhouse	C of Edin	NT2171	55°55·8'	3°15·4'W	T	66
Stenhouse	D & G	NX8093	55°13·3'	3°52·8'W	T	78
Stenhouse Fm	Fife	NT2188	56°5·0'	3°15·7'W	FM	66
Stenhouse Hill	D & G	NX7892	55°12·7'	3°54·6'W	H	78
Stenhousemuir	Falk	NS8783	56°1·9'	3°48·4'W	T	65
Stenhouse Resr	Fife	NT2187	56°4·4'	3°15·7'W	W	66
Stenigot	Lincs	TF2581	53°18·9'	0°7·0'W	T	122
Stenigot Ho	Lincs	TF2581	53°18·9'	0°7·0'W	X	122
Stenkrith Ho	Cumbr	NY7707	54°27·7'	2°20·9'W	X	91
Stenmuir	D & G	NY0287	55°10·3'	3°31·9'W	X	78
Stenmuir	Scot Bord	NT6840	55°39·4'	2°30·1'W	X	74
Stennack	Corn	SW6537	50°11·4'	5°17·2'W	T	203
Stennerskeugh	Cumbr	NY7401	54°24·5'	2°23·6'W	X	91
Stennerskeugh Clouds	Cumbr	NY7400	54°23·9'	2°23·6'W	X	91
Stenness	Orkney	HY3010	58°58·6'	3°12·6'W	X	6
Stenness	Shetld	HU2177	60°28·8'	1°36·6'W	X	3
Stennestwatt	Shetld	HU2351	60°14·8'	1°34·6'W	X	3
Stennett's Fm	Lincs	TF2055	53°5·0'	0°12·1'W	FM	122
Stennie Hill	Orkney	HY5635	59°12·2'	2°45·7'W	H	5,6
Stennies Water	D & G	NY3293	55°13·8'	3°3·7'W	W	79
Stennigor	Orkney	HY2209	58°57·9'	3°20·9'W	X	6,7
Stennishope	Scot Bord	NT5003	55°19·4'	2°46·8'W	X	79
St Enoder	Corn	SW8956	50°22·2'	4°57·7'W	T	200
St Enoder Wood	Corn	SW8852	50°20·0'	4°58·4'W	F	200,204
St Enodoc Church	Corn	SW9377	50°33·6'	4°55·0'W	X	200
Stenor Scar	Cumbr	NY1457	54°54·3'	3°20·0'W	X	85
Stenries	D & G	NY1270	55°1·3'	3°22·2'W	X	85
Stenrieshill	D & G	NY1097	55°15·8'	3°24·5'W	X	78
Stenscholl	Highld	NG4868	57°38·2'	6°12·9'W	T	23
Stensigar	Orkney	HY5390	58°58·7'	2°58·7'W	X	7
Stensley Fm	Heref	SO3239	52°3·0'	2°59·1'W	FM	161
Stenso	Orkney	HY3525	59°6·7'	3°7·6'W	X	6
Stenson	Derby	SK3229	52°51·7'	1°31·1'W	T	128
Stenson Fields	Derby	SK3231	52°52·8'	1°31·5'W	X	128
Stenswall	Shetld	HU3952	60°15·3'	1°17·2'W	T	3
Stent Hill	Somer	SS8347	51°12·9'	3°40·1'W	X	181
Stenton	E Loth	NT6274	55°57·7'	2°36·1'W	T	67
Stenton	Fife	NO5103	56°13·3'	2°47·0'W	X	59
Stenton	Fife	NT2798	56°10·4'	3°10·1'W	T	59
Stenton	Pth & Kin	NO0640	56°32·8'	3°31·3'W	X	52,53
Stentwood	Devon	ST1309	50°52·7'	3°13·8'W	T	192,193
Stenwith	Lincs	SK8336	52°55·1'	0°45·5'W	T	130
Stepaside	Corn	SW9545	50°16·4'	4°52·2'W	T	204
Stepaside	Pemb	SN1307	51°44·1'	4°42·1'W	T	158
Stepaside	Powys	SO0889	52°29·7'	3°20·9'W	T	136
Stepends	D & G	NX8595	55°14·4'	3°48·1'W	X	78
Stepends	D & G	NX9088	55°10·7'	3°43·2'W	X	78
Step Ends	Durham	NY9524	54°36·9'	2°4·2'W	X	91,92
Step Fm	Oxon	SU2796	51°40·0'	1°36·2'W	FM	163
Stepford	D & G	NX8681	55°6·9'	3°46·8'W	X	78
Stephen Gelly	Corn	SX0565	50°27·4'	4°44·5'W	X	200
Stephen Moor	Lancs	SD7454	53°59·1'	2°23·4'W	X	103
Stephen Moor Lodge	Lancs	SD7554	53°59·1'	2°22·5'W	X	103
Stephen Park	Lancs	SD7456	54°0·2'	2°23·4'W	X	103
Stephen's Castle	Dorset	SU0909	50°53·1'	1°51·9'W	X	195
Stephen's Castle Down	Hants	SU5621	50°59·4'	1°11·7'W	X	185
Stephen's Castle (Tumulus)	Dorset	SU0909	50°53·1'	1°51·9'W	A	195
Stephens Fm	Somer	ST2236	51°7·3'	3°6·5'W	FM	182
Stephens Gate	Orkney	HY5836	59°12·8'	2°43·7'W	X	5
Stephen's Grave	Devon	SX5378	50°35·2'	4°4·2'W	X	191,201
Stephen's Green	Pemb	SN0401	51°40·7'	4°49·7'W	X	157,158
Stephen's Hall	Ghead	NZ1563	54°57·9'	1°45·5'W	X	88

Stephenson Ground	Cumbr	SD2393	54°19·9'	3°10·6'W	X	96
Stephensons	Lancs	SD7551	53°57·5'	2°22·4'W	X	103
Stephenson's Cottage	Northum	NZ1265	54°59·0'	1°48·3'W	X	88
Stephenson Wold	E Yorks	SE9150	53°56·5'	0°36·4'W	X	106
Stephney	Cumbr	NY0306	54°26·7'	3°29·3'W	X	89
Stepleton House	Dorset	ST8611	50°54·1'	2°11·6'W	A	194
Stepmoles	Warw	SP2645	52°6·4'	1°36·8'W	X	151
Stepney	Lincs	TA1610	53°34·7'	0°14·5'W	X	113
Stepney	T Ham	TQ3481	51°30·9'	0°3·7'W	T	176,177
Stepper Point	Corn	SW9178	50°34·1'	4°56·7'W	X	200
Steppes Fm	Monm	SO3821	51°53·3'	2°53·7'W	FM	161
Stepping Hill	Stock	SJ9187	53°23·0'	2°7·7'W	T	109
Steppingley	Beds	TL0135	52°0·5'	0°31·3'W	T	153
Steppings	Cumbr	NY5474	55°3·8'	2°42·8'W	X	86
Stepping Stones	N Yks	SE0559	54°1·9'	1°55·0'W	X	104
Steppington Hill	Northnts	SP5257	52°12·8'	1°13·9'W	X	151
Stepple	Shrops	SO3282	52°26·1'	2°59·6'W	X	137
Stepple Hall	Shrops	SO6678	52°24·2'	2°29·6'W	X	138
Steppleknoll	Shrops	SO3282	52°26·1'	2°59·6'W	H	137
Stepps	N Lanak	NS6568	55°53·4'	4°9·1'W	T	64
Steps	Cumbr	NY5906	54°27·1'	2°37·5'W	X	91
Steps	Staffs	SK0859	53°7·9'	1°52·4'W	X	119
Steps Br	Devon	SX8088	50°41·0'	3°41·5'W	X	191
Steps Hall	Cumbr	NY5513	54°30·9'	2°41·3'W	X	90
Steps Hill	Bucks	SP9515	51°49·8'	0°36·9'W	X	165
Steps of Cally	Pth & Kin	NO1251	56°38·8'	3°25·7'W	X	53
Steps of Grace	Northum	NT9855	55°47·5'	2°1·5'W	X	75
Stepstones Fm	N Som	ST4264	51°22·6'	2°49·6'W	FM	172,182
Stepstones Fm	N Som	ST4661	51°21·0'	2°46·1'W	FM	172,182
Stepstones Fm	N Som	ST4661	51°21·0'	2°46·1'W	FM	172,182
Step, The	Cumbr	NY3611	54°29·7'	2°58·9'W	X	90
Sterling Fm	Cambs	TL5763	52°14·8'	0°18·4'E	FM	154
St Erme	Corn	SW8449	50°18·3'	5°1·6'W	T	204
Sterndale Ho	Derby	SK1675	53°16·5'	1°45·2'W	X	119
Sterndale Moor	Derby	SK1068	53°12·8'	1°50·6'W	T	119
St Erney	Corn	SX3759	50°24·7'	4°17·3'W	T	201
Sternfield	Suff	TM3961	52°11·9'	1°30·3'E	T	156
Sternhouse Fm	Norf	TL6990	52°29·1'	0°29·7'E	FM	143
Sterridge Valley	Devon	SS5545	51°11·4'	4°4·1'W	X	180
Stert	Wilts	SU0259	51°20·0'	1°57·9'W	T	173
Stert Barton	Devon	SX7457	50°24·2'	3°46·0'W	X	202
Stert Copse	Wilts	SU2852	51°16·2'	1°35·5'W	F	184
Sterte	Poole	SZ0091	50°43·3'	1°59·6'W	T	195
Stert Flats	Somer	ST2647	51°13·3'	3°3·2'W	X	182
Stert Fm	Wilts	SU0092	51°37·8'	1°59·6'W	FM	163,173
St Erth	Corn	SW5535	50°10·1'	5°25·5'W	T	203
St Erth Praze	Corn	SW5735	50°10·2'	5°23·8'W	T	203
St Erth Sta	Corn	SW5435	50°10·1'	5°26·3'W	X	203
Stert Island	Somer	ST2948	51°13·8'	3°0·6'W	X	182
Stert Point	Somer	ST2847	51°13·3'	3°1·5'W	X	182
St Ervan	Corn	SW8970	50°29·7'	4°58·1'W	T	200
Stetchworth	Cambs	TL6458	52°12·0'	0°24·4'E	T	154
Stetchworth Ley	Cambs	TL6557	52°11·4'	0°25·2'E	X	154
Stetchworth Park	Cambs	TL6459	52°12·5'	0°24·4'E	X	154
Stetchworth Park Fm	Cambs	TL6656	52°10·9'	0°26·1'E	FM	154
Stetfold Rocks	Somer	SS8738	51°8·0'	3°36·5'W	X	181
Steuarthall	Stir	NS8292	56°6·6'	3°53·4'W	X	57
St Eval	Corn	SW8868	50°28·6'	4°58·9'W	T	200
Stevenage	Herts	TL2424	51°54·3'	0°11·5'W	T	166
Stevensburn	Aberd	NJ8749	57°32·1'	2°12·6'W	X	30
Steven's Crouch	E Susx	TQ7115	50°54·8'	0°26·3'E	T	199
Stevens Fm	Essex	TQ8291	51°35·5'	0°38·0'E	FM	178
Stevenshill	Shrops	SJ5503	52°37·6'	2°39·5'W	X	126
Stevenson	Scot Bord	NT1643	55°40·6'	3°19·7'W	X	72
Stevenson Hill	Scot Bord	NT1743	55°40·7'	3°18·8'W	H	72
Stevenson Ho	E Loth	NT5474	55°57·7'	2°43·8'W	X	66
Stevenson Mains	E Loth	NT5474	55°57·7'	2°43·8'W	X	66
Stevenston	E Ayr	NS5121	55°27·9'	4°21·0'W	X	70
Stevenston	N Ayr	NS2642	55°38·7'	4°45·5'W	T	63,70
Stevenstone	Devon	SS5219	50°57·3'	4°6·1'W	T	180
Stevenstone Barton	Devon	SX9099	50°47·0'	3°33·2'W	X	192
Stevenston or Ashgrove Loch	N Ayr	NS2744	55°39·8'	4°44·6'W	W	63,70
Steventon	Hants	SU5447	51°13·4'	1°13·2'W	T	185
Steventon	Oxon	SU4691	51°37·2'	1°19·7'W	T	164,174
Steventon	Shrops	SO5273	52°21·4'	2°41·9'W	T	137,138
Steventon End	Essex	TL5942	52°3·4'	0°19·6'E	T	154
Steventon Field	Oxon	SU4593	51°38·3'	1°20·6'W	X	164,174
Steventon Hill	Oxon	SU4791	51°37·2'	1°18·9'W	X	164,174
Steventon Warren Fm	Hants	SU5345	51°12·3'	1°14·1'W	FM	185
Stevington	Beds	SP9853	52°10·2'	0°33·6'W	T	153
Stewards	Essex	TL4507	51°44·8'	0°6·4'E	T	167
Stewards Elm Fm	Essex	TQ8992	51°35·9'	0°44·1'E	FM	178
Stewards Fm	Suff	TL9537	52°0·1'	0°50·8'E	FM	155
Steward's Green	Essex	TL4600	51°41·0'	0°7·1'E	T	167
Steward Shield Meadow	Durham	NY9843	54°47·2'	2°1·4'W	X	87
Steward's Ho	Northum	NY8875	55°4·4'	2°10·8'W	X	87
Steward's Hyde	Heref	SO6152	52°10·1'	2°33·8'W	X	149
Steward's Ley	Herts	TL3331	51°57·9'	0°3·4'W	F	166
Stewartby	Beds	TL0242	52°4·2'	0°30·3'W	T	153
Stewartby Lake Country Park	Beds	TL0042	52°4·3'	0°32·1'W	X	153
Stewartfield	Aberd	NJ5724	57°18·5'	2°42·4'W	X	37
Stewartfield	Aberd	NJ8657	57°36·4'	2°13·6'W	X	30
Stewartfield	Arg & Bt	NR7555	55°44·4'	5°34·6'W	X	62
Stewartfield	S Lanak	NS6255	55°46·4'	4°11·6'W	X	64
Stewartfield	S Lanak	NS6753	55°45·4'	4°6·7'W	X	64
Stewarthall	Arg & Bt	NS0562	55°49·0'	5°6·3'W	X	63
Stewart Hill	Cumbr	NY3634	54°42·1'	2°59·2'W	X	90
Stewarton	Arg & Bt	NR6919	55°24·9'	5°38·6'W	T	68
Stewarton	D & G	NX4449	54°48·9'	4°25·2'W	X	83
Stewarton	D & G	NX8288	55°10·6'	3°50·7'W	X	78
Stewarton	E Ayr	NS4246	55°41·2'	4°30·4'W	T	64
Stewarton	Scot Bord	NT2145	55°41·8'	3°15·0'W	X	73
Stewarts	Essex	TL5201	51°41·5'	0°12·3'E	X	167
Stewart's Fm	Staffs	SJ9147	53°1·5'	2°7·6'W	FM	118
Stewart Shiels	Northum	NY8698	55°16·8'	2°12·8'W	X	80
Stewartshiels Burn	Northum	NT8600	55°17·9'	2°12·8'W	W	80
Stewartshiels Plantation	Northum	NT8500	55°17·9'	2°13·7'W	F	80
Stewartshill	Pth & Kin	NO2015	56°19·5'	3°17·2'W	X	58

Stewart Tower	Pth & Kin	NO0936	56°30·7'	3°28·3'W	X	52,53
Stewdon Fm	Devon	SS4902	50°48·1'	4°8·2'W	FM	191
Stewdon Moor	Devon	SS4801	50°47·6'	4°9·0'W	X	191
St Ewe	Corn	SW9746	50°17·0'	4°50·6'W	T	204
Stewkley	Bucks	SP8526	51°55·8'	0°45·4'W	T	165
Stewkley Dean	Bucks	SP8326	51°55·8'	0°47·2'W	T	165
Stewley	Somer	ST3118	50°57·7'	2°58·6'W	T	193
Stewner Park Fm	Cumbr	SD2378	54°11·8'	3°10·4'W	FM	96
Stews	Orkney	ND4689	58°47·4'	2°55·6'W	X	7
Stews Taing	Orkney	ND4689	58°47·4'	2°55·6'W	X	7
Stewton	Lincs	TF3686	53°21·4'	0°3·0'E	T	113,122
Stewton Newkin	Lincs	TF3688	53°22·5'	0°3·1'E	X	113,122
Stey Fell	D & G	NX5560	54°55·1'	4°15·3'W	H	83
Steygail	D & G	NS8808	55°21·4'	3°45·6'W	H	71,78
Steyne Cross	I of W	SZ6487	50°41·0'	1°5·3'W	T	196
Steyne Ho	I of W	SZ6487	50°41·0'	1°5·3'W	X	196
Steynes Fm	Hants	SU5820	50°58·8'	1°10·0'W	FM	185
Steyning	W Susx	TQ1711	50°53·4'	0°19·8'W	T	198
Steyning Bowl	W Susx	TQ1609	50°52·4'	0°20·7'W	X	198
Steyning Manor	Somer	ST2242	51°10·6'	3°6·6'W	X	182
Steyning Round Hill	W Susx	TQ1610	50°52·9'	0°20·7'W	X	198
Steynton	Pemb	SM9107	51°43·6'	5°1·2'W	T	157,158
St Fagans	Card	ST1277	51°29·3'	3°15·7'W	T	171
St Faith's Common	Norf	TG1817	52°42·6'	1°14·0'E	X	133,134
St Fergus	Aberd	NK0952	57°33·7'	1°50·5'W	T	30
St Fergus Links	Aberd	NK1151	57°33·2'	1°48·5'W	X	30
St Fergus Moss	Aberd	NK0553	57°34·3'	1°54·5'W	X	30
St Fillans	Pth & Kin	NN6924	56°23·7'	4°6·9'W	T	51
St Fillan's Cave	Fife	NO5402	56°12·8'	2°44·1'W	X	59
St Fillan's Priory	Stir	NN3528	56°25·2'	4°40·1'W	A	50
St Finan's Chapel	Highld	NM7568	56°45·2'	5°40·4'W	A	40
St Fink	Pth & Kin	NO2147	56°36·8'	3°16·8'W	X	53
St Fittick's Church	C of Aber	NJ9604	57°7·9'	2°3·5'W	A	38
St Flanan	E Dunb	NS6874	55°56·7'	4°6·4'W	X	64
St Florence	Pemb	SN0801	51°40·7'	4°46·2'W	T	158
St Ford	Fife	NO4801	56°12·2'	2°49·8'W	X	59
St Ford Links	Fife	NO4600	56°11·6'	2°51·8'W	X	59
St Fort Home Fm	Fife	NO4125	56°25·1'	2°56·9'W	FM	54,59
St Frideswide Fm	Oxon	SP5011	51°48·0'	1°16·1'W	FM	164
St Gabriel's Ho	Dorset	SY4092	50°43·7'	2°50·6'W	X	193
St Gabriels Mouth	Dorset	SY3992	50°43·7'	2°51·5'W	W	193
St Gabriel's (Sch)	W Berks	SU4764	51°22·6'	1°19·1'W	X	174
St Gennys	Corn	SX1497	50°44·8'	4°37·8'W	T	190
St George	C of Bris	ST6273	51°27·5'	2°32·4'W	T	172
St George	Conwy	SH9775	53°16·0'	3°32·3'W	T	116
St George in the East	T Ham	TQ3480	51°30·4'	0°3·8'W	T	176,177
St Georges	Gwyn	SH5910	52°40·4'	4°4·7'W	X	124
St Georges	N Som	ST3762	51°21·5'	2°53·9'W	T	182
St George's	Traf	SJ8297	53°28·4'	2°15·9'W	T	109
St George's	V of Glam	ST0976	51°28·8'	3°18·2'W	T	171
St George's	Wrekin	SJ7010	52°41·5'	2°26·2'W	T	127
St George's Channel		SH1637	52°54·2'	4°43·8'W	W	123
St George's Channel	Pemb	SM8237	51°59·6'	5°10·1'W	W	157
St George's Cross	Somer	ST8050	51°15·2'	2°16·8'W	X	183
St George's Down	I of W	SZ5186	50°40·5'	1°16·3'W	X	196
St George's Fm	Derby	SK3179	53°18·7'	1°31·7'W	FM	119
St George's Hill	Surrey	TQ0762	51°21·0'	0°27·4'W	T	176,187
St George's OR Looe Island	Corn	SX2551	50°20·2'	4°27·2'W	X	201
St George's Retreat	E Susx	TQ3319	50°57·5'	0°6·0'W	X	198
St George's School	Kent	TQ6140	51°8·4'	0°18·5'E	X	188
St George's Well	Corn	SW9176	50°33·0'	4°56·6'W	A	200
St George's Well	Devon	ST0208	50°52·0'	3°23·2'W	T	192
St George's Well	Highld	NH7378	57°46·7'	4°7·7'W	X	21
St Germains	E Loth	NT4274	55°57·6'	2°55·3'W	X	66
St Germans	Corn	SX3557	50°23·6'	4°18·9'W	T	201
St Germans or Lynher River	Corn	SX3955	50°22·6'	4°15·5'W	W	201
St Germans Quay	Corn	SX3657	50°23·6'	4°18·1'W	X	201
St Giles	Camden	TQ3081	51°31·0'	0°7·2'W	T	176,177
St Giles	Essex	TL7702	51°41·6'	0°34·1'E	X	167
St Giles	Lincs	SK9872	53°14·4'	0°31·5'W	T	121
St Giles Fm	N Yks	SE2199	54°23·4'	1°40·2'W	FM	99
St Giles Fm	Warw	SP0962	52°15·6'	1°51·7'W	FM	150
St Giles in the Wood	Devon	SS5318	50°56·8'	4°5·2'W	T	180
St Giles on the Heath	Devon	SX3690	50°41·4'	4°18·9'W	T	190
St Giles's Hill	Hants	SU4929	51°3·7'	1°17·7'W	T	185
St Gluvias	Corn	SW7834	50°10·1'	5°6·2'W	T	204
St Godwalds	Worcs	SO9769	52°19·4'	2°2·2'W	T	139
St Govan's Head	Pemb	SR9792	51°35·7'	4°55·5'W	X	158
St Guthlac's Lodge	Lincs	TF2614	52°42·8'	0°7·7'W	X	131
St Gwenfaen's Well	I of Angl	SH2575	53°14·8'	4°37·0'W	A	114
St Gwynno Forest	Rho Cyn Taf	ST0396	51°39·5'	3°23·8'W	F	170
St Harmon	Powys	SN9872	52°20·4'	3°29·4'W	T	136,147
St Helena	Angus	NO5231	56°28·4'	2°46·3'W	X	54
St Helena	Corn	SW6915	49°59·7'	5°13·0'W	X	203
St Helena	Cumbr	NY0111	54°29·3'	3°31·3'W	X	89
St Helena	E Yorks	SE7321	53°41·1'	0°53·3'W	X	105,106,112
St Helena	N Yks	NZ6803	54°25·3'	0°56·7'W	X	94
St Helena	Suff	TM4671	52°17·1'	1°36·8'E	X	156
St Helena	Warw	SK2601	52°36·6'	1°36·6'W	T	140
St Helena Fm	E Susx	TQ3518	50°57·0'	0°4·3'W	FM	198
St Helena Fm	Lincs	SE9000	53°29·6'	0°38·2'W	FM	112
St Helena Island	D & G	NX1955	54°51·7'	4°48·8'W	X	82
St Helen Auckland	Durham	NZ1827	54°38·5'	1°42·8'W	T	92
St Helen's	Barns	SE3608	53°34·3'	1°27·0'W	T	110,111
St Helens	Cumbr	NY0132	54°40·7'	3°31·7'W	T	89
St Helen's	E Susx	TQ8212	50°52·9'	0°35·6'E	T	199
St Helens	I of W	SZ6289	50°42·1'	1°6·9'W	T	196
St Helen's	I Scilly	SV8917	49°58·6'	6°19·9'W	X	203
St Helens	N Lincs	TA0107	53°33·2'	0°28·1'W	X	112
St Helens	Scot Bord	NT4830	55°33·9'	2°49·0'W	X	73
St Helens	St Hel	SJ5095	53°27·2'	2°44·8'W	T	108
St Helens Canal	Warr	SJ5586	53°22·4'	2°40·2'W	W	108
St Helen's Church	I of W	SZ6389	50°42·1'	1°6·1'W	A	196
St Helen's Cott	N Yks	SE4289	54°17·9'	1°20·9'W	X	99
St Helen's Fm	Cumbr	SD2174	54°9·6'	3°12·2'W	FM	96
St Helen's Fm	E Yorks	SE7739	53°50·7'	0°49·4'W	FM	105,106
St Helen's Fm	N Yks	SE3852	53°58·0'	1°24·8'W	FM	104
St Helen's Fort	I of W	SZ6489	50°42·1'	1°5·2'W	A	196
St Helens Junc Sta	St Hel	SJ5393	53°26·1'	2°42·0'W	X	108
St Helen's Pool	I Scilly	SV9016	49°58·1'	6°19·0'W	W	203
St Helen's Well	N Yks	SD9357	54°0·8'	2°6·0'W	A	103
St Helen's Wood	E Susx	TQ8111	50°52·4'	0°34·7'E	T	199
St Helen's Wood	Lincs	TF2559	53°7·0'	0°7·5'W	F	122
St Helier	Sutton	TQ2766	51°23·0'	0°10·1'W	T	176
St Herbert's Island	Cumbr	NY2621	54°35·0'	3°8·3'W	X	89,90
St Hilary	Corn	SW5531	50°7·9'	5°25·3'W	T	203
St Hilary	V of Glam	ST0173	51°27·1'	3°25·1'W	T	170
St Hilary Down	V of Glam	ST0173	51°27·1'	3°25·1'W	H	170
St Hildas Wold	N Yks	SE9575	54°10·0'	0°32·3'W	X	101
St Huberts	Bucks	TQ0086	51°34·1'	0°33·0'W	X	176
St Hubert's Lodge	I of W	SZ4389	50°42·2'	1°23·1'W	X	196
St Hugh's School	Oxon	SU3297	51°40·5'	1°31·8'W	X	164
Stibb	Corn	SS2210	50°52·0'	4°31·4'W	T	190
Stibbard	Norf	TF9828	52°49·0'	0°56·7'E	T	132
Stibb Cross	Devon	SS4214	50°54·5'	4°14·5'W	T	180,190
Stibbear Fm	Somer	ST3313	50°55·0'	2°56·8'W	FM	193
Stibb Green	Wilts	SU2262	51°21·6'	1°40·7'W	T	174
Stibb Hollow Fm	Devon	SS4313	50°53·9'	4°13·6'W	FM	180,190
Stibbiegill Head	D & G	NY3794	55°14·4'	2°59·0'W	H	79
Stibbiegill Knowe	D & G	NY3793	55°13·9'	2°59·0'W	H	79
Stibbington	Cambs	TL0898	52°34·4'	0°24·0'W	T	142
Stibbington Ho	Cambs	TL0798	52°34·4'	0°24·9'W	X	142
St Ibbs	Herts	TL1926	51°55·4'	0°15·8'W	T	166
Stibbs Wood	W Berks	SU3670	51°25·9'	1°28·5'W	F	174
Sticelett	I of W	SZ4693	50°44·3'	1°20·5'W	X	196
Stichens Green	W Berks	SU5879	51°30·6'	1°9·5'W	X	174
Stichill	Scot Bord	NT7138	55°38·3'	2°27·2'W	T	74
Stichill Eastfield	Scot Bord	NT7339	55°38·9'	2°25·3'W	X	74
Stichill Home Fm	Scot Bord	NT7039	55°38·9'	2°28·2'W	FM	74
Stichill Linn	Scot Bord	NT7037	55°37·8'	2°28·2'W	X	74
Stichill Stables	Scot Bord	NT7039	55°38·9'	2°28·2'W	X	74
Stick Close Beck	Lancs	SD5756	54°0·1'	2°38·9'W	W	102
Sticker	Corn	SW9750	50°19·1'	4°50·7'W	T	200,204
Stickeridge	Devon	SS8710	50°52·9'	3°36·0'W	X	192
Stickford	Lincs	TF3559	53°6·9'	0°1·4'E	T	122
Stickford Ho	Lincs	TF3460	53°7·5'	0°0·6'E	X	122
Stickford Lo	Lincs	TF3660	53°7·4'	0°2·4'E	X	122
Stick Hill	Kent	TQ4643	51°10·3'	0°5·7'E	T	188
Sticking Hill	Thurr	TQ6583	51°31·5'	0°23·1'E	X	177,178
Stickland Hill Fm	Dorset	ST8305	50°50·9'	2°14·1'W	FM	194
Stickleball Hill	Somer	ST5738	51°8·6'	2°36·5'W	X	182,183
Stickle Heaton	Northum	NT8841	55°40·0'	2°11·0'W	X	74
Sticklepath	Devon	SS5532	51°4·4'	4°3·8'W	T	180
Sticklepath	Devon	SX6394	50°44·0'	3°56·1'W	T	191
Sticklepath	Somer	ST0436	51°7·2'	3°21·9'W	T	181
Sticklepath	Somer	ST3012	50°54·4'	2°59·4'W	T	193
Stickle Pike	Cumbr	SD2192	54°19·3'	3°12·5'W	H	96
Stickle Tarn	Cumbr	NY2807	54°27·4'	3°6·2'W	W	89,90
Stickley Fm	Northum	NZ2877	55°5·4'	1°33·2'W	FM	88
Sticklinch	Somer	ST5638	51°8·6'	2°37·4'W	T	182,183
Stickling Green	Essex	TL4732	51°58·2'	0°8·8'E	T	167
Stickney	Lincs	TF3456	53°5·3'	0°0·5'E	T	122
Stickney Grange	Lincs	TF3355	53°4·8'	0°0·5'W	X	122
Sticks Burn	Angus	NO6957	56°42·5'	2°29·9'W	W	54
Sticks Pass	Cumbr	NY3418	54°33·4'	3°0·8'W	X	90
Stickstey Wood	Glos	ST7888	51°35·7'	2°18·7'W	F	162,172
Stickworth Hall	I of W	SZ5385	50°40·0'	1°14·6'W	X	196
Stidcot	S Glos	ST6888	51°35·6'	2°27·3'W	X	162,172
Stiddlehill Common	Northum	NY9285	55°9·8'	2°7·1'W	X	80
Stidriggs	D & G	NY0599	55°16·8'	3°29·3'W	X	78
Stidriggs Burn	D & G	NY2284	55°8·9'	3°13·0'W	W	79
Stidston	Devon	SX7160	50°25·8'	3°48·6'W	X	202
Stiffkey	Norf	TF9743	52°57·1'	0°56·4'E	T	132
Stiffkey Freshes	Norf	TF9845	52°58·2'	0°57·3'E	X	132
Stiffkey Greens	Norf	TF9744	52°57·7'	0°56·4'E	X	132
Stiffkey Salt Marshes	Norf	TF9844	52°57·6'	0°57·3'E	W	132
Stifford Clays Fm	Thurr	TQ6181	51°30·5'	0°19·6'E	FM	177
Stifford's Bridge	Heref	SO7348	52°8·0'	2°23·3'W	X	150
Stiff Street	Kent	TQ8761	51°19·3'	0°41·4'E	T	178
Stiglister	Orkney	HY6540	59°15·0'	2°36·3'W	X	5
Stildon Manor	Worcs	SO7169	52°19·3'	2°25·1'W	X	138
Stile	Somer	SS9342	51°10·3'	3°31·4'W	X	181
Stile Bridge	Kent	TQ7547	51°11·9'	0°30·7'E	X	188
Stilecop Field	Staffs	SK0315	52°44·2'	1°56·9'W	X	128
Stile End	Cumbr	NY2221	54°34·9'	3°12·0'W	X	89,90
Stile End	Cumbr	NY4604	54°26·0'	2°49·5'W	X	90
Stile Fm	Kent	TR0853	51°14·5'	0°59·2'E	FM	179,189
Stile House Fm	Staffs	SK0156	53°6·3'	1°58·7'W	FM	119
Stilesmeadow Fm	Ches	SJ9265	53°11·2'	2°6·8'W	FM	118
Stileway	Somer	ST4641	51°10·2'	2°46·0'W	T	182
Stileway Fm	Somer	ST7327	51°2·7'	2°22·7'W	FM	183
Still	Shetld	HU6490	60°35·6'	0°49·4'W	X	1,2
Stillaig Fm	Arg & Bt	NR9468	55°51·9'	5°17·1'W	FM	62
Stilland Fm	W Susx	SU9532	51°5·0'	0°38·2'W	FM	186
Stillbrook Fm	Somer	ST3522	50°59·9'	2°55·2'W	FM	193
Still Burn	Scot Bord	NT4249	55°44·1'	2°55·0'W	W	73
Stillers Fm	Hants	SU8050	51°14·8'	0°50·8'W	FM	186
Stillingfleet	N Yks	SE5940	53°51·4'	1°5·8'W	T	105
Stillingfleet Beck	N Yks	SE5840	53°51·4'	1°6·7'W	W	105
Stillingfleet Grange	N Yks	SE6041	53°51·9'	1°4·8'W	X	105
Stillingfleet Ho	N Yks	SE5841	53°52·0'	1°6·7'W	X	105
Stillington	N Yks	SE5867	54°6·0'	1°6·4'W	T	100
Stillington	Stock on T	NZ3723	54°36·3'	1°25·2'W	T	93
Stillington Grange	N Yks	SE5568	54°6·5'	1°9·1'W	X	100
Still Loch, The	Arg & Bt	NR8185	56°0·7'	5°30·4'W	W	55
Stillmeadow Fm	E Yorks	TA1635	53°48·1'	0°13·9'W	FM	107
Stillswells	Aberd	NJ8554	57°34·8'	2°14·6'W	X	30
St Illtyd	Blae Gw	SO2101	51°42·4'	3°8·2'W	T	171
St Illtyd's Way	Carm	SN5203	51°42·6'	4°8·1'W	X	159
Stilstead	Kent	TQ6547	51°12·1'	0°22·1'E	X	188
Stilton	Cambs	TL1689	52°29·4'	0°17·1'W	T	142
Stilton Fen	Cambs	TL1889	52°29·4'	0°15·3'W	X	142
Stilton House Fm	N Yks	SE5984	54°15·1'	1°5·2'W	FM	100
Stimmy Fm	Wrex	SJ4738	52°56·4'	2°46·9'W	FM	126
Stinchar Br	S Ayr	NX3995	55°13·6'	4°31·5'W	X	77
Stinchcombe	Glos	ST7398	51°41·0'	2°23·0'W	T	162
Stinchcombe Hill	Glos	ST7498	51°41·0'	2°22·2'W	H	162
Stines Moss	Orkney	HY3108	58°57·5'	3°11·5'W	X	6,7
Sting Bank Burn	E Loth	NT5362	55°51·2'	2°44·6'W	W	66
Sting Burn	Northum	NT9413	55°24·9'	2°5·3'W	W	80
Stinger's Hill	Devon	SX6366	50°28·9'	3°55·5'W	X	202
Sting Head	Northum	NT9312	55°24·4'	2°6·2'W	X	80
Sting Hill	E Loth	NT6967	55°54·0'	2°29·3'W	H	67
Sting Law	Scot Bord	NT6554	55°46·9'	2°33·0'W	X	67,74
Sting Rig	Scot Bord	NT2028	55°32·6'	3°15·6'W	H	73
Stingwern	Powys	SJ1300	52°35·7'	3°16·7'W	X	136
Stingwern Hill	Powys	SJ1301	52°36·2'	3°16·7'W	H	136
Stinkanie Geo	Orkney	HY3835	59°12·1'	3°4·6'W	X	6
Stinking Bay	N Ayr	NS1759	55°47·6'	4°54·7'W	W	63
Stinking Cove	Corn	SW8576	50°32·9'	5°1·7'W	W	200
Stinking Crag	Cumbr	NY0748	54°49·3'	3°26·4'W	X	85
Stinking Goat	Northum	NU1238	55°38·4'	1°48·1'W	W	75
Stinking Rocks	S Ayr	NS3233	55°34·0'	4°39·4'W	X	70
Stinking Stone	Brad	SE0142	53°52·7'	1°58·7'W	X	104
Stinsford	Dorset	SY7191	50°43·3'	2°24·3'W	T	194
Stinton Hall Fm	Norf	TG1125	52°47·1'	1°8·1'E	FM	133
Stints, The	Leic	SK5022	52°47·8'	1°15·1'W	X	129
St Inunger Fm	Corn	SX0563	50°26·3'	4°44·4'W	FM	200
Stiolamair	N Eil	NG2194	57°51·2'	6°41·7'W	X	14
Stiperden Bar Ho	Lancs	SD9128	53°45·1'	2°7·8'W	X	103
Stiperden Moor	Lancs	SD9028	53°45·1'	2°8·7'W	X	103
Stiper's Hill	Worcs	SO6369	52°19·3'	2°32·2'W	X	138
Stiperstones	Shrops	SJ3600	52°35·9'	2°56·3'W	T	126
Stiperstones	Shrops	SO3698	52°34·8'	2°56·3'W	H	137
Stippadon	Devon	SX7062	50°26·8'	3°49·5'W	X	202
St Ippollitts	Herts	TL1927	51°56·0'	0°15·8'W	T	166
Stirch	Northnts	SP5055	52°11·7'	1°15·7'W	X	151
Stirches Mains	Scot Bord	NT4916	55°26·4'	2°47·9'W	X	79
Stirchley	Birm	SP0581	52°25·9'	1°55·2'W	T	139
Stirchley	Wrekin	SJ7006	52°39·3'	2°26·2'W	T	127
Stirkfield	Scot Bord	NT1040	55°39·0'	3°25·4'W	X	72
Stirkfield Hope	Scot Bord	NT1140	55°39·0'	3°24·4'W	H	72
Stirkhill Plantn	Northum	NU1407	55°21·7'	1°46·3'W	F	81
Stirk Ho (Hotel)	Lancs	SD8148	53°55·9'	2°16·9'W	X	103
Stirkoke Ho	Highld	ND3150	58°26·2'	3°10·4'W	X	11,12
Stirkpool	D & G	NY2172	55°2·4'	3°13·7'W	X	85
Stirley Hill	Kirk	SE1413	53°37·0'	1°46·9'W	X	110
Stirling	Aberd	NJ6300	57°5·6'	2°36·2'W	X	37
Stirling	Aberd	NK1242	57°28·3'	1°47·5'W	T	30
Stirling	Stir	NS7993	56°7·1'	3°56·3'W	T	57
Stirling Corner	Barnet	TQ2095	51°38·7'	0°15·5'W	X	166,176
Stirling Hill	Aberd	NK1241	57°27·8'	1°47·5'W	X	30
Stirrup	Stock	SJ9892	53°25·7'	2°1·4'W	X	109
Stirrup Benches	Stock	SJ9891	53°25·2'	2°1·4'W	X	109
Stirrup Crag	Cumbr	NY1709	54°28·4'	3°16·4'W	X	89,90
Stirrup Mark, The	Highld	NG8950	57°29·7'	5°30·8'W	X	24
Stirtloe	Cambs	TL1966	52°17·0'	0°14·9'W	T	153
Stirton	Fife	NO3521	56°22·9'	3°2·7'W	X	54,59
Stirton	N Yks	SD9752	53°58·1'	2°2·3'W	T	103
Stirton Mill	Fife	NO3621	56°22·9'	3°1·7'W	X	54,59
St Ishmael	Carm	SN3608	51°44·4'	4°22·2'W	X	159
St Ishmael's	Pemb	SM8307	51°43·4'	5°8·1'W	T	157
St Issey	Corn	SW9271	50°30·3'	4°55·6'W	T	200
Stisted	Essex	TL8024	51°53·4'	0°37·3'E	T	168
Stitchcombe	Wilts	SU2269	51°25·4'	1°40·6'W	T	174
Stitchel Hill	Scot Bord	NY5398	55°16·7'	2°44·0'W	H	79
Stitches Fm	Cambs	TL4492	52°30·6'	0°7·7'E	FM	142,143
Stitches Fm	E Susx	TQ5533	51°4·7'	0°13·2'E	FM	188
Stitchin's Hill	Worcs	SO7551	52°9·6'	2°21·5'W	T	150
Stitchpool	Devon	SS7233	51°5·2'	3°49·3'W	X	180
Stithians	Corn	SW7336	50°11·1'	5°10·4'W	T	204
Stithians Resr	Corn	SW7136	50°11·0'	5°12·1'W	W	203
Stitley	Highld	ND1468	58°35·8'	3°28·3'W	X	11,12
Stittenham	Highld	NH6574	57°44·4'	4°15·6'W	X	21
Stittenham Wood	Highld	NH6474	57°44·4'	4°16·6'W	F	21
Stittenham Wood	N Yks	SE6767	54°5·9'	0°58·1'W	F	100
Stitt Fms	Shrops	SO4098	52°34·8'	2°52·7'W	FM	137
Stitt Hill	Shrops	SO4097	52°34·3'	2°52·7'W	X	137
Stitworthy Fm	Devon	SS2921	50°58·0'	4°25·7'W	FM	190
Stiughaigh	N Eil	NG1996	57°52·2'	6°43·9'W	X	14
Stiughaigh na Leum	N Eil	NG2095	57°51·7'	6°42·8'W	X	14
Stiva	Shetld	HU3457	60°18·0'	1°22·6'W	X	2,3
Stiva	Shetld	HU4778	60°29·2'	1°8·2'W	X	2,3
St Ive	Corn	SX3067	50°28·9'	4°23·4'W	T	201
St Ive Cross	Corn	SX3167	50°28·9'	4°22·6'W	T	201
Stiver's Wood	E Susx	TQ6434	51°5·1'	0°20·9'E	F	188
St Ives	Brad	SE0938	53°50·5'	1°51·4'W	X	104
St Ives	Cambs	TL3072	52°20·1'	0°5·1'W	T	153
St Ives	Corn	SW5140	50°12·7'	5°29·0'W	T	203
St Ives	Dorset	SU1204	50°50·4'	1°49·4'W	T	195
St Ives Bay	Corn	SW5440	50°12·8'	5°26·5'W	W	203
St Ives Fm	E Susx	TQ4636	51°6·5'	0°5·5'E	FM	188
St Ives Fm	N Yks	NZ9202	54°24·5'	0°34·5'W	FM	94
St Ives Head or The Island	Corn	SW5241	50°13·3'	5°28·2'W	X	203
Stivichall	Cov	SP3376	52°23·1'	1°30·5'W	T	140
Stivichall Common	Cov	SP3276	52°23·1'	1°31·4'W	X	140
Stivi Geo	Shetld	HU5966	60°22·7'	0°55·3'W	X	2
Stivva	Shetld	HU3070	60°25·0'	1°26·8'W	X	3
Stixwould	Lincs	TF1765	53°10·4'	0°14·6'W	T	121
Stixwould Grange	Lincs	TF1763	53°9·3'	0°14·6'W	X	121
Stixwould Wood	Lincs	TF1866	53°10·9'	0°13·6'W	F	122
St Jacob's Hall	Suff	TM3071	52°17·6'	1°22·8'E	X	156
St James	C of West	TQ2980	51°30·5'	0°8·1'W	T	176
St James	Dorset	ST8622	51°0·1'	2°11·6'W	T	183
St James	Norf	TG2720	52°44·0'	1°22·1'E	T	133,134
ST James Chapel	Suff	TL9744	52°3·8'	0°52·8'E	A	155
St James Church	Somer	SS9829	51°3·3'	3°26·9'W	A	181
St Jame's Fm	Suff	TM3081	52°22·9'	1°23·6'E	FM	156
St James's	Aberd	NO4699	57°5·0'	2°53·0'W	X	37,44
St James's Church	Oxon	SU7286	51°34·3'	0°57·3'W	A	175
St James's Common	Dorset	ST8521	50°59·5'	2°12·4'W	X	183
St James's End	Northnts	SP7460	52°14·2'	0°54·6'W	T	152
St James's Fm	Lincs	TF2610	52°40·6'	0°7·8'W	FM	131,142
St James's Lochs	Aberd	NO7471	56°50·0'	2°25·1'W	W	45
St James South Elmham	Suff	TM3281	52°22·9'	1°24·9'E	T	156
St James's Park	C of West	TQ2979	51°29·9'	0°8·1'W	T	176
St James's Stone	Devon	SS1346	51°11·2'	4°40·2'W	X	180
St Jidgey	Corn	SW9469	50°29·3'	4°53·9'W	T	200

St Joan à Gore Fm	Wilts	SU0150	51°15·2′	1°58·8′W	FM	184
St John	Corn	SX4053	50°21·5′	4°14·6′W	T	201
St Johns	Bucks	TQ0181	51°31·4′	0°32·3′W	X	176
St Johns	Devon	SX6888	50°40·8′	3°51·7′W	X	191
St John's	E Susx	TQ5031	51°3·7′	0°8·8′E	T	188
St John's	I of M	SC2781	54°12·0′	4°38·7′W	T	95
St John's	Kent	TQ5256	51°17·2′	0°11·2′E	T	188
St John's	Kent	TQ5570	51°24·7′	0°14·1′E	A	177
St John's	Kent	TQ5841	51°9·0′	0°15·9′E	T	188
St John's	Leeds	SE4337	53°49·9′	1°20·4′W	T	105
St Johns	Lew	TQ3776	51°28·2′	0°1·3′W	T	177
St Johns	Roth	SK5287	53°22·9′	1°12·7′W	X	111,120
St Johns	Scot Bord	NT9357	55°48·6′	2°6·3′W	X	67,74,75
St Johns	Surrey	SU9857	51°18·4′	0°35·3′W	T	175,186
St Johns	Warw	SP2870	52°19·9′	1°34·9′W	T	140
St John's	Worcs	SO8354	52°11·3′	2°14·5′W	T	150
St John's Beck	Cumbr	NY3121	54°35·0′	3°3·6′W	W	90
St John's Br	Oxon	SU2298	51°41·1′	1°40·5′W	X	163
St John's Cairn	Moray	NJ1107	57°9·0′	3°27·8′W	X	36
St John's Castle	Glos	SO8834	52°0·5′	2°10·1′W	A	
St John's Castle	Glos	SO8834	52°0·5′	2°10·1′W	A	150
St John's Chapel	Devon	SS5329	51°2·7′	4°5·4′W	T	180
St John's Chapel	Durham	NY8838	54°44·5′	2°10·8′W	T	91,92
St John's Chapel(ruin)	Highld	NG3043	57°24·1′	6°29·2′W	X	23
St John's Church	Aberd	NJ7964	57°40·2′	2°20·7′W	A	29,30
St John's College Fm	Cambs	TL3467	52°17·3′	0°1·7′W	FM	154
St John's cross	Hants	SU3342	51°10·8′	1°31·3′W	X	185
St John's Fen End	Norf	TF5311	52°40·7′	0°16·2′E	T	131,143
St John's Fm	Cambs	TL5977	52°22·3′	0°20·5′E	FM	143
St John's Fm	Essex	TQ4795	51°38·3′	0°7·9′E	FM	167,177
St Johns Fm	Kent	TR2343	51°8·8′	1°11·7′E	FM	179,189
St John's Fm	Norf	TF7405	52°37·1′	0°34·6′E	FM	143
St John's Fm	Suff	TM0977	52°21·3′	1°4·5′E	FM	144
St John's Fm	Wilts	ST9980	51°31·4′	2°0·5′W	FM	173
St John's Grove	Suff	TM0555	52°9·5′	1°0·2′E	F	155
St John's Hall	Durham	NZ0633	54°41·8′	1°54·0′W	X	92
St John's Hall	Suff	TM3687	52°26·0′	1°28·7′E	X	156
St John's Haven	Northum	NT9856	55°48·1′	2°1·5′W	W	75
St John's Head	Orkney	HY1803	58°54·7′	3°24·9′W	X	7
St John's Highway	Norf	TF5214	52°42·4′	0°15·4′E	T	131
St John's Hill	Aberd	NO8377	56°53·3′	2°16·3′W	H	45
St John's Ho	Hants	SU5530	50°59·9′	1°16·6′W	A	185
St John's in the Vale	Cumbr	NY3122	54°35·6′	3°3·7′W	X	90
St John's Kirk	S Lanak	NS9836	55°36·7′	3°36·7′W	X	72
St John's Knap	Aberd	NO8477	56°53·3′	2°15·3′W	H	45
St John's Lake	Corn	SX4254	50°22·1′	4°12·9′W	W	201
St John's Loch	Highld	ND2272	58°38·0′	3°20·1′W	W	7,12
St Johns Lodge Fm	Suff	TM3587	52°26·0′	1°27·8′E	FM	156
St John's Park	I of W	SZ6092	50°43·7′	1°8·6′W	T	196
St John's Point	Highld	ND3175	58°39·7′	3°10·9′W	X	7,12
St John's Sch	Northnts	SP7051	52°9·4′	0°58·2′W	X	152
St John's Spring	Northnts	SP7665	52°16·9′	0°52·8′W	W	152
St John's Town of Dalry	D & G	NX6281	55°6·5′	4°9·4′W	T	77
St John's Well	Devon	SS5504	50°49·3′	4°3·1′W	A	191
St John's Well Plantn	N Yks	SE6065	54°4·9′	1°4·6′W	F	100
St John's Wells	Aberd	NJ7936	57°25·1′	2°20·5′W	X	29,30
St John's Wood	C of West	TQ2683	51°32·1′	0°10·6′W	T	176
St John's Wood	Herts	TL3025	51°54·7′	0°6·2′W	F	166
St John's Wood Fm	Peterb	TL0399	52°35·0′	0°28·4′W	FM	141
St Joseph's Hospl	Midlo	NT2961	55°50·5′	3°7·6′W	X	66
St Joseph's School	Surrey	TQ0640	51°9·2′	0°28·7′W	X	187
St Judes	I of M	SC3996	54°20·3′	4°28·2′W	T	95
St Jude's Fm	Beds	TL0740	52°3·1′	0°26·0′W	FM	153
St Julians	Herts	TL1405	51°44·2′	0°20·5′W	T	166
St Julian's	Kent	TQ5452	51°15·0′	0°12·8′E	X	188
St Julians	Newp	ST3289	51°36·0′	2°58·5′W	T	171
St Just	Corn	SW3631	50°7·5′	5°41·3′W	T	203
St Justinian	Pemb	SM7225	51°52·9′	5°18·4′W	X	157
St Just in Roseland	Corn	SW8535	50°10·8′	5°0·3′W	T	204
St Just or Land's End Aerodrome	Corn	SW3729	50°6·4′	5°40·3′W	X	203
St Just Pool	Corn	SW8435	50°10·8′	5°1·2′W	W	204
St Katharines	Wilts	SU2564	51°22·7′	1°38·1′W	X	174
ST Katherine Docks	T Ham	TQ3480	51°30·4′	0°3·8′W	X	177
St Katherines	Aberd	NJ7834	57°24·0′	2°21·5′W	T	29,30
St Kenelm's Well	Glos	SP0427	51°56·7′	1°56·1′W	A	163
St Kenox	Pemb	SN0716	51°48·8′	4°47·6′W	X	158
St Keverne	Corn	SW7921	50°3·1′	5°4·9′W	T	204
St Kew	Corn	SX0276	50°33·3′	4°47·3′W	T	200
St Kew Highway	Corn	SX0375	50°32·7′	4°46·5′W	T	200
St Keyne	Corn	SX2460	50°25·0′	4°28·3′W	T	201
St Kilda or Hirta	N Eil	NF0999	57°48·8′	8°34·7′W	X	18
St Lawrence	Corn	SX0466	50°27·9′	4°45·3′W	T	200
ST Lawrence	Essex	TL9505	51°42·8′	0°49·8′E	T	168
St Lawrence	Essex	TL9604	51°42·3′	0°50·6′E	T	168
St Lawrence	I of W	SZ5376	50°35·1′	1°14·7′W	T	196
St Lawrence	Kent	TR3665	51°20·3′	1°23·7′E	T	179
St Lawrence Bay	Essex	TL9605	51°42·8′	0°50·6′E	W	168
St Lawrence Fm	Herts	TL3104	51°43·4′	0°5·8′W	FM	166
St Lawrence's Chapel	Durham	NZ1616	54°32·6′	1°44·7′W	A	92
St Leonards	Bucks	SP9107	51°45·5′	0°40·5′W	T	165
St Leonards	Devon	SS2423	50°59·0′	4°30·1′W	X	190
St Leonards	Dorset	SU1103	50°49·8′	1°50·2′W	T	195
St Leonards	Essex	TL3904	51°43·3′	0°1·1′E	X	166
St Leonards	Essex	TL6200	51°40·7′	0°21·0′E	X	167
St Leonards	E Susx	TQ7909	50°51·4′	0°33·0′E	T	199
St Leonards	Scot Bord	NT4912	55°24·2′	2°47·9′W	X	79
St Leonards	Scot Bord	NT5545	55°42·0′	2°42·5′W	X	73
St Leonards	Win & Maid	SU9374	51°27·7′	0°39·3′W	X	175
St Leonards	W Susx	TQ2031	51°4·2′	0°16·8′W	X	187
St Leonard's Chapel	Kent	TQ6756	51°16·9′	0°24·1′E	A	178,188
St Leonard's Forest	W Susx	TQ2231	51°4·1′	0°15·1′W	F	187
St Leonards Grange	Hants	SZ4098	50°47·0′	1°25·6′W	X	196
St Leonard's Hospital	Northum	NU1814	55°25·4′	1°42·5′W	A	81
St Leonard's Priory	Glos	SO8003	51°43·8′	2°17·0′W	A	162
St Leonard's Park	Scot Bord	NT4811	55°23·7′	2°48·8′W	X	79
St Leonard's Street	Kent	TQ6756	51°16·9′	0°24·1′E	T	178,188
St Leonard's Well	E Yorks	SE7753	53°58·3′	0°49·2′W	W	105,106
St Levan	Corn	SW3822	50°2·7′	5°39·2′W	T	203

St Lois Fm	E Yorks	SE7149	53°56·2′	0°54·7′W	FM	105,106
St Lois Fm	E Yorks	SE7453	53°58·3′	0°51·9′W	FM	105,106
St Lonan's Ch	I of M	SC4279	54°11·2′	4°24·9′W	A	95
St Loy	Corn	SW4223	50°3·3′	5°35·9′W	X	203
St Loy's Cove	Corn	SW4222	50°2·8′	5°35·9′W	W	203
St Luke's	C of Derb	SK3335	52°54·9′	1°30·1′W	T	128
St Lukes	Corn	SX1976	50°33·6′	4°33·0′W	X	201
St Luke's	Isling	TQ3282	51°31·5′	0°5·4′W	T	176,177
St Lythans	V of Glam	ST1072	51°26·6′	3°17·3′W	T	171
St Lythans Down	V of Glam	ST1173	51°27·2′	3°16·5′W	X	171
St Mabyn	Corn	SX0473	50°31·7′	4°45·6′W	T	200
St Machar's Cross & Well	Aberd	NO5099	57°5·0′	2°49·0′W	A	37,44
St Madoes	Pth & Kin	NO1920	56°22·2′	3°18·2′W	T	53,58
St Magnus Bay	Shetld	HU2568	60°24·0′	1°32·3′W	W	3
St Magnus's Ch	Orkney	HY4630	59°9·5′	2°56·2′W	A	5,6
St Margaret's	Beds	TL0726	51°55·6′	0°26·2′W	X	166
St Margarets	Heref	SO3533	51°59·7′	2°56·4′W	T	149,161
St Margarets	Herts	TL0211	51°47·5′	0°30·9′W	X	166
St Margarets	Herts	TL3811	51°47·1′	0°0·4′E	T	166
St Margarets	Kent	TQ5770	51°24·7′	0°15·8′E	X	177
St Margarets	Rich	TQ1774	51°27·4′	0°18·6′W	T	176
St Margaret's at Cliffe	Kent	TR3644	51°9·0′	1°22·9′E	T	179
St Margaret's Bay	Kent	TR3744	51°9·0′	1°23·7′E	W	179
St Margaret's Fm	Herts	TL0111	51°47·5′	0°31·7′W	FM	166
St Margaret's Fm	Northum	NU1509	55°22·7′	1°45·4′W	FM	81
St Margaret's Hope	Fife	NT1081	56°1·1′	3°26·2′W	W	65
St Margaret's Hope	Orkney	ND4493	58°49·5′	2°57·7′W	T	7
St Margaret's Hope	Orkney	ND4494	58°50·1′	2°57·7′W	W	7
St Margaret's Island	Pemb	SS1297	51°38·7′	4°42·6′W	X	158
St Margaret South Elmham	Suff	TM3183	52°24·0′	1°24·1′E	T	156
St Margaret's Stone	Fife	NT1085	56°3·2′	3°26·3′W	X	65
St Mark's	Glos	SO9222	51°54·0′	2°6·6′W	T	163
St Mark's	I of M	SC2974	54°8·3′	4°36·6′W	T	95
St Martha's Hill	Surrey	TQ0248	51°13·6′	0°32·0′W	H	186
St Martin	Corn	SW7323	50°4·1′	5°10·0′W	T	204
St Martin	Corn	SX2655	50°22·4′	4°26·4′W	T	201
St Martin's	E Renf	NS5051	55°44·0′	4°22·9′W	X	64
St Martins	Highld	NH6463	57°38·4′	4°16·2′W	X	21
St Martin's	I Scilly	SV9215	49°57·6′	6°17·3′W	X	203
St Martins	Pth & Kin	NO1530	56°27·5′	3°22·3′W	T	53
St Martin's	Shrops	SJ3236	52°55·3′	3°0·3′W	T	126
St Martin's Bay	I Scilly	SV9216	49°58·1′	6°17·4′W	W	203
St Martins Ch	Dorset	ST8707	50°52·0′	2°10·7′W	A	194
St Martin's Convent	Leic	SP4097	52°34·4′	1°24·2′W	X	140
St Martin's Down	I of W	SZ5680	50°37·2′	1°12·1′W	X	196
St Martin's Flats	I Scilly	SV9215	49°57·6′	6°17·3′W	X	203
St Martin's Fm	Suff	TM2276	52°20·4′	1°15·9′E	FM	156
St Martin's Head	I Scilly	SV9416	49°58·2′	6°15·7′W	X	203
St Martin's Moor	Shrops	SJ3135	52°54·7′	3°1·2′W	T	126
St Martins Plain	Kent	TR1836	51°5·1′	1°7·2′E	X	179,189
St Mary Bourne	Hants	SU4250	51°15·1′	1°23·5′W	T	185
St Marychurch	Torbay	SX9266	50°29·3′	3°31·0′W	T	202
St Mary Church	V of Glam	ST0071	51°26·0′	3°25·9′W	T	170
St Mary Cray	Brom	TQ4667	51°23·2′	0°6·3′E	T	177
St Mary Hall	Essex	TL8039	52°1·4′	0°37·8′E	X	155
St Mary Hill	V of Glam	SS9678	51°29·7′	3°29·5′W	T	170
St Mary Hill Down	V of Glam	SS9678	51°29·7′	3°29·5′W	H	170
St Mary Hoo	Medway	TQ8076	51°27·5′	0°35·9′E	T	178
St Mary in the Marsh	Kent	TR0627	51°0·5′	0°56·6′E	T	189
St Marys	Devon	SY3195	50°45·3′	2°58·3′W	X	193
St Mary's	I Scilly	SV9111	49°55·4′	6°18·0′W	X	203
St Marys	Moray	NJ3255	57°35·1′	3°7·8′W	X	28
St Mary's	Orkney	HY4701	58°53·8′	2°54·7′W	T	6,7
St Mary's Abbey	Gwyn	SH1222	52°46·0′	4°46·8′W	A	123
St Mary's Bay	Kent	TR0827	51°0·5′	0°58·3′E	T	189
St Mary's Bay	Medway	TQ7979	51°29·1′	0°35·1′E	W	178
St Mary's Bay	Orkney	HY4700	58°53·3′	2°54·7′W	W	6,7
St Marys Bay	Torbay	SX9355	50°23·3′	3°29·9′W	W	202
St Mary's Br	Norf	TF5813	52°41·7′	0°20·7′E	X	131,143
St Mary's Chapel	Highld	ND0270	58°36·7′	3°40·7′W	A	12
St Mary's Church	Aberd	NO8887	56°58·7′	2°11·4′W	A	45
St Mary's Church	Cered	SN3444	52°4·4′	4°24·9′W	A	145
St Mary's Church	Durham	NZ0712	54°30·4′	1°53·1′W	A	92
St Mary's Church	Essex	TM1230	51°55·9′	1°5·4′E	A	168,169
St Mary's Church	Kent	TR2269	51°22·8′	1°11·8′E	A	179
St Mary's Church	Shetld	HU5242	60°9·8′	1°3·3′W	A	4
St Mary's Cott	Scot Bord	NT7855	55°47·5′	2°20·6′W	X	67,74
St Mary's Croft	D & G	NX0365	54°56·7′	5°4·1′W	X	82
St Mary's Fm	Essex	TM1121	51°51·1′	1°4·2′E	FM	168,169
St Mary's Fm	E Susx	TQ3410	50°52·7′	0°5·3′W	FM	198
St Mary's Fm	Fife	NO3415	56°19·6′	3°3·6′W	FM	59
St Mary's Fm	Suff	TM4486	52°25·3′	1°35·7′E	FM	156
St Mary's Glebe Fm	Norf	TF7305	52°37·1′	0°33·7′E	FM	143
St Marys Graveyard	Scot Bord	NT2523	55°30·0′	3°10·8′W	X	73
St Mary's Hall	Norf	TF5814	52°42·3′	0°20·7′E	X	131
St Mary's Ho	E Susx	TQ3318	50°57·0′	0°6·0′W	X	198
St Mary's Home	Derby	SK2342	52°58·7′	1°39·0′W	X	119,128
St Mary's Hospital	Northum	NZ1881	55°7·6′	1°42·6′W	X	81
St Mary's Island	Medway	TQ7670	51°24·3′	0°32·2′E	X	178
St Mary's Isle	D & G	NX6749	54°49·3′	4°3·8′W	X	83,84
St Mary's Loch	Scot Bord	NT2422	55°29·4′	3°11·7′W	W	73
St Mary's Marshes	Medway	TQ8078	51°28·6′	0°35·9′E	X	178
St Mary's Mill	Powys	SO2965	52°17·0′	3°2·1′W	X	137,148
St Mary's or Bait Island	N Tyne	NZ3575	55°4·3′	1°26·7′W	X	88
St Mary's or Conister Rock	I of M	SC3875	54°9·0′	4°28·4′W	X	95
St Mary's or Newton Haven	Northum	NU2424	55°30·8′	1°36·8′W	X	75
St Mary's Pool	I Scilly	SV9011	49°55·4′	6°18·8′W	W	203
St Mary's Priory	Oxon	SU2892	51°37·8′	1°35·3′W	X	163,174
St Mary's Sch	Wilts	ST8822	51°0·1′	2°9·9′W	X	183
St Mary's Sound	I Scilly	SV8809	49°54·2′	6°20·4′W	W	203
St Mary's Vale	Cumbr	NY5663	54°57·8′	2°40·8′W	X	86
St Mary's Well	Devon	SS5205	50°49·8′	4°5·7′W	A	191
St Mary's Well	D & G	NX0365	54°56·7′	5°4·1′W	A	82
St Mary's Well	Highld	ND0269	58°36·1′	3°40·7′W	A	12
St Mary's Well	Highld	NH7783	57°49·4′	4°3·8′W	A	21
St Mary's Well Bay	V of Glam	ST1767	51°24·0′	3°11·2′W	W	171
St Maughans	Monm	SO4617	51°51·2′	2°46·6′W	T	161

St Maughans Green	Monm	SO4717	51°51·2′	2°45·8′W	T	161
St Mawes	Corn	SW8433	50°9·7′	5°1·1′W	T	204
St Mawes Castle	Corn	SW8432	50°9·2′	5°1·1′W	A	204
St Mawes Harbour	Corn	SW8432	50°9·2′	5°1·1′W	W	204
St Mawgan	Corn	SW8765	50°27·0′	4°59·7′W	T	200
St Mawgan Airfield	Corn	SW8664	50°26·4′	5°0·5′W	X	200
St Mellion	Corn	SX3865	50°28·0′	4°16·6′W	T	201
St Mellons	Card	ST2381	51°31·6′	3°6·2′W	T	171
St Merin's Church	Gwyn	SH1731	52°51·0′	4°42·7′W	A	123
St Merryn	Corn	SW8873	50°31·3′	4°59·1′W	T	200
St Mewan	Corn	SW9951	50°19·7′	4°49·1′W	T	200,204
St Michael Caerhays	Corn	SW9642	50°14·8′	4°51·3′W	T	204
St Michael Church	Somer	ST3030	51°4·1′	2°59·6′W	T	182
St Michaels	Kent	TQ8835	51°5·2′	0°41·5′E	T	189
St Michaels	Torbay	SX8860	50°26·0′	3°34·2′W	T	202
St Michaels	Worcs	SO5865	52°17·1′	2°36·5′W	T	137,138,149
St Michael's Chapel	Devon	SS4937	51°7·0′	4°9·1′W	A	180
St Michaels Cheshire Home	Somer	ST4354	51°17·2′	2°48·7′W	X	182
St Michael's Court	Kent	TQ8737	51°6·3′	0°40·7′E	X	189
St Michael's Hamlet	Liv	SJ3686	53°22·3′	2°57·3′W	T	108
St Michael's Hill	Somer	ST4917	50°57·2′	2°43·2′W	H	183,193
St Michael's Island	I of M	SC2967	54°4·5′	4°36·4′W	X	95
St Michael's Mead	Herts	TL4720	51°51·8′	0°8·5′E	X	167
St Michael's Mount	Corn	SW5129	50°6·8′	5°28·6′W	X	203
St Michael's on Wyre	Lancs	SD4641	53°52·0′	2°48·9′W	T	102
St Michael South Elmham	Suff	TM3483	52°23·9′	1°26·8′E	T	156
St Michael's Pool	Powys	SO1869	52°19·0′	3°11·8′W	W	136,148
St Michael's Walls	D & G	NY1384	55°8·8′	3°21·5′W	X	78
St Michael's Wood	Fife	NO4423	56°24·0′	2°54·0′W	F	54,59
St Micheal Penkevil	Corn	SW8542	50°14·6′	5°0·6′W	T	204
St Milburga's Priory	Shrops	SJ6200	52°36·0′	2°33·3′W	A	127,138
St Milburgha's Well	Shrops	SO5682	52°26·3′	2°38·4′W	W	137,138
St Mildred's Bay	Kent	TR3270	51°23·1′	1°20·5′E	W	179
St Minver	Corn	SW9677	50°33·7′	4°52·4′W	T	200
St Molnag's Chapel	Highld	NG5436	57°21·1′	6°4·9′W	A	24,32
St Monance	Fife	NO5201	56°12·2′	2°46·0′W	T	59
St Monance Burn	Fife	NO5102	56°12·7′	2°47·0′W	W	59
St Mungo's Ch	D & G	NY1275	55°4·0′	3°22·3′W	A	85
St Mungo's Fm	Pth & Kin	NN9307	56°14·9′	3°43·2′W	FM	58
St Murray	S Ayr	NS3011	55°22·1′	4°40·5′W	X	70
St Nectan's Glen	Corn	SX0788	50°39·8′	4°43·5′W	X	190,200
St Nectan's Kieve	Corn	SX0888	50°39·8′	4°42·6′W	X	190,200
St Neot	Corn	SX1867	50°28·7′	4°33·5′W	T	201
St Neot River or River Loveny	Corn	SX1868	50°29·2′	4°33·6′W	W	201
St Neots	Cambs	TL1860	52°13·8′	0°15·9′W	T	153
St Newlyn East	Corn	SW8256	50°22·0′	5°3·6′W	T	200
St Nicholas	Herts	TL2526	51°55·3′	0°10·5′W	T	166
St Nicholas	Pemb	SM9035	51°58·7′	5°3·1′W	T	157
St Nicholas	V of Glam	ST0974	51°27·7′	3°18·2′W	T	171
St Nicholas at Wade	Kent	TR2666	51°21·1′	1°15·1′E	T	179
St Nicholas Court	Kent	TR2566	51°21·1′	1°14·3′E	X	179
St Nicholas Fm	Wok	SU7972	51°26·7′	0°51·4′W	FM	175
St Nicholas Ho	Lincs	TF2216	52°43·9′	0°11·2′W	X	131
St Nicholas Rock	S Ayr	NS3222	55°28·0′	4°39·0′W	X	70
St Nicholas's Church	Kent	TR3546	51°10·1′	1°22·1′E	A	179
St Nicholas South Elmham	Suff	TM3282	52°23·4′	1°25·0′E	T	156
St Nicolas Park	Warw	SP3793	52°32·3′	1°26·9′W	T	140
St Ninians	Highld	NH5230	57°20·5′	4°27·1′W	X	26
St Ninians	Stir	NS7991	56°6·0′	3°56·3′W	T	57
St Ninian's Bay	Arg & Bt	NS0361	55°48·4′	5°8·2′W	W	63
St Ninian's Bay	Shetld	HU3720	59°58·1′	1°19·7′W	W	4
St Ninian's Cave	D & G	NX4236	54°41·9′	4°26·7′W	A	83
St Ninian's Chapel	D & G	NX4836	54°42·0′	4°21·1′W	A	83
St Ninian's Isle	Shetld	HU3621	59°58·6′	1°20·8′W	X	4
St Ninian's Point	Arg & Bt	NS0361	55°48·4′	5°8·2′W	X	63
St Ninian's Well	Cumbr	NY4251	54°51·3′	2°53·8′W	A	85
St Ninian's Well	D & G	NX4262	54°55·9′	4°27·5′W	A	83
St Nonna's Well	Corn	SX2256	50°22·9′	4°29·8′W	A	201
St Non's Bay	Pemb	SM7524	51°52·4′	5°15·7′W	W	157
Stoaches Fm	W Susx	TQ3826	51°1·2′	0°1·6′W	FM	187,198
Stoak	Ches	SJ4273	53°15·3′	2°51·8′W	T	117
Stoak Grange	Ches	SJ4273	53°15·3′	2°51·8′W	X	117
Stoal	Shetld	HU5487	60°34·0′	1°0·4′W	X	1,2
Stob a Bhiora	Stir	NN4032	56°27·4′	4°35·3′W	X	51
Stob a' Bhruaich Léith	Arg & Bt	NN2045	56°34·0′	4°55·3′W	H	50
Stob a' Chearcaill	Highld	NG8402	57°3·8′	5°33·3′W	X	33
Stob a' Choin	Stir	NN4116	56°18·8′	4°33·8′W	H	56
Stob a Choin Duibh	Stir	NS4396	56°8·1′	4°31·1′W	X	56
Stob á Choire Léith	Highld	NN2573	56°49·2′	4°51·6′W	X	41
Stob a' Choire Mheadhoin	Highld	NN3173	56°49·3′	4°45·7′W	H	41
Stob a' Choire Odhair	Highld	NG8304	57°4·8′	5°34·4′W	X	33
Stob a' Choire Odhair	Highld	NN2546	56°34·7′	4°50·5′W	H	50
Stob a' Chùir	Highld	NM9071	56°47·3′	5°25·8′W	H	40
Stob a' Ghlais Choire	Highld	NN2451	56°37·3′	4°51·7′W	X	41
Stob a' Ghrianain	Highld	NN0882	56°53·6′	5°8·7′W	H	41
Stob an Aonaich Mhóir	Pth & Kin	NN5369	56°47·6′	4°24·0′W	H	42
Stob an Cul Choire	Highld	NN2272	56°48·6′	4°54·5′W	X	41
Stoban Dubha	Arg & Bt	NN2412	56°16·3′	4°50·1′W	H	50,56
Stob an Duibhe	Stir	NN3915	56°18·3′	4°35·7′W	H	50,56
Stob an Duine Ruaidh	Arg & Bt	NN1140	56°31·1′	5°3·9′W	H	50
Stob an Eas	Arg & Bt	NN1807	56°13·5′	4°55·7′W	H	56
Stob an Fhàinne	Stir	NN3511	56°16·0′	4°39·4′W	H	50,56
Stob an Fhithich	Arg & Bt	NN3015	56°18·1′	4°44·4′W	H	50,56
Stob an Fhuarain	Highld	NN1152	56°37·6′	5°4·4′W	H	41
Stob an Tighe Aird	Stir	NN2726	56°23·9′	4°47·7′W	X	50
Stob an t-Sléibhe	Highld	NN3679	56°52·7′	4°41·0′W	H	41
Stob an t-Sluichd	Moray	NJ1102	57°6·3′	3°27·7′W	X	36
Stob an Uillt Dharaich	Highld	NM9265	56°44·1′	5°23·6′W	X	40
Stob an Uillt-fhearna	Highld	NG8001	57°3·1′	5°37·2′W	H	33
Stobars Hall	Cumbr	NY7608	54°28·3′	2°21·8′W	X	91
Stob Bac an Fhurain	Moray	NJ1303	57°6·8′	3°25·7′W	H	36
Stob Bàn	Highld	NN1465	56°44·6′	5°2·0′W	H	41
Stob Bàn	Highld	NN2672	56°48·7′	4°50·6′W	H	41
Stobb Cross	Durham	NZ3133	54°41·7′	1°30·7′W	X	93
Stobb Cross	Northum	NY8654	54°53·1′	2°12·7′W	X	87
Stob Beinn a' Chrulaiste	Highld	NN2356	56°40·0′	4°52·9′W	X	41
Stobb Ho	Darl	NZ2423	54°36·3′	1°37·3′W	X	93
Stobb House	Durham	NZ2240	54°45·5′	1°39·1′W	X	88

Stobbilee Fm	Durham	NZ1344	54°47·7′	1°47·4′W	FM	88
Stobbilee Fm	Durham	NZ2145	54°48·2′	1°40·0′W	FM	88
Stob Binnein	Stir	NN4322	56°22·1′	4°32·1′W	H	51
Stob Breac	Stir	NN4416	56°18·9′	4°30·9′W	H	57
Stobbs	Northum	NY8397	55°16·3′	2°15·6′W	X	80
Stobby Lea	Northum	NY9152	54°52·0′	2°8·0′W	X	87
Stobbylee Burn	Northum	NY9151	54°51·5′	2°8·0′W	W	87
Stob Caol	Stir	NN4922	56°22·2′	4°26·2′W	H	51
Stob Choire Claurigh	Highld	NN2673	56°49·2′	4°50·6′W	H	41
Stob Coir'an Albannaich	Arg & Bt	NN1744	56°33·4′	4°58·2′W	H	50
Stob Coire á Chàirn	Highld	NN1866	56°45·3′	4°58·2′W	X	41
Stob Coire a' Chearcaill	Highld	NN0172	56°48·1′	5°15·1′W	H	41
Stob Coire Altrium	Highld	NN1953	56°38·3′	4°56·6′W	H	41
Stob Coire an Laoigh	Highld	NN2472	56°48·6′	4°52·5′W	H	41
Stob Coire an Lochain	Stir	NN4322	56°22·1′	4°32·1′W	H	51
Stob Coire Bhealaich	Highld	NN2070	56°47·5′	4°56·4′W	X	41
Stob Coire Bhuidhe	Stir	NN4022	56°22·1′	4°35·0′W	H	51
Stob Coire Dheirg	Arg & Bt	NN1342	56°32·2′	5°2·0′W	X	50
Stob Coire Easain	Highld	NN2372	56°48·6′	4°53·5′W	H	41
Stob Coire Easain	Highld	NN3073	56°49·3′	4°46·7′W	H	41
Stob Coire Etchachan	Aberd	NJ0200	57°5·1′	3°36·6′W	X	36
Stob Coire Léith	Highld	NN1458	56°40·9′	5°1·7′W	X	41
Stob Coire na Ceannain	Highld	NN2674	56°49·8′	4°50·6′W	H	41
Stob Coire na h-Eirghe	Highld	NN1664	56°44·1′	5°0·0′W	X	41
Stob Coire nam Beith	Highld	NN1354	56°38·7′	5°2·5′W	X	41
Stob Coire nan Cearc	Highld	NM9385	56°54·9′	5°23·6′W	H	40
Stob Coire nan Lochan	Highld	NN1454	56°38·7′	5°1·6′W	H	41
Stob Coire Raineach	Highld	NN1954	56°38·8′	4°56·7′W	H	41
Stob Coire Sgreamhach	Highld	NN1553	56°38·2′	5°0·5′W	H	41
Stob Coire Sgriodain	Highld	NN3574	56°50·0′	4°41·8′W	H	41
Stob Creagach	Stir	NN4523	56°22·7′	4°30·2′W	H	51
Stob Creag an Fhithich	Stir	NN3519	56°20·3′	4°39·7′W	H	50,56
Stobcross	Pth & Kin	NO2541	56°33·6′	3°12·8′W	X	53
Stob Dearg	Highld	NN2254	56°38·9′	4°53·7′W	H	41
Stob Diamh	Arg & Bt	NN0930	56°25·7′	5°5·4′W	X	50
Stob Dubh	Arg & Bt	NN2426	56°23·9′	4°50·7′W	X	50
Stob Dubh	Highld	NN1648	56°35·5′	4°59·4′W	H	50
Stob Dubh	Highld	NN1753	56°38·2′	4°58·6′W	H	41
Stob Dubh an Eas Bhig	Aberd	NJ1300	57°5·2′	3°25·7′W	X	36
Stoberry Park	Somer	ST5546	51°12·9′	2°38·3′W	X	182,183
Stob Fell	Scot Bord	NY4598	55°16·6′	2°51·5′W	H	79
Stob Gaibhre	Arg & Bt	NN0646	56°34·2′	5°9·0′W	H	50
Stob Garbh	Stir	NN2627	56°24·5′	4°48·8′W	X	50
Stob Garbh	Stir	NN4121	56°21·5′	4°34·0′W	X	51,56
Stob Garbh Leachtir	Pth & Kin	NN4039	56°31·2′	4°35·6′W	H	51
Stob Ghabhar	Arg & Bt	NN2345	56°34·1′	4°52·4′W	H	50
Stob Glas	Stir	NN3619	56°20·4′	4°38·7′W	H	50,56
Stob Glas	Stir	NN4020	56°21·0′	4°34·9′W	H	51,56
Stob Glas Bheag	Stir	NN3919	56°20·4′	4°35·8′W	X	50,56
Stob Gobhlach	Arg & Bt	NS3298	56°9·0′	4°41·8′W	X	56
Stobgreen Plantn	Durham	NZ0023	54°36·4′	1°59·6′W	F	92
Stobhall	Pth & Kin	NO1334	56°29·7′	3°24·3′W	A	53
Stobhill	Midlo	NT3561	55°50·5′	3°1·8′W	X	66
Stob Hill	Northum	NZ0870	55°1·7′	1°52·1′W	X	88
Stobhill	Northum	NZ2084	55°9·2′	1°40·7′W	T	81
Stob Hill	S Ayr	NX3798	55°15·2′	4°33·4′W	H	77
Stobhillgate	Northum	NZ2085	55°9·8′	1°40·7′W	T	81
Stob Ho	Durham	NZ1553	54°52·5′	1°45·5′W	X	88
Stobhorne Fm	N Yks	SE3798	54°22·8′	1°25·4′W	FM	99
Stob House Fm	Hartpl	NZ4527	54°38·4′	1°17·7′W	FM	93
Stobieside	S Lanak	NS6239	55°37·8′	4°11·1′W	X	71
Stobie Slack	Scot Bord	NT3822	55°29·5′	2°58·4′W	X	73
Stobilea	S Lanak	NS9146	55°42·0′	3°43·6′W	X	72
Stob Invercarnaig	Stir	NN4419	56°20·5′	4°31·0′W	H	57
Stobitcote	Scot Bord	NT4607	55°21·5′	2°50·7′W	X	79
Stob Law	Scot Bord	NT2333	55°35·3′	3°12·9′W	H	73
Stob Leacann na Bò Gile	Pth & Kin	NN3951	56°37·7′	4°37·0′W	X	41
Stob Leathad a' Mhadaidh	Pth & Kin	NN5968	56°47·2′	4°18·0′W	H	42
Stob Liath	Arg & Bt	NN1705	56°12·4′	4°56·6′W	H	56
Stob Loch Monaidh	Pth & Kin	NN5568	56°47·1′	4°22·0′W	H	42
Stob Lùib	Stir	NN4826	56°24·4′	4°27·4′W	H	51
Stob Maol	Arg & Bt	NN1330	56°25·8′	5°1·5′W	H	50
Stob Mhic Bheathain	Highld	NM9171	56°47·3′	5°24·9′W	H	40
Stob Mhic Mhartuin	Highld	NN2057	56°40·5′	4°55·8′W	H	41
Stob na Boine Druim-fhinn	Arg & Bt	NN1602	56°10·8′	4°57·4′W	H	56
Stob na Bròige	Highld	NN1952	56°37·8′	4°56·6′W	H	41
Stob na Cruaiche	Pth & Kin	NN3657	56°40·8′	4°40·2′W	H	41
Stob na Doire	Highld	NN2053	56°38·3′	4°55·7′W	H	41
Stob na Muicraidh	Highld	NG8502	57°3·8′	5°32·3′W	X	33
Stob nan Cabar	Highld	NN1955	56°39·4′	4°56·7′W	X	41
Stob nan Clach	Pth & Kin	NN3835	56°29·0′	4°37·4′W	H	50
Stob nan Coinnich Bhacain	Arg & Bt	NN3014	56°17·5′	4°44·4′W	H	50,56
Stob nan Eighrach	Stir	NN3414	56°17·6′	4°40·5′W	H	50,56
Stob nan Losgann	Pth & Kin	NN3457	56°40·8′	4°42·1′W	X	41
Stobo	Scot Bord	NT1837	55°37·4′	3°17·7′W	T	72
Stobo Castle	Scot Bord	NT1736	55°36·9′	3°18·6′W	X	72
Stob Odhar	Arg & Bt	NR8174	55°54·8′	5°29·8′W	H	62
Stobohill	D & G	NY1887	55°10·5′	3°16·8′W	X	79
Stobohope	Scot Bord	NT1537	55°37·4′	3°20·6′W	X	72
Stobo Hopehead	Scot Bord	NT1439	55°38·5′	3°21·5′W	X	72
Stoborough	Dorset	SY9286	50°40·6′	2°6·4′W	T	195
Stoborough Green	Dorset	SY9285	50°40·1′	2°6·4′W	T	195
Stoborough Heath	Dorset	SY9284	50°39·6′	2°6·4′W	X	195
Stob Poite Coire Ardair	Highld	NN4288	56°57·6′	4°35·5′W	H	34,42
Stob Poite Coire Ardair	Highld	NN4289	56°58·2′	4°35·5′W	X	34,42
Stobs	Midlo	NT3561	55°50·5′	3°1·8′W	X	66
Stobs Castle	Scot Bord	NT5008	55°22·1′	2°46·9′W	T	79
Stobs Cross	Northum	NY8658	54°55·2′	2°12·7′W	A	87
Stobshaw Hill	Scot Bord	NT4523	55°30·1′	2°51·8′W	H	73
Stobshiel	E Loth	NT4963	55°51·7′	2°48·5′W	X	66
Stobshiel Resr	E Loth	NT5061	55°50·6′	2°47·5′W	W	66
Stobswood	Northum	NZ2394	55°14·6′	1°37·9′W	T	81
Stobswood	Scot Bord	NT7156	55°48·0′	2°27·3′W	X	67,74
Stob, The	Stir	NN4923	56°22·8′	4°26·3′W	H	51
Stobthorn Fm	N Yks	SE3898	54°22·8′	1°24·5′W	FM	99
Stob Voire Gaibhre	Highld	NN2675	56°50·3′	4°50·7′W	X	41
Stobwood	S Lanak	NS9552	55°45·3′	3°39·9′W	X	65,72
Stòcaidh	N Eil	NF6663	57°32·3′	7°34·5′W	X	22
Stocanais	N Eil	NG4098	57°54·0′	6°22·8′W	X	14

Stocia Fm	Ches	SJ7059	53°7·9′	2°26·5′W	FM	118
Stock	Cumbr	SD3088	54°17·2′	3°4·1′W	X	96,97
Stock	Essex	TQ6899	51°40·1′	0°26·2′E	T	167,177
Stock	Lancs	SD8648	53°55·9′	2°12·4′W	T	103
Stock	N Som	ST4561	51°21·0′	2°47·0′W	T	172,182
Stock-a-Bank	Lancs	SD5160	54°2·3′	2°44·5′W	X	97
Stockadon	Corn	SX4063	50°26·9′	4°14·8′W	X	201
Stockadon	Devon	SS8806	50°50·8′	3°35·1′W	X	192
Stockadon	Devon	SX6949	50°19·8′	3°50·1′W	X	202
Stocka House Fm	Brad	SE1036	53°49·5′	1°50·5′W	FM	104
Stockalls	Herts	TL3623	51°53·6′	0°1·0′W	X	166
Stockarton	D & G	NX7253	54°51·6′	3°59·2′W	X	83,84
Stockastead	Cumbr	NY5676	55°4·8′	2°40·9′W	X	86
Stockaton	Corn	SX3171	50°31·1′	4°22·7′W	X	201
Stockbatch	Shrops	SJ5102	52°37·1′	2°43·0′W	X	126
Stockbeare Fm	Devon	SS5700	50°47·2′	4°1·3′W	FM	191
Stock Beck	Lancs	SD8449	53°56·5′	2°14·2′W	W	103
Stock Beck	N Yks	SE1874	54°9·9′	1°43·0′W	W	99
Stock Beck Moor	N Yks	SE1874	54°9·9′	1°43·0′W	X	99
Stockber	Cumbr	NY7211	54°29·9′	2°25·5′W	X	91
Stockborough Fm	Lincs	TF2272	53°14·1′	0°9·9′W	FM	122
Stock Bottom	Wilts	SU1932	51°5·5′	1°43·3′W	X	184
Stockbridge	Aberd	NK0745	57°30·0′	1°52·5′W	X	30
Stockbridge	Brad	SE0742	53°52·7′	1°53·2′W	T	104
Stockbridge	Cumbr	SD0993	54°19·7′	3°23·5′W	X	96
Stockbridge	D & G	NY1978	55°5·6′	3°15·7′W	X	85
Stockbridge	Donc	SE5706	53°33·1′	1°8·0′W	T	111
Stockbridge	Hants	SU3535	51°7·0′	1°29·6′W	T	185
Stockbridge	Scot Bord	NT7669	55°55·1′	2°22·6′W	X	67
Stockbridge	Stir	NN7601	56°11·4′	3°59·4′W	X	57
Stockbridge	W Susx	SU8503	50°49·4′	0°47·2′W	T	197
Stockbridge Down	Hants	SU3734	51°6·5′	1°27·9′W	X	185
Stockbridge Fms	Dorset	ST6311	50°54·1′	2°31·2′W	FM	194
Stockbridgehill	D & G	NY1979	55°6·2′	3°15·7′W	X	85
Stockbridge Ho	Kent	TR0131	51°2·8′	0°52·4′E	X	189
Stockbridge Ho	N Yks	SE5536	53°49·3′	1°9·5′W	X	105
Stockbridge Oak	Dorset	ST6310	50°53·5′	2°31·2′W	X	194
Stockbridge Pond	Surrey	SU8742	51°10·5′	0°44·9′W	W	186
Stockbridge Village	Know	SJ4293	53°26·1′	2°52·0′W	T	108
Stockbriggs	S Lanak	NS7936	55°36·4′	3°54·8′W	X	71
Stockbury	Kent	TQ8461	51°19·3′	0°38·8′E	T	178,188
Stock Castle	Devon	SS7146	51°12·2′	3°50·4′W	X	180
Stockcleuch Edge	Scot Bord	NY4295	55°15·0′	2°54·3′W	X	79
Stock Close Fm	Wilts	SU2373	51°27·6′	1°39·7′W	FM	174
Stock Common	Devon	SS7246	51°12·2′	3°49·5′W	X	180
Stock Common	Wilts	SU2664	51°22·7′	1°37·2′W	X	174
Stockcross	W Berks	SU4368	51°24·8′	1°22·5′W	T	174
Stockdale	Corn	SW7937	50°11·7′	5°5·4′W	X	204
Stockdale	Cumbr	NY2534	54°42·0′	3°9·4′W	X	89,90
Stockdale	Cumbr	NY4905	54°26·5′	2°46·8′W	X	90
Stock Dale	N Yks	SD8698	54°22·9′	2°12·5′W	X	98
Stockdale Beck	N Yks	NZ6304	54°25·9′	1°1·3′W	W	94
Stockdale Beck	N Yks	SD8563	54°4·0′	2°13·3′W	W	98
Stockdale Fm	N Yks	SD8563	54°4·0′	2°13·3′W	FM	98
Stockdale Hall	Cumbr	NY4955	54°53·5′	2°47·3′W	X	86
Stockdale Head	Cumbr	NY1309	54°28·4′	3°20·1′W	X	89
Stockdale Moor	Cumbr	NY0908	54°27·8′	3°23·8′W	X	89
Stockdale Moor	N Yks	NZ6303	54°25·4′	1°1·3′W	X	94
Stockdale Plantn	Lancs	SD8743	53°53·2′	2°11·5′W	F	103
Stockdalewath	Cumbr	NY3844	54°47·5′	2°57·4′W	T	85
Stockdove Shaw	E Yorks	TA2433	53°46·9′	0°6·7′W	F	107
Stockdove Wood	E Yorks	TA0127	53°44·0′	0°27·7′W	X	106,107
Stock Down	Devon	SS6836	51°6·7′	3°52·8′W	X	180
Stocked Head	Aberd	NJ7564	57°40·2′	2°24·7′W	X	29
Stockeld Grange	N Yks	SE3749	53°56·4′	1°25·8′W	X	104
Stockeld Lodge Fm	N Yks	SE3848	53°55·8′	1°24·9′W	FM	104
Stockeld Park	N Yks	SE3749	53°56·4′	1°25·8′W	X	104
Stocken	Devon	SX5599	50°46·6′	4°3·0′W	X	191
Stocken Bridge Ho	Lancs	SD4540	53°51·4′	2°49·8′W	X	102
Stockend	Glos	SO8409	51°47·0′	2°13·5′W	T	162
Stockendale Fm	N Yks	TA0778	54°11·4′	0°21·2′W	FM	101
Stockenden Fm	Surrey	TQ4150	51°14·1′	0°1·6′E	FM	187
Stockend Fm	Worcs	SO8051	52°9·7′	2°17·1′W	FM	150
Stockend Fm	Worcs	SO8767	52°18·3′	2°11·0′W	FM	150
Stocken Fm	Heref	SO3166	52°17·5′	3°0·3′W	FM	137,148
Stocken Hall Fm	Rut	SK9518	52°45·3′	0°35·1′W	FM	130
Stockenny Fm	Powys	SO2159	52°13·7′	3°9·0′W	FM	148
Stockerlane	Ches	SJ6263	53°10·0′	2°33·7′W	X	118
Stockerley Br	Durham	NZ1348	54°49·8′	1°47·4′W	X	88
Stockerley Burn	Durham	NZ1349	54°50·4′	1°47·4′W	W	88
Stockers Fm	Devon	SY2197	50°46·3′	3°6·8′W	FM	192,193
Stocker's Head	Kent	TQ9650	51°13·2′	0°48·8′E	T	189
Stockers Lake	Hill	TQ0493	51°37·8′	0°29·4′W	W	176
Stocker's Lake	W Susx	SZ7599	50°47·4′	0°55·8′W	W	197
Stockerston	Leic	SP8397	52°34·1′	0°46·1′W	T	141
Stockery Park Fm	Ches	SJ7866	53°11·7′	2°19·4′W	FM	118
Stocketthill	C of Aber	NJ9107	57°9·5′	2°8·5′W	T	38
Stockett's Manor	Surrey	TQ3950	51°14·2′	0°0·1′W	X	187
Stockfield	Birm	SP1284	52°27·5′	1°49·0′W	T	139
Stockfield	I of M	SC3087	54°15·3′	4°36·2′W	X	95
Stockfield	Shrops	SJ3913	52°42·9′	2°53·8′W	X	126
Stockfields	Staffs	SK1401	52°36·6′	1°47·2′W	X	139
Stock Fm	Ches	SJ7684	53°21·4′	2°21·2′W	FM	109
Stock Fm	Devon	SS6736	51°6·7′	3°53·6′W	FM	180
Stock Fm	Hants	SU6626	51°2·0′	1°3·1′W	FM	185,186
Stock Fm	S Glos	ST6090	51°36·7′	2°34·3′W	FM	162,172
Stock Fm	Surrey	SU8738	51°8·3′	0°45·0′W	FM	186
Stock Gaylard Ho	Dorset	ST7213	50°55·2′	2°23·5′W	X	194
Stock Ghyll	Cumbr	NY3906	54°27·0′	2°56·0′W	W	90
Stockghyll Force	Cumbr	NY3804	54°25·9′	2°56·9′W	W	90
Stockgill River	N Eil	NB0330	58°9·8′	7°2·5′W	W	13
Stock Green	Worcs	SO9858	52°13·4′	2°1·4′W	T	150
Stockgrove Country Park	Beds	SP9129	51°57·4′	0°40·1′W	X	165
Stock Hall	Essex	TL5411	51°46·8′	0°14·3′E	X	167
Stock Hall	Shrops	SO6377	52°23·6′	2°32·2′W	X	138
Stock Hall Fm	Essex	TL8209	51°45·2′	0°38·6′E	FM	168
Stockham	Devon	SS7713	50°54·4′	3°44·6′W	X	180
Stockham	Devon	SY2092	50°43·6′	3°7·6′W	X	192,193
Stockham	Somer	SS9229	51°3·2′	3°32·1′W	X	181
Stockham	Somer	ST1533	51°5·6′	3°12·4′W	X	181

Stockham Marsh Fm	Wilts	ST9977	51°29·7′	2°0·5′W	FM	173
Stockham Wood	Devon	SX3298	50°45·7′	4°22·5′W	F	190
Stockheath	Hants	SU7107	50°51·7′	0°59·1′W	T	197
Stockheld Grange Fm	Leeds	SE3837	53°49·9′	1°24·9′W	FM	104
Stock Hill	Dorset	ST6808	50°52·5′	2°26·9′W	X	194
Stock Hill	Leeds	SE2338	53°50·5′	1°38·6′W	X	104
Stock Hill	Northnts	TL0991	52°30·6′	0°23·2′W	X	142
Stock Hill	Scot Bord	NT3203	55°19·2′	3°3·9′W	H	79
Stockhill	S Lanak	NS7834	55°35·3′	3°55·7′W	X	71
Stockhill	Somer	ST5551	51°15·6′	2°38·3′W	F	182,183
Stock Hill	Suff	TL9769	52°17·3′	0°53·7′E	T	155
Stockhill Fm	Notts	SK6445	53°0·1′	1°2·4′W	FM	129
Stockhill Fm	N Yks	SE5079	54°12·5′	1°13·6′W	FM	100
Stockhill Green	N Yks	SE4678	54°12·0′	1°17·3′W	X	100
Stock Hill(Hotel)	Dorset	ST7826	51°2·2′	2°18·4′W	X	183
Stockhill Lodge	Cambs	TL1091	52°30·6′	0°22·3′W	X	142
Stockholes Turbary	N Lincs	SE7607	53°33·5′	0°50·7′W	T	112
Stockholm	D & G	NY0898	55°16·3′	3°26·5′W	X	78
Stockholm Fm	Oxon	SU3088	51°35·6′	1°33·6′W	FM	174
Stockholm Hill Fm	E Yorks	TA2027	53°43·8′	0°10·4′W	FM	107
Stockholt Fm	Bucks	SP7038	52°2·4′	0°58·4′W	FM	152
Stockhow Hall	Cumbr	NY0616	54°32·1′	3°26·7′W	X	89
Stockhurst Fm	E Susx	TQ8422	50°58·3′	0°37·6′E	FM	199
Stockie Muir	Stir	NS4982	56°0·7′	4°24·9′W	X	57,64
Stockiemuir	Stir	NS5083	56°1·2′	4°24·0′W	X	57,64
Stocking	Heref	SO6230	51°58·3′	2°32·8′W	T	149
Stocking Cottage	Shrops	SO5878	52°24·1′	2°36·6′W	X	137,138
Stocking Drove Fm	Cambs	TL3982	52°25·3′	0°3·1′E	FM	142,143
Stocking Farm	C of Leic	SK5807	52°39·7′	1°8·1′W	FM	140
Stocking Fen	Cambs	TL2986	52°27·6′	0°5·7′W	X	142
Stockingfield	Heref	SO4155	52°11·6′	2°51·4′W	X	148,149
Stocking Fm	Heref	SO4464	52°16·5′	2°48·8′W	FM	137,148,149
Stocking Fm	Shrops	SO6897	52°34·4′	2°27·9′W	FM	138
Stockingford	Warw	SP3391	52°31·2′	1°30·4′W	T	140
Stocking Green Fm	Mil Key	SP8047	52°7·2′	0°49·5′W	FM	152
Stocking Green Fm	N Yks	SE5418	53°39·6′	1°10·6′W	FM	111
Stocking Hall	N Yks	SE5571	54°8·2′	1°9·1′W	X	100
Stocking Hill	Herts	TL3130	51°57·4′	0°5·2′W	X	166
Stocking Hill Fm	N Yks	SE6375	54°10·3′	1°1·7′W	FM	100
Stocking Ho	N Yks	NZ6506	54°27·0′	0°59·4′W	X	94
Stocking Ho	N Yks	SE5584	54°15·2′	1°8·9′W	X	100
Stocking Pelham	Herts	TL4529	51°56·7′	0°7·0′E	T	167
Stockings Cote	Staffs	SJ7649	53°2·5′	2°21·1′W	F	118
Stockings Fm	Bucks	SU9694	51°38·4′	0°36·4′W	FM	175,176
Stockings Fm	Northnts	SP5942	52°4·6′	1°7·9′W	FM	152
Stockings Fm	Notts	SK5847	53°1·3′	1°7·7′W	FM	129
Stockings, The	Staffs	SJ8503	52°37·7′	2°12·9′W	X	127,139
Stockings Wood	Kent	TQ8059	51°18·3′	0°35·3′E	F	178,188
Stocking's Wood	Suff	TL9567	52°16·2′	0°51·9′E	F	155
Stocking Wood	Heref	SO3160	52°14·3′	3°0·2′W	F	137,148
Stockingwood Fm	Bucks	SP6830	51°58·1′	1°0·2′W	FM	152,165
Stock-in-Hey Fm	Ches	SJ7982	53°20·3′	2°18·5′W	FM	109
Stockland	Card	ST1078	51°29·9′	3°17·4′W	X	171
Stockland	Devon	ST2404	50°50·1′	3°4·4′W	T	192,193
Stockland Beck	N Yks	SE9193	54°19·7′	0°35·6′W	W	94,101
Stockland Bristol	Somer	ST2443	51°11·1′	3°4·9′W	T	182
Stockland Fm	Devon	ST0704	50°49·9′	3°18·9′W	FM	192
Stockland Fm	E Susx	TQ5224	50°59·9′	0°10·4′E	FM	199
Stockland Great Castle	Devon	ST2202	50°49·0′	3°6·1′W	A	192,193
Stockland Green	Birm	SP0991	52°31·2′	1°51·6′W	T	139
Stockland Green	Kent	TQ5642	51°9·6′	0°14·2′E	T	188
Stockland Hill	Devon	ST2203	50°49·5′	3°6·1′W	X	192,193
Stockland Little Castle	Devon	ST2203	50°49·5′	3°6·1′W	A	192,193
Stockland Lovell Manor	Somer	ST2241	51°10·0′	3°6·6′W	X	182
Stockland Manor	Somer	ST2343	51°11·1′	3°5·7′W	X	182
Stockland Reach	Somer	ST2845	51°12·2′	3°1·5′W	W	182
Stocklands Fm	E Susx	TQ7921	50°57·9′	0°33·3′E	FM	199
Stockleigh Barton	Devon	SS5409	50°52·0′	4°4·1′W	X	191
Stockleigh Court	Devon	SS8406	50°50·7′	3°38·5′W	X	191
Stockleigh English	Devon	SS8506	50°50·8′	3°37·6′W	T	191
Stockleigh Fm	Devon	SS5104	50°49·2′	4°6·5′W	FM	191
Stockleigh Pomeroy	Devon	SS8703	50°49·2′	3°35·9′W	T	192
Stockley	Devon	SX6095	50°44·5′	3°58·7′W	X	191
Stockley	Durham	NZ2137	54°43·9′	1°40·0′W	X	93
Stockley	Wilts	SU0067	51°24·4′	1°59·6′W	T	173
Stockley Beck	Durham	NZ2237	54°43·9′	1°39·1′W	W	93
Stockley Bridge	Cumbr	NY2310	54°29·0′	3°10·9′W	X	89,90
Stockley Copse	Oxon	SP2913	51°49·1′	1°34·4′W	F	164
Stockley Cross	Heref	SO3761	52°14·9′	2°55·0′W	X	137,148,149
Stockley Fell	Durham	NZ1937	54°43·9′	1°41·9′W	X	92
Stockley Fell Plantn	Durham	NZ2037	54°43·9′	1°40·9′W	F	93
Stockley Fm	Ches	SJ6881	53°19·7′	2°28·4′W	FM	109
Stockley Fm	Ches	SJ6881	53°19·7′	2°28·4′W	FM	109
Stockley Fm	Warr	SJ6281	53°19·7′	2°33·8′W	FM	109
Stockley Hamlet	Devon	SX6195	50°44·5′	3°57·8′W	X	191
Stockley Hill	Heref	SO3638	52°2·4′	2°55·6′W	X	149,161
Stockley Inclosure	Hants	SU3402	50°49·2′	1°30·7′W	F	196
Stockley Park	Staffs	SK2025	52°49·6′	1°41·8′W	X	128
Stockley Wood	Powys	SO1040	52°3·3′	3°18·4′W	F	148,161
Stocklinch	Somer	ST3817	50°57·2′	2°52·6′W	T	193
Stocklinch Ottersey	Somer	ST3816	50°56·6′	2°52·6′W	X	193
Stocklinch St Magdalen	Somer	ST3817	50°57·2′	2°52·6′W	X	193
Stocklow Manor	Heref	SO3761	52°14·9′	2°55·0′W	X	137,148,149
Stockman's Coomb Fm	Surrey	TQ1249	51°14·0′	0°23·4′W	FM	187
Stockmeadows	Staffs	SJ9862	53°9·6′	2°1·4′W	X	118
Stockmoor	Cumbr	NY0632	54°40·7′	3°27·0′W	X	89
Stockmoor	Heref	SO3955	52°11·6′	2°53·1′W	X	148,149
Stock Moor	Somer	ST2934	51°6·3′	3°0·5′W	X	182
Stockmoss	D & G	NX7648	54°48·9′	3°55·4′W	X	84
Stockmuir	Pth & Kin	NO2432	56°28·7′	3°13·6′W	X	53
Stockng Green	Essex	TL5938	52°1·3′	0°19·4′E	T	154
Stock Nook	Roch	SD8408	53°34·3′	2°14·1′W	X	109
Stock o' Broom	Stir	NS6897	56°9·1′	4°7·1′W	X	57
Stock Park Fm	Pemb	SM9020	51°50·6′	5°2·5′W	FM	157,158
Stockport	Stock	SJ8990	53°24·6′	2°9·5′W	T	109
Stockport	Wilts	SU1639	51°9·2′	1°45·9′W	X	184
Stock Ridge	N Yks	SE0672	54°8·9′	1°54·1′W	X	99
Stock Ridge Bottom	N Yks	SE0771	54°8·3′	1°53·2′W	X	99
Stocks	Cumbr	SD6294	54°20·8′	2°34·6′W	X	97
Stocks	Herts	SP9613	51°48·7′	0°36·1′W	X	165

Stocks and Kingswood Fms	Surrey	TQ3847	51°12·6′	0°1·1′W	FM	187
Stocksbridge	Sheff	SK2698	53°28·9′	1°36·1′W	T	110
Stocksfield	Northum	NZ0561	54°56·9′	1°54·9′W	T	87
Stocksfield Burn	Northum	NZ0558	54°55·2′	1°54·9′W	W	87
Stocksfield Hall	Northum	NZ0561	54°56·9′	1°54·9′W	X	87
Stocks Fm	E Susx	TQ3316	50°55·9′	0°6·0′W	FM	198
Stocks Fm	E Susx	TQ8516	50°55·0′	0°38·3′E	FM	189,199
Stock's Fm	Hants	SU2003	50°49·8′	1°42·6′W	FM	195
Stocks Fm	Hants	SU6319	50°58·2′	1°5·8′W	FM	185
Stocks Fm	Shrops	SJ4137	52°55·9′	2°52·3′W	FM	126
Stocks Fm	W Berks	SU5280	51°31·2′	1°14·6′W	FM	174
Stocks Fm	Worcs	SO7251	52°9·6′	2°24·2′W	FM	149
Stocks Green	Kent	TQ5547	51°12·3′	0°13·5′E	T	188
Stocks Heath Fm	Lincs	SK9851	53°3·1′	0°31·9′W	FM	121
Stock's Hill	Lincs	TF3224	52°48·1′	0°2·1′W	X	131
Stocks Ho	Lancs	SD8445	53°54·3′	2°14·2′W	X	103
Stocks Ho	Leic	SK4602	52°37·1′	1°18·8′W	X	140
Stocksmoor Sta	Kirk	SE1810	53°35·4′	1°43·3′W	X	110
Stocks Reservoir	Lancs	SD7255	53°59·7′	2°25·2′W	W	103
Stocks, The	Shrops	SJ4236	52°55·3′	2°51·4′W	X	126
Stockstreet	Essex	TL8222	51°52·2′	0°39·0′E	T	168
Stockton	Heref	SO5161	52°14·9′	2°42·7′W	T	137,138,149
Stockton	Leeds	SE3345	53°54·2′	1°29·4′W	X	104
Stockton	Norf	TM3894	52°29·7′	1°30·8′E	T	134
Stockton	Shrops	SJ2601	52°36·3′	3°5·2′W	T	126
Stockton	Shrops	SO7299	52°35·5′	2°24·4′W	T	138
Stockton	Warw	SP4363	52°16·0′	1°21·8′W	T	151
Stockton	Wilts	ST9838	51°8·7′	2°1·3′W	T	184
Stockton	Wrekin	SJ7716	52°44·7′	2°20·0′W	T	127
Stockton Brook	Staffs	SJ9152	53°4·1′	2°7·7′W	T	118
Stockton Buildings	Shrops	SO7399	52°35·5′	2°23·5′W	X	138
Stockton Common	York	SE6558	54°1·1′	1°0·1′W	X	105,106
Stockton Cott	York	SE6559	54°1·6′	1°0·0′W	X	105,106
Stockton Cross	Heref	SO5160	52°14·4′	2°42·7′W	X	137,138,149
Stockton Down	Wilts	ST9536	51°7·6′	2°3·9′W	X	184
Stockton Earthworks	Wilts	ST9636	51°7·6′	2°3·0′W	A	184
Stockton Grange	Wrekin	SJ7716	52°44·7′	2°20·0′W	X	127
Stockton Hall	York	SE6556	54°0·0′	1°0·1′W	X	105,106
Stockton Hall Fm	Ches	SJ4745	53°0·2′	2°47·0′W	FM	117
Stockton Heath	Warr	SJ6186	53°22·4′	2°34·8′W	T	109
Stockton Ho	Warw	SP4362	52°16·6′	1°21·8′W	X	151
Stockton Ho	Wilts	ST9738	51°8·7′	2°2·2′W	A	184
Stockton Locks	Warw	SP4364	52°16·6′	1°21·8′W	X	151
Stockton Moors	Wrekin	SJ7816	52°44·7′	2°19·2′W	X	127
Stockton Old Hall	Norf	TM3994	52°29·7′	1°31·7′E	X	134
Stockton-on-Tees	Stock on T	NZ4320	54°34·6′	1°19·7′W	T	93
Stockton on Teme	Worcs	SO7167	52°18·3′	2°25·1′W	T	138,149
Stockton on the Forest	York	SE6555	53°59·5′	1°0·1′W	T	105,106
Stockton Ride	Heref	SO5162	52°15·5′	2°42·7′W	F	137,138,149
Stockton Stone	Norf	TM3894	52°29·7′	1°30·8′E	X	134
Stockton West Moor	York	SE6454	53°58·9′	1°1·0′W	X	105,106
Stocktonwood	Shrops	SJ2601	52°36·3′	3°5·2′W	T	126
Stockton Wood	Wilts	ST9635	51°7·1′	2°3·0′W	F	184
Stockval	Highld	NG3529	57°16·8′	6°23·4′W	H	32
Stockwell	Devon	SS9702	50°48·7′	3°27·3′W	T	192
Stockwell	Glos	SO9414	51°49·7′	2°4·8′W	T	163
Stockwell	Lam	TQ3075	51°27·8′	0°7·3′W	T	176,177
Stockwell End	Wolv	SJ8800	52°36·1′	2°10·2′W	T	127,139
Stockwell Green	Glos	SO6513	51°49·1′	2°30·1′W	X	162
Stockwell Hall	Cumbr	NY3641	54°45·8′	2°59·3′W	X	85
Stockwell Hall	Essex	TQ6692	51°36·4′	0°24·2′E	A	177,178
Stockwell Heath	Staffs	SK0521	52°47·4′	1°55·1′W	T	128
Stockwell Lane Fm	Bucks	SP7906	51°45·1′	0°50·9′W	FM	165
Stockwitch Cross	Somer	ST5524	51°1·1′	2°38·1′W	T	183
Stockwith Ellers	Lincs	SK7995	53°27·0′	0°48·2′W	X	112
Stockwith Mill Bridge	Lincs	TF3570	53°12·8′	0°1·7′E	X	122
Stockwood	C of Bris	ST6268	51°24·8′	2°32·4′W	T	172
Stock Wood	Cumbr	SD3188	54°17·2′	3°3·2′W	F	96,97
Stockwood	Dorset	ST5806	50°51·4′	2°35·4′W	T	194
Stock Wood	Kent	TQ8958	51°17·6′	0°43·0′E	F	178
Stock Wood	Wilts	ST8930	51°31·4′	2°9·1′W	F	173
Stock Wood	Worcs	SP0058	52°13·4′	1°59·6′W	T	150
Stockwood Fm	E Susx	TQ8021	50°57·8′	0°34·2′E	FM	199
Stockwood Park	Luton	TL0819	51°51·8′	0°25·5′W	X	166
Stockwood Stud	Worcs	SO9959	52°14·0′	2°0·5′W	X	150
Stockwood Vale	Bath & NE Somer	ST6469	51°25·4′	2°30·7′W	T	172
Stockyards Fm	E Susx	TQ5526	51°1·0′	0°13·0′E	FM	188,199
Stocleit an Ear	N Eil	NG1194	57°50·8′	6°51·8′W	H	14
Stocleit an Iar	N Eil	NG1094	57°50·8′	6°52·8′W	H	14
Stoddah Bank	Cumbr	NY4126	54°37·8′	2°54·4′W	X	90
Stoddah Fm	Cumbr	NY4126	54°37·8′	2°54·4′W	FM	90
Stoddard Fm	E Susx	TQ8424	50°59·4′	0°37·7′E	FM	199
Stodday	Lancs	SD4658	54°1·2′	2°49·0′W	T	102
Stodfold	Aberd	NJ5834	57°23·9′	2°41·5′W	X	29
Stodfold	Aberd	NJ9941	57°27·8′	2°0·5′W	X	30
Stodham Park	Hants	SU7726	51°1·9′	0°53·7′W	X	186,197
Stodhoe	Darl	NZ3313	54°30·9′	1°29·0′W	X	93
Stodmarsh	Kent	TR2160	51°18·0′	1°10·6′E	T	179
Stodmarsh National Nature Reserve	Kent	TR2262	51°19·0′	1°11·5′E	X	179
Stodrig	Scot Bord	NT6934	55°36·2′	2°29·1′W	X	74
Stody	Norf	TG0535	52°52·6′	1°3·2′E	T	133
Stoer	Highld	NC0328	58°12·1′	5°20·7′W	T	15
Stoer Ho	Highld	NC0328	58°12·1′	5°20·7′W	X	15
Stoford	Somer	ST5613	50°55·1′	2°37·2′W	T	194
Stoford	Wilts	SU0835	51°7·1′	1°52·8′W	T	184
Stoford Hill Buildings	Wilts	SU0936	51°7·6′	1°51·9′W	X	184
Stoford Water	Devon	ST0708	50°52·1′	3°18·9′W	T	192
Stogumber	Somer	ST0937	51°7·7′	3°17·6′W	T	181
Stogursey	Somer	ST2042	51°10·5′	3°8·3′W	T	182
Stogursey Brook	Somer	ST1941	51°10·0′	3°9·1′W	W	181
Stogursey Brook	Somer	ST2042	51°10·5′	3°8·3′W	W	182
Stoile	N Eil	NF9173	57°38·7′	7°10·3′W	X	18
Stoke	C of Plym	SX4655	50°22·7′	4°9·6′W	T	201
Stoke	Cov	SP3678	52°24·2′	1°27·9′W	T	140
Stoke	Devon	SS2324	50°59·5′	4°31·0′W	T	190
Stoke	Devon	SX6970	50°31·1′	3°50·5′W	T	202
Stoke	Hants	SU4051	51°15·6′	1°25·2′W	T	185
Stoke	Hants	SU7202	50°49·0′	0°58·3′W	T	197
Stoke	Medway	TQ8275	51°26·9′	0°37·5′E	T	178
Stoke	Suff	TM1643	52°2·8′	1°9·4′E	T	169
Stoke Abbott	Dorset	ST4500	50°48·1′	2°46·4′W	T	193
Stoke Albany	Northnts	SP8087	52°28·7′	0°48·9′W	T	141
Stoke Aldermoor	Cov	SP3577	52°23·6′	1°28·7′W	T	140
Stoke Ash	Suff	TM1170	52°17·5′	1°6·0′E	T	144,155
Stoke Bardolph	Notts	SK6441	52°58·0′	1°2·4′W	T	129
Stoke Beach	Devon	SX5646	50°18·0′	4°0·9′W	X	202
Stoke Beara	Devon	SS6535	51°6·1′	3°55·3′W	X	180
Stoke Bishop	C of Bris	ST5675	51°28·6′	2°37·6′W	T	172
Stoke Bliss	Worcs	SO6562	52°15·5′	2°30·4′W	T	138,149
Stoke Bottom Fm	Somer	ST6647	51°13·5′	2°28·8′W	FM	183
Stoke Brook	Derby	SK2375	53°16·5′	1°38·9′W	W	119
Stoke Brook	Shrops	SO5671	52°20·4′	2°38·4′W	W	137,138
Stoke Bruerne	Northnts	SP7449	52°8·3′	0°54·7′W	T	152
Stoke Brunswick	E Susx	TQ4237	51°7·1′	0°2·1′E	X	187
Stoke Bushes	Oxon	SP5629	51°57·6′	1°10·7′W	F	164
Stoke by Clare	Suff	TL7443	52°3·7′	0°32·7′E	T	155
Stoke-by-Nayland	Suff	TL9836	51°59·5′	0°53·4′E	T	155
Stoke Canon	Devon	SX9398	50°46·5′	3°30·7′W	T	192
Stoke Charity	Hants	SU4839	51°9·1′	1°18·4′W	T	185
Stoke Climsland	Corn	SX3674	50°32·8′	4°18·5′W	T	201
Stoke Clump	W Susx	SU8309	50°52·7′	0°48·8′W	F	197
Stoke Common	Bucks	SU9885	51°33·5′	0°34·8′W	F	175,176
Stoke Common	Dorset	ST7506	50°51·4′	2°20·9′W	X	194
Stoke Common	Dorset	SY8786	50°40·6′	2°10·7′W	X	194
Stoke Common	Hants	SU4720	50°58·9′	1°19·4′W	T	185
Stoke Common Fm	Wilts	SU0690	51°36·8′	1°54·4′W	FM	163,173
Stoke Court	Bucks	SU9784	51°33·0′	0°35·7′W	X	175,176
Stoke Court	Shrops	SO5671	52°20·4′	2°38·4′W	A	137,138
Stoke Court	Shrops	SO5782	52°26·3′	2°37·6′W	X	137,138
Stoke Court	Somer	ST2621	50°59·3′	3°2·9′W	X	193
Stoke Court	Worcs	SO9668	52°18·8′	2°3·1′W	X	139
Stoke Cross	Heref	SO6250	52°9·1′	2°32·9′W	T	149
Stoke Cross	Worcs	SO9769	52°19·4′	2°2·2′W	X	139
Stoke D' Abernon	Surrey	TQ1259	51°19·4′	0°23·2′W	T	187
Stoke Down	Wilts	SU0527	51°2·8′	1°55·3′W	X	184
Stoke Down	W Susx	SU8209	50°52·7′	0°49·7′W	X	197
Stoke Doyle	Northnts	TL0286	52°28·0′	0°29·5′W	T	141
Stoke Dry	Rut	SP8596	52°33·5′	0°44·4′W	T	141
Stoke Dry Wood	Rut	SP8497	52°34·1′	0°45·2′W	F	141
Stoke Edith	Heref	SO6040	52°3·7′	2°34·6′W	T	149
Stoke Edith Park	Heref	SO6040	52°3·7′	2°34·6′W	X	149
Stoke Enclosure	Shrops	SO5983	52°26·8′	2°35·8′W	X	137,138
Stoke End	Warw	SP1797	52°34·5′	1°44·5′W	T	139
Stoke Farthing	Wilts	SU0525	51°1·7′	1°55·3′W	T	184
Stoke Ferry	Norf	TF7000	52°34·5′	0°30·9′E	T	143
Stoke Ferry Fen	Norf	TL6897	52°32·9′	0°29·1′E	X	143
Stokefield Fm	Oxon	SU6897	51°40·3′	1°0·6′W	FM	164,165
Stoke Fields Fm	Notts	SK7648	53°1·7′	0°51·6′W	FM	129
Stoke Flat	Derby	SK2576	53°17·1′	1°37·1′W	X	119
Stoke Fleming	Devon	SX8648	50°19·5′	3°35·7′W	T	202
Stoke Fm	Somer	ST7132	51°5·4′	2°24·5′W	FM	183
Stoke Fm	Wilts	SU0525	51°1·7′	1°55·3′W	FM	184
Stoke Ford	Derby	SK2179	53°18·7′	1°40·7′W	X	119
Stokeford	Dorset	SY8687	50°41·2′	2°11·5′W	T	194
Stokeford Heath	Dorset	SY8788	50°41·7′	2°10·7′W	X	194
Stoke Gabriel	Devon	SX8457	50°24·3′	3°37·6′W	T	202
Stokegap Lodge	Northnts	SP7550	52°8·8′	0°53·8′W	X	152
Stoke Gifford	S Glos	ST6280	51°31·3′	2°32·5′W	T	172
Stoke Golding	Leic	SP4097	52°34·4′	1°24·2′W	T	140
Stoke Goldington	Mil Key	SP8348	52°7·7′	0°46·9′W	T	152
Stokegorse	Shrops	SO5683	52°26·8′	2°38·4′W	T	137,138
Stoke Grange	Oxon	SP6700	51°41·9′	1°1·4′W	X	164,165
Stoke Grange	Shrops	SJ6331	52°52·8′	2°32·6′W	X	127
Stoke Green	Bucks	SU9882	51°31·9′	0°34·8′W	T	175,176
Stoke Hall	Ches	SJ6256	53°6·2′	2°33·7′W	X	118
Stoke Hall	Notts	SK7450	53°2·8′	0°53·4′W	X	120
Stokeham	Notts	SK7876	53°16·7′	0°49·4′W	T	120,121
Stoke Hammond	Bucks	SP8829	51°57·4′	0°42·8′W	T	165
Stoke Heath	Cov	SP3580	52°25·2′	1°28·7′W	T	140
Stoke Heath	Dorset	SY8489	50°42·3′	2°13·2′W	X	194
Stoke Heath	Shrops	SJ6529	52°51·7′	2°30·8′W	T	127
Stoke Heath	Worcs	SO9468	52°18·8′	2°4·9′W	T	139
Stokehill	Devon	SX5067	50°29·3′	4°6·5′W	X	201
Stoke Hill	Devon	SX9295	50°44·9′	3°31·5′W	X	192
Stoke Hill	Devon	SX9394	50°44·4′	3°30·6′W	T	192
Stoke Hill	Heref	SO6149	52°8·5′	2°33·8′W	T	149
Stoke Hill	Heref	SO6663	52°16·1′	2°29·5′W	X	138,149
Stoke Hill	Somer	ST2622	50°59·8′	3°2·9′W	X	193
Stoke Hill	Wilts	ST9552	51°16·3′	2°3·9′W	X	184
Stoke Hill Fm	Devon	SX9295	50°44·9′	3°31·5′W	FM	192
Stokehill Fm	Hants	SU3951	51°15·6′	1°26·1′W	FM	185
Stokehill Fm	Wilts	ST9552	51°16·3′	2°3·9′W	FM	184
Stoke Ho	Bucks	SP8309	51°46·6′	0°47·4′W	X	165
Stoke Ho	Bucks	SP8831	51°58·5′	0°42·7′W	X	152,165
Stoke Ho	Devon	SX5646	50°18·0′	4°0·9′W	X	202
Stoke Ho	Northnts	SP8087	52°28·7′	0°48·9′W	X	141
Stoke Ho	Somer	ST2622	50°59·8′	3°2·9′W	X	193
Stoke Holy Cross	Norf	TG2301	52°33·9′	1°17·8′E	T	134
Stokehouse	Devon	SS9805	50°50·4′	3°26·5′W	X	192
Stokeinteignhead	Devon	SX9170	50°31·4′	3°31·9′W	T	202
Stoke Knap	Dorset	ST4401	50°48·6′	2°47·3′W	X	193
Stoke Lacy	Heref	SO6249	52°8·5′	2°32·9′W	T	149
Stoke Lane	Heref	SO6350	52°9·1′	2°32·1′W	T	149
Stokeleigh Camp	N Som	ST5573	51°27·5′	2°38·5′W	A	172
Stoke Little Wood	Oxon	SP5627	51°56·6′	1°10·7′W	F	164
Stokelodge Fm	Mil Key	SP8150	52°8·8′	0°48·6′W	FM	152
Stoke Lodge Fm	Shrops	SO5680	52°25·2′	2°38·4′W	FM	137,138
Stoke Lyne	Oxon	SP5628	51°57·1′	1°10·7′W	T	164
Stoke Mandeville	Bucks	SP8310	51°47·2′	0°47·4′W	T	165
Stoke Mandeville Hospl	Bucks	SP8211	51°47·7′	0°48·3′W	X	165
Stoke Manor	Shrops	SJ6427	52°50·6′	2°31·7′W	X	127
Stoke Marshes	Medway	TQ8475	51°26·9′	0°39·3′E	X	178
Stoke Mill Fm	Dorset	SY4297	50°46·4′	2°49·0′W	FM	193
Stoke Moor	Somer	ST4648	51°14·0′	2°46·0′W	X	182
Stokenbridge	Devon	SX6752	50°21·4′	3°51·8′W	X	202
Stokenchurch	Bucks	SU7696	51°39·7′	0°53·7′W	T	165
Stoke Newington	Hack	TQ3386	51°33·7′	0°4·5′W	T	176,177
Stokenham	Devon	SX8042	50°16·2′	3°40·7′W	T	202
Stoke on Tern	Shrops	SJ6427	52°50·6′	2°31·7′W	T	127
Stoke-on-Trent	C of Stoke	SJ8747	53°1·4′	2°11·2′W	T	118
Stoke Ooze	Medway	TQ8473	51°25·8′	0°39·2′E	X	178
Stoke Orchard	Glos	SO9228	51°57·3′	2°6·6′W	T	150,163
Stoke Park	Bucks	SU9682	51°32·0′	0°36·6′W	X	175,176
Stoke Park	Suff	TM1542	52°2·3′	1°8·5′E	T	169
Stoke Park	Surrey	TQ0050	51°14·7′	0°33·6′W	X	186
Stoke Park Fm	Hants	SU4720	50°58·9′	1°19·4′W	FM	185
Stoke Park Hospl	S Glos	ST6277	51°29·7′	2°32·5′W	X	172
Stoke Park Pavilions	Northnts	SP7448	52°7·8′	0°54·7′W	A	152
Stoke Park Wood	Hants	SU4719	50°58·3′	1°19·4′W	F	185
Stoke Park Wood	Lincs	SK9427	52°50·2′	0°35·9′W	F	130
Stokepark Wood	Mil Key	SP8249	52°8·2′	0°47·7′W	F	152
Stokepark Wood	Northnts	SP7349	52°8·3′	0°55·6′W	F	152
Stoke Pasture	Lincs	SK8827	52°50·2′	0°41·2′W	F	130
Stoke Pero	Somer	SS8743	51°10·7′	3°36·6′W	X	181
Stoke Pero Common	Somer	SS8742	51°10·2′	3°36·6′W	X	181
Stoke Place	Bucks	SU9882	51°31·9′	0°34·8′W	X	175,176
Stoke Plain	Northnts	SP7350	52°8·8′	0°55·6′W	X	152
Stoke Poges	Bucks	SU9883	51°32·5′	0°34·8′W	T	175,176
Stoke Point	Devon	SX5645	50°17·5′	4°0·9′W	X	202
Stoke Point	Devon	SX8456	50°23·8′	3°37·5′W	X	202
Stoke Post	Devon	SX9496	50°45·5′	3°29·8′W	X	192
Stoke Pound	Worcs	SO9667	52°18·3′	2°3·1′W	T	150
Stoke Prior	Heref	SO5256	52°12·2′	2°41·7′W	T	149
Stoke Prior	Worcs	SO9467	52°18·3′	2°4·9′W	T	150
Stoke Priory	Suff	TL9837	52°0·0′	0°53·5′E	X	155
Stoke Ridge	Somer	SS8742	51°10·2′	3°36·6′W	X	181
Stoke Rivers	Devon	SS6335	51°6·1′	3°57·0′W	T	180
Stokeroad Fm	Bucks	SP8528	51°56·9′	0°45·4′W	FM	165
Stoke Rochford	Lincs	SK9127	52°50·2′	0°38·5′W	T	130
Stoke Rochford Hall	Lincs	SK9128	52°50·7′	0°38·5′W	X	130
Stoke Row	Oxon	SU6884	51°33·3′	1°0·8′W	T	175
Stokerow Fm	Oxon	SU6884	51°33·3′	1°0·8′W	FM	175
Stoke Saltings	Medway	TQ8374	51°26·3′	0°38·4′E	W	178
Stokesay	Shrops	SO4381	52°25·7′	2°49·9′W	T	137
Stokesay Court	Shrops	SO4478	52°24·1′	2°49·0′W	X	137,148
Stokes Barns	Warw	SP3958	52°13·4′	1°25·3′W	FM	151
Stokes Bay	Hants	SZ5998	50°46·9′	1°9·4′W	W	196
Stokesby	Norf	TG4310	52°38·2′	1°35·9′E	T	134
Stokes Fm	Norf	TL6389	52°28·7′	0°24·4′E	FM	143
Stokes Fm	Wok	SU8269	51°25·1′	0°48·9′W	FM	175
Stoke's Hall	Essex	TQ9298	51°39·1′	0°46·9′E	X	168
Stokesley	N Yks	NZ5208	54°28·1′	1°11·4′W	T	93
Stokes Marsh Fm	Wilts	ST9456	51°18·4′	2°4·8′W	FM	173
Stoke St Gregory	Somer	ST3427	51°2·5′	2°56·1′W	T	193
Stoke St Mary	Somer	ST2622	50°59·8′	3°2·9′W	T	193
Stoke St Michael	Somer	ST6646	51°13·0′	2°28·8′W	T	183
Stoke St Milborough	Shrops	SO5682	52°26·3′	2°38·4′W	T	137,138
Stoke Sub Hamdon	Somer	ST4717	50°57·2′	2°44·9′W	T	193
Stoke Talmage	Oxon	SU6799	51°41·4′	1°1·4′W	T	164,165
Stoke Trister	Somer	ST7328	51°3·3′	2°22·7′W	T	183
Stoke Tye	Suff	TL9737	52°0·0′	0°52·6′E	X	155
Stoke-upon-Trent	C of Stoke	SJ8745	53°0·4′	2°11·2′W	T	118
Stoke Villice	Bath & NE Somer	ST5560	51°20·5′	2°38·4′W	X	172,182
Stoke Wake	Dorset	ST7606	50°51·4′	2°20·1′W	T	194
Stoke Water	Dorset	ST4600	50°48·1′	2°45·6′W	T	193
Stoke Wharf	Worcs	SO9566	52°17·8′	2°4·0′W	T	150
Stoke Wood	Bucks	SU9785	51°33·6′	0°35·6′W	F	175,176
Stoke Wood	Hants	SU6317	50°57·2′	1°5·8′W	F	185
Stoke Wood	Hants	SU6318	50°57·7′	1°5·8′W	X	185
Stoke Wood	Northnts	SP8086	52°28·2′	0°48·9′W	F	141
Stoke Wood	Northnts	TL0087	52°28·5′	0°31·3′W	F	141
Stoke Wood	Notts	SK7449	53°2·2′	0°53·4′W	F	129
Stoke Wood	Oxon	SP5527	51°56·6′	1°11·6′W	F	164
Stoke Wood	Shrops	SO4281	52°25·7′	2°50·8′W	F	137
Stoke Wood	Surrey	TQ1560	51°19·9′	0°20·6′W	F	176,187
Stokewood Fm	Shrops	SO4479	52°24·6′	2°49·0′W	FM	137,148
Stoke Woods	Devon	SX9396	50°45·5′	3°30·6′W	F	192
Stoke Works	Worcs	SO9466	52°17·8′	2°4·9′W	X	150
Stokke Manor	Wilts	SU2664	51°22·7′	1°37·2′W	X	174
Stokoe	Northum	NY7386	55°10·3′	2°25·0′W	T	80
Stokoe High Crags	Northum	NY7584	55°9·2′	2°23·1′W	H	80
Stokyn Hall	Flint	SJ1777	53°17·3′	3°14·3′W	X	116
St Ola	Orkney	HY4409	58°58·1′	2°57·9′W	X	6,7
St Olaves	Norf	TM4599	52°32·2′	1°37·2′E	T	134
Stolerston Wood	N Yks	SE0697	54°22·4′	1°54·0′W	F	99
Stolford	Somer	ST0332	51°5·0′	3°22·7′W	X	181
Stolford	Somer	ST2345	51°12·2′	3°5·7′W	T	182
Stoliford	Devon	SX6650	50°20·3′	3°52·6′W	X	202
Stollerie's Fm	Norf	TM1081	52°23·4′	1°5·6′E	FM	144
Stonaford	Corn	SX2577	50°34·2′	4°27·9′W	X	201
Stonar Cut	Kent	TR3361	51°18·2′	1°21·0′E	W	179
Stonards Fm	Essex	TL4601	51°41·6′	0°7·1′E	FM	167
Stonard's Fm	Suff	TL7344	52°4·3′	0°31·9′E	FM	155
Stonar School	Wilts	ST8465	51°23·3′	2°13·4′W	X	173
Stondon Hall Fm	Essex	TL5701	51°41·4′	0°16·7′E	FM	167
Stondon Massey	Essex	TL5800	51°40·8′	0°17·5′E	T	167
Stondon Massey Ho	Essex	TL5701	51°41·4′	0°16·7′E	X	167
Stondon Place	Essex	TL5700	51°40·8′	0°16·7′E	X	167
Stone	Bucks	SP7812	51°48·3′	0°51·7′W	T	165
Stone	Devon	SS4021	50°58·2′	4°16·4′W	X	180,190
Stone	Devon	SS4711	50°52·9′	4°10·1′W	X	191
Stone	Devon	SS6433	51°5·0′	3°56·1′W	X	180
Stone	Devon	SS6921	50°58·6′	3°51·6′W	X	180
Stone	Devon	SS6925	51°0·8′	3°51·7′W	X	180
Stone	Devon	SS8128	51°2·6′	3°41·5′W	X	181
Stone	Devon	SS9305	50°50·3′	3°30·8′W	X	192
Stone	Devon	SX3986	50°39·3′	4°16·3′W	X	201
Stone	Devon	SX8286	50°39·9′	3°39·8′W	X	191
Stone	Glos	ST6895	51°39·4′	2°27·4′W	T	162
Stone	Kent	TQ5774	51°26·8′	0°16·0′E	T	177
Stone	Roth	SK5589	53°23·9′	1°10·0′W	T	111,120
Stone	Somer	SS8638	51°8·0′	3°37·4′W	X	181
Stone	Somer	ST5834	51°6·5′	2°35·6′W	T	182,183
Stone	Staffs	SJ9034	52°54·4′	2°8·5′W	T	127
Stone	Worcs	SO8575	52°22·6′	2°12·8′W	T	139
Stonea	Cambs	TL4593	52°31·2′	0°8·6′E	T	143

Stonea Camp	Cambs	TL4493	52°31·2′	0°7·7′E	A	142,143
Stoneacre	Kent	TQ8053	51°15·1′	0°35·2′E	A	188
Stoneacre Fm	Kent	TQ8053	51°15·1′	0°35·2′E	FM	188
Stoneacton	Shrops	SO5093	52°32·2′	2°43·8′W	T	137,138
Stonea Fm	Lincs	TF4593	53°25·1′	0°11·3′E	FM	143
Stonea Grange Fm	Cambs	TL4493	52°31·2′	0°7·7′E	FM	142,143
Stone Allerton	Somer	ST4051	51°15·5′	2°51·2′W	T	182
Stone Arthur	Cumbr	NY3409	54°28·6′	3°0·7′W	X	90
Stone Ash	Devon	SS7908	50°51·8′	3°42·8′W	X	191
Ston Easton	Somer	ST6253	51°16·7′	2°32·3′W	T	183
Stone Avenue	Wilts	SU1069	51°25·4′	1°51·0′W	A	173
Stone Bank	N Yks	SE7297	54°22·0′	0°53·1′W	X	94,100
Stonebarrow Hill	Dorset	SY3893	50°44·2′	2°52·3′W	X	193
Stone Barton	Devon	SS7113	50°54·4′	3°49·7′W	X	180
Stone Beck	N Yks	SE0375	54°10·5′	1°56·8′W	W	98
Stonebeck Gate Fm	N Yks	NZ7105	54°26·4′	0°53·9′W	FM	94
Stonebench	Glos	SO7914	51°49·7′	2°17·9′W	X	162
Stonebow	Worcs	SO9349	52°8·6′	2°5·7′W	T	150
Stonebow Fm	Glos	SO8225	51°55·6′	2°15·3′W	FM	162
Stonebridge	Brent	TQ2083	51°32·2′	0°15·8′W	T	176
Stone Bridge	Durham	NZ2541	54°46·0′	1°36·3′W	X	88
Stonebridge	Essex	TQ9188	51°33·7′	0°45·7′E	T	178
Stonebridge	E Susx	TQ5220	50°57·8′	0°10·3′E	X	199
Stone Bridge	Kent	TQ9426	51°0·3′	0°46·3′E	X	189
Stonebridge	Lincs	TF4299	53°28·3′	0°8·8′E	X	113
Stonebridge	Medway	TQ7672	51°25·4′	0°32·3′E	X	178
Stonebridge	Mil Key	SP8241	52°3·9′	0°47·8′W	X	152
Stonebridge	Norf	TL9290	52°28·7′	0°50·0′E	T	144
Stonebridge	N Som	ST3959	51°19·8′	2°52·1′W	T	182
Stonebridge	Sol	SP2182	52°26·4′	1°41·1′W	T	139
Stonebridge	Surrey	TQ1747	51°12·8′	0°19·1′W	T	187
Stone Bridge Corner	Peterb	TF2700	52°35·2′	0°7·1′W	X	142
Stone Bridge Drain	Lincs	TF3451	53°2·6′	0°3·5′E	W	122
Stonebridge Fm	E Susx	TQ7711	50°52·5′	0°31·3′E	FM	199
Stonebridge Fm	Lincs	TA3502	53°30·1′	0°2·5′E	FM	113
Stone Bridge Fm	Lincs	TF3348	53°1·0′	0°0·6′W	FM	131
Stone Bridge Fm	Peterb	TF1705	52°38·0′	0°15·9′W	FM	142
Stonebridge Fm	Suff	TL7146	52°5·4′	0°30·2′E	FM	154
Stonebridge Green	Kent	TQ9147	51°11·6′	0°44·4′E	T	189
Stonebridge Hill	Essex	TL8429	51°56·0′	0°41·0′E	X	168
Stonebridge Lees	Cumbr	NY5153	54°52·4′	2°45·4′W	X	86
Stonebridge Marshes	Suff	TM3848	52°5·0′	1°28·8′E	X	169
Stonebriggs	Aberd	NJ9165	57°40·7′	2°8·6′W	X	30
Stonebriggs	E Ayr	NS6223	55°29·1′	4°10·6′W	X	71
Stonebroom	Derby	SK4159	53°7·8′	1°22·8′W	T	120
Stonebury Fm	Herts	TL3828	51°56·2′	0°0·8′E	FM	166
Stonebyres	E Renf	NS5949	55°43·1′	4°14·2′W	X	64
Stonebyres Falls	S Lanak	NS8544	55°40·8′	3°49·3′W	W	71,72
Stonebyres Holdings	S Lanak	NS8343	55°40·2′	3°51·2′W	T	71,72
Stonebyres Wood	E Renf	NS5949	55°43·1′	4°14·2′W	F	64
Stonecalsey	S Ayr	NS4032	55°33·6′	4°31·8′W	X	70
Stone Carr	Cumbr	NY4228	54°38·9′	2°53·5′W	X	90
Stone Carr	E Yorks	TA0738	53°49·9′	0°22·0′W	X	107
Stone Carrs	Durham	NY9137	54°43·9′	2°8·0′W	X	91,92
Stone Castle	Kent	TQ5874	51°26·8′	0°16·8′E	X	177
Stone Chair	Cald	SE1127	53°44·6′	1°49·6′W	T	104
Stone Check Hall	Lancs	SD4142	53°52·5′	2°53·4′W	X	102
Stonechester	Durham	NZ1229	54°39·6′	1°48·4′W	X	92
Stonechester	Durham	NZ1736	54°43·4′	1°43·7′W	X	92
Stone Cliff	Kent	TQ9326	51°0·3′	0°45·4′E	X	189
Stonecliff Wood	N Yks	SE4786	54°16·3′	1°16·3′W	F	100
Stone Close Ho	Durham	NZ0311	54°29·9′	1°56·8′W	X	92
Stoneclough	Bolton	SD7505	53°32·7′	2°22·2′W	T	109
Stonecombe	Devon	SS6043	51°10·4′	3°59·8′W	T	180
Stonecombe	Dorset	ST4901	50°48·6′	2°43·0′W	X	193,194
Stone Common	Suff	TM3557	52°9·9′	1°26·6′E	X	156
Stone Copse	W Berks	SU4969	51°25·3′	1°17·3′W	X	174
Stone Corner Fm	Kent	TQ9129	51°1·9′	0°43·8′E	FM	189
Stone Cott	Arg & Bt	NR3562	55°47·0′	6°13·2′W	X	60,61
Stone Cove	Cumbr	NY3510	54°29·1′	2°59·8′W	X	90
Stone Creek	E Yorks	TA2318	53°38·9′	0°7·9′W	W	113
Stone Creek Fm	E Yorks	TA2419	53°39·4′	0°7·0′W	FM	113
Stone Creek Ho	E Yorks	TA2318	53°38·9′	0°7·9′W	X	113
Stonecroft Ho	N Lincs	TA0810	53°34·8′	0°21·7′W	X	112
Stonecroft Ho	Northum	NY8668	55°0·6′	2°12·7′W	X	87
Stonecroft Manor Fm	Somer	ST5020	50°58·9′	2°42·4′W	FM	183
Stone Cross	Cumbr	SD2878	54°11·8′	3°5·8′W	X	96,97
Stone Cross	Devon	SS5409	50°52·0′	4°4·1′W	X	191
Stone Cross	Devon	SS6433	51°5·0′	3°56·1′W	X	180
Stone Cross	Devon	SS6801	50°47·8′	3°52·0′W	X	191
Stone Cross	Durham	NZ0319	54°34·2′	1°56·8′W	X	92
Stone Cross	E Susx	TQ5128	51°2·1′	0°9·6′E	T	188,199
Stone Cross	E Susx	TQ6104	50°49·0′	0°17·5′E	T	199
Stone Cross	E Susx	TQ6431	51°3·5′	0°20·8′E	T	188
Stone Cross	Kent	TQ5238	51°7·5′	0°10·7′E	T	188
Stone Cross	Kent	TR0236	51°5·5′	0°53·5′E	T	189
Stone Cross	Kent	TR3257	51°16·1′	1°19·9′E	T	179
Stone Cross	Sand	SP0094	52°32·9′	1°59·6′W	T	139
Stone Cross	W Susx	TQ3527	51°1·8′	0°4·1′W	X	187,198
Stone Cross Fm	E Susx	TQ5112	50°53·5′	0°9·2′E	FM	199
Stonecross Green	Suff	TL8257	52°11·1′	0°40·1′E	X	155
Stonecrouch	Kent	TQ6933	51°4·5′	0°25·1′E	T	188
Stone Dean Fm	Bucks	SU9790	51°36·3′	0°35·6′W	FM	175,176
Stonedelph Fm	Ches	SJ7284	53°21·4′	2°24·8′W	FM	109
Stonedge	Scot Bord	NT5509	55°22·6′	2°42·2′W	T	80
Stonedge Forest	Scot Bord	NT5408	55°22·1′	2°43·1′W	F	79
Stonedge Hill	Scot Bord	NT5408	55°22·1′	2°43·1′W	H	79
Stonedike	Aberd	NJ5024	57°18·5′	2°49·3′W	X	37
Stoneditch Hill	Devon	SS5845	51°11·4′	4°1·5′W	H	180
Stone Down Hill	Somer	ST5139	51°9·1′	2°41·7′W	H	182,183
Stonedown Wood	Wilts	ST9920	50°59·0′	2°0·5′W	F	184
Stone Dykes	Cumbr	SD2785	54°15·6′	3°6·8′W	X	96,97
Stone Edge	Derby	SK3266	53°11·6′	1°30·9′W	X	119
Stone Edge	Lancs	SD8641	53°52·1′	2°12·4′W	T	103
Stone-edge Batch	N Som	ST4671	51°26·4′	2°46·2′W	T	171,172
Stone Edge Plantation	Derby	SK3467	53°12·2′	1°29·1′W	F	119
Stone End	Glos	SO7718	51°51·8′	2°19·6′W	X	162
Stone End Ho	Glos	SO7926	51°56·2′	2°17·9′W	X	162
Stone Ends	Cumbr	NY3533	54°41·5′	3°0·1′W	X	90
Stonefauld Knowes	D & G	NX7496	55°14·8′	3°58·5′W	X	77
Stone Faulds	Cumbr	NY4345	54°48·0′	2°52·8′W	X	85
Stoneferry	K upon H	TA1031	53°46·1′	0°19·5′W	T	107
Stonefield	Arg & Bt	NM9533	56°26·9′	5°19·1′W	X	49
Stonefield	Arg & Bt	NR8568	55°51·7′	5°25·7′W	X	62
Stonefield	Arg & Bt	NS1186	56°2·0′	5°1·6′W	X	56
Stonefield	Pth & Kin	NN8525	56°24·5′	3°51·4′W	X	52,58
Stonefield	S Lanak	NS6957	55°47·6′	4°4·9′W	T	64
Stonefield	Staffs	SJ8934	52°54·4′	2°9·4′W	T	127
Stonefield	Stir	NN5500	56°10·5′	4°19·7′W	X	57
Stonefield Castle Hotel	Arg & Bt	NR8671	55°53·3′	5°24·9′W	X	62
Stonefieldhill Fm	Midlo	NT3060	55°49·9′	3°6·6′W	FM	66
Stonefield Ho	N Yks	SE5571	54°8·2′	1°9·1′W	X	100
Stoneflatts	Cumbr	NY4566	54°59·4′	2°51·1′W	X	86
Stone Fm	Devon	SS6801	50°47·8′	3°52·0′W	FM	191
Stone Fm	Devon	SS7715	50°55·5′	3°44·6′W	FM	180
Stone Fm	Devon	SX5089	50°41·1′	4°7·0′W	FM	191
Stone Fm	Devon	SX7190	50°42·0′	3°49·2′W	FM	191
Stone Fm	Devon	SX8252	50°21·6′	3°39·2′W	FM	202
Stone Fm	Hants	SZ4599	50°47·6′	1°21·3′W	FM	196
Stone Fm	Heref	SO5155	52°11·7′	2°42·6′W	FM	149
Stone Fm	Heref	SO5852	52°10·1′	2°36·5′W	FM	149
Stone Fm	I of W	SZ5086	50°40·5′	1°17·2′W	FM	196
Stone Fm	Kent	TQ9228	51°1·4′	0°44·7′E	FM	189
Stone Fm	Kent	TQ9832	51°3·4′	0°49·9′E	FM	189
Stone Fm	Kent	TQ9862	51°19·6′	0°50·9′E	FM	178
Stone Fm	Kent	TR1537	51°5·7′	1°4·6′E	FM	179,189
Stone Fm	Lincs	TF1495	53°26·6′	0°16·6′W	FM	113
Stone Fm	Oxon	SU2690	51°36·7′	1°37·1′W	FM	163,174
Stone Fm	Somer	ST5518	50°57·8′	2°38·1′W	FM	183
Stone Fm	Somer	ST5835	51°7·0′	2°35·6′W	FM	182,183
Stone Fm	Suff	TL8838	52°0·7′	0°44·8′E	FM	155
Stone Fm	Suff	TL9256	52°10·4′	0°48·9′E	FM	155
Stone Fm	Suff	TM0950	52°6·8′	1°3·5′E	FM	155
Stone Fm	Suff	TM3262	52°12·7′	1°24·2′E	FM	156
Stone Fm	Suff	TM3556	52°9·4′	1°26·5′E	FM	156
Stone Fm	W Susx	TQ1535	51°6·4′	0°21·0′W	FM	187
Stonefold	Aberd	NJ5913	57°12·6′	2°40·3′W	X	37
Stone Fold	Lancs	SD7047	53°55·3′	2°27·0′W	X	103
Stone Fold	Lancs	SD7825	53°43·5′	2°19·6′W	X	103
Stonefold	N Yks	SE1879	54°12·6′	1°43·0′W	X	99
Stonefold	Scot Bord	NT7442	55°40·5′	2°24·4′W	X	74
Stonefolds	Aberd	NJ8042	57°28·3′	2°19·5′W	X	29,30
Stonefolds	Northum	NY7770	55°1·7′	2°21·2′W	X	86,87
Stonefoot Hill	Durham	NZ1240	54°45·5′	1°48·4′W	X	88
Stone Gap	Red & Cl	NZ6522	54°35·6′	0°59·2′W	X	94
Stone Gappe	N Yks	SD9645	53°54·3′	2°3·2′W	X	103
Stonegarthside	Cumbr	NY4780	55°6·9′	2°49·4′W	X	79
Stonegarthside Hall	Cumbr	NY4881	55°7·5′	2°48·5′W	A	79
Stonegate	E Susx	TQ6628	51°1·9′	0°22·4′E	T	188,199
Stonegate	N Yks	NZ7709	54°28·5′	0°48·3′W	T	94
Stonegate Beck	N Yks	NZ7807	54°27·4′	0°47·4′W	W	94
Stonegate Fm	Kent	TR0135	51°5·0′	0°52·6′E	FM	189
Stonegate Fm	Norf	TG1825	52°46·9′	1°14·4′E	FM	133,134
Stonegate Gill Wood	N Yks	NZ7708	54°27·9′	0°48·3′W	F	94
Stonegate Ho	Lincs	TF4023	52°47·4′	0°5·0′E	X	131
Stonegate Sta	E Susx	TQ6527	51°1·3′	0°21·6′E	X	188,199
Stone Gill Foot	N Yks	SD8285	54°15·9′	2°16·2′W	X	98
Stone Grain	Scot Bord	NT1628	55°32·6′	3°19·4′W	W	72
Stone Grain Rig	Scot Bord	NT1825	55°31·0′	3°17·5′W	H	72
Stonegrave	N Yks	SE6577	54°11·3′	0°59·8′W	T	100
Stonegrave Lodge	N Yks	SE6478	54°11·9′	1°0·7′W	X	100
Stonegravels	Derby	SK3872	53°14·9′	1°25·4′W	T	119
Stonegreen Hall Fm	Kent	TR0438	51°6·5′	0°55·3′E	FM	179,189
Stonegrove	N Yks	SD6967	54°6·1′	2°28·0′W	X	98
Stonegrove Hill	W Berks	SU3269	51°25·4′	1°32·0′W	X	174
Stone Hagg	N Yks	SE6995	54°21·0′	0°55·9′W	X	94,100
Stone Hall	Essex	TL5115	51°49·0′	0°11·8′E	X	167
Stone Hall	Essex	TL5922	51°52·7′	0°19·0′E	X	167
Stone Hall	Kent	TQ8447	51°11·8′	0°38·4′E	X	188
Stone Hall	Kent	TR1345	51°10·1′	1°3·2′E	X	179,189
Stonehall	Kent	TR2645	51°9·8′	1°14·3′E	T	179
Stone Hall	Northum	NY7564	54°58·4′	2°23·0′W	X	86,87
Stone Hall	Northum	NY8357	54°54·7′	2°15·5′W	X	86,87
Stonehall	Orkney	HY5503	58°55·0′	2°46·4′W	X	6
Stone Hall	Pemb	SM9327	51°54·4′	5°0·2′W	X	157,158
Stone Hall	Suff	TM0273	52°19·3′	0°58·2′E	X	144,155
Stone Hall	Suff	TM2753	52°7·9′	1°19·4′E	X	156
Stone Hall	Thurr	TQ6285	51°32·7′	0°20·6′E	X	177
Stonehall	Worcs	SO8848	52°8·0′	2°10·1′W	T	150
Stone Hall	W Susx	TQ3228	51°2·4′	0°6·6′W	A	187,198
Stonehall Common	Worcs	SO8849	52°8·6′	2°10·1′W	X	150
Stone Hall Fm	Essex	TL5212	51°47·4′	0°12·6′E	FM	167
Stonehall Fm	Essex	TM1526	51°53·7′	1°7·9′E	FM	168,169
Stone Hall Fm	Somer	ST2535	51°6·8′	3°3·9′W	FM	182
Stonehall Fm	Suff	TL7760	52°12·8′	0°35·9′E	FM	155
Stoneham Fm	W Berks	SU6574	51°27·9′	1°3·5′W	FM	175
Stoneham Fms	E Susx	TQ4211	50°53·1′	0°1·5′E	FM	198
Stonehanger Copse	Hants	SU3241	51°10·3′	1°32·1′W	F	185
Stonehaugh	Northum	NY7976	55°4·9′	2°19·3′W	T	86,87
Stonehaven	Aberd	NO8786	56°58·2′	2°12·4′W	T	45
Stonehaven Bay	Aberd	NO8786	56°58·2′	2°12·4′W	W	45
Stonehayes	Devon	ST1603	50°49·5′	3°11·2′W	X	192,193
Stonehay Fm	Derby	SK3367	53°12·2′	1°29·9′W	FM	119
Stonehead	Lancs	SD5352	53°58·0′	2°42·6′W	X	102
Stone Head	N Yks	SD9443	53°53·2′	2°5·1′W	T	103
Stonehead	W Loth	NS9462	55°50·6′	3°41·1′W	X	65
Stoneheap	W Loth	NS9661	55°50·1′	3°39·2′W	X	65
Stoneheap Fm	Kent	TR3250	51°12·3′	1°19·7′E	FM	179
Stone Heath	Staffs	SJ9735	52°55·0′	2°2·3′W	T	127
Stonehenge	Wilts	SU1242	51°10·9′	1°49·3′W	A	184
Stonehenge Fm	Oxon	SP4101	51°42·6′	1°24·0′W	FM	164
Stone Hill	Cambs	TL4552	52°9·1′	0°7·6′E	X	154
Stone Hill	Donc	SE6708	53°34·1′	0°58·9′W	T	111
Stonehill	E Susx	TQ5615	50°55·0′	0°13·5′E	A	199
Stone Hill	Kent	TQ9046	51°11·1′	0°43·5′E	T	189
Stone Hill	Kent	TR0938	51°6·4′	0°59·5′E	T	179,189
Stone Hill	Norf	TG1741	52°55·6′	1°14·1′E	X	133
Stone Hill	Norf	TG2041	52°55·5′	1°16·8′E	X	133
Stone Hill	Northnts	SP9892	52°31·3′	0°32·9′W	X	141
Stone Hill	Notts	SK6790	53°24·4′	0°59·1′W	X	111
Stone Hill	Roth	SK4880	53°19·1′	1°16·4′W	X	111,120
Stone Hill	S Glos	ST6471	51°26·4′	2°30·7′W	T	172
Stonehill	S Lanak	NS8321	55°28·4′	3°50·6′W	X	71,72
Stone Hill	S Lanak	NS8936	55°36·6′	3°45·3′W	H	71,72
Stonehill	S Lanak	NS9036	55°36·6′	3°44·3′W	X	71,72
Stonehill	Stir	NN8000	56°10·9′	3°55·6′W	X	57
Stonehill	Surrey	TQ0063	51°21·7′	0°33·4′W	T	176,186
Stone Hill	Wilts	ST9989	51°36·2′	2°0·5′W	X	173
Stonehill Bank	S Lanak	NS8320	55°27·8′	3°50·6′W	H	71,72
Stonehill Copse	Wilts	ST9136	51°7·6′	2°7·3′W	F	184
Stonehill Down	Dorset	SY9282	50°38·5′	2°6·4′W	X	195
Stonehill Fm	Bucks	SP7522	51°53·7′	0°54·2′W	FM	165
Stone Hill Fm	Cambs	TL2054	52°10·5′	0°14·3′W	FM	153
Stonehill Fm	Essex	TL6307	51°44·5′	0°22·1′E	FM	167
Stonehill Fm	E Susx	TQ5615	50°55·0′	0°13·5′E	FM	199
Stonehill Fm	Lincs	TF2768	53°11·9′	0°5·5′W	FM	122
Stonehill Fm	Notts	SK7869	53°13·0′	0°49·5′W	FM	120,121
Stonehill Fm	Wilts	ST9889	51°36·2′	2°1·3′W	FM	173
Stonehill Green	Kent	TQ5070	51°24·8′	0°9·8′E	X	177
Stonehill Ho	Oxon	SU4895	51°39·3′	1°18·0′W	X	164
Stone Hill Ho	W Susx	TQ3834	51°5·5′	0°1·4′W	X	187
Stonehills	Devon	SX7855	50°23·2′	3°42·6′W	X	202
Stonehills	Hants	SU4602	50°49·2′	1°20·4′W	T	196
Stonehills Fm	Norf	TF6302	52°35·7′	0°24·8′E	FM	143
Stonehills Plantn	Notts	SK5358	53°7·2′	1°12·1′W	F	120
Stonehill Wood	Glos	ST8091	51°37·3′	2°16·9′W	F	162,173
Stonehill Wood	Wilts	SU0089	51°36·2′	1°59·6′W	F	173
Stone Ho	Ches	SJ4652	53°4·0′	2°47·9′W	X	117
Stone Ho	Cumbr	NY5157	54°54·6′	2°45·4′W	X	86
Stone Ho	E Susx	TQ6318	50°56·5′	0°19·6′E	X	199
Stone Ho	Kent	TR3969	51°22·4′	1°26·4′E	X	179
Stone Ho	N Yks	NY8500	54°24·0′	2°13·4′W	X	91,92
Stone Ho	N Yks	SE5695	54°21·1′	1°7·9′W	X	100
Stone Ho	Powys	SJ0110	52°41·0′	3°27·5′W	X	125
Stone Ho	Powys	SO2354	52°11·0′	3°7·2′W	X	148
Stone Ho	Shrops	SJ3918	52°45·6′	2°53·8′W	X	126
Stone Ho	Shrops	SJ5419	52°46·2′	2°40·5′W	X	126
Stone Ho	Shrops	SJ5701	52°36·5′	2°37·7′W	X	126
Stone Ho	Shrops	SO2384	52°27·2′	3°7·6′W	X	137
Stone Ho	W Berks	SU5464	51°22·6′	1°13·1′W	X	174
Stone Ho	Win & Maid	SU8786	51°34·2′	0°44·3′W	X	175
Stoneholme	N Lincs	SK9899	53°29·0′	0°31·0′W	X	112
Stone Ho, The	Staffs	SK0217	52°45·3′	1°57·8′W	X	128
Stonehouse	Aberd	NJ8240	57°27·3′	2°17·5′W	X	29,30
Stonehouse	Aberd	NO7787	56°58·7′	2°22·3′W	X	45
Stonehouse	Ches	SJ5070	53°13·7′	2°44·5′W	X	117
Stonehouse	C of Plym	SX4654	50°22·2′	4°9·6′W	T	201
Stone House	Cumbr	SD7785	54°15·9′	2°20·8′W	T	98
Stonehouse	D & G	NX4147	54°47·8′	4°28·0′W	X	83
Stonehouse	D & G	NX8268	54°59·8′	3°50·2′W	X	84
Stonehouse	D & G	NY3067	54°59·8′	3°5·2′W	X	85
Stonehouse	E Susx	TQ4825	51°0·5′	0°7·0′E	X	188,198
Stonehouse	E Susx	TQ7814	50°54·1′	0°32·3′E	X	199
Stonehouse	Glos	SO8005	51°44·8′	2°17·0′W	T	162
Stonehouse	Moray	NJ2657	57°36·1′	3°13·8′W	X	28
Stonehouse	Northum	NY6958	54°55·2′	2°28·6′W	X	86,87
Stone House	Northum	NY8280	55°7·1′	2°16·5′W	X	80
Stone House	N Yks	SD7777	54°11·5′	2°20·7′W	X	98
Stonehouse	Powys	SJ1710	52°41·1′	3°13·3′W	X	125
Stonehouse	Powys	SJ1718	52°45·4′	3°13·4′W	X	125
Stone House	Shrops	SO6677	52°23·6′	2°29·6′W	X	138
Stonehouse	S Lanak	NS7546	55°41·7′	3°58·9′W	T	64
Stonehouse Barn	Powys	SO2353	52°10·4′	3°7·2′W	X	148
Stonehouse Cote	N Yks	SE5699	54°23·2′	1°7·8′W	X	100
Stonehouse Fm	Essex	TL8335	51°59·2′	0°40·3′E	FM	155
Stone House Fm	E Susx	TQ7428	51°1·7′	0°29·3′E	FM	188,199
Stonehouse Fm	Falk	NS9184	56°2·4′	3°44·5′W	FM	65
Stonehouse Fm	Glos	SO6731	51°58·8′	2°28·4′W	FM	149
Stonehouse Fm	Glos	SO8930	51°58·3′	2°9·2′W	FM	150
Stonehouse Fm	Kent	TQ4762	51°20·5′	0°7·0′E	FM	177,188
Stonehouse Fm	Leic	SK3613	52°43·0′	1°27·6′W	FM	128
Stone House Fm	Leic	SK8110	52°41·1′	0°47·7′W	FM	130
Stonehouse Fm	Lincs	TF1813	52°42·3′	0°14·8′W	FM	130,142
Stone House Fm	Medway	TQ7371	51°24·9′	0°29·7′E	FM	178
Stonehouse Fm	Norf	TL9685	52°25·9′	0°53·4′E	FM	144
Stonehouse Fm	Oxon	SP4811	51°48·0′	1°17·8′W	FM	164
Stonehouse Fm	Oxon	SP5219	51°52·3′	1°14·3′W	FM	164
Stone House Fm	Powys	SJ2507	52°39·6′	3°6·1′W	FM	126
Stonehouse Fm	Somer	ST2027	51°2·4′	3°8·1′W	FM	193
Stonehouse Fm	Suff	TL7858	52°11·7′	0°36·7′E	FM	155
Stonehouse Fm	Suff	TM2162	52°12·9′	1°14·5′E	FM	156
Stone House Fm	Suff	TM4273	52°18·3′	1°33·4′E	FM	156
Stone House Fm	Warw	SP3370	52°19·9′	1°30·5′W	FM	140
Stonehouse Fm	Worcs	SP0157	52°12·9′	1°58·7′W	FM	150
Stonehousehill	Aberd	NK0639	57°26·7′	1°53·5′W	X	30
Stone Houses	Durham	NY9025	54°37·4′	2°8·9′W	X	91,92
Stonehouses	Staffs	SJ9740	52°57·7′	2°2·3′W	T	118
Stonehouse Tower	Cumbr	NY4680	55°6·9′	2°50·4′W	A	79
Stone Howe	N Yks	SE6274	54°9·7′	1°2·6′W	A	100
Stonehurst	E Susx	TQ5426	51°1·0′	0°12·1′E	X	188,199
Stonehurst	E Susx	TQ6124	50°59·8′	0°18·1′E	X	199
Stonehurst	Surrey	SU9736	51°7·1′	0°36·5′W	X	186
Stone in Oxney	Kent	TQ9427	51°0·8′	0°46·3′E	T	189
Stone Intake	N Yks	NZ5400	54°23·8′	1°9·7′W	X	93
Stonekiln	Aberd	NJ9942	57°28·4′	2°0·5′W	X	30
Stoneknowe	Cumbr	NY4462	54°57·2′	2°52·0′W	X	85
Stoneknowe	Cumbr	NY5179	55°6·4′	2°45·7′W	X	86
Stoneland Fm	Devon	SS8818	50°57·3′	3°35·3′W	FM	181
Stonelands	N Yks	SD9173	54°9·4′	2°7·9′W	X	98
Stonelands	Oxon	SP2709	51°47·0′	1°36·1′W	X	163
Stonelands	W Susx	TQ3533	51°5·0′	0°4·0′W	X	187
Stoneland's Fm	E Susx	TQ5136	51°6·4′	0°9·8′E	FM	188
Stonelands Fm	E Susx	TQ6315	50°54·9′	0°19·5′E	FM	199
Stonelands Waste	Devon	SX8180	50°36·7′	3°40·5′W	X	191
Stonelaws	E Loth	NT5780	56°0·9′	2°40·9′W	X	67
Stoneleigh	Surrey	TQ2264	51°21·9′	0°14·5′W	T	176,187
Stoneleigh	Warw	SP3372	52°20·9′	1°30·5′W	T	140
Stoneleigh Grange	Warw	SP3373	52°21·5′	1°30·5′W	X	140
Stoneleigh Manor	Devon	SX7552	50°21·5′	3°45·1′W	X	202
Stoneley Green	Ches	SJ6251	53°3·5′	2°33·6′W	T	118

Stonelink Fm	E Susx	TQ8418	50°56·1'	0°37·5'E	FM	199
Stone Lodge	Leic	SK7704	52°37·9'	0°51·3'W	X	141
Stone Lodge	Somer	SS9335	51°6·5'	3°31·3'W	X	181
Stone Lodge Fm	Leic	SK7606	52°39·0'	0°52·2'W	FM	141
Stone Low	Derby	SE1000	53°30·0'	1°50·5'W	X	110
Stone Low	Derby	SK2871	53°14·4'	1°34·4'W	A	119
Stonelow Flat Fm	Derby	SK2972	53°14·9'	1°33·5'W	FM	119
Stone Lud	Highld	ND2261	58°32·1'	3°19·9'W	X	11,12
Stonely	Cambs	TL1067	52°17·6'	0°22·8'W	T	153
Stonelynk Fm	E Susx	TQ8712	50°52·9'	0°39·9'E	FM	199
Stonely Woods	N Yks	SE6591	54°18·9'	0°59·6'W	F	94,100
Stone Marsh	Essex	TM2425	51°52·9'	1°15·7'E	W	169
Stone Marshes	Kent	TQ5675	51°27·4'	0°15·1'E	X	177
Stonemeal Creek	Norf	TF9444	52°57·7'	0°53·7'E	W	132
Stonemill Fm	Devon	SS7213	50°54·4'	3°48·9'W	FM	180
Stone Mill Fm	E Susx	TQ5426	51°1·0'	0°12·1'E	FM	188,199
Stone Moor	Sheff	SK2697	53°28·4'	1°36·1'W	X	110
Stone Moor Cross	Devon	SS7214	50°54·9'	3°48·9'W	X	180
Stone Ness	Thurr	TQ5876	51°27·9'	0°16·9'E	X	177
Stone of Benholm	Aberd	NO7968	56°48·4'	2°20·2'W	X	45
Stone of Comba	Shetld	HU3950	60°14·2'	1°17·2'W	X	3
Stone of Morphie	Aberd	NO7162	56°45·2'	2°28·0'W	X	45
Stone of Setter	Orkney	HY5637	59°13·3'	2°45·8'W	A	5
Stonepark	Staffs	SJ9134	52°54·4'	2°7·6'W	X	127
Stone Pike	Cumbr	NY0707	54°27·2'	3°25·6'W	X	89
Stonepit Fm	Notts	SK5229	52°51·6'	1°13·3'W	FM	129
Stonepit Hill	Norf	TG1538	52°54·0'	1°12·2'E	X	133
Stonepit Hills	Norf	TF7522	52°46·3'	0°36·1'E	X	132
Stonepit Hills	Oxon	SP5219	51°52·3'	1°14·3'W	X	164
Stonepit Hills	Staffs	SK1828	52°51·2'	1°43·6'W	X	128
Stonepit Lee Clough	Kirk	SE0112	53°36·5'	1°58·7'W	X	110
Stonepits	Worcs	SP0056	52°12·4'	1°59·6'W	T	150
Stonepit Spinney	Oxon	SP6233	51°59·8'	1°5·4'W	F	152,165
Stonepitts	Kent	TQ5657	51°17·7'	0°14·6'E	X	188
Stonepit Wood	N Lincs	SE9403	53°31·2'	0°34·5'W	F	112
Stonepit Wood	Suff	TL8280	52°23·5'	0°40·9'E	F	144
Stone Place Fm	I of W	SZ4582	50°38·4'	1°21·4'W	FM	196
Stone Point	Essex	TM2425	51°52·9'	1°15·7'E	X	169
Stone Point	Hants	SZ4598	50°47·0'	1°21·3'W	X	196
Stonequarry	W Susx	TQ4039	51°8·2'	0°0·5'E	T	187
Stone Quarry Bottom	Hants	SU1916	50°56·8'	1°43·4'W	X	184
Stonequarry Fm	Devon	SS4601	50°47·5'	4°10·7'W	FM	190
Stoneraise	Cumbr	NY2645	54°47·9'	3°8·6'W	X	85
Stoneraise	Cumbr	NY3426	54°37·7'	3°0·9'W	X	90
Stone Raise	Cumbr	NY4049	54°50·2'	2°55·6'W	T	85
Stone Raise	Cumbr	NY4049	54°50·2'	2°55·6'W	X	85
Stoneraise Place	Cumbr	NY2745	54°47·9'	3°7·7'W	X	85
Stoner Hill	Hants	SU7225	51°1·4'	0°58·0'W	T	186,197
Stoneridge	Falk	NS8770	55°54·8'	3°48·0'W	X	65
Stoneridge Fm	Hants	SU6816	50°56·6'	1°1·5'W	FM	185
Stone Ridge Plain	N Yks	SE0056	54°0·2'	1°59·6'W	X	104
Stonerigg	Cumbr	NY3355	54°53·4'	3°2·2'W	X	85
Stonerigg	W Loth	NS9367	55°53·3'	3°42·2'W	X	65
Stoneriggs	Cumbr	NY7220	54°34·7'	2°25·6'W	X	91
Stone Riggs	N Yks	NZ3204	54°26·1'	1°30·0'W	X	93
Stone Riggs	York	SE6555	53°59·5'	1°0·1'W	X	105,106
Stone Road End Fm	Notts	SK7569	53°13·0'	0°52·2'W	FM	120
Stoneroad Fm	Norf	TG0212	52°40·3'	0°59·7'E	FM	133
Stonerocks Fm	Kent	TR1861	51°18·6'	1°8·1'E	FM	179
Stone Rook Hill	N Yks	NZ6703	54°25·3'	0°57·6'W	X	94
Stone Ruck	N Yks	NZ7100	54°23·7'	0°54·0'W	X	94
Stone Ruckles	N Yks	SE6390	54°18·3'	1°1·5'W	X	94,100
Stone Ruckles (Cairn)	N Yks	SE6390	54°18·3'	1°1·5'W	A	94,100
Stone Ruck (Tumulus)	N Yks	NZ7100	54°23·7'	0°54·0'W	A	94
Stonerwood Park	Hants	SU7325	51°1·4'	0°57·2'W	X	186,197
Stonery Fm	E Susx	TQ5106	50°50·3'	0°9·1'E	FM	199
Stones	Cald	SD9223	53°42·4'	2°6·9'W	X	103
Stones	Essex	TL6430	51°56·9'	0°23·6'E	X	167
Stones Br	Staffs	SK2611	52°42·0'	1°36·5'W	X	128
Stonesby	Leic	SK8224	52°48·7'	0°46·6'W	T	130
Stonesby Lodge	Leic	SK8323	52°48·1'	0°45·7'W	X	130
Stonesby Spinney	Leic	SK8223	52°48·1'	0°46·6'W	F	130
Stonesdale Beck	N Yks	NY8803	54°25·6'	2°10·7'W	W	91,92
Stonesdale Moor	N Yks	NY8904	54°26·1'	2°9·8'W	X	91,92
Stonesfield	Oxon	SP3917	51°51·2'	1°25·6'W	T	164
Stones Fm	Aberd	NK0436	57°25·1'	1°55·5'W	FM	30
Stone's Fm	Dorset	ST6306	50°51·4'	2°31·2'W	FM	194
Stones Green	Essex	TM1626	51°53·7'	1°8·8'E	T	168,169
Stoneshiel	Scot Bord	NT8760	55°50·2'	2°12·0'W	X	67
Stoneshiel Hill	Scot Bord	NT7758	55°49·1'	2°21·6'W	X	67,74
Stoneshot Common	Essex	TL4007	51°44·9'	0°2·1'E	X	167
Stoneside	S Lanak	NS5733	55°34·4'	4°15·7'W	X	64
Stoneside	S Lanak	NS5753	55°45·2'	4°16·3'W	X	64
Stoneside Hill	Cumbr	SD1489	54°17·6'	3°18·9'W	X	96
Stone Sleights	N Yks	SE8061	54°2·6'	0°46·3'W	X	100
Stones of Stenness	Orkney	HY3012	58°59·6'	3°12·6'W	A	6
Stones of Via	Orkney	HY2516	59°1·7'	3°17·9'W	A	6
Stonestar	Cumbr	SD2091	54°18·7'	3°13·4'W	X	96
Stonesteps	I of W	SZ4287	50°41·1'	1°23·9'W	X	196
Stone Stile	Kent	TQ8245	51°10·7'	0°36·6'E	X	188
Stonestile	Kent	TQ9451	51°13·7'	0°47·1'E	X	189
Stone Stile	Northum	NY8357	54°54·7'	2°15·5'W	X	86,87
Stone Stile Fm	Kent	TR0555	51°15·7'	0°56·7'E	FM	179
Stone Street	Kent	TQ5754	51°16·0'	0°15·4'E	T	188
Stone Street	Suff	TL9639	52°1·1'	0°51·8'E	T	155
Stone Street	Suff	TM3882	52°23·3'	1°30·3'E	T	156
Stonestreet Green	Kent	TR0637	51°5·9'	0°56·9'E	T	179,189
Stone Street (Roman Road)	Kent	TR1345	51°10·1'	1°3·2'E	R	179,189
Stone Street (Roman Road)	Suff	TM3685	52°24·9'	1°28·6'E	R	156
Stonesty Pike	Cumbr	NY2403	54°25·3'	3°9·9'W	X	89,90
Stone, The	Essex	TL9506	51°43·4'	0°49·8'E	X	168
Stone, The	Heref	SO5748	52°8·0'	2°37·3'W	X	149
Stonethwaite	Cumbr	NY2613	54°30·7'	3°8·2'W	T	89,90
Stonethwaite	Cumbr	NY3449	54°50·1'	3°1·2'W	X	85
Stonethwaite Beck	Cumbr	NY2613	54°30·7'	3°8·2'W	W	89,90
Stonethwaite Fell	Cumbr	NY2610	54°29·0'	3°8·1'W	X	89,90
Stonethwaite Fell	Cumbr	NY2713	54°30·7'	3°7·2'W	X	89,90

Stoneton	Warw	SP4654	52°11·2'	1°19·2'W	T	151
Stoneton Moat Fm	Warw	SP4654	52°11·2'	1°19·2'W	FM	151
Stoneton Village	Warw	SP4654	52°11·2'	1°19·2'W	A	151
Stonetor Hill	Devon	SX6485	50°39·2'	3°55·1'W	H	191
Stonewall	E Susx	TQ5633	51°4·7'	0°14·0'E	X	188
Stonewall	Kent	TQ7248	51°12·5'	0°28·1'E	A	188
Stonewall Fm	Suff	TM1554	52°8·8'	1°8·9'E	FM	156
Stonewall Fm	W Susx	SU8204	50°50·0'	0°49·7'W	FM	197
Stonewall Hill	Powys	SO3168	52°18·6'	3°0·3'W	X	137,148
Stonewall Park	Kent	TQ5042	51°9·7'	0°9·1'E	X	188
Stonewells	Aberd	NJ8165	57°40·7'	2°18·7'W	X	29,30
Stonewells	Moray	NJ2865	57°40·4'	3°12·0'W	X	28
Stonewood	Kent	TQ5972	51°25·7'	0°17·6'E	T	177
Stoneyard	Devon	SS5833	51°5·0'	4°1·3'W	X	180
Stoneyard Green	Heref	SO7144	52°5·9'	2°25·0'W	T	149
Stoneyard Wood	Devon	SS5040	51°8·6'	4°8·3'W	F	180
Stoneybank	E Loth	NT3371	55°55·9'	3°3·9'W	T	66
Stoneybeck	D & G	NY2277	55°5·1'	3°12·9'W	X	85
Stoney Br	Leic	SP5092	52°31·6'	1°15·4'W	X	140
Stoney Brook	Staffs	SK0328	52°51·2'	1°56·9'W	W	128
Stoneyburn	S Lanak	NS9619	55°27·5'	3°38·2'W	X	78
Stoneyburn	W Loth	NS9762	55°50·7'	3°38·3'W	T	65
Stoney Carr Fm	E Yorks	SE8631	53°46·3'	0°41·3'W	FM	106
Stoney Cliffe	Staffs	SK0160	53°8·5'	1°58·7'W	X	119
Stoney Comb	Durham	NY8132	54°41·2'	2°17·3'W	X	91,92
Stoneycombe	Devon	SX8667	50°29·7'	3°36·1'W	T	202
Stoney Cove	Leic	SP4994	52°32·7'	1°16·2'W	W	140
Stoneycroft	Cumbr	NY2321	54°34·9'	3°11·1'W	X	89,90
Stoneycroft	Liv	SJ3991	53°25·0'	2°54·7'W	T	108
Stoney Croft Ho	N Som	ST4562	51°21·5'	2°47·0'W	X	172,182
Stoney Cross	Hants	SU2511	50°54·1'	1°38·3'W	T	195
Stoney Cross Plain	Hants	SU2511	50°54·1'	1°38·3'W	X	195
Stoneydale	Aberd	NO7068	56°48·4'	2°29·0'W	X	45
Stoneyfield	Aberd	NJ5837	57°25·5'	2°41·5'W	X	29
Stoneyfield	Aberd	NJ7634	57°24·0'	2°23·5'W	X	29
Stoneyfield	Moray	NJ1357	57°35·9'	3°26·9'W	X	28
Stoneyfield	Roch	SD8912	53°36·5'	2°9·6'W	T	109
Stoney Flatt Fm	Darl	NZ3620	54°34·7'	1°26·2'W	FM	93
Stoney Fm	Devon	SX4997	50°45·4'	4°8·1'W	FM	191
Stoneyfold	Aberd	NJ8942	57°28·3'	2°10·5'W	X	30
Stoneyfold	Staffs	SK0657	53°6·8'	1°54·2'W	X	119
Stoneyford	Derby	SK4449	53°2·4'	1°20·2'W	T	129
Stoney Ford	Devon	SS5418	50°56·8'	4°4·3'W	X	180
Stoneyford	Devon	ST0207	50°51·5'	3°23·2'W	T	192
Stoneyford	Devon	SY0688	50°41·3'	3°19·5'W	X	192
Stoneyford	S Lanak	NS6337	55°36·7'	4°10·1'W	X	71
Stoneygate	Aberd	NK0339	57°26·7'	1°56·5'W	X	30
Stoneygate	C of Leic	SK6002	52°37·0'	1°6·4'W	T	140
Stoney Gill	D & G	NY1697	55°15·9'	3°18·9'W	W	79
Stoneyhall Hill	Fife	NT2388	56°5·0'	3°13·8'W	X	66
Stoneyhill	Aberd	NJ6239	57°26·6'	2°37·5'W	X	29
Stoneyhill	Aberd	NJ6458	57°36·9'	2°35·7'W	X	29
Stoneyhill	Aberd	NK0740	57°27·3'	1°52·5'W	X	30
Stoneyhill	Aberd	NO8793	57°1·9'	2°12·4'W	X	38,45
Stoneyhill	Northum	NU1812	55°24·3'	1°42·5'W	X	81
Stoneyhill	S Lanak	NS6436	55°36·2'	4°9·1'W	X	71
Stoney Hill	Worcs	SO9670	52°19·9'	2°3·1'W	T	139
Stoneyhill Fm	Glos	SO9311	51°48·1'	2°5·7'W	FM	163
Stoneyhills	Essex	TQ9597	51°38·5'	0°49·5'E	T	168
Stoneyholme	Lancs	SD8333	53°47·8'	2°15·1'W	X	103
Stoney Hook Fm	Pemb	SN0126	51°54·1'	4°53·2'W	FM	145,157,158
Stoneykirk	D & G	NX0853	54°50·4'	4°59·0'W	T	82
Stoneylands	Essex	TL8332	51°57·6'	0°40·2'E	X	168
Stoneylane	Shrops	SO5576	52°23·0'	2°39·3'W	T	137,138
Stoney Lane Fm	Worcs	SP0070	52°19·9'	1°59·6'W	FM	139
Stoneylea	D & G	NY3072	55°2·5'	3°5·3'W	X	85
Stoney Low	Staffs	SJ7843	52°59·3'	2°19·3'W	X	118
Stoney Middleton	Derby	SK2275	53°16·5'	1°39·8'W	T	119
Stoney Mountain Plantation	I of M	SC2877	54°9·9'	4°37·7'W	F	95
Stoneypath	E Loth	NT6171	55°56·1'	2°37·0'W	X	67
Stoneypath Tower	E Loth	NT5971	55°56·1'	2°38·9'W	X	67
Stoney Port	N Ayr	NS1851	55°43·4'	4°53·4'W	W	63
Stoney Pound	Shrops	SO2380	52°25·0'	3°7·5'W	H	137
Stoneyquoy	Orkney	ND2991	58°48·3'	3°13·3'W	X	7
Stoney Royd	Cald	SE0924	53°43·0'	1°51·4'W	T	104
Stoney Stanton	Leic	SP4994	52°32·7'	1°16·2'W	T	140
Stoney Stoke	Somer	ST7032	51°5·4'	2°25·3'W	T	183
Stoney Stratton	Somer	ST6539	51°9·2'	2°29·6'W	T	183
Stoney Stretton	Shrops	SJ3809	52°40·8'	2°54·6'W	T	126
Stoney Thorpe Hall	Warw	SP4062	52°15·5'	1°24·4'W	A	151
Stoney Thorpe Home Fm	Warw	SP3962	52°15·5'	1°25·3'W	FM	151
Stoneyton	Moray	NJ3450	57°32·4'	3°5·7'W	X	28
Stoney Ware	Win & Maid	SU8485	51°33·7'	0°46·9'W	X	175
Stoneywath	Cumbr	NY0717	54°32·6'	3°25·8'W	X	89
Stoney Wath Fm	Cumbr	NY4649	54°50·2'	2°50·0'W	FM	86
Stoneywell Wood	Leic	SK4911	52°41·9'	1°16·1'W	F	129
Stoneywood	C of Aber	NJ8911	57°11·6'	2°10·5'W	T	38
Stoneywood	Falk	NS7982	56°1·2'	3°56·0'W	T	57,64
Stoneywood Ho	C of Aber	NJ8911	57°11·6'	2°10·5'W	X	38
Stonga Banks	Shetld	HU2985	60°33·1'	1°27·8'W	X	1,3
Stonganess	Shetld	HP5402	60°42·1'	1°0·1'W	T	1
Stongir Holm	Shetld	HU5994	60°37·8'	0°54·8'W	X	1,2
Stonham Aspal	Suff	TM1359	52°11·5'	1°7·4'E	T	156
Stonieley	Aberd	NJ6758	57°36·9'	2°32·7'W	X	29
Stonieroo	Aberd	NO7075	56°52·2'	2°29·1'W	X	45
Stonish Hill	Notts	SK6662	53°9·3'	1°0·4'W	X	120
Stonnall	Staffs	SK0703	52°37·7'	1°53·4'W	T	139
Stonner Point	Suff	TM2944	52°3·0'	1°20·8'E	X	169
Stonor	Oxon	SU7388	51°35·4'	0°56·4'W	T	175
Stonor Ho	Oxon	SU7489	51°35·9'	0°55·5'W	X	175
Stonor Park	Oxon	SU7388	51°35·4'	0°56·4'W	X	175
Stonton Wood	Leic	SP7496	52°33·6'	0°54·1'W	F	141
Stonton Wyville	Leic	SP7395	52°33·1'	0°55·0'W	T	141
Stony-ayre	Orkney	ND3394	58°50·0'	3°9·2'W	X	7
Stony Batter	Hants	SU2829	51°3·8'	1°35·6'W	T	184
Stony Binks	E Yorks	TA4010	53°34·3'	0°7·3'E	X	113
Stony Br	Corn	SX2664	50°27·2'	4°26·7'W	X	201
Stonybreck	Shetld	HZ2070	59°31·2'	1°38·3'W	T	4
Stony Bridge	Devon	SS6307	50°51·0'	3°56·4'W	X	191

Stony Bridge	Devon	SS7129	51°3·0'	3°50·0'W	X	180
Stonybridge Wood	S Glos	ST7486	51°34·6'	2°22·1'W	F	172
Stonybriggs	Fife	NO2811	56°17·4'	3°9·3'W	X	59
Stonybrigs	Angus	NO5656	56°41·9'	2°42·7'W	X	54
Stony Brook	Heref	SO6742	52°4·8'	2°28·5'W	W	149
Stony Cliffe Wood	Wakf	SE2716	53°38·6'	1°35·1'W	F	110
Stony Corner	Devon	SS6146	51°12·0'	3°59·0'W	X	180
Stony Cove Pike	Cumbr	NY4109	54°28·6'	2°54·2'W	H	90
Stony Crag	Cumbr	SD2780	54°12·9'	3°6·7'W	X	96,97
Stony Cross	Devon	SS5125	51°0·5'	4°7·1'W	T	180
Stony Cross	Heref	SO5466	52°17·7'	2°40·1'W	T	137,138,149
Stony Cross	Heref	SO7247	52°7·5'	2°24·1'W	T	149
Stony Cross	N Yks	SE6684	54°15·1'	0°58·8'W	X	100
Stonycross Fm	Devon	SX5852	50°21·3'	3°59·4'W	FM	202
Stony Dale	Cumbr	SD3981	54°13·5'	2°55·7'W	X	96,97
Stony Dale	Notts	SK7244	52°59·5'	0°55·2'W	T	129
Stonyditch Point	Suff	TM4248	52°4·9'	1°32·3'E	X	169
Stony Down	Somer	ST3011	50°53·9'	2°59·3'W	X	193
Stony Down Plantation	Dorset	SY9696	50°46·0'	2°3·0'W	F	195
Stonyflats	Ches	SJ8062	53°9·5'	2°17·5'W	X	118
Stonyfold	Ches	SJ9167	53°12·2'	2°7·7'W	X	118
Stonyford	Aberd	NJ5104	57°7·7'	2°48·1'W	X	37
Stonyford	Angus	NO5072	56°50·5'	2°48·7'W	X	44
Stonyford	Derby	SK0881	53°19·8'	1°52·4'W	X	110
Stonyford	Hants	SU3215	50°56·2'	1°32·3'W	T	196
Stonyford	Pemb	SN1215	51°48·4'	4°43·2'W	X	158
Stonyford	Staffs	SK1520	52°46·9'	1°46·3'W	X	128
Stonyford	Swan	SS4991	51°36·1'	4°10·4'W	X	159
Stonyford Pond	Hants	SU4104	50°50·3'	1°24·7'W	W	196
Stonygate	Cumbr	NY4578	55°5·9'	2°51·3'W	X	86
Stony Gate	Sund	NZ3551	54°51·4'	1°26·9'W	T	88
Stonygate Moor	N Yks	SE8785	54°15·4'	0°39·4'W	X	94,101
Stonygill	Cumbr	NY5808	54°28·2'	2°38·5'W	X	91
Stony Green	Bucks	SU8699	51°41·2'	0°45·0'W	T	165
Stony Grooves	N Yks	SE0966	54°5·6'	1°51·3'W	X	99
Stonygroves	Angus	NO3433	56°29·3'	3°3·9'W	X	54
Stonyhall	E Ayr	NS5236	55°36·0'	4°20·5'W	X	70
Stony Hard Fm	Hants	SU5522	50°59·9'	1°12·6'W	FM	185
Stony Head	Cumbr	NY6608	54°28·2'	2°31·1'W	X	91
Stony Head	Somer	ST2922	50°59·8'	3°0·3'W	X	193
Stony Heap	Durham	NZ1451	54°51·5'	1°46·5'W	T	88
Stony Heath	Hants	SU5758	51°19·3'	1°10·5'W	T	174
Stony Hill	Aberd	NJ3617	57°14·6'	3°3·2'W	H	37
Stony Hill	Aberd	NJ5932	57°22·9'	2°40·5'W	H	29,37
Stony Hill	Aberd	NO7983	56°56·5'	2°20·3'W	X	45
Stony Hill	E Ayr	NS6229	55°32·4'	4°10·8'W	X	71
Stony Hill	E Ayr	NS7221	55°28·2'	4°1·1'W	H	71
Stony Hill	Moray	NJ2451	57°32·8'	3°15·7'W	X	28
Stony Hill	Surrey	SU8952	51°15·8'	0°43·1'W	X	186
Stony Hill	Wilts	ST9536	51°7·6'	2°3·9'W	X	184
Stony Hill	Wilts	ST9940	51°9·8'	2°0·5'W	X	184
Stonyhill Beck	Norf	TL8792	52°29·9'	0°45·7'E	X	144
Stonyhills	Herts	TL3216	51°49·8'	0°4·7'W	X	166
Stony Houghton	Derby	SK4966	53°11·6'	1°15·6'W	T	120
Stony How	Cumbr	NY0500	54°23·4'	3°27·4'W	X	89
Stonyhurst College	Lancs	SD6939	53°51·0'	2°27·9'W	A	103
Stony Island	I Scilly	SV8812	49°55·8'	6°20·5'W	X	203
Stony Knaps	Dorset	ST3904	50°50·2'	2°51·6'W	T	193
Stony Knowe	Scot Bord	NT3939	55°38·7'	2°57·7'W	H	73
Stony Knowe	Scot Bord	NT4232	55°34·9'	2°54·8'W	X	73
Stony Knowes Hill	E Ayr	NS5505	55°19·3'	4°16·7'W	X	71,77
Stonyland	Devon	SS5329	51°2·7'	4°5·4'W	T	180
Stonylands Fm	Hants	SU6920	50°58·7'	1°0·6'W	FM	197
Stony Leas	N Yks	SE8899	54°23·0'	0°38·3'W	H	94,101
Stony Littleton	Bath & NE Somer	ST7356	51°18·4'	2°22·9'W	T	172
Stony Marl Howes	N Yks	NZ9600	54°23·4'	0°30·9'W	A	94
Stony Marl Moor	N Yks	NZ9500	54°23·4'	0°31·8'W	X	94
Stonymarsh	Hants	SU3326	51°2·2'	1°31·4'W	T	185
Stony Mea	Cumbr	NY7627	54°38·5'	2°21·9'W	X	91
Stony Moor	N Yks	SE5197	54°22·2'	1°12·5'W	X	100
Stony Moor	N Yks	SE8091	54°18·7'	0°45·8'W	X	94,100
Stony Moor Riggs	Northum	NT9655	55°47·5'	2°3·4'W	X	74,75
Stony Muir	Aberd	NO7689	56°59·7'	2°23·2'W	X	45
Stony Park Burn	Scot Bord	NT6953	55°46·4'	2°29·2'W	W	67,74
Stonypath	Scot Bord	NT1453	55°46·0'	3°21·8'W	X	65,72
Stonypath	S Lanak	NT0548	55°43·2'	3°30·3'W	X	72
Stony Raise (Cairn)	N Yks	SD9586	54°16·4'	2°4·2'W	A	98
Stony Reins	N Yks	SE0192	54°19·7'	1°58·7'W	X	98
Stony Ridge	N Yks	NZ6302	54°24·8'	1°1·3'W	H	94
Stony Ridge	Sheff	SK2780	53°19·2'	1°35·3'W	X	110
Stony Rigg	Cumbr	NY6637	54°43·9'	2°31·3'W	X	91
Stony Rigg	N Yks	SE9097	54°21·9'	0°36·5'W	X	94,101
Stony Stratford	Mil Key	SP7940	52°3·4'	0°50·5'W	T	152
Stony Tarn	Cumbr	NY1902	54°24·7'	3°14·5'W	W	89,90
Stonythwaite	Cumbr	SD2196	54°21·5'	3°12·5'W	X	96
Stony Weir	Dorset	SY8587	50°41·2'	2°12·4'W	A	194
Stonywell	Staffs	SK0812	52°42·6'	1°52·5'W	X	128
Stoodham	Somer	ST4317	50°57·2'	2°48·3'W	X	193
Stood Hill	D & G	NS8512	55°23·6'	3°48·5'W	H	71,78
Stoodleigh	Devon	SS6532	51°4·5'	3°55·2'W	X	180
Stoodleigh	Devon	SS9218	50°57·3'	3°31·9'W	T	181
Stoodleigh Barton	Devon	SS6533	51°5·1'	3°55·3'W	X	180
Stoodleigh Beacon	Devon	SS8818	50°57·3'	3°35·3'W	X	181
Stoodleigh Down	Devon	SS6634	51°5·6'	3°54·4'W	X	180
Stoodleighmoor	Devon	SS9219	50°57·9'	3°31·9'W	X	181
Stoodley	Devon	SX7169	50°30·6'	3°48·8'W	X	202
Stoodley Pike Monument	Cald	SD9724	53°43·0'	2°2·3'W	X	103
Stook Ho	Somer	ST3946	51°12·8'	2°52·0'W	X	182
Stool End	Cumbr	NY2705	54°26·4'	3°7·1'W	X	89,90
Stoop	D & G	NX9876	55°4·3'	3°35·4'W	X	84
Stoop Fm	Derby	SK0668	53°12·8'	1°54·2'W	FM	119
Stoop Fm	Derby	SK2338	52°56·6'	1°39·1'W	FM	128
Stoop Hill	Durham	NY9623	54°36·4'	2°3·3'W	X	91,92
Stoop House Fm	N Yks	SE1490	54°18·6'	1°46·7'W	FM	99
Stoop Rigg	Cumbr	NY6160	54°56·2'	2°36·1'W	X	86
Stooprigg	Northum	NY8472	55°2·8'	2°14·6'W	X	86,87
Stoops Barn	N Yks	SD7364	54°4·5'	2°24·3'W	X	98
Stoopshill	N Ayr	NS3048	55°42·0'	4°41·9'W	X	63
Stoops Moss	Cumbr	SD7883	54°14·8'	2°19·8'W	X	98

Stop-and-Call	Pemb	SM9338	52°0·4′	5°0·6′W	T	157
Stope Hill Fm	Lincs	TF0998	53°28·3′	0°21·1′W	FM	112
Stopes	Sheff	SK2888	53°23·5′	1°34·3′W	T	110
Stopgate	Devon	ST2309	50°52·8′	3°5·3′W	T	192,193
Stopgate Cross	Devon	SS7205	50°50·1′	3°48·7′W	X	191
Stopham	W Susx	TQ0219	50°57·9′	0°32·5′W	T	197
Stopham Ho	W Susx	TQ0218	50°57·4′	0°32·5′W	X	197
Stopper Lane	Lancs	SD8145	53°54·3′	2°16·9′W	T	103
Stopsley	Luton	TL1023	51°53·9′	0°23·7′W	T	166
Stopsley Common	Luton	TL0924	51°54·5′	0°24·5′W	X	166
Stopsley Holes Fm	Herts	TL1525	51°54·9′	0°19·3′W	FM	166
Stoptide	Corn	SW9475	50°32·5′	4°54·1′W	T	200
Storakaig	Arg & Bt	NR4061	55°46·6′	6°8·3′W	X	60
Stordon Grange	Leic	SK4119	52°46·3′	1°23·1′W	X	129
Stords	Cumbr	NY0708	54°27·8′	3°25·7′W	X	89
Storefield Lodge	Northnts	SP8584	52°27·1′	0°44·6′W	X	141
Storefield Wood	Northnts	SP8584	52°27·1′	0°44·6′W	F	141
Storehouse	Cered	SN7572	52°20·2′	3°49·7′W	X	135,147
Storehouse Geo	Orkney	HY7037	59°13·4′	2°31·0′W	X	5
Stores Brook	Heref	SO6840	52°3·7′	2°27·6′W	W	149
Storeton	Wirral	SJ3084	53°21·1′	3°2·7′W	T	108
Storeton Hill	Wirral	SJ3184	53°21·1′	3°1·8′W	X	108
Storey Arms Centre (Canolfan Addysg Awyr Agored)	Powys	SN9820	51°52·4′	3°28·5′W	X	160
Storey's Wood	Essex	TL8219	51°50·6′	0°38·9′E	F	168
Storff Burn	Scot Bord	NY5592	55°13·5′	2°42·0′W	W	80
Stories Ho	N Yks	SD9348	53°55·9′	2°6·0′W	X	103
Storiths	N Yks	SE0854	53°59·2′	1°52·3′W	T	104
Stork Hill Fm	E Yorks	TA0541	53°51·5′	0°23·8′W	FM	107
Stork Ho	N Yks	SE6294	54°20·5′	1°2·4′W	X	94,100
St Orland's Stone	Angus	NO4049	56°38·0′	2°58·2′W	A	54
Storling Bank	Powys	SO2067	52°18·0′	3°10·0′W	H	137,148
Stormer Hall	Heref	SO4075	52°22·4′	2°52·5′W	X	137,148
Stormont	Pth & Kin	NO1046	56°36·1′	3°27·5′W	X	53
Stormontfield	Pth & Kin	NO1029	56°26·9′	3°27·2′W	T	53,58
Stormont Loch	Pth & Kin	NO1942	56°34·0′	3°18·6′W	W	53
Stormore	Wilts	ST8449	51°14·6′	2°13·4′W	T	183
Stormsdown	Devon	SX7772	50°32·3′	3°43·8′W	X	191
Storm's Fm	Hants	SU2814	50°55·7′	1°35·7′W	FM	195
Stormy	Brig	SS8481	51°31·2′	3°39·9′W	X	170
Stormy Down	Brig	SS8480	51°30·7′	3°39·9′W	H	170
Stormy Hall	N Yks	NZ6804	54°25·9′	0°56·7′W	X	94
Stornoway (Steòrnabhagh)	N Eil	NB4232	58°12·3′	6°23·0′W	T	8
Storrage Ho	Worcs	SP0571	52°20·5′	1°55·2′W	X	139
Storra Pasture	N Yks	SE2590	54°18·5′	1°36·5′W	X	99
Storrers Fm	E Susx	TQ6729	51°2·4′	0°23·3′E	FM	188,199
Storridge	Heref	SO7548	52°8·0′	2°21·5′W	T	150
Storridge Fm	Wilts	ST8552	51°16·3′	2°12·5′W	FM	183
Storridge Hill	Devon	ST3104	50°50·1′	2°58·4′W	X	193
Storridge Hill	Dorset	ST4900	50°48·1′	2°43·0′W	X	193,194
Storridge Hill	Somer	SS9430	51°3·8′	3°30·4′W	H	181
Storridge Wood	Devon	SX7352	50°21·5′	3°46·8′W	F	202
Storrington	W Susx	TQ0814	50°55·1′	0°27·4′W	T	197
Storr Lochs	Highld	NG5050	57°28·5′	6°9·7′W	W	23,24
Storrs	Cumbr	SD3994	54°20·5′	2°55·9′W	T	96,97
Storrs	Sheff	SK2989	53°24·1′	1°33·4′W	T	110
Storrs Bridge	Sheff	SK2990	53°24·6′	1°33·4′W	X	110
Storrs Cave	N Yks	SD7073	54°9·4′	2°27·1′W	X	98
Storrs Hall	Lancs	SD5771	54°8·2′	2°39·1′W	X	97
Storr, The	Highld	NG4954	57°30·7′	6°11·0′W	H	23
Storry Hill	N Yks	SE9993	54°19·6′	0°28·2′W	X	94,101
Stortford Park	Herts	TL4721	51°52·3′	0°8·5′E	X	167
Storth	Cumbr	SD4779	54°12·5′	2°48·3′W	T	97
Storth End	Cumbr	SD5386	54°16·3′	2°42·9′W	X	97
Storthes	Cumbr	SD1693	54°19·8′	3°17·1′W	X	96
Storthes Hall	Kirk	SE1712	53°36·5′	1°44·2′W	X	110
Storth House Fm	Derby	SK3078	53°18·1′	1°32·6′W	FM	119
Storth House Fm	Leeds	SE1542	53°52·7′	1°45·9′W	FM	104
Storthwaite Hall	N Yks	NZ0102	54°25·1′	1°58·7′W	X	92
Storth Wood	N Yks	SE2079	54°12·6′	1°41·2′W	F	99
Storwood	E Yorks	SE7144	53°53·5′	0°54·8′W	T	105,106
Storwood Grange	E Yorks	SE7144	53°53·5′	0°54·8′W	X	105,106
Story Moats	Beds	TL2051	52°8·9′	0°14·4′W	A	153
Story's Gairs	Northum	NY6282	55°8·1′	2°35·3′W	X	80
St Oswald's	Cumbr	NY3307	54°27·5′	3°1·6′W	X	90
St Oswald's Bay	Dorset	SY8080	50°37·4′	2°16·6′W	W	194
St Osyth	Essex	TM1215	51°47·8′	1°4·9′E	T	168,169
St Osyth Beach	Essex	TM1212	51°46·2′	1°4·8′E	X	168,169
St Osyth Creek	Essex	TM1015	51°47·9′	1°3·1′E	W	168,169
St Osythe	N Yks	NZ1702	54°25·0′	1°43·9′W	X	92
St Osyth Heath	Essex	TM1318	51°49·4′	1°5·9′E	T	168,169
St Osyth Lodge Fm	Essex	TM1315	51°47·8′	1°5·7′E	FM	168,169
St Osyth Marsh	Essex	TM1113	51°46·8′	1°3·9′E	X	168,169
St Osyth Stone Point	Essex	TM0815	51°47·9′	1°1·4′E	X	168,169
St Osyth Wick Fm	Essex	TM1219	51°50·0′	1°5·0′E	FM	168,169
Stot Crags	Northum	NY5983	55°8·6′	2°38·2′W	H	80
Stoterley Hill	Durham	NZ0148	54°49·9′	1°58·6′W	X	87
Stotfaulds	Angus	NO4939	56°32·7′	2°49·3′W	X	54
Stotfield	Moray	NJ2270	57°43·0′	3°18·1′W	T	28
Stotfield Bay	Arg & Bt	NR7168	55°51·3′	5°39·1′W	W	62
Stotfield Hill	Scot Bord	NT7012	55°24·3′	2°28·0′W	H	80
Stotfold	Beds	TL2136	52°0·8′	0°13·8′W	T	153
Stotfold	Donc	SE4706	53°33·1′	1°17·0′W	X	111
Stotfold	Durham	NZ3948	54°49·8′	1°23·1′W	X	88
Stotfold Crest	Hartpl	NZ4529	54°39·5′	1°17·7′W	X	93
Stotfold Moor	Hartpl	NZ4331	54°40·6′	1°19·6′W	X	93
Stotgate	Durham	NZ2443	54°47·1′	1°37·2′W	X	88
Stot Hill	Aberd	NJ5903	57°7·2′	2°40·2′W	H	37
Stot Knowe	D & G	NT0909	55°22·2′	3°25·7′W	X	78
Stotley Grange	Durham	NY9626	54°38·0′	2°3·3′W	X	91,92
Stotley Hall	Durham	NY9625	54°37·5′	2°3·3′W	X	91,92
Stotsfold Fm	Northum	NY9055	54°53·6′	2°8·9′W	FM	87
Stotsfold Hall	Northum	NY9155	54°53·6′	2°8·0′W	X	87
Stott Crags	N Yks	SE0772	54°8·9′	1°53·2′W	X	99
Stottencleugh	E Loth	NT7270	55°55·6′	2°26·4′W	X	67
Stottesdon	Shrops	SO6782	52°26·3′	2°28·7′W	T	138
Stott Fold	N Yks	SE1477	54°11·6′	1°46·7′W	X	99
Stott Ghyll	Cumbr	NY3437	54°43·7′	3°1·1′W	X	90
Stott Hill Moor	N Yks	SD9741	53°52·2′	2°2·3′W	X	103
Stottle Bank Nook	E Yorks	TA2571	54°7·4′	0°4·8′W	X	101
Stoughton	Leic	SK6402	52°37·0′	1°2·9′W	T	140
Stoughton	Surrey	SU9851	51°15·2′	0°35·4′W	T	186
Stoughton	W Susx	SU8011	50°53·8′	0°51·4′W	T	197
Stoughton Cross	Somer	ST4249	51°14·5′	2°49·5′W	T	182
Stoughton Down	W Susx	SU8112	50°54·3′	0°50·5′W	X	197
Stoughton Grange Fm	Leic	SK6202	52°37·0′	1°4·7′W	FM	140
Stoughton Lodge Fm	Leic	SK6302	52°37·0′	1°3·8′W	FM	140
Stoul	Highld	NM7594	56°59·2′	5°41·8′W	X	33,40
Stoulton	Worcs	SO9049	52°8·6′	2°8·4′W	T	150
Stoupdale Crags	Cumbr	SD1587	54°16·5′	3°17·9′W	X	96
Stoup Dub	Cumbr	SD1578	54°11·7′	3°17·8′W	X	96
Stoupe Beck	N Yks	NZ9503	54°25·1′	0°31·7′W	W	94
Stoupe Beck Sands	N Yks	NZ9503	54°25·1′	0°31·7′W	X	94
Stoupe Brow	N Yks	NZ9602	54°24·5′	0°30·8′W	X	94
Stoupe Brow Cottage Fm	N Yks	NZ9503	54°25·1′	0°31·7′W	FM	94
Stoupe Cross Fm	N Yks	NZ9110	54°28·9′	0°35·3′W	FM	94
Stoupersgate Fm	Donc	SE6909	53°34·6′	0°57·1′W	FM	111
Stoupes Fm	Lincs	TF2277	53°16·8′	0°9·8′W	FM	122
Stouphill	Northum	NU1612	55°24·3′	1°44·4′W	X	81
Stouraba	Shetld	HP4905	60°43·8′	1°5·6′W	X	1
Stoura Clett	Shetld	HU5138	60°7·7′	1°4·4′W	X	4
Stouraclev	Shetld	HU4982	60°31·4′	1°5·9′W	X	1,2,3
Stoura Field	Shetld	HU3836	60°6·7′	1°18·5′W	X	4
Stoura Pund	Shetld	HU2577	60°28·8′	1°32·2′W	X	3
Stoura Scord	Shetld	HU5086	60°33·5′	1°4·8′W	X	1,2,3
Stoura Stack	Shetld	HU6971	60°25·3′	0°44·3′W	X	2
Stourbridge	Dudley	SO8883	52°26·9′	2°10·2′W	T	139
Stourbridge Canal	Staffs	SO8885	52°28·0′	2°10·2′W	W	139
Stourbrough Hill	Shetld	HU2152	60°15·4′	1°36·7′W	H	3
Stourcleugh Gair	Cumbr	NY6774	55°3·8′	2°30·6′W	X	86,87
Stourhead	Wilts	ST7734	51°6·5′	2°19·3′W	A	183
Stour Hevda	Shetld	HU5273	60°26·5′	1°2·8′W	X	2,3
Stour Hill	Dorset	ST7722	51°0·0′	2°19·3′W	X	183
Stour Hill	Worcs	SO8373	52°21·5′	2°14·6′W	X	138
Stour Ho	Essex	TM0731	51°56·6′	1°1·1′E	X	168,169
Stouri Croo	Shetld	HU3828	60°2·4′	1°18·6′W	X	4
Stourie	Shetld	HU3789	60°35·2′	1°19·0′W	X	1,2
Stourl	Shetld	HU3784	60°32·5′	1°19·0′W	X	1,2,3
Stour Lodge	Essex	TM1431	51°56·4′	1°7·2′E	X	168,169
Stourpaine	Dorset	ST8609	50°53·1′	2°11·6′W	T	194
Stourpaine Down	Dorset	ST8810	50°53·6′	2°9·9′W	X	194
Stourport-on-Severn	Worcs	SO8171	52°20·4′	2°16·3′W	T	138
Stour Provost	Dorset	ST7921	50°59·5′	2°17·6′W	T	183
Stour Row	Dorset	ST8221	50°59·5′	2°15·0′W	T	183
Stours	Essex	TL7543	52°3·7′	0°33·6′E	X	155
Stourscombe	Corn	SX3483	50°37·6′	4°20·4′W	X	201
Stoursdale	Orkney	HY3210	58°58·6′	3°10·5′W	X	6
Stours Kinora	Orkney	HY1801	58°53·6′	3°24·9′W	X	7
Stourton	Leeds	SE3230	53°46·2′	1°30·5′W	T	104
Stourton	Staffs	SO8685	52°28·0′	2°12·0′W	T	139
Stourton	Warw	SP2936	52°1·5′	1°34·2′W	T	151
Stourton	Wilts	ST7734	51°6·5′	2°19·3′W	T	183
Stourton Barton	Devon	SS8012	50°53·9′	3°42·0′W	X	181
Stourton Caundle	Dorset	ST7115	50°56·3′	2°24·4′W	T	183
Stourton Hill	Warw	SP3035	52°1·0′	1°33·4′W	T	151
Stour Valley Path	Cambs	TL6260	52°13·1′	0°22·7′E	X	154
Stour Valley Walk	Kent	TR0851	51°13·4′	0°59·1′E	X	179
Stour View Ho	Dorset	ST7814	50°55·7′	2°18·4′W	X	194
Stour Wood	Essex	TM1931	51°56·3′	1°11·6′E	F	168,169
Stourwood Fm	Essex	TM1930	51°55·7′	1°11·5′E	FM	168,169
Stouslie	Scot Bord	NT4816	55°26·4′	2°48·9′W	X	79
Stout	Somer	ST4331	51°4·8′	2°48·4′W	T	182
Stout Bay	V of Glam	SS9767	51°23·8′	3°28·4′W	W	170
Stout Fm	Devon	ST2211	50°53·8′	3°6·2′W	FM	192,193
Stout Fm	Devon	SY1698	50°46·8′	3°11·1′W	FM	192,193
Stout Hall	Swan	SS4789	51°35·0′	4°12·1′W	X	159
Stout Point	V of Glam	SS9767	51°23·8′	3°28·4′W	X	170
Stouts Hill	Glos	ST7897	51°40·5′	2°18·7′W	X	162
Stova	Shetld	HU4348	60°13·1′	1°12·9′W	H	3
Stove	Orkney	HY2420	59°3·9′	3°19·0′W	X	6
Stove	Orkney	HY5807	58°57·2′	2°43·3′W	X	6
Stove	Orkney	HY6035	59°12·3′	2°41·5′W	X	5,6
Stove	Shetld	HP6212	60°47·4′	0°51·2′W	T	1
Stove	Shetld	HU4224	60°0·2′	1°14·3′W	T	4
Stoven	Suff	TM4481	52°22·6′	1°35·5′E	T	156
Stoven Wood	Suff	TM4382	52°23·1′	1°34·7′E	F	156
Stover County Park	Devon	SX8375	50°34·0′	3°38·7′W	X	191
Stovern's Hall	Essex	TL8217	51°49·5′	0°38·9′E	X	168
Stover School	Devon	SX8374	50°33·5′	3°38·7′W	X	191
Stow	Lincs	SK8881	53°19·4′	0°40·3′W	T	121
Stow	Scot Bord	NT4644	55°41·4′	2°51·1′W	T	73
Stowbank	Cumbr	NY0716	54°32·1′	3°25·8′W	X	89
Stow Bardolph	Norf	TF6205	52°37·3′	0°24·0′E	T	143
Stow Bardolph Fen	Norf	TF5604	52°36·9′	0°18·7′E	X	143
Stow Barrow	Somer	ST5253	51°16·7′	2°40·9′W	A	182,183
Stow Bedon	Norf	TL9596	52°31·8′	0°52·9′E	T	144
Stowbedon Hall	Norf	TL9694	52°30·7′	0°53·7′E	X	144
Stowborrow Hill	Somer	ST1141	51°9·9′	3°16·0′W	H	181
Stow Br	Glos	SP1723	51°54·6′	1°44·8′W	X	163
Stowbridge	Norf	TF6007	52°38·5′	0°22·3′E	T	143
Stow Creek	Essex	TQ8497	51°37·8′	0°40·0′E	W	168
Stow cum Quy	Cambs	TL5260	52°13·3′	0°13·9′E	T	154
Stow cum Quy Fen	Cambs	TL5162	52°14·4′	0°13·1′E	X	154
Stowe	Glos	SO5606	51°45·3′	2°37·9′W	T	162
Stowe	Heref	SO2847	52°7·2′	3°2·7′W	T	148
Stowe	Shrops	SO3173	52°21·3′	3°0·4′W	T	137,148
Stowe	Staffs	SK1210	52°41·5′	1°48·9′W	T	128
Stowe Avenue	Bucks	SP6835	52°0·8′	1°0·2′W	X	152
Stowe Barton	Corn	SS2111	50°52·5′	4°32·3′W	X	190
Stowe-by-Chartley	Staffs	SK0027	52°50·7′	1°59·6′W	T	128
Stowe Castle Fm	Bucks	SP6837	52°1·9′	1°0·1′W	FM	152
Stowe Cliffs	Corn	SS2010	50°51·9′	4°33·1′W	X	190
Stowe Corner	Bucks	SP6740	52°3·5′	1°1·0′W	X	152
Stowe Fm	Lincs	TF1011	52°41·4′	0°21·9′W	FM	130,142
Stowe Green	Glos	SO5606	51°45·3′	2°37·9′W	T	162
Stowehill	Northnts	SP6458	52°13·2′	1°3·4′W	X	152
Stowehill	Suff	TL8253	52°8·9′	0°40·0′E	X	155
Stowe Ho	Durham	NZ1342	54°46·6′	1°47·4′W	X	88
Stowell	Glos	SP0813	51°49·2′	1°52·6′W	T	163
Stowell	Somer	ST6822	51°0·0′	2°27·0′W	T	183
Stowell Fm	Wilts	ST8772	51°27·0′	2°10·8′W	FM	173
Stowell Grove	Glos	SP0813	51°49·2′	1°52·6′W	F	163
Stowell Park	Glos	SP0813	51°49·2′	1°52·6′W	X	163
Stowell Park	Wilts	SU1461	51°21·1′	1°47·5′W	X	173
Stowe Lodge	Northnts	SP6256	52°12·2′	1°5·2′W	X	152
St Owen's Cross	Heref	SO5324	51°55·0′	2°40·6′W	T	162
Stowe Ollands	Norf	TG0236	52°53·2′	1°0·6′E	X	133
Stowe Park	Bucks	SP6737	52°1·9′	1°1·0′W	X	152
Stower Hill	Northum	NY6485	55°9·7′	2°33·5′W	H	80
Stowe School and Gardens	Bucks	SP6737	52°1·9′	1°1·0′W	X	152
Stowe's Hill	Corn	SX2572	50°31·5′	4°27·8′W	H	201
Stowe's Pound	Corn	SX2572	50°31·5′	4°27·8′W	A	201
Stowe Wood	Corn	SS2211	50°52·5′	4°31·4′W	F	190
Stowe Wood	Northnts	SP6257	52°12·7′	1°5·2′W	F	152
Stowe Woods	Bucks	SP6739	52°3·0′	1°1·0′W	F	152
Stowey	Bath & NE Somer	ST5959	51°20·0′	2°34·9′W	T	172,182
Stowey Castle	Somer	ST1839	51°8·9′	3°10·0′W	A	181
Stowey Fm	Somer	SS9439	51°8·7′	3°30·5′W	FM	181
Stowey Fm	Somer	ST3422	50°59·9′	2°56·0′W	FM	193
Stowey Ridge	Somer	SS8045	51°11·7′	3°42·7′W	X	181
Stow Fen	Cambs	TL4294	52°31·7′	0°6·0′E	X	142,143
Stow Fen	Suff	TM3288	52°26·7′	1°25·2′E	X	156
Stowfield	Glos	SO5917	51°51·2′	2°35·3′W	T	162
Stow Fm	Lincs	TF0934	52°53·8′	0°22·4′W	FM	130
Stowford	Ches	SJ7353	53°4·7′	2°23·8′W	X	118
Stowford	Devon	SS2523	50°59·0′	4°29·2′W	X	190
Stowford	Devon	SS2913	50°53·7′	4°25·5′W	T	190
Stowford	Devon	SS3815	50°54·9′	4°17·9′W	X	190
Stowford	Devon	SS4715	50°55·1′	4°10·2′W	X	180
Stowford	Devon	SS6226	51°1·2′	3°57·7′W	T	180
Stowford	Devon	SS6541	51°9·4′	3°55·4′W	T	180
Stowford	Devon	SX4386	50°39·4′	4°12·9′W	T	201
Stowford	Devon	SX4397	50°45·3′	4°13·2′W	T	190
Stowford	Devon	SY0587	50°40·7′	3°20·3′W	X	192
Stowford	Devon	SY1189	50°41·9′	3°15·2′W	T	192
Stowford	Oxon	SP5508	51°46·3′	1°11·8′W	X	164
Stowford Fm	Wilts	ST8157	51°18·9′	2°16·0′W	FM	173
Stowford Ho	Devon	SX6457	50°24·1′	3°54·4′W	A	202
Stowgate	Lincs	TF1910	52°40·7′	0°14·0′W	T	130,142
Stowgate Fms	Lincs	TF1910	52°40·7′	0°14·0′W	FM	130,142
Stowgill	Cumbr	NY8408	54°28·3′	2°14·4′W	X	91,92
Stow Gill	S Lanak	NS9212	55°23·7′	3°41·9′W	W	71,78
Stowgill Dod	S Lanak	NS9211	55°23·1′	3°41·9′W	H	71,78
Stow Green Hill	Lincs	TF0935	52°54·3′	0°22·4′W	X	130
Stowhall Burn	Arg & Bt	NR9476	55°56·2′	5°17·5′W	W	62
Stow Hill	Norf	TG3135	52°52·0′	1°26·3′E	X	133
Stow Hill	Shrops	SO3074	52°21·8′	3°1·3′W	H	137,148
Stowlangtoft	Suff	TL9568	52°16·8′	0°51·9′E	T	155
Stowlangtoft Park	Suff	TL9668	52°16·7′	0°52·8′E	X	155
Stow Lawn	Wolv	SO9497	52°34·5′	2°4·9′W	T	139
Stow Longa	Cambs	TL1070	52°19·3′	0°22·8′W	T	153
Stow Maries	Essex	TQ8399	51°39·8′	0°39·2′E	T	168
Stowmarket	Suff	TM0558	52°11·2′	1°0·3′E	T	155
Stow-on-the-Wold	Glos	SP1925	51°55·6′	1°43·0′W	T	163
Stow Park	Lincs	SK8679	53°18·3′	0°42·2′W	X	121
Stow Park	Lincs	SK8681	53°19·4′	0°42·1′W	X	121
Stow Park	Newp	ST3087	51°34·9′	3°0·2′W	T	171
Stow Park	Suff	TM3287	52°26·1′	1°25·2′E	X	156
Stow Pasture	Lincs	SK8982	53°19·9′	0°39·4′W	X	121
Stowsdon	Corn	SX3190	50°41·3′	4°23·2′W	X	190
Stows Fm	Essex	TL9803	51°41·7′	0°52·3′E	FM	168
Stow's Hill	Suff	TL9052	52°8·2′	0°47·0′E	X	155
Stowting	Kent	TR1241	51°8·0′	1°2·2′E	T	179,189
Stowting Common	Kent	TR1243	51°9·0′	1°2·3′E	T	179,189
Stowting Court	Kent	TR1141	51°8·0′	1°1·3′E	X	179,189
Stowting Hill	Kent	TR1242	51°8·5′	1°2·2′E	X	179,189
Stowupland	Suff	TM0660	52°12·2′	1°1·3′E	T	155
Stow Well	Glos	SP1926	51°56·2′	1°43·0′W	W	163
Stow Wood	Oxon	SP5510	51°47·4′	1°11·8′W	F	164
St Pancras	Camden	TQ3082	51°31·5′	0°7·2′W	T	176,177
St Pancras Sta	Camden	TQ3082	51°31·5′	0°7·2′W	X	176,177
St Patrick's Br	Wok	SU7676	51°28·9′	0°53·9′W	X	175
St Patrick's Chair	I of M	SC3177	54°9·9′	4°34·9′W	A	95
St Patrick's Chapel	Lancs	SD4161	54°2·7′	2°53·6′W	A	96,97
St Patrick's College	Stir	NS5493	56°6·7′	4°20·4′W	X	57
St Patrick's Isle	I of M	SC2484	54°13·5′	4°41·6′W	X	95
St Patrick's Well	Cumbr	NY3816	54°32·4′	2°57·1′W	A	90
St Paul's	Glos	SO8217	51°51·3′	2°15·3′W	T	162
St Paul's Cray	Brom	TQ4669	51°24·3′	0°6·3′E	T	177
St Paul's Epistle	Glos	SP0018	51°51·9′	1°59·6′W	X	163
St Pauls Priory	Lancs	SD5162	54°3·3′	2°44·5′W	A	97
St Paul's Walden	Herts	TL1922	51°53·3′	0°15·9′W	T	166
St Peter's	Glos	SO9323	51°54·6′	2°5·7′W	T	163
St Peters	Kent	TR3868	51°21·9′	1°25·5′E	T	179
St Peter's	N upon Ty	NZ2763	54°57·9′	1°34·3′W	T	88
St Peter's Abbey	Dorset	SY5785	50°40·0′	2°36·1′W	A	194
St Peter's Bay	Orkney	HY5304	58°55·5′	2°48·5′W	W	6,7
St Peter's Br	Northnts	SP7759	52°13·7′	0°52·0′W	X	152
St Peter's Ch	Aberd	NJ4841	57°27·6′	2°51·5′W	A	28,29
St Peter's Ch	Bucks	SP8015	51°49·9′	0°49·9′W	A	165
St Peter's Chapel	Essex	TM0308	51°44·3′	0°56·8′E	A	168
St Peter's Church	Rho Cyn Taf	SS9985	51°33·5′	3°27·0′W	A	170
St Peter's Flat	Essex	TM0408	51°44·2′	0°57·7′E	X	168
St Peter's Fm	Cambs	TL3399	52°34·6′	0°1·8′W	FM	142
St Peter's Hall	Suff	TM3385	52°25·0′	1°26·0′E	A	156
St Peter's Lodge	Norf	TF5215	52°42·9′	0°15·4′E	X	131
St Peter South Elmham	Suff	TM3384	52°24·5′	1°25·9′E	T	156
St Peter's Pool	Orkney	HY5404	58°55·5′	2°47·5′W	W	6,7
St Peter's Pump	Wilts	ST7635	51°7·1′	2°20·2′W	A	183
St Peter's Way	Essex	TL8802	51°41·3′	0°43·6′E	X	168
St Peter's Way	Essex	TQ6899	51°40·1′	0°26·2′E	X	167,177
St Peter's Way	Kent	TQ6970	51°24·5′	0°26·2′E	X	177,178
St Peter The Great	Worcs	SO8552	52°10·2′	2°12·8′W	T	150
St Petrox	Pemb	SR9797	51°38·4′	4°55·6′W	T	158
St Pierre	Monm	ST5190	51°36·6′	2°42·1′W	A	162,172
St Pierre Fm	Monm	ST5190	51°36·6′	2°42·1′W	FM	162,172
St Pierre Pill	Monm	ST5289	51°36·1′	2°41·2′W	W	162,172

St Pierre's Great Woods	Monm	ST5092	51°37·7'	2°43·0'W	F	162,172
St Pinnock	Corn	SX2063	50°26·6'	4°31·7'W	T	201
St Piran's Oratory	Corn	SW7656	50°21·9'	5°8·6'W	A	200
St Piran's Round	Corn	SW7754	50°20·9'	5°7·7'W	A	200
St Quivox	S Ayr	NS3724	55°29·2'	4°34·4'W	T	70
Straad	Arg & Bt	NS0462	55°48·9'	5°7·3'W	T	63
Straan	Highld	NJ1235	57°24·1'	3°27·4'W	X	28
Straangalls	Moray	NJ1639	57°26·3'	3°23·5'W	X	28
Straanruie	Highld	NH9916	57°13·7'	3°39·9'W	X	36
Straan Wood	Highld	NJ1336	57°24·6'	3°26·4'W	F	28
Strabane	N Ayr	NS0137	55°35·4'	5°9·0'W	X	69
Strabauchlinn Knowe	E Loth	NT4985	56°3·6'	2°48·7'W	X	66
Strabeg	Highld	NC3951	58°25·3'	4°44·9'W	X	9
Strabracken	D & G	NX1475	55°2·3'	4°54·2'W	X	76
Stracathro Ho	Angus	NO6265	56°46·8'	2°36·9'W	X	45
Stracathro Service Area	Angus	NO6264	56°46·2'	2°36·9'W	X	45
Stracey Arms (PH)	Norf	TG4309	52°37·7'	1°35·8'E	X	134
Strachan	Aberd	NO6792	57°1·3'	2°32·2'W	T	38,45
Strachur	Arg & Bt	NN0901	56°10·1'	5°4·1'W	T	56
Strachur Bay	Arg & Bt	NN0801	56°10·0'	5°5·1'W	W	56
Strachur Ho	Arg & Bt	NN0901	56°10·1'	5°4·1'W	X	56
Strachurmore	Arg & Bt	NN1000	56°9·5'	5°3·1'W	X	56
Stradbroke	Suff	TM2374	52°19·3'	1°16·7'E	T	156
Stradbroke Town Fm	Suff	TM4180	52°22·1'	1°32·8'E	FM	156
Stradey Castle	Carm	SN4901	51°41·5'	4°10·7'W	X	159
St Radigund's Abbey	Kent	TR2741	51°7·6'	1°15·0'E	A	179
Stradishall	Suff	TL7452	52°8·6'	0°33·0'E	T	155
Stradland	Pemb	SM9926	51°54·0'	4°54·9'W	X	157,158
Stradmore Mansion	Cered	SN2441	52°2·6'	4°33·6'W	X	145
Stradsett	Norf	TF6605	52°37·3'	0°27·5'E	T	143
Stradsett Park	Norf	TF6606	52°37·8'	0°27·6'E	X	143
Straenia Water	Orkney	HY6021	59°4·7'	2°41·4'W	W	5,6
Strageath Hall	Pth & Kin	NN8818	56°20·7'	3°48·3'W	X	58
Strageath Mains	Pth & Kin	NN8918	56°20·7'	3°47·3'W	X	58
Stragglethorpe	Lincs	SK9152	53°3·7'	0°38·1'W	T	121
Stragglethorpe	Notts	SK6537	52°55·8'	1°1·6'W	X	129
Stragglethorpe Grange	Lincs	SK8952	53°3·7'	0°39·9'W	X	121
Stragglingwath Plantation	D & G	NY0670	55°1·2'	3°27·8'W	F	85
Strahangles Point	Aberd	NJ8765	57°40·7'	2°12·6'W	X	30
Strahanna	D & G	NX6495	55°14·1'	4°7·9'W	X	77
Straid	S Ayr	NX1390	55°10·4'	4°55·8'W	X	76
Straid	Stir	NN6505	56°13·4'	4°10·2'W	X	57
Straid Burn	E Ayr	NS5709	55°21·5'	4°14·9'W	W	71,77
Straid Fm	E Ayr	NS5710	55°22·0'	4°14·9'W	FM	71
Straight Mile	Warw	SP4471	52°20·4'	1°20·9'W	X	140
Straight Mile Fm	Wok	SU8271	51°26·2'	0°48·8'W	FM	175
Straightneck Wood	Durham	NZ1555	54°53·6'	1°45·5'W	F	88
Straight Point	Devon	SY0379	50°36·4'	3°21·9'W	X	192
Straight Soley	Wilts	SU3272	51°27·0'	1°32·0'W	T	174
Straight Stean Beck	N Yks	SE0472	54°8·9'	1°55·9'W	W	98
Straight Step	S Lanak	NT0113	55°24·3'	3°33·4'W	W	78
Straights, The	Northnts	SP6642	52°4·6'	1°1·8'W	F	152
Straitbraes	Aberd	NO7067	56°47·9'	2°29·0'W	X	45
Straitgate Fm	Devon	SY0695	50°45·1'	3°19·6'W	FM	192
Straith	D & G	NX8388	55°10·6'	3°49·8'W	X	78
Strait Hill	D & G	NY4390	55°12·5'	2°53·3'W	X	79
Straiton	Midlo	NT2766	55°53·2'	3°9·6'W	T	66
Straiton	S Ayr	NS3804	55°18·5'	4°32·7'W	T	77
Straiton Hill	Fife	NO4122	56°23·5'	2°56·9'W	X	54,59
Straits Head	Lancs	SD5569	54°7·1'	2°40·9'W	X	97
Straits Inclosure	Hants	SU7939	51°8·9'	0°51·8'W	F	186
Straits of Riggindale	Cumbr	NY4412	54°30·3'	2°51·5'W	X	90
Straloch	Aberd	NJ8621	57°17·0'	2°13·5'W	X	38
Straloch	Pth & Kin	NO0463	56°45·2'	3°33·7'W	T	43
Straloch Ho	Pth & Kin	NO0364	56°45·7'	3°34·8'W	X	43
Stralochy	Pth & Kin	NO0841	56°33·4'	3°29·4'W	X	52,53
Stramollach	Arg & Bt	NR7130	55°30·9'	5°37·2'W	X	68
Stramolloch	S Lanak	NS6747	55°42·1'	4°6·6'W	X	64
Stramshall	Staffs	SK0735	52°55·0'	1°53·3'W	T	128
Stranbrough Plantn	N Yks	NZ2708	54°28·2'	1°34·6'W	F	93
Strancleuch Hill	S Lanak	NS8720	55°27·9'	3°46·8'W	H	71,72
Strancleugh	S Lanak	NS8621	55°28·4'	3°47·8'W	X	71,72
Strand	C of West	TQ3080	51°30·5'	0°7·2'W	T	176,177
Strand	Glos	SO7113	51°49·1'	2°24·9'W	T	162
Strand	Shetld	HU6691	60°36·1'	0°47·2'W	X	1,2
Strand	S Lanak	NS9025	55°30·6'	3°44·1'W	X	71,72
Strand Brook	Shrops	SO5484	52°27·4'	2°40·2'W	W	137,138
Strandburgh Ness	Shetld	HU6792	60°36·6'	0°46·1'W	X	1,2
Strand Foot	Durham	NY9715	54°32·1'	2°2·4'W	X	92
Strand Gate	E Susx	TQ9017	50°55·5'	0°42·6'E	X	189
Strandhall	I of M	SC2368	54°4·9'	4°41·9'W	X	95
Strandhead	S Ayr	NS4326	55°30·4'	4°28·7'W	X	70
Strand Ho	Devon	SS5234	51°5·4'	4°6·4'W	X	180
Strandlands	Essex	TM1831	51°56·3'	1°10·7'E	X	168,169
Strand Loch	Shetld	HU4346	60°12·0'	1°13·0'W	W	4
Strandlud Hill	E Ayr	NS5806	55°19·9'	4°13·9'W	H	71,77
Strands	Cumbr	SD1884	54°15·0'	3°15·1'W	T	96
Strands	N Yks	SD8692	54°19·6'	2°12·5'W	X	98
Strands	N Yks	SD9697	54°22·4'	2°3·3'W	X	98
Strand, The	Arg & Bt	NR3690	56°2·1'	6°13·8'W	X	61
Strand, The	Medway	TQ7869	51°23·7'	0°33·9'E	X	178
Strand, The	Somer	SS9746	51°12·5'	3°28·1'W	X	181
Stranduff	Aberd	NJ5901	57°6·1'	2°40·2'W	X	37
Strand Water	Win & Maid	SU8984	51°33·1'	0°42·6'W	W	175
Strane River	Devon	SX6171	50°31·6'	3°57·3'W	W	202
Stranfasket	D & G	NX5884	55°8·1'	4°13·2'W	X	77
Stranfasket Hill	D & G	NX5784	55°8·0'	4°14·2'W	X	77
Strang	I of M	SC3678	54°10·5'	4°30·3'W	T	95
Stranger Head	Orkney	ND3792	58°48·9'	3°5·0'W	X	7
Strangeways	Man	SJ8499	53°29·5'	2°14·1'W	T	109
Strangeways Fm	Herts	TQ2198	51°40·3'	0°14·6'W	FM	166,176
Strangford	Heref	SO5828	51°57·2'	2°36·3'W	T	149
Stranghow	Red & Cl	NZ6715	54°31·8'	0°57·5'W	T	94
Strangles, The	Corn	SX1295	50°43·7'	4°39·5'W	X	190
Strangquoy Taing	Orkney	HY6037	59°13·3'	2°41·6'W	X	5
Strangways	Dorset	ST7720	50°59·0'	2°19·3'W	X	183
Strangways	Wilts	SU1443	51°11·4'	1°47·6'W	T	184
Strani Field	Shetld	HU4461	60°20·1'	1°11·7'W	X	2,3
Stranlea	Aberd	NJ3100	57°5·4'	3°7·9'W	X	37
Stranndabhal	N Eil	NG0384	57°45·1'	6°59·1'W	H	18
Stranny Point	S Ayr	NX0199	55°15·0'	5°7·4'W	X	76
Stranoch, The	D & G	NX1671	55°0·2'	4°52·2'W	X	76
Stranog	Aberd	NO8696	57°3·5'	2°13·4'W	T	38,45
Stranog Hill	Aberd	NO8696	57°3·5'	2°13·4'W	H	38,45
Stranraer	D & G	NX0560	54°54·1'	5°2·1'W	T	82
Strans Wood	N Yks	SD9178	54°12·1'	2°7·9'W	F	98
Strap Rocks	Corn	SW5741	50°13·4'	5°24·0'W	X	203
Strase Cliff	Corn	SW8466	50°27·5'	5°2·2'W	X	200
Strashleigh	Devon	SX6055	50°22·9'	3°57·8'W	X	202
Strata Florida	Cered	SN7465	52°16·4'	3°50·4'W	T	135,147
Stratfield Fm	Oxon	SP4912	51°48·5'	1°17·0'W	FM	164
Stratfield Mortimer	W Berks	SU6664	51°22·5'	1°2·7'W	T	175,186
Stratfield Saye	Hants	SU6861	51°20·9'	1°1·0'W	T	175,186
Stratfield Saye House	Hants	SU7061	51°20·9'	0°59·3'W	A	175,186
Stratfield Saye Park	Hants	SU7061	51°20·9'	0°59·3'W	X	175,186
Stratfield Turgis	Hants	SU6959	51°19·8'	1°0·2'W	T	175,186
Stratford	Beds	TL1847	52°6·8'	0°16·2'W	T	153
Stratford	Newham	TQ3884	51°32·5'	0°0·2'W	T	177
Stratford	Worcs	SO8838	52°2·7'	2°10·1'W	T	150
Stratford Br	Oxon	SP4418	51°51·8'	1°21·3'W	X	164
Stratford Hall	Suff	TM0534	51°58·2'	0°59·5'E	X	155
Stratford Hills	Suff	TM0435	51°58·8'	0°58·6'E	X	155
Stratford Marsh	T Ham	TQ3783	51°32·0'	0°1·1'W	T	177
Stratford New Town	Newham	TQ3884	51°32·5'	0°0·2'W	T	177
Stratford St Mary	Suff	TM0434	51°58·2'	0°58·6'E	T	155
Stratford Sub Castle	Wilts	SU1332	51°5·5'	1°48·5'W	T	184
Stratford Tony	Wilts	SU0926	51°2·2'	1°51·9'W	T	184
Stratford Tony Down	Wilts	SU0924	51°1·1'	1°51·9'W	X	184
Stratford upon-Avon	Warw	SP1955	52°11·8'	1°42·9'W	T	151
Stratford-upon-Avon Canal	Sol	SP1175	52°22·6'	1°49·9'W	W	139
Stratford-upon-Avon Canal	Warw	SP1661	52°15·1'	1°45·5'W	W	151
Strath	Aberd	NJ7930	57°21·9'	2°20·5'W	X	29,30
Strath	Arg & Bt	NR6819	55°24·9'	5°39·5'W	X	68
Strath	E Ayr	NS5236	55°36·0'	4°20·5'W	X	70
Strath	Highld	ND2552	58°27·3'	3°16·6'W	X	11,12
Strath	Highld	NG7977	57°44·0'	5°42·3'W	T	19
Stràthabhal	N Eil	NB1903	57°55·9'	6°44·4'W	H	13,14
Strathaird	Highld	NG5317	57°10·9'	6°4·8'W	X	32
Strathaird Ho	Highld	NG5518	57°11·5'	6°2·9'W	X	32
Strathairly Ho	Fife	NO4303	56°13·2'	2°54·7'W	X	59
Strathallan	Pth & Kin	NN8508	56°15·3'	3°50·9'W	X	58
Strathallan Airfield	Pth & Kin	NN9216	56°19·6'	3°44·4'W	X	58
Strathallan Castle	Pth & Kin	NN9115	56°19·1'	3°45·3'W	X	58
Strathallan School	Pth & Kin	NO0918	56°21·0'	3°27·9'W	X	58
Strathan	Highld	NC0821	58°8·4'	5°15·2'W	T	15
Strathan	Highld	NC2461	58°30·4'	5°0·8'W	X	9
Strathan	Highld	NC5764	58°32·8'	4°26·9'W	T	10
Strathan	Highld	NG9338	57°23·4'	5°26·2'W	T	25
Strathan	Highld	NM9792	56°58·7'	5°20·0'W	X	33,40
Strathan Allt na Fiacail	Highld	NH4224	57°17·0'	4°36·8'W	X	26
Strath an Loin	Highld	NC4416	58°6·6'	4°38·4'W	X	16
Strathanmore	Highld	NH2954	57°32·9'	4°51·0'W	X	25
Strathan Skerray	Highld	NC6463	58°32·3'	4°19·7'W	T	10
Strathardle	Pth & Kin	NO0955	56°40·9'	3°28·7'W	X	52,53
Strathardle	Pth & Kin	NO1055	56°40·9'	3°27·7'W	X	53
Strath Aulasary	N Eil	NF8171	57°37·2'	7°20·2'W	X	18
Strathaven	S Lanak	NS7044	55°40·6'	4°3·6'W	T	71
Strathavon	Falk	NS8674	55°57·0'	3°49·1'W	X	65
Strath Avon	Moray	NJ1425	57°18·7'	3°25·2'W	X	36
Strathavon	W Loth	NS9372	55°56·0'	3°42·3'W	X	65
Strathavon Lodge	Moray	NJ1421	57°16·6'	3°25·1'W	X	36
Strath Balne	Stir	NS5381	56°0·2'	4°21·0'W	X	64
Strathbalne	Stir	NS5679	55°59·2'	4°18·1'W	T	64
Strath Barragill	Highld	NG4835	57°20·4'	6°10·8'W	X	32
Strath Bay	Highld	NG7977	57°44·0'	5°42·3'W	W	19
Strath Beag	Highld	NH1087	57°50·2'	5°11·6'W	X	19
Strath Beg	Highld	NC8531	58°15·4'	3°57·1'W	X	17
Strathblane Hills	Stir	NS5581	56°0·3'	4°19·1'W	X	64
Strath Bogie	Aberd	NJ5238	57°26·0'	2°47·5'W	X	29
Strathbogie	Aberd	NJ5537	57°25·5'	2°44·5'W	X	29
Strathbogie	S Lanak	NT0642	55°40·0'	3°29·2'W	X	72
Strathbraan	Pth & Kin	NN9739	56°32·2'	3°40·0'W	X	52,53
Strath Bran	Highld	NH1858	57°34·8'	5°2·2'W	X	25
Strath Bran	Highld	NH2461	57°36·5'	4°56·3'W	X	20
Strathbran Lodge	Highld	NH2461	57°36·5'	4°56·3'W	X	20
Strathbran Plantation	Highld	NH2161	57°36·5'	4°59·3'W	F	20
Strath Brora	Highld	NC7408	58°2·9'	4°7·6'W	X	16
Strathbungo	C of Glas	NS5762	55°50·1'	4°16·6'W	T	64
Strathburn	Aberd	NJ7802	57°6·8'	2°21·3'W	X	38
Strathburn	Fife	NO4223	56°24·0'	2°55·9'W	X	54,59
Strath Burn	Highld	ND2551	58°26·7'	3°16·6'W	W	11,12
Strath Canaird	Highld	NC1501	57°57·9'	5°7·2'W	X	15
Strathcanaird	Highld	NC1501	57°57·9'	5°7·2'W	X	15
Strathcarron	Highld	NG9442	57°25·6'	5°25·4'W	T	25
Strathcarron	Highld	NH5092	57°53·8'	4°31·4'W	X	20
Strathcashell Point	Stir	NS3993	56°6·4'	4°34·9'W	X	56
Strathchailleach	Highld	NC2465	58°32·5'	5°1·0'W	X	9
Strath Chailleach	Highld	NC2466	58°33·1'	5°1·0'W	X	9
Strath Cluanie	Highld	NH1311	57°9·4'	5°5·1'W	X	34
Strathclyde Country Park	N Lanak	NS7357	55°47·6'	4°1·1'W	X	64
Strathclyde Loch	N Lanak	NS7257	55°47·6'	4°2·1'W	W	64
Strathcoil	Arg & Bt	NM6830	56°24·6'	5°45·2'W	T	49
Strathconon	Highld	NH3955	57°33·7'	4°41·0'W	X	26
Strathconon Forest	Highld	NH2847	57°29·1'	4°51·7'W	X	25
Strathconon Forest	Highld	NH2853	57°32·3'	4°51·9'W	F	25
Strathconon Forest	Highld	NH3053	57°32·4'	4°49·9'W	F	26
Strathcoul	Highld	ND1155	58°28·7'	3°31·1'W	T	11,12
Strath Croe	Highld	NG9621	57°14·3'	5°22·4'W	X	25,33
Strathcroy	Highld	NC0831	58°13·8'	5°15·7'W	X	15
Strath Cuileannac	Highld	NH4393	57°54·2'	4°38·5'W	X	20
Strathculm	Devon	SS9902	50°48·8'	3°25·6'W	X	192
Strathdearn	Highld	NH7725	57°18·2'	4°2·0'W	X	35
Strathdearn	Highld	NH7732	57°22·0'	4°2·2'W	X	27
Strathdon	Aberd	NJ3512	57°11·9'	3°4·1'W	T	37
Strath Dores	Highld	NH6037	57°24·4'	4°19·4'W	X	26
Strath Duchally Burn	Highld	NC4325	58°11·4'	4°39·8'W	W	16
Strath Eachaig	Arg & Bt	NS1384	56°1·0'	4°59·6'W	X	56
Strathearn	Pth & Kin	NN9717	56°20·3'	3°39·5'W	X	58
Stratheast	Orkney	HY4803	58°54·9'	2°53·7'W	X	6,7
Strathella	Angus	NO6454	56°40·8'	2°34·8'W	X	54
Strathellen Wood	Highld	NG8032	57°19·8'	5°38·8'W	F	24
Strathellie	Aberd	NK0261	57°38·6'	1°57·5'W	X	30
Strathend	Aberd	NK0435	57°24·6'	1°55·5'W	X	30
Strathenry Ho	Fife	NO2201	56°12·0'	3°15·0'W	X	58
Stratherrick	Highld	NH4815	57°12·3'	4°30·5'W	X	34
Stratherrick	Highld	NH5421	57°15·6'	4°24·8'W	X	26,35
Strath Fillan	Stir	NN3628	56°25·2'	4°39·1'W	X	50
Strath Finella	Aberd	NO6979	56°54·3'	2°30·1'W	X	45
Strathfinella Hill	Aberd	NO6878	56°53·8'	2°31·1'W	H	45
Strath Fleet	Highld	NC7102	57°59·6'	4°10·5'W	X	16
Strathgarry	Pth & Kin	NN8863	56°45·0'	3°49·4'W	X	43
Strath Gartney	Stir	NN4310	56°15·7'	4°31·6'W	X	56
Strath Gartney	Stir	NN4711	56°16·3'	4°27·8'W	X	57
Strathgarve Forest	Highld	NH4164	57°38·5'	4°39·4'W	X	20
Strathgarve Lodge	Highld	NH4061	57°36·9'	4°40·2'W	X	20
Strath Ghrùidh or Strath Grudie	Highld	NC5205	58°0·8'	4°29·8'W	X	16
Strathgirnock	Aberd	NO3395	57°2·7'	3°5·8'W	X	37,44
Strathglass	Highld	NH3836	57°23·4'	4°41·3'W	X	26
Strathgroy	Pth & Kin	NN8964	56°45·5'	3°48·5'W	X	43
Strath Grudie or Strath Ghrùidh	Highld	NC5205	58°0·8'	4°29·8'W	X	16
Strathgryfe	Inverc	NS3270	55°53·9'	4°40·8'W	X	63
Strathgryfe	Inverc	NS3370	55°53·9'	4°39·8'W	X	63
Strathgyle	Aberd	NO7992	57°1·4'	2°20·3'W	H	38,45
Strathgyle Wood	Aberd	NO8093	57°1·9'	2°19·3'W	F	38,45
Strath Halladale	Highld	NC8953	58°27·3'	3°53·7'W	X	10
Strath-head	Pth & Kin	NO0136	56°30·6'	3°36·1'W	X	52,53
Strath House	W Loth	NS9272	55°56·0'	3°43·3'W	X	65
Strathie	Aberd	NO7895	57°3·0'	2°21·3'W	X	38,45
Strathie	Highld	NG7932	57°19·8'	5°39·8'W	X	24
Strath Isla	Moray	NJ4149	57°31·9'	2°58·7'W	X	28
Strathkinness	Fife	NO4616	56°20·3'	2°52·0'W	T	59
Strathkyle Ho	Highld	NH5297	57°56·5'	4°29·5'W	X	20
Strathlachlan Forest	Arg & Bt	NS0093	56°5·5'	5°12·5'W	F	55
Strathlachlan River	Arg & Bt	NS0296	56°7·2'	5°10·7'W	W	55
Strathlethan Bay	Aberd	NO8884	56°57·1'	2°11·4'W	W	45
Strathloanhead	W Loth	NS9272	55°56·0'	3°43·3'W	X	65
Strathlunach	Aberd	NJ5417	57°14·7'	2°45·3'W	X	37
Strath Lunndaidh	Highld	NC7800	57°58·6'	4°3·3'W	X	17
Strathlynn	Highld	NH7501	57°5·2'	4°3·3'W	X	35
Strathmaddie	D & G	NX4663	54°56·5'	4°23·8'W	X	83
Strathmarchin Bay	Aberd	NJ6166	57°41·2'	2°38·8'W	W	29
Strathmartine Cas	Angus	NO3736	56°31·0'	3°1·0'W	X	54
Strath Mashie	Highld	NN5892	57°0·1'	4°19·8'W	X	35
Strathmashie Ho	Highld	NN5891	56°59·6'	4°19·8'W	X	35
Strath Melness Burn	Highld	NC5662	58°31·6'	4°27·9'W	W	10
Strath Mhuilich	Highld	NH1144	57°27·1'	5°8·5'W	X	25
Strathmiglo	Fife	NO2110	56°16·8'	3°16·1'W	T	58
Strathmilligan	D & G	NX7794	55°13·7'	3°55·6'W	X	78
Strath Mòr	Highld	NH1041	57°25·4'	5°9·4'W	X	25
Strathmore	Aberd	NJ4903	57°7·2'	2°50·1'W	X	37
Strathmore	Aberd	NO6871	56°50·0'	2°31·0'W	X	45
Strathmore	Angus	NO5965	56°46·7'	2°39·8'W	X	44
Strathmore	Arg & Bt	NR8294	56°5·6'	5°29·8'W	X	55
Strath More	Highld	NC4544	58°21·7'	4°38·5'W	X	9
Strath More	Highld	NH1882	57°47·7'	5°3·3'W	X	20
Strathmore	Pth & Kin	NO2443	56°34·6'	3°13·8'W	X	53
Strathmore Lodge	Highld	ND1047	58°24·4'	3°31·9'W	X	11,12
Strathmore River	Highld	NC4547	58°23·3'	4°38·6'W	W	9
Strath Mulzie	Highld	NH3193	57°53·9'	4°50·6'W	X	20
Strathnacro	Highld	NH4629	57°19·8'	4°33·0'W	X	26
Strathnafanaig	Arg & Bt	NR7756	55°45·0'	5°32·8'W	X	62
Strathnairn	Highld	NH6529	57°20·2'	4°14·1'W	X	26,35
Strath nam Poll Dubh	Highld	NG9353	57°31·5'	5°27·0'W	X	25
Strath na Sealga	Highld	NH0680	57°46·3'	5°15·3'W	X	19
Strath na Seilge	Highld	NC7019	58°8·7'	4°12·0'W	X	16
Strathnasheallag Forest	Highld	NH0483	57°47·9'	5°17·4'W	X	19
Strathnaver	Highld	NC7045	58°22·7'	4°12·9'W	X	10
Strath Nethy	Highld	NJ0207	57°8·9'	3°36·7'W	X	36
Strath of Appin	Arg & Bt	NM9445	56°33·4'	5°20·7'W	X	49
Strath of Arisaig	Highld	NM6685	56°54·1'	5°50·1'W	F	40
Strath of Brydock	Aberd	NJ6559	57°37·4'	2°34·7'W	X	29
Strath of Kildonan or Strath Ullie	Highld	NC9120	58°9·6'	3°50·7'W	X	17
Strath of Orchy	Arg & Bt	NN1627	56°24·2'	4°58·5'W	X	50
Strath of Pitcalnie	Highld	NH8273	57°44·1'	3°58·4'W	X	21
Strath of Watten	Highld	ND2555	58°28·9'	3°16·7'W	X	11,12
Strathord	Aberd	NJ6258	57°36·9'	2°37·7'W	X	29
Strathore	Fife	NT2697	56°9·9'	3°11·1'W	X	59
Strathore	Orkney	HY4919	59°3·6'	2°52·9'W	X	6
Strathore House & Skeddoway	Fife	NT2598	56°10·4'	3°12·0'W	X	59
Strathorn	Aberd	NJ6827	57°20·2'	2°31·4'W	X	38
Strathossian Ho	Highld	NN4073	56°49·5'	4°36·9'W	X	42
Strath Oykel	Highld	NC4201	57°58·5'	4°39·8'W	X	16
Strathpeffer	Highld	NH4858	57°35·5'	4°32·1'W	T	26
Strath Peffer	Highld	NH5159	57°36·1'	4°29·1'W	X	26
Strath Rannoch	Highld	NH3872	57°42·8'	4°42·7'W	X	20
Strathrannock	Highld	NH3874	57°43·9'	4°42·8'W	X	20
Strathray	Aberd	NJ7912	57°12·2'	2°20·4'W	X	38
Strath Rory	Highld	NH6777	57°46·0'	4°13·7'W	X	21
Strathrory	Highld	NH6777	57°46·0'	4°13·7'W	X	21
Strathrory River	Highld	NH6378	57°46·5'	4°17·7'W	W	21
Strathruddie	Fife	NT2197	56°9·8'	3°15·9'W	X	58
Strath Rusdale	Highld	NH5777	57°45·9'	4°23·8'W	X	21
Strath Rusdale Lodge	Highld	NH5777	57°45·9'	4°23·8'W	X	21
Strathseasgaich	Highld	NC3010	58°3·1'	4°52·4'W	X	15
Strath Sgitheach	Highld	NH5263	57°38·2'	4°28·3'W	X	20
Strath Shinary	Highld	NC2461	58°30·4'	5°0·8'W	X	9
Strathside	Aberd	NJ6014	57°13·2'	2°39·3'W	X	37
Strath Skinsdale	Highld	NC7519	58°8·8'	4°6·9'W	X	16
Strath Skinsdale	Highld	NC7620	58°9·4'	4°6·0'W	X	17
Strathspey	Highld	NH7800	57°4·8'	4°0·3'W	X	35
Strathspey	Highld	NJ0629	57°20·8'	3°33·3'W	X	36
Strathspey	Highld	NJ0931	57°21·9'	3°30·3'W	X	27,36
Strathspey	Highld	NJ1437	57°25·2'	3°25·5'W	X	28
Strathspey Railway, The	Highld	NH9116	57°13·6'	3°47·9'W	X	36
Strath Stack	Highld	NC2740	58°19·1'	4°56·7'W	X	9
Strathsteven	Highld	NC8801	57°59·3'	3°53·2'W	X	17

Strathstodley	Aberd	NK0256	57°35·9'	1°57·5'W	X	30
Strath Suardal	Highld	NG6221	57°13·3'	5°56·1'W	X	32
Strathtay	Pth & Kin	NN9053	56°39·6'	3°47·2'W	T	52
Strath Tay	Pth & Kin	NO0143	56°34·4'	3°36·2'W	X	52,53
Strath Tirry	Highld	NC5219	58°8·4'	4°30·4'W	X	16
Strath Tollaidh	Highld	NC6800	57°58·4'	4°13·4'W	X	16
Strath Tollaidh	Highld	NH6999	57°57·9'	4°12·4'W	X	21
Strathtongue	Highld	NC6259	58°30·1'	4°21·6'W	X	10
Strathtyrum Ho	Fife	NO4817	56°20·8'	2°50·0'W	X	59
Strath Ullie or Strath of Kildonan	Highld	NC9120	58°9·6'	3°50·7'W	X	17
Strath Vagastie	Highld	NC5531	58°14·9'	4°27·8'W	X	16
Strath Vaich	Highld	NH3572	57°42·7'	4°45·7'W	X	20
Strathvaich Forest	Highld	NH3076	57°44·8'	4°50·9'W	X	20
Strathvaich Lodge	Highld	NH3474	57°43·8'	4°46·8'W	X	20
Strathwell Park	I of W	SZ5178	50°36·2'	1°16·4'W	X	196
Strathweltie	Aberd	NJ4703	57°7·2'	2°52·1'W	X	37
Strathwhillan	N Ayr	NS0235	55°34·4'	5°8·0'W	T	69
Strathwhillan Burn	N Ayr	NS0134	55°33·8'	5°8·9'W	W	69
Strathwiggan Burn	E Ayr	NS5605	55°19·3'	4°15·7'W	W	71,77
Strath Wood	Aberd	NJ6811	57°11·6'	2°31·3'W	F	38
Strathy	Highld	NC8365	58°33·7'	4°0·2'W	T	10
Strathy	Highld	NH6475	57°44·9'	4°16·6'W	X	21
Strathy	Pth & Kin	NN9916	56°19·8'	3°37·6'W	X	58
Strathy Bay	Highld	NC8366	58°34·2'	4°0·2'W	W	10
Strathy Forest	Highld	NC8155	58°28·3'	4°1·9'W	F	10
Strathy Forest	Highld	NC8161	58°31·5'	4°2·1'W	F	10
Strathy Inn	Highld	NC8365	58°33·7'	4°0·2'W	X	10
Strathy Point	Highld	NC8269	58°35·8'	4°1·3'W	X	10
Strathyre	Stir	NN5617	56°19·7'	4°19·3'W	T	57
Strathyre	Stir	NN5617	56°19·7'	4°19·3'W	X	57
Strathyre Forest	Stir	NN5618	56°20·2'	4°19·3'W	F	57
Strattenborough Castle Fm	Oxon	SU2392	51°37·8'	1°39·7'W	FM	163,174
Stratton	Corn	SS2206	50°49·8'	4°31·3'W	T	190
Stratton	Dorset	SY6593	50°44·4'	2°29·4'W	T	194
Stratton	Glos	SP0103	51°43·8'	1°58·7'W	T	163
Stratton	Highld	NH7045	57°28·9'	4°9·6'W	X	27
Stratton Audley	Oxon	SP6026	51°56·0'	1°7·2'W	T	164,165
Stratton Audley Park	Oxon	SP6127	51°56·5'	1°6·4'W	X	164,165
Stratton Chase	Bucks	SU9894	51°38·4'	0°34·6'W	T	175,176
Stratton Down	Dorset	SY6595	50°45·4'	2°29·4'W	X	194
Stratton Fm	Beds	TL2142	52°4·0'	0°13·7'W	FM	153
Stratton Hall	Suff	TM2438	51°59·9'	1°16·2'E	X	169
Strattonhill Fm	Norf	TG2121	52°44·7'	1°16·9'E	FM	133,134
Stratton Ho	Hants	SU5440	51°9·6'	1°13·3'W	X	185
Stratton Manor	Hants	SU5859	51°19·9'	1°9·7'W	X	174
Stratton Moor	Somer	ST6548	51°14·0'	2°29·7'W	X	183
Stratton-on-the-Fosse	Somer	ST6550	51°15·1'	2°29·7'W	T	183
Strattons	Hants	SU5160	51°20·4'	1°15·7'W	X	174
Stratton St Margaret	Swin	SU1787	51°35·1'	1°44·9'W	T	173
Stratton St Michael	Norf	TM2093	52°29·7'	1°14·9'E	T	134
Stratton Strawless	Norf	TG2220	52°44·1'	1°17·7'E	T	133,134
Stravanan Bay	Arg & Bt	NS0756	55°45·8'	5°4·1'W	W	63
Stravenhouse Fm	S Lanak	NS8151	55°44·5'	3°53·3'W	FM	65,72
St Raven's Edge	Cumbr	NY4008	54°28·1'	2°55·1'W	H	90
Straverron Hill	D & G	NX5082	55°6·8'	4°20·7'W	X	77
Stravithie	Fife	NO5311	56°17·6'	2°45·1'W	T	59
Stravithie Ho	Fife	NO5311	56°17·6'	2°45·1'W	X	59
Stravithie Mains	Fife	NO5312	56°18·1'	2°45·1'W	X	59
Strawarren Fell	S Ayr	NX1679	55°4·5'	4°52·5'W	X	76
Straw Barrow	Dorset	ST9403	50°49·8'	2°4·7'W	A	195
Straw Beck	N Yks	SD9097	54°22·3'	2°8·8'W	W	98
Strawberry Bank	Aberd	NK0447	57°31·0'	1°55·5'W	X	30
Strawberry Bank	Cumbr	SD4189	54°17·8'	2°54·0'W	T	96,97
Strawberry Bank	Cumbr	SD5590	54°18·5'	2°41·1'W	X	97
Strawberry Bank	Devon	SS2900	50°46·7'	4°25·2'W	X	190
Strawberry Bottom	Surrey	SU9159	51°19·6'	0°41·2'W	X	175,186
Strawberry Hall	Lincs	TF4319	52°45·2'	0°7·5'E	X	131
Strawberry Hill	Durham	NZ3439	54°44·9'	1°27·9'W	X	93
Strawberry Hill	E Susx	TQ5637	51°6·9'	0°14·1'E	T	188
Strawberry Hill	Notts	SK5860	53°8·3'	1°7·6'W	X	120
Strawberry Hill	Rich	TQ1572	51°26·3'	0°20·3'W	T	176
Strawberry Hill	Scot Bord	NT1117	55°26·6'	3°24·0'W	X	78
Strawberry Hill	Staffs	SK0019	52°46·4'	1°59·6'W	X	128
Strawberry Hill	Stock	SJ9687	53°23·0'	2°3·2'W	X	109
Strawberry Hill	Surrey	SU9159	51°19·6'	0°41·2'W	X	175,186
Strawberry Hill	Wakf	SE4221	53°41·3'	1°21·4'W	T	105
Strawberry Hill	Wilts	ST9952	51°16·3'	2°0·5'W	X	184
Strawberry Hill Fm	Beds	TL0062	52°15·1'	0°31·7'W	FM	153
Strawberry Hill Fm	E Susx	TQ7621	50°57·9'	0°30·8'E	FM	199
Strawberry Hill Fm	Pemb	SN0102	51°41·1'	4°52·3'W	FM	157,158
Strawberry Hole	E Susx	TQ8224	50°59·4'	0°36·0'E	A	199
Strawberry How	Cumbr	NY1329	54°39·2'	3°20·5'W	X	89
Strawbridge	Devon	SS5304	50°49·3'	4°4·8'W	X	191
Strawbridge's Fm	Somer	ST1916	50°56·5'	3°8·8'W	FM	181,193
Strawearn Burn	Pth & Kin	NO1109	56°16·2'	3°25·8'W	W	58
Straw Hall	Leic	SP5990	52°30·5'	1°7·4'W	X	140
Straw House Fm	N Yks	SE2972	54°8·8'	1°32·9'W	FM	99
Strawlaw	S Lanak	NT0440	55°38·9'	3°31·1'W	X	72
Strawmoor Fm	Staffs	SJ8503	52°37·7'	2°12·9'W	FM	127,139
Stray Fm	E Yorks	SE8439	53°50·7'	0°43·0'W	FM	106
Stray Head	N Yks	NZ8705	54°26·2'	0°39·1'W	X	94
Stray Marshes	Kent	TQ9369	51°23·5'	0°46·8'E	X	178
St Rayn Hill	Somer	ST4009	50°52·9'	2°50·8'W	X	193
Stray, The or Two Hundred Acre	N Yks	SE3054	53°59·1'	1°32·1'W	X	104
Straythe, The	Corn	SW9238	50°12·6'	4°54·5'W	X	204
Stream	Somer	ST0639	51°8·8'	3°20·2'W	X	181
Streamcombe	Somer	SS8927	51°2·1'	3°34·6'W	X	181
Stream Dike	E Yorks	TA1444	53°53·0'	0°15·5'W	W	107
Stream Dike	N Yks	SE4735	53°48·8'	1°16·8'W	W	105
Stream Dyke	E Yorks	TA1654	53°59·3'	0°13·5'W	W	107
Stream Fm	E Susx	TQ5515	50°55·0'	0°12·7'E	FM	199
Stream Fm	E Susx	TQ6518	50°56·5'	0°21·3'E	FM	199
Stream Fm	Hants	SU8338	51°8·3'	0°48·4'W	FM	186
Stream Fm	Kent	TQ7936	51°5·9'	0°33·8'E	FM	188
Stream Fm	Kent	TQ8032	51°3·8'	0°34·5'E	FM	188
Stream Fm	N Yks	SE4834	53°48·2'	1°15·9'W	FM	105
Stream Fm	Somer	ST2432	51°5·2'	3°4·7'W	FM	182

Stream Fm	Surrey	SU9454	51°16·9'	0°38·7'W	FM	186
Stream Fm	W Susx	TQ0718	50°57·3'	0°28·2'W	FM	197
Stream Mill	E Susx	TQ5515	50°55·0'	0°12·7'E	X	199
Stream Sound	Shetld	HU3834	60°5·6'	1°18·5'W	W	4
Stream Taing	Orkney	HY5420	59°4·1'	2°47·7'W	X	5,6
Stream Taing	Shetld	HU3782	60°31·5'	1°19·1'W	X	1,2,3
Stream, The	Glos	SO8126	51°56·2'	2°16·2'W	X	162
Streap	Highld	NM9486	56°55·4'	5°22·6'W	H	40
Streap Comhlaidh	Highld	NM9586	56°55·5'	5°21·7'W	X	40
Streat	E Susx	TQ3515	50°55·3'	0°4·4'W	T	198
Streatham	Lam	TQ3071	51°25·6'	0°7·4'W	T	176,177
Streatham Hill	Lam	TQ3073	51°26·7'	0°7·4'W	T	176,177
Streatham Park	Lam	TQ2971	51°25·6'	0°8·3'W	T	176
Streatham Vale	Lam	TQ2970	51°25·1'	0°8·3'W	T	176
Streathayne Ho	Devon	SY2294	50°44·7'	3°6·0'W	X	192,193
Streathill Fm	E Susx	TQ3512	50°53·7'	0°4·4'W	FM	198
Streatlam Grange	Durham	NZ0720	54°34·8'	1°53·1'W	X	92
Streatlam Grove	Durham	NZ1019	54°34·2'	1°50·3'W	X	92
Streatlam Home Fm	Durham	NZ0919	54°34·2'	1°51·2'W	FM	92
Streatlam Park	Durham	NZ0819	54°34·2'	1°52·2'W	X	92
Streatley	Beds	TL0728	51°56·6'	0°26·2'W	T	166
Streatley	W Berks	SU5980	51°31·2'	1°8·6'W	T	174
Streatley Fm	W Berks	SU5981	51°31·7'	1°8·6'W	FM	174
Streatley Warren	W Berks	SU5580	51°31·2'	1°12·0'W	X	174
Streat Place	E Susx	TQ3515	50°55·3'	0°4·4'W	A	198
Streel Fm	E Susx	TQ5526	51°1·0'	0°13·0'E	FM	188,199
Streens	Highld	NH8638	57°25·3'	3°53·4'W	X	27
Street	Corn	SX2697	50°45·0'	4°27·6'W	X	190
Street	Cumbr	NY2746	54°48·5'	3°7·7'W	X	85
Street	Cumbr	NY6208	54°28·2'	2°34·8'W	T	91
Street	Cumbr	NY7301	54°24·5'	2°24·5'W	X	91
Street	Devon	SY1889	50°41·9'	3°9·3'W	T	192
Street	Lancs	SD5252	53°58·0'	2°43·5'W	T	102
Street	N Yks	NZ7304	54°25·8'	0°52·1'W	T	94
Street	Roth	SK4098	53°28·9'	1°23·4'W	X	111
Street	Somer	ST3507	50°51·8'	2°55·0'W	T	193
Street	Somer	ST4836	51°7·5'	2°44·2'W	T	182
Street Ash	Somer	ST2813	50°55·0'	3°1·1'W	T	193
Street Ashton	Warw	SP4582	52°26·3'	1°19·9'W	T	140
Street Ashton Ho	Warw	SP4582	52°26·3'	1°19·9'W	X	140
Street Br	Lancs	SD5152	53°58·0'	2°44·4'W	X	102
Street Court	Heref	SO4260	52°14·3'	2°50·6'W	X	137,148,149
Street Dinas	Shrops	SJ3338	52°56·4'	2°59·4'W	T	126
Street End	Hants	SU5519	50°58·3'	1°12·6'W	T	185
Street End	Kent	TR1453	51°14·4'	1°4·3'E	T	179,189
Street End	W Susx	SZ8599	50°47·3'	0°47·3'W	T	197
Street End Copse	Hants	SU7256	51°18·1'	0°57·6'W	F	175,186
Street End Fm	E Susx	TQ6023	50°59·3'	0°17·2'E	FM	199
Streetfield	Heref	SO6258	52°13·4'	2°33·0'W	X	149
Streetfield Fm	Warw	SP5182	52°26·2'	1°14·6'W	FM	140
Streetfield Wood	E Susx	TQ7820	50°57·3'	0°32·5'E	F	199
Street Fm	Brad	SE0749	53°56·5'	1°53·2'W	FM	104
Street Fm	Ches	SJ5068	53°12·6'	2°44·5'W	FM	117
Street Fm	E Yorks	SE7356	53°59·9'	0°52·8'W	FM	105,106
Street Fm	Norf	TG3000	52°33·2'	1°24·0'E	FM	134
Street Fm	Suff	TL8251	52°7·9'	0°39·9'E	FM	155
Street Fm	Suff	TL9969	52°17·2'	0°55·5'E	FM	155
Street Fm	Suff	TM2971	52°17·6'	1°21·9'E	FM	156
Street Fm	Suff	TM3361	52°12·1'	1°25·0'E	FM	156
Street Gate	Ghead	NZ2159	54°55·8'	1°39·9'W	T	88
Street Gate	N Yks	SD9065	54°5·1'	2°8·8'W	X	98
Streethay	Staffs	SK1410	52°41·5'	1°47·2'W	T	128
Street Head	Cumbr	NY3338	54°44·2'	3°2·0'W	X	90
Streethead	Cumbr	NY4242	54°46·4'	2°53·7'W	X	85
Street Head	Northum	NY7398	55°16·8'	2°25·1'W	X	80
Street Head	N Yks	SD9647	53°55·4'	2°3·2'W	X	103
Street Heath	Somer	ST4639	51°9·1'	2°45·9'W	X	182
Street Hey	Ches	SJ3378	53°17·9'	2°59·9'W	X	117
Street Hill	Oxon	SP5716	51°50·6'	1°10·0'W	X	164
Streethill Fm	Leic	SK7109	52°40·7'	0°56·6'W	FM	141
Street Ho	Cumbr	NY5157	54°54·6'	2°45·4'W	X	86
Street Ho	Cumbr	NY5447	54°49·2'	2°42·5'W	X	86
Street Ho	Cumbr	NY5723	54°36·3'	2°39·5'W	X	91
Street Ho	Cumbr	NY6024	54°36·3'	2°35·8'W	X	91
Street Ho	Cumbr	NY6325	54°37·4'	2°34·0'W	X	91
Street Ho	Darl	NZ3415	54°32·0'	1°28·1'W	X	93
Street Ho	N Yks	NZ2113	54°31·0'	1°40·1'W	X	93
Street Ho	N Yks	SE2593	54°20·2'	1°36·5'W	X	99
Street Ho	N Yks	SE3185	54°15·8'	1°31·0'W	X	99
Street Ho	N Yks	SE4185	54°15·8'	1°21·8'W	X	99
Street Hos	Northum	NZ1771	55°2·2'	1°43·6'W	X	88
Streethouse	Scot Bord	NT7712	55°24·3'	2°21·4'W	X	80
Streethouse	Wakf	SE3920	53°40·7'	1°24·2'W	T	104
Street House Fm	Derby	SK1167	53°12·2'	1°49·7'W	FM	119
Street House Fm	N Yks	SD7858	54°1·3'	2°19·7'W	FM	103
Street House Fm	N Yks	SE3785	54°15·8'	1°25·5'W	FM	99
Street House Fm	Red & Cl	NZ7419	54°33·9'	0°50·9'W	FM	94
Street Houses	Northum	NZ0970	55°1·7'	1°51·1'W	X	88
Street Houses	N Yks	SE5245	53°54·2'	1°12·1'W	T	105
Streetlam	N Yks	SE3198	54°22·8'	1°30·9'W	T	99
Streetlam Fm	N Yks	SE3198	54°22·8'	1°30·9'W	FM	99
Streetlam Grange	N Yks	NZ3000	54°23·9'	1°31·9'W	X	93
Street Lane	Derby	SK3848	53°1·9'	1°25·6'W	T	119
Streetly	Birm	SP0998	52°35·0'	1°51·6'W	T	139
Street Lydan	Wrex	SJ4339	52°57·0'	2°50·5'W	T	126
Streetly End	Cambs	TL6148	52°6·6'	0°21·5'E	T	154
Streetly Hall	Cambs	TL6048	52°6·7'	0°20·6'E	X	154
Street of Kincardine	Highld	NH9417	57°14·1'	3°44·9'W	X	36
Street on the Fosse	Somer	ST6139	51°9·2'	2°33·1'W	T	183
Streets	N Yks	SD8766	54°5·6'	2°11·5'W	X	98
Streets Farmhouse	Somer	ST2619	50°58·2'	3°2·9'W	X	193
Streetside	Cumbr	SD7298	54°22·8'	2°25·4'W	X	98
Street Side Fm	Durham	NZ0513	54°31·0'	1°54·9'W	FM	92
Street, The	Northum	NT8313	55°24·9'	2°15·7'W	X	80
Street, The	Scot Bord	NT8018	55°27·6'	2°18·5'W	X	80
Streetway Ho	Staffs	SK1205	52°38·8'	1°49·0'W	X	139
Streetway Lane	Dorset	ST7600	50°48·2'	2°20·1'W	X	194
Street Wood	Heref	SO4259	52°13·8'	2°50·6'W	F	148,149
Strefford	Shrops	SO4485	52°27·8'	2°49·1'W	T	137
Strefford Wood	Shrops	SO4485	52°27·8'	2°49·1'W	F	137

Streflyn	Gwyn	SH8836	52°54·8'	3°39·5'W	X	124,125
Streigh Fm	Corn	SX0759	50°24·2'	4°42·6'W	FM	200
Strelitz	Pth & Kin	NO1836	56°30·8'	3°19·5'W	X	53
Strelitz Wood	Pth & Kin	NO1836	56°30·8'	3°19·5'W	F	53
Strelley	Notts	SK5041	52°58·1'	1°14·9'W	T	129
Strelley Hall	Notts	SK5042	52°58·6'	1°14·9'W	X	129
Strelley Park Fm	Notts	SK4943	52°59·2'	1°15·8'W	FM	129
Strem Ness	Shetld	HT9741	60°9·5'	2°2·7'W	X	4
Stremnishmore	Arg & Bt	NR3140	55°35·0'	6°15·7'W	X	60
Strenaby	I of M	SC3781	54°12·2'	4°29·5'W	X	95
Strenaby	I of M	SC4283	54°13·4'	4°25·0'W	X	95
Strensall	York	SE6360	54°2·2'	1°1·9'W	T	100
Strensall Camp	York	SE6359	54°1·6'	1°1·9'W	X	105,106
Strensall Common	York	SE6559	54°1·6'	1°0·0'W	X	105,106
Strensall Common	York	SE6560	54°2·2'	1°0·0'W	X	100
Strensall Forest	York	SE6362	54°3·2'	1°1·8'W	X	100
Strensall New Br	York	SE6260	54°2·2'	1°2·8'W	X	100
Strensham	Worcs	SO9140	52°3·7'	2°7·5'W	T	150
Strensham Service Area	Worcs	SO9039	52°3·2'	2°8·4'W	X	150
Stresa Glebe Fm	Leic	SP5890	52°30·5'	1°8·3'W	FM	140
Stretchacott	Devon	SS4417	50°56·1'	4°12·8'W	X	180,190
Stretch Down	Devon	SS8113	50°54·5'	3°41·2'W	T	181
Stretchford	Devon	SX7664	50°28·0'	3°44·5'W	X	202
Stretchnook Fm	Leic	SK4900	52°36·0'	1°16·2'W	FM	140
Stretcholt	Somer	ST2943	51°11·1'	3°0·6'W	T	182
Strete	Devon	SX8347	50°18·9'	3°38·2'W	T	202
Strete Fm	Devon	SY0495	50°45·0'	3°21·3'W	FM	192
Strete Gate	Devon	SX8345	50°17·8'	3°38·2'W	X	202
Strete Raleigh	Devon	SY0495	50°45·0'	3°21·3'W	T	192
Stretfield Hill	Glos	SO6707	51°45·9'	2°28·3'W	X	162
Stretford	Heref	SO5257	52°12·8'	2°41·8'W	T	149
Stretford	Traf	SJ7994	53°26·8'	2°18·6'W	T	109
Stretford Brook	Heref	SO4254	52°11·1'	2°50·5'W	W	148,149
Stretford Brook	Heref	SO5558	52°13·3'	2°39·1'W	W	149
Stretford Court	Heref	SO4455	52°11·7'	2°48·8'W	T	148,149
Stretford Water	Somer	ST3811	50°53·9'	2°52·5'W	W	193
Strethall	Essex	TL4839	52°2·0'	0°9·9'E	T	154
Strethall Field	Essex	TL4941	52°3·1'	0°10·8'E	X	154
Stretham	Cambs	TL5174	52°20·8'	0°13·4'E	T	143
Stretham Manor	W Susx	TQ2013	50°54·5'	0°17·2'W	X	198
Stretham Mere	Cambs	TL5272	52°19·7'	0°14·2'E	X	154
Stretham Old Engine	Cambs	TL5172	52°19·7'	0°13·4'E	A	154
Strettington	W Susx	SU8907	50°51·6'	0°43·7'W	T	197
Stretton	Ches	SJ4452	53°4·0'	2°49·7'W	T	117
Stretton	Derby	SK3961	53°8·9'	1°24·6'W	T	119
Stretton	Rut	SK9415	52°43·7'	0°36·1'W	T	130
Stretton	Staffs	SJ8811	52°42·0'	2°10·3'W	T	127
Stretton	Staffs	SK2526	52°50·1'	1°37·3'W	T	128
Stretton	Warr	SJ6182	53°20·3'	2°34·7'W	T	109
Stretton Baskerville Village	Warw	SP4291	52°31·2'	1°22·5'W	A	140
Stretton Br	Leic	SK3012	52°42·5'	1°33·0'W	X	128
Stretton Court Fm	Heref	SO4642	52°4·7'	2°46·9'W	FM	148,149,161
Stretton en le Field	Leic	SK3011	52°42·0'	1°33·0'W	T	128
Stretton Fields Fm	Warw	SP4091	52°31·2'	1°24·2'W	FM	140
Stretton Grandison	Heref	SO6344	52°5·8'	2°32·0'W	T	149
Stretton Hall	Ches	SJ4452	53°4·0'	2°49·7'W	X	117
Stretton Hall Fm	Derby	SK3762	53°9·5'	1°26·4'W	FM	119
Stretton Hall (Hospl)	Leic	SP6599	52°35·3'	1°2·0'W	X	141
Stretton Heath	Shrops	SJ3710	52°41·3'	2°55·5'W	X	126
Stretton Hillside	Derby	SK3960	53°8·4'	1°24·6'W	X	119
Stretton Ho	Derby	SK3861	53°8·9'	1°25·5'W	X	119
Stretton Ho	Leic	SP4291	52°31·2'	1°22·5'W	X	140
Stretton Ho	Warr	SJ6281	53°19·7'	2°33·8'W	X	109
Stretton Lodge Fm	Warw	SP3972	52°20·9'	1°25·2'W	FM	140
Stretton Lower Hall	Ches	SJ4453	53°4·5'	2°49·7'W	X	117
Stretton Magna Village	Leic	SK6500	52°35·9'	1°2·0'W	A	141
Stretton Moss	Warr	SJ6382	53°20·3'	2°32·9'W	X	109
Stretton-on-Dunsmore	Warw	SP4072	52°20·9'	1°24·4'W	T	140
Stretton-on-Fosse	Warw	SP2238	52°2·6'	1°40·4'W	T	151
Stretton Sugwas	Heref	SO4642	52°4·7'	2°46·9'W	T	148,149,161
Stretton under Fosse	Warw	SP4581	52°25·7'	1°19·9'W	T	140
Stretton Westwood	Shrops	SO5998	52°34·9'	2°35·9'W	T	137,138
Stretton Wharf	Warw	SP4481	52°25·7'	1°20·8'W	X	140
Stretton Wood	Rut	SK9517	52°44·8'	0°35·2'W	F	130
Stretton Wood	Staffs	SJ8812	52°42·6'	2°10·3'W	F	127
Stribers	Cumbr	SD3581	54°13·5'	2°59·4'W	X	96,97
Stribers Moss	Cumbr	SD3481	54°13·5'	3°0·3'W	F	96,97
Stricegill	Cumbr	NY8312	54°30·4'	2°15·3'W	X	91,92
Strichen	Aberd	NJ9455	57°35·4'	2°5·6'W	T	30
Strichen Mains	Aberd	NJ9353	57°34·3'	2°6·6'W	X	30
Strickland	Cumbr	NY4457	54°54·5'	2°52·0'W	X	85
Strickland Hill	Cumbr	SD4285	54°15·7'	2°53·0'W	X	96,97
Strickland Ledge Fm	Cumbr	NY5621	54°35·2'	2°40·4'W	FM	90
Strickland Manor Fm	Suff	TM3869	52°16·3'	1°29·7'E	FM	156
Strickley	Cumbr	SD5489	54°17·9'	2°42·0'W	X	97
Strickstenning Hall	Heref	SO5130	51°58·2'	2°42·4'W	X	149
Strickstenton	Corn	SX0857	50°23·1'	4°41·7'W	X	200
Strid Cott	N Yks	SE0656	54°0·2'	1°54·1'W	X	104
Stride's Fm	Hants	SU2829	51°3·8'	1°35·6'W	FM	184
Striding Edge	Cumbr	NY3415	54°31·8'	3°0·8'W	X	90
Stridrigg	D & G	NY2285	55°9·4'	3°13·0'W	X	79
Strid, The	N Yks	SE0656	54°0·2'	1°54·1'W	X	104
Strift Ho	Wrex	SJ4743	52°59·1'	2°47·0'W	X	117
Strifts Plantation	Leic	SK8322	52°47·6'	0°45·7'W	F	130
Strine Brook	Wrekin	SJ7017	52°45·2'	2°26·3'W	W	127
Strine Dale	Oldham	SD9506	53°33·3'	2°4·1'W	X	109
Strines	Sheff	SK2290	53°24·6'	1°39·7'W	X	110
Strines	Staffs	SK0361	53°9·0'	1°56·9'W	X	119
Strines	Stock	SJ9786	53°22·5'	2°2·3'W	T	109
Strines Dike	Sheff	SK2190	53°24·6'	1°40·6'W	W	110
Strines Edge	Sheff	SK2189	53°24·1'	1°40·6'W	X	110
Strines Moor	Derby	SK2189	53°24·1'	1°40·6'W	X	110
Strines Resr	Sheff	SK2290	53°24·6'	1°39·7'W	W	110
Stringer's Brook	Wrex	SJ3359	53°7·7'	2°59·7'W	W	117
Stringmans Fm	Kent	TR0254	51°15·2'	0°54·1'E	FM	189
Strings, The	Wilts	SU0277	51°29·7'	1°57·9'W	X	173
Stringston	Somer	ST1742	51°10·5'	3°10·9'W	T	181
String, The	N Ayr	NR9736	55°34·8'	5°12·8'W	X	69
String, The	Orkney	HY4714	59°0·9'	2°54·9'W	W	6
Stripe Head	Durham	NY8439	54°45·0'	2°14·5'W	X	91,92

Stripe Ho	N Yks	NZ3202	54°25·0′	1°30·0′W	X	93
Stripend	Scot Bord	NT7211	55°23·8′	2°26·1′W	X	80
Stripe of Loan	Moray	NJ2050	57°32·2′	3°19·7′W	W	28
Stripes	Cumbr	NY4551	54°51·3′	2°51·0′W	X	86
Stripes	Cumbr	NY7409	54°28·8′	2°23·7′W	X	91
Stripes Fm	N Yks	NZ9209	54°28·3′	0°34·4′W	FM	94
Stripeside	Moray	NJ3549	57°31·9′	3°4·7′W	X	28
Stripeside	Moray	NJ3843	57°28·6′	3°1·6′W	X	28
Stripeside	Moray	NJ4651	57°33·0′	2°53·7′W	X	28,29
Stripeside	Moray	NJ5054	57°34·7′	2°49·7′W	X	29
Stripe Sike	Northum	NY6579	55°6·5′	2°32·5′W	W	86
Stripes, The	N Yks	SE2982	54°14·2′	1°32·9′W	X	99
Stripple Stones	Corn	SX1475	50°32·9′	4°37·2′W	X	200
Stripple Stones (Henge)	Corn	SX1475	50°32·9′	4°37·2′W	A	200
Strip, The	D & G	NY1198	55°16·3′	3°23·6′W	F	78
Strixton	Northnts	SP9061	52°14·6′	0°40·5′W	T	152
Stroan Br	D & G	NX3778	55°4·4′	4°32·8′W	X	77
Stroanfreggan	D & G	NX6491	55°11·9′	4°7·8′W	A	77
Stroanfreggan Bridge	D & G	NX6491	55°11·9′	4°7·8′W	X	77
Stroanfreggan Burn	D & G	NX6692	55°12·5′	4°5·9′W	W	77
Stroanfreggan Craig	D & G	NX6392	55°12·4′	4°8·7′W	X	77
Stroangassel	D & G	NX6086	55°9·2′	4°11·4′W	X	77
Stroangassel Hill	D & G	NX5985	55°8·6′	4°12·3′W	H	77
Stroan Hill	D & G	NX6885	55°8·8′	4°3·8′W	H	77
Stroan Hill	D & G	NX6985	55°8·8′	4°2·9′W	X	77
Stroan Ho	D & G	NX3878	55°4·5′	4°31·8′W	X	77
Stroan Loch	D & G	NX6470	55°0·6′	4°7·2′W	W	77
Stroanpatrick	D & G	NX6491	55°11·9′	4°7·8′W	X	77
Stroans	D & G	NX5053	54°51·2′	4°19·8′W	X	83
Stroanshalloch Burn	D & G	NX6991	55°12·0′	4°3·1′W	W	77
Stroanshalloch Hill	D & G	NX7090	55°11·5′	4°2·1′W	H	77
Stroanshalloch Loch	D & G	NX7090	55°11·5′	4°2·1′W	W	77
Stroan Viaduct	D & G	NX6470	55°0·6′	4°7·2′W	X	77
Stroat	Glos	ST5797	51°40·4′	2°36·9′W	T	162
Stròc-bheinn	Highld	NG4539	57°22·5′	6°14·1′W	H	23,32
Strocherie	Aberd	NJ7355	57°35·3′	2°26·6′W	X	29
St Roche's Hill	W Susx	SU8711	50°53·7′	0°45·4′W	H	197
Strode	Devon	SX6453	50°21·9′	3°54·4′W	X	202
Strode	N Som	ST5361	51°21·0′	2°40·1′W	T	172,182
Strode Fm	Kent	TR1766	51°21·3′	1°7·4′E	FM	179
Strode Manor	Dorset	SY4499	50°47·6′	2°47·3′W	X	193
Strodgemoor Bottom	Hants	SU1803	50°49·8′	1°44·3′W	X	195
Stroin	Aberd	NJ3509	57°10·3′	3°4·0′W	X	37
Stroin Vuigh	I of M	SC2174	54°8·1′	4°44·0′W	X	95
Strollamus	Highld	NG5926	57°15·9′	5°59·4′W	X	32
Strom	N Eil	NF9673	57°38·9′	7°5·3′W	W	18
Strom	Shetld	HU3948	60°13·1′	1°17·3′W	X	3
Stromacleit	N Eil	NB1230	58°10·2′	6°53·4′W	H	13
Stromay	N Eil	NF7665	57°33·8′	7°24·7′W	X	18
Stromay	N Eil	NF9374	57°39·3′	7°8·4′W	X	18
Stromay	N Eil	NF9888	57°47·1′	7°4·4′W	X	18
Stromban	N Eil	NF9068	57°36·0′	7°10·9′W	X	18
Strombery	Orkney	HY4616	59°1·9′	2°56·0′W	X	6
Strom Chaltanais	N Eil	NF8240	57°20·6′	7°16·7′W	W	22
Strome Carronach	Highld	NG8737	57°22·7′	5°32·1′W	X	24
Strome Castle	Highld	NG8635	57°21·6′	5°33·0′W	A	24
Strome Ferry	Highld	NG8634	57°21·0′	5°33·0′W	T	24
Strome Island's	Highld	NG8334	57°21·0′	5°36·0′W	X	24
Stromemore	Highld	NG8635	57°21·6′	5°33·0′W	T	24
Stròm Eòratan	N Eil	NF8550	57°26·1′	7°14·5′W	W	22
Strome Wood	Highld	NG8736	57°22·1′	5°32·1′W	F	24
Stromfirth	Shetld	HU4050	60°14·2′	1°16·2′W	X	3
Stromness	Orkney	HY2509	58°58·0′	3°17·8′W	T	6,7
Strom Ness	Orkney	HY7651	59°20·9′	2°24·8′W	X	5
Strom Ness	Shetld	HU2245	60°11·6′	1°35·7′W	X	4
Strom Ness	Shetld	HU2965	60°22·3′	1°27·9′W	X	3
Stromness	Shetld	HU3845	60°11·5′	1°18·4′W	X	4
Strom Ness	Shetld	HU3846	60°12·1′	1°18·4′W	X	4
Stromness Taing	Orkney	HY4425	59°6·8′	2°58·2′W	X	5,6
Stromness Voe	Shetld	HU3844	60°11·0′	1°18·4′W	W	4
Stronachavie	Moray	NJ1318	57°14·9′	3°26·1′W	X	36
Stronach Hill	D & G	NX0173	55°1·0′	5°6·3′W	X	76,82
Stronach Hill	D & G	NX5358	54°54·0′	4°17·1′W	X	83
Stronachie	Pth & Kin	NO0608	56°15·6′	3°30·6′W	X	58
Stronachlachar	Stir	NN4010	56°15·6′	4°34·5′W	T	56
Stronachroe	Highld	NH4552	57°32·2′	4°34·9′W	X	26
Stronachullin Fm	Arg & Bt	NR8479	55°57·6′	5°27·2′W	FM	62
Stronachullin Lodge	Arg & Bt	NR8479	55°57·6′	5°27·2′W	X	62
Stronacroibh	Arg & Bt	NM8844	56°32·7′	5°26·5′W	X	49
Stronafian	Arg & Bt	NS0281	55°59·1′	5°10·0′W	X	55,63
Stronafyne	Arg & Bt	NN3005	56°12·7′	4°44·0′W	X	56
St Ronan's Bay	Arg & Bt	NM2824	56°20·1′	6°23·6′W	W	48
St Ronan's Wells	Scot Bord	NT3237	55°37·6′	3°4·4′W	X	73
Stronbae Hill	D & G	NX4574	55°2·4′	4°25·1′W	H	77
Stronchreggan	Highld	NN0772	56°48·2′	5°9·2′W	T	41
Stronchrubie	Highld	NC2419	58°7·8′	4°58·9′W	X	15
Stronchullin	Arg & Bt	NS1884	56°1·1′	4°54·8′W	X	56
Stronchullin Burn	Arg & Bt	NR8379	55°57·6′	5°28·1′W	W	62
Stronchullin Hill	Arg & Bt	NS1786	56°2·2′	4°55·8′W	H	56
Strond	N Eil	NG0384	57°45·1′	6°59·1′W	T	18
Strondavon	Arg & Bt	NS0490	56°4·0′	5°8·5′W	X	56
Strondow	Moray	NJ1644	57°29·0′	3°23·6′W	X	28
Strone	Angus	NO4260	56°43·9′	2°56·4′W	X	44
Strone	Arg & Bt	NN2027	56°24·3′	4°54·6′W	X	50
Strone	Arg & Bt	NR5064	55°48·5′	5°59·0′W	X	61
Strone	Arg & Bt	NR6210	55°19·8′	5°44·7′W	X	68
Strone	Arg & Bt	NR7788	56°2·2′	5°34·3′W	X	55
Strone	Arg & Bt	NR9481	55°58·9′	5°17·7′W	X	55
Strone	Arg & Bt	NR9697	56°7·6′	5°16·5′W	X	55
Strone	Arg & Bt	NS0497	56°7·8′	5°8·8′W	X	56
Strone	Arg & Bt	NS1980	55°59·0′	4°53·6′W	T	63
Strone	Highld	NH5228	57°19·4′	4°27·0′W	T	26,35
Strone	Highld	NH5774	57°44·2′	4°23·7′W	X	21
Strone	Highld	NH7100	57°4·6′	4°7·2′W	T	35
Strone	Highld	NN1481	56°53·2′	5°2·7′W	X	34,41
Strone	Inverc	NS2974	55°56·0′	4°43·8′W	T	63
Strone	Pth & Kin	NN9709	56°16·0′	3°39·3′W	X	58
Strone	Stir	NN4510	56°15·7′	4°29·7′W	X	57
Strone Baddoch	Aberd	NO1382	56°55·5′	3°25·3′W	H	43
Strone Br	Pth & Kin	NO1452	56°39·4′	3°23·7′W	X	53

Strone Burn	Arg & Bt	NR9481	55°58·9′	5°17·7′W	W	55
Strone Burn	Stir	NN4412	56°16·7′	4°30·7′W	W	57
Strone Farm	Inverc	NS2877	55°57·6′	4°44·9′W	FM	63
Stronefield	Arg & Bt	NR7274	55°54·6′	5°38·4′W	X	62
Strone Garden	Arg & Bt	NN1810	56°15·1′	4°55·8′W	X	50,56
Strone Geers	Highld	NG2949	57°27·3′	6°30·6′W	H	23
Strone Glen	Arg & Bt	NR6409	55°19·4′	5°42·8′W	X	68
Strone Hill	Aberd	NJ4832	57°22·8′	2°51·4′W	H	29,37
Strone Hill	Aberd	NJ5713	57°12·6′	2°42·3′W	H	37
Strone Hill	Angus	NO2956	56°41·7′	3°9·1′W	H	53
Strone Ho	Pth & Kin	NO1451	56°38·8′	3°23·7′W	X	53
Strone House	Arg & Bt	NS2690	56°4·5′	4°47·3′W	X	56
Stronelairg Lodge	Highld	NH5306	57°7·5′	4°25·2′W	X	35
Stronenaba	Highld	NN2084	56°55·0′	4°57·0′W	T	34,41
Stronend	Stir	NS6289	56°4·7′	4°12·6′W	H	57
Strone Nea	Highld	NH1984	57°48·8′	5°2·3′W	X	20
Strone of Auchinleck	D & G	NX4671	55°0·8′	4°24·1′W	X	77
Strone Point	Arg & Bt	NN1108	56°13·9′	5°2·5′W	X	56
Strone Point	Arg & Bt	NS0771	55°53·9′	5°4·8′W	X	63
Strone Point	Arg & Bt	NS1980	55°59·0′	4°53·6′W	X	63
Strone Point	Highld	NH5328	57°19·4′	4°26·0′W	X	26,35
Strone Saul	Arg & Bt	NS1379	55°58·3′	4°59·4′W	X	63
Stroneskar	Arg & Bt	NM8701	56°9·5′	5°25·4′W	X	55
Stroneslaney	Stir	NN5519	56°20·7′	4°20·3′W	X	57
Stroness	Pth & Kin	NN9227	56°25·6′	3°44·6′W	X	52,58
Strone, The	Aberd	NO2799	57°4·3′	3°11·8′W	X	37,44
Strone, The	Aberd	NO4793	57°1·8′	2°51·9′W	H	37,44
Strone, The	Angus	NO2778	56°53·5′	3°11·4′W	X	44
Strone, The	Arg & Bt	NS2692	56°5·6′	4°47·4′W	H	56
Stronetic	Pth & Kin	NO1454	56°40·4′	3°23·8′W	X	53
Stronetoper	Highld	NN8497	57°3·2′	3°54·3′W	X	35,43
Strone Water	Arg & Bt	NR6409	55°19·4′	5°42·8′W	W	68
Strònfine	Arg & Bt	NM9332	56°26·3′	5°21·0′W	X	49
Strongarbh	Arg & Bt	NM5055	56°37·5′	6°4·1′W	T	47
Strongarve	Highld	NH5764	57°38·9′	4°23·3′W	X	21
Strongford Fm	C of Stoke	SJ8739	52°57·1′	2°11·2′W	FM	127
Stronhavie	Pth & Kin	NO0063	56°45·1′	3°37·7′W	X	43
Stronhavie Craig	Pth & Kin	NN9964	56°45·6′	3°38·7′W	H	43
Stronie	D & G	NW9855	54°51·2′	5°8·4′W	X	82
Stron Lochie	Stir	NN4304	56°12·4′	4°31·4′W	H	56
Stronlonag	Arg & Bt	NS1186	56°2·0′	5°1·6′W	X	56
Stronmacnair	Stir	NN4202	56°11·3′	4°32·3′W	X	56
Stronmagachan	Arg & Bt	NN0814	56°17·0′	5°5·7′W	X	50,56
Stronmilchan	Arg & Bt	NN1528	56°24·7′	4°59·5′W	T	50
Stronord	D & G	NX4564	54°57·0′	4°24·8′W	T	83
Stronsaul	Arg & Bt	NS1379	55°58·3′	4°59·4′W	X	63
Stronsay	Orkney	HY6525	59°6·9′	2°36·2′W	X	5
Stronsay Firth	Orkney	HY5721	59°4·7′	2°44·5′W	W	5,6
Strontian	Highld	NM8161	56°41·6′	5°34·1′W	T	40
Strontian River	Highld	NM8364	56°43·3′	5°32·3′W	W	40
Strontoiller	Arg & Bt	NM9029	56°24·7′	5°23·8′W	X	49
Stronuich	Pth & Kin	NN5041	56°32·5′	4°25·9′W	X	51
Stronuich Reservoir	Pth & Kin	NN5041	56°32·5′	4°25·9′W	W	51
Stronvar	Stir	NN5220	56°21·2′	4°23·3′W	X	51,57
Stronvochlan	Arg & Bt	NS1888	56°3·3′	4°54·9′W	X	56
Stronyaraig	Arg & Bt	NS0975	55°56·1′	5°3·0′W	X	63
Strood	Kent	TQ8532	51°3·7′	0°38·8′E	X	189
Strood	Medway	TQ7269	51°23·9′	0°28·7′E	T	178
Strood Channel	Essex	TM0013	51°47·0′	0°54·4′E	W	168
Strood Fm	E Susx	TQ3520	50°58·0′	0°4·3′W	FM	198
Strood Fm	E Susx	TQ5614	50°54·5′	0°13·5′E	FM	199
Strood Fm	W Susx	SU9819	50°58·0′	0°35·9′W	FM	197
Strood Green	Surrey	TQ2048	51°13·3′	0°16·5′W	T	187
Strood Green	W Susx	TQ0224	51°0·6′	0°32·4′W	T	197
Strood Green	W Susx	TQ1332	51°4·8′	0°22·8′W	T	187
Strood Hall	Essex	TL5921	51°52·1′	0°19·0′E	X	167
Stroods	E Susx	TQ4827	51°1·6′	0°7·0′E	X	188,198
Strood, The	Essex	TM0115	51°48·1′	0°55·3′E	X	168
Strool Bay	D & G	NW9565	54°56·5′	5°11·6′W	W	82
Stroom Dyke	Notts	SK7233	52°53·6′	0°55·4′W	W	129
Stroomfields	Notts	SK7134	52°54·2′	0°56·3′W	X	129
Stropestone	Somer	ST6252	51°16·2′	2°32·3′W	X	183
Stroquhan	D & G	NX8483	55°7·9′	3°48·7′W	X	78
Stroquhan Hill	D & G	NX8382	55°7·4′	3°49·7′W	H	78
Stroquhan Moor	D & G	NX8282	55°7·4′	3°50·6′W	X	78
Strother House Fm	S Tyne	NZ3260	54°56·3′	1°29·6′W	FM	88
Strothers Dale	Northum	NY9757	54°54·7′	2°2·4′W	T	87
Stroud	Glos	SO8405	51°44·8′	2°13·5′W	T	162
Stroud	Hants	SU7223	51°0·3′	0°58·0′W	T	197
Stroud	Surrey	SU9235	51°6·6′	0°40·8′W	T	186
Stroud Br	Dorset	SY8891	50°43·3′	2°9·8′W	X	194
Stroudbridge Fm	Hants	SU7222	50°59·8′	0°58·1′W	FM	197
Stroud Common	S Glos	ST6287	51°35·1′	2°32·5′W	X	172
Stroud Common	Surrey	TQ0442	51°10·3′	0°30·4′W	X	186
Stroud Copse	Oxon	SP4407	51°45·8′	1°21·4′W	F	164
Stroude	Surrey	TQ0068	51°24·4′	0°33·3′W	T	176
Strouden	Bourne	SZ1194	50°45·0′	1°50·3′W	T	195
Stroud Fm	Dorset	ST7213	50°55·2′	2°23·5′W	FM	194
Stroud Fm	Dorset	ST7910	50°53·6′	2°17·5′W	FM	194
Stroud Fm	Hants	SU7223	51°0·3′	0°58·0′W	FM	197
Stroud Fm	Win & Maid	SU9077	51°29·3′	0°41·8′W	FM	175
Stroud Green	Essex	TQ8590	51°34·9′	0°40·6′E	T	178
Stroud Green	Glos	SO8007	51°45·9′	2°17·0′W	T	162
Stroud Green	Hargy	TQ3188	51°34·8′	0°6·2′W	T	176,177
Stroud Green	W Berks	SU4766	51°23·7′	1°19·1′W	X	174
Strouds	W Berks	SU5874	51°27·9′	1°9·5′W	X	174
Stroud Sch	Hants	SU3821	50°59·5′	1°27·1′W	X	185
Stroud's Fm	Somer	ST2720	50°58·7′	3°2·0′W	FM	193
Stroud Slad Fm	Glos	SO8706	51°45·4′	2°10·9′W	FM	162
Stroudwood Dairy Fm	Hants	SU5119	50°58·3′	1°16·0′W	FM	185
Stroudwood Fm	Hants	SU5119	50°58·3′	1°16·0′W	FM	185
Stroul	Arg & Bt	NS2483	56°0·7′	4°49·0′W	T	56
Stroul Bay	Arg & Bt	NS2583	56°0·7′	4°48·0′W	W	56
Stroupster	Highld	ND3366	58°34·9′	3°8·7′W	X	12
Strowan Ho	Pth & Kin	NN8121	56°22·2′	3°55·2′W	X	52,57
Strow Burn	Aberd	NJ5314	57°13·1′	2°46·2′W	W	37
Stroxton	Lincs	SK9031	52°52·4′	0°39·4′W	T	130
Stroxton Lodge	Lincs	SK8931	52°52·4′	0°40·3′W	X	130
Stroxworthy	Devon	SS3419	50°57·0′	4°21·4′W	T	190
Struan	Angus	NO6167	56°47·8′	2°37·9′W	X	45

Struan	Arg & Bt	NM2563	56°40·9′	6°29·0′W	X	46,47
St Ruan	Corn	SW7115	49°59·7′	5°11·3′W	T	203
Struan	Highld	NG3438	57°21·6′	6°24·9′W	T	23,32
Struan	Pth & Kin	NN8065	56°45·9′	3°57·3′W	T	43
Struanmore	Highld	NG3437	57°21·0′	6°24·9′W	T	23,32
St Ruan's Well	Corn	SW7114	49°59·2′	5°11·3′W	A	203
Strubby	Lincs	TF1577	53°16·9′	0°16·1′W	X	121
Strubby	Lincs	TF4582	53°19·1′	0°11·0′E	T	122
Strubby Airfield (dis)	Lincs	TF4481	53°18·6′	0°10·1′E	X	122
Strubby Grange	Lincs	TF4683	53°19·7′	0°11·9′E	X	122
Structon's Heath	Worcs	SO7765	52°17·2′	2°19·8′W	T	138,150
Strudda Bank	Cumbr	NY0508	54°27·8′	3°27·5′W	X	89
Struey Rocks	N Ayr	NR9920	55°26·2′	5°10·2′W	X	69
Struff Wood	N Yks	SE0753	53°58·6′	1°53·2′W	F	104
Strugg's Hill	Lincs	TF2937	52°55·1′	0°4·5′W	T	131
Struidh	Highld	NM4988	56°55·2′	6°7·0′W	X	39
Struie	Highld	NH6585	57°50·3′	4°16·0′W	X	21
Struie Hill	Highld	NH6786	57°50·9′	4°14·0′W	H	21
Struie Hill	Pth & Kin	NO0610	56°16·6′	3°30·6′W	X	58
Struie Wood	Highld	NH6386	57°50·8′	4°18·0′W	F	21
St Rumbald's Well	Northnts	SP5036	52°1·4′	1°15·9′W	X	151
Strumble Head	Pemb	SM8941	52°1·9′	5°4·2′W	X	157
Strumore	N Eil	NF9069	57°36·5′	7°11·0′W	T	18
Strumpshaw	Norf	TG3507	52°36·8′	1°28·7′E	T	134
Strumpshaw Hall	Norf	TG3406	52°36·3′	1°27·8′E	X	134
Strumpshaw Hill	Norf	TG3507	52°36·8′	1°28·7′E	X	134
Strumpshaw Marsh	Norf	TG3306	52°36·3′	1°26·9′E	W	134
St Rumwold's Church	Kent	TR0534	51°4·3′	0°56·0′E	X	179,189
Struncheon Hill Fm	E Yorks	TA0750	53°56·3′	0°21·8′W	FM	107
Struntry Carr	N Yks	NZ8102	54°24·7′	0°44·7′W	X	94
Strùp Arasaig	N Eil	NG1291	57°49·2′	6°50·6′W	X	14
Strutforth Hill	Cumbr	NY7412	54°30·4′	2°23·7′W	H	91
Struthan Bàn	N Eil	NF7642	57°21·5′	7°22·8′W	W	22
Struthan Glac na h-Atha	Arg & Bt	NR5488	56°1·6′	5°56·4′W	W	61
Struthan na Creige Bàin Aird	Highld	NM6248	56°34·1′	5°52·0′W	W	49
Struthen Glac na Dunaich	Arg & Bt	NR6386	56°0·8′	5°47·7′W	W	61
Struther Bog	Northum	NY8195	55°15·2′	2°17·5′W	X	80
Struthers	E Ayr	NS4437	55°36·4′	4°28·1′W	X	70
Struthers	Fife	NO3709	56°16·4′	3°0·6′W	X	59
Struthers Barns	Fife	NO3809	56°16·4′	2°59·6′W	X	59
Struther's Brae	E Ayr	NS6105	55°19·4′	4°11·0′W	H	71,77
Struther, The	Scot Bord	NT3947	55°43·0′	2°57·8′W	H	73
Struthill	Pth & Kin	NN8515	56°19·1′	3°51·1′W	X	58
Struy	Highld	NH3940	57°25·6′	4°40·4′W	T	26
Struy Br	Highld	NH4040	57°25·6′	4°39·4′W	X	26
Struy Forest	Highld	NH3540	57°25·5′	4°44·4′W	X	26
Stryd	I of Angl	SH2482	53°18·6′	4°38·1′W	T	114
Stryd y Facsen	I of Angl	SH3383	53°19·3′	4°30·0′W	T	114
Strypes	Moray	NJ2758	57°36·6′	3°12·8′W	X	28
Strypes, The	Scot Bord	NT1918	55°27·2′	3°16·4′W	H	79
Stryt	Wrex	SJ2751	53°3·3′	3°4·9′W	X	117
Stryt-cae-rhedyn	Flint	SJ2660	53°8·2′	3°6·0′W	X	117
Stryt Fawr	Denb	SJ1162	53°9·1′	3°19·4′W	X	116
Stryt-issa	Wrex	SJ2845	53°0·1′	3°4·0′W	T	117
Stryt-swndwr	Flint	SJ2458	53°7·1′	3°7·7′W	X	117
Stryt-yr-hwch	Wrex	SJ3346	53°0·7′	2°59·5′W	X	117
St Sairs	Aberd	NJ6332	57°22·9′	2°36·5′W	X	29,37
St Scythes	Lincs	TF3161	53°8·0′	0°2·1′W	X	122
St Serf's Island	Pth & Kin	NO1500	56°11·4′	3°21·7′W	X	58
St Stephen	Corn	SW9453	50°20·7′	4°53·4′W	T	200,204
St Stephens	Corn	SX3285	50°38·7′	4°22·2′W	T	201
St Stephens	Corn	SX4158	50°24·3′	4°13·9′W	T	201
St Stephens	Herts	TL1306	51°44·7′	0°21·4′W	T	166
St Stephen's Hill Fm	Staffs	SK0623	52°48·5′	1°54·3′W	FM	128
St Sunday Crag	Cumbr	NY3613	54°30·7′	2°58·9′W	X	90
St Teath	Corn	SX0680	50°35·5′	4°44·1′W	T	200
St Teresa's Convent	Surrey	TQ1151	51°15·1′	0°24·2′W	X	187
St Thomas	Devon	SX9091	50°42·7′	3°33·1′W	T	192
St Thomas	Staffs	SJ9523	52°48·5′	2°4·0′W	X	127
St Thomas	Swan	SS6693	51°37·4′	3°55·8′W	T	159
St Thomas's Bridge	Wilts	SU1632	51°5·5′	1°45·9′W	X	184
St Thomas's Head	N Som	ST3467	51°24·1′	2°56·5′W	X	171,182
St Trinians	N Yks	NZ1901	54°24·5′	1°42·0′W	X	92
St Trinian's Hall	N Yks	NZ1900	54°24·0′	1°42·0′W	X	92
St Tudno's Well	Conwy	SH7783	53°20·0′	3°50·4′W	A	115
St Tudwal's Island East	Gwyn	SH3425	52°48·1′	4°27·3′W	X	123
St Tudwal's Island West	Gwyn	SH3325	52°48·0′	4°28·2′W	X	123
St Tudwal's Road	Gwyn	SH3328	52°49·7′	4°28·3′W	W	123
St Tudy	Corn	SX0676	50°33·3′	4°44·0′W	T	200
St Twynnells	Pemb	SR9497	51°38·3′	4°58·2′W	T	158
Stuabhal	N Eil	NB1312	58°0·5′	6°51·1′W	H	13,14
Stuack	Shetld	HU3795	60°38·5′	1°18·9′W	X	1,2
Stuadh Airigh Alasdair	Arg & Bt	NR8664	55°49·6′	5°24·6′W	X	62
Stuadh Rùnastach	Arg & Bt	NR3072	55°52·2′	6°18·5′W	X	60
Stuaidh	N Eil	NG0483	57°44·6′	6°58·0′W	X	18
Stuartfield	Aberd	NJ9745	57°30·0′	2°2·5′W	T	30
Stuartfield Lodge Plantations	Durham	NZ0745	54°48·2′	1°53·0′W	F	88
Stuartfield Lodge Plantns	Durham	NZ0743	54°47·2′	1°53·0′W	F	88
Stuartslaw	Scot Bord	NT8555	55°47·5′	2°13·9′W	X	67,74
Stubb	Cumbr	NY5278	55°5·9′	2°44·7′W	X	86
Stubb	Norf	TG4122	52°44·7′	1°34·7′E	T	134
Stubb	N Yks	SD8155	53°59·7′	2°17·0′W	X	103
Stubba Water	Shetld	HU3175	60°27·7′	1°25·7′W	W	3
Stubben Edge Hall	Derby	SK3662	53°9·5′	1°27·3′W	X	119
Stubbermere	W Susx	SU7509	50°52·8′	0°55·6′W	T	197
Stubbers Fm	Essex	TL6100	51°40·8′	0°20·1′E	FM	167
Stubber's Green	Wals	SK0401	52°36·6′	1°56·1′W	T	139
Stubbers (Outdoor Pursuits Centre)	Hav	TQ5784	51°32·2′	0°16·2′E	X	177
Stubb Fm	Cumbr	NY4367	54°59·9′	2°53·0′W	FM	85
Stubb Fm	Cumbr	SD5385	54°15·8′	2°42·9′W	FM	97
Stubb Ho	Durham	NZ1215	54°32·1′	1°48·5′W	X	92
Stubb Ho	N Yks	SE3691	54°19·0′	1°26·4′W	X	99
Stubbin Fm	N Yks	SE0198	54°22·9′	1°58·7′W	FM	98
Stubbing	N Yks	SD9643	53°53·2′	2°3·2′W	X	103
Stubbing Court	Derby	SK3567	53°12·2′	1°28·2′W	A	119
Stubbinghill Fm	Notts	SK4760	53°8·3′	1°17·4′W	FM	120

Stubbing Hill Fm	N Yks	SE0043	53°53·2′	1°59·6′W	FM	104
Stubbing Nook	N Yks	SE2187	54°16·9′	1°40·2′W	X	99
Stubbing Rigg	N Yks	SD7795	54°21·2′	2°20·8′W	X	98
Stubbings	N Yks	SE1871	54°8·3′	1°43·1′W	X	99
Stubbings	N Yks	SE2477	54°11·5′	1°37·5′W	X	99
Stubbings	Win & Maid	SU8481	51°31·5′	0°47·0′W	T	175
Stubbings Barn	N Yks	SE3362	54°3·4′	1°29·3′W	X	99
Stubbing's Entry	Suff	TM0674	52°19·7′	1°1·8′E	X	144
Stubbings Fm	Leeds	SE2244	53°53·7′	1°39·5′W	FM	104
Stubbing's Green	Suff	TM0674	52°19·7′	1°1·8′E	T	144
Stubbing's Wood	Suff	TM0675	52°20·3′	1°1·8′E	F	144
Stubbington	Hants	SU5503	50°49·7′	1°12·8′W	T	196
Stubbins	Lancs	SD5042	53°52·6′	2°45·2′W	T	102
Stubbins	Lancs	SD7818	53°39·7′	2°19·6′W	T	109
Stubbins Fm	Notts	SK6852	53°3·9′	0°58·7′W	FM	120
Stubbleborough	Pemb	SN0419	51°50·4′	4°50·3′W	X	157,158
Stubble Close	C of Derb	SK3831	52°52·7′	1°25·7′W	X	128
Stubblefield Ho	Kent	TQ9353	51°14·8′	0°46·3′E	X	189
Stubble Green	Cumbr	SD0599	54°22·9′	3°27·3′W	T	96
Stubble Hill Fm	Leic	SK3700	52°36·0′	1°26·8′W	FM	140
Stubbles	W Berks	SU5776	51°29·0′	1°10·4′W	T	174
Stubb Mill	Norf	TG4321	52°44·1′	1°36·4′E	X	134
Stubbock Hill	Lincs	SK8837	52°55·6′	0°41·0′W	X	130
Stubborn Fm	Devon	SS8412	50°54·0′	3°38·6′W	FM	181
Stubborn Sand	Norf	TF6537	52°54·5′	0°27·6′E	X	132
Stubb Place	Cumbr	SD0890	54°18·1′	3°24·4′W	X	96
Stubbs Br	Donc	SE5010	53°35·3′	1°14·3′W	X	111
Stubbs Br	N Yks	SE5323	53°42·3′	1°11·4′W	X	105
Stubb's Copse	Hants	SU3627	51°2·7′	1°28·8′W	F	185
Stubb's Copse	Hants	SU4354	51°17·2′	1°22·6′W	F	185
Stubb's Copse	Hants	SU5547	51°13·4′	1°12·4′W	F	185
Stubb's Cross	Kent	TQ9838	51°6·6′	0°50·1′E	T	189
Stubbs Fm	Hants	SU7639	51°8·9′	0°54·4′W	FM	186
Stubbsgill	Cumbr	NY1444	54°47·3′	3°19·8′W	X	85
Stubbs Grange	N Yks	SE5716	53°38·5′	1°7·9′W	X	111
Stubb's Green	Norf	TM2598	52°32·2′	1°19·5′E	X	134
Stubbs Green	Norf	TM3597	52°31·4′	1°28·3′E	T	134
Stubbs Hall	Donc	SE4911	53°35·8′	1°15·2′W	X	111
Stubbs Hill Fm	Norf	TL6494	52°31·4′	0°25·4′E	FM	143
Stubbs Wood	Hants	SU3603	50°49·8′	1°28·9′W	F	196
Stubbs Wood	N Yks	SE1349	53°56·5′	1°47·7′W	F	104
Stubbs Wood	N Yks	SE7157	54°0·5′	0°54·6′W	F	105,106
Stubb, The	Powys	SJ2503	52°37·4′	3°6·1′W	X	126
Stubby Copse Inclosure	Hants	SU3204	50°50·3′	1°32·3′W	F	196
Stubby Knowe	D & G	NY3172	55°2·5′	3°4·4′W	X	85
Stubby Leas	Staffs	SK1809	52°40·9′	1°43·6′W	X	128
Stubbylee Park	Lancs	SD8621	53°41·4′	2°12·3′W	X	103
Stubcroft Fm	W Susx	SZ8097	50°46·3′	0°51·5′W	FM	197
Stubdale Fm	Red & Cl	NZ7112	54°30·1′	0°53·8′W	FM	94
Stubden Resr	Brad	SE0633	53°47·8′	1°54·1′W	W	104
Stub Hall Fm	Lancs	SD5066	54°5·5′	2°45·5′W	FM	97
Stubhampton	Dorset	ST9113	50°55·2′	2°7·3′W	T	195
Stubhampton Bottom	Dorset	ST8916	50°56·8′	2°9·0′W	X	184
Stubhampton Down	Dorset	ST9014	50°55·8′	2°8·2′W	X	195
Stub House Fm	Leeds	SE3043	53°53·2′	1°32·2′W	FM	104
Stub House Plantation	Leeds	SE3043	53°53·2′	1°32·2′W	F	104
Stublach Dairy Fm	Ches	SJ7170	53°13·8′	2°25·7′W	FM	118
Stublach Fm	Ches	SJ7270	53°13·8′	2°24·8′W	FM	118
Stublach Grange	Ches	SJ7170	53°13·8′	2°25·7′W	X	118
Stubley Hall	Roch	SD9215	53°38·1′	2°6·8′W	A	109
Stublick Bog	Northum	NY8360	54°56·3′	2°15·5′W	X	86,87
Stublick Fm	Northum	NY8360	54°56·3′	2°15·5′W	FM	86,87
Stublick Hill	Northum	NY8561	54°56·9′	2°13·6′W	X	87
Stublick Moor	Northum	NY8560	54°56·3′	2°13·6′W	X	87
Stublick Sike	Northum	NY8761	54°56·9′	2°11·8′W	W	87
Stub Riding	S Glos	ST7283	51°32·9′	2°23·8′W	X	172
Stubsgill	Cumbr	NY0122	54°35·3′	3°31·5′W	X	89
Stubshaw Cross	Wigan	SD5800	53°29·9′	2°37·6′W	T	108
Stubs Wood	Lancs	SD8045	53°54·3′	2°17·9′W	F	103
Stubthorn Ho	N Yks	SE3486	54°16·4′	1°28·3′W	X	99
Stubton	Lincs	SK8748	53°1·6′	0°41·8′W	T	130
Stubwood	Staffs	SK0939	52°57·1′	1°51·6′W	T	128
Stub Wood	York	SE5843	53°53·0′	1°6·6′W	F	105
Stùc a' Bhuic	Stir	NN3904	56°12·3′	4°35·3′W	X	56
Stùc a' Choire Dhuibh Bhig	Highld	NG9458	57°34·2′	5°26·2′W	H	25
Stùc a' Chroin	Stir	NN6117	56°19·8′	4°14·4′W	H	57
Stùc an t- Iobairt	Arg & Bt	NN3301	56°10·6′	4°41·0′W	X	56
Stùc Bheag	Highld	NH0523	57°16·1′	5°13·5′W	H	25,33
Stuccles Fm	W Susx	TQ2518	50°57·1′	0°12·8′W	FM	198
Stuc Coire an Laoigh	Highld	NG9659	57°34·8′	5°24·3′W	H	25
Stuc Dhubh	Stir	NN5512	56°17·0′	4°20·1′W	H	57
Stùc Gharbh MhÒR	Aberd	NJ1401	57°5·8′	3°24·7′W	H	36
Stuchbury	Northnts	SP5643	52°5·2′	1°10·6′W	X	152
Stùchdan Capuill	Arg & Bt	NS0478	55°57·6′	5°8·0′W	H	63
Stuchd an Lochain	Pth & Kin	NN4841	56°34·1′	4°28·0′W	H	51
Stuchd Bhreac	Arg & Bt	NR8377	55°56·5′	5°28·1′W	X	62
Stuck	Arg & Bt	NS0670	55°53·3′	5°5·7′W	X	63
Stuck	Arg & Bt	NS1393	56°5·9′	4°59·9′W	X	56
Stuckbeg	Arg & Bt	NS2097	56°8·2′	4°53·4′W	X	56
Stuck Chapel Burn	Pth & Kin	NN7835	56°29·7′	3°58·5′W	W	51,52
Stuckendroin	Arg & Bt	NN3214	56°17·6′	4°42·4′W	X	50,56
Stuckenduff	Arg & Bt	NS2586	56°2·4′	4°48·1′W	X	56
Stuckeridge Ho	Devon	SS9221	50°58·9′	3°31·9′W	X	181
Stuckeridge South	Devon	SS9220	50°58·4′	3°31·9′W	X	181
Stuckgowan	Arg & Bt	NN3202	56°11·1′	4°42·0′W	X	56
Stuckiedhu	Arg & Bt	NN3104	56°12·2′	4°43·0′W	X	56
Stuckivoulich	Arg & Bt	NN3203	56°11·7′	4°42·0′W	X	56
Stucko Clett	Shetld	HU2877	60°28·8′	1°28·9′W	X	3
Stuckreoch	Arg & Bt	NS0599	56°8·9′	5°7·9′W	X	56
Stuckton	Hants	SU1613	50°55·2′	1°46·0′W	T	195
Stuckumb Point	Corn	SX0144	50°16·0′	4°47·2′W	X	204
Stùc Loch na Cabhaig	Highld	NG8961	57°35·6′	5°31·4′W	H	19,24
Stuc na Nughinn	Arg & Bt	NN3113	56°17·0′	4°43·4′W	X	50,56
Stuc Odhar	Stir	NN5508	56°14·8′	4°20·0′W	H	57
Stuc Scardan	Arg & Bt	NN1114	56°17·1′	5°2·8′W	H	50,56
Stucscardan	Arg & Bt	NN1213	56°16·6′	5°1·8′W	X	50,56
Studborough Hill	Northnts	SP5359	52°13·8′	1°13·0′W	X	152
Stud Brook	Leic	SK4327	52°50·5′	1°21·3′W	W	129
Studdah	N Yks	SE1490	54°18·6′	1°46·7′W	X	99

Studdal	Kent	TR3149	51°11·8′	1°18·8′E	T	179
Studdens Fm	E Susx	TQ6214	50°54·4′	0°18·6′E	FM	199
Studd Hill	Kent	TR1567	51°21·9′	1°5·7′E	T	179
Studdolph	Pemb	SM9108	51°44·1′	5°1·2′W	X	157,158
Studdon Park	Northum	NY8453	54°52·5′	2°14·5′W	X	86,87
Studdridge Fm	Bucks	SU7594	51°38·6′	0°54·6′W	FM	175
Studdridge Fm	Bucks	SU7595	51°39·2′	0°54·6′W	FM	165
Stud Farm	Lincs	SK8779	53°18·3′	0°41·3′W	FM	121
Stud Fm	Ches	SJ4256	53°6·1′	2°51·6′W	FM	117
Stud Fm	Cumbr	NY0331	54°40·1′	3°29·8′W	FM	89
Stud Fm	D & G	NX9377	55°4·8′	3°40·1′W	FM	84
Stud Fm	Essex	TL8603	51°41·9′	0°41·9′E	FM	168
Stud Fm	E Susx	TQ4601	50°47·6′	0°4·7′E	FM	198
Stud Fm	E Yorks	TA1745	53°53·5′	0°12·8′W	FM	107
Stud Fm	E Yorks	TA2227	53°43·7′	0°8·6′W	FM	107
Stud Fm	Lancs	SD4534	53°48·2′	2°49·7′W	FM	102
Stud Fm	Leic	SK4611	52°41·9′	1°18·8′W	FM	129
Stud Fm	Leic	SK4902	52°37·0′	1°16·2′W	FM	140
Stud Fm	NE Lincs	TA2207	53°33·0′	0°9·1′W	FM	113
Stud Fm	Norf	TG0332	52°51·1′	1°1·3′E	FM	133
Stud Fm	Northnts	SP7667	52°18·0′	0°52·7′W	FM	152
Stud Fm	Notts	SK7864	53°10·3′	0°49·6′W	FM	120,121
Stud Fm	N Yks	SE6535	53°48·7′	1°0·4′W	FM	105,106
Stud Fm	Oxon	SP5221	51°53·3′	1°14·3′W	FM	164
Stud Fm	Oxon	SU2597	51°40·5′	1°37·9′W	FM	163
Stud Fm	Shrops	SO3073	52°21·3′	3°1·3′W	FM	137,148
Stud Fm	Staffs	SK1723	52°48·5′	1°44·5′W	FM	128
Stud Fm	Suff	TM2859	52°11·1′	1°20·5′E	FM	156
Stud Fm	Suff	TM3461	52°12·1′	1°25·9′E	FM	156
Studfold	Cumbr	NY2846	54°48·5′	3°6·8′W	X	85
Studfold	Cumbr	NY7200	54°23·9′	2°25·5′W	X	91
Studfold	Notts	SK5055	53°5·6′	1°14·8′W	X	120
Studfold	N Yks	SD8170	54°7·8′	2°17·0′W	T	98
Studfold	N Yks	SE0254	53°59·2′	1°57·8′W	X	104
Studford Gill	Lancs	SD7757	54°0·8′	2°20·6′W	X	103
Studford Ring	N Yks	SE5879	54°12·4′	1°6·2′W	A	100
Studforth	N Yks	SE4072	54°8·8′	1°22·8′W	X	99
Studforth Hill	N Yks	SE4065	54°5·0′	1°22·9′W	A	99
Studforth Plantn	E Yorks	TA0946	53°54·2′	0°20·0′W	F	107
Stud Green	Ches	SJ7362	53°9·5′	2°23·8′W	T	118
Stud Green	Win & Maid	SU8877	51°29·3′	0°43·6′W	T	175
Studham	Beds	TL0215	51°49·7′	0°30·8′W	T	166
Studham	Devon	SX7698	50°46·3′	3°45·1′W	X	191
Studhayes Fm	Devon	SY2698	50°46·8′	3°2·6′W	FM	192,193
Stud Ho	Dorset	ST9109	50°53·1′	2°7·3′W	X	195
Stud Ho	Rich	TQ1668	51°24·2′	0°19·5′W	X	176
Studholme	Cumbr	NY2556	54°53·8′	3°9·7′W	X	85
Studholme Fm	Suff	TM2772	52°18·2′	1°20·2′E	FM	156
Studholmerigg Wood	Cumbr	NY2843	54°46·9′	3°6·7′W	F	85
Studie Knowe	D & G	NX1574	55°1·8′	4°53·3′W	X	76
Studland	Dorset	SZ0382	50°38·5′	1°57·1′W	T	195
Studland Bay	Dorset	SZ0383	50°39·0′	1°57·1′W	W	195
Studland Heath	Dorset	SZ0284	50°39·6′	1°57·9′W	X	195
Studlands Park	Suff	TL6365	52°15·8′	0°23·7′E	X	154
Studlehurst	Lancs	SD6433	53°47·8′	2°32·4′W	X	102,103
Studley	Shrops	SO6074	52°22·0′	2°34·9′W	X	138
Studley	Warw	SP0763	52°16·1′	1°53·4′W	T	150
Studley	Wilts	ST8665	51°23·3′	2°11·7′W	X	173
Studley	Wilts	ST9671	51°26·5′	2°3·1′W	T	173
Studley Castle	Hants	SU2216	50°56·8′	1°40·8′W	A	184
Studley Fm	Somer	ST7140	51°9·7′	2°24·5′W	FM	183
Studley Green	Bucks	SU7995	51°39·1′	0°51·1′W	T	165
Studley Green	Wilts	ST8356	51°18·4′	2°14·2′W	T	173
Studley Park	N Yks	SE2869	54°7·2′	1°33·9′W	X	99
Studley Priory	Oxon	SP5912	51°48·4′	1°8·3′W	A	164
Studley Roger	N Yks	SE2970	54°7·7′	1°33·0′W	T	99
Studley Royal	N Yks	SE2770	54°7·8′	1°34·8′W	T	99
Studley Wood	Oxon	SP5911	51°47·9′	1°8·3′W	F	164
Studrigg Scar	N Yks	SD7870	54°7·8′	2°19·8′W	X	98
Studstyle Fm	N Yks	SE5895	54°21·1′	1°6·0′W	FM	100
Study, The	Highld	NN1856	56°39·9′	4°57·7′W	X	41
Stuffynwood Fm	Derby	SK5265	53°11·0′	1°12·9′W	FM	120
Stugdale Ho	N Yks	SE6962	54°3·2′	0°56·3′W	X	100
Stuggadhoo	I of M	SC3175	54°8·8′	4°34·8′W	X	95
Stugger Hill	Shetld	HU3077	60°28·8′	1°26·8′W	H	3
Stùic na Cuigealach	Pth & Kin	NN8071	56°49·2′	3°57·5′W	X	43
Stuic, The	Aberd	NO2285	56°57·2′	3°16·5′W	X	44
Stuin, The	Orkney	HY6337	59°13·3′	2°38·4′W	X	5
Stuis of Graveland	Shetld	HU4696	60°38·9′	1°9·0′W	X	1
Stukeley Park	Cambs	TL2274	52°21·3′	0°12·1′W	X	142
Stulabhal	N Eil	NF8024	57°12·0′	7°17·5′W	H	22
Stulaigh	N Eil	NF8323	57°11·6′	7°14·4′W	X	22
Stumblehole Fm	Surrey	TQ2446	51°12·2′	0°13·1′W	FM	187
Stumbleholm Fm	W Susx	TQ2236	51°6·8′	0°15·0′W	FM	187
Stumble, The	Essex	TL9107	51°44·0′	0°46·4′E	X	168
Stumblewood Common	E Susx	TQ4030	51°3·4′	0°0·2′E	X	187
Stump Cross	Cald	SE1026	53°44·1′	1°50·5′W	X	104
Stump Cross	Donc	SK5698	53°28·8′	1°9·0′W	X	111
Stump Cross	Essex	TL5044	52°4·7′	0°11·7′E	X	154
Stump Cross	Herts	TL3236	52°0·6′	0°4·2′W	X	153
Stump Cross	Lancs	SD5737	53°49·9′	2°38·8′W	X	102
Stump Cross	Leic	SK6917	52°45·0′	0°58·3′W	A	129
Stump Cross	Norf	TG1421	52°44·9′	1°10·7′E	A	133
Stump Cross	Norf	TG2636	52°52·7′	1°21·9′E	A	133
Stump Cross	N Yks	NZ7409	54°28·5′	0°51·1′W	A	94
Stump Cross	N Yks	SE6098	54°22·7′	1°4·2′W	A	94,100
Stump Cross	Somer	ST5943	51°11·3′	2°34·8′W	X	182,183
Stump Cross Caverns	N Yks	SE0863	54°4·0′	1°52·2′W	X	99
Stump Fm	Shetld	HU3045	60°11·6′	1°27·0′W	FM	4
Stump Hall	Lancs	SD8037	53°50·0′	2°17·8′W	X	103
Stump Howe	N Yks	NZ7913	54°30·6′	0°46·4′W	X	94
Stump's Cross	Essex	TL7338	52°1·0′	0°31·7′E	X	155
Stumps Cross	Glos	SP0730	51°58·3′	1°53·5′W	T	150
Stumps Fm	Kent	TR0958	51°17·2′	1°0·2′E	FM	179
Stumps Grove	Surrey	TQ0856	51°17·8′	0°26·7′W	F	187
Stumpy Cross	Devon	SS9501	50°48·2′	3°29·0′W	X	192
Stunstead	Lancs	SD9139	53°51·1′	2°7·8′W	X	103
Stuntney	Cambs	TL5578	52°22·9′	0°17·0′E	T	143
Stunts Green	E Susx	TQ6213	50°53·8′	0°18·6′E	T	199
Stup Pill	C of Bris	ST5281	51°31·8′	2°41·1′W	W	172

Stuppington Fm	Kent	TQ9659	51°18·0′	0°49·1′E	FM	178
Stuppington Fm	Kent	TR1455	51°15·5′	1°4·4′E	FM	179
Sturbridge	Staffs	SJ8330	52°52·3′	2°14·2′W	T	127
Sturcombe River	Devon	SS8118	50°57·2′	3°41·3′W	W	181
Sturdon Burn	Scot Bord	NT5441	55°39·9′	2°43·4′W	W	73
Sturdy Beck	Leeds	SE3241	53°52·1′	1°30·4′W	W	104
Sturdy Hill	Aberd	NO5977	56°53·2′	2°39·9′W	H	44
Sturdy Hill	Lincs	TF4185	53°20·8′	0°7·5′E	X	122
Sturdy Ho	N Yks	NZ1305	54°26·7′	1°47·6′W	X	92
Sturdy's	Cumbr	SD3781	54°13·5′	2°57·6′W	X	96,97
Sturdy's Castle (PH)	Oxon	SP4619	51°52·3′	1°19·5′W	X	164
Sturford	Wilts	ST8344	51°11·9′	2°14·2′W	T	183
Sturgate	Lincs	SK8789	53°23·7′	0°41·1′W	T	112,121
Sturgate Airfield	Lincs	SK8787	53°22·6′	0°41·1′W	X	112,121
Sturgeons Fm	Essex	TL6607	51°44·5′	0°24·7′E	FM	167
Sturmer	Essex	TL6943	52°3·8′	0°28·3′E	T	154
Sturminster Common	Dorset	ST7912	50°54·7′	2°17·5′W	T	194
Sturminster Marshall	Dorset	SY9499	50°47·7′	2°4·7′W	T	195
Sturminster Newton	Dorset	ST7814	50°55·7′	2°18·4′W	T	194
Sturrick Fm	Essex	TM1022	51°51·6′	1°3·4′E	FM	168,169
Sturridge	Devon	SS8203	50°49·1′	3°40·1′W	X	191
Stùrr Ruadh	Highld	ND1325	58°12·6′	3°28·4′W	X	17
Sturry	Kent	TR1760	51°18·1′	1°7·2′E	T	179
Stursdon	Corn	SS2413	50°53·6′	4°29·8′W	T	190
Stursdon Cross	Corn	SS2513	50°53·6′	4°28·9′W	X	190
Sturston Carr	Norf	TL8795	52°31·5′	0°45·8′E	F	144
Sturston Hall	Derby	SK2046	53°0·9′	1°41·7′W	X	119,128
Sturston Warren	Norf	TL8893	52°30·4′	0°46·6′E	X	144
Sturt	Angus	NO4457	56°42·3′	2°54·4′W	X	54
Sturt Common	Shrops	SO7277	52°23·7′	2°24·3′W	X	138
Sturt Fm	Dorset	ST7216	50°56·8′	2°23·5′W	FM	183
Sturt Fm And Stud	Oxon	SP2710	51°47·5′	1°36·1′W	FM	163
Sturton	N Lincs	SE9704	53°31·7′	0°31·8′W	T	112
Sturton by Stow	Lincs	SK8980	53°18·8′	0°39·4′W	T	121
Sturton Grange	Leeds	SE4233	53°47·7′	1°21·3′W	X	105
Sturton Grange	Northum	NU2107	55°21·6′	1°39·7′W	X	81
Sturton High Ho	Notts	SK7583	53°20·6′	0°52·0′W	X	120
Sturton le Steeple	Notts	SK7884	53°21·1′	0°49·3′W	T	120,121
Sturt Pond	Hants	SZ2991	50°43·3′	1°35·0′W	W	196
Sturtwood Fm	Surrey	TQ2142	51°10·1′	0°15·8′W	FM	187
Sturzaker House Fm	Lancs	SD5043	53°53·1′	2°45·2′W	FM	102
Stuston	Suff	TM1377	52°21·2′	1°8·1′E	T	144,156
Stuston Common	Suff	TM1378	52°21·7′	1°8·1′E	X	144,156
Stutfall Castle	Kent	TR1134	51°4·2′	1°1·1′E	X	179,189
Stutfall Castle (Roman Fort)	Kent	TR1134	51°4·2′	1°1·1′E	R	179,189
Stutfield Brook	Oxon	SU3491	51°37·2′	1°30·1′W	W	164,174
Stutherhead	S Lanak	NS7241	55°39·0′	4°1·6′W	X	71
Stutton	N Yks	SE4741	53°52·0′	1°16·7′W	T	105
Stutton	Suff	TM1534	51°58·0′	1°8·2′E	T	169
Stutton Hall	Suff	TM1333	51°57·5′	1°6·4′E	A	168,169
Stutton Ho	Suff	TM1634	51°58·0′	1°9·1′E	X	169
Stutton Mill	Suff	TM1333	51°57·5′	1°6·4′E	X	168,169
Stutton Ness	Essex	TM1532	51°56·9′	1°8·1′E	X	168,169
St Veep	Corn	SX1355	50°22·1′	4°37·4′W	T	200
St Vigeans	Angus	NO6342	56°34·4′	2°35·7′W	T	54
St Vincent	Highld	NH7781	57°48·4′	4°3·7′W	X	21
St Vincent	Lincs	SK9235	52°54·5′	0°37·5′W	X	130
St Vincents	Kent	TQ6458	51°18·1′	0°21·5′E	X	188
St Vincent's Cross	Peterb	TF2507	52°39·0′	0°8·7′W	A	142
St Vincent's Hamlet	Essex	TQ5594	51°37·6′	0°14·8′E	T	167,177
St Warna's Well	I Scilly	SV8807	49°53·2′	6°20·3′W	A	203
Stwarth	Cumbr	NY6902	54°25·0′	2°28·2′W	X	91
St Wenn	Corn	SW9664	50°26·7′	4°52·0′W	T	200
St Weonards	Heref	SO4924	51°55·0′	2°44·1′W	T	162
St Winifred's Well	Shrops	SJ3224	52°48·8′	3°0·1′W	A	126
St Winnolls	Corn	SX3455	50°22·5′	4°19·7′W	X	201
St Winnow	Corn	SX1157	50°23·2′	4°39·2′W	T	200
St Wulstans Fm	Heref	SO5117	51°51·2′	2°42·3′W	FM	162
Styal	Ches	SJ8383	53°20·9′	2°14·9′W	T	109
Styal Country Park	Ches	SJ8383	53°20·9′	2°14·9′W	X	109
Styants Bottom	Kent	TQ5756	51°17·1′	0°15·5′E	T	188
Sty Bank	Cumbr	NY8110	54°29·3′	2°17·2′W	X	91,92
Stybarrow Crag	Cumbr	NY3817	54°32·9′	2°57·1′W	X	90
Stybarrow Dodd	Cumbr	NY3418	54°33·4′	3°0·8′W	H	90
Stybeck Fm	Cumbr	NY3118	54°33·4′	3°3·6′W	FM	90
Styche Fm	Shrops	SJ6435	52°54·9′	2°31·7′W	FM	127
Styche Hall	Shrops	SJ6435	52°54·9′	2°31·7′W	T	127
Stydd	Lancs	SD6535	53°48·9′	2°31·5′W	T	102,103
Stydd Hall	Derby	SK1740	52°57·7′	1°44·4′W	A	119,128
Styford Hall	Northum	NZ0162	54°57·4′	1°58·6′W	X	87
Stygate Fm	Leic	SK7912	52°42·2′	0°49·4′W	FM	129
Sty Head	Cumbr	NY2209	54°28·5′	3°11·8′W	X	89,90
Styhead Gill	Cumbr	NY2210	54°29·0′	3°11·8′W	W	89,90
Styhead Tarn	Cumbr	NY2209	54°28·5′	3°11·8′W	W	89,90
Stylemans Middle	Norf	TF6034	52°53·0′	0°23·1′E	X	132
Stylemouth	Pth & Kin	NO0956	56°41·5′	3°28·7′W	X	52,53
Style Place Fm	Kent	TQ6449	51°13·2′	0°21·3′E	FM	188
Styles Fm	Glos	SO8311	51°48·1′	2°14·4′W	FM	162
Styles Lodge	Northnts	SP8281	52°25·5′	0°47·2′W	X	141
Stymilders	Orkney	HY3413	59°0·2′	3°8·5′W	X	6
Styne Fm	Hants	SU7541	51°10·0′	0°55·2′W	FM	186
Stynie	Moray	NJ3360	57°37·8′	3°6·9′W	X	28
Stynie Glebe	Moray	NJ3361	57°38·3′	3°6·9′W	X	28
St y-Nyll	V of Glam	ST0978	51°29·9′	3°18·3′W	T	171
Stype Grange	Wilts	SU3165	51°23·2′	1°32·9′W	X	174
Styperson Park	Ches	SJ9379	53°18·7′	2°5·9′W	X	118
Stype Wood	Wilts	SU3066	51°23·8′	1°33·7′W	F	174
Styrrup	Notts	SK6090	53°24·4′	1°5·4′W	T	111
Styrrup Carr	Notts	SK5990	53°24·4′	1°6·3′W	X	111
Sty Taing	Orkney	HY6129	59°9·0′	2°40·4′W	X	5
Sty Wick	Orkney	HY6838	59°13·9′	2°33·2′W	W	5
Suainaval	N Eil	NB0730	58°10·0′	6°58·5′W	H	13
Suainebost	N Eil	NB5162	58°28·8′	6°15·8′W	T	8
Suardail	N Eil	NB4930	58°11·5′	6°15·8′W	T	8
Suardal	Highld	NG6221	57°13·3′	5°56·1′W	X	32
Suardalan	Highld	NG8817	57°13·3′	5°30·1′W	X	33
Suardal Burn	Highld	NG2451	57°28·2′	6°35·7′W	W	23
Subberthwaite Common	Cumbr	SD2686	54°16·1′	3°7·8′W	X	96,97
Submarine Forest	Somer	SS8747	51°12·9′	3°36·7′W	X	181

Subscription Br	Norf	TF5410	52°40·2′	0°17·1′E	X	131,143
Succoth	Aberd	NJ4235	57°24·4′	2°57·5′W	X	28
Succoth	Arg & Bt	NN2905	56°12·7′	4°45·0′W	T	56
Succoth	Moray	NJ2935	57°24·3′	3°10·4′W	X	28
Succoth	Moray	NJ3933	57°23·3′	3°0·4′W	X	28
Succoth Lodge	Arg & Bt	NN2126	56°23·8′	4°53·6′W	X	50
Succothmore	Arg & Bt	NN1201	56°10·1′	5°1·2′W	X	56
Sucklawridge	Scot Bord	NT6833	55°35·6′	2°30·0′W	X	74
Suckley	Worcs	SO7251	52°9·6′	2°24·2′W	T	149
Suckley Court	Heref	SO7151	52°9·6′	2°25·0′W	X	149
Suckley Green	Worcs	SO7153	52°10·7′	2°25·1′W	T	149
Suckley Hills	Worcs	SO7352	52°10·2′	2°23·3′W	H	150
Suckley Knowl	Worcs	SO7153	52°10·7′	2°25·1′W	T	149
Suckquoy	Orkney	ND4488	58°46·8′	2°57·6′W	X	7
Sucksted Green	Essex	TL5828	51°55·9′	0°18·3′E	T	167
Suck Stone	Monm	SO5314	51°49·6′	2°40·5′W	X	162
Sudborough	Northnts	SP9682	52°25·9′	0°34·9′W	T	141
Sudbourne	Suff	TM4153	52°7·6′	1°31·7′E	T	156
Sudbourne Beach	Suff	TM4553	52°7·5′	1°35·2′E	X	156
Sudbourne Fm	Suff	TM0367	52°16·0′	0°58·9′E	FM	155
Sudbourne Great Wood	Suff	TM4154	52°8·1′	1°31·7′E	F	156
Sudbourne Marshes	Suff	TM4453	52°7·5′	1°34·3′E	X	156
Sudbourne Park	Suff	TM4051	52°6·5′	1°30·7′E	X	156
Sudbrook	Lincs	SK9744	52°59·3′	0°32·9′W	T	130
Sudbrook	Monm	ST5087	51°35·0′	2°42·9′W	X	172
Sudbrooke	Lincs	TF0376	53°16·5′	0°26·9′W	T	121
Sudbrooke Park	Lincs	TF0476	53°16·5′	0°26·0′W	X	121
Sudbrook Hill Fm	Lincs	SK9645	52°59·9′	0°33·8′W	FM	130
Sudbrook Ho	Lincs	SK9846	53°0·4′	0°32·0′W	X	130
Sudbrook Park	Rich	TQ1872	51°26·3′	0°17·7′W	X	176
Sudburn Beck	Durham	NZ1219	54°34·2′	1°48·4′W	W	92
Sudbury	Brent	TQ1685	51°33·3′	0°19·2′W	T	176
Sudbury	Derby	SK1632	52°53·4′	1°45·3′W	T	128
Sudbury	Suff	TL8741	52°2·4′	0°44·0′E	T	155
Sudbury Coppice	Derby	SK1535	52°55·0′	1°46·2′W	F	128
Sudbury Fm	Oxon	SU3999	51°41·5′	1°25·8′W	FM	164
Sudbury Hill Stations	Ealing	TQ1585	51°33·4′	0°20·1′W	X	176
Sudbury's Fm	Essex	TQ7396	51°38·4′	0°30·4′E	FM	167
Sudcott	Corn	SX2296	50°44·4′	4°31·0′W	X	190
Suddell Ho	Lincs	TA1100	53°29·3′	0°19·2′W	X	113
Sudden	Roch	SD8811	53°36·0′	2°10·5′W	T	109
Suddene Park Fm	Wilts	SU2461	51°21·1′	1°38·9′W	FM	174
Suddern Hill	Hants	SU2637	51°8·1′	1°37·3′W	H	184
Suddle Wood	Lincs	TA1709	53°34·1′	0°13·6′W	F	113
Suddon	Devon	SS4111	50°52·8′	4°15·2′W	X	190
Suddon Fm	Devon	SS4614	50°54·5′	4°11·0′W	FM	180,190
Suddon Grange	Somer	ST6928	51°3·3′	2°26·2′W	X	183
Suddon Hall	Suff	TM2065	52°14·6′	1°13·8′E	X	156
Sudeley Castle	Glos	SP0327	51°56·7′	1°57·0′W	A	163
Sudeley Hill	Glos	SP0427	51°56·7′	1°56·1′W	X	163
Sudeley Lodge	Glos	SP0427	51°56·7′	1°56·1′W	X	163
Sudell's Fm	Lancs	SD5935	53°48·8′	2°36·9′W	FM	102
Sudgrove	Glos	SO9307	51°45·9′	2°5·7′W	T	163
Sudlow Fm	Ches	SJ7378	53°18·1′	2°23·9′W	FM	118
Suem	N Eil	NF9985	57°45·5′	7°3·2′W	X	18
Suenish	N Eil	NF8978	57°41·3′	7°12·7′W	X	18
Sueno's Stone	Moray	NJ0459	57°36·9′	3°36·0′W	A	27
Suffenton	Corn	SX0580	50°35·5′	4°44·9′W	X	200
Sufficient Hill	Scot Bord	NY4585	55°9·6′	2°51·4′W	H	79
Suffield	Norf	TG2332	52°50·6′	1°19·1′E	T	133
Suffield	N Yks	SE9890	54°18·0′	0°29·2′W	T	94,101
Suffield Fm	Derby	SK2234	52°54·4′	1°40·0′W	FM	128
Suffield Fm	Surrey	SU9247	51°13·1′	0°40·6′W	FM	186
Suffield Heights	N Yks	SE9789	54°17·5′	0°30·2′W	X	94,101
Suffield Ings	N Yks	SE9889	54°17·5′	0°29·2′W	X	94,101
Suffield Quarry	N Yks	SE9790	54°18·0′	0°30·1′W	X	94,101
Suffolk Coastal Path	Suff	TM4764	52°13·3′	1°37·4′E	X	156
Suffolk Coast and Heaths Path	Suff	TM3439	52°0·2′	1°25·0′E	X	169
Suffolk Showground	Suff	TM2142	52°2·2′	1°13·7′E	X	169
Suffolk Wild Life Country Park	Suff	TM5186	52°25·1′	1°41·9′E	X	156
Sufton	Heref	SO5737	52°2·0′	2°37·2′W	X	149
Sugar Brook	Ches	SJ7782	53°20·3′	2°20·3′W	W	109
Sugar Brook Fm	Ches	SJ7783	53°20·8′	2°20·3′W	FM	109
Sugar Fen	Norf	TF6920	52°45·3′	0°30·7′E	X	132
Sugar Hill	Dorset	SY8892	50°43·9′	2°9·8′W	X	194
Sugar Hill	N Yks	SE1588	54°17·5′	1°45·8′W	X	99
Sugar Hill	N Yks	SE1794	54°20·7′	1°43·9′W	X	99
Sugar Hill	N Yks	SE2273	54°9·4′	1°39·4′W	X	99
Sugar Hill	N Yks	SE4390	54°18·5′	1°19·9′W	X	99
Sugar Hill	Wilts	SU2378	51°30·3′	1°39·7′W	X	174
Sugar Loaf	Carm	SN8342	52°4·1′	3°42·0′W	H	147,160
Sugar Loaf	Devon	SS1444	51°10·1′	4°39·3′W	X	180
Sugarloaf	D & G	NX6543	54°46·1′	4°5·5′W	X	83,84
Sugarloaf	Kent	TQ9935	51°5·0′	0°50·9′E	X	189
Sugar Loaf	Monm	SO2718	51°51·6′	3°3·2′W	H	161
Sugar Loaf	Powys	SO0471	52°20·0′	3°24·1′W	H	136,147
Sugarloaf	Staffs	SK0956	53°6·3′	1°51·5′W	X	119
Sugar Loaf Fm	Staffs	SO8881	52°25·8′	2°10·2′W	FM	139
Sugarloaf Hill	Kent	TR2237	51°5·6′	1°10·6′E	H	179,189
Sugar Loaf Hill	N Yks	SD8363	54°4·0′	2°15·2′W	H	98
Sugarloaf Hill	Somer	SS8049	51°13·9′	3°42·7′W	H	181
Sugar Loaf or Knot	Lancs	SD6750	53°56·9′	2°29·8′W	X	103
Sugarloaf, The	I of M	SC1966	54°3·7′	4°45·5′W	X	95
Sugar Sands	Northum	NU2616	55°26·5′	1°34·9′W	X	81
Sugarswell Fm	Oxon	SP3643	52°5·3′	1°28·1′W	FM	151
Sugdon	Wrekin	SJ6014	52°43·6′	2°35·1′W	X	127
Sugham Fm	Surrey	TQ3844	51°10·9′	0°1·1′W	FM	187
Sugil	Shetld	HU5892	60°36·7′	0°55·9′W	X	1,2
Sug Marsh	N Yks	SE1453	53°58·6′	1°46·8′W	X	104
Sugnall	Staffs	SJ7930	52°52·3′	2°18·3′W	T	127
Sugnall Park	Staffs	SJ7930	52°52·3′	2°18·3′W	X	127
Sugwas Court	Heref	SO4540	52°3·6′	2°47·7′W	X	148,149,161
Sugwas Fm	Heref	SO4541	52°4·1′	2°47·7′W	FM	148,149,161
Sugwas Pool	Heref	SO4541	52°4·1′	2°47·7′W	T	148,149,161
Sugworth Fm	Oxon	SP5100	51°42·0′	1°15·3′W	FM	164
Sugworth Fm	W Susx	TQ3226	51°1·3′	0°6·7′W	FM	187,198
Sugworth Hall	Sheff	SK2389	53°24·1′	1°38·8′W	X	110
Suidh' a' Mhinn	Highld	NG4068	57°37·9′	6°20·9′W	H	23

Suidh' an Fhir-bhig or The Child's Seat	Highld	NC9625	58°12·4′	3°45·7′W	H	17
Suidheacha-sealg	N Eil	NF8967	57°35·4′	7°11·8′W	X	18
Suidhe Beag	Moray	NJ2624	57°18·3′	3°13·2′W	X	37
Suidhe Biorach	Highld	NG5112	57°8·1′	6°6·5′W	X	32
Suidhe Chatain	Arg & Bt	NS0955	55°45·3′	5°2·2′W	H	63
Suidhe Fhearghas	N Ayr	NR9945	55°39·7′	5°11·3′W	X	62,69
Suidhe Ghuirmain	Highld	NH3827	57°18·6′	4°40·9′W	H	26
Suidhe Phadruig	N Ayr	NR9026	55°29·2′	5°19·0′W	X	68,69
Suidh Fhinn	Highld	NG4642	57°24·1′	6°13·2′W	H	23
Suie	Moray	NJ2724	57°18·3′	3°12·2′W	X	37
Suie Burn	Aberd	NJ5521	57°16·9′	2°44·3′W	W	37
Suie Cairn	Aberd	NJ5523	57°18·0′	2°44·4′W	X	37
Suie Foot	Aberd	NJ5424	57°18·5′	2°45·4′W	X	37
Suie Hill	Aberd	NJ5523	57°18·0′	2°44·4′W	H	37
Suie Hill	D & G	NX3585	55°8·2′	4°34·9′W	H	77
Suie Hill	D & G	NX7650	54°50·0′	3°55·4′W	H	84
Sui Fea	Orkney	HY1903	58°54·7′	3°23·9′W	H	7
Suifea Lochs	Orkney	HY1901	58°53·6′	3°23·9′W	W	7
Suil a' Bhadain Duinn	Highld	NC4339	58°19·0′	4°40·3′W	X	16
Sùil á Ghriama	Highld	NC4127	58°12·5′	4°41·9′W	W	16
Sùil a' Ghriama	Highld	NC4130	58°14·1′	4°42·0′W	W	16
Sùil Bó	Arg & Bt	NM5142	56°30·5′	6°2·4′W	X	47,48
Sùileabhaig	Highld	NG2703	57°2·5′	6°29·6′W	W	39
Suileag	Highld	NC1421	58°8·6′	5°9·1′W	X	15
Sùil Ghorm	Arg & Bt	NM2865	56°42·1′	6°26·2′W	X	46,47
Suilven	Highld	NC1517	58°6·5′	5°7·9′W	H	15
Suisgill Burn	Highld	NC9026	58°12·8′	3°51·9′W	W	17
Suisgill Lodge	Highld	NC9023	58°11·2′	3°51·8′W	X	17
Suisnish	Highld	NG5535	57°20·6′	6°3·9′W	T	24,32
Suisnish	Highld	NG5916	57°10·6′	5°58·8′W	T	32
Suisnish Hill	Highld	NG5634	57°20·1′	6°2·8′W	H	24,32
Suisnish Point	Highld	NG5534	57°20·1′	6°3·8′W	X	24,32
Sukers Lodge	Staffs	SK0213	52°43·1′	1°57·8′W	X	128
Sukka Mire	Shetld	HU3148	60°13·2′	1°25·9′W	X	3
Sukka Mires	Shetld	HU5282	60°31·4′	1°2·7′W	X	1,2,3
Sula	Shetld	HP6613	60°47·9′	0°46·7′W	X	1
Suladale	Highld	NG3753	57°29·7′	6°22·9′W	T	23
Sulaisiadar	N Eil	NB5335	58°14·3′	6°12·0′W	T	8
Sula Sgeir	N Eil	HW6230	59°5·7′	6°8·8′W	X	8
Sula Skerry	Highld	NG3138	57°21·4′	6°27·9′W	X	23,32
Sulber	N Yks	SD7873	54°9·4′	2°19·8′W	X	98
Sulber Laithe	N Yks	SD9553	53°58·6′	2°4·2′W	X	103
Sulber Pot	N Yks	SD7773	54°9·4′	2°20·7′W	X	98
Sulbrick	I of M	SC3174	54°8·3′	4°34·8′W	X	95
Sulby	I of M	SC3780	54°11·6′	4°29·5′W	X	95
Sulby	I of M	SC3894	54°19·2′	4°29·0′W	T	95
Sulby Abbey	Northnts	SP6580	52°25·1′	1°2·3′W	X	141
Sulby Bridge	I of M	SC3994	54°19·2′	4°28·1′W	X	95
Sulby Covert	Northnts	SP6681	52°25·6′	1°1·4′W	F	141
Sulby Glen	I of M	SC3891	54°17·6′	4°28·9′W	X	95
Sulby Grange	Northnts	SP6680	52°25·1′	1°1·4′W	X	141
Sulby Lodge	Northnts	SP6682	52°26·2′	1°1·3′W	X	141
Sulby Reservoir	I of M	SC3788	54°16·0′	4°29·8′W	W	95
Sulby Resr	Northnts	SP6581	52°25·6′	1°2·2′W	W	141
Sulby River	I of M	SC3780	54°11·6′	4°29·5′W	W	95
Sulby River	I of M	SC3889	54°16·5′	4°28·9′W	W	95
Sulby River	I of M	SC4094	54°19·2′	4°27·2′W	W	95
Sulby Straight	I of M	SC3894	54°19·2′	4°29·0′W	X	95
Sule Skerry	Orkney	HX6224	59°5·1′	4°24·0′W	X	6
Sule Stack	Orkney	HX5617	59°1·2′	4°30·0′W	X	6
Sulgrave	Northnts	SP5545	52°6·3′	1°11·4′W	T	152
Sulgrave	Sund	NZ3157	54°54·6′	1°30·6′W	T	88
Sulgrave Manor	Northnts	SP5645	52°6·3′	1°10·5′W	A	152
Sulham	W Berks	SU6474	51°27·9′	1°4·3′W	T	175
Sulham Ho	W Berks	SU6474	51°27·9′	1°4·3′W	X	175
Sulhampstead	W Berks	SU6368	51°24·7′	1°5·3′W	T	175
Sulhampstead Abbots	W Berks	SU6467	51°24·1′	1°4·4′W	T	175
Sulhampstead Bannister Upper End	W Berks	SU6368	51°24·7′	1°5·3′W	T	175
Sulham Wood	W Berks	SU6475	51°28·5′	1°4·3′W	F	175
Sulis Manor	Bath & NE Somer	ST7361	51°21·1′	2°22·9′W	X	172
Sullanan Ard	N Eil	NB2419	58°4·7′	6°40·4′W	H	13,14
Sulland	Orkney	HY5040	59°14·9′	2°52·1′W	X	5
Sulland's Geo	Orkney	HY5141	59°15·4′	2°51·1′W	X	5
Sulleys Manor Fm	Suff	TM0438	52°0·4′	0°58·7′E	FM	155
Sullington	W Susx	TQ0913	50°54·6′	0°26·6′W	T	198
Sullington Hill	W Susx	TQ0912	50°54·1′	0°26·6′W	X	198
Sullington Warren	W Susx	TQ0914	50°55·1′	0°26·6′W	T	198
Sullom	Shetld	HU3573	60°26·6′	1°21·3′W	T	2,3
Sullom End	Lancs	SD5243	53°53·1′	2°43·4′W	X	102
Sullom Side	Lancs	SD5244	53°53·6′	2°43·4′W	X	102
Sullom Voe	Shetld	HU3773	60°26·6′	1°19·2′W	W	2,3
Sullom Voe Terminal	Shetld	HU4076	60°28·2′	1°15·9′W	X	2,3
Sully	Somer	SS9439	51°8·7′	3°30·5′W	X	181
Sully	V of Glam	ST1568	51°24·5′	3°12·9′W	T	171
Sully Bay	V of Glam	ST1567	51°24·0′	3°12·9′W	W	171
Sully Brook	V of Glam	ST1669	51°25·1′	3°12·1′W	W	171
Sully Island	V of Glam	ST1667	51°24·0′	3°12·1′W	X	171
Sully-Penarth Cycle Route	V of Glam	ST1768	51°24·5′	3°11·2′W	X	171
Sulma Water	Shetld	HU2555	60°17·0′	1°32·4′W	W	3
Sulock, The	Shetld	HU5383	60°31·9′	1°1·6′W	X	1,2,3
Sulphur Well	Carm	SN6617	51°50·4′	3°56·3′W	W	159
Sultigeo	Orkney	HY3011	58°59·1′	3°12·6′W	X	6
Sumardale	Highld	NG3735	57°20·0′	6°21·8′W	X	32
Sumardale River	Highld	NG3736	57°20·6′	6°21·8′W	W	23,32
Sumburgh	Shetld	HU4009	59°52·1′	1°16·7′W	T	4
Sumburgh Airport	Shetld	HU3910	59°52·7′	1°17·7′W	X	4
Sumburgh Head	Shetld	HU4007	59°51·0′	1°16·7′W	X	4
Sumburgh Ho	Cumbr	NY5647	54°49·2′	2°40·7′W	X	86
Sumburgh Roost	Shetld	HU4007	59°51·0′	1°16·7′W	W	4
Summerbridge	N Yks	SE2062	54°3·5′	1°41·3′W	T	99
Summer Burn	Orkney	ND2295	58°50·4′	3°20·6′W	W	7
Summer Carr	N Yks	SE3988	54°17·4′	1°23·6′W	X	99
Summer Cleuch	D & G	NT2106	55°20·8′	3°14·3′W	X	79
Summer Close	Ches	SJ9877	53°17·6′	2°1·4′W	X	118
Summercourt	Corn	SW8856	50°22·2′	4°58·5′W	T	200
Summercroft Fm	N Lincs	TA0923	53°41·8′	0°20·5′W	FM	107,112
Summer Cross	Derby	SK1475	53°16·5′	1°47·0′W	X	119

Summer Ct	Heref	SO3354	52°11·0′	2°58·4′W	X	148,149
Summerden	Hants	SU8534	51°6·2′	0°46·8′W	X	186
Summerdown	Devon	SY1997	50°46·3′	3°8·5′W	X	192,193
Summer Down	Wilts	ST9148	51°14·1′	2°7·3′W	X	184
Summer Down	Wilts	SU0650	51°15·2′	1°54·5′W	X	184
Summer Down	Wilts	SU2155	51°17·9′	1°41·5′W	X	174
Summer Down Fm	Hants	SU5651	51°15·6′	1°11·5′W	FM	185
Summerend Fm	Norf	TF7515	52°42·5′	0°35·8′E	FM	132
Summerer Fm	Lancs	SD3837	53°49·8′	2°56·1′W	FM	102
Summerfield	D & G	NX9877	55°4·9′	3°35·4′W	X	84
Summerfield	D & G	NY1167	54°59·6′	3°23·0′W	X	85
Summerfield	Kent	TR2755	51°15·2′	1°15·6′E	T	179
Summerfield	Norf	TF7438	52°54·9′	0°35·7′E	T	132
Summerfield	Northum	NZ0551	54°51·5′	1°54·9′W	X	87
Summerfield	N Yks	SE6681	54°13·5′	0°58·8′W	X	100
Summerfield	Pth & Kin	NO1610	56°16·8′	3°21·0′W	X	58
Summerfield	Worcs	SO8373	52°21·5′	2°14·6′W	T	138
Summerfield Fm	N Yks	NZ4501	54°24·4′	1°18·0′W	FM	93
Summerfield Ho	Lancs	SD6177	54°11·5′	2°35·4′W	X	97
Summerfield House Fm	N Yks	NZ3803	54°25·5′	1°24·4′W	FM	93
Summerfield Park	Birm	SP0387	52°29·1′	1°56·9′W	T	139
Summerfields	Derby	SK2215	52°44·2′	1°40·0′W	X	128
Summer Fields	E Susx	TQ8009	50°51·4′	0°33·8′E	X	199
Summerfields Hill	Lincs	SK9144	52°59·4′	0°38·3′W	X	130
Summer Fm	Devon	SS7913	50°54·5′	3°42·9′W	FM	180
Summerford Fm	E Susx	TQ4936	51°6·5′	0°8·1′E	FM	188
Summergangs	K upon H	TA1130	53°45·5′	0°18·6′W	T	107
Summergil Brook	Powys	SO1958	52°13·1′	3°10·7′W	W	148
Summergrove Hall	Cumbr	NX9915	54°31·5′	3°33·2′W	X	89
Summerham Brook	Wilts	ST9560	51°20·6′	2°3·9′W	W	173
Summer Heath	Bucks	SU7490	51°36·5′	0°55·5′W	T	175
Summerhill	Angus	NO5646	56°36·5′	2°42·6′W	X	54
Summerhill	Arg & Bt	NR7221	55°26·0′	5°35·8′W	X	68
Summerhill	C of Aber	NJ9006	57°8·9′	2°9·5′W	T	38
Summer Hill	Cumbr	SD1182	54°13·8′	3°21·5′W	X	96
Summer Hill	Cumbr	SD3083	54°14·5′	3°4·0′W	X	96,97
Summer Hill	Cumbr	SD4482	54°14·1′	2°51·1′W	X	97
Summerhill	D & G	NX6577	55°4·4′	4°6·4′W	X	77,84
Summerhill	D & G	NX6766	54°58·5′	4°4·3′W	X	83,84
Summerhill	D & G	NX7665	54°58·1′	3°55·8′W	X	84
Summerhill	D & G	NX9481	55°7·0′	3°39·3′W	X	78
Summerhill	D & G	NX9576	55°4·3′	3°38·2′W	X	84
Summer Hill	E Loth	NT6464	55°52·3′	2°34·1′W	H	67
Summer Hill	E Susx	TQ5807	50°50·7′	0°15·0′E	T	199
Summerhill	Glos	SP1224	51°55·1′	1°49·1′W	X	163
Summerhill	Heref	SO2343	52°5·0′	3°7·0′W	X	148,161
Summerhill	I of M	SC3897	54°20·8′	4°29·1′W	X	95
Summer Hill	Kent	TQ8931	51°3·1′	0°42·2′E	X	189
Summerhill	Newp	ST3288	51°35·4′	2°58·5′W	T	171
Summerhill	N Lanak	NS7471	55°55·2′	4°0·5′W	X	64
Summerhill	Norf	TF6736	52°54·0′	0°29·4′E	X	132
Summerhill	Pemb	SM8920	51°50·6′	5°3·4′W	X	157,158
Summerhill	Pemb	SN1507	51°44·1′	4°40·4′W	T	158
Summer Hill	Sand	SO9693	52°32·3′	2°3·1′W	T	139
Summerhill	Staffs	SJ8828	52°51·2′	2°10·3′W	X	127
Summerhill	Staffs	SJ9645	53°0·4′	2°3·2′W	X	118
Summerhill	Staffs	SJ9833	52°53·9′	2°1·4′W	X	127
Summerhill	Staffs	SK0062	53°9·5′	1°59·6′W	X	119
Summerhill	Staffs	SK0367	53°12·2′	1°56·9′W	X	119
Summerhill	Staffs	SK0705	52°38·8′	1°53·4′W	T	139
Summer Hill	W Berks	SU3661	51°21·0′	1°28·6′W	X	174
Summerhill	Worcs	SO8176	52°23·1′	2°16·4′W	T	138
Summer Hill	Worcs	SO9363	52°16·1′	2°5·8′W	H	150
Summerhill	Wrekin	SJ7219	52°46·3′	2°24·5′W	T	127
Summerhill	Wrex	SJ3153	53°4·4′	3°1·4′W	T	117
Summerhill Fm	Derby	SK1565	53°11·2′	1°46·1′W	FM	119
Summerhill Fm	Essex	TQ7191	51°35·7′	0°28·5′E	FM	178
Summerhill Fm	Kent	TQ8244	51°10·2′	0°36·6′E	FM	188
Summer Hill Fm	Warw	SP1153	52°10·7′	1°50·0′W	FM	150
Summerhope Burn	Scot Bord	NT2220	55°28·3′	3°13·6′W	W	73
Summer House	Brad	SE0143	53°53·2′	1°58·7′W	X	104
Summerhouse	Darl	NZ2019	54°34·2′	1°41·0′W	T	93
Summerhouse	Falk	NS8972	55°56·0′	3°46·2′W	X	65
Summerhouse Beck	Darl	NZ2018	54°33·7′	1°41·0′W	W	93
Summer House Fm	Cambs	TL3842	52°3·8′	0°1·2′E	FM	154
Summerhouse Fm	Northnts	SP6254	52°11·1′	1°5·2′W	FM	152
Summer House Fm	Wilts	SU0189	51°36·2′	1°58·7′W	FM	173
Summer House Head	Lancs	SD5555	53°59·6′	2°40·8′W	X	102
Summer House Hill	Devon	SS7248	51°13·2′	3°49·6′W	H	180
Summerhouse Hill	Kent	TR1637	51°5·7′	1°5·5′E	H	179,189
Summer House Hill	Norf	TG0340	52°55·4′	1°1·6′E	X	133
Summer House Hill	Somer	ST5615	50°56·2′	2°37·2′W	H	183
Summerhouse Hill	Warw	SP0865	52°17·2′	1°52·6′W	H	150
Summerhouse Point	V of Glam	SS9966	51°23·3′	3°26·7′W	X	170
Summer Isles	Highld	NB9706	58°0·1′	5°25·6′W	X	15
Summerlands	Cumbr	SD5386	54°16·3′	2°42·9′W	T	97
Summerlands	Somer	ST5416	50°56·7′	2°38·9′W	T	183
Summerlands Fm	Wilts	ST9579	51°30·8′	2°3·9′W	FM	173
Summerleaze	Newp	ST4284	51°33·4′	2°49·8′W	T	171,172
Summerleaze Fm	Wilts	ST8929	51°3·8′	2°9·0′W	FM	184
Summerlees	Oxon	SU5590	51°36·6′	1°12·0′W	X	164,174
Summerley	Derby	SK3778	53°18·1′	1°26·3′W	T	119
Summerley	Hants	SU6640	51°9·6′	1°3·0′W	X	185,186
Summerleys	Bucks	SP7903	51°43·4′	0°51·0′W	X	165
Summer Lodge	N Yks	SD9695	54°21·3′	2°3·3′W	X	98
Summer Lodge Beck	N Yks	SD9695	54°21·3′	2°3·3′W	W	98
Summer Lodge Moor	N Yks	SD9595	54°21·3′	2°4·2′W	X	98
Summer Lodge Tarn	N Yks	SD9594	54°20·7′	2°4·2′W	W	98
Summerlug Hill	Dorset	SU0604	50°50·4′	1°54·5′W	X	195
Summer Moor	Devon	SS6227	51°1·8′	3°57·7′W	X	180
Summer of Hoy	Orkney	ND2296	58°50·9′	3°20·6′W	X	6,7
Summerpit Bottom	Suff	TL8178	52°22·4′	0°39·9′E	X	144
Summerpit Fm	Suff	TL8278	52°22·4′	0°40·8′E	FM	144
Summerrods	Northum	NY9063	54°57·9′	2°8·9′W	X	87
Summersbrook Wood	E Susx	TQ5417	50°56·1′	0°11·9′E	F	199
Summersbury	I of W	SZ5482	50°38·3′	1°13·8′W	X	196
Summerscales	N Yks	SE1054	53°59·2′	1°50·4′W	T	104
Summersdale	W Susx	SU8606	50°51·1′	0°46·3′W	T	197
Summerseat	Bury	SD7914	53°37·6′	2°18·6′W	T	109
Summers Fm	Hants	SU7547	51°13·3′	0°55·2′W	FM	186

Summersgill	Lancs	SD6463	54°3·9′	2°32·6′W	X	97
Summersgill Fell	Lancs	SD6361	54°2·9′	2°33·5′W	X	97
Summerside	C of Edin	NT3168	55°54·3′	3°5·8′W	X	66
Summerside	N Lanak	NS8654	55°46·2′	3°48·6′W	X	65,72
Summer Side	N Yks	SE1477	54°11·6′	1°46·7′W	X	99
Summerside	Shetld	HU2450	60°14·3′	1°33·5′W	X	3
Summerside Knowe	Scot Bord	NT1015	55°25·5′	3°24·9′W	X	78
Summer Sides Wood	Cumbr	SD3687	54°16·7′	2°58·6′W	F	96,97
Summerslade Down	Wilts	ST8737	51°8·2′	2°10·8′W	X	183
Summers Place	W Susx	TQ0927	51°2·1′	0°26·3′W	X	187,198
Summerstead Fm	Hants	SU6956	51°18·2′	1°0·2′W	FM	175,186
Summerston	C of Glas	NS5670	55°54·4′	4°17·8′W	T	64
Summerstone Lodge	N Yks	SE0977	54°11·6′	1°51·3′W	X	99
Summerston Fm	C of Glas	NS5772	55°55·4′	4°16·9′W	FM	64
Summerstown	Bucks	SP6522	51°53·8′	1°2·9′W	T	164,165
Summerstown	Wan	TQ2672	51°26·2′	0°10·8′W	T	176
Summerswood Fm	Herts	TQ2199	51°40·8′	0°14·6′W	FM	166,176
Summerton	Highld	NH8581	57°48·5′	3°55·7′W	X	21
Summerton	Orkney	ND4796	58°51·2′	2°54·6′W	X	6,7
Summerton	Pemb	SM9829	51°55·6′	4°55·9′W	X	157,158
Summerton	Pemb	SN0602	51°41·2′	4°48·0′W	X	158
Summertown	Oxon	SP5108	51°46·3′	1°15·3′W	T	164
Summertree Fm	E Susx	TQ6416	50°55·4′	0°20·4′E	FM	199
Summertree Fm	N Yks	SE8279	54°12·2′	0°44·2′W	FM	100
Summerville	D & G	NX9676	55°4·3′	3°37·3′W	T	84
Summerville	Northum	NU0301	55°18·4′	1°56·7′W	X	81
Summerville Fm	Stock on T	NZ4122	54°35·7′	1°21·5′W	FM	93
Summerway	Somer	SS9033	51°5·4′	3°33·9′W	X	181
Summerwell Fm	Devon	SS2719	50°56·9′	4°27·4′W	FM	190
Summerwell Fm	Glos	ST9095	51°39·5′	2°8·3′W	FM	163
Summer Wood Ho	N Yks	SE2264	54°4·5′	1°39·4′W	X	99
Summery	Orkney	ND2790	58°47·7′	3°15·3′W	X	7
Summit	Oldham	SD9009	53°34·9′	2°8·7′W	T	109
Summit	Roch	SD8411	53°36·0′	2°14·1′W	T	109
Summit	Roch	SD9418	53°39·7′	2°5·0′W	T	109
Summit Cottages	Northum	NY9384	55°9·3′	2°6·2′W	X	80
Summit Cotts	Northum	NU1412	55°24·4′	1°46·3′W	X	81
Summit Fm	N Yks	SE9472	54°8·4′	0°33·2′W	FM	101
Summit Ho	E Yorks	SE9153	53°58·1′	0°36·3′W	X	106
Summit Sta	Gwyn	SH6054	53°4·1′	4°5·0′W	X	115
Summit Sta	I of M	SC3987	54°15·5′	4°27·9′W	X	95
Summons Head	Shetld	HT9440	60°8·9′	2°6·0′W	X	4
Sumners	Essex	TL4307	51°44·8′	0°4·7′E	X	167
Sumner's Fm	Essex	TQ5996	51°38·6′	0°18·3′E	FM	167,177
Sumula	N Eil	NL6087	56°51·3′	7°34·3′W	X	31
Sunadale	Arg & Bt	NR8144	55°38·7′	5°28·4′W	X	62,69
Sunadale Cott	Arg & Bt	NR8145	55°39·2′	5°28·4′W	X	62,69
Sunagill	Highld	NG2045	57°24·8′	6°39·3′W	X	23
Sùnam	N Eil	NG0085	57°45·5′	7°2·2′W	X	18
Sùnamul	N Eil	NF8056	57°29·1′	7°20·0′W	X	22
Sunart	Highld	NM7966	56°44·3′	5°36·4′W	X	40
Sun Bank	N Yks	SE1454	53°59·2′	1°46·8′W	X	104
Sun Beck	N Yks	SE4671	54°8·2′	1°17·3′W	W	100
Sunbiggin	Cumbr	NY6508	54°28·2′	2°32·0′W	X	91
Sunbiggin Tarn	Cumbr	NY6707	54°27·7′	2°30·1′W	W	91
Sunbrick	Cumbr	SD2873	54°9·1′	3°5·7′W	T	96,97
Sunbrough	Northum	NU0406	55°21·1′	1°55·8′W	X	81
Sunbury	Surrey	TQ1069	51°24·8′	0°24·7′W	T	176
Sunbury Common	Surrey	TQ0970	51°25·3′	0°25·5′W	T	176
Sunbury Court	Surrey	TQ1169	51°24·8′	0°23·8′W	X	176
Sunbury Lock	Surrey	TQ1068	51°24·2′	0°24·7′W	X	176
Sun Court	Suff	TM0243	52°3·1′	0°57·2′E	A	155
Sunday Burn	Northum	NY6973	55°3·3′	2°28·7′W	W	86,87
Sundayshill	S Glos	ST6793	51°38·3′	2°28·2′W	T	162,172
Sundaysight	Northum	NY8189	55°11·9′	2°17·5′W	X	80
Sundayswells	Aberd	NJ6103	57°7·2′	2°38·2′W	X	37
Sundayswells Croft	Aberd	NJ6002	57°6·7′	2°39·2′W	X	37
Sundaywell	D & G	NX8184	55°8·4′	3°51·6′W	X	78
Sundaywell Moor	D & G	NX7984	55°8·4′	3°53·5′W	X	78
Sunderland	Cumbr	NY1735	54°42·4′	3°16·9′W	T	89,90
Sunderland	Kent	TQ9461	51°19·1′	0°47·4′E	A	178
Sunderland	Lancs	SD4255	53°59·5′	2°52·7′W	T	102
Sunderland	Scot Bord	NT4731	55°34·4′	2°50·0′W	X	73
Sunderland	Sund	NZ3957	54°54·6′	1°23·1′W	T	88
Sunderland Bank	Lancs	SD3956	54°0·0′	2°55·4′W	X	102
Sunderland Bridge	Durham	NZ2637	54°43·9′	1°35·4′W	T	93
Sunderland Brows	Lancs	SD4256	54°0·1′	2°52·7′W	X	102
Sunderland Fm	Arg & Bt	NR2464	55°47·7′	6°23·8′W	FM	60
Sunderland Fm	Durham	NY9439	54°45·0′	2°5·2′W	FM	91,92
Sunderland Fm	E Yorks	TA2729	53°44·7′	0°4·0′W	FM	107
Sunderland Fm	Norf	TF7839	52°55·4′	0°39·3′E	FM	132
Sunderland Fm	Northum	NY9494	55°14·7′	2°5·2′W	FM	80
Sunderland Hall	Lancs	SD6233	53°47·8′	2°34·2′W	X	102,103
Sunderland Hall	Scot Bord	NT4731	55°34·4′	2°50·0′W	X	73
Sunderland Hall Fm	Beds	TL2245	52°5·6′	0°12·7′W	FM	153
Sunderland Heads	Cumbr	NY1735	54°42·4′	3°16·9′W	X	89,90
Sunderland Hill	Arg & Bt	NR2463	55°47·1′	6°23·7′W	H	60
Sunderland Point	Lancs	SD4255	53°59·5′	2°52·7′W	X	102
Sunderlandwick Hall	E Yorks	TA0155	53°59·1′	0°27·2′W	X	106,107
Sunderlandwick Village	E Yorks	TA0155	53°59·1′	0°27·2′W	A	106,107
Sunderleigh Fm	Devon	SS9722	50°59·5′	3°27·7′W	FM	181
Sunderton	Shrops	SJ5316	52°44·6′	2°41·4′W	X	126
Sundey Hill Fm	Wilts	SU0086	51°34·6′	1°59·6′W	FM	173
Sundhope	Scot Bord	NT3325	55°31·1′	3°3·2′W	T	73
Sundhope	Scot Bord	NY5099	55°17·2′	2°46·8′W	X	79
Sundhope Burn	Scot Bord	NT3224	55°30·6′	3°4·2′W	W	73
Sundhope Burn	Scot Bord	NY5099	55°17·2′	2°46·8′W	W	79
Sundhope Flow	Scot Bord	NY4999	55°17·2′	2°47·7′W	X	79
Sundhopehead	Scot Bord	NT3223	55°30·0′	3°4·2′W	X	73
Sundhope Height	Scot Bord	NT3423	55°30·0′	3°2·3′W	H	73
Sundhope Rig	Scot Bord	NT5000	55°17·7′	2°46·8′W	X	79
Sun Dodd	Durham	NY9413	54°31·0′	2°5·1′W	X	91,92
Sundon Hills	Beds	TL0528	51°56·7′	0°27·9′W	X	166
Sundon Park	Luton	TL0525	51°55·0′	0°28·0′W	T	166
Sundorne Fm	Shrops	SJ5215	52°44·1′	2°42·3′W	FM	126
Sundrabister	Shetld	HU4884	60°32·5′	1°7·0′W	X	1,2,3
Sundridge	Brom	TQ4170	51°24·9′	0°2·1′E	T	177
Sundridge	Kent	TQ4855	51°16·7′	0°7·7′E	T	188
Sundridge Hill Fm	Kent	TQ4758	51°18·4′	0°6·9′E	FM	188
Sundridge Park	Brom	TQ4170	51°24·9′	0°2·1′E	X	177
Sundridge Place	Kent	TQ4854	51°16·2′	0°7·7′E	X	188
Sundrum Castle	S Ayr	NS4121	55°27·7′	4°30·5′W	A	70
Sundrum Mains	S Ayr	NS4020	55°27·1′	4°31·4′W	X	70
Sunflower Fm	Bucks	SP6429	51°57·6′	1°3·7′W	FM	164,165
Sunflower Fm	Suff	TM3069	52°16·5′	1°22·7′E	FM	156
Sun Fm	Staffs	SJ9931	52°52·8′	2°0·5′W	FM	127
Sung	Shetld	HU1950	60°14·3′	1°38·9′W	X	3
Sun Green	Tames	SJ9899	53°29·5′	2°1·4′W	T	109
Sun Hill	Cald	SE0133	53°47·8′	1°58·7′W	X	104
Sunhill	Glos	SP1102	51°43·2′	1°50·1′W	T	163
Sunhill	Glos	SP1102	51°43·2′	1°50·1′W	X	163
Sun Hill	N Yks	SE1689	54°18·0′	1°44·8′W	X	99
Sunhill Fm	Stock	SJ9890	53°24·6′	2°1·4′W	FM	109
Sunhoney	Aberd	NJ7105	57°8·4′	2°28·3′W	X	38
Sunilaws	Northum	NT8237	55°37·8′	2°16·7′W	X	74
Sun Inn	Hants	SU5746	51°12·9′	1°10·6′W	X	185
Sunipol	Arg & Bt	NM3753	56°36·0′	6°16·6′W	X	47
Sunisletter	Highld	NM6889	56°56·3′	5°48·4′W	X	40
Sunken Marsh	Essex	TQ8084	51°31·8′	0°36·1′E	T	178
Sunkhead Moss	D & G	NS5301	55°17·1′	4°18·4′W	X	77
Sunkir	Shetld	HU6287	60°34·0′	0°51·6′W	X	1,2
Sunk Island	E Yorks	TA2618	53°38·8′	0°5·2′W	T	113
Sunk Island Drain	E Yorks	TA2721	53°40·4′	0°4·2′W	W	107,113
Sunk Island Sands	E Yorks	TA3116	53°37·7′	0°0·7′W	X	113
Sunk Roads		TA2915	53°37·2′	0°2·6′W	W	113
Sunk Sand		TF6445	52°58·9′	0°27·0′E	X	132
Sunlawshill	Scot Bord	NT7128	55°32·9′	2°27·1′W	X	74
Sunlaws Ho (Hotel)	Scot Bord	NT7029	55°33·5′	2°28·1′W	X	74
Sunlaws Mill	Scot Bord	NT7029	55°33·5′	2°28·1′W	X	74
Sunless Geo	Orkney	ND4397	58°51·7′	2°58·8′W	X	6,7
Sunley Court	N Yks	SE6881	54°13·5′	0°57·0′W	X	100
Sunley Hill	N Yks	SE6882	54°14·0′	0°57·0′W	X	100
Sunley Raynes	N Yks	SE2871	54°8·3′	1°33·9′W	X	99
Sunley Wood	Oxon	SU7698	51°40·8′	0°53·7′W	F	165
Sunley Woods	N Yks	SE5275	54°10·3′	1°11·8′W	X	100
Sun Moor Plantn	N Yks	SD9856	54°0·2′	2°1·4′W	F	103
Sunning Dale	N Yks	SE9573	54°8·9′	0°32·3′W	X	101
Sunningdale	Win & Maid	SU9567	51°23·9′	0°37·7′W	T	175,176
Sunninghill	Win & Maid	SU9368	51°24·4′	0°39·4′W	T	175
Sunninglye Fm	E Susx	TQ6237	51°6·8′	0°19·3′E	FM	188
Sunningwell	Oxon	SP4900	51°42·0′	1°17·1′W	T	164
Sunniside	Durham	NZ1438	54°44·5′	1°46·5′W	T	92
Sunniside	Ghead	NZ2058	54°55·2′	1°40·9′W	T	88
Sunniside	Sund	NZ3350	54°50·9′	1°28·7′W	T	88
Sunniside Fm	Durham	NZ1450	54°50·9′	1°46·5′W	FM	88
Sunniside Fm	S Tyne	NZ3863	54°57·9′	1°24·0′W	FM	88
Sunny Bank	Brad	SE0333	53°47·8′	1°56·9′W	X	104
Sunny Bank	Bury	SD8107	53°33·8′	2°16·8′W	T	109
Sunny Bank	Cald	SE1124	53°43·0′	1°49·6′W	X	104
Sunnybank	Ches	SJ9079	53°18·7′	2°8·6′W	X	118
Sunny Bank	Cumbr	SD2892	54°19·4′	3°6·0′W	X	96,97
Sunnybank	D & G	NY1268	55°0·2′	3°22·1′W	X	85
Sunnybank	E Loth	NT5179	56°0·3′	2°46·7′W	X	66
Sunny Bank	Heref	SO2448	52°7·7′	3°6·2′W	X	148
Sunny Bank	Lancs	SD7233	53°47·8′	2°25·1′W	X	103
Sunnybank	Monm	SO2827	51°56·4′	3°2·5′W	X	161
Sunnybank	Newp	ST2587	51°34·8′	3°4·6′W	X	171
Sunny Bank	N Yks	SD6867	54°6·1′	2°28·9′W	X	98
Sunny Bank	N Yks	SE0390	54°18·6′	1°56·8′W	X	98
Sunnybank	Orkney	HY3821	59°4·6′	3°4·4′W	X	6
Sunnybank	Orkney	HY4210	58°58·7′	3°0·1′W	X	6
Sunnybank	Orkney	HY4944	59°17·0′	2°53·2′W	X	5
Sunnybank	Pemb	SN1015	51°48·3′	4°45·0′W	X	158
Sunnybank	Powys	SO2157	52°12·6′	3°9·0′W	X	148
Sunnybank	Scot Bord	NT4818	55°27·4′	2°48·9′W	X	79
Sunny Bank	Staffs	SK1354	53°5·2′	1°47·9′W	X	119
Sunny Bank	Wrex	SJ2644	52°59·5′	3°5·7′W	X	117
Sunny Bank Fm	Ches	SJ7981	53°19·8′	2°18·5′W	FM	109
Sunny Bank Fm	Heref	SO3331	51°58·6′	2°58·1′W	FM	149,161
Sunny Bank Fm	Lancs	SD5570	54°7·7′	2°40·9′W	FM	97
Sunnybank Fm	Lancs	SD8742	53°52·7′	2°11·5′W	FM	103
Sunnybank Fm	N Yks	SE5389	54°17·9′	1°10·7′W	FM	100
Sunny Bower	Black w Dar	SD7030	53°46·2′	2°26·9′W	T	103
Sunnybrae	Aberd	NJ5403	57°7·2′	2°45·1′W	X	37
Sunnybrae	Aberd	NJ5809	57°10·5′	2°41·2′W	X	37
Sunnybrae	Aberd	NJ8023	57°18·1′	2°19·5′W	X	38
Sunnybrae	Aberd	NJ8861	57°38·6′	2°11·6′W	X	30
Sunnybrae	Aberd	NO7798	57°4·6′	2°22·3′W	X	38,45
Sunnybrae	Orkney	HY4211	58°59·2′	3°0·1′W	X	6
Sunnybrae	Pth & Kin	NO0437	56°31·2′	3°33·2′W	X	52,53
Sunnybraes	Fife	NO3110	56°16·9′	3°6·4′W	X	59
Sunnybraes	Fife	NO5509	56°16·5′	2°43·2′W	X	59
Sunnybrook Fm	Devon	SS8409	50°52·4′	3°38·5′W	FM	191
Sunny Brow	Cumbr	NY3400	54°23·7′	3°0·6′W	X	90
Sunnybrow	Cumbr	SD4495	54°21·1′	2°51·3′W	X	97
Sunny Brow	Durham	NZ1834	54°42·3′	1°42·8′W	T	92
Sunnyclose	Bucks	SU7587	51°34·8′	0°54·7′W	X	175
Sunny Corner	Corn	SW7540	50°13·3′	5°8·9′W	X	204
Sunny Dale	Brad	SE1043	53°53·2′	1°50·5′W	X	104
Sunnydale	Devon	SX8241	50°15·7′	3°39·0′W	X	202
Sunnydale	Orkney	HY3010	58°58·6′	3°12·6′W	X	6
Sunnydale Fm	Staffs	SK0466	53°11·7′	1°56·0′W	FM	119
Sunnydown	Surrey	SU9648	51°13·6′	0°37·1′W	X	186
Sunnyfields	Donc	SE5405	53°32·6′	1°10·7′W	T	111
Sunnygill Beck	Cumbr	NY6136	54°43·3′	2°35·9′W	W	91
Sunny Green	Cumbr	SD4182	54°14·1′	2°53·9′W	X	96,97
Sunnyhall	Angus	NO2938	56°32·0′	3°8·8′W	X	53
Sunnyhall	Aberd	NJ7250	57°32·6′	2°27·6′W	X	29
Sunnyhill	Bucks	SP7831	51°58·6′	0°51·5′W	X	152,165
Sunnyhill	Cered	SN6860	52°13·6′	3°55·6′W	X	146
Sunny Hill	C of Derb	SK3332	52°53·3′	1°30·2′W	T	128
Sunnyhill	D & G	NX9282	55°7·5′	3°41·2′W	X	78
Sunnyhill	Kent	TQ8763	51°20·3′	0°41·5′E	X	178
Sunny Hill	N Yks	SE4087	54°16·9′	1°22·7′W	X	99
Sunnyhill	Pemb	SM9217	51°49·0′	5°0·7′W	X	157,158
Sunnyhill	Shrops	SO3283	52°26·7′	2°59·6′W	H	137
Sunny Hill Fm	Pemb	SS0699	51°39·6′	4°47·9′W	FM	158
Sunnyhill Fm	Wilts	SU1762	51°21·6′	1°45·0′W	FM	173
Sunnyhillock	Highld	NH8255	57°34·4′	3°57·9′W	X	27
Sunny Howe	Cumbr	NY0520	54°34·2′	3°27·7′W	X	89
Sunnyhurst	Black w Dar	SD6822	53°41·9′	2°28·7′W	T	103
Sunnyhurst Hey Resr	Black w Dar	SD6721	53°41·3′	2°29·6′W	W	103
Sunnylaw	Stir	NS7998	56°9·8′	3°56·5′W	T	57
Sunny Leys	Leic	SK6602	52°36·9′	1°1·1′W	F	141
Sunnymead	Devon	SX5498	50°46·0′	4°3·8′W	X	191
Sunnymead	Oxon	SP5009	51°46·9′	1°16·1′W	T	164
Sunnymeads	Win & Maid	TQ0075	51°28·1′	0°33·2′W	T	176
Sunnymede	Essex	TQ6894	51°37·4′	0°26·0′E	T	167,177,178
Sunnymede	Notts	SK7942	52°58·4′	0°49·0′W	X	129
Sunnyrigg	Cumbr	NY4173	55°3·1′	2°55·0′W	X	85
Sunny-Rigg	Northum	NY6965	54°59·0′	2°28·6′W	X	86,87
Sunnyside	Aberd	NJ5367	57°41·7′	2°46·8′W	X	29
Sunnyside	Aberd	NJ5653	57°34·2′	2°43·7′W	X	29
Sunnyside	Aberd	NJ5850	57°32·6′	2°41·6′W	X	29
Sunnyside	Aberd	NJ6024	57°18·5′	2°39·4′W	X	37
Sunnyside	Aberd	NJ6338	57°26·1′	2°36·5′W	X	29
Sunnyside	Aberd	NJ6410	57°11·0′	2°35·3′W	X	37
Sunnyside	Aberd	NJ7230	57°21·8′	2°27·5′W	X	29
Sunnyside	Aberd	NJ7738	57°26·2′	2°22·5′W	X	29,30
Sunnyside	Aberd	NJ7761	57°38·6′	2°22·7′W	X	29,30
Sunnyside	Aberd	NJ8324	57°18·6′	2°16·5′W	X	38
Sunnyside	Aberd	NJ9837	57°25·7′	2°1·5′W	X	30
Sunnyside	Aberd	NO7999	57°5·1′	2°20·3′W	X	38,45
Sunnyside	Aberd	NO8496	57°3·5′	2°15·4′W	X	38,45
Sunnyside	Aberd	NO8998	57°4·6′	2°10·4′W	X	38,45
Sunnyside	D & G	NS7611	55°22·9′	3°57·0′W	X	71,78
Sunnyside	Durham	NZ0512	54°30·4′	1°54·9′W	X	92
Sunnyside	Durham	NZ3832	54°41·1′	1°24·2′W	X	93
Sunnyside	E Ayr	NS5611	55°22·6′	4°15·9′W	X	71
Sunnyside	E Ayr	NS6121	55°28·0′	4°11·5′W	X	71
Sunnyside	E Loth	NT5467	55°53·9′	2°43·7′W	X	66
Sunnyside	E Loth	NT5975	55°58·2′	2°39·0′W	X	67
Sunnyside	Fife	NT0386	56°3·7′	3°33·0′W	X	65
Sunnyside	Heref	SO4828	51°57·1′	2°45·0′W	X	149,161
Sunny Side	Midd	NZ5014	54°31·4′	1°13·2′W	X	93
Sunnyside	N Ayr	NS3548	55°42·1′	4°37·1′W	X	63
Sunnyside	Northum	NY8045	54°48·2′	2°18·2′W	X	86,87
Sunnyside	Northum	NY9562	54°57·4′	2°4·3′W	X	87
Sunnyside	N upon Ty	NZ2070	55°1·7′	1°40·8′W	X	88
Sunny Side	N Yks	NZ4900	54°23·8′	1°14·3′W	X	93
Sunnyside	N Yks	SE5171	54°8·2′	1°12·7′W	X	100
Sunnyside	Orkney	HY4110	58°58·7′	3°1·1′W	X	6
Sunnyside	Orkney	HY6722	59°5·3′	2°34·1′W	X	5
Sunnyside	Pth & Kin	NN9724	56°24·1′	3°39·7′W	X	52,53,58
Sunnyside	Pth & Kin	NT1297	56°9·7′	3°24·6′W	X	58
Sunnyside	Roth	SK4793	53°26·1′	1°17·1′W	T	111
Sunnyside	Scot Bord	NT1751	55°45·0′	3°18·9′W	X	65,66,72
Sunnyside	Scot Bord	NT5213	55°24·8′	2°45·1′W	X	79
Sunnyside	Scot Bord	NT8561	55°50·8′	2°13·9′W	X	67
Sunnyside	S Lanak	NS7451	55°44·4′	4°0·0′W	X	64
Sunnyside	S Lanak	NS8644	55°40·8′	3°48·3′W	X	71,72
Sunnyside	S Lanak	NT0134	55°35·6′	3°33·8′W	X	72
Sunnyside	W Susx	TQ3937	51°7·1′	0°0·4′W	T	187
Sunnyside Fm	Cumbr	SD4479	54°12·5′	2°51·1′W	FM	97
Sunnyside Fm	Devon	SS9708	50°52·0′	3°27·4′W	FM	192
Sunnyside Fm	Durham	NZ0535	54°42·8′	1°54·9′W	FM	92
Sunnyside Fm	Hants	SU2839	51°9·2′	1°35·6′W	FM	184
Sunnyside Fm	Kent	TQ8445	51°10·7′	0°38·3′E	FM	188
Sunnyside Fm	Kent	TR0326	51°0·1′	0°54·0′E	FM	189
Sunnyside Fm	Kirk	SE1312	53°36·5′	1°47·8′W	FM	110
Sunnyside Fm	Lincs	TF0129	52°51·2′	0°29·6′W	FM	130
Sunnyside Fm	Norf	TF6514	52°42·1′	0°26·9′E	FM	132
Sunnyside Fm	Scot Bord	NT5234	55°36·1′	2°45·3′W	FM	73
Sunnyside Hill	Scot Bord	NT8326	55°31·9′	2°15·7′W	H	74
Sunnyside House	Suff	TM0271	52°18·2′	0°58·2′E	X	144,155
Sunnyside of Folla	Aberd	NJ7133	57°23·4′	2°28·5′W	X	29
Sunnythwaite	Cumbr	NY4574	55°3·7′	2°51·2′W	X	86
Sunny Vale	Cumbr	NY3944	54°47·5′	2°56·5′W	X	85
Sunrise Fm	N Yks	SE3350	53°56·9′	1°29·4′W	FM	104
Sun Rising	Warw	SP3645	52°6·4′	1°28·1′W	X	151
Sunrose Fm	Cambs	TL6083	52°25·5′	0°21·6′E	FM	143
Sunset	Heref	SO3056	52°12·1′	3°1·1′W	T	148
Sunside	Aberd	NJ5828	57°20·7′	2°41·4′W	X	37
Sunside	Aberd	NJ7029	57°21·3′	2°29·5′W	X	38
Sun Side	N Yks	SD9696	54°21·8′	2°3·3′W	X	98
Sun Side	N Yks	SE1265	54°5·1′	1°48·6′W	X	99
Sunte Ho	W Susx	TQ3325	51°0·8′	0°5·9′W	X	187,198
Sunt Fm	Surrey	TQ4048	51°13·1′	0°0·7′E	FM	187
Sunton	Wilts	SU2454	51°17·3′	1°39·0′W	T	184
Sunton Heath	Wilts	SU2653	51°16·8′	1°37·2′W	X	184
Sunton Sike	Cumbr	NY0212	54°29·9′	3°30·4′W	W	89
Suntrap	C of Edin	NT1770	55°55·2′	3°19·2′W	X	65,66
Sunwick Fm	Scot Bord	NT8952	55°45·9′	2°10·1′W	FM	67,74
Sun Wood	N Yks	SE2469	54°7·2′	1°37·6′W	F	99
Sunwood Fm	Hants	SU7519	50°58·2′	0°55·5′W	FM	197
Superity Fm	W Berks	SU5180	51°31·2′	1°15·5′W	FM	174
Supperton Fm	Kent	TR2259	51°17·4′	1°11·4′E	FM	179
Supplebank	D & G	NY1873	55°2·9′	3°16·6′W	X	85
Surbiton	King	TQ1767	51°23·6′	0°18·7′W	T	176
Surby	I of M	SC2070	54°5·9′	4°44·8′W	T	95
Sure as Death Bank	Pth & Kin	NO2621	56°22·8′	3°11·5′W	X	53,59
Surfleet	Lincs	TF2528	52°50·3′	0°8·2′W	T	131
Surfleet Fen	Lincs	TF1730	52°51·5′	0°15·3′W	X	130
Surfleet Fen Fm	Lincs	TF1631	52°52·1′	0°16·2′W	FM	130
Surfleet Seas End	Lincs	TF2728	52°50·3′	0°6·5′W	T	131
Surf Point	Devon	SS1443	51°9·6′	4°39·2′W	X	180
Surgate Brow Fm	N Yks	SE9793	54°19·6′	0°30·1′W	FM	94,101
Surge Burn	N Ayr	NS2760	55°48·4′	4°45·2′W	W	63
Surgill Beck	N Yks	SD9545	53°54·3′	2°4·2′W	W	103
Surhoose Taing	Orkney	HY5052	59°21·3′	2°52·3′W	X	5
Surlingham	Norf	TG3106	52°36·4′	1°25·1′E	T	134
Surlingham Broad	Norf	TG3107	52°36·9′	1°25·1′E	W	134
Surman's Fm	Worcs	SO8946	52°7·0′	2°9·2′W	FM	150
Surney Fm	Northnts	SP6165	52°17·0′	1°5·9′W	FM	152
Surney Fm	W Susx	SU9126	51°1·8′	0°41·7′W	FM	186,197
Surprise Hill	Surrey	SU9051	51°15·3′	0°42·2′W	X	186
Surradale	Moray	NJ1665	57°40·3′	3°24·0′W	X	28

Surrells Wood	Win & Maid	SU8273	51°27·2′	0°48·8′W	F	175
Surrendell Fm	Wilts	ST8782	51°32·4′	2°10·9′W	FM	173
Surrendell Wood	Wilts	ST8682	51°32·4′	2°11·7′W	F	173
Surrenden	Kent	TQ9345	51°10·5′	0°46·1′E	X	189
Surrender Moss	N Yks	NY9701	54°24·5′	2°2·4′W	X	92
Surrex	Essex	TL8622	51°52·2′	0°42·5′E	T	168
Surrey Docks	Sthwk	TQ3680	51°30·4′	0°2·0′W	X	177
Surrey Hill	Brackn	SU8864	51°22·3′	0°43·8′W	X	175,186
Surridge Fm	Devon	SS9424	51°0·6′	3°30·3′W	FM	181
Surridge Fm	Somer	SS9727	51°2·2′	3°27·8′W	FM	181
Surridge Fm	Somer	ST0524	51°0·7′	3°20·9′W	FM	181
Surrie Geo	Orkney	HY5337	59°13·3′	2°48·9′W	X	5
Surries	E Susx	TQ4337	51°7·1′	0°3·0′E	X	187
Surrigarth	Orkney	HY4945	59°17·6′	2°53·2′W	X	5
Sursay	N Eil	NF9576	57°40·5′	7°6·5′W	X	18
Sursetter	Shetld	HU4065	60°22·3′	1°16·0′W	X	2,3
Surwood Fm	Suff	TM0867	52°15·9′	1°3·3′E	FM	155
Susacres Fms	N Yks	SE3160	54°2·3′	1°31·2′W	FM	99
Susan's Hill Fm	Kent	TQ9235	51°5·2′	0°44·9′E	FM	189
Suso Burn	Orkney	HY4130	59°9·4′	3°1·4′W	W	5,6
Suspension Bridge	Norf	TL5392	52°30·5′	0°15·7′E	T	143
Sussex Border Path	E Susx	TQ3316	50°55·9′	0°6·0′W	X	198
Sussex Border Path	E Susx	TQ6334	51°5·2′	0°20·0′E	X	188
Sussex Border Path	E Susx	TQ9025	50°59·8′	0°42·9′E	X	189
Sussex Border Path	Hants	SU7311	50°53·9′	0°57·3′W	X	197
Sussex Border Path	Kent	TQ7628	51°1·7′	0°31·0′E	X	188,199
Sussex Border Path	Surrey	TQ2541	51°9·5′	0°12·4′W	X	187
Sussex Border Path	W Susx	SU9130	51°4·0′	0°41·7′W	X	186
Sussex Fm	Cambs	TL3799	52°34·5′	0°1·7′E	FM	142,143
Sussex Fm	Norf	TF8041	52°56·4′	0°41·1′E	FM	132
Sussex Fm	Surrey	TQ0554	51°16·8′	0°29·3′W	FM	187
Sussex House Fm	E Susx	TQ4740	51°8·6′	0°6·5′E	FM	188
Su Stanes	Shetld	HU4163	60°21·2′	1°14·9′W	X	2,3
Sustead	Norf	TG1836	52°52·9′	1°14·8′E	T	133
Susworth	Lincs	SE8302	53°30·7′	0°44·5′W	T	112
Sutch Fm	Ches	SJ7151	53°3·6′	2°25·6′W	FM	118
Sutcliffe Hill	Notts	SK5723	52°48·3′	1°8·9′W	X	129
Sutcombe	Devon	SS3411	50°52·7′	4°21·2′W	T	190
Sutcombemill	Devon	SS3411	50°52·7′	4°21·2′W	T	190
Sutes	Herts	TL3618	51°50·9′	0°1·1′W	A	166
Sutes Woods	Herts	TL3719	51°51·4′	0°0·2′W	F	166
Sutherbruff Rigg	N Yks	SE8686	54°16·0′	0°40·4′W	H	94,101
Sutherland	Orkney	ND4394	58°50·0′	3°8·1′W	X	7
Sutherland	Orkney	ND4895	58°50·6′	2°53·6′W	X	7
Sutherland Beck	N Yks	SE7790	54°18·2′	0°48·6′W	W	94,100
Sutherland Lodge	N Yks	SE7691	54°18·8′	0°49·5′W	X	94,100
Sutherlands Grove	Arg & Bt	NM9642	56°31·8′	5°18·6′W	T	49
Suther Ness	Shetld	HU5565	60°22·2′	0°59·7′W	X	2
Suthra Voe	Shetld	HU2960	60°19·6′	1°28·0′W	W	3
Suton	Norf	TM0998	52°32·6′	1°5·3′E	T	144
Sutor Fm	Somer	ST7226	51°2·2′	2°23·6′W	FM	183
Sutors of Cromarty	Highld	NH8067	57°40·9′	4°0·3′W	X	21,27
Sutors Stacks	Highld	NH8167	57°40·9′	3°59·3′W	X	21,27
Sutterby	Lincs	TF3872	53°13·9′	0°4·5′E	T	122
Sutterton	Lincs	TF2835	52°54·1′	0°5·4′W	T	131
Sutterton Br	Lincs	TF2247	53°0·6′	0°10·5′W	X	131
Sutterton Dowdyke	Lincs	TF2833	52°53·0′	0°5·5′W	T	131
Suttie	Aberd	NJ8116	57°14·3′	2°18·4′W	X	38
Suttieside	Angus	NO4651	56°39·1′	2°52·4′W	T	54
Suttle Ho	Cumbr	NY3754	54°52·9′	2°58·5′W	X	85
Sutton	Beds	TL2247	52°6·7′	0°12·7′W	T	153
Sutton	Bucks	TQ0278	51°29·7′	0°31·4′W	T	176
Sutton	Cambs	TL4479	52°23·6′	0°7·4′E	T	142,143
Sutton	Corn	SX2972	50°31·6′	4°24·4′W	X	201
Sutton	Devon	SS7904	50°49·6′	3°42·7′W	X	191
Sutton	Devon	SX7042	50°16·1′	3°49·1′W	T	202
Sutton	Donc	SE5512	53°36·3′	1°9·7′W	T	111
Sutton	E Susx	TV4999	50°46·5′	0°7·2′E	T	199
Sutton	Kent	TR3349	51°11·8′	1°20·5′E	T	179
Sutton	Lincs	SK8752	53°3·7′	0°41·7′W	T	121
Sutton	Norf	TG3823	52°45·4′	1°32·0′E	T	133,134
Sutton	Notts	SK6884	53°21·1′	0°58·3′W	T	111,120
Sutton	Notts	SK7637	52°55·7′	0°51·8′W	T	129
Sutton	N Yks	SE4925	53°43·4′	1°15·0′W	T	105
Sutton	Oxon	SP4106	51°45·3′	1°24·0′W	T	164
Sutton	Pemb	SM9115	51°47·9′	5°1·5′W	T	157,158
Sutton	Peterb	TL0998	52°34·4′	0°23·1′W	T	142
Sutton	Powys	SO2096	52°33·6′	3°10·4′W	X	137
Sutton	Shrops	SJ3527	52°50·4′	2°57·5′W	T	126
Sutton	Shrops	SJ5010	52°41·4′	2°44·0′W	T	126
Sutton	Shrops	SJ6631	52°52·8′	2°29·9′W	T	127
Sutton	Shrops	SO7286	52°28·5′	2°24·3′W	T	138
Sutton	Somer	ST6233	51°5·9′	2°32·2′W	T	183
Sutton	Staffs	SJ7622	52°47·9′	2°21·0′W	T	127
Sutton	St Hel	SJ5393	53°26·1′	2°42·0′W	T	108
Sutton	Suff	TM3045	52°3·6′	1°21·7′E	T	169
Sutton	Sutton	TQ2564	51°21·9′	0°11·9′W	T	176,187
Sutton	V of Glam	SS9472	51°26·5′	3°31·1′W	A	170
Sutton	V of Glam	ST0869	51°25·0′	3°19·0′W	X	170
Sutton	W Susx	SU9715	50°55·8′	0°36·8′W	T	197
Sutton Abinger	Surrey	TQ1045	51°11·8′	0°25·1′W	T	187
Sutton at Hone	Kent	TQ5570	51°24·7′	0°14·1′E	T	177
Sutton Bank	N Yks	SE5182	54°14·1′	1°12·6′W	X	100
Sutton Baron	Kent	TQ8762	51°19·8′	0°41·4′E	X	178
Sutton Barton	Devon	ST0109	50°52·6′	3°24·0′W	X	192
Sutton Barton	Devon	SY2098	50°46·8′	3°7·7′W	X	192,193
Sutton Bassett	Northnts	SP7790	52°30·4′	0°51·5′W	T	141
Sutton Beck	N Yks	SE4883	54°14·7′	1°15·4′W	W	100
Sutton Beech Wood	Hants	SU6233	51°5·8′	1°6·5′W	F	185
Sutton Benger	Wilts	ST9478	51°30·3′	2°4·8′W	T	173
Sutton Bingham	Somer	ST5411	50°54·0′	2°38·9′W	T	194
Sutton Bingham Reservoir	Somer	ST5410	50°53·5′	2°38·9′W	W	194
Sutton Bonington	Notts	SK5025	52°49·4′	1°15·1′W	T	129
Sutton Bottom	Glos	SO6612	51°48·6′	2°29·2′W	X	162
Sutton Bottom	Wilts	ST8839	51°9·2′	2°9·9′W	X	183
Sutton Bridge	Lincs	TF4721	52°46·2′	0°11·1′E	T	131
Sutton Bridge Fm	Essex	TQ8889	51°34·3′	0°43·2′E	FM	178
Sutton Broad	Norf	TG3723	52°45·4′	1°31·1′E	W	133,134
Sutton Brook	Derby	SK2331	52°52·8′	1°39·1′W	W	128
Sutton Cheney	Leic	SK4100	52°36·0′	1°23·3′W	T	140
Sutton Coldfield	Birm	SP1395	52°33·4′	1°48·1′W	T	139
Sutton Common	Ches	SJ9367	53°12·2′	2°5·9′W	H	118
Sutton Common	Hants	SU7345	51°12·2′	0°56·9′W	X	186
Sutton Common	Suff	TM3247	52°4·6′	1°23·5′E	X	169
Sutton Corner	Lincs	TF4327	52°49·5′	0°7·7′E	T	131
Sutton Court	Bath & NE Somer	ST5960	51°20·5′	2°34·9′W	X	172,182
Sutton Court	Worcs	SO6165	52°17·1′	2°33·9′W	X	138,149
Sutton Courtenay	Oxon	SU5093	51°38·2′	1°16·3′W	T	164,174
Sutton Court Fm	Wok	SU8366	51°23·4′	0°48·0′W	FM	175
Sutton Crosses	Lincs	TF4321	52°46·3′	0°7·6′E	T	131
Sutton Cross Roads	Notts	SK6883	53°20·6′	0°58·3′W	X	111,120
Sutton Down	Wilts	ST9826	51°2·2′	2°1·3′W	X	184
Sutton Down Fm	Hants	SU4537	51°8·1′	1°21·0′W	FM	185
Suttondown Plantn	Corn	SX2995	50°44·0′	4°25·0′W	F	190
Sutton Downs	Kent	TR3348	51°11·2′	1°20·5′E	X	179
Sutton End	Ches	SJ9568	53°12·8′	2°4·1′W	X	118
Sutton End	W Susx	SU9816	50°56·3′	0°35·9′W	T	197
Sutton Farm	Worcs	SO8175	52°22·6′	2°16·3′W	FM	138
Sutton Fen	Cambs	TL3977	52°22·6′	0°2·9′E	X	142,143
Sutton Fields Fm	Ches	SJ5579	53°18·6′	2°40·1′W	FM	117
Sutton Fields Ho	Notts	SK5026	52°50·0′	1°15·1′W	X	129
Sutton Fm	Corn	SX2994	50°43·5′	4°25·0′W	FM	190
Sutton Fm	Devon	SS7202	50°48·4′	3°48·6′W	FM	191
Sutton Fm	E Yorks	SE7045	53°54·0′	0°55·7′W	FM	105,106
Sutton Fm	I of W	SZ4481	50°37·8′	1°22·3′W	FM	196
Sutton Fm	Kent	TR0929	51°1·6′	0°59·2′E	FM	189
Sutton Fm	N Som	ST5061	51°21·0′	2°42·7′W	FM	172,182
Sutton Fm	Somer	ST3837	51°8·0′	2°52·8′W	FM	182
Sutton Fm	Somer	ST6223	51°0·5′	2°32·1′W	FM	183
Sutton Fm	V of Glam	SS8675	51°28·0′	3°38·1′W	FM	170
Sutton Forest Side	Notts	SK5059	53°7·8′	1°14·8′W	T	120
Sutton Gault	Cambs	TL4279	52°23·7′	0°5·6′E	T	142,143
Sutton Grange	Notts	SK6985	53°21·7′	0°57·4′W	X	111,120
Sutton Grange	N Yks	SE2873	54°9·4′	1°33·9′W	X	99
Sutton Grange	N Yks	SE5863	54°3·8′	1°6·4′W	X	100
Sutton Grange	N Yks	SE7970	54°7·4′	0°47·1′W	X	100
Sutton Green	Ches	SJ3776	53°16·9′	2°56·3′W	T	117
Sutton Green	Surrey	TQ0054	51°16·8′	0°33·6′W	T	186
Sutton Green	Wrex	SJ4048	53°1·8′	2°53·3′W	T	117
Sutton Hall	Ches	SJ9271	53°14·4′	2°6·8′W	X	118
Sutton Hall	Essex	TQ8889	51°34·3′	0°43·2′E	X	178
Sutton Hall	E Susx	TQ4318	50°56·8′	0°2·5′E	X	198
Sutton Hall	Norf	TG3924	52°45·9′	1°33·0′E	X	133,134
Sutton Hall	Shrops	SJ7101	52°36·6′	2°25·3′W	T	127
Sutton Hall	Suff	TL9056	52°10·4′	0°47·1′E	X	155
Sutton Hall	Suff	TM3045	52°3·6′	1°21·7′E	X	169
Sutton Hall Fm	Ches	SJ7064	53°10·6′	2°26·5′W	FM	118
Sutton Hall Fm	Thurr	TQ6785	51°32·6′	0°24·9′E	FM	177,178
Sutton Hams	Somer	ST3636	51°7·4′	2°54·5′W	X	182
Sutton Heath	Peterb	TF0800	52°35·5′	0°23·9′W	X	142
Suttonheath	Shrops	SJ6630	52°52·2′	2°29·9′W	X	127
Sutton Heath	St Hel	SJ5093	53°26·1′	2°44·7′W	T	108
Sutton Hill	Bath & NE Somer	ST5958	51°19·4′	2°34·9′W	X	172,182
Sutton Hill	Dorset	ST8815	50°56·3′	2°9·9′W	X	183
Sutton Hill	Heref	SO5445	52°6·3′	2°39·9′W	X	149
Sutton Hill	Kent	TR3350	51°12·3′	1°20·5′E	X	179
Sutton Hill	Shrops	SO5382	52°26·3′	2°41·1′W	X	137,138
Sutton Hill	Wrekin	SJ7003	52°37·7′	2°26·2′W	T	127
Sutton Hill Br	Leic	SP5194	52°32·7′	1°14·5′W	X	140
Sutton Hill Fm	Dorset	ST8816	50°56·8′	2°9·9′W	FM	183
Sutton Hill Fm	Leic	SP5194	52°32·7′	1°14·5′W	FM	140
Suttonhill Ho	Shrops	SJ7002	52°37·1′	2°26·2′W	X	127
Sutton Ho	Shrops	SJ7201	52°36·6′	2°24·4′W	X	127
Sutton Ho	Worcs	SO6165	52°17·1′	2°33·9′W	X	138,149
Sutton Holms	Dorset	SU0509	50°53·1′	1°55·4′W	T	195
Sutton Holwoods	Cambs	TL3978	52°23·2′	0°3·0′E	X	142,143
Sutton Hoo	Suff	TM2849	52°5·8′	1°20·1′E	X	169
Sutton Howgrave	N Yks	SE3179	54°12·6′	1°31·1′W	T	99
Sutton In Ashfield	Notts	SK4958	53°7·3′	1°15·7′W	T	120
Sutton-in-Craven	N Yks	SE0043	53°53·2′	1°59·6′W	T	104
Sutton Ings	K upon H	TA1231	53°46·0′	0°17·6′W	T	107
Sutton Ings	Lincs	TF5080	53°18·0′	0°15·5′E	X	122
Sutton in the Elms	Leic	SP5193	52°32·2′	1°14·5′W	T	140
Sutton Lakes	Heref	SO5446	52°6·9′	2°39·9′W	T	149
Sutton Lane Ends	Ches	SJ9271	53°14·4′	2°6·8′W	T	118
Sutton Lane Fm	Wilts	ST9577	51°29·7′	2°3·9′W	FM	173
Sutton Leach	St Hel	SJ5292	53°25·6′	2°42·9′W	T	108
Sutton Lodge	Leic	SP5192	52°31·6′	1°14·5′W	X	140
Sutton Lodge	Pemb	SM9116	51°48·5′	5°1·5′W	X	157,158
Sutton Lodge Fm	E Yorks	SE6923	53°42·2′	0°56·9′W	FM	105,106
Sutton Lodge Fm	Northnts	SP4938	52°2·5′	1°16·7′W	FM	151
Sutton Maddock	Shrops	SJ7201	52°36·6′	2°24·4′W	T	127
Sutton Mallet	Somer	ST3736	51°7·4′	2°53·6′W	T	182
Sutton Mandeville	Wilts	ST9828	51°3·3′	2°1·3′W	T	184
Sutton Manor	Hants	SU4639	51°9·1′	1°20·1′W	X	185
Sutton Manor	St Hel	SJ5190	53°24·5′	2°43·8′W	T	108
Sutton Marsh	Heref	SO5444	52°5·8′	2°39·9′W	T	149
Sutton Meadlands	Cambs	TL3978	52°23·2′	0°3·0′E	X	142,143
Sutton Mill	N Yks	SE0044	53°53·8′	1°59·6′W	T	104
Sutton Mill	Warw	SP3036	52°1·5′	1°33·4′W	X	151
Sutton Montis	Somer	ST6224	51°1·1′	2°32·1′W	T	183
Sutton Moor	Brad	SE0041	53°52·2′	1°59·6′W	X	104
Sutton Moor	N Yks	SD9941	53°52·2′	2°0·5′W	X	103
Sutton Mountain	Pemb	SM9015	51°47·9′	5°2·3′W	X	157,158
Sutton New Hall	Ches	SJ3676	53°16·9′	2°57·2′W	X	117
Sutton-on-Hull	K upon H	TA1132	53°46·6′	0°18·5′W	T	107
Sutton on Sea	Lincs	TF5281	53°18·5′	0°17·3′E	T	122
Sutton-on-the-Forest	N Yks	SE5864	54°4·4′	1°6·4′W	T	100
Sutton on the Hill	Derby	SK2333	52°53·9′	1°39·1′W	T	128
Sutton on Trent	Notts	SK7965	53°10·8′	0°48·7′W	T	120,121
Sutton Park	Birm	SP0997	52°34·5′	1°51·6′W	X	139
Sutton Park	N Yks	SE5864	54°4·4′	1°6·4′W	X	100
Sutton Park	Worcs	SO6266	52°17·7′	2°33·0′W	X	138,149
Sutton Parkway Station	Notts	SK5057	53°6·7′	1°14·8′W	X	120
Sutton Penn	N Yks	SE2082	54°14·2′	1°41·2′W	X	99
Sutton Place	Kent	TQ5571	51°25·2′	0°14·1′E	X	177
Sutton Place	Surrey	TQ0153	51°16·3′	0°32·7′W	A	186
Sutton Pools	Oxon	SU5094	51°38·8′	1°16·2′W	W	164,174
Sutton Poyntz	Dorset	SY7083	50°39·0′	2°25·1′W	T	194
Sutton Resr	Ches	SJ9170	53°13·9′	2°7·7′W	W	118
Sutton Row	Wilts	ST9728	51°3·3′	2°2·2′W	T	184
Sutton Rush	E Yorks	SE7145	53°54·0′	0°54·7′W	X	105,106
Suttons	Essex	TQ5197	51°39·3′	0°11·4′E	X	167,177
Sutton Scarsdale	Derby	SK4468	53°12·7′	1°20·1′W	T	120
Sutton Scotney	Hants	SU4639	51°9·1′	1°20·1′W	T	185
Sutton's Fm	Essex	TL9128	51°55·3′	0°47·1′E	FM	168
Sutton's Fm	Herts	TL1910	51°46·8′	0°16·1′W	FM	166
Sutton's Fm	Norf	TM4592	52°28·5′	1°36·9′E	FM	134
Sutton Spring Wood	Derby	SK4268	53°12·7′	1°21·9′W	F	120
Sutton St Edmund	Lincs	TF3613	52°42·1′	0°1·2′E	T	131,142
Sutton St Edmund's Common	Cambs	TF3408	52°39·4′	0°0·7′W	X	142
Sutton St James	Lincs	TF3918	52°44·7′	0°4·0′E	T	131
Sutton St Michael	Heref	SO5245	52°6·3′	2°41·7′W	T	149
Sutton St Nicholas	Heref	SO5345	52°6·3′	2°40·8′W	T	149
Sutton Street	Suff	TM3044	52°3·0′	1°21·7′E	T	169
Sutton Thorn	Devon	SY2197	50°46·3′	3°6·8′W	X	192,193
Sutton Town	Corn	SX3190	50°41·3′	4°23·2′W	X	190
Sutton-under-Brailes	Warw	SP2937	52°2·1′	1°34·2′W	T	151
Sutton-under-Whitestonecliffe	N Yks	SE4882	54°14·1′	1°15·4′W	T	100
Sutton upon Derwent	E Yorks	SE7046	53°54·6′	0°55·6′W	T	105,106
Sutton Vale Ho	Kent	TR3349	51°11·8′	1°20·5′E	X	179
Sutton Valence	Kent	TQ8149	51°12·9′	0°35·9′E	T	188
Sutton Veny	Wilts	ST8942	51°10·9′	2°9·1′W	T	184
Sutton Veny Ho	Wilts	ST8942	51°10·9′	2°9·1′W	X	184
Sutton Waldron	Dorset	ST8615	50°56·3′	2°11·6′W	T	183
Sutton Walks	Suff	TM2948	52°5·2′	1°21·0′E	X	169
Sutton Walls	Heref	SO5246	52°6·9′	2°41·7′W	A	149
Sutton Weaver	Ches	SJ5479	53°18·6′	2°41·0′W	T	117
Sutton West Fen	Cambs	TL4179	52°23·7′	0°4·7′E	X	142,143
Sutton Wharf Br	Leic	SP4199	52°35·5′	1°23·3′W	X	140
Sutton Wick	Bath & NE Somer	ST5758	51°19·4′	2°36·6′W	T	172,182
Sutton Wick	Oxon	SU4794	51°38·8′	1°18·8′W	T	164,174
Sutton Wood	E Yorks	SE7048	53°55·6′	0°55·6′W	F	105,106
Sutton Wood	Peterb	TF0901	52°36·0′	0°23·0′W	F	142
Sutton Wood Fm	Shrops	SJ7002	52°37·1′	2°26·2′W	FM	127
Swaa Head	Shetld	HT9740	60°8·9′	2°2·7′W	X	4
Swaba Stacks	Shetld	HU2861	60°20·2′	1°29·1′W	X	3
Swabie Water	Shetld	HU3185	60°33·1′	1°25·6′W	W	1,3
Swabi Stack	Shetld	HU3066	60°22·9′	1°26·9′W	X	3
Swabwall	Shetld	HU2744	60°11·0′	1°30·3′W	X	4
Swaby	Lincs	TF3877	53°16·6′	0°4·6′E	T	122
Swaddledown	Devon	SX4592	50°42·7′	4°11·3′W	A	190
Swading Hill	Beds	TL1848	52°7·3′	0°16·2′W	X	153
Swadlincote	Derby	SK2919	52°46·3′	1°33·8′W	T	128
Swae Field	Shetld	HU2652	60°15·4′	1°31·3′W	X	3
Swaffen Prior Fen	Cambs	TL5467	52°17·0′	0°15·9′E	X	154
Swaffham	Norf	TF8109	52°39·1′	0°41·0′E	T	144
Swaffham Bulbeck	Cambs	TL5562	52°14·3′	0°16·6′E	T	154
Swaffham Bulbeck Fen	Cambs	TL5564	52°15·4′	0°16·7′E	X	154
Swaffham Bulbeck Lode	Cambs	TL5464	52°15·4′	0°15·8′E	W	154
Swaffham Gap	Norf	TL7898	52°33·3′	0°37·9′E	X	144
Swaffham Heath	Norf	TF7807	52°38·1′	0°38·2′E	X	144
Swaffham Plashes	Norf	TF8110	52°39·7′	0°41·0′E	X	132
Swaffham Prior	Cambs	TL5764	52°15·3′	0°18·4′E	T	154
Swaffham Prior Ho	Cambs	TL5663	52°14·8′	0°17·5′E	X	154
Swafield	Norf	TG2832	52°50·5′	1°23·5′E	T	133
Swafield Ho	Norf	TG2833	52°51·0′	1°23·6′E	X	133
Swailend	Aberd	NJ8816	57°14·3′	2°11·5′W	X	38
Swaile's Green	E Susx	TQ7721	50°57·9′	0°31·6′E	T	199
Swainby	N Yks	NZ4702	54°24·9′	1°16·1′W	T	93
Swainby Abbey	N Yks	SE3385	54°15·8′	1°29·2′W	A	99
Swainby Grove	N Yks	SE3385	54°15·8′	1°29·2′W	X	99
Swaines Hill Manor	Hants	SU7143	51°11·1′	0°58·7′W	X	186
Swaine Wood	Leeds	SE2237	53°50·0′	1°39·5′W	F	104
Swain Fm	Kent	TQ9134	51°4·6′	0°44·0′E	FM	189
Swain House	Brad	SE1636	53°49·4′	1°45·0′W	T	104
Swains Fm	Surrey	TQ2346	51°12·2′	0°14·0′W	FM	187
Swains Fm	W Susx	TQ1921	50°58·8′	0°17·9′W	FM	198
Swains Greave	Derby	SK1297	53°28·4′	1°48·7′W	X	110
Swains Head	Derby	SK1398	53°29·0′	1°47·8′W	X	110
Swainshead Hall	Lancs	SD5352	53°58·0′	2°42·6′W	X	102
Swainshill	Heref	SO4641	52°4·1′	2°46·9′W	T	148,149,161
Swainshill Fm	Hants	SU7144	51°11·7′	0°58·6′W	FM	186
Swainsley	Staffs	SK0957	53°6·8′	1°51·5′W	X	119
Swainsmoor	Staffs	SK0261	53°9·0′	1°57·8′W	X	119
Swainson Knott	Cumbr	NY0708	54°27·8′	3°25·7′W	X	89
Swainstead	N Yks	SD7961	54°2·9′	2°18·8′W	X	98
Swainsteads	Cumbr	NY5164	54°58·3′	2°45·5′W	X	86
Swainsthorpe	Norf	TG2100	52°33·4′	1°16·0′E	T	134
Swainston	I of W	SZ4487	50°41·1′	1°22·2′W	X	196
Swainstone	Devon	SX6054	50°22·4′	3°57·8′W	X	202
Swain's Wood	Bucks	SU7392	51°37·6′	0°56·3′W	F	175
Swair Dale	N Yks	SE8689	54°17·6′	0°40·3′W	X	94,101
Swaites	Cumbr	NY5666	54°59·4′	2°40·8′W	X	86
Swaites	S Lanak	NS9641	55°39·3′	3°38·7′W	X	72
Swaites Hill	S Lanak	NS9541	55°39·3′	3°39·7′W	H	72
Swaithe	Barns	SE3704	53°32·1′	1°26·1′W	T	110,111
Swakeleys	Hill	TQ0785	51°33·5′	0°27·0′W	A	176
Swalcliffe	Oxon	SP3737	52°2·0′	1°27·2′W	T	151
Swalcliffe Grange	Oxon	SP3736	52°1·5′	1°27·2′W	X	151
Swalcliffe Lea	Oxon	SP3838	52°2·6′	1°26·4′W	X	151
Swale Bank Fm	Lincs	TF2030	52°51·5′	0°12·7′W	FM	131
Swalecliffe	Kent	TR1367	51°21·9′	1°4·0′E	T	179
Swaledale	N Yks	SE0298	54°22·9′	1°57·7′W	X	98
Swalefields	N Yks	SE3190	54°18·5′	1°31·0′W	X	99
Swale Fm	N Yks	SE0797	54°22·4′	1°53·1′W	FM	99
Swale Hall	N Yks	SE0498	54°22·9′	1°55·9′W	X	98
Swale Heritage Trail	Kent	TQ9763	51°20·1′	0°50·1′E	X	178
Swale Ho	N Yks	SE3783	54°14·7′	1°25·5′W	X	99
Swale Sta	Kent	TQ9169	51°23·5′	0°45·1′E	X	178
Swale, The	Kent	TQ9466	51°21·8′	0°47·6′E	W	178
Swale, The	Kent	TR0567	51°22·1′	0°57·1′E	W	178,179
Swaletree House Fm	N Yks	SE3684	54°15·3′	1°26·4′W	FM	99
Swalland Fm	Dorset	SY9278	50°36·3′	2°6·4′W	FM	195
Swallet Fm	Somer	ST5453	51°16·7′	2°39·2′W	FM	182,183

Swallett Gate	Wilts	ST9980	51°31·4′	2°0·5′W	X	173
Swallick Fm	Hants	SU6448	51°13·9′	1°4·6′W	FM	185
Swallohurst	Cumbr	SD1091	54°18·6′	3°22·6′W	T	96
Swallow	Lincs	TA1703	53°30·9′	0°13·7′W	T	113
Swallow Beck	Lincs	SK9568	53°12·3′	0°34·3′W	T	121
Swallow Cliff	N Som	ST3266	51°23·6′	2°58·3′W	X	171,182
Swallowcliffe	Wilts	ST9626	51°2·2′	2°3·0′W	T	184
Swallowcliffe Down	Wilts	ST9725	51°1·7′	2°2·2′W	X	184
Swallowcliffe Wood	Wilts	ST9627	51°2·8′	2°3·0′W	F	184
Swallow Copse	Glos	SU0099	51°41·6′	1°59·6′W	F	163
Swallow Crags	Northum	NY7369	55°1·1′	2°24·9′W	X	86,87
Swallow Craig	Fife	NT1982	56°1·7′	3°17·5′W	X	65,66
Swallowdale	Ches	SJ9366	53°11·7′	2°5·9′W	X	118
Swallow Falls	Conwy	SH7657	53°6·0′	3°50·7′W	W	115
Swallowfield	Wok	SU7264	51°22·5′	0°57·5′W	T	175,186
Swallowfield	W Susx	TQ2028	51°2·6′	0°16·9′W	X	187,198
Swallowfield Park	Wok	SU7365	51°23·0′	0°56·7′W	X	175
Swallowfields	Devon	SX7961	50°26·4′	3°41·9′W	T	202
Swallow Grove Fm	Herts	TL3310	51°46·6′	0°3·9′W	FM	166
Swallow Hall	York	SE6546	53°54·6′	1°0·2′W	X	105,106
Swallowhayes	Devon	SS9407	50°51·4′	3°30·0′W	X	192
Swallow Head Fm	N Yks	NZ9302	54°24·5′	0°33·6′W	FM	94
Swallowhead Springs	Wilts	SU1068	51°24·9′	1°51·0′W	W	173
Swallow Hill	Barns	SE3209	53°34·8′	1°30·6′W	X	110,111
Swallow Hole Fm	Leic	SK8427	52°50·3′	0°44·8′W	FM	130
Swallow Knowe	Northum	NU0705	55°20·6′	1°52·9′W	H	81
Swallow Mill Fm	Kent	TQ9346	51°11·1′	0°46·1′E	FM	189
Swallow Mire	Cumbr	SD4187	54°16·8′	2°54·0′W	X	96,97
Swallow Moss	Staffs	SK0660	53°8·5′	1°54·2′W	X	119
Swallow Mount	Lincs	TA1604	53°31·4′	0°14·6′W	X	113
Swallow Nest	N Yks	SE5472	54°8·7′	1°10·0′W	X	100
Swallownest	Roth	SK4485	53°21·8′	1°19·9′W	T	111,120
Swallowpits Beck	N Yks	SE7459	54°1·5′	0°51·8′W	W	105,106
Swallow Scars	Lancs	SD7451	53°57·5′	2°23·4′W	X	103
Swallows Cross	Essex	TQ6198	51°39·7′	0°20·1′E	T	167,177
Swallows Fm	W Susx	TQ1520	50°58·3′	0°21·3′W	FM	198
Swallowship Hill	Northum	NY9662	54°57·4′	2°3·3′W	X	87
Swallow Shore	Lancs	SD8326	53°44·0′	2°15·0′W	X	103
Swallow Tree	Devon	SX7296	50°45·2′	3°48·5′W	X	191
Swallow Vale Fm	Lincs	TA1704	53°31·4′	0°13·7′W	FM	113
Swallow Wold	Lincs	TA1604	53°31·4′	0°14·6′W	X	113
Swalwell	Ghead	NZ2062	54°57·4′	1°42·8′W	T	88
Swamp, The	Derby	SK1095	53°27·3′	1°50·6′W	X	110
Swampton	Hants	SU4150	51°15·1′	1°24·4′W	T	185
Swanage	Dorset	SZ0278	50°36·3′	1°57·9′W	T	195
Swanage Bay	Dorset	SZ0379	50°36·9′	1°57·1′W	W	195
Swanage Railway	Dorset	SZ0279	50°36·9′	1°57·9′W	X	195
Swanbach	Ches	SJ6542	52°58·7′	2°30·9′W	T	118
Swan Barn	Lancs	SD7448	53°55·9′	2°23·3′W	X	103
Swanbeck Fm	N Yks	SE9990	54°18·0′	0°28·3′W	FM	94,101
Swanbister	Orkney	HY3405	58°55·4′	3°8·3′W	T	6,7
Swanbister Bay	Orkney	HY3604	58°55·4′	3°6·2′W	W	6,7
Swanbister House	Orkney	HY3505	58°55·9′	3°7·3′W	X	6,7
Swanborough	Swin	SU1891	51°37·3′	1°44·0′W	T	163,173
Swanborough Hill	E Susx	TQ3806	50°50·4′	0°2·0′W	X	198
Swanborough Manor	E Susx	TQ3907	50°51·0′	0°1·1′W	A	198
Swanborough Tump	Wilts	SU1360	51°20·6′	1°48·4′W	A	173
Swan Bottom	Bucks	SP9005	51°44·4′	0°41·4′W	T	165
Swanboune Ho	Bucks	SP7927	51°56·4′	0°50·6′W	X	165
Swanbourne	Bucks	SP8027	51°56·4′	0°49·8′W	T	165
Swanbourne Lake	W Susx	TQ0108	50°52·0′	0°33·5′W	W	197
Swanbridge	V of Glam	ST1667	51°24·0′	3°12·1′W	T	171
Swan Bushes	Leeds	SE3043	53°53·2′	1°32·2′W	F	104
Swancar Fm	Notts	SK4939	52°57·0′	1°15·8′W	FM	129
Swan Carr	Durham	NZ3126	54°37·9′	1°30·8′W	X	93
Swancote	Shrops	SO7494	52°32·8′	2°22·6′W	X	138
Swancote Fm	Worcs	SO9074	52°22·1′	2°8·4′W	FM	139
Swancroft	Lincs	TF4195	53°26·2′	0°7·8′E	X	113
Swandale	Orkney	HY4332	59°10·5′	2°59·3′W	X	5,6
Swan Fm	Kent	TQ7239	51°7·7′	0°27·9′E	FM	188
Swan Fm	Norf	TG3027	52°47·7′	1°25·1′E	FM	133,134
Swanford	Aberd	NJ8245	57°29·9′	2°17·6′W	X	29,30
Swang	Cumbr	NY0401	54°24·0′	3°28·3′W	X	89
Swang	N Yks	NZ0701	54°24·5′	1°53·1′W	X	92
Swangey Fen	Norf	TM0093	52°30·1′	0°57·2′E	X	144
Swangey Fm	Norf	TM0194	52°30·6′	0°58·1′E	FM	144
Swang Fm	N Yks	NZ7605	54°26·3′	0°49·3′W	FM	94
Swang Fm	Somer	ST2338	51°8·4′	3°5·7′W	FM	182
Swangley's Fm	Herts	TL2519	51°51·6′	0°10·7′W	FM	166
Swan Green	Ches	SJ7373	53°15·4′	2°23·9′W	T	118
Swan Green	Suff	TM2974	52°19·2′	1°22·0′E	T	156
Swangrove	S Glos	ST7986	51°34·6′	2°17·8′W	F	172
Swanhall Fm	Oxon	SP3612	51°48·6′	1°28·3′W	FM	164
Swan Hill	E Yorks	TA1532	53°46·5′	0°14·9′W	A	107
Swanhill	Northum	NZ1496	55°15·7′	1°46·4′W	X	81
Swan Hill	Shrops	SO4178	52°24·0′	2°51·6′W	X	137,148
Swan Hill Fm	N Yks	SE9781	54°13·2′	0°30·3′W	FM	101
Swanholme Lakes	Lincs	SK9468	53°12·3′	0°35·1′W	W	121
Swan Hotel	Cumbr	NY2226	54°37·6′	3°12·1′W	X	89,90
Swan House Fm	Darl	NZ2519	54°34·2′	1°36·4′W	FM	93
Swan I	E Yorks	TA1947	53°54·6′	0°10·9′W	X	107
Swanlake Bay	Pemb	SS0497	51°38·5′	4°49·6′W	W	158
Swanland	E Yorks	SE9927	53°44·0′	0°29·5′W	T	106
Swan Lane Fm	Kent	TQ4448	51°13·0′	0°4·1′E	FM	187
Swanlaws	Scot Bord	NT7716	55°26·5′	2°21·4′W	X	80
Swanley	Glos	ST7096	51°40·0′	2°25·6′W	T	162
Swanley	Kent	TQ5168	51°23·7′	0°10·6′E	T	177
Swanley Bar	Herts	TL2502	51°42·4′	0°11·1′W	T	166
Swanley Fm	Kent	TR0072	51°24·9′	0°53·0′E	FM	178
Swanley Hall	Ches	SJ6152	53°4·1′	2°34·5′W	X	118
Swanley Village	Kent	TQ5269	51°24·2′	0°11·5′E	T	177
Swan Loch	E Ayr	NS5022	55°28·4′	4°22·0′W	W	70
Swan Lodge	Norf	TG0641	52°55·8′	1°4·3′E	X	133
Swanmoor	Devon	SS5626	51°1·2′	4°2·8′W	X	180
Swanmore	Hants	SU5716	50°56·7′	1°10·9′W	T	185
Swanmore	I of W	SZ5991	50°43·2′	1°9·5′W	T	196
Swanmore Park Ho	Hants	SU5817	50°57·2′	1°10·1′W	X	185
Swannacott	Corn	SX2497	50°45·0′	4°29·3′W	X	190
Swannacott Wood	Corn	SX2498	50°45·5′	4°29·3′W	F	190
Swannaton	Devon	SS8005	50°50·2′	3°41·9′W	X	191

Swannaton	Devon	SX8750	50°20·6′	3°34·9′W	X	202
Swannay Fm	Orkney	HY2929	59°8·8′	3°14·0′W	FM	6
Swannies Point	Orkney	ND4697	58°51·7′	2°55·7′W	X	6,7
Swannington	Leic	SK4116	52°44·6′	1°23·2′W	T	129
Swannington	Norf	TG1319	52°43·8′	1°9·7′E	T	133
Swannington Bottom Plantation	Norf	TG1517	52°42·7′	1°11·4′E	F	133
Swannington Common	Leic	SK4216	52°44·6′	1°22·3′W	X	129
Swannybrook Fm	Oxon	SU4096	51°39·9′	1°24·9′W	FM	164
Swanpens Fm	Lincs	TF2819	52°45·4′	0°5·8′W	FM	131
Swan Pond	S Ayr	NS2209	55°20·8′	4°48·0′W	W	70,76
Swan Pool	Corn	SW8031	50°8·5′	5°4·4′W	W	204
Swanpool	Lincs	SK9570	53°13·3′	0°34·2′W	T	121
Swan Pool	Sand	SP0292	52°31·8′	1°57·8′W	W	139
Swanpool Beach	Corn	SW8031	50°8·5′	5°4·4′W	X	204
Swan Pool Drain	Carm	SN4001	51°41·3′	4°18·5′W	W	159
Swanpool Point	Corn	SW8031	50°8·5′	5°4·4′W	X	204
Swans	Lancs	SD6563	54°4·0′	2°31·7′W	X	97
Swansbrook Fm	E Susx	TQ5714	50°54·5′	0°14·4′E	FM	199
Swansbrook Fm	Wilts	ST8256	51°18·4′	2°15·1′W	FM	173
Swanscoe Hall	Ches	SJ9375	53°16·6′	2°5·9′W	X	118
Swanscombe	Kent	TQ5974	51°26·8′	0°17·7′E	T	177
Swanscombe Fm	Essex	TL8728	51°55·4′	0°43·6′E	FM	168
Swanscombe Marshes	Kent	TQ6075	51°27·3′	0°18·6′E	X	177
Swansea Airport	Swan	SS5691	51°36·2′	4°4·4′W	X	159
Swansea Bay	Swan	SS6888	51°34·8′	3°53·9′W	W	159
Swansea Bay / Bae Abertawe		SS6988	51°34·8′	3°53·1′W	W	170
Swansea Fm	Somer	SS9933	51°5·5′	3°26·2′W	FM	181
Swansea/Abertawe	Swan	SS6494	51°37·9′	3°57·5′W	T	159
Swansea Valley	Nth Pt Talb	SN7304	51°43·5′	3°49·9′W	X	170
Swansea Valley	Nth Pt Talb	SN7405	51°44·0′	3°49·1′W	X	160
Swansfield	Scot Bord	NT8462	55°51·3′	2°14·9′W	X	67
Swan's Fm	Essex	TL6139	52°1·8′	0°21·2′E	FM	154
Swan's Fm	Hants	SU7652	51°16·0′	0°54·2′W	FM	186
Swan's Hall	Suff	TL7951	52°7·9′	0°37·3′E	X	155
Swan Shank	Northum	NZ7993	55°14·1′	2°19·4′W	X	80
Swan's Hill	Worcs	SP0574	52°22·1′	1°55·2′W	X	139
Swanside	Know	SJ4191	53°25·0′	2°52·9′W	T	108
Swanside	Lancs	SD7946	53°54·8′	2°18·8′W	X	103
Swanside Beck	Lancs	SD7946	53°54·8′	2°18·8′W	W	103
Swansley Wood Fm	Cambs	TL3060	52°13·6′	0°5·4′W	FM	153
Swansmoor	Staffs	SK0124	52°49·1′	1°58·7′W	X	128
Swan's Neck	Worcs	SO9342	52°4·8′	2°5·7′W	W	150
Swansriver	Mil Key	SP9246	52°6·5′	0°39·0′W	X	152
Swanstead	Northum	NZ0978	55°6·0′	1°51·1′W	X	88
Swanstead Hill	Scot Bord	NT4109	55°22·5′	2°55·4′W	H	79
Swanston	C of Edin	NT2368	55°54·2′	3°13·5′W	T	66
Swanston	C of Edin	NT2467	55°53·7′	3°12·5′W	T	66
Swanston Burn	C of Edin	NT2567	55°53·7′	3°11·5′W	W	66
Swanstone	Devon	SS6000	50°47·2′	3°58·8′W	X	191
Swanstone Court	Heref	SO4453	52°10·6′	2°48·7′W	X	148,149
Swanstone Moor	Devon	SS6100	50°47·2′	3°57·9′W	X	191
Swan Street	Essex	TL8927	51°54·8′	0°45·3′E	T	168
Swan Street	Kent	TQ9349	51°12·7′	0°46·2′E	X	189
Swan's Way	Bucks	SP7910	51°47·2′	0°50·9′W	X	165
Swan's Way	Mil Key	SP8343	52°5·0′	0°46·9′W	X	152
Swan's Way	Oxon	SU6691	51°37·1′	1°2·4′W	X	164,175
Swansyard Fm	E Susx	TQ3316	50°55·9′	0°6·0′W	FM	198
Swanthorpe Fm	Hants	SU7747	51°13·2′	0°53·5′W	FM	186
Swanthorpe Ho	Hants	SU7846	51°12·7′	0°52·6′W	X	186
Swanton	Kent	TR2058	51°16·9′	1°9·7′E	X	179
Swanton Abbott	Norf	TG2625	52°46·7′	1°21·5′E	T	133,134
Swanton Court	Kent	TR0339	51°7·1′	0°54·4′E	X	179,189
Swanton Court Fm	Kent	TR2444	51°9·3′	1°12·6′E	FM	179,189
Swanton Fm	Kent	TQ8758	51°17·6′	0°41·3′E	FM	178
Swanton Fm	Kent	TR0235	51°4·9′	0°53·4′E	FM	189
Swanton Great Wood	Norf	TG0131	52°50·6′	0°59·5′E	F	133
Swanton Hill	Norf	TG2626	52°47·3′	1°21·5′E	T	133,134
Swanton Mill	Kent	TR0338	51°6·5′	0°54·4′E	X	179,189
Swanton Morley	Norf	TG0116	52°42·5′	0°58·9′E	T	133
Swanton Morley Airfield (Dis)	Norf	TG0018	52°43·6′	0°58·1′E	X	133
Swanton Morley Ho	Norf	TG0017	52°43·0′	0°58·1′E	X	133
Swanton Novers	Norf	TG0232	52°51·1′	1°0·4′E	T	133
Swanton Street	Kent	TQ8759	51°18·2′	0°41·4′E	T	178
Swanton Valley	Kent	TQ6353	51°15·4′	0°20·6′E	X	188
Swan Village	Sand	SO9892	52°31·8′	2°1·4′W	T	139
Swanwick	Derby	SK4053	53°4·6′	1°23·8′W	T	120
Swanwick	Hants	SU5109	50°52·9′	1°16·1′W	T	196
Swanwick Green	Ches	SJ5547	53°1·3′	2°39·8′W	T	117
Swanwick Hall Fm	Ches	SJ7670	53°13·8′	2°21·2′W	FM	118
Swanwick Sta	Hants	SU5108	50°52·4′	1°16·1′W	X	196
Swan Wood	Oxon	SU6985	51°33·8′	0°59·9′W	F	175
Swape Foot	Durham	NZ1326	54°38·0′	1°47·5′W	X	92
Swap Hill	Somer	SS8142	51°10·1′	3°41·7′W	X	181
Swarbacks Head	Shetld	HU2861	60°20·2′	1°29·1′W	X	3
Swarbacks Minn	Shetld	HU3161	60°20·2′	1°25·8′W	W	3
Swarbacks Skerry	Shetld	HU2962	60°20·7′	1°28·0′W	X	3
Swarble Hill	N Yks	SE1489	54°18·0′	1°46·7′W	X	99
Swarbrick Hall	Lancs	SD3935	53°48·7′	2°55·2′W	X	102
Swarby	Lincs	TF0440	52°57·1′	0°26·7′W	T	130
Swarcliffe	Leeds	SE3636	53°49·4′	1°26·8′W	T	104
Swarcliffe	N Yks	SE2259	54°1·8′	1°39·4′W	X	104
Swardeston	Norf	TG2002	52°34·5′	1°15·2′E	T	134
Sward Field	N Yks	SE1496	54°21·8′	1°46·7′W	X	99
Swardicott	Devon	SS4807	50°50·8′	4°9·2′W	X	191
Sware Brae	D & G	NS5902	55°17·8′	4°12·8′W	X	77
Sware Gill Head	N Yks	SD7473	54°9·4′	2°23·5′W	X	98
Swarf Hill	Scot Bord	NY5187	55°10·7′	2°45·7′W	H	79
Swarf, The	Orkney	HY6032	59°10·6′	2°41·5′W	X	5,6
Swarf, The	Orkney	HY6737	59°13·4′	2°34·2′W	X	5
Swarf, The	Shetld	HU4623	59°59·6′	1°10·0′W	X	4
Swarister	Shetld	HU5284	60°32·4′	1°2·6′W	T	1,2,3
Swarkestone	Derby	SK3728	52°51·1′	1°26·6′W	T	128
Swarkestone Bridge	Derby	SK3727	52°50·6′	1°26·6′W	A	128
Swarkestone Lows	Derby	SK3629	52°51·7′	1°27·5′W	A	128
Swarland	Northum	NU1603	55°19·5′	1°44·4′W	T	81

Swarland Burn	Northum	NU1402	55°19·0′	1°46·3′W	W	81
Swarlanddean	Northum	NU1701	55°18·4′	1°43·5′W	X	81
Swarland Fence	Northum	NU1501	55°18·4′	1°45·4′W	X	81
Swarland Wood	Northum	NU1503	55°19·5′	1°45·4′W	F	81
Swarling Manor Fm	Kent	TR1252	51°13·9′	1°2·6′E	FM	179,189
Swarm Haugh Closes	Cambs	TL4779	52°23·6′	0°10·0′E	X	143
Swarraton	Hants	SU5637	51°8·0′	1°11·6′W	T	185
Swarraton Fm	Hants	SU5736	51°7·5′	1°10·7′W	FM	185
Swarsquoy	Orkney	HY4909	58°58·2′	2°52·7′W	X	6,7
Swarta Fiold	Orkney	HY3928	59°8·3′	3°3·5′W	X	6
Swartafiold	Orkney	HY4232	59°10·5′	3°0·4′W	X	5,6
Swartaquoy	Orkney	HY5119	59°3·6′	2°50·8′W	X	6
Swarta Shun	Shetld	HU4688	60°34·6′	1°9·1′W	W	1,2
Swarta Skerries	Shetld	HU6362	60°20·5′	0°51·0′W	X	2
Swarta Skerry	Shetld	HP6407	60°44·7′	0°49·1′W	X	1
Swarta Skerry	Shetld	HU1559	60°19·2′	1°43·2′W	X	3
Swarta Skerry	Shetld	HU2973	60°26·7′	1°27·9′W	X	3
Swarta Skerry	Shetld	HU3415	59°55·4′	1°23·0′W	X	4
Swarta Skerry	Shetld	HU3443	60°10·5′	1°22·7′W	X	4
Swarta Skerry	Shetld	HU4761	60°20·1′	1°8·4′W	X	2,3
Swarta Skerry	Shetld	HU4868	60°23·8′	1°7·2′W	X	2,3
Swarta Skerry	Shetld	HU5266	60°22·7′	1°2·9′W	X	2,3
Swarta Skerry	Shetld	HU5373	60°26·5′	1°1·7′W	X	2,3
Swarta Skerry	Shetld	HU6493	60°37·2′	0°49·3′W	X	1,2
Swarta Taing	Shetld	HU4078	60°29·3′	1°15·8′W	X	2,3
Swartha	Brad	SE0546	53°54·8′	1°55·0′W	T	104
Swarthbank	Cumbr	NY4419	54°34·0′	2°51·5′W	X	90
Swarthbeck	Cumbr	NY4520	54°34·6′	2°50·6′W	X	90
Swarth Beck	Cumbr	NY7725	54°37·4′	2°21·0′W	W	91
Swarthdale	Lancs	SD5368	54°6·6′	2°42·7′W	X	97
Swart Hellia Geo	Orkney	HY4944	59°17·0′	2°53·2′W	X	5
Swart Helligeo	Orkney	HY5317	59°2·5′	2°48·7′W	X	6
Swarther Plantn	Cumbr	SD5986	54°16·3′	2°37·4′W	F	97
Swarth Fell	Cumbr	NY4519	54°34·0′	2°50·6′W	X	90
Swarth Fell	Cumbr	SD7596	54°21·8′	2°22·7′W	H	98
Swarth Fell Pike	Cumbr	SD7695	54°21·2′	2°21·7′W	H	98
Swarthfield	Cumbr	NY4420	54°34·6′	2°51·6′W	X	90
Swarthgill	N Yks	SD8482	54°14·3′	2°14·3′W	X	98
Swarth Greaves	Cumbr	SD6495	54°21·2′	2°32·8′W	X	97
Swarth Hill	N Yks	SE3050	53°57·0′	1°32·2′W	X	104
Swarth Howe	N Yks	SE9694	54°20·2′	0°31·0′W	A	94,101
Swarthmoor	Cumbr	SD2777	54°11·3′	3°6·7′W	T	96,97
Swarth Moor	N Yks	SD8068	54°6·7′	2°17·9′W	X	98
Swarthoull	Shetld	HU2978	60°29·3′	1°27·8′W	X	3
Swart Houll	Shetld	HU6491	60°36·1′	0°49·4′W	X	1,2
Swarthouse	Highld	ND3246	58°24·1′	3°9·3′W	X	12
Swart Howe	Orkney	HY5003	58°54·9′	2°51·6′W	X	6,7
Swarthy Hill	Cumbr	NY0640	54°45·0′	3°27·2′W	X	85
Swarthy Mere	Durham	NY9622	54°35·8′	2°3·3′W	X	91,92
Swartiebank	Highld	ND2861	58°32·1′	3°13·7′W	X	11,12
Swarti Meadow	Shetld	HU1951	60°14·8′	1°38·9′W	X	3
Swartland	Orkney	HY2721	59°4·5′	3°15·9′W	X	6
Swartland	Orkney	ND3092	58°48·9′	3°12·2′W	X	7
Swarting	Shetld	HP6515	60°49·0′	0°47·8′W	X	1
Swart Skerry	Shetld	HU3511	59°53·2′	1°22·0′W	X	4
Swart Skerry	Shetld	HU4012	59°53·7′	1°16·6′W	X	4
Swartz Geo	Shetld	HZ2170	59°31·2′	1°37·2′W	X	4
Swasedale Fm	Cambs	TL5881	52°24·5′	0°19·8′E	FM	143
Swastika Stone	Brad	SE0946	53°54·8′	1°51·4′W	A	104
Swatchway	Northum	NY1358	54°54·8′	3°21·0′W	W	85
Swath Beck	Cumbr	NY7133	54°41·7′	2°26·6′W	W	91
Swathburn	Cumbr	NY7012	54°30·4′	2°27·4′W	X	91
Swathgill	N Yks	SE6373	54°9·2′	1°1·7′W	X	100
Swathwaite Head	Cumbr	NY4243	54°47·0′	2°53·7′W	X	85
Swathwick	Derby	SK3667	53°12·2′	1°27·3′W	T	119
Swatnage Wood	Wilts	ST9888	51°35·7′	2°1·3′W	F	173
Swaton	Lincs	TF1337	52°55·3′	0°18·7′W	T	130
Swaton Common	Lincs	TF1138	52°55·9′	0°20·5′W	X	130
Swaton Fen	Lincs	TF1536	52°54·8′	0°17·0′W	X	130
Swatte Fell	D & G	NT1111	55°23·3′	3°23·9′W	H	78
Swavesey	Cambs	TL3668	52°17·8′	0°0·1′E	T	154
Swaw Beck	N Yks	SD8062	54°3·5′	2°17·9′W	X	98
Sway	Hants	SZ2798	50°47·1′	1°36·6′W	T	195
Swayfield	Lincs	SK9922	52°47·4′	0°31·5′W	T	130
Swayfield Lodge	Lincs	SK9924	52°48·5′	0°31·5′W	X	130
Swaylands (Sch)	Kent	TQ5343	51°10·2′	0°11·7′E	X	188
Swayne's Firs	Hants	SU0722	51°0·1′	1°53·6′W	F	184
Swayne's Hall	Essex	TL5431	51°57·6′	0°14·9′E	X	167
Swayne's Jumps	Somer	ST4037	51°8·0′	2°51·1′W	X	182
Swaynesland	Surrey	TQ4250	51°14·1′	0°2·4′E	X	187
Swaythling	C of Soton	SU4315	50°56·2′	1°22·9′W	T	196
Swaythorpe	E Yorks	TA0368	54°6·1′	0°25·1′W	X	101
Swaythorpe Plantn	E Yorks	TA0469	54°6·6′	0°24·1′W	F	101
Swaythorpe Village	E Yorks	TA0369	54°6·6′	0°25·0′W	A	101
Swch-cae-rhiw	Wrex	SJ1335	52°54·6′	3°17·2′W	X	125
Swch y Llan	Conwy	SH9348	53°1·4′	3°35·3′W	X	116
Sweare Deep	Hants	SU7304	50°50·1′	0°57·4′W	W	197
Sweat Mere	Shrops	SJ4330	52°52·1′	2°50·4′W	W	126
Sweden Sykes	N Yks	SE3196	54°21·8′	1°31·0′W	X	99
Sweenalay	Orkney	HY3819	59°3·5′	3°4·4′W	X	6
Sweeney Hall Hotel	Shrops	SJ2926	52°49·9′	3°2·8′W	X	126
Sweeney Mountain	Shrops	SJ2725	52°49·3′	3°4·6′W	X	126
Sweep Fm	Leeds	SE4046	53°54·8′	1°23·0′W	FM	105
Sweepstakes Fm	Kent	TQ8363	51°20·4′	0°38·0′E	FM	178,188
Sweerburn	Aberd	NJ6553	57°34·2′	2°34·6′W	X	29
Sweet Appletree	Shrops	SJ6728	52°51·1′	2°29·0′W	X	127
Sweetbit	D & G	NS8502	55°18·2′	3°48·3′W	X	78
Sweetbriar Fm	N Lincs	TA1017	53°38·5′	0°19·8′W	FM	113
Sweetbrier Fm	Beds	TL1245	52°5·7′	0°21·5′W	FM	153
Sweet Burn	Angus	NO4537	56°31·6′	2°53·2′W	W	54
Sweet Clough	Lancs	SD8938	53°50·5′	2°9·6′W	X	103
Sweet Earth	N Yks	SE1461	54°2·9′	1°46·8′W	X	99
Sweetfield	Devon	SS7401	50°47·9′	3°46·9′W	X	191
Sweet Green	Worcs	SO6462	52°15·5′	2°31·2′W	T	138,149
Sweetham	Devon	SX8899	50°47·0′	3°34·9′W	T	192
Sweet Haugh	Northum	NU0230	55°34·1′	1°57·7′W	X	75
Sweethaws	E Susx	TQ5028	51°2·1′	0°8·8′E	T	188,199
Sweethay	Somer	ST2021	50°59·2′	3°8·0′W	T	193
Sweethill Fm	W Susx	TQ1715	50°55·6′	0°19·7′W	FM	198
Sweethillock	Moray	NJ1361	57°38·1′	3°27·0′W	X	28

Sweethillock	Moray	NJ1969	57°42·5′	3°21·1′W	X	28
Sweet Hills	N Lincs	SK9299	53°29·0′	0°36·4′W	X	112
Sweet Hills Fm	N Yks	SE5058	54°1·2′	1°13·8′W	FM	105
Sweetholm	Fife	NO3210	56°16·9′	3°5·5′W	X	59
Sweetholme	Cumbr	NY5518	54°33·6′	2°41·3′W	T	90
Sweethope	Northum	NY9581	55°7·6′	2°4·3′W	X	81
Sweethope	Scot Bord	NT6839	55°38·9′	2°30·1′W	X	74
Sweethope Crags	Northum	NY9681	55°7·6′	2°3·3′W	H	81
Sweethope Hill	Scot Bord	NT6939	55°38·9′	2°29·1′W	H	74
Sweethope Loughs	Northum	NY9482	55°8·2′	2°5·2′W	W	80
Sweetiehillock	Aberd	NJ8754	57°34·8′	2°12·6′W	H	30
Sweetings	Lancs	SD4450	53°56·8′	2°50·8′W	X	102
Sweeting's Green	Norf	TM2187	52°26·4′	1°15·5′E	X	156
Sweeting Thorns	N Lincs	SE9307	53°33·3′	0°35·4′W	F	112
Sweet Knowle Fm	Warw	SP2047	52°7·5′	1°42·1′W	FM	151
Sweetlands Couchman Green	Kent	TQ7945	51°10·8′	0°34·1′E	X	188
Sweetlands Fm	Devon	ST2110	50°53·3′	3°7·0′W	FM	192,193
Sweet Nap Fm	Somer	ST7537	51°8·1′	2°21·1′W	FM	183
Sweetnap Fm	Somer	ST7537	51°8·1′	2°21·1′W	FM	183
Sweet Pits Plantation	Lincs	TF4467	53°11·1′	0°9·7′E	F	122
Sweet Rigg	Northum	NY7570	55°1·7′	2°23·0′W	H	86,87
Sweets	Corn	SX1595	50°43·7′	4°36·9′W	T	190
Sweetshaw Brae	S Lanak	NS9809	55°22·1′	3°36·1′W	X	78
Sweetshaw Burn	S Lanak	NS9908	55°21·6′	3°35·2′W	W	78
Sweetshaw Rig	S Lanak	NS9807	55°21·0′	3°36·1′W	H	78
Sweetshouse	Corn	SX0861	50°25·3′	4°41·8′W	T	200
Sweet Side	N Yks	SD8089	54°18·0′	2°18·0′W	X	98
Sweet Side	N Yks	SD9965	54°5·1′	2°0·5′W	X	98
Sweet Sike	Northum	NY7271	55°2·2′	2°25·9′W	W	86,87
Sweetslade Fm	Glos	SP1418	51°51·9′	1°47·4′W	FM	163
Sweetstone	Devon	SX8250	50°20·5′	3°39·1′W	X	202
Sweetwell	Corn	SX2285	50°38·5′	4°30·7′W	X	201
Sweetwell Fm	Wilts	ST8528	51°3·3′	2°12·5′W	FM	183
Sweetworthy	Somer	SS8842	51°10·2′	3°35·7′W	X	181
Sweffling	Suff	TM3463	52°13·1′	1°26·0′E	T	156
Sweffling Hall	Suff	TM3364	52°13·7′	1°25·1′E	X	156
Sweinna Stack	Shetld	HU4391	60°36·3′	1°12·4′W	X	1,2
Sweinn Geo	Orkney	ND2391	58°48·2′	3°19·5′W	X	7
Swell	Somer	ST3623	51°0·4′	2°54·3′W	T	193
Swellands Resr	Kirk	SE0309	53°34·9′	1°56·9′W	W	110
Swell Buildings Fm	Glos	SP1526	51°56·2′	1°46·5′W	FM	163
Swell Court Farm	Somer	ST3623	51°0·4′	2°54·3′W	A	193
Swellhead	Aberd	NO8897	57°4·1′	2°11·4′W	T	38,45
Swell Hill Fm	Glos	SP1526	51°56·2′	1°46·5′W	FM	163
Swelling Hill	Hants	SU6532	51°5·2′	1°3·9′W	T	185,186
Swell Wold Fm	Glos	SP1326	51°56·2′	1°48·3′W	FM	163
Swenstay	Orkney	HY5331	59°10·1′	2°48·8′W	X	5,6
Swepstone	Leic	SK3610	52°41·4′	1°27·6′W	T	128
Swerbrook Fm	Oxon	SP3933	51°59·9′	1°25·5′W	FM	151
Swerford	Oxon	SP3731	51°58·8′	1°27·3′W	T	151
Swerford Heath	Oxon	SP3831	51°58·8′	1°26·4′W	X	151
Swerford Park	Oxon	SP3631	51°58·8′	1°28·2′W	X	151
Swerves Fm	Wilts	ST9871	51°26·5′	2°1·3′W	FM	173
Swettenham	Ches	SJ8067	53°12·2′	2°17·6′W	T	118
Swettenham Brook	Ches	SJ7967	53°12·2′	2°18·5′W	W	118
Swettenham Hall	Ches	SJ8066	53°11·7′	2°17·6′W	X	118
Swettenham Heath	Ches	SJ8167	53°12·2′	2°16·7′W	X	118
Swetton	N Yks	SE1973	54°9·4′	1°42·1′W	T	99
Swetton Moor	N Yks	SE1872	54°8·9′	1°43·0′W	X	99
Swevers Taing	Shetld	HU5166	60°22·7′	1°4·0′W	X	2,3
Swey	Shetld	HZ2173	59°32·8′	1°37·2′W	X	4
Sweyne's Howes	Swan	SS4289	51°34·9′	4°16·4′W	X	159
Sweyne's Howes (Burial Chambers)	Swan	SS4289	51°34·9′	4°16·4′W	A	159
Sweyney Cliff	Shrops	SJ7001	52°36·6′	2°26·2′W	X	127
Sweyn Holm	Orkney	HY4522	59°5·1′	2°57·1′W	X	5,6
Sweyn Holm	Shetld	HU3520	59°58·1′	1°21·9′W	X	4
Sweyn Ness	Shetld	HU5044	60°10·9′	1°5·4′W	X	4
Swffryd	Blae Gw	ST2199	51°41·3′	3°8·2′W	T	171
Swift Burn	Northum	NY9274	55°3·9′	2°7·1′W	W	87
Swiftsden	E Susx	TQ7228	51°1·8′	0°27·6′E	X	188,199
Swifts Fm	Hants	SU4921	50°59·4′	1°17·7′W	FM	185
Swift's Green	Kent	TQ8744	51°10·1′	0°40·9′E	T	189
Swift's Hill	Glos	SO8706	51°45·4′	2°10·9′W	X	162
Swifts House Fm	Oxon	SP5527	51°56·6′	1°11·6′W	FM	164
Swifts Manor	Suff	TL9549	52°6·5′	0°51·3′E	X	155
Swigshole	Medway	TQ7877	51°28·1′	0°34·2′E	X	178
Swilcarlawn Fm	Staffs	SK1328	52°51·2′	1°48·0′W	FM	128
Swilder Burn	Northum	NZ0382	55°8·2′	1°56·7′W	W	81
Swilebog	Aberd	NJ5555	57°35·2′	2°44·7′W	X	29
Swilkie Point	Highld	ND3579	58°41·9′	3°6·8′W	X	7,12
Swilla Glen	N Yks	SD6974	54°9·9′	2°28·1′W	X	98
Swilland	Suff	TM1852	52°7·6′	1°11·5′E	T	156
Swilland Manor	Suff	TM1853	52°8·2′	1°11·5′E	X	156
Swillbrook	Lancs	SD4834	53°48·2′	2°47·0′W	T	102
Swill Brook	Wilts	SU0293	51°38·4′	1°57·9′W	W	163,173
Swillbrook Fm	Wilts	SU0293	51°38·4′	1°57·9′W	FM	163,173
Swillbrook Ho	Lancs	SD4834	53°48·2′	2°47·0′W	X	102
Swilletts Fm	Dorset	ST4201	50°48·6′	2°49·0′W	FM	193
Swillington	Leeds	SE3830	53°46·1′	1°25·0′W	T	104
Swillington Common	Leeds	SE3832	53°47·2′	1°25·0′W	T	104
Swimbridge	Devon	SS6229	51°2·9′	3°57·7′W	T	180
Swimbridge Newland	Devon	SS6030	51°3·4′	3°59·5′W	T	180
Swim Coots	Norf	TG4121	52°44·2′	1°34·6′E	W	134
Swinabbey	W Loth	NS9765	55°52·3′	3°38·3′W	X	65
Swinacote	N Yks	SD9886	54°16·4′	2°1·4′W	X	98
Swinawe Wood	Northnts	SP8486	52°28·2′	0°45·4′W	F	141
Swinbatch	Shrops	SJ6901	52°36·6′	2°27·1′W	X	127
Swin Ber	Orkney	HY5809	58°58·2′	2°43·3′W	X	6
Swinbrook	Oxon	SP2812	51°48·6′	1°35·2′W	T	163
Swinburne Castle	Northum	NY9375	55°4·4′	2°6·1′W	X	87
Swinburn's Park	Cumbr	NY4221	54°35·1′	2°53·4′W	X	90
Swinchurch Fm	Staffs	SJ8037	52°56·0′	2°17·4′W	FM	127
Swincliffe	Kirk	SE2027	53°44·6′	1°41·4′W	T	104
Swincliffe	N Yks	SE2458	54°1·3′	1°37·6′W	T	104
Swincombe	Devon	SS6941	51°9·4′	3°52·0′W	T	180
Swincombe Head	Devon	SX6369	50°30·5′	3°55·6′W	W	202
Swincombe Rocks	Devon	SS6942	51°10·0′	3°52·0′W	X	180
Swincombe (ruin)	Devon	SX6372	50°32·1′	3°55·6′W	X	191
Swindale Beck	Cumbr	NY5113	54°30·8′	2°45·0′W	W	90
Swindale Beck	Cumbr	NY6928	54°39·0′	2°28·4′W	W	91
Swindale Beck	Cumbr	NY8016	54°32·6′	2°18·1′W	W	91,92
Swindale Common	Cumbr	NY4913	54°30·8′	2°46·8′W	X	90
Swindale Edge	Cumbr	NY7521	54°35·3′	2°22·8′W	X	91
Swindale Fm	Red & Cl	NZ6714	54°31·3′	0°57·5′W	FM	94
Swindale Foot	Cumbr	NY5213	54°30·8′	2°44·1′W	X	90
Swindale Grange	Cumbr	NY8015	54°32·0′	2°18·1′W	X	91,92
Swindale Head	Cumbr	NY5012	54°30·3′	2°45·9′W	X	90
Swindalehead Ho	Cumbr	NY8117	54°33·1′	2°17·2′W	X	91,92
Swinden	Lancs	SD8833	53°47·8′	2°10·5′W	X	103
Swinden	N Yks	SD8654	53°59·2′	2°12·4′W	T	103
Swinden Gill Wood	N Yks	SD8654	53°59·2′	2°12·4′W	F	103
Swinden Moor Head	N Yks	SD8753	53°58·6′	2°11·5′W	X	103
Swinden Quarry	N Yks	SD9761	54°2·9′	2°2·3′W	X	98
Swinden Resrs	Lancs	SD8833	53°47·8′	2°10·5′W	W	103
Swinden Water	Lancs	SD9033	53°47·8′	2°8·7′W	W	103
Swinderby	Lincs	SK8662	53°9·1′	0°42·4′W	T	121
Swinderby Sta	Lincs	SK8664	53°10·2′	0°42·4′W	X	121
Swindon	Glos	SO9325	51°55·6′	2°5·7′W	T	163
Swindon	Northum	NY9799	55°17·4′	2°2·4′W	X	81
Swindon	Scot Bord	NT8220	55°28·7′	2°16·7′W	X	74
Swindon	Staffs	SO8690	52°30·7′	2°12·0′W	T	139
Swindon	Swin	SU1685	51°34·1′	1°45·8′W	T	173
Swindon and Cricklade Railway and Mus	Wilts	SU1089	51°36·2′	1°50·9′W	X	173
Swindon Bank Fm	N Yks	SE3049	53°56·4′	1°32·2′W	FM	104
Swindon Down	Devon	SS5439	51°8·1′	4°4·8′W	H	180
Swindon Grange Fm	N Yks	SE3147	53°55·3′	1°31·3′W	FM	104
Swindon Hall	N Yks	SE3148	53°55·9′	1°31·3′W	X	104
Swindon Hill	Scot Bord	NT8418	55°27·6′	2°14·7′W	H	80
Swindon Lodge	N Yks	SE3148	53°55·9′	1°31·3′W	X	104
Swindon Wood	N Yks	SE3148	53°55·9′	1°31·3′W	F	104
Swindridge Muir	N Ayr	NS3149	55°42·6′	4°41·0′W	X	63
Swine	E Yorks	TA1335	53°48·2′	0°16·6′W	T	107
Swine Beck Knotts	N Yks	SE1069	54°7·2′	1°50·4′W	X	99
Swineburn	C of Edin	NT1076	55°58·4′	3°26·1′W	X	65
Swine Cave	S Ayr	NS0100	55°15·5′	5°7·5′W	X	76
Swinecotte Dale	Notts	SK5454	53°5·1′	1°11·2′W	X	120
Swine Crag	Lancs	SD6055	53°59·6′	2°36·2′W	X	102,103
Swine Crags	Cumbr	NY3608	54°28·0′	2°58·8′W	X	90
Swine Dale	Orkney	HY4245	59°17·5′	3°0·6′W	X	5
Swineden	Aberd	NK0053	57°34·3′	1°59·5′W	X	30
Swinefleet	E Yorks	SE7722	53°41·6′	0°49·6′W	T	105,106,112
Swinefleet Warping Drain	E Yorks	SE7518	53°39·4′	0°51·5′W	W	112
Swineford	S Glos	ST6969	51°25·4′	2°26·4′W	T	172
Swine Gill	Cumbr	NY5828	54°39·0′	2°38·6′W	W	91
Swine Gill	S Lanak	NT0023	55°29·7′	3°34·5′W	W	72
Swineham	Devon	SS8522	50°59·4′	3°37·9′W	X	181
Swineham Fm	Dorset	SY9387	50°41·2′	2°5·6′W	FM	195
Swineham Point	Dorset	SY9487	50°41·2′	2°4·7′W	X	195
Swinehaw Bottom	N Yks	SD9891	54°19·1′	2°1·4′W	X	98
Swine Hill	Lincs	SK8831	52°52·4′	0°41·1′W	X	130
Swine Holes	S Ayr	NS0200	55°15·5′	5°6·5′W	X	76
Swineholes Wood	Staffs	SK0450	53°3·1′	1°56·0′W	F	119
Swine Lairs	N Yks	NZ2314	54°31·5′	1°38·3′W	X	93
Swine Lane Br	Brad	SE0841	53°52·2′	1°52·3′W	X	104
Swineley Ho	N Yks	SD8085	54°15·9′	2°18·0′W	X	98
Swineley Ho	N Yks	SD8085	54°15·9′	2°18·0′W	X	98
Swine Moor	E Yorks	TA0440	53°51·0′	0°24·7′W	X	107
Swine Park	N Yks	NZ4900	54°23·8′	1°14·3′W	X	93
Swinescales	Cumbr	NY4127	54°38·3′	2°54·4′W	X	90
Swineshaw Burn	Northum	NY7980	55°7·1′	2°19·3′W	W	80
Swineshaw Moor	Tames	SE0000	53°30·0′	1°59·6′W	X	110
Swineshaw Reservoirs	Tames	SK0099	53°29·5′	1°59·6′W	W	110
Swineshaw Resr	Derby	SK0495	53°27·3′	1°56·0′W	W	110
Swineshead	Beds	TL0565	52°16·6′	0°27·3′W	T	153
Swineshead	Lincs	TF2340	52°56·8′	0°9·8′W	T	131
Swineshead Bridge	Lincs	TF2143	52°58·5′	0°11·5′W	T	131
Swineshead Sta	Lincs	TF2142	52°57·9′	0°11·5′W	X	131
Swineshead Wood	Beds	TL0666	52°17·1′	0°26·4′W	F	153
Swinesherd	Worcs	SO8753	52°10·7′	2°11·0′W	T	150
Swineside	Cumbr	NY3432	54°41·0′	3°1·0′W	X	90
Swineside	N Yks	SE0682	54°14·3′	1°54·1′W	X	99
Swineside Knott	Cumbr	NY3719	54°34·0′	2°58·0′W	H	90
Swineside Moor	N Yks	SE0682	54°14·3′	1°54·1′W	X	99
Swinesleys Fm	Hants	SU3701	50°48·7′	1°28·1′W	FM	196
Swine Sty	Derby	SK2775	53°16·5′	1°35·3′W	X	119
Swinethorpe	Lincs	SK8769	53°12·9′	0°41·4′W	T	121
Swinewaird	Aberd	NO8580	56°54·9′	2°14·3′W	X	45
Swiney	Highld	ND2335	58°18·1′	3°18·4′W	T	11
Swineyard Hall	Ches	SJ6783	53°20·8′	2°29·3′W	A	109
Swiney Ho	Highld	ND2334	58°17·5′	3°18·3′W	X	11
Swinfen Hall	Staffs	SK1305	52°38·8′	1°48·1′W	X	139
Swinford	Leic	SP5679	52°24·6′	1°10·2′W	T	140
Swinford	Oxon	SP4408	51°46·4′	1°21·3′W	T	164
Swinford Corner	Leic	SP5681	52°25·7′	1°10·2′W	X	140
Swinford Ho	Ches	SJ4871	53°14·3′	2°46·3′W	X	117
Swinford Lodge	Leic	SP5679	52°24·6′	1°10·2′W	X	140
Swinford Manor (Sch)	Kent	TQ9743	51°9·4′	0°49·4′E	X	189
Swinfordmill Fm	Ches	SJ4869	53°13·2′	2°46·3′W	FM	117
Swinga Taing	Shetld	HP4702	60°42·2′	1°7·8′W	X	1
Swingate	Notts	SK5044	52°59·7′	1°14·9′W	T	129
Swingate Cross	Devon	SX3597	50°45·2′	4°20·0′W	X	190
Swingbrow	Cambs	TL3788	52°28·6′	0°1·4′E	T	142,143
Swingdon	Devon	SX3798	50°45·8′	4°18·3′W	X	190
Swinge Hill	Kent	TR2439	51°6·6′	1°12·4′E	X	179,189
Swingen's Wood	Suff	TM0752	52°7·9′	1°1·9′E	F	155
Swingfield Minnis	Kent	TR2142	51°8·3′	1°9·9′E	T	179,189
Swingfield Street	Kent	TR2343	51°8·8′	1°11·7′E	T	179,189
Swin Gill	D & G	NY3595	55°14·9′	3°0·9′W	W	79
Swingill	D & G	NY3694	55°14·4′	3°0·0′W	X	79
Swinging Gate	Cumbr	NY8116	54°32·6′	2°17·2′W	X	91,92
Swingleton Green	Suff	TL9647	52°5·4′	0°52·1′E	T	155
Swinham Wood	N Yks	SE8163	54°3·6′	0°45·3′W	F	100
Swinhay Fm	Glos	ST7393	51°38·3′	2°23·0′W	FM	162,172
Swinhill	S Lanak	NS7748	55°42·8′	3°57·0′W	X	64
Swinhoe	Northum	NU2028	55°33·0′	1°40·5′W	T	75
Swinhoe Burn	Northum	NU2028	55°33·0′	1°40·5′W	W	75
Swinhoe Fm	Northum	NU0834	55°36·2′	1°51·9′W	FM	75
Swinhoe Lakes	Northum	NU0735	55°36·8′	1°52·9′W	W	75
Swinholm	Derby	SK1141	52°58·2′	1°49·8′W	X	119,128
Swinholme	Durham	NY9813	54°31·0′	2°1·4′W	X	92
Swinhope	Lincs	TF2196	53°27·0′	0°10·3′W	T	113
Swin Hope	Northum	NU1209	55°22·7′	1°48·2′W	X	81
Swin Hope	Northum	NY8348	54°49·8′	2°15·5′W	X	86,87
Swinhope Brats	Lincs	TF2395	53°26·5′	0°8·5′W	X	113
Swinhope Burn	Durham	NY9035	54°42·8′	2°8·9′W	W	91,92
Swinhopeburn	Durham	NY9137	54°43·9′	2°8·0′W	X	91,92
Swinhope Burn	Northum	NY8347	54°49·3′	2°15·5′W	W	86,87
Swinhope Head	Durham	NY8933	54°41·8′	2°9·8′W	X	91,92
Swinhopehead Ho	Durham	NY8934	54°42·3′	2°9·8′W	X	91,92
Swinhope Hill	Lincs	TF2194	53°26·0′	0°10·3′W	X	113
Swinhope Moor	Durham	NY8834	54°42·3′	2°10·8′W	X	91,92
Swinhope Moor	Northum	NY8246	54°48·8′	2°16·4′W	X	86,87
Swinhope Shield	Northum	NY8449	54°50·4′	2°14·5′W	X	86,87
Swining	Shetld	HU4566	60°22·8′	1°10·5′W	T	2,3
Swining Burn	Shetld	HU4467	60°23·3′	1°11·6′W	W	2,3
Swining Voe	Shetld	HU4667	60°23·3′	1°9·4′W	W	2,3
Swinister	Shetld	HU3380	60°30·4′	1°23·4′W	T	1,2,3
Swinister	Shetld	HU4124	60°0·2′	1°15·4′W	X	4
Swinister	Shetld	HU4472	60°26·0′	1°11·5′W	X	2,3
Swinister Voe	Shetld	HU4572	60°26·0′	1°10·4′W	W	2,3
Swinithwaite	N Yks	SE0489	54°18·0′	1°55·9′W	T	98
Swinket Mease Rigg	Durham	NY8926	54°38·0′	2°9·8′W	X	91,92
Swinkie Fm	Fife	NO5510	56°17·1′	2°43·2′W	FM	59
Swinklebank	Cumbr	NY4904	54°26·0′	2°46·8′W	X	90
Swinklebank Crag	Cumbr	NY4904	54°26·0′	2°46·8′W	X	90
Swinlees	N Ayr	NS2952	55°44·1′	4°43·0′W	X	63
Swinley Down	Oxon	SU2781	51°31·9′	1°36·3′W	X	174
Swinley Fms	Wilts	ST9179	51°30·8′	2°7·4′W	FM	173
Swinley Green	Worcs	SO8332	51°59·4′	2°14·5′W	X	150
Swinley Park	Brackn	SU8967	51°23·9′	0°42·8′W	X	175
Swinmoor	Heref	SO4240	52°3·6′	2°50·4′W	X	148,149,161
Swinmore Common	Heref	SO6741	52°4·2′	2°28·5′W	T	149
Swinna Ness	Shetld	HP6509	60°45·8′	0°47·9′W	X	1
Swinner Gill	N Yks	NY9100	54°24·0′	2°7·9′W	W	91,92
Swinney Beck	N Yks	SE1882	54°14·2′	1°43·0′W	W	99
Swinney Fm	Shrops	SJ7000	52°36·1′	2°26·2′W	FM	127
Swinneyford Fm	Northnts	SP6847	52°7·3′	1°0·0′W	FM	152
Swinnie	Scot Bord	NT6216	55°26·4′	2°35·6′W	T	80
Swinnie Plantation	Scot Bord	NT6215	55°25·9′	2°35·6′W	F	80
Swinnock Hall	Sheff	SK2994	53°26·8′	1°33·4′W	X	110
Swinnow Hill	Leeds	SE4249	53°56·4′	1°21·2′W	X	105
Swinnow Moor	Leeds	SE2333	53°47·8′	1°38·6′W	T	104
Swinnow Park	Leeds	SE4149	53°56·4′	1°22·1′W	X	105
Swinnow Wood	Notts	SK6392	53°25·5′	1°2·7′W	F	111
Swinn Wood	Lincs	TF4277	53°16·5′	0°8·2′E	F	122
Swinny Knoll	Kirk	SE1209	53°34·9′	1°48·7′W	H	110
Swinscoe	Staffs	SK1348	53°2·0′	1°48·0′W	T	119
Swinshaw Hall	Lancs	SD8126	53°44·0′	2°16·9′W	X	103
Swinshaw Moor	Lancs	SD8225	53°43·5′	2°16·0′W	X	103
Swinside	Cumbr	NY0614	54°31·0′	3°26·7′W	X	89
Swinside	Cumbr	NY1624	54°36·5′	3°17·6′W	X	89
Swinside	Cumbr	NY1723	54°36·0′	3°16·7′W	X	89,90
Swinside	Cumbr	NY2421	54°35·0′	3°10·1′W	T	89,90
Swinside	Cumbr	NY2422	54°35·5′	3°10·1′W	H	89,90
Swinside	Cumbr	SD1788	54°17·1′	3°16·1′W	X	96
Swinside End	Cumbr	NY0514	54°31·0′	3°27·6′W	X	89
Swinside Fell	Cumbr	SD1588	54°17·1′	3°17·9′W	X	96
Swinside Hall	Scot Bord	NT7216	55°26·5′	2°26·1′W	T	80
Swinside Ho	Durham	NY8935	54°42·8′	2°9·8′W	X	91,92
Swinside Townfoot	Scot Bord	NT7216	55°26·5′	2°26·1′W	T	80
Swinstead	Lincs	TF0122	52°47·4′	0°29·7′W	T	130
Swinstie	N Lanak	NS8057	55°47·7′	3°54·4′W	X	65,72
Swinsto Cave	N Yks	SD6977	54°11·5′	2°28·1′W	X	98
Swinsty Fm	Cumbr	NY1750	54°50·5′	3°17·1′W	FM	85
Swinsty Hall	N Yks	SE1953	53°58·6′	1°42·2′W	A	104
Swinsty Moor Plantation	N Yks	SE1853	53°58·6′	1°43·1′W	F	104
Swinsty Reservoir	N Yks	SE1953	53°58·6′	1°42·2′W	W	104
Swint Clough	Derby	SK1290	53°24·6′	1°48·8′W	X	110
Swinthorpe	Lincs	TF0580	53°18·6′	0°25·0′W	X	121
Swintley Lodge	Rut	SK8204	52°37·9′	0°46·9′W	X	141
Swinton	C of Glas	NS6864	55°51·3′	4°6·1′W	T	64
Swinton	N Yks	SE2179	54°12·6′	1°40·3′W	T	99
Swinton	N Yks	SE7573	54°9·1′	0°50·7′W	T	100
Swinton	Roth	SK4598	53°28·8′	1°18·9′W	T	111
Swinton	Salf	SD7701	53°30·6′	2°20·4′W	T	109
Swinton	Scot Bord	NT8347	55°43·2′	2°15·8′W	T	74
Swinton Bridge	Roth	SK4699	53°29·4′	1°18·0′W	T	111
Swinton Grange	N Yks	SE7571	54°8·0′	0°50·7′W	X	100
Swinton Green	N Yks	SE2179	54°12·6′	1°40·3′W	X	99
Swinton Hill	Scot Bord	NT8446	55°42·7′	2°14·8′W	T	74
Swinton Ho	Scot Bord	NT8147	55°43·2′	2°17·7′W	X	74
Swinton Ings	N Yks	SE7774	54°9·6′	0°48·8′W	X	100
Swintonmill	Scot Bord	NT8145	55°42·1′	2°17·7′W	X	74
Swinton Park	N Yks	SE2079	54°12·6′	1°41·2′W	X	99
Swinton Park	Salf	SD7800	53°30·0′	2°19·5′W	T	109
Swinton Quarter	Scot Bord	NT8447	55°43·2′	2°14·8′W	X	74
Swinwood Mill	Scot Bord	NT8962	55°51·3′	2°10·1′W	X	67
Swinyard Hill	Worcs	SO7638	52°2·6′	2°20·6′W	H	150
Swinzie Burn	E Ayr	NS4748	55°42·3′	4°25·7′W	W	64
Swire Hill	N Yks	SD8849	53°56·5′	2°10·6′W	X	103
Swire Knowe	Scot Bord	NT4700	55°17·7′	2°49·7′W	H	79
Swires Fm	Surrey	TQ1844	51°11·2′	0°18·3′W	FM	187
Swire Sike	Scot Bord	NT5903	55°19·4′	2°38·3′W	W	80
Swirl How	Cumbr	NY2700	54°23·7′	3°7·0′W	H	89,90
Swirral Edge	Cumbr	NY3415	54°31·8′	3°0·8′W	X	90
Swiss Cott	Derby	SK2770	53°13·8′	1°35·3′W	X	119
Swiss Cott	I of W	SZ5294	50°44·8′	1°15·4′W	X	196
Swiss Cott	Shrops	SO4490	52°30·5′	2°49·1′W	X	137
Swiss Cottage	N Yks	SE7169	54°7·0′	0°54·4′W	X	100
Swiss Cottage	Suff	TM1666	52°15·2′	1°10·3′E	X	156
Swiss Cottage	Traf	SJ7591	53°25·2′	2°22·2′W	X	109
Swiss Farm Ho	Glos	SP1524	51°55·1′	1°46·5′W	X	163
Swiss Fm	Oxon	SU7683	51°32·7′	0°53·8′W	FM	175
Swiss Garden	Beds	TL1444	52°5·2′	0°19·8′W	X	153
Swiss Valley	Carm	SN5202	51°42·1′	4°8·1′W	T	159
Switchers Fm	N Yks	SD8755	53°59·7′	2°11·5′W	FM	103
Swite's Wood	W Susx	TQ4039	51°8·2′	0°0·5′E	F	187

Switha	Orkney	ND3690	58°47·8′	3°6·0′W	X	7
Switha Sound	Orkney	ND3591	58°48·4′	3°7·0′W	W	7
Swithland	Leic	SK5513	52°42·9′	1°10·7′W	T	129
Swithland Reservoir	Leic	SK5514	52°43·5′	1°10·7′W	W	129
Swithland Wood	Leic	SK5312	52°42·4′	1°12·5′W	F	129
Swmbarch Fm	Pemb	SM9428	51°55·0′	4°59·3′W	FM	157,158
Swndwr	Flint	SJ2568	53°12·5′	3°7·0′W	X	117
Swona	Orkney	ND3884	58°44·6′	3°3·8′W	X	7
Swordale	Highld	NH5765	57°39·4′	4°23·3′W	T	21
Swordale	Highld	NH6191	57°53·5′	4°20·2′W	T	21
Swordale Hill	Highld	NH5666	57°39·9′	4°24·4′W	H	21
Swordie Mains	W Loth	NS9978	55°59·3′	3°36·7′W	X	65
Swordland	Highld	NM7891	56°57·7′	5°38·6′W	X	33,40
Swordland Lodge	Highld	NM7891	56°57·7′	5°38·6′W	X	33,40
Swordle Bay Ho	Highld	NM5470	56°45·7′	6°1·1′W	X	39,47
Swordle Fm	Highld	NM5470	56°45·7′	6°1·1′W	FM	39,47
Swordly	Highld	NC7363	58°32·5′	4°10·4′W	T	10
Swordly Burn	Highld	NC7362	58°31·9′	4°10·4′W	W	10
Swordwell	D & G	NY2166	54°59·2′	3°13·6′W	X	85
Swordwellrigg	D & G	NY2266	54°59·2′	3°12·7′W	X	85
Sworton Heath	Ches	SJ6884	53°21·4′	2°28·4′W	T	109
Swychyrhafod	Conwy	SH8363	53°9·3′	3°44·6′W	X	116
Swyddffynnon	Cered	SN6966	52°16·8′	3°54·8′W	T	135
Swyncombe Downs	Oxon	SU6791	51°37·1′	1°1·5′W	X	164,175
Swyncombe Ho	Oxon	SU6890	51°36·5′	1°0·7′W	X	164,175
Swynnerton	Staffs	SJ8535	52°55·0′	2°13·0′W	T	127
Swynnerton Grange	Staffs	SJ8634	52°54·4′	2°12·1′W	X	127
Swynnerton Old Park	Staffs	SJ8239	52°57·1′	2°15·7′W	X	127
Swynnerton Park	Staffs	SJ8534	52°54·4′	2°13·0′W	X	127
Swyre	D & G	NX8885	55°9·1′	3°45·0′W	X	78
Swyre	Dorset	SY5288	50°41·6′	2°40·4′W	T	194
Swyre Fm	Glos	SP1508	51°46·5′	1°46·6′W	FM	163
Swyre Head	Dorset	SY7980	50°37·4′	2°17·4′W	X	194
Swyre Head	Dorset	SY9378	50°36·3′	2°5·6′W	X	195
Swyre Hill	Dorset	SY5197	50°46·5′	2°41·3′W	H	194
Swythamley Hall	Staffs	SJ9764	53°10·6′	2°2·3′W	X	118
Syart	Scot Bord	NT2122	55°29·4′	3°14·6′W	X	73
Syart Burn	Scot Bord	NT2121	55°28·8′	3°14·6′W	W	73
Syart Law	Scot Bord	NT2022	55°29·4′	3°15·5′W	H	73
Syart Rig	Scot Bord	NT2121	55°28·8′	3°14·6′W	X	73
Sybil Hill	Warw	SP2396	52°33·9′	1°39·2′W	X	139
Sybole Fm	Northnts	SP6180	52°25·1′	1°5·8′W	FM	140
Sycamore	Devon	ST2905	50°50·6′	3°0·1′W	T	193
Sycamore Cross	V of Glam	ST0774	51°27·7′	3°19·9′W	X	170
Sycamore Fm	Cambs	TL1776	52°22·4′	0°16·5′W	FM	142
Sycamore Fm	Kent	TR0225	50°59·6′	0°53·1′E	FM	189
Sycamore Fm	Lincs	SK8829	52°51·3′	0°41·2′W	FM	130
Sycamore Fm	Lincs	TF2292	53°24·9′	0°9·5′W	FM	113
Sycamore Fm	Lincs	TF3219	52°45·4′	0°2·2′W	FM	131
Sycamore Fm	Norf	TM2790	52°27·9′	1°20·9′E	FM	134
Sycamore Fm	Norf	TM3996	52°30·8′	1°31·7′E	FM	134
Sycamore Fm	Peterb	TF3108	52°39·5′	0°3·4′W	FM	142
Sycamore Fm	Somer	ST7328	51°3·3′	2°22·7′W	FM	183
Sycamore Fm	Staffs	SK0845	53°0·4′	1°52·4′W	FM	119,128
Sycamore Fm	Suff	TM1147	52°5·1′	1°5·2′E	FM	155,169
Sycamore Fm	Suff	TM1464	52°14·2′	1°8·5′E	FM	156
Sycamore Fm	Suff	TM1966	52°15·1′	1°12·9′E	FM	156
Sycamore Fm	Suff	TM2050	52°6·5′	1°13·2′E	FM	156
Sycamore Fm Ho	Shrops	SJ3929	52°51·5′	2°54·0′W	X	126
Sycamore Grange	Lincs	TF3211	52°41·1′	0°2·4′W	X	131,142
Sycamore Hill	Staffs	SJ9718	52°45·8′	2°2·3′W	H	127
Sycamore Ho	Lincs	TF1849	53°1·7′	0°14·0′W	X	130
Sycamore Lodge	Cumbr	NY4244	54°47·5′	2°53·7′W	X	85
Sycamore Lodge	Lincs	TF3619	52°45·3′	0°1·3′E	X	131
Sycamores, The	Shrops	SJ3931	52°52·6′	2°54·0′W	X	126
Sycamore Tree Fm	Cumbr	NY7700	54°23·9′	2°20·8′W	FM	91
Sycharth	Powys	SJ2025	52°49·2′	3°10·8′W	X	126
Sychbant	Pemb	SN0435	51°59·0′	4°50·9′W	X	145,157
Sychcwm	Powys	SO1752	52°9·8′	3°12·4′W	X	148
Sychdyn	Denb	SJ0773	53°15·0′	3°23·2′W	X	116
Sychdyn or Soughton	Flint	SJ2466	53°11·4′	3°7·8′W	T	117
Sychnant	Carm	SN3238	52°1·1′	4°26·5′W	X	145
Sychnant	Carm	SN6647	52°6·5′	3°57·0′W	X	146
Sychnant	Carm	SN8023	51°53·8′	3°44·3′W	W	160
Sychnant	Gwyn	SH2130	52°50·5′	4°39·1′W	X	123
Sychnant	Gwyn	SH7039	52°56·2′	3°55·7′W	X	124
Sychnant	Powys	SJ0201	52°36·1′	3°26·4′W	X	136
Sychnant	Powys	SJ1227	52°50·2′	3°18·0′W	X	125
Sychnant	Powys	SN9777	52°23·1′	3°30·4′W	X	136,147
Sychnant	Powys	SO1286	52°28·1′	3°17·3′W	X	136
Sychnant Fm	Carm	SN5907	51°44·9′	4°2·2′W	FM	159
Sychnant Fm	Powys	SO1733	51°59·6′	3°12·1′W	FM	161
Sychnant Pass	Conwy	SH7477	53°16·7′	3°53·0′W	X	115
Sychpant	Carm	SN3225	51°54·1′	4°26·1′W	X	145
Sychpant	Cered	SN3241	52°2·8′	4°26·6′W	X	145
Sychpant	Cered	SN4561	52°13·8′	4°15·8′W	X	146
Sychpant	Pemb	SN0526	51°54·1′	4°49·7′W	X	145,158
Sychpant	Pemb	SN0825	51°53·7′	4°47·0′W	X	145,158
Sychpant	Pemb	SN0838	52°0·7′	4°47·5′W	X	145
Sychpant	Pemb	SN2236	51°59·9′	4°35·2′W	X	145
Sychpwll	Powys	SJ3117	52°45·0′	3°0·9′W	X	126
Sychryd	Rho Cyn Taf	SN9107	51°45·3′	3°34·4′W	W	160
Sychtre	Monm	SO2729	51°57·5′	3°3·4′W	X	161
Sychtyn	Denb	SJ1164	53°10·2′	3°19·5′W	X	116
Sychtyn	Powys	SH9907	52°39·3′	3°29·2′W	X	125
Sydal Lodge	N Yks	NZ4201	54°24·4′	1°20·8′W	X	93
Sydallt	Wrex	SJ3155	53°5·5′	3°1·4′W	T	117
Syd Brook Hall Fm	Lancs	SD5017	53°39·1′	2°45·0′W	FM	108
Sydcombe Fm	Heref	SO2944	52°5·6′	3°1·8′W	FM	148,161
Syddynmelyn	Cered	SN4405	51°43·6′	4°15·1′W	X	159
Syde	Angus	NO6164	56°46·2′	2°37·8′W	X	45
Syde	Glos	SO9410	51°47·6′	2°4·8′W	T	163
Syde	S Lanak	NS9236	55°36·6′	3°42·4′W	X	71,72
Syde Fm	S Lanak	NS6538	55°37·3′	4°8·2′W	FM	71
Sydeham Fm	Devon	SS8719	50°57·8′	3°36·2′W	FM	181
Sydenham	Devon	SX4283	50°37·8′	4°13·7′W	A	201
Sydenham	Oxon	SP7301	51°42·4′	0°56·2′W	T	165
Sydenham	Somer	ST3137	51°7·9′	2°58·8′W	T	182
Sydenham Damerel	Devon	SX4076	50°33·9′	4°15·2′W	T	201
Sydenham Fm	Glos	SP2227	51°56·7′	1°40·4′W	FM	163
Sydenham Grange Fm	Oxon	SP7102	51°43·0′	0°57·9′W	FM	165
Sydenham Ho	Scot Bord	NT7236	55°37·3′	2°26·2′W	X	74
Sydenham Hurst	Oxon	SP7203	51°43·5′	0°57·1′W	F	165
Sydenhams	Glos	SO8907	51°45·9′	2°9·2′W	X	163
Sydenham Wood	Devon	SX4383	50°37·8′	4°12·8′W	F	201
Sydenhurst	Surrey	SU9534	51°6·1′	0°38·2′W	X	186
Syderstone	Norf	TF8332	52°51·5′	0°43·5′E	T	132
Syderstone Common	Norf	TF8231	52°51·0′	0°42·6′E	X	132
Sydham	Devon	SS7014	50°54·9′	3°50·6′W	X	180
Sydling St Nicholas	Dorset	SY6399	50°47·6′	2°31·1′W	T	194
Sydling Water	Dorset	SY6395	50°45·4′	2°31·1′W	W	194
Sydmonton	Hants	SU4857	51°18·8′	1°18·3′W	T	174
Sydmonton Common	Hants	SU4963	51°22·1′	1°17·4′W	F	174
Sydmonton Court	Hants	SU4857	51°18·8′	1°18·3′W	X	174
Sydney	Ches	SJ7256	53°6·3′	2°24·7′W	T	118
Sydney Fm	Surrey	TQ0232	51°4·9′	0°32·2′W	FM	186
Sydnope Hall	Derby	SK2964	53°10·6′	1°33·6′W	X	119
Sydnope Stand	Derby	SK2963	53°10·0′	1°33·6′W	X	119
Sydserf	E Loth	NT5481	56°1·4′	2°43·8′W	X	66
Syerscote Barn	Staffs	SK2206	52°39·3′	1°40·1′W	X	139
Syerscote Manor	Staffs	SK2207	52°39·9′	1°40·1′W	X	139
Syerston	Notts	SK7447	53°1·1′	0°53·4′W	T	129
Syfydrin	Cered	SN7284	52°26·6′	3°52·6′W	X	135
Sygun Copper Mine	Gwyn	SH6048	53°0·9′	4°4·8′W	X	115
Syke	Carm	SN2010	51°45·8′	4°36·1′W	X	158
Syke	Cumbr	SD6394	54°20·7′	2°33·7′W	X	97
Syke	E Ayr	NS5024	55°29·5′	4°22·0′W	X	70
Syke	Roch	SD8915	53°38·1′	2°9·6′W	T	109
Syke	Roch	SD9414	53°37·6′	2°5·0′W	X	109
Syke	W Loth	NS9978	55°59·3′	3°36·7′W	X	65
Syke Beck Fm	Cumbr	SD0987	54°16·5′	3°23·4′W	FM	96
Sykebreck Fm	Notts	SK5954	53°5·0′	1°6·7′W	FM	120
Syke Fm	Cumbr	NY2747	54°49·0′	3°7·7′W	FM	85
Syke Fm	E Yorks	TA1353	53°57·9′	0°16·2′W	FM	107
Syke Fm	Pemb	SM8610	51°45·1′	5°5·6′W	FM	157
Syke Gate	N Yks	SE6375	54°10·3′	1°1·7′W	X	100
Sykehead	Cumbr	NY4767	54°59·9′	2°49·3′W	X	86
Syke Ho	Cumbr	NY5822	54°35·7′	2°38·6′W	X	91
Syke Ho	Lancs	SD5640	53°51·5′	2°39·7′W	X	102
Sykehouse	Donc	SE6316	53°38·4′	1°2·4′W	T	111
Syke House Fm	Brad	SE0751	53°57·5′	1°53·2′W	FM	104
Syke House Fm	E Yorks	SE9038	53°50·1′	0°37·5′W	FM	106
Sykemouth Fm	Lincs	TF2442	52°57·9′	0°8·8′W	FM	131
Sykes	Cumbr	NY2922	54°35·5′	3°5·5′W	X	89,90
Sykes	Lancs	SD6351	53°57·5′	2°33·4′W	T	102,103
Sykes Fell	Lancs	SD6150	53°56·9′	2°35·2′W	X	102,103
Syke's Fm	Lancs	SD5250	53°56·9′	2°43·5′W	FM	102
Sykes Fm	Lincs	SK8876	53°16·7′	0°40·4′W	FM	121
Sykes Fm	N Yks	SE1878	54°12·1′	1°43·0′W	FM	99
Sykes Ho	N Yks	SE6691	54°18·9′	0°58·7′W	X	94,100
Sykes House Fm	Leeds	SE4348	53°55·8′	1°20·3′W	FM	105
Sykeside	Cumbr	NY7412	54°30·4′	2°23·7′W	X	91
Syke Side	Lancs	SD7632	53°47·3′	2°21·4′W	X	103
Sykes Moor	Derby	SK0896	53°27·9′	1°52·4′W	X	110
Sykes Nab	Lancs	SD6351	53°57·5′	2°33·4′W	X	102,103
Sykes, The	N Yks	SE6767	54°5·9′	0°58·1′W	X	100
Syleham	Suff	TM2178	52°21·6′	1°15·1′E	T	156
Syleham Hall	Suff	TM2278	52°21·5′	1°16·0′E	X	156
Syleham Ho	Suff	TM2179	52°22·1′	1°15·2′E	X	156
Syleham Manor	Suff	TM2078	52°21·6′	1°14·3′E	X	156
Sylen	Carm	SN5106	51°44·2′	4°9·1′W	T	159
Sylen Ranch	Carm	SN5206	51°44·2′	4°8·2′W	X	159
Syles Fm	Somer	ST7420	50°59·0′	2°21·8′W	FM	183
Sylfaen	Gwyn	SH6318	52°44·8′	4°1·4′W	X	124
Sylfaen	Powys	SJ1706	52°39·0′	3°13·2′W	X	125
Sylfaen Brook	Powys	SJ1906	52°39·0′	3°11·4′W	W	125
Sylfaen Fm	Flint	SJ2271	53°14·1′	3°9·7′W	FM	117
Sylavethy	Aberd	NJ5717	57°14·8′	2°42·3′W	X	37
Syllenhurst Fm	Shrops	SJ7242	52°58·7′	2°24·6′W	FM	118
Syllodioch	D & G	NX5953	54°51·4′	4°11·4′W	X	83
Symbister	Shetld	HU3729	60°2·9′	1°19·6′W	X	4
Symbister	Shetld	HU5362	60°20·6′	1°1·9′W	T	2,3
Symbister House (Sch)	Shetld	HU5462	60°20·6′	1°0·8′W	X	2
Symbister Ness	Shetld	HU5362	60°20·6′	1°1·9′W	X	2,3
Symblisetter	Shetld	HU3616	59°55·9′	1°20·9′W	X	4
Symbol Stone	Moray	NJ1857	57°36·0′	3°21·9′W	A	28
Symbol Stone	Pth & Kin	NN9209	56°15·9′	3°44·2′W	A	58
Symington	S Ayr	NS3831	55°33·0′	4°33·6′W	T	70
Symington	Scot Bord	NT4348	55°43·6′	2°54·0′W	T	73
Symington	S Lanak	NS9935	55°36·1′	3°35·7′W	T	72
Symington Hill	Scot Bord	NT4147	55°43·0′	2°55·9′W	H	73
Symington Ho	S Lanak	NT0035	55°36·2′	3°34·8′W	X	72
Symington Lo	S Lanak	NT0035	55°36·2′	3°34·8′W	X	72
Symington Mains Fm	S Lanak	NS9934	55°35·6′	3°35·7′W	FM	72
Symington Mill	S Lanak	NT0035	55°36·2′	3°34·8′W	X	72
Symnell	Kent	TR0637	51°5·9′	0°56·9′E	X	179,189
Symondsbury	Dorset	SY4493	50°44·3′	2°47·2′W	T	193
Symond's Fm	Suff	TL7865	52°15·5′	0°36·9′E	FM	155
Symonds Green	Herts	TL2225	51°54·8′	0°13·2′W	T	166
Symonds Hall Fm	Glos	ST7996	51°40·0′	2°17·8′W	FM	162
Symondshyde Fm	Herts	TL1911	51°47·3′	0°16·1′W	FM	166
Symondshyde Great Wood	Herts	TL1910	51°46·8′	0°16·1′W	F	166
Symonds Yat	Heref	SO5516	51°50·7′	2°38·8′W	T	162
Symond's Yat Rock	Heref	SO5616	51°50·7′	2°37·9′W	X	162
Synalds	Shrops	SO4091	52°31·1′	2°52·7′W	X	137
Syndale Bottom	Kent	TQ9156	51°16·5′	0°44·7′E	X	178
Syndale Park Motel	Kent	TQ9960	51°18·5′	0°51·7′E	X	178
Synderborough Fm	Devon	SY1492	50°43·5′	3°12·7′W	FM	192,193
Synderford	Dorset	ST3803	50°49·6′	2°52·4′W	T	193
Synding Hill	Northum	NT8940	55°39·5′	2°10·1′W	H	74
Syningthwaite Fm	N Yks	SE4648	53°55·8′	1°17·5′W	FM	105
Synod Inn	Cered	SN4054	52°9·9′	4°20·0′W	T	146
Synod Mill	Cered	SN3954	52°9·9′	4°20·8′W	X	145
Synton	Scot Bord	NT4822	55°29·6′	2°48·9′W	T	73
Synton Mains	Scot Bord	NT4722	55°29·6′	2°49·9′W	T	73
Syntonmill	Scot Bord	NT4923	55°30·1′	2°48·0′W	X	73
Synton Mossend	Scot Bord	NT4820	55°28·5′	2°48·9′W	X	73
Synton Parkhead	Scot Bord	NT4821	55°29·1′	2°48·9′W	X	73
Synwell	Glos	ST7693	51°38·4′	2°20·4′W	T	162,172
Syon Abbey	Devon	SX7261	50°26·3′	3°47·8′W	X	202
Syon Ho	Devon	SY0784	50°39·1′	3°18·6′W	X	192
Syon Ho	Houns	TQ1776	51°28·5′	0°18·5′W	A	176
Sype Land	N Yks	SE1273	54°9·4′	1°48·6′W	X	99
Sypsies	Fife	NO6007	56°15·5′	2°38·3′W	X	59
Syra Dale	Orkney	HY3515	59°1·3′	3°7·4′W	X	6
Syre	Highld	NC6943	58°21·6′	4°13·9′W	T	10
Syreford	Glos	SP0220	51°52·9′	1°57·9′W	T	163
Syre Lodge	Highld	NC6944	58°22·2′	4°13·9′W	X	10
Syrencot Ho	Wilts	SU1546	51°13·0′	1°46·7′W	X	184
Syresham	Northnts	SP6241	52°4·1′	1°5·3′W	T	152
Syrior	Denb	SJ0038	52°56·0′	3°28·9′W	X	125
Sysonby Grange Fm	Leic	SK7318	52°45·5′	0°54·7′W	FM	129
Sysonby Lodge	Leic	SK7420	52°46·6′	0°53·8′W	X	129
Syster	Highld	ND2668	58°35·9′	3°15·9′W	X	11,12
Syston	Leic	SK6211	52°41·8′	1°4·5′W	T	129
Syston	Lincs	SK9240	52°57·2′	0°37·4′W	T	130
Syston Grange	Leic	SK6310	52°41·3′	1°3·7′W	X	129
Syston Grange	Lincs	SK9540	52°57·2′	0°34·7′W	X	130
Syston Park	Lincs	SK9340	52°57·2′	0°36·5′W	X	130
Sytchampton	Worcs	SO8466	52°17·8′	2°13·7′W	T	138,150
Sytches Fm	Heref	SO4257	52°12·7′	2°50·5′W	FM	148,149
Sytch Ho Green	Shrops	SO7890	52°30·7′	2°19·1′W	T	138
Sytch Lane	Wrekin	SJ6220	52°46·8′	2°33·4′W	T	127
Sytch, The	Shrops	SJ6721	52°47·4′	2°29·0′W	X	127
Sythe Harbour	N Eil	NB0203	57°55·3′	7°1·5′W	W	13,18
Sywell	Northnts	SP8267	52°17·9′	0°47·5′W	T	152
Sywell Grange	Northnts	SP8168	52°18·5′	0°48·3′W	X	152
Sywell Lodge Fm	Northnts	SP8168	52°18·5′	0°48·3′W	FM	152
Sywell Resr	Northnts	SP8365	52°16·8′	0°46·6′W	W	152
Sywell Wood	Northnts	SP8269	52°19·0′	0°47·4′W	F	152

T

Taagan	Highld	NH0163	57°37·1′	5°19·5′W	X	19
Tabbermear's Fm	Leic	SP6085	52°27·8′	1°6·6′W	FM	140
Taberon Law	Scot Bord	NT1428	55°32·5′	3°21·3′W	H	72
Tabhaidh Mhòr	N Eil	NB4222	58°7·0′	6°22·4′W	X	14
Tablehurst Fm	E Susx	TQ4235	51°6·0′	0°2·1′E	FM	187
Table Mountain	Powys	SO2220	51°52·6′	3°7·6′W	H	161
Table Oak Fm	Sol	SP2374	52°22·0′	1°39·3′W	FM	139
Table of Lorn or An Dunan	Highld	NM7343	56°31·7′	5°41·0′W	X	49
Table of Stoo	Shetld	HU4423	59°59·6′	1°12·2′W	X	4
Table Rings	E Loth	NT6363	55°51·8′	2°35·0′W	X	67
Table Rings (Cairn)	E Loth	NT6363	55°51·8′	2°35·0′W	A	67
Table Rock, The	Ches	SJ5257	53°6·7′	2°42·6′W	X	117
Table, The	Highld	NG4569	57°38·6′	6°15·9′W	H	23
Table, The	Pemb	SM7109	51°44·2′	5°18·6′W	X	157
Tableybrook Fm	Ches	SJ7179	53°18·7′	2°25·7′W	FM	118
Tabley Grange	Ches	SJ7176	53°17·1′	2°25·7′W	X	118
Tabley Hall	Ches	SJ7177	53°17·6′	2°25·7′W	A	118
Tabley Hill	Ches	SJ7379	53°18·7′	2°23·9′W	T	118
Tabley Ho	Ches	SJ7277	53°17·6′	2°24·8′W	X	118
Tabley Mere	Ches	SJ7276	53°17·1′	2°24·8′W	W	118
Tabor	Gwyn	SH7517	52°44·4′	3°50·7′W	T	124
Tabor Hill	Devon	SS7532	51°4·7′	3°46·7′W	X	180
Tabost	N Eil	NB3219	58°5·0′	6°32·3′W	T	13,14
Tabost	N Eil	NB5162	58°28·8′	6°15·8′W	T	8
Tabrum's Fm	Essex	TQ7997	51°38·8′	0°35·6′E	FM	167
Tach	Powys	SO0283	52°26·4′	3°26·1′W	X	136
Tachbrook Hill Fm	Warw	SP3060	52°14·5′	1°33·2′W	FM	151
Tachbrook Mallory	Warw	SP3162	52°15·6′	1°32·4′W	T	151
Tacher	Highld	ND1746	58°23·9′	3°24·7′W	X	11,12
Tacher Burn	D & G	NX7949	54°49·5′	3°52·6′W	W	84
Tackbeare Fm	Devon	SS2501	50°47·2′	4°28·6′W	FM	190
Tacker Street	Somer	ST0237	51°7·7′	3°23·6′W	T	181
Tack Fm	Dudley	SO9582	52°26·4′	2°4·0′W	FM	139
Tack Fm	Worcs	SP0167	52°18·3′	1°58·7′W	FM	150
Tackhouse	S Lanak	NS6443	55°39·9′	4°9·3′W	X	71
Tackley	Oxon	SP4720	51°52·8′	1°18·6′W	T	164
Tackley Heath	Oxon	SP4621	51°53·4′	1°19·5′W	X	164
Tackley Park	Oxon	SP4720	51°52·8′	1°18·6′W	X	164
Tackley Wood	Oxon	SP4721	51°53·4′	1°18·6′W	F	164
Tack Wood	Powys	SO2439	52°2·9′	3°6·1′W	F	161
Tacolneston	Norf	TM1494	52°30·3′	1°9·6′E	T	144
Tadbesom Wood	Somer	ST7740	51°9·8′	2°19·3′W	F	183
Tad Brook	Staffs	SK0527	52°50·7′	1°55·1′W	W	128
Tadcaster	N Yks	SE4843	53°53·1′	1°15·8′W	T	105
Tadcaster Ings	N Yks	SE4842	53°52·6′	1°15·8′W	X	105
Tadden	Dorset	ST9801	50°48·7′	2°1·3′W	T	195
Taddiford Fm	Hants	SZ2692	50°43·9′	1°37·5′W	FM	195
Taddington	Derby	SK1471	53°14·4′	1°47·0′W	T	119
Taddington	Glos	SP0831	51°58·9′	1°52·6′W	T	150
Taddington Dale	Derby	SK1671	53°14·4′	1°45·2′W	X	119
Taddington Field	Derby	SK1670	53°13·8′	1°45·2′W	X	119
Taddington Moor	Derby	SK1370	53°13·9′	1°47·9′W	X	119
Taddiport	Devon	SS4818	50°56·7′	4°9·4′W	T	180
Taddiport	Devon	SS6431	51°4·0′	3°56·1′W	X	180
Tadham Moor	Somer	ST4244	51°11·8′	2°49·4′W	X	182
Tadhill	Somer	ST6846	51°13·0′	2°27·1′W	T	183
Tadley	Hants	SU6061	51°20·9′	1°7·9′W	T	175
Tadley	Oxon	SU5388	51°35·5′	1°13·7′W	T	174
Tadley Common	Hants	SU6062	51°21·5′	1°7·9′W	X	175
Tadlow	Cambs	TL2847	52°6·6′	0°7·4′W	T	153
Tadmarton	Oxon	SP3937	52°2·0′	1°25·5′W	T	151
Tadmarton Heath	Oxon	SP3835	52°1·0′	1°26·4′W	X	151
Tadmarton House Fm	Oxon	SP4136	52°1·5′	1°23·8′W	FM	151
Tadmarton Lodge	Oxon	SP4136	52°1·5′	1°23·8′W	X	151
Tadmoor Cott	Surrey	SU8942	51°10·4′	0°43·2′W	X	186
Tadnoll	Dorset	SY7986	50°40·6′	2°17·5′W	T	194
Tadnoll Barrow	Dorset	SY7987	50°41·2′	2°17·5′W	A	194
Tadpole Bridge	Oxon	SP3300	51°42·1′	1°31·0′W	X	164
Tadpole Fm	Swin	SU1189	51°36·2′	1°50·1′W	FM	173
Tadwell Fm	Kent	TQ9672	51°25·0′	0°49·5′E	FM	178

Tadwick	Bath & NE Somer	ST7470	51°25·9′	2°22·1′W	T	172
Tadworth	Surrey	TQ2256	51°17·6′	0°14·6′W	T	187
Tadworth Court	Surrey	TQ2356	51°17·6′	0°13·8′W	A	187
Taeblair	Highld	NH6351	57°32·0′	4°16·8′W	X	26
Taeholm Burn	D & G	NS8203	55°18·7′	3°51·1′W	W	78
Taeweg	Highld	NH6351	57°32·0′	4°16·8′W	X	26
Tafarnaubach	Blae GW	SO1110	51°47·1′	3°17·0′W	T	161
Tafarn-y-Bugail	Cered	SN2546	52°5·3′	4°32·9′W	X	145
Tafarn-y-bwlch	Pemb	SN0833	51°58·0′	4°47·3′W	T	145
Tafarn-y-Garreg (PH)	Powys	SN8417	51°50·6′	3°40·6′W	X	160
Tafarn-y-garth	Denb	SJ2151	53°3·3′	3°10·3′W	X	117
Tafarn-y-Gelyn	Denb	SJ1861	53°8·6′	3°13·2′W	T	116
Taf Fawr	Rho Cyn Taf	SO0013	51°48·6′	3°26·6′W	W	160
Taf Fechan	Merth Tyd	SO0510	51°47·1′	3°22·2′W	W	160
Taf Fechan	Powys	SO0316	51°50·3′	3°24·1′W	W	160
Taf Fechan Forest	Powys	SO0416	51°50·3′	3°23·2′W	F	160
Taff Merthyr Garden Village	Merth Tyd	ST1097	51°40·1′	3°17·7′W	T	171
Taffs Fm	Warw	SP3287	52°29·0′	1°31·3′W	FM	140
Taff's Well	Rho Cyn Taf	ST1283	51°32·6′	3°15·8′W	A	171
Taffs Well	Rho Cyn Taf	ST1283	51°32·6′	3°15·8′W	T	171
Taff Trail	Merth Tyd	ST0897	51°40·1′	3°19·4′W	X	160,170,171
Taff Vale	Rho Cyn Taf	ST1086	51°34·2′	3°17·5′W	X	171
Taff Vale / Cwm Taf	Rho Cyn Taf	ST0892	51°37·4′	3°19·4′W	X	160,170,171
Tafolgraig	Gwyn	SN6597	52°33·5′	3°59·1′W	X	135
Tafolog	Powys	SH8909	52°40·3′	3°38·1′W	X	124,125
Tafolwern	Powys	SH8902	52°36·5′	3°38·0′W	T	135,136
Taftend	Orkney	HY4942	59°16·0′	2°53·2′W	X	5
Taftin Hill	Shetld	HU3574	60°27·2′	1°21·3′W	H	2,3
Taft Leys Fm	Notts	SK5627	52°50·5′	1°9·7′W	FM	129
Taftnica	Orkney	ND4895	58°50·6′	2°53·6′W	X	7
Tag Bale	N Yks	SE0566	54°5·6′	1°55·0′W	X	98
Tagents Fm	W Susx	SU9217	50°56·9′	0°41·0′W	FM	197
Tagley	Essex	TL7138	52°1·1′	0°29·9′E	X	154
Tagmoor Fm	Glos	SP1619	51°52·4′	1°45·7′W	FM	163
Tagon	Shetld	HU4063	60°21·2′	1°16·0′W	X	2,3
Tagon Hill	Shetld	HU4163	60°21·2′	1°14·9′W	H	2,3
Tagsclough Hill	Ches	SJ9867	53°12·2′	2°1·4′W	H	118
Tahall Mains	D & G	NX4052	54°50·5′	4°29·1′W	X	83
Tahaval	N Eil	NB0426	58°7·7′	7°1·2′W	H	13
Tahay	N Eil	NF9675	57°40·0′	7°5·4′W	X	18
Tai	Conwy	SH8670	53°13·1′	3°42·0′W	X	116
Taibach	Nth Pt Talb	SS7789	51°35·4′	3°46·1′W	T	170
Tai-bach	Powys	SJ1528	52°50·8′	3°15·3′W	X	125
Tai Bowen	Flint	SJ2661	53°8·7′	3°6·0′W	X	117
Tai Cochion	Gwyn	SH5843	52°58·2′	4°6·5′W	X	124
Taicochion	I of Angl	SH4765	53°9·9′	4°16·9′W	X	114,115
Tai-croesion	I of Angl	SH3375	53°15·0′	4°29·8′W	X	114
Tai-draw	Conwy	SH9648	53°1·4′	3°32·6′W	X	116
Tai-draw	Gwyn	SH9338	52°56·0′	3°35·1′W	X	125
Tai-duon	Conwy	SH8351	53°2·9′	3°44·3′W	X	116
Tai-duon	Conwy	SH9269	53°12·7′	3°36·6′W	X	116
Taiduon	Gwyn	SH4847	53°0·2′	4°15·5′W	X	115,123
Taigh Bhaltois	N Eil	NB3120	58°5·5′	6°33·4′W	X	13,14
Taigh Iamain	N Eil	NF8343	57°22·3′	7°16·0′W	X	22
Taiglim	E Ayr	NS5816	55°25·3′	4°14·2′W	X	71
Taiglum Burn	E Ayr	NS4718	55°26·2′	4°24·7′W	W	70
Tai-gwynion	Cered	SN5048	52°6·8′	4°11·0′W	X	146
Tai-gwynion	Cered	SN6387	52°28·1′	4°0·6′W	X	135
Tai-hen	I of Angl	SH3891	53°23·7′	4°25·8′W	X	114
Tai-hirion	Conwy	SH8352	53°3·4′	3°44·3′W	X	116
Tai-hirion	I of Angl	SH4570	53°12·5′	4°18·9′W	X	114,115
Taihirion	I of Angl	SH5175	53°15·3′	4°13·6′W	X	114,115
Tai-hirion	Powys	SN9411	51°47·5′	3°31·8′W	X	160
Taihirion-rhos	Cered	SN6465	52°16·2′	3°59·2′W	X	135
Tai-isa	Denb	SJ1056	53°5·9′	3°20·2′W	X	116
Tai-isaf	Denb	SJ0359	53°7·4′	3°26·6′W	X	116
Tail	Pth & Kin	NN9324	56°24·0′	3°43·6′W	X	52,58
Tailabout	Fife	NO3814	56°19·1′	2°59·7′W	X	59
Tailbert	Cumbr	NY5314	54°31·4′	2°43·1′W	X	90
Tailbert Head	Cumbr	NY5214	54°31·4′	2°44·1′W	X	90
Tailbridge Hill	Cumbr	NY8005	54°26·6′	2°18·1′W	H	91,92
Tail Burn	D & G	NT1715	55°25·6′	3°18·3′W	W	79
Tail o' Ling	Cumbr	NY4716	54°32·4′	2°48·7′W	X	90
Tailor's Leap	Arg & Bt	NN0128	56°24·4′	5°13·1′W	X	50
Tailors, The	Glos	SO7827	51°56·7′	2°18·8′W	X	162
Tails of the Tarf, The	Orkney	ND3783	58°44·1′	3°4·8′W	X	7
Tail, The	D & G	NY3879	55°6·3′	2°57·9′W	X	85
Tai-mawr	Conwy	SH9942	52°58·2′	3°29·8′W	X	125
Tai-moelion	I of Angl	SH3772	53°13·4′	4°26·1′W	X	114
Tai-morfa	Gwyn	SH2826	52°48·5′	4°32·7′W	T	123
Tain	Highld	ND2166	58°34·8′	3°21·0′W	X	11,12
Tain	Highld	NH7881	57°48·4′	4°2·7′W	T	21
Tai-nant	Wrex	SJ2746	53°0·6′	3°4·9′W	T	117
Taindore	Highld	NH6751	57°32·0′	4°12·8′W	X	26
Tai-newyddion	Denb	SJ1948	53°1·6′	3°12·1′W	X	116
Tainfield	Highld	NH7778	57°46·8′	4°3·6′W	X	21
Tainfield Park	Somer	ST2228	51°3·0′	3°6·4′W	X	193
Taing	Shetld	HU4860	60°19·5′	1°7·4′W	X	2,3
Taingar	Shetld	HU5493	60°37·3′	1°0·3′W	X	1,2
Tainga Skerries	Shetld	HU2558	60°18·6′	1°32·4′W	X	3
Taing Ayre	Orkney	HY6945	59°17·7′	2°32·2′W	X	5
Taing Head	Orkney	ND3299	58°52·6′	3°10·3′W	X	6,7
Taing of Beeman	Orkney	HY5309	58°58·2′	2°48·6′W	X	6,7
Taing of Blogars-hellia	Shetld	HU4430	60°3·4′	1°12·1′W	X	4
Taing of Brae	Orkney	HY4528	59°8·5′	2°57·2′W	X	5,6
Taing of Corkatae	Orkney	HY6738	59°13·9′	2°34·2′W	X	5
Taing of Crudy	Orkney	HY7043	59°16·6′	2°31·1′W	X	5
Taing of Ham	Shetld	HU4839	60°8·2′	1°7·7′W	X	4
Taing of Helliness	Shetld	HU4628	60°2·3′	1°10·0′W	X	4
Taing of Kelswick	Shetld	HU4969	60°24·4′	1°6·1′W	X	2,3
Taing of Looswick	Shetld	HP6018	60°50·7′	0°53·3′W	X	1
Taing of Maywick	Shetld	HU3725	60°0·8′	1°19·7′W	X	4
Taing of Midgarth	Orkney	HY4023	59°5·6′	3°2·3′W	X	5,6
Taing of Norwick	Shetld	HU3681	60°30·9′	1°20·2′W	X	1,2,3
Taing of Noustigarth	Shetld	HP6300	60°41·0′	0°50·3′W	X	1
Taing of Redbanks	Orkney	HY5110	58°58·7′	2°50·7′W	X	6
Taing of Sandside	Orkney	HY2606	58°56·7′	3°16·7′W	X	6,7
Taing of Selwick	Orkney	HY2205	58°55·8′	3°20·8′W	X	6,7
Taing of Setter	Shetld	HU4581	60°30·9′	1°10·3′W	X	1,2,3
Taing of the Busy	Orkney	HY5421	59°4·7′	2°47·7′W	X	5,6
Taing of the Clett	Orkney	HY4808	58°57·6′	2°53·8′W	X	6,7
Taing of the Pund	Orkney	HY6441	59°15·5′	2°37·4′W	X	5
Taing of Tor Sker	Orkney	HY7245	59°17·7′	2°29·0′W	X	5
Taing of Tratland	Orkney	HY4027	59°7·8′	3°2·4′W	X	5,6
Taing of Trumland	Orkney	HY4227	59°7·8′	3°0·3′W	X	5,6
Taing of Westbank	Orkney	HY4601	58°53·8′	2°55·7′W	X	6,7
Taing of Westove	Orkney	HY6645	59°17·7′	2°35·3′W	X	5
Taing Skerry	Orkney	HY4519	59°3·5′	2°57·1′W	X	6
Taings of Berstane	Orkney	HY5316	59°2·0′	2°48·6′W	X	6
Taing, The	Orkney	HY4225	59°6·7′	3°0·3′W	X	5,6
Taing, The	Orkney	HY4321	59°4·6′	2°59·2′W	X	5,6
Taing, The	Orkney	HY4552	59°21·3′	2°57·6′W	X	5
Taing, The	Shetld	HP6514	60°48·5′	0°47·8′W	X	1
Taing, The	Shetld	HU3344	60°11·0′	1°23·8′W	X	4
Taing, The	Shetld	HU3831	60°4·0′	1°18·5′W	X	4
Taing, The	Shetld	HU4011	59°53·2′	1°16·6′W	X	4
Taing, The	Shetld	HU4038	60°7·7′	1°16·3′W	X	4
Taing, The	Shetld	HU4968	60°23·8′	1°6·2′W	X	2,3
Tai'n Lôn	Gwyn	SH4450	53°1·7′	4°19·2′W	X	115,123
Tain Scalps	Highld	NH7785	57°50·5′	4°3·9′W	X	21
Tai'n-y-foel	Conwy	SH9550	53°2·5′	3°33·6′W	X	116
Tai'n-y-maes	Conwy	SH8350	53°2·3′	3°44·3′W	X	116
Tai'n-y-rhôs	Conwy	SH9447	53°0·8′	3°34·4′W	X	116
Tai'n-y-waens	Conwy	SH9951	53°3·0′	3°30·0′W	X	116
Taipellaf	Conwy	SH8659	53°7·2′	3°41·8′W	X	116
Taipellaf	Conwy	SH9456	53°5·7′	3°34·6′W	X	116
Tairbh	N Eil	NB3242	58°17·4′	6°33·9′W	W	8,13
Tai'r Bull	Powys	SN9925	51°55·1′	3°27·7′W	T	160
Tair Carn Isaf	Carm	SN6816	51°49·9′	3°54·5′W	X	159
Tair Carn Uchaf	Carm	SN6917	51°50·4′	3°53·7′W	H	160
Tair Carreg	Powys	SJ2319	52°46·0′	3°8·1′W	X	126
Tair Croes Down	V of Glam	SS9176	51°28·6′	3°33·8′W	X	170
Taireval	N Eil	NB0024	58°6·5′	7°5·1′W	H	13
Taireval	N Eil	NB0131	58°10·3′	7°4·7′W	X	13
Tair-felin	Gwyn	SH9039	52°56·5′	3°37·8′W	X	125
Tairgwaith	Nth Pt Talb	SN7112	51°47·7′	3°51·8′W	T	160
Tai'r-heol	Caer	ST1094	51°38·5′	3°17·6′W	T	171
Tai'r-heol	Rho Cyn Taf	ST0692	51°37·4′	3°21·1′W	X	170
Tai-rhôs	I of Angl	SH4670	53°12·5′	4°18·0′W	X	114,115
Tairisgir Mòr	N Eil	NB0625	58°7·2′	6°59·1′W	H	13,14
Tairlaw	S Ayr	NS4000	55°16·3′	4°30·7′W	X	77
Tairlaw Plantation	S Ayr	NX4098	55°15·3′	4°30·6′W	F	77
Tairlaw Ring	S Ayr	NX4098	55°15·3′	4°30·6′W	X	77
Tairlaw Toll	S Ayr	NX3999	55°15·8′	4°31·6′W	X	77
Tai'r-meibion	Gwyn	SH6371	53°13·3′	4°2·7′W	X	115
Taironen	Swan	SN6503	51°42·8′	3°56·9′W	X	159
Tair Onen Nursery	V of Glam	ST0374	51°27·6′	3°23·4′W	X	170
Tai'r-waun	Caer	ST1093	51°38·0′	3°17·6′W	X	171
Tai'r-ysgol	Swan	SS6997	51°39·6′	3°53·3′W	T	170
Tais Bheinn	Arg & Bt	NR3669	55°50·8′	6°12·6′W	X	60,61
Tai-tan-lan	Conwy	SH8952	53°3·5′	3°39·0′W	X	116
Taitealach	N Eil	NG0185	57°45·6′	7°1·2′W	X	18
Tai-Têg	Conwy	SH9865	53°10·6′	3°31·2′W	X	116
Tai-teg	Denb	SJ0449	53°2·0′	3°25·5′W	X	116
Taitlands	N Yks	SD8266	54°5·6′	2°16·1′W	X	98
Tait's Hill	Glos	SO7300	51°42·1′	2°23·1′W	X	162
Tai Ucha	Denb	SJ0256	53°5·8′	3°27·4′W	X	116
Tai Uchaf	I of Angl	SH3478	53°16·6′	4°29·0′W	X	114
Tai-uchaf	Powys	SJ0626	52°49·6′	3°23·3′W	X	125
Tai-ucha'n-cwm	Conwy	SH9147	53°0·8′	3°37·1′W	X	116
Takeley	Essex	TL5621	51°52·2′	0°16·4′E	T	167
Takeley Manor	Essex	TL4404	51°43·2′	0°5·5′E	X	167
Takeley Street	Essex	TL5421	51°52·2′	0°14·6′E	T	167
Talachddu	Powys	SO0833	51°59·5′	3°20·0′W	T	160
Talacre	Flint	SJ1284	53°21·0′	3°18·9′W	T	116
Talafon	Gwyn	SH4140	52°56·3′	4°21·6′W	X	123
Talardd	Carm	SN4941	52°3·1′	4°11·7′W	X	146
Talardd	Gwyn	SH8926	52°49·4′	3°38·4′W	T	124,125
Talatoll	Arg & Bt	NR7653	55°43·4′	5°33·6′W	X	62
Talaton	Devon	SY0699	50°47·2′	3°19·6′W	T	192
Talaton Fm	Devon	SY0797	50°46·1′	3°18·8′W	FM	192
Tala Water	Corn	SX3191	50°41·9′	4°23·2′W	W	190
Talbenny	Pemb	SM8311	51°45·6′	5°8·3′W	T	157
Talbontdrain	Powys	SN7795	52°32·6′	3°48·4′W	X	135
Talbot Br	Lancs	SD7044	53°53·7′	2°27·0′W	X	103
Talbot Fm	S Glos	ST7376	51°29·2′	2°22·9′W	FM	172
Talbot Green	Rho Cyn Taf	ST0382	51°32·0′	3°23·5′W	T	170
Talbot Heath	Poole	SZ0693	50°44·4′	1°54·5′W	T	195
Talbot Ho	Wigan	SD5712	53°36·4′	2°38·6′W	X	108
Talbot's End	S Glos	ST7090	51°36·7′	2°25·6′W	T	162,172
Talbots, The	V of Glam	ST0670	51°25·5′	3°20·7′W	X	170
Talbot Village	Bourne	SZ0794	50°45·0′	1°53·7′W	T	195
Talbot Wood	N Yks	SE8394	54°20·3′	0°43·0′W	F	94,100
Talbot Woods	Bourne	SZ0792	50°43·9′	1°53·7′W	T	195
Tal Cefn	Powys	SH9313	52°42·5′	3°34·6′W	X	125
Talcen Eithin	Gwyn	SH8343	52°58·5′	3°44·1′W	X	124,125
Talcen Llwyd	Conwy	SH7946	53°0·1′	3°47·8′W	X	115
Talcen-llwydiarth	Powys	SN9781	52°25·3′	3°30·5′W	X	136
Taldrwst	I of Angl	SH3091	53°23·6′	4°33·0′W	X	114
Taldrwst	I of Angl	SH4172	53°13·5′	4°22·5′W	X	114,115
Taldrwst Mawr	I of Angl	SH4388	53°22·2′	4°21·2′W	X	114
Talebrigg Hill	Cumbr	SD6085	54°15·8′	2°36·4′W	X	97
Taleford	Devon	SY0996	50°45·6′	3°17·0′W	T	192
Talerddig	Powys	SH9300	52°35·5′	3°34·4′W	T	136
Talewater	Devon	SY0899	50°47·2′	3°17·9′W	T	192
Tal-fan	Cered	SN5557	52°11·8′	4°6·9′W	X	146
Talfan Isaf	Carm	SN3222	51°52·5′	4°26·0′W	X	145,159
Talfryn	Cered	SN6267	52°17·3′	4°1·0′W	X	135
Talfryn	Cered	SN7069	52°18·5′	3°54·0′W	X	135,147
Talfryn	Wrex	SJ2239	52°56·8′	3°9·2′W	X	126
Talgarreg	Cered	SN4251	52°8·3′	4°18·1′W	T	146
Talgarth	Cered	SN6872	52°20·1′	3°55·8′W	X	135
Talgarth	Newp	ST4291	51°37·1′	2°49·9′W	X	171,172
Talgarth	Powys	SN9690	52°30·1′	3°31·5′W	X	136
Talgarth	Powys	SO1533	51°59·6′	3°13·9′W	T	161
Talgarth's Well	Swan	SS4288	51°34·4′	4°16·4′W	T	159
Talgoed	Carm	SN4238	52°1·3′	4°17·8′W	X	146
Talgrwn	Cered	SN5247	52°6·3′	4°9·3′W	X	146
Talgrwn	Conwy	SH9673	53°14·9′	3°33·1′W	X	116
Talgwynedd	I of Angl	SH4664	53°9·3′	4°17·8′W	X	114,115
Talhardd	Carm	SN6220	51°51·9′	3°59·9′W	X	159
Taliaris	Carm	SN6428	51°56·3′	3°58·3′W	X	146
Taliaris Park	Carm	SN6328	51°56·3′	3°59·2′W	F	146
Talisker	Highld	NG3230	57°17·2′	6°26·4′W	T	32
Talisker Bay	Highld	NG3130	57°17·1′	6°27·4′W	W	32
Talisker Distillery	Highld	NG3731	57°17·9′	6°21·5′W	X	32
Talisker Point	Highld	NG3129	57°16·6′	6°27·3′W	X	32
Talke	Staffs	SJ8253	53°4·7′	2°15·7′W	T	118
Talke Pits	Staffs	SJ8252	53°4·1′	2°15·7′W	T	118
Talkin	Cumbr	NY5457	54°54·6′	2°42·6′W	T	86
Talkin Fell	Cumbr	NY5756	54°54·1′	2°39·8′W	H	86
Talkin Head Fm	Cumbr	NY5556	54°54·1′	2°41·7′W	FM	86
Talkin Tarn	Cumbr	NY5458	54°55·1′	2°42·6′W	W	86
Talla Bheith Forest	Pth & Kin	NN5567	56°46·6′	4°21·9′W	X	42
Tallabric	Highld	NG2604	57°3·0′	6°30·6′W	H	39
Talladale	Highld	NG9170	57°40·5′	5°29·8′W	T	19
Talladh-a-Bheithe	Pth & Kin	NN5557	56°41·2′	4°21·6′W	X	42,51
Talla East Side	Scot Bord	NT1618	55°27·2′	3°19·3′W	X	79
Talla Linnfoots	Scot Bord	NT1320	55°28·2′	3°22·1′W	T	72
Tallaminnoch	S Ayr	NX4098	55°15·3′	4°30·6′W	X	77
Tallaminnock	S Ayr	NX4096	55°14·2′	4°30·5′W	X	77
Talland	Corn	SX2251	50°20·2′	4°29·7′W	T	201
Talland Bay	Corn	SX2251	50°20·2′	4°29·7′W	W	201
Tallant	Arg & Bt	NR3358	55°44·8′	6°14·8′W	X	60
Tallant	Arg & Bt	NR4550	55°40·8′	6°3·0′W	X	60
Talla Reservoir	Scot Bord	NT1121	55°28·7′	3°24·1′W	W	72
Tallarn Green	Wrex	SJ4444	52°59·7′	2°49·7′W	T	117
Tallash	Staffs	SJ9260	53°8·5′	2°6·8′W	X	118
Talla Water	Scot Bord	NT1518	55°27·2′	3°20·2′W	W	79
Tallentire	Cumbr	NY1035	54°42·4′	3°23·4′W	T	89
Tallentire Hill	Cumbr	NY1235	54°42·4′	3°21·5′W	H	89
Tallents Fm	Herts	TL1517	51°50·6′	0°19·4′W	FM	166
Talley	Carm	SN6332	51°58·4′	3°59·3′W	T	146
Tallin	Gwyn	SH6437	52°55·0′	4°1·0′W	X	124
Tallington	Lincs	TF0908	52°39·8′	0°22·9′W	T	142
Tallington Lakes Leisure Park	Lincs	TF0909	52°40·3′	0°22·9′W	W	142
Tallington Lodge	Lincs	TF0909	52°40·3′	0°22·9′W	X	142
Tallowquhairn	D & G	NX9958	54°54·6′	3°34·1′W	X	84
Tally Ho	Devon	SX8163	50°27·5′	3°40·2′W	X	202
Tally Ho	Glos	SP0923	51°54·6′	1°51·8′W	X	163
Tally-Ho	Pemb	SM9609	51°44·8′	4°56·9′W	X	157,158
Tallyho Covert	Northnts	SP7178	52°24·0′	0°57·0′W	F	141
Tallysow	Highld	NH5255	57°33·9′	4°28·0′W	X	26
Talm	Highld	NM4890	56°56·2′	6°8·1′W	X	39
Talmine	Highld	NC5862	58°31·6′	4°25·8′W	T	10
Talmine Island	Highld	NC5962	58°31·7′	4°24·8′W	X	10
Talog	Carm	SN3325	51°54·2′	4°25·3′W	T	145
Talog	Carm	SN7436	52°0·7′	3°49·8′W	X	146,160
Talrhyn	Carm	SN7335	52°0·2′	3°50·6′W	X	146,160
Talsarn	Carm	SN7726	51°55·4′	3°46·9′W	T	146,160
Tal-sarn	Cered	SN5456	52°11·2′	4°7·8′W	T	146
Talsarn	Gwyn	SH2729	52°50·1′	4°33·7′W	X	123
Talsarn	Powys	SO1623	51°54·2′	3°12·9′W	X	161
Talsarnau	Gwyn	SH6135	52°53·9′	4°3·6′W	T	124
Talskiddy	Corn	SW9165	50°27·1′	4°56·3′W	T	200
Talton Fm	Warw	SP2346	52°6·9′	1°39·4′W	FM	151
Talton Ho	Warw	SP2347	52°7·5′	1°39·4′W	X	151
Taltreuddyn	Gwyn	SH5825	52°48·5′	4°6·0′W	X	124
Tal Trwynau	Powys	SO2224	51°54·8′	3°7·6′W	X	161
Talvan	Corn	SX1755	50°22·2′	4°34·0′W	X	201
Talwen	Powys	SO0633	51°59·5′	3°21·7′W	X	160
Talwrn	Cered	SN5662	52°14·5′	4°6·1′W	X	146
Talwrn	Cered	SN5767	52°17·2′	4°5·4′W	X	135
Talwrn	Cered	SN7464	52°15·8′	3°50·4′W	X	146,147
Talwrn	Flint	SJ2358	53°7·1′	3°8·6′W	X	117
Talwrn	Flint	SJ2958	53°7·1′	3°3·2′W	X	117
Talwrn	I of Angl	SH4977	53°16·4′	4°15·5′W	T	114,115
Talwrn	Powys	SJ1719	52°46·0′	3°13·4′W	X	125
Talwrn	Powys	SJ1927	52°50·3′	3°11·7′W	X	125
Talwrn	Powys	SN9464	52°16·1′	3°32·8′W	X	147
Talwrn	Wrex	SJ2851	53°3·3′	3°4·1′W	T	117
Talwrn	Wrex	SJ2947	53°1·2′	3°3·1′W	T	117
Talwrn	Wrex	SJ3847	53°1·2′	2°55·1′W	X	117
Talwrn-côch	Cered	SN5867	52°17·2′	4°4·5′W	X	135
Talwrn Hogfaen	Cered	SN5867	52°17·2′	4°4·5′W	X	135
Talwrnllyn	Cered	SN5766	52°16·7′	4°5·4′W	X	135
Talwrn-y-glo	Powys	SJ1125	52°49·2′	3°18·8′W	X	125
Tal-y-bidwal bâch	Denb	SJ1247	53°1·0′	3°18·3′W	X	116
Tal-y-bidwal fawr	Denb	SJ1246	53°0·5′	3°18·3′W	X	116
Tal-y-bont	Cered	SN6589	52°29·2′	3°58·9′W	T	135
Tal-y-Bont	Conwy	SH7668	53°11·9′	3°51·0′W	T	115
Tal-y-bont	Gwyn	SH5821	52°46·3′	4°5·9′W	T	124
Talybont	Gwyn	SH5903	52°36·6′	4°4·5′W	X	135
Tal-y-bont	Gwyn	SH6070	53°12·8′	4°5·4′W	T	115
Tal-y-bont	Gwyn	SH8634	52°53·7′	3°41·3′W	X	124,125
Tal-y-bont	Gwyn	SH9038	52°55·9′	3°37·8′W	X	125
Tal -y-bontan	I of Angl	SH4586	53°21·1′	4°19·3′W	X	114
Talybont Forest	Powys	SO0818	51°51·4′	3°19·8′W	F	160
Talybont-on-Usk	Powys	SO1122	51°53·6′	3°17·2′W	T	161
Talybont Reservoir	Powys	SO0918	51°51·4′	3°18·9′W	W	161
Tal-y-braich	Conwy	SH6960	53°7·5′	3°57·1′W	X	115
Tal-y-bryn	Conwy	SH9970	53°13·3′	3°30·4′W	X	116
Tal-y-bryn	Powys	SO1322	51°53·6′	3°15·5′W	X	161
Tal-y-cae	Gwyn	SH6068	53°11·7′	4°5·3′W	X	115
Tal-y-cafn	Conwy	SH7971	53°13·6′	3°48·3′W	T	115
Tal-y-cefn Isaf	Conwy	SH9951	53°3·0′	3°30·0′W	X	116
Tal-y-cefn Uchaf	Conwy	SH9952	53°3·6′	3°30·0′W	X	116
Tal-y-coed	Monm	SO4115	51°50·1′	2°51·0′W	T	161
Talycynllwyn	Swan	SN5905	51°43·8′	4°2·1′W	X	159
Tal-y-fan	Cered	SN6047	52°6·5′	4°2·3′W	X	146
Tal y Fan	Conwy	SH7372	53°14·0′	3°53·8′W	H	115
Tal-y-fan	Gwyn	SH6504	52°37·3′	3°59·3′W	X	135
Tal-y-fan	Monm	SO4508	51°46·3′	2°47·4′W	X	161
Talyfan	Swan	SN5805	51°43·8′	4°3·0′W	X	159
Tal-y-fan-uchaf	Carm	SN3223	51°53·1′	4°26·1′W	X	145,159
Tal-y-fedw	Rho Cyn Taf	ST0485	51°33·6′	3°22·7′W	X	170
Tal y ffnonau	Gwyn	SH6124	52°48·0′	4°3·3′W	X	124

Tal y ffyhonau	Gwyn	SH6124	52°48·0'	4°3·3'W	X	124
Tal y gareg	Gwyn	SH5703	52°36·6'	4°6·3'W	X	135
Talygarn	Rho Cyn Taf	ST0380	51°30·9'	3°23·5'W	X	170
Talygarth	Wrex	SJ2137	52°55·7'	3°10·1'W	X	126
Tal-y-llyn	Conwy	SH7266	53°10·8'	3°54·5'W	X	115
Tal-y-llyn	Conwy	SH7560	53°7·6'	3°51·7'W	X	115
Tal-y-llyn	Gwyn	SH5544	52°58·7'	4°9·2'W	X	124
Tal-y-llyn	Gwyn	SH7109	52°40·0'	3°54·1'W	T	124
Tal-y-llyn	I of Angl	SH3673	53°14·0'	4°27·0'W	X	114
Talyllyn	Powys	SO1027	51°56·3'	3°18·2'W	T	161
Tal-y-llyn Lake	Gwyn	SH7109	52°40·0'	3°54·1'W	W	124
Tal y Llyn Ogwen	Conwy	SH6660	53°7·5'	3°59·8'W	X	115
Talyllyn Railway	Gwyn	SH6102	52°36·1'	4°2·8'W	X	135
Talyllyn Railway	Gwyn	SH6605	52°37·8'	3°58·4'W	X	124
Tal-y-maen	Corn	SW3225	50°4·1'	5°44·4'W	X	203
Tal-y-maes	Powys	SO2226	51°55·9'	3°7·7'W	X	161
Tal y Mieryn	Gwyn	SH8212	52°41·8'	3°44·4'W	H	124,125
Tal-y-mignedd	Gwyn	SH5252	53°2·9'	4°12·1'W	X	115
Talyrnau	Powys	SH8507	52°39·2'	3°41·6'W	X	124,125
Talyrnau	Powys	SJ1906	52°39·0'	3°11·4'W	X	125
Talysarn	Gwyn	SH4853	53°3·4'	4°15·7'W	T	115,123
Talywaen	Gwyn	SH5963	53°9·0'	4°6·1'W	X	114,115
Tal y Waen	Gwyn	SH6917	52°44·3'	3°56·0'W	X	124
Tal-y-waenydd	Gwyn	SH6947	53°0·5'	3°56·7'W	T	115
Talywain	Torf	SO2604	51°44·0'	3°3·9'W	T	171
Tal-y-waun	Conwy	SH7159	53°7·0'	3°55·2'W	X	115
Tal-y-Wern	Powys	SH8200	52°35·3'	3°44·1'W	T	135,136
Tamanaisval	N Eil	NB0423	58°6·1'	7°1·0'W	H	13
Tamanavay	N Eil	NB0227	58°4·5'	7°0·8'W	X	13
Tamano	Pth & Kin	NN8008	56°15·2'	3°55·8'W	X	57
Tamar	Corn	SX1670	50°30·3'	4°35·3'W	X	201
Tamar Br	Devon	SX4358	50°24·3'	4°12·2'W	X	201
Tamar Lakes Water Park	Devon	SS2812	50°53·2'	4°26·3'W	W	190
Tamarstone	Devon	SS2805	50°49·4'	4°26·1'W	X	190
Tamatown	Corn	SX3390	50°41·4'	4°21·5'W	X	190
Tamavoid	Stir	NS5999	56°10·0'	4°15·8'W	X	57
Tambeth	Pth & Kin	NN8705	56°13·7'	3°48·9'W	X	58
Tambowie	E Dunb	NS5275	55°57·0'	4°21·8'W	X	64
Tamduff	Aberd	NJ4624	57°18·5'	2°53·3'W	X	37
Tame Br	N Yks	NZ5108	54°28·1'	1°12·4'W	X	93
Tame Bridge	N Yks	NZ5008	54°28·1'	1°13·3'W	T	93
Tame Lane Cottage	Kent	TR0832	51°3·2'	0°58·5'E	X	189
Tamer Lane End	Wigan	SD6301	53°30·5'	2°33·1'W	T	109
Tamerton Foliot	C of Plym	SX4761	50°26·0'	4°8·9'W	T	201
Tamerton Town	Corn	SX3196	50°44·6'	4°23·3'W	X	190
Tame Valley Canal	Sand	SP0294	52°32·9'	1°57·8'W	W	139
Tame Water	Oldham	SD9806	53°33·3'	2°1·4'W	T	109
Tamfourhill	Falk	NS8580	56°0·2'	3°50·2'W	T	65
Tamhilt	Angus	NO4871	56°49·9'	2°50·7'W	H	44
Tamhnich Burn	Arg & Bt	NS0284	56°0·7'	5°10·1'W	W	55
Tamhorn House Br	Staffs	SK1807	52°39·9'	1°43·6'W	X	139
Tamhorn Park	Staffs	SK1706	52°39·3'	1°44·5'W	X	139
Tamiang	Highld	NH7792	57°54·3'	4°4·1'W	X	21
Ta Mill	Corn	SX1884	50°37·9'	4°34·0'W	X	201
Tammy's Hill	Shetld	HU2484	60°32·6'	1°33·2'W	H	3
Tammy Tiffy	Orkney	HY5905	58°56·1'	2°42·3'W	X	6
Tamna	N Eil	NB1241	58°16·1'	6°54·2'W	X	13
Tamnagorn	Aberd	NJ6407	57°9·4'	2°35·3'W	X	37
Tam na Moin	Moray	NJ1050	57°32·1'	3°29·7'W	X	28
Tamond Heights	D & G	NY4296	55°15·5'	2°54·3'W	H	79
Tam O'Shanter Experience	S Ayr	NS3318	55°25·9'	4°37·9'W	X	70
Tampie	Aberd	NO 946	56°28·3'	7°51·4'W	X	44
Tampie	Aberd	NO4986	56°58·0'	2°49·9'W	H	44
Tamshiel Rig	Scot Bord	NT6406	55°21·1'	2°33·6'W	X	80
Tam's Hill	E Ayr	NS4846	55°41·3'	4°24·6'W	X	64
Tamsquite	Corn	SX0575	50°32·8'	4°44·8'W	X	200
Tam, The	Moray	NJ3650	57°32·4'	3°3·7'W	X	28
Tamworth	Staffs	SK2203	52°37·7'	1°40·1'W	T	139
Tamworth Green	Lincs	TF3842	52°57·7'	0°3·7'E	T	131
Tamworth Service Area	Warw	SK2400	52°36·1'	1°38·3'W	X	139
Tana Leas Fm	Shrops	SO5583	52°26·8'	2°39·3'W	FM	137,138
Tanaraidh	N Eil	NB3922	58°6·9'	6°25·4'W	X	14
Tanat Valley	Powys	SJ0924	52°48·6'	3°20·6'W	X	125
Tan-banc	Cered	SN5961	52°14·0'	4°3·5'W	X	146
Tancnwch	Cered	SN7168	52°17·9'	3°53·1'W	X	135,147
Tancred	N Yks	SE4558	54°1·2'	1°18·4'W	T	105
Tancred Grange	N Yks	SE2499	54°23·4'	1°37·4'W	X	99
Tancredston	Pemb	SM8826	51°53·8'	5°4·5'W	X	157
Tan Dderwen	Denb	SJ0668	53°12·3'	3°24·0'W	X	116
Tandem	Kirk	SE1716	53°38·7'	1°44·2'W	T	110
Tanden	Kent	TQ9138	51°6·8'	0°44·1'E	T	189
Tanderlane	E Loth	NT5871	55°56·1'	2°39·9'W	X	67
Tandlaw	Scot Bord	NT4917	55°26·9'	2°47·9'W	X	79
Tandlehill	Renf	NS4062	55°49·7'	4°32·8'W	T	64
Tandle Hill Country Park	Oldham	SD9008	53°34·4'	2°8·6'W	X	109
Tandlemuir	Renf	NS3361	55°48·9'	4°39·5'W	X	63
Tandleview	N Ayr	NS3852	55°44·3'	4°34·4'W	X	63
Tandoo Point	D & G	NX0052	54°49·6'	5°6·4'W	X	82
Tandridge	Surrey	TQ3750	51°14·2'	0°1·9'W	T	187
Tandridge Court	Surrey	TQ3751	51°14·7'	0°1·8'W	X	187
Tandridge Hill	Surrey	TQ3753	51°15·8'	0°1·8'W	X	187
Tanera Beg	Highld	NB9607	58°0·6'	5°26·7'W	X	15
Tanera Mor	Highld	NB9807	58°0·6'	5°24·7'W	X	15
Tanerdy	Carm	SN4221	51°52·2'	4°17·3'W	T	159
Tanerdy	Carm	SN4923	51°53·3'	4°11·3'W	X	159
Tanfield	Durham	NZ1855	54°53·6'	1°42·7'W	T	88
Tanfield Grange Fm	Durham	NZ1955	54°53·6'	1°41·8'W	FM	88
Tanfield Hall Fm	N Yks	SE2577	54°11·5'	1°36·6'W	FM	99
Tanfield Lea	Durham	NZ1854	54°53·1'	1°42·7'W	T	88
Tanfield Leith Fm	Durham	NZ1854	54°53·1'	1°42·7'W	FM	88
Tanfield Lodge	N Yks	SE2477	54°11·5'	1°37·5'W	X	99
Tanfield Moor	Durham	NZ1855	54°53·6'	1°42·7'W	X	88
Tanfield Railway	Ghead	NZ2057	54°54·7'	1°40·9'W	X	88
Tanfield Stud Fm	Herts	TL3204	51°43·4'	0°4·9'W	FM	166
Tanfield Tye	Essex	TL7201	51°41·1'	0°29·7'E	X	167
Tanforhesgen	Gwyn	SH5834	52°53·3'	4°6·2'W	X	124
Tang	N Yks	SE2357	54°0·8'	1°38·5'W	T	104
Tanga Deas	N Eil	NB4219	58°5·4'	6°22·2'W	X	14
Tangarn	Cered	SN5863	52°15·1'	4°4·4'W	X	146
Tangasdale	N Eil	NF6500	56°58·4'	7°30·4'W	T	31

Tang Hall	N Yks	SE4985	54°15·7'	1°14·4'W	X	100
Tang Hall	York	SE6252	53°57·9'	1°2·9'W	T	105
Tang Hall Beck	York	SE6354	53°58·9'	1°1·9'W	W	105,106
Tangham Ho	Suff	TM3548	52°5·0'	1°26·2'E	X	169
Tang Head	Highld	ND2774	58°39·1'	3°15·0'W	X	7,12
Tang Head	Highld	ND3560	58°31·7'	3°6·5'W	X	12
Tangi	Orkney	HY5906	58°56·6'	2°42·3'W	X	6
Tangier	Hants	SU5853	51°16·6'	1°9·7'W	X	185
Tangier Fm	Hants	SU5317	50°57·2'	1°14·3'W	FM	185
Tangiers	Pemb	SM9518	51°49·6'	4°58·1'W	T	157,158
Tangies	Corn	SW6624	50°4·4'	5°15·9'W	X	203
Tangi Loch	Shetld	HU4678	60°29·2'	1°9·3'W	W	2,3
Tangi Voe	Shetld	HU3539	60°8·3'	1°21·7'W	W	4
Tanglandford	Aberd	NJ8835	57°24·6'	2°11·5'W	X	30
Tangleha'	Aberd	NO7764	56°46·3'	2°22·1'W	X	45
Tangley	Hants	SU3352	51°16·2'	1°31·2'W	T	185
Tangley Bottom	Hants	SU3252	51°16·2'	1°32·1'W	X	185
Tangley Farm	Hants	SU3452	51°16·2'	1°30·4'W	FM	185
Tangley Fm	Oxon	SP5829	51°57·6'	1°9·0'W	FM	164
Tangley Hall	Oxon	SP2316	51°50·8'	1°39·6'W	X	163
Tangley Woods	Oxon	SP2317	51°51·3'	1°39·6'W	F	163
Tanglogau	Cered	SN6169	52°18·3'	4°1·9'W	X	135
Tanglwst	Carm	SN3134	51°59·0'	4°27·3'W	T	145
Tanglwys	Powys	SJ0312	52°42·1'	3°25·7'W	X	125
Tangmere	W Susx	SU9006	50°51·0'	0°42·9'W	T	197
Tangraig	Cered	SN5761	52°14·0'	4°5·2'W	X	146
Tangs Bottom	Somer	SS7540	51°9·0'	3°46·8'W	X	180
Tang, The	Suff	TM3747	52°4·5'	1°27·9'E	W	169
Tang Wick	Shetld	HU2277	60°28·8'	1°35·5'W	W	3
Tangwick	Shetld	HU2377	60°28·8'	1°34·4'W	T	3
Tangy	Arg & Bt	NR6727	55°29·1'	5°40·8'W	X	68
Tangy Burn	Arg & Bt	NR6727	55°29·1'	5°40·8'W	W	68
Tangy Loch	Arg & Bt	NR6927	55°29·2'	5°38·9'W	W	68
Tangy Lodge	Arg & Bt	NR6527	55°29·1'	5°42·7'W	X	68
Tangymoil	Arg & Bt	NR6628	55°29·6'	5°41·8'W	X	68
Tangytavil	Arg & Bt	NR6529	55°30·2'	5°42·8'W	X	68
Tan Hill	D & G	NX8270	55°0·9'	3°50·3'W	H	84
Tan Hill	N Yks	NY8906	54°27·2'	2°9·8'W	X	91,92
Tanhill	S Lanak	NS7744	55°40·7'	3°56·9'W	X	71
Tan Hill	Wilts	SU0864	51°22·7'	1°52·7'W	X	173
Tan-hill Copse	Dorset	ST8113	50°55·2'	2°15·8'W	F	194
Tan Hills	Durham	NZ2547	54°49·3'	1°36·2'W	T	88
Tan Hill Way	Wilts	SU1263	51°22·2'	1°49·3'W	X	173
Tan Hinon	Powys	SN8985	52°27·3'	3°37·6'W	T	135,136
Tan Ho	Heref	SO2448	52°7·7'	3°6·2'W	X	148
Tan Ho	Powys	SJ2216	52°44·4'	3°8·9'W	X	126
Tan Ho	Powys	SO1667	52°17·9'	3°13·5'W	X	136,148
Tan Ho	Powys	SO2691	52°31·0'	3°5·0'W	X	137
Tanholt Fm	Peterb	TF2301	52°35·8'	0°10·6'W	FM	142
Tanhouse	Ches	SJ8764	53°10·6'	2°11·3'W	X	118
Tan House	Kent	TQ4750	51°14·0'	0°6·7'E	X	188
Tanhouse	Lancs	SD4905	53°32·6'	2°45·8'W	T	108
Tan House Fm	Ches	SJ5575	53°16·4'	2°40·1'W	FM	117
Tanhouse Fm	E Susx	TQ8221	50°57·8'	0°35·9'E	FM	199
Tan House Fm	S Glos	ST7185	51°34·0'	2°24·7'W	FM	172
Tanhouse Fm	Wilts	ST9363	51°22·2'	2°5·6'W	FM	173
Tanhouse Wood	Heref	SO3634	52°0·3'	2°55·5'W	F	149,161
Tanhurst	Surrey	TQ1242	51°10·2'	0°23·5'W	X	187
Tanhurst Fm	Surrey	TQ1940	51°9·0'	0°17·5'W	FM	187
Tanis	Wilts	ST9862	51°21·7'	2°1·3'W	T	173
Tankards Fm	Herts	TL1322	51°53·3'	0°21·1'W	FM	166
Tankerness	Orkney	HY5008	58°57·6'	2°51·7'W	X	6,7
Tankersley	Barns	SK3498	53°28·9'	1°28·8'W	X	110,111
Tankersley Park	Sheff	SK3498	53°28·9'	1°28·8'W	X	110,111
Tankerton	Kent	TR1266	51°21·4'	1°3·1'E	T	179
Tankerton Bay	Kent	TR1068	51°22·6'	1°1·4'E	W	179
Tankeylake Moor	Swan	SS4391	51°36·0'	4°15·6'W	X	159
Tank Fm	C of Edin	NT1476	55°58·4'	3°22·2'W	FM	65
Tankins Fm	Corn	SS2600	50°46·6'	4°27·7'W	FM	190
Tank Plantn	E Yorks	SE7747	53°55·0'	0°49·2'W	F	105,106
Tank Wood	Notts	SK6374	53°15·8'	1°2·9'W	F	120
Tan-lan	Conwy	SH7963	53°9·3'	3°48·2'W	T	115
Tan-lan	Conwy	SH7964	53°9·8'	3°48·2'W	X	115
Tanlan	Flint	SJ1282	53°19·9'	3°18·9'W	T	116
Tan-lan	Gwyn	SH6142	52°57·7'	4°3·8'W	T	124
Tan-Lan	I of Angl	SH3485	53°20·4'	4°29·2'W	X	114
Tan Lan	I of Angl	SH4071	53°13·0'	4°23·4'W	X	114,115
Tanlan Banks	Flint	SJ1183	53°20·4'	3°19·8'W	T	116
Tan-lan-fawr	Carm	SN6846	52°6·0'	3°55·2'W	X	146
Tanlawhill	D & G	NY2391	55°12·7'	3°12·2'W	X	79
Tanlaw Naze	Scot Bord	NT3905	55°20·4'	2°57·3'W	H	79
Tan-llan	Cered	SN6576	52°22·2'	3°58·6'W	X	135
Tan Llan	Conwy	SH8676	53°16·4'	3°42·2'W	X	116
Tan-llan	Conwy	SH9871	53°13·8'	3°31·3'W	X	116
Tan-llan	Flint	SJ1571	53°14·0'	3°16·0'W	X	116
Tan-llan	Flint	SJ2657	53°6·5'	3°5·9'W	X	117
Tan-llan	Gwyn	SH2336	52°53·8'	4°37·5'W	X	123
Tanllan	Powys	SJ0717	52°44·8'	3°22·3'W	X	125
Tanlluest	Cered	SN5966	52°16·7'	4°3·6'W	X	135
Tan Llwyn	Powys	SJ1724	52°48·7'	3°13·5'W	X	125
Tannach	Highld	ND3247	58°24·6'	3°9·4'W	T	12
Tannach Hill	Highld	ND3047	58°24·6'	3°11·4'W	H	11,12
Tannachie	Aberd	NO7883	56°56·5'	2°21·2'W	X	45
Tannachy	Highld	NC7507	58°2·3'	4°6·6'W	X	16
Tannacrieff	E Ayr	NS4442	55°39·0'	4°28·3'W	X	70
Tannadice	Angus	NO4758	56°42·9'	2°51·5'W	T	54
Tannadyce Ho	Angus	NO4857	56°42·4'	2°50·5'W	X	54
Tannahill	E Ayr	NS4341	55°38·5'	4°29·2'W	X	70
Tannaraidh	N Eil	NB4023	58°7·4'	6°24·5'W	X	14
Tannerhall	Pth & Kin	NO1207	56°15·1'	3°24·8'W	X	58
Tanner Ho	Kent	TQ7341	51°8·7'	0°28·8'E	X	188
Tanners	Devon	SS5926	51°1·2'	4°0·2'W	X	180
Tanners	Essex	TL6020	51°51·6'	0°19·8'E	X	167
Tanner's	Glos	ST8790	51°36·8'	2°10·9'W	X	162,173
Tanner's Brook	Hants	SU3918	50°57·8'	1°26·3'W	W	185
Tanner's Brook	Surrey	TQ1948	51°13·4'	0°17·4'W	W	187
Tanner's Brook	Worcs	SO7173	52°21·5'	2°25·2'W	W	138
Tanners Cross	Kent	TQ5557	51°17·7'	0°13·8'E	X	188
Tanner's Fm	Oxon	SU7077	51°29·5'	0°59·1'W	FM	175
Tanner's Fm	Wok	SU7465	51°23·0'	0°55·8'W	FM	175

Tanners Fm	W Susx	TQ0624	51°0·6'	0°29·0'W	FM	197
Tanner's Green	Worcs	SP0874	52°22·1'	1°52·6'W	T	139
Tanner's Hall Fm	Durham	NZ1737	54°43·9'	1°43·7'W	FM	92
Tanner's Hatch	Surrey	TQ1451	51°15·0'	0°21·6'W	X	187
Tanners Manor	E Susx	TQ5618	50°56·6'	0°13·6'E	X	199
Tannington	Suff	TM2467	52°15·6'	1°17·3'E	X	156
Tannington Hall	Suff	TM2468	52°16·1'	1°17·4'E	X	156
Tannington Lodge	Suff	TM2567	52°15·5'	1°18·2'E	X	156
Tannington Place	Suff	TM2367	52°15·6'	1°16·5'E	T	156
Tannis Court	Herts	TL3328	51°56·3'	0°3·5'W	X	166
Tannoch	N Lanak	NS7772	55°55·8'	3°57·7'W	X	64
Tannoch Burn	D & G	NX6074	55°2·7'	4°11·0'W	W	77
Tannoch Burn	D & G	NX8759	54°55·0'	3°45·4'W	W	84
Tannoch Burn	D & G	NX9464	54°57·8'	3°38·9'W	W	84
Tannoch Flow	D & G	NX6174	55°2·7'	4°10·1'W	X	77
Tannochside	N Lanak	NS7061	55°49·7'	4°4·1'W	T	64
Tannock Hill	D & G	NX9363	54°57·3'	3°39·8'W	H	84
Tannockhill	S Ayr	NS4526	55°30·4'	4°26·8'W	X	70
Tannylaggie	D & G	NX2872	55°1·0'	4°41·0'W	X	76
Tannylaggie Flow	D & G	NX2771	55°0·5'	4°41·9'W	X	76
Tannymaas	D & G	NX6355	54°52·5'	4°7·7'W	X	83
Tan Office	Suff	TM1063	52°13·7'	1°4·9'E	T	155
Tan Office Fm	Suff	TL8353	52°8·9'	0°40·9'E	FM	155
Tan Office Green	Suff	TL7858	52°11·7'	0°36·7'E	T	155
Tanpencefn	I of Angl	SH4666	53°10·4'	4°17·8'W	X	114,115
Tan Pits Fm	Lancs	SD6213	53°37·0'	2°34·1'W	FM	109
Tanrallt	Cered	SN4555	52°10·5'	4°15·6'W	X	146
Tanrallt	Conwy	SH7870	53°13·0'	3°49·2'W	X	115
Tan Rallt	Conwy	SH9175	53°15·9'	3°37·6'W	X	116
Tan Rallt	I of Angl	SH3675	53°15·0'	4°27·1'W	X	114
Tanrallt	Powys	SN9995	52°32·9'	3°29·0'W	X	136
Tanrallt Fm	Conwy	SH7674	53°15·2'	3°51·1'W	FM	115
Tanrallt-Isaf	Cered	SN6960	52°13·6'	3°54·7'W	X	146
Tansfield	Highld	ND1967	58°35·3'	3°23·1'W	X	11,12
Tanshall	Fife	NO2500	56°11·5'	3°12·1'W	T	59
Tansie Knowes	Shetld	HU4538	60°7·7'	1°10·9'W	X	4
Tanskey Rocks	Wirral	SJ2085	53°21·6'	3°11·7'W	X	108
Tansley	Derby	SK3259	53°7·9'	1°30·9'W	T	119
Tansley Dale	Derby	SK1774	53°16·0'	1°44·3'W	X	119
Tansley Hill	Dudley	SO9589	52°30·2'	2°4·0'W	T	139
Tansley Knoll	Derby	SK3260	53°8·4'	1°30·9'W	X	119
Tansley Moor	Derby	SK3261	53°8·9'	1°30·9'W	X	119
Tansley Rig	D & G	NS9201	55°17·7'	3°41·6'W	X	78
Tansomalia	Powys	SO1680	52°24·9'	3°13·7'W	X	136
Tansor	Northnts	TL0591	52°30·6'	0°26·8'W	T	142
Tansor Grange	Northnts	TL0790	52°30·1'	0°25·0'W	X	142
Tansor Lodge	Northnts	TL0589	52°29·6'	0°26·8'W	X	142
Tansor Wold Fm	Northnts	TL0889	52°29·5'	0°24·2'W	FM	142
Tansterne	E Yorks	TA2237	53°49·1'	0°8·4'W	X	107
Tansy Hill	D & G	NY3284	55°9·0'	3°3·6'W	H	79
Tantah	Scot Bord	NT2439	55°38·6'	3°12·0'W	X	73
Tantallon Castle	E Loth	NT5985	56°3·6'	2°39·1'W	A	67
Tantany Wood	Hants	SU3604	50°50·3'	1°28·9'W	F	196
Tanterton	Lancs	SD5132	53°47·2'	2°44·2'W	T	102
Tan, The	N Ayr	NS1553	55°44·4'	4°56·4'W	W	63
Tantobie	Durham	NZ1754	54°53·1'	1°43·7'W	T	88
Tanton	N Yks	NZ5210	54°29·2'	1°11·4'W	X	93
Tanton Dykes	N Yks	NZ5209	54°28·7'	1°11·4'W	X	93
Tantons	Aberd	NJ8153	57°34·3'	2°18·6'W	X	29,30
Tanton's Plain	Devon	SS4919	50°57·3'	4°8·6'W	X	180
Tantree Bank	Shrops	SJ2905	52°38·5'	3°2·6'W	X	126
Tanvats	Lincs	TF1364	53°9·9'	0°18·2'W	X	121
Tanwood	Worcs	SO9074	52°22·1'	2°8·4'W	T	139
Tanworth-in-Arden	Warw	SP1170	52°19·9'	1°49·9'W	T	139
Tanyard	Kent	TQ8040	51°8·1'	0°34·8'E	X	188
Tanyard	Somer	ST2130	51°4·1'	3°7·3'W	X	182
Tanyard	W Susx	TQ3730	51°3·4'	0°2·3'W	X	187
Tanyard Bay	Cumbr	NX9720	54°34·1'	3°35·2'W	W	89
Tanyard Fm	Ches	SJ7884	53°21·4'	2°19·4'W	FM	109
Tanyard Fm	Ches	SJ8277	53°17·6'	2°15·8'W	FM	118
Tanyard Fm	E Susx	TQ4127	51°1·7'	0°1·0'E	FM	187,198
Tanyard Fm	Kent	TQ6047	51°12·2'	0°17·8'E	FM	188
Tanyard Fm	Kent	TQ7432	51°3·9'	0°29·4'E	FM	188
Tanyard Fm	Kent	TQ9051	51°13·8'	0°43·7'E	FM	189
Tanyard Fm	Pemb	SM9817	51°49·1'	4°55·5'W	FM	157,158
Tan-y-berth	Powys	SN9175	52°22·0'	3°35·7'W	X	136,147
Tan-y-bryn	Conwy	SH7772	53°14·1'	3°50·2'W	X	115
Tan-y-bryn	Conwy	SH9576	53°16·5'	3°34·1'W	X	116
Tan-y-bryn	Denb	SJ0172	53°14·4'	3°28·6'W	X	116
Tan-y-bryn	Denb	SJ0676	53°16·6'	3°24·2'W	X	116
Tan-y-bryn	Gwyn	SH3334	52°52·9'	4°28·5'W	X	123
Tan-y-bryn	Gwyn	SH4652	53°2·8'	4°17·4'W	X	115,123
Tanybryn	Powys	SO1697	52°34·1'	3°14·0'W	X	136
Tanybwlch	Cered	SN5879	52°23·7'	4°4·8'W	X	135
Tan-y-bwlch	Conwy	SH7368	53°11·9'	3°53·7'W	X	115
Tan-y-bwlch	Conwy	SH9352	53°3·5'	3°35·4'W	H	116
Tan-y-bwlch	Denb	SJ0149	53°2·0'	3°28·2'W	X	116
Tan-y-bwlch	Denb	SJ2047	53°1·1'	3°11·2'W	X	117
Tan-y-Bwlch	Gwyn	SH6065	53°10·1'	4°5·3'W	X	115
Tan-y-bwlch	Gwyn	SH6540	52°56·7'	4°0·1'W	T	124
Tan-y-bwlch	Gwyn	SH9124	52°48·4'	3°36·6'W	X	125
Tan-y-bwlch	Wrex	SJ2552	53°3·8'	3°6·7'W	X	117
Tan-y-caeau	Powys	SJ0217	52°44·7'	3°26·7'W	X	125
Tan-y-castell	Denb	SJ2243	52°59·0'	3°9·3'W	X	117
Tan-y-cefn	Powys	SN9966	52°17·2'	3°28·4'W	X	136,147
Tan y clawdd	Powys	SJ1907	52°39·5'	3°11·5'W	X	125
Tan-y-clogwyn	Conwy	SH7752	53°3·3'	3°49·7'W	X	115
Tan-y-coed	Carm	SN6039	52°2·1'	4°2·1'W	F	146
Tan-y-coed	Cered	SN4144	52°4·5'	4°18·8'W	X	146
Tan-y-coed	Denb	SJ1044	52°59·4'	3°20·0'W	X	125
Tan-y-coed	Gwyn	SH5362	53°8·3'	4°11·5'W	X	114,115
Tan-y-coed	Gwyn	SH6505	52°37·8'	3°59·3'W	X	124
Tan y Dderwen	Conwy	SH8775	53°15·8'	3°41·2'W	X	116
Tanyfedw	Powys	SN8825	51°55·0'	3°37·3'W	X	160
Tan-y-ffordd	Conwy	SH9650	53°2·5'	3°32·7'W	X	116
Tan-y-ffridd	Powys	SJ1210	52°41·1'	3°17·7'W	X	125
Tan-y-ffridd	Powys	SJ1211	52°41·6'	3°17·7'W	X	125
Tan-y-ffridd	Powys	SJ1229	52°51·3'	3°18·0'W	X	125
Tan-y-foel	Conwy	SH7276	53°16·2'	3°54·8'W	X	115
Tan-y-foel	Conwy	SH9067	53°11·6'	3°38·4'W	X	116

Tan-y-foel	Conwy	SH9161	53°8·3'	3°37·4'W	X	116
Tan-y-foel	Denb	SJ1546	53°0·5'	3°15·6'W	X	116
Tan-y-foel	Gwyn	SH7520	52°46·0'	3°50·8'W	X	124
Tan-y-Foel	Powys	SJ0510	52°41·0'	3°23·9'W	X	125
Tan y Foel (Hotel)	Conwy	SH8156	53°5·5'	3°46·2'W	X	116
Tan-y-fron	Conwy	SH9564	53°10·0'	3°33·8'W	T	116
Tan y Fron	Denb	SJ2051	53°3·3'	3°11·2'W	X	117
Tan-y-fron	I of Angl	SH6280	53°18·2'	4°3·9'W	X	114,115
Tan-y-fron	Powys	SJ1715	52°43·8'	3°13·3'W	X	125
Tanyfron	Wrex	SJ2952	53°3·9'	3°3·2'W	T	117
Tan-y-gaer	Conwy	SH9772	53°14·3'	3°32·2'W	X	116
Tan-y-gaer	Conwy	SH9848	53°1·4'	3°30·8'W	X	116
Tan-y-gopa	Conwy	SH9377	53°17·0'	3°35·9'W	X	116
Tan-y-graig	Cered	SN5975	52°21·5'	4°3·8'W	X	135
Tan-y-Graig	Conwy	SH8769	53°12·6'	3°41·1'W	X	116
Tan-y-graig	Conwy	SH9068	53°12·1'	3°38·4'W	X	116
Tan-y-graig	Denb	SH9356	53°5·7'	3°35·5'W	X	116
Tan-y-graig	Denb	SJ1440	52°57·3'	3°16·4'W	X	125
Tan-y-graig	Denb	SJ1449	53°2·1'	3°16·5'W	X	116
Tan-y-graig	Denb	SJ2240	52°57·3'	3°9·3'W	X	117
Tan-y-graig	Denb	SJ2246	53°0·6'	3°9·3'W	X	117
Tan-y-graig	Gwyn	SH3138	52°55·0'	4°30·4'W	X	123
Tan-y-graig	Gwyn	SH3837	52°54·6'	4°24·1'W	X	123
Tan-y-graig	Gwyn	SH3946	52°59·5'	4°23·5'W	X	123
Tan-y-graig	Gwyn	SH4660	53°7·1'	4°17·7'W	X	114,115
Tan-y-graig	I of Angl	SH5379	53°17·5'	4°11·9'W	X	114,115
Tan-y-graig	Powys	SJ0603	52°37·2'	3°22·9'W	X	136
Tan-y-graig	Shrops	SJ2329	52°51·4'	3°8·2'W	X	126
Tanygrisiau	Gwyn	SH6845	52°59·4'	3°57·6'W	T	115
Tanygrisiau Resr	Gwyn	SH6744	52°58·9'	3°58·5'W	W	124
Tan-y-groes	Cered	SN2849	52°7·0'	4°30·3'W	T	145
Tan y gyrt	Conwy	SH9670	53°13·3'	3°33·1'W	X	116
Tan-y-gyrt	Denb	SJ0163	53°9·5'	3°28·4'W	X	116
Tan-y-lan	Carm	SN6338	52°1·7'	3°59·4'W	X	146
Tan-y-lan	Carm	SN6923	51°53·7'	3°53·8'W	X	160
Tan-y-lan	Conwy	SH8564	53°9·9'	3°42·8'W	X	116
Tan-y-lan	V of Glam	SS9579	51°30·2'	3°30·4'W	X	170
Tanylan Fm	Carm	SN3707	51°44·5'	4°21·3'W	FM	159
Tanyllwyfan	Conwy	SH8673	53°14·8'	3°42·1'W	X	116
Tan-y-llyn	Denb	SJ2155	53°5·4'	3°10·4'W	X	117
Tan-y-maes	Gwyn	SH5266	53°10·5'	4°12·5'W	X	114,115
Tan-y-mynydd	Conwy	SH9574	53°15·4'	3°34·0'W	X	116
Tan-y-mynydd	Gwyn	SH3230	52°50·7'	4°29·3'W	T	123
Tan-y-mynydd	Gwyn	SH8738	52°55·9'	3°40·5'W	X	124,125
Tan-y-pistyll	Powys	SJ0729	52°51·3'	3°22·5'W	X	125
Tan-yr-allt	Cered	SN5158	52°12·2'	4°10·4'W	X	146
Tan-yr-allt	Cered	SN6174	52°21·0'	4°2·1'W	X	135
Tan-yr-allt	Cered	SN6591	52°30·3'	3°58·9'W	X	135
Tan-yr-allt	Cered	SN6674	52°21·1'	3°57·7'W	X	135
Tan-yr-allt	Denb	SJ0680	53°18·8'	3°24·2'W	T	116
Tan-yr-allt	Flint	SJ1277	53°17·2'	3°18·8'W	X	116
Tan-yr-allt	Gwyn	SH4136	52°54·1'	4°21·4'W	X	123
Tanyrallt	Gwyn	SH4852	53°2·9'	4°15·7'W	X	115,123
Tan-yr-allt	Gwyn	SH5640	52°56·5'	4°8·2'W	X	124
Tan-yr-allt	Gwyn	SH7508	52°39·6'	3°50·5'W	X	124
Tan-yr-allt	I of Angl	SH3183	53°19·3'	4°31·8'W	X	114
Tan-yr-allt	Powys	SN9075	52°22·0'	3°36·5'W	X	136,147
Tanyrallt	Powys	SN9453	52°10·1'	3°32·6'W	X	147
Tanyresgair	Cered	SN6166	52°16·7'	4°1·9'W	X	135
Tan-y-rhiw	Nth Pt Talb	SN7701	51°41·9'	3°46·4'W	X	170
Tan-y-rhiwiau	Conwy	SH9460	53°7·8'	3°34·7'W	X	116
Tanyrhydiau	Cered	SN7369	52°18·5'	3°51·4'W	X	135,147
Tanysgafell	Gwyn	SH6166	53°10·6'	4°4·4'W	T	115
Tan y Waen	Conwy	SH8662	53°8·8'	3°41·9'W	X	116
Tan-y-wal	Flint	SJ2366	53°11·4'	3°8·7'W	X	117
Tanzie	Moray	NJ3146	57°30·2'	3°8·6'W	X	28
Taobh a Deas Loch Aineort	N Eil	NF7628	57°13·9'	7°21·8'W	T	22
Taobh a' Ghlinne	N Eil	NB3715	58°3·0'	6°27·0'W	T	14
Taobh a Tuath Loch Aineort	N Eil	NF7729	57°14·5'	7°20·8'W	T	22
Taobh Deas	N Eil	NF9692	57°49·1'	7°6·7'W	X	18
Taobh Dubh	Highld	NM7857	56°36·9'	5°36·9'W	H	49
Taobh na Coille	Stir	NN4615	56°18·4'	4°28·9'W	H	57
Taobh Siar	N Eil	NB1400	57°54·1'	6°49·2'W	T	14
Taoslin	Arg & Bt	NM3922	56°16·6'	6°12·8'W	X	48
Tape Hill	Somer	ST6349	51°14·6'	2°31·4'W	X	183
Tapeley Park	Devon	SS4729	51°2·6'	4°10·6'W	X	180
Taphland	Orkney	HY4744	59°17·0'	2°55·3'W	X	5
Tapitlaw Fm	Fife	NT0189	56°5·3'	3°35·0'W	FM	65
Taplands	Hants	SU6014	50°55·6'	1°8·4'W	X	196
Taplin's Fm	Hants	SU7655	51°17·6'	0°54·2'W	FM	175,186
Taplow	Bucks	SU9182	51°32·0'	0°40·9'W	T	175
Taplow Ct	Bucks	SU9082	51°32·0'	0°41·8'W	X	175
Taplow Lodge	Bucks	SU9184	51°33·1'	0°40·9'W	X	175
Tap Mawr	Gwyn	SH9118	52°45·2'	3°36·5'W	X	125
Tapnage	Hants	SU5510	50°53·4'	1°12·7'W	X	196
Tapnell Fm	I of W	SZ3786	50°40·6'	1°28·2'W	FM	196
Tapners	Kent	TQ5444	51°10·7'	0°12·6'E	X	188
Tap Nyth-yr-eryr	Gwyn	SH9021	52°46·8'	3°37·4'W	X	125
Tap o' Noth	Aberd	NJ4829	57°21·2'	2°51·4'W	H	37
Tap o' Noth (Fort)	Aberd	NJ4829	57°21·2'	2°51·4'W	A	37
Tapp	Moray	NJ1447	57°30·6'	3°25·7'W	X	28
Tappacks	Aberd	NJ6449	57°32·0'	2°35·6'W	X	29
Tappet Hill	E Ayr	NS5312	55°23·1'	4°18·8'W	X	70
Tappetknowe	Falk	NS7681	56°0·6'	3°58·9'W	X	64
Tappies	Aberd	NJ7213	57°12·7'	2°27·4'W	X	38
Tappington Fm	E Susx	TQ6233	51°4·6'	0°19·2'E	FM	188
Tappington Hall	Kent	TR2046	51°10·5'	1°9·2'E	A	179,189
Tappins, The	S Ayr	NX3596	55°14·1'	4°35·3'W	H	77
Tappoch	Falk	NS8385	56°2·9'	3°52·3'W	X	57,65
Tappoch	Moray	NJ1467	57°41·3'	3°26·1'W	H	28
Tapster Mill	Warw	SP1669	52°19·4'	1°45·5'W	X	139,151
Tapton	Derby	SK3972	53°14·9'	1°24·5'W	T	119
Tapton Grove	Derby	SK4072	53°14·8'	1°23·6'W	X	120
Tapton Hill	Sheff	SK3286	53°22·4'	1°30·7'W	T	110,111
Tapton Ho	Derby	SK3972	53°14·9'	1°24·5'W	X	119
Tap y Gigfran	Powys	SJ0124	52°48·5'	3°27·7'W	X	125
Tara	Bucks	SU9786	51°34·1'	0°35·6'W	X	175,176

Tarabuckle	Angus	NO3667	56°47·7'	3°2·4'W	X	44
Taracliff Bay	Orkney	HY5503	58°55·0'	2°46·4'W	W	6
Tarain	N Eil	NB0427	58°8·2'	7°1·3'W	H	13
Taran Beag	N Eil	NB0415	58°1·8'	7°0·4'W	H	13
Taran Meadhoin	N Eil	NB0415	58°1·8'	7°0·4'W	H	13
Taran Mór	N Eil	NB0315	58°1·8'	7°1·4'W	H	13
Taransay	N Eil	NB0301	57°54·2'	7°0·4'W	X	18
Taransay	N Eil	NB0303	57°55·3'	7°0·5'W	X	13,18
Taransay Glorigs	N Eil	NA9606	57°56·6'	7°7·8'W	X	13
Tarapetmile	Angus	NO2963	56°45·5'	3°9·2'W	H	44
Taraphocain	Arg & Bt	NN0246	56°34·1'	5°12·9'W	X	50
Tara, The	Shetld	HU4525	60°0·7'	1°11·1'W	X	4
Tarbarrel Moss	Cumbr	NY2025	54°37·1'	3°13·9'W	X	89,90
Tar Barrow	Glos	SP0302	51°43·2'	1°57·0'W	A	163
Tarbat Ho	Highld	NH7773	57°44·1'	4°3·5'W	X	21
Tarbat Mains	Highld	NH7673	57°44·0'	4°4·5'W	X	21
Tarbat Ness	Highld	NH9487	57°51·9'	3°46·7'W	X	21
Tarbay Fm	Win & Maid	SU9275	51°28·2'	0°40·1'W	FM	175
Tarbert	Arg & Bt	NR6182	55°58·5'	5°49·4'W	T	61
Tarbert	Arg & Bt	NR6551	55°42·0'	5°44·0'W	X	62
Tarbert	Arg & Bt	NR8668	55°51·7'	5°24·7'W	T	62
Tarbert	Highld	NM6863	56°42·3'	5°47·0'W	X	40
Tarbert Bay	Arg & Bt	NR6081	55°58·0'	5°50·3'W	W	61
Tarbert Bay	Highld	NG2405	57°3·5'	6°32·7'W	W	39
Tarbert Hill	N Ayr	NS2147	55°41·3'	4°50·4'W	H	63
Tarbert or Tairbeart	N Eil	NB1500	57°54·2'	6°48·2'W	T	14
Tarbet	Arg & Bt	NN3104	56°12·2'	4°43·0'W	T	56
Tarbet	Highld	NC1649	58°23·7'	5°8·4'W	T	9
Tarbet	Highld	NG2305	57°3·4'	6°33·7'W	X	39
Tarbet	Highld	NM7992	56°58·2'	5°37·7'W	T	33,40
Tarbet Bay	Highld	NM7992	56°58·2'	5°37·7'W	W	33,40
Tarbet Hole	Fife	NT6599	56°11·2'	2°33·4'W	W	59
Tarbet Isle	Arg & Bt	NN3205	56°12·7'	4°42·1'W	X	56
Tarbock Green	Know	SJ4687	53°22·9'	2°48·3'W	T	108
Tarbock Hall Fm	Know	SJ4688	53°23·4'	2°48·3'W	FM	108
Tarbolton	S Ayr	NS4327	55°30·9'	4°28·8'W	T	70
Tarbothill Fm	C of Aber	NJ9513	57°12·7'	2°4·5'W	FM	38
Tarbrax	Angus	NO3843	56°34·7'	3°0·1'W	X	54
Tarbrax	S Lanak	NT0255	55°47·0'	3°33·3'W	T	65,72
Tarbreoch	D & G	NX7869	55°0·3'	3°54·0'W	X	84
Tarbuckle Hill	Aberd	NJ4937	57°25·5'	2°50·5'W	X	28,29
Tarcoon	D & G	NY3677	55°5·2'	2°59·7'W	X	85
Tarcreish	Scot Bord	NT1537	55°37·4'	3°20·6'W	H	72
Tardd-y-dwr	Flint	SJ1767	53°11·9'	3°14·1'W	X	116
Tardebigge	Worcs	SO9969	52°19·4'	2°0·5'W	T	139
Tardebigge Fm	Worcs	SO9767	52°18·3'	2°2·2'W	FM	150
Tarden	Stock	SJ9888	53°23·6'	2°1·4'W	X	109
Tardoes	E Ayr	NS7028	55°32·0'	4°3·2'W	X	71
Tarduf	Falk	NS9475	55°57·6'	3°41·4'W	X	65
Tarduff Hill	Falk	NS7583	56°1·7'	3°59·9'W	X	57,64
Tarduff Hill	Pth & Kin	NO1915	56°19·5'	3°18·1'W	H	58
Tardy Gate	Lancs	SD5325	53°43·4'	2°42·3'W	T	102
Tarecroft Wood	Essex	TL8217	51°49·1'	0°38·9'E	F	168
Tarelgin	E Ayr	NS4620	55°27·2'	4°25·7'W	X	70
Tareni Gleision	Nth Pt Talb	SN7506	51°44·6'	3°48·2'W	X	160
Tarfat	Aberd	NJ9355	57°35·4'	2°6·6'W	X	30
Tarf Bridge	D & G	NX2564	54°56·7'	4°43·5'W	X	82
Tarf Bridge	D & G	NX2959	54°54·0'	4°39·6'W	X	82
Tarfessock	S Ayr	NX3688	55°9·8'	4°34·0'W	X	77
Tarfessock	S Ayr	NX4088	55°9·9'	4°30·3'W	H	77
Tarff Sta	D & G	NX6856	54°53·1'	4°3·0'W	X	83,84
Tarff Water	D & G	NX6857	54°53·7'	4°3·1'W	W	83,84
Tarfhaugh	Scot Bord	NT1450	55°44·4'	3°21·8'W	X	65,72
Tar Fm	Oxon	SP3807	51°45·9'	1°26·6'W	FM	164
Tarfoot Croft	Aberd	NJ9255	57°35·4'	2°7·6'W	X	30
Tarfside	Angus	NO4979	56°54·2'	2°49·8'W	T	44
Tarf Water	D & G	NX2270	54°59·8'	4°46·5'W	W	76
Tarf Water	D & G	NX2761	54°55·1'	4°41·5'W	W	82
Tarf Water	Pth & Kin	NN9379	56°53·7'	3°44·9'W	W	43
Targate	Pemb	SM9510	51°45·3'	4°57·8'W	X	157,158
Target Hill	Suff	TM2783	52°24·1'	1°20·6'E	H	156
Targies	Shetld	HU2280	60°30·5'	1°35·5'W	X	3
Tar Grove	Shrops	SO5277	52°23·6'	2°41·9'W	F	137,138
Tarhill	Pth & Kin	NO1304	56°13·5'	3°23·7'W	X	58
Tar Hill	Staffs	SJ9619	52°46·4'	2°3·2'W	X	127
Tar Hill	W Loth	NT0673	55°56·7'	3°29·9'W	X	65
Tarholm	S Ayr	NS3922	55°28·2'	4°32·4'W	X	70
Taring of Berstane	Orkney	HY4710	58°58·7'	2°54·8'W	X	6
Tarista	Corn	SX2152	50°20·7'	4°30·6'W	X	201
Tarka Trail	Devon	SS4525	51°0·4'	4°12·2'W	X	180
Tarka Trail	Devon	SS6248	51°13·1'	3°58·2'W	X	180
Tarka Trail	Devon	SS7237	51°7·3'	3°49·4'W	X	180
Tarland	Aberd	NJ4804	57°7·7'	2°51·1'W	T	37
Tarland Burn	Aberd	NJ4903	57°7·2'	2°50·1'W	W	37
Tarland Lodge	Aberd	NJ4805	57°8·2'	2°51·1'W	X	37
Tarleton	Lancs	SD4520	53°40·7'	2°49·5'W	T	102
Tarleton Moss	Lancs	SD4321	53°41·2'	2°51·4'W	T	102
Tarlogie	Highld	NH7583	57°49·4'	4°5·8'W	X	21
Tarlogie Scalps	Highld	NH7485	57°50·5'	4°6·9'W	X	21
Tarlogie Wood	Highld	NH7582	57°48·9'	4°5·8'W	F	21
Tarlscough	Lancs	SD4314	53°37·4'	2°51·3'W	T	108
Tarlton	Glos	ST9599	51°41·6'	2°3·9'W	T	163
Tarlton Down	Glos	ST9499	51°41·6'	2°4·8'W	X	163
Tarmair	Aberd	NJ9262	57°39·1'	2°7·6'W	X	30
Tarmangie Hill	Clackm	NN9401	56°11·6'	3°42·1'W	H	58
Tarmore	Moray	NJ4152	57°33·5'	2°58·7'W	X	28
Tarmore Hill	Arg & Bt	NS0558	55°46·8'	5°6·1'W	H	63
Tarn	Brad	SE1639	53°51·1'	1°45·0'W	T	104
Tarn	Cumbr	SD7197	54°22·3'	2°26·4'W	X	98
Tarnacre Hall Fm	Lancs	SD4642	53°52·5'	2°48·9'W	FM	102
Tarnacre House Fm	Lancs	SD4742	53°52·5'	2°48·0'W	FM	102
Tarnash Fm	Moray	NJ4449	57°31·9'	2°55·7'W	FM	28
Tarn at Leaves	Cumbr	NY2512	54°30·1'	3°9·1'W	W	89,90
Tarn Bank	Cumbr	NY0729	54°39·1'	3°26·1'W	X	89
Tarn Bay	Cumbr	SD0789	54°17·5'	3°25·3'W	W	96
Tarn Beck	Cumbr	NY6178	55°5·9'	2°36·2'W	W	86
Tarn Beck	Cumbr	SD2397	54°22·0'	3°10·7'W	W	96
Tarn Brook	Lancs	SD5563	54°3·9'	2°40·8'W	W	97
Tarnbrook	Lancs	SD5855	53°59·6'	2°38·0'W	T	102
Tarnbrook Fell	Lancs	SD6057	54°0·7'	2°36·2'W	X	102,103

Tarnbrook Wyre	Lancs	SD5855	53°59·6'	2°38·0'W	W	102
Tarn Burn	Northum	NY7396	55°15·7'	2°25·1'W	W	80
Tarn Close	Cumbr	SD4695	54°21·1'	2°49·4'W	X	97
Tarn Crag	Cumbr	NY2907	54°27·5'	3°5·3'W	X	89,90
Tarn Crag	Cumbr	NY3009	54°28·5'	3°4·4'W	H	90
Tarn Crag	Cumbr	NY3512	54°30·2'	2°59·8'W	X	90
Tarn Crag	Cumbr	NY4807	54°27·6'	2°47·7'W	H	90
Tarn Crag	Cumbr	SD1999	54°23·1'	3°14·4'W	X	96
Tarn Crags	Cumbr	NY3013	54°30·7'	3°4·5'W	X	90
Tarn Crags	Cumbr	NY3228	54°38·8'	3°2·8'W	X	90
Tarn Crags	Cumbr	NY3331	54°40·4'	3°1·9'W	X	90
Tarn Dub	Durham	NY8528	54°39·1'	2°13·5'W	W	91,92
Tarner Island	Highld	NG2938	57°21·4'	6°29·9'W	X	23
Tarneybackle	Pth & Kin	NN8607	56°14·8'	3°49·9'W	X	58
Tarneybank Tarn	Cumbr	SD5888	54°17·4'	2°38·3'W	W	97
Tarney Force	N Yks	SD8489	54°18·0'	2°14·3'W	X	98
Tarnflat Hall	Cumbr	NX9414	54°30·9'	3°33·8'W	X	89
Tarn Fm	Lancs	SD4449	53°56·3'	2°50·8'W	FM	102
Tarn Foot	Cumbr	NY3404	54°25·9'	3°0·6'W	X	90
Tarn Gill	Cumbr	NY8019	54°34·2'	2°18·1'W	W	91,92
Tarn Gill	N Yks	SD7987	54°16·9'	2°18·9'W	W	98
Tarn Gill	N Yks	SE1062	54°3·5'	1°50·4'W	W	99
Tarn Hill	Brad	SE0342	53°52·7'	1°56·8'W	X	104
Tarn Hill	Cumbr	SD6990	54°18·5'	2°28·2'W	X	98
Tarn Hill	Cumbr	SD7492	54°19·6'	2°23·6'W	X	98
Tarn Hill	N Yks	SD8194	54°20·7'	2°17·1'W	X	98
Tarn Ho	Brad	SE0342	53°52·7'	1°56·8'W	X	104
Tarn Ho	Cumbr	NY5737	54°43·8'	2°39·6'W	X	91
Tarn Ho	Cumbr	NY6058	54°55·2'	2°37·0'W	A	86
Tarn Ho	Cumbr	NY7403	54°25·6'	2°23·6'W	X	91
Tarn Ho (Hotel)	N Yks	SD9753	53°58·6'	2°2·3'W	X	103
Tarn Hole	N Yks	SE5997	54°22·1'	1°5·1'W	X	100
Tarn Hole Beck	N Yks	SE5997	54°22·1'	1°5·1'W	W	100
Tarnhouse Rigg	Cumbr	NY6059	54°55·7'	2°37·0'W	X	86
Tarnhouse Tarn	Cumbr	SD5783	54°14·7'	2°39·2'W	W	97
Tarn How	Cumbr	NY0602	54°24·5'	3°26·5'W	X	89
Tarnhow Hill	N Yks	NY9708	54°28·3'	2°2·4'W	X	92
Tarn Hows	Cumbr	NY3300	54°23·7'	3°1·5'W	W	90
Tarn Hows	Cumbr	SD3299	54°23·1'	3°2·4'W	X	96,97
Tarn Hows Hotel	Cumbr	SD3399	54°23·2'	3°1·5'W	X	96,97
Tarn Hows Wood	Cumbr	SD3199	54°23·2'	3°3·3'W	F	96,97
Tarnis Burn	D & G	NT0202	55°18·4'	3°32·2'W	W	78
Tarnis Head	D & G	NT0203	55°18·9'	3°32·2'W	H	78
Tarn Lodge	Cumbr	NY5254	54°53·0'	2°44·5'W	X	86
Tarnmonath Fell	Cumbr	NY5854	54°53·0'	2°38·9'W	H	86
Tarn Moor	Cumbr	NY4821	54°35·1'	2°47·9'W	X	90
Tarn Moor	Cumbr	NY6707	54°27·7'	2°30·1'W	X	91
Tarn-moor	Cumbr	NY7213	54°30·9'	2°25·5'W	X	91
Tarn Moss	Cumbr	SD6090	54°18·5'	2°36·5'W	X	97
Tarn Moss	N Yks	NY8402	54°25·0'	2°14·4'W	X	91,92
Tarn Moss	N Yks	SD8866	54°5·6'	2°10·6'W	X	98
Tarnock	Somer	ST3752	51°16·1'	2°53·8'W	T	182
Tarn Rigg	N Yks	SD9594	54°20·7'	2°4·2'W	X	98
Tarn Rigg Hill	Cumbr	SD7491	54°19·1'	2°23·6'W	X	98
Tarnrigg Moor	Cumbr	NY2551	54°51·1'	3°9·7'W	X	85
Tarn Riggs	Cumbr	SD2790	54°18·3'	3°6·9'W	X	96,97
Tarns	Cumbr	NY1147	54°48·8'	3°22·7'W	T	85
Tarns Dub	Cumbr	NY1147	54°48·8'	3°22·7'W	W	85
Tarnside	Cumbr	NY2551	54°51·1'	3°9·7'W	X	85
Tarnside	Cumbr	SD4390	54°18·4'	2°52·1'W	T	97
Tarn Sike	Cumbr	NY6607	54°27·7'	2°31·0'W	W	91
Tarn Sike	Cumbr	NY7403	54°25·6'	2°23·6'W	W	91
Tarns, The	Cumbr	NY1247	54°48·9'	3°21·7'W	X	85
Tarnsyke Barn	Lancs	SD5856	54°0·1'	2°38·0'W	X	102
Tarnsyke Clough	Lancs	SD5956	54°0·1'	2°37·1'W	X	102
Tarn, The	Brad	SE1247	53°55·4'	1°48·6'W	W	104
Tarn, The	Cumbr	SD0789	54°17·5'	3°25·3'W	X	96
Tarn, The	Lancs	SD5148	53°55·8'	2°44·4'W	W	102
Tarn, The	N Yks	SE1967	54°6·2'	1°42·1'W	X	99
Tarn, The	Surrey	SU9145	51°12·0'	0°41·5'W	W	186
Tarporley	Ches	SJ5562	53°9·4'	2°40·0'W	T	117
Tarpots	Essex	TQ7688	51°34·0'	0°32·8'E	T	178
Tarr	Somer	ST1030	51°4·0'	3°16·7'W	X	181
Tarraby	Cumbr	NY4058	54°55·0'	2°55·4'W	T	85
Tarradale Ho	Highld	NH5548	57°30·2'	4°24·7'W	X	26
Tarradale Mains	Highld	NH5549	57°30·7'	4°24·8'W	X	26
Tarrant Abbey House	Dorset	ST9203	50°49·8'	2°6·4'W	A	195
Tarrant Crawford	Dorset	ST9203	50°49·8'	2°6·4'W	T	195
Tarrant Gunville	Dorset	ST9212	50°54·7'	2°6·4'W	T	195
Tarrant Hinton	Dorset	ST9311	50°54·1'	2°5·6'W	T	195
Tarrant Hinton Down	Dorset	ST9511	50°54·1'	2°3·9'W	X	195
Tarrant Keyneston	Dorset	ST9204	50°50·4'	2°6·4'W	T	195
Tarrant Launceston	Dorset	ST9409	50°53·1'	2°4·7'W	T	195
Tarrant Monkton	Dorset	ST9408	50°52·5'	2°4·7'W	T	195
Tarrant Rawston	Dorset	ST9306	50°51·4'	2°5·6'W	X	195
Tarrant Rushton	Dorset	ST9305	50°50·9'	2°5·6'W	T	195
Tarrant, The	Dorset	ST9305	50°50·9'	2°5·6'W	W	195
Tarras	Moray	NJ0659	57°36·9'	3°33·9'W	X	27
Tarrasfoot	D & G	NY3780	55°6·9'	2°58·8'W	X	79
Tarrasfoot Hill	D & G	NY3881	55°7·4'	2°57·9'W	H	79
Tarras Lodge	D & G	NY4087	55°10·7'	2°56·1'W	X	79
Tarras Rig	D & G	NY4086	55°10·1'	2°56·1'W	X	79
Tarras Water	D & G	NY4085	55°9·6'	2°56·1'W	W	79
Tarr Ball Hill	Somer	SS8644	51°11·3'	3°37·5'W	X	181
Tarrcroys	Moray	NJ4053	57°34·0'	2°59·7'W	X	28
Tarrel	Highld	NH8981	57°48·6'	3°51·6'W	X	21
Tarren Bwlch-gwyn	Powys	SN8193	52°31·6'	3°44·8'W	X	135,136
Tarren Cadian	Gwyn	SH7306	52°38·5'	3°52·2'W	H	124
Tarren Cwm-ffernol	Gwyn	SH6602	52°36·2'	3°58·3'W	X	135
Tarren-fach	Gwyn	SH6705	52°37·8'	3°57·5'W	H	124
Tarrenhendre	Gwyn	SH6804	52°37·3'	3°56·6'W	H	135
Tarren Maerdy	Rho Cyn Taf	SS9897	51°40·0'	3°28·1'W	X	170
Tarren Nantymynach	Gwyn	SH6603	52°36·7'	3°58·3'W	X	135
Tarren Rhiw-llech	Nth Pt Talb	SS8696	51°39·3'	3°38·5'W	X	170
Tarren Rhiw-maen	Brig	SS9294	51°38·3'	3°33·3'W	X	170
Tarren Rhosfarch	Gwyn	SH6802	52°36·2'	3°56·6'W	X	135
Tarren Saerbren	Rho Cyn Taf	SS9297	51°39·9'	3°33·3'W	X	170
Tarren Tormwnt	Powys	SO0415	51°49·8'	3°23·2'W	X	160
Tarren Tyn-y-maen	Cered	SN7296	52°33·1'	3°52·9'W	H	135
Tarrenybarcut	Gwyn	SH6403	52°36·7'	4°0·1'W	X	135

Tarren y Bwllfa	Rho Cyn Taf	SS9693	51°37·8′	3°29·8′W	X	170
Tarren y Fforch	Brig	SS9293	51°37·8′	3°33·2′W	X	170
Tarren y Gesail	Gwyn	SH7106	52°38·4′	3°54·0′W	H	124
Tarren yr Esgob	Powys	SO2431	51°58·6′	3°6·0′W	X	161
Tarren y Trwyn	Blae Gw	SO1807	51°45·6′	3°10·9′W	X	161
Tarret Burn	Northum	NY8091	55°13·0′	2°18·4′W	W	80
Tarr Fm	Somer	SS8632	51°4·8′	3°37·3′W	FM	181
Tarr Fm	Somer	ST2129	51°3·5′	3°7·3′W	FM	193
Tarr Fms	Pemb	SN0800	51°40·2′	4°46·2′W	FM	158
Tarri Clett	Orkney	ND4698	58°52·2′	2°55·7′W	X	6,7
Tarriebank	Angus	NO6544	56°35·5′	2°33·7′W	X	54
Tarriebank Home Fm	Angus	NO6444	56°35·4′	2°34·7′W	FM	54
Tarri Geo	Shetld	HU4485	60°33·0′	1°11·4′W	X	1,2,3
Tarri Geos	Shetld	HU5060	60°19·5′	1°5·2′W	X	2,3
Tarring Neville	E Susx	TQ4403	50°48·7′	0°3·0′E	T	198
Tarrington	Heref	SO6140	52°3·7′	2°33·7′W	T	149
Tarrington Common	Heref	SO6139	52°3·1′	2°33·7′W	T	149
Tarristae	Orkney	HY4442	59°15·9′	2°58·5′W	X	5
Tarrnacraig	N Ayr	NR9334	55°33·6′	5°16·5′W	X	68,69
Tarroul	Highld	ND2654	58°28·3′	3°15·6′W	X	11,12
Tarroul Moss	Highld	ND2655	58°28·9′	3°15·7′W	X	11,12
Tarr's Fm	Somer	ST3154	51°17·1′	2°59·0′W	FM	182
Tarr Sgeir	Arg & Bt	NR3842	55°36·3′	6°9·2′W	X	60
Tarr Steps	Somer	SS8632	51°4·8′	3°37·3′W	A	181
Tarry	Northum	NU1020	55°28·7′	1°50·1′W	X	75
Tarry Back	Northum	NY7857	54°54·7′	2°20·2′W	X	86,87
Tarryblake Ho	Moray	NJ5149	57°32·0′	2°48·6′W	X	29
Tarryblake Wood	Moray	NJ5149	57°32·0′	2°48·6′W	F	29
Tarrylaw	Pth & Kin	NO1829	56°27·0′	3°19·4′W	X	53,58
Tarsappie	Pth & Kin	NO1221	56°22·6′	3°25·1′W	X	53,58
Tarsappie Hill	Pth & Kin	NO1320	56°22·1′	3°24·1′W	X	53,58
Tarsbhal	N Eil	NB1505	57°56·9′	6°48·5′W	H	13,14
Tarset Burn	Northum	NY7888	55°11·4′	2°20·3′W	W	80
Tarset Castle (rems of)	Northum	NY7985	55°9·8′	2°19·3′W	A	80
Tarsets	Aberd	NJ9627	57°20·3′	2°3·5′W	X	38
Tarshaw	S Ayr	NS3927	55°30·9′	4°32·6′W	X	70
Tarskavaig	Highld	NG5809	57°6·8′	5°59·4′W	T	32,39
Tarskavaig Bay	Highld	NG5709	57°6·7′	6°0·4′W	W	32,39
Tarskavaig Point	Highld	NG5709	57°6·7′	6°0·4′W	X	32,39
Tar's Mill Fm	Heref	SO5235	52°0·9′	2°41·6′W	FM	149
Tarston Hall	Suff	TM0851	52°7·3′	1°2·7′E	X	155
Tars Wood	Heref	SO4463	52°16·0′	2°48·8′W	F	137,148,149
Tarta Geodha	N Eil	NA9514	58°0·9′	7°9·4′W	X	13
Tartan Hill	Scot Bord	NT4647	55°43·1′	2°51·1′W	X	73
Tartendown Cross	Corn	SX3661	50°25·8′	4°18·2′W	X	201
Tarth Water	Scot Bord	NT1444	55°41·2′	3°21·6′W	W	72
Tarts Hill	Shrops	SJ4338	52°56·4′	2°50·5′W	T	126
Tarty Burn	Aberd	NJ9726	57°19·7′	2°2·5′W	W	38
Tarves	Aberd	NJ8631	57°22·4′	2°13·5′W	T	30
Tarvie	Highld	NH4258	57°35·3′	4°38·1′W	X	26
Tarvie	Pth & Kin	NO0164	56°45·7′	3°36·7′W	X	43
Tarvie Burn	Pth & Kin	NO0165	56°46·2′	3°36·7′W	W	43
Tarvin	Ches	SJ4866	53°11·6′	2°46·3′W	T	117
Tarvin Sands	Ches	SJ4967	53°12·1′	2°45·4′W	T	117
Tarvit Fm	Fife	NO3813	56°18·6′	2°59·7′W	FM	59
Tarvit Mill	Fife	NO3612	56°18·0′	3°1·6′W	X	59
Tarwathie	Moray	NJ4062	57°38·9′	2°59·9′W	X	28
Tar Wood	Oxon	SP3907	51°45·9′	1°25·7′W	F	164
Tasburgh	Norf	TM2095	52°30·7′	1°14·9′E	T	134
Tascott Fm	Corn	SX2892	50°42·4′	4°25·8′W	FM	190
Tascroft Fm	Wilts	ST8444	51°11·9′	2°13·4′W	FM	183
Tashieburn	S Lanak	NS9654	55°46·3′	3°39·0′W	X	65,72
Taska	Shetld	HU4538	60°7·7′	1°10·9′W	X	4
Tasley	Shrops	SO6994	52°32·8′	2°27·0′W	T	138
Tassetshill	Aberd	NK0033	57°23·5′	1°59·5′W	X	30
Taston	Oxon	SP3521	51°53·4′	1°29·1′W	T	164
Tat Bank	Sand	SO9989	52°30·2′	2°0·5′W	T	139
Tatchbury	Hants	SU3314	50°55·7′	1°31·4′W	A	196
Tatchbury Manor Ho	Hants	SU3214	50°55·7′	1°32·3′W	X	196
Tatchbury Mount Hospital	Hants	SU3314	50°55·7′	1°31·4′W	X	196
Tatefield Hall	N Yks	SE2751	53°57·5′	1°34·9′W	X	104
Tate Gallery	C of West	TQ3078	51°29·4′	0°7·3′W	X	176,177
Tatenhill	Staffs	SK2021	52°47·4′	1°41·8′W	T	128
Tatenhill Common	Staffs	SK1922	52°48·0′	1°42·7′W	T	128
Tater-du	Corn	SW4422	50°2·8′	5°34·2′W	X	203
Tates Hill	D & G	NT1900	55°17·5′	3°16·1′W	H	79
Tate's Well	Northum	NT7304	55°20·0′	2°25·1′W	W	80
Tàtha ham Beann	Highld	NC3540	58°19·3′	4°48·6′W	H	9
Tathall End	Mil Key	SP8246	52°6·6′	0°47·8′W	T	152
Tatham	Lancs	SD6069	54°7·2′	2°36·3′W	T	97
Tatham	Somer	ST1728	51°3·0′	3°10·7′W	X	181,193
Tatham Fells	Lancs	SD6763	54°4·0′	2°29·8′W	X	98
Tatham Hall	Lancs	SD6068	54°6·7′	2°36·3′W	X	97
Tathanais	N Eil	NF8344	57°22·8′	7°16·1′W	X	22
Tathas Bheag	N Eil	NB2802	57°55·7′	6°35·2′W	H	14
Tathas Mhòr	N Eil	NB2804	57°56·8′	6°35·3′W	H	13,14
Tathhill	D & G	NY0899	55°16·8′	3°26·5′W	X	78
Tathieknowe Burn	Scot Bord	NT3552	55°45·7′	3°1·7′W	W	66,73
Tathwell	Lincs	TF3282	53°19·3′	0°0·7′W	T	122
Tathwell Grange	Lincs	TF3181	53°18·8′	0°1·6′W	X	122
Tathwell Lodge	Lincs	TF3282	53°19·3′	0°0·7′W	X	122
Tatlingbury	Kent	TQ6444	51°10·5′	0°21·2′E	X	188
Tatling End	Bucks	TQ0187	51°34·6′	0°32·2′W	T	176
Tatman Fm	Kent	TR0829	51°1·6′	0°58·4′E	FM	189
Tatmore Place	Herts	TL1826	51°55·4′	0°16·6′W	X	166
Tatsfield	Surrey	TQ4157	51°17·9′	0°1·7′E	T	187
Tatsfield Court Fm	Surrey	TQ4255	51°16·8′	0°2·6′E	FM	187
Tatson	Devon	SS2701	50°47·2′	4°26·9′W	X	190
Tattenhall	Ches	SJ4858	53°7·2′	2°46·2′W	T	117
Tattenham Corner Sta	Surrey	TQ2258	51°18·7′	0°14·6′W	X	187
Tattenhoe	Mil Key	SP8334	52°0·1′	0°47·1′W	T	152,165
Tattenhoe Park	Mil Key	SP8233	51°59·6′	0°47·9′W	X	152,165
Tatterford	Norf	TF8628	52°49·3′	0°46·0′E	T	132
Tatterford Common	Norf	TF8627	52°48·7′	0°46·0′E	X	132
Tatteridge Hill	Heref	SO4272	52°20·8′	2°50·7′W	X	137,148
Tattersall's Fm	Essex	TL7433	51°58·3′	0°32·4′E	FM	167
Tattersett	Norf	TF8429	52°49·9′	0°44·3′E	T	132
Tattershall	Lincs	TF2158	53°6·6′	0°11·1′W	T	122
Tattershall Bridge	Lincs	TF1956	53°5·5′	0°13·0′W	T	122
Tattershall Ho	Lincs	TF0595	53°26·7′	0°24·7′W	X	112

Tattershall Thorpe	Lincs	TF2159	53°7·1′	0°11·1′W	T	122
Tatterthorn	N Yks	SD6870	54°7·7′	2°29·0′W	X	98
Tattingstone	Suff	TM1337	51°59·7′	1°6·6′E	T	169
Tattingstone Place	Suff	TM1336	51°59·1′	1°6·5′E	X	169
Tattingstone White Horse	Suff	TM1338	52°0·2′	1°6·6′E	T	169
Tattingstone Wonder	Suff	TM1336	51°59·1′	1°6·5′E	X	169
Tattiscombe Fm	Devon	SS6346	51°12·0′	3°57·3′W	FM	180
Tattle Bank	Warw	SP1863	52°16·1′	1°43·8′W	T	151
Tattlebury	Kent	TQ8345	51°10·7′	0°37·5′E	X	188
Tattle Hill	Herts	TL3014	51°48·8′	0°6·5′W	X	166
Tatton Dale	Ches	SJ7482	53°20·3′	2°23·0′W	T	109
Tatton Fm	Dorset	SY6382	50°38·4′	2°31·0′W	FM	194
Tatton Fm	Newp	ST3585	51°33·8′	2°55·9′W	FM	171
Tatton Hall	Ches	SJ7481	53°19·8′	2°23·0′W	A	109
Tatton Ho	Dorset	SY6283	50°39·0′	2°31·9′W	X	194
Tatton Mere	Ches	SJ7579	53°18·7′	2°22·1′W	W	118
Tatton Mere	Ches	SJ7580	53°19·2′	2°22·1′W	W	109
Tatton Park	Ches	SJ7581	53°19·8′	2°22·1′W	X	109
Tatworth	Somer	ST3205	50°50·7′	2°57·6′W	T	193
Tauchers, The	E Ayr	NX4587	55°9·4′	4°25·5′W	X	77
Tauchers Wood	Moray	NJ3649	57°31·9′	3°3·7′W	F	28
Taumberland	Lincs	TF2639	52°56·2′	0°7·1′W	X	131
Taunton	Somer	ST2324	51°0·8′	3°5·5′W	T	193
Taunton	Tames	SD9200	53°30·0′	2°6·8′W	T	109
Taunton Deane Service Area	Somer	ST1920	50°58·7′	3°8·8′W	X	181,193
Tavantaggart	Arg & Bt	NR7046	55°39·4′	5°38·9′W	X	62
Tavelty	Aberd	NJ7817	57°14·8′	2°21·4′W	X	38
Taverham	Norf	TG1614	52°41·1′	1°12·2′E	T	133
Taverham Hall (Sch)	Norf	TG1513	52°40·5′	1°11·2′E	X	133
Taverners Green	Essex	TL5618	51°50·6′	0°16·3′E	T	167
Tavern Fm	Suff	TM2265	52°14·5′	1°15·5′E	FM	156
Tavernspite	Pemb	SN1812	51°46·9′	4°37·9′W	T	158
Tavers Cleugh	E Loth	NT6266	55°53·4′	2°36·0′W	X	67
Taversoe Tuick	Orkney	HY4227	59°7·8′	3°0·3′W	X	5,6
Taversoe Tuick (Chambered Cairn)	Orkney	HY4227	59°7·8′	3°0·3′W	A	5,6
Tavistock	Devon	SX4874	50°33·0′	4°8·4′W	T	191,201
Tavis Vor	Corn	SW4726	50°5·1′	5°31·8′W	X	203
Taviton	Devon	SX5074	50°33·0′	4°6·7′W	X	191,201
Tavool Ho	Arg & Bt	NM4327	56°22·2′	6°9·3′W	X	48
Tavy Br	Devon	SX4561	50°25·9′	4°10·6′W	X	201
Tavy Cleave	Devon	SX5583	50°38·0′	4°2·6′W	X	191
Taw Bridge	Devon	SS6706	50°50·5′	3°53·0′W	X	191
Tawelfan	Powys	SH8700	52°35·4′	3°39·7′W	X	135,136
Tawell Fm	Corn	SX1358	50°23·8′	4°37·5′W	FM	200
Tawells, The	Shetld	HU4864	60°21·7′	1°7·3′W	X	2,3
Taw Green	Devon	SS6606	50°50·5′	3°53·8′W	X	191
Taw Green	Devon	SX6597	50°45·6′	3°54·5′W	T	191
Taw Head	Devon	SX6085	50°39·1′	3°58·4′W	W	191
Taw Ho	Cumbr	NY2101	54°24·1′	3°12·6′W	X	89,90
Taw Marsh	Devon	SX6190	50°41·8′	3°57·7′W	W	191
Tawmill	Devon	SX6599	50°46·7′	3°54·5′W	X	191
Tawna	Corn	SX1367	50°28·6′	4°37·8′W	X	200
Tawna Downs	Corn	SX1366	50°28·1′	4°37·7′W	X	200
Tawnamoor	Corn	SX1066	50°28·0′	4°40·3′W	X	200
Tawnaze Hill	D & G	NY0492	55°13·0′	3°30·1′W	X	78
Tawney Common	Essex	TL4901	51°41·5′	0°9·7′E	X	167
Tawney's Fm	Oxon	SP4205	51°44·8′	1°23·1′W	FM	164
Tawneys Fm	Suff	TM1037	51°59·7′	1°3·9′E	FM	155,169
Tawsmead Copse	Wilts	SU1261	51°21·1′	1°49·3′W	F	173
Tawstock	Devon	SS5529	51°2·8′	4°3·7′W	T	180
Taxal	Derby	SK0079	53°18·7′	1°59·6′W	T	119
Taxal Edge	Ches	SJ9979	53°18·7′	2°0·5′W	X	118
Tax Fm	Derby	SK2963	53°10·0′	1°33·6′W	FM	119
Taxing Stone	D & G	NX0670	54°59·5′	5°1·5′W	A	76
Taxmere Fm	Ches	SJ7862	53°9·5′	2°19·3′W	FM	118
Tayandock	Arg & Bt	NR3163	55°47·4′	6°17·0′W	X	60,61
Taybank	Pth & Kin	NO2522	56°23·3′	3°12·4′W	X	53,59
Tay Bridge	Fife	NO3927	56°26·1′	2°58·9′W	X	54,59
Tayburn	E Ayr	NS5143	55°39·7′	4°21·7′W	X	70
Tay Burn	Scot Bord	NT6668	55°54·5′	2°32·2′W	W	67
Tayfield	Fife	NO4227	56°26·2′	2°56·0′W	X	54,59
Tayfield	Pth & Kin	NO1919	56°21·6′	3°18·2′W	X	58
Tay Fm	Pth & Kin	NO1440	56°32·9′	3°23·5′W	FM	53
Tayinloan	Arg & Bt	NR6946	55°39·4′	5°39·9′W	T	62
Tayinloan Burn	Arg & Bt	NR7146	55°39·5′	5°38·0′W	W	62
Tayinloan Lodge	Highld	NG3753	57°29·7′	6°22·9′W	X	23
Tayintrath	Arg & Bt	NR8293	56°5·1′	5°29·8′W	X	55
Tayloch	Aberd	NJ5328	57°20·7′	2°46·4′W	X	37
Taylorburn	Northum	NY7950	54°50·9′	2°19·2′W	X	86,87
Taylorgill Force	Cumbr	NY2210	54°29·0′	3°11·8′W	W	89,90
Taylor Rigg	Cumbr	NY8907	54°27·7′	2°9·8′W	X	91,92
Taylors	Surrey	TQ1838	51°8·0′	0°18·4′W	X	187
Taylor's Bank	Sefton	SD2504	53°31·9′	3°7·5′W	X	108
Taylor's Cottage	E Susx	TQ7220	50°57·4′	0°27·3′E	X	199
Taylor's Covert	Staffs	SJ8226	52°50·1′	2°15·6′W	F	127
Taylor's Cross	Corn	SS2612	50°53·1′	4°28·0′W	X	190
Taylor's Down	Devon	SS6204	50°49·4′	3°57·2′W	X	191
Taylor's Fm	Essex	TL7814	51°48·0′	0°35·3′E	FM	167
Taylors Fm	Essex	TQ4694	51°37·8′	0°7·0′E	FM	167,177
Taylor's Fm	Lancs	SD3921	53°41·2′	2°55·0′W	FM	102
Taylor's Fm	Lancs	SD5251	53°57·4′	2°43·5′W	FM	102
Taylor's Fm	Rut	SK9912	52°42·0′	0°31·7′W	FM	130
Taylor's Fm	Suff	TL7147	52°5·9′	0°30·2′E	FM	154
Taylor's Grove	Suff	TL9075	52°20·6′	0°47·8′E	F	144
Taylor's Hill	Glos	SP0015	51°50·3′	1°59·6′W	X	163
Taylor Shop	Corn	SX3473	50°32·2′	4°20·2′W	X	201
Taylor's Island	I Scilly	SV9011	49°55·4′	6°18·8′W	X	203
Taylorspark	Aberd	NO7366	56°47·3′	2°26·1′W	X	45
Taymount	Pth & Kin	NO1622	56°23·2′	3°21·2′W	X	53,58
Taymount Ho	Pth & Kin	NO1234	56°29·6′	3°25·3′W	X	53
Taymount Home Fm	Pth & Kin	NO1134	56°29·6′	3°26·3′W	FM	53
Taymount Mains	Pth & Kin	NO1234	56°29·6′	3°25·3′W	X	53
Taymouth Castle	Pth & Kin	NN7846	56°35·7′	3°58·8′W	T	51,52
Tayness	Arg & Bt	NR8197	56°7·2′	5°30·9′W	X	55
Taynish Ho	Arg & Bt	NR7283	55°59·4′	5°38·9′W	X	55
Taynish Island	Arg & Bt	NR7282	55°58·9′	5°38·9′W	X	55
Taynton	Glos	SO7321	51°53·5′	2°23·1′W	T	162
Taynton	Oxon	SP2313	51°49·1′	1°39·6′W	T	163

Taynton Bushes	Oxon	SP2216	51°50·8′	1°40·4′W	F	163
Taynton Court Fm	Glos	SO7423	51°54·5′	2°22·3′W	FM	162
Taynton Ho	Glos	SO7222	51°54·0′	2°24·0′W	X	162
Taynton Pound Fm	Glos	SO7423	51°54·5′	2°22·3′W	FM	162
Taynuilt	Arg & Bt	NN0031	56°26·0′	5°14·2′W	T	50
Tayock	Angus	NO6959	56°43·6′	2°29·9′W	X	54
Tayovullin	Arg & Bt	NR2872	55°52·1′	6°20·4′W	X	60
Tayport	Fife	NO4528	56°26·7′	2°53·1′W	T	54,59
Tay Road Bridge	Fife	NO4129	56°27·2′	2°57·0′W	X	54,59
Taythes	Cumbr	SD7095	54°21·2′	2°27·3′W	X	98
Taythes Beck Wood	Cumbr	SD7095	54°21·2′	2°27·3′W	F	98
Taythes Gill	Cumbr	SD7195	54°21·2′	2°26·4′W	W	98
Tayvallich	Arg & Bt	NR7487	56°1·6′	5°37·2′W	T	55
Tayvullin	Arg & Bt	NR7285	56°0·5′	5°39·0′W	T	55
Teacaddy Fm	Northnts	SP8169	52°19·0′	0°48·3′W	FM	152
Teachatt	Highld	NH5864	57°38·9′	4°22·3′W	X	21
Teachmore Fm	Devon	SS5700	50°47·2′	4°1·3′W	FM	191
Teacoombe	Corn	SX1758	50°23·8′	4°34·1′W	X	201
Tea Green	Herts	TL1323	51°53·9′	0°21·1′W	T	166
Teague's Fm	E Susx	TQ3721	50°58·6′	0°2·5′W	FM	198
Teahaval	N Eil	NB1629	58°9·8′	6°49·3′W	H	13
Teakettle Hall Fm	Peterb	TF2700	52°35·2′	0°7·1′W	FM	142
Teakins	Shrops	SJ5226	52°50·0′	2°42·3′W	X	126
Tealair	N Eil	NB5547	58°20·9′	6°10·7′W	W	8
Tealby	Lincs	TF1590	53°23·9′	0°15·8′W	T	113
Tealby Moor	Lincs	TF1390	53°23·9′	0°17·6′W	X	113
Tealby Thorpe	Lincs	TF1490	53°23·9′	0°16·7′W	X	113
Teal Fm	Wilts	ST9776	51°29·2′	2°2·2′W	FM	173
Tealham Moor	Somer	ST3945	51°12·3′	2°52·0′W	X	182
Tealhole Point	Northum	NU1039	55°38·9′	1°50·0′W	X	75
Tealing	Angus	NO4138	56°32·1′	2°57·1′W	T	54
Tealing Hill	Angus	NO4040	56°33·1′	2°58·1′W	H	54
Tealing Ho	Angus	NO4138	56°32·1′	2°57·1′W	X	54
Team Gate Drain	NE Lincs	TA2304	53°31·3′	0°8·3′W	W	113
Teampall Amhlaigh	N Eil	NB4941	58°17·4′	6°16·5′W	A	8
Teampall Bhuirgh	N Eil	NF7650	57°25·7′	7°23·5′W	A	22
Teampall Challuim Chille	N Eil	NF7854	57°28·0′	7°21·8′W	A	22
Teampall Eoin	N Eil	NB2848	58°20·4′	6°38·4′W	A	8
Teampall Mholuaidh	N Eil	NB5165	58°30·4′	6°16·0′W	A	8
Teampall nan Crò Naomh	N Eil	NB4359	58°26·9′	6°23·8′W	A	8
Teampall Naoimb Ronain	N Eil	HW8032	59°7·3′	5°50·2′W	X	8
Teampall Naomh Mhicheil	N Eil	NF8854	57°28·4′	7°11·8′W	A	22
Teampall na Trionaid	N Eil	NF8160	57°31·3′	7°19·3′W	A	22
Teampall Pheadair	N Eil	NB3754	58°24·0′	6°29·6′W	A	8
Teampuill Chaon	Highld	NG6113	57°9·0′	5°56·6′W	A	32
Teampuill Fraing	Highld	NG6228	57°17·1′	5°56·5′W	A	32
Teampull Drain	N Eil	NF7777	57°40·3′	7°24·6′W	A	18
Teampull Mhóire	N Eil	NF8886	57°45·6′	7°14·3′W	A	18
Teampull Mhuir	N Eil	NF7876	57°39·8′	7°23·5′W	A	18
Teampull Pheadair	N Eil	NB5063	58°29·3′	6°16·9′W	A	8
Teams	Ghead	NZ2362	54°57·4′	1°38·0′W	T	88
Team Valley	Ghead	NZ2460	54°56·3′	1°37·1′W	T	88
Tean	I Scilly	SV9016	49°58·1′	6°19·0′W	X	203
Teanacoil	Highld	NH4941	57°26·3′	4°30·5′W	X	26
Teanacoil Wood	Highld	NH4840	57°25·8′	4°31·4′W	F	26
Teanafruich	Highld	NH4652	57°32·2′	4°33·9′W	X	26
Teanagairn	Highld	NH5958	57°35·7′	4°21·1′W	X	26
Teanahuig	Highld	NH6253	57°33·0′	4°17·9′W	X	26
Teanalick	Highld	NH5248	57°30·1′	4°27·7′W	X	26
Teanchoisin Glen	Arg & Bt	NR7440	55°36·3′	5°34·8′W	X	62
Teandalloch	Highld	NH5148	57°30·1′	4°28·7′W	X	26
Teandore	Highld	NH6150	57°31·4′	4°18·8′W	X	26
Teanford	Staffs	SK0040	52°57·7′	1°59·6′W	T	119,128
Teanga Bhàn	Arg & Bt	NM6526	56°22·3′	5°47·9′W	X	49
Teanga Bheag	Highld	NN3295	57°1·2′	4°45·6′W	H	34
Teanga Brideig	Arg & Bt	NM5630	56°24·2′	5°56·8′W	X	48
Teanga Chorrach	Highld	NM8672	56°47·7′	5°29·8′W	X	40
Teanga Dhubh	Arg & Bt	NM6537	56°28·3′	5°48·5′W	X	49
Teanga Dhubh	Arg & Bt	NN0841	56°31·6′	5°6·8′W	X	50
Teanga Fhraoich	N Ayr	NR9725	55°28·9′	5°12·3′W	X	69
Teanga Fiadhaich	Highld	NG9849	57°29·4′	5°21·8′W	X	25
Teanga gun Urrainn	Highld	NN1597	57°1·9′	5°2·5′W	X	34
Teanga Màm an Tiompain	Arg & Bt	NM5932	56°25·4′	5°54·0′W	X	48
Teanga Mheadhonach	Highld	NM9973	56°48·6′	5°17·1′W	X	40
Teanga Mhór	Highld	NN3395	57°1·2′	4°44·6′W	H	34
Teanga na Comhstri	Highld	NG8122	57°14·4′	5°37·3′W	X	33
Teanga na Feinne	Highld	NH0208	57°7·5′	5°15·8′W	X	33
Teanga nan Allt	Highld	NM5654	56°37·1′	5°58·2′W	X	47
Teanga nan Càiseachan	Highld	NH0974	57°43·2′	5°12·0′W	X	19
Teanga Riabhach	Arg & Bt	NM5033	56°25·6′	6°2·8′W	X	47,48
Teanga Shamhairidh	Highld	NM6449	56°34·7′	5°50·1′W	X	49
Teanga Thunga	N Eil	NB4435	58°14·0′	6°21·2′W	X	8
Teangue	Highld	NG6609	57°7·0′	5°51·5′W	T	32
Teaninich Ho	Highld	NH6568	57°41·2′	4°15·4′W	X	21
Tean Leys Fm	Staffs	SK0138	52°56·6′	1°58·7′W	FM	128
Teanna Mhachair	N Eil	NF7762	57°32·2′	7°23·4′W	X	22
Teanord	Highld	NH5964	57°38·9′	4°21·3′W	X	21
Teanroit	Highld	NH5146	57°29·0′	4°28·7′W	X	26
Tean Sound	I Scilly	SV9116	49°58·1′	6°18·2′W	W	203
Teapot	Stir	NN4403	56°11·9′	4°30·4′W	X	57
Teapot Hall	Lincs	TF5367	53°10·9′	0°17·8′E	X	122
Tearnden Fm	Kent	TQ9040	51°7·9′	0°43·3′E	FM	189
Tearnside Hall	Cumbr	SD5879	54°12·5′	2°38·2′W	X	97
Tearsall Fm	Derby	SK2659	53°7·9′	1°36·3′W	FM	119
Tears Point	Swan	SS4186	51°33·3′	4°17·2′W	X	159
Teasley Mead	E Susx	TQ5039	51°8·1′	0°9·0′E	T	188
Teasses	Fife	NO4008	56°15·9′	2°57·7′W	X	59
Teassesmill	Fife	NO3910	56°17·0′	2°58·7′W	X	59
Teaths	S Lanak	NS8542	55°39·7′	3°49·2′W	X	71,72
Teatle Water	Arg & Bt	NN1424	56°22·6′	5°0·3′W	W	50
Teawig	Highld	NH5145	57°28·5′	4°28·6′W	X	26
Tebay	Cumbr	NY6104	54°26·0′	2°35·7′W	T	91
Tebay Fell	Cumbr	NY6201	54°24·4′	2°34·7′W	H	91
Tebaygill	Cumbr	NY6103	54°25·5′	2°35·6′W	X	91
Tebay Gill	Cumbr	NY6202	54°25·0′	2°34·7′W	X	91
Tebay Service Area	Cumbr	NY6006	54°27·1′	2°36·6′W	X	91
Tebbitt's Br	Cambs	TL2491	52°30·4′	0°10·0′W	X	142
Tebbutt's Fm	Notts	SK5223	52°48·4′	1°13·3′W	FM	129
Tebworth	Beds	SP9926	51°55·7′	0°33·2′W	T	165
Techmuiry	Aberd	NJ9560	57°38·1′	2°4·6′W	X	30

Techon	Carm	SS5499	51°40·5′	4°6·3′W	X	159
Tecket	Northum	NY8672	55°2·8′	2°12·7′W	X	87
Tedbeer	Somer	ST0321	50°59·0′	3°22·5′W	X	181
Tedbridge	Devon	SS9704	50°49·8′	3°27·4′W	X	192
Tedbridge	Devon	SY1795	50°45·2′	3°10·2′W	X	192,193
Tedburn St Mary	Devon	SX8194	50°44·2′	3°40·8′W	T	191
Tedbury	Somer	ST7448	51°14·1′	2°22·0′W	A	183
Tedcastle	Northum	NY8063	54°57·9′	2°18·3′W	X	86,87
Teddesley Park	Staffs	SJ9516	52°44·7′	2°4·0′W	X	127
Teddington	Glos	SO9633	52°0·0′	2°3·1′W	T	150
Teddington	Rich	TQ1670	51°25·3′	0°19·5′W	T	176
Teddington Hands	Glos	SO9634	52°0·5′	2°3·1′W	T	150
Teddington Lock	Rich	TQ1671	51°25·8′	0°19·5′W	X	176
Tedfold	W Susx	TQ0826	51°1·6′	0°27·2′W	X	187,197
Tedgewood	Heref	SO6627	51°56·7′	2°29·3′W	X	162
Tedham	Northum	NY8449	54°50·4′	2°14·5′W	X	86,87
Tedham Moss	Northum	NY8649	54°50·4′	2°12·7′W	X	87
Tedion	Pemb	SN0308	51°44·4′	4°50·8′W	X	157,158
Tedion Mountain	Pemb	SN0308	51°44·4′	4°50·8′W	H	157,158
Tednambury Fm	Herts	TL4916	51°49·6′	0°10·1′E	FM	167
Tedney Bank	Heref	SO7258	52°13·4′	2°24·2′W	X	149
Tedney Ho	Heref	SO7358	52°13·4′	2°23·3′W	X	150
Tedsmore	Shrops	SJ3725	52°49·4′	2°55·7′W	T	126
Tedsmore Hall	Shrops	SJ3625	52°49·4′	2°56·6′W	X	126
Tedstill	Shrops	SO6887	52°29·0′	2°27·9′W	X	138
Tedstone Delamere	Heref	SO6958	52°13·4′	2°26·8′W	T	149
Tedstone Ho	Devon	SY0084	50°39·1′	3°24·5′W	X	192
Tedstone Wafer	Heref	SO6759	52°13·9′	2°28·6′W	T	149
T & EE Aberporth	Cered	SN2452	52°8·5′	4°33·9′W	X	145
Teedleham Fm	Kent	TR2361	51°18·5′	1°12·4′E	FM	179
Teenley Hill	N Yks	SD8157	54°0·8′	2°17·0′W	X	103
Teeny Burn	Pth & Kin	NO1005	56°14·0′	3°26·7′W	W	58
Tees Barrage	Stock on T	NZ4619	54°34·1′	1°16·9′W	X	93
Tees Bay	Red & Cl	NZ5528	54°38·9′	1°8·4′W	W	93
Teesdale	Durham	NY9325	54°37·5′	2°6·1′W	X	91,92
Tees Head	Cumbr	NY6933	54°41·7′	2°28·4′W	X	91
Tees Mouth	Stock on T	NZ5426	54°37·8′	1°9·4′W	W	93
Teesport	Red & Cl	NZ5423	54°36·2′	1°9·4′W	X	93
Teesside Industrial Estate	Stock on T	NZ4514	54°31·4′	1°17·9′W	X	93
Teesside International Airport	Darl	NZ3713	54°30·9′	1°25·3′W	X	93
Teesside Park	Stock on T	NZ4618	54°33·6′	1°16·9′W	X	93
Teesville	Red & Cl	NZ5419	54°34·0′	1°9·5′W	T	93
Teeton	Northnts	SP6970	52°19·7′	0°58·8′W	T	141
Teetotal Channel		TF5532	52°52·0′	0°18·6′E	W	131
Teffont Down	Wilts	ST9934	51°6·5′	2°0·5′W	X	184
Teffont Evias	Wilts	ST9831	51°4·9′	2°1·3′W	T	184
Teffont Field Buildings	Wilts	ST9933	51°6·0′	2°0·5′W	X	184
Teffont Magna	Wilts	ST9832	51°5·5′	2°1·3′W	T	184
Teffont Manor	Wilts	ST9931	51°4·9′	2°0·5′W	A	184
Tefit Hall	Durham	NZ1211	54°29·9′	1°48·5′W	X	92
Tegarmuchd	Pth & Kin	NN7948	56°36·8′	3°57·8′W	X	51,52
Teg Down	Hants	SU4529	51°3·7′	1°21·1′W	X	185
Tegdown Hill	Bri & Hov	TQ3110	50°52·7′	0°7·9′W	X	198
Tegdown Hill	Hants	SU6919	50°58·2′	1°0·7′W	X	197
Tegfan	Cered	SN4157	52°11·5′	4°19·2′W	X	146
Tegfynydd	Carm	SN1420	51°51·1′	4°41·7′W	X	145,158
Tegg's Nose	Ches	SJ9472	53°14·9′	2°5·0′W	X	118
Teglease Down	Hants	SU6519	50°58·2′	1°4·1′W	X	185
Teglease Fm	Hants	SU6518	50°57·7′	1°4·1′W	FM	185
Tegleaze	W Susx	SU9315	50°55·8′	0°40·2′W	F	197
Tegleaze Fm	W Susx	SU9315	50°55·8′	0°40·2′W	FM	197
Tegryn	Pemb	SN2233	51°58·3′	4°35·1′W	T	145
Tehidy Barton	Corn	SW6444	50°15·2′	5°18·3′W	X	203
Tehidy Country Park	Corn	SW6443	50°14·6′	5°18·2′W	X	203
Teigh	Leic	SK8616	52°44·3′	0°43·2′W	T	130
Teigh Lodge	Leic	SK8516	52°44·3′	0°44·1′W	X	130
Teiglum Burn	S Lanak	NS8041	55°39·1′	3°54·0′W	W	71,72
Teigncombe	Devon	SX6787	50°40·3′	3°52·6′W	X	191
Teigngrace	Devon	SX8473	50°33·0′	3°37·9′W	T	191
Teign Head	Devon	SX6184	50°38·6′	3°57·6′W	W	191
Teignhead Fm (ruin)	Devon	SX6384	50°38·6′	3°55·9′W	FM	191
Teignmouth	Devon	SX9473	50°33·1′	3°29·4′W	T	192
Teign Village	Devon	SX8381	50°37·3′	3°38·9′W	T	191
Tèileasbhal	N Eil	NB1209	57°58·9′	6°51·9′W	H	13,14
Teilem Bay	N Eil	NF9174	57°39·3′	7°10·4′W	W	18
Teilem Point	N Eil	NF9175	57°39·8′	7°10·5′W	X	18
Teilia	Flint	SJ0881	53°19·3′	3°22·5′W	X	116
Teiliau	Gwyn	SH7043	52°58·4′	3°55·8′W	X	124
Teindland	Moray	NJ2655	57°35·0′	3°13·8′W	X	28
Teindland Mains	Moray	NJ2856	57°35·6′	3°11·8′W	X	28
Teindland Wood	Moray	NJ2956	57°35·6′	3°10·8′W	F	28
Teindside	Scot Bord	NT4408	55°22·0′	2°52·6′W	X	79
Teindside Burn	Scot Bord	NT4209	55°22·5′	2°54·5′W	W	79
Teindside Lodge	Scot Bord	NT4307	55°21·5′	2°53·5′W	X	79
Teinnasaval	N Eil	NB0425	58°7·2′	7°1·2′W	H	13
Teiran	Denb	SJ1460	53°8·1′	3°16·7′W	X	116
Teirtref	Powys	SJ1213	52°42·7′	3°17·8′W	X	125
Teistie Geo	Shetld	HU5059	60°19·0′	1°5·2′W	X	2,3
Teistie Taing	Orkney	HY5051	59°20·8′	2°52·3′W	X	5
Teisti Geo	Shetld	HU3829	60°2·9′	1°18·6′W	X	4
Telegraph	I Scilly	SV9012	49°55·9′	6°18·8′W	X	203
Telegraph Fm	Kent	TR3151	51°12·9′	1°18·9′E	FM	179
Telegraph Fm	Norf	TM0993	52°29·9′	1°5·2′E	FM	144
Telegraph Hill	Devon	SX8073	50°32·9′	3°41·3′W	H	191
Telegraph Hill	Devon	SX9183	50°38·4′	3°32·1′W	X	192
Telegraph Hill	Dorset	ST6404	50°50·3′	2°30·3′W	X	194
Telegraph Hill	Hants	SU5228	51°3·2′	1°15·1′W	H	185
Telegraph Hill	Herts	TL1128	51°56·6′	0°22·7′W	X	166
Telegraph Hill	Kent	TR3165	51°20·4′	1°19·4′E	X	179
Telegraph Hill	King	TQ1660	51°19·9′	0°19·7′W	X	176,187
Telegraph Hill	Norf	TG1042	52°56·3′	1°7·9′E	X	133
Telegraph Hill	Norf	TM0086	52°26·3′	0°57·0′E	X	144
Telegraph Hill	Scot Bord	NT8570	55°55·6′	2°14·0′W	X	67
Telegraph Hill	Surrey	TQ0858	51°18·9′	0°26·6′W	X	187
Telegraph Hill	Surrey	TQ1564	51°22·0′	0°20·5′W	X	176,187
Telegraph Hill	W Susx	SU7814	50°55·4′	0°53·0′W	H	197
Telegraph Hill	W Susx	SU8726	51°1·8′	0°45·2′W	X	186,197
Telegraph Ho	Lincs	TF2767	53°11·3′	0°5·5′W	X	122

Telegraph Ho	W Susx	SU8017	50°57·0′	0°51·3′W	X	197
Telegraph Plantation	Dorset	SU0911	50°54·1′	1°51·9′W	F	195
Telegraph Plantation	Suff	TL7873	52°19·8′	0°37·1′E	F	144,155
Telegraph Wood	Hants	SU3818	50°57·8′	1°27·1′W	F	185
Telfit	N Yks	NZ0802	54°25·0′	1°52·2′W	X	92
Telford	Wrekin	SJ6909	52°40·9′	2°27·1′W	T	127
Telford Bridge	Moray	NJ2845	57°29·6′	3°11·6′W	X	28
Telford Horsehay Steam Trust	Wrekin	SJ6707	52°39·8′	2°28·9′W	X	127
Telford Memorial	D & G	NY3090	55°12·2′	3°5·6′W	X	79
Telfords	Essex	TL6005	51°43·5′	0°19·4′E	X	167
Telford's Bridge	Glos	SO8119	51°52·4′	2°16·2′W	X	162
Telford Town Park	Wrekin	SJ6908	52°40·4′	2°27·1′W	X	127
Telham	E Susx	TQ7614	50°54·1′	0°30·6′E	T	199
Telham Court (Sch)	E Susx	TQ7514	50°54·2′	0°29·7′E	X	199
Telham Hill	E Susx	TQ7513	50°53·6′	0°29·7′E	X	199
Telham Place	E Susx	TQ7613	50°53·6′	0°30·5′E	X	199
Tellis Coppice	E Susx	TQ7215	50°54·8′	0°27·2′E	F	199
Tellisford	Somer	ST8055	51°17·9′	2°16·8′W	T	173
Tellisford Ho	Somer	ST7955	51°17·9′	2°17·7′W	X	172
Tell's Tower	Wirral	SJ2185	53°21·6′	3°10·8′W	X	108
Telpits Fm	Kent	TQ8748	51°12·3′	0°41·0′E	FM	189
Telpyn Fm	Carm	SN1807	51°44·2′	4°37·8′W	FM	158
Telpyn Pt	Carm	SN1807	51°44·2′	4°37·8′W	X	158
Telscombe	E Susx	TQ4003	50°48·8′	0°0·4′W	T	198
Telscombe Cliffs	E Susx	TQ4001	50°47·7′	0°0·4′W	T	198
Temon	Cumbr	NY6163	54°57·9′	2°36·1′W	A	86
Tempar Burn	Pth & Kin	NN6956	56°40·9′	4°7·9′W	W	42,51
Tempe Fm	Leic	SK3611	52°42·0′	1°27·6′W	FM	128
Temperance Fm	Northum	NY8047	54°49·3′	2°18·3′W	FM	86,87
Temperley Grange	Northum	NY9861	54°56·9′	2°1·4′W	X	87
Temperness	Pemb	SM9014	51°47·4′	5°2·3′W	X	157,158
Temperness	Pemb	SM9115	51°47·9′	5°1·5′W	X	157,158
Templand	Aberd	NJ4727	57°20·1′	2°52·4′W	X	37
Templand	Aberd	NJ7040	57°27·2′	2°29·5′W	X	29
Templand	Cumbr	SD3876	54°10·8′	2°56·6′W	X	96,97
Templand	D & G	NY0886	55°9·8′	3°26·2′W	T	78
Templand	Highld	NH6957	57°35·3′	4°11·0′W	X	26
Templand Hill	D & G	NX9780	55°6·5′	3°36·4′W	X	78
Templand Ho	D & G	NY0885	55°9·3′	3°26·2′W	X	78
Templand Mains	D & G	NX8894	55°13·9′	3°45·2′W	X	78
Templandmuir Fm	N Ayr	NS3148	55°42·0′	4°40·9′W	FM	63
Templandshaw	E Ayr	NS5924	55°29·6′	4°13·5′W	X	71
Templars	Aberd	NO8499	57°5·2′	2°15·4′W	X	38,45
Templars	Essex	TL6328	51°55·8′	0°22·6′E	X	167
Templar's Bath	N Lincs	SE8905	53°32·3′	0°39·0′W	A	112
Templars Fm	W Berks	SU3773	51°27·5′	1°27·7′W	FM	174
Templars' Hall	Sol	SP2075	52°22·6′	1°42·0′W	A	139
Temple	Aberd	NO8576	56°52·8′	2°14·3′W	X	45
Temple	C of Glas	NS5469	55°53·8′	4°19·7′W	T	64
Temple	Corn	SX1473	50°31·9′	4°37·1′W	T	200
Temple	Midlo	NT3158	55°48·9′	3°5·6′W	T	66,73
Temple	Renf	NS3860	55°48·6′	4°34·7′W	X	63
Temple	Wilts	ST8244	51°11·9′	2°15·1′W	T	183
Temple	Win & Maid	SU8484	51°33·1′	0°46·9′W	T	175
Temple Balsall	Sol	SP2075	52°22·6′	1°42·0′W	T	139
Templebank	Aberd	NO7178	56°53·8′	2°28·1′W	X	45
Templebank	Angus	NO4046	56°36·4′	2°58·2′W	X	54
Temple Bar	Carm	SN5817	51°50·3′	4°3·3′W	T	159
Temple Bar	Cered	SN5354	52°10·1′	4°8·6′W	T	146
Temple Bar	Herts	TL3401	51°41·7′	0°3·3′W	A	166
Temple Bar	Pemb	SN0839	52°1·2′	4°47·5′W	X	145
Temple Bar	W Susx	SU8907	50°51·6′	0°43·7′W	T	197
Templeborough	Sheff	SK4091	53°25·1′	1°23·5′W	T	111
Temple Bottom	Wilts	SU1472	51°27·0′	1°47·5′W	X	173
Temple Br	Suff	TL7572	52°19·3′	0°34·5′E	X	155
Temple Brook	Dorset	ST4003	50°49·6′	2°50·7′W	W	193
Temple Bruer	Lincs	TF0053	53°4·1′	0°30·0′W	X	121
Temple Bungalow	Win & Maid	SU9669	51°24·9′	0°36·8′W	X	175,176
Temple Cloud	Bath & NE Somer	ST6257	51°18·9′	2°32·3′W	T	172
Templecombe	Somer	ST7022	51°0·0′	2°25·3′W	T	183
Temple Combe	Wok	SU7881	51°31·6′	0°52·1′W	X	175
Temple Court	Heref	SO6943	52°5·3′	2°26·8′W	X	149
Temple Court	Surrey	TQ0351	51°15·2′	0°31·1′W	X	186
Temple Covert	Suff	TM3572	52°18·0′	1°27·2′E	F	156
Temple Cowley	Oxon	SP5404	51°44·2′	1°12·7′W	T	164
Temple Dinsley	Herts	TL1824	51°54·4′	0°16·7′W	X	166
Temple Druid	Pemb	SN0927	51°54·8′	4°46·2′W	X	145
Temple Druid	Pemb	SN0927	51°54·8′	4°46·2′W	X	145,158
Temple Elfande	Surrey	TQ1939	51°8·5′	0°17·5′W	X	187
Temple End	Essex	TL8243	52°3·6′	0°39·7′E	T	155
Temple End	Herts	TL1627	51°56·0′	0°18·4′W	X	166
Temple End	Suff	TL6650	52°7·6′	0°25·9′E	T	154
Temple Ewell	Kent	TR2844	51°9·2′	1°16·0′E	T	179
Temple Fields	Essex	TL4612	51°47·5′	0°7·4′E	T	167
Temple Fm	Cambs	TL6286	52°27·1′	0°23·4′E	FM	143
Temple Fm	Essex	TL7100	51°40·6′	0°28·8′E	FM	167
Temple Fm	Essex	TQ8888	51°33·8′	0°43·1′E	FM	178
Temple Fm	E Yorks	TA1466	54°4·9′	0°15·0′W	FM	101
Temple Fm	Heref	SO5469	52°19·3′	2°40·1′W	FM	137,138
Temple Fm	Kent	TQ9256	51°16·5′	0°45·6′E	FM	178
Temple Fm	Kent	TR2845	51°9·7′	1°16·1′E	FM	179
Temple Fm	Leic	SK3503	52°37·7′	1°28·6′W	FM	140
Temple Fm	Lincs	TF0053	53°4·1′	0°30·0′W	FM	121
Temple Fm	Midlo	NT3258	55°48·9′	3°4·7′W	FM	66,73
Temple Fm	N Yks	SE0388	54°17·5′	1°56·8′W	FM	98
Temple Fm	Wilts	SU1472	51°27·0′	1°47·5′W	FM	173
Temple Fm	Win & Maid	SU8483	51°32·6′	0°46·9′W	FM	175
Templefold	Aberd	NJ7703	57°7·3′	2°22·3′W	X	38
Temple Gate	Pemb	SN1336	51°59·7′	4°43·0′W	X	145
Temple Grafton	Warw	SP1254	52°11·3′	1°49·1′W	T	150
Temple Grove (Sch)	E Susx	TQ4827	51°1·6′	0°7·0′E	X	188,198
Temple Guiting	Glos	SP0928	51°57·3′	1°51·7′W	T	150,163
Templehall	Angus	NO4935	56°30·5′	2°49·3′W	T	54
Templehall	E Loth	NT4266	55°53·3′	2°55·2′W	X	66
Templehall	Fife	NT2088	56°4·9′	3°16·7′W	X	66
Templehall	Fife	NT2693	56°7·7′	3°11·0′W	T	59
Temple Hall	Leic	SK3602	52°37·1′	1°27·7′W	X	140

Templehall	Orkney	HY6741	59°15·5′	2°34·2′W	X	5
Templehall	Pth & Kin	NO3127	56°26·1′	3°6·7′W	T	53,59
Templehall	Scot Bord	NT5708	55°22·1′	2°40·3′W	X	80
Temple Hall	Scot Bord	NT8965	55°52·9′	2°10·1′W	X	67
Templehall Hill	Scot Bord	NT5606	55°21·0′	2°41·2′W	H	80
Temple Herdewyke	Warw	SP3752	52°10·1′	1°27·1′W	T	151
Temple High Grange Fm	Lincs	TF0257	53°6·3′	0°28·2′W	FM	121
Templehill	E Ayr	NS5538	55°37·1′	4°17·7′W	X	71
Temple Hill	Kent	TQ5575	51°27·4′	0°14·3′E	T	177
Temple Hill	Lincs	SK8847	53°1·0′	0°40·9′W	X	130
Temple Hill	Lincs	SK9220	52°46·4′	0°37·8′W	X	130
Temple Hill	Northnts	SP5757	52°12·7′	1°9·5′W	X	152
Temple Hill	Pth & Kin	NO1009	56°16·2′	3°26·7′W	H	58
Temple Hill	W Loth	NT1161	55°50·3′	3°24·8′W	X	65
Temple Hill Fm	York	SE5746	53°54·7′	1°7·5′W	FM	105
Temple Hirst	N Yks	SE6025	53°43·3′	1°5·0′W	T	105
Temple Ho	C of Edin	NT1364	55°51·9′	3°23·0′W	X	65
Temple Ho	Herts	TL3400	51°41·2′	0°3·3′W	X	166
Temple Ho	Warw	SP3289	52°30·1′	1°31·3′W	X	140
Temple House Fm	N Yks	NZ3003	54°25·5′	1°31·8′W	FM	93
Temple House Fm	Somer	ST6544	51°11·9′	2°29·7′W	FM	183
Temple House, The	Northnts	SP8254	52°10·9′	0°47·6′W	X	152
Temple Island	Wok	SU7784	51°33·2′	0°53·0′W	X	175
Templeland	Aberd	NJ6341	57°27·7′	2°36·5′W	X	29
Templeland	Aberd	NJ6631	57°22·3′	2°33·5′W	X	29
Templelands	Angus	NO3536	56°31·0′	3°2·9′W	X	54
Templelands	Fife	NO2506	56°14·7′	3°12·2′W	X	59
Temple Laugherne	Worcs	SO8256	52°12·4′	2°15·4′W	X	150
Templelea	Stir	NS5290	56°5·1′	4°22·3′W	X	57
Templeman Fm	Wilts	SU2021	50°59·5′	1°42·5′W	FM	184
Temple Manor	Hants	SU7633	51°5·7′	0°54·5′W	X	186
Temple Manor	Medway	TQ7368	51°23·3′	0°29·6′E	X	178
Temple Manor	N Yks	SE5925	53°43·3′	1°5·9′W	A	105
Templeman's Ash	Dorset	ST4000	50°48·0′	2°50·7′W	T	193
Temple Marsh	Medway	TQ7367	51°22·8′	0°29·6′E	X	178
Temple Meads Sta	C of Bris	ST5972	51°27·0′	2°35·0′W	X	172
Templemill	Pth & Kin	NN8718	56°20·7′	3°49·3′W	X	58
Temple Mills	Newham	TQ3785	51°33·1′	0°1·0′W	T	177
Temple New Br	Corn	SX1574	50°32·4′	4°36·3′W	X	201
Temple Newsam	Leeds	SE3532	53°47·2′	1°27·7′W	A	104
Temple Newsam Park	Leeds	SE3531	53°46·7′	1°27·7′W	X	104
Temple Normanton	Derby	SK4167	53°12·1′	1°22·8′W	T	120
Temple of Boclair	C of Glas	NS5772	55°55·4′	4°16·9′W	X	64
Temple of Fiddes	Aberd	NO8181	56°55·5′	2°18·3′W	X	45
Temple of Venus	Leic	SK4919	52°46·2′	1°16·0′W	X	129
Temple Pool	Warw	SP3744	52°5·8′	1°27·2′W	W	151
Templer Way	Devon	SX9172	50°32·5′	3°31·9′W	X	192,202
Temples	E Renf	NS6050	55°43·6′	4°13·3′W	X	64
Temple Sowerby	Cumbr	NY6127	54°38·4′	2°35·8′W	T	91
Templestone	Moray	NJ0656	57°35·3′	3°33·9′W	X	27
Temple Stones	Aberd	NJ9516	57°14·3′	2°4·5′W	A	38
Temples Wood	N Yks	SE6485	54°15·6′	1°0·6′W	F	94,100
Temple, The	Ches	SJ7481	53°19·8′	2°23·0′W	X	109
Temple, The	D & G	NX6054	54°51·9′	4°10·5′W	X	83
Temple, The	Fife	NO3401	56°12·1′	3°3·4′W	X	59
Temple, The	Fife	NT0391	56°6·4′	3°33·1′W	X	58
Temple, The	Hants	SU4560	51°20·5′	1°20·8′W	X	174
Temple, The	Lancs	SD8249	53°56·5′	2°16·0′W	X	103
Temple, The	Midlo	NT3966	55°53·3′	2°58·1′W	X	66
Temple, The	Norf	TF8742	52°56·8′	0°47·4′E	X	132
Temple, The	N Yks	NZ1703	54°25·6′	1°43·9′W	X	92
Temple, The	N Yks	SE4058	54°1·2′	1°23·0′W	X	105
Temple, The	N Yks	SE7269	54°6·9′	0°53·5′W	X	100
Temple, The	Staffs	SK0339	52°57·1′	1°56·9′W	X	128
Temple, The	Suff	TL9078	52°22·2′	0°47·9′E	X	144
Templeton	Aberd	NJ4617	57°14·7′	2°53·2′W	X	37
Templeton	Aberd	NO6791	57°0·8′	2°32·2′W	X	38,45
Templeton	Angus	NO3142	56°34·2′	3°6·9′W	X	53
Templeton	Angus	NO3535	56°30·4′	3°2·9′W	X	54
Templeton	Angus	NO6147	56°37·1′	2°37·7′W	T	54
Templeton	Devon	SS8814	50°55·1′	3°35·2′W	T	181
Templeton	Pemb	SN1111	51°46·2′	4°44·0′W	T	158
Templeton	S Ayr	NS3934	55°34·6′	4°32·8′W	X	70
Templeton	W Berks	SU3566	51°23·7′	1°29·4′W	T	174
Templeton Bridge	Devon	SS8714	50°55·1′	3°36·1′W	T	181
Templetonburn	E Ayr	NS4538	55°36·9′	4°27·2′W	X	70
Templeton Fm	Pth & Kin	NT1197	56°9·7′	3°25·5′W	FM	58
Templeton Woods	C of Dun	NO3634	56°29·9′	3°1·9′W	F	54
Temple Tor	Corn	SX1473	50°31·9′	4°37·1′W	X	200
Templetown	Durham	NZ1049	54°50·4′	1°50·2′W	T	88
Temple Valley	Hants	SU5328	51°3·2′	1°14·2′W	X	185
Templewood	Angus	NO6162	56°45·1′	2°37·8′W	X	45
Temple Wood	Beds	TL0160	52°14·0′	0°30·9′W	F	153
Temple Wood	Lincs	TF0528	52°50·6′	0°26·1′W	F	130
Tempsford	Beds	TL1653	52°10·0′	0°17·8′W	T	153
Tempsford Bridge	Beds	TL1654	52°10·6′	0°17·8′W	X	153
Tempsford Hall	Beds	TL1653	52°10·0′	0°17·8′W	X	153
Temsend	Cumbr	NY4042	54°46·4′	2°55·5′W	X	85
Tenacre	Kent	TQ9561	51°19·1′	0°48·3′E	X	178
Ten Acre Bank	Red & Cl	NZ5516	54°32·4′	1°8·6′W	X	93
Ten Acre Resr	N Yks	SE2453	53°58·6′	1°37·6′W	W	104
Ten Acres	Birm	SP0581	52°25·9′	1°55·2′W	T	139
Ten Acre Wood	Corn	SX2354	50°21·8′	4°28·9′W	F	201
Tenandry	Pth & Kin	NN9161	56°43·9′	3°46·4′W	T	43
Tenanton	Moray	NJ3745	57°29·7′	3°2·6′W	X	28
Tenantrees	Dorset	SY7389	50°42·2′	2°22·6′W	X	194
Tenantry Down	Dorset	SU0112	50°54·7′	1°58·8′W	X	195
Tenantry Down	Wilts	ST9350	51°15·2′	2°5·6′W	X	184
Tenantry Fm	Hants	SU1021	50°59·5′	1°51·1′W	FM	184
Tenantry Ground	E Susx	TQ5402	50°48·0′	0°11·5′E	X	199
Tenants' Cliff	N Yks	TA0684	54°14·7′	0°22·0′W	X	101
Tenant's Hill	Dorset	ST6901	50°48·7′	2°26·0′W	X	194
Tenants Hill	Dorset	SY5788	50°41·6′	2°36·1′W	X	194
Tenants Hill	Kent	TR3754	51°14·4′	1°24·1′E	X	179
Tenants Hill	W Susx	TQ1407	50°51·3′	0°22·4′W	X	198
Tenbury Wells	Worcs	SO5967	52°18·2′	2°35·7′W	T	137,138,149
Tenby (Dinbych-y-pysgod)	Pemb	SN1300	51°40·3′	4°41·9′W	T	158
Tenby Roads	Pemb	SN1301	51°40·8′	4°41·9′W	W	158
Tenchleys Manor	Surrey	TQ4250	51°14·1′	0°2·4′E	X	187
Tenchleys Park	Surrey	TQ4151	51°14·7′	0°1·6′E	X	187

Ten Commandments Stone, The	Devon	SX7373	50°32·8′	3°47·2′W	X	191
Tencreek	Corn	SX1455	50°22·2′	4°36·6′W	X	200
Tencreek	Corn	SX2352	50°20·7′	4°28·9′W	T	201
Tencreek Fm	Corn	SX2663	50°26·7′	4°26·7′W	FM	201
Tendera	Corn	SW7725	50°5·2′	5°6·7′W	X	204
Tendley Hill	Cumbr	NY0828	54°38·6′	3°25·1′W	X	89
Tendring	Essex	TM1424	51°52·6′	1°6·9′E	T	168,169
Tendring Green	Essex	TM1425	51°53·2′	1°7·0′E	T	168,169
Tendring Hall Fm	Suff	TL9935	51°58·9′	0°54·3′E	FM	155
Tendring Heath	Essex	TM1326	51°53·7′	1°6·1′E	T	168,169
Tendring Lodge	Essex	TM1525	51°53·1′	1°7·9′E	X	168,169
Tendring's Fm	Essex	TL5732	51°58·1′	0°17·5′E	FM	167
Tenement	Wrex	SJ3139	52°56·9′	3°1·2′W	X	126
Tenement Fm	Cumbr	SD5196	54°21·7′	2°44·8′W	FM	97
Tenement Fm	Staffs	SK0746	53°0·9′	1°53·3′W	FM	119,128
Tenements Fm	Herts	TL1003	51°43·1′	0°24·1′W	FM	166
Ten End	N Yks	SD8487	54°16·9′	2°14·3′W	X	98
Tenfoot Br	Oxon	SU3599	51°41·6′	1°29·2′W	X	164
Tenga	Arg & Bt	NM5145	56°32·1′	6°2·5′W	X	47,48
Tengore Fm	Somer	ST4427	51°2·6′	2°47·5′W	FM	193
Tenley Fm	N Yks	SD8655	53°59·7′	2°12·4′W	FM	103
Tenments, The	D & G	NX7851	54°50·6′	3°53·6′W	X	84
Ten Mile Bank	Norf	TL6096	52°32·5′	0°22·0′E	T	143
Tennacott	Devon	SS5327	51°1·7′	4°5·4′W	X	180
Tennacott Fm	Devon	SS4624	50°59·9′	4°11·3′W	FM	180,190
Tennant Canal	Nth Pt Talb	SS7093	51°37·5′	3°52·3′W	W	170
Tennant Gill	N Yks	SD8869	54°7·2′	2°10·6′W	W	98
Tennant Gill	N Yks	SD8869	54°7·2′	2°10·6′W	X	98
Tennaton	Devon	SX7455	50°23·1′	3°46·0′W	X	202
Tennersfield	Heref	SO4522	51°53·9′	2°47·6′W	X	161
Tenningshook Wood	Surrey	TQ0945	51°11·9′	0°26·0′W	F	187
Tenniscourt	Orkney	ND4678	58°41·4′	2°55·4′W	X	7
Tennis Plantn	Norf	TL7193	52°30·7′	0°31·6′E	F	143
Tennox	N Ayr	NS3052	55°44·2′	4°42·0′W	X	63
Tennyson Down	I of W	SZ3285	50°40·1′	1°32·4′W	X	196
Tennyson's Monument	I of W	SZ3285	50°40·1′	1°32·4′W	X	196
Tennyson Trail	I of W	SZ3785	50°40·0′	1°28·2′W	X	196
Ten-o'-Clock Barn	Durham	NZ3930	54°40·1′	1°23·3′W	X	93
Tenpenny Brook	Essex	TM0721	51°51·2′	1°0·7′E	W	168,169
Tenpenny Fm	Essex	TM0721	51°51·2′	1°0·7′E	FM	168,169
Ten Rides	Glos	SO9602	51°43·2′	2°3·1′W	X	163
Ten Rood	Moray	NJ3945	57°29·7′	3°0·6′W	X	28
Tenshillingland	S Ayr	NS4316	55°25·0′	4°28·4′W	X	70
Tenston	Orkney	HY2716	59°1·8′	3°15·8′W	T	6
Tenterden	Kent	TQ8833	51°4·2′	0°41·4′E	T	189
Tenterden Ho	Herts	TL1303	51°43·1′	0°21·5′W	X	166
Tenterden Sewer	Kent	TQ9232	51°3·5′	0°44·8′E	W	189
Tenter Hill	N Yks	SE6894	54°20·5′	0°56·8′W	X	94,100
Tenterhill	Staffs	SK0467	53°12·2′	1°56·0′W	X	119
Tent Lodge	Cumbr	SD3197	54°22·1′	3°3·3′W	X	96,97
Tents Muir	Fife	NO4922	56°23·5′	2°49·1′W	F	54,59
Tentsmuir Point Nature Reserve	Fife	NO5028	56°26·7′	2°48·2′W	X	54,59
Tentsmuir Sands	Fife	NO5025	56°25·1′	2°48·2′W	X	54,59
Tentworth	W Susx	SU8524	51°0·8′	0°46·9′W	X	197
Ten Wood	Cambs	TL6655	52°10·3′	0°26·1′E	F	154
Teppermoor	Northum	NY8671	55°2·2′	2°12·7′W	X	87
Terally	D & G	NX1240	54°43·4′	4°54·7′W	X	82
Terally Bay	D & G	NX1241	54°44·0′	4°54·8′W	W	82
Terally Point	D & G	NX1240	54°43·4′	4°54·7′W	X	82
Terchick Burn	Moray	NJ1664	57°39·7′	3°24·0′W	W	28
Tercrosset	Cumbr	NY5768	55°0·5′	2°39·9′W	X	86
Tererran	D & G	NX7592	55°12·6′	3°57·4′W	X	78
Tererran Hill	D & G	NX7692	55°12·7′	3°56·5′W	H	78
Terets, The	Warw	SP1871	52°20·4′	1°43·7′W	X	139
Terfyn	Conwy	SH9177	53°17·0′	3°37·7′W	T	116
Terfyn	Gwyn	SH5961	53°7·9′	4°6·0′W	T	114,115
Ter Hill	Devon	SX6470	50°31·1′	3°54·7′W	X	202
Terhill	Somer	ST1732	51°5·1′	3°10·7′W	T	181
Terley	Devon	SS9104	50°49·8′	3°32·5′W	X	192
Terling	Essex	TL7715	51°48·6′	0°34·5′E	T	167
Terling Hall	Essex	TL7713	51°47·5′	0°34·4′E	X	167
Terlingham	Kent	TR2138	51°6·1′	1°9·8′E	X	179,189
Terling Place	Essex	TL7714	51°48·0′	0°34·4′E	X	167
Termitt's Fm	Essex	TL7913	51°47·4′	0°36·1′E	FM	167
Ternemny	Moray	NJ5552	57°33·6′	2°44·7′W	X	29
Tern Fm	Wrekin	SJ6216	52°44·7′	2°33·4′W	FM	127
Ternhill	Shrops	SJ6332	52°53·3′	2°32·6′W	T	127
Teroy Fort	D & G	NX0964	54°56·3′	4°58·5′W	X	82
Teroy Fort (Broch)	D & G	NX0964	54°56·3′	4°58·5′W	A	82
Terpersie Castle	Aberd	NJ5420	57°16·4′	2°45·3′W	A	37
Terrace Fm	Dorset	ST8022	51°0·1′	2°16·7′W	FM	183
Terrace Fm	Lancs	SD5158	54°1·2′	2°44·5′W	FM	102
Terrace Gill	Brad	SE1048	53°55·9′	1°50·4′W	X	104
Terrace Hill	Wilts	SU2364	51°22·7′	1°39·8′W	X	174
Terrace Hills	Leic	SK7932	52°53·0′	0°49·2′W	X	129
Terrace Hills	Leic	SK8032	52°53·0′	0°48·3′W	X	130
Terrace Hills Fm	Leic	SK7931	52°52·5′	0°49·2′W	FM	129
Terraces, The	Wilts	ST9132	51°5·5′	2°7·3′W	X	184
Terrace, The	Shrops	SJ7506	52°39·3′	2°21·8′W	X	127
Terras	Corn	SW9353	50°20·7′	4°54·2′W	T	200,204
Terraughtie	D & G	NX9375	55°3·7′	3°40·1′W	X	84
Terregles	D & G	NX9377	55°4·8′	3°40·1′W	T	84
Terregles Bank	D & G	NX9376	55°4·3′	3°40·1′W	X	84
Terreglestown	D & G	NX9476	55°4·3′	3°39·2′W	X	84
Terrel Hays	Derby	SK2734	52°54·4′	1°35·5′W	X	128
Terret, The	Derby	SK0371	53°14·4′	1°56·9′W	X	119
Terrible Down	E Susx	TQ4915	50°55·1′	0°7·6′E	T	199
Terrick	Bucks	SP8308	51°46·1′	0°47·4′W	T	165
Terrick Fm	Shrops	SJ5442	52°58·6′	2°40·7′W	FM	117
Terrick Hall (Hotel)	Shrops	SJ5442	52°58·6′	2°40·7′W	X	117
Terrick Ho	Bucks	SP8308	51°46·1′	0°47·4′W	X	165
Terriemore Fm	Highld	NH9737	57°25·0′	3°42·4′W	FM	27
Terriers	Bucks	SU8794	51°38·5′	0°44·2′W	T	175
Terrier's End	Bucks	SP9109	51°46·6′	0°40·5′W	X	165
Terrier's Fm	Essex	TL6232	51°58·0′	0°21·9′E	FM	167
Terrill, The	Wrekin	SJ6419	52°46·3′	2°31·6′W	X	127
Terrington	N Yks	SE6770	54°7·5′	0°58·1′W	T	100
Terrington Ct	Norf	TF5320	52°45·6′	0°16·5′E	X	131
Terrington Land Fm	Cambs	TF3402	52°36·2′	0°0·9′W	FM	142
Terrington Marsh	Norf	TF5423	52°47·2′	0°17·4′E	X	131
Terrington Moor	N Yks	SE6871	54°8·1′	0°57·1′W	X	100
Terrington St Clement	Norf	TF5419	52°45·0′	0°17·3′E	T	131
Terrington St John	Norf	TF5314	52°42·4′	0°16·3′E	T	131
Terrona	D & G	NY3787	55°10·6′	2°58·9′W	X	79
Terrona Burn	D & G	NY3888	55°11·2′	2°58·0′W	W	79
Terrona Hill	D & G	NY3886	55°10·1′	2°58·0′W	H	79
Terry Bank	Cumbr	SD5982	54°14·2′	2°37·3′W	H	97
Terrybank Tarn	Cumbr	SD5982	54°14·2′	2°37·3′W	W	97
Terry Booth Fm	Lincs	TF1951	53°2·8′	0°13·1′W	FM	122
Terryfield	Aberd	NK0453	57°34·3′	1°55·5′W	X	30
Terry Hill	Fife	NT2087	56°4·4′	3°16·7′W	H	66
Terry Hill	Somer	ST7153	51°16·8′	2°24·6′W	H	183
Terryhorn	Aberd	NJ4640	57°27·1′	2°53·5′W	X	28,29
Terry Lug	Leeds	SE4042	53°52·6′	1°23·1′W	X	105
Terry's Cross	W Susx	TQ2314	50°55·0′	0°14·6′W	X	198
Terry's Green	Warw	SP1073	52°21·5′	1°50·8′W	T	139
Terry's Lodge Fm	Kent	TQ5960	51°19·2′	0°17·3′E	FM	177,188
Tersets	Aberd	NO7798	57°4·6′	2°22·3′W	X	38,45
Terstan	Hants	SU3536	51°7·6′	1°29·6′W	X	185
Tertowie Ho	Aberd	NJ8210	57°11·1′	2°17·4′W	X	38
Tervieside	Moray	NJ2330	57°21·5′	3°16·3′W	X	36
Tervine	Arg & Bt	NN0826	56°23·5′	5°6·2′W	X	50
Terwick Common	W Susx	SU8124	51°0·8′	0°50·3′W	T	197
Testaquoy	Orkney	HY4325	59°6·8′	2°59·2′W	X	5,6
Testbourne	Hants	SU4446	51°12·9′	1°21·8′W	X	185
Testcombe	Hants	SU3839	51°9·2′	1°27·0′W	X	185
Testerton Hall	Norf	TF9326	52°48·0′	0°52·2′E	X	132
Teston	Kent	TQ7053	51°15·3′	0°26·6′E	T	188
Test Way	Hants	SU3658	51°19·4′	1°28·6′W	X	174
Test Way	Hants	SU3840	51°9·7′	1°27·0′W	X	185
Testwood	Hants	SU3514	50°55·7′	1°29·7′W	T	196
Testwood Ho	Hants	SU3415	50°56·2′	1°30·6′W	X	196
Testwood Lakes	Hants	SU3415	50°56·2′	1°30·6′W	W	196
Tetbury	Glos	ST8993	51°38·4′	2°9·1′W	T	163,173
Tetbury Upton	Glos	ST8895	51°39·5′	2°10·0′W	T	162
Tetchill	Shrops	SJ3932	52°53·2′	2°54·0′W	T	126
Tetchill Moor	Shrops	SJ3931	52°52·6′	2°54·0′W	X	126
Tetchwick	Bucks	SP6718	51°51·6′	1°1·2′W	T	164,165
Tetcott	Devon	SX3396	50°44·6′	4°21·6′W	T	190
Tetcott Manor	Devon	SX3396	50°44·6′	4°21·6′W	A	190
Tetford	Lincs	TF3374	53°15·0′	0°0·0′E	T	122
Tetford Hill	Lincs	TF3275	53°15·6′	0°0·9′W	H	122
Tetherings	S Lanak	NS6743	55°40·0′	4°6·4′W	X	71
Tet Hill	Somer	ST2041	51°10·0′	3°8·3′W	X	182
Tet Hill	Suff	TM2948	52°5·2′	1°21·0′E	X	169
Tethyknowe	Pth & Kin	NT0195	56°8·5′	3°35·2′W	X	58
Tetley	N Lincs	SE7711	53°35·6′	0°49·8′W	T	112
Tetney	Lincs	TA3101	53°29·6′	0°1·1′W	T	113
Tetney Blow Wells	Lincs	TA3100	53°29·1′	0°1·1′W	W	113
Tetney Haven	Lincs	TA3604	53°31·1′	0°3·5′E	W	113
Tetney High Sands	Lincs	TA3604	53°31·1′	0°3·5′E	X	113
Tetney Lock	Lincs	TA3402	53°30·1′	0°1·6′E	T	113
Tetstill	Shrops	SO6671	52°20·4′	2°29·5′W	X	138
Tetsworth	Oxon	SP6802	51°43·0′	1°0·5′W	T	164,165
Tetsworth Common	Oxon	SP6802	51°43·0′	1°0·5′W	X	164,165
Tettaridge Barton	Devon	SX3586	50°39·3′	4°19·7′W	X	201
Tettenhall	Wolv	SJ8800	52°36·1′	2°10·2′W	T	127,139
Tettenhall Wood	Wolv	SO8799	52°35·6′	2°11·1′W	T	139
Tetton Fm	Somer	ST2130	51°4·1′	3°7·3′W	FM	182
Tetton Hall	Ches	SJ7163	53°10·0′	2°25·6′W	X	118
Tetton Ho	Somer	ST2030	51°4·1′	3°8·1′W	A	182
Tetwell	Devon	SX6849	50°19·8′	3°50·9′W	X	202
Tetworth	Cambs	TL2153	52°9·9′	0°13·5′W	T	153
Tetworth Hall	Win & Maid	SU9369	51°25·0′	0°39·4′W	X	175
Teuchan	Aberd	NK0839	57°26·7′	1°51·5′W	X	30
Teuchar	Aberd	NJ8049	57°32·1′	2°19·6′W	X	29,30
Teuchar Lodge	Aberd	NJ7949	57°32·1′	2°20·6′W	X	29,30
Teuchathaugh	Aberd	NJ7530	57°21·8′	2°24·5′W	X	29
Teuchat Muir	Pth & Kin	NO2642	56°34·1′	3°11·8′W	X	53
Teuchats	Fife	NO4007	56°15·4′	2°57·7′W	X	59
Teversal	Notts	SK4861	53°8·9′	1°16·5′W	T	120
Teversham	Cambs	TL4958	52°12·2′	0°11·2′E	T	154
Teversham Fen	Cambs	TL5058	52°12·2′	0°12·1′E	X	154
Teviot Bank	Scot Bord	NT5518	55°27·5′	2°42·3′W	X	80
Teviotdale	Scot Bord	NT5822	55°29·7′	2°39·5′W	X	73,74
Teviotdale	Scot Bord	NT6123	55°30·2′	2°36·6′W	X	74
Teviothead	Scot Bord	NT4005	55°20·4′	2°56·3′W	X	79
Tewel	Aberd	NO8285	56°57·6′	2°17·3′W	X	45
Tewes Fm	Essex	TL6433	51°58·5′	0°23·7′E	FM	167
Tewet Tarn	Cumbr	NY3023	54°36·1′	3°4·6′W	W	90
Tewfaitegreen	Cumbr	NY3861	54°56·6′	2°57·6′W	X	85
Tewfit Moss	Cumbr	NY1946	54°48·4′	3°15·2′W	X	85
Tewfitt Mires	Cumbr	NY8113	54°31·0′	2°17·2′W	X	91,92
Tewgoed	V of Glam	SS9976	51°28·6′	3°29·5′W	X	170
Tewin	Herts	TL2714	51°48·8′	0°9·1′W	T	166
Tewin Bury Fm	Herts	TL2614	51°48·9′	0°9·9′W	FM	166
Tewin Hill Fm	Herts	TL2715	51°49·4′	0°9·0′W	FM	166
Tewin Mill Ho	Herts	TL2713	51°48·3′	0°9·1′W	X	166
Tewin Water	Herts	TL2514	51°48·9′	0°10·8′W	X	166
Tewin Wood	Herts	TL2716	51°49·9′	0°9·0′W	T	166
Tewit Bogs	N Yks	SE0155	53°59·7′	1°58·7′W	W	104
Tewit Castle	N Yks	NZ3107	54°27·7′	1°30·9′W	X	93
Tewitfield	Lancs	SD5273	54°9·3′	2°43·7′W	T	97
Tewit Fm	N Yks	SE1163	54°4·0′	1°49·5′W	FM	99
Tewit Hall	N Yks	SD7169	54°7·2′	2°26·2′W	X	98
Tewit Hall Fm	Lancs	SD8152	53°58·1′	2°17·0′W	FM	103
Tewit How	Cumbr	NY1412	54°30·0′	3°19·3′W	X	89
Tewit Nest	N Yks	SE4759	54°1·7′	1°16·5′W	X	105
Tewitt Hall Fm	Brad	SE0138	53°50·5′	1°58·7′W	FM	104
Tewitt Ho	Brad	SE1240	53°51·6′	1°48·6′W	X	104
Tewkesbury	Glos	SO8932	51°59·4′	2°9·2′W	T	150
Tewkesbury Park	Glos	SO8831	51°58·9′	2°10·1′W	X	150
Tew's End	Northnts	SP7246	52°6·7′	0°56·5′W	X	152
Tewsgill Hill	S Lanak	NS9623	55°29·6′	3°38·3′W	H	72
Texa	Arg & Bt	NR3943	55°36·9′	6°8·3′W	X	60
Teybrook Fm	Essex	TL8924	51°53·2′	0°45·2′E	FM	168
Teycross Fm	Essex	TL8826	51°54·3′	0°44·4′E	FM	168
Teynham	Kent	TQ9562	51°19·6′	0°48·3′E	T	178
Teynham Court	Kent	TQ9663	51°20·2′	0°49·2′E	X	178
Teynham Level	Kent	TQ9764	51°20·7′	0°50·1′E	X	178
Teynham Street	Kent	TQ9663	51°20·2′	0°49·2′E	T	178
Teyrdan Fm	Conwy	SH8776	53°16·4′	3°41·3′W	FM	116
Tg Newydd Fm	Gwyn	SH2926	52°48·5′	4°31·8′W	FM	123
Thacker Barn	Derby	SK4440	52°57·6′	1°20·3′W	X	129
Thackham's Fm	Hants	SU7158	51°19·2′	0°58·5′W	FM	175,186
Thackley	Brad	SE1738	53°50·5′	1°44·1′W	T	104
Thackley End	Brad	SE1738	53°50·5′	1°44·1′W	T	104
Thackmire	Cumbr	NY3539	54°44·8′	3°0·2′W	X	90
Thack Moor	Cumbr	NY6146	54°48·7′	2°36·0′W	H	86
Thack Moor	Cumbr	NY6435	54°42·8′	2°33·1′W	X	91
Thack Side Ho	N Yks	NZ8101	54°24·1′	0°44·7′W	X	94
Thackson's Well Fm	Lincs	SK8341	52°57·8′	0°45·4′W	FM	130
Thackthwaite	Cumbr	NY1423	54°35·9′	3°19·5′W	T	89
Thackthwaite	Cumbr	NY4225	54°37·3′	2°53·5′W	X	90
Thackthwaite Hall	Cumbr	NY2643	54°46·8′	3°8·6′W	X	85
Thackwood	Cumbr	NY3843	54°46·9′	2°57·4′W	X	85
Thackwood	Cumbr	NY4346	54°48·6′	2°52·8′W	X	85
Thacmyers	Durham	NZ4137	54°43·8′	1°21·4′W	X	93
Thain	Moray	NJ2422	57°17·2′	3°15·2′W	X	36
Thainstone Ho	Aberd	NJ7618	57°15·4′	2°23·4′W	X	38
Thakeham	W Susx	TQ1017	50°56·7′	0°25·7′W	T	198
Thakeham Place	W Susx	TQ1117	50°56·7′	0°24·8′W	X	198
Thalta Sgeir	N Eil	NB1442	58°16·7′	6°52·3′W	X	13
Thamarasaigh	N Eil	NG2194	57°51·2′	6°41·7′W	X	14
Thame	Oxon	SP7005	51°44·6′	0°58·8′W	T	165
Thame Br	Oxon	SP7006	51°45·1′	0°58·8′W	X	165
Thame Park	Oxon	SP7103	51°43·5′	0°57·9′W	X	165
Thames Barrier	Newham	TQ4179	51°29·8′	0°2·3′E	X	177
Thames Ditton	Surrey	TQ1567	51°23·6′	0°20·4′W	T	176
Thames Haven	Thurr	TQ7481	51°30·3′	0°30·8′E	X	178
Thames Head	Glos	ST9899	51°41·6′	2°1·3′W	T	163
Thamesmead	Bexley	TQ4780	51°30·2′	0°7·5′E	T	177
Thames Path	Gren	TQ3978	51°29·3′	0°0·5′E	X	177
Thames Side Fm	Oxon	SP3801	51°42·6′	1°26·6′W	FM	164
Thamna Sgeir	N Eil	HW6230	59°5·7′	6°8·8′W	X	8
Thanckes Lake	Corn	SX4355	50°22·7′	4°12·1′W	W	201
Thane Croft	Fife	NO2316	56°20·1′	3°14·3′W	X	58
Thanes Fm	Dorset	ST8624	51°1·1′	2°11·6′W	FM	183
Thanet Well	Cumbr	NY3935	54°42·6′	2°56·4′W	X	90
Thanington	Kent	TR1356	51°16·0′	1°3·6′E	T	179
Thankerton	S Lanak	NS9738	55°37·7′	3°37·7′W	T	72
Thankerton Ho	N Lanak	NS7560	55°49·3′	3°59·3′W	X	64
Thankerton Moor	S Lanak	NS9538	55°37·7′	3°39·6′W	X	72
Tharbies	Herts	TL4616	51°49·6′	0°7·5′E	X	167
Tharston	Norf	TM1894	52°30·2′	1°13·1′E	T	134
Thatcham	W Berks	SU5167	51°24·2′	1°15·6′W	T	174
Thatcham Ponds Fm	Bucks	SP6540	52°3·5′	1°2·7′W	FM	152
Thatcham Sta	W Berks	SU5266	51°23·7′	1°14·8′W	X	174
Thatch Close	Heref	SO5319	51°52·3′	2°40·6′W	X	162
Thatched House Lodge	Rich	TQ1971	51°25·8′	0°16·9′W	X	176
Thatcher Ho	Lancs	SD4539	53°50·9′	2°49·7′W	X	102
Thatcher Rock	Torbay	SX9462	50°27·1′	3°29·2′W	X	202
Thatcher's Fm	Essex	TL6508	51°45·0′	0°23·8′E	FM	167
Thatchers Wood	Shrops	SO7090	52°30·7′	2°26·1′W	F	138
Thatch Ling	N Yks	SE1253	53°58·6′	1°48·6′W	X	104
Thatchmire Fm	Red & Cl	NZ7114	54°31·2′	0°53·8′W	FM	94
Thatch Mires	Durham	NY8837	54°43·9′	2°10·8′W	X	91,92
Thatchmoor Fm	Staffs	SK1510	52°41·5′	1°46·3′W	FM	128
Thatharsal	N Eil	NF7735	57°17·7′	7°21·3′W	H	22
Thatto Heath	St Hel	SJ5093	53°26·1′	2°44·7′W	T	108
Thatton	Devon	SS4713	50°54·0′	4°10·2′W	X	180
Thaxted	Essex	TL6131	51°57·5′	0°21·0′E	T	167
Theakston	N Yks	SE3085	54°15·8′	1°31·9′W	T	99
Theakston Grange	N Yks	SE3186	54°16·4′	1°31·0′W	X	99
Thealby	N Lincs	SE8917	53°38·8′	0°38·8′W	T	112
The Alders	Staffs	SK1904	52°38·2′	1°42·8′W	T	139
Theale	Devon	SX4578	50°35·1′	4°11·0′W	X	201
Theale	Somer	ST4646	51°12·9′	2°46·0′W	T	182
Theale	W Berks	SU6471	51°26·3′	1°4·4′W	T	175
Theale Fm	W Susx	TQ1231	51°4·3′	0°23·7′W	FM	187
Theamarabhagh	N Eil	NF6360	57°30·5′	7°37·2′W	W	22
The Arms	Norf	TL8798	52°33·1′	0°45·9′E	T	144
Thearnais	N Eil	NF6263	57°32·1′	7°38·5′W	X	22
Thearne	E Yorks	TA0736	53°48·8′	0°22·1′W	T	107
Theats Fm	Somer	ST2727	51°2·5′	3°2·1′W	FM	193
The Bage	Heref	SO2943	52°5·1′	3°1·8′W	T	148,161
The Bank	Ches	SJ8457	53°6·8′	2°13·9′W	T	118
The Banks	Stock	SJ9787	53°23·0′	2°2·3′W	T	109
The Banks	Wilts	SU0179	51°30·8′	1°58·7′W	T	173
The Barony	Ches	SJ6553	53°4·6′	2°30·9′W	T	118
The Barton	Wilts	SU0779	51°30·8′	1°53·6′W	T	173
The Batch	S Glos	ST6672	51°27·0′	2°29·0′W	T	172
The Beeches	Glos	SP0302	51°43·2′	1°57·0′W	T	163
The Bell	Wigan	SD5405	53°32·6′	2°41·2′W	T	108
The Bents	Staffs	SK0234	52°54·4′	1°57·8′W	T	128
Theberton	Suff	TM4365	52°14·0′	1°33·9′E	T	156
Thebertonhall Fm	Suff	TM4366	52°14·5′	1°34·0′E	FM	156
Theberton Ho	Suff	TM4465	52°14·0′	1°34·8′E	X	156
Theberton Woods	Suff	TM4265	52°14·0′	1°33·1′E	F	156
The Black Mountain	Carm	SN6817	51°50·4′	3°54·6′W	H	159
The Blythe	Staffs	SK0428	52°51·2′	1°56·0′W	T	128
The Borough	Sthwk	TQ3279	51°29·9′	0°5·5′W	T	176,177
The Bourne	Surrey	SU8444	51°11·6′	0°47·5′W	T	186
The Bourne	Worcs	SO9856	52°12·4′	2°1·4′W	T	150
The Brand	Leic	SK5313	52°43·0′	1°12·5′W	T	129
The Bratch	Staffs	SO8693	52°32·3′	2°12·0′W	T	139
The Brents	Kent	TR0161	51°19·0′	0°53·5′E	T	178
The Bridge	Dorset	ST7813	50°55·2′	2°18·4′W	T	194
The Brook	Suff	TM0876	52°20·8′	1°3·6′E	T	144
The Brushes	Derby	SK3775	53°16·5′	1°26·3′W	T	119
The Bryn	Monm	SO3309	51°46·8′	2°57·9′W	T	161
The Burf	Worcs	SO8167	52°18·3′	2°16·3′W	T	138,150
The Burn	Aberd	NO5971	56°50·0′	2°39·9′W	X	44
The Burn	Shetld	HU2943	60°10·5′	1°28·1′W	X	4
The Butts	Hants	SU7138	51°8·4′	0°58·7′W	T	186
The Buzzard's	Heref	SO4262	52°15·2′	2°50·6′W	X	137
The Camp	Glos	SO9109	51°47·0′	2°7·4′W	T	163
The Camp	Herts	TL1606	51°44·7′	0°18·8′W	T	166

The Cape	Warw	SP2765	52°17·2′	1°35·9′W	T	151
The Chart	Kent	TQ4652	51°15·1′	0°5·9′E	T	188
The Chequer	Wrex	SJ4940	52°57·5′	2°45·1′W	T	117
The Chuckery	Wals	SP0298	52°35·0′	1°57·8′W	T	139
The City	Bucks	SU7896	51°39·7′	0°51·9′W	T	165
The, Close	W Susx	SU8504	50°50·0′	0°47·2′W	T	197
The Colony	Oxon	SP3437	52°2·1′	1°29·9′W	T	151
The Common	Bath & NE Somer	ST6263	51°22·1′	2°32·4′W	T	172
The Common	Bucks	SP7731	51°58·6′	0°52·3′W	T	152,165
The Common	Dorset	ST7810	50°53·6′	2°18·4′W	T	194
The Common	Shrops	SJ6727	52°50·6′	2°29·0′W	T	127
The Common	Wilts	ST8764	51°22·7′	2°10·8′W	T	173
The Common	Wilts	SU0284	51°33·5′	1°57·9′W	T	173
The Common	W Susx	TQ1631	51°4·2′	0°20·3′W	T	187
The Corner	Kent	TQ7041	51°8·8′	0°26·2′E	T	188
The Cot	Monm	ST5099	51°41·5′	2°43·0′W	T	162
The Cross Hands	Leic	SK3302	52°37·1′	1°30·4′W	T	140
The Cwm	Monm	ST4592	51°37·7′	2°47·3′W	T	171,172
Thedden Copse	Hants	SU6939	51°9·0′	1°0·4′W	F	186
Thedden Grange	Hants	SU6839	51°9·0′	1°1·3′W	X	185,186
Theddingworth	Leic	SP6685	52°27·8′	1°1·3′W	T	141
Theddingworth Lodge	Leic	SP6586	52°28·3′	1°2·2′W	X	141
Theddlethorpe All Saints	Lincs	TF4688	53°22·4′	0°12·1′E	T	113,122
Theddlethorpe St Helen	Lincs	TF4788	53°22·3′	0°13·0′E	T	113,122
The Delves	Wals	SP0196	52°33·9′	1°58·7′W	T	139
The Den	N Ayr	NS3251	55°43·7′	4°40·1′W	T	63
The Dene	Hants	SU3853	51°16·7′	1°26·9′W	T	185
The Down	Kent	TQ6735	51°5·6′	0°23·5′E	T	188
The Downs	Surrey	SU9535	51°6·6′	0°38·2′W	T	186
The Dudd	Shetld	HU3356	60°17·5′	1°23·7′W	H	2,3
The Elgar Centre	Worcs	SO8055	52°11·8′	2°17·2′W	X	150
The Fall	Leeds	SE3025	53°43·5′	1°32·3′W	T	104
The Fence	Glos	SO5405	51°44·7′	2°39·6′W	T	162
The Flat	Glos	SO7515	51°50·2′	2°21·4′W	T	162
The Flourish	Derby	SK4238	52°56·5′	1°22·1′W	T	129
The Folly	Herts	TL1614	51°49·0′	0°18·6′W	T	166
The Folly	S Glos	ST7473	51°27·6′	2°22·1′W	T	172
The Ford	Bucks	SP7703	51°43·5′	0°52·7′W	X	165
The Fording	Heref	SO6525	51°55·6′	2°30·1′W	T	162
The Forstal	Kent	TR0439	51°7·1′	0°55·3′E	T	179,189
The Forties	Derby	SK3419	52°46·3′	1°29·4′W	T	128
The Four Alls	Shrops	SJ6831	52°52·8′	2°28·1′W	T	127
The Fox	Wilts	SU1087	51°35·1′	1°50·9′W	T	173
The Frenches	Hants	SU3022	51°0·0′	1°34·0′W	T	185
The Frythe	Herts	TL2214	51°48·9′	0°13·4′W	T	166
The Gibb	Wilts	ST8379	51°30·8′	2°14·3′W	T	173
The Grange	Fife	NO5115	56°19·7′	2°47·1′W	X	59
The Grange	N Yks	SE5796	54°21·6′	1°6·9′W	T	100
The Green	Barns	SE2402	53°31·1′	1°37·9′W	T	110
The Green	Beds	TL0017	51°50·8′	0°32·5′W	T	166
The Green	Cambs	TL2966	52°16·8′	0°6·1′W	T	153
The Green	Cumbr	SD1784	54°14·9′	3°16·0′W	T	96
The Green	Cumbr	SD3676	54°10·8′	2°58·4′W	T	96,97
The Green	Essex	TL7719	51°50·7′	0°34·6′E	T	167
The Green	Mil Key	SP8743	52°4·9′	0°43·4′W	T	152
The Green	Norf	TG0701	52°34·3′	1°3·7′E	T	144
The Green	Norf	TG0735	52°52·6′	1°5·0′E	T	133
The Green	Northnts	SP7942	52°4·5′	0°50·4′W	T	152
The Green	Oxon	SP4728	51°57·1′	1°18·6′W	T	164
The Green	Warw	SP2159	52°14·0′	1°41·2′W	T	151
The Grove	Durham	NZ0950	54°50·9′	1°51·2′W	T	88
The Grove	Herts	TQ0898	51°40·0′	0°25·9′W	T	166,176
The Gutter	Derby	SK3647	53°1·4′	1°27·4′W	T	119,128
The Gutter	Worcs	SO9577	52°23·7′	2°4·0′W	T	139
The Hacket	S Glos	ST6589	51°36·2′	2°29·9′W	T	162,172
The Hague	Tames	SK0094	53°26·8′	1°59·6′W	T	110
The Hallands	N Lincs	TA0920	53°40·1′	0°20·6′W	T	107,112
The Handfords	Staffs	SJ8722	52°48·0′	2°11·2′W	T	127
The Harbour	Kent	TQ8148	51°12·4′	0°35·9′E	T	188
The Haven	W Susx	TQ0830	51°3·8′	0°27·1′W	T	187
The Headland	Hartpl	NZ5234	54°42·1′	1°11·2′W	T	93
The Heath	Norf	TF9329	52°49·7′	0°52·3′E	T	132
The Heath	Norf	TG1821	52°44·8′	1°14·2′E	T	133,134
The Heath	Norf	TG2321	52°44·7′	1°18·6′E	T	133,134
The Heath	Staffs	SK0834	52°54·4′	1°52·5′W	T	128
The Heath	Suff	TM1236	51°59·1′	1°5·6′E	T	155,169
The Hem	Shrops	SJ7205	52°38·8′	2°24·4′W	T	127
The Hendre	Monm	SO4514	51°49·6′	2°47·5′W	T	161
The Herberts	V of Glam	SS9972	51°26·5′	3°26·8′W	T	170
The Hermitage	Cambs	TL3974	52°21·0′	0°2·9′E	T	142,143
The High	Essex	TL4410	51°46·4′	0°5·6′E	T	167
The Highlands	E Susx	TQ7309	50°51·5′	0°27·9′E	T	199
The Hill	Cumbr	SD1783	54°14·4′	3°16·0′W	T	96
The Hollands	Staffs	SJ9159	53°7·9′	2°7·7′W	T	118
The Holmes	C of Derb	SK3536	52°55·5′	1°28·4′W	T	128
The Holt	Wok	SU8078	51°29·9′	0°51·6′W	T	175
The Hook	Worcs	SO8240	52°3·7′	2°15·4′W	T	150
The Howe	Cumbr	SD4588	54°17·3′	2°50·3′W	T	97
The Humbers	Wrekin	SJ6914	52°43·6′	2°27·1′W	T	127
The Hyde	Brent	TQ2188	51°34·9′	0°14·8′W	T	176
The Hyde	Worcs	SO8340	52°3·7′	2°14·5′W	T	150
The Hythe	Essex	TM0124	51°52·9′	0°55·6′E	T	168
The Inch	C of Edin	NT2770	55°55·3′	3°9·6′W	T	66
Theisteamuil	N Eil	NF7948	57°24·8′	7°20·3′W	X	22
The Itchen Bridge	Hants	SU4311	50°54·0′	1°22·9′W	X	196
The Knap	V of Glam	ST0966	51°23·4′	3°18·1′W	T	171
The Knapp	Heref	SO6554	52°11·2′	2°30·3′W	T	149
The Knapp	S Glos	ST6591	51°37·2′	2°29·9′W	T	162,172
The Knaps	Angus	NO1965	56°46·4′	3°19·1′W	X	43
The Knowle	Sand	SO9687	52°29·1′	2°3·1′W	T	139
The Laches	Staffs	SJ9207	52°39·9′	2°6·7′W	T	127,139
The Lake	D & G	NX6847	54°48·3′	4°2·8′W	T	83,84
The Lakes	Worcs	SO7775	52°22·6′	2°19·9′W	T	138
The Lawe	S Tyne	NZ3667	55°0·0′	1°25·8′W	T	88
The Lawns	E Yorks	TA0933	53°47·2′	0°20·5′W	T	107
Thelbridge	Devon	SS5718	50°56·9′	4°1·8′W	X	180
Thelbridge Barton	Devon	SS7812	50°53·9′	3°43·7′W	X	180
Thelbridge Br	Devon	SS8104	50°49·6′	3°41·0′W	X	191
Thelbridge Cross	Devon	SS7911	50°53·4′	3°42·8′W	X	191
Thelbridge Hall Fm	Devon	SS7913	50°54·5′	3°42·9′W	FM	180
The Leacon	Kent	TQ9833	51°3·9′	0°50·0′E	T	189
The Lee	Bucks	SP9004	51°43·9′	0°41·4′W	T	165
The Lees	Kent	TR0050	51°13·1′	0°52·2′E	T	189
The Leigh	Glos	SO8726	51°56·2′	2°11·0′W	T	162
The Leys	Staffs	SK2004	52°38·2′	1°41·9′W	T	139
The Ling	Norf	TM3098	52°32·1′	1°23·9′E	T	134
The Lings	Norf	TG0306	52°37·1′	1°0·3′E	T	144
The Linleys	Wilts	ST8768	51°24·9′	2°10·8′W	T	173
The Linns	Stir	NN8101	56°11·5′	3°54·6′W	X	57
Thellow Heath Fm	Ches	SJ6478	53°18·1′	2°32·0′W	FM	118
Thelnetham	Suff	TM0178	52°22·0′	0°57·5′E	T	144
Thelsford Brook	Warw	SP2758	52°13·4′	1°35·9′W	W	151
Thelsford Fm	Warw	SP2758	52°13·4′	1°35·9′W	FM	151
The Lunt	Wolv	SO9696	52°33·9′	2°3·1′W	T	139
Thelveton	Norf	TM1681	52°23·3′	1°10·9′E	T	144,156
Thelwall	Warr	SJ6487	53°23·0′	2°32·1′W	T	109
Thelwall Grange	Warr	SJ6586	53°22·4′	2°31·2′W	X	109
Thelwall Heys	Warr	SJ6486	53°22·4′	2°32·1′W	X	109
Thelwall Viaduct	Warr	SJ6688	53°23·5′	2°30·3′W	X	109
The Marsh	Ches	SJ8462	53°9·5′	2°14·0′W	T	118
The Marsh	Shrops	SJ6925	52°49·5′	2°27·2′W	T	127
The Marsh	Staffs	SJ8426	52°50·1′	2°13·8′W	T	127
The Marsh	Suff	TM0877	52°21·3′	1°3·7′E	T	144
The Marsh	Suff	TM1176	52°20·7′	1°6·3′E	T	144
Themelthorpe	Norf	TG0524	52°46·7′	1°2·8′E	T	133
The Middles	Durham	NZ2051	54°51·4′	1°40·9′W	T	88
The Midland	Pemb	SM9329	51°55·5′	5°0·2′W	X	157,158
The Mint	Hants	SU7828	51°3·0′	0°52·8′W	T	186,197
The Moor	Flint	SJ3266	53°11·4′	3°0·7′W	T	117
The Moor	Kent	TQ7529	51°2·2′	0°30·2′E	T	188,199
The Mount	Dorset	SY4896	50°45·9′	2°43·9′W	T	193
The Mount	Hants	SU4361	51°21·0′	1°22·6′W	T	174
The Mount	Read	SU7272	51°26·8′	0°57·4′W	T	175
The Murray	S Lanak	NS6353	55°45·3′	4°10·5′W	T	64
The Mythe	Glos	SO8934	52°0·5′	2°9·2′W	T	150
The Nant	Wrex	SJ2850	53°2·8′	3°4·0′W	T	117
Thenford	Northnts	SP5141	52°4·1′	1°15·0′W	T	151
Thenford Grounds Fm	Northnts	SP5143	52°5·2′	1°14·9′W	FM	151
Thenford Hill	Northnts	SP5243	52°5·2′	1°14·1′W	X	151
The Node	Herts	TL2120	51°52·2′	0°14·2′W	T	166
The Nook	Shrops	SJ5630	52°52·2′	2°38·8′W	T	126
The Nook	Shrops	SJ6724	52°49·0′	2°29·0′W	T	127
The North	Monm	SO5206	51°45·3′	2°41·3′W	T	162
Theobalds	E Susx	TQ3220	50°58·1′	0°6·8′W	X	198
Theobald's Green	Wilts	SU0269	51°25·4′	1°57·9′W	T	173
Theobalds Manor	Herts	TL3300	51°41·2′	0°4·2′W	X	166
Theobalds Park	Herts	TL3400	51°41·2′	0°3·3′W	X	166
The Oval	Bath & NE Somer	ST7363	51°22·2′	2°22·9′W	T	172
The Park	Glos	SO9421	51°53·5′	2°4·8′W	T	163
The Parks	Donc	SE6409	53°34·7′	1°1·6′W	T	111
The Platt	Oxon	SP5901	51°42·5′	1°8·4′W	T	164
The Pleasance	E Loth	NT6675	55°58·3′	2°32·2′W	X	67
The Pludds	Glos	SO6116	51°50·7′	2°33·6′W	T	162
The Point	Devon	SX9980	50°36·9′	3°25·3′W	T	192
The Pole of Itlaw	Aberd	NJ6756	57°35·8′	2°32·7′W	T	29
The Port of Felixstowe	Suff	TM2833	51°57·1′	1°19·5′E	T	169
The Quarry	Glos	ST7399	51°41·6′	2°23·0′W	T	162
The Quarry	Shrops	SJ4812	52°42·4′	2°45·8′W	T	126
The Quarter	Kent	TQ8832	51°3·6′	0°41·4′E	T	189
The Quarter	Kent	TQ8844	51°10·1′	0°41·7′E	T	189
The Rampings	Worcs	SO8534	52°0·5′	2°12·7′W	T	150
Therfield	Herts	TL3337	52°1·2′	0°3·3′W	T	154
Therfield Heath	Herts	TL3339	52°2·2′	0°3·3′W	X	154
The Rhôs	Powys	SO1731	51°58·5′	3°12·1′W	X	161
The Rhydd	Heref	SO4633	51°59·8′	2°46·8′W	T	149,161
The Ridge	Wilts	ST8768	51°24·9′	2°10·8′W	T	173
The Ridges	Wok	SU8063	51°21·9′	0°50·7′W	T	175,186
The Ridgeway	Herts	TL2803	51°42·9′	0°8·4′W	T	166
The Riding	Northum	NY9366	54°59·6′	2°6·1′W	T	87
The Rise	Win & Maid	SU9467	51°23·9′	0°38·5′W	T	175
The Rock	Wrekin	SJ6809	52°40·9′	2°28·0′W	T	127
The Rocks	Kent	TQ7056	51°16·9′	0°26·7′E	T	178,188
The Rocks	S Glos	ST7284	51°33·5′	2°23·8′W	T	172
The Rookery	Herts	TQ1094	51°38·3′	0°24·2′W	T	166,176
The Rookery	Staffs	SJ8555	53°5·8′	2°13·0′W	T	118
The Row	Lancs	SD4775	54°10·3′	2°48·3′W	T	97
The Rowe	Staffs	SJ8238	52°56·6′	2°15·7′W	T	127
The Ryde	Herts	TL2309	51°46·2′	0°12·6′W	T	166
The Sale	Staffs	SK1514	52°43·6′	1°46·3′W	T	128
The Sands	Surrey	SU8846	51°12·6′	0°44·0′W	T	186
The Scarr	Glos	SO7227	51°56·7′	2°24·0′W	T	162
The Shoe	Wilts	ST8074	51°28·1′	2°16·9′W	T	173
The Shruggs	Staffs	SJ9430	52°52·3′	2°4·9′W	T	127
The Slade	W Berks	SU5369	51°25·3′	1°13·9′W	T	174
The Spa	Wilts	ST9162	51°21·7′	2°7·4′W	T	173
The Spring	Warw	SP2873	52°21·5′	1°34·9′W	T	140
The Square	Torf	ST2796	51°39·7′	3°2·9′W	T	171
The Stocks	Kent	TQ9127	51°0·9′	0°43·8′E	T	189
The Stocks	Wilts	ST9260	51°20·6′	2°6·5′W	T	173
The Straits	Dudley	SO9092	52°31·8′	2°8·4′W	T	139
The Straits	Hants	SU7838	51°8·4′	0°52·7′W	T	186
The Strand	Wilts	ST9159	51°20·0′	2°7·4′W	T	173
The Swillett	Herts	TQ0295	51°38·9′	0°31·1′W	T	166,176
The Sydnall	Shrops	SJ6830	52°52·2′	2°28·1′W	T	127
Thetford	Lincs	TF1114	52°43·0′	0°21·0′W	T	130
Thetford	Norf	TL8783	52°25·0′	0°45·4′E	T	144
Thetford Farmhouse	Norf	TM2595	52°30·6′	1°19·3′E	X	134
Thetford Heath	Suff	TL8579	52°22·9′	0°43·5′E	X	144
Thetford Lodge Fm	Suff	TL8285	52°26·2′	0°41·1′E	FM	144
Thetford Warren	Norf	TL8383	52°25·1′	0°41·9′E	F	144
Thetford Warren Lodge	Norf	TL8384	52°25·6′	0°41·9′E	A	144
The Thickets	Somer	ST2533	51°5·7′	3°3·9′W	F	182
The Thrift	Herts	TL3139	52°2·3′	0°5·0′W	T	153
The Throat	Wok	SU8066	51°23·5′	0°50·6′W	T	175
Thethwaite	Cumbr	NY3744	54°47·5′	2°58·4′W	X	85
The Toft	Staffs	SJ9018	52°45·8′	2°8·5′W	T	127
The Towans	Corn	SW5538	50°11·7′	5°25·6′W	T	203
The Town	I Scilly	SV8715	49°57·4′	6°21·5′W	T	203
The Twittocks	Glos	SO8837	52°2·1′	2°10·1′W	T	150
The Tynings	Glos	SO9219	51°52·4′	2°6·6′W	T	163
The Valley	Ches	SJ6955	53°5·7′	2°27·4′W	T	118
The Valley	Kent	TQ9553	51°14·8′	0°48·0′E	T	189
The Valley	Leic	SK7119	52°46·1′	0°56·5′W	T	129
The Village	Dudley	SO8989	52°30·2′	2°9·3′W	T	139
The Village	Newp	ST3490	51°36·5′	2°56·8′W	T	171
The Warren	Kent	TQ9944	51°9·9′	0°51·2′E	T	189
The Warren	Wilts	SU2465	51°23·2′	1°38·9′W	T	174
The Waterwheel	Shrops	SJ3602	52°37·0′	2°56·3′W	T	126
The Wells	Surrey	TQ1960	51°19·8′	0°17·1′W	T	176,187
The Wern	Wrex	SJ2750	53°2·8′	3°4·9′W	T	117
The Willows	NE Lincs	TA2409	53°34·0′	0°7·2′W	T	113
The Wood	Shrops	SJ3022	52°47·7′	3°1·9′W	T	126
The Wood	Shrops	SJ4528	52°51·0′	2°48·6′W	T	126
The Woodlands	Leic	SP6596	52°33·7′	1°2·1′W	T	141
The Woodlands	Lincs	TF5462	53°8·2′	0°18·5′E	X	122
The Woodlands	Suff	TM0540	52°1·5′	0°59·7′E	T	155
The Woodlands	Suff	TM1637	51°59·6′	1°9·2′E	T	169
The Woods	Sand	SP0095	52°33·4′	1°59·6′W	T	139
The World of Robin Hood	Notts	SK6872	53°14·7′	0°58·4′W	X	120
The Wrangle	Bath & NE Somer	ST5456	51°18·3′	2°39·2′W	T	172,182
The Wrythe	Sutton	TQ2765	51°22·4′	0°10·1′W	T	176
The Wyke	Shrops	SJ7306	52°39·3′	2°23·5′W	T	127
Theydon Bois	Essex	TQ4599	51°40·5′	0°6·2′E	T	167,177
Theydon Garnon	Essex	TQ4799	51°40·5′	0°8·0′E	T	167,177
Theydon Hall	Essex	TQ4697	51°39·4′	0°7·0′E	X	167,177
Theydon Mount	Essex	TQ4999	51°40·4′	0°9·7′E	T	167,177
Thick Bank	Lancs	SD9044	53°53·8′	2°8·7′W	X	103
Thickbare Wood	Bucks	SP8033	51°59·6′	0°49·7′W	F	152,165
Thickbroom	Staffs	SK1303	52°37·7′	1°48·1′W	X	139
Thick Cleuch	S Lanak	NS9502	55°18·3′	3°38·8′W	X	78
Thick Cleuch Moss	S Lanak	NS9401	55°17·8′	3°39·7′W	X	78
Thickens Fm	Cambs	TL3691	52°30·2′	0°0·6′E	FM	142
Thicket Copse	Wilts	SU2170	51°25·9′	1°41·5′W	F	174
Thicket Mead	Bath & NE Somer	ST6655	51°17·8′	2°28·9′W	T	172,183
Thicket Priory	N Yks	SE6943	53°53·0′	0°56·6′W	X	105,106
Thickets Ho	Hants	SU5516	50°56·7′	1°12·6′W	X	185
Thicket Wood	Monm	ST4488	51°35·5′	2°48·1′W	F	171,172
Thick Hollins	Kirk	SE1010	53°35·4′	1°50·5′W	T	110
Thick Hollins Moor	Kirk	SE1109	53°34·9′	1°49·6′W	X	110
Thickley	Darl	NZ2224	54°36·9′	1°39·1′W	X	93
Thicknall Fm	Worcs	SO9079	52°24·8′	2°8·4′W	FM	139
Thickpenny Fm	N Yks	SE5356	54°0·1′	1°11·1′W	FM	105
Thickside	D & G	NT2002	55°18·6′	3°15·2′W	H	79
Thickside	Scot Bord	NT6820	55°28·6′	2°29·9′W	X	74
Thicks, The	Norf	TG3400	52°33·1′	1°27·5′E	F	134
Thicks, The	Suff	TM3650	52°6·1′	1°27·2′E	F	156
Thickthorn	Somer	ST3216	50°56·6′	2°57·7′W	X	193
Thickthorn Down	Dorset	ST9612	50°54·7′	2°3·0′W	X	195
Thickthorn Fm	Mil Key	SP9247	52°7·0′	0°39·0′W	FM	152
Thickthorn Fm	Oxon	SP4446	52°6·9′	1°21·0′W	FM	151
Thickthorn Fm	Suff	TM2171	52°17·8′	1°14·9′E	FM	156
Thickthorn Fm	Wilts	SU0477	51°29·7′	1°56·2′W	FM	173
Thickthorn Hall	Norf	TG1705	52°36·2′	1°12·7′E	T	134
Thickthorn Wood	Mil Key	SP9147	52°7·1′	0°39·9′W	F	152
Thickwithers	Ches	SJ9570	53°13·9′	2°4·1′W	X	118
Thick Withins	Staffs	SK0466	53°11·7′	1°56·0′W	X	119
Thickwood	Wilts	ST8272	51°27·0′	2°15·2′W	T	173
Thiefhole Fm	N Yks	SE3988	54°17·4′	1°23·6′W	FM	99
Thieflinn Knowe	D & G	NY2191	55°12·7′	3°14·1′W	H	79
Thief Sand	Lincs	TF5433	52°52·6′	0°17·7′E	X	131
Thiefsbush Hill	Moray	NJ3125	57°18·9′	3°8·3′W	H	37
Thiefs Cave	Pth & Kin	NN8230	56°27·1′	3°54·4′W	X	52
Thief's Hill	Moray	NJ3654	57°34·6′	3°3·7′W	H	28
Thief's Hill	W Dunb	NS4779	55°59·0′	4°26·7′W	X	64
Thief's Hole	Shetld	HU4227	60°1·8′	1°14·3′W	X	4
Thief's House	Shetld	HU3413	59°54·3′	1°23·0′W	X	4
Thiefside Cottages	Cumbr	NY4841	54°45·9′	2°48·1′W	X	86
Thief Sike	Scot Bord	NY4993	55°14·0′	2°47·7′W	W	79
Thiefsike Head	Scot Bord	NY4894	55°14·5′	2°48·6′W	X	79
Thief's Road	Scot Bord	NT1630	55°33·6′	3°19·5′W	X	72
Thiernswood Hall	N Yks	SE0199	54°23·4′	1°58·7′W	X	98
Thieveley Pike	Lancs	SD8727	53°44·6′	2°11·4′W	H	103
Thieveley Pike (Beacon)	Lancs	SD8727	53°44·6′	2°11·4′W	A	103
Thieveley Scout	Lancs	SD8727	53°44·6′	2°11·4′W	H	103
Thieves Dikes	N Yks	SE9792	54°19·1′	0°30·1′W	A	94,101
Thieves Gill	N Yks	SE2095	54°21·3′	1°41·1′W	W	99
Thieves Gill Fm	N Yks	SE2773	54°9·4′	1°34·8′W	FM	99
Thieves Holm	Orkney	HY4614	59°0·8′	2°55·9′W	X	6
Thieves Knowes	Shetld	HU3867	60°23·4′	1°18·1′W	X	2,3
Thieves, The	D & G	NX4071	55°0·7′	4°29·7′W	X	77
Thieves, The (Standing Stones)	D & G	NX4071	55°0·7′	4°29·7′W	A	77
Thieves Wood	Notts	SK5456	53°6·1′	1°11·2′W	F	120
Thimbleby	Lincs	TF2369	53°12·5′	0°9·1′W	T	122
Thimbleby	N Yks	SE4495	54°21·2′	1°19·0′W	T	99
Thimbleby Grange	N Yks	SE4494	54°20·6′	1°19·0′W	X	99
Thimbleby Hall	N Yks	SE4596	54°21·7′	1°18·0′W	X	99
Thimbleby Hill	Durham	NY9937	54°43·9′	2°0·5′W	X	92
Thimbleby Ho	Lincs	TF2570	53°13·0′	0°7·3′W	X	122
Thimbleby Ho	Lincs	TF4132	52°52·2′	0°6·1′E	X	131
Thimbleby Moor	N Yks	SE4695	54°21·1′	1°17·1′W	X	100
Thimble End	Birm	SP1394	52°32·9′	1°48·1′W	T	139
Thimble Hall	Lancs	SD6367	54°6·1′	2°33·5′W	X	97
Thimble Stones	Brad	SE1045	53°54·3′	1°50·5′W	X	104
Thinacre Muir	S Lanak	NS7349	55°43·3′	4°0·9′W	X	64
Thinacres	S Lanak	NS7350	55°43·9′	4°0·9′W	X	64
Thinford	Durham	NZ2834	54°42·3′	1°33·5′W	T	93
Thinfords	Aberd	NJ8557	57°36·4′	2°14·6′W	X	30
Thing-hill Court	Heref	SO5644	52°5·8′	2°38·1′W	X	149
Thing-hill Grange	Heref	SO5545	52°6·3′	2°39·0′W	X	149
Thingley	Wilts	ST8970	51°26·0′	2°9·1′W	T	173
Thingwall	Wirral	SJ2784	53°21·1′	3°5·4′W	T	108
Thinhope Burn	Northum	NY6553	54°52·5′	2°32·3′W	W	86
Thin Oaks Wood	N Yks	SE6786	54°16·2′	0°57·9′W	F	94,100
Thinwood Fm	Corn	SX2398	50°45·5′	4°30·2′W	FM	190
Third	D & G	NY0687	55°10·4′	3°28·1′W	X	78

Third	Scot Bord	NT6135	55°36·7'	2°36·7'W	X	74
Third	Stir	NS4486	56°2·7'	4°29·8'W	X	57
Third Hill	Pth & Kin	NO0106	56°14·4'	3°35·4'W	X	58
Third Hill Fm	Lincs	TF0468	53°12·2'	0°26·2'W	FM	121
Third House Fm	Northum	NZ2888	55°11·4'	1°33·2'W	FM	81
Third Inchna Burn	Stir	NS8499	56°10·4'	3°51·7'W	W	58
Thirdpart	E Ayr	NS5221	55°27·9'	4°20·0'W	X	70
Thirdpart	Fife	NO5806	56°14·9'	2°40·2'W	X	59
Thirdpart	N Ayr	NS1849	55°42·3'	4°53·4'W	T	63
Thirdpart	N Ayr	NS1965	55°50·9'	4°53·0'W	X	63
Thirdpart	N Ayr	NS2650	55°43·0'	4°45·8'W	X	63
Thirdpart Hall	Renf	NS3961	55°49·2'	4°33·8'W	X	63
Thirds	Stir	NS5893	56°6·8'	4°16·6'W	X	57
Third Slip	Suff	TL7977	52°21·9'	0°38·1'E	F	144
Thirds Wood	Bucks	SU7994	51°38·6'	0°51·1'W	F	175
Thirkelow	Derby	SK0468	53°12·8'	1°56·0'W	X	119
Thirkleby Barugh	N Yks	SE4777	54°11·4'	1°16·4'W	X	100
Thirkleby Beck	N Yks	SE4677	54°11·4'	1°17·3'W	W	100
Thirkleby Manor	N Yks	SE9168	54°6·2'	0°36·1'W	X	101
Thirkleby Warren	N Yks	SE9170	54°7·3'	0°36·0'W	X	101
Thirkleby Wold	N Yks	SE9367	54°5·7'	0°34·3'W	X	101
Thirlby	N Yks	SE4884	54°15·2'	1°15·4'W	T	100
Thirle Door	Highld	ND4072	58°38·2'	3°1·5'W	X	7,12
Thirlestane	Scot Bord	NT5647	55°43·1'	2°41·6'W	T	73
Thirlestane	Scot Bord	NT8028	55°33·0'	2°18·6'W	X	74
Thirlestane Castle	Scot Bord	NT5347	55°43·1'	2°44·5'W	A	73
Thirlestane Hill	Scot Bord	NT2816	55°26·2'	3°7·8'W	H	79
Thirlestane Hill	Scot Bord	NT8029	55°33·5'	2°18·6'W	H	74
Thirlestanehope	Scot Bord	NT2816	55°26·2'	3°7·8'W	X	79
Thirlestone Burn	Scot Bord	NT2519	55°27·8'	3°10·7'W	W	79
Thirley Cote Fm	N Yks	SE9795	54°20·7'	0°30·0'W	FM	94,101
Thirlings	Northum	NT9532	55°35·1'	2°4·3'W	X	74,75
Thirlmere	Cumbr	NY3116	54°32·3'	3°3·6'W	W	90
Thirl Moor	Northum	NT8008	55°22·2'	2°18·5'W	H	80
Thirlsey	N Yks	SE9791	54°18·6'	0°30·1'W	X	94,101
Thirlspot	Cumbr	NY3117	54°32·9'	3°3·6'W	X	90
Thirl Stane	D & G	NX9956	54°53·6'	3°34·1'W	X	84
Thirlstane	Scot Bord	NT8028	55°33·0'	2°18·6'W	X	74
Thirl, The	Highld	ND1872	58°38·0'	3°24·3'W	X	7,12
Thirlwall Castle	Northum	NY6566	54°59·5'	2°32·4'W	A	86
Thirlwall Common (North Side)	Northum	NY6769	55°1·1'	2°30·5'W	X	86,87
Thirlwall Common (South Side)	Northum	NY6364	54°58·4'	2°34·3'W	X	86
Thirn	N Yks	SE2185	54°15·9'	1°40·2'W	T	99
Thirn Grange	N Yks	SE2186	54°16·4'	1°40·2'W	X	99
Thirn Moor Fm	N Yks	SE2285	54°15·9'	1°39·3'W	FM	99
Thirsk	N Yks	SE4282	54°14·2'	1°20·9'W	T	99
Thirsk Lodge	N Yks	SE4183	54°14·7'	1°21·8'W	X	99
Thirsk Sta	N Yks	SE4081	54°13·6'	1°22·8'W	X	99
Thirstane Hill	D & G	NS8709	55°22·0'	3°46·5'W	X	71,78
Thirsting Castle Lodge	N Yks	SE1585	54°15·9'	1°45·8'W	X	99
Thirstlet Creek	Essex	TL9407	51°43·9'	0°49·0'E	W	168
Thirstone	S Lanak	NS8926	55°31·2'	3°45·1'W	X	71,72
Thirston New Hos	Northum	NZ1899	55°17·3'	1°42·6'W	X	81
Thirteen Hundred Down	Wilts	ST8949	51°14·6'	2°9·1'W	X	184
Thirties Fm	Cambs	TL4497	52°33·3'	0°7·8'E	FM	142,143
Thirties Fm	Cambs	TL4595	52°32·2'	0°8·7'E	FM	143
Thirtleby	E Yorks	TA1734	53°47·6'	0°13·0'W	T	107
Thirtover	W Berks	SU5070	51°25·8'	1°16·5'W	X	174
Thirty Acre Barn	Surrey	TQ1956	51°17·7'	0°17·2'W	X	187
Thirty Acres	Lancs	SD7141	53°52·1'	2°26·0'W	X	103
Thistlebottom	Cumbr	NY2839	54°44·7'	3°6·7'W	X	89,90
Thistle Brook	Bucks	SP8717	51°50·9'	0°43·8'W	W	165
Thistlebrook Fm	Bucks	SP8717	51°50·9'	0°43·8'W	FM	165
Thistle Flat	Moray	NJ1556	57°35·4'	3°24·9'W	X	28
Thistleford Br	Shrops	SJ5428	52°51·1'	2°40·6'W	X	126
Thistle Green	Durham	NY8428	54°39·1'	2°14·5'W	X	91,92
Thistle Grove	N Yks	NZ8507	54°27·3'	0°40·9'W	X	94
Thistle Head	I of M	SC2383	54°13·0'	4°42·5'W	H	95
Thistle Hill	Cambs	TL1868	52°18·1'	0°15·8'W	X	153
Thistle Hill	Dorset	SY3594	50°44·8'	2°54·9'W	X	193
Thistle Hill	Lancs	SD6962	54°3·4'	2°28·0'W	X	98
Thistle Hill	N Yks	SE3555	53°59·6'	1°27·6'W	X	104
Thistle Hill	N Yks	SE4780	54°13·1'	1°16·3'W	X	100
Thistle Hill Fm	N Yks	SE3555	53°59·6'	1°27·6'W	FM	104
Thistle Hill Plantn	Cambs	TL2255	52°11·0'	0°12·5'W	F	153
Thistlemark Hill	D & G	NX7695	55°14·3'	3°56·6'W	H	78
Thistlemoor Wood	Peterb	TF1400	52°35·4'	0°18·6'W	F	142
Thistle Rigg Fm	Northum	NY9167	55°0·1'	2°8·0'W	FM	87
Thistleton	Cumbr	NY0904	54°25·6'	3°23·7'W	X	89
Thistleton	Lancs	SD4037	53°49·8'	2°54·3'W	T	102
Thistleton	Northum	NU0108	55°22·2'	1°58·6'W	X	81
Thistleton	Rut	SK9117	52°44·8'	0°38·7'W	T	130
Thistleton Brook	Lancs	SD4038	53°50·3'	2°54·3'W	W	102
Thistleton Lodge	Lancs	SD4037	53°49·8'	2°54·3'W	X	102
Thistlewood	Cumbr	NY3943	54°46·9'	2°56·5'W	A	85
Thistlewood Fm	Durham	NZ0738	54°44·5'	1°53·1'W	FM	92
Thistleworth Fm	W Susx	TQ1518	50°57·2'	0°21·4'W	FM	198
Thistleycrook	Aberd	NJ6402	57°6·7'	2°35·2'W	X	37
Thistleyfield Covert	Staffs	SJ7721	52°47·4'	2°20·1'W	F	127
Thistley Green	Essex	TL7019	51°50·8'	0°28·5'E	T	167
Thistley Green	Suff	TL6776	52°21·6'	0°27·6'E	T	143
Thistley Hall	Essex	TL5531	51°57·6'	0°15·8'E	X	167
Thistleyhaugh	Northum	NZ1398	55°16·8'	1°47·3'W	X	81
Thistley Hill	Glos	SP1443	52°5·3'	1°47·3'W	X	151
Thistley Hillock	Aberd	NK0452	57°33·7'	1°55·5'W	X	30
Thistley Vale	Herts	TL3429	51°56·8'	0°2·6'W	X	166
Thistly Coppice	Notts	SK6649	53°2·3'	1°0·5'W	F	129
Thistlyhill Fm	Aberd	NJ9123	57°18·1'	2°8·5'W	FM	38
Thixendale	N Yks	SE8461	54°2·5'	0°42·6'W	T	100
Thixendale Grange	N Yks	SE8160	54°2·0'	0°45·4'W	X	100
Thixendale Wold	N Yks	SE8460	54°2·0'	0°42·6'W	X	100
Thoby Priory	Essex	TQ6298	51°39·7'	0°20·9'E	X	167,177
Thockrington	Northum	NY9579	55°6·6'	2°4·3'W	T	87
Thockrington Crags	Northum	NY9579	55°6·6'	2°4·3'W	X	87
Tholmair	N Eil	NF8342	57°21·7'	7°15·9'W	X	22
Tholomas Drove	Cambs	TF4006	52°38·2'	0°4·5'E	T	142,143
Tholt-e-Will Glen	I of M	SC3789	54°16·5'	4°29·8'W	X	95
Tholt-e-Will Plantation	I of M	SC3789	54°16·5'	4°29·8'W	F	95
Tholthorpe	N Yks	SE4766	54°5·5'	1°16·5'W	T	100
Tholthorpe Moor	N Yks	SE4867	54°6·0'	1°15·5'W	X	100
Thomanean	Pth & Kin	NO0904	56°13·4'	3°27·6'W	X	58
Thomarston	E Ayr	NS5820	55°27·5'	4°14·3'W	X	71
Thomas Carlyle's Birthplace	D & G	NY1974	55°3·5'	3°15·7'W	X	85
Thomas Chapel	Pemb	SN1008	51°44·6'	4°44·7'W	T	158
Thomas Close	Cumbr	NY4340	54°45·4'	2°52·7'W	T	85
Thomas Hall	Devon	SX9194	50°44·4'	3°32·3'W	X	192
Thomas Hill	Rut	SK8414	52°43·3'	0°45·0'W	X	130
Thomason Foss	N Yks	NZ8202	54°24·6'	0°43·8'W	W	94
Thomason's Hollow	Derby	SK0992	53°25·7'	1°51·5'W	X	110
Thomas's Covert	Suff	TM3472	52°18·0'	1°26·3'E	F	156
Thomaston	S Ayr	NS2409	55°20·9'	4°46·1'W	X	70,76
Thomastown	Aberd	NJ5736	57°25·0'	2°42·5'W	X	29
Thomastown	Aberd	NJ7243	57°28·8'	2°27·6'W	X	29
Thomastown	Rho Cyn Taf	ST0087	51°34·6'	3°26·2'W	T	170
Thomas Wood	Heref	SO5918	51°51·8'	2°35·3'W	F	162
Thomley Hall Fm	Oxon	SP6308	51°46·3'	1°4·8'W	FM	164,165
Thompson	Norf	TL9196	52°31·9'	0°49·4'E	T	144
Thompson	Staffs	SJ9463	53°10·1'	2°5·0'W	X	118
Thompson Common	Norf	TL9395	52°31·3'	0°51·1'E	F	144
Thompson Fold	Cumbr	SD5680	54°13·1'	2°40·1'W	X	97
Thompsonhall Plantn	Norf	TL9295	52°31·4'	0°50·2'E	F	144
Thompson Hole Ridge	N Yks	SE0365	54°5·1'	1°56·8'W	X	98
Thompson's Bottom	Lincs	TF0155	53°5·2'	0°29·1'W	X	121
Thompson's Holme	Cumbr	SD3997	54°22·1'	2°55·9'W	X	96,97
Thompson's Rigg	N Yks	SE8792	54°19·2'	0°39·3'W	X	94,101
Thompson Water	Norf	TL9194	52°30·8'	0°49·3'E	W	144
Thomsford	Fife	NO3904	56°13·7'	2°58·6'W	X	59
Thomshill	Moray	NJ2157	57°36·0'	3°18·8'W	T	28
Thomson's Hill	Orkney	ND3295	58°50·5'	3°10·2'W	X	7
Thomsons Walls	Northum	NT8630	55°34·1'	2°12·9'W	X	74
Thong	Kent	TQ6770	51°24·5'	0°24·5'E	T	177,178
Thonglands	Shrops	SO5489	52°30·1'	2°40·3'W	X	137,138
Thongsbridge	Kirk	SE1509	53°34·9'	1°46·0'W	T	110
Thongsleigh	Devon	SS9011	50°53·5'	3°33·5'W	X	192
Thonock Grove	Lincs	SK8391	53°24·8'	0°44·7'W	X	112
Thonock Lane Fm	Lincs	SK8292	53°25·3'	0°45·6'W	FM	112
Thoragill Beck Ho	N Yks	SD8870	54°7·8'	2°10·6'W	X	98
Thoralby	N Yks	SE0086	54°16·4'	1°59·6'W	T	98
Thoralby Common	N Yks	SD9484	54°15·3'	2°5·1'W	X	98
Thoralby Hall	E Yorks	SE7758	54°1·0'	0°49·1'W	X	105,106
Thoraldby Fm	N Yks	NZ4907	54°27·6'	1°14·2'W	FM	93
Thorax	Aberd	NJ5854	57°34·7'	2°41·7'W	X	29
Thoresby	Notts	SK6371	53°14·2'	1°3·0'W	T	120
Thoresby Br	Lincs	TF3399	53°28·5'	0°0·7'E	X	113
Thoresby Home Fm	Notts	SK6471	53°14·2'	1°2·1'W	FM	120
Thoresby Lake	Notts	SK6270	53°13·6'	1°3·9'W	W	120
Thoresby Park	Notts	SK6471	53°14·2'	1°2·1'W	X	120
Thoresthorpe	Lincs	TF4577	53°16·4'	0°10·9'E	T	122
Thoresway	Lincs	TF1696	53°27·1'	0°14·8'W	T	113
Thoresway Grange	Lincs	TF1697	53°27·7'	0°14·8'W	X	113
Thoresway North Wold	Lincs	TF1597	53°27·7'	0°15·7'W	X	113
Thorganby	Lincs	TF2097	53°27·6'	0°11·1'W	T	113
Thorganby	N Yks	SE6941	53°51·9'	0°56·6'W	T	105,106
Thorganby Hall	Lincs	TF2098	53°28·1'	0°11·1'W	X	113
Thorganby Lodge	N Yks	SE6740	53°51·4'	0°58·5'W	X	105,106
Thorgill	N Yks	SE7096	54°21·5'	0°54·9'W	T	94,100
Thorgill Fm	N Yks	SE7196	54°21·5'	0°54·0'W	FM	94,100
Thorgill Ho	N Yks	SE7195	54°21·0'	0°54·0'W	X	94,100
Thorington	Suff	TM4274	52°18·9'	1°33·4'E	T	156
Thorington Hall	Suff	TM0135	51°58·8'	0°56·0'E	X	155
Thorington Hall	Suff	TM1441	52°1·8'	1°7·6'E	X	169
Thorington Hall	Suff	TM4273	52°18·3'	1°33·4'E	X	156
Thorington Hall Fm	Suff	TM4173	52°18·4'	1°32·5'E	FM	156
Thorington Street	Suff	TM0135	51°58·8'	0°56·0'E	T	155
Thorlby	N Yks	SD9652	53°58·1'	2°3·2'W	T	103
Thorlby Ho	N Yks	SD9753	53°58·6'	2°2·3'W	X	103
Thorley	Herts	TL4719	51°51·2'	0°8·5'E	T	167
Thorley	I of W	SZ3788	50°41·7'	1°28·2'W	T	196
Thorley Brook	I of W	SZ3888	50°41·7'	1°27·3'W	W	196
Thorley Houses	Herts	TL4620	51°51·8'	0°7·6'E	T	167
Thorley Street	Herts	TL4819	51°51·2'	0°9·3'E	T	167
Thorley Street	I of W	SZ3788	50°41·7'	1°28·2'W	T	196
Thorley Wash	Herts	TL4818	51°50·7'	0°9·3'E	X	167
Thorlieshope	Scot Bord	NY5796	55°15·6'	2°40·2'W	X	80
Thorlieshope Heights	Scot Bord	NY5895	55°15·1'	2°39·2'W	H	80
Thorlieshope Pike	Scot Bord	NY5896	55°15·6'	2°39·2'W	H	80
Thormanby	N Yks	SE4974	54°9·8'	1°14·6'W	T	100
Thormanby Hill Fm	N Yks	SE4974	54°9·8'	1°14·6'W	FM	100
Thormanby Stud	Suff	TL7372	52°19·4'	0°32·7'E	X	155
Thorn	Beds	TL0024	51°54·6'	0°32·4'W	X	166
Thorn	Devon	SX4385	50°38·8'	4°12·9'W	X	201
Thorn	Devon	SX5449	50°19·6'	4°2·7'W	X	201
Thorn	Devon	SX6886	50°39·8'	3°51·7'W	T	191
Thorn	Devon	SX7285	50°39·3'	3°48·3'W	X	191
Thorn	Devon	SX8047	50°18·9'	3°40·8'W	X	202
Thorn	Devon	SX8649	50°20·0'	3°35·7'W	X	202
Thorn	D & G	NX7449	54°49·5'	3°57·3'W	X	83,84
Thorn	E Ayr	NS4444	55°40·1'	4°28·4'W	X	70
Thorn	Orkney	HY4846	59°18·1'	2°54·3'W	X	5
Thorn	Powys	SO2763	52°15·9'	3°3·8'W	T	137,148
Thorn	Pth & Kin	NN9223	56°23·5'	3°44·5'W	X	52,58
Thorn	Pth & Kin	NN9612	56°17·6'	3°40·4'W	X	58
Thorn	Pth & Kin	NO2247	56°36·8'	3°15·8'W	X	53
Thorn	S Lanak	NS8751	55°44·6'	3°47·6'W	X	65,72
Thorn	Worcs	SP0155	52°11·8'	1°58·7'W	X	150
Thornaby-on-Tees	Stock on T	NZ4516	54°32·5'	1°17·8'W	T	93
Thornaby Wood	Stock on T	NZ4415	54°31·9'	1°18·8'W	F	93
Thornage	Norf	TG0536	52°53·2'	1°3·2'E	T	133
Thornbank	Cumbr	NY0702	54°24·5'	3°25·6'W	X	89
Thornbank Fm	Staffs	SK0353	53°4·7'	1°56·9'W	FM	119
Thornbarrow	Cumbr	NY4734	54°42·1'	2°48·9'W	X	90
Thorn Barrow	Devon	SX4195	50°44·2'	4°14·8'W	A	190
Thornber	N Yks	SD6770	54°7·7'	2°29·9'W	X	98
Thornberry Hill Fm	Cambs	TL3551	52°8·7'	0°1·2'W	FM	154
Thornborough	Bucks	SP7433	51°59·7'	0°54·9'W	T	152,165
Thornborough	Leic	SK4215	52°44·1'	1°22·3'W	X	129
Thornborough	N Yks	SE2979	54°12·6'	1°32·9'W	T	99
Thornborough Br	Bucks	SP7233	51°59·7'	0°56·7'W	A	152,165
Thornborough Fm	Leic	SP5585	52°27·8'	1°11·0'W	FM	140
Thornborough Fm	N Yks	SE3890	54°18·5'	1°24·5'W	FM	99
Thornborough Mill	Bucks	SP7335	52°0·7'	0°55·8'W	X	152
Thornbridge Hall	Derby	SK1970	53°13·8'	1°42·5'W	X	119
Thornbroke	S Ayr	NS2908	55°20·4'	4°41·4'W	X	70,76
Thornbrough	Northum	NZ0064	54°58·5'	1°59·6'W	X	87
Thornbrough	N Yks	SE2299	54°23·4'	1°39·3'W	X	99
Thornbrough High Barns	Northum	NZ0165	54°59·0'	1°58·6'W	X	87
Thornbrough Ho	N Yks	SE4284	54°15·2'	1°20·9'W	X	99
Thornbrough Kiln Ho	Northum	NZ0165	54°59·0'	1°58·6'W	X	87
Thornburrow Hill	Northnts	SP6665	52°17·0'	1°1·5'W	X	152
Thornbury	Brad	SE1934	53°48·4'	1°42·3'W	T	104
Thornbury	Devon	SS4008	50°51·2'	4°16·0'W	T	190
Thornbury	Devon	SX7093	50°43·6'	3°50·1'W	X	191
Thornbury	Heref	SO6259	52°13·9'	2°33·0'W	T	149
Thornbury	Powys	SO2099	52°35·2'	3°10·5'W	X	137
Thornbury	S Glos	ST6490	51°36·7'	2°30·8'W	T	162,172
Thornbury Court	Heref	SO6160	52°14·4'	2°33·9'W	X	138,149
Thornbury Hall	Lincs	TF2712	52°41·7'	0°6·8'W	X	131,142
Thornbury Hill	Lincs	TF3569	53°12·3'	0°1·7'E	X	122
Thornbury Hill	Roth	SK5789	53°23·9'	1°8·2'W	X	111,120
Thornbush	Lancs	SD5964	54°4·5'	2°37·2'W	X	97
Thornbush	Pemb	SM9121	51°51·2'	5°1·7'W	X	157,158
Thornbush Fm	Suff	TM1258	52°11·0'	1°6·5'E	FM	155
Thornbush Hall	Suff	TM1145	52°4·0'	1°5·1'E	X	155,169
Thornby	Cumbr	NY2952	54°51·7'	3°5·9'W	T	85
Thornby	Northnts	SP6675	52°22·4'	1°1·4'W	T	141
Thornby End	Cumbr	NY2046	54°48·4'	3°14·3'W	X	85
Thornby Grange	Northnts	SP6574	52°21·8'	1°2·3'W	X	141
Thornby Villa	Cumbr	NY2852	54°51·7'	3°6·9'W	X	85
Thorncliff	Kirk	SE2113	53°37·0'	1°40·5'W	T	110
Thorncliffe	Staffs	SK0158	53°7·4'	1°58·7'W	T	119
Thorncliffe Hall	Tames	SK0096	53°27·9'	1°59·6'W	X	110
Thorncombe	Dorset	ST3703	50°49·6'	2°53·3'W	T	193
Thorncombe Barrow	Somer	ST1239	51°8·8'	3°15·1'W	A	181
Thorncombe Beacon	Dorset	SY4391	50°43·2'	2°48·1'W	X	193
Thorncombe Fm	Dorset	ST7300	50°48·2'	2°22·6'W	FM	194
Thorncombe Hill	Somer	ST1339	51°8·9'	3°14·2'W	H	181
Thorncombe Ho	Somer	ST1238	51°8·3'	3°15·1'W	X	181
Thorncombe Park	Surrey	TQ0042	51°10·3'	0°33·8'W	X	186
Thorncombe Street	Surrey	SU9942	51°10·3'	0°34·6'W	T	186
Thorn Corner	Devon	SS6805	50°50·0'	3°52·1'W	X	191
Thorncote Green	Beds	TL1547	52°6·8'	0°18·8'W	T	153
Thorn Cottage	Cumbr	NY5401	54°24·4'	2°42·1'W	X	90
Thorn Covert	Glos	ST8991	51°37·3'	2°9·1'W	F	163,173
Thorn Crag	Lancs	SD5957	54°0·7'	2°37·1'W	X	102
Thorncroft Fm	Lincs	SK9794	53°26·3'	0°32·0'W	FM	112
Thorn Cross	Devon	ST0321	50°59·0'	3°22·5'W	X	181
Thorncross	I of W	SZ4381	50°37·9'	1°23·1'W	T	196
Thorn Ct	Suff	TL8853	52°8·8'	0°45·3'E	X	155
Thorndale	Glos	SP0117	51°51·3'	1°58·7'W	X	163
Thorndale Plantn	Notts	SK6150	53°2·9'	1°5·0'W	F	120
Thorndale Shaft	N Yks	NZ7918	54°33·3'	0°46·3'W	X	94
Thorn Dene	Worcs	SP0155	52°11·8'	1°58·7'W	X	150
Thornden Fm	E Susx	TQ6716	50°55·4'	0°23·0'E	FM	199
Thornden Fm	Kent	TQ8646	51°11·2'	0°40·1'E	FM	189
Thornden Wood	Kent	TR1463	51°19·8'	1°4·7'E	F	179
Thorndon	Devon	SS3202	50°47·8'	4°22·7'W	X	190
Thorndon	Devon	SX4094	50°43·7'	4°15·6'W	X	190
Thorndon	Suff	TM1369	52°16·9'	1°7·8'E	T	156
Thorndon Cross	Devon	SX5393	50°43·3'	4°4·6'W	T	191
Thorndon Down	Devon	SX5293	50°43·3'	4°5·4'W	X	191
Thorndon Fm	Devon	SX5192	50°42·7'	4°6·3'W	FM	191
Thorndon Hall	Essex	TQ6191	51°35·9'	0°19·9'E	A	177
Thorndon Hill	Suff	TM1569	52°16·8'	1°9·5'E	X	156
Thorndon Ho	Devon	SX4094	50°43·7'	4°15·6'W	X	190
Thorndon Park	Essex	TQ6191	51°35·9'	0°19·9'E	X	177
Thorndykes	Scot Bord	NT6148	55°43·7'	2°36·8'W	X	74
Thorne	Corn	SS2104	50°48·7'	4°32·1'W	T	190
Thorne	Corn	SS2510	50°52·0'	4°28·8'W	X	190
Thorne	Corn	SS2604	50°48·8'	4°27·8'W	X	190
Thorne	Corn	SX2799	50°46·1'	4°26·8'W	X	190
Thorne	Devon	SS3808	50°51·2'	4°17·7'W	X	190
Thorne	Devon	SS4714	50°54·5'	4°10·2'W	X	180
Thorne	Devon	SS7300	50°47·4'	3°47·7'W	X	191
Thorne	Devon	SS7403	50°49·0'	3°46·9'W	X	191
Thorne	Devon	SX3988	50°40·4'	4°16·3'W	X	190
Thorne	Donc	SE6813	53°36·8'	0°57·9'W	T	111
Thorne	Pemb	SR9496	51°37·7'	4°58·2'W	X	158
Thorne	Somer	SS8438	51°8·0'	3°39·1'W	X	181
Thorne	Somer	SS9138	51°8·1'	3°33·1'W	X	181
Thorne Barton	Bucks	SP9704	51°43·8'	0°35·3'W	X	165
Thorne Coffin	Somer	ST5217	50°57·3'	2°40·6'W	T	183
Thornecroft	Devon	SX7766	50°29·1'	3°43·7'W	X	202
Thorne Cross	Devon	SX7493	50°43·6'	3°46·7'W	X	191
Thorn Edge	Lancs	SD9239	53°51·1'	2°6·9'W	X	103
Thorne Fm	Devon	SS3005	50°49·4'	4°24·4'W	FM	190
Thorne Fm	Devon	SS4219	50°57·2'	4°14·6'W	FM	180,190
Thorne Fm	Devon	SS7024	51°0·3'	3°50·8'W	FM	180
Thorne Fm	Devon	SS7304	50°49·5'	3°47·8'W	FM	191
Thorne Fm	Devon	SS8911	50°53·5'	3°34·3'W	FM	192
Thorne Fm	Devon	SS8919	50°57·8'	3°34·5'W	FM	181
Thorne Fm	Devon	SX6890	50°41·9'	3°51·8'W	FM	191
Thorne Fm	E Susx	TQ7110	50°52·1'	0°26·2'E	FM	199
Thorne Fm	Kent	TR3364	51°19·9'	1°21·1'E	FM	179
Thorne Fm	Pemb	SN0607	51°43·9'	4°48·2'W	FM	158
Thornehillhead	Devon	SS4116	50°55·5'	4°15·4'W	T	180,190
Thornemead	Somer	SS8038	51°8·0'	3°42·5'W	X	181
Thornemoor	Devon	SS3005	50°49·4'	4°24·4'W	X	190
Thorne Moor	Devon	SS4116	50°55·5'	4°15·4'W	X	180,190
Thorne Moor	Devon	SX3889	50°40·9'	4°17·2'W	T	190
Thorne Moors or Waste	Donc	SE7215	53°37·8'	0°54·3'W	X	112
Thornend	Wilts	ST9778	51°30·3'	2°2·2'W	T	173
Thorne Park	Devon	SS3406	50°50·0'	4°21·1'W	X	190
Thorner	Leeds	SE3740	53°51·5'	1°25·8'W	T	104
Thornery	Devon	SS3222	50°58·6'	4°23·2'W	X	190
Thornes	Staffs	SK0703	52°37·7'	1°53·4'W	T	139
Thornes	Wakf	SE3219	53°40·2'	1°30·5'W	T	110,111
Thornes Field	N Yks	SD9643	53°53·2'	2°3·2'W	X	103

Thorness	Orkney	HY6643	59°16·6′	2°35·3′W	X	5
Thorness Bay	I of W	SZ4694	50°44·9′	1°20·5′W	W	196
Thorne St Margaret	Somer	ST0921	50°59·1′	3°17·4′W	T	181
Thornes Wood	Devon	SS9810	50°53·1′	3°26·6′W	F	192
Thorne, The	E Susx	TQ7210	50°52·1′	0°27·1′E	X	199
Thornet Wood	Surrey	TQ1154	51°16·7′	0°24·1′W	F	187
Thorne Waste or Moors	Donc	SE7215	53°37·8′	0°54·3′W	X	112
Thorney	Bucks	TQ0479	51°30·2′	0°29·7′W	T	176
Thorney	Notts	SK8572	53°14·5′	0°43·2′W	T	121
Thorney	Peterb	TF2804	52°37·4′	0°6·1′W	T	142
Thorney	Pth & Kin	NO0834	56°29·6′	3°29·2′W	X	52,53
Thorney	Somer	ST4222	50°59·9′	2°49·2′W	T	193
Thorneybank	Aberd	NJ6840	57°27·2′	2°31·5′W	X	29
Thorney Bank	Cumbr	NY5512	54°30·3′	2°41·3′W	X	90
Thorney Bay	Essex	TQ7982	51°30·7′	0°35·2′E	W	178
Thorney Brow	N Yks	NZ9401	54°24·0′	0°32·7′W	X	94
Thorneyburn Common	Northum	NY7587	55°10·8′	2°23·1′W	H	80
Thorneyburn Common	Northum	NY7687	55°10·9′	2°22·2′W	X	80
Thorney Channel	W Susx	SU7702	50°49·0′	0°54·0′W	W	197
Thorney Close	Sund	NZ3654	54°53·0′	1°25·9′W	T	88
Thorney Close Fm	Stock on T	NZ4223	54°36·3′	1°20·6′W	FM	93
Thorney Croft	Cumbr	NY5820	54°34·7′	2°38·6′W	X	91
Thorney Crofts	E Yorks	TA2123	53°41·6′	0°9·6′W	X	107,113
Thorney Cross	Devon	SX3896	50°44·7′	4°17·4′W	X	190
Thorneyd Fm	Dorset	ST9915	50°56·3′	2°0·5′W	FM	184
Thorney Fields Fm	Leic	SP4796	52°33·8′	1°18·0′W	FM	140
Thorneyfields Fm	Staffs	SJ9020	52°46·9′	2°8·5′W	FM	127
Thorneyfold Fm	E Susx	TQ6415	50°54·9′	0°20·4′E	FM	199
Thorneyford	Northum	NZ1577	55°5·5′	1°45·5′W	X	88
Thorney Gale	Cumbr	NY8213	54°31·0′	2°16·3′W	X	91,92
Thorney Green	Suff	TM0660	52°12·2′	1°1·3′E	T	155
Thorney Hill	Cambs	TL5779	52°23·4′	0°18·8′E	X	143
Thorney Hill	Hants	SZ2099	50°47·6′	1°42·6′W	T	195
Thorney Hill	Notts	SK6273	53°15·3′	1°3·8′W	F	120
Thorney Hill Holms	Hants	SU2000	50°48·2′	1°42·6′W	X	195
Thorneyhirst	Northum	NY8678	55°6·0′	2°12·7′W	X	87
Thorney Ho	Bucks	TQ0379	51°30·3′	0°30·6′W	X	176
Thorneyholme	Lancs	SD6649	53°56·4′	2°30·7′W	X	103
Thorney Island	W Susx	SU7503	50°49·5′	0°55·7′W	T	197
Thorneyknowe	Cumbr	NY4474	55°3·7′	2°52·2′W	X	85
Thorney Mire Ho	N Yks	SD8589	54°18·0′	2°13·4′W	X	98
Thorney Moor	Somer	ST4223	51°0·4′	2°49·2′W	X	193
Thorney Rig	N Yks	SD6977	54°11·5′	2°28·1′W	X	98
Thorney River	Peterb	TF2702	52°36·3′	0°7·1′W	W	142
Thorney Scale	Cumbr	NY8112	54°30·4′	2°17·2′W	X	91,92
Thorneythwaite Fm	Cumbr	NY2413	54°30·6′	3°10·0′W	FM	89,90
Thorney Toll	Cambs	TF3403	52°36·7′	0°0·8′W	T	142
Thorneywaite	N Yks	NZ7706	54°26·9′	0°48·3′W	X	94
Thorneywood	Notts	SK5941	52°58·0′	1°6·9′W	T	129
Thornfalcon	Somer	ST2823	51°0·3′	3°1·2′W	T	193
Thornfield Ho	N Yks	SE5423	53°42·3′	1°10·5′W	X	105
Thornflatt	Cumbr	SD0897	54°21·9′	3°24·5′W	X	96
Thornflatt Fm	N Yks	NZ4300	54°23·9′	1°19·8′W	FM	93
Thorn Fleet	Essex	TL9912	51°46·5′	0°53·5′E	W	168
Thorn Fm	Clackm	NS9898	56°10·1′	3°38·1′W	FM	58
Thorn Fm	Devon	SX7557	50°24·2′	3°45·2′W	FM	202
Thorn Fm	E Ayr	NS3748	55°42·1′	4°35·2′W	FM	63
Thorn Fm	N Yks	NZ4503	54°25·5′	1°18·0′W	FM	93
Thorn Fm	S Lanak	NS6549	55°43·2′	4°8·5′W	FM	64
Thorn Fm	Worcs	SO6563	52°16·1′	2°30·4′W	FM	138,149
Thornford	Dorset	ST6013	50°55·1′	2°33·8′W	T	194
Thorngarth Hill	Durham	NY9620	54°34·8′	2°3·3′W	X	91,92
Thorngill	N Yks	SE0986	54°16·4′	1°51·3′W	X	99
Thorngrafton	Northum	NY7865	54°59·0′	2°20·2′W	T	86,87
Thorngrafton Common	Northum	NY7866	54°59·5′	2°20·2′W	X	86,87
Thorngreen	Pth & Kin	NO1345	56°35·6′	3°24·6′W	X	53
Thorngreen	Pth & Kin	NO1831	56°28·1′	3°19·4′W	X	53
Thorngrove	Dorset	ST7925	51°1·7′	2°17·6′W	X	183
Thorngrove	Somer	ST3632	51°5·3′	2°54·4′W	T	182
Thorngrove	Worcs	SO8260	52°14·5′	2°15·4′W	X	138,150
Thorngumbald	E Yorks	TA2026	53°43·2′	0°10·5′W	T	107
Thorngumbald Drain	E Yorks	TA1825	53°42·7′	0°12·3′W	W	107,113
Thorn Hall	Cambs	TL5571	52°19·1′	0°16·9′E	X	154
Thorn Hall	E Yorks	TA2026	53°43·2′	0°10·5′W	X	107
Thornham	Devon	SS7318	50°57·1′	3°48·1′W	X	180
Thornham	Devon	SS7715	50°55·5′	3°44·6′W	X	180
Thornham	Devon	SX6454	50°22·4′	3°54·4′W	X	202
Thornham	Donc	SE6504	53°32·0′	1°0·7′W	X	111
Thornham	Norf	TF7343	52°57·6′	0°35·0′E	T	132
Thornham Corner	Norf	TF7439	52°55·4′	0°35·7′E	X	132
Thornham Down	Wilts	SU0951	51°15·7′	1°51·9′W	X	184
Thornham Fm	Norf	TL7295	52°31·8′	0°32·5′E	FM	143
Thornham Fold	Roch	SD8909	53°34·9′	2°9·6′W	T	109
Thornham Hill	Northum	NZ0570	55°1·7′	1°54·9′W	X	87
Thornham Magna	Suff	TM1070	52°17·5′	1°5·2′E	T	144,155
Thornham Park	Suff	TM1071	52°18·0′	1°5·2′E	X	144,155
Thornham Parva	Suff	TM1072	52°18·6′	1°5·2′E	T	144,155
Thornham Walks	Suff	TM1072	52°18·6′	1°5·2′E	X	144
Thornham Walks	Suff	TM1072	52°18·6′	1°5·2′E	X	144,155
Thornhaugh	Peterb	TF0600	52°35·5′	0°25·7′W	T	142
Thornhill	Aberd	NJ8050	57°32·6′	2°19·6′W	X	29,30
Thornhill	Caer	ST1584	51°33·1′	3°13·2′W	T	171
Thorn Hill	Cambs	TL3651	52°8·7′	0°0·3′W	X	154
Thornhill	Card	ST1782	51°32·1′	3°11·4′W	T	171
Thornhill	Carm	SN5711	51°47·0′	4°4·0′W	X	159
Thornhill	C of Soton	SU4612	50°54·6′	1°20·4′W	T	196
Thornhill	Cumbr	NY0108	54°27·7′	3°31·2′W	T	89
Thornhill	Derby	SK1983	53°20·9′	1°42·5′W	T	110
Thornhill	D & G	NX8795	55°14·4′	3°46·2′W	T	78
Thornhill	E Ayr	NS4347	55°41·7′	4°29·4′W	X	64
Thornhill	E Susx	TQ4337	51°7·1′	0°3·0′E	X	187
Thorn Hill	Kent	TR0171	51°24·4′	0°53·8′E	X	178
Thornhill	Kirk	SE2518	53°39·7′	1°36·9′W	T	110
Thornhill	Moray	NJ2558	57°36·6′	3°14·9′W	X	28
Thorn Hill	N Yks	NZ4602	54°24·9′	1°17·0′W	X	93
Thorn Hill	N Yks	NZ7807	54°27·4′	0°47·4′W	X	94
Thornhill	N Yks	NZ8400	54°23·6′	0°42·0′W	X	94
Thorn Hill	N Yks	NZ8804	54°25·7′	0°38·2′W	X	94
Thorn Hill	N Yks	SE1170	54°7·8′	1°49·5′W	X	99
Thorn Hill	N Yks	SE4879	54°12·5′	1°15·4′W	X	100

Thorn Hill	Oxon	SP5706	51°45·2′	1°10·1′W	X	164
Thornhill	Pth & Kin	NN9421	56°22·4′	3°42·5′W	X	52,53,58
Thorn Hill	Roth	SK4293	53°26·2′	1°21·7′W	T	111
Thorn Hill	Somer	SS7243	51°10·6′	3°49·5′W	X	180
Thorn Hill	Somer	ST2823	51°0·3′	3°1·2′W	H	193
Thornhill	Stir	NS6699	56°10·1′	4°9·0′W	T	57
Thornhill	Torf	ST2795	51°39·2′	3°2·9′W	T	171
Thorn Hill	Warw	SP3753	52°10·7′	1°27·1′W	X	151
Thorn Hill	W Berks	SU5378	51°30·1′	1°13·8′W	X	174
Thornhill	Wilts	SU0778	51°30·3′	1°53·6′W	T	173
Thorn Hill	Wilts	SU1165	51°23·3′	1°50·1′W	X	173
Thornhill Brink	Derby	SK1785	53°21·9′	1°44·3′W	X	110
Thornhill Copse	W Berks	SU3377	51°29·7′	1°31·1′W	F	174
Thornhill Down	Wilts	SU2255	51°17·9′	1°40·7′W	X	174
Thornhill Edge	Kirk	SE2417	53°39·2′	1°37·8′W	T	110
Thornhill Fm	Glos	SP1800	51°42·1′	1°44·0′W	FM	163
Thorn Hill Fm	Leic	SP5494	52°32·7′	1°11·8′W	FM	140
Thornhill Fm	N Yks	NZ6609	54°28·6′	0°58·5′W	FM	94
Thornhill Fm	N Yks	SE5070	54°7·6′	1°13·7′W	FM	100
Thornhill Fm	N Yks	SE6070	54°7·6′	1°4·5′W	FM	100
Thornhill Fm	N Yks	SE6640	53°51·4′	0°59·4′W	FM	105,106
Thornhill Fm	Oxon	SP5707	51°45·8′	1°10·0′W	FM	164
Thornhill Fm	Somer	ST6937	51°8·1′	2°26·2′W	FM	183
Thornhill Fm	Warw	SP0556	52°12·4′	1°55·2′W	FM	150
Thornhill Fm	Wilts	ST9286	51°34·6′	2°6·5′W	FM	173
Thornhill Fm	Wilts	ST9476	51°29·2′	2°4·8′W	FM	173
Thorn Hill Head	N Yks	SE8894	54°20·3′	0°38·4′W	X	94,101
Thornhill Ho	Dorset	ST7414	50°55·7′	2°21·8′W	X	194
Thornhill Lees	Kirk	SE2419	53°40·3′	1°37·8′W	T	110
Thornhill Lodge	Pth & Kin	NN8221	56°22·3′	3°54·2′W	X	52,57
Thornhill Park	C of Soton	SU4713	50°55·1′	1°19·5′W	T	196
Thornhills	Cald	SE1523	53°42·4′	1°46·0′W	T	104
Thorn Hills	Norf	TM3088	52°26·7′	1°23·5′E	X	156
Thornhill Wood	Warw	SP0556	52°12·4′	1°55·2′W	F	150
Thornholme	Cumbr	NY0608	54°27·8′	3°26·6′W	X	89
Thornholme	E Yorks	TA1163	54°3·3′	0°17·8′W	T	101
Thornholme Field	E Yorks	TA1164	54°3·8′	0°17·8′W	X	101
Thornholme Moor	E Yorks	TA1161	54°2·2′	0°17·9′W	X	101
Thornhome	S Lanak	NS8751	55°44·6′	3°47·6′W	X	65,72
Thornhope Beck	Durham	NZ0538	54°44·5′	1°54·9′W	W	92
Thornhope Burn	Northum	NY6850	54°50·9′	2°29·5′W	W	86,87
Thornhope Fell	Northum	NY6649	54°50·3′	2°31·3′W	X	86
Thorn House Fm	N Yks	SE6669	54°7·0′	0°59·0′W	FM	100
Thornhurst	Leeds	SE3744	53°53·7′	1°25·8′W	T	104
Thornicombe	Dorset	ST8703	50°49·8′	2°10·7′W	T	194
Thornicombe Fm	Dorset	ST8502	50°49·3′	2°12·4′W	FM	194
Thorniebrae	Aberd	NJ5439	57°26·6′	2°45·5′W	X	29
Thorniecleuch Hill	Scot Bord	NT3416	55°26·3′	3°2·2′W	H	79
Thorniehill	D & G	NX6676	55°3·9′	4°5·5′W	X	77,84
Thorniehill	D & G	NX8754	54°52·3′	3°45·2′W	X	84
Thornielaw	Scot Bord	NT5729	55°33·4′	2°40·5′W	X	73,74
Thorniethwaite	D & G	NY0779	55°6·1′	3°27·0′W	X	85
Thorniewhats	D & G	NY3878	55°5·8′	2°57·9′W	X	85
Thorninghurst Fm	Donc	SE6614	53°37·3′	0°59·7′W	FM	111
Thornington	Northum	NT8833	55°35·7′	2°11·0′W	X	74
Thorn Island	Pemb	SM8403	51°41·3′	5°7·1′W	X	157
Thorn Isle	Arg & Bt	NR7725	55°28·3′	5°31·3′W	X	68,69
Thorn Key Howes	N Yks	NZ9103	54°25·1′	0°35·4′W	A	94
Thornland	Devon	ST0321	50°59·0′	3°22·5′W	X	181
Thornleigh Park	Flint	SJ3666	53°11·5′	2°57·1′W	X	117
Thornley	Durham	NZ1137	54°43·9′	1°49·3′W	T	92
Thornley	Durham	NZ3639	54°44·9′	1°26·0′W	T	93
Thornley Bank	Ghead	NZ1660	54°56·3′	1°44·6′W	X	88
Thornley Beck	Durham	NZ1136	54°43·4′	1°49·3′W	W	92
Thornley Gate	Northum	NY8356	54°54·2′	2°15·5′W	X	86,87
Thornley Hall	Durham	NZ3638	54°44·4′	1°26·0′W	X	93
Thornley Hall	Lancs	SD6341	53°52·1′	2°33·3′W	X	102,103
Thornley Manor	I of W	SZ3689	50°42·2′	1°29·0′W	X	196
Thornley Woodlands Centre	Ghead	NZ1859	54°55·8′	1°42·7′W	X	88
Thornliebank	E Renf	NS5559	55°48·4′	4°18·4′W	T	64
Thornliemuir	Renf	NS4659	55°48·2′	4°27·0′W	X	64
Thornlybank Hill	Renf	NS3363	55°50·1′	4°39·6′W	X	63
Thornly Park	Renf	NS4862	55°49·9′	4°25·2′W	T	64
Thorn Marsh Fm	E Yorks	TA2024	53°42·2′	0°10·5′W	FM	107,113
Thorn Moor	Cumbr	SD6483	54°14·7′	2°32·7′W	X	97
Thornmuir	S Lanak	NS8852	55°45·2′	3°46·6′W	X	65,72
Thornpark Cross	Devon	SS6635	51°6·2′	3°54·5′W	X	180
Thorn Park Fm	N Yks	SE9888	54°16·9′	0°29·3′W	FM	94,101
Thorn Platt Fm	Lancs	SD6034	53°48·3′	2°36·0′W	FM	102,103
Thorn Point	Devon	SX4462	50°26·5′	4°11·4′W	X	201
Thornroan	Aberd	NJ8632	57°23·0′	2°13·5′W	T	30
Thorn Rock	Pemb	SM7408	51°43·8′	5°16·0′W	X	157
Thorns	D & G	NY1870	55°1·3′	3°16·5′W	X	85
Thorns	N Yks	NY8800	54°24·0′	2°10·7′W	T	91,92
Thorns	N Yks	SD7879	54°12·6′	2°19·8′W	X	98
Thorns	Suff	TL7455	52°10·2′	0°33·1′E	T	155
Thorn's Beach	Corn	SX1597	50°44·8′	4°37·0′W	X	190
Thorns Beach	Hants	SZ3996	50°46·0′	1°26·4′W	X	196
Thornsby Ho	N Yks	SE7891	54°18·8′	0°47·6′W	X	94,100
Thornsdale	E Susx	TQ9225	50°59·8′	0°44·6′E	X	189
Thornseat	Sheff	SK2492	53°25·7′	1°37·9′W	T	110
Thornseat Delf	Sheff	SK2292	53°25·7′	1°39·7′W	X	110
Thornsett	Derby	SK0187	53°23·0′	1°58·7′W	T	110
Thornsett Fields Fm	Derby	SK0188	53°23·6′	1°58·7′W	FM	110
Thornsett Fm	Ches	SJ9575	53°16·6′	2°4·1′W	FM	118
Thorn's Fm	Hants	SU7747	51°13·2′	0°53·5′W	FM	186
Thorns Fm	Hants	SZ3897	50°46·5′	1°27·3′W	FM	196
Thorns Fm	Lincs	SK8838	52°56·2′	0°41·0′W	FM	130
Thorns Fm	Lincs	TF0840	52°57·0′	0°23·1′W	FM	130
Thornsgill Beck	Cumbr	NY3723	54°36·1′	2°58·1′W	W	90
Thorns Green	Ches	SJ7984	53°21·4′	2°18·5′W	T	109
Thornship	Cumbr	NY5514	54°31·4′	2°41·3′W	X	90
Thornship Gill	Cumbr	NY5513	54°30·9′	2°41·3′W	W	90
Thorn, The	Heref	SO4554	52°11·1′	2°47·9′W	X	148,149
Thorn, The	Heref	SO5521	51°53·4′	2°38·8′W	X	162
Thornthorpe Ho	N Yks	SE7967	54°5·8′	0°47·1′W	X	100
Thornthwaite	Cumbr	NY2225	54°37·1′	3°12·1′W	T	89,90
Thornthwaite	Cumbr	NY2741	54°45·8′	3°7·6′W	X	85
Thornthwaite	Cumbr	NY8016	54°32·6′	2°18·1′W	X	91,92

Thornthwaite	N Yks	SE1758	54°1·3′	1°44·0′W	T	104
Thornthwaite Beck	Cumbr	NY2742	54°46·3′	3°7·7′W	W	85
Thornthwaite Crag	Cumbr	NY4309	54°28·6′	2°52·4′W	H	90
Thornthwaite Hall	Cumbr	NY5116	54°32·5′	2°45·0′W	X	90
Thornton	Angus	NO3946	56°36·4′	2°59·2′W	T	54
Thornton	Brad	SE1032	53°47·3′	1°50·5′W	T	104
Thornton	Bucks	SP7535	52°0·7′	0°54·0′W	T	152
Thornton	Corn	SX3267	50°29·0′	4°21·7′W	X	201
Thornton	E Loth	NT7473	55°57·2′	2°24·5′W	X	67
Thornton	E Yorks	SE7545	53°54·0′	0°51·1′W	T	105,106
Thornton	Fife	NO3423	56°23·9′	3°3·7′W	X	54,59
Thornton	Fife	NT2897	56°9·9′	3°9·1′W	T	59
Thornton	Lancs	SD3442	53°52·4′	2°59·8′W	T	102
Thornton	Leic	SK4607	52°39·8′	1°18·8′W	T	140
Thornton	Lincs	TF2467	53°11·4′	0°8·2′W	T	122
Thornton	Midd	NZ4713	54°30·8′	1°16·0′W	T	93
Thornton	Midlo	NT2961	55°50·5′	3°7·6′W	X	66
Thornton	Moray	NJ4851	57°33·0′	2°51·7′W	X	28,29
Thornton	Northum	NT9547	55°43·2′	2°4·3′W	T	74,75
Thornton	Pemb	SM9007	51°43·6′	5°2·1′W	T	157,158
Thornton	Pth & Kin	NO0740	56°32·8′	3°30·3′W	X	52,53
Thornton	Sefton	SD3300	53°29·8′	3°0·2′W	T	108
Thornton	S Lanak	NS5954	55°45·8′	4°14·4′W	X	64
Thornton Abbey	N Lincs	TA1118	53°39·0′	0°18·8′W	A	113
Thornton Barn	Lancs	SD5024	53°42·8′	2°45·0′W	X	102
Thornton Beck	N Yks	SE2462	54°3·4′	1°37·6′W	W	99
Thornton Beck	N Yks	SE8381	54°13·3′	0°43·2′W	W	100
Thornton Burn	E Loth	NT7474	55°57·8′	2°24·5′W	W	67
Thornton Carrs	Lincs	TF0296	53°27·3′	0°27·4′W	X	112
Thornton College	Bucks	SP7536	52°1·3′	0°54·0′W	X	152
Thornton Cottage	Northum	NT9448	55°43·8′	2°5·3′W	X	74,75
Thornton Curtis	N Lincs	TA0817	53°38·5′	0°21·6′W	T	112
Thornton Dale	N Yks	SE8586	54°16·0′	0°41·3′W	X	94,100
Thornton Field Ho	N Yks	SE6864	54°4·3′	0°57·2′W	X	100
Thornton Fields	Red & Cl	NZ6118	54°33·5′	1°3·0′W	X	94
Thornton Fm	Kent	TR2952	51°13·5′	1°17·2′E	FM	179
Thornton Fm	Wirral	SJ3180	53°19·0′	3°1·7′W	FM	108
Thornton Force	N Yks	SD6975	54°10·4′	2°28·1′W	W	98
Thornton Grange	E Yorks	SE7546	53°54·5′	0°51·1′W	X	105,106
Thornton Grange	N Yks	SE1888	54°17·5′	1°43·0′W	X	99
Thornton Grange	N Yks	SE2562	54°3·4′	1°36·7′W	X	99
Thornton Grange	Stock on T	NZ4713	54°30·8′	1°16·0′W	X	93
Thornton Grange Fm	N Yks	SE6764	54°4·3′	0°58·1′W	FM	100
Thornton Green Ho	Ches	SJ4473	53°15·3′	2°50·0′W	X	117
Thornton Grove	N Yks	SE2663	54°4·0′	1°35·7′W	X	99
Thornton Hall	Bucks	SP7635	52°0·7′	0°53·2′W	X	152
Thornton Hall	Darl	NZ2317	54°33·1′	1°38·2′W	A	93
Thornton Hall	N Lincs	TA0918	53°39·1′	0°20·6′W	A	112
Thornton Hall	N Yks	SD6974	54°9·9′	2°28·1′W	X	98
Thorntonhall	S Lanak	NS5955	55°46·3′	4°14·4′W	T	64
Thornton Heath	Croy	TQ3168	51°24·0′	0°6·6′W	T	176,177
Thorntonhill	Pth & Kin	NO0302	56°12·3′	3°33·4′W	X	58
Thornton Hill	Pth & Kin	NO0303	56°12·8′	3°33·4′W	X	58
Thornton Hill Fm	N Yks	SE5373	54°9·2′	1°10·9′W	FM	100
Thornton Ho	E Yorks	SE8427	53°44·2′	0°43·2′W	X	106
Thornton Ho	Lincs	TF2653	53°3·8′	0°6·8′W	X	122
Thornton Ho	Northum	NZ0986	55°10·3′	1°51·1′W	X	81
Thornton Ho	N Yks	SE3889	54°18·0′	1°24·5′W	X	99
Thornton Home Fm	Aberd	NO6871	56°50·0′	2°31·0′W	FM	45
Thornton Hough	Wirral	SJ3081	53°19·5′	3°2·7′W	T	108
Thornton House Fm	E Yorks	SE7447	53°55·1′	0°52·0′W	FM	105,106
Thornton-in-Craven	N Yks	SD9048	53°55·9′	2°8·7′W	T	103
Thornton in Lonsdale	N Yks	SD6873	54°9·4′	2°29·0′W	T	98
Thornton Lands	E Yorks	SE8524	53°42·6′	0°42·3′W	X	106,112
Thornton-le-Beans	N Yks	SE3990	54°18·5′	1°23·6′W	T	99
Thornton-le-Clay	N Yks	SE6865	54°4·8′	0°57·2′W	T	100
Thornton-le-Dale	N Yks	SE8382	54°13·9′	0°43·2′W	T	100
Thornton le Moor	Lincs	TF0596	53°27·3′	0°24·7′W	T	112
Thornton-le-Moor	N Yks	SE3988	54°17·4′	1°23·6′W	T	99
Thornton-le-Moors	Ches	SJ4474	53°15·8′	2°50·0′W	T	117
Thornton-le-Street	N Yks	SE4186	54°16·3′	1°21·8′W	T	99
Thornton Le Street Stud	N Yks	SE3985	54°15·8′	1°23·7′W	X	99
Thorntonloch	E Loth	NT7574	55°57·8′	2°23·6′W	T	67
Thornton Lodge	N Yks	SE1889	54°18·0′	1°43·0′W	X	99
Thornton Lodge Fm	Lincs	TF2567	53°11·4′	0°7·3′W	FM	122
Thornton Lodge Fm	N Yks	SE5372	54°8·7′	1°10·9′W	FM	100
Thornton Low Moor	Stock on T	NZ4812	54°30·3′	1°15·1′W	X	93
Thornton Mains	Northum	NT9647	55°43·2′	2°3·4′W	X	74,75
Thornton Manor	N Yks	SE4371	54°8·2′	1°20·1′W	X	99
Thornton Manor	Wirral	SJ3081	53°19·5′	3°2·7′W	X	108
Thornton Moor	Cald	SE0532	53°47·3′	1°55·0′W	X	104
Thornton Moor	Northum	NZ0987	55°10·9′	1°51·1′W	X	81
Thornton Moor	N Yks	SD9346	53°54·8′	2°6·0′W	X	103
Thornton Moor	N Yks	SE6763	54°3·8′	0°58·2′W	X	100
Thornton Moor Fm	N Yks	SE2763	54°4·0′	1°34·8′W	FM	99
Thornton Moor Resr	Brad	SE0533	53°47·8′	1°55·0′W	W	104
Thornton Park	Northum	NT9448	55°43·8′	2°5·3′W	X	74,75
Thornton Resr	Leic	SK4707	52°39·8′	1°17·9′W	W	140
Thornton Rust	N Yks	SD9788	54°17·5′	2°2·3′W	T	98
Thornton Rust Moor	N Yks	SD9587	54°17·0′	2°4·2′W	X	98
Thornton's Br	Norf	TF5713	52°41·7′	0°19·8′E	X	131,143
Thornton Steward	N Yks	SE1787	54°16·9′	1°43·9′W	T	99
Thornton Steward Resr	N Yks	SE1888	54°17·5′	1°43·0′W	W	99
Thornton Village	N Yks	SE5374	54°9·8′	1°10·9′W	A	100
Thornton Village	Warw	SP2750	52°9·1′	1°35·9′W	A	151
Thornton Watlass	N Yks	SE2385	54°15·9′	1°38·4′W	T	99
Thornton Wood	E Yorks	SE7844	53°53·4′	0°48·4′W	F	105,106
Thornton Wood	Fife	NT1293	56°7·6′	3°24·5′W	F	58
Thornton Wood	Lincs	TF2266	53°10·9′	0°10·1′W	F	122
Thornton Wood	Warw	SP2750	52°9·1′	1°35·9′W	F	151
Thorntoun	E Ayr	NS3838	55°36·8′	4°33·9′W	X	70
Thorntree	Derby	SK1863	53°10·1′	1°43·4′W	X	119
Thorntree	Stir	NS6093	56°6·8′	4°14·7′W	X	57
Thorntree Fm	N Yks	NZ4101	54°24·4′	1°21·7′W	FM	93
Thorntree Fm	N Yks	NZ4400	54°23·9′	1°18·9′W	FM	93
Thorntree Fm	N Yks	SE3895	54°21·2′	1°24·5′W	FM	99
Thorn Tree Fm	N Yks	SE6274	54°9·7′	1°2·6′W	FM	100
Thorntree Hill	Wakf	SE3617	53°39·1′	1°26·9′W	X	110,111
Thorntree Hill	York	SE6552	53°57·8′	1°0·1′W	X	105,106
Thorntree Ho	N Yks	NZ3106	54°27·1′	1°30·9′W	X	93

Thorn Villa	E Yorks	TA1927	53°43·8′	0°11·4′W	X	107
Thornwell	Monm	ST5391	51°37·2′	2°40·3′W	X	162,172
Thornwick Bay	E Yorks	TA2372	54°8·0′	0°6·6′W	W	101
Thornwick Nab	E Yorks	TA2372	54°8·0′	0°6·6′W	X	101
Thorn Wold	Cumbr	SD7588	54°17·5′	2°22·6′W	X	98
Thornwood Common	Essex	TL4704	51°43·2′	0°8·1′E	T	167
Thornworthy	Devon	SS7045	51°11·6′	3°51·2′W	X	180
Thornworthy Tor	Devon	SX6685	50°39·2′	3°53·4′W	H	191
Thorny Abbey Fm	Notts	SK6753	53°4·4′	0°59·6′W	FM	120
Thornybank	Cumbr	SD5298	54°22·8′	2°43·9′W	X	97
Thorny Bank	Midlo	NT3467	55°53·8′	3°2·9′W	X	66
Thornybank	Moray	NJ4262	57°38·9′	2°57·8′W	X	28
Thorny Beck	N Yks	SE9897	54°21·8′	0°29·1′W	W	94,101
Thorny Brown	Notts	SK8671	53°14·0′	0°42·3′W	F	121
Thorny Cleuch	Scot Bord	NT2723	55°30·0′	3°8·9′W	X	73
Thorny Cleugh	Durham	NZ0326	54°38·0′	1°56·8′W	W	92
Thorny Cliff	Corn	SW7316	50°0·3′	5°9·7′W	X	204
Thornycroft Hall	Ches	SJ8671	53°14·4′	2°12·2′W	X	118
Thorny Down	Wilts	SU2034	51°6·5′	1°42·5′W	X	184
Thorny Down Wood	Hants	SU5539	51°9·1′	1°12·4′W	F	185
Thornyedge	Staffs	SJ9450	53°3·1′	2°5·0′W	X	118
Thornyfields	Cumbr	SD4393	54°20·0′	2°52·2′W	X	97
Thornyfields Fm	Ches	SJ7256	53°6·3′	2°24·7′W	FM	118
Thornyflat Fm	S Ayr	NS3622	55°28·1′	4°35·2′W	FM	70
Thorny Grane Gill	N Yks	SE1079	54°12·6′	1°50·4′W	W	99
Thorny Grane Moor	N Yks	SE1079	54°12·6′	1°50·4′W	X	99
Thornyhaugh	Northum	NZ1098	55°16·8′	1°50·1′W	X	81
Thornyhill	Aberd	NO6372	56°50·5′	2°35·9′W	T	45
Thorny Hill	D & G	NX5388	55°10·1′	4°18·0′W	X	77
Thorny Hill	D & G	NX6362	54°56·3′	4°7·9′W	H	83
Thornyhill	Fife	NT0691	56°6·4′	3°30·2′W	X	58
Thorny Hill	Lancs	SD7952	53°58·1′	2°18·8′W	X	103
Thorny Hill	Scot Bord	NT8014	55°25·4′	2°18·5′W	X	80
Thornyhills Fm	S Lanak	NS9039	55°38·2′	3°44·4′W	FM	71,72
Thornyhive Bay	Aberd	NO8882	56°56·0′	2°11·4′W	W	45
Thorny Knowe	Northum	NU1308	55°22·2′	1°47·3′W	X	81
Thornyland	Cumbr	NY4573	55°3·2′	2°51·2′W	X	86
Thornylea	Aberd	NO7674	56°51·7′	2°23·2′W	X	45
Thorny Lee	Derby	SK0278	53°18·2′	1°57·8′W	H	119
Thornylee	Scot Bord	NT4136	55°37·1′	2°55·8′W	T	73
Thornylee Craigs	Scot Bord	NT4037	55°37·6′	2°56·7′W	X	73
Thornyleigh	Staffs	SJ9762	53°9·5′	2°2·3′W	X	118
Thornyside	N Ayr	NS2852	55°44·1′	4°43·9′W	X	63
Thornyslack Fm	Cumbr	SD5297	54°22·2′	2°43·9′W	FM	97
Thornythwaite	Cumbr	NY3922	54°35·6′	2°56·2′W	X	90
Thornythwaite Fell	Cumbr	NY2412	54°30·1′	3°10·0′W	H	89,90
Thoroton	Notts	SK7642	52°58·4′	0°51·7′W	T	129
Thoroughfare Farmhouse	NE Lincs	TA2500	53°29·1′	0°6·6′W	X	113
Thorough Mea	Cumbr	SD7584	54°15·3′	2°22·6′W	X	98
Thoroughway Ho	N Yks	SE2790	54°18·5′	1°34·7′W	X	99
Thorp	Oldham	SD9108	53°34·4′	2°7·7′W	T	109
Thorp Arch	Leeds	SE4345	53°54·2′	1°20·3′W	T	105
Thorpe	Cumbr	NY4926	54°37·8′	2°47·0′W	T	90
Thorpe	Derby	SK1550	53°3·1′	1°46·2′W	T	119
Thorpe	E Yorks	SE9946	53°54·3′	0°29·2′W	T	106
Thorpe	Lincs	TF4982	53°19·1′	0°14·6′E	T	122
Thorpe	Norf	TM4398	52°31·8′	1°35·4′E	T	134
Thorpe	Notts	SK7649	53°2·2′	0°51·6′W	T	129
Thorpe	N Yks	SE0161	54°2·9′	1°58·7′W	T	98
Thorpe	Surrey	TQ0168	51°24·3′	0°32·5′W	T	176
Thorpe Abbotts	Norf	TM1979	52°22·1′	1°13·4′E	T	156
Thorpe Abbotts Place	Norf	TM1979	52°22·1′	1°13·4′E	X	156
Thorpe Acre	Leic	SK5120	52°46·7′	1°14·2′W	T	129
Thorpe Arnold	Leic	SK7720	52°46·6′	0°51·1′W	T	129
Thorpe Audlin	Wakf	SE4716	53°38·5′	1°16·9′W	T	111
Thorpe Bassett	N Yks	SE8673	54°9·0′	0°40·6′W	T	101
Thorpe Bassett Wold	N Yks	SE8472	54°8·5′	0°42·4′W	X	100
Thorpe Bay	Sou-on-Sea	TQ9185	51°32·1′	0°45·6′E	T	178
Thorpe Br	Lincs	TF3860	53°7·4′	0°4·1′E	X	122
Thorpe Bulmer Fm	Hartpl	NZ4535	54°42·7′	1°17·7′W	FM	93
Thorpe by Water	Rut	SP8996	52°33·5′	0°40·8′W	T	141
Thorpe Carr	Suff	TL9273	52°19·5′	0°49·5′E	F	144,155
Thorpe Cloud	Derby	SK1550	53°3·1′	1°46·2′W	X	119
Thorpe Common	Roth	SK5279	53°18·6′	1°12·8′W	X	120
Thorpe Common	Suff	TM2637	51°59·3′	1°17·9′E	T	169
Thorpe Constantine	Staffs	SK2508	52°40·4′	1°37·4′W	T	128,140
Thorpe Cott	N Yks	SE3169	54°7·2′	1°31·1′W	X	99
Thorpe Cross	Essex	TM1921	51°50·9′	1°11·2′E	X	168,169
Thorpe Culvert	Lincs	TF4760	53°7·2′	0°12·2′E	T	122
Thorpe Dales	Lincs	TF4461	53°7·8′	0°9·5′E	X	122
Thorpe Edge	Brad	SE1837	53°50·0′	1°43·2′W	T	104
Thorpe End	Norf	TG2811	52°39·1′	1°22·7′E	T	133,134
Thorpe Fell Top	N Yks	SE0059	54°1·9′	1°59·6′W	H	104
Thorpe Fen	Lincs	TF4360	53°7·3′	0°8·6′E	X	122
Thorpe Fendykes	Lincs	TF4560	53°7·3′	0°10·4′E	T	122
Thorpefield	N Yks	SE4179	54°12·5′	1°21·9′W	X	99
Thorpefield Fm	E Yorks	SE8244	53°53·4′	0°44·7′W	FM	106
Thorpe Field Fm	Notts	SK8457	53°6·4′	0°44·3′W	FM	121
Thorpe Fm	Derby	SK2282	53°20·3′	1°39·8′W	FM	110
Thorpe Fm	Durham	NZ0912	54°30·4′	1°51·2′W	FM	92
Thorpe Fm	Leeds	SE1742	53°52·7′	1°44·1′W	FM	104
Thorpe Fm	Lincs	TF3088	53°22·6′	0°2·3′W	FM	113,122
Thorpe Fm	Lincs	TF4269	53°12·2′	0°8·0′E	FM	122
Thorpe Fm	Norf	TL9090	52°28·7′	0°48·3′E	FM	144
Thorpe Fm	N Yks	NZ3504	54°26·1′	1°27·2′W	FM	93
Thorpe Fox Covert	Northnts	TL0381	52°25·3′	0°28·7′W	F	141
Thorpe Garth	E Yorks	TA2538	53°49·6′	0°5·6′W	X	107
Thorpe Grange	Donc	SE5811	53°35·8′	1°7·0′W	X	111
Thorpe Grange	E Yorks	SE8629	53°45·3′	0°41·3′W	X	106
Thorpe Grange	N Yks	SE2275	54°10·5′	1°39·4′W	X	99
Thorpe Grange	N Yks	SE4660	54°2·3′	1°17·4′W	X	100
Thorpe Grange	N Yks	SE5777	54°11·4′	1°7·2′W	X	100
Thorpe Grange Fm	Lincs	SK9164	53°10·2′	0°37·9′W	FM	121
Thorpe Great Heath	Norf	TL8989	52°28·2′	0°47·4′E	X	144
Thorpe Green	Essex	TM1723	51°52·0′	1°9·5′E	T	168,169
Thorpe Green	Lancs	SD5923	53°42·4′	2°36·9′W	T	102
Thorpe Green	Suff	TL9354	52°9·3′	0°49·7′E	T	155
Thorpe Green	Surrey	TQ0168	51°24·3′	0°32·5′W	T	176
Thorpe Hall	Durham	NZ1014	54°31·5′	1°50·3′W	X	92
Thorpe Hall	Essex	TM1821	51°50·9′	1°10·3′E	X	168,169
Thorpe Hall	E Yorks	SE7529	53°45·4′	0°51·3′W	X	105,106
Thorpe Hall	E Yorks	TA1067	54°5·5′	0°18·7′W	X	101
Thorpe Hall	N Yks	SE5731	53°46·6′	1°7·7′W	X	105
Thorpe Hall	N Yks	SE5776	54°10·8′	1°7·2′W	X	100
Thorpe Hall	Peterb	TL1798	52°34·3′	0°16·0′W	A	142
Thorpe Hall	Staffs	SK2508	52°40·4′	1°37·4′W	X	128,140
Thorpe Hall	Suff	TM2062	52°13·0′	1°13·6′E	X	156
Thorpe Hall	Suff	TM2173	52°18·9′	1°14·9′E	A	156
Thorpe Hall	Suff	TM2780	52°22·5′	1°20·5′E	X	156
Thorpe Hall Fm	Suff	TM2350	52°6·4′	1°15·8′E	FM	156
Thorpe Hamlet	Norf	TG2408	52°37·6′	1°19·0′E	T	134
Thorpe Hesley	Roth	SK3796	53°27·8′	1°26·2′W	T	110,111
Thorpe Hill Fm	N Yks	SE4559	54°1·7′	1°18·4′W	FM	105
Thorpe Hindles	Leic	SK7722	52°47·6′	0°51·1′W	X	129
Thorpe in Balne	Donc	SE5910	53°35·2′	1°6·1′W	T	111
Thorpe Lane Fm	Lincs	SK9280	53°18·8′	0°36·7′W	FM	121
Thorpe Langton	Leic	SP7492	52°31·5′	0°54·2′W	T	141
Thorpe Larches	Durham	NZ3826	54°37·9′	1°24·3′W	T	93
Thorpe Latimer	Lincs	TF1339	52°56·4′	0°18·7′W	T	130
Thorpe Lea	Surrey	TQ0270	51°25·4′	0°31·6′W	T	176
Thorpe Lea West	Durham	NZ4245	54°48·1′	1°20·4′W	X	88
Thorpe Leazes	Stock on T	NZ3824	54°36·8′	1°24·3′W	X	93
Thorpe le Fallows	Lincs	SK9180	53°18·8′	0°37·6′W	X	121
Thorpe le Glebe Village	Notts	SK6025	52°49·4′	1°6·2′W	A	129
Thorpe-le-Soken	Essex	TM1822	51°51·5′	1°10·3′E	T	168,169
Thorpe le Street	E Yorks	SE8344	53°53·4′	0°43·8′W	T	106
Thorpe le Vale	Lincs	TF2090	53°23·8′	0°11·3′W	T	113
Thorpe Lodge	Essex	TM1823	51°52·0′	1°10·4′E	X	168,169
Thorpe Lodge	Notts	SK7749	53°2·2′	0°50·7′W	X	129
Thorpe Lodge	N Yks	SE3168	54°6·7′	1°31·1′W	X	99
Thorpe Lodge Fm	Cambs	TL1570	52°19·2′	0°18·4′W	FM	153
Thorpe Lodge Fm	Northnts	SP5244	52°5·7′	1°14·1′W	FM	151
Thorpe Lodge Fm	Notts	SK6126	52°49·9′	1°5·3′W	FM	129
Thorpe Lubenham	Northnts	SP7086	52°28·3′	0°57·8′W	X	141
Thorpe Malsor	Northnts	SP8379	52°24·4′	0°46·4′W	T	141
Thorpe Malsor Resr	Northnts	SP8279	52°24·4′	0°47·3′W	W	141
Thorpe Mandeville	Northnts	SP5344	52°5·7′	1°13·2′W	T	152
Thorpe Manor	Wakf	SE4815	53°38·0′	1°16·0′W	X	111
Thorpe Market	Norf	TG2435	52°52·2′	1°20·1′E	T	133
Thorpe Marriott	Norf	TG1714	52°41·0′	1°13·0′E	T	133,134
Thorpe Marsh	Donc	SE6009	53°34·7′	1°5·2′W	X	111
Thorpe Marshes	Norf	TM4498	52°31·7′	1°36·2′E	X	134
Thorpe Morieux	Suff	TL9453	52°8·7′	0°50·5′E	T	155
Thorpeness	Suff	TM4759	52°10·7′	1°37·2′E	T	156
Thorpe Ness	Suff	TM4760	52°11·2′	1°37·2′E	X	156
Thorpe on The Hill	Leeds	SE3126	53°44·0′	1°31·4′W	T	104
Thorpe on the Hill	Lincs	SK9065	53°10·7′	0°38·8′W	T	121
Thorpe Park	Essex	TM1821	51°50·9′	1°10·3′E	X	168,169
Thorpe Park	Surrey	TQ0368	51°24·3′	0°30·8′W	X	176
Thorpe Parva Hall	Norf	TM1679	52°22·2′	1°10·8′E	X	144,156
Thorpe Pasture	Derby	SK1551	53°3·6′	1°46·2′W	X	119
Thorpe Rise Fm	E Yorks	SE8443	53°52·8′	0°42·9′W	FM	106
Thorpe Row	Norf	TF9608	52°38·3′	0°54·2′E	T	144
Thorpes	Kent	TQ7629	51°2·2′	0°31·0′E	X	188,199
Thorpe Salvin	Roth	SK5281	53°19·6′	1°12·7′W	T	111,120
Thorpe Satchville	Leic	SK7311	52°41·7′	0°54·8′W	T	129
Thorpes Fm	Cambs	TL3666	52°16·7′	0°0·0′E	FM	154
Thorpe Spring	N Yks	SE5677	54°11·4′	1°8·1′W	X	100
Thorpe St Andrew	Norf	TG2609	52°38·1′	1°20·8′E	T	134
Thorpe St Peter	Lincs	TF4860	53°7·2′	0°13·1′E	T	122
Thorpe Street	Suff	TM0277	52°21·5′	0°58·4′E	T	144
Thorpe Thewles	Stock on T	NZ4023	54°36·3′	1°22·4′W	T	93
Thorpe Tilney	Lincs	TF1157	53°6·2′	0°20·1′W	T	121
Thorpe Tilney Dales	Lincs	TF1858	53°6·6′	0°13·8′W	X	122
Thorpe Tilney Fen	Lincs	TF1558	53°6·6′	0°16·5′W	X	121
Thorpe under Stone	N Yks	NZ1200	54°24·0′	1°48·5′W	X	92
Thorpe Underwood	Northnts	SP7881	52°25·5′	0°50·8′W	T	141
Thorpe Underwood	N Yks	SE4659	54°1·7′	1°17·4′W	T	105
Thorpe Waterville	Northnts	TL0281	52°25·3′	0°29·6′W	T	141
Thorpe Whin	E Yorks	SE8343	53°52·8′	0°43·8′W	X	106
Thorpe Willoughby	N Yks	SE5731	53°46·6′	1°7·7′W	T	105
Thorpe Wood	N Yks	SE5832	53°47·1′	1°6·8′W	T	105
Thorpe Wood	Suff	TL9455	52°9·8′	0°50·6′E	F	155
Thorpewood Fm	Northnts	SP7452	52°9·9′	0°54·7′W	FM	152
Thorpe Woodlands	Norf	TL9484	52°25·4′	0°51·6′E	X	144
Thorphinsty Hall	Cumbr	SD4186	54°16·2′	2°53·9′W	X	96,97
Thorpland	Norf	TF6108	52°39·0′	0°23·2′E	T	143
Thorpland Hall	Norf	TF9332	52°51·3′	0°52·4′E	A	132
Thorpland Lodge Fm	Norf	TF9331	52°50·7′	0°52·4′E	FM	132
Thorp Perrow	N Yks	SE2685	54°15·8′	1°35·6′W	X	99
Thorp's Fm	E Yorks	TA2627	53°43·7′	0°5·0′W	FM	107
Thorp's Plantn	E Yorks	TA2924	53°42·0′	0°2·3′W	F	107,113
Thorpville	Aberd	NJ6729	57°21·3′	2°32·4′W	X	38
Thorrington	Essex	TM0920	51°50·6′	1°2·4′E	T	168,169
Thors Cave	Staffs	SK0954	53°5·2′	1°51·5′W	A	119
Thorseby Hall	Donc	SE6217	53°39·0′	1°3·3′W	X	111
Thors Fm	Essex	TM0819	51°50·1′	1°1·5′E	FM	168,169
Thorsgill Beck	Durham	NZ0314	54°31·5′	1°56·8′W	W	92
Thorsgill Fm	Durham	NZ0415	54°32·1′	1°55·9′W	FM	92
Thorswood Ho	Staffs	SK1147	53°1·4′	1°49·8′W	X	119,128
Thorter Br	Pth & Kin	NO0211	56°17·1′	3°34·5′W	X	58
Thorter Burn	E Loth	NT5969	55°55·0′	2°38·9′W	W	67
Thorter Burn	E Loth	NT6070	55°55·5′	2°38·0′W	W	67
Thorter Burn	Pth & Kin	NO0110	56°16·6′	3°35·5′W	W	58
Thorter Fell	D & G	NX9263	54°57·2′	3°40·8′W	X	84
Thorter Hill	Aberd	NO6580	56°54·9′	2°34·0′W	X	45
Thorton Fm	Dorset	ST8017	50°57·4′	2°16·7′W	FM	183
Thort Rig	D & G	NS7918	55°26·7′	3°54·3′W	X	71,78
Thorverton	Devon	SS9202	50°48·7′	3°31·6′W	T	192
Thougritstane	E Ayr	NS4050	55°43·3′	4°32·4′W	X	64
Thoulstone	Wilts	ST8348	51°14·1′	2°14·2′W	T	183
Thowliestane Hill	Scot Bord	NT7619	55°28·1′	2°22·3′W	H	80
Thrales End	Beds	TL1116	51°50·1′	0°22·9′W	X	166
Thrandeston	Suff	TM1176	52°20·7′	1°6·3′E	T	144
Thrang Crag	Cumbr	NY4317	54°33·0′	2°52·5′W	X	90
Thrang Crag Wood	Cumbr	SD2891	54°18·8′	3°6·0′W	F	96,97
Thrang End Fm	Lancs	SD4976	54°10·9′	2°46·5′W	FM	97
Thrang Fm	Cumbr	NY3105	54°26·4′	3°3·4′W	FM	90
Thrang, The	Cumbr	NY7800	54°23·9′	2°19·9′W	X	91
Thrapston	Northnts	SP9978	52°23·7′	0°32·3′W	T	141
Thrashbush	N Lanak	NS7666	55°52·5′	3°58·5′W	T	64
Thrashie Burn	Scot Bord	NT4047	55°43·0′	2°56·9′W	W	73
Thrashy Knowe	E Ayr	NS5341	55°38·7′	4°19·7′W	X	70
Thrawparts	Pth & Kin	NO2635	56°30·3′	3°11·7′W	X	53
Threadbare Hall Fm	Suff	TM3672	52°17·9′	1°28·1′E	FM	156
Threadgold's Fm	Essex	TL8413	51°47·3′	0°40·5′E	FM	168
Threap Green	Lancs	SD7552	53°58·1′	2°22·5′W	X	103
Threaphaw Fell	Lancs	SD6254	53°59·1′	2°34·4′W	X	102,103
Threapland	Cumbr	NY1539	54°44·6′	3°18·8′W	T	89
Threapland	Moray	NJ2861	57°38·3′	3°11·9′W	X	28
Threapland	N Yks	SD9860	54°2·4′	2°1·4′W	T	98
Threapland Lees	Cumbr	NY1638	54°44·0′	3°17·9′W	X	89
Threapland Moss	Cumbr	NY1736	54°43·0′	3°16·9′W	X	89,90
Threaplands	Cumbr	NY5917	54°33·0′	2°37·6′W	X	91
Threapmuir	Pth & Kin	NT0698	56°10·2′	3°30·4′W	X	58
Threaprig	Falk	NS8374	55°56·9′	3°52·0′W	X	65
Threapthwaite	Cumbr	NY0116	54°32·0′	3°31·4′W	X	89
Threapwood	Ches	SJ4445	53°0·2′	2°49·7′W	T	117
Threapwood	Staffs	SK0442	52°58·8′	1°56·0′W	T	119,128
Threap Wood	Staffs	SK0443	52°59·3′	1°56·0′W	F	119,128
Threave	S Ayr	NS3306	55°19·4′	4°37·5′W	X	70,76
Threave Gardens	D & G	NX7560	54°55·4′	3°56·6′W	X	84
Threave Island	D & G	NX7462	54°56·5′	3°57·6′W	X	83,84
Threave Mains	D & G	NX7362	54°56·4′	3°58·5′W	X	83,84
Three Ashes	Glos	SO7127	51°56·7′	2°24·9′W	X	162
Three Ashes	Hants	SU6361	51°20·9′	1°5·3′W	T	175
Three Ashes	Heref	SO5123	51°54·4′	2°42·3′W	T	162
Three Ashes	Shrops	SO3778	52°24·0′	2°55·2′W	T	137,148
Three Ashes	Somer	ST6228	51°3·2′	2°32·1′W	X	183
Three Ashes	Somer	ST6546	51°13·0′	2°29·7′W	T	183
Three Ashes Fm	Essex	TL7516	51°49·1′	0°32·7′E	FM	167
Three Ash Fm	Suff	TM3487	52°26·1′	1°27·0′E	FM	156
Three Barrows	Devon	SX4697	50°45·4′	4°10·6′W	A	190
Three Barrows	Devon	SX6562	50°26·8′	3°53·7′W	A	202
Three Barrows	Dorset	SY9384	50°39·6′	2°5·6′W	A	195
Three Barrows	Hants	SU5044	51°11·8′	1°16·7′W	A	185
Three Barrows Down	Kent	TR2449	51°12·0′	1°12·8′E	X	179,189
Three Birches	Shrops	SO2385	52°27·7′	3°7·6′W	X	137
Three Brethren	D & G	NX5848	54°48·7′	4°12·2′W	X	83
Three Brethren	Scot Bord	NT4331	55°34·4′	2°53·8′W	H	73
Three Bridge Mill	Bucks	SP6726	51°55·9′	1°1·1′W	X	164,165
Three Bridges	Arg & Bt	NN0812	56°16·0′	5°5·6′W	X	50,56
Three Bridges	Lincs	TF3230	52°51·3′	0°2·0′W	X	131
Three Bridges	Lincs	TF4388	53°22·4′	0°9·4′E	T	113,122
Three Bridges	W Susx	TQ2837	51°7·3′	0°9·9′W	T	187
Three Bridges Fm	Somer	ST1722	50°59·7′	3°10·6′W	FM	181,193
Three Brothers	Lancs	SD4973	54°9·3′	2°46·4′W	X	97
Three Brothers of Grugith	Corn	SW7619	50°2·0′	5°7·3′W	A	204
Threeburnford	Scot Bord	NT4652	55°45·8′	2°51·2′W	X	66,73
Three Burn Grange	Scot Bord	NT8665	55°52·9′	2°13·0′W	X	67
Three Burnshead How	Moray	NJ4129	57°21·1′	2°58·4′W	X	37
Three Burrows	Corn	SW7446	50°16·5′	5°9·9′W	T	204
Three Cairns	D & G	NX8957	54°54·0′	3°43·4′W	X	84
Three Castles Path	Bucks	SU9485	51°33·6′	0°38·2′W	X	175,176,186
Three Chimneys	Durham	NY9120	54°34·8′	2°7·9′W	X	91,92
Three Chimneys	Kent	TQ8238	51°7·0′	0°36·4′E	T	188
Three Chimneys	Northnts	SP8278	52°23·9′	0°47·3′W	X	141
Three Chimneys Fm	Essex	TL7140	52°2·1′	0°30·0′E	FM	154
Three Chimneys Fm	Kent	TQ7234	51°5·0′	0°27·7′E	FM	188
Threecliff Bay	Swan	SS5387	51°34·0′	4°6·9′W	W	159
Three Cocked Hat	Norf	TM4196	52°30·7′	1°33·5′E	T	134
Three Cocks	Powys	SO1737	52°1·8′	3°12·2′W	T	161
Three Comb	Durham	NY8434	54°42·3′	2°14·5′W	X	91,92
Three Corner Hat	Wilts	SU2241	51°10·3′	1°40·7′W	X	184
Three Counties Showground	Worcs	SO7842	52°4·8′	2°18·9′W	X	150
Three Crofts	D & G	NX8772	55°2·0′	3°45·7′W	T	84
Three Crosses	Swan	SS5794	51°37·8′	4°3·6′W	T	159
Three Crossways, The	Suff	TM1459	52°11·5′	1°8·3′E	X	156
Three Cups Corner	E Susx	TQ6320	50°57·6′	0°19·7′E	T	199
Three Curricks	Durham	NY8843	54°47·2′	2°10·8′W	X	87
Three Dikes	N Yks	SE8068	54°6·3′	0°46·2′W	A	100
Three Dubs Crags	Cumbr	SD3897	54°22·1′	2°56·8′W	X	96,97
Three Dubs Tarn	Cumbr	SD3797	54°22·1′	2°57·8′W	W	96,97
Three Farms	Northum	NY9883	55°8·7′	2°1·5′W	FM	81
Three Fingers	Wrex	SJ4541	52°58·1′	2°48·7′W	T	117
Three Fingers Rock	Shrops	SO4794	52°32·7′	2°46·5′W	X	137,138
Threefords	Fife	NO4511	56°17·6′	2°52·9′W	X	59
Three Forests Way	Essex	TL5418	51°50·6′	0°14·5′E	X	167
Three Forests Way	Redbr	TQ4793	51°37·2′	0°7·8′E	X	177
Three Forest Way	Essex	TQ4593	51°37·3′	0°6·1′E	X	177
Three Gates	Devon	SS9819	50°57·9′	3°26·8′W	X	181
Three Gates	Dorset	ST6307	50°51·9′	2°31·2′W	T	194
Three Gates	Leic	SP7198	52°34·7′	0°56·7′W	X	141
Three Gates	Shrops	SO2785	52°27·7′	3°4·1′W	X	137
Three Gates	Worcs	SO6862	52°15·6′	2°27·7′W	X	138,149
Three Gates Bottom	Bucks	SP9105	51°44·4′	0°40·5′W	X	165
Three Gates Cross	Somer	SS9027	51°2·1′	3°33·7′W	X	181
Three Gates Fm	E Susx	TQ7128	51°1·8′	0°26·7′E	FM	188,199
Three Gates Fm	Hartpl	NZ4530	54°40·0′	1°17·7′W	FM	93
Three Gates Fm	I of W	SZ4389	50°42·2′	1°23·1′W	FM	196
Three Gates Stud	Warw	SP3154	52°11·2′	1°32·4′W	X	151
Three Grains	S Lanak	NT0125	55°30·8′	3°33·6′W	W	72
Three Graves, The	Wilts	SU0256	51°18·4′	1°57·9′W	X	173
Threehammer Common	Norf	TG3419	52°43·3′	1°28·3′E	T	133,134
Three Hammers	Corn	SX2287	50°39·6′	4°30·7′W	T	190
Three Hammers	Devon	SS7611	50°53·3′	3°45·4′W	X	191
Three Hills	Northnts	SP9576	52°22·7′	0°35·9′W	X	141
Three Hills (Tumuli)	Northnts	SP9576	52°22·7′	0°35·9′W	A	141
Three Holes	Norf	TF5000	52°34·9′	0°13·2′E	T	143
Three Holes Cross	Corn	SX0173	50°31·6′	4°48·1′W	T	200
Threehope Height	D & G	NS8609	55°22·0′	3°47·5′W	H	71,78
Three Horse Shoes Fm	Hants	SU6527	51°2·5′	1°4·0′W	FM	185,186
Three Households	Bucks	SU9793	51°37·9′	0°35·5′W	X	175,176
Three Houses Fm	Herts	TL2020	51°52·2′	0°15·0′W	FM	166
Three Howes	N Yks	NZ6810	54°29·1′	0°56·6′W	A	94
Three Howes	N Yks	NZ7901	54°24·1′	0°46·6′W	A	94
Three Howes	N Yks	SE6398	54°22·7′	1°1·4′W	A	94,100
Three Howes	N Yks	SE7194	54°20·4′	0°54·1′W	A	94,100
Three Howes	N Yks	SE9697	54°21·8′	0°30·9′W	A	94,101

Three Hundreds of Aylesbury, The	Bucks	SP8506	51°45·0'	0°45·7'W	X	165
Threekingham	Lincs	TF0836	52°54·9'	0°23·2'W	T	130
Three Kings	Northum	NT7700	55°17·9'	2°21·3'W	X	80
Three Kings (Stone Circle)	Northum	NT7700	55°17·9'	2°21·3'W	A	80
Three Knights	Northum	NY7255	54°53·6'	2°25·8'W	X	86,87
Three Knowes	D & G	NY2095	55°14·8'	3°15·1'W	H	79
Three Lane Ends	Roch	SD8309	53°34·9'	2°15·0'W	X	109
Three Lanes End	Wirral	SJ2488	53°23·2'	3°8·2'W	X	108
Three Leaps, The	I of Angl	SH5278	53°16·9'	4°12·8'W	X	114,115
Three Leaps, The (Standing Stones)	I of Angl	SH5278	53°16·9'	4°12·8'W	A	114,115
Three Leg Cross	E Susx	TQ6831	51°3·4'	0°24·2'E	T	188
Three Legged Cross	Dorset	SU0805	50°50·9'	1°52·8'W	T	195
Three Legs Ho	Hants	SU4257	51°18·9'	1°23·5'W	X	174
Three Locks	Bucks	SP8928	51°56·8'	0°41·9'W	X	165
Three Lords	Carm	SN2410	51°45·9'	4°32·6'W	X	158
Three Lords' Barrow	Dorset	SY9184	50°39·6'	2°7·3'W	A	195
Threelows	Staffs	SK0746	53°0·9'	1°53·3'W	T	119,128
Three Maypoles	Sol	SP1177	52°23·7'	1°49·9'W	T	139
Three Men of Gragareth	Lancs	SD6779	54°12·6'	2°29·9'W	X	98
Three Merkland	D & G	NX8067	54°59·2'	3°52·1'W	X	84
Three Mile Bottom	Glos	SO9601	51°42·7'	2°3·1'W	F	163
Three Mile Cross	Lancs	SD5833	53°47·7'	2°37·8'W	X	102
Three Mile Cross	Wok	SU7167	51°24·1'	0°58·4'W	T	175
Three Mile Ho	Cumbr	SD6088	54°17·4'	2°36·5'W	X	97
Three Mile Ho	Norf	TG5009	52°37·5'	1°42·0'E	X	134
Threemilestone	Corn	SW7844	50°15·5'	5°6·5'W	T	204
Threemiletown	W Loth	NT0575	55°57·8'	3°30·9'W	T	65
Three Mullach Hill	D & G	NY1697	55°15·9'	3°18·9'W	H	79
Three Oak Hill Wood	Warw	SP0658	52°13·4'	1°54·3'W	F	150
Three Oaks	Devon	SX4474	50°32·9'	4°11·7'W	X	201
Three Oaks	E Susx	TQ8414	50°54·0'	0°37·4'E	T	199
Three Oaks Fm	Heref	SO2834	52°0·2'	3°2·5'W	FM	161
Three Old Maids, The	Highld	NM7272	56°47·3'	5°43·5'W	X	40
Three Parks Wood	Bucks	SP6539	52°3·0'	1°2·7'W	F	152
Threepen Burn	D & G	NT0102	55°18·4'	3°33·1'W	W	78
Threepgrass Wood	E Renf	NS4558	55°47·7'	4°27·9'W	F	64
Threep Head	Scot Bord	NT4417	55°26·9'	2°52·7'W	X	79
Threep Hill	D & G	NY2788	55°11·1'	3°8·4'W	H	79
Three Pikes	Durham	NY8334	54°42·3'	2°15·4'W	H	91,92
Three Pikes	Northum	NY6351	54°51·4'	2°34·2'W	H	86
Three Pikes	Northum	NY6695	55°15·1'	2°31·7'W	H	80
Threepland	E Renf	NS6049	55°43·1'	4°13·3'W	X	64
Threepland Backshaw	Scot Bord	NT0434	55°35·7'	3°31·0'W	X	72
Threepland Burn	E Renf	NS5949	55°43·1'	4°14·2'W	W	64
Threeply Fm	Renf	NS3766	55°51·8'	4°35·8'W	FM	63
Threep Moor	S Lanak	NS9911	55°23·2'	3°35·2'W	X	78
Threepneuk	D & G	NX8677	55°4·7'	3°46·7'W	X	84
Three Points	Bucks	SP6520	51°52·7'	1°2·9'W	X	164,165
Three Pools Waterway	Sefton	SD3718	53°39·5'	2°56·8'W	W	108
Three Pots (PH)	Leic	SP4391	52°31·1'	1°21·6'W	X	140
Threepsikes	Fife	NT0294	56°8·0'	3°34·2'W	X	58
Threepwood	E Ayr	NS5134	55°34·8'	4°21·4'W	X	70
Threepwood	N Ayr	NS3955	55°46·0'	4°33·5'W	X	63
Threepwood	Northum	NY8563	54°57·9'	2°13·6'W	X	87
Threepwood	Scot Bord	NT5142	55°40·4'	2°46·3'W	T	73
Threepwood	S Lanak	NS8147	55°42·4'	3°53·2'W	X	72
Threepwood Moss	Scot Bord	NT5142	55°40·4'	2°46·3'W	X	73
Three Riggles	Powys	SO1862	52°15·2'	3°11·7'W	X	148
Three Rivers	N Lincs	SE8110	53°35·1'	0°46·2'W	W	112
Three Shire Ash	Warw	SP2351	52°9·6'	1°39·4'W	X	151
Three Shire Heads	Staffs	SK0168	53°12·8'	1°58·7'W	X	119
Threeshire Hill	D & G	NS7427	55°27·7'	3°59·1'W	X	71
Three Shire Ho	Northnts	TL0470	52°19·3'	0°28·0'W	X	141,153
Three Shire Oak	Lincs	SK8242	52°58·4'	0°46·3'W	X	130
Three Shires	Northnts	SP4652	52°10·1'	1°19·2'W	X	151
Three Shire Stone	Cumbr	NY2702	54°24·7'	3°7·1'W	X	89,90
Three Shire Stones	S Glos	ST7970	51°26·0'	2°17·7'W	X	172
Threeshire Wood	Mil Key	SP9155	52°11·4'	0°39·7'W	F	152
Three Sisters	Denb	SJ0961	53°8·5'	3°21·2'W	T	116
Three Sisters	Wigan	SD5801	53°30·5'	2°37·6'W	X	108
Three Sisters, The	Highld	NN1656	56°39·8'	4°59·7'W	H	41
Three Sisters, The	N Ayr	NS1750	55°42·8'	4°54·3'W	X	63
Threestane Hill	Aberd	NO6387	56°58·6'	2°36·1'W	X	45
Threestoneburn Ho	Northum	NT9720	55°28·7'	2°2·4'W	X	75
Threestoneburn Wood	Northum	NT9619	55°28·1'	2°3·4'W	F	81
Three Stone Oar or The Wra	Corn	SW3736	50°10·2'	5°40·6'W	X	203
Three Tarns	Cumbr	NY2406	54°26·9'	3°9·9'W	W	89,90
Three Thorn Hollow Fm	Notts	SK5758	53°7·2'	1°8·5'W	FM	120
Threethorns	S Ayr	NS3504	55°18·4'	4°35·5'W	X	77
Three Towns Fm	Kent	TQ6441	51°8·9'	0°21·1'E	FM	188
Three Tremblers	N Yks	SE9387	54°16·4'	0°33·9'W	X	94,101
Three Tremblers (Tumulus)	N Yks	SE9387	54°16·4'	0°33·9'W	A	94,101
Threewater Foot	D & G	NT0902	55°18·5'	3°25·6'W	X	78
Threewaters	Corn	SX0366	50°27·9'	4°46·2'W	T	200
Three-well-brae	D & G	NY1475	55°4·0'	3°20·4'W	X	85
Three Wells	Aberd	NO8172	56°50·6'	2°18·2'W	X	45
Three Wells	Ches	SJ6942	52°58·7'	2°27·3'W	X	118
Three Wells	Pemb	SN1711	51°46·3'	4°38·8'W	X	158
Three Wells	Powys	SO0658	52°13·0'	3°22·2'W	X	147
Threip Moor	D & G	NX9595	55°14·5'	3°38·7'W	X	78
Threipmuir Reservoir	C of Edin	NT1763	55°51·4'	3°19·1'W	W	65,66
Threlkeld	Cumbr	NY3125	54°37·2'	3°3·7'W	T	90
Threlkeld Common	Cumbr	NY3424	54°36·7'	3°0·9'W	X	90
Threlkeld Knotts	Cumbr	NY3223	54°36·1'	3°2·7'W	X	90
Threlkeld Leys	Cumbr	NY1127	54°38·1'	3°22·3'W	X	89
Threlkeld Side	Cumbr	NY7127	54°38·5'	2°26·5'W	X	91
Thremhall Priory Fm	Essex	TL5321	51°52·2'	0°13·7'E	FM	167
Threpwood Hill	Northum	NY8777	55°5·5'	2°11·8'W	X	87
Threshelfords Fm	Essex	TL8719	51°50·5'	0°43·3'E	FM	168
Threshers Bush	Essex	TL4909	51°45·8'	0°9·9'E	T	167
Threshfield	N Yks	SD9863	54°4·0'	2°1·4'W	T	98
Threshfield Moor	N Yks	SD9663	54°4·0'	2°3·3'W	X	98
Thresholds	Shrops	SO4199	52°35·4'	2°51·9'W	X	137
Threshthwaite Cove	Cumbr	NY4210	54°29·2'	2°53·3'W	X	90
Threshthwaite Mouth	Cumbr	NY4210	54°29·2'	2°53·3'W	X	90
Threxton Hill	Norf	TF8800	52°34·1'	0°46·8'E	X	144
Threxton Ho	Norf	TL8898	52°33·1'	0°46·8'E	X	144
Thriepig	Northum	NT9040	55°39·5'	2°9·1'W	X	74,75
Thriepland	Aberd	NJ6364	57°40·1'	2°36·8'W	X	29
Thriepland	Aberd	NO8080	56°54·9'	2°19·3'W	X	45
Thriepley	Angus	NO3038	56°32·0'	3°7·8'W	X	53
Thrift Cottage	Kent	TQ9731	51°2·9'	0°49·0'E	X	189
Thrift Covert	Suff	TL6863	52°14·6'	0°28·0'E	F	154
Thrift Fm	Essex	TL7004	51°42·8'	0°28·0'E	FM	167
Thrift Fm	Essex	TL9733	51°57·9'	0°52·5'E	FM	168
Thrift Fm	Heref	SO7059	52°13·9'	2°26·0'W	FM	149
Thrift Fm	Suff	TL6954	52°9·7'	0°28·7'E	FM	154
Thrift Hill	Herts	TL3138	52°1·7'	0°5·0'W	X	153
Thrifts Hall Fm	Essex	TQ4598	51°39·9'	0°6·2'E	FM	167,177
Thrift, The	Shrops	SO5683	52°26·8'	2°38·4'W	X	137,138
Thrift, The	Worcs	SO9866	52°17·8'	2°1·4'W	F	150
Thrift Wood	Bucks	SP8132	51°59·1'	0°48·8'W	F	152,165
Thrift Wood	Essex	TL7901	51°41·0'	0°35·8'E	F	167
Thrift Wood	Essex	TL8005	51°43·1'	0°36·7'E	F	168
Thrift Wood	Worcs	SO9155	52°11·8'	2°7·5'W	F	150
Thrigby	Norf	TG4612	52°39·2'	1°38·6'E	T	134
Thrimby	Cumbr	NY5520	54°34·6'	2°41·3'W	X	90
Thrimby Grange	Cumbr	NY5519	54°34·1'	2°41·3'W	X	90
Thrimby Hall	Cumbr	NY5520	54°34·6'	2°41·3'W	X	90
Thringarth	Durham	NY9323	54°36·4'	2°6·1'W	T	91,92
Thringill	Cumbr	NY7706	54°27·2'	2°20·9'W	X	91
Thringstone	Leic	SK4217	52°45·2'	1°22·3'W	T	129
Thrintoft	N Yks	SE3293	54°20·1'	1°30·1'W	T	99
Thrintoft Park	N Yks	SE3194	54°20·7'	1°31·0'W	X	99
Thripland	Scot Bord	NT0435	55°36·2'	3°31·0'W	X	72
Thriple Burn	S Lanak	NT0032	55°34·5'	3°34·7'W	W	72
Thriplow	Cambs	TL4346	52°5·9'	0°5·7'E	T	154
Thripskin Fm	Suff	TM0177	52°21·5'	0°57·5'E	FM	144
Thrislington Plantn	Durham	NZ3132	54°41·2'	1°30·7'W	F	93
Thristley House Fm	Sund	NZ3751	54°51·4'	1°25·0'W	FM	88
Thriverton	Devon	SS3514	50°54·4'	4°20·4'W	X	190
Throapham	Roth	SK5387	53°22·9'	1°11·8'W	T	111,120
Throckenholt	Lincs	TF3509	52°39·9'	0°0·2'E	T	142
Throcking	Herts	TL3330	51°57·4'	0°3·5'W	T	166
Throckley	N upon Ty	NZ1566	54°59·5'	1°45·5'W	T	88
Throckley Ho	N upon Ty	NZ1566	54°59·5'	1°45·5'W	X	88
Throckley Marsh	Northum	NZ1569	55°1·2'	1°45·5'W	X	88
Throckmorton	Worcs	SO9849	52°8·6'	2°1·4'W	T	150
Throgmall Fm	Kent	TQ8563	51°20·4'	0°39·8'E	FM	178
Throlam	E Yorks	SE8235	53°48·5'	0°44·9'W	X	106
Throne of Gargrie	D & G	NX2852	54°50·3'	4°40·3'W	X	82
Throop	Dorset	SY8293	50°44·4'	2°14·9'W	T	194
Throop Clump	Dorset	SY8292	50°43·9'	2°14·9'W	F	194
Throope Hill	Wilts	SU0825	51°1·7'	1°52·8'W	H	184
Throope Manor Ho	Wilts	SU0826	51°2·2'	1°52·8'W	X	184
Throop Heath	Dorset	SY8191	50°43·3'	2°15·8'W	X	194
Throp	Cumbr	NY6265	54°58·9'	2°35·2'W	X	86
Thrope Fm	N Yks	SE1075	54°10·5'	1°50·4'W	FM	99
Thrope Plantn	N Yks	SE1074	54°9·9'	1°50·4'W	F	99
Throphill	Northum	NZ1385	55°9·8'	1°47·3'W	T	81
Thropton	Northum	NU0202	55°19·0'	1°57·7'W	T	81
Throsk	Stir	NS8591	56°6·1'	3°50·5'W	T	58
Throsk Ho	Stir	NS8591	56°6·1'	3°50·5'W	X	58
Thross Burn	Northum	NY7077	55°5·4'	2°27·8'W	W	86,87
Throstle Bank	Derby	SK0383	53°20·9'	1°56·9'W	X	110
Throstle Garth	Cumbr	NY2203	54°25·2'	3°11·7'W	X	89,90
Throstle Gill	N Yks	NZ0803	54°25·6'	1°52·2'W	W	92
Throstle Gill	N Yks	NZ1107	54°27·7'	1°49·4'W	X	92
Throstle Hall	Cumbr	NY3339	54°44·7'	3°2·0'W	X	90
Throstle Hill	N Yks	SE1177	54°11·6'	1°49·5'W	X	99
Throstle Nest	Brad	SE0848	53°55·9'	1°52·3'W	X	104
Throstle Nest	Darl	NZ2319	54°34·2'	1°38·2'W	X	93
Throstle Nest	E Yorks	SE8248	53°55·5'	0°44·7'W	X	106
Throstle Nest	Lancs	SD4648	53°55·8'	2°48·9'W	X	102
Throstle Nest	Lancs	SD5441	53°52·0'	2°41·6'W	X	102
Throstle Nest	Lancs	SD7854	53°59·1'	2°19·7'W	X	103
Throstle Nest	N Yks	NZ8706	54°26·8'	0°39·1'W	X	94
Throstle Nest	N Yks	SD9156	54°0·2'	2°7·8'W	X	103
Throstle Nest	N Yks	SD9889	54°18·0'	2°1·4'W	X	98
Throstle Nest	N Yks	SE2060	54°2·4'	1°41·3'W	X	99
Throstle Nest	N Yks	SE3560	54°2·3'	1°27·5'W	X	99
Throstle Nest	N Yks	SE3790	54°18·5'	1°25·5'W	X	99
Throstle Nest	N Yks	SE4873	54°9·3'	1°15·5'W	X	100
Throstle Nest	N Yks	SE5173	54°9·3'	1°12·7'W	X	100
Throstle Nest	N Yks	SE6280	54°13·0'	1°2·5'W	X	100
Throstle Nest	Red & Cl	NZ6915	54°31·8'	0°55·6'W	X	94
Throstle Nest Fm	Durham	NZ1545	54°48·2'	1°45·6'W	FM	88
Throstle Nest Fm	E Yorks	TA0550	53°56·4'	0°23·6'W	FM	107
Throstle Nest Fm	Leeds	SE4035	53°48·8'	1°23·1'W	FM	105
Throstle Nest Fm	N Yks	SE3753	53°58·5'	1°25·7'W	FM	104
Throstle Nest Fm	N Yks	SE4073	54°9·3'	1°22·8'W	FM	99
Throstle Nest Plantn	Darl	NZ2419	54°34·2'	1°37·3'W	F	93
Throstles Nest Fm	N Yks	SD9769	54°7·3'	2°2·3'W	FM	98
Throstles Nest Fm	N Yks	SD9869	54°7·3'	2°1·4'W	FM	98
Throstle Wood	E Yorks	SE8347	53°55·0'	0°43·8'W	F	106
Throston Grange	Hartpl	NZ4934	54°42·2'	1°14·0'W	X	93
Througham	Glos	SO9207	51°45·9'	2°6·6'W	T	163
Througham Slad	Glos	SO9206	51°45·4'	2°6·6'W	A	163
Through Gang Point	Aberd	NO9395	57°3·0'	2°6·5'W	X	38,45
Throughgate	D & G	NX8784	55°8·5'	3°45·9'W	X	78
Through Hill	Northum	NT8707	55°21·7'	2°11·9'W	H	80
Throwcombe	Devon	SS8819	50°58·0'	3°35·3'W	X	181
Throwleigh	Devon	SX6690	50°41·9'	3°53·5'W	T	191
Throwleigh Common	Devon	SX6490	50°41·9'	3°55·2'W	X	191
Throwley	Kent	TQ9955	51°15·8'	0°51·5'E	T	178
Throwley Cottage	Staffs	SK1051	53°3·6'	1°50·6'W	X	119
Throwley Forstal	Kent	TQ9854	51°15·3'	0°50·6'E	T	189
Throwley Hall	Staffs	SK1152	53°4·1'	1°49·7'W	X	119
Throwley Ho (Hotel)	Kent	TR0156	51°16·3'	0°53·3'E	X	178
Throwmires	E Yorks	SE7152	53°57·8'	0°54·7'W	X	105,106
Throwmires Beck	E Yorks	SE7152	53°57·8'	0°54·7'W	W	105,106
Throws	Essex	TL6522	51°52·6'	0°24·2'E	X	167
Throxenby	N Yks	TA0189	54°17·4'	0°26·5'W	T	101
Thrum Mill	Northum	NU0601	55°18·4'	1°53·9'W	X	81
Thrumpton	Notts	SK5031	52°52·7'	1°15·0'W	T	129
Thrumpton	Notts	SK7080	53°19·0'	0°56·5'W	T	120
Thrumster	Highld	ND3345	58°23·6'	3°8·3'W	T	12
Thrumster Little	Highld	ND3345	58°23·6'	3°8·3'W	X	12
Thrunton	Northum	NU0810	55°23·3'	1°52·0'W	T	81
Thrunton Crag	Northum	NU0709	55°22·7'	1°52·9'W	X	81
Thrunton Mill	Northum	NU0811	55°23·8'	1°52·0'W	X	81
Thrunton Red Ho	Northum	NU0809	55°22·7'	1°52·0'W	X	81
Thrunton Wood	Northum	NU0709	55°22·7'	1°52·9'W	F	81
Thrupe	Somer	ST6045	51°12·4'	2°34·0'W	T	183
Thrupemarsh Fm	Somer	ST6046	51°12·9'	2°34·0'W	FM	183
Thrupp	Glos	SO8603	51°43·8'	2°11·8'W	T	162
Thrupp	Oxon	SP4815	51°50·1'	1°17·8'W	T	164
Thrupp	Oxon	SU2998	51°41·0'	1°34·4'W	T	164
Thrupp End Fm	Beds	SP9839	52°2·7'	0°33·9'W	FM	153
Thrupp Grounds	Northnts	SP6065	52°17·0'	1°6·8'W	X	152
Thrupp Lodge	Northnts	SP5965	52°17·0'	1°7·7'W	X	152
Thrupp Wharf	Northnts	SP7843	52°5·0'	0°51·3'W	X	152
Thruscross	N Yks	SE1558	54°1·3'	1°45·8'W	T	104
Thruscross Reservoir	N Yks	SE1458	54°1·3'	1°46·8'W	W	104
Thrush Clough	Lancs	SD5956	54°0·1'	2°37·1'W	X	102
Thrushelton	Devon	SX4487	50°39·9'	4°12·1'W	T	190
Thrushgill Fell	Lancs	SD6461	54°2·9'	2°32·6'W	X	97
Thrush Ho	N Yks	SE5964	54°4·4'	1°5·5'W	X	100
Thrushlands	D & G	NS8703	55°18·7'	3°46·4'W	X	78
Thrushwood Fm	Red & Cl	NZ6020	54°34·5'	1°3·9'W	FM	94
Thrussington	Leic	SK6415	52°44·0'	1°2·7'W	T	129
Thrussington Grange	Leic	SK6418	52°45·6'	1°2·7'W	X	129
Thrussington Lodge	Leic	SK6516	52°44·5'	1°1·8'W	X	129
Thruxted	Kent	TR1053	51°14·5'	1°0·9'E	X	179,189
Thruxton	Hants	SU2945	51°12·4'	1°34·7'W	T	185
Thruxton	Heref	SO4334	52°0·3'	2°49·4'W	T	149,161
Thruxton Aerodrome and Motor Racing Circuit	Hants	SU2845	51°12·4'	1°35·6'W	X	184
Thruxton Fm	Hants	SU2443	51°11·4'	1°39·0'W	FM	184
Thruxton Hill	Hants	SU2543	51°11·4'	1°38·1'W	H	184
Thruxton Vallets	Heref	SO4333	51°59·8'	2°49·4'W	F	149,161
Thrybergh	Roth	SK4695	53°27·2'	1°18·0'W	T	111
Thrybergh Park	Roth	SK4696	53°27·8'	1°18·0'W	X	111
Thrybergh Resr	Roth	SK4795	53°27·2'	1°17·1'W	W	111
Thuborough Barton	Devon	SS3410	50°52·2'	4°21·2'W	X	190
Thuisgeirean	N Eil	NF5763	57°31·9'	7°43·5'W	X	22
Thulachan	Highld	ND1140	58°20·6'	3°30·7'W	X	11,12
Thule	Devon	SX6688	50°40·8'	3°53·4'W	X	191
Thulston	Derby	SK4031	52°52·7'	1°23·9'W	T	129
Thulston Fields Fm	Derby	SK3931	52°52·7'	1°24·8'W	FM	128
Thunacar Knott	Cumbr	NY2708	54°28·0'	3°7·2'W	X	89,90
Thunder Bridge	Kirk	SE1811	53°36·0'	1°43·3'W	T	110
Thunder Brook	Wilts	SU0583	51°33·0'	1°55·3'W	W	173
Thundercliffe Grange	Roth	SK3793	53°26·2'	1°26·2'W	X	110,111
Thunderfield Grove	Herts	TL3305	51°43·9'	0°4·0'W	F	166
Thundergay	N Ayr	NR8846	55°39·9'	5°21·8'W	X	62,69
Thunderheads	N Yks	SE6893	54°19·9'	0°56·8'W	X	94,100
Thunder Hill	Norf	TG4418	52°42·5'	1°37·1'E	T	134
Thunders Barrow	W Susx	TQ2208	50°51·7'	0°15·6'W	A	198
Thundersbarrow Hill	W Susx	TQ2208	50°51·7'	0°15·6'W	X	198
Thunder's Hill	E Susx	TQ5513	50°54·0'	0°12·6'E	T	199
Thunderslap Hill	Moray	NJ3033	57°23·2'	3°9·4'W	H	28
Thundersley	Essex	TQ7888	51°34·0'	0°34·5'E	T	178
Thunder Stone	Cumbr	NY5515	54°31·9'	2°41·3'W	A	90
Thunder Stone	Cumbr	NY6410	54°29·3'	2°32·9'W	X	91
Thunderton	Aberd	NK0646	57°30·5'	1°53·5'W	X	30
Thundridge	Herts	TL3517	51°50·3'	0°2·0'W	T	166
Thundry Fm	Surrey	SU9044	51°11·5'	0°42·3'W	FM	186
Thunker Hollow	Lincs	TF3069	53°12·4'	0°2·8'W	X	122
Thura Mains	Highld	ND2461	58°32·1'	3°17·8'W	X	11,12
Thurba	Swan	SS4286	51°33·3'	4°16·4'W	X	159
Thurcaston	Leic	SK5610	52°41·3'	1°9·9'W	T	129
Thurcroft	Roth	SK4988	53°23·4'	1°15·4'W	T	111,120
Thurcroft Hall	Roth	SK5089	53°24·0'	1°14·5'W	A	111,120
Thurdistoft	Highld	ND2067	58°35·3'	3°22·1'W	X	11,12
Thurdon	Corn	SS2811	50°52·6'	4°26·3'W	T	190
Thurgarton	Norf	TG1834	52°51·8'	1°14·7'E	T	133
Thurgarton	Notts	SK6949	53°2·3'	0°57·8'W	T	129
Thurgarton Old Hall	Norf	TG1736	52°52·9'	1°13·9'E	X	133
Thurgarton Quarters Fm	Notts	SK6551	53°3·4'	1°1·4'W	FM	120
Thurgoland	Barns	SE2801	53°30·5'	1°34·3'W	T	110
Thurgoods Fm	Essex	TL9225	51°53·7'	0°47·8'E	FM	168
Thurland Castle	Lancs	SD6173	54°9·3'	2°35·4'W	X	97
Thurlaston	Leic	SP5099	52°35·4'	1°15·3'W	T	140
Thurlaston	Warw	SP4671	52°20·3'	1°19·1'W	T	140
Thurlaston Br	Warw	SP4668	52°18·7'	1°19·1'W	X	151
Thurlaston Brook	Leic	SP5197	52°34·3'	1°14·4'W	W	140
Thurlaston Grange	Warw	SP4570	52°19·8'	1°20·0'W	X	140
Thurlaston Lodge Fm	Leic	SK5001	52°36·5'	1°15·3'W	FM	140
Thurlbear	Somer	ST2621	50°59·3'	3°2·9'W	T	193
Thurlbeck Dyke	Notts	SK6236	52°55·3'	1°4·3'W	W	129
Thurlby	Lincs	SK9061	53°8·5'	0°38·9'W	T	121
Thurlby	Lincs	TF0916	52°44·1'	0°22·7'W	T	130
Thurlby	Lincs	TF4975	53°15·3'	0°14·4'E	T	122
Thurlby Fen	Lincs	TF1117	52°44·6'	0°20·9'W	X	130
Thurlby Wood	Lincs	SK8487	53°22·6'	0°43·8'W	F	112,121
Thurle	Devon	SS6915	50°55·4'	3°51·5'W	X	180
Thurle Down	W Berks	SU5781	51°31·7'	1°10·3'W	X	174
Thurle Grange	W Berks	SU5781	51°31·7'	1°10·3'W	X	174
Thurleigh	Beds	TL0558	52°12·8'	0°27·4'W	T	153
Thurlescombe	Devon	SS9811	50°53·6'	3°26·6'W	X	192
Thurlestone	Devon	SX6743	50°16·6'	3°51·6'W	T	202
Thurlestone Grange	Derby	SK4131	52°52·7'	1°23·0'W	X	129
Thurlestone Rock	Devon	SX6741	50°15·5'	3°51·6'W	X	202
Thurleston Lodge	Suff	TM1548	52°5·5'	1°8·7'E	X	169
Thurley Fm	Wok	SU6966	51°23·6'	1°0·1'W	FM	175
Thurlibeer	Corn	SS2504	50°48·8'	4°28·7'W	X	190
Thurloxton	Somer	ST2730	51°4·1'	3°2·1'W	T	182
Thurlstone	Barns	SE2303	53°31·6'	1°38·8'W	T	110
Thurlstone Moors	Barns	SE1702	53°31·1'	1°44·2'W	X	110
Thurlton	Norf	TM4198	52°31·8'	1°33·6'E	T	134
Thurlton Links	Norf	TM4197	52°31·3'	1°33·6'E	T	134
Thurlton Marshes	Norf	TM4399	52°32·3'	1°35·4'E	X	134
Thurlwood	Ches	SJ8057	53°6·8'	2°17·5'W	T	118
Thurlwood Ho	Herts	TQ0696	51°39·4'	0°27·7'W	X	166,176
Thurmaston	Leic	SK6109	52°40·8'	1°5·5'W	T	140

Thurnby	Leic	SK6404	52°38·0'	1°2·9'W	T	140
Thurne	Norf	TG4015	52°41·0'	1°33·5'E	T	134
Thurne Mouth	Norf	TG3915	52°41·0'	1°32·6'E	W	133,134
Thurnham	Kent	TQ8057	51°17·2'	0°35·3'E	T	178,188
Thurnham Keep Fm	Kent	TQ8157	51°17·2'	0°36·1'E	FM	178,188
Thurnholmes Fm	N Lincs	SK7998	53°28·6'	0°48·2'W	FM	112
Thurning	Norf	TG0829	52°49·3'	1°5·6'E	T	133
Thurning	Northnts	TL0883	52°26·3'	0°24·3'W	T	142
Thurning Lodge	Northnts	TL0882	52°25·7'	0°24·3'W	X	142
Thurnscoe	Barns	SE4505	53°32·6'	1°18·8'W	T	111
Thurnscoe East	Barns	SE4605	53°32·6'	1°17·9'W	T	111
Thurnwood Fms	Dorset	ST7204	50°50·3'	2°23·5'W	FM	194
Thurot Cottage	I of M	NX4301	54°23·1'	4°24·6'W	X	95
Thurrigair	Orkney	ND4584	58°44·7'	2°56·5'W	X	7
Thurrish Rough	Cald	SD9933	53°47·8'	2°0·5'W	X	103
Thurrocks	Essex	TL4533	51°58·8'	0°7·1'E	X	167
Thurrock Services	Thurr	TQ5779	51°29·5'	0°16·1'E	X	177
Thursby	Cumbr	NY3250	54°50·7'	3°3·1'W	T	85
Thursden	Lancs	SD9034	53°48·4'	2°8·7'W	X	103
Thursden Brook	Lancs	SD8934	53°48·4'	2°9·6'W	W	103
Thursfield Lodge	Staffs	SJ8655	53°5·8'	2°12·1'W	X	118
Thursford	Norf	TF9734	52°52·3'	0°56·0'E	T	132
Thursford Common	Norf	TF9735	52°52·8'	0°56·1'E	X	132
Thursford Green	Norf	TF9734	52°52·3'	0°56·0'E	T	132
Thursford Old Hall	Norf	TF9833	52°51·7'	0°56·9'E	X	132
Thursgill	Cumbr	SD6893	54°20·1'	2°29·1'W	X	98
Thursland Hill	Lancs	SD4453	53°58·4'	2°50·8'W	X	102
Thursley	Surrey	SU9039	51°8·8'	0°42·4'W	T	186
Thursley Common	Surrey	SU9040	51°9·4'	0°42·4'W	X	186
Thursley Lake	Surrey	SU9239	51°8·8'	0°40·7'W	W	186
Thurso	Highld	ND1168	58°35·7'	3°31·4'W	T	11,12
Thurso Bay	Highld	ND1169	58°36·3'	3°31·4'W	W	12
Thurso East	Highld	ND1268	58°35·7'	3°30·4'W	T	11,12
Thurstaston	Wirral	SJ2484	53°21·1'	3°8·1'W	T	108
Thurstaston Common	Wirral	SJ2485	53°21·6'	3°8·1'W	X	108
Thurstaston Hill	Wirral	SJ2484	53°21·1'	3°8·1'W	H	108
Thurston	Cumbr	SD3196	54°21·5'	3°3·3'W	X	96,97
Thurston	Derby	SK3131	52°52·8'	1°32·0'W	X	128
Thurston	E Loth	NT7174	55°57·7'	2°27·4'W	X	67
Thurston	Pemb	SM9707	51°43·7'	4°56·0'W	X	157,158
Thurston	Suff	TL9265	52°15·2'	0°49·2'E	T	155
Thurston Clough	Oldham	SD9707	53°33·8'	2°2·3'W	T	109
Thurston End	Suff	TL7951	52°7·9'	0°37·3'E	T	155
Thurstonfield	Cumbr	NY3156	54°53·9'	3°4·1'W	T	85
Thurstonfield Lough	Cumbr	NY3156	54°53·9'	3°4·1'W	W	85
Thurston Fm	Essex	TL7136	52°0·0'	0°29·9'E	FM	154
Thurston Fold	Bury	SD8207	53°33·8'	2°15·9'W	X	109
Thurston Ho	Suff	TL9264	52°14·7'	0°49·1'E	X	155
Thurstonland	Kirk	SE1610	53°35·4'	1°45·1'W	T	110
Thurston Mains	E Loth	NT7173	55°57·2'	2°27·4'W	X	67
Thurston Mains Burn	E Loth	NT7173	55°57·2'	2°27·4'W	W	67
Thurston Manor	E Loth	NT7174	55°57·7'	2°27·4'W	X	67
Thurston Planche	Suff	TL9364	52°14·6'	0°50·0'E	X	155
Thurston Ville	Cumbr	SD3084	54°15·1'	3°4·0'W	X	96,97
Thurtle Wood	N Yks	SE6972	54°8·6'	0°56·2'W	F	100
Thurton	Norf	TG3200	52°33·1'	1°25·7'E	T	134
Thurvaston	Derby	SK1338	52°56·6'	1°48·0'W	T	128
Thurvaston	Derby	SK2437	52°56·0'	1°38·2'W	T	128
Thurvoe	Orkney	ND3094	58°49·9'	3°12·3'W	X	7
Thuster	Highld	ND2851	58°26·7'	3°13·5'W	X	11,12
Thuster Ho	Highld	ND3051	58°26·8'	3°11·5'W	X	11,12
Thuxton	Norf	TG0307	52°37·6'	1°0·4'E	T	144
Thwaite	Cumbr	SD6294	54°20·7'	2°34·7'W	X	97
Thwaite	D & G	NY0967	54°59·6'	3°24·9'W	X	85
Thwaite	Durham	NZ0311	54°29·9'	1°56·8'W	X	92
Thwaite	N Yks	SD7570	54°7·8'	2°22·5'W	X	98
Thwaite	N Yks	SD8998	54°22·9'	2°9·7'W	T	98
Thwaite	Suff	TM1168	52°16·4'	1°6·0'E	T	155
Thwaite Beck	Durham	NZ0311	54°29·9'	1°56·8'W	W	92
Thwaite Beck	N Yks	SD8697	54°22·3'	2°12·5'W	W	98
Thwaite Br Ho	N Yks	SD8292	54°19·6'	2°16·2'W	X	98
Thwaite Bridge Common	N Yks	SD8193	54°20·2'	2°17·1'W	X	98
Thwaite Burn	D & G	NY0968	55°0·1'	3°24·9'W	W	85
Thwaite Common	Norf	TG1932	52°50·7'	1°15·5'E	X	133
Thwaite Common	N Yks	SD8697	54°22·3'	2°12·5'W	X	98
Thwaite Flat	Cumbr	SD2174	54°9·6'	3°12·2'W	T	96
Thwaite Fm	Warw	SP4780	52°25·2'	1°18·1'W	FM	140
Thwaite Hall	Cumbr	NY3735	54°42·6'	2°58·2'W	X	90
Thwaite Hall	Durham	NZ0020	54°34·8'	1°59·6'W	X	92
Thwaite Hall	Lincs	TF4669	53°12·1'	0°11·6'E	X	122
Thwaite Hall	Norf	TG1932	52°50·7'	1°15·5'E	X	133
Thwaite Head	Cumbr	SD3490	54°18·3'	3°0·4'W	T	96,97
Thwaite Head	N Yks	SE8589	54°17·6'	0°41·2'W	X	94,100
Thwaite Head Fell	Cumbr	SD3591	54°18·9'	2°59·5'W	X	96,97
Thwaitehill	Cumbr	NY4521	54°35·1'	2°50·6'W	X	90
Thwaite Hill Fm	Norf	TG1833	52°51·2'	1°14·7'E	FM	133
Thwaite Ho	N Yks	SE1076	54°11·0'	1°50·4'W	X	99
Thwaite Ho	N Yks	SE2074	54°9·9'	1°41·2'W	X	99
Thwaite Holme	N Yks	SD9590	54°18·6'	2°4·2'W	X	98
Thwaite House Fm	Lancs	SD4969	54°7·1'	2°46·4'W	FM	97
Thwaite House Fm	Roth	SK5587	53°22·9'	1°10·0'W	FM	111,120
Thwaite Moss	Cumbr	SD3389	54°17·8'	3°1·3'W	F	96,97
Thwaite Moss	Lancs	SD6566	54°5·6'	2°31·7'W	X	97
Thwaite Plantation	N Yks	SD7569	54°7·2'	2°22·5'W	F	98
Thwaites	Brad	SE0741	53°52·2'	1°53·2'W	T	104
Thwaites	Cumbr	NY3443	54°46·9'	3°1·1'W	X	85
Thwaites	Cumbr	NY5248	54°49·7'	2°44·4'W	X	86
Thwaites Brow	Brad	SE0740	53°51·6'	1°53·2'W	T	104
Thwaites Fell	Cumbr	SD1790	54°18·2'	3°16·1'W	X	96
Thwaites Head	Cumbr	SD7290	54°18·5'	2°25·4'W	X	98
Thwaites Ho	N Yks	NZ5202	54°24·9'	1°11·5'W	X	93
Thwaite Side	N Yks	SD8897	54°22·3'	2°10·7'W	X	98
Thwaite St Mary	Norf	TM3394	52°29·9'	1°26·4'E	T	134
Thwaite Yeat	Cumbr	SD1888	54°17·1'	3°15·2'W	X	96
Thwartergill Head	Scot Bord	NY5185	55°9·7'	2°45·7'W	X	79
Thwing	E Yorks	TA0570	54°7·1'	0°23·2'W	T	101
Thybergh Country Park	Roth	SK4796	53°27·8'	1°17·1'W	T	111
Tianavaig Bay	Highld	NG5138	57°22·1'	6°8·0'W	W	23,24,32
Tibberchindy	Aberd	NJ5215	57°13·7'	2°47·2'W	X	37
Tibbermore	Pth & Kin	NO0523	56°23·6'	3°31·9'W	T	52,53,58
Tibbers	D & G	NX8696	55°15·0'	3°47·2'W	X	78
Tibbers Castle	D & G	NX8698	55°16·0'	3°47·2'W	A	78
Tibbers Wood	D & G	NX8597	55°15·5'	3°48·1'W	F	78
Tibberton	Glos	SO7621	51°53·5'	2°20·5'W	T	162
Tibberton	Worcs	SO9057	52°12·9'	2°8·4'W	T	150
Tibberton	Wrekin	SJ6820	52°46·8'	2°28·1'W	T	127
Tibberton Grange	Wrekin	SJ6818	52°45·8'	2°28·1'W	X	127
Tibberton Manor	Wrekin	SJ6919	52°46·3'	2°27·2'W	X	127
Tibberton Moor	Wrekin	SJ6818	52°45·8'	2°28·1'W	X	127
Tibbett's Hill	Devon	SS1346	51°11·2'	4°40·2'W	H	180
Tibbett's Point	Devon	SS1446	51°11·2'	4°39·3'W	X	180
Tibbie Shiels Inn	Scot Bord	NT2420	55°28·3'	3°11·7'W	X	73
Tibbitts Fm	Cambs	TL4270	52°18·8'	0°5·4'E	FM	154
Tibb's Court	Kent	TQ6740	51°8·3'	0°23·6'E	X	188
Tibby Head	Norf	TG0145	52°58·1'	1°0·0'E	X	133
Tibenham	Norf	TM1389	52°27·7'	1°8·5'E	T	144,156
Tibertich	Arg & Bt	NM8402	56°10·0'	5°28·3'W	X	55
Tibhall	Heref	SO3855	52°11·6'	2°54·0'W	X	148,149
Tib Hall Fm	Warw	SP2395	52°33·4'	1°39·2'W	FM	139
Tibridge	Devon	SX4484	50°38·3'	4°12·0'W	X	201
Tibshelf	Derby	SK4360	53°8·4'	1°21·0'W	T	120
Tibshelf Wharf	Notts	SK4561	53°8·9'	1°19·2'W	T	120
Tibthorpe	E Yorks	SE9655	53°59·2'	0°31·7'W	T	106
Tibthorpe Grange	E Yorks	SE9557	54°0·3'	0°32·6'W	X	106
Tibthorpe Ho	E Yorks	SE9456	53°59·7'	0°33·5'W	X	106
Tibthorpe Lodge Fm	E Yorks	SE9556	53°59·7'	0°32·6'W	FM	106
Tibthorpe Manor	E Yorks	SE9355	53°59·2'	0°34·5'W	X	106
Tibthorpe Wold	E Yorks	SE9456	53°59·7'	0°33·5'W	X	106
Ticehurst	E Susx	TQ6930	51°2·9'	0°25·1'E	T	188
Ticehurst Ho	E Susx	TQ6830	51°2·9'	0°24·2'E	X	188
Tich Barrow	Corn	SX1488	50°40·0'	4°37·5'W	A	190,200
Tichborne	Hants	SU5730	51°4·2'	1°10·8'W	T	185
Tichborne Down	Hants	SU5831	51°4·8'	1°9·9'W	X	185
Tichborne Park	Hants	SU5730	51°4·2'	1°10·8'W	X	185
Tichfield Hill	Notts	SK5873	53°15·3'	1°7·4'W	F	120
Tickencote	Rut	SK9809	52°40·4'	0°32·6'W	T	141
Tickencote Laund	Rut	SK9810	52°41·0'	0°32·6'W	F	130
Tickencote Lodge Fm	Rut	SK9709	52°40·4'	0°33·5'W	FM	141
Tickencote Park	Rut	SK9809	52°40·4'	0°32·6'W	X	141
Tickencote Warren	Rut	SK9711	52°41·5'	0°33·5'W	X	130
Tickenham	N Som	ST4471	51°26·3'	2°48·0'W	T	171,172
Tickenham Hill	N Som	ST4472	51°26·9'	2°48·0'W	X	171,172
Tickenham Moor	N Som	ST4470	51°25·8'	2°47·9'W	X	171,172
Tickenhurst	Kent	TR2854	51°14·6'	1°16·4'E	X	179
Tickerage Wood	E Susx	TQ5120	50°57·8'	0°9·4'E	F	199
Ticketwood	Devon	SX7343	50°16·6'	3°46·6'W	T	202
Tick Fen	Cambs	TL3484	52°26·5'	0°1·3'W	X	142
Tickfold Fm	W Susx	TQ1636	51°6·9'	0°20·2'W	FM	187
Tickford Abbey	Mil Key	SP8844	52°5·5'	0°42·5'W	X	152
Tickford End	Mil Key	SP8843	52°4·9'	0°42·5'W	T	152
Tickford Lodge Fm	Mil Key	SP9043	52°4·9'	0°40·8'W	FM	152
Tickford Park	Mil Key	SP9142	52°4·4'	0°39·9'W	X	152
Tickham	Kent	TQ9560	51°18·6'	0°48·3'E	X	178
Tickhill	Donc	SK5993	53°26·1'	1°6·3'W	T	111
Tickhill	Staffs	SJ9544	52°59·8'	2°4·1'W	X	118
Tickhill Fm	N Yks	SE3755	53°59·6'	1°25·7'W	FM	104
Tickhill Grange	Donc	SK6293	53°26·0'	1°3·6'W	X	111
Tickhill High Common	Donc	SK6194	53°26·6'	1°4·5'W	X	111
Tickhill Low Common	Donc	SK6092	53°25·5'	1°5·4'W	X	111
Ticklas Point	Pemb	SM8212	51°46·1'	5°9·2'W	X	157
Tick Law	Northum	NU0821	55°29·2'	1°52·0'W	H	75
Tickleback Row	Brackn	SU8672	51°26·7'	0°45·4'W	T	175
Ticklerton	Shrops	SO4890	52°30·6'	2°45·6'W	T	137,138
Tickmorend	Glos	ST8398	51°41·1'	2°14·4'W	T	162
Ticknall	Derby	SK3523	52°48·4'	1°28·4'W	T	128
Tickton	E Yorks	TA0641	53°51·5'	0°22·9'W	T	107
Tickton Grange (Hotel)	E Yorks	TA0742	53°52·0'	0°22·0'W	X	107
Tickton Hall	E Yorks	TA0542	53°52·1'	0°23·8'W	X	107
Tick Wood	Shrops	SJ6403	52°37·7'	2°31·5'W	F	127
Tickwood Hall	Shrops	SJ6402	52°37·1'	2°31·5'W	X	127
Tidal Observatory	Corn	SW4628	50°6·1'	5°32·8'W	X	203
Tidbatch	Heref	SO7059	52°13·9'	2°26·0'W	X	149
Tidbury Common	Hants	SU4441	51°10·2'	1°21·8'W	X	185
Tidbury Fm	Hants	SU4542	51°10·8'	1°21·0'W	FM	185
Tidbury Green	Sol	SP0975	52°22·6'	1°51·7'W	T	139
Tidbury Ring	Hants	SU4642	51°10·8'	1°20·1'W	A	185
Tidcombe	Wilts	SU2958	51°19·5'	1°34·6'W	T	174
Tidcombe Down	Wilts	SU2858	51°19·5'	1°35·5'W	X	174
Tidderson	Devon	SS8616	50°56·2'	3°37·0'W	X	181
Tiddesley Wood	Worcs	SO9245	52°6·4'	2°6·6'W	F	150
Tiddington	Oxon	SP6504	51°44·1'	1°3·1'W	T	164,165
Tiddington	Warw	SP2255	52°11·8'	1°40·3'W	T	151
Tiddle Brook	Shrops	SO6893	52°32·3'	2°27·9'W	W	138
Tidebrook	E Susx	TQ6129	51°2·5'	0°18·2'E	T	188,199
Tidebrook Manor	E Susx	TQ6129	51°2·5'	0°18·2'E	X	188,199
Tideford	Corn	SX3459	50°24·7'	4°19·8'W	T	201
Tideford Cross	Corn	SX3461	50°25·8'	4°19·9'W	T	201
Tide Mill	Hants	SU3612	50°54·6'	1°28·9'W	X	196
Tide Mills	E Susx	TQ4600	50°47·1'	0°4·7'E	X	198
Tidenham	Glos	ST5595	51°39·4'	2°38·6'W	T	162
Tidenham Chase	Glos	ST5598	51°41·0'	2°38·7'W	T	162
Tides Low	Derby	SK1477	53°17·6'	1°47·0'W	A	119
Tideslow Fm	Derby	SK1578	53°18·2'	1°46·1'W	FM	119
Tideswell	Derby	SK1575	53°16·5'	1°46·1'W	T	119
Tideswell Dale	Derby	SK1574	53°16·0'	1°46·1'W	X	119
Tideswell Moor	Derby	SK1478	53°18·2'	1°47·0'W	X	119
Tidgrove Warren Fm	Hants	SU5254	51°17·2'	1°14·9'W	FM	185
Tidicombe Fm	Devon	SS6339	51°8·3'	3°57·1'W	FM	180
Tidkinhow Fm	Red & Cl	NZ6414	54°31·3'	1°0·3'W	FM	94
Tidlake	Devon	SS7321	50°58·7'	3°48·2'W	X	180
Tidley Hill	Hants	SU5844	51°11·8'	1°9·8'W	X	185
Tidmarsh	W Berks	SU6374	51°27·9'	1°5·2'W	T	175
Tidmarsh Manor	W Berks	SU6274	51°27·9'	1°6·1'W	X	175
Tidmington	Warw	SP2538	52°2·6'	1°37·7'W	T	151
Tidna, The	Corn	SS2014	50°54·1'	4°33·2'W	W	190
Tidnock Wood	Ches	SJ8669	53°13·3'	2°12·2'W	F	118
Tidnor	Heref	SO5539	52°3·1'	2°39·0'W	T	149
Tidpit	Hants	SU0719	50°58·5'	1°53·6'W	T	184
Tidpit Common Down	Hants	SU0617	50°57·4'	1°54·5'W	X	184
Tidwell Ho	Devon	SY0583	50°38·6'	3°20·2'W	X	192
Tidworth Ho	Wilts	SU2347	51°13·5'	1°39·8'W	X	184
Tiel Burn	Fife	NT2590	56°6·1'	3°11·9'W	W	59
Tiers Cross	Pemb	SM9010	51°45·2'	5°2·2'W	T	157,158
Tierson	Pemb	SM9009	51°44·7'	5°2·1'W	X	157,158
Tiervaagain	Arg & Bt	NR3864	55°48·2'	6°10·4'W	X	60,61
Tiffenden Manor Fm	Kent	TQ9036	51°5·7'	0°43·2'E	FM	189
Tiffenthwaite	Cumbr	NY2647	54°49·0'	3°8·7'W	X	85
Tiffery	Aberd	NK0445	57°30·0'	1°55·5'W	X	30
Tiffield	Northnts	SP6951	52°9·4'	0°59·1'W	T	152
Tiffyhall	Orkney	HY5705	58°56·1'	2°44·3'W	X	6
Tifty	Aberd	NJ7740	57°27·2'	2°22·5'W	T	29,30
Tifty Burn	Aberd	NJ7844	57°29·4'	2°21·6'W	W	29,30
Tiger Hill	Suff	TL9235	51°59·0'	0°48·2'E	X	155
Tiger Holt	Lincs	SK8585	53°21·5'	0°43·0'W	F	112,121
Tigerton	Angus	NO5464	56°46·2'	2°44·7'W	T	44
Tighachrochadair	Highld	NH4348	57°30·0'	4°36·7'W	X	26
Tigh a Ghobhainn	Fife	NO5808	56°16·0'	2°40·2'W	X	59
Tigh-a'-mholain	Highld	NG9420	57°13·7'	5°24·3'W	X	25,33
Tigh-an-Ab	Highld	NC9021	58°10·1'	3°51·7'W	X	17
Tigh an Fhraoich	Stir	NN4628	56°25·4'	4°29·4'W	X	51
Tigh-an-rathaid	Arg & Bt	NR9378	55°57·3'	5°18·5'W	X	62
Tigh a' Phuirt	Stir	NN4026	56°24·2'	4°35·1'W	X	51
Tigharry	N Eil	NF7171	57°36·8'	7°30·1'W	T	18
Tighchoie	Arg & Bt	NM2843	56°30·3'	6°24·8'W	X	46,47,48
Tighchuig	Highld	NH3937	57°24·0'	4°40·3'W	X	26
Tighcladich	Arg & Bt	NN1308	56°13·9'	5°0·6'W	X	56
Tighcreag	Highld	NC6209	58°3·2'	4°19·8'W	X	16
Tigh Ghardail	Highld	NM8254	56°37·9'	5°32·8'W	X	49
Tigh Ghlinnegabhar	Highld	NM9563	56°43·1'	5°20·6'W	X	40
Tigh Mor	Arg & Bt	NN1528	56°24·7'	4°59·5'W	A	50
Tighmore	Pth & Kin	NN7460	56°43·1'	4°3·1'W	X	42
Tigh Mór na Seilge	Highld	NH1316	57°12·1'	5°5·3'W	H	34
Tigh-na-Blair	Pth & Kin	NN7716	56°19·5'	3°58·9'W	X	57
Tighnabruaich	Arg & Bt	NR9773	55°54·7'	5°14·4'W	T	62
Tighnacachla	Arg & Bt	NR2965	55°48·4'	6°19·1'W	X	60
Tigh na Caillich	Arg & Bt	NM3542	56°30·0'	6°17·9'W	X	47,48
Tigh-na-Coille	Pth & Kin	NO1465	56°46·4'	3°24·0'W	X	43
Tighnacomaire	Highld	NM9369	56°46·3'	5°22·8'W	X	40
Tighnacraig	Highld	NH5569	57°41·5'	4°25·5'W	X	21
Tigh na Craig	Stir	NN5534	56°28·8'	4°20·8'W	X	51
Tigh na Cruaiche	Pth & Kin	NN3754	56°39·2'	4°39·1'W	X	41
Tighnafiline	Highld	NG8789	57°50·7'	5°34·9'W	X	19
Tigh-na-gaoith	Arg & Bt	NR7168	55°51·3'	5°39·1'W	X	62
Tigh-na-geat	Midlo	NT2565	55°52·6'	3°11·5'W	X	66
Tigh-na-Geat	Pth & Kin	NN9160	56°43·4'	3°46·4'W	X	43
Tighnahinch	Highld	NH5657	57°35·1'	4°24·1'W	X	26
Tighnahoran	Arg & Bt	NR7675	55°55·2'	5°34·7'W	X	62
Tighnaleac	Highld	NH4644	57°27·9'	4°33·6'W	X	26
Tigh nam Bodach	Pth & Kin	NN3842	56°32·8'	4°37·7'W	A	50
Tigh-na-sleubhaich	Highld	NN1364	56°44·1'	5°3·0'W	X	41
Tighnaspeur	Arg & Bt	NR4150	55°40·7'	6°6·8'W	X	60
Tighness	Arg & Bt	NN2903	56°11·6'	4°44·9'W	T	56
Tigh-phuirt	Highld	NN0958	56°40·7'	5°6·6'W	X	41
Tigh-Sith	Shetld	HU6389	60°35·0'	0°50·5'W	X	1,2
Tigh Talamhanta	N Eil	NF6702	56°59·6'	7°28·6'W	X	31
Tigh Talamhanta (Aisled House)	N Eil	NF6702	56°59·6'	7°28·6'W	A	31
Tighvein	N Ayr	NR9927	55°30·0'	5°10·5'W	H	69
Tigley	Devon	SX7560	50°25·8'	3°45·2'W	T	202
Tignals	Hants	SU8237	51°7·8'	0°49·3'W	X	186
Tigwell Fm	Hants	SU6824	51°0·9'	1°1·4'W	FM	185
Tilberthwaite Fells	Cumbr	NY2801	54°24·2'	3°6·1'W	X	89,90
Tilberthwaite High Fells	Cumbr	NY2801	54°24·2'	3°6·1'W	X	89,90
Tilbouries	Aberd	NO8398	57°4·6'	2°16·4'W	X	38,45
Tilbrook	Cambs	TL0769	52°18·8'	0°25·4'W	T	153
Tilbrook Bushes	Cambs	TL0767	52°17·7'	0°25·5'W	F	153
Tilbrook Grange	Cambs	TL0871	52°19·8'	0°24·5'W	X	153
Tilbrook Mill	Cambs	TL0769	52°18·8'	0°25·4'W	X	153
Tilburstow Hill	Surrey	TQ3450	51°14·2'	0°4·4'W	X	187
Tilburstowhill Common	Surrey	TQ3550	51°14·2'	0°3·6'W	X	187
Tilbury	Thurr	TQ6476	51°27·8'	0°22·0'E	T	177
Tilbury Court	Essex	TL7639	52°1·5'	0°34·3'E	X	155
Tilbury Fm	Oxon	SP4806	51°45·3'	1°17·9'W	FM	164
Tilbury Green	Essex	TL7440	52°2·1'	0°32·6'E	T	155
Tilbury Hall	Essex	TL7540	52°2·1'	0°33·5'E	X	155
Tilbury Hollow	Glos	SP1237	52°2·1'	1°49·1'W	X	150
Tilbury Juxta Claire	Essex	TL7640	52°2·1'	0°34·4'E	T	155
Tilbury Ness	Thurr	TQ6275	51°27·3'	0°20·3'E	X	177
Tilden	Kent	TQ8345	51°10·7'	0°37·5'E	X	188
Tilden Fm	Kent	TQ7732	51°3·8'	0°32·0'E	FM	188
Tile Barn	E Susx	TQ5101	50°47·6'	0°8·9'E	X	199
Tile Barn	Northnts	SP5551	52°9·5'	1°11·4'W	X	152
Tile Barn	Oxon	SU4984	51°33·4'	1°17·2'W	X	174
Tile Barn	Surrey	TQ3445	51°11·5'	0°4·5'W	X	187
Tilebarn Fm	E Susx	TQ8422	50°58·3'	0°37·6'E	FM	199
Tile Barn Fm	Hants	SU7147	51°13·3'	0°58·6'W	FM	186
Tile Barn Fm	Kent	TQ8442	51°9·1'	0°38·3'E	FM	188
Tile Barn Fm	Medway	TQ7873	51°25·9'	0°34·0'E	FM	178
Tile Br	N Yks	SE5636	53°49·3'	1°8·5'W	X	105
Tile Cross	Birm	SP1686	52°28·5'	1°45·5'W	T	139
Tile Fm	Norf	TF5803	52°36·3'	0°20·4'E	FM	143
Tilegate Green	Essex	TL5008	51°45·3'	0°10·8'E	T	167
Tile Hill	Cov	SP2878	52°24·2'	1°34·9'W	T	140
Tilehill Wood	Cov	SP2878	52°24·2'	1°34·9'W	F	140
Tile Ho	Bucks	TQ0389	51°35·7'	0°30·4'W	X	176
Tile House Beck	Lincs	TF1271	53°13·7'	0°18·9'W	X	121
Tilehouse Br	N Yks	SE6785	54°15·6'	0°57·9'W	X	94,100
Tile House Fm	Bucks	SP6939	52°2·9'	0°59·2'W	FM	152
Tile House Fm	Essex	TL9729	51°55·7'	0°52·3'E	FM	168
Tilehouse Green	Sol	SP1776	52°23·1'	1°44·6'W	T	139
Tilehouse Wood	Bucks	SP6839	52°2·9'	1°0·1'W	F	152
Tilehurst	Essex	TQ6598	51°39·6'	0°23·5'E	X	167,177
Tile Hurst	E Susx	TQ5709	50°51·8'	0°14·2'E	X	199
Tilehurst	Read	SU6673	51°27·4'	1°2·6'W	T	175
Tilehurst Fm	Surrey	TQ1748	51°13·4'	0°19·1'W	FM	187
Tilehurst Sta	Read	SU6775	51°28·4'	1°1·7'W	X	175
Tilekiln	Essex	TL7032	51°57·9'	0°28·9'E	X	167
Tilekiln Cott	Cumbr	NY1241	54°45·6'	3°21·6'W	X	85
Tilekiln Fm	Essex	TL8628	51°55·4'	0°42·7'E	FM	168
Tilekiln Fm	Herts	TL2528	51°56·4'	0°10·5'W	FM	166

Tilekiln Green	Essex	TL5221	51°52·2'	0°12·9'E	T	167
Tile Kiln Wood	Notts	SK5573	53°15·3'	1°10·1'W	F	120
Tile Lodge	Kent	TQ9349	51°12·7'	0°46·2'E	X	189
Tile Lodge Fm	Kent	TR1962	51°19·1'	1°9·0'E	FM	179
Tilement Fm	E Susx	TQ6017	50°56·0'	0°17·0'E	FM	199
Tilery Fm, The	Cumbr	NY4334	54°42·1'	2°52·6'W	FM	90
Tile's Fm	Bucks	SP9404	51°43·8'	0°37·9'W	FM	165
Tiles Fm	E Susx	TQ6415	50°54·9'	0°20·4'E	FM	199
Tilesford Fm	Worcs	SO9650	52°9·1'	2°3·1'W	FM	150
Tileshed Fm	N Yks	SE6442	53°52·5'	1°1·2'W	FM	105,106
Tile Sheds	Northum	NU0028	55°33·0'	1°59·6'W	X	75
Tilesheds	Northum	NY8592	55°13·6'	2°13·7'W	X	80
Tile Sheds	Northum	NZ1082	55°8·2'	1°50·2'W	X	81
Tilesheds Wood	Northum	NU0734	55°36·2'	1°52·9'W	F	75
Tiley	Dorset	ST6706	50°51·4'	2°27·7'W	T	194
Tilford	Surrey	SU8743	51°11·0'	0°44·9'W	T	186
Tilford Common	Surrey	SU8742	51°10·5'	0°44·9'W	T	186
Tilford Reeds	Surrey	SU8643	51°11·0'	0°45·8'W	T	186
Tilgate	W Susx	TQ2735	51°6·2'	0°10·8'W	T	187
Tilgate Forest	W Susx	TQ2733	51°5·2'	0°10·8'W	F	187
Tilgate Forest Lodge	W Susx	TQ2631	51°4·1'	0°11·7'W	X	187
Tilgate Forest Row	W Susx	TQ2632	51°4·6'	0°11·7'W	T	187
Tilgate Park	W Susx	TQ2734	51°5·7'	0°10·8'W	X	187
Tilgate Wood	W Susx	TQ3231	51°4·0'	0°6·6'W	F	187
Tilham Fm	Somer	ST5535	51°7·0'	2°38·2'W	FM	182,183
Tilhill Ho	Surrey	SU8744	51°11·5'	0°44·9'W	X	186
Tilkey	Essex	TL8423	51°52·7'	0°40·8'E	T	168
Tilkhurst Fm	W Susx	TQ3637	51°7·2'	0°3·0'W	FM	187
Tillan Burn	N Lanak	NS8060	55°49·4'	3°54·5'W	W	65
Tilland	Corn	SX3261	50°25·7'	4°21·5'W	T	201
Tilland Road Fm	Corn	SX3262	50°26·3'	4°21·6'W	FM	201
Tillathrowie	Aberd	NJ4735	57°24·4'	2°52·5'W	X	28,29
Till Bridge Fm	Lincs	SK9079	53°18·3'	0°38·6'W	FM	121
Till Bridge Lane Ho	Lincs	SK9378	53°17·7'	0°35·9'W	X	121
Tillbrook Mill Fm	Cambs	TL0770	52°19·3'	0°25·4'W	FM	153
Tillenhilt	Aberd	NJ6605	57°8·3'	2°33·3'W	X	38
Tillenteach	Aberd	NO6195	57°2·9'	2°38·1'W	X	37,45
Tillenturk	Aberd	NJ6504	57°7·8'	2°34·2'W	X	38
Tillers End Fm	Herts	TL3625	51°54·6'	0°1·0'W	FM	166
Tillers' Green	Glos	SO6932	51°59·4'	2°26·7'W	T	149
Tillerton	Devon	SX7995	50°44·8'	3°42·5'W	X	191
Tillery	Aberd	NJ9122	57°17·6'	2°8·5'W	X	38
Tilley	Shrops	SJ5027	52°50·5'	2°44·1'W	T	126
Tilley Fm	E Susx	TQ6612	50°53·2'	0°22·0'E	FM	199
Tilley Green	Shrops	SJ5127	52°50·5'	2°43·2'W	T	126
Tilley Park	Shrops	SJ4926	52°50·0'	2°45·0'W	X	126
Till Ho	Lancs	SD7647	53°55·4'	2°21·5'W	X	103
Tillicoultry	Clackm	NS9197	56°9·5'	3°44·9'W	T	58
Tilliehashlach	Aberd	NJ6718	57°15·3'	2°32·4'W	X	38
Tillietudlem	S Lanak	NS8045	55°41·3'	3°54·1'W	T	72
Tilliglens	Moray	NJ0047	57°30·4'	3°39·7'W	X	27
Tillinamolt	Aberd	NJ8958	57°37·0'	2°10·6'W	X	30
Tilling Bourne	Surrey	TQ0647	51°13·0'	0°28·5'W	W	187
Tillingdown Fm	Surrey	TQ3455	51°16·9'	0°4·3'W	FM	187
Tillingham	Essex	TL9903	51°41·6'	0°53·2'E	T	168
Tillingham Fm	E Susx	TQ8820	50°57·1'	0°41·0'E	FM	189,199
Tillingham Hall	Thurr	TQ6287	51°33·7'	0°20·6'E	X	177
Tillingham Marshes	Essex	TM0202	51°41·0'	0°55·7'E	X	168
Tillinghurst Fm	W Susx	TQ3330	51°3·5'	0°5·7'W	FM	187
Tillington	Heref	SO4645	52°6·3'	2°46·9'W	T	148,149
Tillington	Staffs	SJ9124	52°49·0'	2°7·6'W	T	127
Tillington	W Susx	SU9621	50°59·0'	0°37·6'W	T	197
Tillington Ho	W Susx	SU9621	50°59·0'	0°37·6'W	X	197
Tillinton Common	Heref	SO4546	52°6·8'	2°47·8'W	T	148,149
Tilloch	Aberd	NJ7305	57°8·4'	2°26·3'W	X	38
Tillislow	Devon	SX3893	50°43·1'	4°17·3'W	T	190
Tillmire Fm	York	SE6247	53°55·2'	1°2·9'W	FM	105
Tillmire Fm	York	SE6448	53°55·7'	1°1·1'W	FM	105,106
Tillmouth Fm	Northum	NT8844	55°41·6'	2°11·0'W	FM	74
Tillputsend Cott	Glos	SO6933	51°59·9'	2°26·7'W	X	149
Till's Fm	Lancs	SD5455	53°59·6'	2°41·7'W	FM	102
Tills Fm	Suff	TL9840	52°1·6'	0°53·6'E	FM	155
Till's Hole	Cumbr	NY4805	54°26·5'	2°47·7'W	X	90
Tillworth	Devon	ST3300	50°48·0'	2°56·7'W	T	193
Tillyarblet	Angus	NO5267	56°47·8'	2°46·7'W	X	44
Tillybardine	Angus	NO4873	56°51·0'	2°50·7'W	X	44
Tillybin	Aberd	NJ7513	57°12·7'	2°24·4'W	X	38
Tillybirloch	Aberd	NJ6707	57°9·4'	2°32·3'W	X	38
Tillybirnie	Angus	NO5166	56°47·2'	2°47·7'W	X	44
Tillybo	Aberd	NJ7759	57°37·5'	2°22·6'W	X	29,30
Tillyboy	Aberd	NJ7206	57°8·9'	2°27·3'W	X	38
Tillybrack	Aberd	NJ6520	57°16·4'	2°34·4'W	X	38
Tillybreak	Aberd	NO7888	56°59·2'	2°21·3'W	X	45
Tillybreen	Aberd	NJ5401	57°6·1'	2°45·1'W	X	37
Tillybrex	Aberd	NK0034	57°24·0'	1°59·5'W	X	30
Tillycairn	Aberd	NJ8331	57°22·4'	2°16·5'W	X	29,30
Tillycairn	Aberd	NO4697	57°3·9'	2°53·0'W	X	37,44
Tillycairn Castle	Aberd	NJ6611	57°11·6'	2°33·3'W	A	38
Tillychardoch	Aberd	NJ5005	57°8·2'	2°49·1'W	X	37
Tillychetly	Aberd	NJ5713	57°12·6'	2°42·3'W	X	37
Tillyching	Aberd	NJ5904	57°7·8'	2°40·2'W	X	37
Tillycorthie Fm	Aberd	NJ9022	57°17·6'	2°9·5'W	FM	38
Tillycorthie Mansion Ho	Aberd	NJ9023	57°18·1'	2°9·5'W	X	38
Tillycroy	Aberd	NJ5508	57°9·9'	2°44·2'W	X	37
Tillycroy	Aberd	NO6193	57°1·8'	2°38·1'W	X	37,45
Tillydesk	Aberd	NJ9536	57°25·1'	2°4·5'W	X	30
Tillydovie	Angus	NO5569	56°48·9'	2°43·8'W	X	44
Tilly Down	Hants	SU3049	51°14·6'	1°33·8'W	T	185
Tillydown	Moray	NJ5749	57°32·0'	2°42·6'W	X	29
Tillydrine	Aberd	NO6098	57°4·5'	2°39·1'W	X	37,45
Tillydrone	C of Aber	NJ9308	57°10·0'	2°6·5'W	T	38
Tillyduff	Aberd	NK0655	57°35·4'	1°53·5'W	X	30
Tillyduke	Aberd	NJ3809	57°10·3'	3°1·1'W	X	37
Tillyeve	Aberd	NJ8922	57°17·6'	2°10·5'W	X	38
Tillyfar	Aberd	NJ7152	57°33·7'	2°28·6'W	X	29
Tillyfar	Aberd	NJ8544	57°29·4'	2°14·6'W	X	30
Tillyfar	Aberd	NJ8638	57°26·2'	2°13·5'W	X	30
Tillyfar	Aberd	NJ9127	57°20·3'	2°8·5'W	X	38
Tillyfauld	Aberd	NK0557	57°36·4'	1°54·5'W	X	30
Tillyfoddie	Aberd	NJ7409	57°10·5'	2°25·3'W	X	38
Tillyfour	Aberd	NJ5910	57°11·0'	2°40·2'W	X	37
Tillyfour	Aberd	NJ9223	57°18·1'	2°7·5'W	X	38
Tillyfourie	Aberd	NJ6412	57°12·1'	2°35·3'W	T	37
Tillyfourie	Aberd	NJ6512	57°12·1'	2°34·3'W	X	38
Tillyfourie Hill	Aberd	NJ6413	57°12·6'	2°35·3'W	H	37
Tillyfro	Aberd	NJ6408	57°9·9'	2°35·3'W	X	37
Tillyfruskie	Aberd	NO6292	57°1·3'	2°37·1'W	X	45
Tillygloom	Angus	NO6161	56°44·6'	2°37·8'W	X	45
Tillygownie	Aberd	NO6593	57°1·9'	2°34·1'W	X	38,45
Tillygrain	Aberd	NO8070	56°49·5'	2°19·2'W	X	45
Tillygreig	Aberd	NJ8822	57°17·6'	2°11·5'W	X	38
Tillyhermack	Aberd	NJ4602	57°6·6'	2°53·0'W	X	37
Tillyhilt	Aberd	NJ8532	57°22·9'	2°14·5'W	X	30
Tillyhiot	Angus	NO5543	56°34·9'	2°43·5'W	X	54
Tillyhowes	Aberd	NJ9201	57°6·2'	2°7·5'W	X	38
Tillykerrie	Aberd	NJ4307	57°9·3'	2°56·1'W	X	37
Tillykerrie	Aberd	NJ8321	57°17·0'	2°16·5'W	X	38
Tillylair	Aberd	NO6494	57°2·4'	2°35·1'W	X	37,45
Tillylodge	Aberd	NJ5206	57°8·8'	2°47·1'W	X	37
Tillyloss	Angus	NO3854	56°40·7'	3°0·3'W	T	54
Tillymair	Aberd	NJ6112	57°12·1'	2°38·3'W	X	37
Tillymaud	Aberd	NJ8825	57°19·2'	2°11·5'W	X	38
Tillymaud Croft	Aberd	NK1038	57°26·2'	1°49·5'W	X	30
Tillymauld	Aberd	NJ8054	57°34·8'	2°19·6'W	X	29,30
Tillyminate	Aberd	NJ4932	57°22·8'	2°50·4'W	X	29,37
Tillynarb	Aberd	NO6996	57°3·5'	2°30·2'W	X	38,45
Tillynaught	Aberd	NJ5961	57°38·5'	2°40·7'W	X	29
Tillyneckle	Aberd	NJ6001	57°6·2'	2°39·2'W	X	37
Tillyochie	Pth & Kin	NO0702	56°12·3'	3°29·5'W	X	58
Tillyochie Mains	Pth & Kin	NO0702	56°12·3'	3°29·5'W	X	58
Tillyorn	Aberd	NJ5307	57°9·3'	2°46·2'W	X	37
Tillyorn	Aberd	NO5990	57°0·2'	2°40·0'W	X	44
Tillyorn Cott	Aberd	NJ7502	57°6·8'	2°24·3'W	X	38
Tillypestle	Aberd	NJ9349	57°32·1'	2°6·6'W	X	30
Tillypronie	Aberd	NJ4307	57°9·3'	2°56·1'W	X	37
Tillyrie Hill	Pth & Kin	NO1008	56°15·6'	3°26·7'W	H	58
Tilly's Hill	Dorset	ST5715	50°56·2'	2°36·3'W	H	183
Tillyshogle	Aberd	NJ7503	57°7·3'	2°24·3'W	X	38
Tillyskukie	Aberd	NJ5407	57°9·4'	2°45·2'W	X	37
Tillysnaught	Aberd	NJ9237	57°25·7'	2°7·5'W	X	30
Tillytarmont	Aberd	NJ5246	57°30·4'	2°47·6'W	X	29
Tilly Tenant	Aberd	NO8990	57°0·3'	2°10·4'W	X	38,45
Tillytoghills	Aberd	NO6271	56°50·0'	2°36·9'W	X	45
Tillywhally	Pth & Kin	NO1105	56°14·0'	3°25·7'W	X	58
Tillywhandland	Angus	NO5254	56°40·8'	2°46·6'W	X	54
Tilly Whim	Dorset	SY6691	50°43·3'	2°29·4'W	X	194
Tilly Whim Caves	Dorset	SZ0376	50°35·3'	1°57·1'W	X	195
Tilmanstone	Kent	TR3051	51°12·9'	1°18·0'E	T	179
Tilmore Brook	Hants	SU7623	51°0·3'	0°54·6'W	W	197
Tiln	Notts	SK7084	53°21·1'	0°56·5'W	X	120
Tilney All Saints	Norf	TF5617	52°43·9'	0°19·0'E	T	131
Tilney cum Islington	Norf	TF5713	52°41·7'	0°19·8'E	T	131,143
Tilney Fen End	Norf	TF5411	52°40·7'	0°17·1'E	T	131,143
Tilney High End	Norf	TF5617	52°43·9'	0°19·0'E	T	131
Tilney St Lawrence	Norf	TF5413	52°41·8'	0°17·1'E	T	131,143
Tiln Holt	Notts	SK7184	53°21·1'	0°55·6'W	F	120
Tilphoudie	Aberd	NJ5500	57°5·6'	2°44·1'W	X	37
Tilquhillie Castle	Aberd	NO7294	57°2·4'	2°27·2'W	A	38,45
Tilquhillie Cott	Aberd	NO7094	57°2·4'	2°29·2'W	X	38,45
Tilsden	Kent	TQ7835	51°5·4'	0°32·9'E	X	188
Tilsdown	Glos	ST7499	51°41·6'	2°22·2'W	T	162
Tilsey Fm	Surrey	TQ0240	51°9·2'	0°32·1'W	FM	186
Tilshead	Wilts	SU0347	51°13·6'	1°57·0'W	T	184
Tilshead Down	Wilts	SU0247	51°13·6'	1°57·9'W	X	184
Tilsmore	E Susx	TQ5721	50°58·2'	0°14·6'E	T	199
Tilsop	Shrops	SO6172	52°20·9'	2°34·0'W	T	138
Tilstock	Shrops	SJ5437	52°55·9'	2°40·7'W	T	126
Tilstockroad Fm	Shrops	SJ5439	52°57·0'	2°40·7'W	FM	126
Tilston	Ches	SJ4551	53°3·4'	2°48·8'W	T	117
Tilstone Bank	Ches	SJ5659	53°7·8'	2°39·1'W	T	117
Tilstone Fearnall	Ches	SJ5660	53°8·4'	2°39·1'W	T	117
Tilstone Hall	Ches	SJ5760	53°8·4'	2°38·2'W	X	117
Tilstone Lodge	Ches	SJ5661	53°8·9'	2°39·1'W	X	117
Tilsworth	Beds	SP9824	51°54·6'	0°34·1'W	T	165
Tilton	E Susx	TQ7112	50°53·2'	0°26·3'E	X	199
Tilton Fm	E Susx	TQ4906	50°50·3'	0°7·4'E	FM	199
Tilton Grange	Leic	SK7504	52°37·9'	0°53·1'W	X	141
Tilton on the Hill	Leic	SK7405	52°38·5'	0°54·0'W	T	141
Tilton Wood	Leic	SK7504	52°37·9'	0°53·1'W	F	141
Tilts	Donc	SE5709	53°34·7'	1°7·9'W	T	111
Tilts Hills	Donc	SE5609	53°34·7'	1°8·8'W	X	111
Tiltup	Glos	SP1903	51°43·8'	1°43·1'W	X	163
Tiltups End	Glos	ST8497	51°40·5'	2°13·5'W	T	162
Tilty	Essex	TL5926	51°54·8'	0°19·1'E	T	167
Tilty Hill Fm	Essex	TL5927	51°55·4'	0°19·1'E	FM	167
Tilwick Fm	Beds	TL0756	52°11·7'	0°25·7'W	FM	153
Timaru Fm	N Lincs	TA0210	53°34·8'	0°27·1'W	FM	112
Tima Water	Scot Bord	NT2709	55°22·4'	3°8·7'W	W	79
Timbercombe	Somer	ST2033	51°5·7'	3°8·2'W	X	182
Timberden Bottom	Kent	TQ5162	51°20·4'	0°10·5'E	T	177,188
Timberford	Aberd	NJ4036	57°24·9'	2°59·5'W	X	28
Timber Hill	Dorset	SY3493	50°44·2'	2°55·7'W	X	193
Timber Hill	Pemb	SM8714	51°47·3'	5°4·9'W	H	157
Timber Hill Fm	Glos	SO6929	51°57·8'	2°26·7'W	FM	149
Timber Holme	N Yks	SE5690	54°18·4'	1°7·9'W	X	100
Timberhonger	Worcs	SO9270	52°19·9'	2°6·6'W	T	139
Timberland	Lincs	TF1258	53°6·7'	0°19·2'W	T	121
Timberland Dales	Lincs	TF1760	53°7·7'	0°14·7'W	X	121
Timberland Delph	Lincs	TF1560	53°7·7'	0°16·5'W	W	121
Timberland Fen	Lincs	TF1559	53°7·2'	0°16·5'W	X	121
Timberley Fm	W Susx	TQ0214	50°55·2'	0°32·5'W	FM	197
Timberline Wood	Heref	SO3837	52°1·9'	2°53·8'W	F	149,161
Timbersbrook	Ches	SJ8962	53°9·5'	2°9·5'W	T	118
Timberscombe	Somer	SS9542	51°10·3'	3°29·7'W	T	181
Timbers Hill	Somer	ST8044	51°11·9'	2°16·8'W	X	183
Timberth	Shrops	SO2596	52°33·6'	3°6·0'W	X	137
Timberwood Hill	Leic	SK4714	52°43·5'	1°17·8'W	X	129
Timble	N Yks	SE1752	53°58·1'	1°44·0'W	T	104
Timble Gill Beck	N Yks	SE1852	53°58·1'	1°43·1'W	W	104
Timble Ings	N Yks	SE1552	53°58·1'	1°45·9'W	X	104
Timbold Hill	Kent	TQ9056	51°16·5'	0°43·8'E	T	178
Timbrelham	Corn	SX3680	50°36·0'	4°18·7'W	T	201
Timbridge Fm	Wilts	SU2467	51°24·3'	1°38·9'W	FM	174
Timewell	Devon	SS9625	51°1·1'	3°28·6'W	X	181
Tim Lodge	Derby	SK0873	53°15·5'	1°52·4'W	X	119
Timm's Grove	Warw	SP0860	52°14·5'	1°52·6'W	F	150
Timoneer, The	E Yorks	TA2369	54°6·4'	0°6·7'W	X	101
Timpendean	Scot Bord	NT6223	55°30·2'	2°35·7'W	X	74
Timperley	Traf	SJ7889	53°24·1'	2°19·4'W	T	109
Timperley Brook	Traf	SJ7887	53°23·0'	2°19·4'W	W	109
Timpton Hill	Durham	NZ0413	54°31·0'	1°55·9'W	X	92
Timsbury	Bath & NE Somer	ST6658	51°19·4'	2°28·9'W	T	172
Timsbury	Hants	SU3424	51°1·1'	1°30·5'W	T	185
Timsbury Bottom	Bath & NE Somer	ST6558	51°19·4'	2°29·8'W	X	172
Timsbury Manor	Hants	SU3424	51°1·1'	1°30·5'W	X	185
Timsgarry	N Eil	NB0534	58°12·0'	7°0·8'W	T	13
Timwood	Somer	ST0335	51°6·6'	3°22·8'W	X	181
Timworth	Suff	TL8669	52°17·5'	0°44·0'E	T	155
Timworth Green	Suff	TL8569	52°17·5'	0°43·2'E	T	155
Timworth Hall	Suff	TL8769	52°17·5'	0°44·9'E	X	155
Timworth Heath	Suff	TL8768	52°16·9'	0°44·9'E	X	155
Tinacre	Devon	SS3600	50°46·8'	4°19·2'W	X	190
Tincleton	Dorset	SY7791	50°43·3'	2°19·2'W	T	194
Tincorn Hill	E Ayr	NS5727	55°31·2'	4°15·5'W	H	71
Tinda	Shetld	HU4537	60°7·2'	1°10·9'W	X	4
Tindale	Cumbr	NY6159	54°55·7'	2°36·1'W	T	86
Tindale Crescent	Durham	NZ1927	54°38·5'	1°41·9'W	T	92
Tindale Fells	Cumbr	NY6057	54°54·6'	2°37·0'W	X	86
Tindale Hill	Northum	NZ1893	55°14·1'	1°42·6'W	X	81
Tindale Tarn	Cumbr	NY6058	54°55·2'	2°37·0'W	W	86
Tindal Ho	Northum	NT9241	55°40·0'	2°7·2'W	X	74,75
Tindall Hall	Norf	TM3393	52°29·3'	1°26·3'E	X	134
Tindall Wood	Norf	TM3293	52°29·4'	1°25·4'E	F	134
Tindon End	Essex	TL6134	51°59·1'	0°21·1'E	T	154
Tind, The	Shetld	HU6790	60°35·5'	0°46·1'W	X	1,2
Tinga Skerry	Shetld	HU4180	60°30·4'	1°14·7'W	X	1,2,3
Tingates	Essex	TL5927	51°55·4'	0°19·1'E	X	167
Tingewick	Bucks	SP6532	51°59·2'	1°2·8'W	T	152,165
Tingewick Mill	Bucks	SP6634	52°0·3'	1°1·9'W	X	152,165
Tingewick Wood	Bucks	SP6531	51°58·7'	1°2·8'W	F	152,165
Tingle Stone, The	Glos	ST8898	51°41·1'	2°10·0'W	X	162
Tingle Stone, The (Long Barrow)	Glos	ST8898	51°41·1'	2°10·0'W	A	162
Tingley	Leeds	SE2826	53°44·0'	1°34·1'W	T	104
Tingley Wood	Herts	TL1330	51°57·6'	0°20·9'W	F	166
Tingly Loup	Orkney	HY7038	59°13·9'	2°31·1'W	X	5
Ting Mound	Cumbr	NY2902	54°24·8'	3°5·2'W	H	89,90
Tingon	Shetld	HU2482	60°31·5'	1°33·3'W	X	3
Tingrith	Beds	TL0032	51°58·9'	0°32·2'W	T	166
Tingwall	Orkney	HY4022	59°5·1'	3°2·3'W	X	5,6
Tingwall Airport	Shetld	HU4245	60°11·5'	1°14·1'W	X	4
Tinhay	Devon	SX3985	50°38·8'	4°16·3'W	T	201
Tinhead Hill	Wilts	ST9352	51°16·3'	2°5·6'W	X	184
Tin Hill	Heref	SO3545	52°6·2'	2°56·5'W	X	148,149
Tinkerbarn	Wilts	SU2556	51°18·4'	1°38·1'W	X	174
Tinker Hill	Barns	SE1603	53°31·6'	1°45·1'W	H	110
Tinker's Barn	Suff	TM4875	52°19·2'	1°38·8'E	X	156
Tinker's Barrow	Dorset	SY7787	50°41·2'	2°19·2'W	A	194
Tinkers' Cross	Worcs	SO7856	52°12·3'	2°18·9'W	X	150
Tinkers End	Bucks	SP7627	51°56·4'	0°53·3'W	T	165
Tinkers Green	Essex	TL6636	52°0·1'	0°25·5'E	X	154
Tinkers Hatch	E Susx	TQ5621	50°58·3'	0°13·7'E	X	199
Tinker's Hill	Glos	SO8719	51°52·4'	2°10·9'W	X	162
Tinker's Hill	Hants	SU3947	51°13·5'	1°26·1'W	X	185
Tinkers Hill	Shrops	SO5272	52°20·9'	2°41·9'W	X	137,138
Tinker's Hill	Somer	ST7528	51°3·3'	2°21·0'W	X	183
Tinker's Ho	Suff	TM4775	52°19·3'	1°37·9'E	X	156
Tinkersley	Derby	SK2665	53°11·1'	1°36·2'W	X	119
Tinker's Lodge	Herts	SP9509	51°46·5'	0°37·0'W	X	165
Tinker's Marshes	Suff	TM4875	52°19·2'	1°38·8'E	X	156
Tinker's Walks	Suff	TM4774	52°18·7'	1°37·8'E	X	156
Tinker's Wood	Suff	TL9260	52°12·5'	0°49·0'E	F	155
Tinkinswood	V of Glam	ST0973	51°27·2'	3°18·2'W	X	171
Tinklee Geo	Shetld	HU3429	60°2·9'	1°22·9'W	X	4
Tinkler Hall	N Yks	NZ8707	54°27·3'	0°39·1'W	X	94
Tinklers Fm	Lancs	SD7352	53°58·0'	2°24·3'W	FM	103
Tinkler's Hill	I Scilly	SV9116	49°58·1'	6°18·2'W	X	203
Tinkley Fm	Glos	SO8200	51°42·1'	2°15·2'W	FM	162
Tinkwood	Ches	SJ4446	53°0·7'	2°49·7'W	X	117
Tinlaw	D & G	NY0478	55°5·5'	3°29·8'W	H	84
Tinlee Stone	Scot Bord	NT4803	55°19·4'	2°48·7'W	A	79
Tinley Lodge Fm	Kent	TQ5851	51°14·4'	0°16·2'E	FM	188
Tinnell	Corn	SX4263	50°27·0'	4°13·2'W	X	201
Tinner's Hut	Devon	SX6187	50°40·2'	3°57·6'W	A	191
Tinney	Devon	SX2999	50°46·2'	4°25·1'W	X	190
Tinneyhall	Corn	SX2780	50°35·9'	4°26·3'W	X	201
Tinney's Firs	Wilts	SU2019	50°58·4'	1°42·5'W	F	184
Tinnis Burn	Scot Bord	NY4583	55°8·5'	2°51·3'W	W	79
Tinnisburn Forest	D & G	NY4382	55°8·0'	2°53·2'W	F	79
Tinnis Castle	Scot Bord	NT1434	55°35·8'	3°21·5'W	A	72
Tinnis Fm	Scot Bord	NT3728	55°32·8'	2°59·5'W	FM	73
Tinnishall	D & G	NY3874	55°3·6'	2°57·8'W	X	85
Tinnis Hill	Scot Bord	NY4385	55°9·6'	2°53·2'W	H	79
Tinny Bank	S Lanak	NT0213	55°24·3'	3°32·4'W	H	78
Tinsey Head	Devon	SX8139	50°14·6'	3°39·8'W	X	202
Tinshill	Leeds	SE2539	53°51·0'	1°36·8'W	T	104
Tinside Rigg	Cumbr	NY7719	54°34·2'	2°20·9'W	X	91
Tinsley	Sheff	SK3990	53°24·6'	1°24·4'W	T	110,111
Tinsley	Sheff	SK4090	53°24·6'	1°23·5'W	T	111
Tinsley Fm	Essex	TL7300	51°40·6'	0°30·5'E	FM	167
Tinsley Green	W Susx	TQ2839	51°8·4'	0°9·8'W	T	187
Tinsley Park	Sheff	SK4088	53°23·5'	1°23·5'W	X	111,120
Tintagel	Corn	SX0588	50°39·8'	4°45·2'W	T	200
Tintagel Head	Corn	SX0488	50°39·8'	4°46·0'W	X	200
Tinten Manor	Corn	SX0675	50°32·8'	4°43·9'W	X	200
Tintern Abbey	Monm	SO5300	51°42·0'	2°40·4'W	A	162
Tintern Cross	Monm	SO5000	51°42·0'	2°43·0'W	X	162
Tintern Parva	Monm	SO5200	51°42·0'	2°41·3'W	T	162

Tintinhull	Somer	ST4919	50°58·3'	2°43·2'W	T	183,193
Tintinhull Ho	Somer	ST5019	50°58·3'	2°42·3'W	X	183
Tinto	S Lanak	NS9534	55°35·6'	3°39·5'W	H	72
Tintock	E Dunb	NS6874	55°56·7'	4°6·4'W	X	64
Tinto End	S Lanak	NS9034	55°35·5'	3°44·3'W	X	71,72
Tintoside	S Lanak	NS9733	55°35·0'	3°37·6'W	X	72
Tintum	D & G	NX6970	55°0·7'	4°2·5'W	X	77,84
Tintwistle	Derby	SK0297	53°28·4'	1°57·8'W	T	110
Tintwistle Knarr	Derby	SK0399	53°29·5'	1°56·9'W	X	110
Tintwistle Low Moor	Derby	SK0298	53°29·0'	1°57·8'W	X	110
Tinwald	D & G	NY0081	55°7·1'	3°33·6'W	T	78
Tinwald Ho	D & G	NY0180	55°6·5'	3°32·7'W	X	78
Tinwald Parks	D & G	NY0080	55°6·5'	3°33·6'W	X	78
Tinwald Shaws	D & G	NY0180	55°6·5'	3°32·7'W	X	78
Tinwell	Rut	TF0006	52°38·8'	0°30·9'W	T	141
Tinwell Lodge Fm	Rut	SK9906	52°38·8'	0°31·8'W	FM	141
Tiogra Beag	N Eil	NB0612	58°0·3'	6°58·2'W	H	13,14
Tiogra Mòr	N Eil	NB0511	57°59·7'	6°59·1'W	H	13,14
Tipalt Burn	Northum	NY6764	54°58·4'	2°30·5'W	W	86,87
Tipalt Burn	Northum	NY7068	55°0·6'	2°27·7'W	W	86,87
Tiphams	Surrey	TQ1639	51°8·5'	0°20·1'W	X	187
Tiphayes Fm	Devon	ST2009	50°52·7'	3°7·8'W	FM	192,193
Tip Head	Essex	TM0308	51°44·3'	0°56·8'E	X	168
Tip Hill	Cumbr	NY6572	55°2·7'	2°32·4'W	X	86
Tip Ho	Shrops	SO7381	52°25·8'	2°23·4'W	X	138
Tiplady Fm	N Yks	SE1765	54°5·1'	1°44·0'W	FM	99
Tipner	C of Port	SU6303	50°49·6'	1°5·9'W	T	196
Tippacott	Devon	SS7647	51°12·8'	3°46·1'W	T	180
Tippacott Ridge	Devon	SS7646	51°12·2'	3°46·1'W	X	180
Tippercowan	Aberd	NJ8155	57°35·3'	2°18·6'W	X	29,30
Tipper's Hill	Warw	SP2888	52°29·6'	1°34·9'W	T	140
Tippertait	Moray	NJ3164	57°39·9'	3°8·9'W	X	28
Tipperton Moss	Fife	NT0895	56°8·6'	3°28·4'W	X	58
Tipperty	Aberd	NJ6660	57°38·0'	2°33·7'W	X	29
Tipperty	Aberd	NJ9626	57°19·7'	2°3·5'W	T	38
Tipperty	Aberd	NO7282	56°56·0'	2°27·2'W	X	45
Tipperweir	Aberd	NO6885	56°57·6'	2°31·1'W	H	45
Tippetcraig	Falk	NS8377	55°58·6'	3°52·1'W	X	65
Tippet Hill	S Lanak	NS9916	55°25·9'	3°35·3'W	X	78
Tippethill	W Loth	NS9465	55°52·2'	3°41·2'W	X	65
Tippet Knowe	S Lanak	NT0430	55°33·5'	3°30·9'W	H	72
Tippet's Belt	D & G	NY0993	55°13·6'	3°25·4'W	F	78
Tippet's Brook	Heref	SO4056	52°12·2'	2°52·3'W	W	148,149
Tippetts Shop	Corn	SW9342	50°14·7'	4°53·8'W	X	204
Tipping's Fm	Lancs	SD6833	53°47·8'	2°28·7'W	FM	103
Tipping's Lodge	Leic	SK8529	52°51·3'	0°43·9'W	X	130
Tipple Cross	Devon	SX3587	50°39·8'	4°19·7'W	T	190
Tipples' Fm	Norf	TG0230	52°50·0'	1°0·3'E	FM	133
Tipps End	Norf	TL5095	52°32·2'	0°13·1'E	T	143
Tipsage Fm	Worcs	SO6570	52°19·9'	2°30·4'W	FM	138
Tip's Cross	Essex	TL5800	51°40·8'	0°17·5'E	T	167
Tips Cross	Kent	TQ5448	51°12·8'	0°12·7'E	X	188
Tips of Clunymore	Moray	NJ3441	57°27·5'	3°5·5'W	H	28
Tips of Corsemaul	Moray	NJ3939	57°26·5'	3°0·5'W	H	28
Tips, The	Suff	TM2945	52°3·6'	1°20·8'E	X	169
Tipta Skerry	Shetld	HP6019	60°51·2'	0°53·2'W	X	1
Tiptoby	Shetld	HU6090	60°35·6'	0°53·8'W	X	1,2
Tiptoe	Hants	SZ2597	50°46·6'	1°38·3'W	T	195
Tiptoe	Northum	NT9041	55°40·0'	2°9·1'W	X	74,75
Tiptoft Fm	Essex	TL5637	52°0·8'	0°16·8'E	FM	154
Tiptoft's Fm	Suff	TM0168	52°16·6'	0°57·2'E	FM	155
Tipton	Sand	SO9592	52°31·8'	2°4·0'W	T	139
Tipton Cross	Devon	SY0592	50°43·4'	3°20·4'W	X	192
Tipton Green	Sand	SO9592	52°31·8'	2°4·0'W	T	139
Tipton Hall	Heref	SO6959	52°13·9'	2°26·8'W	X	149
Tipton St John	Devon	SY0991	50°42·9'	3°17·0'W	T	192
Tiptree	Essex	TL8916	51°48·9'	0°44·9'E	T	168
Tiptree Fm	Suff	TM0462	52°13·3'	0°59·6'E	FM	155
Tiptreehall	Corn	SX1572	50°31·3'	4°36·2'W	X	201
Tiptree Hall	Essex	TL8914	51°47·8'	0°44·9'E	X	168
Tiptree Heath	Essex	TL8815	51°48·3'	0°44·0'E	T	168
Tiptree Priory	Essex	TL8714	51°47·8'	0°43·1'E	X	168
Tipwell	Corn	SX3867	50°29·1'	4°16·6'W	X	201
Tirabad	Powys	SN8741	52°3·6'	3°38·5'W	T	147,160
Tir Abad	V of Glam	SS9568	51°24·3'	3°30·2'W	X	170
Tiraghoil	Arg & Bt	NM3522	56°19·2'	6°16·7'W	X	48
Tir-Aluinn Hotel	Highld	NH1689	57°51·4'	5°5·6'W	X	20
Tir Artair	Pth & Kin	NN5834	56°28·9'	4°17·9'W	X	51
Tir-bâch	Carm	SN5116	51°49·6'	4°9·3'W	X	159
Tir-bâch	Carm	SN5124	51°53·9'	4°9·5'W	X	159
Tir Bach	Gwyn	SH3141	52°56·6'	4°30·5'W	X	123
Tirbach	Pemb	SN1228	51°55·4'	4°43·7'W	X	145,158
Tir Bach	Powys	SO0838	52°2·2'	3°20·1'W	X	160
Tir-bâch	Swan	SN6104	51°43·3'	4°0·4'W	X	159
Tir Bach Fm	Pemb	SN1026	51°54·3'	4°45·3'W	FM	145,158
Tir Barwn	Denb	SJ0246	53°0·4'	3°27·2'W	X	116
Tir Bill Fm	Heref	SO2931	51°58·6'	3°1·6'W	FM	161
Tircanol	Swan	SS6798	51°40·1'	3°55·0'W	T	159
Tircapel	Powys	SN8827	51°56·1'	3°37·4'W	X	160
Tircelyn	Powys	SO0745	52°6·0'	3°21·1'W	X	147
Tirchardie	Pth & Kin	NN8340	56°32·5'	3°53·7'W	X	52
Tircoch	Swan	SS6393	51°37·2'	4°7·0'W	X	159
Tircoed	Swan	SN6100	51°41·1'	4°0·3'W	X	159
Tir-Cook	Merth Tyd	ST0899	51°41·2'	3°19·5'W	X	170
Tirdeunaw	Swan	SS6597	51°39·6'	3°56·7'W	T	159
Tir Dhubh	N Ayr	NR9732	55°32·6'	5°12·6'W	X	69
Tirdu	Powys	SJ0811	52°41·6'	3°21·3'W	X	125
Tir-dyweunydd	Powys	SN9411	51°47·5'	3°31·8'W	X	160
Tire Beggar Hill	Aberd	NO6785	56°57·6'	2°32·1'W	H	45
Tiree	Arg & Bt	NL9944	56°29·8'	6°53·0'W	X	46
Tiree Airport	Arg & Bt	NM0045	56°30·3'	6°52·1'W	X	46
Tirefour Castle	Arg & Bt	NM8642	56°31·5'	5°28·3'W	X	49
Tirefour Castle (Broch)	Arg & Bt	NM8642	56°31·5'	5°28·3'W	A	49
Tir-eithin	Rho Cyn Taf	SS9781	51°31·3'	3°28·7'W	X	170
Tiresford	Ches	SJ5561	53°8·9'	2°40·0'W	X	117
Tiretigan	Arg & Bt	NR7162	55°48·1'	5°38·8'W	X	62
Tirfergus Burn	Arg & Bt	NR6618	55°24·3'	5°41·3'W	W	68
Tirfergus Hill	Arg & Bt	NR6617	55°23·7'	5°41·3'W	H	68
Tir Fhearagain	Arg & Bt	NM3318	56°17·0'	6°18·4'W	X	48
Tirfogrean	Highld	NH8639	57°25·9'	3°53·5'W	X	27
Tirfogrein	Highld	NH8050	57°31·7'	3°59·8'W	X	27
Tir Glyn	Gwyn	SH1525	52°47·7'	4°44·2'W	X	123
Tir Gunter	Monm	SO2215	51°49·9'	3°7·5'W	X	161
Tir-Gwallter	Powys	SO1237	52°1·7'	3°16·6'W	X	161
Tir Gwyn	Powys	SN8484	52°26·7'	3°42·0'W	X	135,136
Tir-Howel	Carm	SN7525	51°54·8'	3°48·7'W	X	146,160
Tir-Ifan-Ddu	Carm	SN5728	51°56·2'	4°4·4'W	X	146
Tirindrish	Highld	NN2382	56°54·0'	4°53·9'W	X	34,41
Tirinie	Pth & Kin	NN7948	56°36·8'	3°57·8'W	X	51,52
Tirinie	Pth & Kin	NN8867	56°47·1'	3°49·5'W	T	43
Tir-isaf	Carm	SN5709	51°45·9'	4°3·9'W	X	159
Tir-isaf Fm	Nth Pt Talb	SN7801	51°41·9'	3°45·5'W	FM	170
Tirlan	Carm	SN5134	51°59·3'	4°9·8'W	X	146
Tirlan	Nth Pt Talb	SN7602	51°42·4'	3°47·3'W	X	170
Tirlan Fm	Carm	SN5507	51°44·8'	4°5·6'W	FM	159
Tirlan Fm	Merth Tyd	ST0999	51°41·2'	3°18·6'W	FM	171
Tirlasgoch	Flint	SJ2666	53°11·4'	3°6·0'W	X	117
Tirle Brook	Glos	SO9132	51°59·4'	2°7·5'W	W	150
Tirley	Glos	SO8328	51°57·2'	2°14·4'W	T	150
Tirley Court	Glos	SO8228	51°57·2'	2°15·3'W	X	150
Tirley Fm	Ches	SJ5466	53°11·6'	2°40·9'W	FM	117
Tirley Garth	Ches	SJ5466	53°11·6'	2°40·9'W	X	117
Tirley Knowle	Glos	SO8229	51°57·8'	2°15·3'W	T	150
Tirlot	Orkney	HY4444	59°17·0'	2°58·5'W	X	5
Tirmawr	Carm	SN7226	51°55·3'	3°51·3'W	X	146,160
Tirmawr	Powys	SN9512	51°48·0'	3°31·0'W	X	160
Tirmawr	Powys	SN9729	51°57·2'	3°29·5'W	X	160
Tir Morfa	Carm	SS5398	51°39·9'	4°7·1'W	X	159
Tir Mostyn	Denb	SH9958	53°6·8'	3°30·1'W	H	116
Tirmynydd Fm	Swan	SS7199	51°40·7'	3°51·6'W	FM	170
Tirnewydd	Powys	SJ1810	52°41·1'	3°12·4'W	X	125
Tiroran	Arg & Bt	NM4727	56°22·3'	6°5·4'W	X	48
Tirpant	Carm	SN6029	51°56·8'	4°1·8'W	X	146
Tirpaun	Carm	SN7627	51°55·9'	3°47·8'W	X	146,160
Tir-pentwys	Torf	ST2499	51°41·3'	3°5·6'W	H	171
Tirphil	Caer	SO1303	51°43·4'	3°15·2'W	T	171
Tir Rhiwiog	Powys	SH9216	52°44·1'	3°35·6'W	H	125
Tir Rhiwiog	Powys	SH9315	52°43·6'	3°34·7'W	H	125
Tirril	Cumbr	NY5026	54°37·8'	2°46·1'W	T	90
Tirry, River	Highld	NC5123	58°10·5'	4°31·5'W	W	16
Tirryside	Highld	NC5611	58°4·1'	4°26·0'W	T	16
Tirsa Water	Shetld	HU4150	60°14·2'	1°15·1'W	W	3
Tir Stent	Gwyn	SH7516	52°43·9'	3°50·7'W	H	124
Tirtopyn	Gwyn	SH1830	52°50·5'	4°41·7'W	X	123
Tir Twyn Fm	Caer	ST1393	51°38·0'	3°15·0'W	FM	171
Tirvister	Shetld	HU3578	60°29·3'	1°21·3'W	T	2,3
Tir-y-berth	Caer	ST1596	51°39·6'	3°13·3'W	T	171
Tir-y-coed	Flint	SJ2159	53°7·6'	3°10·4'W	F	117
Tir-y-coed	Shrops	SJ3219	52°46·1'	3°0·1'W	X	126
Tir-y-coed Fm	Flint	SJ2160	53°8·1'	3°10·4'W	FM	117
Tir-y-cwm	Powys	SN7913	51°48·4'	3°44·9'W	X	160
Tir-y-dail	Carm	SN6213	51°48·2'	3°59·7'W	T	159
Tir-y-felin	Caer	SO1201	51°42·3'	3°16·0'W	X	171
Tir-y-felin	Powys	SN9632	51°58·8'	3°30·5'W	X	160
Tir-y-fron	Flint	SJ2959	53°7·6'	3°3·3'W	X	117
Tirygoitre	Carm	SN6418	51°50·9'	3°58·1'W	X	159
Tir-y-graig	Powys	SN9427	51°56·1'	3°32·1'W	X	160
Tir-y-lan	Carm	SN6622	51°53·1'	3°56·4'W	X	159
Tirymynach	Powys	SH9301	52°36·0'	3°34·4'W	X	136
Tirymynach	Powys	SJ2612	52°42·3'	3°5·3'W	X	126
Tir-y-mynydd	Carm	SN6225	51°54·6'	4°0·0'W	X	146
Tir-y-rhen	Caer	ST1297	51°40·1'	3°16·0'W	X	171
Tir-yr-onen	Powys	SN9612	51°48·1'	3°30·1'W	X	160
Tisbury	Wilts	ST9429	51°3·9'	2°4·8'W	T	184
Tiscott	Corn	SS2208	50°50·9'	4°31·3'W	X	190
Tisman's	W Susx	TQ0633	51°5·4'	0°28·8'W	X	187
Tisman's Common	W Susx	TQ0732	51°4·9'	0°28·0'W	T	187
Tissington	Derby	SK1752	53°4·1'	1°44·4'W	T	119
Tissington Spires	Derby	SK1452	53°4·1'	1°47·1'W	X	119
Tissington Trail	Derby	SK1555	53°5·8'	1°46·2'W	X	119
Tister	Highld	ND1961	58°32·0'	3°23·0'W	X	11,12
Titaboutie	Aberd	NJ5103	57°7·2'	2°48·1'W	X	37
Tit Brook	Cambs	TL3955	52°10·8'	0°2·4'E	W	154
Titchberry	Devon	SS2427	51°1·2'	4°30·2'W	T	190
Titchborne Fm	Wilts	SU2221	50°59·5'	1°40·8'W	FM	184
Titchcombe	Somer	SS7440	51°9·0'	3°47·7'W	X	180
Titchen Fm	Corn	SX1995	50°43·8'	4°33·5'W	FM	190
Titchfield	Hants	SU5305	50°50·8'	1°14·4'W	T	196
Titchfield Common	Hants	SU5206	50°51·3'	1°15·3'W	T	196
Titchfield Haven	Hants	SU5303	50°49·7'	1°14·5'W	W	196
Titchfield Park	Hants	SU5307	50°51·8'	1°14·4'W	T	196
Titch Hill Fm	W Susx	TQ1606	50°50·7'	0°20·7'W	FM	198
Titchmarsh	Northnts	TL0279	52°24·2'	0°29·6'W	T	141
Titchmarsh Wood	Northnts	SP9783	52°26·4'	0°34·0'W	F	141
Titchwell	Norf	TF7543	52°57·6'	0°36·7'E	T	132
Titcomb	W Berks	SU3765	51°23·2'	1°27·7'W	T	174
Titcomb Manor	W Berks	SU3765	51°23·2'	1°27·7'W	X	174
Tites Point	Glos	SO6904	51°44·3'	2°26·5'W	X	162
Tithby	Notts	SK6936	52°55·3'	0°58·0'W	T	129
Tithe Barn	Glos	SO9926	51°56·2'	2°0·5'W	A	163
Tithe Barn	Hill	TQ0577	51°29·2'	0°28·9'W	A	176
Tithebarn	Staffs	SK0741	52°58·2'	1°53·3'W	T	119,128
Tithe Barn	Worcs	SO7853	52°10·7'	2°18·9'W	A	150
Tithebarn Fm	Cambs	TL3984	52°26·4'	0°3·1'E	FM	142,143
Tithebarn Fm	Staffs	SK0123	52°48·5'	1°58·7'W	FM	128
Tithe Barn Hill	Lancs	SD4455	53°59·5'	2°50·8'W	X	102
Tithe Barn Hillock	St Hel	SJ5599	53°29·4'	2°40·3'W	T	108
Tithe Farm	Beds	TL0225	51°55·1'	0°30·6'W	FM	166
Tithe Fm	Beds	SP9851	52°9·1'	0°33·7'W	FM	153
Tithe Fm	Beds	TL1457	52°12·2'	0°19·5'W	FM	153
Tithe Fm	Bucks	SU9683	51°32·5'	0°36·5'W	FM	175,176
Tithe Fm	Cambs	TL2160	52°13·7'	0°13·3'W	FM	153
Tithe Fm	Derby	SK2157	53°6·8'	1°40·8'W	FM	119
Tithe Fm	E Yorks	SE7030	53°45·9'	0°55·9'W	FM	105,106
Tithe Fm	E Yorks	SE9926	53°43·5'	0°29·6'W	FM	106
Tithe Fm	Leic	SK5818	52°45·6'	1°8·0'W	FM	129
Tithe Fm	Lincs	TF1211	52°41·3'	0°20·2'W	FM	130,142
Tithe Fm	Norf	TF7321	52°45·8'	0°34·2'E	FM	132
Tithe Fm	Northnts	SP6868	52°18·6'	0°59·8'W	FM	152
Tithe Fm	Northnts	SP7968	52°18·5'	0°50·1'W	FM	152
Tithe Fm	Oxon	SP4040	52°3·6'	1°24·6'W	FM	151
Tithe Fm	Oxon	SU2591	51°37·3'	1°37·9'W	FM	163,174
Tithe Fm	Suff	TM2677	52°20·9'	1°19·5'E	FM	156
Tithe Fm	Suff	TM3684	52°24·4'	1°28·6'E	FM	156
Tithe Fm	Suff	TM3685	52°24·9'	1°28·6'E	FM	156
Tithe Fm	Warw	SP2348	52°8·0'	1°39·4'W	FM	151
Tithe Fm	Warw	SP2893	52°32·3'	1°34·8'W	FM	140
Tithe Fm	Warw	SP4067	52°18·2'	1°24·4'W	FM	151
Tithe Hall Fm	Corn	SX1563	50°26·5'	4°36·0'W	FM	201
Tithe Hill	Northum	NT8636	55°37·3'	2°12·9'W	X	74
Tithe Platts Fm	Warw	SP4886	52°28·4'	1°17·2'W	FM	140
Tithe Top Fm	E Yorks	SE9153	53°58·1'	0°36·3'W	FM	106
Tithe Ward	Kent	TQ6348	51°12·7'	0°20·4'E	X	188
Tithill	Somer	ST1627	51°2·4'	3°11·5'W	X	181,193
Titkill Br	Norf	TF5107	52°38·6'	0°14·3'E	X	143
Titley	Heref	SO3360	52°14·3'	2°58·5'W	T	137,148,149
Titley Hill	Suff	TM0853	52°8·4'	1°2·8'E	X	155
Titley Mill	Heref	SO3258	52°13·2'	2°59·3'W	X	148
Titling Cairn	Scot Bord	NT5857	55°48·5'	2°39·8'W	A	67,73,74
Titlington	Northum	NU0915	55°26·0'	1°51·0'W	T	81
Titlington Burn	Northum	NU1116	55°26·5'	1°49·1'W	W	81
Titlington Mount	Northum	NU0916	55°26·5'	1°51·0'W	X	81
Titlington Pike	Northum	NU0816	55°26·5'	1°52·0'W	H	81
Titlington Wood	Northum	NU0916	55°26·5'	1°51·0'W	F	81
Titmore Green	Herts	TL2126	51°55·4'	0°14·0'W	T	166
Titness Park	Win & Maid	SU9568	51°24·4'	0°37·7'W	X	175,176
Titrail	Shrops	SO5974	52°22·0'	2°35·7'W	X	137,138
Titsal Wood	Suff	TM4283	52°23·7'	1°33·8'E	F	156
Titsey	Surrey	TQ4054	51°16·3'	0°0·8'E	T	187
Titsey Park	Surrey	TQ4054	51°16·3'	0°0·8'E	X	187
Titsey Wood	Surrey	TQ4254	51°16·3'	0°2·5'E	F	187
Titson	Corn	SS2401	50°47·1'	4°29·4'W	T	190
Tittenhurst	Win & Maid	SU9568	51°24·4'	0°37·7'W	T	175,176
Tittenley Fm	Shrops	SJ6437	52°56·0'	2°31·7'W	FM	127
Tittensor	Staffs	SJ8738	52°56·6'	2°11·2'W	T	127
Tittensor Chase	Staffs	SJ8736	52°55·5'	2°11·2'W	X	127
Titterhill	Shrops	SO5080	52°25·2'	2°43·7'W	T	137,138
Tittershall Wood	Bucks	SP6718	51°51·6'	1°1·2'W	F	164,165
Titters Hill	S Glos	ST6090	51°36·7'	2°34·3'W	X	162,172
Titterstone Clee Hill	Shrops	SO5977	52°23·6'	2°35·8'W	H	137,138
Tittesworth Reservoir	Staffs	SJ9959	53°7·9'	2°0·5'W	W	118
Tittle Path Hill	Wilts	ST8925	51°1·7'	2°9·0'W	H	184
Tittle Row	Win & Maid	SU8680	51°31·0'	0°45·2'W	T	175
Tittleshall	Norf	TF8921	52°45·4'	0°48·5'E	T	132
Tittleshall Hill	Norf	TF9020	52°44·9'	0°49·3'E	X	132
Titton	Worcs	SO8269	52°19·4'	2°15·4'W	T	138
Titty Hill	W Susx	SU8525	51°1·3'	0°46·9'W	T	186,197
Tittynans Hill	Shetld	HP5200	60°41·1'	1°2·4'W	H	1
Titus' Well	Pth & Kin	NN8212	56°17·4'	3°53·9'W	X	57
Titwood	E Ayr	NS4349	55°42·8'	4°29·5'W	X	64
Titwood	E Renf	NS5453	55°45·2'	4°19·1'W	X	64
Titwood	N Ayr	NS4043	55°39·5'	4°32·2'W	X	70
Tiumpan	N Eil	NB1945	58°18·5'	6°47·4'W	X	8
Tivaka Taing	Shetld	HU3777	60°28·8'	1°19·1'W	X	2,3
Tiverton	Ches	SJ5560	53°8·4'	2°40·0'W	T	117
Tiverton	Devon	SS9512	50°54·1'	3°29·2'W	T	181
Tiverton Fm	Ches	SJ5260	53°8·3'	2°42·6'W	FM	117
Tiverton Hall	Ches	SJ5460	53°8·4'	2°40·9'W	X	117
Tiverton Parkway	Devon	ST0413	50°54·7'	3°21·6'W	X	181
Tivetshall St Margaret	Norf	TM1686	52°26·0'	1°11·1'E	T	144,156
Tivetshall St Mary	Norf	TM1686	52°26·0'	1°11·1'E	T	144,156
Tivey's Fm	Leic	SK3707	52°39·8'	1°26·8'W	FM	140
Tividale	Sand	SO9690	52°30·7'	2°3·1'W	T	139
Tivington	Somer	SS9345	51°11·9'	3°31·5'W	T	181
Tivington Common	Somer	SS9444	51°11·4'	3°30·6'W	F	181
Tivington Heights	Somer	SS9345	51°11·9'	3°31·5'W	X	181
Tivington Knowle	Somer	SS9344	51°11·3'	3°31·5'W	T	181
Tivoli	Brad	SE1049	53°56·5'	1°50·4'W	X	104
Tivoli	Cumbr	NX9920	54°34·2'	3°33·3'W	T	89
Tivy Dale	Barns	SE2707	53°33·8'	1°35·1'W	T	110
Tixall	Staffs	SJ9722	52°48·0'	2°2·3'W	T	127
Tixall Fm	Staffs	SJ9823	52°48·5'	2°1·4'W	FM	127
Tixall Heath Fm	Staffs	SJ9623	52°48·5'	2°3·2'W	FM	127
Tixover	Rut	SK9700	52°35·6'	0°33·7'W	T	141
Tixover Grange	Rut	SK9701	52°36·1'	0°33·7'W	X	141
Toab	Orkney	HY5106	58°56·6'	2°50·6'W	X	6,7
Toab	Shetld	HU3811	59°53·2'	1°18·8'W	T	4
Toab Skerry	Orkney	HY5107	58°57·1'	2°50·6'W	X	6,7
Toad Hall Fm	N Yks	NZ7008	54°28·0'	0°54·8'W	FM	94
Toad Hole	N Yks	SE6297	54°22·1'	1°2·3'W	X	94,100
Toad Hole	N Yks	SE6696	54°21·6'	0°58·6'W	X	94,100
Toad Hole Fm	Ches	SJ7753	53°4·7'	2°20·2'W	FM	118
Toadhole Furnace	Derby	SK3956	53°6·2'	1°24·6'W	X	119
Toadmoor	Derby	SK3550	53°3·0'	1°28·3'W	T	119
Toadpool	Cumbr	SD4995	54°21·1'	2°46·7'W	X	97
Toad Rock	Kent	TQ5639	51°8·0'	0°14·2'E	X	188
Toad Row	Suff	TM5086	52°25·1'	1°41·0'E	T	156
Toadsmoor Valley	Glos	SO8804	51°44·3'	2°10·0'W	X	162
Toadsmoor Woods	Glos	SO8804	51°44·3'	2°10·0'W	F	162
Toad's Mouth	Sheff	SK2680	53°19·2'	1°36·2'W	X	110
Toa Mór	N Eil	NB0837	58°13·8'	6°58·0'W	H	13
Toan	N Eil	NF9686	57°45·9'	7°6·3'W	X	18
Toardy, Burn	Angus	NO4367	56°47·7'	2°55·5'W	W	44
Toardy Hill	Angus	NO4268	56°48·3'	2°56·5'W	H	44
Toat Hill	W Susx	TQ1229	51°3·2'	0°23·7'W	X	187,198
Toathmain	Cumbr	NY5216	54°32·5'	2°44·1'W	X	90
Toat Ho	W Susx	TQ0421	50°59·0'	0°30·7'W	X	197
Toatley	Devon	SS7010	50°52·7'	3°50·5'W	X	191
Toat Monument	W Susx	TQ0421	50°59·0'	0°30·7'W	X	197
Toba	Arg & Bt	NM3121	56°18·6'	6°20·5'W	X	48
Tobacco Rock	Orkney	HY7843	59°16·6'	2°22·7'W	X	5
Tobar a' Ghreip	Highld	NG4573	57°40·7'	6°16·2'W	W	23
Tobar Alain	Highld	NH9930	57°21·2'	3°40·3'W	X	27,36
Tobar an Ime	Arg & Bt	NM4842	56°30·4'	6°5·3'W	W	47,48
Tobar Ashik	Highld	NG6824	57°15·1'	5°50·3'W	A	32
Tobar Ceann	Highld	NG5619	57°12·1'	6°1·9'W	A	32
Tobar Chaluim Chille	N Eil	NF8775	57°39·6'	7°14·5'W	A	18
Tobar Cleap	Highld	NG4766	57°37·0'	6°13·7'W	W	23
Tobar Fuar	Aberd	NJ2410	57°10·7'	3°15·0'W	W	36
Tobar Fuar	Arg & Bt	NR3593	56°3·6'	6°15·0'W	X	61

Tobar Mheasain	Highld	NC9313	58°5·9′	3°48·4′W	A	17
Tobarn	Corn	SX1994	50°43·3′	4°33·5′W	X	190
Tobar na Cachlaidh Mòire	Highld	NM6965	56°43·4′	5°46·1′W	W	40
Tobar na Curra	Highld	NG4568	57°38·1′	6°15·9′W	W	23
Tobar na h-Annait	Highld	NG5820	57°12·7′	6°0·0′W	A	32
Tobar na Lagaig	Highld	NM8470	56°46·6′	5°31·7′W	X	40
Tobar nan Ceann	Highld	NN3099	57°3·3′	4°47·7′W	A	34
Tobar nan Uaislean	Highld	NG4527	57°16·0′	6°13·3′W	W	32
Tobar na Slàinte	Highld	NG4668	57°38·1′	6°14·9′W	W	23
Tobar Oran	Arg & Bt	NR3996	56°5·4′	6°11·3′W	A	61
Tòb a Tuath na Ceanna Mhòire	N Eil	NB2107	57°58·2′	6°42·6′W	W	13,14
Tobban Horse	Corn	SW6847	50°16·9′	5°15·0′W	X	203
Tòb Bhreascleit	N Eil	NB2134	58°12·7′	6°44·5′W	W	8,13
Tòb Bhrolluim	N Eil	NB3103	57°56·4′	6°32·2′W	W	13,14
Tob Cheann Tarabhaigh	N Eil	NB2317	58°3·6′	6°41·3′W	W	13,14
Tòb Chollabhig	N Eil	NB2032	58°11·5′	6°45·4′W	W	8,13
Tobees	Angus	NO4656	56°41·8′	2°52·5′W	X	54
Tòb Eisgein	N Eil	NB3211	58°0·7′	6°31·8′W	W	13,14
Toberaie	Highld	NJ0618	57°14·8′	3°33·0′W	X	36
Toberchurn	Highld	NH6162	57°37·9′	4°19·2′W	X	21
Toberchurn	Highld	NH6263	57°38·4′	4°18·2′W	X	21
Tobermory	Arg & Bt	NM5055	56°37·5′	6°4·1′W	T	47
Tobermory River	Arg & Bt	NM4954	56°36·9′	6°5·0′W	W	47
Toberonochy	Arg & Bt	NM7408	56°12·9′	5°38·2′W	T	55
Tobha Aisgeirnis	N Eil	NF7323	57°11·1′	7°24·3′W	X	22
Tobha Beag	N Eil	NF7535	57°17·7′	7°23·3′W	T	22
Tobha Bhornais	N Eil	NF7330	57°14·9′	7°24·9′W	X	22
Tobha Dhiobadail	N Eil	NB4661	58°28·1′	6°20·9′W	X	8
Tobha Ghabhsainn	N Eil	NB4560	58°27·5′	6°21·8′W	X	8
Tobhaidh Bheag	N Eil	NB4122	58°6·9′	6°23·4′W	X	14
Tobha Mòr	N Eil	NF7536	57°18·2′	7°23·4′W	T	22
Tobha Rònaidh	N Eil	HW8132	59°7·4′	5°49·1′W	H	8
Tobha Tholastaidh	N Eil	NB5244	58°19·1′	6°13·6′W	X	8
Tobhta nan Druidhean	Highld	NG5258	57°32·9′	6°8·2′W	X	23,24
Tobhtaral	N Eil	NB1833	58°12·0′	6°47·5′W	T	8,13
Tob Leireabhaigh	N Eil	NB4229	58°10·7′	6°22·8′W	W	8
Tòb Mhic Colla	N Eil	NB2716	58°3·2′	6°37·2′W	W	13,14
Tòb na Gile Mòire	N Eil	NB3310	58°0·2′	6°30·7′W	W	13,14
Tòb na Surraig	N Eil	NB0117	58°2·7′	7°3·6′W	W	13
Tòb Smuaisibhig	N Eil	NB2704	57°56·8′	6°36·4′W	W	13,14
Tobson	N Eil	NB1338	58°14·5′	6°53·0′W	T	13
Tòb Stiomrabhaigh	N Eil	NB3411	58°0·8′	6°29·8′W	W	13,14
Tòb Valasay	N Eil	NB1437	58°14·0′	6°51·9′W	W	13
Toby's Bottom	Dorset	SU0415	50°56·3′	1°56·2′W	X	184
Toby's Hill	Lincs	TF4594	53°25·6′	0°11·4′E	T	113
Toby's Point	Devon	SX6445	50°17·6′	3°54·2′W	X	202
Toby's Walks	Suff	TM4474	52°18·8′	1°35·2′E	X	156
Tocher	Aberd	NJ6932	57°22·9′	2°30·5′W	T	29
Tocherford	Aberd	NJ6933	57°23·4′	2°30·5′W	X	29
Tochie Burn	Pth & Kin	NN7910	56°16·3′	3°56·8′W	W	57
Tochieneal	Moray	NJ5265	57°40·6′	2°47·8′W	X	29
Tocia	Gwyn	SH2030	52°50·5′	4°40·0′W	X	123
Tockenham	Wilts	SU0379	51°30·8′	1°57·0′W	T	173
Tockenham Court Fm	Wilts	SU0378	51°30·3′	1°57·0′W	FM	173
Tockenham Wick	Wilts	SU0381	51°31·9′	1°57·0′W	T	173
Tocketts Fm	Red & Cl	NZ6117	54°32·9′	1°3·0′W	FM	94
Tocketts Fm	Red & Cl	NZ6217	54°32·9′	1°2·1′W	FM	94
Tocketts Mill	Red & Cl	NZ6218	54°33·4′	1°2·1′W	X	94
Tockholes	Black w Dar	SD6623	53°42·4′	2°30·5′W	T	103
Tockington	S Glos	ST6086	51°34·5′	2°34·2′W	T	172
Tockington Park Fm	S Glos	ST6285	51°34·0′	2°32·5′W	FM	172
Tockley	Devon	SS5510	50°52·5′	4°3·3′W	X	191
Tocknells Court	Glos	SO8811	51°48·1′	2°10·0′W	A	162
Tockwith	N Yks	SE4652	53°58·0′	1°17·5′W	T	105
Tockwith Lodge	N Yks	SE4553	53°58·5′	1°18·4′W	X	105
Todbank	Cumbr	NY5841	54°46·0′	2°38·7′W	X	86
Todber	Dorset	ST7920	50°59·0′	2°17·6′W	T	183
Todber	Lancs	SD8346	53°54·8′	2°15·1′W	X	103
Todburn	Northum	NZ1195	55°15·2′	1°49·2′W	X	81
Tod Burn	Northum	NZ1196	55°15·7′	1°49·2′W	W	81
Todburn Moor	Northum	NZ1294	55°14·6′	1°48·2′W	X	81
Todburn Steel	Northum	NY9859	54°55·8′	2°1·4′W	X	87
Todcastle	S Lanak	NS6642	55°39·4′	4°7·4′W	X	71
Tod Crag	Cumbr	NY5584	55°9·1′	2°41·9′W	X	80
Tod Crag	Cumbr	NY5879	55°6·5′	2°39·1′W	X	86
Todcrags	Cumbr	NY5210	54°29·2′	2°44·0′W	X	90
Tod Craig Hill	D & G	NX9499	55°16·7′	3°39·7′W	H	78
Todd Brook	Ches	SJ9878	53°18·2′	2°1·4′W	W	118
Toddbrook Resr	Derby	SK0080	53°19·3′	1°59·6′W	W	110
Todd Crag	Cumbr	NY3603	54°25·4′	2°58·8′W	H	90
Todden Hill	D & G	NS5303	55°18·2′	4°18·5′W	H	77
Todderstaffe Hall	Lancs	SD3636	53°49·2′	2°57·9′W	X	102
Todd Fall Fm	Darl	NZ2223	54°36·3′	1°39·1′W	FM	93
Todd Fell	Cumbr	NY5101	54°24·4′	2°44·9′W	H	90
Todd Hill	Northum	NZ1589	55°11·9′	1°45·4′W	H	81
Toddington	Beds	TL0028	51°56·7′	0°32·3′W	T	166
Toddington	Glos	SP0332	51°59·4′	1°57·0′W	T	150
Toddington	W Susx	TQ0303	50°49·3′	0°31·9′W	T	197
Toddington Manor	Beds	TL0029	51°57·3′	0°32·3′W	X	166
Toddington Park	Beds	SP9929	51°57·3′	0°33·2′W	X	165
Toddington Service Area	Beds	TL0228	51°56·7′	0°30·6′W	X	166
Todd Intake Moor	N Yks	SE5999	54°23·2′	1°5·1′W	X	100
Toddle Burn	Scot Bord	NT4351	55°45·2′	2°54·1′W	W	66,73
Toddlehills	Aberd	NJ9537	57°25·7′	2°4·5′W	X	30
Toddlehills	Aberd	NK0645	57°30·0′	1°53·5′W	T	30
Toddle Knowe	D & G	NT3002	55°18·7′	3°5·7′W	H	79
Toddle Moss	S Lanak	NS9317	55°26·4′	3°41·0′W	X	71,78
Toddley Hill	Aberd	NJ7433	57°23·5′	2°25·5′W	X	29
Todd's Burn	Northum	NY7758	54°55·2′	2°21·1′W	X	86,87
Todd's Green	Herts	TL2226	51°55·4′	0°13·2′W	T	166
Todd's Ho	Cumbr	NY8216	54°32·6′	2°16·3′W	X	91,92
Todd's Hole	Angus	NO7153	56°40·3′	2°27·9′W	X	54
Todd's Lodge	Lincs	SK9522	52°47·5′	0°35·1′W	X	130
Todd's Wood	N Yks	SD9378	54°12·1′	2°6·0′W	F	98
Toddy Bridge	Fife	NO3603	56°13·2′	3°1·5′W	X	59
Toddy Burn	S Ayr	NS3002	55°17·2′	4°40·2′W	W	76
Toddygill Hall	Cumbr	NY7515	54°32·0′	2°22·8′W	X	91
Toddy Park	Corn	SX1876	50°33·6′	4°33·8′W	X	201
Todenham	Glos	SP2436	52°1·5′	1°38·6′W	T	151
Tod Fell	D & G	NX7959	54°54·9′	3°52·8′W	H	84
Todfold	Aberd	NJ7413	57°12·7′	2°25·4′W	X	38
Todgill	Cumbr	NY4022	54°35·6′	2°55·3′W	X	90
Todhall Fm	Fife	NO3916	56°20·2′	2°58·8′W	FM	59
Todhead Point	Aberd	NO8776	56°52·8′	2°12·3′W	X	45
Todheugh	Scot Bord	NT8356	55°48·1′	2°15·8′W	X	67,74
Tod Hill	Arg & Bt	NR7211	55°20·7′	5°35·3′W	H	68
Tod Hill	Falk	NS8483	56°1·8′	3°51·2′W	X	65
Todhill	Northum	NZ1377	55°5·5′	1°47·4′W	X	88
Tod Hill	Scot Bord	NT3504	55°19·8′	3°1·0′W	H	79
Todhill Brae	D & G	NY3087	55°10·6′	3°5·5′W	H	79
Todhillmuir	D & G	NY0884	55°8·8′	3°26·2′W	X	78
Todhill Rig	Scot Bord	NT3504	55°19·8′	3°1·0′W	X	79
Todhillrig	Scot Bord	NT8443	55°41·1′	2°14·8′W	X	74
Todhillrigg Fm	Cumbr	NY4372	55°2·6′	2°53·1′W	FM	85
Todhills	Aberd	NJ6460	57°38·0′	2°35·7′W	X	29
Todhills	Angus	NO4239	56°32·6′	2°56·1′W	T	54
Todhills	C of Edin	NT3068	55°54·3′	3°6·7′W	X	66
Todhills	Cumbr	NY3663	54°57·7′	2°59·5′W	T	85
Todhills	Cumbr	NY6138	54°44·4′	2°35·9′W	X	91
Todhills	Durham	NZ2133	54°41·7′	1°40·0′W	T	93
Todhills Moss	E Ayr	NS5444	55°40·3′	4°18·9′W	X	70
Todhillwood	D & G	NY3873	55°3·1′	2°57·8′W	X	85
Todhillwood	Northum	NY7259	54°55·7′	2°25·8′W	X	86,87
Todhillwood	Northum	NY7260	54°56·3′	2°25·8′W	X	86,87
Todhole	Cumbr	NY0722	54°35·3′	3°25·9′W	X	89
Todholes	Aberd	NJ8457	57°36·4′	2°15·6′W	X	29,30
Todholes	D & G	NS7314	55°24·5′	3°59·9′W	X	71
Todholes	D & G	NY2567	54°59·8′	3°9·9′W	X	85
Todholes	Moray	NJ1054	57°34·3′	3°29·8′W	X	28
Todholes	Moray	NJ3632	57°22·7′	3°3·4′W	X	37
Todholes	Northum	NY6464	54°58·4′	2°33·3′W	X	86
Todholes	Northum	NY9492	55°13·6′	2°5·2′W	X	80
Todholes	Stir	NS6786	56°3·2′	4°7·7′W	X	57
Todholes	Stir	NS7588	56°4·4′	4°0·0′W	X	57
Todholes Fm	Highld	ND1264	58°33·6′	3°30·3′W	FM	11,12
Todholes Hill	D & G	NS7415	55°25·0′	3°59·0′W	H	71
Todhunter Grain	Scot Bord	NY4484	55°9·1′	2°52·3′W	W	79
Todhurst Fm	W Susx	SU9704	50°49·9′	0°37·0′W	FM	197
Tod Knowe	D & G	NY4290	55°12·3′	2°54·3′W	X	79
Tod Knowe	Northum	NY7699	55°17·3′	2°22·2′W	H	80
Tod Knowe	Northum	NY9894	55°14·7′	2°1·5′W	H	81
Tod Knowes	E Ayr	NS5441	55°38·7′	4°18·8′W	X	70
Todlachie	Aberd	NJ6513	57°12·6′	2°34·3′W	X	38
Todlaw	Aberd	NJ6952	57°33·7′	2°30·6′W	X	29
Tod Law	Northum	NT7700	55°17·9′	2°21·3′W	H	80
Tod Law	Northum	NY8397	55°16·3′	2°15·6′W	H	80
Todlaw	Scot Bord	NT6419	55°28·1′	2°33·7′W	X	80
Tod Law	S Lanak	NS7735	55°35·8′	3°56·7′W	H	71
Todlaw	S Lanak	NS7735	55°35·8′	3°56·7′W	X	71
Todlaw Rig	S Lanak	NT0127	55°31·9′	3°33·7′W	X	72
Todlaw Wood	Aberd	NJ6953	57°34·2′	2°30·6′W	F	29
Tod-le-Moor	Northum	NU0208	55°22·2′	1°57·7′W	X	81
Todleth Hill	Powys	SO2894	52°32·6′	3°3·3′W	H	137
Todley Hill	Brad	SE0141	53°52·2′	1°58·7′W	X	104
Tod Moor	Devon	SX6253	50°21·9′	3°56·0′W	X	202
Todmorden	Cald	SD9424	53°43·0′	2°5·0′W	T	103
Todmorden Edge	Cald	SD9224	53°43·0′	2°6·9′W	X	103
Todmorden Moor	Cald	SD8924	53°43·0′	2°9·6′W	X	103
Todpark	Pth & Kin	NO2647	56°36·8′	3°11·9′W	X	53
Todpool	Corn	SW7443	50°14·9′	5°9·8′W	T	204
Todridge	Northum	NY9971	55°2·3′	2°0·5′W	X	87
Todridge	Northum	NZ0585	55°9·8′	1°54·9′W	X	81
Todridge Fell	Northum	NY9972	55°2·8′	2°0·5′W	X	87
Tod Rig	Scot Bord	NT4202	55°18·8′	2°54·4′W	H	79
Todrig	Scot Bord	NT4219	55°27·9′	2°54·6′W	A	79
Tod Rig	Scot Bord	NT4220	55°28·5′	2°54·6′W	H	73
Todrig	Scot Bord	NT7043	55°41·0′	2°28·2′W	X	74
Todrig	Scot Bord	NT7942	55°40·5′	2°19·6′W	X	74
Todrig Burn	Scot Bord	NT4118	55°27·4′	2°55·5′W	W	79
Todrigs Burn	S Ayr	NS3934	55°34·6′	4°32·8′W	W	70
Todrigshiel	Scot Bord	NT4219	55°27·9′	2°54·6′W	X	79
Todsbughts	Falk	NS8272	55°55·9′	3°52·9′W	X	65
Tod's Gote	Highld	ND3544	58°23·0′	3°6·2′W	W	12
Todshawhaugh	Scot Bord	NT4513	55°24·7′	2°51·7′W	X	79
Todshawhaugh Hill	Scot Bord	NT4513	55°24·7′	2°51·7′W	H	79
Todshawhill	D & G	NY2293	55°13·8′	3°13·2′W	X	79
Todshaw Hill	Scot Bord	NT3916	55°26·3′	2°57·4′W	H	79
Todshawhill	Scot Bord	NT4512	55°24·2′	2°51·7′W	X	79
Tods Hill	D & G	NX6184	55°8·1′	4°10·4′W	X	77
Tods Knowe	Scot Bord	NT1623	55°29·9′	3°19·3′W	H	72
Tod Slack	D & G	NX9594	55°14·0′	3°38·6′W	H	78
Todstead	Northum	NZ1298	55°16·8′	1°48·2′W	X	81
Todston	Pth & Kin	NN9621	56°22·5′	3°40·6′W	X	52,53,58
Todstone	D & G	NX6184	55°8·1′	4°10·4′W	X	77
Tòdun	N Eil	NB2102	57°55·5′	6°42·3′W	H	14
Todwell Ho	Durham	NZ1621	54°35·3′	1°44·7′W	X	92
Todwick	Roth	SK4984	53°21·3′	1°15·4′W	T	111,120
Todwick Grange	Roth	SK4985	53°21·8′	1°15·4′W	X	111,120
Toecroft Fm	Donc	SE5202	53°31·0′	1°12·5′W	FM	111
Toe Head	N Eil	NF9594	57°50·2′	7°7·9′W	X	18
Toffit Ing	N Yks	SE1057	54°0·8′	1°50·4′W	W	104
Toffling Fm	E Yorks	TA3324	53°42·0′	0°1·3′E	FM	107,113
Toft	Cambs	TL3656	52°11·4′	0°0·2′W	T	154
Toft	Devon	SX4292	50°42·6′	4°13·9′W	X	190
Toft	Lincs	TF0617	52°44·6′	0°25·4′W	T	130
Toft	Shetld	HU4376	60°28·2′	1°12·6′W	X	2,3
Toft	Warw	SP4770	52°19·8′	1°18·2′W	T	140
Tofta Fm	N Yks	SE9898	54°22·3′	0°29·1′W	FM	94,101
Tofta Ho	N Yks	NZ1407	54°27·7′	1°46·6′W	X	92
Toftbarns	Scot Bord	NT5326	55°31·8′	2°44·2′W	X	73
Toftcarl	Highld	ND3446	58°24·1′	3°7·3′W	X	12
Toftcombs Fm	S Lanak	NT0639	55°38·4′	3°29·2′W	FM	72
Tofte Manor	Beds	SP9860	52°14·0′	0°33·5′W	X	153
Toft Fm	Lincs	TF4450	53°1·9′	0°9·3′E	FM	122
Toft Fm	Warw	SP4869	52°19·3′	1°17·3′W	FM	151
Toft Gate	N Yks	SE1364	54°4·5′	1°47·7′W	X	99
Toft Grange	Lincs	TF2661	53°8·1′	0°6·6′W	X	122
Toftgreen Fm	Staffs	SJ9064	53°10·6′	2°8·6′W	FM	118
Toft Hall	Ches	SJ7576	53°17·1′	2°22·1′W	X	118
Toft Hall	Northum	NZ0278	55°6·0′	1°57·7′W	X	87
Toft Hill	Durham	NZ1528	54°39·1′	1°45·6′W	T	92
Toft Hill	Lincs	TF2462	53°8·7′	0°8·4′W	T	122
Toft Hill	Northum	NT9143	55°41·1′	2°8·2′W	H	74,75
Toft Hill	Northum	NZ0680	55°7·1′	1°53·9′W	X	81
Toft Hill	N upon Ty	NZ2072	55°2·8′	1°40·8′W	X	88
Toft Hill	N Yks	NZ4604	54°26·0′	1°17·0′W	X	93
Toft Hill	N Yks	NZ5404	54°26·0′	1°9·6′W	X	93
Tofthill	Pth & Kin	NO1721	56°22·7′	3°20·2′W	X	53,58
Tofthill	Scot Bord	NT8554	55°47·0′	2°13·9′W	X	67,74
Toft Hill Hall	Durham	NZ1428	54°39·1′	1°46·6′W	X	92
Tofthills	Aberd	NJ5526	57°19·6′	2°44·4′W	X	37
Tofthills	Aberd	NJ8015	57°13·8′	2°19·4′W	X	38
Toft Ho	Lincs	TF4451	53°2·4′	0°9·3′E	X	122
Toft Ho	Northum	NY8699	55°17·3′	2°12·8′W	X	80
Toft Ho	N Yks	SE8364	54°4·2′	0°43·5′W	X	100
Toftholm Sike	Scot Bord	NY4995	55°15·0′	2°47·7′W	W	79
Toft House Fm	E Yorks	SE7945	53°53·9′	0°47·4′W	FM	105,106
Tofthouse Fm	Lincs	TF4450	53°1·9′	0°9·3′E	FM	122
Toft House Fm	Lincs	TF4957	53°5·6′	0°13·9′E	FM	122
Toft House Fm	N Yks	NZ8608	54°27·8′	0°40·0′W	FM	94
Toftingall	Highld	ND1754	58°28·2′	3°24·9′W	X	11,12
Toftley's Fm	Lincs	TF0688	53°22·9′	0°24·0′W	FM	112,121
Toft Lodge	Lincs	TF0719	52°45·7′	0°24·5′W	X	130
Toft Monks	Norf	TM4294	52°29·6′	1°34·3′E	T	134
Toft Monks Ho	Norf	TM4395	52°30·1′	1°35·2′E	X	134
Toft Ness	Shetld	HU4476	60°28·2′	1°11·5′W	X	2,3
Toft next Newton	Lincs	TF0488	53°23·0′	0°25·8′W	T	112,121
Toftrees	Norf	TF8927	52°48·7′	0°48·7′E	T	132
Tofts	Cumbr	SD6887	54°16·9′	2°29·1′W	X	98
Tofts	Essex	TL7808	51°44·8′	0°35·1′E	X	167
Tofts	Hartpl	NZ5128	54°38·9′	1°12·2′W	X	93
Tofts	Highld	ND3668	58°36·0′	3°5·6′W	X	12
Tofts	Northum	NY8365	54°59·0′	2°15·5′W	X	86,87
Tofts	Northum	NY8592	55°13·6′	2°13·7′W	X	80
Tofts	Orkney	HY3732	59°10·5′	3°5·6′W	A	6
Tofts	Orkney	HY4309	58°58·1′	2°59·0′W	X	6,7
Tofts	Orkney	HY7446	59°18·2′	2°26·9′W	X	5
Tofts	Orkney	ND4797	58°51·7′	2°54·6′W	X	6,7
Tofts	Pth & Kin	NN9423	56°23·5′	3°42·6′W	X	52,53,58
Tofts	Scot Bord	NT1144	55°41·1′	3°24·5′W	X	72
Toft Sand	Lincs	TF4440	52°56·5′	0°9·0′E	X	131
Tofts Burn	Northum	NY8691	55°13·0′	2°12·8′W	W	80
Tofts Dale	Norf	TF7730	52°50·5′	0°38·1′E	F	132
Tofts Fm	Hartpl	NZ4427	54°38·4′	1°18·7′W	FM	93
Tofts Fm	N Yks	SE7980	54°12·8′	0°46·9′W	FM	100
Tofts Fm	Red & Cl	NZ6421	54°35·1′	1°0·2′W	FM	94
Tofts Fm	S Lanak	NS8534	55°35·4′	3°49·1′W	FM	71,72
Toftsgate	S Lanak	NS8534	55°35·4′	3°49·1′W	X	71,72
Toftshaw	Brad	SE1829	53°45·7′	1°43·2′W	T	104
Tofts Hill	Norf	TF7731	52°51·1′	0°38·1′E	X	132
Toftsholm	Scot Bord	NY5094	55°14·5′	2°46·8′W	X	79
Tofts Ness	Orkney	HY7547	59°18·8′	2°25·9′W	X	5
Tofts Voe	Shetld	HU4475	60°27·6′	1°11·5′W	W	2,3
Toft, The	Staffs	SJ8439	52°57·1′	2°13·9′W	X	127
Toftwood	Norf	TF9911	52°39·8′	0°57·0′E	T	132
Tog Dale	E Yorks	TA0268	54°6·1′	0°26·0′W	X	101
Togdale Fm	E Yorks	TA0268	54°6·1′	0°26·0′W	FM	101
Toggs	Herts	TL2831	51°58·0′	0°7·8′W	X	166
Tog Hill	S Glos	ST7372	51°27·0′	2°22·9′W	X	172
Toghill Fm	S Glos	ST7272	51°27·0′	2°23·8′W	FM	172
Togston	Northum	NU2401	55°18·4′	1°36·9′W	T	81
Togston Barns	Northum	NU2501	55°18·4′	1°35·9′W	X	81
Togston East Fm	Northum	NU2601	55°18·4′	1°35·0′W	FM	81
Togston Hall	Northum	NU2502	55°18·9′	1°35·9′W	X	81
Toigal	Highld	NM6792	56°57·9′	5°49·5′W	X	40
Toils Fm	Brad	SE1241	53°52·1′	1°48·6′W	FM	104
Toisland Fm	N Yks	SE8363	54°3·6′	0°43·5′W	FM	100
Tokavaig	Highld	NG6011	57°7·9′	5°57·5′W	X	32
Toke Fm	E Susx	TQ8716	50°55·0′	0°40·0′E	FM	189,199
Tokenbury Corner	Corn	SX2869	50°30·0′	4°25·1′W	X	201
Tokenbury Manor	Corn	SX2870	50°30·5′	4°25·2′W	X	201
Tokenspire Park	E Yorks	TA0538	53°49·9′	0°23·9′W	X	107
Tokers Green	Oxon	SU6977	51°29·5′	1°0·0′W	T	175
Tokka	Shetld	HU2975	60°27·7′	1°27·9′W	X	3
Tokyngton	Brent	TQ1984	51°32·8′	0°16·6′W	T	176
Tolain	Highld	NM4789	56°55·7′	6°9·0′W	X	39
Tolastadh Chaolais	N Eil	NB1938	58°14·7′	6°46·9′W	T	8,13
Tolborough	Corn	SX1777	50°34·1′	4°34·7′W	T	201
Tolborough Tor	Corn	SX1777	50°34·1′	4°34·7′W	H	201
Tolcarne	Corn	SW4529	50°6·6′	5°33·6′W	X	203
Tolcarne	Corn	SW6538	50°12·0′	5°17·2′W	T	203
Tolcarne	Corn	SW6834	50°9·9′	5°14·5′W	T	203
Tolcarne	Corn	SW8251	50°19·4′	5°3·4′W	X	200,204
Tolcarne	Corn	SW8438	50°12·4′	5°1·3′W	X	204
Tolcarne	Corn	SX2478	50°34·8′	4°28·8′W	X	201
Tolcarne Merock	Corn	SW8566	50°27·5′	5°1·4′W	X	200
Tolcarne Tor	Corn	SX2578	50°34·8′	4°27·9′W	X	201
Tolcarne Wartha	Corn	SW6835	50°10·4′	5°14·6′W	T	203
Tolchmoor Gate	Devon	SX5861	50°26·1′	3°59·6′W	X	202
Tolcis Fm	Devon	ST2700	50°47·9′	3°1·8′W	FM	193
Toldavas Fm	Corn	SW4226	50°4·9′	5°36·0′W	FM	203
Toldhu	Aberd	NO3491	57°0·6′	3°4·8′W	X	44
Toldhu	Corn	SW6617	50°0·7′	5°15·6′W	W	203
Toldish	Corn	SW9259	50°23·9′	4°55·2′W	T	200
Toldrie	Fife	NO5808	56°16·0′	2°40·2′W	X	59
Toldrum	N Yks	SE2471	54°8·3′	1°37·5′W	X	99
Tolduquhill	Aberd	NJ3115	57°13·5′	3°8·1′W	X	37
Toledo Fm	Denb	SJ0874	53°15·5′	3°22·3′W	FM	116
Tolehurst Fm	Kent	TQ7840	51°8·1′	0°33·0′E	FM	188
Tolethorpe Hall	Rut	TF0210	52°40·9′	0°29·1′W	X	130
Tolethorpe Oaks	Rut	TF0212	52°42·0′	0°29·0′W	F	130
Tolgans	Shetld	HU6187	60°34·0′	0°52·7′W	X	1,2
Tolgarrick	Corn	SW9352	50°20·1′	4°54·2′W	X	200,204
Tolgroggan	Corn	SW8151	50°19·3′	5°4·2′W	X	200,204
Tolgullow	Corn	SW7343	50°14·8′	5°10·7′W	X	204
Tolgus Mount	Corn	SW6842	50°14·2′	5°14·8′W	T	203
Tolhurst	E Susx	TQ6730	51°2·9′	0°23·3′E	T	188

Toll a' Bhuic	Arg & Bt	NS2091	56°4·9′	4°53·1′W	W	56
Toll a' Choin	Highld	NH1345	57°27·7′	5°6·6′W	X	25
Tolladine	Worcs	SO8655	52°11·8′	2°11·9′W	T	150
Tollafraick	Aberd	NJ4017	57°14·6′	2°59·2′W	X	37
Toll a' Ghobhain	Highld	NH1250	57°30·3′	5°7·8′W	X	25
Toll Ainich	Highld	NG9982	57°47·2′	5°22·4′W	X	19
Toll a' Meitheach	Highld	NG9357	57°33·6′	5°27·2′W	X	25
Toll a' Mhadaidh Mor	Highld	NG8660	57°35·0′	5°34·3′W	X	19
Toll a' Mhuic	Highld	NH2342	57°26·3′	4°56·5′W	X	25
Tolland	Somer	ST1032	51°5·1′	3°16·7′W	T	181
Tolland Down	Somer	ST1032	51°5·1′	3°16·7′W	X	181
Toll a' Phuinsin	N Eil	NF9893	57°49·7′	7°4·8′W	W	18
Tollard Farnham	Dorset	ST9415	50°56·3′	2°4·7′W	T	184
Tollard Green	Wilts	ST9216	50°56·8′	2°6·4′W	X	184
Tollard Park	Wilts	ST9317	50°57·4′	2°5·6′W	X	184
Tollard Royal	Wilts	ST9417	50°57·4′	2°4·7′W	T	184
Toll a' Roimh	N Eil	NG4298	57°54·1′	6°20·8′W	X	14
Toll Bàn	Highld	NG8751	57°30·2′	5°32·9′W	X	24
Toll Bar	Donc	SE5607	53°33·6′	1°8·9′W	T	111
Toll Bar	Rut	TF0008	52°39·9′	0°30·9′W	T	141
Toll Bar	St Hel	SJ4994	53°26·7′	2°45·7′W	T	108
Toll Bar Cott	D & G	NX8767	54°59·3′	3°45·5′W	X	84
Tollbar End	Cov	SP3675	52°22·5′	1°27·9′W	T	140
Toll Bar Fm	Notts	SK7042	52°58·5′	0°57·0′W	FM	129
Toll Bar Fm	Notts	SK7657	53°6·5′	0°51·5′W	FM	120
Toll Beag	Highld	NH1566	57°39·0′	5°5·6′W	X	20
Toll Beag	Highld	NH1662	57°36·9′	5°4·4′W	X	20
Toll Creagach	Highld	NH1928	57°18·7′	4°59·9′W	H	25
Tollcross Park	C of Glas	NS6363	55°50·7′	4°10·8′W	X	64
Toll-dhoire	Arg & Bt	NM5438	56°28·5′	5°59·2′W	X	47,48
Tolldish	Staffs	SK0023	52°48·5′	1°59·6′W	X	128
Toll Doire	Arg & Bt	NM5641	56°30·1′	5°57·5′W	X	47,48
Toll Easach	Highld	NH1114	57°10·9′	5°7·2′W	X	34
Toll Eilean a' Chléirich	Highld	NB9202	57°57·8′	5°30·5′W	X	15
Tollemache Hall	Suff	TM0450	52°6·9′	0°59·2′E	X	155
Toll End	Sand	SO9792	52°31·8′	2°2·3′W	T	139
Toller Down	Dorset	ST5102	50°49·2′	2°41·4′W	X	194
Toller Down Gate	Dorset	ST5203	50°49·7′	2°40·5′W	X	194
Tollerford	Dorset	SY5997	50°46·5′	2°34·5′W	T	194
Toller Fratrum	Dorset	SY5797	50°46·5′	2°36·2′W	T	194
Toller Porcorum	Dorset	SY5698	50°47·0′	2°37·1′W	T	194
Tollers Fm	Croy	TQ3057	51°18·1′	0°7·7′W	FM	187
Tollerton	Notts	SK6034	52°54·2′	1°6·1′W	T	129
Tollerton	N Yks	SE5164	54°4·4′	1°12·8′W	T	100
Tollerton Forest	N Yks	SE5264	54°4·4′	1°11·9′W	X	100
Toller Whelme	Dorset	ST5101	50°48·6′	2°41·3′W	T	194
Tollesbury	Essex	TL9510	51°45·5′	0°49·9′E	T	168
Tollesbury Fleet	Essex	TL9711	51°46·0′	0°51·7′E	W	168
Tollesburys Fm	Essex	TL6726	51°54·7′	0°26·1′E	FM	167
Tollesbury Wick Marshes	Essex	TL9710	51°45·5′	0°51·7′E	X	168
Tollesby	Midd	NZ5115	54°31·9′	1°12·3′W	T	93
Tolleshunt D'Arcy	Essex	TL9211	51°46·1′	0°47·4′E	T	168
Tolleshunt Knights	Essex	TL9114	51°47·7′	0°46·6′E	T	168
Tolleshunt Major	Essex	TL9011	51°46·1′	0°45·6′E	T	168
Tolleshunts Fm	Essex	TL9111	51°46·1′	0°46·5′E	FM	168
Toll Fm	Cambs	TL3286	52°27·6′	0°3·0′W	FM	142
Toll Fm	Cambs	TL4381	52°24·7′	0°6·6′E	FM	142,143
Toll Fm	Cambs	TL4688	52°28·5′	0°9·4′E	FM	143
Tollgate	Corn	SX1360	50°24·8′	4°37·6′W	X	200
Tollgate Fm	Herts	TL2105	51°44·1′	0°14·5′W	FM	166
Tollgate Fm	Norf	TF9901	52°34·4′	0°56·6′E	FM	144
Tollgate Fm	Norf	TG0611	52°39·7′	1°3·2′E	FM	133
Tollgate Fm	Suff	TM1164	52°14·2′	1°5·8′E	FM	155
Tollgate Fm	Warw	SP3159	52°13·9′	1°32·4′W	FM	151
Tollhurst Fm	E Susx	TQ4940	51°8·6′	0°8·2′E	FM	188
Tollie	Highld	NH5256	57°34·5′	4°28·0′W	X	26
Tollie Bay	Highld	NG8778	57°44·7′	5°34·3′W	W	19
Tollie Fm	Highld	NG8678	57°44·7′	5°35·3′W	FM	19
Tollie Hill	Fife	NT1693	56°7·6′	3°20·6′W	H	58
Tollingham	E Yorks	SE8335	53°48·5′	0°44·0′W	X	106
Tollishill	Scot Bord	NT5157	55°48·5′	2°46·5′W	X	66,73
Toll Lochan	Highld	NH3388	57°51·3′	4°48·4′W	W	20
Toll Mór	Highld	NH1562	57°36·9′	5°5·4′W	X	20
Toll na Feurstaig	Highld	NH1333	57°21·2′	5°6·0′W	X	25
Toll nam Muc	Arg & Bt	NS2093	56°6·0′	4°53·2′W	W	56
Tollo	Aberd	NJ6644	57°29·4′	2°33·6′W	X	29
Toll Odhar	Highld	NH1818	57°13·3′	5°0·4′W	X	34
Toll Odhar	Highld	NH2229	57°19·3′	4°56·9′W	X	25
Toll Odhar Mór	Highld	NH2335	57°22·5′	4°56·2′W	X	25
Toll of Birness	Aberd	NK0034	57°24·0′	1°59·5′W	X	30
Tollohill	Aberd	NJ9202	57°6·8′	2°7·5′W	X	38
Tollohill Lodge	Aberd	NJ9101	57°6·2′	2°8·5′W	X	38
Tollomill	Aberd	NJ6645	57°29·9′	2°33·6′W	X	29
Tollomuick Forest	Highld	NH3380	57°47·0′	4°48·1′W	X	20
Toll Point	Corn	SW7826	50°5·8′	5°5·9′W	X	204
Toll's Hill	Norf	TG2440	52°54·9′	1°20·3′E	X	133
Toll's Island	I Scilly	SV9311	49°55·5′	6°16·3′W	X	203
Toll Slagan Neisdeil	N Eil	NB5646	58°20·3′	6°9·7′W	X	8
Tollslye	Kent	TQ6337	51°6·8′	0°20·1′E	X	188
Tollsworth Manor	Surrey	TQ3054	51°16·4′	0°7·8′W	X	187
Tolm	N Eil	NB0402	57°54·8′	6°59·4′W	X	18
Tolm	N Eil	NB4531	58°11·9′	6°19·9′W	T	8
Tolmachan	N Eil	NB0905	57°56·6′	6°54·6′W	X	13,14
Tolman Point	I Scilly	SV9109	49°54·3′	6°17·9′W	X	203
Tolmare Fm	W Susx	TQ1008	50°51·9′	0°25·8′W	FM	198
Tolm Bùirich	Aberd	NJ2112	57°11·8′	3°18·0′W	H	36
Tolmers	Herts	TL3003	51°42·9′	0°6·7′W	T	166
Tòl Mòr	N Eil	NB3552	58°22·8′	6°31·5′W	X	8
Tolmount	Angus	NO2079	56°54·0′	3°18·4′W	H	44
Tolpits Ho	Herts	TQ0894	51°38·3′	0°26·0′W	X	166,176
Tolpuddle	Dorset	SY7994	50°44·9′	2°17·5′W	T	194
Tolpuddle Ball	Dorset	SY8094	50°44·9′	2°16·6′W	X	194
Tolquhon Castle	Aberd	NJ8728	57°20·8′	2°12·5′W	A	38
Tolraggott Fm	Corn	SW9978	50°34·3′	4°49·9′W	FM	200
Tolroy	Corn	SW5635	50°10·1′	5°24·6′W	X	203
Tolsford Hill	Kent	TR1538	51°6·3′	1°4·7′E	X	179,189
Tolskithy	Corn	SW6841	50°13·6′	5°14·8′W	T	203
Tolson Hall	Cumbr	SD4995	54°21·1′	2°46·7′W	X	97
Tolstadh bho Thuath	N Eil	NB5347	58°20·8′	6°12·8′W	T	8
Tolsta Head (Ceann or Rubha Tholastaidh)	N Eil	NB5647	58°20·9′	6°9·7′W	X	8
Tolvaddon Downs	Corn	SW6542	50°14·1′	5°17·4′W	T	203
Tolvah	Highld	NN8499	57°4·3′	3°54·3′W	T	35,43
Tolvan	Corn	SW7028	50°6·7′	5°12·7′W	X	203
Tolvan Cross	Corn	SW7027	50°6·2′	5°12·6′W	X	203
Tolver	Corn	SW4932	50°8·3′	5°30·4′W	X	203
Tolverne	Corn	SW8539	50°13·0′	5°0·5′W	X	204
Tolworth	King	TQ1965	51°22·5′	0°17·0′W	T	176
Tom	N Eil	NB0233	58°11·4′	7°3·8′W	X	13
Tom	N Eil	NB2432	58°11·7′	6°41·4′W	X	8,13
Tom a' Bhiorain	Arg & Bt	NS0795	56°6·8′	5°5·8′W	H	56
Tom a' Bhuachaille	Arg & Bt	NN1514	56°17·2′	4°58·9′W	H	50,56
Tom a' Bhùraich	Aberd	NJ3108	57°9·7′	3°8·0′W	H	37
Tom a' Chadail	Highld	NM6161	56°41·0′	5°53·7′W	X	40
Tom a' Chadalair	Moray	NJ1819	57°15·5′	3°21·1′W	X	36
Tom a' Chait	Highld	NJ1533	57°23·0′	3°24·4′W	H	28
Tom a' Char	Aberd	NJ4304	57°7·7′	2°56·0′W	X	37
Tomachar	Moray	NJ2432	57°22·6′	3°15·4′W	H	36
Tomachar	Moray	NJ2732	57°22·6′	3°12·4′W	X	37
Tomacharich	Highld	NN1478	56°51·6′	5°2·6′W	X	41
Tom a' Charraigh	Aberd	NJ3511	57°11·4′	3°4·1′W	H	37
Tom a' Chatha	Aberd	NJ2704	57°7·5′	3°11·9′W	X	37
Tomachlaggan	Moray	NJ1522	57°17·1′	3°24·1′W	X	36
Tom a' Choilich	Arg & Bt	NM5125	56°21·4′	6°1·4′W	X	48
Tomachoin	Highld	NH5437	57°24·3′	4°25·3′W	X	26
Tom a' Chòinich	Highld	NH1627	57°18·1′	5°2·8′W	H	25
Tom a' Chòinnich	Highld	NH4669	57°41·3′	4°34·5′W	H	20
Tom a' Chor	Moray	NJ1624	57°18·2′	3°23·2′W	H	36
Tom a'Chrochaidh	Arg & Bt	NM8322	56°20·7′	5°30·2′W	H	49
Tom a' Chrochaidh	Highld	NM4964	56°42·3′	6°5·6′W	X	47
Tom a' Chrochain	Arg & Bt	NN1607	56°13·5′	4°57·6′W	X	56
Tom a' Chrochaire	Arg & Bt	NM5442	56°30·6′	5°59·5′W	X	47,48
Tomachrochar	Highld	NH9821	57°16·4′	3°41·0′W	X	36
Tom a' Chruachain	Arg & Bt	NM8418	56°18·6′	5°29·1′W	H	55
Tom a' Chuir	Aberd	NJ1901	57°5·8′	3°19·8′W	X	36
Tom a' Ghealagaidh	Highld	NH8232	57°22·1′	3°57·3′W	H	27
Tomaig	Arg & Bt	NR7019	55°24·9′	5°37·6′W	X	68
Tomaig Glen	Arg & Bt	NR7118	55°24·4′	5°36·6′W	X	68
Tom Airigh an Tailleir	N Eil	NB4648	58°21·1′	6°20·0′W	X	8
Tomaknock	Pth & Kin	NN8721	56°22·3′	3°49·3′W	T	52,58
Tomalienan	Moray	NJ2220	57°16·1′	3°17·1′W	X	36
Tom Allt na Mèinne	Highld	NM8046	56°33·5′	5°34·4′W	H	49
Tom a' Mhaide	N Eil	NL5583	56°48·9′	7°38·8′W	H	31
Tom a' Mhile	N Eil	NB4357	58°25·8′	6°23·7′W	H	8
Tom a' Mhinisteir	N Eil	NB3752	58°22·9′	6°29·5′W	X	8
Tomamhoid	Highld	NH3807	57°7·8′	4°40·1′W	X	34
Tom a Mhorair	Stir	NS4293	56°6·5′	4°32·0′W	X	56
Tom an Aighe	Arg & Bt	NN1219	56°19·8′	5°2·0′W	X	50,56
Tom an Aighe	N Eil	NB3542	58°17·5′	6°30·8′W	X	8
Toman Biorach	Arg & Bt	NN2521	56°21·2′	4°49·5′W	H	50,56
Tomanbuidhe	Pth & Kin	NN7359	56°42·6′	4°4·0′W	X	42,51,52
Toman Dubh	Arg & Bt	NS0376	55°56·5′	5°8·8′W	H	63
Toman Dunaiche	Arg & Bt	NR9497	56°7·5′	5°18·4′W	X	55
Tom an Eich Bhàin	Arg & Bt	NN0117	56°18·5′	5°12·6′W	X	50,55
Tom an Eite	Highld	NN2369	56°47·0′	4°53·4′W	X	41
Tom an Eòin	Highld	NN3265	56°45·0′	4°44·4′W	X	41
Tom an Fhéidh	Arg & Bt	NN0917	56°18·7′	5°4·8′W	X	50,56
Tom an Fheidh	Highld	NH9141	57°27·0′	3°48·5′W	X	27
Tom an Fhiodha	Highld	NH0772	57°42·0′	5°13·9′W	X	19
Tom an Fhithich	Arg & Bt	NM8812	56°15·5′	5°24·9′W	H	55
Tom an Fhuadain	N Eil	NB3914	58°2·6′	6°24·9′W	T	14
Tom an Ime	Highld	NJ1634	57°23·6′	3°23·4′W	X	28
Tom an Inbhire	Highld	NM6659	56°40·1′	5°48·7′W	X	49
Tom an Lagain	Aberd	NO3294	57°2·2′	3°6·8′W	H	37,44
Tom an Neòil	Highld	NM8096	57°0·4′	5°36·9′W	H	33,40
Tomanour	Pth & Kin	NN7320	56°21·6′	4°2·9′W	X	51,52,57
Tomanraid	Pth & Kin	NN8663	56°44·9′	3°51·4′W	X	43
Tom an Riseal	N Eil	NB4040	58°16·6′	6°25·6′W	H	8
Tom an Sgalaig	Arg & Bt	NN0602	56°10·5′	5°7·1′W	X	56
Tom an Teine	Highld	NN2179	56°52·3′	4°55·8′W	X	41
Tom Anthon	Aberd	NO0988	56°58·7′	3°29·4′W	H	43
Tom an t-Saighdeir	Arg & Bt	NM9715	56°17·3′	5°16·4′W	H	55
Tom an t-Saoir	Arg & Bt	NM9112	56°15·5′	5°22·0′W	H	55
Tom an t-Sealgair	N Eil	NB3840	58°16·5′	6°27·6′W	X	8
Tom an t-Seallaidh	Arg & Bt	NM9249	56°35·5′	5°22·8′W	H	49
Tom an-t-Seallaidh	Arg & Bt	NM9908	56°13·6′	5°14·1′W	H	55
Tóm an t-Sealltair	Arg & Bt	NM6729	56°24·0′	5°46·1′W	X	49
Tom an t-Sidhean	Highld	NM8261	56°41·7′	5°33·2′W	X	40
Tom an t-Sionnaich	Arg & Bt	NM5345	56°32·2′	6°0·6′W	X	47,48
Tom an t-Suidhe Mhóir	Highld	NJ1118	57°14·9′	3°28·0′W	H	36
Tom an Uird	Highld	NJ0930	57°21·3′	3°30·3′W	H	27,36
Tom Aonghais Ruaidh	Highld	NM7356	56°38·7′	5°41·7′W	X	49
Tom a' Phiobaire	Arg & Bt	NN1717	56°18·9′	4°57·1′W	H	50,56
Tom Apigill	Highld	NC7056	58°28·6′	4°13·3′W	H	10
Tom Ard	Arg & Bt	NM8833	56°26·8′	5°25·9′W	H	49
Tom a' Reithean	N Eil	NL5684	56°49·5′	7°37·9′W	H	31
Tom a' Thomaidh Mór	Highld	NH9124	57°17·9′	3°48·1′W	H	36
Tomatin	Highld	NH8028	57°19·9′	3°59·1′W	T	35
Tomatin Ho	Highld	NH8129	57°20·4′	3°58·2′W	X	35
Tom a Voan	Moray	NJ2520	57°16·1′	3°14·2′W	H	37
Tomb	Pth & Kin	NO1270	56°49·0′	3°26·0′W	X	43
Tom Bad a' Mhonaidh	Aberd	NO2891	57°0·5′	3°10·7′W	H	44
Tombae	Aberd	NO4396	57°3·4′	2°55·9′W	X	37,44
Tombae	Moray	NJ2125	57°18·8′	3°18·2′W	X	36
Tom Bailgeann	Highld	NH5829	57°20·0′	4°21·1′W	H	26,35
Tombain	Highld	NH8606	57°8·1′	3°52·6′W	X	35,36
Tombain	Highld	NJ0333	57°22·9′	3°36·3′W	X	27
Tombain	Moray	NJ0044	57°28·8′	3°39·6′W	X	27
Tombain	Moray	NJ3346	57°30·2′	3°6·6′W	X	28
Tombain	Moray	NJ3831	57°22·2′	3°1·4′W	X	37
Tom Bàn	Highld	NN4283	56°54·9′	4°35·3′W	H	34,42
Tomban	Pth & Kin	NN8265	56°46·0′	3°55·4′W	X	43
Tom Bàn Beag	Highld	NH3173	57°43·2′	4°49·8′W	X	20
Tombane	Pth & Kin	NN8215	56°19·0′	3°54·0′W	X	57
Tombane	Pth & Kin	NN9552	56°39·1′	3°42·3′W	X	52,53
Tombane Burn	Pth & Kin	NN9241	56°33·2′	3°45·0′W	W	52
Tom Bàn Mór	Highld	NH3175	57°44·2′	4°49·9′W	H	20
Tom Baraidh	Highld	NH7501	57°5·2′	4°3·3′W	X	35
Tombay	Angus	NO2860	56°43·8′	3°10·2′W	H	44
Tom Beag	Moray	NJ1319	57°15·5′	3°26·1′W	H	36
Tombeg	Aberd	NJ6814	57°13·2′	2°31·3′W	X	38
Tom Beith	Aberd	NJ4212	57°12·0′	2°57·1′W	H	37
Tom Beith	Pth & Kin	NN9757	56°41·9′	3°40·5′W	H	52,53
Tombeithe	Pth & Kin	NN8963	56°45·0′	3°48·5′W	X	43
Tombeth Hill	Pth & Kin	NO0809	56°16·1′	3°28·7′W	X	58
Tomb Fm	W Berks	SU5978	51°30·1′	1°8·6′W	FM	174
Tom Bharra	Arg & Bt	NN0318	56°19·1′	5°10·7′W	X	50,55
Tom Bhataleòis	N Eil	NB5153	58°23·9′	6°15·2′W	X	8
Tom Bheithe	Aberd	NO2997	57°3·8′	3°9·8′W	X	37,44
Tombrake	Stir	NS5490	56°5·1′	4°20·3′W	X	57
Tom Breac	Aberd	NJ3714	57°13·0′	3°2·1′W	H	37
Tom Breac	Aberd	NO2299	57°4·8′	3°16·8′W	H	36,44
Tombreck	Highld	NH6934	57°22·9′	4°10·3′W	X	26
Tombreck	Moray	NJ1218	57°14·9′	3°27·0′W	X	36
Tombreck	Moray	NJ1452	57°33·3′	3°25·8′W	X	28
Tombreck	Moray	NJ1935	57°24·2′	3°20·4′W	X	28
Tombreck	Moray	NJ2241	57°27·4′	3°17·5′W	X	28
Tombreck	Pth & Kin	NN6537	56°30·6′	4°11·2′W	X	51
Tombreck	Pth & Kin	NN7756	56°41·0′	4°0·0′W	X	42,51,52
Tombreckachie	Moray	NJ2029	57°20·9′	3°19·3′W	X	36
Tombreck Hill	Aberd	NJ5313	57°12·6′	2°46·2′W	H	37
Tombreck Wood	Moray	NJ3947	57°30·8′	3°0·6′W	W	28
Tom Buidhe	Angus	NO2178	56°53·5′	3°17·4′W	H	44
Tombuidhe	Arg & Bt	NN0900	56°9·5′	5°4·1′W	X	56
Tom Buidhe	Arg & Bt	NS2595	56°7·2′	4°48·5′W	H	56
Tombuie	Pth & Kin	NN8651	56°38·5′	3°51·1′W	X	52
Tombuie Cottage	Pth & Kin	NN7844	56°34·6′	3°58·7′W	X	51,52
Tom Cave	Highld	NG5142	57°24·3′	6°8·3′W	X	23,24
Tomchrasky	Highld	NH2512	57°10·2′	4°53·2′W	X	34
Tomchulan	Pth & Kin	NO0264	56°45·7′	3°35·7′W	X	43
Tomcluich	Highld	NH8848	57°30·8′	3°51·7′W	X	27
Tomcork	Moray	NJ0446	57°29·9′	3°35·7′W	X	27
Tomcork	Moray	NJ1349	57°31·6′	3°26·7′W	X	28
Tomcraggach	Pth & Kin	NN7364	56°45·3′	4°4·2′W	X	42
Tom Cross Rigg	N Yks	SE8597	54°21·9′	0°41·1′W	X	94,100
Tom Cuaiche	Arg & Bt	NR9695	56°6·5′	5°16·4′W	H	55
Tom Cullach	Moray	NJ2529	57°21·0′	3°14·3′W	X	37
Tomdachoille	Pth & Kin	NN9555	56°40·8′	3°42·4′W	X	52,53
Tom Darrach	Angus	NO5679	56°54·3′	2°42·9′W	X	44
Tomdhu	Highld	NH9720	57°15·8′	3°42·0′W	X	36
Tomdoun	Highld	NH1501	57°4·0′	5°2·6′W	X	34
Tomdow	Moray	NJ0044	57°28·8′	3°39·6′W	X	27
Tom Dubh	Aberd	NJ3104	57°7·6′	3°7·9′W	X	37
Tom Dubh	Aberd	NJ4109	57°10·3′	2°58·1′W	H	37
Tom Dubh	Arg & Bt	NM8206	56°12·1′	5°30·4′W	X	55
Tom Dubh	Arg & Bt	NN1508	56°14·0′	4°58·6′W	X	56
Tom Dubh	Highld	NN4394	57°0·9′	4°34·7′W	X	34
Tom Dubh	Highld	NN9295	57°2·3′	3°46·3′W	H	36,43
Tom Dubh	Pth & Kin	NN9855	56°40·8′	3°39·4′W	H	52,53
Tom Dubh	Stir	NN6409	56°15·5′	4°11·3′W	H	57
Tomdubh Burn	Aberd	NJ4109	57°10·3′	2°58·1′W	W	37
Tom Dubh-mór	Highld	NN3453	56°38·6′	4°42·0′W	X	41
Tom Dubh nan Caorach	Stir	NN4301	56°10·8′	4°31·3′W	H	56
Tom Dunan	Aberd	NJ2109	57°10·2′	3°17·9′W	H	36
Tom Earsail	N Eil	NB5158	58°26·6′	6°15·5′W	H	8
Tom Eas	Stir	NN3600	56°10·1′	4°38·0′W	X	56
Tom Eileatier	N Eil	NB4651	58°22·7′	6°20·2′W	X	8
Tomen Bedd Ugre	Powys	SO1069	52°18·9′	3°18·8′W	A	136,148
Tomen Castell	Conwy	SH7252	53°3·2′	3°54·2′W	A	115
Tomen Castell	Conwy	SH8152	53°3·4′	3°46·1′W	X	116
Tomen Castle	Powys	SO1758	52°13·1′	3°12·5′W	A	148
Tomen Fawr	Gwyn	SH4537	52°54·7′	4°17·9′W	A	123
Tomen Lâs	Gwyn	SH6900	52°35·2′	3°55·6′W	A	135
Tomenlawddog	Carm	SN3536	52°0·1′	4°23·8′W	A	145
Tomen Llanio	Cered	SN6657	52°11·9′	3°57·2′W	A	146
Tomen Rhyd-Owen	Cered	SN4444	52°4·6′	4°16·2′W	A	146
Tomenseba	Carm	SN3237	52°0·6′	4°26·5′W	A	145
Tomen y Bala	Gwyn	SH9230	52°51·6′	3°35·8′W	A	125
Tomen y Faerdre	Denb	SJ1956	53°5·9′	3°12·2′W	A	116
Tomen y Gwyddel	Wrex	SJ1735	52°54·6′	3°13·7′W	A	125
Tomen y Meirw	Wrex	SJ1638	52°56·2′	3°14·6′W	A	125
Tomen y Rhos	Carm	SN8029	51°57·0′	3°44·4′W	A	160
Tom Fade	Highld	NH9149	57°31·3′	3°48·7′W	X	27
Tomfarclas	Moray	NJ2037	57°25·2′	3°19·5′W	X	28
Tomfarclas Wood	Moray	NJ2037	57°25·2′	3°19·5′W	F	28
Tom Fithich	Stir	NN3601	56°10·7′	4°38·1′W	X	56
Tomfyne	N Lanak	NS7679	55°59·5′	3°58·8′W	X	64
Tom Garbh-bheinne	Moray	NJ2314	57°12·9′	3°16·0′W	H	36
Tom Garchory	Aberd	NJ3502	57°6·5′	3°3·9′W	X	37
Tom Garlet	Moray	NJ2115	57°13·4′	3°18·0′W	X	36
Tomgarrow	Pth & Kin	NO0040	56°32·7′	3°37·1′W	X	52,53
Tom Giubhais	Aberd	NO4691	57°0·7′	2°52·9′W	H	44
Tomhay Wood	Staffs	SK1113	52°43·1′	1°49·8′W	F	128
Tom Heights	Cumbr	NY3200	54°23·7′	3°2·4′W	H	90
Tom Hill	Sheff	SK2789	53°24·1′	1°35·2′W	X	110
Tomhommie	Highld	NH8254	57°33·9′	3°57·9′W	X	27
Tom Hurd Rock	Cumbr	NX9618	54°33·0′	3°36·1′W	X	89
Tomibeg	E Dunb	NS5077	55°58·0′	4°23·8′W	X	64
Tomich	Highld	NC6005	58°1·0′	4°21·7′W	X	16
Tomich	Highld	NC8026	58°12·7′	4°2·1′W	H	17
Tomich	Highld	NH3027	57°18·4′	4°48·9′W	T	26
Tomich	Highld	NH7071	57°42·9′	4°10·5′W	X	21
Tomich Ho	Highld	NH5347	57°29·6′	4°26·7′W	X	26
Tominachty	Moray	NJ2945	57°29·6′	3°10·6′W	X	28
Tominteold	Pth & Kin	NN8250	56°37·9′	3°55·0′W	X	52
Tomintianda	Pth & Kin	NN8160	56°43·3′	3°56·2′W	X	43,52
Tomintoul	Aberd	NO1490	56°59·8′	3°24·5′W	T	43
Tomintoul	Highld	NH6628	57°19·6′	4°13·1′W	X	26,35
Tomintoul	Moray	NJ1618	57°15·0′	3°23·1′W	T	36
Tomintuigle	Moray	NJ1741	57°27·4′	3°22·5′W	X	28
Tomkin's Fm	Notts	SK8367	53°11·9′	0°45·0′W	FM	121
Tomlachlan Burn	Highld	NH9337	57°24·9′	3°46·4′W	W	27
Tomlay	Highld	NJ1222	57°17·1′	3°27·1′W	X	36
Tomle	Wrex	SJ0833	52°53·4′	3°21·6′W	H	125
Tomlea	Moray	NJ1740	57°26·8′	3°22·5′W	X	28
Tomlea	Moray	NJ2444	57°29·1′	3°15·6′W	X	28
Tomleuchar Burn	D & G	NT2305	55°20·2′	3°12·4′W	W	79
Tomley Hall Fm	Leic	SP5579	52°24·6′	1°11·1′W	FM	140
Tom Liath	Aberd	NJ3203	57°7·0′	3°6·9′W	H	37

Tom Liath	Arg & Bt	NN2242	56°32·4'	4°53·3'W	X	50
Tom Liath	Highld	NH7924	57°17·7'	4°0·0'W	X	35
Tom Liath	Highld	NJ0725	57°18·6'	3°32·2'W	H	36
Tom Liath	Highld	NM7167	56°44·6'	5°44·2'W	X	40
Tom Liath	Highld	NM7367	56°44·6'	5°42·3'W	H	40
Tom Liath	Moray	NJ2833	57°23·2'	3°11·4'W	X	28
Tom Liath	Pth & Kin	NN8880	56°54·1'	3°49·9'W	H	43
Tomlin	Cumbr	NX9412	54°29·8'	3°37·8'W	X	89
Tomling Cote	Brad	SE0545	53°54·3'	1°55·0'W	X	104
Tomlin's Hill	Heref	SO5266	52°17·6'	2°41·8'W	X	137,138,149
Tomlinson's Corner	Staffs	SK1227	52°50·7'	1°48·9'W	X	128
Tomlin's Pond	Surrey	SU8858	51°19·1'	0°43·8'W	W	175,186
Tomlin Wood	Northnts	TL0094	52°32·3'	0°31·1'W	F	141
Tomloan	Highld	NH9048	57°30·8'	3°49·7'W	X	27
Tom Lomaidean	N Eil	NB4559	58°27·0'	6°21·8'W	H	8
Tomlow	Warw	SP4563	52°16·0'	1°20·0'W	T	151
Tomlow Fm	Warw	SP4563	52°16·0'	1°20·0'W	FM	151
Tomluncart	Highld	NH8452	57°32·9'	3°55·8'W	X	27
Tommacneil	Pth & Kin	NN9162	56°44·5'	3°46·5'W	X	43
Tom Meadhoin	Highld	NN0862	56°42·9'	5°7·8'W	H	41
Tom Molach	Arg & Bt	NS2196	56°7·6'	4°52·4'W	H	56
Tom Mór	Arg & Bt	NS1180	55°58·8'	5°1·3'W	X	63
Tom Mór	Highld	NH8926	57°18·9'	3°50·1'W	H	35
Tom Mór	Highld	NJ0733	57°22·9'	3°32·4'W	H	27
Tom Mór	Highld	NM5849	56°34·5'	5°56·0'W	X	47,48
Tom Mór	Highld	NM5858	56°39·3'	5°56·5'W	X	47
Tom Mór	Highld	NM6347	56°33·6'	5°51·0'W	X	49
Tom Mór	Highld	NN3686	56°56·4'	4°41·3'W	X	34,41
Tom Mór	Moray	NJ1320	57°16·0'	3°26·1'W	H	36
Tom Mór	Moray	NJ4038	57°26·0'	2°59·5'W	H	28
Tom Mór	Stir	NS3898	56°9·1'	4°36·0'W	X	56
Tommore	Moray	NJ1935	57°24·2'	3°20·4'W	X	28
Tommy Hall's Barn	N Yks	SD8258	54°1·3'	2°16·1'W	X	103
Tommy's Belt	Norf	TL8892	52°29·8'	0°46·6'E	F	144
Tommy's Fell	Cumbr	NY5182	55°8·0'	2°45·7'W	X	79
Tom na Bat	Moray	NJ1716	57°13·9'	3°22·0'W	H	36
Tom na Bent	Moray	NJ2540	57°26·9'	3°14·5'W	X	28
Tomnabhal	N Eil	NB1607	57°58·0'	6°47·7'W	H	13,14
Tom na Brataich	Highld	NN1779	56°52·2'	4°59·7'W	H	41
Tomnabrilach	Moray	NJ1731	57°22·0'	3°22·3'W	X	36
Tomnabroilach	Pth & Kin	NN9366	56°46·7'	3°44·6'W	X	43
Tom na Caillich	Highld	NH4365	57°39·1'	4°37·4'W	H	20
Tom na Callain	Stir	NN5031	56°27·1'	4°25·6'W	X	51
Tom na Cathaig	Arg & Bt	NN1214	56°17·1'	5°1·8'W	H	50,56
Tom na Cloiche Glaise	Highld	NN1977	56°51·2'	4°57·7'W	X	41
Tom na Cona	Arg & Bt	NS3490	56°4·7'	4°39·6'W	X	56
Tom na Còrr Laraich	Highld	NM7048	56°34·3'	5°44·2'W	X	49
Tom na Creige	Arg & Bt	NS0287	56°2·4'	5°10·3'W	X	55
Tom na Crìor	Arg & Bt	NR3256	55°43·7'	6°15·7'W	X	60
Tom na Croich	Highld	NH5928	57°19·5'	4°20·0'W	X	26,35
Tom na Croiche	Highld	NM6346	56°33·0'	5°50·9'W	X	49
Tomnacross	Highld	NH5141	57°26·4'	4°28·5'W	X	26
Tom na Cruaiche	Highld	NM9299	57°2·4'	5°25·2'W	X	33,40
Tom na Cùile Riabhaich	Highld	NM6891	56°59·7'	4°9·9'W	H	35
Tom na Dalach	Highld	NM5368	56°44·6'	6°1·9'W	X	47
Tom na Dubh Ghlaic	Highld	NM7049	56°34·9'	5°44·3'W	H	49
Tom na Eun	Moray	NJ3034	57°23·7'	3°9·4'W	X	28
Tom na Faire	Arg & Bt	NM7836	56°28·1'	5°35·8'W	X	49
Tom na Fianaig	Highld	NJ0915	57°13·3'	3°30·0'W	X	36
Tom na Gabhar	Aberd	NJ3615	57°13·5'	3°3·1'W	H	37
Tom na Gainmheich	Highld	NM5467	56°44·0'	6°0·9'W	X	47
Tomnagairn	Pth & Kin	NN9439	56°32·1'	3°43·0'W	X	52,53
Tom na Gaoithe	Arg & Bt	NN1529	56°25·3'	4°59·5'W	X	50
Tomnagee	Highld	NH9550	57°31·9'	3°44·8'W	X	27
Tom na Glas	Arg & Bt	NS3394	56°6·8'	4°40·7'W	X	56
Tom na Gobhair	Arg & Bt	NN1914	56°17·3'	4°55·0'W	X	50,56
Tomnagowhan	Highld	NH9615	57°13·1'	3°42·9'W	X	36
Tomnagrew	Pth & Kin	NN9439	56°32·1'	3°43·0'W	X	52,53
Tom na Gruagaich	Highld	NG8560	57°35·0'	5°35·3'W	H	19,24
Tóm na Gualainne	Arg & Bt	NM6230	56°24·4'	5°51·0'W	X	49
Tom na h-Aire	Highld	NM9082	56°53·2'	5°26·4'W	X	40
Tom na h-Airigh Duibhe	Highld	NM6257	56°38·9'	5°52·5'W	X	49
Tom na h-Eilde	Highld	NM8147	56°34·1'	5°33·4'W	H	49
Tom na h-Eilrig	Aberd	NO1896	57°3·1'	3°20·7'W	X	36,43
Tom na h-Innse	Arg & Bt	NN3211	56°16·0'	4°42·3'W	X	50,56
Tom na h-Iolaire	Arg & Bt	NR9484	56°0·5'	5°17·8'W	H	55
Tom na h-Iolaire	Highld	NC9221	58°10·1'	3°49·7'W	X	17
Tóm na h-Iolaire	Arg & Bt	NM9828	56°24·3'	5°16·0'W	H	49
Tom na h-Ulaidh	Highld	NH7831	57°21·5'	4°1·2'W	H	27
Tomnakeist	Aberd	NO4098	57°4·4'	2°58·9'W	X	37,44
Tom na Laimh	Highld	NJ1033	57°23·0'	3°29·4'W	H	28
Tom na Liach	Moray	NJ2128	57°20·4'	3°18·3'W	X	36
Tom nam Broc	Stir	NS4793	56°6·5'	4°27·2'W	X	57
Tom nam Buachaille	Arg & Bt	NM8225	56°22·3'	5°31·4'W	H	49
Tom nam Buachaillean	Arg & Bt	NN0405	56°12·1'	5°9·1'W	X	56
Tom nam Fitheach	Arg & Bt	NM4648	56°33·6'	6°7·6'W	H	47,48
Tom nam Meann	Highld	NH9242	57°27·6'	3°47·6'W	H	27
Tom nam Mòine	Arg & Bt	NR9585	56°1·1'	5°16·9'W	X	55
Tom na Mòine	Highld	NH7827	57°19·3'	4°1·1'W	H	35
Tom na Mòine	Pth & Kin	NN6960	56°43·1'	4°8·0'W	X	42
Tom na Moine	Pth & Kin	NN7542	56°33·5'	4°1·6'W	X	51,52
Tom-na Moine Shuas	Pth & Kin	NN7341	56°32·9'	4°3·5'W	X	51,52
Tomnamoon	Moray	NJ0450	57°32·1'	3°35·7'W	X	27
Tom nan Aighean	Arg & Bt	NN0129	56°24·9'	5°13·1'W	H	50
Tom nan Caorach	N Eil	NB0917	58°3·1'	6°55·5'W	X	13,14
Tom nan Clach	Highld	NH8634	57°23·2'	3°53·3'W	X	27
Tom nan Cliath	Highld	NH8329	57°20·5'	3°56·2'W	H	35
Tom nan Con	Arg & Bt	NS1788	56°3·3'	4°55·9'W	X	56
Tom nan Cuileag	Arg & Bt	NN2242	56°32·4'	4°53·3'W	X	50
Tom nan Eildean	Highld	NM6057	56°38·9'	5°54·4'W	H	49
Tom nan Eun	Moray	NJ3034	57°23·7'	3°9·4'W	H	28
Tom nan Gamhna	Arg & Bt	NN2100	56°9·8'	4°52·5'W	H	56
Tom nan Naoi-uairean	Highld	NN1587	56°56·5'	5°2·0'W	X	34,41
Tom nan Ragh	Arg & Bt	NS1481	55°59·4'	4°58·5'W	X	63
Tomnanuan	Moray	NJ1346	57°30·0'	3°26·6'W	X	28
Tom na Pàirce	Arg & Bt	NN3647	56°35·4'	4°39·8'W	X	50
Tom na Pìoghaide	Arg & Bt	NR6694	56°5·2'	5°45·2'W	H	55,61
Tomnareave	Moray	NJ2331	57°22·0'	3°16·4'W	X	36
Tomnarieve	Moray	NJ2321	57°16·6'	3°16·2'W	X	36
Tomnarroch Fm	Highld	NH9644	57°28·7'	3°43·6'W	FM	27

Tom na Seilg	Highld	NM7962	56°42·1'	5°36·2'W	X	40
Tom na Slaite	Highld	NH8234	57°23·1'	3°57·3'W	H	27
Tom na Sròin	Highld	NN2175	56°50·2'	4°55·6'W	X	41
Tomnauld	Pth & Kin	NN9855	56°40·8'	3°39·4'W	X	52,53
Tomnaven	Moray	NJ4033	57°23·3'	2°59·4'W	X	28
Tomnavey	Aberd	NJ3001	57°5·9'	3°8·9'W	X	37
Tomnavoulin	Moray	NJ2126	57°19·3'	3°18·3'W	T	36
Tomnavoun	Moray	NJ3731	57°22·2'	3°2·4'W	X	37
Tomneen	Moray	NJ2644	57°29·1'	3°13·6'W	X	28
Tomnoan	Moray	NJ3338	57°25·9'	3°6·5'W	X	28
Tomnun	Angus	NO2764	56°46·0'	3°11·2'W	X	44
Tomocrocher	Pth & Kin	NN6035	56°29·4'	4°16·0'W	X	51
Tom Odhar	Aberd	NJ2603	57°7·0'	3°12·9'W	H	37
Tom Odhar	Arg & Bt	NR9767	55°51·5'	5°14·2'W	X	62
Tom Odhar	Arg & Bt	NS1577	55°57·3'	4°57·4'W	X	63
Tom Odhar	Highld	NM7781	56°52·3'	5°39·1'W	H	40
Tom Odhar	Stir	NN6514	56°18·2'	4°10·5'W	H	57
Tom of Ruthrie	Moray	NJ2538	57°25·8'	3°14·5'W	X	28
Tomont End	N Ayr	NS1759	55°47·6'	4°54·7'W	X	63
Tomont Hill	S Lanak	NS9812	55°23·7'	3°36·2'W	H	78
Tomore	Moray	NJ2043	57°28·5'	3°19·6'W	X	28
Tom Osgro	N Eil	NB4650	58°22·2'	6°20·1'W	X	8
Tomperrow	Corn	SW7744	50°15·5'	5°7·3'W	T	204
Tomphubil	Pth & Kin	NN7754	56°40·0'	4°0·0'W	X	42,51,52
Tompkin	Staffs	SJ9451	53°3·6'	2°5·0'W	T	118
Tompset's Bank	E Susx	TQ4233	51°4·9'	0°2·0'E	T	187
Tom Reamhar	Highld	NN8188	56°58·3'	3°57·0'W	H	43
Tom Rostain	N Eil	NB3023	58°7·1'	6°34·6'W	X	13,14
Tom Rostal	N Eil	NB2830	58°10·8'	6°37·1'W	X	8,13
Tom Ruadh	Moray	NJ1757	57°36·0'	3°22·9'W	X	28
Tom Rudd Beck	Cumbr	NY1529	54°39·2'	3°18·6'W	W	89
Tom Ruisg	N Eil	NB1511	58°0·1'	6°49·0'W	H	13,14
Tom's Cairn	Aberd	NO6194	57°2·4'	2°38·1'W	H	37,45
Tom's Down	Hants	SU4501	50°48·6'	1°21·3'W	X	196
Tom's Forest	Aberd	NJ7517	57°14·8'	2°24·4'W	F	38
Tomshielburn	D & G	NY3477	55°5·2'	3°1·6'W	X	85
Tom's Hill	Aberd	NJ7056	57°35·8'	2°29·7'W	X	29
Tom's Hill	Herts	SP9611	51°47·6'	0°36·1'W	X	165
Tomshogle	Highld	NH9050	57°31·9'	3°49·8'W	X	27
Tom's Howe	Cumbr	NY4804	54°26·0'	2°47·7'W	X	90
Tomsléibhe	Arg & Bt	NM6137	56°28·1'	5°52·4'W	X	49
Tom Smith's Cross	N Yks	SE5781	54°13·5'	1°7·1'W	X	100
Tom Smith's Stone	Northum	NY6546	54°48·7'	2°32·3'W	X	86
Tom Soilleir	Arg & Bt	NM8409	56°13·7'	5°28·6'W	H	55
Tom Soilleir	Arg & Bt	NM9500	56°9·2'	5°17·6'W	X	55
Tom Soilleir	Arg & Bt	NS0092	56°5·0'	5°12·4'W	H	55
Tom Soilleir	Arg & Bt	NS1491	56°4·8'	4°58·9'W	X	56
Tom Soilleir	Stir	NS4095	56°7·5'	4°34·0'W	X	56
Tom's Wood	Peterb	TF0902	52°36·5'	0°23·0'W	F	142
Tomtain	N Lanak	NS7281	56°0·5'	4°2·7'W	H	64
Tom Tallon's Crag	Northum	NT9328	55°33·0'	2°6·2'W	H	74,75
Tom, The	Aberd	NJ3403	57°7·1'	3°4·9'W	H	37
Tom, The	Arg & Bt	NS1470	55°53·5'	4°58·0'W	X	63
Tom, The	Arg & Bt	NS1674	55°55·7'	4°56·3'W	H	63
Tomthorn	Derby	SK0775	53°16·6'	1°53·3'W	T	119
Tom Titlach	Angus	NO3876	56°52·5'	3°0·6'W	X	44
Tomtit's Bottom	Glos	SO9714	51°49·7'	2°2·2'W	F	163
Tom Trumper	Moray	NJ2318	57°15·0'	3°16·1'W	H	36
Tom Uaine	Highld	NM9566	56°44·7'	5°20·7'W	H	40
Tomvaich	Highld	NJ0630	57°21·3'	3°33·3'W	X	27,36
Tom Waring's Well	Lancs	SD5849	53°56·4'	2°38·0'W	W	102
Tomwell Fm	Oxon	SP4530	51°58·2'	1°20·3'W	FM	151
Ton	Monm	SO3613	51°49·0'	2°55·3'W	X	161
Ton	Monm	ST3696	51°39·8'	2°55·1'W	T	171
Tonacheois	N Eil	NF7942	57°21·6'	7°19·9'W	X	22
Tonacombe	Corn	SS2014	50°54·1'	4°33·2'W	A	190
Tòn Airigh Sgallaidh	Arg & Bt	NR1755	55°42·6'	6°29·9'W	X	60
Tonasdale	Shetld	HU4763	60°21·2'	1°8·4'W	X	2,3
Ton Breigam	V of Glam	SS9979	51°30·3'	3°26·9'W	T	170
Tonbridge	Kent	TQ5946	51°11·7'	0°16·9'E	T	188
Tonburn	Aberd	NJ4627	57°20·1'	2°53·4'W	X	37
Ton Burn	Aberd	NJ6913	57°12·7'	2°30·3'W	W	38
Tonderghie	D & G	NX4435	54°41·4'	4°24·8'W	X	83
Tonderghie Burn	D & G	NX4973	55°2·0'	4°21·3'W	W	77
Tondu	Brig	SS8984	51°32·9'	3°35·7'W	T	170
Tòn Dubh-sgairt	Arg & Bt	NM4129	56°23·2'	6°11·3'W	X	48
Tondu House Fm	Brig	SS8884	51°32·9'	3°36·5'W	FM	170
Tone	Somer	ST1221	50°59·1'	3°14·8'W	T	181,193
Tonedale	Somer	ST1221	50°59·1'	3°14·8'W	T	181,193
Tone Fm	Somer	ST0233	51°5·5'	3°23·6'W	FM	181
Tone Green	Somer	ST1723	51°0·3'	3°10·6'W	T	181,193
Tone Hall	Northum	NY9080	55°7·1'	2°9·0'W	X	80
Toneham Fm	Peterb	TF2703	52°36·8'	0°7·0'W	FM	142
Tòn Eich	Pth & Kin	NN8029	56°26·5'	3°56·3'W	H	52
Ton-eithin	Caer	ST1992	51°37·5'	3°9·8'W	X	171
Tonerspuddle Heath	Dorset	SY8291	50°43·3'	2°14·9'W	X	194
Tone Vale	Somer	ST1627	51°2·4'	3°11·5'W	X	181,193
Toney's Fm	Glos	SO7434	52°0·5'	2°22·3'W	FM	150
Tonfanau	Gwyn	SH5603	52°36·6'	4°7·2'W	X	135
Ton Fm	Brig	SS8777	51°29·1'	3°37·3'W	FM	170
Ton Fm	Heref	SO2545	52°6·1'	3°5·3'W	FM	148
Ton Fm,The	Monm	SO3905	51°44·7'	2°52·6'W	FM	161
Tonford Manor	Kent	TR1257	51°16·6'	1°2·8'E	X	179
Tong	Brad	SE2230	53°46·2'	1°39·6'W	T	104
Tong	Kent	TQ8346	51°11·3'	0°37·5'E	T	188
Tong	Shrops	SJ7907	52°39·9'	2°18·2'W	T	127
Tonga	Shetld	HP5005	60°43·8'	1°4·5'W	X	1
Tonga	Shetld	HP5814	60°48·5'	0°55·5'W	X	1
Tonga	Shetld	HU3808	59°51·6'	1°18·8'W	X	4
Tonga Brae	Orkney	HY4430	59°9·5'	2°58·3'W	X	5,6
Tonga Field	Shetld	HP5001	60°41·6'	1°4·6'W	H	1
Tonga Lees	Shetld	HP5814	60°48·5'	0°55·5'W	X	1
Tongan Swarta	Shetld	HU3090	60°35·8'	1°26·6'W	X	1
Tonga Stack	Shetld	HP5714	60°48·6'	0°56·6'W	X	1
Tonga Water	Shetld	HU3387	60°34·2'	1°23·4'W	W	1,2
Tonge	Leic	SK4123	52°48·4'	1°23·1'W	T	129
Tonge Corner	Kent	TQ9365	51°21·3'	0°46·7'E	T	178
Tonge Fm	Lincs	TF1860	53°7·7'	0°13·8'W	FM	122
Tonge Fold	Bolton	SD7309	53°34·9'	2°24·1'W	T	109
Tonge Hall	Roch	SD8705	53°32·7'	2°11·4'W	A	109

Tonge Moor	Bolton	SD7210	53°35·4'	2°25·0'W	T	109
Tonge's Fm	Lincs	SK8960	53°8·0'	0°39·8'W	FM	121
Tong Fm	N Eil	NB4436	58°14·6'	6°21·3'W	FM	8
Tong Forge	Shrops	SJ7808	52°40·4'	2°19·1'W	T	127
Tong Green	Kent	TQ9854	51°15·3'	0°50·6'E	T	189
Tongham	Surrey	SU8849	51°14·2'	0°44·0'W	T	186
Tong Hill Fm	Shrops	SJ8007	52°39·9'	2°17·3'W	FM	127
Tong Ho	Kent	TQ9556	51°16·4'	0°48·1'E	X	178
Tong Knoll	Staffs	SJ8009	52°40·9'	2°17·3'W	X	127
Tongland	D & G	NX6954	54°52·1'	4°2·1'W	T	83,84
Tongland Br	D & G	NX6953	54°51·5'	4°2·0'W	X	83,84
Tongland Loch	D & G	NX7056	54°53·2'	4°1·2'W	W	83,84
Tong Lodge	Shrops	SJ7806	52°39·3'	2°19·1'W	X	127
Tong Norton	Shrops	SJ7908	52°40·4'	2°18·2'W	T	127
Tong Park	Brad	SE1639	53°51·1'	1°45·0'W	T	104
Tong Park Fm	Shrops	SJ8006	52°39·3'	2°17·3'W	FM	127
Tong Priory	Shrops	SJ7907	52°39·9'	2°18·2'W	X	127
Tong Rough	Shrops	SJ8208	52°40·4'	2°15·6'W	F	127
Tongs Fm	Brom	TQ4468	51°23·8'	0°4·6'E	FM	177
Tongside	Highld	ND1057	58°29·8'	3°32·2'W	X	11,12
Tong Street	Brad	SE1930	53°46·2'	1°42·3'W	T	104
Tongue	Cumbr	NY2307	54°27·4'	3°10·8'W	X	89,90
Tongue	Cumbr	NY4324	54°36·7'	2°52·5'W	X	90
Tongue	E Ayr	NS5232	55°33·8'	4°20·4'W	X	70
Tongue	E Ayr	NS5938	55°37·2'	4°13·9'W	X	71
Tongue	Highld	NC5956	58°28·4'	4°24·6'W	T	10
Tongue	N Yks	SD8497	54°22·3'	2°14·4'W	X	98
Tongue Bay	Highld	NC6061	58°31·1'	4°23·7'W	W	10
Tongue Burn	D & G	NS7606	55°20·2'	3°56·9'W	W	71,78
Tongue Burn	Scot Bord	NY4798	55°16·6'	2°49·6'W	W	79
Tongue End	Lincs	TF1618	52°45·1'	0°16·5'W	T	130
Tongue Field	Shetld	HU4131	60°4·0'	1°15·3'W	H	4
Tongue Gill	Cumbr	NY3410	54°29·1'	3°0·7'W	W	90
Tongue Glen	D & G	NX1569	54°59·1'	4°53·1'W	X	82
Tongue Head	Cumbr	NY2408	54°27·9'	3°9·9'W	X	89,90
Tongue Hill	D & G	NS8214	55°24·6'	3°51·4'W	H	71,78
Tongue Hill	N Yks	NZ0602	54°25·0'	1°54·0'W	X	92
Tongue Ho	Cumbr	SD2397	54°22·0'	3°10·7'W	X	96
Tongue Ho (ruin)	Cumbr	NY4506	54°27·0'	2°50·5'W	X	90
Tongue House	Highld	NC5958	58°29·5'	4°24·7'W	X	10
Tongue House High Close	Cumbr	SD2497	54°22·0'	3°9·8'W	X	96
Tongue How	Cumbr	NY0709	54°28·3'	3°25·7'W	X	89
Tongue Lodge	Highld	NC5858	58°29·5'	4°25·7'W	X	10
Tongue Moor	Cumbr	NY1603	54°25·2'	3°17·3'W	X	89
Tongue Moor	Cumbr	NY1703	54°25·2'	3°16·3'W	X	89,90
Tongue of Gangsta	Orkney	HY4503	58°54·9'	2°56·8'W	X	6,7
Tongue of Westerbister	Orkney	HY4502	58°54·4'	2°56·8'W	X	6,7
Tongue Rigg	Cumbr	NY5210	54°29·2'	2°44·0'W	H	90
Tongues Fm	Lancs	SD3748	53°55·7'	2°57·2'W	FM	102
Tongues Fm	Northum	NZ0376	55°5·0'	1°56·8'W	FM	87
Tongues of Clatto	Fife	NO4515	56°19·7'	2°52·9'W	X	59
Tongue, The	Cumbr	NY3430	54°39·9'	3°1·0'W	H	90
Tongue, The	Cumbr	NY3513	54°30·7'	2°59·8'W	X	90
Tongue, The	Cumbr	NY4206	54°27·0'	2°53·3'W	H	90
Tongue, The	N Ayr	NS2860	55°48·4'	4°44·2'W	X	63
Tongue Vale	Orkney	ND2695	58°50·4'	3°16·4'W	X	7
Tonguey Faulds	Pth & Kin	NO0208	56°15·5'	3°34·5'W	X	58
Tongwell	Mil Key	SP8741	52°3·9'	0°43·5'W	T	152
Tongwynlais	Card	ST1382	51°32·0'	3°14·9'W	T	171
Tòn Lagain	Arg & Bt	NR2169	55°50·3'	6°26·9'W	X	60
Tonley	Aberd	NJ6113	57°12·6'	2°38·3'W	X	37
Tonmawr	Nth Pt Talb	SS8096	51°39·2'	3°43·7'W	T	170
Ton Mawr Fm	Nth Pt Talb	SS8286	51°33·9'	3°41·8'W	FM	170
Tòn Mhór	Arg & Bt	NR2371	55°51·4'	6°25·2'W	X	60
Tonn	Carm	SN7635	52°0·2'	3°48·0'W	X	146,160
Tonna	Nth Pt Talb	SS7799	51°40·8'	3°46·4'W	T	170
Tonnachrae	D & G	NX1358	54°53·2'	4°54·5'W	X	82
Tonnel Hill	N Ayr	NS1757	55°46·6'	4°54·6'W	X	63
Ton Pentre	Rho Cyn Taf	SS9695	51°38·9'	3°29·8'W	T	170
Ton Philip	Brig	SS8684	51°32·8'	3°38·3'W	X	170
Tonrioch	Arg & Bt	NR6919	55°24·9'	5°38·6'W	X	68
Tonspyddaden	Powys	SN8612	51°47·9'	3°38·8'W	X	160
Tontearie	Highld	NH9716	57°13·7'	3°41·9'W	X	36
Ton-teg	Rho Cyn Taf	ST0986	51°34·2'	3°18·4'W	T	171
Tontine	Lancs	SD5204	53°32·1'	2°43·0'W	T	108
Tontine Fm	Kent	TR0933	51°3·7'	0°59·4'E	FM	179,189
Tòn Tire	Arg & Bt	NM6020	56°19·0'	5°52·4'W	X	49
Ton-ty'r-bel	Caer	ST2099	51°41·3'	3°9·0'W	X	171
Tonwell	Herts	TL3317	51°50·4'	0°3·8'W	T	166
Tonyfield Fm	Devon	SS7110	50°52·7'	3°49·6'W	FM	191
Tonyfildre	Powys	SN8610	51°46·9'	3°38·8'W	X	160
Ton-y-gilfach	Nth Pt Talb	SN8908	51°45·8'	3°36·1'W	X	160
Tonypandy	Rho Cyn Taf	SS9992	51°37·3'	3°27·2'W	T	170
Ton-y-pistyll	Caer	ST1996	51°39·7'	3°9·9'W	T	171
Tonyrefail	Rho Cyn Taf	ST0188	51°35·2'	3°25·4'W	T	170
Too	Orkney	HY3833	59°11·0'	3°4·6'W	X	6
Too Brekk	Shetld	HU3269	60°24·5'	1°24·6'W	X	3
Too Field	Shetld	HU2946	60°12·1'	1°28·1'W	X	4
Toog	Shetld	HU4377	60°28·7'	1°12·6'W	X	2,3
Toogood Fm	Lancs	SD5213	53°36·9'	2°43·1'W	FM	108
Toogoods Fm	Dorset	ST7918	50°57·9'	2°17·6'W	FM	183
Toogs	Shetld	HU3243	60°10·5'	1°24·9'W	X	4
Toogs	Shetld	HU3733	60°5·1'	1°19·6'W	T	4
Toogs	Shetld	HU4234	60°5·6'	1°14·2'W	X	4
Tooin of Rusht	Orkney	HY3520	59°4·0'	3°7·5'W	X	6
Tookey Fm	Cambs	TL1191	52°30·6'	0°21·5'W	FM	142
Tookeys Fm	Worcs	SP0361	52°15·1'	1°57·0'W	FM	150
Tooley Fm	Leic	SP4799	52°35·4'	1°18·0'W	FM	140
Tooley's Fm	Essex	TL6523	51°53·1'	0°24·2'E	FM	167
Tooleyshaw Moor	Derby	SE0802	53°31·1'	1°52·4'W	X	110
Tooleyshaw Moss	Derby	SE0804	53°32·2'	1°52·3'W	X	110
Tooley Spinneys	Leic	SK4700	52°36·0'	1°18·0'W	F	140
Toolie	Shetld	HP5916	60°49·6'	0°54·4'W	X	1
Toombers Wood	Norf	TF6506	52°37·8'	0°26·7'E	F	143
Toomer Fm	Somer	ST7019	50°58·4'	2°25·3'W	FM	183
Toomer Hill	Somer	ST6919	50°58·4'	2°26·1'W	H	183
Toon's Lodge	Cambs	TL1493	52°31·6'	0°18·8'W	X	142
Too of the Head	Orkney	ND1998	58°52·0'	3°23·8'W	X	7
Toot Baldon	Oxon	SP5600	51°42·0'	1°11·0'W	T	164
Toot Hill	Cald	SE0222	53°41·9'	1°57·8'W	X	104

Toothill	Cald	SE1421	53°41·4′	1°46·9′W	T	104
Toot Hill	Ches	SJ9671	53°14·4′	2°3·2′W	X	118
Toot Hill	Derby	SK0883	53°20·9′	1°52·4′W	X	110
Toot Hill	Essex	TL5102	51°42·0′	0°11·5′E	T	167
Toothill	Hants	SU3718	50°57·8′	1°28·0′W	T	185
Toot Hill	Herts	TL1431	51°58·2′	0°20·0′W	X	166
Toot Hill	Lincs	TF4281	53°18·6′	0°8·3′E	X	122
Toot Hill	Notts	SK6939	52°56·9′	0°58·0′W	X	129
Toot Hill	Notts	SK7045	53°0·1′	0°57·0′W	X	129
Toot Hill	Staffs	SK0537	52°56·1′	1°55·1′W	X	128
Toot Hill	Staffs	SK0642	52°58·8′	1°54·2′W	T	119,128
Toothill	Swin	SU1283	51°33·0′	1°49·2′W	T	173
Toothill Fm	Derby	SK2482	53°20·3′	1°38·0′W	FM	110
Toot Hill (Motte and Bailey)	Herts	TL1431	51°58·2′	0°20·0′W	A	166
Toot Hill (Motte and Bailey)	Lincs	TF4281	53°18·6′	0°8·3′E	A	122
Tooting Bec Common	Wan	TQ2972	51°26·2′	0°8·3′W	X	176
Tooting Graveney	Wan	TQ2771	51°25·7′	0°10·0′W	T	176
Tootle Bridge Fm	Somer	ST5532	51°5·4′	2°38·2′W	FM	182,183
Tootle Hall	Lancs	SD5545	53°54·2′	2°40·7′W	X	102
Toovies Fm	W Susx	TQ2939	51°8·4′	0°9·0′W	FM	187
Topan-bach	Conwy	SH8272	53°14·2′	3°45·7′W	X	116
Top Barn Fm	Worcs	SO8261	52°15·0′	2°15·4′W	FM	138,150
Top Brackendale Fm	Notts	SK6938	52°56·3′	0°58·0′W	FM	129
Top Bridge Fm	N Yks	SE8380	54°12·8′	0°43·2′W	FM	100
Top Buildings	Lincs	TF1396	53°27·2′	0°17·5′W	X	113
Top Castle	Carm	SN1907	51°44·2′	4°36·9′W	A	158
Topcliffe	Leeds	SE2726	53°44·0′	1°35·0′W	T	104
Topcliffe	N Yks	SE4076	54°10·9′	1°22·8′W	T	99
Topcliffe Airfield	N Yks	SE4079	54°12·6′	1°22·8′W	X	99
Topcliffe Manor Fm	N Yks	SE4175	54°10·4′	1°21·9′W	FM	99
Topcliffe Parks	N Yks	SE3978	54°12·0′	1°23·7′W	X	99
Topcliffe Parks	N Yks	SE4077	54°11·5′	1°22·8′W	X	99
Topclose Fm	Ches	SJ9572	53°14·9′	2°4·1′W	FM	118
Topcroft	Norf	TM2692	52°29·0′	1°20·1′E	T	134
Topcroft Street	Norf	TM2691	52°28·4′	1°20·1′E	T	134
Top End	Beds	TL0362	52°15·0′	0°29·1′W	T	153
Top Farm	Notts	SK6777	53°17·4′	0°59·3′W	FM	120
Topfauld	Pth & Kin	NN8708	56°15·3′	3°49·0′W	X	58
Topfaulds Hill	E Renf	NS5348	55°42·4′	4°19·9′W	X	64
Topfield Fm	Cambs	TL2868	52°17·9′	0°7·0′W	FM	153
Topfield Fm	Leic	SK6713	52°42·9′	1°0·1′W	FM	129
Topfield Fm	Notts	SK7045	53°0·1′	0°57·0′W	FM	129
Top Flash	Ches	SJ6764	53°10·6′	2°29·2′W	W	118
Top Fm	Beds	TL1557	52°12·2′	0°18·6′W	FM	153
Top Fm	Beds	TL1956	52°11·6′	0°15·1′W	FM	153
Top Fm	Cambs	TL1483	52°26·2′	0°19·0′W	FM	142
Top Fm	Cambs	TL1977	52°22·9′	0°14·7′W	FM	142
Top Fm	Cambs	TL2087	52°28·3′	0°13·6′W	FM	142
Top Fm	Cambs	TL2367	52°17·5′	0°11·4′W	FM	153
Top Fm	Cambs	TL2948	52°7·1′	0°6·6′W	FM	153
Top Fm	Ches	SJ5146	53°0·8′	2°43·4′W	FM	117
Top Fm	Ches	SJ6258	53°7·3′	2°33·7′W	FM	118
Top Fm	Glos	SP1240	52°3·7′	1°49·1′W	FM	150
Top Fm	Leic	SK6120	52°46·7′	1°5·3′W	FM	129
Top Fm	Lincs	SK8794	53°26·4′	0°41·0′W	FM	112
Top Fm	Lincs	SK9784	53°20·9′	0°32·2′W	FM	121
Top Fm	Lincs	TA0309	53°34·3′	0°26·3′W	FM	112
Top Fm	Lincs	TF0183	53°20·3′	0°28·6′W	FM	121
Top Fm	Lincs	TF0494	53°26·2′	0°25·7′W	FM	112
Top Fm	Lincs	TF0793	53°25·6′	0°23·0′W	FM	112
Top Fm	Lincs	TF0887	53°22·4′	0°22·2′W	FM	112,121
Top Fm	Lincs	TF1886	53°21·7′	0°13·2′W	FM	113,122
Top Fm	Lincs	TF2695	53°26·4′	0°5·8′W	FM	113
Top Fm	Lincs	TF2794	53°25·9′	0°4·9′W	FM	113
Top Fm	Mil Key	SP9150	52°8·7′	0°39·8′W	FM	152
Top Fm	N Lincs	SE9306	53°32·8′	0°35·4′W	FM	112
Top Fm	N Lincs	TA0713	53°36·4′	0°22·6′W	FM	112
Top Fm	Norf	TF8911	52°40·1′	0°48·1′E	FM	132
Top Fm	Norf	TF9434	52°52·3′	0°53·4′E	FM	132
Top Fm	Norf	TL9396	52°31·9′	0°51·1′E	FM	144
Top Fm	Northnts	SP7151	52°9·4′	0°57·3′W	FM	152
Top Fm	Notts	SK7744	52°59·5′	0°50·8′W	FM	129
Top Fm	N Yks	SD8074	54°9·9′	2°18·0′W	FM	98
Top Fm	Staffs	SJ8045	53°0·4′	2°17·5′W	FM	118
Top Fm	Staffs	SK1063	53°10·1′	1°50·6′W	FM	119
Top Fm	Suff	TM3082	52°23·5′	1°23·2′E	FM	156
Top Fm	Warw	SP1945	52°6·4′	1°43·0′W	FM	151
Top Fm	Warw	SP3793	52°32·3′	1°26·9′W	FM	140
Top Fm	Warw	SP4167	52°18·2′	1°23·5′W	FM	151
Top Fm	Win & Maid	SU8281	51°31·5′	0°48·7′W	FM	175
Top Fm	Wrex	SJ3442	52°58·5′	2°58·6′W	FM	117
Top Fox Covert	Lincs	SK8486	53°22·1′	0°43·8′W	F	112,121
Top Green	Notts	SK7645	53°0·1′	0°51·6′W	T	129
Top Hake's Fm	Cambs	TL3795	52°32·4′	0°1·6′E	FM	142,143
Top Hall	Roth	SK5380	53°19·1′	1°11·9′W	X	111,120
Top Hall	Rut	SK9004	52°37·8′	0°39·8′W	X	141
Topham	Donc	SE6217	53°39·0′	1°3·3′W	T	111
Tophead	Aberd	NJ9859	57°37·5′	2°1·5′W	X	30
Tophead	Aberd	NK0755	57°35·4′	1°52·5′W	X	30
Tophead	Pth & Kin	NO0731	56°28·0′	3°30·1′W	X	52,53
Tophill Fm	Caer	ST1297	51°40·1′	3°16·0′W	FM	171
Tophill Fm	Derby	SK2457	53°6·8′	1°38·1′W	FM	119
Top Hill Fm	E Susx	TQ4937	51°7·0′	0°8·1′E	FM	188
Top Hill Fm	Kent	TQ5338	51°7·5′	0°11·6′E	FM	188
Tophill Fm	Kent	TQ9053	51°14·9′	0°43·7′E	FM	189
Tophill Fm	Kent	TQ9126	51°0·3′	0°43·7′E	FM	189
Tophill Low	E Yorks	TA0748	53°55·3′	0°21·8′W	X	107
Top Ho	Ches	SJ4348	53°1·8′	2°50·6′W	X	117
Top Ho	E Yorks	SE7019	53°40·0′	0°56·0′W	X	112
Top Ho	Shrops	SJ4733	52°53·8′	2°46·9′W	X	126
Top House Fm	Ches	SJ6446	53°0·8′	2°31·8′W	FM	118
Top House Fm	Derby	SK1838	52°56·6′	1°43·5′W	FM	128
Tophouse Fm	Leic	SP6287	52°28·9′	1°4·8′W	FM	140
Tophouse Fm	Notts	SK5748	53°1·8′	1°8·6′W	FM	129
Top House Fm	N Yks	SE5828	53°44·9′	1°6·8′W	FM	105
Top House Fm	Shrops	SJ4128	52°51·0′	2°52·2′W	FM	126
Toplands Fm	Wilts	ST8474	51°28·1′	2°13·4′W	FM	173
Top Lane Fm	Wilts	ST7633	51°6·0′	2°20·2′W	FM	183

Topleigh	W Susx	SU9118	50°57·5′	0°41·9′W	T	197
Topler's Hill	Beds	TL2140	52°2·9′	0°13·7′W	X	153
Topley	Shrops	SO5290	52°30·6′	2°42·0′W	X	137,138
Topley Fm	Notts	SK7389	53°23·8′	0°53·7′W	FM	112,120
Topley Head Fm	Derby	SK1172	53°14·9′	1°49·7′W	FM	119
Topley Pike	Derby	SK1072	53°14·9′	1°50·6′W	X	119
Top Lock	Wigan	SD6006	53°33·2′	2°35·8′W	T	109
Top Lodge	Northnts	SP7579	52°24·5′	0°53·4′W	X	141
Top Lodge	Northnts	SP9798	52°34·5′	0°33·7′W	X	141
Top Lodge Fm	Cambs	TL1276	52°22·5′	0°20·9′W	FM	142
Top Lodge Fm	Northnts	SP8859	52°13·6′	0°42·3′W	FM	152
Top Lodge Fm	Peterb	TF1001	52°36·0′	0°22·1′W	FM	142
Top Low	Staffs	SK1249	53°2·5′	1°48·9′W	A	119
Top Mere	N Yks	SD9775	54°10·5′	2°2·3′W	X	98
Top Merril Grange	Leic	SK4321	52°47·3′	1°21·3′W	X	129
Top Moor	Cambs	TL4868	52°17·6′	0°10·6′E	X	154
Top Moss	Shrops	SJ5726	52°50·0′	2°37·9′W	F	126
Topmuir	D & G	NY1269	55°0·7′	3°22·1′W	X	85
Top of Blaze Moss	Lancs	SD6152	53°58·0′	2°35·3′W	H	102,103
Top of Ecton	Staffs	SK1057	53°6·8′	1°50·6′W	X	119
Top of Hebers	Roch	SD8607	53°33·8′	2°12·3′W	T	109
Top of Pike	Roch	SD8617	53°39·2′	2°12·3′W	X	109
Top of Ramsgreave	Lancs	SD6631	53°46·7′	2°30·5′W	X	103
Top of South House Moor	N Yks	SD7575	54°10·5′	2°22·6′W	X	98
Top of the Battery or Carn Damhaireach	Aberd	NO0585	56°57·1′	3°33·3′W	H	43
Top of the Town	Ches	SJ6346	53°0·8′	2°32·7′W	X	118
Top o' Selside	Cumbr	SD3091	54°18·8′	3°4·1′W	H	96,97
Top o'th' Hill	Ches	SJ8979	53°18·7′	2°9·5′W	X	118
Top o' th' Knotts	Bolton	SD7413	53°37·0′	2°23·2′W	X	109
Top o'th' Lane	Lancs	SD5923	53°42·4′	2°36·9′W	T	102
Top o' th' Meadows	Oldham	SD9606	53°33·3′	2°3·2′W	T	109
Topperfettle	Highld	NJ0525	57°18·6′	3°34·2′W	X	36
Toppesfield	Essex	TL7337	52°0·5′	0°31·6′E	T	155
Toppesfield Hall	Essex	TL7437	52°0·5′	0°32·5′E	X	155
Toppin Castle	Cumbr	NY4957	54°54·6′	2°47·3′W	X	86
Topping Hall	D & G	NY2167	54°59·7′	3°13·7′W	X	85
Toppinghoe Hall	Essex	TL7711	51°46·4′	0°34·3′E	X	167
Toppinghoehall Wood	Essex	TL7612	51°47·0′	0°33·5′E	F	167
Topping Riggs Wood	N Yks	NZ8908	54°27·8′	0°37·2′W	F	94
Toppings	Bolton	SD7213	53°37·0′	2°25·0′W	T	109
Toppinhill	Cumbr	NY4445	54°48·1′	2°51·8′W	X	85
Toppin Rays	Cumbr	SD3081	54°13·4′	3°4·0′W	X	96,97
Top Plantn	E Yorks	SE9530	53°45·7′	0°33·1′W	F	106
Topples Wood	Oxon	SP3716	51°50·7′	1°27·4′W	F	164
Top Pool	Shrops	SJ5207	52°39·8′	2°42·2′W	W	126
Topps, The	Ches	SJ7769	53°17·6′	2°14·0′W	X	118
Topps, The	Falk	NS7584	56°2·2′	3°59·9′W	X	57,64
Top-rhiw-fawr	Powys	SJ1117	52°44·8′	3°18·7′W	X	125
Top Road Fm	Lincs	TF0791	53°24·5′	0°23·0′W	FM	112
Toprow	Norf	TM1698	52°32·4′	1°11·5′E	T	144
Topsham	Devon	SX9688	50°41·2′	3°28·0′W	T	192
Topsham Br	Devon	SX7351	50°20·9′	3°46·7′W	X	202
Topshill Fm	Derby	SK2650	53°3·0′	1°36·3′W	FM	119
Tops Hill Fm	Norf	TG2335	52°52·2′	1°19·2′E	FM	133
Tops of Craigeazle	D & G	NX4983	55°7·4′	4°21·7′W	H	77
Tops of Fichell	Angus	NO3868	56°48·2′	3°0·5′W	H	44
Topstone Fm	N Yks	NZ8307	54°27·3′	0°42·8′W	FM	94
Top Stydd	Derby	SK1640	52°57·7′	1°45·3′W	X	119,128
Top, The	Aberd	NJ4909	57°10·4′	2°50·2′W	X	37
Topthorn	Cumbr	SD5598	54°22·8′	2°41·1′W	X	97
Top Tieb	Corn	SW5230	50°7·3′	5°27·8′W	X	203
Top Tor	Devon	SX7376	50°34·4′	3°47·2′W	H	191
Top Valley	C of Nott	SK5545	53°0·2′	1°10·4′W	T	129
Top Wighay Fm	Notts	SK5251	53°3·5′	1°13·0′W	FM	120
Top Windmill	Rut	SK8105	52°38·4′	0°47·8′W	F	141
Top Wood	Lincs	SK8986	53°22·0′	0°39·3′W	F	112,121
Top Wood	Notts	SK6377	53°17·4′	1°2·9′W	F	120
Top Wood	Powys	SJ1213	52°42·7′	3°17·8′W	F	125
Topwood Fm	Ches	SJ4445	53°0·2′	2°49·7′W	FM	117
Top Yard	Lincs	TF1583	53°20·1′	0°16·0′W	X	121
Top-y-fron	Flint	SJ2769	53°13·0′	3°5·2′W	X	117
Top-y-Glol	Conwy	SH9574	53°15·4′	3°34·0′W	X	116
Top-y-rhos	Flint	SJ2558	53°7·1′	3°6·8′W	X	117
Top-y-rhos Fm	Flint	SJ2858	53°7·1′	3°4·1′W	FM	117
Tor	Corn	SX1080	50°35·6′	4°40·7′W	X	200
Tor	Corn	SX3665	50°27·9′	4°18·3′W	X	201
Tor	Devon	SX4771	50°31·4′	4°9·1′W	X	201
Torachilty	Highld	NH4555	57°33·8′	4°35·0′W	X	26
Tora-cleit	N Eil	NG0586	57°46·3′	6°57·2′W	X	14,18
Tor an Eas	Highld	NN1983	56°54·4′	4°57·9′W	H	34,41
Toranore	Arg & Bt	NR2166	55°48·7′	6°26·8′W	X	60
Torasclett	N Eil	NB1701	57°54·8′	6°46·2′W	H	14
Torasdaidh	N Eil	NB3819	58°5·2′	6°26·2′W	X	14
Torastan	Arg & Bt	NM2261	56°39·8′	6°31·8′W	X	46,47
Toravaig House Hotel	Highld	NG6709	57°7·0′	5°50·5′W	X	32
Torbain	Moray	NJ1613	57°12·3′	3°23·0′W	X	36
Torbain Fm	Fife	NT2493	56°7·7′	3°12·9′W	FM	59
Tor Balk	Corn	SW6813	49°58·6′	5°13·8′W	X	203
Torbank	Scot Bord	NT1840	55°39·1′	3°17·8′W	X	72
Torbank Hill	Scot Bord	NT1740	55°39·0′	3°18·7′W	H	72
Torbant	Pemb	SM8430	51°55·8′	5°8·1′W	X	157
Torbay	D & G	NX8554	54°52·3′	3°47·1′W	X	84
Torbay	Moray	NJ3344	57°29·1′	3°6·6′W	X	28
Torbay	Torbay	SX8961	50°26·5′	3°33·4′W	T	202
Tor Bay	Torbay	SX9260	50°26·0′	3°30·9′W	W	202
Torbeckhill	D & G	NY2379	55°6·2′	3°12·0′W	X	85
Torbeckhill Reservoir	D & G	NY2379	55°6·2′	3°12·0′W	W	85
Torbeg	Aberd	NJ3200	57°5·4′	3°6·9′W	X	37
Torbeg	N Ayr	NR9029	55°30·8′	5°19·1′W	T	68,69
Torberry Hill	W Susx	SU7720	50°58·7′	0°53·8′W	H	197
Torberry Hill (Fort)	W Susx	SU7720	50°58·7′	0°53·8′W	A	197
Torbhain Mór	Arg & Bt	NM7928	56°23·8′	5°34·4′W	H	49
Torbhlaren	Arg & Bt	NR8694	56°5·7′	5°26·0′W	X	55
Torboll Fm	Highld	NH7599	57°58·0′	4°6·3′W	FM	21
Torbothie	N Lanak	NS8959	55°48·9′	3°45·8′W	T	65,72
Tor Bracken	Renf	NS4060	55°48·7′	4°32·8′W	X	64
Torbraehead	D & G	NX7896	55°14·8′	3°54·7′W	H	78
Torbreck	Highld	NC7003	58°0·1′	4°11·5′W	X	16
Torbreck	Highld	NH6440	57°26·1′	4°15·5′W	X	26

Torbreck	Highld	NH8302	57°5·9′	3°55·4′W	X	35
Torbreck Burn	Highld	NC7006	58°1·7′	4°11·6′W	W	16
Torbreck Ho	Highld	NC0824	58°10·1′	5°15·4′W	X	15
Torbrex	N Lanak	NS7971	55°55·3′	3°55·7′W	X	64
Torbrex	Stir	NS7892	56°6·6′	3°57·3′W	T	57
Torbryan	Devon	SX8266	50°29·2′	3°39·4′W	T	202
Tor Burn	Falk	NS8485	56°2·9′	3°51·3′W	W	65
Torbush	N Lanak	NS8355	55°46·7′	3°51·5′W	T	65,72
Torcastle	Highld	NN1378	56°51·6′	5°3·6′W	X	41
Torc-choire	Highld	NM8499	57°2·2′	5°33·1′W	X	33,40
Torchastle	Moray	NJ1352	57°33·2′	3°26·8′W	X	28
Torchoillean	Arg & Bt	NR6619	55°24·8′	5°41·4′W	X	68
Torchuaig Hill	Pth & Kin	NO0039	56°32·2′	3°37·1′W	H	52,53
Tor Clunes	Highld	NH5442	57°27·0′	4°25·5′W	X	26
Torcoed	Carm	SN4914	51°48·5′	4°11·0′W	X	159
Torcoed Fawr	Carm	SN4814	51°48·5′	4°11·9′W	X	159
Torcraik	Midlo	NT3659	55°49·5′	3°0·9′W	X	66,73
Torcross	Devon	SX8242	50°16·2′	3°39·0′W	T	202
Torcross	S Ayr	NS4127	55°30·9′	4°30·7′W	X	70
Torcroy	Highld	NN7799	57°4·2′	4°1·3′W	X	35
Torcuileainn	Highld	NG8100	57°2·6′	5°36·2′W	X	33
Tordarroch	Highld	NH6733	57°22·3′	4°12·2′W	X	26
Tordean	Devon	SX7262	50°26·9′	3°47·8′W	X	202
Tor Dhamh	Arg & Bt	NM9025	56°22·5′	5°23·6′W	H	49
Tordown	Devon	SS6331	51°4·0′	3°56·9′W	X	180
Tor Down	Devon	SX6194	50°44·0′	3°57·8′W	X	191
Tor Down Fm	Devon	SS6103	50°48·8′	3°58·0′W	FM	191
Tor-Du'	Highld	NC8530	58°14·9′	3°57·1′W	X	17
Torduff Point	D & G	NY2663	54°57·6′	3°8·9′W	X	85
Torduff Resr	C of Edin	NT2067	55°53·6′	3°16·3′W	W	66
Tore	Highld	NH6052	57°32·5′	4°19·9′W	T	26
Torebane	Highld	NM9679	56°51·7′	5°20·3′W	X	40
Tore Burn	Aberd	NJ8363	57°39·7′	2°16·6′W	W	29,30
Tore Croft	Highld	NH5958	57°35·7′	4°21·1′W	X	26
Toreduff	Moray	NJ1260	57°37·5′	3°27·9′W	X	28
Tore Hill	Highld	NH9817	57°14·2′	3°40·9′W	H	36
Torehill Cottage	Highld	NH9916	57°13·7′	3°39·9′W	X	36
Tor Elick	Moray	NJ3131	57°22·1′	3°8·4′W	H	37
Tore Lodge	Aberd	NJ8163	57°39·6′	2°18·6′W	X	29,30
Toremore	Highld	ND1730	58°15·3′	3°24·4′W	X	11
Tor End	Lancs	SD7720	53°40·8′	2°20·5′W	X	103
Tore of Troup	Aberd	NJ8362	57°39·1′	2°16·6′W	X	29,30
Torepark	Highld	NH6053	57°33·0′	4°19·9′W	X	26
Tores, The	S Ayr	NX3889	55°10·4′	4°32·2′W	X	77
Tore, The	Moray	NJ3524	57°18·4′	3°4·3′W	X	37
Torfichen Hill	Midlo	NT3353	55°46·2′	3°3·6′W	H	66,73
Tor Fm	Devon	SX7769	50°30·7′	3°43·7′W	FM	202
Tor Fm	Sheff	SK2491	53°25·2′	1°37·9′W	FM	110
Torfoot Fm	S Lanak	NS6438	55°37·3′	4°9·1′W	FM	71
Torfrey	Corn	SX1154	50°21·6′	4°39·1′W	T	200
Torgalter	Aberd	NO2895	57°2·7′	3°10·7′W	X	37,44
Torgarrow	Highld	NH9140	57°26·5′	3°48·5′W	X	27
Torgate	Ches	SJ9872	53°14·9′	2°1·4′W	X	118
Torgate Fm	Lincs	SK9259	53°7·4′	0°37·1′W	FM	121
Torgelli	Rho Cyn Taf	ST0081	51°31·4′	3°26·1′W	X	170
Tor Glas	Powys	SO0319	51°51·9′	3°24·1′W	X	160
Torglass Hill	D & G	NX6655	54°52·6′	4°4·9′W	X	83,84
Torglass Hill	D & G	NX7858	54°54·4′	3°53·7′W	H	84
Torgorm	Highld	NH5554	57°33·4′	4°24·9′W	X	26
Torgormack	Highld	NH4844	57°27·9′	4°31·6′W	X	26
Tor-gro	Swan	SS4593	51°37·1′	4°13·9′W	X	159
Torgulbin	Highld	NN4382	56°54·4′	4°34·2′W	T	34,42
Torgur	Shetld	HU3938	60°7·7′	1°17·4′W	X	4
Torgyle Bridge	Highld	NH3012	57°10·3′	4°48·3′W	X	34
Torheads	S Lanak	NS6953	55°45·4′	4°4·8′W	X	64
Tor Hill	Aberd	NO6171	56°50·0′	2°37·9′W	X	45
Torhill	Devon	SX6890	50°41·9′	3°51·8′W	X	191
Tor Hill	Glos	ST7692	51°37·8′	2°20·4′W	X	162,172
Tor Hill	Lancs	SD7720	53°40·8′	2°20·5′W	H	103
Torhill	Pth & Kin	NO0715	56°19·4′	3°29·8′W	X	58
Tor Hill	Scot Bord	NT2738	55°38·1′	3°9·1′W	H	73
Tor Hill	Wilts	ST9077	51°29·7′	2°8·4′W	X	173
Torhill Fm	Devon	SX7381	50°37·1′	3°47·3′W	FM	191
Tor Ho	Corn	SX1570	50°30·3′	4°36·2′W	X	201
Tor Hole	Somer	ST5752	51°16·2′	2°36·6′W	X	182,183
Torhousekie Fm	D & G	NX3756	54°52·6′	4°32·0′W	FM	83
Torhouse Mill	D & G	NX3955	54°52·1′	4°30·1′W	X	83
Torhousemuir	D & G	NX3957	54°53·2′	4°30·2′W	X	83
Torhousemuir House	D & G	NX3956	54°52·6′	4°30·1′W	X	83
Torinturk	Arg & Bt	NR8165	55°50·0′	5°29·4′W	T	62
Torinturk Fm	Arg & Bt	NM9028	56°24·1′	5°23·7′W	FM	49
Torispardon	Highld	NH9623	57°17·4′	3°43·1′W	X	36
Torkatrine	D & G	NX8364	54°57·7′	3°49·2′W	X	84
Torkington	Stock	SJ9386	53°22·5′	2°5·9′W	T	109
Torkington Lodge	Northnts	SP6471	52°20·2′	1°3·2′W	X	140
Torkirra	D & G	NX8664	54°57·7′	3°46·4′W	X	84
Torksey	Lincs	SK8378	53°17·8′	0°44·9′W	T	121
Torksey Lock	Lincs	SK8378	53°17·8′	0°44·9′W	X	121
Torlands	Corn	SX1187	50°39·4′	4°40·1′W	X	190,200
Torleehouse	Northum	NT9128	55°33·0′	2°8·1′W	X	74,75
Torllwyn	I of Angl	SH4094	53°25·4′	4°24·1′W	X	114
Torlochan	Arg & Bt	NM5540	56°29·6′	5°58·4′W	X	47,48
Torloisk	Fife	NO3405	56°14·2′	3°3·4′W	X	59
Torloisk Ho	Arg & Bt	NM4145	56°31·8′	6°12·3′W	X	47,48
Torlum	N Eil	NF7850	57°25·8′	7°21·5′W	T	22
Torlum	Pth & Kin	NN8119	56°21·2′	3°55·1′W	H	57
Torlum Wood	Pth & Kin	NN8218	56°20·6′	3°54·1′W	F	57
Torlundy	Highld	NN1476	56°50·6′	5°2·5′W	T	41
Tormarton	S Glos	ST7678	51°30·3′	2°20·4′W	T	172
Tormaukin	Pth & Kin	NN9904	56°13·3′	3°37·3′W	H	58
Tor Mere Top	N Yks	SD9776	54°11·0′	2°2·3′W	X	98
Tormisdale	Arg & Bt	NR1958	55°44·3′	6°28·2′W	X	60
Tormiston	Orkney	HY2626	59°7·1′	3°17·1′W	X	6
Tormiston Mill	Orkney	HY3112	58°59·6′	3°11·6′W	X	6
Tormitchell	S Ayr	NX2394	55°12·8′	4°46·5′W	X	76
Tormollan Hill	D & G	NX6466	54°58·5′	4°7·1′W	H	83
Tormore	Highld	NG6101	57°2·6′	5°55·9′W	T	32
Tormore	Highld	NJ1535	57°24·1′	3°24·4′W	X	28
Tormore	N Ayr	NR8932	55°32·4′	5°20·2′W	T	68,69
Tormsdale	Highld	ND1350	58°26·0′	3°28·9′W	X	11,12

Tormuick	Highld	NH5052	57°32·3'	4°29·9'W	X	26
Tormusk	N Ayr	NR9429	55°30·9'	5°15·3'W	H	68,69
Tormwnt	Powys	SO0314	51°49·2'	3°24·1'W	X	160
Tornagawn	Aberd	NJ3414	57°13·0'	3°5·1'W	X	37
Tornagrain	Highld	NH7649	57°31·1'	4°3·8'W	T	27
Tornagrain Wood	Highld	NH7650	57°31·7'	4°3·8'W	F	27
Tornahaish	Aberd	NJ2908	57°9·7'	3°10·0'W	X	37
Tornahatnach	Aberd	NJ4215	57°13·6'	2°57·2'W	X	37
Tornameal	Highld	ND0757	58°29·7'	3°35·3'W	X	11,12
Tornamean	Aberd	NJ6803	57°7·3'	2°31·3'W	X	38
Tornapress	Highld	NG8342	57°25·3'	5°36·4'W	X	24
Tornauran	Aberd	NO2894	57°2·1'	3°10·7'W	X	37,44
Tornaveen	Aberd	NJ6106	57°8·9'	2°38·2'W	T	37
Tornaveen Ho	Aberd	NJ6105	57°8·3'	2°38·2'W	X	37
Torne Br	Donc	SE6703	53°31·4'	0°59·0'W	X	111
Torness	Arg & Bt	NM6432	56°25·5'	5°49·2'W	X	49
Torness	Highld	NH5827	57°19·0'	4°21·0'W	T	26,35
Torness	Highld	NN1883	56°54·4'	4°58·9'W	X	34,41
Tor Ness	Orkney	HY4219	59°3·5'	3°0·2'W	X	6
Tor Ness	Orkney	HY6520	59°4·2'	2°36·1'W	X	5
Tor Ness	Orkney	HY6742	59°16·1'	2°34·2'W	X	5
Tor Ness	Orkney	HY7555	59°23·1'	2°25·9'W	X	5
Tor Ness	Orkney	ND2588	58°46·7'	3°17·3'W	X	7
Torness Point	E Loth	NT7575	55°58·3'	2°23·6'W	X	67
Tornewton	Devon	SX8167	50°29·7'	3°40·3'W	X	202
Torney Court Fm	S Glos	ST7370	51°25·9'	2°22·9'W	FM	172
Torney's Fell	Northum	NY8770	55°1·7'	2°11·8'W	X	87
Torniechelt	Moray	NJ3728	57°20·5'	3°2·3'W	X	37
Tor Noon	Corn	SW4034	50°9·2'	5°38·0'W	X	203
Torns	Shetld	HU5989	60°35·1'	0°54·9'W	X	1,2
Tor of Craigoch	D & G	NX0064	54°56·1'	5°6·9'W	X	82
Tor of Suie	Moray	NJ2826	57°19·4'	3°11·3'W	X	37
Torogay	N Eil	NF7774	57°38·7'	7°24·4'W	X	18
Torogay	N Eil	NF9178	57°41·4'	7°10·7'W	X	18
Toroghas	N Eil	NF7670	57°36·5'	7°25·1'W	X	18
Toronto	Durham	NZ1930	54°40·1'	1°41·9'W	T	92
Torosay Castle	Arg & Bt	NM7235	56°27·4'	5°41·6'W	X	49
Torpantau	Powys	SO0417	51°50·8'	3°23·2'W	X	160
Tor Park	Corn	SX2386	50°39·0'	4°29·9'W	X	201
Torpel Way	Peterb	TF1204	52°37·6'	0°20·3'W	X	142
Torpenhow	Cumbr	NY2039	54°44·6'	3°14·1'W	T	89,90
Torphichen	W Loth	NS9672	55°56·0'	3°39·4'W	T	65
Torphin	C of Edin	NT2067	55°53·6'	3°16·3'W	T	66
Torphins	Aberd	NJ6201	57°6·2'	2°37·2'W	T	37
Tor Pike	N Yks	SD9875	54°10·5'	2°1·4'W	A	98
Torpoint	Corn	SX4355	50°22·7'	4°12·1'W	T	201
Tor Point	Highld	NH5935	57°23·3'	4°20·3'W	X	26
Torquay	Torbay	SX9165	50°28·7'	3°31·8'W	T	202
Torquhan	Scot Bord	NT4447	55°43·0'	2°53·0'W	T	73
Torquhandallochy	Aberd	NO5896	57°3·4'	2°41·1'W	X	37,44
Torr	Arg & Bt	NM4452	56°35·7'	6°9·8'W	X	47
Torr	Arg & Bt	NS2784	56°1·3'	4°46·1'W	X	56
Torr	Devon	SX5851	50°20·7'	3°59·4'W	T	202
Torr	Devon	SX6160	50°25·6'	3°57·0'W	T	202
Torr	D & G	NX7952	54°51·1'	3°52·7'W	X	84
Torr	S Ayr	NS3813	55°23·3'	4°33·0'W	X	70
Torra	Arg & Bt	NR3454	55°42·6'	6°13·7'W	X	60
Tòrr a' Bhacain	Arg & Bt	NM3821	56°18·8'	6°13·8'W	X	48
Torr a' Bhalbhain	Highld	NM7999	57°2·0'	5°38·1'W	X	33,40
Torr a' Bhealaidh	Highld	NH3756	57°34·1'	4°43·1'W	H	26
Torr a' Bheannain	N Ayr	NR9922	55°27·3'	5°10·3'W	H	69
Torr a' Bhlàir	Arg & Bt	NM5137	56°27·8'	6°2·1'W	X	47,48
Torr a' Bhreitheimh	Highld	NM7370	56°46·2'	5°42·4'W	X	40
Torr Achilty	Highld	NH4455	57°33·8'	4°36·0'W	H	26
Torrachilty Wood	Highld	NH4355	57°33·7'	4°37·0'W	F	26
Torr a Choilich	Highld	NM6058	56°39·4'	5°54·5'W	X	49
Torr a' Choiltreich	Highld	NH3607	57°7·7'	4°42·1'W	H	34
Torr a' Choit	Highld	NG9307	57°6·7'	5°24·7'W	X	33
Torr a' Chonnaidh	Highld	NM7693	56°58·7'	5°40·7'W	X	33,40
Torr a Chreamha	Arg & Bt	NR3141	55°35·6'	6°15·7'W	H	60
Torr a' Chruidh	Highld	NG3656	57°31·3'	6°24·1'W	H	23
Torr a' Chuilinn	Highld	NM6168	56°44·8'	5°54·1'W	X	40
Torra Duncan	Aberd	NJ5439	57°26·6'	2°45·5'W	X	29
Torr a' Ghoai	Arg & Bt	NM5728	56°23·2'	5°55·8'W	X	48
Torr a' Ghobhainn	Arg & Bt	NR7736	55°34·3'	5°31·8'W	X	68,69
Torr a' Ghuilbinn	Highld	NN4381	56°53·9'	4°34·2'W	H	34,42
Torrain Dubha	Arg & Bt	NR3969	55°50·9'	6°9·8'W	X	60,61
Torr a' Mhuilt	Highld	NN1788	56°57·1'	5°0·1'W	X	34,41
Torran	Aberd	NJ3001	57°5·9'	3°8·9'W	X	37
Torran	Arg & Bt	NM8704	56°11·1'	5°25·5'W	X	55
Torran	Arg & Bt	NR2065	55°48·1'	6°27·7'W	X	60
Torran	Highld	ND0554	58°28·1'	3°37·2'W	X	11,12
Torran	Highld	NG5949	57°28·3'	6°0·7'W	T	24
Torran	Highld	NH7175	57°45·0'	4°9·6'W	X	21
Torran	Highld	NM7367	56°44·6'	5°42·3'W	X	40
Torran a' Bhuachaille	Highld	NG8617	57°11·9'	5°32·1'W	X	33
Torr an Aird	Arg & Bt	NM4243	56°30·8'	6°11·2'W	X	47,48
Torr-an-Arbhain	Arg & Bt	NM5440	56°29·5'	5°59·3'W	X	47,48
Torrance	E Dunb	NS6274	55°56·6'	4°12·1'W	T	64
Torrance	N Lanak	NS8365	55°52·1'	3°51·7'W	X	65
Torrance	Stir	NN7502	56°11·9'	4°0·4'W	X	57
Torran Ceann Liath	Highld	NH1546	57°28·3'	5°4·6'W	X	25
Torran Ceann Liath	Highld	NH2247	57°29·0'	4°57·7'W	X	25
Torrance Fm	N Lanak	NS9066	55°52·7'	3°45·1'W	FM	65
Torrance Ho	S Lanak	NS6552	55°44·8'	4°8·6'W	X	64
Torran Clachach	N Ayr	NS0323	55°27·9'	5°6·5'W	X	69
Torrancroy	Aberd	NJ3315	57°13·5'	3°6·1'W	X	37
Torran-cuilinn	Highld	NH0255	57°32·8'	5°18·1'W	X	25
Torr an da Choille	Arg & Bt	NM3954	56°36·6'	6°14·8'W	X	47
Torr an Daimh	Arg & Bt	NM4342	56°30·3'	6°10·1'W	X	47,48
Torr an Daimh	Arg & Bt	NM4454	56°36·7'	6°9·9'W	X	47
Torr an Daimh	Highld	NN3581	56°53·7'	4°42·1'W	X	34,41
Torr an Daimh	N Ayr	NR9125	55°28·7'	5°18·0'W	X	68,69
Torr an Daraich	Highld	NN0376	56°50·3'	5°13·3'W	X	41
Torrandhu	Aberd	NJ3211	57°11·3'	3°7·1'W	X	37
Torran Dubha	Arg & Bt	NR3453	55°42·1'	6°13·6'W	X	60
Torr an Eas	Highld	NH2814	57°11·3'	4°50·3'W	H	34
Torraneidhinn	Highld	NM6256	56°38·4'	5°52·4'W	X	49
Torr an Eilein	Highld	NC1924	58°10·3'	5°4·2'W	X	15
Torranerrick	Highld	NH5239	57°25·3'	4°27·4'W	X	26

Torr an Fhamhair	Highld	NM9358	56°40·3'	5°22·3'W	H	49
Torrangorm	Highld	NH5238	57°24·8'	4°27·4'W	X	26
Torran Iamhair	Highld	NM6567	56°44·4'	5°50·1'W	X	40
Tòrr an Lochain	Arg & Bt	NR5885	56°0·1'	5°52·4'W	W	61
Torran nam Crann	Highld	NM9673	56°48·5'	5°20·0'W	H	40
Torran nam Meirleach	Highld	NM6889	56°56·3'	5°48·4'W	X	40
Torran nam Mial	Highld	NM7868	56°45·3'	5°37·4'W	H	40
Torran na Mòintich	Highld	NM9256	56°39·2'	5°23·1'W	X	49
Torran nan Coisichean	Highld	NH1342	57°26·1'	5°6·5'W	X	25
Torr an Ogha	Arg & Bt	NM4044	56°31·2'	6°13·2'W	X	47,48
Torranreach	Highld	ND2836	58°18·7'	3°13·3'W	X	11
Torran Rocks	Arg & Bt	NM2813	56°14·2'	6°22·9'W	X	48
Torran Ruadh	Highld	NH1867	57°39·6'	5°2·6'W	H	20
Torrans	Arg & Bt	NM4825	56°21·3'	6°4·3'W	X	48
Torrans	Moray	NJ1419	57°15·5'	3°25·1'W	X	36
Torran Sgoilte	Arg & Bt	NM2712	56°13·6'	6°23·8'W	X	48
Torr an Sgrithinn	Arg & Bt	NM6224	56°21·2'	5°50·7'W	X	49
Torranshondall	Highld	ND1256	58°29·3'	3°30·1'W	X	11,12
Torr an t-Sagairt	Highld	NM6785	56°54·1'	5°49·1'W	H	40
Torr an t-Saothaid	Arg & Bt	NM2713	56°14·1'	6°23·9'W	X	48
Torr-an-tuirc	Arg & Bt	NM9027	56°23·6'	5°23·7'W	X	49
Tòrr-an-tuirc	Arg & Bt	NR3895	56°4·8'	6°12·2'W	X	61
Torr an Tuirc	Highld	NG7912	57°9·0'	5°38·8'W	X	33
Torran Tuirc	Highld	NM8198	57°1·5'	5°36·1'W	X	33,40
Torran Tùrach	Arg & Bt	NS0070	55°53·2'	5°11·4'W	H	63
Torran Water	Highld	ND0553	58°27·6'	3°37·2'W	W	11,12
Torranyard	N Ayr	NS3544	55°39·9'	4°37·0'W	T	63,70
Torra River	Arg & Bt	NR3554	55°42·7'	6°12·7'W	W	60
Torr á Sonn	Highld	NN3991	56°59·2'	4°38·5'W	H	34
Torrax	Angus	NO2755	56°41·1'	3°11·1'W	X	53
Tòrr Beag	Highld	NG5333	57°19·5'	6°5·7'W	X	24,32
Torr Beag	Highld	NG8816	57°11·4'	5°30·1'W	H	33
Torr Beag	N Ayr	NR9525	55°28·8'	5°14·2'W	X	68,69
Torr Beithe	Highld	NM6269	56°45·4'	5°53·2'W	H	40
Torr Bhruaich	N Ayr	NR9425	55°28·8'	5°15·2'W	X	68,69
Torrbrach	Highld	NC9626	58°12·9'	3°45·7'W	X	17
Torr Breac	Highld	NH4063	57°38·0'	4°40·3'W	X	20
Torr Breac	N Ayr	NR9551	55°42·8'	5°15·4'W	X	62,69
Torr Breac	N Ayr	NR9837	55°35·3'	5°11·9'W	X	69
Torr Brook	Devon	SX7449	50°19·9'	3°45·8'W	W	202
Torr Carbh	Highld	NH7003	57°6·2'	4°8·3'W	X	35
Torr Clawdd	Swan	SN6606	51°44·4'	3°56·1'W	X	159
Torr Cruinn	Highld	NM8495	57°0·0'	5°32·9'W	X	33,40
Torr Daraich	Arg & Bt	NM7125	56°22·0'	5°42·0'W	X	49
Torr Dearg	Highld	NH9914	57°12·6'	3°39·9'W	H	36
Torr Dhùin	Highld	NH3406	57°7·2'	4°44·1'W	H	34
Torr Down	Devon	SX6248	50°19·2'	3°55·9'W	X	202
Torr Dubh	Arg & Bt	NR3947	55°39·0'	6°8·5'W	X	60
Torr Dubh	Arg & Bt	NR6207	55°18·2'	5°44·6'W	X	68
Torr Dubh	Pth & Kin	NN7463	56°44·8'	4°3·2'W	X	42
Torr Dubh Mór	Highld	ND0153	58°27·5'	3°41·3'W	H	11,12
Torr Dubh Mór	N Ayr	NR9823	55°27·8'	5°11·3'W	H	69
Torre	Somer	ST0440	51°9·3'	3°22·0'W	T	181
Torre	Torbay	SX9064	50°28·2'	3°32·6'W	T	202
Torre Abbey	Torbay	SX9063	50°27·6'	3°32·6'W	A	202
Torre Fm	Somer	SS8937	51°7·5'	3°34·8'W	FM	181
Torrell's Hall Fm	Essex	TL6008	51°45·1'	0°19·5'E	FM	167
Torrent Walk	Gwyn	SH7518	52°45·0'	3°50·7'W	X	124
Torr Fada	Arg & Bt	NM3219	56°17·5'	6°19·4'W	H	48
Torr Fhionn	Highld	NG8130	57°18·7'	5°37·7'W	X	24
Torr Fm	Corn	SX2761	50°25·6'	4°25·8'W	FM	201
Torr Fm	Devon	SX8048	50°19·4'	3°40·8'W	FM	202
Torr Forret	Fife	NO3719	56°21·8'	3°0·7'W	X	59
Torr Garbh	Highld	NH0688	57°50·6'	5°15·6'W	X	19
Tòrr Gauscavaig	Highld	NG5910	57°7·3'	5°58·4'W	H	32
Torr Hall	Renf	NS3666	55°51·8'	4°36·8'W	X	63
Torr Hill	D & G	NX8152	54°51·2'	3°50·8'W	H	84
Torr Ho	D & G	NX8052	54°51·2'	3°51·7'W	X	84
Torrich	Highld	NH8751	57°32·4'	3°52·8'W	X	27
Torridge Br	Devon	SS4627	51°1·5'	4°11·4'W	X	180
Torridon	Highld	NG8956	57°33·0'	5°31·1'W	T	24
Torridon	Highld	NG9055	57°32·4'	5°30·1'W	T	25
Torridon Forest	Highld	NG8958	57°34·0'	5°31·2'W	F	24
Torridon Forest	Highld	NG9058	57°34·1'	5°30·2'W	X	25
Torridon Ho	Highld	NG8657	57°33·4'	5°34·2'W	X	24
Torrie Cott	Stir	NN6405	56°13·3'	4°11·2'W	X	57
Torriegorrie	Highld	NH3763	57°37·9'	4°43·3'W	X	20
Torrie Ho	Fife	NT0186	56°3·7'	3°35·0'W	X	65
Torries	Aberd	NJ6113	57°12·6'	2°38·3'W	T	37
Torries	Aberd	NJ6825	57°19·1'	2°31·4'W	X	38
Torrieston	Moray	NJ1658	57°36·5'	3°23·9'W	T	28
Torrin	Highld	NG5720	57°12·6'	6°1·0'W	T	32
Torrinch	W Dunb	NS4089	56°4·3'	4°33·8'W	X	56
Torrisdale	Arg & Bt	NR7736	55°34·3'	5°31·8'W	X	68,69
Torrisdale	Highld	NC6761	58°31·3'	4°16·5'W	T	10
Torrisdale Bay	Arg & Bt	NR7935	55°33·8'	5°29·9'W	W	68,69
Torrisdale Bay	Highld	NC6862	58°31·8'	4°15·5'W	W	10
Torrisdale Castle	Arg & Bt	NR7936	55°34·3'	5°29·9'W	X	68,69
Torrisdale Square	Arg & Bt	NR7936	55°34·3'	5°29·9'W	X	68,69
Torrisdale Water	Arg & Bt	NR7836	55°34·3'	5°30·9'W	W	68,69
Torrish	Highld	NC9718	58°8·6'	3°44·5'W	X	17
Torrish Burn	Highld	NC9622	58°10·7'	3°45·6'W	W	17
Torrisholme	Lancs	SD4564	54°4·4'	2°50·0'W	T	97
Torr Lane	D & G	NX3979	55°5·0'	4°30·9'W	W	77
Torrlaoighseach	Highld	NG9516	57°11·6'	5°23·1'W	X	33
Torr Leathann	Highld	NH6178	57°46·5'	4°19·8'W	H	21
Torr Liath-bheag	Arg & Bt	NN3446	56°34·9'	4°41·7'W	X	50
Torr Loisgte	Arg & Bt	NM8425	56°22·3'	5°29·4'W	X	49
Torr Meadhonach	N Ayr	NR9551	55°42·8'	5°15·4'W	H	62,69
Torr Mhaoile	N Ayr	NR9626	55°29·4'	5°13·3'W	X	68,69
Torr Mhurchaidh	Highld	NM6791	56°57·4'	5°49·5'W	X	40
Torr Molach	Highld	NM6762	56°41·8'	5°47·9'W	X	40
Torr Molach	Highld	NM7048	56°34·3'	5°44·2'W	X	49
Torr Mór	Arg & Bt	NM3221	56°18·6'	6°19·6'W	H	48
Torr Mór	Arg & Bt	NM3640	56°28·9'	6°16·8'W	H	47,48
Torr Mór	Arg & Bt	NM3736	56°26·8'	6°15·6'W	H	47,48
Torr Mór	Arg & Bt	NM3819	56°17·7'	6°13·6'W	H	48
Torr Mór	Arg & Bt	NM3824	56°20·4'	6°13·9'W	X	48
Torr Mór	Arg & Bt	NM4038	56°28·0'	6°12·8'W	X	47,48
Torr Mór	Arg & Bt	NM4123	56°20·0'	6°11·0'W	X	48

Torr Mór	Arg & Bt	NM8425	56°22·3'	5°29·4'W	X	49
Torr Mór	Arg & Bt	NR5907	55°18·1'	5°47·4'W	H	68
Tòrr Mór	Arg & Bt	NR7487	56°1·6'	5°37·2'W	H	55
Torr Mor	Arg & Bt	NR8039	55°36·0'	5°29·1'W	X	68,69
Torr Mór	Arg & Bt	NS1052	55°43·7'	5°1·1'W	H	63,69
Tòrr Mór	Highld	NG5333	57°19·5'	6°5·7'W	X	24,32
Torr Mór	Highld	NG6216	57°10·6'	5°55·8'W	X	32
Torr Mor	Highld	NG7143	57°25·4'	5°48·4'W	H	24
Torr Mór	Highld	NG7201	57°2·9'	5°45·1'W	H	33
Torr Mór	Highld	NG8132	57°19·8'	5°37·8'W	X	24
Torr Mor	Highld	NG9591	57°52·0'	5°26·9'W	H	19
Torr Mór	Highld	NH4843	57°27·4'	4°31·6'W	H	26
Torr Mór	Highld	NH5339	57°25·3'	4°26·4'W	H	26
Torr Mór	Highld	NH8324	57°17·8'	3°56·0'W	X	35
Torr Mór	Highld	NM6385	56°54·0'	5°53·1'W	H	40
Torr Mór	Highld	NM6670	56°46·0'	5°49·3'W	H	40
Torr Mór	Pth & Kin	NN9640	56°32·7'	3°41·0'W	X	52,53
Torr Mór a' Chonairst	Arg & Bt	NM3118	56°17·0'	6°20·3'W	X	48
Torr Mór Ghaoideil	Highld	NM6784	56°53·6'	5°49·1'W	H	40
Torr na Bà	Highld	NM7092	56°58·0'	5°46·6'W	H	33,40
Torr na Baoileig	N Ayr	NS0324	55°28·5'	5°6·6'W	X	69
Torr na Bithe	Highld	NC4560	58°30·3'	4°39·1'W	H	9
Torr na Carraidh	Highld	NH1901	57°4·1'	4°58·7'W	X	34
Torr na Carraige	Arg & Bt	NR4347	55°39·2'	6°4·7'W	X	60
Torr na Craoibhe	Highld	NC8532	58°16·0'	3°57·1'W	X	17
Torr na Dòilinne	Highld	NM6058	56°39·4'	5°54·5'W	X	49
Torr na Duile	Highld	NM8146	56°33·6'	5°33·4'W	H	49
Torr na h-Innse	Highld	NG7001	57°2·8'	5°47·1'W	H	33
Torr na h-Iolaire	Highld	NG8319	57°12·9'	5°35·2'W	H	33
Torr na h-Iolaire	Highld	NG9244	57°26·6'	5°27·5'W	X	25
Torr na h-Uamha	Arg & Bt	NM5533	56°25·8'	5°58·0'W	X	47,48
Torr nam Braonan	Highld	NH2339	57°24·7'	4°56·3'W	H	25
Torr nam Broc	Highld	NM6257	56°38·9'	5°52·5'W	X	49
Torr nam Fiann	Arg & Bt	NM5341	56°30·0'	6°0·4'W	X	47,48
Torr nam Freumh	N Ayr	NR9537	55°35·3'	5°14·7'W	X	68,69
Torr na Mòine	Highld	NM5562	56°41·4'	5°59·6'W	X	47
Torr na Mòine	Highld	NM6861	56°41·3'	5°46·9'W	H	40
Torr na Muic	Highld	NH2725	57°17·2'	4°51·8'W	X	25
Torr nan Caorach	N Ayr	NR8740	55°36·7'	5°22·5'W	X	62,69
Torr nan Ceann	Highld	NM8460	56°41·2'	5°31·2'W	X	40
Torr nan Clach	Arg & Bt	NM5441	56°30·1'	5°59·4'W	X	47,48
Torr nan Con	Highld	NM5858	56°39·3'	5°56·5'W	X	47
Torr nan Damh	Arg & Bt	NM4453	56°36·2'	6°9·8'W	X	47
Torr nan Damh	Highld	NN5487	56°57·3'	4°23·6'W	X	42
Torr nan Dearc	N Ayr	NR9833	55°33·2'	5°11·7'W	X	69
Torr nan Gabhar	Highld	NC9326	58°12·9'	3°48·8'W	X	17
Torr nan Gabhar	Highld	NG9178	57°44·8'	5°30·3'W	H	19
Torr nan Gamhainn	Highld	NM7694	56°59·2'	5°40·8'W	X	33,40
Torr nan Uain	N Ayr	NR9720	55°26·2'	5°12·1'W	X	69
Torr na Sealga	Arg & Bt	NM3617	56°16·6'	6°15·4'W	X	48
Torr na Sean Airigh	Arg & Bt	NM3720	56°18·2'	6°14·7'W	X	48
Torr na Slinndrich	Highld	NM7366	56°44·1'	5°42·2'W	X	40
Torr Nead an Eoin	N Ayr	NR9549	55°41·7'	5°15·3'W	H	62,69
Torroble	Highld	NC5804	58°0·4'	4°23·7'W	T	16
Tor Rock	Derby	SK0667	53°12·2'	1°54·2'W	X	119
Tor Rock	Devon	SX6349	50°19·7'	3°55·1'W	X	202
Tor Rocks	Devon	SX6459	50°25·1'	3°54·5'W	X	202
Torr of Kedlock	Fife	NO3719	56°21·8'	3°0·7'W	X	59
Torr of Moonzie	Fife	NO3517	56°20·7'	3°2·7'W	X	59
Torrorie	D & G	NX9557	54°54·1'	3°37·8'W	X	84
Torrovaich	Highld	ND0357	58°29·7'	3°39·4'W	X	11,12
Torrovaich	Highld	ND2637	58°19·2'	3°15·3'W	X	11
Torroy	Highld	NH5497	57°56·6'	4°27·5'W	T	21
Torr Royal	Devon	SX5973	50°32·6'	3°59·0'W	X	191
Torr Pàiteag	Highld	NH4715	57°12·3'	4°31·5'W	H	34
Torr Port a' Bhàta	Highld	NM6872	56°47·2'	5°47·5'W	H	40
Torr Quarry	Devon	SX7448	50°19·3'	3°45·8'W	X	202
Torr Reamhar	N Ayr	NR9947	55°40·8'	5°11·4'W	X	62,69
Torr Righ Beag	N Ayr	NR8931	55°31·9'	5°20·2'W	X	68,69
Torr Righ Mór	N Ayr	NR8830	55°31·3'	5°21·1'W	H	68,69
Torrs	D & G	NX5289	55°10·6'	4°19·0'W	H	77
Torrs	D & G	NX6845	54°47·2'	4°2·7'W	X	83,84
Torrs	D & G	NX7761	54°56·0'	3°54·8'W	X	84
Torrs	S Lanak	NS9905	55°20·0'	3°35·1'W	X	78
Torrs Fm	S Glos	ST5684	51°33·4'	2°37·7'W	FM	172
Torrshelly	Highld	NH5723	57°16·8'	4°21·9'W	X	26,35
Torrs Moor	D & G	NX6846	54°47·7'	4°2·8'W	X	83,84
Torr Solais	Highld	NM4963	56°41·7'	6°5·5'W	X	47
TÒRR Sonnachain	Highld	NN1778	56°51·7'	4°59·7'W	X	41
Torrs Park	Devon	SS5047	51°12·4'	4°8·5'W	X	180
Torrs Point	D & G	NX6744	54°46·7'	4°3·6'W	X	83,84
Torrs, The	D & G	NX8854	54°52·3'	3°44·3'W	X	84
Torrs, The	Northum	NU2614	55°25·4'	1°34·9'W	X	81
Torrs Warren	D & G	NX1555	54°51·6'	4°52·5'W	X	82
Torr, The	N Ayr	NR9125	55°28·7'	5°18·0'W	H	68,69
Torr Wood	Arg & Bt	NS1058	55°46·9'	5°1·4'W	F	63
Torry	Aberd	NJ4340	57°27·1'	2°56·5'W	X	28
Torry	C of Aber	NJ9505	57°8·4'	2°4·5'W	T	38
Torry Bay	Fife	NT0185	56°3·1'	3°34·9'W	W	65
Torryburn	Aberd	NJ7815	57°13·8'	2°21·4'W	X	38
Torryburn	Fife	NT0286	56°3·7'	3°34·0'W	T	65
Torrycrien	Aberd	NJ4311	57°11·4'	2°56·1'W	X	37
Torry Hill	Kent	TQ9057	51°17·0'	0°43·9'E	X	178
Torrylinn	N Ayr	NR9521	55°26·7'	5°14·0'W	T	68,69
Torrylinnwater Foot	N Ayr	NR9520	55°26·1'	5°14·0'W	X	68,69
Torsa	Arg & Bt	NM7613	56°15·7'	5°36·6'W	X	55
Torsa Beag	Arg & Bt	NM7512	56°15·1'	5°37·5'W	X	55
Torscaram	N Eil	NB2104	57°56·5'	6°42·4'W	H	13,14
Torside Castle	Derby	SK0796	53°27·9'	1°53·3'W	X	110
Torside Clough	Derby	SK0797	53°28·4'	1°53·3'W	X	110
Torside Naze	Derby	SK0797	53°28·4'	1°53·3'W	X	110
Torside Reservoir	Derby	SK0698	53°29·0'	1°54·2'W	W	110
Torsker	Orkney	HY7344	59°17·2'	2°27·9'W	X	5
Torsonce	Scot Bord	NT4543	55°40·9'	2°52·0'W	T	73
Torsonce Hill	Scot Bord	NT4642	55°40·4'	2°51·1'W	H	73
Torsonce Mains	Scot Bord	NT4543	55°40·9'	2°52·0'W	T	73
Torston	Aberd	NJ6056	57°35·8'	2°39·7'W	X	29
Torterston	Aberd	NK0747	57°31·0'	1°52·5'W	T	30
Torthorwald	D & G	NY0378	55°5·5'	3°30·8'W	T	84
Tortie	Cumbr	NY5662	54°57·3'	2°40·8'W	A	86

Tortie	Cumbr	NY5857	54°54·6′	2°38·9′W	X	86
Torties	Cumbr	NY5769	55°1·1′	2°39·9′W	X	86
Tortington	W Susx	TQ0005	50°50·4′	0°34·4′W	T	197
Tortington Common	W Susx	SU9906	50°50·9′	0°35·2′W	F	197
Tortoiseshell Rocks	Devon	SY1186	50°40·2′	3°15·2′W	X	192
Tortoiseshell Wood	Lincs	SK9619	52°45·8′	0°34·2′W	X	130
Tortolocate	Cumbr	NY0409	54°28·3′	3°28·5′W	X	89
Torton	Worcs	SO8472	52°21·0′	2°13·7′W	T	138
Tortown	Devon	SX5175	50°33·6′	4°5·8′W	X	191,201
Tortworth	S Glos	ST7093	51°38·3′	2°25·6′W	T	162,172
Torvaig	Highld	NG4944	57°25·3′	6°10·4′W	T	23
Torvald's Geo	Shetld	HU4739	60°8·2′	1°8·7′W	X	4
Torvean	Highld	NH6443	57°27·7′	4°15·6′W	X	26
Torver	Cumbr	SD2894	54°20·4′	3°6·0′W	T	96,97
Torver Back Common	Cumbr	SD2993	54°19·9′	3°5·1′W	X	96,97
Torver Common Wood	Cumbr	SD2994	54°20·4′	3°5·1′W	F	96,97
Torver High Common	Cumbr	SD2695	54°21·0′	3°7·9′W	H	96,97
Torver Low Common	Cumbr	SD2792	54°19·3′	3°6·9′W	X	96,97
Torwatletie	D & G	NX6579	55°5·5′	4°6·5′W	X	77,84
Torweaving Hill	W Loth	NT0757	55°48·1′	3°28·6′W	X	65,72
Torweston Fm	Somer	ST0940	51°9·4′	3°17·7′W	FM	181
Torwilkie	D & G	NX6579	55°5·5′	4°6·5′W	X	77,84
Torwinny	Moray	NJ1348	57°31·1′	3°26·7′W	X	28
Tor Wood	Devon	SX5389	50°41·2′	4°4·5′W	F	191
Torwood	D & G	NY1283	55°8·3′	3°22·4′W	X	78
Tor Wood	Falk	NS8384	56°2·3′	3°52·2′W	F	57,65
Torwood	Falk	NS8484	56°2·3′	3°51·3′W	T	65
Torwood Castle	Falk	NS8384	56°2·3′	3°52·2′W	A	57,65
Torwoodlee	Scot Bord	NT4737	55°37·7′	2°50·1′W	A	73
Torwoodlee Mains	Scot Bord	NT4637	55°37·7′	2°51·0′W	T	73
Torwood Lodge	D & G	NY1282	55°7·7′	3°22·4′W	X	78
Torwood Plantn	D & G	NY1282	55°7·7′	3°22·4′W	F	78
Torworth	Notts	SK6586	53°22·2′	1°1·0′W	T	111,120
Tory Brook	Devon	SX5558	50°24·5′	4°2·1′W	W	202
Tor-y-coed	Rho Cyn Taf	ST0682	51°32·0′	3°20·9′W	X	170
Tor y Foel	Powys	SO1119	51°52·0′	3°17·2′W	H	161
Tor-y-fron	Brig	SS8888	51°35·0′	3°36·6′W	X	170
Tosaby	I of M	SC2975	54°8·8′	4°36·7′W	X	95
Tosberry	Devon	SS2621	50°58·0′	4°28·3′W	T	190
Tosberry Moor	Devon	SS2620	50°57·4′	4°28·3′W	X	190
Tosca	Cumbr	SD5881	54°13·6′	2°38·2′W	X	97
Toscaig	Highld	NG7138	57°23·0′	5°48·1′W	T	24
Toseland	Cambs	TL2362	52°14·8′	0°11·5′W	T	153
Tosh	Fife	NO5210	56°17·1′	2°46·1′W	X	59
Tosnos Point	Devon	SX7440	50°15·0′	3°45·7′W	X	202
Tossbeck	Cumbr	SD6285	54°15·8′	2°34·6′W	X	97
Tossell Barton	Devon	SS6634	51°5·6′	3°54·4′W	X	180
Tossels Fm	Wilts	ST9968	51°24·9′	2°0·5′W	FM	173
Tosside	Lancs	SD7656	54°0·2′	2°21·6′W	T	103
Tosside Beck	Lancs	SD7754	53°59·1′	2°20·6′W	W	103
Tosside Fold	N Yks	SD7755	53°59·7′	2°20·6′W	X	103
Tosson Hill	Northum	NZ0098	55°16·8′	1°59·6′W	H	81
Tostary	Arg & Bt	NM3945	56°31·7′	6°14·2′W	T	47,48
Tostock	Suff	TL9563	52°14·1′	0°51·7′E	T	155
Tostock Ho	Suff	TL9563	52°14·1′	0°51·7′E	X	155
Tostock Old Hall	Suff	TL9664	52°14·6′	0°52·7′E	A	155
Tostock Place	Suff	TL9563	52°14·1′	0°51·7′E	X	155
Toston Hill	Leic	SK8037	52°55·7′	0°48·2′W	X	130
Totachocaire	Highld	NG2549	57°27·1′	6°34·6′W	X	23
Totag	Highld	NC0329	58°12·6′	5°20·7′W	X	15
Tota Hunder	N Eil	NF9064	57°33·8′	7°10·6′W	X	18
Totaig	Highld	NG1950	57°27·5′	6°40·7′W	T	23
Totaig	Highld	NG8725	57°16·2′	5°31·5′W	X	33
Totamore	Arg & Bt	NM1756	56°36·9′	6°36·3′W	X	46
Totamore	Arg & Bt	NM1758	56°38·0′	6°36·5′W	X	46
Totardor	Highld	NG3739	57°22·2′	6°22·0′W	T	23,32
Tota Rebein	N Eil	NF8886	57°45·6′	7°14·3′W	X	18
Tota Tarra	Highld	NG2405	57°3·5′	6°32·7′W	X	39
Tota-thaoig	Highld	NG4740	57°23·1′	6°12·1′W	X	23
Tote	Highld	NG4149	57°27·7′	6°18·7′W	T	23
Totegan	Highld	NC8268	58°35·3′	4°1·3′W	T	10
Tote Hill	Hants	SU3024	51°1·1′	1°34·0′W	T	185
Tote Hill	W Susx	SU8624	51°0·8′	0°46·1′W	T	197
Tote Ho	Highld	NG4149	57°27·7′	6°18·7′W	X	23
Totford	Hants	SU5737	51°8·0′	1°10·7′W	T	185
Totford Fm	Hants	SU5738	51°8·5′	1°10·7′W	FM	185
Totham Cartach	N Eil	NB1001	57°54·5′	6°53·3′W	X	14
Totham Hill	Essex	TL8712	51°46·7′	0°43·0′E	T	168
Totham Lodge	Essex	TL8510	51°45·7′	0°41·2′E	X	168
Totham Plains	Essex	TL8812	51°46·7′	0°43·9′E	T	168
Tothan Cartach	N Eil	NB1000	57°54·0′	6°53·2′W	X	14
Tothby Manor	Lincs	TF4476	53°15·9′	0°10·0′E	X	122
Totherick, The	E Ayr	NS4451	55°43·9′	4°28·6′W	X	64
Totherin Hill	S Lanak	NS9535	55°36·1′	3°39·6′W	H	72
Tot Hill	Hants	SU4662	51°21·5′	1°20·0′W	T	174
Tothill	Lincs	TF4181	53°18·7′	0°7·4′E	T	122
Tot Hill	Suff	TM0360	52°12·3′	0°58·7′E	X	155
Tothill Fm	Heref	SO2852	52°9·9′	3°2·8′W	FM	148
Tothill Wood	Lincs	TF4181	53°18·7′	0°7·4′E	F	122
Totland	I of W	SZ3286	50°40·6′	1°32·4′W	T	196
Totland Bay	I of W	SZ3186	50°40·6′	1°33·3′W	W	196
Totleigh Barton	Devon	SS5006	50°50·3′	4°7·4′W	X	191
Totley	Sheff	SK3079	53°18·7′	1°32·6′W	T	119
Totley Bents	Sheff	SK3080	53°19·2′	1°32·6′W	X	110,111
Totley Brook	Sheff	SK3180	53°19·2′	1°31·7′W	T	110,111
Totley Moor	Derby	SK2779	53°18·7′	1°35·3′W	X	119
Totley Moss	Derby	SK2779	53°18·7′	1°35·3′W	X	119
Totley Rise	Sheff	SK3280	53°19·2′	1°30·8′W	T	110,111
Totleys Fm	E Yorks	TA2327	53°43·7′	0°7·7′W	FM	107
Totley Tunnel	Derby	SK2779	53°18·7′	1°35·3′W	X	119
Totleywells	W Loth	NT0976	55°58·4′	3°27·0′W	X	65
Totmonslow	Staffs	SJ9939	52°57·1′	2°0·5′W	T	127
Totnell	Dorset	ST6208	50°52·4′	2°32·0′W	T	194
Totnes	Devon	SX8060	50°25·9′	3°41·0′W	T	202
Totnes Cross	Devon	SX7852	50°21·6′	3°42·5′W	X	202
Totney Fm	Somer	ST3947	51°13·4′	2°52·0′W	FM	182
Totnor	Heref	SO5931	51°58·8′	2°35·4′W	T	149
Toton	Notts	SK5034	52°54·3′	1°15·0′W	T	129
Totridge	Lancs	SD6349	53°56·4′	2°33·4′W	H	102,103
Totronald	Arg & Bt	NM1656	56°36·8′	6°37·3′W	X	46

Totscore	Highld	NG3866	57°36·7′	6°22·8′W	T	23
Tottenham	Hargy	TQ3390	51°35·8′	0°4·4′W	T	176,177
Tottenham Hale	Hargy	TQ3489	51°35·3′	0°3·5′W	T	176,177
Tottenham House	Wilts	SU2463	51°22·2′	1°38·9′W	A	174
Tottenham Park	Wilts	SU2464	51°22·7′	1°38·9′W	X	174
Tottenhill	Norf	TF6410	52°40·0′	0°25·9′E	T	132,143
Tottenhill Row	Norf	TF6312	52°41·1′	0°25·1′E	T	132,143
Totterdale Fm	Wilts	ST9427	51°2·8′	2°4·7′W	FM	184
Totterdown Fm	Somer	SS9642	51°10·3′	3°28·9′W	FM	181
Totterdown Ho	W Berks	SU3465	51°23·2′	1°30·3′W	X	174
Tottergill	Cumbr	NY5454	54°53·0′	2°42·6′W	X	86
Totteridge	Barnet	TQ2494	51°38·1′	0°12·1′W	T	166,176
Totteridge	Bucks	SU8893	51°38·0′	0°43·3′W	T	175
Totteridge Fm	Wilts	SU1861	51°21·1′	1°44·1′W	FM	173
Totteridge Park	Barnet	TQ2394	51°38·1′	0°13·0′W	X	166,176
Totterie	Aberd	NO7567	56°47·9′	2°24·1′W	X	45
Totternhoe	Beds	SP9821	51°53·0′	0°34·2′W	T	165
Totteroak	S Glos	ST7484	51°33·5′	2°22·1′W	T	172
Totterton	Shrops	SO3687	52°28·9′	2°56·1′W	T	137
Totterton Hall	Shrops	SO3687	52°28·9′	2°56·1′W	X	137
Totties	Kirk	SE1508	53°34·3′	1°46·0′W	T	110
Tottiford Reservoir	Devon	SX8083	50°38·3′	3°41·4′W	W	191
Tottington	Bury	SD7712	53°36·5′	2°20·4′W	T	109
Tottington	Norf	TL8995	52°31·4′	0°47·6′E	T	144
Tottington Barn	W Susx	TQ2210	50°52·8′	0°15·6′W	X	198
Tottington Manor Fm	W Susx	TQ2111	50°53·4′	0°16·4′W	FM	198
Tottington Warren	Norf	TL8797	52°32·5′	0°45·9′E	X	144
Tottlebank	Cumbr	SD2688	54°17·2′	3°7·8′W	X	96,97
Tottlebank	Cumbr	SD3184	54°15·1′	3°3·1′W	T	96,97
Tottlehams Glen	D & G	NX7769	55°0·3′	3°55·0′W	X	84
Tottleworth	Lancs	SD7331	53°46·7′	2°24·2′W	T	103
Totto Hill	Scot Bord	NT3045	55°41·9′	3°6·4′W	H	73
Totton	Hants	SU3513	50°55·2′	1°29·7′W	T	196
Tottrome	Highld	NG5054	57°30·7′	6°10·0′W	X	23,24
Totty Pot	Somer	ST4853	51°16·7′	2°44·3′W	X	182
Touby	Shetld	HU4053	60°15·8′	1°16·1′W	X	3
Touchadam Muir	Stir	NS7189	56°4·8′	4°3·9′W	X	57
Touchbridge	Bucks	SP6414	51°49·5′	1°3·9′W	X	164,165
Touch Burn	Stir	NS7492	56°6·5′	4°1·1′W	W	57
Touchen-end	Win & Maid	SU8776	51°28·8′	0°44·4′W	T	175
Touch Hills	Stir	NS7291	56°5·9′	4°3·0′W	H	57
Touch Ho	Stir	NS7592	56°6·5′	4°0·2′W	A	57
Touch Home Fm	Stir	NS7593	56°7·1′	4°0·2′W	FM	57
Touchie	Pth & Kin	NO0605	56°14·0′	3°30·5′W	X	58
Touchill	Shrops	SO2699	52°35·3′	3°5·1′W	X	137
Touch Mollar	Stir	NS7591	56°6·0′	4°0·1′W	X	57
Touch Muir	Stir	NS7291	56°5·9′	4°3·0′W	X	57
Toucks	Aberd	NO8484	56°57·1′	2°15·3′W	X	45
Toulbrick	Lancs	SD3741	53°51·9′	2°57·1′W	X	102
Toull	D & G	NX8258	54°54·4′	3°50·0′W	X	84
Toulston	N Yks	SE4544	53°53·7′	1°18·5′W	T	105
Toulton	Somer	ST1931	51°4·6′	3°9·0′W	T	181
Toulvaddie	Highld	NH8880	57°48·0′	3°52·6′W	T	21
Tounafield	Shetld	HT9538	60°7·9′	2°4·9′W	X	4
Tour	E Ayr	NS4140	55°37·9′	4°31·1′W	X	70
Tourgill	N Ayr	NS2264	55°50·4′	4°50·1′W	X	63
Tourgill Burn	N Ayr	NS2263	55°49·9′	4°50·1′W	W	63
Tournaig	Highld	NG8783	57°47·4′	5°34·5′W	T	19
Tournaig Fm	Highld	NG8783	57°47·4′	5°34·5′W	FM	19
Tourner Bury	Hants	SZ7399	50°47·4′	0°57·5′W	A	197
Tout Hill	Dorset	SY5992	50°43·8′	2°34·5′W	H	194
Tout Hill	Dorset	SY8487	50°41·2′	2°13·2′W	X	194
Touting Birk's Hill	Scot Bord	NT4833	55°35·5′	2°49·1′W	H	73
Touting Hill	Durham	NY8031	54°40·7′	2°18·2′W	X	91,92
Toux	Aberd	NJ9850	57°32·7′	2°1·5′W	X	30
Touxhill	Aberd	NJ8941	57°27·8′	2°10·5′W	X	30
Tovil	Kent	TQ7554	51°15·7′	0°30·9′E	T	188
Tow	Shetld	HU4329	60°2·9′	1°13·2′W	X	4
Tow	Shetld	HU5288	60°34·6′	1°2·6′W	X	1,2
Towan	Corn	SW8774	50°31·9′	5°0·0′W	T	200
Towan	Corn	SX0149	50°18·7′	4°47·3′W	X	204
Towan Beach	Corn	SW8732	50°9·2′	4°58·5′W	X	204
Towan Cross	Corn	SW7048	50°17·5′	5°13·4′W	T	203
Towan Head	Corn	SW7962	50°25·2′	5°6·5′W	X	200
Towans, The	Corn	SW6620	50°2·3′	5°15·7′W	X	203
Toward	Arg & Bt	NS1368	55°52·4′	4°59·0′W	T	63
Toward Castle	Arg & Bt	NS1167	55°51·8′	5°0·8′W	A	63
Toward Fm	Arg & Bt	NS1268	55°52·4′	4°59·9′W	FM	63
Toward Hill	Arg & Bt	NS1270	55°53·4′	4°59·9′W	H	63
Toward Nuilt	Arg & Bt	NS1369	55°52·9′	4°58·9′W	W	63
Toward Point	Arg & Bt	NS1367	55°51·9′	4°58·9′W	X	63
Toward Quay	Arg & Bt	NS1167	55°51·8′	5°0·8′W	X	63
Toward Taynuilt	Arg & Bt	NS1268	55°52·4′	4°58·9′W	X	63
Tow Barrow	Wilts	SU2757	51°18·9′	1°36·4′W	H	174
Tow Barrow (Long						
Barrow)	Wilts	SU2757	51°18·9′	1°36·4′W	A	174
Towbury Hill	Glos	SO8836	52°1·6′	2°10·1′W	X	150
Towbury Hill (Towbury)	Glos	SO8836	52°1·6′	2°10·1′W	A	150
Towcester	Northnts	SP6948	52°7·8′	0°59·1′W	T	152
Towcett	Cumbr	NY5718	54°33·6′	2°39·5′W	X	91
Towdy Potts	Durham	NZ0636	54°43·4′	1°54·0′W	X	92
Towednack	Corn	SW4838	50°11·5′	5°31·5′W	T	203
Towell Fm	Devon	SS5313	50°54·1′	4°5·1′W	FM	180
Tower	D & G	NX7511	55°22·9′	3°57·9′W	X	71,78
Tower	D & G	NX6381	55°6·5′	4°8·4′W	X	77
Tower	N Ayr	NS2747	55°41·4′	4°44·7′W	X	63
Tower	Orkney	HY3818	59°2·9′	3°4·4′W	X	6
Towerage	Bucks	SU8293	51°38·0′	0°48·5′W	T	175
Tower Beck	N Yks	NZ6705	54°26·4′	0°57·6′W	W	94
Tower Br	T Ham	TQ3380	51°30·4′	0°4·6′W	X	176,177
Tower Brae	Cumbr	NY5672	55°2·7′	2°40·9′W	X	86
Tower Burn	D & G	NS7512	55°23·4′	3°58·0′W	W	71,78
Tower Burn	Scot Bord	NT3725	55°31·1′	2°59·4′W	W	73
Towerburn	Scot Bord	NT5818	55°27·5′	2°39·4′W	X	80
Tower End	Norf	TF6617	52°43·7′	0°27·9′E	T	132
Tower Fm	Cambs	TL2290	52°29·9′	0°11·8′W	FM	142
Tower Fm	Cambs	TL5184	52°26·2′	0°13·7′E	FM	143
Tower Fm	Devon	SS6428	51°2·4′	3°56·0′W	FM	180
Tower Fm	Kent	TR0151	51°13·6′	0°53·1′E	FM	189
Tower Fm	Leic	SP5784	52°27·3′	1°9·3′W	FM	140

Tower Fm	Lincs	SK9274	53°15·5′	0°36·8′W	FM	121
Tower Fm	Norf	TG0222	52°45·7′	1°0·0′E	FM	133
Tower Fm	Oxon	SP5330	51°58·2′	1°13·3′W	FM	152
Tower Fm	Scot Bord	NT7869	55°55·1′	2°20·7′W	FM	67
Tower Fm	S Lanak	NS8636	55°36·5′	3°48·1′W	FM	71,72
Tower Fm	Warw	SP3291	52°31·2′	1°31·3′W	FM	140
Tower Hamlets	Kent	TR3041	51°7·5′	1°17·6′E	T	179
Towerhead	N Som	ST4159	51°19·9′	2°50·4′W	T	172,182
Towerhead Brook	N Som	ST4060	51°20·4′	2°51·3′W	W	172,182
Tower Hill	Aberd	NJ5857	57°36·3′	2°41·7′W	H	29
Tower Hill	Birm	SP0592	52°31·8′	1°55·2′W	T	139
Tower Hill	Brackn	SU9066	51°23·4′	0°42·0′W	X	175
Tower Hill	Cald	SE0526	53°44·1′	1°55·0′W	X	104
Towerhill	Cered	SN4855	52°10·6′	4°13·0′W	X	146
Tower Hill	Ches	SJ9475	53°16·6′	2°5·0′W	T	118
Tower Hill	Devon	SX3790	50°41·4′	4°18·1′W	T	190
Towerhill	D & G	NS7612	55°23·4′	3°57·0′W	X	71,78
Tower Hill	Essex	TM2632	51°56·7′	1°17·7′E	T	169
Tower Hill	E Susx	TQ7315	50°54·7′	0°28·0′E	X	199
Tower Hill	Hants	SU2438	51°8·7′	1°39·0′W	H	184
Tower Hill	Heref	SO5939	52°3·1′	2°35·5′W	X	149
Tower Hill	Herts	TL0302	51°42·7′	0°30·2′W	T	166
Towerhill	Highld	ND1368	58°35·7′	3°29·3′W	X	11,12
Tower Hill	Inverc	NS2377	55°57·5′	4°49·7′W	H	63
Tower Hill	Kent	TQ6556	51°17·0′	0°22·4′E	X	178,188
Tower Hill	Know	SD4100	53°29·8′	2°53·0′W	T	108
Tower Hill	Lancs	SD7542	53°52·7′	2°22·4′W	X	103
Tower Hill	Lincs	SK9022	52°47·5′	0°39·5′W	A	130
Tower Hill	Medway	TQ7570	51°24·3′	0°31·4′E	X	178
Tower Hill	N Yks	SE2475	54°10·5′	1°37·5′W	X	99
Towerhill	Orkney	HY4609	58°58·2′	2°55·9′W	X	6,7
Towerhill	Orkney	HY5101	58°53·9′	2°50·5′W	X	6,7
Tower Hill	Oxon	SU2883	51°32·9′	1°35·4′W	X	174
Tower Hill	Somer	ST5650	51°15·1′	2°37·4′W	X	182,183
Tower Hill	Surrey	TQ1648	51°13·4′	0°19·9′W	T	187
Tower Hill	W Susx	SP7818	50°57·6′	0°53·0′W	H	197
Tower Hill	W Susx	TQ1629	51°3·1′	0°20·3′W	T	187,198
Tower Ho	E Susx	TQ7016	50°55·3′	0°25·5′E	X	199
Tower Ho	E Yorks	TA2326	53°43·2′	0°7·7′W	X	107
Tower Ho	Hants	SU4260	51°20·5′	1°23·4′W	X	174
Tower Ho	W Susx	TQ3025	51°0·8′	0°8·4′W	X	187,198
Towerims Craig	Highld	ND2374	58°39·1′	3°19·1′W	X	7,12
Tower Knowe	Scot Bord	NT3935	55°36·5′	2°57·7′W	X	73
Tower Lodge	Lancs	SD6053	53°58·5′	2°36·2′W	X	102,103
Tower Mains	Highld	NH4652	57°32·2′	4°33·9′W	X	26
Tower Martin	Northum	NU0026	55°31·9′	1°59·6′W	X	75
Tower Moor	Devon	SS6327	51°1·8′	3°56·8′W	X	180
Tower of Johnston	Aberd	NO7269	56°49·0′	2°27·1′W	X	45
Tower of Johnston (Cairn)	Aberd	NO7269	56°49·0′	2°27·1′W	A	45
Tower of Lethendy	Pth & Kin	NO1441	56°33·4′	3°23·5′W	A	53
Tower-of-Sark	D & G	NY3375	55°4·1′	3°2·5′W	X	85
Tower of Ward Hill	Shetld	HZ2073	59°32·8′	1°38·3′W	X	4
Tower on the Moor	Lincs	TF2063	53°9·3′	0°11·9′W	A	122
Tower Point	Pemb	SM7810	51°44·9′	5°12·6′W	X	157
Tower Rock	N Som	ST2360	51°20·3′	3°5·9′W	X	182
Towersey	Oxon	SP7305	51°44·6′	0°56·2′W	T	165
Towers Fm	Cambs	TF3703	52°36·7′	0°1·8′E	FM	142,143
Towers of Kirkconnell	D & G	NX6659	54°54·7′	4°5·0′W	H	83,84
Towers, The	Essex	TL5737	52°0·8′	0°17·7′E	X	154
Towers, The	Somer	ST6832	51°5·4′	2°27·0′W	X	183
Towers Yard Fm	Ches	SJ9284	53°21·4′	2°6·8′W	FM	109
Tower, The	Derby	SK1391	53°25·2′	1°47·9′W	X	110
Tower, The	D & G	NX8249	54°49·6′	3°49·8′W	X	84
Tower, The	Glos	SO8101	51°42·7′	2°16·1′W	X	162
Tower, The	Norf	TG1628	52°48·6′	1°12·7′E	X	133
Tower, The	N Yks	SE2767	54°6·1′	1°34·8′W	A	99
Tower, The	Powys	SO1024	51°54·7′	3°18·1′W	A	161
Tower, The	Shrops	SJ8009	52°40·9′	2°17·3′W	X	127
Tower, The	Staffs	SJ9504	52°38·3′	2°4·0′W	X	127,139
Tower, The	T Ham	TQ3380	51°30·4′	0°4·6′W	A	176,177
Tower Tye	Northum	NY8971	55°2·3′	2°9·9′W	X	87
Tower Wood	Devon	SX8785	50°39·5′	3°35·5′W	F	192
Tow Ford	Scot Bord	NT7613	55°24·9′	2°22·3′W	X	80
Towhaugh	Aberd	NJ6022	57°17·5′	2°39·4′W	X	37
Tow Hill	N Yks	SD8286	54°16·4′	2°16·2′W	X	98
Tow House	Northum	NY7664	54°58·5′	2°22·1′W	T	86,87
Towie	Aberd	NJ4312	57°12·0′	2°56·1′W	T	37
Towie	Aberd	NJ5327	57°20·1′	2°46·4′W	X	37
Towie	Aberd	NJ8763	57°39·7′	2°12·6′W	X	30
Towie Barclay Castle	Aberd	NJ7443	57°28·8′	2°25·6′W	A	29
Towiemore	Moray	NJ3945	57°29·7′	3°0·6′W	T	28
Towie Turner	Aberd	NJ7442	57°28·3′	2°25·6′W	X	29
Towie Wood	Aberd	NJ5363	57°39·7′	2°46·8′W	F	29
Tow Law	Durham	NZ1138	54°44·5′	1°49·3′W	T	92
Towler Hill	Durham	NZ0317	54°33·1′	1°56·8′W	X	92
Towler Hill	N Yks	SE1479	54°12·6′	1°46·7′W	X	99
Towleys	Aberd	NJ6023	57°18·0′	2°39·4′W	X	37
Towmill	Aberd	NJ6121	57°16·9′	2°38·4′W	X	37
Town Bank	Cumbr	NY0710	54°28·9′	3°25·7′W	X	89
Town Bar	Corn	SW9275	50°32·5′	4°55·8′W	X	200
Town Barton	Devon	SX8094	50°44·2′	3°41·7′W	T	191
Townburn Wood	D & G	NX9193	55°13·4′	3°42·4′W	F	78
Town Centre	Lancs	SD4806	53°33·1′	2°46·7′W	T	108
Town Centre	Wrekin	SJ6908	52°40·4′	2°27·1′W	T	127
Town Common	Dorset	SZ1396	50°46·0′	1°48·6′W	X	195
Town Coppice	Worcs	SO7676	52°23·1′	2°20·8′W	F	138
Towncroft	Renf	NS4069	55°53·5′	4°33·1′W	X	64
Towncroft Fm	Lancs	SD5041	53°52·0′	2°45·2′W	FM	102
Town Ditch	Wrex	SJ3258	53°7·1′	3°0·6′W	X	117
Towneley Hall	Lancs	SD8530	53°46·2′	2°13·2′W	A	103
Town End	Bucks	SU7897	51°40·2′	0°51·9′W	T	165
Town End	Cambs	TL4195	52°32·3′	0°5·1′E	T	142,143
Town End	Cumbr	NY0308	54°27·7′	3°29·4′W	X	89
Town End	Cumbr	NY3406	54°27·0′	3°0·7′W	T	90
Townend	Cumbr	NY3635	54°42·6′	2°59·2′W	X	90
Town End	Cumbr	NY4002	54°24·8′	2°55·1′W	T	90
Townend	Cumbr	NY4002	54°24·8′	2°55·1′W	X	90
Townend	Cumbr	NY4633	54°41·6′	2°49·8′W	X	90
Town End	Cumbr	NY5326	54°37·9′	2°43·3′W	X	90
Town End	Cumbr	NY5623	54°36·3′	2°40·4′W	X	90

Town End	Cumbr	NY6325	54°37·4'	2°34·0'W	T	91
Town End	Cumbr	SD3598	54°22·6'	2°59·6'W	T	96,97
Town End	Cumbr	SD3687	54°16·7'	2°58·6'W	T	96,97
Town End	Cumbr	SD3795	54°21·0'	2°57·7'W	X	96,97
Town End	Cumbr	SD4483	54°14·6'	2°51·1'W	T	97
Town End	Cumbr	SD6282	54°14·2'	2°34·6'W	T	97
Townend	Derby	SK0681	53°19·8'	1°54·2'W	T	110
Town End	Derby	SK1575	53°16·5'	1°46·1'W	T	119
Townend	E Ayr	NS4644	55°40·2'	4°26·5'W	X	70
Town End	E Yorks	SE7053	53°58·3'	0°55·6'W	T	105,106
Town End	Kirk	SE0915	53°38·1'	1°51·4'W	T	110
Town End	Know	SJ4988	53°23·4'	2°45·6'W	T	108
Town End	Lancs	SD6243	53°53·2'	2°34·3'W	X	102,103
Town End	N Yks	NZ3801	54°24·4'	1°24·5'W	X	93
Townend	S Ayr	NS3731	55°33·0'	4°34·6'W	X	70
Townend	S Ayr	NS4331	55°33·1'	4°28·9'W	X	70
Townend	S Lanak	NS7442	55°39·6'	3°59·7'W	X	71
Townend	Staffs	SJ9537	52°56·1'	2°4·1'W	T	127
Townend	Staffs	SK1160	53°8·5'	1°49·7'W	X	119
Townend	W Dunb	NS4076	55°57·3'	4°33·3'W	T	64
Town End Farm	Sund	NZ3459	54°55·7'	1°27·7'W	FM	88
Townend Fm	Derby	SK0774	53°16·0'	1°53·3'W	FM	119
Townend Fm	Derby	SK1169	53°13·3'	1°49·7'W	FM	119
Townend Fm	Derby	SK1468	53°12·8'	1°47·0'W	FM	119
Town End Fm	E Yorks	SE7153	53°58·3'	0°54·6'W	FM	105,106
Townend Fm	E Yorks	SE8738	53°50·1'	0°40·3'W	FM	106
Townend Fm	N Yks	SE2548	53°55·9'	1°36·7'W	FM	104
Town End Hall	N Yks	SE0399	54°23·4'	1°56·8'W	X	98
Townend of Caprington	E Ayr	NS4034	55°34·7'	4°31·9'W	X	70
Town End Plantn	E Yorks	SE7152	53°57·8'	0°54·7'W	F	105,106
Townend Wood	E Yorks	SE8850	53°56·6'	0°39·1'W	F	106
Town Farm	Northum	NT9945	55°42·2'	2°0·5'W	FM	75
Town Fen	Suff	TM4480	52°22·0'	1°35·5'E	X	156
Townfield	Durham	NY9548	54°49·9'	2°4·2'W	T	87
Townfield Fm	Ches	SJ6162	53°9·5'	2°34·6'W	FM	118
Townfield Head	Sheff	SK2887	53°23·0'	1°34·3'W	X	110
Townfield Lands	Ches	SJ4158	53°7·2'	2°52·5'W	X	117
Town Fields	Ches	SJ5461	53°8·9'	2°40·9'W	X	117
Town Fields	Ches	SJ6465	53°11·1'	2°31·9'W	T	118
Town Fm	Beds	SP9933	51°59·4'	0°33·1'W	FM	165
Town Fm	Beds	TL0053	52°10·2'	0°31·9'W	FM	153
Town Fm	Bucks	SP6308	51°46·3'	1°4·8'W	FM	164,165
Town Fm	Bucks	SP9516	51°50·3'	0°36·9'W	FM	165
Town Fm	Bucks	SU9092	51°37·4'	0°41·6'W	FM	175
Town Fm	Ches	SJ5673	53°15·4'	2°39·2'W	FM	117
Town Fm	Devon	SS6337	51°7·2'	3°57·1'W	FM	180
Town Fm	Devon	SS8327	51°2·1'	3°39·7'W	FM	181
Town Fm	Devon	SX3499	50°46·2'	4°20·9'W	FM	190
Town Fm	Dorset	SU0016	50°56·8'	1°59·6'W	FM	184
Town Fm	Essex	TL5316	51°49·5'	0°13·6'E	FM	167
Town Fm	Heref	SO2835	52°0·8'	3°2·6'W	FM	161
Town Fm	Heref	SO5363	52°16·0'	2°40·9'W	FM	137,138,149
Town Fm	Norf	TF7908	52°38·6'	0°39·2'E	FM	144
Town Fm	Norf	TF8608	52°38·5'	0°45·4'E	FM	144
Town Fm	Norf	TL9985	52°25·8'	0°56·0'E	FM	144
Town Fm	Norf	TM3291	52°28·3'	1°25·4'E	FM	134
Town Fm	Suff	TM0371	52°18·2'	0°59·1'E	FM	144,155
Town Fm	Suff	TM1572	52°18·5'	1°9·6'E	FM	144,156
Town Fm	Suff	TM1974	52°19·4'	1°13·2'E	FM	156
Town Fm	Suff	TM2169	52°16·7'	1°14·8'E	FM	156
Town Fm	Suff	TM3076	52°20·3'	1°23·0'E	FM	156
Town Fm	Suff	TM3478	52°21·2'	1°26·6'E	FM	156
Town Fm	Suff	TM3966	52°14·6'	1°30·5'E	FM	156
Town Fm	Wilts	SU3361	51°21·1'	1°31·2'W	FM	174
Townfoot	Cumbr	NY5247	54°49·2'	2°44·4'W	X	86
Townfoot	D & G	NX9082	55°7·5'	3°43·1'W	X	78
Townfoot	D & G	NX9197	55°15·6'	3°42·5'W	X	78
Townfoot	D & G	NX9968	55°0·0'	3°34·3'W	X	84
Townfoot	D & G	NY0187	55°10·3'	3°32·8'W	X	78
Townfoot	D & G	NY0672	55°2·3'	3°27·8'W	X	85
Townfoot	Northum	NU2009	55°22·7'	1°40·6'W	X	81
Town Foot	Northum	NY7164	54°58·4'	2°26·8'W	X	86,87
Townfoot	Northum	NY9857	54°54·7'	2°1·4'W	X	87
Townfoot	S Lanak	NT0234	55°35·6'	3°32·9'W	X	72
Townfoot	S Lanak	NT0945	55°41·7'	3°26·4'W	X	72
Townfoot	Stir	NS7484	56°2·2'	4°0·9'W	X	57,64
Town Foot Fm	Cumbr	NY3949	54°50·2'	2°56·6'W	FM	85
Townfoot Fm	S Lanak	NT0034	55°35·6'	3°34·8'W	FM	72
Townfoot Hill	Scot Bord	NT7318	55°27·6'	2°25·2'W	H	80
Townfoot of Netherton	S Lanak	NS9141	55°39·3'	3°43·5'W	X	71,72
Towngate	Cumbr	NY5246	54°48·6'	2°44·4'W	T	86
Towngate	Lincs	TF1310	52°40·8'	0°19·3'W	T	130,142
Town Green	Lancs	SD4005	53°32·5'	2°53·9'W	T	108
Town Green	Norf	TG3612	52°39·5'	1°29·8'E	T	133,134
Town Green	Northum	NY6753	54°52·5'	2°30·4'W	X	86,87
Town Green	Wigan	SJ5899	53°29·4'	2°37·6'W	T	108
Townhead	Aberd	NJ5700	57°5·6'	2°42·1'W	X	37
Townhead	Aberd	NJ8241	57°27·8'	2°17·5'W	X	29,30
Townhead	Aberd	NJ8900	57°5·7'	2°10·4'W	X	38
Townhead	Aberd	NJ9133	57°23·5'	2°8·5'W	X	30
Townhead	Aberd	NO7775	56°52·2'	2°22·2'W	X	45
Townhead	Aberd	NO8272	56°50·6'	2°17·3'W	T	45
Townhead	Arg & Bt	NS0863	55°49·6'	5°3·5'W	T	63
Townhead	Arg & Bt	NS3182	56°0·3'	4°42·2'W	X	56
Townhead	Barns	SE1602	53°31·1'	1°45·1'W	T	110
Town Head	Brad	SE0446	53°54·9'	1°55·9'W	T	104
Townhead	C of Glas	NS5965	55°51·7'	4°14·7'W	T	64
Townhead	Cumbr	NY0735	54°42·3'	3°26·2'W	T	89
Town Head	Cumbr	NY2538	54°44·1'	3°9·5'W	X	89,90
Town Head	Cumbr	NY3142	54°46·3'	3°3·9'W	X	85
Townhead	Cumbr	NY3239	54°44·7'	3°3·0'W	X	90
Townhead	Cumbr	NY3248	54°49·6'	3°3·1'W	X	85
Town Head	Cumbr	NY3309	54°28·6'	3°1·6'W	T	90
Town Head	Cumbr	NY4103	54°25·4'	2°54·1'W	T	90
Townhead	Cumbr	NY5157	54°54·6'	2°45·4'W	X	86
Townhead	Cumbr	NY5247	54°49·2'	2°44·4'W	X	86
Townhead	Cumbr	NY5439	54°44·9'	2°42·5'W	T	90
Townhead	Cumbr	NY5649	54°50·3'	2°40·7'W	X	86
Town Head	Cumbr	NY5825	54°37·4'	2°38·6'W	T	91
Town Head	Cumbr	NY6022	54°35·7'	2°36·7'W	T	91
Town Head	Cumbr	NY6214	54°31·4'	2°34·8'W	T	91
Townhead	Cumbr	NY6334	54°42·2'	2°34·0'W	T	91
Town Head	Cumbr	NY6425	54°37·4'	2°33·0'W	T	91
Town Head	Cumbr	NY6712	54°30·4'	2°30·2'W	T	91
Town Head	Cumbr	NY6924	54°36·9'	2°28·4'W	T	91
Town Head	Cumbr	SD3887	54°16·7'	2°56·7'W	X	96,97
Town Head	Derby	SK1269	53°13·3'	1°48·8'W	X	119
Town Head	Derby	SK1576	53°17·1'	1°46·1'W	T	119
Townhead	Derby	SK1684	53°21·4'	1°45·2'W	X	110
Townhead	D & G	NX6255	54°52·5'	4°8·6'W	X	83
Townhead	D & G	NX6946	54°47·8'	4°1·8'W	T	83,84
Townhead	D & G	NX8090	55°11·6'	3°52·7'W	X	78
Townhead	D & G	NX8298	55°16·0'	3°51·0'W	X	78
Townhead	D & G	NX8982	55°7·5'	3°44·0'W	X	78
Townhead	D & G	NX9198	55°16·1'	3°42·5'W	X	78
Townhead	D & G	NY0081	55°7·1'	3°33·6'W	X	78
Townhead	D & G	NY0088	55°10·8'	3°33·8'W	X	78
Townhead	E Ayr	NS5122	55°28·4'	4°21·0'W	X	70
Townhead	E Loth	NT5568	55°54·4'	2°42·8'W	X	66
Townhead	Lancs	SD7152	53°58·0'	2°26·1'W	X	103
Townhead	N Lanak	NS7166	55°52·5'	4°3·3'W	T	64
Townhead	N Lanak	NS7478	55°59·0'	4°0·7'W	X	64
Townhead	Northum	NY8774	55°3·9'	2°11·8'W	X	87
Townhead	Northum	NY8893	55°14·1'	2°10·9'W	T	80
Townhead	Northum	NY9087	55°10·9'	2°9·0'W	X	80
Townhead	Northum	NY9757	54°54·7'	2°2·4'W	X	87
Town Head	N Yks	SD7768	54°6·7'	2°20·7'W	T	98
Town Head	N Yks	SD8258	54°1·3'	2°16·1'W	T	103
Town Head	N Yks	SD9846	53°54·9'	2°1·4'W	X	103
Town Head	N Yks	SE1748	53°55·9'	1°44·0'W	X	104
Townhead	Pth & Kin	NN8306	56°14·2'	3°52·8'W	X	57
Townhead	Pth & Kin	NO1729	56°27·0'	3°20·3'W	X	53,58
Townhead	S Ayr	NS2103	55°17·6'	4°48·7'W	T	76
Townhead	S Ayr	NS4125	55°29·8'	4°30·6'W	X	70
Townhead	Sheff	SK3081	53°19·7'	1°32·6'W	T	110,111
Townhead	S Lanak	NS8835	55°36·0'	3°46·2'W	X	71,72
Townhead	S Lanak	NS9842	55°39·9'	3°36·9'W	X	72
Townhead	S Lanak	NT0945	55°41·7'	3°26·4'W	X	72
Town Head	Staffs	SK0449	53°2·5'	1°56·0'W	T	119
Townhead	Staffs	SK0658	53°7·4'	1°54·2'W	X	119
Townhead	Stir	NS6093	56°6·8'	4°14·7'W	X	57
Townhead	Stir	NS6485	56°2·6'	4°10·6'W	X	57
Townhead	Stir	NS7489	56°4·9'	4°1·0'W	X	57
Townhead Cott	D & G	NX7973	55°2·5'	3°53·2'W	X	84
Townhead Cottage	S Lanak	NS8328	55°32·2'	3°50·8'W	X	71,72
Town Head Fm	Cumbr	NY4134	54°42·1'	2°54·5'W	FM	90
Townhead Fm	Derby	SK0297	53°28·4'	1°57·8'W	FM	110
Townhead Fm	D & G	NY0673	55°2·8'	3°27·8'W	FM	85
Townhead Fm	E Ayr	NS4833	55°34·3'	4°24·2'W	FM	70
Townhead Fm	Northum	NZ1390	55°12·5'	1°47·3'W	FM	81
Townhead of Blacklaw	E Ayr	NS4650	55°43·4'	4°26·7'W	X	64
Townhead of Culloch	D & G	NX8364	54°57·7'	3°49·2'W	X	84
Townhead of Grange	E Ayr	NS4452	55°44·4'	4°28·7'W	X	64
Townhead of Gree	E Ayr	NS4646	55°41·2'	4°26·5'W	X	64
Townhead of Greenlaw	D & G	NX7464	54°57·5'	3°57·6'W	T	83,84
Townhead of Greenock	E Ayr	NS6427	55°31·3'	4°8·8'W	X	71
Townhead of Hairshaw	E Ayr	NS4547	55°41·8'	4°27·5'W	X	64
Townhead of Killymingan	D & G	NX8567	54°59·3'	3°47·4'W	X	84
Townhead of Lambroughton	N Ayr	NS4043	55°39·5'	4°32·2'W	X	70
Townhead Wood	D & G	NX8298	55°16·0'	3°51·0'W	F	78
Townhead Wood	D & G	NX8882	55°7·4'	3°45·0'W	F	78
Townhead Wood	S Lanak	NS8329	55°32·7'	3°50·8'W	F	71,72
Townhill	Fife	NT1089	56°5·4'	3°26·3'W	T	65
Town Hill	Oxon	SU5994	51°38·7'	1°8·4'W	H	164,174
Town Hill	Powys	SO2195	52°33·1'	3°9·5'W	X	137
Townhill	Swan	SS6393	51°37·4'	3°58·4'W	T	159
Town Hill Fm	Dorset	SY6192	50°43·8'	2°32·8'W	FM	194
Townhill Park	C of Soton	SU4514	50°55·7'	1°21·2'W	T	196
Townhill Wood	Fife	NT1089	56°5·4'	3°26·3'W	F	65
Town Ho	Cumbr	SD5789	54°17·9'	2°39·2'W	X	97
Townhouse	Ches	SJ6844	52°59·8'	2°28·2'W	X	118
Townhouse	Staffs	SJ7951	53°3·6'	2°18·4'W	X	118
Townhouse Barton	Devon	SS6826	51°1·3'	3°52·5'W	X	180
Townhouse Farm Ho	W Susx	TQ1232	51°4·8'	0°23·7'W	X	187
Town House Fm	Ches	SJ7552	53°4·1'	2°22·0'W	FM	118
Town House Fm	W Susx	TQ1017	50°56·7'	0°25·7'W	FM	198
Town House Fruit Fm	Suff	TM0441	52°2·0'	0°58·8'E	FM	155
Townings Fm	E Susx	TQ3720	50°58·0'	0°2·5'W	FM	198
Townings Place	E Susx	TQ3420	50°58·1'	0°5·1'W	X	198
Town Kelloe	Durham	NZ3536	54°43·2'	1°27·0'W	T	93
Townlake	Devon	SX4074	50°32·9'	4°15·1'W	T	201
Townland Green	Kent	TQ9434	51°4·6'	0°46·6'E	T	189
Town Lane	Wigan	SJ6999	53°29·5'	2°27·6'W	T	109
Town Law	Northum	NU0331	55°34·6'	1°56·7'W	X	75
Town Law	Scot Bord	NT4048	55°43·6'	2°56·9'W	H	73
Townlaw Cairn	Northum	NU1411	55°23·8'	1°46·3'W	X	81
Town Leat	Devon	SS9717	50°56·8'	3°27·6'W	W	181
Townleigh Fm	Devon	SX4287	50°39·9'	4°13·8'W	FM	190
Townley Fm	Ches	SJ5746	53°0·8'	2°38·1'W	FM	117
Town Littleworth	E Susx	TQ4118	50°56·9'	0°0·8'E	T	198
Town Loch	Fife	NT0989	56°5·4'	3°27·3'W	W	65
Town Loch	Shetld	HU3065	60°22·3'	1°26·9'W	W	3
Town Marshes	Suff	TM4350	52°5·9'	1°33·3'E	X	156
Town Marshes	Suff	TM5075	52°19·2'	1°40·5'E	X	156
Town Mills	Devon	SS5018	50°56·8'	4°7·7'W	X	180
Town Moor	Devon	SS7714	50°55·0'	3°44·6'W	X	180
Town Moor	N upon Ty	NZ2466	54°59·5'	1°37·1'W	X	88
Town Moor	N Yks	SD7956	54°0·2'	2°18·8'W	X	103
Townmoor Fm	Suff	TL6681	52°24·3'	0°26·8'E	FM	143
Town of Inchinnan	Renf	NS4868	55°53·1'	4°25·4'W	X	64
Town of Lowton	Wigan	SJ6095	53°27·3'	2°35·7'W	T	109
Town-o'-rule	Scot Bord	NT5813	55°24·8'	2°39·4'W	X	80
Town Park	Essex	TL4510	51°46·4'	0°6·5'E	X	167
Town Park	Halton	SJ5481	53°19·7'	2°41·0'W	X	108
Town Park	Wrekin	SJ6908	52°40·4'	2°27·1'W	T	127
Town Place	Kent	TQ9856	51°16·3'	0°50·7'E	X	178
Town Place	W Susx	TQ3825	51°0·7'	0°1·6'W	X	187,198
Town Quay	Hants	SU4110	50°53·5'	1°24·6'W	X	196
Town Quay	Hants	SU5705	50°50·7'	1°11·0'W	X	196
Town Row	E Susx	TQ5630	51°3·1'	0°13·9'E	T	188
Townscliffe Fm	Stock	SJ9788	53°23·6'	2°2·3'W	FM	109
Town's Close Lodge	Northnts	SP8384	52°27·1'	0°46·3'W	X	141
Town's Common	E Ayr	NS4805	55°19·2'	4°23·3'W	X	70,77
Townsdales	Lancs	SD3944	53°53·6'	2°55·3'W	X	102
Townsend	Bath & NE Somer	ST5756	51°18·3'	2°36·6'W	T	172,182
Town's End	Bucks	SP6422	51°53·8'	1°3·8'W	T	164,165
Townsend	Bucks	SP7409	51°46·7'	0°55·2'W	T	165
Townsend	C of Stoke	SJ9147	53°1·5'	2°7·6'W	T	118
Townsend	Devon	SS6325	51°0·7'	3°56·8'W	T	180
Town's End	Dorset	ST5707	50°51·9'	2°36·3'W	T	194
Towns End	Dorset	ST7219	50°58·4'	2°23·5'W	T	183
Town's End	Dorset	SY8595	50°45·5'	2°12·4'W	T	194
Town's End	Dorset	SY9681	50°38·0'	2°3·0'W	T	195
Towns End	Hants	SU5658	51°19·3'	1°11·4'W	T	174
Townsend	Herts	TL1408	51°45·8'	0°20·5'W	T	166
Townsend	Orkney	HY5331	59°10·1'	2°48·8'W	X	5,6
Townsend	Oxon	SU3887	51°35·1'	1°26·7'W	T	174
Townsend	Pemb	SM8106	51°42·8'	5°9·8'W	T	157
Townsend	Somer	ST5251	51°15·6'	2°40·9'W	T	182,183
Town's End	Somer	ST6847	51°13·5'	2°27·1'W	T	183
Townsend	Wilts	ST9658	51°19·5'	2°3·1'W	T	173
Townsend	Wilts	SU0456	51°18·4'	1°56·2'W	T	173
Towns End Field	Cambs	TL4874	52°20·9'	0°10·8'E	X	143
Townsend Field	Cambs	TL4973	52°20·3'	0°11·6'E	X	154
Townsend Fm	Ches	SJ8157	53°6·8'	2°16·6'W	FM	118
Towns End Fm	Dorset	ST7007	50°51·9'	2°25·2'W	FM	194
Townsend Fm	Heref	SO5926	51°56·1'	2°35·4'W	FM	162
Townsend Fm	Heref	SO6457	52°12·8'	2°31·2'W	FM	149
Townsend Fm	Norf	TF5506	52°38·0'	0°17·8'E	FM	143
Townsend Fm	Oxon	SP6206	51°45·2'	1°5·7'W	FM	164,165
Townsend Fm	Somer	ST0042	51°10·3'	3°25·4'W	FM	181
Townsend Fm	Somer	ST1342	51°10·5'	3°14·3'W	FM	181
Townsend Fm	Suff	TL8251	52°7·9'	0°39·9'E	FM	155
Townsend Fm	Wilts	SU0563	51°22·2'	1°55·3'W	FM	173
Townsend Fold	Lancs	SD8021	53°41·3'	2°17·8'W	T	103
Townsend's Fm	Lancs	SD4713	53°36·9'	2°47·7'W	FM	108
Towns Fell	Cumbr	SD6985	54°15·8'	2°28·1'W	X	98
Towns Green	Ches	SJ6061	53°8·9'	2°35·5'W	X	118
Townshayne Common	Devon	SY1997	50°46·3'	3°8·5'W	X	192,193
Townshend	Corn	SW5932	50°8·6'	5°22·0'W	T	203
Townshield Bank	Northum	NY8173	55°3·3'	2°17·4'W	X	86,87
Town Shields	Northum	NY8171	55°2·2'	2°17·4'W	X	86,87
Townson Hill	Lancs	SD3948	53°55·7'	2°55·3'W	X	102
Town Street	Glos	SO8429	51°57·8'	2°13·6'W	T	150
Town Thorns	Warw	SP4479	52°24·7'	1°20·8'W	X	140
Town Thorns Fm	Warw	SP4578	52°24·1'	1°19·9'W	FM	140
Townthwaite Beck	Cumbr	NY2743	54°46·8'	3°7·7'W	W	85
Town Tree Fm	Somer	ST4421	50°59·4'	2°47·5'W	FM	193
Townwell	S Glos	ST6990	51°36·7'	2°26·5'W	T	162,172
Town Wood	Cumbr	NY6023	54°36·3'	2°36·7'W	F	91
Town Wood	Northnts	SP9496	52°33·5'	0°36·4'W	F	141
Town Yeat	Cumbr	SD4591	54°18·9'	2°50·3'W	X	97
Town Yetholm	Scot Bord	NT8128	55°33·0'	2°17·6'W	T	74
Towranna Fm	Suff	TM3375	52°19·6'	1°25·6'E	FM	156
Tows Bank	Northum	NY6857	54°54·6'	2°29·5'W	X	86,87
Tow Scar	N Yks	SD6875	54°10·4'	2°29·0'W	X	98
Towthorpe	E Yorks	SE9062	54°3·0'	0°37·1'W	T	101
Towthorpe	York	SE6358	54°1·1'	1°1·9'W	T	105,106
Towthorpe Common	York	SE6458	54°1·1'	1°1·0'W	X	105,106
Towthorpe Corner	E Yorks	SE8844	53°53·3'	0°39·2'W	X	106
Towthorpe Field	E Yorks	SE9062	54°3·0'	0°37·1'W	X	101
Towthorpe Plantn	E Yorks	SE9064	54°4·1'	0°37·1'W	F	101
Towthorpe Village	E Yorks	SE8643	53°52·8'	0°41·1'W	A	106
Towthorpe Village	E Yorks	SE8962	54°3·0'	0°38·0'W	A	101
Towthorpe Wold	E Yorks	SE8963	54°3·6'	0°38·0'W	X	101
Towton	N Yks	SE4839	53°50·9'	1°15·8'W	T	105
Tow Top	N Yks	SD9646	53°54·9'	2°3·2'W	X	103
Towtop Kirk	Cumbr	NY4917	54°33·0'	2°46·9'W	A	90
Tow Top Plantn	Cumbr	SD4183	54°14·6'	2°53·9'W	F	96,97
Towy Castle	Carm	SN4014	51°48·3'	4°18·9'W	X	159
Towyn	Conwy	SH9779	53°18·1'	3°32·3'W	T	116
Towyn	Gwyn	SH2337	52°54·3'	4°37·5'W	X	123
Towyn	Gwyn	SH2827	52°49·0'	4°32·7'W	X	123
Towyn Warren	Cered	SN1649	52°6·8'	4°40·8'W	X	145
Toxside	Midlo	NT2854	55°46·7'	3°8·4'W	X	66,73
Toxsidehill	Midlo	NT2854	55°46·7'	3°8·4'W	X	66,73
Toxside Moss	Midlo	NT2753	55°46·1'	3°9·4'W	X	66,73
Toxteth	Liv	SJ3588	53°23·3'	2°58·2'W	T	108
Toyd Clump	Wilts	SU0822	51°0·1'	1°52·8'W	F	184
Toyd Down	Hants	SU0819	50°58·5'	1°52·8'W	X	184
Toyd Fm	Hants	SU0820	50°59·0'	1°52·8'W	FM	184
Toy Ness	Orkney	HY3504	58°55·4'	3°7·3'W	X	6,7
Toynton All Saints	Lincs	TF3963	53°9·0'	0°5·1'E	T	122
Toynton Fen Side	Lincs	TF3962	53°8·5'	0°5·1'E	T	122
Toynton Ings	Lincs	TF4162	53°8·4'	0°6·9'E	X	122
Toynton St Peter	Lincs	TF4063	53°9·0'	0°6·0'E	T	122
Toy's Hill	Kent	TQ4751	51°14·6'	0°6·8'E	T	188
Toytop Plantn	Darl	NZ2122	54°35·8'	1°40·1'W	F	93
Trabboch	E Ayr	NS4321	55°27·7'	4°28·6'W	T	70
Trabbochburn	E Ayr	NS4621	55°27·8'	4°25·7'W	X	70
Trabboch Burn	E Ayr	NS4721	55°27·8'	4°24·8'W	W	70
Trabboch Ho	E Ayr	NS4321	55°27·7'	4°28·6'W	X	70
Trabboch Mains	E Ayr	NS4522	55°28·3'	4°26·7'W	X	70
Trabeattie	D & G	NY0377	55°4·9'	3°30·7'W	X	84
Traboe	Corn	SW7421	50°3·0'	5°9·1'W	T	204
Traboe Cross	Corn	SW7320	50°2·4'	5°9·9'W	X	204
Traboyack	S Ayr	NX2591	55°11·2'	4°44·5'W	X	76
Traboyack Burn	S Ayr	NX2591	55°11·2'	4°44·5'W	W	76
Trabroun	E Loth	NT4674	55°57·6'	2°51·5'W	X	66
Trabrown	Scot Bord	NT5049	55°44·2'	2°47·3'W	T	73
Trabrown Hill	Scot Bord	NT5048	55°43·6'	2°47·3'W	H	73
Trabrownhill	Scot Bord	NT5048	55°43·6'	2°47·3'W	X	73
Tracebridge	Somer	ST0621	50°59·1'	3°20·0'W	T	181
Tracentree	Cumbr	NY3045	54°47·9'	3°4·9'W	X	85
Tracey	Devon	ST1501	50°48·4'	3°12·0'W	X	192,193
Tracey Fm	Oxon	SP3926	51°56·1'	1°25·6'W	FM	164
Traceys Fm	Essex	TQ5299	51°40·4'	0°12·3'E	FM	167,177
Tracy Park	S Glos	ST7171	51°26·5'	2°24·6'W	X	172

Tracy's Dell	Hants	SU4345	51°12·4'	1°22·7'W	X	185
Tradespark	Highld	NH8656	57°35·0'	3°53·9'W	T	27
Tradespark	Orkney	HY4508	58°57·6'	2°56·9'W	T	6,7
Tradunnock	S Ayr	NS3004	55°18·3'	4°40·3'W	X	76
Traed y Milwyr	Caer	SO0911	51°47·7'	3°18·8'W	X	161
Trae Geo	Orkney	ND4678	58°41·4'	2°55·4'W	X	7
Traeth Abermenai	I of Angl	SH4462	53°8·2'	4°19·5'W	X	114,115
Traeth Bach	Gwyn	SH5735	52°53·9'	4°7·2'W	X	124
Traeth Bach	V of Glam	SS8971	51°25·9'	3°35·4'W	X	170
Traeth Bychan	I of Angl	SH5184	53°20·2'	4°13·9'W	X	114,115
Traeth-coch or Red Wharf Bay	I of Angl	SH5480	53°18·1'	4°11·0'W	W	114,115
Traeth Crigyll	I of Angl	SH3173	53°13·9'	4°31·5'W	X	114
Traeth Crugan	Gwyn	SH3533	52°52·4'	4°26·7'W	X	123
Traeth Cymyran	I of Angl	SH3074	53°14·4'	4°32·4'W	X	114
Traeth Dulas	I of Angl	SH4888	53°22·3'	4°16·7'W	X	114
Traeth Gwyllt	I of Angl	SH4864	53°9·3'	4°16·0'W	X	114,115
Traeth Lafan or Lavan Sands	Gwyn	SH6376	53°16·0'	4°2·8'W	X	114,115
Traeth Lligwy	I of Angl	SH4987	53°21·7'	4°15·7'W	X	114
Traeth Llydan	I of Angl	SH3272	53°13·4'	4°30·6'W	X	114
Traeth Llyfn	Pemb	SM8031	51°56·3'	5°11·6'W	X	157
Traeth Maelgwyn	Cered	SN6294	52°31·8'	4°1·7'W	X	135
Traeth Mawr	Gwyn	SH6040	52°56·6'	4°4·6'W	X	124
Traeth Mawr	I of Angl	SH3567	53°10·7'	4°27·7'W	X	114
Traeth Mawr	Powys	SN9625	51°55·1'	3°30·3'W	W	160
Traeth Mawr	V of Glam	SS9070	51°25·3'	3°34·5'W	X	170
Traeth-Penbryn	Cered	SN2952	52°8·6'	4°29·6'W	X	145
Traeth Penllech	Gwyn	SH2034	52°52·6'	4°40·1'W	X	123
Traethy Coubal	Cered	SN3759	52°12·6'	4°22·7'W	X	145
Traeth y Gribin	I of Angl	SH2881	53°18·1'	4°34·5'W	X	114
Traeth yr Afon	Brig	SS8576	51°28·5'	3°39·0'W	X	170
Traeth yr Ora	I of Angl	SH4988	53°22·3'	4°15·8'W	X	114
Traeth-yr-ynys	Cered	SN3155	52°10·3'	4°27·9'W	X	145
Trafalgar	Corn	SX1291	50°41·5'	4°39·3'W	X	190
Trafalgar	E Loth	NT5267	55°53·9'	2°45·6'W	X	66
Trafalgar Fm	Glos	SP1129	51°57·8'	1°50·0'W	FM	150,163
Trafalgar Ho	Wilts	SU1823	51°0·6'	1°44·2'W	A	184
Trafel-gwyn	Powys	SN8975	52°22·0'	3°37·4'W	X	135,136,147
Trafel-y-pwll	Carm	SN3330	51°56·8'	4°25·4'W	X	145
Trafel-yr-ych	Carm	SN2821	51°51·9'	4°29·5'W	X	145,158
Trafford Br	Northnts	SP5147	52°7·4'	1°14·9'W	X	151
Trafford Bridge Fm	Northnts	SP5147	52°7·4'	1°14·9'W	FM	151
Trafford Hill	Stock on T	NZ3711	54°29·8'	1°25·3'W	X	93
Trafford Ho	Lincs	TF4116	52°43·6'	0°5·7'E	X	131
Trafford Ho	Norf	TF5110	52°40·2'	0°14·4'E	X	131,143
Trafford Ho	Northnts	SP5248	52°7·9'	1°14·0'W	X	151
Trafford Park	Traf	SJ7896	53°27·9'	2°19·5'W	T	109
Traffwll	I of Angl	SH3276	53°15·5'	4°30·7'W	X	114
Trafle	Powys	SN9860	52°14·0'	3°29·2'W	X	147
Trafle	Swan	SS5996	51°38·9'	4°1·9'W	X	159
Trago	Corn	SX1170	50°30·2'	4°39·5'W	X	200
Trago Fm	Corn	SX1864	50°27·1'	4°33·5'W	FM	201
Trago Mills	Corn	SX1764	50°27·1'	4°34·3'W	X	201
Trahenna Hill	Scot Bord	NT1337	55°37·4'	3°22·5'W	H	72
Traian	Conwy	SH9851	53°3·0'	3°30·9'W	X	116
Traian	Gwyn	SH3236	52°54·0'	4°29·5'W	X	123
Traian	Gwyn	SH5444	52°58·7'	4°10·1'W	X	124
Traie Cabbag	I of M	SC2281	54°11·9'	4°43·3'W	X	95
Traie Cronkan	I of M	SC2280	54°11·3'	4°43·3'W	X	95
Traie ny Halsall	I of M	SC4788	54°16·1'	4°20·6'W	X	95
Traie ny Unaig	I of M	SC4889	54°16·7'	4°19·7'W	X	95
Tràigh Allt Chàilgeag	Highld	NC4465	58°33·0'	4°40·4'W	X	9
Tràigh a' Mhachaire	Arg & Bt	NR3249	55°39·9'	6°15·3'W	X	60
Tràigh an Luig	Arg & Bt	NR2763	55°47·3'	6°20·9'W	X	60
Tràigh an Taoibh Thuath	N Eil	NF9891	57°48·7'	7°4·6'W	X	18
Tràigh an t-Seana-chaisteil	N Eil	NF8986	57°45·6'	7°13·3'W	X	18
Tràigh a' Siar	N Eil	NB0001	57°54·1'	7°3·4'W	X	18
Tràigh Bad na Bàighe	Highld	NC2247	58°22·8'	5°2·2'W	W	9
Tràigh Bail'-a-mhuilinn	Arg & Bt	NL9547	56°31·2'	6°57·1'W	X	46
Tràigh Baile Aonghais	Arg & Bt	NR3273	55°52·8'	6°16·7'W	X	60,61
Tràigh Baile Fo Thuath	N Eil	NF9087	57°46·2'	7°12·4'W	X	18
Tràigh Bàn	Arg & Bt	NR4098	56°6·5'	6°10·5'W	X	61
Tràigh Bhàigh	Arg & Bt	NM0043	56°29·3'	6°52·0'W	X	46
Tràigh Bhàn	Arg & Bt	NM3938	56°28·0'	6°13·8'W	X	47,48
Tràigh Bhàn	Arg & Bt	NM4318	56°17·4'	6°8·7'W	X	48
Tràigh Bhàn	Arg & Bt	NR2169	55°50·3'	6°26·9'W	X	60
Tràigh Bhàn	Arg & Bt	NR8265	55°50·0'	5°28·4'W	X	62
Tràigh Bhàn	N Eil	NF7309	57°3·6'	7°23·2'W	X	31
Tràigh Bhàn na Sgùrra	Arg & Bt	NM4218	56°17·3'	6°9·7'W	X	48
Tràigh Bhi	Arg & Bt	NL9440	56°27·4'	6°57·6'W	X	46
Tràigh Bhuidhe	Highld	ND1223	58°11·5'	3°29·3'W	X	17
Tràigh Cadh' an Easa'	Arg & Bt	NM4719	56°18·0'	6°4·9'W	X	48
Tràigh Chornaig	Arg & Bt	NL9748	56°31·8'	6°55·2'W	X	46
Tràigh Chrois	N Eil	NB4962	58°28·7'	6°17·9'W	X	8
Tràigh Chuil	N Eil	NB4638	58°15·7'	6°19·4'W	X	8
Tràigh Chumil	N Eil	NB4963	58°29·2'	6°17·9'W	X	8
Tràigh Cill an Rubha	Arg & Bt	NR3262	55°46·9'	6°16·0'W	X	60,61
Tràigh Cille-bharra	N Eil	NF7106	57°1·9'	7°25·0'W	X	31
Tràigh Dhail	N Eil	NB4862	58°28·7'	6°18·9'W	X	8
Tràigh Doire Dhubhaig	Arg & Bt	NM4936	56°27·2'	6°4·0'W	X	47,48
Tràigh Eachcamais	N Eil	NF7960	57°31·2'	7°21·3'W	X	22
Tràigh Eais	N Eil	NF6906	57°1·8'	7°26·9'W	X	31
Tràigh Ear	N Eil	NF8276	57°40·0'	7°19·5'W	X	18
Tràigh Flèisgein Bheag	Arg & Bt	NR2067	55°49·2'	6°27·8'W	X	60
Tràigh Gheal	Arg & Bt	NM2919	56°17·4'	6°22·3'W	X	48
Tràigh Gheal	Arg & Bt	NM3417	56°16·5'	6°17·4'W	X	48
Tràigh Ghearadha	N Eil	NB5349	58°21·9'	6°12·9'W	X	8
Tràigh Ghioradail	N Eil	NB5446	58°20·3'	6°11·7'W	X	8
Tràigh Ghriais	N Eil	NB4941	58°17·4'	6°16·5'W	X	8
Tràigh Ghrianal	Arg & Bt	NL9344	56°29·5'	6°58·9'W	X	46
Tràigh Ghruineart	Arg & Bt	NR2867	55°49·4'	6°20·1'W	X	60
Tràigh Himiligh	N Eil	NF7876	57°39·8'	7°23·5'W	X	18
Tràigh Ho	Highld	NM6590	56°56·8'	5°51·4'W	X	40
Tràigh Hough	Arg & Bt	NL9346	56°30·6'	6°59·0'W	X	46
Tràigh Iar	N Eil	NF6969	57°35·6'	7°32·0'W	X	18
Tràigh Iar	N Eil	NG0396	57°51·6'	7°0·0'W	X	18
Tràigh Iar	N Eil	NF8176	57°39·9'	7°20·5'W	X	18
Tràigh Leathann	N Eil	NF7763	57°32·8'	7°23·5'W	X	18
Tràigh Losgaintir	N Eil	NG0797	57°52·2'	6°56·0'W	X	14,18
Tràigh man Gilean	Arg & Bt	NL9341	56°27·9'	6°58·6'W	X	46
Tràigh Mhachir	Arg & Bt	NR2063	55°47·0'	6°27·5'W	X	60
Tràigh Mhealaboist	N Eil	NB4535	58°14·1'	6°20·2'W	X	8
Tràigh Mheilein	N Eil	NA9914	58°1·1'	7°5·4'W	X	13
Tràigh Mhòr	Arg & Bt	NM0547	56°31·6'	6°47·4'W	X	46
Tràigh Mhòr	Arg & Bt	NM2823	56°19·5'	6°23·5'W	X	48
Tràigh Mhòr	Arg & Bt	NM3723	56°19·8'	6°14·8'W	X	48
Tràigh Mhòr	N Eil	NB5448	58°21·4'	6°11·8'W	X	8
Tràigh Mhòr	N Eil	NF7005	57°1·3'	7°25·9'W	X	31
Tràigh na Berie	N Eil	NB1035	58°12·8'	6°55·8'W	X	13
Tràigh na Cille	Arg & Bt	NM4045	56°31·8'	6°13·2'W	X	47,48
Tràigh na Cleavag	N Eil	NF9891	57°48·7'	7°4·6'W	X	18
Tràigh na Doirlinn	N Eil	NF7317	57°7·9'	7°23·9'W	X	31
Tràigh na Lùibe	N Eil	NF8581	57°42·8'	7°16·9'W	X	18
Tràigh na Margaidh	Arg & Bt	NM3324	56°20·2'	6°18·8'W	X	48
Tràigh nam Bàrc	Arg & Bt	NR3591	56°2·6'	6°14·9'W	X	61
Tràigh nam Beach	Arg & Bt	NM4624	56°20·7'	6°6·2'W	X	48
Tràigh nam Faoghailean	N Eil	NF7070	57°36·2'	7°31·1'W	X	18
Tràigh nam Musgan	Arg & Bt	NM8008	56°13·1'	5°32·5'W	X	55
Tràigh nan Cisteachan	Arg & Bt	NR2973	55°52·7'	6°19·5'W	X	60
Tràigh na Reill	N Eil	NF7208	57°3·0'	7°24·1'W	X	31
Tràigh Nisabost	N Eil	NG0497	57°52·1'	6°59·1'W	X	18
Tràigh Nòstaig	Arg & Bt	NR2873	55°52·7'	6°20·5'W	X	60
Tràigh Rèbac	N Eil	NB4940	58°16·9'	6°16·4'W	X	8
Tràigh Rosamol	N Eil	NB0600	57°53·8'	6°57·3'W	X	14,18
Tràigh Scarasta	N Eil	NG0093	57°49·8'	7°2·8'W	X	18
Tràigh Scurrival	N Eil	NF7008	57°3·0'	7°26·1'W	X	31
Tràigh Shanndaig	N Eil	NB1837	58°14·2'	6°47·8'W	X	8,13
Tràigh Shanndaigh	N Eil	NB5164	58°29·9'	6°15·9'W	X	8
Tràigh Sheileboist	N Eil	NG0698	57°52·7'	6°57·1'W	X	14,18
Tràigh Shorobaidh	Arg & Bt	NL9842	56°28·7'	6°53·9'W	X	46
Tràigh Shuaineboist	N Eil	NB5063	58°29·3'	6°16·9'W	X	8
Tràigh Stir	N Eil	NF7172	57°37·3'	7°30·2'W	X	18
Tràigh Thodhrasdail	Arg & Bt	NL9344	56°29·5'	6°58·9'W	X	46
Traighuaine	Arg & Bt	NM8009	56°13·6'	5°32·5'W	X	55
Tràigh Uamha Seilbhe	Arg & Bt	NR3687	56°0·5'	6°13·7'W	X	61
Tràigh Udal	N Eil	NF8278	57°41·0'	7°19·7'W	X	18
Tràigh Varlish	N Eil	NL6197	56°56·7'	7°34·1'W	X	31
Tràigh Verral	N Eil	NF7173	57°37·9'	7°30·3'W	X	18
Trailflat	D & G	NY0485	55°9·3'	3°30·0'W	X	78
Trailflat Church	D & G	NY0484	55°8·7'	3°29·9'W	A	78
Trailholme	Lancs	SD4257	54°0·6'	2°52·7'W	X	102
Trail Isle	N Ayr	NS1551	55°43·3'	4°56·3'W	X	63,69
Traillisker	N Eil	NF7208	57°3·0'	7°24·1'W	X	31
Trailtrow	D & G	NY1471	55°1·8'	3°20·3'W	X	85
Trainlands	Cumbr	NY6317	54°33·1'	2°33·9'W	X	91
Trainriggs	Cumbr	NY5715	54°32·0'	2°39·4'W	X	91
Trainriggs	Cumbr	NY7610	54°29·3'	2°21·8'W	X	91
Traitor's Ford	Warw	SP3336	52°1·5'	1°30·7'W	X	151
Tralee	Arg & Bt	NM8939	56°30·0'	5°25·3'W	X	49
Trallong	Powys	SN9629	51°57·2'	3°30·4'W	T	160
Trallwm	Carm	SN4811	51°46·9'	4°11·8'W	X	159
Trallwm	Powys	SN8754	52°10·6'	3°38·8'W	X	147
Trallwn	Rho Cyn Taf	ST0790	51°36·3'	3°20·2'W	T	170
Trallwn	Swan	SS6996	51°39·1'	3°53·2'W	T	170
Trallwng or Welshpool	Powys	SJ2207	52°39·5'	3°8·8'W	T	126
Trallwyn Hall	Gwyn	SH3841	52°56·8'	4°24·3'W	X	123
Tralodden Cott	S Ayr	NX2296	55°13·8'	4°47·5'W	X	76
Tralorg Hill	S Ayr	NX2297	55°14·4'	4°47·6'W	X	76
Tramagenna	Corn	SX0982	50°36·6'	4°41·6'W	T	200
Tramaig Bay	Arg & Bt	NR6588	56°1·9'	5°45·9'W	W	55,61
Tram Inn	Heref	SO4633	51°59·8'	2°46·8'W	T	149,161
Trammins	S Ayr	NX0299	55°15·0'	5°6·5'W	X	76
Tran	Rho Cyn Taf	SS9988	51°35·1'	3°27·1'W	X	170
Tra na h-Uil	Arg & Bt	NS0159	55°47·3'	5°10·0'W	X	63
Tranch	Torf	SO2700	51°41·9'	3°3·0'W	T	171
Trancie Hill	Aberd	NJ4512	57°12·0'	2°54·2'W	H	37
Tranearth	Cumbr	SD2895	54°21·0'	3°6·0'W	X	96,97
Tranent	E Loth	NT4072	55°56·5'	2°57·2'W	T	66
Tranent Mains	E Loth	NT4073	55°57·0'	2°57·2'W	X	66
Tranew	S Ayr	NS3507	55°20·0'	4°35·6'W	X	70,77
Tranew Linn	S Ayr	NS3506	55°19·5'	4°35·6'W	W	70,77
Tranmere	Wirral	SJ3287	53°22·8'	3°0·9'W	T	108
Tranmere Plantn	E Yorks	TA0165	54°4·5'	0°27·0'W	F	101
Tranmire	N Yks	NZ7710	54°29·0'	0°48·3'W	X	94
Tranmire	N Yks	SE1582	54°14·3'	1°45·8'W	X	99
Tranmire Grange	N Yks	NZ7711	54°29·5'	0°48·3'W	X	94
Tranmire Hill	N Yks	SE1483	54°14·8'	1°46·7'W	H	99
Tranmire Moor	N Yks	NZ7711	54°29·5'	0°48·3'W	X	94
Tranmire Plain	N Yks	SE7391	54°18·8'	0°52·3'W	X	94,100
Tranmoor	Cumbr	NY6904	54°26·1'	2°28·3'W	X	91
Tranmoor	Donc	SE6110	53°35·2'	1°4·3'W	X	111
Trannack	Corn	SW5633	50°9·0'	5°24·6'W	X	203
Trannack	Corn	SW6630	50°7·7'	5°16·1'W	X	203
Trannack Downs	Corn	SW6630	50°7·7'	5°16·1'W	H	203
Trannack Fm	Corn	SW4130	50°7·1'	5°37·0'W	FM	203
Tranno	Corn	SW6127	50°5·9'	5°20·2'W	X	203
Trannon	Powys	SN9095	52°32·7'	3°36·9'W	X	136
Trannon	Powys	SN9096	52°33·3'	3°37·0'W	X	136
Transporter Br	Midd	NZ5021	54°35·1'	1°13·2'W	X	93
Transporter Br	Newp	ST3186	51°34·4'	2°59·3'W	X	171
Tranthwaite Hall	Cumbr	SD4693	54°20·0'	2°49·4'W	X	97
Trantlebeg	Highld	NC8953	58°27·3'	3°53·7'W	T	10
Trantlebeg Burn	Highld	NC9153	58°27·4'	3°51·6'W	W	10
Trantlemore	Highld	NC8853	58°27·3'	3°54·7'W	T	10
Tranwell	Northum	NZ1883	55°8·7'	1°42·6'W	T	81
Traolaistoc	N Eil	NB5143	58°18·6'	6°14·6'W	X	8
Trapnell Br	Shrops	SO6372	52°20·9'	2°32·2'W	X	138
Trapnell Brook	Worcs	SO6371	52°20·4'	2°32·2'W	W	138
Trapp	Carm	SN6518	51°50·9'	3°57·2'W	T	159
Trapps Fm	Pemb	SM8818	51°49·5'	5°4·2'W	FM	157
Traprain	E Loth	NT5975	55°58·2'	2°39·0'W	T	67
Traprain Law	E Loth	NT5874	55°57·7'	2°39·9'W	H	67
Traprain Law (Fort)	E Loth	NT5874	55°57·7'	2°39·9'W	A	67
Traps Coppice	Shrops	SJ6202	52°37·1'	2°33·3'W	F	127
Trap's Green	Warw	SP1069	52°19·4'	1°50·8'W	T	139
Trapshill	W Berks	SU3763	51°22·1'	1°27·7'W	T	174
Trap Street	Ches	SJ8268	53°12·8'	2°15·8'W	X	118
Trap, The	Corn	TF4942	52°57·5'	0°13·5'E	X	131
Traquair	Scot Bord	NT3334	55°36·0'	3°3·4'W	T	73
Traquair Bank	Scot Bord	NT3235	55°36·5'	3°4·3'W	X	73
Traquair Ho	Scot Bord	NT3235	55°36·5'	3°4·3'W	A	73
Trasbwll	Conwy	SH7366	53°10·8'	3°53·6'W	X	115
Trash Green	W Berks	SU6569	51°25·2'	1°3·5'W	T	175
Trashy Hill	Lancs	SD4444	53°53·6'	2°50·7'W	X	102
Trasnagh	Scot Bord	NT8244	55°41·6'	2°16·7'W	X	74
Tratland	Orkney	HY4027	59°7·8'	3°2·4'W	X	5,6
Travebank	Angus	NO5235	56°30·5'	2°46·3'W	X	54
Travel	Pemb	SN1128	51°55·3'	4°44·5'W	X	145,158
Traveller's Hill	Suff	TL8474	52°20·2'	0°42·5'E	X	144
Traveller's Hill (Tumulus)	Suff	TL8474	52°20·2'	0°42·5'E	A	144
Travellers' Rest	Carm	SN3819	51°51·0'	4°20·7'W	T	159
Travellers' Rest	Dorset	ST8407	50°52·0'	2°13·3'W	X	194
Travellers Rest	N Yks	SE5169	54°7·1'	1°12·8'W	X	100
Traveller's Rest Fm	N Yks	NZ7810	54°29·0'	0°47·3'W	FM	94
Travers Fm	Hants	SU7747	51°13·2'	0°53·5'W	FM	186
Travley	Powys	SO1742	52°4·4'	3°12·3'W	X	148,161
Trawden	Lancs	SD9138	53°50·5'	2°7·8'W	T	103
Trawler's Fm	W Susx	TQ1424	51°0·5'	0°22·1'W	FM	198
Trawsallt	Cered	SN7770	52°19·1'	3°47·9'W	H	135,147
Trawscoed	Carm	SN5637	52°1·0'	4°5·5'W	X	146
Trawscoed	Gwyn	SH8432	52°52·6'	3°43·0'W	X	124,125
Trawscoed	Powys	SN9332	51°58·8'	3°33·1'W	X	160
Trawscoed	Powys	SN9795	52°32·8'	3°30·7'W	X	136
Trawscoed	Powys	SO0688	52°29·2'	3°22·7'W	X	136
Trawscoed	Powys	SO0834	52°0·0'	3°20·0'W	T	160
Trawscoed	Powys	SO1071	52°20·0'	3°18·9'W	X	136,148
Trawscoed Fm	Powys	SJ2112	52°42·2'	3°9·8'W	FM	126
Trawscoed Hall	Powys	SJ2011	52°41·7'	3°10·6'W	X	126
Trawscoed-hen Fm	Powys	SJ2112	52°42·2'	3°9·8'W	FM	126
Trawsdir	Gwyn	SH5919	52°45·3'	4°5·0'W	X	124
Trawsdre	Carm	SN5415	51°49·1'	4°6·7'W	X	159
Trawsfynydd	Gwyn	SH6410	52°40·5'	4°0·3'W	H	124
Trawsfynydd	Gwyn	SH7035	52°54·0'	3°55·6'W	T	124
Trawsgelli	Powys	SO0699	52°35·1'	3°22·8'W	X	136
Trawsgoed	Cered	SN6773	52°20·6'	3°56·7'W	X	135
Trawsmawr	Carm	SN3724	51°53·7'	4°21·7'W	X	145,159
Trawsnant	Cered	SN3855	52°10·4'	4°21·8'W	X	145
Trawsnant	Cered	SN5666	52°16·6'	4°6·3'W	T	135
Trawsnant	Conwy	SH8043	52°58·5'	3°46·8'W	X	124,125
Trawsnant	Denb	SJ0256	53°5·8'	3°27·4'W	X	116
Trawsnant	Denb	SJ0735	52°54·5'	3°22·6'W	X	125
Trawsnant	Powys	SN9092	52°31·1'	3°36·9'W	W	136
Trawstir	Powys	SO0047	52°7·0'	3°27·2'W	X	147
Trayhill	Devon	SS4828	51°2·1'	4°9·7'W	X	180
Traylesfield Fm	Beds	TL0555	52°11·2'	0°27·4'W	FM	153
Trayne	Devon	SS5446	51°11·9'	4°5·0'W	X	180
Trayne Hills	Devon	SS5346	51°11·9'	4°5·9'W	H	180
Tre Abbot	Flint	SJ1078	53°17·7'	3°20·6'W	X	116
Treable Fm	Devon	SX7192	50°43·0'	3°49·3'W	FM	191
Treadam	Monm	SO3815	51°50·0'	2°53·6'W	T	161
Treaddow	Heref	SO5424	51°55·0'	2°39·7'W	T	162
Treago	Corn	SW7860	50°24·1'	5°7·1'W	X	200
Treago	Heref	SO4923	51°54·4'	2°44·1'W	A	162
Treak Cliff Cavern	Derby	SK1383	53°20·9'	1°47·9'W	X	110
Treal	Corn	SW7116	50°0·2'	5°11·4'W	T	203
Trealabhal	N Eil	NB2623	58°6·9'	6°38·7'W	H	13,14
Trealaw	Rho Cyn Taf	SS9992	51°37·3'	3°27·2'W	T	170
Trealbhan	Arg & Bt	NM3838	56°27·9'	6°14·8'W	X	47,48
Treales	Lancs	SD4432	53°47·1'	2°50·6'W	T	102
Treales Cottage	Lancs	SD4532	53°47·1'	2°49·7'W	X	102
Trealy	Monm	SO4709	51°46·9'	2°45·7'W	X	161
Treamble	Corn	SW7856	50°22·0'	5°6·9'W	T	200
Treanay	N Eil	NF8963	57°33·3'	7°11·5'W	X	18
Trean Fm	Stir	NN6208	56°14·9'	4°13·2'W	FM	57
Tre-Angharad	I of Angl	SH3379	53°17·1'	4°29·9'W	X	114
Tre Anna	I of Angl	SH4566	53°10·4'	4°18·7'W	X	114,115
Trearddur	I of Angl	SH2579	53°17·0'	4°37·1'W	T	114
Trearddur Bay	I of Angl	SH2578	53°16·5'	4°37·1'W	W	114
Treasbeare Fm	Devon	SY0094	50°44·5'	3°24·7'W	FM	192
Treaserth	I of Angl	SH4468	53°11·4'	4°19·7'W	X	114,115
Treasgell	Carm	SN2720	51°51·3'	4°30·3'W	X	145,158
Treaslane	Highld	NG3952	57°29·2'	6°20·9'W	X	23
Treaslane River	Highld	NG3950	57°28·2'	6°20·7'W	W	23
Treasonfield	Cumbr	SD6183	54°14·7'	2°35·5'W	X	97
Treassowe Manor	Corn	SW4933	50°8·9'	5°30·4'W	X	203
Treasurer's House	Somer	ST4619	50°58·3'	2°45·8'W	X	193
Treath	Corn	SW7626	50°5·7'	5°7·6'W	T	204
Treathro	Pemb	SM8939	52°0·8'	5°4·1'W	X	157
Treaton	Fife	NO3202	56°12·6'	3°5·3'W	X	59
Treator	Corn	SW9075	50°32·5'	4°57·5'W	T	200
Tre-Aubrey	V of Glam	ST0372	51°26·6'	3°23·4'W	T	170
Treavarran	Highld	NH5237	57°24·2'	4°27·3'W	X	26
Treave	Corn	SW3827	50°5·4'	5°39·4'W	X	203
Trea Wick	Shetld	HU2859	60°19·1'	1°29·1'W	W	3
Treawick	Shetld	HU5763	60°21·1'	0°57·5'W	X	2
Treb	Orkney	HY7553	59°22·0'	2°25·9'W	X	5
Trebah	Corn	SW7727	50°6·3'	5°6·8'W	X	204
Treban	I of Angl	SH3677	53°16·1'	4°27·1'W	X	114
Trebandy Ho Fm	Heref	SO5420	51°52·8'	2°39·7'W	FM	162
Trebanog	Rho Cyn Taf	SN9407	51°45·3'	3°31·8'W	X	160
Trebanog	Rho Cyn Taf	ST0190	51°36·2'	3°25·4'W	T	170
Trebanog Isaf	Rho Cyn Taf	SN9207	51°45·3'	3°33·5'W	X	160
Trebanos	Nth Pt Talb	SN7103	51°42·9'	3°51·6'W	T	170
Trebant	Corn	SX2380	50°35·8'	4°29·7'W	X	201
Trebant Water	Corn	SX1556	50°22·7'	4°35·7'W	W	201
Trebarber	Corn	SW8662	50°25·4'	5°0·4'W	T	200
Trebared	Cered	SN1747	52°5·7'	4°39·9'W	X	145
Trebarfoote	Corn	SX1899	50°46·0'	4°34·5'W	X	190
Trebarret	Corn	SX1559	50°24·3'	4°35·8'W	X	201
Trebarried	Powys	SO1135	52°0·6'	3°17·4'W	A	161
Trebarrow	Corn	SX2896	50°44·5'	4°25·9'W	X	190
Trebartha	Corn	SX2677	50°34·2'	4°27·1'W	T	201
Trebartha Barton	Corn	SX2677	50°34·2'	4°27·1'W	X	201
Trebarvah	Corn	SW5429	50°6·8'	5°26·1'W	X	203
Trebarvah	Corn	SW7030	50°7·8'	5°12·7'W	X	203
Trebarveth	Corn	SW7920	50°2·6'	5°4·8'W	X	204
Trebarwith	Corn	SX0586	50°38·7'	4°45·1'W	T	200
Trebarwith Strand	Corn	SX0486	50°38·7'	4°46·0'W	T	200

Trebathevy	Corn	SX1055	50°22·1'	4°39·9'W	X	200
Trebblehayes	Devon	ST2606	50°51·2'	3°2·7'W	X	192,193
Trebeath	Corn	SX2587	50°39·6'	4°28·2'W	T	190
Trebedw	Cered	SN3640	52°2·3'	4°23·1'W	X	145
Tre-Beferad	V of Glam	SS9868	51°24·3'	3°27·6'W	T	170
Trebehor	Corn	SW3724	50°3·7'	5°40·1'W	X	203
Trebeigh	Corn	SX3067	50°28·9'	4°23·4'W	X	201
Trebeigh Wood	Corn	SX2966	50°28·4'	4°24·2'W	F	201
Tre-beirdd	Flint	SJ2362	53°9·2'	3°8·7'W	X	117
Trebela	Monm	ST4298	51°40·9'	2°49·9'W	X	171
Trebella	Monm	SO4219	51°52·2'	2°50·2'W	X	161
Trebellan	Corn	SW7857	50°22·5'	5°7·0'W	X	200
Trebell Green	Corn	SX0562	50°25·8'	4°44·4'W	T	200
Trebelsue Fm	Corn	SW8464	50°26·4'	5°2·1'W	FM	200
Tre-berfe	Pemb	SM9731	51°56·7'	4°56·8'W	X	157
Treberfedd	Cered	SN5054	52°10·1'	4°11·2'W	X	146
Treberfydd	Powys	SO1225	51°55·2'	3°16·4'W	T	161
Treberon	Heref	SO5025	51°55·5'	2°43·2'W	X	162
Treberran Fm	Monm	SO4311	51°47·9'	2°49·2'W	FM	161
Treberrick	Corn	SW9543	50°15·3'	4°52·2'W	X	204
Trebersed	Carm	SN3820	51°51·5'	4°20·8'W	X	145,159
Treberth	Pemb	SN1306	51°43·5'	4°42·1'W	X	158
Trebetherick	Corn	SW9378	50°34·1'	4°55·0'W	T	200
Trebetherick Point	Corn	SW9277	50°33·6'	4°55·8'W	X	200
Trebettyn	V of Glam	SS9976	51°28·7'	3°26·9'W	X	170
Trebick	Devon	SX4689	50°41·1'	4°10·4'W	X	190
Trebiffin	Corn	SX1290	50°41·0'	4°39·3'W	X	190
Trebilcock	Corn	SW9960	50°24·6'	4°49·4'W	T	200
Trebinnick	Corn	SX1870	50°30·3'	4°33·6'W	X	201
Trebinshwm Fm	Powys	SO1324	51°54·7'	3°15·5'W	FM	161
Trebisken	Corn	SW7857	50°22·5'	5°7·0'W	X	200
Trebister	Shetld	HU4438	60°7·7'	1°12·0'W	X	4
Trebithick	Corn	SX3277	50°34·4'	4°22·0'W	X	201
Treblary	Corn	SX1587	50°39·4'	4°36·7'W	X	190
Treble House Fm	N Som	ST3868	51°24·7'	2°53·1'W	FM	171,182
Trebler's Fm	E Susx	TQ5428	51°2·1'	0°12·2'E	FM	188,199
Treble's Holford	Somer	ST1533	51°5·6'	3°12·4'W	T	181
Treble Sykes Fm	N Yks	SE4370	54°7·7'	1°20·1'W	FM	99
Treblethick	Corn	SX0573	50°31·7'	4°44·7'W	X	200
Tre-boeth	Pemb	SM9434	51°58·2'	4°59·6'W	X	157
Treboeth	Powys	SO0874	52°21·6'	3°20·7'W	X	136,147
Tre-boeth	Powys	SO2069	52°19·0'	3°10·0'W	X	137,148
Tre-boeth	Rho Cyn Taf	ST0288	51°35·2'	3°24·5'W	X	170
Tre-boeth	Swan	SS6596	51°39·0'	3°56·7'W	T	159
Treborough	Somer	ST0136	51°7·1'	3°24·5'W	T	181
Treborough Common	Somer	ST0035	51°6·6'	3°25·3'W	X	181
Treborough Lodge Fm	Somer	ST0137	51°7·7'	3°24·5'W	FM	181
Treborth Hall	Gwyn	SH5570	53°12·7'	4°9·9'W	X	114,115
Trebost	Corn	SW7438	50°12·2'	5°9·7'W	X	204
Treboul	Corn	SX3457	50°23·6'	4°19·8'W	X	201
Trebover	Pemb	SM9635	51°58·8'	4°57·8'W	X	157
Trebowland	Corn	SW7338	50°12·1'	5°10·5'W	X	204
Trebray	Corn	SX1982	50°36·8'	4°33·1'W	X	201
Trebreak	Corn	SX2190	50°41·2'	4°31·7'W	X	190
Trebrodier	Shrops	SO1980	52°25·0'	3°11·1'W	X	136
Trebrowen	Pemb	SR9199	51°39·3'	5°0·9'W	X	158
Trebrown	Corn	SX3363	50°26·8'	4°20·8'W	X	201
Trebrownbridge Wood	Corn	SX2959	50°24·6'	4°24·0'W	F	201
Tre-bryn	Brig	SS9482	51°31·9'	3°31·3'W	X	170
Tre-brys	Powys	SJ1525	52°49·2'	3°15·3'W	X	125
Trebrython	Pemb	SM9334	51°58·2'	5°0·4'W	X	157
Trebudannon	Corn	SW8961	50°24·9'	4°57·8'W	T	200
Trebullett	Corn	SX3278	50°34·9'	4°22·0'W	T	201
Treburgett	Corn	SX0579	50°34·9'	4°44·9'W	T	200
Treburgie	Corn	SX2064	50°27·1'	4°31·8'W	T	201
Treburick Fm	Corn	SW8972	50°30·8'	4°58·2'W	FM	200
Treburland	Corn	SX2379	50°35·3'	4°29·7'W	X	201
Treburley	Corn	SX3477	50°34·4'	4°20·3'W	T	201
Treburrick	Corn	SW8670	50°29·7'	5°0·7'W	T	200
Treburrow	Corn	SX2587	50°39·6'	4°28·2'W	X	190
Trebursye Manor	Corn	SX3083	50°37·6'	4°23·8'W	X	201
Trebursye Oak	Corn	SX3084	50°38·1'	4°23·9'W	X	201
Treburthes	Corn	SW9140	50°13·6'	4°55·4'W	X	204
Treburtle	Corn	SX2488	50°40·1'	4°29·1'W	X	190
Treburvaugh	Powys	SO2369	52°19·1'	3°7·4'W	X	137,148
Trebwl	Carm	SN4227	51°55·4'	4°17·5'W	X	146
Trebwlch	Pemb	SN0835	51°59·1'	4°47·4'W	X	145
Trebyan	Corn	SX0763	50°26·3'	4°42·7'W	T	200
Treby Fm	Devon	SX5953	50°21·8'	3°58·6'W	FM	202
Trebyla Fm	Corn	SX1192	50°42·1'	4°40·2'W	FM	190
Tre-Cadifor	Heref	SO3335	52°0·8'	2°58·2'W	X	149,161
Trecadifor	Pemb	SN0237	52°0·0'	4°52·7'W	X	145,157
Trecadwgan	Pemb	SM8125	51°53·1'	5°10·5'W	X	157
Trecagal	Cered	SN3841	52°2·9'	4°21·4'W	X	145
Trecaine	Corn	SW9647	50°17·5'	4°51·5'W	X	204
Trecangate	Corn	SX1659	50°24·4'	4°35·0'W	X	201
Trecarne	Corn	SX0980	50°35·5'	4°41·5'W	X	200
Trecarne	Corn	SX2468	50°29·4'	4°28·5'W	X	201
Trecarne Fm	Corn	SX0585	50°38·2'	4°45·1'W	FM	200
Trecarrell Br	Corn	SX3277	50°34·4'	4°22·0'W	X	201
Trecarrell Manor	Corn	SX3178	50°34·9'	4°22·9'W	A	201
Trecastell	I of Angl	SH3370	53°12·3'	4°29·6'W	X	114
Tre-castell	I of Angl	SH6178	53°17·1'	4°4·7'W	X	114,115
Trecastell	Rho Cyn Taf	ST0181	51°31·4'	3°25·2'W	X	170
Trecastle	Monm	SO4506	51°45·2'	2°47·4'W	X	161
Trecastle	Powys	SN8829	51°57·1'	3°37·4'W	T	160
Trecco Bay	Brig	SS8376	51°28·5'	3°40·7'W	W	170
Trecefel	Cered	SN6658	52°12·5'	3°57·3'W	X	146
Tre-cefn	Cered	SN2050	52°7·4'	4°37·4'W	X	145
Trecenydd	Caer	ST1487	51°34·8'	3°14·1'W	T	171
Treclago	Corn	SX1082	50°36·6'	4°40·8'W	X	200
Treclyn	Pemb	SN1438	52°0·8'	4°42·2'W	X	145
Trecoed	Pemb	SM9232	51°57·1'	5°1·2'W	X	157
Trecoed	Powys	SO0555	52°11·3'	3°23·0'W	X	147
Trecoll	Cered	SN6462	52°14·6'	3°59·1'W	X	146
Trecollas Fm	Corn	SX2083	50°37·4'	4°32·3'W	FM	201
Trecombe	Corn	SW7629	50°7·4'	5°7·7'W	X	204
Trecombe	Corn	SX3777	50°34·4'	4°17·7'W	X	201
Trecongdon	Corn	SX2982	50°37·0'	4°24·7'W	X	201
Trecor	Carm	SN3710	51°46·1'	4°21·4'W	X	159
Trecorme	Corn	SX3264	50°27·3'	4°21·6'W	X	201
Trecorner	Corn	SX2480	50°35·8'	4°28·8'W	X	201
Trecott	Devon	SS6300	50°47·2'	3°56·2'W	T	191
Trecregyn	Cered	SN2551	52°8·0'	4°33·0'W	X	145
Trecregyn Fm	Cered	SN3354	52°9·8'	4°26·1'W	FM	145
Trecrogo	Corn	SX3080	50°35·9'	4°23·8'W	X	201
Tre-cŵm	Pemb	SN1540	52°1·9'	4°41·4'W	X	145
Trecwn	Pemb	SM9632	51°57·2'	4°57·7'W	T	157
Trecwn	Pemb	SM9732	51°57·2'	4°56·9'W	T	157
Trecwn Isaf	Pemb	SN1447	52°5·6'	4°42·5'W	X	145
Trecynon	Rho Cyn Taf	SN9903	51°43·2'	3°27·3'W	T	170
Trecyrn	Carm	SN2426	51°54·5'	4°33·1'W	X	145,158
Tredafydd	Pemb	SM9333	51°57·7'	5°0·4'W	X	157
Tredafydd	Pemb	SN0234	51°58·4'	4°52·6'W	X	145,157
Tredallett	Corn	SX2456	50°22·9'	4°28·2'W	X	201
Tredannick	Corn	SX0171	50°30·5'	4°48·0'W	T	200
Tredarras	Corn	SX2080	50°35·8'	4°32·2'W	X	201
Tredarren	Carm	SN4029	51°56·4'	4°19·3'W	T	146
Tredarrup	Corn	SX0779	50°35·0'	4°43·2'W	X	200
Tredarrup	Corn	SX1990	50°41·1'	4°33·4'W	X	190
Tredarrup Fm	Corn	SX1666	50°28·1'	4°35·2'W	FM	201
Tredaule	Corn	SX2381	50°36·3'	4°29·7'W	T	201
Tredavoe	Corn	SW4528	50°6·1'	5°33·6'W	T	203
Treddafydd	Cered	SN3051	52°8·1'	4°28·6'W	X	145
Tre-Ddafydd-isaf	I of Angl	SH3871	53°12·9'	4°25·2'W	X	114
Tre-Ddafydd-uchaf	I of Angl	SH3870	53°12·4'	4°25·1'W	X	114
Treddiog	Pemb	SM8828	51°54·9'	5°4·6'W	X	157
Treddolphin	I of Angl	SH3675	53°15·0'	4°27·1'W	X	114
Tredean	Monm	ST4799	51°41·5'	2°45·6'W	X	171
Tredean Fm	Monm	SO4700	51°42·0'	2°45·6'W	FM	171
Tredefaid	Pemb	SN1643	52°3·5'	4°40·6'W	X	145
Tre-deg	Powys	SN7511	51°47·3'	3°48·3'W	X	160
Tredegar	Blae Gw	SO1409	51°46·6'	3°14·4'W	T	161
Tredegar-fawr	Swan	SS6399	51°40·6'	3°58·5'W	X	159
Tredegar House Country Park	Newp	ST2885	51°33·8'	3°1·9'W	X	171
Tredegar Patch	Blae Gw	SO1209	51°46·6'	3°16·1'W	X	161
Tredellans	Corn	SW8537	50°11·9'	5°0·4'W	X	204
Tredenham	Corn	SX0463	50°26·3'	4°45·2'W	X	200
Tre-derwen	Powys	SJ2319	52°46·0'	3°8·1'W	T	126
Trederwen	Powys	SJ2715	52°43·9'	3°4·5'W	T	126
Trederwen Feibion Gwnwas	Powys	SJ2616	52°44·4'	3°5·4'W	X	126
Trederwen Hall	Powys	SJ2615	52°43·9'	3°5·4'W	X	126
Tredethick	Corn	SX1158	50°23·7'	4°39·2'W	X	200
Tredethy	Corn	SX0671	50°30·6'	4°43·8'W	T	200
Tredidon Barton	Corn	SX2784	50°38·0'	4°26·4'W	X	201
Tredilion Park	Monm	SO3114	51°49·5'	2°59·7'W	X	161
Tredington	Glos	SO9029	51°57·8'	2°8·3'W	T	150,163
Tredington	Warw	SP2543	52°5·3'	1°37·7'W	T	151
Tredington Court	Glos	SO9029	51°57·8'	2°8·3'W	A	150,163
Tredington Hills	Warw	SP2542	52°4·8'	1°37·7'W	H	151
Tredinney	Corn	SW3928	50°5·9'	5°38·6'W	X	203
Tredinnick	Corn	SW4434	50°9·3'	5°34·7'W	T	203
Tredinnick	Corn	SW9242	50°14·7'	4°54·7'W	X	204
Tredinnick	Corn	SW9270	50°29·8'	4°55·6'W	T	200
Tredinnick	Corn	SX0459	50°24·1'	4°45·1'W	T	200
Tredinnick	Corn	SX0473	50°31·7'	4°45·6'W	X	200
Tredinnick	Corn	SX0762	50°25·8'	4°42·7'W	X	200
Tredinnick	Corn	SX1666	50°28·1'	4°35·2'W	T	201
Tredinnick	Corn	SX2357	50°23·4'	4°29·0'W	T	201
Tredinnick	Corn	SX2957	50°23·5'	4°24·0'W	X	201
Tredinnick	Corn	SX3559	50°24·7'	4°19·0'W	X	201
Tredinnick Fm	Corn	SW8656	50°22·1'	5°0·2'W	FM	200
Tredis	Corn	SX3555	50°22·5'	4°18·9'W	X	201
Tredivett	Corn	SX3481	50°36·5'	4°20·4'W	X	201
Tre-Dodridge	V of Glam	ST0577	51°29·3'	3°21·7'W	X	170
Tredogan	V of Glam	ST0767	51°23·9'	3°19·8'W	T	170
Tredole Fm	Corn	SX0989	50°40·4'	4°41·8'W	FM	190,200
Tredomen	Caer	ST1394	51°38·5'	3°15·0'W	T	171
Tre-domen	Carm	SN6041	52°3·2'	4°2·1'W	X	146
Tredomen	Pemb	SN7624	51°54·3'	3°47·8'W	X	160
Tredomen	Powys	SO1231	51°58·5'	3°16·5'W	T	161
Tredomen Court	Powys	SO1231	51°58·5'	3°16·5'W	X	161
Tredon Fm	Cambs	TL3971	52°19·4'	0°2·8'E	FM	154
Tredore	Corn	SW9272	50°30·9'	4°55·7'W	X	200
Tredorn Fm	Corn	SX1089	50°40·4'	4°41·0'W	FM	190,200
Tredower	Corn	SW9775	50°32·6'	4°51·5'W	X	200
Tredown	Corn	SX2091	50°41·7'	4°32·5'W	X	190
Tredown	Devon	SS2318	50°56·3'	4°30·8'W	T	190
Tredown	Devon	SS3802	50°47·9'	4°17·6'W	X	190
Tredown	Devon	SX3980	50°36·1'	4°16·1'W	X	201
Tredown	Devon	SX4092	50°42·6'	4°15·6'W	X	190
Tredrea Manor	Corn	SW5434	50°9·5'	5°26·3'W	X	203
Tredrizzick	Corn	SW9576	50°33·1'	4°53·3'W	T	200
Tredrossel	Corn	SX3555	50°22·5'	4°18·9'W	X	201
Tredruston Fm	Corn	SW9671	50°30·4'	4°52·3'W	FM	200
Tre-Drŵy	I of Angl	SH4667	53°10·9'	4°17·9'W	X	114,115
Tredudwell	Corn	SX1552	50°20·6'	4°35·6'W	X	201
Tredundle	Corn	SX2684	50°38·0'	4°27·3'W	X	201
Tredunnock	Heref	SO5220	51°52·8'	2°41·4'W	X	162
Tredunnock	Monm	ST3794	51°38·7'	2°54·2'W	T	171
Tredurn	Powys	SO1134	52°0·1'	3°17·4'W	X	161
Tredustan	Powys	SO1332	51°59·0'	3°15·6'W	T	161
Tredwen Barton	Corn	SX1785	50°38·4'	4°34·9'W	X	201
Tredworth	Glos	SO8417	51°51·3'	2°13·5'W	T	162
Tree	Devon	SS8009	50°52·3'	3°41·9'W	X	191
Tree Beech	Devon	SS6333	51°5·0'	3°57·0'W	X	180
Tree Bridge Fm	N Yks	NZ5412	54°30·3'	1°9·5'W	FM	93
Tree Cathedral	Beds	TL0018	51°51·3'	0°32·5'W	X	166
Tre-Eden-Owain	Flint	SJ1577	53°17·2'	3°16·1'W	X	116
Tree Fm	Suff	TL6478	52°22·8'	0°25·0'E	FM	143
Tree Geo	Highld	ND3677	58°40·8'	3°5·7'W	X	7,12
Treehead	Aberd	NO7672	56°50·6'	2°23·2'W	X	45
Treehill Fm	Pemb	SM7708	51°43·8'	5°13·4'W	FM	157
Treemans	W Susx	TQ3726	51°1·2'	0°2·4'W	A	187,198
Treen	Corn	SW3923	50°3·2'	5°38·4'W	T	203
Treen	Corn	SW4337	50°10·9'	5°35·6'W	T	203
Treeroot	Aberd	NJ7943	57°28·9'	2°20·6'W	X	29,30
Trees	Aberd	NO8294	57°2·5'	2°17·3'W	X	38,45
Trees	Cumbr	NY2055	54°53·3'	3°14·4'W	X	85
Trees	N Yks	SD7755	53°59·7'	2°20·6'W	X	103
Trees	S Ayr	NS2711	55°22·0'	4°43·4'W	X	70
Trees	S Ayr	NS3818	55°26·0'	4°33·2'W	X	70
Treesbank Fm	N Lanak	NS8864	55°51·6'	3°46·9'W	FM	65
Treesbank Ho	E Ayr	NS4234	55°34·7'	4°30·0'W	X	70
Trees Fm	E Ayr	NS4433	55°34·2'	4°28·0'W	FM	70
Trees Fm	Lancs	SD3744	53°53·5'	2°57·1'W	FM	102
Trees Fm	W Loth	NS9467	55°53·3'	3°41·3'W	FM	65
Treeshill	E Ayr	NS5222	55°28·4'	4°20·1'W	X	70
Trees House Fm	Durham	NZ0512	54°30·4'	1°54·9'W	FM	92
Treesmax	E Ayr	NS4618	55°26·2'	4°25·6'W	X	70
Treesmill	Corn	SX0855	50°22·1'	4°41·6'W	T	200
Tre Essey	Heref	SO5021	51°53·4'	2°43·2'W	X	162
Tre Essey Cross	Heref	SO5021	51°53·4'	2°43·2'W	X	162
Treeton	Highld	NH7853	57°33·3'	4°1·9'W	X	27
Treeton	Roth	SK4387	53°22·9'	1°20·8'W	T	111,120
Tree Tops Fm	Lincs	TF2577	53°16·7'	0°7·1'W	FM	122
Treeve Fm	Corn	SW5839	50°12·3'	5°23·1'W	FM	203
Trefach	Carm	SN1927	51°55·0'	4°37·5'W	X	145,158
Trefach	Carm	SN2226	51°54·5'	4°34·9'W	X	145,158
Trefach	Pemb	SN0635	51°59·0'	4°49·1'W	X	145
Trefach	Pemb	SN0841	52°2·3'	4°47·6'W	X	145
Trefach	Pemb	SN1429	51°55·9'	4°41·9'W	X	145,158
Trefach	Pemb	SN1736	51°59·8'	4°39·6'W	X	145
Trefadog	I of Angl	SH2986	53°20·8'	4°33·7'W	X	114
Tre-faes	Cered	SN6073	52°20·5'	4°2·9'W	X	135
Trefaes	Gwyn	SH2532	52°51·7'	4°35·6'W	T	123
Trefaes-Fach	Cered	SN2746	52°5·4'	4°31·1'W	X	145
Trefaes Fawr	Gwyn	SH2531	52°51·1'	4°35·5'W	X	123
Trefaes Ganol	Pemb	SN1142	52°2·9'	4°45·0'W	X	145
Trefaes Isaf	Pemb	SN1243	52°3·5'	4°44·1'W	X	145
Trefaldu	Monm	SO4608	51°46·3'	2°46·6'W	X	161
Trefan	Gwyn	SH4839	52°55·9'	4°15·3'W	X	123
Trefan	Powys	SN9352	52°9·6'	3°33·5'W	X	147
Trefaner	Pemb	SM8526	51°53·7'	5°7·1'W	X	157
Trefanny Hill	Corn	SX2057	50°23·4'	4°31·6'W	T	201
Trefarclawdd	Shrops	SJ2627	52°50·4'	3°5·5'W	X	126
Trefasser	Pemb	SM8937	51°59·7'	5°4·0'W	T	157
Tre-fawr	Carm	SN8439	52°2·5'	3°41·1'W	X	160
Tre fawr	Pemb	SN2230	51°56·6'	4°35·0'W	X	145
Trefayog	Pemb	SM9037	51°59·7'	5°3·2'W	X	157
Trefcaereinion	Powys	SH8309	52°40·2'	3°43·4'W	X	124,125
Trefdraeth	I of Angl	SH4070	53°12·4'	4°23·3'W	T	114,115
Trefeca	Powys	SO1432	51°59·0'	3°14·7'W	T	161
Trefecca fawr	Powys	SO1431	51°58·5'	3°14·7'W	A	161
Tre-fechan	Carm	SN3920	51°51·6'	4°19·9'W	X	145,159
Trefechan	Cered	SN5881	52°24·8'	4°4·9'W	T	135
Trefechan	Merth Tyd	SO0308	51°46·0'	3°24·0'W	T	160
Trefechan	Wrex	SJ2645	53°0·1'	3°5·8'W	T	117
Trefeddian Fm	Gwyn	SN6096	52°32·9'	4°3·5'W	FM	135
Trefedlin	Cered	SN5875	52°21·5'	4°4·7'W	X	135
Trefeglwys	Powys	SN9790	52°30·1'	3°30·6'W	T	136
Trefeiddan	Pemb	SM7325	51°52·9'	5°17·5'W	X	157
Trefeilir	I of Angl	SH4071	53°13·0'	4°23·4'W	X	114,115
Trefeiliw	Powys	SJ1524	52°48·7'	3°15·3'W	X	125
Trefeinon Fm	Powys	SO1330	51°57·9'	3°15·6'W	FM	161
Trefeitha	Powys	SO1031	51°58·5'	3°18·2'W	T	161
Trefelgarn	Pemb	SM9135	51°58·7'	5°2·2'W	X	157
Trefelyn	Pemb	SM8632	51°57·0'	5°6·5'W	X	157
Trefenter	Cered	SN6068	52°17·8'	4°2·8'W	T	135
Trefenty	Carm	SN2913	51°47·6'	4°28·4'W	X	159
Treferanon Fm	Heref	SO4724	51°55·0'	2°45·8'W	FM	161
Trefere	Cered	SN2149	52°6·9'	4°36·5'W	X	145
Treferig Ho	Rho Cyn Taf	ST0387	51°34·6'	3°23·6'W	X	170
Treferwydd	I of Angl	SH3779	53°17·2'	4°26·3'W	X	114
Tre-ferwydd	I of Angl	SH4670	53°12·5'	4°18·0'W	X	114,115
Tref-erwyn	Gwyn	SH2637	52°54·4'	4°34·8'W	X	123
Treferyn	Pemb	SM7929	51°55·2'	5°12·4'W	X	157
Treffgarne	Pemb	SM9523	51°52·3'	4°58·3'W	T	157,158
Treffgarne	Pemb	SN1513	51°47·3'	4°40·6'W	X	158
Treffos	I of Angl	SH5475	53°15·4'	4°10·9'W	X	114,115
Treffry	Corn	SW8645	50°16·2'	4°59·8'W	X	204
Treffry	Corn	SX0763	50°26·3'	4°42·7'W	X	200
Treffry Viaduct	Corn	SX0557	50°23·1'	4°44·2'W	X	200
Treffynnon	Pemb	SM8428	51°54·8'	5°8·0'W	T	157
Treffynnon or Holywell	Flint	SJ1875	53°16·2'	3°13·4'W	T	116
Treffgarn Owen	Pemb	SM8625	51°53·2'	5°6·2'W	T	157
Trefgraig	Gwyn	SH1931	52°51·0'	4°40·9'W	X	123
Trefigin	Pemb	SN1443	52°3·5'	4°42·4'W	X	145
Trefil	Blae Gw	SO1212	51°48·2'	3°16·2'W	T	161
Trefilan	Cered	SN5457	52°11·8'	4°7·8'W	T	146
Trefil Ddu	Blae Gw	SO1113	51°48·8'	3°17·1'W	X	161
Trefil Las	Blae Gw	SO1213	51°48·8'	3°16·2'W	X	161
Trefin	Pemb	SM8332	51°56·9'	5°9·1'W	T	157
Trefinnick	Corn	SX3274	50°32·7'	4°21·9'W	X	201
Treflach	Shrops	SJ2625	52°49·3'	3°5·5'W	T	126
Treflach Fm	Shrops	SJ2725	52°49·3'	3°4·6'W	FM	126
Treflach Hall	Shrops	SJ2725	52°49·3'	3°4·6'W	X	126
Treflan-isaf	Gwyn	SH5358	53°6·2'	4°11·3'W	X	115
Treflech	Conwy	SH9568	53°12·2'	3°33·9'W	X	116
Treflesg	I of Angl	SH3077	53°16·0'	4°32·5'W	X	114
Trefloyne	Pemb	SS1099	51°39·7'	4°44·4'W	X	158
Treflyn	Cered	SN6962	52°14·7'	3°54·7'W	X	146
Treflyn	Powys	SO0164	52°16·2'	3°26·7'W	X	147
Treflys	Cered	SN5869	52°18·3'	4°4·6'W	X	135
Tref-nannau Bank	Powys	SJ2316	52°44·4'	3°8·0'W	X	126
Trefnanney	Powys	SJ2015	52°43·8'	3°10·7'W	T	126
Trefnanney Fm	Powys	SJ1915	52°43·8'	3°11·6'W	FM	125
Trefnant	Denb	SJ0570	53°13·4'	3°25·0'W	T	116
Trefnant	I of Angl	SH4971	53°13·1'	4°15·3'W	X	114,115
Trefnant	Powys	SJ1809	52°40·6'	3°12·4'W	X	125
Trefnant Hall	Powys	SJ1803	52°37·4'	3°12·3'W	A	136
Trefnant Hall Fm	Shrops	SJ3010	52°41·2'	3°1·7'W	FM	126
Trefochlyd Fm	Pemb	SM8129	51°55·2'	5°10·7'W	FM	157
Tre-foel	Powys	SO1379	52°24·4'	3°16·3'W	X	136,148
Trefollwyn	Gwyn	SH2637	52°49·0'	4°34·5'W	X	123
Trefollwyn	I of Angl	SH4577	53°16·3'	4°19·1'W	X	114,115
Trefonen	Shrops	SJ2526	52°49·8'	3°6·4'W	T	126
Trefonen Hall	Shrops	SJ2426	52°49·8'	3°7·3'W	X	126

Trefor	Gwyn	SH3746	52°59·4′	4°25·3′W	T	123
Trefor	I of Angl	SH3780	53°17·8′	4°26·3′W	T	114
Trefor	I of Angl	SH5477	53°16·4′	4°11·0′W	X	114,115
Treforda	Corn	SX0781	50°36·0′	4°43·3′W	T	200
Treforda	Corn	SX0988	50°39·9′	4°41·8′W	X	190,200
Treforda	Corn	SX2096	50°44·4′	4°32·7′W	X	190
Treforest	Rho Cyn Taf	ST0888	51°35·2′	3°19·3′W	T	170
Treforest Industrial Estate	Rho Cyn Taf	ST1086	51°34·2′	3°17·5′W	X	171
Treforgan	Cered	SN2046	52°5·2′	4°37·2′W	T	145
Tre-Forgan	Nth Pt Talb	SN7906	51°44·6′	3°44·8′W	T	160
Treforis Fach	Carm	SN3809	51°45·6′	4°20·5′W	X	159
Treforris Fawr	Carm	SN3809	51°45·6′	4°20·5′W	X	159
Trefran	Cered	SN5757	52°11·8′	4°5·1′W	X	146
Tre-Frân	Rho Cyn Taf	SS9880	51°30·8′	3°27·8′W	X	170
Trefranck	Corn	SX2084	50°37·9′	4°32·3′W	X	201
Trefrane	Pemb	SM8620	51°50·5′	5°6·0′W	X	157
Trefrawl	Corn	SX1654	50°21·7′	4°34·8′W	X	201
Trefreock	Corn	SW9979	50°34·8′	4°50·0′W	X	200
Trefresa Fm	Corn	SW9475	50°32·5′	4°54·1′W	FM	200
Trefrew	Corn	SX1084	50°37·7′	4°40·8′W	X	200
Trefri	Gwyn	SN6396	52°32·9′	4°0·8′W	X	135
Trefri	I of Angl	SH3666	53°10·2′	4°26·8′W	X	114
Trefrida	Corn	SX1996	50°44·4′	4°33·5′W	X	190
Trefrifawr	Gwyn	SN6397	52°33·5′	4°0·9′W	X	135
Trefriw	Conwy	SH7863	53°9·3′	3°49·1′W	T	115
Trefriw-fawr	Cered	SN6970	52°19·0′	3°54·9′W	X	135
Trefrize	Corn	SX3076	50°33·8′	4°23·6′W	T	201
Trefronick Fm	Corn	SW8251	50°19·4′	5°3·4′W	FM	200,204
Trefrouse	Corn	SX2398	50°45·5′	4°30·2′W	X	190
Trefrwd	Flint	SJ2259	53°7·6′	3°9·5′W	X	117
Trefuge	Corn	SX2877	50°34·3′	4°25·4′W	X	201
Trefula	Corn	SW7142	50°14·3′	5°12·3′W	X	203
Trefullock Fms	Corn	SW8955	50°21·7′	4°57·6′W	FM	200
Trefursdon	Corn	SX2293	50°42·8′	4°30·9′W	X	190
Trefusis	Corn	SW8134	50°10·2′	5°3·6′W	X	204
Trefusis Fm	Somer	ST1623	51°0·3′	3°11·5′W	FM	181,193
Trefusis Point	Corn	SW8133	50°9·6′	5°3·6′W	X	204
Trefwrdan	Pemb	SN0942	52°2·9′	4°46·7′W	X	145
Trefwtial	Cered	SN2348	52°6·4′	4°34·7′W	X	145
Trefwynt Fm	Pemb	SN0818	51°49·9′	4°46·8′W	FM	158
Tref-y-Clawdd or Knighton	Powys	SO2872	52°20·7′	3°3·0′W	T	137,148
Trefydd Bychain	Denb	SJ2050	53°2·7′	3°11·2′W	X	117
Tref-y-nant	Denb	SJ2742	52°58·5′	3°4·8′W	X	117
Tre-fynor	Cered	SN5756	52°11·3′	4°5·1′W	X	146
Trefynwy or Monmouth	Monm	SO5012	51°48·5′	2°43·1′W	T	162
Trefynys	Carm	SN4224	51°53·8′	4°17·4′W	X	159
Tregada	Corn	SX3481	50°36·5′	4°20·4′W	T	201
Tregaddick	Corn	SX0873	50°31·8′	4°42·2′W	X	200
Tregaddock	Corn	SX0573	50°31·7′	4°44·7′W	X	200
Tregaddra	Corn	SW7021	50°2·9′	5°12·4′W	X	203
Tregadgwith	Corn	SW4225	50°4·4′	5°36·0′W	T	203
Tregadillett	Corn	SX2983	50°37·5′	4°24·7′W	T	201
Tregadjack	Corn	SW4933	50°8·9′	5°30·4′W	X	203
Tregadjack	Corn	SW7022	50°3·5′	5°12·4′W	X	203
Tregaer	Powys	SO0724	51°54·6′	3°20·7′W	X	160
Tre-gagle	Monm	SO5207	51°45·8′	2°41·3′W	T	162
Tregaian	I of Angl	SH4579	53°17·4′	4°19·1′W	T	114,115
Tregain	Corn	SW9747	50°17·5′	4°50·6′W	X	204
Tregaina	Corn	SX0989	50°40·4′	4°41·8′W	X	190,200
Tregairewoon Fm	Corn	SW8738	50°12·5′	4°58·7′W	FM	204
Tregair Fm	Corn	SW8258	50°23·1′	5°3·6′W	FM	200
Tregajorran	Corn	SW6740	50°13·1′	5°15·6′W	T	203
Tregaller	Corn	SX3182	50°37·0′	4°23·0′W	X	201
Tregallet	Pemb	SN1209	51°45·1′	4°43·0′W	X	158
Tregallon	D & G	NX9374	55°3·2′	3°40·1′W	X	84
Tregamellyn	Corn	SX1753	50°21·1′	4°34·0′W	X	201
Tregamenna Manor Fm	Corn	SW9138	50°12·5′	4°55·4′W	FM	204
Tregamere	Corn	SW9264	50°26·6′	4°55·4′W	T	200
Tregaminion	Corn	SW7922	50°3·7′	5°4·9′W	X	204
Tregaminion	Corn	SX0952	50°20·5′	4°40·7′W	X	200,204
Tregamman	Pemb	SN1042	52°2·9′	4°45·9′W	X	145
Tregandanel	Corn	SW9851	50°19·7′	4°49·9′W	X	200,204
Treganhoe	Corn	SW4229	50°6·5′	5°36·1′W	X	203
Treganoon	Corn	SX0658	50°23·6′	4°43·4′W	X	200
Tregantallan	Corn	SW7132	50°8·9′	5°12·0′W	X	203
Tregantle Cliff	Corn	SX3852	50°21·0′	4°16·3′W	X	201
Tregantle Fm	Corn	SX0659	50°24·2′	4°43·4′W	FM	200
Tregantle Fort	Corn	SX3853	50°21·5′	4°16·3′W	A	201
Tregarden	Corn	SX0272	50°31·1′	4°47·2′W	A	200
Tregardock	Corn	SX0483	50°37·1′	4°45·9′W	T	200
Tregardock Beach	Corn	SX0484	50°37·6′	4°45·9′W	X	200
Tregardock Cliff	Corn	SX0483	50°37·1′	4°45·9′W	X	200
Tregare	Monm	SO4110	51°47·4′	2°50·9′W	T	161
Tregargus	Corn	SW9453	50°20·7′	4°53·4′W	T	200,204
Tregarland	Corn	SX2557	50°23·4′	4°27·3′W	T	201
Tregarlandbridge	Corn	SX2457	50°23·4′	4°28·2′W	T	201
Tregarne	Corn	SW7822	50°3·6′	5°5·7′W	T	204
Tregarnedd	Gwyn	SH2535	52°53·3′	4°35·7′W	X	123
Tregarnedd Fawr	I of Angl	SH4775	53°15·2′	4°17·2′W	X	114,115
Tregaron	Cered	SN6759	52°13·0′	3°56·4′W	T	146
Tregarrick	Corn	SX0776	50°33·4′	4°43·1′W	X	200
Tregarrick Fm	Corn	SX1955	50°22·3′	4°32·3′W	FM	201
Tregarrick Mill	Corn	SX2057	50°23·4′	4°31·6′W	T	201
Tregarrick Tor	Corn	SX2471	50°31·0′	4°28·6′W	X	201
Tregarrick Wood	Corn	SX2056	50°22·8′	4°31·5′W	F	201
Tregartha	Corn	SX2765	50°27·8′	4°25·9′W	X	201
Tregarthen	Corn	SW4932	50°8·3′	5°30·4′W	X	203
Tregarton Fm	Corn	SW9843	50°15·4′	4°49·7′W	FM	204
Tregassa	Corn	SW8735	50°10·8′	4°58·6′W	X	204
Tregassick	Corn	SW8634	50°10·3′	4°59·4′W	X	204
Tregasso	Corn	SW7824	50°4·7′	5°5·8′W	X	204
Tregassow	Corn	SW8548	50°17·8′	5°0·8′W	X	204
Tregastick	Corn	SX2859	50°24·6′	4°24·9′W	X	201
Tregaswith	Corn	SW8962	50°25·4′	4°57·9′W	X	200
Tregate Bridge	Monm	SO4717	51°51·2′	2°45·8′W	X	161
Tregate Fm	Heref	SO4817	51°51·2′	2°44·9′W	FM	161
Tregath	Corn	SX1084	50°37·7′	4°40·8′W	X	200
Tregath	Gwyn	SH6067	53°11·1′	4°5·3′W	T	115
Tregathenan	Corn	SW6530	50°7·6′	5°16·9′W	X	203
Tregatherall Fm	Corn	SX1189	50°40·4′	4°40·1′W	FM	190,200

Tregatillian	Corn	SW9263	50°26·0′	4°55·4′W	T	200
Tregatta	Corn	SX0587	50°39·2′	4°45·1′W	T	200
Tregavarah	Corn	SW4429	50°6·6′	5°34·5′W	T	203
Tregavarras	Corn	SW9841	50°14·3′	4°49·6′W	X	204
Tregaverne	Corn	SX0180	50°35·4′	4°48·3′W	X	200
Tregavethan Manor	Corn	SW7847	50°17·1′	5°6·6′W	X	204
Tregavithick	Corn	SX1752	50°20·6′	4°33·9′W	X	201
Tregavone Fm	Corn	SW8973	50°31·4′	4°58·2′W	FM	200
Tregawn	Corn	SX0778	50°34·4′	4°43·2′W	X	200
Tregawne	Corn	SX0066	50°27·8′	4°48·7′W	X	200
Tregays	Corn	SX1257	50°23·2′	4°38·3′W	X	200
Tregeagle	Corn	SW8647	50°17·3′	4°59·9′W	X	204
Tregeague Fm	Corn	SW7421	50°3·0′	5°9·1′W	FM	204
Tregear	Corn	SW6923	50°4·0′	5°13·3′W	T	203
Tregear	Corn	SW8650	50°18·9′	5°0·0′W	X	200,204
Tregear	Corn	SW9744	50°15·9′	4°50·5′W	X	204
Tregeare	Corn	SX2486	50°39·1′	4°29·0′W	T	201
Tregeare Down	Corn	SX2586	50°39·1′	4°28·2′W	X	201
Tregearedown Beacon	Corn	SX2586	50°39·1′	4°28·2′W	H	201
Tregeare Rounds	Corn	SX0380	50°35·4′	4°46·6′W	A	200
Tregear Fm	Corn	SW6434	50°9·8′	5°17·9′W	FM	203
Tregear Vean	Corn	SW8434	50°10·2′	5°1·1′W	X	204
Tregedna Fm	Corn	SW7830	50°7·9′	5°6·0′W	FM	204
Tregeen	Corn	SX1688	50°40·0′	4°35·8′W	X	190
Tregeiriog	Monm	SO4504	51°44·2′	2°47·4′W	X	171
Tregeiriog	Wrex	SJ1733	52°53·5′	3°13·6′W	T	125
Tregele	I of Angl	SH3592	53°24·2′	4°28·5′W	T	114
Tregella	Corn	SW9073	50°31·4′	4°57·4′W	X	200
Tregellas	Corn	SW9149	50°18·5′	4°55·7′W	X	204
Tregellast Barton	Corn	SW7920	50°2·6′	5°4·8′W	X	204
Tregellist	Corn	SX0077	50°33·7′	4°49·1′W	T	200
Tregembo	Corn	SW5731	50°8·0′	5°23·7′W	X	203
Tregendeg	Pemb	SN0921	51°51·5′	4°46·0′W	X	145,158
Tregender Manor	Corn	SW5134	50°9·5′	5°28·8′W	X	203
Tregenhorne	Corn	SW5634	50°9·6′	5°24·6′W	X	203
Tregenna	Corn	SW8562	50°25·3′	5°1·2′W	X	200
Tregenna	Corn	SW8743	50°15·2′	4°58·9′W	X	204
Tregenna	Corn	SW9440	50°13·7′	4°52·9′W	X	204
Tregenna	Corn	SW9948	50°18·1′	4°49·0′W	X	204
Tregenna	Corn	SX0973	50°31·8′	4°41·3′W	X	200
Tregenna	Corn	SX1455	50°22·2′	4°36·6′W	X	200
Tregenna	Corn	SX2087	50°39·5′	4°32·4′W	X	190
Tregenna Fm	Corn	SW9674	50°32·0′	4°52·3′W	FM	200
Tregerest	Corn	SW4032	50°8·1′	5°37·9′W	X	203
Tregerrick	Corn	SW8745	50°16·2′	4°59·0′W	X	204
Tregerrick	Corn	SW9943	50°15·4′	4°48·8′W	X	204
Tregerthen	Corn	SW4639	50°12·0′	5°33·2′W	X	203
Tregeseal	Corn	SW3732	50°8·0′	5°40·5′W	T	203
Tregevis Fm	Corn	SW7423	50°4·1′	5°9·1′W	FM	204
Tregew	Corn	SW6227	50°6·0′	5°19·3′W	X	203
Tregew	Corn	SW8034	50°10·1′	5°4·5′W	T	204
Tregew	Corn	SW8240	50°13·4′	5°3·0′W	X	204
Tre-Gibbon	Rho Cyn Taf	SN9905	51°44·3′	3°27·4′W	T	160
Tregibby Fm	Cered	SN1847	52°5·7′	4°39·0′W	FM	145
Tregidden	Corn	SW7523	50°4·1′	5°8·3′W	T	204
Tregiddle	Corn	SW6723	50°3·9′	5°15·0′W	X	203
Tregidgeo Fm	Corn	SW9647	50°17·5′	4°51·5′W	FM	204
Tregidreg Fm	Pemb	SM8630	51°55·9′	5°6·4′W	FM	157
Tregiffian	Corn	SW3627	50°5·3′	5°41·1′W	X	203
Tregilders	Corn	SX0274	50°32·2′	4°47·3′W	X	200
Tregildren Ho	Corn	SX0379	50°34·9′	4°46·6′W	X	200
Tregilgas	Corn	SW9744	50°15·9′	4°50·5′W	X	204
Tregilliowe Fm	Corn	SW5333	50°9·0′	5°27·1′W	FM	203
Tregillis	Corn	SX2981	50°36·5′	4°24·6′W	X	201
Tregingey Fm	Corn	SW9071	50°30·3′	4°57·3′W	FM	200
Treginnis	Pemb	SM7224	51°52·3′	5°18·3′W	T	157
Tregirls	Corn	SX2280	50°35·8′	4°30·5′W	X	201
Tregirls Fm	Corn	SW9176	50°33·0′	4°56·6′W	FM	200
Tregiskey	Corn	SX0146	50°17·1′	4°47·2′W	X	204
Tregisswyn	Corn	SW9041	50°14·1′	4°56·3′W	X	204
Tregithew	Corn	SW7524	50°4·6′	5°8·3′W	X	204
Tregithey	Corn	SW7724	50°4·7′	5°6·6′W	X	204
Treglai	Carm	SN6721	51°52·5′	3°55·5′W	X	159
Treglasta Fm	Corn	SX1886	50°39·0′	4°34·1′W	FM	201
Tregleath	Corn	SX0269	50°29·5′	4°47·1′W	X	200
Treglemais	Pemb	SM8128	51°54·7′	5°10·7′W	T	157
Treglidgwith	Corn	SW7429	50°7·3′	5°9·3′W	X	204
Treglines Fm	Corn	SW9578	50°34·2′	4°53·3′W	FM	200
Treglinnick	Corn	SW8870	50°29·7′	4°59·0′W	X	200
Treglisson	Corn	SW5836	50°10·7′	5°23·0′W	X	203
Treglith	Corn	SX2188	50°40·1′	4°31·6′W	X	190
Tre-glog	Carm	SN6035	52°0·0′	4°2·0′W	X	146
Treglossick	Corn	SW7823	50°4·2′	5°5·8′W	X	204
Treglyn Down	Corn	SW9777	50°33·7′	4°51·6′W	X	200
Treglyn Fm	Corn	SW9776	50°33·1′	4°51·6′W	FM	200
Tregoad	Corn	SX2755	50°22·4′	4°25·6′W	X	201
Tregodva	Shrops	SO2177	52°23·4′	3°9·3′W	X	137,148
Tregoiffe	Corn	SX3176	50°33·8′	4°22·8′W	X	201
Tregolds	Corn	SW8872	50°30·8′	4°59·0′W	X	200
Tregolds	Corn	SW9171	50°30·3′	4°56·5′W	X	200
Tregole	Corn	SX1998	50°45·4′	4°33·6′W	X	190
Tregolls	Corn	SW7336	50°11·1′	5°10·4′W	T	204
Tregolls	Corn	SW9866	50°27·8′	4°50·4′W	X	200
Tregona	Corn	SW8569	50°29·1′	5°1·5′W	T	200
Tregonan Fm	Corn	SW9545	50°16·4′	4°52·2′W	FM	204
Tregonce	Corn	SW9273	50°31·4′	4°55·7′W	T	200
Tregondale Fm	Corn	SX2964	50°27·3′	4°24·2′W	FM	201
Tregondean Fm	Corn	SW9844	50°15·9′	4°49·7′W	FM	204
Tregonebris	Corn	SW4128	50°6·0′	5°36·9′W	X	203
Tregonetha	Corn	SW9563	50°26·1′	4°52·8′W	T	200
Tregonetha Downs	Corn	SW9562	50°25·6′	4°52·8′W	X	200
Tregonger	Corn	SX1884	50°37·9′	4°34·0′W	X	201
Tregongon	Corn	SW9141	50°14·2′	4°55·5′W	X	204
Tregonhawke	Corn	SX4051	50°20·5′	4°14·5′W	X	201
Tregonhaye	Corn	SW7733	50°9·5′	5°7·0′W	X	204
Tregonhay Fm	Corn	SW9960	50°24·6′	4°49·4′W	FM	200
Tregonhayne	Corn	SW9345	50°16·4′	4°53·9′W	X	204
Tregonian	Corn	SW8542	50°14·6′	5°0·6′W	X	204
Tregoninny	Corn	SW8546	50°16·7′	5°0·7′W	X	204
Tregonjohn Fm	Corn	SW9447	50°17·5′	4°53·2′W	FM	204

Tregonna	Corn	SW9172	50°30·9′	4°56·5′W	T	200
Tregonnett	Corn	SX3270	50°30·6′	4°21·8′W	X	201
Tregonnick Tail	Corn	SX0384	50°37·6′	4°46·7′W	X	200
Tregonning	Corn	SW8658	50°23·2′	5°0·3′W	T	200
Tregonning	Corn	SX0557	50°23·1′	4°44·2′W	X	200
Tregonning Hill	Corn	SW6029	50°7·0′	5°21·1′W	H	203
Tregonwell	Corn	SW7524	50°4·6′	5°8·3′W	X	204
Tregony	Corn	SW9245	50°16·3′	4°54·8′W	T	204
Tregooden	Corn	SX0675	50°32·8′	4°43·9′W	X	200
Tregoodwell	Corn	SX1183	50°37·2′	4°39·9′W	T	200
Tregoose	Corn	SW6429	50°7·1′	5°17·7′W	X	203
Tregoose	Corn	SW6824	50°4·5′	5°14·2′W	X	203
Tregoose	Corn	SW6928	50°6·7′	5°13·5′W	X	203
Tregoose	Corn	SW8039	50°12·8′	5°4·7′W	X	204
Tregoose	Corn	SW8861	50°24·9′	4°58·7′W	X	200
Tregoose	Corn	SW9148	50°17·9′	4°55·7′W	X	204
Tregorden	Corn	SX0074	50°32·1′	4°49·0′W	T	200
Tregorland	Corn	SW8536	50°11·3′	5°0·4′W	X	204
Tregorrick	Corn	SX0151	50°19·8′	4°47·4′W	T	200,204
Tregoss	Corn	SW9660	50°24·5′	4°51·9′W	T	200
Tregoss Moor	Corn	SW9760	50°24·5′	4°51·0′W	X	200
Tregotha Fm	Corn	SW5936	50°10·7′	5°22·2′W	FM	203
Tregothnan	Corn	SW8541	50°14·0′	5°0·5′W	X	204
Tre-gout	Monm	SO4419	51°52·2′	2°48·4′W	X	161
Tregowris	Corn	SW7722	50°3·6′	5°6·6′W	X	204
Tregoyd	Powys	SO1937	52°1·8′	3°10·4′W	X	161
Tregoyd Common	Powys	SO2036	52°1·2′	3°9·6′W	X	161
Tregoyd Mill	Powys	SO1837	52°1·8′	3°11·3′W	T	161
Tregragon	Corn	SX0483	50°37·1′	4°45·9′W	X	200
Tre-graig	Powys	SO1622	51°53·7′	3°12·9′W	X	161
Tregreenwell	Corn	SX0780	50°35·5′	4°43·2′W	T	200
Tregrehan	Corn	SX0553	50°20·9′	4°44·1′W	X	200,204
Tregrehan Mills	Corn	SX0453	50°20·9′	4°44·9′W	T	200,204
Tregrenna	Corn	SX2379	50°35·3′	4°29·7′W	X	201
Tregrill	Corn	SX2863	50°26·7′	4°25·0′W	X	201
Tregroes	Cered	SN4044	52°4·5′	4°19·7′W	T	146
Tre-groes	Pemb	SM9436	51°59·3′	4°59·6′W	X	157
Tregroes Moor	Pemb	SM9335	51°58·7′	5°0·5′W	X	157
Tregrugyn	Powys	SO1567	52°17·9′	3°14·4′W	X	136,148
Tregrylls	Corn	SX1289	50°40·5′	4°39·3′W	X	190,200
Treguddick	Corn	SX2782	50°37·0′	4°26·4′W	X	201
Tregue	Corn	SX1851	50°20·1′	4°33·1′W	X	201
Tregue	Corn	SX2083	50°37·4′	4°32·3′W	X	201
Treguff	V of Glam	ST0371	51°26·0′	3°23·3′W	X	170
Tregulland	Corn	SX1985	50°38·4′	4°33·2′W	X	201
Tregullas	Corn	SW8141	50°13·9′	5°3·9′W	X	204
Tregullon	Corn	SX0664	50°26·9′	4°43·6′W	T	200
Tregullow	Corn	SW7243	50°14·8′	5°11·5′W	X	204
Tregune	Corn	SX2279	50°35·3′	4°30·5′W	X	201
Tregunna	Corn	SW9673	50°31·5′	4°52·3′W	T	200
Tregunnick	Corn	SX3055	50°22·5′	4°23·1′W	X	201
Tregunno Fm	Corn	SW6127	50°5·9′	5°20·2′W	FM	203
Tregunnon	Corn	SX2283	50°37·4′	4°30·6′W	X	201
Tregunter Fm	Powys	SO1333	51°59·6′	3°15·6′W	FM	161
Tregurno	Corn	SW8747	50°17·3′	4°59·0′W	X	204
Tregurnog Fm	Card	ST1078	51°29·9′	3°17·4′W	FM	171
Tregurra	Corn	SW8346	50°16·7′	5°2·4′W	X	204
Tregurrian	Corn	SW8565	50°27·0′	5°1·3′W	T	200
Tregurrian or Watergate Beach	Corn	SW8364	50°26·4′	5°3·0′W	X	200
Tregurtha Downs	Corn	SW5331	50°7·9′	5°27·0′W	T	203
Tregurtha Fm	Corn	SW9564	50°26·6′	4°52·9′W	FM	200
Tregustick	Corn	SW9866	50°27·8′	4°50·4′W	X	200
Tregustick Fm	Corn	SW8463	50°25·9′	5°2·1′W	FM	200
Tregwarmond	Corn	SW9876	50°33·2′	4°50·7′W	X	200
Tregwhelydd	I of Angl	SH3482	53°18·8′	4°29·1′W	X	114
Tregwindles	Corn	SW9869	50°29·4′	4°50·5′W	X	200
Tregwm	Gwyn	SH2333	52°52·2′	4°37·4′W	X	123
Tre-gwynt	Powys	SJ0306	52°38·8′	3°25·6′W	X	125
Tregwynt Fm	Pemb	SM8834	51°58·1′	5°4·8′W	FM	157
Tregydd	Pemb	SM7927	51°54·1′	5°12·4′W	X	157
Tregyddulan	Pemb	SM8936	51°59·2′	5°4·0′W	T	157
Tregye	Corn	SW8040	50°13·4′	5°4·7′W	X	204
Tregynan	Cered	SN5471	52°19·3′	4°8·1′W	X	135
Tre-Gynon	Pemb	SM8230	51°55·8′	5°9·9′W	X	157
Tregynon	Pemb	SN0534	51°58·5′	4°50·0′W	X	145
Tregynon	Powys	SO0998	52°34·6′	3°20·2′W	T	136
Tregynrig	I of Angl	SH4093	53°24·8′	4°24·0′W	X	114
Tre-gynwer	Carm	SN4119	51°51·1′	4°18·1′W	T	159
Trehafod	Rho Cyn Taf	ST0491	51°36·8′	3°22·8′W	T	170
Trehafren	Powys	SO0990	52°30·3′	3°20·0′W	T	136
Trehale Fm	Pemb	SM8828	51°54·9′	5°4·6′W	FM	157
Trehan	Corn	SX4057	50°23·7′	4°14·7′W	T	201
Trehane	Corn	SX1487	50°39·4′	4°37·5′W	X	190,200
Trehane	Corn	SX2864	50°27·3′	4°25·0′W	X	201
Trehane Barton	Corn	SW8648	50°17·8′	4°59·9′W	X	204
Trehane Fm	Corn	SX0989	50°40·4′	4°41·8′W	FM	190,200
Trehane Vean	Corn	SW8649	50°18·4′	5°0·0′W	X	204
Trehane Wood	Corn	SW8548	50°17·8′	5°0·8′W	F	204
Trehannick Fm	Corn	SX0679	50°34·9′	4°44·0′W	FM	200
Treharris	Merth Tyd	ST0997	51°40·1′	3°18·6′W	T	171
Treharrock	Corn	SX0178	50°34·3′	4°48·2′W	X	200
Trehausa	Corn	SX2197	50°44·9′	4°31·9′W	X	190
Trehawke	Corn	SX3162	50°26·2′	4°22·4′W	X	201
Treheli	Gwyn	SH2328	52°49·5′	4°37·2′W	X	123
Trehelig	Powys	SJ2103	52°37·4′	3°9·6′W	X	126
Trehelig-gro	Powys	SJ2102	52°36·8′	3°9·6′W	X	126
Trehemborne	Corn	SW8773	50°31·3′	4°59·9′W	T	200
Trehenry	Pemb	SN2130	51°56·6′	4°35·9′W	X	145
Trehenry	Powys	SO0934	52°0·1′	3°19·1′W	X	161
Treherbert	Rho Cyn Taf	SS9498	51°40·5′	3°31·6′W	T	170
Trehere	Corn	SX2660	50°25·1′	4°26·6′W	X	201
Treheslog Fm	Powys	SN9468	52°18·2′	3°32·9′W	FM	136,147
Treheveras	Corn	SW8146	50°16·6′	5°4·1′W	X	204
Trehill	Corn	SX3864	50°27·4′	4°16·6′W	X	201
Trehill	Corn	SX4169	50°30·2′	4°14·2′W	X	201
Trehill	Devon	SX9184	50°39·0′	3°32·1′W	A	192
Tre-hill	V of Glam	ST0874	51°27·7′	3°19·1′W	T	170
Trehill Fm	Corn	SX3967	50°29·1′	4°15·8′W	FM	201
Trehill Fm	Devon	SX6397	50°45·6′	3°56·2′W	FM	191

Trehilyn	Pemb	SM9038	52°0·3'	5°3·2'W	X	157
Trehingsta	Corn	SX3376	50°33·8'	4°21·1'W	X	201
Trehir Uchaf	Carm	SN1825	51°53·9'	4°38·3'W	X	145,158
Trehole Fm	Corn	SX1495	50°43·7'	4°37·8'W	FM	190
Treholford	Powys	SO1425	51°55·3'	3°14·6'W	X	161
Trehoose	Carm	SN2424	51°53·4'	4°33·1'W	X	145,158
Tre-Howel	Pemb	SM9139	52°0·8'	5°2·4'W	X	157
Trehowel	Pemb	SN1828	51°55·5'	4°38·4'W	X	145,158
Trehowell	Shrops	SJ2836	52°55·2'	3°3·9'W	X	126
Tre-huddion	Carm	SN3413	51°47·7'	4°24·0'W	X	159
Trehudreth	Corn	SX1172	50°31·3'	4°39·6'W	X	200
Trehudreth Downs	Corn	SX1272	50°31·3'	4°38·8'W	X	200
Trehumfrey	Heref	SO5222	51°53·9'	2°41·5'W	X	162
Trehummer	Corn	SX2488	50°40·1'	4°29·1'W	X	190
Trehunist	Corn	SX3163	50°26·8'	4°22·4'W	T	201
Trehunsey Barton	Corn	SX3065	50°27·8'	4°23·3'W	X	201
Trehunsey Br	Corn	SX2965	50°27·8'	4°24·2'W	X	201
Trehurst	Corn	SX3462	50°26·3'	4°19·9'W	X	201
Tre Hwfa	I of Angl	SH3579	53°17·2'	4°28·1'W	X	114
Trehwfa Fawr	I of Angl	SH4375	53°15·2'	4°20·8'W	X	114,115
Treiago Fm	Pemb	SM7728	51°54·6'	5°14·1'W	FM	157
Treial	Pemb	SN1739	52°1·4'	4°39·6'W	X	145
Treicert	Pemb	SN0942	52°2·9'	4°46·7'W	X	145
Treiddon	I of Angl	SH3770	53°12·4'	4°26·0'W	X	114
Tre-Ifor	Rho Cyn Taf	SN9905	51°44·3'	3°27·4'W	T	160
Tre Iorwerth	I of Angl	SH3580	53°17·7'	4°28·1'W	X	114
Treiorwg	Carm	SN6520	51°52·0'	3°57·3'W	X	159
Treire Fm	Corn	SX1555	50°22·2'	4°35·7'W	FM	201
Treisaac Fm	Corn	SW8662	50°25·4'	5°0·4'W	FM	200
Treiva	Pemb	SM8427	51°54·2'	5°8·0'W	X	157
Trekee	Corn	SX0479	50°34·9'	4°45·7'W	X	200
Trekeek	Corn	SX1186	50°38·8'	4°40·0'W	X	200
Trekeivesteps	Corn	SX2270	50°30·4'	4°30·2'W	T	201
Trekelland	Corn	SX2979	50°35·4'	4°24·6'W	X	201
Trekelland	Corn	SX3480	50°36·0'	4°20·4'W	X	201
Trekennard	Corn	SX2099	50°46·0'	4°32·8'W	X	190
Trekenner	Corn	SX2483	50°37·4'	4°28·9'W	X	201
Trekenner	Corn	SX3478	50°34·9'	4°20·3'W	T	201
Trekennick	Corn	SX2181	50°36·3'	4°31·4'W	X	201
Trekennick Tor	Corn	SX2181	50°36·3'	4°31·4'W	X	201
Trekenning	Corn	SW9062	50°25·5'	4°57·0'W	T	200
Trekenning Ho	Corn	SW9162	50°25·5'	4°56·2'W	X	200
Trekernell	Corn	SX2578	50°34·8'	4°27·9'W	X	201
Trekillick Fm	Corn	SX0565	50°27·4'	4°44·5'W	FM	200
Tre-Knoll Fm	Corn	SW8949	50°18·4'	4°57·4'W	FM	204
Treknow	Corn	SX0586	50°38·7'	4°45·1'W	T	200
Trela	Corn	SX1186	50°38·8'	4°40·0'W	X	200
Trelabe	Corn	SX3175	50°33·3'	4°22·8'W	X	201
Trelach-ddu	Heref	SO2930	51°58·1'	3°1·6'W	X	161
Trelagossick	Corn	SW9241	50°14·2'	4°54·6'W	X	204
Trelaminney	Corn	SW7422	50°3·5'	5°9·1'W	X	204
Trelan	Corn	SW7418	50°1·4'	5°8·9'W	T	204
Tre-lan	Flint	SJ1765	53°10·8'	3°14·1'W	T	116
Trelana	Devon	SS2901	50°47·2'	4°25·2'W	X	190
Trelandon	Heref	SO3426	51°56·0'	2°57·2'W	X	161
Trelanvean	Corn	SW7519	50°2·0'	5°8·1'W	X	204
Trelasdee Fm	Heref	SO5023	51°54·4'	2°43·2'W	FM	162
Trelash	Corn	SX1890	50°41·1'	4°34·2'W	T	190
Trelaske	Corn	SW7956	50°22·0'	5°6·1'W	X	200
Trelaske	Corn	SX2253	50°21·2'	4°29·8'W	X	201
Trelaske Ho	Corn	SX2880	50°35·9'	4°25·4'W	X	201
Trelasker	Corn	SW9043	50°15·2'	4°56·4'W	X	204
Trelassick	Corn	SW8752	50°20·0'	4°59·2'W	X	200,204
Trelavour Downs	Corn	SW9557	50°22·9'	4°52·6'W	X	200
Trelawder	Corn	SW9775	50°32·6'	4°51·5'W	X	200
Trelawne	Corn	SX2154	50°21·8'	4°30·6'W	X	201
Trelawne Manor	Corn	SX2254	50°21·8'	4°29·8'W	A	201
Trelawney	Corn	SX2182	50°36·9'	4°31·4'W	X	201
Trelawnyd	Flint	SJ0879	53°18·2'	3°22·4'W	T	116
Trelay	Corn	SS2302	50°47·7'	4°30·3'W	X	190
Trelay	Corn	SX1787	50°39·5'	4°35·0'W	X	190
Trelay	Monm	ST4198	51°40·9'	2°50·8'W	X	171
Trelay Fm	Corn	SX1796	50°44·3'	4°35·2'W	FM	190
Trelay Fm	Corn	SX2154	50°21·8'	4°30·6'W	FM	201
Treleague	Corn	SW7115	49°59·7'	5°11·3'W	X	203
Treleague	Corn	SW7821	50°3·1'	5°5·7'W	X	204
Trelean	Corn	SW5734	50°9·6'	5°23·8'W	X	203
Trelease	Corn	SW7017	50°0·8'	5°12·3'W	X	203
Trelease Fm	Corn	SW7621	50°3·1'	5°7·4'W	FM	204
Trelease Mill	Corn	SW7521	50°3·0'	5°8·2'W	X	204
Treleathick	Corn	SX2266	50°28·2'	4°30·1'W	X	201
Treleaven Fm	Corn	SX0045	50°16·5'	4°48·0'W	FM	204
Treleaver	Corn	SW7716	50°0·4'	5°6·4'W	X	204
Treleaver Cliff	Corn	SW7716	50°0·4'	5°6·4'W	X	204
Trelech	Carm	SN2830	51°56·8'	4°29·0'W	T	145
Treleddyd-fawr	Pemb	SM7527	51°54·0'	5°15·8'W	T	157
Treleddyn	Pemb	SM7325	51°52·9'	5°17·5'W	X	157
Treleddyn	Pemb	SN1740	52°1·9'	4°39·7'W	X	145
Treleidir	Pemb	SM7628	51°54·6'	5°15·0'W	X	157
Treleigh	Corn	SW7043	50°14·8'	5°13·2'W	T	203
Treleigh Fm	Corn	SW9071	50°30·3'	4°57·3'W	FM	200
Trelenny	Monm	ST5192	51°37·7'	2°42·1'W	X	162,172
Trelerney	Shrops	SO2885	52°27·7'	3°3·2'W	X	137
Trelerw	Pemb	SM7724	51°52·4'	5°14·0'W	X	157
Trelessy Fm	Pemb	SN1708	51°44·7'	4°38·7'W	FM	158
Trelew	Corn	SW8135	50°10·7'	5°3·7'W	T	204
Trelewack	Corn	SW9746	50°17·0'	4°50·6'W	X	204
Trelew Fm	Corn	SW4227	50°5·5'	5°36·1'W	FM	203
Trelewis	Merth Tyd	ST1097	51°40·1'	3°17·7'W	T	171
Trelewyd	Pemb	SM7527	51°54·0'	5°15·8'W	X	157
Treliever	Corn	SW7635	50°10·6'	5°7·9'W	X	204
Treligga	Corn	SX0584	50°37·6'	4°45·1'W	T	200
Treliggon	Corn	SX0564	50°26·8'	4°44·4'W	X	200
Trelights	Corn	SW9979	50°34·8'	4°50·0'W	T	200
Trelil	Corn	SW6728	50°6·6'	5°15·2'W	X	203
Trelill	Corn	SX0478	50°34·4'	4°45·7'W	T	200
Trelinnoe	Corn	SX3181	50°36·5'	4°22·9'W	X	201
Trelion	Corn	SW9352	50°20·1'	4°54·2'W	T	200,204
Treliske	Corn	SW8045	50°16·1'	5°4·9'W	T	204
Trelissa	Corn	SW8638	50°12·4'	4°59·6'W	X	204
Trelissick	Corn	SW6228	50°6·5'	5°19·4'W	X	203
Trelissick	Corn	SW8339	50°12·9'	5°2·1'W	T	204
Trelissick	Corn	SW9644	50°15·9'	4°51·4'W	X	204
Treliver	Corn	SW9260	50°24·4'	4°55·3'W	X	200
Treliver	Corn	SW9865	50°27·2'	4°50·4'W	T	200
Tre-llan	Pemb	SM9836	51°59·4'	4°56·1'W	X	157
Trellech	Monm	SO5005	51°44·7'	2°43·1'W	T	162
Trelleck Common	Monm	SO5006	51°45·3'	2°43·1'W	X	162
Trelleck Cross	Monm	SO4904	51°44·2'	2°43·9'W	X	162
Trelleck Grange	Monm	SO4901	51°42·6'	2°43·9'W	T	162
Trelleck Hill	Monm	SO5006	51°45·3'	2°43·1'W	X	162
Trellick	Devon	SS2323	50°59·0'	4°30·9'W	X	190
Trellwydion	Powys	SO0973	52°21·1'	3°19·8'W	X	136,147
Trellwyn	Pemb	SN0035	51°58·9'	4°54·4'W	X	145,157
Trellyffaint	Pemb	SN0842	52°2·8'	4°47·6'W	X	145
Trellys-y-Cnwc	Pemb	SM8935	51°58·6'	5°4·0'W	X	157
Trellys-y-Coed	Pemb	SM9034	51°58·1'	5°3·0'W	X	157
Treloan	Corn	SW8734	50°10·3'	4°58·6'W	X	204
Treloar	Kent	TR0728	51°1·1'	0°57·5'E	X	189
Trelogan	Flint	SJ1180	53°18·8'	3°19·7'W	T	116
Trelogan	Flint	SJ1380	53°18·8'	3°17·9'W	X	116
Trelong Bay	Aberd	NO8778	56°53·8'	2°12·4'W	W	45
Treloank	Corn	SW8941	50°14·1'	4°57·2'W	X	204
Treloquithack	Corn	SW6929	50°7·2'	5°13·5'W	T	203
Treloskan	Corn	SW6823	50°3·9'	5°14·1'W	X	203
Trelough	Heref	SO4331	51°58·7'	2°49·4'W	X	149,161
Trelowarren	Corn	SW7223	50°4·0'	5°10·8'W	A	204
Trelowarren Mill	Corn	SW7124	50°4·6'	5°11·7'W	X	203
Trelow Downs	Corn	SW9268	50°28·7'	4°55·5'W	H	200
Trelower	Corn	SW9850	50°19·2'	4°49·9'W	X	200,204
Trelowgoed Mill	Powys	SO0963	52°15·7'	3°19·6'W	X	147
Trelowia	Corn	SX2956	50°23·0'	4°23·9'W	T	201
Trelowsa Fm	Corn	SW8974	50°31·9'	4°58·3'W	FM	200
Trelowth	Corn	SW9951	50°19·7'	4°49·1'W	T	200,204
Trelowthas	Corn	SW8846	50°16·8'	4°58·2'W	X	204
Treloy	Corn	SW8562	50°25·3'	5°1·2'W	X	200
Treluckey	Corn	SW9443	50°15·3'	4°53·0'W	X	204
Treludderow Manor	Corn	SW8155	50°21·5'	5°4·4'W	X	200
Treludick	Corn	SX2588	50°40·2'	4°28·2'W	X	190
Trelugga	Corn	SW7016	50°0·2'	5°12·2'W	X	203
Treluggan	Corn	SW8838	50°12·5'	4°57·9'W	X	204
Treluggan Manor	Corn	SX3759	50°24·7'	4°17·3'W	X	201
Trelung Ness	Aberd	NO8881	56°55·5'	2°11·4'W	X	45
Treluswell	Corn	SW7736	50°11·2'	5°7·1'W	X	204
Trelydan	Powys	SJ2310	52°41·2'	3°7·9'W	X	126
Trelyll Fm	Corn	SW9771	50°30·5'	4°51·4'W	FM	200
Trelyn	Corn	SX2082	50°36·8'	4°32·3'W	X	201
Trelystan	Powys	SJ2603	52°37·4'	3°5·2'W	T	126
Trelywarch	I of Angl	SH3084	53°19·8'	4°32·8'W	X	114
Tremabe	Corn	SX2566	50°28·3'	4°27·6'W	X	201
Tremabyn	Corn	SX0564	50°26·8'	4°44·4'W	X	200
Tremadart Wood	Corn	SX2158	50°23·9'	4°30·7'W	F	201
Tremaddock Fm	Corn	SX1868	50°29·2'	4°33·6'W	FM	201
Tremadoc Bay		SH5333	52°52·7'	4°10·7'W	W	124
Tremadog	Gwyn	SH5640	52°56·5'	4°8·2'W	T	124
Tremadog Bay		SH5333	52°52·7'	4°10·7'W	W	124
Tremaen	Powys	SO0752	52°9·7'	3°21·2'W	X	147
Tremaenhir	Pemb	SM8226	51°53·6'	5°9·7'W	X	157
Tremahaid	Heref	SO4918	51°51·7'	2°44·0'W	X	162
Tremail	Corn	SX1686	50°38·9'	4°35·8'W	T	201
Tremain	Cered	SN2348	52°6·4'	4°34·7'W	T	145
Tremaine	Corn	SX1956	50°22·8'	4°32·4'W	X	201
Tremaine	Corn	SX2388	50°40·1'	4°29·9'W	T	190
Tremains	Brig	SS9179	51°30·2'	3°33·8'W	T	170
Tremar	Corn	SX2568	50°29·4'	4°27·7'W	T	201
Trematon	Corn	SX3959	50°24·8'	4°15·6'W	T	201
Trematon Castle	Corn	SX4157	50°23·7'	4°13·9'W	T	201
Tremayna	Corn	SX1696	50°44·3'	4°36·1'W	X	190
Tremayne	Corn	SW4231	50°7·6'	5°36·2'W	X	203
Tremayne	Corn	SW6435	50°10·3'	5°17·9'W	T	203
Tremayne	Corn	SW7325	50°5·1'	5°10·0'W	X	204
Tremayne	Corn	SW9364	50°26·6'	4°54·6'W	X	200
Trembleath	Corn	SW8865	50°27·0'	4°58·8'W	X	200
Trembleathe Barton	Corn	SW8869	50°29·2'	4°58·9'W	X	200
Trembraze	Corn	SW7821	50°3·1'	5°5·7'W	X	204
Trembraze	Corn	SX2565	50°27·8'	4°27·6'W	T	201
Trembroath	Corn	SW7237	50°11·6'	5°11·3'W	X	204
Trembyd	Powys	SN9861	52°14·5'	3°29·2'W	X	147
Tremeale	Corn	SX3183	50°37·6'	4°23·0'W	X	201
Tremearne	Corn	SW4632	50°8·3'	5°32·9'W	X	203
Tremearne	Corn	SW6126	50°5·4'	5°20·1'W	X	203
Tremedda	Corn	SW4639	50°12·0'	5°33·2'W	T	203
Tremeer	Corn	SX0676	50°33·3'	4°44·0'W	X	200
Tremeere Manor	Corn	SX0464	50°26·8'	4°45·3'W	X	200
Tremeer Fm	Corn	SX1652	50°20·6'	4°34·8'W	FM	201
Tremeirchion	Denb	SJ0873	53°15·0'	3°22·3'W	T	116
Tremelling	Corn	SW5534	50°9·6'	5°25·4'W	X	203
Tremenheere	Corn	SW6728	50°6·6'	5°15·2'W	X	203
Tremethick Cross	Corn	SW4430	50°7·1'	5°34·5'W	T	203
Tremle	Carm	SN4435	51°59·7'	4°15·9'W	X	146
Tremoan	Corn	SX3965	50°28·0'	4°15·7'W	X	201
Tremoilet Fm	Carm	SN2209	51°45·3'	4°34·4'W	FM	158
Tremollet Down	Corn	SX3375	50°33·3'	4°21·1'W	X	201
Tremollett	Corn	SX2975	50°33·2'	4°24·5'W	X	201
Tremore	Corn	SX0164	50°26·8'	4°47·8'W	T	200
Tremorebridge	Corn	SX0064	50°26·7'	4°48·6'W	T	200
Tremorfa	Card	ST2077	51°29·4'	3°8·7'W	T	171
Tremorfa	Conwy	SH7873	53°14·6'	3°49·3'W	X	115
Tremorithic	Heref	SO3531	51°58·7'	2°56·4'W	X	149,161
Tremorle	Corn	SX1291	50°41·5'	4°39·3'W	X	190
Tre-Mostyn	Flint	SJ1479	53°18·3'	3°17·0'W	T	116
Tremough	Corn	SW7734	50°10·1'	5°7·0'W	X	204
Tremount	Corn	SW9068	50°28·7'	4°57·2'W	X	200
Tremoutha Haven	Corn	SX1396	50°44·2'	4°38·6'W	W	190
Tremuda Bay	Aberd	NO8882	56°56·0'	2°11·4'W	W	45
Tremvan Hall	Gwyn	SH3231	52°51·3'	4°29·3'W	X	123
Tremynydd Fawr	Pemb	SM7729	51°55·1'	5°14·2'W	X	157
Trenabie	Orkney	HY4451	59°20·8'	2°58·6'W	X	5
Trenache Fm	Nth Pt Talb	SN7401	51°41·9'	3°49·0'W	FM	170
Trenadlyn	Corn	SX0955	50°22·1'	4°40·8'W	X	200
Trenain Fm	Corn	SW9377	50°33·6'	4°55·0'W	FM	200
Trenake	Corn	SX1955	50°22·3'	4°32·3'W	X	201
Trenale	Corn	SX0687	50°39·3'	4°44·3'W	X	200
Trena Loch	Orkney	ND4685	58°45·2'	2°55·5'W	W	7
Trenance	Corn	SW8022	50°3·7'	5°4·1'W	X	204
Trenance	Corn	SW8161	50°24·7'	5°4·6'W	T	200
Trenance	Corn	SW8457	50°22·6'	5°1·9'W	X	200
Trenance	Corn	SW8567	50°28·0'	5°1·4'W	T	200
Trenance	Corn	SW9271	50°30·3'	4°55·6'W	T	200
Trenance	Corn	SW9864	50°26·7'	4°50·3'W	T	200
Trenance Downs	Corn	SX0054	50°21·4'	4°48·3'W	H	200
Trenance Fm	Corn	SW6718	50°1·2'	5°14·8'W	FM	203
Trenance Point	Corn	SW8468	50°28·6'	5°2·3'W	X	200
Trenance Rock	Corn	SW8467	50°28·0'	5°2·3'W	X	200
Trenannick	Corn	SX1992	50°42·2'	4°33·4'W	X	190
Trenant	Corn	SW9479	50°34·7'	4°54·2'W	X	200
Trenant	Corn	SW9972	50°31·0'	4°49·7'W	T	200
Trenant	Corn	SX1052	50°20·5'	4°39·8'W	X	200,204
Trenant	Corn	SX2168	50°29·3'	4°31·0'W	T	201
Trenant	Corn	SX2964	50°27·3'	4°24·2'W	X	201
Trenant Brook	Heref	SO3337	52°1·9'	2°58·2'W	W	149,161
Trenant Cross	Corn	SX2355	50°22·3'	4°29·0'W	X	201
Trenant Park	Corn	SX2455	50°22·4'	4°28·1'W	X	201
Trenant Wood	Corn	SX2454	50°21·8'	4°28·1'W	F	201
Trenarlet Fm	Corn	SX0874	50°32·3'	4°42·2'W	FM	200
Trenarren	Corn	SX0348	50°18·2'	4°45·6'W	T	204
Trenarrett	Corn	SX2382	50°36·9'	4°29·7'W	X	201
Trenarth	Corn	SW7528	50°6·8'	5°8·5'W	X	204
Trenault	Corn	SX2683	50°37·5'	4°27·2'W	X	201
Trenay	Corn	SX1666	50°28·1'	4°35·2'W	T	201
Trench	Shrops	SJ3937	52°55·9'	2°54·0'W	X	126
Trench	Wrekin	SJ6912	52°42·5'	2°27·1'W	T	127
Trench	Wrex	SJ3839	52°56·9'	2°55·0'W	X	126
Trenchard Fm	Devon	SS6809	50°52·2'	3°52·2'W	FM	191
Trenches Fm	Bucks	TQ0080	51°30·8'	0°33·1'W	FM	176
Trench Fm	Kent	TQ5749	51°13·3'	0°15·3'E	FM	188
Trench Fm	Shrops	SJ3937	52°55·9'	2°54·0'W	FM	126
Trenchford Reservoir	Devon	SX8082	50°37·8'	3°41·4'W	W	191
Trench Green	Oxon	SU6877	51°29·5'	1°0·8'W	T	175
Trench Hall	Ghead	NZ2259	54°55·8'	1°39·0'W	X	88
Trench Hall	Shrops	SJ5126	52°50·0'	2°43·2'W	X	126
Trench Pt	Arg & Bt	NR7320	55°25·5'	5°34·8'W	X	68
Trench, The	Glos	SO9204	51°44·3'	2°6·6'W	X	163
Trench, The	Northum	NZ0989	55°12·0'	1°51·1'W	X	81
Trenchway Wood	Corn	SX2060	50°25·0'	4°31·6'W	F	201
Trench Wood	Kent	TQ5948	51°12·8'	0°17·0'E	T	188
Trench Wood (Nature Reserve)	Worcs	SO9258	52°13·4'	2°6·6'W	X	150
Trencreek	Corn	SW8260	50°24·2'	5°3·7'W	T	200
Trencreek	Corn	SW9343	50°15·3'	4°53·9'W	X	204
Trencreek	Corn	SX1071	50°30·7'	4°40·4'W	X	200
Trencreek	Corn	SX1896	50°44·3'	4°34·4'W	X	190
Trencreek Fm	Corn	SW9648	50°18·0'	4°51·5'W	FM	204
Trencrom	Corn	SW5136	50°10·5'	5°28·9'W	T	203
Trencrom Hill	Corn	SW5136	50°10·5'	5°28·9'W	H	203
Trencrom Hill (Fort)	Corn	SW5136	50°10·5'	5°28·9'W	A	203
Trendeal	Corn	SW8952	50°20·0'	4°57·5'W	T	200,204
Trendeal Hill	Corn	SW8853	50°20·6'	4°58·4'W	X	200,204
Trendlebere Down	Devon	SX7779	50°36·1'	3°43·9'W	H	191
Trendle Ring	Somer	ST1139	51°8·8'	3°16·0'W	X	181
Trendle Ring (Settlement)	Somer	ST1139	51°8·8'	3°16·0'W	A	181
Trendrean	Corn	SW8357	50°22·6'	5°2·8'W	X	200
Trendrennen	Corn	SW3823	50°3·2'	5°39·2'W	X	203
Trendrine	Corn	SW4739	50°12·1'	5°32·4'W	X	203
Trendrine Hill	Corn	SW4738	50°11·5'	5°32·3'W	H	203
Treneague	Corn	SW9871	50°30·5'	4°50·6'W	X	200
Trenean Fms	Corn	SX2857	50°23·5'	4°24·8'W	FM	201
Trenear	Corn	SW6831	50°8·3'	5°14·4'W	T	203
Trenearne	Corn	SW8974	50°31·9'	4°58·3'W	X	200
Trenear's Rock	I Scilly	SV9212	49°56·0'	6°17·2'W	X	203
Trenedden	Corn	SX1754	50°21·7'	4°34·0'W	X	201
Treneddyn Fm	Carm	SN5707	51°44·8'	4°3·9'W	FM	159
Trenedros	Corn	SW5534	50°9·6'	5°25·4'W	X	203
Treneglos	Corn	SX2088	50°40·1'	4°32·5'W	T	190
Trenemene	I Scilly	SV8405	49°51·9'	6°23·5'W	X	203
Trenerry	Corn	SW8352	50°19·9'	5°2·6'W	X	200,204
Trenerth	Corn	SW6035	50°10·2'	5°21·3'W	T	203
Trenestrall	Corn	SW8839	50°13·0'	4°57·9'W	X	204
Trenethans	Corn	SX0360	50°24·6'	4°46·0'W	X	200
Trenethick Barton	Corn	SW6629	50°7·1'	5°16·0'W	A	203
Trenet Laithe	N Yks	SD9151	53°57·5'	2°7·8'W	X	103
Trenewan	Corn	SX1753	50°21·1'	4°34·0'W	T	201
Trenewth	Corn	SX0778	50°34·4'	4°43·2'W	X	200
Trenewydd	Carm	SN3016	51°49·2'	4°27·6'W	X	159
Trenewydd	Carm	SN3623	51°53·1'	4°22·6'W	X	145,159
Trenewydd	Cered	SN1444	52°4·0'	4°42·4'W	X	145
Trenewydd	Heref	SO2550	52°8·8'	3°5·4'W	X	148
Trenewydd	Pemb	SM9139	52°0·8'	5°2·4'W	X	157
Trenewydd	Pemb	SM9936	51°59·4'	4°55·3'W	X	157
Trenewydd	Pemb	SN1610	51°45·7'	4°39·6'W	X	158
Trenewydd	Powys	SO2035	52°0·7'	3°9·5'W	X	161
Trenewydd Fawr	Pemb	SM8429	51°55·3'	5°8·1'W	X	157
Trengale	Corn	SX2167	50°28·8'	4°31·0'W	T	201
Trengayor	Corn	SX1797	50°44·9'	4°35·3'W	X	190
Trengoffe	Corn	SX1567	50°28·7'	4°36·1'W	X	201
Trengothal Fm	Corn	SW3724	50°3·7'	5°40·1'W	FM	203
Trengrouse Fm	Corn	SW9241	50°14·2'	4°54·6'W	FM	204
Trengrove Fm	Corn	SX2766	50°28·3'	4°25·9'W	FM	201
Trengune	Corn	SX1893	50°42·7'	4°34·3'W	T	190
Trengwainton Carn	Corn	SW4432	50°8·2'	5°34·6'W	X	203
Trengwainton Ho	Corn	SW4431	50°7·7'	5°34·5'W	X	203
Trenhayle	Corn	SW5635	50°10·1'	5°24·6'W	X	203
Trenholme Fm	N Yks	NZ4402	54°24·9'	1°18·9'W	FM	93
Trenholme Stell	N Yks	NZ4502	54°24·9'	1°18·0'W	W	93
Trenholm Ho	N Yks	SE4697	54°22·2'	1°17·1'W	X	100
Trenhorne	Corn	SX2778	50°34·8'	4°26·2'W	T	201
Trenichol	Pemb	SM8527	51°54·2'	5°7·1'W	X	157
Treniffle	Corn	SX3583	50°37·6'	4°19·6'W	X	201
Trenilk	Corn	SX2279	50°35·3'	4°30·5'W	X	201
Treningle	Corn	SX0465	50°27·4'	4°45·3'W	T	200

Treninick	Corn	SW9942	50°14·9'	4°48·8'W	X	204
Treninnick	Corn	SW8160	50°24·2'	5°4·5'W	T	200
Treninnow	Corn	SX4151	50°20·5'	4°13·7'W	X	201
Trenissick	Corn	SW7958	50°23·1'	5°6·2'W	X	200
Trenithan Bennett	Corn	SW9049	50°18·5'	4°56·6'W	X	204
Trenithan Chancellor	Corn	SW9048	50°17·9'	4°56·6'W	X	204
Trenithon	Corn	SW7521	50°3·0'	5°8·2'W	X	204
Trenithon	Corn	SW8955	50°21·7'	4°57·6'W	T	200
Trenley Fm	Kent	TQ7532	51°3·9'	0°30·2'E	FM	188
Trenley Ho	Glos	SO7701	51°42·7'	2°19·6'W	X	162
Trenleypark Wood	Kent	TR1959	51°17·5'	1°8·9'E	F	179
Trennet Bank	N Yks	SE5598	54°22·7'	1°8·8'W	X	100
Trennick	Corn	SW8344	50°15·6'	5°2·3'W	X	204
Trenodden	Corn	SX3062	50°26·2'	4°23·3'W	X	201
Trenode	Corn	SX2858	50°24·0'	4°24·8'W	X	201
Trenoeth	Carm	SN3128	51°55·7'	4°27·1'W	X	145
Trenoon	Corn	SW7018	50°1·3'	5°12·3'W	T	203
Trenorgan	Pemb	SR9495	51°37·2'	4°58·2'W	X	158
Trenos Fm	Rho Cyn Taf	SS9882	51°31·9'	3°27·8'W	FM	170
Trenouth	Corn	SX2668	50°29·4'	4°26·8'W	X	201
Trenouth Fm	Corn	SX0685	50°38·2'	4°44·2'W	FM	200
Trenovissick Fm	Corn	SX0653	50°20·9'	4°43·2'W	FM	200,204
Trenow Cove	Corn	SW5329	50°6·8'	5°26·9'W	W	203
Trenower Fm	Corn	SW9961	50°25·1'	4°49·4'W	FM	200
Trenoweth	Corn	SW7533	50°9·5'	5°8·6'W	T	204
Trenoweth	Corn	SW8022	50°3·7'	5°4·1'W	X	204
Trenoweth Fm	Corn	SW6522	50°3·3'	5°16·6'W	FM	203
Trenoweth Fm	Corn	SX0458	50°23·6'	4°45·1'W	FM	200
Trenowin	Corn	SW4934	50°9·4'	5°30·5'W	X	203
Trenowin	Corn	SW6038	50°11·8'	5°21·4'W	X	203
Trenowin Downs	Corn	SW4835	50°9·9'	5°31·4'W	X	203
Trenowth	Corn	SW9250	50°19·0'	4°54·9'W	X	200,204
Trenowth Ho	Corn	SW9350	50°19·1'	4°54·1'W	X	200,204
Trent	Dorset	ST5918	50°57·8'	2°34·6'W	T	183
Trentabank Reservoir	Ches	SJ9671	53°14·4'	2°3·2'W	W	118
Trent and Mersey Canal	Staffs	SJ9231	52°52·8'	2°6·7'W	W	127
Trent Barrow	Dorset	ST6118	50°57·8'	2°32·9'W	X	183
Trent Brook	Dorset	ST5818	50°57·8'	2°35·5'W	W	183
Trent College	Derby	SK4833	52°53·8'	1°16·8'W	X	129
Trent Contry Park	Enf	TQ2897	51°39·7'	0°8·6'W	X	166,176
Trent Falls	E Yorks	SE8623	53°42·0'	0°41·4'W	W	106,112
Trentfield Fm	Notts	SK8177	53°17·3'	0°46·7'W	FM	121
Trent Fm	Lancs	SD8942	53°52·7'	2°9·6'W	FM	103
Trentham	C of Stoke	SJ8741	52°58·2'	2°11·2'W	T	118
Trentham	Highld	NH7893	57°54·8'	4°3·1'W	X	21
Trentham Gdns	Staffs	SJ8640	52°57·7'	2°12·1'W	X	118
Trent Hills	Notts	SK7147	53°1·2'	0°56·1'W	X	129
Trent Hills Fm	Notts	SK7246	53°0·6'	0°55·2'W	FM	129
Trentinney	Corn	SX0077	50°33·7'	4°49·1'W	X	200
Trentishoe	Devon	SS6448	51°13·1'	3°56·5'W	T	180
Trentishoe Down	Devon	SS6247	51°12·6'	3°58·2'W	H	180
Trentishoe Manor	Devon	SS6346	51°12·0'	3°57·3'W	X	180
Trentlock	Derby	SK4831	52°52·7'	1°16·8'W	T	129
Trent & Mersey Canal	Ches	SJ5877	53°17·5'	2°37·4'W	W	117
Trent & Mersey Canal	Ches	SJ6075	53°16·5'	2°35·6'W	W	118
Trent & Mersey Canal	Ches	SJ7164	53°10·6'	2°25·6'W	W	118
Trent & Mersey Canal	C of Stoke	SJ8842	52°58·8'	2°10·3'W	W	118
Trent & Mersey Canal	Derby	SK4228	52°51·1'	1°22·2'W	W	129
Trent & Mersey Canal	Staffs	SK1514	52°43·6'	1°46·3'W	W	128
Trent Port	Lincs	SK8381	53°19·4'	0°44·8'W	X	121
Trent Vale	C of Stoke	SJ8643	52°59·3'	2°12·1'W	T	118
Trent Vale Fm	Dorset	SY8790	50°42·8'	2°10·7'W	FM	194
Trent Valley	Staffs	SJ9429	52°51·7'	2°4·9'W	X	127
Trent Valley	Staffs	SK0120	52°46·9'	1°58·7'W	X	128
Trent Valley or Lichfield Sta	Staffs	SK1309	52°40·9'	1°48·1'W	X	128
Trent Valley Way	Notts	SK8363	53°9·7'	0°45·1'W	X	121
Trentworthy Fm	Devon	SS2815	50°54·8'	4°26·4'W	FM	190
Trenuggo	Corn	SW4227	50°5·5'	5°36·1'W	X	203
Trenute	Corn	SX3378	50°34·9'	4°21·2'W	X	201
Trenuth Fm	Corn	SX1284	50°37·8'	4°39·1'W	FM	200
Trenwheal	Corn	SW6132	50°8·6'	5°20·3'W	T	203
Trenwick	E Yorks	SE8344	53°53·4'	0°43·8'W	X	106
Trenython Manor	Corn	SX1054	50°21·6'	4°39·9'W	X	200
Treoes	V of Glam	SS9478	51°29·7'	3°31·2'W	T	170
Treoffal	Corn	SW8257	50°22·6'	5°3·6'W	X	200
Treorchy / Treorci	Rho Cyn Taf	SS9596	51°39·4'	3°30·7'W	T	170
Treore Fm	Corn	SX0280	50°35·4'	4°47·5'W	FM	200
Treovis	Corn	SX2874	50°32·7'	4°25·3'W	X	201
Treowen	Caer	ST2098	51°40·7'	3°9·0'W	T	171
Treowen	Monm	SO4611	51°47·9'	2°46·6'W	A	161
Treowen	Powys	SO1191	52°30·8'	3°18·3'W	T	136
Trepant	Pemb	SN0431	51°56·8'	4°50·7'W	X	145,157
Treparcau	Carm	SN2827	51°55·1'	4°29·7'W	X	145,158
Trephillip	Powys	SO1234	52°0·1'	3°16·5'W	X	161
Tre-pit	V of Glam	SS9172	51°26·4'	3°33·7'W	T	170
Trepoyle	Corn	SX3097	50°45·1'	4°24·2'W	X	190
Treprenal	Shrops	SJ2821	52°47·1'	3°3·7'W	X	126
Treprior	Cered	SN2348	52°6·4'	4°34·7'W	X	145
Tre-Prysg	Pemb	SN1144	52°4·0'	4°45·1'W	X	145
Tre-pys-llygod	Conwy	SH8868	53°12·1'	3°40·2'W	H	116
Trequean	Corn	SW6027	50°5·9'	5°21·0'W	X	203
Trequite	Corn	SX0276	50°33·3'	4°47·3'W	T	200
Trequites	Corn	SX0672	50°31·2'	4°43·8'W	X	200
Treragin	Corn	SX4069	50°30·2'	4°15·0'W	X	201
Trerair Fm	Corn	SW8769	50°29·2'	4°59·8'W	FM	200
Trerank	Corn	SW9859	50°24·0'	4°50·2'W	X	200
Trerank Moor	Corn	SW9859	50°24·0'	4°50·2'W	X	200
Trerathick Point	Corn	SW8468	50°28·6'	5°2·3'W	X	200
Treravel	Corn	SW8970	50°29·7'	4°58·1'W	X	200
Treravel Fm	Corn	SW9073	50°31·4'	4°57·4'W	FM	200
Treraven	Corn	SW9971	50°30·5'	4°49·7'W	X	200
Treraven	Corn	SX1984	50°37·9'	4°33·2'W	X	201
Tre'r Ceiri	Gwyn	SH3744	52°58·4'	4°25·2'W	X	123
Tre'r Ceiri (Fort)	Gwyn	SH3744	52°58·4'	4°25·2'W	A	123
Tre'r-ddôl	Cered	SN6692	52°30·8'	3°58·1'W	T	135
Tre'r-ddôl	I of Angl	SH3981	53°18·3'	4°24·6'W	A	114
Trereece	Heref	SO5220	51°52·8'	2°41·4'W	X	162
Trereen Dinas	Corn	SW4338	50°11·4'	5°35·7'W	A	203
Trerefters	Corn	SX3276	50°33·8'	4°22·0'W	X	201

Trereife	Corn	SW4529	50°6·6'	5°33·6'W	X	203
Trerethern	Corn	SW9173	50°31·4'	4°56·5'W	X	200
Trerew Fm	Corn	SW8158	50°23·1'	5°4·5'W	FM	200
Trer-gôf	I of Angl	SH4174	53°14·6'	4°22·6'W	X	114,115
Tre-rhew Brook	Monm	SO3717	51°51·1'	2°54·5'W	W	161
Tre-rhiwarth	Powys	SJ0229	52°51·2'	3°26·9'W	X	125
Trerhos Fm	Pemb	SM9227	51°54·4'	5°1·0'W	FM	157,158
Trerhyngyll	V of Glam	ST0076	51°28·7'	3°26·0'W	T	170
Tre-Rhys	Pemb	SN1146	52°5·0'	4°45·1'W	X	145
Treribble	Heref	SO5122	51°53·9'	2°42·3'W	X	162
Trerice	Corn	SW8251	50°19·4'	5°3·4'W	X	200,204
Trerice	Corn	SW8458	50°23·2'	5°1·9'W	A	200
Trerice	Corn	SW9969	50°29·4'	4°49·7'W	X	200
Trerice Fm	Corn	SW9357	50°22·8'	4°54·3'W	FM	200
Trerieve	Corn	SX3054	50°21·9'	4°23·0'W	X	201
Treriffith	Pemb	SN1044	52°4·0'	4°45·9'W	X	145
Treriffri	I of Angl	SH3881	53°18·3'	4°25·5'W	X	114
Treringey	Corn	SW8060	50°24·2'	5°5·4'W	X	200
Treringey Round	Corn	SW8160	50°24·2'	5°4·5'W	A	200
Trerise	Corn	SW7117	50°0·8'	5°11·4'W	T	203
Trerithick	Corn	SX2482	50°36·9'	4°28·9'W	X	201
Tre'r-llan	Denb	SJ0336	52°55·0'	3°26·2'W	X	125
Tre'r-llan	Gwyn	SH9737	52°55·5'	3°31·5'W	X	125
Treroosel	Corn	SX0580	50°35·5'	4°44·9'W	X	200
Trerose	Corn	SW7827	50°6·3'	5°5·9'W	T	204
Tre'r-parc	Denb	SJ0756	53°5·8'	3°22·9'W	X	116
Trerubies Cove	Corn	SX0383	50°37·0'	4°46·7'W	W	200
Treruffydd	I of Angl	SH3572	53°13·4'	4°27·9'W	X	114
Trerulefoot	Corn	SX3258	50°24·1'	4°21·5'W	T	201
Treryn Dinas	Corn	SW4022	50°2·7'	5°37·5'W	A	203
Tresaddern	Corn	SW9362	50°25·5'	4°54·5'W	X	200
Tresaddern Fm	Corn	SW7116	50°0·2'	5°11·4'W	FM	203
Tresahor	Corn	SW7430	50°7·9'	5°9·4'W	X	204
Tresaison	Monm	SO3311	51°47·9'	2°57·9'W	X	161
Tresaith	Cered	SN2751	52°8·1'	4°31·3'W	T	145
Tresallack	Corn	SX3475	50°33·3'	4°20·2'W	X	201
Tresallyn Fm	Corn	SW8973	50°31·4'	4°58·2'W	FM	200
Tresamble	Corn	SW7539	50°12·7'	5°8·9'W	T	204
Tresare Fm	Pemb	SM8531	51°56·4'	5°7·3'W	FM	157
Tresarrett	Corn	SX0873	50°31·8'	4°42·2'W	T	200
Tresavean	Corn	SW7239	50°12·7'	5°11·4'W	T	204
Tresawle	Corn	SW8946	50°16·8'	4°57·3'W	T	204
Tresawle	Corn	SW8963	50°26·0'	4°57·9'W	X	200
Tresawna	Corn	SW8958	50°23·3'	4°57·7'W	X	200
Tresawsan	Corn	SW8643	50°15·1'	4°59·7'W	X	204
Tresawsen	Corn	SW7849	50°18·2'	5°6·7'W	T	204
Tresawson	Corn	SX1856	50°22·8'	4°33·2'W	X	201
Tresco	I Scilly	SV8914	49°56·9'	6°19·8'W	X	203
Tresco Flats	I Scilly	SV8813	49°56·4'	6°20·6'W	W	203
Trescoll	Corn	SX0361	50°25·2'	4°46·0'W	T	200
Trescore Islands	Corn	SW8472	50°30·7'	5°2·4'W	X	200
Trescott	Staffs	SO8497	52°34·5'	2°13·8'W	T	138
Trescott Grange	Staffs	SO8596	52°33·9'	2°12·9'W	X	139
Trescowe	Corn	SW5730	50°7·5'	5°23·6'W	T	203
Trescowe	Corn	SX0471	50°30·6'	4°45·5'W	X	200
Trescowe Brake	Corn	SX0470	50°30·1'	4°45·5'W	F	200
Trescowthick	Corn	SW8157	50°22·6'	5°4·4'W	X	200
Tresdale	Highld	ND3471	58°37·6'	3°7·7'W	X	7,12
Tresean	Corn	SW7858	50°23·0'	5°7·0'W	T	200
Treseat Fm	Corn	SX1887	50°39·5'	4°34·1'W	FM	190
Tresenny	Monm	SO4024	51°54·9'	2°51·9'W	X	161
Tresevern Croft	Corn	SW7137	50°11·6'	5°12·1'W	T	203
Tresewig	Pemb	SM8328	51°54·7'	5°8·9'W	X	157
Tresgyrch Fawr	Nth Pt Talb	SN6809	51°46·1'	3°54·4'W	X	159
Tresham	Glos	ST7991	51°37·3'	2°17·8'W	T	162,172
Treshnish	Arg & Bt	NM3548	56°33·2'	6°18·3'W	X	47,48
Treshnish Isles	Arg & Bt	NM2741	56°29·2'	6°25·6'W	X	46,47,48
Treshnish Point	Arg & Bt	NM3348	56°33·1'	6°20·2'W	X	47,48
Treshwood Scar	Cumbr	SD2565	54°4·8'	3°8·4'W	X	96
Tresibbett	Corn	SX2282	50°36·9'	4°30·6'W	X	201
Tresidder	Corn	SW3924	50°3·8'	5°38·5'W	X	203
Tresilian	V of Glam	SS9467	51°23·8'	3°31·0'W	X	170
Tresilian Bay	V of Glam	SS9467	51°23·8'	3°31·0'W	W	170
Tresillian	Corn	SW8646	50°16·7'	4°59·8'W	T	204
Tresillian Ho	Corn	SW8558	50°23·2'	5°1·1'W	X	200
Tresillian River	Corn	SW8544	50°15·6'	5°0·6'W	W	204
Tresinney	Corn	SX1081	50°36·1'	4°40·7'W	T	200
Tresinwen	Pemb	SM9040	52°1·4'	5°3·3'W	X	157
Tresior	Pemb	SM9435	51°58·8'	4°59·6'W	X	157
Tresisslit	Pemb	SM8935	51°58·6'	5°4·0'W	X	157
Tresithick	Corn	SW8039	50°12·8'	5°4·7'W	X	204
Tresithick	Corn	SW8449	50°18·3'	5°1·6'W	X	204
Tresithney	Corn	SW9059	50°23·8'	4°56·9'W	X	200
Tresivick	N Eil	NL6295	56°55·6'	7°32·9'W	X	31
Treskellow	Corn	SX1988	50°40·0'	4°33·3'W	X	190
Treskerby	Corn	SW7143	50°14·8'	5°12·4'W	T	203
Treskewes	Corn	SW7820	50°2·6'	5°5·7'W	X	204
Treskillard	Corn	SW6739	50°12·5'	5°15·6'W	T	203
Treskilling	Corn	SX0357	50°23·0'	4°45·9'W	T	200
Treskinnick Cross	Corn	SX2098	50°45·5'	4°32·7'W	T	190
Treslay	Corn	SX1388	50°39·9'	4°38·4'W	X	190,200
Treslea	Corn	SX1368	50°29·2'	4°37·8'W	X	200
Treslea Downs	Corn	SX1468	50°29·2'	4°36·9'W	X	200
Treslothan	Corn	SW6537	50°11·4'	5°17·2'W	T	203
Tresmaine	Corn	SX2281	50°36·3'	4°30·6'W	X	201
Tresmarrow	Corn	SX3183	50°37·6'	4°23·0'W	X	201
Tresmeake	Corn	SX2082	50°36·8'	4°32·3'W	X	201
Tresmeer	Corn	SX2387	50°39·6'	4°29·9'W	T	190
Tresmorn	Corn	SX1597	50°44·8'	4°37·0'W	X	190
Tresmorn Village	Corn	SX1697	50°44·8'	4°36·1'W	A	190
Tresness	Orkney	HY7038	59°13·9'	2°31·1'W	X	5
Tres Ness	Orkney	HY7137	59°13·4'	2°30·0'W	X	5
Tresoke	Corn	SX1687	50°39·5'	4°35·8'W	X	190
Tresooth Fm	Corn	SW7631	50°8·4'	5°7·7'W	FM	204
Tresowes Green	Corn	SW5929	50°7·0'	5°21·9'W	T	203
Tresoweshill	Corn	SW6029	50°7·0'	5°21·1'W	T	203
Tresowga	Corn	SW8847	50°17·3'	4°58·2'W	X	204
Tresparrett	Corn	SX1491	50°41·6'	4°37·6'W	T	190
Tresparrett Down	Corn	SX1492	50°42·1'	4°37·7'W	X	190
Tresparrett Posts	Corn	SX1493	50°42·7'	4°37·7'W	T	190

Trespearne	Corn	SX2383	50°37·4'	4°29·8'W	X	201
Tresprison Fm	Corn	SW6727	50°6·1'	5°15·1'W	FM	203
Tresprisson	Corn	SW6818	50°1·3'	5°14·0'W	X	203
Tresquare	Corn	SX0674	50°32·3'	4°43·9'W	X	200
Tressady	Highld	NC6904	58°0·6'	4°12·6'W	T	16
Tressady Lodge	Highld	NC7004	58°0·6'	4°11·5'W	X	16
Tressair	Pth & Kin	NN8160	56°43·3'	3°56·2'W	T	43,52
Tressait	Pth & Kin	NN8160	56°43·3'	3°56·2'W	T	43,52
Tressa Ness	Shetld	HU6194	60°37·7'	0°52·6'W	X	1,2
Tressellern	Corn	SX2376	50°33·7'	4°29·6'W	X	201
Tresta	Shetld	HU3651	60°14·8'	1°20·5'W	T	3
Tresta	Shetld	HU6190	60°35·6'	0°52·7'W	X	1,2
Tresta Voe	Shetld	HU3550	60°14·2'	1°21·6'W	W	3
Trestle Cairn	Scot Bord	NT7516	55°26·5'	2°23·3'W	A	80
Trestrayle	Corn	SW9046	50°16·8'	4°56·5'W	X	204
Tresuck	Corn	SX1091	50°41·5'	4°41·0'W	X	190
Tresungers	Corn	SX0079	50°34·8'	4°49·1'W	A	200
Tresungers Point	Corn	SX0081	50°35·9'	4°49·2'W	X	200
Tresvennack	Corn	SW4428	50°6·1'	5°34·4'W	X	203
Tresvennack Pillar	Corn	SW4427	50°5·5'	5°34·4'W	A	203
Treswallen	Corn	SW9547	50°17·5'	4°52·3'W	X	204
Treswallock	Corn	SX1078	50°34·5'	4°40·6'W	X	200
Treswallock Downs	Corn	SX1178	50°34·5'	4°39·8'W	X	200
Treswarrow Fm	Corn	SW9878	50°34·2'	4°50·8'W	FM	200
Tresweeta	Corn	SW9353	50°20·7'	4°54·2'W	X	200,204
Treswell	Notts	SK7879	53°18·4'	0°49·4'W	T	120,121
Treswell Wood	Notts	SK7679	53°18·4'	0°51·2'W	F	120
Treswen	Corn	SX2190	50°41·2'	4°31·7'W	X	190
Treswigga	Corn	SX1274	50°32·4'	4°38·8'W	X	200
Treswithian	Corn	SW6340	50°13·0'	5°19·0'W	T	203
Treswithian	Corn	SW9141	50°14·2'	4°55·5'W	X	204
Treswithian Downs	Corn	SW6341	50°13·5'	5°19·0'W	T	203
Treswny Moor	Pemb	SM7325	51°52·9'	5°17·5'W	X	157
Tre Taliesin	Cered	SN6591	52°30·3'	3°58·9'W	T	135
Tretawn Fm	Corn	SX0375	50°32·7'	4°46·5'W	FM	200
Trethake Fm	Corn	SX1552	50°20·6'	4°35·6'W	FM	201
Tretharrup	Corn	SW7422	50°3·5'	5°9·1'W	X	204
Trethawle Fm	Corn	SX2662	50°26·2'	4°26·6'W	FM	201
Tretheague	Corn	SW7236	50°11·0'	5°11·3'W	X	204
Tretheake Manor	Corn	SW9341	50°14·2'	4°53·8'W	X	204
Trethella	Corn	SW8941	50°14·1'	4°57·2'W	X	204
Trethellan Water	Corn	SW7138	50°12·1'	5°12·2'W	T	203
Trethem	Corn	SW8536	50°11·3'	5°0·4'W	X	204
Trethem Mill	Corn	SW8636	50°11·4'	4°59·5'W	X	204
Trethennal Manor	Corn	SW9340	50°13·7'	4°53·8'W	X	204
Trethern Fm	Corn	SX0984	50°37·7'	4°41·7'W	FM	200
Tretherres	Corn	SW8150	50°18·8'	5°4·2'W	X	200,204
Trethevan Fm	Corn	SX0374	50°32·2'	4°46·4'W	FM	200
Trethevey	Corn	SX0657	50°23·1'	4°43·4'W	X	200
Trethevy	Corn	SX0373	50°31·7'	4°46·4'W	X	200
Trethevy	Corn	SX0789	50°40·4'	4°43·5'W	T	190,200
Trethevy	Corn	SX2881	50°36·4'	4°25·5'W	X	201
Trethevy Quoit	Corn	SX2568	50°29·4'	4°27·7'W	A	201
Trethew	Corn	SX0758	50°23·6'	4°42·6'W	X	200
Trethewell	Corn	SW8535	50°10·8'	5°0·3'W	T	204
Trethewell Fm	Corn	SW8770	50°29·7'	4°59·8'W	FM	200
Trethewey	Corn	SW3823	50°3·2'	5°39·2'W	T	203
Trethewey	Corn	SW7323	50°4·1'	5°10·0'W	X	204
Trethewey	Corn	SW9072	50°30·8'	4°57·4'W	X	200
Trethewey Fm	Corn	SW9143	50°15·2'	4°55·5'W	FM	204
Trethias Fm	Corn	SW8673	50°31·3'	5°0·8'W	FM	200
Trethias Island	Corn	SW8573	50°31·3'	5°1·6'W	X	200
Trethick Fm	Corn	SX0472	50°31·1'	4°45·5'W	FM	200
Trethiggy Fm	Corn	SW8459	50°23·7'	5°2·0'W	FM	200
Trethill	Corn	SX3754	50°22·0'	4°17·1'W	X	201
Trethill Cliffs	Corn	SX3753	50°21·5'	4°17·1'W	X	201
Trethillick	Corn	SW9075	50°32·5'	4°57·5'W	T	200
Trethin	Corn	SX1081	50°36·1'	4°40·7'W	X	200
Trethingey Fm	Corn	SW5736	50°10·7'	5°23·8'W	FM	203
Trethinna	Corn	SX2482	50°36·9'	4°28·9'W	X	201
Trethinnick	Corn	SX2367	50°28·8'	4°29·3'W	X	201
Trethomas	Caer	ST1888	51°35·3'	3°10·6'W	T	171
Trethorne Leisure Fm	Corn	SX2883	50°37·5'	4°25·5'W	FM	201
Trethosa	Corn	SW9454	50°21·2'	4°53·4'W	T	200
Trethowa	Corn	SW8848	50°17·9'	4°58·2'W	X	204
Trethowel	Corn	SX0153	50°20·8'	4°47·5'W	T	200,204
Trethowell	Corn	SW8242	50°14·5'	5°3·1'W	X	204
Trethullan Castle	Corn	SW9751	50°19·7'	4°50·8'W	A	200,204
Trethurgy	Corn	SX0355	50°22·0'	4°45·8'W	T	200
Trethvas Fm	Corn	SW7013	49°58·6'	5°12·1'W	FM	203
Tretio	Pemb	SM7828	51°54·6'	5°13·3'W	T	157
Tretio Common	Pemb	SM7828	51°54·6'	5°13·3'W	X	157
Tretire	Heref	SO5223	51°54·4'	2°41·5'W	T	162
Treto	Carm	SN2730	51°56·7'	4°30·6'W	X	145
Tretoil	Corn	SX0663	50°26·3'	4°43·6'W	X	200
Tretower	Powys	SO1821	51°53·1'	3°11·1'W	T	161
Tretton Manor Fm	Lincs	TF4217	52°44·1'	0°6·6'E	FM	131
Treuddyn	Flint	SJ2558	53°7·1'	3°6·8'W	T	117
Trevabyn	Corn	SW5431	50°7·9'	5°26·2'W	X	203
Trevaccoon	Pemb	SM8130	51°55·8'	5°10·7'W	X	157
Treva Croft Wood	Corn	SW5336	50°10·6'	5°27·2'W	F	203
Trevaddra	Corn	SW7523	50°4·1'	5°8·3'W	X	204
Trevadlock	Corn	SX2679	50°35·3'	4°27·1'W	T	201
Trevadoc	Heref	SO2541	52°4·0'	3°5·3'W	X	148,161
Trevague	Corn	SX2379	50°35·3'	4°29·7'W	X	201
Treval	Powys	SO0267	52°17·8'	3°25·8'W	X	136,147
Trevales	Corn	SW7435	50°10·6'	5°9·5'W	X	204
Trevalfry	Corn	SX1756	50°22·8'	4°34·1'W	X	201
Trevalga	Corn	SX0890	50°40·9'	4°42·7'W	T	190
Trevalgan	Corn	SW4940	50°12·6'	5°30·7'W	T	203
Trevallack	Corn	SW7821	50°3·1'	5°5·7'W	X	204
Trevallen	Pemb	SR9793	51°36·2'	4°55·5'W	X	158
Trevallen Downs	Pemb	SR9693	51°36·2'	4°56·4'W	X	158
Trevallett	Corn	SX2884	50°38·1'	4°25·6'W	X	201
Trevalso	Corn	SW8152	50°19·9'	5°4·3'W	X	200,204
Trevalsoe	Corn	SW7919	50°2·0'	5°4·8'W	X	204
Trevalyn	Wrex	SJ3756	53°6·1'	2°56·1'W	T	117
Trevalyn Fm	Wrex	SJ3857	53°6·6'	2°55·2'W	FM	117
Trevalyn Hall	Wrex	SJ3656	53°6·1'	2°56·9'W	A	117
Trevalyn Meadows	Wrex	SJ3956	53°6·1'	2°54·3'W	X	117

Trevance	Corn	SW9371	50°30·4′	4°54·8′W	T	200
Trevane	Pemb	SN0410	51°45·5′	4°50·0′W	X	157,158
Trevanger	Corn	SW9577	50°33·6′	4°53·3′W	T	200
Trevanney Fm	Corn	SX0556	50°22·5′	4°44·2′W	FM	200
Trevan Point	Corn	SW9680	50°35·3′	4°52·5′W	X	200
Trevanson	Corn	SW9772	50°31·0′	4°51·4′W	T	200
Trevan Wood	Corn	SW9350	50°19·1′	4°54·1′W	F	200,204
Trevarder	Corn	SX1651	50°20·0′	4°34·8′W	X	201
Trevarner	Corn	SX0072	50°31·1′	4°48·9′W	X	200
Trevarno	Corn	SW6430	50°7·6′	5°17·8′W	X	203
Trevarnon	Corn	SW5939	50°12·4′	5°22·3′W	X	203
Trevarnon Round	Corn	SW5840	50°12·9′	5°23·2′W	A	203
Trevarrack	Corn	SW4831	50°7·8′	5°31·2′W	T	203
Trevarrack	Corn	SW5137	50°11·1′	5°28·9′W	X	203
Trevarren	Corn	SW9160	50°24·4′	4°56·1′W	T	200
Trevarrian	Corn	SW8566	50°27·5′	5°1·4′W	T	200
Trevarrick	Corn	SW9843	50°15·4′	4°49·7′W	T	204
Trevarth	Corn	SW7240	50°13·2′	5°11·4′W	T	204
Trevartha	Corn	SX2764	50°27·3′	4°25·9′W	X	201
Trevarthain	Corn	SW8458	50°23·2′	5°1·9′W	X	200
Trevarth Fm	Corn	SW7340	50°13·2′	5°10·6′W	FM	204
Trevarthian Fm	Corn	SW5332	50°8·4′	5°27·0′W	FM	203
Trevascus	Corn	SW9744	50°15·9′	4°50·5′W	X	204
Trevase Fm	Heref	SO5125	51°55·5′	2°42·4′W	FM	162
Trevashmond	Corn	SX3562	50°26·3′	4°19·0′W	X	201
Trevaskis	Corn	SW7646	50°16·5′	5°8·3′W	X	204
Trevassack	Corn	SW7122	50°3·5′	5°11·6′W	X	203
Trevassack	Corn	SW7228	50°6·7′	5°11·0′W	X	204
Trevathan	Corn	SW9977	50°33·7′	4°49·9′W	X	200
Trevaughan	Carm	SN2015	51°48·5′	4°36·3′W	T	158
Trevaughan	Carm	SN3921	51°52·1′	4°19·9′W	T	145,159
Tre-vaughan	Carm	SN4021	51°52·1′	4°19·0′W	T	159
Trevaughan	Powys	SO0847	52°7·1′	3°20·2′W	X	147
Trevaunance Cove	Corn	SW7251	50°19·1′	5°11·8′W	W	204
Trevawden	Corn	SX1958	50°23·9′	4°32·4′W	X	201
Trevaylor	Corn	SW4632	50°8·3′	5°32·9′W	X	203
Trevaylor Stream	Corn	SW4632	50°8·3′	5°32·9′W	W	203
Trevayne	Pemb	SN1403	51°41·9′	4°41·1′W	X	158
Treveador	Corn	SW7425	50°5·2′	5°9·2′W	X	204
Treveague Fm	Corn	SX0041	50°14·3′	4°47·9′W	FM	204
Treveal	Corn	SW4740	50°12·6′	5°32·4′W	T	203
Treveal	Corn	SW7858	50°23·0′	5°7·0′W	T	200
Treveale	Corn	SW8751	50°19·5′	4°59·2′W	X	200,204
Trevean	Corn	SW4135	50°9·7′	5°37·2′W	X	203
Trevean	Corn	SW7620	50°2·5′	5°7·3′W	X	204
Trevean	Corn	SW7920	50°2·6′	5°4·8′W	X	204
Trevean	Corn	SW8441	50°14·0′	5°1·4′W	X	204
Trevean	Corn	SW8658	50°23·2′	5°0·3′W	X	200
Trevean	Corn	SW8772	50°30·8′	4°59·9′W	X	200
Trevean Cove	Corn	SW5428	50°6·3′	5°26·1′W	W	203
Trevean Fm	Corn	SW5428	50°6·3′	5°26·1′W	FM	203
Treveans	Corn	SX0782	50°36·6′	4°43·3′W	X	200
Trevear	Corn	SW3726	50°4·8′	5°40·2′W	X	203
Trevear	Corn	SW8773	50°31·3′	4°59·9′W	X	200
Trevear Fm	Corn	SW9471	50°30·4′	4°53·9′W	FM	200
Trevease Fm	Corn	SW7231	50°8·4′	5°11·1′W	FM	204
Trevedda Fm	Corn	SX1453	50°21·1′	4°36·5′W	FM	200
Treveddoe	Corn	SX1569	50°29·7′	4°36·1′W	X	201
Treveddon	Corn	SW7115	49°59·7′	5°11·3′W	X	203
Treveddw	Monm	SO3221	51°53·2′	2°58·9′W	X	161
Trevedra Fm	Corn	SW3627	50°5·3′	5°41·1′W	FM	203
Trevedran	Corn	SW4123	50°3·3′	5°36·7′W	X	203
Trevedras	Corn	SW8866	50°27·6′	4°58·8′W	X	200
Trevegean	Corn	SW3629	50°6·4′	5°41·2′W	T	203
Treveglos	Corn	SX0473	50°31·7′	4°45·6′W	X	200
Trevego	Corn	SX1359	50°24·3′	4°37·5′W	X	200
Treveigan Fm	Corn	SX0270	50°30·0′	4°47·1′W	FM	200
Treveighan	Corn	SX0779	50°35·0′	4°43·2′W	T	200
Trevelgue	Corn	SW8363	50°25·8′	5°3·0′W	X	200
Trevelgue Head	Corn	SW8263	50°25·8′	5°3·8′W	X	200
Trevell	Corn	SX2581	50°36·4′	4°28·0′W	X	201
Trevella	Corn	SW7960	50°24·1′	5°6·2′W	X	200
Trevella	Corn	SW8450	50°18·9′	5°1·7′W	X	200,204
Trevellan	Corn	SW8148	50°17·7′	5°4·1′W	X	204
Trevellas	Corn	SW7452	50°19·7′	5°10·2′W	T	204
Trevellas Coombe	Corn	SW7251	50°19·1′	5°11·8′W	X	204
Trevellas Porth	Corn	SW7252	50°19·7′	5°11·8′W	W	204
Trevella Stream	Corn	SW8547	50°17·3′	5°0·7′W	W	204
Trevelloe Fm	Corn	SW4425	50°4·4′	5°34·3′W	FM	203
Trevelmond	Corn	SX2063	50°26·6′	4°31·7′W	T	201
Trevelog	Monm	SO2729	51°57·5′	3°3·4′W	X	161
Trevelver	Corn	SW9574	50°32·0′	4°53·2′W	T	200
Trevelyan	Corn	SX1554	50°21·6′	4°35·7′W	X	201
Trevemedar	Corn	SW8571	50°30·2′	5°1·5′W	X	200
Trevemper	Corn	SW8159	50°23·6′	5°4·5′W	T	200
Treven	Corn	SW5734	50°9·6′	5°23·8′W	X	203
Treven	Corn	SX0587	50°39·2′	4°45·1′W	T	200
Treven	Corn	SX1884	50°37·9′	4°34·0′W	X	201
Treven	Corn	SX2184	50°37·9′	4°31·5′W	X	201
Treven	Corn	SX3373	50°32·2′	4°21·0′W	X	201
Trevena	Corn	SW6128	50°6·5′	5°20·2′W	T	203
Treveneague	Corn	SW5432	50°8·5′	5°26·2′W	X	203
Trevenen	Corn	SW6829	50°7·2′	5°14·4′W	T	203
Trevenen Bal	Corn	SW6729	50°7·2′	5°15·2′W	T	203
Trevengenow	Corn	SW8969	50°29·2′	4°58·1′W	X	200
Trevenna	Corn	SX0955	50°22·1′	4°40·8′W	X	200
Trevenna	Corn	SX1768	50°29·2′	4°34·4′W	X	201
Trevennel Fm	Corn	SW8534	50°10·3′	5°0·3′W	FM	204
Trevennen Fm	Corn	SW9743	50°15·4′	4°50·5′W	FM	204
Trevenn Fm	Corn	SX1491	50°41·6′	4°37·6′W	FM	190
Trevenning	Corn	SX0777	50°33·9′	4°43·1′W	T	200
Trevenwith	Corn	SW7417	50°0·9′	5°8·9′W	X	204
Treveor	Corn	SW8744	50°15·7′	4°58·9′W	X	204
Treveor	Corn	SW9841	50°14·3′	4°49·6′W	T	204
Treverbyn	Corn	SW8849	50°18·4′	4°58·3′W	X	204
Treverbyn	Corn	SX0156	50°22·5′	4°47·5′W	T	200
Treverbyn	Corn	SX0356	50°22·5′	4°45·9′W	T	200
Treverbyn	Corn	SX2067	50°28·7′	4°31·8′W	T	201
Treverbyn Mill	Corn	SX2067	50°28·7′	4°31·8′W	T	201
Treverbyn Vean	Corn	SX1865	50°27·6′	4°33·5′W	X	201

Trevereux	Surrey	TQ4350	51°14·1′	0°3·3′E	X	187
Treverras	Corn	SW8438	50°12·4′	5°1·3′W	X	204
Treverry Fm	Corn	SW6925	50°5·0′	5°13·4′W	FM	203
Treverva	Corn	SW7531	50°8·4′	5°8·6′W	T	204
Treverven	Heref	SO5320	51°52·8′	2°40·6′W	X	162
Treverven Fm	Corn	SW4123	50°3·3′	5°36·7′W	FM	203
Treverven Ho	Corn	SW4023	50°3·3′	5°37·6′W	X	203
Treverward Ho	Shrops	SO2878	52°24·0′	3°3·1′W	X	137,148
Trevescan	Corn	SW3524	50°3·7′	5°41·8′W	T	203
Trevessa Fm	Corn	SW4839	50°12·1′	5°31·5′W	FM	203
Trevessa Fm	Corn	SW5433	50°9·0′	5°26·2′W	FM	203
Trevessa Fm	Corn	SW8655	50°21·6′	5°0·2′W	FM	200
Trevesson Fm	Corn	SW9941	50°14·3′	4°48·8′W	FM	204
Trevethan	Corn	SW7241	50°13·7′	5°11·4′W	X	204
Trevethan	Corn	SW8571	50°30·2′	5°1·5′W	X	200
Trevethin	Torf	SO2702	51°43·0′	3°3·0′W	T	171
Trevethoe	Corn	SW5337	50°11·1′	5°27·2′W	X	203
Trevethoe Fm	Lincs	TF3732	52°52·3′	0°2·5′E	FM	131
Trevia	Corn	SX0983	50°37·2′	4°41·6′W	T	200
Treviades	Corn	SW7428	50°6·8′	5°9·3′W	X	204
Trevibban	Corn	SW9169	50°29·2′	4°56·4′W	X	200
Trevider	Corn	SW4326	50°4·9′	5°35·2′W	X	203
Trevidgeowe Fm	Corn	SW9964	50°26·7′	4°49·5′W	FM	200
Trevigan	Pemb	SM8329	51°55·3′	5°9·0′W	X	157
Trevigo	Corn	SW9679	50°34·7′	4°52·5′W	X	200
Trevigro	Corn	SX3369	50°30·1′	4°20·9′W	T	201
Trevigue	Corn	SX1395	50°43·7′	4°38·6′W	X	190
Trevilder	Corn	SX0272	50°31·1′	4°47·2′W	T	200
Treviles	Corn	SW8940	50°13·6′	4°57·1′W	X	204
Trevilgan Fm	Corn	SW6926	50°5·6′	5°13·4′W	FM	203
Trevilges Fm	Corn	SW6828	50°6·6′	5°14·3′W	FM	203
Trevilgus Fm	Corn	SW9372	50°30·9′	4°54·8′W	FM	200
Trevilla	Corn	SW8239	50°12·9′	5°3·0′W	T	204
Trevilla	Corn	SX1491	50°41·6′	4°37·6′W	X	190
Trevilla	Corn	SX3274	50°32·7′	4°21·9′W	X	201
Trevillador	Corn	SW9170	50°29·8′	4°56·4′W	X	200
Trevilla Down	Corn	SX1590	50°41·1′	4°36·8′W	X	190
Trevilla Park	Corn	SX1186	50°38·8′	4°40·0′W	X	200
Trevilledor	Corn	SW8867	50°28·1′	4°58·9′W	X	200
Trevilley	Corn	SW3524	50°3·7′	5°41·8′W	X	203
Trevilley	Corn	SW8359	50°23·7′	5°2·8′W	X	200
Trevilley Fm	Corn	SX0681	50°36·0′	4°44·1′W	FM	200
Trevillian	Corn	SX1892	50°42·2′	4°34·3′W	X	190
Trevillian's Gate	Corn	SX1683	50°37·3′	4°35·7′W	X	201
Trevillick	Corn	SW9349	50°18·5′	4°54·1′W	X	204
Trevillies	Corn	SX2361	50°25·6′	4°29·1′W	X	201
Trevillis	Corn	SX1861	50°25·5′	4°33·4′W	X	201
Trevillis Wood	Corn	SX1961	50°25·5′	4°32·5′W	F	201
Trevillyn	Corn	SX0461	50°25·2′	4°45·2′W	X	200
Trevilson	Corn	SW8455	50°21·6′	5°1·8′W	T	200
Trevilvas	Corn	SW9247	50°17·4′	4°54·8′W	X	204
Trevilveth	Corn	SW9442	50°14·8′	4°53·0′W	X	204
Trevince	Corn	SW7340	50°13·2′	5°10·6′W	X	204
Trevine	Corn	SW9976	50°33·2′	4°49·9′W	T	200
Trevinert	Pemb	SM7625	51°53·0′	5°14·9′W	X	157
Trevinnick	Corn	SX0178	50°34·3′	4°48·2′W	X	200
Trevio	Corn	SW8771	50°30·2′	4°59·9′W	X	200
Treviscoe	Corn	SW9456	50°22·3′	4°53·4′W	T	200
Treviscoe Barton	Corn	SW9356	50°22·3′	4°54·3′W	X	200
Trevisick	Corn	SX1999	50°46·0′	4°33·6′W	X	190
Trevisker Fm	Corn	SW8769	50°29·2′	4°59·8′W	FM	200
Trevisker Fm	Corn	SW9072	50°30·8′	4°57·4′W	FM	200
Treviskey	Corn	SW7239	50°12·7′	5°11·4′W	T	204
Treviskey	Corn	SW9340	50°13·7′	4°53·8′W	X	204
Trevispian-Vean	Corn	SW8450	50°18·9′	5°1·7′W	X	200,204
Trevisquite Manor	Corn	SX0474	50°32·2′	4°45·6′W	X	200
Trevissick	Corn	SX0248	50°18·2′	4°46·5′W	X	204
Trevissick	Corn	SX0972	50°31·2′	4°41·3′W	X	200
Trevissick Fm	Corn	SW7047	50°16·9′	5°13·3′W	FM	203
Trevissome	Corn	SW7547	50°17·0′	5°9·1′W	X	204
Trevissome Ho	Corn	SW7934	50°10·1′	5°5·3′W	X	204
Trevithal	Corn	SW4626	50°5·0′	5°32·7′W	T	203
Trevithel	Powys	SO1536	52°1·2′	3°13·9′W	X	161
Trevithian	Corn	SW7620	50°2·5′	5°7·3′W	X	204
Trevithick	Corn	SW8862	50°25·4′	4°58·7′W	X	200
Trevithick East Fm	Corn	SW9363	50°26·1′	4°54·5′W	FM	200
Trevithick Fm	Corn	SW9645	50°16·4′	4°51·4′W	FM	204
Trevithick Manor	Corn	SW8259	50°23·7′	5°3·7′W	X	200
Trevivian	Corn	SX1785	50°38·4′	4°34·9′W	X	201
Trevol	Powys	SO1368	52°18·4′	3°16·2′W	X	136,148
Trevoll	Corn	SW8358	50°23·1′	5°2·8′W	T	200
Trevolland	Corn	SW9248	50°18·0′	4°54·9′W	X	204
Trevollard	Corn	SX1656	50°22·7′	4°34·9′W	X	201
Trevollard	Corn	SX3858	50°24·2′	4°16·4′W	X	201
Trevone	Corn	SW8975	50°32·4′	4°58·3′W	T	200
Trevone Bay	Corn	SW8876	50°33·0′	4°59·2′W	W	200
Trevone Fm	Corn	SW7432	50°8·9′	5°9·4′W	FM	204
Trevonny	Monm	SO4421	51°53·3′	2°48·4′W	X	161
Trevoole	Corn	SW6337	50°11·4′	5°18·9′W	X	203
Trevor	Denb	SJ2742	52°58·5′	3°4·8′W	T	117
Trevorder	Corn	SW9870	50°29·9′	4°50·5′W	X	200
Trevorder	Corn	SX1467	50°28·6′	4°36·9′W	X	200
Trevorgans	Corn	SW4025	50°4·3′	5°37·7′W	X	203
Trevorgey	Corn	SW8670	50°29·7′	5°0·7′W	X	200
Trevorgus	Corn	SW8873	50°31·3′	4°59·1′W	X	200
Trevor Hall	Denb	SJ2542	52°58·4′	3°6·6′W	A	117
Trevornick	Corn	SW7758	50°23·0′	5°7·8′W	X	200
Trevornick	Corn	SW9265	50°27·1′	4°55·4′W	X	200
Trevorrian	Corn	SW3726	50°4·8′	5°40·2′W	X	203
Trevorrian	Corn	SX0479	50°34·9′	4°45·7′W	X	200
Trevorrian Fm	Corn	SW4126	50°4·9′	5°36·9′W	FM	203
Trevorrick	Corn	SW8672	50°30·8′	5°0·7′W	X	200
Trevorrick	Corn	SW9273	50°31·4′	4°55·7′W	T	200
Trevor Rocks	Denb	SJ2343	52°59·0′	3°8·4′W	X	117
Trevorrow Fm	Corn	SW5233	50°8·9′	5°27·9′W	FM	203
Trevorry	Corn	SX0857	50°23·1′	4°41·7′W	X	200
Trevors Close Fm	Ches	SJ8771	53°14·4′	2°11·3′W	FM	118
Trevor Tower	Denb	SJ2543	52°59·0′	3°6·6′W	X	117
Trevor Uchaf	Denb	SJ2442	52°58·4′	3°7·5′W	T	117
Trevorva	Corn	SW8946	50°16·8′	4°57·3′W	X	204

Trevose Fm	Corn	SW8675	50°32·4′	5°0·8′W	FM	200
Trevose Head	Corn	SW8576	50°32·9′	5°1·7′W	X	200
Trevoulter Fm	Corn	SX1999	50°46·0′	4°33·6′W	FM	190
Trevowah	Corn	SW7959	50°23·6′	5°6·2′W	T	200
Trevowhan	Corn	SW4035	50°9·7′	5°38·1′W	T	203
Trevoyan	Corn	SW8672	50°30·8′	5°0·7′W	X	200
Trevozah Barton	Corn	SX3380	50°36·0′	4°21·2′W	X	201
Trevuzza	Corn	SW8958	50°23·3′	4°57·7′W	X	200
Trevyr	Monm	SO3922	51°53·8′	2°52·8′W	X	161
Trew	Corn	SW6129	50°7·0′	5°20·2′W	T	203
Trew	Corn	SX2287	50°39·6′	4°30·7′W	X	190
Trew	Devon	SS4704	50°49·2′	4°9·9′W	X	191
Trew	Devon	SS8503	50°49·1′	3°37·6′W	X	191
Trewadoc	Heref	SO4423	51°54·4′	2°48·4′W	X	161
Trewalder	Corn	SX0782	50°36·6′	4°43·3′W	T	200
Trewalkin	Powys	SO1531	51°58·5′	3°13·9′W	X	161
Trewall	Corn	SX3254	50°22·0′	4°21·4′W	X	201
Trewalla	Corn	SX2471	50°31·0′	4°28·6′W	X	201
Trewalter	Powys	SO1229	51°57·4′	3°16·4′W	X	161
Trewandra Fm	Corn	SX3561	50°25·8′	4°19·0′W	FM	201
Trewane	Corn	SX0378	50°34·3′	4°46·6′W	A	200
Trewan Hall	Corn	SW9164	50°26·6′	4°56·2′W	A	200
Trewannett	Corn	SX1191	50°41·5′	4°40·2′W	X	190
Trewannion	Corn	SX1390	50°41·0′	4°38·5′W	X	190
Trewanta Hall Fm	Corn	SX2680	50°35·9′	4°27·1′W	FM	201
Trewardale	Corn	SX1071	50°30·7′	4°40·4′W	X	200
Trewardreva	Corn	SW7230	50°7·8′	5°11·0′W	X	204
Trewarlett	Corn	SX3380	50°36·0′	4°21·2′W	X	201
Trewarlett Cross	Corn	SX3280	50°36·0′	4°22·1′W	X	201
Trewarmenna	Corn	SW9447	50°17·5′	4°53·2′W	X	204
Trewarmett	Corn	SX0686	50°38·7′	4°44·3′W	T	200
Trewarne	Heref	SO5217	51°51·2′	2°41·4′W	X	162
Trewarnevas	Corn	SW7824	50°4·7′	5°5·8′W	X	204
Trewarren	Pemb	SM8207	51°43·4′	5°9·0′W	X	157
Trewarren Fm	Corn	SW9052	50°20·1′	4°56·7′W	FM	200,204
Trewartha	Corn	SW5137	50°11·1′	5°28·9′W	T	203
Trewartha	Corn	SW9239	50°13·1′	4°54·6′W	T	204
Trewarthenick	Corn	SW9044	50°15·8′	4°56·4′W	X	204
Trewarveneth	Corn	SW4627	50°5·6′	5°32·7′W	X	203
Trewashford	Corn	SX3664	50°27·4′	4°18·3′W	X	201
Trewassa	Corn	SX1486	50°38·9′	4°37·5′W	T	200
Trewaters Fm	Corn	SW8553	50°20·5′	5°0·9′W	FM	200,204
Trewaugh	Heref	SO5122	51°53·9′	2°42·3′W	X	162
Trewaun	Cered	SN6460	52°13·5′	3°59·1′W	X	146
Trewavas	Corn	SW5926	50°5·4′	5°21·8′W	X	203
Trewavas Head	Corn	SW5926	50°5·4′	5°21·8′W	X	203
Treway Fm	Corn	SW9450	50°19·1′	4°53·3′W	FM	200,204
Treway Fm	Corn	SX1491	50°41·6′	4°37·6′W	FM	190
Treweatha	Corn	SX2167	50°28·8′	4°31·0′W	X	201
Treweatha	Corn	SX2965	50°27·8′	4°24·2′W	X	201
Treween	Corn	SX2282	50°36·9′	4°30·6′W	T	201
Treweers	Corn	SX1952	50°20·6′	4°32·3′W	X	201
Trewellard	Corn	SW3733	50°8·6′	5°40·5′W	T	203
Trewellard Zawn	Corn	SW3734	50°9·1′	5°40·5′W	W	203
Trewellwell	Pemb	SM7926	51°53·6′	5°12·3′W	X	157
Trewen	Corn	SX0883	50°37·1′	4°42·5′W	T	200
Trewen	Corn	SX1959	50°24·4′	4°32·5′W	X	201
Trewen	Corn	SX2583	50°37·5′	4°28·1′W	T	201
Trewen	Gwyn	SH2630	52°50·6′	4°34·6′W	X	123
Trewen	Heref	SO5318	51°51·8′	2°40·6′W	X	162
Trewen	Monm	ST4590	51°36·6′	2°47·3′W	T	171,172
Trewen Fm	Corn	SW7731	50°8·5′	5°6·9′W	FM	204
Trewen Fm	Corn	SX0576	50°33·3′	4°44·8′W	FM	200
Trewenfron	Pemb	SN1341	52°2·4′	4°43·2′W	X	145
Trewennack	Corn	SW6828	50°6·6′	5°14·3′W	T	203
Trewennan	Corn	SX0681	50°36·0′	4°44·1′W	T	200
Trewent Point	Pemb	SS0297	51°38·5′	4°51·3′W	X	158
Tre-wern	Card	ST1080	51°30·9′	3°17·4′W	X	171
Trewern	Carm	SN6532	51°58·4′	3°57·5′W	X	146
Trewern	Corn	SW4232	50°8·2′	5°36·3′W	X	203
Trewern	Heref	SO3230	51°58·1′	2°59·0′W	X	161
Trewern	Pemb	SN0332	51°57·3′	4°51·6′W	X	145,157
Trewern	Pemb	SN0838	52°0·7′	4°47·5′W	X	145
Trewern	Pemb	SN1208	51°44·6′	4°43·0′W	X	158
Trewern	Pemb	SN1717	51°49·5′	4°38·9′W	X	158
Tre-wern	Powys	SJ1326	52°49·7′	3°17·1′W	X	125
Trewern	Powys	SJ2811	52°41·8′	3°3·5′W	T	126
Trewern	Powys	SO1462	52°15·2′	3°15·2′W	X	148
Trewern	Powys	SO2257	52°12·6′	3°8·1′W	X	148
Tre-wern	Shrops	SJ2932	52°53·1′	3°2·9′W	X	126
Trewern-fawr	Cered	SN6560	52°13·5′	3°58·2′W	X	146
Trewern Fm	Powys	SJ2712	52°42·3′	3°4·4′W	FM	126
Trewern Hall	Powys	SJ2611	52°41·7′	3°5·3′W	A	126
Trewern Hill	Powys	SO1243	52°4·9′	3°16·7′W	X	148,161
Trewern Round	Corn	SW4331	50°7·6′	5°35·4′W	A	203
Trewerry Mill	Corn	SW8358	50°23·1′	5°2·8′W	X	200
Trewetha	Corn	SX0080	50°35·4′	4°49·2′W	T	200
Trewether	Corn	SX0479	50°34·9′	4°45·7′W	T	200
Trewethern	Corn	SX1158	50°23·7′	4°39·2′W	X	200
Trewethern	Corn	SX0076	50°33·2′	4°49·0′W	T	200
Trewey	Corn	SW4538	50°11·5′	5°34·0′W	T	203
Trewey Common	Corn	SW4636	50°10·4′	5°33·1′W	X	203
Trew Fm	Devon	SS2921	50°58·0′	4°25·7′W	FM	190
Trew Fm	Devon	SX4699	50°46·4′	4°10·7′W	FM	190
Trewhella Fm	Corn	SW5532	50°8·5′	5°25·4′W	FM	203
Trewhiddle	Corn	SX0051	50°19·7′	4°48·2′W	X	200,204
Trewhitt Hall	Northum	NU0006	55°21·1′	1°59·6′W	X	81
Trewhitt Moor	Northum	NT9804	55°20·1′	2°1·5′W	X	81
Trewhitt Steads	Northum	NU0006	55°21·1′	1°59·6′W	X	81
Trewidden	Corn	SW4429	50°6·6′	5°34·5′W	X	203
Trewidland	Corn	SX2559	50°24·5′	4°27·4′W	T	201
Trewidwal	Pemb	SN1245	52°4·5′	4°44·2′W	X	145
Trewiggett	Corn	SX0379	50°34·9′	4°46·6′W	X	200
Trewillis	Corn	SW7717	50°0·9′	5°6·4′W	X	204
Tre-Wilmot	I of Angl	SH2281	53°18·0′	4°39·9′W	X	114
Trewilym	Pemb	SM8827	51°54·3′	5°5·6′W	X	157
Trewilym	Pemb	SN1440	52°1·9′	4°42·3′W	X	145
Trewin	Corn	SX3555	50°22·5′	4°18·9′W	X	201
Trewince	Corn	SW7322	50°3·5′	5°9·9′W	X	204
Trewince	Corn	SW7335	50°10·5′	5°10·4′W	X	204

Trewince	Corn	SW7528	50°6·8′	5°8·5′W	X	204
Trewince	Corn	SW8563	50°25·9′	5°1·3′W	X	200
Trewince	Corn	SW8633	50°9·7′	4°59·4′W	X	204
Trewince	Corn	SW9150	50°19·0′	4°55·8′W	X	200,204
Trewince	Corn	SW9371	50°30·4′	4°54·8′W	X	200
Trewindle	Corn	SX1462	50°25·9′	4°36·8′W	T	200
Trewindsor	Cered	SN2247	52°5·8′	4°35·5′W	X	145
Trewinnard Manor	Corn	SW5434	50°9·5′	5°26·3′W	X	203
Trewinney	Corn	SX0145	50°16·5′	4°47·2′W	X	204
Trewinnick	Corn	SW8969	50°29·2′	4°58·1′W	X	200
Trewinnick	Corn	SX0888	50°39·8′	4°42·6′W	X	190,200
Trewinnion	Corn	SW8857	50°22·7′	4°58·5′W	X	200
Trewinnow	Corn	SW9549	50°18·6′	4°52·4′W	X	204
Trewinnow	Corn	SX1686	50°38·9′	4°35·8′W	X	201
Trewinnow	Corn	SX2978	50°34·8′	4°24·5′W	X	201
Trewinnow Cross	Corn	SX2979	50°35·4′	4°24·6′W	X	201
Trewint	Corn	SW9477	50°33·6′	4°54·1′W	X	200
Trewint	Corn	SX1072	50°31·3′	4°40·4′W	X	200
Trewint	Corn	SX1080	50°35·6′	4°40·7′W	X	200
Trewint	Corn	SX1897	50°44·9′	4°34·4′W	T	190
Trewint	Corn	SX2280	50°35·8′	4°30·5′W	T	201
Trewint	Corn	SX2963	50°26·8′	4°24·1′W	T	201
Trewint	Corn	SX3759	50°24·7′	4°17·3′W	X	201
Trewint Downs	Corn	SX2080	50°35·8′	4°32·2′W	X	201
Trewinte	Corn	SW9879	50°34·8′	4°50·8′W	X	200
Trewirgie	Corn	SW8845	50°16·3′	4°58·1′W	X	204
Trewiston Fm	Corn	SW9477	50°33·6′	4°54·1′W	FM	200
Trewithen	Corn	SW9147	50°17·4′	4°55·7′W	X	204
Trewithen Fm	Corn	SW8973	50°31·4′	4°58·2′W	FM	200
Trewithen Moor	Corn	SW7238	50°12·1′	5°11·3′W	X	204
Trewithey	Corn	SX2876	50°33·7′	4°25·3′W	X	201
Trewithian	Corn	SW8737	50°11·9′	4°58·7′W	T	204
Trewithick	Corn	SW6127	50°5·9′	5°20·2′W	X	203
Trewithick	Corn	SX2985	50°38·6′	4°24·7′W	T	201
Trewitten	Corn	SX0888	50°39·8′	4°42·6′W	X	190,200
Trewolla	Corn	SW8057	50°22·5′	5°5·3′W	X	200
Trewollack	Corn	SW8534	50°10·3′	5°0·3′W	X	204
Trewollack	Corn	SW9666	50°27·7′	4°52·1′W	X	200
Trewollack Fm	Corn	SW8461	50°24·8′	5°2·0′W	FM	200
Trewollack Plantn	Corn	SW9666	50°27·7′	4°52·1′W	F	200
Trewollock	Corn	SX0042	50°14·9′	4°47·9′W	T	204
Trewolsta	Corn	SX3461	50°25·8′	4°19·9′W	X	201
Trewolvas	Corn	SW9363	50°26·1′	4°54·5′W	X	200
Trewonnal	Corn	SW8742	50°14·6′	4°58·9′W	X	204
Trewonnard	Corn	SX1989	50°40·6′	4°33·3′W	X	190
Trewoodloe	Corn	SX3271	50°31·1′	4°21·8′W	T	201
Trewoofe	Corn	SW4325	50°4·4′	5°35·1′W	X	203
Trewoon	Corn	SW6819	50°1·8′	5°14·0′W	T	203
Trewoon	Corn	SW7522	50°3·6′	5°8·3′W	X	204
Trewoon	Corn	SW7631	50°8·4′	5°7·7′W	X	204
Trewoon	Corn	SW9952	50°20·3′	4°49·1′W	T	200,204
Trewoone	Corn	SW5736	50°10·7′	5°23·8′W	X	203
Treworder	Corn	SW7846	50°16·6′	5°6·6′W	X	204
Treworder	Corn	SX0172	50°31·1′	4°48·1′W	X	200
Treworga	Corn	SW8940	50°13·6′	4°57·1′W	T	204
Treworgan	Corn	SW8349	50°18·3′	5°2·5′W	X	204
Treworgan	Heref	SO5119	51°52·3′	2°42·3′W	X	162
Treworgan Common	Monm	SO4205	51°44·7′	2°50·0′W	T	161
Treworgans	Corn	SW7858	50°23·0′	5°7·0′W	X	200
Treworgey	Corn	SX2456	50°22·9′	4°28·2′W	X	201
Treworgey Manor	Corn	SX2466	50°28·3′	4°28·4′W	X	201
Treworgie	Corn	SW7623	50°4·1′	5°7·4′W	X	204
Treworgie Barton	Corn	SX1796	50°44·3′	4°35·2′W	X	190
Treworlas	Corn	SW8938	50°12·5′	4°57·1′W	T	204
Treworld	Corn	SX1190	50°41·0′	4°40·2′W	T	190
Trewornan	Corn	SW9874	50°32·1′	4°50·7′W	T	200
Treworra	Corn	SX1586	50°38·9′	4°36·6′W	X	201
Treworrick	Corn	SW9744	50°15·9′	4°50·5′W	X	204
Treworrick	Corn	SX2368	50°29·3′	4°29·3′W	T	201
Trewortha	Corn	SX2475	50°33·1′	4°28·7′W	X	201
Treworthal	Corn	SW8058	50°23·1′	5°5·3′W	X	200
Treworthal	Corn	SW8838	50°12·5′	4°57·9′W	T	204
Trewortha Tor	Corn	SX2475	50°33·1′	4°28·7′W	X	201
Trewortha Village	Corn	SX2276	50°33·6′	4°30·4′W	A	201
Treworthen Fm	Corn	SW7856	50°22·0′	5°6·9′W	FM	200
Treworvack	Corn	SW7332	50°8·9′	5°10·3′W	X	204
Treworval Fm	Corn	SW7629	50°7·4′	5°7·7′W	FM	204
Treworyan	Corn	SW8950	50°19·0′	4°57·5′W	X	200,204
Trewothack	Corn	SW7724	50°4·7′	5°6·6′W	X	204
Trewrach	Pemb	SM9938	52°0·5′	4°55·3′W	X	157
Trewrickle Fm	Corn	SX3554	50°22·0′	4°18·8′W	FM	201
Trewrong Fm	Corn	SX0953	50°21·0′	4°40·7′W	FM	200,204
Trewsbury Ho	Glos	ST9899	51°41·6′	2°1·3′W	X	163
Trewylan Hall	Powys	SJ2217	52°44·9′	3°8·9′W	X	126
Trewylan Ho	Powys	SJ2218	52°45·5′	3°8·9′W	X	126
Trewylan Isaf	Powys	SJ2118	52°45·5′	3°9·8′W	X	126
Trewyn	Devon	SS3304	50°48·9′	4°21·9′W	T	190
Tre-ŵyn	I of Angl	SH4585	53°20·6′	4°19·3′W	X	114
Tre-wyn	Monm	SO3222	51°53·8′	2°58·9′W	T	161
Trewysgoed	Monm	SO2720	51°52·7′	3°3·2′W	X	161
Trewythen	Powys	SO0090	52°30·2′	3°28·0′W	X	136
Treyarnon	Corn	SW8673	50°31·3′	5°0·8′W	T	200
Treyarnon Bay	Corn	SW8574	50°31·8′	5°1·6′W	W	200
Treyarnon Point	Corn	SW8574	50°31·8′	5°1·6′W	X	200
Treyeo	Corn	SS2704	50°48·8′	4°27·0′W	X	190
Treyew Mills	Corn	SW8044	50°15·5′	5°4·8′W	X	204
Treyford	W Susx	SU8218	50°57·6′	0°49·6′W	T	197
Treyford Hill	W Susx	SU8217	50°57·0′	0°49·6′W	H	197
Tre-y-llan	Powys	SJ0427	52°50·2′	3°25·1′W	X	125
Treyone	Corn	SX3156	50°23·0′	4°22·3′W	X	201
Treyscaw	Pemb	SM8428	51°54·8′	5°8·0′W	X	157
Tre-Ysgawen	I of Angl	SH4581	53°18·4′	4°19·2′W	X	114,115
Treza	Corn	SW6227	50°6·0′	5°19·3′W	X	203
Trezaise	Corn	SW9959	50°24·0′	4°49·3′W	T	200
Trezance	Corn	SX1269	50°29·7′	4°38·7′W	X	200
Trezare Fm	Corn	SX1153	50°21·0′	4°39·0′W	FM	200,204
Trezebel	Corn	SW7623	50°4·1′	5°7·4′W	X	204
Trezelah	Corn	SW4733	50°8·8′	5°32·1′W	T	203
Trezelland	Corn	SX1978	50°34·7′	4°33·0′W	X	201
Trezibbett	Corn	SX2075	50°33·1′	4°32·1′W	X	201

Trezise	Corn	SW7222	50°3·5′	5°10·8′W	X	204
Triallabreac	N Eil	NF8546	57°24·0′	7°14·2′W	X	22
Triallabreac Mòr	N Eil	NF8156	57°29·2′	7°19·0′W	X	22
Trian	Pth & Kin	NN7618	56°20·5′	3°59·9′W	X	57
Triangle	Cald	SE0422	53°41·9′	1°56·0′W	T	104
Triangle	Glos	SO5401	51°42·6′	2°39·6′W	T	162
Triangle	Staffs	SK0259	53°7·9′	1°57·8′W	X	119
Triangle	Staffs	SK0507	52°39·9′	1°55·2′W	T	139
Triangle Covert	Norf	TL9984	52°25·3′	0°56·0′E	F	144
Triangle Fm	Dorset	ST7518	50°57·9′	2°21·0′W	FM	183
Triangle Plantn	Suff	TL8578	52°22·4′	0°43·5′E	F	144
Triasamol	N Eil	NB0333	58°11·4′	7°2·8′W	X	13
Tribbens, The	Corn	SW3426	50°4·7′	5°42·7′W	W	203
Tribley Fm	Durham	NZ2451	54°51·4′	1°37·1′W	FM	88
Trichrug	Carm	SN6922	51°53·1′	3°53·8′W	H	160
Trichrug	Cered	SN5460	52°13·4′	4°7·9′W	H	146
Tri Chrugiau	Powys	SN9343	52°4·7′	3°33·3′W	A	147,160
Trickett's Cross	Dorset	SU0801	50°48·7′	1°52·8′W	T	195
Trickey Warren	Somer	ST1915	50°56·0′	3°8·8′W	F	181,193
Trickey Warren Fm	Somer	ST2014	50°55·4′	3°7·9′W	FM	193
Trickley Coppice	Warw	SP1599	52°35·6′	1°46·3′W	F	139
Trickley Wood	Northum	NU0226	55°31·9′	1°57·7′W	F	75
Tricombe	Devon	SY2096	50°45·7′	3°7·7′W	T	192,193
Tridley Foot	Devon	SS8108	50°51·8′	3°41·1′W	X	191
Triermain	Cumbr	NY5966	54°59·5′	2°38·0′W	X	86
Triffle	Corn	SX3354	50°22·0′	4°20·5′W	X	201
Triffleton	Pemb	SM9724	51°52·9′	4°56·6′W	T	157,158
Triffrwd	Powys	SO0737	52°1·7′	3°20·9′W	X	160
Triffrwd	Powys	SO1136	52°1·2′	3°17·4′W	W	161
Triggabrowne	Corn	SX1551	50°20·0′	4°35·6′W	X	201
Trigger Castle	N Yks	SE7571	54°8·0′	0°50·7′W	X	100
Trigg's Fm	Kent	TQ7237	51°6·6′	0°27·8′E	FM	188
Trigon Fm	Dorset	SY8888	50°41·7′	2°9·8′W	FM	194
Trigon Hill	Dorset	SY8989	50°42·3′	2°9·0′W	X	195
Trigony Ho	D & G	NX8893	55°13·4′	3°45·2′W	X	78
Triley Mill	Monm	SO3117	51°51·1′	2°59·7′W	X	161
Trill	Devon	SY2895	50°45·2′	3°0·9′W	T	193
Trillacott	Corn	SX2689	50°40·7′	4°27·4′W	T	190
Trill Br	Dorset	ST7820	50°59·0′	2°18·4′W	X	183
Trilleachan Beag	N Eil	NB2008	57°58·7′	6°43·7′W	X	13,14
Trilleachan-Mòr	N Eil	NB2007	57°58·1′	6°43·6′W	X	13,14
Trilleachan Slabs	Highld	NN0944	56°33·2′	5°6·0′W	X	50
Trill Fm	Corn	SX0852	50°20·4′	4°41·5′W	FM	200,204
Trill Fm	Dorset	ST5912	50°54·6′	2°34·6′W	FM	194
Trillinghurst Farmhouse	Kent	TQ7136	51°6·1′	0°26·9′E	X	188
Trillis Cottage	Glos	SO9203	51°43·8′	2°6·6′W	X	163
Trillow	Devon	SX8793	50°43·8′	3°35·7′W	X	192
Trilly	Devon	SS7449	51°13·8′	3°47·9′W	H	180
Tri Maen-trai	Pemb	SM8838	52°0·2′	5°4·9′W	X	157
Trimdon	Durham	NZ3633	54°41·7′	1°26·1′W	T	93
Trimdon Colliery	Durham	NZ3835	54°42·8′	1°24·2′W	T	93
Trimdon East Ho	Durham	NZ3833	54°41·7′	1°24·2′W	X	93
Trimdon Grange	Durham	NZ3735	54°42·8′	1°25·1′W	T	93
Trimdon Ho	Durham	NZ3633	54°41·7′	1°26·1′W	X	93
Trimingham	Norf	TG2738	52°53·7′	1°22·9′E	T	133
Trimley Lower Street	Suff	TM2636	51°58·8′	1°17·9′E	T	169
Trimley Marshes	Suff	TM2535	51°58·3′	1°16·9′E	X	169
Trimley St Martin	Suff	TM2737	51°59·3′	1°18·8′E	T	169
Trimley St Mary	Suff	TM2836	51°58·8′	1°19·6′E	T	169
Trimpley	Worcs	SO7978	52°24·2′	2°18·1′W	T	138
Trimsaran	Carm	SN4504	51°43·0′	4°14·2′W	T	159
Trims Green	Herts	TL4717	51°50·2′	0°8·4′E	T	167
Trimstone	Devon	SS5043	51°10·2′	4°8·4′W	T	180
Trimworth Manor	Kent	TR0649	51°12·4′	0°57·3′E	X	179,189
Trinafour	Pth & Kin	NN7264	56°45·3′	4°5·2′W	T	42
Trinant	Caer	ST2099	51°41·3′	3°9·0′W	T	171
Trinant	Gwyn	SH8242	52°58·0′	3°45·0′W	W	124,125
Trinant	Powys	SN8223	51°53·8′	3°42·5′W	W	160
Trinant Hall	Caer	SO2100	51°41·8′	3°8·2′W	X	171
Trindalls Fm	Oxon	SP6403	51°43·6′	1°4·0′W	FM	164,165
Trinder's Barn	Glos	SP1212	51°48·6′	1°49·2′W	X	163
Trindledown Copse	W Berks	SU3876	51°29·1′	1°26·8′W	F	174
Trindledown Fm	W Berks	SU3977	51°29·7′	1°25·9′W	FM	174
Trindlegreen	E Ayr	NS4250	55°43·3′	4°30·5′W	X	64
Tring	Herts	SP9211	51°47·6′	0°39·6′W	T	165
Tringford	Herts	SP9113	51°48·7′	0°40·4′W	T	165
Tring Grange Fm	Herts	SP9407	51°45·5′	0°37·9′W	FM	165
Tring Park	Herts	SP9210	51°47·1′	0°39·6′W	X	165
Tring Sta	Herts	SP9512	51°48·1′	0°36·9′W	X	165
Tring Wharf	Herts	SP9212	51°48·2′	0°39·5′W	T	165
Trinity	Angus	NO6062	56°45·1′	2°38·8′W	T	45
Trinity	C of Edin	NT2476	55°58·5′	3°12·6′W	T	66
Trinity	Devon	SS9905	50°50·4′	3°25·7′W	T	192
Trinity Channel		TA3913	53°35·9′	0°6·4′E	W	113
Trinity College Fm	Cambs	TL3766	52°16·7′	0°0·9′E	FM	154
Trinity College Fm	Cambs	TL3773	52°20·5′	0°1·1′E	FM	154
Trinity Conduit Head	Cambs	TL4259	52°12·9′	0°5·1′E	A	154
Trinity Fields	Staffs	SJ9125	52°49·6′	2°7·6′W	T	127
Trinity Fm	Cambs	TL3849	52°7·6′	0°1·4′E	FM	154
Trinity Fm	Suff	TM3588	52°26·6′	1°27·9′E	FM	156
Trinity Gask	Pth & Kin	NN9618	56°20·8′	3°40·5′W	T	58
Trinity Hall	Beds	SP9825	51°55·1′	0°34·1′W	X	165
Trinity Hall	Norf	TF5211	52°40·8′	0°15·3′E	X	131,143
Trinity Hill	Devon	SY3095	50°45·3′	2°59·2′W	X	193
Trinity Ho Fm	E Yorks	TA3522	53°40·9′	0°3·1′E	FM	107,113
Trinity House Fm	E Yorks	SE9827	53°44·0′	0°30·4′W	FM	106
Trinity House Fm	E Yorks	SE9930	53°45·7′	0°29·5′W	FM	106
Trinity Leigh	Devon	SS7005	50°50·0′	3°50·4′W	X	191
Trinity Sands	E Yorks	TA3615	53°37·1′	0°3·8′E	X	113
Trink	Corn	SW5137	50°11·1′	5°28·9′W	X	203
Trinkeld Fm	Cumbr	SD2776	54°10·7′	3°6·7′W	FM	96,97
Trinket, The	Northum	NY7577	55°5·5′	2°23·1′W	X	86,87
Trink Hill	Corn	SW5037	50°11·1′	5°29·8′W	H	203
Trink Hill (Tumulus)	Corn	SW5037	50°11·1′	5°29·8′W	A	203
Trinks o' Clave, The	Shetld	HP5708	60°45·3′	0°56·7′W	X	1
Trinlaymire	W Loth	NT0675	55°57·8′	3°29·9′W	X	65
Trinloist	Highld	NH5220	57°15·1′	4°26·7′W	X	26,35
Trinnant	Powys	SO0179	52°24·2′	3°26·9′W	X	136,147
Trinneabhal	N Eil	NF7726	57°12·9′	7°20·6′W	H	22
Triol	Carm	SN3432	51°57·9′	4°24·6′W	X	145

Triolbrith	Carm	SN3935	51°59·6′	4°20·3′W	X	145
Triolmaengwyn	Carm	SN3934	51°59·1′	4°20·3′W	X	145
Tripcock Ness or Margaret	Gren	TQ4581	51°30·8′	0°5·8′E	X	177
Triple Buttress	Highld	NG9460	57°35·2′	5°26·3′W	X	19
Tripontivm (Roman Settlement)	Shrops	SO5379	52°24·7′	2°41·1′W	R	137,138
Tripp Barrow	Somer	ST0333	51°5·5′	3°22·7′W	A	181
Tripp Bottom	Somer	ST0433	51°5·5′	3°21·9′W	X	181
Trippenkennet	Heref	SO5022	51°53·9′	2°43·2′W	X	162
Tripp Fm	Somer	ST0432	51°5·0′	3°21·9′W	FM	181
Tripphill Fm	W Susx	TQ0017	50°56·9′	0°34·2′W	FM	197
Trippleton	Heref	SO4173	52°21·4′	2°51·6′W	X	137,148
Trippling Hows	N Lincs	SE8605	53°32·3′	0°41·7′W	X	112
Tripsdale	N Yks	SE5898	54°22·7′	1°6·0′W	X	100
Tripsdale Beck	N Yks	SE5898	54°22·7′	1°6·0′W	W	100
Tripsdale Head	N Yks	NZ5900	54°23·8′	1°5·1′W	X	93
Trip's Fm	Dorset	ST6816	50°56·8′	2°26·9′W	FM	183
Trip, The	Shetld	HU2981	60°31·0′	1°27·8′W	X	1,3
Trisant	Cered	SN7175	52°21·7′	3°53·3′W	T	135,147
Triscombe	Somer	ST1535	51°6·7′	3°12·5′W	T	181
Triscombe Fm	Somer	SS9237	51°7·6′	3°32·2′W	FM	181
Triscombe Ho	Somer	ST1534	51°6·2′	3°12·5′W	X	181
Triscombe Stone	Somer	ST1635	51°6·7′	3°11·6′W	X	181
Trislaig	Highld	NN0874	56°49·3′	5°8·3′W	T	41
Trispen	Corn	SW8450	50°18·9′	5°1·7′W	T	200,204
Triss Combe	Devon	SS8129	51°3·1′	3°41·5′W	X	181
Tristan Stone	Corn	SX1152	50°20·5′	4°39·0′W	A	200,204
Tristford Ho	Devon	SX7759	50°25·3′	3°43·5′W	X	202
Tristis Rock	Devon	SX6360	50°25·7′	3°55·4′W	X	202
Tritchayne	Devon	SY2395	50°45·2′	3°5·1′W	X	192,193
Tritchmarsh	Devon	SY2495	50°45·2′	3°4·3′W	X	192,193
Tri-thy	Flint	SJ2758	53°7·1′	3°5·0′W	X	117
Tritlington	Northum	NZ2092	55°13·6′	1°40·7′W	T	81
Tritlington Broom	Northum	NZ1992	55°13·6′	1°41·6′W	X	81
Trittencott	Devon	SS7521	50°58·7′	3°46·5′W	X	180
Triuirebheinn	N Eil	NF8121	57°10·4′	7°16·3′W	H	31
Triumphal Arch	Norf	TF8839	52°55·2′	0°48·2′E	X	132
Trivor	Monm	SO4617	51°51·2′	2°46·6′W	X	161
Troakes Fm	Somer	ST2535	51°6·8′	3°3·9′W	FM	182
Troan	Corn	SW8957	50°22·7′	4°57·7′W	T	200
Troax	S Ayr	NX1187	55°8·7′	4°57·5′W	X	76
Trobridge Ho	Devon	SX8397	50°45·9′	3°39·2′W	X	191
Trobus Fm	Corn	SW8850	50°18·9′	4°58·3′W	FM	200,204
Trochail	Moray	NJ2257	57°36·0′	3°17·8′W	X	28
Trochelhill	Moray	NJ3158	57°36·7′	3°8·8′W	T	28
Trochrague	S Ayr	NS2100	55°16·0′	4°48·6′W	X	76
Trochry	Pth & Kin	NN9740	56°32·7′	3°40·1′W	T	52,53
Trochry Hill	Pth & Kin	NN9838	56°31·6′	3°39·0′W	H	52,53
Troearhiwgwair	Blae Gw	SO1506	51°45·0′	3°13·5′W	T	161
Troedrhiw	Powys	SN9253	52°10·1′	3°34·4′W	X	147
Troedrhiwbeynon	Carm	SN7545	52°5·6′	3°49·1′W	X	146,147
Troed-rhiw-cymmer	Cered	SN7648	52°7·2′	3°48·3′W	X	146,147
Troedrhiwdalar	Powys	SN9553	52°10·2′	3°31·7′W	T	147
Troed-rhiw-draen	Powys	SN8967	52°17·6′	3°37·3′W	X	135,136,147
Troedrhiwfach	Powys	SN9346	52°6·4′	3°33·3′W	X	147
Troedrhiwfelen	Cered	SN7173	52°20·6′	3°53·2′W	X	135,147
Troedrhiwffenyd	Cered	SN4042	52°3·4′	4°19·6′W	T	146
Troedrhiwfuwch	Caer	SO1304	51°43·9′	3°15·2′W	T	171
Troedrhiwlas	Cered	SN6779	52°23·8′	3°56·9′W	X	135
Troedrhiwlasgrug	Cered	SN6280	52°24·3′	4°1·3′W	X	135
Troed-rhiw-ruddwen	Cered	SN7747	52°6·7′	3°47·4′W	X	146,147
Troedrhiwseiri	Cered	SN6785	52°27·0′	3°57·0′W	X	135
Troed-y-bryn	Carm	SN6545	52°5·5′	3°57·8′W	X	146
Troed-y-foel	Gwyn	SH9019	52°45·7′	3°37·4′W	X	125
Troedyraur	Cered	SN3245	52°4·9′	4°26·7′W	T	145
Troed-yr-esgair	Powys	SN8879	52°24·1′	3°38·4′W	X	135,136,147
Troedyrharn	Powys	SO0630	51°57·9′	3°21·7′W	X	160
Troed-yr-harn	Powys	SO1632	51°59·0′	3°13·0′W	X	161
Troed-yr-Henriw	Cered	SN7480	52°24·5′	3°50·7′W	X	135
Troedyrhiw	Carm	SN2619	51°50·8′	4°31·2′W	X	158
Troed-y-rhiw	Carm	SN6836	52°0·6′	3°55·0′W	X	146
Troed-y-rhiw	Carm	SN7035	52°0·1′	3°53·2′W	X	146,160
Troed-y-rhiw	Carm	SN7446	52°6·1′	3°50·0′W	X	146,147
Troed-y-rhiw	Carm	SN7537	52°1·3′	3°48·9′W	X	146,160
Troedyrhiw	Cered	SN2049	52°6·8′	4°37·3′W	X	145
Troed-y-rhiw	Cered	SN2550	52°7·5′	4°33·0′W	X	145
Troedyrhiw	Cered	SN2842	52°3·2′	4°30·1′W	X	145
Troed-y-rhiw	Cered	SN4952	52°9·0′	4°12·0′W	X	146
Troed-y-rhiw	Cered	SN5267	52°17·1′	4°9·8′W	X	135
Troed-y-rhiw	Cered	SN7666	52°16·9′	3°48·7′W	X	135,147
Troedyrhiw	Merth Tyd	SO0702	51°42·8′	3°20·4′W	T	170
Troed-y-rhiw	Nth Pt Talb	SS8385	51°33·3′	3°40·9′W	X	170
Troed-y-rhiw	Nth Pt Talb	SS8497	51°39·8′	3°40·2′W	X	170
Troed-y-rhiw	Pemb	SM8624	51°52·7′	5°6·2′W	X	157
Troedyrhiw	Pemb	SN1933	51°58·2′	4°37·7′W	X	145
Troed-y-rhiw	Powys	SN7398	52°34·1′	3°52·0′W	X	135
Troedyrhiw	Powys	SN9547	52°6·9′	3°31·6′W	X	147
Troedyryrfa	Carm	SN4427	51°55·4′	4°15·7′W	X	146
Trofarth	Conwy	SH8570	53°13·1′	3°42·9′W	X	116
Trofarth	Conwy	SH8571	53°13·7′	3°43·0′W	T	116
Trofarth Gorse	Conwy	SH8569	53°12·6′	3°42·9′W	H	116
Trogog	I of Angl	SH4292	53°24·3′	4°22·2′W	X	114
Trohoughton	D & G	NY0072	55°2·2′	3°33·5′W	X	84
Troilhoulland	Shetld	HU3051	60°14·8′	1°27·0′W	X	3
Troisgeach	Stir	NN2919	56°20·2′	4°45·5′W	H	50,56
Troisgeach Bheag	Stir	NN3119	56°20·3′	4°43·6′W	X	50,56
Trolaisgeir	N Eil	NF7227	57°13·2′	7°25·6′W	X	22
Trolamul	N Eil	NB2001	57°54·9′	6°43·2′W	H	14
Trolamul	N Eil	NF8149	57°25·4′	7°18·4′W	X	22
Trolane	D & G	NX6481	55°6·5′	4°7·5′W	X	77
Trolane Burn	D & G	NX6382	55°7·1′	4°8·5′W	W	77
Trolladale Water	Shetld	HU3273	60°26·6′	1°24·6′W	W	3
Trollakeldas Houlla	Shetld	HU5094	60°37·8′	1°4·7′W	H	1,2
Trollaman	N Eil	NF9674	57°39·5′	7°5·4′W	X	18
Trolla Skerry	Shetld	HP6302	60°42·0′	0°50·3′W	X	1
Trolla Stack	Shetld	HU3782	60°31·5′	1°19·1′W	X	1,2,3
Trollaval	Highld	NM3795	56°58·5′	6°19·2′W	H	39
Trolla Vatn	Orkney	HY7856	59°23·6′	2°22·8′W	W	5
Trolla Water	Shetld	HU4150	60°14·2′	1°15·1′W	W	3

Trollers Gill	N Yks	SE0661	54°2·9'	1°54·1'W	X	99
Trolligarts	Shetld	HU2452	60°15·4'	1°33·5'W	X	3
Trolliloes	E Susx	TQ6214	50°54·4'	0°18·6'E	T	199
Trollochy	Aberd	NO8879	56°54·4'	2°11·4'W	W	45
Troloss	S Lanak	NS9108	55°21·5'	3°42·7'W	X	71,78
Trolway	Heref	SO4623	51°54·4'	2°46·7'W	X	161
Tromba of Griskerry	Shetld	HU3623	59°59·7'	1°20·8'W	X	4
Tromie Bridge	Highld	NN7899	57°4·2'	4°0·3'W	X	35
Tromie Mills	Highld	NN7899	57°4·2'	4°0·3'W	X	35
Tromode	I of M	SC3777	54°10·0'	4°29·4'W	T	95
Tronach Head	Moray	NJ4768	57°42·2'	2°52·9'W	X	28,29
Trona Dale	Shetld	HP5804	60°43·2'	0°55·7'W	X	1
Trona Dale	Shetld	HU4996	60°38·9'	1°5·7'W	X	1
Tronafirth	Shetld	HU4446	60°12·0'	1°11·9'W	X	4
Trona Scord	Shetld	HU2155	60°17·0'	1°36·7'W	X	3
Trona Water	Shetld	HU4995	60°38·4'	1°5·7'W	W	1,2
Trondavoe	Shetld	HU3770	60°25·0'	1°19·2'W	T	2,3
Trondra	Shetld	HU3937	60°7·2'	1°17·4'W	X	4
Troneyhill	Scot Bord	NT5723	55°30·2'	2°40·4'W	H	73,74
Tronister	Shetld	HU4566	60°22·8'	1°10·5'W	X	2,3
Tronshaw Hill	Scot Bord	NT7717	55°27·0'	2°21·4'W	H	80
Tronston	Orkney	HY2520	59°3·9'	3°18·0'W	T	6
Troon	Corn	SW6638	50°12·0'	5°16·4'W	T	203
Troon	S Ayr	NS3230	55°32·3'	4°39·3'W	T	70
Trooper's Inn	Pemb	SM9610	51°45·3'	4°57·0'W	T	157,158
Tropical Bird Park	I of W	SZ5276	50°35·1'	1°15·5'W	X	196
Tropueer	D & G	NX9775	55°3·8'	3°36·3'W	T	84
Troquhain	D & G	NX6879	55°5·5'	4°3·7'W	X	77,84
Troquhain	S Ayr	NS3709	55°21·1'	4°33·8'W	X	70,77
Troquhain Hill	D & G	NX6981	55°6·6'	4°2·8'W	X	77
Trosaraidh	N Eil	NF7516	57°7·5'	7°21·8'W	X	31
Troserch	Carm	SN5503	51°42·7'	4°5·5'W	X	159
Trosgiche	Arg & Bt	NN2318	56°19·5'	4°51·3'W	X	50,56
Trosley Country Park	Kent	TQ6461	51°19·7'	0°21·6'E	X	177,188
Trosnant	Powys	SO0425	51°55·2'	3°23·4'W	X	160
Trossachs, The	Stir	NN5007	56°14·2'	4°24·8'W	X	57
Trossell	Corn	SX2490	50°41·2'	4°29·1'W	X	190
Trostan Burn	D & G	NX4479	55°5·1'	4°26·2'W	W	77
Trostan Hill	D & G	NS6101	55°17·3'	4°10·9'W	H	77
Trostan Hill	S Ayr	NS4002	55°17·4'	4°30·8'W	H	77
Troston	D & G	NX6889	55°10·9'	4°4·0'W	X	77
Troston	D & G	NX9268	54°59·9'	3°40·9'W	X	84
Troston	Suff	TL8972	52°19·0'	0°46·8'E	T	144,155
Troston Hill	D & G	NX6990	55°11·5'	4°3·0'W	X	77
Troston Hill	D & G	NX7099	55°16·3'	4°2·3'W	X	77
Troston Hill	D & G	NX9368	55°0·0'	3°39·9'W	H	84
Troston Loch	D & G	NX7090	55°11·5'	4°2·1'W	W	77
Troston Mount	Suff	TL8974	52°20·1'	0°46·8'E	X	144
Troston Mount (Tumulus)	Suff	TL8974	52°20·1'	0°46·8'E	A	144
Trostra	Monm	SO3100	51°41·9'	2°59·5'W	X	171
Trostre	Carm	SS5299	51°40·5'	4°8·0'W	T	159
Trostrey Common	Monm	SO3804	51°44·1'	2°53·5'W	T	171
Trostrey Court	Monm	SO3604	51°44·1'	2°55·2'W	X	171
Trostrey Hill	Monm	SO3605	51°44·6'	2°55·2'W	H	161
Trostrey Lodge	Monm	SO3507	51°45·7'	2°56·1'W	X	161
Trostrey Wood	Monm	SO3604	51°44·1'	2°55·2'W	F	171
Trostrie	D & G	NX6557	54°53·6'	4°5·9'W	X	83,84
Troswell	Corn	SX2591	50°41·8'	4°28·3'W	T	190
Tros Wick	Shetld	HU4016	59°55·9'	1°16·6'W	W	4
Troswick	Shetld	HU4016	59°55·9'	1°16·6'W	X	4
Troswickness	Shetld	HU4017	59°56·4'	1°16·6'W	T	4
Troswick Ness	Shetld	HU4117	59°56·4'	1°15·5'W	X	4
Tros y marian	I of Angl	SH6181	53°18·7'	4°4·8'W	A	114,115
Tros-y-waen	Gwyn	SH5666	53°10·5'	4°8·9'W	X	114,115
Trota Stack	Shetld	HU6165	60°22·1'	0°53·1'W	X	2
Trothland	Heref	SO4722	51°53·9'	2°45·8'W	X	161
Trotshill	Worcs	SO8855	52°11·8'	2°10·1'W	T	150
Trottenden Fm	Kent	TQ7138	51°7·2'	0°27·0'E	FM	188
Trotten Marsh	W Susx	SU8225	51°1·3'	0°49·5'W	T	186,197
Trotters	Essex	TQ9187	51°33·2'	0°45·7'E	X	178
Trotters Fm	N Yks	SE4955	53°59·6'	1°14·7'W	FM	105
Trotters' Rest	Essex	TL7726	51°54·5'	0°34·8'E	X	167
Trottick	C of Dun	NO4033	56°29·4'	2°58·0'W	T	54
Trottingshaw	Scot Bord	NT6458	55°49·1'	2°34·0'W	X	67,74
Trottiscliffe	Kent	TQ6460	51°19·2'	0°21·6'E	T	177,188
Trotton	W Susx	SU8322	50°59·7'	0°48·6'W	T	197
Trotton Common	W Susx	SU8421	50°59·2'	0°47·8'W	X	197
Trotts	Hants	SU3711	50°54·1'	1°28·0'W	X	196
Trottsford Fm	Hants	SU8038	51°8·4'	0°51·0'W	FM	186
Troublehouse Covert	Glos	ST9195	51°39·5'	2°7·4'W	F	163
Troudale Burn	D & G	NX7853	54°51·7'	3°53·6'W	W	84
Trough Burn	E Ayr	NS5003	55°18·2'	4°21·3'W	W	77
Troughend	Northum	NY8692	55°13·6'	2°12·8'W	X	80
Troughend Common	Northum	NY8591	55°13·0'	2°13·7'W	X	80
Troughfoot	Cumbr	NY4642	54°46·4'	2°49·9'W	X	86
Troughfoot	Cumbr	NY4974	55°3·7'	2°47·5'W	X	86
Trough Gate	Lancs	SD8821	53°41·4'	2°10·5'W	T	103
Trough Head	Cumbr	NY4775	55°4·2'	2°49·4'W	X	86
Trough Heads	Durham	NY9611	54°29·9'	2°3·3'W	X	91,92
Trough Ho	Lancs	SD6836	53°49·4'	2°28·8'W	X	103
Trough Ho	N Yks	NZ7001	54°24·2'	0°54·9'W	X	94
Trough Hope	D & G	NY3095	55°14·9'	3°5·6'W	W	79
Trough of Bowland	Lancs	SD6253	53°58·5'	2°34·3'W	X	102,103
Troughstone Fm	Staffs	SJ9059	53°7·9'	2°8·6'W	FM	118
Troughton Hall	Cumbr	SD2591	54°18·8'	3°8·8'W	X	96
Troughton Ho	Cumbr	NY0116	54°32·0'	3°31·4'W	X	89
Troulligarth	Shetld	HU2149	60°13·8'	1°36·8'W	X	3
Troup Head	Aberd	NJ8267	57°41·8'	2°17·7'W	X	29,30
Troup House	Aberd	NJ8265	57°40·7'	2°17·6'W	X	29,30
Troupsmill	Aberd	NJ5839	57°26·6'	2°41·5'W	X	29
Trously	Scot Bord	NT3845	55°41·9'	2°58·8'W	X	73
Troustan	Arg & Bt	NS0776	55°56·6'	5°5·0'W	X	63
Troustrie	Fife	NO5907	56°15·5'	2°39·3'W	X	59
Troutal	Cumbr	SD2398	54°22·5'	3°10·7'W	X	96
Troutal Fell	Cumbr	SD2599	54°23·1'	3°8·9'W	X	96
Troutal Tongue	Cumbr	SD2398	54°22·5'	3°10·7'W	X	96
Trout Beck	Cumbr	NY3826	54°37·8'	2°57·2'W	W	90
Troutbeck	Cumbr	NY3826	54°37·8'	2°57·2'W	X	90
Troutbeck	Cumbr	NY4002	54°24·8'	2°55·1'W	T	90
Trout Beck	Cumbr	NY4104	54°25·9'	2°54·2'W	W	90
Troutbeck	Cumbr	NY4856	54°54·0'	2°48·2'W	X	86
Trout Beck	Cumbr	NY4956	54°54·0'	2°47·3'W	W	86
Trout Beck	Cumbr	NY6071	55°2·2'	2°37·1'W	W	86
Trout Beck	Cumbr	NY6524	54°36·8'	2°32·1'W	W	91
Trout Beck	Cumbr	NY7432	54°41·2'	2°23·8'W	W	91
Trout Beck	D & G	NY2083	55°8·3'	3°14·9'W	W	79
Troutbeck Bridge	Cumbr	NY4000	54°23·8'	2°55·0'W	T	90
Troutbeck Park	Cumbr	NY4205	54°26·5'	2°53·2'W	X	90
Troutbeck Park	Cumbr	NY4207	54°27·6'	2°53·3'W	H	90
Troutdale Cottages	Cumbr	NY2517	54°32·8'	3°9·1'W	X	89,90
Trout Fm	Inverc	NS3667	55°52·4'	4°36·8'W	FM	63
Trout Fm	Lincs	TF4077	53°16·5'	0°6·4'E	FM	122
Trout Fm	Lincs	TF4282	53°19·2'	0°8·3'E	FM	122
Trout Fm	W Berks	SU3468	51°24·8'	1°30·3'W	FM	174
Trout Hall	Red & Cl	NZ6618	54°33·4'	0°58·3'W	X	94
Trout Hill	Somer	SS7842	51°10·1'	3°44·3'W	H	180
Trouting,The	Northum	NT6502	55°18·9'	2°32·7'W	X	80
Trout Inn	Oxon	SP4809	51°46·9'	1°17·9'W	X	164
Trouts	Kent	TQ9972	51°24·9'	0°52·1'E	X	178
Trouts Dale	N Yks	SE9288	54°17·0'	0°34·8'W	X	94,101
Troutsdale Beck	N Yks	SE9287	54°16·5'	0°34·8'W	W	94,101
Troutsdale Fm	Staffs	SJ9958	53°7·4'	2°0·5'W	FM	118
Troutsdale Low Hall	N Yks	SE9389	54°17·5'	0°33·9'W	X	94,101
Troutsdale Moor	N Yks	SE9188	54°17·0'	0°35·7'W	X	94,101
Trouts Fm	Surrey	TQ1642	51°10·2'	0°20·1'W	FM	187
Troves	Moray	NJ2459	57°37·5'	3°15·9'W	X	28
Trow	Devon	SY1589	50°41·9'	3°11·8'W	T	192
Trowan	Corn	SW4940	50°12·6'	5°30·7'W	X	203
Trowan	Pth & Kin	NN8221	56°22·3'	3°54·2'W	X	52,57
Troway	Derby	SK3979	53°18·6'	1°24·5'W	T	119
Trowbridge	Card	ST2380	51°31·1'	3°6·2'W	T	171
Trowbridge	Wilts	ST8557	51°18·9'	2°12·5'W	T	173
Trowbridge Fm	N Yks	SE6881	54°13·5'	0°57·0'W	FM	100
Trow Brook	Shrops	SO5590	52°30·6'	2°39·4'W	W	137,138
Trowdale	D & G	NX7669	55°0·3'	3°55·9'W	X	84
Trow Down	Wilts	ST9621	50°59·5'	2°3·0'W	X	184
Troweir Hill	S Ayr	NX2196	55°13·8'	4°48·5'W	H	76
Trowel Covert	Glos	SP1312	51°48·6'	1°48·3'W	F	163
Trowell	Notts	SK4839	52°57·0'	1°16·7'W	T	129
Trowell Fm	Somer	ST0426	51°1·8'	3°21·8'W	FM	181
Trowell Hall	Notts	SK4939	52°57·0'	1°15·8'W	X	129
Trowell Moor	Notts	SK5040	52°57·5'	1°14·9'W	X	129
Trowell Service Area	Notts	SK4940	52°57·5'	1°15·8'W	X	129
Trow Fm	Devon	SY0297	50°45·9'	3°23·0'W	FM	192
Trow Fm	Wilts	ST9622	51°0·1'	2°3·0'W	FM	184
Trow Gill	N Yks	SD7571	54°8·3'	2°22·5'W	X	98
Trowgrain Middle	D & G	NT2015	55°25·6'	3°15·4'W	H	79
Trow Green	Glos	SO5706	51°45·3'	2°37·0'W	T	162
Trow Hall	Devon	SY1489	50°41·9'	3°12·7'W	X	192
Trow Hill	Scot Bord	NT5453	55°46·3'	2°43·6'W	X	66,73
Trow Hill	S Lanak	NS9923	55°29·7'	3°35·5'W	H	72
Trowie Glen	Orkney	HY2300	58°53·1'	3°19·7'W	X	6,7
Trow Knowes	Scot Bord	NT5216	55°26·4'	2°45·1'W	X	79
Trowland Creek	Norf	TF8245	52°58·5'	0°43·0'E	W	132
Trowle Common	Wilts	ST8358	51°19·5'	2°14·3'W	T	173
Trowle Fm	Wilts	ST8258	51°19·5'	2°15·1'W	FM	173
Trowlesworthy Tors	Devon	SX5764	50°27·7'	4°0·5'W	X	202
Trowlesworthy Warren	Devon	SX5764	50°27·7'	4°0·5'W	X	202
Trowley	Powys	SO1446	52°6·6'	3°15·0'W	X	148
Trowley Bottom	Herts	TL0713	51°48·6'	0°26·5'W	T	166
Trow Point	S Tyne	NZ3866	54°59·5'	1°23·9'W	X	88
Trows	Northum	NT8512	55°24·4'	2°13·8'W	X	80
Trows	Scot Bord	NT6832	55°35·1'	2°30·0'W	X	74
Trows Burn	Northum	NT8513	55°24·9'	2°13·8'W	W	80
Trowse Newton	Norf	TG2406	52°36·6'	1°18·9'E	T	134
Trowstree	Wrex	SJ4443	52°59·1'	2°49·6'W	X	117
Trowswell	Kent	TQ7238	51°7·1'	0°27·9'E	X	188
Trowup Burn	Northum	NT8726	55°31·9'	2°11·9'W	W	74
Trowupburn	Northum	NT8726	55°31·9'	2°11·9'W	X	74
Troyan	Pemb	SN2029	51°56·1'	4°36·7'W	X	145,158
Troydale	Leeds	SE2332	53°47·3'	1°38·6'W	T	104
Troy Fm	Oxon	SP5127	51°56·6'	1°15·1'W	FM	164
Troy Ho	Monm	SO5011	51°48·0'	2°43·1'W	X	162
Troypark Wood	Monm	SO5110	51°47·4'	2°42·2'W	F	162
Troys Fm	Essex	TL7916	51°49·1'	0°36·2'E	FM	167
Troys Hall	Essex	TL7716	51°49·1'	0°34·5'E	X	167
Troys Wood	Essex	TL7816	51°49·1'	0°35·4'E	F	167
Troytes Fm	Somer	SS9345	51°11·9'	3°31·5'W	FM	181
Troy Town	Kent	TQ4247	51°12·5'	0°2·4'E	T	187
Troy Town	Kent	TR0744	51°9·7'	0°58·0'E	T	179,189
Troy Town	Medway	TQ7467	51°22·7'	0°30·4'E	T	178
Troy Town Fm	Dorset	SY7394	50°44·9'	2°22·6'W	FM	194
Troy Wood	Fife	NO5608	56°16·0'	2°42·2'W	F	59
Troy Wood	Lincs	TF2558	53°6·5'	0°7·5'W	F	122
Truagh Mheall	Highld	NG3821	57°12·6'	6°19·9'W	H	32
Truas	Corn	SX0687	50°39·3'	4°44·3'W	T	200
Trub	Roch	SD8809	53°34·9'	2°10·5'W	T	109
Truckett's Hall	Suff	TL8150	52°7·3'	0°39·0'E	X	155
Truckham Fm	Devon	SS6145	51°11·5'	3°59·0'W	FM	180
Truckle Crags	N Yks	SE0759	54°1·9'	1°53·2'W	X	104
Truckle Hill	Wilts	ST8375	51°28·7'	2°14·3'W	H	173
Trudernish	Arg & Bt	NR4652	55°42·0'	6°2·1'W	X	60
Trudernish Point	Arg & Bt	NR4652	55°42·0'	6°2·1'W	X	60
Truderscaig	Highld	NC7034	58°16·8'	4°12·5'W	X	16
Trudgian	Corn	SW9747	50°17·5'	4°50·6'W	X	204
Trudgwell	Corn	SW7625	50°5·2'	5°7·5'W	X	204
Trudoxhill	Somer	ST7443	51°11·4'	2°21·9'W	T	183
Truelove	Devon	SX5560	50°25·6'	4°2·1'W	X	202
Trueman's Heath	Worcs	SP0977	52°23·7'	1°51·7'W	T	139
Truesdale Lodge	Lincs	TF1112	52°41·9'	0°21·0'W	X	130,142
True Street	Devon	SX8260	50°25·9'	3°39·3'W	T	202
Trugger's Fm	Kent	TQ4943	51°10·2'	0°8·3'E	FM	188
Truggles Water	Shetld	HU3754	60°16·4'	1°19·4'W	W	3
Trugo Fm	Corn	SW8960	50°24·4'	4°57·8'W	FM	200
Truleigh Hill	W Susx	TQ2210	50°52·8'	0°15·6'W	X	198
Truleigh Manor Fm	W Susx	TQ2211	50°53·4'	0°15·5'W	FM	198
Truleigh Sands	W Susx	TQ2212	50°53·9'	0°15·5'W	X	198
Trull	Somer	ST2122	50°59·8'	3°7·2'W	T	193
Trull Ho	Glos	ST9296	51°40·0'	2°6·5'W	X	163
Truly	Flint	SJ1473	53°15·1'	3°16·9'W	X	116
Truman	Carm	SN7420	51°52·1'	3°49·4'W	X	160
Truman	Cered	SN7776	52°22·3'	3°48·0'W	H	135,147
Trumans Fm	Cambs	TL3796	52°32·9'	0°1·6'E	FM	142,143
Truman's Lodge	Notts	SK6075	53°16·4'	1°5·6'W	X	120
Trumau	Powys	SN8667	52°17·6'	3°39·9'W	X	135,136,147
Trumba	Shetld	HU3528	60°2·4'	1°21·8'W	X	4
Trumba	Shetld	HU3779	60°29·8'	1°19·1'W	X	2,3
Trumba	Shetld	HU3893	60°37·4'	1°17·8'W	X	1,2
Trumba	Shetld	HU4431	60°3·9'	1°12·1'W	X	4
Trumfleet	Donc	SE6011	53°35·8'	1°5·2'W	T	111
Trumfleet Grange	Donc	SE6012	53°36·3'	1°5·2'W	X	111
Trum Gelli	Gwyn	SH6501	52°35·6'	3°59·2'W	H	135
Trumisgarry	N Eil	NF8674	57°39·0'	7°15·4'W	T	18
Trumland Ho	Orkney	HY4227	59°7·8'	3°0·3'W	X	5,6
Trumley Copse	W Susx	SU8408	50°52·2'	0°48·0'W	F	197
Trumley Fm	Lancs	SD4257	54°0·6'	2°52·7'W	FM	102
Trum Nant-fach	Gwyn	SH8945	52°59·7'	3°38·8'W	H	116
Trumpan	Highld	NG2261	57°33·5'	6°38·4'W	X	23
Trumpet	Heref	SO6539	52°3·1'	2°30·2'W	T	149
Trumpets Hill	Surrey	TQ2349	51°13·8'	0°13·9'W	X	187
Trumpington	Cambs	TL4454	52°10·2'	0°6·7'E	T	154
Trumpington Hall	Cambs	TL4455	52°10·7'	0°6·8'E	X	154
Trumpingtons Fm	Essex	TL8724	51°53·2'	0°43·4'E	FM	168
Trumpletts Fm	W Berks	SU5175	51°28·5'	1°15·5'W	FM	174
Trumps	Devon	ST0416	50°56·4'	3°21·6'W	X	181
Trumps Fm	Surrey	TQ0066	51°23·3'	0°33·4'W	FM	176
Trumps Green	Surrey	SU9967	51°23·8'	0°34·2'W	T	175,176
Trum y Ddysgl	Gwyn	SH5451	53°2·4'	4°10·3'W	X	115
Trum y Fawnog	Powys	SJ0026	52°49·6'	3°28·6'W	X	125
Trum y Gŵr	Powys	SN8271	52°19·7'	3°43·5'W	H	135,136,147
Trum y Sarn	Gwyn	SH9930	52°51·7'	3°29·6'W	H	125
Trunch	Norf	TG2834	52°51·5'	1°23·6'E	T	133
Truncheaunts	Hants	SU7237	51°7·9'	0°57·9'W	X	186
Trunch Ho	Norf	TM2887	52°26·2'	1°21·7'E	X	156
Trundlebeer	Devon	SX6694	50°44·0'	3°53·6'W	X	191
Trundle Mere	Cambs	TL1990	52°29·9'	0°14·4'W	X	142
Trundlemoor Fm	Devon	SS8809	50°52·4'	3°35·1'W	FM	192
Trundle, The	W Susx	SU8711	50°53·7'	0°45·4'W	A	197
Trundle Wood	Kent	TQ8858	51°17·6'	0°42·2'E	F	178
Trundley Wood	Suff	TL6949	52°7·0'	0°28·5'E	F	154
Trunkwell Ho	W Berks	SU6964	51°22·5'	1°0·1'W	X	175,186
Trunla Allotment	N Yks	SE0765	54°5·1'	1°53·2'W	X	99
Trunla Gill	N Yks	SE0765	54°5·1'	1°53·2'W	W	99
Trunnah	Lancs	SD3343	53°53·0'	3°0·7'W	T	102
Trunnelmire Plantn	Durham	NZ1723	54°36·4'	1°43·8'W	F	92
Truro	Corn	SW8244	50°15·6'	5°3·1'W	T	204
Truro River	Corn	SW8442	50°14·5'	5°1·4'W	W	204
Truscott	Corn	SX3085	50°38·6'	4°23·9'W	T	201
Trusham	Devon	SX8582	50°37·8'	3°37·2'W	T	191
Trusler's Hill Fm	W Susx	TQ2416	50°56·0'	0°13·7'W	FM	198
Trusley	Derby	SK2535	52°54·9'	1°37·3'W	T	128
Trusley Brook Fm	Derby	SK2534	52°54·4'	1°37·3'W	FM	128
Trusleywood Ho	Derby	SK2537	52°56·0'	1°37·3'W	X	128
Trusmadoor	Cumbr	NY2733	54°41·5'	3°7·5'W	X	89,90
Trussall	Corn	SW6929	50°7·2'	5°13·5'W	T	203
Trussel Br	Corn	SX2462	50°26·1'	4°28·3'W	X	201
Trussell	Corn	SX2289	50°40·6'	4°30·8'W	X	190
Truss Gap	Cumbr	NY5113	54°30·8'	2°45·0'W	X	90
Trusta	Angus	NO4865	56°46·7'	2°50·6'W	X	44
Trustach Cott	Aberd	NO6496	57°3·5'	2°35·2'W	X	37,45
Trustan's Fm	Suff	TM4069	52°16·2'	1°31·5'E	FM	156
Trust Fm	Suff	TM3765	52°14·1'	1°28·7'E	FM	156
Trust Fm	Suff	TM4266	52°14·6'	1°33·1'E	FM	156
Trusthorpe	Lincs	TF5183	53°19·6'	0°16·4'E	T	122
Trusthorpe Hall	Lincs	TF5082	53°19·1'	0°15·5'E	X	122
Trusty Burn	Angus	NO4368	56°48·3'	2°55·6'W	W	44
Truthall	Corn	SW6530	50°7·6'	5°16·9'W	X	203
Truthan	Corn	SW8351	50°19·4'	5°2·5'W	T	200,204
Truthwall	Corn	SW5232	50°8·4'	5°27·9'W	T	203
Trutons	Essex	TL6220	51°51·5'	0°21·5'E	X	167
Truxford	Surrey	SU8940	51°9·4'	0°43·3'W	X	186
Trwstllewelyn	Powys	SO1898	52°34·7'	3°12·2'W	T	136
Trwyn Bendro	Pemb	SM6923	51°51·7'	5°20·9'W	X	157
Trwynbychan	I of Angl	SH4094	53°25·4'	4°24·1'W	X	114
Trwyn Bychestyn	Gwyn	SH1524	52°47·2'	4°44·2'W	X	123
Trwyn Carreg-y-tir	Gwyn	SH2824	52°47·4'	4°32·6'W	X	123
Trwyncastell	Pemb	SM7931	51°56·3'	5°12·5'W	X	157
Trwyn Cemlyn	I of Angl	SH3394	53°25·2'	4°30·4'W	X	114
Trwyn Cilan	Gwyn	SH2922	52°46·4'	4°31·7'W	X	123
Trwyn Crou	Cered	SN3355	52°10·3'	4°26·1'W	X	145
Trwyn Cynddeiriog	Pemb	SM7423	51°51·8'	5°16·6'W	X	157
Trwyn Dinmor	I of Angl	SH6381	53°18·7'	4°3·0'W	X	114,115
Trwyn-drain-du	Pemb	SM6924	51°52·2'	5°21·0'W	X	157
Trwyn Dwlban	I of Angl	SH5381	53°18·6'	4°12·0'W	X	114,115
Trwyn Elen	Pemb	SM8132	51°56·8'	5°10·8'W	X	157
Trwyn Ffynnon-y-Sais	I of Angl	SH3863	53°8·6'	4°24·9'W	X	114
Trwyn Glas	Gwyn	SH1630	52°50·4'	4°43·5'W	X	123
Trwyn Hwch	Pemb	SN2036	51°59·8'	4°36·9'W	X	145
Trwynhwrddyn	Pemb	SM7327	51°54·0'	5°17·6'W	X	157
Trwyn Isaac	Pemb	SN0140	52°1·6'	4°53·7'W	X	145,157
Trwyn Llanbedrog	Gwyn	SH3330	52°50·7'	4°28·4'W	X	123
Trwyn Llech-y-doll	Gwyn	SH3023	52°46·9'	4°30·8'W	X	123
Trwynllundain	Pemb	SM6923	51°51·7'	5°20·9'W	X	157
Trwyn-llwyd	Pemb	SM7328	51°54·5'	5°17·6'W	X	157
Trwyn Llwyd	Pemb	SM8332	51°56·9'	5°9·1'W	X	157
Trwyn Llwyd	Pemb	SM8736	51°59·1'	5°5·7'W	X	157
Trwyn Llwynog	Pemb	SM8634	51°58·0'	5°6·5'W	X	157
Trwyn Maen Dylan	Gwyn	SH4252	53°2·8'	4°21·0'W	X	115,123
Trwyn Maen Melyn	Gwyn	SH1325	52°47·7'	4°46·0'W	X	123
Trwynmynachdy	Pemb	SM6922	51°51·2'	5°20·9'W	X	157
Trwyn Ogof Hen	Pemb	SM7024	51°52·3'	5°20·1'W	X	157
Trwyn Penmon	I of Angl	SH6481	53°18·8'	4°2·1'W	X	114,115
Trwyn Porth Dinllaen	Gwyn	SH2741	52°56·6'	4°34·1'W	X	123
Trwyn-Siôn-Owen	Pemb	SM7025	51°52·8'	5°20·1'W	X	157
Trwyn Swch	Conwy	SH8064	53°9·8'	3°47·3'W	X	116
Trwyn Swch	Conwy	SH9159	53°7·3'	3°37·3'W	X	116
Trwyn Talfarach	Gwyn	SH2125	52°47·8'	4°38·9'W	X	123
Trwyn-y-bryn	Powys	SH9706	52°38·8'	3°30·9'W	X	125
Trwyn y Bwa	Pemb	SN0542	52°2·8'	4°50·2'W	X	145
Trwyn y Ffosle	Gwyn	SH2824	52°47·4'	4°32·6'W	X	123

Trwyn y Fulfran	Gwyn	SH2823	52°46·9'	4°32·6'W	X	123
Trwyn y Gader or Carmel Head	I of Angl	SH2993	53°24·6'	4°34·0'W	X	114
Trwyn-y-garnedd	Gwyn	SH6340	52°56·6'	4°1·9'W	X	124
Trwynygogarth	Conwy	SH7583	53°20·0'	3°52·2'W	X	115
Trwyn y Gorlech	Gwyn	SH1122	52°46·0'	4°47·7'W	X	123
Trwyn y Gorlech	Gwyn	SH3445	52°58·8'	4°28·0'W	X	123
Trwyn y Gwyddel	Gwyn	SH1424	52°47·1'	4°45·1'W	X	123
Trwyn y Penrhyn	Gwyn	SH1825	52°47·8'	4°41·6'W	X	123
Trwynypenrhyn	Gwyn	SH5837	52°54·9'	4°6·3'W	X	124
Trwyn y Penrhyn	I of Angl	SH6279	53°17·6'	4°3·8'W	X	114,115
Trwyn yr Wylfa	Gwyn	SH3224	52°47·5'	4°29·1'W	X	123
Trwyn Ysgwrfa	Powys	SO2221	51°53·2'	3°7·6'W	X	161
Trwyn y Tâl	Gwyn	SH3647	53°0·0'	4°26·2'W	X	123
Trwyn y Witch	V of Glam	SS8872	51°26·4'	3°36·3'W	X	170
Tryal	Cered	SN5768	52°17·7'	4°5·4'W	X	135
Tryal-Bach	Cered	SN5265	52°16·0'	4°9·7'W	X	135
Tryal Manor	Cered	SN4853	52°9·5'	4°12·9'W	X	146
Trychiad	Gwyn	SH6005	52°37·7'	4°3·7'W	X	124
Trychrug	Carm	SN2931	51°57·3'	4°28·9'W	A	145
Tryddyn Cottage	Flint	SJ2456	53°6·0'	3°7·7'W	X	117
Trye Fm	Corn	SW4535	50°9·8'	5°33·9'W	FM	203
Tryfan	Conwy	SH6659	53°6·9'	3°59·7'W	H	115
Tryfan	Conwy	SH9766	53°11·1'	3°32·1'W	X	116
Tryfan Hall	Gwyn	SH4856	53°5·0'	4°15·8'W	X	115,123
Tryfel	Powys	SH9716	52°44·2'	3°31·1'W	X	125
Tryfil	I of Angl	SH4081	53°18·4'	4°23·7'W	T	114,115
Trygarn	Gwyn	SH2431	52°51·1'	4°36·4'W	X	123
Trygill	Northum	NY9755	54°53·6'	2°2·4'W	X	87
Tryndehayes	Essex	TQ7993	51°36·7'	0°35·5'E	X	178
Tryock Burn	D & G	NX1871	55°0·3'	4°50·3'W	W	76
Trysglwyn	I of Angl	SH4489	53°22·7'	4°20·3'W	X	114
Trysgol	Powys	SN8554	52°10·6'	3°40·5'W	X	147
Trysull	Staffs	SO8594	52°32·9'	2°12·9'W	T	139
Trythall	Corn	SW4433	50°8·7'	5°34·6'W	X	203
Trythance	Corn	SW7920	50°2·6'	5°4·8'W	X	204
Trythogga	Corn	SW4731	50°7·7'	5°32·0'W	T	203
Try Valley	Corn	SW4535	50°9·8'	5°33·9'W	X	203
Trywell Lodge	Cumbr	NY6163	54°57·9'	2°36·1'W	X	86
TT Course	I of M	SC3477	54°10·0'	4°32·2'W	X	95
Tua	Shetld	HU4663	60°21·2'	1°9·5'W	X	2,3
Tuach Hill	Aberd	NJ7915	57°13·8'	2°20·4'W	X	38
Tuaks of the Boy	Orkney	HY1700	58°53·0'	3°25·9'W	X	7
Tuan	Orkney	HY4845	59°17·6'	2°54·3'W	X	5
Tuarach Cottage	Stir	NN4719	56°20·6'	4°28·1'W	X	57
Tuarie Burn	Highld	NC8220	58°9·5'	3°59·8'W	W	17
Tubbon Hill	Corn	SW7437	50°11·6'	5°9·6'W	X	204
Tubb's Bottom	S Glos	ST6882	51°32·4'	2°27·3'W	X	172
Tubb's Fm	Cambs	TL4078	52°23·2'	0°3·8'E	FM	142,143
Tubbs Mill	Corn	SW9643	50°15·3'	4°51·3'W	T	204
Tubby's Head	Corn	SW6950	50°18·5'	5°14·3'W	X	203
Tubeg	Highld	NC6563	58°32·3'	4°18·7'W	X	10
Tubhailt Mhic'ic Eoghain or Maclean's Towel	Highld	NM9964	56°43·7'	5°16·7'W	W	40
Tubney	Oxon	SU4398	51°41·0'	1°22·3'W	T	164
Tubney Lodge	Oxon	SU4399	51°41·5'	1°22·3'W	X	164
Tubney Manor Fm	Oxon	SP4400	51°42·1'	1°21·4'W	FM	164
Tubney Wood	Oxon	SP4400	51°42·1'	1°21·4'W	F	164
Tubslake	Kent	TQ7633	51°4·4'	0°31·1'E	T	188
Tubwell Fm	E Susx	TQ5329	51°2·6'	0°11·3'E	FM	188,199
Tuchethill	Pth & Kin	NN9020	56°21·8'	3°46·4'W	X	52,58
Tuckenhay	Devon	SX8155	50°23·2'	3°40·1'W	T	202
Tucker Fm	Kent	TQ9734	51°4·5'	0°49·1'E	FM	189
Tuckermarsh	Devon	SX4467	50°29·2'	4°11·6'W	T	201
Tucker's Cross	Dorset	ST6017	50°57·3'	2°33·8'W	X	183
Tucker's Fm	Devon	ST0916	50°56·4'	3°17·3'W	FM	181
Tucker's Grave Inn (PH)	Somer	ST7555	51°17·8'	2°21·1'W	X	172
Tucker's Hill Fm	Wigan	SD6010	53°35·3'	2°35·8'W	FM	109
Tucker's Hill Stud	Hants	SU5461	51°21·0'	1°13·1'W	X	174
Tucker's Moor	Devon	SS8623	50°59·9'	3°37·1'W	X	181
Tuckerton	Somer	ST2929	51°3·6'	3°0·4'W	T	193
Tuckett's Fm	Essex	TL9013	51°47·2'	0°45·7'E	FM	168
Tuckey Fm	Bucks	SP7526	51°55·9'	0°54·2'W	FM	165
Tuckhill	Shrops	SO7888	52°29·6'	2°19·0'W	T	138
Tuckingmill	Bath & NE Somer	ST6563	51°22·1'	2°29·8'W	X	172
Tucking Mill	Bath & NE Somer	ST7661	51°21·1'	2°20·3'W	T	172
Tuckingmill	Corn	SW6640	50°13·1'	5°16·4'W	T	203
Tuckingmill	Corn	SX0977	50°33·9'	4°41·4'W	T	200
Tuckingmill	Corn	SX2291	50°41·7'	4°30·8'W	X	190
Tuckingmill	Devon	SS4022	50°58·7'	4°16·4'W	X	180,190
Tuckingmill	Devon	SS7203	50°49·0'	3°48·6'W	X	191
Tuckingmill	Wilts	ST9329	51°3·8'	2°5·6'W	T	184
Tuckmans Fm	W Susx	TQ1723	50°59·9'	0°19·6'W	FM	198
Tuck Mill	Heref	SO4539	52°3·0'	2°47·7'W	X	149,161
Tuckmill Fm	Devon	ST0701	50°48·3'	3°18·8'W	FM	192
Tuckmill Fm	Devon	ST3501	50°48·5'	2°55·0'W	FM	193
Tuck Mill Fm	Worcs	SP0838	52°2·7'	1°52·6'W	FM	150
Tuck's Fm	Norf	TF8814	52°41·7'	0°47·3'E	FM	132
Tuckton	Bourne	SZ1492	50°43·9'	1°47·7'W	T	195
Tuc Memorial Cottages	Dorset	SY7894	50°44·9'	2°18·3'W	X	194
Tucoyse	Corn	SW9645	50°16·4'	4°51·4'W	X	204
Tudball	Somer	ST2033	51°5·7'	3°8·2'W	X	182
Tudbeer Fm	Somer	ST3409	50°52·8'	2°55·9'W	FM	193
Tuddenham	Suff	TL7371	52°18·8'	0°32·7'E	T	155
Tuddenham	Suff	TM1948	52°5·4'	1°12·2'E	T	169
Tuddenham Corner	Suff	TL7467	52°16·6'	0°33·4'E	X	155
Tuddenham Hall	Suff	TM1948	52°5·4'	1°12·2'E	X	169
Tuddenham Heath	Suff	TL7472	52°19·3'	0°33·6'E	X	155
Tudeley	Kent	TQ6245	51°11·1'	0°19·5'E	T	188
Tudeley Hale	Kent	TQ6246	51°11·6'	0°19·5'E	T	188
Tudhay	Devon	ST3200	50°48·0'	2°57·5'W	T	193
Tudhoe	Durham	NZ2635	54°42·8'	1°35·4'W	T	93
Tudhoe Grange	Durham	NZ2534	54°42·3'	1°36·3'W	T	93
Tudhope	Scot Bord	NT6420	55°28·6'	2°33·7'W	X	74
Tudhope Hill	D & G	NY4399	55°17·2'	2°53·4'W	H	79
Tudor Fm	Bucks	SP6721	51°53·2'	1°1·2'W	FM	164,165
Tudor Fm	Medway	TQ8174	51°26·4'	0°36·7'E	FM	178
Tudor Fm	Oxon	SU2897	51°40·5'	1°35·3'W	FM	163
Tudor Grange Park	Sol	SP1479	52°24·8'	1°47·3'W	X	139
Tudor Hill	Birm	SP1196	52°33·9'	1°49·9'W	T	139
Tudor Ho	Shrops	SO7882	52°26·3'	2°19·0'W	X	138
Tudor House	Heref	SO4863	52°16·0'	2°45·3'W	A	137,138,148
Tudor Lodge	Suff	TL9966	52°15·6'	0°55·4'E	X	155
Tudor Rocks	E Susx	TQ4925	51°0·5'	0°7·8'E	X	188,199
Tudor Stud	Herts	TL3528	51°56·3'	0°1·8'W	X	166
Tudorville	Heref	SO5922	51°53·9'	2°35·4'W	T	162
Tudweiliog	Gwyn	SH2336	52°53·8'	4°37·5'W	T	123
Tudwick Hall Fm	Essex	TL8913	51°47·2'	0°44·8'E	FM	168
Tudworth Green Fm	Donc	SE6810	53°35·2'	0°58·0'W	FM	111
Tudworth Hall Fm	Donc	SE6810	53°35·2'	0°58·0'W	FM	111
Tuebrook	Liv	SJ3892	53°25·5'	2°55·6'W	T	108
Tuell	Devon	SX4177	50°34·5'	4°14·4'W	X	201
Tuelldown	Devon	SX4278	50°35·1'	4°13·5'W	X	201
Tuelmenna	Corn	SX2265	50°27·7'	4°30·1'W	T	201
Tuesley	Surrey	SU9641	51°9·8'	0°37·2'W	T	186
Tuesnoad	Kent	TQ9042	51°9·0'	0°43·4'E	T	189
Tuetoes Hills	Lincs	SE8401	53°30·2'	0°43·6'W	X	112
Tuffland	Devon	SX6648	50°19·2'	3°52·6'W	X	202
Tuffley	Glos	SO8315	51°50·2'	2°14·4'W	T	162
Tuffley Fm	Glos	SO8214	51°49·7'	2°15·3'W	FM	162
Tufnell Park	Camden	TQ2985	51°33·2'	0°8·0'W	T	176
Tufta	Orkney	HY2720	59°3·9'	3°15·9'W	X	6
Tufta	Orkney	HY2724	59°6·1'	3°16·0'W	X	6
Tufter	Orkney	HY4443	59°16·5'	2°58·5'W	X	5
Tufthill Fm	E Yorks	TA0865	54°4·4'	0°20·5'W	FM	101
Tuft House Fm	N Yks	SE6876	54°10·8'	0°57·1'W	FM	100
Tufton	Hants	SU4546	51°12·9'	1°21·0'W	T	185
Tufton	Pemb	SN0428	51°55·2'	4°50·6'W	T	145,157,158
Tufton Lodge	Cumbr	NY8410	54°29·4'	2°14·4'W	X	91,92
Tufton Place	E Susx	TQ8123	50°58·9'	0°35·1'E	X	199
Tufton Warren Fm	Hants	SU4744	51°11·8'	1°19·3'W	FM	185
Tufts, The	Glos	SO6105	51°44·8'	2°33·5'W	X	162
Tugby	Leic	SK7600	52°35·8'	0°52·3'W	T	141
Tugby Wood	Leic	SK7602	52°36·9'	0°52·2'W	F	141
Tugford	Shrops	SO5587	52°29·0'	2°39·4'W	T	137,138
Tuggall Grange	Northum	NU2027	55°32·4'	1°40·6'W	X	75
Tuggall Hall	Northum	NU2126	55°31·9'	1°39·6'W	X	75
Tughall	Northum	NU2126	55°31·9'	1°39·6'W	T	75
Tughall Burn	Northum	NU2027	55°32·4'	1°40·6'W	W	75
Tughall Covert	Northum	NU2026	55°31·9'	1°40·6'W	F	75
Tughall Mill	Northum	NU2227	55°32·4'	1°38·6'W	X	75
Tugley Wood	Surrey	SU9833	51°5·5'	0°35·6'W	F	186
Tugnet	Moray	NJ3465	57°40·5'	3°5·9'W	T	28
Tuhwnt i' Ffawnog	Conwy	SH8066	53°10·9'	3°47·3'W	X	116
Tu-hwnt-i'r-afon	Conwy	SH8167	53°11·5'	3°46·5'W	X	116
Tu-hwnt-ir-afon	Conwy	SH8759	53°7·2'	3°40·9'W	X	116
Tu-hwnt-i'r-afon	Conwy	SH8768	53°12·1'	3°41·1'W	X	116
Tuhwntir Afon	Wrex	SJ1334	52°54·0'	3°17·2'W	X	125
Tuhwnt-i'r-mynydd-isaf	Gwyn	SH4544	52°58·5'	4°18·1'W	X	123
Tu-hwynt-i'r-nant	Conwy	SH8667	53°11·5'	3°42·0'W	X	116
Tuiffit Manor	N Yks	SE7678	54°11·8'	0°49·7'W	X	100
Tuilyies	Fife	NT0286	56°3·7'	3°34·0'W	X	65
Tuilyies (Standing Stone)	Fife	NT0286	56°3·7'	3°34·0'W	A	65
Tuiteam Tarbhach	Highld	NC4301	57°58·5'	4°38·8'W	X	16
Tulach Hill	Pth & Kin	NN8564	56°45·5'	3°52·4'W	H	43
Tulchan	Pth & Kin	NN9528	56°26·2'	3°41·7'W	X	52,53,58
Tulchan Ho	Pth & Kin	NN9528	56°26·2'	3°41·7'W	X	52,53,58
Tulchan Lodge	Angus	NO1872	56°50·2'	3°20·2'W	X	43
Tulchan Lodge	Highld	NJ1235	57°24·1'	3°27·4'W	X	28
Tulip Hill	Norf	TF8515	52°42·3'	0°44·7'E	X	132
Tulkie	Shetld	HU3348	60°13·2'	1°23·8'W	T	3
Tulk's Hill	Dorset	SY5486	50°40·5'	2°38·7'W	X	194
Tullach Ard	Pth & Kin	NO2131	56°28·1'	3°16·5'W	X	53
Tulla Cottage	Arg & Bt	NN3144	56°33·7'	4°44·6'W	X	50
Tullaghmore	E Susx	TQ5518	50°56·7'	0°12·8'E	X	199
Tullecombe	W Susx	SU8025	51°1·4'	0°51·2'W	T	186,197
Tulleys Fm	W Susx	TQ3235	51°6·2'	0°6·5'W	FM	187
Tulleys Wells Fm	E Susx	TQ3913	50°54·2'	0°1·0'W	FM	198
Tulliallan Castle	Fife	NS9388	56°4·6'	3°42·7'W	X	65
Tullibardine	Pth & Kin	NN9214	56°18·6'	3°44·3'W	T	58
Tullibardine Chapel	Pth & Kin	NN9013	56°18·1'	3°46·2'W	A	58
Tullibardine Wood	Pth & Kin	NN9112	56°17·5'	3°45·2'W	X	58
Tullibody	Clackm	NS8695	56°8·3'	3°49·6'W	T	58
Tullibody Inch	Clackm	NS8692	56°6·7'	3°49·6'W	X	58
Tullibole Castle	Pth & Kin	NO0500	56°11·2'	3°31·4'W	A	58
Tullich	Arg & Bt	NM8312	56°15·3'	5°29·8'W	X	55
Tullich	Arg & Bt	NM8527	56°23·4'	5°28·6'W	X	49
Tullich	Arg & Bt	NN0815	56°17·6'	5°5·7'W	X	50,56
Tullich	Highld	NC5200	57°58·1'	4°29·7'W	X	16
Tullich	Highld	NG9142	57°25·5'	5°28·4'W	X	25
Tullich	Highld	NH6328	57°19·6'	4°16·1'W	X	26,35
Tullich	Highld	NH6554	57°33·6'	4°14·9'W	X	26
Tullich	Moray	NJ2225	57°18·8'	3°17·2'W	X	36
Tullich	Moray	NJ3242	57°28·1'	3°7·6'W	X	28
Tullich	Stir	NN5136	56°29·8'	4°24·8'W	X	51
Tullich Burn	Aberd	NO3799	57°4·9'	3°1·9'W	W	37,44
Tullichewan Fm	W Dunb	NS3781	55°59·9'	4°36·4'W	FM	63
Tullich Fm	Arg & Bt	NS3099	56°9·5'	4°43·8'W	FM	56
Tullich Fm	Highld	NH8576	57°45·8'	3°55·5'W	FM	21
Tullichglass	Pth & Kin	NN7238	56°31·3'	4°4·4'W	X	51,52
Tullich Hill	Arg & Bt	NN2900	56°10·0'	4°44·8'W	H	56
Tullich Hill	Pth & Kin	NN7036	56°30·1'	4°6·3'W	H	51,52
Tullich Muir	Highld	NH7373	57°44·0'	4°7·5'W	T	21
Tullichuil	Pth & Kin	NN8047	56°36·2'	3°56·8'W	X	52
Tullich Wood	Highld	NH7274	57°44·5'	4°8·5'W	F	21
Tulliemet	Pth & Kin	NN9952	56°39·2'	3°38·4'W	T	52,53
Tulliemet Burn	Pth & Kin	NO0053	56°39·7'	3°37·4'W	W	52,53
Tulliemet Ho	Pth & Kin	NN9953	56°39·7'	3°38·4'W	X	52,53
Tullieroch	Aberd	NJ6249	57°32·0'	2°37·6'W	X	29
Tulliesfield	D & G	NY2467	54°59·8'	3°10·9'W	X	85
Tullikera	Aberd	NK0259	57°37·5'	1°57·5'W	X	30
Tullis Cote	N Yks	SE0790	54°18·6'	1°53·1'W	X	99
Tullithwaite Hall	Cumbr	SD4790	54°18·4'	2°48·5'W	X	97
Tullo	Aberd	NJ8031	57°22·4'	2°19·5'W	X	29,30
Tullo	Aberd	NO7671	56°50·0'	2°23·1'W	X	45
Tulloch	Aberd	NJ5218	57°15·3'	2°47·3'W	X	37
Tulloch	Aberd	NJ5405	57°8·3'	2°45·1'W	X	37
Tulloch	Aberd	NJ6317	57°14·8'	2°36·3'W	X	37
Tulloch	Aberd	NJ6806	57°8·9'	2°31·3'W	X	38
Tulloch	Aberd	NJ7931	57°22·4'	2°20·5'W	X	29,30
Tulloch	Angus	NO2162	56°44·8'	3°17·1'W	X	44
Tulloch	C of Aber	NJ8409	57°10·5'	2°15·4'W	X	38
Tulloch	E Ayr	NS5836	55°36·1'	4°14·8'W	X	71
Tulloch	Highld	NH6192	57°54·0'	4°20·3'W	T	21
Tulloch	Highld	NH9816	57°13·7'	3°40·9'W	T	36
Tulloch	Highld	NN3280	56°53·1'	4°45·0'W	X	34,41
Tulloch	Moray	NJ0855	57°34·8'	3°31·9'W	X	27
Tulloch	Moray	NJ3860	57°37·8'	3°1·8'W	X	28
Tulloch	Pth & Kin	NO0925	56°24·8'	3°28·0'W	T	52,53,58
Tulloch	Stir	NN5120	56°21·2'	4°24·2'W	X	51,57
Tullochallum	Moray	NJ3439	57°26·5'	3°5·5'W	X	28
Tullochan	W Dunb	NS4185	56°2·1'	4°32·7'W	X	56
Tullochbeg	Aberd	NJ5138	57°26·0'	2°48·5'W	X	29
Tullochcan	Stir	NN6434	56°29·0'	4°12·1'W	X	51
Tulloch Castle	Highld	NH5460	57°36·6'	4°26·2'W	X	21
Tullochclury	Highld	NH7833	57°22·5'	4°1·3'W	X	27
Tullochcoy	Aberd	NO2394	57°2·1'	3°15·7'W	X	36,44
Tullochcurran	Pth & Kin	NO0660	56°43·6'	3°31·7'W	X	43
Tullochcurran Burn	Pth & Kin	NO0560	56°43·6'	3°32·7'W	W	43
Tullochgorm	Arg & Bt	NR9695	56°6·5'	5°16·4'W	T	55
Tullochgorum	Highld	NH9621	57°16·3'	3°43·0'W	X	36
Tullochgribban High	Highld	NH9425	57°18·5'	3°45·1'W	X	36
Tulloch Hill	Angus	NO3761	56°44·4'	3°1·3'W	H	44
Tulloch Hill	E Ayr	NS5835	55°35·5'	4°14·8'W	H	71
Tulloch Hill	Highld	NH5361	57°37·2'	4°27·2'W	X	20
Tulloch Ho	Aberd	NJ7931	57°22·4'	2°20·5'W	X	29,30
Tullochleys	Aberd	NJ5324	57°18·5'	2°46·4'W	X	37
Tullochmacarrick	Aberd	NJ2701	57°5·9'	3°11·8'W	X	37
Tullochroam	Highld	NN5189	56°58·4'	4°26·6'W	X	42
Tullochroisk	Pth & Kin	NN7157	56°41·5'	4°5·9'W	X	42,51,52
Tullochs	Aberd	NJ4948	57°31·4'	2°50·6'W	X	28,29
Tulloch Sta	Highld	NN3580	56°53·2'	4°42·0'W	X	34,41
Tullochvenus	Aberd	NJ5807	57°9·4'	2°41·2'W	X	37
Tulloch Wood	Moray	NJ3342	57°28·1'	3°6·6'W	F	28
Tullock Fm	W Berks	SU4072	51°27·0'	1°25·1'W	FM	174
Tullo Fm	Angus	NO5366	56°47·2'	2°45·7'W	FM	44
Tulloford	Aberd	NJ8033	57°23·5'	2°19·5'W	X	29,30
Tullo Hill	Angus	NO4964	56°46·1'	2°49·6'W	H	44
Tullo' of Benholm	Aberd	NO7970	56°49·5'	2°20·2'W	X	45
Tullos	Aberd	NJ7021	57°17·0'	2°29·4'W	X	38
Tullos	C of Aber	NJ9403	57°7·3'	2°5·5'W	T	38
Tullos Cairn	C of Aber	NJ9504	57°7·9'	2°4·5'W	A	38
Tullos Ho	Aberd	NJ7021	57°17·0'	2°29·4'W	A	38
Tullybaccart	Pth & Kin	NO2636	56°30·9'	3°11·7'W	X	53
Tullybannocher	Pth & Kin	NN7521	56°22·1'	4°1·0'W	T	51,52,57
Tullybelton Ho	Pth & Kin	NO0333	56°29·0'	3°34·1'W	X	52,53
Tullybothy Craigs	Fife	NO6310	56°17·1'	2°35·4'W	X	59
Tullybreck	Fife	NT3198	56°10·4'	3°6·2'W	X	59
Tullycross	Stir	NS4686	56°2·8'	4°27·9'W	T	57
Tullygarth	Clackm	NS9292	56°6·8'	3°43·8'W	X	58
Tullylumb Plantn	Fife	NT2393	56°7·7'	3°13·9'W	F	58
Tullymoran	Pth & Kin	NN9729	56°26·8'	3°39·8'W	X	52,53,58
Tullymurdoch	Pth & Kin	NO1952	56°39·4'	3°18·8'W	X	53
Tullyneddie	Pth & Kin	NO1244	56°35·0'	3°25·5'W	X	53
Tullynessle	Aberd	NJ5519	57°15·8'	2°44·3'W	T	37
Tullypowrie	Pth & Kin	NN9154	56°40·2'	3°46·3'W	X	52
Tullypowrie Burn	Pth & Kin	NN9054	56°40·1'	3°47·2'W	W	52
Tullythwaite Ho	Cumbr	SD4791	54°19·0'	2°48·5'W	X	97
Tulm Bay	Highld	NG4075	57°41·6'	6°21·3'W	W	23
Tulm Island	Highld	NG4074	57°41·1'	6°21·3'W	X	23
Tulmore	Stir	NS6992	56°6·4'	4°5·9'W	X	57
Tulse Hill	Lam	TQ3173	51°26·7'	0°6·5'W	T	176,177
Tulwick Fm	Oxon	SU4190	51°36·7'	1°24·1'W	FM	164,174
Tumble	Carm	SN5411	51°47·0'	4°6·6'W	T	159
Tumble Beacon	Surrey	TQ2359	51°19·2'	0°13·7'W	A	187
Tumbler's Green	Essex	TL8025	51°53·9'	0°37·4'E	T	168
Tumblers, The	Northum	NU2132	55°35·1'	1°39·6'W	X	75
Tumble, The	Monm	SO2511	51°47·8'	3°4·9'W	X	161
Tumbley Hill	Norf	TF7716	52°43·0'	0°37·6'E	X	132
Tumblin	Shetld	HU3353	60°15·9'	1°23·7'W	X	3
Tumby	Lincs	TF2359	53°7·1'	0°9·3'W	T	122
Tumby Gates	Lincs	TF2560	53°7·6'	0°7·5'W	X	122
Tumby Ho	Lincs	TF2758	53°6·5'	0°5·8'W	X	122
Tumby Lawn	Lincs	TF2460	53°7·6'	0°8·4'W	X	122
Tumby Woodside	Lincs	TF2657	53°6·0'	0°6·7'W	T	122
Tumley Hill	Warw	SP4679	52°24·7'	1°19·0'W	X	140
Tummel Bridge	Pth & Kin	NN7659	56°42·6'	4°1·1'W	T	42,51,52
Tummel Forest	Pth & Kin	NN7661	56°43·7'	4°1·1'W	F	42
Tummer Hill Marsh	Cumbr	SD1867	54°5·8'	3°14·8'W	W	96
Tummer Hill Scar	Cumbr	SD1767	54°5·8'	3°15·7'W	X	96
Tumore	Highld	NC1826	58°11·4'	5°5·3'W	X	15
Tumore	Highld	NC5235	58°17·0'	4°31·0'W	X	16
Tump	Monm	SO3519	51°52·2'	2°56·3'W	X	161
Tump Bew Hill	Worcs	SP1145	52°6·4'	1°50·0'W	X	150
Tump Covert	Glos	ST8493	51°38·4'	2°13·5'W	F	162,173
Tump Fm	Glos	ST5594	51°38·8'	2°38·6'W	FM	162,172
Tump Fm	Monm	ST4096	51°39·8'	2°51·7'W	FM	171
Tump Fm	Powys	SO2146	52°6·6'	3°8·8'W	FM	148
Tump Fm, The	Heref	SO5418	51°51·8'	2°39·7'W	FM	162
Tump Plantn	Glos	ST9397	51°40·5'	2°5·7'W	F	163
Tump Terret	Monm	SO4905	51°44·7'	2°43·9'W	A	162
Tump, The	Glos	SP1625	51°55·6'	1°45·6'W	A	163
Tumpy Green	Glos	SO7201	51°42·7'	2°23·9'W	T	162
Tumpy Lakes	Heref	SO5447	52°7·4'	2°39·9'W	T	149
Tumrose	Corn	SX1073	50°31·8'	4°40·5'W	X	200
Tun Bridge	Bath & NE Somer	ST5762	51°21·6'	2°36·7'W	A	172,182
Tunbridge Hill	Medway	TQ8074	51°26·4'	0°35·8'E	T	178
Tun Brook	Lancs	SD6034	53°48·3'	2°36·0'W	W	102,103
Tundergarth Mains	D & G	NY1780	55°6·7'	3°17·6'W	X	79
Tundry Pond	Hants	SU7752	51°15·9'	0°53·4'W	W	186
Tunehead	Cumbr	NY7638	54°44·4'	2°21·9'W	X	91
Tunga	N Eil	NB4436	58°14·6'	6°21·3'W	T	8
Tunga	Orkney	HY2223	59°5·5'	3°21·2'W	X	6
Tungadal River	Highld	NG4139	57°22·3'	6°18·0'W	W	23,32
Tungate	Norf	TG2629	52°48·9'	1°21·6'E	T	133,134
Tungli Geo	Shetld	HU4281	60°30·9'	1°13·6'W	X	1,2,3
Tun Hill	D & G	NX7655	54°52·7'	3°55·5'W	H	84

Tunlands Fm	Hants	SU2938	51°8·7′	1°34·7′W	FM	185
Tunley	Bath & NE Somer	ST6959	51°20·0′	2°26·3′W	T	172
Tunley	Glos	SO9304	51°44·3′	2°5·7′W	T	163
Tunley Fm	Bath & NE Somer	ST6859	51°20·0′	2°27·2′W	FM	172
Tunman Wood	Lincs	SK8864	53°10·2′	0°40·6′W	F	121
Tunnel End	Kirk	SE0411	53°36·0′	1°56·0′W	X	110
Tunneley Wood	Rut	SK9312	52°42·1′	0°37·0′W	F	130
Tunnel Fm	Northnts	SP5871	52°20·3′	1°8·5′W	FM	140
Tunnel Hill	Surrey	SU9155	51°17·4′	0°41·3′W	X	175,186
Tunnel Hill	Worcs	SO8440	52°3·7′	2°13·6′W	T	150
Tunnel Hill	Worcs	SP0247	52°7·5′	1°57·9′W	X	150
Tunnel Hill Fm	Northnts	SP7352	52°9·9′	0°55·6′W	FM	152
Tunnel How Hill	Leeds	SE2938	53°50·5′	1°33·1′W	X	104
Tunnel Pits	N Lincs	SE7304	53°31·9′	0°53·5′W	T	112
Tunnel, The	Warw	SP4352	52°10·1′	1°21·9′W	X	151
Tunningham Fm	Northnts	SP5953	52°10·6′	1°7·8′W	FM	152
Tunnoch	S Ayr	NS3009	55°21·0′	4°40·4′W	X	70,76
Tunns	Arg & Bt	NR9295	56°6·4′	5°20·3′W	X	55
Tunshill	Roch	SD9413	53°37·1′	2°5·0′W	T	109
Tunskeen (Bothy)	S Ayr	NX4290	55°11·0′	4°28·5′W	X	77
Tunskeen Lane	S Ayr	NX4390	55°11·0′	4°27·5′W	W	77
Tunstall	C of Stoke	SJ8651	53°3·6′	2°12·1′W	T	118
Tunstall	E Yorks	TA3031	53°45·8′	0°1·3′W	T	107
Tunstall	Kent	TQ8961	51°19·2′	0°43·1′E	T	178
Tunstall	Lancs	SD6073	54°9·3′	2°36·3′W	T	97
Tunstall	Norf	TG4107	52°36·7′	1°34·0′E	T	134
Tunstall	N Yks	SE2195	54°21·2′	1°40·2′W	T	99
Tunstall	Staffs	SJ7727	52°50·6′	2°20·1′W	T	127
Tunstall	Suff	TM3655	52°8·8′	1°27·4′E	T	156
Tunstall	Sund	NZ3853	54°52·5′	1°24·0′W	T	88
Tunstall Beck	N Yks	SE2396	54°21·8′	1°38·3′W	W	99
Tunstall Br	Norf	TG4209	52°37·7′	1°35·0′E	X	134
Tunstall Burn	Durham	NZ0441	54°46·1′	1°55·8′W	W	87
Tunstall Common	Suff	TM3754	52°8·2′	1°28·2′E	X	156
Tunstall Drain	E Yorks	TA3130	53°45·2′	0°0·4′W	W	107
Tunstall Fm	E Susx	TQ7221	50°58·0′	0°27·4′E	FM	199
Tunstall Fm	Shrops	SJ6326	52°50·1′	2°32·6′W	FM	127
Tunstall Forest	Suff	TM3854	52°8·2′	1°29·1′E	F	156
Tunstall Grange	N Yks	SE1995	54°21·3′	1°42·0′W	X	99
Tunstall Hall	Shrops	SJ6835	52°54·9′	2°28·2′W	A	127
Tunstall Hills	Sund	NZ3954	54°53·0′	1°23·1′W	H	88
Tunstall Ho	Durham	NZ0641	54°46·1′	1°54·0′W	X	87
Tunstall Ho	Lancs	SD6566	54°5·6′	2°31·7′W	X	97
Tunstall Lodge Fm	Sund	NZ3852	54°51·9′	1°24·1′W	FM	88
Tunstall Reservoir	Durham	NZ0641	54°46·1′	1°54·0′W	W	87
Tunstall Wood	Shrops	SJ6226	52°50·1′	2°33·4′W	F	127
Tunstead	Derby	SK0279	53°18·7′	1°57·8′W	X	119
Tunstead	Derby	SK1175	53°16·6′	1°49·7′W	T	119
Tunstead	Norf	TG2921	52°44·5′	1°24·0′E	T	133,134
Tunstead	Oldham	SE0004	53°32·2′	1°59·6′W	T	110
Tunstead	Staffs	SK0865	53°11·2′	1°52·4′W	X	119
Tunstead Ho	Derby	SK0586	53°22·5′	1°55·1′W	X	110
Tunsteads	Lancs	SD5236	53°49·3′	2°43·3′W	X	102
Tunworth	Hants	SU6748	51°13·9′	1°2·0′W	T	185,186
Tunworth Ho	Hants	SU6749	51°14·4′	1°2·0′W	X	185,186
Tuperee	Northum	NT8933	55°35·7′	2°10·0′W	X	74
Tupgill Park	N Yks	SE0986	54°16·4′	1°51·3′W	X	99
Tup Hag Wood	N Yks	SE5687	54°16·8′	1°8·0′W	F	100
Tupholme Hall Fm	Lincs	TF1468	53°12·0′	0°17·2′W	FM	121
Tup Knowe	D & G	NY4197	55°16·1′	2°55·3′W	H	79
Tuppark Linn	D & G	NX9989	55°11·4′	3°34·8′W	W	78
Tuppenhurst	Staffs	SK0915	52°44·2′	1°51·6′W	X	128
Tupsley	Heref	SO5340	52°3·6′	2°40·7′W	T	149
Tup Stones	Derby	SE0901	53°30·6′	1°51·4′W	X	110
Tupton	Derby	SK3965	53°11·1′	1°24·6′W	T	119
Tupton	Shetld	HP6313	60°48·0′	0°50·0′W	X	1
Tuquoy	Orkney	HY4543	59°16·5′	2°57·4′W	X	5
Turbary Common	Poole	SZ0594	50°45·0′	1°55·4′W	T	195
Turbary Pasture	N Yks	SD6979	54°12·6′	2°28·1′W	X	98
Turbiskill	Arg & Bt	NR7386	56°1·0′	5°38·1′W	X	55
Turbitail	Orkney	HY4032	59°10·5′	3°2·5′W	X	5,6
Turbot Point	Corn	SX0242	50°14·9′	4°46·3′W	X	204
Turchington	Devon	SX3883	50°37·7′	4°17·1′W	X	201
Turclossie	Aberd	NJ8857	57°36·4′	2°11·6′W	X	30
Turdale	Shetld	HU1950	60°14·3′	1°38·9′W	X	3
Turdale Water	Shetld	HU3052	60°15·3′	1°27·0′W	W	3
Turdees	N Lanak	NS8063	55°51·0′	3°54·6′W	X	65
Turf	Devon	SX9686	50°40·1′	3°27·9′W	X	192
Turfachie	Angus	NO4158	56°42·9′	2°57·4′W	X	54
Turfbeg	Angus	NO4451	56°39·1′	2°54·4′W	X	54
Turfcraig	Aberd	NO8497	57°4·1′	2°15·4′W	X	38,45
Turf Croft	Hants	SU2005	50°50·9′	1°42·6′W	X	195
Turfdown	Corn	SX0965	50°27·5′	4°41·1′W	T	200
Turf Fen	Cambs	TL2483	52°26·1′	0°10·2′W	X	142
Turf Fen	Cambs	TL3282	52°25·4′	0°3·1′W	X	142
Turf Fen	Cambs	TL3389	52°29·2′	0°2·1′W	X	142
Turf Fen	Cambs	TL3989	52°29·1′	0°3·2′E	X	142,143
Turf Fen	Norf	TG3618	52°42·7′	1°30·0′E	W	133,134
Turf Fen	Suff	TL7082	52°24·8′	0°30·4′E	X	143
Turf Fen	Suff	TL7473	52°19·9′	0°33·6′E	X	155
Turf Fen Br	Cambs	TF3505	52°37·8′	0°0·1′E	X	142
Turf Fen Fm	Norf	TL6393	52°30·9′	0°24·5′E	FM	143
Turfgate	Aberd	NO5992	57°1·3′	2°40·1′W	X	44
Turfgraft Wood	E Yorks	SE7838	53°50·2′	0°48·5′W	F	105,106
Turf Hill	Aberd	NJ4526	57°19·5′	2°54·3′W	H	37
Turf Hill	Aberd	NJ6420	57°16·4′	2°35·4′W	H	37
Turf Hill	Aberd	NJ6548	57°31·5′	2°34·6′W	H	29
Turfhill	Aberd	NJ8747	57°31·0′	2°12·6′W	T	30
Turf Hill	Aberd	NO7184	56°57·0′	2°28·2′W	H	45
Turf Hill	Angus	NO3561	56°44·4′	3°3·3′W	X	44
Turf Hill	Angus	NO4874	56°51·5′	2°50·7′W	X	44
Turf Hill	D & G	NY1398	55°16·4′	3°21·7′W	H	78
Turf Hill	Hants	SU2102	50°49·3′	1°41·7′W	X	195
Turf Hill	Roch	SD9011	53°36·0′	2°8·7′W	T	109
Turf Hill	S Ayr	NX0575	55°2·1′	5°2·7′W	X	76
Turf Hill	Scot Bord	NT3608	55°22·0′	3°0·2′W	H	79
Turf Hill Inclosure	Hants	SU2017	50°57·4′	1°42·5′W	F	184
Turfhillock	Moray	NJ4044	57°29·2′	2°59·6′W	X	28

Turfhill of Auchtylair	Aberd	NJ9743	57°28·9′	2°2·5′W	X	30
Turfhills Fm	Pth & Kin	NO1002	56°12·4′	3°26·6′W	FM	58
Turf Ho	Northum	NY9155	54°53·6′	2°8·0′W	X	87
Turfholm	S Lanak	NS8139	55°38·1′	3°53·0′W	T	71,72
Turfhouse	Devon	ST1708	50°52·2′	3°10·4′W	X	192,193
Turfland	Ches	SJ5779	53°18·6′	2°38·3′W	X	117
Turf Law	Scot Bord	NT4756	55°47·9′	2°50·3′W	X	66,73
Turf Lea Fm	Stock	SJ9686	53°22·5′	2°3·2′W	FM	109
Turflundie	Pth & Kin	NO1914	56°18·9′	3°18·1′W	X	58
Turfmoor	Devon	ST2701	50°48·5′	3°1·8′W	T	193
Turf Moor	Lancs	SD8217	53°39·2′	2°15·9′W	X	109
Turf Moor	N Yks	NY9902	54°25·1′	2°0·5′W	X	92
Turfmoor	Shrops	SJ3518	52°45·6′	2°57·4′W	T	126
Turf Moor Fm	Notts	SK8558	53°7·0′	0°43·4′W	FM	121
Turf Nest Fm	Wigan	SJ6998	53°28·9′	2°27·6′W	FM	109
Turf Pits	Tames	SD9900	53°30·0′	2°0·5′W	X	109
Turfpits Fm	Lincs	TF2714	52°42·8′	0°6·8′W	FM	131
Turf Rigg	N Yks	NZ9100	54°23·5′	0°35·5′W	X	94
Turgeny	S Ayr	NS4305	55°19·1′	4°28·0′W	H	70,77
Tur Geo	Orkney	ND5399	58°52·8′	2°48·4′W	X	6,7
Turgis Green	Hants	SU6959	51°19·8′	1°0·2′W	T	175,186
Turgy	Powys	SO1584	52°27·1′	3°14·6′W	X	136
Turin Hill	Angus	NO5153	56°40·2′	2°47·5′W	H	54
Turin House	Angus	NO5452	56°39·7′	2°44·6′W	X	54
Turkdean	Glos	SP1017	51°51·3′	1°50·9′W	T	163
Turker Beck	N Yks	SE3894	54°20·6′	1°24·5′W	W	99
Turkers	E Yorks	TA0956	53°59·5′	0°19·8′W	X	107
Turkers Wood	York	SE6554	53°58·9′	1°0·1′W	F	105,106
Turkey Cott	Somer	ST3328	51°3·1′	2°57·0′W	X	193
Turkey Farmhouse	Kent	TQ7344	51°10·4′	0°28·9′E	X	188
Turkey Fields Fm	Notts	SK4942	52°58·6′	1°15·8′W	FM	129
Turkey Fm	Warw	SP2567	52°18·3′	1°37·6′W	FM	151
Turkey Hall	Cumbr	NY5557	54°54·6′	2°41·7′W	X	86
Turkey Hall	Suff	TM2980	52°22·4′	1°22·3′E	X	156
Turkey Hall	Suff	TM3173	52°18·6′	1°23·7′E	X	156
Turkey Hall Fm	Medway	TQ8075	51°26·9′	0°35·8′E	FM	178
Turkey Hill	S Lanak	NT0131	55°34·0′	3°33·8′W	H	72
Turkey Island	Hants	SU5613	50°55·1′	1°11·8′W	T	196
Turkey Island	W Susx	SU7919	50°58·1′	0°52·1′W	T	197
Turkey Tump	Heref	SO5028	51°57·1′	2°43·3′W	T	149
Turkington Hill	Cambs	TL3778	52°23·2′	0°1·2′E	X	142,143
Turk's Br	E Susx	TQ6325	51°0·3′	0°19·8′E	X	188,199
Turks Castle	Pemb	SM9701	51°40·5′	4°55·8′W	X	157,158
Turk's Fm	Wilts	ST9888	51°35·7′	2°1·3′W	FM	173
Turks Head	Cumbr	NY7715	54°32·0′	2°20·9′W	X	91
Turks Head Fm	Kent	TQ8838	51°6·8′	0°41·6′E	FM	189
Turk, The	Fife	NO2319	56°21·7′	3°14·3′W	X	58
Turla	Shetld	HU3797	60°39·5′	1°18·9′W	X	1
Tur Langton	Leic	SP7194	52°32·6′	0°56·8′W	T	141
Turleigh	Wilts	ST8060	51°20·6′	2°16·8′W	T	173
Turley Down	Devon	SS9910	50°53·1′	3°25·8′W	X	192
Turleygreen	Shrops	SO7685	52°28·0′	2°20·8′W	T	138
Turley Holes and Higher House Moor	Cald	SD9821	53°41·4′	2°1·4′W	X	103
Turley Holes Edge	Cald	SD9822	53°41·9′	2°1·4′W	X	103
Turlin Moor	Poole	SY9891	50°43·3′	2°1·3′W	T	195
Turlow Fields	Derby	SK2449	53°2·5′	1°38·1′W	X	119
Turls Head	Shetld	HU2886	60°33·7′	1°28·9′W	X	1,3
Turl Stack	Shetld	HU2658	60°18·6′	1°31·3′W	X	3
Turmar Fm	E Yorks	TA2734	53°47·4′	0°3·9′W	FM	107
Turmer	Hants	SU1309	50°53·1′	1°48·5′W	T	195
Turmer Hall	E Yorks	TA1533	53°47·1′	0°14·9′W	X	107
Tùr Mór	Arg & Bt	NM5545	56°32·3′	5°58·7′W	H	47,48
Turn	Lancs	SD8118	53°39·7′	2°16·8′W	T	109
Turnabrain	Angus	NO5078	56°53·7′	2°48·8′W	X	44
Turnaichaidh	Arg & Bt	NR2162	55°46·5′	6°26·5′W	H	60
Turnalief	Aberd	NK0938	57°26·2′	1°50·5′W	X	30
Turnalt	Arg & Bt	NM8407	56°12·7′	5°28·5′W	X	55
Turnant	Heref	SO3028	51°57·0′	3°0·7′W	X	161
Turnastone	Heref	SO3536	52°1·4′	2°56·4′W	T	149,161
Turnave Hill	Renf	NS3260	55°48·5′	4°40·4′W	X	63
Turnave Hill	Renf	NS3360	55°48·5′	4°39·5′W	X	63
Turnaware Point	Corn	SW8338	50°12·4′	5°2·1′W	X	204
Turnbank	Cumbr	NY6119	54°34·1′	2°35·8′W	X	91
Turn Beck	N Yks	SE0583	54°14·8′	1°55·0′W	W	98
Turnberry	S Ayr	NS2005	55°18·6′	4°49·7′W	T	70,76
Turnberry Bay	S Ayr	NS1906	55°19·1′	4°50·7′W	W	70,76
Turnberry Ho	Cumbr	NY5551	54°51·4′	2°41·6′W	X	86
Turnberry Point	S Ayr	NS1906	55°19·1′	4°50·7′W	X	70,76
Turnbridge Fm	E Yorks	SE6621	53°41·1′	0°59·6′W	FM	105,106
Turnchapel	C of Plym	SX4952	50°21·1′	4°7·0′W	T	201
Turncliff	Derby	SK0470	53°13·9′	1°56·0′W	X	119
Turncole Fm	Essex	TQ9998	51°39·0′	0°53·0′E	FM	168
Turncroft	Notts	SK6554	53°5·0′	1°1·4′W	X	120
Turnditch	Derby	SK2946	53°0·9′	1°33·7′W	T	119,128
Turn Edge	Staffs	SK0167	53°12·2′	1°58·7′W	H	119
Turned Hill	N Yks	SD8794	54°20·7′	2°11·6′W	X	98
Turner	Stir	NN5194	56°7·2′	4°23·4′W	X	57
Turner Cleuch Law	Scot Bord	NT2820	55°28·4′	3°7·9′W	H	73
Turner Fold	Lancs	SD6840	53°51·6′	2°28·8′W	X	103
Turnerford	N Yks	SD7266	54°5·6′	2°25·3′W	X	98
Turner Green	Lancs	SD6130	53°46·1′	2°35·1′W	T	102,103
Turnerhall	Aberd	NO4098	57°4·4′	2°58·9′W	X	37,44
Turner Hall Fm	Cumbr	SD2396	54°21·5′	3°10·7′W	FM	96
Turner Ho	Cumbr	SD7893	54°20·2′	2°19·9′W	X	98
Turnerhill	E Ayr	NS4924	55°29·4′	4°23·0′W	X	70
Turner Ing	N Yks	SE2158	54°1·3′	1°40·4′W	X	104
Turner Lodge Fm	Derby	SK0675	53°16·6′	1°54·2′W	FM	119
Turners	Durham	NY9427	54°38·5′	2°5·2′W	X	91,92
Turner's Boat	Heref	SO3145	52°6·2′	3°0·1′W	X	148
Turners Court	Oxon	SU6488	51°35·5′	1°4·2′W	T	175
Turner's Court Fm	Somer	ST6149	51°14·6′	2°33·1′W	FM	183
Turner's Fm	E Susx	TQ6719	50°57·0′	0°23·0′E	FM	199
Turner's Fm	Wilts	ST9561	51°21·1′	2°3·9′W	FM	173
Turner's Green	E Susx	TQ6319	50°57·1′	0°19·6′E	T	199
Turner's Green	E Susx	TQ6332	51°4·1′	0°20·0′E	T	188
Turner's Green	Warw	SP1969	52°19·4′	1°42·9′W	T	139,151
Turner's Green	W Berks	SU5368	51°24·7′	1°13·9′W	T	174
Turner's Hall Fm	Herts	TL0915	51°49·6′	0°24·7′W	FM	166
Turners Hall Fm	Herts	TL1516	51°50·1′	0°19·5′W	FM	166

Turner's Hill	Sand	SO9688	52°29·6′	2°3·1′W	H	139
Turners Hill	W Susx	TQ3435	51°6·1′	0°4·8′W	T	187
Turner's Monument	D & G	NX8276	55°4·1′	3°50·4′W	X	84
Turner's Pool	Staffs	SJ9763	53°10·1′	2°2·3′W	W	118
Turners Puddle	Dorset	SY8393	50°44·4′	2°14·1′W	T	194
Turner's Tump	Glos	SO6217	51°51·3′	2°32·7′W	X	162
Turnerwood	Roth	SK5481	53°19·6′	1°10·9′W	T	111,120
Tur Ness	Shetld	HU2876	60°28·3′	1°28·9′W	X	3
Tur Ness	Shetld	HU6199	60°40·4′	0°52·5′W	X	1
Turney Shield	Northum	NY8049	54°50·4′	2°18·3′W	X	86,87
Turnford	Herts	TL3604	51°43·3′	0°1·5′W	T	166
Turnham	Devon	ST0419	50°58·0′	3°21·6′W	X	181
Turnham Hall	N Yks	SE6431	53°46·5′	1°1·3′W	X	105,106
Turnham Wood	Wilts	ST9974	51°28·1′	2°0·5′W	F	173
Turnhead Fm	N Yks	SE6335	53°48·7′	1°2·2′W	FM	105,106
Turnhigh	W Loth	NS9363	55°51·2′	3°42·1′W	X	65
Turn Hill	Somer	ST4131	51°4·8′	2°50·2′W	H	182
Turnhouse	C of Edin	NT1674	55°57·4′	3°20·3′W	T	65,66
Turnhouse Fm	Lincs	SK9986	53°21·9′	0°30·3′W	FM	112,121
Turnhouse Hill	Midlo	NT2162	55°50·9′	3°15·3′W	X	66
Turnhurst	Ches	SJ9366	53°11·7′	2°5·9′W	X	118
Turnhurst	C of Stoke	SJ8653	53°4·7′	2°12·1′W	T	118
Turniedykes	Midlo	NT3863	55°51·6′	2°59·0′W	X	66
Turniemoon	W Loth	NT0362	55°50·7′	3°32·5′W	X	65
Tùrnigil	Arg & Bt	NR3592	56°3·1′	6°14·9′W	X	61
Turning Hill	Shetld	HU2682	60°31·5′	1°31·1′W	H	3
Turnings	Cumbr	NY7341	54°46·0′	2°24·8′W	X	86,87
Turningshaw Fm	Renf	NS4267	55°52·5′	4°31·1′W	FM	64
Turnlaw	S Lanak	NS6458	55°48·0′	4°9·7′W	X	64
Turnley's	Lancs	SD6239	53°51·0′	2°34·2′W	X	102,103
Turnock Fm	Ches	SJ8370	53°13·8′	2°14·9′W	FM	118
Turnours Hall	Essex	TQ4595	51°38·3′	0°6·1′E	X	167,177
Turnover Hall	Lancs	SD4541	53°52·0′	2°49·8′W	X	102
Turnpike Corner	Somer	ST6053	51°16·7′	2°34·0′W	X	183
Turnpike Cross	Devon	SS4843	51°10·2′	4°10·1′W	X	180
Turnpike Fm	Beds	TL0419	51°51·8′	0°29·0′W	FM	166
Turnpike Fm	Wilts	ST9866	51°23·8′	2°1·3′W	FM	173
Turnpike Top Fm	N Lincs	TA0314	53°37·0′	0°26·2′W	FM	112
Turnpole Wood	Rut	TF0013	52°42·6′	0°30·8′W	F	130
Turnpost Fm	Leic	SK6224	52°48·8′	1°4·4′W	FM	129
Turnshaw	Cumbr	NY4551	54°51·3′	2°51·0′W	X	86
Turnshawhead	D & G	NY1772	55°2·4′	3°17·5′W	X	85
Turn Slack Clough	Roch	SD9218	53°39·7′	2°6·9′W	X	109
Turnstead Milton	Derby	SK0380	53°19·3′	1°56·9′W	T	110
Turnworth	Dorset	ST8107	50°52·0′	2°15·8′W	T	194
Turnworth Clump	Dorset	ST8008	50°52·5′	2°16·7′W	F	194
Turnworth Down	Dorset	ST8108	50°52·5′	2°15·8′W	X	194
Turnworth Ho	Dorset	ST8108	50°52·5′	2°15·8′W	X	194
Turpin Fm	Lincs	SK9185	53°21·5′	0°37·5′W	FM	112,121
Turpin Lair	N Yks	SE2057	54°0·8′	1°41·3′W	X	104
Turpin's Hill	Northum	NZ1068	55°0·6′	1°50·2′W	X	88
Turpit Gate Ho	Lancs	SD8749	53°56·5′	2°11·5′W	X	103
Turra Field	Shetld	HU6191	60°36·1′	0°52·7′W	X	1,2
Turrastane	Aberd	NJ8137	57°25·6′	2°18·5′W	X	29,30
Turrerich	Pth & Kin	NN8538	56°31·5′	3°51·7′W	X	52
Turrerich Burn	Pth & Kin	NN8639	56°32·0′	3°50·8′W	W	52
Turret Bridge	Highld	NN3391	56°59·1′	4°44·4′W	X	34
Turret Burn	Pth & Kin	NN7930	56°27·1′	3°57·3′W	W	51,52
Turret Burn	Pth & Kin	NN8424	56°23·9′	3°52·3′W	W	52,58
Turret, The	Hants	SU3337	51°8·1′	1°31·3′W	X	185
Turr Geo	Shetld	HU3060	60°19·6′	1°26·9′W	X	3
Turrieday	Orkney	HY3512	58°59·7′	3°7·4′W	X	6
Turriff	Aberd	NJ7250	57°32·6′	2°27·6′W	T	29
Turrifield	Shetld	HU2056	60°17·5′	1°37·8′W	X	3
Turri Geo	Shetld	HU1859	60°19·1′	1°39·9′W	X	3
Turrill Hill Fm	Hants	SU5048	51°14·0′	1°16·6′W	FM	185
Turri Ness	Shetld	HU4529	60°2·9′	1°11·0′W	X	4
Turri Water	Shetld	HU2745	60°11·6′	1°30·3′W	W	4
Tursdale	Durham	NZ3035	54°42·8′	1°31·6′W	T	93
Tursdale Ho	Durham	NZ2937	54°43·9′	1°32·6′W	X	93
Turtle Hill Fm	E Yorks	TA1160	54°1·7′	0°17·9′W	FM	101
Turtleton	Scot Bord	NT8153	55°46·4′	2°17·7′W	X	67,74
Turton and Entwistle Resr	Black w Dar	SD7117	53°39·2′	2°25·9′W	W	109
Turton Bottoms	Black w Dar	SD7315	53°38·1′	2°24·1′W	T	109
Turton Heights	Black W Dar	SD7016	53°38·6′	2°26·8′W	H	109
Turton Moor	Black w Dar	SD6818	53°39·7′	2°28·6′W	X	109
Turton's Covert	N Lincs	TA0118	53°39·2′	0°27·9′W	F	112
Turton Tower	Black w Dar	SD7315	53°38·1′	2°24·1′W	A	109
Turtory	Moray	NJ5949	57°32·0′	2°40·6′W	X	29
Turvalds Head	Shetld	HU3268	60°23·9′	1°24·7′W	X	3
Turvelaws Fm	Northum	NT9929	55°33·5′	2°0·5′W	FM	75
Turves	Cambs	TL3396	52°33·0′	0°1·9′W	T	142
Turves Green	Birm	SP0278	52°24·2′	1°57·8′W	T	139
Turves, The	Cambs	TL3396	52°33·0′	0°1·9′W	X	142
Turvey	Beds	SP9452	52°9·7′	0°37·1′W	T	153
Turvey Abbey	Beds	SP9452	52°9·7′	0°37·1′W	X	153
Turvey Cott	Beds	SP9351	52°9·2′	0°38·0′W	X	153
Turvey Ho	Beds	SP9353	52°10·3′	0°38·0′W	X	153
Turville	Bucks	SU7691	51°37·0′	0°53·7′W	T	175
Turville Court	Bucks	SU7590	51°36·5′	0°54·6′W	X	175
Turville Grange	Bucks	SU7491	51°37·0′	0°55·5′W	X	175
Turville Heath	Bucks	SU7491	51°37·0′	0°55·5′W	T	175
Turville Hill	Bucks	SU7691	51°37·0′	0°53·7′W	X	175
Turville Park	Bucks	SU7391	51°37·0′	0°56·3′W	X	175
Turvin Clough	Cald	SD9820	53°40·8′	2°1·4′W	X	103
Turvins Fm	Kent	TQ4957	51°17·8′	0°8·6′E	FM	188
Turweston	Bucks	SP6037	52°1·9′	1°7·1′W	T	152
Turwhappie	Angus	NO4347	56°36·9′	2°55·3′W	X	54
Turzes Fm	E Susx	TQ6826	51°0·8′	0°24·1′E	FM	188,199
Tus Brook	Warw	SP2841	52°4·2′	1°35·1′W	W	151
Tusbrook Fm	Warw	SP3041	52°4·2′	1°33·3′W	FM	151
Tusdale	Highld	NG3525	57°14·6′	6°23·1′W	X	32
Tusdale Burn	Highld	NG3526	57°15·1′	6°23·2′W	W	32
Tushielaw	Scot Bord	NT2917	55°26·8′	3°6·9′W	H	79
Tushielaw	Scot Bord	NT3018	55°27·3′	3°6·0′W	T	79

Tushielaw Burn	Scot Bord	NT2819	55°27·8′	3°7·9′W	W	79
Tushingham Hall	Ches	SJ5245	53°0·3′	2°42·5′W	X	117
Tushingham Ho	Ches	SJ5244	52°59·8′	2°42·5′W	X	117
Tuskerbister	Orkney	HY3509	58°58·1′	3°7·3′W	X	6,7
Tusker Rock	Pemb	SM7509	51°44·3′	5°15·1′W	X	157
Tusker Rock	V of Glam	SS8474	51°27·4′	3°39·8′W	X	170
Tusmore Ho	Oxon	SP5630	51°58·2′	1°10·7′W	X	152
Tusmore Park	Oxon	SP5630	51°58·2′	1°10·7′W	X	152
Tuston	Heref	SO6341	52°4·2′	2°32·0′W	X	149
Tutbury	Staffs	SK2028	52°51·2′	1°41·8′W	T	128
Tute Hill	Durham	NY9714	54°31·5′	2°2·4′W	X	92
Tutehill Fm	Cumbr	NY0220	54°34·2′	3°30·5′W	FM	89
Tutehill Moss	Northum	NY9793	55°14·1′	2°2·4′W	X	81
Tuters Hill	Staffs	SO8199	52°35·5′	2°16·4′W	X	138
Tut Hill	Northum	NZ0288	55°11·4′	1°57·7′W	X	81
Tut Hill Fm	Dorset	ST6814	50°55·7′	2°26·9′W	FM	194
Tuthill Fm	Heref	SO6251	52°9·6′	2°32·9′W	FM	149
Tutim Burn	Highld	NC4203	57°59·6′	4°39·9′W	X	16
Tutnall	Worcs	SO9870	52°19·9′	2°1·4′W	T	139
Tutnalls	Glos	SO6402	51°43·2′	2°30·9′W	T	162
Tutsham Hall	Kent	TQ7052	51°14·7′	0°26·5′E	X	188
Tutshill	Devon	SS5535	51°6·0′	4°3·9′W	X	180
Tutshill	Glos	ST5494	51°38·8′	2°39·5′W	T	162,172
Tutshill Ear	N Som	ST3865	51°23·1′	2°53·1′W	X	171,182
Tutt	Swan	SS6287	51°34·1′	3°59·1′W	X	159
Tutta Beck	Durham	NZ0513	54°31·0′	1°54·9′W	W	92
Tutta Beck Fm	Durham	NZ0613	54°31·0′	1°54·0′W	FM	92
Tutt Hill	Kent	TQ9746	51°11·0′	0°49·5′E	T	189
Tutt Hill	Norf	TL8881	52°23·9′	0°46·2′E	X	144
Tutt Hill (Tumulus)	Norf	TL8881	52°23·9′	0°46·2′E	A	144
Tuttington	Norf	TG2227	52°47·9′	1°18·0′E	T	133,134
Tuttle Fm	Norf	TF9321	52°45·4′	0°52·0′E	FM	132
Tuttles Wood	Suff	TM4578	52°20·9′	1°36·2′E	F	156
Tutton's Fm	Somer	ST2236	51°7·3′	3°6·5′W	FM	182
Tutts Clump	W Berks	SU5871	51°26·3′	1°9·5′W	T	174
Tutts Fm	E Susx	TQ4119	50°57·4′	0°0·8′E	FM	198
Tutwell	Corn	SX3975	50°33·4′	4°16·0′W	T	201
Tuxford	Notts	SK7370	53°13·6′	0°54·0′W	T	120
Tuxton Fm	Devon	SX5654	50°22·3′	4°1·1′W	FM	202
Tuxwell Fm	Somer	ST2037	51°7·8′	3°8·2′W	FM	182
Twa Havens	Aberd	NK1036	57°25·1′	1°49·6′W	W	30
Twarri Field	Shetld	HU3919	59°57·5′	1°17·6′W	H	4
Twart Burn	Shetld	HU2552	60°15·4′	1°32·4′W	W	3
Twart Burn	Shetld	HU2681	60°31·0′	1°31·1′W	W	3
Twart Burn	Shetld	HU2878	60°29·4′	1°28·9′W	W	3
Twartquoy	Orkney	HY4007	58°57·0′	3°2·1′W	X	6,7
Twathats	D & G	NY1070	55°1·2′	3°24·0′W	X	85
Twatley Manor Fm	Wilts	ST8987	51°35·1′	2°9·1′W	FM	173
Twatt	Orkney	HY2724	59°6·1′	3°16·0′W	T	6
Twatt	Shetld	HU3253	60°15·9′	1°24·8′W	T	3
Twatt Hill	Shetld	HU2951	60°14·8′	1°28·1′W	H	3
Twdin	Powys	SN9152	52°9·6′	3°35·2′W	A	147
Twdin	Powys	SN9250	52°8·5′	3°34·3′W	A	147
Twdin	Powys	SN9252	52°9·6′	3°34·3′W	A	147
Twechar	E Dunb	NS6975	55°57·3′	4°5·4′W	T	64
Tweddle Black Halls	Durham	NZ4637	54°43·8′	1°16·7′W	X	93
Tweedale	Wrekin	SJ7004	52°38·2′	2°26·2′W	T	127
Tweedbank	Scot Bord	NT5134	55°36·1′	2°46·2′W	X	73
Tweed-dale	Aberd	NJ7820	57°16·5′	2°21·4′W	X	38
Tweeddaleburn	Midlo	NT2752	55°45·6′	3°9·4′W	T	66,73
Tweeddaleburn	Midlo	NT2752	55°45·6′	3°9·4′W	X	66,73
Tweeddale Burn	Scot Bord	NT2749	55°44·0′	3°9·3′W	W	73
Tweeddale Burn	Scot Bord	NT2752	55°45·6′	3°9·4′W	W	66,73
Tweeden Burn	Scot Bord	NY5186	55°10·2′	2°45·7′W	W	79
Tweedenhead	Scot Bord	NY5287	55°10·7′	2°44·8′W	X	79
Tweeden Plantation	Scot Bord	NY4886	55°10·2′	2°48·6′W	F	79
Tweedhill	Scot Bord	NT9251	55°45·4′	2°7·2′W	X	67,74,75
Tweedhopefoot	Scot Bord	NT0517	55°26·5′	3°29·7′W	X	78
Tweedhopefoot Rig	Scot Bord	NT0516	55°26·0′	3°29·6′W	H	78
Tweediehall	S Lanak	NS7243	55°40·1′	4°1·7′W	X	71
Tweedieside	S Lanak	NS7242	55°39·5′	4°1·6′W	X	71
Tweedmill	Scot Bord	NT8643	55°41·1′	2°12·9′W	X	74
Tweedmouth	Northum	NT9952	55°45·9′	2°0·5′W	T	75
Tweedmouthmoor	Northum	NT9949	55°44·3′	2°0·5′W	X	75
Tweed River	Leic	SP4297	52°34·4′	1°22·4′W	W	140
Tweedsmuir	Scot Bord	NT0924	55°30·3′	3°26·0′W	T	72
Tweed's Well or Source of River Tweed	Scot Bord	NT0514	55°24·9′	3°29·6′W	W	78
Tweedy Hill	Cumbr	NY5867	55°0·0′	2°39·0′W	X	86
Tween Bridge Moors	Donc	SE7014	53°37·3′	0°56·1′W	X	112
Tweenhills Fm	Glos	SO7924	51°55·1′	2°17·9′W	FM	162
Tween the Wicks	Orkney	ND3896	58°51·1′	3°4·0′W	X	6,7
Twelmlow Hall	Ches	SJ7868	53°12·8′	2°19·4′W	X	118
Twelve Acre Fm	Oxon	SP4109	51°46·9′	1°23·9′W	FM	164
Twelve Acres	Ches	SJ6763	53°10·0′	2°29·2′W	X	118
Twelve Acre Wood	Essex	TL7840	52°2·0′	0°36·1′E	F	155
Twelve Apostles	Brad	SE1245	53°54·3′	1°48·6′W	X	104
Twelve Apostles	D & G	NX9479	55°5·9′	3°39·2′W	X	84
Twelve Apostles	Staffs	SK1451	53°3·6′	1°47·1′W	X	119
Twelve Apostles (Stone Circle)	Brad	SE1245	53°54·3′	1°48·6′W	A	104
Twelve Apostles (Stone Circle)	D & G	NX9479	55°5·9′	3°39·2′W	A	84
Twelve Foot Cut	N Yks	SE7781	54°13·4′	0°48·7′W	W	100
Twelve Foot Drain	Suff	TL7085	52°26·4′	0°30·5′E	W	143
Twelveheads	Corn	SW7642	50°14·4′	5°8·1′W	T	204
Twelve Hours Tower	Orkney	HY3931	59°9·9′	3°3·5′W	H	6
Twelve Men's Moor	Corn	SX2575	50°33·2′	4°27·8′W	X	201
Twelve Months Carr	Donc	SE6400	53°29·8′	1°1·7′W	X	111
Twelve Oaks	E Susx	TQ6820	50°57·5′	0°23·9′E	T	199
Twelve Oaks	Surrey	SU9463	51°21·7′	0°38·6′W	X	175,186
Twelve Oaks Fm	Devon	SX8573	50°33·0′	3°37·0′W	FM	191
Twelvewoods	Corn	SX2065	50°27·7′	4°31·8′W	T	201
Twemlow Green	Ches	SJ7868	53°12·8′	2°19·4′W	T	118
Twemlows Big Wood	Shrops	SJ5636	52°55·4′	2°38·9′W	F	126
Twemlows Hall	Shrops	SJ5637	52°56·0′	2°38·9′W	X	126
Twemlows, The	Shrops	SJ5737	52°56·0′	2°38·0′W	X	126
Twenties	Kent	TR3469	51°22·5′	1°22·1′E	T	179
Twenty	Lincs	TF1520	52°46·2′	0°17·3′W	T	130
Twenty	Pth & Kin	NN7622	56°22·7′	4°0·0′W	X	51,52
Twenty Acre Hill	Suff	TL7766	52°16·0′	0°36·0′E	X	155
Twenty Acre Plantation	Somer	ST1833	51°5·7′	3°9·9′W	F	181
Twenty Acres	Devon	ST0711	50°53·7′	3°19·0′W	X	192
Twenty Foot Drain or Fenton Lode	Cambs	TL3581	52°24·8′	0°0·5′W	W	142
Twenty Foot River	Cambs	TL3599	52°34·6′	0°0·1′W	W	142
Twentyshilling	D & G	NS8006	55°20·3′	3°53·1′W	X	71,78
Twentyshilling Burn	D & G	NS7905	55°19·7′	3°54·0′W	W	71,78
Twentyshilling Hill	D & G	NS7904	55°19·2′	3°54·0′W	H	78
Twerlow Fm	Staffs	SJ9532	52°53·4′	2°4·1′W	FM	127
Twerton	Bath & NE Somer	ST7264	51°22·7′	2°23·8′W	T	172
Tweseldown Hill	Hants	SU8251	51°15·4′	0°49·1′W	X	186
Twice Brewed	Northum	NY7567	55°0·1′	2°23·0′W	X	86,87
Twichills	Staffs	SK1518	52°45·8′	1°46·3′W	X	128
Twickenham	Rich	TQ1573	51°26·9′	0°20·3′W	T	176
Twigbeare	Devon	SS4712	50°53·5′	4°10·1′W	X	180
Twiglees	D & G	NY2294	55°14·3′	3°13·2′W	X	79
Twiglees Burn	D & G	NY2295	55°14·8′	3°13·2′W	W	79
Twigmoor Grange	N Lincs	SE9205	53°32·3′	0°36·3′W	X	112
Twigmoor Hall	N Lincs	SE9206	53°32·8′	0°36·3′W	X	112
Twigmoor Woods	N Lincs	SE9305	53°32·2′	0°35·4′W	F	112
Twig Side	Bucks	SU7592	51°37·5′	0°54·6′W	X	175
Twigworth	Glos	SO8422	51°54·0′	2°13·6′W	T	162
Twiland Wood	Worcs	SO9780	52°25·3′	2°2·2′W	F	139
Twineham	W Susx	TQ2519	50°57·6′	0°12·8′W	T	198
Twineham Court Fm	W Susx	TQ2420	50°58·2′	0°13·6′W	FM	198
Twineham Grange	W Susx	TQ2420	50°58·2′	0°13·6′W	X	198
Twineham Green	W Susx	TQ2520	50°58·2′	0°12·8′W	T	198
Twineham Place	W Susx	TQ2419	50°57·6′	0°13·7′W	X	198
Twi Ness	Orkney	HY4616	59°1·9′	2°56·0′W	X	6
Twiness	Orkney	HY4941	59°15·4′	2°53·2′W	X	5
Twin Hill	Notts	SK5555	53°5·6′	1°10·3′W	X	120
Twinhills Wood	Somer	ST5543	51°11·3′	2°38·2′W	F	182,183
Twinhoe	Bath & NE Somer	ST7459	51°20·0′	2°22·0′W	T	172
Twining Hill	Wrex	SJ3443	52°59·1′	2°58·6′W	X	117
Twin Law	Scot Bord	NT6254	55°46·9′	2°35·9′W	X	67,74
Twinlaw Cairns	Scot Bord	NT6254	55°46·9′	2°35·9′W	A	67,74
Twin Laws	S Lanak	NT0352	55°45·4′	3°32·3′W	X	65,72
Twinley Manor	Hants	SU4852	51°16·1′	1°18·3′W	X	185
Twinney Creek	Kent	TQ8669	51°23·6′	0°40·8′E	W	178
Twin Oak Fm	Suff	TM3168	52°15·9′	1°23·5′E	FM	156
Twinsburn Fm	Darl	NZ2421	54°35·3′	1°37·3′W	FM	93
Twin Standing Stones	N Yks	SE1280	54°13·2′	1°48·5′W	X	99
Twinstead	Essex	TL8636	51°59·7′	0°43·0′E	T	155
Twinstead Green	Essex	TL8536	51°59·7′	0°42·1′E	T	155
Twinway Fm	Bath & NE Somer	ST6062	51°21·6′	2°34·1′W	FM	172
Twin Wood	Beds	TL0354	52°10·7′	0°29·2′W	F	153
Twinwood Coppice	Dorset	ST7815	50°56·3′	2°18·4′W	F	183
Twinwood Fm	Beds	TL0354	52°10·7′	0°29·2′W	FM	153
Twinyards Fm	Derby	SK4558	53°7·3′	1°19·2′W	FM	120
Twinyeo Fm	Devon	SX8476	50°34·6′	3°37·9′W	FM	191
Twinyess	Orkney	HY7452	59°21·5′	2°27·0′W	X	5
Twiscob	Powys	SO2366	52°17·4′	3°7·3′W	X	137,148
Twiscombe	Devon	SX8495	50°44·8′	3°38·3′W	X	191
Twisden Fm	Kent	TQ8634	51°4·7′	0°39·7′E	FM	189
Twislehope	Scot Bord	NY4496	55°15·6′	2°52·4′W	X	79
Twislehope Burn	Scot Bord	NY4395	55°15·0′	2°53·4′W	W	79
Twislehope Hope	Scot Bord	NY4395	55°15·0′	2°53·4′W	X	79
Twisleton	N Yks	SD7176	54°11·0′	2°26·2′W	X	98
Twisleton Dale Ho	N Yks	SD7175	54°10·4′	2°26·2′W	X	98
Twisleton Hall	N Yks	SD7075	54°10·4′	2°27·2′W	X	98
Twisleton Scar End	N Yks	SD7075	54°10·4′	2°27·2′W	X	98
Twisleton Scars	N Yks	SD7176	54°11·0′	2°26·2′W	X	98
Twisly	E Susx	TQ7212	50°53·1′	0°27·1′E	X	199
Twiss Green	Warr	SJ6595	53°27·3′	2°31·2′W	T	109
Twist	Devon	ST2803	50°49·6′	3°1·0′W	T	193
Twist Castle	Lancs	SD8833	53°47·8′	2°10·5′W	A	103
Twisted Oak	Devon	SX7994	50°44·2′	3°42·5′W	X	191
Twistgates Fm	Devon	ST2209	50°52·7′	3°6·1′W	FM	192,193
Twistgreen	Staffs	SK0655	53°5·8′	1°54·2′W	X	119
Twisting Nevi	Orkney	HY5909	58°58·2′	2°42·3′W	X	6
Twistin Hill	Stir	NN3720	56°20·9′	4°37·8′W	H	50,56
Twiston	Lancs	SD8143	53°53·2′	2°16·9′W	T	103
Twiston Moor	Lancs	SD8242	53°52·7′	2°16·0′W	X	103
Twist, The	Herts	SP9310	51°47·1′	0°38·7′W	X	165
Twist, The	Staffs	SK0656	53°6·3′	1°54·2′W	X	119
Twist Wood	Suff	TL8062	52°13·8′	0°38·5′E	F	155
Twitchen	Devon	SS5043	51°10·2′	4°8·4′W	X	180
Twitchen	Devon	SS5223	50°59·5′	4°6·2′W	X	180
Twitchen	Devon	SS6416	50°55·9′	3°55·7′W	X	180
Twitchen	Devon	SS6440	51°8·8′	3°56·3′W	X	180
Twitchen	Devon	SS6941	51°9·4′	3°52·0′W	X	180
Twitchen	Devon	SS7830	51°3·6′	3°44·1′W	T	180
Twitchen	Shrops	SO3779	52°24·6′	2°55·2′W	T	137,148
Twitchen Barrows	Devon	SS8032	51°4·7′	3°42·4′W	A	181
Twitchen Fm	Devon	SS8628	51°2·6′	3°37·2′W	FM	181
Twitchen Ho	Devon	SS4644	51°10·7′	4°11·8′W	X	180
Twitchen Mill	Devon	SS7830	51°3·6′	3°44·1′W	T	180
Twitchen Ridge	Devon	SS7932	51°4·7′	3°43·3′W	H	180
Twitchen Ridge	Devon	SS8032	51°4·7′	3°42·4′W	X	181
Twitchill Fm	Derby	SK1784	53°21·4′	1°44·3′W	FM	110
Twite's Fm	Suff	TL7863	52°14·4′	0°36·8′E	FM	155
Twitham	Kent	TR2656	51°15·7′	1°14·8′E	T	179
Twitton	Kent	TQ5159	51°18·8′	0°10·4′E	T	188
Twitty Fee	Essex	TL7906	51°43·7′	0°35·9′E	X	167
Twizel	Northum	NT8743	55°41·1′	2°12·0′W	X	74
Twizel Bridge	Northum	NT8843	55°41·1′	2°11·0′W	A	74
Twizell	Northum	NU1228	55°33·0′	1°48·2′W	X	75
Twizell Burn	Durham	NZ2251	54°51·4′	1°39·0′W	W	88
Twizell Fm	Northum	NZ1578	55°6·0′	1°45·5′W	FM	88
Twizell Hall	Durham	NZ2151	54°51·4′	1°39·9′W	X	88
Twizell Ho	Northum	NU1328	55°33·0′	1°47·2′W	X	75
Twizel Mill	Northum	NT8842	55°40·5′	2°11·0′W	X	74
Twizle Head Moss	Kirk	SE1003	53°31·7′	1°50·5′W	X	110
Twizziegill Fm	Red & Cl	NZ7518	54°33·3′	0°50·0′W	FM	94
Twizzlefoot Bridge	Essex	TQ9797	51°38·5′	0°51·2′E	X	168
Twizzle, The	Essex	TM2423	51°51·9′	1°15·6′E	W	169
Twlc Pt	Swan	SS4193	51°37·0′	4°17·4′W	X	159
Twll Du or Devil's Kitchen	Gwyn	SH6458	53°6·4′	4°1·5′W	X	115
Twll-y-clawdd	I of Angl	SH5073	53°14·2′	4°14·5′W	X	114,115
Twllydarren	Gwyn	SH6308	52°39·4′	4°1·1′W	H	124
Twmbarlwm	Caer	ST2492	51°37·5′	3°5·5′W	H	171
Twmpa or Lord Hereford's Knob	Powys	SO2234	52°0·2′	3°7·8′W	X	161
Twmpath	Powys	SO0743	52°4·9′	3°21·0′W	X	147,160
Twmpath	V of Glam	SS9576	51°28·6′	3°30·3′W	X	170
Twmpath Diwlith	Nth Pt Talb	SS8388	51°35·0′	3°40·9′W	A	170
Twmpath Melyn	Powys	SH9602	52°36·6′	3°31·8′W	X	136
Twnan Uchaf	Conwy	SH8875	53°15·9′	3°40·3′W	X	116
Two Acre Belt	Suff	TL7467	52°16·6′	0°33·4′E	F	155
Two Ash Hill	Somer	ST3206	50°51·2′	2°57·6′W	X	193
Two Barns Fm	Cambs	TL2595	52°32·5′	0°9·0′W	FM	142
Two Barrows	Devon	SX7079	50°36·0′	3°49·8′W	A	191
Two Bit Fm	Cambs	TL4768	52°17·7′	0°9·7′E	FM	154
Two Bridges	Corn	SX2781	50°36·4′	4°26·3′W	X	201
Two Bridges	Devon	SX6075	50°33·7′	3°58·2′W	T	191
Two Bridges	Glos	SO6608	51°46·4′	2°29·2′W	T	162
Two Bridges Fm	Somer	ST3421	50°59·3′	2°56·0′W	FM	193
Two Burrows	Corn	SW7346	50°16·5′	5°10·8′W	T	204
Two Castles	Orkney	HY6823	59°5·8′	2°33·0′W	X	5
Two Chimneys	Kent	TR3268	51°22·0′	1°20·4′E	X	179
Two Crosses	Shrops	SO2386	52°28·2′	3°7·6′W	X	137
Twodale Barn	Derby	SK1956	53°6·3′	1°42·6′W	X	119
Two Dale Fm	Notts	SK4853	53°4·6′	1°16·6′W	FM	120
Two Dales	Derby	SK2862	53°9·5′	1°34·5′W	T	119
Twofords Br	Dorset	ST7513	50°55·2′	2°21·0′W	X	194
Two Gates	Dorset	SY5593	50°44·3′	2°37·9′W	X	194
Two Gates	Staffs	SK2101	52°36·6′	1°41·0′W	T	139
Two Gates Cross	Devon	SS8618	50°57·2′	3°37·0′W	X	181
Two Gates Fm	Kent	TQ7272	51°25·5′	0°28·8′E	FM	178
Two Howes	N Yks	SE8299	54°23·0′	0°43·8′W	A	94,100
Two Howes Rigg	N Yks	SE8299	54°23·0′	0°43·8′W	X	94,100
Two Hundred Acre or The Stray	N Yks	SE3054	53°59·1′	1°32·1′W	X	104
Two Hundreds Fm	Lincs	TF2446	53°0·0′	0°8·7′W	FM	131
Twolads' Crag	Cumbr	NY5980	55°7·0′	2°38·1′W	X	80
Two Meres	Derby	SK2558	53°7·4′	1°37·2′W	W	119
Twomerkland	D & G	NX7688	55°10·5′	3°56·4′W	X	78
Two Mile Ash	Mil Key	SP8138	52°2·3′	0°48·7′W	T	152
Two Mile Ash	W Susx	TQ1427	51°2·1′	0°22·1′W	T	187,198
Two Mile Bank	Lincs	TF4487	53°21·8′	0°10·3′E	X	113,122
Two Mile Bottom	Norf	TL8487	52°27·2′	0°42·9′E	X	144
Two Mile Down	Wilts	ST8933	51°6·0′	2°9·0′W	X	184
Two Mile Hill	C of Bris	ST6374	51°28·1′	2°31·6′W	T	172
Two Mile Ho	Ches	SJ3862	53°9·3′	2°55·2′W	X	117
Twomile Ho	Pth & Kin	NO1525	56°24·8′	3°22·2′W	X	53,58
Two Mile Oak Cross	Devon	SX8468	50°30·3′	3°37·8′W	T	202
Two Mills	Ches	SJ3573	53°15·2′	2°58·1′W	T	117
Two Mills Fm	Ches	SJ3473	53°15·2′	2°59·0′W	FM	117
Two Moors Way	Devon	SX6465	50°28·4′	3°54·6′W	X	202
Two Moors Way	Devon	SX7392	50°43·1′	3°47·6′W	X	191
Two Moors Way	Somer	SS7442	51°10·0′	3°47·7′W	X	180
Two Moors Way	Somer	SS7542	51°10·1′	3°46·9′W	X	180
Two Moor Ways	Devon	SS8527	51°2·1′	3°38·0′W	X	181
Two Oaks Fm	Notts	SK5357	53°6·7′	1°12·1′W	FM	120
Twopenny Knowe	E Ayr	NS6232	55°34·0′	4°10·9′W	X	71
Two Post Cross	Devon	SX6796	50°45·1′	3°52·7′W	X	191
Two Pots	Devon	SS5344	51°10·8′	4°5·8′W	T	180
Two Pots House Farm	Cambs	TL3459	52°13·0′	0°1·9′W	FM	154
Two Ridges	Beds	SP9124	51°54·7′	0°40·2′W	X	165
Two Ridges Link	Bucks	SP9221	51°53·0′	0°39·4′W	X	165
Two Rivers Way	Bath & NE Somer	ST5562	51°21·6′	2°38·4′W	X	172,182
Two Saints Fm	Norf	TG3019	52°43·4′	1°24·8′E	FM	133,134
Two Stones	Devon	SX8136	50°13·0′	3°39·7′W	X	202
Two Thorn Fields Fm	Derby	SK1787	53°23·0′	1°44·3′W	FM	110
Twotop Hill	Cumbr	NY6341	54°46·0′	2°34·1′W	X	86
Two Tree Hill	Worcs	SO9666	52°17·8′	2°3·1′W	H	150
Two Tree Island	Sou-on-Sea	TQ8285	51°32·3′	0°37·9′E	X	178
Two Waters	Herts	TL0505	51°44·3′	0°28·4′W	T	166
Two Waters Fm	Somer	ST3014	50°55·5′	2°59·4′W	FM	193
Two Waters Foot	Corn	SX1864	50°27·1′	4°33·5′W	X	201
Twr	I of Angl	SH2282	53°18·5′	4°39·9′W	T	114
Twrch Fechan	Carm	SN7819	51°51·6′	3°45·9′W	W	160
Twt Hill	Denb	SJ0277	53°17·1′	3°27·8′W	A	116
Twycross	Leic	SK3304	52°38·2′	1°30·3′W	T	140
Twycross Hill	Leic	SK3304	52°38·2′	1°30·3′W	X	140
Twycross Zoo	Leic	SK3106	52°39·3′	1°32·1′W	X	140
Twydall	Medway	TQ7966	51°22·1′	0°34·7′E	T	178
Twyford	Bucks	SP6626	51°55·9′	1°2·0′W	T	164,165
Twyford	Derby	SK3228	52°51·1′	1°31·1′W	T	128
Twyford	Dorset	ST8518	50°57·9′	2°12·4′W	T	183
Twyford	Hants	SU4824	51°1·0′	1°18·6′W	T	185
Twyford	Heref	SO3959	52°13·8′	2°53·2′W	X	148,149
Twyford	Heref	SO5034	52°0·4′	2°43·3′W	X	149
Twyford	Leic	SK7210	52°41·2′	0°55·7′W	T	129
Twyford	Norf	TG0124	52°46·8′	0°59·2′E	T	133
Twyford	Oxon	SP4736	52°1·5′	1°18·5′W	T	151
Twyford	Shrops	SJ3426	52°49·9′	2°58·4′W	T	126
Twyford	Wok	SU7975	51°28·3′	0°51·4′W	T	175
Twyford	Worcs	SP0446	52°7·0′	1°56·1′W	T	150
Twyford Common	Heref	SO5135	52°0·9′	2°42·4′W	T	149
Twyford Down	Hants	SU4827	51°2·6′	1°18·5′W	X	185
Twyford Lodge	Bucks	SP6525	51°55·4′	1°2·9′W	X	164,165
Twyford Lodge	E Susx	TQ3930	51°3·4′	0°0·6′W	X	187
Twyford Lodge	Hants	SU4825	51°1·6′	1°18·5′W	X	185
Twyford Mill	Bucks	SP6527	51°56·5′	1°2·9′W	X	164,165
Twyford Moors	Hants	SU4723	51°0·5′	1°19·4′W	X	185
Twyford Wood	Lincs	SK9423	52°48·0′	0°35·9′W	F	130
Twyi Forest	Cered	SN7761	52°14·2′	3°47·7′W	F	146,147
Twyn	Cered	SN7365	52°16·4′	3°51·3′W	X	135,147
Twyn	Powys	SN8626	51°55·5′	3°39·1′W	X	160
Twyn	Powys	SO0325	51°55·1′	3°24·2′W	X	160
Twyn	Powys	SO2120	51°52·6′	3°8·5′W	X	161
Twyn	Swan	SN6202	51°42·2′	3°59·4′W	X	159
Twyn Abertyswg	Caer	SO1206	51°45·0′	3°16·1′W	H	161

Twyn-Allws	Monm	SO2513	51°48·9′	3°4·9′W	T	161
Twynau Gwynion	Merth Tyd	SO0610	51°47·1′	3°21·4′W	H	160
Twynau Gwynion	Powys	SO0812	51°48·2′	3°19·7′W	X	160
Twyn Brynbychan	Rho Cyn Taf	ST0698	51°40·6′	3°21·2′W	H	170
Twyn Brynffaldau	Powys	SN8613	51°48·5′	3°38·8′W	X	160
Twyn Brynhicet	Powys	SN8832	51°58·8′	3°37·5′W	X	160
Twyn Bryn-march	Blae Gw	SO1412	51°48·2′	3°14·4′W	X	161
Twyn Cae Hugh	Caer	ST1791	51°36·9′	3°11·5′W	A	171
Twyn Calch	Torf	ST2699	51°41·3′	3°3·8′W	X	171
Twyn Carncanddo	Blae Gw	SO2010	51°47·2′	3°9·2′W	X	161
Twyn Cecil	Monm	SO3304	51°44·1′	2°57·8′W	X	171
Twyn Ceilog	Blae Gw	SO0912	51°48·2′	3°18·8′W	X	161
Twyn Cerrig-cadarn	Powys	SN9438	52°2·1′	3°32·3′W	A	160
Twyn-cil-rhew	Powys	SO0124	51°54·6′	3°26·0′W	X	160
Twyn Cornicyll	Caer	SO1304	51°43·9′	3°15·2′W	X	171
Twyn Corrwg Fechan	Nth Pt Talb	SN8802	51°42·6′	3°36·9′W	X	170
Twyn Croes	Merth Tyd	SO0413	51°48·7′	3°23·2′W	H	160
Twyn Croes Gwallter	Powys	SN9514	51°49·1′	3°31·0′W	X	160
Twyn Disgwylfa	Powys	SN9531	51°58·3′	3°31·3′W	H	160
Twyn-Du	Powys	SO0820	51°52·5′	3°19·8′W	X	160
Twyn Du	Powys	SO2226	51°55·9′	3°7·7′W	X	161
Twyn Du	Torf	SO2305	51°44·5′	3°6·5′W	X	161
Twyn Dysgwylfa	Rho Cyn Taf	SS9891	51°36·8′	3°28·0′W	X	170
Twyn Eithinog	Powys	SN8009	51°46·2′	3°44·0′W	X	160
Twynersh Ho	Surrey	TQ0367	51°23·8′	0°30·8′W	X	176
Twynffrwd	Powys	SO1827	51°56·4′	3°11·2′W	X	161
Twyn Ffynhonnau Goerion	Torf	SO2308	51°46·2′	3°6·6′W	H	161
Twyn Fm	Carm	SN5321	51°52·3′	4°7·7′W	FM	159
Twyn Fm	Monm	SO3708	51°46·3′	2°54·4′W	FM	161
Twyn Garreg-wen	Powys	SN9816	51°50·2′	3°28·4′W	X	160
Twyn Garwa	Caer	ST1485	51°33·7′	3°14·1′W	H	171
Twyn-giden	Merth Tyd	SO1000	51°41·7′	3°17·7′W	X	171
Twyn Gwryd	Blae Gw	SO2207	51°45·6′	3°7·4′W	X	161
Twyn-gwyn	Caer	SO1701	51°42·3′	3°11·7′W	X	171
Twyn-gwyn	Caer	ST2097	51°40·2′	3°9·0′W	X	171
Twyn Gwyn	Nth Pt Talb	SN8803	51°43·1′	3°36·9′W	X	170
Twyn-gwyn	Torf	SO2901	51°42·4′	3°1·3′W	X	171
Twynholm	D & G	NX6654	54°52·0′	4°4·9′W	T	83,84
Twyn Hywel	Caer	ST1091	51°36·9′	3°17·6′W	H	171
Twyni Bâch	Cered	SN6094	52°31·8′	4°3·4′W	X	135
Twyni Mawr	Cered	SN6093	52°31·3′	4°3·4′W	X	135
Twyning	Glos	SO8936	52°1·6′	2°9·2′W	T	150
Twyning Green	Glos	SO9036	52°1·6′	2°8·3′W	T	150
Twynllanan	Carm	SN7524	51°54·3′	3°48·6′W	T	160
Twyn Maes-y-grug	Rho Cyn Taf	ST0687	51°34·7′	3°21·0′W	X	170
Twyn Mawr	Powys	SO2030	51°58·0′	3°9·5′W	X	161
Twyn Mwyalchod	Powys	SO0217	51°50·8′	3°25·0′W	X	160
Twynmynydd	Carm	SN6614	51°48·8′	3°56·2′W	T	159
Twyn Pen-rhiw	Powys	SO1716	51°50·4′	3°11·9′W	X	161
Twyn Pentre	Blae Gw	SO2205	51°44·5′	3°7·4′W	X	161
Twyn Pwll Morlais	Powys	SO0811	51°47·6′	3°19·7′W	X	160
Twyn Rhondda Fach	Rho Cyn Taf	SN9501	51°42·1′	3°30·8′W	X	170
Twyn Rhyd-car	Powys	SN9642	52°4·2′	3°30·6′W	H	147,160
Twyn Shôn-Ifan	Caer	ST1593	51°38·0′	3°13·3′W	T	171
Twyn-Swnd	Carm	SN7720	51°52·1′	3°46·8′W	H	160
Twyn Talycefn	Powys	SO2232	51°59·1′	3°7·8′W	X	161
Twyn Tudur	Caer	ST1993	51°38·0′	3°9·8′W	A	171
Twyn-tyle	Swan	SN6205	51°43·8′	3°59·5′W	X	159
Twyn Wenallt	Monm	SO2413	51°48·9′	3°5·8′W	X	161
Twyn y Beddau	Powys	SO2438	52°2·4′	3°6·1′W	A	161
Twyn y Bloedd	Rho Cyn Taf	SN9302	51°42·6′	3°32·5′W	X	170
Twyn-y-Briddallt	Rho Cyn Taf	ST0098	51°40·6′	3°26·4′W	H	170
Twyn-y-Briddallt (Roman Camp)	Rho Cyn Taf	ST0098	51°40·6′	3°26·4′W	R	170
Twyn y Crug	Nth Pt Talb	SN8700	51°41·5′	3°37·7′W	X	170
Twyn y Fidffawydd	Caer	SO1102	51°42·8′	3°16·9′W	H	171
Twyn y Gaer	Monm	SO2921	51°53·2′	3°1·5′W	A	161
Twyn-y-gaer	Powys	SN9630	51°57·8′	3°30·4′W	A	160
Twyn y Gaer	Powys	SN9928	51°56·8′	3°27·8′W	X	160
Twyn-y-gaer	Powys	SO0535	52°0·6′	3°22·7′W	A	160
Twyn y Garth	Powys	SO1043	52°4·9′	3°18·4′W	H	148,161
Twyn-y-Glog	Rho Cyn Taf	SN9508	51°45·9′	3°30·9′W	X	160
Twyn y glog	Rho Cyn Taf	SO0593	51°37·9′	3°22·0′W	H	170
Twyn-y-gnol	Caer	ST2296	51°39·7′	3°7·3′W	H	171
Twyn y Gregen	Monm	SO3609	51°46·8′	2°55·3′W	A	161
Twyn-y-gwynt	Rho Cyn Taf	ST0991	51°36·9′	3°18·5′W	H	171
Twyn-y-post	Powys	SO0240	52°3·2′	3°25·4′W	X	147,160
Twyn-yr-allt	Monm	SO2916	51°50·5′	3°1·4′W	X	161
Twyn-yr-argoed	Monm	SO4207	51°45·8′	2°50·0′W	X	161
Twyn yr Arian	Caer	SO1009	51°46·6′	3°17·9′W	X	161
Twyn yr Esgair	Carm	SN8023	51°53·8′	3°44·3′W	X	160
Twyn-yr-hydd	Nth Pt Talb	SS8185	51°33·3′	3°42·6′W	X	170
Twyn yr Hyddod	Blae Gw	SO1405	51°44·5′	3°14·3′W	H	161
Twynyrodyn	Merth Tyd	SO0505	51°44·4′	3°22·2′W	T	160
Twyn-yr-odyn	V of Glam	ST1173	51°27·2′	3°16·5′W	X	171
Twyn yr Oerfel	Caer	ST1890	51°36·4′	3°10·7′W	H	171
Twyn-y-Sheriff	Monm	SO4005	51°44·7′	2°51·8′W	T	161
Twyn y Waun	Merth Tyd	SO0807	51°45·5′	3°19·6′W	X	160
Twysden	Kent	TQ7035	51°5·6′	0°26·1′E	X	188
Twyssenden Manor	Kent	TQ7135	51°5·6′	0°26·9′E	X	188
Twywell	Northnts	SP9578	52°23·7′	0°35·8′W	T	141
Tyacaochan	Highld	NH4350	57°31·0′	4°36·8′W	X	26
Ty-ar-y-Graig	Powys	SJ0514	52°43·2′	3°24·0′W	X	125
Ty-bach	Heref	SO3130	51°58·1′	2°59·9′W	X	161
Ty Bach	Powys	SJ0201	52°36·1′	3°26·4′W	X	136
Ty-bach	Powys	SN9145	52°5·8′	3°35·1′W	X	147
Ty Bach	Powys	SN9457	52°12·3′	3°32·7′W	X	147
Tŷ-Bain	Powys	SJ1921	52°47·1′	3°11·7′W	X	125
Tyberton	Heref	SO3839	52°3·0′	2°53·9′W	T	149,161
Ty Brickly	Wrex	SJ2637	52°55·8′	3°5·6′W	X	126
Ty-Brîth	Denb	SJ0857	53°6·4′	3°22·1′W	X	116
Tŷ-brith	Denb	SJ1152	53°3·7′	3°19·3′W	X	116
Tŷ-brith	Denb	SJ1955	53°5·4′	3°12·2′W	X	116
Ty-brith	Powys	SJ0523	52°48·0′	3°24·1′W	X	125
Tybrith	Powys	SJ0802	52°36·7′	3°21·1′W	X	136
Tŷ-brith	Powys	SJ1018	52°45·4′	3°19·6′W	X	125
Tŷ-brith	Powys	SJ1526	52°49·7′	3°15·3′W	X	125
Ty-brith	Powys	SJ1909	52°40·6′	3°11·5′W	X	125
Tybroughton Hall	Wrex	SJ4643	52°59·1′	2°47·9′W	X	117
Ty-brŷch	Carm	SN7522	51°53·2′	3°48·6′W	X	160

Ty Bryn	Swan	SS4889	51°35·0′	4°11·2′W	X	159
Ty-Bryn	V of Glam	SS9173	51°27·0′	3°33·7′W	X	170
Tyburn	Birm	SP1391	52°31·2′	1°48·1′W	T	139
Tyby	Norf	TG0827	52°48·3′	1°5·6′E	T	133
Tŷ Calch	I of Angl	SH4171	53°13·0′	4°22·5′W	X	114,115
Tycam	Cered	SN5770	52°18·8′	4°5·5′W	X	135
Tycam	Cered	SN6879	52°23·8′	3°56·0′W	X	135
Tycam Fm	Cered	SN4944	52°4·7′	4°11·8′W	FM	146
Ty-canol	Caer	ST1889	51°35·9′	3°10·6′W	X	171
Ty Canol	Carm	SN3115	51°48·7′	4°26·7′W	X	159
Tycanol	Carm	SN4416	51°49·5′	4°15·4′W	X	159
Ty-canol	Carm	SN5907	51°44·9′	4°2·2′W	X	159
Ty-canol	Conwy	SH9470	53°13·2′	3°34·9′W	X	116
Ty-canol	Denb	SJ1444	52°59·4′	3°16·5′W	X	125
Ty Canol	Denb	SJ2247	53°1·1′	3°9·4′W	A	117
Tycanol	Heref	SO3427	51°56·5′	2°57·2′W	X	161
Ty-canol	Monm	SO3614	51°49·5′	2°55·3′W	X	161
Tycanol	Nth Pt Talb	SS8295	51°38·7′	3°41·9′W	X	170
Tycanol	Pemb	SN0439	52°1·1′	4°51·0′W	X	145,157
Tycanol	Pemb	SN0936	51°59·6′	4°46·5′W	X	145
Tŷ-canol	Pemb	SN1434	51°58·6′	4°42·1′W	X	145
Ty-canol	Powys	SJ1721	52°47·1′	3°13·4′W	X	125
Ty Canol	Powys	SN9771	52°19·9′	3°30·3′W	X	136,147
Ty-Canol	Shrops	SJ2425	52°49·3′	3°7·3′W	X	126
Ty Canol	Torf	ST2694	51°38·6′	3°3·8′W	X	171
Ty Canol	Wrex	SJ2746	53°0·6′	3°4·9′W	X	117
Ty-cant	Pemb	SM9228	51°54·9′	5°1·1′W	X	157,158
Ty Caradog	Heref	SO3232	51°59·2′	2°59·0′W	X	161
Ty Celyn	Conwy	SH8574	53°15·3′	3°43·0′W	X	116
Ty Celyn	Conwy	SH8663	53°9·4′	3°41·9′W	X	116
Ty Celyn	Conwy	SH9172	53°14·3′	3°37·6′W	X	116
Ty-celyn	Conwy	SH9264	53°10·0′	3°36·5′W	X	116
Ty-celyn	Conwy	SH9864	53°10·0′	3°31·1′W	X	116
Ty-celyn	Conwy	SJ0068	53°12·2′	3°29·4′W	X	116
Ty Celyn	Denb	SJ0676	53°16·6′	3°24·2′W	X	116
Ty-cerig	Denb	SJ0545	52°59·9′	3°24·5′W	X	116
Tycerrig	Carm	SN6648	52°7·1′	3°57·0′W	X	146
Ty Cerrig	Conwy	SH9864	53°10·0′	3°31·1′W	X	116
Ty-cerrig	Denb	SJ0246	53°0·4′	3°27·2′W	X	116
Ty-cerrig	Denb	SJ1748	53°1·6′	3°13·8′W	X	116
Ty-cerrig	Denb	SJ1941	52°57·9′	3°12·0′W	X	125
Ty Cerrig	Gwyn	SH2028	52°49·4′	4°39·9′W	X	123
Tŷ Cerrig	Gwyn	SH4942	52°57·5′	4°14·5′W	X	123
Ty Cerrig	Gwyn	SH5834	52°53·3′	4°6·2′W	X	124
Ty-cerrig	Gwyn	SH6933	52°53·0′	3°56·4′W	X	124
Ty-cerrig	Gwyn	SH7620	52°46·0′	3°49·9′W	X	124
Ty-cerrig	Gwyn	SH9142	52°58·1′	3°37·0′W	X	125
Ty cerrig	Gwyn	SH9735	52°54·4′	3°31·5′W	X	125
Ty Cerrig	Powys	SJ0821	52°47·0′	3°21·4′W	X	125
Tycerrig	Powys	SJ1410	52°41·1′	3°15·9′W	X	125
Tycerrig	Powys	SJ1621	52°47·0′	3°14·3′W	X	125
Ty Cerrig	Wrex	SJ2952	53°3·9′	3°3·2′W	X	117
Ty Cerrig Isaf	Gwyn	SH8734	52°53·7′	3°40·4′W	X	124,125
Ty-Charles	Brig	SS9784	51°33·0′	3°28·7′W	X	170
Tychat	Highld	NH5330	57°20·5′	4°26·1′W	X	26
Ty-chwith	Brig	SS9783	51°32·4′	3°28·7′W	X	170
Ty-chwith	V of Glam	ST0177	51°29·2′	3°25·2′W	X	170
Ty-côch	Carm	SN4506	51°44·1′	4°14·3′W	X	159
Ty-côch	Carm	SN5424	51°54·0′	4°6·9′W	X	159
Tŷ Coch	Carm	SN6530	51°57·4′	3°57·5′W	X	146
Tŷ-coch	Cered	SN4757	52°11·6′	4°13·9′W	X	146
Ty Coch	Conwy	SH7752	53°3·3′	3°49·7′W	X	115
Ty Coch	Denb	SJ0577	53°17·1′	3°25·1′W	X	116
Ty-coch	Denb	SJ0764	53°10·1′	3°23·1′W	X	116
Ty-côch	Denb	SJ0770	53°13·4′	3°23·2′W	X	116
Tŷ-côch	Denb	SJ0963	53°9·6′	3°21·3′W	X	116
Tŷ-côch	Denb	SJ1263	53°9·7′	3°18·6′W	X	116
Tŷ-côch	Flint	SJ2359	53°7·6′	3°8·6′W	X	117
Tŷ-côch	Gwyn	SH5356	53°5·1′	4°11·3′W	X	115
Tycoch	Heref	SO2440	52°3·4′	3°6·1′W	X	148,161
Ty Coch	I of Angl	SH4866	53°10·4′	4°16·0′W	X	114,115
Tŷ-coch	I of Angl	SH5076	53°15·8′	4°14·5′W	X	114,115
Ty-coch	Monm	SO2822	51°53·8′	3°2·4′W	X	161
Ty-côch	Newp	ST2781	51°31·6′	3°2·8′W	X	171
Tŷ-coch	Powys	SH9012	52°41·9′	3°37·3′W	X	125
Tŷ-coch	Powys	SJ1719	52°46·0′	3°13·4′W	X	125
Ty-coch	Powys	SJ2619	52°46·1′	3°5·4′W	X	126
Ty Coch	Powys	SN8298	52°34·3′	3°44·1′W	X	135,136
Ty-Coch	Powys	SN9462	52°15·0′	3°32·8′W	X	147
Ty-coch	Swan	SS6293	51°37·4′	3°59·2′W	T	159
Ty Coch Fm	Brig	SS8279	51°30·1′	3°41·6′W	FM	170
Tycoch Fm	Carm	SN4722	51°52·8′	4°13·0′W	FM	159
Tycoch Fm	Shrops	SJ2823	52°48·2′	3°3·7′W	FM	126
Tŷ-coed	Pemb	SN2132	51°57·7′	4°35·9′W	X	145
Ty Cooke	Monm	SO3005	51°44·6′	3°0·4′W	X	161
Tŷ-cornel	Powys	SJ1517	52°44·9′	3°15·2′W	X	125
Ty-cornel	Powys	SO1187	52°28·7′	3°18·2′W	X	136
Ty Cornel Fm	Carm	SN4204	51°43·0′	4°16·8′W	FM	159
Ty Corniog	Gwyn	SH3539	52°55·6′	4°26·9′W	X	123
Tycribwr Fm	Brig	SS8883	51°32·3′	3°36·5′W	FM	170
Ty Cristion	I of Angl	SH3380	53°17·7′	4°29·9′W	X	114
Tycroes	Carm	SN6010	51°46·5′	4°1·4′W	T	159
Ty Croes	I of Angl	SH2985	53°20·3′	4°33·7′W	X	114
Tŷ-croes	I of Angl	SH3183	53°19·3′	4°31·8′W	X	114
Ty Croes	I of Angl	SH3472	53°13·4′	4°28·8′W	T	114
Ty-croes	I of Angl	SH3782	53°18·8′	4°26·4′W	X	114
Ty Croes	I of Angl	SH4083	53°19·4′	4°23·7′W	X	114,115
Ty Croes Mawr	Gwyn	SH2227	52°48·9′	4°38·1′W	X	123
Tycrwyn	Powys	SJ1018	52°45·4′	3°19·6′W	X	125
Tycwtta	Powys	SO0060	52°14·0′	3°27·5′W	X	147
Ty Cwyfan	I of Angl	SH3368	53°11·2′	4°29·6′W	X	114
Ty-Cynfin	Powys	SO1822	51°53·7′	3°11·1′W	X	161
Tŷ-dabuan	Powys	SN9960	52°14·0′	3°28·3′W	X	147
Tydd Gote	Lincs	TF4517	52°44·1′	0°9·3′E	T	131
Tyddn-y-pandy	I of Angl	SH3989	53°22·6′	4°24·8′W	X	114
Tyddn-ysgubor	Gwyn	SJ0040	52°57·1′	3°28·9′W	X	125
Tydd St Giles	Cambs	TF4216	52°43·6′	0°6·6′E	T	131
Tydd St Giles Fen	Cambs	TF3914	52°42·6′	0°3·9′E	X	131
Tydd St Mary	Lincs	TF4418	52°44·7′	0°8·4′E	T	131
Tydd St Mary's Fen	Lincs	TF3811	52°41·0′	0°2·9′E	X	131,142,143

Tydd St Mary's Marsh	Lincs	TF4619	52°45·2′	0°10·2′E	X	131
Tyddu Fm	Powys	SO1266	52°17·3′	3°17·0′W	FM	136,148
Tyddyn	Carm	SN7129	51°56·9′	3°52·2′W	X	146,160
Tyddyn	Gwyn	SH2236	52°53·8′	4°38·4′W	X	123
Tyddyn	Gwyn	SH3739	52°55·7′	4°25·1′W	X	123
Tyddyn	Gwyn	SH4739	52°55·8′	4°16·2′W	X	123
Tyddyn	I of Angl	SH3969	53°11·9′	4°24·2′W	X	114
Tyddyn	I of Angl	SH5174	53°14·8′	4°13·6′W	X	114,115
Tyddyn	Pemb	SN2733	51°58·4′	4°30·7′W	X	145
Tyddyn	Powys	SJ0909	52°40·5′	3°20·4′W	X	125
Tyddyn	Powys	SJ0921	52°47·0′	3°20·6′W	X	125
Tyddyn	Powys	SJ2212	52°42·2′	3°8·9′W	X	126
Tyddyn	Powys	SN9987	52°28·5′	3°28·8′W	T	136
Tyddyn-adi	Gwyn	SH5438	52°55·4′	4°9·9′W	X	124
Tyddyn Amlwg	Powys	SH9915	52°43·6′	3°29·3′W	X	125
Tyddyn Angharad	Denb	SJ0745	52°59·9′	3°22·7′W	T	116
Tyddyn Bach	Conwy	SH7570	53°13·0′	3°51·9′W	X	115
Tyddyn-bach	Conwy	SH8568	53°12·0′	3°42·9′W	X	116
Tyddyn-bach	Denb	SJ0247	53°0·9′	3°27·2′W	X	116
Tyddyn-bach	Gwyn	SH6026	52°49·0′	4°4·2′W	X	124
Tyddyn Bach	Gwyn	SH7133	52°53·0′	3°54·6′W	X	124
Tyddyn Bartley	Conwy	SJ0070	53°13·3′	3°29·5′W	X	116
Tyddyn-barwn	Gwyn	SH9834	52°53·9′	3°30·6′W	X	125
Tyddyn Berth	Gwyn	SH4337	52°54·7′	4°19·7′W	X	123
Tyddynbriddell Hill	Gwyn	SN6498	52°34·0′	4°0·0′W	H	135
Tyddyn Cae	Gwyn	SH3337	52°54·5′	4°28·6′W	X	123
Tyddyn-cae	Gwyn	SH5162	53°8·3′	4°13·2′W	X	114,115
Tyddyncaled	Gwyn	SH3433	52°52·4′	4°27·6′W	X	123
Tyddyn Cestyll	Gwyn	SH3641	52°56·7′	4°26·0′W	X	123
Tyddyncethin	Conwy	SH7951	53°2·8′	3°47·9′W	X	115
Tyddyn-Cethin	Gwyn	SH4343	52°57·9′	4°19·9′W	X	123
Tyddyn cethin	Gwyn	SH4940	52°56·4′	4°14·4′W	X	123
Tyddyn Cook	Denb	SJ0856	53°5·8′	3°22·0′W	X	116
Tyddyn-copyn	I of Angl	SH5478	53°17·0′	4°11·0′W	X	114,115
Tyddyn-copyn	I of Angl	SH5478	53°17·0′	4°11·0′W	X	114,115
Tyddyn Corn Fm	Gwyn	SH2429	52°50·0′	4°36·4′W	FM	123
Tyddyn Dai	I of Angl	SH4391	53°23·8′	4°21·3′W	T	114
Tyddyn Dauddwr	Powys	SJ2317	52°44·9′	3°8·0′W	X	126
Tyddyn-dedwydd	Wrex	SJ2748	53°1·7′	3°4·9′W	X	117
Tyddyn-du	Cered	SN4853	52°9·5′	4°12·9′W	X	146
Tyddyn Du	Gwyn	SH7615	52°43·4′	3°49·8′W	X	124
Tyddyn Dyfi	Gwyn	SJ0041	52°57·7′	3°28·9′W	X	125
Tyddyn-Ednyfed	Gwyn	SH7316	52°43·8′	3°52·4′W	X	124
Tyddyn Elen	Gwyn	SH4860	53°7·2′	4°15·9′W	X	114,115
Tyddyn Eli	Conwy	SH9643	52°58·7′	3°32·5′W	X	125
Tyddyn-Fadog	I of Angl	SH5170	53°12·6′	4°13·5′W	X	114,115
Tyddynfari	Carm	SN2629	51°56·2′	4°31·5′W	X	145,158
Tyddyn Felin	Gwyn	SH6029	52°50·7′	4°4·3′W	X	124
Tyddyn Fm	Flint	SJ2563	53°9·8′	3°6·9′W	FM	117
Tyddyn Forgan	Gwyn	SH5567	53°11·1′	4°9·8′W	X	114,115
Tyddyn-graig	Gwyn	SH5143	52°58·1′	4°12·7′W	X	124
Tyddyn Gwydd	Gwyn	SH5059	53°6·7′	4°14·1′W	X	115
Tyddyn Gwyn	Gwyn	SH2929	52°50·1′	4°31·9′W	X	123
Tyddyn Gwyn	Gwyn	SH6242	52°57·7′	4°2·9′W	X	124
Tyddyn Gwynt	Gwyn	SH6030	52°51·2′	4°4·4′W	X	124
Tyddyn-Heilyn	Gwyn	SH5668	53°11·6′	4°8·9′W	X	114,115
Tyddyn-hen	Gwyn	SH2533	52°52·2′	4°35·6′W	X	123
Tyddyn-Hen	Gwyn	SH4048	53°0·6′	4°22·7′W	X	115,123
Tyddyn Hywel	I of Angl	SH3573	53°14·0′	4°27·9′W	X	114
Tyddyn-igin	I of Angl	SH4689	53°22·8′	4°18·5′W	X	114
Tyddyninco	Gwyn	SH9936	52°55·0′	3°29·7′W	X	125
Tyddyn-Iolyn	Gwyn	SH5140	52°56·4′	4°12·6′W	X	124
Tyddyn Isaf	I of Angl	SH4887	53°21·7′	4°16·6′W	X	114
Tyddyn Llewelyn	Gwyn	SH3434	52°52·9′	4°27·6′W	X	123
Tyddynllwyn Fm	Gwyn	SH7717	52°44·4′	3°48·9′W	FM	124
Tyddyn Llywarch	Conwy	SH8257	53°6·1′	3°45·3′W	X	116
Tyddynllywarch	Gwyn	SH8629	52°51·0′	3°41·2′W	X	124,125
Tyddyn Lunt	Denb	SJ0569	53°12·8′	3°25·0′W	X	116
Tyddyn Maen	Powys	SJ1627	52°50·3′	3°14·4′W	X	125
Tyddyn-mawr	Gwyn	SH4344	52°58·5′	4°19·9′W	X	123
Tyddyn-mawr	Gwyn	SH5348	53°0·8′	4°11·1′W	X	115
Tyddyn-mawr	Gwyn	SH5544	52°58·7′	4°9·2′W	X	124
Tyddyn-mawr	Gwyn	SH7015	52°43·3′	3°55·1′W	X	124
Tyddyn-mawr	Gwyn	SH7130	52°51·4′	3°54·6′W	X	124
Tyddyn-mawr	Gwyn	SH7528	52°50·3′	3°50·9′W	X	124
Tyddyn Mawr	I of Angl	SH4773	53°14·2′	4°17·1′W	X	114,115
Tyddyn Norbury	Denb	SJ1462	53°9·1′	3°16·8′W	X	116
Tyddyn-onn	Flint	SJ1669	53°12·9′	3°15·1′W	X	116
Tyddyn Parthle	Gwyn	SH4959	53°6·7′	4°15·0′W	X	115,123
Tyddyn Phillip	I of Angl	SH4882	53°19·0′	4°16·5′W	X	114,115
Tyddyn-Prŷs	I of Angl	SH3790	53°23·1′	4°26·6′W	X	114
Tyddyn-Roger	Denb	SJ0857	53°6·4′	3°22·1′W	X	116
Tyddyn Sadler	I of Angl	SH4173	53°14·1′	4°22·5′W	X	114,115
Tyddyn Sais	Gwyn	SH7033	52°53·0′	3°55·5′W	X	124
Tyddyn Sieffre	Gwyn	SH6213	52°42·1′	4°2·1′W	X	124
Tyddyn Siencyn	I of Angl	SH4178	53°16·8′	4°22·7′W	X	114,115
Tyddyn Singrig	Gwyn	SH3035	52°53·4′	4°31·2′W	X	123
Tyddyn Starkey	Flint	SJ2469	53°13·0′	3°7·9′W	X	117
Tyddyn-tlodion	Denb	SJ1753	53°4·3′	3°13·9′W	X	116
Tyddyn Tudur	Conwy	SH9849	53°2·0′	3°30·9′W	X	116
Tyddyn-twll	Conwy	SH8272	53°14·2′	3°45·7′W	X	116
Tyddyn Tyfod	Gwyn	SH9841	52°57·6′	3°30·7′W	X	125
Tyddyn Ucha	Conwy	SH8373	53°14·7′	3°44·8′W	X	116
Tyddyn Ucha	Denb	SJ0342	52°58·2′	3°26·3′W	X	125
Tyddyn Uchaf	Conwy	SH8261	53°8·2′	3°45·4′W	X	116
Tyddyn Uchaf	Conwy	SH8766	53°11·0′	3°41·1′W	X	116
Tyddyn-uchaf	Conwy	SH8863	53°9·4′	3°40·1′W	X	116
Tyddyn-uchaf	Conwy	SH9376	53°16·5′	3°35·9′W	X	116
Tyddyn-uchaf	Denb	SJ0862	53°9·1′	3°22·1′W	X	116
Tyddynuchaf	Flint	SJ2365	53°10·8′	3°8·7′W	X	117
Tyddyn Uchaf	Gwyn	SH3440	52°56·2′	4°27·8′W	X	123
Tyddyn-uchaf	Wrex	SJ2645	53°0·1′	3°5·8′W	X	117
Tyddyn Ucha Fm	Wrex	SJ3141	52°58·0′	3°1·2′W	FM	117
Tyddyn Waen	Denb	SJ2155	53°5·4′	3°10·4′W	X	117
Tyddyn Whisgin	Gwyn	SH5161	53°7·8′	4°13·2′W	X	114,115
Tyddyn-Wilym	Conwy	SH7665	53°10·3′	3°50·9′W	X	115
Tyddyn-y-Berth	Gwyn	SN6297	52°33·4′	4°1·7′W	X	135
Tyddyn-y-fawd	I of Angl	SH4267	53°10·8′	4°21·5′W	X	114,115
Tyddyn-y-felin	Gwyn	SH4440	52°56·3′	4°18·9′W	X	123
Tyddyn-y-felin	Gwyn	SH8629	52°51·0′	3°41·2′W	X	124,125

Tyddyn-y-felin	I of Angl	SH5272	53°13·7′	4°12·6′W	X	114,115
Tyddyn-y-graig	Conwy	SH8474	53°15·3′	3°43·9′W	X	116
Tyddyn-y-gwynt	Flint	SJ2167	53°11·9′	3°10·6′W	X	117
Tyddyn-yr-haint	Gwyn	SH3033	52°52·3′	4°31·2′W	X	123
Ty-derlwyn	Monm	SO3322	51°53·8′	2°58·0′W	X	161
Ty Draw	Brig	SS8180	51°30·6′	3°42·5′W	X	170
Ty-draw	Caer	ST1193	51°38·0′	3°16·8′W	X	171
Tŷ-draw	Conwy	SH8659	53°7·2′	3°41·8′W	X	116
Tŷ-draw	Denb	SJ1059	53°7·5′	3°20·3′W	X	116
Ty-draw	Denb	SJ1071	53°13·9′	3°20·5′W	X	116
Ty-Draw	Monm	SO3203	51°43·5′	2°58·7′W	X	171
Tŷ-draw	Powys	SJ1526	52°49·7′	3°15·3′W	X	125
Ty-draw	Powys	SJ2032	52°53·0′	3°10·9′W	X	126
Tydraw	Rho Cyn Taf	SS9199	51°41·0′	3°34·2′W	X	170
Ty-draw	Rho Cyn Taf	ST0588	51°35·2′	3°21·9′W	X	170
Ty-draw	Swan	SS6894	51°38·0′	3°54·1′W	T	159
Ty-draw	V of Glam	SS9475	51°28·1′	3°31·2′W	X	170
Ty-draw	V of Glam	ST0372	51°26·6′	3°23·4′W	X	170
Ty-draw Fm	Monm	SO3314	51°49·5′	2°57·9′W	FM	161
Ty Draw Fm	Rho Cyn Taf	SN9205	51°44·2′	3°33·5′W	FM	160
Tydraw Fm	V of Glam	ST0070	51°25·4′	3°25·9′W	FM	170
Ty-du	Cered	SN6087	52°28·0′	4°3·3′W	X	135
Tŷ-du	Conwy	SH9069	53°12·6′	3°38·4′W	X	116
Tŷ-du	Conwy	SH9448	53°1·4′	3°34·4′W	X	116
Tŷ-du	Conwy	SH9568	53°12·2′	3°33·9′W	X	116
Tŷ-du	I of Angl	SH3994	53°25·3′	4°25·0′W	X	114
Ty Du	I of Angl	SH5880	53°18·1′	4°7·5′W	X	114,115
Ty-du	Monm	SO3812	51°48·4′	2°53·6′W	X	161
Tŷ-du	Powys	SJ1927	52°50·3′	3°11·7′W	X	125
Tŷ-du	Powys	SN9838	52°2·1′	3°28·8′W	X	160
Tŷ-du	Powys	SO0039	52°2·7′	3°27·1′W	X	160
Ty-du	Rho Cyn Taf	ST0281	51°31·4′	3°24·4′W	X	170
Ty-du	Wrex	SJ1834	52°54·1′	3°12·7′W	X	125
Tydu Fm	Card	ST1079	51°30·4′	3°17·4′W	FM	171
Ty Du Isaf	Gwyn	SH3638	52°55·1′	4°26·0′W	X	123
Ty Du Uchaf	Gwyn	SH3639	52°55·6′	4°26·0′W	X	123
Tye	Hants	SU7302	50°49·0′	0°57·4′W	T	197
Tyeantore	Highld	NH5634	57°22·7′	4°23·2′W	X	26
Tye Common	Essex	TQ6693	51°36·9′	0°24·3′E	T	177,178
Tye Fm	Devon	ST0303	50°49·3′	3°22·2′W	FM	192
Tye Fm	Essex	TM0524	51°52·8′	0°59·1′E	FM	168
Tye Fm	E Susx	TQ4838	51°7·6′	0°7·3′E	FM	188
Tyegate Green	Norf	TG3613	52°40·0′	1°29·8′E	T	133,134
Tye Green	Essex	TL4508	51°45·3′	0°6·4′E	T	167
Tye Green	Essex	TL5424	51°53·8′	0°14·7′E	T	167
Tye Green	Essex	TL5935	51°59·7′	0°19·4′E	T	154
Tye Green	Essex	TL6212	51°47·2′	0°21·3′E	T	167
Tye Green	Essex	TL7820	51°51·2′	0°35·5′E	T	167
Tye Green	Essex	TQ6899	51°40·1′	0°26·2′E	T	167,177
Tye Hall	Essex	TL6308	51°45·0′	0°22·1′E	X	167
Tye Hill	E Susx	TQ5407	50°50·7′	0°11·6′E	X	199
Tye Ho	Suff	TM0947	52°5·1′	1°3·4′E	X	155,169
Tye Homestead	Essex	TM1220	51°50·5′	1°5·1′E	X	168,169
Tyelaw Burn	Northum	NU2108	55°22·2′	1°39·7′W	W	81
Tŷ Elltud	Powys	SO0926	51°55·7′	3°19·0′W	X	161
Tŷ Elltud (Long Barrow)	Powys	SO0926	51°55·7′	3°19·0′W	A	161
Tŷ Engan	Gwyn	SH2431	52°51·1′	4°36·4′W	X	123
Tye Rocks	Corn	SW6325	50°4·9′	5°18·4′W	X	203
Tyersal	Brad	SE1932	53°47·3′	1°42·3′W	T	104
Tyersal Beck	Leeds	SE2033	53°47·8′	1°41·4′W	W	104
Tyersal Gate	Brad	SE1931	53°46·7′	1°42·3′W	X	104
Tyersal Hall	Leeds	SE2032	53°47·3′	1°41·4′W	X	104
Tyers Hall	Barns	SE3906	53°33·2′	1°24·3′W	X	110,111
Tyes Cross	W Susx	TQ3832	51°4·5′	0°1·4′W	X	187
Tyes Place	W Susx	TQ2828	51°2·4′	0°10·1′W	X	187,198
Tyfaenor Park	Powys	SO0771	52°20·0′	3°21·5′W	X	136,147
Tyfos	Denb	SJ0238	52°56·1′	3°27·1′W	X	125
Tŷ-fry	Caer	ST1286	51°34·2′	3°15·8′W	X	171
Tŷ-fry	I of Angl	SH5176	53°15·9′	4°13·6′W	A	114,115
Ty-fry	Monm	ST4397	51°40·4′	2°49·1′W	T	171
Ty-Fry	V of Glam	ST0476	51°28·7′	3°22·6′W	X	170
Tyfry Fm	Brig	SS8582	51°31·8′	3°39·1′W	FM	170
Tŷ-fy-nain	Denb	SJ1761	53°8·6′	3°14·0′W	X	116
Tyganol	V of Glam	ST0372	51°26·6′	3°23·4′W	T	170
Tyglyn	Cered	SN4959	52°12·8′	4°12·2′W	X	146
Tygrug	Pemb	SM9830	51°56·2′	4°55·9′W	X	157
Ty gwyn	Caer	ST1591	51°36·9′	3°13·3′W	X	171
Ty-gwyn	Carm	SN4603	51°42·5′	4°13·3′W	X	159
Tygwyn	Carm	SN4615	51°49·0′	4°13·7′W	X	159
Ty-gwyn	Carm	SN5609	51°45·9′	4°4·8′W	X	159
Tygwyn	Cered	SN1748	52°6·2′	4°39·9′W	X	145
Ty Gwyn	Cered	SN1951	52°7·9′	4°38·3′W	X	145
Tygwyn	Cered	SN5264	52°15·5′	4°9·7′W	X	146
Tygwyn	Cered	SN6079	52°23·7′	4°3·1′W	X	135
Tŷ-gwyn	Conwy	SH7971	53°13·6′	3°48·3′W	X	115
Tŷ-gwyn	Conwy	SH8277	53°16·9′	3°45·8′W	X	116
Ty Gwyn	Conwy	SH8665	53°10·4′	3°41·9′W	X	116
Ty Gwyn	Conwy	SH9570	53°13·2′	3°34·0′W	X	116
Ty-gwyn	Conwy	SH9745	52°59·8′	3°31·7′W	X	116
Tŷ-gwyn	Conwy	SJ0168	53°12·2′	3°28·5′W	X	116
Ty Gwyn	Denb	SJ0774	53°15·5′	3°23·2′W	X	116
Tŷ-gwyn	Flint	SJ1569	53°12·9′	3°16·0′W	X	116
Ty-gwyn	Flint	SJ1666	53°11·3′	3°15·0′W	X	116
Tŷ Gwyn	Gwyn	SH6462	53°8·5′	4°1·6′W	X	115
Tŷ-gwyn	Gwyn	SH8937	52°55·4′	3°38·7′W	X	124,125
Tŷ-gwyn	I of Angl	SH4476	53°15·7′	4°19·9′W	X	114,115
Ty-gwyn	Monm	SO2514	51°49·4′	3°4·9′W	X	161
Ty Gwyn	Monm	SO3107	51°45·7′	2°59·6′W	X	161
Ty-gwyn	Nth Pt Talb	SN8900	51°41·5′	3°36·0′W	X	170
Ty Gwyn	Pemb	SN0234	51°58·4′	4°52·6′W	X	145,157
Ty-gwyn	Pemb	SN0533	51°57·9′	4°49·9′W	X	145
Tygwyn	Pemb	SN1635	51°59·2′	4°40·4′W	X	145
Tygwyn	Pemb	SN1741	52°2·5′	4°39·7′W	X	145
Tygwyn	Powys	SJ1115	52°43·8′	3°18·7′W	X	125
Ty-gwyn	Powys	SJ1730	52°51·9′	3°13·6′W	X	125
Tŷ-gwyn	Powys	SJ2024	52°48·7′	3°10·8′W	X	126
Tŷ-gwyn	Powys	SJ2521	52°47·1′	3°6·3′W	X	126
Ty-gwyn	Powys	SN8848	52°7·4′	3°37·8′W	X	147
Tŷ-gwyn	Powys	SN9796	52°33·4′	3°30·8′W	X	136
Tygwyn	Powys	SO0758	52°13·0′	3°21·3′W	X	147
Ty-Gwyn	Powys	SO1126	51°55·8′	3°17·3′W	X	161
Ty-gwyn	Powys	SO1553	52°10·4′	3°14·2′W	X	148
Ty-gwyn	Swan	SS5893	51°37·3′	4°2·7′W	X	159
Tygwyn Fm	Pemb	SN1614	51°47·9′	4°39·7′W	FM	158
Ty-Gwyn Hall	Monm	SO3016	51°50·5′	3°0·6′W	X	161
Tygwyn Sta	Gwyn	SH6034	52°53·4′	4°4·5′W	X	124
Ty Harry	Monm	SO4407	51°45·8′	2°48·3′W	X	161
Ty-Helyg	Denb	SJ1549	53°2·1′	3°15·7′W	X	116
Ty Hen	Carm	SN1219	51°50·5′	4°43·4′W	X	158
Ty-hên	Carm	SN3024	51°53·6′	4°27·8′W	X	145,159
Tyhen	Cered	SN1948	52°6·3′	4°38·2′W	X	145
Tyhen	Cered	SN2846	52°5·4′	4°30·2′W	X	145
Ty Hen	Cered	SN3655	52°10·4′	4°23·5′W	X	145
Tyhen	Cered	SN5668	52°17·7′	4°6·3′W	X	135
Ty-hên	Cered	SN6663	52°15·2′	3°57·4′W	X	146
Tŷ-hen	Gwyn	SH1731	52°51·0′	4°42·7′W	X	123
Ty-hên	Gwyn	SH8936	52°54·8′	3°38·6′W	X	124,125
Ty Hen	I of Angl	SH3180	53°17·6′	4°31·7′W	X	114
Ty Hên	I of Angl	SH3578	53°16·6′	4°28·1′W	X	114
Tŷ-Hen Fm	Cered	SN2851	52°8·1′	4°30·4′W	FM	145
Ty-hen Fm	Pemb	SN1840	52°2·0′	4°38·8′W	FM	145
Ty-Hen Newydd	I of Angl	SH4382	53°18·9′	4°21·0′W	X	114,115
Ty Hewell	Carm	SN6331	51°57·9′	3°59·3′W	X	146
Tyhir	Carm	SN2639	52°1·6′	4°31·8′W	X	145
Tyhir	Carm	SN4718	51°50·6′	4°12·9′W	X	159
Tyhir	Cered	SN1546	52°5·1′	4°41·6′W	X	145
Ty-hîr	Cered	SN6794	52°31·9′	3°57·2′W	X	135
Tŷ-hir	Conwy	SH8664	53°9·9′	3°41·9′W	X	116
Tŷ-hir	Gwyn	SH4239	52°55·8′	4°20·6′W	X	123
Ty-hîr	Gwyn	SH7621	52°46·6′	3°49·9′W	X	124
Ty-hir	Monm	SO3213	51°48·9′	2°58·8′W	X	161
Tŷ-Hir Fm	Wrex	SJ2452	53°3·8′	3°7·6′W	FM	117
Tŷ-hwnt	Cered	SN6292	52°30·7′	4°1·6′W	X	135
Tyhwnt	Powys	SN7812	51°47·8′	3°45·8′W	X	160
Ty'h-y-ffos	Powys	SN9650	52°8·6′	3°30·8′W	X	147
Ty-hyll	Conwy	SH7557	53°6·0′	3°51·6′W	X	115
Ty Isa	Denb	SJ1250	53°2·6′	3°18·4′W	X	116
Ty-isa	Shrops	SJ2426	52°49·8′	3°7·3′W	X	126
Ty Isa Cefn	Conwy	SH8663	53°9·4′	3°41·9′W	X	116
Ty-isa-cwm	Conwy	SH9247	53°0·8′	3°36·2′W	X	116
Ty Isaf	Brig	SS8887	51°34·5′	3°36·6′W	X	170
Ty-isaf	Carm	SN5709	51°45·9′	4°3·9′W	X	159
Ty-isaf	Carm	SN6217	51°50·3′	3°59·8′W	X	159
Tŷ-isaf	Carm	SS5099	51°40·4′	4°9·8′W	T	159
Ty Isaf	Cered	SN6076	52°22·1′	4°3·0′W	X	135
Tŷ-isaf	Conwy	SH9356	53°5·7′	3°35·5′W	X	116
Ty-isaf	Denb	SJ0176	53°16·5′	3°28·7′W	X	116
Tŷ-isaf	Denb	SJ0340	52°57·2′	3°26·2′W	X	125
Ty Isaf	Denb	SJ0348	53°1·5′	3°26·4′W	X	116
Tŷ-isaf	Denb	SJ1070	53°13·4′	3°20·5′W	X	116
Tŷ-isaf	Denb	SJ1346	53°0·5′	3°17·4′W	X	116
Ty-isaf	Denb	SJ1452	53°3·7′	3°16·6′W	X	116
Ty-isaf	Flint	SJ1867	53°11·9′	3°13·2′W	X	116
Ty-isaf	Flint	SJ2459	53°7·6′	3°7·7′W	X	117
Ty-isaf	Flint	SJ2757	53°6·6′	3°5·0′W	X	117
Ty-isaf	Gwyn	SH1728	52°49·4′	4°42·6′W	X	123
Ty Isaf	Gwyn	SH3134	52°52·9′	4°30·3′W	X	123
Ty-isaf	Gwyn	SH9031	52°52·2′	3°37·7′W	X	125
Tŷ-isaf	Gwyn	SH9535	52°54·4′	3°33·3′W	X	125
Tŷ-isaf	Gwyn	SH9838	52°56·0′	3°30·7′W	X	125
Tŷ-isaf	Gwyn	SJ0243	52°58·8′	3°27·2′W	X	125
Tŷ-isaf	Powys	SJ0513	52°42·6′	3°24·0′W	X	125
Ty isaf	Powys	SJ0704	52°37·8′	3°22·0′W	X	136
Ty-isaf	Powys	SJ1130	52°51·9′	3°18·9′W	X	125
Ty Isaf	Powys	SN8798	52°34·3′	3°39·6′W	X	135,136
Ty-isaf	Powys	SO2527	51°56·4′	3°5·1′W	X	161
Tŷ-isaf	Shrops	SJ2323	52°48·2′	3°8·1′W	X	126
Ty-isaf	Wrex	SJ1736	52°55·1′	3°13·7′W	X	125
Ty-isaf Fm	Powys	SO0942	52°4·4′	3°19·3′W	FM	147,161
Ty Isa Fm	Denb	SJ0575	53°16·1′	3°25·1′W	FM	116
Ty Isa Gell	Conwy	SH8569	53°12·6′	3°42·9′W	X	116
Tyisha	Powys	SN9927	51°56·2′	3°27·8′W	X	160
Tyisha	Powys	SO1828	51°56·9′	3°11·2′W	X	161
Ty-isha	V of Glam	ST0475	51°28·2′	3°22·5′W	X	170
Ty-issa	Powys	SJ2321	52°47·1′	3°8·1′W	X	126
Tyla	Monm	SO2413	51°48·9′	3°5·8′W	T	161
Tylacoch Fm	Brig	SS8987	51°34·5′	3°35·7′W	FM	170
Tyla Du	Caer	SO1104	51°43·9′	3°16·9′W	X	171
Tyla Fm	Brig	SS8878	51°29·6′	3°36·4′W	FM	170
Tyla Fm	Newp	ST2482	51°32·1′	3°5·4′W	FM	171
Tylaglas	Merth Tyd	SO1001	51°42·3′	3°17·8′W	X	171
Tyla Gwyn	V of Glam	SS9680	51°30·8′	3°29·5′W	X	170
Tyla-Morris	Card	ST1180	51°31·0′	3°16·6′W	X	171
Tyland Fm	Kent	TQ7559	51°18·4′	0°31·0′E	FM	178,188
Tylas Fm	N Yks	SE5686	54°16·2′	1°8·0′W	FM	100
Tylau	Cered	SN5860	52°13·4′	4°4·3′W	X	146
Tylcau Hill	Powys	SO1476	52°22·8′	3°15·4′W	H	136,148
Tylcha Fach	Rho Cyn Taf	ST0187	51°34·6′	3°25·3′W	X	170
Tylcha-fawr	Rho Cyn Taf	ST0187	51°34·6′	3°25·3′W	X	170
Tylcha-ganol	Rho Cyn Taf	ST0187	51°34·6′	3°25·3′W	X	170
Tyldesley	Wigan	SD7001	53°30·5′	2°26·7′W	T	109
Tyle	Carm	SN5724	51°54·0′	4°4·3′W	X	159
Tyle	Carm	SN6726	51°55·2′	3°55·6′W	T	146
Tyle Brith	Powys	SN9919	51°51·9′	3°27·6′W	X	160
Tylebychan	Powys	SN9326	51°55·6′	3°33·0′W	X	160
Tyle-Clydach	Powys	SO0921	51°53·0′	3°18·9′W	X	161
Tyle Coch	Nth Pt Talb	SN7301	51°41·8′	3°49·9′W	X	170
Tyle Coch	Rho Cyn Taf	SS9496	51°39·4′	3°31·6′W	X	170
Tyle-coch	Swan	SN6407	51°45·0′	3°57·8′W	X	159
Tyle Cott	Angus	NO3635	56°30·4′	3°1·9′W	X	54
Tylecrwn	Powys	SO0932	51°59·0′	3°19·1′W	X	161
Tyle Du	Carm	SN7319	51°51·5′	3°50·3′W	X	160
Tyle Du	Carm	SN7722	51°53·2′	3°46·8′W	H	160
Tyle Fforest	Rho Cyn Taf	SS9499	51°41·0′	3°31·6′W	F	170
Tyle Garw	Powys	SN7716	51°50·0′	3°46·7′W	X	160
Tyle-garw	Powys	SN9220	51°52·3′	3°33·7′W	X	160
Tyle-garw	Rho Cyn Taf	ST0281	51°31·4′	3°24·4′W	T	170
Tyleglas	Powys	SN9320	51°52·3′	3°32·9′W	X	160
Tyle-glas	Powys	SO1736	52°1·2′	3°12·2′W	X	161
Tyle Hall	Essex	TQ8998	51°39·2′	0°44·3′E	X	168
Tyleheulog	Powys	SO0841	52°3·8′	3°20·1′W	X	147,160
Tyle-llwyd	Powys	SO0423	51°54·1′	3°23·3′W	X	160
Tyle Mawr	Nth Pt Talb	SS8598	51°40·4′	3°39·4′W	X	170
Tyle-mawr	Powys	SO1542	52°4·4′	3°14·0′W	X	148,161
Tyle Mill	W Berks	SU6269	51°25·2′	1°6·1′W	X	175
Tyle Pen-lan	Nth Pt Talb	SN7312	51°47·8′	3°50·1′W	X	160
Tyle'r-fedwen	Nth Pt Talb	SS7792	51°37·0′	3°46·2′W	X	170
Tyler Hill	Kent	TR1460	51°18·2′	1°4·6′E	T	179
Tylers Causeway	Herts	TL2905	51°44·0′	0°7·5′W	T	166
Tylers Common	Hav	TQ5690	51°35·5′	0°15·5′E	X	177
Tylers Copse	Hants	SZ3999	50°47·6′	1°26·4′W	F	196
Tylers Green	Bucks	SU9094	51°38·5′	0°41·6′W	T	175
Tyler's Green	Essex	TL5005	51°43·6′	0°10·7′E	T	167
Tyler's Green	Surrey	TQ3552	51°15·3′	0°3·5′W	T	187
Tylers Green Fm	S Glos	ST7585	51°34·0′	2°21·3′W	FM	172
Tyler's Hill	Bucks	SP9801	51°42·2′	0°34·5′W	T	165
Tyle'r waun	Nth Pt Talb	SS8398	51°40·4′	3°41·1′W	X	170
Tyley Bottom	Glos	ST7894	51°38·9′	2°18·7′W	X	162,172
Tylissa	Powys	SJ0906	52°38·9′	3°20·3′W	X	125
Ty-Llangenny	Powys	SO2319	51°52·1′	3°6·7′W	X	161
Tyllicci	Powys	SO0837	52°1·7′	3°20·1′W	X	160
Tyllosg	Pemb	SN0630	51°56·3′	4°48·9′W	X	145
Tyllwyd	Carm	SN4520	51°51·7′	4°14·7′W	X	159
Ty-llwyd	Carm	SN4715	51°49·0′	4°12·8′W	X	159
Tyllwyd	Carm	SN4829	51°56·6′	4°12·3′W	X	146
Ty-Llwyd	Carm	SN5002	51°42·0′	4°9·9′W	X	159
Tyllwyd	Carm	SN5706	51°44·3′	4°3·9′W	X	159
Tyllwyd	Carm	SN5718	51°50·8′	4°4·2′W	X	159
Tyllwyd	Carm	SN6946	52°6·1′	3°54·4′W	X	146
Tyllwyd	Carm	SN7133	51°59·1′	3°52·3′W	X	146,160
Tyllwyd	Cered	SN2848	52°6·5′	4°30·3′W	X	145
Ty-llŵyd	Cered	SN5548	52°6·9′	4°6·7′W	X	146
Tyllwyd	Cered	SN5977	52°22·6′	4°3·9′W	X	135
Tyllwyd	Cered	SN8275	52°21·9′	3°43·6′W	X	135,136,147
Ty-llŵyd	Gwyn	SH9039	52°56·5′	3°37·8′W	X	125
Ty-Llwyd	Monm	SO4301	51°42·5′	2°49·1′W	X	171
Ty-Llwyd	Pemb	SM8428	51°54·8′	5°8·0′W	X	157
Tyllwyd	Pemb	SN1236	51°59·7′	4°43·9′W	X	145
Tŷ-llwyd	Powys	SJ0221	52°46·9′	3°26·8′W	X	125
Ty-llwyd	Swan	SN6102	51°42·2′	4°0·3′W	X	159
Ty-llwyd	Torf	ST3194	51°38·7′	2°59·4′W	X	171
Tŷllwyd-mawr	Carm	SN4319	51°51·1′	4°16·4′W	X	159
Ty Llwyn	Blae Gw	SO1708	51°46·1′	3°11·8′W	T	161
Tylney Hall (Hotel)	Hants	SU7055	51°17·6′	0°59·4′W	X	175
Tylney Ho	Hants	SU7155	51°17·6′	0°58·5′W	X	175,186
Tylorstown	Rho Cyn Taf	ST0095	51°38·9′	3°26·3′W	T	170
Tylwch	Powys	SN9680	52°24·7′	3°31·3′W	T	136
Tymaen	Brig	SS8977	51°29·1′	3°35·5′W	X	170
Tymaen	Carm	SN3936	52°0·2′	4°20·3′W	X	145
Tymaen	V of Glam	ST0178	51°29·8′	3°25·2′W	X	170
Ty-maen	Wrex	SJ2941	52°57·9′	3°3·0′W	X	117
Ty Mawr	Carm	SN4103	51°42·4′	4°17·7′W	X	159
Ty-mawr	Carm	SN5006	51°44·2′	4°10·0′W	X	159
Ty Mawr	Carm	SN5443	52°4·2′	4°7·4′W	X	146
Ty Mawr	Cered	SN5159	52°12·8′	4°10·5′W	X	146
Ty Mawr	Cered	SN6292	52°30·7′	4°1·6′W	X	135
Tymawr	Cered	SN6557	52°11·9′	3°58·1′W	X	146
Tymawr	Cered	SN7579	52°23·9′	3°49·8′W	X	135,147
Tŷ-Mawr	Cered	SN8174	52°21·3′	3°44·4′W	X	135,136,147
Ty Mawr	Conwy	SH7752	53°3·3′	3°49·7′W	A	115
Tŷ-mawr	Conwy	SH8168	53°12·0′	3°46·5′W	X	116
Ty-Mawr	Conwy	SH8259	53°7·2′	3°45·4′W	X	116
Ty Mawr	Conwy	SH8350	53°2·3′	3°44·3′W	X	116
Tŷ-mawr	Conwy	SH8773	53°14·8′	3°41·2′W	X	116
Ty Mawr	Conwy	SH8877	53°16·9′	3°40·4′W	X	116
Ty-mawr	Conwy	SH9679	53°18·1′	3°33·2′W	T	116
Tŷ-mawr	Conwy	SH9747	53°0·9′	3°31·7′W	X	116
Tŷ-mawr	Denb	SJ0773	53°15·0′	3°23·2′W	X	116
Ty-mawr	Denb	SJ0860	53°8·0′	3°22·1′W	X	116
Tŷ-mawr	Denb	SJ1145	52°59·9′	3°19·2′W	X	116
Ty Mawr	Denb	SJ1343	52°58·9′	3°17·3′W	X	125
Tŷ-mawr	Denb	SJ1648	53°1·6′	3°14·7′W	X	116
Tŷ-mawr	Gwyn	SH1731	52°51·0′	4°42·7′W	X	123
Tŷ-mawr	Gwyn	SH2135	52°53·2′	4°39·2′W	X	123
Ty Mawr	Gwyn	SH2528	52°49·5′	4°35·4′W	X	123
Ty Mawr	Gwyn	SH4354	53°3·9′	4°20·2′W	X	115,123
Ty Mawr	Gwyn	SH4557	53°5·5′	4°18·5′W	X	115,123
Ty-Mawr	Gwyn	SH5053	53°3·4′	4°13·9′W	A	115
Ty-mawr	Gwyn	SH5566	53°10·5′	4°9·8′W	X	114,115
Ty-mawr	Gwyn	SH5900	52°35·0′	4°4·5′W	X	135
Ty-mawr	Gwyn	SH6006	52°38·3′	4°3·7′W	X	124
Tŷ-mawr	Gwyn	SH6140	52°56·6′	4°3·7′W	X	124
Ty-mawr	Gwyn	SH6146	52°59·8′	4°3·9′W	A	115
Tŷ-mawr	Gwyn	SH6405	52°37·8′	4°0·2′W	X	124
Ty-mawr	Gwyn	SH8022	52°47·2′	3°46·4′W	X	124,125
Ty-mawr	Gwyn	SH8412	52°41·8′	3°42·6′W	X	124,125
Ty Mawr	Heref	SO3226	51°55·9′	2°58·9′W	X	161
Tŷ-mawr	I of Angl	SH2181	53°18·0′	4°40·8′W	X	114
Tŷ-mawr	I of Angl	SH2280	53°17·5′	4°39·8′W	X	114
Ty-mawr	I of Angl	SH2978	53°16·5′	4°33·5′W	X	114
Ty Mawr	I of Angl	SH3087	53°21·4′	4°32·9′W	X	114
Ty Mawr	I of Angl	SH3575	53°15·0′	4°28·0′W	X	114
Ty-mawr	I of Angl	SH3584	53°19·9′	4°28·3′W	X	114
Ty-mawr	I of Angl	SH3671	53°12·9′	4°27·0′W	X	114
Ty Mawr	I of Angl	SH3775	53°15·1′	4°26·2′W	X	114
Ty Mawr	I of Angl	SH3969	53°11·9′	4°24·2′W	X	114
Ty-mawr	I of Angl	SH4266	53°10·3′	4°21·4′W	X	114,115
Ty Mawr	I of Angl	SH4478	53°16·8′	4°20·0′W	X	114,115
Ty-mawr	I of Angl	SH4785	53°20·6′	4°17·5′W	X	114
Ty Mawr	I of Angl	SH4867	53°10·9′	4°16·1′W	X	114,115
Ty Mawr	I of Angl	SH4969	53°12·0′	4°15·2′W	X	114,115
Ty-mawr	I of Angl	SH5479	53°17·5′	4°11·0′W	X	114,115
Ty Mawr	Monm	SO4309	51°46·8′	2°49·2′W	X	161
Ty-mawr	Monm	SO5007	51°45·8′	2°43·1′W	X	162
Ty-mawr	Pemb	SN1027	51°54·8′	4°45·4′W	X	145,158
Ty-mawr	Pemb	SN2734	51°58·9′	4°30·8′W	X	145
Ty-mawr	Powys	SH7706	52°38·5′	3°48·7′W	X	124
Ty-mawr	Powys	SH8510	52°40·8′	3°41·7′W	X	124,125
Tŷ-mawr	Powys	SH9002	52°36·5′	3°37·1′W	X	136
Tŷ-mawr	Powys	SJ0108	52°39·9′	3°27·4′W	X	125

Tŷ-mawr	Powys	SJ0328	52°50·7'	3°26·0'W	X	125
Ty-mawr	Powys	SJ0802	52°36·7'	3°21·1'W	X	136
Tymawr	Powys	SJ1015	52°43·8'	3°19·6'W	X	125
Ty-mawr	Powys	SJ1200	52°35·7'	3°17·6'W	X	136
Tŷ-mawr	Powys	SJ1528	52°50·8'	3°15·3'W	X	125
Ty-mawr	Powys	SJ1704	52°37·9'	3°13·2'W	A	136
Ty-mawr	Powys	SJ2018	52°45·5'	3°10·7'W	X	126
Tŷ-mawr	Powys	SJ2129	52°51·4'	3°10·0'W	X	126
Tymawr	Powys	SN8099	52°34·8'	3°45·9'W	X	135,136
Tŷ-mawr	Powys	SN8553	52°10·0'	3°40·5'W	X	147
Ty-mawr	Powys	SN8780	52°24·6'	3°39·3'W	X	135,136
Tymawr	Powys	SN9273	52°20·9'	3°34·7'W	X	136,147
Ty-mawr	Powys	SN9411	51°47·5'	3°31·8'W	X	160
Ty-Mawr	Powys	SN9528	51°56·7'	3°31·3'W	X	160
Ty-Mawr	Powys	SN9589	52°29·6'	3°32·4'W	A	136
Ty-mawr	Powys	SN9651	52°9·1'	3°30·8'W	X	147
Ty Mawr	Powys	SN9857	52°12·3'	3°29·2'W	X	147
Ty-mawr	Powys	SO0140	52°3·2'	3°26·2'W	X	147,160
Ty Mawr	Rho Cyn Taf	ST0883	51°32·5'	3°19·2'W	X	170
Ty-mawr	Torf	SO3101	51°42·4'	2°59·5'W	X	171
Ty Mawr Cwm	Conwy	SH9047	53°0·8'	3°38·0'W	X	116
Tymawr Fm	Newp	ST2682	51°32·2'	3°3·6'W	FM	171
Tymawr Fm	Powys	SO1226	51°55·8'	3°16·4'W	FM	161
Ty Mawr Gell	Conwy	SH8570	53°13·1'	3°42·9'W	X	116
Ty-mawr Hill	Powys	SJ1201	52°36·2'	3°17·6'W	H	136
Ty mawr Llanddewi	Monm	ST3198	51°40·8'	2°59·5'W	X	171
Ty-Mawr Prion	Denb	SJ0663	53°9·6'	3°23·9'W	X	116
Ty Mawr Resr	Wrex	SJ2748	53°1·7'	3°4·9'W	W	117
Ty Mawr School	Monm	SO2515	51°50·0'	3°4·9'W	X	161
Ty Meinor	Brig	SS9092	51°37·2'	3°34·9'W	X	170
Ty-Melin Uchaf	Swan	SN6806	51°44·5'	3°54·3'W	X	159
Ty-moel	I of Angl	SH4375	53°15·2'	4°20·8'W	X	114,115
Tympanheck	D & G	NY3274	55°3·6'	3°3·4'W	X	85
Tymparon Hall	Cumbr	NY4630	54°40·0'	2°49·8'W	X	90
Tynabeinne	Arg & Bt	NR2663	55°47·2'	6°21·8'W	X	60
Tynacoille	Arg & Bt	NR2763	55°47·3'	6°20·9'W	X	60
Tynaherrick	Highld	NH4924	57°17·2'	4°29·9'W	X	26
Tynant	Carm	SN6746	52°6·0'	3°56·1'W	X	146
Ty-nant	Cered	SN5058	52°12·2'	4°11·3'W	X	146
Ty-nant	Cered	SN6272	52°20·0'	4°1·1'W	X	135
Tŷnant	Cered	SN6461	52°14·1'	3°59·1'W	X	146
Tynant	Cered	SN6988	52°28·7'	3°55·3'W	X	135
Ty Nant	Conwy	SH8349	53°1·8'	3°44·3'W	X	116
Ty Nant	Conwy	SH8448	53°1·2'	3°43·4'W	X	116
Ty-nant	Conwy	SH9944	52°59·3'	3°29·9'W	T	125
Ty-nant	Conwy	SJ0050	53°2·5'	3°29·1'W	X	116
Tŷ-nant	Denb	SJ0746	53°0·4'	3°22·8'W	X	116
Tŷ-nant	Gwyn	SH8442	52°58·0'	3°43·2'W	X	124,125
Ty-nant	Gwyn	SH8738	52°55·9'	3°40·5'W	X	124,125
Tŷ-nant	Gwyn	SH9026	52°49·5'	3°37·6'W	X	125
Ty-nant	Gwyn	SH9037	52°55·4'	3°37·8'W	X	125
Tŷ-nant	Gwyn	SH9338	52°56·0'	3°35·1'W	X	125
Tŷ-nant	Gwyn	SH9537	52°55·5'	3°33·3'W	X	125
Tŷ-nant	Powys	SJ1723	52°48·1'	3°13·5'W	X	125
Tynant	Rho Cyn Taf	ST0685	51°33·6'	3°21·0'W	T	170
Ty Nant Gell	Conwy	SH8469	53°12·6'	3°43·8'W	X	116
Ty-nant-llwyn	Conwy	SH9843	52°58·7'	3°30·7'W	X	125
Tynaspirit	Stir	NN6604	56°12·8'	4°9·2'W	X	57
Tynayare	Pth & Kin	NN7346	56°35·6'	4°3·6'W	X	51,52
Tynbedw	Cered	SN4961	52°13·8'	4°12·3'W	X	146
Tynbedw	Cered	SN6971	52°19·5'	3°54·9'W	X	135
Tynbeili	Cered	SN5669	52°18·3'	4°6·3'W	X	135
Tynberllan	Cered	SN6573	52°20·6'	3°58·5'W	X	135
Tyn Beudy	I of Angl	SH4878	53°16·9'	4°16·4'W	X	114,115
Ty'n Buarth	I of Angl	SH5073	53°14·2'	4°14·5'W	X	114,115
Tynbwlch	Cered	SN5573	52°20·4'	4°7·3'W	X	135
Tynbwlch	Cered	SN6770	52°19·0'	3°56·7'W	X	135
Tyncae	Cered	SN6957	52°12·0'	3°54·6'W	X	146
Tyn Cae	I of Angl	SH4972	53°13·7'	4°15·3'W	X	114,115
Tyncelyn	Cered	SN6463	52°15·1'	3°59·1'W	X	146
Tyn Celyn	Conwy	SH7966	53°10·9'	3°48·2'W	X	115
Tyn Celyn	Denb	SJ0344	52°59·3'	3°26·3'W	X	125
Tyncelyn	Denb	SJ0545	52°59·9'	3°24·5'W	X	116
Ty'n-Celyn	Denb	SJ2340	52°57·4'	3°8·4'W	X	117
Tyncelyn	Powys	SJ2129	52°51·4'	3°10·0'W	X	126
Tyncoed	Cered	SN7061	52°14·2'	3°53·8'W	X	146,147
Tyn Coed	Gwyn	SH3840	52°56·2'	4°24·2'W	X	123
Tyn Coed	I of Angl	SH3774	53°14·5'	4°26·2'W	X	114
Tyn Coed	I of Angl	SH4580	53°17·9'	4°19·1'W	X	114,115
Ty'n-Coed	I of Angl	SH4676	53°15·8'	4°18·1'W	X	114,115
Tyncoed	Powys	SN9176	52°22·5'	3°35·7'W	X	136,147
Tyncoed	Powys	SN9652	52°9·6'	3°30·8'W	X	147
Tyncoed	Powys	SO0355	52°11·3'	3°24·7'W	X	147
Tyncwm	Carm	SN6335	52°0·0'	3°59·4'W	X	146
Tyncwm	Cered	SN6482	52°25·4'	3°59·6'W	X	135
Tyncwm	Cered	SN7765	52°16·4'	3°47·8'W	X	135,147
Tyndales	Essex	TL8004	51°42·6'	0°36·7'E	X	168
Tynddol	Cered	SN7667	52°17·5'	3°48·7'W	X	135,147
Ty'n-ddol	Conwy	SH8672	53°14·2'	3°42·1'W	X	116
Tyn Ddol	Conwy	SH8765	53°10·5'	3°41·0'W	X	116
Tynddol	Gwyn	SH9138	52°55·9'	3°36·9'W	X	125
Tynddraenen	Cered	SN6966	52°16·8'	3°54·8'W	X	135
Ty'n-dolau	Cered	SN6566	52°16·8'	3°58·3'W	X	135
Ty'n-domen	Carm	SN6711	51°47·2'	3°55·3'W	X	159
Tyndrain	Gwyn	SH6934	52°53·5'	3°56·4'W	X	124
Tyndrum	Highld	NH5220	57°15·1'	4°26·7'W	X	26,35
Tyndrum	Stir	NN3330	56°26·2'	4°42·1'W	T	50
Tyn Dryfol	I of Angl	SH3973	53°14·0'	4°24·3'W	X	114
Tyndwr Hall	Denb	SJ2341	52°57·9'	3°8·4'W	X	117
Tynebank	Midlo	NT3862	55°51·1'	2°59·0'W	X	66
Tyne Dock	S Tyne	NZ3565	54°58·9'	1°26·8'W	T	88
Tynefield	E Loth	NT6277	55°59·3'	2°36·1'W	X	67
Tyne Green	Northum	NY9364	54°58·5'	2°6·1'W	X	87
Tyne Green Riverside Park	Northum	NY9364	54°58·5'	2°6·1'W	X	87
Tyneham	Dorset	SY8880	50°37·4'	2°9·8'W	T	194
Tyneham Cap	Dorset	SY8979	50°36·9'	2°8·9'W	H	195
Tyne Head	Cumbr	NY7536	54°43·3'	2°22·9'W	X	91
Tynehead	Midlo	NT3959	55°49·5'	2°58·0'W	T	66,73
Tynehead Fell	Cumbr	NY7635	54°42·8'	2°21·9'W	H	91
Tyne Hill	Oxon	SP3638	52°2·6'	1°28·1'W	X	151
Tyne Hill Fm	Oxon	SP3638	52°2·6'	1°28·1'W	FM	151
Tyneholme	Suff	TM3981	52°22·7'	1°31·1'E	X	156
Tyneholm Ho	E Loth	NT4468	55°54·4'	2°53·3'W	X	66
Tynely	Northum	NU1723	55°30·3'	1°43·4'W	X	75
Tynemead Fm	Somer	ST7441	51°10·3'	2°21·9'W	FM	183
Tynemount	E Loth	NT4068	55°54·3'	2°57·1'W	X	66
Tyne Mouth	E Loth	NT6480	56°0·9'	2°34·2'W	W	67
Tynemouth	N Tyne	NZ3569	55°1·1'	1°26·7'W	T	88
Tyne, River	E Loth	NT5071	55°56·0'	2°47·6'W	W	66
Tyne Riverside Country Park	Northum	NZ0863	54°57·9'	1°52·1'W	X	88
Tyne Riverside Country Park	N upon Ty	NZ1665	54°59·0'	1°44·6'W	X	88
Tyne Sands	E Loth	NT6380	56°0·9'	2°35·2'W	X	67
Tyne Water	Midlo	NT3966	55°53·3'	2°58·1'W	W	66
Tynewydd	Brig	SS9584	51°32·9'	3°30·5'W	X	170
Tynewydd	Caer	ST1799	51°41·3'	3°11·7'W	X	171
Tynewydd	Card	ST1177	51°29·3'	3°16·5'W	X	171
Tynewydd	Card	ST1182	51°32·0'	3°16·6'W	X	171
Tynewydd	Carm	SN2016	51°49·1'	4°36·3'W	X	158
Tŷnewydd	Carm	SN3621	51°52·1'	4°22·5'W	X	145,159
Tynewydd	Carm	SN4322	51°52·7'	4°16·5'W	X	159
Ty-Newydd	Carm	SN4438	52°1·4'	4°16·0'W	X	146
Tynewydd	Cered	SN2347	52°5·8'	4°34·7'W	T	145
Ty-Newydd	Cered	SN5468	52°17·7'	4°8·1'W	T	135
Ty-newydd	Cered	SN5972	52°19·9'	4°3·8'W	X	135
Tynewydd	Cered	SN7973	52°20·7'	3°46·2'W	X	135,147
Tynewydd	Conwy	SH8456	53°5·6'	3°43·5'W	X	116
Ty-newydd	Conwy	SH8575	53°15·8'	3°43·0'W	X	116
Ty-newydd	Conwy	SH8576	53°16·4'	3°43·1'W	X	116
Tŷ-newydd	Conwy	SH8670	53°13·1'	3°42·0'W	X	116
Ty Newydd	Denb	SH9959	53°7·4'	3°30·2'W	X	116
Ty Newydd	Denb	SJ0569	53°12·8'	3°25·0'W	X	116
Ty-newydd	Denb	SJ0749	53°2·1'	3°22·8'W	X	116
Ty Newydd	Denb	SJ0757	53°6·4'	3°22·9'W	X	116
Ty Newydd	Denb	SJ0779	53°18·2'	3°23·3'W	X	116
Ty-newydd	Denb	SJ0952	53°3·7'	3°21·1'W	X	116
Ty-newydd	Denb	SJ1072	53°14·5'	3°20·5'W	X	116
Ty-newydd	Denb	SJ1144	52°59·4'	3°19·2'W	X	125
Ty Newydd	Denb	SJ1542	52°58·4'	3°15·5'W	X	125
Ty Newydd	Flint	SJ2458	53°7·1'	3°7·7'W	X	117
Ty-newydd	Flint	SJ2461	53°8·7'	3°7·8'W	X	117
Tynewydd	Gwyn	SH2733	52°52·2'	4°33·8'W	X	123
Tynewydd	Gwyn	SH6224	52°48·0'	4°2·4'W	X	124
Tŷ-newydd	Gwyn	SH9737	52°55·5'	3°31·5'W	X	125
Ty Newydd	I of Angl	SH3474	53°14·5'	4°28·9'W	X	114
Tynewydd	newp	ST2482	51°32·1'	3°5·4'W	X	171
Tynewydd	Nth Pt Talb	SN8209	51°46·3'	3°42·2'W	T	160
Tynewydd	Pemb	SM9737	51°59·9'	4°57·0'W	X	157
Ty-newydd	Pemb	SN1835	51°59·3'	4°38·6'W	X	145
Tynewydd	Pemb	SS0699	51°39·6'	4°47·9'W	X	158
Ty-newydd	Powys	SH8106	52°38·6'	3°45·1'W	X	124,125
Tŷ-newydd	Powys	SJ0313	52°42·6'	3°25·7'W	X	125
Tŷ newydd	Powys	SJ0825	52°49·1'	3°21·5'W	X	125
Ty-newydd	Powys	SJ1318	52°45·4'	3°16·9'W	X	125
Tŷ-newydd	Powys	SJ1529	52°51·3'	3°15·3'W	X	125
Tynewydd	Powys	SJ2027	52°50·3'	3°10·9'W	X	126
Tynewydd	Powys	SN8399	52°34·8'	3°43·2'W	X	135,136
Ty-newydd	Powys	SN9124	51°54·5'	3°34·7'W	X	160
Tynewydd	Powys	SN9351	52°9·1'	3°33·4'W	X	147
Tynewydd	Powys	SN9826	51°55·6'	3°28·6'W	X	160
Tynewydd	Powys	SO0826	51°55·7'	3°19·9'W	X	160
Ty-newydd	Powys	SO1025	51°55·2'	3°18·1'W	X	161
Tynewydd	Powys	SO1037	52°1·7'	3°18·3'W	X	161
Tynewydd	Rho Cyn Taf	SS9398	51°40·5'	3°32·5'W	T	170
Tynewydd	Rho Cyn Taf	SS9787	51°34·6'	3°28·8'W	X	170
Tŷ-newydd	Wrex	SJ1833	52°53·5'	3°12·7'W	X	125
Tynewydd Fm	Monm	SO3811	51°47·9'	2°53·6'W	FM	161
Tynewydd Fm	Pemb	SM9535	51°58·8'	4°58·7'W	FM	157
Tynewydd Fm	Powys	SO0336	52°1·1'	3°24·4'W	FM	160
Tynewydd Gosen	Powys	SJ0007	52°39·3'	3°28·3'W	X	125
Ty-newydd-grûg	Pemb	SM9228	51°54·9'	5°1·1'W	X	157,158
Ty-newydd-gwyllt	Gwyn	SH7225	52°48·7'	3°53·5'W	X	124
Ty Newydd (Hotel)	Rho Cyn Taf	SN9406	51°44·8'	3°31·7'W	X	160
Ty Newydd Isa	Conwy	SH8762	53°8·8'	3°41·0'W	X	116
Ty-newydd-y-mynydd	Gwyn	SH7925	52°48·8'	3°47·3'W	X	124
Ty'n Fedw	Gwyn	SH9839	52°56·6'	3°30·7'W	X	125
Ty'n Fflat	I of Angl	SH4269	53°11·9'	4°21·5'W	X	114,115
Ty'n-ffynnon	Cered	SN5060	52°13·3'	4°11·4'W	X	146
Ty'n Fron	Cered	SN5776	52°22·0'	4°5·6'W	X	135
Tynfron	Cered	SN7568	52°18·0'	3°49·6'W	X	135,147
Tyngrug-uchaf	Cered	SN4846	52°5·7'	4°12·7'W	X	146
Tyngwndwn	Cered	SN5362	52°14·4'	4°8·8'W	X	146
Tyngwndwn	Cered	SN5873	52°20·4'	4°4·7'W	X	135
Tyning	Bath & NE Somer	ST6658	51°19·4'	2°28·9'W	T	172
Tyning	Bath & NE Somer	ST6955	51°17·8'	2°26·3'W	T	172,183
Tyning Fm	S Glos	ST7278	51°30·2'	2°23·8'W	FM	172
Tyninghame	E Loth	NT6079	56°0·4'	2°38·0'W	T	67
Tyninghame Ho	E Loth	NT6179	56°0·4'	2°37·1'W	X	67
Tyninghame Links	E Loth	NT6280	56°0·9'	2°36·1'W	X	67
Tyning's Fm	Somer	ST4756	51°18·3'	2°45·2'W	FM	172,182
Tyning,The	S Glos	ST7982	51°32·4'	2°17·8'W	F	172
Tyning Wood	Glos	SP1706	51°45·4'	1°44·8'W	F	163
Tyning Wood	Wilts	ST7739	51°9·2'	2°19·3'W	F	183
Ty'n-llan	I of Angl	SH3083	53°19·2'	4°32·7'W	X	114
Tyn Llan	I of Angl	SH3293	53°24·7'	4°31·3'W	X	114
Tynllan	I of Angl	SH4379	53°17·3'	4°20·9'W	X	114,115
Ty'n-Llanfair	Denb	SJ1351	53°3·2'	3°17·5'W	X	116
Tyn-llechwedd	Denb	SJ0248	53°1·5'	3°27·3'W	X	116
Tyn-llechwedd	Denb	SJ0746	53°0·4'	3°22·8'W	X	116
Tyn Llidiart	Gwyn	SH2534	52°52·7'	4°35·6'W	X	123
Ty'n-llidiart	Gwyn	SH6715	52°43·2'	3°57·8'W	X	124
Tynllidiart	Powys	SN9066	52°17·1'	3°36·4'W	X	136,147
Tyn Llwydan	I of Angl	SH3666	53°10·2'	4°26·8'W	X	114
Tynllwyn	Cered	SN6271	52°19·4'	4°1·1'W	X	135
Tynllwyn	Cered	SN6453	52°9·8'	3°58·9'W	X	146
Ty'n Llwyn	Conwy	SH8650	53°2·4'	3°41·6'W	X	116
Ty'n-llwyn	Denb	SJ1541	52°57·8'	3°15·5'W	X	125
Tyn-llwŷn	Gwyn	SH4752	53°2·8'	4°16·5'W	X	115,123
Tŷ'n-llwyn	Gwyn	SH5667	53°11·1'	4°8·9'W	X	114,115
Ty'n-llwyn	Gwyn	SH9237	52°55·4'	3°36·0'W	X	125
Tyn Llwyn	I of Angl	SH4070	53°12·4'	4°23·3'W	X	114,115
Tyn Llwyn	I of Angl	SH5880	53°18·1'	4°7·5'W	X	114,115
Tynllwyn	Powys	SH8504	52°37·5'	3°41·5'W	X	135,136
Tynllwyn	Powys	SJ1932	52°53·0'	3°11·8'W	X	125
Tynllwyn	Powys	SJ2108	52°40·1'	3°9·7'W	X	126
Tynllwyn	Powys	SN9354	52°10·7'	3°33·5'W	X	147
Tynllwyn	Powys	SN9863	52°15·6'	3°29·3'W	X	147
Tynllwyn	Powys	SO0624	51°54·6'	3°21·6'W	X	160
Tynllwyn	Powys	SO0651	52°9·2'	3°22·0'W	X	147
Tynllwyn Fm	Conwy	SH8374	53°15·3'	3°44·8'W	FM	116
Tynllwyn-hen	Gwyn	SH6202	52°36·1'	4°1·9'W	X	135
Tynllwyni	Powys	SN9044	52°5·2'	3°35·9'W	X	147,160
Ty'n-llyn	Conwy	SH8956	53°5·6'	3°39·1'W	X	116
Tynllyn	Gwyn	SH7134	52°53·5'	3°54·6'W	X	124
Tyn-llyn	Powys	SJ1728	52°50·8'	3°13·5'W	X	125
Tynllyne	Powys	SO2039	52°2·9'	3°9·6'W	X	161
Tŷ'n Lôn	Denb	SJ0769	53°12·8'	3°23·2'W	X	116
Tyn-lôn	Gwyn	SH1525	52°47·7'	4°44·2'W	X	123
Tyn Lôn	Gwyn	SH3035	52°53·4'	4°31·2'W	X	123
Tyn Lon	Gwyn	SH4341	52°56·9'	4°19·8'W	X	123
Tyn-lon	Gwyn	SH4657	53°5·5'	4°17·6'W	T	115,123
Tyn Lôn	I of Angl	SH6178	53°17·1'	4°4·7'W	X	114,115
Tynlône	Carm	SN7228	51°56·4'	3°51·3'W	X	146,160
Ty'n-lôn Fm	Gwyn	SH1929	52°49·9'	4°40·8'W	FM	123
Tyn'n-y-llechwedd	Gwyn	SH8732	52°52·7'	3°40·3'W	X	124,125
Tynohir	Powys	SN7098	52°34·1'	3°54·7'W	X	135
Tyn Pwll	I of Angl	SH4368	53°11·4'	4°20·6'W	X	114,115
Ty'n Pwll	I of Angl	SH5078	53°16·9'	4°14·6'W	X	114,115
Tynpynfarch	Cered	SN6584	52°26·5'	3°58·8'W	X	135
Tynreithyn	Cered	SN6268	52°17·8'	4°1·0'W	X	135
Tynreoch	Pth & Kin	NN7123	56°23·2'	4°4·9'W	X	51,52
Tynrhelyg	Cered	SN6689	52°29·2'	3°58·0'W	X	135
Tynrhos	Cered	SN6258	52°12·4'	4°0·8'W	X	146
Ty'n-rhos	Cered	SN6385	52°27·0'	4°0·6'W	X	135
Tyn-rhos	I of Angl	SH3873	53°14·0'	4°25·2'W	X	114
Tynrhos	Powys	SJ0910	52°41·0'	3°20·4'W	X	125
Tynrhos	Powys	SO0041	52°3·7'	3°27·1'W	X	147,160
Tyn-rhos-fawr	Gwyn	SH3838	52°55·1'	4°24·2'W	X	123
Tyn-rhos-ganol	I of Angl	SH3872	53°13·5'	4°25·2'W	X	114
Tyn-rhos-uchaf	I of Angl	SH3871	53°12·9'	4°25·2'W	X	114
Tynribbie	Arg & Bt	NM9346	56°33·9'	5°21·7'W	X	49
Tynrich	Highld	NH6326	57°18·5'	4°16·0'W	X	26,35
Tynron	D & G	NX8093	55°13·3'	3°52·8'W	T	78
Tynron Doon	D & G	NX8193	55°13·3'	3°51·8'W	H	78
Tynshimley	Powys	SN9770	52°19·3'	3°30·3'W	X	136,147
Tyn Simdda	Gwyn	SH2634	52°52·8'	4°34·7'W	X	123
Tyntesfield	N Som	ST5071	51°26·4'	2°42·8'W	T	172
Tyntesfield Plantn	N Som	ST5171	51°26·4'	2°41·9'W	F	172
Tyntetown	Rho Cyn Taf	ST0696	51°39·5'	3°21·1'W	T	170
Tynton	Nth Pt Talb	SS8095	51°38·7'	3°43·7'W	X	170
Tyn-twll	Conwy	SH7861	53°8·2'	3°49·0'W	X	115
Tyn-twll	Conwy	SH8764	53°9·9'	3°41·0'W	X	116
Ty'n-twll	Denb	SJ0161	53°8·5'	3°28·4'W	X	116
Ty'n-Twll	Denb	SJ1055	53°5·3'	3°20·2'W	X	116
Tyn Twll	Gwyn	SH6835	52°54·0'	3°57·3'W	X	124
Tyntwll	Powys	SH8001	52°35·9'	3°45·9'W	X	135,136
Ty'n'twll	Powys	SJ1320	52°46·5'	3°17·0'W	X	125
Tyn-twll	Wrex	SJ1234	52°54·0'	3°18·1'W	X	125
Tyn Twll Fm	Denb	SJ1855	53°5·4'	3°13·1'W	FM	116
Tyn Twll Fm	Flint	SJ2075	53°16·2'	3°11·6'W	FM	117
Tyn-twll Fm	Wrex	SJ3551	53°3·4'	2°57·8'W	FM	117
Tyntyle	Rho Cyn Taf	SS9995	51°38·9'	3°27·2'W	X	170
Tynwald Hill	I of M	SC2781	54°12·0'	4°38·7'W	A	95
Tynwald (site of)	I of M	SC3682	54°12·7'	4°30·5'W	A	95
Tynwaun	Cered	SN6664	52°15·7'	3°57·4'W	X	146
Tynwaun	Powys	SO0039	52°2·7'	3°27·1'W	X	160
Tynwern	Cered	SN5769	52°18·3'	4°5·4'W	X	135
Tynwtra	Powys	SH8505	52°38·1'	3°41·6'W	X	124,125
Ty'n-y-banadi	Powys	SO1196	52°33·5'	3°18·4'W	X	136
Tynybedw	Carm	SN7036	52°0·7'	3°53·3'W	X	146,160
Tyn-y-bedw	Conwy	SH9672	53°14·3'	3°33·1'W	X	116
Ty'n-y-berth	Cered	SN6663	52°15·2'	3°57·4'W	X	146
Ty'n-y-berth	Powys	SO0673	52°21·1'	3°22·4'W	X	136,147
Ty'n-y-bonau	Swan	SN5904	51°43·3'	4°2·1'W	X	159
Tyn-y-bont	Gwyn	SH8940	52°57·0'	3°38·7'W	X	124,125
Ty'n-y-braich	Conwy	SH9046	53°0·2'	3°38·0'W	X	116
Ty'n-y-braich	Gwyn	SH8315	52°43·4'	3°43·5'W	X	124,125
Ty'n-y-brŵyn	Newp	ST2683	51°32·7'	3°3·6'W	X	171
Ty'n-y-bryn	Conwy	SH8358	53°6·6'	3°44·5'W	X	116
Tyn-y-bryn	Conwy	SH8551	53°2·9'	3°42·5'W	X	116
Ty'n-y-bryn	Conwy	SJ0045	52°59·8'	3°29·0'W	X	116
Ty'n-y-bryn	Gwyn	SH6507	52°38·9'	3°59·3'W	X	124
Tyn-y-bryn	Powys	SJ0405	52°38·3'	3°24·7'W	X	125
Ty'n y Bryn	Powys	SO0997	52°34·0'	3°20·2'W	X	136
Ty'n-y-bryn	Rho Cyn Taf	ST0087	51°34·6'	3°26·2'W	T	170
Tynybryniau	Powys	SO1278	52°23·8'	3°17·2'W	X	136,148
Tynybryniau Hill	Powys	SO1378	52°23·8'	3°16·3'W	X	136,148
Tynybwlch	Gwyn	SH6234	52°53·4'	4°2·7'W	X	124
Ty'n-y-bwlch	Gwyn	SH8431	52°52·1'	3°43·0'W	X	124,125
Tyn-y-bwlch	Gwyn	SJ0042	52°58·2'	3°28·9'W	X	125
Tynybwlch	Powys	SJ1223	52°48·1'	3°17·9'W	X	125
Tyn-y-byrwydd	Powys	SJ1205	52°38·4'	3°17·6'W	X	125
Tyn-y-cablyd	Powys	SJ0126	52°49·6'	3°27·8'W	X	125
Tyn-y-cae	Powys	SJ1230	52°51·9'	3°18·0'W	X	125
Ty'n-y-caeau	Brig	SS8379	51°30·1'	3°40·8'W	X	170
Ty'n-y-caeau	Brig	SS8582	51°31·8'	3°39·1'W	X	170
Tyn-y-caeau	Conwy	SH8768	53°12·1'	3°41·1'W	X	116
Ty'n-y-caeau	Conwy	SH8864	53°9·9'	3°40·1'W	X	116
Ty'n-y-caeau	Conwy	SH9969	53°12·8'	3°30·3'W	X	116
Tyn-y-caeau	Denb	SJ0162	53°9·0'	3°28·4'W	X	116
Tyn-y-caeau	Denb	SJ0441	52°57·7'	3°25·4'W	X	125
Ty'n-y-caeau	Denb	SJ1059	53°7·5'	3°20·3'W	X	116
Ty'n-y-caeau	Denb	SJ1064	53°10·2'	3°20·4'W	X	116
Tyn-y-caeau	Denb	SJ1262	53°9·1'	3°18·6'W	X	116
Ty'n-y-caeau	Flint	SJ1081	53°19·3'	3°20·7'W	X	116
Ty'n-y-caeau	Flint	SJ1766	53°11·3'	3°14·1'W	X	116

Tyn-y-caeau	Flint	SJ2367	53°11·9′	3°8·8′W	X	117
Ty'n-y-caeau	Monm	SO3300	51°41·9′	2°57·8′W	X	171
Ty'n-y-caeau	Powys	SO0728	51°56·8′	3°20·8′W	X	160
Ty'n-y-caeau	V of Glam	SS9169	51°24·8′	3°33·7′W	X	170
Tyn-y-Caeau	V of Glam	SS9478	51°29·7′	3°31·2′W	X	170
Ty'n-y-caeau	V of Glam	ST0073	51°27·1′	3°26·0′W	X	170
Ty'n-y-caeau Hill	Monm	ST3598	51°40·9′	2°56·0′W	H	171
Ty'n y Caeu	Gwyn	SH5967	53°11·1′	4°6·2′W	X	114,115
Tynycaia	V of Glam	SS9472	51°26·5′	3°31·1′W	X	170
Tynycaia Fm	V of Glam	SS8975	51°28·0′	3°35·5′W	FM	170
Ty'n-y-castell	Cered	SN7277	52°22·8′	3°52·4′W	X	135,147
Ty'n-y-cefn	Denb	SJ0643	52°58·8′	3°23·6′W	X	125
Tyn-y-cefn	Gwyn	SH6943	52°58·3′	3°56·6′W	X	124
Ty'n-y-celyn	Denb	SJ0854	53°4·8′	3°22·0′W	X	116
Ty'n-y-celyn	Denb	SJ0956	53°5·9′	3°21·1′W	X	116
Ty'n-y-celyn	Denb	SJ1069	53°12·9′	3°20·5′W	X	116
Ty'n-y-celyn	Denb	SJ1456	53°5·9′	3°16·7′W	X	116
Tyn-y-Celyn	Denb	SJ1462	53°9·1′	3°16·8′W	X	116
Ty'n-y-celyn	Denb	SJ1548	53°1·6′	3°15·6′W	X	116
Ty'n-y-celyn	Gwyn	SH8415	52°43·5′	3°42·7′W	X	124,125
Ty'n-y-celyn	Gwyn	SH9338	52°56·0′	3°35·1′W	X	125
Tyn-y-celyn	Powys	SJ0828	52°50·7′	3°21·6′W	X	125
Ty'n-y-celyn	Powys	SJ1026	52°49·7′	3°19·7′W	X	125
Tyn-y-celyn	Powys	SJ1127	52°50·2′	3°18·9′W	X	125
Tyn-y-celyn	Powys	SJ1626	52°49·7′	3°14·4′W	X	125
Tyn-y-celyn	Wrex	SJ1737	52°55·7′	3°13·7′W	X	125
Ty'n-y-cerrig	Gwyn	SH8739	52°56·4′	3°40·5′W	X	124,125
Tynyceunant	Gwyn	SH6815	52°43·2′	3°56·9′W	X	124
Ty'n-y-clawdd	Gwyn	SH7517	52°44·4′	3°50·7′W	X	124
Tŷ'n-y-coed	Card	ST0882	51°32·0′	3°19·2′W	F	170
Tyn-y-coed	Carm	SN7737	52°1·3′	3°47·2′W	X	146,160
Ty'n-y-coed	Carm	SN8236	52°0·8′	3°42·8′W	X	160
Ty'n-y-coed	Cered	SN6148	52°7·0′	4°1·4′W	X	146
Tyn-y-coed	Conwy	SH7979	53°17·9′	3°48·5′W	X	115
Ty'n-y-coed	Conwy	SH8072	53°14·1′	3°47·5′W	X	116
Ty'n-y-coed	Denb	SJ0072	53°14·4′	3°29·5′W	X	116
Tyn-y-coed	Denb	SJ0336	52°55·0′	3°26·2′W	X	125
Ty'n-y-coed	Flint	SJ2569	53°13·0′	3°7·0′W	X	117
Tyn-y-coed	Gwyn	SH2331	52°51·1′	4°37·3′W	X	123
Ty'n-y-Coed	Gwyn	SH4250	53°1·7′	4°21·0′W	X	115,123
Ty'n-y-coed	Gwyn	SH8716	52°44·0′	3°40·0′W	X	124,125
Ty'n-y-Coed	Heref	SO4162	52°15·4′	2°51·5′W	X	137,148,149
Ty'n-y-Coed	I of Angl	SH3869	53°11·9′	4°25·1′W	X	114
Ty'n-y-Coed	I of Angl	SH4869	53°12·0′	4°16·1′W	X	114,115
Tyn-y-coed	Powys	SH8702	52°36·5′	3°39·7′W	X	135,136
Tyn-y-coed	Powys	SJ0603	52°37·2′	3°22·9′W	X	136
Ty'n-y-coed	Powys	SN9466	52°17·2′	3°32·8′W	X	136,147
Ty'n-y-coed	Powys	SO1354	52°10·9′	3°16·0′W	X	148
Ty'n-y-coed	Rho Cyn Taf	SS9884	51°33·0′	3°27·9′W	X	170
Ty'n-y-coed	Rho Cyn Taf	ST0186	51°34·1′	3°25·3′W	X	170
Ty'n-y-coed	Shrops	SJ2322	52°47·6′	3°8·1′W	X	126
Ty'n-y-coed	Shrops	SJ2324	52°48·7′	3°8·1′W	X	126
Tyn-y-coed	Shrops	SJ2528	52°50·9′	3°6·4′W	T	126
Ty'n-y-coed	V of Glam	ST0673	51°27·1′	3°20·8′W	X	170
Ty'n-y-coedcae	Caer	ST1988	51°35·3′	3°9·8′W	T	171
Ty'n-y-coed Fm	Denb	SJ0372	53°14·4′	3°26·8′W	FM	116
Tynycoed Fm	Powys	SN9548	52°7·5′	3°31·6′W	FM	147
Ty'n-y-cornel	Cered	SN7553	52°9·9′	3°49·3′W	X	146,147
Tyn-y-cornel	Gwyn	SH6307	52°38·9′	4°1·1′W	X	124
Tynycornel	Gwyn	SN6199	52°34·5′	4°2·7′W	X	135
Tyn-y-cornel Isaf	Gwyn	SH6907	52°38·9′	3°55·8′W	X	124
Ty'n-y-Cwm	Brig	SS9785	51°33·5′	3°28·8′W	X	170
Ty'n-y-cwm	Carm	SN4909	51°45·8′	4°10·9′W	X	159
Ty'n-y-cwm	Conwy	SH7349	53°1·6′	3°53·2′W	X	115
Tyn-y-cwm	Gwyn	SH9533	52°53·3′	3°33·2′W	X	125
Tyn-y-cwm	Powys	SO1583	52°26·5′	3°14·6′W	X	136
Tyn-y-cwm	Powys	SO2049	52°8·2′	3°9·7′W	X	148
Tyn-y-cwm	Swan	SN6302	51°42·2′	3°58·6′W	T	159
Ty'n-y-cyl	Powys	SJ0715	52°43·7′	3°22·2′W	X	125
Ty'n-y-cyll	Conwy	SH9069	53°12·6′	3°38·4′W	X	116
Ty'n-y-ddôl	Conwy	SH8963	53°9·4′	3°39·2′W	X	116
Ty'n-y-ddôl	Denb	SJ0245	52°59·8′	3°27·2′W	X	116
Tyn-y-ddôl	Denb	SJ0337	52°55·5′	3°26·2′W	X	125
Tyn-y-ddôl	Gwyn	SH6709	52°40·0′	3°57·6′W	X	124
Tyn-y-ddôl	Gwyn	SH9736	52°54·9′	3°31·5′W	X	125
Tynydrain	Shrops	SJ2432	52°53·0′	3°7·4′W	X	126
Tynyfach	Gwyn	SH6709	52°40·0′	3°57·6′W	X	124
Tynyfawnog	Powys	SJ0604	52°37·8′	3°22·9′W	X	136
Tynyfedw	Conwy	SH9566	53°11·1′	3°33·9′W	T	116
Tyn-y-fedw	Denb	SJ0341	52°57·7′	3°26·2′W	X	125
Ty'n-y-fedw	Gwyn	SH9026	52°49·5′	3°37·6′W	X	125
Tyn'y-fedw	Wrex	SJ1632	52°53·0′	3°14·5′W	X	125
Tyn-y-fedwen	Powys	SJ1031	52°52·4′	3°19·8′W	X	125
Ty'n-y-felin	I of Angl	SH2876	53°15·4′	4°34·3′W	X	114
Ty'n-y-ffnonydd	Powys	SJ0328	52°50·7′	3°26·0′W	X	125
Tynyffordd	Cered	SN7579	52°23·9′	3°49·8′W	X	135,147
Ty'n-y-ffordd	Conwy	SH8665	53°10·4′	3°41·9′W	X	116
Ty'n-y-ffordd	Denb	SJ0272	53°14·4′	3°27·7′W	T	116
Tynyffridd	Gwyn	SH5868	53°11·7′	4°7·1′W	X	114,115
Tynyffridd	Gwyn	SH5868	53°11·7′	4°7·1′W	X	114,115
Ty'n-y-ffridd	Gwyn	SH8938	52°55·9′	3°38·7′W	X	124,125
Tyn-y-ffridd	Gwyn	SH9739	52°56·6′	3°31·6′W	X	125
Tyn-y-ffridd	Powys	SJ1130	52°51·9′	3°18·9′W	X	125
Tyn-y-ffridd	Powys	SJ1627	52°50·3′	3°14·4′W	X	125
Ty'n-y-ffrîth	Conwy	SH7375	53°15·7′	3°53·8′W	X	115
Ty'n y-ffrith	Conwy	SH9270	53°13·2′	3°36·6′W	X	116
Ty'n-y-ffynnon	Cered	SN6587	52°28·1′	3°58·8′W	X	135
Ty'n-y-ffynnon	Conwy	SH8563	53°9·3′	3°42·8′W	X	116
Ty'n-y-ffynnon	Denb	SJ0160	53°7·9′	3°28·4′W	X	116
Ty'nyfron	Cered	SN5155	52°10·6′	4°10·4′W	X	146
Tyn-y-fron	Gwyn	SH9025	52°48·9′	3°37·5′W	X	125
Tyn-y-fron	Gwyn	SJ0142	52°58·2′	3°28·0′W	X	125
Tyn-y-fron	Powys	SJ1529	52°51·3′	3°15·3′W	X	125
Tynyfron	Powys	SJ2131	52°52·5′	3°10·0′W	X	126
Ty'n-y-garn	Brig	SS8982	51°31·8′	3°35·6′W	T	170
Ty'n-y-garreg	Conwy	SH8851	53°2·9′	3°39·8′W	X	116
Tynygarreg	Powys	SJ0120	52°46·4′	3°27·7′W	X	125
Tyn-y-garth	Cered	SN6994	52°31·9′	3°55·5′W	X	135
Ty'n-y-gilfach	Conwy	SH9450	53°2·5′	3°34·5′W	X	116
Tynygongl	I of Angl	SH5182	53°19·1′	4°13·8′W	T	114,115
Tyn-y-gors	Gwyn	SH3843	52°57·8′	4°24·3′W	X	123
Tynygraig	Cered	SN6969	52°18·5′	3°54·9′W	T	135
Ty'n-y-graig	Conwy	SH9251	53°3·0′	3°36·3′W	X	116
Tyn-y-graig	Denb	SJ0037	52°55·5′	3°28·9′W	X	125
Tyn-y-graig	Denb	SJ1541	52°57·8′	3°15·5′W	X	125
Tyn y Graig	Gwyn	SH2228	52°49·5′	4°38·1′W	X	123
Tyn-y-graig	Gwyn	SH6817	52°44·3′	3°56·9′W	X	124
Ty'n-y-graig	I of Angl	SH3379	53°17·1′	4°29·9′W	X	114
Tyn-y-graig	Powys	SJ1625	52°49·2′	3°14·4′W	X	125
Tyn-y-graig	Powys	SO0149	52°8·1′	3°26·4′W	X	147
Tynygraig Fm	Cered	SN6690	52°29·7′	3°58·0′W	FM	135
Ty'n-y-groes	Conwy	SH7771	53°13·6′	3°50·1′W	T	115
Tynygroes	Powys	SJ2031	52°52·5′	3°10·9′W	X	126
Tyn-y-groes	Wrex	SJ2639	52°56·8′	3°5·7′W	X	126
Ty'n-y-groesffordd	Denb	SJ1359	53°7·5′	3°17·6′W	X	116
Ty'n-y-groes Hotel	Gwyn	SH7223	52°47·6′	3°53·5′W	X	124
Ty'n y Llidiart	Conwy	SH8553	53°4·0′	3°42·6′W	X	116
Ty'n-y-llidiart	Denb	SJ1951	53°3·3′	3°12·1′W	X	116
Ty'n-y-llŵyn	Denb	SJ1058	53°6·9′	3°20·3′W	X	116
Ty'n y Llwyn	Gwyn	SH7121	52°46·5′	3°54·3′W	X	124
Tynyllwyn	Powys	SJ0606	52°38·9′	3°23·0′W	X	125
Tyn-y-llwyn	Powys	SJ0928	52°50·8′	3°20·7′W	X	125
Ty'n-y-llyn	Denb	SH9977	53°17·1′	3°30·5′W	X	116
Ty'n-y-lôn	Cered	SN4649	52°7·3′	4°14·6′W	X	146
Ty'n y-Maes	Conwy	SH8651	53°2·9′	3°41·6′W	X	116
Ty'n-y-maes	Gwyn	SH6363	53°9·0′	4°2·5′W	X	115
Ty'n-y-maes	Gwyn	SH7311	52°41·2′	3°52·3′W	X	124
Ty'n-y-maes	Gwyn	SH8618	52°45·1′	3°40·9′W	X	124,125
Tynymaes	Powys	SJ0418	52°45·3′	3°24·9′W	X	125
Tyn-y-maes	Powys	SJ1325	52°49·2′	3°17·1′W	X	125
Ty'n-y-maes	Powys	SN8645	52°5·7′	3°39·5′W	X	147
Tyn-y-Morfa	Flint	SJ1084	53°21·0′	3°20·7′W	X	116
Ty'n y Mynydd	Conwy	SH8455	53°5·0′	3°43·5′W	X	116
Ty'n-y-mynydd	Conwy	SH9748	53°1·4′	3°31·7′W	X	116
Tyn-y-mynydd	Denb	SJ0753	53°4·2′	3°22·9′W	X	116
Tynymynydd	Denb	SJ2252	53°3·8′	3°9·4′W	X	117
Tyn-y-mynydd	Gwyn	SH5360	53°7·3′	4°11·4′W	X	114,115
Ty'n-y-mynydd	I of Angl	SH5579	53°17·5′	4°10·1′W	X	114,115
Tyn-y-pant	Conwy	SH8553	53°4·0′	3°42·6′W	X	116
Ty'n-y-pant	Gwyn	SH8838	52°55·9′	3°39·6′W	X	124,125
Tyn-y-pant	Gwyn	SJ0036	52°55·0′	3°28·8′W	X	125
Tyn-y-pant	Powys	SJ1303	52°37·3′	3°16·7′W	X	136
Tynypant	Powys	SN8948	52°7·4′	3°36·9′W	X	147
Ty'n-y-pant	Powys	SN9952	52°9·7′	3°28·2′W	X	147
Tynypant	Powys	SO0875	52°22·2′	3°20·7′W	X	136,147
Tyn-y-parc	Cered	SN6287	52°28·1′	4°1·5′W	X	135
Tyn-y-parc	Gwyn	SH2429	52°50·0′	4°36·4′W	X	123
Tyn-y-Pistyll	Conwy	SH9845	52°59·8′	3°30·8′W	X	116
Tyn-y-Pistyll	Flint	SJ2074	53°15·7′	3°11·6′W	X	117
Tyn-y-pistyll	Powys	SJ1521	52°47·0′	3°15·2′W	X	125
Ty'n-y-pistyll	Wrex	SJ1736	52°55·1′	3°13·7′W	X	125
Ty'n-y-pwll	Denb	SJ0457	53°6·3′	3°25·6′W	X	116
Ty'n-y-pwll	Denb	SJ1751	53°3·2′	3°13·9′W	X	116
Tyn-y-pwll	Powys	SJ1206	52°38·9′	3°17·6′W	X	125
Ty'n-y-pwll	V of Glam	ST0675	51°28·2′	3°20·8′W	X	170
Ty'n-yr-acrau	Gwyn	SH5833	52°52·8′	4°6·2′W	X	124
Tynyraelgerth	Gwyn	SH5758	53°6·2′	4°7·8′W	X	115
Ty'n-yr-eithin	Cered	SN6662	52°14·6′	3°57·4′W	X	146
Tynyreithin	Powys	SN9396	52°33·3′	3°34·3′W	X	136
Tynyreithin Hall	Powys	SO1093	52°31·9′	3°19·2′W	X	136
Ty'n-y-rhedyn	Powys	SJ0823	52°48·0′	3°21·5′W	X	125
Ty'n-yr-helyg	Cered	SN6088	52°28·6′	4°3·3′W	X	135
Ty'n-yr-hendre	Gwyn	SH6271	53°13·3′	4°3·6′W	X	115
Tynyrhos	Cered	SN5753	52°9·6′	4°5·0′W	X	146
Tyn-y-rhos	Conwy	SH8947	53°0·8′	3°38·9′W	X	116
Ty'n-y-rhos	Denb	SJ0745	52°59·9′	3°22·7′W	X	116
Tyn-y-rhos	Denb	SJ1548	53°1·6′	3°15·6′W	X	116
Tyn-y-rhos	Gwyn	SH8736	52°54·8′	3°40·4′W	X	124,125
Ty'n-y-rhôs	I of Angl	SH3787	53°21·5′	4°26·6′W	X	114
Ty'n-y-rhôs	I of Angl	SH4677	53°16·3′	4°18·2′W	X	114,115
Tyn-y-rhos	Powys	SJ1819	52°46·0′	3°12·5′W	X	125
Tyn-y-rhos	Powys	SJ1825	52°49·2′	3°12·6′W	X	125
Ty'n-y-rhos	Powys	SN8781	52°25·2′	3°39·3′W	X	135,136
Tyn-y-Rhos	Shrops	SJ2736	52°55·2′	3°4·7′W	X	126
Ty'n-y-rhŷd	Cered	SN7276	52°22·3′	3°52·4′W	X	135,147
Tyn-y-rhyd	Powys	SJ0711	52°41·6′	3°22·2′W	X	125
Tyn-y-rhyd	Wrex	SJ2334	52°54·1′	3°8·3′W	X	126
Tynyronen	I of Angl	SH4379	53°17·3′	4°20·9′W	X	114,115
Tynyrwtra	Powys	SJ0517	52°44·8′	3°24·0′W	X	125
Tynyrwtra	Powys	SN8885	52°27·3′	3°38·5′W	T	135,136
Tyn yr ynn	Powys	SO1576	52°22·8′	3°14·5′W	X	136,148
Ty'n-y-sarn	Gwyn	SH8837	52°55·4′	3°39·6′W	X	124,125
Ty'n-y-sŵydd	Cered	SN6662	52°14·6′	3°57·4′W	X	146
Tynytranch Fm	V of Glam	ST0079	51°30·3′	3°26·1′W	FM	170
Ty'n-y-twll	Gwyn	SH8518	52°45·1′	3°41·8′W	X	124,125
Ty'n-y-twll	Powys	SJ0312	52°42·1′	3°25·7′W	X	125
Ty'n-y-waen	Conwy	SH9150	53°2·4′	3°37·1′W	X	116
Tynywain	Powys	SO1668	52°18·5′	3°13·5′W	X	136,148
Ty'n-y-waun	Brig	SS8688	51°35·0′	3°38·3′W	X	170
Tyn-y-waun	Brig	SS9585	51°33·5′	3°30·5′W	X	170
Ty'n-y-waun	Carm	SN5222	51°52·9′	4°8·6′W	X	159
Tynywaun	Carm	SN5704	51°43·2′	4°3·8′W	X	159
Tynywaun	Carm	SN6820	51°52·0′	3°54·6′W	X	159
Ty'n-y-waun	Carm	SN7640	52°2·9′	3°48·1′W	X	146,147,160
Ty'n-y-waun	Powys	SN9467	52°17·7′	3°32·9′W	X	136,147
Ty'n-y-waun	Powys	SO0347	52°7·0′	3°24·6′W	X	147
Ty'n-y-waun	Powys	SO0783	52°26·5′	3°21·7′W	X	136
Ty'n-y-waun	Rho Cyn Taf	ST0181	51°31·4′	3°25·2′W	X	170
Tynywern	Cered	SN6078	52°23·2′	4°3·0′W	X	135
Tyn-y-wern	Denb	SJ0337	52°55·5′	3°26·2′W	X	125
Tyn-y-wern	Denb	SJ0344	52°59·3′	3°26·3′W	X	125
Tyn-y-wern	Denb	SJ0441	52°57·7′	3°25·4′W	X	125
Ty'n-y-wern	Denb	SJ1256	53°5·9′	3°18·5′W	X	116
Ty'n-y-wern	Denb	SJ1446	53°0·5′	3°16·5′W	X	116
Ty'n-y-wern	Powys	SH8507	52°39·2′	3°41·6′W	X	124,125
Tyn-y-wern	Powys	SJ0828	52°50·7′	3°21·6′W	X	125
Ty'n-y-wern	Powys	SN9942	52°4·3′	3°28·0′W	X	147,160
Ty'n-y-wern	Rho Cyn Taf	ST0694	51°38·5′	3°21·1′W	X	170
Tŷ-obry	Gwyn	SH6039	52°56·1′	4°4·6′W	X	124
Type Knowes	D & G	NT0409	55°22·2′	3°30·5′W	X	78
Type Knowes	S Lanak	NS9806	55°20·5′	3°36·1′W	H	78
Ty Pella	Powys	SH8802	52°36·5′	3°38·8′W	X	135,136
Ty Pellaf	Gwyn	SH1121	52°45·5′	4°47·7′W	X	123
Ty Pengam	Monm	SO3406	51°45·2′	2°57·0′W	X	161
Typica Fm	Brig	SS9285	51°33·5′	3°33·1′W	FM	170
Typicca	Carm	SN5420	51°51·8′	4°6·8′W	X	159
Typoeth	Cered	SN2644	52°4·3′	4°31·9′W	X	145
Typoeth	Powys	SH8406	52°38·6′	3°42·5′W	X	124,125
Ty-poeth Fm	Torf	SO3001	51°42·4′	3°0·4′W	FM	171
Ty'r Abby	Cered	SN6084	52°26·4′	4°3·2′W	X	135
Ty-Rachel	Powys	SO1818	51°51·5′	3°11·1′W	X	161
Ty'r-ali	Denb	SJ0875	53°16·1′	3°22·4′W	X	116
Ty-rarlwydd	Rho Cyn Taf	ST0687	51°34·7′	3°21·0′W	X	170
Tyrau Wood	Nth Pt Talb	SN8403	51°43·1′	3°40·4′W	F	170
Tŷ'r-bont	Gwyn	SH6138	52°55·5′	4°3·7′W	X	124
Ty'r Dewin	Gwyn	SH4645	52°59·1′	4°17·2′W	X	115,123
Tyrebagger	C of Aber	NJ8411	57°11·6′	2°15·4′W	X	38
Tyrebagger Hill	C of Aber	NJ8412	57°12·2′	2°15·4′W	H	38
Tyreglwys Fm	Carm	SN5503	51°42·7′	4°5·5′W	FM	159
Tyre Hill	Worcs	SO8041	52°4·3′	2°17·1′W	X	150
Tyrellcote Fm	Bucks	SP7634	52°0·2′	0°53·2′W	FM	152,165
Tyrells End	Beds	SP9833	51°59·4′	0°34·0′W	T	165
Tyrell's Wood	Surrey	TQ1855	51°17·1′	0°18·1′W	T	187
Tyrer Fm	Lancs	SD4647	53°55·2′	2°48·9′W	FM	102
Tyrewen Fm	Monm	SO2715	51°50·0′	3°3·2′W	FM	161
Tŷ'r-felin-isaf	Conwy	SH8863	53°9·4′	3°40·1′W	T	116
Ty'r Gate	Carm	SN2915	51°48·7′	4°28·4′W	X	159
Ty'rgawen	Gwyn	SH6206	52°38·3′	4°2·0′W	X	124
Tyrgof	Swan	SN6005	51°43·8′	4°1·2′W	X	159
Ty'r Heol	Carm	SN4517	51°50·0′	4°14·6′W	X	159
Tyrheol	Carm	SN6534	51°59·5′	3°57·6′W	X	146
Tyrhester	Swan	SS6294	51°37·9′	3°59·2′W	X	159
Ty Rhiw	Rho Cyn Taf	ST1283	51°32·6′	3°15·8′W	T	171
Tyrhos	Carm	SN3725	51°54·2′	4°21·8′W	X	145
Ty-rhôs	Cered	SN3759	52°12·6′	4°22·7′W	X	145
Tyrhos	Pemb	SN1940	52°2·0′	4°37·9′W	X	145
Ty-rhŷg	Pemb	SN0429	51°55·7′	4°50·7′W	X	145,157,158
Tyrie	Aberd	NJ9262	57°39·1′	2°7·6′W	T	30
Tyrie	Fife	NT2789	56°5·5′	3°10·0′W	X	66
Tyrie Mains	Aberd	NJ9363	57°39·7′	2°6·6′W	X	30
Tyries	Aberd	NJ4618	57°15·2′	2°53·2′W	X	37
Tyringham	Mil Key	SP8547	52°7·1′	0°45·1′W	T	152
Tyringham Hall	Mil Key	SP8547	52°7·1′	0°45·1′W	X	152
Tyrley Castle Fm	Shrops	SJ6733	52°53·8′	2°29·0′W	FM	127
Tyrley Locks	Staffs	SJ6832	52°53·3′	2°28·1′W	X	127
Tyrmynydd	Carm	SN5208	51°45·3′	4°8·3′W	X	159
Ty'r-mynydd	V of Glam	ST0276	51°28·7′	3°24·3′W	X	170
Tyrnest	Carm	SN4016	51°49·4′	4°18·9′W	X	159
Tyronhill	Aberd	NJ9964	57°40·2′	2°0·5′W	X	30
Tyrosser	Powys	SN9453	52°10·1′	3°32·6′W	X	147
Ty'r-pâb	Carm	SN5625	51°54·5′	4°5·2′W	X	146
Tyrpark	Carm	SN3629	51°56·4′	4°22·8′W	X	145
Tyrrau Mawr	Gwyn	SH6713	52°42·1′	3°57·7′W	X	124
Tyrrells	Essex	TQ6698	51°39·6′	0°24·4′E	X	167,177
Tyrrell's Ford (Hotel)	Hants	SZ1499	50°47·7′	1°47·7′W	X	195
Tyr Sais Fm	Caer	SO1800	51°41·8′	3°10·8′W	FM	171
Tyruched	Powys	SO1839	52°2·8′	3°11·4′W	X	161
Tyrwhitt Ho	Surrey	TQ1558	51°18·8′	0°20·6′W	X	187
Ty'r Yet	Cered	SN1850	52°7·3′	4°39·1′W	X	145
Tyryet	Pemb	SN0233	51°57·9′	4°52·5′W	X	145,157
Tyseahill Fm	Essex	TQ5195	51°38·2′	0°11·3′E	FM	167,177
Tysegur	Powys	SN9651	52°9·1′	3°30·8′W	X	147
Tyseley	Birm	SP1184	52°27·5′	1°49·9′W	T	139
Ty-Sheriff	Powys	SO1518	51°51·5′	3°13·7′W	X	161
Ty-Sign	Caer	ST2490	51°36·5′	3°5·5′W	T	171
Tysoe Hill	Warw	SP3443	52°5·3′	1°29·8′W	X	151
Tysoe Vale Fm	Warw	SP3446	52°6·9′	1°29·8′W	FM	151
Tytandderwen	Conwy	SH9943	52°58·7′	3°29·9′W	X	125
Tŷ-tan-derw	Denb	SJ1447	53°1·0′	3°16·5′W	X	116
Ty Tanglwyst Fm	Brig	SS8280	51°30·6′	3°41·6′W	FM	170
Ty-tan-y-dderwen	Powys	SJ1617	52°44·9′	3°14·3′W	X	125
Ty-tan-y-ffordd	Conwy	SH9942	52°58·2′	3°29·8′W	X	125
Ty-tan-y-graig	Conwy	SH9449	53°1·9′	3°34·4′W	X	116
Tŷ-tan-y-graig	Gwyn	SH9635	52°54·4′	3°32·4′W	X	125
Tyte Fm, The	Shrops	SO7798	52°35·0′	2°20·0′W	FM	138
Tythby Grange	Notts	SK7137	52°55·8′	0°56·2′W	X	129
Tythebarns Fm	Surrey	TQ0454	51°16·8′	0°30·1′W	FM	186
Tythecott	Devon	SS4117	50°56·1′	4°15·4′W	T	180,190
Tythe Fm	Beds	TL0047	52°7·0′	0°32·0′W	FM	153
Tythe Fm	E Yorks	TA0656	53°59·6′	0°22·6′W	FM	107
Tythe Fm	Norf	TF8322	52°46·1′	0°43·2′E	FM	132
Tythe Fm	Warw	SP4881	52°25·7′	1°17·2′W	FM	140
Tythegston	Brig	SS8578	51°29·6′	3°39·0′W	T	170
Tythehouse	Scot Bord	NT5708	55°22·1′	2°40·3′W	X	80
Tytherington	Ches	SJ9175	53°16·6′	2°7·7′W	T	118
Tytherington	S Glos	ST6788	51°35·6′	2°28·2′W	T	162,172
Tytherington	Somer	ST7645	51°12·5′	2°20·2′W	T	183
Tytherington	Wilts	ST9141	51°10·3′	2°7·3′W	T	184
Tytherington Hill	S Glos	ST6788	51°35·6′	2°28·2′W	X	162,172
Tytherington Hill	Wilts	ST9139	51°9·2′	2°7·3′W	X	184
Tytherleigh	Devon	ST3103	50°49·6′	2°58·4′W	T	193
Tytherley Common	Hants	SU2628	51°3·3′	1°37·4′W	F	184
Tytherley Fm	Bath & NE Somer	ST7658	51°19·5′	2°20·3′W	FM	172
Tytherton Lucas	Wilts	ST9474	51°28·1′	2°4·8′W	T	173
Tythorn Hill	Leic	SP6296	52°33·7′	1°4·7′W	X	140
Tythrop Ho	Bucks	SP7307	51°45·6′	0°56·1′W	X	165
Tyting Fm	Surrey	TQ0248	51°13·6′	0°32·0′W	FM	186
Ty-tomaen	Monm	SO3007	51°45·7′	3°0·5′W	X	161
Ty-to-maen Fm	Card	ST2378	51°30·0′	3°6·2′W	FM	171
Tyttenhanger	Herts	TL1805	51°44·1′	0°17·1′W	T	166
Tyttenhanger Fm	Herts	TL1905	51°44·1′	0°16·2′W	FM	166
Tyttenhanger Park	Herts	TL1904	51°43·6′	0°16·2′W	A	166
Tytton Hall	Lincs	TF3241	52°57·2′	0°1·7′W	X	131
Tytup Hall	Cumbr	SD2375	54°10·1′	3°10·4′W	X	96
Tytywyrch	Denb	SJ0077	53°17·1′	3°29·6′W	X	116
Tŷ Ucha	Conwy	SH7471	53°13·5′	3°52·8′W	X	115
Ty Ucha	Conwy	SH9948	53°1·4′	3°29·9′W	X	116
Ty-ucha	Denb	SJ2341	52°57·9′	3°8·4′W	X	117
Ty Ucha	Gwyn	SH8629	52°51·0′	3°41·2′W	X	124,125

Tŷ-uchaf	Conwy	SH8171	53°13·6′	3°46·6′W	X	116
Ty Uchaf	Conwy	SH8350	53°2·3′	3°44·3′W	X	116
Ty-uchaf	Conwy	SH9065	53°10·5′	3°38·3′W	X	116
Tŷ-uchaf	Conwy	SH9853	53°4·1′	3°30·9′W	X	116
Ty-uchaf	Denb	SJ0438	52°56·1′	3°25·3′W	X	125
Ty-uchaf	Denb	SJ2152	53°3·8′	3°10·3′W	X	117
Ty-uchaf	Flint	SJ1867	53°11·9′	3°13·2′W	X	116
Ty Uchaf	Flint	SJ2856	53°6·0′	3°4·1′W	X	117
Ty Uchaf	Gwyn	SH4659	53°6·6′	4°17·6′W	X	115,123
Tŷ-uchaf	Gwyn	SH9739	52°56·6′	3°31·6′W	X	125
Tyuchaf	Heref	SO2839	52°2·9′	3°2·6′W	X	161
Ty-uchaf	Monm	SO2214	51°49·4′	3°7·5′W	X	161
Ty Uchaf	Monm	SO3108	51°46·2′	2°59·6′W	X	161
Ty-uchaf	Powys	SH8802	52°36·5′	3°38·8′W	X	135,136
Tŷ-uchaf	Powys	SH9921	52°46·9′	3°29·4′W	X	125
Ty-uchaf	Powys	SJ1717	52°44·9′	3°13·4′W	X	125
Tŷ-uchaf	Powys	SJ2231	52°52·5′	3°9·1′W	X	126
Ty-uchaf	Powys	SN9144	52°5·3′	3°35·1′W	X	147,160
Tŷ-uchaf	Powys	SO0199	52°35·0′	3°27·3′W	X	136
Ty-uchaf	Powys	SO1825	51°55·3′	3°11·2′W	X	161
Tyuchaf	Rho Cyn Taf	ST0783	51°32·5′	3°20·1′W	X	170
Ty-Uchaf	Wrex	SJ1636	52°55·1′	3°14·6′W	X	125
Ty Uchaf	Wrex	SJ1834	52°54·1′	3°12·7′W	X	125
Ty-Uchaf-Cwm	Swan	SN6805	51°43·9′	3°54·3′W	X	159
Ty-uchaf Fm	V of Glam	ST0473	51°27·1′	3°22·5′W	FM	170
Ty-Ucha Fm	Denb	SJ0575	53°16·1′	3°25·1′W	FM	116
Ty-Ucha Fm	Gwyn	SH9534	52°53·8′	3°33·3′W	FM	125
Ty-ucha'r-llyn	Denb	SJ0748	53°1·5′	3°22·8′W	X	116
Tywardreath	Corn	SX0854	50°21·5′	4°41·6′W	T	200
Tywardreath Highway	Corn	SX0755	50°22·0′	4°42·5′W	T	200
Ty Wian	I of Angl	SH3291	53°23·6′	4°31·2′W	X	114
Tywi Fechan	Cered	SN7861	52°14·3′	3°46·8′W	W	146,147
Tywi Forest	Powys	SN8151	52°8·9′	3°44·0′W	F	147
Ty-Wilson	Monm	ST4199	51°41·4′	2°50·8′W	X	171
Tywyllnodwydd	Gwyn	SH7102	52°36·3′	3°53·9′W	X	135
Tywyn	Conwy	SH7878	53°17·3′	3°49·4′W	T	115
Tywyn	Gwyn	SH5800	52°35·0′	4°5·4′W	T	135
Tywyn Aberffraw	I of Angl	SH3668	53°11·3′	4°26·9′W	X	114
Tywyn Fferam	I of Angl	SH3371	53°12·8′	4°29·7′W	X	114
Tywyn Hir	I of Angl	SH2884	53°19·7′	4°34·6′W	X	114
Tywyn Llyn	I of Angl	SH3272	53°13·4′	4°30·6′W	X	114
Tywyn or The Burrows	Pemb	SM7326	51°53·4′	5°17·5′W	X	157
Tywyn Point	Carm	SN3506	51°43·9′	4°23·0′W	X	159
Tywyn Trewan Common (Cyttir Tywyn Trewan)	I of Angl	SH3275	53°15·0′	4°30·7′W	X	114
Tywysog	Conwy	SJ0066	53°11·1′	3°29·4′W	X	116
Ty-yr-heol	Rho Cyn Taf	ST0287	51°34·6′	3°24·5′W	X	170

U

Uabhal Beag	N Eil	NG1395	57°51·4′	6°49·8′W	X	14
Uabhal Mòr	N Eil	NG1296	57°51·9′	6°50·9′W	H	14
Uachdar	N Eil	NF8055	57°28·6′	7°19·9′W	T	22
Uags	Highld	NG7234	57°20·6′	5°46·9′W	X	24
Uaigh Dhiarmaid	Highld	NC5851	58°25·7′	4°25·4′W	X	10
Uair, The	Highld	NC8254	58°27·8′	4°0·9′W	W	10
Uamascleit	N Eil	NG1399	57°53·6′	6°50·1′W	H	14
Uamh	N Eil	NG0584	57°45·2′	6°57·1′W	X	18
Uamh a' Choilich	Highld	NM8347	56°34·1′	5°31·5′W	X	49
Uamha na Creadha	Highld	NM5262	56°41·3′	6°2·5′W	F	47
Uamh an Dùnain	Arg & Bt	NM5621	56°19·4′	5°56·3′W	X	48
Uamhannan Donna	Arg & Bt	NR3676	55°54·5′	6°13·0′W	X	60,61
Uamh an Tartair	Highld	NC2109	58°2·3′	5°1·5′W	X	15
Uamh a' Phrionnsa	N Eil	NF8331	57°15·8′	7°15·1′W	X	22
Uamha Thuill	Arg & Bt	NM8026	56°22·8′	5°33·4′W	X	49
Uamh Bheag	Stir	NN6911	56°16·7′	4°6·5′W	H	57
Uamh Bhiogadail	N Eil	NB1511	58°0·1′	6°49·0′W	X	13,14
Uamh Bhreacain	Arg & Bt	NM6800	56°8·4′	5°43·6′W	X	55,61
Uamh Capuill	Arg & Bt	NS0952	55°43·7′	5°2·1′W	X	63,69
Uamh Chaol	Highld	NC8368	58°35·3′	4°0·3′W	X	10
Uamh Chluanaidh or Cluny's Cave	Highld	NN6796	57°2·4′	4°11·1′W	X	35
Uamh Fhliuch	Arg & Bt	NM8029	56°24·4′	5°33·5′W	X	49
Uamh Fhraing	Highld	NG4783	56°52·4′	6°8·7′W	X	39
Uamh Liath	Arg & Bt	NM5019	56°18·1′	6°2·0′W	X	48
Uamh Mhòr	Highld	NG6051	57°29·4′	5°59·8′W	X	24
Uamh Mhòr	Stir	NN6811	56°16·6′	4°7·5′W	X	57
Uamh nan Calman	Arg & Bt	NM8029	56°24·4′	5°33·5′W	X	49
Uamh nan Calmon	Arg & Bt	NM4029	56°23·2′	6°12·3′W	X	48
Uamh nan Daoine	Highld	NG5851	57°29·3′	6°1·8′W	X	24
Uamh na Nighinn	Arg & Bt	NM7429	56°24·2′	5°39·3′W	X	49
Uamh nan Tàillearan	Arg & Bt	NM5823	56°20·5′	5°54·5′W	X	48
Uamh Oir	Highld	NG3771	57°39·4′	6°24·1′W	X	23
Uamh Ròn	Highld	ND1730	58°15·3′	3°24·4′W	X	11
Uamh Ropa (cave)	Arg & Bt	NR5915	55°22·4′	5°47·8′W	X	68
Uamh Ruaidhridh	Highld	NC2333	58°15·3′	5°0·5′W	X	15
Uamh Showhairle (Cave)	Highld	NN1668	56°46·3′	5°0·2′W	X	41
Uamh Tarskavaig	Highld	NG5811	57°7·8′	5°59·5′W	X	32
Uamh Tom a' Mhòr-fhir	Pth & Kin	NN7053	56°39·3′	4°6·8′W	X	42,51,52
Uasaig River	N Eil	NB0933	58°11·7′	6°56·7′W	W	13
Uath Lochan	Highld	NH8301	57°5·4′	3°55·4′W	W	35
Ubberley	C of Stoke	SJ9146	53°0·9′	2°7·6′W	T	118
Ubbeston	Suff	TM3272	52°18·0′	1°24·6′E	X	156
Ubbeston Green	Suff	TM3272	52°18·0′	1°24·6′E	X	156
Ubley	Bath & NE Somer	ST5258	51°19·4′	2°40·9′W	T	172,182
Ubley Drove Fm	Somer	ST5156	51°18·3′	2°41·8′W	FM	172,182
Ubley Park Ho	Bath & NE Somer	ST5359	51°19·9′	2°40·1′W	X	172,182
Ubley Warren Fm	Somer	ST5155	51°17·8′	2°41·8′W	FM	172,182

Uchd a' Chlàrsair	Pth & Kin	NN8181	56°54·6′	3°56·8′W	H	43
Uchd Mór	Highld	NG3833	57°19·0′	6°20·6′W	H	32
Uchd na Féithe-seileach	Highld	NH0969	57°40·5′	5°11·7′W	X	19
Uchd na h-Anaile	Pth & Kin	NO0866	56°46·8′	3°29·9′W	X	43
Uchd nan Carn	Pth & Kin	NO0967	56°47·4′	3°28·9′W	H	43
Ucheldre	Gwyn	SH9144	52°59·2′	3°37·0′W	X	125
Ucheldre	Powys	SO1398	52°34·6′	3°16·6′W	X	136
Ucheldref	Denb	SJ0445	52°59·9′	3°25·4′W	X	116
Ucheldref	I of Angl	SH5577	53°16·5′	4°10·1′W	X	114,115
Ucheldref Goed	I of Angl	SH3487	53°21·5′	4°29·3′W	X	114
Ucheldref Uchaf	I of Angl	SH3487	53°21·5′	4°29·3′W	X	114
Uchtubeg	Highld	NJ0431	57°21·8′	3°35·3′W	X	27,36
Uchtugorm	Highld	NJ0332	57°22·3′	3°36·3′W	X	27,36
Uckerby	N Yks	NZ2402	54°25·0′	1°37·4′W	T	93
Uckerby Fox Covert	N Yks	NZ2603	54°25·5′	1°35·5′W	F	93
Uckerby Mill	N Yks	NZ2402	54°25·0′	1°37·4′W	X	93
Uckfield	E Susx	TQ4721	50°58·4′	0°6·0′E	T	198
Uckinghall	Worcs	SO8638	52°2·6′	2°11·9′W	T	150
Uckington	Glos	SO9124	51°55·1′	2°7·5′W	T	163
Uckington	Shrops	SJ5709	52°40·9′	2°37·8′W	T	126
Udairn	Highld	NG5142	57°24·3′	6°8·3′W	X	23,24
Udal	N Eil	NF8277	57°40·5′	7°19·6′W	X	18
Udale Bay	Highld	NH7166	57°40·2′	4°9·3′W	W	21,27
Udale Beck	Lancs	SD5660	54°2·3′	2°39·9′W	W	97
Udale Fm	Highld	NH7264	57°39·1′	4°8·2′W	FM	21,27
Uddens Plantn	Dorset	SU0501	50°48·7′	1°55·4′W	F	195
Uddens Water	Dorset	SU0602	50°49·3′	1°54·5′W	W	195
Uddingston	S Lanak	NS6960	55°49·2′	4°5·0′W	T	64
Uddington	S Lanak	NS8633	55°34·9′	3°48·1′W	T	71,72
Udford	Cumbr	NY5730	54°40·0′	2°39·6′W	X	91
Udford Ho	Cumbr	NY5730	54°40·0′	2°39·6′W	X	91
Udiam	E Susx	TQ7724	50°59·5′	0°31·7′E	X	199
Udimore	E Susx	TQ8618	50°56·1′	0°39·2′E	T	189,199
Udley	N Som	ST4663	51°22·0′	2°46·2′W	T	172,182
Udlington	Shrops	SJ4514	52°43·5′	2°48·5′W	X	126
Udny Castle	Aberd	NJ8826	57°19·7′	2°11·5′W	A	38
Udny Green	Aberd	NJ8826	57°19·7′	2°11·5′W	T	38
Udny Links	Aberd	NK0025	57°19·2′	1°59·5′W	X	38
Udny Station	Aberd	NJ9024	57°18·6′	2°9·5′W	T	38
Udraclete	N Eil	NA1505	57°52·4′	8°29·3′W	X	18
Udrigle	Highld	NG8993	57°52·9′	5°33·1′W	X	19
Udston	S Lanak	NS6955	55°46·5′	4°4·9′W	T	64
Udston	S Lanak	NS7545	55°41·2′	3°58·9′W	X	64
Udstonhead	S Lanak	NS7046	55°41·7′	4°3·7′W	T	64
Uffcott	Wilts	SU1277	51°29·7′	1°49·2′W	T	173
Uffcott Down	Wilts	SU1376	51°29·2′	1°48·4′W	X	173
Uffculme	Devon	ST0612	50°54·2′	3°19·8′W	T	181
Uffington	Lincs	TF0607	52°39·3′	0°25·6′W	T	142
Uffington	Oxon	SU3089	51°36·2′	1°33·6′W	T	174
Uffington	Shrops	SJ5213	52°43·0′	2°42·2′W	T	126
Uffington Castle	Oxon	SU2986	51°34·6′	1°34·5′W	X	174
Uffington Castle (Fort)	Oxon	SU2986	51°34·6′	1°34·5′W	A	174
Uffington Court	Kent	TR2454	51°14·7′	1°13·0′E	X	179,189
Uffington Down	Oxon	SU3085	51°33·4′	1°33·6′W	X	174
Uffington Park	Lincs	TF0607	52°39·3′	0°25·6′W	X	142
Uffmoor Fm	Dudley	SO9581	52°25·9′	2°4·0′W	FM	139
Uffmoor Wood	Worcs	SO9581	52°25·9′	2°4·0′W	F	139
Ufford	Peterb	TF0904	52°37·6′	0°23·0′W	T	142
Ufford	Suff	TM2952	52°7·4′	1°21·1′E	T	156
Ufford Hall	Suff	TM2774	52°19·2′	1°20·3′E	X	156
Uffords	Herts	TL4318	51°50·8′	0°5·0′E	X	167
Ufford Thicks	Suff	TM2853	52°7·9′	1°20·3′E	F	156
Ufnell Bridge	Worcs	SO9347	52°7·5′	2°5·7′W	X	150
Ufshins	Shetld	HT9438	60°7·9′	2°6·0′W	X	4
Ufton	Warw	SP3762	52°15·5′	1°27·1′W	T	151
Ufton Br	W Berks	SU6168	51°24·7′	1°7·0′W	X	175
Ufton Court	Heref	SO5435	52°0·9′	2°39·8′W	X	149
Ufton Court	W Berks	SU6266	51°23·6′	1°6·1′W	A	175
Ufton Cross Roads	Warw	SP3861	52°15·0′	1°26·2′W	X	151
Ufton Fields	Derby	SK3955	53°5·7′	1°24·6′W	X	119
Ufton Fields Fm	Derby	SK3956	53°6·2′	1°24·6′W	FM	119
Ufton Green	W Berks	SU6268	51°24·7′	1°6·1′W	T	175
Ufton Hill Fm	Warw	SP3861	52°15·0′	1°26·2′W	FM	151
Ufton Nervet	W Berks	SU6367	51°24·1′	1°5·3′W	T	175
Ufton Wood	Warw	SP3862	52°15·5′	1°26·2′W	F	151
Ufton Wood	W Berks	SU6170	51°25·8′	1°7·0′W	F	175
Ugadale	Arg & Bt	NR7728	55°30·0′	5°31·4′W	X	68,69
Ugadale Point	Arg & Bt	NR7828	55°30·0′	5°30·5′W	X	68,69
Ugag	Arg & Bt	NM4054	56°36·6′	6°13·8′W	W	47
Ugasta	Shetld	HU5792	60°36·7′	0°57·0′W	X	1,2
Ugborough	Devon	SX6755	50°23·0′	3°51·9′W	T	202
Ugborough Beacon	Devon	SX6659	50°25·2′	3°52·8′W	H	202
Ugborough Moor	Devon	SX6562	50°26·8′	3°53·7′W	X	202
Ugbrooke Ho	Devon	SX8778	50°35·7′	3°35·4′W	X	192
Ugford	Wilts	SU0831	51°4·9′	1°52·8′W	T	184
Uggaton Fm	Devon	ST0903	50°49·4′	3°17·1′W	FM	192
Uggeshall	Suff	TM4480	52°22·0′	1°35·5′E	T	156
Uggeshall Hall	Suff	TM4581	52°22·6′	1°36·4′E	X	156
Ugglebarnby	N Yks	NZ8807	54°27·3′	0°38·1′W	T	94
Ugglebarnby Moor	N Yks	NZ8805	54°26·2′	0°38·2′W	X	94
Ugg Mere	Cambs	TL2486	52°27·7′	0°10·1′W	X	142
Ughill	Sheff	SK2590	53°24·6′	1°37·0′W	T	110
Ughill Moors	Sheff	SK2389	53°24·1′	1°38·8′W	X	110
Ugiebrae	Aberd	NJ9256	57°35·9′	2°7·6′W	X	30
Ugley	Essex	TL5228	51°56·0′	0°13·1′E	T	167
Ugley Green	Essex	TL5227	51°55·5′	0°13·0′E	T	167
Ugly Grain	Scot Bord	NT1827	55°32·0′	3°17·5′W	W	72
Ugston	E Loth	NT4974	55°57·6′	2°48·6′W	X	66
Ugthorpe	N Yks	NZ7911	54°29·5′	0°46·4′W	T	94
Ugthorpe Grange	N Yks	NZ7909	54°28·5′	0°46·4′W	X	94
Ugthorpe Lodge	N Yks	NZ7811	54°29·5′	0°47·3′W	X	94
Ugthorpe Moor	N Yks	NZ7710	54°29·0′	0°48·3′W	X	94
Ugworthy Barrows	Devon	SS3207	50°50·5′	4°22·8′W	A	190
Ugworthy Barton	Devon	SS3207	50°50·5′	4°22·8′W	X	190
Uidh	N Eil	NL6595	56°55·8′	7°30·0′W	T	31
Uidh an Leothaidh	Highld	NC1828	58°12·5′	5°5·4′W	W	15
Uidh an Tuim	Highld	NC2948	58°23·5′	4°55·1′W	W	9
Uidh Fhearna	Highld	NC1415	58°5·4′	5°8·8′W	W	15
Uidh Loch na Gaineimh	Highld	NC7331	58°15·2′	4°9·4′W	W	16
Uidh nan Con Luatha	Highld	NC8459	58°30·5′	3°59·0′W	W	10

Uidh Rabhain	Highld	NC7557	58°29·3′	4°8·2′W	W	10
Uig	Arg & Bt	NM1654	56°35·8′	6°37·2′W	T	46
Uig	Arg & Bt	NS1484	56°1·0′	4°58·6′W	X	56
Uig	Highld	NG1952	57°28·5′	6°40·8′W	T	23
Uig	Highld	NG3963	57°35·2′	6°21·6′W	T	23
Uig	Highld	NH5767	57°40·5′	4°23·4′W	X	21
Uig Bay	Highld	NG3862	57°34·6′	6°22·5′W	W	23
Uigen	N Eil	NB0934	58°12·2′	6°56·8′W	T	13
Uiginish	Highld	NG2448	57°26·6′	6°35·5′W	X	23
Uiginish Point	Highld	NG2349	57°27·1′	6°36·6′W	X	23
Uigle	Arg & Bt	NR6916	55°23·3′	5°38·4′W	X	68
Uig Lodge	N Eil	NB0533	58°11·5′	7°0·7′W	X	13
Uig Sands	N Eil	NB0432	58°10·9′	7°1·7′W	X	13
Uigshader	Highld	NG4246	57°26·1′	6°17·5′W	T	23
Uileann	Highld	NM7450	56°35·5′	5°40·4′W	X	49
Uillain	Arg & Bt	NR8692	56°4·6′	5°25·9′W	X	55
Uillt Gharbha	Arg & Bt	NM5927	56°22·7′	5°53·8′W	W	48
Uillt Ghobhlach	Highld	NH0300	57°3·5′	5°14·4′W	X	33
Uillt na Teanga	Highld	NG4026	57°15·3′	6°18·2′W	X	32
Uillt Ruadha	Arg & Bt	NR3957	55°44·4′	6°9·1′W	X	60
Uinaby Beck	Darl	NZ2315	54°32·0′	1°38·3′W	W	93
Uinessan	N Eil	NL6695	56°55·8′	7°29·0′W	X	31
Uirigh Bheithe	Arg & Bt	NM6420	56°19·1′	5°48·5′W	X	49
Uirigh Ghlas	Arg & Bt	NR6799	56°7·9′	5°44·5′W	X	55,61
Uirigh na Salach	Arg & Bt	NM6320	56°19·0′	5°49·5′W	X	49
Uisaed	Arg & Bt	NR6220	55°25·2′	5°45·2′W	X	68
Uiseabhal	N Eil	NG2298	57°53·4′	6°41·0′W	H	14
Uisg a' Chaime	Highld	NH4501	57°4·7′	4°33·0′W	W	34
Uisg an t-Suidhe	Arg & Bt	NR2863	55°47·3′	6°19·9′W	W	60
Uisgeabhagh	N Eil	NF8650	57°26·2′	7°13·5′W	X	22
Uisgeacha Geala	Arg & Bt	NM5830	56°24·3′	5°54·9′W	W	48
Uisge Dubh	Highld	NH7130	57°20·8′	4°8·2′W	W	27
Uisge Dubh	Highld	NN2085	56°55·5′	4°57·0′W	W	34,41
Uisge Dubh	Highld	NN6199	57°3·9′	4°17·1′W	W	35
Uisge Dubh or Black Water	Highld	NH0038	57°23·6′	5°19·2′W	W	25
Uisge Dubh Poll a' Choin	Highld	NJ0508	57°9·4′	3°33·8′W	W	36
Uisge Faur	Arg & Bt	NR3751	55°41·1′	6°10·6′W	W	60
Uisge Fealasgaig	Arg & Bt	NM5324	56°20·9′	5°59·4′W	W	48
Uisge Geal	Highld	NN5986	56°56·9′	4°18·6′W	W	42
Uisge Gleann a' Chromain	Arg & Bt	NR3753	55°42·2′	6°10·7′W	W	60
Uisge Labhair	Highld	NN4471	56°48·5′	4°32·9′W	W	42
Uisge Misgeach	Highld	NH1938	57°24·0′	5°0·3′W	W	25
Uisge na Cràlaig	Highld	NH1116	57°12·0′	5°7·3′W	W	34
Uisge na Criche	Arg & Bt	NR3252	55°41·5′	6°15·4′W	W	60
Uisge nam Fichead	Highld	NN3888	56°57·6′	4°39·4′W	W	34,41
Uisge Toll a' Mhadaidh	Highld	NG9783	57°47·7′	5°24·5′W	W	19
Uisgneabhal	N Eil	NB1109	57°58·8′	6°52·9′W	X	13,14
Uisgneabhal Beag	N Eil	NB1108	57°58·3′	6°52·8′W	H	13,14
Uisgneabhal Mòr	N Eil	NB1208	57°58·3′	6°51·8′W	H	13,14
Uisinis	N Eil	NB3306	57°58·1′	6°30·4′W	H	13,14
Uisinis	N Eil	NF8635	57°18·1′	7°12·4′W	X	22
Uisken	Arg & Bt	NM3819	56°17·7′	6°13·6′W	T	48
Uiskentuie	Arg & Bt	NR2964	55°47·9′	6°19·0′W	X	60
Ukna Skerry	Shetld	HU3531	60°4·0′	1°21·8′W	X	4
Ulaw	Aberd	NJ9429	57°21·3′	2°5·5′W	X	38
Ulbster	Highld	ND3240	58°20·9′	3°9·2′W	T	12
Ulcat Row	Cumbr	NY4022	54°35·6′	2°55·3′W	T	90
Ulceby	Lincs	TF4272	53°13·8′	0°8·1′E	T	122
Ulceby	N Lincs	TA1014	53°36·9′	0°19·8′W	T	113
Ulceby Carr	N Lincs	TA1216	53°37·9′	0°18·0′W	X	113
Ulceby Carr Fm	N Lincs	TA1115	53°37·4′	0°18·9′W	FM	113
Ulceby Chase Fm	N Lincs	TA1012	53°35·8′	0°19·9′W	FM	113
Ulceby Cross	Lincs	TF4173	53°14·3′	0°7·2′E	X	122
Ulceby Grange	Lincs	TF4273	53°14·3′	0°8·1′E	X	122
Ulceby Grange	N Lincs	TA1014	53°36·9′	0°19·8′W	X	113
Ulceby Lodge	Lincs	TF4274	53°14·9′	0°8·1′E	X	122
Ulceby Skitter	N Lincs	TA1215	53°37·4′	0°18·0′W	T	113
Ulceby Sta	N Lincs	TA1215	53°37·4′	0°18·0′W	X	113
Ulcombe	Kent	TQ8449	51°12·9′	0°38·5′E	T	188
Uldale	Cumbr	NY2436	54°43·0′	3°10·4′W	T	89,90
Uldale	Cumbr	SD7496	54°21·8′	2°23·6′W	X	98
Uldale Beck	Cumbr	NY6401	54°24·4′	2°32·9′W	W	91
Uldale Beck	N Yks	NY8103	54°25·6′	2°17·2′W	W	91,92
Uldale Fells	Cumbr	NY2734	54°42·0′	3°7·5′W	X	89,90
Uldale Fm	Cumbr	NY0412	54°29·6′	3°28·5′W	FM	89
Uldale Gill Head	N Yks	NY8002	54°25·0′	2°18·1′W	X	91,92
Uldale Head	Cumbr	NY6400	54°23·9′	2°32·9′W	X	91
Uldale Ho	Cumbr	SD7396	54°21·8′	2°24·5′W	X	98
Uldale Mill Fm	Cumbr	NY2337	54°43·6′	3°11·3′W	FM	89,90
Ulehams Fm	Essex	TQ8798	51°39·2′	0°42·6′E	FM	168
Uley	Glos	ST7898	51°41·1′	2°18·7′W	T	162
Uley Bury	Glos	ST7898	51°41·1′	2°18·7′W	A	162
Ulfers Gill	N Yks	SE0982	54°14·3′	1°51·3′W	W	99
Ulfhart Point	Highld	NG4716	57°10·2′	6°10·7′W	X	32
Ulgary	Highld	NM7776	56°49·6′	5°38·8′W	X	40
Ulgham	Northum	NZ2392	55°13·5′	1°37·9′W	T	81
Ulgham Broom Fm	Northum	NZ2291	55°13·0′	1°38·8′W	FM	81
Ulgham Fence Fm	Northum	NZ2291	55°13·0′	1°38·8′W	FM	81
Ulgham Grange Fm	Northum	NZ2492	55°13·5′	1°36·9′W	FM	81
Ulgham Park	Northum	NZ2293	55°14·1′	1°38·8′W	X	81
Ulgill	Cumbr	NX9821	54°34·7′	3°34·3′W	X	89
Ulgill Rigg	Cumbr	SD6498	54°22·8′	2°32·8′W	X	97
Ulgraves	Cumbr	SD5199	54°23·3′	2°44·9′W	H	97
Ullabhal	N Eil	NB0811	57°59·8′	6°56·1′W	H	13,14
Ullacombe Fm	Devon	SX7877	50°35·0′	3°43·0′W	FM	191
Ulladale	Highld	NH4758	57°35·4′	4°33·1′W	X	26
Ullapool	Highld	NH1294	57°54·0′	5°9·9′W	T	19
Ullapool Point	Highld	NH1293	57°53·5′	5°9·8′W	X	19
Ullapool River	Highld	NH1495	57°54·6′	5°7·9′W	W	20
Ullapow	Orkney	ND5199	58°52·8′	2°50·5′W	X	6,7
Ullardhall Fm	Ches	SJ7476	53°17·1′	2°23·0′W	FM	118
Ullathorns	Cumbr	SD6286	54°16·3′	2°34·6′W	X	97
Ullcombe	Devon	ST2109	50°52·7′	3°7·0′W	T	192,193
Ullenhall	Warw	SP1267	52°18·3′	1°49·0′W	T	150
Ullenwood	Glos	SO9416	51°50·8′	2°4·8′W	X	163
Ullerbank	Cumbr	NY5557	54°54·6′	2°41·7′W	X	86
Ullermire	Cumbr	NY4666	54°59·4′	2°50·2′W	X	86
Ulleskelf	N Yks	SE5139	53°50·9′	1°13·1′W	T	105
Ullesthorpe	Leic	SP5087	52°29·0′	1°15·4′W	T	140

Ullesthorpe Court	Leic	SP5088	52°29·5'	1°15·4'W	X	140
Ulley	Roth	SK4687	53°22·9'	1°18·1'W	T	111,120
Ulley Beeches	Roth	SK4787	53°22·9'	1°17·2'W	X	111,120
Ulley Country Park	Roth	SK4587	53°22·9'	1°19·0'W	T	111,120
Ulley Resr	Roth	SK4587	53°22·9'	1°19·0'W	W	111,120
Ullingswick	Heref	SO5949	52°8·5'	2°35·6'W	T	149
Ullington	Worcs	SP1047	52°7·5'	1°50·8'W	T	150
Ullinish	Highld	NG3238	57°21·5'	6°26·9'W	T	23,32
Ullinish Lodge (Hotel)	Highld	NG3237	57°20·9'	6°26·9'W	X	23,32
Ullinish Point	Highld	NG3136	57°20·4'	6°27·8'W	X	23,32
Ullins Water	Shetld	HU5240	60°8·7'	1°3·3'W	W	4
Ulloch	D & G	NX6968	54°59·6'	4°2·4'W	X	83,84
Ulloch Hill	D & G	NX6867	54°59·1'	4°3·3'W	H	83,84
Ullock	Cumbr	NY0723	54°35·9'	3°25·9'W	T	89
Ullock	Cumbr	NY2423	54°36·0'	3°10·2'W	T	89,90
Ullock Pike	Cumbr	NY2428	54°38·7'	3°10·2'W	X	89,90
Ullscarf	Cumbr	NY2912	54°30·1'	3°5·4'W	H	89,90
Ullscarf Gill	Cumbr	NY3013	54°30·7'	3°4·5'W	W	90
Ullsmoor	Cumbr	NY5613	54°30·9'	2°40·4'W	X	90
Ull Stone	Cumbr	NY4508	54°28·1'	2°50·5'W	X	90
Ullswater	Cumbr	NY4420	54°34·6'	2°51·6'W	W	90
Ulluva	Highld	NG8233	57°20·4'	5°36·9'W	X	24
Ulnaby Hall	Darl	NZ2217	54°33·1'	1°39·2'W	X	93
Ulnaby Village	Darl	NZ2217	54°33·1'	1°39·2'W	A	93
Ulpha	Cumbr	SD1993	54°19·8'	3°14·3'W	T	96
Ulpha	Cumbr	SD4581	54°13·6'	2°50·2'W	X	97
Ulpha Fell	Cumbr	NY2502	54°24·7'	3°8·9'W	X	89,90
Ulpha Fell	Cumbr	SD1795	54°20·9'	3°16·2'W	X	96
Ulpha Fell	Cumbr	SD4581	54°13·6'	2°50·2'W	X	97
Ulpha Park	Cumbr	SD1990	54°18·2'	3°14·3'W	F	96
Ulrome	E Yorks	TA1656	53°59·5'	0°13·4'W	T	107
Ulrome Grange	E Yorks	TA1557	54°0·0'	0°14·3'W	X	107
Ulrome Sands	E Yorks	TA1757	54°0·0'	0°12·5'W	X	107
Ulshaw	N Yks	SE1487	54°16·9'	1°46·7'W	T	99
Ulsta	Shetld	HU4680	60°30·3'	1°9·2'W	T	1,2,3
Ulsta House	Shetld	HU4680	60°30·3'	1°9·2'W	X	1,2,3
Ulston	Scot Bord	NT6621	55°29·1'	2°31·8'W	X	74
Ulston Moor	Scot Bord	NT6821	55°29·2'	2°30·0'W	X	74
Ulthwaite Rigg	Cumbr	NY5109	54°28·7'	2°45·0'W	X	90
Ulting	Essex	TL8008	51°44·7'	0°36·8'E	X	168
Ulting Grove	Essex	TL8109	51°45·2'	0°37·7'E	X	168
Ulting Hall	Essex	TL8109	51°45·2'	0°37·7'E	A	168
Uluvalt	Arg & Bt	NM5429	56°23·6'	5°58·7'W	X	48
Ulva	Arg & Bt	NM4139	56°28·6'	6°11·9'W	X	47,48
Ulva Ho	Arg & Bt	NM4439	56°28·7'	6°9·0'W	X	47,48
Ulva Islands	Arg & Bt	NR7282	55°58·9'	5°38·9'W	X	55
Ulverley Green	Sol	SP1381	52°25·8'	1°48·1'W	T	139
Ulverscroft Cottage Fm	Leic	SK4910	52°41·4'	1°16·1'W	FM	129
Ulverscroft Grange	Leic	SK4811	52°41·9'	1°17·0'W	X	129
Ulverscroft Lodge Fm	Leic	SK4913	52°43·0'	1°16·1'W	FM	129
Ulverston	Cumbr	SD2878	54°11·8'	3°5·8'W	T	96,97
Ulverston Channel	Cumbr	SD3277	54°8·6'	3°2·0'W	W	96,97
Ulverston Sands	Cumbr	SD3074	54°9·7'	3°3·9'W	X	96,97
Ulveston Hall	Suff	TM1463	52°13·6'	1°8·4'E	X	156
Ulwell	Dorset	SZ0280	50°37·4'	1°57·9'W	T	195
Ulwith	N Yks	SE1796	54°21·8'	1°43·9'W	X	99
Ulzieside	D & G	NS7708	55°21·3'	3°56·0'W	X	71,78
Ulzieside Plantn	D & G	NS7507	55°20·7'	3°57·8'W	F	71,78
Umachan	Highld	NG6049	57°28·3'	5°59·7'W	X	24
Umberleigh	Devon	SS6023	50°59·6'	3°59·3'W	T	180
Umberleigh Ho	Devon	SS5924	51°0·1'	4°0·2'W	X	180
Umberley Brook	Derby	SK2871	53°14·4'	1°34·4'W	W	119
Umberley Sick	Derby	SK2969	53°13·3'	1°33·5'W	W	119
Umberslade Park	Warw	SP1371	52°20·5'	1°48·2'W	A	139
Umborne	Devon	SY2397	50°46·3'	3°5·1'W	T	192,193
Umborne Brook	Devon	SY2298	50°46·8'	3°6·0'W	W	192,193
Unapool	Highld	NC2332	58°14·7'	5°0·5'W	T	15
Unapool Burn	Highld	NC2330	58°13·7'	5°0·4'W	W	15
Unapool Ho	Highld	NC2332	58°14·7'	5°0·5'W	X	15
Unasaraidh	N Eil	NF7627	57°13·4'	7°21·7'W	X	22
Uncleby	E Yorks	SE8159	54°1·5'	0°45·4'W	X	106
Uncleby Wold	E Yorks	SE8259	54°1·5'	0°44·5'W	X	106
Uncllys	Worcs	SO7675	52°22·6'	2°20·8'W	X	138
Underbank	Cumbr	SD6692	54°19·6'	2°30·9'W	X	98
Under Bank	Kirk	SE1407	53°33·8'	1°46·9'W	T	110
Underbank	Northum	NY7049	54°50·3'	2°27·6'W	X	86,87
Underbank	S Lanak	NS8345	55°41·3'	3°51·2'W	X	72
Underbank Hall	Barns	SK2599	53°29·5'	1°37·0'W	X	110
Underbank Resr	Sheff	SK2499	53°29·5'	1°37·9'W	W	110
Underbarrow	Cumbr	SD4692	54°19·5'	2°49·4'W	T	97
Under Brae Lane	D & G	NX8671	55°1·5'	3°46·6'W	W	84
Under Burnmouth	Scot Bord	NY4783	55°8·6'	2°49·5'W	X	79
Undercleave	Devon	SS5116	50°55·7'	4°6·8'W	X	180
Undercleave Fm	Devon	ST2901	50°48·5'	3°0·1'W	FM	193
Undercliff	S Tyne	NZ3962	54°57·3'	1°23·0'W	X	88
Undercliffe	Brad	SE1734	53°48·4'	1°44·1'W	T	104
Undercliff, The	I of W	SZ3982	50°38·4'	1°26·5'W	X	196
Undercliff, The	I of W	SZ5376	50°35·1'	1°14·7'W	X	196
Undercrag	Cumbr	NY3630	54°39·9'	2°59·1'W	X	90
Under Crag	Cumbr	SD2396	54°21·5'	3°10·7'W	X	96
Under Crag	Cumbr	SD2794	54°20·4'	3°7·0'W	H	96,97
Undercraig	Renf	NS3772	55°55·1'	4°36·1'W	X	63
Under Craigs	D & G	NX9974	55°3·3'	3°34·4'W	X	84
Under Croft	Lancs	SD5053	53°58·5'	2°45·3'W	X	102
Underdale	Shrops	SJ5013	52°43·0'	2°44·0'W	T	126
Underdown	Devon	SS6100	50°47·2'	3°57·9'W	X	191
Underdown	Devon	SX7091	50°42·5'	3°50·1'W	X	191
Underdown	Devon	SX8885	50°39·5'	3°34·7'W	T	192
Underdown	Heref	SO7136	52°1·5'	2°25·0'W	X	149
Underdown Fm	Devon	ST2005	50°50·6'	3°7·8'W	FM	192,193
Underdown Fm	Devon	ST2307	50°51·7'	3°5·3'W	FM	192,193
Underfell	Cumbr	SD6382	54°14·2'	2°33·6'W	X	97
Undergrove	Carm	SN4941	52°3·1'	4°11·7'W	X	146
Underhand	Lancs	SD7048	53°56·1'	2°27·0'W	X	103
Underheugh	Cumbr	NY6166	54°59·5'	2°36·1'W	X	86
Underheugh	Inverc	NS2075	55°56·3'	4°52·5'W	X	63
Underhill	Barnet	TQ2595	51°38·6'	0°11·2'W	T	166,176
Underhill	Corn	SX3093	50°42·9'	4°24·1'W	X	190
Underhill	Derby	SK0966	53°11·7'	1°51·5'W	X	119
Underhill	Heref	SO5929	51°57·7'	2°35·4'W	X	149
Underhill	N Ayr	NS2148	55°41·8'	4°50·5'W	X	63
Underhill	Pth & Kin	NN8616	56°19·6'	3°50·2'W	X	58
Underhill	Shrops	SJ2630	52°52·0'	3°5·6'W	X	126
Underhill	Wilts	ST8730	51°4·4'	2°10·7'W	T	183
Underhill Fm	Devon	SY3291	50°43·1'	2°57·4'W	FM	193
Underhill Fm	N Yks	NZ5103	54°25·4'	1°12·4'W	FM	93
Underhill Fm	N Yks	SE6894	54°20·5'	0°56·8'W	FM	94,100
Underhill Fm	Somer	ST2517	50°57·1'	3°3·7'W	FM	193
Underhill Fm	Somer	ST5628	51°3·2'	2°37·3'W	FM	183
Under Hill Fm	Staffs	SK0266	53°11·7'	1°57·8'W	FM	119
Underhill Fm	Surrey	TQ2251	51°14·9'	0°14·7'W	FM	187
Underhill Fm	Worcs	SO7639	52°3·2'	2°20·6'W	FM	150
Underhill Fm	Worcs	SO7933	51°59·9'	2°18·0'W	FM	150
Underhill Hall	Shrops	SJ4300	52°35·9'	2°50·1'W	X	126
Under Hill Head	Scot Bord	NT3210	55°23·0'	3°4·0'W	H	79
Underhills	S Ayr	NS4030	55°32·5'	4°31·7'W	X	70
Underhoull	Shetld	HP5704	60°43·2'	0°56·8'W	T	1
Under Howe	Cumbr	NY3728	54°38·8'	2°58·2'W	X	90
Underlaid Wood	Cumbr	SD4879	54°12·5'	2°47·4'W	F	97
Underlaw	E Ayr	NS5938	55°37·2'	4°13·9'W	X	71
Underley	Heref	SO6561	52°15·0'	2°30·4'W	X	138,149
Underley Grange	Cumbr	SD6180	54°13·1'	2°35·5'W	X	97
Underley Hall School	Cumbr	SD6180	54°13·1'	2°35·5'W	X	97
Underlining Green	Kent	TQ7546	51°11·4'	0°30·7'E	T	188
Undermillbeck Common	Cumbr	SD4295	54°21·1'	2°53·1'W	X	96,97
Under Millsteads	D & G	NY4279	55°6·4'	2°54·1'W	X	85
Under Park	N Yks	NZ7707	54°27·4'	0°48·3'W	X	94
Under Pendle	Lancs	SD8040	53°51·6'	2°17·8'W	X	103
Underriver	Kent	TQ5552	51°15·0'	0°13·7'E	T	188
Underriver Fm	Kent	TQ5651	51°14·4'	0°14·5'E	FM	188
Underriver Ho	Kent	TQ5652	51°15·0'	0°14·5'E	T	188
Underscar (Hotel)	Cumbr	NY2725	54°37·1'	3°7·4'W	X	89,90
Under Shieldhill	S Lanak	NS8349	55°43·5'	3°51·3'W	X	72
Under Stenniesweater	D & G	NY3294	55°14·4'	3°3·7'W	X	79
Undertakers, The	Cambs	TL4970	52°18·7'	0°11·5'E	X	154
Under the Brae	D & G	NX8771	55°1·5'	3°45·6'W	X	84
Under the Hill	Staffs	SK0865	53°11·2'	1°52·4'W	X	119
Under the Wood	Kent	TR2266	51°21·2'	1°11·7'E	T	179
Under Thorn	S Lanak	NS8751	55°44·6'	3°47·6'W	X	65,72
Under Tofts	Sheff	SK3087	53°23·0'	1°32·5'W	T	110,111
Underton	Shrops	SO6892	52°31·7'	2°27·9'W	T	138
Undertown	Corn	SX3578	50°34·9'	4°19·5'W	X	201
Undertrees Fm	Kent	TR2261	51°18·5'	1°11·5'E	FM	179
Under Wetton	Staffs	SK1156	53°6·3'	1°49·7'W	X	119
Under Whitle	Staffs	SK1063	53°10·1'	1°50·6'W	X	119
Underwinder	Cumbr	SD6492	54°19·6'	2°32·8'W	X	97
Underwood	Bucks	SU9292	51°37·4'	0°39·9'W	X	175
Underwood	C of Plym	SX5355	50°22·8'	4°3·7'W	T	201
Underwood	Corn	SS2405	50°49·3'	4°29·5'W	X	190
Underwood	Cumbr	NY1024	54°36·4'	3°23·2'W	X	89
Underwood	Cumbr	NY4223	54°36·2'	2°53·4'W	X	90
Underwood	Cumbr	NY5577	55°5·4'	2°41·9'W	X	86
Underwood	Cumbr	NY6430	54°40·1'	2°33·1'W	X	91
Underwood	Cumbr	SD6887	54°16·9'	2°29·1'W	X	144
Underwood	D & G	NX6855	54°52·6'	4°3·0'W	X	83,84
Underwood	Newp	ST3888	51°35·5'	2°53·3'W	T	171
Underwood	Notts	SK4750	53°2·9'	1°17·5'W	T	120
Underwood	Pemb	SM9811	51°45·9'	4°55·3'W	T	157,158
Underwood	S Ayr	NS3829	55°31·9'	4°33·6'W	X	70
Underwood Fm	Corn	SX3087	50°39·7'	4°23·9'W	FM	190
Underwood Fm	Derby	SK1948	53°2·0'	1°42·6'W	FM	119
Underwood Grange	Suff	TM0349	52°6·3'	0°58·3'E	X	155
Underwood Hall	Cambs	TL6157	52°11·5'	0°21·7'E	X	154
Underwood Ho	Falk	NS8079	55°59·6'	3°55·0'W	X	65
Underwood Lodge	Leic	SK6713	52°42·9'	1°0·1'W	X	129
Underwood Mains	S Ayr	NS3829	55°31·9'	4°33·6'W	X	70
Underwood Plantn	N Yks	SE4184	54°15·2'	1°21·8'W	F	99
Underwood's Fm	Cambs	TL2692	52°30·9'	0°8·2'W	FM	142
Underwood's Fm	E Susx	TQ7025	51°0·2'	0°25·8'E	FM	188,199
Underwood's Grounds	Cambs	TL2794	52°32·0'	0°7·3'W	X	142
Undley	Suff	TL6981	52°24·3'	0°29·5'E	T	143
Undley Common	Suff	TL7080	52°23·7'	0°30·3'E	X	143
Undraynian Point	Arg & Bt	NS0768	55°52·3'	5°4·6'W	X	63
Undy	Monm	ST4386	51°34·4'	2°49·0'W	T	171,172
Uneval	N Eil	NF8067	57°35·0'	7°20·8'W	H	18
Ungam	Shetld	HU3874	60°27·1'	1°18·1'W	X	2,3
Ungeshader	N Eil	NB1229	58°9·6'	6°53·3'W	X	13
Ungirsta	Shetld	HP6213	60°48·0'	0°51·1'W	X	1
Ungla Skerry	Shetld	HU5961	60°20·0'	0°55·4'W	X	2
Unhill Bottom	Oxon	SU5582	51°32·3'	1°12·0'W	X	174
Unhill Bottom	Oxon	SU5683	51°32·8'	1°11·2'W	X	174
Unhill Wood	Oxon	SU5682	51°32·3'	1°11·2'W	F	174
Uni Firth	Shetld	HU2856	60°17·5'	1°29·1'W	W	3
Unifirth	Shetld	HU2856	60°17·5'	1°29·1'W	T	3
Unigarth	Orkney	HY2417	59°2·3'	3°19·0'W	X	6
Union	Fife	NO3808	56°15·9'	2°59·6'W	X	59
Union	Stir	NN6301	56°11·2'	4°12·0'W	X	57
Union Bank Fm	St Hel	SJ5190	53°24·5'	2°43·8'W	FM	108
Union Bay	Arg & Bt	NR9693	56°5·4'	5°16·3'W	W	55
Union Br	Scot Bord	NT9351	55°45·4'	2°6·3'W	X	67,74,75
Union Canal	C of Edin	NT1670	55°55·2'	3°20·2'W	W	65,66
Union Canal	W Loth	NT0776	55°58·3'	3°29·0'W	W	65
Union Channel	E Susx	TQ9322	50°58·1'	0°45·3'E	W	189
Union Cott	Aberd	NO8290	57°0·3'	2°17·3'W	X	38,45
Union Croft	Aberd	NJ6160	57°38·0'	2°38·7'W	X	29
Union Fm	Ches	SJ5778	53°18·1'	2°38·3'W	FM	117
Union Fm	Norf	TF9716	52°42·6'	0°55·4'E	FM	132
Union Fm	Suff	TM4476	52°19·9'	1°35·3'E	FM	156
Union Gorse Covert	Glos	ST8595	51°39·4'	2°12·6'W	F	162
Union Hall	Durham	NZ2945	54°48·2'	1°32·5'W	X	88
Union Ho	N Yks	NZ2001	54°24·5'	1°41·1'W	X	93
Union Mills	I of M	SC3577	54°10·0'	4°31·2'W	T	95
Union Street	E Susx	TQ7031	51°3·4'	0°25·9'E	T	188
Unish	Highld	NG2365	57°35·7'	6°37·2'W	X	23
United Downs	Corn	SW7441	50°13·8'	5°9·8'W	T	204
Unity	Cumbr	NY5359	54°55·7'	2°43·6'W	X	86
Unity Fm	Somer	ST2953	51°16·5'	3°0·7'W	FM	182
University Fm	Oxon	SP3205	51°44·8'	1°31·8'W	FM	164
University of Essex	Essex	TM0223	51°52·4'	0°56·5'E	X	168
University of Lancaster	Lancs	SD4857	54°0·6'	2°47·2'W	X	102
University of Stirling	Stir	NS8096	56°8·8'	3°55·4'W	X	57
University of Sussex	Bri & Hov	TQ3409	50°52·1'	0°5·4'W	X	198
Unst	Shetld	HP6109	60°45·8'	0°52·3'W	X	1
Unsted Park	Surrey	SU9944	51°11·4'	0°34·6'W	X	186
Unstone	Derby	SK3777	53°17·6'	1°26·3'W	T	119
Unstone Grange	Derby	SK3877	53°17·6'	1°25·4'W	X	119
Unstone Green	Derby	SK3776	53°17·0'	1°26·3'W	T	119
Unsworth	Bury	SD8107	53°33·8'	2°16·8'W	T	109
Unthank	Angus	NO6061	56°44·6'	2°38·8'W	X	45
Unthank	Cumbr	NY3948	54°49·6'	2°56·5'W	T	85
Unthank	Cumbr	NY4536	54°43·2'	2°50·8'W	T	90
Unthank	Cumbr	NY6040	54°45·4'	2°36·9'W	T	86
Unthank	Derby	SK3076	53°17·0'	1°32·6'W	T	119
Unthank	D & G	NY3894	55°14·4'	2°58·1'W	X	79
Unthank	Durham	NY8231	54°40·7'	2°16·3'W	X	91,92
Unthank	Durham	NY9938	54°44·5'	2°0·5'W	X	92
Unthank	Moray	NJ1767	57°41·4'	3°23·1'W	X	28
Unthank	Northum	NU0111	55°23·8'	1°58·6'W	X	81
Unthank	Northum	NZ0454	54°53·1'	1°55·8'W	X	87
Unthank	S Lanak	NT0132	55°34·6'	3°33·8'W	X	72
Unthank Blue Ho	Northum	NT9848	55°43·8'	2°1·5'W	X	75
Unthank Burn	D & G	NY3994	55°14·4'	2°57·1'W	W	79
Unthank End	Cumbr	NY4535	54°42·7'	2°50·8'W	X	90
Unthank Fm	Northum	NT9848	55°43·8'	2°1·5'W	FM	75
Unthank Fm	N Yks	SE1790	54°18·6'	1°43·9'W	FM	99
Unthank Hall	Northum	NY7262	54°57·4'	2°25·8'W	X	86,87
Unthank Ho	Cumbr	NY4436	54°43·2'	2°51·7'W	X	90
Unthank Moor	Northum	NT9848	55°43·8'	2°1·5'W	X	75
Unthank Pikes	D & G	NY4194	55°14·5'	2°55·2'W	H	79
Unthank Square	Northum	NT9848	55°43·8'	2°1·5'W	X	75
Upavon	Wilts	SU1355	51°17·9'	1°48·4'W	T	173
Upavon Airfield	Wilts	SU1554	51°17·3'	1°46·7'W	X	184
Upavon Down	Wilts	SU1654	51°17·3'	1°45·8'W	X	184
Upavon Hill	Wilts	SU1455	51°17·9'	1°47·6'W	H	173
Upbank Wood	N Yks	SE2380	54°13·2'	1°38·4'W	F	99
Up Cerne	Dorset	ST6502	50°49·2'	2°29·4'W	T	194
Upchurch	Kent	TQ8467	51°22·6'	0°39·0'E	T	178
Upcot	Dorset	SY3992	50°43·7'	2°51·5'W	X	193
Upcote Fm	Glos	SP0216	51°50·8'	1°57·9'W	FM	163
Upcott	Corn	SX3875	50°33·4'	4°16·8'W	X	201
Upcott	Devon	SS2417	50°55·8'	4°29·9'W	T	190
Upcott	Devon	SS3511	50°52·7'	4°20·3'W	X	190
Upcott	Devon	SS3804	50°49·0'	4°17·6'W	X	190
Upcott	Devon	SS4421	50°58·3'	4°12·9'W	X	180,190
Upcott	Devon	SS4425	51°0·4'	4°13·0'W	X	180,190
Upcott	Devon	SS4839	51°8·0'	4°10·0'W	T	180
Upcott	Devon	SS5541	51°9·2'	4°4·0'W	X	180
Upcott	Devon	SS5703	50°48·8'	4°1·4'W	X	191
Upcott	Devon	SS5709	50°52·0'	4°1·6'W	T	191
Upcott	Devon	SS5838	51°7·7'	4°1·4'W	X	180
Upcott	Devon	SS6107	50°51·0'	3°58·1'W	X	191
Upcott	Devon	SS6118	50°56·9'	3°58·3'W	X	180
Upcott	Devon	SS6226	51°1·2'	3°57·7'W	X	180
Upcott	Devon	SS6509	50°52·1'	3°54·7'W	T	191
Upcott	Devon	SS6902	50°48·4'	3°51·2'W	X	191
Upcott	Devon	SS7507	50°51·2'	3°46·2'W	X	191
Upcott	Devon	SS7529	51°3·0'	3°46·6'W	X	180
Upcott	Devon	SS8212	50°54·0'	3°40·3'W	X	181
Upcott	Devon	SX4498	50°45·9'	4°12·3'W	X	190
Upcott	Devon	SY0494	50°44·5'	3°21·3'W	X	192
Upcott	Heref	SO3250	52°8·9'	2°59·2'W	T	148
Upcott	Somer	SS9025	51°1·1'	3°33·7'W	X	181
Upcott	Somer	SS9135	51°6·5'	3°33·0'W	X	181
Upcott	Somer	ST1924	51°0·8'	3°8·9'W	T	181,193
Upcott Barton	Devon	SS4707	50°50·8'	4°10·0'W	T	191
Upcott Barton	Devon	SS5615	50°55·2'	4°2·5'W	X	180
Upcott Barton	Devon	SS8608	50°51·9'	3°36·8'W	A	191
Upcott Barton	Devon	SS9204	50°49·8'	3°31·6'W	X	192
Upcott Barton	Devon	SX3990	50°41·5'	4°16·4'W	X	190
Upcott Cross	Devon	SS3704	50°49·0'	4°18·5'W	X	190
Upcott Cross	Devon	SX4397	50°45·3'	4°13·2'W	X	190
Upcott Fm	Devon	SS4604	50°49·1'	4°10·8'W	FM	190
Upcott Fm	Devon	SS5430	51°3·3'	4°4·6'W	FM	180
Upcott Fm	Devon	SS5927	51°1·7'	4°0·3'W	FM	180
Upcott Fm	Devon	SS6632	51°4·5'	3°54·4'W	FM	180
Upcott Fm	Devon	SS9021	50°58·9'	3°33·6'W	FM	181
Upcott Fm	Devon	ST0905	50°50·5'	3°17·2'W	FM	192
Upcott Fm	Devon	ST1017	50°57·0'	3°16·5'W	FM	181,193
Upcott Fm	Somer	ST0126	51°1·7'	3°24·3'W	FM	181
Upcott Ho	Devon	SS5435	51°6·0'	4°4·7'W	X	180
Upcott Wood	Devon	SS4608	50°51·3'	4°10·9'W	F	190
Upcott Wood	Devon	SS4708	50°51·3'	4°10·0'W	F	191
Upcott Wood	Devon	SX3990	50°41·5'	4°16·4'W	F	190
Updown Fm	Kent	TR3153	51°14·0'	1°18·9'E	FM	179
Updown Ho	Kent	TR3153	51°14·0'	1°18·9'E	X	179
Updown Ho	Kent	TR3669	51°22·5'	1°23·9'E	X	179
Upend	Cambs	TL6958	52°11·9'	0°28·8'E	T	154
Up End	Mil Key	SP9245	52°6·0'	0°39·0'W	T	152
Upend Green	Cambs	TL6958	52°11·9'	0°28·8'E	X	154
Up Exe	Devon	SS9402	50°48·7'	3°29·9'W	T	192
Upfields	Staffs	SK1908	52°40·4'	1°42·7'W	X	128
Upfolds Fm	Surrey	TQ1143	51°10·8'	0°24·3'W	FM	187
Upgang Beach	N Yks	NZ8812	54°30·0'	0°38·0'W	X	94
Upgate	Norf	TG1418	52°43·3'	1°10·5'E	T	133
Upgate Green Fm	Norf	TM2598	52°32·2'	1°19·5'E	FM	134
Upgate Ho	Norf	TG1417	52°42·7'	1°10·5'E	X	133
Upgate Street	Norf	TM0992	52°29·4'	1°5·1'E	T	144
Upgate Street	Norf	TM2891	52°28·4'	1°21·8'E	T	134
Up Green	Hants	SU7960	51°20·2'	0°51·6'W	T	175,186
Uphall	Dorset	ST5502	50°49·2'	2°37·9'W	T	194
Uphall	W Loth	NT0571	55°55·6'	3°30·8'W	T	65
Uphall Fm	Norf	TM0184	52°25·2'	0°57·8'E	FM	144
Uphall Grange	Norf	TF8705	52°36·9'	0°46·1'E	X	144
Uphall Station	W Loth	NT0670	55°55·1'	3°29·8'W	T	65
Upham	Devon	SS8808	50°51·9'	3°35·1'W	T	192
Upham	Hants	SU5320	50°58·8'	1°14·3'W	T	185
Upham Fm	Devon	SS8808	50°51·9'	3°35·1'W	FM	192
Upham Fm	Devon	SY0290	50°42·3'	3°22·9'W	FM	192
Upham Fm	Hants	SU5220	50°58·9'	1°15·2'W	FM	185
Uphampton	Heref	SO3963	52°15·9'	2°53·2'W	T	137,148,149

Uphampton	Worcs	SO8364	52°16·7'	2°14·6'W	T	138,150
Uphampton Fm	Heref	SO5758	52°13·3'	2°37·4'W	FM	149
Uphams Plantation	Devon	SY0486	50°40·2'	3°21·1'W	F	192
Upham Village	Wilts	SU2277	51°29·7'	1°40·6'W	A	174
Up Hatherley	Glos	SO9120	51°52·9'	2°7·5'W	T	163
Uphay Fm	Devon	SY2999	50°47·4'	3°0·1'W	FM	193
Uphempston	Devon	SX8263	50°27·5'	3°39·4'W	T	202
Uphill	Corn	SX2974	50°32·7'	4°24·4'W	X	201
Uphill	Devon	SX5065	50°28·2'	4°6·4'W	X	201
Uphill	N Som	ST3158	51°19·3'	2°59·0'W	T	182
Uphill Manor	N Som	ST3259	51°19·8'	2°58·2'W	T	182
Uphoe Manor Ho	Mil Key	SP9253	52°10·3'	0°38·9'W	X	152
Up Holland	Lancs	SD5105	53°32·6'	2°44·0'W	T	108
Upholland Sta	Lancs	SD5103	53°31·5'	2°43·9'W	X	108
Uphouse	Shetld	HU4369	60°24·4'	1°12·7'W	X	2,3
Uphouse	Shetld	HU5041	60°9·3'	1°5·5'W	X	4
Uphouse Fm	Norf	TF8723	52°46·6'	0°46·8'E	FM	132
Upland	Carm	SN4013	51°47·8'	4°18·8'W	X	159
Upland Fm	Norf	TM4093	52°29·1'	1°32·5'E	FM	134
Upland Fm	Suff	TM0861	52°12·7'	1°3·1'E	FM	155
Upland Hall	Suff	TM3388	52°26·6'	1°26·1'E	X	156
Uplandhall Fm	Suff	TM3387	52°26·1'	1°26·1'E	FM	156
Uplands	Bath & NE Somer	ST6666	51°23·8'	2°28·9'W	X	172
Uplands	Bucks	SU8796	51°39·6'	0°44·1'W	X	165
Uplands	E Yorks	TA0560	54°1·8'	0°23·4'W	X	101
Uplands	Glos	SO8505	51°44·8'	2°12·6'W	T	162
Uplands	Monm	ST4398	51°40·9'	2°49·1'W	X	171
Uplands	N Som	ST4663	51°22·0'	2°46·2'W	X	172,182
Uplands	Shrops	SO7189	52°30·1'	2°25·2'W	X	138
Uplands	Swan	SS6392	51°36·8'	3°58·3'W	T	159
Uplands	Torf	ST2897	51°40·3'	3°2·1'W	X	171
Uplands	Worcs	SP0172	52°21·0'	1°58·7'W	X	139
Uplands Fm	Hants	SU5113	50°55·1'	1°16·1'W	FM	196
Uplands Fm	Heref	SO7040	52°3·7'	2°25·9'W	FM	149
Uplands Fm	Northnts	SP8078	52°23·9'	0°49·1'W	FM	141
Uplands Fm	Suff	TM1673	52°19·0'	1°10·6'E	FM	144,156
Uplands Fm	Tames	SJ9692	53°25·7'	2°3·2'W	FM	109
Uplands Fm	Warw	SP3746	52°6·9'	1°27·2'W	FM	151
Uplands Stables	W Berks	SU5379	51°30·7'	1°13·8'W	X	174
Uplands, The	Warw	SP2888	52°29·6'	1°34·9'W	X	140
Uplawmoor	E Renf	NS4355	55°46·0'	4°29·7'W	T	64
Upleadon	Glos	SO7526	51°56·2'	2°21·4'W	T	162
Upleadon Court	Glos	SO7626	51°56·2'	2°20·6'W	T	162
Upleadon Court	Heref	SO6642	52°4·8'	2°29·4'W	X	149
Upleadon Fm	Heref	SO6742	52°4·8'	2°28·5'W	FM	149
Upleatham	Red & Cl	NZ6319	54°34·0'	1°1·1'W	T	94
Uplees	Kent	TQ9964	51°20·6'	0°51·8'E	X	178
Uploders	Dorset	SY5093	50°44·3'	2°42·1'W	T	194
Uplowman	Devon	ST0115	50°55·8'	3°24·1'W	T	181
Uplyme	Devon	SY3293	50°44·2'	2°57·4'W	T	193
Upmanhowe	Cumbr	NY8412	54°30·4'	2°14·4'W	X	91,92
Up Marden	W Susx	SU7914	50°55·4'	0°52·2'W	T	197
Upminster	Hav	TQ5687	51°33·8'	0°15·4'E	T	177
Up Mudford	Somer	ST5718	50°57·8'	2°36·4'W	T	183
Up Nately	Hants	SU6951	51°15·5'	1°0·3'W	T	186
Upnor Reach	Medway	TQ7670	51°24·3'	0°32·2'E	W	178
Upottery	Devon	ST2007	50°51·7'	3°7·8'W	T	192,193
Uppacott	Devon	SS5528	51°2·2'	4°3·7'W	T	180
Uppacott	Devon	SS7521	50°58·7'	3°46·5'W	X	180
Uppacott Down	Devon	SX7389	50°41·4'	3°47·5'W	H	191
Uppacott Fm	Corn	SS2713	50°53·7'	4°27·2'W	FM	190
Uppacott Fm	Devon	SX7388	50°40·9'	3°47·5'W	FM	191
Uppark	W Susx	SU7717	50°57·1'	0°53·8'W	A	197
Up Park	W Susx	SU7817	50°57·1'	0°53·0'W	X	197
Uppat	Highld	NC8602	57°59·8'	3°55·2'W	T	17
Uppaton	Devon	SX4380	50°36·2'	4°12·7'W	X	201
Uppaton	Devon	SX4969	50°30·3'	4°7·4'W	X	201
Uppaton Fm	Devon	SX4968	50°29·8'	4°7·4'W	FM	201
Uppat Wood	Highld	NC8702	57°59·8'	3°54·2'W	F	17
Uppend	Essex	TL4626	51°55·0'	0°7·8'E	T	167
Upper Abbey	Suff	TM4564	52°13·4'	1°35·6'E	X	156
Upper Achairn (ruin)	Highld	ND2747	58°24·6'	3°14·5'W	X	11,12
Upper Achies	Highld	ND1354	58°28·2'	3°29·0'W	X	11,12
Upper Achnacroish	Arg & Bt	NM7234	56°26·8'	5°41·5'W	X	49
Upper Ackergill	Highld	ND3553	58°27·9'	3°6·4'W	X	12
Upper Acre	Staffs	SK0458	53°7·4'	1°56·0'W	X	119
Upper Adhurst Fm	Hants	SU7725	51°1·4'	0°53·7'W	FM	186,197
Upper Affcot	Shrops	SO4486	52°28·4'	2°49·1'W	T	137
Upper Affloch	Aberd	NJ7708	57°10·0'	2°22·4'W	X	38
Upper Altgaltraig	Arg & Bt	NS0473	55°54·9'	5°7·7'W	X	63
Upper Anguston	C of Aber	NJ8002	57°6·8'	2°19·4'W	X	38
Upper Appleford Fm	I of W	SZ4980	50°37·3'	1°18·1'W	FM	196
Upper Ardchronie	Highld	NH6088	57°51·8'	4°21·1'W	T	21
Upper Ardgrain	Aberd	NJ9534	57°24·0'	2°4·5'W	X	30
Upper Ardroscadale	Arg & Bt	NS0364	55°50·0'	5°8·3'W	X	63
Upper Arley	Worcs	SO7680	52°25·3'	2°20·8'W	T	138
Upper Armley	Leeds	SE2634	53°48·3'	1°35·9'W	T	104
Upper Arncott	Oxon	SP6117	51°51·1'	1°6·5'W	T	164,165
Upper Arthrath	Aberd	NJ9636	57°25·1'	2°3·5'W	X	30
Upper Ashe	Hants	SU5348	51°14·0'	1°14·1'W	X	185
Upper Ashentilly	Aberd	NO8197	57°4·1'	2°18·3'W	X	38,45
Upper Ashop	Derby	SK1489	53°24·1'	1°47·0'W	X	110
Upper Ashton Fm	Heref	SO5164	52°16·6'	2°42·7'W	FM	137,138,149
Upper Astley	Shrops	SJ5318	52°45·7'	2°41·4'W	T	126
Upper Aston	Shrops	SO8193	52°32·3'	2°16·4'W	T	138
Upper Astrop	Northnts	SP5137	52°2·0'	1°15·0'W	T	151
Upper Auchairn	Aberd	NJ4646	57°30·3'	2°53·6'W	X	28,29
Upper Auchenreath	Moray	NJ3862	57°38·9'	3°1·9'W	X	28
Upper Auchenreoch	D & G	NX8170	55°0·9'	3°51·2'W	X	84
Upper Auchinlay	Stir	NN7703	56°12·5'	3°58·5'W	X	57
Upper Auchmill	Aberd	NJ5544	57°29·3'	2°44·6'W	X	29
Upper Auchnagorth	Aberd	NJ8356	57°35·9'	2°16·6'W	X	29,30
Upper Auchnamoon	Aberd	NJ8255	57°35·3'	2°17·6'W	X	29,30
Upper Austby	N Yks	SE1050	53°57·0'	1°50·4'W	X	104
Upper Austin Lodge	Kent	TQ5462	51°20·4'	0°13·1'E	X	177,188
Upper Avenue	Staffs	SJ8707	52°39·9'	2°11·1'W	X	127,139
Upper Aynho Grounds	Northnts	SP5232	51°59·3'	1°14·2'W	X	151
Upper Backieley	Aberd	NJ6254	57°34·7'	2°37·7'W	X	29
Upper Bacombe	Bucks	SP8506	51°45·0'	0°45·7'W	X	165
Upper Badcall	Highld	NC1541	58°19·4'	5°9·1'W	T	9
Upper Badrain	Highld	NH6359	57°36·3'	4°17·1'W	X	26
Upper Bainshole	Aberd	NJ6135	57°24·5'	2°38·5'W	X	29
Upper Balannan	D & G	NX7059	54°54·8'	4°1·3'W	X	83,84
Upper Balblair	Aberd	NJ7006	57°8·9'	2°29·3'W	X	38
Upper Balfour	Aberd	NJ5317	57°14·7'	2°46·3'W	X	37
Upper Balfour	Aberd	NO7896	57°3·5'	2°21·3'W	X	38,45
Upper Balgray	Angus	NO3458	56°42·8'	3°4·2'W	X	54
Upper Ballaclucas	I of M	SC3479	54°11·0'	4°32·2'W	X	95
Upper Ballaird	Stir	NS5591	56°5·6'	4°19·4'W	X	57
Upper Ballavarkish	I of M	SC2571	54°6·6'	4°40·2'W	X	95
Upper Ballunie	Pth & Kin	NO2639	56°32·5'	3°11·8'W	X	53
Upper Ballywilline	Arg & Bt	NR7123	55°27·1'	5°36·9'W	X	68
Upper Balquhindochy	Aberd	NJ7647	57°31·0'	2°23·6'W	X	29
Upper Balwill	Stir	NS5492	56°6·2'	4°20·4'W	X	57
Upper Bangor	Gwyn	SH5772	53°13·8'	4°8·1'W	T	114,115
Upper Barden Resr	N Yks	SE0157	54°0·8'	1°58·7'W	W	104
Upper Bardley	Shrops	SO6980	52°25·3'	2°27·0'W	X	138
Upper Barn	Shrops	SO4286	52°28·4'	2°50·8'W	X	137
Upper Barn	Shrops	SO5591	52°31·1'	2°39·4'W	X	137,138
Upper Barn	Shrops	SO5692	52°31·7'	2°38·5'W	X	137,138
Upper Barnbow Fm	Leeds	SE3935	53°48·8'	1°24·0'W	FM	104
Upper Barn Fm	Bucks	SP7118	51°51·6'	0°57·7'W	FM	165
Upper Barn Fm	Surrey	TQ3545	51°11·5'	0°3·7'W	FM	187
Upper Barns Fm	Glos	ST7490	51°36·7'	2°22·1'W	FM	162,172
Upper Barpham	W Susx	TQ0608	50°51·9'	0°29·2'W	X	197
Upper Barr	Arg & Bt	NR6837	55°34·5'	5°40·4'W	X	68
Upper Barr	D & G	NX4162	54°55·9'	4°28·5'W	X	83
Upper Barr	D & G	NX7678	55°5·1'	3°56·1'W	X	84
Upper Barr	S Ayr	NX2895	55°13·4'	4°41·8'W	X	76
Upper Basildon	W Berks	SU5976	51°29·0'	1°8·6'W	T	174
Upper Batley	Kirk	SE2425	53°43·5'	1°37·8'W	T	104
Upper Battlefield	Shrops	SJ5117	52°45·1'	2°43·2'W	T	126
Upper Baulk	Aberd	NO8086	56°58·1'	2°19·3'W	X	45
Upper Baynton Fm	Wilts	ST9453	51°16·8'	2°4·8'W	FM	184
Upper Beakley Fm	Essex	TL8029	51°55·8'	0°37·5'E	FM	168
Upper Beanshill	C of Aber	NJ8402	57°6·8'	2°15·4'W	X	38
Upper Beeding	W Susx	TQ1910	50°52·9'	0°18·1'W	T	198
Upper Bench	S Glos	ST5690	51°36·7'	2°37·7'W	X	162,172
Upper Benefield	Northnts	SP9889	52°29·6'	0°33·0'W	T	141
Upper Bentley	Worcs	SO9966	52°17·8'	2°0·5'W	T	150
Upper Bentley Fm	Worcs	SO9965	52°17·2'	2°0·5'W	FM	150
Upper Beoch	E Ayr	NS5210	55°22·0'	4°19·7'W	X	70
Upper Berrow Fm	Worcs	SO9962	52°15·6'	2°0·5'W	FM	150
Upper Berryhill	Orkney	HY4108	58°57·6'	3°1·1'W	X	6,7
Upper Berthlwyd	Monm	SO3705	51°44·6'	2°54·4'W	X	161
Upper Berwick	Shrops	SJ4715	52°44·0'	2°46·7'W	X	126
Upper Bettws	Powys	SO2246	52°6·6'	3°7·9'W	X	148
Upper Bevendean	Bri & Hov	TQ3506	50°50·5'	0°4·6'W	X	198
Upper Bigging	Orkney	HY3219	59°3·4'	3°10·7'W	X	6
Upper Bighouse	Highld	NC8857	58°29·5'	3°54·8'W	T	10
Upper Billesley	Warw	SP1556	52°12·4'	1°46·4'W	X	151
Upper Billown	I of M	SC2670	54°6·0'	4°39·3'W	X	95
Upper Birch Fm	Worcs	SO7980	52°25·3'	2°18·1'W	FM	138
Upper Birchitt	Derby	SK3379	53°18·7'	1°29·9'W	X	119
Upper Birchwood	Derby	SK4354	53°5·1'	1°21·1'W	T	120
Upper Birnie	Aberd	NO7969	56°49·0'	2°20·2'W	X	45
Upper Bisterne Fm	Hants	SU1501	50°48·7'	1°46·8'W	FM	195
Upper Bittell Resr	Worcs	SP0175	52°22·6'	1°58·7'W	W	139
Upper Blackgrove Fm	Bucks	SP7718	51°51·5'	0°52·5'W	FM	165
Upper Blaen	Heref	SO2733	51°59·7'	3°3·4'W	X	161
Upper Blainslie	Scot Bord	NT5344	55°41·5'	2°44·4'W	T	73
Upper Blairmaud	Aberd	NJ6159	57°37·4'	2°38·7'W	X	29
Upper Blairmore	Stir	NS4989	56°4·5'	4°25·1'W	X	57
Upper Blairnain	Moray	NJ2738	57°25·8'	3°12·5'W	X	28
Upper Blairock	Moray	NJ5062	57°39·0'	2°49·8'W	X	29
Upper Blakenhall	Staffs	SK1518	52°45·8'	1°46·3'W	X	128
Upper Boat	Rho Cyn Taf	ST1087	51°34·7'	3°17·5'W	T	171
Upper Boddam	Aberd	NJ6230	57°21·8'	2°37·4'W	T	29,37
Upper Boddington	Northnts	SP4853	52°10·6'	1°17·5'W	T	151
Upper Bogrow	Highld	NH7081	57°48·2'	4°10·8'W	X	21
Upper Bogside	Moray	NJ2057	57°36·0'	3°19·9'W	X	28
Upper Bolney Ho	Oxon	SU7579	51°30·5'	0°54·8'W	X	175
Upper Bolstone Wood	Heref	SO5433	51°59·8'	2°39·8'W	F	149
Upper Bolton	E Loth	NT5069	55°54·9'	2°47·6'W	X	66
Upper Bonchurch	I of W	SZ5778	50°36·2'	1°11·3'W	T	196
Upper Booth	Derby	SK1085	53°21·9'	1°50·6'W	T	110
Upper Borth	Cered	SN6088	52°28·6'	4°3·3'W	T	135
Upper Bottom Ho	Bucks	SU9794	51°38·4'	0°35·5'W	X	175,176
Upper Bowden Fm	W Berks	SU6175	51°28·5'	1°6·9'W	FM	175
Upper Boyndlie	Aberd	NJ9062	57°39·1'	2°9·6'W	T	30
Upper Brailes	Warw	SP3039	52°3·1'	1°33·4'W	T	151
Upper Brandon Parva	Norf	TG0408	52°38·1'	1°1·3'E	T	144
Upper Breakish	Highld	NG6823	57°14·6'	5°50·3'W	T	32
Upper Breinton	Heref	SO4640	52°3·6'	2°46·9'W	T	148,149,161
Upper Brick Yard	Torf	SO2510	51°47·3'	3°4·9'W	X	161
Upper Broadmoor	Glos	SP1616	51°50·8'	1°45·7'W	X	163
Upper Brockholes	Cald	SE0629	53°45·7'	1°54·1'W	X	104
Upper Brogan	Aberd	NK0230	57°21·9'	1°57·5'W	X	30
Upper Brook Ho	Staffs	SK1130	52°52·3'	1°49·8'W	X	128
Upper Brookhouse Fm	E Susx	TQ4919	50°57·3'	0°7·7'E	FM	199
Upper Broombriggs	Leic	SK5113	52°43·0'	1°14·3'W	X	129
Upper Broomhill	Aberd	NJ6007	57°9·4'	2°39·2'W	X	37
Upper Broomhills	Aberd	NJ7207	57°9·4'	2°27·3'W	X	38
Upper Brotherstone	Scot Bord	NT4256	55°47·9'	2°55·1'W	X	66,73
Upper Broughton	Notts	SK6826	52°49·9'	0°59·0'W	T	129
Upper Broughton	Shrops	SO3090	52°30·4'	3°1·5'W	X	137
Upper Brownhill	Aberd	NK0432	57°23·0'	1°55·6'W	X	30
Upper Broxwood	Heref	SO3653	52°10·5'	2°55·8'W	T	148,149
Upper Bruntingthorpe	Leic	SP6088	52°29·4'	1°6·6'W	T	140
Upper Bruntlands	Moray	NJ1943	57°28·5'	3°20·6'W	X	28
Upper Brydekirk	D & G	NY1872	55°4·5'	3°16·6'W	X	85
Upper Brynamman	Carm	SN7114	51°48·8'	3°51·9'W	T	160
Upper Brynkyn	Powys	SO2895	52°33·1'	3°2·6'W	X	137
Upper Bryn-y-groes	Powys	SJ1410	52°41·1'	3°15·9'W	X	125
Upper Buckenhill	Heref	SO5933	51°59·9'	2°35·4'W	T	149
Upper Bucklebury	W Berks	SU5468	51°24·7'	1°13·0'W	T	174
Upper Bullington	Hants	SU4641	51°10·2'	1°20·1'W	T	185
Upper Bunction Ho	W Susx	TQ1414	50°55·1'	0°22·3'W	X	198
Upper Bunzion	Fife	NO3408	56°15·9'	3°3·5'W	X	59
Upper Burgate	Hants	SU1516	50°56·8'	1°46·8'W	T	184
Upper Burnhaugh	Aberd	NO8394	57°2·5'	2°16·4'W	X	38,45
Upper Burnside	Aberd	NJ6509	57°10·5'	2°34·3'W	X	38
Upper Bush	Medway	TQ6966	51°22·3'	0°26·1'E	T	177,178
Upperby	Cumbr	NY4053	54°52·3'	2°55·7'W	T	85
Upper Cabra	Aberd	NJ9751	57°33·2'	2°2·5'W	X	30
Upper Cadley's	Oxon	SU6282	51°32·2'	1°6·0'W	X	175
Upper Cae Garw	Monm	SO4805	51°44·7'	2°44·8'W	X	161
Upper Cae-glas	Powys	SO1376	52°22·7'	3°16·3'W	X	136,148
Upper Caerfaelog	Powys	SO1174	52°21·7'	3°18·0'W	X	136,148
Upper Cairn	Scot Bord	NT1050	55°44·4'	3°25·6'W	A	65,72
Upper Cairnie	Pth & Kin	NO0319	56°21·5'	3°33·7'W	X	58
Upper Caldecote	Beds	TL1645	52°5·7'	0°18·0'W	T	153
Upper Callowhill	Staffs	SK0527	52°50·7'	1°55·1'W	X	128
Upper Cam	Glos	ST7599	51°41·6'	2°21·3'W	T	162
Upper Campsfield Fm	Oxon	SP4616	51°50·7'	1°19·5'W	FM	164
Upper Camster	Highld	ND2641	58°21·3'	3°15·4'W	X	11,12
Upper Canada	Aberd	NJ6424	57°18·6'	2°35·4'W	X	37
Upper Canada	N Som	ST3658	51°19·3'	2°54·7'W	T	182
Upper Canfold Wood	Surrey	TQ0840	51°9·2'	0°27·0'W	F	187
Upper Canterton	Hants	SU2612	50°54·6'	1°37·4'W	T	195
Upper Cantref Fm	Powys	SO0525	51°55·2'	3°22·5'W	FM	160
Upper Carbarns	N Lanak	NS7753	55°45·5'	3°57·2'W	X	64
Upper Carlestoun	E Dunb	NS6275	55°57·2'	4°12·2'W	X	64
Upper Carr Fm	N Yks	SE8081	54°13·3'	0°46·0'W	FM	100
Upper Carvan	Pemb	SN1713	51°47·4'	4°38·8'W	X	158
Upper Carwood	Shrops	SO4085	52°27·8'	2°52·6'W	X	137
Upper Castle Ely	Carm	SN1910	51°45·8'	4°37·0'W	X	158
Upper Castleton	Moray	NJ1928	57°20·4'	3°20·3'W	X	36
Upper Castleton Fm	Heref	SO2745	52°6·2'	3°3·6'W	FM	148
Upper Caswell Fm	N Som	ST4874	51°28·0'	2°44·5'W	FM	171,172
Upper Catesby	Northnts	SP5259	52°13·8'	1°13·9'W	T	151
Upper Cathedine	Powys	SO1424	51°54·7'	3°14·6'W	X	161
Upper Catshill	Worcs	SO9674	52°22·1'	2°3·1'W	T	139
Upper Cefn	Heref	SO3530	51°58·1'	2°56·4'W	X	149,161
Upper Cefnwern	Powys	SO1528	51°56·9'	3°13·8'W	X	161
Upper Chalkley Fm	S Glos	ST7685	51°34·0'	2°20·4'W	FM	172
Upper Challoch	D & G	NX0163	54°55·6'	5°5·9'W	X	82
Upper Chance Fm	Oxon	SU5284	51°33·4'	1°14·6'W	FM	174
Upper Chancton Fm	W Susx	TQ1314	50°55·1'	0°23·2'W	FM	198
Upper Chapel	Powys	SO0040	52°3·2'	3°27·1'W	T	147,160
Upper Chatto	Scot Bord	NT7617	55°27·0'	2°22·3'W	X	80
Upper Cheddon	Somer	ST2328	51°3·0'	3°5·5'W	T	193
Upper Chelmscote	Warw	SP3141	52°4·2'	1°32·5'W	X	151
Upper Chicksgrove	Wilts	ST9629	51°3·9'	2°3·0'W	T	184
Upper Church Fm	Suff	TL9054	52°9·3'	0°47·1'E	FM	155
Upper Church Fm	W Berks	SU6065	51°23·1'	1°7·9'W	FM	175
Upper Church Village	Rho Cyn Taf	ST0886	51°34·2'	3°19·3'W	T	170
Upper Chute	Wilts	SU2953	51°16·8'	1°34·7'W	T	185
Upper Circourt Fm	Oxon	SU3791	51°37·2'	1°27·5'W	FM	164,174
Upper Clapton	Hack	TQ3487	51°34·2'	0°3·6'W	T	176,177
Upper Clare Fm	Hants	SU8047	51°13·2'	0°50·9'W	FM	186
Upper Clatford	Hants	SU3543	51°11·3'	1°29·6'W	T	185
Upper Clay Hill Fm	E Susx	TQ4414	50°54·7'	0°3·3'E	FM	198
Uppercleuch	D & G	NY1187	55°10·4'	3°23·4'W	X	78
Upper Cliff	Staffs	SK0314	52°43·7'	1°56·9'W	H	128
Upper Clifton	D & G	NX9057	54°54·0'	3°42·5'W	X	84
Upper Cloan	Pth & Kin	NN9610	56°16·5'	3°40·3'W	X	58
Upper Clochforbie	Aberd	NJ8058	57°37·0'	2°19·6'W	X	29,30
Upper Clopton	Warw	SP1744	52°5·9'	1°44·7'W	X	151
Upper Cluden	D & G	NX9379	55°5·9'	3°40·2'W	X	84
Upper Clydach River	Nth Pt Talb	SN7006	51°44·5'	3°52·6'W	W	160
Upper Clydd	Monm	SO3223	51°54·3'	2°58·9'W	X	161
Upper Clyth	Highld	ND2737	58°19·2'	3°14·3'W	X	11
Upper Coberley	Glos	SO9715	51°50·3'	2°2·2'W	T	163
Upper Cog	D & G	NS8115	55°25·1'	3°52·4'W	X	71,78
Upper College	Shrops	SJ5734	52°54·3'	2°38·0'W	T	126
Upper Collinhirst	D & G	NY1775	55°4·0'	3°17·6'W	X	85
Upper Colwall	Heref	SO7643	52°5·3'	2°20·6'W	T	150
Upper Common	Hants	SU6345	51°12·3'	1°5·5'W	T	185
Upper Common	Suff	TL7645	52°4·7'	0°34·5'E	X	155
Upper Common	W Berks	SU5369	51°25·3'	1°13·9'W	X	174
Upper Common Fm	Roth	SK4884	53°21·3'	1°16·3'W	FM	111,120
Upper Commons	Sheff	SK2196	53°27·9'	1°40·6'W	X	110
Upper Conheath	D & G	NY0070	55°1·1'	3°33·4'W	X	84
Upper Cook	Aberd	NJ8056	57°35·9'	2°19·6'W	X	29,30
Upper Coomb Craig	D & G	NT1212	55°23·9'	3°22·9'W	X	78
Upper Copcourt Fm	Oxon	SP7000	51°41·9'	0°58·8'W	FM	165
Upper Coquet Dale	Northum	NT8807	55°21·7'	2°10·9'W	X	80
Upper Coscombe	Glos	SP0730	51°58·3'	1°53·5'W	X	150
Upper Coston	Shrops	SO3880	52°25·1'	2°54·3'W	X	137
Upper Cotburn	Aberd	NJ7653	57°34·2'	2°23·6'W	X	29
Upper Cotton	Staffs	SK0547	53°1·5'	1°55·1'W	T	119,128
Upper Cottown	Aberd	NJ7615	57°13·8'	2°23·4'W	X	38
Upper Coul	Pth & Kin	NN9712	56°17·6'	3°39·4'W	X	58
Upper Coullie	Aberd	NJ7016	57°14·3'	2°29·4'W	X	38
Upper Coullie	Aberd	NO7177	56°53·3'	2°28·1'W	X	45
Upper Cound	Shrops	SJ5504	52°38·2'	2°39·5'W	T	126
Upper Court	Monm	SO3310	51°47·3'	2°57·9'W	X	161
Upper Court Fm	Oxon	SP3222	51°54·0'	1°31·7'W	FM	164
Upper Cowley	Staffs	SJ8219	52°46·3'	2°15·6'W	X	127
Upper Cragabus	Arg & Bt	NR3244	55°37·2'	6°15·0'W	X	60
Upper Craggan	Highld	NJ0126	57°19·1'	3°38·2'W	X	36
Upper Craigenbay	D & G	NX5578	55°4·8'	4°15·9'W	X	77
Upper Craighill	Aberd	NO7466	56°47·3'	2°25·1'W	X	45
Upper Craighill	Aberd	NO7976	56°52·8'	2°20·2'W	H	45
Upper Craigmaud	Aberd	NJ8758	57°37·0'	2°12·6'W	X	30
Upper Craigton	Aberd	NJ5900	57°5·6'	2°40·1'W	X	37
Upper Craigwell	Aberd	NO8394	57°2·5'	2°16·4'W	X	38,45
Upper Cranbourne Fm	Hants	SU4842	51°10·7'	1°18·4'W	FM	185
Upper Cranhill Fm	Warw	SP1252	52°10·2'	1°49·1'W	FM	150
Upper Crannabog	Aberd	NJ6454	57°34·7'	2°35·7'W	X	29
Upper Crannel Fm	Somer	ST4941	51°10·2'	2°43·4'W	FM	182,183
Upper Crichie	Aberd	NJ9544	57°29·4'	2°4·5'W	X	30
Upper Criftin	Shrops	SO3891	52°31·0'	2°54·4'W	X	137
Upper Criggie	Aberd	NO8383	56°56·5'	2°16·3'W	X	45
Upper Croxley	Somer	ST5343	51°11·3'	2°40·0'W	T	182,183
Upper Cudworth	Barns	SE3809	53°34·8'	1°25·2'W	T	110,111
Upper Cufaude Fm	Hants	SU6557	51°18·7'	1°3·7'W	FM	175,186
Upper Culham Fm	Wok	SU7982	51°32·1'	0°51·3'W	FM	175

Upper Cullernie	Highld	NH7347	57°30·0′	4°6·7′W	X	27
Upper Culphin	Aberd	NJ6058	57°36·9′	2°39·7′W	X	29
Upper Cumberworth	Kirk	SE2108	53°34·3′	1°40·6′W	T	110
Upper Cuts	Cambs	TL4871	52°19·3′	0°10·7′E	X	154
Upper Cuttlehill	Aberd	NJ4947	57°30·9′	2°50·6′W	X	28,29
Upper Cwmbran	Torf	ST2796	51°39·7′	3°2·9′W	T	171
Upper Cwmbran	Torf	ST2993	51°38·1′	3°1·2′W	T	171
Upper Cwmbrith	Powys	SO1060	52°14·1′	3°18·7′W	X	148
Upper Cwmcadarn	Powys	SO1935	52°0·7′	3°10·4′W	X	161
Upper Dagie	Aberd	NJ6007	57°9·4′	2°39·2′W	X	37
Upperdale	Derby	SK1772	53°14·9′	1°44·3′W	T	119
Upperdale	Shetld	HU1953	60°15·9′	1°38·9′W	T	3
Upper Dalguhurn	W Dunb	NS3878	55°58·3′	4°35·3′W	X	63
Upper Dalhousie	Midlo	NT3163	55°51·6′	3°5·7′W	X	66
Upper Dallachy	Aberd	NJ6365	57°40·7′	2°36·8′W	X	29
Upper Dallachy	Moray	NJ3662	57°38·9′	3°3·9′W	T	28
Upper Dalveen	D & G	NS9008	55°21·5′	3°43·7′W	X	71,78
Upper Darley	Aberd	NJ7239	57°26·7′	2°27·5′W	X	29
Upper Dead Edge	Barns	SE1301	53°30·6′	1°47·8′W	X	110
Upper Deal	Kent	TR3651	51°12·8′	1°23·1′E	T	179
Upper Dean	Beds	TL0467	52°17·7′	0°28·1′W	T	153
Upper Dean	Devon	SX7264	50°27·9′	3°47·8′W	T	202
Upper Dean Park	C of Edin	NT1664	55°52·0′	3°20·1′W	X	65,66
Upper Dearham's Fm	Bucks	SU9091	51°36·9′	0°41·6′W	FM	175
Upper Dell	Highld	NJ0816	57°13·8′	3°31·0′W	X	36
Upper Delphs	Cambs	TL4073	52°20·5′	0°3·7′E	X	154
Upper Denby	Kirk	SE2207	53°33·8′	1°39·7′W	T	110
Upper Denby	Kirk	SE2316	53°38·6′	1°38·7′W	T	110
Upper Denton	Cumbr	NY6165	54°58·9′	2°36·1′W	T	86
Upper Derraid	Highld	NJ0233	57°22·9′	3°37·3′W	X	27
Upper Derwent Valley	Derby	SK1790	53°24·6′	1°44·2′W	X	110
Upper Diabaig	Highld	NG8160	57°34·9′	5°39·3′W	T	19,24
Upper Dicker	E Susx	TQ5510	50°52·3′	0°12·6′E	T	199
Upper Diddlesfold Fm	W Susx	SU9429	51°3·4′	0°39·1′W	FM	186,197
Upper Dinchope	Shrops	SO4583	52°26·8′	2°48·2′W	T	137,138
Upper Dinmore	Heref	SO4850	52°9·0′	2°45·2′W	X	148,149
Upper Dinvin	D & G	NX0156	54°51·8′	5°5·6′W	X	82
Upper Ditchford Village	Glos	SP1936	52°1·6′	1°43·0′W	A	151
Upper Dochcarty	Highld	NH5360	57°36·6′	4°27·2′W	X	20
Upper Dod	D & G	NX9796	55°15·1′	3°36·8′W	H	78
Upper Dods Fm	Suff	TL8356	52°10·5′	0°41·0′E	FM	155
Upper Dolwilkin	Powys	SO2472	52°20·7′	3°6·5′W	X	137,148
Upper Dormington	Heref	SO5839	52°3·1′	2°36·4′W	T	149
Upper Dormont	D & G	NY1075	55°3·9′	3°24·1′W	X	85
Upper Dornford Fm	Oxon	SP4521	51°53·4′	1°20·4′W	FM	164
Upper Dounreay	Highld	ND0065	58°34·0′	3°42·7′W	T	11,12
Upper Dovercourt	Essex	TM2330	51°55·7′	1°15·0′E	T	169
Upper Dowdeswell	Glos	SP0019	51°52·4′	1°59·6′W	T	163
Upper Down	Shrops	SO6374	52°22·0′	2°32·2′W	X	138
Upper Drakemyres	Moray	NJ3954	57°34·6′	3°0·7′W	X	28
Upper Drayton	Heref	SO5366	52°17·6′	2°41·0′W	X	137,138,149
Upper Drochil	Scot Bord	NT1543	55°40·6′	3°20·7′W	X	72
Upper Drostre	Powys	SO0930	51°57·9′	3°19·1′W	X	161
Upper Druimfin	Arg & Bt	NM5253	56°36·5′	6°2·0′W	X	47
Upper Drumallochy	Aberd	NJ4614	57°13·1′	2°53·2′W	X	37
Upper Drumbane	Stir	NN6606	56°13·9′	4°9·3′W	X	57
Upper Drumbuie	Highld	NH5131	57°21·0′	4°28·1′W	X	26
Upper Drummond	Highld	NH6643	57°27·7′	4°13·6′W	T	26
Upper Dullarg	D & G	NX6875	55°3·4′	4°3·6′W	X	77,84
Upper Dumball	Glos	SO7511	51°48·1′	2°21·4′W	X	162
Upper Dunsforth	N Yks	SE4463	54°3·9′	1°19·2′W	T	99
Upper Dunsley	Herts	SP9311	51°47·6′	0°38·7′W	T	165
Upper Dyffryn	Monm	SO4223	51°54·4′	2°50·2′W	X	161
Upper Dysart	Angus	NO6853	56°40·3′	2°30·9′W	X	54
Upper Earlscourt Fm	Swin	SU2284	51°33·5′	1°40·6′W	FM	174
Upper Earnstrey Park	Shrops	SO5887	52°29·0′	2°36·7′W	X	137,138
Upper Eashing	Surrey	SU9543	51°10·9′	0°38·1′W	T	186
Upper Eastern Green	Cov	SP2780	52°25·3′	1°35·8′W	T	140
Upper Eastwood	Cald	SD9625	53°43·5′	2°3·2′W	X	103
Upper Eathie	Highld	NH7663	57°38·7′	4°4·2′W	X	21,27
Upper Edge	Derby	SK0768	53°12·8′	1°53·3′W	X	119
Upper Edgebold	Shrops	SJ4511	52°41·9′	2°48·4′W	X	126
Upper Edindurno	Aberd	NJ6214	57°13·2′	2°37·3′W	X	37
Upper Edmonton	Enf	TQ3492	51°36·9′	0°3·5′W	T	176,177
Upper Egleton	Heref	SO6344	52°5·8′	2°32·0′W	T	149
Upper Elkstone	Staffs	SK0558	53°7·4′	1°55·1′W	T	119
Upper Ellastone	Staffs	SK1143	52°59·3′	1°49·8′W	T	119,128
Upper Elmers End	Brom	TQ3667	51°23·4′	0°2·3′W	T	177
Upper End	Derby	SK0876	53°17·1′	1°52·4′W	T	119
Upper End	Glos	SP0006	51°45·4′	1°59·6′W	T	163
Upper End	Glos	SP1213	51°49·2′	1°49·2′W	T	163
Upper End	Leic	SK7414	52°43·2′	0°53·9′W	T	129
Upper Enham	Hants	SU3649	51°14·6′	1°28·7′W	T	185
Upper Ensign	Kent	TR0656	51°16·2′	0°57·6′E	X	179
Upper Esgair Hill	Powys	SO0273	52°21·0′	3°25·9′W	X	136,147
Upper Esgair-rhiw	Powys	SN9967	52°17·8′	3°28·5′W	X	136,147
Upper Ettrick	Arg & Bt	NS0367	55°51·6′	5°8·4′W	X	63
Upper Fall	Highld	NH4919	57°14·5′	4°29·7′W	W	34
Upper Farmcote	Shrops	SO7791	52°31·2′	2°19·9′W	T	138
Upper Farm Down	Wilts	SU0335	51°7·1′	1°57·0′W	X	184
Upper Farringdon	Hants	SU7135	51°6·8′	0°58·8′W	T	186
Upper Faulds	Orkney	ND4896	58°51·2′	2°53·6′W	X	6,7
Upper Fea	Orkney	HY4507	58°57·1′	2°56·9′W	X	6,7
Upper Feorlig	Highld	NG2944	57°24·6′	6°30·3′W	T	23
Upper Fernoch	Arg & Bt	NN0020	56°20·1′	5°13·7′W	X	50
Upper Fernoch	Arg & Bt	NR7285	56°0·5′	5°39·0′W	X	55
Upper Ffynnonau	Powys	SO1854	52°10·9′	3°11·6′W	X	148
Upper Field	Heref	SO5020	51°52·8′	2°43·2′W	X	162
Upperfield Fm	Derby	SK2551	53°3·6′	1°37·2′W	FM	119
Upperfield Fm	Oxon	SP5902	51°43·0′	1°8·4′W	FM	164
Upper Fields	Leic	SK3711	52°42·0′	1°26·7′W	X	128
Upper Fields Fm	Glos	SP1931	51°58·9′	1°43·0′W	FM	151
Upper Finlarig	Highld	NH9925	57°18·5′	3°40·1′W	X	36
Upper Firth	Midlo	NT2658	55°48·8′	3°10·4′W	X	66,73
Upper Fivehead	Somer	ST3423	51°0·4′	2°56·1′W	T	193
Upper Fleet Green	Staffs	SK0561	53°9·0′	1°55·1′W	X	119
Upper Fm	Bucks	SP6707	51°45·7′	1°1·4′W	FM	164,165
Upper Fm	Dorset	SU0611	50°54·1′	1°54·5′W	FM	195
Upper Fm	Essex	TL7441	52°2·6′	0°32·6′E	FM	155
Upper Fm	N Som	ST5472	51°26·9′	2°39·3′W	FM	172

Upper Fm	Oxon	SP5524	51°54·9′	1°11·6′W	FM	164
Upper Fm	Oxon	SP7602	51°42·9′	0°53·6′W	FM	165
Upper Fm	Oxon	SU4785	51°33·9′	1°18·9′W	FM	174
Upper Fm	Oxon	SU5499	51°41·5′	1°12·7′W	FM	164
Upper Fm	Powys	SJ2813	52°42·8′	3°3·5′W	FM	126
Upper Fm	Powys	SO1769	52°19·0′	3°12·7′W	FM	136,148
Upper Fm	Staffs	SJ9127	52°50·7′	2°7·6′W	FM	127
Upper Fm	Suff	TM4381	52°22·6′	1°34·6′E	FM	156
Upper Fm	Wilts	ST9074	51°28·1′	2°8·2′W	FM	173
Upper Fm	Wilts	SU0470	51°26·0′	1°56·2′W	FM	173
Upper Foker	Staffs	SJ9758	53°7·4′	2°2·3′W	X	118
Upper Forge	Glos	SO6305	51°44·8′	2°31·8′W	X	162
Upper Forge	Shrops	SO7289	52°30·1′	2°24·4′W	T	138
Upper Fowle Hall Fm	Kent	TQ6945	51°11·0′	0°25·5′E	FM	188
Upper Fowlis	Aberd	NJ5511	57°11·5′	2°44·2′W	X	37
Upper Fowlwood	Moray	NJ5252	57°33·6′	2°47·7′W	X	29
Upper Foxhall	Heref	SO6325	51°55·6′	2°31·9′W	X	162
Upper Framilode	Glos	SO7510	51°47·5′	2°21·4′W	T	162
Upper Frithfold Fm	W Susx	SU9829	51°3·3′	0°35·7′W	FM	186,197
Upper Froyle	Hants	SU7542	51°10·6′	0°55·2′W	T	186
Upper Gambolds	Worcs	SO9768	52°18·8′	2°2·2′W	T	139
Upper Garreg Lwyd	Powys	SJ2215	52°43·9′	3°8·9′W	X	126
Upper Gartally	Highld	NH4831	57°20·9′	4°31·1′W	X	26
Upper Gartness	Stir	NS4986	56°2·8′	4°25·0′W	X	57
Upper Gate Clough	Derby	SK0991	53°25·2′	1°51·5′W	X	110
Upper Gatehampton Fm	Oxon	SU6180	51°31·2′	1°6·9′W	FM	175
Upper Gatton Park	Surrey	TQ2653	51°16·0′	0°11·2′W	X	187
Upper Gillock	Highld	ND3452	58°27·3′	3°7·4′W	X	12
Upper Gills	Highld	ND3271	58°37·6′	3°9·8′W	T	7,12
Upper Glandulas	Powys	SN9483	52°26·3′	3°33·2′W	X	136
Upper Glasslaw	Aberd	NJ8559	57°37·5′	2°14·6′W	X	30
Upper Glebe Fm	Cambs	TL1386	52°27·8′	0°19·8′W	FM	142
Upperglen	Highld	NG3151	57°28·4′	6°28·8′W	X	23
Upper Glendessarry	Highld	NM9593	56°59·2′	5°22·0′W	X	33,40
Upper Glendevon Reservoir	Pth & Kin	NN9004	56°13·2′	3°46·0′W	W	58
Upper Glenfintaig	Highld	NN2588	56°57·3′	4°52·2′W	X	34,41
Upper Glenlair	D & G	NX7371	55°1·3′	3°58·8′W	X	77,84
Upper Glenton	Aberd	NJ6612	57°12·1′	2°33·3′W	X	38
Upper Godney	Somer	ST4842	51°10·7′	2°44·2′W	T	182
Upper Goldstone	Kent	TR2960	51°17·8′	1°17·5′E	T	179
Upper Goosehill Fm	Worcs	SO9461	52°15·1′	2°4·9′W	FM	150
Upper Gordonsburn	Aberd	NJ4637	57°25·5′	2°53·5′W	X	28,29
Upper Gore Fm	Lancs	SD3603	53°31·4′	2°57·5′W	FM	108
Upper Gornal	Dudley	SO9292	52°31·8′	2°6·7′W	T	139
Upper Gothens	Pth & Kin	NO1641	56°33·5′	3°21·6′W	X	53
Upper Goytre	Monm	SO3522	51°53·8′	2°56·3′W	X	161
Upper Grain	D & G	NY1898	55°16·4′	3°17·0′W	W	79
Upper Grange	Heref	SO3632	51°59·2′	2°55·5′W	X	149,161
Upper Grange	Monm	ST4288	51°35·5′	2°49·8′W	X	171,172
Upper Grange	Oxon	SU6096	51°39·8′	1°7·6′W	X	164,165
Upper Grange Fm	Leic	SK4312	52°42·5′	1°21·4′W	FM	129
Upper Grange Fm	Leic	SK6522	52°47·7′	1°1·8′W	FM	129
Upper Gravenhurst	Beds	TL1136	52°0·9′	0°22·6′W	T	153
Upper Green	Essex	TL4434	51°59·4′	0°6·2′E	T	154
Upper Green	Leeds	SE2725	53°43·5′	1°35·0′W	T	104
Upper Green	Monm	SO3818	51°51·7′	2°53·6′W	T	161
Upper Green	Staffs	SK0458	53°7·4′	1°56·0′W	X	119
Upper Green	Suff	TL7464	52°15·0′	0°33·3′E	T	155
Upper Green	W Berks	SU3663	51°22·1′	1°28·6′W	T	174
Upper Greenburn	Aberd	NJ9259	57°37·5′	2°7·6′W	X	30
Upper Greenfield	Aberd	NJ8147	57°31·0′	2°18·6′W	X	29,30
Upper Green Fm	Norf	TM2989	52°27·3′	1°22·6′E	FM	156
Upper Green Lane	Heref	SO3247	52°7·3′	2°59·2′W	X	148
Upper Green Quarries	Cumbr	NY3345	54°48·0′	3°2·1′W	X	85
Upper Grimmer	Shrops	SJ3403	52°37·5′	2°58·1′W	X	126
Upper Grounds	Kent	TR2166	51°21·2′	1°10·8′E	X	179
Upper Grove	Monm	SO4518	51°51·7′	2°47·5′W	X	161
Upper Grove Common	Heref	SO5526	51°56·1′	2°38·9′W	T	162
Upper Grove Fm	Suff	TM3566	52°14·7′	1°27·0′E	FM	156
Upper Grove Mill	Oxon	SP4537	52°2·0′	1°20·2′W	X	151
Upper Guist	Norf	TG0026	52°47·9′	0°58·4′E	T	133
Upper Gylen	Arg & Bt	NM8126	56°22·8′	5°32·4′W	X	49
Upper Hackney	Derby	SK2961	53°9·0′	1°33·6′W	T	119
Upper Hairshaw	E Ayr	NS4548	55°42·3′	4°27·6′W	X	64
Upper Hale	Surrey	SU8449	51°14·3′	0°47·4′W	T	186
Upper Halistra	Highld	NG2459	57°32·5′	6°36·3′W	T	23
Upper Hall	E Ayr	NS6828	55°31·9′	4°5·1′W	X	71
Upper Hall	Essex	TL5406	51°44·1′	0°14·2′E	X	167
Upper Hall	Glos	SO6914	51°49·7′	2°26·6′W	X	162
Upper Hall	Powys	SJ1310	52°41·1′	3°16·8′W	X	125
Upper Hallfields	Derby	SK2148	53°2·0′	1°40·8′W	X	119
Upper Halliford	Surrey	TQ0968	51°24·3′	0°25·6′W	T	176
Upper Halling	Medway	TQ6964	51°21·2′	0°26·0′E	T	177,178,188
Upper Ham	Worcs	SO8539	52°3·2′	2°12·7′W	T	150
Upper Ham	Worcs	SO8549	52°8·6′	2°12·8′W	X	150
Upper Hambleton	Rut	SK9007	52°39·4′	0°39·8′W	T	141
Upper Ham Fm	Wilts	SU0779	51°30·8′	1°53·6′W	FM	173
Upper Hamnish	Heref	SO5459	52°13·9′	2°40·0′W	T	149
Upper Handwick	Angus	NO3642	56°34·2′	3°2·0′W	T	54
Upper Harbledown	Kent	TR1158	51°17·1′	1°1·9′E	T	179
Upper Harcourt	Shrops	SO6982	52°26·3′	2°27·0′W	X	138
Upper Hardacre	N Yks	SD7168	54°6·7′	2°26·2′W	X	98
Upper Hardland	D & G	NX6580	55°6·0′	4°6·5′W	X	77
Upper Hardres Court	Kent	TR1550	51°12·7′	1°5·1′E	T	179,189
Upper Hardres Wood	Kent	TR1449	51°12·2′	1°4·2′E	F	179,189
Upper Hardwick	Heref	SO4057	52°12·7′	2°52·3′W	T	148,149
Upper Harford	Glos	SP1221	51°53·5′	1°49·1′W	X	163
Upper Hartfield	E Susx	TQ4634	51°5·4′	0°5·5′E	T	188
Upper Hartshay	Derby	SK3850	53°3·0′	1°25·6′W	T	119
Upper Harveys	Essex	TL6415	51°48·8′	0°23·1′E	X	167
Upper Haselor	Worcs	SP0141	52°4·3′	1°58·7′W	T	150
Upper Hassiewells	Aberd	NJ6539	57°26·7′	2°34·5′W	X	29
Upper Hatton	Staffs	SJ8337	52°56·0′	2°14·8′W	T	127
Upper Hattons	Staffs	SJ8804	52°38·3′	2°10·2′W	X	127,139
Upper Haugh	Roth	SK4297	53°28·3′	1°21·6′W	T	111
Upper Haughton Ho	Staffs	SJ8719	52°46·3′	2°11·2′W	X	127
Upper Hawkhillock	Aberd	NK0039	57°26·7′	1°59·5′W	X	30
Upper Hay Corner	Staffs	SK0560	53°8·5′	1°55·1′W	X	119

Upper Hayes	Bath & NE Somer	ST3758	51°19·5′	2°22·9′W	X	172
Upper Hayesden	Kent	TQ5644	51°10·7′	0°14·3′E	T	188
Upper Hayston	Angus	NO4045	56°35·8′	2°58·2′W	X	54
Upper Haythog	Pemb	SM9921	51°51·3′	4°54·7′W	X	157,158
Upper Hayton	Shrops	SO5181	52°25·7′	2°42·8′W	T	137,138
Upper Haywood	S Lanak	NS9655	55°46·9′	3°39·1′W	X	65,72
Upper Headley	Brad	SE0932	53°47·3′	1°51·4′W	A	104
Upper Heads	N Yks	NZ7700	54°23·6′	0°48·4′W	X	94
Upper Heath	Shrops	SO5685	52°27·9′	2°38·5′W	X	137,138
Upper Heathfield	Aberd	NJ6238	57°26·1′	2°37·5′W	X	29
Upper Heaton	Kirk	SE1819	53°40·3′	1°43·2′W	T	110
Upper Heilar	E Ayr	NS5925	55°30·2′	4°13·5′W	X	71
Upper Heldre	Powys	SJ2709	52°40·7′	3°4·4′W	X	126
Upper Hellesdon	Norf	TG2211	52°39·3′	1°17·3′E	T	133,134
Upper Helmsley	N Yks	SE6956	54°0·0′	0°56·4′W	T	105,106
Upper Helmsley Common	N Yks	SE6857	54°0·5′	0°57·3′W	X	105,106
Upper Hendre	Monm	SO3207	51°45·7′	2°58·7′W	X	161
Upper Hengoed	Shrops	SJ2834	52°54·2′	3°3·8′W	T	126
Upper Hentland	Pemb	SM9102	51°40·9′	5°1·0′W	X	157,158
Upper Herdswick Fm	Wilts	SU1576	51°29·2′	1°46·6′W	FM	173
Upper Hergest	Heref	SO2654	52°11·0′	3°4·5′W	T	148
Upper Hesleden	N Yks	SD8674	54°9·9′	2°12·4′W	X	98
Upper Hexgreave	Notts	SK6558	53°7·1′	1°1·3′W	X	120
Upper Hey	Sheff	SK1894	53°26·8′	1°43·3′W	H	110
Upper Heyden	Derby	SE0903	53°31·7′	1°51·4′W	X	110
Upper Heyford	Northnts	SP6659	52°13·7′	1°1·6′W	T	152
Upper Heyford	Oxon	SP4926	51°56·1′	1°16·8′W	T	164
Upper Heyford Airfield	Oxon	SP5126	51°56·0′	1°15·1′W	X	164
Upper Hiendly Fm	Wakf	SE3913	53°37·0′	1°24·2′W	FM	110,111
Upperhill	Aberd	NJ6308	57°9·9′	2°36·3′W	X	37
Upper Hill	D & G	NS5800	55°16·7′	4°13·7′W	H	77
Upper Hill	D & G	NY3895	55°15·0′	2°58·1′W	H	79
Upper Hill	Heref	SO4753	52°10·6′	2°46·1′W	T	148,149
Upper Hill	S Glos	ST6596	51°39·9′	2°30·0′W	T	162
Upper Hill Fm	Essex	TL9322	51°52·0′	0°48·6′E	FM	168
Upper Hill Fm	Glos	SO9924	51°55·1′	2°0·5′W	FM	163
Upperhill Fm	Kent	TQ8549	51°12·8′	0°39·3′E	FM	189
Upper Hill Fm	Pemb	SN0018	51°49·7′	4°53·8′W	FM	157,158
Upper Hill Fm	Shrops	SO5696	52°33·8′	2°38·5′W	FM	137,138
Upper Hill Ho	Shrops	SO5884	52°27·4′	2°36·7′W	X	137,138
Upper Hilton	Aberd	NJ4241	57°27·6′	2°57·5′W	X	28
Upper Hindhope	Scot Bord	NT7609	55°22·7′	2°22·3′W	T	80
Upper Hlcombe Fm	Glos	SO8511	51°48·1′	2°12·7′W	FM	162
Upper Ho	Derby	SK0687	53°23·0′	1°54·2′W	A	110
Upper Ho	Heref	SO5454	52°11·2′	2°40·0′W	X	149
Upper Ho	Monm	SO2823	51°54·3′	3°2·4′W	X	161
Upper Ho	Monm	SO3820	51°52·7′	2°53·7′W	X	161
Upper Ho	Monm	SO4215	51°50·1′	2°50·1′W	X	161
Upper Ho	Monm	ST4099	51°41·4′	2°51·7′W	X	171
Upper Ho	Powys	SO0756	52°11·9′	3°21·2′W	X	147
Upper Ho	Powys	SO1499	52°35·2′	3°15·8′W	X	136
Upper Ho	Shrops	SO6581	52°25·8′	2°30·5′W	X	138
Upper Ho	Shrops	SO7079	52°24·7′	2°26·1′W	X	138
Upper Ho	Staffs	SJ8938	52°56·6′	2°9·4′W	X	127
Upper Ho	Surrey	TQ0039	51°8·7′	0°33·8′W	X	186
Upper Ho	Surrey	TQ0342	51°10·3′	0°31·2′W	X	186
Upper Ho	Worcs	SO6165	52°17·1′	2°33·9′W	X	138,149
Upper Ho	Worcs	SO7152	52°10·2′	2°25·0′W	X	149
Upper Hockenden	Brom	TQ4969	51°24·3′	0°8·9′E	X	177
Upper Ho Fm	Shrops	SO6592	52°31·7′	2°30·6′W	FM	138
Upper Hogstow	Shrops	SJ3504	52°38·0′	2°57·2′W	X	126
Upper Hollesley Common	Suff	TM3347	52°4·6′	1°24·4′E	X	169
Upper Holloway	Camden	TQ2986	51°33·7′	0°7·9′W	T	176
Upper Holt	Somer	ST7538	51°8·7′	2°21·1′W	X	183
Upper Holton	Suff	TM4078	52°21·1′	1°31·9′E	T	156
Upper Honeydon Fm	Beds	TL1259	52°13·3′	0°21·2′W	FM	153
Upper Hopton	Kirk	SE1918	53°39·7′	1°42·3′W	T	110
Upper Horns Fm	Hants	SU3359	51°20·0′	1°31·2′W	FM	174
Upper Horsebridge	E Susx	TQ5811	50°52·8′	0°15·2′E	T	199
Upper Horsehall Hill Fm	Wilts	SU2666	51°23·8′	1°37·2′W	FM	174
Upper Horton Fm	Kent	TR1254	51°15·0′	1°2·7′E	FM	179,189
Upper Horton Fm	W Susx	TQ2011	50°53·4′	0°17·2′W	FM	198
Upper House Fm	Derby	SK1189	53°24·1′	1°49·7′W	FM	110
Upperhouse Fm	Derby	SK1859	53°7·9′	1°43·5′W	FM	119
Upper House Fm	Essex	TL6942	52°3·3′	0°28·3′E	FM	154
Upper House Fm	E Susx	TQ6211	50°52·8′	0°18·6′E	FM	199
Upper House Fm	Hants	SU5260	51°20·4′	1°14·8′W	FM	174
Upper House Fm	Heref	SO2834	52°0·2′	3°2·5′W	FM	161
Upper House Fm	Heref	SO3526	51°56·0′	2°56·3′W	FM	161
Upper House Fm	Heref	SO6661	52°15·0′	2°29·5′W	FM	138,149
Upper House Fm	Norf	TF8223	52°46·7′	0°42·3′E	FM	132
Upper House Fm	Oxon	SU6686	51°34·4′	1°2·5′W	FM	175
Upper House Fm	Oxon	SU7381	51°31·6′	0°56·5′W	FM	175
Upper House Fm	Shrops	SO6179	52°24·7′	2°34·0′W	FM	138
Upper House Fm	Shrops	SO6590	52°30·6′	2°30·6′W	FM	138
Upper House Fm	Warw	SP1799	52°35·5′	1°44·5′W	FM	139
Upper House Fm	Worcs	SO6663	52°16·1′	2°29·5′W	FM	138,149
Upper Houses	Durham	NZ1446	54°48·8′	1°46·5′W	X	88
Upper Houses	Essex	TL8339	52°1·4′	0°40·4′E	X	155
Upper Howbog	Moray	NJ4026	57°19·5′	2°59·3′W	X	37
Upper Howe	I of M	SC3774	54°8·4′	4°29·3′W	X	95
Upper Howecleugh	S Lanak	NT0014	55°24·8′	3°34·3′W	X	78
Upper Howsell	Worcs	SO7748	52°8·0′	2°19·8′W	T	150
Upper Hoyland	Barns	SE3501	53°30·5′	1°27·9′W	T	110,111
Upper Hulme	Staffs	SK0160	53°8·5′	1°58·7′W	T	119
Upper Hulme Fm	Ches	SJ8560	53°8·5′	2°13·0′W	FM	118
Upper Hurst	Staffs	SK1158	53°7·4′	1°49·7′W	X	119
Upper Hurst Fm	Derby	SK2283	53°20·8′	1°39·8′W	FM	110
Upper Hyde	I of W	SZ5781	50°37·8′	1°11·3′W	T	196
Upper Hyde	Worcs	SO8870	52°19·9′	2°10·2′W	X	139
Upper Ifield	Kent	TQ6871	51°25·0′	0°25·4′E	X	177,178
Upper Ifold	Surrey	TQ0033	51°5·5′	0°33·9′W	T	186
Upper Inglesham	Swin	SU2096	51°40·0′	1°42·3′W	T	163
Upper Ingleston	D & G	NX8769	55°0·4′	3°45·6′W	X	84
Upper Ings	Notts	SK8184	53°21·0′	0°46·6′W	X	121
Upper Inverbrough	Highld	NH8130	57°21·0′	3°58·2′W	X	27
Upper Inverichnie	Aberd	NJ7060	57°38·0′	2°29·7′W	X	29
Upper Ironside	Aberd	NJ8852	57°33·7′	2°11·6′W	X	30
Upper Jubidee	Orkney	HY3724	59°6·2′	3°5·5′W	X	6

Upper Kebbaty	Aberd	NJ6608	57°10·0′	2°33·3′W	X	38
Upper Keith	E Loth	NT4562	55°51·1′	2°52·3′W	X	66
Upper Keithack	Moray	NJ3437	57°25·4′	3°5·5′W	X	28
Upper Kenley	Fife	NO5611	56°17·6′	2°42·2′W	T	59
Upper Kergord	Shetld	HU4056	60°17·4′	1°16·1′W	T	2,3
Upper Kidston	Scot Bord	NT2242	55°40·2′	3°14·0′W	T	73
Upper Kilchàttan	Arg & Bt	NR3795	56°4·8′	6°13·2′W	T	61
Upper Kilcott	Glos	ST7988	51°35·7′	2°17·8′W	T	162,172
Upper Killay	Swan	SS5892	51°36·8′	4°2·7′W	T	159
Upper Killeyan	Arg & Bt	NR2841	55°35·5′	6°18·6′W	X	60
Upper Kinchrackine	Arg & Bt	NN1527	56°24·2′	4°59·4′W	X	50
Upper Kingston Fm	Hants	SU1603	50°49·8′	1°46·0′W	FM	195
Upper Kinkell	Aberd	NJ7820	57°16·5′	2°21·4′W	X	38
Upper Kinmonth	Aberd	NO7782	56°56·0′	2°22·2′W	X	45
Upper Kinneil	Falk	NS9779	55°59·8′	3°38·6′W	X	65
Upper Kinsham	Heref	SO3665	52°17·0′	2°55·9′W	T	137,148,149
Upper Knarr Fen	Peterb	TF2902	52°36·3′	0°5·3′W	X	142
Upper Knockando	Moray	NJ1843	57°28·5′	3°21·6′W	T	28
Upper Knockans	Moray	NJ1643	57°28·4′	3°23·6′W	X	28
Upper Knockchoilum	Highld	NH4913	57°11·2′	4°29·5′W	X	34
Upper Knowe	Scot Bord	NT6157	55°48·5′	2°36·9′W	X	67,74
Upper Knox	Aberd	NO8071	56°50·1′	2°19·2′W	X	45
Upper Lacon Fm	Shrops	SJ5331	52°52·7′	2°41·5′W	FM	126
Upper Lady Meadows	Staffs	SK0252	53°4·2′	1°57·8′W	X	119
Upper Lairdmannoch	D & G	NX6761	54°55·8′	4°4·1′W	X	83,84
Upper Lake	Aberd	NJ8734	57°24·0′	2°12·5′W	W	30
Upper Lake	Notts	SK5353	53°4·5′	1°12·1′W	W	120
Upper Lake	Wakf	SE3917	53°39·1′	1°24·2′W	W	110,111
Upper Lambourn	W Berks	SU3180	51°31·3′	1°32·8′W	T	174
Upper Landywood	Staffs	SJ9805	52°38·8′	2°1·4′W	T	127,139
Upper Langdales Fm	Suff	TM0958	52°11·1′	1°3·8′E	FM	155
Upper Langford	N Som	ST4659	51°19·9′	2°46·1′W	T	172,182
Upper Langley	Shrops	SO6473	52°21·5′	2°31·3′W	X	138
Upper Langridge Fm	Bath & NE Somer	ST7368	51°24·9′	2°22·9′W	FM	172
Upper Langwith	Derby	SK5169	53°13·2′	1°13·8′W	T	120
Upper Lanham Fm	Hants	SU6136	51°7·4′	1°7·3′W	FM	185
Upper Lanrick	Stir	NN6702	56°11·8′	4°8·2′W	X	57
Upper Larel	Highld	ND1857	58°29·9′	3°23·9′W	X	11,12
Upper Largie	Arg & Bt	NM8300	56°8·9′	5°29·2′W	X	55
Upper Largo or Kirkton of Largo	Fife	NO4203	56°13·2′	2°55·7′W	T	59
Upper Latheron	Highld	ND1731	58°15·9′	3°24·4′W	X	11
Upper Latheron	Highld	ND1935	58°18·0′	3°22·4′W	X	11
Upper Layham	Suff	TM0340	52°1·5′	0°57·9′E	T	155
Upper Lea Fm	Oxon	SP3938	52°2·6′	1°25·5′W	FM	151
Upper Ledwyche	Shrops	SO5579	52°24·7′	2°39·3′W	X	137,138
Upper Leigh	Staffs	SK0136	52°55·5′	1°58·7′W	T	128
Upper Leigh Fm	Wilts	ST8829	51°3·8′	2°9·9′W	FM	183
Upper Leighs	Leic	SP8192	52°31·4′	0°48·0′W	X	141
Upper Lemington Village	Glos	SP2134	52°0·5′	1°41·2′W	A	151
Upper Lenie	Highld	NH5127	57°18·8′	4°28·0′W	X	26,35
Upper Letters	Highld	NH3495	57°55·1′	4°47·7′W	X	20
Upper Ley	Glos	SO7217	51°51·3′	2°24·0′W	X	162
Upper Leys Fm	N Yks	SD9745	53°54·3′	2°2·3′W	FM	103
Upper Lhergydhoo	I of M	SC2884	54°13·6′	4°37·9′W	X	95
Upper Linklater	Orkney	HY2621	59°4·4′	3°17·0′W	X	6
Upper Linn	E Ayr	NS6415	55°24·9′	4°8·5′W	X	71
Upper Linnay	Orkney	HY7554	59°22·6′	2°25·9′W	X	5
Upper Littleton	N Som	ST5564	51°22·6′	2°38·4′W	T	172,182
Upper Litton	Powys	SO2567	52°18·0′	3°5·6′W	X	137,148
Upper Llaithddu	Powys	SO0679	52°24·3′	3°22·5′W	X	136,147
Upper Llangoed	Powys	SO1139	52°2·8′	3°17·5′W	X	161
Upper Llanover	Monm	SO2908	51°46·2′	3°1·3′W	X	161
Upper Llantydwell	Pemb	SN1712	51°46·8′	4°38·8′W	X	158
Upper Lliedi Redr	Carm	SN5104	51°43·1′	4°9·0′W	W	159
Upper Lliw Resr	Swan	SN6606	51°44·4′	3°56·1′W	W	159
Upper Loads	Derby	SK3169	53°13·3′	1°31·7′W	T	119
Upper Loch	Arg & Bt	NR6350	55°41·4′	5°45·8′W	W	62
Upper Loch	D & G	NX5881	55°6·4′	4°13·1′W	W	77
Upper Loch	D & G	NY0783	55°8·2′	3°27·1′W	W	78
Upper Lochan Sligeanach	Highld	NM7174	56°48·3′	5°44·6′W	W	40
Upper Locharwoods	D & G	NY0367	54°59·5′	3°30·5′W	X	84
Upper Loch Aulasary	N Eil	NF9372	57°38·3′	7°8·2′W	W	18
Upper Loch Kildonan	N Eil	NF7328	57°13·8′	7°24·7′W	W	22
Upper Loch of Brouster	Shetld	HU2652	60°15·4′	1°31·3′W	W	3
Upper Loch of Setter	Shetld	HU3792	60°36·8′	1°18·9′W	W	1,2
Upper Lochton	Aberd	NO6997	57°4·0′	2°30·2′W	T	38,45
Upper Loch Torridon	Highld	NG8456	57°32·8′	5°36·1′W	W	24
Upper Lode	Worcs	SO8833	52°0·0′	2°10·1′W	T	150
Upper Lodge	Northnts	SP7783	52°26·6′	0°51·6′W	X	141
Upper Lodge	Suff	TM0164	52°14·5′	0°57·0′E	X	155
Upper Lodge	W Susx	SU8726	51°1·8′	0°45·2′W	X	186,197
Upper Lodge Farm	E Susx	TQ4814	50°54·6′	0°6·7′E	FM	198
Upper Lodge Fm	Cambs	TL1594	52°32·1′	0°17·9′W	FM	142
Upper Longdon	Staffs	SK0514	52°43·7′	1°55·2′W	T	128
Upper Ludstone	Shrops	SO8095	52°33·4′	2°17·3′W	T	138
Upper Lurg	Aberd	NJ6905	57°8·3′	2°30·3′W	X	38
Upper Lutheredge Fm	Glos	ST8198	51°41·1′	2°16·1′W	FM	162
Upper Lybster	Highld	ND2537	58°19·2′	3°16·3′W	T	11
Upper Lydbrook	Glos	SO6015	51°50·2′	2°34·4′W	T	162
Upper Lyde	Heref	SO4944	52°5·8′	2°44·3′W	T	148,149
Upper Lye	Heref	SO3965	52°17·0′	2°53·3′W	T	137,148,149
Upper Lyne	Moray	NJ2639	57°26·4′	3°13·5′W	X	28
Upper Lynemore	Moray	NJ4043	57°28·7′	2°59·6′W	X	28
Upper Maenllwyd	Powys	SO1692	52°31·4′	3°13·9′W	X	136
Upper Maes-coed	Heref	SO3334	52°0·3′	2°58·2′W	T	149,161
Upper Magus	Fife	NO4414	56°19·2′	2°53·9′W	X	59
Upper Maidensgrove	Oxon	SU7089	51°36·0′	0°59·0′W	X	175
Upper Mains	Aberd	NJ7048	57°31·5′	2°29·6′W	X	29
Upper Mains	Aberd	NJ7306	57°8·9′	2°26·3′W	X	38
Upper Mains	D & G	NY1369	55°0·7′	3°21·2′W	X	85
Upper Mains of Crichie	Aberd	NJ9544	57°29·4′	2°4·5′W	X	30
Upper Manbeen	Moray	NJ1857	57°36·0′	3°21·9′W	X	28
Upper Marsh	Brad	SE0236	53°49·5′	1°57·8′W	T	104
Upper Marshes	Shrops	SO6478	52°24·2′	2°31·4′W	X	138
Upper Marston	Heref	SO3558	52°13·2′	2°56·7′W	X	148,149
Upper Maudlin Fm	W Susx	TQ1709	50°52·3′	0°19·8′W	FM	198
Upper Medhurst Green Fm	Ches	SJ8162	53°9·5′	2°16·6′W	FM	118
Upper Mickle Hey	Black w Dar	SD6931	53°46·7′	2°27·8′W	X	103
Upper Middleton	Angus	NO3743	56°34·7′	3°1·1′W	X	54
Upper Midhope	Sheff	SK2199	53°29·5′	1°40·6′W	T	110
Upper Midway	Derby	SK3020	52°46·8′	1°32·9′W	T	128
Upper Mill	Aberd	NJ5514	57°13·1′	2°44·3′W	X	37
Uppermill	Aberd	NJ7044	57°29·4′	2°29·6′W	X	29
Upper Mill	Aberd	NJ7714	57°13·2′	2°22·4′W	X	38
Uppermill	Aberd	NK0537	57°25·7′	1°54·5′W	X	30
Uppermill	Aberd	NO6474	56°51·6′	2°35·0′W	X	45
Upper Mill	Aberd	NO8273	56°51·1′	2°17·3′W	X	45
Uppermill	Oldham	SD9905	53°32·7′	2°0·5′W	T	109
Upper Mill Fm	Glos	SU0196	51°40·0′	1°58·7′W	FM	163
Upper Millichope	Shrops	SO5289	52°30·0′	2°42·0′W	X	137,138
Upper Mill of Byth	Aberd	NJ8352	57°33·7′	2°16·6′W	X	29,30
Uppermill of Tillyhilt	Aberd	NJ8431	57°22·4′	2°15·5′W	X	29,30
Uppermills	Aberd	NO7597	57°4·1′	2°24·3′W	X	38,45
Upper Millsteads	D & G	NY4281	55°7·4′	2°54·1′W	X	79
Upper Milovaig	Highld	NG1549	57°26·8′	6°44·6′W	T	23
Upper Milton	Oxon	SP2517	51°51·3′	1°37·8′W	T	163
Upper Milton	Somer	ST5447	51°13·5′	2°39·1′W	T	182,183
Upper Minety	Wilts	SU0091	51°37·3′	1°59·6′W	T	163,173
Upper Minmore	Aberd	NJ5013	57°12·6′	2°49·2′W	X	37
Upper Minnydow	D & G	NX7971	55°1·4′	3°53·1′W	X	84
Upper Mitchell Fm	Heref	SO7239	52°3·2′	2°24·1′W	FM	149
Upper Moat	Shrops	SJ4503	52°37·6′	2°48·4′W	X	126
Upper Monksfields	Powys	SJ2807	52°39·6′	3°3·5′W	X	126
Upper Monynut	Scot Bord	NT6966	55°53·4′	2°29·3′W	X	67
Uppermoor	D & G	NY1571	55°1·8′	3°19·4′W	X	85
Upper Moor	Worcs	SO9747	52°7·5′	2°2·2′W	T	150
Upper Moorcroft Fm	Glos	SO7918	51°51·8′	2°17·9′W	FM	162
Upper Moorend Fm	Worcs	SO6971	52°20·4′	2°26·9′W	FM	138
Uppermoor Fm	Derby	SK1757	53°6·8′	1°44·4′W	FM	119
Upper Moor Side	Leeds	SE2430	53°46·2′	1°37·7′W	T	104
Upper Moraston	Heref	SO5626	51°56·1′	2°38·0′W	X	162
Upper Moreton	Staffs	SK0222	52°48·0′	1°57·8′W	X	128
Upper Morton	Notts	SK6677	53°17·4′	1°0·2′W	X	120
Upper Morton	S Glos	ST6591	51°37·2′	2°29·9′W	T	162,172
Upper Mossend	Aberd	NK0439	57°26·7′	1°55·5′W	X	30
Upper Mouson	Devon	SX7794	50°44·2′	3°44·2′W	X	191
Upper Muckovie	Highld	NH7143	57°27·8′	4°8·6′W	X	27
Uppermuir	Aberd	NJ7108	57°10·0′	2°28·3′W	X	38
Upper Muirskie	Aberd	NO8295	57°3·0′	2°17·3′W	X	38,45
Upper Mulben	Moray	NJ3652	57°33·5′	3°3·7′W	X	28
Upper Mumbie	D & G	NY3880	55°6·9′	2°57·9′W	X	79
Upper Murthat	D & G	NT0900	55°17·4′	3°25·5′W	X	78
Upper Musden	Staffs	SK1250	53°3·1′	1°48·9′W	X	119
Upper Mystole Park Fm	Kent	TR0952	51°14·0′	1°0·0′E	FM	179,189
Upper Nash	Pemb	SN0202	51°41·2′	4°51·5′W	T	157,158
Upper Neepaback	Shetld	HU5280	60°30·3′	1°2·7′W	T	1,2,3
Upper Neeston	Pemb	SM8707	51°43·5′	5°4·7′W	X	157
Upper Netchwood	Shrops	SO6092	52°31·7′	2°35·0′W	T	138
Upper Newbold	Derby	SK3573	53°15·4′	1°28·1′W	T	119
Upper Newby	Scot Bord	NT2637	55°37·5′	3°10·1′W	X	73
Upper Newlands	Kent	TQ9661	51°19·1′	0°49·2′E	X	178
Upper Newton Fm	Pemb	SM9426	51°53·9′	4°59·3′W	FM	157,158
Upper Nisbet	Scot Bord	NT6727	55°32·4′	2°30·9′W	X	74
Upper Nisbet Moor	Scot Bord	NT6628	55°32·9′	2°31·9′W	X	74
Upper Nisthouse	Orkney	HY3411	58°59·1′	3°8·4′W	X	6
Upper Nobut	Staffs	SK0435	52°55·0′	1°56·0′W	T	128
Upper Norncott	Shrops	SO5685	52°27·9′	2°38·5′W	X	137,138
Upper North Dean	Bucks	SU8498	51°40·7′	0°46·7′W	T	165
Upper North Park Fm	W Susx	SU8727	51°2·4′	0°45·2′W	FM	186,197
Upper Norton	Heref	SO6858	52°13·4′	2°27·7′W	X	149
Upper Norton Fm	Hants	SU4742	51°10·7′	1°19·3′W	FM	185
Upper Norwood	Croy	TQ3369	51°24·5′	0°4·9′W	T	176,177
Upper Norwood	W Susx	SU9317	50°56·9′	0°40·2′W	T	197
Upper Nut Hurst	Birm	SP1097	52°34·5′	1°50·7′W	F	139
Upper Obney	Pth & Kin	NO0336	56°30·6′	3°34·1′W	X	52,53
Upper Ochrwyth	Caer	ST2389	51°35·9′	3°6·3′W	T	171
Upper Oddington	Glos	SP2225	51°55·6′	1°40·4′W	T	163
Upper Oldmill	Aberd	NJ7346	57°30·5′	2°26·6′W	X	29
Upper Old Park	Surrey	SU8248	51°13·7′	0°49·1′W	X	186
Upper Oldwhat	Aberd	NJ8552	57°33·7′	2°14·6′W	X	30
Upper Oliver Dod	Scot Bord	NT0825	55°30·9′	3°27·0′W	H	72
Upper Ollach	Highld	NG5136	57°21·1′	6°7·9′W	T	23,24,32
Upper Onston	Orkney	HY2811	58°59·1′	3°14·7′W	X	6
Upper Ord	Aberd	NJ4827	57°20·1′	2°51·4′W	X	37
Upper Otterpool	Kent	TR1136	51°5·3′	1°1·2′E	X	179,189
Upper Outwoods Fm	Staffs	SK2225	52°49·6′	1°40·0′W	FM	128
Upper Padley	Derby	SK2479	53°18·7′	1°38·0′W	T	119
Upper Pandy	Powys	SJ1600	52°35·7′	3°14·0′W	X	136
Upper Park	Aberd	NO7697	57°4·1′	2°23·3′W	X	38,45
Upper Park	Brig	SS8580	51°30·7′	3°39·0′W	X	170
Upper Park	Pth & Kin	NN8951	56°38·5′	3°48·2′W	X	52
Upper Park Fm	Kent	TR0835	51°4·8′	0°58·6′E	FM	179,189
Upper Park Fm	Powys	SJ1911	52°41·7′	3°11·5′W	FM	125
Upper Parrock	E Susx	TQ4534	51°5·4′	0°4·6′E	X	188
Upper Pennington	Hants	SZ3095	50°45·5′	1°34·1′W	X	196
Upper Penrhuddlan	Powys	SO0085	52°27·5′	3°27·9′W	X	136
Upper Pentre	Powys	SO2194	52°32·5′	3°9·5′W	X	137
Upper Persley	C of Aber	NJ8910	57°11·1′	2°10·5′W	T	38
Upper Pertwood Bushes	Wilts	ST8835	51°7·1′	2°9·9′W	X	183
Upper Pertwood Bushes	Wilts	ST8935	51°7·1′	2°9·0′W	X	184
Upper Pickwick	Wilts	ST8571	51°26·5′	2°12·6′W	T	173
Upper Pikeley	Brad	SE0934	53°48·4′	1°51·4′W	X	104
Upper Pirriesmill	Aberd	NJ5339	57°26·6′	2°46·5′W	X	29
Upper Pitforthie	Aberd	NO8179	56°54·4′	2°18·3′W	X	45
Upper Pitglassie	Aberd	NJ6943	57°28·8′	2°30·6′W	X	29
Upper Pitkerrie	Highld	NH8679	57°47·4′	3°54·6′W	X	21
Upper Pitts Fm	Powys	SO3171	52°20·2′	3°0·4′W	FM	137,148
Upper Pollicott	Bucks	SP7013	51°48·9′	0°58·7′W	T	165
Upper Poppleton	York	SE5554	53°59·0′	1°9·3′W	T	105
Upper Port	Highld	NJ0529	57°20·8′	3°34·3′W	X	36
Upper Porterbelly	D & G	NX8565	54°58·2′	3°47·4′W	X	84
Upper Postern	Kent	TQ6146	51°11·7′	0°18·6′E	T	188
Upper Powburn	Aberd	NO7474	56°51·7′	2°25·1′W	X	45
Upper Prestwood Fm	W Susx	TQ2339	51°8·4′	0°14·1′W	FM	187
Upper Quinton	Warw	SP1746	52°7·0′	1°44·7′W	T	151
Upper Quoigs	Pth & Kin	NN8206	56°14·2′	3°53·8′W	X	57
Upper Quoy	Orkney	ND3295	58°50·5′	3°10·2′W	X	7
Upper Rabber	Powys	SO2455	52°11·5′	3°6·3′W	X	148
Upper Race	Torf	ST2799	51°41·3′	3°3·0′W	T	171
Upper Radbourne Fm	Warw	SP4458	52°13·3′	1°21·0′W	FM	151
Upper Raddery	Highld	NH7060	57°36·9′	4°10·1′W	X	21,27
Upper Ratley	Hants	SU3223	51°0·6′	1°32·2′W	T	185
Upper Raypitts Fm	Essex	TQ8995	51°37·5′	0°44·2′E	FM	168
Upper Rectory Fm	Leic	SK3208	52°40·4′	1°31·2′W	FM	128,140
Upper Redhall	Stir	NS7294	56°7·6′	4°3·1′W	X	57
Upper Rerrick	D & G	NX7547	54°48·4′	3°56·3′W	X	84
Upper Resr	Arg & Bt	NS1053	55°44·2′	5°1·2′W	W	63
Upper Reule Fm	Staffs	SJ8420	52°46·9′	2°13·8′W	FM	127
Upper Rhynd	Pth & Kin	NN8610	56°16·4′	3°50·0′W	W	58
Upper Ridinghill	Aberd	NK0254	57°34·8′	1°57·5′W	X	30
Upper Rig	D & G	NX9191	55°12·3′	3°42·3′W	X	78
Upper Ringorm	Moray	NJ2644	57°29·1′	3°13·6′W	X	28
Upper Roadstead	Highld	NC3955	58°27·5′	4°45·1′W	W	9
Upper Rochford	Worcs	SO6267	52°18·2′	2°33·0′W	T	138,149
Upper Rodmersham	Kent	TQ9260	51°18·6′	0°45·7′E	T	178
Upper Row Fm	Hants	SU3358	51°19·4′	1°31·2′W	FM	174
Upper Rusko	D & G	NX5661	54°55·6′	4°14·4′W	X	83
Upper Rusko Burn	D & G	NX5560	54°55·1′	4°15·3′W	W	83
Upper Rusko Cott	D & G	NX5662	54°56·2′	4°14·4′W	X	83
Upper Ruthven	Aberd	NJ4502	57°6·6′	2°54·0′W	X	37
Upper Samieston	Scot Bord	NT7220	55°28·6′	2°26·1′W	X	74
Upper Sampshill Fm	Beds	TL0532	51°58·8′	0°27·9′W	FM	166
Upper Sandaig	Highld	NG7814	57°10·1′	5°39·9′W	X	33
Upper Sanday	Orkney	HY5403	58°55·0′	2°47·4′W	T	6,7
Upper Sands	E Yorks	SE7823	53°42·1′	0°48·7′W	X	105,106,112
Upper Sapey	Heref	SO6863	52°16·1′	2°27·7′W	T	138,149
Upper Sauchen	Aberd	NJ6710	57°11·0′	2°32·3′W	X	38
Upper Scapa	Orkney	HY4309	58°58·1′	2°59·0′W	X	6,7
Upper Scolton	Pemb	SM9822	51°51·8′	4°55·6′W	X	157,158
Upper Scotstown	Aberd	NJ6233	57°23·4′	2°37·5′W	X	29
Upper Scoveston	Pemb	SM9207	51°43·6′	5°0·3′W	X	157,158
Upper Seagry	Wilts	ST9480	51°31·4′	2°4·8′W	T	173
Upper Seatter	Orkney	ND2992	58°48·8′	3°13·3′W	X	7
Upper Senwick	D & G	NX6546	54°47·7′	4°5·6′W	X	83,84
Upper Seven Mile Ho	Norf	TG0244	52°57·5′	1°0·9′E	X	134
Upper Shadymoor Fm	Shrops	SJ4502	52°37·0′	2°48·3′W	FM	126
Upper Shampher	Aberd	NO6693	57°1·9′	2°33·2′W	X	38,45
Upper Shelton	Beds	SP9943	52°4·8′	0°32·9′W	T	153
Upper Sheringham	Norf	TG1441	52°55·6′	1°11·4′E	T	133
Upper Shirley	C of Soton	SU4014	50°55·7′	1°25·5′W	T	196
Upper Shirley	Croy	TQ3564	51°21·8′	0°3·3′W	T	177,187
Upper Short Ditch	Shrops	SO1986	52°28·2′	3°11·1′W	A	136
Upper Shuckburgh	Warw	SP4961	52°14·9′	1°16·5′W	X	151
Upper Siddington	Glos	SU0299	51°41·6′	1°57·9′W	T	163
Upper Side	Midlo	NT2955	55°47·2′	3°7·5′W	X	66,73
Upper Skelmorlie	N Ayr	NS1967	55°52·0′	4°53·1′W	T	63
Upper Skilts Fm	Warw	SP0967	52°18·3′	1°51·7′W	FM	150
Upper Slackbuie	Highld	NH6741	57°26·7′	4°12·5′W	X	26
Upper Slackstead	Hants	SU3926	51°2·2′	1°26·2′W	T	185
Upper Slatepits	Glos	SP1032	51°59·4′	1°50·9′W	F	150
Upper Slaughter	Glos	SP1523	51°54·6′	1°46·5′W	T	163
Upper Slope End Fm	Wilts	SU3265	51°23·2′	1°32·0′W	FM	174
Upper Small Clough	Derby	SK1496	53°27·9′	1°46·9′W	X	110
Upper Smiddyseat	Aberd	NJ7449	57°32·1′	2°25·6′W	X	29
Upper Smite Village	Warw	SP4282	52°26·3′	1°22·5′W	A	140
Upper Snead	Powys	SO3193	52°32·1′	3°0·6′W	X	137
Upper Solva	Pemb	SM7924	51°52·5′	5°12·3′W	T	157
Upper Sonachan	Arg & Bt	NN0621	56°20·8′	5°7·9′W	X	50,56
Upper Soroba	Arg & Bt	NM8627	56°23·5′	5°27·6′W	X	49
Upper Soudley	Glos	SO6510	51°47·5′	2°30·1′W	T	162
Upper Souldern Grounds Fm	Oxon	SP5130	51°58·2′	1°15·1′W	FM	151
Uppersound	Shetld	HU4540	60°8·8′	1°10·9′W	T	4
Upper Sour	Highld	ND1160	58°31·4′	3°31·2′W	X	11,12
Upper Southmead Fm	Glos	SO9007	51°45·9′	2°8·3′W	FM	163
Upper Sower	Orkney	HY2906	58°56·4′	3°13·5′W	X	6,7
Upper Spernall Fm	Warw	SP1061	52°15·1′	1°50·8′W	FM	150
Upper Spittalton	Stir	NS6999	56°10·2′	4°6·2′W	X	57
Upper Spoad	Shrops	SO2481	52°25·5′	3°6·7′W	X	137
Upper Spond	Heref	SO3153	52°10·5′	3°0·1′W	X	148
Upper Springs Fm	Shrops	SJ5700	52°36·0′	2°37·7′W	FM	126
Upper Standen Fm	Kent	TR2340	51°7·2′	1°11·6′E	FM	179,189
Upper Stanton Drew	Bath & NE Somer	ST6062	51°21·6′	2°34·1′W	T	172
Upper Staploe	Beds	TL1459	52°13·3′	0°19·5′W	T	153
Upper Stennieswater	D & G	NY3395	55°14·9′	3°2·8′W	X	79
Upper Stoke	Cov	SP3580	52°25·2′	1°28·7′W	T	140
Upper Stoke	Norf	TG2502	52°34·4′	1°19·6′E	T	134
Upper Stondon	Beds	TL1435	52°0·3′	0°20·0′W	T	153
Upper Stonehurst Fm	Surrey	TQ4241	51°9·3′	0°2·2′E	FM	187
Upper Stoneymollan	W Dunb	NS3781	55°59·9′	4°36·4′W	X	63
Upper Stony Holes	Northum	NT6501	55°18·4′	2°32·7′W	X	80
Upper Stowe	Northnts	SP6456	52°12·1′	1°3·4′W	T	152
Upper Stratton	Swin	SU1687	51°35·1′	1°45·8′W	T	173
Upper Street	Hants	SU1518	50°57·9′	1°46·8′W	T	184
Upper Street	Norf	TG2536	52°52·7′	1°21·0′E	T	133
Upper Street	Norf	TG3024	52°46·1′	1°25·0′E	T	133,134
Upper Street	Norf	TG3217	52°42·3′	1°26·5′E	T	133,134
Upper Street	Norf	TG3517	52°42·2′	1°29·1′E	T	133,134
Upper Street	Norf	TM1780	52°22·7′	1°11·7′E	T	156
Upper Street	Suff	TL7851	52°7·9′	0°36·4′E	T	155
Upper Street	Suff	TM1051	52°7·3′	1°4·5′E	T	155
Upper Street	Suff	TM1434	51°58·0′	1°7·3′E	T	169
Upper Strensham	Worcs	SO9039	52°3·2′	2°8·4′W	T	150
Upper Stroquhan Hill	D & G	NX8281	55°6·8′	3°50·6′W	H	78
Upper Strowan	Pth & Kin	NN8220	56°21·7′	3°54·2′W	X	52,57
Upper Studley	Wilts	ST8456	51°18·4′	2°13·4′W	T	173
Upper Studley Fm	Wilts	SU1082	51°32·4′	1°51·0′W	FM	173
Upper Succoth	Arg & Bt	NN1302	56°10·7′	5°0·3′W	X	56
Upper Suisgill	Highld	NC8925	58°12·3′	3°52·9′W	X	17
Upper Sundon	Beds	TL0427	51°56·1′	0°28·8′W	T	166
Upper Swainswick	Bath & NE Somer	ST7568	51°24·9′	2°21·2′W	T	172
Upper Swanmore	Hants	SU5817	50°57·2′	1°10·1′W	T	185
Upper Sweeney	Shrops	SJ2825	52°49·3′	3°3·7′W	X	126
Upper Swell	Glos	SP1726	51°56·2′	1°44·8′W	T	163

Upper Swineseye Fm	Stock	SJ9082	53°20·3′	2°8·6′W	FM	109
Upper Swithen	Barns	SE2911	53°35·9′	1°33·3′W	X	110
Upper Swydd	Powys	SO1364	52°16·3′	3°16·1′W	X	148
Upper Sydenham	Lew	TQ3471	51°25·6′	0°4·0′W	T	176,177
Upper Tack	Aberd	NJ8916	57°14·3′	2°10·5′W	X	38
Uppertack	Aberd	NJ9053	57°34·3′	2°9·6′W	X	30
Upper Talcoed	Powys	SO0666	52°17·3′	3°22·3′W	X	136,147
Upper Tamar Lake	Devon	SS2812	50°53·2′	4°26·3′W	W	190
Upper Tankersley	Barns	SK3499	53°29·4′	1°28·8′W	T	110,111
Upper Tarnberry	D & G	NT1714	55°25·0′	3°18·2′W	H	79
Upper Tarr	Stir	NN6201	56°11·2′	4°13·0′W	X	57
Upper Tarr	Stir	NN6300	56°10·6′	4°12·0′W	X	57
Upper Tas Valley Walk	Norf	TM1491	52°28·7′	1°9·5′E	X	144
Upper Tas Valley Walk	Norf	TM1898	52°32·4′	1°13·3′E	X	134
Upper Taylorton	Stir	NS8193	56°7·2′	3°54·4′W	X	57
Upper Tean	Staffs	SK0139	52°57·1′	1°58·7′W	T	128
Upper Terryvale	Aberd	NJ7809	57°10·5′	2°21·4′W	X	38
Upper Thainston	Aberd	NO6275	56°52·1′	2°37·0′W	X	45
Upperthird	Aberd	NJ6839	57°26·7′	2°31·5′W	X	29
Upperthong	Kirk	SE1308	53°34·3′	1°47·8′W	T	110
Upperthorpe	Derby	SK4680	53°19·1′	1°18·2′W	T	111,120
Upperthorpe	N Lincs	SE7500	53°29·7′	0°51·8′W	T	112
Upper Threapwood	Ches	SJ4445	53°0·2′	2°49·7′W	T	117
Upper Throughburn	S Lanak	NS9352	55°45·2′	3°41·9′W	X	65,72
Upper Thruxted Fm	Kent	TR0951	51°13·4′	1°0·0′E	FM	179,189
Upper Thurnham	Lancs	SD4554	53°59·0′	2°49·9′W	T	102
Upper Tillygarmond	Aberd	NO6293	57°1·8′	2°37·1′W	X	37,45
Upper Tillylair	Aberd	NJ5401	57°6·1′	2°45·1′W	X	37
Upper Tillyrie	Pth & Kin	NO1106	56°14·5′	3°25·7′W	X	58
Upper Tittesworth	Staffs	SK0058	53°7·4′	1°59·6′W	X	119
Upper Toes	Kent	TQ8965	51°21·4′	0°43·3′E	X	178
Upper Tofts	Scot Bord	NT5413	55°24·8′	2°43·2′W	X	79
Upper Tomdhu	Moray	NJ1842	57°27·9′	3°21·6′W	X	28
Upper Tomvaich Wood	Highld	NJ0530	57°21·3′	3°34·3′W	F	27,36
Upperton	Aberd	NJ3617	57°14·6′	3°3·2′W	X	37
Upperton	Aberd	NJ7943	57°28·9′	2°20·6′W	X	29,30
Upperton	Aberd	NJ8446	57°30·5′	2°15·6′W	X	29,30
Upperton	Aberd	NO7372	56°50·6′	2°26·1′W	X	45
Upperton	Aberd	NO7392	57°1·4′	2°26·2′W	X	38,45
Upperton	Devon	SX7690	50°42·0′	3°45·0′W	X	191
Upperton	E Susx	TQ6000	50°46·9′	0°16·6′E	T	199
Upperton	Heref	SO3947	52°7·3′	2°53·1′W	X	148,149
Upperton	Highld	NH3931	57°20·7′	4°40·1′W	X	26
Upperton	Oxon	SU6594	51°38·7′	1°3·2′W	T	164,175
Upperton	Shetld	HU4020	59°58·0′	1°16·5′W	X	4
Upperton	W Susx	SU7821	50°59·2′	0°52·9′W	X	197
Upperton	W Susx	SU9522	50°59·6′	0°38·4′W	T	197
Upperton Common	W Susx	SU9523	51°0·1′	0°38·4′W	F	197
Upperton Fm	Devon	SX7990	50°42·1′	3°42·4′W	FM	191
Upperton of Gask	Aberd	NJ7248	57°31·5′	2°27·6′W	X	29
Upper Tooting	Wan	TQ2772	51°26·2′	0°10·0′W	T	176
Upper Tor	Derby	SK1187	53°23·0′	1°49·7′W	X	110
Upper Torrs	D & G	NX7762	54°56·5′	3°54·8′W	X	84
Upper Tote	Highld	NG5159	57°33·4′	6°9·3′W	X	23,24
Upper Toucks	Aberd	NO8383	56°56·5′	2°16·3′W	X	45
Upper Towie	Aberd	NJ4411	57°11·4′	2°55·1′W	X	37
Upper Town	Brad	SE0234	53°48·4′	1°57·8′W	T	104
Uppertown	Cumbr	NY4467	54°59·9′	2°52·1′W	X	85
Upper Town	Derby	SK2351	53°3·6′	1°39·0′W	T	119
Upper Town	Derby	SK2461	53°9·0′	1°38·1′W	X	119
Upper Town	Derby	SK2758	53°7·3′	1°35·4′W	T	119
Uppertown	Derby	SK3264	53°10·6′	1°30·9′W	T	119
Upper Town	Durham	NZ0737	54°43·9′	1°53·1′W	T	92
Upper Town	Heref	SO5849	52°8·5′	2°36·4′W	T	149
Uppertown	Highld	ND3576	58°40·3′	3°6·8′W	T	7,12
Uppertown	Highld	NH4431	57°20·8′	4°35·1′W	X	26
Uppertown	Moray	NJ2740	57°26·9′	3°12·5′W	X	28
Uppertown	Northum	NY8672	55°2·8′	2°12·7′W	T	87
Upper Town	N Som	ST5266	51°23·7′	2°41·0′W	T	172,182
Uppertown	Orkney	HY3907	58°57·0′	3°3·1′W	X	6,7
Uppertown	Orkney	ND4193	58°49·5′	3°0·8′W	X	7
Upper Town	Suff	TL9267	52°16·3′	0°49·2′E	T	155
Upper Town	Wilts	ST9779	51°30·8′	2°2·2′W	T	173
Upper Towthorpe	N Yks	SE6267	54°5·9′	1°2·7′W	X	100
Upper Transfield Fm	Brad	SE0840	53°51·6′	1°52·3′W	FM	104
Upper Trefeen	Powys	SO1790	52°30·3′	3°13·0′W	X	136
Upper Trelowgoed	Powys	SO0863	52°15·7′	3°20·5′W	X	147
Upper Trench	Shrops	SJ5126	52°50·0′	2°43·2′W	X	126
Upper Treverward	Shrops	SO2778	52°23·9′	3°4·0′W	T	137,148
Upper Tullich	Highld	NH7373	57°44·0′	4°7·5′W	T	21
Upper Tullochgrue	Highld	NH9109	57°9·8′	3°47·7′W	X	36
Upper Tulloes	Angus	NO5146	56°36·5′	2°47·4′W	X	54
Upper Twatt	Orkney	HY3211	58°59·1′	3°10·5′W	X	6
Upper Tysoe	Warw	SP3343	52°5·3′	1°30·7′W	T	151
Upper Underley	Heref	SO6562	52°15·5′	2°30·4′W	X	138,149
Upper Unsted Fm	Surrey	SU9945	51°12·0′	0°34·6′W	FM	186
Upper Unthank	Moray	NJ2965	57°40·4′	3°11·0′W	X	28
Upper Up	Wilts	SU0496	51°40·0′	1°56·1′W	T	163
Upper Upham	Wilts	SU2277	51°29·7′	1°40·6′W	T	174
Upper Upnor	Medway	TQ7570	51°24·3′	0°31·4′E	T	178
Upper Urafirth	Shetld	HU3078	60°29·3′	1°26·7′W	T	3
Upper Urquhart	Fife	NO1908	56°15·7′	3°18·0′W	X	58
Upper Vaunce's Fm	Norf	TM1984	52°24·8′	1°13·6′E	FM	156
Upper Venn Fm	Heref	SO6651	52°9·6′	2°29·4′W	FM	149
Upper Vert Wood	E Susx	TQ5114	50°54·6′	0°9·3′E	F	199
Upper Vicar's Fm	Oxon	SU7296	51°39·7′	0°57·1′W	FM	165
Upper Vicarwood	Derby	SK3139	52°57·1′	1°31·9′W	X	128
Upper Victoria	Angus	NO5336	56°31·1′	2°45·4′W	X	54
Upper Vobster	Somer	ST7049	51°14·6′	2°25·4′W	T	183
Upper Wain	Shrops	SO2180	52°25·0′	3°9·3′W	X	137
Upper Walthamstow	Wal F	TQ3889	51°35·2′	0°0·1′W	T	177
Upper Wardington	Oxon	SP4946	52°6·8′	1°16·7′W	T	151
Upper Wardley	W Susx	SU8428	51°2·9′	0°47·7′W	T	186,197
Upper Warroch	Pth & Kin	NO0505	56°13·9′	3°31·5′W	X	58
Upper Watchingwell	I of W	SZ4488	50°41·6′	1°22·2′W	X	196
Upper Water Mouth	Notts	SK7753	53°4·4′	0°50·6′W	W	120
Upper Wawensmoor	Warw	SP1264	52°16·7′	1°49·0′W	X	150
Upper Weald	Mil Key	SP8037	52°1·8′	0°49·6′W	T	152
Upper Wealthieston	Angus	NO6057	56°42·4′	2°38·8′W	X	54
Upper Weedon	Northnts	SP6258	52°13·2′	1°5·1′W	T	152

Upper Welland	Worcs	SO7740	52°3·7′	2°19·7′W	T	150
Upper Wellingham	E Susx	TQ4313	50°54·1′	0°2·4′E	T	198
Upper Wellwood	E Ayr	NS6725	55°30·3′	4°5·9′W	X	71
Upper Welson	Heref	SO2951	52°9·4′	3°1·9′W	T	148
Upper Westholme	Somer	ST5740	51°9·7′	2°36·5′W	T	182,183
Upper Weston	Bath & NE Somer	ST7267	51°24·3′	2°23·8′W	T	172
Upper Weston	Powys	SO2170	52°19·6′	3°9·2′W	X	137,148
Upper Westown	Aberd	NO8280	56°54·9′	2°17·3′W	X	45
Upper Wetmoor	S Glos	ST7387	51°35·1′	2°23·0′W	F	172
Upper Weybread	Suff	TM2379	52°22·0′	1°16·9′E	T	156
Upper Whiston	Roth	SK4589	53°24·0′	1°19·0′W	T	111,120
Upper Whitcastles	D & G	NY2386	55°10·0′	3°12·1′W	X	79
Upper Whitecleuch	S Lanak	NS8219	55°27·3′	3°51·5′W	X	71,78
Upper Whitehaugh	E Ayr	NS6230	55°32·9′	4°10·8′W	X	71
Upper Whitehill Fm	Hants	SU5146	51°12·9′	1°15·8′W	FM	185
Upper Whiteside Moor	D & G	NX8082	55°7·3′	3°52·5′W	X	78
Upper Whiteston	Stir	NN8004	56°13·1′	3°55·7′W	X	57
Upper White Well	Brad	SE0550	53°57·0′	1°55·0′W	X	104
Upper Whitfield	Scot Bord	NT1753	55°46·0′	3°18·9′W	X	65,66,72
Upper Whitle	Staffs	SK1064	53°10·6′	1°50·6′W	X	119
Upper Whitley Edge	Barns	SE1904	53°32·2′	1°42·4′W	H	110
Upper Whitley Fm	Oxon	SP4504	51°44·2′	1°20·5′W	FM	164
Upper Wick	Glos	ST7196	51°40·0′	2°24·8′W	T	162
Upper Wick	Worcs	SO8253	52°10·7′	2°15·4′W	T	150
Upper Widhill Fm	Swin	SU1390	51°36·8′	1°48·3′W	FM	163,173
Upper Wield	Hants	SU6238	51°8·5′	1°6·4′W	T	185
Upper Wigginton	Shrops	SJ3335	52°54·7′	2°59·4′W	T	126
Upper Wilting Fm	E Susx	TQ7710	50°52·0′	0°31·3′E	FM	199
Upper Winchendon	Bucks	SP7414	51°49·4′	0°55·2′W	T	165
Upper Wingbury Fm	Bucks	SP8720	51°52·5′	0°43·8′W	FM	165
Upper Winskill	N Yks	SD8266	54°5·6′	2°16·1′W	X	98
Upper Wintercott	Heref	SO4754	52°11·1′	2°46·1′W	X	148,149
Upper Withers	Heref	SO5264	52°16·6′	2°41·8′W	X	137,138,149
Upper Witton	Birm	SP0892	52°31·8′	1°52·5′W	T	139
Upper Wolvercote	Oxon	SP4909	51°46·9′	1°17·0′W	T	164
Upper Wolverton	Worcs	SO9150	52°9·1′	2°7·5′W	T	150
Upperwood	Derby	SK2957	53°6·8′	1°33·6′W	T	119
Upper Wood	Oxon	SU2881	51°31·9′	1°35·4′W	F	174
Upper Woodbatch	Shrops	SO2989	52°29·9′	3°2·4′W	X	137
Upper Woodcott Down	Hants	SU4455	51°17·8′	1°21·7′W	X	174,185
Upper Wooden	Scot Bord	NT7024	55°30·8′	2°28·1′W	X	74
Upper Woodend	Aberd	NJ6619	57°15·9′	2°33·4′W	T	38
Upper Woodend Fm	Bucks	SU7588	51°35·4′	0°54·6′W	FM	175
Upper Wood Fm	Herts	TL0612	51°48·0′	0°27·4′W	FM	166
Upper Woodford	Wilts	SU1237	51°8·2′	1°49·3′W	T	184
Upper Woodhill Fm	Surrey	TQ0444	51°11·4′	0°30·3′W	FM	186
Upperwood Ho	Oldham	SE0205	53°32·7′	1°57·8′W	X	110
Upperwood Ho	Wok	SU7469	51°25·1′	0°55·8′W	X	175
Upper Woodlands Fm	Somer	ST5537	51°8·1′	2°38·2′W	FM	182,183
Upper Woolhampton	W Berks	SU5767	51°24·2′	1°10·4′W	T	174
Upper Woolwich	Kent	TQ8531	51°3·1′	0°38·8′E	X	189
Upper Wootton	Hants	SU5754	51°17·2′	1°10·6′W	T	185
Upper Wraxall	Wilts	ST8074	51°28·1′	2°16·9′W	T	173
Upper Wyche	Worcs	SO7743	52°5·3′	2°19·7′W	T	150
Upper Wyke	Hants	SU4050	51°15·1′	1°25·2′W	X	185
Upper Wyndings	Aberd	NO8085	56°57·6′	2°19·3′W	X	45
Upper Wythall	Heref	SO5920	51°52·9′	2°35·3′W	A	162
Upper Yeldham Hall	Essex	TL7838	52°0·9′	0°36·0′E	X	155
Upp Hall	Herts	TL4024	51°54·0′	0°2·5′E	A	167
Upp Hall	Lancs	SD5374	54°9·8′	2°42·8′W	X	97
Upp Hall Fm	Essex	TL8823	51°52·7′	0°44·3′E	FM	168
Upphall Fm	Lincs	TF3985	53°20·8′	0°5·7′E	FM	122
Uppincott	Devon	SS8802	50°48·6′	3°35·0′W	T	192
Uppincott	Devon	SS9006	50°50·8′	3°33·4′W	X	192
Upping Copse	Hants	SU3842	51°10·8′	1°27·0′W	F	185
Uppingham	Rut	SP8699	52°35·2′	0°43·4′W	T	141
Uppings Fm	Bucks	SP8018	51°51·5′	0°49·9′W	FM	165
Uppington	Dorset	SU0106	50°51·4′	1°58·8′W	T	195
Uppington	Shrops	SJ5909	52°40·9′	2°36·0′W	T	126
Uppington	Shrops	SJ6009	52°40·9′	2°35·1′W	T	127
Uppington	Somer	SS8535	51°6·4′	3°38·2′W	X	181
Uppington Ho	Wilts	SU0738	51°8·7′	1°53·6′W	X	184
Uppper Longwood	Shrops	SJ6007	52°39·8′	2°35·1′W	T	127
Upr Cwm Fm	Heref	SO3033	51°59·7′	3°0·8′W	FM	161
Upright Cliff	Devon	SS2226	51°0·6′	4°31·9′W	X	190
Upsall	N Yks	SE4587	54°16·8′	1°18·1′W	T	99
Upsall Carrs Plantn	Red & Cl	NZ5514	54°31·3′	1°8·6′W	F	93
Upsall Castle	N Yks	SE4586	54°16·3′	1°18·1′W	X	99
Upsall Hall	Red & Cl	NZ5415	54°31·9′	1°9·5′W	X	93
Upsettlington	Scot Bord	NT8846	55°42·7′	2°11·0′W	X	74
Upsher Green	Suff	TL9143	52°3·4′	0°47·6′E	T	155
Upshire	Essex	TL4100	51°41·1′	0°2·8′E	T	167
Upsland	N Yks	SE3080	54°13·1′	1°32·0′W	X	99
Upsland Fm	N Yks	SE3079	54°12·6′	1°32·0′W	FM	99
Upsland Stell	N Yks	SE3178	54°12·1′	1°31·1′W	W	99
Up Somborne	Hants	SU3932	51°5·4′	1°26·2′W	T	185
Upstreet	Kent	TR2263	51°19·6′	1°11·6′E	T	179
Upswall	Shetld	HP6307	60°44·7′	0°50·2′W	X	1
Upswall	Shetld	HU4135	60°6·1′	1°15·3′W	X	4
Up Sydling	Dorset	ST6201	50°48·7′	2°32·0′W	T	194
Upthorpe	Glos	SO7500	51°42·1′	2°21·3′W	T	162
Upthorpe	Suff	TL9772	52°18·9′	0°53·8′E	T	144,155
Upthorpe Lodge	Cambs	TL1271	52°19·8′	0°21·0′W	X	153
Upton	Bucks	SP7711	51°47·8′	0°52·6′W	T	165
Upton	Cambs	TL1778	52°23·5′	0°16·4′W	T	142
Upton	Ches	SJ4068	53°12·6′	2°53·5′W	T	117
Upton	Corn	SS2004	50°48·7′	4°32·9′W	T	190
Upton	Corn	SX0585	50°38·2′	4°45·1′W	X	200
Upton	Corn	SX2772	50°31·6′	4°26·1′W	T	201
Upton	Cumbr	NY3239	54°44·7′	3°3·0′W	T	90
Upton	Devon	ST0902	50°48·9′	3°17·1′W	T	192
Upton	Devon	SX7043	50°16·6′	3°49·1′W	T	202
Upton	Dorset	SY7483	50°39·0′	2°21·7′W	X	194
Upton	Dorset	SY9893	50°44·4′	2°1·3′W	T	195
Upton	E Yorks	TA1454	53°58·4′	0°15·3′W	T	107
Upton	Halton	SJ4887	53°22·9′	2°46·5′W	T	108
Upton	Hants	SU3655	51°17·8′	1°28·6′W	T	174,185
Upton	Hants	SU3717	50°57·3′	1°28·0′W	T	185
Upton	I of W	SZ5890	50°42·6′	1°10·3′W	T	196

Upton	Kent	TR3867	51°21·3′	1°25·5′E	T	179
Upton	Leic	SP3699	52°35·5′	1°27·7′W	T	140
Upton	Lincs	SK8686	53°22·1′	0°42·0′W	T	112,121
Upton	Newham	TQ4084	51°32·5′	0°1·5′E	T	177
Upton	Norf	TG3912	52°39·4′	1°32·4′E	T	133,134
Upton	Northnts	SP7160	52°14·2′	0°57·2′W	T	152
Upton	Notts	SK7354	53°4·9′	0°54·2′W	T	120
Upton	Notts	SK7476	53°16·8′	0°53·0′W	T	120
Upton	Oxon	SP2412	51°48·6′	1°38·7′W	T	163
Upton	Oxon	SU5186	51°34·5′	1°15·5′W	T	174
Upton	Pemb	SN0104	51°42·2′	4°52·4′W	X	157,158
Upton	Peterb	TF1000	52°35·4′	0°22·2′W	T	142
Upton	Red & Cl	NZ7319	54°33·9′	0°51·8′W	X	94
Upton	Shrops	SJ7506	52°39·3′	2°21·8′W	X	127
Upton	Slough	SU9879	51°30·3′	0°34·9′W	T	175,176
Upton	Somer	SS9928	51°2·8′	3°26·1′W	T	181
Upton	Somer	ST4526	51°2·1′	2°46·7′W	T	193
Upton	Wakf	SE4713	53°36·9′	1°17·0′W	T	111
Upton	Warw	SP1257	52°12·9′	1°49·1′W	T	150
Upton	Wilts	ST8732	51°5·5′	2°10·8′W	T	183
Upton	Wirral	SJ2788	53°23·3′	3°5·5′W	T	108
Upton Barton	Corn	SX2479	50°35·3′	4°28·8′W	X	201
Upton Beacon	Wakf	SE4713	53°36·9′	1°17·0′W	X	111
Upton Bishop	Heref	SO6527	51°56·7′	2°30·2′W	T	162
Upton Broad	Norf	TG3813	52°40·0′	1°31·6′E	W	133,134
Upton Cheyney	S Glos	ST6969	51°25·4′	2°26·4′W	T	172
Upton Country Park	Poole	SY9992	50°43·9′	2°0·5′W	X	195
Upton Court	Heref	SO5566	52°17·7′	2°39·2′W	X	137,138,149
Upton Court	Heref	SO6528	51°57·2′	2°30·2′W	X	149
Upton Cow Down	Wilts	ST8749	51°14·6′	2°10·8′W	H	183
Upton Cressett	Shrops	SO6592	52°31·7′	2°30·6′W	T	138
Upton Cressett Hall	Shrops	SO6592	52°31·7′	2°30·6′W	A	138
Upton Crews	Heref	SO6427	51°56·7′	2°31·0′W	T	162
Upton Cross	Corn	SX2872	50°31·6′	4°25·2′W	T	201
Upton Down	Oxon	SP2211	51°48·1′	1°40·5′W	X	163
Upton End	Beds	TL1234	51°59·8′	0°21·7′W	T	153
Upton Field	Notts	SK7154	53°4·9′	0°56·0′W	T	120
Upton Fm	Devon	ST0200	50°47·7′	3°23·1′W	FM	192
Upton Fm	Somer	SS9729	51°3·3′	3°27·8′W	FM	181
Upton Fm	Surrey	TQ0857	51°18·3′	0°26·6′W	FM	187
Upton Fm	Worcs	SO8769	52°19·4′	2°11·0′W	FM	139
Upton Fms	Devon	ST0306	50°51·0′	3°22·3′W	FM	192
Upton Fold Fm	Ches	SJ9367	53°12·2′	2°5·9′W	FM	118
Upton Forge	Shrops	SJ5511	52°41·9′	2°39·6′W	X	126
Upton Grange	Lincs	SK8987	53°22·6′	0°39·3′W	X	112,121
Upton Great Barrow	Wilts	ST9542	51°10·9′	2°3·9′W	A	184
Upton Green	Norf	TG3912	52°39·4′	1°32·4′E	T	133,134
Upton Grey	Hants	SU6948	51°13·8′	1°0·3′W	T	186
Upton Grey Ho	Hants	SU6948	51°13·8′	1°0·3′W	X	186
Upton Grove	Glos	ST8894	51°38·9′	2°10·0′W	X	162,173
Upton Grove Fm	Lincs	SK8487	53°22·6′	0°43·8′W	FM	112,121
Upton Hall	Ches	SJ9075	53°16·6′	2°8·6′W	X	118
Upton Hall Fm	N Yks	NZ8313	54°30·6′	0°42·7′W	FM	94
Upton Heath	Ches	SJ4169	53°13·1′	2°52·6′W	T	117
Upton Heath	Dorset	SY9894	50°45·0′	2°1·3′W	X	195
Upton Hellions	Devon	SS8403	50°49·1′	3°38·4′W	T	191
Upton Ho	Kent	TR3355	51°15·0′	1°20·7′E	X	179
Upton Ho	Poole	SY9993	50°44·4′	2°0·5′W	X	195
Upton Ho	Warw	SP3645	52°6·4′	1°28·1′W	X	151
Upton Lake	Bucks	TQ0084	51°33·0′	0°33·1′W	W	176
Upton Lea	Slough	SU9881	51°31·4′	0°34·9′W	T	175,176
Upton Lodge	Northnts	SP7160	52°14·2′	0°57·2′W	X	152
Upton Lodge	Notts	SK7355	53°5·5′	0°54·2′W	X	120
Upton Lodge	Oxon	SU5186	51°34·5′	1°15·5′W	X	174
Upton Lodge	Peterb	TL1099	52°34·9′	0°22·2′W	X	142
Upton Lodge Fm	Cambs	TL1679	52°24·0′	0°17·3′W	FM	142
Upton Lodge Fm	Leic	SP3698	52°35·0′	1°27·7′W	FM	140
Upton Lovell	Wilts	ST9440	51°9·8′	2°4·8′W	T	184
Upton Magna	Shrops	SJ5512	52°42·5′	2°39·6′W	T	126
Upton Manor	Hants	SU3555	51°17·8′	1°29·5′W	X	174,185
Upton Marshes	Norf	TG3913	52°39·9′	1°32·5′E	W	133,134
Upton Mill	Northnts	SP7259	52°13·7′	0°56·4′W	X	152
Upton Mill	Notts	SK7253	53°4·4′	0°55·1′W	X	120
Upton Noble	Somer	ST7139	51°9·2′	2°24·5′W	T	183
Upton Park	Leic	SP3798	52°34·9′	1°26·8′W	X	140
Upton Park	Newham	TQ4183	51°31·9′	0°2·4′E	T	177
Upton Park	Shrops	SO6491	52°31·2′	2°31·4′W	X	138
Upton Pyne	Devon	SX9197	50°46·0′	3°32·4′W	T	192
Upton Rocks	Halton	SJ5087	53°22·9′	2°44·7′W	T	108
Upton Scudamore	Wilts	ST8647	51°13·6′	2°11·6′W	T	183
Upton Snodsbury	Worcs	SO9454	52°11·3′	2°4·9′W	T	150
Upton Sta	Wirral	SJ2888	53°23·3′	3°4·5′W	X	108
Upton St Leonards	Glos	SO8614	51°49·7′	2°11·8′W	T	162
Upton Towans	Corn	SW5739	50°12·3′	5°24·0′W	X	203
Upton upon Severn	Worcs	SO8540	52°3·7′	2°12·7′W	T	150
Upton Village	Glos	SP1534	52°0·5′	1°46·5′W	A	151
Upton Warren	Worcs	SO9367	52°18·3′	2°5·8′W	T	150
Upton-Wold Fm	Glos	SP1434	52°0·5′	1°47·4′W	FM	151
Upton Wood	Cambs	TL1879	52°24·0′	0°15·5′W	F	142
Upton Wood	Kent	TR2646	51°10·3′	1°14·4′E	F	179
Upwaltham	W Susx	SU9413	50°54·8′	0°39·4′W	T	197
Upwaltham Hill	W Susx	SU9412	50°54·2′	0°39·4′W	X	197
Upware	Cambs	TL5370	52°18·6′	0°15·1′E	T	154
Upwell	Norf	TF4902	52°35·9′	0°12·4′E	T	143
Upwell Fen	Cambs	TL4895	52°32·2′	0°11·3′E	X	143
Upwell Fen	Norf	TL5599	52°34·2′	0°17·6′E	X	143
Upwey	Dorset	SY6684	50°39·5′	2°28·5′W	T	194
Upwey Manor	Dorset	SY6684	50°39·5′	2°28·5′W	A	194
Upwick Green	Herts	TL4524	51°54·0′	0°6·8′E	T	167
Upwick Hall	Herts	TL4524	51°54·0′	0°6·8′E	X	167
Upwood	Brad	SE0943	53°53·2′	1°51·4′W	X	104
Upwood	Cambs	TL2582	52°25·5′	0°9·3′W	T	142
Upwood	Dorset	ST9918	50°57·9′	2°0·5′W	X	184
Up Wood	Norf	TG1337	52°53·5′	1°10·4′E	F	133
Upwood Fm	Brad	SE0435	53°48·9′	1°55·9′W	FM	104
Upwood Park	Oxon	SP4500	51°42·0′	1°20·5′W	X	164
Upwoods Fm	Derby	SK1135	52°55·0′	1°49·8′W	FM	128
Ura	Shetld	HP6317	60°50·1′	0°50·0′W	X	1
Urabug	Shetld	HU4487	60°34·1′	1°11·3′W	X	1,2
Uradale	Shetld	HU4037	60°7·2′	1°16·3′W	X	4

Ura Firth	Shetld	HU2977	60°28·8'	1°27·8'W	W	3
Urafirth	Shetld	HU3078	60°29·3'	1°26·7'W	T	3
Uragaig	Arg & Bt	NR3898	56°6·4'	6°12·4'W	T	61
Uralee	Shetld	HU5289	60°35·1'	1°2·6'W	X	1,2
Uras	Aberd	NO8781	56°55·5'	2°12·4'W	X	45
Uras Knaps	Aberd	NO8780	56°54·9'	2°12·4'W	X	45
Ura Stack	Shetld	HU5057	60°17·9'	1°5·2'W	X	2,3
Urban Fm	Know	SJ4399	53°29·3'	2°51·1'W	FM	108
Urban Fm	Leeds	SE2936	53°49·4'	1°33·2'W	FM	104
Urchair Fhada	Highld	NM6486	56°54·6'	5°52·1'W	X	40
Urchany and Farley Forest	Highld	NH4647	57°29·5'	4°33·7'W	X	26
Urchfont	Wilts	SU0457	51°19·0'	1°56·2'W	T	173
Urchfont Down	Wilts	SU0552	51°16·3'	1°55·3'W	X	184
Urchfont Hill	Wilts	SU0455	51°17·9'	1°56·2'W	H	173
Urchinrigg Fm	Cumbr	SD5486	54°16·3'	2°42·0'W	FM	97
Urchinwood Manor	N Som	ST4463	51°22·0'	2°47·9'W	X	172,182
Urdd Centre	Cered	SN3254	52°9·8'	4°27·0'W	X	145
Urdimarsh	Heref	SO5248	52°7·9'	2°41·7'W	T	149
Ure	Shetld	HU2280	60°30·5'	1°35·5'W	T	3
Ure Bank	N Yks	SE3172	54°8·8'	1°31·1'W	T	99
Ure Head	N Yks	SD8096	54°21·8'	2°18·0'W	X	98
Urgashay	Somer	ST5624	51°1·1'	2°37·3'W	T	183
Urgha	N Eil	NG1799	57°53·7'	6°46·1'W	T	14
Urgha Beag	N Eil	NB1700	57°54·2'	6°46·2'W	T	14
Urgles	Devon	SX5364	50°27·7'	4°3·9'W	X	201
Urie Lingey	Shetld	HU5995	60°38·3'	0°54·8'W	X	1,2
Urie Loch	N Ayr	NS0028	55°30·5'	5°9·6'W	W	69
Urie Ness	Shetld	HU5994	60°37·8'	0°54·8'W	X	1,2
Urie The	N Ayr	NS0028	55°30·5'	5°9·6'W	H	69
Urioch	D & G	NX6866	54°58·5'	4°3·3'W	X	83,84
Urishay Castle	Heref	SO3237	52°1·9'	2°59·1'W	X	161
Urit Hill	S Lanak	NS7626	55°31·0'	3°57·4'W	H	71
Urlar	Pth & Kin	NN8446	56°35·8'	3°52·9'W	X	52
Urlar Burn	Pth & Kin	NN8345	56°35·2'	3°53·9'W	W	52
Urlarmore	Moray	NJ1420	57°16·0'	3°25·1'W	X	36
Urlay Nook	Stock on T	NZ4014	54°31·4'	1°22·5'W	T	93
Urless Fm	Dorset	ST5103	50°49·7'	2°41·4'W	FM	194
Urloxhey Fm	Worcs	SO8969	52°19·4'	2°9·3'W	FM	139
Urmston	Traf	SJ7494	53°26·8'	2°23·1'W	T	109
Urpeth	Durham	NZ2554	54°53·1'	1°36·2'W	T	88
Urquhart	Fife	NT0786	56°3·7'	3°29·2'W	X	65
Urquhart	Highld	NH5858	57°35·6'	4°22·1'W	X	26
Urquhart	Moray	NJ2862	57°38·8'	3°11·9'W	T	28
Urquhart Bay	Highld	NH5229	57°19·9'	4°27·1'W	W	26,35
Urquhart Castle	Highld	NH5328	57°19·4'	4°26·0'W	A	26,35
Urra	N Yks	NZ5701	54°24·3'	1°6·9'W	T	93
Urrall	D & G	NX2969	54°59·4'	4°39·9'W	X	82
Urrall Fell	D & G	NX2970	55°0·0'	4°40·0'W	H	76
Urrall Loch	D & G	NX2869	54°59·4'	4°40·9'W	W	82
Urra Moor	N Yks	NZ5801	54°24·3'	1°6·0'W	X	93
Urrard Ho	Pth & Kin	NN9063	56°45·0'	3°47·5'W	X	43
Urr Water	D & G	NX7582	55°7·3'	3°57·2'W	W	78
Urr Water	D & G	NX7669	55°0·3'	3°55·9'W	W	84
Urr Waterfoot	D & G	NX8551	54°50·7'	3°47·0'W	W	84
Urswick Tarn	Cumbr	SD2774	54°9·6'	3°6·7'W	W	96,97
Urvaig	Arg & Bt	NM0850	56°33·2'	6°44·7'W	X	46
Ury Ho	Aberd	NO8587	56°58·7'	2°14·4'W	X	45
Ury Home Fm	Aberd	NO8588	56°59·2'	2°14·4'W	FM	45
Uryside	Aberd	NJ7722	57°17·5'	2°22·4'W	X	38
Usan	Angus	NO7254	56°40·9'	2°27·0'W	X	54
Usan Ho	Angus	NO7255	56°41·4'	2°27·0'W	X	54
Usha Gap	N Yks	SD9097	54°22·3'	2°8·8'W	X	98
Ushat Head	Highld	ND0371	58°37·2'	3°39·7'W	X	12
Ushaw College	Durham	NZ2143	54°47·1'	1°40·0'W	X	88
Ushaw Fm	Durham	NZ2143	54°47·1'	1°40·0'W	FM	88
Ushaw Moor	Durham	NZ2242	54°46·6'	1°39·1'W	T	88
Ushercombe Fm	Oxon	SP3935	52°1·0'	1°25·5'W	FM	151
Usher Fm	Leic	SP5786	52°28·4'	1°9·2'W	FM	140
Usherwoods	Lancs	SD6666	54°5·6'	2°30·8'W	X	98
Uskie Geo	Shetld	HU2047	60°12·7'	1°37·8'W	X	3
Uskmouth	Newp	ST3383	51°32·8'	2°57·6'W	X	171
Usk or Brynbuga	Monm	SO3700	51°41·9'	2°54·3'W	T	171
Usk Patch		ST3580	51°31·1'	2°55·8'W	X	171
Usk Reservoir	Carm	SN8228	51°56·5'	3°42·6'W	W	160
Usk Valley Walk	Monm	SO3409	51°46·8'	2°57·0'W	X	161
Usk Valley Walk	Monm	ST3895	51°39·3'	2°53·4'W	X	171
Usselby	Lincs	TF0993	53°25·6'	0°21·2'W	T	112
Usselby Moor	Lincs	TF1092	53°25·0'	0°20·3'W	X	113
Usselby Plantn	Lincs	TF1092	53°25·0'	0°20·3'W	F	113
Ussel Croft	N Yks	NZ3906	54°27·1'	1°23·5'W	X	93
Ussie	Highld	NH5157	57°35·0'	4°29·1'W	X	26
Ussie, Loch	Highld	NH5057	57°35·0'	4°30·1'W	W	26
Usta Ness	Shetld	HU3841	60°9·4'	1°18·4'W	X	4
Ustaness	Shetld	HU3843	60°10·4'	1°18·4'W	X	4
Usway Burn	Northum	NT8710	55°23·3'	2°11·9'W	W	80
Usway Burn	Northum	NT8815	55°26·0'	2°10·9'W	W	80
Uswayford	Northum	NT8814	55°25·4'	2°10·9'W	X	80
Usworth	Sund	NZ3058	54°55·2'	1°31·5'W	T	88
Usworth Hall	Sund	NZ3158	54°55·2'	1°30·6'W	X	88
Utcoate Grange	Beds	SP9332	51°59·0'	0°38·4'W	X	165
Uthrogle	Fife	NO3313	56°18·5'	3°4·5'W	X	59
Utica	Gwyn	SH6938	52°55·7'	3°56·5'W	X	124
Utkinton	Ches	SJ5464	53°10·5'	2°40·9'W	T	117
Utkinton Hall	Ches	SJ5564	53°10·5'	2°40·0'W	A	117
Utley	Brad	SE0542	53°52·7'	1°55·0'W	T	104
Utnabrake	Shetld	HU4040	60°8·8'	1°16·3'W	X	4
Uton	Devon	SX8298	50°46·4'	3°40·0'W	T	191
Utstabi	Shetld	HU2176	60°28·3'	1°36·6'W	X	3
Utterby	Lincs	TF3093	53°25·3'	0°2·2'W	T	113
Utterby Ho	Lincs	TF3093	53°25·3'	0°2·2'W	X	113
Uttershill Castle	Midlo	NT2359	55°49·3'	3°13·3'W	A	66,73
Uttoxeter	Staffs	SK0933	52°53·9'	1°51·6'W	T	128
Uttworth Manor	Surrey	TQ0438	51°8·1'	0°30·4'W	X	186
Uwchafon	Gwyn	SH9029	52°51·1'	3°37·6'W	X	125
Uwchlaw'r-coed	Gwyn	SH6025	52°48·5'	4°4·2'W	X	124
Uwchlaw'r-rhos	Gwyn	SH4754	53°3·9'	4°16·6'W	X	115,123
Uwchmynydd	Gwyn	SH1525	52°47·7'	4°44·2'W	T	123
Uwch-mynydd	Gwyn	SH6519	52°45·3'	3°59·6'W	X	124
Uwch-Mynydd	Gwyn	SH8239	52°56·4'	3°45·0'W	X	124,125
Uwch-y-coed	Powys	SN8294	52°32·1'	3°44·0'W	X	135,136
Uwchygarreg	Gwyn	SH6710	52°40·5'	3°57·6'W	X	124
Uwch-y-llan	Powys	SJ1403	52°37·3'	3°15·8'W	X	136
Uwch-y-nant	Flint	SJ1666	53°11·3'	3°15·0'W	X	116
Uxbridge	Hill	TQ0583	51°32·4'	0°28·8'W	T	176
Uxbridge Common	Hill	TQ0685	51°33·5'	0°27·9'W	X	176
Uxbridge Moor	Hill	TQ0583	51°32·4'	0°28·8'W	T	176
Uxmore Fm	Oxon	SU6784	51°33·3'	1°1·6'W	FM	175
Uxna Geo	Shetld	HU4628	60°2·3'	1°10·0'W	X	4
Ux Ness	Shetld	HU3835	60°6·1'	1°18·5'W	X	4
Uyea	Shetld	HU3192	60°36·9'	1°25·5'W	X	1
Uyea	Shetld	HU3291	60°36·3'	1°24·4'W	X	1
Uyea	Shetld	HU6099	60°40·4'	0°53·6'W	X	1
Uyea Scord	Shetld	HU3383	60°32·0'	1°23·4'W	X	1,2,3
Uyea Sound	Shetld	HP5800	60°41·0'	0°55·8'W	W	1
Uyeasound	Shetld	HP5901	60°41·5'	0°54·7'W	T	1
Uyea Sound	Shetld	HU3160	60°19·6'	1°25·8'W	W	3
Uyea Sound	Shetld	HU4480	60°30·3'	1°11·4'W	W	1,2,3
Uynarey (Nature Reserve)	Shetld	HU4481	60°30·9'	1°11·4'W	X	1,2,3
Uzmaston	Pemb	SM9714	51°47·5'	4°56·2'W	T	157,158
Uzzicar	Cumbr	NY2321	54°34·9'	3°11·1'W	X	89,90
Uzzles Hill	Durham	NY9248	54°49·9'	2°7·0'W	X	87

V

Vaa Geo	Shetld	HU3611	59°53·2'	1°20·9'W	X	4
Vaakel Craigs	Shetld	HU4013	59°54·3'	1°16·6'W	X	4
Vaasetter	Shetld	HZ2071	59°31·7'	1°38·3'W	X	4
Vaava Runs, The	Shetld	HU3074	60°27·2'	1°26·8'W	X	3
Vacam Island	N Eil	NF9982	57°43·9'	7°3·0'W	X	18
Vaccasay	N Eil	NF9774	57°39·5'	7°4·4'W	X	18
Vachelich	Pemb	SM7725	51°53·0'	5°14·0'W	T	157
Vacherie Ho	Lincs	TF1652	53°3·4'	0°15·7'W	X	121
Vachery Ho	Surrey	TQ0737	51°7·6'	0°27·9'W	X	187
Vachery Pond	Surrey	TQ0637	51°7·6'	0°28·7'W	W	187
Vache, The	Bucks	SU9994	51°38·4'	0°33·8'W	X	175,176
Vacquoy	Orkney	HY3932	59°10·5'	3°3·5'W	X	6
Vacsay	N Eil	NB1136	58°13·3'	6°54·9'W	X	13
Vacye	Corn	SX3198	50°45·7'	4°23·4'W	X	190
Vad	N Eil	NF9073	57°38·7'	7°11·3'W	X	18
Vaddicott	Devon	SS4210	50°52·3'	4°14·4'W	X	190
Vadill of Garth	Shetld	HU4754	60°16·3'	1°8·5'W	W	3
Vadills,The	Shetld	HU2955	60°17·0'	1°28·0'W	W	3
Vadill, The	Shetld	HU4759	60°19·0'	1°8·5'W	W	2,3
Vadlure	Shetld	HU2448	60°13·2'	1°33·5'W	X	3
Vadna Taing	Shetld	HP6616	60°49·5'	0°46·7'W	X	1
Vady	Orkney	HY4628	59°8·4'	2°56·1'W	X	5,6
Vagar Hill	Heref	SO2939	52°2·9'	3°1·7'W	X	161
Vagastie	Highld	NC5328	58°13·2'	4°29·7'W	X	16
Vagg	Somer	ST5218	50°57·8'	2°40·6'W	T	183
Vagg Fm	Somer	ST5318	50°57·8'	2°39·8'W	FM	183
Vagg's Hill	Wilts	ST8055	51°17·9'	2°16·8'W	H	173
Vaglefield	Devon	SS3606	50°50·1'	4°19·4'W	X	190
Vagniacis	Kent	TQ6172	51°25·7'	0°19·4'E	R	177
Vagwr Eilw	Pemb	SM8127	51°54·2'	5°10·6'W	X	157
Vagwrlas	Pemb	SN0332	51°57·3'	4°51·6'W	X	145,157
Vaila Sound	Shetld	HU2347	60°12·7'	1°34·6'W	W	3
Vain Fm	Heref	SO6218	51°51·8'	2°32·7'W	FM	162
Vaiseys Fm	Suff	TL9347	52°5·5'	0°49·4'E	FM	155
Vaish Moar Fm	I of M	SC2884	54°13·6'	4°37·9'W	FM	95
Vaitam	N Eil	NF9380	57°42·6'	7°8·8'W	X	18
Vai Voe	Shetld	HU5766	60°22·7'	0°57·5'W	W	2
Vaivoe	Shetld	HU5766	60°22·7'	0°57·5'W	X	2
Valaberg	Shetld	HP5712	60°47·5'	0°56·7'W	X	1
Valance	Essex	TL4633	51°58·8'	0°8·0'E	X	167
Valance-end Fm	Beds	SP9918	51°51·3'	0°33·4'W	FM	165
Valance Fm	Cambs	TL4841	52°3·1'	0°9·9'E	FM	154
Valasay	N Eil	NB1436	58°13·5'	6°51·8'W	T	13
Valast Hill Fm	Pemb	SR9696	51°37·8'	4°56·5'W	FM	158
Valbrook Fm	Beds	TL0662	52°15·0'	0°26·4'W	FM	153
Valder, The	Shetld	HU4333	60°5·0'	1°13·1'W	X	4
Valdigar	Orkney	HY4908	58°57·6'	2°52·7'W	X	6,7
Valdoe, The	W Susx	SU8708	50°52·1'	0°45·4'W	F	197
Vald Skerries	Shetld	HU4572	60°26·0'	1°10·4'W	X	2,3
Vale	Cald	SD9126	53°44·1'	2°7·8'W	T	103
Vale Acre Fm	Dorset	SU0811	50°54·1'	1°52·8'W	FM	195
Vale Down	Devon	SX5286	50°39·5'	4°5·3'W	T	191,201
Vale Fm	Dorset	ST8416	50°56·8'	2°13·3'W	FM	183
Vale Fm	Hants	SU4444	51°11·8'	1°21·8'W	FM	185
Vale Fm	Herts	TL0105	51°44·3'	0°31·8'W	FM	166
Vale Fm	Kent	TR1662	51°19·2'	1°6·4'E	FM	179
Vale Fm	Lincs	TF3967	53°11·1'	0°5·2'E	FM	122
Vale Fm	Norf	TF9617	52°43·1'	0°54·5'E	FM	132
Vale Fm	Norf	TF9713	52°41·0'	0°55·3'E	FM	132
Vale Fm	Norf	TG0822	52°45·6'	1°5·4'E	FM	133
Vale Fm	Northnts	SP6976	52°22·9'	0°58·8'W	FM	141
Vale Fm	Notts	SK8354	53°4·8'	0°45·2'W	FM	121
Vale Fm	Shrops	SJ5831	52°52·7'	2°37·0'W	FM	126
Vale Fm	Somer	ST5826	51°2·1'	2°35·6'W	FM	183
Vale Fm	Suff	TM0634	51°58·2'	1°0·3'E	FM	155
Vale Fm	Suff	TM1156	52°9·9'	1°5·5'E	FM	155
Vale Fm	Suff	TM1335	51°58·6'	1°6·5'E	FM	169
Vale Fm	Suff	TM3145	52°3·5'	1°22·6'E	FM	169
Vale Fm	Suff	TM3469	52°16·4'	1°26·2'E	FM	156
Vale Fm	Suff	TM4066	52°14·6'	1°31·3'E	FM	156
Vale Fm	Suff	TM4880	52°21·9'	1°39·0'E	FM	156
Vale Fm	Surrey	TQ1248	51°13·4'	0°23·4'W	FM	187
Vale Fm	Wilts	SU0680	51°31·4'	1°54·4'W	FM	173
Vale Fm	W Susx	TQ3821	50°58·5'	0°1·7'W	FM	198
Vale Fm, The	Suff	TM1835	51°58·5'	1°10·8'E	FM	169
Valehead	Aberd	NO8780	56°54·9'	2°12·4'W	X	45
Vale Ho	Lancs	SD5245	53°54·2'	2°43·4'W	X	102
Vale Ho	Leic	SK7734	52°54·1'	0°50·9'W	X	129
Vale Ho	Norf	TF9009	52°39·0'	0°48·9'E	X	144
Valehouse Fm	Dorset	SY3997	50°46·4'	2°51·5'W	FM	193
Vale House Fm	Durham	NY9412	54°30·4'	2°5·1'W	FM	91,92
Vale House Fm	Durham	NY9417	54°33·1'	2°5·1'W	FM	91,92
Vale House Fm	N Lincs	TA1013	53°36·4'	0°19·8'W	FM	113
Valehouse Resr	Derby	SK0397	53°28·4'	1°56·9'W	W	110
Vale Lodge	Surrey	TQ1655	51°17·2'	0°19·8'W	X	187
Valence Ho	Bark & Dag	TQ4886	51°33·4'	0°8·5'E	A	177
Valence Lodge	Durham	NY8531	54°40·7'	2°13·5'W	X	91,92
Valence School	Kent	TQ4554	51°16·2'	0°5·1'E	X	188
Valentine Ho	Lancs	SD5031	53°46·6'	2°45·1'W	X	102
Valentine's Fm	Devon	ST1811	50°53·8'	3°9·6'W	FM	192,193
Valentine's Fm	Herts	TQ2298	51°40·3'	0°13·7'W	FM	166,176
Valentines Park	Redbr	TQ4387	51°34·0'	0°4·2'E	X	177
Vale of Belvoir	Notts	SK7737	52°55·7'	0°50·9'W	X	129
Vale of Berkeley	Glos	SO7001	51°42·7'	2°25·7'W	X	162
Vale of Catmose	Rut	SK8609	52°40·5'	0°43·3'W	X	141
Vale of Clwyd	Denb	SJ0770	53°13·4'	3°23·2'W	X	116
Vale of Edale	Derby	SK1284	53°21·4'	1°48·8'W	X	110
Vale of Evesham	Worcs	SP0441	52°4·3'	1°56·1'W	X	150
Vale of Ewyas	Monm	SO2630	51°58·1'	3°4·2'W	X	161
Vale of Ewyas	Monm	SO2824	51°54·8'	3°2·4'W	X	161
Vale of Ffestiniog	Gwyn	SH6640	52°56·7'	3°59·3'W	X	124
Vale of Gloucester	Glos	SO8219	51°52·4'	2°15·3'W	X	162
Vale of Gloucester	Glos	SO8928	51°57·3'	2°9·2'W	X	150,163
Vale of Health	Camden	TQ2686	51°33·8'	0°10·5'W	T	176
Vale of Lanherne or Mawgan	Corn	SW8765	50°27·0'	4°59·7'W	X	200
Vale of Leven	W Dunb	NS3877	55°57·8'	4°35·3'W	X	63
Vale of Llangollen	Denb	SJ2641	52°57·9'	3°5·7'W	X	117
Vale of Mawgan or Lanherne	Corn	SW8765	50°27·0'	4°59·7'W	X	200
Vale of Neath or Cwm Nedd	Nth Pt Talb	SN8303	51°43·1'	3°41·2'W	X	170
Vale of Pewsey	Wilts	SU1158	51°19·5'	1°50·1'W	X	173
Vale of Rheidol Rly	Cered	SN6678	52°23·3'	3°57·7'W	X	135
Vale of Taunton Deane	Somer	ST1526	51°1·9'	3°12·3'W	X	181,193
Vale of White Horse	Oxon	SU3291	51°37·2'	1°31·9'W	X	164,174
Vale Royal	Ches	SJ6369	53°13·2'	2°32·8'W	A	118
Valeroyal	Ches	SJ9574	53°16·0'	2°4·1'W	X	118
Valeroyal Cut	Ches	SJ6469	53°13·3'	2°31·9'W	W	118
Vales Hall	Suff	TM2578	52°21·5'	1°18·7'E	X	156
Vales Moor	Hants	SU1904	50°50·3'	1°43·4'W	X	195
Vale's Rock	Worcs	SO8282	52°26·4'	2°15·5'W	X	138
Vales Wood	Shrops	SJ3920	52°46·7'	2°53·9'W	F	126
Valeswood	Shrops	SJ3920	52°46·7'	2°53·9'W	T	126
Vale, The	Birm	SP0584	52°27·5'	1°55·2'W	T	139
Vale, The	Lincs	TA1704	53°31·4'	0°13·7'W	F	113
Vale, The	Powys	SO0335	52°0·5'	3°24·4'W	X	160
Vale, The	W Susx	TQ1207	50°51·3'	0°24·1'W	X	198
Valewood Fm	Ches	SJ7880	53°19·2'	2°19·4'W	FM	109
Valewood Ho	W Susx	SU9030	51°4·0'	0°42·5'W	X	186
Valiants	Essex	TL8632	51°57·5'	0°42·8'E	X	168
Valla Dale	Shetld	HU3077	60°28·8'	1°26·8'W	X	3
Valla Field	Shetld	HP5806	60°44·2'	0°55·7'W	H	1
Vallafield	Shetld	HP5908	60°45·3'	0°54·5'W	X	1
Valla Kames	Shetld	HU2986	60°33·7'	1°27·8'W	X	1,3
Valla Ness	Shetld	HU5058	60°18·4'	1°5·2'W	X	2,3
Vallaquie Island	N Eil	NF9167	57°35·5'	7°9·8'W	X	18
Vallaquie Strand	N Eil	NF8575	57°39·5'	7°16·5'W	X	18
Vallay	N Eil	NF7776	57°39·7'	7°24·5'W	X	18
Vallay	N Eil	NG0582	57°44·1'	6°56·9'W	X	18
Vallay House	N Eil	NF7775	57°39·2'	7°24·5'W	X	18
Vallay Sound	N Eil	NF7575	57°39·1'	7°26·5'W	W	18
Vallay Strand	N Eil	NF7875	57°39·2'	7°23·5'W	X	18
Vallen	Pemb	SN0408	51°44·4'	4°49·9'W	X	157,158
Vallets	Heref	SO4771	52°20·3'	2°46·3'W	X	137,138,148
Vallets, The	Heref	SO4332	51°59·2'	2°49·4'W	X	149,161
Valley	D & G	NY3070	55°1·4'	3°5·3'W	X	85
Valley	Orkney	HY3705	58°55·9'	3°5·2'W	X	6,7
Valley Airfield	I of Angl	SH3075	53°14·9'	4°32·5'W	X	114
Valley Barn	W Susx	TQ1807	50°51·3'	0°19·0'W	X	198
Valleybottom Fm	Herts	TL0614	51°49·1'	0°27·3'W	FM	166
Valley Bottom or The Pools	Cambs	TL5077	52°22·5'	0°12·6'E	X	143
Valley Brook	Ches	SJ7553	53°4·7'	2°22·0'W	W	118
Valley Burn	Durham	NZ2535	54°42·8'	1°36·3'W	W	93
Valley End	Surrey	SU9564	51°22·3'	0°37·7'W	X	175,176,186
Valley End Fm	Oxon	SU7286	51°34·3'	0°57·3'W	FM	175
Valleyfield	D & G	NW9868	54°58·2'	5°8·9'W	X	82
Valleyfield	D & G	NX6855	54°52·6'	4°3·0'W	X	83,84
Valleyfield	D & G	NX7665	54°58·1'	3°55·8'W	X	84
Valleyfield Fm	Pth & Kin	NO2426	56°25·5'	3°13·5'W	FM	53,59
Valley Fields Fm	Warw	SP4866	52°17·6'	1°17·4'W	FM	151
Valley Fm	Bucks	SP8925	51°55·2'	0°42·0'W	FM	165
Valley Fm	Cambs	TL2153	52°9·9'	0°13·5'W	FM	153
Valley Fm	Cambs	TL3248	52°7·1'	0°3·9'W	FM	153
Valley Fm	Cambs	TL3251	52°8·7'	0°3·9'W	FM	153
Valley Fm	Cambs	TL5253	52°9·5'	0°13·7'E	FM	154
Valley Fm	Ches	SJ6075	53°16·5'	2°35·6'W	FM	118
Valley Fm	Ches	SJ7752	53°4·1'	2°20·2'W	FM	118
Valley Fm	Devon	SX8170	50°31·3'	3°40·3'W	FM	202
Valley Fm	Durham	NY9212	54°30·4'	2°7·0'W	FM	91,92
Valley Fm	Essex	TL7229	51°56·2'	0°30·5'E	FM	167
Valley Fm	Essex	TM1723	51°52·0'	1°9·5'E	FM	168,169
Valley Fm	Glos	SO9407	51°45·9'	2°4·8'W	FM	163
Valley Fm	Herts	TQ0299	51°41·1'	0°31·1'W	FM	166,176
Valley Fm	Kent	TQ9955	51°15·8'	0°51·5'E	FM	178
Valley Fm	Leic	SK3415	52°44·1'	1°29·4'W	FM	128
Valley Fm	Leic	SK3510	52°41·4'	1°28·5'W	FM	128
Valley Fm	Leic	SP6285	52°27·8'	1°4·8'W	FM	140
Valley Fm	Lincs	SK9842	52°58·2'	0°32·0'W	FM	130

Valley Fm	Lincs	TF1678	53°17·4′	0°15·2′W	FM	121
Valley Fm	Lincs	TF2672	53°14·0′	0°6·3′W	FM	122
Valley Fm	Lincs	TF3878	53°17·1′	0°4·6′E	FM	122
Valley Fm	Norf	TF7524	52°47·3′	0°36·1′E	FM	132
Valley Fm	Norf	TF7943	52°57·5′	0°40·3′E	FM	132
Valley Fm	Norf	TF8503	52°35·8′	0°44·3′E	FM	144
Valley Fm	Norf	TG0720	52°44·5′	1°4·4′E	FM	133
Valley Fm	Norf	TG5200	52°32·6′	1°43·4′E	FM	134
Valley Fm	Norf	TM0781	52°23·5′	1°2·9′E	FM	144
Valley Fm	Norf	TM2598	52°32·2′	1°19·5′E	FM	134
Valley Fm	N Yks	NZ3500	54°23·9′	1°27·2′W	FM	93
Valley Fm	N Yks	NZ3702	54°25·0′	1°25·4′W	FM	93
Valley Fm	N Yks	SE0143	53°53·2′	1°58·7′W	FM	104
Valley Fm	N Yks	SE2752	53°58·0′	1°34·9′W	FM	104
Valley Fm	N Yks	SE6273	54°9·2′	1°2·6′W	FM	100
Valley Fm	Pemb	SN0117	51°49·2′	4°52·9′W	FM	157,158
Valley Fm	S Glos	ST5887	51°35·1′	2°36·0′W	FM	172
Valley Fm	Staffs	SJ9118	52°45·8′	2°7·6′W	FM	127
Valley Fm	Suff	TL8947	52°5·6′	0°45·9′E	FM	155
Valley Fm	Suff	TL9041	52°2·3′	0°46·6′E	FM	155
Valley Fm	Suff	TL9353	52°8·7′	0°49·6′E	FM	155
Valley Fm	Suff	TL9446	52°4·9′	0°50·3′E	FM	155
Valley Fm	Suff	TL9459	52°11·9′	0°50·7′E	FM	155
Valley Fm	Suff	TM0036	51°59·4′	0°55·2′E	FM	155
Valley Fm	Suff	TM0057	52°10·7′	0°55·9′E	FM	155
Valley Fm	Suff	TM0156	52°10·2′	0°56·8′E	FM	155
Valley Fm	Suff	TM0442	52°2·6′	0°58·9′E	FM	155
Valley Fm	Suff	TM0457	52°10·6′	0°59·4′E	FM	155
Valley Fm	Suff	TM0549	52°6·3′	1°0·0′E	FM	155
Valley Fm	Suff	TM0553	52°8·5′	1°0·2′E	FM	155
Valley Fm	Suff	TM0746	52°4·6′	1°1·6′E	FM	155,169
Valley Fm	Suff	TM1143	52°2·9′	1°5·0′E	FM	155,169
Valley Fm	Suff	TM1177	52°21·2′	1°6·3′E	FM	144
Valley Fm	Suff	TM1552	52°7·7′	1°8·9′E	FM	156
Valley Fm	Suff	TM1849	52°6·0′	1°11·4′E	FM	169
Valley Fm	Suff	TM1958	52°10·8′	1°12·6′E	FM	156
Valley Fm	Suff	TM1960	52°11·9′	1°12·7′E	FM	156
Valley Fm	Suff	TM2173	52°18·9′	1°14·9′E	FM	156
Valley Fm	Suff	TM2269	52°16·7′	1°15·7′E	FM	156
Valley Fm	Suff	TM2343	52°2·7′	1°15·5′E	FM	169
Valley Fm	Suff	TM2355	52°9·1′	1°16·0′E	FM	156
Valley Fm	Suff	TM2770	52°17·1′	1°20·1′E	FM	156
Valley Fm	Suff	TM2884	52°24·6′	1°21·5′E	FM	156
Valley Fm	Suff	TM2956	52°9·5′	1°21·3′E	FM	156
Valley Fm	Suff	TM3141	52°1·4′	1°22·4′E	FM	169
Valley Fm	Suff	TM3172	52°18·1′	1°23·7′E	FM	156
Valley Fm	Suff	TM3284	52°24·5′	1°25·1′E	FM	156
Valley Fm	Suff	TM3376	52°20·2′	1°25·6′E	FM	156
Valley Fm	Suff	TM3473	52°18·5′	1°26·4′E	FM	156
Valley Fm	Suff	TM3570	52°16·9′	1°27·1′E	FM	156
Valley Fm	Suff	TM3579	52°21·7′	1°27·5′E	FM	156
Valley Fm	Suff	TM3647	52°4·5′	1°27·0′E	FM	169
Valley Fm	Suff	TM3673	52°18·5′	1°28·1′E	FM	156
Valley Fm	Suff	TM3675	52°19·6′	1°28·2′E	FM	156
Valley Fm	Suff	TM3959	52°10·9′	1°30·2′E	FM	156
Valley Fm	Suff	TM3978	52°21·1′	1°31·0′E	FM	156
Valley Fm	Suff	TM4288	52°26·4′	1°34·0′E	FM	156
Valley Fm	Suff	TM4353	52°7·5′	1°33·4′E	FM	156
Valley Fm	Suff	TM4378	52°21·0′	1°34·5′E	FM	156
Valley Fm	Suff	TM4686	52°25·2′	1°37·5′E	FM	156
Valley Fm	Suff	TM4881	52°22·5′	1°39·0′E	FM	156
Valley Fm	Warw	SP1973	52°21·5′	1°42·9′W	FM	139
Valley Fm	Warw	SP3649	52°8·5′	1°28·0′W	FM	151
Valley Fm	Warw	SP4246	52°6·9′	1°22·8′W	FM	151
Valley Fm	Wilts	ST9843	51°11·4′	2°1·3′W	FM	184
Valley Fm	Worcs	SO8568	52°18·8′	2°12·8′W	FM	139
Valley Fm	Worcs	SO9473	52°21·5′	2°4·9′W	FM	139
Valley Fm	W Susx	TQ2518	50°57·1′	0°12·8′W	FM	198
Valley Fm, The	Essex	TL8836	51°59·7′	0°44·7′E	FM	155
Valley Fm, The	Leic	SK3701	52°36·6′	1°26·8′W	FM	140
Valley Gardens	Surrey	SU9769	51°24·9′	0°35·9′W	X	175,176
Valley Green Fm	Essex	TL8932	51°57·5′	0°45·4′E	FM	168
Valley Ho	Essex	TM0234	51°58·3′	0°56·9′E	X	155
Valley of Balmule	Fife	NT0991	56°6·4′	3°27·4′W	X	58
Valley of Desolation	N Yks	SE0856	54°0·2′	1°52·3′W	X	104
Valley of Keelhamar	Shetld	HU4645	60°11·5′	1°9·7′W	X	4
Valley of Kergord	Shetld	HU4058	60°18·5′	1°16·1′W	X	2,3
Valley of Koam	Shetld	HU1560	60°19·7′	1°43·2′W	X	3
Valley of Rocks, The	Devon	SS7049	51°13·8′	3°51·3′W	X	180
Valley of Stones	Dorset	SY5987	50°41·1′	2°34·4′W	X	194
Valley or Dyffryn	I of Angl	SH2979	53°17·1′	4°33·5′W	T	114
Valleys	I of W	SZ4887	50°41·1′	1°18·8′W	X	196
Valley Springs	Devon	SX7845	50°17·8′	3°42·4′W	X	202
Valleys, The	Norf	TG1941	52°55·5′	1°15·9′E	X	133
Valley, The	Lincs	SK9842	52°58·2′	0°32·0′W	X	130
Valley, The	NE Lincs	TF2596	53°27·0′	0°6·6′W	F	113
Valley, The	Pemb	SN0914	51°47·8′	4°45·8′W	X	158
Valley, The	Pemb	SN1205	51°43·0′	4°42·9′W	T	158
Valley, The	Shetld	HU3613	59°54·3′	1°20·9′W	X	4
Valley Truckle	Corn	SX0982	50°36·6′	4°41·6′W	T	200
Valley View Fm	Beds	SP9454	52°10·8′	0°37·1′W	FM	153
Valley Walk, The	Essex	TL8542	52°3·0′	0°42·3′E	X	155
Valleywood	Surrey	SU9663	51°21·7′	0°36·9′W	X	175,176,186
Valley Wood	Swan	SS6398	51°40·1′	3°58·5′W	F	159
Vallis Fm	Somer	ST7549	51°14·6′	2°21·1′W	FM	183
Vallis Vale	Somer	ST7549	51°14·6′	2°21·1′W	X	183
Valtoes	Shetld	HP6613	60°47·9′	0°46·7′W	X	1
Valtos	Highld	NG5163	57°35·6′	6°9·5′W	T	23,24
Valtos	N Eil	NB0937	58°13·8′	6°57·0′W	X	13
Vamh	Orkney	ND4192	58°49·0′	3°0·8′W	X	7
Van	Caer	ST1686	51°34·2′	3°12·3′W	T	171
Van	Powys	SN9587	52°28·5′	3°32·4′W	T	136
Vancelette's Fm	Wilts	ST8588	51°35·7′	2°12·6′W	FM	162,173
Van Common	W Susx	SU8929	51°3·4′	0°43·4′W	X	186,197
Vane Court	E Susx	TQ9522	50°58·1′	0°47·0′E	X	189
Vane Court	Kent	TQ8540	51°8·0′	0°39·0′E	X	189
Vane Farm Nature Centre	Pth & Kin	NT1699	56°10·8′	3°20·7′W	X	58
Van Fm	Carm	SN4511	51°46·8′	4°14·4′W	FM	159
Van Fm	Durham	NZ1013	54°31·0′	1°50·3′W	FM	92
Vange	Essex	TQ7287	51°33·6′	0°29·3′E	T	178

Vange Creek	Essex	TQ7385	51°32·5′	0°30·1′E	W	178
Vange Marshes	Essex	TQ7286	51°33·0′	0°29·2′E	X	178
Vanguard Way	E Susx	TQ4829	51°2·7′	0°7·1′E	X	188,198
Vanguard Way	E Susx	TQ5416	50°55·6′	0°11·9′E	X	199
Vanguard Way	Surrey	TQ3661	51°20·1′	0°2·5′W	X	177,187
Vanlop	Shetld	HU3718	59°57·0′	1°19·8′W	T	4
Vann	Surrey	SU9837	51°7·7′	0°35·6′W	X	186
Vann Copse	Surrey	SU9737	51°7·7′	0°36·4′W	F	186
Vanner's Fm	W Berks	SU4264	51°22·6′	1°23·4′W	FM	174
Vann Fm	Hants	SU7330	51°4·1′	0°57·1′W	FM	186
Vann Hill	Surrey	SU9738	51°8·2′	0°36·4′W	X	186
Vann Ho	Surrey	TQ1539	51°8·5′	0°21·0′W	X	187
Van Post	Devon	SS9718	50°57·4′	3°27·6′W	X	181
Vantage	Fife	NT1585	56°3·3′	3°21·5′W	X	65
Van, The	Powys	SO1658	52°13·1′	3°13·4′W	H	148
Varaquoy	Orkney	HY4531	59°10·0′	2°57·2′W	X	5,6
Varchoel	Powys	SJ2312	52°42·3′	3°8·0′W	T	126
Varden House Fm	Ches	SJ8580	53°19·2′	2°13·1′W	FM	109
Vardentown	Ches	SJ8775	53°16·6′	2°11·3′W	X	118
Varfell	Corn	SW5032	50°8·4′	5°29·6′W	T	203
Varish Veg	I of M	SC2984	54°13·6′	4°37·0′W	X	95
Varle Hill	Somer	SS8831	51°4·3′	3°35·5′W	H	181
Varley Field	Lancs	SD8551	53°57·5′	2°13·3′W	X	103
Varley Fm	Devon	SS5436	51°6·5′	4°4·8′W	FM	180
Varley Head	Corn	SW9881	50°35·9′	4°50·9′W	X	200
Varlish	N Eil	NF7174	57°38·4′	7°30·4′W	X	18
Varmady	Orkney	HY4127	59°7·8′	3°1·4′W	X	5,6
Varragill River	Highld	NG4737	57°21·5′	6°11·9′W	W	23,32
Varrinish	N Eil	NF7719	57°9·2′	7°20·1′W	X	31
Varsity Mink Fm	Cambs	TL5069	52°18·1′	0°12·4′E	FM	154
Varteg	Powys	SN7808	51°45·7′	3°45·7′W	X	160
Varteg	Torf	SO2606	51°45·1′	3°3·9′W	T	161
Varteg Hill	Nth Pt Talb	SN7707	51°45·1′	3°46·5′W	H	160
Vartenham Hill	Somer	ST6618	50°57·9′	2°28·7′W	H	183
Vasa Loch	Orkney	HY4718	59°3·0′	2°54·9′W	W	6
Vassa	Shetld	HU4653	60°15·8′	1°9·6′W	T	3
Vassa Voe	Shetld	HU4652	60°15·2′	1°9·6′W	W	3
Vastern	Wilts	SU0581	51°31·9′	1°55·3′W	T	173
Vat Burn	Aberd	NO4299	57°5·0′	2°57·0′W	W	37,44
Vatches, The	Bucks	SP8612	51°48·2′	0°44·8′W	X	165
Vatchley	Shetld	HU3916	59°55·9′	1°17·6′W	X	4
Vatch, The	Glos	SO8706	51°45·4′	2°10·9′W	X	162
Vatem	N Eil	NG0079	57°42·3′	7°1·7′W	X	18
Vatersay	N Eil	NL6394	56°55·1′	7°31·9′W	T	31
Vatersay	N Eil	NL6395	56°55·7′	7°32·0′W	X	31
Vatersay Bay	N Eil	NL6495	56°55·7′	7°31·0′W	W	31
Vat of Kirbuster (Group)	Orkney	HY6823	59°5·8′	2°33·0′W	X	5
Vatsetter	Shetld	HU3723	59°59·7′	1°19·7′W	X	4
Vatsetter	Shetld	HU5389	60°35·1′	1°1·5′W	T	1,2
Vats Houll	Shetld	HU3956	60°17·4′	1°17·2′W	X	2,3
Vatsie	Shetld	HU5288	60°34·6′	1°2·6′W	X	1,2
Vatster	Shetld	HU4248	60°13·1′	1°14·0′W	X	3
Vats Wick	Shetld	HU5278	60°29·2′	1°2·7′W	W	2,3
Vatten	Highld	NG2843	57°24·0′	6°31·2′W	T	23
Vat, The	Aberd	NO4299	57°5·0′	2°57·0′W	X	37,44
Vauce, The	Northum	NY8062	54°57·4′	2°18·3′W	X	86,87
Vauce Wood	Northum	NY8062	54°57·4′	2°18·3′W	F	86,87
Vaugh Steel	Cumbr	NY4918	54°33·5′	2°46·9′W	X	90
Vaul	Arg & Bt	NM0448	56°32·1′	6°48·4′W	T	46
Vaul Bay	Arg & Bt	NM0548	56°32·1′	6°47·5′W	W	46
Vauld, The	Heref	SO5349	52°8·5′	2°40·8′W	T	149
Vault Beach or Bow	Corn	SX0040	50°13·8′	4°47·9′W	X	204
Vault Hill	Suff	TM4667	52°15·0′	1°36·6′E	X	156
Vaulty Manor	Essex	TL8807	51°44·0′	0°43·8′E	X	168
Vauterhill	Devon	SS5919	50°57·4′	4°0·1′W	X	180
Vauxhall	Birm	SP0887	52°29·1′	1°52·5′W	T	139
Vauxhall	C of West	TQ3078	51°29·4′	0°7·3′W	T	176,177
Vauxhall	Liv	SJ3491	53°24·9′	2°59·2′W	T	108
Vauxhall	Suff	TM0740	52°1·4′	1°1·4′E	X	155,169
Vauxhall	Wrekin	SJ7318	52°45·8′	2°23·6′W	X	127
Vauxhall Br	C of West	TQ3078	51°29·4′	0°7·3′W	X	176,177
Vaval	Orkney	HY4451	59°20·8′	2°58·6′W	X	5
Vayne	Angus	NO4960	56°44·0′	2°49·6′W	X	44
Vaynol Hall	Gwyn	SH5369	53°12·1′	4°11·6′W	T	114,115
Vaynor	Merth Tyd	SO0410	51°47·1′	3°23·1′W	T	160
Vaynor	Pemb	SN0917	51°49·4′	4°45·9′W	X	158
Vaynor	Pemb	SN2342	52°3·1′	4°34·5′W	X	145
Vaynor	Powys	SO0169	52°18·9′	3°26·7′W	X	136,147
Vaynor Fm	Carm	SN2413	51°47·5′	4°32·7′W	FM	158
Vaynor isaf	Pemb	SN0330	51°56·3′	4°51·6′W	X	145,157
Vaynor Park	Powys	SJ1700	52°35·7′	3°13·1′W	X	136
Vayres Fm	I of W	SZ4886	50°40·5′	1°18·9′W	FM	196
Veal's Fm	Hants	SU3909	50°53·0′	1°26·4′W	FM	196
Vean	Orkney	HY3109	58°58·0′	3°11·5′W	X	6,7
Veantrow Bay	Orkney	HY5020	59°4·1′	2°51·8′W	W	5,6
Vearndon	Devon	SX3495	50°44·1′	4°20·8′W	X	190
Vearse Fm	Dorset	SY4592	50°43·7′	2°46·4′W	FM	193
Veaullt	Powys	SO1951	52°9·3′	3°10·6′W	X	148
Vedders Geo	Shetld	HU6791	60°36·1′	0°46·1′W	X	1,2
Veddertownmail	Orkney	HY5009	58°58·2′	2°51·7′W	X	6,7
Vedwllwyd	Powys	SO2078	52°23·9′	3°10·2′W	X	137,148
Veeda Stack	Shetld	HU5662	60°20·6′	0°58·6′W	X	2
Veensgarth	Shetld	HU4244	60°11·1′	1°14·1′W	T	4
Vee Taing	Shetld	HU5999	60°40·5′	0°54·7′W	X	1
Veet Mill Fm	Devon	SX7391	50°42·5′	3°47·5′W	FM	191
Vegadal	Shetld	HU4684	60°32·5′	1°9·2′W	X	1,2,3
Vehicle Proving Ground	Warw	SP3453	52°10·7′	1°29·8′W	X	151
Veilish Point	N Eil	NF8178	57°41·0′	7°20·7′W	X	18
Velator	Devon	SS4835	51°5·9′	4°9·9′W	T	180
Velcourt	Glos	SO6734	52°0·4′	2°28·5′W	X	149
Veldo	Heref	SO5543	52°5·2′	2°39·0′W	T	149
Velindra	Heref	SO4922	51°53·9′	2°44·1′W	X	162
Velindre	Pemb	SM8936	51°59·2′	5°4·0′W	X	157
Velindre	Pemb	SN0425	51°53·6′	4°50·5′W	X	145,157,158
Velindre	Powys	SO1836	52°1·2′	3°11·3′W	T	161
Vellaford Fm	Devon	SS5705	50°49·8′	4°1·5′W	FM	191
Vellake	Devon	SS8305	50°50·2′	3°39·3′W	X	191
Vellake Corner	Devon	SX5590	50°41·7′	4°2·8′W	W	191
Vellan Drang	Corn	SW7011	49°57·5′	5°12·0′W	X	203
Vellan Head	Corn	SW6614	49°59·1′	5°15·5′W	X	203

Vellanoweth	Corn	SW5033	50°8·9′	5°29·6′W	T	203
Vellore	Falk	NS9476	55°58·2′	3°41·5′W	X	65
Vellow	Somer	ST0938	51°8·3′	3°17·7′W	T	181
Vellow Wood Fm	Somer	ST0938	51°8·3′	3°17·7′W	FM	181
Velly	Devon	SS2924	50°59·6′	4°25·8′W	T	190
Velmead Fm	Hants	SU8051	51°15·4′	0°50·8′W	FM	186
Velmore Fm	Hants	SU4219	50°58·4′	1°23·7′W	FM	185
Velt Hevda	Shetld	HU3794	60°37·9′	1°18·9′W	X	1,2
Velthouse	Glos	SO6917	51°51·3′	2°26·6′W	X	162
Velthouse Fm	Glos	SO7714	51°49·7′	2°19·6′W	FM	162
Veltie Skerry	Orkney	HY6331	59°10·1′	2°38·3′W	X	5
Veltigar	Orkney	HY5005	58°56·0′	2°51·6′W	X	6,7
Velvains	Devon	SS9414	50°55·2′	3°30·1′W	X	181
Velvet Bottom	Somer	ST4955	51°17·7′	2°43·5′W	X	172,182
Velvet Hall	Northum	NT9448	55°43·8′	2°5·3′W	X	74,75
Velwell	Devon	SX7663	50°27·5′	3°44·4′W	X	202
Velzian	Orkney	HY2317	59°2·3′	3°20·0′W	X	6
Velzian	Orkney	HY2921	59°4·5′	3°13·8′W	X	6
Velzie	Shetld	HU6091	60°36·1′	0°53·8′W	X	1,2
Vementry	Shetld	HU2960	60°19·6′	1°28·0′W	X	3
Vementry	Shetld	HU3059	60°19·1′	1°26·9′W	T	3
Ven	Somer	ST6818	50°57·9′	2°27·0′W	A	183
Venbridge Ho	Devon	SX7794	50°44·2′	3°44·2′W	X	191
Venchen	Scot Bord	NT8229	55°33·5′	2°16·7′W	X	74
Venchen Hill	Scot Bord	NT8229	55°33·5′	2°16·7′W	H	74
Vencroft Fm	Somer	ST1815	50°56·0′	3°9·6′W	FM	181,193
Vendown	Corn	SX1088	50°39·9′	4°40·9′W	X	190,200
Vendra Stacks	Shetld	HP6516	60°49·6′	0°47·8′W	X	1
Ve Ness	Orkney	HY3705	58°55·9′	3°5·2′W	X	6,7
Veness	Orkney	HY5729	59°9·0′	2°44·6′W	T	5,6
Veness Hill	Orkney	HY3705	58°55·9′	3°5·2′W	H	6,7
Venetian Lodge	Cambs	TL1591	52°30·5′	0°17·9′W	X	142
Venford	Devon	SS8629	51°3·2′	3°37·2′W	X	181
Venford Resr	Devon	SX6870	50°31·1′	3°51·3′W	W	202
Venhay	Devon	SS7918	50°57·2′	3°43·0′W	X	180
Veniekelday	Orkney	HY5304	58°55·5′	2°48·5′W	X	6,7
Ven Law	Scot Bord	NT2541	55°39·7′	3°11·1′W	H	73
Venmans	Devon	SS9821	50°59·0′	3°26·8′W	X	181
Venmore	Heref	SO4354	52°11·1′	2°49·6′W	X	148,149
Venmore Fm	Devon	SY0086	50°40·1′	3°24·5′W	FM	192
Venn	Devon	SS2806	50°49·9′	4°26·2′W	X	190
Venn	Devon	SS3220	50°57·5′	4°23·2′W	X	190
Venn	Devon	SS3716	50°55·5′	4°18·8′W	X	190
Venn	Devon	SS3811	50°52·8′	4°17·8′W	X	190
Venn	Devon	SS5830	51°3·3′	4°1·2′W	X	180
Venn	Devon	SS6805	50°50·0′	3°52·1′W	X	191
Venn	Devon	SS7705	50°50·1′	3°44·4′W	X	191
Venn	Devon	SS8302	50°48·6′	3°39·3′W	X	191
Venn	Devon	SS8806	50°50·8′	3°35·1′W	X	192
Venn	Devon	SX4576	50°34·0′	4°10·9′W	X	201
Venn	Devon	SX7046	50°18·2′	3°49·2′W	T	202
Venn	Devon	SX7969	50°30·7′	3°42·0′W	X	202
Venn	Devon	SX8549	50°20·0′	3°36·6′W	X	202
Venn	Dorset	ST3903	50°49·6′	2°51·6′W	X	193
Venn	Somer	SS9530	51°3·8′	3°29·5′W	X	181
Venn Barton	Devon	SX4995	50°44·3′	4°8·0′W	X	191
Vennbridge Fm	Devon	SX9681	50°37·4′	3°27·8′W	FM	192
Venncott	Devon	SS4013	50°53·9′	4°16·1′W	X	180,190
Venn Cross	Somer	ST0324	51°0·7′	3°22·6′W	X	181
Venn Down	Devon	SX5094	50°43·8′	4°7·1′W	H	191
Venne Cott	Somer	SS9930	51°3·9′	3°26·1′W	X	181
Vennel	D & G	NS7214	55°24·4′	4°0·9′W	X	71
Venner's Fm	Somer	ST2916	50°56·6′	3°0·3′W	FM	193
Venner's Water	Somer	ST3016	50°56·6′	2°59·4′W	W	193
Venney Fm	Norf	TL5697	52°33·1′	0°18·5′E	FM	143
Venn Fm	Corn	SS2608	50°51·0′	4°27·9′W	FM	190
Venn Fm	Devon	SS4013	50°53·9′	4°16·1′W	FM	180,190
Venn Fm	Devon	ST0208	50°52·0′	3°23·9′W	FM	192
Venn Fm	Devon	ST0313	50°54·7′	3°22·4′W	FM	181
Venn Fm	Devon	SX3791	50°42·0′	4°18·1′W	FM	190
Venn Fm	Devon	SX8386	50°40·0′	3°39·0′W	FM	191
Venn Fm	Devon	SX9274	50°33·6′	3°31·1′W	FM	192
Venn Fm	Dorset	SY4194	50°44·8′	2°49·8′W	FM	193
Venn Fm	Dorset	SY4299	50°47·5′	2°49·0′W	FM	193
Venn Fm	Pemb	SM9205	51°42·6′	5°0·3′W	FM	157,158
Venn Fm	Somer	SS8825	51°1·0′	3°35·4′W	FM	181
Venngreen	Devon	SS3711	50°52·8′	4°18·6′W	T	190
Venn Hill	Dorset	ST3803	50°49·6′	2°52·4′W	X	193
Venn Ho	Devon	SX6856	50°23·6′	3°51·0′W	X	202
Vennie	Aberd	NK1040	57°27·3′	1°49·5′W	X	30
Vennington	Shrops	SJ3309	52°40·7′	2°59·1′W	T	126
Venn Lodge (Hotel)	Devon	SX9275	50°34·1′	3°31·1′W	X	192
Venn Mill	Devon	SX4888	50°40·5′	4°8·7′W	X	191
Venn Mill	Oxon	SU4394	51°38·8′	1°22·3′W	X	164,174
Vennmills	Devon	SS3918	50°56·6′	4°17·1′W	X	190
Vennmoor Plantn	Devon	SX3890	50°41·5′	4°17·2′W	F	190
Venn Ottery	Devon	SY0791	50°42·9′	3°18·7′W	T	192
Venn Ottery Common	Devon	SY0691	50°42·9′	3°19·5′W	X	192
Venns Fm	Suff	TM1749	52°6·0′	1°10·5′E	FM	169
Venn's Green	Heref	SO5348	52°7·9′	2°40·8′W	T	149
Venns, The	Shrops	SO5571	52°20·4′	2°39·2′W	X	137,138
Venn, The	Heref	SO6650	52°9·1′	2°29·4′W	X	149
Vennwood	Heref	SO5448	52°7·9′	2°39·9′W	X	149
Venny Tedburn	Devon	SX8297	50°45·9′	3°40·0′W	T	191
Venonis	Warw	SP4788	52°29·5′	1°18·1′W	R	140
Vensilly Hill	Orkney	ND4591	58°48·4′	2°56·6′W	X	7
Venson Fm	Kent	TR2952	51°13·5′	1°17·2′E	FM	179
Venta Icenorum (Roman Town)	Norf	TG2303	52°35·0′	1°17·9′E	R	134
Venta Silvrvm (Caerwent)	Monm	ST4690	51°36·6′	2°46·4′W	R	171,172
Venta (Winchester)	Hants	SU4829	51°3·7′	1°18·5′W	R	185
Venterdon	Corn	SX3574	50°32·8′	4°19·4′W	T	201
Venters	W Susx	TQ2137	51°7·4′	0°15·9′W	X	187
Vent Ho	Kent	TQ9451	51°13·7′	0°47·1′E	X	189
Vention	Devon	SS4540	51°8·5′	4°12·6′W	T	180
Ventners Hall	Northum	NY7268	55°0·6′	2°25·8′W	X	86,87
Ventnor	I of W	SZ5677	50°35·6′	1°12·1′W	T	196
Ventnor Bay	I of W	SZ5677	50°35·6′	1°12·1′W	W	196
Venton	Corn	SX3199	50°46·2′	4°23·4′W	X	190
Venton	Devon	SS4822	50°58·9′	4°9·5′W	X	180

Venton	Devon	SS5004	50°49·2′	4°7·4′W	X	191
Venton	Devon	SS5612	50°53·6′	4°2·5′W	X	180
Venton	Devon	SX4967	50°29·2′	4°7·3′W	X	201
Venton	Devon	SX5856	50°23·4′	3°59·5′W	T	202
Venton	Devon	SX6991	50°42·5′	3°50·9′W	X	191
Venton	Devon	SX7276	50°34·4′	3°48·1′W	X	191
Venton	Devon	SX7560	50°25·8′	3°45·2′W	X	202
Venton Cross	Devon	SS5003	50°48·7′	4°7·4′W	X	191
Venton Fm	Devon	SS4420	50°57·7′	4°12·9′W	FM	180,190
Venton Fm	Devon	SS6011	50°53·1′	3°59·0′W	FM	191
Ventongimps	Corn	SW7851	50°19·3′	5°6·8′W	T	200,204
Ventongimps Fms	Corn	SW7950	50°18·7′	5°5·9′W	FM	200,204
Venton Hill Point	Corn	SW6911	49°57·5′	5°12·9′W	X	203
Venton Ho	Corn	SX2866	50°28·4′	4°25·1′W	X	201
Ventonleague	Corn	SW5738	50°11·8′	5°23·9′W	T	203
Venton Moor	Devon	SS6011	50°53·1′	3°59·0′W	X	191
Venton Vaise	Corn	SW7750	50°18·7′	5°7·6′W	X	200,204
Venton Vedna	Corn	SW6426	50°5·5′	5°17·6′W	X	203
Venton Veor	Corn	SX2266	50°28·2′	4°30·1′W	X	201
Ventonwyn	Corn	SW9646	50°17·0′	4°51·4′W	X	204
Ventonwyn Fm	Corn	SW9550	50°19·1′	4°52·4′W	FM	200,204
Ventown	Devon	SX6298	50°46·1′	3°57·0′W	X	191
Venus Bank	Shrops	SJ3501	52°36·4′	2°57·2′W	A	126
Venusbank	Shrops	SJ5505	52°38·7′	2°39·5′W	X	126
Venus Hill	Herts	TL0101	51°42·1′	0°31·9′W	T	166
Venus Wood	W Susx	SU8516	50°56·5′	0°47·0′W	F	197
Veraby	Devon	SS7726	51°1·4′	3°44·8′W	T	180
Verandah, The	I of M	SC4088	54°16·0′	4°27·0′W	X	95
Ver-Colne Valley Walk	Herts	TL1111	51°47·4′	0°23·0′W	X	166
Vercovicivm (Roman Fort)	Northum	NY7868	55°0·6′	2°20·2′W	R	86,87
Verdley Fm	W Susx	SU9025	51°1·3′	0°42·6′W	FM	186,197
Verdley Place	W Susx	SU9027	51°2·3′	0°42·6′W	X	186,197
Verdley Wood	W Susx	SU9025	51°1·3′	0°42·6′W	F	186,197
Verdon's Fm	Suff	TM2673	52°18·7′	1°19·3′E	FM	156
Vereley	Hants	SU2005	50°50·9′	1°42·6′W	X	195
Vere Lodge	Norf	TF8724	52°47·1′	0°46·8′E	X	132
Verely Hill	Hants	SU1904	50°50·3′	1°43·4′W	X	195
Vere Point	Orkney	HY4550	59°20·2′	2°57·5′W	X	5
Vere, The	Shetld	HP5505	60°43·7′	0°59·0′W	X	1
Vere, The	Shetld	HP6403	60°42·6′	0°49·1′W	X	1
Verge Fm	Glos	SP1100	51°42·2′	1°50·1′W	FM	163
Ver Geo	Orkney	HY6124	59°6·3′	2°40·4′W	X	5
Verigens	Orkney	HY3617	59°2·4′	3°6·4′W	W	6
Vermuden's Drain or Forty Foot	Cambs	TL4087	52°28·0′	0°4·1′E	W	142,143
Vernal Fm	Hants	SU5731	51°4·8′	1°10·8′W	FM	185
Vernatt's Drain	Lincs	TF2323	52°47·7′	0°10·1′W	W	131
Verndtich Chase	Wilts	SU0321	50°59·5′	1°57·0′W	F	184
Verne, The	Dorset	SY6973	50°33·6′	2°25·9′W	X	194
Verne Yeates	Dorset	SY6973	50°33·6′	2°25·9′W	X	194
Verney Junction	Bucks	SP7327	51°56·4′	0°55·9′W	X	165
Vernham Bank	Hants	SU3356	51°18·4′	1°31·2′W	T	174
Vernham Dean	Hants	SU3456	51°18·4′	1°30·3′W	T	174
Vernham Manor	Hants	SU3556	51°18·4′	1°29·5′W	X	174
Vernham Row	Hants	SU3357	51°18·9′	1°31·2′W	T	174
Vernham Street	Hants	SU3457	51°18·9′	1°30·3′W	T	174
Vernham Wood	Bath & NE Somer	ST7361	51°21·1′	2°22·9′W	F	172
Vern Leaze	Wilts	ST9970	51°26·0′	2°0·5′W	X	173
Vernolds Common	Shrops	SO4780	52°25·2′	2°46·4′W	T	137,138
Vernon Hill Ho	Hants	SU5518	50°57·8′	1°12·6′W	X	185
Vernon's Oak Fm	Derby	SK1536	52°55·5′	1°46·2′W	FM	128
Vernon Wood	Norf	TG2430	52°49·5′	1°19·9′E	F	133
Vern, The	Heref	SO5150	52°9·0′	2°42·6′W	X	149
Verona	Ches	SJ6155	53°5·7′	2°34·5′W	X	118
Verrington	Somer	ST7029	51°3·8′	2°25·3′W	X	183
Versa Geo	Orkney	HY7856	59°23·6′	2°22·8′W	X	5
Verteris (Roman Fort)	Cumbr	NY7914	54°31·5′	2°19·0′W	R	91
Vertish Hill	Scot Bord	NT4912	55°24·2′	2°47·9′W	H	79
Verville	V of Glam	SS8977	51°29·1′	3°35·5′W	X	170
Vervlamivm (Roman Town)	Herts	TL1307	51°45·2′	0°21·4′W	R	166
Verwill Fm	Devon	SS6246	51°12·0′	3°58·1′W	FM	180
Verwood	Dorset	SU0808	50°52·5′	1°52·8′W	T	195
Veryan	Corn	SW9139	50°13·1′	4°55·4′W	T	204
Veryan Bay	Corn	SW9639	50°13·2′	4°51·2′W	W	204
Veryan Green	Corn	SW9240	50°13·6′	4°54·6′W	T	204
Verzons, The	Heref	SO6639	52°3·1′	2°29·4′W	X	149
Veshels, The	Aberd	NK0731	57°22·4′	1°52·6′W	X	30
Ve Skerries	Shetld	HU1065	60°22·4′	1°48·6′W	X	3
Vesper Hawk Fm	Kent	TQ8841	51°8·5′	0°41·6′E	FM	189
Vesquoy	Shetld	HU2149	60°13·8′	1°36·8′W	X	3
Vessacks	Corn	SW3721	50°2·1′	5°40·0′W	X	203
Vessey Pasture	N Yks	SE8262	54°3·1′	0°44·4′W	X	100
Vessons	Shrops	SJ3801	52°36·4′	2°54·5′W	X	126
Vesta Skerry	Shetld	HP6019	60°51·2′	0°53·2′W	X	1
Vestinore	Shetld	HU4227	60°1·8′	1°14·3′W	X	4
Vest Ness	Orkney	HY4848	59°19·2′	2°54·3′W	X	5
Vestness	Orkney	HY4849	59°19·7′	2°54·3′W	X	5
Vestra Fiold	Orkney	HY2322	59°4·9′	3°20·1′W	H	6
Vestry Fm	Heref	SO2757	52°12·6′	3°3·7′W	FM	148
Vetquoy	Orkney	HY2718	59°2·8′	3°15·9′W	X	6
Vexour	Kent	TQ5145	51°11·3′	0°10·0′E	X	188
Via	Orkney	HY2516	59°1·7′	3°17·9′W	X	6
Via	Orkney	HY4953	59°21·9′	2°53·3′W	X	5
Viaduct Plantation	Highld	NH2661	57°36·6′	4°54·3′W	F	20
Via Gellia	Derby	SK2656	53°6·3′	1°36·3′W	X	119
Vianshill	V of Glam	ST1074	51°27·7′	3°17·3′W	X	171
Vian, The	Orkney	HY4652	59°21·3′	2°56·5′W	W	5
Vicarage	Devon	SY2088	50°41·4′	3°7·6′W	T	192
Vicarage Cliff	Corn	SS1915	50°54·6′	4°34·1′W	X	190
Vicarage Fm	Beds	TL0148	52°7·5′	0°31·1′W	FM	153
Vicarage Fm	Beds	TL0157	52°12·3′	0°30·9′W	FM	153
Vicarage Fm	Beds	TL0643	52°4·7′	0°26·8′W	FM	153
Vicarage Fm	Beds	TL2350	52°8·3′	0°11·8′W	FM	153
Vicarage Fm	Bucks	SP8626	51°55·8′	0°44·6′W	FM	165
Vicarage Fm	Bucks	SP9317	51°50·9′	0°38·6′W	FM	165
Vicarage Fm	Cambs	TL5862	52°14·2′	0°19·2′E	FM	154
Vicarage Fm	Cambs	TL7056	52°10·8′	0°29·6′E	FM	154
Vicarage Fm	Cumbr	NY4945	54°48·1′	2°47·2′W	FM	86
Vicarage Fm	E Yorks	SE9548	53°55·4′	0°32·8′W	FM	106

Vicarage Fm	Leeds	SE3444	53°53·7′	1°28·5′W	FM	104
Vicarage Fm	Lincs	TF1728	52°50·4′	0°15·4′W	FM	130
Vicarage Fm	Lincs	TF2148	53°1·2′	0°11·4′W	FM	131
Vicarage Fm	Norf	TG3015	52°41·3′	1°24·6′E	FM	133,134
Vicarage Fm	Northnts	SP6561	52°14·8′	1°2·5′W	FM	152
Vicarage Fm	Northnts	SP9064	52°16·2′	0°40·5′W	FM	152
Vicarage Fm	Notts	SK7972	53°14·6′	0°48·6′W	FM	120,121
Vicarage Fm	N Yks	SE6960	54°2·1′	0°56·4′W	FM	100
Vicarage Fm	N Yks	TA1175	54°9·8′	0°17·6′W	FM	101
Vicarage Fm	Oxon	SP4819	51°52·3′	1°17·8′W	FM	164
Vicarage Fm	Suff	TL8967	52°16·3′	0°46·6′E	FM	155
Vicarage Fm	Suff	TM1254	52°8·8′	1°6·3′E	FM	155
Vicarage Fm	Suff	TM3277	52°20·7′	1°24·8′E	FM	156
Vicarage Fm	Suff	TM3589	52°27·1′	1°27·9′E	FM	156
Vicarage Fm	Warw	SP4376	52°23·1′	1°21·7′W	FM	140
Vicarage Fm	Worcs	SO9665	52°17·2′	2°3·1′W	FM	150
Vicarage Wood	Corn	SX3165	50°27·9′	4°22·5′W	F	201
Vicargate	Cumbr	NY3836	54°43·2′	2°57·3′W	X	90
Vicar's Allotment	Monm	SO5106	51°45·3′	2°42·2′W	X	162
Vicar's Allotment	N Yks	SE0150	53°57·0′	1°58·7′W	X	104
Vicar's Br	Clackm	NS9898	56°10·1′	3°38·1′W	X	58
Vicar's Coppice	Staffs	SK1113	52°43·1′	1°49·8′W	F	128
Vicars Croft	Notts	SK7338	52°56·3′	0°54·4′W	X	129
Vicarscross	Ches	SJ4466	53°11·5′	2°49·9′W	T	117
Vicarsford	Fife	NO4524	56°24·6′	2°53·0′W	X	54,59
Vicarsford Cottages	Fife	NO4525	56°25·1′	2°53·0′W	X	54,59
Vicar's Green	N Yks	NZ1300	54°24·0′	1°47·6′W	X	92
Vicars Hill	Hants	SZ3297	50°46·5′	1°32·4′W	X	196
Vicars Lot	Cald	SE0717	53°39·2′	1°53·2′W	X	110
Vicar's Moor	N Yks	SE3884	54°15·3′	1°24·6′W	X	99
Vicar Water	Notts	SK5862	53°9·4′	1°7·5′W	W	120
Vickers Fm	Lincs	TF3329	52°50·8′	0°1·1′W	FM	131
Vickerstown	Cumbr	SD1868	54°6·3′	3°14·8′W	T	96
Victoria	Barns	SE1705	53°32·7′	1°44·2′W	T	110
Victoria	Corn	SW9861	50°25·1′	4°50·2′W	T	200
Victoria	Pth & Kin	NN8415	56°19·1′	3°52·1′W	X	58
Victoria Bay	Cumbr	NY2520	54°34·4′	3°9·2′W	W	89,90
Victoria Br	Arg & Bt	NN2742	56°32·6′	4°48·4′W	X	50
Victoria Br	Highld	NN1275	56°50·0′	5°4·4′W	X	41
Victoria Br	Worcs	SO7679	52°24·7′	2°20·8′W	X	138
Victoria Bridge	Aberd	NO1089	56°59·3′	3°28·4′W	X	43
Victoria Cave	N Yks	SD8365	54°5·1′	2°15·2′W	A	98
Victoria Falls	Highld	NG8971	57°41·0′	5°31·9′W	W	19
Victoria Fm	Lincs	SK9349	53°2·0′	0°36·4′W	FM	130
Victoria Fm	Lincs	TF2414	52°42·8′	0°9·5′W	FM	131
Victoria Fm	Sol	SP2578	52°24·2′	1°37·6′W	FM	140
Victoria Hall Fm	Cambs	TL4597	52°33·3′	0°8·7′E	FM	143
Victoria Lodge	Scot Bord	NT1023	55°29·8′	3°25·0′W	X	72
Victoria Park	Bucks	SP8313	51°48·8′	0°47·4′W	T	165
Victoria Park	C of Glas	NS5467	55°52·7′	4°19·6′W	X	64
Victoria Park	C of Leic	SK5903	52°37·5′	1°7·3′W	X	140
Victoria Park	T Ham	TQ3684	51°32·5′	0°1·9′W	X	177
Victoria Park	Warr	SJ6187	53°22·9′	2°34·8′W	X	109
Victoria Pier	K upon H	TA1028	53°44·4′	0°19·5′W	X	107
Victoria Sta	C of West	TQ2878	51°29·4′	0°9·0′W	X	176
Victoria Sta	Man	SJ8499	53°29·5′	2°14·1′W	X	109
Victoria Sta	Sou-on-Sea	TQ8886	51°32·7′	0°43·1′E	X	178
Victoria Wells	Powys	SN8646	52°6·3′	3°39·5′W	X	147
Victoria Wharf	Shrops	SJ6735	52°54·9′	2°29·0′W	X	127
Victors Barns	Northnts	SP7469	52°19·1′	0°54·5′W	X	152
Victory Fm	Lincs	TF2918	52°44·9′	0°4·9′W	FM	131
Victory Gardens	Renf	NS5066	55°52·1′	4°23·4′W	T	64
Vidigill Burn	Highld	NG3936	57°20·7′	6°19·8′W	W	23,32
Vidigill Burn	Highld	NG4138	57°21·8′	6°18·0′W	W	23,32
Vidle Van Fm	Hants	SZ3091	50°43·3′	1°34·1′W	FM	196
Vidlin	Shetld	HU4765	60°22·2′	1°8·4′W	T	2,3
Vidlin Ness	Shetld	HU4766	60°22·8′	1°8·4′W	X	2,3
Vidlin Voe	Shetld	HU4866	60°22·8′	1°7·3′W	W	2,3
Vielstone	Devon	SS4117	50°56·1′	4°15·4′W	X	180,190
Viewbank	Aberd	NJ9253	57°34·3′	2°7·6′W	X	30
Viewbank	Pth & Kin	NO2442	56°34·1′	3°13·8′W	X	53
View Edge or Weo Edge	Shrops	SO4280	52°25·1′	2°50·8′W	X	137
Viewfield	Aberd	NJ6346	57°30·4′	2°36·6′W	X	29
Viewfield	Aberd	NJ6608	57°10·0′	2°33·3′W	X	38
Viewfield	Angus	NO3753	56°40·1′	3°1·2′W	X	54
Viewfield	D & G	NX6378	55°4·9′	4°8·3′W	X	77
Viewfield	Fife	NT1291	56°6·5′	3°24·5′W	X	58
Viewfield	Highld	ND0767	58°35·1′	3°35·5′W	X	11,12
Viewfield	Highld	NH7681	57°48·4′	4°4·7′W	X	21
Viewfield	Moray	NJ2864	57°39·9′	3°11·9′W	X	28
Viewfield	Orkney	HY4610	58°58·7′	2°55·9′W	X	6
Viewfield	Orkney	HY6427	59°8·0′	2°37·3′W	X	5
Viewfield	Scot Bord	NT7242	55°40·5′	2°26·3′W	X	74
Viewfield	S Lanak	NS7051	55°44·4′	4°3·8′W	X	64
Viewfield	S Lanak	NT0156	55°47·5′	3°34·3′W	X	65,72
Viewfield Ho	Highld	NG4743	57°24·7′	6°12·3′W	X	23
View Fm	Devon	SS4002	50°48·0′	4°15·9′W	FM	190
Viewhill	Highld	NH7954	57°33·9′	4°0·9′W	X	27
Viewhill	Moray	NJ1655	57°34·9′	3°23·8′W	X	28
Viewing Hill	Durham	NY7833	54°41·7′	2°20·1′W	H	91
Viewlaw	Northum	NZ1394	55°14·6′	1°47·3′W	X	81
Viewley	Northum	NY9355	54°53·6′	2°6·1′W	X	87
Viewley Hill	N Yks	NZ3808	54°28·2′	1°24·4′W	X	93
Viewley Hill Fm	Darl	NZ3321	54°35·2′	1°28·9′W	FM	93
Viewley Hill Fm	Stock on T	NZ3817	54°33·1′	1°24·3′W	FM	93
Viewly Grange	Durham	NZ2747	54°49·3′	1°34·4′W	X	88
Viewly Hill	Durham	NZ1039	54°45·0′	1°50·3′W	X	92
Viewly Hill	N Yks	NZ5105	54°26·5′	1°12·4′W	X	93
Viewly Hill	N Yks	SE3986	54°16·3′	1°23·6′W	X	99
Viewly Hill	Stock on T	NZ4323	54°36·3′	1°19·6′W	X	93
Viewly Hill Fm	N Yks	SE3592	54°19·6′	1°27·3′W	FM	99
Viewly Hill Fm	N Yks	SE3597	54°22·3′	1°27·3′W	FM	99
Viewly Hill Fm	N Yks	SE6175	54°10·3′	1°3·5′W	FM	100
Viewmont	E Loth	NT4977	55°59·2′	2°48·6′W	X	66
Viewpark	N Lanak	NS7161	55°49·8′	4°3·1′W	T	64
Views, The	Oxon	SP6202	51°43·0′	1°5·8′W	X	164,165
Views,The	Oxon	SU4692	51°37·7′	1°19·7′W	X	164,174
Views Wood	E Susx	TQ4822	50°58·9′	0°6·9′E	F	198
View, The	Powys	SO2793	52°32·0′	3°4·2′W	X	137
Viewy Knowe	D & G	NY3279	55°6·3′	3°3·5′W	H	85

Vigga	Orkney	HY5001	58°53·9′	2°51·6′W	X	6,7
Viggar	Orkney	HY6543	59°16·6′	2°36·4′W	X	5
Viggay	Orkney	HY7652	59°21·5′	2°24·8′W	X	5
Vigo	Wals	SK0402	52°37·2′	1°56·1′W	T	139
Vigo	Worcs	SO9871	52°20·5′	2°1·4′W	X	139
Vigo Fm	Surrey	TQ1744	51°11·2′	0°19·2′W	FM	187
Vigon	Shetld	HP4804	60°43·2′	1°6·7′W	X	1
Vigo Village	Kent	TQ6361	51°19·7′	0°20·8′E	T	177,188
Vigrind	Shetld	HU5998	60°39·9′	0°54·7′W	X	1
Vig Vishins	Shetld	HU3285	60°33·1′	1°24·5′W	X	1,3
Vikings' Mound	Norf	TM0287	52°26·8′	0°58·8′E	A	144
Viking Way	Lincs	SK9769	53°12·8′	0°32·4′W	X	121
Viking Way	Lincs	TF1293	53°25·5′	0°18·5′W	X	113
Viking Way	Lincs	TF2872	53°14·0′	0°4·5′W	X	122
Viking Way	Rut	SK8708	52°40·0′	0°42·4′W	X	141
Viking Way, The	Lincs	SK8727	52°50·2′	0°42·1′W	X	130
Viking Way,The	N Lincs	TA0023	53°41·9′	0°28·7′W	X	106,107,112
Vikisgill Burn	Highld	NG4030	57°17·5′	6°18·5′W	W	32
Villabank	Angus	NO5742	56°34·3′	2°41·5′W	X	54
Villa Fm	Ches	SJ6843	52°59·2′	2°28·2′W	FM	118
Villa Fm	Ches	SJ7278	53°18·1′	2°24·8′W	FM	118
Villa Fm	E Yorks	TA1926	53°43·2′	0°11·4′W	FM	107
Villa Fm	Glos	SO9126	51°56·2′	2°7·5′W	FM	163
Villa Fm	Lincs	TF4957	53°5·6′	0°13·9′E	FM	122
Villa Fm	Northum	NU1704	55°20·0′	1°43·5′W	FM	81
Villa Fm	N Yks	NZ5308	54°28·1′	1°10·5′W	FM	93
Villa Fm	Shrops	SO5770	52°19·8′	2°37·5′W	FM	137,138
Villa Fm	Staffs	SJ8028	52°51·2′	2°17·4′W	FM	127
Villa Fm	Suff	TM2156	52°9·7′	1°14·3′E	FM	156
Village Bay or Loch Hirta	N Eil	NF1098	57°48·4′	8°33·6′W	W	18
Village Earthworks	Heref	SO5160	52°14·4′	2°42·7′W	A	137,138,149
Village Fm	Hants	SU5647	51°13·4′	1°11·5′W	FM	185
Village Fm	Leic	SK6807	52°39·6′	0°59·3′W	FM	141
Village Fm	Notts	SK6726	52°49·9′	0°59·9′W	FM	129
Village Fm	Oxon	SP5027	51°56·6′	1°16·0′W	FM	164
Village Fm	Warw	SP3754	52°11·2′	1°27·1′W	FM	151
Village, The	Win & Maid	SU9572	51°26·6′	0°37·6′W	T	175,176
Village Wood	Red & Cl	NZ6319	54°34·0′	1°1·1′W	F	94
Villa Real Fm	Notts	SK6166	53°11·5′	1°4·8′W	FM	120
Villa, The	Dorset	SZ0288	50°41·7′	1°57·9′W	X	195
Villa, The	Lincs	TF2240	52°56·8′	0°10·6′W	X	131
Villa, The	N Yks	SE7576	54°10·7′	0°50·6′W	X	100
Villa, The	Shrops	SO4397	52°34·3′	2°50·1′W	X	137
Villa, The	Shrops	SO5094	52°32·7′	2°43·8′W	X	137,138
Villaton	Corn	SX3862	50°26·4′	4°16·5′W	X	201
Villaton Fm	Corn	SX2894	50°43·4′	4°25·8′W	FM	190
Villavin	Devon	SS3103	50°48·4′	4°23·5′W	X	190
Villavin	Devon	SS5816	50°55·8′	4°0·9′W	X	180
Villians of Hamnavoe	Shetld	HU2481	60°31·0′	1°33·3′W	X	3
Villians of Ure	Shetld	HU2179	60°29·9′	1°36·6′W	X	3
Villigar	Orkney	ND3795	58°50·5′	3°5·0′W	W	7
Vilner Fm	S Glos	ST6489	51°36·2′	2°30·8′W	FM	162,172
Vimy Ridge Fm	Notts	SK6631	52°52·6′	1°0·8′W	FM	129
Vince Moor	N Yks	NZ2807	54°27·7′	1°33·7′W	X	93
Vincent Fm	Kent	TR3467	51°21·4′	1°22·1′E	FM	179
Vincent Hills	Norf	TF6926	52°48·5′	0°30·8′E	X	132
Vincent Ho	Derby	SK1363	53°10·1′	1°47·9′W	X	119
Vincent Plantn	Notts	SK5651	53°3·4′	1°9·5′W	F	120
Vincent's Fm	Somer	ST2921	50°59·3′	3°0·3′W	FM	193
Vincent's Fm	Suff	TL8258	52°11·6′	0°40·2′E	FM	155
Vinden	Orkney	HY3615	59°1·3′	3°6·4′W	X	6
Vindobala (Roman Fort)	Northum	NZ1167	55°0·1′	1°49·3′W	R	88
Vindolanda (Roman Fort)	Northum	NY7766	54°59·5′	2°21·1′W	R	86,87
Vindomora (Roman Fort)	Durham	NZ1055	54°53·6′	1°50·2′W	R	88
Vine Fm	Essex	TL8911	51°46·2′	0°44·8′E	FM	168
Vine Fm	E Susx	TQ4916	50°55·7′	0°7·6′E	FM	199
Vine Fm	Norf	TM1284	52°25·0′	1°7·5′E	FM	144
Vinegar Hill	Cambs	TL1877	52°22·9′	0°15·6′W	X	142
Vinegar Hill	Glos	SO8108	51°46·5′	2°16·1′W	X	162
Vinegar Hill	Monm	ST4387	51°35·0′	2°49·0′W	T	171,172
Vinegar Hill	Pth & Kin	NN6980	56°53·8′	4°8·6′W	X	42
Vinegar Hill	Somer	SS9843	51°10·9′	3°27·2′W	X	181
Vinegar Middle	Norf	TF6024	52°47·6′	0°22·8′E	X	132
Vine Geo	Shetld	HU2445	60°11·6′	1°33·5′W	X	4
Vine Hall	Kent	TQ9438	51°6·7′	0°46·7′E	X	189
Vinehall (Sch)	E Susx	TQ7520	50°57·4′	0°29·9′E	X	199
Vinehall Street	E Susx	TQ7520	50°57·4′	0°29·9′E	T	199
Vine Ho	Durham	NZ1239	54°45·0′	1°48·4′W	X	92
Vine Ho	Lincs	TF0057	53°6·3′	0°30·0′W	X	121
Vine Hotel	Lincs	TF5661	53°7·6′	0°20·3′E	X	122
Vine House Fm	Warw	SP3045	52°6·4′	1°33·3′W	FM	151
Vinepark Fm	Norf	TF9634	52°52·3′	0°55·1′E	FM	132
Vineries, The	Lincs	TF3241	52°57·2′	0°1·7′W	X	131
Viners Fm	Essex	TL9016	51°48·8′	0°45·8′E	FM	168
Vines	Kent	TQ5650	51°13·9′	0°14·5′E	X	188
Vines Brake	Wilts	SU0897	51°40·5′	1°52·7′W	F	163
Vines Cross	E Susx	TQ5917	50°56·1′	0°16·2′E	T	199
Vine's Down Bldgs	Dorset	SY8283	50°39·0′	2°14·9′W	X	194
Vines Fm	Oxon	SU7079	51°30·6′	0°59·1′W	FM	175
Vines Gate	Kent	TQ4653	51°15·7′	0°5·9′E	X	188
Vinesse Fm	Essex	TL9530	51°56·3′	0°50·6′E	FM	168
Vine, The	Worcs	SO6164	52°16·6′	2°33·9′W	X	138,149
Viney	Glos	SO6606	51°45·3′	2°29·2′W	X	162
Vineyard	Shrops	SJ5340	52°57·6′	2°41·6′W	X	117
Vineyard Fm	Heref	SO3424	51°54·9′	2°57·2′W	FM	161
Vineyard Hill	W Susx	TQ1407	50°51·3′	0°22·4′W	X	198
Vineyards Fm	Glos	SO9718	51°51·9′	2°2·2′W	FM	163
Vineyard, The	Essex	TL5339	52°1·9′	0°14·2′E	X	154
Vineyard, The	Heref	SO7133	51°59·9′	2°25·0′W	X	149
Vineyard, The	Herts	TL2409	51°46·2′	0°11·8′W	X	166
Vineyard, The	Norf	TM0594	52°30·5′	1°1·7′E	X	144
Viney Hill	Glos	SO6506	51°45·3′	2°30·0′W	T	162
Vining Station	N Yks	SE5327	53°44·4′	1°11·4′W	X	105
Vinnals, The	Shrops	SJ4504	52°38·1′	2°48·4′W	X	126
Vinnetrow Fm	W Susx	SU8803	50°49·4′	0°44·6′W	FM	197
Vinney Copse	Hants	SU7345	51°12·2′	0°56·9′W	F	186
Vinney Cross	Dorset	SY5192	50°43·8′	2°41·3′W	X	194
Vinney Green	S Glos	ST6677	51°29·7′	2°29·0′W	T	172
Vinney Ridge Inclosure	Hants	SU2605	50°50·9′	1°37·5′W	F	195
Vinnicombe	Somer	SS9434	51°6·0′	3°30·5′W	X	181

Vinnybank Fm	Angus	NO5146	56°36·5′	2°47·4′W	FM	54
Vinovia (Roman Fort)	Durham	NZ2131	54°40·7′	1°40·0′W	R	93
Vinquin Hill	Orkney	HY3228	59°8·3′	3°10·8′W	H	6
Vinquoy Hill	Orkney	HY5638	59°13·8′	2°45·8′W	H	5
Vins Taing	Shetld	HU4321	59°58·6′	1°13·3′W	X	4
Vinters Park	Kent	TQ7756	51°16·8′	0°32·7′E	X	178,188
Violetbank	D & G	NY1867	54°59·7′	3°16·5′W	X	85
Violet Grange	E Yorks	SE7932	53°46·9′	0°47·6′W	X	105,106
Violet Grange	N Yks	NZ2105	54°26·6′	1°40·1′W	X	93
Violet Hill	Hants	SU4127	51°2·7′	1°24·5′W	H	185
Violet Hill	Notts	SK5747	53°1·3′	1°8·6′W	X	129
Violets Fm	W Susx	TQ1032	51°4·8′	0°25·4′W	FM	187
Viol Moor	Cumbr	NY5940	54°45·4′	2°37·8′W	X	86
Viol Moor	Cumbr	NY5941	54°46·0′	2°37·8′W	X	86
Virda	Shetld	HU3631	60°4·0′	1°20·7′W	X	4
Virda	Shetld	HU5065	60°22·2′	1°5·1′W	X	2,3
Virdack	Shetld	HU4331	60°4·0′	1°13·2′W	X	4
Virda Dale	Shetld	HP5301	60°41·6′	1°1·3′W	X	1
Virda Field	Shetld	HP6206	60°44·2′	0°51·3′W	X	1
Virda Field	Shetld	HU1562	60°20·8′	1°43·2′W	H	3
Virda Lee	Shetld	HU4237	60°7·2′	1°14·2′W	X	4
Virda Loch	Shetld	HU2251	60°14·8′	1°35·7′W	W	3
Virda Pund	Shetld	HP5811	60°46·9′	0°55·6′W	X	1
Virda Vatn	Shetld	HU3529	60°2·9′	1°21·8′W	W	4
Virdick	Shetld	HU5240	60°8·7′	1°3·3′W	H	4
Virdi Field	Shetld	HU4018	59°57·0′	1°16·5′W	H	4
Virdik	Shetld	HP6517	60°50·1′	0°47·8′W	X	1
Virdins	Shetld	HU3368	60°23·9′	1°23·6′W	X	2,3
Virdins	Shetld	HU3575	60°27·7′	1°21·3′W	H	2,3
Virdins of Hamar	Shetld	HU3176	60°28·3′	1°25·7′W	X	3
Virdi Point	Shetld	HP5400	60°41·0′	1°0·2′W	X	1
Virdi Taing	Shetld	HU5693	60°37·3′	0°58·1′W	X	1,2
Virdi Water	Shetld	HU4593	60°37·3′	1°10·2′W	W	1,2
Virginia	I of M	SC3479	54°11·0′	4°32·2′W	X	95
Virginia	Orkney	HY3213	59°0·2′	3°10·5′W	X	6
Virginia Water	Surrey	SU9768	51°24·4′	0°35·9′W	W	175,176
Virginia Water	Surrey	SU9967	51°23·8′	0°34·2′W	T	175,176
Virgin Moss	N Yks	SD9994	54°20·7′	2°0·5′W	X	98
Virginstow	Devon	SX3792	50°42·5′	4°18·1′W	T	190
Virley Channel	Essex	TM0011	51°45·9′	0°54·3′E	W	168
Viroconivm (Roman Town)	Shrops	SJ5608	52°40·3′	2°38·6′W	R	126
Virosidvm (Roman Fort)	N Yks	SD9390	54°18·6′	2°6·0′W	R	98
Virtle Rock	Dorset	SY3391	50°43·1′	2°56·6′W	X	193
Virtue's Fm	Suff	TM3443	52°2·4′	1°25·1′E	FM	169
Virworthy	Devon	SS3110	50°52·1′	4°23·7′W	X	190
Viscar	Corn	SW7133	50°9·4′	5°12·0′W	T	203
Vishall Hill	Orkney	HY3824	59°6·2′	3°4·5′W	H	6
Vishwell Fm	V of Glam	ST1272	51°26·6′	3°15·6′W	FM	171
Vision Fm, The	Monm	SO2631	51°58·6′	3°4·2′W	FM	161
Vissitt Manor	Wakf	SE4112	53°36·4′	1°22·4′W	X	111
Vistla Fm	V of Glam	SS9776	51°28·7′	3°28·6′W	FM	170
Vitower Ho	Dorset	SY9886	50°40·6′	2°1·3′W	X	195
Vitters Oak	Kent	TQ9440	51°7·8′	0°46·8′E	X	189
Vittlefields Fm	I of W	SZ4589	50°42·2′	1°21·4′W	FM	196
Viveham Fms	Devon	SS5739	51°8·2′	4°2·3′W	FM	180
Viver	Cumbr	SD5184	54°15·2′	2°44·7′W	X	97
Viverdon Down	Corn	SX3767	50°29·0′	4°17·5′W	X	201
Vivian's Covert	Northnts	SP8669	52°19·0′	0°43·9′W	F	152
Vivilie Loch	Shetld	HU2645	60°11·6′	1°31·4′W	W	4
Vivod	Denb	SJ1942	52°58·4′	3°12·0′W	X	125
Vivod Mountain	Wrex	SJ1739	52°56·8′	3°13·7′W	H	125
Vixen Tor	Devon	SX5474	50°33·1′	4°3·3′W	X	191,201
Viza	Devon	SX3796	50°44·7′	4°18·2′W	X	190
Voaker Burn	Highld	NG3639	57°22·2′	6°23·0′W	W	23,32
Vobster	Somer	ST7049	51°14·6′	2°25·4′W	T	183
Voe	Shetld	HU3381	60°30·9′	1°23·4′W	T	1,2,3
Voe	Shetld	HU4015	59°55·3′	1°16·6′W	W	4
Voe	Shetld	HU4062	60°20·7′	1°16·0′W	T	2,3
Voehead	Shetld	HU3555	60°16·9′	1°21·5′W	X	3
Voe-head	Shetld	HU4249	60°13·7′	1°14·0′W	X	3
Voelas	Cered	SN6996	52°33·0′	3°55·5′W	X	135
Voelas	Conwy	SH8551	53°2·9′	3°42·5′W	X	116
Voe of Browland	Shetld	HU2650	60°14·3′	1°31·3′W	W	3
Voe of Clousta	Shetld	HU2957	60°18·0′	1°28·0′W	W	3
Voe of Cullingsburgh	Shetld	HU5242	60°9·8′	1°3·3′W	W	4
Voe of Dale	Shetld	HU1751	60°14·8′	1°41·1′W	W	3
Voe of Footabrough	Shetld	HU1949	60°13·8′	1°38·9′W	W	3
Voe of Leiraness	Shetld	HU4941	60°9·3′	1°6·5′W	W	4
Voe of North Ho	Shetld	HU3731	60°4·0′	1°19·6′W	W	4
Voe of Scatsta	Shetld	HU3973	60°26·6′	1°17·0′W	W	2,3
Voe of Snarraness	Shetld	HU2356	60°17·5′	1°34·5′W	W	3
Voe of Sound	Shetld	HU4639	60°8·2′	1°9·8′W	W	4
Voe of the Brig	Shetld	HU3584	60°32·5′	1°21·2′W	W	1,2,3
Voe of the Mels	Shetld	HU5340	60°8·7′	1°2·2′W	W	4
Voesgarth	Shetld	HP6108	60°45·3′	0°52·3′W	T	1
Vogans Voe	Shetld	HU6872	60°25·8′	0°45·4′W	W	2
Vogar	Pemb	SN0212	51°46·5′	4°51·8′W	X	157,158
Voggis Hill Fm	Devon	SY1590	50°42·4′	3°11·8′W	FM	192,193
Vognacott	Devon	SS3307	50°50·5′	4°21·9′W	X	190
Vogrie Burn	Midlo	NT3763	55°51·6′	3°0·0′W	W	66
Vogrie Grange	Midlo	NT3762	55°51·1′	2°59·9′W	X	66
Vogrie Ho	Midlo	NT3863	55°51·6′	2°59·0′W	X	66
Vogue	Corn	SW7242	50°14·3′	5°11·5′W	T	204
Vogwell Fm	Devon	SX7281	50°37·1′	3°48·2′W	FM	191
Voiskinish	N Eil	NF9073	57°38·7′	7°11·3′W	X	18
Vola	Orkney	HY3114	59°0·7′	3°11·6′W	X	6
Voldigarth	Orkney	HY4745	59°17·6′	2°55·3′W	X	5
Vole	Somer	ST3649	51°14·4′	2°54·6′W	T	182
Vole Fm	Somer	ST3549	51°14·4′	2°55·5′W	FM	182
Volehouse Fm	Devon	SS3416	50°55·4′	4°21·3′W	FM	190
Voley	Devon	SS6445	51°11·5′	3°56·4′W	X	180
Voley Castle	Devon	SS6546	51°12·1′	3°55·6′W	X	180
Volis Cross	Somer	ST2330	51°4·1′	3°5·6′W	X	182
Volis Fm	Somer	ST2329	51°3·5′	3°5·5′W	FM	193
Volla Wood	N Yks	SE2564	54°4·5′	1°36·7′W	F	99
Vollister	Shetld	HU4793	60°37·3′	1°8·0′W	X	1,2
Volta Fm	N Yks	SE1858	54°1·3′	1°43·1′W	FM	104
Von Barrow	Dorset	SY8692	50°43·9′	2°11·5′W	A	194
Vongs	Shetld	HU6370	60°24·8′	0°50·9′W	X	2
Vord Hill	Shetld	HP6103	60°42·6′	0°52·4′W	H	1

Vord Hill	Shetld	HU6293	60°37·2′	0°51·5′W	H	1,2
Voreda (Roman Fort)	Cumbr	NY4938	54°44·3′	2°47·1′W	R	90
Vorlan	Pemb	SN0826	51°54·2′	4°47·1′W	X	145,158
Vorogay	N Eil	NF7864	57°33·3′	7°22·6′W	X	18
Vorvas	Corn	SW5138	50°11·6′	5°29·0′W	X	203
Voscombe	Devon	SS5128	51°2·2′	4°7·1′W	X	180
Vose	Corn	SW9545	50°16·4′	4°52·2′W	X	204
Voss	Devon	SX5755	50°22·9′	4°0·3′W	X	202
Voter Run	Corn	SX1294	50°43·2′	4°39·4′W	X	190
Votersay	N Eil	NF9476	57°40·5′	7°7·5′W	X	18
Votes Court	Kent	TQ6553	51°15·4′	0°22·3′E	A	188
Votty	Powys	SJ1131	52°52·4′	3°18·9′W	X	125
Voucher's Fm	Essex	TL8811	51°46·2′	0°43·9′E	FM	168
Voulsdon Cross	Devon	SX4693	50°43·2′	4°10·5′W	X	190
Vowchurch	Heref	SO3636	52°1·4′	2°55·6′W	T	149,161
Vowchurch Common	Heref	SO3737	52°1·9′	2°54·7′W	T	149,161
Vowley Fm	Wilts	SU0980	51°31·4′	1°51·8′W	FM	173
Vow Randie	Orkney	ND2699	58°52·6′	3°16·5′W	X	6,7
Voxhills Fm	Glos	SO9908	51°46·5′	2°0·5′W	FM	163
Voxmoor	Somer	ST1418	50°57·5′	3°13·1′W	T	181,193
Voxter Centre	Shetld	HU3770	60°25·0′	1°19·2′W	X	2,3
Voxter Ness	Shetld	HU3670	60°25·0′	1°20·3′W	X	2,3
Voxter Voe	Shetld	HU3669	60°24·5′	1°20·3′W	W	2,3
Voy	Orkney	HY2514	59°0·7′	3°17·9′W	T	6
Vriskaig Point	Highld	NG4842	57°24·2′	6°11·3′W	X	23
Vroe	Heref	SO3826	51°56·0′	2°53·7′W	X	161
Vron	Shrops	SO1782	52°26·0′	3°12·9′W	X	136
Vron	Shrops	SO3275	52°22·4′	2°59·5′W	X	137,148
Vron Fm	Powys	SO1959	52°13·6′	3°10·8′W	FM	148
Vronganllwyd	Powys	SO1372	52°20·6′	3°16·2′W	X	136,148
Vron Gate	Shrops	SJ3209	52°40·7′	2°59·9′W	T	126
Vronlace	Powys	SO1563	52°15·8′	3°14·3′W	X	148
Vron, The	Powys	SO1252	52°9·8′	3°16·8′W	X	148
Vron Vyrnwy	Powys	SJ2018	52°45·5′	3°10·7′W	X	126
Vugga Cove	Corn	SW7760	50°24·1′	5°7·9′W	W	200
Vuggles Fm	E Susx	TQ4319	50°57·4′	0°2·6′E	FM	198
Vuia Beag	N Eil	NB1233	58°11·8′	6°53·6′W	X	13
Vuia Mór	N Eil	NB1234	58°12·3′	6°53·7′W	X	13
Vulcan Village	St Hel	SJ5893	53°26·2′	2°37·5′W	T	108
Vulscombe	Devon	SS8911	50°53·5′	3°34·3′W	X	192
Vyne Lodge Fm	Hants	SU6457	51°18·7′	1°4·5′W	FM	175
Vyne Park	Hants	SU6356	51°18·2′	1°5·4′W	X	175
Vyne, The	Hants	SU6356	51°18·2′	1°5·4′W	A	175

W

Waas	Highld	ND0766	58°34·6′	3°35·5′W	X	11,12
Waberthwaite	Cumbr	SD1093	54°19·7′	3°22·6′W	X	96
Waberthwaite Fell	Cumbr	SD1393	54°19·8′	3°19·9′W	X	96
Wabi Fm	Wilts	SU0459	51°20·0′	1°56·2′W	FM	173
Wackerfield	Durham	NZ1522	54°35·8′	1°45·6′W	T	92
Wackland	I of W	SZ5584	50°39·4′	1°12·9′W	X	196
Wackley Fm	Shrops	SJ4427	52°50·5′	2°49·5′W	FM	126
Wackley Lodge	Shrops	SJ4427	52°50·5′	2°49·5′W	X	126
Wacton	Heref	SO6157	52°12·8′	2°33·9′W	T	149
Wacton	Norf	TM1791	52°28·6′	1°12·1′E	T	134
Wacton Common	Norf	TM1889	52°27·5′	1°12·9′E	T	156
Wacton Common	Norf	TM1890	52°28·1′	1°13·0′E	X	134
Wadbister	Shetld	HU3946	60°12·1′	1°17·3′W	X	4
Wadbister	Shetld	HU4349	60°13·6′	1°12·9′W	T	3
Wadbister Ness	Shetld	HU4449	60°13·6′	1°11·8′W	X	3
Wadbister Voe	Shetld	HU4350	60°14·2′	1°12·9′W	W	3
Wadborough	Worcs	SO9047	52°7·5′	2°8·4′W	T	150
Wadborough Park Fm	Worcs	SO8948	52°8·0′	2°9·2′W	FM	150
Wadbrook	Devon	ST3201	50°48·5′	2°57·5′W	T	193
Wadbury	Somer	ST7348	51°14·1′	2°22·8′W	A	183
Wadcrag	Cumbr	NY1829	54°39·2′	3°15·8′W	X	89,90
Wad Dale	N Yks	SE9571	54°7·8′	0°32·4′W	X	101
Waddelscairn Moor	Scot Bord	NT5458	55°49·0′	2°43·6′W	X	66,73
Waddels Loch	D & G	NS8602	55°18·2′	3°47·3′W	W	78
Wadden	Devon	SY2193	50°44·1′	3°6·8′W	X	192,193
Wadden Fm	Staffs	SJ9827	52°50·7′	2°1·4′W	FM	127
Waddenhall Fm	Kent	TR1248	51°11·7′	1°2·5′E	FM	179,189
Waddenhall Wood	Kent	TR1349	51°12·2′	1°3·3′E	F	179,189
Waddenshope Burn	Scot Bord	NT2535	55°36·4′	3°11·0′W	W	73
Waddesdon	Bucks	SP7416	51°50·5′	0°55·2′W	T	165
Waddesdon Hill	Bucks	SP7515	51°49·9′	0°54·3′W	H	165
Waddesdon Manor	Bucks	SP7316	51°50·5′	0°56·0′W	X	165
Waddeton	Devon	SX8756	50°23·8′	3°35·0′W	T	202
Waddeton Court	Devon	SX8756	50°23·8′	3°35·0′W	X	202
Waddicar	Sefton	SJ3999	53°29·3′	2°54·8′W	T	108
Waddicombe	Devon	SS8627	51°2·1′	3°37·2′W	T	181
Waddingham	Lincs	SK9896	53°27·3′	0°31·0′W	T	112
Waddingham Carrs	Lincs	TF0096	53°27·3′	0°29·2′W	X	112
Waddingham Grange	Lincs	SK9796	53°27·3′	0°31·9′W	X	112
Waddingham Ho	Lincs	SK9895	53°26·8′	0°31·1′W	X	112
Waddington	Devon	SS6918	50°57·0′	3°51·5′W	X	180
Waddington	Lancs	SD7243	53°53·2′	2°25·1′W	T	103
Waddington	Lincs	SK9864	53°10·1′	0°31·6′W	T	121
Waddington Fell	Lancs	SD7147	53°55·3′	2°26·1′W	H	103
Waddington Heath	Lincs	SK9863	53°9·5′	0°31·6′W	X	121
Waddingworth	Lincs	TF1871	53°13·6′	0°13·5′W	T	122
Waddles Down	Devon	SX8694	50°44·3′	3°36·6′W	X	191
Waddock Fm	Dorset	SY7990	50°42·8′	2°17·5′W	FM	194
Waddock Lake	Pemb	SN0409	51°45·0′	4°50·0′W	W	157,158
Waddock Lake	Pemb	SN0508	51°44·4′	4°49·1′W	W	158

Waddon	Croy	TQ3164	51°21·8′	0°6·7′W	T	176,177,187
Waddon	Devon	SX8879	50°36·2′	3°34·6′W	T	192
Waddon	Dorset	SY6185	50°40·0′	2°32·7′W	X	194
Waddon Brakes	Devon	SX8980	50°36·8′	3°33·8′W	X	192
Waddon Fm	Somer	ST6435	51°7·0′	2°30·5′W	FM	183
Waddon Hill	Dorset	ST4401	50°48·6′	2°47·3′W	H	193
Waddon Hill	Dorset	SY4994	50°44·8′	2°43·0′W	H	193,194
Waddon Hill (Roman Fort)	Dorset	ST4401	50°48·6′	2°47·3′W	R	193
Waddon House	Dorset	SY6185	50°40·0′	2°32·7′W	A	194
Waddow Hall	Lancs	SD7342	53°52·7′	2°24·2′W	X	103
Waddow Lodge	Lancs	SD7243	53°53·2′	2°25·1′W	X	103
Waddyside Rig	Scot Bord	NT2129	55°33·2′	3°14·7′W	X	73
Wadebridge	Corn	SW9872	50°31·0′	4°50·6′W	T	200
Wade Bridge	Highld	NN6382	56°54·8′	4°14·6′W	X	42
Wade Brook	Ches	SJ6874	53°16·0′	2°28·4′W	W	118
Wadeford	Somer	ST3010	50°53·3′	2°59·3′W	T	193
Wade Hall	Lancs	SD5221	53°41·2′	2°43·2′W	T	102
Wade Hall	Suff	TM4790	52°27·3′	1°38·5′E	X	134
Wade Hill	Oldham	SD9805	53°32·7′	2°1·4′W	X	109
Wade Hill Fm	Hants	SU3416	50°56·8′	1°30·6′W	FM	185
Wadeley	Shrops	SO7086	52°28·5′	2°26·1′W	X	138
Wade Marsh	Kent	TR2668	51°22·2′	1°15·2′E	X	179
Waden Hill	Wilts	SU1069	51°25·4′	1°51·0′W	H	173
Wadenhoe	Northnts	TL0183	52°26·4′	0°30·4′W	T	141
Wadenhoe Lodge	Northnts	SP9984	52°26·9′	0°32·2′W	X	141
Wade Park Fm	Hants	SU3216	50°56·8′	1°32·3′W	FM	185
Wades Fm	Cambs	TL5680	52°24·0′	0°18·0′E	FM	143
Wades Green	Ches	SJ6560	53°8·4′	2°31·0′W	T	118
Wade's Green Hall	Ches	SJ6559	53°7·9′	2°31·0′W	A	118
Wade's Hall	Essex	TL5027	51°55·5′	0°11·3′E	X	167
Wadesmill	Herts	TL3517	51°50·3′	0°2·0′W	T	166
Wades Stone	N Yks	NZ8214	54°31·1′	0°43·6′W	A	94
Wade's Stone	N Yks	NZ8312	54°30·0′	0°42·7′W	A	94
Wade Stone, The	Pth & Kin	NN6971	56°49·0′	4°8·3′W	X	42
Wade, The	Essex	TM2323	51°51·9′	1°14·7′E	W	169
Wadfast	Corn	SX2697	50°45·0′	4°27·6′W	X	190
Wadfield	Glos	SP0226	51°56·2′	1°57·9′W	X	163
Wadge Head	Northum	NY7985	55°9·8′	2°19·3′W	X	80
Wadgell's Fm	Suff	TL7051	52°8·1′	0°29·4′E	FM	154
Wadgell's Wood	Suff	TL6951	52°8·1′	0°28·6′E	F	154
Wadgett's Copse	Hants	SU6741	51°10·1′	1°2·1′W	F	185,186
Wadground Barn	Northnts	SP5247	52°7·4′	1°14·0′W	X	151
Wadham	Devon	SS8123	50°59·9′	3°41·4′W	X	181
Wadham Park Fm	Essex	TQ8293	51°36·6′	0°38·1′E	FM	178
Wadham Rocks	Devon	SX5846	50°18·0′	3°59·3′W	X	202
Wadhayes	Devon	ST1303	50°49·4′	3°13·7′W	X	192,193
Wadhead Scar	Cumbr	SD3174	54°9·7′	3°3·0′W	X	96,97
Wad House Fm	Leic	SK6624	52°48·8′	1°0·8′W	FM	129
Wadhurst	E Susx	TQ6431	51°3·5′	0°20·8′E	T	188
Wadhurst Castle	E Susx	TQ6331	51°3·5′	0°20·0′E	X	188
Wadhurst Park	E Susx	TQ6328	51°1·9′	0°19·9′E	X	188,199
Wadhurst Sta	E Susx	TQ6232	51°4·1′	0°19·1′E	X	188
Wadill, The	Shetld	HU3688	60°34·7′	1°20·1′W	X	1,2
Wadland Barton	Devon	SX5096	50°44·9′	4°7·2′W	A	191
Wadland Down Plantations	Devon	SX5195	50°44·4′	4°6·3′W	F	191
Wadley	Durham	NZ1334	54°42·3′	1°47·5′W	X	92
Wadley Hill	Oxon	SP5509	51°46·8′	1°11·8′W	X	164
Wadley Manor	Oxon	SU3196	51°39·9′	1°32·7′W	X	164
Wadlow Fm	Cambs	TL5854	52°9·9′	0°19·0′E	FM	154
Wadman's Coppice	Wilts	ST9449	51°14·6′	2°4·8′W	F	184
Wadmill Fm	Dorset	ST8119	50°58·4′	2°15·9′W	FM	183
Wadshelf	Derby	SK3170	53°13·8′	1°31·7′W	T	119
Wad's Howe	Cumbr	NY4903	54°25·4′	2°46·7′W	X	90
Wadsley	Sheff	SK3190	53°24·6′	1°31·6′W	T	110,111
Wadsley Bridge	Sheff	SK3391	53°25·1′	1°29·8′W	T	110,111
Wadstray Ho	Devon	SX8251	50°21·1′	3°39·1′W	X	202
Wadswick	Wilts	ST8467	51°24·3′	2°13·4′W	T	173
Wadsworth Banks Fields	Cald	SE0126	53°44·1′	1°58·7′W	X	104
Wadsworth Fm	Durham	NZ1831	54°40·7′	1°42·8′W	FM	92
Wadsworth Moor	Cald	SD9733	53°47·8′	2°2·3′W	X	103
Wadwick	Hants	SU4353	51°16·7′	1°22·6′W	T	185
Wadworth	Donc	SK5697	53°28·2′	1°9·0′W	T	111
Wadworth Bar	Donc	SK5895	53°27·2′	1°7·2′W	X	111
Wadworth Carr	Donc	SK5897	53°28·2′	1°7·2′W	X	111
Wadworth Hill	Donc	SK5797	53°28·2′	1°8·1′W	X	111
Wadworth Hill	E Yorks	TA2329	53°44·8′	0°7·7′W	X	107
Wadworth Wood	Donc	SK5597	53°28·2′	1°9·9′W	F	111
Waen	Denb	SH9962	53°9·0′	3°30·2′W	T	116
Waen	Denb	SJ1065	53°10·7′	3°20·4′W	T	116
Waen	Flint	SJ1573	53°15·1′	3°16·0′W	T	116
Waen	Gwyn	SH2433	52°52·2′	4°36·5′W	X	123
Waen	Gwyn	SH5906	52°38·2′	4°4·6′W	X	124
Waen	Powys	SN9591	52°30·6′	3°32·4′W	T	136
Waen	Powys	SO1195	52°33·0′	3°18·4′W	X	136
Waen	Powys	SO1282	52°26·0′	3°17·3′W	X	136
Waen	Shrops	SJ3222	52°47·7′	3°0·1′W	X	126
Waen Aberwheeler	Denb	SJ0969	53°12·9′	3°21·4′W	T	116
Waen-dyllog	Denb	SJ2056	53°6·0′	3°11·3′W	X	117
Waen-dymarch	Flint	SJ1570	53°13·5′	3°16·0′W	X	116
Waenfach	Gwyn	SH5904	52°37·2′	4°4·6′W	X	135
Waen-fâch	Powys	SJ2017	52°44·9′	3°10·7′W	T	126
Waen Fawr	Conwy	SJ0065	53°10·6′	3°29·4′W	X	116
Waen Fawr	Denb	SJ0444	52°59·3′	3°25·4′W	X	125
Waen Fechan	Conwy	SH8171	53°13·6′	3°46·6′W	X	116
Waen Fechan	Gwyn	SH6816	52°43·8′	3°56·9′W	X	124
Waen Fm	Conwy	SH8774	53°15·3′	3°41·2′W	FM	116
Waen Fm	Flint	SJ1577	53°17·2′	3°16·1′W	FM	116
Waen Fm	Flint	SJ2461	53°8·7′	3°7·8′W	FM	117
Waen Ganol	Denb	SJ0453	53°4·2′	3°25·6′W	X	116
Waen Gate	Denb	SJ0674	53°15·5′	3°24·1′W	X	116
Waenglapiau	Powys	SJ0504	52°37·8′	3°23·8′W	X	136
Waen Goleugoed	Denb	SJ0673	53°15·0′	3°24·1′W	X	116
Waen Hilin	Denb	SJ0974	53°15·6′	3°21·4′W	X	116
Waenhir	Conwy	SH7358	53°6·5′	3°53·4′W	X	115
Waenllefenni	Gwyn	SH7612	52°41·7′	3°49·7′W	X	124
Waen Llywarch	Powys	SN9716	51°50·2′	3°29·3′W	X	160
Waen Lych	I of Angl	SH3191	53°23·6′	4°32·1′W	X	114
Waenoleu	Powys	SJ1222	52°47·5′	3°17·9′W	X	125
Waen-pentir	Gwyn	SH5766	53°10·6′	4°8·0′W	T	114,115

Waenreef	Wrex	SJ4841	52°58·1'	2°46·1'W	X	117
Waen-Rydd	Powys	SN8745	52°5·7'	3°38·6'W	X	147
Waen Tincer	Powys	SN9615	51°49·7'	3°30·2'W	X	160
Waen Uchaf	Denb	SJ0353	53°4·2'	3°26·5'W	X	116
Waen-wen	Gwyn	SH5768	53°11·6'	4°8·0'W	T	114,115
Waen Wen	Merth Tyd	SO0214	51°49·2'	3°24·9'W	X	160
Waen Wen	Shrops	SJ2822	52°47·7'	3°3·7'W	X	126
Waen y Bala	Gwyn	SH8837	52°55·4'	3°39·6'W	X	124,125
Waen-y-gittin	Powys	SN9091	52°30·6'	3°36·9'W	X	136
Waen y gorlan	Powys	SO0618	51°51·4'	3°21·5'W	X	160
Waen-y-pant	Powys	SO0697	52°34·0'	3°22·8'W	X	136
Waffapool	Devon	SS3916	50°55·5'	4°17·1'W	X	190
Waffrons, The	Surrey	TQ1664	51°22·0'	0°19·6'W	X	176,187
Wag	Highld	ND0126	58°13·0'	3°40·6'W	X	17
Wagaford Water	Devon	SS4701	50°47·5'	4°9·9'W	W	191
Wagbeach	Shrops	SJ3602	52°37·0'	2°56·3'W	T	126
Wagborough Bush	Glos	SP1422	51°54·0'	1°47·4'W	X	163
Wagborough Bush (Tumulus)	Glos	SP1422	51°54·0'	1°47·4'W	A	163
Wag Burn	Highld	ND1032	58°16·3'	3°31·6'W	W	11,17
Wager Head	Durham	NZ0133	54°41·8'	1°58·6'W	X	92
Wager Ho	Northum	NY8255	54°53·6'	2°16·4'W	X	86,87
Wagg	Somer	ST4326	51°2·1'	2°48·4'W	T	193
Waggadon	Devon	SS5122	50°58·9'	4°7·0'W	X	180
Wagger Fm	Suff	TL9648	52°6·0'	0°52·1'E	FM	155
Waggersley	Staffs	SJ8737	52°56·1'	2°11·2'W	T	127
Waggle Hill	Aberd	NJ8046	57°30·5'	2°19·6'W	X	29,30
Waggles	Angus	NO5776	56°52·7'	2°41·9'W	X	44
Waggoners Wells	Hants	SU8534	51°6·2'	0°46·8'W	W	186
Waggon Low	Derby	SK1164	53°10·6'	1°49·7'W	X	119
Waggs Plot	Devon	ST3101	50°48·5'	2°58·4'W	T	193
Wag Hill	Highld	ND1032	58°16·3'	3°31·6'W	H	11,17
Wag Hill	Lancs	SD4643	53°53·1'	2°48·9'W	X	102
Wagland	Devon	SX7654	50°22·6'	3°44·3'W	X	202
Wagmore Rigg	Highld	NC9926	58°12·9'	3°42·7'W	X	17
Wagstaff	Kent	TQ8739	51°7·4'	0°40·7'E	X	189
Wagstaff Fm	Warw	SP2589	52°30·1'	1°37·5'W	FM	140
Wagtail	Durham	NY9348	54°49·9'	2°6·1'W	X	87
Wagtail	Kent	TR2467	51°21·7'	1°13·5'E	X	179
Wagtail Fm	Northum	NU0700	55°17·9'	1°53·0'W	FM	81
Waie	Devon	SS7203	50°49·0'	3°48·6'W	X	191
Wainbody Wood Fm	Warw	SP3174	52°22·0'	1°32·3'W	FM	140
Wain Br	Leic	SP6396	52°33·7'	1°3·8'W	X	140
Wain Common	Shrops	SO2179	52°24·4'	3°9·3'W	X	137,148
Wainddu	Powys	SO1062	52°15·2'	3°18·7'W	X	148
Wainfelin	Torf	SO2701	51°42·4'	3°3·0'W	T	171
Wainfleet All Saints	Lincs	TF4959	53°6·7'	0°14·0'E	T	122
Wainfleet Bank	Lincs	TF4759	53°6·7'	0°12·2'E	T	122
Wainfleet Clough	Lincs	TF5459	53°6·6'	0°18·5'E	X	122
Wainfleet Common	Lincs	TF4759	53°6·7'	0°12·2'E	X	122
Wainfleet Harbour	Lincs	TF5557	53°5·5'	0°19·3'E	W	122
Wainfleet Haven or Steeping River	Lincs	TF5259	53°6·6'	0°16·7'E	W	122
Wainfleet Road	Lincs	TF5758	53°6·0'	0°21·1'E	W	122
Wainfleet Sand	Lincs	TF5356	53°5·0'	0°17·5'E	X	122
Wainfleet St Mary	Lincs	TF4958	53°6·1'	0°13·9'E	T	122
Wainfleet St Mary Fen	Lincs	TF4558	53°6·2'	0°10·4'E	X	122
Wainfleet Swatchway	Lincs	TF5656	53°4·9'	0°20·2'E	W	122
Wainfleet Tofts	Lincs	TF4857	53°5·6'	0°13·0'E	T	122
Wain Fm	Heref	SO3330	51°58·1'	2°58·1'W	FM	149,161
Wainford	Norf	TM3490	52°27·7'	1°27·1'E	T	134
Wainfordrigg	Northum	NY9196	55°15·7'	2°8·1'W	X	80
Wain Gap	Cumbr	NY6505	54°26·6'	2°32·0'W	X	91
Waingap	Cumbr	SD4596	54°21·6'	2°50·4'W	X	97
Waingatehead	Cumbr	NY4569	55°1·0'	2°51·2'W	X	86
Waingates Fm	N Yks	SE3764	54°4·5'	1°25·7'W	FM	99
Waingroves	Derby	SK4149	53°2·4'	1°22·9'W	T	129
Waingroves Hall	Derby	SK4148	53°1·9'	1°22·9'W	X	129
Wainherbert	Heref	SO3332	51°59·2'	2°58·1'W	X	149,161
Wain Hill	Bucks	SP7700	51°41·8'	0°52·8'W	H	165
Wain Hill	Shrops	SO5681	52°25·8'	2°38·4'W	X	137,138
Wainhir	Powys	SO0586	52°28·1'	3°23·5'W	X	136
Wain Ho	Shrops	SJ5226	52°50·0'	2°42·3'W	X	126
Wainhope	Northum	NY6792	55°13·5'	2°30·7'W	X	80
Wainhope	Northum	NY6793	55°14·1'	2°30·7'W	X	80
Wainhouse Corner	Corn	SX1895	50°43·8'	4°34·4'W	T	190
Wain Lee	Staffs	SJ8655	53°5·8'	2°12·1'W	T	118
Wainlode Hill	Glos	SO8525	51°55·6'	2°12·7'W	X	162
Wain Rigg	Northum	NY6462	54°57·3'	2°33·3'W	X	86
Wainscott	Medway	TQ7471	51°24·9'	0°30·5'E	T	178
Wainsford Ho	Hants	SZ2995	50°45·5'	1°34·9'W	X	196
Wain's Hill	N Som	ST3970	51°25·8'	2°52·3'W	H	171,172
Wain's Hill (Fort)	N Som	ST3970	51°25·8'	2°52·3'W	A	171,172
Wainstalls	Cald	SE0428	53°45·1'	1°55·9'W	T	104
Wainstones	Derby	SK0277	53°17·6'	1°57·8'W	X	119
Wain Stones	Derby	SK0995	53°27·3'	1°51·5'W	X	110
Wain Stones	N Yks	NZ5503	54°25·4'	1°8·7'W	X	93
Wain Wath Force	N Yks	NY8701	54°24·5'	2°11·6'W	W	91,92
Wain wen	Powys	SO2154	52°11·0'	3°8·9'W	X	148
Wain Wood	Herts	TL1725	51°54·9'	0°17·5'W	F	166
Wain-y-parc Fm	Monm	SO5001	51°42·6'	2°43·0'W	FM	162
Waird	Orkney	HY2921	59°4·5'	3°13·8'W	X	6
Wairdlaw	W Loth	NS9973	55°56·6'	3°36·6'W	X	65
Waird of the Cairn	Aberd	NO6681	56°55·4'	2°33·1'W	X	45
Wairds of Alpity	Aberd	NO7977	56°53·2'	2°20·2'W	X	45
Waistland	E Ayr	NS6613	55°23·8'	4°6·5'W	X	71
Waitby	Cumbr	NY7508	54°28·3'	2°22·7'W	T	91
Waitby Common	Cumbr	NY7406	54°27·2'	2°23·6'W	X	91
Waitefield	Cumbr	NY1554	54°52·7'	3°19·1'W	X	85
Waite Fm	Devon	SS4210	50°52·3'	4°14·4'W	FM	190
Waite Fm	Lincs	TF2652	53°3·3'	0°6·8'W	FM	122
Waite Fm	Norf	TF9206	52°37·3'	0°50·6'E	FM	144
Waite Hill Fm	Wilts	SU0180	51°31·4'	1°58·7'W	FM	173
Waite's Fm	Lincs	TF3856	53°5·2'	0°4·0'E	FM	122
Waites House Fm	N Yks	NZ6503	54°25·3'	0°59·5'W	FM	94
Waites Moor	N Yks	NZ6602	54°24·8'	0°58·6'W	X	94
Waitham Hill	Cumbr	SD2284	54°15·0'	3°11·4'W	X	96
Waithe	Lincs	TA2800	53°29·1'	0°3·8'W	T	113
Waithe Beck	NE Lincs	TA2401	53°29·7'	0°7·4'W	W	113
Waithe House Fm	Lincs	TF2899	53°28·6'	0°3·9'W	FM	113
Waithe Top	Lincs	TA2700	53°29·1'	0°4·7'W	X	113
Wait Hill	D & G	NT1204	55°19·6'	3°22·8'W	H	78
Waithwith Bank	N Yks	SE1497	54°22·3'	1°46·6'W	X	99
Waithwith Bank Fm	N Yks	SE1498	54°22·9'	1°46·6'W	FM	99
Wait's Fm	Essex	TL8140	52°2·0'	0°38·7'E	FM	155
Waits Fm	Hants	SU5261	51°21·0'	1°14·8'W	FM	174
Waits Wood	Wilts	SU0289	51°36·2'	1°57·9'W	F	173
Wakebarrow	Cumbr	SD4487	54°16·8'	2°51·2'W	X	97
Wakebarrow Scar	Cumbr	SD6087	54°16·9'	2°36·4'W	X	97
Wakebridge	Derby	SK3355	53°5·7'	1°30·0'W	X	119
Wakefield	Aberd	NO6869	56°48·9'	2°31·0'W	X	45
Wakefield	Scot Bord	NT1254	55°46·5'	3°23·7'W	X	65,72
Wakefield	Wakf	SE3320	53°40·8'	1°29·6'W	T	104
Wakefield Fm	Norf	TG0426	52°47·8'	1°2·0'E	FM	133
Wakefield Fm	Northnts	SP7443	52°5·1'	0°54·8'W	FM	152
Wakefield Lawn	Northnts	SP7342	52°4·5'	0°55·7'W	X	152
Wakefield Lodge	Northnts	SP7342	52°4·5'	0°55·7'W	X	152
Wake Green	Birm	SP0882	52°26·4'	1°52·5'W	T	139
Wakeham	Devon	SX6849	50°19·8'	3°50·9'W	X	202
Wakeham Fm	W Susx	SU8122	50°59·7'	0°50·4'W	FM	197
Wakehams Fm	E Susx	TQ8712	50°52·9'	0°39·9'E	FM	199
Wakehams Green Fm	W Susx	TQ3038	51°7·8'	0°8·1'W	FM	187
Wake Hill	N Yks	SE1970	54°7·8'	1°42·1'W	T	99
Wakehill	Somer	ST3713	50°55·0'	2°53·4'W	X	193
Wakehurst Place	W Susx	TQ3331	51°4·0'	0°5·7'W	A	187
Wakelands	E Susx	TQ4611	50°53·0'	0°4·9'E	X	198
Wakeland's Fm	Essex	TL6839	52°1·7'	0°27·3'E	FM	154
Wakeley	Herts	TL3426	51°55·2'	0°2·7'W	T	166
Wakeley Fm	Leic	SP5884	52°27·3'	1°8·4'W	FM	140
Wakeley Village	Herts	TL3426	51°55·2'	0°2·7'W	A	166
Wakelyns	Suff	TM2878	52°21·4'	1°21·3'E	X	156
Wakering's Fm	Essex	TL7314	51°48·1'	0°30·9'E	FM	167
Wakering Stairs	Essex	TQ9787	51°33·1'	0°50·9'E	X	178
Wakerley	Northnts	SP9599	52°35·1'	0°35·5'W	T	141
Wakerley Great Wood	Northnts	SP9698	52°34·5'	0°34·6'W	F	141
Wakerley Oaks	Northnts	SP9699	52°35·1'	0°34·6'W	F	141
Wakes Colne	Essex	TL8928	51°55·3'	0°45·3'E	T	168
Wakes Colne Green	Essex	TL8930	51°56·4'	0°45·4'E	T	168
Wakes End Fm	Beds	SP9934	52°0·0'	0°33·1'W	FM	153,165
Wakes Hall	Essex	TL8828	51°55·3'	0°44·4'E	X	168
Wakeshall Fm	Essex	TL7741	52°2·6'	0°35·3'E	FM	155
Wakeswood	Hants	SU4151	51°15·6'	1°24·4'W	X	185
Wake Wood	N Yks	SE5020	53°40·7'	1°14·2'W	F	105
Wakey Hill	Cumbr	NY4875	55°4·3'	2°48·4'W	H	86
Walberswick	Suff	TM4974	52°18·7'	1°39·6'E	T	156
Walberswick Common	Suff	TM4875	52°19·2'	1°38·8'E	X	156
Walberswick Nature Reserve	Suff	TM4674	52°18·8'	1°37·0'E	X	156
Walberton	W Susx	SU9606	50°51·0'	0°37·8'W	T	197
Walberton Fm	W Susx	SU9705	50°50·4'	0°37·0'W	FM	197
Walbottle	N upon Ty	NZ1766	54°59·5'	1°43·6'W	T	88
Walburn Hall	N Yks	SE1195	54°21·3'	1°49·4'W	A	99
Walburn Moor	N Yks	SE1095	54°21·3'	1°50·3'W	X	99
Walbury Hill	W Berks	SU3761	51°21·0'	1°27·7'W	H	174
Walbury Hill (Fort)	W Berks	SU3761	51°21·0'	1°27·7'W	A	174
Walbut Bridge	E Yorks	SE7744	53°53·4'	0°49·3'W	X	105,106
Walbutt	D & G	NX7468	54°59·7'	3°57·7'W	X	83,84
Walbutts	York	SE6462	54°3·2'	1°0·9'W	X	100
Walby	Cumbr	NY4360	54°56·1'	2°53·0'W	T	85
Walcombe	Somer	ST5547	51°13·5'	2°38·3'W	T	182,183
Walcombe Wood	Somer	ST5548	51°14·0'	2°38·3'W	F	182,183
Walcot	Bath & NE Somer	ST7565	51°23·2'	2°21·2'W	T	172
Walcot	Lincs	TF0635	52°54·4'	0°25·0'W	T	130
Walcot	N Lincs	SE8821	53°40·9'	0°39·6'W	T	106,112
Walcot	Oxon	SP3419	51°52·3'	1°30·0'W	T	164
Walcot	Shrops	SO2699	52°35·3'	3°5·1'W	X	137
Walcot	Shrops	SO3484	52°27·2'	2°57·9'W	X	137
Walcot	Swin	SU1684	51°33·5'	1°45·8'W	T	173
Walcot	Worcs	SO9448	52°8·1'	2°4·9'W	T	150
Walcot	Wrekin	SJ5911	52°41·9'	2°36·0'W	T	126
Walcote	Leic	SP5683	52°26·8'	1°10·2'W	T	140
Walcote	Warw	SP1258	52°13·4'	1°49·1'W	T	150
Walcote Fields	Leic	SP5883	52°26·7'	1°8·4'W	X	140
Walcot Green	Norf	TM1280	52°22·8'	1°7·3'E	T	144
Walcot Green Fm	Norf	TM1381	52°23·4'	1°8·2'E	FM	144,156
Walcot Hall	Peterb	TF0804	52°37·6'	0°23·9'W	X	142
Walcot Lodge	Lincs	TF0534	52°53·8'	0°25·9'W	X	130
Walcot Park	Shrops	SO3483	52°26·7'	2°57·9'W	X	137
Walcott	Lincs	TF1356	53°5·6'	0°18·3'W	T	121
Walcott	Norf	TG3632	52°50·2'	1°30·6'E	T	133
Walcott Dales	Lincs	TF1857	53°6·1'	0°13·8'W	X	122
Walcott Fen	Lincs	TF1557	53°6·1'	0°16·5'W	X	121
Walcott Gap	Norf	TG3533	52°50·8'	1°29·8'E	X	133
Walcott Hall	Norf	TG3630	52°49·2'	1°30·6'E	X	133
Walcott Ho	Norf	TG3630	52°49·2'	1°30·6'E	X	133
Walcott Hurn	Lincs	TF1657	53°6·1'	0°15·6'W	X	121
Walcott's Hall	Essex	TL8825	51°53·7'	0°44·3'E	X	168
Walcot Waste	Shrops	SJ5811	52°41·9'	2°36·9'W	X	126
Waldegrave Fm	Suff	TL8453	52°8·9'	0°41·8'E	FM	155
Waldegraves	Essex	TL5332	51°58·2'	0°14·0'E	X	167
Waldegraves Fm	Essex	TM0313	51°47·0'	0°57·0'E	FM	168
Walden	N Yks	SE0182	54°14·3'	1°58·7'W	T	98
Walden Beck	N Yks	SE0184	54°15·3'	1°58·7'W	W	98
Walden Head	N Yks	SD9880	54°13·2'	2°1·4'W	X	98
Walden Ho	Wilts	SU2027	51°2·8'	1°42·5'W	X	184
Walden Manor	Brom	TQ4867	51°23·2'	0°8·0'E	X	177
Walden Moor	N Yks	SD9779	54°12·6'	2°2·3'W	X	98
Waldens	Essex	TQ9090	51°34·8'	0°44·9'E	X	178
Walden Stubbs	N Yks	SE5516	53°38·5'	1°9·7'W	T	111
Walderchain Wood	Kent	TR2048	51°11·5'	1°9·3'E	F	179,189
Waldergrove Fm	W Susx	SU8326	51°1·9'	0°48·6'W	FM	186,197
Waldersea Ho	Cambs	TF4504	52°37·1'	0°8·9'E	X	143
Waldersey	Cambs	TF4203	52°36·6'	0°6·2'E	X	142,143
Waldershaigh	Sheff	SK2696	53°27·8'	1°36·1'W	T	110
Waldershare Ho	Kent	TR2848	51°11·4'	1°16·2'E	A	179
Walderslade	Kent	TQ7562	51°20·0'	0°31·1'E	T	178,188
Walders Low	Sheff	SK2796	53°27·8'	1°35·2'W	A	110
Walderton	W Susx	SU7810	50°53·3'	0°53·1'W	T	197
Walderton Down	W Susx	SU7910	50°53·3'	0°52·2'W	X	197
Walditch	Dorset	SY4892	50°43·8'	2°43·8'W	T	193
Waldley	Derby	SK1236	52°55·4'	1°48·9'W	T	128
Waldon Fm	Devon	SS3610	50°52·2'	4°19·5'W	FM	190
Waldons	Devon	SS5706	50°50·4'	4°1·5'W	X	191
Waldridge	Durham	NZ2550	54°50·9'	1°36·2'W	T	88
Waldridge Fell	Durham	NZ2449	54°50·4'	1°37·2'W	X	88
Waldridge Manor	Bucks	SP7807	51°45·6'	0°51·8'W	X	165
Waldridge Village	Bucks	SP7807	51°45·6'	0°51·8'W	A	165
Waldringfield	Suff	TM2844	52°3·1'	1°19·9'E	T	169
Waldringfield Heath	Suff	TM2644	52°3·1'	1°18·2'E	T	169
Waldron	E Susx	TQ5419	50°57·2'	0°11·9'E	T	199
Waldron Down	E Susx	TQ5321	50°58·3'	0°11·1'E	T	199
Waldron Gill	E Susx	TQ5719	50°57·2'	0°14·5'E	W	199
Waldron Ho	E Susx	TQ5419	50°57·2'	0°11·9'E	X	199
Waldron's Fm	Somer	ST0422	50°59·6'	3°21·7'W	FM	181
Wald Taing	Orkney	HY3917	59°2·4'	3°3·3'W	X	6
Walducks Fm	Bucks	SP8625	51°55·2'	0°44·6'W	FM	165
Wales	Roth	SK4782	53°20·2'	1°17·2'W	T	111,120
Wales	Somer	ST5824	51°1·1'	2°35·5'W	T	183
Wales Bar	Roth	SK4683	53°20·8'	1°18·1'W	T	111,120
Walesby	Lincs	TF1392	53°25·0'	0°17·6'W	T	113
Walesby	Notts	SK6870	53°13·6'	0°58·5'W	T	120
Walesby Grange	Lincs	TF1190	53°23·9'	0°19·4'W	T	113
Walesby Moor	Lincs	TF1191	53°24·5'	0°19·4'W	F	113
Walesby Top Fm	Lincs	TF1492	53°25·0'	0°16·7'W	FM	113
Wales End	Suff	TL7949	52°6·8'	0°37·3'E	T	155
Wales Field	Durham	NZ1127	54°38·5'	1°49·4'W	X	92
Wales Fm	E Susx	TQ3513	50°54·3'	0°4·4'W	FM	198
Walesley	S Lanak	NS7042	55°39·5'	4°3·5'W	X	71
Waleswood	Roth	SK4583	53°20·8'	1°19·0'W	T	111,120
Waleys	Surrey	TQ1538	51°8·0'	0°21·0'W	X	187
Walford	Heref	SO3972	52°20·8'	2°53·3'W	T	137,148
Walford	Heref	SO5820	51°52·9'	2°36·2'W	T	162
Walford	Shrops	SJ4320	52°46·7'	2°50·3'W	T	126
Walford	Somer	ST2728	51°3·0'	3°2·1'W	T	193
Walford	Staffs	SJ8133	52°53·9'	2°16·5'W	T	127
Walford Court	Heref	SO5820	51°52·9'	2°36·2'W	X	162
Walford Hall Fm	Sol	SP1880	52°25·3'	1°43·7'W	FM	139
Walford Heath	Shrops	SJ4519	52°46·2'	2°48·5'W	T	126
Walford Ho	Heref	SO5921	51°53·4'	2°35·4'W	X	162
Walford Ho	Kent	TQ8741	51°8·5'	0°40·8'E	X	189
Walford Ho	Shrops	SJ4703	52°37·6'	2°46·6'W	X	126
Walford Ho	Somer	ST2728	51°3·0'	3°2·1'W	X	193
Walfords' Gibbet	Somer	ST1739	51°8·9'	3°10·8'W	X	181
Walgherton	Ches	SJ6948	53°1·9'	2°27·3'W	T	118
Wal-goch	Flint	SJ1669	53°12·9'	3°15·1'W	A	116
Walgrave	Northnts	SP8072	52°20·6'	0°49·1'W	T	141
Walgrave Lodge	Northnts	SP8073	52°21·2'	0°49·1'W	X	141
Walhalla	Corn	SW9162	50°25·5'	4°56·2'W	X	200
Walham	Glos	SO8220	51°52·9'	2°15·3'W	T	162
Walham Green	Ham & Ful	TQ2577	51°28·9'	0°11·6'W	T	176
Walhampton	Hants	SZ3395	50°45·4'	1°31·5'W	T	196
Walhampton School	Hants	SZ3396	50°46·0'	1°31·5'W	X	196
Walkbarn Fm	Suff	TM4568	52°15·6'	1°35·8'E	FM	156
Walkden	Salf	SD7303	53°31·6'	2°24·0'W	T	109
Walkden House Fm	Lancs	SD4401	53°30·4'	2°50·3'W	FM	108
Walkend	Aberd	NJ7212	57°12·1'	2°27·4'W	X	38
Walken Park Fm	Herts	TL3124	51°54·2'	0°5·4'W	FM	166
Walker	N upon Ty	NZ2964	54°58·4'	1°32·4'W	T	88
Walker Barn	Ches	SJ9573	53°15·5'	2°4·1'W	T	118
Walker Burn	Scot Bord	NT3538	55°38·1'	3°1·5'W	W	73
Walkerburn	Scot Bord	NT3637	55°37·6'	3°0·5'W	T	73
Walkerdales	Moray	NJ4262	57°38·9'	2°57·8'W	X	28
Walkerdyke	S Lanak	NS7146	55°41·7'	4°2·7'W	X	64
Walker Fold	Bolton	SD6712	53°36·5'	2°29·5'W	X	109
Walker Fold	Lancs	SD6741	53°52·1'	2°29·7'W	T	103
Walker Hall	Durham	NZ1217	54°33·1'	1°48·4'W	X	92
Walkerhill	Aberd	NJ7857	57°36·4'	2°21·6'W	X	29,30
Walkerhill	D & G	NX6480	55°6·0'	4°7·5'W	X	77
Walkerhill Fm	Aberd	NJ7656	57°35·9'	2°23·6'W	FM	29
Walker Ho	Cumbr	NY2559	54°55·5'	3°9·8'W	X	85
Walker Ho	Sheff	SK2591	53°25·2'	1°37·0'W	X	110
Walkeridge Fm	Hants	SU5255	51°17·7'	1°14·9'W	FM	174,185
Walkeringham	Notts	SK7692	53°25·4'	0°51·0'W	T	112
Walkerith	Notts	SK7892	53°25·4'	0°49·2'W	T	112
Walkern	Herts	TL2926	51°55·3'	0°7·1'W	T	166
Walkern Bury Fm	Herts	TL3026	51°55·3'	0°6·2'W	FM	166
Walkern Hall	Herts	TL3024	51°54·2'	0°6·2'W	X	166
Walkers	Lancs	SD7156	54°0·2'	2°26·1'W	X	103
Walkers Fm	Essex	TL5714	51°48·4'	0°17·0'E	FM	167
Walker's Fm	Glos	SO8028	51°57·2'	2°17·1'W	FM	150
Walker's Green	Ches	SJ7365	53°11·1'	2°23·8'W	X	118
Walkersgreen	Ches	SJ9478	53°18·2'	2°5·0'W	X	118
Walker's Green	Heref	SO5247	52°7·4'	2°41·7'W	T	149
Walker's Heath	Birm	SP0578	52°24·2'	1°55·2'W	T	139
Walkersheath	Ches	SJ8770	53°13·9'	2°11·3'W	X	118
Walker's Hill	Oxon	SP4030	51°58·3'	1°24·7'W	X	151
Walker's Hill	Wilts	SU1163	51°22·2'	1°50·1'W	H	173
Walkersknowe	Scot Bord	NT6623	55°30·2'	2°31·9'W	X	74
Walkerslow Fm	Shrops	SO6586	52°28·5'	2°30·5'W	FM	138
Walkers Marsh	Norf	TF5424	52°47·7'	0°17·5'E	X	131
Walkerstrough	Moray	NJ3955	57°35·1'	3°0·8'W	X	28
Walker's Wood	Notts	SK6780	53°19·0'	0°59·2'W	F	111,120
Walkerville	N Yks	SE2098	54°22·9'	1°41·1'W	T	99
Walkerwalls	Northum	NT9825	55°31·4'	2°1·5'W	X	75
Walkerwood Resr	Tames	SJ9899	53°29·5'	2°1·4'W	W	109
Walk Fm	E Yorks	SE9933	53°47·3'	0°29·4'W	FM	106
Walk Fm	Lincs	SK8587	53°22·6'	0°42·9'W	FM	112,121
Walk Fm	Lincs	TF4286	53°21·3'	0°8·4'E	FM	113,122
Walk Fm	NE Lincs	TA2004	53°31·4'	0°11·0'W	FM	113
Walk Fm	Norf	TM1888	52°27·0'	1°12·9'E	FM	156
Walk Fm	Oxon	SP3329	51°57·7'	1°30·8'W	FM	164
Walk Fm	Rut	TF0111	52°41·5'	0°29·9'W	FM	130
Walk Fm	Somer	ST7233	51°6·0'	2°23·6'W	FM	183
Walk Fm	Somer	ST7641	51°10·3'	2°20·2'W	FM	183
Walk Fm	Staffs	SK0947	53°1·5'	1°51·5'W	FM	119,128
Walk Fm	Suff	TM2539	52°0·4'	1°17·1'E	FM	169
Walk Fm	Worcs	SO8038	52°2·6'	2°17·1'W	FM	150
Walkford	Dorset	SZ2194	50°44·9'	1°41·8'W	T	195
Walkford Brook	Hants	SZ2295	50°45·5'	1°40·9'W	W	195

Walkham Head	Devon	SX5881	50°36·9′	4°0·1′W	X	191
Walkhampton	Devon	SX5369	50°30·4′	4°4·0′W	T	201
Walkhampton Common	Devon	SX5772	50°32·1′	4°0·7′W	H	191
Walkhamwood Fm	Shrops	SO6588	52°29·6′	2°30·5′W	FM	138
Walk House	N Lincs	SE9417	53°38·7′	0°34·3′W	X	112
Walk House	N Lincs	TA0718	53°39·1′	0°22·5′W	X	112
Walk House Fm	E Yorks	SE9244	53°53·3′	0°35·6′W	FM	106
Walkhurst Fm	Kent	TQ8133	51°4·3′	0°35·4′E	FM	188
Walkingham Hill	N Yks	SE3461	54°2·9′	1°28·4′W	X	99
Walkington	E Yorks	SE9937	53°49·4′	0°29·3′W	T	106
Walkington Wold Fm	E Yorks	SE9637	53°49·5′	0°32·1′W	FM	106
Walkley	Sheff	SK3388	53°23·5′	1°29·8′W	T	110,111
Walk Mill	Cumbr	NY7416	54°32·6′	2°23·7′W	X	91
Walk Mill	Lancs	SD8630	53°46·2′	2°12·3′W	T	103
Walkmill	Northum	NU2204	55°20·0′	1°38·8′W	X	81
Walkmill	Northum	NZ0084	55°9·3′	1°59·6′W	X	81
Walkmill	Powys	SO1296	52°33·5′	3°17·5′W	X	136
Walkmill	Shrops	SO3792	52°31·6′	2°55·3′W	T	137
Walkmills	Shrops	SO4699	52°35·4′	2°47·4′W	T	137,138
Walks Fm	Lincs	TF1546	53°0·2′	0°16·8′W	FM	130
Walks, The	E Yorks	TA1063	54°3·3′	0°18·8′W	X	101
Walks, The	Suff	TM4661	52°11·8′	1°36·4′E	X	156
Walk, The	Staffs	SK0846	53°0·9′	1°52·4′W	X	119,128
Walk Wood	Herts	TL1822	51°53·3′	0°16·7′W	F	166
Walk Wood	Herts	TL3936	52°0·5′	0°1·9′E	F	154
Walkwood	Worcs	SP0364	52°16·7′	1°57·0′W	X	150
Wall	Corn	SW6036	50°10·8′	5°21·3′W	T	203
Wall	Dorset	ST4201	50°48·6′	2°49·0′W	X	193
Wall	Northum	NY9168	55°0·6′	2°8·0′W	T	87
Wall	Staffs	SK0906	52°39·3′	1°51·6′W	T	139
Walla Brook	Devon	SX6387	50°40·2′	3°55·9′W	W	191
Walla Brook	Devon	SX6776	50°34·4′	3°52·3′W	W	191
Wallabrook Fm	Devon	SX4778	50°35·1′	4°9·3′W	FM	191,201
Walla Brook Head	Devon	SX6285	50°39·1′	3°56·8′W	W	191
Wallace Field	Cumbr	NY5049	54°50·2′	2°46·3′W	X	86
Wallace Fm	N Ayr	NS3256	55°46·3′	4°40·3′W	FM	63
Wallacegill Muir	E Ayr	NS5440	55°38·2′	4°18·7′W	X	70
Wallacehall	D & G	NX8487	55°10·1′	3°48·8′W	X	78
Wallacehall	D & G	NY2877	55°5·2′	3°7·3′W	X	85
Wallace Hill	Bucks	SU7495	51°39·2′	0°55·4′W	X	165
Wallace Lane	Cumbr	NY2943	54°46·9′	3°5·8′W	X	85
Wallacenick	Scot Bord	NT7232	55°35·1′	2°26·2′W	X	74
Wallace's Cast	S Lanak	NS9626	55°31·3′	3°38·4′W	X	72
Wallace's Cave	E Ayr	NS4923	55°28·9′	4°22·9′W	X	70
Wallace's Cave	Midlo	NT2863	55°51·5′	3°8·6′W	A	66
Wallace's Cave	W Loth	NS9473	55°56·6′	3°41·4′W	X	65
Wallace's Crags	Northum	NY6956	54°54·1′	2°28·6′W	X	86,87
Wallace's Fm	Essex	TL7932	51°57·7′	0°36·7′E	FM	167
Wallace's Hill	Scot Bord	NT3036	55°37·0′	3°6·3′W	H	73
Wallace's House	D & G	NY0390	55°11·9′	3°31·0′W	X	78
Wallace's House (Fort)	D & G	NY0390	55°11·9′	3°31·0′W	A	78
Wallace's Isle	Arg & Bt	NN3209	56°14·9′	4°42·2′W	X	56
Wallace's Putting Stone	Scot Bord	NT4635	55°36·6′	2°51·0′W	X	73
Wallace's Statue	Scot Bord	NT5932	55°35·0′	2°38·6′W	X	73,74
Wallace's Stone	S Ayr	NS3316	55°24·8′	4°37·9′W	A	70
Wallacestone	Falk	NS9177	55°58·7′	3°44·4′W	T	65
Wallaceton	Arg & Bt	NS3577	55°57·7′	4°38·2′W	X	63
Wallaceton	D & G	NX8487	55°10·1′	3°48·8′W	T	78
Wallaceton	E Ayr	NS6021	55°28·0′	4°12·4′W	X	71
Wallacetown	Pth & Kin	NO1518	56°21·1′	3°22·1′W	X	58
Wallacetown	S Ayr	NS2702	55°17·2′	4°43·0′W	T	76
Wallacetown	S Ayr	NS3422	55°28·1′	4°37·1′W	T	70
Wallacetown	Shetld	HU3052	60°15·3′	1°27·0′W	X	3
Walla Crag	Cumbr	NY2721	54°35·0′	3°7·3′W	X	89,90
Wallacre	Staffs	SK0856	53°6·3′	1°52·4′W	X	119
Wallaford	Devon	SX7265	50°28·5′	3°47·9′W	X	202
Wallaford Down	Devon	SX7065	50°28·5′	3°49·5′W	H	202
Walla' Kirk	Aberd	NJ4237	57°25·4′	2°57·5′W	X	28
Walland	Devon	SS3522	50°58·7′	4°20·6′W	X	190
Walland	Devon	SS4011	50°52·8′	4°16·1′W	X	190
Walland	Devon	SS6832	51°4·6′	3°52·7′W	X	180
Walland Fm	Somer	ST2315	50°56·0′	3°5·4′W	FM	193
Walland Manor	E Susx	TQ6430	51°3·0′	0°20·8′E	X	188
Walland Marsh	Kent	TQ9923	50°58·5′	0°50·5′E	X	189
Wallands Park	E Susx	TQ4010	50°52·6′	0°0·2′W	T	198
Wallange Fm, The	Ches	SJ6865	53°11·1′	2°28·3′W	FM	118
Wallasea Island	Essex	TQ9693	51°36·3′	0°50·2′E	X	178
Wallasea Ness	Essex	TQ9894	51°36·8′	0°52·0′E	X	168,178
Wallasey	Wirral	SJ3092	53°25·5′	3°2·8′W	T	108
Wallas Fach	V of Glam	SS9175	51°28·0′	3°33·8′W	X	170
Wallas Fm	V of Glam	SS9175	51°28·0′	3°33·8′W	FM	170
Wallash	Staffs	SK1545	53°0·4′	1°46·2′W	X	119,128
Wallaston Cross	Pemb	SM9201	51°40·4′	5°0·1′W	X	157,158
Wallaston Green	Pemb	SM9200	51°39·9′	5°0·1′W	X	157,158
Wallaton Cross	Devon	SX7948	50°19·4′	3°41·6′W	X	202
Wallbank	Lancs	SD8717	53°39·2′	2°11·4′W	T	109
Wall Bank	Shrops	SO5092	52°31·7′	2°43·8′W	T	137,138
Wallbank	Stock	SJ9085	53°21·9′	2°8·6′W	X	109
Wallberry Fm	I of M	SC3674	54°8·4′	4°30·2′W	FM	95
Wallberry Hill	I of M	SC3673	54°7·9′	4°30·2′W	H	95
Wall Bowers	Cumbr	NY5965	54°58·9′	2°38·0′W	X	86
Wallbrook	Dudley	SO9493	52°32·3′	2°4·9′W	T	139
Wall Brook	Somer	ST3711	50°53·9′	2°53·4′W	W	193
Wallbrook Fm	Heref	SO4435	52°0·9′	2°48·6′W	FM	149,161
Wallbrook Wood	Heref	SO5132	51°59·3′	2°42·4′W	F	149
Wallbury	Essex	TL4917	51°50·1′	0°10·2′E	A	167
Wall Cliff	Derby	SK1477	53°17·6′	1°47·0′W	H	119
Wallclough	Lancs	SD6041	53°52·1′	2°36·1′W	X	102,103
Wall Common	Somer	ST2545	51°12·2′	3°4·0′W	X	182
Wall Covert	Suff	TL9779	52°22·6′	0°54·1′E	F	144
Wallcrouch	E Susx	TQ6630	51°2·9′	0°22·5′E	T	188
Walldub	Cumbr	NY4260	54°56·1′	2°53·9′W	X	85
Wallemoore Brook	Shrops	SO6184	52°27·4′	2°34·0′W	W	138
Wallen Barton	Devon	SS8804	50°49·7′	3°35·0′W	X	192
Wall End	Cumbr	NY2805	54°26·4′	3°6·2′W	X	89,90
Wall End	Cumbr	NY3913	54°30·8′	2°56·1′W	X	90
Wall End	Cumbr	SD2287	54°16·6′	3°11·5′W	X	96
Wall End	Cumbr	SD2383	54°14·5′	3°10·5′W	T	96
Wall End	Heref	SO4457	52°12·7′	2°48·8′W	X	148,149
Wallend	Kent	TQ9371	51°24·5′	0°46·9′E	X	178
Wall End	Kent	TR2363	51°19·6′	1°12·4′E	T	179
Wallend	Newham	TQ4383	51°31·9′	0°4·1′E	T	177
Wallenrigg	Cumbr	SD2289	54°17·7′	3°11·5′W	X	96
Waller House Fm	N Yks	SE4748	53°55·8′	1°16·6′W	FM	105
Wallers Ash	Hants	SU4836	51°7·5′	1°18·5′W	X	185
Waller's Green	Heref	SO6739	52°3·1′	2°28·5′W	T	149
Waller's Haven	E Susx	TQ6608	50°51·1′	0°21·9′E	W	199
Wallerthwaite Village	N Yks	SE2964	54°4·5′	1°33·0′W	A	99
Wallet Knowe	Scot Bord	NT3543	55°40·8′	3°1·6′W	H	73
Wallett Court	Kent	TQ8646	51°11·2′	0°40·1′E	X	189
Wallett's Ct	Kent	TR3444	51°9·1′	1°21·2′E	X	179
Walley's Green	Ches	SJ6861	53°9·0′	2°28·3′W	T	118
Walley Thorn	Northum	NY9059	54°55·8′	2°8·9′W	X	87
Wallfauld	Pth & Kin	NN9415	56°19·2′	3°42·4′W	X	58
Wall Fen Fm	Northum	NY9568	55°0·6′	2°4·3′W	FM	87
Wallfield	Moray	NJ2965	57°40·4′	3°11·0′W	X	28
Wall Fm	Glos	SP1510	51°47·5′	1°46·6′W	FM	163
Wall Fm	Lancs	SD4140	53°51·4′	2°53·4′W	FM	102
Wallfoot (Hotel)	Cumbr	NY4359	54°55·6′	2°52·9′W	X	85
Wall Furlong Fm	Shrops	SO6685	52°28·0′	2°29·6′W	FM	138
Wall Grange Fm	Staffs	SJ9754	53°5·2′	2°2·3′W	FM	118
Wall Hall College	Herts	TQ1399	51°40·9′	0°21·5′W	X	166,176
Wall Head	Cumbr	NY4560	54°56·1′	2°51·1′W	X	86
Wall Heath	Dudley	SO8789	52°30·2′	2°11·1′W	T	139
Wall Hill	Cov	SP2983	52°26·9′	1°34·0′W	X	140
Wall Hill	D & G	NX7344	54°46·7′	3°58·1′W	H	83,84
Wall Hill	Oldham	SD9706	53°33·3′	2°2·3′W	T	109
Wallhill	Staffs	SJ9363	53°10·1′	2°5·9′W	X	118
Wallhill Fm	Ches	SJ6877	53°17·6′	2°28·4′W	FM	118
Wallhill Fm	Ches	SJ8262	53°9·5′	2°15·7′W	FM	118
Wallhill Fm	E Susx	TQ4235	51°6·0′	0°2·1′E	FM	187
Wall Hills	Heref	SO6359	52°13·9′	2°32·1′W	A	149
Wall Hills	Heref	SO6838	52°2·6′	2°27·6′W	X	149
Wallhills	Heref	SO6938	52°2·6′	2°26·7′W	X	149
Wall Hills Fm	Heref	SO6360	52°14·5′	2°32·1′W	FM	138,149
Wall Ho	Northum	NZ0053	54°52·6′	1°59·6′W	X	87
Wallholme	Cumbr	NY5864	54°58·4′	2°38·9′W	X	86
Wallhouse Fm	W Loth	NS9572	55°56·0′	3°40·4′W	FM	65
Wallhouse Fm	Worcs	SO9964	52°16·7′	2°0·5′W	FM	150
Wall Houses	Northum	NZ0368	55°0·6′	1°56·8′W	X	87
Wallhurst Manor	W Susx	TQ2223	50°59·8′	0°15·3′W	X	198
Walling Fen	E Yorks	SE8829	53°45·2′	0°39·5′W	X	106
Wallingfen House Fm	E Yorks	SE8630	53°45·8′	0°41·3′W	FM	106
Wallingford	Oxon	SU6089	51°36·0′	1°7·6′W	T	175
Wallington	Hants	SU5806	50°51·3′	1°10·2′W	T	196
Wallington	Herts	TL2933	51°59·1′	0°6·9′W	T	166
Wallington	Northum	NZ0284	55°9·3′	1°57·7′W	X	81
Wallington	Sutton	TQ2964	51°21·8′	0°8·4′W	T	176,187
Wallington Bury	Herts	TL2933	51°59·1′	0°6·9′W	X	166
Wallington Hall	Norf	TF6207	52°38·4′	0°24·1′E	A	143
Wallington Heath	Wals	SJ9902	52°37·2′	2°0·5′W	T	127,139
Wallington Newhouses	Northum	NZ0484	55°9·3′	1°55·8′W	X	81
Wallington River	Hants	SU5909	50°52·9′	1°9·3′W	W	196
Wallingwells	Notts	SK5784	53°21·2′	1°8·2′W	T	111,120
Wallingwells Wood	Notts	SK5884	53°21·2′	1°7·3′W	F	111,120
Wallis	Pemb	SN0125	51°53·5′	4°53·1′W	X	145,157,158
Wallisdown	Poole	SZ0593	50°44·4′	1°55·4′W	T	195
Wallis Grange	E Yorks	SE9343	53°52·7′	0°34·7′W	X	106
Wallish Walls	Northum	NZ0650	54°50·9′	1°54·0′W	X	87
Wallis Moor	Pemb	SN0126	51°54·1′	4°53·2′W	X	145,157,158
Walliswood	Surrey	TQ1138	51°8·1′	0°24·4′W	T	187
Walliswood Fm	Surrey	TQ1138	51°8·1′	0°24·4′W	FM	187
Walliwall	Orkney	HY4310	58°58·7′	2°59·0′W	X	6
Wall Lands	Derby	SK2352	53°4·1′	1°39·0′W	X	119
Wallmarsh Fm	Somer	ST8048	51°14·1′	2°16·8′W	FM	183
Wall Mead	Bath & NE Somer	ST6759	51°20·0′	2°28·0′W	T	172
Wallmead Fm	Wilts	ST9428	51°3·3′	2°4·8′W	FM	184
Wall Nook	Cumbr	NY4839	54°44·8′	2°48·0′W	X	90
Wall Nook	Cumbr	SD3780	54°13·0′	2°57·5′W	X	96,97
Wallnook	Derby	SK0368	53°12·8′	1°56·9′W	X	119
Wall Nook	Durham	NZ2145	54°48·2′	1°40·0′W	T	88
Wallog	Cered	SN5985	52°26·9′	4°4·1′W	X	135
Wallon	Devon	SX7790	50°42·0′	3°44·1′W	X	191
Wallop Brook	Hants	SU3231	51°4·9′	1°32·2′W	W	185
Walloper Well	Lancs	SD7148	53°55·9′	2°26·1′W	W	103
Wallop Hall Fm	Shrops	SJ3107	52°39·6′	3°0·8′W	FM	126
Wallop Ho	Hants	SU2936	51°7·6′	1°34·7′W	X	185
Wallops Wood Fm	Hants	SU6318	50°57·7′	1°5·8′W	FM	185
Wallover Barton	Devon	SS6838	51°7·8′	3°52·8′W	X	180
Wallover Down	Devon	SS6939	51°8·4′	3°52·0′W	X	180
Walloway	Cumbr	NY4125	54°37·3′	2°54·4′W	X	90
Wallowbarrow	Cumbr	SD2196	54°21·5′	3°12·5′W	X	96
Wallowbarrow Heald	Cumbr	SD2197	54°22·0′	3°12·5′W	X	96
Wallow Crag	Cumbr	NY4915	54°31·9′	2°46·9′W	X	90
Wallow Fm	Suff	TM0349	52°6·3′	0°58·3′E	FM	155
Wallow Green	Glos	ST8398	51°41·1′	2°14·4′W	T	162
Wall Pool Br	Lancs	SD4140	53°51·4′	2°53·4′W	X	102
Wallridge	Northum	NZ0576	55°5·0′	1°54·9′W	T	87
Wallrudding Fm	Notts	SK8872	53°14·5′	0°40·5′W	FM	121
Walls	Cumbr	SD0895	54°20·8′	3°24·5′W	X	96
Walls	Shetld	HU2449	60°13·7′	1°33·5′W	T	3
Walls Br	Powys	SJ2620	52°46·6′	3°5·4′W	X	126
Walls Burn	D & G	NX7586	55°9·4′	3°57·3′W	W	78
Walls Close Ho	N Yks	SE4159	54°1·8′	1°22·0′W	X	105
Walls Copse	W Berks	SU3075	51°28·6′	1°33·7′W	F	174
Wallsend	N Tyne	NZ2966	54°59·5′	1°32·4′W	T	88
Walls Fm	E Susx	TQ5014	50°54·6′	0°8·4′E	FM	199
Wall's Green	Essex	TL6106	51°44·0′	0°20·3′E	X	167
Wallsgrove Ho	Essex	TQ4097	51°39·5′	0°1·8′E	X	167,177
Wall Shield	Northum	NY7169	55°1·1′	2°26·8′W	X	86,87
Walls Hill	Renf	NS4158	55°47·6′	4°31·7′W	X	64
Walls Hill	Torbay	SX9365	50°28·7′	3°30·1′W	X	202
Walls Hill (Fort)	Renf	NS4158	55°47·6′	4°31·7′W	A	64
Walls Pit Ho	Warr	SJ6181	53°19·7′	2°34·7′W	X	109
Wallstale	Stir	NS7790	56°5·5′	3°58·2′W	X	57
Walls, The	Derby	SK5077	53°17·5′	1°14·6′W	X	120
Walls, The	Shrops	SO7896	52°33·9′	2°19·1′W	A	138
Walls, The	V of Glam	ST0166	51°23·3′	3°25·0′W	X	170
Wallston	V of Glam	ST1273	51°27·2′	3°15·6′W	T	171
Wallstone	Ches	SJ5651	53°3·5′	2°39·0′W	X	117
Wallstone Fm	Derby	SK2949	53°2·5′	1°33·6′W	FM	119
Wallstone Fm	Monm	ST5189	51°36·1′	2°42·1′W	FM	162,172
Wallstych Fm	Heref	SO2857	52°12·6′	3°2·8′W	FM	148
Wallsuches	Bolton	SD6511	53°35·9′	2°31·3′W	T	109
Wallsworth	Glos	SO8423	51°54·6′	2°13·6′W	T	162
Wallthwaite	Cumbr	NY3526	54°37·7′	3°0·0′W	X	90
Walltower	Midlo	NT2457	55°48·3′	3°12·3′W	X	66,73
Walltown	Northum	NY6766	54°59·5′	2°30·5′W	X	86,87
Wall Town	Shrops	SO6978	52°24·2′	2°26·9′W	X	138
Walltree Fm	Northnts	SP5437	52°2·0′	1°12·4′W	FM	152
Wall under Heywood	Shrops	SO5092	52°31·7′	2°43·8′W	T	137,138
Wall Wood	Essex	TL5218	51°50·6′	0°12·8′E	F	167
Wallyford	E Loth	NT3672	55°56·5′	3°1·0′W	T	66
Walman's Green	Herts	TL3024	51°54·2′	0°6·2′W	X	166
Walmer	Kent	TR3750	51°12·2′	1°24·0′E	T	179
Walmer Bridge	Lancs	SD4724	53°42·8′	2°47·8′W	T	102
Walmer Fm	Worcs	SO9264	52°16·7′	2°6·6′W	FM	150
Walmersley	Bury	SD8013	53°37·0′	2°17·7′W	T	109
Walmer Sta	Kent	TR3650	51°12·2′	1°23·1′E	X	179
Walmersyke	Cumbr	NY5545	54°48·1′	2°41·6′W	X	86
Walmestone	Kent	TR2559	51°17·4′	1°14·0′E	X	179
Walmgate	Cumbr	NY5117	54°33·0′	2°45·0′W	X	90
Walmgate Head	Cumbr	NY5116	54°32·5′	2°45·0′W	H	90
Walmgate Stray	York	SE6150	53°56·8′	1°3·8′W	T	105
Walm How	Cumbr	NY5117	54°33·0′	2°45·0′W	X	90
Walmley	Birm	SP1393	52°32·3′	1°48·1′W	T	139
Walmore Common	Glos	SO7415	51°50·2′	2°22·2′W	X	162
Walmsgate	Lincs	TF3678	53°17·1′	0°2·8′E	T	122
Walmsley Br	Lancs	SD5341	53°52·0′	2°42·5′W	X	102
Walna Scar	Cumbr	SD2596	54°21·5′	3°8·8′W	H	96
Walna Scar Road	Cumbr	SD2696	54°21·5′	3°7·9′W	X	96,97
Walner Fm	Devon	SS6446	51°12·1′	3°56·4′W	FM	180
Walney Airfield	Cumbr	SD1771	54°7·9′	3°15·8′W	X	96
Walney Channel	Cumbr	SD1967	54°5·8′	3°13·9′W	W	96
Walney Island	Cumbr	SD1865	54°4·7′	3°14·8′W	X	96
Walney Meetings	Cumbr	SD1871	54°7·9′	3°14·9′W	W	96
Walning Fm	S Glos	ST5786	51°34·5′	2°36·8′W	FM	172
Walnut Fm	Lincs	SK8955	53°5·3′	0°39·9′W	FM	121
Walnut Fm	Norf	TG4524	52°45·7′	1°38·3′E	FM	134
Walnut Grove	Pth & Kin	NO1322	56°23·2′	3°24·1′W	T	53,58
Walnuts Fm	Cambs	TL4298	52°33·9′	0°6·1′E	FM	142,143
Walnuts, The	Mil Key	SP8543	52°5·0′	0°45·2′W	X	152
Walnut Tree	Mil Key	SP8936	52°1·1′	0°41·8′W	T	152
Walnut Tree Cottage	Oxon	SP4916	51°50·7′	1°16·9′W	X	164
Walnut Tree Fm	Bath & NE Somer	ST5361	51°21·0′	2°40·1′W	FM	172,182
Walnut Tree Fm	Ches	SJ4974	53°15·9′	2°45·5′W	FM	117
Walnut Tree Fm	Ches	SJ7653	53°4·7′	2°21·1′W	FM	118
Walnut Tree Fm	Ches	SJ8975	53°16·6′	2°9·5′W	FM	118
Walnut Tree Fm	Essex	TL6811	51°46·6′	0°26·5′E	FM	167
Walnut Tree Fm	Herts	TL1431	51°58·2′	0°20·0′W	FM	166
Walnut Tree Fm	Medway	TQ7975	51°27·0′	0°35·0′E	FM	178
Walnut Tree Fm	Monm	ST3396	51°39·8′	2°57·7′W	FM	171
Walnut Tree Fm	Norf	TM0480	52°23·0′	1°0·3′E	FM	144
Walnut Tree Fm	Suff	TM0175	52°20·4′	0°57·4′E	FM	144
Walnut Tree Fm	Suff	TM0760	52°12·2′	1°2·2′E	FM	155
Walnut Tree Fm	Suff	TM1253	52°8·3′	1°6·3′E	FM	155
Walnut-tree Fm	Suff	TM1348	52°5·6′	1°7·0′E	FM	169
Walnut Tree Fm	Suff	TM1937	51°59·5′	1°11·8′E	FM	169
Walnut Tree Fm	Suff	TM2171	52°17·8′	1°14·9′E	FM	156
Walnut Tree Fm	Suff	TM3169	52°16·5′	1°23·6′E	FM	156
Walnut-tree Fm	Suff	TM3444	52°2·9′	1°25·2′E	FM	169
Walnut Tree Fm	Suff	TM3477	52°20·7′	1°26·5′E	FM	156
Walnut Tree Fm	Suff	TM3661	52°12·0′	1°27·6′E	FM	156
Walnut Tree Fm	Suff	TM3775	52°19·5′	1°29·1′E	FM	156
Walnut Tree Fm	Suff	TM4173	52°18·4′	1°32·5′E	FM	156
Walnut Tree Fm	Suff	TM5085	52°24·6′	1°41·0′E	FM	156
Walnut Tree Fm	Warr	SJ6281	53°19·7′	2°33·8′W	FM	109
Walnuttree Green	Herts	TL4523	51°53·4′	0°6·8′E	T	167
Walnut Tree Ho	W Susx	SZ7899	50°47·3′	0°53·2′W	X	197
Walpan	I of W	SZ4778	50°36·2′	1°19·8′W	X	196
Walpole	Somer	ST3041	51°10·1′	2°59·7′W	T	182
Walpole	Suff	TM3674	52°19·0′	1°28·2′E	T	156
Walpole Cross Keys	Norf	TF5119	52°45·1′	0°14·6′E	T	131
Walpole Gate	Norf	TF5211	52°40·8′	0°15·3′E	X	131,143
Walpole Hatch Fm	Suff	TM3774	52°19·0′	1°29·0′E	FM	156
Walpole Highway	Norf	TF5113	52°41·8′	0°14·5′E	T	131,143
Walpole Ho	Norf	TF5119	52°45·1′	0°14·6′E	X	131
Walpole Marsh	Norf	TF4817	52°44·1′	0°11·9′E	T	131
Walpole Rocks	Kent	TR3671	51°23·6′	1°23·9′E	X	179
Walpole St Andrew	Norf	TF5017	52°44·0′	0°13·7′E	T	131
Walpole St Peter	Norf	TF5016	52°43·5′	0°13·7′E	T	131
Walreddon	Devon	SX4771	50°31·4′	4°9·1′W	A	201
Walrond's Park	Somer	ST3720	50°58·8′	2°53·5′W	X	193
Walrow	Somer	ST3347	51°13·3′	2°57·2′W	T	182
Walsal End	Sol	SP2079	52°24·8′	1°42·0′W	T	139
Walsall	Wals	SP0198	52°35·0′	1°58·7′W	T	139
Walsall Wood	Wals	SK0403	52°37·7′	1°56·1′W	T	139
Walsbatch Manor	Shrops	SO6790	52°30·7′	2°28·8′W	X	138
Walscombe Fm	Somer	ST3409	50°52·8′	2°55·9′W	FM	193
Walscott	Devon	SS7032	51°4·6′	3°51·0′W	X	180
Walsden	Cald	SD9322	53°41·9′	2°5·9′W	T	103
Walsden Moor	Cald	SD9421	53°41·4′	2°5·0′W	X	103
Walsey Hills	Norf	TG0644	52°57·5′	1°4·4′E	X	133
Walsgrave Hill	Warw	SP3980	52°25·2′	1°25·2′W	X	140
Walsgrave on Sowe	Cov	SP3881	52°25·8′	1°26·1′W	T	140
Walsgrove Hill	Worcs	SO7465	52°17·2′	2°22·5′W	H	138,150
Walsham Hall	Suff	TM2883	52°24·1′	1°21·5′E	X	156
Walsham Le Willows	Suff	TM0071	52°18·3′	0°56·4′E	T	144,155
Walsham Wood	Norf	TG3412	52°39·5′	1°28·0′E	F	133,134
Walshaw	Bury	SD7711	53°35·9′	2°20·4′W	T	109
Walshaw	Cald	SD9731	53°46·8′	2°2·3′W	X	103
Walshaw Dean	Cald	SD9635	53°48·9′	2°3·2′W	X	103
Walshaw Dean Reservoirs	Cald	SD9633	53°47·8′	2°3·2′W	W	103
Walshes, The	Worcs	SO8070	52°19·9′	2°17·2′W	T	138
Walsh Fold	Bolton	SD7414	53°37·6′	2°23·2′W	X	109
Walshford	N Yks	SE4153	53°58·5′	1°22·1′W	T	105
Walsh Hall	Lancs	SD3806	53°33·1′	2°55·7′W	X	108
Walsh Hall	Sol	SP2582	52°26·4′	1°37·5′W	A	140

Walsingham Wood	Herts	TL2103	51°43·0′	0°14·5′W	F	166
Walsis Hill	Norf	TG0818	52°43·4′	1°5·2′E	X	133
Walsoken	Norf	TF4710	52°40·3′	0°10·9′E	T	131,143
Walson	Monm	SO4320	51°52·8′	2°49·3′W	T	161
Walson Barton	Devon	SS6205	50°49·9′	3°57·2′W	X	191
Walson Barton	Devon	SS7300	50°47·4′	3°47·7′W	X	191
Walsopthorne	Heref	SO6542	52°4·8′	2°30·2′W	A	149
Walstead Clough	Lancs	SD8619	53°40·3′	2°12·3′W	X	109
Walstead Fm	W Susx	TQ3624	51°0·2′	0°3·3′W	FM	198
Walstead Place Fm	W Susx	TQ3524	51°0·2′	0°4·2′W	FM	198
Walston	E Ayr	NS4640	55°38·0′	4°26·3′W	X	70
Walston	S Ayr	NS4225	55°29·9′	4°29·6′W	X	70
Walston	S Lanak	NT0545	55°41·6′	3°30·2′W	T	72
Walston Braehead	S Lanak	NT0444	55°41·1′	3°31·2′W	X	72
Walstone	Midlo	NT1858	55°48·8′	3°18·1′W	X	65,66,72
Walston Mill	S Lanak	NT0345	55°41·6′	3°32·2′W	X	72
Walsworth	Herts	TL1930	51°57·6′	0°15·7′W	T	166
Walter Hill Plantn	Lancs	SD8448	53°55·9′	2°14·2′W	F	103
Walter Ho	Kent	TQ9533	51°4·0′	0°47·4′E	X	189
Walter's Ash	Bucks	SU8498	51°40·7′	0°46·7′W	T	165
Walter's Fm	E Susx	TQ7422	50°58·5′	0°29·1′E	FM	199
Walter's Fm	Oxon	SP6404	51°44·1′	1°4·0′W	FM	164,165
Walters Fm	Somer	ST7237	51°8·1′	2°23·6′W	FM	183
Walters Fm	V of Glam	ST0968	51°24·5′	3°18·1′W	FM	171
Walter's Green	Kent	TQ5140	51°8·6′	0°9·9′E	T	188
Waltersmuir Resr	Stir	NN8100	56°10·9′	3°54·6′W	W	57
Walter's Sheds	Norf	TF7406	52°37·7′	0°34·7′E	X	143
Walterstead	Scot Bord	NT8746	55°42·7′	2°12·0′W	X	74
Walterston	Pemb	SM8927	51°54·3′	5°3·7′W	X	157,158
Walterston	Swan	SS5189	51°35·0′	4°8·7′W	X	159
Walterston	V of Glam	ST0671	51°26·0′	3°20·8′W	T	170
Walterstone	Heref	SO3425	51°55·4′	2°57·2′W	T	161
Walterstone Common	Heref	SO3525	51°55·4′	2°56·3′W	X	161
Waltham	Kent	TR1048	51°11·8′	1°0·7′E	T	179,189
Waltham	NE Lincs	TA2603	53°30·7′	0°5·6′W	T	113
Waltham Abbey	Essex	TL3800	51°41·1′	0°0·2′E	T	166
Waltham Bury	Essex	TL6814	51°48·2′	0°26·6′E	X	167
Waltham Chase	Hants	SU5615	50°56·1′	1°11·8′W	T	196
Waltham Cross	Herts	TL3500	51°41·2′	0°2·4′W	T	166
Waltham Ct	Kent	TR1149	51°12·3′	1°1·6′E	X	179,189
Waltham Down	W Susx	SU9314	50°55·3′	0°40·2′W	X	197
Waltham Hall	Essex	TL5624	51°53·8′	0°16·4′E	X	167
Waltham Hall	Suff	TM1162	52°13·2′	1°5·7′E	X	155
Waltham Ho	Essex	TL7014	51°48·2′	0°28·3′E	X	167
Waltham Ho	Leic	SK7924	52°48·7′	0°49·3′W	X	129
Waltham House Fm	NE Lincs	TA2803	53°30·7′	0°3·8′W	FM	113
Waltham on the Wolds	Leic	SK8025	52°49·2′	0°48·4′W	T	130
Waltham Pasture Fm	Leic	SK8122	52°47·6′	0°47·5′W	FM	130
Waltham Place	Win & Maid	SU8577	51°29·4′	0°46·2′W	X	175
Waltham's Cross	Essex	TL6930	51°56·8′	0°27·9′E	T	167
Waltham St Lawrence	Win & Maid	SU8277	51°29·4′	0°48·7′W	T	175
Walthamstow	Wal F	TQ3789	51°35·2′	0°1·0′W	T	177
Waltham Trinleys	Hants	SU5444	51°11·8′	1°13·2′W	F	185
Waltham Windmill	NE Lincs	TA2503	53°30·8′	0°6·5′W	X	113
Walthwaite	Cumbr	NY3205	54°26·4′	3°2·5′W	X	90
Walthwaite	Cumbr	SD2577	54°11·2′	3°8·5′W	X	96
Waltness	Orkney	HY4819	59°3·6′	2°53·9′W	X	6
Walton	Arg & Bt	NS3577	55°57·7′	4°38·2′W	X	63
Walton	Bucks	SP8213	51°48·8′	0°48·2′W	T	165
Walton	Cumbr	NY5264	54°58·3′	2°44·6′W	T	86
Walton	Derby	SK3669	53°13·2′	1°27·2′W	T	119
Walton	E Renf	NS4855	55°46·1′	4°24·9′W	X	64
Walton	Falk	NT0279	55°59·9′	3°33·8′W	X	65
Walton	Leeds	SE4447	53°55·3′	1°19·4′W	T	105
Walton	Leic	SP5987	52°28·9′	1°5·8′W	T	140
Walton	Liv	SJ3694	53°26·6′	2°57·4′W	T	108
Walton	Mil Key	SP8936	52°1·1′	0°41·8′W	T	152
Walton	Peterb	TF1702	52°36·4′	0°15·9′W	T	142
Walton	Powys	SO2559	52°13·7′	3°5·5′W	T	148
Walton	Shrops	SO4679	52°24·6′	2°47·2′W	T	137,138,148
Walton	Shrops	SO6781	52°25·8′	2°28·7′W	X	138
Walton	S Lanak	NT0949	55°43·8′	3°26·5′W	X	72
Walton	Somer	ST4636	51°7·5′	2°45·9′W	T	182
Walton	Staffs	SJ8527	52°50·7′	2°13·0′W	T	127
Walton	Staffs	SJ8933	52°53·9′	2°9·4′W	T	127
Walton	Suff	TM2935	51°58·2′	1°20·4′E	T	169
Walton	Wakf	SE3517	53°39·1′	1°27·8′W	T	110,111
Walton	Warw	SP2853	52°10·7′	1°35·0′W	T	151
Walton	Wrekin	SJ5818	52°45·7′	2°36·9′W	T	126
Waltonbank	Staffs	SJ8627	52°50·7′	2°12·1′W	X	127
Walton Bay	N Som	ST4274	51°28·0′	2°49·7′W	W	171,172
Walton Burn	E Renf	NS4954	55°45·6′	4°24·0′W	W	64
Walton Burn	N Lanak	NS7976	55°58·0′	3°55·9′W	W	64
Walton Burn	N Lanak	NS8076	55°58·0′	3°54·9′W	W	65
Walton Cardiff	Glos	SO9032	51°59·4′	2°8·3′W	T	150
Walton Channel	Essex	TM2424	51°52·4′	1°15·6′E	W	169
Walton Common	Norf	TF7316	52°43·1′	0°34·1′E	X	132
Walton Court	Bucks	SP8112	51°48·3′	0°49·1′W	T	165
Walton Court Fm	Powys	SO2659	52°13·7′	3°4·6′W	FM	148
Walton Dam	E Renf	NS4955	55°46·1′	4°24·0′W	W	64
Walton Down	N Som	ST4274	51°28·0′	2°49·7′W	X	171,172
Walton Downs	Surrey	TQ2257	51°18·2′	0°14·6′W	X	187
Walton East	Pemb	SN0223	51°52·5′	4°52·2′W	T	145,157,158
Walton Elm	Dorset	ST7817	50°57·4′	2°18·5′W	T	183
Walton Fields	Staffs	SJ8116	52°44·7′	2°16·5′W	X	127
Walton Fm	Falk	NS7977	55°58·5′	3°55·9′W	FM	64
Walton Fm	Somer	ST6951	51°15·7′	2°26·3′W	FM	183
Walton Grange	Leic	SK5719	52°46·2′	1°8·9′W	X	129
Walton Grange	Pemb	SN0222	51°51·9′	4°52·2′W	X	145,157,158
Walton Grange	Shrops	SO6298	52°34·9′	2°33·3′W	X	138
Walton Grange	Staffs	SJ8017	52°45·3′	2°17·4′W	X	127
Walton Green	Powys	SO2659	52°13·7′	3°4·6′W	X	148
Walton Grounds	Northnts	SP5034	52°0·4′	1°15·9′W	T	151
Walton Hall	Cumbr	SD3678	54°11·9′	2°58·4′W	X	96,97
Walton Hall	Derby	SK2117	52°45·2′	1°40·9′W	X	128
Walton Hall	Essex	TL8201	51°40·9′	0°38·4′E	X	168
Walton Hall	Essex	TM2623	51°51·8′	1°17·3′E	X	169
Walton Hall	Norf	TG3919	52°43·2′	1°32·7′E	X	133,134
Walton Hall	Warr	SJ6084	53°21·3′	2°35·7′W	X	109
Walton Hall (Hotel)	Wakf	SE3616	53°38·6′	1°26·9′W	X	110,111
Walton Hall (Hotel)	Warw	SP2852	52°10·2′	1°35·0′W	X	151
Walton Hall Sch	Staffs	SJ8528	52°51·2′	2°13·0′W	X	127
Walton Heath	Hants	SU6109	50°52·9′	1°7·6′W	T	196
Walton Heath	Somer	ST4539	51°9·1′	2°46·8′W	X	182
Walton Heath	Staffs	SJ8832	52°53·4′	2°10·3′W	X	127
Walton Heath	Surrey	TQ2253	51°16·0′	0°14·7′W	X	187
Walton High Rigg	Cumbr	NY5265	54°58·9′	2°44·6′W	X	86
Walton Highway	Norf	TF4912	52°41·3′	0°12·7′E	T	131,143
Walton Hill	Cambs	TL2080	52°24·5′	0°13·7′W	X	142
Waltonhill	Fife	NO3609	56°16·4′	3°1·6′W	X	59
Walton Hill	Fife	NO3610	56°16·9′	3°1·6′W	H	59
Walton Hill	Powys	SJ2705	52°38·5′	3°4·3′W	X	126
Walton Hill	Somer	ST4635	51°6·9′	2°45·9′W	H	182
Walton Hill	Worcs	SO9479	52°24·8′	2°4·9′W	H	139
Walton Hill Fm	Derby	SK2217	52°45·2′	1°40·0′W	FM	128
Walton Hill Fm	Glos	SO8928	51°57·3′	2°9·2′W	FM	150,163
Walton Hill Fm	Warw	SP2852	52°10·2′	1°34·2′W	FM	151
Walton Hill Ho	Staffs	SJ8933	52°53·9′	2°9·4′W	X	127
Walton Ho	Worcs	SO9378	52°24·2′	2°5·8′W	X	139
Walton Hole	Brad	SE0449	53°56·5′	1°55·9′W	X	104
Walton Holt	Leic	SP6186	52°28·3′	1°5·7′W	X	140
Waltonhurst	Staffs	SJ8527	52°50·7′	2°13·0′W	X	127
Walton-in-Gordano	N Som	ST4273	51°27·4′	2°49·7′W	T	171,172
Walton-le-Dale	Lancs	SD5527	53°44·5′	2°40·5′W	T	102
Walton Lees Fm	Derby	SK3267	53°12·2′	1°30·8′W	FM	119
Walton Lodge	Derby	SK3468	53°12·7′	1°29·0′W	X	119
Walton Lodge	Leeds	SE4547	53°55·3′	1°18·5′W	X	105
Walton Lodge	Leic	SP6085	52°27·8′	1°6·6′W	X	140
Walton Manor	Oxon	SP5007	51°45·8′	1°16·1′W	T	164
Walton Mill	Pemb	SN0323	51°52·5′	4°51·3′W	X	145,157,158
Walton Moor	N Som	ST4372	51°26·9′	2°48·8′W	F	171,172
Walton Moss	Cumbr	NY5066	54°59·4′	2°46·5′W	X	86
Walton-on-Thames	Surrey	TQ1066	51°23·2′	0°24·8′W	T	176
Walton-on-the-Hill	Staffs	SJ9520	52°46·9′	2°4·0′W	T	127
Walton on the Hill	Surrey	TQ2254	51°16·6′	0°14·7′W	T	187
Walton-On-The-Naze	Essex	TM2521	51°50·8′	1°16·4′E	T	169
Walton on the Wolds	Leic	SK5919	52°46·2′	1°7·1′W	T	129
Walton-on-Trent	Derby	SK2118	52°45·8′	1°40·9′W	T	128
Walton Park	D & G	NX7670	55°0·8′	3°55·9′W	X	84
Walton Park	Mil Key	SP8935	52°0·6′	0°41·8′W	X	152
Walton Park Fm	D & G	NX7671	55°1·3′	3°56·0′W	FM	84
Walton Pool	Worcs	SO9378	52°24·2′	2°5·8′W	X	139
Waltons	Essex	TL5942	52°3·4′	0°19·6′E	X	154
Waltons Fm	Lincs	TF3313	52°42·1′	0°1·5′W	FM	131,142
Walton's Rough	Staffs	SJ8325	52°49·6′	2°14·7′W	F	127
Walton St Mary	N Som	ST4172	51°26·9′	2°50·6′W	T	171,172
Walton Summit	Lancs	SD5725	53°43·4′	2°38·7′W	T	102
Walton's Wood	Staffs	SJ7846	53°0·9′	2°19·3′W	T	118
Walton Thorns	Leic	SK6220	52°46·7′	1°4·4′W	X	129
Walton Warren	Norf	TF7415	52°42·5′	0°34·9′E	T	132
Walton West	Pemb	SM8612	51°46·2′	5°5·7′W	T	157
Walton Wood	Cumbr	NY5465	54°58·9′	2°42·7′W	F	86
Walton Wood	Derby	SK2116	52°44·7′	1°40·9′W	F	128
Walton Wood	Derby	SK3668	53°12·7′	1°27·2′W	F	119
Walton Wood	Leeds	SE4648	53°55·8′	1°17·5′W	F	105
Walton Wood	Norf	TF7315	52°42·5′	0°34·1′E	F	132
Walton Wood	Warw	SP2851	52°9·6′	1°35·0′W	F	151
Walton Woodhead	Cumbr	NY5566	54°59·4′	2°41·8′W	X	86
Walton Wood Ho	Wakf	SE4914	53°37·5′	1°15·1′W	X	111
Waltwood Hill	Newp	ST3888	51°35·5′	2°53·3′W	H	171
Walverden Resr	Lancs	SD8736	53°49·4′	2°11·4′W	W	103
Walves Resr	Black w Dar	SD7415	53°38·1′	2°23·2′W	W	109
Walwen	Flint	SJ1179	53°18·3′	3°19·7′W	T	116
Walwen	Flint	SJ1771	53°14·0′	3°14·2′W	T	116
Walwen	Flint	SJ2076	53°16·7′	3°11·6′W	T	117
Walwick	Northum	NY9070	55°1·7′	2°9·0′W	T	87
Walwick Fell	Northum	NY8870	55°1·7′	2°10·8′W	X	87
Walwick Grange	Northum	NY9069	55°1·2′	2°9·0′W	X	87
Walwick Hall	Northum	NY8970	55°1·7′	2°9·9′W	X	87
Walworth	Darl	NZ2318	54°33·6′	1°38·2′W	T	93
Walworth	Sthwk	TQ3278	51°29·4′	0°5·5′W	T	176,177
Walworth Fm	Warw	SP3858	52°13·4′	1°26·2′W	FM	151
Walworth Gate	Darl	NZ2320	54°34·7′	1°38·2′W	T	93
Walworth Grange	Darl	NZ2318	54°33·6′	1°38·2′W	X	93
Walworth Moor Fm	Darl	NZ2321	54°35·3′	1°38·2′W	FM	93
Walworth Village	Darl	NZ2319	54°34·2′	1°38·2′W	A	93
Walwyn's Castle	Pemb	SM8711	51°45·7′	5°4·8′W	T	157
Wambarrows	Somer	SS8734	51°5·9′	3°36·4′W	A	181
Wambrook	Somer	ST2907	50°51·7′	3°0·1′W	T	193
Wambs Fm	Lancs	SD8725	53°43·5′	2°11·4′W	FM	103
Wamil Hall	Suff	TL6974	52°20·5′	0°29·3′E	A	143
Wampford	Devon	SS6922	50°59·2′	3°51·6′W	X	180
Wamphray	E Loth	NT5683	56°2·5′	2°41·9′W	X	67
Wamphraygate	D & G	NY1296	55°15·3′	3°22·6′W	X	78
Wamphray Water	D & G	NT1401	55°18·0′	3°20·8′W	W	78
Wamphray Water	D & G	NT1502	55°18·5′	3°19·9′W	W	79
Wamphray Water	D & G	NY1396	55°15·3′	3°21·7′W	W	78
Wampool	Cumbr	NY2454	54°52·7′	3°10·6′W	T	85
Wanbarrow Fm	W Susx	TQ2715	50°55·5′	0°11·2′W	FM	198
Wanborough	Surrey	SU9348	51°13·6′	0°39·7′W	T	186
Wanborough	Swin	SU2082	51°32·4′	1°42·3′W	T	174
Wanborough Ho	Swin	SU1984	51°33·5′	1°43·2′W	X	173
Wanborough Manor	Surrey	SU9348	51°13·6′	0°39·7′W	X	186
Wanborough Plain	Swin	SU2280	51°31·3′	1°40·6′W	X	174
Wanborough Plain Farm	Swin	SU2480	51°31·3′	1°38·9′W	FM	174
Wanborough Sta	Surrey	SU9350	51°14·7′	0°39·7′W	X	186
Wanborough Wood	Surrey	SU9249	51°14·2′	0°40·5′W	F	186
Wanborough Youth Ho	Surrey	SU9450	51°14·2′	0°38·8′W	X	186
Wancombe Hill	Dorset	ST6402	50°49·2′	2°30·3′W	X	194
Wandale	N Yks	SE7174	54°9·7′	0°54·3′W	X	100
Wandale Beck	Cumbr	SD7198	54°22·8′	2°26·4′W	W	98
Wandale Fm	E Yorks	TA1567	54°5·4′	0°14·1′W	FM	101
Wandale Fm	E Yorks	TA2073	54°8·6′	0°9·4′W	FM	101
Wandale Hill	Cumbr	SD7098	54°22·8′	2°27·3′W	H	98
Wandales	N Yks	SE8360	54°2·0′	0°43·5′W	X	100
Wandel	S Lanak	NS9427	55°31·8′	3°40·3′W	X	71,72
Wandel Burn	S Lanak	NS9626	55°31·3′	3°38·4′W	W	72
Wandel Cottages	S Lanak	NS9527	55°31·8′	3°39·4′W	X	72
Wandel Dyke	S Lanak	NS9526	55°31·2′	3°39·4′W	T	72
Wandel Hill	S Lanak	NS9526	55°31·2′	3°39·4′W	H	72
Wanden	Kent	TQ8845	51°10·6′	0°41·8′E	X	189
Wandershiell	Angus	NO5657	56°42·4′	2°42·7′W	X	54
Wanders Knowe	Scot Bord	NT3731	55°34·4′	2°59·5′W	H	73
Wand Hill Fm	N Yks	NZ4603	54°25·5′	1°17·0′W	FM	93
Wand Hills	Red & Cl	NZ6719	54°33·9′	0°57·4′W	X	94
Wandlebury	Cambs	TL4953	52°9·5′	0°11·1′E	A	154
Wandle Park	Croy	TQ3165	51°22·4′	0°6·7′W	T	176,177
Wandles Fm	N Yks	SE7083	54°14·5′	0°55·1′W	FM	100
Wandley Gill	N Yks	SE1774	54°9·9′	1°44·0′W	W	99
Wandmire Fm	N Yks	SE6066	54°5·4′	1°4·5′W	FM	100
Wandon	Northum	NU0328	55°33·0′	1°56·7′W	X	75
Wandon	Staffs	SK0314	52°43·7′	1°56·9′W	X	128
Wandon End	Herts	TL1322	51°53·3′	0°21·1′W	T	166
Wandon Green Fm	Herts	TL1420	51°52·2′	0°20·3′W	FM	166
Wandope	Cumbr	NY1819	54°33·8′	3°15·7′W	H	89,90
Wandsworth	Wan	TQ2575	51°27·8′	0°11·6′W	T	176
Wandsworth Br	Wan	TQ2575	51°27·8′	0°11·6′W	X	176
Wandsworth Common	Wan	TQ2773	51°26·7′	0°10·0′W	X	176
Wandylaw	Northum	NU1425	55°31·4′	1°46·3′W	X	75
Wandylaw Bog	Northum	NU1324	55°30·8′	1°47·2′W	X	75
Wandylaw Moor	Northum	NU1325	55°31·4′	1°47·2′W	X	75
Wandy Marsh	Northum	NU0806	55°21·1′	1°52·0′W	X	81
Wandystead	Northum	NU0906	55°21·1′	1°51·1′W	X	81
Wane Cleuch	Scot Bord	NT5701	55°18·3′	2°40·2′W	X	80
Waneham Fm	Lincs	TF0562	53°8·9′	0°25·4′W	FM	121
Wan Fell	Cumbr	NY5236	54°43·3′	2°44·3′W	H	90
Wanfield Hall	Staffs	SK0429	52°51·7′	1°56·0′W	X	128
Wanford	Aberd	NJ7061	57°38·5′	2°29·7′W	X	29
Wangfield Fm	Hants	SU5214	50°55·6′	1°15·2′W	FM	196
Wangford	Suff	TL7483	52°25·3′	0°33·9′E	X	143
Wangford	Suff	TM4679	52°21·4′	1°37·2′E	T	156
Wangford Common Covert	Suff	TM4677	52°20·4′	1°37·1′E	F	156
Wangford Hill	Suff	TM4778	52°20·9′	1°38·0′E	X	156
Wangford Warren	Suff	TL7682	52°24·7′	0°35·7′E	F	143
Wangford Warren	Suff	TL7782	52°24·7′	0°36·5′E	X	144
Wangford Woods	Suff	TL7881	52°24·1′	0°37·4′E	F	144
Wanlass	N Yks	SE0689	54°18·0′	1°54·0′W	X	99
Wanlass Howe	Cumbr	NY3703	54°25·4′	2°57·8′W	X	90
Wanlass Park	N Yks	SE0589	54°18·0′	1°55·0′W	X	98
Wanless	Lancs	SD9138	53°50·5′	2°7·8′W	X	103
Wanlip	Leic	SK6010	52°41·3′	1°6·3′W	T	129
Wanlip Hill	Leic	SK5911	52°41·8′	1°7·2′W	X	129
Wanlock Dod	D & G	NS8713	55°24·1′	3°46·6′W	H	71,78
Wanlockhead	D & G	NS8712	55°23·6′	3°46·6′W	T	71,78
Wanlock Water	D & G	NS8416	55°25·7′	3°49·6′W	W	71,78
Wannage Fm	Norf	TL6391	52°29·8′	0°24·5′E	FM	143
Wannerton Fm	Worcs	SO8678	52°24·2′	2°11·9′W	FM	139
Wannock	E Susx	TQ5703	50°48·5′	0°14·1′E	T	199
Wansdyke	Bath & NE Somer	ST6963	51°22·1′	2°26·3′W	A	172
Wansdyke	Wilts	SU1064	51°22·7′	1°51·0′W	A	173
Wansdyke Ho	Bath & NE Somer	ST6663	51°22·1′	2°28·9′W	X	172
Wansdyke Path	Wilts	SU1164	51°22·7′	1°50·1′W	X	173
Wansfell	Cumbr	NY3904	54°25·9′	2°56·0′W	H	90
Wansfell Holme	Cumbr	NY3802	54°24·8′	2°56·9′W	X	90
Wansfell Pike	Cumbr	NY3904	54°25·9′	2°56·0′W	H	90
Wansford	E Yorks	TA0656	53°59·6′	0°22·6′W	T	107
Wansford	Peterb	TL0799	52°34·9′	0°24·8′W	T	142
Wansford Sta	Cambs	TL0997	52°33·8′	0°23·1′W	X	142
Wans Ho	Wilts	ST9667	51°24·4′	2°3·1′W	X	173
Wanshurst Green	Kent	TQ7645	51°10·8′	0°31·5′E	T	188
Wanside	E Loth	NT4962	55°51·2′	2°48·4′W	X	66
Wanside Rig	E Loth	NT6064	55°52·3′	2°37·9′W	X	67
Wansley Barton	Devon	SS5617	50°56·3′	4°2·6′W	X	180
Wansley Hall	Notts	SK4651	53°3·5′	1°18·4′W	X	120
Wanson	Corn	SS1900	50°46·5′	4°33·7′W	T	190
Wanson Mouth	Corn	SS1901	50°47·1′	4°33·7′W	W	190
Wanson Water	Corn	SS1900	50°46·5′	4°33·7′W	W	190
Wanstead	Redbr	TQ4088	51°34·6′	0°1·6′E	T	177
Wanstead Flats	Wal F	TQ4086	51°33·6′	0°1·6′E	X	177
Wanstead Fm	Hants	SU6409	50°52·8′	1°5·0′W	FM	196
Wanstead Park	Redbr	TQ4187	51°34·1′	0°2·5′E	X	177
Wanstone Fm	Kent	TR3543	51°8·5′	1°22·0′E	FM	179
Wanstrow	Somer	ST7141	51°10·3′	2°24·5′W	T	183
Wanswell	Glos	SO6801	51°42·6′	2°27·4′W	T	162
Wanswell Court Fm	Glos	SO6901	51°42·6′	2°26·5′W	FM	162
Wantage	Oxon	SU4087	51°35·1′	1°25·0′W	T	174
Wantage Field	Oxon	SU4086	51°34·5′	1°25·0′W	X	174
Wanthwaite	Cumbr	NY3123	54°36·1′	3°3·7′W	X	90
Wanthwaite Crags	Cumbr	NY3222	54°35·6′	3°2·7′W	X	90
Wantisden Corner	Suff	TM3651	52°6·6′	1°27·2′E	X	156
Wantisden Hall	Suff	TM3652	52°7·2′	1°27·2′E	X	156
Wanton Walls	Scot Bord	NT5448	55°43·6′	2°43·5′W	X	73
Wantonwells	Aberd	NJ6227	57°20·2′	2°37·4′W	X	37
Wantonwells	Aberd	NJ7708	57°10·0′	2°22·4′W	X	38
Wants Green	Worcs	SO7657	52°12·9′	2°20·7′W	T	150
Wantsley Fm	Dorset	ST4502	50°49·1′	2°46·5′W	FM	193
Wantsum Walk	Kent	TR2364	51°20·1′	1°12·5′E	X	179
Wantyn Dyke	Powys	SO2088	52°29·3′	3°10·3′W	A	137
Wantyn's Dike	Powys	SO1890	52°30·3′	3°12·1′W	A	136
Wantz Corner	Essex	TL7200	51°40·6′	0°29·7′E	X	167
Wanwood Hill	Cumbr	NY7047	54°49·3′	2°27·6′W	H	86
Wapley	S Glos	ST7179	51°30·8′	2°24·7′W	T	172
Wapley Common	S Glos	ST7180	51°31·3′	2°24·7′W	X	172
Wapley Hill	Heref	SO3462	52°15·4′	2°57·6′W	H	137,148,149
Waplington Hall	E Yorks	SE7746	53°54·5′	0°49·3′W	X	105,106
Wappenbury	Warw	SP3769	52°19·3′	1°27·0′W	A	151
Wappenbury	Warw	SP3769	52°19·3′	1°27·0′W	T	151
Wappenbury Wood	Warw	SP3770	52°19·8′	1°27·0′W	F	140
Wappenham	Northnts	SP6245	52°6·2′	1°5·3′W	T	152
Wappenham Lodge Fm	Northnts	SP6344	52°5·7′	1°4·4′W	FM	152
Wappenshall	Wrekin	SJ6615	52°44·1′	2°31·6′W	X	127
Wappenshall Moor	Wrekin	SJ6615	52°44·1′	2°29·8′W	X	127
Wapping	T Ham	TQ3480	51°30·4′	0°3·8′W	T	176,177
Wappingthorn	W Susx	TQ1613	50°54·5′	0°20·6′W	X	198
Wappingthorn Wood	W Susx	TQ1713	50°54·5′	0°19·8′W	F	198
Wapsbourne Fm	E Susx	TQ3923	50°59·6′	0°0·8′W	FM	198

Wapshott Fm	Surrey	SU9960	51°20·1'	0°34·3'W	FM	175,176,186
Wapsworthy	Devon	SX5380	50°36·3'	4°4·3'W	X	191,201
Warathwaite Head	Cumbr	NY4749	54°50·2'	2°49·1'W	X	86
Warbanks, The	Suff	TL8853	52°8·8'	0°45·3'E	A	155
Warbister Hill	Orkney	ND3884	58°46·8'	3°3·8'W	H	7
Warb Law	D & G	NY3583	55°8·5'	3°0·8'W	H	79
Warblebank	Cumbr	NY2846	54°48·5'	3°6·8'W	X	85
Warbleton	E Susx	TQ6018	50°56·6'	0°17·0'E	T	199
Warblington	Hants	SU7206	50°51·2'	0°58·2'W	T	197
Warborne	Hants	SZ3297	50°46·5'	1°32·4'W	X	196
Warboro Fm	Warw	SP2464	52°16·7'	1°38·5'W	FM	151
Warborough	Oxon	SU5993	51°38·2'	1°8·5'W	T	164,174
Warborough Fm	Oxon	SU3885	51°34·0'	1°26·7'W	FM	174
Warborough Hill	Norf	TF9643	52°57·1'	0°55·5'E	X	132
Warborough Hill	Norf	TG0843	52°56·9'	1°6·2'E	X	133
Warboys	Cambs	TL3080	52°24·4'	0°4·9'W	T	142
Warboys Heath	Cambs	TL3280	52°24·4'	0°3·2'W	X	142
Warboys High Fen	Cambs	TL3583	52°25·9'	0°0·5'W	X	142
Warboys Wood	Cambs	TL3081	52°24·9'	0°4·9'W	F	142
Warbraham Mains Fm	Cambs	TL5963	52°14·8'	0°20·1'E	FM	154
Warbreck	Blackp	SD3238	53°50·3'	3°1·6'W	T	102
Warbrick's Loch	Highld	NN2459	56°41·6'	4°52·0'W	W	41
Warbrook	Hants	SU7761	51°20·8'	0°53·3'W	X	175,186
War Brook	Shrops	SJ4321	52°47·3'	2°50·3'W	W	126
Warbstow	Corn	SX2090	50°41·1'	4°32·5'W	T	190
Warbstow Bury	Corn	SX2090	50°41·1'	4°32·5'W	A	190
Warbstow Cross	Corn	SX2090	50°41·1'	4°32·5'W	T	190
Warburton	Aberd	NO7363	56°45·7'	2°26·0'W	X	45
Warburton	Traf	SJ6989	53°24·1'	2°27·6'W	T	109
Warburton Green	Traf	SJ7984	53°21·4'	2°18·5'W	T	109
Warburton Park	Traf	SJ7090	53°24·6'	2°26·7'W	X	109
War Carr	Northum	NY6567	55°0·0'	2°32·4'W	X	86
Warcombe	Devon	SX7347	50°18·8'	3°46·6'W	X	202
Warcop	Cumbr	NY7415	54°32·0'	2°23·7'W	T	91
Warcop Fell	Cumbr	NY7820	54°34·7'	2°20·0'W	X	91
Ward	Aberd	NK0531	57°22·4'	1°54·6'W	X	30
Ward	Devon	SS5523	50°59·5'	4°3·6'W	X	180
Ward	E Ayr	NS5316	55°25·2'	4°18·9'W	X	70
Ward	Renf	NS3463	55°50·2'	4°38·6'W	X	63
Ward	Stir	NS5394	56°7·2'	4°21·4'W	X	57
Wardale	N Yks	SE8570	54°7·4'	0°41·5'W	X	100
Wardale	Shrops	SJ6729	52°51·7'	2°29·0'W	X	127
Ward Br	Devon	SX5472	50°32·0'	4°3·2'W	X	191,201
Ward Burn	D & G	NX1766	54°57·6'	4°51·1'W	W	82
Ward Burn	E Ayr	NS5317	55°25·7'	4°19·0'W	W	70
Warddykes	Angus	NO6442	56°34·4'	2°34·7'W	X	54
Wardell Ho	N Yks	SE2291	54°19·1'	1°39·3'W	X	99
Warden	Devon	SS6701	50°47·8'	3°52·9'W	X	191
Warden	Kent	TR0271	51°24·3'	0°54·7'E	T	178
Warden	Northum	NY9166	54°59·6'	2°8·0'W	T	87
Warden	Powys	SO3064	52°16·4'	3°1·2'W	T	137,148
Wardend	Aberd	NJ5721	57°16·9'	2°42·3'W	X	37
Wardend	Aberd	NJ6045	57°29·9'	2°39·6'W	X	29
Wardend	Aberd	NJ6661	57°38·5'	2°33·7'W	X	29
Wardend	Aberd	NO7593	57°1·9'	2°24·3'W	X	38,45
Wardend	Angus	NO3054	56°40·6'	3°8·1'W	X	53
Ward End	Birm	SP1188	52°29·6'	1°49·9'W	T	139
Wardend	Moray	NJ2255	57°35·0'	3°17·8'W	X	28
Wardend Ho	Moray	NJ0454	57°34·2'	3°35·8'W	X	27
Warden Grange	Northnts	SP5150	52°9·0'	1°14·9'W	X	151
Warden Great Wood	Beds	TL1042	52°4·2'	0°23·3'W	F	153
Warden Hill	Beds	TL0926	51°55·5'	0°24·5'W	H	166
Warden Hill	Beds	TL1951	52°8·9'	0°15·2'W	X	153
Warden Hill	Durham	NY9138	54°44·5'	2°8·0'W	X	91,92
Warden Hill	Glos	SO9320	51°52·9'	2°5·7'W	T	163
Warden Hill	Lincs	TF3473	53°14·5'	0°0·9'E	X	122
Warden Hill	Northnts	SP5150	52°9·0'	1°14·9'W	X	151
Warden Law	Sund	NZ3649	54°50·3'	1°25·9'W	X	88
Warden Law	Sund	NZ3750	54°50·9'	1°25·0'W	X	88
Warden Little Wood	Beds	TL1043	52°4·7'	0°23·3'W	F	153
Warden Point	I of W	SZ3287	50°41·1'	1°32·4'W	T	196
Warden Point	Kent	TR0272	51°24·9'	0°54·7'E	X	178
Warden's Down	Wilts	ST9050	51°15·2'	2°8·2'W	X	184
Warden's Fm	Essex	TL9000	51°40·2'	0°45·3'E	FM	168
Warden's Hall	Essex	TL5907	51°44·6'	0°18·6'E	X	167
Warden Street	Beds	TL1244	52°5·2'	0°21·5'W	T	153
Warden Warren	Beds	TL1443	52°4·6'	0°19·8'W	F	153
Wardes	Aberd	NJ7612	57°12·1'	2°23·4'W	X	38
Wardfall	Lancs	SD6935	53°48·9'	2°27·8'W	X	103
Ward Fm	Devon	SS5321	50°58·4'	4°5·2'W	FM	180
Ward Fm	N Ayr	NS2651	55°43·5'	4°45·8'W	FM	63
Wardfold	Aberd	NJ4802	57°6·6'	2°51·1'W	X	37
Wardford	Aberd	NJ8438	57°26·2'	2°15·5'W	X	29,30
Ward Green	Barns	SE3404	53°32·1'	1°28·8'W	T	110,111
Ward Green	Suff	TM0463	52°13·9'	0°59·6'E	T	155
Ward Green Cross	Lancs	SD6337	53°49·9'	2°33·3'W	T	102,103
Wardhall Common	Cumbr	NY1437	54°43·5'	3°19·7'W	X	89
Wardhall Guards	Cumbr	NY1338	54°44·0'	3°20·6'W	X	89
Wardhaugh	Aberd	NJ6247	57°31·0'	2°37·6'W	X	29
Wardhead	Aberd	NJ5403	57°7·2'	2°45·1'W	X	37
Wardhead	Aberd	NJ5621	57°16·9'	2°43·3'W	X	37
Wardhead	Aberd	NJ9135	57°24·6'	2°8·5'W	X	30
Wardhead	Aberd	NJ9254	57°34·8'	2°7·6'W	X	30
Wardhead	Aberd	NJ9432	57°23·0'	2°5·5'W	X	30
Wardhead	Aberd	NJ9620	57°16·5'	2°3·5'W	X	38
Wardhead	Aberd	NK0156	57°35·9'	1°58·5'W	X	30
Wardhead	Aberd	NO8475	56°52·2'	2°15·3'W	X	45
Wardhead	C of Aber	NJ8704	57°7·9'	2°12·4'W	X	38
Wardhead	E Ayr	NS4144	55°40·1'	4°31·2'W	X	70
Wardhead	Moray	NJ3142	57°28·0'	3°8·6'W	X	28
Wardhead	N Lanak	NS7371	55°55·2'	4°1·5'W	X	64
Wardheads	Pth & Kin	NO2424	56°24·4'	3°13·4'W	X	53,59
Wardhedges	Beds	TL0635	52°0·4'	0°26·9'W	T	153
Wardhill	Angus	NO6161	56°44·6'	2°37·8'W	X	45
Ward Hill	D & G	NY2787	55°10·6'	3°8·3'W	H	79
Ward Hill	Heref	SO6748	52°8·0'	2°28·5'W	X	149
Ward Hill	Orkney	HY2202	58°54·2'	3°20·8'W	H	6,7
Ward Hill	Orkney	HY2218	59°2·8'	3°21·1'W	X	6
Wardhill	Orkney	HY2510	58°58·5'	3°17·8'W	X	6
Ward Hill	Orkney	HY3308	58°57·5'	3°9·4'W	H	6,7

Ward Hill	Orkney	HY3830	59°9·4'	3°4·6'W	H	6
Ward Hill	Orkney	HY5017	59°2·5'	2°51·8'W	X	6
Ward Hill	Orkney	HY5530	59°9·5'	2°46·7'W	H	5,6
Wardhill	Orkney	HY6525	59°6·9'	2°36·2'W	T	5
Ward Hill	Orkney	ND4588	58°46·8'	2°56·6'W	H	7
Ward Hill	Shetld	HU3912	59°53·7'	1°17·7'W	X	4
Ward Hill	Shetld	HZ2073	59°32·8'	1°38·3'W	H	4
Wardhillock	Aberd	NJ9220	57°16·5'	2°7·5'W	X	38
Ward Holm	Orkney	HY5901	58°53·9'	2°42·2'W	X	6
Wardhouse	Aberd	NJ5630	57°21·8'	2°43·4'W	X	29,37
Wardhouse Hill	Aberd	NJ5631	57°22·3'	2°43·4'W	H	29,37
Wardington	Oxon	SP4946	52°6·8'	1°16·7'W	T	151
Wardington Gate Fm	Northnts	SP4947	52°7·4'	1°16·7'W	FM	151
Wardlaw	D & G	NT0401	55°17·9'	3°30·3'W	X	78
Wardlaw	D & G	NX9488	55°10·7'	3°39·4'W	H	78
Ward Law	D & G	NY0266	54°59·0'	3°31·5'W	X	84
Wardlaw	E Ayr	NS3746	55°41·1'	4°35·1'W	X	63
Wardlaw	N Ayr	NS2451	55°43·5'	4°47·7'W	X	63
Ward Law	Northum	NT8613	55°24·9'	2°12·8'W	H	80
Ward Law	Scot Bord	NT2616	55°26·2'	3°9·7'W	H	79
Ward Law	Scot Bord	NT2725	55°31·1'	3°8·9'W	H	73
Wardlaw	Scot Bord	NT2916	55°26·2'	3°6·9'W	T	79
Ward Law	S Lanak	NT0229	55°32·9'	3°32·8'W	H	72
Wardlaw Hill	E Ayr	NS6822	55°28·7'	4°4·9'W	H	71
Wardle	Ches	SJ6157	53°6·8'	2°34·6'W	T	118
Wardle	Roch	SD9116	53°38·7'	2°7·8'W	T	109
Wardle Bank	Ches	SJ6158	53°7·3'	2°34·6'W	T	118
Wardle Bridge Fm	Ches	SJ6057	53°6·8'	2°35·4'W	FM	118
Wardle Green	N Yks	SE8296	54°21·4'	0°43·9'W	X	94,100
Wardle Hill	Ches	SJ5957	53°6·8'	2°36·3'W	X	117
Wardle Rigg	N Yks	SE8195	54°20·9'	0°44·8'W	X	94,100
Wardless	Cumbr	NY4303	54°25·4'	2°52·3'W	X	90
Wardley	Ghead	NZ2961	54°56·8'	1°32·4'W	T	88
Wardley	Rut	SK8300	52°35·7'	0°46·1'W	T	141
Wardley	Salf	SD7602	53°31·1'	2°21·3'W	T	109
Wardley	W Susx	SU8427	51°2·4'	0°47·7'W	T	186,197
Wardley Hall	Salf	SD7502	53°31·1'	2°22·2'W	A	109
Wardley Wood	Rut	SP8499	52°35·2'	0°45·2'W	F	141
Wardlow	Derby	SK1874	53°16·0'	1°43·4'W	T	119
Wardlow	Staffs	SK0847	53°1·5'	1°52·4'W	X	119,128
Wardlow Hay	Derby	SK1874	53°16·0'	1°43·4'W	X	119
Wardlow Mires	Derby	SK1775	53°16·5'	1°44·3'W	X	119
Wardly Hill	Norf	TM3693	52°29·3'	1°29·0'E	X	134
Ward Marsh	Norf	TG3715	52°41·1'	1°30·8'E	W	133,134
Wardmill	Aberd	NJ8101	57°6·2'	2°18·4'W	X	38
Wardmill	Angus	NO4554	56°40·7'	2°53·4'W	X	54
Wardmoor Hill	Scot Bord	NT6006	55°21·0'	2°37·4'W	H	80
Wardneuk Fm	Angus	NO5343	56°34·9'	2°45·5'W	FM	54
Ward Odds	Cumbr	NY7805	54°26·6'	2°19·9'W	X	91
Ward of Arisdale	Shetld	HU4983	60°31·9'	1°5·9'W	X	1,2,3
Ward of Bressay	Shetld	HU5038	60°7·7'	1°5·5'W	H	4
Ward of Brough	Shetld	HU4754	60°16·3'	1°8·5'W	H	3
Ward of Browland	Shetld	HU2651	60°14·8'	1°31·3'W	H	3
Ward of Burraland	Shetld	HU4423	59°59·6'	1°12·2'W	H	4
Ward of Cairnlea	S Ayr	NX2281	55°5·7'	4°46·9'W	X	76
Ward of Challister	Shetld	HU5766	60°22·7'	0°57·5'W	X	2
Ward of Clett	Shetld	HU5561	60°20·0'	0°59·7'W	H	2
Ward of Clugan	Shetld	HP6407	60°44·7'	0°49·1'W	X	1
Ward of Copister	Shetld	HU4879	60°29·8'	1°7·1'W	H	2,3
Ward of Culswick	Shetld	HU2645	60°11·6'	1°31·4'W	H	4
Ward of Dragon-ness	Shetld	HU5064	60°21·7'	1°5·1'W	H	2,3
Ward of Greenmow	Shetld	HU4528	60°2·3'	1°11·0'W	X	4
Ward of Grimsetter	Shetld	HP5300	60°41·0'	1°1·3'W	H	1
Ward of Hevdafield	Shetld	HU5561	60°20·0'	0°59·7'W	X	2
Ward of Houlland	Shetld	HP5809	60°45·9'	0°55·6'W	X	1
Ward of Housebay	Orkney	HY6721	59°4·7'	2°34·1'W	X	5
Ward of Housebay (Chambered Mound)	Orkney	HY6721	59°4·7'	2°34·1'W	A	5
Ward of Kirkbuddo	Angus	NO5043	56°34·8'	2°48·4'W	X	54
Ward of Laxfirth	Shetld	HU4347	60°12·6'	1°13·0'W	H	3
Ward of Norwick	Shetld	HP6415	60°49·0'	0°48·9'W	H	1
Ward of Otterswick	Shetld	HU5085	60°33·0'	1°4·8'W	X	1,2,3
Ward of Outrabister	Shetld	HU5172	60°26·0'	1°3·9'W	H	2,3
Ward of Petester	Shetld	HP5811	60°46·9'	0°55·6'W	X	1
Ward of Reawick	Shetld	HU3244	60°11·0'	1°24·9'W	H	4
Ward of Redland	Orkney	HY3617	59°2·4'	3°6·4'W	H	6
Ward of Runafirth	Shetld	HU3467	60°23·4'	1°22·5'W	X	2,3
Ward of Scollan	Shetld	HU2556	60°17·5'	1°32·4'W	H	3
Ward of Scousburgh	Shetld	HU3818	59°57·0'	1°18·7'W	H	4
Ward of Setter	Shetld	HU4870	60°24·9'	1°7·2'W	H	2,3
Ward of Silwick	Shetld	HU2942	60°10·0'	1°28·2'W	X	4
Ward of Symbister	Shetld	HU3730	60°3·4'	1°19·6'W	H	4
Ward of Tumblin	Shetld	HU3452	60°15·3'	1°22·6'W	H	3
Ward of Veester	Shetld	HU4126	60°1·3'	1°15·4'W	H	4
Ward of Virdaskule	Shetld	HU3354	60°16·4'	1°23·7'W	H	3
Ward of Wick	Shetld	HU4339	60°8·3'	1°13·1'W	H	4
Wardon Hill	Dorset	ST6102	50°49·2'	2°32·8'W	H	194
Wardoughan	Northum	NY6365	54°58·9'	2°34·3'W	X	86
Wardour	Wilts	ST9227	51°2·8'	2°6·5'W	X	184
Wardour Castle	Wilts	ST9226	51°2·2'	2°6·5'W	X	184
War Down	Hants	SU7219	50°58·2'	0°58·1'W	X	197
Wardpark	D & G	NY1472	55°2·4'	3°20·3'W	X	85
Wardpark	N Lanak	NS7777	55°58·5'	3°57·8'W	T	64
Ward Point	Orkney	ND4798	58°52·2'	2°54·7'W	X	6,7
Wardrew Fm	Northum	NY6468	55°0·6'	2°33·3'W	FM	86
Wardrobes	Bucks	SP8101	51°42·3'	0°49·3'W	T	165
Wardropers	Essex	TQ6596	51°38·5'	0°23·5'E	X	167,177
Wards	D & G	NX4439	54°43·6'	4°24·9'W	X	83
Wards	Fife	NO4722	56°23·5'	2°51·1'W	X	54,59
Wards	Moray	NJ1265	57°40·2'	3°28·1'W	X	28
Wards	Moray	NJ1562	57°38·7'	3°25·0'W	X	28
Wards	Moray	NJ1656	57°35·4'	3°23·8'W	X	28
Wards	Orkney	ND3190	58°47·8'	3°11·2'W	X	7
Wards	W Dunb	NS4487	56°3·3'	4°29·9'W	X	57
Wardsbrook Fm	E Susx	TQ6829	51°2·4'	0°24·2'E	FM	188,199
Ward's Coombe	Bucks	SP9715	51°49·7'	0°35·1'W	X	165
Wardsend	Ches	SJ9282	53°20·3'	2°6·8'W	T	109
Ward's End	Lancs	SD6145	53°54·2'	2°35·2'W	X	102,103
Wards End	N Yks	SD6570	54°7·7'	2°31·7'W	X	97
Wards End	N Yks	SE1051	53°57·5'	1°50·4'W	X	104

Wardses	Cumbr	SD6996	54°21·8'	2°28·2'W	X	98
Ward's Fm	Essex	TL6303	51°42·3'	0°21·9'E	FM	167
Ward's Fm	Essex	TL8127	51°54·9'	0°38·3'E	FM	168
Ward's Fm	Herts	TL1127	51°56·1'	0°22·7'W	FM	166
Wards Fm	Lincs	TF2009	52°40·2'	0°13·1'W	FM	142
Wards Fm	Lincs	TF4231	52°51·7'	0°7·0'E	FM	131
Ward's Fm	Surrey	TQ3740	51°8·8'	0°2·1'W	FM	187
Ward's Fm	Worcs	SO9660	52°14·5'	2°3·1'W	FM	150
Wards Hill	Northum	NZ0896	55°15·7'	1°52·0'W	X	81
Ward's Hill	Warw	SP2447	52°7·5'	1°38·6'W	X	151
Ward's Hill	Warw	SP3097	52°34·4'	1°33·0'W	X	140
Ward's Ho	Lancs	SD4731	53°46·6'	2°47·8'W	X	102
Ward's Hurst Fm	Bucks	SP9715	51°49·7'	0°35·1'W	FM	165
Ward's Knob	Ches	SJ9472	53°14·9'	2°5·0'W	X	118
Wards of Afforsk	Aberd	NJ7862	57°39·1'	2°21·7'W	X	29,30
Wards of Goodie	Stir	NS6499	56°10·1'	4°11·0'W	X	57
Ward's Piece	Derby	SK1585	53°21·9'	1°46·1'W	X	110
Wards Resr	Black w Dar	SD6615	53°38·1'	2°30·4'W	W	109
Ward's Stone	Lancs	SD5958	54°1·2'	2°37·1'W	H	102
Ward's Stone Breast	Lancs	SD5858	54°1·2'	2°38·0'W	X	102
Wards, The	Glos	SO6604	51°44·3'	2°29·2'W	X	162
Wards, The	Orkney	HY3425	59°6·7'	3°8·7'W	H	6
Wards, The	Shetld	HU2656	60°17·5'	1°31·3'W	H	3
Wardstone Barrow	Dorset	SY7981	50°37·9'	2°17·4'W	A	194
Ward's Wood	Herts	TL1026	51°55·5'	0°23·6'W	F	166
Ward, The	Aberd	NJ5139	57°26·6'	2°48·5'W	X	29
Ward, The	Orkney	HY5607	58°57·1'	2°45·4'W	X	6
Ward, The	Pth & Kin	NO1044	56°35·0'	3°27·5'W	A	53
Ward, The	Renf	NS3259	55°48·0'	4°40·4'W	X	63
Ward, The	Shetld	HU6099	60°40·4'	0°53·6'W	X	1
Ward, The (Burnt Mound)	Orkney	HY5607	58°57·1'	2°45·4'W	A	6
Wardwarrow	Cumbr	NY0801	54°24·0'	3°24·6'W	X	89
Wardwell	Aberd	NJ6148	57°31·5'	2°38·6'W	X	29
Wardy Hill	Cambs	TL4782	52°25·2'	0°10·1'E	T	143
Ware	Devon	SX7466	50°29·1'	3°46·2'W	X	202
Ware	Devon	SY3291	50°43·1'	2°57·4'W	T	193
Ware	Herts	TL3614	51°48·7'	0°1·2'W	T	166
Ware	Kent	TR2760	51°17·8'	1°15·8'E	T	179
Ware Ball	Somer	SS8040	51°9·0'	3°42·6'W	X	181
Warebanks	Orkney	ND4798	58°52·2'	2°54·7'W	X	6,7
Ware Barton	Devon	SX8872	50°32·5'	3°34·5'W	X	192
Warebeth	Orkney	HY2308	58°57·4'	3°19·8'W	W	6,7
Ware Wood	Flint	SJ2667	53°11·9'	3°6·1'W	F	117
Ware Fm	Devon	SY1295	50°45·1'	3°14·5'W	FM	192,193
Ware Geo	Orkney	HY4820	59°4·1'	2°53·9'W	X	5,6
Ware Geos	Orkney	HY5422	59°5·2'	2°47·7'W	X	5,6
Wareham	Dorset	SY9287	50°41·2'	2°6·4'W	T	195
Wareham Channel	Dorset	SY9890	50°42·8'	2°1·3'W	W	195
Wareham Forest	Dorset	SY8792	50°43·9'	2°10·7'W	F	194
Wareham Forest	Dorset	SY8991	50°43·3'	2°9·0'W	F	195
Wareham Point	Devon	SX7440	50°15·0'	3°45·7'W	X	202
Wareham Wood	Corn	SX3877	50°34·5'	4°16·9'W	F	201
Warehead Fm	W Susx	SU9108	50°52·1'	0°42·0'W	FM	197
Warehill Br	N Yks	SE5263	54°3·9'	1°11·9'W	X	100
Warehorn	Kent	TR2567	51°21·7'	1°14·3'E	X	179
Warehorne	Kent	TQ9832	51°3·4'	0°49·9'E	T	189
Warehouse	Highld	ND3041	58°21·4'	3°11·3'W	X	11,12
Warehouse Hill	Highld	ND3041	58°21·4'	3°11·3'W	H	11,12
Wareland	Aberd	NJ8863	57°39·7'	2°11·6'W	X	30
Waren Burn	Northum	NU1530	55°34·1'	1°45·3'W	W	75
Warenford	Northum	NU1328	55°33·0'	1°47·2'W	T	75
Waren Mill	Northum	NU1434	55°36·2'	1°46·2'W	T	75
Warennes Wood	W Berks	SU6565	51°23·0'	1°3·6'W	X	175
Warenne, The	W Susx	TQ2914	50°54·9'	0°9·5'W	X	198
Warenton	Northum	NU1030	55°34·1'	1°50·1'W	X	75
Ware Park Fm	Herts	TL3314	51°48·8'	0°3·8'W	FM	166
Wares	Essex	TL6311	51°46·7'	0°22·2'E	X	167
Wareside	Herts	TL3915	51°49·2'	0°1·4'E	T	166
Waresley	Cambs	TL2554	52°10·4'	0°9·9'W	T	153
Waresley	Worcs	SO8470	52°19·9'	2°13·7'W	T	138
Waresley Park	Cambs	TL2454	52°10·4'	0°10·8'W	X	153
Waresley Wood	Cambs	TL2654	52°10·4'	0°9·0'W	F	153
Ware Street	Kent	TQ7956	51°16·7'	0°34·4'E	T	178,188
Warey Haven	Pemb	SM8011	51°45·5'	5°10·9'W	W	157
Warfield	Brackn	SU8772	51°26·6'	0°44·5'W	T	175
Warfield Hall	Brackn	SU8671	51°26·1'	0°45·4'W	X	175
Warfield Ho	Brackn	SU8871	51°26·1'	0°43·6'W	X	175
Warfield Park	Brackn	SU8870	51°25·6'	0°43·7'W	X	175
Warfleet	Devon	SX8750	50°20·6'	3°34·9'W	T	202
Warford Hall	Ches	SJ8176	53°17·1'	2°16·7'W	X	118
Warford Ho	Ches	SJ8078	53°18·2'	2°17·6'W	X	118
Wargate	Lincs	TF2330	52°51·4'	0°10·0'W	T	131
Wargery	Devon	SS2323	50°59·0'	4°30·9'W	X	190
Wargrave	St Hel	SJ5894	53°26·7'	2°37·5'W	T	108
Wargrave	Wok	SU7878	51°30·0'	0°52·2'W	T	175
Wargrave Manor	Wok	SU7879	51°30·5'	0°52·2'W	X	175
Warham	Devon	SS5314	50°54·6'	4°5·1'W	X	180
Warham	Heref	SO4839	52°3·1'	2°45·1'W	T	149,161
Warham	Norf	TF9441	52°56·1'	0°53·6'E	T	132
Warham Fm	E Yorks	SE7833	53°47·5'	0°48·5'W	FM	105,106
Warham Greens	Norf	TF9443	52°57·2'	0°53·7'E	X	132
Warham Hole	Norf	TF9846	52°58·7'	0°57·4'E	X	132
Warhams	W Susx	TQ0832	51°4·9'	0°27·1'W	X	187
Warham Salt Marshes	Norf	TF9444	52°57·7'	0°53·7'E	W	132
War Hill	Staffs	SJ7839	52°57·1'	2°19·2'W	H	127
Warhill	Tames	SJ9995	53°27·3'	2°0·5'W	T	109
Warhurst Fold Fm	Derby	SJ9993	53°26·3'	2°0·5'W	FM	109
Warie Gill	Shetld	HU2383	60°32·1'	1°34·3'W	W	3
Waring's Green	Sol	SP1274	52°22·1'	1°49·0'W	T	139
Warins Barn	Oxon	SP6129	51°57·6'	1°6·3'W	X	164,165
Warish Hall Fm	Essex	TL5622	51°52·7'	0°16·4'E	FM	167
Wark	Northum	NT8238	55°38·4'	2°16·7'W	T	74
Wark	Northum	NY8677	55°5·5'	2°12·7'W	T	87
Wark Common	Northum	NT8236	55°37·3'	2°16·7'W	T	74
Wark Common	Northum	NY8378	55°6·0'	2°15·6'W	X	86,87
Wark Common Fm	Northum	NT8136	55°37·3'	2°17·7'W	FM	74
Wark Fm	Aberd	NJ5209	57°10·4'	2°47·2'W	FM	37
Wark Forest	Northum	NY7377	55°5·5'	2°25·0'W	F	86,87
Warklaw Hill	C of Edin	NT1967	55°53·6'	3°17·3'W	X	65,66

Warkleigh	Devon	SS6422	50°59·1'	3°55·9'W	T	180
Warkleigh Ho	Devon	SS6522	50°59·1'	3°55·0'W	X	180
Warks Burn	Northum	NY8077	55°5·5'	2°18·4'W	W	86,87
Warksfield Head	Northum	NY8478	55°6·0'	2°14·6'W	X	86,87
Warks Haugh	Northum	NY8676	55°4·9'	2°12·7'W	X	87
Warkshaugh Bank	Northum	NY8677	55°5·5'	2°12·7'W	X	87
Warkswood	Northum	NY8478	55°6·0'	2°14·6'W	X	86,87
Warkton	Northnts	SP8979	52°24·3'	0°41·1'W	T	141
Wark Westcommon	Northum	NT8035	55°36·7'	2°18·6'W	X	74
Warkworth	Northnts	SP4840	52°3·6'	1°17·6'W	T	151
Warkworth	Northum	NU2406	55°21·1'	1°36·9'W	T	81
Warkworth Hall Fm	Northnts	SP4839	52°3·1'	1°17·6'W	FM	151
Warkworth Harbour	Northum	NU2604	55°20·0'	1°35·0'W	W	81
Warkworthlane Cott	Northum	NZ2792	55°13·5'	1°34·1'W	X	81
Warkworth Moor	Northum	NU2304	55°20·0'	1°37·8'W	X	81
Warlaby	N Yks	SE3491	54°19·0'	1°28·2'W	T	99
Warlaby Nook	N Yks	SE3590	54°18·5'	1°27·3'W	X	99
Warland	Cald	SD9420	53°40·8'	2°5·0'W	T	103
Warland	Durham	NZ2148	54°49·8'	1°40·0'W	X	88
Warland Drain	Cald	SD9621	53°41·4'	2°3·2'W	W	103
Warland Green	Durham	NZ2148	54°49·8'	1°40·0'W	X	88
Warland Resr	Cald	SD9520	53°40·8'	2°4·1'W	W	103
Warlands	I of W	SZ4188	50°41·6'	1°24·8'W	X	196
War Law	Northum	NY9453	54°52·6'	2°5·2'W	X	87
Warlawbank	Scot Bord	NT8361	55°50·8'	2°15·9'W	X	67
Warlaw Hill	S Lanak	NS7937	55°36·9'	3°54·8'W	H	71
Warldsend	Aberd	NJ8934	57°24·0'	2°10·5'W	X	30
Warle	Powys	SO0632	51°59·0'	3°21·7'W	X	160
Warleggan	Corn	SX1569	50°29·7'	4°36·1'W	T	201
Warleggan Down	Corn	SX1569	50°29·7'	4°36·1'W	X	201
Warleggan River or River Bedalder	Corn	SX1471	50°30·8'	4°37·0'W	W	200
Warleigh	Bath & NE Somer	ST7964	51°22·7'	2°17·7'W	T	172
Warleigh Ho	Devon	SX4561	50°25·9'	4°10·6'W	A	201
Warleigh Manor	Bath & NE Somer	ST7964	51°22·7'	2°17·7'W	X	172
Warleigh Point	Devon	SX4461	50°25·9'	4°11·4'W	X	201
Warleigh Wood	Bath & NE Somer	ST7963	51°22·2'	2°17·7'W	F	172
Warley	Essex	TQ5992	51°36·5'	0°18·2'E	T	177
Warleycross Hill	E Yorks	TA1250	53°56·3'	0°17·2'W	H	107
Warley Moor	Cald	SE0330	53°46·2'	1°56·9'W	X	104
Warley Moor Resr	Cald	SE0331	53°46·8'	1°56·9'W	W	104
Warley Town	Cald	SE0525	53°43·5'	1°55·0'W	T	104
Warley Wise	N Yks	SD9443	53°53·2'	2°5·1'W	X	103
Warley Woods	Sand	SP0186	52°28·6'	1°58·7'W	T	139
Warlies Park	Essex	TL4101	51°41·6'	0°2·8'E	X	167
Warlingham	Surrey	TQ3558	51°18·5'	0°3·4'W	T	187
Warlow Fm	Heref	SO4339	52°3·0'	2°49·5'W	FM	149,161
Warmanbie (Hotel)	D & G	NY1968	55°0·2'	3°15·6'W	X	85
Warmark Fm	Beds	SP9928	51°56·7'	0°33·2'W	FM	165
Warmbrook	Derby	SK2853	53°4·6'	1°34·5'W	T	119
Warm Burn	Aberd	NO5984	56°57·0'	2°40·0'W	W	44
War Memorial Park	Cov	SP3277	52°23·6'	1°31·4'W	X	140
Warmfield	Wakf	SE3720	53°40·7'	1°26·0'W	T	104
Warmhill Fm	Devon	SX8380	50°36·7'	3°38·8'W	FM	191
Warmingham	Ches	SJ7061	53°9·0'	2°26·5'W	T	118
Warminghurst	W Susx	TQ1116	50°56·2'	0°24·8'W	T	198
Warmington	Devon	SS4725	51°0·5'	4°10·5'W	X	180
Warmington	Northnts	TL0791	52°30·6'	0°25·0'W	T	142
Warmington	Warw	SP4147	52°7·4'	1°23·7'W	T	151
Warmington Grange	Northnts	TL0592	52°31·2'	0°26·7'W	X	142
Warminster	Wilts	ST8745	51°12·5'	2°10·8'W	T	183
Warminster Common	Wilts	ST8644	51°11·9'	2°11·6'W	T	183
Warminster Down	Wilts	ST8948	51°14·1'	2°9·1'W	X	184
Warminster Training Centre	Wilts	ST8846	51°13·0'	2°9·9'W	X	183
Warmlake	Kent	TQ8149	51°12·9'	0°35·9'E	T	188
Warmleigh Fm	Devon	SS2823	50°59·1'	4°26·7'W	FM	190
Warmley	S Glos	ST6773	51°27·5'	2°28·1'W	T	172
Warmleybury	Herts	TL3505	51°43·9'	0°2·3'W	A	166
Warmley Hill	S Glos	ST6573	51°27·5'	2°29·8'W	T	172
Warmley Tower	S Glos	ST6672	51°27·0'	2°29·0'W	T	172
Warmonds Hill	Northnts	SP9568	52°18·3'	0°36·0'W	T	153
Warmore	Devon	SS9425	51°1·1'	3°30·3'W	X	181
Warmscombe Fm	Devon	SS5345	51°11·4'	4°5·8'W	FM	180
Warmsworth	Donc	SE5400	53°29·9'	1°10·7'W	T	111
Warmwell	Dorset	SY7585	50°40·1'	2°20·8'W	T	194
Warmwell Down Barn	Dorset	SY7385	50°40·1'	2°22·5'W	X	194
Warmwell Fm	Dorset	SY9596	50°46·0'	2°3·9'W	FM	195
Warmwell Heath	Dorset	SY7586	50°40·6'	2°20·8'W	X	194
Warmwell Ho	Dorset	SY7585	50°40·1'	2°20·8'W	A	194
Warnborough Green	Hants	SU7252	51°16·0'	0°57·7'W	T	186
Warndon	Worcs	SO8756	52°12·4'	2°11·0'W	T	150
Warndon	Worcs	SO8856	52°12·4'	2°10·1'W	T	150
Warnell Fell	Cumbr	NY3341	54°45·8'	3°2·1'W	H	85
Warnell Hall	Cumbr	NY3541	54°45·8'	3°0·2'W	X	85
Warners	Oxon	SP4008	51°46·4'	1°24·8'W	X	164
Warners End	Herts	TL0307	51°45·4'	0°30·1'W	T	166
Warner's Fm	Cambs	TL3679	52°23·8'	0°0·3'E	FM	142
Warner's Fm	Essex	TL6915	51°48·7'	0°27·5'E	FM	167
Warners Fm	Hants	SU3119	50°58·4'	1°33·1'W	FM	185
War Ness	Orkney	HY5528	59°8·5'	2°46·7'W	X	5,6
Warnford	Hants	SU6223	51°0·4'	1°6·6'W	T	185
Warnford Court	N Yks	SE0086	54°16·4'	1°59·6'W	X	98
Warnford Park	Hants	SU6222	50°59·9'	1°6·6'W	X	185
Warnham	W Susx	TQ1533	51°5·3'	0°21·1'W	T	187
Warnham Court School	W Susx	TQ1533	51°5·3'	0°21·1'W	X	187
Warnham Lodge	W Susx	TQ1434	51°5·9'	0°21·8'W	X	187
Warnham Mill Pond	W Susx	TQ1732	51°4·7'	0°19·4'W	W	187
Warnicombe	Devon	SS9710	50°53·1'	3°27·5'W	X	192
Warningcamp	W Susx	TQ0307	50°51·4'	0°31·8'W	T	197
Warningcamp Hill	W Susx	TQ0407	50°51·4'	0°31·0'W	X	197
Warninglid	W Susx	TQ2526	51°1·4'	0°12·7'W	T	187,198
Warningore Fm	E Susx	TQ3713	50°54·2'	0°2·7'W	FM	198
Warningore Ho	E Susx	TQ3713	50°54·2'	0°2·7'W	X	198
Warningore Wood	E Susx	TQ3814	50°54·8'	0°1·8'W	F	198
Warnockland	E Ayr	NS4744	55°40·2'	4°25·5'W	X	70
Warnscale Bottom	Cumbr	NY1913	54°30·6'	3°14·6'W	X	89,90
Warp Fm	Lincs	SK8192	53°25·4'	0°46·5'W	FM	112
Warp Fm	Lincs	SK8296	53°27·5'	0°45·5'W	FM	112
Warping Drain	N Lincs	SE8112	53°36·1'	0°46·1'W	W	112
Warping Drain	N Lincs	SE8510	53°35·0'	0°42·5'W	W	112
Warping Drain	N Lincs	SK7398	53°28·7'	0°53·6'W	W	112
Warpings, The	N Lincs	SE7614	53°37·3'	0°50·6'W	X	112
Warp Mill	Notts	SK5450	53°2·9'	1°11·3'W	X	120
Warpsgrove	Oxon	SU6498	51°40·9'	1°4·1'W	T	164,165
Warra	Corn	SX3288	50°40·3'	4°22·3'W	X	190
Warracott	Devon	SX4282	50°37·2'	4°13·6'W	X	201
Warrage, The	Monm	SO4209	51°46·8'	2°50·1'W	X	161
Warr Br	Dorset	ST7314	50°55·7'	2°22·7'W	X	194
Warrells, The	Bucks	SP6716	51°50·5'	1°1·3'W	W	164,165
Warren	Angus	NO3848	56°37·4'	3°0·2'W	X	54
Warren	Cered	SN5550	52°8·0'	4°6·7'W	X	146
Warren	Ches	SJ8870	53°13·9'	2°10·4'W	T	118
Warren	Dorset	SY8591	50°43·3'	2°12·4'W	T	194
Warren	Pemb	SR9397	51°38·3'	4°59·1'W	T	158
Warren	Sheff	SK3597	53°28·4'	1°28·0'W	T	110,111
Warren Bank	Flint	SJ3263	53°9·8'	3°0·6'W	X	117
Warren Bank	Powys	SO1470	52°19·5'	3°15·3'W	X	136,148
Warren Bank	Powys	SO1678	52°23·9'	3°13·7'W	H	136,148
Warren Barn	Dorset	SY6986	50°40·6'	2°25·9'W	X	194
Warren Barn	S Glos	ST7980	51°31·3'	2°17·8'W	X	172
Warren Bay	Somer	ST0643	51°10·9'	3°20·3'W	W	181
Warren Bottom Copse	Hants	SU5554	51°17·2'	1°12·3'W	F	185
Warren Brook	Powys	SO1878	52°23·9'	3°11·9'W	W	136,148
Warrenby	Red & Cl	NZ5825	54°37·3'	1°5·7'W	T	93
Warren Corner	Hants	SU7227	51°2·5'	0°58·0'W	T	186,197
Warren Corner	Hants	SU8149	51°14·3'	0°50·0'W	T	186
Warren Cott	Suff	TL8979	52°22·8'	0°47·0'E	X	144
Warren Cottage	Devon	SX5346	50°18·0'	4°3·5'W	X	201
Warren Cove	Corn	SW8573	50°31·3'	5°1·6'W	W	200
Warrendale Fms	E Yorks	SE8350	53°56·6'	0°43·7'W	FM	106
Warrendale Plantn	E Yorks	SE8350	53°56·6'	0°43·7'W	F	106
Warrendale Plantn	E Yorks	SE8747	53°54·9'	0°40·1'W	F	106
Warren Dingle	Flint	SJ3262	53°9·3'	3°0·6'W	W	117
Warren Down	W Berks	SU3680	51°31·3'	1°28·5'W	X	174
Warren Down	Wilts	SU0451	51°15·7'	1°56·2'W	X	184
Warren Down	Wilts	SU0929	51°3·8'	1°51·9'W	X	184
Warren Down	W Susx	SU7512	50°54·4'	0°55·6'W	X	197
Warrener's Bottom	N Yks	SE2483	54°14·8'	1°37·5'W	F	99
Warreners Ho	Northum	NZ1888	55°11·4'	1°42·6'W	X	81
Warren Farm	Wok	SU8171	51°26·2'	0°49·7'W	FM	175
Warren Farm Cottages	E Yorks	SE7646	53°54·5'	0°50·2'W	X	105,106
Warren Fm	Bark & Dag	TQ4889	51°35·0'	0°8·6'E	FM	177
Warren Fm	Barns	SE3211	53°35·9'	1°30·6'W	FM	110,111
Warren Fm	Beds	TL0034	52°0·0'	0°32·2'W	FM	153
Warren Fm	Beds	TL0133	51°59·4'	0°31·3'W	FM	166
Warren Fm	Beds	TL0138	52°2·1'	0°31·3'W	FM	153
Warren Fm	Beds	TL0937	52°1·5'	0°24·3'W	FM	153
Warren Fm	Beds	TL2048	52°7·3'	0°14·4'W	FM	153
Warren Fm	Bucks	SP7932	51°59·1'	0°50·6'W	FM	152,165
Warren Fm	Bucks	SP8524	51°54·7'	0°45·5'W	FM	165
Warren Fm	Bucks	SU9995	51°38·9'	0°33·7'W	FM	165,176
Warren Fm	Bucks	TQ0190	51°36·2'	0°32·1'W	FM	176
Warren Fm	Derby	SK2118	52°45·8'	1°40·9'W	FM	128
Warren Fm	Devon	SS4903	50°48·6'	4°8·2'W	FM	191
Warren Fm	Essex	TL6807	51°44·4'	0°26·4'E	FM	167
Warren Fm	Essex	TL7807	51°44·2'	0°35·1'E	FM	167
Warren Fm	Essex	TL8016	51°49·0'	0°37·1'E	FM	168
Warren Fm	Essex	TM1215	51°47·8'	1°4·9'E	FM	168,169
Warren Fm	E Susx	TQ5222	50°58·9'	0°10·3'E	FM	199
Warren Fm	E Susx	TQ5535	51°5·8'	0°13·2'E	FM	188
Warren Fm	E Yorks	SE8451	53°57·1'	0°42·8'W	FM	106
Warren Fm	E Yorks	SE9562	54°2·9'	0°32·5'W	FM	101
Warren Fm	Glos	SO7909	51°47·0'	2°17·9'W	FM	162
Warren Fm	Glos	SP0231	51°58·9'	1°57·9'W	FM	150
Warren Fm	Glos	ST9095	51°39·5'	2°8·3'W	FM	163
Warren Fm	Gwyn	SH4359	53°6·6'	4°20·3'W	FM	115,123
Warren Fm	Hants	SU2633	51°6·0'	1°37·3'W	FM	184
Warren Fm	Hants	SU2822	51°0·0'	1°35·7'W	FM	184
Warren Fm	Hants	SU3821	50°59·5'	1°27·1'W	FM	185
Warren Fm	Hants	SU5142	51°10·7'	1°15·8'W	FM	185
Warren Fm	Hants	SU5225	51°1·5'	1°15·1'W	FM	185
Warren Fm	Hants	SU6940	51°9·5'	1°0·4'W	FM	186
Warren Fm	Hants	SU7228	51°3·0'	0°58·0'W	FM	186,197
Warren Fm	Hants	SZ4197	50°46·5'	1°24·7'W	FM	196
Warren Fm	Herts	TL2005	51°44·1'	0°15·3'W	FM	166
Warren Fm	Herts	TL2112	51°47·8'	0°14·3'W	FM	166
Warren Fm	Herts	TL4519	51°51·3'	0°6·7'E	FM	167
Warren Fm	I of W	SZ3185	50°40·1'	1°33·3'W	FM	196
Warren Fm	Kent	TR0348	51°11·9'	0°54·7'E	FM	179,189
Warren Fm	Kent	TR0725	50°59·4'	0°57·4'E	FM	189
Warren Fm	Leeds	SE2644	53°53·7'	1°35·8'W	FM	104
Warren Fm	Leeds	SE4332	53°47·2'	1°20·4'W	FM	105
Warren Fm	Leic	SK4729	52°51·6'	1°17·7'W	FM	129
Warren Fm	Leic	SP5583	52°26·8'	1°11·0'W	FM	140
Warren Fm	Leic	SP6287	52°28·9'	1°4·8'W	FM	140
Warren Fm	Lincs	SE8500	53°29·6'	0°42·7'W	FM	112
Warren Fm	Lincs	TF0217	52°44·7'	0°28·9'W	FM	130
Warren Fm	Lincs	TF1879	53°17·9'	0°13·4'W	FM	122
Warren Fm	Lincs	TF2686	53°21·6'	0°6·0'W	FM	113,122
Warren Fm	Lincs	TF4396	53°26·7'	0°9·6'E	FM	113
Warren Fm	Merton	TQ2171	51°25·7'	0°15·2'W	FM	176
Warren Fm	Norf	TF6621	52°45·9'	0°28·0'E	FM	132
Warren Fm	Norf	TF7815	52°42·4'	0°38·5'E	FM	132
Warren Fm	Norf	TF7901	52°34·9'	0°38·9'E	FM	144
Warren Fm	Norf	TG1040	52°55·2'	1°7·8'E	FM	133
Warren Fm	Norf	TG4524	52°45·7'	1°38·3'E	FM	134
Warren Fm	Norf	TM0299	52°33·3'	0°59·2'E	FM	144
Warren Fm	Northnts	SP5333	51°59·8'	1°13·3'W	FM	152
Warren Fm	Northnts	SP6042	52°4·6'	1°7·1'W	FM	152
Warren Fm	Notts	SK5663	53°9·9'	1°9·3'W	FM	120
Warren Fm	N Yks	NZ6209	54°28·6'	1°2·2'W	FM	94
Warren Fm	N Yks	SE3361	54°2·9'	1°29·3'W	FM	99
Warren Fm	N Yks	SE8491	54°18·7'	0°42·1'W	FM	94,100
Warren Fm	Oxon	SP2218	51°51·8'	1°40·4'W	FM	163
Warren Fm	Oxon	SP5907	51°45·7'	1°8·3'W	FM	164
Warren Fm	Oxon	SP6013	51°49·0'	1°7·4'W	FM	164,165
Warren Fm	Oxon	SP6233	51°59·8'	1°5·4'W	FM	152,165
Warren Fm	Oxon	SU5196	51°39·9'	1°15·4'W	FM	164
Warren Fm	Rut	SK8914	52°43·2'	0°40·5'W	FM	130
Warren Fm	Shrops	SJ6530	52°52·2'	2°30·8'W	FM	127
Warren Fm	Somer	SS7940	51°9·0'	3°43·4'W	FM	180
Warren Fm	Somer	ST0543	51°10·9'	3°21·2'W	FM	181
Warren Fm	Somer	ST2956	51°18·2'	3°0·7'W	FM	182
Warren Fm	Somer	ST4954	51°17·2'	2°43·5'W	FM	182,183
Warren Fm	Somer	ST6146	51°12·9'	2°33·1'W	FM	183
Warren Fm	Stock on T	NZ4325	54°37·3'	1°19·6'W	FM	93
Warren Fm	Suff	TL7069	52°17·8'	0°30·0'E	FM	154
Warren Fm	Suff	TL9962	52°13·4'	0°55·2'E	FM	155
Warren Fm	Surrey	TQ1152	51°15·6'	0°24·2'W	FM	187
Warren Fm	Surrey	TQ1853	51°16·1'	0°18·1'W	FM	187
Warren Fm	V of Glam	ST0475	51°28·2'	3°22·5'W	FM	170
Warren Fm	Warw	SP2172	52°21·0'	1°41·1'W	FM	139
Warren Fm	W Berks	SU3581	51°31·8'	1°29·3'W	FM	
Warren Fm	W Berks	SU3581	51°31·8'	1°29·3'W	FM	174
Warren Fm	W Berks	SU5481	51°31·7'	1°12·9'W	FM	174
Warren Fm	W Berks	SU5681	51°31·7'	1°11·2'W	FM	174
Warren Fm	Wilts	SU2172	51°27·0'	1°41·5'W	FM	174
Warren Fm	W Susx	TQ3929	51°2·8'	0°0·6'W	FM	187,198
Warrengate Fm	Herts	TL2302	51°42·4'	0°12·8'W	FM	166
Warrengate Fm	Herts	TL2713	51°48·3'	0°9·1'W	FM	166
Warren Gutter	Corn	SS2011	50°52·5'	4°33·1'W	X	190
Warren Hall	Donc	SE6417	53°39·0'	1°1·5'W	X	111
Warren Hall	Flint	SJ3262	53°9·3'	3°0·6'W	X	117
Warrenhall	Orkney	HY5332	59°10·6'	2°48·9'W	X	5,6
Warren Heath	Dorset	SY8491	50°43·3'	2°13·2'W	X	194
Warren Heath	Hants	SU7759	51°19·7'	0°53·7'W	F	175,186
Warren Heath	Suff	TM2042	52°2·2'	1°12·9'E	T	169
Warren Hill	Cambs	TL1068	52°18·2'	0°22·8'W	X	153
Warren Hill	Cambs	TL6563	52°14·7'	0°25·4'E	X	154
Warren Hill	Donc	SE6308	53°34·1'	1°2·5'W	X	111
Warren Hill	Dorset	SY5299	50°47·5'	2°40·5'W	H	194
Warren Hill	E Susx	TV5897	50°45·3'	0°14·8'E	X	199
Warren Hill	Hants	SU7829	51°3·5'	0°52·8'W	X	186,197
Warren Hill	Leic	SK5211	52°41·9'	1°13·4'W	X	129
Warren Hill	Lincs	TF1879	53°17·9'	0°13·4'W	X	122
Warren Hill	Norf	TF7301	52°35·0'	0°33·6'E	X	143
Warren Hill	Northnts	SP7680	52°25·0'	0°52·6'W	X	141
Warren Hill	Notts	SK6255	53°5·6'	1°4·0'W	X	120
Warren Hill	Oxon	SU6485	51°33·8'	1°4·2'W	X	175
Warren Hill	Oxon	SU6588	51°35·5'	1°3·3'W	X	175
Warren Hill	Oxon	SU7394	51°38·6'	0°56·3'W	X	175
Warren Hill	Powys	SO1477	52°23·3'	3°15·4'W	H	136,148
Warrenhill	S Lanak	NS9438	55°37·7'	3°40·6'W	X	71,72
Warren Hill	Somer	ST4010	50°53·4'	2°50·8'W	X	193
Warren Hill	Somer	ST6426	51°2·2'	2°30·4'W	X	183
Warren Hill	Staffs	SJ9715	52°44·2'	2°2·3'W	H	127
Warren Hill	Wilts	SU2547	51°13·5'	1°38·1'W	X	184
Warren Hill Copse	Devon	SY1793	50°44·1'	3°10·2'W	F	192,193
Warren Hill Fm	E Yorks	SE8834	53°47·9'	0°39·4'W	FM	106
Warren Hill Fm	Northnts	SP7680	52°25·0'	0°52·6'W	FM	141
Warrenhill Fm	Suff	TM1477	52°21·2'	1°8·9'E	FM	144,156
Warrenhill Ho	Suff	TL6763	52°14·6'	0°27·2'E	X	154
Warrenhill Pin Covert	Suff	TL8068	52°17·1'	0°38·7'E	F	155
Warren Hills	Leic	SK4514	52°43·5'	1°19·6'W	X	129
Warren Hills	Norf	TM3697	52°31·4'	1°29·1'E	X	134
Warren Hills	Suff	TM1478	52°21·7'	1°9·0'E	X	144,156
Warren Ho	Bucks	TQ0283	51°32·4'	0°31·4'W	X	176
Warren Ho	Cumbr	NY5461	54°56·7'	2°42·7'W	X	86
Warren Ho	Devon	SX8950	50°20·6'	3°33·2'W	X	202
Warren Ho	Herts	TL3108	51°45·5'	0°5·7'W	X	166
Warren Ho	King	TQ2070	51°25·2'	0°16·1'W	X	176
Warren Ho	Norf	TF6710	52°39·9'	0°28·6'E	X	132,143
Warren Ho	Norf	TG1625	52°47·0'	1°12·6'E	X	133
Warren Ho	Norf	TL7493	52°30·7'	0°34·2'E	X	143
Warren Ho	Northum	NY7062	54°57·4'	2°27·7'W	X	86,87
Warren Ho	N Som	ST4765	51°23·1'	2°45·3'W	X	171,172,182
Warren Ho	N Yks	SD9889	54°18·0'	2°1·4'W	X	98
Warren Ho	N Yks	SE1882	54°14·2'	1°43·0'W	X	99
Warren Ho	N Yks	SE2265	54°5·1'	1°39·4'W	X	99
Warren Ho	N Yks	SE2892	54°19·6'	1°33·7'W	X	99
Warren Ho	N Yks	SE6073	54°9·2'	1°4·5'W	X	100
Warren Ho	N Yks	SE8784	54°14·9'	0°39·5'W	X	101
Warren Ho	N Yks	SE9875	54°9·9'	0°29·5'W	X	101
Warren Ho	Red & Cl	NZ7316	54°32·3'	0°51·9'W	X	94
Warren Ho	Shrops	SJ5537	52°56·0'	2°39·8'W	X	126
Warren Ho	Somer	ST4558	51°19·3'	2°47·0'W	X	172,182
Warren Ho	Suff	TM5180	52°21·9'	1°41·6'E	X	156
Warren Ho	Warw	SK2703	52°37·7'	1°35·7'W	X	140
Warren Ho Fm	Leeds	SE2141	53°52·1'	1°40·4'W	FM	104
Warren Ho, The	Essex	TL8006	51°43·7'	0°36·8'E	X	168
Warren House Fm	Donc	SE5113	53°36·9'	1°13·3'W	FM	111
Warren House Fm	Donc	SK6398	53°28·7'	1°2·6'W	FM	111
Warren House Fm	E Yorks	SE9247	53°54·9'	0°35·5'W	FM	106
Warren House Fm	N Yks	SE4640	53°51·5'	1°17·6'W	FM	105
Warren House Fm	York	SE6544	53°53·5'	1°0·2'W	FM	105,106
Warren House Inn	Devon	SX6780	50°36·5'	3°52·4'W	X	191
Warren Houses	Lincs	TF0254	53°4·6'	0°28·2'W	X	121
Warren Knoll	Beds	SP9724	51°54·6'	0°35·0'W	X	165
Warren Lodge	Derby	SK2574	53°16·0'	1°37·1'W	X	119
Warren Lodge	Norf	TL7594	52°31·2'	0°35·2'E	X	143
Warren Lodge	Suff	TL7580	52°23·6'	0°34·7'E	X	143
Warren Lodge	Suff	TL8064	52°14·9'	0°38·6'E	X	155
Warren Lodge	W Berks	SU4664	51°22·6'	1°20·0'W	X	174
Warren Lodge	Wok	SU7964	51°22·4'	0°51·5'W	X	175,186
Warren Mere	Surrey	SU9140	51°9·3'	0°41·5'W	X	186
Warren Moor	N Yks	NZ6208	54°28·1'	1°2·2'W	X	94
Warren Mountain	Flint	SJ3163	53°9·8'	3°1·5'W	X	117
Warren Parc	Powys	SH7701	52°35·8'	3°48·6'W	X	135
Warren Park Fm	Dorset	SU1211	50°54·1'	1°49·4'W	FM	195
Warren Park Fm	Essex	TL7118	51°50·3'	0°29·3'E	FM	167
Warren Place	Suff	TL6663	52°14·6'	0°26·3'E	X	154
Warren Plantation	Powys	SO1861	52°14·7'	3°11·7'W	F	148
Warren Plantn	Cumbr	NY4046	54°48·6'	2°55·6'W	F	85
Warren Point	C of Plym	SX4460	50°25·4'	4°11·4'W	X	201
Warren Point	Devon	SX5347	50°18·5'	4°3·5'W	X	201
Warren Point	Devon	SX5550	50°20·2'	4°1·9'W	X	202

Warren Point	Devon	SX6444	50°17·1'	3°54·2'W	X	202
Warren Point	Devon	SX6642	50°16·0'	3°52·4'W	X	202
Warren Point	Somer	SS9846	51°12·5'	3°27·2'W	X	181
Warren Pond	Surrey	SU9046	51°12·6'	0°42·3'W	W	186
Warren Row	Win & Maid	SU8180	51°31·0'	0°49·6'W	T	175
Warrens	Hants	SU2715	50°56·3'	1°36·6'W	X	184
Warrens	Herts	TL4517	51°50·2'	0°6·7'E	X	167
Warren's Cross	Devon	SX5173	50°32·5'	4°5·8'W	X	191,201
Warren's Cross Fm	Glos	SU1999	51°41·6'	1°43·1'W	FM	163
Warren's Fm	Essex	TM1123	51°52·2'	1°4·3'E	FM	168,169
Warren's Fm	Hants	SU2714	50°55·7'	1°36·6'W	FM	195
Warrens Fm	Monm	SO5006	51°45·3'	2°43·1'W	FM	162
Warren's Green	Herts	TL2628	51°56·4'	0°9·6'W	T	166
Warrens, The	E Yorks	SE9432	53°46·8'	0°34·0'W	X	106
Warren Street	Kent	TQ9253	51°14·9'	0°45·5'E	T	189
Warren, The	Caer	ST1685	51°33·7'	3°12·3'W	F	171
Warren,The	Devon	SS2225	51°0·1'	4°31·8'W	X	190
Warren, The	Devon	SS5938	51°7·7'	4°0·5'W	X	180
Warren, The	Devon	SX5346	50°18·0'	4°3·5'W	X	201
Warren, The	Devon	SX7036	50°12·8'	3°49·0'W	X	202
Warren, The	Devon	SY0488	50°41·3'	3°21·2'W	X	192
Warren, The	Devon	SY0783	50°38·6'	3°18·5'W	X	192
Warren, The	Donc	SK6299	53°29·3'	1°3·5'W	X	111
Warren, The	Dorset	SY7880	50°37·4'	2°18·3'W	X	194
Warren, The	Essex	TL4300	51°41·1'	0°4·5'E	F	167
Warren, The	Essex	TQ4095	51°38·4'	0°1·8'E	F	167,177
Warren, The	E Susx	TQ4021	50°58·5'	0°0·0'E	X	198
Warren, The	E Susx	TQ5536	51°6·4'	0°13·2'E	F	188
Warren, The	Flint	SJ1084	53°21·0'	3°20·7'W	X	116
Warren, The	Glos	SO5803	51°43·7'	2°36·1'W	X	162
Warren, The	Glos	SP0506	51°45·4'	1°55·3'W	X	163
Warren, The	Glos	SP1430	51°58·3'	1°47·4'W	F	151
Warren, The	Gwyn	SH3129	52°50·2'	4°30·1'W	X	123
Warren, The	Hants	SU7228	51°3·0'	0°58·0'W	F	186,197
Warren, The	Hants	SU7735	51°6·8'	0°53·6'W	X	186
Warren, The	Heref	SO3168	52°18·6'	3°0·3'W	H	137,148
Warren, The	Herts	TL4023	51°53·5'	0°2·5'E	X	167
Warren, The	Kent	TR2437	51°5·5'	1°12·3'E	X	179,189
Warren, The	Monm	ST4197	51°40·4'	2°50·8'W	X	171
Warren, The	Norf	TF9017	52°43·3'	0°49·2'E	X	132
Warren, The	Norf	TG2440	52°54·9'	1°20·3'E	X	133
Warren, The	N Som	ST4271	51°26·3'	2°49·7'W	X	171,172
Warren, The	Oxon	SP3522	51°54·0'	1°29·1'W	F	164
Warren, The	Oxon	SU3287	51°35·1'	1°31·9'W	X	174
Warren, The	Oxon	SU4383	51°32·9'	1°22·4'W	F	174
Warren, The	Pemb	SM8834	51°58·1'	5°4·8'W	X	157
Warren, The	Powys	SJ0215	52°43·7'	3°26·7'W	X	125
Warren, The	Powys	SJ1911	52°41·7'	3°11·5'W	F	125
Warren, The	Powys	SN9746	52°6·4'	3°29·8'W	X	147
Warren, The	Staffs	SK0625	52°49·6'	1°54·3'W	X	128
Warren, The	Suff	TM4767	52°15·0'	1°37·5'E	F	156
Warren, The	Suff	TM5280	52°21·8'	1°42·5'E	X	156
Warren, The	Warw	SP3440	52°3·7'	1°29·8'W	F	151
Warren, The	Wilts	ST8632	51°5·5'	2°11·6'W	X	183
Warren, The	Wilts	ST9568	51°24·9'	2°3·9'W	F	173
Warren, The	Wilts	SU0051	51°15·7'	1°59·6'W	F	184
Warren, The	W Susx	TQ2209	50°52·3'	0°15·6'W	X	198
Warren, The	W Susx	TQ2428	51°2·5'	0°13·5'W	X	187,198
Warren, The	W Susx	TQ3232	51°4·6'	0°6·6'W	F	187
Warren Wood	Aberd	NO8096	57°3·5'	2°19·3'W	F	38,45
Warren Wood	Beds	TL0837	52°1·5'	0°25·2'W	F	153
Warren Wood	Hants	SU4335	51°7·0'	1°22·8'W	F	185
Warren Wood	Kent	TQ8453	51°15·0'	0°38·6'E	F	188
Warren Wood	Lincs	SK8288	53°23·2'	0°45·6'W	F	112,121
Warren Wood	Lincs	TF1388	53°22·8'	0°17·7'W	F	113,121
Warren Wood	Norf	TL8485	52°26·1'	0°42·8'E	F	144
Warren Wood	N Yks	SE4891	54°19·0'	1°15·3'W	F	100
Warren Wood	W Susx	TQ2429	51°3·0'	0°13·5'W	F	187,198
Warrenwood Park	Herts	TL2606	51°44·5'	0°10·1'W	X	166
Warridge Lodge Fm	Worcs	SO9370	52°19·9'	2°5·8'W	FM	139
Warrilowhead Fm	Ches	SJ9573	53°15·5'	2°4·1'W	FM	118
Warriner's Wood	Cumbr	SD4990	54°18·4'	2°46·6'W	F	97
Warrington	Mil Key	SP8954	52°10·9'	0°41·5'W	T	152
Warrington	Warr	SJ6088	53°23·5'	2°35·7'W	T	109
Warrington Lodge	Mil Key	SP8855	52°11·4'	0°42·4'W	X	152
Warriors Lodge Fm	Warw	SP2572	52°21·0'	1°37·6'W	FM	140
Warrior Stone, The	Northum	NZ0474	55°3·9'	1°55·8'W	A	87
Warriston	C of Edin	NT1668	55°54·1'	3°20·2'W	X	65,66
Warriston	C of Edin	NT2575	55°58·0'	3°11·7'W	T	66
Warrix	N Ayr	NS3337	55°36·1'	4°38·6'W	X	70
Warroch East Burn	Pth & Kin	NO0506	56°14·5'	3°31·5'W	W	58
Warroch Hill	Pth & Kin	NO0405	56°13·9'	3°32·5'W	H	58
Warroch Ho	Pth & Kin	NO0604	56°13·4'	3°30·5'W	X	58
Warroch West Burn	Pth & Kin	NO0405	56°13·9'	3°32·5'W	W	58
Warr's Fm	E Susx	TQ3922	50°59·1'	0°0·8'W	FM	198
Warrs Fm	Northnts	SP6248	52°7·8'	1°5·3'W	FM	152
Warry's Plantations	Dorset	ST6909	50°53·0'	2°26·1'W	F	194
Warsash	Hants	SU4906	50°51·3'	1°17·8'W	T	196
Warse	Highld	ND3372	58°38·1'	3°8·8'W	T	7,12
Warsett	Orkney	HY4629	59°8·9'	2°56·2'W	X	5,6
Warsetter	Orkney	HY6237	59°13·3'	2°39·5'W	X	5
Warsett Hill	Red & Cl	NZ6921	54°35·0'	0°55·5'W	H	94
Warsill	N Yks	SE2265	54°5·1'	1°39·4'W	T	99
Warsill Hall Fm	N Yks	SE2365	54°5·1'	1°38·5'W	FM	99
Warslow	Staffs	SK0858	53°7·4'	1°52·4'W	T	119
Warslow Brook	Staffs	SK0757	53°6·8'	1°53·3'W	W	119
Warslow Hall	Staffs	SK0959	53°7·9'	1°51·5'W	X	119
Warsman Head	N Yks	SE9294	54°20·2'	0°34·7'W	X	94,101
Warson	Devon	SX4885	50°38·9'	4°8·6'W	X	191,201
Warsop Cottage Fm	Notts	SK5368	53°12·6'	1°12·0'W	FM	120
Warsop Vale	Notts	SK5467	53°12·1'	1°11·1'W	T	120
Warsop Wood	Notts	SK5569	53°13·1'	1°10·2'W	F	120
Warstock	Birm	SP0979	52°24·8'	1°51·7'W	T	139
Warstone	Staffs	SJ9705	52°38·8'	2°2·3'W	T	127,139
War Stone	Staffs	SO8392	52°31·8'	2°14·6'W	A	138
Warstone Fm	Worcs	SO9881	52°25·9'	2°1·4'W	FM	139
Wart	Shetld	HU4939	60°8·2'	1°6·6'W	X	4
Wartches	Cumbr	NY4620	54°34·6'	2°49·7'W	X	90
Warter	E Yorks	SE8650	53°56·6'	0°41·0'W	T	106
Warter Farm Ho	E Yorks	SE9050	53°56·5'	0°37·3'W	X	106
Warter Priory	E Yorks	SE8549	53°56·0'	0°41·9'W	X	106
Warter Wold	E Yorks	SE8751	53°57·1'	0°40·0'W	X	106
Warth	Cumbr	SD5584	54°15·2'	2°41·0'W	X	97
Warth	Orkney	HY2721	59°4·5'	3°15·9'W	X	6
Warthermarske	N Yks	SE2078	54°12·1'	1°41·2'W	T	99
Warth Hill	Cumbr	SD5684	54°15·2'	2°40·1'W	H	97
Warth Hill	Highld	ND3769	58°36·5'	3°4·6'W	H	12
Warth Ho	N Yks	SD6872	54°8·8'	2°29·0'W	X	98
Warthill	N Yks	SE6755	53°59·4'	0°58·3'W	X	105,106
Warthill	Orkney	HY5201	58°53·9'	2°49·5'W	X	6,7
Wart Hill	Shrops	SO4084	52°27·3'	2°52·6'W	H	137
Warthill Common	N Yks	SE6756	54°0·0'	0°58·3'W	X	105,106
Warthill Fm	Shrops	SO5677	52°23·6'	2°38·4'W	FM	137,138
Warthill Ho	Aberd	NJ7131	57°22·4'	2°28·5'W	X	29
Warth Lodge	Northnts	SP7679	52°24·5'	0°52·6'W	X	141
Wart Holm	Orkney	HY4838	59°13·8'	2°54·2'W	X	5
Warth's Hundred Fm	Cambs	TL4486	52°27·4'	0°7·6'E	FM	142,143
Warth, The	Glos	SO7204	51°44·3'	2°23·9'W	X	162
Wartle	Aberd	NJ5404	57°7·7'	2°45·1'W	X	37
Wartle Moss	Aberd	NJ7232	57°22·9'	2°27·5'W	X	29
Wartling	E Susx	TQ6509	50°51·6'	0°21·1'E	T	199
Wartling Wood	E Susx	TQ6510	50°52·2'	0°21·1'E	F	199
Wartnaby	Leic	SK7123	52°48·2'	0°56·4'W	T	129
Warton	Lancs	SD4128	53°44·9'	2°53·3'W	T	102
Warton	Lancs	SD5072	54°8·7'	2°45·5'W	T	97
Warton	Northum	NU0002	55°19·0'	1°59·6'W	T	81
Warton	Warw	SK2803	52°37·7'	1°34·8'W	T	140
Warton Aerodrome	Lancs	SD4127	53°44·4'	2°53·3'W	X	102
Warton Bank	Lancs	SD4027	53°44·4'	2°54·2'W	T	102
Warton Crag	Lancs	SD4973	54°9·3'	2°46·4'W	X	97
Warton Grange	Staffs	SJ7622	52°47·9'	2°21·0'W	X	127
Warton Hall	Lancs	SD3828	53°44·9'	2°56·0'W	X	102
Warton Sands	Lancs	SD4572	54°8·7'	2°50·1'W	X	97
Wart, The	Orkney	HY6237	59°13·3'	2°39·5'W	X	5
Wart, The	Orkney	ND4393	58°49·5'	2°58·7'W	H	7
Wart, The	Shetld	HU4323	59°59·6'	1°13·3'W	X	4
Warwick	Warw	SP2865	52°17·2'	1°35·0'W	T	151
Warwick Bridge	Cumbr	NY4756	54°54·0'	2°49·2'W	T	86
Warwickdale	N Ayr	NS3639	55°37·3'	4°35·8'W	X	70
Warwick Fm	Cambs	TF3600	52°35·1'	0°0·8'E	FM	142
Warwick Hall	Cumbr	NY1343	54°46·7'	3°20·7'W	X	85
Warwick Hall	Cumbr	NY4656	54°54·0'	2°50·1'W	X	86
Warwickhill	N Ayr	NS3739	55°37·3'	4°34·9'W	X	70
Warwick Ho	E Yorks	SE8126	53°43·7'	0°45·9'W	X	106
Warwick Holme	Cumbr	NY4458	54°55·1'	2°52·0'W	X	85
Warwick Mains	N Ayr	NS3739	55°37·3'	4°34·9'W	X	70
Warwick Moor Wood	Cumbr	NY4555	54°53·5'	2°51·0'W	F	86
Warwick-on-Eden	Cumbr	NY4656	54°54·0'	2°50·1'W	T	86
Warwick Resr	Wal F	TQ3488	51°34·7'	0°3·6'W	W	176,177
Warwicks	E Yorks	SE8227	53°44·2'	0°45·0'W	X	106
Warwick Slade	Hants	SU2706	50°51·4'	1°36·6'W	X	195
Warwicksland	Cumbr	NY4477	55°5·3'	2°52·2'W	T	85
Warwick Wold	Surrey	TQ3152	51°15·4'	0°7·0'W	T	187
Warylip	Aberd	NJ6464	57°40·1'	2°35·7'W	X	29
Wasbister	Orkney	HY2814	59°0·7'	3°14·7'W	X	6
Wasbister	Orkney	HY3932	59°10·5'	3°3·5'W	T	6
Wasbister	Orkney	ND4490	58°47·9'	2°57·7'W	X	7
Wasdale	Orkney	HY3414	59°0·7'	3°8·5'W	X	6
Wasdale Beck	Cumbr	NY5608	54°28·2'	2°40·3'W	W	90
Wasdale Fell	Cumbr	NY1909	54°28·4'	3°14·6'W	X	89,90
Wasdale Hall	Cumbr	NY1404	54°25·7'	3°19·1'W	X	89
Wasdale Head	Cumbr	NY1808	54°27·9'	3°15·5'W	T	89,90
Wasdale Head	Cumbr	NY5408	54°28·2'	2°42·2'W	X	90
Wasdale Head Hall Fm	Cumbr	NY1806	54°26·8'	3°15·5'W	FM	89,90
Wasdale Pike	Cumbr	NY5308	54°28·2'	2°43·1'W	H	90
Waseley Hill	Worcs	SO9777	52°23·7'	2°2·2'W	H	139
Wash	Derby	SK0682	53°20·3'	1°54·2'W	T	110
Wash	Devon	SX7665	50°28·5'	3°44·5'W	X	202
Washall Green	Herts	TL4430	51°57·2'	0°6·1'E	T	167
Washaway	Corn	SX0369	50°29·5'	4°46·3'W	T	200
Washbattle Br	Somer	ST0528	51°2·8'	3°20·9'W	X	181
Wash Beck	Durham	NZ1029	54°39·6'	1°50·3'W	X	92
Wash Beck	N Yks	NZ8704	54°25·7'	0°39·1'W	W	94
Wash Beck	N Yks	NZ9007	54°27·3'	0°36·3'W	W	94
Washbeerhayes Fm	Devon	ST0102	50°48·8'	3°23·9'W	FM	192
Washbourne	Devon	SX7954	50°22·6'	3°41·7'W	T	202
Wash Br	Notts	SK6547	53°1·2'	1°1·5'W	X	129
Wash Brook	Derby	SK1650	53°3·1'	1°45·3'W	W	119
Washbrook	Somer	ST4250	51°15·0'	2°49·5'W	T	182
Washbrook	Suff	TM1142	52°2·4'	1°5·0'E	T	155,169
Washbrook Fm	Suff	TM4178	52°21·0'	1°32·7'E	FM	156
Washbrooks Fm	W Susx	TQ2716	50°56·0'	0°11·2'W	FM	198
Washbrook Street	Suff	TM1142	52°2·4'	1°5·0'E	T	155,169
Wash Common	W Berks	SU4564	51°22·6'	1°20·8'W	T	174
Wash Common Fm	W Berks	SU4564	51°22·6'	1°20·8'W	FM	174
Wash Dale	Staffs	SJ9036	52°55·5'	2°8·5'W	X	127
Wash Dike	Lincs	TF1445	52°59·6'	0°17·7'W	X	130
Wash Dub Wood	Lancs	SD5574	54°9·8'	2°40·9'W	F	97
Wash Dyke	Norf	TF5016	52°43·5'	0°13·7'E	T	131
Washdyke Br	Lincs	TF4779	53°17·5'	0°12·7'E	X	122
Washdyke Fm	Lincs	TF2334	52°53·6'	0°9·9'W	FM	131
Washdyke Plantn	E Yorks	SE8838	53°50·1'	0°39·4'W	F	106
Washenden Manor	Kent	TQ8638	51°6·9'	0°39·8'E	X	189
Washer Gill	N Yks	SD7995	54°21·3'	2°19·0'W	W	98
Washers Pit	Dorset	ST8916	50°56·8'	2°9·0'W	X	184
Washer's Wood	Beds	SP9931	51°58·3'	0°33·1'W	F	165
Washerwall	Staffs	SJ9347	53°1·5'	2°5·9'W	T	118
Washer Willy's	Fife	NO4427	56°26·2'	2°54·0'W	X	54,59
Washfield	Devon	SS9315	50°55·7'	3°31·0'W	T	181
Wash Fm	Ches	SJ7376	53°17·1'	2°23·9'W	FM	118
Wash Fm	Essex	TL9127	51°54·7'	0°47·0'E	FM	168
Wash Fm	Norf	TF5703	52°36·4'	0°19·5'E	FM	143
Wash Fm	Suff	TM2967	52°15·4'	1°21·7'E	FM	156
Washfold	N Yks	NY8602	54°25·0'	2°12·5'W	X	91,92
Washfold	N Yks	NZ0502	54°25·0'	1°55·0'W	T	92
Washfold Fm	N Yks	SE0992	54°19·7'	1°51·3'W	FM	99
Washfold Pot	N Yks	SD7776	54°11·0'	2°20·7'W	X	98
Washford	Somer	ST0441	51°9·8'	3°22·0'W	T	181
Washford	Worcs	SP0765	52°17·2'	1°53·4'W	T	150
Washford Cross	Somer	ST0540	51°9·3'	3°21·1'W	X	181
Washford Moor	Devon	SS8111	50°53·4'	3°41·1'W	X	191
Washford Pyne	Devon	SS8111	50°53·4'	3°41·1'W	T	191
Washford River	Somer	ST0541	51°9·9'	3°21·1'W	W	181
Wash Hall	Ches	SJ3768	53°12·6'	2°56·2'W	X	117
Washingborough	Lincs	TF0270	53°13·3'	0°27·9'W	T	121
Washingborough Fen	Lincs	TF0370	53°13·3'	0°27·0'W	X	121
Washingborough Top Fm	Lincs	TF0168	53°12·2'	0°28·9'W	FM	121
Washing Burn	Scot Bord	NT5147	55°43·1'	2°46·4'W	W	73
Washingdales	Angus	NO4344	56°35·3'	2°55·2'W	X	54
Washing Dales Fm	NE Lincs	TA1806	53°32·5'	0°12·7'W	FM	113
Washingford Fm	Norf	TM3399	52°32·6'	1°26·6'E	FM	134
Washingford Ho	Norf	TG3101	52°33·7'	1°24·9'E	X	134
Washingley	Cambs	TL1389	52°29·5'	0°19·7'W	T	142
Washingpool	Somer	ST5946	51°12·9'	2°34·8'W	X	182,183
Washingpool Fm	S Glos	ST5783	51°32·9'	2°36·8'W	FM	172
Washing Rocks	Corn	SX1250	50°19·4'	4°38·1'W	X	200
Washington	Sund	NZ3157	54°54·6'	1°30·6'W	T	88
Washington	W Susx	TQ1212	50°54·0'	0°24·0'W	T	198
Washington Birtley Service Area	Ghead	NZ2855	54°53·6'	1°33·4'W	X	88
Washington Common	W Susx	TQ1114	50°55·1'	0°24·9'W	X	198
Washington Village	Sund	NZ3056	54°54·1'	1°31·5'W	T	88
Washingwells	Ghead	NZ2160	54°56·3'	1°39·9'W	X	88
Washingwells	Highld	NH9356	57°35·1'	3°46·9'W	X	27
Washmere Green	Suff	TL9147	52°5·5'	0°47·7'E	T	155
Wash Meres	Norf	TF7729	52°50·0'	0°38·1'E	X	132
Washmore Hill	W Berks	SU3680	51°31·3'	1°28·5'W	X	174
Washneys, The	Kent	TQ4660	51°19·4'	0°6·1'E	X	177,188
Washpit	Kirk	SE1406	53°33·3'	1°46·9'W	T	110
Washpit Fm	Norf	TF8119	52°44·5'	0°41·3'E	FM	132
Washpit Plantn	Norf	TG0630	52°49·9'	1°3·9'E	F	133
Wash, The		TF5442	52°57·4'	0°18·0'E	W	131
Wash, The	Cambs	TL2799	52°34·7'	0°7·1'W	X	142
Wash, The	Pemb	SR9194	51°36·6'	5°0·7'W	W	158
Wash, The	Peterb	TF1908	52°39·6'	0°14·0'W	X	142
Wash, The	Staffs	SK0166	53°11·7'	1°58·7'W	X	119
Wash, The	Suff	TL7760	52°12·8'	0°35·9'E	X	155
Wash, The	Suff	TL9452	52°8·2'	0°50·5'E	X	155
Wash, The	Suff	TM1469	52°16·9'	1°8·6'E	X	156
Washwalk	Devon	SX7950	50°20·5'	3°41·7'W	X	202
Wash Water	W Berks	SU4563	51°22·1'	1°20·8'W	T	174
Washwood Heath	Birm	SP1088	52°29·6'	1°50·8'W	T	139
Wasing	W Berks	SU5764	51°22·6'	1°10·5'W	T	174
Wasing Fm	W Berks	SU5764	51°22·6'	1°10·5'W	FM	174
Wasing Lower Fm	W Berks	SU5765	51°23·1'	1°10·5'W	FM	174
Wasing Park	W Berks	SU5764	51°22·6'	1°10·5'W	X	174
Wasing Wood	W Berks	SU5763	51°22·0'	1°10·5'W	F	174
Waskerley	Durham	NZ0545	54°48·2'	1°54·9'W	T	87
Waskerley Beck	Durham	NZ0344	54°47·7'	1°56·8'W	W	87
Waskerley Beck	Durham	NZ0639	54°45·0'	1°54·0'W	W	92
Waskerleyedge Plantn	Northum	NZ0754	54°53·1'	1°53·0'W	F	88
Waskerley Park	Durham	NZ0143	54°47·2'	1°58·6'W	X	87
Waskerley Reservoir	Durham	NZ0244	54°47·7'	1°57·7'W	W	87
Waskerley Way	Durham	NZ0545	54°48·2'	1°54·9'W	X	87
Waskerley Way	Durham	NZ0847	54°49·3'	1°52·1'W	X	88
Waskew Head	Cumbr	NY6203	54°25·5'	2°34·7'W	X	91
Wasperton	Warw	SP2658	52°13·4'	1°36·8'W	T	151
Wasperton Fm	Warw	SP2760	52°14·5'	1°35·9'W	FM	151
Wasperton Hill	Warw	SP2859	52°13·9'	1°35·0'W	X	151
Wasp Green	Surrey	TQ3245	51°11·6'	0°6·3'W	T	187
Waspley Fm	Devon	SS8819	50°57·8'	3°35·3'W	FM	181
Wasps Nest	Lincs	TF0864	53°10·0'	0°22·7'W	T	121
Wass	N Yks	SE5579	54°12·5'	1°9·0'W	T	100
Wassall Ho	Kent	TQ8429	51°2·1'	0°37·9'E	X	188,199
Wassand Hall	E Yorks	TA1746	53°54·1'	0°12·7'W	X	107
Wassell	Heref	SO4175	52°22·4'	2°51·6'W	X	137,148
Wassell Grove	Worcs	SO9382	52°26·4'	2°5·8'W	X	139
Wassell Wood	Worcs	SO7977	52°23·7'	2°18·1'W	F	138
Wasses	Suff	TM0235	51°58·8'	0°56·9'E	X	155
Wasset Fell	N Yks	SD9883	54°14·8'	2°1·4'W	X	98
Wass Grange	N Yks	SE5678	54°11·9'	1°8·1'W	X	100
Wass Ho	N Yks	SE5589	54°17·9'	1°8·9'W	X	100
Wass Moor	N Yks	SE5680	54°13·0'	1°8·1'W	X	100
Wasso	Orkney	HY7037	59°13·4'	2°31·0'W	X	5
Wasso (Broch)	Orkney	HY7037	59°13·4'	2°31·0'W	A	5
Wass Wick	Orkney	HY4122	59°5·1'	3°1·3'W	W	5,6
Waste Barn	Glos	ST8289	51°36·2'	2°15·2'W	X	162,173
Waste Fm	Staffs	SK0943	52°59·3'	1°51·6'W	FM	119,128
Waste Fm	Warw	SP2497	52°34·5'	1°38·4'W	FM	139
Waste Green	Warw	SP2469	52°19·3'	1°38·5'W	T	139,151
Waste Hill	Warw	SP2898	52°35·0'	1°34·8'W	X	140
Wasters Plantn	E Yorks	TA1372	54°8·1'	0°15·8'W	F	101
Waste Wood	E Susx	TQ5223	50°59·4'	0°10·3'E	F	199
Waste Wood	N Yks	SE2391	54°19·1'	1°38·4'W	F	99
Wast Hills	Worcs	SP0376	52°23·2'	1°57·0'W	X	139
Wastlee Moor	Orkney	ND2588	58°46·7'	3°17·3'W	X	7
Wastor	Devon	SX6449	50°19·7'	3°54·3'W	T	202
Wastor Fm	Devon	SX4982	50°37·3'	4°7·7'W	FM	191,201
Wast Water	Cumbr	NY1605	54°26·3'	3°17·3'W	W	89
Watbridge Fm	Bucks	SP7214	51°49·4'	0°56·9'W	FM	165
Watcarrick	D & G	NY2496	55°15·4'	3°11·3'W	X	79
Watch	Conwy	SH9575	53°15·9'	3°34·1'W	A	116
Watchbury Hill	Warw	SP2860	52°14·5'	1°35·0'W	X	151
Watchclose	Cumbr	NY4760	54°56·2'	2°49·2'W	X	86
Watchcombe	Devon	SY2397	50°46·3'	3°5·1'W	T	192,193
Watch Crags	Northum	NY7882	55°8·2'	2°20·3'W	H	80
Watch Craig	Aberd	NJ6522	57°17·5'	2°34·4'W	H	38
Watch Craig	D & G	NT2404	55°19·7'	3°11·4'W	H	79
Watch Croft	Corn	SW4235	50°9·8'	5°36·4'W	H	203
Watch Cross	Cumbr	NY4759	54°55·6'	2°49·2'W	X	86
Watch Currick Fm	Northum	NY8962	54°57·4'	2°9·9'W	FM	87
Watcher's Hill	Cumbr	NY6644	54°47·6'	2°31·3'W	X	86
Watchet	Somer	ST0743	51°11·0'	3°19·5'W	T	181
Watchet Hill	Devon	SX6193	50°43·4'	3°57·8'W	H	191
Watchfield	Oxon	SU2490	51°36·7'	1°38·8'W	T	163,174
Watchfield	Somer	ST3447	51°13·3'	2°56·3'W	T	182
Watch Folly	Oxon	SU6184	51°33·3'	1°6·8'W	X	175
Watchford Fm	Devon	ST2211	50°53·8'	3°6·2'W	FM	192,193
Watchgate	Cumbr	SD5299	54°23·3'	2°43·9'W	T	97
Watch Hill	Arg & Bt	NS0364	55°50·0'	5°8·3'W	X	63

Watch Hill	Cumbr	NY0021	54°34·7′	3°32·4′W	H	89
Watch Hill	Cumbr	NY1431	54°40·3′	3°19·6′W	H	89
Watchhill	Cumbr	NY1842	54°46·2′	3°16·1′W	T	85
Watch Hill	Cumbr	NY1954	54°52·7′	3°15·3′W	X	85
Watch Hill	Cumbr	NY2745	54°47·9′	3°7·7′W	X	85
Watch Hill	Cumbr	NY3159	54°55·5′	3°4·2′W	X	85
Watch Hill	Cumbr	NY6245	54°48·2′	2°35·0′W	H	86
Watchhill	D & G	NY0682	55°7·7′	3°28·0′W	X	78
Watch Hill	D & G	NY4390	55°12·3′	2°53·3′W	H	79
Watch Hill	Northum	NT9526	55°31·9′	2°4·3′W	H	74,75
Watch Hill	Northum	NY6669	55°1·1′	2°31·5′W	X	86
Watch Hill	Northum	NZ0557	54°54·7′	1°54·9′W	X	87
Watch Hill	Northum	NZ1581	55°7·6′	1°45·5′W	X	81
Watch Hill	Notts	SK6159	53°7·7′	1°4·9′W	X	120
Watch Hill	Shetld	HU2578	60°29·4′	1°32·2′W	H	3
Watch Ho	E Susx	TQ9217	50°55·4′	0°44·3′E	X	189
Watch Ho	Kent	TQ8643	51°9·6′	0°40·0′E	X	189
Watch-house	Shetld	HU4657	60°17·9′	1°9·6′W	X	2,3
Watch House Gap	Norf	TG3533	52°50·8′	1°29·8′E	X	133
Watch House Green	Essex	TL6921	51°51·9′	0°27·7′E	T	167
Watch House Point	Pemb	SM8306	51°42·9′	5°8·1′W	X	157
Watch House Point	V of Glam	ST0465	51°22·8′	3°22·4′W	X	170
Watchill	D & G	NY2066	54°59·2′	3°14·6′W	T	85
Watch Knowe	D & G	NT1816	55°26·1′	3°17·3′W	H	79
Watch Knowe	D & G	NX7486	55°9·4′	3°58·2′W	A	77
Watch Knowe	D & G	NY4293	55°13·9′	2°54·3′W	X	79
Watch Knowe	Scot Bord	NT6116	55°26·4′	2°36·6′W	X	80
Watch Knowe	Scot Bord	NY5489	55°11·8′	2°42·9′W	H	79
Watchknowe	S Lanak	NS8837	55°37·1′	3°46·3′W	X	71,72
Watch Knowe (Settlement)	D & G	NX7486	55°9·4′	3°58·2′W	A	77
Watch Law	E Loth	NT6570	55°55·6′	2°33·2′W	H	67
Watchlaw	Northum	NT9639	55°38·9′	2°3·4′W	X	74,75
Watch Law	Scot Bord	NT2221	55°28·8′	3°13·6′W	H	73
Watchman Hill	D & G	NX9391	55°12·4′	3°40·5′W	H	78
Watchman Hill	S Lanak	NS9415	55°25·3′	3°40·1′W	X	71,78
Watchman Moor	D & G	NX9687	55°10·2′	3°37·5′W	X	78
Watchman's Brae	S Lanak	NS9506	55°20·5′	3°38·9′W	X	78
Watchmoor Wood	Dorset	SU1305	50°50·9′	1°48·5′W	F	195
Watchoak	Shrops	SJ5806	52°39·2′	2°36·9′W	X	126
Watch Rigg	Cumbr	NY5778	55°5·9′	2°40·0′W	X	86
Watch Rigg	Cumbr	NY6372	55°2·7′	2°34·3′W	X	86
Watch, The	D & G	NY3788	55°11·2′	2°58·9′W	H	79
Watch Trees	Northum	NY6860	54°56·3′	2°29·5′W	X	86,87
Watch Water	Scot Bord	NT6355	55°47·5′	2°35·0′W	W	67,74
Watch Water Resr	Scot Bord	NT6656	55°48·0′	2°32·1′W	W	67,74
Watcombe	E Susx	TQ8522	50°58·3′	0°38·5′E	X	189,199
Watcombe	Torbay	SX9167	50°29·8′	3°31·8′W	T	202
Watcombe Bottom	Dorset	ST7102	50°49·2′	2°24·3′W	X	194
Watcombe Head	Torbay	SX9267	50°29·8′	3°31·0′W	X	202
Watcombe Manor	Oxon	SU6894	51°38·7′	1°0·6′W	X	164,175
Watendlath	Cumbr	NY2716	54°32·3′	3°7·3′W	T	89,90
Watendlath Beck	Cumbr	NY2617	54°32·8′	3°8·2′W	W	89,90
Watendlath Fell	Cumbr	NY2814	54°31·2′	3°6·3′W	X	89,90
Watendlath Tarn	Cumbr	NY2716	54°32·3′	3°7·3′W	W	89,90
Water	Devon	SX7580	50°36·6′	3°45·6′W	T	191
Water	Lancs	SD8425	53°43·5′	2°14·1′W	T	103
Water Barrows	Dorset	SY8681	50°37·9′	2°11·5′W	A	194
Waterbeach	Cambs	TL4965	52°16·0′	0°11·4′E	T	154
Waterbeach	W Susx	SU8908	50°52·1′	0°43·7′W	T	197
Waterbeck	D & G	NY2477	55°5·1′	3°11·0′W	T	85
Water Beck	D & G	NY2479	55°6·2′	3°11·0′W	W	85
Water Beck Fm	N Yks	NZ5605	54°26·5′	1°7·8′W	FM	93
Waterblean	Cumbr	SD1782	54°13·9′	3°16·0′W	X	96
Water-break-its-neck	Powys	SO1860	52°14·2′	3°11·7′W	W	148
Water Bridge Cross	Devon	SS7503	50°49·0′	3°46·1′W	X	191
Waterbrook	Kent	TR0240	51°7·6′	0°53·6′E	X	189
Waterbrooks Fm	Devon	SS7628	51°2·5′	3°45·7′W	FM	180
Watercombe	Devon	SX6261	50°26·2′	3°56·2′W	X	202
Watercombe	Dorset	SY7584	50°39·5′	2°20·8′W	X	194
Watercombe	Somer	SS9239	51°8·6′	3°32·3′W	X	181
Watercombe Fm	Glos	SO9413	51°49·2′	2°4·8′W	FM	163
Watercombe Fm	Glos	SO9710	51°47·6′	2°2·2′W	FM	163
Water Crag	Cumbr	SD1597	54°21·9′	3°18·1′W	H	96
Water Crag	N Yks	NY9204	54°26·1′	2°7·0′W	H	91,92
Water Crag	N Yks	SD9958	54°1·3′	2°0·5′W	X	103
Watercress Line	Hants	SU6635	51°6·9′	1°3·0′W	X	185,186
Watercroft Fm	Bucks	SU7993	51°38·0′	0°51·1′W	FM	175
Water Cut or Mill Race	N Yks	SD6776	54°11·0′	2°29·9′W	W	98
Waterdale	Herts	TL1102	51°42·6′	0°23·7′W	T	166
Water Dale	N Yks	SE8261	54°2·5′	0°44·4′W	X	100
Water Dean Bottom	Wilts	SU1052	51°16·3′	1°51·0′W	X	184
Waterdell Ho	Herts	TQ0796	51°39·4′	0°26·8′W	X	166,176
Waterden	Norf	TF8836	52°53·5′	0°48·1′E	X	132
Waterden Fen	Cambs	TL5682	52°25·1′	0°18·0′E	X	143
Waterden Fm	Norf	TF8836	52°53·5′	0°48·1′E	FM	132
Waterditch	Hants	SZ1896	50°46·0′	1°44·3′W	T	195
Waterditch Fm	Dorset	SZ1895	50°45·5′	1°44·3′W	FM	195
Waterditch Fm	Kent	TQ9352	51°14·2′	0°46·3′E	FM	189
Water Eaton	Mil Key	SP8732	51°59·0′	0°43·6′W	T	152,165
Water Eaton	Oxon	SP5112	51°48·5′	1°15·2′W	T	164
Water Eaton	Staffs	SJ9011	52°42·0′	2°8·5′W	X	127
Water Eaton Copse	Wilts	SU1493	51°38·4′	1°47·5′W	F	163,173
Water Eaton Ho	Wilts	SU1293	51°38·4′	1°49·2′W	X	163,173
Wateredge Fm	Glos	SO9111	51°48·1′	2°7·4′W	FM	163
Water End	Beds	TL0637	52°1·5′	0°26·9′W	T	153
Water End	Beds	TL1047	52°6·9′	0°23·2′W	T	153
Water End	Beds	TL2547	52°6·7′	0°10·1′W	T	153
Waterend	Bucks	SU7896	51°39·7′	0°51·9′W	T	165
Waterend	Cumbr	NY1122	54°35·4′	3°22·2′W	T	89
Water End	Essex	TL5840	52°2·4′	0°18·6′E	T	154
Water End	E Yorks	SE7838	53°50·2′	0°48·5′W	T	105,106
Waterend	Glos	SO7514	51°49·7′	2°21·4′W	T	162
Water End	Hants	SU6953	51°16·5′	1°0·3′W	T	186
Water End	Herts	TL0310	51°47·0′	0°30·0′W	T	166
Waterend	Herts	TL2013	51°48·4′	0°15·2′W	T	166
Water End	Herts	TL2204	51°43·5′	0°13·6′W	T	166
Water End Fm	Essex	TL5404	51°43·0′	0°14·2′E	FM	167
Waterend Fm	Glos	SO7502	51°43·2′	2°21·3′W	FM	162
Water End Fm	Norf	TF8401	52°34·8′	0°43·3′E	FM	144
Waterend Fm	Norf	TF9202	52°35·1′	0°50·5′E	FM	144
Waterend Fm	Norf	TL8595	52°31·5′	0°44·0′E	FM	144
Watererne	Aberd	NJ4507	57°9·3′	2°54·1′W	X	37
Waterfall	Staffs	SK0851	53°3·6′	1°52·4′W	T	119
Waterfall Beck	N Yks	NZ2008	54°28·3′	1°41·1′W	W	93
Waterfall Cross	Staffs	SK0651	53°3·6′	1°54·2′W	X	119
Waterfall Fm	Derby	SK1976	53°17·1′	1°42·5′W	FM	119
Waterfall Fm	Norf	TG0118	52°43·6′	0°59·0′E	FM	133
Waterfall Fm	Red & Cl	NZ6316	54°32·4′	1°1·2′W	FM	94
Waterfall Gill Beck	N Yks	SE0272	54°8·9′	1°57·7′W	W	98
Waterfall Low	Staffs	SK0852	53°4·1′	1°52·4′W	X	119
Waterfalls	Northum	NY9181	55°7·6′	2°8·0′W	X	80
Waterfall Wood	Red & Cl	NZ6316	54°32·4′	1°1·2′W	F	94
Waterfield Barn Fm	Suff	TL6653	52°9·2′	0°26·0′E	FM	154
Waterfield Fm	Notts	SK6064	53°10·4′	1°5·7′W	FM	120
Water Flash	N Yks	SE8895	54°20·8′	0°38·4′W	X	94,101
Waterflosh	Cumbr	NY2854	54°52·8′	3°6·9′W	X	85
Water Fm	Kent	TR1040	51°7·5′	1°0·5′E	FM	179,189
Water Fm	Somer	ST1136	51°7·2′	3°15·9′W	FM	181
Water Fm	Somer	ST1943	51°11·1′	3°9·2′W	FM	181
Waterfoot	Arg & Bt	NR8037	55°34·9′	5°29·0′W	T	68,69
Waterfoot	Cumbr	NY4524	54°36·7′	2°50·7′W	T	90
Waterfoot	D & G	NY1964	54°58·1′	3°15·5′W	X	85
Waterfoot	E Renf	NS5654	55°45·7′	4°17·3′W	T	64
Waterfoot	E Renf	NS5654	55°45·7′	4°17·3′W	T	64
Waterfoot	Lancs	SD8321	53°41·4′	2°15·0′W	T	103
Waterford	Hants	SZ3394	50°44·9′	1°31·5′W	T	196
Waterford	Herts	TL3114	51°48·8′	0°5·6′W	T	166
Waterford Fm	Moray	NJ0259	57°36·9′	3°38·0′W	FM	27
Waterford Hall Fm	Herts	TL3115	51°49·3′	0°5·6′W	FM	166
Waterforth	N Yks	SE0685	54°15·9′	1°54·1′W	W	99
Water Fryston	Wakf	SE4626	53°43·9′	1°17·7′W	T	105
Watergall Fox Covert	Warw	SP4154	52°11·2′	1°23·6′W	F	151
Water Garth	N Yks	SD7562	54°3·4′	2°22·5′W	X	98
Water Garth Nook	Cumbr	SD1867	54°5·8′	3°14·8′W	T	96
Watergate	Corn	SX1181	50°36·1′	4°39·9′W	T	200
Watergate	Corn	SX2354	50°21·8′	4°28·9′W	T	201
Watergate	Devon	SS6125	51°0·7′	3°58·5′W	X	180
Watergate	Devon	SX5087	50°40·0′	4°7·0′W	X	191
Watergate	Northum	NY8179	55°6·6′	2°17·4′W	X	86,87
Watergate	N Yks	SE2665	54°5·1′	1°35·7′W	X	99
Water Gate	N Yks	SE5877	54°11·4′	1°6·2′W	X	100
Watergate	W Susx	SU7811	50°53·8′	0°53·1′W	X	197
Watergate Bay	Corn	SW8365	50°26·9′	5°3·0′W	W	200
Watergate Br	Devon	SS4617	50°56·2′	4°11·1′W	X	180,190
Watergate Fm	Beds	SP9828	51°56·7′	0°34·1′W	FM	165
Watergate Fm	Bucks	SP6229	51°57·6′	1°5·5′W	FM	164,165
Watergate Fm	Cumbr	NY1221	54°34·8′	3°21·3′W	FM	89
Watergate Fm	N Yks	NZ8107	54°27·4′	0°44·6′W	FM	94
Watergate Fm	N Yks	SE3891	54°19·0′	1°24·5′W	FM	99
Watergate Fm	Oxon	SP5726	51°56·0′	1°9·9′W	FM	164
Watergate Hanger	W Susx	SU7712	50°54·4′	0°53·9′W	F	197
Watergate Moor	Northum	NY8078	55°6·0′	2°18·4′W	X	86,87
Watergate or Tregurrian Beach	Corn	SW8364	50°26·4′	5°3·0′W	X	200
Watergate Sike	Northum	NY7979	55°6·5′	2°19·3′W	W	86,87
Water Glen	Orkney	HY2202	58°54·2′	3°20·8′W	W	6,7
Watergore	Somer	ST4315	50°56·1′	2°48·3′W	T	193
Watergrove Resr	Roch	SD9017	53°39·2′	2°8·7′W	W	109
Watergrove	Derby	SK1875	53°16·5′	1°43·4′W	X	119
Waterhales	Essex	TQ5395	51°38·2′	0°13·1′E	T	167,177
Waterhall	Bri & Hov	TQ2808	50°51·7′	0°10·5′W	X	198
Water Hall	Cambs	TL6766	52°16·2′	0°27·3′E	X	154
Water Hall	N Yks	SE4488	54°17·4′	1°19·0′W	X	99
Water Hall	N Yks	SE4883	54°14·7′	1°15·4′W	X	100
Waterhall	Orkney	HY6540	59°15·0′	2°36·3′W	X	5
Waterhall Fm	Cambs	TL6767	52°16·8′	0°27·3′E	FM	154
Water Hall Fm	Essex	TL5831	51°57·5′	0°18·4′E	FM	167
Water Hall Fm	Herts	TL2909	51°46·1′	0°7·4′W	FM	166
Water Hall Fm	Suff	TL7043	52°3·8′	0°29·2′E	FM	154
Waterham	Kent	TR0762	51°19·4′	0°58·7′E	T	179
Waterhatch	Glos	SP0325	51°55·6′	1°57·0′W	X	163
Waterhay	Wilts	SU0693	51°38·4′	1°54·4′W	T	163,173
Waterhay Br	Wilts	SU0693	51°38·4′	1°54·4′W	X	163,173
Waterhead	Angus	NO4671	56°49·9′	2°52·6′W	X	44
Waterhead	Cumbr	NY3703	54°25·4′	2°57·8′W	T	90
Waterhead	Cumbr	SD3197	54°22·1′	3°3·3′W	X	96,97
Waterhead	Devon	SX6847	50°18·7′	3°50·9′W	T	202
Waterhead	Devon	SX7638	50°14·0′	3°43·9′W	X	202
Waterhead	D & G	NX5499	55°16·1′	4°17·4′W	X	77
Waterhead	D & G	NX7483	55°7·8′	3°58·1′W	X	77
Waterhead	D & G	NY1894	55°14·3′	3°16·9′W	X	79
Waterhead	E Ayr	NS5411	55°22·5′	4°17·8′W	X	70
Waterhead	E Ayr	NS6930	55°33·0′	4°4·2′W	X	71
Waterhead	E Dunb	NS6583	56°1·5′	4°9·5′W	X	57,64
Waterhead	N Lanak	NS7673	55°56·3′	3°58·7′W	X	64
Waterhead	Northum	NY7466	54°59·5′	2°24·0′W	X	86,87
Waterhead	Northum	NY7690	55°12·5′	2°22·2′W	X	80
Waterhead	S Ayr	NX4300	55°16·4′	4°27·9′W	X	77
Waterhead	S Ayr	NX4495	55°13·7′	4°26·7′W	X	77
Waterhead	S Lanak	NS6135	55°35·6′	4°11·9′W	X	71
Waterhead	S Lanak	NS7737	55°36·9′	3°56·7′W	X	71
Water Head	S Lanak	NS8817	55°26·3′	3°45·8′W	H	71,78
Waterhead	S Lanak	NS8818	55°26·8′	3°45·8′W	X	71,78
Waterhead Brake	Devon	SX8951	50°21·1′	3°33·2′W	X	202
Waterhead Common	Cumbr	NY6168	55°0·6′	2°36·2′W	F	86
Waterhead Hill	D & G	NS5700	55°16·7′	4°14·6′W	H	77
Waterhead Moor	S Ayr	NS2562	55°49·4′	4°47·2′W	X	63
Waterhead on Minnoch	S Ayr	NX3691	55°11·4′	4°34·1′W	X	77
Water Head or Shielhope Head	Scot Bord	NT1925	55°31·0′	3°16·5′W	H	72
Waterheads	Scot Bord	NT2450	55°44·5′	3°12·2′W	T	66,73
Waterheath	Norf	TM4494	52°29·6′	1°36·1′E	T	134
Water Hill	Aberd	NO8276	56°52·8′	2°17·3′W	H	45
Water Hill	Devon	SX6781	50°37·0′	3°52·4′W	H	191
Waterhill of Bruxie	Aberd	NJ9447	57°31·0′	2°5·6′W	X	30
Water Hills	Lincs	TA1101	53°29·9′	0°19·2′W	X	113
Waterholmes	N Yks	SE7078	54°11·8′	0°55·2′W	X	100
Waterhouse	Devon	SS5401	50°47·6′	4°3·9′W	X	191
Waterhouse	Devon	SS5903	50°48·8′	3°59·7′W	X	191
Waterhouse	Devon	SS7525	51°0·9′	3°46·5′W	X	180
Waterhouse	Staffs	SK0355	53°5·8′	1°56·9′W	X	119
Waterhouse	Wilts	ST7861	51°21·1′	2°18·6′W	X	172
Waterhouse Cross	Devon	SS8607	50°51·3′	3°36·8′W	X	191
Waterhouse Fm	Devon	ST0023	51°0·1′	3°25·1′W	FM	181
Waterhouse Fm	Devon	ST2603	50°49·5′	3°2·7′W	FM	192,193
Waterhouse Fm	Essex	TM0728	51°54·9′	1°1·0′E	FM	168,169
Waterhouse Fm	Norf	TF9232	52°51·3′	0°51·5′E	FM	132
Waterhouse Fm	Somer	SS8335	51°6·4′	3°39·9′W	FM	181
Waterhouse Fm	Staffs	SK0963	53°10·1′	1°51·5′W	FM	119
Water House Fm	Suff	TM0339	52°1·0′	0°57·9′E	FM	155
Water House Fm	Surrey	TQ3451	51°14·8′	0°4·4′W	FM	187
Water Houses	Cumbr	NY7110	54°29·3′	2°26·4′W	X	91
Waterhouses	Durham	NZ1841	54°46·1′	1°42·8′W	T	88
Water Houses	N Yks	SD8867	54°6·2′	2°10·6′W	T	98
Waterhouses	Staffs	SK0850	53°3·1′	1°52·4′W	T	119
Water Houses	Suff	TM1070	52°17·5′	1°5·2′E	X	144,155
Waterhouses Wood	Durham	NZ1840	54°45·5′	1°42·8′W	F	88
Wateridgemuir	Aberd	NJ6908	57°10·0′	2°30·3′W	X	38
Wateridgemuir	Aberd	NJ9526	57°19·7′	2°4·5′W	X	38
Wateries	Orkney	HY3327	59°7·7′	3°9·8′W	X	6
Wateringbury	Kent	TQ6953	51°15·3′	0°25·7′E	T	188
Watering Dyke Houses	Lincs	SK9777	53°17·1′	0°32·3′W	X	121
Watering Fm	Norf	TG0011	52°39·8′	0°57·9′E	FM	133
Watering Fm	Norf	TG2402	52°34·4′	1°18·8′E	FM	134
Watering Fm	Norf	TL9194	52°30·8′	0°49·3′E	FM	144
Watering Fm	Suff	TM0856	52°10·0′	1°2·9′E	FM	155
Waterings Fm, The	Staffs	SK1249	53°2·5′	1°48·9′W	FM	119
Water Knott	Durham	NY9217	54°33·1′	2°7·0′W	X	91,92
Waterlair	Aberd	NO7574	56°51·7′	2°24·2′W	X	45
Waterlake	Devon	SS5236	51°6·5′	4°6·5′W	X	180
Waterlake	Kent	TQ4947	51°12·4′	0°8·4′E	X	188
Water Lake Bottom	Dorset	SU0314	50°55·8′	1°57·1′W	X	195
Waterlands	S Lanak	NS8252	55°45·1′	3°52·4′W	X	65,72
Waterlands Fm	Oxon	SP7303	51°43·5′	0°56·2′W	FM	165
Waterlane	Glos	SO9204	51°44·3′	2°6·6′W	T	163
Waterlane Fm	Kent	TQ8243	51°9·7′	0°36·6′E	FM	188
Waterlane Fm	Kent	TQ8552	51°14·5′	0°39·4′E	FM	189
Water Lane Fm	Know	SJ4688	53°23·4′	2°48·3′W	FM	108
Waterlea	Renf	NS3967	55°52·4′	4°34·0′W	X	63
Water Lees	Derby	SK1571	53°14·4′	1°46·1′W	X	119
Waterless Brook	Ches	SJ5063	53°9·9′	2°44·5′W	W	117
Waterley Bottom	Glos	ST7695	51°39·4′	2°20·4′W	X	162
Water Ling Pasture	N Yks	SD9486	54°16·4′	2°5·1′W	X	98
Waterlip	Somer	ST6644	51°11·9′	2°28·8′W	T	183
Waterloo	Aberd	NK0135	57°24·6′	1°58·5′W	X	30
	Black w Dar	SD6625	53°43·5′	2°30·5′W	T	103
Waterloo	Ches	SJ5373	53°15·4′	2°41·9′W	X	117
Waterloo	Corn	SX1072	50°31·3′	4°40·4′W	T	200
Waterloo	Corn	SX2887	50°39·7′	4°25·6′W	X	190
Waterloo	Cumbr	NY1128	54°38·6′	3°22·3′W	X	89
Waterloo	Derby	SK4163	53°10·0′	1°22·8′W	T	120
Waterloo	Heref	SO3447	52°7·3′	2°57·4′W	X	148,149
Waterloo	Highld	ND3351	58°26·8′	3°8·4′W	X	12
Waterloo	Highld	NG6623	57°14·5′	5°52·2′W	T	32
Waterloo	Highld	NH9056	57°35·1′	3°49·9′W	X	27
Waterloo	N Lanak	NS8053	55°45·6′	3°54·3′W	T	65,72
Waterloo	Norf	TG2219	52°43·6′	1°17·7′E	T	133,134
Waterloo	Norf	TM1479	52°22·3′	1°9·0′E	X	144,156
Waterloo	Norf	TM4293	52°29·1′	1°34·3′E	T	134
Waterloo	Northum	NY6663	54°57·9′	2°31·4′W	X	86
Waterloo	Northum	NZ0373	55°3·3′	1°56·8′W	X	87
Waterloo	N Yks	SE2965	54°5·0′	1°33·0′W	X	99
Waterloo	Pemb	SM9703	51°41·6′	4°55·8′W	T	157,158
Waterloo	Poole	SZ0194	50°45·0′	1°58·8′W	T	195
Waterloo	Powys	SJ1920	52°46·5′	3°11·6′W	X	125
Waterloo	Pth & Kin	NO0536	56°30·6′	3°32·2′W	T	52,53
Waterloo	Sefton	SJ3198	53°28·7′	3°2·0′W	T	108
Waterloo	Shetld	HU2448	60°13·2′	1°33·5′W	X	3
Waterloo	Shrops	SJ4933	52°53·8′	2°45·1′W	T	126
Waterloo	Tames	SD9300	53°30·0′	2°5·9′W	T	109
Waterloo	Wrekin	SJ7220	52°46·9′	2°24·5′W	X	127
Waterloo Barn	Northnts	SP6356	52°12·1′	1°4·3′W	X	152
Waterloo Br	Conwy	SH7955	53°5·0′	3°48·0′W	X	115
Waterloo Carn	Highld	NH8708	57°9·2′	3°51·6′W	X	35,36
Waterloo Crescent	Somer	ST6622	51°0·0′	2°28·7′W	X	183
Waterloo Cross	Devon	ST0514	50°55·3′	3°20·7′W	X	181
Waterlooe Lodge Fm	Leic	SK6808	52°40·2′	0°59·3′W	FM	141
Waterloo Farmhouse	Essex	TL5512	51°47·3′	0°15·2′E	X	167
Waterloo Fm	Beds	TL1851	52°8·9′	0°16·1′W	FM	153
Waterloo Fm	Beds	TL2037	52°1·3′	0°14·7′W	FM	153
Waterloo Fm	Bucks	SP8923	51°54·1′	0°42·0′W	FM	165
Waterloo Fm	Cambs	TL2072	52°20·2′	0°13·9′W	FM	153
Waterloo Fm	Cambs	TL2366	52°16·9′	0°11·4′W	FM	153
Waterloo Fm	Devon	SS3504	50°49·0′	4°20·2′W	FM	190
Waterloo Fm	Devon	SS7218	50°57·1′	3°49·0′W	FM	180
Waterloo Fm	Dorset	ST8224	51°1·1′	2°15·0′W	FM	183
Waterloo Fm	E Yorks	SE7333	53°47·5′	0°53·1′W	FM	105,106
Waterloo Fm	E Yorks	TA0644	53°53·1′	0°22·8′W	FM	107
Waterloo Fm	Flint	SJ3468	53°12·5′	2°58·9′W	FM	117
Waterloo Fm	Hants	SU3033	51°6·0′	1°33·9′W	FM	185
Waterloo Fm	Lincs	SK9251	53°3·1′	0°37·2′W	FM	121
Waterloo Fm	Lincs	SK9943	52°58·7′	0°31·1′W	FM	130
Waterloo Fm	Lincs	TF1964	53°9·8′	0°12·8′W	FM	122
Waterloo Fm	N Yks	NZ2507	54°27·7′	1°36·4′W	FM	93
Waterloo Fm	N Yks	SE1585	54°15·9′	1°45·8′W	FM	99
Waterloo Fm	N Yks	SE5781	54°13·5′	1°7·1′W	FM	100
Waterloo Fm	Oxon	SP2613	51°49·1′	1°37·0′W	FM	163
Waterloo Fm	Oxon	SP5927	51°56·5′	1°8·1′W	FM	164
Waterloo Fm	Staffs	SK0635	52°55·0′	1°54·2′W	FM	128
Waterloo Fm	Suff	TM4684	52°24·1′	1°37·4′E	FM	156
Waterloo Fm	Surrey	TQ0855	51°17·3′	0°26·7′W	FM	187
Waterloo Fm	W Susx	SU8006	50°51·1′	0°51·4′W	FM	197
Waterloo Lodge	Leic	SK8016	52°44·4′	0°48·5′W	X	130
Waterloo Lodge	Northnts	SP7483	52°26·6′	0°54·3′W	X	141
Waterloo Mon	D & G	NX9565	54°58·4′	3°38·0′W	X	84
Waterloo Monument	Scot Bord	NT6526	55°31·8′	2°32·8′W	X	74
Waterloo Park	Sefton	SJ3298	53°28·7′	3°1·1′W	T	108
Waterloo Plantation	Norf	TG2725	52°46·7′	1°22·4′E	F	133,134
Waterloo Plantn	Northum	NZ2375	55°4·4′	1°38·0′W	F	88

Wat's Dyke	Wrex	SJ3352	53°3·9'	2°59·6'W	X	117
Wats Ness	Shetld	HU1750	60°14·3'	1°41·1'W	X	3
Watsness	Shetld	HU1750	60°14·3'	1°41·1'W	X	3
Watsonburn	E Ayr	NS6316	55°25·4'	4°9·4'W	X	71
Watson Field Ho	N Yks	NZ3502	54°25·0'	1°27·2'W	X	93
Watsonfoot	N Lanak	NS8455	55°46·7'	3°50·5'W	X	65,72
Watsonhead	N Lanak	NS8454	55°46·2'	3°50·5'W	X	65,72
Watson Hill	Cumbr	NX9811	54°29·3'	3°34·1'W	X	89
Watson Ho	N Yks	NZ0200	54°24·0'	1°57·7'W	X	92
Watson Ho	N Yks	SD7365	54°5·1'	2°24·3'W	X	98
Watson Ho	Stir	NS6994	56°7·5'	4°6·0'W	X	57
Watsonmids	N Lanak	NS8454	55°46·2'	3°50·5'W	X	65,72
Watson's Br	Durham	NY9130	54°40·1'	2°7·9'W	X	91,92
Watson's Corner	Suff	TL9840	52°1·6'	0°53·6'E	X	155
Watson's Dodd	Cumbr	NY3319	54°34·0'	3°1·8'W	H	90
Watson's Fm	Lancs	SD6520	53°40·8'	2°31·4'W	FM	102,103
Watson's Fm	Suff	TM2976	52°20·3'	1°22·1'E	FM	156
Watson's Walls	Northum	NY7881	55°7·6'	2°20·3'W	X	80
Watson's Well	Northum	NY8152	54°52·0'	2°17·3'W	W	86,87
Wat Stock	Kent	TQ5043	51°10·2'	0°9·1'E	X	188
Watston	E Ayr	NS4921	55°27·8'	4°22·9'W	X	70
Watston	E Ayr	NS5917	55°25·9'	4°13·3'W	X	71
Watston	Stir	NN7100	56°10·8'	4°4·2'W	X	57
Watston Burn	E Ayr	NS5217	55°25·7'	4°19·9'W	W	70
Watstone	S Lanak	NS7646	55°41·8'	3°57·9'W	X	64
Watstone Hill	E Ayr	NS5934	55°35·0'	4°13·8'W	H	71
Wattaman	D & G	NY3277	55°5·2'	3°3·5'W	X	85
Watt Crag	N Yks	SD9958	54°1·3'	2°0·5'W	X	103
Watten	Highld	ND2354	58°28·3'	3°18·7'W	T	11,12
Watten	Orkney	HY4731	59°10·0'	2°55·1'W	X	5,6
Watten Lodge	Highld	ND2455	58°28·9'	3°17·7'W	X	11,12
Wattie's Ship	Orkney	HY4526	59°7·3'	2°57·2'W	X	5,6
Wattisfield	Suff	TM0174	52°19·9'	0°57·4'E	T	144
Wattisham	Suff	TM0151	52°7·5'	0°56·6'E	T	155
Wattisham Airfield	Suff	TM0251	52°7·4'	0°57·5'E	X	155
Wattisham Stone	Suff	TM0051	52°7·5'	0°55·7'E	T	155
Wattle	Orkney	HY2627	59°7·7'	3°17·1'W	X	6
Wattlefield	Norf	TM1196	52°31·5'	1°7·0'E	T	144
Wattlehurst Fm	Surrey	TQ1637	51°7·5'	0°20·2'W	FM	187
Wattlesborough Hall	Shrops	SJ3512	52°42·3'	2°57·3'W	X	126
Wattlesborough Heath	Shrops	SJ3511	52°41·8'	2°57·3'W	T	126
Wattles Hill	Somer	ST5247	51°13·4'	2°40·9'W	H	182,183
Wattle Syke	Leeds	SE3946	53°54·8'	1°24·0'W	X	104
Watton	Dorset	SY4591	50°43·2'	2°46·4'W	T	193
Watton	E Yorks	TA0150	53°56·4'	0°27·3'W	T	106,107
Watton	Norf	TF9100	52°34·1'	0°49·5'E	T	144
Watton Abbey	E Yorks	TA0249	53°55·9'	0°26·4'W	A	106,107
Watton at Stone	Herts	TL2919	51°51·5'	0°7·2'W	T	166
Watton Beck	E Yorks	TA0548	53°55·3'	0°23·7'W	W	107
Watton Carrs	E Yorks	TA0549	53°55·8'	0°23·6'W	X	107
Watton Fm	Devon	ST0112	50°54·2'	3°24·1'W	FM	181
Watton Grange	E Yorks	TA0150	53°56·4'	0°27·3'W	X	106,107
Watton Green	Norf	TF9201	52°34·6'	0°50·4'E	T	144
Watton Hill	Dorset	SY4793	50°44·3'	2°44·7'W	H	193
Watton Ho	Herts	TL3019	51°51·5'	0°6·3'W	X	166
Watton's Green	Essex	TQ5295	51°38·2'	0°12·2'E	T	167,177
Watt's Burn	Scot Bord	NY5195	55°15·1'	2°45·8'W	W	79
Watts Common	Hants	SU8552	51°15·9'	0°46·5'W	X	186
Watt's Hall Fm	Norf	TG3811	52°38·9'	1°31·5'E	FM	133,134
Watts Hill	Surrey	TQ4252	51°15·2'	0°2·5'E	X	187
Watts Hill Fm	E Susx	TQ8023	50°58·9'	0°34·3'E	FM	199
Watts Ho	Somer	ST1630	51°4·0'	3°11·5'W	X	181
Watts Lodge Fm	Northnts	SP6378	52°24·0'	1°4·0'W	FM	140
Wattston	N Lanak	NS7770	55°54·7'	3°57·6'W	T	64
Wattstown	Rho Cyn Taf	ST0193	51°37·9'	3°25·4'W	T	170
Wattsville	Caer	ST2091	51°37·0'	3°8·9'W	T	171
Watty Bell's Cairn	Northum	NT8901	55°18·4'	2°10·0'W	X	80
Watwick Bay	Pemb	SM8104	51°41·8'	5°9·8'W	W	157
Watwick Point	Pemb	SM8204	51°41·8'	5°8·9'W	X	157
Wauchan	Highld	NM9681	56°52·8'	5°20·4'W	X	40
Wauchope Burn	Scot Bord	NT5605	55°20·5'	2°41·2'W	W	80
Wauchope Common	Scot Bord	NT5706	55°21·0'	2°40·3'W	X	80
Wauchope Fm	Scot Bord	NT5808	55°22·1'	2°39·3'W	FM	80
Wauchope Forest	Scot Bord	NT6004	55°20·0'	2°37·4'W	X	80
Wauchope Water	D & G	NY3382	55°7·9'	3°2·6'W	W	79
Waud Ho	Northum	NT9827	55°32·5'	2°1·5'W	X	75
Waughold Holme	Northum	NY6758	54°55·2'	2°30·5'W	X	86,87
Waughslea	D & G	NY3275	55°4·1'	3°3·5'W	X	85
Waughton	E Loth	NT5680	56°0·9'	2°41·9'W	X	67
Waughton Castle	E Loth	NT5680	56°0·9'	2°41·9'W	A	67
Waughton Hill	Aberd	NJ9657	57°36·4'	2°3·6'W	H	30
Waughtonhill	Aberd	NJ9758	57°37·0'	2°2·6'W	X	30
Waukenwae	S Lanak	NS6851	55°44·3'	4°5·7'W	X	64
Waukers	E Renf	NS5852	55°44·7'	4°15·3'W	X	64
Wauk Hill	D & G	NX8490	55°11·7'	3°48·9'W	H	78
Waukmill	D & G	NX6277	55°4·4'	4°9·3'W	X	77
Waukmill	Fife	NT3098	56°10·4'	3°7·2'W	X	59
Waukmill	Highld	NH9250	57°31·9'	3°47·8'W	X	27
Waukmill	Moray	NJ2362	57°38·7'	3°16·9'W	X	28
Waukmill	S Lanak	NS7144	55°40·6'	4°2·6'W	X	71
Waukmill Hill	Aberd	NJ6125	57°19·1'	2°38·4'W	H	37
Wauldby Manor Fm	E Yorks	SE9629	53°45·1'	0°32·2'W	FM	106
Wauldby Scrogs	E Yorks	SE9830	53°45·7'	0°30·4'W	X	106
Waulkmill	Aberd	NJ5507	57°9·4'	2°44·2'W	X	37
Waulkmill	Aberd	NJ5710	57°11·0'	2°42·2'W	X	37
Waulkmill	Aberd	NJ5928	57°20·7'	2°40·4'W	X	37
Waulkmill	Aberd	NJ6201	57°6·2'	2°37·2'W	X	37
Waulkmill	Aberd	NJ6433	57°23·4'	2°35·5'W	X	29
Waulkmill	Aberd	NJ6752	57°33·7'	2°32·6'W	X	29
Waulkmill	Aberd	NJ6910	57°11·0'	2°30·3'W	X	38
Waulkmill	Aberd	NJ7335	57°24·5'	2°26·5'W	X	29
Waulkmill	Aberd	NJ8151	57°33·2'	2°18·6'W	X	29,30
Waulkmill	Aberd	NJ8850	57°32·7'	2°11·6'W	X	30
Waulkmill	Aberd	NJ8915	57°13·8'	2°10·5'W	X	38
Waulkmill	Aberd	NJ9232	57°23·0'	2°7·5'W	X	30
Waulkmill	Aberd	NK0029	57°21·3'	1°59·5'W	X	38
Waulkmill	Aberd	NO6492	57°1·3'	2°35·1'W	X	45
Waulkmill	Aberd	NO6596	57°3·5'	2°34·2'W	X	38,45
Waulkmill	Aberd	NO7074	56°51·6'	2°29·1'W	X	45
Waulkmill	Aberd	NO7294	57°2·4'	2°27·2'W	X	38,45

Waulkmill	Angus	NO6349	56°38·1'	2°35·7'W	T	54
Waulkmill	Arg & Bt	NR9982	55°59·6'	5°12·9'W	X	55
Waulkmill	D & G	NX4347	54°47·9'	4°26·1'W	T	83
Waulkmill	Fife	NT0584	56°2·6'	3°31·1'W	X	65
Waulkmill	Moray	NJ5148	57°31·4'	2°48·6'W	X	29
Waulkmill	Pth & Kin	NO1028	56°26·4'	3°27·1'W	T	53,58
Waulkmill	S Ayr	NX2481	55°5·8'	4°45·1'W	X	76
Waulkmill	S Lanak	NT0149	55°43·7'	3°34·1'W	X	72
Waulkmill Bay	Orkney	HY3806	58°56·5'	3°4·2'W	W	6,7
Waulkmill Fm	Pth & Kin	NO0905	56°14·0'	3°27·6'W	FM	58
Waulkmill Glen Resr	E Renf	NS5257	55°47·3'	4°21·2'W	W	64
Waulkmill Lodge	Orkney	HY3806	58°56·5'	3°4·2'W	X	6,7
Waulkmill of Auchnagatt	Aberd	NJ9339	57°26·7'	2°6·5'W	X	30
Waulkmills	Angus	NO6344	56°35·4'	2°35·7'W	T	54
Waulud's Bank	Luton	TL0624	51°54·5'	0°27·1'W	A	166
Waun	Carm	SN2322	51°52·4'	4°33·9'W	X	145,158
Waun	Carm	SN3017	51°49·8'	4°27·6'W	X	159
Waun	Gwyn	SH5564	53°9·4'	4°9·7'W	T	114,115
Waun	Powys	SH8504	52°37·5'	3°41·5'W	X	135,136
Waun	Powys	SJ1102	52°36·8'	3°18·5'W	X	136
Waun	Powys	SJ2319	52°46·0'	3°8·1'W	T	126
Waun	Powys	SN8859	52°13·3'	3°38·0'W	X	147
Waun	Powys	SN9982	52°25·8'	3°28·7'W	X	136
Waun	Powys	SO0176	52°22·6'	3°26·9'W	X	136,147
Waun Afon	Torf	SO2210	51°47·2'	3°7·5'W	X	161
Waunarlwydd	Swan	SS6095	51°38·4'	4°1·0'W	T	159
Waun-arw	Monm	ST4188	51°35·5'	2°50·7'W	X	171,172
Waun Baglam	Carm	SN4403	51°42·5'	4°15·1'W	X	159
Waunbant	Carm	SN6246	52°5·9'	4°0·5'W	X	146
Waunbayvil	Pemb	SN1041	52°2·3'	4°45·8'W	X	145
Waun Beddau	Pemb	SM7729	51°55·1'	5°14·2'W	T	157
Waun Brwynant	Pemb	SN1134	51°58·6'	4°44·7'W	X	145
Waun Brynmeinog	Cered	SN6653	52°9·8'	3°57·2'W	X	146
Waun-ceiliogau	Carm	SN3031	51°57·3'	4°28·1'W	X	145
Waun Claerddu	Cered	SN7969	52°18·6'	3°46·1'W	X	135,147
Waun-clawdd	Cered	SN6755	52°10·9'	3°56·3'W	X	146
Wauncleddau	Pemb	SN1631	51°57·1'	4°40·3'W	X	145
Wauncllunda	Carm	SN6831	51°57·9'	3°54·9'W	X	146
Waun Coli	Powys	SN8446	52°6·3'	3°41·2'W	X	147
Waun Croes Hywel	Powys	SO2136	52°1·2'	3°8·7'W	X	161
Waun Cwmcalch	Powys	SN9097	52°33·8'	3°37·0'W	X	136
Waun-Cynydd	Cered	SN6850	52°8·2'	3°55·3'W	X	146
Waundas	Carm	SN3515	51°48·8'	4°23·2'W	X	159
Waundbwll	Carm	SN1928	51°55·5'	4°37·6'W	X	145,158
Waun Ddu	Carm	SN8230	51°57·6'	3°42·7'W	W	160
Waun Ddubarthog	Powys	SO0381	52°25·3'	3°25·2'W	X	136
Waundeg	Carm	SN3630	51°56·9'	4°22·8'W	X	145
Waundwrgi	Pemb	SN1716	51°49·0'	4°38·9'W	X	158
Wauneos	Conwy	SH8757	53°6·1'	3°40·9'W	W	116
Waunewydd	Powys	SN8623	51°53·9'	3°39·0'W	X	160
Waun-fâch	Carm	SN1421	51°51·6'	4°41·7'W	X	145,158
Waun Fach	Pemb	SM9029	51°55·4'	5°2·9'W	X	157,158
Waun Fach	Powys	SO2129	51°57·5'	3°8·6'W	H	161
Waunfawr	Carm	SN3535	51°59·6'	4°23·8'W	X	145
Waunfawr	Cered	SN3248	52°6·5'	4°26·8'W	X	145
Waun-fawr	Cered	SN5764	52°15·6'	4°5·3'W	X	146
Waun Fawr	Cered	SN6081	52°24·8'	4°3·1'W	T	135
Waunfawr	Cered	SN6558	52°12·5'	3°58·1'W	X	146
Waunfawr	Gwyn	SH5359	53°6·7'	4°11·4'W	T	115
Waun Fawr	Pemb	SM7626	51°53·5'	5°14·9'W	X	157
Waun Fawr	Pemb	SM8328	51°54·7'	5°8·9'W	X	157
Waun Fawr	Powys	SH8704	52°37·6'	3°39·8'W	X	135,136
Waunffrwd	Carm	SN1521	51°51·7'	4°40·8'W	X	145,158
Waun Ffyrdd	Swan	SN6400	51°41·2'	3°57·7'W	X	159
Waun-garanod	Carm	SN5225	51°54·5'	4°8·7'W	X	146
Waun Garno	Powys	SN9594	52°32·3'	3°32·5'W	X	136
Waun Gaseg	Powys	SO0672	52°20·5'	3°22·4'W	X	136,147
Waun-gau	Powys	SH8806	52°38·7'	3°38·9'W	X	124,125
Waungelod	Cered	SN1648	52°6·2'	4°40·8'W	X	145
Waungilwen	Carm	SN3439	52°1·7'	4°24·8'W	T	145
Waungoch	Powys	SN9023	51°53·9'	3°35·5'W	X	160
Waungochen	Carm	SN3423	51°53·1'	4°24·3'W	X	145,159
Waungrechydd	Carm	SN5004	51°43·1'	4°9·9'W	X	159
Waun-gron	Carm	SN5241	52°3·1'	4°9·1'W	X	146
Waungron	Pemb	SN1915	51°48·5'	4°37·1'W	X	158
Waungron	Swan	SN5902	51°42·2'	4°2·0'W	T	159
Waun Gynllwch	Powys	SO0641	52°3·8'	3°21·9'W	X	147,160
Waun Haffes	Powys	SN8219	51°51·7'	3°42·4'W	X	160
Waunhall	Powys	SO0678	52°23·8'	3°22·5'W	X	136,147
Waun Hesgog	Cered	SN7289	52°29·3'	3°52·7'W	X	135
Waun-hir	Carm	SN6611	51°47·1'	3°56·2'W	X	159
Waun Hir	Gwyn	SH6023	52°47·4'	4°4·2'W	X	124
Waun Hirwaun	Powys	SO0545	52°6·0'	3°22·8'W	X	147
Waun Hoscyn	Torf	SO2507	51°45·6'	3°4·8'W	X	161
Waunifor	Cered	SN4541	52°3·0'	4°15·2'W	X	146
Waun Isaf	Pemb	SN1429	51°55·9'	4°41·9'W	X	145,158
Waun Lefrith	Carm	SN7921	51°52·7'	3°45·1'W	H	160
Waun Leuci	Powys	SN8621	51°52·8'	3°39·0'W	X	160
Waunllanau	Carm	SN4022	51°52·7'	4°19·1'W	X	159
Waun Llech	Powys	SO1617	51°51·0'	3°12·8'W	X	161
Waun Llechwedd Llyfn	Cered	SN7186	52°27·6'	3°53·5'W	X	135
Waun Llinau	Powys	SH8709	52°40·3'	3°39·9'W	X	124,125
Waun Lluestowain	Powys	SO0484	52°27·0'	3°24·4'W	X	136
Waun Lluest-wen	Brig	SS8389	51°35·5'	3°41·0'W	X	170
Waun-Lwyd	Blae Gw	SO1706	51°45·1'	3°11·8'W	T	161
Waun Lwyd	Carm	SN4236	52°0·2'	4°17·7'W	X	146
Waun Lwyd	Carm	SN8124	51°54·4'	3°43·4'W	H	160
Waun Lwyd	Pemb	SN1531	51°57·0'	4°41·1'W	X	145
Waun Lwyd	Powys	SN8490	52°30·0'	3°42·1'W	X	135,136
Waun lwyd	Powys	SN9160	52°13·9'	3°35·4'W	X	147
Waun-lwyd-fach	Carm	SN7018	51°51·0'	3°52·9'W	X	160
Waunlwyd Fm	Pemb	SN2336	51°59·9'	4°34·3'W	FM	145
Waun Lydan	Powys	SN8761	52°14·4'	3°38·9'W	X	147
Waun Lysiog	Powys	SO0116	51°50·3'	3°25·8'W	X	160
Waun Lywd	Powys	SH9209	52°40·3'	3°35·4'W	X	125
Waun Maenllwyd	Cered	SN6753	52°9·8'	3°56·3'W	X	146
Waun-Maes	Pemb	SN0632	51°57·4'	4°49·0'W	X	145
Waun Marteg	Powys	SO0176	52°22·6'	3°26·9'W	X	136,147
Waun Mawn	Pemb	SN0834	51°58·5'	4°47·3'W	H	145
Waun-meindy	Cered	SN3150	52°7·6'	4°27·7'W	X	145

Waunmeirch	Carm	SN4036	52°0·2'	4°19·5'W	X	146
Waun-oer	Gwyn	SH7814	52°42·8'	3°48·0'W	H	124
Waun Oer	Powys	SH9613	52°42·5'	3°32·0'W	X	125
Waunoleu	Carm	SN2823	51°53·0'	4°29·6'W	X	145,158
Waunorfa	Pemb	SN0337	52°0·0'	4°51·8'W	X	145,157
Waun Rydd	Powys	SO0620	51°52·5'	3°21·5'W	X	160
Waun Rydd	Powys	SO0714	51°49·3'	3°20·6'W	X	160
Waun Sarn	Powys	SN9361	52°14·4'	3°33·6'W	X	147
Waun Sarnau	Cered	SN7285	52°27·1'	3°52·6'W	X	135
Waun Twmpath	Carm	SN4602	51°42·0'	4°13·3'W	A	159
Waun Tynewydd	Brig	SS8991	51°36·7'	3°35·8'W	X	170
Waun-Tysswg	Caer	SO1306	51°45·0'	3°15·2'W	X	161
Waun-uchaf	Pemb	SN0736	51°59·6'	4°48·3'W	X	145
Waun Vachelich	Pemb	SM7826	51°53·5'	5°13·2'W	X	157
Waun Wen	Brig	SS9485	51°33·5'	3°31·4'W	X	170
Waun-wen	Denb	SJ1164	53°10·2'	3°19·5'W	X	116
Waun Wen	Monm	SO2211	51°47·8'	3°7·5'W	X	161
Waun Wen	Torf	SO2304	51°44·0'	3°6·5'W	H	171
Waunwen Fm	Carm	SN5416	51°49·7'	4°6·7'W	FM	159
Waunwhiod	Pemb	SN1445	52°4·6'	4°42·5'W	X	145
Waun y Clyn	Carm	SN4504	51°43·0'	4°14·2'W	T	159
Waun y Ddraenen	Carm	SN7515	51°49·4'	3°48·4'W	X	160
Waun y Gadair	Powys	SN9188	52°29·0'	3°35·9'W	H	136
Waun y Gadfa	Powys	SH9223	52°47·9'	3°35·7'W	X	125
Waun y Gilfach	Brig	SS8488	51°35·0'	3°40·1'W	T	170
Waun y Griafolen	Gwyn	SH8129	52°51·0'	3°45·6'W	X	124,125
Waun y Gwair	Powys	SO0811	51°47·6'	3°19·7'W	X	160
Waun-y-Llyn Country Park	Flint	SJ2858	53°7·1'	3°4·1'W	X	117
Waun-y-mer	Brig	SS8080	51°30·6'	3°43·4'W	X	170
Waun-y-mynach Common	Powys	SO0929	51°57·4'	3°19·1'W	X	161
Waun y Pound	Blae Gw	SO1510	51°47·2'	3°13·5'W	X	161
Waun-y-pwll	Torf	ST3195	51°39·2'	2°59·5'W	X	171
Waun-yr-hyddod	Carm	SN2125	51°53·9'	4°35·7'W	X	145,158
Waun y Sarn	Powys	SH9406	52°38·7'	3°33·6'W	W	125
Waupley Moor	Red & Cl	NZ7212	54°30·1'	0°52·9'W	X	94
Waupley Wood	Red & Cl	NZ7215	54°31·8'	0°52·8'W	F	94
Wavendon	Mil Key	SP9037	52°1·7'	0°40·9'W	T	152
Wavendon Fields	Mil Key	SP9136	52°1·1'	0°40·0'W	X	152
Wavendon Gate	Mil Key	SP9036	52°1·1'	0°40·9'W	T	152
Wavendon Grange	Leic	SK6722	52°47·7'	1°0·0'W	X	129
Wavendon Ho	Mil Key	SP9237	52°1·7'	0°39·1'W	X	152
Wavendon Tower	Mil Key	SP9037	52°1·7'	0°40·9'W	X	152
Wavendon Wood	Mil Key	SP9135	52°0·6'	0°40·1'W	F	152
Waveney Forest	Norf	TG4600	52°32·8'	1°38·1'E	F	134
Waveney Grange Fm	Suff	TM4896	52°30·5'	1°39·7'E	FM	134
Waveney Ho	Suff	TM2581	52°23·1'	1°18·8'E	X	156
Waveney Ho	Suff	TM2782	52°23·6'	1°20·6'E	X	156
Waveney Lodge	Suff	TM0774	52°19·7'	1°2·7'E	X	144
Waver Bank	Cumbr	NY2243	54°46·8'	3°12·3'W	X	85
Waverbridge	Cumbr	NY2249	54°50·0'	3°12·4'W	T	85
Waverbridge Mill	Cumbr	NY2148	54°49·5'	3°13·4'W	X	85
Wavergillhead	Cumbr	NY3041	54°45·8'	3°4·9'W	X	85
Waverhead Fm	Cumbr	NY3041	54°45·8'	3°4·9'W	FM	85
Waveridge Sand	Glos	SO6804	51°44·3'	2°27·4'W	X	162
Wavering Down	Somer	ST4055	51°17·7'	2°51·2'W	H	172,182
Waverley Abbey	Surrey	SU8645	51°12·1'	0°45·8'W	A	186
Waverley Abbey Ho	Surrey	SU8645	51°12·1'	0°45·8'W	X	186
Waverley Fm	Glos	SO9307	51°45·9'	2°5·7'W	FM	163
Waverley Fm	Warw	SP3471	52°20·4'	1°29·7'W	FM	140
Waverley Sta	C of Edin	NT2573	55°56·9'	3°11·6'W	X	66
Waverley Wood	Warw	SP3570	52°19·9'	1°28·8'W	F	140
Waverton	Ches	SJ4564	53°10·5'	2°49·0'W	T	117
Waverton	Cumbr	NY2247	54°49·0'	3°12·4'W	T	85
Waverton Approach	Ches	SJ4461	53°8·8'	2°49·8'W	X	117
Waverton Stud	Glos	SP1631	51°58·9'	1°45·6'W	X	151
Wavertree	Liv	SJ3889	53°23·9'	2°55·5'W	T	108
Wavertree Park	Liv	SJ3790	53°24·4'	2°56·5'W	X	108
Wavery Gill	N Yks	SD8498	54°22·9'	2°14·4'W	W	98
Waves Fm	Lincs	SK9473	53°15·0'	0°35·1'W	FM	121
Wawcott	W Berks	SU3968	51°24·8'	1°26·0'W	T	174
Wawne	E Yorks	TA0836	53°48·8'	0°21·2'W	T	107
Wawne Common	E Yorks	TA1038	53°49·8'	0°19·3'W	X	107
Wawne Drain	K upon H	TA0934	53°47·7'	0°20·3'W	W	107
Wawne Grange	E Yorks	TA0938	53°49·8'	0°20·2'W	X	107
Wax Hall	Shrops	SO2976	52°22·9'	3°2·2'W	X	137,148
Waxham	Norf	TG4326	52°46·8'	1°36·6'E	T	134
Waxholme	E Yorks	TA3229	53°44·7'	0°0·5'E	T	107
Waxway	Devon	SY1192	50°43·5'	3°15·3'W	X	192,193
Way	Devon	SS9309	50°52·5'	3°30·9'W	X	192
Way	Kent	TR3265	51°20·4'	1°20·3'E	T	179
Way Barton	Devon	SS5520	50°57·9'	4°3·5'W	X	180
Way Barton Fm	Devon	SX4989	50°41·1'	4°7·9'W	FM	191
Waybench	Pemb	SM7309	51°44·3'	5°16·9'W	X	157
Waydalehill	Northnts	SP6563	52°15·9'	1°2·5'W	X	152
Way Down	Devon	SX6889	50°41·4'	3°51·7'W	X	191
Waydown Plantn	Devon	SS4908	50°51·3'	4°8·3'W	F	191
Waye	Devon	SX7771	50°31·8'	3°43·8'W	T	202
Waye Barton	Devon	SX6886	50°39·8'	3°51·7'W	X	191
Waye Barton	Devon	SX8364	50°28·1'	3°38·5'W	X	202
Waye Fm	Devon	SX6052	50°21·3'	3°57·7'W	FM	202
Waye Fm	Devon	SX7868	50°30·2'	3°42·8'W	FM	202
Wayend Street	Heref	SO7436	52°1·5'	2°22·3'W	T	150
Wayfarer's Walk	Hants	SU4060	51°20·5'	1°25·2'W	X	174
Wayfarer's Walk	Hants	SU5633	51°5·8'	1°11·6'W	X	185
Wayfarer's Walk	Hants	SU6413	50°55·0'	1°5·0'W	X	196
Wayfarer's Walk	Hants	SU7405	50°50·6'	0°56·5'W	X	197
Wayfield	Medway	TQ7565	51°21·6'	0°31·2'E	T	178
Wayfield Ho	Warw	SP2059	52°14·0'	1°42·0'W	X	151
Way Fm	Corn	SX3097	50°45·1'	4°24·2'W	FM	190
Way Fm	Devon	SS9305	50°50·3'	3°30·8'W	FM	192
Way Fm	Devon	SX6889	50°41·4'	3°51·7'W	FM	191
Way Fm	Devon	SX8294	50°44·3'	3°40·0'W	FM	191
Way Fm	Devon	SX8893	50°43·8'	3°34·8'W	FM	192
Wayford	Somer	ST4006	50°51·3'	2°50·8'W	T	193
Wayford Br	Norf	TG3424	52°46·0'	1°28·5'E	X	133,134
Wayford Br	Shrops	SJ4703	52°37·6'	2°46·6'W	X	126
Waygateshaw House	S Lanak	NS8248	55°42·9'	3°52·3'W	X	72
Way Gill	N Yks	SD9360	54°2·4'	2°6·0'W	X	98
Waygill Hill	Cumbr	NY5556	54°54·1'	2°41·7'W	X	86
Way Head	Cambs	TL4883	52°25·7'	0°11·0'E	X	143

Wayhouse Fm	Oxon	SP4536	52°1·5′	1°20·3′W	FM	151
Wayland	Corn	SX2868	50°29·4′	4°25·1′W	X	201
Wayland	Devon	SS9212	50°54·1′	3°31·8′W	X	181
Wayland Fm	Devon	SX8394	50°44·3′	3°39·1′W	FM	191
Wayland Fm	Norf	TF9801	52°34·5′	0°55·7′E	FM	144
Wayland's Smithy	Oxon	SU2885	51°34·0′	1°35·4′W	X	174
Wayland's Smithy (Long Barrow)	Oxon	SU2885	51°34·0′	1°35·4′W	A	174
Wayland Wood	Norf	TL9299	52°33·5′	0°50·4′E	F	144
Wayletts	Essex	TQ5299	51°40·4′	0°12·3′E	X	167,177
Way Mill	Devon	SS9909	50°52·5′	3°25·8′W	X	192
Waymills	Shrops	SJ5541	52°58·1′	2°39·8′W	T	117
Wayne	Monm	SO4118	51°51·7′	2°51·0′W	X	161
Wayne Green	Monm	SO4118	51°51·7′	2°51·0′W	T	161
Waynflete's Tower	Surrey	TQ1365	51°22·6′	0°22·2′W	A	176
Wayoh Fm	Black w Dar	SD7218	53°39·7′	2°25·0′W	FM	109
Wayoh Resr	Black w Dar	SD7316	53°38·6′	2°24·1′W	W	109
Waypost Fm	Cambs	TL3087	52°28·2′	0°4·8′W	FM	142
Wayrham Fm	E Yorks	SE8357	54°0·4′	0°43·6′W	FM	106
Way's Green	Ches	SJ6465	53°11·1′	2°31·9′W	T	118
Wayshaw Bogs	N Yks	SE0055	53°59·7′	1°59·6′W	W	104
Way's Hill	Dorset	SY4995	50°45·4′	2°43·0′W	H	193,194
Wayshill	Somer	ST0937	51°7·7′	3°17·6′W	X	181
Wayside	E Susx	TQ6118	50°56·6′	0°17·9′E	X	199
Wayside Farm Ho	Beds	SP9323	51°54·1′	0°38·5′W	X	165
Wayside Gardens	Leeds	SE3642	53°52·6′	1°26·7′W	X	104
Way Stone	Cald	SD9914	53°37·6′	2°0·5′W	X	109
Way Stone Edge	Cald	SD9914	53°37·6′	2°0·5′W	X	109
Way Stone Edge	Kirk	SE0014	53°37·6′	1°59·6′W	X	110
Waystrode Manor	Kent	TQ4540	51°8·7′	0°4·8′E	A	188
Waytes Court	I of W	SZ4282	50°38·4′	1°24·0′W	X	196
Wayting Hill	Herts	TL0930	51°57·7′	0°24·4′W	X	166
Wayton	Corn	SX4263	50°27·0′	4°13·2′W	X	201
Waytown	Devon	SS3622	50°58·7′	4°19·8′W	T	190
Waytown	Devon	SS5733	51°4·9′	4°2·1′W	T	180
Waytown	Devon	SS6144	51°10·9′	3°58·9′W	X	180
Waytown	Devon	SX5497	50°45·5′	4°3·8′W	X	191
Waytown	Devon	SX7967	50°29·7′	3°42·0′W	X	202
Waytown	Dorset	SY4697	50°46·4′	2°45·6′W	T	193
Waytown Fm	Devon	SS5836	51°6·6′	4°1·3′W	FM	180
Way to Wooler	Northum	NU0028	55°33·0′	1°59·6′W	X	75
Way Village	Devon	SS8810	50°53·0′	3°35·1′W	T	192
Way Wick	N Som	ST3862	51°21·5′	2°53·0′W	T	182
Wayworth	N Yks	NZ6409	54°28·6′	1°0·3′W	X	94
Wayworth Moor	N Yks	NZ6310	54°29·1′	1°1·2′W	X	94
W Camps	Fife	NT0488	56°4·8′	3°32·1′W	X	65
Weach Barton Fm	Devon	SS4826	51°1·0′	4°9·6′W	FM	180
Weachyburn	Aberd	NJ6356	57°35·8′	2°36·7′W	X	29
Weacombe	Somer	ST1140	51°9·4′	3°16·0′W	T	181
Weags Br	Staffs	SK1054	53°5·2′	1°50·6′W	X	119
Weaklaw Rocks	E Loth	NT5086	56°4·1′	2°47·7′W	X	66
Weald	Oxon	SP3002	51°43·2′	1°33·5′W	T	164
Weald Barkfold	W Susx	TQ0031	51°4·4′	0°34·0′W	X	186
Weald Br	Essex	TL5106	51°44·2′	0°11·6′E	X	167
Weald Brook	Hav	TQ5593	51°37·1′	0°14·7′E	W	177
Wealden Forest Park	Kent	TR1663	51°19·7′	1°6·4′E	X	179
Weald Fm	Cambs	TL2259	52°13·2′	0°12·4′W	FM	153
Weald Hall	Essex	TL4805	51°43·7′	0°9·0′E	X	167
Weald Lodge	Essex	TL5107	51°44·7′	0°11·6′E	X	167
Weald Moors, The	Wrekin	SJ6617	52°45·2′	2°29·8′W	X	127
Wealdmore Lodge Fm	Lincs	SK8831	52°52·4′	0°41·1′W	FM	130
Weald Park (Country Park)	Essex	TQ5694	51°37·6′	0°15·6′E	X	167,177
Weald Place	Kent	TQ5252	51°15·0′	0°11·1′E	X	188
Wealdside	Essex	TQ5594	51°37·6′	0°14·8′E	X	167,177
Wealdstone	Harrow	TQ1589	51°35·5′	0°20·0′W	T	176
Weald, The	E Susx	TQ7029	51°2·3′	0°25·9′E	X	188,199
Weald Village	Cambs	TL2359	52°13·2′	0°11·6′W	A	153
Wealdway	E Susx	TQ4725	51°0·6′	0°6·1′E	X	187,198,199
Wealdway	E Susx	TQ5036	51°6·4′	0°9·0′E	X	188
Wealdway	E Susx	TQ5117	50°56·2′	0°9·3′E	X	199
Wealdway	Kent	TQ5744	51°10·6′	0°15·2′E	X	188
Wealdway	Kent	TQ6765	51°21·8′	0°24·3′E	X	177,178
Wealside	Northum	NY7368	55°0·6′	2°24·9′W	X	86,87
Wealtheston	Angus	NO6056	56°41·9′	2°38·7′W	X	54
Wealth of Waters	E Ayr	NS5428	55°31·7′	4°18·3′W	X	70
Weam Common Hill	Dorset	ST6501	50°48·7′	2°29·4′W	H	194
Weaners Fm	Suff	TL9148	52°6·1′	0°47·7′E	FM	155
Wear Cliffs	Dorset	SY4092	50°43·7′	2°50·6′W	X	193
Weardale	Durham	NY9038	54°44·5′	2°8·9′W	X	91,92
Weardale Forest	Durham	NY8242	54°46·6′	2°16·4′W	F	86,87
Weardale Way	Durham	NY8244	54°47·7′	2°16·4′W	X	86,87
Weardale Way	Durham	NY8541	54°46·1′	2°13·6′W	X	87
Weardale Way	Durham	NY8938	54°44·5′	2°9·8′W	X	91,92
Weardale Way	Durham	NZ2335	54°42·8′	1°38·2′W	X	93
Weardale Way	Durham	NZ3152	54°52·0′	1°30·6′W	X	88
Wearde	Corn	SX4258	50°24·3′	4°13·0′W	T	201
Wearde Quay	Corn	SX4257	50°23·7′	4°13·0′W	X	201
Weardeth	Orkney	HY2513	59°0·1′	3°17·8′W	X	6
Weardley	Leeds	SE2944	53°53·7′	1°33·1′W	T	104
Weare	Somer	ST4152	51°16·1′	2°50·4′W	T	182
Weare Giffard	Devon	SS4721	50°58·3′	4°10·4′W	T	180
Wear Fm	Devon	SX8873	50°33·0′	3°34·5′W	FM	192
Wearhead	Durham	NY8539	54°45·0′	2°13·6′W	T	91,92
Wearne	Somer	ST4228	51°3·1′	2°49·3′W	T	193
Wear Point	Pemb	SM9304	51°42·0′	4°59·4′W	X	157,158
Wears Fm	Dorset	SY5686	50°40·6′	2°37·0′W	FM	194
Wears Hill	Dorset	SY5686	50°40·6′	2°37·0′W	H	194
Weary	Pemb	SM9028	51°54·9′	5°2·8′W	X	157,158
Wearyall Hill	Somer	ST4938	51°8·6′	2°43·4′W	H	182,183
Weary Bank Wood	Stock on T	NZ4509	54°28·7′	1°17·9′W	F	93
Weary Hall	Cumbr	NY1548	54°49·4′	3°19·0′W	X	85
Weary Hall	Cumbr	NY2141	54°45·7′	3°13·2′W	X	85
Weasdale	Cumbr	NY6903	54°25·5′	2°28·2′W	T	91
Weasdale Beck	Cumbr	NY6802	54°25·0′	2°29·2′W	W	91
Weasel Green	N Yks	SD9746	53°54·9′	2°2·3′W	X	103
Weasel Hill	Scot Bord	NT6208	55°22·1′	2°35·5′W	H	80
Weasenham All Saints	Norf	TF8421	52°45·5′	0°44·0′E	T	132
Weasenham Lyngs	Norf	TF8519	52°44·4′	0°44·8′E	X	132
Weasenham St Peter	Norf	TF8522	52°46·1′	0°44·9′E	T	132
Weaste	Salf	SJ8098	53°28·9′	2°17·7′W	T	109
Weatherall Fm	Norf	TF5222	52°46·7′	0°15·6′E	FM	131
Weather Beds	Durham	NY9230	54°40·1′	2°7·0′W	X	91,92
Weatherby Castle	Dorset	SY8096	50°46·0′	2°16·6′W	X	194
Weatherby Castle (fort)	Dorset	SY8096	50°46·0′	2°16·6′W	A	194
Weathercalf Moss	Cumbr	SD6599	54°23·4′	2°31·9′W	X	97
Weathercock	Essex	TM0213	51°47·0′	0°56·1′E	X	168
Weathercock Fm	Suff	TL7049	52°7·0′	0°29·4′E	FM	154
Weather Cock Fm	Suff	TL9977	52°21·5′	0°55·8′E	FM	144
Weathercock Hill	Oxon	SU2982	51°32·4′	1°34·5′W	X	174
Weathercote	N Yks	SD7377	54°11·5′	2°24·4′W	X	98
Weatherdon Hill	Devon	SX6558	50°24·6′	3°53·6′W	X	202
Weathergrove Fm	Somer	ST6121	50°59·5′	2°33·0′W	FM	183
Weatherham Fm	Somer	SS9330	51°3·8′	3°31·2′W	FM	181
Weather Head	Northum	NZ0197	55°16·3′	1°58·6′W	H	81
Weather Heath	Suff	TL7877	52°22·0′	0°37·3′E	X	144
Weather Hill	Cumbr	NY6303	54°25·5′	2°33·8′W	X	91
Weatherhill	Surrey	TQ3143	51°10·5′	0°7·2′W	T	187
Weather Hill	Wilts	SU2051	51°15·7′	1°42·4′W	H	184
Weatherhill Engine	Durham	NY9942	54°46·6′	2°0·5′W	X	87
Weather Hill Firs	Wilts	SU2052	51°16·2′	1°42·4′W	F	184
Weather Hill Fm	E Yorks	TA1845	53°53·5′	0°11·8′W	FM	107
Weather Hill Fm	Suff	TL7872	52°19·3′	0°37·1′E	FM	144,155
Weather Hill Ho	Durham	NZ1938	54°44·4′	1°41·9′W	X	92
Weather Hill Wood	Durham	NZ1939	54°45·0′	1°41·9′W	F	92
Weatherhouse	Scot Bord	NT4226	55°31·7′	2°54·7′W	X	73
Weather Law	Durham	NZ0341	54°46·1′	1°56·8′W	X	87
Weather Law	E Loth	NT7171	55°56·1′	2°27·4′W	X	67
Weather Law	Scot Bord	NT3746	55°42·5′	2°59·7′W	H	73
Weather Ling Hill	Cumbr	SD6786	54°16·4′	2°30·0′W	X	98
Weatherly	E Loth	NT6771	55°56·1′	2°31·3′W	X	67
Weather Ness	Orkney	HY5240	59°14·9′	2°50·0′W	X	5
Weatherness Sound	Orkney	HY5240	59°14·9′	2°50·0′W	W	5
Weatheroak Hill	Worcs	SP0574	52°22·1′	1°55·2′W	T	139
Weatherslade	Somer	SS8436	51°6·9′	3°39·1′W	X	181
Weatherwick	Essex	TM0105	51°42·7′	0°55·0′E	X	168
Weathery Crook	Cumbr	NY5920	54°34·7′	2°37·6′W	X	91
Weaveley Fms	Oxon	SP4618	51°51·8′	1°19·5′W	FM	164
Weaveley Wood	Cambs	TL2254	52°10·5′	0°12·6′W	F	153
Weaven, The	Heref	SO5431	51°58·8′	2°39·8′W	T	149
Weaver	Devon	ST0403	50°49·4′	3°21·4′W	X	192
Weaver	Heref	SO4274	52°21·9′	2°50·7′W	H	137,148
Weaver Bank	Ches	SJ6762	53°9·5′	2°29·2′W	X	118
Weaver Fm	Ches	SJ5551	53°3·5′	2°39·9′W	FM	117
Weavergrove	Ches	SJ6564	53°10·6′	2°31·0′W	X	118
Weaver Hall	Ches	SJ6664	53°10·6′	2°30·1′W	X	118
Weaverham	Ches	SJ6174	53°15·9′	2°34·7′W	T	118
Weaver Hills	Staffs	SK0946	53°0·9′	1°51·5′W	H	119,128
Weavering Street	Kent	TQ7856	51°16·7′	0°33·5′E	T	178,188
Weaver Navigation	Ches	SJ5477	53°17·5′	2°41·0′W	W	117
Weaver Navigation	Ches	SJ6572	53°14·9′	2°31·1′W	W	118
Weavern Fm	Wilts	ST8471	51°26·5′	2°13·4′W	FM	173
Weaver Park Fm	Ches	SJ6562	53°9·5′	2°31·0′W	FM	118
Weavers	Lancs	SD4948	53°55·8′	2°46·2′W	X	102
Weaver's Castle	N Eil	NF7807	57°2·8′	7°18·2′W	A	31
Weaver's Cottage	Renf	NS4063	55°50·3′	4°32·9′W	X	64
Weavers Down	Hants	SU8030	51°4·1′	0°51·1′W	X	186
Weaver's Fm	E Susx	TQ8522	50°58·3′	0°38·5′E	FM	189,199
Weavers Hill	Staffs	SJ7920	52°46·9′	2°18·3′W	X	127
Weaverslake	Staffs	SK1319	52°46·3′	1°48·0′W	T	128
Weaver Sluices	Ches	SJ4980	53°19·1′	2°45·5′W	X	108
Weaver's Point	N Eil	NF9569	57°36·7′	7°6·0′W	X	18
Weaver's Way	Norf	TG2428	52°48·4′	1°19·8′E	X	133,134
Weavers' Way	Norf	TG4306	52°36·1′	1°35·7′E	X	134
Weaverthorpe	N Yks	SE9670	54°7·3′	0°31·5′W	T	101
Weaverthorpe Pasture	N Yks	SE9768	54°6·2′	0°30·6′W	X	101
Weaverthorpe Slack	N Yks	SE9772	54°8·3′	0°30·5′W	X	101
Weaverwood Fm	Ches	SJ6663	53°10·0′	2°30·1′W	FM	118
Webber Hill Fm	Devon	SX6096	50°45·0′	3°58·7′W	FM	191
Webber's Post	Somer	SS9043	51°10·8′	3°34·0′W	X	181
Webberton Cross	Devon	SX8787	50°40·5′	3°35·6′W	X	192
Webbery	Devon	SS5026	51°1·1′	4°7·9′W	X	180
Webbery	Devon	SS7724	51°0·4′	3°44·8′W	X	180
Webb Hill	Somer	ST1426	51°1·9′	3°13·2′W	X	181,193
Webbhouse Fm	Worcs	SO9464	52°16·7′	2°4·9′W	FM	150
Webbington	Somer	ST3855	51°17·7′	2°53·0′W	T	182
Webble Fm	Devon	ST2605	50°50·6′	3°2·7′W	FM	192,193
Webb's Covert	Norf	TF8924	52°47·1′	0°48·6′E	X	132
Webbs Down	Corn	SX2078	50°34·7′	4°32·2′W	X	201
Webb's Fm	Essex	TL7618	51°50·2′	0°33·7′E	FM	167
Webbs Green Fm	Hants	SU6115	50°56·1′	1°7·5′W	FM	196
Webb's Heath	S Glos	ST6873	51°27·5′	2°27·2′W	X	172
Webbs Land	Hants	SU5610	50°53·4′	1°11·8′W	X	196
Webb's Wood	Wilts	SU0485	51°34·1′	1°56·1′W	F	173
Webby's Fm	Devon	SX8891	50°42·7′	3°34·8′W	FM	192
Webheath	Worcs	SP0166	52°17·8′	1°58·7′W	T	150
Webland	Devon	SS9218	50°57·3′	3°31·9′W	X	181
Webland Fm	Devon	SX7159	50°25·2′	3°48·6′W	FM	202
Webscott	Shrops	SJ4722	52°47·8′	2°46·8′W	T	126
Webscott Fm	Shrops	SJ4722	52°47·8′	2°46·8′W	FM	126
Websdill Wood	Norf	TM2890	52°27·8′	1°21·8′E	F	134
Websley Fm	Dorset	ST8507	50°52·0′	2°12·4′W	FM	194
Websters	Lancs	SD5150	53°56·9′	2°44·4′W	X	102
Webster's Meadow	Lancs	SD5948	53°55·8′	2°37·1′W	X	102
Webton Court	Heref	SO4236	52°1·5′	2°50·3′W	X	149,161
Webtree	Heref	SO4737	52°2·0′	2°46·0′W	X	149,161
Webworthy	Corn	SX2692	50°42·3′	4°27·5′W	X	190
Wecock	Hants	SU6811	50°53·9′	1°1·6′W	T	196
Wedacre	Lancs	SD8448	53°55·9′	2°14·2′W	X	103
Weddel	Orkney	ND3393	58°49·4′	3°9·1′W	X	7
Weddell	Orkney	ND4798	58°52·2′	2°54·7′W	X	6,7
Weddell Point	Orkney	ND4798	58°52·2′	2°54·7′W	X	6,7
Weddell Sound	Orkney	ND4798	58°52·2′	2°54·7′W	W	6,7
Weddell Sound	Orkney	ND3394	58°50·0′	3°9·2′W	W	7
Wedderburn	Aberd	NJ5935	57°24·5′	2°40·5′W	X	29
Wedderburn Castle	Scot Bord	NT8052	55°45·9′	2°18·7′W	X	67,74
Wedder Dod	D & G	NS8215	55°25·1′	3°51·4′W	H	71,78
Wedder Dod	S Lanak	NS7521	55°28·3′	3°58·2′W	H	71
Wedderhill	Aberd	NO8797	57°4·1′	2°12·4′W	X	38,45
Wedder Hill	E Ayr	NS5930	55°32·9′	4°13·7′W	H	71
Wedder Hill	E Ayr	NS6302	55°17·8′	4°9·0′W	H	77
Wedder Hill	Highld	NC9043	58°22·0′	3°52·3′W	X	10
Wedder Hill	Northum	NT7911	55°23·8′	2°19·5′W	H	80
Wedder Hill	S Lanak	NS7624	55°29·9′	3°57·3′W	X	71
Wedder Hill	S Lanak	NS7730	55°33·1′	3°56·6′W	X	71
Wedder Holm	Shetld	HU6197	60°39·4′	0°52·5′W	X	1
Wedderlairs	Aberd	NJ8532	57°22·9′	2°14·5′W	T	30
Wedder Lairs	Northum	NY6482	55°8·1′	2°33·5′W	X	80
Wedder Lairs	Scot Bord	NT3417	55°26·8′	3°2·2′W	H	79
Wedder Lairs	Scot Bord	NT5857	55°48·5′	2°39·8′W	X	67,73,74
Wedder Law	D & G	NS9302	55°18·3′	3°40·7′W	H	78
Wedder Law	Scot Bord	NT2613	55°24·6′	3°9·7′W	H	79
Wedder Law	Scot Bord	NT5656	55°48·0′	2°41·7′W	X	67,73
Wedder Law	S Lanak	NS8828	55°32·2′	3°46·1′W	H	71,72
Wedderleys	Angus	NO3644	56°35·3′	3°2·1′W	X	54
Wedderlie	Scot Bord	NT6451	55°45·3′	2°34·0′W	X	67,74
Wedderlie Burn	Scot Bord	NT6452	55°45·9′	2°34·0′W	W	67,74
Wedderlie House	Scot Bord	NT6351	55°45·3′	2°34·9′W	A	67,74
Weddersbie	Fife	NO2613	56°18·5′	3°11·3′W	X	59
Weddersbie Hill	Fife	NO2514	56°19·0′	3°12·3′W	H	59
Weddicar Hall	Cumbr	NY0117	54°32·6′	3°31·4′W	X	89
Weddicar Rig	Cumbr	NY0118	54°33·1′	3°31·4′W	X	89
Weddicott	Devon	SX7085	50°39·2′	3°50·0′W	X	191
Weddington	Kent	TR2959	51°17·3′	1°17·4′E	T	179
Weddington	Warw	SP3692	52°31·7′	1°27·8′W	T	140
Weddington Hill	Warw	SP4057	52°12·8′	1°24·5′W	X	151
Wedd's Fm	E Susx	TQ6729	51°2·4′	0°23·3′E	FM	188,199
Wedfield	Devon	SS3517	50°56·0′	4°20·5′W	X	190
Wedge's Fm	W Susx	TQ1128	51°2·7′	0°24·6′W	FM	187,198
Wedge's Mills	Staffs	SJ9608	52°40·4′	2°3·1′W	X	127
Wedgewood's Monument	Staffs	SJ8251	53°3·6′	2°15·7′W	X	118
Wedgnock Park Fm	Warw	SP2666	52°17·7′	1°36·7′W	FM	151
Wedgwood Sta	Staffs	SJ8839	52°57·1′	2°10·3′W	X	127
Wedhampton	Wilts	SU0657	51°19·0′	1°54·4′W	T	173
Wedholme Flow	Cumbr	NY2153	54°52·2′	3°13·4′W	X	85
Wedholme Hill	Cumbr	NY2251	54°51·1′	3°12·5′W	X	85
Wedholme Ho	Cumbr	NY2052	54°51·6′	3°14·4′W	X	85
Wedlake	Devon	SX5377	50°34·7′	4°4·2′W	X	191,201
Wedlock Fms	Pemb	SN0902	51°41·3′	4°45·4′W	FM	158
Wedmore	Somer	ST4347	51°13·4′	2°48·6′W	T	182
Wedmore Moor	Somer	ST4548	51°13·9′	2°46·9′W	X	182
Wednesbury	Sand	SO9895	52°33·4′	2°1·4′W	T	139
Wednesbury Oak	Sand	SO9694	52°32·9′	2°3·1′W	T	139
Wednesfield	Wolv	SJ9400	52°36·1′	2°4·9′W	T	127,139
Wee Berbeth Loch	E Ayr	NS4703	55°18·1′	4°24·2′W	W	77
Wee Bridge Fm	Ches	SJ7880	53°19·2′	2°19·4′W	FM	109
Wee Burn	S Ayr	NX2784	55°7·5′	4°42·4′W	W	76
Weecar	Notts	SK8266	53°11·3′	0°46·0′W	T	121
Weecher Flat	Brad	SE1242	53°52·7′	1°48·6′W	X	104
Wee Chirmorie	S Ayr	NX1976	55°3·0′	4°49·6′W	X	76
Wee Craigenlee	D & G	NX2070	54°59·8′	4°48·4′W	X	76
Weed Acre	Lancs	SD6541	53°52·1′	2°31·5′W	X	102,103
Weedley	E Yorks	SE9532	53°46·8′	0°33·1′W	X	106
Weedon	Bucks	SP8118	51°51·5′	0°49·0′W	T	165
Weedon Bec	Northnts	SP6259	52°13·8′	1°5·1′W	T	152
Weedon Hill	Bucks	SP8116	51°50·4′	0°49·1′W	X	165
Weedon Hill Fm	Bucks	SU9399	51°41·2′	0°38·9′W	FM	165
Weedon Hill Fm	Northnts	SP6258	52°13·2′	1°5·1′W	FM	152
Weedonhill Wood	Bucks	SU9499	51°41·1′	0°38·0′W	F	165
Weedon Lodge	Northnts	SP6157	52°12·7′	1°6·0′W	X	152
Weedon Lois	Northnts	SP6047	52°7·3′	1°7·0′W	T	152
Wee Fea	Orkney	ND2894	58°49·9′	3°14·3′W	X	7
Wee Fell	S Ayr	NX1878	55°4·0′	4°50·6′W	X	76
Weeford	Staffs	SK1403	52°37·7′	1°47·2′W	T	139
Weeford Park	Staffs	SK1401	52°36·6′	1°47·2′W	F	139
Weeford Park Fm	Birm	SK1300	52°36·1′	1°48·1′W	FM	139
Wee Hill	S Lanak	NS7426	55°30·9′	3°59·3′W	X	71
Wee Hill	S Lanak	NS9734	55°35·6′	3°37·6′W	H	72
Wee Hill of Craigmulloch	E Ayr	NX4895	55°13·8′	4°23·0′W	H	77
Wee Hill of Glenmount	E Ayr	NS4501	55°17·0′	4°26·0′W	H	77
Week	Devon	SS5606	50°50·4′	4°2·3′W	X	191
Week	Devon	SS5627	51°1·7′	4°2·8′W	T	180
Week	Devon	SS6118	50°56·9′	3°58·3′W	X	180
Week	Devon	SS6501	50°47·8′	3°54·6′W	X	191
Week	Devon	SS7316	50°56·0′	3°48·1′W	X	180
Week	Devon	SS7823	50°59·8′	3°43·9′W	X	180
Week	Devon	ST0307	50°51·5′	3°22·3′W	X	192
Week	Devon	SX4581	50°36·7′	4°11·1′W	T	201
Week	Devon	SX7862	50°26·9′	3°42·7′W	T	202
Week	Somer	SS9133	51°5·4′	3°33·0′W	X	181
Weekaborough	Devon	SX8464	50°28·1′	3°37·7′W	X	202
Week Barton	Devon	SS4612	50°53·5′	4°11·0′W	X	180,190
Week Common	Dorset	SZ1399	50°47·7′	1°48·5′W	X	195
Week Down	Devon	SS6017	50°56·4′	3°59·2′W	X	180
Week Down	I of W	SZ5377	50°35·6′	1°14·7′W	X	196
Weeke	Devon	SS7606	50°50·7′	3°45·3′W	T	191
Weeke	Devon	SX7047	50°18·8′	3°49·2′W	X	202
Weeke	Hants	SU4630	51°4·3′	1°20·2′W	T	185
Weeke Barton	Devon	SX8287	50°40·5′	3°39·8′W	X	191
Weeke Fm	Devon	SS8511	50°53·5′	3°37·7′W	FM	191
Weeke Fm	Devon	SX6653	50°21·9′	3°52·7′W	FM	202
Weeke Fm	Devon	SX7097	50°45·7′	3°50·2′W	FM	191
Weekefield Fm	Somer	SS9434	51°6·0′	3°30·5′W	FM	181
Week Fm	Bath & NE Somer	ST7260	51°20·5′	2°23·7′W	FM	172
Week Fm	Devon	SX5191	50°42·2′	4°6·2′W	FM	191
Week Fm	Dorset	SU1300	50°48·2′	1°48·5′W	FM	195
Week Fm	I of W	SZ5377	50°35·6′	1°14·7′W	FM	196
Week Fm	Somer	ST0532	51°5·0′	3°21·0′W	FM	181
Week Green	Corn	SX2397	50°45·0′	4°30·2′W	T	190
Week Green Fm	Hants	SU7226	51°2·0′	0°58·0′W	FM	186,197
Weekhayne	Devon	SY2092	50°43·6′	3°7·6′W	X	192,193
Weekley	Northnts	SP8880	52°24·9′	0°42·0′W	T	141
Weekley Hall Wood	Northnts	SP8782	52°26·0′	0°42·8′W	F	141
Weekmoor	Somer	ST1325	51°1·3′	3°14·0′W	T	181,193
Week Orchard	Corn	SS2300	50°46·6′	4°30·3′W	X	190
Weekpark Plantn	Devon	SS4202	50°48·0′	4°14·2′W	F	190
Weeks	I of W	SZ5991	50°43·2′	1°9·5′W	T	196
Weeks Fm	Wilts	ST9985	51°34·1′	2°0·5′W	FM	173

Weeks-in-the-Moor	Devon	SX5194	50°43·8′	4°6·3′W	X	191
Week St Mary	Corn	SX2397	50°45·0′	4°30·2′W	T	190
Week Street Down	Dorset	ST9613	50°55·2′	2°3·0′W	X	195
Weel	E Yorks	TA0639	53°50·4′	0°22·9′W	T	107
Wee Lanes	S Ayr	NX2598	55°15·0′	4°44·8′W	X	76
Weel Carr	E Yorks	TA0739	53°50·4′	0°22·0′W	X	107
Wee Leith Hill	S Ayr	NX0872	55°0·6′	4°59·7′W	X	76
Weeley	Essex	TM1422	51°51·6′	1°6·9′E	T	168,169
Weeleyhall Wood	Essex	TM1520	51°50·5′	1°7·7′E	F	168,169
Weeley Heath	Essex	TM1520	51°50·5′	1°7·7′E	T	168,169
Weeley Lodge	Essex	TM1621	51°51·0′	1°8·6′E	X	168,169
Weel Fm	Devon	SS5119	50°57·3′	4°6·9′W	FM	180
Weelie's Taing	Orkney	HY5053	59°21·9′	2°52·3′W	X	5
Weels	Renf	NS3462	55°49·6′	4°38·6′W	X	63
Weelsby	NE Lincs	TA2808	53°33·4′	0°3·6′W	T	113
Weelsby Woods	NE Lincs	TA2807	53°32·9′	0°3·7′W	F	113
Weem	Pth & Kin	NN8449	56°37·4′	3°53·0′W	T	52
Wee Meaul	D & G	NX5699	55°16·1′	4°15·6′W	X	77
Weem Hill	Pth & Kin	NN8251	56°38·4′	3°55·0′W	H	52
Weens Ho	Scot Bord	NT5812	55°24·3′	2°39·4′W	X	80
Weensmoor	Scot Bord	NT5712	55°24·3′	2°40·3′W	X	80
Weeping Cross	Shrops	SJ5110	52°41·4′	2°43·1′W	X	126
Weeping Cross	Staffs	SJ9421	52°47·4′	2°4·9′W	T	127
Wee Queensbury	D & G	NX9897	55°15·7′	3°35·9′W	H	78
Weetfoot Bog	Scot Bord	NT6752	55°45·9′	2°31·1′W	X	67,74
Weeth	Corn	SW6527	50°6·0′	5°16·8′W	X	203
Weethick Fm	Orkney	HY4909	58°58·2′	2°52·7′W	FM	6,7
Weethick Head	Orkney	HY4909	58°58·2′	2°52·7′W	X	6,7
Weethick Point	Orkney	HY4909	58°58·2′	2°52·7′W	X	6,7
Weethley	Warw	SP0555	52°11·8′	1°55·2′W	T	150
Weethley Bank	Warw	SP0554	52°11·3′	1°55·2′W	T	150
Weethley Fm	Warw	SP0555	52°11·8′	1°55·2′W	FM	150
Weethley Gate	Warw	SP0554	52°11·3′	1°55·2′W	T	150
Weethley Wood	Warw	SP0455	52°11·8′	1°56·1′W	F	150
Weeting	Norf	TL7789	52°28·4′	0°36·8′E	T	144
Weetingshill	Aberd	NJ9050	57°32·7′	2°9·6′W	X	30
Weeton	E Yorks	TA3520	53°39·8′	0°3·0′E	T	107,113
Weeton	Lancs	SD3834	53°48·2′	2°56·1′W	T	102
Weeton	N Yks	SE2846	53°54·8′	1°34·0′W	T	104
Weeton Camp	Lancs	SD3836	53°49·2′	2°56·1′W	X	102
Weeton Lane Heads	Lancs	SD3934	53°48·2′	2°55·2′W	X	102
Weeton Sta	N Yks	SE2747	53°55·3′	1°34·9′W	X	104
Weets	Aberd	NJ5730	57°21·8′	2°42·4′W	X	29,37
Weets Hill	Lancs	SD8544	53°53·8′	2°13·3′W	H	103
Weets Ho	Lancs	SD8544	53°53·8′	2°13·3′W	X	103
Weets, The	N Yks	SD9263	54°4·0′	2°6·9′W	X	98
Weetwood	Leeds	SE2737	53°50·0′	1°35·0′W	T	104
Weet Wood	Leeds	SE4434	53°48·3′	1°19·5′W	F	105
Weetwood Common	Ches	SJ5266	53°11·6′	2°42·7′W	T	117
Weetwood Hall	Leeds	SE2638	53°50·5′	1°35·9′W	X	104
Weetwood Hall	Northum	NU0129	55°33·5′	1°58·6′W	X	75
Weetwood Hill	Northum	NU0129	55°33·5′	1°58·6′W	H	75
Weetwood Moor	Northum	NU0128	55°33·0′	1°58·6′W	X	75
Weetyfoot	Moray	NJ5151	57°33·0′	2°48·7′W	X	29
Weftmuir	C of Edin	NT1076	55°58·4′	3°26·1′W	X	65
Wegnall	Powys	SO3263	52°15·9′	2°59·4′W	A	137,148
Weighton Clay Field	E Yorks	SE8742	53°52·3′	0°40·2′W	X	106
Weighton Common	E Yorks	SE8640	53°51·2′	0°41·1′W	X	106
Weighton Lock	E Yorks	SE8725	53°43·1′	0°40·5′W	X	106
Weighton Wold Ho	E Yorks	SE8941	53°51·7′	0°38·4′W	X	106
Weights Fm	Worcs	SP0369	52°19·4′	1°57·0′W	FM	139
Weights Wood	E Susx	TQ8225	51°0·0′	0°36·0′E	F	188,199
Weinnia Ness	Shetld	HU1653	60°15·9′	1°42·2′W	X	3
Weir	Essex	TQ8089	51°34·5′	0°36·3′E	T	178
Weirbrook	Shrops	SJ3424	52°48·8′	2°58·4′W	T	126
Weird Law	Scot Bord	NT0723	55°29·8′	3°27·9′W	H	72
Weird's Wood	E Loth	NT5170	55°55·5′	2°46·6′W	F	66
Weir Dyke	N Lincs	SE9713	53°36·5′	0°31·6′W	W	112
Weirend	Heref	SO5723	51°54·5′	2°37·1′W	X	162
Weirglodd-ddu	Gwyn	SH8441	52°57·5′	3°43·2′W	X	124,125
Weir Green	Glos	SO7915	51°50·2′	2°17·9′W	X	162
Weir Ho	Somer	SS9326	51°1·6′	3°31·2′W	X	181
Weiris Wood	Angus	NO5161	56°44·5′	2°47·6′W	F	44
Weirmarsh Fm	Devon	SS6121	50°58·5′	3°58·4′W	FM	180
Weir Mill Fm	Devon	ST0410	50°53·1′	3°21·5′W	FM	192
Weiroch	Moray	NJ1839	57°26·3′	3°21·5′W	X	28
Weir Point	Corn	SW8136	50°11·2′	5°3·7′W	X	204
Weir Point	Corn	SX4361	50°25·9′	4°12·3′W	X	201
Weir Quay	Corn	SX4364	50°27·5′	4°12·3′W	T	201
Weirs Combe	Devon	SS7039	51°8·4′	3°51·1′W	X	180
Weirstock Fm	Essex	TL8831	51°57·0′	0°44·5′E	FM	168
Weir, The	Heref	SO4341	52°4·1′	2°49·5′W	X	148,149,161
Weir, The	Wilts	SU1177	51°29·7′	1°50·1′W	X	173
Weir Water	Somer	SS8345	51°11·8′	3°40·1′W	W	181
Weirwood Common	Somer	SS8346	51°12·3′	3°40·1′W	F	181
Weir Wood Resr	E Susx	TQ3934	51°5·5′	0°0·5′W	W	187
Weisdale	Shetld	HU3953	60°15·8′	1°17·2′W	T	3
Weisdale Hill	Shetld	HU3852	60°15·3′	1°18·3′W	H	3
Weisdale Voe	Shetld	HU3848	60°13·1′	1°18·4′W	W	3
Weitshaw	E Ayr	NS5529	55°32·2′	4°17·4′W	X	71
Weitshaw Muir	E Ayr	NS5730	55°32·8′	4°15·6′W	X	71
Weland	Orkney	HY4919	59°3·6′	2°52·9′W	X	6
Welbatch	Shrops	SJ4508	52°40·3′	2°48·4′W	X	126
Welbeck Abbey	Notts	SK5674	53°15·8′	1°9·2′W	A	120
Welbeck Fm	Norf	TG2800	52°33·2′	1°22·2′E	FM	134
Welbeck Hill	NE Lincs	TA2104	53°31·4′	0°10·1′W	X	113
Welbeck Park	Notts	SK5673	53°15·3′	1°9·2′W	X	120
Welbeck Woodhouse	Notts	SK5774	53°15·8′	1°8·3′W	X	120
Welborne	Norf	TG0609	52°38·6′	1°3·1′E	T	144
Welbourn	Lincs	SK9654	53°4·7′	0°33·6′W	T	121
Welbourne Common	Norf	TG0509	52°38·6′	1°2·2′E	T	144
Welbourne Fm	Lincs	TF5469	53°12·0′	0°18·7′E	FM	122
Welbourn Heath	Lincs	SK9853	53°4·1′	0°31·8′W	X	121
Welbourn Low Fields	Lincs	SK9454	53°4·7′	0°35·4′W	X	121
Welburn	N Yks	SE6884	54°15·1′	0°57·0′W	T	100
Welburn	N Yks	SE7267	54°5·9′	0°53·5′W	T	100
Welburn Grange	N Yks	SE6882	54°14·0′	0°57·0′W	X	100
Welburn Hall Sch	N Yks	SE6884	54°15·1′	0°57·0′W	X	100
Welbury	N Yks	NZ3902	54°25·0′	1°23·5′W	T	93
Welbury Grange	N Yks	NZ3900	54°23·9′	1°23·5′W	X	93
Welby	Lincs	SK9738	52°56·1′	0°33·0′W	T	130
Welby Fm	Lincs	TF4125	52°48·5′	0°5·9′E	FM	131
Welby Grange	Leic	SK7321	52°47·1′	0°54·7′W	X	129
Welby Heath	Lincs	SK9736	52°55·0′	0°33·0′W	X	130
Welby Ho	Lincs	TF4327	52°49·5′	0°7·7′E	X	131
Welby Lodge Fm	Lincs	SK9837	52°55·5′	0°32·1′W	FM	130
Welby Pastures	Lincs	SK9740	52°57·1′	0°33·0′W	X	130
Welby Village	Leic	SK7220	52°46·6′	0°55·6′W	A	129
Welby Warren	Lincs	SK9535	52°54·5′	0°34·8′W	X	130
Welches	Essex	TM1318	51°49·4′	1°5·9′E	X	168,169
Welches Dam	Cambs	TL4686	52°27·4′	0°9·3′E	X	143
Welches Fm	Herts	TL2617	51°50·5′	0°9·9′W	FM	166
Welcombe	Devon	SS2218	50°56·3′	4°31·6′W	T	190
Welcombe	Devon	SS5921	50°58·5′	4°0·1′W	X	180
Welcombe	Devon	SS6833	51°5·1′	3°52·7′W	X	180
Welcombe Cross	Devon	SS2617	50°55·8′	4°28·2′W	X	190
Welcombe Hills Country Park	Warw	SP2157	52°12·9′	1°41·2′W	X	151
Welcombe (Hotel)	Warw	SP2056	52°12·3′	1°42·0′W	X	151
Welcombe Mouth	Devon	SS2118	50°56·3′	4°32·5′W	W	190
Welcome Hill	Dorset	SY5095	50°45·4′	2°42·1′W	X	194
Welcome Nook	Cumbr	SD1193	54°19·7′	3°21·7′W	X	96
Weld Bank	Lancs	SD5816	53°38·6′	2°37·7′W	T	108
Weld House Fm	Ches	SJ8661	53°9·0′	2°12·2′W	FM	118
Weldon	Northnts	SP9289	52°29·7′	0°38·3′W	T	141
Weldon	Northum	NZ1398	55°16·8′	1°47·3′W	T	81
Weldon Fm	Notts	SK7051	53°3·3′	0°56·9′W	FM	120
Weldon Lodge	Northnts	SP9191	52°30·8′	0°39·1′W	X	141
Weldon Park	Northnts	SP9490	52°30·2′	0°36·5′W	F	141
Weldon's Plantation	E Yorks	TA3125	53°42·5′	0°0·5′W	F	107,113
Welford	Northnts	SP6480	52°25·1′	1°3·1′W	T	140
Welford	V of Glam	ST0868	51°24·5′	3°19·0′W	X	170
Welford	W Berks	SU4073	51°27·5′	1°25·1′W	T	174
Welford Hill	Warw	SP1550	52°9·1′	1°46·4′W	H	151
Welford Lodge	Northnts	SP6579	52°24·5′	1°2·3′W	X	141
Welford Lodge Fm	Northnts	SP6478	52°24·0′	1°3·2′W	FM	140
Welford-on-Avon	Warw	SP1451	52°9·7′	1°47·3′W	T	151
Welford Park	W Berks	SU4073	51°27·5′	1°25·1′W	X	174
Welford Pasture Fm	Warw	SP1251	52°9·7′	1°49·1′W	FM	150
Welford Resr	Northnts	SP6481	52°25·6′	1°3·1′W	W	140
Welham	Leic	SP7692	52°31·5′	0°52·4′W	T	141
Welham	Notts	SK7282	53°20·0′	0°54·7′W	T	120
Welham	Somer	ST6631	51°4·9′	2°28·7′W	T	183
Welhambridge	E Yorks	SE7934	53°48·0′	0°47·6′W	T	105,106
Welham Bridge Fm	E Yorks	SE7934	53°48·0′	0°47·6′W	FM	105,106
Welham Green	Herts	TL2305	51°44·0′	0°12·7′W	T	166
Welham Hall	Notts	SK7281	53°19·5′	0°54·7′W	X	120
Welham Hall Fm	N Yks	SE7869	54°6·9′	0°48·0′W	FM	100
Welham Lodge	Leic	SP7593	52°32·0′	0°53·3′W	X	141
Welham's Fm	Essex	TM1026	51°53·8′	1°3·5′E	FM	168,169
Welham Wold Fm	N Yks	SE7868	54°6·4′	0°48·0′W	FM	100
Well	Hants	SU7646	51°12·7′	0°54·3′W	T	186
Well	Lincs	TF4473	53°14·3′	0°9·9′E	T	122
Well	N Yks	SE2681	54°13·7′	1°35·7′W	T	99
Well	Somer	SS9639	51°8·7′	3°28·8′W	X	181
Wellacres Fm	Glos	SP1736	52°1·6′	1°44·7′W	FM	151
Welland	Worcs	SO7939	52°3·2′	2°18·0′W	T	150
Welland Court	Worcs	SO8139	52°3·2′	2°16·2′W	X	150
Welland Down	Devon	SS8106	50°50·7′	3°41·0′W	X	191
Welland Fm	Lincs	TF2517	52°44·4′	0°8·5′W	FM	131
Welland Ho	Lincs	TF3326	52°49·1′	0°1·2′W	X	131
Welland House Fm	Lincs	TF2828	52°50·3′	0°5·6′W	FM	131
Welland House Fm	Lincs	TF2930	52°51·4′	0°4·6′W	FM	131
Welland Lodge	Worcs	SO8139	52°3·2′	2°16·2′W	X	150
Wellands	Devon	ST2701	50°48·5′	3°1·8′W	X	193
Wellands Fm	S Tyne	NZ4062	54°57·3′	1°22·1′W	FM	88
Welland Stone	Worcs	SO8138	52°2·6′	2°16·2′W	T	150
Well Bands	Cumbr	SD7496	54°21·8′	2°23·6′W	X	98
Wellbank	Aberd	NK1043	57°28·9′	1°49·5′W	X	30
Wellbank	Angus	NO4059	56°43·4′	2°58·4′W	X	54
Wellbank	Angus	NO4637	56°31·6′	2°52·2′W	T	54
Wellbank	Angus	NO4736	56°31·0′	2°51·2′W	T	54
Wellbank	Highld	NH5247	57°29·6′	4°27·7′W	X	26
Well Bank	Lancs	SD7823	53°42·4′	2°19·6′W	X	103
Wellbank	Pth & Kin	NO2732	56°28·7′	3°10·7′W	X	53
Well Barn	Oxon	SU5782	51°32·3′	1°10·3′W	X	174
Wellbeck Fm	Lincs	SK8662	53°9·1′	0°42·4′W	FM	121
Well Beck Fm	Lincs	TF4574	53°14·8′	0°10·8′E	FM	122
Well Bottom	Dorset	ST9116	50°56·8′	2°7·3′W	T	184
Well Bottom	E Susx	TQ4505	50°49·8′	0°3·9′E	X	198
Well Bottom	Wilts	ST9237	51°8·2′	2°6·5′W	X	184
Well Bottom	Wilts	SU1148	51°14·1′	1°50·2′W	X	184
Well Bottom Down	Dorset	SY6898	50°47·1′	2°26·9′W	X	194
Wellbottom Down	W Berks	SU3183	51°32·9′	1°32·8′W	X	174
Wellbrae	S Lanak	NS9640	55°38·8′	3°38·7′W	X	72
Wellbrae Resrs	S Lanak	NS6853	55°45·4′	4°5·8′W	W	64
Wellbrook	E Susx	TQ5726	51°0·9′	0°14·7′E	T	188,199
Wellbrook Fm	Kent	TR0459	51°17·8′	0°56·0′E	FM	178,179
Wellbrook Manor	Heref	SO3538	52°2·4′	2°56·5′W	A	149,161
Wellburn	Northum	NZ0863	54°57·9′	1°52·1′W	X	88
Wellburn	Pth & Kin	NO1801	56°11·9′	3°18·9′W	X	58
Wellburn	S Lanak	NS8041	55°39·1′	3°54·0′W	X	71,72
Wellbury Ho	Herts	TL1329	51°57·1′	0°20·9′W	X	166
Wellbutts	S Lanak	NT0643	55°40·5′	3°29·2′W	X	72
Well Chapel	Corn	SX3769	50°30·1′	4°17·5′W	A	201
Wellcleuch Plantn	Scot Bord	NT6105	55°20·5′	2°36·5′W	F	80
Well Close Fm	N Yks	SE1893	54°20·2′	1°43·0′W	FM	99
Well Close Fm	N Yks	SE5265	54°4·9′	1°11·9′W	FM	100
Wellcoombe	Devon	SS8805	50°50·3′	3°35·1′W	X	192
Well Copse	Hants	SU4230	51°4·3′	1°23·6′W	F	185
Well Copse	W Berks	SU3879	51°30·7′	1°26·8′W	F	174
Well Court	Kent	TR1361	51°18·7′	1°3·8′E	X	179
Well Covert	Devon	SX8776	50°34·6′	3°35·4′W	F	192
Well Creek	Norf	TF5401	52°35·3′	0°16·8′E	W	143
Well Cross	Devon	SX6855	50°23·0′	3°51·0′W	X	202
Wellcross Grange	W Susx	TQ1330	51°3·7′	0°22·9′W	X	187
Welldale	D & G	NY1866	54°59·2′	3°16·5′W	T	85
Welldale Beck	N Yks	SE9181	54°13·2′	0°35·8′W	W	101
Welldale Fm	Notts	SK5629	52°51·6′	1°9·7′W	FM	129
Welldale Fm	N Yks	SE9182	54°13·8′	0°35·8′W	FM	101
Welldean Hill	Scot Bord	NT3429	55°33·3′	3°2·3′W	H	73
Wellees Fm	Renf	NS3968	55°53·0′	4°34·0′W	FM	63
Wellees Rig	D & G	NX5869	55°0·0′	4°12·8′W	H	83
Well End	Bucks	SU8888	51°35·3′	0°43·4′W	T	175
Well End	Herts	TQ2098	51°40·3′	0°15·5′W	T	166,176
Weller's Town	Kent	TQ5044	51°10·8′	0°9·2′E	T	188
Wellesbourne	Warw	SP2755	52°11·8′	1°35·9′W	T	151
Wellesbourne Wood	Warw	SP2653	52°10·7′	1°36·8′W	F	151
Welleslea	N Lanak	NS8763	55°51·1′	3°47·9′W	X	65
Wellesley Fm	Devon	SS5926	51°1·2′	4°0·2′W	FM	180
Wellesley Fm	Somer	ST5543	51°11·3′	2°38·2′W	FM	182,183
Wellesley Ho	Kent	TQ8650	51°13·4′	0°40·2′E	X	189
Well Fen Fm	Cambs	TL4797	52°33·3′	0°10·5′E	FM	143
Wellfield	Aberd	NO8492	57°1·4′	2°15·4′W	X	38,45
Wellfield	Fife	NO1909	56°16·3′	3°18·0′W	X	58
Wellfield Fm	Devon	SY3799	50°47·5′	2°53·2′W	FM	193
Well Field Fm	N Yks	SE6368	54°6·5′	1°1·8′W	FM	100
Wellfield Fm	Shrops	SJ4533	52°53·7′	2°48·7′W	FM	126
Wellfield Ho	N Yks	SE3689	54°18·0′	1°26·4′W	X	99
Wellfield Ho	Pth & Kin	NO1616	56°20·0′	3°21·1′W	X	58
Wellfield Ho	Somer	ST3748	51°13·9′	2°53·8′W	X	182
Wellfield Steading	Fife	NO1910	56°16·8′	3°18·1′W	X	58
Well Fm	Bucks	SP9915	51°49·7′	0°33·4′W	FM	165
Well Fm	Devon	SS9309	50°52·5′	3°30·9′W	FM	192
Well Fm	Devon	SX4565	50°28·1′	4°10·7′W	FM	201
Well Fm	Devon	SX6890	50°41·9′	3°51·8′W	FM	191
Well Fm	Devon	SX7768	50°30·2′	3°43·7′W	FM	202
Well Fm	Herts	TL0805	51°44·2′	0°25·8′W	FM	166
Well Fm	N Yks	NZ5506	54°27·0′	1°8·7′W	FM	93
Well Fm	Shrops	SO6481	52°25·8′	2°31·4′W	FM	138
Well Fm	Somer	SS9442	51°10·3′	3°30·6′W	FM	181
Well Fm	Staffs	SK0062	53°9·5′	1°59·6′W	FM	119
Well Foot	Cumbr	NY4903	54°25·4′	2°46·7′W	X	90
Wellford	Angus	NO4860	56°44·0′	2°50·5′W	X	44
Wellgill	Cumbr	NY7744	54°47·7′	2°21·0′W	X	86,87
Wellgrain Dod	S Lanak	NS9017	55°26·3′	3°43·9′W	H	71,78
Well Grange	Lincs	TF4374	53°14·9′	0°9·0′E	X	122
Wellgreen	S Lanak	NS7148	55°42·8′	4°2·8′W	X	64
Well Green	Traf	SJ7886	53°22·5′	2°19·4′W	T	109
Wellgreens	Highld	NH5792	57°53·9′	4°24·3′W	X	21
Wellground Fm	Bucks	SU7494	51°38·6′	0°55·4′W	FM	175
Wellground Fm	Bucks	SU7495	51°39·2′	0°55·4′W	FM	165
Wellhall	Clackm	NS9796	56°9·0′	3°39·0′W	X	58
Well Hall	Gren	TQ4275	51°27·6′	0°3·0′E	X	177
Well Hall	Norf	TF7220	52°45·2′	0°33·3′E	X	132
Wellham Fm	Somer	ST5128	51°3·2′	2°41·6′W	FM	183
Wellhams Brook	Somer	ST4917	50°57·2′	2°43·2′W	W	183,193
Wellham's Mill	Somer	ST4818	50°57·8′	2°44·0′W	X	193
Wellham Wood	Kent	TQ8948	51°12·2′	0°42·7′E	F	189
Wellhanger Copse	W Susx	SU8614	50°55·4′	0°46·2′W	F	197
Wellhaugh	Northum	NY6489	55°11·9′	2°33·5′W	X	80
Wellhaugh Point	Northum	NU2704	55°20·0′	1°34·0′W	X	81
Wellhayes Fm	Devon	ST0223	51°0·1′	3°23·4′W	FM	181
Wellhayes Fm	Devon	ST2103	50°49·5′	3°6·9′W	FM	192,193
Wellhead	Aberd	NJ7400	57°5·7′	2°25·3′W	X	38
Wellhead	Aberd	NJ9736	57°25·1′	2°2·5′W	X	30
Well Head	Beds	SP9920	51°52·4′	0°33·3′W	X	165
Well Head	Cumbr	NY8116	54°32·6′	2°17·2′W	X	91,92
Wellhead	Herts	TL1727	51°56·0′	0°17·5′W	X	166
Well-head	Highld	NH7162	57°38·0′	4°9·2′W	X	21,27
Well Head	N Yks	SD9542	53°52·7′	2°4·1′W	X	103
Well Head	N Yks	SD9945	53°54·3′	2°0·5′W	X	103
Well Head	Oxon	SP2608	51°46·4′	1°37·0′W	W	163
Wellhead	S Lanak	NS9046	55°42·0′	3°44·6′W	X	72
Well Head Laithe	N Yks	SD9057	54°0·8′	2°8·7′W	X	103
Wellheads	Aberd	NJ4839	57°26·6′	2°51·5′W	X	28,29
Wellheads	Aberd	NJ5815	57°13·7′	2°41·3′W	X	37
Wellheads	Aberd	NJ5962	57°39·0′	2°40·8′W	X	29
Well Heads	Brad	SE0833	53°47·8′	1°52·3′W	T	104
Well Heads	Cumbr	SD5186	54°16·3′	2°44·7′W	X	97
Wellheads	Moray	NJ3860	57°37·8′	3°1·8′W	X	28
Well Heads	Moray	NJ5551	57°33·1′	2°44·7′W	X	29
Wellheads	W Loth	NT0664	55°51·9′	3°29·7′W	X	65
Wellheads Hush	Durham	NY8240	54°45·5′	2°16·4′W	X	86,87
Wellhill	Angus	NO6860	56°44·1′	2°30·9′W	X	45
Well Hill	D & G	NS6907	55°20·6′	4°3·5′W	H	71,77
Well Hill	D & G	NS8314	55°24·6′	3°50·4′W	H	71,78
Well Hill	D & G	NS9106	55°20·4′	3°42·7′W	H	71,78
Wellhill	D & G	NX7773	55°2·4′	3°55·1′W	X	84
Wellhill	E Ayr	NS5814	55°24·2′	4°14·1′W	X	71
Well Hill	Kent	TQ4963	51°21·0′	0°8·8′E	T	177,188
Wellhill	Moray	NJ0061	57°37·9′	3°40·0′W	X	27
Well Hill	Northum	NZ1882	55°8·2′	1°42·6′W	X	81
Wellhill	Pth & Kin	NO0215	56°19·3′	3°34·6′W	X	58
Wellhill Fm	Leeds	SE4242	53°52·6′	1°21·3′W	FM	105
Wellhill Plantation	Glos	SO9903	51°43·8′	2°0·5′W	F	163
Well Ho	Ches	SJ4657	53°6·7′	2°48·0′W	X	117
Well Ho	Cumbr	NY6920	54°34·7′	2°28·4′W	X	91
Well Ho	Cumbr	SD2185	54°15·5′	3°12·3′W	X	96
Well Ho	Cumbr	SD2782	54°14·0′	3°6·8′W	X	96,97
Well Ho	D & G	NX3261	54°55·2′	4°36·9′W	X	82
Well Ho	Lancs	SD7554	53°59·1′	2°22·5′W	X	103
Well Ho	Northum	NY7368	55°0·6′	2°24·9′W	X	86,87
Well Ho	Northum	NY9674	55°3·9′	2°3·3′W	X	87
Well Ho	N Yks	SE0481	54°13·7′	1°55·9′W	X	98
Well Ho	N Yks	SE0874	54°9·9′	1°52·2′W	X	99
Well Ho	N Yks	SE2361	54°2·9′	1°38·5′W	X	99
Well Ho Fm	Flint	SJ3664	53°10·4′	2°57·0′W	FM	117
Wellhope	Durham	NY8241	54°46·1′	2°16·4′W	X	86,87
Wellhope	Northum	NU1105	55°20·6′	1°49·2′W	X	81
Wellhope Burn	Durham	NY8141	54°46·1′	2°17·3′W	W	86,87
Wellhope Burn	Northum	NY7749	54°50·4′	2°21·1′W	W	86,87
Wellhope Knowe	Northum	NU0905	55°20·6′	1°51·1′W	X	81
Wellhope Moor	Durham	NY8041	54°46·1′	2°18·2′W	X	86,87
Well Ho, The	E Susx	TQ6510	50°52·2′	0°21·1′E	X	199
Well Ho, The	Suff	TL9753	52°8·6′	0°53·1′E	X	155
Wellhouse	Aberd	NJ5515	57°13·7′	2°44·3′W	X	37
Wellhouse	D & G	NX0070	54°59·3′	5°7·1′W	X	76,82
Well House	Essex	TL4630	51°57·2′	0°7·9′E	A	167
Wellhouse	Highld	NH5651	57°31·8′	4°23·8′W	X	26

Wellhouse	Highld	NH5755	57°34·0′	4°23·0′W	X	26
Wellhouse	Kirk	SE0914	53°37·6′	1°51·4′W	T	110
Wellhouse	Northum	NZ0283	55°8·7′	1°57·7′W	X	81
Wellhouse	W Berks	SU5272	51°26·9′	1°14·7′W	T	174
Wellhouse Bay	Glos	SO6603	51°43·7′	2°29·1′W	W	162
Wellhouse Fm	Cumbr	SD2974	54°9·7′	3°4·8′W	FM	96,97
Wellhouse Fm	Essex	TL9131	51°56·9′	0°47·2′E	FM	168
Wellhouse Fm	Essex	TM0113	51°47·0′	0°55·2′E	FM	168
Wellhouse Fm	E Susx	TQ3217	50°56·5′	0°6·9′W	FM	198
Wellhouse Fm	Hants	SU4760	51°20·5′	1°19·1′W	FM	174
Well House Fm	Hants	SU7563	51°21·9′	0°55·0′W	FM	175,186
Well House Fm	Leeds	SE4333	53°47·7′	1°20·4′W	FM	105
Well House Fm	Northum	NT9405	55°20·6′	2°5·2′W	FM	80
Well House Fm	Northum	NZ0466	54°59·6′	1°55·8′W	FM	87
Wellhouse Fm	Sheff	SK2798	53°28·9′	1°35·2′W	X	110
Wellhouse Fm	Wilts	SU1227	51°2·8′	1°49·3′W	FM	184
Wellhowe	Aberd	NJ9151	57°33·2′	2°8·6′W	X	30
Wellinditch	Essex	TQ8198	51°39·3′	0°37·4′E	X	168
Welling	Bexley	TQ4675	51°27·5′	0°6·5′E	T	177
Wellingborough	Northnts	SP8967	52°17·9′	0°41·3′W	T	152
Wellingborough Grange	Northnts	SP8669	52°19·0′	0°43·9′W	X	152
Wellingham	Norf	TF8722	52°46·0′	0°46·7′E	T	132
Wellingham Ho	E Susx	TQ4313	50°54·1′	0°2·4′E	X	198
Wellingley	Donc	SK5996	53°27·7′	1°6·3′W	X	111
Wellingore	Lincs	SK9856	53°5·8′	0°31·8′W	T	121
Wellingore Heath	Lincs	SK9955	53°5·2′	0°30·9′W	X	121
Wellingore Low Fields	Lincs	SK9655	53°5·2′	0°33·6′W	X	121
Wellings, The	Staffs	SJ7638	52°56·6′	2°21·0′W	X	127
Wellington	Aberd	NK1044	57°29·4′	1°49·5′W	X	30
Wellington	Cumbr	NY0704	54°25·6′	3°25·6′W	T	89
Wellington	Cumbr	NY1029	54°39·1′	3°23·3′W	X	89
Wellington	Heref	SO4948	52°7·9′	2°44·3′W	T	148,149
Wellington	Somer	ST1420	50°58·6′	3°13·1′W	T	181,193
Wellington	Wrekin	SJ6411	52°42·0′	2°31·6′W	T	127
Wellington Brook	Heref	SO4748	52°7·9′	2°46·1′W	W	148,149
Wellington Coll	Brackn	SU8363	51°21·8′	0°48·1′W	X	175,186
Wellington Coppice	Heref	SO4835	52°0·9′	2°45·1′W	F	149,161
Wellington Country Park	Hants	SU7262	51°21·4′	0°57·6′W	X	175,186
Wellington Farm	Cumbr	NY1543	54°46·7′	3°18·9′W	FM	85
Wellington Fm	N Yks	NZ4402	54°24·9′	1°18·9′W	FM	93
Wellington Fm	Somer	ST4853	51°16·7′	2°44·3′W	FM	182
Wellington Fm	Staffs	SK0256	53°6·3′	1°57·8′W	FM	119
Wellington Heath	Heref	SO7140	52°3·7′	2°25·0′W	T	149
Wellington Hill	Leeds	SE3538	53°50·5′	1°27·7′W	T	104
Wellington Hill	Somer	ST1317	50°57·0′	3°13·9′W	X	181,193
Wellington Ho	Midlo	NT3269	55°54·8′	3°4·8′W	X	66
Wellington House Fm	Cambs	TL2487	52°28·2′	0°10·1′W	FM	142
Wellington Marsh	Heref	SO4947	52°7·4′	2°44·3′W	X	148,149
Wellington Monument	Hants	SU7161	51°20·8′	0°58·4′W	X	175,186
Wellington Monument	Somer	ST1317	50°57·0′	3°13·9′W	X	181,193
Wellington Sch	Midlo	NT2356	55°47·7′	3°13·3′W	X	66,73
Wellington's Monument	Derby	SK2673	53°15·4′	1°36·2′W	X	119
Wellington Wood	Heref	SO4849	52°8·4′	2°45·2′W	F	148,149
Wellisford	Somer	ST0921	50°59·1′	3°17·4′W	T	181
Well Isle	D & G	NW9872	55°0·3′	5°9·1′W	X	76,82
Well Knowe	Cumbr	SD3779	54°12·4′	2°57·5′W	X	96,97
Wellknowe Rigg	Cumbr	NY4369	55°1·0′	2°53·1′W	X	85
Well Land Fm	W Susx	TQ1821	50°58·8′	0°18·8′W	FM	198
Wellmarsh Creek	Kent	TQ9567	51°22·3′	0°48·5′E	W	178
Wellmore	Bucks	SP7035	52°0·8′	0°58·4′W	X	152
Welloe	Corn	SW5825	50°4·8′	5°22·6′W	X	203
Well of Cardowan	Aberd	NO6278	56°53·8′	2°37·0′W	W	45
Well of Don	Aberd	NJ1906	57°8·5′	3°19·9′W	W	36
Well of the Lecht	Moray	NJ2315	57°13·4′	3°16·1′W	W	36
Wellow	Bath & NE Somer	ST7358	51°19·5′	2°22·9′W	T	172
Wellow	I of W	SZ3888	50°41·7′	1°27·3′W	T	196
Wellow	NE Lincs	TA2608	53°33·4′	0°5·5′W	T	113
Wellow	Notts	SK6766	53°11·4′	0°59·4′W	T	120
Wellow Brook	Bath & NE Somer	ST7558	51°19·5′	2°21·1′W	W	172
Wellow Park	Notts	SK6867	53°12·0′	0°58·5′W	F	120
Wellow Wood	Hants	SU2921	50°59·5′	1°34·8′W	T	185
Wellparks	Devon	SX8499	50°47·0′	3°38·4′W	X	191
Well Place	Oxon	SU6585	51°33·8′	1°3·3′W	T	175
Well Place Fm	Kent	TQ5344	51°10·7′	0°11·7′E	FM	188
Well Plantn	Scot Bord	NT4013	55°24·7′	2°56·4′W	F	79
Wellpond Green	Herts	TL4121	51°52·4′	0°3·3′E	T	167
Well Rash	Cumbr	NY2441	54°45·7′	3°10·4′W	X	85
Wellrig	Scot Bord	NT5928	55°32·9′	2°38·6′W	X	73,74
Wellrig Burn	Scot Bord	NT7653	55°46·4′	2°22·5′W	W	67,74
Well Rigg	Northum	NY8271	55°2·2′	2°16·5′W	H	86,87
Wellriggs	S Lanak	NS8449	55°43·5′	3°50·4′W	X	72
Wellroyd	Leeds	SE2137	53°50·0′	1°40·4′W	T	104
Wells	Somer	ST5445	51°12·4′	2°39·1′W	T	182,183
Wellsborough	Leic	SK3602	52°37·1′	1°27·7′W	T	140
Wells' Br	Cambs	TL3088	52°28·7′	0°4·7′W	X	142
Wells Cleugh	Northum	NY7578	55°6·0′	2°23·1′W	X	86,87
Well's Copse	Hants	SU5850	51°15·0′	1°9·7′W	F	185
Wells Corner	Suff	TM2771	52°17·6′	1°20·1′E	X	156
Wellsden	Angus	NO5665	56°46·7′	2°42·8′W	X	44
Wells Fm	Cambs	TL4649	52°7·4′	0°8·4′E	FM	154
Well's Fm	Essex	TL6002	51°41·9′	0°19·3′E	FM	167
Wells Fm	Herts	TL3002	51°42·3′	0°6·7′W	FM	166
Wells Fm	NE Lincs	TA1909	53°34·1′	0°11·8′W	FM	113
Wells Fm	Notts	SK7871	53°14·1′	0°49·5′W	FM	120,121
Wells Folly	Glos	SP2231	51°58·9′	1°40·4′W	X	151
Wellsforest	Aberd	NK0941	57°27·8′	1°50·5′W	X	30
Wells Green	Ches	SJ6853	53°4·6′	2°28·3′W	T	118
Wellsgreen Fm	Fife	NT3398	56°10·5′	3°4·3′W	FM	59
Wells Hall	Suff	TL9447	52°5·5′	0°50·3′E	X	155
Wellshead	Somer	SS8239	51°8·5′	3°40·8′W	X	181
Wellshead Allotment	Somer	SS8341	51°9·6′	3°40·0′W	X	181
Wellshields	S Lanak	NS8739	55°38·1′	3°47·3′W	X	71,72
Wells Hill Bottom Fm	Somer	ST5949	51°14·6′	2°34·9′W	FM	182,183
Wells Hill Fm	Hants	SU7247	51°13·3′	0°57·7′W	FM	186
Wellshot	N Lanak	NS7177	55°58·4′	4°3·6′W	X	64
Wellshot Hill	S Lanak	NS9617	55°26·4′	3°38·2′W	H	78
Wellshurst	E Susx	TQ5814	50°54·5′	0°15·2′E	X	199
Wellside	Aberd	NJ6124	57°18·6′	2°38·4′W	X	37
Wellside	Moray	NJ4355	57°35·1′	2°56·7′W	X	28
Wellside Fm	Moray	NJ0161	57°37·9′	3°39·0′W	FM	27
Wellsies	Pth & Kin	NO1937	56°31·3′	3°18·5′W	X	53
Well Sike	Cumbr	NY3864	54°58·3′	2°57·7′W	W	85
Wells-Next-The-Sea	Norf	TF9143	52°57·2′	0°51·0′E	T	132
Wells of Dee	Highld	NN9398	57°3·9′	3°45·4′W	W	36,43
Wells of Newton	Aberd	NJ8838	57°26·2′	2°11·5′W	X	30
Wells of Rothie	Aberd	NJ7137	57°25·6′	2°28·5′W	X	29
Wells of the Rees, The	D & G	NX2272	55°0·9′	4°46·6′W	A	76
Wells Park	Devon	ST0008	50°52·0′	3°24·9′W	X	192
Wellspring Fm	Derby	SK3374	53°16·0′	1°29·9′W	FM	119
Well Spring Fm	Somer	ST4607	50°51·8′	2°45·7′W	FM	193
Wellsprings	Somer	ST2226	51°1·9′	3°6·4′W	T	193
Wellsprings Drain	E Yorks	SE9953	53°58·1′	0°29·0′W	W	106
Wellsprings Fm	Durham	NZ2446	54°48·7′	1°37·2′W	FM	88
Well Springs Plantn	D & G	NY1280	55°6·6′	3°22·3′W	F	78
Wells Salt Marshes	Norf	TF9244	52°57·8′	0°51·9′E	W	132
Well's Green	Norf	TF8414	52°41·8′	0°43·8′E	X	132
Wells & Sheds	Essex	TL6402	51°41·8′	0°22·8′E	X	167
Wells Spa	Conwy	SH7865	53°10·3′	3°49·1′W	X	115
Wells Stables	Scot Bord	NT5917	55°27·0′	2°38·5′W	X	80
Wells, The	Heref	SO6253	52°10·7′	2°32·9′W	X	149
Wellston (ruin)	Shetld	HP6516	60°49·6′	0°47·8′W	X	1
Well Street	Kent	TQ6956	51°16·9′	0°25·8′E	T	178,188
Wellstye Green	Essex	TL6418	51°50·4′	0°23·2′E	T	167
Wellswood	Torbay	SX9264	50°28·2′	3°30·9′W	T	202
Wellsworth	Hants	SU7311	50°53·9′	0°57·3′W	X	197
Wellsyke Fm	Lincs	TF2363	53°9·2′	0°9·2′W	FM	122
Well, The	Lincs	TF5949	53°1·1′	0°22·6′E	W	131
Welltown	Corn	SX1367	50°28·6′	4°37·8′W	T	200
Well Town	Devon	SS9009	50°52·4′	3°33·4′W	T	192
Welltown	Devon	SX5470	50°30·9′	4°3·2′W	X	201
Welltown Fm	Devon	SX3585	50°38·7′	4°19·7′W	FM	201
Welltown Manor	Corn	SX0890	50°40·9′	4°42·7′W	A	190
Welltree	Fife	NO2906	56°14·7′	3°8·3′W	X	59
Welltree	Pth & Kin	NN9622	56°23·0′	3°40·6′W	X	52,53,58
Welltrees	E Ayr	NS6324	55°29·7′	4°9·7′W	X	71
Welltrees Hill	D & G	NS7504	55°19·1′	3°57·8′W	X	78
Welltrees Tappin	D & G	NS7504	55°19·1′	3°57·8′W	H	78
Welltrough Hall Fm	Ches	SJ8168	53°12·8′	2°16·7′W	FM	118
Well Turn	Lincs	TF4574	53°14·8′	0°10·8′E	X	122
Well Vale	Lincs	TF4373	53°14·3′	0°9·0′E	F	122
Well Vale Hall (School)	Lincs	TF4473	53°14·3′	0°9·9′E	X	122
Wellwick Fm	Bucks	SP8507	51°45·5′	0°45·7′W	FM	165
Wellwick Fm	Essex	TM1217	51°48·9′	1°4·9′E	FM	168,169
Wellwood	Aberd	NJ6306	57°8·9′	2°36·2′W	X	37
Well Wood	Corn	SX1566	50°28·1′	4°36·0′W	F	201
Well Wood	Cumbr	SD2486	54°16·1′	3°9·6′W	X	96
Wellwood	Fife	NT0989	56°5·4′	3°27·3′W	T	65
Well Wood	Herts	TL2703	51°42·9′	0°9·3′W	F	166
Wellwood Fm	Dorset	ST4703	50°49·7′	2°44·8′W	FM	193
Welmore Fm	Oxon	SU3697	51°40·5′	1°28·4′W	FM	164
Welney	Norf	TL5294	52°31·6′	0°14·8′E	T	143
Welney House Fm	Norf	TL5295	52°32·1′	0°14·9′E	FM	143
Welsbere Barton	Devon	SS8408	50°51·8′	3°38·5′W	X	191
Welsdale Bottom	Lincs	TF2584	53°20·5′	0°6·9′W	X	122
Welsford	Devon	SS2721	50°58·0′	4°27·4′W	T	190
Welsford Moor	Devon	SS2720	50°57·4′	4°27·4′W	X	190
Welshampton	Shrops	SJ4334	52°54·3′	2°50·4′W	T	126
Welsh Bicknor	Glos	SO5917	51°51·2′	2°35·3′W	T	162
Welshbury	Glos	SO6715	51°50·2′	2°28·3′W	A	162
Welshbury Wood	Glos	SO6715	51°50·2′	2°28·3′W	F	162
Welsh Court	Heref	SO6430	51°58·3′	2°31·0′W	X	149
Welshcroft Hill	Oxon	SP4039	52°3·1′	1°24·6′W	X	151
Welsh End	Shrops	SJ5135	52°54·9′	2°43·3′W	T	126
Welsh Folk Museum	Card	ST1177	51°29·3′	3°16·5′W	X	171
Welsh Frankton	Shrops	SJ3632	52°53·1′	2°56·7′W	T	126
Welsh Grounds	Newp	ST4381	51°31·7′	2°48·9′W	X	171,172
Welsh Harp	Brent	TQ2186	51°33·8′	0°14·9′W	T	176
Welsh Harp Fm	Powys	SJ2708	52°40·1′	3°4·4′W	FM	126
Welsh Hawking Centre	V of Glam	ST0969	51°25·0′	3°18·1′W	X	171
Welsh Highland Rly	Gwyn	SH5739	52°56·0′	4°7·3′W	X	124
Welsh Ho	Glos	SO7230	51°58·3′	2°24·1′W	X	149
Welsh Hook	Pemb	SM9327	51°54·4′	5°0·2′W	T	157,158
Welshie Law	Scot Bord	NT3329	55°33·3′	3°3·3′W	H	73
Welshman's Bay	Pemb	SM7904	51°41·7′	5°11·5′W	W	157
Welshman's Rock	Highld	NM4195	56°58·7′	6°15·3′W	X	39
Welsh Moor	Swan	SS5292	51°36·7′	4°7·9′W	X	159
Welsh Myers Fm	Leic	SK7502	52°36·9′	0°53·1′W	FM	141
Welsh Newton	Heref	SO5017	51°51·2′	2°43·2′W	T	162
Welsh Newton Common	Heref	SO5117	51°51·2′	2°42·3′W	T	162
Welshpool and Llanfair Railway	Powys	SJ1407	52°39·5′	3°15·9′W	X	125
Welshpool & Llanfair Light Rly	Powys	SJ2107	52°39·5′	3°9·7′W	X	126
Welshpool or Trallwng	Powys	SJ2207	52°39·5′	3°8·8′W	T	126
Welsh Road	Northnts	SP5049	52°8·5′	1°15·8′W	X	151
Welsh Road	Warw	SP3467	52°18·2′	1°29·7′W	X	151
Welsh Road	Warw	SP4359	52°13·9′	1°21·8′W	X	151
Welsh Road Fm	Warw	SP3764	52°16·6′	1°27·1′W	FM	151
Welsh's Fm	Lincs	TF4255	53°4·6′	0°7·6′E	FM	122
Welsh St Donats	V of Glam	ST0276	51°28·7′	3°24·3′W	T	170
Welsh Way	Glos	SP0505	51°44·9′	1°55·3′W	X	163
Welshwood Fm	Heref	SO2749	52°8·3′	3°3·6′W	FM	148
Welshwood Park	Essex	TM0226	51°54·0′	0°56·6′E	T	168
Welston	Pemb	SN0302	51°41·2′	4°50·6′W	X	157,158
Welstor	Devon	SX7473	50°32·8′	3°46·3′W	T	191
Weltmore Fm	Cambs	TL6085	52°26·6′	0°21·7′E	FM	143
Welton	Angus	NO4749	56°38·0′	2°51·4′W	X	54
Welton	Bath & NE Somer	ST6655	51°17·8′	2°28·9′W	T	172,183
Welton	Bath & NE Somer	ST6754	51°17·3′	2°28·0′W	T	183
Welton	Cumbr	NY3544	54°47·5′	3°0·2′W	T	85
Welton	E Ayr	NS5027	55°31·1′	4°22·1′W	T	70
Welton	E Yorks	SE9627	53°44·1′	0°32·3′W	T	106
Welton	Lincs	TF0179	53°18·2′	0°29·0′W	T	121
Welton	Northnts	SP5866	52°17·6′	1°8·6′W	T	152
Welton Beck	Lincs	TF4867	53°11·0′	0°13·3′E	W	122
Welton Cliff	Lincs	SK9779	53°18·2′	0°32·3′W	X	121
Welton Dale	E Yorks	SE9628	53°44·6′	0°32·2′W	X	106
Welton Fields	Northnts	SP5867	52°18·1′	1°8·6′W	X	152
Welton Fm	Northum	NZ0667	55°0·1′	1°53·9′W	FM	87
Welton Grange	Northnts	SP5966	52°17·6′	1°7·7′W	X	152
Welton Hall	Northum	NZ0667	55°0·1′	1°53·9′W	A	87
Welton High Wood	Lincs	TF4569	53°12·1′	0°10·7′E	F	122
Welton Hill	Lincs	TF0481	53°19·2′	0°25·9′W	T	121
Welton Hythe	Northnts	SP5966	52°17·6′	1°7·7′W	X	152
Welton le Marsh	Lincs	TF4768	53°11·6′	0°12·4′E	T	122
Welton le Wold	Lincs	TF2787	53°22·1′	0°5·1′W	T	113,122
Welton Lodge Fm	Northnts	SP5967	52°18·1′	1°7·7′W	FM	152
Welton Low Wood	Lincs	TF4670	53°12·7′	0°11·6′E	F	122
Welton Manor	Northnts	SP5865	52°17·0′	1°8·6′W	X	152
Welton Mill	E Yorks	SE9627	53°44·1′	0°32·3′W	X	106
Welton of Creuchies	Pth & Kin	NO2150	56°38·4′	3°16·8′W	X	53
Welton Place	Northnts	SP5766	52°17·6′	1°9·5′W	X	152
Welton, The	Angus	NO3055	56°41·1′	3°8·1′W	X	53
Welton, The	Pth & Kin	NO1944	56°35·1′	3°18·7′W	X	53
Welton Wold	E Yorks	SE9728	53°44·6′	0°31·3′W	X	106
Welton Wold Fm	E Yorks	SE9729	53°45·1′	0°31·3′W	FM	106
Welwick	E Yorks	TA3421	53°40·3′	0°2·1′E	T	107,113
Welwyn	Herts	TL2216	51°50·0′	0°13·4′W	T	166
Welwyn Garden City	Herts	TL2413	51°48·3′	0°11·7′W	T	166
Welwyn North Sta	Herts	TL2415	51°49·4′	0°11·6′W	X	166
Wem	Shrops	SJ5129	52°51·6′	2°43·3′W	T	126
Wembdon	Somer	ST2837	51°7·9′	3°1·4′W	T	182
Wembdon Fm	Somer	ST2838	51°8·4′	3°1·4′W	FM	182
Wemberham Cott	N Som	ST4065	51°23·1′	2°51·3′W	X	171,172,182
Wembley	Brent	TQ1785	51°33·3′	0°18·3′W	T	176
Wembley Fm	Notts	SK6029	52°51·5′	1°6·1′W	FM	129
Wembley Lodge	Notts	SK6029	52°51·5′	1°6·1′W	X	129
Wembley Park	Brent	TQ1986	51°33·8′	0°16·6′W	T	176
Wem Brook	Warw	SP3789	52°30·1′	1°26·9′W	W	140
Wembsworthy	Devon	SS2419	50°56·9′	4°30·0′W	X	190
Wembury	Devon	SX5248	50°19·0′	4°4·4′W	T	201
Wembury Bay	Devon	SX5147	50°18·5′	4°5·2′W	W	201
Wembury Ho	Devon	SX5349	50°19·6′	4°3·5′W	X	201
Wembury Point	Devon	SX5047	50°18·5′	4°6·0′W	X	201
Wembury Wood	Devon	SX5350	50°20·1′	4°3·6′W	F	201
Wembworthy	Devon	SS6609	50°52·1′	3°53·9′W	T	191
Wemmergill Hall	Durham	NY9021	54°35·3′	2°8·9′W	X	91,92
Wem Moss	Shrops	SJ4734	52°54·3′	2°46·9′W	F	126
Wems, The	Shrops	SJ6739	52°57·1′	2°29·1′W	X	127
Wemyss	Angus	NO4952	56°39·7′	2°49·5′W	X	54
Wemyss Bay	Inverc	NS1969	55°53·1′	4°53·2′W	T	63
Wemyss Bay	N Ayr	NS1968	55°52·5′	4°53·2′W	W	63
Wemyss Castle	Fife	NT3295	56°8·8′	3°5·2′W	A	59
Wemysshill	N Lanak	NS7952	55°45·0′	3°55·2′W	X	64
Wemyss Point	Inverc	NS1870	55°53·6′	4°54·2′W	X	63
Wemyss Wood	Fife	NT3298	56°10·4′	3°5·3′W	F	59
Wenallt	Carm	SN3218	51°50·4′	4°25·9′W	X	159
Wenallt	Carm	SN4209	51°45·7′	4°17·0′W	F	159
Wenallt	Carm	SN4320	51°51·6′	4°16·4′W	X	159
Wenallt	Carm	SN4825	51°54·4′	4°12·2′W	X	146
Wenallt	Carm	SN5418	51°50·7′	4°6·8′W	X	159
Wenallt	Carm	SN5840	52°2·7′	4°3·8′W	X	146
Wenallt	Cered	SN6771	52°19·5′	3°56·7′W	T	135
Wenallt	Conwy	SH8670	53°13·1′	3°42·0′W	X	116
Wenallt	Conwy	SH9663	53°9·5′	3°32·9′W	X	116
Wenallt	Gwyn	SH7317	52°44·4′	3°52·5′W	T	124
Wenallt	Gwyn	SH8123	52°47·7′	3°45·5′W	X	124,125
Wenallt	Gwyn	SH8818	52°45·1′	3°39·2′W	X	124,125
Wenallt	Gwyn	SH9021	52°46·8′	3°37·4′W	H	125
Wenallt	Gwyn	SH9842	52°58·2′	3°30·7′W	X	125
Wenallt	Powys	SH8300	52°35·4′	3°43·2′W	X	135,136
Wenallt	Powys	SJ1825	52°49·2′	3°12·6′W	X	125
Wenallt	Powys	SO0124	51°54·6′	3°26·0′W	X	160
Wenallt	Powys	SO1121	51°53·1′	3°17·2′W	X	161
Wenallt	Powys	SO2238	52°2·3′	3°7·8′W	X	161
Wenallt Fm	Nth Pt Talb	SS7899	51°40·8′	3°45·5′W	FM	170
Wenallt Wood	Nth Pt Talb	SS7899	51°40·8′	3°45·5′W	F	170
Wenalt	Gwyn	SH9234	52°53·8′	3°35·9′W	X	125
Wenbans	E Susx	TQ6329	51°2·5′	0°19·9′E	X	188,199
Wenchly Top	Inverc	NS2369	55°53·2′	4°49·4′W	H	63
Wendens Ambo	Essex	TL5136	52°0·3′	0°12·4′E	T	154
Wendlebury	Oxon	SP5619	51°52·2′	1°10·8′W	T	164
Wendling	Norf	TF9313	52°41·0′	0°51·7′E	T	132
Wendling Carr	Norf	TF9413	52°41·0′	0°52·6′E	X	132
Wendover	Bucks	SP8608	51°46·1′	0°44·8′W	T	165
Wendover Dean	Bucks	SP8704	51°43·9′	0°44·0′W	T	165
Wendover Lodge	Bucks	SP8605	51°44·5′	0°44·9′W	X	165
Wendover Woods	Bucks	SP8808	51°46·1′	0°43·1′W	F	165
Wendron	Corn	SW6731	50°8·2′	5°15·3′W	T	203
Wendy	Cambs	TL3247	52°6·6′	0°3·9′W	T	153
Wenffrwd	Cered	SN6793	52°31·4′	3°57·2′W	X	135
Wenffrwd	Powys	SJ2028	52°50·9′	3°10·9′W	X	126
Wenfordbridge	Corn	SX0875	50°32·8′	4°42·2′W	T	200
Wenham Grange	Suff	TM0740	52°1·4′	1°1·4′E	X	155,169
Wenham Hill	Suff	TM0737	51°59·8′	1°1·3′E	X	155,169
Wenham Manor Fm	W Susx	SU7823	51°0·3′	0°52·9′W	FM	197
Wenham Place	Suff	TM0737	51°59·8′	1°1·3′E	X	155,169
Wenham Thicks	Suff	TM0840	52°1·4′	1°2·3′E	F	155,169
Wenhaston	Suff	TM4275	52°19·4′	1°33·5′E	T	156
Wenhaston Black Heath	Suff	TM4174	52°18·9′	1°32·6′E	T	156
Wenhaston Grange	Suff	TM3875	52°19·5′	1°30·0′E	X	156
Wenlli	Conwy	SH8366	53°10·9′	3°44·6′W	X	116
Wenlli	Conwy	SH8465	53°10·4′	3°43·7′W	X	116
Wenlock	Dorset	ST6614	50°55·7′	2°28·6′W	X	194
Wenlock Edge	Shrops	SO5190	52°30·6′	2°42·9′W	X	137,138
Wenlock's Fm	Essex	TL6001	51°41·3′	0°19·3′E	FM	167
Wenlock Walton	Shrops	SO6398	52°35·0′	2°32·4′W	X	138
Wenmouth	Corn	SX1967	50°28·7′	4°32·7′W	X	201
Wenmouth Cross	Corn	SX1968	50°29·3′	4°32·7′W	X	201
Wennallt	Powys	SN9357	52°12·3′	3°33·6′W	X	147
Wennallt	Powys	SN9678	52°23·7′	3°31·3′W	H	136,147
Wennallt	Powys	SO0371	52°20·0′	3°25·0′W	H	136,147
Wenningber	N Yks	SD8757	54°0·8′	2°11·5′W	X	103
Wenning Side	N Yks	SD7267	54°6·1′	2°25·3′W	X	98
Wennington	Cambs	TL2379	52°23·9′	0°11·1′W	T	142

Wennington	Hav	TQ5480	51°30·1'	0°13·5'E	T	177
Wennington	Lancs	SD6170	54°7·7'	2°35·4'W	T	97
Wennington Lodge Fm	Cambs	TL2279	52°24·0'	0°12·0'W	FM	142
Wennington Marshes	Hav	TQ5380	51°30·1'	0°12·7'E	X	177
Wennington Old Fm	Lancs	SD6169	54°7·2'	2°35·4'W	FM	97
Wennington Wood	Cambs	TL2478	52°23·4'	0°10·3'W	F	142
Wenny	Cambs	TL4184	52°26·4'	0°4·9'E	X	142,143
Wensley	Derby	SK2661	53°9·0'	1°36·3'W	T	119
Wensley	N Yks	SE0989	54°18·0'	1°51·3'W	T	99
Wensley Dale	Derby	SK2560	53°8·4'	1°37·2'W	X	119
Wensleydale	N Yks	SD9789	54°18·0'	2°2·3'W	X	98
Wensleydale	N Yks	SE0689	54°18·0'	1°54·0'W	X	99
Wensor Br	Notts	SK7845	53°0·0'	0°49·9'W	X	129
Wensor Castle Fm	Lincs	TF1712	52°41·8'	0°15·7'W	FM	130,142
Wensor Fm	Lincs	TF1913	52°42·3'	0°13·9'W	FM	130,142
Wensum Fm	Norf	TG0417	52°43·0'	1°1·6'E	FM	133
Wentbank Ho	N Yks	SE5416	53°38·5'	1°10·6'W	X	111
Went Br	Donc	SE5616	53°38·5'	1°8·8'W	X	111
Wentbridge	Wakf	SE4817	53°39·1'	1°16·0'W	T	111
Wentcliff Brook	N Yks	SD9247	53°55·4'	2°6·9'W	W	103
Went Fm	Donc	SE5816	53°38·5'	1°6·9'W	FM	111
Went Fm	Kent	TQ5540	51°8·5'	0°13·3'E	FM	188
Wentford	Suff	TL7646	52°5·3'	0°34·5'E	X	155
Wentford Fm	Suff	TL7646	52°5·3'	0°34·5'E	FM	155
Went Hill	E Susx	TV5596	50°44·8'	0°12·2'E	X	199
Wentlooge Level	Newp	ST2781	51°31·6'	3°2·8'W	X	171
Wentnor	Shrops	SO3892	52°31·6'	2°54·4'W	T	137
Wentnor Prolley Moor	Shrops	SO3993	52°32·1'	2°53·6'W	X	137
Went's Fm	Norf	TL7496	52°32·3'	0°34·3'E	FM	143
Wentsford House Fm	E Yorks	SE7138	53°50·2'	0°54·8'W	FM	105,106
Wentwood	Monm	ST4294	51°38·7'	2°49·9'W	F	171,172
Wentwood-gate	Newp	ST4092	51°37·7'	2°51·6'W	X	171,172
Wentwood Resr	Newp	ST4293	51°38·2'	2°49·9'W	W	171,172
Wentworth	Cambs	TL4778	52°23·0'	0°10·0'E	T	143
Wentworth	Roth	SK3898	53°28·9'	1°25·2'W	T	110,111
Wentworth Castle	Barns	SE3203	53°31·6'	1°30·6'W	X	110,111
Wentworth Club	Surrey	SU9867	51°23·8'	0°35·1'W	X	175,176
Wentworth Park	Roth	SK3997	53°28·3'	1°24·3'W	X	110,111
Wentworth Place	Northum	NY8355	54°53·6'	2°15·5'W	X	86,87
Wentworth Sedge Fen	Cambs	TL4980	52°24·1'	0°11·8'E	X	143
Wentworth Woodhouse	Roth	SK3997	53°28·3'	1°24·3'W	A	110,111
Wenvoe	V of Glam	ST1272	51°26·6'	3°15·6'W	T	171
Wenvoe Castle	V of Glam	ST1271	51°26·1'	3°15·6'W	X	171
Weobley	Heref	SO4051	52°9·5'	2°52·2'W	T	148,149
Weobley Castle	Swan	SS4792	51°36·6'	4°12·2'W	A	159
Weobley Fm	Shrops	SJ6226	52°50·1'	2°33·4'W	FM	127
Weobley Marsh	Heref	SO4151	52°9·5'	2°51·4'W	T	148,149
Weo Fm	Shrops	SO4180	52°25·1'	2°51·7'W	FM	137
Weoley Castle	Birm	SP0282	52°26·4'	1°57·8'W	T	139
Wepham	W Susx	TQ0408	50°52·0'	0°30·9'W	T	197
Wepham Down	W Susx	TQ0610	50°53·0'	0°29·2'W	X	197
Wepham Wood	W Susx	TQ0507	50°51·4'	0°30·1'W	F	197
Wephurst Park	W Susx	TQ0228	51°2·8'	0°32·3'W	X	186,197
Wephurst Wood	W Susx	TQ0229	51°3·3'	0°32·3'W	F	186,197
Weppons	W Susx	TQ1412	50°54·0'	0°22·3'W	X	198
Wepre	Flint	SJ2969	53°13·0'	3°3·4'W	T	117
Wepre Brook	Flint	SJ2968	53°12·5'	3°3·4'W	W	117
Wepre Park	Flint	SJ2967	53°12·0'	3°3·4'W	X	117
Wereham	Norf	TF6801	52°35·1'	0°29·2'E	T	143
Wereham Row	Norf	TF6700	52°34·6'	0°28·3'E	T	143
Werescote	Somer	ST0918	50°57·5'	3°17·4'W	X	181
Wereton	Staffs	SJ7950	53°3·1'	2°18·4'W	T	118
Werfa	Brig	SS9194	51°38·3'	3°34·1'W	H	170
Werganrows Fm	Swan	SS5790	51°35·7'	4°3·5'W	FM	159
Wergins Br	Heref	SO5244	52°5·8'	2°41·6'W	X	149
Wergins Stone	Heref	SO5243	52°5·2'	2°41·6'W	A	149
Werglodd	Gwyn	SH8731	52°52·1'	3°40·5'W	X	124,125
Wergs	Wolv	SJ8700	52°36·1'	2°11·1'W	T	127,139
Wergs Copse	W Berks	SU3865	51°23·2'	1°26·8'W	F	174
Wergs Fm	Hants	SU4758	51°19·4'	1°19·1'W	FM	174
Wern	Carm	SN4110	51°46·2'	4°17·9'W	X	159
Wern	Carm	SN5118	51°50·7'	4°9·4'W	X	159
Wern	Carm	SN5940	52°2·7'	4°3·0'W	X	146
Wern	Carm	SN7235	52°0·2'	3°51·5'W	X	146,160
Wern	Conwy	SH7772	53°14·1'	3°50·2'W	X	115
Wern	Denb	SJ1052	53°3·7'	3°20·2'W	X	116
Wern	Denb	SJ1359	53°7·5'	3°17·6'W	X	116
Wern	Denb	SJ1757	53°6·5'	3°14·0'W	X	116
Wern	Flint	SJ1274	53°15·6'	3°18·7'W	X	116
Wern	Gwyn	SH3141	52°56·6'	4°30·5'W	X	123
Wern	Gwyn	SH5061	53°7·8'	4°14·1'W	X	114,115
Wern	Gwyn	SH5439	52°56·0'	4°9·9'W	T	124
Wern	Gwyn	SH5859	53°6·8'	4°6·9'W	X	115
Wern	Gwyn	SH6242	52°57·7'	4°2·9'W	X	124
Wern	Heref	SO2448	52°7·7'	3°6·2'W	X	148
Wern	I of Angl	SH5474	53°14·8'	4°10·9'W	X	114,115
Wern	I of Angl	SH6080	53°18·2'	4°5·7'W	X	114,115
Wern	Monm	SO4502	51°43·1'	2°47·4'W	X	171
Wern	Pemb	SN1229	51°55·9'	4°43·7'W	X	145,158
Wern	Powys	SH9612	52°42·0'	3°31·9'W	X	125
Wern	Powys	SJ0707	52°39·4'	3°22·1'W	X	125
Wern	Powys	SJ2513	52°42·8'	3°6·2'W	T	126
Wern	Powys	SJ2520	52°46·6'	3°6·3'W	T	126
Wern	Powys	SN8732	51°58·7'	3°38·3'W	X	160
Wern	Powys	SN9890	52°30·1'	3°29·8'W	X	136
Wern	Powys	SO0363	52°15·6'	3°24·9'W	X	147
Wern	Powys	SO0730	51°57·9'	3°20·6'W	X	160
Wern	Powys	SO1117	51°50·9'	3°17·1'W	T	161
Wern	Powys	SO1645	52°6·1'	3°13·2'W	X	148
Wern	Powys	SO1822	52°10·4'	3°13·3'W	X	148
Wern	Powys	SO1824	51°54·7'	3°11·1'W	X	161
Wern	Shrops	SJ2734	52°54·2'	3°4·7'W	T	126
Wern	Swan	SS5394	51°37·8'	4°7·0'W	T	159
Wern	Wrex	SJ4147	53°1·3'	2°52·4'W	X	117
Wern	Wrex	SJ4440	52°57·5'	2°49·6'W	A	117
Wernberni	Carm	SN2124	51°53·4'	4°35·7'W	X	145,158
Wern Birs	Monm	SO4400	51°42·0'	2°48·2'W	F	171
Wern-blaidd	Powys	SO1058	52°13·0'	3°18·6'W	X	148
Werncoli	Cered	SN6453	52°9·8'	3°58·9'W	X	146
Werndansey	Powys	SO1257	52°12·5'	3°16·9'W	X	148
Werndofn	Pemb	SN2136	51°59·7'	4°36·1'W	X	145
Wern Ddu	Caer	ST1785	51°33·7'	3°11·5'W	X	171
Wern Ddu	Carm	SN3717	51°49·9'	4°21·5'W	X	159
Wernddu	Carm	SN7337	52°1·3'	3°50·7'W	X	146,160
Wern-ddu	Cered	SN3744	52°4·5'	4°22·3'W	X	145
Wern-ddu	Cered	SN5154	52°10·1'	4°10·3'W	X	146
Wernddu	Cered	SN5162	52°14·4'	4°10·5'W	X	146
Wern-ddu	Cered	SN6279	52°23·7'	4°1·3'W	X	135
Wern Ddu	Denb	SJ0573	53°15·0'	3°25·0'W	X	116
Wern-ddu	Denb	SJ0647	53°1·0'	3°23·7'W	X	116
Wern ddu	Denb	SJ1644	52°59·4'	3°14·7'W	X	125
Wern ddu	Flint	SJ2769	53°13·0'	3°5·2'W	X	117
Wern-ddu	Heref	SO3529	51°57·6'	2°56·4'W	X	149,161
Wern-ddu	Monm	SO3215	51°50·0'	2°58·8'W	X	161
Wernddu	Nth Pt Talb	SN7302	51°42·4'	3°49·9'W	X	170
Wern Ddu	Pemb	SN1335	51°59·2'	4°43·0'W	X	145
Wern ddu	Powys	SJ0724	52°48·6'	3°22·4'W	X	125
Wernddu	Powys	SO0326	51°55·7'	3°24·3'W	X	160
Wern-ddu	Powys	SO1424	51°54·7'	3°14·6'W	X	161
Wernddu	Powys	SO2693	52°32·0'	3°5·1'W	X	137
Wern ddu	Shrops	SJ2326	52°49·8'	3°8·2'W	T	126
Wernddyfwg	Powys	SO0735	52°0·6'	3°20·9'W	X	160
Werndeg	Cered	SN6888	52°28·7'	3°56·2'W	X	135
Werndew	Pemb	SN0238	52°0·6'	4°52·7'W	X	145,157
Wern Dolau	Carm	SN5818	51°50·8'	4°3·3'W	X	159
Wern Dover	Powys	SO1540	52°3·4'	3°14·0'W	F	148,161
Wern-drefi	Carm	SN4822	51°52·8'	4°12·1'W	X	159
Werneth	Oldham	SD9104	53°32·2'	2°7·7'W	T	109
Werneth Hall Fm	Stock	SJ9592	53°25·7'	2°4·1'W	FM	109
Werneth Low	Tames	SJ9592	53°25·7'	2°4·1'W	T	109
Werneth Low Country Park	Tames	SJ9693	53°26·3'	2°3·2'W	X	109
Wern Fach	Cered	SN3442	52°3·3'	4°24·9'W	X	145
Wern-fâch	Gwyn	SH6833	52°52·9'	3°57·3'W	X	124
Wern Farm, The	Powys	SO1157	52°12·5'	3°17·8'W	X	148
Wern-fawr	Conwy	SH8168	53°12·0'	3°46·5'W	X	116
Wern-fawr	Denb	SJ1362	53°9·1'	3°17·7'W	X	116
Wern Fawr	Gwyn	SH3233	52°52·3'	4°29·4'W	X	123
Wern Fawr	Gwyn	SH9140	52°57·0'	3°36·9'W	X	125
Wern Fawr	Monm	SO3205	51°44·6'	2°58·7'W	F	161
Wern Fawr	Monm	SO3207	51°45·7'	2°58·7'W	F	161
Wern-fawr	Powys	SN9322	51°53·4'	3°32·9'W	X	160
Wernfawr	Powys	SN9727	51°56·2'	3°29·5'W	X	160
Wernfawr	Powys	SO0150	52°8·6'	3°26·4'W	X	147
Wern-fawr	Powys	SO0457	52°12·4'	3°23·9'W	X	147
Wern-fawr	Powys	SO1633	51°59·6'	3°13·0'W	X	161
Wern-fawr	Powys	SO1846	52°6·6'	3°11·5'W	X	148
Wern-fawr	Swan	SS5992	51°36·8'	4°1·8'W	X	159
Wern Fawr	V of Glam	ST0278	51°29·8'	3°24·3'W	X	170
Wern Fawr Covert	Gwyn	SH9140	52°57·0'	3°36·9'W	F	125
Wernfelig	Cered	SN5353	52°9·6'	4°8·5'W	X	146
Wernffrwd	Swan	SS5194	51°37·7'	4°8·8'W	T	159
Wernfigin	Powys	SN9430	51°57·7'	3°32·2'W	X	160
Wern Fm	Carm	SN3218	51°50·4'	4°25·9'W	FM	159
Wern Fm	Carm	SN4512	51°47·4'	4°14·5'W	FM	159
Wern Fm	Carm	SN5516	51°49·7'	4°5·9'W	FM	159
Wern Fm	Flint	SJ1380	53°18·8'	3°17·9'W	FM	116
Wern Fm	Heref	SO4917	51°51·2'	2°44·0'W	FM	162
Wern Fm	I of Angl	SH5680	53°18·1'	4°9·3'W	FM	114,115
Wern Fm	Powys	SJ2413	52°42·8'	3°7·1'W	FM	126
Wern Fm	Powys	SO1953	52°10·4'	3°10·7'W	FM	148
Wern Fm	Powys	SO2455	52°11·5'	3°6·3'W	FM	148
Wern Fm	Torf	SO3001	51°42·4'	3°0·4'W	FM	171
Wern-Frank	Powys	SO1933	51°59·6'	3°10·4'W	X	161
Wern Gadno	Cered	SN3045	52°4·9'	4°28·5'W	X	145
Wern Ganol	Flint	SJ2554	53°4·9'	3°6·8'W	X	117
Wern-gerhynt	Powys	SN8999	52°34·9'	3°37·9'W	X	135,136
Wern-Gifford	Monm	SO3321	51°53·2'	2°58·0'W	T	
Werngochlyn Fm	Monm	SO3315	51°50·0'	2°58·0'W	FM	161
Werngof	Powys	SO0031	51°58·3'	3°27·0'W	X	160
Wern-gounsel	Monm	SO3522	51°53·8'	2°56·3'W	X	161
Werngronllwyd	Powys	SO0363	52°15·6'	3°24·9'W	X	147
Wern-halog	Swan	SS5093	51°37·2'	4°9·6'W	X	159
Wernham Fm	Wilts	SU1866	51°23·8'	1°44·1'W	FM	173
Wern-heulog	Powys	SO0853	52°10·3'	3°20·3'W	X	147
Wernhir	Powys	SO0160	52°14·0'	3°26·6'W	X	147
Wern Iago	Powys	SO1938	52°2·3'	3°10·5'W	F	161
Wern Isaf	Denb	SH9860	53°7·9'	3°31·1'W	X	116
Wern Isaf	Denb	SJ2242	52°58·4'	3°9·3'W	X	117
Wernished Fm	Powys	SO1138	52°2·2'	3°17·5'W	FM	161
Wern-las	Powys	SJ1625	52°49·2'	3°14·4'W	X	125
Wernlas	Rho Cyn Taf	SN9609	51°46·4'	3°30·1'W	X	160
Wernlas	Shrops	SJ3120	52°46·6'	3°1·0'W	T	126
Wernlas-deg	Gwyn	SH5849	53°1·4'	4°6·6'W	X	115
Wernlaswen	Gwyn	SH4958	53°6·1'	4°14·9'W	X	115,123
Wernllaeth	Cered	SN5165	52°16·0'	4°10·6'W	X	135
Wernllath	Swan	SS5890	51°35·7'	4°2·6'W	X	159
Wernllwyd	Powys	SJ2002	52°36·8'	3°10·5'W	X	126
Wernlygoes	Carm	SN1620	51°51·1'	4°39·9'W	X	145,158
Wern-Meirch	Cered	SN4863	52°14·9'	4°13·2'W	X	146
Wern-neidr	Denb	SJ0763	53°9·6'	3°23·1'W	X	116
Wernnewydd	Powys	SN9665	52°16·6'	3°31·1'W	X	136,147
Wern-newydd	Powys	SO1845	52°6·1'	3°11·4'W	X	148
Wernolau	Carm	SN3617	51°49·9'	4°22·4'W	X	159
Wern-olau	Swan	SS5695	51°38·4'	4°4·5'W	T	159
Wern-oleu	Powys	SJ1924	52°48·7'	3°11·7'W	X	125
Wernoleu Fawr	Carm	SN2124	51°53·4'	4°35·7'W	X	145,158
Wernoog	Powys	SO1945	52°6·1'	3°10·6'W	X	148
Wernos	Powys	SO0940	52°3·3'	3°19·2'W	X	147,161
Wernpennant	Powys	SJ1822	52°47·6'	3°12·6'W	X	125
Wern Phillip	Cered	SN6282	52°25·4'	4°1·4'W	X	135
Wernrheolydd	Monm	SO3912	51°48·4'	2°52·7'W	T	161
Wern-scadog	Powys	SJ1023	52°48·1'	3°19·7'W	X	125
Wern Tarw	Brig	SS9684	51°33·0'	3°29·6'W	T	170
Wern, The	Powys	SO1748	52°7·7'	3°12·4'W	X	148
Wern, The	Powys	SO2219	51°52·1'	3°7·6'W	X	161
Wern, The	Powys	SO2651	52°9·4'	3°4·5'W	X	148
Werntoe	Powys	SO0737	52°1·7'	3°20·9'W	X	160
Wern Tower	Wrex	SJ2539	52°56·8'	3°6·6'W	X	126
Wern-uchaf	Conwy	SJ0043	52°58·7'	3°29·0'W	X	125
Wern Uchaf	Denb	SH9860	53°7·9'	3°31·1'W	X	116
Wern-Watkin	Powys	SO2115	51°49·9'	3°8·4'W	X	161
Wern-Wgan	Carm	SN6819	51°51·5'	3°54·6'W	X	159
Wern-y-cwm	Monm	SO3417	51°51·1'	2°57·1'W	X	161
Wern-y-cwm	Monm	ST4697	51°40·4'	2°46·5'W	F	171
Wern-y-cwrt	Monm	SO3908	51°46·3'	2°52·7'W	T	161
Wern-y-gaer	Flint	SJ2069	53°13·0'	3°11·5'W	T	117
Wernygeufron	Powys	SO2276	52°22·8'	3°8·4'W	X	137,148
Wernygeufron Hill	Powys	SO2275	52°22·3'	3°8·3'W	H	137,148
Wern-y-melyn	Monm	SO4111	51°47·9'	2°50·9'W	X	161
Wernynad	Cered	SN2246	52°5·3'	4°35·5'W	X	145
Wernypentre	Powys	SO2145	52°6·1'	3°8·8'W	X	148
Wern-y-wig	Powys	SJ0712	52°42·1'	3°22·2'W	X	125
Werrar Fm	I of W	SZ5092	50°43·8'	1°17·1'W	FM	196
Werrington	Corn	SX3287	50°39·7'	4°22·2'W	T	190
Werrington	Peterb	TF1603	52°37·0'	0°16·8'W	T	142
Werrington	Staffs	SJ9447	53°1·5'	2°5·0'W	T	118
Werrington End Fm	Peterb	TF1704	52°37·5'	0°15·9'W	FM	142
Werrington Mansion	Corn	SX3387	50°39·8'	4°21·4'W	A	190
Werrington Park	Corn	SX3386	50°39·2'	4°21·4'W	X	201
Werthyr	I of Angl	SH4192	53°24·3'	4°23·1'W	X	114
Wervil Grange	Cered	SN3452	52°8·7'	4°25·2'W	X	145
Wervin	Ches	SJ4271	53°14·2'	2°51·7'W	T	117
Wescoe	Cumbr	NY3025	54°37·2'	3°4·6'W	X	90
Wescoe Hill	N Yks	SE2746	53°54·8'	1°34·9'W	T	104
Wesham	Lancs	SD4232	53°47·1'	2°52·4'W	T	102
Wesham Ho	Lancs	SD4133	53°47·6'	2°53·3'W	X	102
Wesley Cottage	Corn	SX2280	50°35·8'	4°30·5'W	X	201
Wesley End	Essex	TL7239	52°1·6'	0°30·8'E	X	154
Wessenden	Kirk	SE0508	53°34·4'	1°55·1'W	X	110
Wessenden Head	Kirk	SE0707	53°33·8'	1°53·2'W	X	110
Wessenden Head Moor	Kirk	SE0605	53°32·7'	1°54·2'W	X	110
Wessenden Moor	Kirk	SE0608	53°34·4'	1°54·2'W	X	110
Wessenden Resr	Kirk	SE0508	53°34·4'	1°55·1'W	W	110
Wessington	Derby	SK3757	53°6·8'	1°26·4'W	T	119
Wessington Ct	Heref	SO6035	52°1·0'	2°34·6'W	X	149
Wessington Fm	Heref	SO6034	52°0·4'	2°34·6'W	FM	149
Wessington Green	Derby	SK3657	53°6·8'	1°27·3'W	X	119
West Aberthaw	V of Glam	ST0266	51°23·3'	3°24·1'W	T	170
West Achath	Aberd	NJ7210	57°11·1'	2°27·3'W	X	38
Westacombe	Devon	SX5598	50°46·0'	4°3·0'W	X	191
Westacombe Fm	Devon	SX7990	50°42·1'	3°42·4'W	FM	191
Westacot	Devon	SX7922	50°59·3'	3°43·1'W	X	180
Westacott	Devon	SS4126	51°0·9'	4°15·6'W	X	180,190
Westacott	Devon	SS5008	50°51·4'	4°7·5'W	X	191
Westacott	Devon	SS5300	50°47·1'	4°4·7'W	X	191
Westacott	Devon	SS5827	51°1·7'	4°1·1'W	X	180
Westacott	Devon	SS5832	51°4·4'	4°1·2'W	T	180
Westacott	Devon	SS6203	50°48·8'	3°57·2'W	X	191
Westacott	Devon	SS6730	51°3·5'	3°53·5'W	X	180
Westacott	Devon	SS6807	50°51·1'	3°52·1'W	X	191
Westacott Barton	Devon	SS5913	50°54·2'	3°59·9'W	X	180
Westacott Barton	Devon	SS6802	50°48·4'	3°52·0'W	X	191
Westacott Cotts	Devon	SS8500	50°47·5'	3°37·5'W	X	191
Westacott Fm	Devon	SS7421	50°58·7'	3°47·3'W	FM	180
West Acre	Norf	TF7715	52°42·4'	0°37·6'E	T	132
West Acre Gdns	Norf	TF7918	52°44·0'	0°39·5'E	X	132
West Acre Lodge	N Yks	SE4886	54°16·3'	1°15·4'W	X	100
West Acres	Norf	TM0483	52°24·6'	1°0·4'E	X	144
West Acton	Ealing	TQ1981	51°31·1'	0°16·7'W	T	176
West Adamston	Aberd	NJ5637	57°25·5'	2°43·5'W	X	29
West Adamston	Angus	NO3235	56°30·4'	3°5·8'W	X	53
West Adderbury	Oxon	SP4635	52°0·9'	1°19·4'W	T	151
West-a-Firth	Shetld	HP4904	60°43·2'	1°5·6'W	X	1
West Agra	N Yks	SE1481	54°13·7'	1°46·7'W	X	99
West Allerdean	Northum	NT9646	55°42·7'	2°3·4'W	X	74,75
West Allerton Station	Liv	SJ3986	53°22·3'	2°54·6'W	X	108
West Allotment	N Tyne	NZ3070	55°1·7'	1°31·4'W	T	88
West Alvington	Devon	SX7243	50°16·6'	3°47·4'W	T	202
West Amesbury	Wilts	SU1441	51°10·3'	1°47·6'W	T	184
West Angle Bay	Pemb	SM8403	51°41·3'	5°7·1'W	W	157
West Anstey	Devon	SS8527	51°2·1'	3°38·0'W	T	181
West Anstey Barrows	Devon	SS8529	51°3·2'	3°38·1'W	A	181
West Anstey Common	Devon	SS8429	51°3·2'	3°38·9'W	X	181
West Appleton	N Yks	SE2194	54°20·7'	1°40·2'W	T	99
West Aquhorthies	Aberd	NJ7119	57°15·9'	2°28·4'W	X	38
West Ardhu	Arg & Bt	NM4251	56°35·1'	6°11·7'W	X	47
West Ardler	Pth & Kin	NO2541	56°33·6'	3°12·8'W	X	53
West Ardsley	Leeds	SE2825	53°43·5'	1°34·1'W	T	104
West Arnecliff Wood	N Yks	NZ7804	54°25·8'	0°47·4'W	F	94
West Arson	Devon	SS6015	50°55·3'	3°59·1'W	X	180
West Arthurlie	E Renf	NS4958	55°47·8'	4°24·1'W	T	64
West Ash	Devon	SS3216	50°55·4'	4°23·0'W	X	190
West Ashby	Lincs	TF2672	53°14·0'	0°6·3'W	T	122
West Ashey Fm	I of W	SZ5788	50°41·6'	1°11·2'W	FM	196
West Ashford	Devon	SS5235	51°6·0'	4°6·4'W	T	180
West Ashgill	Cumbr	NY7539	54°45·0'	2°22·9'W	X	91
West Ashling	W Susx	SU8007	50°51·6'	0°51·4'W	T	197
West Ashton	Wilts	ST8755	51°17·9'	2°10·8'W	T	173
West Auchavaich	Moray	NJ2420	57°16·1'	3°15·2'W	X	36
West Auchmaliddie	Aberd	NJ8744	57°29·4'	2°12·6'W	X	30
West Auckland	Durham	NZ1826	54°38·0'	1°42·8'W	T	92
Westaway	Devon	SS5634	51°5·5'	4°3·0'W	X	180
West Axnoller Fm	Dorset	ST4804	50°50·2'	2°43·9'W	FM	193
West Ayre	Orkney	HY7244	59°17·2'	2°29·0'W	X	5
Westayre Loch	Orkney	HY7244	59°17·2'	2°29·0'W	W	5
West Ayton	N Yks	SE9884	54°14·8'	0°29·3'W	T	101
West Backs	Arg & Bt	NR6821	55°25·9'	5°39·6'W	X	68
West Backstone	Devon	SS8319	50°57·7'	3°39·6'W	X	181
West Backwear	Somer	ST4840	51°9·6'	2°44·2'W	X	182
West Badallan	N Lanak	NS9158	55°48·4'	3°43·9'W	X	65,72
West Bagborough	Somer	ST1733	51°5·7'	3°10·7'W	T	181
West Balbairdie	Fife	NT2289	56°5·5'	3°14·8'W	X	66
West Balbarton	Fife	NT2391	56°6·6'	3°13·8'W	X	58
West Baldwin	I of M	SC3582	54°12·7'	4°31·4'W	X	95
West Baldwin Resr	I of M	SC3683	54°13·2'	4°30·5'W	W	95
West Balgonar	Fife	NT0193	56°7·4'	3°35·1'W	X	58
West Balgothrie	Fife	NO2203	56°13·0'	3°15·0'W	X	58
West Balgray	N Ayr	NS3542	55°38·9'	4°36·9'W	X	63,70
West Balhagarty	Aberd	NO7569	56°49·0'	2°24·1'W	X	45

West Balmirmer	Angus	NO5738	56°32·2′	2°41·5′W	T	54
West Balnakelly	Aberd	NJ4910	57°10·9′	2°50·2′W	X	37
West Balquhain	Aberd	NJ7223	57°18·1′	2°27·4′W	X	38
West Balsdon	Corn	SX2798	50°45·6′	4°26·8′W	X	190
West Bandodle	Aberd	NJ6506	57°8·9′	2°34·3′W	X	38
Westbank	Angus	NO4680	56°54·7′	2°52·8′W	X	44
West Bank	Blae Gw	SO2105	51°44·5′	3°8·3′W	T	161
Westbank	Derby	SK3649	53°2·5′	1°27·4′W	T	119
West Bank	E Loth	NT4371	55°56·0′	2°54·3′W	X	66
West Bank	Halton	SJ5183	53°20·7′	2°43·8′W	T	108
West Bank	Lincs	TF4783	53°19·6′	0°12·8′E	X	122
West Bank	Pth & Kin	NN9419	56°21·3′	3°42·5′W	X	58
West Bank	Pth & Kin	NO3129	56°27·1′	3°6·7′W	X	53,59
West Bank Burn	Pth & Kin	NO1307	56°15·1′	3°23·8′W	W	58
West Bank Ho	N Yks	SE6224	53°42·8′	1°3·2′W	X	105
West Barcloy	D & G	NX8553	54°51·8′	3°47·1′W	X	84
West Barkwith	Lincs	TF1580	53°18·5′	0°16·0′W	T	121
West Barn	Lincs	TF2181	53°19·0′	0°10·6′W	X	122
West Barnby	N Yks	NZ8112	54°30·1′	0°44·5′W	T	94
West Barnes	Merton	TQ2267	51°23·6′	0°14·4′W	T	176
West Barn Fms	Somer	ST7340	51°9·7′	2°22·8′W	FM	183
West Barnley	Durham	NZ0022	54°35·8′	1°59·6′W	X	92
West Barns	E Loth	NT6578	55°59·9′	2°33·2′W	T	67
West Barr	D & G	NX3146	54°47·1′	4°37·3′W	X	82
West Barsham	Norf	TF9033	52°51·9′	0°49·8′E	T	132
West Barton	Devon	SS5027	51°1·6′	4°8·0′W	X	180
West Barton	Devon	SS8226	51°1·5′	3°40·6′W	X	181
West Barton Fm	Devon	SS9209	50°52·5′	3°31·7′W	FM	192
West Batter Law Fm	Durham	NZ4045	54°48·1′	1°22·2′W	FM	88
West Baugh Fell	Cumbr	SD7394	54°20·7′	2°24·5′W	X	98
West Baugh Fell Tarn	Cumbr	SD7293	54°20·2′	2°25·4′W	W	98
West Bay	Arg & Bt	NS1776	55°56·8′	4°55·4′W	W	63
West Bay	Dorset	SY4690	50°42·7′	2°45·5′W	T	193
West Bay	Dorset	SY6773	50°33·6′	2°27·6′W	W	194
West Bay	Inverc	NS2377	55°57·5′	4°49·7′W	W	63
West Beacon Point	Pemb	SS1296	51°38·1′	4°42·6′W	X	158
West Bearford	E Loth	NT5473	55°57·1′	2°43·8′W	X	66
West Beck	Durham	NY8534	54°42·3′	2°13·5′W	W	91,92
West Beck	N Yks	NZ5305	54°26·5′	1°10·5′W	X	93
West Beck	N Yks	NZ8200	54°23·6′	0°43·8′W	X	94
West Beck	N Yks	SD9788	54°17·5′	2°2·3′W	W	98
West Beck	N Yks	SE1648	53°55·9′	1°45·0′W	W	104
West Beck	N Yks	SE2449	53°56·4′	1°37·6′W	W	104
West Beckham	Norf	TG1339	52°54·0′	1°10·5′E	T	133
West Bedfont	Surrey	TQ0773	51°27·0′	0°27·2′W	T	176
Westbeech	Staffs	SJ8200	52°36·1′	2°15·5′W	X	127
West Beer	Devon	SX7794	50°44·2′	3°44·2′W	X	191
West Begbeer	Devon	SX7199	50°46·8′	3°49·4′W	X	191
West Belsay Fm	Northum	NZ0778	55°6·0′	1°53·0′W	FM	88
West Benhar	N Lanak	NS8863	55°51·1′	3°46·9′W	T	65
West Bennan	N Ayr	NR9821	55°26·7′	5°11·2′W	T	69
West Benridge	Northum	NZ1687	55°10·9′	1°44·5′W	X	81
West Benula Forest	Highld	NH0827	57°17·9′	5°10·7′W	X	25,33
Westbere	Kent	TR1961	51°18·6′	1°8·9′E	T	179
Westbere Marshes	Kent	TR1960	51°18·0′	1°8·9′E	W	179
West Bergholt	Essex	TL9627	51°54·6′	0°51·4′E	T	168
West Bexington	Dorset	SY5386	50°40·5′	2°39·5′W	T	194
West Bight	Orkney	HY5239	59°14·4′	2°50·0′W	W	5
West Bilney	Norf	TF7115	52°42·6′	0°32·3′E	T	132
West Bilney Hall	Norf	TF7014	52°42·0′	0°31·4′E	X	132
West Bilney Wood	Norf	TF6913	52°41·5′	0°30·4′E	F	132,143
West Binny	W Loth	NT0372	55°56·1′	3°32·7′W	X	65
West Blackbyre	E Ayr	NS4943	55°39·7′	4°23·6′W	X	70
West Blackdene	Durham	NY8639	54°45·0′	2°12·6′W	T	91,92
West Blackdown	Devon	SX4981	50°36·8′	4°7·7′W	T	191,201
West Blagdon	Dorset	SU0416	50°56·8′	1°56·2′W	X	184
West Blairshinnoch	Aberd	NJ6361	57°38·5′	2°36·7′W	X	29
West Blanerne	Scot Bord	NT8256	55°48·1′	2°16·8′W	X	67,74
West Blatchington	Bri & Hov	TQ2706	50°50·6′	0°11·4′W	T	198
West Blean Ho	Kent	TR1763	51°19·7′	1°7·3′E	X	179
West Blean Wood	Kent	TR1664	51°20·3′	1°6·5′E	F	179
West Blockhouse Point	Pemb	SM8103	51°41·2′	5°9·7′W	X	157
West Board	E Dunb	NS7074	55°56·7′	4°4·5′W	X	64
West Boat	Northum	NY9165	54°59·0′	2°8·2′W	X	87
West Bog	Angus	NO4155	56°41·2′	2°57·3′W	X	54
West Boghead	Angus	NO6746	56°36·5′	2°31·8′W	X	54
West Bogton	Aberd	NO7383	56°56·5′	2°26·2′W	X	45
West Bold	Scot Bord	NT3636	55°37·1′	3°0·5′W	T	73
West Boldon	S Tyne	NZ3561	54°56·8′	1°26·8′W	T	88
West Bolton	Northum	NU1013	55°24·9′	1°50·1′W	X	81
West Bolton	N Yks	SE0291	54°19·1′	1°57·7′W	X	98
West Bolton Moor	N Yks	SD9893	54°20·2′	2°1·4′W	X	98
West Bonhard	Fife	NT0389	56°5·3′	3°33·1′W	X	65
West Boonraw	Scot Bord	NT4917	55°26·9′	2°47·9′W	X	79
West Border	Angus	NO5949	56°38·1′	2°39·7′W	X	54
Westborough	Lincs	SK8544	52°59·4′	0°43·6′W	T	130
Westborough Lodge	Lincs	SK8646	53°0·5′	0°42·7′W	X	130
West Borronhead	N Yks	SD7066	54°5·6′	2°27·1′W	X	98
Westbourne	Bourne	SZ0791	50°43·3′	1°53·7′W	T	195
Westbourne	Suff	TM1445	52°3·9′	1°7·7′E	T	169
Westbourne	W Susx	SU7507	50°51·7′	0°55·7′W	T	197
Westbourne Green	C of West	TQ2582	51°31·6′	0°11·5′W	T	176
Westbourn Fm	Cambs	TL4955	52°10·6′	0°11·1′E	FM	154
West Bourton	Dorset	ST7629	51°3·8′	2°20·2′W	T	183
West Bovey	Somer	ST0424	51°0·7′	3°21·7′W	X	181
West Bowers Hall	Essex	TL7907	51°44·2′	0°35·9′E	A	167
West Bowhill	D & G	NY1470	55°1·3′	3°20·3′W	X	85
West Bowling	Brad	SE1631	53°46·7′	1°45·0′W	T	104
West Brachmont	Aberd	NO8194	57°2·5′	2°18·3′W	X	38,45
West Brackley	Pth & Kin	NT1498	56°10·3′	3°22·7′W	X	58
West Bradford	Lancs	SD7444	53°53·7′	2°23·3′W	T	103
West Bradieston	Aberd	NO7368	56°48·4′	2°26·1′W	X	45
West Bradley	Devon	SS8914	50°55·1′	3°34·4′W	X	181
West Bradley	Somer	ST5536	51°7·5′	2°38·2′W	T	182,183
West Brandon	Durham	NZ1939	54°45·0′	1°41·9′W	X	92
West Brant Syke	Lincs	SK9157	53°6·4′	0°38·0′W	W	121
West Brathens	Aberd	NO6698	57°4·6′	2°33·2′W	X	38,45
Westbreck	Shetld	HP5909	60°45·8′	0°54·5′W	X	1
West Breckan	Orkney	HY4801	58°53·9′	2°53·7′W	X	6,7
Westbrecks Fm	Notts	SK8079	53°18·3′	0°47·6′W	FM	121

West Bretton	D & G	NY2271	55°1·9′	3°12·8′W	X	85
West Bretton	Wakf	SE2813	53°37·0′	1°34·2′W	T	110
West Bridgford	Notts	SK5836	52°55·3′	1°7·8′W	T	129
West Briggs	Norf	TF6510	52°40·0′	0°26·8′E	X	132,143
West Briggs Lodge	Norf	TF6411	52°40·5′	0°26·0′E	X	132,143
Westbriggs Wood	Norf	TF6510	52°40·0′	0°26·8′E	F	132,143
West Brimmondside	C of Aber	NJ8508	57°10·0′	2°14·4′W	X	38
West Briscoe	Durham	NY9619	54°34·2′	2°3·3′W	X	91,92
West Brizlee	Northum	NU1414	55°25·4′	1°46·3′W	X	81
West Broadlaw	W Loth	NT0373	55°56·7′	3°32·7′W	X	65
West Broadmoss	E Ayr	NS4446	55°41·2′	4°28·5′W	X	64
Westbroke Ho	Kent	TR0321	50°57·4′	0°53·8′E	X	189
West Brompton	Ham & Ful	TQ2577	51°28·9′	0°11·6′W	T	176
West Bromwich	Sand	SO9992	52°31·8′	2°0·5′W	T	139
West Brook	Cambs	TL3068	52°17·9′	0°5·2′W	W	153
West Brook	Derby	SK2412	52°42·5′	1°38·3′W	W	128
Westbrook	Devon	SX9475	50°34·1′	3°29·4′W	X	192
Westbrook	Heref	SO2843	52°5·1′	3°2·7′W	T	148,161
Westbrook	Kent	TR3470	51°23·1′	1°22·2′E	T	179
Westbrook	Surrey	SU8943	51°11·0′	0°43·2′W	X	186
Westbrook	Surrey	SU9643	51°10·9′	0°37·2′W	T	186
Westbrook	Warr	SJ5790	53°24·5′	2°38·4′W	T	108
Westbrook	W Berks	SU4271	51°26·4′	1°23·4′W	T	174
Westbrook	Wilts	ST9565	51°23·3′	2°3·9′W	T	173
Westbrook Fm	Derby	SK2312	52°42·5′	1°39·2′W	FM	128
Westbrook Fm	Devon	SS9322	50°59·5′	3°31·1′W	FM	181
Westbrook Fm	Dorset	ST7825	51°1·7′	2°18·4′W	FM	183
Westbrook Fm	Kent	TR0322	50°57·9′	0°53·9′E	FM	189
Westbrook Fm	Oxon	SP7303	51°43·5′	0°56·2′W	FM	165
Westbrook Fm	Somer	ST6338	51°8·6′	2°31·4′W	FM	183
Westbrook Fm	W Berks	SU4272	51°27·0′	1°23·3′W	FM	174
Westbrook Green	Norf	TM1181	52°23·4′	1°6·5′E	T	144
Westbrook Hall	W Susx	TQ1334	51°5·9′	0°22·8′W	X	187
Westbrook Hay	Herts	TL0205	51°44·3′	0°31·0′W	T	166
Westbrook Ho	Dorset	SY6684	50°39·5′	2°28·5′W	X	194
Westbrook Ho	Worcs	SO5567	52°18·2′	2°39·2′W	X	137,138,149
Westbrooks Fm	Somer	ST0926	51°1·8′	3°17·5′W	FM	181
Westbrook Wood	Devon	SS9321	50°58·9′	3°31·1′W	F	181
Westbrough	Orkney	HY6642	59°16·1′	2°35·3′W	X	5
West Broughton	Derby	SK1433	52°53·9′	1°47·1′W	T	128
West Browncastle	S Lanak	NS6243	55°39·9′	4°11·2′W	X	71
West Brownrigg	Cumbr	NY5137	54°43·8′	2°45·2′W	X	90
West Broyle Ho	W Susx	SU8406	50°51·1′	0°48·0′W	X	197
West Brucehill	Aberd	NJ8547	57°31·0′	2°14·6′W	X	30
West Brunton Fm	N upon Ty	NZ2170	55°1·7′	1°39·9′W	FM	88
West Brushford Fm	Devon	SS6607	50°51·1′	3°53·8′W	FM	191
West Bu	Orkney	HY4603	58°54·9′	2°55·8′W	X	6,7
West Buckland	Devon	SS6531	51°4·0′	3°55·2′W	T	180
West Buckland	Somer	ST1720	50°58·6′	3°10·6′W	T	181,193
West Buckland School	Devon	SS6631	51°4·0′	3°54·4′W	X	180
West Bucknowle Ho	Dorset	SY9481	50°38·0′	2°4·7′W	X	195
Westburn	Aberd	NJ9420	57°16·5′	2°5·5′W	X	38
West Burn	Angus	NO3169	56°48·7′	3°7·4′W	W	44
West Burn	Angus	NO4373	56°51·0′	2°55·6′W	W	44
West Burn	D & G	NT1906	55°20·7′	3°16·2′W	W	79
West Burn	E Ayr	NS5211	55°22·5′	4°19·7′W	W	70
West Burn	E Ayr	NS5644	55°40·3′	4°16·9′W	W	71
West Burn	E Ayr	NS6035	55°35·6′	4°12·9′W	W	71
West Burn	E Loth	NT6468	55°54·5′	2°34·1′W	W	67
West Burn	N Ayr	NS2551	55°43·5′	4°46·8′W	W	63
West Burn	Northum	NT8912	55°24·4′	2°10·0′W	W	80
Westburn	Pth & Kin	NN9915	56°19·3′	3°37·5′W	X	58
West Burn	Scot Bord	NT5730	55°34·0′	2°40·5′W	W	73,74
Westburn	S Lanak	NS6660	55°49·1′	4°7·9′W	T	64
West Burn	S Lanak	NS9532	55°34·5′	3°39·5′W	W	72
West Burn	Stir	NS7392	56°6·5′	4°2·1′W	W	57
West Burn	W Loth	NT0857	55°48·1′	3°27·6′W	W	65,72
West Burnhead	E Ayr	NS5233	55°34·3′	4°20·4′W	X	70
Westburnhope	Northum	NY8854	54°53·1′	2°10·8′W	X	87
Westburnhope Moor	Northum	NY8755	54°53·6′	2°11·7′W	X	87
West Burn of Builg	Aberd	NO6984	56°57·0′	2°30·1′W	W	45
West Burn of Glenmoye	Angus	NO4067	56°47·7′	2°58·5′W	W	44
West Burnside	Aberd	NO6572	56°50·5′	2°34·0′W	X	45
West Burnside	Aberd	NO7070	56°49·5′	2°29·0′W	T	45
West Burnside	Orkney	HY4707	58°57·1′	2°54·8′W	X	6,7
West Burra	Shetld	HU3632	60°4·5′	1°20·7′W	X	4
West Burrafirth	Shetld	HU2556	60°17·5′	1°32·4′W	T	3
West Burra Firth	Shetld	HU2557	60°18·0′	1°32·4′W	W	3
West Burton	Notts	SK7885	53°21·6′	0°49·3′W	X	112,120,121
West Burton	N Yks	SE0186	54°16·4′	1°58·7′W	T	98
West Burton	W Susx	SU9913	50°54·7′	0°35·1′W	T	197
West Burton Fm	Dorset	SY8285	50°40·1′	2°14·9′W	FM	194
Westburton Hill	W Susx	SU9912	50°54·2′	0°35·1′W	H	197
West Burton Village	Notts	SK7985	53°21·6′	0°48·4′W	A	112,120,121
Westbury	Bucks	SP6235	52°0·8′	1°5·4′W	T	152
Westbury	Shrops	SJ3509	52°40·7′	2°57·3′W	T	126
Westbury	Wilts	ST8650	51°15·2′	2°11·6′W	T	183
Westbury Beacon	Somer	ST5050	51°15·1′	2°42·6′W	H	182,183
Westbury Court Fm	Bucks	SP6323	51°54·3′	1°4·7′W	FM	164,165
Westbury Fm	Dorset	ST9112	50°54·7′	2°7·3′W	FM	195
Westbury Fm	Hav	TQ5887	51°33·8′	0°17·2′E	FM	177
Westbury Fm	Mil Key	SP8235	52°0·7′	0°47·9′W	FM	152
Westbury Fm	Somer	ST4815	50°56·2′	2°44·0′W	FM	193
Westbury Fm	W Berks	SU6576	51°29·0′	1°3·4′W	FM	175
Westbury Hill	Wilts	ST8951	51°15·7′	2°9·1′W	X	184
Westbury Ho	Hants	SU6523	51°0·4′	1°4·0′W	X	185
Westbury Leigh	Wilts	ST8650	51°15·2′	2°11·6′W	T	183
Westbury Moor	Somer	ST4847	51°13·4′	2°44·3′W	X	182
Westbury-on-Severn	Glos	SO7114	51°49·7′	2°24·9′W	T	162
Westbury on Trym	C of Bris	ST5677	51°29·6′	2°37·6′W	T	172
Westbury Park	C of Bris	ST5775	51°28·6′	2°36·8′W	T	172
Westbury-sub-Mendip	Somer	ST5048	51°14·0′	2°42·6′W	T	182,183
Westbury White Horse	Wilts	ST8951	51°15·7′	2°9·1′W	X	184
Westbury Wood	Herts	TL1425	51°54·9′	0°20·2′W	F	166
West Butsfield	Durham	NZ1044	54°47·7′	1°50·2′W	T	88
West Buttergask	Pth & Kin	NO2034	56°29·7′	3°17·5′W	X	53
West Butterwick	N Lincs	SE8305	53°32·3′	0°44·4′W	T	112
Westby	Lancs	SD3831	53°46·5′	2°56·0′W	T	102
Westby	Lincs	SK9728	52°50·7′	0°33·2′W	T	130
West Byfleet	Surrey	TQ0460	51°20·0′	0°30·0′W	T	176,186

Westby Hall Fm	Lancs	SD8248	53°55·9′	2°16·0′W	FM	103
West Byres	E Loth	NT4067	55°53·8′	2°57·1′W	X	66
West Cairnbeg	Aberd	NO7076	56°52·7′	2°29·1′W	X	45
West Cairncake	Aberd	NJ8249	57°32·1′	2°17·6′W	X	29,30
West Cairnhill	Aberd	NJ6633	57°23·4′	2°33·5′W	X	29
West Cairn Hill	W Loth	NT1058	55°48·7′	3°25·7′W	H	65,72
West Cairns	W Loth	NT0860	55°49·7′	3°27·7′W	X	65
West Cairns Plantation	W Loth	NT0859	55°49·2′	3°27·7′W	F	65,72
West Caister	Norf	TG5011	52°38·6′	1°42·1′E	T	134
West Calder	Highld	ND0962	58°32·5′	3°33·3′W	X	11,12
West Calder	W Loth	NT0163	55°51·3′	3°34·5′W	T	65
West Calder Burn	W Loth	NT0263	55°51·3′	3°33·5′W	W	65
West Caldhame	Aberd	NO6668	56°48·4′	2°33·0′W	X	45
West Caldhame	Angus	NO4748	56°37·5′	2°51·4′W	X	54
West Calthorpe Heath	Suff	TL8377	52°21·9′	0°41·7′E	X	144
West Camel	Somer	ST5724	51°1·1′	2°36·4′W	T	183
West Campsie	Angus	NO2853	56°40·1′	3°10·0′W	X	53
West Canisbay	Highld	ND3471	58°37·6′	3°7·7′W	X	7,12
West Cannahars	Aberd	NJ9121	57°17·0′	2°8·5′W	X	38
Westcar	Norf	TM0294	52°30·6′	0°59·0′E	X	144
West Carlton	E Yorks	TA2138	53°49·7′	0°9·3′W	X	107
West Carlton	Leeds	SE2042	53°52·7′	1°41·3′W	T	104
West Carne	Corn	SX2082	50°36·8′	4°32·3′W	X	201
West Carr	Durham	NZ1141	54°46·1′	1°49·3′W	X	88
West Carr	K upon H	TA0932	53°46·6′	0°20·3′W	T	107
West Carr	N Lincs	SE7407	53°33·5′	0°52·6′W	T	112
West Carr	Scot Bord	NT9661	55°50·8′	2°3·4′W	X	67
West Carrabus	Arg & Bt	NR3063	55°47·4′	6°18·0′W	X	60
West Carr Houses	N Lincs	SE7306	53°33·0′	0°53·5′W	X	112
West Carrside Fm	Durham	NZ3733	54°41·7′	1°25·1′W	FM	93
West Carse	Stir	NS7394	56°7·6′	4°2·1′W	X	57
West Carsebank	Angus	NO4853	56°40·2′	2°50·5′W	X	54
West Carswell	E Renf	NS4552	55°44·5′	4°27·7′W	X	64
West Cassingray	Fife	NO4707	56°15·4′	2°50·9′W	X	59
West Cauldcoats	S Lanak	NS6840	55°38·4′	4°5·4′W	X	71
West Cawledge Park	Northum	NU1810	55°23·3′	1°42·5′W	X	81
West Centry	Devon	SS7721	50°58·8′	3°44·7′W	X	180
West Cevidley	Aberd	NJ5918	57°15·3′	2°40·3′W	X	37
West Chadsmoor	Staffs	SJ9812	52°42·6′	2°1·4′W	T	127
West Chaldon	Dorset	SY7782	50°38·5′	2°19·1′W	X	194
West Challoch	D & G	NX1557	54°52·7′	4°52·6′W	X	82
West Challow	Oxon	SU3688	51°35·6′	1°28·4′W	T	174
West Challow Field	Oxon	SU3687	51°35·1′	1°28·4′W	X	174
West Channel	D & G	NX4752	54°50·6′	4°22·5′W	W	83
West Chapple	Devon	SS6108	50°51·5′	3°58·1′W	X	191
West Charity Fm	Durham	NY9712	54°30·4′	2°2·4′W	FM	92
West Charleton	Devon	SX7542	50°16·1′	3°44·9′W	T	202
West Chase Fm	Dorset	ST9819	50°58·5′	2°1·3′W	FM	184
West Chelborough	Dorset	ST5405	50°50·8′	2°38·8′W	T	194
West Chevin Fm	Leeds	SE1844	53°53·8′	1°43·2′W	FM	104
West Chevington	Northum	NZ2297	55°16·2′	1°38·8′W	T	81
West Chiltington	W Susx	TQ0918	50°57·3′	0°26·5′W	T	198
West Chiltington Common	W Susx	TQ0817	50°56·8′	0°27·4′W	T	197
West Chinnock	Somer	ST4613	50°55·1′	2°45·7′W	T	193
West Chinnock Hill	Somer	ST4612	50°54·5′	2°45·7′W	X	193
West Chirton	N Tyne	NZ3368	55°0·6′	1°28·6′W	T	88
West Chisenbury	Wilts	SU1352	51°16·3′	1°48·4′W	T	184
West Clandon	Surrey	TQ0452	51°15·7′	0°30·2′W	T	186
West Cleish	Pth & Kin	NT0597	56°9·6′	3°31·3′W	X	58
West Cleugh	Northum	NY7376	55°4·9′	2°24·9′W	X	86,87
West Cliff	Bourne	SZ0790	50°42·8′	1°53·7′W	T	195
West Cliff	Devon	SX6938	50°13·9′	3°49·8′W	X	202
West Cliff	Dorset	SY4590	50°42·7′	2°46·4′W	X	193
West Cliff	Dorset	SY6872	50°33·0′	2°26·7′W	X	194
West Cliff	Kent	TR3764	51°19·8′	1°24·5′E	X	179
West Cliff	N Yks	NZ6804	54°25·9′	0°56·7′W	X	94
West Cliff	N Yks	NZ8811	54°29·4′	0°38·1′W	T	94
West Cliffe	Kent	TR3444	51°9·1′	1°21·2′E	T	179
Westcliff-on-Sea	Sou-on-Sea	TQ8685	51°32·2′	0°41·3′E	T	178
West Clifton	C of Edin	NT1069	55°54·6′	3°25·9′W	X	65
West Close	Durham	NZ2831	54°40·6′	1°33·5′W	X	93
West Close	Lancs	SD8036	53°49·4′	2°17·8′W	X	103
West Close	Lancs	SD8045	53°54·3′	2°17·9′W	X	103
Westclose Hill	Somer	ST4949	51°14·5′	2°43·5′W	H	182,183
West Close Pasture	N Yks	SD7379	54°12·6′	2°24·4′W	X	98
West Clyne	Highld	NC8805	58°1·5′	3°53·3′W	T	17
West Clyst	Devon	SX9795	50°45·0′	3°27·2′W	X	192
West Clyth Fm	Highld	ND2636	58°18·6′	3°15·3′W	FM	11
West Cocklake	Cumbr	NY7547	54°49·3′	2°22·9′W	X	86,87
West Coker	Somer	ST5113	50°55·1′	2°41·4′W	T	194
West Coldside	Northum	NZ1583	55°8·7′	1°45·5′W	X	81
West Coldstream	S Lanak	NS8749	55°43·5′	3°47·5′W	X	72
West Collary	E Ayr	NS4943	55°39·7′	4°23·6′W	X	70
West Colwell	Devon	SY1998	50°46·8′	3°8·6′W	X	192,193
West Comalegy	Aberd	NJ5738	57°26·1′	2°42·5′W	X	29
West Combe	Devon	SS6030	51°3·4′	3°59·5′W	X	180
Westcombe	Devon	SS9920	50°58·5′	3°25·9′W	X	181
Westcombe	Devon	SX7662	50°26·9′	3°44·4′W	X	202
Westcombe	Somer	ST2016	50°56·5′	3°7·9′W	X	193
Westcombe	Somer	ST4629	51°3·7′	2°45·9′W	T	193
Westcombe	Somer	ST6739	51°9·2′	2°27·9′W	T	183
Westcombe	Wilts	ST8739	51°9·2′	2°10·8′W	X	183
Westcombe Beach	Devon	SX6345	50°17·6′	3°55·0′W	X	202
Westcombe Coppice	Dorset	ST5201	50°48·6′	2°40·5′W	F	194
Westcombe Fm	Northnts	SP5757	52°12·7′	1°9·5′W	FM	152
West Common	Durham	NY8131	54°40·7′	2°17·3′W	X	91,92
West Common	Hants	SU4400	50°48·1′	1°22·2′W	T	196
West Common	Lincs	SK9672	53°14·4′	0°33·3′W	X	121
West Compton	Dorset	SY5694	50°44·9′	2°37·0′W	T	194
West Compton	Somer	ST5942	51°10·8′	2°34·8′W	T	182,183
West Conland	Fife	NO2504	56°13·6′	3°12·1′W	X	59
West Coombe	Corn	SX1651	50°20·0′	4°34·8′W	X	201
West Coombe	Devon	SS3703	50°48·5′	4°18·4′W	X	190
West Coombe	Devon	SX5388	50°40·6′	4°4·5′W	X	191
West Coombeshead	Corn	SX3473	50°32·2′	4°20·2′W	X	201
West Corncatterach	Aberd	NJ5434	57°23·9′	2°45·5′W	X	29
West Cornforth	Durham	NZ3133	54°41·7′	1°30·7′W	T	93
West Corrie	Angus	NO2578	56°53·5′	3°13·4′W	X	44
West Corrie	Angus	NO4672	56°50·4′	2°52·7′W	X	44
Westcot	Oxon	SU3387	51°35·1′	1°31·0′W	T	174

Westcot Down	Oxon	SU3283	51°32·9′	1°31·9′W	X	174
West Cote	Scot Bord	NT5316	55°26·4′	2°44·1′W	X	79
Westcote Brook	Oxon	SP2421	51°53·5′	1°38·7′W	W	163
Westcote Farm	Warw	SP3547	52°7·4′	1°28·9′W	FM	151
Westcote Fm	N Yks	NZ5400	54°23·8′	1°9·7′W	FM	93
Westcote Hill	Glos	SP2119	51°52·4′	1°41·3′W	X	163
Westcote Manor	Warw	SP3646	52°6·9′	1°28·1′W	X	151
Westcotes	C of Leic	SK5703	52°37·5′	1°9·1′W	T	140
West Cotes	Northum	NZ1374	55°3·9′	1°47·4′W	X	88
West Cot Ho	Durham	NZ0249	54°50·4′	1°57·7′W	X	87
West Cotside	Angus	NO5233	56°29·5′	2°46·3′W	X	54
Westcott	Bucks	SP7117	51°51·1′	0°57·8′W	T	165
Westcott	Corn	SX2389	50°40·7′	4°29·9′W	X	190
Westcott	Corn	SX2596	50°44·5′	4°28·4′W	X	190
Westcott	Corn	SX2895	50°44·0′	4°25·9′W	X	190
Westcott	Corn	SX3099	50°46·2′	4°24·3′W	X	190
Westcott	Corn	SX3768	50°29·6′	4°17·5′W	X	201
Westcott	Devon	SS8011	50°53·4′	3°42·0′W	X	191
Westcott	Devon	ST0204	50°49·9′	3°23·1′W	T	192
Westcott	Devon	SX4681	50°36·7′	4°10·2′W	X	201
Westcott	Devon	SX7886	50°39·9′	3°43·2′W	X	191
Westcott	Devon	SY0599	50°47·2′	3°20·5′W	X	192
Westcott	Shrops	SJ4001	52°36·4′	2°52·8′W	T	126
Westcott	Surrey	TQ1448	51°13·4′	0°21·7′W	T	187
Westcott Barton	Devon	SS5338	51°7·6′	4°5·7′W	X	180
Westcott Barton	Oxon	SP4225	51°55·5′	1°23·0′W	T	164
Westcott Brake	Somer	SS8446	51°12·3′	3°39·2′W	F	181
Westcott Fm	Corn	SS2015	50°54·6′	4°33·2′W	FM	190
Westcott Fm	Devon	SS8720	50°58·3′	3°36·2′W	FM	181
Westcott Fm	Devon	ST0516	50°56·4′	3°20·7′W	FM	181
Westcott Fm	Devon	ST1108	50°52·1′	3°15·5′W	FM	192,193
Westcott Fm	Somer	ST0323	51°0·1′	3°22·6′W	FM	181
Westcott Fm	Somer	ST0731	51°4·5′	3°19·3′W	FM	181
Westcott Heath	Surrey	TQ1348	51°13·4′	0°22·5′W	X	187
Westcott Hill	Shrops	SJ4001	52°36·4′	2°52·8′W	X	126
Westcott Ho	Devon	SY0293	50°43·9′	3°22·9′W	X	192
Westcott Mill	Shrops	SJ7028	52°51·2′	2°26·3′W	X	127
Westcott Plantn	Corn	SX3099	50°46·2′	4°24·3′W	F	190
West Coullie	Aberd	NJ8725	57°19·2′	2°12·5′W	X	38
West Court	Hants	SU7641	51°10·0′	0°54·4′W	X	186
West Court	I of W	SZ4582	50°38·4′	1°21·4′W	A	196
West Court	Kent	TQ6673	51°26·1′	0°23·7′E	X	177,178
Westcourt	Wilts	SU2261	51°21·1′	1°40·7′W	T	174
West Court	Wok	SU7763	51°21·9′	0°53·2′W	X	175,186
West Court Downs	Kent	TR2448	51°11·5′	1°12·7′E	X	179,189
West Court Fm	Kent	TR2447	51°10·9′	1°12·7′E	FM	179,189
West Court Fm	Medway	TQ7275	51°27·1′	0°28·9′E	FM	178
West Court Fm	S Glos	ST6771	51°26·5′	2°28·1′W	FM	172
West Cowick	E Yorks	SE6421	53°41·1′	1°1·4′W	T	105,106
West Craig	Aberd	NJ8925	57°19·2′	2°10·5′W	X	38
West Craig	Angus	NO4548	56°37·5′	2°53·3′W	X	54
West Craig	Angus	NO4973	56°51·0′	2°49·7′W	X	44
West Craig	I of M	SC3896	54°20·3′	4°29·1′W	X	95
West Craigford	Aberd	NJ6427	57°20·2′	2°35·4′W	X	37
West Craigie Fm	C of Edin	NT1576	55°58·4′	3°21·3′W	FM	65
West Craigs	C of Edin	NT1773	55°56·8′	3°19·3′W	X	65,66
Westcraigs	W Loth	NS9067	55°53·3′	3°45·1′W	X	65
West Crannow	Corn	SX1697	50°44·8′	4°36·1′W	X	190
West Creech	Dorset	SY8982	50°38·5′	2°9·0′W	X	195
West Creech Hill	Dorset	SY8981	50°37·9′	2°9·0′W	X	195
West Crichie	Aberd	NJ9643	57°28·9′	2°3·5′W	X	30
West Croachy	Highld	NH6427	57°19·1′	4°15·0′W	X	26,35
West Croft	Cumbr	NY0021	54°34·7′	3°32·4′W	X	89
Westcroft	Mil Key	SP8234	52°0·1′	0°47·9′W	T	152,165
Westcroft	Wolv	SJ9302	52°37·2′	2°5·8′W	T	127,139
Westcroft Fm	Staffs	SO8796	52°33·9′	2°11·1′W	FM	139
West Croftmore	Highld	NH9315	57°13·1′	3°45·9′W	X	36
Westcroft Park	Surrey	SU9563	51°21·7′	0°37·7′W	X	175,176,186
Westcroft Stables	Bucks	SU8399	51°41·2′	0°47·6′W	X	165
West Cross	Kent	TQ8331	51°3·2′	0°37·1′E	T	188
West Cross	Swan	SS6189	51°35·2′	4°0·0′W	T	159
West Crudwell	Wilts	ST9493	51°38·4′	2°4·8′W	T	163,173
West Cullery	Aberd	NJ7603	57°7·3′	2°23·3′W	X	38
West Cult	Pth & Kin	NO0642	56°33·9′	3°31·3′W	X	52,53
West Culvennan	D & G	NX2965	54°57·3′	4°39·8′W	X	82
West Curry	Corn	SX2893	50°42·9′	4°25·8′W	T	190
West Curthwaite	Cumbr	NY3248	54°49·6′	3°3·1′W	T	85
West Dairy	Pemb	SN0118	51°49·8′	4°52·9′W	X	157,158
West Dale	E Yorks	TA0375	54°9·9′	0°24·9′W	X	101
West Dale	Orkney	ND2595	58°50·4′	3°17·5′W	X	7
Westdale Bay	Pemb	SM7905	51°42·3′	5°11·5′W	W	157
Westdale Fm	Leic	SP5894	52°32·7′	1°8·3′W	FM	140
West Darlochan	Arg & Bt	NR6723	55°27·0′	5°40·6′W	X	68
West Dart Head	Devon	SX6081	50°37·0′	3°58·4′W	W	191
West Dart Head	Devon	SX6081	50°37·0′	3°58·4′W	W	191
West Dart River	Devon	SX6174	50°33·2′	3°57·4′W	W	191
West Davoch	Aberd	NJ4606	57°8·8′	2°53·1′W	X	37
Westdean	E Susx	TV5299	50°46·5′	0°9·7′E	T	199
West Dean	Wilts	SU2527	51°2·7′	1°38·2′W	T	184
West Dean	W Susx	SU8612	50°54·3′	0°46·2′W	T	197
West Dean Fm	Wilts	SU2326	51°2·2′	1°39·9′W	FM	184
West Deanraw	Northum	NY8162	54°57·4′	2°17·4′W	X	86,87
Westdean Woods	W Susx	SU8415	50°55·9′	0°47·9′W	F	197
West Deeping	Lincs	TF1108	52°39·7′	0°21·1′W	T	142
West Denant	Pemb	SM9013	51°46·8′	5°2·3′W	T	157,158
West Denbie Fm	D & G	NY0873	55°2·8′	3°26·0′W	FM	85
Westdene	Bri & Hov	TQ2908	50°51·7′	0°9·6′W	T	198
West Denmore	Aberd	NJ8940	57°27·3′	2°10·5′W	X	30
West Denside	Angus	NO4638	56°32·1′	2°52·2′W	T	54
West Denton	N upon Ty	NZ1866	54°59·5′	1°42·7′W	T	88
West Derby	Liv	SJ3993	53°26·1′	2°54·7′W	T	108
West Dereham	Norf	TF6601	52°35·1′	0°27·4′E	T	143
West Devon Way	Devon	SX5490	50°41·7′	4°3·7′W	X	191
West Dhuloch	D & G	NW9865	54°56·6′	5°8·8′W	X	82
West Didsbury	Man	SJ8391	53°25·2′	2°14·9′W	T	109
West Dipton burn	Northum	NY9161	54°56·9′	2°8·0′W	W	87
West Ditchburn	Northum	NU1320	55°28·7′	1°47·2′W	X	75
West Dougliehill	Inverc	NS3173	55°55·5′	4°41·9′W	X	63
West Down	Devon	SS2914	50°54·2′	4°25·5′W	X	190
West Down	Devon	SS5142	51°9·7′	4°7·5′W	T	180
Westdown	Devon	SS5601	50°47·7′	4°2·2′W	X	191
West Down	Devon	SX4099	50°46·3′	4°15·8′W	X	190
West Down	Devon	SX4870	50°30·8′	4°8·3′W	X	201
West Down	Devon	SX5463	50°27·2′	4°3·0′W	X	201
West Down	Devon	SX7695	50°44·7′	3°45·1′W	X	191
Westdown	Devon	SX8149	50°20·0′	3°39·9′W	X	202
West Down	Devon	SY0481	50°37·5′	3°21·1′W	H	192
West Down	Dorset	SY8497	50°46·6′	2°13·2′W	X	194
West Down	Glos	SP0024	51°55·1′	1°59·6′W	X	163
West Down	Hants	SU3838	51°8·6′	1°27·0′W	T	185
West Down	Kent	TR0945	51°10·2′	0°59·8′E	X	179,189
West Down	Wilts	SU0548	51°14·1′	1°55·3′W	X	184
West Down	Wilts	SU0768	51°24·9′	1°53·6′W	X	173
Westdown Artillery Range	Wilts	SU0451	51°15·7′	1°56·2′W	X	184
Westdown Camp	Wilts	SU0447	51°13·6′	1°56·2′W	T	184
Westdownend	Corn	SX2585	50°38·5′	4°28·1′W	X	201
West Down Fm	Devon	SY0380	50°36·9′	3°21·9′W	FM	192
West Down Fm	Dorset	SY8181	50°37·9′	2°15·7′W	FM	194
Westdown Fm	E Susx	TQ6422	50°58·7′	0°20·6′E	FM	199
Westdown Fm	Somer	ST7245	51°12·4′	2°23·7′W	FM	183
West Down Plantation	Wilts	SU0449	51°14·6′	1°56·2′W	F	184
West Downs	Corn	SX0364	50°26·8′	4°46·1′W	T	200
Westdowns	Corn	SX0582	50°36·5′	4°45·0′W	T	200
Westdown Wood	Corn	SX2965	50°27·8′	4°24·2′W	F	201
West Drain	N Lincs	SE9615	53°37·6′	0°32·5′W	W	112
West Drayton	Hill	TQ0679	51°30·2′	0°28·0′W	T	176
West Drayton	Notts	SK7074	53°15·7′	0°56·6′W	T	120
West Drip	Stir	NS7595	56°8·1′	4°0·2′W	X	57
West Drive	Corn	SX1360	50°24·8′	4°37·6′W	F	200
West Dron	Pth & Kin	NO1215	56°19·4′	3°24·9′W	X	58
West Dron Hill	Pth & Kin	NO1115	56°19·4′	3°25·9′W	H	58
West Drove Fm	Norf	TF5012	52°41·3′	0°13·6′E	FM	131,143
West Drumlemble	Arg & Bt	NR6619	55°24·8′	5°41·4′W	X	68
West Drumloch	S Lanak	NS6750	55°43·8′	4°6·6′W	X	64
West Drums	Angus	NO5857	56°42·4′	2°40·7′W	X	54
West Duddo	Northum	NZ1879	55°6·6′	1°42·6′W	X	88
West Duerley Pasture	N Yks	SD8685	54°15·9′	2°12·5′W	X	98
West Dullater	Stir	NN5805	56°13·2′	4°17·0′W	X	57
West Dulwich	Lam	TQ3272	51°26·1′	0°5·7′W	T	176,177
West Dun Hill	Cumbr	NY6252	54°51·9′	2°35·1′W	X	86
West Dunley Fm	Wilts	ST8481	51°31·9′	2°13·4′W	FM	173
West Dunnet	Highld	ND2171	58°37·5′	3°21·1′W	T	7,12
West Dykehead Fm	S Lanak	NS6639	55°37·8′	4°7·3′W	FM	71
West Dykes	S Lanak	NS6639	55°37·8′	4°7·3′W	X	71
West Ealing	Ealing	TQ1680	51°30·6′	0°19·3′W	T	176
Wested Fm	Kent	TQ5166	51°22·6′	0°10·6′E	FM	177
West Edge	Derby	SK3363	53°10·0′	1°30·0′W	T	119
West Edge Fm	C of Edin	NT2867	55°53·7′	3°8·6′W	FM	66
West Edge Fm	Northum	NT9555	55°47·5′	2°4·3′W	FM	67,74,75
West Edington	Northum	NZ1582	55°8·2′	1°45·5′W	X	81
West Edmondsley	Durham	NZ2249	54°50·4′	1°39·0′W	X	88
West Ednie	Aberd	NK0750	57°32·7′	1°52·5′W	X	30
West Ella	E Yorks	TA0029	53°45·1′	0°28·6′W	T	106,107
West Ella Grange	E Yorks	TA0128	53°44·6′	0°27·7′W	X	106,107
West Emlett	Devon	SS8008	50°51·8′	3°41·9′W	X	191
West End	Beds	SP9853	52°10·2′	0°33·6′W	T	153
West End	Beds	TL0962	52°15·0′	0°23·8′W	T	153
West End	Brackn	SU8671	51°26·1′	0°45·4′W	T	175
West End	Caer	ST2195	51°39·1′	3°8·1′W	T	171
West End	Ches	SJ6754	53°5·2′	2°29·2′W	X	118
West End	Cumbr	NY2849	54°50·1′	3°6·8′W	X	85
West End	Cumbr	NY3258	54°55·0′	3°3·2′W	T	85
West End	Donc	SE6115	53°37·9′	1°4·2′W	X	111
West End	Donc	SE6607	53°33·6′	0°59·8′W	T	111
West End	Dorset	ST9002	50°49·3′	2°8·1′W	T	195
West End	Durham	NY9820	54°34·8′	2°1·4′W	X	92
West End	E Yorks	SE9130	53°45·7′	0°36·8′W	T	106
West End	E Yorks	TA0564	54°3·9′	0°23·3′W	T	101
West End	E Yorks	TA1656	53°59·5′	0°13·4′W	T	107
West End	E Yorks	TA1730	53°45·4′	0°13·1′W	T	107
West End	E Yorks	TA2727	53°43·7′	0°4·1′W	T	107
Westend	Glos	SO7806	51°45·4′	2°18·7′W	X	162
West End	Glos	ST8797	51°40·5′	2°10·9′W	T	162
West End	Hants	SU4614	50°55·6′	1°20·3′W	T	196
West End	Hants	SU5605	50°50·7′	1°11·9′W	T	196
West End	Hants	SU6335	51°6·9′	1°5·6′W	T	185
West End	Herts	TL2608	51°45·6′	0°10·1′W	T	166
Westend	Herts	TL2814	51°48·8′	0°8·2′W	X	166
West End	Kent	TQ9257	51°17·0′	0°45·6′E	T	178
West End	Kent	TR1565	51°20·8′	1°5·6′E	T	179
West End	Kirk	SE1825	53°43·5′	1°43·2′W	T	104
West End	Lancs	SD4363	54°3·8′	2°51·8′W	T	97
West End	Lancs	SD7328	53°45·1′	2°24·2′W	T	103
West End	Leeds	SE2338	53°50·5′	1°38·6′W	T	104
West End	Leic	SK4219	52°46·3′	1°22·2′W	T	129
West End	Lincs	TF3598	53°27·9′	0°2·4′E	T	113
West End	Lincs	TF3846	52°59·8′	0°3·8′E	T	131
West End	Monm	ST4496	51°39·8′	2°48·2′W	T	171
West End	Norf	TF9009	52°39·0′	0°48·9′E	T	144
West End	Norf	TG4911	52°38·6′	1°41·2′E	T	134
West End	Norf	TM3892	52°28·7′	1°30·7′E	X	134
West End	Northum	NY8445	54°48·2′	2°14·5′W	X	86,87
West End	N Som	ST4469	51°25·3′	2°47·9′W	T	171,172,182
West End	N Yks	SD7895	54°21·2′	2°19·9′W	X	98
West End	N Yks	SE1457	54°0·8′	1°46·8′W	T	104
West End	N Yks	SE2348	53°55·9′	1°38·6′W	X	104
West End	N Yks	SE5140	53°51·5′	1°13·1′W	T	105
West End	N Yks	SE5718	53°39·6′	1°7·8′W	X	111
West End	N Yks	SE5835	53°48·7′	1°6·7′W	T	105
Westend	Oxon	SP3222	51°54·0′	1°31·7′W	T	164
West End	Oxon	SP4204	51°44·2′	1°23·1′W	T	164
West End	Oxon	SU5886	51°34·4′	1°9·4′W	T	174
West End	Pemb	SN0516	51°48·8′	4°49·3′W	X	158
Westend	S Glos	ST6092	51°37·8′	2°34·3′W	T	162,172
West End	S Glos	ST7188	51°35·6′	2°24·7′W	T	162,172
Westend	S Lanak	NS5852	55°44·7′	4°15·3′W	X	64
West End	S Lanak	NS9646	55°42·0′	3°38·9′W	T	72
West End	Somer	ST5652	51°16·2′	2°37·5′W	T	182,183
West End	Somer	ST6734	51°6·5′	2°27·9′W	T	183
West End	Suff	TM4683	52°23·6′	1°37·3′E	T	156
West End	Surrey	SU8242	51°10·5′	0°49·2′W	T	186
West End	Surrey	SU9460	51°20·1′	0°38·6′W	T	175,186
West End	Surrey	TQ1263	51°21·5′	0°23·1′W	T	176,187
West End	Wilts	ST9123	51°0·6′	2°7·3′W	T	184
West End	Wilts	ST9777	51°29·7′	2°2·2′W	T	173
West End	Wilts	ST9824	51°1·2′	2°1·3′W	T	184
West End	Win & Maid	SU8275	51°28·3′	0°48·8′W	T	175
West End	Worcs	SP0936	52°1·6′	1°51·7′W	T	150
West End	W Susx	TQ2016	50°56·1′	0°17·1′W	T	198
Westend Common	Surrey	SU9160	51°20·1′	0°41·2′W	X	175,186
West End Common	Surrey	TQ1263	51°21·5′	0°23·1′W	X	176,187
Westend Down	Hants	SU6418	50°57·7′	1°4·9′W	X	185
West End Fm	Beds	SP9747	52°7·0′	0°34·6′W	FM	153
Westend Fm	Beds	SP9855	52°11·3′	0°33·6′W	FM	153
West End Fm	Beds	TL0640	52°3·1′	0°26·8′W	FM	153
Westend Fm	E Yorks	SE9759	54°1·3′	0°30·7′W	FM	106
West End Fm	Hants	SU6364	51°22·5′	1°5·3′W	FM	175
West End Fm	Heref	SO5557	52°12·8′	2°39·1′W	FM	149
Westend Fm	Herts	TL1427	51°56·0′	0°20·1′W	FM	166
West End Fm	Herts	TL1612	51°47·9′	0°18·7′W	FM	166
West End Fm	Lincs	TF4391	53°24·0′	0°9·5′E	FM	113
West End Fm	N Som	ST3559	51°19·8′	2°55·6′W	FM	182
West End Fm	N Yks	SD6469	54°7·2′	2°32·6′W	FM	97
West End Fm	N Yks	SE6639	53°50·8′	0°59·4′W	FM	105,106
West End Fm	Somer	ST3338	51°8·5′	2°57·1′W	FM	182
Westend Fm	Suff	TM0355	52°9·6′	0°58·5′E	FM	155
West End Fm	Suff	TM0873	52°19·2′	1°3·5′E	FM	144,155
Westend Fm	Suff	TM4285	52°24·8′	1°33·9′E	FM	156
West End Fm	Surrey	SU9334	51°6·1′	0°39·9′W	FM	186
West End Green	Hants	SU6661	51°20·9′	1°2·7′W	T	175,186
Westend Head	Derby	SK1195	53°27·3′	1°49·7′W	X	110
Westend Hill	Bucks	SP9116	51°50·3′	0°40·4′W	H	165
West End Lathe	N Yks	SE0773	54°9·4′	1°53·2′W	X	99
Westend Moor	Derby	SK1393	53°26·3′	1°47·8′W	X	110
Westend Moor	Northum	NY8344	54°47·7′	2°15·4′W	X	86,87
Westend Moss	Derby	SE0801	53°30·6′	1°52·4′W	H	110
West End or Marian-y-mor	Gwyn	SH3634	52°53·0′	4°25·8′W	T	123
Westend Town	Northum	NY7765	54°59·0′	2°21·1′W	T	86,87
West-end Town	V of Glam	SS9668	51°24·3′	3°29·3′W	T	170
Westend Town Fm	S Glos	ST7674	51°28·1′	2°20·3′W	FM	172
West End Wood	Somer	ST7537	51°8·1′	2°21·1′W	F	183
Westenhanger	Kent	TR1137	51°5·8′	1°1·2′E	A	179,189
Westenhanger	Kent	TR1237	51°5·8′	1°2·1′E	T	179,189
West Enoch	S Ayr	NS2810	55°21·5′	4°42·4′W	X	70
Wester	Highld	ND2372	58°38·0′	3°19·1′W	X	7,12
Wester	Highld	NH1464	57°37·9′	5°6·5′W	X	20
Wester Aberchalder	Highld	NH5519	57°14·6′	4°23·7′W	T	35
Wester Achnacloich	Highld	NH6674	57°44·4′	4°14·6′W	X	21
Wester Achtuie	Highld	NH5231	57°21·0′	4°27·1′W	X	26
Wester Aikengall	E Loth	NT7070	55°55·6′	2°28·4′W	X	67
Wester Aldie	Pth & Kin	NT0397	56°9·6′	3°33·3′W	X	58
Wester Alemoor	Scot Bord	NT4015	55°25·8′	2°56·5′W	X	79
Wester Alves	Moray	NJ1262	57°38·6′	3°28·0′W	X	28
Wester Arboll	Highld	NH8781	57°48·5′	3°53·6′W	T	21
Wester Aucheen	Angus	NO5279	56°54·2′	2°46·8′W	X	44
Wester Auchendennan	Arg & Bt	NS3584	56°1·5′	4°38·4′W	X	56
Wester Auchentroig	Stir	NS5493	56°6·7′	4°20·4′W	X	57
Wester Auchinloch	N Lanak	NS6570	55°54·5′	4°9·1′W	T	64
Wester Auchnagallin	Highld	NJ0533	57°22·9′	3°34·3′W	X	27
Wester Badentyre	Aberd	NJ7652	57°33·7′	2°23·6′W	X	29
Wester Badgrinnan	Highld	NH6359	57°36·3′	4°17·1′W	X	26
Wester Balbeggie	Fife	NT2796	56°9·3′	3°10·1′W	X	59
Wester Balgair	Stir	NS5989	56°4·6′	4°15·5′W	X	57
Wester Balgarvie	Fife	NO3415	56°19·6′	3°3·6′W	X	59
Wester Balgedie	Pth & Kin	NO1604	56°13·5′	3°20·8′W	T	58
Wester Balgersho	Pth & Kin	NO2138	56°31·9′	3°16·6′W	X	53
Wester Balgour	Pth & Kin	NO0016	56°19·8′	3°36·6′W	X	58
Wester Balloan	Highld	NH4753	57°32·7′	4°32·9′W	X	26
Wester Balloch	Angus	NO3479	56°54·1′	3°4·6′W	H	44
Wester Balrymonth	Fife	NO5014	56°19·2′	2°48·1′W	X	59
Wester Banchory	Pth & Kin	NO1840	56°32·9′	3°19·6′W	X	53
Wester Bankhead	Pth & Kin	NO0409	56°16·1′	3°32·6′W	X	58
Wester Barevan	Highld	NH8246	57°29·6′	3°57·7′W	X	27
Wester Barnego	Falk	NS7884	56°2·3′	3°57·0′W	X	57,64
Wester Bauds	Moray	NJ3059	57°37·2′	3°9·9′W	X	28
Wester Bavelaw	C of Edin	NT1562	55°50·9′	3°21·0′W	X	65
Wester Beck	Durham	NY9030	54°40·1′	2°8·9′W	W	91,92
Wester Beltie	Aberd	NJ6102	57°6·7′	2°38·2′W	X	37
Wester Biggs	Pth & Kin	NN8606	56°14·2′	3°49·9′W	X	58
Wester Blackwells	Highld	NH5358	57°35·6′	4°27·1′W	X	26
Wester Blair	Aberd	NJ8420	57°16·5′	2°15·5′W	X	38
Wester Blairgorts	Stir	NS5993	56°6·8′	4°15·6′W	X	57
Wester Bleaton	Pth & Kin	NO1159	56°43·1′	3°26·8′W	X	53
Wester Bogie	Fife	NT2493	56°7·7′	3°12·9′W	X	59
Wester Bonhard	Pth & Kin	NO1526	56°25·4′	3°22·2′W	X	53,58
Wester Bows	Stir	NN7306	56°14·0′	4°2·5′W	X	57
Wester Bracco	N Lanak	NS8165	55°52·1′	3°53·7′W	X	65
Wester Bracklinn	Stir	NN6508	56°15·0′	4°10·3′W	X	57
Wester Brae	Highld	NH6562	57°37·9′	4°15·2′W	X	21
Wester Brae of Cantray	Highld	NH7847	57°30·1′	4°1·7′W	X	27
Wester Braikie	Angus	NO6251	56°39·2′	2°36·7′W	X	54
Wester Breich	W Loth	NT0064	55°51·8′	3°35·4′W	X	65
Wester Broomhouse	E Loth	NT6776	55°58·8′	2°31·3′W	T	67
Wester Bullaford Moor	Devon	SS8025	51°0·9′	3°42·3′W	X	181
Wester Burn	Scot Bord	NT3915	55°25·8′	2°57·4′W	W	79
Wester Burn	Scot Bord	NT5855	55°47·4′	2°39·8′W	W	67,73,74
Wester Burn	Scot Bord	NT6559	55°49·6′	2°33·1′W	W	67,74
Westerby Fm	Norf	TF5404	52°36·9′	0°16·9′E	FM	143
Wester Cairnie	Pth & Kin	NO0318	56°20·9′	3°33·7′W	X	58
Wester Calcots	Moray	NJ2463	57°39·3′	3°16·0′W	X	28
Wester Calrichie	Highld	NH7073	57°43·9′	4°10·5′W	X	21
Wester Cambushinnie	Stir	NN7806	56°14·1′	3°57·7′W	X	57
Wester Cambushinnie	Stir	NN7906	56°14·1′	3°56·7′W	X	57
Wester Cameron	Stir	NS4583	56°1·1′	4°28·8′W	X	57,64
Wester Campfield	Aberd	NJ6500	57°5·6′	2°34·2′W	X	38
Wester Cardean	Angus	NO2946	56°36·3′	3°8·9′W	X	53
Wester Cardno	Aberd	NJ9664	57°40·2′	2°3·6′W	X	30
Wester Carmuirs	Falk	NS8480	56°0·2′	3°51·2′W	X	65
Wester Cash	Fife	NO2209	56°16·3′	3°15·1′W	X	58
Wester Caulan	Highld	NH6836	57°24·0′	4°11·3′W	X	26

Wester Causewayend	W Loth	NT0860	55°49·7′	3°27·7′W	X	65
Wester Chalder	Moray	NJ4047	57°30·8′	2°59·6′W	X	28
Wester Claggan	Moray	NJ2126	57°19·3′	3°18·3′W	X	36
Wester Clova	Aberd	NJ4519	57°15·8′	2°54·3′W	X	37
Wester Clune	Aberd	NO5991	57°0·8′	2°40·1′W	X	44
Wester Clune	Highld	NH9451	57°32·5′	3°45·8′W	X	27
Wester Clunes	Highld	NH5340	57°25·9′	4°26·4′W	X	26
Wester Clunie	Pth & Kin	NN9159	56°42·9′	3°46·4′W	X	52
Wester Clunie	Pth & Kin	NO2117	56°20·6′	3°16·2′W	X	58
Wester Cochno	W Dunb	NS4974	55°56·4′	4°24·6′W	X	64
Wester Coillechat	Stir	NN6804	56°12·9′	4°7·3′W	X	57
Wester Cornhill	Clackm	NS9799	56°10·6′	3°39·1′W	X	58
Wester Corse	Aberd	NJ5307	57°9·3′	2°46·2′W	X	37
Wester Corskie	Aberd	NJ6253	57°34·2′	2°37·7′W	X	29
Wester Coul	Angus	NO2757	56°42·2′	3°11·1′W	X	53
Wester Coull	Aberd	NJ4702	57°6·6′	2°52·0′W	X	37
Wester Cowden	Midlo	NT3567	55°53·8′	3°1·9′W	X	66
Wester Coxton	Moray	NJ2560	57°37·7′	3°14·9′W	X	28
Wester Craggach	Highld	NH5643	57°27·5′	4°23·6′W	X	26
Wester Craggan	Highld	NJ0126	57°19·1′	3°38·2′W	X	36
Wester Craigfoodie	Fife	NO4017	56°20·7′	2°57·8′W	X	59
Wester Craiglands	Highld	NH7057	57°35·3′	4°10·0′W	X	27
Wester Croft	S Ayr	NS3631	55°33·0′	4°35·5′W	X	70
Wester Cudrish	Highld	NH5034	57°22·6′	4°29·2′W	X	26
Wester Culbeuchly	Aberd	NJ6462	57°39·0′	2°35·7′W	X	29
Wester Culbowie	Stir	NS5792	56°6·2′	4°17·5′W	X	57
Wester Culbo Wood	Highld	NH6459	57°36·3′	4°16·1′W	F	26
Wester Culfoich Fm	Highld	NJ0832	57°22·4′	3°31·3′W	FM	27,36
Wester Cultmalundie	Pth & Kin	NO0322	56°23·1′	3°33·8′W	X	52,53,58
Wester Culvie	Aberd	NJ5854	57°34·7′	2°41·7′W	X	29
Wester Daldowie	C of Glas	NS6662	55°50·2′	4°7·9′W	X	64
Westerdale	Highld	ND1251	58°26·6′	3°30·0′W	T	11,12
Westerdale	N Yks	NZ6605	54°26·4′	0°58·5′W	T	94
Westerdale	N Yks	NZ6606	54°26·9′	0°58·5′W	X	94
Westerdale	N Yks	SE7469	54°6·9′	0°51·7′W	X	100
Westerdale Moor	N Yks	NZ6602	54°24·8′	0°58·6′W	X	94
Westerdale Moor	N Yks	NZ6607	54°27·5′	0°58·5′W	X	94
Wester Dalinch	Angus	NO3365	56°46·6′	3°5·3′W	X	44
Wester Dalvoult	Highld	NH9417	57°14·1′	3°44·9′W	X	36
Wester Dalziel	Highld	NH7550	57°31·6′	4°4·8′W	X	27
Wester Darbreich	Moray	NJ4862	57°39·0′	2°51·8′W	X	28,29
Wester Dawyck	Scot Bord	NT1534	55°35·8′	3°20·5′W	X	72
Wester Deans	Scot Bord	NT2151	55°45·0′	3°15·1′W	X	66,73
Wester Dechmont	W Loth	NT0270	55°55·0′	3°33·6′W	T	65
Wester Delfour	Highld	NH8408	57°9·2′	3°54·6′W	X	35
Wester Delnies	Highld	NH8355	57°34·5′	3°56·9′W	X	27
Wester Deloraine	Scot Bord	NT3320	55°28·4′	3°3·2′W	T	73
Wester Denhead	Pth & Kin	NO2340	56°33·0′	3°14·7′W	X	53
Wester Denoon	Angus	NO3443	56°34·7′	3°4·0′W	X	54
Wester Derry	Angus	NO2354	56°40·5′	3°15·0′W	X	53
Wester Deuglie	Pth & Kin	NO1011	56°17·2′	3°26·8′W	X	58
Wester Dod	E Loth	NT7168	55°54·5′	2°27·4′W	X	67
Wester Dollerie	Pth & Kin	NN8921	56°22·4′	3°47·4′W	X	52,58
Wester Dounie	Highld	NH5590	57°52·8′	4°26·2′W	X	21
Wester Dron	Fife	NO4116	56°20·2′	2°56·8′W	X	59
Wester Drumcross	W Loth	NS9970	55°55·0′	3°36·5′W	X	65
Wester Drummond	Highld	NH4613	57°11·2′	4°32·4′W	X	34
Wester Drumquhassle	Stir	NS4887	56°3·4′	4°26·0′W	X	57
Wester Duncanstone	Aberd	NJ5626	57°19·6′	2°43·4′W	X	37
Wester Dundurn	Pth & Kin	NN7023	56°23·1′	4°5·9′W	X	51,52
Wester Dunidea	Pth & Kin	NO1059	56°43·1′	3°27·8′W	X	53
Wester Dunsyston	N Lanak	NS7963	55°51·0′	3°55·5′W	X	64
Wester Durie	Fife	NO3602	56°12·6′	3°1·5′W	X	59
Wester Durris	Aberd	NO7696	57°3·5′	2°23·3′W	X	38,45
Wester Earshaig	D & G	NT0402	55°18·4′	3°30·3′W	X	78
Wester Eggie	Angus	NO3570	56°49·3′	3°3·4′W	T	44
Wester Elchies	Moray	NJ2542	57°28·0′	3°14·6′W	X	28
Wester Ellister	Arg & Bt	NR1852	55°41·0′	6°28·8′W	X	60
Wester Emmetts	Somer	SS7437	51°7·3′	3°47·6′W	X	180
Wester Erchite	Highld	NH5730	57°20·5′	4°22·1′W	X	26
Wester Essendy	Pth & Kin	NO1343	56°34·5′	3°24·5′W	T	53
Wester Essenside	Scot Bord	NT4420	55°28·5′	2°52·7′W	T	73
Wester Fearn	Highld	NH6287	57°51·3′	4°19·1′W	X	21
Wester Fearn Burn	Highld	NH6086	57°50·8′	4°21·1′W	W	21
Wester Fearn Point	Highld	NH6388	57°51·9′	4°18·1′W	X	21
Wester Feddal	Pth & Kin	NN8208	56°15·2′	3°53·8′W	X	57
Westerfield	Shetld	HU3551	60°14·8′	1°21·6′W	T	3
Westerfield	Suff	TM1747	52°4·9′	1°10·4′E	T	169
Westerfield Hall Fm	Suff	TM1748	52°5·5′	1°10·5′E	FM	169
Westerfield Ho	Suff	TM1847	52°4·9′	1°11·3′E	X	169
Wester Filla Burn	Shetld	HU4161	60°20·1′	1°14·9′W	W	2,3
Wester Fintray	Aberd	NJ8116	57°14·3′	2°18·4′W	X	38
Wester Floors	Aberd	NO5290	57°0·2′	2°47·0′W	X	44
Wester Fodderlee	Scot Bord	NT6014	55°25·3′	2°37·5′W	X	80
Wester Foffarty	Angus	NO4145	56°35·8′	2°57·2′W	T	54
Westerfolds	Moray	NJ1967	57°41·4′	3°21·1′W	X	28
Wester Forret	Fife	NO3820	56°22·4′	2°59·8′W	X	54,59
Wester Fowlis	Aberd	NJ5411	57°11·5′	2°45·2′W	X	37
Wester Frew	Stir	NS6696	56°8·5′	4°9·0′W	X	57
Wester Friarton	Fife	NO4225	56°25·1′	2°56·0′W	X	54,59
Wester Galcantray	Highld	NH8047	57°30·1′	3°59·7′W	X	27
Wester Gallovie	Highld	NH9523	57°17·4′	3°44·1′W	X	36
Wester Gartshore	E Dunb	NS6873	55°56·2′	4°6·4′W	X	64
Westergate	W Susx	SU9305	50°50·4′	0°40·4′W	T	197
Wester Gatherleys	Pth & Kin	NO0411	56°17·2′	3°32·6′W	X	58
Wester Gauldwell	Moray	NJ3044	57°29·1′	3°9·6′W	X	28
Wester Gaulrig	Moray	NJ1513	57°12·3′	3°24·0′W	X	36
Wester Gavin	Renf	NS3758	55°47·5′	4°35·6′W	X	63
Wester Gellet	Fife	NT0984	56°2·7′	3°27·2′W	X	65
Wester Geo	Shetld	HU6670	60°24·8′	0°47·6′W	X	2
Wester Glasslie	Fife	NO2305	56°14·1′	3°14·1′W	X	58
Wester Glenerney	Moray	NJ0045	57°29·3′	3°39·6′W	X	27
Westerglen Fm	Falk	NS8777	55°58·6′	3°48·2′W	FM	65
Wester Glen Quoich Burn	Highld	NG9909	57°7·9′	5°18·8′W	W	33
Wester Glensherup	Pth & Kin	NN9605	56°13·8′	3°40·2′W	X	58
Wester Glentore	N Lanak	NS7872	55°55·8′	3°56·7′W	X	64
Wester Gorton	Highld	NJ0128	57°20·2′	3°38·2′W	X	36
Wester Gospetry	Fife	NO1606	56°14·6′	3°20·9′W	X	58
Wester Greens	Moray	NJ0349	57°31·5′	3°36·7′W	X	27
Wester Greenskares	Aberd	NJ7763	57°39·6′	2°22·7′W	X	29,30
Wester Gruinards	Highld	NH5192	57°53·8′	4°30·4′W	T	20
Wester Hailes	C of Edin	NT2069	55°54·7′	3°16·4′W	T	66
Westerhall	Clackm	NN9800	56°11·2′	3°38·2′W	X	58
Westerhall	D & G	NY3189	55°11·7′	3°4·6′W	X	79
Wester Hall	Northum	NY9172	55°2·8′	2°8·0′W	X	87
Westerham	Kent	TQ4454	51°16·2′	0°4·2′E	T	187
Westerham Wood	Kent	TQ4354	51°16·3′	0°3·4′E	F	187
Wester Happrew	Scot Bord	NT1741	55°39·6′	3°18·7′W	X	72
Wester Hassockrigg	N Lanak	NS8763	55°51·1′	3°47·9′W	X	65
Wester Hatton	Aberd	NJ9515	57°13·8′	2°4·5′W	X	38
Wester Haven	Highld	ND2874	58°39·1′	3°14·0′W	W	7,12
Wester Herricks	Moray	NJ4549	57°31·9′	2°54·7′W	X	28,29
Westerheugh	Northum	NZ0773	55°3·3′	1°53·0′W	X	88
Westerheugh	Northum	NZ1097	55°16·3′	1°50·1′W	X	81
Wester Hevda Wick	Shetld	HU4479	60°29·8′	1°11·4′W	W	2,3
Westerhill	Arg & Bt	NS3576	55°57·2′	4°38·1′W	X	63
Wester Hill	D & G	NX9398	55°16·1′	3°40·6′W	X	78
Westerhill	E Dunb	NS6370	55°54·5′	4°11·1′W	X	64
Wester Hill	Northum	NT8733	55°35·7′	2°11·9′W	X	74
Westerhill Fm	Kent	TQ7450	51°13·6′	0°29·9′E	FM	188
Wester Hillhead	Falk	NS9273	55°56·5′	3°43·3′W	X	65
Wester Hillhouse	W Loth	NS9270	55°54·9′	3°43·2′W	X	65
Wester Hoevdi	Shetld	HT9339	60°8·4′	2°7·1′W	X	4
Westerhope	N upon Ty	NZ1967	55°0·1′	1°41·8′W	T	88
Wester Hope Burn	Scot Bord	NT1123	55°29·8′	3°24·1′W	W	72
Westerhope Fm	Devon	ST1206	50°51·0′	3°14·6′W	FM	192,193
Wester Houran	Shetld	HU2953	60°15·9′	1°28·1′W	H	3
Westerhouse	Shetld	HP6300	60°41·0′	0°50·3′W	X	1
Westerhouse	Shetld	HU5197	60°39·4′	1°3·5′W	X	1
Westerhouse	S Lanak	NS8851	55°44·6′	3°46·6′W	X	65,72
Wester Housebyres	Scot Bord	NT5336	55°37·2′	2°44·3′W	T	73
Westerhouses	Scot Bord	NT6212	55°24·3′	2°35·6′W	X	80
Wester Howlaws	Scot Bord	NT7242	55°40·5′	2°26·3′W	X	74
Wester Jaw	Falk	NS8573	55°56·4′	3°50·0′W	X	65
Wester Jawcraig	Falk	NS8375	55°57·5′	3°52·0′W	X	65
Wester Kame	Shetld	HU3788	60°34·7′	1°19·0′W	X	1,2
Wester Keilhill	Aberd	NJ7160	57°38·0′	2°28·7′W	X	29
Wester Keillour	Pth & Kin	NN9725	56°24·6′	3°39·7′W	X	52,53,58
Wester Keith	Angus	NO2837	56°31·4′	3°9·8′W	X	53
Wester Kellie	Fife	NO5105	56°14·4′	2°47·0′W	X	59
Wester Keltie	Pth & Kin	NO0013	56°18·2′	3°36·5′W	X	58
Westerker Rig	D & G	NY2993	55°13·8′	3°6·6′W	H	79
Wester Kershope	Scot Bord	NT3626	55°31·7′	3°0·4′W	T	73
Wester Kichanroy	Highld	NJ0333	57°22·9′	3°36·3′W	X	27
Wester Kilgour	Fife	NO2108	56°15·7′	3°16·1′W	X	58
Wester Kilmany	Fife	NO3821	56°22·9′	2°59·8′W	X	54,59
Wester Kilwhiss	Fife	NO2510	56°16·8′	3°12·2′W	X	59
Wester Kincraigie	Aberd	NJ5604	57°7·7′	2°43·2′W	X	37
Wester Kinleith	C of Edin	NT1866	55°53·1′	3°18·2′W	X	65,66
Wester Kinloch	Pth & Kin	NN8737	56°30·9′	3°49·7′W	X	52
Wester Kinnear	Fife	NO4022	56°23·4′	2°57·9′W	X	54,59
Wester Kinsleith	Fife	NO3119	56°21·8′	3°6·6′W	X	59
Wester Kirkhill	Highld	NH5445	57°28·6′	4°25·6′W	X	26
Westerkirk Mains	D & G	NY2991	55°12·7′	3°6·5′W	X	79
Wester Knockbae	Pth & Kin	NN8224	56°23·9′	3°54·3′W	H	52
Wester Laggan	Highld	NH9925	57°18·5′	3°40·1′W	X	36
Wester Lairgs	Highld	NH7034	57°22·9′	4°9·3′W	X	27
Westerlake Fm	Corn	SX2171	50°30·9′	4°31·1′W	FM	201
Westerland	Devon	SX8662	50°27·0′	3°36·0′W	X	202
Westerlands Stud	W Susx	SU9418	50°57·5′	0°39·3′W	X	197
Wester Land Taing	Shetld	HU4379	60°29·8′	1°12·5′W	X	2,3
Wester Lathallan	Fife	NO4406	56°14·8′	2°53·8′W	X	59
Wester Lawrenceton	Moray	NJ0758	57°36·4′	3°32·9′W	X	27
Wester Lealty	Highld	NH6073	57°43·8′	4°20·6′W	X	21
Wester Leckie	Stir	NS6894	56°7·5′	4°7·0′W	X	57
Wester Lednathie	Angus	NO3263	56°45·5′	3°6·3′W	X	44
Wester Lee of Gloup	Shetld	HP5003	60°42·7′	1°4·5′W	X	1
Westerleigh	S Glos	ST6979	51°30·8′	2°26·4′W	T	172
Westerleigh Common	S Glos	ST7081	51°31·9′	2°25·6′W	X	172
Westerleigh Hill	S Glos	ST7079	51°30·8′	2°25·5′W	T	172
Wester Lennieston	Stir	NN6201	56°11·2′	4°13·0′W	X	57
Wester Leochel	Aberd	NJ5309	57°10·4′	2°46·2′W	X	37
Wester Leochel Wood	Aberd	NJ5310	57°11·0′	2°46·2′W	F	37
Wester Letter	Aberd	NJ7511	57°11·6′	2°24·4′W	X	38
Wester Limekilns	Highld	NH9935	57°23·9′	3°40·4′W	X	27
Wester Lix	Stir	NN5429	56°26·1′	4°21·6′W	X	51
Wester Loanrigg	Falk	NS8673	55°56·4′	3°49·1′W	X	65
Westerloch	Highld	ND3258	58°30·6′	3°9·5′W	X	12
Wester Lochend	Highld	NH8152	57°32·8′	3°58·8′W	X	27
Wester Loch of Daldorn	Stir	NN6703	56°12·3′	4°8·2′W	W	57
Wester Logie	Angus	NO3851	56°39·1′	3°0·2′W	X	54
Wester Logie	Pth & Kin	NO1046	56°36·1′	3°27·5′W	X	53
Wester Lonvine	Highld	NH7172	57°43·4′	4°9·5′W	X	21
Wester Lovat	Highld	NH5346	57°29·1′	4°26·7′W	X	26
Wester Lownie Fm	Angus	NO4948	56°37·5′	2°49·4′W	FM	54
Wester Lumbennie	Fife	NO2215	56°19·5′	3°15·2′W	X	58
Wester Lundie	Stir	NN7204	56°12·9′	4°3·4′W	X	57
Wester Mains	Aberd	NJ6501	57°6·2′	2°34·2′W	X	38
Wester Mains	Highld	NH4240	57°25·6′	4°37·4′W	X	26
Wester Manbeen	Moray	NJ1960	57°37·6′	3°20·9′W	X	28
Wester Mandally	Highld	NH2900	57°3·8′	4°48·8′W	X	34
Wester Marchhead	Moray	NJ1660	57°37·6′	3°23·9′W	X	28
Wester Meathie	Angus	NO4546	56°36·4′	2°53·3′W	T	54
Wester Melville	Midlo	NT2966	55°53·2′	3°7·7′W	X	66
Wester Memus	Angus	NO4359	56°43·4′	2°55·4′W	X	54
Wester Micras	Aberd	NO2895	57°2·7′	3°10·7′W	X	37,44
Wester Millbuies	Moray	NJ2456	57°35·5′	3°15·8′W	X	28
Westermill Fm	Somer	SS8239	51°8·5′	3°40·8′W	FM	181
Wester Milltown	Aberd	NJ7343	57°28·8′	2°26·6′W	X	29
Wester Milton	Highld	NH9552	57°33·0′	3°44·8′W	X	27
Wester Moss	Clackm	NO0000	56°11·2′	3°36·2′W	X	58
Wester Mosshat	S Lanak	NS9955	55°46·9′	3°36·2′W	X	65,72
Wester Mosshead	Aberd	NJ5437	57°25·5′	2°45·5′W	X	29
Wester Moy	Highld	NH4755	57°33·8′	4°33·0′W	X	26
Wester Moy	Moray	NJ0159	57°36·9′	3°39·0′W	X	27
Wester Muckersie	Pth & Kin	NO0615	56°19·3′	3°30·8′W	X	58
Wester Muirdean	Scot Bord	NT6834	55°36·2′	2°30·0′W	X	74
Wester Muirhouse	Falk	NS9979	55°59·9′	3°36·7′W	X	65
Wester Murnich	Highld	NH5119	57°14·5′	4°27·7′W	X	35
Wester Mye	Stir	NS5794	56°7·3′	4°17·6′W	X	57
Western	Devon	SS8823	51°0·0′	3°35·4′W	X	181
Western Ball	Devon	SS7831	51°4·2′	3°44·1′W	X	180
Western Bank	Cumbr	NY2448	54°49·5′	3°10·6′W	T	85
Western Beacon	Devon	SX6557	50°24·1′	3°53·6′W	X	202
Western Blackapit	Corn	SX0991	50°41·5′	4°41·9′W	X	190
Western Brockholes	Somer	SS9149	51°14·0′	3°33·3′W	X	181
Western Channel	Falk	NS9382	56°1·4′	3°42·6′W	W	65
Western Cleddau	Pemb	SM8831	51°56·5′	5°4·7′W	W	157
Western Cleddau	Pemb	SM9421	51°51·2′	4°59·1′W	W	157,158
Western Cleddau	Pemb	SM9912	51°46·5′	4°54·4′W	W	157,158
Westerncombe	Devon	SX7539	50°14·5′	3°44·8′W	X	202
Western Common	Devon	SS7336	51°6·8′	3°48·5′W	X	180
Western Court	Hants	SU6032	51°5·3′	1°8·2′W	X	185
Western Cressar	Corn	SW4830	50°7·2′	5°31·2′W	X	203
Western Docks	Kent	TR3240	51°7·0′	1°19·3′E	X	179
Western Docks Sta	Kent	TR3240	51°7·0′	1°19·3′E	X	179
Western Downs	Staffs	SJ9021	52°47·4′	2°8·5′W	T	127
Western End	N Yks	SD8289	54°18·0′	2°16·2′W	X	98
Wester Newbigging	Aberd	NJ5337	57°25·5′	2°46·5′W	X	29
Wester Newburn	Fife	NO4405	56°14·3′	2°53·8′W	X	59
Wester Newforres	Moray	NJ0657	57°35·9′	3°33·9′W	X	27
Wester New Moor	Devon	SS8225	51°1·0′	3°40·6′W	X	181
Western Fm	Leic	SP5891	52°31·1′	1°8·3′W	FM	140
Western Fm	Suff	TM3181	52°22·9′	1°24·1′E	FM	156
Western Green Fm	Bucks	SP7333	51°59·7′	0°55·8′W	FM	152,165
Western Haven	I of W	SZ4090	50°42·7′	1°25·6′W	W	196
Western Heights	Kent	TR3140	51°7·0′	1°18·4′E	T	179
Western Hill	Durham	NZ2642	54°46·6′	1°35·3′W	T	88
Westernhope Burn	Durham	NY9235	54°42·8′	2°7·0′W	W	91,92
Westernhopeburn	Durham	NY9337	54°43·9′	2°6·1′W	A	91,92
Westernhope Moor	Durham	NY9133	54°41·8′	2°8·0′W	X	91,92
Western Horn	Orkney	HY2505	58°55·8′	3°17·7′W	X	6,7
Western Howes	N Yks	NZ6702	54°24·8′	0°57·6′W	A	94
Western King Point	C of Plym	SX4653	50°21·6′	4°9·5′W	X	201
Western Ledges	Dorset	SY6777	50°35·7′	2°27·6′W	X	194
Western Meadows	Northum	NY8948	54°49·8′	2°9·8′W	X	87
Western Meres Fm	Staffs	SJ7937	52°56·0′	2°18·3′W	FM	127
Western Park	C of Leic	SK5604	52°38·1′	1°9·9′W	T	140
Western Patches	Dorset	SY4091	50°43·2′	2°50·6′W	X	193
Western Ridge	Cumbr	NY5057	54°54·6′	2°46·4′W	X	86
Western Rocks	I Scilly	SV8306	49°52·5′	6°24·4′W	X	203
Wester Ochiltree	W Loth	NT0374	55°57·2′	3°32·8′W	X	65
Wester Offerance	Stir	NS5795	56°7·8′	4°17·6′W	X	57
Wester Olrig	Highld	ND2164	58°33·7′	3°21·0′W	X	11,12
Wester Ord	Aberd	NJ8204	57°7·9′	2°17·4′W	X	38
Westerpark	Aberd	NJ4338	57°26·0′	2°56·5′W	X	28
Wester Park	Scot Bord	NT8340	55°39·4′	2°15·8′W	X	74
Wester Parkgate	D & G	NY0288	55°10·8′	3°31·9′W	T	78
Wester Parkhead	Pth & Kin	NO2143	56°34·6′	3°16·7′W	X	53
Wester Pearsie	Angus	NO3458	56°42·8′	3°4·2′W	X	54
Wester Peathaugh	Angus	NO2357	56°42·2′	3°15·0′W	X	53
Wester Pettymarcus	Aberd	NK0042	57°28·4′	1°59·5′W	X	30
Wester Pirleyhill	Falk	NS8977	55°58·6′	3°46·3′W	X	65
Wester Pitscottie	Fife	NO4012	56°18·1′	2°57·7′W	X	59
Wester Quarff	Shetld	HU4035	60°6·1′	1°16·3′W	T	4
Wester Raddery	Highld	NH6958	57°35·8′	4°11·1′W	X	26
Wester Rarichie	Highld	NH8374	57°44·7′	3°57·5′W	X	21
Wester Rhynd	Pth & Kin	NO1718	56°21·1′	3°20·1′W	X	58
Wester Rig	Scot Bord	NT3806	55°20·9′	2°58·2′W	H	79
Wester Rig	Scot Bord	NT4216	55°26·3′	2°54·6′W	H	79
Wester Rochelhill	Angus	NO3644	56°35·3′	3°2·1′W	X	54
Wester Rora	Aberd	NK0549	57°32·1′	1°54·5′W	X	30
Wester Ross	Highld	NH0964	57°37·8′	5°11·5′W	X	19
Wester Rossie	Fife	NO2512	56°17·9′	3°12·3′W	X	59
Wester Row	Stir	NS7399	56°10·3′	4°2·3′W	X	57
Wester Rynaballoch	Highld	NJ1028	57°20·3′	3°29·3′W	X	36
Wester Sand	Orkney	HY5000	58°53·3′	2°51·6′W	X	6,7
Wester Scord	Shetld	HU3967	60°23·4′	1°17·0′W	X	2,3
Wester Seafield	Highld	NH9082	57°49·1′	3°50·6′W	X	21
Westerseat	Highld	ND3552	58°27·4′	3°6·4′W	X	12
Wester Shenalt	Aberd	NJ2002	57°6·4′	3°18·8′W	W	36
Wester Shian	Pth & Kin	NN8440	56°32·5′	3°52·7′W	X	52
Wester Shieldhill Lands	Falk	NS8876	55°58·1′	3°47·2′W	X	65
Wester Shoals	Orkney	ND4578	58°41·4′	2°56·5′W	X	7
Wester Shore Wood	W Loth	NT0679	55°59·9′	3°30·0′W	F	65
Westerside	Moray	NJ4564	57°40·0′	2°54·9′W	X	28,29
Westerside	Scot Bord	NT8868	55°54·5′	2°11·1′W	X	67
Wester Silverford	Aberd	NJ7663	57°39·6′	2°23·7′W	X	29
Wester Skeld	Shetld	HU2943	60°10·5′	1°28·1′W	T	4
Wester Skerry	Shetld	HU4327	60°1·8′	1°13·2′W	X	4
Wester Skuiley	Angus	NO3977	56°53·1′	2°59·6′W	X	44
Wester Sleach Burn	Aberd	NJ2501	57°5·9′	3°13·8′W	W	37
Wester Softlaw	Scot Bord	NT7330	55°34·0′	2°25·3′W	X	74
Wester Sound	Shetld	HU2146	60°12·1′	1°36·8′W	W	3,4
Wester Stonyfield	Highld	NH6973	57°43·9′	4°11·5′W	X	21
Wester Strath	Highld	NH6658	57°35·8′	4°14·1′W	X	26
Wester Third	Stir	NS5296	56°8·3′	4°22·5′W	X	57
Wester Thomaston	Falk	NS7779	55°59·5′	3°57·9′W	X	64
Wester Tillathrowie	Aberd	NJ4634	57°23·9′	2°53·5′W	X	28,29
Wester Tillyshogle	Aberd	NJ7403	57°7·3′	2°25·3′W	X	38
Wester Toberandonich	Pth & Kin	NN8853	56°39·6′	3°49·2′W	X	52
Wester Tolmauds	Aberd	NJ6007	57°9·4′	2°39·2′W	X	37
Westerton	Aberd	NJ5041	57°27·7′	2°49·5′W	X	29
Westerton	Aberd	NJ5700	57°5·6′	2°42·1′W	X	37
Westerton	Aberd	NJ6927	57°20·2′	2°30·4′W	X	38
Westerton	Aberd	NJ7018	57°15·4′	2°29·4′W	X	38
Westerton	Aberd	NJ7044	57°29·4′	2°29·6′W	X	29
Westerton	Aberd	NJ7602	57°6·8′	2°23·3′W	X	38
Westerton	Aberd	NK0848	57°31·6′	1°51·5′W	X	30
Westerton	Aberd	NO6173	56°51·1′	2°37·9′W	X	45
Westerton	Aberd	NO7174	56°51·6′	2°28·1′W	X	45
Westerton	Aberd	NO7391	57°0·8′	2°26·2′W	X	38,45
Westerton	Angus	NO2859	56°43·3′	3°10·1′W	X	53
Westerton	Angus	NO5352	56°39·7′	2°45·6′W	X	54
Westerton	Durham	NZ2331	54°40·7′	1°38·2′W	T	93
Westerton	E Dunb	NS6377	55°58·2′	4°11·3′W	X	64
Westerton	Fife	NO2101	56°12·0′	3°16·0′W	X	58
Westerton	Fife	NT1892	56°7·1′	3°18·7′W	X	58
Westerton	Moray	NJ1965	57°40·3′	3°21·0′W	X	28
Westerton	Moray	NJ3156	57°35·6′	3°8·8′W	X	28

Westerton	Moray	NJ3644	57°29·2'	3°3·6'W	X	28
Westerton	Pemb	SN1310	51°45·7'	4°42·2'W	X	158
Westerton	Pth & Kin	NN8710	56°16·4'	3°49·0'W	X	58
Westerton	Pth & Kin	NN8714	56°18·6'	3°49·1'W	X	58
Westerton	Pth & Kin	NN9714	56°18·7'	3°39·5'W	X	58
Westerton	Pth & Kin	NO0132	56°28·4'	3°36·0'W	X	52,53
Westerton	Stir	NS5284	56°1·8'	4°22·1'W	X	57,64
Westerton	Stir	NS6594	56°7·4'	4°9·9'W	X	57
Westerton	Stir	NS7997	56°9·3'	3°56·4'W	X	57
Westerton	Stir	NS8389	56°5·0'	3°52·4'W	X	57,65
Westerton	W Dunb	NS4183	56°1·1'	4°32·6'W	X	56,64
Westerton	W Susx	SU8807	50°51·6'	0°44·6'W	T	197
Westerton Fm	Aberd	NK0135	57°24·6'	1°58·5'W	FM	30
Westerton Ho	Pth & Kin	NN8223	56°23·3'	3°54·2'W	X	52
Westerton of New Rayne	Aberd	NJ6729	57°21·3'	2°32·4'W	X	38
Westerton of Rossie	Angus	NO6654	56°40·8'	2°32·8'W	X	54
Westerton of Runavey	Pth & Kin	NO1269	56°48·5'	3°26·0'W	T	43
Westerton of Stracathro	Angus	NO6164	56°46·2'	2°37·8'W	X	45
Westerton, The	Pth & Kin	NO1461	56°44·2'	3°23·9'W	X	43
Westerton Wood	Stir	NN7303	56°12·4'	4°2·4'W	F	57
Westertoun Fm	S Lanak	NS6239	55°37·8'	4°11·1'W	FM	71
Westertown	Aberd	NJ5944	57°29·3'	2°40·6'W	X	29
Westertown	Aberd	NJ7033	57°23·4'	2°29·5'W	X	29
Westertown	Aberd	NJ7531	57°22·4'	2°24·5'W	X	29
Westertown	Moray	NJ1925	57°18·8'	3°20·2'W	X	36
Westertown	Moray	NJ5055	57°35·2'	2°49·7'W	X	29
Westertown	S Lanak	NS9150	55°44·1'	3°43·7'W	X	65,72
Westertown Fm	Moray	NJ3142	57°28·0'	3°8·6'W	FM	28
Westertown of Memsie	Aberd	NJ9661	57°38·6'	2°3·6'W	X	30
Wester Tullich	Pth & Kin	NN6837	56°30·7'	4°8·3'W	X	51
Wester Urray	Highld	NH5052	57°32·3'	4°29·9'W	X	26
Wester Walston	S Lanak	NT0545	55°41·6'	3°30·2'W	X	72
Wester Water	Shetld	HU3376	60°28·1'	1°23·5'W	W	2,3
Wester Waterlair	Aberd	NO7574	56°51·7'	2°24·2'W	X	45
Wester Watten	Highld	ND2254	58°28·3'	3°19·8'W	X	11,12
Wester Watten Moss	Highld	ND2151	58°26·7'	3°20·7'W	X	11,12
Wester Whale Geo	Highld	ND3240	58°20·9'	3°9·2'W	X	12
Wester Whin	Falk	NS8668	55°53·8'	3°48·9'W	X	65
Wester Whitefield	Fife	NT1189	56°5·4'	3°25·4'W	X	65
Wester Whyntie	Aberd	NJ6264	57°40·1'	2°37·8'W	X	29
Wester Wick	Shetld	HU2842	60°10·0'	1°29·2'W	W	4
Westerwick	Shetld	HU2842	60°10·0'	1°29·2'W	T	4
Wester Wick of Copister	Shetld	HU4778	60°29·2'	1°8·2'W	W	2,3
Wester Wood	E Loth	NT5366	55°53·3'	2°44·6'W	F	66
Westerwood	N Lanak	NS7677	55°58·5'	3°58·8'W	X	64
Wester Wooden	Scot Bord	NT7025	55°31·3'	2°28·1'W	X	74
Wester Woodside	W Loth	NS9673	55°56·6'	3°39·5'W	X	65
Wester Yardhouses	S Lanak	NT0050	55°44·2'	3°35·1'W	X	65,72
West Everleigh Down	Wilts	SU1855	51°17·9'	1°44·1'W	X	173
West Ewell	Surrey	TQ2063	51°21·4'	0°16·2'W	T	176,187
West Fallodon	Northum	NU1922	55°29·7'	1°41·5'W	X	75
West Fannyside	N Lanak	NS8072	55°55·8'	3°54·8'W	X	65
West Farleigh	Devon	SS9007	50°51·4'	3°32·4'W	X	192
West Farleigh	Kent	TQ7152	51°14·7'	0°27·4'E	T	188
West Farleigh Hall	Kent	TQ7152	51°14·7'	0°27·4'E	A	188
West Farndon	Northnts	SP5251	52°9·5'	1°14·0'W	T	151
West Feal	Pth & Kin	NO2003	56°13·0'	3°17·0'W	X	58
West Fell	Cumbr	NY3335	54°42·6'	3°2·0'W	H	90
West Fell	Cumbr	NY6601	54°24·4'	2°31·0'W	H	91
West Fell	Northum	NY9862	54°57·4'	2°1·4'W	X	87
West Fell	N Yks	SD7278	54°12·1'	2°25·3'W	X	98
West Fell	N Yks	SD9282	54°14·3'	2°6·9'W	X	98
West Felton	Shrops	SJ3425	52°49·4'	2°58·4'W	T	126
West Fen	Cambs	TL3696	52°32·9'	0°0·7'E	X	142
West Fen	Cambs	TL3699	52°34·5'	0°0·8'E	X	142
West Fen	Cambs	TL5182	52°25·1'	0°13·6'E	X	143
West Fen	Cambs	TL6169	52°18·0'	0°22·1'E	X	154
West Fen Catchwater Drain	Lincs	TF3358	53°6·4'	0°0·4'W	W	122
West Fen Drain	Lincs	TF2951	53°2·7'	0°4·1'W	W	122
West Fen Drain	Lincs	TF3248	53°1·0'	0°1·5'W	W	131
West Fen Fm	Cambs	TL3698	52°34·0'	0°0·8'E	FM	142
West Fen Fm	Cambs	TL3896	52°32·9'	0°2·5'E	FM	142,143
West Fen Fm	Cambs	TL5181	52°24·6'	0°13·6'E	FM	143
West Fen Fm	Lincs	TF3059	53°7·0'	0°3·0'W	FM	122
West Fenton	E Loth	NT4981	56°1·5'	2°48·7'W	X	66
West Fenton	Northum	NT9633	55°35·7'	2°3·4'W	X	74,75
West Ferry	C of Dun	NO4431	56°28·3'	2°54·1'W	T	54
Westfield	Aberd	NJ5207	57°9·3'	2°47·2'W	X	37
Westfield	Aberd	NJ5826	57°19·6'	2°41·4'W	X	37
Westfield	Aberd	NJ6224	57°18·6'	2°37·4'W	X	37
Westfield	Aberd	NJ6444	57°29·3'	2°35·6'W	X	29
Westfield	Aberd	NJ6936	57°25·1'	2°30·5'W	X	29
Westfield	Aberd	NJ7457	57°36·4'	2°25·6'W	X	29
Westfield	Aberd	NJ9420	57°16·5'	2°5·5'W	X	38
Westfield	Aberd	NJ9624	57°18·7'	2°3·5'W	X	38
Westfield	Aberd	NK0029	57°21·3'	1°59·5'W	X	38
Westfield	Angus	NO4449	56°38·0'	2°54·3'W	T	54
Westfield	Angus	NO6248	56°37·6'	2°36·7'W	X	54
Westfield	Bath & NE Somer	ST6754	51°17·3'	2°28·0'W	T	183
West Field	Brad	SE0238	53°50·5'	1°57·8'W	X	104
Westfield	C of Aber	NJ8503	57°7·3'	2°14·4'W	X	38
Westfield	Cumbr	NX9927	54°37·9'	3°33·5'W	T	89
Westfield	Derby	SK2082	53°20·3'	1°41·6'W	X	110
Westfield	Durham	NZ0715	54°32·1'	1°53·1'W	X	92
Westfield	E Loth	NT4971	55°56·0'	2°48·5'W	X	66
Westfield	E Susx	TQ8115	50°54·6'	0°34·9'E	T	199
West Field	E Yorks	SE8654	53°58·7'	0°40·9'W	X	106
Westfield	E Yorks	SE8860	54°1·9'	0°39·0'W	X	101
West Field	E Yorks	SE9560	54°1·9'	0°32·6'W	X	101
Westfield	E Yorks	TA1048	53°55·2'	0°19·1'W	X	107
Westfield	Falk	NS8887	56°4·0'	3°47·5'W	X	65
Westfield	Falk	NS9080	56°0·3'	3°45·4'W	X	65
Westfield	Fife	NO2307	56°15·2'	3°14·1'W	X	58
Westfield	Fife	NO4910	56°17·0'	2°49·0'W	X	59
Westfield	Glos	SP0821	51°53·5'	1°52·6'W	X	163
Westfield	Hants	SZ7199	50°47·4'	0°59·2'W	T	197
Westfield	Heref	SO7247	52°7·5'	2°24·1'W	T	149
Westfield	Highld	ND0564	58°33·5'	3°37·5'W	T	11,12
Westfield	Kirk	SE2124	53°43·0'	1°40·5'W	T	104
Westfield	Lancs	SD4942	53°52·5'	2°46·1'W	X	102
Westfield	Lancs	SD5337	53°49·9'	2°42·4'W	X	102
Westfield	Leeds	SE1940	53°51·6'	1°42·3'W	T	104
Westfield	Leic	SP6794	52°32·6'	1°0·3'W	X	141
Westfield	Moray	NJ1665	57°40·3'	3°24·0'W	X	28
Westfield	N Lanak	NS7273	55°56·2'	4°2·5'W	T	64
Westfield	N Lanak	NS8361	55°49·9'	3°51·6'W	X	65
West Field	N Lincs	TA1219	53°39·6'	0°17·9'W	T	113
Westfield	Norf	TF9909	52°38·8'	0°56·9'E	T	144
West Field	Northum	NZ3073	55°3·3'	1°31·4'W	X	88
West Field	Notts	SK7067	53°12·0'	0°56·7'W	X	120
Westfield	N Yks	SD9543	53°53·2'	2°4·1'W	X	103
Westfield	N Yks	SE0890	54°18·6'	1°52·2'W	X	99
Westfield	N Yks	SE2575	54°10·5'	1°36·6'W	X	99
Westfield	N Yks	SE4555	53°59·6'	1°18·4'W	X	105
West Field	N Yks	SE5665	54°4·9'	1°8·2'W	X	100
Westfield	N Yks	SE5763	54°3·8'	1°7·3'W	X	100
West Field	N Yks	SE6137	53°49·8'	1°4·0'W	X	105
Westfield	N Yks	SE8979	54°12·2'	0°37·7'W	X	101
West Field	Oxon	SU5492	51°37·7'	1°12·8'W	X	164,174
Westfield	Pth & Kin	NO0604	56°13·4'	3°30·5'W	X	58
Westfield	Pth & Kin	NO2348	56°37·3'	3°14·8'W	X	53
Westfield	Red & Cl	NZ5924	54°36·7'	1°4·8'W	T	93
Westfield	S Ayr	NS4227	55°30·9'	4°29·7'W	X	70
Westfield	Scot Bord	NT6335	55°36·7'	2°34·8'W	X	74
Westfield	Sheff	SK4381	53°19·7'	1°20·9'W	T	111,120
Westfield	S Lanak	NT0747	55°42·7'	3°28·4'W	X	72
Westfield	Surrey	TQ0056	51°17·9'	0°33·5'W	T	186
Westfield	W Loth	NS8567	55°53·2'	3°49·9'W	X	65
Westfield	W Loth	NS9372	55°56·0'	3°42·3'W	T	65
Westfield	W Loth	NT0463	55°51·3'	3°31·6'W	X	65
West Field	York	SE5650	53°56·8'	1°8·4'W	T	105
Westfield Barn	Glos	ST8697	51°40·5'	2°11·8'W	X	162
Westfield Brake	Glos	SO6700	51°42·1'	2°28·3'W	F	162
Westfield Brook	Lancs	SD5437	53°49·9'	2°41·5'W	W	102
Westfield Bury	Herts	TL4221	51°52·4'	0°4·2'E	X	167
Westfield Common	Herts	TL2830	51°57·5'	0°7·8'W	X	166
Westfield Fm	Beds	TL1737	52°1·4'	0°17·3'W	FM	153
Westfield Fm	Brad	SE0135	53°48·9'	1°58·7'W	FM	104
Westfield Fm	Bucks	SP6609	51°46·8'	1°2·2'W	FM	164,165
Westfield Fm	Bucks	SP6728	51°57·0'	1°1·1'W	FM	164,165
Westfield Fm	Bucks	SP8931	51°58·5'	0°41·9'W	FM	152,165
Westfield Fm	Bucks	SU7984	51°33·2'	0°51·2'W	FM	175
Westfield Fm	Cambs	TL3854	52°10·2'	0°1·5'E	FM	154
Westfield Fm	C of Edin	NT1076	55°56·7'	3°26·1'W	FM	65
Westfield Fm	Derby	SK4676	53°17·0'	1°18·2'W	FM	120
Westfield Fm	E Yorks	SE7445	53°54·0'	0°52·0'W	FM	105,106
Westfield Fm	E Yorks	SE7548	53°55·6'	0°51·1'W	FM	105,106
Westfield Fm	E Yorks	SE9353	53°58·1'	0°34·5'W	FM	106
Westfield Fm	E Yorks	SE9551	53°57·0'	0°32·7'W	FM	106
Westfield Fm	E Yorks	SE9837	53°49·4'	0°30·3'W	FM	106
West Field Fm	E Yorks	SE9928	53°44·6'	0°29·5'W	FM	106
Westfield Fm	E Yorks	SE9967	54°5·6'	0°28·8'W	FM	101
Westfield Fm	E Yorks	TA0032	53°46·7'	0°28·5'W	FM	106,107
Westfield Fm	E Yorks	TA0163	54°3·4'	0°27·0'W	FM	101
Westfield Fm	E Yorks	TA0373	54°8·8'	0°25·0'W	FM	101
Westfield Fm	E Yorks	TA0558	54°0·7'	0°23·4'W	FM	107
Westfield Fm	E Yorks	TA1154	53°58·4'	0°18·0'W	FM	107
Westfield Fm	E Yorks	TA1630	53°45·4'	0°14·0'W	FM	107
Westfield Fm	E Yorks	TA1847	53°54·6'	0°11·8'W	FM	107
Westfield Fm	Glos	SO7602	51°43·2'	2°20·5'W	FM	162
Westfield Fm	Hants	SU5728	51°3·1'	1°10·8'W	FM	185
Westfield Fm	Leic	SK3804	52°38·2'	1°25·9'W	FM	140
Westfield Fm	Leic	SP4698	52°34·9'	1°18·9'W	FM	140
Westfield Fm	Lincs	SK8591	53°24·8'	0°42·9'W	FM	112
Westfield Fm	Lincs	SK9967	53°11·7'	0°30·7'W	FM	121
Westfield Fm	Lincs	TF0199	53°28·9'	0°28·3'W	FM	112
Westfield Fm	Lincs	TF0273	53°14·9'	0°27·9'W	FM	121
Westfield Fm	Lincs	TF0348	53°1·4'	0°27·5'W	FM	130
Westfield Fm	Lincs	TF1244	52°59·1'	0°19·5'W	FM	130
Westfield Fm	Lincs	TF1927	52°49·9'	0°13·6'W	FM	130
Westfield Fm	Lincs	TF2467	53°11·4'	0°8·2'W	FM	122
Westfield Fm	Lincs	TF2697	53°27·5'	0°5·7'W	FM	113
Westfield Fm	Lincs	TF3295	53°26·3'	0°0·4'W	FM	113
West Field Fm	Lincs	TF3486	53°21·5'	0°1·2'E	FM	122
West Field Fm	Lincs	TF3586	53°21·5'	0°2·1'E	FM	113
Westfield Fm	Lincs	TF4685	53°20·7'	0°12·0'E	FM	122
Westfield Fm	N Lincs	TA1416	53°37·9'	0°16·1'W	FM	113
Westfield Fm	Norf	TG0223	52°46·2'	1°0·1'E	FM	133
Westfield Fm	Northum	NU2031	55°34·6'	1°40·5'W	FM	75
Westfield Fm	Notts	SK8261	53°8·6'	0°46·0'W	FM	121
West Field Fm	N Yks	SE2394	54°20·7'	1°38·4'W	FM	99
Westfield Fm	N Yks	SE6365	54°4·9'	1°1·8'W	FM	100
Westfield Fm	N Yks	SE7381	54°13·4'	0°52·4'W	FM	100
Westfield Fm	N Yks	SE8170	54°7·4'	0°45·2'W	FM	100
Westfield Fm	N Yks	SE9476	54°10·5'	0°33·2'W	FM	101
Westfield Fm	Oxon	SP3704	51°44·2'	1°27·5'W	FM	164
Westfield Fm	Oxon	SU5492	51°37·7'	1°12·8'W	FM	164,174
Westfield Fm	Oxon	SU5785	51°33·9'	1°10·3'W	FM	174
Westfield Fm	Somer	ST3337	51°7·9'	2°57·1'W	FM	182
Westfield Fm	Somer	ST5312	50°54·6'	2°39·7'W	FM	194
Westfield Fm	Suff	TL8665	52°15·3'	0°43·9'E	FM	155
Westfield Fm	W Berks	SU3576	51°29·1'	1°29·4'W	FM	174
Westfield Fm	Wilts	ST8078	51°30·3'	2°16·9'W	FM	173
Westfield Fm	Wilts	SU0896	51°40·0'	1°52·7'W	FM	163
Westfield Fm	Wilts	SU1139	51°9·2'	1°50·2'W	FM	184
Westfield Fm	W Loth	NS9472	55°56·0'	3°41·4'W	FM	65
Westfield Ho	Cumbr	NY2554	54°52·8'	3°9·7'W	X	85
Westfield Ho	Cumbr	NY2561	54°56·5'	3°9·8'W	X	85
Westfield Ho	Cumbr	NY4873	55°3·2'	2°48·4'W	X	86
Westfield Ho	Donc	SE6214	53°37·4'	1°3·3'W	X	111
West Field Ho	Durham	NZ0637	54°43·9'	1°54·0'W	X	92
Westfield Ho	E Yorks	SE9858	54°0·8'	0°29·9'W	X	106
Westfield Ho	E Yorks	TA0671	54°7·7'	0°22·3'W	X	101
Westfield Ho	Kent	TQ7344	51°10·4'	0°28·9'E	X	188
Westfield Ho	Lancs	SD4966	54°5·5'	2°46·4'W	X	97
Westfield Ho	Lancs	SD5357	54°0·7'	2°42·6'W	X	102
Westfield Ho	Leic	SP6192	52°31·6'	1°5·6'W	X	140
Westfield Ho	N Lincs	TA0122	53°41·3'	0°27·8'W	X	106,107,112
Westfield Ho	Northum	NY9267	55°0·1'	2°7·1'W	X	87
Westfield Ho	Notts	SK5665	53°11·0'	1°9·3'W	X	120
Westfield Ho	N Yks	NZ2802	54°25·0'	1°33·7'W	X	93
Westfield Ho	N Yks	SE1366	54°5·6'	1°47·7'W	X	99
Westfield Ho	N Yks	SE7587	54°16·6'	0°50·5'W	X	94,100
Westfield Ho	N Yks	TA0273	54°8·8'	0°25·9'W	X	101
Westfield Ho	Wilts	ST9474	51°28·1'	2°4·8'W	X	173
Westfield House Fm	Northum	NU0103	55°19·5'	1°58·6'W	FM	81
Westfield Lodge	Northnts	SP9072	52°20·6'	0°40·3'W	X	141
West Field Lodge	Northnts	SP9369	52°18·9'	0°37·7'W	X	153
Westfield Lodge	N Yks	SE7089	54°17·7'	0°55·0'W	X	94,100
Westfield of Pitlochie	Fife	NO1609	56°16·2'	3°20·9'W	X	58
Westfield Place	E Susx	TQ8017	50°55·7'	0°34·1'E	X	199
Westfield Point	Cumbr	SD2266	54°5·3'	3°11·1'W	X	96
Westfields	Dorset	ST7206	50°51·4'	2°23·5'W	T	194
Westfields	Heref	SO4942	52°4·7'	2°44·3'W	T	148,149
Westfields	Heref	SO5651	52°9·6'	2°38·2'W	X	149
Westfields	N Yks	NZ3207	54°27·7'	1°30·0'W	X	93
Westfields	Pemb	SN0110	51°45·4'	4°52·6'W	X	157,158
West Fields	W Berks	SU4666	51°23·7'	1°19·9'W	T	174
Westfields Fm	Beds	SP9954	52°10·8'	0°32·7'W	FM	153
Westfields Fm	Herts	TL1205	51°44·2'	0°22·3'W	FM	166
Westfields Fm	Kent	TQ6458	51°18·1'	0°21·5'E	FM	188
Westfields Fm	N Yks	NZ8113	54°30·6'	0°44·5'W	FM	94
Westfields Fm	Warw	SP3255	52°11·8'	1°31·5'W	FM	151
Westfields Fm	Warw	SP3561	52°15·0'	1°28·8'W	FM	151
Westfields Fm	Wilts	SU1974	51°28·1'	1°43·2'W	FM	173
Westfields Fm	Worcs	SO9263	52°16·1'	2°6·6'W	FM	150
Westfields of Rattray	Pth & Kin	NO1846	56°36·2'	3°19·7'W	T	53
Westfield Sole	Kent	TQ7761	51°19·5'	0°32·8'E	T	178,188
Westfield Stables	Oxon	SU5784	51°33·4'	1°10·3'W	X	174
Westfield Wold	N Yks	SE9475	54°10·0'	0°33·2'W	X	101
Westfield Wood	Lincs	TF0448	53°1·4'	0°26·6'W	F	130
Westfield Wood	N Yks	SE7089	54°17·7'	0°55·0'W	F	94,100
West Firle	E Susx	TQ4707	50°50·9'	0°5·7'E	T	198
West Firsby Village	Lincs	SK9985	53°21·4'	0°30·3'W	A	112,121
West Fishwick	Scot Bord	NT9050	55°44·8'	2°9·1'W	X	67,74,75
West Fleet	Dorset	SY5982	50°38·4'	2°34·4'W	W	194
West Fleet Fm	Dorset	SY6281	50°37·9'	2°31·9'W	FM	194
West Fleetham	Northum	NU1928	55°33·0'	1°41·5'W	T	75
West Float	Wirral	SJ3090	53°24·4'	3°2·8'W	W	108
West Flodden	Northum	NT9134	55°36·2'	2°8·1'W	T	74,75
West Flotmanby	N Yks	TA0779	54°12·0'	0°21·2'W	X	101
West Flotmanby Wold Fm	N Yks	TA0778	54°11·4'	0°21·2'W	FM	101
West Fm	Cambs	TL2369	52°18·5'	0°11·3'W	FM	153
West Fm	C of Edin	NT0973	55°56·7'	3°27·0'W	FM	65
West Fm	Dorset	ST4405	50°50·7'	2°47·3'W	FM	193
West Fm	Dorset	ST8415	50°56·3'	2°13·3'W	FM	183
West Fm	Dorset	SY8399	50°47·7'	2°14·1'W	FM	194
West Fm	Durham	NZ0921	54°35·3'	1°51·2'W	FM	92
West Fm	E Yorks	TA2519	53°39·4'	0°6·1'W	FM	113
West Fm	Hants	SU5544	51°11·8'	1°12·4'W	FM	185
West Fm	Lincs	TF0317	52°44·7'	0°28·0'W	FM	130
West Fm	Lincs	TF0993	53°25·6'	0°21·2'W	FM	112
West Fm	Norf	TF5501	52°35·3'	0°17·7'E	FM	143
West Fm	Norf	TL9492	52°29·7'	0°51·9'E	FM	144
West Fm	Northum	NU2018	55°27·6'	1°40·6'W	FM	81
West Fm	Northum	NY9861	54°56·9'	2°1·4'W	FM	87
West Fm	N Yks	SE3298	54°22·8'	1°30·0'W	FM	99
West Fm	N Yks	SE4395	54°21·2'	1°19·9'W	FM	99
West Fm	N Yks	SE7077	54°11·3'	0°55·2'W	FM	100
West Fm	N Yks	SE7777	54°11·2'	0°48·8'W	FM	100
West Fm	N Yks	SE8186	54°16·0'	0°45·0'W	FM	94,100
West Fm	N Yks	SE8677	54°11·1'	0°40·5'W	FM	101
West Fm	N Yks	SE8974	54°9·5'	0°37·8'W	FM	101
West Fm	Somer	ST5423	51°0·5'	2°39·0'W	FM	183
West Fm	Somer	ST6349	51°14·6'	2°31·4'W	FM	183
West Fm	Suff	TL8576	52°21·3'	0°43·4'E	FM	144
West Fm	Suff	TM3163	52°13·2'	1°23·3'E	FM	156
West Fm	Wilts	ST9442	51°10·9'	2°4·8'W	FM	184
West Fm	Wilts	SU0028	51°3·3'	1°59·6'W	FM	184
Westfolds	Aberd	NJ4341	57°27·6'	2°56·5'W	X	28
West Ford	Devon	SS7027	51°1·9'	3°50·9'W	X	180
West Ford	Devon	SX7191	50°42·5'	3°49·2'W	X	191
Westford	Highld	NH6469	57°41·7'	4°16·4'W	T	21
Westford	Somer	ST1220	50°58·6'	3°14·8'W	T	181,193
West Ford Fm	Devon	SS4716	50°55·6'	4°10·2'W	FM	180
West Foredibban Hill	E Ayr	NS6918	55°26·6'	4°3·8'W	H	71
West Forest	Northum	NZ1995	55°15·2'	1°41·6'W	X	81
West Fornet	Aberd	NJ7711	57°11·6'	2°22·4'W	X	38
West Forth	S Lanak	NS9353	55°45·8'	3°41·9'W	X	65,72
West Forthar	Fife	NO2906	56°14·7'	3°8·3'W	X	59
West Fortune	E Loth	NT5379	56°0·4'	2°44·8'W	X	66
West Foscote Fm	Wilts	ST8578	51°30·3'	2°12·6'W	FM	173
West Fossil Fm	Dorset	SY7985	50°40·1'	2°17·4'W	FM	194
West Foulden	Scot Bord	NT9155	55°47·5'	2°8·2'W	X	67,74,75
West Foulshiels	W Loth	NS9663	55°51·2'	3°39·2'W	X	65
West Freugh Airfield	D & G	NX1154	54°51·0'	4°56·2'W	X	82
West Frostybrae	Aberd	NJ9346	57°30·5'	2°6·6'W	X	30
West Fulton	Renf	NS4265	55°51·4'	4°31·0'W	X	64
West Funach	Aberd	NO7594	57°2·4'	2°24·3'W	X	38,45
West Galdenoch	D & G	NX0956	54°52·0'	4°58·2'W	X	82
West Gallaton	Aberd	NO8682	56°56·0'	2°13·4'W	X	45
West Garforth	Leeds	SE3932	53°47·2'	1°24·1'W	T	104
West Garland Fm	Devon	SS7017	50°56·5'	3°50·6'W	FM	180
West Garland Moor	Devon	SS7118	50°57·1'	3°49·8'W	X	180
West Garleton Ho	E Loth	NT4976	55°58·7'	2°48·6'W	X	66
Westgarth	Cumbr	NY5057	54°54·6'	2°46·4'W	X	86
Westgarth Hill	Cumbr	NY5542	54°46·5'	2°41·5'W	X	86
West Garty	Highld	NC9912	58°5·4'	3°42·3'W	X	17
Westgate	Devon	SY1298	50°46·7'	3°14·5'W	X	192,193
Westgate	Durham	NY9038	54°44·5'	2°8·9'W	T	91,92
Westgate	Fife	NO3000	56°11·5'	3°7·2'W	X	59
Westgate	N Lincs	SE7707	53°33·5'	0°49·8'W	T	112
Westgate	Norf	TF9740	52°55·5'	0°56·3'E	T	132
Westgate	Northum	NZ1275	55°4·4'	1°48·3'W	X	88
Westgate	N Yks	SD6774	54°9·9'	2°29·9'W	X	98
Westgate	S Lanak	NS9238	55°37·7'	3°42·5'W	X	71,72
Westgate Carr	N Yks	SE7782	54°13·9'	0°48·7'W	X	100

Westgate Fm	Norf	TF8100	52°34·3′	0°40·7′E	FM	144
Westgate Fm	Norf	TF8141	52°56·4′	0°42·0′E	FM	132
Westgate Fm	N Yks	NZ6609	54°28·6′	0°58·5′W	FM	94
Westgate Fm	Staffs	SJ9738	52°56·6′	2°2·3′W	FM	127
Westgate Fm	Stock on T	NZ3714	54°31·4′	1°25·3′W	FM	93
Westgate Fm	Suff	TM4175	52°19·4′	1°32·6′E	FM	156
Westgate Hill	Brad	SE2029	53°45·7′	1°41·4′W	T	104
Westgate Hill	Devon	SY1296	50°45·6′	3°14·5′W	X	192,193
Westgate on Sea	Kent	TR3270	51°23·1′	1°20·5′E	T	179
West Gates	Durham	NY9812	54°30·4′	2°1·4′W	X	92
Westgate Street	Norf	TG1921	52°44·8′	1°15·1′E	T	133,134
West Geo	Orkney	ND3388	58°46·7′	3°9·0′W	X	7
West Ghyll End Fm	Cumbr	NX9924	54°36·3′	3°33·4′W	FM	89
West Gibseat	Aberd	NJ9341	57°27·8′	2°6·5′W	X	30
Westgill	D & G	NY2167	54°59·7′	3°13·7′W	X	85
West Gill	N Yks	SD8295	54°21·3′	2°16·2′W	W	98
West Gill	N Yks	SE0079	54°12·6′	1°59·6′W	W	98
West Gill	N Yks	SE6596	54°21·6′	0°59·6′W	X	94,100
West Gill Beck	N Yks	SE6695	54°21·0′	0°58·7′W	W	94,100
West Gill Dike	N Yks	SE0374	54°10·0′	1°56·8′W	W	98
West Gill Head	N Yks	SD8197	54°22·3′	2°17·1′W	X	98
West Gill Head	N Yks	SE6497	54°22·1′	1°0·5′W	X	94,100
Westgillsyke	D & G	NY3370	55°1·5′	3°2·5′W	X	85
West Gilston Mains	Fife	NO4307	56°15·4′	2°54·8′W	X	59
West Ginge	Oxon	SU4486	51°34·5′	1°21·5′W	T	174
West Ginge Down	Oxon	SU4483	51°32·9′	1°21·5′W	X	174
West Girt Hill	N Ayr	NS2762	55°49·5′	4°45·3′W	H	63
West Glen	Arg & Bt	NR9974	55°55·3′	5°12·6′W	X	62
West Glenan Burn	Arg & Bt	NR9272	55°54·0′	5°19·2′W	W	62
West Glenarm	D & G	NX8269	55°0·3′	3°50·3′W	X	84
West Glen Fm	Renf	NS3770	55°54·0′	4°36·0′W	FM	63
West Glengyre	D & G	NW9864	54°56·0′	5°8·8′W	X	82
West Glen River	Lincs	TF0020	52°46·3′	0°30·7′W	W	130
West Glen River	Lincs	TF0711	52°41·4′	0°24·6′W	W	130,142
West Glenshinnoch	Renf	NS4170	55°54·1′	4°32·2′W	X	64
West Gogar	Stir	NS8395	56°8·3′	3°52·5′W	X	57
West Gormack	Pth & Kin	NO1447	56°36·7′	3°23·6′W	X	53
West Gorton	Man	SJ8696	53°27·9′	2°12·2′W	T	109
West Gotten	Highld	ND1528	58°14·2′	3°26·4′W	W	17
Westgouch Plantn	Suff	TL8178	52°22·4′	0°39·9′E	F	144
West Grafton	Wilts	SU2460	51°20·5′	1°38·9′W	T	174
West Grain	Angus	NO4587	56°58·5′	2°53·8′W	W	44
West Grain	Cumbr	NY6901	54°24·5′	2°28·2′W	X	91
West Grain	Durham	NY8736	54°43·4′	2°11·7′W	W	91,92
West Grange	Durham	NZ2939	54°45·0′	1°32·5′W	X	93
West Grange	Fife	NS9889	56°5·2′	3°37·9′W	X	65
West Grange	N Lincs	SE8504	53°31·8′	0°42·6′W	X	112
West Grange	Northum	NZ0486	55°10·3′	1°55·8′W	X	81
West Grange	Northum	NZ1075	55°4·4′	1°50·2′W	X	88
West Grange	N Yks	SE4650	53°56·9′	1°17·5′W	X	105
West Grange	N Yks	SE6641	53°51·9′	0°59·4′W	X	105,106
West Grange	Pth & Kin	NO2625	56°24·9′	3°11·5′W	X	53,59
West Grange	Stir	NS8194	56°7·7′	3°54·4′W	X	57
West Grange Fm	E Ayr	NS4352	55°44·4′	4°29·6′W	FM	64
West Grange of Aberbothrie	Pth & Kin	NO2244	56°35·1′	3°15·7′W	X	53
West Grange of Conon	Angus	NO5844	56°35·4′	2°40·6′W	X	54
West Green	Barns	SE3708	53°34·3′	1°26·1′W	T	110,111
West Green	Hants	SU7456	51°18·1′	0°55·9′W	T	175,186
West Green	Hargy	TQ3289	51°35·3′	0°5·3′W	T	176,177
West Green	W Susx	TQ2637	51°7·3′	0°11·6′W	T	187
West Greenburn	Aberd	NJ5808	57°9·9′	2°41·2′W	X	37
West Green Ho	Hants	SU7456	51°18·1′	0°55·9′W	X	175,186
West Greenland	Highld	ND2267	58°35·3′	3°20·0′W	X	11,12
West Greenside	Pth & Kin	NO2016	56°20·0′	3°17·2′W	X	58
West Greylake	Devon	SS5522	50°59·0′	4°3·6′W	X	180
West Grimstead	Wilts	SU2126	51°2·2′	1°41·6′W	T	184
West Grinstead	W Susx	TQ1720	50°58·3′	0°19·6′W	T	198
West Grinstead Lodge	W Susx	TQ1721	50°58·8′	0°19·6′W	X	198
West Grinstead Park	W Susx	TQ1721	50°58·8′	0°19·6′W	X	198
West Grove	Corn	SS2204	50°48·7′	4°31·2′W	X	190
West Grove	Pemb	SM9501	51°40·5′	4°57·5′W	X	157,158
West Haddlesey	N Yks	SE5626	53°43·9′	1°8·7′W	T	105
West Haddon	Northnts	SP6371	52°20·2′	1°4·1′W	T	140
West Haddon Grange	Northnts	SP6272	52°20·8′	1°5·0′W	X	140
West Hagbourne	Oxon	SU5187	51°35·0′	1°15·4′W	T	174
West Hagbourne Field	Oxon	SU5088	51°35·5′	1°16·3′W	X	174
West Hagginton	Devon	SS5446	51°11·9′	4°5·0′W	X	180
West Hagley	Worcs	SO9080	52°25·3′	2°8·4′W	T	139
West Haigh Wood	Barns	SE4208	53°34·3′	1°21·5′W	F	111
West Hale Fm	N Lincs	SE7407	53°33·5′	0°52·6′W	FM	112
Westhall	Aberd	NJ5900	57°5·6′	2°40·1′W	X	37
Westhall	Aberd	NJ6726	57°19·7′	2°32·4′W	A	38
Westhall	Angus	NO4535	56°30·5′	2°53·2′W	X	54
West Hall	Cumbr	NY5667	55°0·0′	2°40·8′W	X	86
West Hall	Dorset	ST6512	50°54·6′	2°29·5′W	A	194
West Hall	Durham	NZ0314	54°31·5′	1°56·8′W	X	92
West Hall	Essex	TQ9193	51°36·4′	0°45·9′E	X	178
Westhall	Fife	NO3314	56°19·1′	3°4·5′W	X	59
West Hall	Hants	SU5320	50°58·8′	1°14·3′W	X	185
West Hall	Lincs	SK9979	53°18·2′	0°30·5′W	X	121
West Hall	Norf	TL7994	52°31·1′	0°38·7′E	X	144
West Hall	Northnts	SP7853	52°10·4′	0°51·2′W	X	152
Westhall	Northum	NU1034	55°36·2′	1°50·0′W	X	75
West Hall	N Yks	SE0850	53°57·0′	1°52·3′W	X	104
Westhall	Pth & Kin	NO0916	56°19·9′	3°27·9′W	X	58
Westhall	S Lanak	NT0447	55°42·7′	3°31·2′W	X	72
West Hall	S Tyne	NZ3961	54°56·8′	1°23·0′W	X	88
West Hall	Suff	TM0273	52°19·3′	0°58·2′E	X	144,155
Westhall	Suff	TM4181	52°22·7′	1°32·9′E	T	156
West Hall	Surrey	TQ0560	51°20·0′	0°29·2′W	X	176,187
West Hallam	Derby	SK4341	52°58·1′	1°21·2′W	T	129
West Hall Cottage	Durham	NZ2246	54°48·7′	1°39·0′W	X	88
West Hall Fm	Lancs	SD5975	54°10·4′	2°37·3′W	FM	97
Westhall Fm	Suff	TM4380	52°22·1′	1°34·6′E	FM	156
Westhall Hill	Oxon	SP2612	51°48·6′	1°37·0′W	T	163
Westhall Hill	Pth & Kin	NO0915	56°19·4′	3°27·8′W	X	58
West Hall Park	Lancs	SD5875	54°10·4′	2°38·2′W	F	97
Westhall Terrace	Angus	NO4436	56°31·0′	2°54·2′W	X	54
Westhall Wood	Suff	TM0273	52°19·3′	0°58·2′E	F	144,155
West Halse	Devon	SS7301	50°47·9′	3°47·8′W	X	191
West Halton	N Lincs	SE9020	53°40·4′	0°37·8′W	T	106,112
Westham	Dorset	SY6679	50°36·8′	2°28·5′W	T	194
Westham	E Susx	TQ6304	50°49·0′	0°19·2′E	T	199
West Ham	Hants	SU6152	51°16·1′	1°7·1′W	T	185
West Ham	Newham	TQ4083	51°31·9′	0°1·5′E	T	177
West Ham	Shetld	HU3526	60°1·3′	1°21·8′W	W	4
West Ham	Shetld	HU4524	60°0·2′	1°11·1′W	W	4
Westham	Somer	ST4046	51°12·8′	2°51·2′W	T	182
West Hamarsland	Shetld	HU4047	60°12·6′	1°16·2′W	X	3
Westham Ho	Warw	SP2660	52°14·5′	1°36·8′W	X	151
West Ham Park	Newham	TQ4084	51°32·5′	0°1·5′E	X	177
Westhampnett	W Susx	SU8806	50°51·0′	0°44·6′W	T	197
West Hampstead	Camden	TQ2585	51°33·2′	0°11·4′W	T	176
West Handaxwood	W Loth	NS9459	55°49·0′	3°41·1′W	X	65,72
West Handley	Derby	SK3977	53°17·5′	1°24·5′W	T	119
West Hanney	Oxon	SU4092	51°37·8′	1°24·9′W	T	164,174
West Hanningfield	Essex	TQ7399	51°40·0′	0°30·5′E	T	167
West Hanningfield Hall	Essex	TL7100	51°40·6′	0°28·8′E	X	167
West Happas	Angus	NO4441	56°33·7′	2°54·2′W	X	54
West Hardwick	Wakf	SE4118	53°39·7′	1°22·4′W	T	111
West Harle	Northum	NY9982	55°8·2′	2°0·5′W	X	81
West Harling Common	Norf	TL9585	52°25·9′	0°52·5′E	F	144
West Harling Heath	Norf	TL9683	52°24·8′	0°53·3′E	F	144
West Harlsey	N Yks	SE4198	54°22·8′	1°21·7′W	T	99
West Harptree	Bath & NE Somer	ST5656	51°18·3′	2°37·5′W	T	172,182
West Harrow	Harrow	TQ1487	51°34·4′	0°20·9′W	T	176
West Harrowbarrow	Corn	SX3869	50°30·1′	4°16·7′W	X	201
West Hartburn Village	Darl	NZ3514	54°31·4′	1°27·1′W	A	93
West Hartford Fm	Northum	NZ2579	55°6·5′	1°36·1′W	FM	88
West Harting	W Susx	SU7821	50°59·2′	0°52·9′W	T	197
West Harting Down	W Susx	SU7617	50°57·1′	0°54·7′W	F	197
West Hartley	Devon	SX8052	50°21·6′	3°40·8′W	X	202
West Harton	S Tyne	NZ3664	54°58·4′	1°25·8′W	T	88
West Harwood	W Loth	NT0160	55°49·6′	3°34·4′W	X	65
West Harwood Fm	Somer	SS9340	51°9·2′	3°31·4′W	FM	181
West Hatch	Somer	ST2821	50°59·3′	3°1·2′W	T	193
West Hatch	Wilts	ST9227	51°2·8′	2°6·5′W	T	184
West Hatton	C of Aber	NJ8506	57°8·9′	2°14·4′W	X	38
Westhaugh	Pth & Kin	NO1439	56°32·4′	3°23·5′W	X	53
West Haugh	Pth & Kin	NO1944	56°35·1′	3°18·7′W	X	53
West Haven	Aberd	NK0365	57°40·7′	1°56·5′W	W	30
West Haven	Angus	NO5734	56°30·0′	2°41·5′W	X	54
West Hawkwell Fm	Somer	SS9038	51°8·1′	3°33·9′W	FM	181
Westhay	Devon	ST3500	50°48·0′	2°55·0′W	X	193
West Hay	N Som	ST4663	51°22·0′	2°46·2′W	X	172,182
Westhay	Somer	ST4342	51°10·7′	2°48·5′W	T	182
Westhay Bridge	Somer	ST4342	51°10·7′	2°48·5′W	X	182
Westhayes	Devon	SY2891	50°43·1′	3°0·8′W	X	193
Westhay Fm	Dorset	SY3892	50°43·7′	2°52·3′W	FM	193
Westhay Fm	Northnts	TL0199	52°35·0′	0°30·2′W	FM	141
Westhay Fm	Somer	ST2315	50°56·0′	3°5·4′W	FM	193
Westhay Heath	Somer	ST4241	51°10·2′	2°49·4′W	X	182
Westhay Level	Somer	ST4242	51°10·7′	2°49·4′W	X	182
Westhay Lodge	Northnts	TL0199	52°35·0′	0°30·2′W	X	141
Westhay Moor	Somer	ST4544	51°11·8′	2°46·8′W	X	182
Westhay Wood	Northnts	SP9897	52°34·0′	0°32·8′W	F	141
West Head	Aberd	NJ5767	57°41·7′	2°42·8′W	X	29
Westhead	Lancs	SD4307	53°33·6′	2°51·2′W	T	108
West Head	Norf	TF5705	52°37·4′	0°19·6′E	T	143
West Head Coll	N Yks	TA0091	54°18·5′	0°27·4′W	X	101
West Head of Papa	Shetld	HU3538	60°7·8′	1°21·7′W	X	4
West Heads	E Ayr	NS5338	55°37·1′	4°19·6′W	X	70
West Heanton	Devon	SS4709	50°51·9′	4°10·1′W	X	191
West Heath	Bexley	TQ4777	51°28·6′	0°7·4′E	T	177
West Heath	Birm	SP0277	52°23·7′	1°57·8′W	T	139
West Heath	Ches	SJ7449	53°2·5′	2°22·9′W	X	118
West Heath	Ches	SJ8463	53°10·1′	2°14·0′W	T	118
West Heath	Hants	SU5958	51°19·3′	1°8·8′W	T	174
West Heath	Hants	SU8556	51°18·0′	0°46·5′W	T	175,186
West Heath Common	W Susx	SU7822	50°59·8′	0°52·9′W	X	197
West Heath Fm	Norf	TF7822	52°46·2′	0°38·7′E	FM	132
West Helmsdale	Highld	ND0115	58°7·0′	3°40·4′W	T	17
West Hendon	Brent	TQ2188	51°34·9′	0°14·8′W	T	176
West Hendred	Oxon	SU4488	51°35·6′	1°21·5′W	T	174
West Heogaland	Shetld	HU2278	60°29·4′	1°35·5′W	T	3
West Hepple	Northum	NT9700	55°17·9′	2°2·4′W	X	81
West Herrington	Sund	NZ3453	54°52·5′	1°27·8′W	T	88
West Heslerton	N Yks	SE9175	54°10·0′	0°35·9′W	T	101
West Heslerton Carr	N Yks	SE9177	54°11·1′	0°35·9′W	X	101
West Heslerton Wold	N Yks	SE9173	54°8·9′	0°36·0′W	X	101
West Hewish	N Som	ST3964	51°22·5′	2°52·2′W	T	182
Westhey Manor	Beds	TL0932	51°58·8′	0°24·4′W	X	166
Westhide	Heref	SO5844	52°5·8′	2°36·4′W	T	149
Westhide Wood	Heref	SO5843	52°5·3′	2°36·4′W	F	149
West High Ho	Northum	NZ1885	55°9·8′	1°42·6′W	X	81
West Highland Way	Stir	NN3329	56°25·7′	4°42·0′W	X	50
West Highland Way	Stir	NN3403	56°11·7′	4°40·1′W	X	56
West Highland Way	Stir	NS5378	55°58·6′	4°20·9′W	X	64
West Highland Way, The	Highld	NN2059	56°41·5′	4°55·9′W	X	41
West Highridge	Northum	NY8181	55°7·6′	2°17·4′W	X	80
West High Wood	Durham	NZ0623	54°36·4′	1°54·0′W	X	92
Westhill	Aberd	NJ8206	57°8·9′	2°17·4′W	T	38
Westhill	Angus	NO3149	56°37·9′	3°7·0′W	X	53
West Hill	Cambs	TL4047	52°6·4′	0°3·1′E	X	154
West Hill	Cambs	TL5475	52°21·3′	0°16·1′E	X	143
West Hill	Devon	SX6197	50°45·6′	3°57·9′W	X	191
West Hill	Devon	SY0694	50°44·5′	3°19·6′W	T	192
West Hill	D & G	NX9474	55°3·2′	3°39·1′W	X	84
West Hill	Dorset	ST7002	50°49·2′	2°25·2′W	H	194
West Hill	Dorset	SY5387	50°41·1′	2°39·5′W	X	194
West Hill	Dorset	SY9577	50°35·8′	2°3·9′W	X	195
West Hill	Dorset	SY9582	50°38·5′	2°3·9′W	H	195
West Hill	E Susx	TQ8210	50°51·9′	0°35·6′E	T	199
West Hill	E Yorks	TA1666	54°4·8′	0°13·2′W	T	101
Westhill	E Yorks	TA2239	53°50·2′	0°8·3′W	T	107
West Hill	Glos	ST7899	51°41·6′	2°18·7′W	X	162
Westhill	Highld	NH7144	57°28·3′	4°8·6′W	T	27
West Hill	Northum	NT8921	55°29·2′	2°10·0′W	H	74
West Hill	Northum	NT9029	55°33·5′	2°9·1′W	H	74,75
West Hill	Northum	NU0214	55°25·4′	1°57·7′W	H	81
West Hill	Notts	SK6979	53°18·4′	0°57·5′W	X	120
West Hill	N Som	ST4576	51°29·1′	2°47·1′W	T	171,172
West Hill	N Som	ST4872	51°26·9′	2°44·5′W	X	171,172
West Hill	Orkney	HY2505	58°55·8′	3°17·7′W	H	6,7
West Hill	Orkney	ND3593	58°49·4′	3°7·1′W	H	7
Westhill	Pth & Kin	NN9018	56°20·8′	3°46·3′W	X	58
West Hill	Scot Bord	NT4959	55°49·5′	2°48·4′W	H	66,73
West Hill	Shetld	HU3258	60°18·6′	1°24·8′W	H	3
West Hill	Shetld	HU4782	60°31·4′	1°8·1′W	H	1,2,3
West Hill	Shetld	HU5039	60°8·2′	1°5·5′W	H	4
West Hill	Somer	ST1241	51°9·9′	3°15·1′W	X	181
West Hill	Somer	ST7028	51°3·3′	2°25·3′W	T	183
West Hill	Staffs	SJ9912	52°42·6′	2°0·5′W	T	127
West Hill	Surrey	SU9656	51°17·9′	0°37·0′W	X	175,186
West Hill	Wan	TQ2474	51°27·3′	0°12·5′W	T	176
West Hill	Warw	SP3268	52°18·8′	1°31·4′W	X	151
West Hill	Wilts	ST8766	51°23·8′	2°10·8′W	T	173
West Hill	Wilts	SU0135	51°7·1′	1°58·8′W	X	184
West Hill	Wilts	SU2253	51°16·8′	1°40·7′W	X	184
West Hill	W Susx	TQ2711	50°53·3′	0°11·3′W	X	198
West Hill	W Susx	TQ3230	51°3·5′	0°6·6′W	T	187
Westhill Cott	Aberd	NO7799	57°5·1′	2°22·3′W	X	38,45
West Hill Edge	N Yks	SE2271	54°8·3′	1°39·4′W	X	99
West Hill Fm	Bucks	SP7029	51°57·5′	0°58·5′W	FM	165
Westhill Fm	Devon	SS9321	50°58·9′	3°31·1′W	FM	181
West Hill Fm	Devon	SY3093	50°44·2′	2°59·1′W	FM	193
Westhill Fm	Dorset	SY9578	50°36·3′	2°3·9′W	FM	195
Westhill Fm	Oxon	SP5605	51°44·7′	1°10·9′W	FM	164
West Hill Fm	Oxon	SP5812	51°48·4′	1°9·1′W	FM	164
West Hill Fm	Pemb	SS0199	51°39·5′	4°52·2′W	FM	158
West Hill Fm	Suff	TM2461	52°12·3′	1°17·1′E	FM	156
West Hill Fm	Wilts	ST8432	51°5·5′	2°13·3′W	FM	183
West Hill Fm	Wilts	ST9344	51°11·9′	2°5·6′W	FM	184
West Hillhead	Angus	NO5039	56°32·7′	2°48·3′W	X	54
West Hillhead	E Ayr	NS4239	55°37·4′	4°30·1′W	X	70
Westhill Lodge	Dorset	ST6414	50°55·7′	2°30·4′W	X	194
West Hill of Burrafirth	Shetld	HU3659	60°19·1′	1°20·4′W	H	2,3
West Hill of Grunnafirth	Shetld	HU4460	60°19·6′	1°11·7′W	H	2,3
West Hill of Ham	Shetld	HU2964	60°21·8′	1°28·0′W	H	3
West Hill of Weisdale	Shetld	HU3854	60°16·4′	1°18·3′W	H	3
Westhills	Aberd	NJ4923	57°17·9′	2°50·3′W	X	37
Westhills	Aberd	NJ9317	57°14·9′	2°6·5′W	X	38
West Hills	Angus	NO5344	56°35·4′	2°45·5′W	T	54
Westhills	D & G	NY2765	54°58·7′	3°8·0′W	X	85
Westhills	Renf	NS3358	55°47·4′	4°39·4′W	X	63
Westhills	Renf	NS3457	55°46·9′	4°38·4′W	X	63
West Hillside	Aberd	NJ5009	57°10·4′	2°49·2′W	X	37
Westhills Moss	D & G	NY2665	54°58·7′	3°8·9′W	X	85
Westhill Wood	Scot Bord	NT1534	55°35·8′	3°20·5′W	F	72
West Hill Wood	Somer	SS9729	51°3·3′	3°27·8′W	F	181
West Ho	Cumbr	NY0834	54°41·8′	3°25·2′W	X	89
West Ho	Cumbr	NY1148	54°49·4′	3°22·7′W	X	85
West Ho	Cumbr	NY1939	54°44·6′	3°15·1′W	X	89,90
West Ho	Darl	NZ3722	54°35·8′	1°25·2′W	X	93
West Ho	N Yks	NZ0003	54°25·6′	1°59·6′W	X	92
West Ho	N Yks	NZ0604	54°26·1′	1°54·0′W	X	92
West Ho	N Yks	NZ6309	54°28·6′	1°1·2′W	X	94
West Ho	Suff	TL9870	52°17·8′	0°54·6′E	X	144,155
West Hoathly	W Susx	TQ3632	51°4·5′	0°3·1′W	T	187
West Holme	Dorset	SY8885	50°40·1′	2°9·8′W	T	194
Westholme	Notts	SK7781	53°19·5′	0°50·2′W	X	120
Westholme	N Yks	SE4377	54°11·5′	1°20·0′W	X	99
Westholme Hall	Durham	NZ1318	54°33·7′	1°47·5′W	A	92
West Holme Heath	Dorset	SY8884	50°39·6′	2°9·8′W	X	194
West Holme Ho	Durham	NZ0219	54°34·2′	1°57·7′W	X	92
West Holmes	Lincs	TF0299	53°28·9′	0°27·4′W	X	112
Westholme (Sch)	Black w Dar	SD6528	53°45·1′	2°31·4′W	X	102,103
West Holway	Dorset	ST5701	50°48·6′	2°36·2′W	X	194
West Holywell	N Tyne	NZ3072	55°2·7′	1°31·4′W	T	88
West Hope	Durham	NZ0309	54°28·8′	1°56·8′W	X	92
Westhope	Heref	SO4651	52°9·5′	2°47·0′W	T	148,149
Westhope	Shrops	SO4786	52°28·4′	2°46·4′W	T	137,138
Westhope Hill	Heref	SO4652	52°10·1′	2°47·0′W	X	148,149
West Hopes	E Loth	NT5562	55°51·2′	2°42·7′W	X	66
Westhope Wood	Heref	SO4551	52°9·5′	2°47·8′W	F	148,149
West Hoppyland	Durham	NZ0931	54°40·7′	1°51·2′W	X	92
West Horndon	Essex	TQ6288	51°34·3′	0°20·7′E	T	177
Westhorp	Northnts	SP5153	52°10·6′	1°14·9′W	T	151
Westhorpe	Lincs	TF2231	52°52·0′	0°10·9′W	T	131
Westhorpe	Notts	SK6852	53°3·9′	0°58·7′W	T	120
Westhorpe	N Yks	NZ3403	54°25·5′	1°28·1′W	X	93
Westhorpe	Suff	TM0469	52°17·1′	0°59·9′E	T	155
Westhorpe Dumble	Notts	SK6752	53°3·9′	0°59·6′W	W	120
Westhorpe Ho	Bucks	SU8687	51°34·7′	0°45·1′W	X	175
Westhorpe Lodge Fm	Suff	TM0470	52°17·6′	0°59·9′E	FM	144,155
West Horrington	Somer	ST5747	51°13·5′	2°36·6′W	T	182,183
West Horsley	Surrey	TQ0752	51°15·7′	0°27·6′W	T	187
West Horsley Place	Surrey	TQ0853	51°16·2′	0°26·7′W	A	187
West Horton	Northum	NU0230	55°34·1′	1°57·7′W	T	75
West Horton Fm	Hants	SU4717	50°57·3′	1°19·5′W	FM	185
West Hos	Northum	NZ1572	55°2·8′	1°45·5′W	X	88
West Hotbank	Northum	NY7669	55°1·1′	2°22·1′W	X	86,87
West Hougham	Kent	TR2640	51°7·1′	1°14·2′E	T	179
Westhoughton	Bolton	SD6505	53°32·7′	2°31·3′W	T	109
West Houlland	Shetld	HU2750	60°14·3′	1°30·2′W	T	3
West House	Durham	NZ3525	54°37·4′	1°27·1′W	X	93
Westhouse	N Yks	SD6774	54°9·9′	2°29·9′W	T	98
Westhouse	S Lanak	NS6941	55°38·9′	4°4·5′W	X	71
West House Fm	Brad	SE0137	53°50·0′	1°58·7′W	FM	104
Westhouse Fm	Derby	SK4258	53°7·3′	1°21·9′W	FM	120
West House Fm	Durham	NZ3432	54°41·2′	1°27·9′W	FM	93
Westhouse Fm	Essex	TL9726	51°54·1′	0°52·2′E	FM	168
West House Fm	Essex	TM0220	51°50·7′	0°56·4′E	FM	168
West House Fm	Northum	NZ1480	55°7·1′	1°46·4′W	FM	81
West House Fm	Northum	NZ2079	55°6·5′	1°40·8′W	FM	88
West House Fm	Notts	SK5548	53°1·8′	1°10·4′W	FM	129
West House Fm	N Yks	SE1072	54°8·9′	1°50·4′W	FM	99

West House Fm	N Yks	SE2460	54°2·4′	1°37·6′W	FM	99
West House Fm	S Tyne	NZ3361	54°56·8′	1°28·7′W	FM	88
Westhouse Fm	Suff	TM4163	52°13·0′	1°32·1′E	FM	156
West House Fm	W Susx	TQ2516	50°56·0′	0°12·9′W	FM	198
Westhouses	Derby	SK4257	53°6·7′	1°21·9′W	T	120
West Houses	Lincs	TF3354	53°4·2′	0°0·5′W	T	122
West Howcreek	D & G	NY1065	54°58·5′	3°23·9′W	X	85
West Howdens	Northum	NZ1698	55°16·8′	1°44·5′W	X	81
West Howe	Bourne	SZ0595	50°45·5′	1°55·4′W	T	195
West Howetown	Somer	SS9134	51°5·9′	3°33·0′W	T	181
West Howmuir	Angus	NO4957	56°42·4′	2°49·5′W	X	54
West Hoy Fm	Kent	TQ8642	51°9·0′	0°40·0′E	FM	189
Westhumble	Surrey	TQ1651	51°15·0′	0°19·9′W	T	187
West Hunton	E Yorks	TA1670	54°7·0′	0°13·1′W	X	101
West Huntspill	Somer	ST3044	51°11·7′	2°59·7′W	T	182
West Hurlett Ho	E Renf	NS5160	55°48·9′	4°23·2′W	X	64
West Hurn	Dorset	SZ1196	50°46·0′	1°50·3′W	T	195
West Hyde	Beds	TL1117	51°50·7′	0°22·9′W	X	166
West Hyde	Essex	TL9703	51°41·7′	0°51·4′E	X	168
West Hyde	Herts	TQ0391	51°36·7′	0°30·4′W	T	176
West Hynish	Arg & Bt	NL9639	56°27·0′	6°55·6′W	T	46
West Hythe	Kent	TR1234	51°4·2′	1°2·0′E	T	179,189
West Idvies	Angus	NO5347	56°37·0′	2°45·5′W	X	54
West Ilkerton	Devon	SS7046	51°12·1′	3°51·3′W	T	180
West Ilkerton Common	Devon	SS6946	51°12·1′	3°52·1′W	X	180
West Ilsley	W Berks	SU4782	51°32·3′	1°18·9′W	T	174
West Inch	Angus	NO3655	56°41·2′	3°2·2′W	X	54
West India Docks	T Ham	TQ3780	51°30·4′	0°1·2′W	X	177
Westing	Cumbr	NY3729	54°39·4′	2°58·2′W	X	90
Westing	Shetld	HP5705	60°43·7′	0°56·8′W	T	1
West Ings	N Yks	SE6884	54°15·1′	0°57·0′W	X	100
Westington	Glos	SP1438	52°2·6′	1°47·4′W	T	151
Westington Court	Heref	SO5856	52°12·3′	2°36·5′W	X	149
Westington Hill	Glos	SP1437	52°2·1′	1°47·4′W	X	151
West Irishborough	Devon	SS6328	51°2·3′	3°56·9′W	X	180
West Itchenor	W Susx	SU7901	50°48·4′	0°52·3′W	T	197
West Jesmond	N upon Ty	NZ2566	54°59·5′	1°36·1′W	T	88
West Jordanston	Pemb	SN0501	51°40·7′	4°48·8′W	X	158
West Kaim	Renf	NS3561	55°49·1′	4°38·6′W	X	63
West Kame	Shetld	HU3959	60°19·1′	1°17·1′W	H	2,3
West Keal	Lincs	TF3663	53°9·0′	0°2·4′E	T	122
West Kellow	Corn	SX1952	50°20·6′	4°32·3′W	X	201
West Kennett	Wilts	SU1168	51°24·9′	1°50·1′W	T	173
West Kennett Long Barrow	Wilts	SU1067	51°24·3′	1°51·0′W	A	173
West Kensington	Ham & Ful	TQ2478	51°29·5′	0°12·4′W	T	176
West Kielder Moor	Northum	NY6499	55°17·3′	2°33·6′W	X	80
West Kilbride	Arg & Bt	NS3086	56°2·5′	4°43·5′W	X	56
West Kilbride	Inverc	NS3371	55°54·4′	4°39·9′W	X	63
West Kilbride	N Ayr	NS2048	55°41·8′	4°51·4′W	T	63
West Kilbride	N Eil	NF7514	57°6·4′	7°21·6′W	T	31
West Kilburn	Ken & Ch	TQ2482	51°31·6′	0°12·4′W	T	176
West Kimber	Devon	SX4898	50°45·9′	4°8·9′W	X	191
West Kimmeragh	I of M	NX4400	54°22·4′	4°25·9′W	X	95
West Kingsdown	Kent	TQ5763	51°20·9′	0°15·7′E	T	177,188
West Kingsmill	Corn	SX4162	50°26·4′	4°14·0′W	X	201
West Kingston	W Susx	TQ0801	50°48·1′	0°27·7′W	T	197
West Kington	Wilts	ST8077	51°29·7′	2°16·9′W	T	173
West Kington Wick	Wilts	ST8176	51°29·2′	2°16·0′W	T	173
West Kinharrachie	Aberd	NJ9231	57°22·4′	2°7·5′W	X	30
West Kinmonth	Aberd	NO7781	56°55·4′	2°22·2′W	X	45
West Kinnernie	Aberd	NJ7110	57°11·1′	2°28·3′W	X	38
West Kinnochtry	Pth & Kin	NO2136	56°30·8′	3°16·6′W	X	53
West Kintrockat	Angus	NO5659	56°43·5′	2°42·7′W	X	54
West Kinwhirrie	Angus	NO3758	56°42·8′	3°1·3′W	X	54
West Kip	Midlo	NT1760	55°49·5′	3°19·1′W	H	65,66
West Kirby	Wirral	SJ2186	53°22·1′	3°10·8′W	T	108
West Kirkcarswell	D & G	NX7549	54°49·5′	3°56·3′W	X	84
West Kirkland	D & G	NX4356	54°52·7′	4°26·4′W	X	83
West Kirkton	Pth & Kin	NN9414	56°18·7′	3°42·4′W	X	58
West Knapton	N Yks	SE8775	54°10·0′	0°39·6′W	T	101
West Knighton	Dorset	SY7387	50°41·2′	2°22·6′W	T	194
West Knock	Aberd	NJ9845	57°30·0′	2°1·5′W	X	30
West Knock	Angus	NO4775	56°52·1′	2°51·7′W	H	44
West Knock	Sou-on-Sea	TQ9282	51°30·5′	0°46·4′E	X	178
West Knockbrex	D & G	NX3964	54°56·9′	4°30·4′W	X	83
West Knowe	Cumbr	NY4865	54°58·9′	2°48·3′W	X	86
West Knowle	Somer	SS8925	51°1·1′	3°34·6′W	X	181
West Knoyle	Wilts	ST8532	51°5·5′	2°12·5′W	T	183
West Kyloe	Northum	NU0440	55°39·5′	1°55·8′W	X	75
West Kyo	Durham	NZ1752	54°52·0′	1°43·7′W	T	88
West Kype	S Lanak	NS7041	55°39·0′	4°3·5′W	X	71
West Lairo	Orkney	HY5018	59°3·0′	2°51·8′W	X	6
Westlake	Devon	SX6194	50°44·0′	3°57·8′W	X	191
Westlake	Devon	SX6253	50°21·9′	3°56·0′W	T	202
Westlake Fm	Devon	SX5498	50°46·0′	4°3·8′W	FM	191
Westlake's Plantns	Devon	SX4397	50°45·3′	4°13·2′W	F	190
Westlakes Science Park	Cumbr	NX9914	54°30·9′	3°33·2′W	X	89
West Lambrook	Somer	ST4118	50°57·7′	2°50·0′W	T	193
West Lambroughton	N Ayr	NS3943	55°39·5′	4°33·1′W	X	63,70
West Lambston	Pemb	SM8916	51°48·4′	5°3·3′W	X	157,158
Westland	Arg & Bt	NS0765	55°50·6′	5°4·5′W	X	63
Westland	Devon	SS6542	51°9·9′	3°55·5′W	X	180
Westland	Devon	SS8411	50°53·4′	3°38·6′W	X	191
Westland	Devon	SX8191	50°42·6′	3°40·7′W	X	191
Westland	D & G	NX7980	55°6·2′	3°53·4′W	X	78
West Land Ends	Northum	NY8363	54°57·9′	2°15·5′W	X	86,87
Westland Fm	Herts	SP9512	51°48·1′	0°36·9′W	FM	165
Westland Green	Herts	TL4221	51°52·4′	0°4·2′E	T	167
Westlands	Cambs	TL5388	52°28·3′	0°15·6′E	X	143
Westlands	E Yorks	SE9128	53°44·7′	0°36·8′W	X	106
Westlands	E Yorks	TA1840	53°50·8′	0°12·0′W	X	107
Westlands	Staffs	SJ8444	52°59·8′	2°13·9′W	T	118
Westlands	Worcs	SO8864	52°16·7′	2°10·2′W	T	150
Westlands	W Susx	TQ2023	50°59·9′	0°17·0′W	X	198
Westlands	W Susx	TQ3930	51°3·4′	0°0·6′W	X	187
Westlands Fm	Essex	TQ6597	51°39·1′	0°23·5′E	FM	167,177
Westlands Fm	Kent	TQ6058	51°18·1′	0°18·1′E	FM	188
Westlands Fm	W Susx	SU8100	50°47·9′	0°50·7′W	FM	197
Westlands Fm	W Susx	TQ0623	51°0·0′	0°29·0′W	FM	197
Westlands Plantation	E Yorks	TA2722	53°41·0′	0°4·2′W	F	107,113
Westland Wood	Rut	SK9212	52°42·1′	0°37·9′W	F	130
Westlane Barn	Surrey	TQ1147	51°12·9′	0°24·3′W	X	187
West Lanegate	D & G	NY0084	55°8·7′	3°33·7′W	X	78
West Lane Ho	N Yks	SD9784	54°15·3′	2°2·3′W	X	98
West Langapool	Orkney	HY4006	58°56·5′	3°2·1′W	X	6,7
West Langarth	Corn	SW7745	50°16·0′	5°7·4′W	X	204
West Langdon	Corn	SX1993	50°42·7′	4°33·5′W	X	190
West Langdon	Kent	TR3147	51°10·8′	1°18·7′E	T	179
West Langton	E Ayr	NS4050	55°43·3′	4°32·4′W	X	64
West Langton Lodge	Leic	SP7291	52°31·0′	0°55·9′W	X	141
West Langwell	Highld	NC6908	58°2·8′	4°12·7′W	T	16
West Lanyon Quoit	Corn	SW4233	50°8·7′	5°36·3′W	A	203
West Laughton	Lincs	TF0731	52°52·2′	0°24·2′W	X	130
West Lavington	Wilts	SU0052	51°16·3′	1°59·6′W	T	184
West Lavington	W Susx	SU8920	50°58·6′	0°43·5′W	T	197
West Lavington Down	Wilts	ST9949	51°14·6′	2°0·5′W	X	184
West Lawn	Heref	SO3040	52°3·5′	3°0·9′W	X	148,161
West Lawn Wood	E Yorks	TA1367	54°5·4′	0°15·9′W	F	101
West Layton	N Yks	NZ1410	54°29·4′	1°46·6′W	T	92
West Layton Fm	Durham	NZ3726	54°37·9′	1°25·2′W	FM	93
West Lea	Durham	NZ4049	54°50·3′	1°22·2′W	T	88
Westlea	Herts	TL3306	51°44·4′	0°4·0′W	X	166
Westlea	Northum	NZ2481	55°7·6′	1°37·0′W	T	81
Westlea	Swin	SU1284	51°33·5′	1°49·2′W	T	173
West Leake	Notts	SK5226	52°50·0′	1°13·3′W	T	129
West Leake Hills	Notts	SK5328	52°51·0′	1°12·4′W	H	129
West Learmouth	Northum	NT8437	55°37·8′	2°14·8′W	T	74
West Learney	Aberd	NJ6203	57°7·2′	2°37·2′W	X	37
West Leas	N Yks	SE2473	54°9·4′	1°37·5′W	X	99
Westleaze	Swin	SU1383	51°33·0′	1°48·4′W	X	173
Westleaze Cottages	Oxon	SU7185	51°33·8′	0°58·1′W	X	175
Westleaze Fm	Somer	ST6929	51°3·8′	2°26·2′W	FM	183
West Lees	N Yks	NZ4702	54°24·9′	1°16·1′W	X	93
West Lees	Scot Bord	NT5117	55°26·9′	2°46·0′W	X	79
West Lees	Scot Bord	NT5915	55°25·9′	2°38·4′W	X	80
Westlees Fm	Surrey	TQ1447	51°12·9′	0°21·7′W	FM	187
Westleigh	Devon	SS4728	51°2·1′	4°10·5′W	T	180
West Leigh	Devon	SS6805	50°50·0′	3°52·1′W	T	191
Westleigh	Devon	ST0617	50°56·9′	3°19·9′W	T	181
West Leigh	Devon	SX6852	50°21·4′	3°51·0′W	X	202
West Leigh	Devon	SX7557	50°24·2′	3°45·2′W	X	202
West Leigh	Hants	SU7208	50°52·2′	0°58·2′W	T	197
Westleigh	Lancs	SD4931	53°46·6′	2°46·0′W	X	102
West Leigh	Somer	ST1130	51°4·0′	3°15·8′W	T	181
Westleigh	Wigan	SD6401	53°30·5′	2°32·2′W	T	109
Westleigh Fm	Devon	SS6045	51°11·5′	3°59·8′W	FM	180
Westleigh Fm	Somer	ST2132	51°5·1′	3°7·3′W	FM	182
West Leith	Herts	SP9110	51°47·1′	0°40·4′W	X	165
West Lesses	Orkney	HY5640	59°14·9′	2°45·8′W	X	5
West Lethans	Fife	NT0594	56°8·0′	3°31·3′W	X	58
Westleton	Suff	TM4469	52°16·1′	1°35·0′E	T	156
Westleton Common	Suff	TM4368	52°15·6′	1°34·1′E	X	156
Westleton Heath	Suff	TM4569	52°16·1′	1°35·9′E	X	156
Westleton Walks	Suff	TM4668	52°15·5′	1°36·7′E	X	156
West Lexham	Norf	TF8417	52°43·4′	0°43·9′E	T	132
Westley	Shrops	SJ3606	52°39·1′	2°56·4′W	T	126
Westley	Shrops	SJ4606	52°39·2′	2°47·5′W	X	126
Westley	Suff	TL8264	52°14·9′	0°40·4′E	T	155
Westley Bank	Northum	NY8365	54°59·0′	2°15·5′W	X	86,87
Westley Bank Cotts	Cumbr	NY6423	54°36·3′	2°33·0′W	X	91
Westley Bottom	Cambs	TL5957	52°11·5′	0°20·0′E	X	154
Westley Bottom Fm	Suff	TL8263	52°14·3′	0°40·3′E	FM	155
Westley Br	Warw	SP3173	52°21·5′	1°32·3′W	X	140
Westley Fm	Essex	TL5340	52°2·5′	0°14·2′E	FM	154
Westley Fm	Glos	SO9102	51°43·2′	2°7·4′W	FM	163
Westleygreen Fm	Suff	TM0949	52°6·2′	1°3·5′E	FM	155,169
Westley Heights	Essex	TQ6857	51°33·1′	0°25·8′E	T	177,178
Westley Manor Fm	Devon	SX9280	50°36·8′	3°31·2′W	FM	192
Westleymill	Brackn	SU8674	51°27·7′	0°45·3′W	X	175
Westleys	Stir	NS7796	56°8·7′	3°58·3′W	X	57
Westley Waterless	Cambs	TL6256	52°10·9′	0°22·6′E	T	154
Westley Wood	Dorset	ST9200	50°48·2′	2°6·4′W	F	195
West Lilling	N Yks	SE6465	54°4·9′	1°0·9′W	T	100
Westlinbank	S Lanak	NS6640	55°38·4′	4°7·3′W	X	71
West Lindsaylands	S Lanak	NT0236	55°36·7′	3°32·9′W	X	72
West Linga	Shetld	HU5264	60°21·7′	1°2·9′W	X	2,3
West Lingo	Fife	NO4908	56°16·0′	2°49·0′W	X	59
Westlington	Bucks	SP7610	51°47·2′	0°53·5′W	T	165
Westlington Ho	Bucks	SP7510	51°47·2′	0°54·4′W	X	165
West Linkhall	Northum	NU1721	55°29·2′	1°43·4′W	X	75
West Links	E Loth	NT4984	56°3·0′	2°48·7′W	X	66
West Links	E Loth	NT5485	56°3·6′	2°43·9′W	X	66
West Linnbridgeford	D & G	NY2679	55°6·2′	3°9·2′W	X	85
Westlinton	Cumbr	NY3964	54°58·3′	2°56·7′W	T	85
West Linton	Scot Bord	NT1551	55°44·9′	3°20·8′W	T	65,72
West Linton Fm	E Yorks	SE7928	53°44·8′	0°47·7′W	FM	105,106
West Liss	Hants	SU7728	51°3·0′	0°53·7′W	T	186,197
West Littleton	S Glos	ST7675	51°28·6′	2°20·3′W	T	172
West Littleton Down	S Glos	ST7677	51°29·7′	2°20·4′W	X	172
West Loanend	Northum	NT9451	55°45·4′	2°5·3′W	X	67,74,75
Westloch	Scot Bord	NT2551	55°45·0′	3°11·3′W	X	66,73
West Loch	Scot Bord	NT8968	55°54·5′	2°10·1′W	X	67
West Loch	Shetld	HU2177	60°28·8′	1°36·6′W	W	3
West Loch	Shetld	HU3540	60°8·8′	1°21·7′W	W	4
West Loch of Skaw	Shetld	HU5766	60°22·7′	0°57·5′W	W	2
West Loch Roag	N Eil	NB0940	58°15·4′	6°57·2′W	W	13
West Lochside	Angus	NO3554	56°40·7′	3°3·2′W	X	54
West Loch Tarbert	Arg & Bt	NR8062	55°48·3′	5°30·2′W	W	62
West Lockinge	Oxon	SU4287	51°35·0′	1°23·2′W	T	174
West Lodge	Dorset	ST8915	50°56·3′	2°9·0′W	X	184
West Lodge	Dorset	SY7988	50°41·7′	2°17·5′W	X	194
West Lodge	Hants	SU5912	50°54·5′	1°9·3′W	X	196
West Lodge	Leic	SK7821	52°47·1′	0°50·2′W	X	129
West Lodge	Northnts	SP6674	52°21·8′	1°1·4′W	X	141
West Lodge	Northnts	SP7453	52°10·4′	0°54·7′W	X	152
West Lodge	N Yks	SE3082	54°14·2′	1°32·0′W	X	99
West Lodge	N Yks	SE3877	54°11·5′	1°24·6′W	X	99
West Lodge	Pth & Kin	NO0363	56°45·2′	3°34·7′W	X	43
West Lodge	Suff	TL9059	52°12·0′	0°47·2′E	X	155
West Lodge Fm	Cambs	TL1173	52°20·9′	0°21·8′W	FM	153
West Lodge Fm	Northnts	SP8184	52°27·1′	0°48·1′W	FM	141
West Lodge Fm	Worcs	SO9268	52°18·8′	2°6·6′W	FM	139
West Lodge Park	Enf	TQ2798	51°40·2′	0°9·4′W	X	166,176
West Logan	D & G	NX8063	54°57·1′	3°52·0′W	X	84
West Lomond	Fife	NO1906	56°14·6′	3°18·0′W	H	58
West Longridge	Northum	NT9549	55°44·3′	2°4·3′W	X	74,75
West Looe	Corn	SX2553	50°21·3′	4°27·2′W	T	201
West Looe River	Corn	SX2159	50°24·5′	4°30·8′W	W	201
West Lowfield Fm	N Yks	SE2994	54°20·7′	1°32·8′W	FM	99
West Low Grounds	Lincs	TF2041	52°57·4′	0°12·4′W	X	131
West Low Ho	Northum	NZ1480	55°7·1′	1°46·4′W	X	81
West Luccombe	Somer	SS8946	51°12·4′	3°35·0′W	T	181
West Lulworth	Dorset	SY8280	50°37·4′	2°14·9′W	T	194
West Lunna Voe	Shetld	HU4869	60°24·4′	1°7·2′W	W	2,3
West Lutton	N Yks	SE9369	54°6·7′	0°34·2′W	T	101
West Lydford	Somer	ST5631	51°4·8′	2°37·3′W	T	182,183
West Lydiatt	Heref	SO5543	52°5·2′	2°39·0′W	T	149
West Lyham	Northum	NU0530	55°34·1′	1°54·8′W	X	75
West Lyn	Devon	SS7248	51°13·2′	3°49·6′W	T	180
West Lyng	Somer	ST3128	51°3·1′	2°58·7′W	T	193
West Lynn	Norf	TF6120	52°45·4′	0°23·6′E	T	132
West Lynn	N Yks	NZ3807	54°27·7′	1°24·4′W	X	93
West Lyn River	Devon	SS7145	51°11·6′	3°50·4′W	W	180
West Machrihanish	Arg & Bt	NR6520	55°25·3′	5°42·4′W	X	68
West Mains	Aberd	NJ5402	57°6·7′	2°45·1′W	X	37
West Mains	Aberd	NJ7112	57°12·1′	2°28·3′W	X	38
West Mains	Aberd	NJ7205	57°8·4′	2°27·3′W	X	38
West Mains	Aberd	NJ8563	57°39·7′	2°14·6′W	X	30
West Mains	Aberd	NJ9043	57°28·9′	2°9·5′W	X	30
West Mains	Aberd	NO8378	56°53·8′	2°16·3′W	X	45
West Mains	Angus	NO3137	56°31·5′	3°6·8′W	X	53
West Mains	Angus	NO4245	56°35·9′	2°56·2′W	X	54
West Mains	Angus	NO6946	56°36·5′	2°29·9′W	X	54
West Mains	D & G	NY0475	55°3·9′	3°29·8′W	X	84
West Mains	E Loth	NT3770	55°55·4′	3°0·1′W	X	66
West Mains	E Loth	NT5772	55°56·6′	2°40·9′W	X	67
West Mains	Falk	NS9081	56°0·8′	3°45·4′W	X	65
West Mains	Fife	NO4411	56°17·5′	2°53·8′W	X	59
West Mains	Moray	NJ1866	57°40·8′	3°22·0′W	X	28
West Mains	Pth & Kin	NN9117	56°20·2′	3°45·3′W	X	58
West Mains	Pth & Kin	NN9208	56°15·4′	3°44·2′W	X	58
West Mains	Pth & Kin	NO0724	56°24·2′	3°30·0′W	X	52,53,58
West Mains	Pth & Kin	NO0943	56°34·5′	3°28·4′W	X	52,53
West Mains	Pth & Kin	NO2728	56°26·6′	3°10·6′W	X	53,59
West Mains	Scot Bord	NT1554	55°46·6′	3°20·9′W	X	65,72
West Mains	Scot Bord	NT5546	55°42·6′	2°42·5′W	T	73
West Mains	Scot Bord	NT6442	55°40·5′	2°33·9′W	X	74
West Mains	S Lanak	NS6254	55°45·8′	4°11·5′W	T	64
West Mains	S Lanak	NS7446	55°41·7′	3°59·8′W	X	64
West Mains	S Lanak	NS9549	55°43·6′	3°39·9′W	X	72
West Mains	S Lanak	NT0146	55°42·1′	3°34·1′W	X	72
West Mains	W Loth	NS9567	55°53·3′	3°40·3′W	X	65
West Mains	W Loth	NT0061	55°50·2′	3°35·4′W	X	65
West Mainshill	S Ayr	NS3311	55°22·1′	4°37·7′W	X	70
West Mains Inn	Northum	NU0542	55°40·5′	1°54·8′W	X	75
Westmains Moor	Scot Bord	NT9157	55°48·6′	2°8·2′W	X	67,74,75
West Mains of Auchmithie	Angus	NO6644	56°35·5′	2°32·8′W	X	54
West Mains of Colliston	Angus	NO6046	56°36·5′	2°38·7′W	X	54
West Mains of Dunnichen	Angus	NO5048	56°37·5′	2°48·4′W	X	54
West Mains of Finavon	Angus	NO4856	56°41·8′	2°50·5′W	X	54
West Mains of Gagie	Angus	NO4535	56°30·5′	2°53·2′W	X	54
West Mains of Gardyne	Angus	NO5648	56°37·6′	2°42·6′W	X	54
West Mains of Hedderwick	Angus	NO6860	56°44·1′	2°30·9′W	X	45
West Mains of Rossie	Angus	NO6754	56°40·9′	2°31·9′W	X	54
West Mains of Turin	Angus	NO5153	56°40·2′	2°47·5′W	X	54
West Malling	Kent	TQ6857	51°17·5′	0°25·0′E	T	178,188
West Malling Aerodrome	Kent	TQ6755	51°16·4′	0°24·0′E	X	178,188
West Malvern	Worcs	SO7646	52°6·9′	2°20·6′W	T	150
West Man	Dorset	SY9775	50°34·7′	2°2·2′W	X	195
Westmancote	Worcs	SO9337	52°2·1′	2°5·7′W	T	150
Westmanton	Devon	SX3994	50°43·6′	4°16·5′W	X	190
West Manywells Fm	Brad	SE0635	53°48·9′	1°54·1′W	FM	104
West Marden	W Susx	SU7713	50°54·9′	0°53·9′W	T	197
West Marina	E Susx	TQ7808	50°50·9′	0°32·1′E	T	199
Westmark Fm	Hants	SU7624	51°0·8′	0°54·6′W	FM	197
West Markham	Notts	SK7272	53°14·6′	0°54·9′W	T	120
West Marsh	Carm	SN2508	51°44·8′	4°31·7′W	X	158
Westmarsh	Kent	TR2761	51°18·4′	1°15·8′E	T	179
West Marsh	NE Lincs	TA2509	53°34·0′	0°6·3′W	T	113
Westmarsh Fm	Wilts	ST8428	51°3·3′	2°13·3′W	FM	183
Westmarsh Point	Essex	TM0716	51°48·5′	1°0·6′E	X	168,169
West Marton	N Yks	SD8950	53°57·0′	2°9·6′W	T	103
West Mathers	Aberd	NO7665	56°46·8′	2°23·1′W	X	45
Westmead Fm	Carm	SN2509	51°45·4′	4°31·7′W	FM	158
Westmeadow Brook	Leic	SK4522	52°47·9′	1°19·6′W	W	129
West Meadows	Hartpl	NZ4827	54°38·4′	1°15·0′W	X	93
West Melbury	Dorset	ST8620	50°59·0′	2°11·6′W	T	183
West Mellwaters	Durham	NY9512	54°30·4′	2°4·2′W	X	91,92
West Melton	Roth	SE4200	53°29·9′	1°21·6′W	T	111
West Mendip Way	N Som	ST3756	51°18·2′	2°53·8′W	X	182
West Mendip Way	Somer	ST4557	51°18·8′	2°47·0′W	X	172,182
West Mendip Way	Somer	ST5051	51°15·6′	2°42·6′W	X	182,183
West Meon	Hants	SU6424	51°0·9′	1°4·9′W	T	185
West Meon Hut	Hants	SU6526	51°2·0′	1°4·0′W	X	185,186
West Meon Woodlands	Hants	SU6426	51°2·0′	1°4·8′W	T	185
Westmere	Devon	SS9915	50°55·8′	3°25·9′W	X	181
West Mere	Norf	TL8896	52°32·0′	0°46·7′E	W	144
Westmere Fm	Cambs	TL5470	52°18·6′	0°15·9′E	FM	154
Westmere Fm	Lincs	TF4722	52°46·8′	0°11·2′E	FM	131
Westmere Fm	Norf	TL8896	52°32·0′	0°46·7′E	FM	144
Westmere House Fm	Lincs	TF4723	52°47·3′	0°11·2′E	FM	131
West Merkland	Highld	NC3832	58°15·1′	4°45·2′W	X	16
West Mersea	Essex	TM0112	51°46·5′	0°55·2′E	T	168
Westmeston	E Susx	TQ3313	50°54·3′	0°6·1′W	T	198
Westmeston Place	E Susx	TQ3314	50°54·8′	0°6·1′W	A	198
West Mey	Highld	ND2873	58°38·6′	3°13·9′W	X	7,12
West Middles	Scot Bord	NT5324	55°30·7′	2°44·2′W	X	73
West Middleton	Devon	SS6445	51°11·5′	3°56·4′W	X	180

West Middleton Fm	Darl	NZ3611	54°29·8′	1°26·2′W	FM	93
West Migvie	Angus	NO4778	56°53·7′	2°51·7′W	X	44
Westmill	Herts	TL1730	51°57·6′	0°17·4′W	T	166
Westmill	Herts	TL3627	51°55·7′	0°0·9′W	T	166
West Mill	Pth & Kin	NO2044	56°35·1′	3°17·7′W	X	53
Westmill	S Lanak	NT1046	55°42·2′	3°25·5′W	X	72
Westmill Fm	Herts	TL3315	51°49·3′	0°3·8′W	FM	166
Westmill Fm	Oxon	SU2390	51°36·7′	1°39·7′W	FM	163,174
West Mill Fm	W Susx	TQ2113	50°54·5′	0°16·4′W	FM	198
West Mill Ho	N Yks	SE6866	54°5·4′	0°57·2′W	X	100
West Mill of Colliston	Angus	NO5945	56°36·0′	2°39·6′W	X	54
West Mills	Dorset	SY9187	50°41·2′	2°7·3′W	X	195
West Mill Tor	Devon	SX5890	50°41·8′	4°0·3′W	H	191
Westmiln	Pth & Kin	NO1016	56°19·9′	3°26·9′W	X	58
West Milton	Dorset	SY5096	50°45·9′	2°42·2′W	T	194
West Milton Burn	Aberd	NO3099	57°4·9′	3°8·8′W	W	37,44
West Minley Fm	Hants	SU8158	51°19·1′	0°49·9′W	FM	175,186
Westminster	C of West	TQ2979	51°29·9′	0°8·1′W	T	176
West Minster	Kent	TQ9173	51°25·6′	0°45·2′E	T	178
West Minsteracres	Northum	NZ0155	54°53·6′	1°58·6′W	X	87
Westminster Fm	Worcs	SO9980	52°25·3′	2°0·5′W	FM	139
West Mitchelton	Renf	NS3660	55°48·6′	4°36·6′W	X	63
West Molesey	Surrey	TQ1368	51°24·2′	0°22·1′W	T	176
West Molland Barton	Devon	SS7928	51°2·6′	3°43·2′W	X	180
West Monar Forest	Highld	NH0842	57°25·9′	5°11·4′W	X	25
West Mondynes	Aberd	NO7679	56°54·4′	2°23·2′W	X	45
West Moneylaws	Northum	NT8735	55°36·8′	2°11·9′W	X	74
West Monkseaton	N Tyne	NZ3371	55°2·2′	1°28·6′W	T	88
West Monkton	Somer	ST2628	51°3·0′	3°3·0′W	T	193
West Moor	Cambs	TL3786	52°27·5′	0°1·4′E	X	142,143
Westmoor	Corn	SW4024	50°3·8′	5°37·6′W	X	203
West Moor	Corn	SX1880	50°35·7′	4°33·9′W	X	201
West Moor	Devon	SS3319	50°57·0′	4°22·3′W	X	190
West Moor	Donc	SE6406	53°33·0′	1°1·6′W	X	111
Westmoor	Heref	SO4045	52°6·2′	2°52·2′W	X	148,149
Westmoor	Lancs	SD7651	53°57·5′	2°21·5′W	X	103
West Moor	Northum	NZ1294	55°14·6′	1°48·2′W	X	81
West Moor	Northum	NZ1798	55°16·8′	1°43·5′W	X	81
West Moor	N Tyne	NZ2770	55°1·7′	1°34·2′W	T	88
West Moor	N Yks	NY9405	54°26·7′	2°5·1′W	X	91,92
West Moor	N Yks	NY9508	54°28·3′	2°4·2′W	X	91,92
West Moor	N Yks	SD8579	54°12·6′	2°13·4′W	X	98
West Moor	N Yks	SD9071	54°8·3′	2°8·8′W	X	98
West Moor	N Yks	SE4871	54°8·2′	1°15·5′W	X	100
West Moor	N Yks	SE6471	54°8·1′	1°0·8′W	X	100
West Moor	Pth & Kin	NN8910	56°16·4′	3°47·1′W	X	58
West Moor	Somer	ST2925	51°1·4′	3°0·4′W	X	193
West Moor	Somer	ST3537	51°8·0′	2°55·4′W	X	182
West Moor	Somer	ST4121	50°59·4′	2°50·1′W	X	193
West Moor	Stock on T	NZ3614	54°31·4′	1°26·2′W	X	93
West Moor	Stock on T	NZ3912	54°30·4′	1°23·4′W	X	93
West Moor Cliff	Pemb	SS0398	51°39·0′	4°50·5′W	X	158
Westmoor Common	Cambs	TL5084	52°26·2′	0°12·8′E	X	143
West Moorehouses	Northum	NZ0469	55°1·2′	1°55·8′W	X	87
Westmoor End	Cumbr	NY1039	54°44·5′	3°23·5′W	T	89
Westmoor Fen	Cambs	TL5289	52°28·9′	0°14·7′E	X	143
Westmoor Fm	Cambs	TL3786	52°27·5′	0°1·4′E	FM	142,143
West Moor Fm	Donc	SE6406	53°33·0′	1°1·6′W	FM	111
Westmoor Fm	Durham	NZ3942	54°46·5′	1°23·2′W	FM	88
West Moor Fm	Lincs	TF0891	53°24·5′	0°22·1′W	FM	112
Westmoor Fm	Lincs	TF1059	53°7·2′	0°21·0′W	FM	121
West Moor Fm	Midd	NZ5214	54°31·4′	1°11·4′W	FM	93
West Moor Fm	Northum	NZ2791	55°13·0′	1°34·1′W	FM	81
West Moor Fm	N Yks	NZ4206	54°27·1′	1°20·7′W	FM	93
Westmoor Fm	Rut	SK8310	52°41·1′	0°45·9′W	FM	130
Westmoor Fm	Staffs	SJ9829	52°51·7′	2°1·4′W	FM	127
West Moor Fm	Sund	NZ3358	54°55·2′	1°28·7′W	FM	88
Westmoorgate	Corn	SX2080	50°35·8′	4°32·2′W	X	201
Westmoor Ho	Lancs	SD4258	54°1·1′	2°52·7′W	X	102
West Moor Ho	N Yks	SE1250	53°57·0′	1°48·6′W	X	104
West Moor House Fm	Durham	NZ3944	54°47·6′	1°23·2′W	FM	88
West Moor Plantn	Durham	NZ0832	54°41·2′	1°52·1′W	F	92
Westmoor Plantn	Northum	NT9044	55°41·6′	2°9·1′W	F	74,75
West Moors	Dorset	SU0802	50°49·2′	1°52·8′W	T	195
West Moors Plantation	Dorset	SU0903	50°49·8′	1°51·9′W	F	195
West Morden	Dorset	SY9095	50°45·5′	2°8·1′W	T	195
Westmorelands	Lincs	TF1547	53°0·7′	0°16·7′W	X	130
West Morham	E Loth	NT5471	55°56·0′	2°43·7′W	X	66
West Morriston	Scot Bord	NT6040	55°39·4′	2°37·7′W	X	74
West Morton	Brad	SE0942	53°52·7′	1°51·4′W	T	104
West Moss	N Yks	SD7378	54°12·1′	2°24·4′W	X	98
West Mosside	E Ayr	NS4435	55°35·3′	4°28·1′W	X	70
West Moss-side	Stir	NS6499	56°10·1′	4°11·0′W	X	57
West Mostard	Cumbr	SD7090	54°18·5′	2°27·2′W	X	98
Westmoston	Aberd	NO6876	56°52·7′	2°31·1′W	X	45
West Moulie Geo	Shetld	HU2940	60°8·9′	1°28·2′W	X	4
West Mouse or Maen y Bugael	I of Angl	SH3094	53°25·2′	4°33·1′W	X	114
West Muck	Moray	NJ4266	57°41·1′	2°57·9′W	X	28
West Muckcroft	E Dunb	NS6376	55°57·7′	4°11·2′W	X	64
West Mudford	Somer	ST5620	50°58·9′	2°37·2′W	T	183
Westmuir	Angus	NO3652	56°39·6′	3°2·2′W	T	54
West Muir	Angus	NO5661	56°44·6′	2°42·7′W	T	44
Westmuir	D & G	NX9266	54°58·9′	3°40·8′W	X	84
Westmuir	Pth & Kin	NO0221	56°22·5′	3°34·8′W	X	52,53,58
Westmuir	Pth & Kin	NS9997	56°9·6′	3°37·1′W	X	58
West Muir	W Loth	NT0162	55°50·7′	3°34·4′W	X	65
West Muircambus	Fife	NO4701	56°12·2′	2°50·8′W	X	59
West Muirhouse	Angus	NO5847	56°37·0′	2°40·6′W	X	54
West Muirhouse	N Ayr	NS3250	55°43·1′	4°40·0′W	X	63
West Muirside	Angus	NO5664	56°46·2′	2°42·7′W	X	44
West Muirton	Aberd	NJ6810	57°11·0′	2°31·3′W	X	38
West Mulloch	Aberd	NO7292	57°1·4′	2°27·2′W	X	38,45
West Muntloch	D & G	NX1134	54°40·2′	4°55·4′W	X	82
West Murkle	Highld	ND1569	58°36·3′	3°27·3′W	X	12
West Myreriggs	Pth & Kin	NO2042	56°34·0′	3°17·7′W	X	53
West Myroch	D & G	NX1141	54°44·0′	4°55·7′W	X	82
West Nab	Kirk	SE0708	53°34·4′	1°53·2′W	H	110
West Nab	Sheff	SK2694	53°26·8′	1°36·1′W	X	110
West Nappin	I of M	SC3598	54°21·3′	4°31·9′W	X	95
West Neap	Shetld	HU5890	60°35·6′	0°56·0′W	X	1,2
West Ness	Fife	NO6106	56°14·9′	2°37·3′W	X	59
West Ness	Fife	NT1382	56°1·6′	3°23·3′W	X	65
West Ness	N Yks	SE6979	54°12·4′	0°56·1′W	T	100
Westness	Orkney	HY7655	59°23·1′	2°24·9′W	X	5
Westness Fm	Orkney	HY3828	59°8·3′	3°4·5′W	FM	6
West Nevay	Angus	NO3243	56°34·7′	3°6·0′W	X	53
West Newbiggin	Darl	NZ3518	54°33·6′	1°27·1′W	X	93
West Newbiggin	Northum	NT8945	55°42·1′	2°10·1′W	X	74
West Newhall	Fife	NO5910	56°17·1′	2°39·3′W	X	59
West Newham	Northum	NZ0976	55°4·9′	1°51·1′W	X	88
West Newlands	Durham	NZ0437	54°43·9′	1°55·8′W	X	92
West Newlands	Essex	TL9502	51°41·2′	0°49·7′E	X	168
West Newlandside	Durham	NY9737	54°43·9′	2°2·4′W	X	92
West Newton	Aberd	NJ9942	57°28·4′	2°0·5′W	X	30
Westnewton	Cumbr	NY1344	54°47·3′	3°20·8′W	T	85
West Newton	E Ayr	NS5139	55°37·6′	4°21·6′W	X	70
West Newton	E Yorks	TA1937	53°49·2′	0°11·1′W	T	107
West Newton	Norf	TF6927	52°49·1′	0°30·9′E	T	132
Westnewton	Northum	NT9030	55°34·1′	2°9·1′W	T	74,75
West Newton	Scot Bord	NT8449	55°44·3′	2°14·9′W	X	74
West Newton	S Lanak	NS6843	55°40·0′	4°5·5′W	X	71
West Newton	Somer	ST2829	51°3·6′	3°1·3′W	T	193
West Newton Belts	E Yorks	TA1837	53°49·2′	0°12·0′W	F	107
West Newton Grange	N Yks	SE6380	54°13·0′	1°1·6′W	X	100
West Newton Ho	Angus	NO6546	56°36·5′	2°33·8′W	X	54
West Newtonleys	Aberd	NO8683	56°56·5′	2°13·4′W	X	45
West Nichold	Northum	NY6468	55°0·6′	2°33·3′W	X	86
West Nisbet	Scot Bord	NT6725	55°31·3′	2°30·9′W	X	74
Westnors End Fm	Heref	SO6231	51°58·8′	2°32·8′W	FM	149
Westnorth Fm	Corn	SX2458	50°24·0′	4°28·2′W	FM	201
West Norwood	Lam	TQ3271	51°25·6′	0°5·7′W	T	176,177
West Nubbock	Northum	NY8862	54°57·4′	2°10·8′W	X	87
West Nymph	Devon	SX6695	50°44·6′	3°53·6′W	X	191
Westock's Fm	Essex	TL7618	51°50·2′	0°33·7′E	FM	167
Westoe	S Tyne	NZ3766	54°59·5′	1°24·9′W	T	88
Westoe Fm	Cambs	TL5944	52°4·5′	0°19·6′E	FM	154
West Ogwell	Devon	SX8270	50°31·3′	3°39·5′W	T	202
West Okement Head	Devon	SX6085	50°39·1′	3°58·4′W	W	191
West Okement River	Devon	SX5689	50°41·2′	4°1·9′W	W	191
Westol Hall Fm	Worcs	SP0054	52°11·3′	1°59·6′W	FM	150
Weston	Bath & NE Somer	ST7266	51°23·8′	2°23·8′W	T	172
Weston	Ches	SJ7352	53°4·1′	2°23·8′W	X	118
Weston	Ches	SJ8972	53°14·9′	2°9·5′W	T	118
Weston	C of Soton	SU4410	50°53·5′	1°22·1′W	T	196
Weston	Corn	SX2988	50°40·2′	4°24·8′W	X	190
Weston	Devon	ST1400	50°47·8′	3°12·8′W	T	192,193
Weston	Devon	SY1688	50°41·4′	3°11·0′W	T	192
Weston	Dorset	ST5005	50°50·8′	2°42·2′W	T	194
Weston	Dorset	SY6871	50°32·5′	2°26·7′W	T	194
Weston	Halton	SJ5080	53°19·1′	2°44·6′W	T	108
Weston	Hants	SU7221	50°59·3′	0°58·1′W	T	197
Weston	Heref	SO3656	52°12·1′	2°55·8′W	T	148,149
Weston	Herts	TL2630	51°57·5′	0°9·6′W	T	166
Weston	Highld	NH7058	57°35·9′	4°10·0′W	X	27
Weston	Lincs	TF2824	52°48·1′	0°5·7′W	T	131
Weston	Moray	NJ4962	57°39·0′	2°50·8′W	X	28,29
Weston	Northnts	SP5846	52°6·8′	1°8·8′W	T	152
Weston	Notts	SK7767	53°11·9′	0°50·4′W	T	120
Weston	N Yks	SE1746	53°54·8′	1°44·1′W	T	104
Weston	Pemb	SN0210	51°45·5′	4°51·8′W	T	157,158
Weston	Shrops	SJ2927	52°50·4′	3°2·8′W	T	126
Weston	Shrops	SJ5628	52°51·1′	2°38·8′W	T	126
Weston	Shrops	SO2781	52°25·6′	3°4·0′W	X	137
Weston	Shrops	SO3273	52°21·3′	2°59·5′W	T	137,148
Weston	Shrops	SO5992	52°31·7′	2°35·9′W	T	137,138
Weston	S Lanak	NS8229	55°32·7′	3°51·8′W	X	71,72
Weston	S Lanak	NT0347	55°42·7′	3°32·2′W	T	72
Weston	Staffs	SJ9727	52°50·7′	2°2·3′W	T	127
Weston	Suff	TM4287	52°25·9′	1°34·0′E	T	156
Weston	W Berks	SU3973	51°27·5′	1°26·1′W	T	174
Weston Bampfylde	Somer	ST6124	51°1·1′	2°33·0′W	T	183
Weston Bay	N Som	ST3060	51°20·3′	2°59·9′W	W	182
Weston Beggard	Heref	SO5841	52°4·2′	2°36·4′W	T	149
Westonbirt	Glos	ST8589	51°36·2′	2°12·6′W	T	162,173
Westonbirt School	Glos	ST8689	51°36·2′	2°11·7′W	X	173
Weston Burn	Scot Bord	NT1537	55°37·4′	3°20·6′W	W	72
Weston Bury	Herts	TL2630	51°57·5′	0°9·6′W	X	166
Westonbury Fm	Heref	SO3756	52°12·2′	2°54·9′W	FM	148,149
Westonby Ho	N Yks	NZ7907	54°27·4′	0°46·5′W	X	94
Westonby Moor Plantn	N Yks	NZ7808	54°27·9′	0°47·4′W	F	94
Weston by Welland	Northnts	SP7791	52°30·9′	0°51·5′W	T	141
Weston Cliff	Devon	SY1788	50°41·4′	3°10·1′W	X	192
Weston Colley	Hants	SU5039	51°9·1′	1°16·7′W	T	185
Weston Colville	Cambs	TL6153	52°9·3′	0°21·6′E	T	154
Weston Combe	Devon	SY1688	50°41·4′	3°11·0′W	X	192
Weston Common	C of Soton	SU4611	50°54·0′	1°20·4′W	T	196
Weston Common	Hants	SU6944	51°11·7′	1°0·4′W	F	186
Westoncommon	Shrops	SJ4226	52°49·9′	2°51·3′W	T	126
Weston Corbett	Hants	SU6847	51°13·3′	1°1·2′W	T	185,186
Weston Court Fm	Shrops	SO5872	52°20·9′	2°36·6′W	FM	137,138
Weston Coyney	C of Stoke	SJ9344	52°59·8′	2°5·9′W	T	118
Weston Ditch	Suff	TL6777	52°22·2′	0°27·6′E	T	143
Weston Down	N Som	ST4374	51°28·0′	2°48·8′W	X	171,172
Weston Ebb	Devon	SY1787	50°40·8′	3°10·1′W	X	192
Weston Favell	Northnts	SP7962	52°15·3′	0°50·2′W	T	152
Weston Fen	Lincs	TF2716	52°43·8′	0°6·7′W	X	131
Weston Fen	Suff	TL9878	52°22·1′	0°54·9′E	X	144
Weston Fields Fm	Derby	SK3929	52°51·7′	1°24·8′W	FM	128
Weston Fields Fm	Warw	SP3670	52°19·8′	1°27·9′W	FM	140
Weston Fm	Oxon	SU2197	51°40·5′	1°41·4′W	FM	163
Weston Fm	Shrops	SO6975	52°22·6′	2°26·9′W	FM	138
Weston Fm	Somer	ST2909	50°52·8′	3°0·2′W	A	193
Weston Fm	Somer	ST5510	50°53·5′	2°38·0′W	FM	194
Weston Fm	Worcs	SO5863	52°16·1′	2°36·5′W	FM	137,138,149
Weston Gardens	Warw	SP2735	52°1·0′	1°36·0′W	X	151
Weston Grange	Derby	SK4128	52°51·1′	1°23·1′W	X	129
Weston Green	Cambs	TL6252	52°8·8′	0°22·5′E	T	154
Weston Green	Norf	TG1014	52°41·2′	1°6·8′E	T	133
Weston Green	Surrey	TQ1566	51°23·1′	0°20·4′W	T	176
Weston Hall	Ches	SJ7351	53°3·6′	2°23·8′W	X	118
Weston Hall	Derby	SK4028	52°51·1′	1°24·0′W	A	129
Weston Hall	Essex	TL8345	52°4·6′	0°40·6′E	X	155
Weston Hall	Norf	TG1017	52°42·8′	1°6·9′E	X	133
Weston Hall	Staffs	SJ8036	52°55·5′	2°17·4′W	X	127
Weston Hall	Staffs	SJ9627	52°50·7′	2°3·2′W	A	127
Weston Hall (Hotel)	Warw	SP3887	52°29·0′	1°26·0′W	X	140
Weston Heath	Shrops	SJ5627	52°50·6′	2°38·8′W	X	126
Weston Heath	Shrops	SJ7713	52°43·1′	2°20·0′W	T	127
Weston Heath Coppice	Shrops	SJ5627	52°50·6′	2°38·8′W	F	126
Weston Hill	Shrops	SO2781	52°25·6′	3°4·0′W	H	137
Weston Hill	Shrops	SO5582	52°26·3′	2°39·3′W	H	137,138
Weston Hill	Warw	SP1550	52°9·1′	1°46·4′W	X	151
Weston Hills	Herts	TL2532	51°58·6′	0°10·4′W	X	166
Weston Hills	Lincs	TF2820	52°46·0′	0°5·8′W	T	131
Westonhill Wood	Heref	SO3145	52°6·2′	3°0·1′W	F	148
Weston Hindle Fm	Suff	TL9975	52°20·4′	0°55·7′E	FM	144
Weston Ho	Devon	SX8160	50°25·9′	3°40·2′W	X	202
Weston Ho	Norf	TG1017	52°42·8′	1°6·9′E	X	133
Weston Ho	Shrops	SJ4325	52°49·4′	2°50·4′W	X	126
Weston House Fm	Shrops	SO2998	52°34·8′	3°2·5′W	FM	137
Weston House Fm	Staffs	SJ8036	52°55·5′	2°17·4′W	FM	127
Weston House Fm	Suff	TM2982	52°23·5′	1°22·3′E	FM	156
Weston in Arden	Warw	SP3887	52°29·0′	1°26·0′W	T	140
Westoning	Beds	TL0332	51°58·8′	0°29·6′W	T	166
Weston-in-Gordano	N Som	ST4474	51°28·0′	2°48·0′W	T	171,172
Weston Jones	Staffs	SJ7624	52°49·0′	2°21·0′W	T	127
Weston Jones Mill	Staffs	SJ7523	52°48·5′	2°21·8′W	X	127
Weston Level	Somer	ST3433	51°5·8′	2°56·2′W	X	182
Weston Lodge	Derby	SK2942	52°58·7′	1°33·7′W	X	119,128
Weston Lodge	Herts	TL2728	51°56·4′	0°8·7′W	X	166
Weston Lodge	Shrops	SJ2835	52°54·7′	3°3·8′W	X	126
Weston Longville	Norf	TG1115	52°41·7′	1°7·8′E	T	133
Weston Lullingfields	Shrops	SJ4224	52°48·9′	2°51·2′W	T	126
Weston Madoc	Powys	SO2294	52°32·5′	3°8·6′W	X	137
Weston Manor	I of W	SZ3286	50°40·6′	1°32·4′W	T	196
Weston Manor	N Yks	SE1847	53°55·4′	1°43·1′W	X	104
Weston Marsh	Lincs	TF2928	52°50·3′	0°4·7′W	X	131
Weston Mead Fm	Bucks	SP8513	51°48·8′	0°45·6′W	FM	165
Weston Mill	C of Plym	SX4557	50°23·8′	4°10·5′W	T	201
Weston Mill	Warw	SP2736	52°1·5′	1°36·0′W	X	151
Weston Mill Lake	C of Plym	SX4457	50°23·8′	4°11·3′W	W	201
Weston Moor	N Som	ST4473	51°27·4′	2°48·0′W	X	171,172
Weston Moor	N Yks	SE1849	53°56·4′	1°43·1′W	X	104
Weston Mouth	Devon	SY1687	50°40·8′	3°11·0′W	X	192
Weston-on-Avon	Warw	SP1551	52°9·7′	1°46·4′W	T	151
Weston-on-the-Green	Oxon	SP5318	51°51·7′	1°13·4′W	T	164
Weston-on-Trent	Derby	SK4028	52°51·1′	1°24·0′W	T	129
Weston Park	Bath & NE Somer	ST7366	51°23·8′	2°22·9′W	T	172
Weston Park	Glos	SP1238	52°2·7′	1°49·1′W	X	150
Weston Park	Herts	TL2629	51°56·9′	0°9·6′W	X	166
Weston Park	N Yks	SE1846	53°54·8′	1°43·1′W	X	104
Weston Park	Shrops	SJ8009	52°40·9′	2°17·3′W	X	127
Weston Park	Warw	SP2834	52°0·5′	1°35·1′W	X	151
Weston Park Fm	Oxon	SP5418	51°51·7′	1°12·6′W	FM	164
Weston Park Fm	Staffs	SJ8210	52°41·5′	2°15·6′W	FM	127
Weston Patrick	Hants	SU6946	51°12·8′	1°0·3′W	T	186
Weston Point	Ches	SJ4981	53°19·7′	2°45·5′W	T	108
Weston Rhyn	Shrops	SJ2835	52°54·7′	3°3·8′W	T	126
Westons	W Susx	SU7621	50°59·2′	0°54·6′W	X	197
Weston Sands	Warw	SP1651	52°9·7′	1°45·6′W	X	151
Weston's Fm	W Susx	TQ1329	51°3·2′	0°22·9′W	FM	187,198
Westons Place	W Susx	TQ1633	51°5·3′	0°20·2′W	X	187
Weston-sub-Edge	Glos	SP1241	52°4·3′	1°49·1′W	T	150
Weston-super-Mare	N Som	ST3261	51°20·9′	2°58·7′W	T	182
Weston, The	Heref	SO3245	52°6·2′	2°59·2′W	X	148
Weston Town	Somer	ST7041	51°10·3′	2°25·4′W	T	183
Weston Turvill	Bucks	SP8510	51°47·2′	0°45·7′W	T	165
Weston Turville Resr	Bucks	SP8609	51°46·6′	0°44·8′W	W	165
Weston Under Lizard	Staffs	SJ8010	52°41·5′	2°17·4′W	T	127
Weston under Penyard	Heref	SO6223	51°54·5′	2°32·8′W	T	162
Weston under Wetherley	Warw	SP3669	52°19·3′	1°27·9′W	T	151
Weston Underwood	Derby	SK2942	52°58·7′	1°33·7′W	T	119,128
Weston Underwood	Mil Key	SP8650	52°8·7′	0°44·2′W	T	152
Westonwharf	Shrops	SJ4225	52°49·4′	2°51·2′W	T	126
Weston Wood	Oxon	SP5417	51°51·2′	1°12·6′W	F	164
Weston Woods	N Som	ST3262	51°21·4′	2°58·2′W	F	182
Weston Woods Fm	Cambs	TL6350	52°7·7′	0°23·3′E	FM	154
Westonzoyland	Somer	ST3534	51°6·3′	2°55·3′W	T	182
West Orchard	Dorset	ST8216	50°56·8′	2°15·0′W	T	183
West Orchard Fm	Dorset	SY9480	50°37·4′	2°4·7′W	FM	195
West Ord	Northum	NT9551	55°45·4′	2°4·3′W	X	67,74,75
Westover	Devon	SS4706	50°50·2′	4°10·0′W	X	191
Westover	I of W	SZ4286	50°40·6′	1°24·0′W	X	196
Westover Down	I of W	SZ4184	50°39·5′	1°24·8′W	X	196
Westover Fm	Dorset	SU1404	50°50·4′	1°47·7′W	FM	195
Westover Fm	Dorset	SY3595	50°45·3′	2°54·9′W	FM	193
Westover Fm	Hants	SU3640	51°9·7′	1°28·7′W	FM	185
Westover Fm	I of W	SZ4186	50°40·6′	1°24·8′W	FM	196
Westover Fm	Somer	ST4224	51°1·0′	2°49·2′W	FM	193
Westover Plantation	I of W	SZ4185	50°40·0′	1°24·8′W	F	196
West Overton	Wilts	SU1367	51°24·3′	1°48·4′W	T	173
Westow	N Yks	SE7565	54°4·8′	0°50·8′W	T	100
Westowe	Somer	ST1232	51°5·1′	3°15·0′W	T	181
Westow Fm	Corn	SW9054	50°21·1′	4°56·8′W	FM	200
Westow Grange	N Yks	SE7665	54°4·8′	0°49·9′W	X	100
Westow Low Grange	N Yks	SE7664	54°4·2′	0°49·9′W	X	100
Westown	Devon	ST1113	50°54·8′	3°15·6′W	T	181,193
Westown	Pth & Kin	NO2527	56°26·0′	3°12·5′W	T	53,59
Westown	S Lanak	NS7644	55°40·7′	3°57·9′W	X	71
West Panson	Devon	SX3491	50°41·9′	4°20·7′W	T	190
West Park	Aberd	NO7697	57°4·1′	2°23·3′W	X	38,45
West Park	Bucks	SP8620	51°52·5′	0°44·6′W	X	165
Westpark	Corn	SX1960	50°25·0′	4°32·5′W	X	201
Westpark	Devon	SS5608	50°51·5′	4°2·4′W	X	191
West Park	Devon	SS7229	51°3·0′	3°49·2′W	X	180
West Park	Devon	SS8326	51°1·5′	3°39·7′W	X	181

West Park	Durham	NY9919	54°34·2′	2°0·5′W	X	92
West Park	Durham	NZ1237	54°43·9′	1°48·4′W	X	92
West Park	Hants	SU1116	50°56·8′	1°50·2′W	X	184
West Park	Hartpl	NZ4832	54°41·1′	1°14·9′W	T	93
West Park	K upon H	TA0728	53°44·5′	0°22·2′W	T	107
West Park	Leeds	SE2637	53°50·0′	1°35·9′W	T	104
West Park	N Yks	SE4979	54°12·5′	1°14·5′W	X	100
West Park	Pth & Kin	NN8913	56°18·0′	3°47·2′W	X	58
Westpark	S Ayr	NS3919	55°26·6′	4°32·3′W	X	70
Westpark	S Lanak	NS6943	55°40·0′	4°4·5′W	X	71
West Park	St Hel	SJ4995	53°27·2′	2°45·7′W	T	108
West Park	S Tyne	NZ3665	54°58·9′	1°25·8′W	T	88
West Park	Surrey	TQ3441	51°9·4′	0°4·6′W	X	187
West Park	Wolv	SO9099	52°35·6′	2°8·5′W	X	139
West Parkfergus	Arg & Bt	NR6520	55°25·3′	5°42·4′W	X	68
West Park Fm	Beds	TL0641	52°3·7′	0°26·8′W	FM	153
West Park Fm	Corn	SW9470	50°29·9′	4°53·9′W	FM	200
West Park Fm	Dorset	SY9296	50°46·0′	2°6·4′W	FM	195
West Park Fm	E Ayr	NS6112	55°23·2′	4°11·2′W	FM	71
West Park Fm	Hants	SU1215	50°56·3′	1°49·4′W	FM	184
West Park Fm	Kent	TQ6359	51°18·6′	0°20·7′E	FM	188
West Park Fm	King	TQ1861	51°20·4′	0°18·0′W	FM	176,187
West Park Fm	Northnts	SP6843	52°5·1′	1°0·1′W	FM	152
West Park Fm	Somer	ST4537	51°8·0′	2°46·8′W	FM	182
West Park Fm	Wilts	ST9184	51°33·5′	2°7·4′W	FM	173
West Park Fm	Wilts	SU0055	51°17·9′	1°59·6′W	FM	173
West Parkgate	Ches	SJ9581	53°19·8′	2°4·1′W	X	109
West Park Wood	Brad	SE1348	53°55·9′	1°47·7′W	F	104
West Park Wood	Wilts	ST9184	51°33·5′	2°7·4′W	F	173
West Parley	Dorset	SZ0897	50°46·6′	1°52·8′W	T	195
West Pasture	Durham	NY9422	54°35·8′	2°5·1′W	T	91,92
West Pasture	N Yks	SE2389	54°18·0′	1°38·4′W	X	99
West Pastures	Hartpl	NZ4628	54°38·9′	1°16·8′W	X	93
West Peckham	Kent	TQ6452	51°14·8′	0°21·4′E	T	188
West Peeke	Devon	SX3493	50°43·0′	4°20·7′W	X	190
West Pelton	Durham	NZ2353	54°52·5′	1°38·1′W	T	88
West Pennard	Somer	ST5438	51°8·6′	2°39·1′W	T	182,183
West Pentire	Corn	SW7760	50°24·1′	5°7·9′W	T	200
West Perry	Cambs	TL1466	52°17·0′	0°19·3′W	T	153
West Petherwin	Corn	SX3082	50°37·0′	4°23·8′W	X	201
West Pickard Bay	Pemb	SM8601	51°40·3′	5°5·3′W	W	157
West Pier	Bri & Hov	TQ3003	50°48·9′	0°8·9′W	X	198
West Pier	N Yks	NZ8911	54°29·4′	0°37·1′W	X	94
West Pier	Swan	SS6692	51°36·9′	3°55·7′W	X	159
West Pill	Monm	ST4686	51°34·5′	2°46·4′W	W	171,172
West Pill	Pemb	SM8503	51°41·3′	5°6·3′W	X	157
West Pinford	Somer	SS7941	51°9·6′	3°43·4′W	X	180
West Pitcorthie	Fife	NO5706	56°14·9′	2°41·2′W	X	59
West Pitmillan	Aberd	NJ9725	57°19·2′	2°2·5′W	X	38
West Pitt Fm	Devon	SS9610	50°53·0′	3°28·3′W	FM	192
West Pitton	Devon	SX5854	50°22·4′	3°59·4′W	X	202
Westplace Burn	Pth & Kin	NN9706	56°14·4′	3°39·3′W	W	58
West Plain Fm	Cumbr	SD3674	54°9·7′	2°58·4′W	FM	96,97
West Plaistow	Devon	SS5638	51°7·6′	4°3·1′W	X	180
West Plann	E Ayr	NS3939	55°37·3′	4°33·0′W	X	70
West Plean	Stir	NS8187	56°3·9′	3°54·2′W	X	57,65
West Point	Essex	TL9006	51°43·5′	0°45·5′E	X	168
West Point	Kent	TQ9071	51°24·6′	0°44·3′E	X	178
West Point	Medway	TQ7979	51°29·1′	0°35·1′E	X	178
West Polquhirter	E Ayr	NS6313	55°23·8′	4°9·4′W	X	71
West Pontnewydd	Torf	ST2896	51°39·7′	3°2·1′W	T	171
West Pool	Carm	SN2110	51°45·8′	4°35·3′W	X	158
West Pool	Shetld	HU4623	59°59·6′	1°10·0′W	W	4
West Poringland	Norf	TG2600	52°33·3′	1°20·4′E	T	134
West Porlock	Somer	SS8747	51°12·9′	3°36·7′W	T	181
Westport	Aberd	NO8889	56°59·8′	2°11·4′W	X	45
Westport	Arg & Bt	NR6526	55°28·5′	5°42·7′W	X	68
West Port	Highld	NJ0628	57°20·2′	3°33·2′W	X	36
Westport	Somer	ST3819	50°58·3′	2°52·6′W	T	193
Westport Canal	Somer	ST3920	50°58·8′	2°51·8′W	W	193
Westport Lake	C of Stoke	SJ8550	53°3·1′	2°13·0′W	W	118
West Porton	Renf	NS4371	55°54·6′	4°30·3′W	T	64
West Prawle	Devon	SX7637	50°13·4′	3°43·9′W	X	202
West Preston	D & G	NX9555	54°53·0′	3°37·8′W	X	84
West Printonan	Scot Bord	NT7846	55°42·7′	2°20·6′W	X	74
West Pulham	Dorset	ST7008	50°52·5′	2°25·2′W	T	194
West Putford	Devon	SS3515	50°54·9′	4°20·5′W	T	190
West Quantoxhead	Somer	ST1141	51°9·9′	3°16·0′W	T	181
Westquarter	Falk	NS9178	55°59·2′	3°44·4′W	T	65
West Quarter	S Lanak	NS8650	55°44·1′	3°48·5′W	X	65,72
Westquarter Burn	Falk	NS8876	55°58·1′	3°47·2′W	W	65
Westquarter Ho	S Lanak	NS7146	55°41·7′	4°2·7′W	X	64
Westra	V of Glam	ST1471	51°26·1′	3°13·8′W	T	171
West Raddon	Devon	SS8902	50°48·7′	3°34·2′W	X	192
West Raedykes	Aberd	NO8390	57°0·3′	2°16·3′W	X	38,45
West Raffles	D & G	NY0872	55°2·3′	3°25·9′W	X	85
West Rainton	Durham	NZ3246	54°48·7′	1°29·7′W	T	88
West Rasen	Lincs	TF0689	53°23·5′	0°24·0′W	T	112,121
West Rattenraw	Northum	NY8364	54°58·5′	2°15·5′W	X	86,87
West Ravendale	NE Lincs	TF2299	53°28·6′	0°9·3′W	T	113
West Raw	Northum	NZ0999	55°17·3′	1°51·1′W	X	81
Westraw	S Lanak	NS9442	55°39·9′	3°40·7′W	X	71,72
Westraw Mains	S Lanak	NS9343	55°40·4′	3°41·6′W	X	71,72
Westray	Cumbr	NY1530	54°39·7′	3°18·6′W	X	89
Westray	Orkney	HY4446	59°18·1′	2°58·5′W	X	5
Westray Firth	Orkney	HY4536	59°12·7′	2°57·3′W	W	5
Westray Firth	Orkney	HY4834	59°11·6′	2°54·1′W	W	5,6
West Raynham	Norf	TF8725	52°47·6′	0°46·8′E	T	132
West Raynham Airfield	Norf	TF8524	52°47·1′	0°45·0′E	X	132
West Reef	Arg & Bt	NM2413	56°14·0′	6°26·8′W	X	48
West Regwm	Carm	SN2117	51°49·6′	4°35·5′W	X	158
West Retford	Notts	SK6981	53°19·5′	0°57·4′W	T	111,120
West Revoch	E Renf	NS5550	55°43·6′	4°18·1′W	X	64
West Riddens	W Susx	TQ2922	50°59·2′	0°9·3′W	X	198
Westridge Down	I of W	SZ4784	50°39·5′	1°19·7′W	X	196
Westridge Green	W Berks	SU5679	51°30·7′	1°11·2′W	T	174
Westridge Wood	Glos	ST7595	51°39·4′	2°21·3′W	F	162
West Riding	Northum	NZ0759	54°55·8′	1°53·0′W	X	88
Westrigg Burn	Pth & Kin	NN9507	56°14·9′	3°41·2′W	W	58
West Rigg	C of Edin	NT1562	55°50·9′	3°21·0′W	X	65
Westrigg	W Loth	NS9067	55°53·3′	3°45·1′W	T	65
West Ringuinea	D & G	NX0747	54°47·1′	4°59·7′W	X	82
Westrip	Glos	SO8205	51°44·8′	2°15·3′W	T	162
West Ripe	Kent	TR0319	50°56·3′	0°53·8′E	X	189
Westrip Farm Ho	Glos	ST8998	51°41·1′	2°9·2′W	X	163
West Riskpark	D & G	NX6277	55°4·4′	4°9·3′W	X	77
West Road	Kent	TR0015	50°54·2′	0°51·1′E	W	189
Westrop	Wilts	ST8870	51°26·0′	2°10·0′W	T	173
Westrop Fm	W Berks	SU5170	51°25·8′	1°15·6′W	FM	174
Westrop Green	W Berks	SU5271	51°26·4′	1°14·7′W	T	174
West Rose	Carm	SN1912	51°46·9′	4°37·1′W	X	158
West Roucan	D & G	NY0278	55°5·5′	3°31·7′W	X	84
West Roughlea Fm	Durham	NZ2731	54°40·6′	1°34·5′W	FM	93
West Rounton	N Yks	NZ4103	54°25·5′	1°21·7′W	T	93
West Rounton Grange	N Yks	NZ4102	54°24·9′	1°21·7′W	X	93
Westrow	Dorset	ST6910	50°53·6′	2°26·1′W	X	194
West Row	Suff	TL6775	52°21·1′	0°27·5′E	T	143
West Rowhorne	Devon	SX8794	50°44·3′	3°35·7′W	X	192
Westrow Reach	Suff	TM4555	52°8·6′	1°35·2′E	W	156
West Royd	Brad	SE1637	53°50·0′	1°45·0′W	T	104
West Ruckham	Devon	SS8711	50°53·5′	3°36·0′W	X	192
West Rudham	Norf	TF8127	52°48·8′	0°41·6′E	T	132
West Rudham Common	Norf	TF8224	52°47·2′	0°42·3′E	F	132
West Ruffside	Durham	NY9750	54°50·9′	2°2·4′W	X	87
West Ruislip	Hill	TQ0886	51°34·0′	0°26·1′W	T	176
Westrum	Lincs	TA0006	53°32·7′	0°29·0′W	T	112
West Runton	Norf	TG1842	52°56·1′	1°15·0′E	T	133
Westruther	Scot Bord	NT6350	55°44·8′	2°34·9′W	T	67,74
Westruther Burn	S Lanak	NT0248	55°43·2′	3°33·2′W	W	72
Westruther Burn	S Lanak	NT0451	55°44·8′	3°31·3′W	W	65,72
Westruther Mains	Scot Bord	NT6449	55°44·2′	2°34·0′W	X	74
Westry	Cambs	TL3998	52°34·0′	0°3·5′E	T	142,143
Westry Fm	Cambs	TL4098	52°33·9′	0°4·3′E	FM	142,143
West Saline	Fife	NS9894	56°7·9′	3°38·0′W	X	58
West Saltoun	E Loth	NT4667	55°53·8′	2°51·4′W	T	66
West Sand	Norf	TF9645	52°58·2′	0°55·5′E	X	132
West Sandend	Aberd	NK0732	57°23·0′	1°52·6′W	X	30
West Sandford	Devon	SS8102	50°48·6′	3°41·0′W	T	191
West Sands	Fife	NO5018	56°21·4′	2°48·1′W	X	59
West Sands	Norf	TF8845	52°58·4′	0°48·4′E	X	132
West Sandwick	Shetld	HU4488	60°34·7′	1°11·3′W	T	1,2
West Sand Wick	Shetld	HU4489	60°35·2′	1°11·3′W	W	1,2
West Scale Park	N Yks	SD9774	54°10·0′	2°2·3′W	X	98
West Scales	D & G	NY2767	54°59·8′	3°8·0′W	X	85
West Scar	Red & Cl	NZ6026	54°37·8′	1°3·8′W	X	94
West Scar Ho	Cumbr	SD7690	54°18·5′	2°21·7′W	X	98
West Scholes	Brad	SE0931	53°46·8′	1°51·4′W	T	104
West Scrafton	N Yks	SE0783	54°14·8′	1°53·1′W	T	99
West Scrafton Moor	N Yks	SE0781	54°13·7′	1°53·1′W	X	99
West Scryne	Angus	NO5737	56°31·6′	2°41·5′W	X	54
Westseat	Aberd	NJ5232	57°22·8′	2°47·4′W	X	29,37
West Seaton	Angus	NO6541	56°33·8′	2°33·7′W	X	54
West Sedge Moor	Somer	ST3625	51°1·5′	2°54·4′W	X	193
West Sevington Fm	Wilts	ST8678	51°30·3′	2°11·7′W	FM	173
West Shaftoe	Northum	NZ0481	55°7·6′	1°55·8′W	X	81
West Shaird	Orkney	ND4389	58°47·4′	2°58·7′W	X	7
West Shambellie	D & G	NX9567	54°59·4′	3°38·0′W	X	84
West Shaw	N Yks	SD8687	54°17·0′	2°12·5′W	X	98
West Shaws	Durham	NZ0815	54°32·1′	1°52·2′W	X	92
West Shaws	Northum	NY9264	54°58·5′	2°7·1′W	X	87
West Shebster	Highld	ND0163	58°32·9′	3°41·6′W	X	11,12
West Shepton	Somer	ST6143	51°11·3′	2°33·1′W	T	183
West Sherford	Devon	SX5453	50°21·8′	4°2·8′W	X	201
Westshield	S Lanak	NS9449	55°43·6′	3°40·8′W	X	72
West Shield Hill	Northum	NZ1988	55°11·4′	1°41·7′W	X	81
West Shields	Durham	NZ1141	54°46·1′	1°49·4′W	X	88
Westshiels	Scot Bord	NT6206	55°21·0′	2°35·5′W	X	80
West Shinness Lodge	Highld	NC5315	58°6·2′	4°29·2′W	X	16
West Shipley Fm	Durham	NZ1033	54°41·8′	1°50·3′W	FM	92
Westside	Aberd	NJ4716	57°14·2′	2°52·2′W	X	37
Westside	Aberd	NJ5309	57°10·4′	2°46·2′W	X	37
Westside	Aberd	NJ5764	57°40·1′	2°42·8′W	X	29
Westside	Aberd	NJ6225	57°19·1′	2°37·4′W	X	37
Westside	Aberd	NJ6513	57°12·6′	2°34·3′W	X	38
Westside	Aberd	NJ7221	57°17·0′	2°27·4′W	X	38
Westside	Aberd	NJ8105	57°8·4′	2°18·4′W	X	38
Westside	Aberd	NJ8820	57°16·5′	2°11·5′W	X	38
Westside	Aberd	NO8596	57°3·5′	2°14·0′W	X	38,45
Westside	Angus	NO6066	56°47·3′	2°38·8′W	X	45
West Side	Blae Gw	SO1907	51°45·6′	3°10·0′W	T	161
Westside	Cumbr	NY3816	54°32·4′	2°57·1′W	X	90
Westside	Midlo	NT1859	55°49·3′	3°18·1′W	X	65,66,72
Westside	Northum	NY7857	54°54·7′	2°20·2′W	X	86,87
West Side	Northum	NZ0074	55°3·9′	1°59·6′W	X	87
West Side	N Yks	SD8195	54°21·3′	2°17·1′W	X	98
West Side	N Yks	SD8893	54°20·2′	2°10·7′W	X	98
West Side	N Yks	SD9182	54°14·3′	2°7·9′W	X	98
Westside	Orkney	HY2824	59°6·1′	3°14·9′W	X	6
Westside	Orkney	HY3729	59°8·9′	3°5·6′W	X	6
Westside	Orkney	HY5332	59°10·6′	2°48·9′W	T	5,6
Westside	S Lanak	NS9834	55°35·6′	3°36·7′W	X	72
West Side	Staffs	SK1058	53°7·4′	1°50·6′W	X	119
Westside Fm	Cambs	TL5970	52°18·5′	0°20·3′E	FM	154
Westside Fm	I of W	SZ4778	50°36·2′	1°19·8′W	FM	196
West Side Ho	Durham	NZ1420	54°34·7′	1°46·6′W	X	92
Westside Ho	N Yks	SD8567	54°6·2′	2°13·3′W	X	98
Westside of Carnousie	Aberd	NJ6551	57°33·1′	2°34·6′W	X	29
Westside of Dalhaikie	Aberd	NO6398	57°4·5′	2°36·2′W	X	37,45
Westside of Kingsford	Aberd	NJ5613	57°12·6′	2°43·2′W	X	37
West Sidewood	S Lanak	NS9751	55°44·7′	3°38·0′W	X	65,72
West Skelston	D & G	NX8285	55°9·0′	3°50·7′W	T	78
West Skerry	Shetld	HU3533	60°5·1′	1°21·8′W	X	4
West Skichen	Angus	NO5141	56°33·8′	2°47·4′W	X	54
West Skilmafilly	Aberd	NJ8939	57°26·7′	2°10·5′W	X	30
West Sleekburn	Northum	NZ2885	55°9·8′	1°33·7′W	T	81
West Somerset Railway	Somer	ST1039	51°8·8′	3°16·8′W	X	181
West Somerton	Norf	TG4619	52°43·0′	1°39·0′E	T	134
West Sous	Orkney	HY4939	59°14·3′	2°53·1′W	X	5
West Southbourne	Bourne	SZ1392	50°43·9′	1°48·6′W	T	195
West Spring Wood	N Yks	SE1593	54°20·2′	1°45·7′W	F	99
West Spurway	Devon	SS8821	50°58·9′	3°35·4′W	X	181
West Stack	Shetld	HU1849	60°13·8′	1°40·0′W	X	3
West Stafford	Dorset	SY7289	50°42·2′	2°23·4′W	T	194
West Steel	E Loth	NT6869	55°55·0′	2°30·3′W	X	67
West Stell	Fife	NT2983	56°2·3′	3°7·9′W	X	66
West Stobswood	Northum	NZ2195	55°15·2′	1°39·7′W	X	81
West Stockwith	Notts	SK7995	53°27·0′	0°48·2′W	T	112
West Stoke	Somer	ST4717	50°57·2′	2°44·9′W	T	193
West Stoke	W Susx	SU8208	50°52·2′	0°49·7′W	T	197
West Stoke Fm	Hants	SU4737	51°8·0′	1°19·3′W	FM	185
West Stoke Ho	W Susx	SU8208	50°52·2′	0°49·7′W	X	197
West Stonesdale	N Yks	NY8802	54°25·0′	2°10·7′W	T	91,92
West Stones Dale	N Yks	NY8803	54°25·6′	2°10·7′W	X	91,92
West Stonesdale Out Pasture	N Yks	NY8703	54°25·6′	2°11·6′W	X	91,92
West Stoneyhill	Aberd	NO8694	57°2·5′	2°13·4′W	X	38,45
West Stoney Keld	Durham	NY9715	54°32·1′	2°2·4′W	X	92
West Stotley	Durham	NY9625	54°37·5′	2°3·3′W	X	91,92
West Stoughton	Somer	ST4149	51°14·5′	2°50·3′W	T	182
West Stour	Dorset	ST7822	51°0·1′	2°18·4′W	T	183
West Stourmouth	Kent	TR2562	51°19·0′	1°14·1′E	T	179
West Stove	Orkney	HY2320	59°3·9′	3°20·1′W	X	6
West Stow	Suff	TL8170	52°18·1′	0°39·7′E	T	144,155
West Stowell	Wilts	SU1362	51°21·6′	1°48·4′W	T	173
West Stow Field	Suff	TL8072	52°19·2′	0°38·9′E	F	144,155
West Stowford Barton	Devon	SS5342	51°9·7′	4°5·8′W	X	180
West Stow Heath	Suff	TL8071	52°18·7′	0°38·8′E	F	144,155
Weststow Long Plantation	Suff	TL8073	52°19·8′	0°38·9′E	F	144,155
West Strath	Aberd	NJ6014	57°13·2′	2°39·3′W	X	37
West Strathan	Highld	NC5663	58°32·1′	4°27·9′W	T	10
West Stratton	Hants	SU5240	51°9·6′	1°15·0′W	T	185
West Street	Kent	TQ9054	51°15·4′	0°44·0′E	T	189
West Street	Kent	TR3254	51°14·5′	1°19·8′E	T	179
West Street	Medway	TQ7376	51°27·6′	0°29·8′E	T	178
West Street	Suff	TL9870	52°17·8′	0°54·6′E	T	144,155
West Street Fm	E Susx	TQ5714	50°54·5′	0°14·4′E	FM	199
West Street Fm	Suff	TM0274	52°19·8′	0°58·3′E	FM	144
West Studdal Fm	Kent	TR3049	51°11·9′	1°17·9′E	FM	179
West Summer Side	N Yks	SE1376	54°11·0′	1°47·6′W	X	99
West Sunderland Fm	Beds	TL2145	52°5·6′	0°13·6′W	FM	153
West Swainsford Fm	Wilts	ST8130	51°4·4′	2°15·9′W	FM	183
West Swale	Kent	TQ9072	51°25·1′	0°44·4′E	W	178
West Swilletts	Dorset	ST4205	50°50·7′	2°49·0′W	X	193
Westsyde	Inverc	NS3269	55°53·3′	4°40·7′W	X	63
West Syke Green Fm	N Yks	SE2357	54°0·8′	1°38·5′W	FM	104
West Syme	N Yks	SE9695	54°20·7′	0°31·0′W	X	94,101
West Taing	Orkney	HY4117	59°2·4′	3°1·2′W	X	6
West Taing	Shetld	HU4470	60°25·0′	1°11·6′W	X	2,3
West Tamana	N Eil	NB0020	58°4·3′	7°4·8′W	X	13
West Tanfield	N Yks	SE2678	54°12·1′	1°35·7′W	T	99
West Taphouse	Corn	SX1563	50°26·5′	4°36·0′W	T	201
West Tapps	Devon	SS8923	51°0·0′	3°34·5′W	X	181
West Tarbert	Arg & Bt	NR8467	55°51·1′	5°26·6′W	T	62
West Tarbert Bay	Arg & Bt	NR6453	55°43·0′	5°45·0′W	W	62
West Tarbet	D & G	NX1330	54°38·1′	4°53·4′W	X	82
West Tarbrax	Angus	NO4341	56°33·7′	2°55·2′W	X	54
West Tarbrax	N Lanak	NS8658	55°48·4′	3°48·7′W	X	65,72
West Tarring	W Susx	TQ1303	50°49·2′	0°23·4′W	T	198
West Tarwathie	Aberd	NJ9458	57°37·0′	2°5·6′W	X	30
West Tayloch	Aberd	NJ5228	57°20·7′	2°47·4′W	X	37
West Tees Br	Durham	NZ1517	54°33·1′	1°45·7′W	X	92
West Tempar	Pth & Kin	NN6857	56°41·4′	4°8·9′W	X	42,51
West Teuchan	Aberd	NK0738	57°26·2′	1°52·5′W	X	30
West, The	Pemb	SN0123	51°52·4′	4°53·1′W	X	145,157,158
West Third	Fife	NO4617	56°20·8′	2°52·0′W	X	59
West Third	Pth & Kin	NN8406	56°14·2′	3°51·8′W	X	58
West Third	Pth & Kin	NN9113	56°18·1′	3°45·2′W	X	58
West Third	Scot Bord	NT6436	55°37·2′	2°33·9′W	T	74
West Thirston	Northum	NU1800	55°17·9′	1°42·6′W	T	81
West Thirston	Northum	NZ1899	55°17·3′	1°42·6′W	T	81
West Thorn	Northum	NZ1476	55°4·9′	1°46·4′W	X	88
West Thornber	N Yks	SD8154	53°59·1′	2°17·0′W	X	103
West Thorney	W Susx	SU7602	50°49·0′	0°54·9′W	T	197
Westthorpe	Derby	SK4579	53°18·6′	1°19·1′W	T	120
West Thorpe	Durham	NZ0914	54°31·5′	1°51·2′W	X	92
West Thunderton	Aberd	NK0746	57°30·5′	1°52·5′W	X	30
West Thurrock	Thurr	TQ5878	51°29·0′	0°16·9′E	T	177
West Thurrock Marshes	Thurr	TQ5777	51°28·4′	0°16·0′E	X	177
West Tilbury	Thurr	TQ6678	51°28·8′	0°23·8′E	T	177,178
West Tilbury Marshes	Thurr	TQ6676	51°27·7′	0°23·8′E	X	177,178
West Tisted	Hants	SU6529	51°3·6′	1°4·0′W	T	185,186
West Tisted Common	Hants	SU6730	51°4·2′	1°2·2′W	X	185,186
West Tober	Corn	SX1676	50°33·5′	4°35·5′W	X	201
West Toe	Orkney	HY5640	59°14·9′	2°45·8′W	X	5
West Tofts	Norf	TL8392	52°29·9′	0°42·2′E	T	144
West Tofts	Pth & Kin	NO1134	56°29·6′	3°26·3′W	X	53
West Tofts Heath	Norf	TL8490	52°28·8′	0°43·0′E	X	144
West Tofts Mere	Norf	TL8491	52°29·4′	0°43·0′E	W	144
West Tolgus	Corn	SW6742	50°14·2′	5°15·7′W	T	203
West Torphin	W Loth	NT0360	55°49·7′	3°32·5′W	X	65
West Torrie	Stir	NN6404	56°12·8′	4°11·1′W	X	57
West Torrington	Lincs	TF1382	53°19·6′	0°17·8′W	T	121
West Torrington Grange	Lincs	TF1481	53°19·1′	0°16·9′W	X	121
West Toun	S Lanak	NS8233	55°34·8′	3°51·9′W	X	71,72
West Tower (Hotel)	Lancs	SD3805	53°32·5′	2°55·7′W	X	108
West-town	Aberd	NJ8921	57°17·0′	2°10·5′W	X	38
West Town	Aberd	NO8379	56°54·4′	2°16·3′W	X	45
West Town	Devon	SS3221	50°58·1′	4°23·2′W	T	190
West Town	Devon	SX8593	50°43·7′	3°37·4′W	X	191
West Town	Devon	SX8797	50°45·9′	3°35·8′W	T	192
Westtown	E Ayr	NS5627	55°31·2′	4°16·4′W	X	71
West Town	Hants	SZ7199	50°47·4′	0°59·2′W	T	197
West Town	Heref	SO4461	52°14·9′	2°48·8′W	T	137,148,149
West Town	N Som	ST4868	51°24·8′	2°44·5′W	T	171,172,182
West Town	S Lanak	NS9342	55°39·8′	3°41·6′W	X	71,72
West Town	Somer	ST5160	51°20·5′	2°41·8′W	T	172,182
West Town	Somer	ST5335	51°7·0′	2°39·9′W	T	182,183
West Town	W Susx	TQ2716	50°56·0′	0°11·2′W	T	198
West Town Fm	Bucks	SU9280	51°30·9′	0°40·1′W	FM	175
West Town Fm	Devon	SX8890	50°42·2′	3°34·8′W	FM	192

West-town of Nemphlar	S Lanak	NS8445	55°41·3′	3°50·3′W	X	72
West Trelowthas	Corn	SW8846	50°16·8′	4°58·2′W	X	204
West Tremabe	Corn	SX2164	50°27·1′	4°30·9′W	X	201
West Trodigal	Arg & Bt	NR6420	55°25·3′	5°43·3′W	X	68
West Tullyfergus	Pth & Kin	NO2148	56°37·3′	3°16·8′W	X	53
West Tump	Glos	SO9113	51°49·2′	2°7·4′W	A	163
West Tump	Pemb	SM5909	51°43·9′	5°29·0′W	X	157
West Tytherley	Hants	SU2729	51°3·8′	1°36·5′W	T	184
West Unthank	Northum	NY7263	54°57·9′	2°25·8′W	X	86,87
Westup Fm	W Susx	TQ2930	51°3·5′	0°9·2′W	FM	187
West Uplaw	E Renf	NS4354	55°45·5′	4°29·7′W	X	64
West Usk Lighthouse	Newp	ST3182	51°32·2′	2°59·3′W	X	171
West Vale	Cald	SE0921	53°41·4′	1°51·4′W	T	104
Westvale	Know	SJ4098	53°28·8′	2°53·8′W	T	108
West Venn	Devon	SX3796	50°44·7′	4°18·2′W	X	190
West View	Cumbr	NY7815	54°32·0′	2°20·0′W	X	91
West View	Cumbr	SD5399	54°23·3′	2°43·0′W	X	97
West View	Cumbr	SD5685	54°15·8′	2°40·1′W	X	97
West View	Hartpl	NZ4835	54°42·7′	1°14·9′W	T	93
West View	Lancs	SD4960	54°2·3′	2°46·3′W	X	97
West View	Warw	SP4367	52°18·2′	1°21·8′W	X	151
West View Fm	Derby	SK2613	52°43·1′	1°36·5′W	FM	128
West View Fm	Lincs	TF1416	52°44·0′	0°18·3′W	FM	130
West View Fm	Notts	SK8263	53°9·7′	0°46·0′W	FM	121
West Village	V of Glam	SS9974	51°27·6′	3°26·8′W	T	170
Westville	Devon	SX7344	50°17·2′	3°46·6′W	T	202
Westville	Notts	SK5147	53°1·3′	1°14·0′W	T	129
Westville Fm	Lincs	TF2952	53°3·2′	0°4·1′W	FM	122
Westville Fm	Lincs	TF3051	53°2·7′	0°3·2′W	FM	122
West Voe	Shetld	HU1761	60°20·2′	1°41·0′W	W	3
West Voe	Shetld	HU3630	60°3·5′	1°20·7′W	W	4
West Voe	Shetld	HU6771	60°25·3′	0°46·5′W	W	2
West Voe of Quarff	Shetld	HU4035	60°6·1′	1°16·3′W	W	4
West Voe of Skellister	Shetld	HU4655	60°16·9′	1°9·6′W	W	3
West Voe of Sumburgh	Shetld	HU3909	59°52·1′	1°17·7′W	W	4
West Vows	Fife	NT2888	56°5·0′	3°9·0′W	X	66
West Vows	Fife	NT4799	56°11·1′	2°50·8′W	X	59
West Walk	Hants	SU5912	50°54·5′	1°9·3′W	F	196
West Walkinshaw Fm	Renf	NS4666	55°52·0′	4°27·2′W	FM	64
West Walton	E Renf	NS4854	55°45·6′	4°24·9′W	X	64
West Walton	Norf	TF4713	52°41·9′	0°10·9′E	T	131,143
West Wantley Fm	W Susx	TQ0815	50°55·7′	0°27·4′W	FM	197
Westward	Cumbr	NY2744	54°47·4′	3°7·7′W	T	85
West Ward	Shetld	HU2245	60°11·6′	1°35·7′W	X	4
Westward Ho!	Devon	SS4329	51°2·6′	4°14·0′W	T	180
Westward Park	Cumbr	NY2844	54°47·4′	3°6·8′W	X	85
West Water	Angus	NO5269	56°48·9′	2°46·7′W	W	44
Westwater	D & G	NY3082	55°7·9′	3°5·4′W	X	79
West Water	Scot Bord	NT1351	55°44·9′	3°22·7′W	W	65,72
West Water	S Lanak	NT0018	55°27·0′	3°34·4′W	W	78
West Water	S Lanak	NT0851	55°44·9′	3°27·5′W	W	65,72
West Water	Somer	SS8433	51°5·3′	3°39·0′W	W	181
Westwater Allotment	Somer	SS8433	51°5·3′	3°39·0′W	X	181
Westwater Br	Angus	NO6065	56°46·7′	2°38·8′W	X	45
Westwater Fm	Somer	SS8433	51°5·3′	3°39·0′W	FM	181
West Watergate	Corn	SX2153	50°21·2′	4°30·6′W	T	201
West Waterhall	Orkney	HY4707	58°57·1′	2°54·8′W	X	6,7
West Water Reservoir	Scot Bord	NT1152	55°45·4′	3°24·7′W	W	65,72
West Watford	Herts	TQ1095	51°38·8′	0°24·2′W	T	166,176
Westway	Devon	SS8710	50°52·9′	3°36·0′W	X	192
Westway Fm	Devon	SS8213	50°54·5′	3°40·3′W	FM	181
West Weare	Dorset	SY6872	50°33·0′	2°26·7′W	X	194
West Webburn River	Devon	SX6976	50°34·4′	3°50·6′W	W	191
Westweek	Devon	SX4193	50°43·1′	4°14·8′W	X	190
Westweek Barton	Devon	SX4193	50°43·1′	4°14·8′W	X	190
Westweekmoor	Devon	SX4093	50°43·1′	4°15·6′W	T	190
West Weetwood	Northum	NU0028	55°33·0′	1°59·6′W	X	75
Westwell	Kent	TQ9847	51°11·5′	0°50·4′E	T	189
Westwell	Oxon	SP2210	51°47·5′	1°40·5′W	T	163
Westwell Copse	Oxon	SP2109	51°47·0′	1°41·3′W	F	163
Westwell Leacon	Kent	TQ9647	51°11·5′	0°48·7′E	T	189
West Wellow	Hants	SU2919	50°58·4′	1°34·8′W	T	185
West Wellow Common	Hants	SU2818	50°57·9′	1°35·7′W	X	184
Westwells	Wilts	ST8568	51°24·9′	2°12·6′W	T	173
West Wemyss	Fife	NT3294	56°8·3′	3°5·2′W	T	59
West Whitefield	Pth & Kin	NO1634	56°29·7′	3°21·4′W	T	53
West Whitehill	Northum	NY9985	55°9·8′	2°0·5′W	X	81
West Whitelee	E Ayr	NS4549	55°42·8′	4°27·6′W	X	64
West Whiteside	Aberd	NJ9856	57°35·9′	2°1·5′W	X	30
West Whitnole	Devon	SS8818	50°57·3′	3°35·3′W	X	181
Westwick	Cambs	TL4265	52°16·1′	0°5·3′E	T	154
Westwick	Durham	NZ0715	54°32·1′	1°53·1′W	T	92
West Wick	Essex	TQ9796	51°37·9′	0°51·2′E	X	168
Westwick	Norf	TG2726	52°47·3′	1°22·4′E	T	133,134
West Wick	N Som	ST3661	51°20·9′	2°54·8′W	T	182
Westwick	N Yks	SE3466	54°5·6′	1°28·4′W	X	99
Westwick Field	Cambs	TL4266	52°16·7′	0°5·3′E	X	154
Westwick Fm	Derby	SK3370	53°13·8′	1°29·9′W	FM	119
Westwick Fm	Essex	TL9907	51°43·8′	0°53·3′E	FM	168
Westwick Fm	Suff	TM1171	52°18·0′	1°6·1′E	FM	144,155
West Wick Fm	Wilts	SU1762	51°21·6′	1°45·0′W	FM	173
Westwick Hall	Herts	TL1006	51°44·7′	0°24·0′W	X	166
Westwick Hall Fm	N Yks	SE3566	54°5·6′	1°27·5′W	FM	99
West Wickham	Brom	TQ3865	51°22·3′	0°0·7′W	T	177
West Wickham	Cambs	TL6149	52°7·2′	0°21·5′E	T	154
Westwick Hill	Norf	TG2727	52°47·8′	1°22·4′E	X	133,134
Westwick Ho	Norf	TG2826	52°47·2′	1°23·3′E	X	133,134
Westwick Moor	Durham	NZ0817	54°33·1′	1°52·2′W	X	92
Westwick Row	Herts	TL0906	51°44·8′	0°24·9′W	X	166
West Wilkwood	Northum	NT8703	55°19·5′	2°11·9′W	X	80
West Williamston	Pemb	SN0305	51°42·8′	4°50·7′W	T	157,158
West Willoughby	Lincs	SK9643	52°58·8′	0°33·8′W	T	130
West Winch	Norf	TF6215	52°42·7′	0°24·3′E	T	132
Westwinds	E Yorks	SE9929	53°45·1′	0°29·5′W	X	106
West Windygoul	E Loth	NT4072	55°56·5′	2°57·2′W	X	66
West Wini Skerry	Orkney	ND3883	58°44·1′	3°3·8′W	X	7
West Winner	C of Port	SZ6898	50°46·9′	1°1·7′W	X	196
West Winterslow	Wilts	SU2332	51°5·4′	1°39·9′W	T	184
West Wirren	Angus	NO5174	56°51·5′	2°47·8′W	H	44
West Withens Clough	Derby	SE1102	53°31·1′	1°49·6′W	X	110
West Withy Fm	Somer	ST0030	51°3·9′	3°25·2′W	FM	181
West Wittering	W Susx	SZ7798	50°46·8′	0°54·1′W	T	197
West Witton	N Yks	SE0688	54°17·5′	1°54·1′W	T	99
West Witton Moor	N Yks	SE0587	54°17·0′	1°55·0′W	X	98
West Witton Moor	N Yks	SE0687	54°17·0′	1°54·1′W	X	99
West Witton Row	Durham	NZ1429	54°39·6′	1°46·6′W	X	92
West Wold Fm	N Yks	SE8068	54°6·3′	0°46·2′W	FM	100
West Wolves Fm	W Susx	TQ1216	50°56·2′	0°24·0′W	FM	198
West Wong	Leic	SK8133	52°53·5′	0°47·4′W	X	130
West Wood	Aberd	NJ6733	57°23·4′	2°32·5′W	X	29
West Wood	Barns	SK3398	53°28·9′	1°29·8′W	F	110,111
West Wood	Beds	SP9962	52°15·1′	0°32·6′W	F	153
West Wood	Brad	SE1441	53°52·1′	1°46·8′W	F	104
West Wood	Cambs	TL1569	52°18·7′	0°18·4′W	F	153
West Wood	Derby	SK4172	53°14·8′	1°22·7′W	F	120
Westwood	Devon	SS7423	50°59·8′	3°47·4′W	X	180
Westwood	Devon	SX5499	50°46·6′	4°3·9′W	X	191
Westwood	Devon	SX7195	50°44·7′	3°49·3′W	X	191
Westwood	Devon	SX8791	50°42·7′	3°35·7′W	X	192
Westwood	Devon	SX9680	50°36·9′	3°27·8′W	T	192
Westwood	Devon	SY0198	50°46·6′	3°23·9′W	T	192
Westwood	D & G	NY1580	55°6·7′	3°19·5′W	X	79
West Wood	Dorset	ST8918	50°57·9′	2°9·0′W	F	184
Westwood	Durham	NZ0315	54°32·1′	1°56·8′W	X	92
West Wood	Durham	NZ1739	54°45·0′	1°43·7′W	F	92
West Wood	Essex	TQ8088	51°34·0′	0°36·2′E	F	178
West Wood	E Susx	TQ3419	50°57·5′	0°5·1′W	F	198
West Wood	E Yorks	SE7658	54°1·0′	0°50·0′W	F	105,106
Westwood	E Yorks	TA0239	53°50·5′	0°26·6′W	X	106,107
West Wood	Fife	NO4406	56°14·8′	2°53·8′W	F	59
West Wood	Glos	SP0223	51°54·6′	1°57·9′W	F	163
West Wood	Glos	ST8092	51°37·8′	2°16·9′W	F	162,173
West Wood	Hants	SU4129	51°3·8′	1°24·5′W	F	185
West Wood	Hants	SU5547	51°13·4′	1°12·4′W	F	185
West Wood	Hants	SU5825	51°1·5′	1°10·0′W	F	185
West Wood	Herts	TL1625	51°54·9′	0°18·4′W	F	166
Westwood	I of W	SZ5392	50°43·7′	1°14·6′W	X	196
Westwood	Kent	TQ5970	51°24·6′	0°17·6′E	X	177
Westwood	Kent	TR1343	51°9·0′	1°3·1′E	FM	179,189
Westwood	Kent	TR1749	51°12·2′	1°6·8′E	T	179,189
Westwood	Kent	TR3668	51°21·9′	1°23·8′E	T	179
West Wood	Leeds	SE1937	53°50·0′	1°42·3′W	F	104
Westwood	Leeds	SE3847	53°55·3′	1°24·9′W	X	104
Westwood	N Lincs	SE9509	53°34·4′	0°33·5′W	F	112
West Wood	Norf	TF9526	52°48·0′	0°54·0′E	F	132
West Wood	Northum	NT9204	55°20·0′	2°7·1′W	F	80
Westwood	Northum	NY9165	54°59·0′	2°8·0′W	X	87
West Wood	Notts	SK4551	53°3·5′	1°19·3′W	T	120
West Wood	Notts	SK5678	53°18·0′	1°9·2′W	F	120
Westwood	Notts	SK7170	53°13·6′	0°55·8′W	X	120
West Wood	Notts	SK8472	53°14·5′	0°44·1′W	F	121
West Wood	N Yks	NY9001	54°24·5′	2°8·8′W	F	91,92
West Wood	N Yks	SE0689	54°18·0′	1°54·0′W	F	99
West Wood	N Yks	SE1367	54°6·2′	1°47·7′W	F	99
West Wood	N Yks	SE1799	54°23·4′	1°43·9′W	F	99
Westwood	N Yks	SE2578	54°12·1′	1°36·6′W	X	99
West Wood	N Yks	SE7173	54°9·1′	0°54·4′W	F	100
Westwood	Peterb	TL1699	52°34·8′	0°16·9′W	T	142
Westwood	Pth & Kin	NO0833	56°29·1′	3°29·2′W	X	52,53
Westwood	S Lanak	NS6253	55°45·3′	4°11·5′W	T	64
West Wood	Somer	ST1042	51°10·4′	3°16·9′W	F	181
West Wood	Somer	ST4529	51°3·7′	2°46·7′W	F	193
West Wood	Somer	ST6921	50°59·5′	2°26·1′W	F	183
Westwood	Stir	NS7494	56°7·6′	4°1·2′W	X	57
Westwood	Wilts	ST8059	51°20·0′	2°16·8′W	T	173
Westwood	Wilts	SU1131	51°4·9′	1°50·2′W	T	184
West Wood	W Susx	SU9513	50°54·7′	0°38·5′W	F	197
West Wooda	Devon	SS5416	50°55·6′	4°12·0′W	X	180,190
Westwood Belt	Norf	TF7327	52°49·0′	0°34·4′E	F	132
Westwood Brook	Derby	SK4360	53°8·4′	1°21·0′W	W	120
West Woodburn	Durham	NZ3935	54°42·8′	1°23·3′W	X	93
West Woodburn	Northum	NY8986	55°10·3′	2°9·9′W	T	80
Westwood Common	Surrey	TQ2046	51°12·3′	0°16·8′W	X	187
Westwood Coppice	Birm	SP0896	52°33·9′	1°52·5′W	F	139
Westwood Cottage	Pth & Kin	NO1623	56°23·8′	3°21·2′W	X	53,58
Westwood Country Park	Sheff	SK3398	53°28·9′	1°29·8′W	X	110,111
Westwood Court	Kent	TR0259	51°17·9′	0°54·2′E	X	178
West Woodend	Pth & Kin	NO1337	56°31·3′	3°24·4′W	X	53
Westwood Fm	Devon	SS8603	50°49·2′	3°36·7′W	FM	191
Westwood Fm	Devon	ST2004	50°50·0′	3°7·8′W	FM	192,193
Westwood Fm	Dorset	SY9880	50°37·4′	2°1·3′W	FM	195
Westwood Fm	Essex	TL8330	51°56·5′	0°40·1′E	FM	168
Westwood Fm	Ghead	NZ1162	54°57·4′	1°49·3′W	FM	88
Westwood Fm	Heref	SO6059	52°13·9′	2°34·7′W	FM	149
Westwood Fm	Notts	SK7066	53°11·4′	0°56·7′W	FM	120
Westwood Fm	Notts	SK7170	53°13·6′	0°55·8′W	FM	120
Westwood Fm	N Yks	NZ5704	54°25·9′	1°6·9′W	FM	93
Westwood Fm	N Yks	SE2577	54°11·5′	1°36·6′W	FM	99
Westwood Fm	Shrops	SO7091	52°31·2′	2°26·1′W	FM	138
Westwood Fm	Surrey	TQ4253	51°15·7′	0°2·5′E	FM	187
Westwood Fm	Wilts	ST8070	51°26·0′	2°16·9′W	FM	173
Westwood Fm	Wilts	ST8825	51°1·7′	2°9·9′W	FM	183
Westwood Fm	Wok	SU7664	51°22·4′	0°54·1′W	FM	175,186
Westwood Fm	Worcs	SO6771	52°20·4′	2°28·7′W	FM	138
Westwood Fm	Worcs	SO8763	52°16·1′	2°11·0′W	FM	150
Westwood Grange	Ches	SJ2979	53°18·4′	3°3·5′W	X	117
Westwood Hall	Suff	TM1062	52°13·2′	1°4·9′E	X	155
Westwood Hall Sch	Staffs	SJ9656	53°6·3′	2°3·2′W	X	118
West Woodhay	W Berks	SU3963	51°22·1′	1°26·0′W	T	174
West Woodhay Down	W Berks	SU3861	51°21·0′	1°26·9′W	X	174
West Woodhay Ho	W Berks	SU3863	51°22·1′	1°26·9′W	A	174
Westwood Heath	Cov	SP2876	52°23·1′	1°34·9′W	T	140
Westwood Ho	E Yorks	SE9443	53°52·7′	0°33·8′W	X	106
West Wood Ho	N Yks	SE1368	54°6·7′	1°47·7′W	X	99
Westwood Ho	Worcs	SO8763	52°16·1′	2°11·0′W	A	150
West Woodlands	Somer	ST7743	51°11·4′	2°19·4′W	T	183
Westwood Lane	Stir	NS7495	56°8·1′	4°1·2′W	X	57
Westwood Lo	Northnts	SP9990	52°30·2′	0°32·1′W	X	141
Westwood Lodge	Suff	TM4673	52°18·2′	1°36·9′E	X	156
Westwood Manor Fm	Oxon	SU7088	51°35·4′	0°59·0′W	FM	175
Westwood Marshes	Suff	TM4773	52°18·2′	1°37·8′E	W	156
Westwood Park	Essex	TL9630	51°56·3′	0°51·5′E	T	168
Westwood Park	Heref	SO6060	52°14·4′	2°34·8′W	X	138,149
Westwood Park	Salf	SJ7599	53°29·5′	2°22·2′W	T	109
Westwood Place	Surrey	SU9250	51°14·7′	0°40·5′W	X	186
Westwoods	Devon	SS9724	51°0·6′	3°27·7′W	X	181
West Woods	Leeds	SE4043	53°53·1′	1°23·1′W	F	105
West Woods	Wilts	SU1566	51°23·8′	1°46·7′W	F	173
West Woods Fm	Dorset	ST5703	50°49·7′	2°36·3′W	FM	194
West Woods Fm	Leeds	SE4143	53°53·1′	1°22·2′W	FM	105
West Woodside	Cumbr	NY3049	54°50·1′	3°5·0′W	X	85
Westwoodside	N Lincs	SK7499	53°29·2′	0°52·7′W	T	112
West Woods of Ethie	Angus	NO6545	56°36·0′	2°33·8′W	F	54
West Woodyates Manor	Dorset	SU0119	50°58·5′	1°58·8′W	X	184
West Worldham	Hants	SU7436	51°7·3′	0°56·2′W	T	186
West Worlington	Devon	SS7613	50°54·4′	3°45·4′W	T	180
West Worsall	N Yks	NZ3706	54°27·1′	1°25·3′W	X	93
West Worthele	Devon	SX6254	50°22·4′	3°56·1′W	X	202
Westworth Fm	Dorset	SU0710	50°53·6′	1°53·6′W	FM	195
West Worthing	W Susx	TQ1302	50°48·6′	0°23·4′W	T	198
Westworth Wood	Red & Cl	NZ6313	54°30·7′	1°1·2′W	F	94
Westworthy	Devon	SS6703	50°48·9′	3°52·9′W	X	191
West Wotton	Devon	SX7498	50°46·3′	3°46·8′W	X	191
West Wotton	Devon	SX7598	50°46·3′	3°46·0′W	X	191
West Wratting	Cambs	TL6051	52°8·3′	0°20·7′E	T	154
West Wratting Park	Cambs	TL6151	52°8·3′	0°21·6′E	X	154
West Wratting Valley Fm	Cambs	TL5654	52°10·0′	0°17·3′E	FM	154
West Wycombe	Bucks	SU8294	51°38·6′	0°48·5′W	T	175
West Wycombe Ho	Bucks	SU8294	51°38·6′	0°48·5′W	X	175
West Wyke	Devon	SX6592	50°43·0′	3°54·4′W	X	191
West Wykeham Village	Lincs	TF2188	53°22·7′	0°10·4′W	A	113,122
West Wylam	Northum	NZ1063	54°57·9′	1°50·2′W	T	88
Westy	Warr	SJ6287	53°23·0′	2°33·9′W	T	109
West Yard	Devon	SS4814	50°54·6′	4°9·3′W	X	180
Westyard	Devon	SS6213	50°54·2′	3°57·4′W	X	180
West Yarde	Devon	SS7234	51°5·7′	3°49·3′W	X	180
West Yatton	Wilts	ST8574	51°28·1′	2°12·6′W	T	173
West Yatton Down	Wilts	ST8575	51°28·7′	2°12·6′W	X	173
Westy Bank Wood	N Yks	SE0654	53°59·2′	1°54·1′W	F	104
West Yell	Shetld	HU4582	60°31·4′	1°10·3′W	T	1,2,3
West Yeo	Devon	SS7814	50°55·0′	3°43·8′W	X	180
West Yeo	Somer	ST3330	51°4·2′	2°57·0′W	T	182
West Yeo Moor	Devon	SS7916	50°56·1′	3°42·9′W	X	180
Westyett Fm	S Lanak	NS9449	55°43·6′	3°40·8′W	FM	72
West Yoke	Kent	TQ5965	51°21·9′	0°17·4′E	T	177
West Youlstone	Corn	SS2615	50°54·7′	4°28·1′W	T	190
Wet Car Wood	N Yks	SE2566	54°5·6′	1°36·6′W	X	99
Weterton Ho	Durham	NZ3630	54°40·1′	1°26·1′W	X	93
Wet Furrows Fm	Red & Cl	NZ6718	54°33·4′	0°57·4′W	FM	94
Wet Gate Fm	Warr	SJ7087	53°23·0′	2°26·7′W	FM	109
Wetham Green	Kent	TQ8468	51°23·1′	0°39·1′E	T	178
Wetheral	Cumbr	NY4654	54°52·9′	2°50·1′W	T	86
Wetheral Pasture	Cumbr	NY4553	54°52·4′	2°51·0′W	X	86
Wetheral Plain	Cumbr	NY4655	54°53·5′	2°50·1′W	T	86
Wetheral Shield	Cumbr	NY4652	54°51·8′	2°50·1′W	X	86
Wetherby	Leeds	SE4048	53°55·8′	1°23·0′W	T	105
Wetherby Grange	Leeds	SE4146	53°54·8′	1°22·1′W	X	105
Wether Cairn	Northum	NT9411	55°23·8′	2°5·3′W	H	80
Wethercote	N Yks	SE5286	54°16·3′	1°11·7′W	X	100
Wethercote Fm	N Yks	SE5692	54°19·5′	1°7·9′W	FM	100
Wether Cote Fm	N Yks	SE6489	54°17·8′	1°0·6′W	FM	94,100
Wethercotes	Derby	SK0187	53°23·0′	1°58·7′W	X	110
Wetherden	Suff	TM0062	52°13·4′	0°56·1′E	T	155
Wetherden Hall	Suff	TL9751	52°7·6′	0°53·1′E	X	155
Wetherden Hall Fm	Suff	TM0164	52°14·5′	0°57·0′E	FM	155
Wetherden Upper Town	Suff	TM0165	52°15·0′	0°57·1′E	T	155
Wether Down	Hants	SU6719	50°58·2′	1°2·4′W	H	185
Wether Down	Oxon	SU4384	51°33·4′	1°22·4′W	X	174
Wether Down	W Berks	SU3281	51°31·9′	1°31·9′W	X	174
Wether Fell	N Yks	SD8787	54°17·0′	2°11·6′W	X	98
Wether Fell Side	N Yks	SD8787	54°17·0′	2°11·6′W	X	98
Wetherham	Corn	SX0575	50°32·8′	4°44·8′W	X	200
Wether Hill	Aberd	NJ5654	57°34·7′	2°43·7′W	H	29
Wether Hill	Aberd	NJ6337	57°25·6′	2°36·5′W	H	29
Wether Hill	Cumbr	NY3463	54°57·7′	3°1·4′W	X	85
Wether Hill	Cumbr	NY4516	54°32·4′	2°50·6′W	H	90
Wether Hill	Cumbr	NY7404	54°26·1′	2°23·6′W	X	91
Wether Hill	D & G	NS6901	55°17·4′	4°3·3′W	X	77
Wether Hill	D & G	NS7301	55°17·5′	3°59·6′W	H	77
Wether Hill	D & G	NS7703	55°18·6′	3°55·8′W	H	78
Wether Hill	D & G	NS8411	55°23·0′	3°49·4′W	H	71,78
Wether Hill	D & G	NS8809	55°22·0′	3°45·6′W	H	71,78
Wether Hill	D & G	NX7087	55°9·9′	4°2·0′W	H	77
Wether Hill	D & G	NX7094	55°13·6′	4°2·2′W	H	77
Wether Hill	Dorset	ST6403	50°49·8′	2°30·3′W	X	194
Wether Hill	Durham	NZ1017	54°33·1′	1°50·3′W	X	92
Wether Hill	Fife	NT0495	56°8·5′	3°32·3′W	H	58
Wether Hill	Northum	NT9012	55°24·4′	2°9·0′W	H	80
Wether Hill	Northum	NU0114	55°25·4′	1°58·6′W	H	81
Wether Hill	Northum	NY9190	55°12·5′	2°8·1′W	H	80
Wether Hill	N Yks	SE6499	54°23·2′	1°0·4′W	X	94,100
Wether Hill	Pth & Kin	NN9106	56°14·3′	3°45·1′W	H	58
Wetherhill Cairn	E Ayr	NS7230	55°33·1′	4°1·3′W	A	71
Wether Holm	Shetld	HU4672	60°26·0′	1°9·4′W	X	2,3
Wether Holm	Shetld	HU5365	60°22·2′	1°1·8′W	X	2,3
Wether Holm	Shetld	HU6872	60°25·8′	0°45·4′W	X	2
Wetherhorn Hill	Scot Bord	NY4394	55°14·5′	2°53·4′W	H	79
Wetherhouse Moor	N Yks	SE5594	54°20·6′	1°8·8′W	X	100
Wetheriggs	Cumbr	NY5526	54°37·9′	2°41·4′W	X	90
Wetheringsett	Suff	TM1266	52°15·3′	1°6·8′E	T	155
Wetheringsett Hall	Suff	TM1366	52°15·3′	1°7·6′E	X	156
Wether Lair	Northum	NY7096	55°15·7′	2°27·9′W	H	80
Wether Lair	Northum	NY7695	55°15·2′	2°22·2′W	H	80
Wetherlam	Cumbr	NY2801	54°24·2′	3°6·1′W	H	89,90
Wether Law	D & G	NY4195	55°15·0′	2°55·3′W	X	79
Wether Law	Pth & Kin	NO0411	56°17·2′	3°32·6′W	X	58
Wether Law	Scot Bord	NT1241	55°39·5′	3°23·5′W	H	72
Wether Law	Scot Bord	NT1358	55°48·7′	3°22·9′W	H	65,72
Wether Law	Scot Bord	NT1948	55°43·4′	3°16·9′W	H	72
Wether Law	Scot Bord	NT4200	55°17·7′	2°54·4′W	H	79

Wether Law	Scot Bord	NT6560	55°50·2'	2°33·1'W	X	67
Wethersfield	Essex	TL7131	51°57·3'	0°29·7'E	T	167
Wethersfield Airfield	Essex	TL7233	51°58·6'	0°30·6'E	X	167
Wethersta	Shetld	HU3665	60°22·3'	1°20·3'W	T	2,3
Wetherstaness	Shetld	HU3565	60°22·3'	1°21·4'W	X	2,3
Wetherup Street	Suff	TM1364	52°14·2'	1°7·6'E	T	156
Wetlands Woods	W Susx	TQ3127	51°1·9'	0°7·5'W	F	187,198
Wet Level	E Susx	TQ8627	51°1·0'	0°39·5'E	X	189,199
Wet Level	E Susx	TQ8726	51°0·4'	0°40·3'E	X	199
Wetley Abbey	Staffs	SJ9648	53°2·0'	2°3·2'W	X	118
Wetleyhay Wood	Staffs	SK1611	52°42·0'	1°45·4'W	F	128
Wetley Moor	Staffs	SJ9248	53°2·0'	2°6·8'W	X	118
Wetley Rocks	Staffs	SJ9649	53°2·5'	2°3·2'W	T	118
Wetley's Wood	Northnts	SP6641	52°4·0'	1°1·8'W	F	152
Wet Moor	Somer	ST4524	51°1·0'	2°46·7'W	X	193
Wetmoor Hall Fm	Staffs	SK2525	52°49·6'	1°37·3'W	FM	128
Wetmore	Heref	SO4477	52°23·5'	2°49·0'W	X	137,148
Wetmore	Staffs	SK2524	52°49·0'	1°37·3'W	T	128
Wetmore Barn	Heref	SO4376	52°23·0'	2°49·9'W	X	137,148
Wetmore Fm	Shrops	SO5089	52°30·0'	2°43·8'W	FM	137,138
Wet Moss	Lancs	SD7619	53°40·3'	2°21·4'W	X	109
Wetness	Aberd	NK0361	57°38·6'	1°56·5'W	X	30
Wetreins Green	Ches	SJ4353	53°4·5'	2°50·6'W	X	117
Wetreins, The	Ches	SJ4452	53°4·0'	2°49·7'W	X	117
Wetshaw Hope	Northum	NY8589	55°12·0'	2°13·7'W	X	80
Wetshod	E Dunb	NS6475	55°57·2'	4°10·2'W	X	64
Wet Side Edge	Cumbr	NY2702	54°24·7'	3°7·1'W	X	89,90
Wet Slack	D & G	NT1700	55°17·5'	3°18·0'W	X	79
Wet Slack	D & G	NT1800	55°17·5'	3°17·0'W	X	79
Wet Slack Ridge	Sheff	SK2293	53°26·2'	1°39·7'W	X	110
Wet Sleddale Reservoir	Cumbr	NY5411	54°29·8'	2°42·2'W	W	90
Wettenhall	Ches	SJ6261	53°8·9'	2°33·7'W	T	118
Wettenhall Brook	Ches	SJ5761	53°8·9'	2°38·2'W	W	117
Wettenhall Brook	Ches	SJ6161	53°8·9'	2°34·6'W	W	118
Wettenhall Green	Ches	SJ6260	53°8·4'	2°33·7'W	T	118
Wettenhall Hall	Ches	SJ6262	53°9·5'	2°33·7'W	X	118
Wettles	Shrops	SO4386	52°28·4'	2°50·0'W	T	137
Wetton	Heref	SO3753	52°10·5'	2°54·9'W	X	148,149
Wetton	Staffs	SK1055	53°5·8'	1°50·6'W	T	119
Wetton Hill	Staffs	SK1056	53°6·3'	1°50·6'W	H	119
Wetton Low	Staffs	SK1154	53°5·2'	1°49·7'W	X	119
Wettonmill	Staffs	SK0956	53°6·3'	1°51·5'W	X	119
Wettyfoot	Aberd	NJ6349	57°32·0'	2°36·6'W	X	29
Wetwang	E Yorks	SE9359	54°1·4'	0°34·4'W	T	106
Wetwang Grange	E Yorks	SE9460	54°1·9'	0°33·5'W	X	101
Wet Wood	D & G	NX8097	55°15·4'	3°52·9'W	F	78
Wet Wood	E Susx	TQ6811	50°52·7'	0°23·7'E	F	199
Wetwood	Staffs	SJ7733	52°53·9'	2°20·1'W	T	127
Wetwood	Staffs	SJ9761	53°9·0'	2°2·3'W	X	118
Wetwood Hill	D & G	NT2102	55°18·6'	3°14·2'W	H	79
Wetwood Rig	D & G	NT2201	55°18·1'	3°13·3'W	X	79
Wexcombe	Wilts	SU2759	51°20·0'	1°36·4'W	T	174
Wexcombe Down	Wilts	SU2757	51°18·9'	1°36·4'W	X	174
Wexland Fm	Wilts	SU1348	51°14·1'	1°48·4'W	FM	184
Wexland Hanging	Wilts	SU1148	51°14·1'	1°50·2'W	X	184
Wey and Arun Canal	Surrey	TQ0337	51°7·6'	0°31·3'W	W	186
Weybeards Fm	Hill	TQ0491	51°36·7'	0°29·5'W	FM	176
Weybourne	Norf	TG1142	52°56·3'	1°8·8'E	T	133
Weybourne	Surrey	SU8549	51°14·3'	0°46·6'W	T	186
Weybourne Heath	Norf	TG1241	52°55·7'	1°9·7'E	X	133
Weybourne Hope	Norf	TG1143	52°56·8'	1°8·8'E	X	133
Weybread	Suff	TM2480	52°22·6'	1°17·9'E	T	156
Weybread Ho	Suff	TM2481	52°23·1'	1°17·9'E	X	156
Weybridge	Surrey	TQ0864	51°22·1'	0°26·5'W	T	176,187
Weybridge Fm	Cambs	TL1873	52°20·8'	0°15·7'W	FM	153
Weycock Hill	Win & Maid	SU8277	51°29·4'	0°48·7'W	X	175
Weycroft	Devon	SY3099	50°47·4'	2°59·2'W	T	193
Weydale	Highld	ND1465	58°34·1'	3°28·2'W	X	11,12
Weydale Fm	N Yks	TA0185	54°15·3'	0°26·6'W	FM	101
Weydale Moss	Highld	ND1365	58°34·1'	3°29·3'W	X	11,12
Weydown Common	Surrey	SU9034	51°6·1'	0°42·5'W	X	186
Weyhill	Hants	SU3146	51°13·0'	1°33·0'W	T	185
Weyhill Service Area	Hants	SU3246	51°13·0'	1°32·1'W	X	185
Wey Ho	Somer	ST1826	51°1·9'	3°9·8'W	X	181,193
Weyland	Orkney	HY4731	59°10·0'	2°55·1'W	X	5,6
Weylands Fm	Suff	TM0036	51°59·4'	0°55·2'E	FM	155
Weyman's Wood	Worcs	SO7262	52°15·6'	2°24·2'W	F	138,149
Weymouth	Dorset	SY6779	50°36·8'	2°27·6'W	T	194
Weymouth	Staffs	SJ7440	52°57·6'	2°22·8'W	X	118
Weymouth Bay	Dorset	SY6980	50°37·4'	2°25·9'W	W	194
Wey-South Path	Surrey	TQ0242	51°10·3'	0°32·1'W	X	186
Wey-South Path	W Susx	TQ0316	50°56·3'	0°31·7'W	X	197
Wey-South Path	W Susx	TQ0628	51°2·7'	0°28·9'W	X	187,197
Wey Street Fm	Kent	TR0231	51°2·8'	0°53·3'E	FM	189
Wey Street Fm	Kent	TR0561	51°18·9'	0°56·9'E	FM	179
Weythel	Powys	SO2357	52°12·6'	3°7·2'W	T	148
Wgi-fawr	Powys	SN9795	52°32·8'	3°30·7'W	X	136
Whaa Field	Shetld	HU4055	60°16·9'	1°16·1'W	X	3
Whaal Voe	Shetld	HU2958	60°18·6'	1°28·0'W	W	3
Whaddon	Bucks	SP8034	52°0·2'	0°49·7'W	T	152,165
Whaddon	Cambs	TL3546	52°6·0'	0°1·3'W	T	154
Whaddon	Glos	SO8313	51°49·2'	2°14·4'W	T	162
Whaddon	Glos	SO9622	51°54·0'	2°3·1'W	T	163
Whaddon	Wilts	ST8761	51°21·1'	2°10·8'W	T	173
Whaddon	Wilts	SU1926	51°2·2'	1°43·4'W	T	184
Whaddon Chase	Bucks	SP8032	51°59·1'	0°49·7'W	X	152,165
Whaddon Common	Wilts	SU2026	51°2·2'	1°42·5'W	X	184
Whaddonfield Fm	Bucks	SP7211	51°47·8'	0°57·0'W	FM	165
Whaddon Fm	Bucks	SP9221	51°53·0'	0°39·4'W	FM	165
Whaddon Fm	Hants	SU5122	50°59·9'	1°16·0'W	FM	185
Whaddon Fm	Warw	SP2441	52°4·2'	1°38·6'W	FM	151
Whaddon Gap	Cambs	TL3446	52°6·0'	0°2·2'W	T	154
Whaddon Grove Fm	Wilts	ST8861	51°21·1'	2°10·0'W	FM	173
Whaddon Hill Fm	Bucks	SP7813	51°48·8'	0°51·7'W	FM	165
Whaddon Ho	Somer	ST6836	51°7·6'	2°27·1'W	X	183
Wha House Fm	Cumbr	NY2000	54°23·6'	3°13·5'W	FM	89,90
Whaick	Pth & Kin	NN8806	56°14·3'	3°48·0'W	X	58
Whaiff Ho	Lincs	TF3162	53°8·6'	0°2·1'W	X	122
Whaitber	N Yks	SD9673	54°9·3'	2°31·7'W	X	97
Whale	Cumbr	NY5221	54°35·2'	2°44·1'W	T	90
Whale Back	Shetld	HP6204	60°43·1'	0°51·3'W	X	1
Whaleback	Shetld	HZ2170	59°31·2'	1°37·2'W	X	4
Whalebone Fm	Ches	SJ6776	53°17·0'	2°29·3'W	FM	118
Whalebone Fm	Wrex	SJ4343	52°59·1'	2°50·5'W	FM	117
Whalebone Marshes	Medway	TQ7677	51°28·1'	0°32·4'E	X	178
Whale Chine	I of W	SZ4678	50°36·2'	1°20·6'W	X	196
Whalecombe Fm	Pemb	SN0005	51°42·7'	4°53·3'W	FM	157,158
Whale Cottage	Highld	NH5093	57°54·3'	4°31·4'W	X	20
Whale Firth	Shetld	HU4693	60°37·3'	1°9·1'W	W	1,2
Whale Geo	Orkney	HY5140	59°14·9'	2°51·1'W	X	5
Whale Geo	Orkney	HY6921	59°4·8'	2°32·0'W	X	5
Whale Geo	Shetld	HU3517	59°56·5'	1°21·9'W	X	4
Whale Geo	Shetld	HU4493	60°37·3'	1°11·3'W	X	1,2
Whale Geo	Shetld	HU5698	60°39·9'	0°58·0'W	X	1
Whale Geo	Shetld	HU6792	60°36·6'	0°46·1'W	X	1,2
Whale Gill	Cumbr	NY3939	54°44·8'	2°56·4'W	W	90
Whale Island	C of Port	SU6302	50°49·1'	1°6·0'W	X	196
Whalemoor	Cumbr	NY5320	54°34·6'	2°43·2'W	X	90
Whale Point	Orkney	HY6545	59°17·7'	2°36·4'W	X	5
Whale Rock	Corn	SW7113	49°58·6'	5°11·3'W	X	203
Whalesborough	Corn	SS2103	50°48·2'	4°32·0'W	X	190
Whales Wick	Shetld	HU3412	59°53·8'	1°23·0'W	W	4
Whale Wick	Shetld	HU3632	60°4·5'	1°20·7'W	W	4
Whaley	Derby	SK5171	53°14·3'	1°13·7'W	T	120
Whaley Bridge	Derby	SK0181	53°19·8'	1°58·7'W	T	110
Whaley Common	Derby	SK5171	53°14·3'	1°13·7'W	X	120
Whaley Hall	Derby	SK5072	53°14·8'	1°14·6'W	X	120
Whaley Moor	Ches	SJ9981	53°19·8'	2°0·5'W	X	109
Whaley Thorns	Derby	SK5371	53°14·2'	1°11·9'W	T	120
Whal Geo	Shetld	HU1751	60°14·8'	1°41·1'W	X	3
Whal Geo	Shetld	HU2860	60°19·7'	1°29·1'W	X	3
Whal Horn	Shetld	HU2784	60°32·6'	1°30·0'W	X	3
Whaligoe	Highld	ND3240	58°20·9'	3°9·2'W	X	12
Whalley	Lancs	SD7336	53°49·4'	2°24·2'W	T	103
Whalley Banks	Lancs	SD7335	53°48·9'	2°24·2'W	T	103
Whalleybourne Fm	Shrops	SJ4204	52°38·1'	2°51·0'W	FM	126
Whalley Fm	Glos	SP0021	51°53·5'	1°59·6'W	FM	163
Whalley Fm	Norf	TF6725	52°48·0'	0°29·0'E	FM	132
Whalley Range	Man	SJ8294	53°26·8'	2°15·9'W	T	109
Whalleys	Lancs	SD4808	53°34·2'	2°46·7'W	T	108
Whallyden	Fife	NO3504	56°13·7'	3°2·5'W	X	59
Whalplaw Burn	Scot Bord	NT5455	55°47·4'	2°43·6'W	W	66,73
Whalsay	Shetld	HU5663	60°21·1'	0°58·6'W	X	2
Whalsies Ayre	Shetld	HU3834	60°5·6'	1°18·5'W	X	4
Whalton	Northum	NZ1381	55°7·6'	1°47·3'W	T	81
Whal Wick	Shetld	HU2381	60°31·0'	1°34·4'W	W	3
Whal Wick	Shetld	HU4036	60°6·7'	1°16·3'W	W	4
Whalwick Taing	Shetld	HU2381	60°31·0'	1°34·4'W	X	3
Wham	N Yks	SD7762	54°3·5'	2°20·7'W	X	98
Wham Bottom	N Yks	NY9203	54°25·6'	2°7·0'W	X	91,92
Whamlands	Northum	NY7854	54°53·1'	2°20·2'W	X	86,87
Whamoss Rigg	Cumbr	NY6261	54°56·8'	2°35·2'W	X	86
Wham Rig	D & G	NS6905	55°19·6'	4°3·5'W	X	71,77
Whams Fm	Lancs	SD4116	53°38·5'	2°53·1'W	FM	108
Whams, The	N Yks	SE0058	54°1·3'	1°59·6'W	X	104
Wham, The	N Yks	SE1491	54°19·1'	1°46·7'W	F	99
Whamthorn Plantn	Cumbr	NY6032	54°41·1'	2°36·8'W	F	91
Whamtown	Cumbr	NY4063	54°57·7'	2°55·8'W	X	85
Whaness Burn	Orkney	HY2402	58°54·2'	3°18·7'W	W	6,7
Whangie, The	Stir	NS4980	55°59·6'	4°24·8'W	H	64
Whangs	Cumbr	NX9911	54°29·3'	3°33·1'W	X	89
Whanland	Angus	NO6254	56°40·8'	2°36·8'W	X	54
Whan Scar	D & G	NY2164	54°58·1'	3°13·6'W	X	85
Whaplode	Lincs	TF3224	52°48·1'	0°2·1'W	T	131
Whaplode Drove	Lincs	TF3113	52°42·2'	0°3·3'W	T	131,142
Whaplode Fen	Lincs	TF3220	52°45·9'	0°2·2'W	X	131
Whaplode Manor	Lincs	TF3427	52°49·7'	0°0·3'W	X	131
Whaplode Marsh	Lincs	TF3329	52°50·8'	0°1·1'W	X	131
Whaplode River	Lincs	TF3428	52°50·2'	0°0·2'W	W	131
Whaplode St Catherine	Lincs	TF3320	52°45·9'	0°1·3'W	X	131
Whapweasel Burn	Northum	NY8756	54°54·2'	2°11·7'W	W	87
Whare Burn	Scot Bord	NT7464	55°52·4'	2°24·5'W	W	67
Whare Burn	Scot Bord	NT7464	55°52·4'	2°24·5'W	W	67
Wharf	Warw	SP4353	52°10·6'	1°21·9'W	T	151
Wharfe	N Yks	SD7869	54°7·2'	2°19·8'W	T	98
Wharfedale	Brad	SE1248	53°55·9'	1°48·6'W	X	104
Wharfe Dale	Leeds	SE3645	53°54·2'	1°26·7'W	X	104
Wharfedale	N Yks	SD9770	54°7·8'	2°2·3'W	X	98
Wharfedale Grange Fm	Brad	SE1446	53°54·8'	1°46·8'W	FM	104
Wharfedale Grange Fm	N Yks	SE3046	53°54·8'	1°32·2'W	FM	104
Wharfe Ings	N Yks	SE5638	53°50·4'	1°8·5'W	X	105
Wharfe's Mouth	N Yks	SE5738	53°50·3'	1°7·6'W	W	105
Wharfe Wood	N Yks	SD7868	54°6·7'	2°19·8'W	F	98
Wharf Fm	N Som	ST3767	51°24·1'	2°54·0'W	FM	171,182
Wharf Fm	Oxon	SP4931	51°58·8'	1°16·8'W	FM	151
Wharf Fm	Swin	SU1282	51°32·4'	1°49·2'W	FM	173
Wharf Ho	Shrops	SO6670	52°19·9'	2°29·5'W	X	138
Wharf Inn	Staffs	SJ7526	52°50·1'	2°21·9'W	X	127
Wharf, The	Leic	SK8816	52°44·3'	0°41·4'W	X	130
Wharlawhill	Pth & Kin	NO0502	56°12·3'	3°31·4'W	X	58
Wharles	Lancs	SD4435	53°48·7'	2°50·6'W	T	102
Wharleycroft	Cumbr	NY6924	54°36·9'	2°28·4'W	X	91
Wharley End	Beds	SP9342	52°4·3'	0°38·2'W	T	153
Wharley Fm	Beds	SP9443	52°4·9'	0°37·3'W	FM	153
Wharley Hall	Sol	SP1979	52°24·8'	1°42·8'W	X	139
Wharley Point	Carm	SN3409	51°45·5'	4°23·9'W	X	159
Wharmley	Northum	NY8866	54°59·6'	2°10·8'W	T	87
Wharncliffe Chase	Barns	SK3196	53°27·8'	1°31·6'W	X	110,111
Wharncliffe Crags	Sheff	SK2997	53°28·4'	1°33·4'W	X	110
Wharncliffe Lodge	Sheff	SK3095	53°27·3'	1°32·5'W	X	110
Wharncliffe Resr	Barns	SK3097	53°28·4'	1°32·5'W	W	110,111
Wharncliffe Side	Sheff	SK2994	53°26·8'	1°33·4'W	T	110
Wharncliffe Wood	Barns	SK3194	53°26·8'	1°31·6'W	F	110,111
Wharnley Burn	Durham	NZ0749	54°50·4'	1°53·0'W	X	88
Wharram Grange Fm	N Yks	SE8565	54°4·7'	0°41·6'W	FM	100
Wharram le Street	N Yks	SE8666	54°5·2'	0°40·7'W	T	101
Wharram Percy	N Yks	SE8564	54°4·1'	0°41·6'W	T	100
Wharram Percy Fm	N Yks	SE8463	54°3·6'	0°42·6'W	FM	100
Wharram Percy Village	N Yks	SE8564	54°4·1'	0°41·6'W	A	100
Wharrels Hill	Cumbr	NY1738	54°44·1'	3°16·9'W	H	89,90
Wharry Burn	Stir	NN8100	56°10·9'	3°54·6'W	W	57
Wharth	Orkney	ND3492	58°48·9'	3°8·1'W	X	7
Wharton	Ches	SJ6666	53°11·6'	2°30·1'W	T	118
Wharton	Heref	SO5055	52°11·7'	2°43·5'W	T	149
Wharton	Lincs	SK8493	53°25·9'	0°43·7'W	T	112
Wharton Court	Heref	SO5155	52°11·7'	2°42·6'W	A	149
Wharton Dikes	Cumbr	NY7605	54°26·6'	2°21·8'W	X	91
Wharton Fell	Cumbr	NY7603	54°25·6'	2°21·8'W	X	91
Wharton Green	Ches	SJ6667	53°12·2'	2°30·1'W	T	118
Wharton Hall	Cumbr	NY7706	54°27·2'	2°20·9'W	A	91
Wharton Ho	Cumbr	NY3737	54°43·7'	2°58·3'W	X	90
Wharton Lodge	Heref	SO6422	51°54·0'	2°31·0'W	X	162
Wharton Lodge	N Yks	SE4550	53°56·9'	1°18·4'W	X	105
Wharton's Lock	Ches	SJ5360	53°8·3'	2°41·8'W	X	117
Wharton Wood	Lincs	SK8492	53°25·3'	0°43·7'W	F	112
Whasdike	Cumbr	SD4397	54°22·2'	2°52·2'W	X	97
Whashton	N Yks	NZ1506	54°27·2'	1°45·7'W	T	92
Whashton Green	N Yks	NZ1405	54°26·7'	1°46·6'W	X	92
Whashton Hag	N Yks	NZ1505	54°26·7'	1°45·7'W	X	92
Whashton Springs	N Yks	NZ1404	54°26·1'	1°46·6'W	X	92
Whasset	Cumbr	SD5081	54°13·6'	2°45·6'W	T	97
Wha Taing	Orkney	ND4496	58°51·1'	2°57·8'W	X	6,7
Whatbarns Fm	Herts	TL3527	51°55·7'	0°1·8'W	FM	166
Whatborough Fm	Leic	SK7705	52°38·5'	0°51·3'W	FM	141
Whatborough Hill	Leic	SK7606	52°39·0'	0°52·2'W	H	141
What Close	Lancs	SD8347	53°55·4'	2°15·1'W	X	103
Whatcomb Bottom	Wilts	ST9339	51°9·2'	2°5·6'W	X	184
Whatcombe	W Berks	SU3978	51°30·2'	1°25·9'W	X	174
Whatcombe Down	Dorset	ST8501	50°48·7'	2°12·4'W	X	194
Whatcombe Down	Dorset	SY5789	50°42·2'	2°36·2'W	X	194
Whatcombe Ho	Dorset	ST8301	50°48·7'	2°14·1'W	X	194
Whatcombe Village	W Berks	SU3978	51°30·2'	1°25·9'W	A	174
Whatcombe Wood	Dorset	ST8202	50°49·3'	2°14·9'W	F	194
Whatcote	Warw	SP2944	52°5·8'	1°34·2'W	T	151
Whatcroft Hall	Ches	SJ6869	53°13·3'	2°28·3'W	X	118
Whateley	Warw	SP2299	52°35·5'	1°40·1'W	T	139
Whatfield	Suff	TM0246	52°4·8'	0°57·3'E	T	155
Whatfield Hall	Suff	TM0147	52°5·3'	0°56·4'E	X	155
Whatley	Somer	ST3606	50°51·2'	2°54·2'W	T	193
Whatley	Somer	ST7347	51°13·5'	2°22·8'W	T	183
Whatley Bottom	Somer	ST7348	51°14·1'	2°22·8'W	X	183
Whatlington	E Susx	TQ7518	50°56·3'	0°29·8'E	T	199
Whatmore	Shrops	SO6171	52°20·4'	2°33·9'W	T	138
Whatoff Lodge	Leic	SK5416	52°44·6'	1°11·6'W	X	129
Whatriggs	E Ayr	NS5139	55°37·6'	4°21·6'W	X	70
Whatshaw Common	Cumbr	NY5405	54°26·5'	2°42·1'W	X	90
Whatside Hills	N Ayr	NS2255	55°45·6'	4°49·8'W	X	63
Whatsill	Shrops	SO6176	52°23·1'	2°34·0'W	X	138
Whatsole Street	Kent	TR1144	51°9·6'	1°1·5'E	T	179,189
Whatstandwell	Derby	SK3354	53°5·2'	1°30·0'W	T	119
Whattal	Shrops	SJ4330	52°52·1'	2°50·4'W	X	126
Whattal Moss	Shrops	SJ4330	52°52·1'	2°50·4'W	F	126
Whatton	Notts	SK7439	52°56·8'	0°53·5'W	T	129
Whatton Fields	Notts	SK7237	52°55·8'	0°55·3'W	X	129
Whatton Ho	Leic	SK4924	52°48·9'	1°16·0'W	X	129
Whatton Lodge Fm	Notts	SK7438	52°56·3'	0°53·5'W	FM	129
Whatton Manor	Notts	SK7438	52°56·3'	0°53·5'W	X	129
Whauphill	D & G	NX4049	54°48·9'	4°29·0'W	T	83
Whaup Knowe	D & G	NX9793	55°13·5'	3°36·7'W	H	78
Whaup Knowe	S Lanak	NS9154	55°46·3'	3°43·8'W	X	65,72
Whaup Moor	Northum	NT8631	55°34·6'	2°12·9'W	X	74
Whaup Moss	Northum	NY9587	55°10·9'	2°4·3'W	X	81
Whaupshaw	Scot Bord	NT3813	55°24·7'	2°58·3'W	X	79
Whaw	N Yks	NY9804	54°26·1'	2°1·4'W	T	92
Whaw Edge	N Yks	NY9603	54°25·6'	2°3·3'W	X	91,92
Whaw Moor	N Yks	NY9603	54°25·6'	2°3·3'W	X	91,92
Whaypules	Essex	TL5910	51°46·2'	0°18·7'E	X	167
Wheadon Fm	Devon	SS7917	50°56·6'	3°43·0'W	FM	180
Wheal Alfred	Corn	SW5736	50°10·7'	5°23·8'W	T	203
Wheal Baddon	Corn	SW7742	50°14·4'	5°7·3'W	T	204
Wheal Bal Hill	Corn	SW3833	50°8·6'	5°39·7'W	H	203
Wheal Bassett Fm	Corn	SW7046	50°16·4'	5°13·3'W	FM	203
Wheal Betsy	Devon	SX5081	50°36·8'	4°6·8'W	A	191,201
Wheal Buller	Corn	SW4031	50°7·6'	5°37·9'W	X	203
Wheal Busy	Corn	SW7444	50°15·4'	5°9·9'W	T	204
Wheal Edward Zawn	Corn	SW3532	50°8·0'	5°42·1'W	W	203
Wheal Frances	Corn	SW7852	50°19·8'	5°6·8'W	T	200,204
Wheal Kitty	Corn	SW7251	50°19·1'	5°11·8'W	T	204
Wheal Plenty	Corn	SW7045	50°15·8'	5°13·3'W	X	203
Wheal Rose	Corn	SW7144	50°15·3'	5°12·4'W	T	203
Wheal Vor	Corn	SW6230	50°7·6'	5°19·4'W	X	203
Wheatacre	Norf	TM4693	52°29·0'	1°37·8'E	T	134
Wheatacre Fm	St Hel	SJ5592	53°25·6'	2°40·2'W	FM	108
Wheatacre Marshes	Norf	TM4795	52°30·0'	1°38·8'E	X	134
Wheat Bank	N Yks	NZ7406	54°26·9'	0°51·1'W	X	94
Wheat Beck	N Yks	SE5094	54°20·6'	1°13·4'W	W	100
Wheatcases	Cambs	TL4157	52°11·8'	0°4·2'E	X	154
Wheatclose	N Yks	SE6766	54°5·4'	0°58·1'W	X	100
Wheatclose Cross	Devon	SS7931	51°4·2'	3°43·2'W	X	180
Wheat Common	Shrops	SO5170	52°19·8'	2°42·7'W	X	137,138
Wheatcroft	Derby	SK3557	53°6·8'	1°28·2'W	T	119
Wheatcroft	D & G	NX7463	54°57·0'	3°57·6'W	X	83,84
Wheatcroft Fm	Devon	ST0305	50°50·4'	3°22·3'W	FM	192
Wheatcroft Fm	Norf	TG5002	52°33·7'	1°41·7'E	FM	134
Wheatcroft Fm	Warw	SP3891	52°31·2'	1°26·0'W	FM	140
Wheat Ends	N Yks	SE7189	54°17·7'	0°54·1'W	X	94,100
Wheatenhurst	Glos	SO7608	51°46·4'	2°20·5'W	T	162
Wheatfield	Oxon	SU6899	51°41·4'	1°0·6'W	X	164,165
Wheathall	Shrops	SJ4903	52°37·6'	2°44·8'W	T	126
Wheatham Fm	Hants	SU7527	51°2·5'	0°55·4'W	FM	186,197
Wheatham Hill	Hants	SU7427	51°2·5'	0°56·3'W	X	186,197
Wheathampstead	Herts	TL1714	51°49·0'	0°17·8'W	T	166
Wheat Hill	Devon	SY1188	50°41·3'	3°15·2'W	X	192
Wheat Hill	Herts	TL3035	52°0·1'	0°6·0'W	X	153
Wheathill	Northum	NY9474	55°3·9'	2°5·2'W	X	87
Wheathill	Shrops	SO6282	52°26·3'	2°33·1'W	T	138
Wheathill	Somer	ST5830	51°4·3'	2°35·6'W	T	182,183
Wheathill Brook	Shrops	SO6282	52°26·3'	2°33·1'W	W	138
Wheathill Fm	Derby	SK2937	52°56·0'	1°33·7'W	FM	128
Wheathill Fm	Know	SJ4389	53°23·9'	2°51·0'W	FM	108

Wheathill Fm	Shrops	SJ5810	52°41·4'	2°36·9'W	FM	126
Wheathills	N Yks	SE7459	54°1·5'	0°51·8'W	X	105,106
Wheat Hold	Hants	SU5560	51°20·4'	1°12·2'W	T	174
Wheatholme	Notts	SK8370	53°13·5'	0°45·0'W	X	121
Wheating Hill	Worcs	SP0261	52°15·1'	1°57·8'W	X	150
Wheatland	Devon	SS9019	50°57·8'	3°33·6'W	X	181
Wheatland	Devon	SX8550	50°20·6'	3°36·6'W	X	202
Wheatland Fm	Devon	SS6410	50°52·6'	3°55·6'W	FM	191
Wheatland Fm	Suff	TM0536	51°59·3'	0°59·5'E	FM	155
Wheatlands	C of Edin	NT1474	55°57·3'	3°22·2'W	X	65
Wheatlands Fm	Devon	SS7029	51°3·0'	3°50·9'W	FM	180
Wheatlands Fm	N Yks	SE3665	54°5·0'	1°26·6'W	FM	99
Wheatlands Manor	Wok	SU7763	51°21·9'	0°53·2'W	X	175,186
Wheatlawn Fm	Somer	ST5829	51°3·8'	2°35·6'W	FM	183
Wheat Leasows	Wrekin	SJ6713	52°43·1'	2°28·9'W	X	127
Wheatley	Cald	SE0726	53°44·1'	1°53·2'W	T	104
Wheatley	Devon	SX4588	50°40·5'	4°11·2'W	X	190
Wheatley	Devon	SX8991	50°42·7'	3°34·0'W	X	192
Wheatley	Donc	SE5804	53°32·0'	1°7·1'W	T	111
Wheatley	Hants	SU7840	51°9·5'	0°52·7'W	T	186
Wheatley	Lancs	SD8148	53°55·9'	2°16·9'W	X	103
Wheatley	Oxon	SP5905	51°44·7'	1°8·3'W	T	164
Wheatley	Shrops	SJ5317	52°45·2'	2°41·4'W	X	126
Wheatley Field	Notts	SK7485	53°21·6'	0°52·9'W	X	112,120
Wheatley Fm	Lancs	SD6239	53°51·0'	2°34·2'W	FM	102,103
Wheatley Fm	Notts	SK8460	53°8·1'	0°44·3'W	FM	121
Wheatley Grange	Durham	NZ0842	54°46·6'	1°52·1'W	X	88
Wheatley Grange	Notts	SK7587	53°22·7'	0°51·9'W	X	112,120
Wheatley Green Fm	Durham	NZ2149	54°50·4'	1°40·0'W	FM	88
Wheatley Hill	Durham	NZ1949	54°50·4'	1°41·8'W	X	88
Wheatley Hill	Durham	NZ3738	54°44·4'	1°25·1'W	T	93
Wheatley Hill	Notts	SK8360	53°8·1'	0°45·2'W	X	121
Wheatley Hill Fm	Kirk	SE2509	53°34·9'	1°36·9'W	FM	110
Wheatley Hills	Donc	SE6004	53°32·0'	1°5·3'W	T	111
Wheatley Lane	Lancs	SD8338	53°50·5'	2°15·1'W	T	103
Wheatley Park	Donc	SE5905	53°32·5'	1°6·2'W	T	111
Wheatley Park Fm	Devon	SX4588	50°40·5'	4°11·2'W	FM	190
Wheatley's Drain	Cambs	TL2283	52°26·1'	0°11·9'W	W	142
Wheatley Wood	Durham	NZ0823	54°36·4'	1°52·1'W	F	92
Wheatley Wood	Notts	SK7588	53°23·2'	0°51·9'W	F	112,120
Wheatley Wood Fm	Notts	SK7687	53°22·7'	0°51·0'W	FM	112,120
Wheatlow Brook	Staffs	SJ9733	52°53·9'	2°2·3'W	W	127
Wheat Lund	N Yks	SE7091	54°18·8'	0°55·0'W	X	94,100
Wheatmoor Fm	Birm	SP1397	52°34·5'	1°48·1'W	FM	139
Wheaton Aston	Staffs	SJ8512	52°42·6'	2°12·9'W	T	127
Wheaton Aston Hall	Staffs	SJ8310	52°41·5'	2°14·7'W	X	127
Wheatrig	E Loth	NT4675	55°58·2'	2°51·5'W	X	66
Wheatrig	N Ayr	NS4042	55°39·0'	4°32·1'W	X	70
Wheat's Fm	W Berks	SU6664	51°22·5'	1°2·7'W	FM	175,186
Wheatsheaf Common	W Susx	SU8329	51°3·5'	0°48·6'W	X	186,197
Wheat Sheaf Hill	Somer	ST6321	50°59·5'	2°31·2'W	H	183
Wheatsheaf Hotel	Surrey	SU9768	51°24·4'	0°35·9'W	X	175,176
Wheat Stack	Scot Bord	NT8671	55°56·2'	2°13·0'W	X	67
Wheats, The	Staffs	SJ9118	52°45·8'	2°7·6'W	X	127
Wheatstone Park	Staffs	SJ8504	52°38·3'	2°12·9'W	X	127,139
Wheatyfauld	N Ayr	NS3250	55°43·1'	4°40·0'W	X	63
Wheddon Cross	Somer	SS9238	51°8·1'	3°32·2'W	T	181
Wheddon Fms	Somer	SS9238	51°8·1'	3°32·2'W	FM	181
Wheeb	S Ayr	NX1783	55°6·7'	4°51·7'W	X	76
Wheedale Plantation	N Yks	SE7799	54°23·1'	0°48·4'W	F	94,100
Wheedlemont	Aberd	NJ4726	57°19·5'	2°52·4'W	X	37
Wheedlemont Hill	Aberd	NJ4626	57°19·5'	2°53·3'W	H	37
Wheelbarrow Town	Kent	TR1545	51°10·0'	1°4·9'E	T	179,189
Wheelabout Wood	Lincs	TF3665	53°10·1'	0°2·5'E	F	122
Wheelam Rock	N Yks	SE0352	53°58·1'	1°56·8'W	X	104
Wheelbarrow Castle	Heref	SO5157	52°12·8'	2°42·6'W	X	149
Wheelbarrow Castle	Warw	SP2631	51°58·8'	1°36·9'W	X	151
Wheelbarrow Hall	Cumbr	NY4356	54°54·0'	2°52·9'W	X	85
Wheelbirks	Northum	NZ0458	54°55·2'	1°55·8'W	X	87
Wheel Brook	Somer	ST7653	51°16·8'	2°20·3'W	W	183
Wheel Burn	Scot Bord	NT5651	55°45·3'	2°41·6'W	W	67,73
Wheelburn Law	Scot Bord	NT5651	55°45·3'	2°41·6'W	X	67,73
Wheel Causeway	Scot Bord	NT6102	55°18·9'	2°36·4'W	A	80
Wheeldale Beck	N Yks	SE8197	54°22·0'	0°44·8'W	W	94,100
Wheeldale Gill	N Yks	SE7899	54°23·1'	0°47·5'W	W	94,100
Wheeldale Howe	N Yks	SE7699	54°23·1'	0°49·4'W	A	94,100
Wheeldale Lodge	N Yks	SE8198	54°22·5'	0°44·8'W	X	94,100
Wheeldale Moor	N Yks	SE7898	54°22·5'	0°47·5'W	X	94,100
Wheeldon	Devon	SX7454	50°22·6'	3°45·9'W	X	202
Wheeldon Trees	Derby	SK1066	53°11·7'	1°50·6'W	X	119
Wheeler End	Bucks	SU8093	51°38·0'	0°50·3'W	T	175
Wheelers Cross	Devon	SS3514	50°54·4'	4°20·4'W	X	190
Wheelers Fm	Essex	TL5112	51°47·4'	0°11·8'E	FM	167
Wheeler's Fm	Hants	SU7125	51°1·4'	0°58·9'W	FM	186,197
Wheeler's Stone	Devon	SS4241	51°9·0'	4°15·2'W	X	180
Wheelerstreet	Surrey	SU9440	51°9·3'	0°39·0'W	T	186
Wheeley Fm	Worcs	SP0072	52°21·0'	1°59·6'W	FM	139
Wheeley Moor Fm	Warw	SP1987	52°29·1'	1°42·8'W	FM	139
Wheel Fell	Cumbr	NY0707	54°27·2'	3°25·6'W	X	89
Wheel Fm	Ches	SJ7673	53°15·4'	2°21·2'W	FM	118
Wheel Fm	Devon	SS5744	51°10·9'	4°2·4'W	FM	180
Wheel Green	Ches	SJ7144	52°59·8'	2°25·5'W	X	118
Wheel Hall	N Yks	SE6038	53°50·3'	1°4·9'W	X	105
Wheelock	Ches	SJ7459	53°7·9'	2°22·9'W	T	118
Wheelock Hall	Ches	SJ7458	53°7·4'	2°22·9'W	X	118
Wheelock Heath	Ches	SJ7557	53°6·8'	2°22·0'W	T	118
Wheelrig Head	Scot Bord	NT6101	55°18·3'	2°36·4'W	H	80
Wheelright Fm	N Yks	SD8855	53°59·7'	2°10·6'W	FM	103
Wheelsgate	Kent	TR0224	50°59·0'	0°53·1'E	X	189
Wheel Stones	Derby	SK2088	53°23·5'	1°41·5'W	X	110
Wheelton	Lancs	SD6021	53°41·3'	2°35·9'W	T	102,103
Wheelton Moor	Lancs	SD6319	53°40·2'	2°33·2'W	X	109
Wheely Down	Hants	SU6123	51°0·4'	1°7·4'W	X	185
Wheely Fm	Hants	SU6124	51°1·0'	1°7·4'W	FM	185
Wheems, The	Orkney	HY6340	59°15·0'	2°38·4'W	X	5
Wheen	Angus	NO3670	56°49·3'	3°2·5'W	X	44
Wheen Cottage	Angus	NO3571	56°49·8'	3°3·5'W	X	44
Wheldale	Wakf	SE4526	53°43·9'	1°18·7'W	T	105
Wheldrake	York	SE6845	53°54·0'	0°57·5'W	T	105,106
Wheldrake Grange	York	SE6643	53°53·0'	0°59·3'W	X	105,106

Wheldrake Ings	York	SE7043	53°52·9'	0°55·7'W	X	105,106
Wheldrake Wood	York	SE6546	53°54·6'	1°0·2'W	F	105,106
Wheler Lodge	Leic	SP6482	52°26·2'	1°3·1'W	X	140
Whelford	Glos	SU1698	51°41·1'	1°45·7'W	T	163
Whelky Geo	Orkney	HY5238	59°13·8'	2°50·0'W	X	5
Whelley	Wigan	SD5906	53°33·2'	2°36·7'W	T	108
Whelly Hill Fm	Hartpl	NZ4534	54°42·2'	1°17·7'W	FM	93
Whelmstone Barton	Devon	SS7500	50°47·4'	3°46·0'W	X	191
Whelphill	S Lanak	NS9920	55°28·1'	3°35·4'W	X	72
Whelphill Hope	S Lanak	NT0020	55°28·1'	3°34·5'W	X	72
Whelpley Fm	Wilts	SU2324	51°1·1'	1°39·9'W	FM	184
Whelpley Hill	Bucks	SP9904	51°43·8'	0°33·6'W	T	165
Whelpley Level	E Susx	TQ6110	50°52·2'	0°17·7'E	X	199
Whelpo	Cumbr	NY3039	54°44·7'	3°4·8'W	T	90
Whelprigg	Cumbr	SD6381	54°13·6'	2°33·6'W	X	97
Whelpshead Crag	Cumbr	SD2183	54°14·4'	3°12·3'W	X	96
Whelpside	C of Edin	NT1365	55°52·5'	3°23·0'W	X	65
Whelp Side	Cumbr	NY3314	54°31·3'	3°1·7'W	X	90
Whelpside	Cumbr	NY5500	54°23·9'	2°41·2'W	X	90
Whelp Stone Crag	Lancs	SD7659	54°1·8'	2°21·6'W	X	103
Whelpstone Lodge	N Yks	SD7659	54°1·8'	2°21·6'W	X	103
Whelp Street	Suff	TL9449	52°6·5'	0°50·4'E	T	155
Whelsiegeo Stacks	Shetld	HU5965	60°22·1'	0°55·3'W	X	2
Whelston	Flint	SJ2176	53°16·7'	3°10·7'W	T	117
Whelter Bottom	Cumbr	NY4613	54°30·8'	2°49·6'W	X	90
Whelter Crags	Cumbr	NY4613	54°30·8'	2°49·6'W	X	90
Whemley Burn	Northum	NZ1594	55°14·6'	1°45·4'W	X	81
Whempstead	Herts	TL3120	51°52·0'	0°5·4'W	T	166
Whenby	N Yks	SE6369	54°7·0'	1°1·8'W	T	100
Whenby Lodge	N Yks	SE6369	54°7·0'	1°1·8'W	X	100
Whepstead	Suff	TL8358	52°11·6'	0°41·0'E	T	155
Whernalls	Warw	SP1159	52°14·0'	1°49·9'W	X	150
Whernside	Cumbr	SD7382	54°14·2'	2°24·4'W	H	98
Whernside	N Yks	SD9975	54°10·5'	2°0·5'W	X	98
Whernside Manor	Cumbr	SD7285	54°15·8'	2°25·4'W	X	98
Whernside Pasture	N Yks	SE0073	54°9·4'	1°59·6'W	X	98
Whernside Tarns	Cumbr	SD7483	54°14·8'	2°23·5'W	W	98
Wherry Town	Corn	SW4629	50°6·6'	5°32·8'W	T	203
Wherstead	Suff	TM1540	52°1·2'	1°8·4'E	T	169
Wherstead Park	Suff	TM1540	52°1·2'	1°8·4'E	X	169
Wherwell	Hants	SU3840	51°9·7'	1°27·0'W	T	185
Whessoe Cott	Darl	NZ2718	54°33·6'	1°34·5'W	X	93
Whessoe Grange	Darl	NZ2718	54°33·6'	1°34·5'W	X	93
Wheston	Derby	SK1376	53°17·1'	1°47·9'W	T	119
Whetcombe	Devon	SX7055	50°23·1'	3°49·3'W	X	202
Whetcombe Barton	Devon	SX8481	50°37·3'	3°38·0'W	X	191
Whetham	Wilts	ST9768	51°24·9'	2°2·2'W	X	173
Whetham Fm	Dorset	ST4103	50°49·6'	2°49·9'W	FM	193
Whetley	Dorset	SY5396	50°45·9'	2°39·6'W	X	194
Whetley Cross	Dorset	ST4504	50°50·2'	2°46·5'W	T	193
Whetley Fm	Dorset	ST4504	50°50·2'	2°46·5'W	FM	193
Whetshaw Bottom	N Yks	NY9702	54°25·1'	2°2·4'W	W	92
Whetsted	Kent	TQ6545	51°11·0'	0°22·0'E	T	188
Whetstone	Barnet	TQ2693	51°37·5'	0°10·4'W	T	176
Whetstone	Cumbr	SD5483	54°14·7'	2°41·9'W	X	97
Whet Stone	Heref	SO2656	52°12·1'	3°4·6'W	X	148
Whetstone	Leic	SP5597	52°34·3'	1°10·9'W	T	140
Whetstone Allotment	Brad	SE0945	53°54·3'	1°51·4'W	X	104
Whetstone Brook	Leic	SP5693	52°32·2'	1°10·1'W	W	140
Whetstone Fm	Leeds	SE2339	53°51·0'	1°38·6'W	FM	104
Whetstone Gate	Brad	SE1045	53°54·3'	1°50·5'W	X	104
Whetstone Gill	N Yks	SD9361	54°2·9'	2°6·0'W	W	98
Whetstone Gorse	Leic	SP5693	52°32·2'	1°10·1'W	X	140
Whetstone Ho	Northum	NY9286	55°10·3'	2°7·1'W	X	80
Whetstone Pastures	Leic	SP5693	52°32·2'	1°10·1'W	X	140
Whetstone Ridge	Ches	SK0170	53°13·9'	1°58·7'W	X	119
Whettleton	Shrops	SO4482	52°26·2'	2°49·0'W	T	137
Whews, The	Norf	TL9796	52°31·8'	0°54·7'E	X	144
Whey Carr Platn	N Yks	SE6959	54°1·6'	0°56·4'W	F	105,106
Whey Curd Fm	Norf	TF9439	52°55·0'	0°53·5'E	FM	132
Whey Fm	Devon	SS6124	51°0·2'	3°58·5'W	FM	180
Whey Geo	Orkney	HY4144	59°17·0'	3°1·6'W	X	5
Whey Knowe	D & G	NT2505	55°20·3'	3°10·5'W	X	79
Wheyrigg Fm	Cumbr	NY1948	54°49·5'	3°15·2'W	FM	85
Wheyside Ho	Durham	NY8529	54°39·6'	2°13·5'W	X	91,92
Wheywells	Aberd	NO7895	57°3·0'	2°21·3'W	X	38,45
Whibbersley Cross	Derby	SK2972	53°14·9'	1°33·5'W	A	119
Whicham	Cumbr	SD1382	54°13·8'	3°19·7'W	T	96
Whicham Beck	Cumbr	SD1583	54°14·4'	3°17·8'W	W	96
Whicham Hall	Cumbr	SD1482	54°13·8'	3°18·7'W	X	96
Whicham Mill	Cumbr	SD1585	54°15·5'	3°17·9'W	X	96
Whicham Valley	Cumbr	SD1583	54°14·4'	3°17·8'W	X	96
Whichford	Warw	SP3134	52°0·4'	1°32·5'W	T	151
Whichford Hill Fm	Warw	SP3233	51°59·9'	1°31·6'W	FM	151
Whichford Mill	Warw	SP3136	52°1·5'	1°32·5'W	X	151
Whichford Wood	Warw	SP3034	52°0·5'	1°33·4'W	F	151
Whickham	Ghead	NZ2060	54°56·3'	1°40·8'W	T	88
Whickham Grange	Durham	NZ0946	54°48·8'	1°51·2'W	X	88
Whickham Hill	Ghead	NZ2260	54°56·3'	1°39·0'W	X	88
Whickham Thorns	Ghead	NZ2261	54°56·8'	1°39·0'W	X	88
Whickhope Nick	Northum	NY6681	55°7·6'	2°31·6'W	X	80
Whiclath	Orkney	HY2826	59°7·2'	3°15·0'W	X	6
Whidana Wood	S Ayr	NX0572	55°0·5'	5°2·5'W	F	76
Whidcombe Brake	Bath & NE Somer	ST6461	51°21·1'	2°30·6'W	X	172
Whiddon	Devon	SS5538	51°7·6'	4°3·9'W	T	180
Whiddon	Devon	SS5731	51°3·9'	4°2·1'W	X	180
Whiddon	Devon	SX3997	50°45·3'	4°16·6'W	X	190
Whiddon	Devon	SX4799	50°46·5'	4°9·8'W	X	191
Whiddon	Devon	SX7289	50°41·4'	3°48·4'W	X	191
Whiddon	Devon	SX8667	50°29·7'	3°36·1'W	X	202
Whiddon Down	Devon	SX6892	50°43·0'	3°51·8'W	T	191
Whiddon Fm	Devon	SX8889	50°41·6'	3°34·8'W	FM	192
Whiddon Fms	Devon	SX7672	50°32·3'	3°44·6'W	FM	191
Whiddon Moor	Devon	SS4600	50°47·0'	4°10·7'W	X	190
Whiddon Wood	Devon	SX7389	50°41·4'	3°47·5'W	F	191
Whifflet	N Lanak	NS7364	55°51·4'	4°1·3'W	T	64
Whigabuts	Aberd	NJ8130	57°21·9'	2°18·5'W	X	29,30
Whiggs, The	Northum	NY9970	55°1·7'	2°0·5'W	X	87
Whigstreet	Angus	NO4844	56°35·4'	2°50·4'W	T	54

Whiley-Hill Fm	Darl	NZ2720	54°34·7'	1°34·5'W	FM	93
Whilgarn	Cered	SN4451	52°8·4'	4°16·4'W	A	146
Whiligh	E Susx	TQ6531	51°3·5'	0°21·7'E	X	188
Whilkie Stack	Shetld	HP4806	60°44·3'	1°6·7'W	X	1
Whilk Isle	S Ayr	NX1189	55°9·8'	4°57·6'W	X	76
Whilk, The	S Ayr	NX1188	55°9·3'	4°57·6'W	X	76
Whillan Beck	Cumbr	NY1802	54°24·7'	3°15·4'W	W	89,90
Whilse Sound	Shetld	HU2076	60°28·3'	1°37·7'W	W	3
Whilton	Northnts	SP6364	52°16·5'	1°4·2'W	T	152
Whilton Locks	Northnts	SP6164	52°16·5'	1°6·0'W	T	152
Whilton Lodge	Northnts	SP6164	52°16·5'	1°6·0'W	X	152
Whimberry Hill	Black w Dar	SD6814	53°37·5'	2°28·6'W	H	109
Whimble	Devon	SS3402	50°47·9'	4°21·0'W	T	190
Whimble	Powys	SO2062	52°15·3'	3°9·9'W	H	137,148
Whim Fm	Scot Bord	NT2153	55°46·1'	3°15·1'W	FM	66,73
Whim Plantn	Pth & Kin	NN8567	56°47·1'	3°52·5'W	F	43
Whimple	Devon	SY0497	50°46·1'	3°21·3'W	T	192
Whimple Wood	Devon	SY0596	50°45·6'	3°20·4'W	X	192
Whim Pond	Scot Bord	NT2154	55°46·6'	3°15·1'W	W	66,73
Whimpton Moor	Notts	SK7874	53°15·7'	0°49·4'W	X	120,121
Whimpton Village	Notts	SK7973	53°15·1'	0°48·5'W	A	120,121
Whimpwell Green	Norf	TG3829	52°48·6'	1°32·3'E	T	133,134
Whimsey Hill	Cumbr	NY7745	54°48·2'	2°21·0'W	H	86,87
Whim, The	Derby	SK1357	53°6·8'	1°47·9'W	X	119
Whim, The	Derby	SK1366	53°11·7'	1°47·9'W	X	119
Whinash	Cumbr	NY5705	54°26·6'	2°39·4'W	H	91
Whinbank	Cumbr	NY1445	54°47·8'	3°19·8'W	X	85
Whinberry Hill	E Yorks	SE7352	53°57·8'	0°52·8'W	X	105,106
Whinbrae	Aberd	NJ5934	57°23·9'	2°40·5'W	X	29
Whin Burn	Aberd	NJ6343	57°28·8'	2°36·6'W	W	29
Whinbush Fm	S Lanak	NT0343	55°40·5'	3°32·1'W	FM	72
Whin Castle Fm	N Yks	SE1749	53°56·5'	1°44·0'W	FM	104
Whinchat Hall	N Yks	SE6441	53°51·9'	1°1·2'W	X	105,106
Whinclose	Cumbr	NY1554	54°52·7'	3°19·1'W	X	85
Whin Close Villa	Norf	TF8736	52°53·6'	0°47·2'E	X	132
Whin Common	Norf	TF6100	52°34·7'	0°23·0'E	X	143
Whincop	Cumbr	SD1799	54°23·0'	3°16·3'W	X	96
Whincover Fm	N Yks	SE5574	54°9·8'	1°9·0'W	FM	100
Whin Covert	Donc	SE6900	53°29·8'	0°57·2'W	F	111
Whin Covert	N Yks	SE4945	53°54·2'	1°14·8'W	F	105
Whin Covert	Scot Bord	NT8155	55°47·5'	2°17·7'W	F	67,74
Whin Covert	Suff	TM2960	52°11·7'	1°21·4'E	F	156
Whin Covert	Suff	TM3659	52°10·9'	1°27·5'E	F	156
Whindrove Fm	Norf	TF6401	52°35·2'	0°25·7'E	FM	143
Whineray Ground	Cumbr	SD2090	54°18·2'	3°13·3'W	X	96
Whin Fell	Cumbr	NY1325	54°37·0'	3°20·4'W	H	89
Whin Fell	Cumbr	NY5643	54°47·0'	2°40·6'W	H	86
Whin Fell	D & G	NY3898	55°16·6'	2°58·1'W	H	79
Whin Fell	Lancs	SD6453	53°58·6'	2°32·5'W	X	102,103
Whinfell Beacon	Cumbr	NY5700	54°23·9'	2°39·3'W	H	91
Whinfell Common	Cumbr	NY5601	54°24·4'	2°40·3'W	X	90
Whinfell Common	Cumbr	NY5701	54°24·4'	2°39·3'W	X	91
Whinfell Forest	Cumbr	NY5727	54°38·4'	2°39·6'W	F	91
Whinfell Hall	Cumbr	NY1425	54°37·0'	3°19·5'W	X	89
Whinfell Ho	Cumbr	NY5828	54°39·0'	2°38·6'W	X	91
Whinfell Park	Cumbr	NY5528	54°39·0'	2°41·4'W	X	90
Whinfell Tarn	Cumbr	SD5598	54°22·8'	2°41·1'W	W	97
Whinfield	Cumbr	SD2576	54°10·7'	3°8·5'W	X	96
Whinfield	Darl	NZ3117	54°33·1'	1°30·8'W	T	93
Whinfield	Scot Bord	NT4822	55°29·6'	2°48·9'W	X	73
Whinfield	Scot Bord	NT5628	55°32·9'	2°41·4'W	X	73
Whinfield Ho	Durham	NZ3022	54°35·8'	1°31·7'W	X	93
Whinflower Hall	N Yks	SE8172	54°8·5'	0°45·2'W	X	100
Whing	D & G	NS7506	55°20·2'	3°57·8'W	X	71,78
Whing Garth	Cumbr	NY0805	54°26·2'	3°24·7'W	X	89
Whing Burn	D & G	NS7607	55°20·7'	3°56·9'W	W	71,78
Whing Head	D & G	NS7505	55°19·6'	3°57·8'W	X	71,78
Whingill	Cumbr	NY7809	54°28·8'	2°20·0'W	X	91
Whingreen	Devon	SX6158	50°24·6'	3°57·0'W	X	202
Whingroves	N Yks	NZ5502	54°24·9'	1°8·7'W	X	93
Whinhall	N Lanak	NS7565	55°52·0'	3°59·4'W	T	64
Whin Hall	N Yks	SD9599	54°23·4'	2°4·2'W	X	98
Whinhaugh	N Yks	SE1055	53°59·7'	1°50·4'W	X	104
Whin Hill	Aberd	NJ8750	57°32·7'	2°12·6'W	H	30
Whinhill	Aberd	NJ8750	57°32·7'	2°12·6'W	X	30
Whin Hill	Cumbr	NY5155	54°53·5'	2°45·4'W	X	86
Whinhill	Highld	NH8649	57°31·3'	3°53·7'W	X	27
Whinhill	Inverc	NS2774	55°55·9'	4°45·7'W	X	63
Whin Hill	Norf	TF8738	52°54·6'	0°47·3'E	X	132
Whin Hill	Notts	SK6382	53°20·1'	1°2·8'W	F	111,120
Whinhill Fm	E Yorks	TA0457	54°0·1'	0°24·4'W	FM	107
Whinhill Fm	E Yorks	TA2725	53°42·6'	0°4·1'W	FM	107,113
Whin-Hill Fm	N Yks	SE2354	53°59·1'	1°38·7'W	FM	104
Whinhill Ho	Arg & Bt	NR7020	55°25·5'	5°37·7'W	X	68
Whinhill Resr	Inverc	NS2774	55°55·9'	4°45·7'W	W	63
Whinhill Station	Inverc	NS2875	55°56·5'	4°44·8'W	X	63
Whinhowe	Cumbr	NY5905	54°26·6'	2°37·5'W	X	91
Whinhowe Gill	Cumbr	SD5798	54°22·8'	2°39·3'W	W	97
Whinkerstones	Scot Bord	NT7647	55°43·2'	2°22·5'W	X	74
Whinknowe	S Lanak	NS7244	55°40·6'	4°1·7'W	X	71
Whin Lane End	Lancs	SD3941	53°51·9'	2°55·2'W	T	102
Whin Lane Fm	N Yks	SE3649	53°56·4'	1°26·7'W	FM	104
Whinlatter	Cumbr	NY1925	54°37·1'	3°14·8'W	H	89,90
Whinlatter Forest Park	Cumbr	NY2125	54°37·1'	3°13·0'W	F	89,90
Whinlatter Forest Park	Cumbr	NY2125	54°37·1'	3°13·0'W	X	89,90
Whinlatter Pass	Cumbr	NY1924	54°36·5'	3°14·8'W	X	89,90
Whinleys Fm	Notts	SK7481	53°19·5'	0°52·9'W	FM	120
Whinleys House Fm	Notts	SK7482	53°20·0'	0°52·9'W	FM	120
Whinmere Fm	Norf	TG4024	52°45·8'	1°33·9'E	FM	134
Whinmoor	Leeds	SE3636	53°49·4'	1°26·8'W	T	104
Whinmoor	Leeds	SE3637	53°49·9'	1°26·8'W	X	104
Whin Moor	N Yks	SE9272	54°8·4'	0°35·1'W	X	101
Whinnah	Cumbr	NY0720	54°34·3'	3°25·9'W	X	89
Whinna Skerry	Shetld	HU4838	60°7·7'	1°7·7'W	X	4
Whinnerah	Cumbr	NY0805	54°26·2'	3°24·7'W	X	89
Whinnerston	Renf	NS3864	55°50·8'	4°34·8'W	X	63
Whinnet Hill	Shrops	SJ4028	52°51·0'	2°53·1'W	X	126
Whinnetley Fm	Northum	NY8165	54°59·0'	2°17·4'W	FM	86,87
Whinnetley Moss	Northum	NY8166	54°59·5'	2°17·4'W	X	86,87

Whinney	Northum	NU1619	55°28·1'	1°44·4'W	X	81
Whinney Fell	Cumbr	NY5657	54°54·6'	2°40·8'W	H	86
Whinneyfield Fm	Lancs	SD4934	53°48·2'	2°46·1'W	FM	102
Whinney Hill	Lancs	SD5467	54°6·1'	2°41·8'W	X	97
Whinney Hill	Northum	NZ1292	55°13·6'	1°48·3'W	X	81
Whinney Hill	Notts	SK5563	53°9·9'	1°10·2'W	X	120
Whinney Hill	Roth	SK4594	53°26·7'	1°18·9'W	T	111
Whinney Hill Fm	Northum	NZ1878	55°6·1'	1°42·6'W	FM	88
Whinney Hill Fm	Northum	NZ2584	55°9·2'	1°36·0'W	FM	81
Whinney Mire	N Yks	SD7070	54°7·7'	2°27·1'W	X	98
Whinneymoor Fm	E Yorks	SE9228	53°44·7'	0°35·9'W	FM	106
Whinney Nab	N Yks	SE8694	54°20·3'	0°40·2'W	X	94,101
Whinney, The	Scot Bord	NT6523	55°30·2'	2°32·8'W	X	74
Whinnieliggate	D & G	NX7152	54°51·0'	4°0·1'W	T	83,84
Whinnow Beck	Cumbr	NY2950	54°50·6'	3°5·9'W	W	85
Whinnybank	Fife	NO2316	56°20·1'	3°14·3'W	X	58
Whinnybrae	Scot Bord	NT0838	55°37·9'	3°27·2'W	X	72
Whinny Brow	Cumbr	NY4870	55°1·6'	2°48·4'W	X	86
Whinny Crag	Cumbr	NY4520	54°34·6'	2°50·6'W	X	90
Whinnyfield Wood	Suff	TL9841	52°2·1'	0°53·6'E	F	155
Whinnyfold	Aberd	NK0733	57°23·5'	1°52·6'W	T	30
Whinnyforth	E Yorks	TA0450	53°56·4'	0°24·5'W	X	107
Whinnyhall	Fife	NT1292	56°7·0'	3°24·5'W	X	58
Whinnyhall	Fife	NT2298	56°10·4'	3°14·9'W	X	58
Whinny Haw	Cumbr	SD6293	54°20·1'	2°34·6'W	X	97
Whinny Heights	Black w Dar	SD6926	53°44·0'	2°27·8'W	T	103
Whinny Hill	Brad	SE0434	53°48·4'	1°55·9'W	X	104
Whinny Hill	D & G	NX9569	55°0·5'	3°38·1'W	H	84
Whinnyhill	D & G	NX9669	55°0·5'	3°37·1'W	X	84
Whinny Hill	Northum	NU2120	55°28·6'	1°39·6'W	X	75
Whinny Hill	N Yks	SE1796	54°21·8'	1°43·9'W	X	99
Whinny Hill	Renf	NS3670	55°54·0'	4°36·9'W	H	63
Whinny Hill	Stock on T	NZ3819	54°34·1'	1°24·3'W	T	93
Whinny Hill Fm	N Yks	SE7286	54°16·1'	0°53·2'W	FM	94,100
Whinny Hills	York	SE5844	53°53·6'	1°6·6'W	X	105
Whinnyhouse	Scot Bord	NT7425	55°31·3'	2°24·3'W	X	74
Whinny Moor Plantn	Stock on T	NZ4427	54°38·4'	1°18·7'W	F	93
Whinny Oaks Covert	N Yks	SE5773	54°9·2'	1°7·2'W	F	100
Whinny Rein Plantn	N Yks	NZ3308	54°28·2'	1°29·0'W	F	93
Whinnyrig	D & G	NY2064	54°58·1'	3°14·6'W	X	85
Whinnyrig	D & G	NY3169	55°0·9'	3°4·3'W	X	85
Whinpark	E Ayr	NS4439	55°37·4'	4°28·2'W	X	70
Whin Plantn	Suff	TM1358	52°11·0'	1°7·3'E	F	156
Whinrig	Scot Bord	NT6756	55°48·0'	2°31·1'W	X	67,74
Whin Rigg	Cumbr	NY1503	54°25·2'	3°18·2'W	H	89
Whinrigg	N Lanak	NS7670	55°54·7'	3°58·6'W	X	64
Whinrig Hill	Scot Bord	NT6657	55°48·6'	2°32·1'W	X	67,74
Whins	Aberd	NO6670	56°49·5'	2°33·0'W	X	45
Whins	Cumbr	NY0025	54°36·9'	3°32·5'W	X	89
Whins	Cumbr	NY0916	54°32·1'	3°24·0'W	X	89
Whin's	Cumbr	SD6397	54°22·3'	2°33·8'W	X	97
Whins	D & G	NY1972	55°2·4'	3°15·6'W	X	85
Whins Beck	Cumbr	SD2683	54°14·5'	3°7·7'W	W	96,97
Whins Brow	Lancs	SD6353	53°58·5'	2°33·4'W	X	102,103
Whinscales	Cumbr	NY1903	54°25·2'	3°14·5'W	X	89,90
Whins End	Cumbr	SD6397	54°22·3'	2°33·8'W	X	97
Whinsfield	Cumbr	NY5531	54°40·6'	2°41·4'W	X	90
Whins Fm	Durham	NZ2132	54°41·2'	1°40·0'W	FM	93
Whins of Fordie	Pth & Kin	NO0741	56°33·4'	3°30·3'W	X	52,53
Whins of Milton	Stir	NS7990	56°5·5'	3°56·2'W	T	57
Whins Pond	Cumbr	NY5530	54°40·1'	2°41·4'W	W	90
Whins, The	Lancs	SD7737	53°50·0'	2°20·6'W	X	103
Whin Stone Gill	Cumbr	SD7495	54°21·2'	2°23·6'W	W	98
Whinstone Lee Tor	Derby	SK2087	53°23·0'	1°41·5'W	X	110
Whinstone Ridge	N Yks	NZ8701	54°24·1'	0°39·2'W	X	94
Whins Wood	Brad	SE0538	53°50·5'	1°55·0'W	T	104
Whin, The	Scot Bord	NT4739	55°38·8'	2°50·1'W	X	73
Whintingstown	Cumbr	NY5275	55°4·3'	2°44·7'W	X	86
Whinyard Rocks	Powys	SO2062	52°15·3'	3°9·9'W	X	137,148
Whin Yeats	Cumbr	SD5579	54°12·5'	2°41·0'W	X	97
Whip Corrie	Highld	NC6332	58°15·6'	4°19·6'W	X	16
Whipcott	Devon	ST0718	50°57·5'	3°19·1'W	T	181
Whipley Manor	Surrey	SU9452	51°15·8'	0°38·8'W	X	186
Whipley Manor	Surrey	TQ0341	51°9·8'	0°31·2'W	X	186
Whippance Fm	I of W	SZ4693	50°44·3'	1°20·5'W	FM	196
Whippendell Botton	Herts	TL0502	51°42·6'	0°28·4'W	T	166
Whippendell Wood	Herts	TQ0797	51°39·9'	0°26·8'W	F	166,176
Whippenscott	Devon	SS7721	50°58·7'	3°44·7'W	X	180
Whipper Slack	Cumbr	NY6274	55°3·8'	2°35·3'W	X	86
Whippielaw	Midlo	NT3963	55°51·6'	2°58·0'W	X	66
Whippingham	I of W	SZ5193	50°44·3'	1°16·3'W	T	196
Whipps Cross Hospl	Wal F	TQ3888	51°34·5'	0°0·1'W	X	177
Whip Ridding	Notts	SK6759	53°7·7'	0°59·5'W	X	120
Whip Ridding Fm	Notts	SK6759	53°7·7'	0°59·5'W	FM	120
Whipsiderry	Corn	SW8363	50°25·8'	5°3·0'W	T	200
Whipsnade	Beds	TL0018	51°51·3'	0°32·5'W	T	166
Whipsnade Heath	Beds	TL0118	51°51·3'	0°31·6'W	X	166
Whipsnade Park Zoo	Beds	TL0017	51°50·8'	0°32·5'W	X	166
Whip, The	Highld	NC6232	58°15·6'	4°20·6'W	H	16
Whipton	Devon	SX9493	50°43·9'	3°29·7'W	T	192
Whirl Burn	D & G	NY2098	55°16·4'	3°15·1'W	W	79
Whirlbush Fm	Bucks	SP7606	51°45·1'	0°53·5'W	FM	165
Whirleybarn	Ches	SJ8874	53°16·0'	2°10·4'W	X	118
Whirley Fm	Ches	SJ8774	53°16·0'	2°11·3'W	FM	118
Whirley Gill	N Yks	SD9793	54°20·2'	2°2·3'W	W	98
Whirley Grove	Ches	SJ8875	53°16·6'	2°10·4'W	T	118
Whirley Hall	Ches	SJ8774	53°16·0'	2°11·3'W	X	118
Whirleyshaws	Northum	NU2003	55°19·5'	1°40·7'W	X	81
Whirl Howe	Cumbr	NY4905	54°26·5'	2°46·8'W	X	90
Whirlow	Sheff	SK3182	53°20·3'	1°31·7'W	T	110,111
Whirlow Brook	Sheff	SK3182	53°20·3'	1°31·7'W	T	110,111
Whirlpippin	Cumbr	SD1685	54°15·5'	3°17·0'W	X	96
Whirl Pool	Corn	SW4136	50°10·3'	5°37·3'W	W	203
Whirlpool	D & G	NX0649	54°48·2'	5°0·7'W	X	82
Whirl Rig	D & G	NY2098	55°16·4'	3°15·1'W	H	79
Whirls End	S Glos	ST5591	51°37·2'	2°38·6'W	X	162,172
Whirls Water	Shetld	HU4147	60°12·6'	1°15·1'W	W	3
Whirly	Shetld	HU4980	60°30·3'	1°6·0'W	X	1,2,3
Whirly Gill	D & G	NT1313	55°24·4'	3°22·0'W	X	78
Whirly Kips	Fife	NO3019	56°21·7'	3°7·5'W	X	59
Whirly Knowe	Shetld	HT9537	60°7·3'	2°4·9'W	X	4
Whirrieston	Stir	NN6601	56°11·2'	4°9·1'W	X	57
Whirstone Hill	D & G	NX6961	54°55·8'	4°2·2'W	H	83,84
Whisby	Lincs	SK9067	53°11·8'	0°38·8'W	T	121
Whiscombe Hill	Somer	ST4629	51°3·7'	2°45·9'W	X	193
Whisgills	Scot Bord	NY4583	55°8·5'	2°51·3'W	X	79
Whisgills Edge	Scot Bord	NY4483	55°8·5'	2°52·3'W	X	79
Whisker Hill	Notts	SK6979	53°18·4'	0°57·5'W	X	120
Whiskershiel Farm	Northum	NY9593	55°14·1'	2°4·3'W	FM	81
Whislebare	Shetld	HU1956	60°17·5'	1°38·9'W	X	3
Whisper Dales	N Yks	SE9592	54°19·1'	0°31·9'W	X	94,101
Whisperdales	N Yks	SE9693	54°19·7'	0°31·0'W	X	94,101
Whisperdales Beck	N Yks	SE9592	54°19·1'	0°31·9'W	W	94,101
Whispering Knights	Oxon	SP3030	51°58·3'	1°33·4'W	X	151
Whispering Knights (Burial Chamber)	Oxon	SP3030	51°58·3'	1°33·4'W	A	151
Whissendine	Rut	SK8214	52°43·3'	0°46·8'W	T	130
Whissendine Lodge	Rut	SK8014	52°43·3'	0°48·5'W	X	130
Whissenthorpe	Rut	SK8014	52°43·3'	0°48·5'W	X	130
Whisslewell Fm	Devon	SX7977	50°35·0'	3°42·2'W	FM	191
Whissonsett	Norf	TF9123	52°46·5'	0°50·3'E	T	132
Whisterfield	Ches	SJ8271	53°14·4'	2°15·8'W	T	118
Whistle Bare	Northum	NT9742	55°40·5'	2°2·4'W	X	75
Whistlebare	Orkney	HY4629	59°8·9'	2°56·2'W	X	5,6
Whistleberry	Aberd	NO8575	56°52·2'	2°14·3'W	X	45
Whistleberry Castle	Aberd	NO8675	56°52·2'	2°13·3'W	A	45
Whistle Br	Somer	ST5612	50°54·6'	2°37·2'W	X	194
Whistlebrae	Pth & Kin	NN8209	56°15·8'	3°53·9'W	X	57
Whistle Brook	Bucks	SP9417	51°50·9'	0°37·7'W	W	165
Whistle Brook Fm	Bucks	SP9420	51°52·5'	0°37·7'W	FM	165
Whistlefield	Arg & Bt	NS1493	56°5·9'	4°59·0'W	X	56
Whistlefield	Arg & Bt	NS2392	56°5·5'	4°50·3'W	T	56
Whistle Ho	N Yks	SE2153	53°58·6'	1°40·4'W	X	104
Whistle Lodge	W Loth	NT0561	55°50·2'	3°30·6'W	X	65
Whistlers	Kent	TQ4646	51°11·9'	0°5·8'E	X	188
Whistler's Fm	Hants	SU3553	51°16·7'	1°29·5'W	FM	185
Whistley Fm	Dorset	ST7828	51°3·3'	2°18·4'W	FM	183
Whistley Fm	Wilts	ST9859	51°20·0'	2°1·3'W	FM	173
Whistley Green	Wok	SU7974	51°27·8'	0°51·4'W	T	175
Whistley Hill	Devon	SX7669	50°30·7'	3°44·6'W	X	202
Whistley Mill Fm	Wok	SU7874	51°27·8'	0°52·2'W	FM	175
Whistley Wood	Northnts	SP6141	52°4·1'	1°6·2'W	F	152
Whistling Green	Cumbr	SD1992	54°19·3'	3°14·3'W	X	96
Whistlow	Oxon	SP4525	51°55·5'	1°20·3'W	T	164
Whiston	Know	SJ4791	53°25·0'	2°47·4'W	T	108
Whiston	Northnts	SP8460	52°14·1'	0°45·8'W	T	152
Whiston	Roth	SK4590	53°24·5'	1°19·0'W	T	111
Whiston	Staffs	SJ8914	52°43·7'	2°9·4'W	T	127
Whiston	Staffs	SK0347	53°1·5'	1°56·9'W	T	119,128
Whiston Brook	Staffs	SJ8714	52°43·6'	2°11·1'W	W	127
Whiston Common	Staffs	SK0447	53°1·5'	1°56·0'W	X	119,128
Whiston Cross	Know	SJ4691	53°25·0'	2°48·3'W	T	108
Whiston Cross	Shrops	SJ7903	52°37·7'	2°18·2'W	T	127
Whiston Eaves	Staffs	SK0446	53°0·9'	1°56·0'W	X	119,128
Whiston Hall	Shrops	SJ7902	52°37·2'	2°18·2'W	X	127
Whiston Priory	Shrops	SJ3912	52°42·4'	2°53·8'W	X	126
Whitacre Fields	Warw	SP2592	52°31·8'	1°37·5'W	X	140
Whitacre Fm	Staffs	SK0705	52°38·8'	1°53·4'W	FM	139
Whitacre Hall	Warw	SP2493	52°32·3'	1°38·4'W	X	139
Whitacre Heath	Warw	SP2192	52°31·8'	1°41·0'W	T	139
Whita Hill	D & G	NY3784	55°9·0'	2°58·9'W	H	79
Whitaker Channel	Essex	TR0999	51°39·3'	1°1·7'E	W	168
Whitaloo Point	Orkney	HY2628	59°8·2'	3°17·1'W	X	6
Whita Rig	D & G	NY3991	55°12·8'	2°57·1'W	X	79
Whitaside Moor	N Yks	SD9895	54°21·3'	2°1·4'W	X	98
Whitaside Tarn	N Yks	SD9795	54°21·3'	2°2·4'W	W	98
Whitbarrow	Cumbr	SD4486	54°16·2'	2°51·2'W	H	97
Whitbarrow Scar	Cumbr	SD4487	54°16·8'	2°51·2'W	X	97
Whitbarrow Village	Cumbr	NY4028	54°38·9'	2°55·4'W	T	90
Whitbatch Fm	Shrops	SO5177	52°23·6'	2°42·8'W	FM	137,138
Whit Beck	Cumbr	NY1725	54°37·0'	3°16·7'W	W	89,90
Whit Beck	Cumbr	NY2825	54°37·2'	3°6·5'W	W	89,90
Whitbeck	Cumbr	SD1184	54°14·9'	3°21·5'W	T	96
Whitbeck	Cumbr	SD7090	54°18·5'	2°27·2'W	X	98
Whit Beck	N Yks	SE0872	54°8·9'	1°52·2'W	W	99
Whitbeck Fm	N Yks	SE0973	54°9·4'	1°51·3'W	FM	99
Whitbeck Manor	N Yks	SE1648	53°55·9'	1°45·0'W	X	104
Whitberry Burn	Cumbr	NY5273	55°3·2'	2°44·7'W	W	86
Whitbourne	Heref	SO7256	52°12·3'	2°24·2'W	T	149
Whitbourne Ford	Heref	SO7258	52°13·4'	2°24·2'W	X	149
Whitbourne Hall	Heref	SO7056	52°12·3'	2°25·9'W	X	149
Whitbourne Moor	Wilts	ST8245	51°12·5'	2°15·1'W	T	183
Whitbourne Springs	Wilts	ST8344	51°11·9'	2°14·2'W	X	183
Whitburgh Ho	Midlo	NT4263	55°51·7'	2°55·2'W	X	66
Whitburgh Mains	Midlo	NT4063	55°51·6'	2°57·1'W	X	66
Whitburn	S Tyne	NZ4062	54°57·3'	1°22·1'W	T	88
Whitburn	W Loth	NS9464	55°51·7'	3°41·2'W	T	65
Whitburn Bay	Sund	NZ4060	54°56·2'	1°22·1'W	W	88
Whitburn Colliery	S Tyne	NZ4063	54°57·8'	1°22·1'W	T	88
Whitby	Ches	SJ3975	53°16·4'	2°54·5'W	T	117
Whitby	N Yks	NZ8910	54°28·9'	0°37·2'W	T	94
Whitbyheath	Ches	SJ3974	53°15·8'	2°54·5'W	T	117
Whitby Sands	N Yks	NZ8811	54°29·4'	0°38·1'W	X	94
Whitby Steads	Cumbr	NY5022	54°35·7'	2°46·0'W	X	90
Whitcalls Fm	Oxon	SU6785	51°33·8'	1°1·6'W	FM	175
Whitcastles	D & G	NY2387	55°10·5'	3°12·1'W	X	79
Whitcastles Hill	D & G	NY2287	55°10·5'	3°13·1'W	H	79
Whitchester	Northum	NY7263	54°57·9'	2°25·8'W	X	86,87
Whitchester	Northum	NY7783	55°8·7'	2°21·2'W	X	80
Whitchester	Northum	NZ0968	55°0·6'	1°51·1'W	X	88
Whitchester	Scot Bord	NT7158	55°49·1'	2°27·3'W	X	67,74
Whitchester Moor	Northum	NY7882	55°8·2'	2°20·3'W	X	80
Whitchesters	Scot Bord	NT4611	55°23·7'	2°50·7'W	X	79
Whitchurch	Bath & NE Somer	ST6167	51°24·3'	2°33·3'W	T	172
Whitchurch	Bucks	SP8020	51°52·6'	0°49·9'W	T	165
Whitchurch	Card	ST1479	51°30·4'	3°14·0'W	T	171
Whitchurch	Devon	SX4973	50°32·5'	4°7·5'W	T	191,201
Whitchurch	Hants	SU4648	51°14·0'	1°20·1'W	T	185
Whitchurch	Heref	SO5417	51°51·2'	2°39·7'W	T	162
Whitchurch	Pemb	SM8025	51°53·1'	5°11·4'W	T	157
Whitchurch	Shrops	SJ5441	52°58·1'	2°40·7'W	T	117
Whitchurch	Somer	ST7220	50°59·0'	2°23·5'W	T	183
Whitchurch Canonicorum	Dorset	SY3995	50°45·3'	2°51·5'W	T	193
Whitchurch Common	Devon	SX5374	50°33·1'	4°4·1'W	X	191,201
Whitchurch Down	Devon	SX5073	50°32·5'	4°6·6'W	X	191,201
Whitchurch Fm	Somer	ST6353	51°16·7'	2°31·4'W	FM	183
Whitchurch Fm	Warw	SP2248	52°8·0'	1°40·3'W	FM	151
Whitchurch Hill	Oxon	SU6479	51°30·6'	1°4·3'W	T	175
Whitchurch-on-Thames	Oxon	SU6377	51°29·5'	1°5·2'W	T	175
Whitcliffe	N Yks	SE3069	54°7·2'	1°32·0'W	X	99
Whitcliffe	Shrops	SO5074	52°21·9'	2°43·7'W	X	137,138
Whitcliffe Scar	N Yks	NZ1302	54°25·0'	1°47·6'W	X	92
Whitcliffe Wood	N Yks	NZ1401	54°24·5'	1°46·6'W	F	92
Whitcliff Park (Deer Park)	Glos	ST6697	51°40·5'	2°29·1'W	X	162
Whitcombe	Devon	SS9312	50°54·1'	3°30·9'W	X	181
Whitcombe	Devon	SX9284	50°39·0'	3°31·3'W	X	192
Whitcombe	Dorset	SY7188	50°41·7'	2°24·3'W	T	194
Whitcombe	Somer	ST6323	51°0·5'	2°31·3'W	T	183
Whitcombe Barn	Dorset	SY7086	50°40·6'	2°25·1'W	X	194
Whitcombe Hill	Dorset	SY7399	50°47·6'	2°22·6'W	X	194
Whitcombe Manor	Dorset	SY7187	50°41·1'	2°24·2'W	X	194
Whitcombe Vale	Dorset	SY8087	50°41·2'	2°16·6'W	X	194
Whit Coombe	W Berks	SU3083	51°32·9'	1°33·6'W	X	174
Whitcot	Shrops	SO3791	52°31·0'	2°55·3'W	T	137
Whitcott	Devon	SS7728	51°2·5'	3°44·9'W	X	180
Whitcott Evan	Shrops	SO2781	52°25·6'	3°4·0'W	X	137
Whitcott Keysett	Shrops	SO2782	52°26·1'	3°4·0'W	T	137
White Abbey	Shrops	SJ3715	52°44·0'	2°55·6'W	X	126
Whiteacen	Moray	NJ2546	57°30·1'	3°14·6'W	X	28
Whiteacre	Kent	TR1147	51°11·2'	1°1·6'E	T	179,189
Whiteacres Fm	Worcs	SO8246	52°7·0'	2°15·4'W	FM	150
Whiteacres Hill	Scot Bord	NT5212	55°24·2'	2°45·0'W	X	79
Whiteadder Resr	E Loth	NT6563	55°51·8'	2°33·1'W	W	67
Whiteadder Water	E Loth	NT6465	55°52·9'	2°34·1'W	W	67
Whiteadder Water	Scot Bord	NT7759	55°49·7'	2°21·6'W	W	67,74
Whiteadder Water	Scot Bord	NT7857	55°48·6'	2°20·6'W	W	67,74
Whiteadder Water	Scot Bord	NT7857	55°48·6'	2°20·6'W	W	67,74
White Alice	Corn	SW6934	50°9·9'	5°13·7'W	X	203
White Anthony Fm	Powys	SO2573	52°21·2'	3°5·7'W	FM	137,148
Whiteash Green	Essex	TL7930	51°56·6'	0°36·7'E	T	167
Whiteash Hill	Moray	NJ3857	57°36·2'	3°1·8'W	H	28
Whiteash Hill Wood	Moray	NJ3758	57°36·7'	3°2·8'W	F	28
White Averham	N Yks	SE6860	54°2·1'	0°57·3'W	X	100
White Ayre	Shetld	HU4844	60°10·9'	1°7·6'W	X	4
White Ball	Somer	ST0919	50°58·0'	3°17·4'W	T	181
White Ball Hill	Somer	ST0918	50°57·5'	3°17·4'W	X	181
White Band	Durham	NY8322	54°35·8'	2°15·4'W	X	91,92
Whitebank	Pth & Kin	NO0025	56°24·7'	3°36·8'W	X	52,53,58
White Barn	Essex	TL8520	51°51·1'	0°41·6'E	X	168
Whitebarn	Oxon	SP4703	51°43·7'	1°18·8'W	X	164
Whitebarn Fm	Suff	TM1367	52°15·8'	1°7·7'E	FM	156
Whitebarns	Herts	TL4329	51°56·7'	0°5·2'E	X	167
White Barony	Scot Bord	NT2646	55°42·4'	3°10·2'W	X	73
White Barrow	Devon	SX5679	50°35·8'	4°1·7'W	A	191
White Barrow	Hants	SU5851	51°15·5'	1°9·7'W	A	185
White Barrow	Wilts	SU0346	51°13·0'	1°57·0'W	X	184
Whitebarrow Downs	Corn	SX1970	50°30·3'	4°32·8'W	X	201
Whitebarrow Fm	Corn	SX1970	50°30·3'	4°32·8'W	FM	201
White Barrow (Long Barrow)	Wilts	SU0346	51°13·0'	1°57·0'W	A	184
White Barrows	Devon	SX6665	50°28·4'	3°52·9'W	A	202
White Bay	N Ayr	NS1759	55°47·6'	4°54·7'W	W	63
White Beacon Hags	N Yks	SD8995	54°21·3'	2°9·7'W	X	98
Whitebear	Devon	SS3911	50°52·8'	4°16·9'W	X	190
Whitebeck	Cumbr	NY5674	55°3·8'	2°40·9'W	X	86
Whitebeck	Cumbr	SD4589	54°17·9'	2°50·3'W	X	97
White Beck	N Yks	SE9290	54°18·1'	0°34·8'W	W	94,101
White Beech	Surrey	SU9836	51°7·1'	0°35·6'W	X	186
White Bents	Angus	NO3076	56°52·5'	3°8·5'W	H	44
White Birch Cott	N Yks	SD7895	54°21·2'	2°19·9'W	X	98
Whitebirk	Black w Dar	SD7028	53°45·1'	2°26·9'W	T	103
White Birks Common	N Yks	SD7794	54°20·7'	2°20·8'W	X	98
White Birren	D & G	NY2791	55°12·7'	3°8·4'W	X	79
White Birren (Settlement)	D & G	NY2791	55°12·7'	3°8·4'W	A	79
Whitebog	Aberd	NJ8548	57°31·6'	2°14·6'W	X	30
Whitebog	Aberd	NJ9359	57°37·5'	2°6·6'W	X	30
White Bog	Cumbr	NY4617	54°33·0'	2°49·7'W	X	90
Whitebog	Highld	NH7260	57°37·0'	4°8·1'W	X	21,27
White Bog	Midlo	NT2963	55°51·6'	3°7·6'W	X	66
White Borran	Cumbr	SD2689	54°17·7'	3°7·8'W	A	96,97
White Br	Bucks	SP7129	51°57·5'	0°57·6'W	X	165
White Br	Lancs	SD4615	53°38·0'	2°48·6'W	X	108
White Br	Norf	TF9904	52°36·1'	0°56·7'E	X	144
White Br	Somer	ST6454	51°17·3'	2°30·6'W	X	183
White Brackens Ho	Cumbr	NY7704	54°26·1'	2°20·9'W	X	91
Whitebrae	Angus	NO5043	56°34·8'	2°48·4'W	X	54
White Brae	Cumbr	NY6277	55°5·4'	2°35·3'W	X	86
White Brae	D & G	NY4191	55°12·8'	2°55·2'W	X	79
White Brae Top	D & G	NX4380	55°5·6'	4°27·2'W	X	77
White Breast	Orkney	HY2701	58°53·7'	3°15·5'W	X	6,7
Whitebrick Moor	Derby	SK4977	53°17·5'	1°15·5'W	X	120
White Bridge	Aberd	NO0188	56°58·6'	3°37·3'W	X	43
Whitebridge	Highld	ND2672	58°38·0'	3°16·0'W	X	7,12
Whitebridge	Highld	ND3550	58°26·3'	3°6·3'W	X	12
White Bridge	Highld	NH2801	57°4·3'	4°49·8'W	X	34
Whitebridge	Highld	NH4815	57°12·3'	4°30·5'W	T	34
White Bridge	Pth & Kin	NN7753	56°39·4'	3°59·9'W	X	42,51,52
White Bridge	Somer	ST4740	51°9·6'	2°45·1'W	X	182
Whitebridge Bay	Arg & Bt	NS0199	56°8·8'	5°11·8'W	W	55
Whitebridge Fm	Wilts	ST8727	51°2·8'	2°10·7'W	FM	183
Whitebridge Plantation	Highld	NH4715	57°12·3'	4°31·5'W	F	34
Whitebrook	Monm	SO5306	51°45·3'	2°40·5'W	T	162
Whitebrook	Newp	ST4292	51°37·7'	2°49·9'W	X	171,172
White Brook	Win & Maid	SU9084	51°33·1'	0°41·7'W	W	175
Whitebrow	Aberd	NJ5928	57°20·7'	2°40·4'W	X	37
White Brow	Cumbr	NY8911	54°29·9'	2°9·8'W	X	91,92
White Brow	Derby	SK0588	53°23·6'	1°55·1'W	X	110

Whiteburn	Aberd	NJ5628	57°20·7′	2°43·4′W	X	37
Whiteburn	Aberd	NJ9638	57°26·2′	2°3·5′W	X	30
White Burn	Angus	NO4161	56°44·5′	2°57·4′W	W	44
Whiteburn	Angus	NO4260	56°43·9′	2°56·4′W	X	44
White Burn	Angus	NO5483	56°56·4′	2°44·9′W	W	44
White Burn	D & G	NX5772	55°1·6′	4°13·8′W	W	77
White Burn	D & G	NX7299	55°16·4′	4°0·5′W	W	77
White Burn	D & G	NX7382	55°7·2′	3°59·1′W	W	77
White Burn	Northum	NT9010	55°23·3′	2°9·0′W	W	80
Whiteburn	Scot Bord	NT5947	55°43·1′	2°38·7′W	X	73,74
White Burn	Scot Bord	NT6109	55°22·7′	2°36·5′W	W	80
Whiteburn	Scot Bord	NT6209	55°22·7′	2°35·5′W	X	80
Whiteburn	Scot Bord	NT7664	55°52·4′	2°22·6′W	X	67
White Burn	S Lanak	NS6143	55°39·9′	4°12·2′W	W	71
White Burn	S Lanak	NS9906	55°20·5′	3°35·1′W	W	78
Whiteburnshank	Northum	NT8912	55°24·4′	2°10·0′W	X	80
Whitebushes	Surrey	TQ2847	51°12·7′	0°9·7′W	T	187
White Cairn	Angus	NO4882	56°55·8′	2°50·8′W	A	44
White Cairn	D & G	NX0966	54°57·4′	4°58·6′W	A	82
Whitecairn	D & G	NX2059	54°53·9′	4°48·0′W	X	82
White Cairn	D & G	NX2554	54°51·3′	4°43·1′W	A	82
White Cairn	D & G	NX2667	54°58·3′	4°42·7′W	A	82
White Cairn	D & G	NX3479	55°4·9′	4°35·6′W	A	76
White Cairn	D & G	NX3655	54°52·0′	4°32·9′W	A	83
White Cairn	D & G	NX4959	54°54·4′	4°20·9′W	A	83
White Cairn	D & G	NX5274	55°2·6′	4°18·6′W	A	77
White Cairn	D & G	NX6883	55°7·7′	4°3·8′W	A	77
Whitecairn	D & G	NX7868	54°59·8′	3°54·0′W	X	84
White Cairn	D & G	NX8297	55°15·4′	3°51·0′W	A	78
White Cairn	D & G	NX8587	55°10·1′	3°47·9′W	A	78
Whitecairn	D & G	NY1374	55°3·4′	3°21·3′W	X	85
White Cairn	S Ayr	NX2278	55°4·1′	4°46·8′W	A	76
White Cairn	S Ayr	NX2282	55°6·3′	4°47·0′W	X	76
Whitecairns	Aberd	NJ8752	57°33·7′	2°12·6′W	X	30
Whitecairns	Aberd	NJ9217	57°14·9′	2°7·5′W	T	38
Whitecairns	Aberd	NK0362	57°39·1′	1°56·5′W	X	30
Whitecamp Brae	S Lanak	NT0421	55°28·7′	3°30·7′W	H	72
White Carr	Lancs	SD4951	53°57·4′	2°46·2′W	X	102
Whitecarr Beck	N Yks	SE6164	54°4·3′	1°3·6′W	W	100
Whitecarr Beck	N Yks	SE7461	54°2·6′	0°51·8′W	W	100
Whitecarr Fm	Derby	SK3659	53°7·9′	1°27·3′W	FM	119
White Carr Fm	Lancs	SD4335	53°48·7′	2°51·5′W	FM	102
White Carr Fm	N Yks	SE6164	54°4·3′	1°3·6′W	FM	100
White Carr Fm	York	SE6850	53°56·7′	0°57·4′W	FM	105,106
Whitecarr Ings	N Yks	SE6164	54°4·3′	1°3·6′W	X	100
White Carr Nooking	York	SE6660	54°2·1′	0°59·1′W	F	100
White Cart Water	C of Glas	NS5761	55°49·5′	4°16·5′W	W	64
White Castle	E Loth	NT6168	55°54·5′	2°37·0′W	X	67
White Castle	Monm	SO3716	51°50·6′	2°54·5′W	A	161
White Castle	Monm	SO3816	51°50·6′	2°53·6′W	X	161
Whitecastle	S Lanak	NT0141	55°39·4′	3°34·0′W	X	72
White Castle (Fort)	E Loth	NT6168	55°54·5′	2°37·0′W	A	67
Whitecastle Hill	S Lanak	NS9138	55°37·7′	3°43·4′W	H	71,72
White Cast Marshes	Suff	TM5092	52°28·3′	1°41·3′E	W	134
White Caterthun	Angus	NO5466	56°47·3′	2°44·7′W	X	44
White Caterthun (Fort)	Angus	NO5466	56°47·3′	2°44·7′W	A	44
White Cawsey	Devon	SS6240	51°8·8′	3°58·0′W	H	180
Whitechapel	C of Lon	TQ3381	51°31·0′	0°4·6′W	T	176,177
Whitechapel	Lancs	SD5541	53°52·0′	2°40·6′W	T	102
Whitechapel	Northum	NY8064	54°58·5′	2°18·3′W	X	86,87
Whitechapel Hill	Northum	NY8065	54°59·0′	2°18·3′W	X	86,87
Whitechapel Manor (Hotel)	Devon	SS7527	51°2·0′	3°46·6′W	A	180
Whitechapel Moors	Devon	SS7526	51°1·4′	3°46·6′W	X	180
Whitechaple Fm	Somer	ST7950	51°15·2′	2°17·7′W	FM	183
White Chest	Orkney	ND2096	58°50·9′	3°22·7′W	X	7
Whitechurch	Devon	SX6739	50°14·4′	3°51·5′W	X	202
Whitechurch Maund	Heref	SO5649	52°8·5′	2°38·2′W	T	149
White Clauchrie	S Ayr	NX2986	55°8·6′	4°40·6′W	X	76
Whitecleat	Orkney	HY5108	58°57·6′	2°50·6′W	X	6,7
Whitecleat	Orkney	HY5219	59°3·6′	2°49·7′W	X	6
Whitecleuch	S Lanak	NS8219	55°27·3′	3°51·5′W	X	71,78
Whitecleuch Fell	D & G	NY3186	55°10·1′	3°4·6′W	H	79
White Cleuch Hill	Scot Bord	NT2229	55°33·2′	3°13·8′W	H	73
White Cleugh	Scot Bord	NT6868	55°54·5′	2°30·3′W	X	67
Whitecleugh	S Lanak	NS9252	55°45·2′	3°42·8′W	X	65,72
Whitecleugh Outdoor Centre	S Lanak	NS8220	55°27·8′	3°51·5′W	X	71,72
Whitecliff	Glos	SO5610	51°47·5′	2°37·9′W	T	162
White Cliff	Wilts	ST9151	51°15·7′	2°7·4′W	X	184
Whitecliff Bay	I of W	SZ6486	50°40·4′	1°5·3′W	W	196
Whitecliff Down	Wilts	ST8338	51°8·7′	2°14·2′W	X	183
White Cliffe Fm	Derby	SK1757	53°6·8′	1°44·4′W	FM	119
Whitecliffe Fm	Derby	SK2557	53°6·8′	1°37·2′W	FM	119
Whitecliff Fm	Dorset	SZ0280	50°37·4′	1°57·9′W	FM	195
Whitecliff Fm	Wilts	ST8538	51°8·7′	2°12·5′W	FM	183
Whitecliff Ledge	I of W	SZ6385	50°39·9′	1°6·1′W	X	196
White Cliff Rigg	N Yks	SE8685	54°15·4′	0°40·4′W	H	94,101
White Cliffs Country Trail	Kent	TR3248	51°11·3′	1°19·6′E	X	179
Whiteclose	Cumbr	NY4670	55°1·5′	2°50·3′W	X	86
White Close	Cumbr	NY5069	55°1·0′	2°46·5′W	X	86
Whiteclosegate	Cumbr	NY4157	54°54·5′	2°54·8′W	T	85
White Close Hill	Durham	NZ0112	54°30·4′	1°58·7′W	X	92
Whitecloserigg	Cumbr	NY4570	55°1·5′	2°51·2′W	X	86
White Colne	Essex	TL8729	51°55·9′	0°43·6′E	T	168
White Combe	Cumbr	SD1586	54°16·0′	3°17·9′W	X	96
White Coomb	D & G	NT1615	55°25·6′	3°19·2′W	H	79
White Coppice	Lancs	SD6118	53°39·7′	2°35·0′W	T	109
White Corries	Highld	NN2652	56°37·9′	4°49·8′W	X	41
Whitecote	Leeds	SE2436	53°49·4′	1°37·7′W	T	104
White Cove	D & G	NY4091	55°12·8′	2°56·1′W	X	79
White Cow Wood	Aberd	NJ9551	57°33·2′	2°4·6′W	F	30
White Crag	Cumbr	NY2612	54°30·1′	3°8·1′W	X	89,90
White Crag	Durham	NY9809	54°28·8′	2°1·4′W	X	92
White Crag	Lancs	SD6155	53°59·6′	2°35·3′W	X	102,103
White Crag Moss	Durham	NY9808	54°28·3′	2°1·4′W	X	92
White Crag Plantn	Brad	SE0646	53°54·8′	1°54·1′W	F	104
White Crags	Northum	NT6901	55°18·4′	2°28·9′W	X	80
Whitecraig	E Loth	NT3570	55°55·4′	3°2·0′W	T	66
White Craig	Fife	NO2317	56°20·6′	3°14·3′W	X	58
Whitecraig	N Ayr	NS2751	55°43·5′	4°44·8′W	X	63
White Craig	S Ayr	NS2915	55°24·2′	4°41·6′W	X	70
White Craig	S Lanak	NT0753	55°45·9′	3°28·5′W	H	65,72
Whitecraig Head	D & G	NX8099	55°16·5′	3°52·9′W	X	78
Whitecraighead	N Lanak	NS7957	55°47·7′	3°55·4′W	X	64
Whitecraigs	E Renf	NS5557	55°47·3′	4°18·3′W	T	64
White Craigs	Pth & Kin	NO1803	56°13·0′	3°18·9′W	X	58
Whitecraigs	S Lanak	NS7147	55°42·2′	4°2·7′W	X	64
White Creek	Cumbr	SD4377	54°11·4′	2°52·0′W	W	97
White Creich Hill	Pth & Kin	NN9905	56°13·9′	3°37·3′W	H	58
Whitecroft	Devon	SS3701	50°47·4′	4°18·4′W	X	190
White Croft	D & G	NX9058	54°54·5′	3°42·5′W	X	84
Whitecroft	D & G	NY1072	55°2·3′	3°24·1′W	X	85
Whitecroft	Glos	SO6106	51°45·3′	2°33·5′W	T	162
Whitecroft	I of W	SZ4986	50°40·5′	1°18·0′W	X	196
Whitecroft	Somer	ST6240	51°9·7′	2°32·2′W	X	183
White Crofts	Thurr	TQ6480	51°29·9′	0°22·2′E	X	177
Whitecrook	D & G	NX1656	54°52·2′	4°51·6′W	X	82
Whitecrook	W Dunb	NS5069	55°53·7′	4°23·5′W	T	64
Whitecross	Aberd	NJ7122	57°17·5′	2°28·4′W	X	38
White Cross	Bath & NE Somer	ST5958	51°19·4′	2°34·9′W	T	172,182
White Cross	Bath & NE Somer	ST6256	51°18·3′	2°32·3′W	T	172
Whitecross	Corn	SW5234	50°9·5′	5°28·0′W	T	203
White Cross	Corn	SW6821	50°2·9′	5°14·1′W	T	203
White Cross	Corn	SW8959	50°23·8′	4°57·8′W	T	200
Whitecross	Corn	SW9672	50°31·0′	4°52·3′W	T	200
Whitecross	Corn	SX1072	50°31·3′	4°40·4′W	X	200
Whitecross	Corn	SX1352	50°20·5′	4°37·3′W	T	200
White Cross	Darl	NZ1916	54°32·6′	1°42·0′W	X	92
White Cross	Devon	SS8706	50°50·8′	3°35·9′W	X	192
White Cross	Devon	SY0290	50°42·3′	3°22·9′W	X	192
White Cross	Devon	SY1192	50°43·5′	3°15·3′W	X	192,193
Whitecross	Dorset	SY4699	50°47·5′	2°45·6′W	T	193
Whitecross	Falk	NS9676	55°58·2′	3°39·5′W	T	65
White Cross	Heref	SO4940	52°3·6′	2°44·2′W	T	148,149
White Cross	Kirk	SE2512	53°36·5′	1°36·9′W	X	110
White Cross	Norf	TG0404	52°36·0′	1°1·1′E	X	144
White Cross	Norf	TG2225	52°46·8′	1°17·9′E	X	133,134
White Cross	Northum	NU1914	55°25·4′	1°41·6′W	A	81
White Cross	N Yks	NZ6710	54°29·1′	0°57·5′W	A	94
White Cross	N Yks	NZ6801	54°24·2′	0°56·7′W	A	94
White Cross	N Yks	SE2489	54°18·0′	1°37·5′W	A	99
White Cross	Oxon	SU6088	51°35·5′	1°7·6′W	X	175
Whitecross	Scot Bord	NT9064	55°52·4′	2°9·2′W	X	67
White Cross	Somer	SS8338	51°8·0′	3°40·0′W	X	181
White Cross	Somer	ST3449	51°14·4′	2°56·3′W	T	182
Whitecross	Somer	ST4024	51°1·0′	2°50·9′W	T	193
Whitecross	Staffs	SJ8622	52°48·0′	2°12·1′W	T	127
White Cross	Staffs	SO8191	52°31·2′	2°16·4′W	X	138
White Cross	Wilts	ST7732	51°5·4′	2°19·3′W	T	183
White Cross Bay	Cumbr	NY3900	54°23·8′	2°56·0′W	W	90
White Cross Clough	Lincs	TF4558	53°6·2′	0°10·4′E	X	122
White Cross Clough	Lincs	TF4658	53°6·2′	0°11·3′E	X	122
White Crosses	Lancs	SD4239	53°50·9′	2°52·5′W	X	102
White Cross Field	Cambs	TL5175	52°21·4′	0°13·4′E	X	143
White Cross Fm	Bath & NE Somer	ST5557	51°18·9′	2°38·4′W	FM	172,182
Whitecross Fm	Heref	SO5724	51°55·0′	2°37·1′W	FM	162
White Cross Fm	Lincs	TF4218	52°44·7′	0°6·6′E	FM	131
White Cross Fm	Suff	TM3755	52°8·8′	1°28·2′E	FM	156
Whitecross Green	Oxon	SP5915	51°50·1′	1°8·2′W	X	164
Whitecross Green Wood	Oxon	SP6014	51°49·5′	1°7·4′W	F	164,165
White Cross Hill	Cambs	TL4975	52°21·4′	0°11·7′E	T	143
Whitecross Stone	Cambs	TL3097	52°33·5′	0°4·5′W	A	142
White Culphin	Aberd	NJ5960	57°37·9′	2°40·7′W	X	29
Whitedale	E Yorks	TA1740	53°50·8′	0°12·9′W	X	107
Whitedale Ho	Hants	SU6515	50°56·1′	1°4·1′W	X	196
Whitedell Fm	Hants	SU5908	50°52·3′	1°9·3′W	FM	196
Whitedell Fm	Herts	TL0200	51°41·6′	0°31·1′W	FM	166
Whitedge Fm	Sefton	SD3004	53°31·9′	3°3·0′W	FM	108
Whitedike	D & G	NX8685	55°9·0′	3°46·9′W	X	78
Whiteditch Fm	Essex	TL5134	51°59·3′	0°12·3′E	FM	154
White Dod	D & G	NS8511	55°23·0′	3°48·5′W	H	71,78
Whitedown	Hants	SU5854	51°17·2′	1°9·7′W	X	185
White Down	Somer	ST3609	50°52·9′	2°54·2′W	X	193
White Down Copse	Devon	ST0001	50°48·2′	3°24·8′W	F	192
White Downs	Corn	SW4235	50°9·8′	5°36·4′W	X	203
White Downs	Surrey	TQ1249	51°14·0′	0°23·4′W	X	187
White Dyke	D & G	NX3452	54°50·4′	4°34·7′W	X	82
White Dyke Fm	E Susx	TQ6008	50°51·2′	0°16·8′E	FM	199
Whitedyke Fm	Norf	TL6989	52°28·6′	0°29·7′E	FM	143
White Edge	Derby	SK2054	53°5·2′	1°41·7′W	X	119
White Edge	Derby	SK2676	53°17·1′	1°36·2′W	X	119
White Edge	Durham	NY8039	54°45·0′	2°18·2′W	X	91,92
White Edge	Durham	NY8941	54°46·1′	2°9·8′W	X	87
White Edge Moor	Derby	SK2678	53°18·1′	1°36·2′W	X	119
White Elm Fm	Essex	TL7902	51°41·5′	0°35·8′E	FM	167
White End	Glos	SO8125	51°55·6′	2°16·2′W	X	162
White End	Worcs	SO7834	52°0·5′	2°18·8′W	T	150
White End Park	Bucks	SP9800	51°41·6′	0°34·5′W	X	165
White Esk	D & G	NT2401	55°18·1′	3°11·4′W	W	79
White Falls	Highld	NN3993	57°0·3′	4°38·6′W	W	34
Whitefarland	N Ayr	NR8642	55°37·7′	5°23·5′W	T	62,69
Whitefarland Bay	Arg & Bt	NR4471	55°52·1′	6°5·1′W	W	60,61
Whitefarland Point	N Ayr	NR8642	55°37·7′	5°23·5′W	X	62,69
Whitefauld Hill	D & G	NY0293	55°13·5′	3°32·0′W	X	78
Whitefaulds	S Ayr	NS2909	55°21·0′	4°41·4′W	T	70,76
White Fell	Cumbr	SD6596	54°21·7′	2°31·9′W	X	97
White Fell	D & G	NX1973	55°1·4′	4°49·5′W	H	76
Whitefell Plantation	S Ayr	NX2583	55°6·9′	4°44·2′W	F	76
White Fen	Cambs	TL3492	52°30·8′	0°1·1′W	X	142
White Fen	Suff	TL7184	52°25·9′	0°31·3′E	X	143
White Fen Fm	Cambs	TL3490	52°29·7′	0°1·2′W	FM	142
White Fen Fm	Cambs	TL3592	52°30·8′	0°0·2′W	FM	142
Whitefield	Aberd	NJ5417	57°14·7′	2°45·3′W	X	37
Whitefield	Aberd	NJ7927	57°20·2′	2°20·5′W	X	38
Whitefield	Aberd	NO7874	56°51·7′	2°21·2′W	X	45
Whitefield	Bury	SD8106	53°33·3′	2°16·8′W	T	109
Whitefield	Cumbr	NY5565	54°58·9′	2°41·8′W	X	86
Whitefield	Devon	SS7035	51°6·2′	3°51·0′W	X	180
Whitefield	D & G	NX2354	54°51·2′	4°45·0′W	X	82
Whitefield	Dorset	SY9094	50°45·0′	2°8·1′W	T	195
Whitefield	Fife	NO2815	56°19·6′	3°9·4′W	X	59
Whitefield	Highld	ND1065	58°34·1′	3°32·4′W	X	11,12
Whitefield	Highld	ND1966	58°34·7′	3°23·1′W	X	11,12
Whitefield	Highld	ND2653	58°27·8′	3°15·6′W	X	11,12
Whitefield	Highld	ND3353	58°27·9′	3°8·4′W	X	12
Whitefield	Highld	NH5528	57°19·4′	4°24·0′W	X	26,35
Whitefield	Moray	NJ1760	57°37·6′	3°22·9′W	X	28
Whitefield	Moray	NJ4461	57°38·4′	2°55·8′W	X	28
Whitefield	Northum	NZ2386	55°10·3′	1°37·9′W	X	81
Whitefield	Scot Bord	NT3427	55°32·2′	3°2·3′W	X	73
Whitefield	Scot Bord	NT5937	55°37·7′	2°38·6′W	X	73,74
Whitefield	Somer	ST0729	51°3·4′	3°19·2′W	T	181
Whitefield Barton	Devon	SS5539	51°8·2′	4°4·0′W	X	180
Whitefield Barton	Devon	SS6741	51°9·4′	3°53·7′W	X	180
Whitefield Bottom	Dorset	SU1211	50°54·1′	1°49·4′W	X	195
Whitefield Castle	Pth & Kin	NO0861	56°44·2′	3°29·8′W	A	43
Whitefield Croft	Moray	NJ1761	57°38·1′	3°22·9′W	X	28
Whitefield Down	Devon	SS5639	51°8·2′	4°3·1′W	X	180
Whitefield Down	Devon	SS7136	51°6·8′	3°50·2′W	X	180
Whitefield Edge	Northum	NU0803	55°19·5′	1°52·0′W	X	81
Whitefield Fm	Devon	SS8424	51°0·5′	3°38·8′W	FM	181
Whitefield Fm	Hants	SU4400	50°48·1′	1°22·2′W	FM	196
Whitefield Fm	I of W	SZ5989	50°42·1′	1°9·5′W	FM	196
Whitefield Fm	Wilts	SU1976	51°29·2′	1°43·2′W	FM	173
Whitefield Hall	Oldham	SD9310	53°35·4′	2°5·9′W	X	109
Whitefield Hill	Hants	SU1800	50°48·2′	1°44·3′W	X	195
Whitefield Hill	Northum	NY9897	55°16·3′	2°1·5′W	H	81
Whitefield Hill	Pth & Kin	NO0862	56°44·7′	3°29·8′W	H	43
Whitefield Hill	Wilts	SU2076	51°29·2′	1°42·3′W	X	174
Whitefield Ho	Northum	NZ2598	55°16·8′	1°36·0′W	X	81
Whitefield Ho	Suff	TL9560	52°12·4′	0°51·6′E	X	155
Whitefield Lane End	Know	SJ4589	53°23·9′	2°49·2′W	T	108
Whitefield Loch	D & G	NX2355	54°51·8′	4°45·1′W	W	82
Whitefield of Dun	Angus	NO6462	56°45·2′	2°34·9′W	X	45
Whitefield Plantn	Hants	SU1709	50°53·0′	1°45·1′W	F	195
Whitefields	Aberd	NK0231	57°22·4′	1°57·5′W	X	30
Whitefields	Aberd	NK0331	57°22·4′	1°56·6′W	X	30
Whitefields Fm	Notts	SK7038	52°56·3′	0°57·1′W	FM	129
Whitefields Fm	N Yks	NZ1801	54°24·5′	1°42·9′W	FM	92
Whitefields Fm	Shrops	SO4990	52°30·6′	2°44·7′W	FM	137,138
Whitefields Fm	V of Glam	ST0175	51°28·2′	3°25·1′W	FM	170
Whitefields Fm	Wrekin	SJ6011	52°42·0′	2°35·1′W	FM	127
Whitefield Wood	I of W	SZ6089	50°42·1′	1°8·6′W	F	196
Whiteflat	E Ayr	NS5225	55°30·0′	4°20·2′W	T	70
White Fm	Dorset	ST9807	50°52·0′	2°1·3′W	FM	195
White Fm	E Yorks	SE7542	53°52·4′	0°51·1′W	FM	105,106
White Fm	Staffs	SJ7630	52°52·3′	2°21·0′W	FM	127
Whitefold	Highld	NH8944	57°28·6′	3°50·6′W	X	27
White Fold	Lancs	SD6239	53°51·0′	2°34·2′W	X	102,103
Whitefold	Pth & Kin	NN9414	56°18·7′	3°42·4′W	X	58
Whitefold Moss	Cumbr	NY6301	54°24·4′	2°33·8′W	X	91
Whitefolds	Moray	NJ2425	57°18·8′	3°15·2′W	X	36
White Force	Durham	NY8527	54°38·5′	2°13·5′W	W	91,92
Whiteford	Aberd	NJ7126	57°19·7′	2°28·4′W	T	38
Whiteford Burrows	Swan	SS4495	51°38·2′	4°14·9′W	X	159
Whiteford Fm	Corn	SX3573	50°32·2′	4°19·3′W	FM	201
Whiteford Hall	Norf	TG2402	52°34·4′	1°18·8′E	X	134
Whitefordhill	S Ayr	NS3720	55°27·1′	4°34·2′W	X	70
Whiteford Point	Swan	SS4496	51°38·7′	4°14·9′W	X	159
Whiteford Sands	Swan	SS4495	51°38·2′	4°14·9′W	X	159
Whitefowl Hill	Orkney	ND2196	58°50·9′	3°21·7′W	X	6,7
Whitefowl Nevi	Orkney	HY4911	58°59·3′	2°52·8′W	X	6
Whitefowl Nevi	Orkney	HY5904	58°55·5′	2°42·2′W	X	6
White Fowl Nevi	Orkney	HY5908	58°57·7′	2°42·3′W	X	6
Whitefurrows	Derby	SK4441	52°58·1′	1°20·3′W	X	129
White Gables	Ches	SJ8977	53°17·6′	2°9·5′W	X	118
White Gables Fm	Leic	SP3697	52°34·4′	1°27·7′W	FM	140
Whitegar	Highld	ND2461	58°32·1′	3°17·8′W	X	11,12
Whitegate	Ches	SJ6269	53°13·2′	2°33·7′W	T	118
White Gate	Kent	TR2041	51°7·8′	1°9·1′E	X	179,189
White Gate	Kirk	SE1205	53°32·7′	1°48·7′W	X	110
Whitegate	Moray	NJ4361	57°38·4′	2°56·8′W	X	28
White Gate	Oldham	SD8903	53°31·7′	2°9·5′W	T	109
White Gate	Oldham	SD9902	53°31·1′	2°0·5′W	X	109
White Gate	Shetld	HU5139	60°8·2′	1°4·4′W	X	4
White Gate	Somer	ST3406	50°51·2′	2°55·9′W	T	193
Whitegate Cottage	Cumbr	NY5171	55°2·1′	2°45·6′W	X	86
White Gate Fm	Cambs	TL4580	52°24·2′	0°8·3′E	FM	143
Whitegate Fm	Ches	SJ6249	53°2·5′	2°33·6′W	FM	118
Whitegate Fm	Norf	TG4311	52°38·8′	1°35·9′E	FM	134
White Gate Fm	Norf	TG4317	52°42·0′	1°36·2′E	FM	134
Whitegate Fm	Red & Cl	NZ5612	54°30·3′	1°7·7′W	FM	93
Whitegate Fm	Staffs	SJ8510	52°41·5′	2°12·9′W	FM	127
Whitegate Fm	Suff	TM1257	52°10·5′	1°6·4′E	FM	155
Whitegate Hill	Lincs	TA1200	53°29·3′	0°18·3′W	X	113
Whitegates	Pth & Kin	NS9997	56°9·6′	3°37·1′W	X	58
White Gates	Suff	TL9966	52°15·6′	0°55·4′E	X	155
Whitegates Fm	Ches	SJ5047	53°1·3′	2°44·3′W	FM	117
White Gates Fm	E Susx	TQ6233	51°4·6′	0°19·2′E	FM	188
White Gates Fm	Northnts	SP8583	52°26·5′	0°44·6′W	FM	141
Whitegates Fm	Sefton	SD4001	53°30·4′	2°53·9′W	FM	108
Whitegates Fm	Shrops	SJ6322	52°47·9′	2°32·5′W	FM	127
Whitegates Fm	Warw	SP3659	52°13·9′	1°28·0′W	FM	151
Whitegate Way	Ches	SJ5969	53°13·2′	2°36·4′W	X	117
Whitegate Way	Ches	SJ6068	53°12·7′	2°35·5′W	X	118
White Geese	Aberd	NJ4231	57°22·2′	2°57·4′W	X	37
White Gill	S Lanak	NS9921	55°28·6′	3°35·4′W	W	72
Whitegill Crag	Cumbr	NY2907	54°27·5′	3°5·3′W	X	89,90
White Gill Wood	S Lanak	NT0021	55°28·6′	3°34·5′W	F	72
White Glen	Angus	NO2371	56°49·7′	3°15·3′W	X	44
White Glen	Orkney	HY2401	58°53·6′	3°18·6′W	X	6,7
Whitegorse Fm	Lincs	TF0939	52°56·5′	0°22·3′W	FM	130
White Grain	Scot Bord	NT2328	55°32·6′	3°12·8′W	W	73
Whitegrain Fell	Scot Bord	NT5602	55°18·9′	2°41·2′W	X	80
Whitegrain Rig	Scot Bord	NT2328	55°32·6′	3°12·8′W	H	73
White Green	Cumbr	SD7297	54°22·3′	2°25·4′W	X	98

White Grit	Powys	SO3198	52°34·8'	3°0·7'W	T	137
Whitegrounds	N Yks	SE7868	54°6·4'	0°48·0'W	X	100
White Grunafirth	Shetld	HU2780	60°30·4'	1°30·0'W	H	3
White Haggle	Shetld	HP6314	60°48·5'	0°50·0'W	X	1
White Hagmark	Shetld	HP5907	60°44·8'	0°54·6'W	X	1
Whitehall	Aberd	NJ6428	57°20·7'	2°35·4'W	X	37
Whitehall	Angus	NO6145	56°36·0'	2°37·7'W	X	54
Whitehall	Beds	TL0934	51°59·9'	0°24·3'W	X	153
Whitehall	Black w Dar	SD6920	53°40·8'	2°27·7'W	T	103
Whitehall	Caer	ST0994	51°38·5'	3°18·5'W	X	171
White Hall	Cambs	TF4407	52°38·7'	0°8·1'E	X	142,143
Whitehall	Cambs	TL1781	52°25·1'	0°16·4'W	X	142
White Hall	Cambs	TL2460	52°13·7'	0°10·7'W	X	153
White Hall	Carm	SN4914	51°48·5'	4°11·0'W	X	159
White Hall	Ches	SJ7557	53°6·8'	2°22·0'W	X	118
Whitehall	C of Bris	ST6174	51°28·1'	2°33·3'W	T	172
Whitehall	Cumbr	NY2041	54°45·7'	3°14·2'W	A	85
Whitehall	Cumbr	NY7844	54°47·7'	2°20·1'W	X	86,87
White Hall	Cumbr	SD6191	54°19·0'	2°35·6'W	X	97
Whitehall	Devon	SS5337	51°7·0'	4°5·6'W	T	180
Whitehall	Devon	ST1214	50°55·4'	3°14·7'W	T	181,193
Whitehall	Devon	SX7145	50°17·7'	3°48·3'W	X	202
Whitehall	D & G	NX9685	55°9·2'	3°37·5'W	X	78
Whitehall	Dorset	ST8619	50°58·4'	2°11·6'W	X	183
Whitehall	Dorset	SY9082	50°38·5'	2°8·1'W	X	195
White Hall	Durham	NY9138	54°44·5'	2°8·0'W	X	91,92
Whitehall	Durham	NZ0847	54°49·3'	1°52·1'W	X	88
White Hall	Essex	TL5912	51°47·3'	0°18·7'E	X	167
White Hall	Essex	TM1622	51°51·5'	1°8·6'E	X	168,169
White Hall	E Yorks	TA0337	53°49·4'	0°25·7'W	X	107
White Hall	E Yorks	TA2923	53°41·5'	0°2·4'W	X	107,113
Whitehall	Fife	NO5509	56°16·5'	2°43·2'W	X	59
Whitehall	Hants	SU7452	51°16·0'	0°56·0'W	T	186
White Hall	Herts	TL2821	51°52·6'	0°8·0'W	T	166
Whitehall	Herts	TL3331	51°57·9'	0°3·4'W	T	166
Whitehall	Herts	TL4822	51°52·8'	0°9·4'E	X	167
Whitehall	Kent	TQ8257	51°17·2'	0°37·0'E	X	178,188
White Hall	Kent	TR2039	51°6·7'	1°9·0'E	X	179,189
White Hall	Lancs	SD4341	53°52·0'	2°51·6'W	X	102
White Hall	Lancs	SD7546	53°54·8'	2°22·4'W	X	103
Whitehall	Lincs	SK9768	53°12·2'	0°32·5'W	X	121
Whitehall	Monm	ST3397	51°40·3'	2°57·7'W	X	171
White Hall	Norf	TF8432	52°51·5'	0°44·4'E	X	132
White Hall	Norf	TF9001	52°34·6'	0°48·7'E	X	144
White Hall	Northnts	SP6458	52°13·2'	1°3·4'W	X	152
Whitehall	Northum	NT8826	55°31·9'	2°11·0'W	X	74
White Hall	Northum	NY9154	54°53·1'	2°8·0'W	X	87
Whitehall	Orkney	HY6428	59°8·5'	2°37·3'W	X	5
Whitehall	Scot Bord	NT8755	55°47·5'	2°12·0'W	X	67,74
Whitehall	Shrops	SJ3327	52°50·4'	2°59·3'W	X	126
White Hall	Shrops	SJ3918	52°45·6'	2°53·8'W	X	126
White Hall	Suff	TL9939	52°1·0'	0°54·4'E	X	155
White Hall	Suff	TM0561	52°12·8'	1°0·4'E	X	155
White Hall	Suff	TM1562	52°13·1'	1°9·3'E	X	156
White Hall	Suff	TM2843	52°2·5'	1°19·9'E	X	169
Whitehall	Surrey	TQ0737	51°7·6'	0°27·9'W	X	187
Whitehall	W Susx	TQ1321	50°58·9'	0°23·0'W	T	198
White Hall Centre	Derby	SK0376	53°17·1'	1°56·9'W	X	119
Whitehall Fm	Black w Dar	SD6819	53°40·2'	2°28·7'W	FM	109
White Hall Fm	Cambs	TL2393	52°31·5'	0°10·8'W	FM	142
White Hall Fm	Cambs	TL2877	52°22·8'	0°6·8'W	FM	142
Whitehall Fm	Cambs	TL3249	52°7·6'	0°3·9'W	FM	153
Whitehall Fm	Cambs	TL5888	52°28·3'	0°20·0'E	FM	143
White Hall Fm	Cambs	TL6276	52°21·7'	0°23·2'E	FM	143
White Hall Fm	Devon	ST1804	50°50·0'	3°9·5'W	FM	192,193
White Hall Fm	Durham	NZ2351	54°51·4'	1°38·1'W	FM	88
White Hall Fm	Essex	TL7332	51°57·8'	0°31·5'E	FM	167
Whitehall Fm	Glos	SO7100	51°42·1'	2°24·8'W	FM	162
White Hall Fm	Glos	SO7621	51°53·5'	2°20·5'W	FM	162
Whitehall Fm	Glos	SO9023	51°54·6'	2°8·3'W	FM	163
Whitehall Fm	Glos	SP0122	51°54·0'	1°58·7'W	FM	163
Whitehall Fm	Herts	TL1623	51°53·8'	0°18·4'W	FM	166
Whitehall Fm	Kent	TQ9929	51°1·8'	0°50·7'E	FM	189
Whitehall Fm	Lincs	TA0508	53°33·7'	0°24·5'W	FM	112
White Hall Fm	Norf	TF5714	52°42·3'	0°19·8'E	FM	131
White Hall Fm	Norf	TF5801	52°35·3'	0°20·3'E	FM	143
Whitehall Fm	Norf	TG0803	52°35·3'	1°4·6'E	FM	144
Whitehall Fm	Norf	TM0095	52°31·2'	0°57·3'E	FM	144
White Hall Fm	Northnts	SP5271	52°20·3'	1°13·8'W	FM	140
White Hall Fm	Northum	NZ2476	55°4·9'	1°37·0'W	FM	88
White Hall Fm	N Yks	SE8779	54°12·2'	0°39·6'W	FM	101
White Hall Fm	N Yks	SE9998	54°22·3'	0°28·1'W	FM	94,101
White Hall Fm	Oxon	SP3010	51°47·5'	1°33·5'W	FM	164
Whitehall Fm	Pemb	SM9728	51°55·1'	4°56·7'W	FM	157,158
White Hall Fm	Powys	SO2093	52°32·0'	3°10·4'W	FM	137
White Hall Fm	Shrops	SJ6528	52°51·1'	2°30·8'W	FM	127
White Hall Fm	Stock on T	NZ4510	54°29·2'	1°17·9'W	FM	93
White Hall Fm	Suff	TL9042	52°2·9'	0°46·6'E	FM	155
White Hall Fm	Surrey	TQ2753	51°15·9'	0°10·4'W	FM	187
White Hall Fm	Thurr	TQ7185	51°32·5'	0°28·4'E	FM	178
White Hall Fm	Warw	SP3295	52°33·3'	1°31·3'W	FM	140
Whitehall Fm	Warw	SP4868	52°18·7'	1°17·4'W	FM	151
White Hall Fm	Wilts	SU0891	51°37·3'	1°52·7'W	FM	163,173
Whitehall Fm	Worcs	SO9479	52°24·8'	2°4·9'W	FM	139
Whitehall Moss	Durham	NZ0747	54°49·3'	1°53·0'W	X	88
White Hall, The	Ches	SJ5866	53°11·6'	2°37·3'W	X	117
Whitehall Village	Orkney	HY6528	59°8·5'	2°36·2'W	T	5
White Hamar	Shetld	HU5380	60°30·3'	1°1·6'W	X	1,2,3
Whitehams	Devon	ST1316	50°56·4'	3°13·9'W	X	181,193
Whitehanger	W Susx	SU8930	51°4·0'	0°43·4'W	X	186
White Hart	Conwy	SH7370	53°13·0'	3°53·7'W	X	115
Whitehart Covert	Staffs	SJ8727	52°50·7'	2°11·2'W	F	127
White Hart Fm	Peterb	TF2805	52°37·9'	0°6·1'W	FM	142
Whitehaugh	Aberd	NJ7218	57°15·4'	2°27·4'W	X	38
Whitehaugh	Angus	NO2974	56°51·4'	3°9·4'W	X	44
Whitehaugh	Scot Bord	NT4815	55°25·8'	2°48·9'W	X	79
Whitehaugh	Scot Bord	NY5291	55°12·9'	2°44·8'W	X	79

Whitehaugh Burn	E Ayr	NS6130	55°32·9'	4°11·8'W	W	71
Whitehaugh Fm	Scot Bord	NT2639	55°38·6'	3°10·1'W	FM	73
Whitehaugh Ho	Aberd	NJ5917	57°14·8'	2°40·3'W	X	37
Whitehaughmoor	Scot Bord	NT4717	55°26·9'	2°49·8'W	X	79
Whitehaugh Water	E Ayr	NS6128	55°31·8'	4°11·7'W	W	71
White Hause	Cumbr	NY2732	54°40·9'	3°7·5'W	X	89,90
Whitehaven	Ches	SJ6053	53°4·6'	2°35·4'W	X	118
Whitehaven	Cumbr	NX9718	54°33·1'	3°35·1'W	T	89
Whitehaven	Shrops	SJ2624	52°48·8'	3°5·5'W	T	126
Whitehawk	Bri & Hov	TQ3304	50°49·4'	0°6·3'W	T	198
Whitehawk Camp	Bri & Hov	TQ3304	50°49·4'	0°6·3'W	A	198
White Haywood Fm	Heref	SO2934	52°0·2'	3°1·7'W	FM	161
Whitehead Hill	Cumbr	NY5152	54°51·9'	2°45·4'W	X	86
Whiteheads	Corn	SX1276	50°33·4'	4°38·9'W	X	200
Whiteheads	Essex	TL5618	51°50·6'	0°16·3'E	X	167
Whitehead's Fm	Essex	TL8017	51°49·6'	0°37·1'E	FM	168
Whiteheathfield Barton	Devon	ST0102	50°48·8'	3°23·9'W	X	192
Whiteheath Fm	Wilts	ST9284	51°33·5'	2°6·5'W	FM	173
Whiteheath Gate	Sand	SO9787	52°29·1'	2°2·3'W	T	139
Whiteheigh Crag	Northum	NY7694	55°14·6'	2°22·2'W	X	80
White Helliacks	Shetld	HU3181	60°31·0'	1°25·6'W	X	1,3
White Hemmels	Northum	NY9960	54°56·3'	2°0·5'W	X	87
White Hill	Aberd	NJ3618	57°15·2'	3°3·2'W	H	37
White Hill	Aberd	NJ4011	57°11·4'	2°59·1'W	H	37
Whitehill	Aberd	NJ4326	57°19·5'	2°56·3'W	X	37
Whitehill	Aberd	NJ5145	57°29·8'	2°48·6'W	X	29
White Hill	Aberd	NJ5744	57°29·3'	2°42·6'W	H	29
White Hill	Aberd	NJ6410	57°11·0'	2°35·3'W	H	37
White Hill	Aberd	NJ6750	57°32·6'	2°32·6'W	X	29
Whitehill	Aberd	NJ8952	57°33·7'	2°10·6'W	X	30
Whitehill	Aberd	NJ9256	57°35·9'	2°7·6'W	X	30
White Hill	Aberd	NK1144	57°29·4'	1°48·5'W	X	30
White Hill	Aberd	NO4592	57°1·2'	2°53·9'W	X	44
White Hill	Aberd	NO5388	56°59·1'	2°46·0'W	X	44
Whitehill	Aberd	NO8088	56°59·2'	2°19·3'W	X	45
White Hill	Aberd	NO8689	56°59·8'	2°13·4'W	H	45
White Hill	Angus	NO3675	56°52·0'	3°2·5'W	X	44
White Hill	Angus	NO4073	56°50·9'	2°58·6'W	H	44
White Hill	Bath & NE Somer	ST5857	51°18·9'	2°35·8'W	H	172,182
White Hill	Bath & NE Somer	ST7156	51°18·4'	2°24·6'W	T	172
White Hill	Brad	SE0040	53°51·6'	1°59·6'W	T	104
White Hill	Bucks	SP9905	51°44·3'	0°33·6'W	X	165
White Hill	Cambs	TL4653	52°9·6'	0°8·5'E	X	154
Whitehill	Cumbr	NY1854	54°52·7'	3°16·3'W	X	85
White Hill	Cumbr	NY4564	54°58·3'	2°51·1'W	X	86
White Hill	Cumbr	NY5365	54°58·9'	2°43·6'W	X	86
White Hill	Devon	SX5383	50°37·9'	4°4·3'W	H	191,201
White Hill	Devon	SX6391	50°42·4'	3°56·0'W	H	191
Whitehill	Devon	SX8558	50°24·9'	3°36·7'W	X	202
White Hill	D & G	NS5503	55°18·2'	4°16·6'W	H	77
White Hill	D & G	NS6810	55°22·2'	4°4·5'W	X	71
White Hill	D & G	NS7420	55°27·7'	3°59·1'W	H	71
White Hill	D & G	NT1508	55°21·8'	3°20·0'W	X	79
White Hill	D & G	NX1238	54°42·4'	4°54·7'W	X	82
Whitehill	D & G	NX1372	55°0·7'	4°55·0'W	X	76
White Hill	D & G	NX2574	55°2·0'	4°43·9'W	X	76
White Hill	D & G	NX4577	55°4·1'	4°25·2'W	H	77
Whitehill	D & G	NX6146	54°47·6'	4°9·3'W	X	83
Whitehill	D & G	NX7070	55°0·7'	4°1·6'W	X	77,84
Whitehill	D & G	NX7856	54°53·3'	3°53·7'W	X	84
White Hill	D & G	NX8753	54°51·8'	3°45·2'W	H	84
White Hill	D & G	NX9393	55°13·4'	3°40·5'W	H	78
White Hill	D & G	NX9490	55°11·8'	3°39·5'W	H	78
White Hill	D & G	NY0482	55°7·6'	3°29·9'W	X	78
White Hill	D & G	NY1474	55°3·4'	3°20·4'W	X	85
White Hill	D & G	NY1788	55°11·0'	3°17·8'W	X	79
White Hill	D & G	NY2077	55°5·1'	3°14·8'W	X	85
White Hill	D & G	NY3993	55°13·9'	2°57·1'W	H	79
White Hill	Dorset	SY5786	50°40·6'	2°36·1'W	H	194
White Hill	Dorset	SY5989	50°42·2'	2°34·5'W	X	194
White Hill	Durham	NY9830	54°40·1'	2°1·4'W	H	92
Whitehill	E Ayr	NS4010	55°21·7'	4°31·0'W	X	70
White Hill	E Ayr	NS4406	55°19·7'	4°27·1'W	H	70,77
Whitehill	E Ayr	NS4617	55°25·6'	4°25·6'W	X	70
Whitehill	E Ayr	NS5217	55°25·7'	4°19·9'W	X	70
Whitehill	E Ayr	NS5711	55°22·6'	4°15·0'W	X	71
Whitehill	E Dunb	NS6375	55°57·2'	4°11·2'W	X	64
Whitehill	E Susx	TQ5129	51°2·7'	0°9·6'E	T	188,199
Whitehill	E Yorks	TA2240	53°50·7'	0°8·3'W	X	107
Whitehill	Falk	NS7680	56°0·1'	3°58·9'W	X	64
Whitehill	Fife	NO3812	56°18·0'	2°59·7'W	X	59
Whitehill	Fife	NT1885	56°3·3'	3°18·6'W	X	65,66
White Hill	Hants	SU5147	51°13·4'	1°15·8'W	X	185
White Hill	Hants	SU5156	51°18·3'	1°15·7'W	X	174
White Hill	Hants	SU5931	51°4·7'	1°9·1'W	X	185
White Hill	Hants	SU6347	51°13·4'	1°5·5'W	X	185
Whitehill	Hants	SU7934	51°6·2'	0°51·9'W	T	186
Whitehill	Heref	SO3852	52°10·0'	2°54·0'W	X	148,149
White Hill	Heref	SO5943	52°5·3'	2°35·5'W	H	149
White Hill	Herts	TQ0792	51°37·2'	0°26·9'W	X	176
White Hill	Inverc	NS2168	55°52·6'	4°51·2'W	X	63
White Hill	Kent	TR0059	51°17·9'	0°52·5'E	T	178
White Hill	Lancs	SD5840	53°51·5'	2°37·9'W	X	102
White Hill	Lancs	SD6758	54°1·3'	2°29·8'W	H	103
White Hill	Lancs	SD7736	53°49·4'	2°20·6'W	X	103
White Hill	Leic	SK4811	52°41·9'	1°17·0'W	X	129
White Hill	Midlo	NT3566	55°53·2'	3°1·9'W	T	66
Whitehill	Moray	NJ1059	57°37·0'	3°29·9'W	X	28
White Hill	Moray	NJ3924	57°18·4'	3°0·3'W	H	37
White Hill	Moray	NJ5354	57°34·7'	2°46·7'W	T	29
White Hill	Northum	NT8732	55°35·1'	2°11·9'W	H	74
White Hill	Northum	NT8929	55°33·5'	2°10·0'W	H	74
White Hill	Northum	NT9635	55°36·8'	2°3·4'W	H	74,75
White Hill	Northum	NU1138	55°38·4'	1°49·1'W	X	75
Whitehill	Northum	NY6777	55°5·4'	2°30·6'W	F	86,87
White Hill	Northum	NY7488	55°11·4'	2°24·1'W	H	80
White Hill	Northum	NY7550	54°50·9'	2°22·9'W	X	86,87
White Hill	Northum	NY7776	55°4·9'	2°21·2'W	H	86,87

White Hill	Northum	NY8548	54°49·8'	2°13·6'W	X	87
White Hill	Oldham	SD9913	53°37·1'	2°0·5'W	H	109
White Hill	Oxon	SU6084	51°33·3'	1°7·7'W	X	175
White Hill	Oxon	SU6186	51°34·4'	1°6·8'W	X	175
Whitehill	Pemb	SN0504	51°42·3'	4°48·9'W	X	158
Whitehill	Pth & Kin	NN9116	56°19·7'	3°45·3'W	X	58
White Hill	Pth & Kin	NO0401	56°11·8'	3°32·4'W	H	58
White Hill	Pth & Kin	NO0531	56°28·0'	3°32·1'W	X	52,53
Whitehill	Pth & Kin	NO0810	56°16·7'	3°28·7'W	X	58
Whitehill	S Ayr	NS3933	55°34·1'	4°32·8'W	X	70
Whitehill	S Ayr	NS4016	55°25·0'	4°31·2'W	X	70
White Hill	Scot Bord	NT0533	55°35·1'	3°30·0'W	H	72
White Hill	Scot Bord	NT3305	55°20·3'	3°2·9'W	H	79
White Hill	Scot Bord	NT3619	55°27·9'	3°0·3'W	H	79
White Hill	Scot Bord	NT4151	55°45·2'	2°56·0'W	X	66,73
White Hill	Scot Bord	NT4301	55°18·2'	2°53·4'W	H	79
White Hill	Scot Bord	NT4806	55°21·0'	2°48·8'W	H	79
White Hill	Scot Bord	NT5209	55°22·6'	2°45·0'W	H	79
White Hill	Scot Bord	NT5212	55°24·2'	2°45·0'W	X	79
White Hill	Scot Bord	NT5737	55°37·7'	2°40·5'W	H	73,74
Whitehill	Scot Bord	NT5831	55°34·5'	2°39·5'W	X	73,74
Whitehill	Scot Bord	NT6350	55°44·8'	2°34·9'W	X	67,74
Whitehill	Scot Bord	NT6609	55°22·7'	2°31·8'W	H	80
Whitehill	Scot Bord	NT6838	55°38·3'	2°30·1'W	X	74
White Hill	Shetld	HU4844	60°10·9'	1°7·6'W	H	4
Whitehill	S Lanak	NS7057	55°47·6'	4°4·0'W	T	64
Whitehill	S Lanak	NS7346	55°41·7'	4°0·8'W	X	64
Whitehill	S Lanak	NS7745	55°41·2'	3°57·0'W	X	64
White Hill	S Lanak	NS8420	55°27·9'	3°49·7'W	X	71,72
White Hill	S Lanak	NS8820	55°27·9'	3°45·9'W	X	71,72
White Hill	S Lanak	NS9416	55°25·8'	3°40·1'W	H	71,78
White Hill	S Lanak	NS9425	55°30·7'	3°40·3'W	H	71,72
White Hill	S Lanak	NS9612	55°23·7'	3°38·1'W	H	78
White Hill	S Lanak	NT0846	55°42·2'	3°27·4'W	H	72
White Hill	Somer	ST1231	51°4·5'	3°15·0'W	X	181
Whitehill	Staffs	SJ8454	53°5·2'	2°13·9'W	T	118
Whitehill	Stir	NS5897	56°8·9'	4°16·7'W	X	57
Whitehill	Stir	NS8587	56°4·0'	3°50·4'W	X	65
White Hill	Surrey	SU9060	51°20·1'	0°42·1'W	X	175,186
White Hill	Surrey	TQ1151	51°15·1'	0°24·2'W	X	187
White Hill	Surrey	TQ1853	51°16·1'	0°18·1'W	X	187
White Hill	Surrey	TQ3253	51°15·9'	0°6·1'W	X	187
White Hill	Wilts	ST8130	51°4·4'	2°15·9'W	T	183
White Hill	Wilts	SU0051	51°15·7'	1°59·6'W	X	184
White Hill	Wilts	SU1467	51°24·3'	1°47·5'W	X	173
Whitehill	W Loth	NT1168	55°54·1'	3°25·0'W	X	65
Whitehill Aisle	Midlo	NT3261	55°50·5'	3°4·7'W	X	66
Whitehill Croft	Aberd	NJ9055	57°35·4'	2°9·6'W	X	30
Whitehill Down	Carm	SN2912	51°47·1'	4°28·4'W	X	159
Whitehill Fm	Arg & Bt	NR7122	55°26·6'	5°36·8'W	FM	68
Whitehill Fm	Beds	TL1025	51°55·0'	0°23·6'W	FM	166
Whitehill Fm	E Ayr	NS4833	55°34·3'	4°24·2'W	FM	70
Whitehill Fm	E Dunb	NS5173	55°55·9'	4°22·7'W	FM	64
Whitehill Fm	Glos	SP0423	51°54·6'	1°56·1'W	FM	163
Whitehill Fm	Herts	TL2215	51°49·4'	0°13·4'W	FM	166
Whitehill Fm	Herts	TL3421	51°52·5'	0°2·8'W	FM	166
Whitehill Fm	Oxon	SP2611	51°48·1'	1°37·0'W	FM	163
Whitehill Fm	S Ayr	NS2801	55°16·6'	4°42·0'W	FM	76
White Hill Fm	Staffs	SO8384	52°27·5'	2°14·6'W	FM	138
Whitehill Fm	Warw	SP2150	52°9·1'	1°41·2'W	FM	151
Whitehillfoot	Scot Bord	NT7129	55°33·5'	2°27·2'W	X	74
Whitehill Head	Northum	NU1027	55°32·4'	1°50·1'W	X	75
Whitehill Head	Pth & Kin	NO0710	56°16·7'	3°29·7'W	H	58
Whitehill Ho	Devon	SX8572	50°32·4'	3°37·0'W	X	191
White Hill Ho	Lancs	SD7457	54°0·7'	2°23·4'W	X	103
Whitehill Ho	Scot Bord	NT6640	55°39·4'	2°32·0'W	X	74
Whitehill Ho	Warw	SP3146	52°6·9'	1°32·4'W	X	151
White Hill Lodge	Northnts	SP8377	52°23·3'	0°46·4'W	X	141
Whitehill Mains	Midlo	NT3171	55°55·9'	3°5·8'W	X	66
Whitehill Moor	Northum	NY6878	55°6·0'	2°29·7'W	X	86,87
Whitehillock	Aberd	NJ3717	57°14·6'	3°2·2'W	X	37
Whitehillock	Aberd	NJ4425	57°19·0'	2°55·3'W	X	37
Whitehillock	Aberd	NJ9042	57°28·3'	2°9·5'W	X	30
Whitehillock	Aberd	NK0258	57°37·0'	1°57·5'W	X	30
Whitehillock	Moray	NJ2645	57°29·6'	3°13·6'W	X	28
Whitehillock	Moray	NJ3253	57°34·0'	3°7·7'W	X	28
Whitehillock	Moray	NJ3826	57°19·5'	3°1·3'W	X	37
Whitehillock Fm	Moray	NJ4445	57°29·8'	2°55·6'W	FM	28
Whitehillocks	Angus	NO3667	56°47·7'	3°2·4'W	X	44
Whitehillocks	Angus	NO4579	56°54·2'	2°53·7'W	X	44
Whitehill of Balmaghie	D & G	NX7261	54°55·9'	3°59·4'W	X	83,84
White Hill of Bogs	Aberd	NJ4426	57°19·5'	2°55·3'W	H	37
White Hill of Vatsetter	Shetld	HU5488	60°34·6'	1°0·4'W	X	1,2
Whitehills	Aberd	NJ6413	57°12·6'	2°35·3'W	X	37
Whitehills	Aberd	NJ6565	57°40·7'	2°34·7'W	T	29
Whitehills	Angus	NO2259	56°43·2'	3°16·0'W	X	53
Whitehills	Angus	NO4651	56°39·1'	2°52·4'W	T	54
Whitehills	Ches	SJ9772	53°14·9'	2°2·3'W	X	118
Whitehills	Derby	SK0478	53°18·2'	1°56·0'W	X	119
Whitehills	D & G	NX4067	54°58·6'	4°29·6'W	X	83
Whitehills	D & G	NX4546	54°47·4'	4°24·2'W	X	83
Whitehills	Fife	NS9690	56°5·7'	3°39·9'W	X	58
Whitehills	Ghead	NZ2860	54°56·3'	1°33·4'W	T	88
White Hills	Hants	SU5320	50°58·8'	1°14·3'W	H	185
White Hills	Highld	NH6670	57°42·3'	4°14·5'W	X	21
White Hills	Northnts	SP7464	52°16·4'	0°54·5'W	T	152
White Hills	N Yks	NZ2501	54°24·5'	1°36·5'W	X	93
Whitehills	Pth & Kin	NN8911	56°17·0'	3°47·1'W	X	58
Whitehills	Pth & Kin	NO2431	56°28·2'	3°13·6'W	X	53
Whitehills	S Lanak	NS6352	55°44·8'	4°10·5'W	T	64
Whitehills Fm	Notts	SK5424	52°48·9'	1°11·5'W	FM	129
White Hills Fm	Oxon	SP2510	51°47·5'	1°37·9'W	FM	163
Whitehillshiel	Scot Bord	NT3618	55°27·4'	3°0·3'W	X	79
Whitehillshiel	Scot Bord	NY5595	55°15·1'	2°42·0'W	X	80
Whitehillshiel Sike	Scot Bord	NT3517	55°26·8'	3°1·4'W	W	79
Whitehills Plantation	Devon	SS6827	51°1·9'	3°52·6'W	F	180
White Hills Wood	Norf	TF6924	52°47·5'	0°30·8'E	F	132
Whitehill Tor	Devon	SX5761	50°26·1'	4°0·4'W	X	202
Whitehill Wood	D & G	NY3894	55°14·4'	2°58·1'W	F	79
Whitehill Wood	E Susx	TQ5735	51°5·8'	0°14·9'E	F	188

Whitehill Wood	Kent	TR1653	51°14·3'	1°6·1'E	F	179,189
Whitehill Wood	Warw	SP2464	52°16·7'	1°38·5'W	F	151
Whitehill Wood	W Berks	SU3373	51°27·5'	1°31·1'W	F	174
White Ho	Cambs	TL6086	52°27·1'	0°21·7'E	X	143
White Ho	Cumbr	NY7248	54°49·8'	2°25·7'W	X	86,87
White Ho	Denb	SJ1165	53°10·7'	3°19·5'W	X	116
White Ho	Derby	SK2352	53°4·1'	1°39·0'W	X	119
White Ho	Devon	SS4633	51°4·8'	4°11·5'W	X	180
White Ho	Durham	NY9638	54°44·5'	2°3·3'W	X	91,92
White Ho	Durham	NZ0223	54°36·4'	1°57·7'W	X	92
White Ho	Durham	NZ1227	54°38·5'	1°48·4'W	X	92
White Ho	Durham	NZ1237	54°43·9'	1°48·4'W	X	92
White Ho	Durham	NZ1527	54°38·5'	1°45·6'W	X	92
White Ho	Durham	NZ1847	54°49·3'	1°42·8'W	X	88
White Ho	Durham	NZ2951	54°51·4'	1°32·5'W	X	88
White Ho	Durham	NZ3638	54°44·4'	1°26·0'W	X	93
White Ho	Essex	TM1728	51°54·7'	1°9·7'E	X	168,169
White Ho	Essex	TM2023	51°52·0'	1°12·1'E	X	169
White Ho	Essex	TQ9395	51°37·5'	0°47·7'E	X	168,178
White Ho	Glos	SO6735	52°1·0'	2°28·5'W	X	149
White Ho	Glos	SO6926	51°56·1'	2°26·7'W	X	162
White Ho	Glos	SO7403	51°43·7'	2°22·2'W	X	162
White Ho	Heref	SO3435	52°0·8'	2°57·3'W	X	149,161
White Ho	Heref	SO3868	52°18·6'	2°54·2'W	X	137,148
White Ho	Heref	SO5124	51°55·0'	2°42·4'W	X	162
White Ho	Heref	SO5961	52°15·0'	2°35·6'W	X	137,138,149
White Ho	Heref	SO6543	52°5·3'	2°30·3'W	X	149
White Ho	Herts	TQ0598	51°40·5'	0°28·5'W	X	166,176
White Ho	Kent	TR0632	51°3·2'	0°56·8'E	X	189
White Ho	Lancs	SD4439	53°50·9'	2°50·7'W	X	102
White Ho	Lancs	SD6017	53°39·1'	2°35·9'W	X	109
White Ho	Leeds	SE2044	53°53·7'	1°41·3'W	X	104
White Ho	Leic	SK7631	52°52·5'	0°51·8'W	X	129
White Ho	Lincs	TF0949	53°1·9'	0°22·1'W	X	130
White Ho	Lincs	TF1742	52°58·0'	0°15·1'W	X	130
White Ho	Lincs	TF2135	52°54·2'	0°11·7'W	X	131
White Ho	Lincs	TF2432	52°52·5'	0°9·0'W	X	131
White Ho	Monm	SO4519	51°52·2'	2°47·5'W	X	161
White Ho	N Lincs	SE8309	53°34·5'	0°44·4'W	X	112
White Ho	Norf	TM1586	52°26·0'	1°10·2'E	X	144,156
White Ho	Northum	NU0039	55°38·9'	1°59·6'W	X	75
White Ho	Northum	NU1617	55°27·0'	1°44·4'W	X	81
White Ho	Northum	NY8358	54°55·2'	2°15·5'W	X	86,87
White Ho	Northum	NY9380	55°7·1'	2°6·2'W	X	80
White Ho	Northum	NY9656	54°54·2'	2°3·3'W	X	87
White Ho	Northum	NZ0179	55°6·6'	1°58·6'W	X	87
White Ho	Northum	NZ0980	55°7·1'	1°51·1'W	X	81
White Ho	N Yks	NZ0400	54°24·0'	1°55·9'W	X	92
White Ho	N Yks	NZ1411	54°29·9'	1°46·6'W	X	92
White Ho	N Yks	NZ2906	54°27·2'	1°32·7'W	X	93
White Ho	N Yks	NZ3204	54°26·1'	1°30·0'W	X	93
White Ho	N Yks	NZ3509	54°28·8'	1°27·2'W	X	93
White Ho	N Yks	NZ4807	54°27·6'	1°15·2'W	X	93
White Ho	N Yks	SE7596	54°21·5'	0°50·3'W	X	94,100
White Ho	Renf	NS4163	55°50·3'	4°31·9'W	X	64
White Ho	Shrops	SO4478	52°24·1'	2°49·0'W	X	137,148
White Ho	Staffs	SJ8505	52°38·8'	2°12·9'W	X	127,139
White Ho	Staffs	SJ9916	52°44·7'	2°0·5'W	X	127
White Ho	Stir	NS7693	56°7·1'	3°59·2'W	X	57
White Ho	Stock on T	NZ4313	54°30·9'	1°19·7'W	X	93
White Ho	Suff	TM1261	52°12·6'	1°6·6'E	X	155
White Ho	Suff	TM2274	52°19·4'	1°15·9'E	X	156
White Ho	Suff	TM3066	52°14·9'	1°22·6'E	X	156
White Ho	Suff	TM3880	52°22·2'	1°30·2'E	X	156
White Ho	Suff	TM3889	52°27·0'	1°30·6'E	X	156
White Ho	Warw	SP3440	52°3·7'	1°29·8'W	X	151
White Ho	Worcs	SO7252	52°10·2'	2°24·2'W	X	149
White Ho	Worcs	SP0264	52°16·7'	1°57·8'W	X	150
White Ho	Wrex	SJ3545	53°0·1'	2°57·7'W	X	117
White Ho	W Susx	TQ2928	51°2·4'	0°9·2'W	X	187,198
White Hoe	I of M	SC3674	54°8·4'	4°30·2'W	X	95
White House Fm	N Lincs	SK9296	53°27·4'	0°36·5'W	FM	112
White Ho Fm	Norf	TF5416	52°43·4'	0°17·2'E	FM	131
White Ho Fm	N Yks	SE6530	53°46·0'	1°0·4'W	FM	105,106
White Ho Fm	Suff	TM3562	52°12·6'	1°26·8'E	FM	156
White Ho Fm, The	Norf	TG3111	52°39·1'	1°25·3'E	FM	133,134
White Hole Burn	D & G	NY2099	55°17·0'	3°15·1'W	W	79
Whitehole Fm	Somer	ST6848	51°14·1'	2°27·1'W	FM	183
Whiteholm	E Ayr	NS6219	55°27·0'	4°10·5'W	X	71
Whiteholm	E Ayr	NS6518	55°26·5'	4°7·6'W	X	71
White Holm	Scot Bord	NT3304	55°19·8'	3°2·9'W	X	79
Whiteholme	Blackp	SD3241	53°51·9'	3°1·6'W	T	102
White Holme	Lancs	SD6633	53°47·8'	2°30·6'W	X	103
Whiteholme	Lancs	SD7151	53°57·5'	2°26·1'W	X	103
White Holme Drain	Cald	SD9820	53°40·8'	2°1·4'W	W	103
White Holme Resr	Cald	SD9719	53°40·3'	2°2·3'W	W	109
Whitehook	Pemb	SN0720	51°51·0'	4°47·7'W	X	145,158
Whitehope	Scot Bord	NT3243	55°40·8'	3°4·4'W	X	73
Whitehope Burn	Scot Bord	NT0814	55°24·9'	3°26·8'W	W	78
Whitehope Burn	Scot Bord	NT2826	55°31·6'	3°8·0'W	W	73
Whitehope Burn	Scot Bord	NT3328	55°32·7'	3°3·3'W	W	73
White Hope Edge	D & G	NY3397	55°16·0'	3°2·8'W	H	79
Whitehope Fm	Scot Bord	NT3527	55°32·2'	3°1·4'W	FM	73
Whitehope Heights	D & G	NT0913	55°24·4'	3°25·8'W	H	78
Whitehope Knowe	Scot Bord	NT0914	55°24·9'	3°25·8'W	H	78
Whitehope Law	Scot Bord	NT3344	55°41·3'	3°3·5'W	H	73
Whitehope Rig	Scot Bord	NT2927	55°32·1'	3°7·1'W	H	73
Whitehope Rig	Scot Bord	NT3931	55°34·4'	2°57·6'W	H	73
Whitehorn Fm	Bucks	SP8309	51°46·6'	0°47·4'W	FM	165
Whitehorn Fm	Devon	ST1901	50°48·4'	3°8·6'W	FM	192,193
White Horse	Aberd	NJ9656	57°35·9'	2°3·6'W	H	30
White Horse	Corn	SW6231	50°8·1'	5°19·5'W	X	203
White Horse	Dorset	SY7184	50°39·5'	2°24·2'W	A	194
White Horse	E Susx	TQ5100	50°47·0'	0°8·9'E	X	199
White Horse	N Yks	SE5181	54°13·6'	1°12·6'W	X	100
White Horse	Oxon	SU3086	51°34·6'	1°33·6'W	A	174
White Horse	Wilts	SU0469	51°25·4'	1°56·2'W	X	173
White Horse	Wilts	SU0978	51°30·3'	1°51·8'W	X	173
White Horse	Wilts	SU1063	51°22·2'	1°51·0'W	X	173
White Horse	Wilts	SU1274	51°28·1'	1°49·2'W	X	173

White Horse	Wilts	SU1758	51°19·5'	1°45·0'W	X	173
White Horse	Wilts	SU1868	51°24·9'	1°44·1'W	X	173
White Horse Bent	Cumbr	NY3428	54°38·8'	3°0·9'W	X	90
White Horse Common	Norf	TG3029	52°48·8'	1°25·2'E	X	133,134
White Horse Fm	Derby	SK3148	53°1·9'	1°31·9'W	FM	119
White Horse Fm	Dorset	SY7183	50°39·0'	2°24·2'W	FM	194
Whitehorse Fm	Essex	TL8811	51°46·2'	0°43·9'E	FM	168
Whitehorse Hill	Devon	SX6185	50°39·1'	3°57·6'W	H	191
White Horse Hill	Dorset	SY7184	50°39·5'	2°24·2'W	X	194
Whitehorse Hill	Oxon	SU3086	51°34·6'	1°33·6'W	H	174
White Horse of Stouri- croo	Shetld	HU3828	60°2·4'	1°18·6'W	X	4
White Horse Stone	Kent	TQ7560	51°19·0'	0°31·1'E	A	178,188
Whitehorse Wood	Kent	TQ6561	51°19·7'	0°22·5'E	F	177,178,188
White Ho, The	Norf	TG1933	52°51·2'	1°15·6'E	X	133
White Ho, The	Powys	SJ2305	52°38·5'	3°7·9'W	X	126
White Ho, The	Somer	ST2622	50°59·8'	3°2·9'W	X	193
White Ho, The	Suff	TM3964	52°13·6'	1°30·4'E	X	156
White Ho, The	Suff	TM4253	52°7·6'	1°32·5'E	X	156
Whitehough	Derby	SK0382	53°20·3'	1°56·9'W	T	110
White Hough	Lancs	SD8340	53°51·6'	2°15·1'W	X	103
Whitehough	Staffs	SK0151	53°3·6'	1°58·7'W	X	119
Whitehouse	Aberd	NJ5504	57°7·7'	2°44·1'W	X	37
Whitehouse	Aberd	NJ5718	57°15·3'	2°42·3'W	X	37
Whitehouse	Aberd	NJ6214	57°13·2'	2°37·3'W	T	37
Whitehouse	Aberd	NJ6214	57°13·2'	2°37·3'W	X	37
Whitehouse	Aberd	NO8270	56°49·5'	2°17·2'W	X	45
Whitehouse	Angus	NO4238	56°32·1'	2°56·1'W	X	54
Whitehouse	Arg & Bt	NN1527	56°24·2'	4°59·4'W	X	50
Whitehouse	Arg & Bt	NR8161	55°47·8'	5°29·2'W	T	62
Whitehouse	Bucks	SP6939	52°2·9'	0°59·2'W	X	152
Whitehouse	Devon	SS6110	50°52·6'	3°58·2'W	X	191
Whitehouse	Devon	ST2905	50°50·6'	3°0·1'W	X	193
Whitehouse	I of M	SC3290	54°16·9'	4°34·4'W	X	95
Whitehouse	Moray	NJ2639	57°26·4'	3°13·5'W	X	28
White House	Northum	NZ0167	55°0·1'	1°58·6'W	X	87
Whitehouse	Pth & Kin	NO1153	56°39·9'	3°26·7'W	X	53
Whitehouse	Pth & Kin	NO1560	56°43·7'	3°22·9'W	X	43
Whitehouse	Scot Bord	NT6124	55°30·7'	2°36·6'W	X	74
Whitehouse	Scot Bord	NT6333	55°35·6'	2°34·8'W	X	74
Whitehouse	Staffs	SK0259	53°7·9'	1°57·8'W	X	119
White House	Suff	TM1346	52°4·5'	1°6·9'E	T	169
Whitehouse Bay	Arg & Bt	NR8358	55°58·7'	5°26·3'W	W	55
Whitehouse Burn	Arg & Bt	NR8461	55°47·9'	5°26·3'W	W	62
Whitehouse Common	Birm	SP1397	52°34·5'	1°48·1'W	T	139
White House Common	Dorset	ST6308	50°52·5'	2°31·2'W	X	194
White House Corner	Suff	TM1465	52°14·7'	1°8·5'E	X	156
White House Fm	Bucks	SP6519	51°52·2'	1°3·0'W	FM	164,165
White House Fm	Bucks	SP7233	51°59·7'	0°56·7'W	FM	152,165
White House Fm	Bucks	SP9400	51°41·7'	0°38·0'W	FM	165
White House Fm	Cambs	TF4400	52°35·0'	0°7·9'E	FM	142,143
White House Fm	Cambs	TL2481	52°25·0'	0°10·2'W	FM	142
Whitehouse Fm	Ches	SJ3373	53°15·2'	2°59·8'W	FM	117
White House Fm	Ches	SJ7176	53°17·1'	2°25·7'W	FM	118
White House Fm	Ches	SJ8766	53°11·7'	2°11·3'W	FM	118
White House Fm	Darl	NZ2223	54°36·3'	1°39·1'W	FM	93
White House Fm	Darl	NZ3515	54°32·0'	1°27·1'W	FM	93
White House Fm	Derby	SK4143	52°59·2'	1°22·9'W	FM	129
White House Fm	Dorset	ST6309	50°53·0'	2°31·2'W	FM	194
Whitehouse Fm	Dorset	ST8424	51°1·1'	2°13·3'W	FM	183
White House Fm	Durham	NZ1534	54°42·3'	1°45·6'W	FM	92
White House Fm	Durham	NZ2150	54°50·9'	1°40·0'W	FM	88
White House Fm	Essex	TL6725	51°54·1'	0°26·0'E	FM	167
White House Fm	Essex	TL6939	52°1·6'	0°28·2'E	FM	154
White House Fm	Essex	TL7314	51°48·1'	0°30·9'E	FM	167
White House Fm	Essex	TL7942	52°3·1'	0°37·0'E	FM	155
White House Fm	Essex	TL8107	51°44·2'	0°37·7'E	FM	168
White House Fm	Essex	TL8311	51°46·3'	0°39·5'E	FM	168
White House Fm	Essex	TL8703	51°41·9'	0°42·8'E	FM	168
Whitehouse Fm	Essex	TL9221	51°51·5'	0°47·7'E	FM	168
White House Fm	Essex	TL9310	51°45·5'	0°48·2'E	FM	168
White House Fm	Essex	TL9426	51°54·1'	0°49·6'E	FM	168
White House Fm	Essex	TM0920	51°50·6'	1°2·4'E	FM	168,169
White House Fm	Essex	TQ8994	51°37·0'	0°44·2'E	FM	168,178
White House Fm	E Yorks	SE7254	53°58·9'	0°53·7'W	FM	105,106
White House Fm	E Yorks	SE7842	53°52·3'	0°48·4'W	FM	105,106
White House Fm	E Yorks	SE8829	53°45·2'	0°39·5'W	FM	106
White House Fm	E Yorks	TA2423	53°41·6'	0°6·9'W	FM	107,113
White House Fm	E Yorks	TA2618	53°38·8'	0°5·2'W	FM	113
Whitehouse Fm	Flint	SJ2663	53°9·8'	3°6·0'W	FM	117
White House Fm	Glos	SO8919	51°52·4'	2°9·2'W	FM	163
White House Fm	Hants	SU4961	51°21·0'	1°17·4'W	FM	174
White House Fm	Heref	SO4525	51°55·5'	2°47·6'W	FM	161
Whitehouse Fm	Heref	SO7146	52°6·9'	2°25·0'W	FM	149
White House Fm	Herts	TL1104	51°43·7'	0°23·2'W	FM	166
White House Fm	I of W	SZ4591	50°43·2'	1°21·4'W	FM	196
White House Fm	Kent	TQ7172	51°25·5'	0°28·0'E	FM	178
White House Fm	Kent	TQ8239	51°7·5'	0°36·4'E	FM	188
White House Fm	Kent	TQ9724	50°59·1'	0°48·8'E	FM	189
White House Fm	Leic	SK7231	52°52·5'	0°55·4'W	FM	129
White House Fm	Leic	SK7508	52°40·1'	0°53·1'W	FM	141
White House Fm	Lincs	SK8146	53°0·5'	0°47·2'W	FM	130
White House Fm	Lincs	SK9693	53°25·7'	0°32·9'W	FM	112
White House Fm	Lincs	TA0702	53°30·5'	0°22·8'W	FM	112
White House Fm	Lincs	TF0567	53°11·6'	0°25·3'W	FM	121
White House Fm	Lincs	TF1647	53°0·7'	0°15·9'W	FM	130
White House Fm	Lincs	TF3071	53°13·4'	0°2·8'W	FM	122
White House Fm	Lincs	TF3134	52°53·5'	0°2·8'W	FM	131
White House Fm	Lincs	TF3152	53°3·2'	0°2·3'W	FM	122
White House Fm	Lincs	TF3229	52°50·8'	0°2·0'W	FM	131
White House Fm	Lincs	TF4221	52°46·3'	0°6·7'E	FM	131
White House Fm	Lincs	TF4552	53°3·0'	0°10·2'E	FM	122
White House Fm	Lincs	TF5159	53°6·6'	0°15·8'E	FM	122
White House Fm	Lincs	TF5367	53°10·9'	0°17·8'E	FM	122
White House Fm	Lincs	TF5668	53°11·4'	0°20·5'E	FM	122
White House Fm	Mil Key	SP8137	52°1·8'	0°48·8'W	FM	152
White House Fm	Monm	SO2810	51°47·3'	3°2·2'W	FM	161
White House Fm	Monm	SO3708	51°46·3'	2°54·4'W	FM	161
White House Fm	Monm	SO4214	51°49·5'	2°50·1'W	FM	161
White House Fm	Monm	SO4321	51°53·3'	2°49·3'W	FM	161

White House Fm	Monm	SO4908	51°46·3'	2°44·0'W	FM	162
Whitehouse Fm	Monm	ST3596	51°39·8'	2°56·0'W	FM	171
White House Fm	Norf	TF4816	52°43·5'	0°11·9'E	FM	131
White House Fm	Norf	TF5412	52°41·3'	0°17·1'E	FM	131,143
White House Fm	Norf	TF6217	52°43·8'	0°24·4'E	FM	132
White House Fm	Norf	TF6601	52°35·1'	0°27·4'E	FM	143
Whitehouse Fm	Norf	TF6618	52°44·3'	0°27·9'E	FM	132
White House Fm	Norf	TF7200	52°34·5'	0°32·7'E	FM	143
White House Fm	Norf	TF9118	52°43·8'	0°50·1'E	FM	132
White House Fm	Norf	TF9411	52°39·9'	0°52·5'E	FM	132
Whitehouse Fm	Norf	TG0212	52°40·3'	0°59·7'E	FM	133
Whitehouse Fm	Norf	TG0614	52°41·3'	1°3·3'E	FM	133
Whitehouse Fm	Norf	TG0708	52°38·0'	1°3·9'E	FM	144
White House Fm	Norf	TG1630	52°49·7'	1°12·8'E	FM	133
White House Fm	Norf	TG1923	52°45·8'	1°15·2'E	FM	133,134
White House Fm	Norf	TG2612	52°39·7'	1°20·9'E	FM	133,134
White House Fm	Norf	TM1187	52°26·6'	1°6·7'E	FM	144
Whitehouse Fm	Norf	TM2890	52°27·8'	1°21·8'E	FM	134
White House Fm	Northnts	SP6473	52°21·3'	1°3·2'W	FM	140
White House Fm	Northnts	SP9058	52°13·0'	0°40·6'W	FM	152
White House Fm	N Yks	NZ5108	54°28·1'	1°12·4'W	FM	93
White House Fm	N Yks	NZ5507	54°27·6'	1°8·7'W	FM	93
White House Fm	N Yks	SE1660	54°2·4'	1°44·9'W	FM	99
White House Fm	N Yks	SE2655	53°59·7'	1°35·8'W	FM	104
White House Fm	N Yks	SE3098	54°22·8'	1°31·9'W	FM	99
White House Fm	N Yks	SE3699	54°23·4'	1°26·3'W	FM	99
White House Fm	N Yks	SE4697	54°22·2'	1°17·1'W	FM	100
White House Fm	N Yks	SE7478	54°11·8'	0°51·5'W	FM	100
White House Fm	N Yks	SE7979	54°12·3'	0°46·9'W	FM	100
White House Fm	N Yks	SE9281	54°13·2'	0°34·9'W	FM	101
White House Fm	Oxon	SP3910	51°47·5'	1°25·7'W	FM	164
White House Fm	Oxon	SP4223	51°54·5'	1°23·0'W	FM	164
White House Fm	Oxon	SP6219	51°52·2'	1°5·6'W	FM	164,165
White House Fm	Oxon	SU4084	51°33·4'	1°25·0'W	FM	174
Whitehouse Fm	Oxon	SU6494	51°38·7'	1°4·1'W	FM	164,175
Whitehouse Fm	S Glos	ST5584	51°33·4'	2°38·6'W	FM	172
Whitehouse Fm	S Glos	ST6585	51°34·0'	2°29·9'W	FM	172
White House Fm	Somer	ST3655	51°17·7'	2°54·7'W	FM	182
White House Fm	Somer	ST4449	51°14·5'	2°47·7'W	FM	182
White House Fm	Somer	ST7033	51°6·0'	2°25·3'W	FM	183
Whitehouse Fm	Staffs	SJ8413	52°43·1'	2°13·8'W	FM	127
Whitehouse Fm	Staffs	SK1206	52°39·3'	1°49·0'W	FM	139
White House Fm	Stock on T	NZ3813	54°30·9'	1°24·4'W	FM	93
White House Fm	Stock on T	NZ4222	54°35·7'	1°20·6'W	FM	93
White House Fm	Stock on T	NZ4324	54°36·8'	1°19·6'W	FM	93
White House Fm	Stock on T	NZ4612	54°30·3'	1°17·0'W	FM	93
White House Fm	Suff	TL9658	52°11·3'	0°52·4'E	FM	155
White House Fm	Suff	TL9676	52°21·0'	0°53·1'E	FM	144
White House Fm	Suff	TL9964	52°14·5'	0°55·3'E	FM	155
White House Fm	Suff	TM0053	52°8·6'	0°55·8'E	FM	155
White House Fm	Suff	TM0346	52°4·7'	0°58·2'E	FM	155
White House Fm	Suff	TM0961	52°12·7'	1°4·0'E	FM	155
White House Fm	Suff	TM1066	52°15·3'	1°5·0'E	FM	155
White House Fm	Suff	TM1335	51°58·6'	1°6·5'E	FM	169
White House Fm	Suff	TM1475	52°20·1'	1°8·9'E	FM	144,156
White House Fm	Suff	TM1558	52°10·9'	1°9·1'E	FM	156
White House Fm	Suff	TM1567	52°15·8'	1°9·4'E	FM	156
White House Fm	Suff	TM1670	52°17·4'	1°10·4'E	FM	144,156
White House Fm	Suff	TM1837	51°59·5'	1°10·9'E	FM	169
White House Fm	Suff	TM1851	52°7·1'	1°11·5'E	FM	156
Whitehouse Fm	Suff	TM1972	52°18·4'	1°13·1'E	FM	156
White House Fm	Suff	TM2151	52°7·0'	1°14·1'E	FM	156
White House Fm	Suff	TM2364	52°14·0'	1°16·3'E	FM	156
Whitehouse Fm	Suff	TM2475	52°19·9'	1°17·7'E	FM	156
White House Fm	Suff	TM2755	52°9·0'	1°19·5'E	FM	156
White House Fm	Suff	TM2766	52°14·9'	1°19·9'E	FM	156
White House Fm	Suff	TM3060	52°11·6'	1°22·3'E	FM	156
White House Fm	Suff	TM3074	52°19·2'	1°22·9'E	FM	156
White House Fm	Suff	TM3271	52°17·5'	1°24·5'E	FM	156
White House Fm	Suff	TM3274	52°19·1'	1°24·7'E	FM	156
White House Fm	Suff	TM3372	52°18·0'	1°25·4'E	FM	156
White House Fm	Suff	TM3480	52°22·3'	1°26·7'E	FM	156
White House Fm	Suff	TM3566	52°14·7'	1°27·0'E	FM	156
White House Fm	Suff	TM3667	52°15·3'	1°27·9'E	FM	156
Whitehouse Fm	Suff	TM3679	52°21·7'	1°28·4'E	FM	156
White House Fm	Suff	TM3683	52°23·9'	1°28·5'E	FM	156
White House Fm	Suff	TM3775	52°19·5'	1°29·1'E	FM	156
White House Fm	Suff	TM3790	52°27·6'	1°29·7'E	FM	134
White House Fm	Suff	TM4070	52°16·8'	1°31·5'E	FM	156
White House Fm	Suff	TM4279	52°21·6'	1°33·7'E	FM	156
White House Fm	Suff	TM4581	52°22·6'	1°36·4'E	FM	156
White House Fm	Suff	TM4683	52°23·6'	1°37·3'E	FM	156
White House Fm	Suff	TM4880	52°21·9'	1°39·0'E	FM	156
Whitehouse Fm	Suff	TM4883	52°23·5'	1°39·1'E	FM	156
White House Fm	Suff	TM4986	52°25·1'	1°40·1'E	FM	156
White House Fm	Suff	TM5188	52°26·2'	1°42·0'E	FM	156
White House Fm	Suff	TM5196	52°30·5'	1°42·3'E	FM	134
White House Fm	Suff	TM5297	52°31·0'	1°43·3'E	FM	134
White House Fm	Surrey	TQ0055	51°17·3'	0°33·6'W	FM	186
White House Fm	Surrey	TQ0253	51°16·2'	0°31·9'W	FM	186
White House Fm	Surrey	TQ3443	51°10·5'	0°4·6'W	FM	187
White House Fm	Surrey	TQ4048	51°13·1'	0°0·7'E	FM	187
Whitehouse Fm	Traf	SJ7389	53°24·1'	2°24·0'W	FM	109
White House Fm	Warr	SJ6485	53°21·9'	2°32·1'W	FM	109
White House Fm	Warw	SP2392	52°31·8'	1°39·3'W	FM	139
White House Fm	Warw	SP2685	52°28·0'	1°36·6'W	FM	140
White House Fm	Warw	SP2744	52°5·9'	1°36·0'W	FM	151
Whitehouse Fm	Wilts	SU2027	51°2·8'	1°42·5'W	FM	184
White House Fm	Wok	SU7065	51°23·0'	0°59·3'W	FM	175
White House Fm	Worcs	SO7636	52°1·6'	2°20·6'W	FM	150
White House Fm	Worcs	SO8245	52°6·4'	2°15·4'W	FM	150
White House Fm	Worcs	SO8679	52°24·8'	2°12·0'W	FM	139
White House Fm	York	SE6161	54°2·7'	1°3·7'W	FM	100
White House Fm	York	SE6247	53°55·2'	1°2·9'W	FM	105
White House Fm	York	SE6548	53°55·7'	1°0·2'W	FM	105,106
White House Fm, The	Leic	SK6905	52°38·5'	0°58·4'W	FM	141
White House Folly	Northum	NU1618	55°27·6'	1°44·4'W	X	81
Whitehouse Green	W Berks	SU6568	51°24·7'	1°3·5'W	T	175
Whitehouse of Aros	Arg & Bt	NM5645	56°32·3'	5°57·7'W	X	47,48
Whitehouse of Dunira	Pth & Kin	NN7423	56°23·2'	4°2·0'W	X	51,52

Whitehouse Plain	Essex	TQ4096	51°38·9′	0°1·8′E	X	167,177
Whitehouse Plantation	Staffs	SO8490	52°30·7′	2°13·7′W	F	138
Whitehouse Point	C of Edin	NT1479	56°0·0′	3°22·3′W	X	65
White House Rhyne	Somer	ST2742	51°10·6′	3°2·3′W	W	182
White Houses	Notts	SK7179	53°18·4′	0°55·7′W	T	120
White Houses	N Yks	SE1965	54°5·1′	1°42·2′W	X	99
White House, The	Roch	SD9617	53°39·2′	2°3·2′W	X	109
White House, The (Mus)	Shrops	SO5086	52°28·4′	2°43·8′W	X	137,138
White Howe	Cumbr	NY3807	54°27·5′	2°57·0′W	X	90
White Howe	Cumbr	NY5204	54°26·0′	2°44·0′W	H	90
Whitehow Head	Cumbr	NY0309	54°28·3′	3°29·4′W	X	89
Whitehurst	Staffs	SJ9745	53°0·4′	2°2·3′W	X	118
White Hurworth	Durham	NZ4034	54°42·2′	1°22·3′W	X	93
Whiteinch	C of Glas	NS5366	55°52·1′	4°20·5′W	T	64
Whiteinches	Aberd	NJ7129	57°21·3′	2°28·5′W	X	38
White Island	D & G	NX3585	55°8·2′	4°34·9′W	X	77
White Island	I Scilly	SV8712	49°55·8′	6°21·3′W	X	203
White Island	I Scilly	SV9217	49°58·7′	6°17·4′W	X	203
Whitekeld Dale	E Yorks	SE8253	53°58·2′	0°44·6′W	X	106
White Kemp Sewer	Kent	TQ9624	50°59·1′	0°47·9′E	W	189
White Kennels	Dorset	ST9312	50°54·7′	2°5·6′W	X	195
White Kielder Burn	Northum	NY6799	55°17·3′	2°30·7′W	W	80
White Kip	Scot Bord	NT3727	55°32·2′	2°59·5′W	X	73
Whitekirk	E Loth	NT5981	56°1·5′	2°39·0′W	T	67
Whitekirk Br	E Loth	NT6081	56°1·5′	2°38·1′W	X	67
Whitekirk Covert	E Loth	NT5982	56°2·0′	2°39·0′W	F	67
White Kirkley	Durham	NZ0235	54°42·8′	1°57·7′W	X	92
Whiteknights	Read	SU7372	51°26·8′	0°56·6′W	T	175
White Knott	Cumbr	NY4621	54°35·1′	2°49·7′W	X	90
Whiteknowe	Cumbr	NY4678	55°5·9′	2°50·3′W	X	86
White Knowe	D & G	NS7010	55°22·3′	4°2·7′W	X	71
White Knowe	D & G	NS7203	55°18·5′	4°0·6′W	H	77
White Knowe	D & G	NT2205	55°20·2′	3°13·4′W	H	79
Whiteknowe	D & G	NY2183	55°8·4′	3°13·9′W	X	79
White Knowe	E Ayr	NS5715	55°24·7′	4°15·1′W	X	71
White Knowe	E Ayr	NS5941	55°38·8′	4°14·0′W	X	71
White Knowe	Scot Bord	NT1746	55°42·3′	3°18·8′W	X	72
White Knowe	Scot Bord	NT3402	55°18·7′	3°2·0′W	X	79
White Knowe	Scot Bord	NT4016	55°26·3′	2°56·5′W	H	79
White Knowe	Scot Bord	NT6852	55°45·9′	2°30·2′W	X	67,74
White Knowe	Scot Bord	NT8617	55°27·0′	2°12·8′W	H	80
White Knowe	Scot Bord	NY5399	55°17·2′	2°44·0′W	H	79
White Knowe Head	Scot Bord	NT0623	55°29·8′	3°28·8′W	H	72
Whiteknowe Head	Scot Bord	NT2629	55°33·2′	3°9·9′W	H	73
Whiteknowes	Aberd	NJ5308	57°9·9′	2°46·2′W	X	37
Whiteknowes	D & G	NY0592	55°13·0′	3°29·2′W	X	78
White Knowes	E Ayr	NS6104	55°18·9′	4°11·0′W	H	77
Whiteknowes	Moray	NJ4861	57°38·4′	2°51·8′W	X	28,29
White Knowes	S Ayr	NX2792	55°11·8′	4°42·7′W	X	76
White Knowe Sike	Northum	NY6497	55°16·2′	2°33·6′W	W	80
White Knowl Fm	Derby	SK0583	53°20·9′	1°55·1′W	FM	110
White Lackington	Dorset	SY7198	50°47·1′	2°24·3′W	T	194
Whitelackington	Somer	ST3815	50°56·1′	2°52·6′W	T	193
White Ladies Aston	Worcs	SO9252	52°10·2′	2°6·6′W	T	150
White Ladies Fm	Shrops	SJ8206	52°39·3′	2°15·6′W	FM	127
White Ladies Priory	Shrops	SJ8207	52°39·9′	2°15·6′W	A	127
White Lady Shieling	Highld	NH9905	57°7·8′	3°39·7′W	X	36
White Laggan (Bothy)	D & G	NX4677	55°4·1′	4°24·3′W	X	77
White Laggan Burn	D & G	NX4677	55°4·1′	4°24·3′W	W	77
Whitelaird	D & G	NY0581	55°7·1′	3°28·9′W	X	78
Whitelake	Somer	ST5640	51°9·7′	2°37·4′W	W	182,183
Whiteland Head	Aberd	NO9193	57°1·9′	2°8·4′W	X	38,45
Whiteland Head	Devon	SS5313	50°54·1′	4°5·1′W	X	180
Whitelands	Essex	TL7813	51°47·5′	0°35·3′E	X	167
Whitelands	W Berks	SU4478	51°30·2′	1°21·6′W	X	174
Whitelands	W Susx	TQ3113	50°54·3′	0°7·8′W	X	198
Whitelands Downs	Dorset	SY7799	50°47·6′	2°19·2′W	X	194
Whitelands Fm	Oxon	SP5622	51°53·9′	1°10·8′W	FM	164
Whitelands Fm	Wilts	ST9178	51°30·3′	2°7·4′W	FM	173
Whitelands Fm	W Susx	TQ1315	50°55·6′	0°23·1′W	FM	198
Whiteland Wood	E Susx	TQ8014	50°54·1′	0°34·0′E	F	199
White Lane Fm	Surrey	SU9048	51°13·7′	0°42·3′W	FM	186
Whitelaw	E Loth	NT5671	55°56·1′	2°41·8′W	X	67
Whitelaw	Midlo	NT3656	55°47·8′	3°0·8′W	X	66,73
White Law	Northum	NT9428	55°33·0′	2°5·3′W	H	74,75
White Law	Northum	NT9706	55°21·1′	2°2·4′W	X	81
White Law	Northum	NU0333	55°35·7′	1°56·7′W	X	75
White Law	Scot Bord	NT2823	55°30·0′	3°8·0′W	H	73
White Law	Scot Bord	NT5130	55°33·9′	2°46·2′W	H	73
White Law	Scot Bord	NT8320	55°28·7′	2°15·7′W	H	74
Whitelaw	Scot Bord	NT8352	55°45·9′	2°15·8′W	X	67,74
White Law	Scot Bord	NT8526	55°31·9′	2°13·8′W	H	74
Whitelaw	S Lanak	NS6443	55°39·9′	4°9·3′W	X	71
White Law	S Lanak	NS9214	55°24·7′	3°41·9′W	X	71,78
Whitelaw	W Loth	NS9969	55°54·5′	3°36·5′W	X	65
Whitelaw Brae	Scot Bord	NT0718	55°27·1′	3°27·8′W	H	78
Whitelaw Brae	S Lanak	NT0025	55°30·8′	3°34·6′W	H	72
Whitelaw Burn	Scot Bord	NT2247	55°42·9′	3°14·1′W	X	73
Whitelaw Burn	S Lanak	NT0223	55°29·7′	3°32·6′W	W	72
Whitelaw Cleugh	Midlo	NT3655	55°47·3′	3°0·8′W	X	66,73
Whitelaw Hill	E Loth	NT5771	55°56·1′	2°40·9′W	H	67
Whitelaw Hill	Scot Bord	NT1935	55°36·4′	3°16·7′W	H	72
Whitelaw Hill	Shetld	HU3553	60°15·8′	1°21·5′W	H	3
Whitelaw Loch	Shetld	HU3554	60°16·4′	1°21·5′W	W	3
Whitelaws	Aberd	NO6379	56°54·3′	2°36·0′W	H	45
White Lea	Durham	NZ4344	54°47·6′	1°19·4′W	X	88
White Lea	Northum	NY7249	54°50·4′	2°25·7′W	X	86,87
White Lea	Surrey	TQ0434	51°6·0′	0°30·5′W	X	186
Whitelea Burn	W Loth	NT0660	55°49·7′	3°29·6′W	W	65
Whiteleaf	Bucks	SP8104	51°44·0′	0°49·2′W	T	165
Whiteleaf Cross	Bucks	SP8204	51°44·0′	0°48·4′W	A	165
White Lea Fm	Durham	NZ1537	54°43·9′	1°45·6′W	FM	92
White Lea Fm	Staffs	SK0256	53°6·3′	1°57·8′W	FM	119
Whiteleas	S Tyne	NZ3663	54°57·9′	1°25·8′W	T	88
White Leas Fm	N Yks	SE2865	54°5·1′	1°33·9′W	FM	99
Whiteleaved Oak	Worcs	SO7535	52°1·0′	2°21·5′W	T	150
Whitelee	Ches	SJ9564	53°10·6′	2°4·1′W	X	118
Whitelee	Derby	SK0981	53°19·8′	1°51·5′W	X	110
White Lee	Kirk	SE2225	53°43·5′	1°39·6′W	T	104
White Lee	Lancs	SD5542	53°52·6′	2°40·7′W	X	102
Whitelee	Northum	NT7105	55°20·5′	2°27·0′W	T	80
Whitelee	Northum	NU1032	55°35·1′	1°50·0′W	X	75
Whitelee	Scot Bord	NT4639	55°38·7′	2°51·0′W	X	73
Whitelee	Scot Bord	NT5630	55°34·0′	2°41·4′W	T	73
White Lee Fm	Sheff	SK2695	53°27·3′	1°36·1′W	FM	110
Whitelee Forest	E Ayr	NS5443	55°39·8′	4°18·8′W	F	70
Whitelee Forest	E Ayr	NS5643	55°39·8′	4°16·9′W	F	71
Whitelee Forest	E Ayr	NS5944	55°40·4′	4°14·1′W	F	71
Whiteleehill	E Ayr	NS5442	55°39·2′	4°18·8′W	H	70
White Lee Moor	Sheff	SK2694	53°26·8′	1°36·1′W	F	110
Whiteleen	Highld	ND3242	58°21·9′	3°9·3′W	X	12
Whitelees	Cumbr	NY1242	54°46·2′	3°21·6′W	X	85
Whitelees	Durham	NY9246	54°48·8′	2°7·0′W	X	87
Whitelees	S Ayr	NS3931	55°33·0′	4°32·7′W	T	70
Whitelees	S Lanak	NS9147	55°42·5′	3°43·6′W	X	72
Whitelees Cottage	Inverc	NS2773	55°55·4′	4°45·7′W	X	63
White Lees Fm	Oxon	SU5591	51°37·1′	1°11·9′W	FM	164,174
Whitelees Moor	Inverc	NS2773	55°55·4′	4°45·7′W	X	63
White-le-Head	Durham	NZ1754	54°53·1′	1°43·7′W	T	88
Whiteleigh Meadow	Devon	SS4102	50°48·0′	4°15·0′W	X	190
Whiteleigh Water	Devon	SS4303	50°48·6′	4°13·3′W	W	190
Whiteless Breast	Cumbr	NY1818	54°33·3′	3°15·7′W	X	89,90
Whiteless Pike	Cumbr	NY1818	54°33·3′	3°15·7′W	H	89,90
Whitelet	Orkney	HY5040	59°14·9′	2°52·1′W	X	5
Whitelett	Orkney	HY4728	59°8·4′	2°55·1′W	X	5,6
Whiteley	Aberd	NJ4803	57°7·2′	2°51·1′W	X	37
Whiteley	Aberd	NJ6213	57°12·6′	2°37·3′W	X	37
Whiteley	Aberd	NJ7328	57°20·8′	2°26·5′W	X	38
Whiteley	Moray	NJ5256	57°35·7′	2°47·7′W	X	29
Whiteley Bank	I of W	SZ5581	50°37·8′	1°13·0′W	T	196
Whiteley Fm	Devon	SX4084	50°38·3′	4°15·4′W	FM	201
Whiteley Fm	Devon	SX7760	50°25·9′	3°43·5′W	FM	202
Whiteley Green	Ches	SJ9278	53°18·2′	2°6·8′W	T	118
Whiteley Hill	Herts	TL3739	52°2·2′	0°0·2′E	X	154
Whiteley Nab	Derby	SK0292	53°25·7′	1°57·8′W	X	110
Whiteleys	Aberd	NJ5537	57°25·5′	2°44·5′W	X	29
White Leys	Derby	SK3623	52°48·4′	1°27·6′W	X	128
Whiteleys	D & G	NX0657	54°52·5′	5°1·0′W	X	82
Whiteleys	D & G	NY2478	55°5·7′	3°11·0′W	X	85
Whiteleys	Pemb	SN0616	51°48·8′	4°48·5′W	X	158
Whiteleys	S Ayr	NS3215	55°24·3′	4°38·8′W	X	70
Whiteleys	Stir	NS5792	56°6·2′	4°17·5′W	X	57
Whiteleys	W Dunb	NS3876	55°57·2′	4°35·2′W	X	63
Whiteley Shield	Northum	NY8048	54°49·8′	2°18·3′W	X	86,87
Whiteley Village	Surrey	TQ0962	51°21·0′	0°25·7′W	T	176,187
Whiteley Wood	Sheff	SK3084	53°21·4′	1°32·5′W	X	110,111
Whitelillies Fm	Essex	TQ7197	51°39·0′	0°28·7′E	FM	167
White Lily	N Yks	SE7777	54°11·2′	0°48·8′W	X	100
Whitelimes	Kent	TQ7433	51°4·4′	0°29·4′E	X	188
White Links	Aberd	NK0464	57°40·2′	1°55·5′W	X	30
Whitelinks Bay	Aberd	NK0564	57°40·2′	1°54·5′W	W	30
White Lion	Herts	SP9917	51°50·8′	0°33·4′W	X	165
White Lion Pond	E Susx	TQ4505	50°49·8′	0°3·9′E	W	198
White Lo	Bucks	TQ0282	51°31·9′	0°31·4′W	X	176
White Loaf Hall	Lincs	TF3943	52°58·2′	0°4·6′E	X	131
White Loch	S Ayr	NX2079	55°4·6′	4°48·8′W	W	76
White Loch	D & G	NX1061	54°54·7′	4°57·4′W	W	82
White Loch	D & G	NX2755	54°51·8′	4°41·3′W	W	82
White Loch	D & G	NX3456	54°52·5′	4°34·8′W	W	82
White Loch	D & G	NX4044	54°46·2′	4°28·8′W	W	83
White Loch	D & G	NX8654	54°52·3′	3°46·2′W	W	84
White Loch	E Renf	NS4852	55°44·5′	4°24·8′W	W	64
White Loch	Pth & Kin	NO1642	56°34·0′	3°21·6′W	W	53
White Loch	S Lanak	NS9647	55°42·6′	3°38·9′W	W	72
White Lochan of Drigmorn	D & G	NX4675	55°3·0′	4°24·2′W	W	77
White Loch of Myrton	D & G	NX3543	54°45·5′	4°33·4′W	W	83
White Lodge	Derby	SK4276	53°17·0′	1°21·8′W	X	120
White Lodge	Leic	SK7015	52°43·9′	0°57·4′W	X	129
White Lodge	Leic	SK7827	52°50·3′	0°50·1′W	X	129
White Lodge	Norf	TG0302	52°34·9′	1°0·2′E	X	144
White Lodge	Northnts	SP8174	52°21·7′	0°48·2′W	X	141
White Lodge	Notts	SK6569	53°13·1′	1°1·2′W	X	120
White Lodge	Rich	TQ2073	51°26·8′	0°16·0′W	X	176
White Lodge	Wilts	SU0689	51°36·2′	1°54·4′W	X	173
White Lodge	Wrekin	SJ5718	52°45·7′	2°37·8′W	X	126
White Lodge Crags	N Yks	SE1575	54°10·5′	1°45·8′W	X	99
White Lodge Fm	Leic	SK7223	52°48·2′	0°55·5′W	FM	129
White Lodge Fm	Northnts	SP8384	52°27·1′	0°46·3′W	FM	141
White Lodge Fm	Worcs	SO9278	52°24·2′	2°6·7′W	FM	139
White Low	Derby	SE0802	53°31·1′	1°52·4′W	X	110
Whitelow	Sheff	SK2881	53°19·7′	1°34·4′W	X	110
Whitelow Fm	Powys	SO1630	51°58·0′	3°13·0′W	FM	161
Whitelumbs	Aberd	NJ5232	57°22·8′	2°47·4′W	X	29,37
Whitelums	Aberd	NJ8121	57°17·0′	2°18·5′W	X	38
White Lund	Lancs	SD4462	54°3·3′	2°50·9′W	T	97
White Lund Fm	Lancs	SD4462	54°3·3′	2°50·9′W	FM	97
Whitely	Devon	SS3215	50°54·8′	4°23·0′W	X	190
Whitelye	Monm	SO5101	51°42·6′	2°42·2′W	T	162
Whitely Hill	W Susx	TQ3034	51°5·7′	0°8·2′W	X	187
White Lyne	Cumbr	NY5473	55°3·2′	2°42·8′W	W	86
White Lyne	Cumbr	NY5780	55°7·0′	2°40·0′W	W	80
Whitelyne Common	Cumbr	NY5880	55°7·0′	2°39·1′W	X	80
White Man's Dam	Know	SJ4594	53°26·6′	2°49·3′W	W	108
Whitemans Green	W Susx	TQ3025	51°0·8′	0°8·4′W	T	187,198
White Mare	Derby	SK0797	53°28·4′	1°53·3′W	X	110
White Mark	Oxon	SU7093	51°38·1′	0°58·9′W	X	175
Whitemaw Bay	Orkney	HY5429	59°9·0′	2°47·8′W	W	5,6
Whitemaw Hill	Orkney	HY5432	59°10·6′	2°47·8′W	X	5,6
White Mead	Dorset	SY7690	50°42·8′	2°20·0′W	X	194
White Meadow	Derby	SK1953	53°4·7′	1°42·6′W	X	119
Whitemeadows	Orkney	HY4031	59°10·0′	3°2·5′W	X	5,6
White Meldon	Scot Bord	NT2142	55°40·2′	3°14·9′W	H	73
White Mere	Durham	NY8831	54°40·7′	2°10·7′W	X	91,92
White Mere	N Yks	SE1263	54°4·0′	1°48·6′W	X	99
White Mere	Shrops	SJ4132	52°53·2′	2°52·6′W	W	126
Whitemere Fm	Staffs	SK1421	52°47·4′	1°47·1′W	FM	128
White Mill	Carm	SN4621	51°52·2′	4°13·8′W	T	159
White Mill	Dorset	ST9500	50°48·2′	2°3·9′W	X	195
Whitemill Bay	Orkney	HY6946	59°18·2′	2°32·2′W	W	5
Whitemill Point	Orkney	HY7046	59°18·2′	2°31·1′W	X	5
Whitemire	Moray	NH9754	57°34·1′	3°42·9′W	T	27
Whitemire	Orkney	HY3226	59°7·2′	3°10·8′W	X	6
Whitemire	Scot Bord	NT8454	55°47·0′	2°14·9′W	X	67,74
White Moor	Brad	SE0332	53°47·3′	1°56·9′W	X	104
White Moor	Cambs	TL3898	52°34·0′	0°2·6′E	X	142,143
Whitemoor	Ches	SJ9168	53°12·8′	2°7·7′W	X	118
Whitemoor	C of Nott	SK5442	52°58·6′	1°11·3′W	T	129
Whitemoor	Corn	SW9757	50°22·9′	4°51·0′W	T	200
Whitemoor	Corn	SX1697	50°44·8′	4°36·1′W	X	190
White Moor	Derby	SK3648	53°1·9′	1°27·4′W	T	119
Whitemoor	Devon	SS5708	50°51·5′	4°1·5′W	X	191
Whitemoor	Devon	SS5730	51°3·3′	4°2·0′W	X	180
White Moor	Devon	SS8130	51°3·7′	3°41·5′W	X	181
White Moor	Devon	SS8624	51°0·5′	3°37·1′W	X	181
Whitemoor	Devon	SX6049	50°19·7′	3°57·6′W	X	202
White Moor	Hants	SU2702	50°49·2′	1°36·6′W	X	195
White Moor	Hants	SU2707	50°51·9′	1°36·6′W	X	195
White Moor	Hants	SU3108	50°52·5′	1°33·2′W	X	196
White Moor	Lancs	SD6054	53°59·1′	2°36·2′W	X	102,103
White Moor	Lancs	SD8644	53°53·8′	2°12·4′W	X	103
White Moor	N Yks	SE7699	54°23·1′	0°49·4′W	X	94,100
White Moor	Somer	SS9337	51°7·6′	3°31·4′W	X	181
White Moor	Swan	SS4290	51°35·4′	4°16·5′W	X	159
Whitemoor	Warw	SP2972	52°21·0′	1°34·1′W	T	140
Whitemoor Fm	Devon	SX8686	50°40·0′	3°36·4′W	FM	191
Whitemoor Fm	N Yks	SE6635	53°48·7′	0°59·4′W	FM	105,106
Whitemoor Hall	Derby	SK3648	53°1·9′	1°27·4′W	X	119
Whitemoor Haye	Staffs	SK1713	52°43·1′	1°44·6′W	X	128
Whitemoor Hill	Ches	SJ9167	53°12·2′	2°7·7′W	H	118
Whitemoor Ho	Notts	SK6570	53°13·6′	1°1·2′W	X	120
White Moor Mill	N Yks	NZ9005	54°26·2′	0°36·3′W	X	94
Whitemoor Resr	Lancs	SD8743	53°53·2′	2°11·5′W	W	103
White Moors	Leic	SP3898	52°34·9′	1°25·9′W	X	140
White Moor Stone	Devon	SX6389	50°41·3′	3°56·0′W	A	191
Whitemoor, The	Staffs	SJ8508	52°40·4′	2°12·9′W	X	127
Whitemore	Staffs	SJ8860	53°8·5′	2°10·4′W	T	118
Whitemore Heath	Staffs	SJ7941	52°58·2′	2°18·4′W	X	118
White Moss	Ches	SJ7755	53°5·7′	2°20·2′W	X	118
Whitemoss	C of Edin	NT1165	55°52·5′	3°24·9′W	X	65
White Moss	Cumbr	NY4660	54°56·2′	2°50·1′W	X	86
White Moss	Cumbr	SD2285	54°15·5′	3°11·4′W	X	96
White Moss	Cumbr	SD3480	54°12·9′	3°0·3′W	X	96,97
White Moss	D & G	NY2767	54°59·8′	3°8·0′W	X	85
White Moss	Kirk	SE0407	53°33·8′	1°56·0′W	X	110
White Moss	Lancs	SD5076	54°10·9′	2°45·5′W	X	97
White Moss	Lancs	SD5750	53°56·9′	2°38·9′W	X	102
White Moss	Lancs	SD6364	54°4·5′	2°33·5′W	X	97
White Moss	Lancs	SD7954	53°59·1′	2°18·8′W	X	103
White Moss	Orkney	HY4805	58°56·0′	2°53·7′W	X	6,7
White Moss	Scot Bord	NT1449	55°43·9′	3°21·7′W	X	72
Whitemoss Burn	D & G	NY1596	55°15·3′	3°19·8′W	W	79
White Moss Common	Cumbr	NY3406	54°27·0′	3°0·7′W	X	90
Whitemoss Dam	Renf	NS4171	55°54·6′	4°32·2′W	W	64
White Moss Fm	Lancs	SD4704	53°32·0′	2°47·6′W	FM	108
Whitemoss Fm	Renf	NS4171	55°54·6′	4°32·2′W	FM	64
White Moss Gate	Lancs	SD5739	53°51·0′	2°38·8′W	X	102
White Moss Lock	Pth & Kin	NN9914	56°18·7′	3°37·5′W	W	58
White Mounth	Aberd	NO2383	56°56·2′	3°15·5′W	H	44
Whitemuir	Aberd	NJ6051	57°33·1′	2°39·6′W	X	29
White Muir	Pth & Kin	NN9010	56°16·4′	3°46·1′W	X	58
Whitemyre	Aberd	NO7175	56°52·2′	2°28·1′W	X	45
White Myre	Angus	NO5756	56°41·9′	2°41·7′W	X	54
Whitemyre	Pth & Kin	NO2028	56°26·5′	3°17·4′W	X	53,58
Whitemyres	Aberd	NJ7430	57°21·8′	2°25·5′W	T	29
White Nab	N Yks	TA0586	54°15·8′	0°22·9′W	X	101
White Nancy	Ches	SJ9377	53°17·6′	2°5·9′W	X	118
Whitenap	Hants	SU3720	50°58·9′	1°28·0′W	T	185
Whitendale	Lancs	SD6655	53°59·6′	2°30·7′W	X	103
Whitendale Fell	Lancs	SD6655	53°59·6′	2°30·7′W	X	103
Whitendale Hanging Stones	Lancs	SD6456	54°0·2′	2°32·5′W	X	102,103
Whitendale River	Lancs	SD6555	53°59·6′	2°31·6′W	W	102,103
White Ness	Highld	NH8186	57°51·1′	3°59·8′W	X	21
White Ness	Kent	TR3971	51°23·5′	1°26·5′E	X	179
White Ness	Shetld	HU3844	60°11·0′	1°18·4′W	T	4
Whiteness	Shetld	HU4147	60°12·6′	1°15·1′W	X	3
Whiteness Head	Highld	NH8058	57°36·0′	4°0·0′W	X	27
Whiteness Sands	Highld	NH8386	57°51·2′	3°57·8′W	X	21
Whiteness Taing	Orkney	HY5227	59°7·9′	2°49·8′W	X	5,6
Whiteness Voe	Shetld	HU3943	60°10·4′	1°17·3′W	W	4
Whiteneuk	D & G	NX7665	54°58·1′	3°55·8′W	X	84
Whiteneuk Hill	D & G	NX7581	55°6·7′	3°57·2′W	X	78
Whiten Head or An Ceann Geal	Highld	NC5068	58°34·7′	4°34·3′W	X	9
Whiten Hill	Wilts	ST8940	51°9·8′	2°9·1′W	H	184
Whitening Ho	Ches	SJ7564	53°10·6′	2°22·0′W	X	118
White Nothe	Dorset	SY7780	50°37·4′	2°19·1′W	X	194
White Notley	Essex	TL7818	51°50·2′	0°35·4′E	T	167
Whitens	Pth & Kin	NN9705	56°13·8′	3°39·2′W	X	58
Whitensmere Fm	Cambs	TL6043	52°4·0′	0°20·5′E	FM	154
White Oak	Kent	TQ5069	51°24·2′	0°9·8′E	T	177
Whiteoak Beck	Cumbr	NY1219	54°33·8′	3°21·2′W	W	89
White Oak Fm	Shrops	SJ8209	52°40·9′	2°15·6′W	FM	127
White Oak Fm	Suff	TM1164	52°14·2′	1°5·8′E	FM	155
Whiteoak Green	Oxon	SP3414	51°49·6′	1°30·0′W	T	164
White Oak Ho	Hants	SU4460	51°20·5′	1°21·7′W	X	174
Whiteoak Moss	Cumbr	NY1217	54°32·7′	3°21·2′W	X	89
White Ollands Fm	Norf	TG0733	52°51·5′	1°4·9′E	FM	133
White Otter Fm	Lancs	SD3211	53°35·7′	3°1·2′W	FM	108
White-oxen Manor	Devon	SX7261	50°26·3′	3°47·8′W	X	202
White Ox Mead	Bath & NE Somer	ST7258	51°19·5′	2°23·7′W	T	172
Whiteparish	Wilts	SU2423	51°0·6′	1°39·1′W	T	184
Whiteparish Common	Wilts	SU2522	51°0·0′	1°38·2′W	X	184
White Park	D & G	NX1059	54°53·6′	4°57·3′W	X	82
Whitepark	D & G	NX7661	54°55·9′	3°55·7′W	X	84
Whitepark Fm	Essex	TL9733	51°57·9′	0°52·5′E	FM	168
Whitepatch Hill	Surrey	SU9252	51°15·8′	0°40·5′W	X	186
White Path Moss	Derby	SK2583	53°20·8′	1°37·1′W	X	110

White Pike	Cumbr	NY3323	54°36·1'	3°1·8'W	X	90
White Pike	Cumbr	SD1595	54°20·9'	3°18·0'W	X	96
White Pike	Cumbr	SD2495	54°20·9'	3°9·7'W	H	96
White Pit	Lincs	TF3777	53°16·6'	0°3·7'E	T	122
Whitepits	Wilts	ST8437	51°8·2'	2°13·3'W	T	183
White Place Fm	Win & Maid	SU9084	51°33·1'	0°41·7'W	FM	175
Whiteplot Fm	Norf	TL6992	52°30·2'	0°29·8'E	FM	143
White Point	N Ayr	NS0530	55°31·7'	5°4·9'W	X	69
Whitepond Fm	Oxon	SU7389	51°35·9'	0°56·4'W	FM	175
White Port	Arg & Bt	NS1154	55°44·8'	5°0·2'W	W	63
White Port	D & G	NX4740	54°44·2'	4°22·2'W	W	83
White Port	D & G	NX7243	54°46·2'	3°59·0'W	W	83,84
White Port	D & G	NX8451	54°50·7'	3°48·0'W	W	84
White Post	Devon	SS8131	51°4·2'	3°41·5'W	X	181
White Post	Dorset	ST6020	50°58·9'	2°33·8'W	X	183
White Post	Kent	TQ5041	51°9·1'	0°9·1'E	T	188
White Post	Kent	TQ8556	51°16·6'	0°39·5'E	X	178
White Post	Notts	SK6257	53°6·6'	1°4·0'W	T	120
White Post	Somer	ST6652	51°16·2'	2°28·9'W	X	183
White Post	Surrey	TQ3350	51°14·2'	0°5·3'W	X	187
Whitepost Corner	Suff	TM2062	52°13·0'	1°13·6'E	X	156
White Post Fm	Hav	TQ5985	51°32·7'	0°18·0'E	FM	177
White Post Fm	N Yks	NZ5505	54°26·5'	1°8·7'W	FM	93
Whitepost Fm	Peterb	TF2103	52°36·9'	0°12·4'W	FM	142
White Post Fm	Suff	TM2775	52°19·8'	1°20·3'E	FM	156
White Post Fm	Suff	TM3872	52°17·9'	1°29·8'E	FM	156
White Preston	Cumbr	NY5977	55°5·4'	2°38·1'W	X	86
White Pump Fm	Staffs	SJ8510	52°41·5'	2°12·9'W	FM	127
White Quarry Fm	N Yks	SE4640	53°51·5'	1°17·6'W	FM	105
Whitequarry Hill	Oxon	SP2626	51°56·1'	1°36·9'W	X	163
Whiterails	Norf	TG1305	52°36·3'	1°9·1'E	X	144
Whiterake	Derby	SK1478	53°18·2'	1°47·0'W	X	119
White Rake	Derby	SK1874	53°16·0'	1°43·4'W	X	119
Whiterashes	Aberd	NJ7353	57°34·2'	2°26·6'W	X	29
Whiterashes	Aberd	NJ7840	57°27·2'	2°21·5'W	X	29,30
Whiterashes	Aberd	NJ8523	57°18·1'	2°14·5'W	T	38
Whiterashes	Aberd	NJ9560	57°38·1'	2°4·6'W	X	30
White Ridge	Devon	SX6482	50°37·5'	3°55·0'W	X	191
White Ridge	Northum	NY8447	54°49·3'	2°14·5'W	X	86,87
White Rig	Scot Bord	NT2150	55°44·5'	3°15·1'W	X	66,73
White Rig	Scot Bord	NT3532	55°34·9'	3°1·4'W	X	73
Whiterig	Scot Bord	NT9258	55°49·2'	2°7·2'W	X	67,74,75
White Rig	S Lanak	NS8123	55°29·3'	3°52·6'W	H	71,72
White Rig	S Lanak	NS9026	55°31·2'	3°44·1'W	X	71,72
White Rigg	Cumbr	NY5971	55°2·2'	2°38·1'W	X	86
White Rigg	Durham	NY8727	54°38·5'	2°11·7'W	X	91,92
Whiterigg	Falk	NS9375	55°57·6'	3°42·4'W	X	65
White Rigg	Northum	NY6770	55°1·7'	2°30·5'W	X	86,87
Whiterigg	Pth & Kin	NO0004	56°13·3'	3°36·3'W	X	58
Whiterigg	Scot Bord	NT5631	55°34·5'	2°41·4'W	T	73
Whiteriggs	Aberd	NO7575	56°52·2'	2°24·2'W	X	45
White Riggs	Northum	NZ0073	55°3·3'	1°59·6'W	X	87
Whiterock	Brig	SS9078	51°29·7'	3°34·7'W	T	
White Rock	Devon	SX8456	50°23·8'	3°37·5'W	X	202
White Rocks	Heref	SO4324	51°54·9'	2°49·3'W	T	161
Whiterocks Down	Devon	SS8729	51°3·2'	3°36·4'W	X	181
White Roding or White Roothing	Essex	TL5613	51°47·9'	0°16·1'E	T	167
White Roothing or White Roding	Essex	TL5613	51°47·9'	0°16·1'E	T	167
White Rose Centre	Leeds	SE2728	53°45·1'	1°35·0'W	X	104
Whiterow	Devon	SX4588	50°40·5'	4°11·2'W	X	190
Whiterow	Highld	ND3548	58°25·2'	3°6·3'W	T	12
Whiterow	Moray	NJ0257	57°35·8'	3°37·9'W	X	27
Whiterow	N Yks	SE0183	54°14·8'	1°58·7'W	X	98
White Row	S Ayr	NX3495	55°13·5'	4°36·2'W	X	76
Whiterow Burn	S Ayr	NX3495	55°13·5'	4°36·2'W	W	76
Whiterow Scaurs	S Ayr	NX3496	55°14·1'	4°36·2'W	X	76
White's	Somer	ST3131	51°4·7'	2°58·7'W	X	182
Whitesand Bay	Corn	SW3527	50°5·3'	5°41·9'W	W	203
White Sands	E Loth	NT7177	55°59·4'	2°27·5'W	X	67
White Sands	Flint	SJ2772	53°14·6'	3°5·2'W	X	117
Whitesands Bay Porth-mawr	Pemb	SM7226	51°53·4'	5°18·4'W	W	157
White Sark	Orkney	HY4502	58°54·4'	2°56·8'W	X	6,7
White's Barn	Leic	SK7007	52°39·6'	0°57·5'W	X	141
White Scar	Cumbr	SD4585	54°15·7'	2°50·2'W	X	97
White Scar Cave	N Yks	SD7174	54°9·9'	2°26·2'W	X	98
White Scar Plantn	N Yks	SE8060	54°2·0'	0°46·3'W	F	100
White Scars	N Yks	SD7273	54°9·4'	2°25·3'W	X	98
White Scaurins	S Ayr	NX3399	55°15·7'	4°37·3'W	X	76
Whitesfield Fm	Bucks	SP7718	51°51·5'	0°52·5'W	FM	165
White's Fm	Essex	TL8831	51°57·0'	0°44·5'E	FM	168
White's Fm	Norf	TG3810	52°38·4'	1°31·5'E	FM	133,134
White's Fm	Somer	ST0430	51°3·9'	3°21·8'W	FM	181
White's Fm	Somer	ST1918	50°57·6'	3°8·8'W	FM	181,193
White's Fm	Somer	ST2815	50°56·0'	3°1·1'W	FM	193
White's Fm	Surrey	SU9555	51°17·4'	0°37·9'W	FM	175,186
White's Fm	Warw	SP2697	52°34·4'	1°36·6'W	FM	140
White's Fm	Wilts	SU0283	51°33·0'	1°57·9'W	FM	173
White's Fm	Wok	SU7566	51°23·5'	0°54·9'W	FM	175
White's Fm	W Susx	TQ0526	51°1·7'	0°29·8'W	FM	187,197
White's Green	W Susx	SU9425	51°1·2'	0°39·2'W	T	186,197
White Shank	D & G	NT1608	55°21·8'	3°19·1'W	H	79
White Shank	D & G	NT2006	55°20·7'	3°15·3'W	H	79
Whiteshard Bottom	Wilts	SU2273	51°27·6'	1°40·6'W	X	174
White Shaw Moss	Cumbr	SD7281	54°13·7'	2°25·4'W	X	98
White Sheet Downs	Wilts	ST8035	51°7·1'	2°16·8'W	H	183
White Sheet Hill	Dorset	ST4902	50°49·2'	2°43·1'W	X	193,194
Whitesheet Hill	Dorset	SY5898	50°47·0'	2°35·4'W	H	194
White Sheet Hill	Wilts	ST8034	51°6·5'	2°16·8'W	H	183
White Sheet Hill	Wilts	ST9424	51°1·2'	2°4·7'W	H	184
White Sheet Plantation	Dorset	SU0503	50°49·8'	1°55·4'W	F	195
Whiteshell Point	Swan	SS5986	51°33·6'	4°1·7'W	X	159
Whiteshill	Glos	SO8407	51°45·9'	2°13·5'W	T	162
Whiteshill	S Glos	ST6479	51°30·8'	2°30·7'W	T	172
White's Hill	Wilts	SU2571	51°26·5'	1°38·0'W	X	174
White's Hill	W Susx	SU9632	51°5·0'	0°37·4'W	X	186
Whiteshill Fm	Essex	TL8222	51°52·2'	0°39·0'E	FM	168
Whiteshoot Hill	Hants	SU2833	51°6·0'	1°35·6'W	X	184
Whiteshoot Hill	Hants	SU2933	51°6·0'	1°34·8'W	X	185
White Shute	W Berks	SU3277	51°29·7'	1°32·0'W	X	174
Whiteside	Aberd	NJ5719	57°15·8'	2°42·3'W	X	37
Whiteside	Aberd	NJ9956	57°35·9'	2°0·5'W	X	30
Whiteside	Cumbr	NY1621	54°34·9'	3°17·6'W	H	89
White Side	Cumbr	NY3317	54°32·9'	3°1·7'W	X	90
White Side	Cumbr	NY6672	55°2·7'	2°31·5'W	X	86
Whiteside	D & G	NS8811	55°23·1'	3°45·6'W	H	71,78
Whiteside	D & G	NX5556	54°52·9'	4°15·2'W	X	83
Whiteside	D & G	NX8083	55°7·9'	3°52·5'W	X	78
Whiteside	D & G	NX8867	54°59·4'	3°44·6'W	X	84
Whiteside	N Lanak	NS8668	55°53·8'	3°48·9'W	X	65
Whiteside	Northum	NY7069	55°1·1'	2°27·7'W	X	86,87
White Side	Northum	NY7185	55°9·8'	2°26·9'W	H	80
White Side	Northum	NY7576	55°4·9'	2°23·1'W	X	86,87
Whiteside	Northum	NY9280	55°7·1'	2°7·1'W	X	80
Whiteside	Northum	NZ1280	55°7·1'	1°48·3'W	X	81
Whiteside	Pth & Kin	NO2249	56°37·8'	3°15·8'W	X	53
Whiteside	Scot Bord	NT1646	55°42·3'	3°19·8'W	X	72
Whiteside	Scot Bord	NT7146	55°42·6'	2°27·3'W	X	74
Whiteside	S Lanak	NS7937	55°36·9'	3°54·8'W	X	71
Whiteside	W Loth	NS9567	55°53·3'	3°40·3'W	X	65
Whiteside	W Loth	NS9667	55°53·4'	3°39·3'W	T	65
Whiteside Burn	D & G	NX5555	54°52·4'	4°15·2'W	W	83
Whiteside Burn	Durham	NZ2048	54°49·8'	1°40·9'W	W	88
Whiteside Edge	Scot Bord	NT2645	55°41·8'	3°10·2'W	H	73
Whiteside End	Cumbr	NY5877	55°5·4'	2°39·1'W	X	86
Whiteside Fm	Aberd	NO8695	57°3·0'	2°13·4'W	FM	38,45
Whiteside Fm	Durham	NZ2048	54°49·8'	1°40·9'W	FM	88
Whiteside Hill	D & G	NS7105	55°19·6'	4°1·6'W	H	71,77
Whiteside Hill	D & G	NS8318	55°26·8'	3°50·5'W	X	71,78
Whiteside Hill	D & G	NS9804	55°19·4'	3°36·0'W	H	78
Whiteside Hill	D & G	NT0111	55°23·2'	3°33·3'W	X	78
Whiteside Hill	D & G	NX8082	55°7·3'	3°52·5'W	H	78
Whiteside Hill	D & G	NY0477	55°4·9'	3°29·8'W	H	84
Whiteside Hill	N Ayr	NS2252	55°44·0'	4°49·7'W	X	63
Whiteside Hill	Scot Bord	NT0821	55°28·7'	3°26·9'W	H	72
Whiteside Hill	Scot Bord	NT1645	55°41·7'	3°19·7'W	H	72
Whiteside Hill	Scot Bord	NT7708	55°22·2'	2°21·3'W	H	80
Whiteside Hill	S Lanak	NS8933	55°34·9'	3°45·2'W	X	71,72
Whiteside Hill	S Lanak	NS9602	55°18·3'	3°37·9'W	X	78
Whiteside Hill	S Lanak	NS9627	55°31·8'	3°38·4'W	H	72
Whiteside Law	Northum	NY9775	55°4·4'	2°2·4'W	X	87
Whiteside Law	Scot Bord	NT3550	55°44·6'	3°1·7'W	H	66,73
White Side of Tarnbrook Fell	Lancs	SD6056	54°0·2'	2°36·2'W	X	102,103
White Side Pasture	N Yks	SD7080	54°13·1'	2°27·2'W	X	98
Whiteside Pike	Cumbr	NY5201	54°24·4'	2°43·9'W	H	90
Whiteside Rig	Scot Bord	NY5388	55°11·3'	2°43·9'W	X	79
White Sike	Northum	NY6884	55°9·2'	2°29·7'W	W	80
White Sitch	Staffs	SJ7912	52°42·6'	2°18·2'W	X	127
White Slea	Norf	TG4221	52°44·2'	1°35·5'E	W	134
White Sleight Fm	Somer	ST6441	51°10·3'	2°30·5'W	FM	183
Whitesmith	E Susx	TQ5213	50°54·0'	0°10·1'E	T	199
Whitesmuir	E Ayr	NS5317	55°25·7'	4°19·0'W	X	70
Whites Ness	Shetld	HU2447	60°12·7'	1°33·5'W	X	3
Whitesness	Shetld	HU2447	60°12·7'	1°33·5'W	X	3
White Snout	D & G	NS9100	55°17·2'	3°42·5'W	X	78
White's Place	Essex	TL6702	51°41·7'	0°25·4'E	X	167
Whitespot	N Ayr	NS3450	55°43·2'	4°38·1'W	X	63
White Spot	Northum	NT8604	55°20·0'	2°12·8'W	X	80
Whitespots	D & G	NX9089	55°11·2'	3°43·2'W	T	78
Whitespout Gutter	Lancs	SD5859	54°1·8'	2°38·1'W	W	102
Whitespout Gutter	Lancs	SD5860	54°2·3'	2°38·1'W	W	97
Whitespout Lane	E Ayr	NX4593	55°12·7'	4°25·7'W	W	77
White's Rock	Arg & Bt	NM3516	56°16·0'	6°16·4'W	X	48
White Stake	Lancs	SD5225	53°43·4'	2°43·2'W	T	102
White Stane	Shetld	HU4226	60°1·3'	1°14·3'W	X	4
White Stane of Erne's Gill	Shetld	HU4027	60°1·8'	1°16·4'W	X	4
White Stane of Housifield	Shetld	HP6313	60°48·0'	0°50·0'W	X	1
White Stane of Willies	Shetld	HU4428	60°2·3'	1°12·1'W	X	4
Whitestanes	D & G	NX9788	55°10·8'	3°36·6'W	X	78
Whitestanes	N Ayr	NS3352	55°44·2'	4°39·2'W	X	63
Whitestanes Moor	D & G	NX9888	55°10·8'	3°37·6'W	X	78
Whitestaunton	Somer	ST2810	50°53·3'	3°1·0'W	T	193
White Stean Well	N Yks	SE0571	54°8·3'	1°55·0'W	W	98
White Stitch	Warw	SP2483	52°26·9'	1°38·4'W	X	140
Whitestock Hall	Cumbr	SD3289	54°17·8'	3°2·3'W	X	96,97
Whitestone	Aberd	NJ8006	57°8·9'	2°19·4'W	X	38
Whitestone	Aberd	NO6392	57°1·3'	2°36·1'W	X	45
Whitestone	Arg & Bt	NR7933	55°32·7'	5°29·8'W	X	68,69
White Stone	Cumbr	NY5720	54°34·7'	2°39·5'W	X	91
White Stone	Cumbr	NY6020	54°34·7'	2°36·7'W	X	91
Whitestone	Devon	SX8693	50°43·8'	3°36·5'W	T	191
White Stone	Heref	SO5642	52°4·7'	2°38·1'W	T	149
White Stone	Shetld	HU3759	60°19·1'	1°19·3'W	X	2,3
WHITESTONE	Warw	SP3889	52°30·1'	1°26·0'W	T	140
Whitestone	W Susx	TQ3630	51°3·4'	0°3·2'W	X	187
Whitestone Cairn	E Loth	NT5662	55°51·2'	2°41·7'W	A	67
Whitestone Cliff	N Yks	SE5083	54°14·7'	1°13·5'W	X	100
Whitestone Cross	Devon	SX8146	50°18·4'	3°39·9'W	X	202
Whitestone Enclosure	Cumbr	SD3885	54°15·7'	2°56·7'W	X	96,97
Whitestone Fm	Brad	SD9837	53°50·0'	2°1·4'W	FM	103
Whitestone Fm	Devon	SS4946	51°11·8'	4°9·3'W	FM	180
Whitestone Fm	Devon	SX8456	50°23·8'	3°37·5'W	FM	202
Whitestone Fm	W Susx	SZ8299	50°47·3'	0°49·8'W	FM	197
White Stone Gill	Durham	NY9109	54°28·8'	2°7·9'W	W	91,92
Whitestone Hill	Aberd	NJ9739	57°26·7'	2°2·5'W	H	30
Whitestone Hill	Scot Bord	NT7915	55°26·0'	2°19·5'W	H	80
Whitestone Ho	Durham	NY8241	54°46·1'	2°16·4'W	X	86,87
White Stone Hole	N Yks	NZ9507	54°27·2'	0°31·7'W	W	94
Whitestone Moor	Cumbr	NY4720	54°34·6'	2°48·8'W	X	90
White Stone of Toufield	Shetld	HU4137	60°7·2'	1°15·2'W	X	4
Whitestones	Aberd	NJ4735	57°24·4'	2°52·5'W	X	28,29
Whitestones	Aberd	NJ7262	57°39·1'	2°27·7'W	X	29
Whitestones	Aberd	NJ7514	57°13·2'	2°24·4'W	X	38
Whitestones	Aberd	NJ8452	57°33·7'	2°15·6'W	X	29,30
White Stones	Brad	SE1243	53°53·2'	1°48·6'W	X	104
Whitestones	Cumbr	NY6711	54°29·8'	2°30·2'W	X	91
Whitestones	Cumbr	SD1193	54°19·7'	3°21·7'W	X	96
White Stones	Derby	SK1197	53°28·4'	1°49·6'W	X	110
White Stones	N Yks	SE0155	53°59·7'	1°58·7'W	X	104
Whitestones	N Yks	SE4993	54°20·1'	1°14·4'W	X	100
White Stones	Red & Cl	NZ7420	54°34·4'	0°50·9'W	X	94
White Stones	Sheff	SK2584	53°21·4'	1°37·1'W	X	110
Whitestones (Cairns)	N Yks	SE4993	54°20·1'	1°14·4'W	A	100
Whitestone Scar	N Yks	SE4892	54°19·5'	1°15·3'W	X	100
Whitestones Fm	Durham	NY8639	54°45·0'	2°12·6'W	FM	91,92
Whitestone Wood	Devon	SX8695	50°44·8'	3°36·6'W	X	191
Whitestown Fm	Somer	ST5255	51°17·8'	2°40·9'W	FM	172,182
White Strand	I of M	SC2685	54°14·1'	4°39·8'W	X	95
Whitestreet	Corn	SW7449	50°18·1'	5°10·0'W	X	204
Whitestreet Green	Suff	TL9739	52°1·1'	0°52·7'E	T	155
Whitestripe	Aberd	NJ9456	57°35·9'	2°5·6'W	X	30
Whitestripes Fm	C of Aber	NJ9111	57°11·6'	2°8·5'W	FM	38
White's Wood	Bucks	SP9300	51°41·7'	0°38·9'W	F	165
White's Wood Fm	Lincs	SK8390	53°24·3'	0°44·7'W	FM	112
Whitesyke	Cumbr	NY4067	54°59·9'	2°55·8'W	X	85
White Syke	Lancs	SD7058	54°1·3'	2°27·1'W	W	103
White Syke Fm	N Yks	SE6758	54°1·1'	0°58·2'W	FM	105,106
White Syke Hill	N Yks	SD7362	54°3·4'	2°24·3'W	X	98
White Sykes	N Yks	SE6592	54°19·4'	0°59·6'W	X	94,100
Whitesytch Fm	Staffs	SJ9433	52°53·9'	2°4·9'W	FM	127
Whitethorn	Devon	SX7394	50°44·1'	3°47·6'W	X	191
Whitethorn	N Yks	SE7688	54°17·2'	0°49·5'W	X	94,100
Whitethorn	N Yks	SE8690	54°18·1'	0°40·3'W	X	94,101
Whitethorn Clough	Derby	SK0491	53°25·2'	1°56·0'W	X	110
White Thorn Fm	N Yks	SE7282	54°14·0'	0°53·3'W	FM	100
White Top	Angus	NO4360	56°43·9'	2°55·4'W	H	44
White Top of Culreoch	D & G	NX6063	54°56·8'	4°10·7'W	H	83
White Tor	Derby	SK1988	53°23·5'	1°42·4'W	X	110
White Tor	Devon	SX4280	50°36·1'	4°13·6'W	X	201
White Tor	Devon	SX5478	50°35·2'	4°3·4'W	H	191,201
Whitetree	Moray	NJ1156	57°35·4'	3°28·9'W	X	28
Whitevine Fm	Somer	ST5008	50°52·4'	2°42·3'W	FM	194
Whitewall	Cumbr	NY6612	54°30·4'	2°31·1'W	X	91
Whitewall Common	Monm	ST4286	51°34·4'	2°49·8'W	T	171,172
Whitewall Corner	N Yks	SE7970	54°7·4'	0°47·1'W	T	100
Whitewalls	Angus	NO4035	56°30·5'	2°58·0'W	X	54
White Walls	Herts	TL0915	51°49·6'	0°24·7'W	X	166
Whitewalls	Swan	SS5693	51°37·3'	4°4·4'W	X	159
Whitewalls Burn	Northum	NY7651	54°51·4'	2°22·0'W	W	86,87
White Waltham	Win & Maid	SU8577	51°29·4'	0°46·2'W	T	175
White Water	Angus	NO2576	56°52·4'	3°13·4'W	W	44
Whitewater	Notts	SK6670	53°13·6'	1°0·3'W	W	120
White Water	Somer	ST7938	51°7·9'	3°43·4'W	W	180
Whitewater Br	Notts	SK6670	53°13·6'	1°0·3'W	X	120
Whitewater Common	Notts	SK6088	53°23·4'	1°5·5'W	X	111,120
Whitewater Dash (Waterfall)	Cumbr	NY2731	54°40·4'	3°7·5'W	W	89,90
Whitewater Fm	Corn	SW9065	50°27·1'	4°57·1'W	FM	200
Whitewater Fm	Glos	ST8291	51°37·3'	2°15·2'W	FM	162,173
Whitewater Fm	Notts	SK6569	53°13·1'	1°1·2'W	FM	120
White Water Reservoir	Northnts	TF0303	52°37·1'	0°28·3'W	W	141
Whiteway	Bath & NE Somer	ST7163	51°22·2'	2°24·6'W	T	172
Whiteway	Dorset	SY8782	50°38·5'	2°10·6'W	T	194
Whiteway	Glos	SO9110	51°47·5'	2°7·4'W	T	163
White Way	Glos	SP0311	51°48·1'	1°57·0'W	A	163
Whiteway	Glos	ST7696	51°40·0'	2°20·4'W	X	162
Whiteway	Glos	ST8498	51°41·1'	2°13·5'W	T	162
Whiteway Barton	Devon	SX8875	50°34·1'	3°34·5'W	X	192
Whiteway Bottom	E Susx	TQ3905	50°49·9'	0°1·2'W	X	198
Whiteway Bottom	Herts	TL1520	51°52·2'	0°19·4'W	X	166
Whiteway Fm	Dorset	SY9281	50°37·9'	2°6·4'W	FM	195
Whiteway Fm	Glos	SP0303	51°43·8'	1°57·0'W	FM	163
Whiteway Fm	Hants	SU5540	51°9·6'	1°12·4'W	FM	185
Whiteway Head	Heref	SO4567	52°18·1'	2°48·0'W	X	137,138,148
Whitewayhead	Shrops	SO5774	52°22·0'	2°37·5'W	X	137,138
White Way Hill	Dorset	ST7917	50°57·4'	2°17·6'W	H	183
Whiteway Hill	Dorset	SY8781	50°37·9'	2°10·6'W	H	194
Whiteway Ho	Devon	SX8782	50°37·8'	3°35·5'W	A	192
Whiteways Lodge	W Susx	TQ0010	50°53·1'	0°34·3'W	X	197
Whiteway Wood	Devon	SX8783	50°38·4'	3°35·5'W	F	192
Whitewebbs Park	Enf	TQ3299	51°40·7'	0°5·1'W	X	166,176,177
Whitewell	Aberd	NJ7021	57°17·0'	2°29·4'W	X	38
Whitewell	Aberd	NJ9461	57°38·6'	2°5·6'W	X	30
Whitewell	Angus	NO4349	56°38·0'	2°55·3'W	X	54
Whitewell	Corn	SX0580	50°35·5'	4°44·9'W	T	200
White Well	Durham	NY8328	54°39·1'	2°15·4'W	X	91,92
Whitewell	Highld	NH9108	57°9·3'	3°47·7'W	X	36
Whitewell	Lancs	SD6546	53°54·8'	2°31·6'W	T	102,103
Whitewell	Pemb	SS0999	51°39·7'	4°45·3'W	A	158
Whitewell	V of Glam	ST0672	51°26·6'	3°20·8'W	X	170
Whitewell	Wrex	SJ4941	52°58·1'	2°45·2'W	T	117
Whitewell Bottom	Lancs	SD8323	53°42·4'	2°15·0'W	T	103
Whitewell Fm	Cumbr	NY7346	54°48·7'	2°24·8'W	FM	86,87
Whitewell Fm	Leeds	SE4139	53°51·0'	1°22·2'W	FM	105
Whitewell Folds	Cumbr	SD5498	54°22·8'	2°42·1'W	X	97
Whitewell Ho	Heref	SO5129	51°57·7'	2°42·4'W	X	149
Whitewell Oasts	Kent	TQ7737	51°6·5'	0°32·1'E	X	188
White Wells	Brad	SE1146	53°54·8'	1°49·5'W	X	104
Whitewells Bush	D & G	NT1611	55°23·4'	3°19·1'W	X	79
White Wells Fm	Derby	SK3350	53°3·0'	1°30·1'W	FM	119
Whitewells Fm	Heref	SO7147	52°7·5'	2°25·0'W	FM	149
White Wells Fm	V of Glam	ST0776	51°28·8'	3°20·0'W	FM	170
Whitewick Fm	Somer	ST2345	51°12·2'	3°5·7'W	FM	182
White Wife	Shetld	HU5385	60°33·0'	1°1·5'W	X	1,2,3
Whitewisp Hill	Clackm	NN9501	56°11·7'	3°41·1'W	H	58
White Wood	Beds	TL2152	52°9·4'	0°13·5'W	F	153
Whitewood	Staffs	SK1520	52°46·9'	1°46·3'W	X	128
Whitewood	Surrey	TQ3445	51°11·5'	0°4·5'W	X	187
Whitewood Fm	Bath & NE Somer	ST6066	51°23·7'	2°34·1'W	FM	172
Whitewood House Fm	Surrey	TQ3444	51°11·0'	0°4·6'W	FM	187
Whitewood Fm	Hants	SU6521	50°59·3'	1°4·0'W	FM	185
Whiteworks	Devon	SX6170	50°31·0'	3°57·3'W	X	202
Whitewreath	Moray	NJ2357	57°36·0'	3°16·8'W	X	28
Whiteyard	D & G	NX8872	55°2·0'	3°44·7'W	X	84
Whiteyards	E Ayr	NS6522	55°28·6'	4°7·7'W	X	71

Whiteyett	D & G	NY2494	55°14·3′	3°11·3′W	X	79
Whitey Top	Dorset	SU0418	50°57·9′	1°56·2′W	X	184
Whitfell	Cumbr	SD1592	54°19·2′	3°18·0′W	H	96
Whit Fell	N Yks	SE0894	54°20·7′	1°52·2′W	H	99
Whitfield	C of Dun	NO4333	56°29·4′	2°55·1′W	X	54
Whitfield	C of Stoke	SJ8852	53°4·1′	2°10·3′W	X	118
Whitfield	Heref	SO4233	51°59·8′	2°50·3′W	X	149,161
Whitfield	Heref	SO5521	51°53·4′	2°38·8′W	X	162
Whitfield	Kent	TR3044	51°9·2′	1°17·7′E	T	179
Whitfield	Northnts	SP6039	52°3·0′	1°7·1′W	T	152
Whitfield	Northum	NY7758	54°55·2′	2°21·1′W	T	86,87
Whitfield	Northum	NY9083	55°8·7′	2°9·0′W	X	80
Whitfield	Scot Bord	NT1653	55°46·0′	3°19·9′W	X	65,66,72
Whitfield	Scot Bord	NT4616	55°26·3′	2°50·8′W	X	79
Whitfield	Scot Bord	NT9063	55°51·9′	2°9·1′W	X	67
Whitfield	S Glos	ST6791	51°37·2′	2°28·2′W	T	162,172
Whitfield Brow	Durham	NZ0034	54°42·3′	1°59·6′W	X	92
Whitfield Court	Surrey	SU9659	51°19·5′	0°36·9′W	T	175,186
Whitfield Fell	N Yks	SD9393	54°20·2′	2°6·0′W	X	98
Whitfield Fm	Dorset	ST6110	50°53·5′	2°32·9′W	FM	194
Whitfield Fm	Warw	SP2650	52°9·1′	1°36·8′W	FM	151
Whitfield Gill Force	N Yks	SD9392	54°19·7′	2°6·0′W	W	98
Whitfield Hall	Northum	NY7756	54°54·1′	2°21·1′W	T	86,87
Whitfield Law	Northum	NY7253	54°52·5′	2°25·8′W	H	86,87
Whitfield Lough	Northum	NY7254	54°53·0′	2°25·8′W	W	86,87
Whitfield Moor	Northum	NY7353	54°52·5′	2°24·8′W	X	86,87
Whitfield's Tump	Glos	SO8501	51°42·7′	2°12·6′W	X	162
Whitfield's Tump (Long Barrow)	Glos	SO8501	51°42·7′	2°12·6′W	A	162
Whitfield Wood	Bucks	SP6439	52°3·0′	1°3·6′W	F	152
Whitfield Woods	Dorset	ST6110	50°53·5′	2°32·9′W	F	194
Whitfold Hill	Scot Bord	NT2642	55°40·2′	3°10·2′W	H	73
Whitford	Devon	SY2595	50°45·2′	3°3·4′W	T	192,193
Whitford Br	Norf	TG0612	52°40·2′	1°3·2′E	X	133
Whitford Bridge	Worcs	SO9667	52°18·3′	2°3·1′W	X	150
Whitford (Chwitffordd)	Flint	SJ1478	53°17·8′	3°17·0′W	T	116
Whitfurrows Fm	Worcs	SP0741	52°4·3′	1°53·5′W	FM	150
Whitgift	E Yorks	SE8122	53°41·5′	0°46·0′W	T	106,112
Whitgift Ness	E Yorks	SE8023	53°42·1′	0°46·9′W	X	106,112
Whitgreave	Staffs	SJ8928	52°51·2′	2°9·4′W	T	127
Whitgreave Manor	Staffs	SJ9027	52°50·7′	2°8·5′W	X	127
Whithaugh	Scot Bord	NY4988	55°11·3′	2°47·6′W	T	79
Whithcote Hall	Leic	SK7905	52°38·5′	0°49·5′W	X	141
Whithebeir	Orkney	HY5634	59°11·7′	2°45·7′W	T	5,6
Whithill	N Yks	SE0661	54°2·9′	1°54·1′W	X	99
Whithope	Scot Bord	NT4413	55°24·7′	2°52·6′W	X	79
Whithope Burn	Scot Bord	NT2417	55°26·7′	3°11·7′W	W	79
Whithorn	D & G	NX4440	54°44·1′	4°25·0′W	T	83
Whithorn Moss	D & G	NX4042	54°45·1′	4°28·7′W	X	83
Whithurst	N Ayr	NS2844	55°39·8′	4°43·6′W	X	63,70
Whiting Bay	N Ayr	NS0425	55°29·2′	5°5·7′W	T	69
Whiting Bay	N Ayr	NS0526	55°29·6′	5°4·8′W	W	69
Whiting Fms	Worcs	SO7834	52°0·5′	2°18·8′W	FM	150
Whiting Hole	Devon	SS4241	51°9·0′	4°15·2′W	X	180
Whiting Ness	Angus	NO6641	56°33·8′	2°32·7′W	X	54
Whiting Point	Orkney	ND3396	58°51·0′	3°9·2′W	X	6,7
Whitings	Essex	TL8227	51°54·9′	0°39·2′E	X	168
Whitings Fm	Dorset	ST8420	50°59·0′	2°13·3′W	FM	183
Whiting Shoal	Norf	TF5232	52°52·1′	0°15·9′E	X	131
Whitington	Norf	TL7199	52°33·9′	0°31·8′E	T	143
Whitkirk	Leeds	SE3633	53°47·8′	1°26·8′W	T	104
Whitlam	Aberd	NJ8821	57°17·0′	2°11·5′W	X	38
Whitland	Carm	SN2016	51°49·1′	4°36·3′W	T	158
Whitland Abbey	Carm	SN2018	51°50·1′	4°36·4′W	X	158
Whitlands	Devon	SY3091	50°43·1′	2°59·1′W	X	193
Whitlaw	Scot Bord	NT4947	55°43·1′	2°48·3′W	T	73
Whitlawside	D & G	NY4480	55°6·9′	2°52·2′W	X	79
Whitlawside Burn	D & G	NY4380	55°6·9′	2°53·2′W	W	79
Whitle	Derby	SJ9986	53°22·5′	2°0·5′W	X	109
Whitleather Lodge	Cambs	TL1472	52°20·3′	0°19·2′W	X	153
Whitlee Burn	Shetld	HU2582	60°31·5′	1°32·2′W	W	3
Whitlees	N Ayr	NS2443	55°39·2′	4°47·4′W	X	63,70
Whitlees	Northum	NY9692	55°13·6′	2°3·3′W	X	81
Whitleigh	C of Plym	SX4760	50°25·4′	4°8·9′W	T	201
Whitlenge Ho	Worcs	SO8571	52°20·4′	2°12·8′W	X	139
Whitlera	Carm	SN5524	51°54·0′	4°6·1′W	X	159
Whitler Hill	Shetld	HU3190	60°35·8′	1°25·5′W	X	1
Whitletts	S Ayr	NS3523	55°28·6′	4°36·2′W	T	70
Whitley	Corn	SX0768	50°29·0′	4°42·9′W	X	200
Whitley	Cov	SP3577	52°23·6′	1°28·7′W	T	140
Whitley	Devon	SX6944	50°17·1′	3°50·0′W	X	202
Whitley	Hants	SU5209	50°52·9′	1°15·3′W	X	196
Whitley	N Yks	SE5621	53°41·2′	1°8·7′W	T	105
Whitley	Read	SU7170	51°25·7′	0°58·3′W	T	175
Whitley	Sheff	SK3494	53°26·7′	1°28·9′W	T	110,111
Whitley	Shrops	SO2496	52°33·6′	3°6·9′W	X	137
Whitley	Wigan	SD5807	53°33·7′	2°37·6′W	T	108
Whitley	Wilts	ST8866	51°23·8′	2°10·0′W	T	173
Whitley Batts	Bath & NE Somer	ST6262	51°21·6′	2°32·4′W	X	172
Whitley Bay	N Tyne	NZ3572	55°2·7′	1°26·7′W	T	88
Whitley Bridge	N Yks	SE5522	53°41·7′	1°9·6′W	T	105
Whitley Brook	Ches	SJ6178	53°18·1′	2°34·7′W	W	118
Whitley Brook Fm	Ches	SJ6981	53°19·7′	2°27·5′W	FM	109
Whitley Castle	Northum	NY6948	54°49·8′	2°28·5′W	X	86,87
Whitley Castle (Roman Fort)	Northum	NY6948	54°49·8′	2°28·5′W	R	86,87
Whitley Chapel	Northum	NY9257	54°54·7′	2°7·1′W	T	87
Whitley Common	Barns	SE1905	53°32·7′	1°42·4′W	X	110
Whitley Common	Northum	NY6747	54°49·3′	2°30·4′W	X	86,87
Whitley Court	Glos	SO8714	51°49·7′	2°10·9′W	X	162
Whitleyeaves	Staffs	SJ8126	52°50·1′	2°16·5′W	X	127
Whitley Fm	Devon	SY1797	50°46·2′	3°10·2′W	FM	192,193
Whitley Fm	Pemb	SN1215	51°48·4′	4°43·2′W	FM	158
Whitley Fm	Somer	ST4536	51°7·5′	2°46·8′W	FM	182
Whitley Fm	Wilts	ST9973	51°27·6′	2°0·5′W	FM	173
Whitleyford Br	Wrekin	SJ7423	52°48·5′	2°22·7′W	X	127
Whitley Forest	Kent	TQ5053	51°15·6′	0°9·4′E	F	188
Whitley Grange	N Yks	SE3787	54°16·9′	1°25·5′W	X	99
Whitley Grange	Shrops	SJ4059	52°40·8′	2°48·4′W	X	126
Whitley Hall	Ches	SJ6178	53°18·1′	2°34·7′W	X	118
Whitley Head	Brad	SE0343	53°53·2′	1°56·8′W	T	104
Whitley Heath	Staffs	SJ8126	52°50·1′	2°16·5′W	T	127
Whitley House Fm	Ches	SJ6278	53°18·1′	2°33·8′W	FM	118
Whitley Lower	Kirk	SE2217	53°39·2′	1°39·6′W	T	110
Whitley Manor Fm	Wrekin	SJ7423	52°48·5′	2°22·7′W	FM	127
Whitley Mill	Northum	NY9258	54°55·2′	2°7·1′W	X	87
Whitley Park	Kirk	SE2116	53°38·6′	1°40·5′W	X	110
Whitley Pike	Northum	NY8291	55°13·0′	2°16·5′W	H	80
Whitley Reed	Ches	SJ6481	53°19·7′	2°32·0′W	T	109
Whitley Ridge Hotel	Hants	SU3102	50°49·2′	1°33·2′W	X	196
Whitley Row	Kent	TQ4952	51°15·1′	0°8·5′E	T	188
Whitleys	Essex	TL6836	52°0·0′	0°27·2′E	X	154
Whitleys	Essex	TL7241	52°2·7′	0°30·9′E	X	154
Whitley Sands	N Tyne	NZ3573	55°3·3′	1°26·7′W	T	88
Whitley Thorpe	N Yks	SE5520	53°40·7′	1°9·6′W	T	105
Whitley Wood	Hants	SU2905	50°50·9′	1°34·9′W	F	196
Whitley Wood	Read	SU7269	51°25·2′	0°57·5′W	T	175
Whitlingham Marsh	Norf	TG2807	52°37·0′	1°22·5′E	W	134
Whitlock's End	Sol	SP1076	52°23·2′	1°50·8′W	T	139
Whitlock's End Fm	Sol	SP1177	52°23·7′	1°49·9′W	FM	139
Whitlocksworthy	Devon	SX6842	50°16·0′	3°50·8′W	X	202
Whitlow	Northum	NY6948	54°49·8′	2°28·5′W	X	86,87
Whitlow	Pemb	SN0311	51°46·0′	4°50·9′W	X	157,158
Whitman's Hill Coppice	Heref	SO7448	52°8·0′	2°22·4′W	F	150
Whitminster	Glos	SO7708	51°46·4′	2°19·6′W	T	162
Whitminster Ho	Glos	SO7609	51°47·0′	2°20·5′W	X	162
Whitmoor	Devon	ST0710	50°53·2′	3°18·9′W	T	192
Whitmoor	Devon	SY1893	50°44·1′	3°9·3′W	X	192,193
Whit Moor	Lancs	SD5864	54°4·5′	2°38·1′W	X	97
Whit Moor	N Yks	SE1358	54°1·3′	1°47·7′W	X	104
Whitmoor	Somer	ST1427	51°2·4′	3°13·2′W	X	181,193
Whit Moor	Somer	ST4424	51°1·0′	2°47·5′W	X	193
Whitmoor Bog	Brackn	SU8968	51°24·5′	0°42·8′W	X	175
Whitmoor Common	Surrey	SU9853	51°16·3′	0°35·3′W	X	186
Whitmoor Fm	Devon	SS8424	51°0·5′	3°38·8′W	FM	181
Whitmoor Fm	N Yks	SE1458	54°1·3′	1°46·8′W	FM	104
Whitmoor Fm	Somer	ST1132	51°5·1′	3°15·9′W	FM	181
Whitmoor Ho	Surrey	TQ0054	51°16·8′	0°33·6′W	X	186
Whitmoor Vale	Hants	SU8536	51°7·2′	0°46·7′W	X	186
Whitmore	Devon	SS6520	50°58·1′	3°55·0′W	X	180
Whitmore	Dorset	SU0509	50°53·1′	1°55·7′W	T	195
Whitmore	Lancs	SD6348	53°55·9′	2°33·4′W	X	102,103
Whitmore	Staffs	SJ8140	52°57·7′	2°16·6′W	T	118
Whitmore Bay	V of Glam	ST1166	51°23·4′	3°16·4′W	W	171
Whitmore Bottom	Dorset	SY9194	50°45·0′	2°7·3′W	X	195
Whitmore Coppice	Dorset	ST7710	50°53·6′	2°19·2′W	F	194
Whitmore Hall	Staffs	SJ8141	52°58·2′	2°16·6′W	A	118
Whitmore Park	Cov	SP3382	52°26·3′	1°30·5′W	T	140
Whitmore Wood	Staffs	SJ7941	52°58·2′	2°18·4′W	F	118
Whitmuir	Scot Bord	NT1951	55°45·0′	3°17·0′W	X	65,66,72
Whitmuir	Scot Bord	NT4926	55°31·8′	2°48·0′W	X	73
Whitmuir Hall	Scot Bord	NT5027	55°32·3′	2°47·1′W	X	73
Whitmuirhaugh	Scot Bord	NT7535	55°36·7′	2°23·4′W	X	74
Whitnage	Devon	ST0215	50°55·8′	3°23·3′W	T	181
Whitnal	Hants	SU4851	51°15·6′	1°18·3′W	X	185
Whitnash	Warw	SP3263	52°16·1′	1°31·5′W	T	151
Whitnell	Somer	ST2139	51°8·9′	3°7·4′W	T	182
Whitnell Corner	Somer	ST5948	51°14·0′	2°34·8′W	X	182,183
Whitnell Fm	Somer	ST6049	51°14·6′	2°34·0′W	FM	183
Whitnell Ho	Somer	ST6048	51°14·0′	2°34·0′W	X	183
Whitners Fm	Shrops	SJ3333	52°53·7′	2°59·4′W	FM	126
Whitney Bottom	Somer	ST3213	50°55·0′	2°57·7′W	T	193
Whitney Court	Heref	SO2647	52°7·2′	3°4·5′W	X	148
Whitney Fm	Brig	SS8778	51°29·6′	3°37·3′W	FM	170
Whitney-on-Wye	Heref	SO2647	52°7·2′	3°4·5′W	T	148
Whitney's Fm, The	Shrops	SJ5438	52°56·5′	2°40·7′W	FM	126
Whitray	Lancs	SD6662	54°3·4′	2°30·7′W	X	98
Whitray Beck	Lancs	SD6761	54°2·9′	2°29·8′W	W	98
Whitray Fell	Lancs	SD6761	54°2·9′	2°29·8′W	X	98
Whitridge	Northum	NZ0688	55°11·4′	1°53·9′W	X	81
Whitridge Well	Northum	NY9984	55°9·3′	2°0·5′W	X	81
Whitrig	Scot Bord	NT7841	55°40·0′	2°20·5′W	X	74
Whitrigg	Cumbr	NY2038	54°44·1′	3°14·1′W	T	89,90
Whitrigg	Cumbr	NY2257	54°54·3′	3°12·6′W	T	85
Whitrigg	Cumbr	NY4735	54°42·7′	2°48·9′W	X	90
Whitrigg	Cumbr	NY8012	54°30·4′	2°18·1′W	X	91,92
Whitrigg Ho	Cumbr	NY2358	54°54·9′	3°11·6′W	X	85
Whitrigg Ho	Cumbr	NY4461	54°56·7′	2°52·0′W	X	85
Whitrigglees	Cumbr	NY2457	54°54·4′	3°10·7′W	X	85
Whitrigglees Moss	Cumbr	NY2458	54°54·9′	3°10·7′W	X	85
Whitriggmoor Ho	Cumbr	NY2359	54°55·4′	3°11·7′W	X	85
Whitriggs	Cumbr	NY0400	54°23·4′	3°28·6′W	X	89
Whitriggs	Scot Bord	NT5615	55°25·9′	2°41·3′W	T	80
Whitriggs Scar	Cumbr	NY0300	54°23·4′	3°29·2′W	X	89
Whitrighill	Scot Bord	NT6234	55°36·1′	2°35·8′W	X	74
Whitrope Burn	Scot Bord	NY5198	55°16·7′	2°45·9′W	W	79
Whitrope Cottages	Scot Bord	NT5200	55°17·8′	2°44·9′W	X	79
Whitrope Edge	Scot Bord	NY5199	55°17·2′	2°45·9′W	X	79
Whitropefoot	Scot Bord	NY5198	55°16·7′	2°45·9′W	X	79
Whitrow Beck	Cumbr	SD1393	54°19·8′	3°19·9′W	W	96
Whitsam	Devon	SX4366	50°28·6′	4°12·4′W	X	201
Whitsand Bay	Corn	SX3951	50°20·5′	4°15·4′W	W	201
Whitsburn Hill	Shrops	SJ3202	52°36·9′	2°59·9′W	X	126
Whitsburn Hill (Earthwork)	Shrops	SJ3202	52°36·9′	2°59·9′W	A	126
Whitsbury	Hants	SU1219	50°58·4′	1°49·4′W	T	184
Whitsbury Common	Hants	SU1318	50°57·9′	1°48·5′W	X	184
Whitsbury Down	Hants	SU1121	50°59·5′	1°50·2′W	X	184
Whitsford	Devon	SS6533	51°5·1′	3°55·3′W	X	180
Whitshaw Wood	Suff	TL8361	52°13·2′	0°41·1′E	F	155
Whitshields	Northum	NY7965	54°59·0′	2°19·3′W	X	86,87
Whitshiels Bog	D & G	NY3786	55°10·1′	2°58·9′W	X	79
Whitshiels Knowe	D & G	NY3785	55°9·6′	2°58·9′W	H	79
Whitslade	Scot Bord	NT1135	55°36·3′	3°24·3′W	X	72
Whitslade	Scot Bord	NT4218	55°27·4′	2°54·6′W	X	79
Whitslade Hill	Scot Bord	NT1034	55°35·7′	3°25·3′W	H	72
Whitslaid	Scot Bord	NT5644	55°41·5′	2°41·6′W	T	73
Whitslaid Faulds	Scot Bord	NT4217	55°26·9′	2°54·6′W	X	79
Whitslaid Hill	Scot Bord	NT4218	55°27·4′	2°54·6′W	X	79
Whitsley Barton	Devon	SS5517	50°56·3′	4°3·4′W	X	180
Whitsome	Scot Bord	NT8650	55°44·8′	2°12·9′W	T	67,74
Whitsomehill	Scot Bord	NT8649	55°44·3′	2°12·9′W	T	74
Whitsome Laws	Scot Bord	NT8350	55°44·8′	2°15·8′W	X	67,74
Whitson	Newp	ST3783	51°32·8′	2°54·1′W	T	171
Whitson Court	Newp	ST3784	51°33·3′	2°54·1′W	X	171
Whitstable	Kent	TR1166	51°21·5′	1°2·2′E	T	179
Whitstable Bay	Kent	TR0766	51°21·5′	0°58·8′E	W	179
Whitstable Street	Kent	TR1167	51°22·0′	1°2·3′E	X	179
Whitstone	Corn	SX2698	50°45·6′	4°27·6′W	T	190
Whitstone	Devon	SS6526	51°1·3′	3°55·1′W	X	180
Whitstone	Devon	SX8179	50°36·2′	3°40·5′W	X	191
Whitstone Fm	Devon	SX4681	50°36·7′	4°10·2′W	FM	201
Whitstone Head	Corn	SX2598	50°45·6′	4°28·5′W	X	190
Whitstonehill	D & G	NY2182	55°7·8′	3°13·9′W	X	79
Whitstone Hill Fm	Somer	ST6341	51°10·3′	2°31·4′W	FM	183
Whit Stones	Somer	SS8546	51°12·3′	3°38·4′W	X	181
Whitsun Dale	N Yks	NY8404	54°26·1′	2°14·4′W	X	91,92
Whitsundale Beck	N Yks	NY8404	54°26·1′	2°14·4′W	W	91,92
Whitsunden	Kent	TQ8039	51°7·5′	0°34·7′E	X	188
Whitsundoles Fm	Beds	SP9240	52°3·3′	0°39·1′W	FM	152
Whitsunn Brook	Worcs	SO9951	52°9·7′	2°0·5′W	W	150
Whits Wood	Somer	SS9742	51°10·3′	3°28·0′W	F	181
Whittaborough Fm	Devon	SX5361	50°26·1′	4°3·8′W	FM	201
Whittaker	Roch	SD9415	53°38·1′	2°5·0′W	X	109
Whittakers	Lancs	SD7445	53°54·3′	2°23·3′W	X	103
Whittaker's Green	Ches	SJ6945	53°0·3′	2°27·3′W	X	118
Whittam Ho	Lancs	SD4262	54°3·3′	2°52·7′W	X	96,97
Whittamoors, The	Staffs	SJ9116	52°44·7′	2°7·6′W	X	127
Whittas Park	Cumbr	NY2136	54°43·0′	3°13·2′W	X	89,90
Whitten Bottom	Hants	SU2000	50°48·2′	1°42·6′W	X	195
Whittenhays	Devon	SS9821	50°59·0′	3°26·8′W	X	181
Whitterleys, The	Powys	SO2773	52°21·3′	3°3·9′W	X	137,148
Whitterns Hill Fm	Wilts	SU2320	50°59·0′	1°40·0′W	FM	184
Whittern, The	Heref	SO3357	52°12·7′	2°58·4′W	X	148,149
Whitters Hill	Lancs	SD4647	53°55·2′	2°48·9′W	X	102
Whittimere	Staffs	SO8292	52°31·8′	2°15·5′W	X	138
Whittingehame Ho	E Loth	NT6073	55°57·2′	2°38·0′W	X	67
Whittingehame Mains	E Loth	NT5973	55°57·2′	2°39·0′W	X	67
Whittingehame Water	E Loth	NT6173	55°57·2′	2°37·0′W	W	67
Whittingham	Northum	NU0611	55°23·8′	1°53·9′W	T	81
Whittingham Carr	Northum	NU2426	55°31·9′	1°36·8′W	X	75
Whittingham Hall	Suff	TM2778	52°21·4′	1°20·4′E	X	156
Whittingham Ho	Lancs	SD5436	53°49·3′	2°41·5′W	X	102
Whittingham Lane	Northum	NU0711	55°23·8′	1°52·9′W	X	81
Whittingham Wood	Northum	NU0511	55°23·8′	1°54·8′W	F	81
Whittingslow	Shrops	SO4388	52°29·5′	2°50·0′W	T	137
Whittington	Glos	SP0121	51°53·5′	1°58·7′W	T	163
Whittington	Lancs	SD6076	54°10·9′	2°36·4′W	T	97
Whittington	Shrops	SJ3231	52°52·6′	3°0·2′W	T	126
Whittington	Staffs	SJ7933	52°53·9′	2°18·3′W	T	127
Whittington	Staffs	SK1608	52°40·4′	1°45·4′W	T	128
Whittington	Staffs	SO8582	52°26·4′	2°12·8′W	T	139
Whittington	Warw	SP2999	52°35·5′	1°33·9′W	T	140
Whittington	Worcs	SO8752	52°10·2′	2°11·0′W	T	150
Whittington Common	Staffs	SO8682	52°26·4′	2°12·0′W	X	139
Whittington Court	Glos	SP0120	51°52·9′	1°58·7′W	A	163
Whittington Fell	Northum	NY9769	55°1·2′	2°2·4′W	X	87
Whittington Grange	Leic	SK4808	52°40·3′	1°17·0′W	X	140
Whittington Heath	Staffs	SK1407	52°39·9′	1°47·2′W	X	139
Whittington Hurst Fm	Staffs	SK1610	52°41·5′	1°45·4′W	FM	128
Whittington Moor	Derby	SK3873	53°15·4′	1°25·4′W	T	119
Whittington White Ho	Northum	NZ0172	55°2·8′	1°58·6′W	X	87
Whittle	Northum	NZ0204	55°20·1′	1°57·7′W	X	81
Whittle Brook	Bury	SD8307	53°33·8′	2°15·0′W	W	109
Whittle Brook	Warr	SJ5689	53°24·0′	2°39·3′W	W	108
Whittle Burn	Northum	NZ0765	54°59·0′	1°53·0′W	W	88
Whittlebury	Northnts	SP6943	52°5·1′	0°59·2′W	T	152
Whittle Car	Leeds	SE4040	53°51·5′	1°23·1′W	F	105
Whittle Colliery	Northum	NU1706	55°21·1′	1°43·5′W	X	81
Whittle Fm	Northum	NZ0765	54°59·0′	1°53·0′W	FM	88
Whittle Hall	Lancs	SD7133	53°47·8′	2°26·0′W	X	103
Whittle Hall	Warr	SJ5689	53°24·0′	2°39·3′W	A	108
Whittle Hill	Lancs	SD8218	53°39·7′	2°15·9′W	H	109
Whittle Hill	Leic	SK4916	52°44·6′	1°16·0′W	X	129
Whittle Hill	Roch	SD8307	53°33·8′	2°15·0′W	H	109
Whittle Hill Fm	Bolton	SD7115	53°38·1′	2°25·9′W	FM	109
Whittle Hole	Cumbr	SD6579	54°12·6′	2°31·8′W	X	97
Whittle-le-Woods	Lancs	SD5821	53°41·3′	2°37·7′W	T	102
Whittlesey	Cambs	TL2797	52°33·6′	0°7·2′W	T	142
Whittlesey Dike	Cambs	TL3195	52°32·5′	0°3·7′W	W	142
Whittlesey Mere	Cambs	TL2290	52°29·9′	0°11·8′W	X	142
Whittles Fm	Oxon	SU6778	51°30·0′	1°1·7′W	FM	175
Whittle's Fm	Somer	ST3219	50°58·2′	2°57·7′W	FM	193
Whittlesford	Cambs	TL4748	52°6·9′	0°9·2′E	T	154
Whittlesford Sta	Cambs	TL4847	52°6·3′	0°10·1′E	X	154
Whittlestone Head	Black w Dar	SD7219	53°40·2′	2°25·0′W	T	109
Whittlewood Forest	Northnts	SP7242	52°4·5′	0°56·6′W	F	152
Whittlieburn	N Ayr	NS2163	55°49·9′	4°51·0′W	X	63
Whittliemuir Midton Loch	Renf	NS4158	55°47·6′	4°31·7′W	W	64
Whittocks End	Heref	SO6629	51°57·7′	2°29·3′W	X	149
Whitton	Heref	SO4174	52°21·9′	2°51·6′W	T	137,148
Whitton	N Lincs	SE9024	53°42·5′	0°37·8′W	T	106,112
Whitton	Northum	NU0501	55°18·4′	1°54·8′W	T	81
Whitton	Powys	SO2767	52°18·0′	3°3·8′W	T	137,148
Whitton	Rich	TQ1473	51°26·9′	0°21·2′W	T	176
Whitton	Scot Bord	NT7622	55°29·7′	2°22·4′W	T	74
Whitton	Shrops	SO5772	52°20·9′	2°37·5′W	T	137,138
Whitton	Stock on T	NZ3822	54°35·7′	1°24·3′W	T	93
Whitton	Suff	TM1447	52°5·0′	1°7·8′E	T	169
Whitton Beck	Stock on T	NZ3822	54°35·7′	1°24·3′W	W	93
Whitton Bush	V of Glam	ST0771	51°26·1′	3°19·9′W	X	170
Whitton Channel	N Lincs	SE8924	53°42·5′	0°38·7′W	W	106,112
Whitton Chase	Shrops	SO5771	52°20·4′	2°37·5′W	X	137,138
Whitton Court	Shrops	SO5773	52°21·4′	2°37·5′W	A	137,138
Whittondean	Northum	NU0500	55°17·9′	1°54·8′W	X	81
Whittonditch	Wilts	SU2872	51°27·0′	1°35·4′W	T	174
Whitton Edge	Scot Bord	NT7418	55°27·6′	2°24·2′W	X	80
Whitton Fm	Shrops	SJ3409	52°40·7′	2°58·2′W	FM	126
Whitton Glebe Fm	Northum	NU0500	55°17·9′	1°54·8′W	FM	81

Whitton Grange	Shrops	SJ3308	52°40·2′	2°59·0′W	X	126
Whitton Hall	Shrops	SJ3409	52°40·7′	2°58·2′W	A	126
Whitton Hill	Northum	NT9234	55°36·2′	2°7·2′W	X	74,75
Whitton Hillhead	Northum	NZ0499	55°17·4′	1°55·8′W	X	81
Whitton Ho	Shrops	SO5673	52°21·4′	2°38·4′W	X	137,138
Whitton Loch	Scot Bord	NT7419	55°28·1′	2°24·2′W	W	80
Whitton Mawr	V of Glam	ST0871	51°26·1′	3°19·0′W	X	170
Whitton Ness	N Lincs	SE9125	53°43·0′	0°36·8′W	X	106
Whitton Rosser Fm	V of Glam	ST0772	51°26·6′	3°19·9′W	FM	170
Whitton Sand	E Yorks	SE8825	53°43·1′	0°39·6′W	X	106
Whittonstall	Northum	NZ0757	54°54·7′	1°53·0′W	T	88
Whittonstall Hall Fm	Northum	NZ0756	54°54·2′	1°53·0′W	FM	88
Whittonstall Sproats	Northum	NZ0656	54°54·2′	1°54·0′W	X	87
Whitton Three Gates	Stock on T	NZ3724	54°36·8′	1°25·2′W	X	93
Whitty	Somer	ST2718	50°57·6′	3°2·0′W	X	193
Whitty Hill	Devon	SY3295	50°45·3′	2°57·5′W	X	193
Whittytree	Shrops	SO4478	52°24·1′	2°49·0′W	T	137,148
Whitway	Hants	SU4559	51°19·9′	1°20·9′W	T	174
Whitwell	Derby	SK5276	53°16·9′	1°12·8′W	T	120
Whitwell	Herts	TL1821	51°52·7′	0°16·7′W	T	166
Whitwell	I of W	SZ5277	50°35·7′	1°15·5′W	T	196
Whitwell	N Yks	SE2481	54°13·7′	1°37·5′W	X	99
Whitwell	N Yks	SE2899	54°23·4′	1°33·7′W	T	99
Whitwell	Rut	SK9208	52°39·9′	0°38·0′W	T	141
Whitwell Common	Derby	SK5177	53°17·5′	1°13·7′W	X	120
Whitwell Common	Norf	TG0820	52°44·5′	1°5·3′E	X	133
Whitwell Coppice	Shrops	SJ6102	52°37·1′	2°34·2′W	F	127
Whitwell East House Fm	Durham	NZ3140	54°45·5′	1°30·7′W	FM	88
Whitwell Fm	Cambs	TL4058	52°12·4′	0°3·3′E	FM	154
Whitwell Fm	Devon	SY2392	50°43·6′	3°5·1′W	FM	192,193
Whitwell Fm	Herts	SP8817	51°50·9′	0°43·0′W	FM	165
Whitwell Grange	Durham	NZ3041	54°46·0′	1°31·6′W	X	88
Whitwell Grange	N Yks	SE2799	54°23·4′	1°34·6′W	X	99
Whitwell Grange	N Yks	SE7166	54°5·3′	0°54·5′W	X	100
Whitwell Hall	Norf	TG0821	52°45·0′	1°5·3′E	X	133
Whitwell Hall Fm	Norf	TG2425	52°46·8′	1°19·7′E	FM	133,134
Whitwell Ho	Durham	NZ3040	54°45·5′	1°31·6′W	X	88
Whitwell House Fm	Leeds	SE3746	53°54·8′	1°25·8′W	FM	104
Whitwell Moor	Sheff	SK2597	53°28·4′	1°37·0′W	X	110
Whitwell-on-the-Hill	N Yks	SE7265	54°4·8′	0°53·6′W	T	100
Whitwell South Fm	Durham	NZ3038	54°44·4′	1°31·6′W	FM	93
Whitwell Street	Norf	TG1022	52°45·5′	1°7·1′E	T	133
Whitwell Wood	Derby	SK5278	53°18·0′	1°12·8′W	F	120
Whitwham	Northum	NY6756	54°54·1′	2°30·5′W	X	86,87
Whitwick	Leic	SK4316	52°44·6′	1°21·4′W	T	129
Whitwick Manor	Heref	SO6145	52°6·4′	2°33·8′W	X	149
Whitwood	Wakf	SE4024	53°42·9′	1°23·2′W	T	105
Whitworth	Durham	NZ2622	54°35·8′	1°35·4′W	X	93
Whitworth	Lancs	SD8818	53°39·7′	2°10·5′W	T	109
Whitworth Hall	Durham	NZ2334	54°42·3′	1°38·2′W	X	93
Whity Cross	Corn	SX3959	50°24·8′	4°15·6′W	X	201
Whity Gill	N Yks	SD9194	54°20·7′	2°7·9′W	X	98
Whity Knots	Cumbr	NY6045	54°48·1′	2°36·9′W	X	86
Whixall	Shrops	SJ5134	52°54·3′	2°43·3′W	T	126
Whixall Moss	Shrops	SJ4835	52°54·8′	2°46·0′W	X	126
Whixley	N Yks	SE4458	54°1·2′	1°19·3′W	T	105
Whixley Cut	N Yks	SE4558	54°1·2′	1°18·4′W	W	105
Whixley Field Ho	N Yks	SE4557	54°0·7′	1°18·4′W	X	105
Whixley Grange Fm	N Yks	SE4459	54°1·7′	1°19·3′W	FM	105
Whixley Lodge	N Yks	SE4356	54°0·1′	1°20·2′W	X	105
Whoals Dale	Shetld	HU5188	60°34·6′	1°3·7′W	X	1,2
Whoap	Cumbr	NY0913	54°30·5′	3°23·9′W	X	89
Whoberley	Cov	SP3078	52°24·2′	1°33·1′W	T	140
Wholeflats	Falk	NS9380	56°0·3′	3°42·5′W	T	65
Whole Ho	Powys	SO1530	51°58·0′	3°13·8′W	X	161
Wholehope	Northum	NT9009	55°22·7′	2°9·0′W	X	80
Wholehope Burn	Northum	NT8909	55°22·7′	2°10·0′W	W	80
Wholehope Knowe	Northum	NT8909	55°22·7′	2°10·0′W	H	80
Wholestone Moor	Kirk	SE0716	53°38·7′	1°53·2′W	H	110
Wholhope Burn	Northum	NT9311	55°23·8′	2°6·2′W	W	80
Wholhope Hill	Northum	NT9311	55°23·8′	2°6·2′W	X	80
W Holling Carr	Durham	NZ3933	54°41·7′	1°23·3′W	X	93
Wholsea Fm	E Yorks	SE8433	53°47·4′	0°43·1′W	FM	106
Wholsea Grange	E Yorks	SE8434	53°48·0′	0°43·1′W	X	106
Whome	Orkney	ND3693	58°49·5′	3°6·0′W	X	7
Whoofer Fm	Lincs	SK8196	53°27·5′	0°46·4′W	FM	112
Whooff Ho	Cumbr	NY4456	54°54·0′	2°52·0′W	X	85
Whooping Rock	Devon	SX7282	50°37·7′	3°48·2′W	X	191
Whorlands	Durham	NY9912	54°30·4′	2°0·5′W	X	92
Whorl Hill	N Yks	NZ4902	54°24·9′	1°14·3′W	H	93
Whorls Fm	Brad	SE0241	53°52·2′	1°57·8′W	FM	104
Whorlton	Durham	NZ1014	54°31·5′	1°50·3′W	T	92
Whorlton	N Yks	NZ4802	54°24·9′	1°15·2′W	T	93
Whorlton Beck	Durham	NZ1015	54°32·1′	1°50·3′W	W	92
Whorlton Grange	Durham	NZ1015	54°32·1′	1°50·3′W	X	92
Whorlton Grange	N upon Ty	NZ1967	55°0·1′	1°41·8′W	X	88
Whorlton Hall	N upon Ty	NZ1868	55°0·6′	1°42·7′W	X	88
Whorlton High Grange	Durham	NZ1016	54°32·6′	1°50·3′W	X	92
Whorlton Ho	N Yks	NZ4801	54°24·4′	1°15·2′W	X	93
Whorlton Lido	Durham	NZ1014	54°31·5′	1°50·3′W	X	92
Whorlton Moor	N Yks	SE5098	54°22·7′	1°13·4′W	X	100
Whorney Side	Cumbr	NY2505	54°26·3′	3°9·0′W	X	89,90
Whorridge Fm	Devon	ST0105	50°50·4′	3°24·0′W	FM	192
Whyburn House Fm	Notts	SK5150	53°2·9′	1°13·9′W	FM	120
Whydown	E Susx	TQ7009	50°51·6′	0°25·3′E	T	199
Whyers Hall Fm	Essex	TM1214	51°47·3′	1°4·8′E	FM	168,169
Whygate	Northum	NY7776	55°4·9′	2°21·2′W	T	86,87
Whygill	Cumbr	NY6913	54°30·9′	2°28·3′W	X	91
Whygill Head	Cumbr	NY7010	54°29·3′	2°27·4′W	X	91
Whyke	W Susx	SU8604	50°50·0′	0°46·3′W	T	197
Whyle	Heref	SO5560	52°14·4′	2°39·1′W	T	137,138,149
Whympston	Devon	SX6650	50°20·3′	3°52·6′W	X	202
Whynietown	Aberd	NJ8944	57°29·4′	2°10·6′W	X	30
Whyntie Head	Aberd	NJ6265	57°40·7′	2°37·8′W	X	29
Whyntie Wood	Aberd	NJ6263	57°39·6′	2°37·7′W	F	29
Whyr Fm	Wilts	SU0874	51°28·1′	1°52·7′W	FM	173
Whytbank	Scot Bord	NT4436	55°37·1′	2°52·9′W	X	73
Whytbank Tower	Scot Bord	NT4437	55°37·7′	2°52·9′W	A	73
Whyte Acre	Lincs	TF3356	53°5·3′	0°0·4′W	X	122
Whyteleafe	Surrey	TQ3358	51°18·6′	0°5·1′W	T	187
Whyteleafe South Sta	Surrey	TQ3457	51°18·0′	0°4·3′W	X	187
Whytha	Lancs	SD8244	53°53·8′	2°16·0′W	X	103
Whytings Fm	W Susx	TQ1928	51°2·6′	0°17·8′W	FM	187,198
Wiay	Highld	NG2936	57°20·3′	6°29·8′W	X	23
Wibben Hill	Derby	SK1852	53°4·1′	1°43·5′W	H	119
Wibbertons Fields	N Yks	SD9573	54°9·4′	2°4·2′W	X	98
Wibble Fm	Somer	ST1041	51°9·9′	3°16·8′W	FM	181
Wibdon	Glos	ST5697	51°40·4′	2°37·8′W	T	162
Wiblings Fm	W Susx	SU9218	50°57·5′	0°41·0′W	FM	197
Wibsey	Brad	SE1430	53°46·2′	1°46·8′W	T	104
Wibtoft	Warw	SP4787	52°29·0′	1°18·1′W	T	140
Wicca	Corn	SW4739	50°12·1′	5°32·4′W	X	203
Wicca Pool	Corn	SW4640	50°12·6′	5°33·2′W	W	203
Wichcot Dingle	Shrops	SO5381	52°25·7′	2°41·1′W	X	137,138
Wichenford	Worcs	SO7860	52°14·5′	2°18·9′W	T	138,150
Wichenford Court	Worcs	SO7859	52°14·0′	2°18·9′W	A	150
Wichling	Kent	TQ9256	51°16·5′	0°45·6′E	T	178
Wichling Wood	Kent	TQ9155	51°15·9′	0°44·7′E	F	178
Wick	Bourne	SZ1591	50°43·3′	1°46·9′W	T	195
Wick	Devon	ST1703	50°49·5′	3°10·3′W	T	192,193
Wick	Essex	TM0217	51°49·1′	0°56·3′E	X	168
Wick	Highld	ND3650	58°26·3′	3°5·3′W	T	12
Wick	S Glos	ST7073	51°27·5′	2°25·5′W	T	172
Wick	Shetld	HP5603	60°42·6′	0°57·9′W	X	1
Wick	Shetld	HU4439	60°8·3′	1°12·0′W	X	4
Wick	Somer	ST2144	51°11·6′	3°7·4′W	T	182
Wick	Somer	ST3253	51°16·6′	2°58·1′W	T	182
Wick	Somer	ST4026	51°2·0′	2°51·0′W	T	193
Wick	Somer	ST5239	51°9·1′	2°40·8′W	X	182,183
Wick	V of Glam	SS9272	51°26·4′	3°32·8′W	T	170
Wick	Wilts	SU1621	50°59·5′	1°45·9′W	T	184
Wick	Worcs	SO9645	52°6·4′	2°3·1′W	T	150
Wick	W Susx	TQ0203	50°49·3′	0°32·7′W	T	197
Wick Airport	Highld	ND3652	58°27·4′	3°5·3′W	X	12
Wick Ball Camp	Wilts	ST9931	51°4·9′	2°0·5′W	A	184
Wick Bay	Highld	ND3750	58°26·3′	3°4·3′W	W	12
Wick Bottom	Bri & Hov	TQ3504	50°49·4′	0°4·6′W	X	198
Wick Copse	Oxon	SP5509	51°46·8′	1°11·8′W	F	164
Wick Court	Glos	SO7310	51°47·5′	2°23·1′W	A	162
Wickcroft	W Berks	SU6371	51°26·3′	1°5·2′W	X	175
Wick Down	Wilts	SU1321	50°59·5′	1°48·5′W	X	184
Wick Down	Wilts	SU2552	51°16·2′	1°38·1′W	X	184
Wick Down Fm	Wilts	SU1373	51°27·6′	1°48·4′W	FM	173
Wicken	Cambs	TL5670	52°18·6′	0°17·7′E	T	154
Wicken	Northnts	SP7439	52°2·9′	0°54·9′W	T	152
Wicken Bonhunt	Essex	TL4933	51°58·8′	0°10·6′E	T	167
Wickenby	Lincs	TF0881	53°19·1′	0°22·3′W	T	121
Wickenby Airport	Lincs	TF1081	53°19·1′	0°20·5′W	X	121
Wickenby Wood	Lincs	TF0782	53°19·7′	0°23·2′W	F	121
Wickenden Fm	W Susx	TQ3831	51°3·9′	0°1·4′W	FM	187
Wick End Fm	Beds	SP9850	52°8·6′	0°33·7′W	FM	153
Wicken Fen	Cambs	TL5570	52°18·6′	0°16·8′E	X	154
Wicken Fm	Norf	TF8117	52°43·4′	0°41·2′E	FM	132
Wicken Fm	Norf	TF9120	52°44·9′	0°50·2′E	FM	132
Wicken Lode	Cambs	TL5569	52°18·1′	0°16·8′E	W	154
Wicken Lowe	Roch	SD9519	53°40·3′	2°4·1′W	X	109
Wicken Park	Northnts	SP7438	52°2·4′	0°54·9′W	X	152
Wickenpond Fm	Norf	TF8331	52°51·0′	0°43·5′E	FM	132
Wickens	Kent	TQ4841	51°9·2′	0°7·4′E	X	188
Wicken, The	Derby	SK1289	53°24·1′	1°48·8′W	X	110
Wicken Walls	Staffs	SK0167	53°12·2′	1°58·7′W	X	119
Wicken Water	Essex	TL4933	51°58·8′	0°10·6′E	X	167
Wicken Wood	Northnts	SP7340	52°3·4′	0°55·7′W	F	152
Wick Episcopi	Worcs	SO8353	52°10·7′	2°14·5′W	T	150
Wickerfield	Cumbr	NY6319	54°34·1′	2°33·9′W	X	91
Wickeridge	Devon	SX7869	50°30·7′	3°42·9′W	X	202
Wickerslack	Cumbr	NY6015	54°32·0′	2°36·7′W	X	91
Wickersley	Roth	SK4891	53°25·1′	1°16·3′W	T	111
Wicker Street Green	Suff	TL9741	52°2·2′	0°52·7′E	T	155
Wickerthwaite	Cumbr	NY4975	55°4·3′	2°47·5′W	X	86
Wicker Well	Suff	TM4896	52°30·5′	1°39·7′E	W	134
Wicket Nook	Derby	SK3520	52°46·8′	1°28·5′W	X	128
Wickets Beer	Somer	ST5311	50°54·0′	2°39·7′W	X	194
Wicketslap	Aberd	NJ7529	57°21·3′	2°24·5′W	X	38
Wicketwalls	Aberd	NJ8622	57°17·6′	2°13·5′W	X	38
Wicketwood Hill	Notts	SK6244	52°59·6′	1°4·2′W	X	129
Wickey Fm, The	Beds	TL1061	52°14·4′	0°22·9′W	FM	153
Wickfield Copse	W Berks	SU3771	51°26·4′	1°27·7′W	F	174
Wickfield Fm	W Berks	SU3873	51°27·5′	1°26·8′W	FM	174
Wickfield Fm	Wilts	SU0982	51°32·4′	1°51·8′W	FM	173
Wickfields Fm	Glos	SO9828	51°57·3′	2°1·4′W	FM	150,163
Wickfield Wood	Glos	ST9296	51°40·0′	2°6·5′W	F	163
Wick Fm	Bath & NE Somer	ST6562	51°21·6′	2°29·8′W	FM	172
Wick Fm	Essex	TL9026	51°54·2′	0°46·1′E	FM	168
Wick Fm	Essex	TL9317	51°49·3′	0°48·4′E	FM	168
Wick Fm	Essex	TM0329	51°55·6′	0°57·5′E	FM	168
Wick Fm	E Susx	TQ3213	50°54·3′	0°7·0′W	FM	198
Wick Fm	Glos	SO8627	51°56·7′	2°11·8′W	FM	162
Wick Fm	Hants	SU7213	50°54·9′	0°58·2′W	FM	197
Wick Fm	Herts	SP9309	51°46·5′	0°38·7′W	FM	165
Wick Fm	Kent	TQ8443	51°9·6′	0°38·3′E	FM	188
Wick Fm	Kent	TR1842	51°8·4′	1°7·4′E	FM	179,189
Wick Fm	Norf	TL9099	52°33·6′	0°48·6′E	FM	144
Wick Fm	Oxon	SP5508	51°46·3′	1°11·8′W	FM	164
Wick Fm	Somer	ST1827	51°2·4′	3°9·8′W	FM	181,193
Wick Fm	Somer	ST3154	51°17·1′	2°59·0′W	FM	182
Wick Fm	Somer	ST7857	51°18·9′	2°18·6′W	FM	172
Wick Fm	Suff	TM0134	51°58·3′	0°56·0′E	FM	155
Wick Fm	Wilts	ST8284	51°33·5′	2°15·2′W	FM	173
Wick Fm	Wilts	ST9762	51°21·7′	2°2·2′W	FM	173
Wick Fm	W Susx	TQ2415	50°55·5′	0°13·8′W	FM	198
Wick Fms	Wilts	ST9357	51°19·0′	2°5·6′W	FM	173
Wickford	Essex	TQ7493	51°36·8′	0°31·2′E	T	178
Wick Hall	Oxon	SU5197	51°40·4′	1°15·4′W	X	164
Wickham	Hants	SU5711	50°54·0′	1°11·0′W	T	196
Wickham	W Berks	SU3971	51°26·4′	1°25·9′W	T	174
Wickham Abbey Fm	Suff	TM0868	52°16·5′	1°3·3′E	FM	155
Wickham Bishops	Essex	TL8412	51°46·8′	0°40·4′E	T	168
Wickhambreaux	Kent	TR2258	51°16·9′	1°11·4′E	T	179
Wickhambrook	Suff	TL7455	52°10·2′	0°33·1′E	T	155
Wickham Bushes	Kent	TR2445	51°9·8′	1°12·6′E	X	179,189
Wickham Common	Hants	SU5810	50°53·4′	1°10·1′W	X	196
Wickham Court	Brom	TQ3864	51°21·7′	0°0·7′W	A	177,187
Wickham Fell	Ghead	NZ2059	54°55·8′	1°40·8′W	T	88
Wickham Field	Kent	TQ5159	51°18·8′	0°10·4′E	X	188
Wickhamford	Worcs	SP0641	52°4·3′	1°54·4′W	T	150
Wickham Green	Suff	TM0969	52°17·0′	1°4·2′E	T	155
Wickham Green	W Berks	SU3971	51°26·4′	1°25·9′W	T	174
Wickham Green Fm	Wilts	SU0257	51°19·0′	1°57·9′W	FM	173
Wickham Hall	Essex	TL8310	51°45·7′	0°39·5′E	X	168
Wickham Hall	Herts	TL4723	51°53·4′	0°8·6′E	X	167
Wickham Heath	W Berks	SU4269	51°25·3′	1°23·4′W	T	174
Wickham Ho	Suff	TL7753	52°9·0′	0°35·6′E	X	155
Wickham Manor	E Susx	TQ8916	50°55·0′	0°41·7′E	A	189
Wickham Market	Suff	TM3055	52°8·9′	1°22·1′E	T	156
Wickham Market Sta	Suff	TM3255	52°8·9′	1°23·9′E	X	156
Wickham Place	Essex	TL8211	51°46·3′	0°38·7′E	X	168
Wickhampton	Norf	TG4205	52°35·6′	1°34·8′E	T	134
Wickham's Cross	Somer	ST5032	51°5·3′	2°42·5′W	T	182,183
Wickham's Fm	Essex	TL8002	51°41·5′	0°36·7′E	FM	168
Wickham Skeith	Suff	TM0969	52°17·0′	1°4·2′E	T	155
Wickham St Paul	Essex	TL8336	51°59·8′	0°40·3′E	T	155
Wickham Street	Suff	TL7554	52°9·6′	0°33·9′E	T	155
Wickham Street	Suff	TM0869	52°17·0′	1°3·4′E	T	155
Wick Hill	Brackn	SU8770	51°25·6′	0°44·5′W	T	175
Wick Hill	Kent	TQ8441	51°8·5′	0°38·2′E	T	188
Wick Hill	Wilts	ST9773	51°27·6′	2°2·2′W	H	173
Wick Hill	Wok	SU8064	51°22·4′	0°50·6′W	T	175,186
Wick Hill Fm	Hants	SU7535	51°6·8′	0°55·3′W	FM	186
Wickhurst	Kent	TQ5247	51°12·3′	0°10·9′E	T	188
Wickhurst Barns	W Susx	TQ2511	50°53·3′	0°13·0′W	X	198
Wickhurst Fm	E Susx	TQ6335	51°5·7′	0°20·1′E	FM	188
Wickhurst Manor	Kent	TQ5151	51°14·5′	0°10·2′E	X	188
Wickinford Fm	Ches	SJ9674	53°16·0′	2°3·2′W	FM	118
Wickington	Devon	SX6596	50°45·1′	3°54·4′W	X	191
Wickins Lane End	Lancs	SD5744	53°53·7′	2°38·8′W	X	102
Wickland Fm	Surrey	TQ1141	51°9·7′	0°24·4′W	FM	187
Wicklands	E Susx	TQ4617	50°56·3′	0°5·1′E	X	198
Wicklane	Bath & NE Somer	ST6958	51°19·4′	2°26·3′W	T	172
Wickleshamlodge Fm	Oxon	SU2994	51°38·9′	1°34·5′W	FM	164,174
Wicklewood	Norf	TG0702	52°34·8′	1°3·7′E	T	144
Wick Marsh	Essex	TM0316	51°48·6′	0°57·1′E	X	168
Wickmere	Norf	TG1733	52°51·3′	1°13·8′E	T	133
Wick Moor	Somer	ST2145	51°12·2′	3°7·5′W	X	182
Wick of Aith	Shetld	HU6489	60°35·0′	0°49·4′W	W	1,2
Wick of Belmont	Shetld	HP5600	60°41·0′	0°58·0′W	W	1
Wick of Breckon	Shetld	HP5205	60°43·7′	1°2·3′W	W	1
Wick of Collaster	Shetld	HP5707	60°44·8′	0°56·8′W	W	1
Wick of Copister	Shetld	HU4878	60°29·2′	1°7·1′W	W	2,3
Wick of Glachon	Shetld	HU5273	60°26·5′	1°2·8′W	W	2,3
Wick of Gossabrough	Shetld	HU5283	60°31·9′	1°2·6′W	W	1,2,3
Wick of Gruting	Shetld	HU6592	60°36·6′	0°48·3′W	W	1,2
Wick of Gutcher	Shetld	HU5499	60°40·5′	1°0·2′W	W	1
Wick of Hagdale	Shetld	HP6410	60°46·3′	0°49·0′W	W	1
Wick of Houbie	Shetld	HU6290	60°35·6′	0°51·6′W	W	1,2
Wick of Lamba	Shetld	HU3881	60°30·9′	1°18·0′W	W	1,2,3
Wick of Neap	Shetld	HU5058	60°18·4′	1°5·2′W	W	2,3
Wick of North Garth	Shetld	HP5400	60°41·0′	1°0·2′W	W	1
Wick of Sandsayre	Shetld	HU4325	60°0·7′	1°13·2′W	W	4
Wick of Shunni	Shetld	HU3515	59°55·4′	1°21·9′W	W	4
Wick of Skaw	Shetld	HP6616	60°49·5′	0°46·7′W	W	1
Wick of Smirgirt	Shetld	HP6203	60°42·6′	0°51·3′W	W	1
Wick of Tresta	Shetld	HU6288	60°34·5′	0°51·6′W	W	1,2
Wick of Trutis	Shetld	HP5005	60°43·8′	1°4·5′W	W	1
Wick of Vatsetter	Shetld	HU5389	60°35·1′	1°1·5′W	W	1,2
Wick of Watsness	Shetld	HU1750	60°14·3′	1°41·1′W	W	3
Wick of Whallerie	Shetld	HP5005	60°43·8′	1°4·5′W	W	1
Wickor Point	W Susx	SU7403	50°49·5′	0°56·6′W	X	197
Wick Pond	Surrey	SU9869	51°24·9′	0°35·1′W	W	175,176
Wickridge Hill	Glos	SO8607	51°45·9′	2°11·8′W	X	162
Wickridge Street	Glos	SO8127	51°56·7′	2°16·2′W	T	162
Wick River	Highld	ND3152	58°27·3′	3°10·5′W	W	11,12
Wick Rocks	S Glos	ST7073	51°27·5′	2°25·5′W	T	172
Wickselm	Glos	SO6800	51°42·1′	2°27·4′W	X	162
Wicks Fm	W Susx	SU9903	50°49·3′	0°35·3′W	FM	197
Wicks Green Fm	Glos	SO7614	51°49·7′	2°20·5′W	FM	162
Wicks Hill	Oxon	SU6386	51°34·4′	1°5·1′W	X	175
Wickslett Copse	W Berks	SU4480	51°31·3′	1°21·6′W	F	174
Wicks Manor Fm	Essex	TL8912	51°46·7′	0°44·8′E	FM	168
Wickson's Fm	Northnts	SP5844	52°5·7′	1°8·8′W	FM	152
Wicks's Fm	Suff	TM0865	52°14·9′	1°3·2′E	FM	155
Wicksted Hall	Ches	SJ5544	52°59·7′	2°39·8′W	X	117
Wicksted Old Hall	Ches	SJ5544	52°59·7′	2°39·8′W	X	117
Wicksteed Park	Northnts	SP8876	52°22·7′	0°42·0′W	X	141
Wicksters Brook	Glos	SO7505	51°44·8′	2°21·3′W	W	162
Wicks, The	E Susx	TR0118	50°55·8′	0°52·0′E	W	189
Wick St Lawrence	N Som	ST3665	51°23·1′	2°54·8′W	T	171,182
Wickstreet	E Susx	TQ5308	50°51·3′	0°10·8′E	T	199
Wick Street	Glos	SO8607	51°45·9′	2°11·8′W	T	162
Wicks Wood	Oxon	SU6487	51°34·9′	1°4·2′W	F	175
Wick, The	Pemb	SM7208	51°43·7′	5°17·7′W	W	157
Wickton Ct	Heref	SO5254	52°11·2′	2°41·7′W	X	149
Wickwar	S Glos	ST7288	51°35·6′	2°23·9′W	T	162,172
Wick Warth	N Som	ST3566	51°23·6′	2°55·7′W	X	171,182
Wick Wood	Hants	SU2609	50°53·0′	1°37·4′W	F	195
Wickwood Fm	Oxon	SU3093	51°38·3′	1°33·6′W	FM	164,174
Wicton Fm	Heref	SO6255	52°11·8′	2°33·0′W	FM	149
Widbrook	Wilts	ST8359	51°20·0′	2°14·3′W	T	173
Widbrook Common	Win & Maid	SU8984	51°33·1′	0°42·6′W	X	175
Widcombe	Bath & NE Somer	ST7663	51°22·2′	2°20·3′W	T	172
Widcombe Barton FM	Devon	SY1894	50°44·6′	3°9·4′W	X	192,193
Widcombe Moor	Somer	ST2016	50°56·5′	3°7·9′W	X	193
Widcombe Wood	Devon	SY1894	50°44·6′	3°9·4′W	F	192,193
Widdacombe	Devon	SX4687	50°40·0′	4°10·4′W	X	190
Widdale	N Yks	SD8288	54°17·5′	2°16·2′W	X	98
Widdale Beck	N Yks	SD8187	54°16·9′	2°17·1′W	W	98

Widdale Fell	N Yks	SD8088	54°17·5'	2°18·0'W	H	98
Widdale Fell	N Yks	SD8088	54°17·5'	2°18·0'W	H	98
Widdale Foot	N Yks	SD8287	54°16·9'	2°16·2'W	X	98
Widdale Ghyll Ho	N Yks	SD8489	54°18·0'	2°14·3'W	X	98
Widdale Great Tarn	Cumbr	SD7987	54°16·9'	2°18·9'W	W	98
Widdale Head	N Yks	SD8085	54°15·9'	2°18·0'W	X	98
Widdale Head	N Yks	SD8085	54°15·9'	2°18·0'W	X	98
Widdale Little Tarn	Cumbr	SD7988	54°17·5'	2°18·9'W	W	98
Widdale Side	N Yks	SD8288	54°17·5'	2°16·2'W	X	98
Widdale Side Allotments	N Yks	SD8289	54°18·0'	2°16·2'W	X	98
Widden Bottom	Hants	SZ2899	50°47·6'	1°35·8'W	X	195
Widdenham Fm	Wilts	ST8370	51°26·0'	2°14·3'W	FM	173
Widdenhill Fm	S Glos	ST7684	51°33·5'	2°20·4'W	FM	172
Widdens Hill	Cambs	TL4481	52°24·7'	0°7·4'E	X	142,143
Widder's Fm	Norf	TF5503	52°36·4'	0°17·7'E	FM	143
Widdicombe Fm	Devon	SX8764	50°28·1'	3°35·2'W	FM	202
Widdicombe Ho	Devon	SX8141	50°15·7'	3°39·8'W	X	202
Widdiman Pasture	N Yks	SE0983	54°14·8'	1°51·3'W	X	99
Widdington	Essex	TL5331	51°57·6'	0°14·0'E	T	167
Widdington Fm	Wilts	SU1253	51°16·8'	1°49·3'W	FM	184
Widdington Grange	N Yks	SE5059	54°1·7'	1°13·8'W	X	105
Widdington Hall Fm	N Yks	SE4959	54°1·7'	1°14·7'W	FM	105
Widdington Manor	N Yks	SE4859	54°1·7'	1°15·6'W	X	105
Widdop	Cald	SD9333	53°47·8'	2°6·0'W	X	103
Widdop Gate	Cald	SD9631	53°46·8'	2°3·2'W	X	103
Widdop Lodge	Cald	SD9333	53°47·8'	2°6·0'W	X	103
Widdop Moor	Cald	SD9333	53°47·8'	2°6·0'W	X	103
Widdop Resr	Cald	SD9332	53°47·3'	2°6·0'W	W	103
Widdowshill Plantn	Norf	TL8694	52°31·0'	0°44·9'E	F	144
Widdowson Spring Wood	Derby	SK3668	53°12·7'	1°27·2'W	F	119
Widdrington	Northum	NZ2595	55°15·2'	1°36·0'W	T	81
Widdrington Fm	Hav	TQ5393	51°37·1'	0°13·0'E	FM	177
Widdrington Station	Northum	NZ2494	55°14·6'	1°36·9'W	T	81
Widdybank Fell	Durham	NY8230	54°40·1'	2°16·3'W	X	91,92
Widdy Bank Fm	Durham	NY8329	54°39·6'	2°15·4'W	FM	91,92
Widdy Field	N Yks	NZ9309	54°28·3'	0°33·5'W	X	94
Widecleugh Rig	Scot Bord	NT5455	55°47·4'	2°43·6'W	X	66,73
Widecombe in the Moor	Devon	SX7176	50°34·4'	3°48·9'W	T	191
Wide Eals	Northum	NY8058	54°55·2'	2°18·3'W	X	86,87
Widefield	Devon	SX5596	50°45·0'	4°2·9'W	X	191
Widefield Wood	Bucks	SU8185	51°33·7'	0°49·5'W	F	175
Wide Firth	Orkney	HY4315	59°1·4'	2°59·1'W	W	6
Wideford	Orkney	HY4608	58°57·6'	2°55·8'W	X	6,7
Wideford Hill	Orkney	HY4111	58°59·2'	3°1·1'W	H	6
Widegate	Swan	SS5688	51°34·6'	4°4·3'W	X	159
Widegates	Corn	SX2857	50°23·5'	4°24·8'W	T	201
Wide Haugh	Northum	NY9664	54°58·5'	2°3·3'W	X	87
Wide Hope	E Loth	NT7069	55°55·0'	2°28·4'W	X	67
Wide Hope	Northum	NU1208	55°22·2'	1°48·2'W	X	81
Widehope Fm	Durham	NZ2024	54°36·9'	1°41·0'W	FM	93
Wide Hope Shank	Scot Bord	NT1844	55°41·2'	3°17·8'W	H	72
Widehurst	Kent	TQ7543	51°9·8'	0°30·6'E	X	188
Widemarsh	Heref	SO5041	52°4·1'	2°43·4'W	T	149
Widemouth Bay	Corn	SS2002	50°47·6'	4°32·9'W	T	190
Widemouth Fms	Corn	SS2001	50°47·1'	4°32·8'W	FM	190
Widemouth Sand	Corn	SS1902	50°47·6'	4°33·7'W	X	190
Wide Open	Northum	NU1339	55°38·9'	1°47·2'W	X	75
Wide Open	N Tyne	NZ2372	55°2·8'	1°38·0'W	T	88
Wideopen	Scot Bord	NT8130	55°34·0'	2°17·6'W	X	74
Wide open Dykes	Cumbr	NY4162	54°57·2'	2°54·8'W	X	85
Wide Open Fm	York	SE5757	54°0·6'	1°7·4'W	FM	105
Wideopen Moor	Scot Bord	NT8131	55°34·6'	2°17·6'W	X	74
Wideopen Plantn	Northum	NT8944	55°41·6'	2°10·1'W	F	74
Widepot	Cumbr	NY5209	54°28·7'	2°44·0'W	X	90
Widewall	Orkney	ND4391	58°48·4'	2°58·7'W	X	7
Widewall Bay	Orkney	ND4292	58°49·0'	2°59·8'W	W	7
Widewalls Fm	Corn	SX1180	50°35·6'	4°39·8'W	FM	200
Widewath	Cumbr	NY5021	54°35·2'	2°46·0'W	X	90
Widewell	C of Plym	SX4961	50°26·0'	4°7·2'W	T	201
Widewell	Devon	SX8142	50°16·2'	3°39·8'W	X	202
Widford	Essex	TL6905	51°43·3'	0°27·2'E	T	167
Widford	Herts	TL4215	51°49·2'	0°4·0'E	T	167
Widford	Oxon	SP2711	51°48·1'	1°36·1'W	X	163
Widford Village	Oxon	SP2712	51°48·6'	1°36·1'W	A	163
Widgeon Hill	Heref	SO5259	52°13·9'	2°41·8'W	X	149
Widgerly Down	Wilts	SU2551	51°15·7'	1°38·1'W	X	184
Widgery Cross	Devon	SX5385	50°39·0'	4°4·4'W	X	191,201
Widgham Green	Cambs	TL6655	52°10·3'	0°26·1'E	T	154
Widham	Wilts	SU0988	51°35·7'	1°51·8'W	T	173
Widhayes Fm	Devon	ST0014	50°55·2'	3°25·0'W	FM	181
Widlake	Somer	SS9234	51°5·9'	3°32·2'W	X	181
Widley	C of Port	SU6706	50°51·2'	1°2·5'W	T	196
Widley Copse	Oxon	SP2714	51°49·7'	1°36·1'W	F	163
Widley Fm	C of Port	SU6606	50°51·2'	1°3·4'W	FM	196
Widley's Fm	Wilts	ST8584	51°33·5'	2°12·6'W	FM	173
Widmere Fm	Bucks	SU8389	51°35·9'	0°47·7'W	FM	175
Widmer End	Bucks	SU8896	51°39·6'	0°43·3'W	T	165
Widmer Fm	Bucks	SU9692	51°37·3'	0°36·4'W	FM	175,176
Widmerpool	Notts	SK6328	52°51·0'	1°3·5'W	T	129
Widmoor	Bucks	SU9186	51°34·2'	0°40·8'W	T	175
Widmore	Brom	TQ4169	51°24·4'	0°2·0'E	T	177
Widmore Fm	Bucks	SP9404	51°43·8'	0°37·9'W	FM	165
Widmore Fm	Herts	TL0313	51°48·6'	0°30·0'W	FM	166
Widmore Fm	Oxon	SP6232	51°59·2'	1°5·4'W	FM	152,165
Widmouth	Devon	SS5448	51°13·0'	4°5·0'W	X	180
Widmouth Head	Devon	SS5448	51°13·0'	4°5·0'W	X	180
Widmouth Hill	Devon	SS5447	51°12·5'	4°5·0'W	H	180
Widnes	Halton	SJ5185	53°21·8'	2°43·8'W	T	108
Widnes Sta	Halton	SJ5187	53°22·9'	2°43·8'W	X	108
Widney Manor Sta	Sol	SP1577	52°23·7'	1°46·4'W	X	139
Widow Feilds Fm	Staffs	SJ9246	53°0·9'	2°6·7'W	FM	118
Widow Hause	Cumbr	NY1826	54°37·6'	3°15·8'W	X	89,90
Widow Howe	N Yks	SE8599	54°23·0'	0°41·1'W	A	94,100
Widow Howe Moor	N Yks	NZ8600	54°23·5'	0°40·1'W	X	94
Widowscroft Fm	Tames	SK0097	53°28·4'	1°59·6'W	FM	110
Widows Fm	W Berks	SU4676	51°29·1'	1°19·9'W	FM	174
Widow's Knowe	Scot Bord	NT5060	55°50·1'	2°47·5'W	X	66
Widow's Loch	E Ayr	NS4401	55°17·0'	4°26·9'W	W	77
Widworthy	Devon	SY2199	50°47·3'	3°6·9'W	T	192,193
Widworthy Court	Devon	SY2099	50°47·3'	3°7·7'W	X	192,193

Widworthy Hill	Devon	SY2198	50°46·8'	3°6·9'W	H	192,193
Wield Wood	Hants	SU6138	51°8·5'	1°7·3'W	F	185
Wierston	D & G	NX0065	54°56·6'	5°6·9'W	X	82
Wierton	Kent	TQ7849	51°13·0'	0°33·3'E	T	188
Wife Geo	Highld	ND3969	58°36·5'	3°2·5'W	X	12
Wife's Geo	Orkney	ND4995	58°50·6'	2°52·5'W	X	7
Wife's Water	Shetld	HU3047	60°12·6'	1°27·0'W	W	3
Wifford	Devon	SX8277	50°35·1'	3°39·6'W	X	191
Wig	Carm	SN5315	51°49·1'	4°7·6'W	X	159
Wig	Gwyn	SH6372	53°13·9'	4°2·7'W	X	115
Wig	Powys	SJ0812	52°42·1'	3°21·3'W	X	125
Wig	Powys	SN8897	52°33·8'	3°38·7'W	X	135,136
Wig	Powys	SO1187	52°28·7'	3°18·2'W	T	136
Wigan	Wigan	SD5805	53°32·6'	2°37·6'W	T	108
Wigan's Fm	Bucks	SU7899	51°41·3'	0°51·9'W	FM	165
Wiganthorpe	N Yks	SE6672	54°8·6'	0°59·0'W	T	100
Wigber Low	Derby	SK2051	53°3·5'	1°41·7'W	X	119
Wigbeth	Dorset	SU0407	50°52·0'	1°56·2'W	T	195
Wigborough	Somer	ST4415	50°56·1'	2°47·4'W	T	193
Wigborough Manor	Somer	ST4415	50°56·1'	2°47·4'W	A	193
Wigboro Wick Fm	Essex	TM1114	51°47·3'	1°4·0'E	FM	168,169
Wig Br	Powys	SO0192	52°31·3'	3°27·1'W	X	136
Wigdan Walls	Durham	NZ1828	54°39·1'	1°42·8'W	X	92
Wigdwr	Powys	SN9986	52°28·0'	3°28·8'W	X	136
Wigdwr Brook	Powys	SN9887	52°28·5'	3°29·7'W	W	136
Wigfa	Nth Pt Talb	SN7504	51°43·5'	3°48·2'W	X	170
Wig Fach	Brig	SS8477	51°29·0'	3°39·9'W	T	170
Wigfair	Denb	SJ0271	53°13·9'	3°27·7'W	X	116
Wigford	Devon	SX7251	50°20·9'	3°47·6'W	X	202
Wigford Down	Devon	SX5464	50°27·7'	4°3·0'W	X	201
Wigga	Heref	SO3628	51°57·0'	2°55·5'W	X	149,161
Wiggall	Heref	SO6256	52°12·3'	2°33·0'W	X	149
Wiggaton	Corn	SX2390	50°41·2'	4°30·0'W	X	190
Wiggaton	Devon	SY1093	50°44·0'	3°16·1'W	T	192,193
Wigg Burn	Scot Bord	NT5804	55°19·9'	2°39·3'W	W	80
Wiggenhall St Germans	Norf	TF5914	52°42·2'	0°21·6'E	T	131
Wiggenhall St Mary Magdalen	Norf	TF5911	52°40·6'	0°21·5'E	T	131,143
Wiggenhall St Mary the Virgin	Norf	TF5813	52°41·7'	0°20·7'E	T	131,143
Wiggenhall St Peter	Norf	TF6013	52°41·7'	0°22·5'E	T	132,143
Wiggens Green	Essex	TL6642	52°3·3'	0°25·7'E	T	154
Wiggerland Wood Fm	Warw	SP3159	52°13·9'	1°32·4'W	FM	151
Wiggington	Staffs	SK2006	52°39·3'	1°41·9'W	T	139
Wiggington Fields	Staffs	SK2007	52°39·9'	1°41·9'W	X	139
Wiggin Hill Fm	Cambs	TL3174	52°21·1'	0°4·2'W	FM	142
Wiggins Hill Fm	Birm	SP1693	52°32·4'	1°45·4'W	FM	139
Wigginstall	Staffs	SK0960	53°8·5'	1°51·5'W	T	119
Wigginton	Herts	SP9310	51°47·1'	0°38·7'W	T	165
Wigginton	Oxon	SP3833	51°59·9'	1°26·4'W	T	151
Wigginton	Shrops	SJ3335	52°54·7'	2°59·4'W	T	126
Wigginton	York	SE5958	54°1·1'	1°5·6'W	T	105
Wigginton Bottom	Herts	SP9309	51°46·5'	0°38·7'W	T	165
Wigginton Cott	York	SE5956	54°0·0'	1°5·6'W	X	105
Wigginton Grange	York	SE5858	54°1·1'	1°6·5'W	X	105
Wigginton Heath	Oxon	SP3835	52°1·0'	1°26·4'W	T	151
Wigginton Lodge	York	SE5956	54°0·0'	1°5·6'W	X	105
Wigginton Moor	York	SE5859	54°1·7'	1°6·5'W	X	105
Wigg Island	Halton	SJ5384	53°21·3'	2°42·0'W	X	108
Wigg Knowe	Scot Bord	NT5704	55°19·9'	2°40·2'W	H	80
Wiggle	Corn	SX4250	50°20·0'	4°12·8'W	X	201
Wigglesworth	N Yks	SD8056	54°0·2'	2°17·9'W	T	103
Wigglesworth Hall Fm	N Yks	SD8157	54°0·8'	2°17·0'W	FM	103
Wigglesworth Row	N Yks	SD8156	54°0·2'	2°17·0'W	X	103
Wiggold	Glos	SP0404	51°44·3'	1°56·1'W	X	163
Wiggonby	Cumbr	NY2953	54°52·3'	3°6·0'W	T	85
Wiggonholt	W Susx	TQ0616	50°56·2'	0°29·1'W	T	197
Wiggonholt Common	W Susx	TQ0516	50°56·3'	0°29·9'W	X	197
Wiggonlea Fm	Derby	SK3351	53°3·6'	1°30·0'W	FM	119
Wiggon Rigg	Cumbr	NY3152	54°51·7'	3°4·1'W	X	85
Wigg's Carr	Norf	TG4204	52°35·0'	1°34·7'E	F	134
Wiggs Fm	Leic	SK4208	52°40·3'	1°22·3'W	FM	140
Wig Hall	N Yks	SE3787	54°16·9'	1°25·5'W	X	99
Wigham	Devon	SS7508	50°51·7'	3°46·2'W	X	191
Wighay	Notts	SK5250	53°2·9'	1°13·1'W	X	120
Wighill	N Yks	SE4746	53°54·7'	1°16·7'W	T	105
Wighill Grange	N Yks	SE4647	53°55·3'	1°17·6'W	X	105
Wighill Lodge	N Yks	SE4648	53°55·8'	1°17·5'W	X	105
Wightfield Manor	Glos	SO8628	51°57·3'	2°11·8'W	A	150
Wightman Hill	E Loth	NT7268	55°54·5'	2°26·4'W	X	67
Wighton	Norf	TF9439	52°55·0'	0°53·5'E	T	132
Wightwick Manor	Wolv	SO8698	52°35·0'	2°12·0'W	T	139
Wigland Hall	Ches	SJ4944	52°59·7'	2°45·2'W	X	117
Wigley	Derby	SK3171	53°14·3'	1°31·7'W	T	119
Wigley	Hants	SU3216	50°56·8'	1°32·3'W	T	185
Wigley	Shrops	SJ3708	52°40·2'	2°55·5'W	X	126
Wigley	Shrops	SO5276	52°23·0'	2°41·9'W	X	137,138
Wigley Cross	Devon	SS5437	51°7·1'	4°4·8'W	X	180
Wigleymeadow Fm	Derby	SK2458	53°7·4'	1°38·1'W	FM	119
Wigman Hall	York	SE6445	53°54·1'	1°1·1'W	X	105,106
Wigmarsh	Shrops	SJ3725	52°49·4'	2°55·7'W	T	126
Wigmore	Heref	SO4169	52°19·2'	2°51·5'W	T	137,148
Wigmore	Medway	TQ8064	51°21·0'	0°35·5'E	T	178,188
Wigmore	Surrey	TQ1742	51°10·1'	0°19·2'W	X	187
Wigmore Abbey	Heref	SO4171	52°20·3'	2°51·6'W	A	137,148
Wigmore Fm	Devon	SS5842	51°9·8'	4°1·5'W	FM	180
Wigmore Fm	Hants	SU6762	51°21·4'	1°1·9'W	FM	175,186
Wigmore Fm	Somer	ST5552	51°16·2'	2°38·3'W	FM	182,183
Wigmore Hall Fm	Luton	TL1222	51°53·3'	0°22·0'W	FM	166
Wigmore Moor	Heref	SO4070	52°19·7'	2°52·4'W	X	137,148
Wigmore Rolls	Heref	SO3969	52°19·2'	2°53·3'W	X	137,148
Wigmore Wood	Shrops	SJ8306	52°39·3'	2°14·7'W	F	127
Wignell Hill	Leic	SP8393	52°32·5'	0°46·2'W	X	141
Wigney Wood	Beds	TL0357	52°12·3'	0°29·2'W	F	153
Wigpool Common	Heref	SO6159	52°13·9'	2°33·9'W	F	149
Wigsley	Notts	SK8670	53°13·4'	0°42·3'W	T	121
Wigsley Drain	Notts	SK8671	53°14·0'	0°42·3'W	W	121
Wigsley Wood	Notts	SK8470	53°13·5'	0°44·1'W	F	121
Wigsthorpe	Northnts	TL0482	52°25·8'	0°27·8'W	T	141
Wigston	Leic	SP6099	52°35·4'	1°6·5'W	T	140

Wig Stones Allotments	N Yks	SE0766	54°5·6'	1°53·2'W	X	99
Wigston Hill	Warw	SP2796	52°33·9'	1°35·7'W	X	140
Wigston Magna	Leic	SP6098	52°34·8'	1°6·5'W	T	140
Wigston Magna	Leic	SP6197	52°34·3'	1°5·6'W	T	140
Wigston Parva	Leic	SP4689	52°30·1'	1°18·9'W	T	140
Wig, The	D & G	NX0367	54°57·8'	5°4·2'W	W	82
Wig, The	Wilts	SU1847	51°13·5'	1°44·1'W	F	184
Wigthorpe	Notts	SK5983	53°20·7'	1°6·4'W	T	111,120
Wigtoft	Lincs	TF2636	52°54·6'	0°7·2'W	T	131
Wigtoft Marsh Fm	Lincs	TF2534	52°53·6'	0°8·1'W	FM	131
Wigton	Cumbr	NY2548	54°49·5'	3°9·6'W	T	85
Wigton Moor	Leeds	SE3240	53°51·6'	1°30·4'W	X	104
Wigtown	D & G	NX4355	54°52·2'	4°26·4'W	T	83
Wigtown Sands	D & G	NX4556	54°52·7'	4°24·5'W	X	83
Wigtwizzle	Sheff	SK2495	53°27·3'	1°37·9'W	T	110
Wigwell Grange	Derby	SK3054	53°5·2'	1°32·7'W	X	119
Wigwellnook	Derby	SK3055	53°5·7'	1°32·7'W	X	119
Wig-wen	Cered	SN4760	52°13·3'	4°14·0'W	X	146
Wigwig	Shrops	SJ6001	52°36·6'	2°35·0'W	X	127
Wig Wood	Heref	SO5153	52°10·6'	2°42·6'W	F	149
Wike	Leeds	SE3342	53°52·6'	1°29·5'W	T	104
Wikefield Fm	Leeds	SE3142	53°52·6'	1°31·3'W	FM	104
Wike Head	Barns	SE1301	53°30·6'	1°48·6'W	X	110
Wike Ridge	Leeds	SE3341	53°52·1'	1°29·5'W	X	104
Wike Well End	Donc	SE6912	53°36·2'	0°57·0'W	T	111
Wike Whin	Leeds	SE3442	53°52·6'	1°28·6'W	X	104
Wilbarston	Northnts	SP8188	52°29·3'	0°48·0'W	T	141
Wilbees Fm	E Susx	TQ5407	50°50·7'	0°11·6'E	FM	199
Wilberfoss	E Yorks	SE7350	53°56·7'	0°52·9'W	T	105,106
Wilberlee	Kirk	SE0614	53°37·6'	1°54·1'W	T	110
Wilbey Hill Fm	Cambs	TL4880	52°24·1'	0°10·9'E	FM	143
Wilbraham Temple	Cambs	TL5557	52°11·6'	0°16·5'E	X	154
Wilbrighton Hall	Staffs	SJ7918	52°45·8'	2°18·3'W	X	127
Wilburton	Cambs	TL4874	52°20·9'	0°10·8'E	T	143
Wilburton Fm	Devon	SX6052	50°21·3'	3°57·7'W	FM	202
Wilbury Fm	Beds	TL1933	51°59·2'	0°15·6'W	FM	166
Wilburyhill Fm	Herts	TL2032	51°58·6'	0°14·8'W	FM	166
Wilbury Ho	Wilts	SU2241	51°10·3'	1°40·7'W	X	184
Wilby	Norf	TM0389	52°27·9'	0°59·7'E	T	144
Wilby	Northnts	SP8666	52°17·4'	0°43·9'W	T	152
Wilby	Suff	TM2472	52°18·2'	1°17·5'E	T	156
Wilby Green	Suff	TM2470	52°17·2'	1°17·5'E	X	156
Wilby Hall	Norf	TM0390	52°28·4'	0°59·7'E	A	144
Wilby Hall	Northnts	SP8468	52°18·5'	0°45·7'W	X	152
Wilby Hall	Suff	TM2672	52°18·2'	1°19·3'E	X	156
Wilcock's Fm	Lancs	SD6315	53°38·1'	2°33·2'W	FM	109
Wilcot	Wilts	SU1460	51°20·6'	1°47·6'W	T	173
Wilcote Grange	Oxon	SP3715	51°50·2'	1°27·4'W	X	164
Wilcote Ho	Oxon	SP3715	51°50·2'	1°27·4'W	X	164
Wilcote Manor	Oxon	SP3715	51°50·2'	1°27·4'W	X	164
Wilcott	Shrops	SJ3718	52°45·6'	2°55·6'W	T	126
Wilcott Marsh	Shrops	SJ3817	52°45·1'	2°54·7'W	T	126
Wilcove	Corn	SX4356	50°23·2'	4°12·1'W	T	201
Wilcrick	Newp	ST4088	51°35·5'	2°51·6'W	T	171,172
Wilcrick Hill	Newp	ST4187	51°35·0'	2°50·7'W	H	171,172
Wilcrick Hill (Fort)	Newp	ST4187	51°35·0'	2°50·7'W	A	171,172
Wilcroft	Heref	SO5641	52°4·2'	2°38·1'W	X	149
Wilday Green	Derby	SK3274	53°16·0'	1°30·8'W	T	119
Wild Bank	Tames	SJ9898	53°29·0'	2°1·4'W	X	109
Wildboarclough	Ches	SJ9868	53°12·8'	2°1·4'W	T	118
Wildboar Clough	Derby	SK0897	53°28·4'	1°52·4'W	X	110
Wild Boar Fell	Cumbr	SD7598	54°22·9'	2°22·7'W	H	98
Wild Boar Fm	Lancs	SD4441	53°52·0'	2°50·7'W	FM	102
Wildboar Scar	Cumbr	NY6732	54°41·2'	2°30·3'W	X	91
Wild Carr	Suff	TM4490	52°27·4'	1°35·9'E	F	134
Wildcat Gate	Scot Bord	NT6620	55°28·6'	2°31·8'W	X	74
Wild Church Bottom	Dorset	SU0909	50°53·1'	1°51·9'W	X	195
Wild Duck Hall	Lancs	SD4868	54°6·6'	2°47·3'W	X	97
Wildecroft	Surrey	TQ2151	51°14·9'	0°15·6'W	X	187
Wildemere Fm	Suff	TL7178	52°22·6'	0°31·1'E	FM	143
Wilden	Beds	TL0955	52°11·2'	0°23·9'W	T	153
Wilden	Heref	SO5764	52°16·6'	2°37·4'W	X	137,138,149
Wilden	Worcs	SO8272	52°21·0'	2°15·5'W	T	138
Wilden Beck	Durham	NZ0020	54°34·8'	1°59·6'W	W	92
Wilden Pool	Worcs	SO8272	52°21·0'	2°15·5'W	W	138
Wilder Bottom	N Yks	SE0982	54°14·3'	1°51·3'W	X	99
Widerhope Manor	Shrops	SO5492	52°31·7'	2°40·3'W	A	137,138
Wilderley Hall	Shrops	SJ4301	52°36·5'	2°50·1'W	X	126
Wilderley Hill	Shrops	SO4199	52°35·4'	2°51·9'W	X	137
Wildern	Hants	SU4813	50°55·1'	1°18·6'W	T	196
Wilderness	Notts	SK5673	53°15·3'	1°9·2'W	F	120
Wilderness	Oldham	SE0201	53°30·6'	1°57·8'W	X	110
Wilderness	Orkney	HY3121	59°4·5'	3°11·7'W	X	6
Wildernesse	Kent	TQ5455	51°16·6'	0°12·9'E	T	188
Wilderness Fm	E Susx	TQ5323	50°59·4'	0°11·2'E	FM	199
Wilderness Fm	Kent	TQ4843	51°10·2'	0°7·4'E	FM	188
Wilderness Plantn	E Dunb	NS5971	55°54·9'	4°14·9'W	F	64
Wilderness, The	Arg & Bt	NM4029	56°23·2'	6°12·3'W	X	48
Wilderness, The	Essex	TL8106	51°43·6'	0°37·6'E	F	168
Wilderness, The	Fife	NO3210	56°16·9'	3°5·5'W	X	59
Wilderness, The	Glos	SO6617	51°51·3'	2°29·2'W	X	162
Wilderness, The	Highld	NH7375	57°45·1'	4°7·6'W	F	21
Wilderness, The	Norf	TG2116	52°42·0'	1°16·7'E	F	133,134
Wilderness, The	Shrops	SO4895	52°33·3'	2°45·6'W	X	137,138
Wilderness, The	Suff	TM4269	52°16·2'	1°33·2'E	F	156
Wilderness, The	W Berks	SU3967	51°24·3'	1°26·0'W	X	174
Wilderness Wood	E Susx	TQ5323	50°59·4'	0°11·2'E	F	199
Wilderness Wood	N Yks	SE3176	54°11·0'	1°31·1'W	F	99
Wilderspool	Warr	SJ6186	53°22·4'	2°34·8'W	T	109
Wilderswood	Bolton	SD6412	53°36·4'	2°32·2'W	T	109
Wilderwick Ho	Surrey	TQ4040	51°8·8'	0°0·5'E	X	187
Wilde Street	Suff	TL7078	52°22·6'	0°30·3'E	T	143
Wildfield Copse	Surrey	SU9549	51°14·2'	0°38·0'W	F	186
Wild Fm	Essex	TQ8698	51°39·2'	0°41·7'E	FM	168
Wild Fm	Herts	TL1701	51°42·0'	0°18·0'W	FM	166
Wildfowl Trust, The	Glos	SO7204	51°44·3'	2°23·9'W	X	162
Wild Goose Carr	York	SE6559	54°1·6'	1°0·0'W	X	105,106
Wildgoose Fm	Notts	SK7087	53°22·7'	0°56·5'W	FM	112,120
Wildgoose Hill	Scot Bord	NT8425	55°31·4'	2°14·8'W	H	74
Wild Goose Leys	Cambs	TL2376	52°22·3'	0°11·2'W	X	142

Wildgoose Race	Pemb	SM7004	51°41·5'	5°19·3'W	W	157
Wild Grove Fm	Leeds	SE2033	53°47·8'	1°41·4'W	FM	104
Wildhams Wood	W Susx	SU8113	50°54·9'	0°50·5'W	F	197
Wildhay	Staffs	SK1145	53°0·4'	1°49·8'W	X	119,128
Wildhern	Hants	SU3550	51°15·1'	1°29·5'W	T	185
Wildhill	Herts	TL2606	51°44·5'	0°10·1'W	T	166
Wild Hill	N Yks	SE1891	54°19·1'	1°43·0'W	X	99
Wild House Fm	Northnts	SP6343	52°5·1'	1°4·4'W	FM	152
Wildicote	Shrops	SJ8001	52°36·6'	2°17·3'W	X	127
Wildings	E Susx	TQ8325	50°59·9'	0°36·9'E	X	188,199
Wilding's Fm	Essex	TL6739	52°1·7'	0°26·5'E	FM	154
Wilding Wood	E Susx	TQ4018	50°56·9'	0°0·0'W	F	198
Wildlife Park	I of M	SC3694	54°19·2'	4°30·9'W	X	95
Wildmanbridge	S Lanak	NS8353	55°45·6'	3°51·4'W	T	65,72
Wild Mill	Brig	SS9080	51°30·7'	3°34·7'W	T	170
Wild Mill	Brig	SS9081	51°31·3'	3°34·7'W	T	170
Wild Moor	Derby	SK0274	53°16·0'	1°57·8'W	X	119
Wildmoor	Hants	SU6856	51°18·2'	1°1·1'W	T	175,186
Wildmoor	Oxon	SU4998	51°40·9'	1°17·1'W	T	164
Wild Moor	Shrops	SO4196	52°33·8'	2°51·8'W	X	137
Wildmoor	Worcs	SO9575	52°22·6'	2°4·0'W	T	139
Wildmoor, The	Warw	SP1655	52°11·8'	1°45·6'W	X	151
Wildmore Fen	Lincs	TF2552	53°3·3'	0°7·7'W	X	122
Wildmore Park	Lincs	TF2553	53°3·8'	0°7·7'W	X	122
Wildon Grange	Durham	NY9921	54°35·3'	2°0·5'W	X	92
Wildon Grange	N Yks	SE5178	54°12·0'	1°12·7'W	X	100
Wildon Hill Fm	N Yks	SE5177	54°11·4'	1°12·7'W	FM	100
Wildpark	Derby	SK2741	52°58·2'	1°35·5'W	F	119,128
Wild Pear Beach	Devon	SS5747	51°12·5'	4°2·4'W	X	180
Wildperry Fm	Heref	SO6659	52°13·9'	2°29·5'W	FM	149
Wildridings	Brackn	SU8668	51°24·5'	0°45·4'W	T	175
Wildriggs	Cumbr	NY4929	54°39·5'	2°47·0'W	X	90
Wild Road		SJ1484	53°21·0'	3°17·1'W	W	116
Wild Share	N Yks	SD8461	54°2·9'	2°14·2'W	F	98
Wildshaw Hill	S Lanak	NS9028	55°32·3'	3°44·1'W	H	71,72
Wild Slack	N Yks	NZ7506	54°26·9'	0°50·2'W	X	94
Wild's Lodge	Leic	SK7815	52°43·9'	0°50·3'W	X	129
Wild's Lodge	Rut	SK9708	52°39·9'	0°33·5'W	X	141
Wildstone Rock	Staffs	SK0166	53°11·7'	1°58·7'W	X	119
Wildsworth	Lincs	SK8097	53°28·1'	0°47·3'W	T	112
Wild Tor	Devon	SX6287	50°40·2'	3°56·8'W	H	191
Wildway Ho	Somer	ST2708	50°52·2'	3°1·9'W	X	193
Wild Wood	Northnts	SP6743	52°5·1'	1°0·9'W	F	152
Wild Wood	N Yks	SE1891	54°19·1'	1°43·0'W	F	99
Wildwood	Staffs	SJ9420	52°46·9'	2°4·9'W	T	127
Wildwoods	Enf	TQ3299	51°40·7'	0°5·1'W	X	166,176,177
Wildwoods Fm	Devon	SX8562	50°27·0'	3°36·8'W	FM	202
Wileirog	Cered	SN6085	52°26·9'	4°3·2'W	X	135
Wiles Fm	Lincs	TF4330	52°51·1'	0°7·8'E	FM	131
Wileycat Wood	Red & Cl	NZ6415	54°31·8'	1°0·2'W	F	94
Wiley Gill	Cumbr	NY2931	54°40·4'	3°5·6'W	W	89,90
Wiley Sike	Cumbr	NY6370	55°1·6'	2°34·3'W	X	86
Wileysike Ho	Cumbr	NY6670	55°1·7'	2°31·5'W	X	86
Wilfholme	E Yorks	TA0448	53°55·3'	0°24·6'W	X	107
Wilfholme Fm	E Yorks	TA0348	53°55·3'	0°25·5'W	FM	107
Wilfholme Landing	E Yorks	TA0647	53°54·7'	0°22·8'W	X	107
Wilford	C of Nott	SK5637	52°55·9'	1°9·6'W	T	129
Wilford Br	Suff	TM2950	52°6·3'	1°21·0'E	X	156
Wilford Hill	Notts	SK5835	52°54·8'	1°7·8'W	X	129
Wilgate Green	Kent	TQ9957	51°16·9'	0°51·6'E	T	178
Wilhoull	Shetld	HU4429	60°2·9'	1°12·1'W	X	4
Wilkesley	Ches	SJ6241	52°58·1'	2°33·5'W	T	118
Wilkhaven	Highld	NH9486	57°51·6'	3°46·7'W	X	21
Wilkhaven Muir	Highld	NH9387	57°51·8'	3°47·7'W	X	21
Wilkie Down Fm	Corn	SX3290	50°41·4'	4°22·3'W	FM	190
Wilkieston	Fife	NO4412	56°18·1'	2°53·9'W	X	59
Wilkieston	W Loth	NT1268	55°54·1'	3°24·0'W	T	65
Wilkieston Burn	Fife	NO4411	56°17·5'	2°53·8'W	W	59
Wilkin Heys	Lancs	SD7637	53°50·0'	2°21·5'W	X	103
Wilkin Ho	Derby	SK3165	53°11·1'	1°31·8'W	X	119
Wilkins Barne	W Berks	SU4579	51°30·7'	1°20·7'W	X	174
Wilkins Fm	Hants	SU1601	50°48·7'	1°46·0'W	FM	195
Wilkinson Park	Northum	NT9406	55°21·1'	2°5·2'W	X	80
Wilkins's Coomb	Hants	SU1215	50°56·3'	1°49·4'W	F	184
Wilkinsyke Fm	Cumbr	NY1716	54°32·2'	3°16·5'W	FM	89,90
Wilkin Throop	Somer	ST6823	51°0·6'	2°27·0'W	T	183
Wilksby	Lincs	TF2862	53°8·6'	0°4·8'W	T	122
Wilks Fm	N Yks	NZ7809	54°28·5'	0°47·4'W	FM	94
Wilk's Hill	Durham	NZ1744	54°47·7'	1°43·7'W	X	88
Wilks Plantn	N Yks	SE6661	54°2·7'	0°59·1'W	F	100
Wilks Rigg	N Yks	NZ7909	54°28·5'	0°46·4'W	X	94
Wilkswood Fm	Dorset	SY9979	50°36·9'	2°0·5'W	FM	195
Wilksworth Fm	Dorset	SU0001	50°48·7'	1°59·6'W	FM	195
Wilkwood Burn	Northum	NT8703	55°19·5'	2°11·9'W	W	80
Wilkwood East	Northum	NT8902	55°19·0'	2°10·0'W	X	80
Will	Somer	ST1132	51°5·1'	3°15·9'W	X	181
Willacy Lane End	Lancs	SD4735	53°48·8'	2°47·9'W	T	102
Willake	Corn	SX1557	50°23·3'	4°35·8'W	X	201
Willa-mina Hoga	Shetld	HU4885	60°33·0'	1°7·0'W	X	1,2,3
Willand	Devon	ST0310	50°53·1'	3°22·4'W	T	192
Willand	Somer	ST1913	50°54·9'	3°8·8'W	T	181,193
Willand Moor	Devon	ST0411	50°53·7'	3°21·5'W	T	192
Willand Wood	W Susx	SU9727	51°2·3'	0°36·6'W	F	186,197
Willanslea	Aberd	NJ9052	57°33·7'	2°9·6'W	X	30
Willanyards	Angus	NO6253	56°40·3'	2°36·8'W	X	54
Willapark	Corn	SX0689	50°40·3'	4°44·4'W	X	200
Willapark	Corn	SX0891	50°41·5'	4°42·7'W	X	190
Willard's Hill	E Susx	TQ7124	50°59·6'	0°26·6'E	T	199
Willaston	Ches	SJ3377	53°17·4'	2°59·9'W	T	117
Willaston	Ches	SJ6752	53°4·1'	2°29·1'W	T	118
Willaston	I of M	SC3877	54°10·0'	4°28·5'W	X	95
Willaston	Shrops	SJ5935	52°54·9'	2°36·2'W	T	126
Willaston Fm	Oxon	SP6029	51°57·6'	1°7·2'W	FM	164,165
Willaston Village	Oxon	SP6029	51°57·6'	1°7·2'W	A	164,165
Willa Water	Shetld	HU6590	60°35·6'	0°48·3'W	W	1,2
Willcross	Lancs	SD8449	53°56·5'	2°14·2'W	X	103
Willdale	Cumbr	NY4817	54°33·0'	2°47·8'W	X	90
Willen	Mil Key	SP8741	52°3·9'	0°43·5'W	T	152
Willenhall	Cov	SP3676	52°23·1'	1°27·9'W	T	140
Willenhall	Wals	SO9698	52°35·0'	2°3·1'W	T	139

Willen Lake	Mil Key	SP8839	52°2·8'	0°42·6'W	W	152
Willen Park	Mil Key	SP8740	52°3·3'	0°43·5'W	X	152
Willerby	E Yorks	TA0230	53°45·6'	0°26·8'W	T	106,107
Willerby	N Yks	TA0079	54°12·1'	0°27·6'W	X	101
Willerby Carr	N Yks	TA0079	54°12·1'	0°27·6'W	X	101
Willerby Carr Fm	K upon H	TA0530	53°45·6'	0°24·0'W	FM	107
Willerby Wold Fm	N Yks	TA0176	54°10·4'	0°26·7'W	FM	101
Willersey	Glos	SP1039	52°3·2'	1°50·9'W	T	150
Willersey Hill	Glos	SP1138	52°2·7'	1°50·0'W	X	150
Willersley	Heref	SO3147	52°7·3'	3°0·1'W	T	148
Willersley Castle	Derby	SK2957	53°6·8'	1°33·6'W	X	119
Willesborough	Kent	TR0241	51°8·2'	0°53·6'E	T	189
Willesborough Lees	Kent	TR0342	51°8·7'	0°54·5'E	T	179,189
Willesden	Brent	TQ2284	51°32·7'	0°14·0'W	T	176
Willesden Green	Brent	TQ2283	51°32·2'	0°14·1'W	T	176
Willesleigh Fm	Devon	SS6033	51°5·0'	3°59·5'W	FM	180
Willesley	Devon	SX4280	50°36·1'	4°13·6'W	X	201
Willesley	Leic	SK3414	52°43·6'	1°29·4'W	T	128
Willesley	Wilts	ST8588	51°35·7'	2°12·6'W	T	162,173
Willesley Warren Fm	Hants	SU5052	51°16·1'	1°16·6'W	FM	185
Willestrew	Devon	SX4378	50°35·1'	4°12·7'W	X	201
Willett	Somer	ST1033	51°5·6'	3°16·7'W	T	181
Willett Hill	Somer	ST0933	51°5·6'	3°17·6'W	H	181
Willett Ho	Somer	ST1134	51°6·1'	3°15·9'W	X	181
Willett's Fm	E Susx	TQ5039	51°8·1'	0°9·0'E	FM	188
Willetts Fm	W Susx	TQ0920	50°58·4'	0°26·5'W	FM	198
Willey	Devon	SX6495	50°44·6'	3°55·3'W	X	191
Willey	Shrops	SO6799	52°35·5'	2°28·8'W	T	138
Willey	Warw	SP4984	52°27·3'	1°16·3'W	T	140
Willey Fields Fm	Warw	SP4885	52°27·9'	1°17·2'W	FM	140
Willey Fm, The	Ches	SJ5347	53°1·3'	2°41·6'W	FM	117
Willey Green	Surrey	SU9351	51°15·3'	0°39·6'W	T	186
Willey Hall	Heref	SO3267	52°18·1'	2°59·4'W	X	137,148
Willey Lodge	Heref	SO3369	52°19·1'	2°58·6'W	X	137,148
Willey Moor	Ches	SJ5346	53°0·8'	2°41·6'W	X	117
Willey Park	Shrops	SO6699	52°35·5'	2°29·7'W	X	138
Willey Place	Surrey	SU8145	51°12·1'	0°50·0'W	X	186
Willey Spring	Notts	SK4749	53°2·4'	1°17·5'W	F	129
Willey Spring	Notts	SK4750	53°2·9'	1°17·5'W	F	120
Willey Wood Fm	Notts	SK4749	53°2·4'	1°17·5'W	FM	129
Willgate Fm	Staffs	SJ9558	53°7·4'	2°4·1'W	FM	118
Will Hall Fm	Hants	SU7039	51°9·0'	0°59·6'W	FM	186
Willhayne	Devon	SY2394	50°44·7'	3°5·1'W	X	192,193
Willhayne	Somer	ST3110	50°53·4'	2°58·5'W	T	193
Will Houll	Shetld	HU4940	60°8·8'	1°6·6'W	X	4
William Beck Fm	N Yks	SE5699	54°23·2'	1°7·8'W	FM	100
William Clough	Derby	SK0689	53°24·1'	1°54·2'W	X	110
Williamcraigs	W Loth	NS9875	55°57·7'	3°37·6'W	X	65
Williamfield	Pth & Kin	NN8507	56°14·8'	3°50·9'W	X	58
Williamgill	Cumbr	NY5759	54°55·7'	2°39·8'W	X	86
William Gill	N Yks	NY9206	54°27·2'	2°7·0'W	W	91,92
William Girling Reservoir	Enf	TQ3694	51°37·9'	0°1·7'W	W	166,177
Williamhope	Scot Bord	NT4133	55°35·5'	2°55·7'W	T	73
William Law	Scot Bord	NT4739	55°38·8'	2°50·1'W	H	73
Williamlaw	Scot Bord	NT4739	55°38·8'	2°50·1'W	X	73
Williamrig Cottage	Scot Bord	NT5926	55°31·8'	2°38·5'W	X	73,74
William's Cleugh	Northum	NY6499	55°17·3'	2°33·6'W	X	80
Williamscot	Oxon	SP4845	52°6·3'	1°17·6'W	T	151
Williamscot Ho	Oxon	SP4745	52°6·3'	1°18·4'W	A	151
Williamsetter	Shetld	HU3821	59°58·6'	1°18·7'W	T	4
Williamsfield	D & G	NX9282	55°7·5'	3°41·2'W	X	78
Williamsfield	D & G	NY2970	55°1·4'	3°6·2'W	X	85
William's Fm	Essex	TL6424	51°53·6'	0°23·4'E	FM	167
William's Fm	Essex	TL8913	51°47·2'	0°44·8'E	FM	168
Williamsgate	Cumbr	NY1334	54°41·9'	3°20·6'W	X	89
Williamsgill	Cumbr	NY6228	54°39·0'	2°34·9'W	X	91
William's Green	Suff	TL9842	52°2·7'	0°53·6'E	T	155
Williams Hill	N Yks	SE1287	54°17·0'	1°48·5'W	X	99
William's Hill (Motte & Bailey)	N Yks	SE1287	54°17·0'	1°48·5'W	A	99
Williamsland Fm	Lancs	SD4664	54°4·4'	2°49·1'W	FM	97
Williamslee	Scot Bord	NT3143	55°40·8'	3°5·4'W	T	73
Williamslee Burn	Scot Bord	NT3144	55°41·3'	3°5·4'W	W	73
Williamson	D & G	NY0893	55°13·6'	3°26·4'W	X	78
Williamson Br	N Yks	SD9151	53°57·5'	2°7·8'W	X	103
Williamson Park	Lancs	SD4861	54°2·8'	2°47·2'W	X	97
Williamson's Monument	Cumbr	NY4500	54°23·8'	2°50·4'W	X	90
Williams's Wood	Staffs	SJ8624	52°49·0'	2°12·1'W	F	127
Williamston	Moray	NJ1669	57°42·4'	3°24·1'W	X	28
Williamston	Northum	NY6851	54°51·4'	2°29·5'W	X	86,87
Williamston	Pemb	SM9806	51°43·2'	4°55·1'W	X	157,158
Williamston	Pth & Kin	NN9722	56°23·0'	3°39·6'W	X	52,53,58
Williamston	Pth & Kin	NO1330	56°27·5'	3°24·3'W	X	53
Williamston Common	Northum	NY6953	54°52·5'	2°28·6'W	H	86,87
Williamstone Fm	E Loth	NT5384	56°3·0'	2°44·8'W	FM	66
Williamston Fm	Pth & Kin	NN9528	56°26·2'	3°41·7'W	FM	52,53,58
Williamston Ho	Aberd	NJ6431	57°22·3'	2°35·5'W	X	29,37
Williamstown	Aberd	NJ5560	57°37·9'	2°44·8'W	X	29
Williamstown	Rho Cyn Taf	ST0090	51°36·2'	3°26·2'W	T	170
Williamstrip Fm	Glos	SP1606	51°45·4'	1°45·7'W	FM	163
Williamstrip Park	Glos	SP1505	51°44·8'	1°46·6'W	X	163
Williamthorpe	Derby	SK4265	53°11·1'	1°21·9'W	T	120
Williamwood	D & G	NY2071	55°1·9'	3°14·7'W	X	85
Williamwood	E Renf	NS5657	55°47·3'	4°17·4'W	T	64
William Wood	Notts	SK4951	53°3·5'	1°15·7'W	F	120
William Wood Fm	Notts	SK5468	53°12·6'	1°11·1'W	FM	120
Willian	Herts	TL2230	51°57·5'	0°13·1'W	T	166
Willicote Pastures	Warw	SP1749	52°8·6'	1°44·7'W	X	151
Willicroft Fm	Devon	SS8717	50°56·7'	3°36·1'W	FM	181
Willicroft Moor	Devon	SS8718	50°57·3'	3°36·1'W	X	181
Willieanna	D & G	NX5795	55°14·0'	4°14·5'W	H	77
Williekeld Sike	Cumbr	NY5931	54°40·6'	2°37·7'W	W	91
Willie Law	Northum	NU0926	55°31·9'	1°51·0'W	H	75
Williemont Hass	S Lanak	NT0114	55°24·8'	3°33·4'W	H	78
Williescrook	Scot Bord	NT6421	55°29·1'	2°33·7'W	X	74
Willie's Law	Scot Bord	NT5660	55°50·1'	2°41·7'W	H	67
Willie's Taing	Shetld	HU1862	60°20·8'	1°39·9'W	X	3
Williestruther Loch	Scot Bord	NT4911	55°23·7'	2°47·9'W	W	79
Willie Wife Moor	Cumbr	NY3312	54°30·2'	3°1·7'W	X	90
Williford	Staffs	SK1610	52°41·5'	1°45·4'W	X	128

Willimontswick	Northum	NY7763	54°57·9'	2°21·1'W	A	86,87
Willingale	Essex	TL5907	51°44·6'	0°18·6'E	T	167
Willingcott	Devon	SS4843	51°10·2'	4°10·1'W	T	180
Willingdon	E Susx	TQ5802	50°48·0'	0°14·9'E	T	199
Willingdon Hill	E Susx	TQ5700	50°46·9'	0°14·0'E	X	199
Willing Fm	Devon	SX7561	50°26·4'	3°45·2'W	FM	202
Willingford	Somer	SS8133	51°5·3'	3°41·6'W	X	181
Willingford Fm	E Susx	TQ6522	50°58·6'	0°21·4'E	FM	199
Willingham	Cambs	TL4070	52°18·8'	0°3·6'E	T	154
Willingham	Suff	TM4384	52°24·2'	1°34·8'E	T	156
Willingham by Stow	Lincs	SK8784	53°21·0'	0°41·2'W	T	121
Willingham Fen	Lincs	TF0271	53°13·8'	0°27·9'W	X	121
Willingham Forest	Lincs	TF1191	53°24·5'	0°19·4'W	F	113
Willingham Green	Cambs	TL6254	52°9·9'	0°22·5'E	T	154
Willingham Hall	Suff	TM4586	52°25·2'	1°36·6'E	X	156
Willingham Woods	Lincs	TF1388	53°22·8'	0°17·7'W	F	113,121
Willinghurst Ho	Surrey	TQ0542	51°10·3'	0°29·5'W	X	187
Willingstone	Devon	SX7588	50°40·9'	3°45·8'W	X	191
Willings Walls Warren	Devon	SX5865	50°28·3'	3°59·7'W	X	202
Willington	Beds	TL1149	52°7·9'	0°22·3'W	T	153
Willington	Derby	SK2928	52°51·2'	1°33·8'W	T	128
Willington	Durham	NZ1935	54°42·8'	1°41·9'W	T	92
Willington	Kent	TQ7853	51°15·1'	0°33·4'E	T	188
Willington	N Tyne	NZ3167	55°0·0'	1°30·5'W	T	88
Willington	Warw	SP2639	52°3·2'	1°36·9'W	T	151
Willington Corner	Ches	SJ5366	53°11·6'	2°41·8'W	T	117
Willington Court	Glos	SO8323	51°54·6'	2°14·4'W	X	162
Willington Cross	Wrex	SJ4442	52°58·6'	2°49·6'W	X	117
Willington Down Fm	Oxon	SU5491	51°37·1'	1°12·8'W	FM	164,174
Willington Hall	Ches	SJ5366	53°11·6'	2°41·8'W	X	117
Willington Quay	N Tyne	NZ3266	54°59·5'	1°29·6'W	T	88
Willingtons, The	Ches	SJ5466	53°11·6'	2°40·9'W	X	117
Willis Elm	Glos	ST6597	51°40·5'	2°30·0'W	X	162
Willis Fm	W Berks	SU3276	51°29·2'	1°32·0'W	FM	174
Willisham	Suff	TM0750	52°6·8'	1°1·8'E	T	155
Willisham Tye	Suff	TM0651	52°7·4'	1°1·0'E	T	155
Willishayes Fm	Devon	SS9425	51°1·1'	3°30·3'W	FM	181
Willis Hill	Monm	ST5092	51°37·7'	2°43·0'W	X	162,172
Willis's Cross	Devon	SX7975	50°34·0'	3°42·1'W	X	191
Willitoft	E Yorks	SE7435	53°48·6'	0°52·2'W	T	105,106
Williton	Somer	ST0741	51°9·9'	3°19·4'W	T	181
Will Moor	Lancs	SD9136	53°49·5'	2°7·8'W	X	103
Willochsheuch Moss	S Lanak	NS6938	55°37·3'	4°4·4'W	X	71
Willot Hall	Ches	SJ3880	53°19·2'	2°10·4'W	X	109
Willott's Hill	Staffs	SJ9561	53°9·0'	2°4·1'W	X	118
Willoughbridge	Staffs	SJ7440	52°57·6'	2°22·8'W	X	118
Willoughbridge Fm	Staffs	SJ7439	52°57·1'	2°22·8'W	FM	127
Willoughbridge Lodge	Staffs	SJ7338	52°56·6'	2°23·7'W	X	127
Willoughbridge Wells	Staffs	SJ7439	52°57·1'	2°22·8'W	X	127
Willoughby	Lincs	TF4671	53°13·2'	0°11·6'E	T	122
Willoughby	Warw	SP5167	52°18·2'	1°14·7'W	T	151
Willoughby Fields Fm	Leic	SK6422	52°47·7'	1°2·6'W	FM	129
Willoughby Fm	Lincs	TF2842	52°57·8'	0°5·2'W	FM	131
Willoughby Fm	Notts	SK7763	53°9·7'	0°50·5'W	FM	120
Willoughby Fm	Notts	SK7862	53°9·2'	0°49·6'W	FM	120,121
Willoughby Gorse	Lincs	TF0842	52°58·1'	0°23·1'W	F	130
Willoughby Hall	Durham	NY9518	54°33·7'	2°4·2'W	X	91,92
Willoughby Heath	Lincs	SK9642	52°58·2'	0°33·8'W	X	130
Willoughby Hedge	Wilts	ST8733	51°6·0'	2°10·8'W	X	183
Willoughby High Drain	Lincs	TF5271	53°13·1'	0°17·0'E	W	122
Willoughby Hills	Lincs	TF3445	52°59·4'	0°0·2'E	T	131
Willoughby Ho	Lincs	TF1541	52°57·5'	0°16·9'W	X	130
Willoughby Ho	Lincs	TF2023	52°47·7'	0°12·8'W	X	131
Willoughby Ho	Lincs	TF2839	52°56·2'	0°5·3'W	X	131
Willoughby Ho	Warw	SP5166	52°17·6'	1°14·7'W	X	151
Willoughby Lodge	Leic	SK6421	52°47·2'	1°2·7'W	X	129
Willoughby Lodge	Notts	SK6326	52°49·9'	1°3·5'W	X	129
Willoughby Lodge	Warw	SP5368	52°18·7'	1°13·0'W	X	152
Willoughby Lodge Fm	Leic	SP5791	52°31·1'	1°9·2'W	FM	140
Willoughby-on-the-Wolds	Notts	SK6325	52°49·4'	1°3·5'W	T	129
Willoughbys	Wigan	SD6009	53°34·8'	2°35·8'W	X	109
Willoughby's Fm	Essex	TL7725	51°53·9'	0°34·8'E	FM	167
Willoughby Walks	Lincs	TF0342	52°58·2'	0°27·6'W	X	130
Willoughby Waterleys	Leic	SP5792	52°31·6'	1°9·2'W	T	140
Willoughby Wood	Lincs	TF4670	53°12·7'	0°11·6'E	F	122
Willoughton	Lincs	SK9393	53°25·8'	0°35·6'W	T	112
Willoughton Cliff	Lincs	SK9492	53°25·2'	0°34·7'W	X	112
Willoughton Grange	Lincs	SK9092	53°25·3'	0°38·3'W	X	112
Willoughton Manor	Lincs	SK9393	53°25·8'	0°35·6'W	X	112
Willoughton Wood	Lincs	SK8588	53°23·2'	0°42·9'W	F	112,121
Willowbank	Aberd	NK0747	57°31·0'	1°52·5'W	X	30
Willowbank	Bucks	TQ0585	51°33·5'	0°28·7'W	T	176
Willow Bank	Cumbr	NY4365	54°58·8'	2°53·0'W	X	85
Willowbank	D & G	NX6865	54°58·0'	4°3·3'W	X	83,84
Willowbank	Stir	NS8690	56°5·6'	3°49·5'W	X	58
Willow Beck	N Yks	SE4376	54°10·9'	1°20·0'W	W	99
Willowbed Fm	Kent	TQ9939	51°7·2'	0°51·0'E	FM	189
Willowbog	Northum	NY5989	55°11·9'	2°38·2'W	X	80
Willowbog	Northum	NY7975	55°4·4'	2°19·3'W	X	86,87
Willow Br	N Yks	NZ2410	54°29·3'	1°37·3'W	X	93
Willow Bridge	N Yks	SE7261	54°2·6'	0°53·6'W	X	100
Willowbridge Wood	N Yks	SE7262	54°3·2'	0°53·6'W	F	100
Willow Brook	Northnts	SP9996	52°33·4'	0°32·0'W	W	141
Willow Brook	Northnts	TL0693	52°31·7'	0°25·8'W	W	142
Willowbrook Fm	Bucks	SP8320	51°52·6'	0°47·3'W	FM	165
Willowbrow Fm	Wirral	SJ3179	53°18·5'	3°1·7'W	FM	117
Willow Burn	D & G	NY0668	55°0·1'	3°27·7'W	W	85
Willow Burn	Northum	NT8436	55°37·3'	2°14·8'W	W	74
Willowfield	Lincs	TF1412	52°41·9'	0°18·4'W	X	130,142
Willow Fm	Bucks	SP9817	51°50·8'	0°34·2'W	FM	165
Willow Fm	Cambs	TF3706	52°38·3'	0°1·9'E	FM	142,143
Willow Fm	Cambs	TL3395	52°32·4'	0°1·9'W	FM	142
Willow Fm	Cambs	TL4884	52°26·3'	0°11·0'E	FM	143
Willow Fm	Cambs	TL4990	52°29·5'	0°12·1'E	FM	143
Willow Fm	Cambs	TL6175	52°21·2'	0°22·2'E	FM	143
Willow Fm	Ches	SJ6553	53°4·6'	2°30·9'W	FM	118
Willow Fm	Essex	TM1818	51°49·3'	1°10·2'E	FM	168,169
Willow Fm	E Yorks	SE7637	53°49·6'	0°50·3'W	FM	105,106
Willow Fm	E Yorks	SE7740	53°51·3'	0°49·3'W	FM	105,106
Willow Fm	Flint	SJ3469	53°13·1'	2°58·9'W	FM	117

Willow Fm	Kent	TQ4956	51°17·2′	0°8·6′E	FM	188
Willow Fm	Kent	TQ9330	51°2·4′	0°45·6′E	FM	189
Willow Fm	Kent	TR0529	51°1·6′	0°55·8′E	FM	189
Willow Fm	Leic	SK4509	52°40·8′	1°19·7′W	FM	140
Willow Fm	Leic	SK7530	52°52·0′	0°52·7′W	FM	129
Willow Fm	Leic	SP5696	52°33·8′	1°10·0′W	FM	140
Willow Fm	Leic	SP5789	52°30·0′	1°9·2′W	FM	140
Willow Fm	Lincs	TF0194	53°26·2′	0°28·4′W	FM	112
Willow Fm	Lincs	TF1463	53°9·3′	0°17·3′W	FM	121
Willow Fm	Lincs	TF2733	52°53·0′	0°6·3′W	FM	131
Willow Fm	Lincs	TF4782	53°19·1′	0°12·8′E	FM	122
Willow Fm	Lincs	TF4977	53°16·4′	0°14·5′E	FM	122
Willow Fm	Norf	TF9112	52°40·5′	0°49·9′E	FM	132
Willow Fm	Norf	TG0414	52°41·3′	1°1·5′E	FM	133
Willow Fm	Norf	TL5998	52°33·6′	0°21·1′E	FM	143
Willow Fm	Norf	TM0180	52°23·1′	0°57·6′E	FM	144
Willow Fm	Norf	TM0193	52°30·1′	0°58·1′E	FM	144
Willow Fm	Norf	TM1185	52°25·6′	1°6·6′E	FM	144
Willow Fm	Norf	TM2082	52°23·7′	1°14·4′E	FM	156
Willow Fm	Norf	TM4399	52°32·3′	1°35·4′E	FM	134
Willow Fm	N Yks	SE8373	54°9·0′	0°43·3′W	FM	100
Willow Fm	Suff	TL7761	52°13·4′	0°35·9′E	FM	155
Willow Fm	Suff	TM0767	52°16·0′	1°2·4′E	FM	155
Willow Fm	Suff	TM0973	52°19·1′	1°4·4′E	FM	144,155
Willow Fm	Suff	TM3472	52°18·0′	1°26·3′E	FM	156
Willowford	Cumbr	NY6266	54°59·5′	2°35·2′W	X	86
Willowford Burn	Scot Bord	NT6415	55°25·9′	2°33·7′W	W	80
Willow Garth	Leeds	SE3245	53°54·3′	1°30·4′W	F	104
Willow Garth	N Yks	SE1489	54°18·0′	1°46·7′W	X	99
Willowgarth Plantn	N Yks	SE4350	53°56·9′	1°20·3′W	F	105
Willow Gill	N Yks	SE1695	54°21·3′	1°44·8′W	W	99
Willowgrain Hill	D & G	NS8412	55°23·5′	3°49·5′W	H	71,78
Willow Grange	Norf	TF9319	52°44·3′	0°51·9′E	X	132
Willow Grange	N Yks	SE8480	54°12·8′	0°42·3′W	X	100
Willow Grange Fm	Cambs	TL4971	52°19·2′	0°11·6′E	FM	154
Willow Green	Ches	SJ6076	53°17·0′	2°35·6′W	T	118
Willow Green	Worcs	SO7658	52°13·4′	2°20·7′W	T	150
Willow Grove	York	SE6454	53°58·9′	1°1·0′W	X	105,106
Willow Grove Fm	Leeds	SE4126	53°44·0′	1°22·3′W	FM	105
Willow Hall	Essex	TM1729	51°55·3′	1°9·7′E	X	168,169
Willow Hall	Peterb	TF2401	52°35·8′	0°9·8′W	X	142
Willow Hall	Suff	TM1168	52°16·4′	1°6·0′E	X	155
Willow Hall Fm	Cambs	TL4175	52°21·5′	0°4·6′E	FM	142,143
Willow Hill	Ches	SJ5255	53°5·6′	2°42·6′W	X	117
Willow Hill	Cumbr	NY4165	54°58·8′	2°54·9′W	X	85
Willowhill Fm	Beds	TL1249	52°7·9′	0°21·4′W	FM	153
Willow Hill Fm	N Yks	SE1449	53°56·5′	1°46·8′W	FM	104
Willow Ho	N Yks	SE2155	53°59·7′	1°40·4′W	X	104
Willow Holme	Cumbr	NY3956	54°54·0′	2°56·6′W	T	85
Willow Holt	Notts	SK5985	53°21·8′	1°6·4′W	F	111,120
Willow House Fm	E Yorks	TA3125	53°42·5′	0°0·5′W	FM	107,113
Willow House Fm	N Yks	SE2373	54°9·4′	1°38·5′W	FM	99
Willowlands Laithe	N Yks	SD9758	54°1·3′	2°2·3′W	X	103
Willow Lodge	Lincs	TF5165	53°9·9′	0°15·9′E	X	122
Willowmoor	Wrekin	SJ6408	52°40·4′	2°31·5′W	X	127
Willowmore Hill	Staffs	SJ8819	52°46·3′	2°10·3′W	H	127
Willowpark	Devon	SS9200	50°47·6′	3°31·6′W	X	192
Willow Pool	Cumbr	NY3973	55°3·1′	2°56·9′W	W	85
Willow Row Drain	Norf	TL5893	52°30·9′	0°20·1′E	W	143
Willow Row Farms	Cambs	TL5890	52°29·3′	0°20·0′E	FM	143
Willows	Bolton	SD7008	53°34·3′	2°26·8′W	T	109
Willows Fm	Herts	TL4428	51°56·1′	0°6·1′E	FM	167
Willows Fm	Lincs	TF3347	53°0·5′	0°0·7′W	FM	131
Willows Fm	Norf	TG0815	52°41·8′	1°5·1′E	FM	133
Willows Fm	Suff	TM2979	52°21·9′	1°22·2′E	FM	156
Willows Green	Essex	TL7219	51°50·8′	0°30·2′E	T	167
Willow's Green Inclosure	Hants	SU8141	51°10·0′	0°51·1′W	F	186
Willows, The	Ches	SJ3870	53°13·6′	2°55·3′W	X	117
Willows, The	Heref	SO4371	52°20·3′	2°49·8′W	X	137,148
Willows, The	Leic	SK4428	52°51·1′	1°20·4′W	X	129
Willows, The	Leic	SK7424	52°48·7′	0°53·7′W	X	129
Willows, The	Lincs	TF2352	53°3·3′	0°9·5′W	X	122
Willows, The	N Yks	TA1274	54°9·2′	0°16·7′W	X	101
Willows, The	Peterb	TF2008	52°39·6′	0°13·1′W	X	142
Willows, The	Suff	TM3359	52°11·0′	1°24·9′E	X	156
Willow Toft	E Yorks	TA2532	53°46·4′	0°5·8′W	X	107
Willow Toft Fox Covert	E Yorks	TA2532	53°46·4′	0°5·8′W	F	107
Willowtops Ho	Lincs	SK8740	52°57·3′	0°41·9′W	X	130
Willowtown	Blae Gw	SO1610	51°47·2′	3°12·7′W	T	161
Willow Tree	N Yks	SD6567	54°6·1′	2°31·7′W	X	97
Willow Tree	N Yks	SD7664	54°4·5′	2°21·6′W	X	98
Willowtree Fm	Ches	SJ6459	53°7·9′	2°31·9′W	FM	118
Willow Tree Fm	Lincs	SK8147	53°1·1′	0°47·1′W	FM	130
Willow Tree Fm	Lincs	TF2217	52°44·4′	0°11·2′W	FM	131
Willow Tree Fm	Lincs	TF3597	53°27·4′	0°2·4′E	FM	113
Willow Tree Fm	Lincs	TF4320	52°45·7′	0°7·6′E	FM	131
Willow Tree Fm	N Yks	NZ5706	54°27·0′	1°6·8′W	FM	93
Willowtree Fm	N Yks	SE3396	54°21·7′	1°29·1′W	FM	99
Willow Tree Fm	Suff	TL9337	52°0·1′	0°49·1′E	FM	155
Willow Tree Ho	Lincs	TF3732	52°52·3′	0°2·5′E	X	131
Willow Tree Ho	Lincs	TF3798	53°27·9′	0°4·2′E	X	113
Willow Wood	Suff	TM0065	52°15·0′	0°56·2′E	X	155
Willoxton	E Ayr	NS5124	55°29·5′	4°21·1′W	X	70
Willoxton Fm	Swan	SS5490	51°35·6′	4°6·1′W	FM	159
Will Pitts	Donc	SE7415	53°37·8′	0°52·4′W	F	112
Will Row	Lincs	TF4586	53°21·3′	0°11·1′E	T	113,122
Will's Ayley	Essex	TL5738	52°1·3′	0°17·7′E	X	154
Willsbridge	S Glos	ST6670	51°25·9′	2°29·0′W	T	172
Willsbury Fm	Glos	SO5804	51°44·2′	2°36·1′W	FM	162
Wills Cleuch Head	S Lanak	NT0320	55°28·1′	3°31·6′W	H	72
Willsfield	Falk	NS8085	56°2·8′	3°55·2′W	T	57,65
Will's Fm	Kent	TR0431	51°2·7′	0°55·0′E	FM	189
Wills Fm	Rut	SK8302	52°36·8′	0°46·0′W	FM	141
Wills Fm	Somer	ST5252	51°16·1′	2°40·9′W	FM	182,183
Will's Knowe	Northum	NY6184	55°9·2′	2°36·3′W	X	80
Willsland	Corn	SX1554	50°21·6′	4°35·7′W	X	201
Willslock	Staffs	SK0730	52°52·3′	1°53·4′W	T	128
Wills Neck	Somer	ST1635	51°6·7′	3°11·6′W	H	181
Wills Pastures	Warw	SP4356	52°12·3′	1°21·8′W	X	151
Will's Rock	Corn	SW8572	50°30·7′	5°1·6′W	X	200

Will's Strand	I of M	SC2686	54°14·7′	4°39·8′W	X	95
Willstock Fm	Somer	ST2934	51°6·3′	3°0·5′W	FM	182
Willstone	Shrops	SO4995	52°33·3′	2°44·7′W	T	137,138
Willstone Hill	Shrops	SO4894	52°32·7′	2°45·6′W	H	137,138
Will's Wood	Aberd	NO8073	56°51·1′	2°19·2′W	F	45
Willswood Fm	Hants	SU3312	50°54·6′	1°31·5′W	FM	196
Willsworthy	Corn	SX2896	50°44·5′	4°25·9′W	X	190
Willsworthy	Devon	SX5381	50°36·8′	4°4·3′W	X	191,201
Willsworthy Artillery Range	Devon	SX5583	50°38·0′	4°2·6′W	X	191
Willsworthy Cross	Corn	SX2796	50°44·5′	4°26·7′W	X	190
Willsworthy Fm	Devon	SX9484	50°39·0′	3°29·6′W	FM	192
Willsworthy Range	Devon	SX5483	50°37·9′	4°3·5′W	X	191,201
Willtown	Devon	SX4091	50°42·0′	4°15·6′W	X	190
Willwick Hill Plantn	N Lincs	SE8923	53°42·0′	0°38·7′W	F	106,112
Willwife Wood	Lancs	SD6233	53°47·8′	2°34·2′W	F	102,103
Willy Howe	E Yorks	SE9565	54°4·6′	0°32·5′W	A	101
Willy Howe	E Yorks	TA0672	54°8·2′	0°22·2′W	A	101
Willy Howe Fm	E Yorks	TA0572	54°8·2′	0°23·2′W	FM	101
Willy Knot	Cumbr	NY2936	54°43·1′	3°5·7′W	X	89,90
Willypark Wood	Shrops	SJ6700	52°36·0′	2°28·8′W	F	127
Willyshaw Rigg	Northum	NY7351	54°51·4′	2°24·8′W	X	86,87
Wilmans	Lancs	SD7550	53°57·0′	2°22·4′W	X	103
Wilma Skerry	Shetld	HU1559	60°19·2′	1°43·2′W	X	3
Wilmaston Fm	Heref	SO3440	52°3·5′	2°57·4′W	FM	148,149,161
Wilmcote	Warw	SP1658	52°13·4′	1°45·5′W	T	151
Wilmcote Manor	Warw	SP1657	52°12·9′	1°45·6′W	X	151
Wilmere Ho	Halton	SJ5189	53°24·0′	2°43·8′W	X	108
Wilmersham	Somer	SS8743	51°10·7′	3°36·6′W	X	181
Wilmersham Common	Somer	SS8642	51°10·2′	3°37·5′W	X	181
Wilmingham	I of W	SZ3687	50°41·1′	1°29·0′W	X	196
Wilmington	Bath & NE Somer	ST6962	51°21·6′	2°26·3′W	T	172
Wilmington	Devon	SY2199	50°47·3′	3°6·9′W	T	192,193
Wilmington	E Susx	TQ5404	50°49·1′	0°11·6′E	T	199
Wilmington	Kent	TQ5371	51°25·3′	0°12·4′E	T	177
Wilmington	Shrops	SJ2901	52°36·4′	3°2·5′W	X	126
Wilmington Fm	Kent	TR0245	51°10·3′	0°53·8′E	FM	189
Wilmington Green	E Susx	TQ5405	50°49·7′	0°11·6′E	T	199
Wilmington Wood	E Susx	TQ5708	50°51·2′	0°14·2′E	F	199
Wilminstone	Devon	SX4976	50°34·1′	4°7·6′W	T	191,201
Wilmire Ho	Stock on T	NZ4324	54°36·8′	1°19·6′W	X	93
Wilmot Hill	Kent	TQ5753	51°15·5′	0°15·4′E	X	188
Wilmshurst	E Susx	TQ4226	51°1·2′	0°1·9′E	X	187,198
Wilmslow	Ches	SJ8480	53°19·2′	2°14·0′W	T	109
Wilmslow Park	Ches	SJ8581	53°19·8′	2°13·1′W	T	109
Wilna Geo	Shetld	HP6018	60°50·7′	0°53·3′W	X	1
Wilnecote	Staffs	SK2201	52°36·6′	1°40·1′W	T	139
Wilney Green	Norf	TM0681	52°23·5′	1°2·1′E	T	144
Wilobe Fm	Cambs	TL3378	52°23·2′	0°2·3′W	FM	142
Wilpol	I of Angl	SH3984	53°20·0′	4°24·7′W	X	114
Wilpshire	Lancs	SD6832	53°47·2′	2°28·7′W	T	103
Wilrack Fm	Shrops	SJ4300	52°35·9′	2°50·1′W	FM	126
Wilsden	Brad	SE0936	53°49·5′	1°51·4′W	T	104
Wilsden Hill	Brad	SE0836	53°49·5′	1°52·3′W	T	104
Wilsey Down	Corn	SX1987	50°39·5′	4°33·3′W	X	190
Wilsford	Lincs	TF0043	52°58·7′	0°30·2′W	T	130
Wilsford	Wilts	SU1057	51°19·0′	1°51·0′W	T	173
Wilsford	Wilts	SU1339	51°9·2′	1°48·5′W	T	184
Wilsford Down	Wilts	SU0853	51°16·8′	1°52·7′W	X	184
Wilsford Down	Wilts	SU1040	51°9·8′	1°51·0′W	X	184
Wilsford Group	Wilts	SU1139	51°9·2′	1°50·2′W	X	184
Wilsford Group (Tumuli)	Wilts	SU1139	51°9·2′	1°50·2′W	A	184
Wilsford Heath	Lincs	SK9941	52°57·7′	0°31·2′W	X	130
Wilsford Heath Fm	Lincs	SK9741	52°57·7′	0°32·9′W	FM	130
Wilsford Hill	Wilts	SU0955	51°17·9′	1°51·9′W	X	173
Wilsford Warren	Lincs	TF0343	52°58·7′	0°27·5′W	X	130
Wilsham	Devon	SS7548	51°13·3′	3°47·0′W	T	180
Wilshaw	Kirk	SE1109	53°34·9′	1°49·6′W	T	110
Wilsic	Donc	SK5696	53°27·7′	1°9·0′W	T	111
Wilsic Hall	Donc	SK5695	53°27·2′	1°9·0′W	X	111
Wilsill	N Yks	SE1864	54°4·5′	1°43·1′W	T	99
Wilsley Green	Kent	TQ7736	51°6·0′	0°32·1′E	T	188
Wilsley Pound	Kent	TQ7837	51°6·5′	0°33·0′E	T	188
Wilsmere Down Fm	Cambs	TL3850	52°8·1′	0°1·4′E	FM	154
Wilson	Hants	SU7239	51°9·0′	0°57·8′W	T	186
Wilson	Devon	SS7814	50°55·0′	3°43·8′W	X	180
Wilson	Heref	SO5523	51°54·3′	2°38·9′W	T	162
Wilson	Leic	SK4024	52°49·0′	1°24·0′W	T	129
Wilson Burn	Scot Bord	NT3715	55°25·7′	2°59·3′W	W	79
Wilson Fm	Devon	SS8317	50°56·7′	3°39·5′W	FM	181
Wilsonhall	Angus	NO5239	56°32·7′	2°46·4′W	T	54
Wilson Hall Fm	Leic	SK4125	52°49·5′	1°23·1′W	FM	129
Wilson Ho	Cumbr	SD4281	54°13·5′	2°53·0′W	X	96,97
Wilson Ho	Durham	NZ0811	54°29·9′	1°52·2′W	X	92
Wilson Ho	N Yks	SE6597	54°22·1′	0°59·6′W	X	94,100
Wilson Knowl	Staffs	SK0266	53°11·7′	1°57·8′W	X	119
Wilson Park	Cumbr	NY0321	54°34·7′	3°29·6′W	X	89
Wilson Place	Cumbr	NY3103	54°25·3′	3°3·4′W	X	90
Wilsons	Lancs	SD6746	53°54·8′	2°29·7′W	X	103
Wilson Scar	Cumbr	NY5417	54°33·0′	2°42·2′W	X	90
Wilsons Fm	Devon	SS9324	51°0·6′	3°31·1′W	FM	181
Wilson's Noup	Shetld	HU3071	60°25·6′	1°26·8′W	X	3
Wilson's Pike	Scot Bord	NY5589	55°11·8′	2°42·0′W	H	80
Wilson's Plantn	N Yks	SE2260	54°2·4′	1°39·4′W	F	99
Wilson's Plantn	York	SE6953	53°58·3′	0°56·5′W	F	105,106
Wilson's Wold Fm	N Yks	SE9872	54°8·3′	0°29·6′W	FM	101
Wilsontown	S Lanak	NS9455	55°46·9′	3°41·0′W	T	65,72
Wilson Wood	N Yks	SD6872	54°8·8′	2°29·0′W	X	98
Wilstead	Beds	TL0643	52°4·7′	0°26·8′W	T	153
Wilstead Wood	Beds	TL0742	52°4·2′	0°25·9′W	F	153
Wilster Copse	Hants	SU3656	51°18·3′	1°28·6′W	F	174
Wilsthorpe	Derby	SK4733	52°53·8′	1°17·7′W	T	129
Wilsthorpe	E Yorks	TA1664	54°3·8′	0°13·2′W	X	101
Wilsthorpe	Lincs	TF0913	52°42·5′	0°22·8′W	T	130,142
Wilsthorpe Village	E Yorks	TA1664	54°3·8′	0°13·2′W	A	101
Wilstone	Herts	SP9014	51°49·3′	0°41·3′W	T	165
Wilstone Green	Herts	SP9013	51°48·7′	0°41·3′W	T	165
Wilstone Resr	Herts	SP9013	51°48·7′	0°41·3′W	W	165
Wilstrop Grange	N Yks	SE4854	53°59·0′	1°15·7′W	X	105

Wilstrop Hall	N Yks	SE4855	53°59·6′	1°15·7′W	X	105
Wilstrop Village	N Yks	SE4855	53°59·6′	1°15·7′W	A	105
Wilstrop Wood	N Yks	SE4853	53°58·5′	1°15·7′W	F	105
Wilsummer Wood	Suff	TL7762	52°13·9′	0°35·9′E	F	155
Wilthorpe	Barns	SE3207	53°33·8′	1°30·6′W	T	110,111
Wilton	Cumbr	NY0311	54°29·4′	3°29·4′W	T	89
Wilton	Devon	SX7739	50°14·5′	3°43·1′W	X	202
Wilton	Heref	SO5824	51°55·0′	2°36·2′W	T	162
Wilton	N Yks	SE8682	54°13·8′	0°40·4′W	T	101
Wilton	Red & Cl	NZ5819	54°34·0′	1°5·8′W	T	93
Wilton	Scot Bord	NT4915	55°25·8′	2°47·9′W	T	79
Wilton	Somer	ST2223	51°0·3′	3°6·3′W	T	193
Wilton	Wilts	SU0931	51°4·9′	1°51·9′W	T	184
Wilton	Wilts	SU2661	51°21·1′	1°37·2′W	T	174
Wilton Br	Suff	TL7286	52°26·9′	0°32·3′E	X	143
Wilton Brail	Wilts	SU2762	51°21·6′	1°36·3′W	F	174
Wilton Burn	Scot Bord	NT4714	55°25·3′	2°49·8′W	W	79
Wiltonburn Hill	Scot Bord	NT4715	55°25·8′	2°49·8′W	H	79
Wilton Carr	N Yks	SE8680	54°12·7′	0°40·5′W	X	101
Wilton Castle	Red & Cl	NZ5819	54°34·0′	1°5·8′W	X	93
Wilton Common	Wilts	SU2762	51°21·6′	1°36·3′W	X	174
Wilton Dean	Scot Bord	NT4814	55°25·3′	2°48·9′W	X	79
Wilton Down	Wilts	SU2862	51°21·6′	1°35·5′W	X	174
Wilton Fm	Bucks	SU8788	51°35·3′	0°44·3′W	FM	175
Wilton Fm	Corn	SX1861	50°25·5′	4°33·4′W	FM	201
Wilton Fm	Corn	SX3158	50°24·1′	4°22·3′W	FM	201
Wilton Fm	Norf	TL7388	52°28·0′	0°33·2′E	FM	143
Wilton Grange	N Yks	SE8781	54°13·3′	0°39·5′W	X	101
Wilton Heights Plantn	N Yks	SE8584	54°14·9′	0°41·3′W	F	100
Wilton Hill	Cumbr	NY3628	54°38·8′	2°59·1′W	X	90
Wilton Hills	Lancs	SD7351	53°57·5′	2°24·3′W	X	103
Wiltonhill Wood	Suff	TL7585	52°26·3′	0°34·9′E	F	143
Wilton Ho	Wilts	SU0930	51°4·4′	1°51·9′W	A	184
Wilton Lodge	E Yorks	SE7953	53°58·3′	0°47·3′W	X	105,106
Wilton Moor Plantn	Red & Cl	NZ5718	54°33·5′	1°6·7′W	F	93
Wilton Park	Bucks	SU9690	51°36·3′	0°36·4′W	T	175,176
Wilton Park	Kirk	SE2325	53°43·5′	1°38·7′W	X	104
Wilton Park	Wilts	SU0930	51°4·4′	1°51·9′W	X	184
Wilton Place	Glos	SO7032	51°59·4′	2°25·8′W	X	149
Wilton Water	Wilts	SU2662	51°21·6′	1°37·2′W	W	174
Wilton Works (Chemicals)	Red & Cl	NZ5722	54°35·6′	1°6·6′W	X	93
Wiltown	Devon	ST1716	50°56·5′	3°10·5′W	T	181,193
Wiltown	Somer	ST3824	51°1·0′	2°52·6′W	T	193
Wiltown Valley	Devon	ST1716	50°56·5′	3°10·5′W	X	181,193
Wiltshire Coppice	Wilts	ST9217	50°57·4′	2°6·4′W	F	184
Wilverley Inclosure	Hants	SU2400	50°48·2′	1°39·2′W	F	195
Wilverley Plain	Hants	SU2501	50°48·7′	1°38·3′W	X	195
Wilverley Post	Hants	SU2402	50°49·3′	1°39·2′W	X	195
Wilway	Somer	SS9027	51°2·1′	3°33·7′W	X	181
Wilyrigg Strips	Scot Bord	NT7021	55°29·2′	2°28·1′W	W	74
Wimberry Moss	Ches	SJ9676	53°17·1′	2°3·2′W	X	118
Wimberry Moss	Oldham	SE0102	53°31·1′	1°58·7′W	X	110
Wimberry Slade	Glos	SO5912	51°48·5′	2°35·3′W	F	162
Wimbish	Essex	TL5936	52°0·2′	0°19·4′E	T	154
Wimbish Green	Essex	TL6035	51°59·6′	0°20·2′E	T	154
Wimbish Hall	Essex	TL5836	52°0·2′	0°18·5′E	X	154
Wimble	Suff	TM0864	52°14·3′	1°3·2′E	X	155
Wimbleball Lake	Somer	SS9730	51°3·8′	3°27·8′W	W	181
Wimblebury	Staffs	SK0111	52°42·0′	1°58·7′W	T	128
Wimbledon	Merton	TQ2471	51°25·7′	0°12·6′W	T	176
Wimbledon Common	Merton	TQ2271	51°25·7′	0°14·3′W	X	176
Wimbledon Park	Merton	TQ2472	51°26·2′	0°12·6′W	X	176
Wimble Hill	Hants	SU8046	51°12·7′	0°50·9′W	T	186
Wimblestone	Somer	ST4358	51°19·3′	2°48·7′W	A	172,182
Wimble Toot	Somer	ST5627	51°2·7′	2°37·3′W	A	183
Wimblington	Cambs	TL4192	52°30·7′	0°5·1′E	T	142,143
Wimblington Common	Cambs	TL4390	52°29·6′	0°6·8′E	X	142,143
Wimblington Fen	Cambs	TL4489	52°29·0′	0°7·6′E	X	142,143
Wimboldsley Hall	Ches	SJ6862	53°9·5′	2°28·3′W	X	118
Wimbolds Trafford	Ches	SJ4472	53°14·8′	2°49·9′W	T	117
Wimborne Minster	Dorset	SU0100	50°48·2′	1°58·8′W	T	195
Wimborne St Giles	Dorset	SU0312	50°54·7′	1°57·1′W	T	195
Wimbotsham	Norf	TF6105	52°37·4′	0°23·1′E	T	143
Wimbotsham Plantn	Norf	TL8199	52°33·7′	0°40·6′E	F	144
Wimland Fm	W Susx	TQ2034	51°5·8′	0°16·8′W	FM	187
Wimley Hill	Glos	ST7794	51°38·9′	2°19·6′W	X	162,172
Wimperhill Wood	Shrops	SO7476	52°23·1′	2°22·5′W	F	138
Wimpole Hall	Cambs	TL3350	52°8·2′	0°3·0′W	A	154
Wimpole Lodge	Cambs	TL3348	52°7·1′	0°3·0′W	X	154
Wimpole Way	Cambs	TL3351	52°8·7′	0°3·0′W	X	154
Wimpole Way	Cambs	TL3958	52°12·4′	0°2·5′E	X	154
Wimpson	C of Soton	SU3814	50°55·7′	1°27·2′W	T	196
Wimpstone	Warw	SP2148	52°8·0′	1°41·2′W	T	151
Wimpstone Fields Fm	Warw	SP2147	52°7·5′	1°41·2′W	FM	151
Winacre Fm	Lancs	SD3917	53°39·0′	2°55·0′W	FM	108
Winaway	Somer	SS7142	51°10·0′	3°50·3′W	H	180
Winbrook	Devon	SX3982	50°37·2′	4°16·2′W	X	201
Winburgh	Norf	TG0009	52°38·7′	0°57·8′E	T	144
Wincanton	Somer	ST7128	51°3·3′	2°24·4′W	T	183
Winceby	Lincs	TF3168	53°11·8′	0°1·9′W	A	122
Winceby	Lincs	TF3168	53°11·8′	0°1·9′W	T	122
Wincelow Hall	Essex	TL6338	52°1·2′	0°22·9′E	X	154
Wincham	Ches	SJ6775	53°16·5′	2°29·3′W	T	118
Wincham Brook	Ches	SJ6975	53°16·5′	2°27·5′W	W	118
Wincham Hall (Hotel)	Ches	SJ6875	53°16·5′	2°28·4′W	X	118
Winchatt	N Yks	NZ4300	54°23·9′	1°19·8′W	X	93
Winchbottom Fm	Bucks	SU8690	51°36·4′	0°45·1′W	FM	175
Winchburgh	W Loth	NT0874	55°57·3′	3°28·0′W	T	65
Winchcombe	Glos	SP0228	51°57·3′	1°57·9′W	T	150,163
Winchcombe Fm	Kent	TR0849	51°12·4′	0°59·1′E	FM	179,189
Winchcombe Fm	W Berks	SU5469	51°25·3′	1°13·0′W	FM	174
Winchells Fm	Dorset	ST8316	50°56·8′	2°14·1′W	FM	183
Winchelsea	E Susx	TQ9017	50°55·5′	0°42·6′E	T	189
Winchelsea Beach	E Susx	TQ9116	50°54·9′	0°43·4′E	T	189
Winchester	Fife	NO5513	56°18·7′	2°43·2′W	X	59
Winchester	Hants	SU4829	51°3·7′	1°18·5′W	T	185
Winchester Hill	Norf	TF8315	52°42·3′	0°42·9′E	X	132
Winchester's Pond	E Susx	TQ5301	50°47·5′	0°10·6′E	W	199
Winchester Wood	Hants	SU6831	51°4·7′	1°1·4′W	F	185,186
Winchestown	Blae Gw	SO1810	51°47·2′	3°10·9′W	T	161

Winchet Hill	Kent	TQ7340	51°8·2′	0°28·8′E	T	188
Winchfield	Hants	SU7654	51°17·0′	0°54·2′W	T	186
Winchfield Ho	Hants	SU7655	51°17·6′	0°54·2′W	X	175,186
Winchfield Hurst	Hants	SU7753	51°16·5′	0°53·4′W	T	186
Winch Hill Fm	Herts	TL1321	51°52·8′	0°21·1′W	FM	166
Winchmore Hill	Bucks	SU9395	51°39·0′	0°39·0′W	T	165
Winchmore Hill	Enf	TQ3194	51°38·0′	0°6·0′W	T	166,176,177
Winckley Hall	Lancs	SD7038	53°50·5′	2°26·9′W	X	103
Wincle	Ches	SJ9566	53°11·7′	2°4·1′W	T	118
Wincle Grange	Ches	SJ9565	53°11·2′	2°4·1′W	X	118
Wincle Minn	Ches	SJ9466	53°11·7′	2°5·0′W	X	118
Wincobank	Sheff	SK3891	53°25·1′	1°25·3′W	T	110,111
Wincombe	Wilts	ST8924	51°1·1′	2°9·0′W	X	184
Wincombe Park	Wilts	ST8724	51°1·1′	2°10·7′W	X	183
Wincote Fm	Staffs	SJ8227	52°50·7′	2°15·6′W	FM	127
Wincot Fm	Warw	SP1849	52°8·6′	1°43·8′W	FM	151
Wind Bay	Pemb	SR8896	51°37·6′	5°3·4′W	W	158
Windberry Top	Pemb	SN1108	51°44·6′	4°43·9′W	X	158
Windbow	Devon	SS9116	50°56·2′	3°32·7′W	X	181
Windbreck	Orkney	HY2425	59°6·6′	3°19·1′W	X	6
Windbreck	Orkney	HY2605	58°55·8′	3°16·6′W	X	6,7
Windbreck	Orkney	HY5505	58°56·1′	2°46·4′W	X	6
Windbreck	Orkney	ND4695	58°50·6′	2°55·7′W	X	7
Wind Burn	E Ayr	NS6329	55°32·4′	4°9·8′W	W	71
Wind Burn	Northum	NY8197	55°16·3′	2°17·5′W	W	80
Windbury Point	Devon	SS2826	51°0·7′	4°26·7′W	X	190
Windcatch Fm	Lincs	TF2721	52°46·5′	0°6·6′W	FM	131
Windcross Fm	Glos	SO6932	51°59·4′	2°26·7′W	FM	149
Windcutter Hill	Devon	SS4845	51°11·3′	4°10·1′W	H	180
Wind Down	Somer	ST2234	51°6·2′	3°6·5′W	X	182
Windedge	Pth & Kin	NO1529	56°27·0′	3°22·3′W	X	53,58
Winden Wood	W Susx	SU8316	50°56·5′	0°48·7′W	F	197
Winder	Cumbr	NY0417	54°32·6′	3°28·6′W	T	89
Winder	Cumbr	SD6593	54°20·1′	2°31·9′W	H	97
Winder	Lancs	SD5963	54°3·9′	2°37·2′W	X	97
Winder Brow	Cumbr	NY0417	54°32·6′	3°28·6′W	X	89
Windergill Beck	Cumbr	NY0417	54°32·6′	3°28·6′W	W	89
Winder Green	Cumbr	NY4923	54°36·2′	2°46·9′W	X	90
Winder Hall Fm	Cumbr	NY4924	54°36·8′	2°47·0′W	FM	90
Windermere	Cumbr	NY3800	54°23·7′	2°56·9′W	W	90
Windermere	Cumbr	SD3894	54°20·5′	2°56·8′W	W	96,97
Windermere	Cumbr	SD4198	54°22·7′	2°54·1′W	T	96,97
Winder Moor	Cumbr	SD3775	54°10·3′	2°57·5′W	X	96,97
Winders Hill	Surrey	TQ3553	51°15·8′	0°3·5′W	X	187
Winderton	Warw	SP3240	52°3·7′	1°31·6′W	T	151
Winderwath	Cumbr	NY5929	54°39·5′	2°37·7′W	X	91
Winderwath Fm	Cumbr	NY5928	54°39·0′	2°37·7′W	FM	91
Winder Wood	Lancs	SD5963	54°3·9′	2°37·2′W	F	97
Windfallwood Common	W Susx	SU9227	51°2·3′	0°40·9′W	X	186,197
Wind Fell	D & G	NT1706	55°20·7′	3°18·1′W	H	79
Wind Fm	Hants	SU5824	51°1·0′	1°10·0′W	FM	185
Windfold	Aberd	NJ9941	57°27·8′	2°0·5′W	X	30
Wind Gap	Cumbr	NY1611	54°29·5′	3°17·4′W	X	89
Windgate	Devon	SY1086	50°40·2′	3°16·0′W	X	192
Windgate Bank	S Lanak	NT0126	55°31·3′	3°33·7′W	H	72
Windgate Edge	Derby	SE0300	53°30·0′	1°56·9′W	X	110
Windgate Fm	Devon	ST1503	50°49·5′	3°12·0′W	FM	192,193
Windgate House	S Lanak	NT0127	55°31·9′	3°33·7′W	A	72
Windgate Nick	Brad	SE0647	53°55·4′	1°54·1′W	X	104
Windgather Rocks	Ches	SJ9978	53°18·2′	2°0·5′W	X	118
Windgill	S Lanak	NT0230	55°33·5′	3°32·8′W	X	72
Wind Hall	Cumbr	NY0704	54°25·6′	3°25·6′W	X	89
Wind Hamars	Shetld	HU4140	60°8·8′	1°15·2′W	X	4
Wind Hill	Aberd	NJ9546	57°30·5′	2°4·5′W	H	30
Windhill	Aberd	NJ9546	57°30·5′	2°4·5′W	X	30
Windhill	Brad	SE1537	53°50·0′	1°45·9′W	T	104
Wind Hill	Cumbr	SD2771	54°8·0′	3°6·6′W	T	96,97
Wind Hill	Devon	SS7349	51°13·8′	3°48·8′W	H	180
Windhill	Donc	SE4800	53°29·9′	1°16·2′W	T	111
Windhill	Highld	NH5348	57°30·2′	4°26·7′W	T	26
Wind Hill	Northum	NY6888	55°11·4′	2°29·7′W	H	80
Wind Hill	N Yks	NZ7606	54°26·9′	0°49·3′W	X	94
Wind Hill	Pemb	SS0798	51°39·1′	4°47·0′W	T	158
Windhill	S Lanak	NS7242	55°39·5′	4°1·6′W	X	71
Windhill Fm	E Renf	NS5654	55°45·7′	4°17·3′W	FM	64
Wind Hill Fm	Roch	SD8314	53°37·6′	2°15·0′W	FM	109
Windhill Fm	Worcs	SO6871	52°20·4′	2°27·8′W	FM	138
Windhill Gate	Devon	SX8187	50°40·5′	3°40·7′W	X	191
Windhouse	Shetld	HU4991	60°36·2′	1°5·8′W	T	1,2
Windicott	Staffs	SJ9546	53°0·9′	2°4·1′W	X	118
Winding Banks	Cumbr	NY1651	54°51·1′	3°18·1′W	X	85
Winding Bottom	W Susx	TQ1808	50°51·8′	0°19·0′W	X	198
Winding Cairn	Scot Bord	NT8166	55°53·5′	2°17·8′W	A	67
Windinglake Fm	Somer	ST6039	51°9·2′	2°33·9′W	FM	183
Winding Law	E Loth	NT5468	55°54·4′	2°43·7′W	X	66
Winding Shoot	Hants	SU2506	50°51·4′	1°38·3′W	X	195
Windings, The	Wrekin	SJ7211	52°42·0′	2°24·5′W	X	127
Winding Wood	W Berks	SU3870	51°25·9′	1°26·8′W	T	174
Windle Beck Fm	N Yks	SE9978	54°11·5′	0°28·5′W	FM	101
Windle Brook	Surrey	SU9262	51°21·2′	0°40·3′W	W	175,186
Windlebrook Fm	Surrey	SU9362	51°21·2′	0°39·5′W	FM	175,186
Windleden Resrs	Barns	SE1501	53°30·6′	1°46·0′W	W	110
Windle Field	Lancs	SD9246	53°54·8′	2°6·9′W	X	103
Windle Fm	Derby	SK2435	52°55·0′	1°38·2′W	FM	128
Windle Fm	St Hel	SJ4897	53°28·3′	2°46·6′W	FM	108
Windle Hall	St Hel	SJ4997	53°28·3′	2°45·7′W	X	108
Windle Hill	Ches	SJ3077	53°17·4′	3°2·6′W	T	117
Windle Hills	Norf	TM4294	52°29·6′	1°34·3′E	X	134
Windle House Fm	Brad	SE0135	53°48·9′	1°58·7′W	FM	104
Windlehurst	Stock	SJ9586	53°22·5′	2°4·1′W	T	109
Windle Park	Heref	SO2744	52°5·6′	3°3·5′W	X	148,161
Windlesham	Surrey	SU9363	51°21·7′	0°39·5′W	T	175,186
Windlesham Court	Surrey	SU9365	51°22·8′	0°39·4′W	X	175
Windlesham Hall	Surrey	SU9265	51°22·8′	0°40·3′W	X	175
Windlesham Park	Surrey	SU9463	51°21·7′	0°38·6′W	X	175,186
Windlesham (Sch)	W Susx	TQ1111	50°53·5′	0°24·9′W	X	198
Windle Side	N Yks	SD9777	54°11·6′	2°2·3′W	X	98
Windlestone Grange	Durham	NZ2528	54°39·0′	1°36·3′W	X	93
Windlestone Hall	Durham	NZ2628	54°39·0′	1°35·4′W	X	93
Windlestone Park	Durham	NZ2628	54°39·0′	1°35·4′W	X	93
Windlestraw Law	Scot Bord	NT3743	55°40·8′	2°59·7′W	H	73
Windleway	Carm	SN2411	51°46·4′	4°32·7′W	X	158
Windley	Derby	SK3045	53°0·3′	1°32·8′W	T	119,128
Windleyhill Fm	Derby	SK3144	52°59·8′	1°31·9′W	FM	119,128
Windley Meadows	Derby	SK3244	52°59·8′	1°31·0′W	X	119,128
Wind Low	Derby	SK1175	53°16·6′	1°49·7′W	A	119
Windmill	Corn	SW8974	50°31·9′	4°58·3′W	T	200
Windmill	Derby	SK1677	53°17·6′	1°45·2′W	X	119
Wind Mill	Durham	NZ1328	54°39·1′	1°47·5′W	X	92
Windmill	Flint	SJ1971	53°14·0′	3°12·4′W	T	116
Windmill	Flint	SJ2071	53°14·0′	3°11·5′W	T	117
Windmill Bank	Staffs	SJ7918	52°45·8′	2°18·3′W	H	127
Windmill Barrow	Dorset	SY9397	50°46·6′	2°5·6′W	A	195
Windmill Creek	Kent	TQ9668	51°22·9′	0°49·4′E	W	178
Windmill Cross	Devon	SS5224	51°0·0′	4°6·2′W	X	180
Windmill Down	Devon	SX7959	50°25·3′	3°41·8′W	X	202
Windmill Down	Hants	SU6415	50°56·1′	1°5·0′W	X	196
Windmill Down	Hants	SU6416	50°56·6′	1°5·0′W	X	185
Windmill Fm	Bucks	SU9991	51°36·8′	0°33·8′W	FM	175,176
Windmill Fm	Ches	SJ5057	53°6·7′	2°44·4′W	FM	117
Windmill Fm	Corn	SW6915	49°59·7′	5°13·0′W	FM	203
Windmill Fm	Derby	SK1643	52°59·3′	1°45·3′W	FM	119,128
Windmill Fm	Essex	TL6008	51°45·1′	0°19·5′E	FM	167
Windmill Fm	E Susx	TQ5937	51°6·8′	0°16·7′E	FM	188
Windmill Fm	Kent	TQ6737	51°6·7′	0°23·5′E	FM	188
Windmill Fm	Lancs	SD4215	53°37·9′	2°52·2′W	FM	108
Windmill Fm	Leic	SK4824	52°48·9′	1°16·9′W	FM	129
Windmill Fm	Leic	SP5985	52°27·8′	1°7·5′W	FM	140
Windmill Fm	Lincs	TF1417	52°44·5′	0°18·3′W	FM	130
Windmill Fm	N Yks	SE7974	54°9·6′	0°47·0′W	FM	100
Windmill Fm	Shrops	SJ3413	52°42·9′	2°58·2′W	FM	126
Windmill Fm	Somer	ST5017	50°57·2′	2°42·3′W	FM	183
Windmill Fm	Staffs	SK1905	52°38·8′	1°42·7′W	FM	139
Windmill Fm	Swan	SS4792	51°36·6′	4°12·2′W	FM	159
Windmill Fm	V of Glam	SS9978	51°29·8′	3°26·9′W	FM	170
Windmill Fm	Warw	SP3247	52°7·5′	1°31·6′W	FM	151
Windmill Fm	Warw	SP4771	52°20·3′	1°18·2′W	FM	140
Windmill Fm	W Berks	SU3077	51°29·7′	1°33·7′W	FM	174
Windmill Hill	Barns	SE4110	53°35·3′	1°22·4′W	X	111
Windmill Hill	Bucks	SP6624	51°54·9′	1°2·0′W	X	164,165
Windmill Hill	Ches	SJ3561	53°8·8′	2°57·9′W	X	117
Windmill Hill	C of Bris	ST5971	51°26·4′	2°35·0′W	T	172
Windmill Hill	Derby	SK4380	53°19·1′	1°20·9′W	X	111,120
Windmill Hill	Devon	SY0190	50°42·3′	3°23·7′W	H	192
Windmill Hill	Donc	SK5696	53°27·7′	1°9·0′W	X	111
Windmill Hill	Dorset	ST6221	50°59·5′	2°32·1′W	X	183
Windmill Hill	Essex	TL8816	51°48·9′	0°44·0′E	X	168
Windmill Hill	E Susx	TQ6412	50°53·3′	0°20·3′E	T	199
Windmill Hill	Glos	SO7815	51°50·2′	2°18·8′W	X	162
Windmill Hill	Halton	SJ5582	53°20·2′	2°40·1′W	T	108
Windmill Hill	Hants	SU0819	50°58·5′	1°52·8′W	H	184
Windmill Hill	Hants	SU4034	51°6·5′	1°25·3′W	X	185
Windmill Hill	Hants	SU6144	51°11·7′	1°7·2′W	X	185
Windmill Hill	Hants	SU7116	50°56·6′	0°59·0′W	H	197
Windmill Hill	Heref	SO5227	51°56·6′	2°41·5′W	X	162
Windmill Hill	Heref	SO6048	52°8·0′	2°34·7′W	X	149
Windmill Hill	Heref	SO6144	52°5·8′	2°33·8′W	X	149
Windmill Hill	Herts	TL2632	51°58·6′	0°9·5′W	X	166
Windmill Hill	Kent	TQ8367	51°22·6′	0°38·2′E	T	178
Windmill Hill	Lancs	SD6125	53°43·4′	2°35·1′W	X	102,103
Windmill Hill	Leic	SK4521	52°47·3′	1°19·6′W	X	129
Windmill Hill	Leic	SK8228	52°50·8′	0°46·5′W	X	130
Windmill Hill	Northum	NU0445	55°42·2′	1°55·7′W	X	75
Windmill Hill	Notts	SK5157	53°6·7′	1°13·9′W	X	120
Windmill Hill	Notts	SK5928	52°51·0′	1°7·0′W	X	129
Windmill Hill	Notts	SK6352	53°3·9′	1°3·2′W	X	120
Windmill Hill	Notts	SK6435	52°54·8′	1°2·5′W	X	129
Windmill Hill	N Som	ST5074	51°28·0′	2°42·8′W	H	172
Windmill Hill	Oxon	SU3787	51°35·1′	1°27·6′W	X	174
Windmill Hill	Oxon	SU3798	51°41·0′	1°27·5′W	X	164
Windmill Hill	Oxon	SU5598	51°40·9′	1°11·9′W	H	164
Windmill Hill	Oxon	SU7087	51°34·9′	0°59·0′W	X	175
Windmill Hill	Pemb	SM9700	51°40·0′	4°55·7′W	X	158
Windmill Hill	Somer	ST3116	50°56·6′	2°58·5′W	T	193
Windmill Hill	Somer	ST3327	51°2·5′	2°57·0′W	X	193
Windmill Hill	Somer	ST4948	51°14·0′	2°43·4′W	H	182,183
Windmill Hill	Somer	ST5111	50°54·0′	2°41·4′W	X	194
Windmill Hill	Somer	ST5129	51°3·7′	2°41·6′W	X	183
Windmill Hill	Somer	ST5435	51°7·0′	2°39·0′W	H	182,183
Windmill Hill	Somer	ST6723	51°0·6′	2°27·8′W	H	183
Windmill Hill	Somer	ST7021	50°59·5′	2°25·3′W	X	183
Windmill Hill	Somer	ST7129	51°3·8′	2°24·4′W	H	183
Windmill Hill	Torbay	SX8762	50°27·1′	3°35·1′W	H	202
Windmill Hill	Wakf	SE3818	53°39·7′	1°25·1′W	T	110,111
Windmill Hill	Warw	SP0960	52°14·5′	1°51·7′W	X	150
Windmill Hill	Warw	SP2042	52°4·8′	1°42·1′W	X	151
Windmill Hill	Warw	SP2393	52°32·3′	1°39·3′W	X	139
Windmill Hill	Warw	SP3047	52°7·5′	1°33·3′W	X	151
Windmill Hill	Warw	SP3161	52°15·0′	1°32·4′W	X	151
Windmill Hill	Warw	SP3342	52°4·8′	1°30·7′W	X	151
Windmill Hill	Warw	SP3459	52°13·9′	1°29·7′W	X	151
Windmill Hill	Warw	SP4170	52°19·8′	1°23·5′W	X	140
Windmill Hill	Warw	SP4259	52°13·9′	1°22·7′W	X	151
Windmill Hill	Warw	SP4350	52°9·0′	1°21·9′W	X	151
Windmill Hill	Wilts	ST9623	51°0·6′	2°3·0′W	H	184
Windmill Hill	Wilts	SU0576	51°29·2′	1°55·3′W	X	173
Windmill Hill	Wilts	SU0871	51°26·5′	1°52·7′W	H	173
Windmill Hill	Wilts	SU1083	51°33·0′	1°51·0′W	X	173
Windmill Hill	Worcs	SO9149	52°8·6′	2°7·5′W	T	150
Windmill Hill	Worcs	SO9777	52°23·7′	2°2·2′W	H	139
Windmill Hill (Causewayed Enclosure)	Wilts	SU0871	51°26·5′	1°52·7′W	A	173
Windmill Hill Clump	Devon	SX8559	50°25·4′	3°36·8′W	H	202
Windmillhill Down	Wilts	SU2451	51°15·7′	1°39·0′W	X	184
Windmill Hill Fm	Bucks	SP7227	51°56·4′	0°56·8′W	FM	165
Windmill Hill Fm	Bucks	SP7315	51°50·0′	0°56·0′W	FM	165
Windmill Hill Fm	Warw	SP3459	52°13·9′	1°29·7′W	FM	151
Windmill Hill Place	E Susx	TQ6511	50°52·7′	0°21·1′E	X	199
Windmill Ho	Cumbr	NY2755	54°53·3′	3°7·9′W	X	85
Windmill Ho	W Berks	SU4881	51°31·8′	1°18·1′W	X	174
Windmill Lodge	Leic	SK8007	52°39·5′	0°48·6′W	X	141
Windmill Naps	Warw	SP0972	52°21·0′	1°51·7′W	F	139
Windmill Park	Pemb	SM8110	51°45·0′	5°10·0′W	X	157
Windmills	Hants	SU3752	51°16·2′	1°27·8′W	X	185
Windmill, The	Cumbr	NY1252	54°51·6′	3°21·8′W	X	85
Windmill, The	Oxon	SP3103	51°43·7′	1°32·7′W	X	164
Windmill Tump	Glos	ST9397	51°40·5′	2°5·7′W	X	163
Windmill Tump	Worcs	SO8635	52°1·0′	2°11·8′W	X	150
Windmill Tump (Long Barrow)	Glos	ST9397	51°40·5′	2°5·7′W	A	163
Windmill Whin	E Yorks	SE9847	53°54·8′	0°30·1′W	X	106
Wind Mill Wood Fm	Swan	SS5692	51°36·7′	4°4·4′W	FM	159
Windmore End	Cumbr	NY8117	54°33·1′	2°17·2′W	X	91,92
Windmore End Fm	Cumbr	NY8216	54°32·6′	2°16·3′W	FM	91,92
Windmore Green	Cumbr	NY8216	54°32·6′	2°16·3′W	X	91,92
Windolphs Fm	Suff	TL7853	52°9·0′	0°36·5′E	FM	155
Windout Fm	Devon	SX8191	50°42·6′	3°40·7′W	FM	191
Windover Hill	E Susx	TQ5403	50°48·6′	0°11·5′E	X	199
Wind Pump Fm	Rut	SK9309	52°40·5′	0°37·1′W	FM	141
Windridge Fm	Herts	TL1205	51°44·2′	0°22·3′W	FM	166
Windrigg Hill	Cumbr	NY5817	54°33·0′	2°38·5′W	H	91
Windros Laithe	N Yks	SD9359	54°1·9′	2°6·0′W	X	103
Windrow Burn	S Lanak	NS8129	55°32·7′	3°52·7′W	W	71,72
Windrow Hill	S Lanak	NS8030	55°33·2′	3°53·7′W	X	71,72
Windrow Wood	S Lanak	NS8129	55°32·7′	3°52·7′W	F	71,72
Windrush	Glos	SP1913	51°49·2′	1°43·1′W	T	163
Windrush Camp	Glos	SP1812	51°48·6′	1°43·9′W	A	163
Windrush Fm	Glos	SP1321	51°53·5′	1°48·3′W	FM	163
Windrush Hill	Glos	SP0723	51°54·6′	1°53·5′W	X	163
Wind Scarth	Cumbr	SD6598	54°22·8′	2°31·9′W	X	97
Winds'ee	Aberd	NJ4706	57°8·8′	2°52·1′W	X	37
Wind's Eye	Aberd	NJ5534	57°23·9′	2°44·5′W	H	29
Windshiel	Scot Bord	NT7458	55°49·1′	2°24·5′W	X	67,74
Windshield Hill	D & G	NY1398	55°16·4′	3°21·7′W	X	78
Windshields	E Ayr	NS5839	55°37·7′	4°14·9′W	X	71
Windshiel Grain	D & G	NY2699	55°17·0′	3°9·5′W	W	79
Windshielknowe	Scot Bord	NT5200	55°17·8′	2°44·9′W	X	79
Windshiels Cott	D & G	NY1692	55°13·2′	3°18·8′W	X	79
Windside Hill	Scot Bord	NT3343	55°40·8′	3°3·5′W	H	73
Windsoer	Moray	NJ3862	57°38·9′	3°1·9′W	X	28
Windsole	Aberd	NJ5560	57°37·9′	2°44·8′W	X	29
Windsor	Corn	SX1851	50°20·1′	4°33·1′W	X	201
Windsor	N Lincs	SE7612	53°36·2′	0°50·7′W	T	112
Windsor	Win & Maid	SU9676	51°28·7′	0°36·7′W	T	175,176
Windsor Castle	Win & Maid	SU9777	51°29·2′	0°35·8′W	A	175,176
Windsoredge	Glos	SO8400	51°42·1′	2°13·5′W	T	162
Windsor Fm	Cumbr	NY1205	54°26·2′	3°21·0′W	FM	89
Windsor Fm	Devon	ST1311	50°53·8′	3°13·8′W	FM	192,193
Windsor Fm	Devon	ST1506	50°51·1′	3°12·1′W	FM	192,193
Windsor Fm	Leeds	SE4240	53°51·5′	1°21·3′W	FM	105
Windsor Fm	Lincs	TF3668	53°11·7′	0°2·6′E	FM	122
Windsor Fm	Lincs	TF5361	53°7·7′	0°17·6′E	FM	122
Windsor Fm	Pemb	SN0101	51°40·6′	4°52·3′W	FM	157,158
Windsor Fm	Somer	ST6023	51°0·5′	2°33·8′W	FM	183
Windsor Forest	Win & Maid	SU9372	51°26·6′	0°39·3′W	F	175
Windsor Great Park	Win & Maid	SU9672	51°26·6′	0°36·7′W	X	175,176
Windsor Green	Suff	TL8954	52°9·3′	0°46·2′E	T	155
Windsor Hill	Bucks	SP8202	51°42·9′	0°48·4′W	X	165
Windsor Hill	Leic	SK8132	52°53·0′	0°47·4′W	X	130
Windsor Hill	Somer	ST6145	51°12·4′	2°33·1′W	X	183
Windsor Hill Fm	Pemb	SM9902	51°41·1′	4°54·1′W	FM	157,158
Windsor Lodge	N Yks	NZ0807	54°27·7′	1°52·2′W	X	92
Windsor Ride	Brackn	SU8763	51°21·8′	0°44·6′W	X	175,186
Windsor Wood	Corn	SX2459	50°24·5′	4°28·2′W	F	201
Windsor Wood	Suff	TL8064	52°14·9′	0°38·6′E	F	155
Windsover Fm	N Yks	SE1150	53°57·0′	1°49·5′W	FM	104
Windsworth	Corn	SX2854	50°21·9′	4°24·7′W	X	201
Wind Tor	Devon	SX7075	50°33·9′	3°49·8′W	H	191
Windward Fm	Fife	NO4715	56°19·7′	2°51·0′W	FM	59
Windwhistle	Devon	ST1116	50°56·4′	3°15·6′W	X	181,193
Windwhistle	Somer	ST3709	50°52·9′	2°53·3′W	T	193
Windwhistle	Wilts	SU0728	51°3·3′	1°53·6′W	X	184
Windwhistle Fm	Devon	ST0806	50°51·0′	3°18·0′W	FM	192
Windwhistle Fm	Somer	ST3809	50°52·9′	2°52·5′W	FM	193
Windwhistle Fm	Suff	TM2263	52°13·4′	1°15·4′E	FM	156
Windwick	Orkney	ND4586	58°45·8′	2°56·6′W	X	7
Wind Wick	Orkney	ND4687	58°46·3′	2°55·5′W	W	7
Windy Arbor	Know	SJ4689	53°23·9′	2°48·3′W	T	108
Windy Arbour	Derby	SK2740	52°57·6′	1°35·5′W	X	119,128
Windy Arbour	Staffs	SJ7745	53°0·3′	2°20·2′W	X	118
Windy Arbour	Warw	SP2971	52°20·4′	1°34·1′W	T	140
Windyates	Lancs	SD7049	53°56·4′	2°27·0′W	X	103
Windy Bank	Durham	NZ0930	54°40·1′	1°51·2′W	X	92
Windy Bank	Lancs	SD8426	53°44·1′	2°14·1′W	X	103
Windy Bank Fm	Wigan	SJ6897	53°28·4′	2°28·5′W	FM	109
Windy Brow	Cumbr	NY7638	54°44·4′	2°21·9′W	X	91
Windy Cleuch	Scot Bord	NY4998	55°16·7′	2°47·7′W	X	79
Windy Clough	Lancs	SD5360	54°2·3′	2°42·6′W	X	97
Windy Corner	I of M	SC3984	54°13·8′	4°27·8′W	X	95
Windy Crag	Northum	NT7705	55°20·6′	2°21·3′W	X	80
Windy Cross	Devon	SS3907	50°50·6′	4°16·8′W	X	190
Windy Cross	Devon	SS5235	51°6·0′	4°6·4′W	X	180
Windy Cross	Devon	SX8688	50°41·1′	3°36·4′W	A	191
Windy Dod	S Lanak	NS8419	55°27·3′	3°49·6′W	H	71,78
Windydoors	Scot Bord	NT4339	55°38·7′	2°53·9′W	T	73
Windyeats Fm	Wilts	SU2118	50°57·9′	1°41·7′W	FM	184
Windyedge	Aberd	NO8993	57°1·9′	2°10·4′W	T	38,45
Windyedge	Angus	NO6359	56°43·5′	2°35·8′W	X	54
Windyedge	Fife	NT1392	56°7·0′	3°23·5′W	X	58
Windyedge	N Ayr	NS2751	55°43·5′	4°44·8′W	X	63
Windy Edge	Northum	NY8076	55°4·9′	2°18·4′W	X	86,87
Windyedge	Pth & Kin	NO0521	56°22·6′	3°31·9′W	X	52,53,58
Windy Edge	Scot Bord	NT4600	55°17·7′	2°50·6′W	X	79
Windy Edge	Scot Bord	NY4384	55°9·1′	2°53·2′W	X	79
Windyedge	S Lanak	NS6744	55°40·5′	4°6·5′W	X	71
Windyfield	Aberd	NJ4927	57°20·1′	2°50·4′W	X	37
Windy Fields	Staffs	SJ9935	52°55·0′	2°0·5′W	X	127
Windyfold	Aberd	NJ8020	57°16·5′	2°19·4′W	X	38
Windy Gap	Cumbr	NY2110	54°29·0′	3°12·7′W	X	89,90
Windygate	Stir	NS5399	56°9·9′	4°21·6′W	X	57

Windygates	Fife	NO3400	56°11·5′	3°3·4′W	T	59
Windygates	Fife	NO4008	56°15·9′	2°57·7′W	X	59
Windygates	S Lanak	NT0048	55°43·2′	3°35·1′W	X	72
Windygates	Staffs	SK0061	53°9·0′	1°59·6′W	X	119
Windy Geo	Shetld	HU2775	60°27·7′	1°30·0′W	X	3
Windy Gyle	Northum	NT8515	55°26·0′	2°13·8′W	H	80
Windyhall	Arg & Bt	NS0963	55°49·6′	5°2·5′W	X	63
Windyharbour	Ches	SJ8270	53°13·8′	2°15·8′W	T	118
Windy Harbour	Lancs	SD6044	53°53·7′	2°36·1′W	X	102,103
Windy Harbour	Lancs	SD6121	53°41·3′	2°35·0′W	X	102,103
Windy Harbour	Staffs	SK0648	53°2·0′	1°54·2′W	X	119
Windyharbour	Staffs	SK0841	52°58·2′	1°52·4′W	X	119,128
Windy Harbour Fm	Lancs	SD4129	53°45·5′	2°53·3′W	FM	102
Windy Harbour Fm	Lancs	SD8141	53°52·1′	2°16·9′W	FM	103
Windyhaugh	Northum	NT8610	55°23·3′	2°12·8′W	X	80
Windyhaugh Ho	Bucks	SU8295	51°39·1′	0°48·5′W	X	165
Windyheads	Aberd	NJ8660	57°38·0′	2°13·6′W	X	30
Windyheads Hill	Aberd	NJ8561	57°38·6′	2°14·6′W	H	30
Windy Hill	Aberd	NJ9341	57°27·8′	2°6·5′W	H	30
Windy Hill	Arg & Bt	NS0469	55°52·7′	5°7·6′W	H	63
Windy Hill	D & G	NX9692	55°12·9′	3°37·6′W	X	78
Windyhill	D & G	NX9692	55°12·9′	3°37·6′W	X	78
Windy Hill	E Ayr	NS5044	55°40·2′	4°22·7′W	X	70
Windyhill	E Ayr	NS5236	55°36·0′	4°20·5′W	X	70
Windyhill	E Dunb	NS5273	55°55·9′	4°21·7′W	X	64
Windy Hill	Highld	NC8524	58°11·7′	3°56·9′W	X	17
Windy Hill	N Yks	NZ4808	54°28·1′	1°15·1′W	X	93
Windy Hill	Pemb	SN0130	51°56·2′	4°53·3′W	X	145,157
Windy Hill	Renf	NS3163	55°50·1′	4°41·5′W	H	63
Windyhill	Renf	NS4056	55°46·5′	4°32·6′W	X	64
Windyhill	Renf	NS4361	55°49·3′	4°29·9′W	X	64
Windy Hill	Roch	SD9714	53°37·6′	2°2·3′W	X	109
Windy Hill	Wrex	SJ3054	53°5·0′	3°2·3′W	T	117
Windyhill Burn	D & G	NX9692	55°12·9′	3°37·6′W	W	78
Windyhill Dam	E Ayr	NS5045	55°40·8′	4°22·7′W	X	64
Windy Hill Fm	Cumbr	SD5491	54°19·0′	2°42·0′W	FM	97
Windyhill Fm	Fife	NS9489	56°5·2′	3°41·8′W	FM	65
Windy Hill Fm	Red & Cl	NZ6421	54°35·1′	1°0·2′W	FM	94
Windy Hill Ho	N Yks	SE1457	54°0·8′	1°46·8′W	X	104
Windyhill Rig	D & G	NX9592	55°12·9′	3°38·6′W	X	78
Windyhills	Aberd	NJ7229	57°21·3′	2°27·5′W	X	38
Windyhills	Aberd	NJ7939	57°26·7′	2°20·5′W	X	29,30
Windy Hills	Aberd	NJ8039	57°26·7′	2°19·5′W	X	29,30
Windyhills	Angus	NO6743	56°34·9′	2°31·8′W	X	54
Windy House	Scot Bord	NT2820	55°28·4′	3°7·9′W	X	73
Windy Knoll	Derby	SK1282	53°20·3′	1°48·8′W	X	110
Windy Knoll	S Lanak	NS9013	55°24·2′	3°43·8′W	X	71,78
Windyknowe	D & G	NY2070	55°1·3′	3°14·7′W	X	85
Windy Knowe	Scot Bord	NT3649	55°44·1′	3°0·7′W	H	73
Windy Knowe	Scot Bord	NY5897	55°16·2′	2°39·2′W	H	80
Windyknowe	W Loth	NS9668	55°53·9′	3°39·4′W	T	65
Windy Law	E Loth	NT4961	55°50·6′	2°48·4′W	X	66
Windy Law	Midlo	NT3658	55°48·9′	3°0·8′W	X	66,73
Windy Law	Northum	NT9037	55°37·8′	2°9·1′W	X	74,75
Windy Law	Scot Bord	NT5258	55°49·0′	2°45·5′W	X	66,73
Windy Law	Scot Bord	NT7918	55°27·6′	2°19·5′W	H	80
Windylaw Loch	Scot Bord	NT3614	55°25·2′	3°0·0′W	W	79
Windylaws	Scot Bord	NT2444	55°41·3′	3°12·1′W	X	73
Windyleys	Aberd	NJ8228	57°20·8′	2°17·5′W	X	38
Windy Mains	E Loth	NT4364	55°52·2′	2°54·2′W	X	66
Windy Mill	Angus	NO4236	56°31·0′	2°56·1′W	X	54
Windy Mount	Donc	SE5108	53°34·2′	1°13·4′W	X	111
Windy Nook	Ghead	NZ2760	54°56·3′	1°34·3′W	T	88
Windy Oak	Wrekin	SJ6123	52°48·4′	2°34·3′W	X	127
Windy Pike	Lancs	SD8150	53°57·0′	2°17·0′W	X	103
Windy Pike	N Yks	SD9061	54°2·9′	2°8·7′W	X	98
Windyraw	Aberd	NJ4144	57°29·2′	2°58·6′W	X	28
Windyridge	Essex	TL9733	51°57·9′	0°52·5′E	X	168
Windyridge	Moray	NJ2367	57°41·4′	3°17·0′W	T	28
Windyridge	N Lanak	NS7671	55°55·2′	3°58·6′W	X	64
Windyridge	Notts	SK6026	52°49·9′	1°6·2′W	X	129
Windyridge Fm	Leic	SK7114	52°43·4′	0°56·5′W	FM	129
Windy Rig	Scot Bord	NT8415	55°26·0′	2°14·7′W	X	80
Windyrigg	Falk	NS9174	55°57·1′	3°44·3′W	X	65
Windyrise	N Ayr	NS2660	55°48·4′	4°46·1′W	X	63
Windy Scord	Shetld	HU2256	60°17·5′	1°35·6′W	X	3
Windyshields	S Lanak	NS9246	55°42·0′	3°42·7′W	X	72
Windy Slack	Cumbr	SD1788	54°17·1′	3°16·1′W	X	96
Windy Slack	Scot Bord	NT3552	55°45·7′	3°1·7′W	X	66,73
Windy Slack	Scot Bord	NT5103	55°19·4′	2°45·9′W	X	79
Windy Stacks	Shetld	HU3514	59°54·8′	1°22·0′W	X	4
Windy Standard	D & G	NS6201	55°17·3′	4°10·0′W	H	77
Windy Standard	E Ayr	NS5204	55°18·7′	4°19·5′W	H	77
Windywall	Orkney	HY5236	59°13·6′	2°50·0′W	X	5
Windy Walls	Northum	NZ1071	55°2·3′	1°50·2′W	X	88
Windywalls	Orkney	HY4551	59°20·8′	2°57·5′W	X	5
Windywalls	Scot Bord	NT7533	55°35·7′	2°23·4′W	X	74
Windyway Ho	Ches	SJ9573	53°15·5′	2°4·1′W	X	118
Windy-Yett	E Ayr	NS4750	55°43·4′	4°25·7′W	T	64
Windy-yett	Falk	NS8973	55°56·5′	3°46·2′W	X	65
Winebeck Fm	Brad	SE0750	53°57·0′	1°53·2′W	FM	104
Wine Cove	Aberd	NO8881	56°55·5′	2°11·4′W	W	45
Wineham	W Susx	TQ2320	50°58·2′	0°14·5′W	T	198
Wine Port	N Ayr	NS0238	55°36·0′	5°8·1′W	W	69
Winestead	E Yorks	TA2924	53°42·0′	0°2·3′W	T	107,113
Winestead Drain	E Yorks	TA2921	53°40·4′	0°2·4′W	W	107,113
Winestead Fm	E Yorks	TA2720	53°39·9′	0°4·3′W	FM	107,113
Winestead Grange	E Yorks	TA2822	53°41·0′	0°3·3′W	X	107,113
Winewall	Lancs	SD9139	53°51·1′	2°7·8′W	T	103
Winewell	Highld	NH9051	57°32·4′	3°49·8′W	X	27
Winfarthing	Norf	TM1085	52°25·6′	1°5·7′E	T	144
Winfield	Scot Bord	NT9051	55°45·4′	2°9·1′W	X	67,74,75
Winfield Fm	Kent	TQ6155	51°16·5′	0°18·9′E	FM	188
Winfield Fm	Scot Bord	NT8950	55°44·8′	2°10·1′W	FM	67,74
Winfold Fell	Lancs	SD6253	53°58·5′	2°34·3′W	X	102,103
Winford	I of W	SZ5684	50°39·4′	1°12·1′W	T	196
Winford	N Som	ST5465	51°23·2′	2°39·3′W	T	172,182
Winford Manor	N Som	ST5364	51°22·6′	2°40·1′W	X	172,182
Winforton	Heref	SO2947	52°7·2′	3°1·8′W	T	148
Winforton Wood Fm	Heref	SO2947	52°7·2′	3°1·8′W	FM	148
Winfrith Heath	Dorset	SY8086	50°40·6′	2°16·6′W	X	194
Winfrith Hill	Dorset	SY8082	50°38·5′	2°16·6′W	H	194
Winfrith Newburgh	Dorset	SY8084	50°39·6′	2°16·6′W	T	194
Wing	Bucks	SP8822	51°53·6′	0°42·9′W	T	165
Wing	Rut	SK8903	52°37·3′	0°40·7′W	T	141
Wingate	Durham	NZ4037	54°43·8′	1°22·3′W	T	93
Wingate Fm	Devon	SS7848	51°13·3′	3°44·4′W	FM	180
Wingate Fm	Kent	TR1945	51°10·0′	1°8·3′E	FM	179,189
Wingate Fm	N Yks	SE3453	53°58·6′	1°28·5′W	FM	104
Wingate Grange Fm	Durham	NZ3837	54°43·8′	1°24·2′W	FM	93
Wingate Hill	N Yks	SE4741	53°52·0′	1°16·7′W	F	105
Wingate Ho	Durham	NZ3736	54°43·3′	1°25·1′W	X	93
Wingates	Bolton	SD6507	53°33·8′	2°31·3′W	T	109
Wingates	Northum	NZ0995	55°15·2′	1°51·1′W	T	81
Wingates Moor Fm	Northum	NZ0993	55°14·1′	1°51·1′W	FM	81
Wingates Wholme	Northum	NZ1094	55°14·7′	1°50·1′W	X	81
Wingate Wood	Medway	TQ6965	51°21·8′	0°26·0′E	F	177,178
Wing Burrows	Rut	SK8801	52°36·2′	0°41·6′W	X	141
Wingerworth	Derby	SK3767	53°12·2′	1°26·4′W	T	119
Wingfield	Beds	TL0026	51°55·6′	0°32·3′W	T	166
Wingfield	Roth	SK4095	53°27·3′	1°23·4′W	T	111
Wingfield	Suff	TM2276	52°20·4′	1°15·9′E	T	156
Wingfield	Wilts	ST8256	51°18·4′	2°15·1′W	T	173
Wingfield Fm	Kent	TQ9555	51°15·9′	0°48·1′E	FM	178
Wingfield Green	Suff	TM2177	52°21·0′	1°15·1′E	T	156
Wingfield Hall	Suff	TM2475	52°19·9′	1°17·7′E	X	156
Wingfield Ho	Wilts	ST8258	51°19·5′	2°15·1′W	X	173
Wingfield Manor Ho	Derby	SK3754	53°5·2′	1°26·4′W	A	119
Wingfield Park	Derby	SK3752	53°4·1′	1°26·5′W	X	119
Wingfield Park	Derby	SK3753	53°4·6′	1°26·5′W	T	119
Wing Grange	Rut	SK8802	52°36·8′	0°41·6′W	X	141
Winghale Priory	Lincs	TF0296	53°27·3′	0°27·4′W	X	112
Wingham	Kent	TR2457	51°16·3′	1°13·1′E	T	179
Wingham Barton Mr	Kent	TR2761	51°18·4′	1°15·8′E	X	179
Wingham Green	Kent	TR2357	51°16·3′	1°12·2′E	T	179
Wingham Well	Kent	TR2356	51°15·8′	1°12·2′E	T	179
Wing Ho	Staffs	SJ8636	52°55·5′	2°12·1′W	X	127
Wingland Grange	Lincs	TF5122	52°46·7′	0°14·7′E	X	131
Wingland Marsh	Lincs	TF4921	52°46·2′	0°12·9′E	X	131
Wingletang Bay	I Scilly	SV8807	49°53·2′	6°20·3′W	W	203
Wingmoor Fm	Glos	SO9327	51°56·7′	2°5·7′W	FM	163
Wingmore	Kent	TR1846	51°10·5′	1°7·5′E	T	179,189
Wing Park Fm	Bucks	SP8822	51°53·6′	0°42·9′W	FM	165
Wingrave	Bucks	SP8618	51°51·5′	0°44·7′W	T	165
Wingrave Cross Roads	Bucks	SP8519	51°52·0′	0°45·5′W	X	165
Win Green	Wilts	ST9220	50°59·0′	2°6·5′W	H	184
Wings Fm	Bucks	SP7624	51°54·8′	0°53·3′W	FM	165
Wings Law	N Ayr	NS2859	55°47·9′	4°44·2′W	X	63
Wingstone Fm	Devon	SX7481	50°37·1′	3°46·5′W	FM	191
Wing, The	Norf	TG0541	52°55·9′	1°3·4′E	F	133
Wing, The	Orkney	ND4383	58°44·1′	2°58·6′W	X	7
Winham	Devon	ST0203	50°49·3′	3°23·1′W	X	192
Win Hill	Derby	SK1885	53°21·9′	1°43·4′W	H	110
Winkburn	Notts	SK7158	53°7·1′	0°55·9′W	T	120
Winkelbury	Wilts	ST9521	50°59·5′	2°3·9′W	A	184
Winkenhurst	E Susx	TQ5814	50°54·5′	0°15·2′E	X	199
Winkfield	Brackn	SU9072	51°26·6′	0°41·9′W	T	175
Winkfield Lodge	Brackn	SU9271	51°26·1′	0°40·2′W	X	175
Winkfield Manor	Brackn	SU9070	51°25·5′	0°41·9′W	X	175
Winkfield Place	Brackn	SU9273	51°27·1′	0°40·2′W	T	175
Winkfield Row	Brackn	SU8970	51°25·5′	0°42·8′W	T	175
Winkford Fm	Surrey	SU9339	51°8·8′	0°39·8′W	FM	186
Winkhill	Lincs	TF1445	52°59·6′	0°17·7′W	X	130
Winkhill	Staffs	SK0651	53°3·6′	1°54·2′W	T	119
Wink Ho	Donc	SE4508	53°34·2′	1°18·8′W	X	111
Winkhurst Green	Kent	TQ4949	51°13·5′	0°8·4′E	T	188
Winkinfield	E Ayr	NS6038	55°37·2′	4°13·0′W	X	71
Winking Hill	Notts	SK5129	52°51·6′	1°14·1′W	X	129
Winking Hill Fm	Notts	SK5029	52°51·6′	1°15·0′W	FM	129
Winkland Oaks Fm	Kent	TR3448	51°11·2′	1°21·3′E	FM	179
Winklebury	Hants	SU6152	51°16·1′	1°7·1′W	T	185
Winkleigh	Devon	SS6308	50°51·6′	3°56·4′W	T	191
Winkleigh Wood	Devon	SS6408	50°51·6′	3°55·6′W	F	191
Winksetter	Orkney	HY3416	59°1·8′	3°8·5′W	X	6
Winksley	N Yks	SE2571	54°8·3′	1°36·6′W	T	99
Winksley Banks	N Yks	SE2471	54°8·3′	1°37·5′W	X	99
Winkston Fm	Scot Bord	NT2443	55°40·7′	3°12·1′W	FM	73
Wink, The	Notts	SK7158	53°7·1′	0°55·9′W	W	120
Winkton	Dorset	SZ1696	50°46·0′	1°46·0′W	T	195
Winkton Common	Dorset	SZ1595	50°45·5′	1°46·9′W	X	195
Winkworth Arboretum	Surrey	SU9941	51°9·8′	0°34·7′W	F	186
Winkworth Fm	Surrey	SU9940	51°9·3′	0°34·7′W	FM	186
Winkworth Fm	Wilts	ST9786	51°34·6′	2°2·2′W	FM	173
Winlaton	Ghead	NZ1862	54°57·4′	1°42·7′W	T	88
Winlaton Mill	Ghead	NZ1860	54°56·3′	1°42·7′W	T	88
Winlea	N Yks	SE9280	54°12·7′	0°34·9′W	X	101
Winless	Highld	ND3054	58°28·4′	3°11·5′W	X	11,12
Winley Fm	Heref	SO7059	52°13·9′	2°26·0′W	FM	149
Winley Hill Fm	N Yks	NZ5309	54°28·7′	1°10·5′W	FM	93
Winllan	Cered	SN6889	52°29·2′	3°56·2′W	X	135
Winllan	Conwy	SH9965	53°10·6′	3°30·3′W	X	116
Winllan	Powys	SJ2121	52°47·1′	3°9·9′W	T	126
Winllan Hill	Powys	SJ2121	52°47·1′	3°9·9′W	H	126
Winmarleigh	Lancs	SD4647	53°55·2′	2°48·9′W	X	102
Winmarleigh Moss	Lancs	SD4447	53°55·2′	2°50·7′W	T	102
Winnacott	Corn	SX2590	50°41·2′	4°28·3′W	X	190
Winnal	Heref	SO4534	52°0·3′	2°47·7′W	T	149,161
Winnal Common	Heref	SO4534	52°0·3′	2°47·7′W	T	149,161
Winnal Fm	Shrops	SO7280	52°25·3′	2°24·3′W	FM	138
Winnall	Hants	SU4930	51°4·3′	1°17·6′W	T	185
Winnall	Worcs	SO8167	52°18·3′	2°16·3′W	T	138,150
Winnall Down Fm	Hants	SU5029	51°3·7′	1°16·8′W	FM	185
Winna Ness	Shetld	HU6098	60°39·9′	0°53·6′W	X	1
Winnard's Perch	Corn	SW9266	50°27·7′	4°55·5′W	T	200
Winnats	Derby	SK1382	53°20·3′	1°47·9′W	X	110
Winn Brook	Somer	SS8735	51°6·4′	3°36·5′W	W	181
Winner Hill	Glos	ST7790	51°36·7′	2°19·5′W	X	162,172
Winneries	Shetld	HU5173	60°26·5′	1°3·9′W	X	2,3
Winnersh	Wok	SU7770	51°25·7′	0°53·2′W	T	175
Winneygreen Fm	Suff	TM0850	52°6·8′	1°2·7′E	FM	155
Winneyhill	Derby	SK2749	53°2·5′	1°35·4′W	X	119
Winney's Down	Devon	SX6282	50°37·5′	3°56·7′W	H	191
Winn Fm	Derby	SK2251	53°3·6′	1°39·9′W	FM	119
Winn Ho	Lancs	SD5441	53°52·0′	2°41·6′W	X	102
Winnia Ness	Shetld	HU4775	60°27·6′	1°8·2′W	X	2,3
Winnianton Fm	Corn	SW6620	50°2·3′	5°15·7′W	FM	203
Winnick	Corn	SX1657	50°23·3′	4°34·9′W	X	201
Winning Foot Hill	Northnts	SP9986	52°28·0′	0°32·2′W	X	141
Winnington	Ches	SJ6474	53°15·9′	2°32·0′W	T	118
Winnington	Shrops	SJ3110	52°41·2′	3°0·8′W	X	126
Winnington	Staffs	SJ7238	52°56·6′	2°24·6′W	T	127
Winnington Green	Shrops	SJ3111	52°41·8′	3°0·9′W	T	126
Winnington Lodge Fm	Shrops	SJ3009	52°40·7′	3°1·7′W	FM	126
Winningtonrig	Scot Bord	NT4909	55°22·6′	2°47·9′W	X	79
Winnold Ho	Norf	TF6803	52°36·2′	0°29·3′E	X	143
Winnothdale	Staffs	SK0340	52°57·7′	1°56·9′W	T	119,128
Winnowshill	Northum	NY9952	54°52·0′	2°0·5′W	X	87
Winnycroft Fm	Glos	SO8514	51°49·7′	2°12·7′W	FM	162
Winny Stone	Cald	SE0131	53°46·8′	1°58·7′W	X	104
Winsbury	Shrops	SO2498	52°34·7′	3°6·9′W	X	137
Winsbury Hill	Bath & NE Somer	ST6763	51°22·1′	2°28·1′W	H	172
Winscales	Cumbr	NY0209	54°28·3′	3°30·3′W	X	89
Winscales	Cumbr	NY0226	54°37·4′	3°30·7′W	T	89
Winscar Resr	Barns	SE1502	53°31·1′	1°46·0′W	W	110
Winscombe	Devon	SX7392	50°43·1′	3°47·6′W	X	191
Winscombe	N Som	ST4257	51°18·8′	2°49·5′W	T	172,182
Winscote Hills	Shrops	SO7297	52°34·4′	2°24·4′W	X	138
Winscott	Bucks	SP8726	51°55·8′	0°43·7′W	X	165
Winscott	Devon	SS3301	50°47·3′	4°21·8′W	X	190
Winscott Barton	Devon	SS4124	50°59·8′	4°15·6′W	X	180,190
Winscott Barton	Devon	SS5518	50°56·8′	4°3·5′W	X	180
Winscott Barton	Devon	SX8998	50°46·5′	3°34·1′W	X	192
Winscott Cross	Devon	SS3401	50°47·3′	4°20·9′W	X	190
Winsdon	Corn	SX2891	50°41·8′	4°25·8′W	X	190
Winsdon Hill	Luton	TL0721	51°52·9′	0°26·3′W	T	166
Winsetts	E Yorks	TA3818	53°38·7′	0°5·7′E	X	113
Winsey Fm	Beds	SP9960	52°14·0′	0°32·6′W	FM	153
Winsey Fm	Essex	TL6041	52°2·9′	0°20·4′E	FM	154
Winsford	Ches	SJ6566	53°11·6′	2°31·0′W	T	118
Winsford	Corn	SW8652	50°20·0′	5°0·1′W	X	200,204
Winsford	Devon	SS4326	51°1·0′	4°13·9′W	X	180,190
Winsford	Devon	SS4501	50°47·5′	4°11·6′W	X	190
Winsford	Somer	SS9034	51°5·9′	3°33·9′W	T	181
Winsford Hall	Norf	TG4411	52°38·7′	1°36·8′E	X	134
Winsford Hill	Somer	SS8734	51°5·9′	3°36·4′W	H	181
Winsham	Devon	SS4938	51°7·5′	4°9·1′W	T	180
Winsham	Somer	ST3706	50°51·2′	2°53·3′W	T	193
Winsham Down Ho	Devon	SS5039	51°8·1′	4°8·3′W	X	180
Winshaw	N Yks	SD7880	54°13·2′	2°19·8′W	X	98
Winshields	Northum	NY7466	54°59·5′	2°24·0′W	X	86,87
Winshill	Staffs	SK2623	52°48·5′	1°36·5′W	T	128
Winsh-wen	Swan	SS6896	51°39·1′	3°54·1′W	T	159
Winsick	Derby	SK4068	53°12·7′	1°23·7′W	T	120
Winskill	Cumbr	NY5834	54°42·2′	2°38·7′W	T	91
Winskill Stones	N Yks	SD8366	54°5·6′	2°15·2′W	X	98
Winslade	Corn	SX3275	50°33·3′	4°21·9′W	X	201
Winslade	Devon	SS3818	50°56·6′	4°18·0′W	T	190
Winslade	Devon	SX4090	50°41·5′	4°15·5′W	X	190
Winslade	Hants	SU6548	51°13·9′	1°3·8′W	T	185,186
Winslade Fm	Devon	SX7742	50°16·1′	3°43·2′W	FM	202
Winslade Park	Devon	SX9790	50°42·3′	3°27·1′W	X	192
Winslakefoot	Devon	SX8193	50°43·7′	3°40·8′W	X	191
Winsle	Pemb	SM8309	51°44·5′	5°8·2′W	X	157
Winsley	N Yks	SE2361	54°2·9′	1°38·5′W	T	99
Winsley	Wilts	ST7960	51°20·6′	2°17·7′W	T	172
Winsley Hall	N Yks	SE2461	54°2·9′	1°37·6′W	X	99
Winsley Hall	Shrops	SJ3507	52°39·7′	2°57·3′W	X	126
Winsley Hill	Heref	SO4952	52°10·1′	2°44·3′W	X	148,149
Winsley Ho	Heref	SO4852	52°10·1′	2°45·2′W	A	148,149
Winsleyhurst	N Yks	SE2261	54°2·9′	1°39·4′W	X	99
Winslow	Bucks	SP7627	51°56·4′	0°53·3′W	T	165
Winslow	Heref	SO6153	52°10·7′	2°33·8′W	X	149
Winslowe Ho	Hants	SU4715	50°56·2′	1°19·5′W	X	196
Winslow Grange	Heref	SO6357	52°12·8′	2°32·1′W	X	149
Winslow Mill	Heref	SO6236	52°1·5′	2°32·8′W	T	149
Winson	Devon	SS6424	51°0·2′	3°55·9′W	X	180
Winson	Glos	SP0908	51°46·5′	1°51·8′W	T	163
Winson Green	Birm	SP0488	52°29·6′	1°56·1′W	T	139
Winson Hill	Notts	SK7068	53°12·5′	0°56·7′W	X	120
Winsor	Devon	SX5953	50°21·8′	3°58·6′W	X	202
Winsor	Hants	SU3114	50°55·7′	1°33·1′W	T	196
Winspit	Dorset	SY9776	50°35·3′	2°2·2′W	X	195
Winspurs Fm	Norf	TG2337	52°53·3′	1°19·3′E	FM	133
Winstanley	Wigan	SD5503	53°31·5′	2°40·3′W	T	108
Winstanley Hall	Wigan	SD5403	53°31·5′	2°41·2′W	A	108
Winstanleys	Wigan	SD5809	53°34·8′	2°37·7′W	T	108
Winster	Cumbr	SD4193	54°20·0′	2°54·0′W	T	96,97
Winster	Derby	SK2460	53°8·4′	1°38·1′W	T	119
Winster Ho	Cumbr	SD4192	54°19·5′	2°54·0′W	X	96,97
Winstermoor Fm	Derby	SK2459	53°7·9′	1°38·1′W	FM	119
Winstitchen	Somer	SS7938	51°7·9′	3°43·4′W	X	180
Winstitchen Fm	Somer	SS7838	51°7·9′	3°44·2′W	FM	180
Winstode	Devon	SX7997	50°45·8′	3°42·6′W	X	191
Winston	Devon	SX5551	50°20·7′	4°1·9′W	X	202
Winston	Durham	NZ1316	54°32·6′	1°47·5′W	T	92
Winston	Shrops	SJ3832	52°53·2′	2°54·9′W	X	126
Winston	Suff	TM1861	52°12·5′	1°11·8′E	T	156
Winston Court	Monm	SO3517	51°51·1′	2°56·2′W	X	161
Winstone	Glos	SO9609	51°47·0′	2°3·1′W	T	163
Winstone Fm	I of W	SZ5581	50°37·8′	1°13·0′W	FM	196
Winston Game Fm	Norf	TM4092	52°28·6′	1°32·5′E	FM	134
Winston Grange	Suff	TM1862	52°13·0′	1°11·9′E	X	156
Winston Green	Suff	TM1661	52°12·5′	1°10·1′E	X	156
Winswell	Devon	SS4913	50°54·0′	4°8·5′W	T	180
Winswell Moor	Devon	SS4913	50°54·0′	4°8·5′W	X	180
Winswood	Devon	SS6415	50°55·3′	3°55·7′W	X	180
Winswood	Devon	SS7313	50°54·4′	3°48·0′W	X	180
Winswood Moor	Devon	SS7414	50°54·9′	3°47·2′W	X	180
Winter Beck	E Yorks	SE7455	53°59·4′	0°51·9′W	W	105,106

Winter Beck	Notts	SK7839	52°56·8′	0°49·9′W	W	129
Winterborne Came	Dorset	SY7088	50°41·7′	2°25·1′W	T	194
Winterborne Clenston	Dorset	ST8302	50°49·3′	2°14·1′W	T	194
Winterborne Herringston	Dorset	SY6888	50°41·7′	2°26·8′W	T	194
Winterborne Houghton	Dorset	ST8104	50°50·3′	2°15·8′W	T	194
Winterborne Kingston	Dorset	SY8697	50°46·6′	2°11·5′W	T	194
Winterborne Monkton	Dorset	SY6787	50°41·1′	2°27·6′W	T	194
Winterborne Muston	Dorset	SY8797	50°46·6′	2°10·7′W	T	194
Winterborne Stickland	Dorset	ST8304	50°50·3′	2°14·1′W	T	194
Winterborne Tomson	Dorset	SY8897	50°46·6′	2°9·8′W	T	194
Winterborne Whitechurch	Dorset	ST8300	50°48·2′	2°14·1′W	T	194
Winterborne Zelston	Dorset	SY8997	50°46·6′	2°9·0′W	T	195
Winterbottom	Ches	SJ7081	53°19·7′	2°26·6′W	X	109
Winterbottom Fm	Ches	SJ7671	53°14·4′	2°21·2′W	FM	118
Winterbourne	Kent	TR0657	51°16·7′	0°57·6′E	T	179
Winterbourne	S Glos	ST6580	51°31·3′	2°29·9′W	T	172
Winterbourne	W Berks	SU4572	51°26·9′	1°20·8′W	T	174
Winterbourne Abbas	Dorset	SY6190	50°42·7′	2°32·8′W	T	194
Winterbourne Bassett	Wilts	SU1074	51°28·1′	1°51·0′W	T	173
Winterbourne Dauntsey	Wilts	SU1734	51°6·5′	1°45·0′W	T	184
Winterbourne Down	S Glos	ST6579	51°30·8′	2°29·9′W	T	172
Winterbourne Down	Wilts	SU2133	51°6·0′	1°41·6′W	X	184
Winterbourne Earls	Wilts	SU1734	51°6·5′	1°45·0′W	T	184
Winterbourne Faringdon Village	Dorset	SY6988	50°41·7′	2°26·0′W	A	194
Winterbourne Gunner	Wilts	SU1835	51°7·1′	1°44·2′W	T	184
Winterbourne Holt	W Berks	SU4571	51°26·4′	1°20·8′W	X	174
Winterbourne Manor	W Berks	SU4471	51°26·4′	1°21·6′W	X	174
Winterbourne Monkton	Wilts	SU0971	51°26·5′	1°51·8′W	T	173
Winterbourne Steepleton	Dorset	SY6289	50°42·2′	2°31·9′W	T	194
Winterbourne Stoke	Wilts	SU0741	51°10·3′	1°53·6′W	T	184
Winterbourne Stoke Down	Wilts	SU0942	51°10·9′	1°51·9′W	X	184
Winterbourne Stoke Group	Wilts	SU1041	51°10·3′	1°51·0′W	X	184
Winterbourne Stoke Group (Tumuli)	Wilts	SU1041	51°10·3′	1°51·0′W	A	184
Winterbrook	Oxon	SU6088	51°35·5′	1°7·6′W	T	175
Winterburn	N Yks	SD9358	54°1·3′	2°6·0′W	T	103
Winterburn Beck	N Yks	SD9359	54°1·9′	2°6·0′W	W	103
Winterburn Brook	Shrops	SO6587	52°29·0′	2°30·5′W	W	138
Winterburn Moor	N Yks	SD9361	54°2·9′	2°6·0′W	X	98
Winterburn Reservoir	N Yks	SD9460	54°2·4′	2°5·1′W	W	98
Winterburn Wood Fm	N Yks	SD9359	54°1·9′	2°6·0′W	FM	103
Wintercleuch Burn	S Lanak	NS9711	55°23·2′	3°37·1′W	W	78
Wintercleuch Fell	S Lanak	NS9910	55°22·7′	3°35·2′W	H	78
Wintercleugh	S Lanak	NS9610	55°22·6′	3°38·0′W	X	78
Winter Corrie	Angus	NO2774	56°51·4′	3°11·4′W	X	44
Winter Covert	Arg & Bt	NR3263	55°47·4′	6°16·1′W	F	60,61
Winter Crag	Cumbr	NY4318	54°33·5′	2°52·5′W	X	90
Winter Down Copse	Hants	SU3833	51°5·9′	1°27·1′W	F	185
Winterdown Fm	Kent	TR2043	51°8·9′	1°9·1′E	FM	179,189
Winterdyne Fm	Staffs	SK2108	52°40·4′	1°41·0′W	FM	128
Winterfield	Bath & NE Somer	ST6555	51°17·8′	2°29·7′W	T	172,183
Winterfield Fm	N Yks	NZ3708	54°28·2′	1°25·3′W	FM	93
Winterfield Ho	N Yks	SE2394	54°20·7′	1°38·4′W	X	99
Winterflood's Fm	Essex	TL9120	51°51·0′	0°46·8′E	FM	168
Winterfold Heath	Surrey	TQ0642	51°10·3′	0°28·6′W	F	187
Winterfold Ho	Surrey	TQ0741	51°9·7′	0°27·8′W	X	187
Winterfold Ho	Worcs	SO8773	52°21·5′	2°11·1′W	X	139
Winterfold Wood	Surrey	TQ0643	51°10·8′	0°28·6′W	F	187
Winterford Fm	Ches	SJ5762	53°9·4′	2°38·2′W	FM	117
Winter Gardens	Essex	TQ7984	51°31·8′	0°35·2′E	T	178
Wintergill Head	D & G	NT1302	55°18·5′	3°21·8′W	H	78
Wintergill Plantn	N Yks	NZ7502	54°24·7′	0°50·2′W	F	94
Winter Hall	Pemb	SN0102	51°41·1′	4°52·3′W	X	157,158
Winterhay Green	Somer	ST3515	50°56·1′	2°55·1′W	T	193
Winterhays	Dorset	ST5909	50°53·0′	2°34·6′W	X	194
Winterhead	Somer	ST4357	51°18·8′	2°48·7′W	T	172,182
Winterhead Hill	Somer	ST4356	51°18·3′	2°48·7′W	X	172,182
Winter Hill	Black w Dar	SD6623	53°42·4′	2°30·5′W	H	103
Winter Hill	Lancs	SD6514	53°37·5′	2°31·3′W	H	109
Winter Hill	Win & Maid	SU8786	51°34·2′	0°44·3′W	X	175
Winter Ho	Cumbr	NY6023	54°36·3′	2°36·7′W	X	91
Winterhope	D & G	NY2782	55°7·9′	3°8·3′W	X	79
Winterhope Burn	Scot Bord	NT1818	55°27·2′	3°17·4′W	W	79
Winterhopeburn	Scot Bord	NT1819	55°27·7′	3°17·4′W	X	79
Winterhopeburn	Scot Bord	NT1820	55°28·3′	3°17·4′W	X	72
Winterhope Reservoir	D & G	NY2782	55°7·9′	3°8·3′W	W	79
Winteringham	N Lincs	SE9222	53°41·4′	0°36·0′W	T	106,112
Winteringham Grange	N Lincs	SE9421	53°40·9′	0°34·2′W	X	106,112
Winteringham Haven	N Lincs	SE9323	53°41·9′	0°35·1′W	X	106,112
Winteringham Ings	N Lincs	SE9620	53°40·3′	0°32·4′W	X	106,112
Winterings	N Yks	SD9499	54°23·4′	2°5·1′W	X	98
Winterings Edge	N Yks	NY9400	54°24·0′	2°5·1′W	X	91,92
Winterlands Fm	E Susx	TQ3914	50°54·7′	0°1·0′W	FM	198
Winterley	Ches	SJ7457	53°6·8′	2°22·9′W	T	118
Winterley Cobba	N Yks	SD8854	53°59·2′	2°10·6′W	X	103
Winterley Ho	Ches	SJ7456	53°6·3′	2°22·9′W	X	118
Wintermuir Fm	S Lanak	NT0639	55°38·4′	3°29·2′W	FM	72
Winter Noust	Orkney	HY5115	59°1·4′	2°50·7′W	X	6
Winterpick Fm	W Susx	TQ2228	51°2·5′	0°15·2′W	FM	187,198
Winters	Essex	TQ8890	51°34·9′	0°43·2′E	X	178
Winters	Somer	ST0229	51°3·4′	3°23·5′W	X	181
Winterscales	N Yks	SD7580	54°13·2′	2°22·6′W	X	98
Winterscales Beck	N Yks	SD7579	54°12·6′	2°22·6′W	W	98
Winterscales Pasture	N Yks	SD7581	54°13·7′	2°22·6′W	X	98
Winter's Cross	Heref	SO5525	51°55·5′	2°38·9′W	X	162
Winters Down	Hants	SU5921	50°59·4′	1°9·2′W	X	185
Winterseeds	Cumbr	NY3308	54°28·0′	3°1·6′W	X	90
Wintersell Fm	Surrey	TQ4147	51°12·5′	0°1·5′E	FM	187
Wintersett	Wakf	SE3815	53°38·0′	1°25·1′W	T	110,111
Wintersett Resr	Wakf	SE3714	53°37·5′	1°26·0′W	W	110,111
Winterseugh	D & G	NY1569	55°0·7′	3°19·3′W	X	85
Winters Fm	Kent	TQ9340	51°7·8′	0°45·9′E	FM	189
Winter's Fm	Kent	TR1555	51°15·4′	1°5·3′E	FM	179
Winter's Gibbet	Northum	NY9690	55°12·5′	2°3·3′W	X	81
Winter's Grove	Norf	TM2694	52°30·0′	1°20·2′E	F	134
Wintershall	Surrey	TQ0141	51°9·8′	0°32·9′W	X	186
Wintershead Fm	Somer	SS7736	51°6·8′	3°45·1′W	FM	180
Wintersheugh Plantn	D & G	NY1570	55°1·3′	3°19·3′W	F	85
Wintershields	Cumbr	NY5572	55°2·7′	2°41·8′W	X	86
Wintershill	Hants	SU5218	50°57·8′	1°15·2′W	T	185
Wintershill Hall	Hants	SU5218	50°57·8′	1°15·2′W	X	185
Winterside Fm	Ches	SJ9578	53°18·2′	2°4·1′W	FM	118
Winterside Fm	Hants	SU3458	51°19·4′	1°30·3′W	FM	174
Winter's Penning	Wilts	SU1857	51°18·9′	1°44·1′W	X	173
Wintertarn	Cumbr	NY5717	54°33·0′	2°39·5′W	X	91
Winterton	Aberd	NJ5459	57°37·4′	2°45·7′W	X	29
Winterton	N Lincs	SE9218	53°39·3′	0°36·1′W	T	112
Winterton	Pemb	SM8008	51°43·9′	5°10·8′W	X	157
Winterton Beck	N Lincs	SE9017	53°38·7′	0°37·9′W	W	112
Winterton Carrs	N Lincs	SE9619	53°39·8′	0°32·4′W	X	112
Winterton Dunes (Nature Reserve)	Norf	TG4920	52°43·4′	1°41·7′E	X	134
Winterton Fm	Sol	SP1375	52°22·6′	1°48·1′W	FM	139
Winterton Holmes	Norf	TG4721	52°44·0′	1°39·9′E	X	134
Winterton Ings	N Lincs	SE9519	53°39·8′	0°33·3′W	X	112
Winterton Ness	Norf	TG4821	52°44·0′	1°40·8′E	X	134
Winterton-on-Sea	Norf	TG4919	52°42·9′	1°41·6′E	T	134
Winter Tor	Devon	SX6091	50°42·3′	3°58·6′W	X	191
Winter Well	Somer	ST2520	50°58·7′	3°3·7′W	T	193
Winterwell Barn	Glos	SP1013	51°49·2′	1°50·9′W	X	163
Winterwell Fm	Glos	SP1013	51°49·2′	1°50·9′W	FM	163
Winthank	Fife	NO4713	56°18·6′	2°51·0′W	X	59
Winthill Fm	Heref	SO7249	52°8·6′	2°24·2′W	FM	149
Winthill Ho	N Som	ST3958	51°19·3′	2°52·1′W	X	182
Winthorpe	Lincs	TF5665	53°9·8′	0°20·4′E	T	122
Winthorpe	Notts	SK8156	53°5·9′	0°47·0′W	T	121
Winthorpe Lake	Notts	SK8057	53°6·5′	0°47·9′W	W	121
Wintles, The	Shrops	SO3189	52°29·9′	3°0·6′W	X	137
Wintofts Fm	N Yks	SE7880	54°12·8′	0°47·8′W	FM	100
Winton	Bourne	SZ0893	50°44·4′	1°52·8′W	T	195
Winton	Cumbr	NY7810	54°29·3′	2°20·0′W	T	91
Winton	E Susx	TQ5203	50°48·6′	0°9·8′E	T	199
Winton	N Yks	SE4196	54°21·7′	1°21·7′W	T	99
Winton	Salf	SJ7598	53°28·9′	2°22·2′W	T	109
Winton Beck	N Yks	SE4097	54°22·3′	1°22·6′W	W	99
Winton Fell	Cumbr	NY8307	54°27·7′	2°15·3′W	X	91,92
Winton Field	Cumbr	NY7710	54°29·3′	2°20·9′W	X	91
Winton Fm	Kent	TQ8631	51°3·1′	0°39·6′E	FM	189
Winton Grange	N Yks	SE4096	54°21·7′	1°22·6′W	X	99
Wintonhill	E Loth	NT4370	55°55·4′	2°54·3′W	X	66
Winton Ho	E Loth	NT4369	55°54·9′	2°54·3′W	X	66
Winton Lea	E Loth	NT4270	55°55·4′	2°55·3′W	X	66
Winton Manor Fm	N Yks	SE4096	54°21·7′	1°22·6′W	FM	99
Winton West Mains	E Loth	NT4269	55°54·9′	2°55·2′W	X	66
Wintour's Leap	Glos	ST5496	51°39·9′	2°39·5′W	X	162
Wintrick	Northum	NZ1998	55°16·8′	1°41·6′W	X	81
Wintringham	N Yks	SE8873	54°9·0′	0°38·7′W	T	101
Wintringham Hall	Cambs	TL2159	52°13·2′	0°13·3′W	X	153
Wintry Park Fm	Essex	TL4603	51°42·6′	0°7·2′E	FM	167
Wintylow	N Yks	SE2096	54°21·8′	1°41·1′W	X	99
Winwick	Cambs	TL1080	52°24·6′	0°22·6′W	T	142
Winwick	Northnts	SP6273	52°21·3′	1°5·0′W	T	140
Winwick	Warr	SJ6092	53°25·6′	2°35·7′W	T	109
Winwick Grange	Northnts	SP6174	52°21·9′	1°5·8′W	X	140
Winwick Lodge	Northnts	SP6274	52°21·9′	1°5·0′W	X	140
Winwick Manor Fm	Northnts	SP6175	52°22·4′	1°5·8′W	FM	140
Winwick Quay	Warr	SJ6091	53°25·1′	2°35·7′W	T	109
Winwick Warren	Northnts	SP6474	52°21·9′	1°3·2′W	X	140
Winwoods	Shrops	SO7277	52°23·7′	2°24·3′W	X	138
Winyard's Gap	Dorset	ST4906	50°51·3′	2°43·1′W	T	193,194
Winyards Nick	Sheff	SK2581	53°19·8′	1°37·1′W	X	110
Winyates	Worcs	SP0767	52°18·3′	1°53·4′W	T	150
Winyates Green	Worcs	SP0867	52°18·3′	1°52·6′W	T	150
Wion	Carm	SN6135	52°0·0′	4°1·1′W	X	146
Wiral	Monm	SO2928	51°57·0′	3°1·6′W	X	161
Wirchet	Northum	NY6297	55°16·2′	2°35·5′W	X	80
Wire Hill	Lincs	TF1578	53°17·4′	0°16·1′W	X	121
Wirelock	Lincs	SK9359	53°7·4′	0°36·2′W	X	121
Wire Stone	Derby	SK3263	53°10·0′	1°30·9′W	X	119
Wirksworth	Derby	SK2853	53°4·6′	1°34·5′W	T	119
Wirksworth Moor	Derby	SK3054	53°5·2′	1°32·7′W	T	119
Wirlie	Shetld	HU4663	60°21·2′	1°9·5′W	X	2,3
Wirral	Wirral	SJ3181	53°19·5′	3°1·8′W	X	108
Wirral Country Park	Wirral	SJ2482	53°20·0′	3°8·1′W	X	108
Wirral Country Park, The	Ches	SJ3277	53°17·4′	3°0·8′W	X	117
Wirral Way	Ches	SJ3377	53°17·4′	2°59·9′W	X	117
Wirrvie Brecks	Shetld	HZ2173	59°32·8′	1°37·2′W	X	4
Wirswall	Ches	SJ5444	52°59·7′	2°40·7′W	T	117
Wisbech	Cambs	TF4609	52°39·8′	0°9·9′E	T	143
Wisbech Channel		TF4934	52°53·2′	0°13·3′E	W	131
Wisbech High Fen	Cambs	TF3704	52°37·2′	0°1·8′E	X	142,143
Wisbech St Mary	Cambs	TF4208	52°39·3′	0°6·4′E	T	142,143
Wisborough Green	W Susx	TQ0426	51°1·7′	0°30·6′W	T	186,197
Wisbridge Fm	Herts	TL3636	52°0·6′	0°0·7′W	FM	154
Wiscombe Park	Devon	SY1893	50°44·1′	3°9·3′W	X	192,193
Wisdome Fm	Devon	SX6160	50°25·6′	3°57·0′W	FM	202
Wisdomhow	Aberd	NO4298	57°4·3′	2°56·9′W	X	37,44
Wiseburrow Fm	Devon	ST0819	50°58·0′	3°18·2′W	FM	181
Wise Een Tarn	Cumbr	SD3797	54°22·1′	2°57·8′W	W	96,97
Wisefield Fm	E Yorks	TA1353	53°57·9′	0°16·2′W	FM	107
Wiselawmill	Scot Bord	NT5151	55°45·2′	2°46·4′W	X	66,73
Wiseman's Br	Pemb	SN1406	51°43·6′	4°41·2′W	X	158
Wisemans' Oby Mill	Norf	TG4013	52°39·9′	1°33·4′E	X	134
Wisenholme Beck	Cumbr	NY0920	54°34·3′	3°24·0′W	W	89
Wiserley Hall	Durham	NZ0836	54°43·4′	1°52·1′W	X	92
Wiseton	Notts	SK7189	53°23·8′	0°55·5′W	T	112,120
Wise Warren	Leeds	SE4442	53°52·6′	1°19·4′W	X	105
Wishach Hill	Aberd	NJ5733	57°23·4′	2°42·5′W	H	29
Wishanger	Glos	SO9209	51°47·1′	2°6·6′W	T	163
Wishanger Lodge	Hants	SU8339	51°8·9′	0°48·4′W	X	186
Wishaw	N Lanak	NS7955	55°46·6′	3°55·3′W	T	64
Wishaw	Northum	NY9487	55°10·9′	2°5·2′W	X	80
Wishaw	Warw	SP1794	52°32·9′	1°44·6′W	T	139
Wishaw Hall Fm	Warw	SP1795	52°33·4′	1°44·6′W	FM	139
Wishaw Pike	Northum	NY9388	55°11·4′	2°6·2′W	H	80
Wishfields Fm	Essex	TQ5897	51°39·2′	0°17·4′E	FM	167,177
Wishford Fm	Devon	SX9995	50°45·0′	3°25·5′W	FM	192
Wishmoor Bottom	Brackn	SU8762	51°21·3′	0°44·6′W	X	175,186
Wishmoor Cross	Surrey	SU8863	51°21·8′	0°43·8′W	X	175,186
Wish Tower	E Susx	TV6198	50°45·8′	0°17·4′E	X	199
Wishworthy	Corn	SX3683	50°37·7′	4°18·8′W	X	201
Wising Gill	N Yks	SE0773	54°9·4′	1°53·2′W	W	99
Wiske Bank Plantn	N Yks	NZ4202	54°24·9′	1°20·7′W	F	93
Wiske Fm	N Yks	NZ3504	54°26·1′	1°27·2′W	FM	93
Wiske Fm	N Yks	NZ3603	54°25·5′	1°26·3′W	FM	93
Wiske Ho	N Yks	NZ3302	54°25·0′	1°29·1′W	X	93
Wiske Moor	N Yks	SE3597	54°22·3′	1°27·3′W	X	99
Wiskett's Wood	Kent	TQ6734	51°5·1′	0°23·5′E	F	188
Wisley	Surrey	TQ0659	51°19·4′	0°28·3′W	T	187
Wisley Common	Surrey	TQ0758	51°18·9′	0°27·5′W	F	187
Wisp	Scot Bord	NT3700	55°17·7′	2°59·1′W	X	79
Wisp Hill	D & G	NY2699	55°17·0′	3°9·5′W	H	79
Wisp Hill	D & G	NY3899	55°17·1′	2°58·1′W	H	79
Wisp Hill	Lancs	SD5560	54°2·3′	2°40·8′W	X	97
Wispington	Lincs	TF2071	53°13·6′	0°11·7′W	T	122
Wisplaw	Northum	NU1919	55°28·1′	1°41·5′W	X	81
Wissenden	Kent	TQ9041	51°8·4′	0°43·4′E	T	189
Wissett	Suff	TM3679	52°21·7′	1°28·4′E	T	156
Wissett Hall	Suff	TM3878	52°21·1′	1°30·1′E	X	156
Wissett Lodge	Suff	TM3678	52°21·2′	1°28·3′E	X	156
Wissett's Wood	Worcs	SO6772	52°20·9′	2°28·7′W	F	138
Wissington	Suff	TL9533	51°57·9′	0°50·7′E	X	168
Wissington Grange	Suff	TL9534	51°58·4′	0°50·7′E	X	155
Wissington Grove	Suff	TL9334	51°58·5′	0°49·0′E	X	155
Wiss, The	Scot Bord	NT2620	55°28·3′	3°9·8′W	H	73
Wistanstow	Shrops	SO4385	52°27·8′	2°49·9′W	T	137
Wistanswick	Shrops	SJ6628	52°51·1′	2°29·9′W	T	127
Wistaston	Ches	SJ6853	53°4·6′	2°28·3′W	T	118
Wistaston	Heref	SO4250	52°9·0′	2°50·5′W	X	148,149
Wistaston Green	Ches	SJ6854	53°5·2′	2°28·3′W	T	118
Wistlandpound	Devon	SS6442	51°9·9′	3°56·3′W	X	180
Wistlandpound Resr	Devon	SS6441	51°9·4′	3°56·3′W	W	180
Wistley Hill	Glos	SO9718	51°51·9′	2°2·2′W	H	163
Wistman's Wood	Devon	SX6177	50°34·8′	3°57·4′W	F	191
Wiston	Devon	SS8522	50°59·4′	3°37·9′W	X	181
Wiston	Pemb	SN0218	51°49·8′	4°52·0′W	T	157,158
Wiston	S Lanak	NS9532	55°34·5′	3°39·5′W	T	72
Wiston	W Susx	TQ1414	50°55·1′	0°22·3′W	T	198
Wiston Barn	W Susx	TQ1511	50°53·4′	0°21·5′W	X	198
Wiston House	W Susx	TQ1512	50°54·0′	0°21·5′W	A	198
Wiston Lodge	S Lanak	NS9532	55°34·5′	3°39·5′W	X	72
Wiston Mains	S Lanak	NS9531	55°33·9′	3°39·5′W	T	72
Wiston Park	W Susx	TQ1512	50°54·0′	0°21·5′W	X	198
Wiston Wood	Pemb	SN0216	51°48·7′	4°52·0′W	F	157,158
Wistow	Cambs	TL2780	52°24·4′	0°7·6′W	T	142
Wistow	Leic	SP6495	52°33·2′	1°3·0′W	T	140
Wistow	N Yks	SE5935	53°48·7′	1°5·8′W	T	105
Wistow Fen	Cambs	TL3183	52°26·0′	0°4·0′W	X	142
Wistow Grange	Leic	SP6594	52°32·6′	1°2·1′W	X	141
Wiswell	Lancs	SD7437	53°50·0′	2°23·3′W	T	103
Wiswell Eaves	Lancs	SD7537	53°50·0′	2°22·4′W	X	103
Wiswell Moor Fm	Lancs	SD7536	53°49·4′	2°22·4′W	FM	103
Wiswell Moor Houses	Lancs	SD7537	53°50·0′	2°22·4′W	X	103
Witcha Fm	Wilts	SU2973	51°27·5′	1°34·6′W	FM	174
Witcham	Cambs	TL4679	52°23·6′	0°9·1′E	T	143
Witcham Fm	Cambs	TL4787	52°27·9′	0°10·2′E	FM	143
Witcham Hythe	Cambs	TL4581	52°24·7′	0°8·3′E	X	143
Witcham Meadlands	Cambs	TL4483	52°25·8′	0°7·5′E	X	142,143
Witchampton	Dorset	ST9806	50°51·4′	2°1·3′W	T	195
Witchburn	Arg & Bt	NR7120	55°25·5′	5°36·7′W	X	68
Witch Burn	E Renf	NS4557	55°47·1′	4°27·9′W	W	64
Witchcleuch Burn	Scot Bord	NT8426	55°31·9′	2°14·8′W	W	74
Witchcombe	Devon	SX6954	50°22·5′	3°50·2′W	X	202
Witchcot	Shrops	SO5381	52°25·7′	2°41·1′W	X	137,138
Witch Crags	Northum	NT8705	55°20·6′	2°11·9′W	H	80
Witchery Hole	Worcs	SO7262	52°15·6′	2°24·2′W	X	138,149
Witches Br	S Ayr	NX3493	55°12·5′	4°36·1′W	X	76
Witches' Cairn	Scot Bord	NT6667	55°53·9′	2°32·2′W	A	67
Witches' Knowe	Scot Bord	NT9557	55°48·6′	2°4·4′W	H	67,74,75
Witchford	Cambs	TL5078	52°23·0′	0°12·6′E	T	143
Witch-hill	Aberd	NJ9863	57°39·7′	2°1·6′W	X	30
Witchie Knowe	Scot Bord	NT3725	55°31·1′	2°59·4′W	X	73
Witch Knowe	Pth & Kin	NN9919	56°21·4′	3°37·6′W	X	58
Witch Knowe (Roman Signal Station)	Pth & Kin	NN9919	56°21·4′	3°37·6′W	R	58
Witch Lodge	Somer	ST2519	50°58·2′	3°3·7′W	X	193
Witchshaw Rig	D & G	NY1990	55°12·1′	3°15·9′W	H	79
Witch's Stone	Pth & Kin	NO0437	56°31·2′	3°33·2′W	A	52,53
Witch Well	Scot Bord	NT2745	55°41·8′	3°9·3′W	W	73
Witcombe	Somer	ST4721	50°59·4′	2°44·9′W	T	193
Witcombe Bottom	Somer	ST4723	51°0·5′	2°44·9′W	X	193
Witcombe Park	Glos	SO9014	51°49·7′	2°8·3′W	X	163
Witcombe Wood	Glos	SO9113	51°49·2′	2°7·4′W	F	163
Witcomb Fm	Wilts	SU0275	51°28·7′	1°57·9′W	FM	173
Witford Point	Nth Pt Talb	SS7291	51°36·4′	3°50·5′W	X	170
Withacott	Devon	SS4315	50°55·0′	4°13·6′W	T	180,190
Witham	Essex	TL8114	51°47·9′	0°37·9′E	T	168
Witham Brewery	Lincs	TF2251	53°2·8′	0°10·4′W	X	122
Witham Common	Lincs	SK9320	52°46·4′	0°36·9′W	X	130
Witham Fm	Lincs	SK9160	53°8·0′	0°38·0′W	FM	121
Witham Friary	Somer	ST7441	51°10·3′	2°21·9′W	T	183
Witham Hall	Stock on T	NZ4215	54°32·0′	1°20·6′W	X	93
Witham Hall Fm	Somer	ST7541	51°10·3′	2°21·1′W	FM	183
Witham House Fm	Lincs	TF1956	53°5·5′	0°13·0′W	FM	122
Witham on the Hill	Lincs	TF0516	52°44·1′	0°26·3′W	T	130
Witham Park	Somer	ST7638	51°8·7′	2°20·2′W	F	183
Witham Park Fm	Somer	ST7639	51°9·2′	2°20·2′W	FM	183
Witham's Fm	Suff	TL7558	52°11·8′	0°34·0′E	FM	155
Withan	Corn	SW7424	50°4·6′	5°9·2′W	X	204
Withaquoy	Orkney	HY4602	58°54·4′	2°55·8′W	X	6,7
Withcall	Lincs	TF2883	53°19·9′	0°4·3′W	T	122
Withcall Village	Lincs	TF2883	53°19·9′	0°4·3′W	A	122
Withcote Lodge	Leic	SK8004	52°37·9′	0°48·7′W	X	141
Withdean	Bri & Hov	TQ3007	50°51·1′	0°8·8′W	T	198
Withe Bottom	Cumbr	SD1593	54°19·8′	3°18·0′W	X	96
Withecombe	Devon	SX6989	50°41·4′	3°50·9′W	X	191

Withen Fm	Devon	SY0290	50°42·3′	3°22·9′W	FM	192
Withens Brook	Derby	SE1101	53°30·6′	1°49·6′W	W	110
Withens Edge	Derby	SE1102	53°31·1′	1°49·6′W	X	110
Withenshaw	Ches	SJ9468	53°12·8′	2°5·0′W	X	118
Withens Moor	Derby	SE1101	53°30·6′	1°49·6′W	X	110
Witherden Fm	Kent	TQ8445	51°10·7′	0°38·3′E	FM	188
Witherdens Hall	Kent	TR2456	51°15·8′	1°13·0′E	X	179
Witherdon	Devon	SX4394	50°43·7′	4°13·1′W	X	190
Witherdon Wood	Devon	SX4395	50°44·2′	4°13·1′W	F	190
Withered Howe	Cumbr	NY4606	54°27·0′	2°49·5′W	X	90
Witherenden Fm	E Susx	TQ6527	51°1·3′	0°21·6′E	FM	188,199
Witherenden Hill	E Susx	TQ6426	51°0·8′	0°20·7′E	T	188,199
Withergate	Norf	TG2927	52°47·7′	1°24·2′E	T	133,134
Witherholme Hall	N Yks	SE6370	54°7·6′	1°1·7′W	X	100
Witherhurst	E Susx	TQ6624	50°59·7′	0°22·3′E	X	199
Witheridge	Devon	SS8014	50°55·0′	3°42·0′W	T	181
Witheridge	Devon	SX8270	50°31·3′	3°39·5′W	X	202
Witheridge Fm	Somer	SS9234	51°5·9′	3°32·2′W	FM	181
Witheridge Hill	Oxon	SU6984	51°33·3′	0°59·9′W	T	175
Witheridge Moor	Devon	SS8515	50°55·6′	3°37·8′W	X	181
Witheridge Moor Fm	Devon	SS8514	50°55·1′	3°37·8′W	FM	181
Witheridge Wood	Bucks	SU9293	51°37·9′	0°39·8′W	F	175
Witherington Down	Wilts	SU2024	51°1·1′	1°42·5′W	X	184
Witherington Fm	Wilts	SU1824	51°1·1′	1°44·2′W	FM	184
Witherley	Leic	SP3297	52°34·4′	1°31·3′W	T	140
Witherley Fields Fm	Leic	SP3298	52°35·0′	1°31·3′W	FM	140
Withermarsh Green	Suff	TM0137	51°59·9′	0°56·1′E	T	155
Withern	Lincs	TF4382	53°19·2′	0°9·2′E	T	122
Withernick Grange	E Yorks	TA1741	53°51·4′	0°12·9′W	X	107
Withernsea	E Yorks	TA3427	53°43·6′	0°2·3′E	T	107
Withernwick	E Yorks	TA1940	53°50·8′	0°11·1′W	T	107
Withersdale Hall	Suff	TM2880	52°22·5′	1°21·4′E	X	156
Withersdale Street	Suff	TM2781	52°23·0′	1°20·5′E	T	156
Withersdane	Kent	TR0545	51°10·3′	0°56·3′E	T	179,189
Withersdane Hall	Kent	TR0646	51°10·8′	0°57·2′E	X	179,189
Withersfield	Suff	TL6547	52°6·0′	0°24·9′E	T	154
Withers Fm	Hants	SU2914	50°55·7′	1°34·9′W	FM	196
Withers Fm	W Berks	SU5371	51°26·4′	1°13·9′W	FM	174
Witherslack	Cumbr	SD4384	54°15·2′	2°52·1′W	T	97
Witherslack Hall (Sch)	Cumbr	SD4386	54°16·2′	2°52·1′W	X	97
Witherstone	Heref	SO5531	51°58·8′	2°38·9′W	X	149
Witherwack	Sund	NZ3759	54°55·7′	1°24·9′W	T	88
Witherwin Fm	Warr	SJ6285	53°21·9′	2°33·9′W	FM	109
Witheven	Corn	SX2194	50°43·3′	4°31·8′W	X	190
Witheven	Corn	SX2292	50°42·3′	4°30·9′W	X	190
Withey Brook	Corn	SX2474	50°32·6′	4°28·7′W	W	201
Witheybrook	Devon	SX6398	50°46·2′	3°56·2′W	X	191
Witheybrook Marsh	Corn	SX2572	50°31·5′	4°27·8′W	X	201
Withgill	Lancs	SD7041	53°52·1′	2°27·0′W	X	103
Withial	Somer	ST5736	51°7·5′	2°36·5′W	T	182,183
Withiel	Corn	SW9965	50°27·3′	4°49·5′W	T	200
Withiel Florey	Somer	SS9833	51°5·5′	3°27·0′W	T	181
Withiel Fm	Somer	SS9833	51°5·5′	3°27·0′W	FM	181
Withiel Fm	Somer	ST2439	51°8·9′	3°4·8′W	FM	182
Withielgoose	Corn	SX0065	50°27·3′	4°48·7′W	T	200
Withielgoose Mills	Corn	SX0065	50°27·3′	4°48·7′W	T	200
Withies	Heref	SO5542	52°4·7′	2°39·0′W	X	149
Withies Green Fm	Essex	TL7922	51°52·3′	0°36·4′E	FM	167
Withi Gill	Orkney	ND2496	58°51·0′	3°18·5′W	H	6,7
Withill	Devon	SX5472	50°32·0′	4°3·2′W	X	191,201
Within Clough	Derby	SK0791	53°25·2′	1°53·3′W	X	110
Withington	Glos	SP0315	51°50·7′	1°57·0′W	T	163
Withington	Heref	SO5643	52°5·3′	2°38·1′W	T	149
Withington	Man	SJ8592	53°25·7′	2°13·1′W	T	109
Withington	Shrops	SJ5713	52°43·0′	2°37·8′W	T	126
Withington	Staffs	SK0335	52°55·0′	1°56·9′W	T	128
Withington Green	Ches	SJ8071	53°14·4′	2°17·6′W	T	118
Withington Hall	Ches	SJ8172	53°14·9′	2°16·7′W	X	118
Withington Marsh	Heref	SO5544	52°5·8′	2°39·0′W	T	149
Withington Woods	Glos	SP0314	51°49·7′	1°57·0′W	F	163
Withinlee Fm	Ches	SJ8876	53°17·1′	2°10·4′W	FM	118
Withinreap Fm	Lancs	SD5939	53°51·0′	2°37·0′W	FM	102
Withins	Brad	SD9835	53°48·9′	2°1·4′W	X	103
Withins Clough Reservoir	Cald	SD9822	53°41·9′	2°1·4′W	W	103
Withins Flat	Brad	SD9835	53°48·9′	2°1·4′W	X	103
Withins Height	Cald	SD9734	53°48·4′	2°2·3′W	H	103
Withins Moor	Cald	SD9722	53°41·9′	2°2·3′W	X	103
Withins Slack	Brad	SD9835	53°48·9′	2°1·4′W	X	103
Withins, The	Lancs	SD3205	53°32·5′	3°1·2′W	X	108
Withinstreet Fm	Ches	SJ7162	53°9·5′	2°25·6′W	FM	118
Withins Wood	Shrops	SO3284	52°27·2′	2°59·6′W	F	137
Withleigh	Devon	SS9012	50°54·1′	3°33·5′W	T	181
Withleigh Goodman	Devon	SS9111	50°53·5′	3°32·6′W	X	192
Withmale Park Wood	Northnts	SP8371	52°20·1′	0°46·5′W	F	141
Withnell	Lancs	SD6322	53°41·8′	2°33·2′W	T	102,103
Withnell Fold	Lancs	SD6123	53°42·4′	2°35·0′W	T	102,103
Withnell Moor	Lancs	SD6419	53°40·2′	2°32·3′W	X	109
Withnell Moor	Lancs	SD6420	53°40·8′	2°32·3′W	X	102,103
Withnoe	Corn	SX4052	50°21·0′	4°14·6′W	X	201
Withstocks Wood	Herts	TL1320	51°52·3′	0°21·1′W	F	166
Withybed Bottom	Hants	SU2510	50°53·6′	1°38·3′W	X	195
Withybed Green	Worcs	SP0172	52°21·0′	1°58·7′W	T	139
Withybed Wood	Shrops	SO7577	52°23·7′	2°21·6′W	F	138
Withy Bridge	Glos	SO9024	51°55·1′	2°8·3′W	X	163
Withybrook	Somer	ST6547	51°13·5′	2°29·7′W	T	183
Withybrook	Warw	SP4384	52°27·4′	1°21·6′W	T	140
Withybrook Grange	Warw	SP4485	52°27·9′	1°20·7′W	X	140
Withybrook Spinney	Warw	SP4485	52°27·9′	1°20·7′W	F	140
Withybush	Pemb	SM9617	51°49·1′	4°57·2′W	T	157,158
Withycombe	Devon	SS6842	51°10·0′	3°52·9′W	X	180
Withycombe	Somer	SS8238	51°8·0′	3°40·8′W	X	181
Withycombe	Somer	ST0141	51°9·8′	3°24·6′W	T	181
Withycombe Farm Ho	Oxon	SP4340	52°3·6′	1°22·0′W	X	151
Withycombe Fm	Devon	SX7993	50°43·7′	3°42·5′W	FM	191
Withycombe Fm	Oxon	SP3734	52°0·4′	1°27·3′W	FM	151
Withycombe Fm	Somer	SS8835	51°6·4′	3°35·6′W	FM	181
Withycombe Fm	Somer	ST0527	51°2·3′	3°20·9′W	FM	181
Withycombe Hill	Somer	ST0041	51°9·8′	3°25·4′W	H	181
Withycombe Raleigh	Devon	SY0181	50°37·5′	3°23·6′W	T	192
Withycombe Ridge	Devon	SS7745	51°11·7′	3°45·2′W	X	180

Withycombe Scruffets	Somer	SS9840	51°9·2′	3°27·1′W	X	181
Withycombe Wood	Warw	SP1457	52°12·9′	1°47·3′W	F	151
Withy Copse	Oxon	SU6880	51°31·1′	1°0·8′W	F	175
Withy Cross	Devon	SS5619	50°57·4′	4°2·6′W	X	180
Withyditch	Bath & NE Somer	ST7059	51°20·0′	2°25·4′W	T	172
Withy Fm	Somer	ST3243	51°11·2′	2°58·0′W	FM	182
Withygate	Devon	SS7034	51°5·7′	3°51·0′W	X	180
Withy Grove Fm	Somer	ST3244	51°11·7′	2°58·0′W	FM	182
Withyham	E Susx	TQ4935	51°5·9′	0°8·1′E	T	188
Withy Hill Fm	Birm	SP1497	52°34·5′	1°47·2′W	FM	139
Withy Mills	Bath & NE Somer	ST6657	51°18·9′	2°28·9′W	T	172
Withymoor Fm	Ches	SJ6040	52°57·6′	2°35·3′W	FM	118
Withymoor Fm	Heref	SO6723	51°54·5′	2°28·4′W	FM	162
Withymoor Village	Dudley	SO9186	52°28·5′	2°7·6′W	T	139
Withymore Fm	Devon	SX7040	50°15·0′	3°49·0′W	FM	202
Withypitts Fm	W Susx	TQ3435	51°6·1′	0°4·8′W	FM	187
Withypool	Somer	SS8435	51°6·4′	3°39·0′W	T	181
Withypool Common	Somer	SS8234	51°5·8′	3°40·7′W	H	181
Withypool Cross	Somer	SS8033	51°5·3′	3°42·4′W	X	181
Withypool Fm	Shrops	SO6475	52°22·5′	2°31·3′W	FM	138
Withypool Hill	Somer	SS8334	51°5·8′	3°39·9′W	H	181
Withysitch Fm	Staffs	SJ9833	52°53·9′	2°1·4′W	FM	127
Withyslade Fm	Wilts	ST9528	51°3·3′	2°3·9′W	FM	184
Withystakes	Staffs	SJ9548	53°2·0′	2°4·1′W	T	118
Withy Trees	Lancs	SD5736	53°49·4′	2°38·8′W	X	102
Withy Wells	Worcs	SO8955	52°11·8′	2°9·3′W	X	150
Withywine	Devon	SS9626	51°1·7′	3°28·6′W	X	181
Withywood	C of Bris	ST5767	51°24·3′	2°36·7′W	T	172,182
Witley	Surrey	SU9439	51°8·8′	0°39·0′W	T	186
Witley Common	Surrey	SU9240	51°9·3′	0°40·7′W	F	186
Witley Court	Worcs	SO7664	52°16·7′	2°20·7′W	A	138,150
Witley Fm	Surrey	SU9136	51°7·2′	0°41·6′W	FM	186
Witley Park	Surrey	SU9239	51°8·8′	0°40·7′W	X	186
Witley Sta	Surrey	SU9437	51°7·7′	0°39·0′W	X	186
Witnells End	Worcs	SO7981	52°25·8′	2°18·1′W	T	138
Witnesham	Suff	TM1850	52°6·5′	1°11·4′E	T	156
Witnesham Thicks	Suff	TM1651	52°7·1′	1°9·7′E	F	156
Witney	Oxon	SP3509	51°46·9′	1°29·2′W	T	164
Witney Green	Essex	TL5806	51°44·1′	0°17·7′E	X	167
Witney Lane Fm	Ches	SJ4949	53°2·4′	2°45·2′W	FM	117
Witsetts, The	Heref	SO5355	52°11·7′	2°40·9′W	X	149
Wittenham Clumps	Oxon	SU5692	51°37·7′	1°11·1′W	F	164,174
Wittensford	Hants	SU2813	50°55·2′	1°35·7′W	T	195
Witterage, The	Shrops	SJ4824	52°48·9′	2°45·9′W	X	126
Wittering	Peterb	TF0502	52°36·6′	0°26·6′W	T	142
Wittering Airfield	Peterb	TF0302	52°36·6′	0°28·3′W	X	141
Wittering Coppice	Peterb	TF0200	52°35·5′	0°29·3′W	F	141
Wittering Grange	Peterb	TF0500	52°35·5′	0°26·6′W	X	142
Wittering Lodge	Peterb	TF0300	52°35·5′	0°28·4′W	X	141
Wittersham	Kent	TQ8927	51°0·9′	0°42·1′E	T	189
Wittersham Manor	Kent	TQ8826	51°0·4′	0°41·2′E	X	189,199
Wittersham Road Sta	Kent	TQ8628	51°1·5′	0°39·5′E	X	189,199
Witter, The	Aberd	NO3179	56°54·1′	3°7·5′W	X	44
Witter,The	Orkney	HY2204	58°55·2′	3°20·8′W	A	6,7
Witter, The	Orkney	ND2789	58°47·2′	3°15·3′W	X	7
Witton	Angus	NO5670	56°49·4′	2°42·8′W	X	44
Witton	Birm	SP0891	52°31·2′	1°52·5′W	T	139
Witton	Norf	TG3109	52°38·0′	1°25·2′E	T	134
Witton	Worcs	SO8962	52°15·6′	2°9·3′W	T	150
Witton Br	Norf	TG3209	52°38·0′	1°26·1′E	X	134
Witton Bridge	Norf	TG3431	52°49·8′	1°28·8′E	T	133
Witton Castle	Durham	NZ1530	54°40·1′	1°45·6′W	A	92
Witton Country Park	Black w Dar	SD6527	53°44·5′	2°31·4′W	X	102,103
Witton Fell	N Yks	SE1385	54°15·9′	1°47·6′W	H	99
Witton Gilbert	Durham	NZ2346	54°48·7′	1°38·1′W	T	88
Witton Hall	Norf	TG3231	52°49·8′	1°27·1′E	X	133
Witton Heath	Norf	TG3130	52°49·3′	1°26·1′E	X	133
Witton Hill	Worcs	SO7661	52°15·0′	2°20·7′W	T	138,150
Witton Ho	Norf	TG3009	52°38·0′	1°24·3′E	X	134
Witton Lakes	Birm	SP0892	52°31·8′	1°52·5′W	W	139
Witton-le-Wear	Durham	NZ1431	54°40·7′	1°46·5′W	T	92
Witton Moor	N Yks	SE1483	54°14·8′	1°46·7′W	X	99
Witton Park	Durham	NZ1730	54°40·1′	1°43·8′W	T	92
Wittons Fm	Lancs	SD7752	53°58·1′	2°20·6′W	FM	103
Witton Shields	Northum	NZ1290	55°12·5′	1°48·3′W	X	81
Wittonstone	Northum	NZ0888	55°11·4′	1°52·0′W	X	81
Witts End	Beds	SP9832	51°58·9′	0°34·0′W	X	165
Wiveliscombe	Somer	ST0827	51°2·3′	3°18·4′W	T	181
Wivelrod	Hants	SU6738	51°8·5′	1°2·1′W	T	185,186
Wivelscombe	Corn	SX3957	50°23·7′	4°15·5′W	X	201
Wiveliscombe Barrow	Somer	ST0034	51°6·0′	3°25·3′W	A	181
Wivelsden Fm	E Susx	TQ3620	50°58·0′	0°3·4′W	FM	198
Wivelsfield	E Susx	TQ3420	50°58·1′	0°5·1′W	T	198
Wivelsfield Green	E Susx	TQ3520	50°58·0′	0°4·3′W	T	198
Wivelsfield Hall	E Susx	TQ3520	50°58·0′	0°4·3′W	X	198
Wivelsfield Sta	W Susx	TQ3219	50°57·5′	0°6·8′W	X	198
Wivenhoe	Essex	TM0422	51°51·8′	0°58·2′E	T	168
Wivenhoe Lodge	Essex	TM0323	51°52·3′	0°57·3′E	X	168
Wiverton	Devon	SX5654	50°22·3′	4°1·1′W	X	202
Wiverton Hall	Notts	SK7136	52°55·2′	0°56·2′W	X	129
Wiveton	Norf	TG0443	52°57·0′	1°2·6′E	T	133
Wiveton Downs	Norf	TG0342	52°56·4′	1°1·7′E	X	133
Wiveton Hall	Norf	TG0344	52°57·5′	1°1·7′E	X	133
Wix	Essex	TM1628	51°54·7′	1°8·8′E	T	168,169
Wix Abbey	Essex	TM1628	51°54·7′	1°8·8′E	X	168,169
Wix Fm	Surrey	TQ0752	51°15·7′	0°27·6′W	FM	187
Wixford	Warw	SP0854	52°11·3′	1°52·6′W	T	150
Wixford Lodge	Warw	SP0953	52°10·7′	1°51·7′W	X	150
Wixhill	Shrops	SJ5628	52°51·1′	2°38·8′W	T	126
Wixland	Devon	SS5922	50°59·0′	4°0·1′W	X	180
Wix Lodge	Essex	TM1428	51°54·8′	1°7·1′E	X	168,169
Wixoe	Essex	TL7142	52°3·2′	0°30·0′E	T	154
Wixoldbury Fm	S Glos	ST7087	51°35·1′	2°25·6′W	FM	172
Wixon Fm	Devon	SS7216	50°56·0′	3°48·9′W	FM	180
Wix's Fm	Kent	TQ9938	51°6·6′	0°51·0′E	FM	189
Wiza Beck	Cumbr	NY2645	54°47·9′	3°8·6′W	W	85
Wiza Fm	Cumbr	NY2545	54°47·9′	3°9·6′W	FM	85

Wizaller	Devon	SX7051	50°20·9′	3°49·3′W	X	202
Wizard Lodge	Norf	TF7217	52°43·6′	0°33·2′E	X	132
Wizard, The	Ches	SJ8677	53°17·6′	2°12·2′W	X	118
W Mill Loch of Hamar	Shetld	HU3075	60°27·7′	1°26·8′W	W	3
Woad Fm	Lincs	TF3541	52°57·2′	0°1·0′E	FM	131
Woad Fm	Lincs	TF4219	52°45·2′	0°6·7′E	FM	131
Woad Fm	Mil Key	SP8147	52°7·2′	0°48·6′W	FM	152
Woad Fm	Mil Key	SP8744	52°5·5′	0°43·4′W	FM	152
Woad Hill	Bucks	SP7521	51°53·2′	0°54·2′W	X	165
Woadmill Fm	Oxon	SP4138	52°2·6′	1°23·7′W	FM	151
Wobage Fm	Heref	SO6327	51°56·7′	2°31·9′W	FM	162
Woburn	Beds	SP9433	51°59·5′	0°37·5′W	T	165
Woburn Abbey	Beds	SP9632	51°58·9′	0°35·7′W	X	165
Woburn Experimental Fm	Beds	SP9636	52°1·1′	0°35·7′W	FM	153
Woburn Park	Beds	SP9633	51°59·5′	0°35·7′W	X	165
Woburn Park	Beds	SP9634	52°0·0′	0°35·7′W	X	153,165
Woburn Park	Surrey	TQ0565	51°22·7′	0°29·1′W	X	176
Woburn Sands	Mil Key	SP9235	52°0·6′	0°39·2′W	T	152
Wodehouse, The	Staffs	SO8893	52°32·3′	2°10·2′W	A	139
Woden Croft	Durham	NZ0020	54°34·8′	1°59·6′W	X	92
Woden Law	Scot Bord	NT7612	55°24·3′	2°22·3′W	H	80
Woeful Lake Fm	Glos	SP1513	51°49·2′	1°46·5′W	FM	163
Wofferwood Common	Heref	SO6951	52°9·6′	2°26·8′W	T	149
Wogaston	Pemb	SM9100	51°39·8′	5°0·9′W	X	157,158
Wogden Clough	Barns	SE1701	53°30·6′	1°44·2′W	X	110
Wogle	Aberd	NJ8011	57°11·6′	2°19·4′W	X	38
Wokefield Common	W Berks	SU6566	51°23·6′	1°3·6′W	X	175
Wokefield Park	W Berks	SU6765	51°23·0′	1°1·8′W	X	175
Woking	Surrey	TQ0058	51°19·0′	0°33·5′W	T	186
Wokingham	Wok	SU8068	51°24·6′	0°50·6′W	T	175
Wokingpark Fm	Surrey	TQ0357	51°18·4′	0°30·9′W	FM	186
Wolborough	Devon	SX8570	50°31·3′	3°37·0′W	T	202
Woldale Lodge	Lincs	TF2677	53°16·7′	0°6·2′W	X	122
Wold Barn	N Yks	SE8669	54°6·8′	0°40·6′W	X	101
Wold Cottage, The	E Yorks	TA0472	54°8·8′	0°24·1′W	X	101
Wold Dyke Fm	E Yorks	SE9248	53°55·4′	0°35·5′W	FM	106
Wold End Moss	Cumbr	SD6885	54°15·8′	2°29·1′W	X	98
Wold Fell	Cumbr	SD7885	54°15·9′	2°19·8′W	H	98
Wold Fell Bents	Cumbr	SD7884	54°15·3′	2°19·8′W	X	98
Wold Fm	E Yorks	SE8349	53°56·1′	0°43·7′W	FM	106
Wold Fm	E Yorks	SE9159	54°1·4′	0°36·2′W	FM	106
Wold Fm	E Yorks	SE9442	53°52·2′	0°33·8′W	FM	106
Wold Fm	E Yorks	TA2172	54°8·0′	0°8·5′W	FM	101
Wold Fm	N Yks	SE8060	54°2·0′	0°46·3′W	FM	100
Wold Fm	N Yks	SE8764	54°4·1′	0°39·8′W	FM	101
Wold Fm	N Yks	SE9174	54°9·5′	0°36·0′W	FM	101
Wold Gate	E Yorks	TA1166	54°4·9′	0°17·8′W	X	101
Woldgill Burn	Cumbr	NY6645	54°48·2′	2°31·3′W	W	86
Woldgill Moss	Cumbr	NY6745	54°48·2′	2°30·4′W	X	86,87
Wold Haven	E Yorks	SE8048	53°55·6′	0°46·5′W	X	106
Wold Ho	E Yorks	TA0066	54°5·0′	0°27·9′W	X	101
Wold Ho	E Yorks	TA0560	54°1·8′	0°23·4′W	X	101
Wold Ho	N Yks	SE8462	54°3·1′	0°42·6′W	X	100
Wold Ho	N Yks	SE8570	54°7·4′	0°41·5′W	X	100
Wold Hos	N Yks	SE6795	54°21·0′	0°57·7′W	X	94,100
Wold House Fm	E Yorks	SE8657	54°0·3′	0°40·9′W	FM	106
Wold House Fm	E Yorks	SE9042	53°52·2′	0°37·5′W	FM	106
Wold House Fm	E Yorks	SE9048	53°55·5′	0°37·4′W	FM	106
Wold House Fm	E Yorks	SE9235	53°48·4′	0°35·8′W	FM	106
Wold House Fm	E Yorks	TA0061	54°2·4′	0°28·0′W	FM	101
Woldhurst	W Susx	SU8801	50°48·3′	0°44·7′W	T	197
Woldingham	Surrey	TQ3756	51°17·4′	0°1·7′W	T	187
Woldingham Garden Village	Surrey	TQ3656	51°17·4′	0°2·6′W	T	187
Wold Newton	E Yorks	TA0473	54°8·8′	0°24·0′W	T	101
Wold Newton	NE Lincs	TF2496	53°27·0′	0°7·6′W	T	113
Wold Newton Field	E Yorks	TA0573	54°8·8′	0°23·1′W	X	101
Wold Newton Grange	E Yorks	TA0573	54°8·8′	0°23·1′W	X	101
Woldringfold	W Susx	TQ2024	51°0·4′	0°17·0′W	X	198
Wold Sea Fm	Lincs	TF5276	53°15·8′	0°17·1′E	FM	122
Wolds Fm	Leic	SK6322	52°47·7′	1°3·5′W	FM	129
Wolds Fm	Leic	SK6420	52°46·7′	1°2·7′W	FM	129
Wolds Fm	Leic	SK7425	52°49·3′	0°53·7′W	FM	129
Wolds Fm	Notts	SK5925	52°49·4′	1°7·1′W	FM	129
Wolds Fm	Notts	SK6526	52°49·9′	1°1·7′W	FM	129
Wolds Fm	Notts	SK6532	52°53·1′	1°1·6′W	FM	129
Wolds Hill	Notts	SK6533	52°53·7′	1°1·6′W	X	129
Woldside	N Yks	SD8883	54°14·8′	2°10·6′W	X	98
Wolds Remand Prison	E Yorks	SE8931	53°46·3′	0°38·6′W	X	106
Wolds, The	E Yorks	SE9457	54°0·3′	0°33·5′W	X	106
Wolds, The	E Yorks	SE9763	54°3·5′	0°30·7′W	H	101
Wolds, The	Lincs	TF2389	53°23·2′	0°8·6′W	X	113
Wolds, The	Lincs	TF2685	53°21·0′	0°6·0′W	H	122
Wolds Way	E Yorks	SE9142	53°52·2′	0°36·5′W	X	106
Wolds Way	E Yorks	TA0125	53°42·9′	0°27·8′W	X	106,107
Wolds Way	N Yks	SE8362	54°3·1′	0°43·5′W	X	100
Wold, The	Northnts	SP8454	52°10·9′	0°45·9′W	X	152
Wolfa	Cumbr	NY5335	54°42·7′	2°43·3′W	X	90
Wolf Burn	Aberd	NO5686	56°58·0′	2°43·0′W	W	44
Wolfcleuch Burn	Scot Bord	NT3107	55°21·4′	3°4·9′W	W	79
Wolfcleuchhead	Scot Bord	NT3207	55°21·4′	3°3·9′W	X	79
Wolfcleugh	Northum	NY7949	54°50·4′	2°19·2′W	X	86,87
Wolf Cleugh	Scot Bord	NT3447	55°43·0′	3°2·6′W	X	73
Wolf Cleugh	Scot Bord	NT8267	55°54·0′	2°16·8′W	X	67
Wolfcleugh Common	Durham	NY8843	54°47·2′	2°10·8′W	X	87
Wolf Cleugh Fm	Durham	NY9042	54°46·6′	2°8·9′W	FM	87
Wolfclyde	S Lanak	NT0236	55°36·7′	3°32·9′W	X	72
Wolf Crags	Cumbr	NY3522	54°35·6′	2°59·9′W	X	90
Wolf Craig	Angus	NO3882	56°55·8′	3°0·7′W	H	44
Wolf Craigs	W Loth	NT0956	55°47·6′	3°26·6′W	X	65,72
Wolfcrooks	S Lanak	NS8635	55°36·0′	3°48·1′W	X	71,72
Wolf-Dale	Staffs	SJ9461	53°9·0′	2°5·0′W	X	118
Wolf Edge	Staffs	SK0267	53°12·2′	1°57·8′W	X	119
Wolfe Hall	Suff	TL7762	52°13·9′	0°35·9′E	X	155
Wolfehopelee	Scot Bord	NT5808	55°22·1′	2°39·3′W	X	80
Wolfelee	Scot Bord	NT5809	55°22·6′	2°39·3′W	X	80
Wolfelee Hill	Scot Bord	NT5908	55°22·1′	2°38·4′W	H	80
Wolfen Hall	Lancs	SD6044	53°53·7′	2°36·1′W	X	102,103
Wolferd Green	Norf	TM2599	52°32·8′	1°19·5′E	T	134
Wolferlow	Heref	SO6661	52°15·0′	2°29·5′W	T	138,149

Wolferlow Park	Heref	SO6663	52°16·1′	2°29·5′W	X	138,149
Wolfershiel	Northum	NU0100	55°17·9′	1°58·6′W	X	81
Wolferton	Norf	TF6528	52°49·7′	0°27·4′E	T	132
Wolferton Creek	Norf	TF6432	52°51·9′	0°26·6′E	W	132
Wolferton Ho	Norf	TF8510	52°39·6′	0°44·5′E	X	132
Wolferton Wood	Norf	TF6627	52°49·1′	0°28·2′E	F	132
Wolfeton Clump	Dorset	SY6995	50°45·5′	2°26·0′W	F	194
Wolfeton Eweleaze	Dorset	SY6893	50°44·4′	2°26·8′W	X	194
Wolfeton Ho	Dorset	SY6792	50°43·8′	2°27·7′W	A	194
Wolf Fell	Lancs	SD6045	53°54·2′	2°36·1′W	X	102,103
Wolfgar Fm	Devon	SX7595	50°44·7′	3°45·9′W	FM	191
Wolf Grain	Aberd	NO4388	56°59·0′	2°55·8′W	W	44
Wolfhall	Wilts	SU2461	51°21·1′	1°38·9′W	X	174
Wolfhampcote	Warw	SP5265	52°17·1′	1°13·9′W	T	151
Wolfhanger Fm	Hants	SU6328	51°3·1′	1°5·7′W	FM	185
Wolf Hill	Aberd	NO5982	56°55·9′	2°40·0′W	X	44
Wolf Hill	Angus	NO3377	56°53·0′	3°5·5′W	H	44
Wolfhill	Pth & Kin	NO1433	56°29·1′	3°23·3′W	X	53
Wolfhill	Pth & Kin	NO1533	56°29·1′	3°22·4′W	T	53
Wolf Hills	Northum	NY7258	54°55·2′	2°25·8′W	X	86,87
Wolfhills Burn	Northum	NY7357	54°54·7′	2°24·8′W	W	86,87
Wolf Hole	Northum	NU0903	55°19·5′	1°51·1′W	X	81
Wolfhole Crag	Lancs	SD6357	54°0·7′	2°33·5′W	X	102,103
Wolfhope Burn	D & G	NY3593	55°13·9′	3°0·9′W	W	79
Wolfin Fm	Devon	SS7504	50°49·6′	3°46·1′W	FM	191
Wolflaw	Angus	NO4455	56°41·3′	2°54·4′W	X	54
Wolford Fields	Warw	SP2636	52°1·5′	1°36·9′W	X	151
Wolford Fm	Devon	ST1304	50°50·0′	3°13·7′W	FM	192,193
Wolford Lodge	Devon	ST1305	50°50·5′	3°13·8′W	X	192,193
Wolford Wood	Warw	SP2333	51°59·9′	1°39·5′W	F	151
Wolf Pit	N Yks	NZ7003	54°25·3′	0°54·8′W	X	94
Wolfpits	Powys	SO2158	52°13·1′	3°9·0′W	X	148
Wolf Pit (Tumulus)	N Yks	NZ7003	54°25·3′	0°54·8′W	A	94
Wolfridge Fm	Dorset	ST8327	51°2·8′	2°14·2′W	FM	183
Wolf Rig	Scot Bord	NT2427	55°32·1′	3°11·8′W	H	73
Wolf Rock	Corn	SW2620	50°1·3′	5°49·2′W	X	203
Wolf's Castle	Pemb	SM9526	51°53·9′	4°58·4′W	T	157,158
Wolfscote Dale	Staffs	SK1357	53°6·8′	1°47·9′W	X	119
Wolfscote Grange	Derby	SK1358	53°7·4′	1°47·9′W	X	119
Wolfscote Hill	Derby	SK1358	53°7·4′	1°47·9′W	H	119
Wolfsdale	Pemb	SM9321	51°51·2′	5°0·0′W	T	157,158
Wolfsdale Hill	Pemb	SM9322	51°51·7′	5°0·0′W	T	157,158
Wolfsgrove	Devon	SX8974	50°33·5′	3°33·6′W	X	192
Wolfshead	Shrops	SJ3620	52°46·7′	2°56·5′W	X	126
Wolf Slock, The	E Ayr	NX4589	55°10·5′	4°25·6′W	X	77
Wolfstar	E Loth	NT4168	55°54·3′	2°56·2′W	X	66
Wolf Stones	Lancs	SD9639	53°51·1′	2°3·2′W	X	103
Wolfstones Height	Kirk	SE1209	53°34·9′	1°48·7′W	X	110
Wolgarston	Staffs	SJ9314	52°43·7′	2°5·8′W	X	127
Woll	Scot Bord	NT4622	55°29·6′	2°50·8′W	T	73
Wolla Bank	Lincs	TF5574	53°14·7′	0°19·8′E	X	122
Wolland Fm	Devon	SS8906	50°50·8′	3°34·2′W	FM	192
Wollaston	Dudley	SO8884	52°27·5′	2°10·2′W	T	139
Wollaston	Northnts	SP9162	52°15·1′	0°39·6′W	T	152
Wollaston	Shrops	SJ3212	52°42·3′	3°0·0′W	T	126
Wollaton	C of Nott	SK5239	52°57·0′	1°13·2′W	T	129
Wollaton	Corn	SX3865	50°28·0′	4°16·6′W	X	201
Wollaton	Devon	SX5552	50°21·2′	4°1·9′W	X	202
Wollaton Park	C of Nott	SK5339	52°57·0′	1°12·3′W	X	129
Woll Burn	Scot Bord	NT4522	55°29·6′	2°51·8′W	W	73
Wolleigh	Devon	SX8080	50°36·7′	3°41·4′W	X	191
Wollerton	Shrops	SJ6230	52°52·2′	2°33·5′W	T	127
Wollerton Wood	Shrops	SJ6131	52°52·7′	2°34·4′W	T	127
Wollescote	Dudley	SO9283	52°26·9′	2°6·7′W	T	139
Wolleux	Corn	SX2285	50°38·5′	4°30·7′W	X	201
Woll Rig	Scot Bord	NT4423	55°30·1′	2°52·8′W	X	73
Wollrig	Scot Bord	NT4522	55°29·6′	2°51·8′W	X	73
Wolsdon Ho	Corn	SX4054	50°22·1′	4°14·6′W	X	201
Wolseley Garden Park	Staffs	SK0220	52°46·9′	1°57·8′W	X	128
Wolseley Park	Staffs	SK0119	52°46·4′	1°58·7′W	F	128
Wolseley Park Ho	Staffs	SK0118	52°45·8′	1°58·7′W	X	128
Wolseley Plain	Staffs	SK0018	52°45·8′	1°59·6′W	X	128
Wolsey Br	Suff	TM4776	52°19·8′	1°37·9′E	X	156
Wolseyhouse Fm	Suff	TM3868	52°15·7′	1°29·7′E	FM	156
Wolsey's Fm	Essex	TL6027	51°55·3′	0°20·0′E	FM	167
Wolsingham	Durham	NZ0737	54°43·9′	1°53·1′W	T	92
Wolsingham North Moor	Durham	NZ0840	54°45·5′	1°52·1′W	X	88
Wolsingham Park Moor	Durham	NZ0340	54°45·5′	1°56·8′W	X	87
Wolstanton	Staffs	SJ8548	53°2·0′	2°13·0′W	T	118
Wolstenholme	Roch	SD8515	53°38·1′	2°13·2′W	T	109
Wolston	Warw	SP4175	52°22·5′	1°23·5′W	T	140
Wolstonbury	W Susx	TQ2813	50°54·4′	0°10·4′W	H	198
Wolstonbury Hill	W Susx	TQ2813	50°54·4′	0°10·4′W	H	198
Wolston Grange	Warw	SP4473	52°21·4′	1°20·8′W	X	140
Wolsty	Cumbr	NY1050	54°50·5′	3°23·7′W	T	85
Wolsty Hall	Cumbr	NY1050	54°50·5′	3°23·7′W	X	85
Wolterton	Norf	TG1631	52°50·2′	1°12·8′E	T	133
Wolterton Park	Norf	TG1631	52°50·2′	1°12·8′E	X	133
Wolvercote	Oxon	SP4809	51°46·9′	1°17·9′W	T	164
Wolverham	Ches	SJ4075	53°16·4′	2°53·6′W	T	117
Wolverhampton	Wolv	SO9198	52°35·0′	2°7·6′W	T	139
Wolverley	Shrops	SJ4731	52°52·7′	2°46·8′W	T	126
Wolverley	Worcs	SO8379	52°24·8′	2°14·6′W	T	138
Wolverley Court	Worcs	SO8378	52°24·2′	2°14·6′W	X	138
Wolvers	Surrey	TQ2445	51°11·7′	0°13·1′W	X	187
Wolvershill Manor	N Som	ST3761	51°20·9′	2°53·9′W	X	182
Wolversleigh Fm	Devon	SY1495	50°45·1′	3°12·8′W	FM	192,193
Wolverstone	Devon	ST1204	50°50·0′	3°14·6′W	T	192,193
Wolverstone Fm	W Susx	SU8715	50°55·9′	0°45·3′W	FM	197
Wolverstone Moor	Devon	ST1204	50°50·0′	3°14·6′W	X	192,193
Wolverton	Hants	SU5558	51°19·3′	1°12·3′W	X	174
Wolverton	Kent	TR2642	51°8·2′	1°14·2′E	T	179
Wolverton	Mil Key	SP8140	52°3·4′	0°48·7′W	T	152
Wolverton	Shrops	SO4687	52°28·9′	2°47·3′W	T	137,138
Wolverton	Warw	SP2062	52°15·6′	1°42·0′W	T	151
Wolverton	Wilts	ST7831	51°4·9′	2°18·5′W	T	183
Wolverton Common	Hants	SU5659	51°19·9′	1°11·4′W	T	174
Wolverton Ho	Hants	SU5558	51°19·3′	1°12·3′W	X	174
Wolverton Manor	I of W	SZ4582	50°38·4′	1°21·4′W	A	196
Wolverton Mill	Mil Key	SP8040	52°3·4′	0°49·6′W	X	152
Wolverton Village	Mil Key	SP8041	52°3·9′	0°49·6′W	A	152
Wolverton Wood	Hants	SU5658	51°19·3′	1°11·4′W	F	174
Wolverton Wood	Shrops	SO4787	52°28·9′	2°46·4′W	F	137,138
Wolvesacre Hall	Wrex	SJ5042	52°58·6′	2°44·3′W	X	117
Wolvesacre Mill	Wrex	SJ5043	52°59·2′	2°44·3′W	X	117
Wolves Fm	Suff	TM0443	52°3·1′	0°58·9′E	FM	155
Wolves Hall Fm	Essex	TM1525	51°53·1′	1°7·9′E	FM	168,169
Wolvesnewton	Monm	ST4599	51°41·5′	2°47·4′W	T	171
Wolves, The	V of Glam	ST2065	51°22·9′	3°8·6′W	X	171,182
Wolves Wood (Nature Reserve)	Suff	TM0543	52°3·1′	0°59·8′E	F	155
Wolvey	Warw	SP4287	52°29·0′	1°22·5′W	T	140
Wolvey Fields Fm	Warw	SP4386	52°28·4′	1°21·6′W	FM	140
Wolvey Heath	Warw	SP4388	52°29·5′	1°21·6′W	T	140
Wolvey Lodge Fm	Warw	SP4487	52°29·0′	1°20·7′W	FM	140
Wolvey Villa Fm	Warw	SP4286	52°28·5′	1°22·5′W	FM	140
Wolvey Wolds	Warw	SP4586	52°28·4′	1°19·8′W	X	140
Wolviston	Stock on T	NZ4525	54°37·3′	1°17·8′W	T	93
Womack Water	Norf	TG3917	52°42·1′	1°32·7′E	W	133,134
Womaston	Powys	SO2660	52°14·2′	3°4·6′W	T	137,148
Womblehill	Aberd	NJ7814	57°13·2′	2°21·4′W	X	38
Wombleton	N Yks	SE6783	54°14·5′	0°57·9′W	T	100
Wombleton Grange	N Yks	SE6682	54°14·0′	0°58·8′W	X	100
Wombourne	Staffs	SO8792	52°31·8′	2°11·1′W	T	139
Wombridge	Wrekin	SJ6911	52°42·0′	2°27·1′W	T	127
Wombwell	Barns	SE3902	53°31·0′	1°24·3′W	T	110,111
Wombwell's Fm	Bucks	SP6910	51°47·3′	0°59·6′W	FM	165
Wombwell Wood	Barns	SE3702	53°31·0′	1°26·1′W	F	110,111
Womenswold	Kent	TR2250	51°12·6′	1°11·1′E	T	179,189
Womersley	N Yks	SE5319	53°40·1′	1°11·5′W	T	111
Womerton	Shrops	SO4597	52°34·3′	2°48·3′W	T	137,138
Womni Geo	Shetld	HU3530	60°3·5′	1°21·8′W	X	4
Wonastow	Monm	SO4810	51°47·4′	2°44·8′W	T	161
Wonder Bank	Pth & Kin	NO2118	56°21·1′	3°16·3′W	X	58
Wonders Corner	Devon	SS4315	50°55·0′	4°13·6′W	X	180,190
Wonderstone	N Som	ST3456	51°18·2′	2°56·4′W	T	182
Wonder, The	Heref	SO6336	52°1·5′	2°32·0′W	X	149
Wonder, The (Landslip AD 1575)	Heref	SO6236	52°1·5′	2°32·8′W	A	149
Wonderwest World	S Ayr	NS3018	55°25·8′	4°40·8′W	X	70
Wondrum Hill	Scot Bord	NT8119	55°28·1′	2°17·6′W	H	80
Wonersh	Surrey	TQ0145	51°11·9′	0°32·9′W	T	186
Wonersh Common	Surrey	TQ0246	51°12·5′	0°32·0′W	X	186
Wonford	Devon	SS3709	50°51·7′	4°18·6′W	X	190
Wonford	Devon	SX9492	50°43·3′	3°29·7′W	T	192
Wonford Moor Fm	Devon	SS3708	50°51·2′	4°18·6′W	FM	190
Wong Fm	Lincs	TF1152	53°3·5′	0°20·2′W	FM	121
Wong Fm	Norf	TG1304	52°35·7′	1°9·1′E	FM	144
Wonham	Devon	SS8010	50°52·9′	3°42·0′W	X	191
Wonham Ho	Devon	SS9221	50°58·9′	3°31·9′W	X	181
Wonham Manor	Surrey	TQ2249	51°13·9′	0°14·8′W	X	187
Wonnacott	Devon	SX4489	50°41·0′	4°12·1′W	X	190
Wonson	Devon	SX6789	50°41·4′	3°52·6′W	T	191
Wonston	Dorset	ST7408	50°52·5′	2°21·8′W	T	194
Wonston	Hants	SU4739	51°9·1′	1°19·3′W	T	185
Wonston Grange	Hants	SU4739	51°9·1′	1°19·3′W	X	185
Wonston Manor Fm	Hants	SU4738	51°8·6′	1°19·3′W	FM	185
Wontley Fm	Glos	SP0024	51°55·1′	1°59·6′W	FM	163
Wonton	Devon	SX7259	50°25·2′	3°47·7′W	X	202
Wonwell Beach	Devon	SX6147	50°18·6′	3°56·8′W	X	202
Wonwell Court Fm	Devon	SX6247	50°18·6′	3°55·9′W	FM	202
Wonwood	Devon	SX4277	50°34·5′	4°13·5′W	X	201
Woo	Orkney	HY4331	59°10·0′	2°59·3′W	X	5,6
Woo	Orkney	HY6645	59°17·7′	2°35·3′W	X	5
Wooburn	Bucks	SU9087	51°34·7′	0°41·7′W	T	175
Woo Burn	Scot Bord	NT4619	55°28·0′	2°50·8′W	W	79
Wooburn Green	Bucks	SU9188	51°35·2′	0°40·8′W	T	175
Wood	Devon	ST0116	50°56·3′	3°24·2′W	X	181
Wood	Devon	SX8973	50°33·0′	3°33·6′W	X	192
Wood	Pemb	SM8521	51°51·0′	5°6·9′W	T	157
Wood	Somer	ST3117	50°57·1′	2°58·6′W	T	193
Wooda	Corn	SX1568	50°29·2′	4°36·1′W	X	201
Wooda	Corn	SX1594	50°43·2′	4°36·9′W	X	190
Wooda	Devon	SS4906	50°50·3′	4°8·3′W	X	191
Wooda	Devon	SS6718	50°57·0′	3°53·2′W	X	180
Wooda Br	Corn	SX3476	50°33·8′	4°20·3′W	X	201
Woodacott	Devon	SS3807	50°50·6′	4°17·7′W	T	190
Woodacott Cross	Devon	SS3807	50°50·6′	4°17·7′W	T	190
Woodacre Hall	Lancs	SD5047	53°55·2′	2°45·3′W	X	102
Woodacre Pasture	Lancs	SD5147	53°55·3′	2°44·4′W	X	102
Wooda Cross	Corn	SX1356	50°22·7′	4°37·4′W	X	200
Woodadvent Fm	Somer	ST0337	51°7·7′	3°22·8′W	FM	181
Wooda Fm	Corn	SS2308	50°50·9′	4°30·5′W	FM	190
Wooda Fm	Corn	SX1356	50°22·7′	4°37·4′W	FM	200
Wooda Fm	Devon	SS3009	50°51·6′	4°24·6′W	FM	190
Wooda Fm	Devon	SX4685	50°38·9′	4°10·3′W	FM	201
Woodah Fm	Devon	SX8486	50°40·0′	3°38·1′W	FM	191
Woo Dale	Derby	SK0973	53°15·5′	1°51·5′W	X	119
Woodale	N Yks	SD9993	54°20·2′	2°0·5′W	X	98
Woodale	N Yks	SE0279	54°12·6′	1°57·7′W	T	98
Woodale Fm	E Yorks	SE9330	53°45·7′	0°34·9′W	FM	106
Woodale Moor	N Yks	SE0080	54°13·2′	1°59·6′W	X	98
Woodale Scar	N Yks	SE0876	54°11·0′	1°52·2′W	X	99
Woodall	Roth	SK4880	53°19·1′	1°16·4′W	X	111,120
Woodall Service Area	Roth	SK4780	53°19·1′	1°17·3′W	X	111,120
Woodbank	Devon	SX6595	50°44·6′	3°54·4′W	X	191
Woodbank	Aberd	NJ5837	57°25·5′	2°41·5′W	X	29
Woodbank	Arg & Bt	NR6816	55°23·2′	5°39·3′W	X	68
Wood Bank	Brad	SE0938	53°50·5′	1°51·4′W	X	104
Woodbank	Ches	SJ3573	53°15·2′	2°58·1′W	T	117
Woodbank	Fife	NT3398	56°10·5′	3°4·3′W	X	59
Woodbank	Monm	ST3592	51°37·6′	2°56·0′W	X	171
Woodbank	Shrops	SO5885	52°27·9′	2°36·7′W	T	137,138
Wood Bank	Staffs	SJ9315	52°44·2′	2°5·8′W	X	127
Woodbank	W Loth	NS9470	55°54·9′	3°41·3′W	X	65
Woodbank Fm	Lincs	SK9172	53°14·5′	0°37·8′W	FM	121
Woodbank Hill	Worcs	SO6464	52°16·6′	2°31·3′W	X	138,149
Woodbank Ho	Cumbr	NY4152	54°51·8′	2°54·7′W	X	85
Woodbank Park	Stock	SJ9190	53°24·6′	2°7·7′W	X	109
Wood Bar Looe	Dorset	SY9690	50°42·8′	2°3·0′W	W	195
Wood Barn	Notts	SK6848	53°1·7′	0°58·8′W	X	129
Wood Barn	Pemb	SN0116	51°48·7′	4°52·8′W	X	157,158
Woodbarn Fm	Bath & NE Somer	ST5761	51°21·0′	2°36·7′W	FM	172,182
Wood Barn Fm	Cambs	TL3557	52°11·9′	0°1·1′W	FM	154
Wood Barn Fm	Notts	SK6246	53°0·7′	1°4·1′W	FM	129
Wood Barn Plantn	Notts	SK5873	53°15·3′	1°7·4′W	F	120
Wood Barns Fm	Essex	TL6100	51°40·8′	0°20·1′E	FM	167
Wood Barrow	Devon	SS7142	51°10·0′	3°50·3′W	A	180
Wood Barton	Devon	SS5805	50°49·9′	4°0·6′W	X	191
Wood Barton	Devon	SS7707	50°51·2′	3°44·5′W	X	191
Wood Barton	Devon	SX7349	50°19·9′	3°46·7′W	A	202
Woodbarton Fm	Devon	ST0508	50°52·1′	3°20·6′W	FM	192
Woodbastwick	Norf	TG3315	52°41·2′	1°27·3′E	T	133,134
Woodbastwick Fens & Marshes	Norf	TG3316	52°41·7′	1°27·3′E	W	133,134
Woodbeare	Devon	ST0504	50°49·9′	3°20·6′W	X	192
Woodbeck	Notts	SK7778	53°17·8′	0°50·3′W	T	120
Woodbecks Fm	Lincs	TF2270	53°13·0′	0°10·0′W	FM	122
Woodbeer	Devon	SS8107	50°51·3′	3°41·1′W	X	191
Woodbeer Court	Devon	ST0604	50°49·9′	3°19·7′W	X	192
Wood Bevington	Warw	SP0553	52°10·7′	1°55·2′W	T	150
Woodbine	Pemb	SM9513	51°46·9′	4°57·9′W	X	157,158
Woodbine Barn	Wilts	ST9534	51°6·5′	2°3·9′W	X	184
Woodbine Cott	E Yorks	TA0066	54°5·0′	0°27·9′W	X	101
Woodbine Fm	Lincs	SK9419	52°45·9′	0°36·0′W	FM	130
Woodbine Fm	N Yks	SE5268	54°6·6′	1°11·9′W	FM	100
Woodbine Fm	Warw	SP4765	52°17·1′	1°18·3′W	FM	151
Woodbine Grange	N Yks	SE5439	53°50·9′	1°10·3′W	X	105
Woodbine Ho	Lincs	TF1931	52°52·0′	0°13·5′W	X	130
Woodbine Ho	NE Lincs	TF2398	53°28·1′	0°8·4′W	X	113
Woodbirds Hill	Somer	ST4429	51°3·7′	2°47·6′W	X	193
Woodborough	Notts	SK6347	53°1·2′	1°3·2′W	T	129
Woodborough	Wilts	SU1159	51°20·0′	1°50·1′W	T	173
Woodborough Fm	Bath & NE Somer	ST7055	51°17·8′	2°25·4′W	FM	172
Woodborough Hill	Wilts	SU1161	51°21·1′	1°50·1′W	H	173
Woodborough Ho	Bath & NE Somer	ST6956	51°18·4′	2°26·3′W	X	172
Woodborough Park	Notts	SK6147	53°1·2′	1°5·0′W	X	129
Woodbottom Fm	Norf	TF9104	52°36·2′	0°49·6′E	FM	144
Woodbottom Fm	N Yks	SE2448	53°55·9′	1°37·7′W	FM	104
Wood Br	Leic	SP5284	52°27·3′	1°13·7′W	X	140
Wood Br	Wilts	SU1357	51°18·9′	1°48·4′W	X	173
Wood Brae	Scot Bord	NT1519	55°27·7′	3°20·2′W	X	79
Woodbridge	Devon	SY1895	50°45·2′	3°9·4′W	T	192,193
Woodbridge	Dorset	ST7112	50°54·6′	2°24·4′W	X	194
Woodbridge	Dorset	ST8518	50°57·9′	2°12·4′W	T	183
Woodbridge	Glos	SP0314	51°49·7′	1°57·0′W	T	163
Woodbridge	Northum	NT9533	55°35·7′	2°4·3′W	X	74,75
Woodbridge	Northum	NZ2888	55°11·4′	1°33·2′W	T	81
Woodbridge	Suff	TM2649	52°5·8′	1°18·4′E	T	169
Woodbridge Airfield	Suff	TM3348	52°5·1′	1°24·5′E	X	169
Woodbridge Brook	Wilts	ST9985	51°34·1′	2°0·5′W	W	173
Woodbridge Fm	Bath & NE Somer	ST5358	51°19·4′	2°40·1′W	FM	172,182
Woodbridge Fm	Wilts	ST9955	51°17·9′	2°0·5′W	FM	173
Woodbridge Haven	Suff	TM3336	51°58·6′	1°24·0′E	W	169
Woodbridge Hill	Surrey	SU9850	51°14·7′	0°35·4′W	T	186
Woodbridge Walk	Suff	TM3545	52°3·4′	1°26·1′E	T	169
Woodbrook	Heref	SO3054	52°11·0′	3°1·0′W	X	148
Wood Brook	Leic	SK5117	52°45·1′	1°14·3′W	W	129
Woodbrooke	Devon	SX7790	50°42·0′	3°44·1′W	X	191
Woodbrook Fm	Somer	ST2018	50°57·6′	3°8·0′W	FM	193
Woodbrooks Fm	E Susx	TQ3916	50°55·8′	0°0·9′W	FM	198
Wood Broughton	Cumbr	SD3781	54°13·5′	2°57·6′W	X	96,97
Wood Burcote	Northnts	SP6946	52°6·7′	0°59·1′W	T	152
Woodburn	Devon	SS8623	50°59·9′	3°37·1′W	X	181
Wood Burn	E Ayr	NS6029	55°32·3′	4°12·7′W	W	71
Woodburn	E Dunb	NS6777	55°58·3′	4°7·4′W	X	64
Woodburn	Highld	NH5299	57°57·6′	4°29·6′W	X	20
Woodburn	Orkney	HY3312	58°59·7′	3°9·5′W	X	6
Woodburn	Pth & Kin	NN9119	56°21·3′	3°45·4′W	X	58
Wood Burn	Scot Bord	NT4111	55°23·6′	2°55·5′W	W	79
Woodburn	Scot Bord	NT4112	55°24·2′	2°55·5′W	X	79
Woodburn Common	Bucks	SU9287	51°34·7′	0°39·9′W	T	175
Woodburnden	Aberd	NO7673	56°51·1′	2°23·2′W	X	45
Woodburn Fm	Devon	SX6057	50°24·0′	3°57·8′W	FM	202
Woodburnhead	Pth & Kin	NO2329	56°27·1′	3°14·5′W	X	53,58
Woodburn Moor	Bucks	SU9190	51°36·3′	0°40·8′W	T	175
Woodburn Resr	E Dunb	NS6678	55°58·8′	4°8·4′W	W	64
Woodbury	Corn	SW8442	50°14·5′	5°1·4′W	X	204
Woodbury	Devon	SX8451	50°21·1′	3°37·5′W	A	202
Woodbury	Devon	SY0187	50°40·7′	3°23·7′W	T	192
Woodbury	Heref	SO6044	52°5·8′	2°34·6′W	X	149
Woodbury	Worcs	SO7564	52°16·7′	2°21·6′W	A	138,150
Woodbury Castle	Devon	SY0387	50°40·7′	3°22·0′W	X	192
Woodbury Castle (Fort)	Devon	SY0387	50°40·7′	3°22·0′W	A	192
Woodbury Common	Devon	SY0386	50°40·2′	3°22·0′W	X	192
Woodbury Fm	Devon	SX8451	50°21·1′	3°37·5′W	FM	202
Woodbury Fm	Heref	SO3541	52°4·1′	2°56·5′W	FM	148,149,161
Woodbury Hall	Beds	TL2052	52°9·4′	0°14·3′W	X	153
Woodbury Hill	Dorset	SY8594	50°45·0′	2°12·4′W	H	194
Woodbury Hill	Worcs	SO7464	52°16·6′	2°22·5′W	H	138,150
Woodbury Hill (Fort)	Dorset	SY8594	50°45·0′	2°12·4′W	A	194
Woodbury Hill Wood	Heref	SO3441	52°4·0′	2°57·4′W	F	148,149,161
Woodbury Hollow	Essex	TQ4297	51°39·5′	0°3·6′E	F	167,177
Woodbury Lodge Fm	Beds	TL1853	52°10·0′	0°16·1′W	FM	153
Woodbury Low Fm	Beds	TL1953	52°10·0′	0°15·2′W	FM	153
Woodbury Salterton	Devon	SY0189	50°41·8′	3°23·7′W	T	192
Wood Cairn	D & G	NX2568	54°58·8′	4°43·7′W	A	82
Woodcarr Fm	N Lincs	SE7508	53°34·0′	0°51·6′W	FM	112
Woodcastle Fm	Powys	SO0258	52°12·9′	3°25·7′W	FM	147
Woodchester	Glos	SO8402	51°43·2′	2°13·5′W	T	162
Woodchester Park	Glos	SO8101	51°42·7′	2°16·1′W	X	162
Woodchurch	Kent	TQ9434	51°4·6′	0°46·6′E	T	189
Woodchurch	Wirral	SJ2887	53°22·7′	3°4·5′W	T	108
Wood Cleugh	Scot Bord	NT6257	55°48·5′	2°35·9′W	X	67,74
Wood Close	Cumbr	NY4137	54°43·7′	2°54·5′W	X	90

Woodclose	Devon	SX5894	50°43·9'	4°0·4'W	X	191
Wood Close Fm	Durham	NZ4234	54°42·2'	1°20·5'W	FM	93
Wood Close Fm	Notts	SK6965	53°10·9'	0°57·6'W	FM	120
Woodclose Gill	Durham	NZ0408	54°28·3'	1°55·9'W	W	92
Woodcoates	Notts	SK7871	53°14·1'	0°49·5'W	X	120,121
Woodcock	Glos	ST8098	51°41·1'	2°17·0'W	X	162
Woodcock	N Yks	SE4581	54°13·6'	1°18·2'W	X	99
Woodcock	Wilts	ST8844	51°11·9'	2°9·9'W	T	183
Woodcock Air	D & G	NY1772	55°2·4'	3°17·5'W	H	85
Woodcockdale	W Loth	NS9776	55°58·2'	3°38·6'W	X	65
Woodcock Downs	Somer	ST2537	51°7·9'	3°3·9'W	X	182
Woodcockfauld	Falk	NS8185	56°2·8'	3°54·2'W	X	57,65
Woodcock Fm	Derby	SK0594	53°26·8'	1°55·1'W	FM	110
Woodcock Fm	E Susx	TQ4426	51°1·1'	0°3·6'E	FM	187,198
Woodcock Fold	Lancs	SD5619	53°40·2'	2°39·5'W	X	108
Woodcock Hall	Lancs	SD4809	53°34·7'	2°46·7'W	X	108
Woodcock Heath	Staffs	SK0529	52°51·7'	1°55·1'W	T	128
Woodcock Hill	Birm	SP0181	52°25·9'	1°58·7'W	T	139
Woodcock Hill	Black w Dar	SD6327	53°44·5'	2°33·2'W	X	102,103
Woodcock Hill	Devon	SX5587	50°40·1'	4°2·7'W	H	191
Woodcock Hill	Heref	SO4768	52°18·7'	2°46·2'W	X	137,138,148
Woodcock Hill	Herts	TQ0692	51°37·2'	0°27·7'W	T	176
Woodcock Hill	Herts	TL1995	51°38·7'	0°16·4'W	X	166,176
Woodcock Hill	Highld	NC8848	58°24·6'	3°54·5'W	X	10
Woodcock Hill	Monm	ST4490	51°36·6'	2°48·1'W	X	171,172
Woodcock Hill	Norf	TL9292	52°29·8'	0°50·1'E	F	144
Woodcock Lodge	Herts	TL2906	51°44·5'	0°7·5'W	X	166
Woodcock Lodge Fm	Herts	TL2906	51°44·5'	0°7·5'W	FM	166
Woodcocks Ley	Somer	SS8845	51°11·8'	3°35·8'W	X	181
Woodcock Wood	Norf	TF6827	52°49·1'	0°30·0'E	F	132
Woodcombe	Devon	SX7837	50°13·5'	3°42·2'W	X	202
Woodcombe	Somer	SS9546	51°12·5'	3°29·8'W	T	181
Woodcombe Bottom	Wilts	ST8339	51°9·2'	2°14·2'W	X	183
Wood Corner	Essex	TL8206	51°43·6'	0°38·5'E	X	168
Woodcorner Fm	Surrey	SU9854	51°16·8'	0°35·3'W	FM	186
Wood Corner Fm	Warw	SP2586	52°28·5'	1°37·5'W	FM	140
Woodcot	Hants	SU5703	50°49·7'	1°11·1'W	T	196
Woodcote	Croy	TQ3061	51°20·2'	0°7·6'W	T	176,177,187
Woodcote	Dorset	SY3598	50°46·9'	2°54·9'W	X	193
Woodcote	Hants	SU5421	50°59·4'	1°13·4'W	X	185
Woodcote	Oxon	SU6481	51°31·7'	1°4·3'W	T	175
Woodcote	Shrops	SJ4511	52°41·9'	2°48·4'W	X	126
Woodcote	Surrey	TQ2059	51°19·3'	0°16·3'W	T	187
Woodcote	Warw	SP2869	52°19·3'	1°35·0'W	X	151
Woodcote	Wrekin	SJ7615	52°44·2'	2°20·9'W	T	127
Woodcote	W Susx	SU8807	50°51·6'	0°44·6'W	X	197
Woodcote Fm	Oxon	SU6482	51°32·2'	1°4·2'W	FM	175
Woodcote Fm	Wakf	SE3312	53°36·5'	1°29·7'W	FM	110,111
Woodcote Fm	W Susx	SU9117	50°56·9'	0°41·9'W	FM	197
Woodcote Green	Sutton	TQ2962	51°20·8'	0°8·5'W	T	176,187
Woodcote Green	Worcs	SO9172	52°21·0'	2°7·5'W	T	139
Woodcote Grove Ho	Croy	TQ2860	51°19·7'	0°9·4'W	X	176,187
Woodcote Lodge	Surrey	TQ0750	51°14·6'	0°27·6'W	X	187
Woodcote Mains	Midlo	NT4560	55°50·1'	2°52·2'W	X	66
Woodcote Manor Ho	Hants	SU6227	51°2·6'	1°6·5'W	X	185
Woodcote Manor Ho	Worcs	SO9272	52°21·0'	2°6·6'W	X	139
Woodcote Park	Midlo	NT4560	55°50·1'	2°52·2'W	X	66
Woodcote Park	Surrey	TQ2058	51°18·7'	0°16·3'W	X	187
Woodcotes	Herts	TL3235	52°0·1'	0°4·2'W	X	153
Woodcote Stud	Surrey	TQ1959	51°19·3'	0°17·1'W	X	187
Wood Cott	Derby	SK1289	53°24·1'	1°48·8'W	X	110
Woodcott	Hants	SU4354	51°17·2'	1°22·6'W	T	185
Wood Cott	Northum	NU1625	55°31·4'	1°44·4'W	X	75
Wood Cottage	Kirk	SE1008	53°34·4'	1°50·5'W	X	110
Woodcotthill Fm	Ches	SJ6047	53°1·4'	2°35·4'W	FM	118
Woodcott Ho	Ches	SJ6048	53°1·9'	2°35·4'W	X	118
Woodcott Ho	Hants	SU4454	51°17·2'	1°21·8'W	X	185
Woodcourt	Devon	SX7755	50°23·2'	3°43·4'W	X	202
Wood Crates	Hants	SU2708	50°52·5'	1°36·6'W	F	195
Woodcray Manor Fm	Wok	SU8066	51°23·5'	0°50·6'W	FM	175
Woodcroft	Aberd	NJ7043	57°28·8'	2°29·6'W	X	29
Wood Croft	Aberd	NO5897	57°4·0'	2°41·1'W	X	37,44
Woodcroft	Devon	SS6105	50°49·9'	3°58·1'W	X	191
Woodcroft	Glos	ST5495	51°39·4'	2°39·5'W	T	162
Woodcroft	Heref	SO4971	52°20·3'	2°44·5'W	X	137,138,148
Woodcroft Castle	Peterb	TF1304	52°37·6'	0°19·4'W	A	142
Woodcroft Fm	D & G	NX9669	55°0·5'	3°37·1'W	FM	84
Woodcroft Fm	Hants	SU7316	50°56·6'	0°57·3'W	FM	197
Woodcroft Fms	Heref	SO6845	52°6·4'	2°27·6'W	FM	149
Woodcroft Hall	Suff	TM2064	52°14·0'	1°13·7'E	X	156
Woodcroft Lodge	Peterb	TF1303	52°37·0'	0°19·4'W	X	142
Wood Cross	Pemb	SN1112	51°46·7'	4°44·0'W	X	158
Woodcut Fm	Kent	TQ8155	51°16·1'	0°36·1'E	FM	178,188
Woodcutts	Dorset	ST9717	50°57·4'	2°2·2'W	T	184
Woodcutts Common	Dorset	ST9617	50°57·4'	2°3·0'W	X	184
Woodcutts Fm	Dorset	SU0104	50°50·4'	1°58·8'W	FM	195
Wooddale Fm	W Susx	TQ1026	51°1·6'	0°25·5'W	FM	187,198
Wood Dale Plantn	E Yorks	SE9564	54°4·0'	0°32·5'W	F	101
Wood Dalling	Norf	TG0927	52°48·2'	1°6·4'E	T	133
Wood Dalling Hall	Norf	TG0727	52°48·3'	1°4·7'E	X	133
Woodditton	Cambs	TL6658	52°11·9'	0°26·1'E	T	154
Woodeaton	Oxon	SP5311	51°47·9'	1°13·5'W	T	164
Wood Eaton	Staffs	SJ8417	52°45·3'	2°13·8'W	T	127
Woodeaton Wood	Oxon	SP5411	51°47·9'	1°12·6'W	F	164
Wood Eaves	E Susx	TQ4831	51°3·8'	0°7·1'E	F	188
Woodeaves	Staffs	SJ9039	52°57·1'	2°8·5'W	X	127
Woodeaves Fm	Derby	SK1850	53°3·1'	1°43·5'W	FM	119
Wood Edge	Cumbr	SD4979	54°12·5'	2°46·5'W	X	97
Wooden	Pemb	SN1105	51°43·0'	4°43·8'W	T	158
Woodenbreck	Shetld	HU6589	60°35·0'	0°48·3'W	X	1,2
Woodend	Aberd	NJ4606	57°8·8'	2°53·1'W	X	37
Woodend	Aberd	NJ5516	57°14·2'	2°44·3'W	X	37
Woodend	Aberd	NJ5605	57°8·3'	2°43·2'W	X	37
Woodend	Aberd	NJ6608	57°10·0'	2°33·3'W	X	38
Woodend	Aberd	NJ6921	57°17·0'	2°30·4'W	X	38
Woodend	Aberd	NJ7113	57°12·7'	2°28·4'W	X	38
Woodend	Aberd	NJ7127	57°20·2'	2°28·4'W	F	38
Woodend	Aberd	NJ7544	57°29·4'	2°24·6'W	X	29
Woodend	Aberd	NJ8720	57°16·5'	2°12·5'W	X	38
Woodend	Aberd	NK0234	57°24·0'	1°57·5'W	X	30
Woodend	Aberd	NO5891	57°0·8'	2°41·0'W	X	44
Woodend	Aberd	NO6296	57°3·5'	2°37·1'W	X	37,45
Woodend	Aberd	NO7297	57°4·0'	2°27·3'W	X	38,45
Woodend	Aberd	NO7695	57°3·0'	2°23·3'W	X	38,45
Woodend	Aberd	NO8593	57°1·9'	2°14·4'W	X	38,45
Woodend	Arg & Bt	NR3966	55°49·3'	6°9·6'W	X	60,61
Wood End	Beds	SP9741	52°3·8'	0°34·7'W	T	153
Wood End	Beds	TL0046	52°6·4'	0°32·0'W	T	153
Wood End	Beds	TL0131	51°58·3'	0°31·4'W	X	166
Wood End	Beds	TL0555	52°11·2'	0°27·4'W	T	153
Wood End	Beds	TL0865	52°16·6'	0°24·6'W	T	153
Wood End	Bucks	SP7833	51°59·6'	0°51·4'W	T	152,165
Wood End	Bucks	SP7930	51°58·0'	0°50·6'W	X	152,165
Woodend	Ches	SJ6944	52°59·8'	2°27·3'W	X	118
Woodend	Ches	SJ9785	53°22·0'	2°2·3'W	T	109
Woodend	C of Aber	NJ8301	57°6·2'	2°16·4'W	X	38
Wood End	Cov	SP3682	52°26·3'	1°27·8'W	T	140
Woodend	Cumbr	NX9814	54°30·9'	3°34·1'W	X	89
Woodend	Cumbr	NY0012	54°29·9'	3°32·2'W	T	89
Woodend	Cumbr	NY0721	54°34·8'	3°25·9'W	T	89
Woodend	Cumbr	NY2127	54°38·2'	3°13·0'W	T	89,90
Woodend	Cumbr	NY6259	54°55·7'	2°35·2'W	X	86
Wood End	Cumbr	SD1099	54°23·0'	3°22·7'W	X	96
Woodend	Cumbr	SD1696	54°21·4'	3°17·1'W	T	96
Wood End	Derby	SK3057	53°6·8'	1°32·7'W	X	119
Woodend	D & G	NS7900	55°17·0'	3°53·9'W	X	78
Woodend	D & G	NX5856	54°53·0'	4°12·4'W	X	83
Woodend	D & G	NX8992	55°12·8'	3°44·2'W	X	78
Woodend	D & G	NY1095	55°14·7'	3°24·5'W	X	78
Woodend	E Ayr	NS5913	55°23·7'	4°13·1'W	X	71
Woodend	E Loth	NT5370	55°55·5'	2°44·7'W	X	66
Woodend	E Loth	NT6172	55°56·6'	2°37·0'W	X	67
Woodend	Essex	TL5610	51°46·2'	0°16·1'E	T	167
Woodend	Falk	NS9078	55°59·2'	3°45·4'W	X	65
Woodend	Fife	NO5312	56°18·1'	2°45·1'W	X	59
Woodend	Fife	NT2096	56°9·3'	3°16·8'W	T	58
Woodend	Hants	SU5913	50°55·0'	1°9·3'W	X	196
Wood End	Heref	SO6341	52°4·2'	2°32·0'W	T	149
Wood End	Herts	TL3225	51°54·7'	0°4·5'W	T	166
Woodend	Highld	NC5959	58°30·1'	4°24·7'W	X	10
Woodend	Highld	NH5027	57°18·8'	4°29·0'W	X	26,35
Woodend	Highld	NH5436	57°23·7'	4°25·3'W	X	26
Woodend	Highld	NH5851	57°31·9'	4°21·8'W	X	26
Woodend	Highld	NH7926	57°18·8'	4°0·1'W	X	35
Woodend	Highld	NH8051	57°32·3'	3°59·8'W	X	27
Woodend	Highld	NH9457	57°35·7'	3°45·9'W	X	27
Woodend	Highld	NM7860	56°41·0'	5°37·0'W	X	40
Wood End	Hill	TQ0981	51°31·3'	0°25·3'W	X	176
Wood End	Lancs	SD8235	53°48·9'	2°16·0'W	X	103
Wood End	Lancs	SD8844	53°53·8'	2°10·5'W	X	103
Woodend	Moray	NJ2222	57°17·2'	3°17·2'W	X	36
Woodend	Moray	NJ3844	57°29·2'	3°1·6'W	X	28
Woodend	N Lanak	NS7067	55°53·0'	4°4·3'W	X	64
Woodend	N Lanak	NS7270	55°54·6'	4°2·4'W	X	64
Woodend	N Lanak	NS7377	55°58·4'	4°1·7'W	X	64
Woodend	Northnts	SP6149	52°8·4'	1°6·1'W	T	152
Woodend	Northum	NT9641	55°40·0'	2°3·4'W	X	74,75
Woodend	Notts	SK4660	53°8·3'	1°18·3'W	T	120
Woodend	Notts	SK5471	53°14·2'	1°11·0'W	X	120
Wood End	N Yks	SD7869	54°7·2'	2°19·8'W	X	98
Wood End	N Yks	SD9998	54°22·9'	2°0·5'W	X	98
Wood End	N Yks	SE0590	54°18·6'	1°55·0'W	X	98
Wood End	N Yks	SE4773	54°9·3'	1°16·4'W	X	100
Wood End	Oldham	SD9309	53°34·9'	2°5·9'W	T	109
Woodend	Pth & Kin	NN7147	56°36·1'	4°5·6'W	X	51,52
Woodend	Pth & Kin	NN8465	56°46·0'	3°53·4'W	X	43
Woodend	Pth & Kin	NN9322	56°22·9'	3°43·5'W	X	52,58
Woodend	Pth & Kin	NN9512	56°17·6'	3°41·3'W	X	58
Woodend	Pth & Kin	NO0332	56°28·5'	3°34·0'W	X	52,53
Woodend	Scot Bord	NT1231	55°34·1'	3°23·3'W	X	72
Woodend	Scot Bord	NT3038	55°38·1'	3°6·3'W	X	73
Woodend	Scot Bord	NT3824	55°30·6'	2°58·5'W	X	73
Wood End	Scot Bord	NT4835	55°36·6'	2°49·1'W	X	73
Woodend	Scot Bord	NT6521	55°29·1'	2°32·8'W	X	74
Woodend	Scot Bord	NT7551	55°45·4'	2°23·5'W	X	67,74
Woodend	Scot Bord	NT7970	55°55·6'	2°19·7'W	X	67
Woodend	Shrops	SO5988	52°29·5'	2°35·8'W	X	137,138
Woodend	S Lanak	NS8744	55°40·8'	3°47·4'W	X	71,72
Woodend	S Lanak	NS9436	55°36·6'	3°40·5'W	X	71,72
Woodend	S Lanak	NS9648	55°43·1'	3°38·9'W	X	72
Woodend	Staffs	SK1726	52°50·1'	1°44·5'W	T	128
Woodend	Stir	NS5694	56°7·3'	4°18·5'W	X	57
Woodend	Stock on T	NZ4026	54°37·9'	1°22·4'W	X	93
Wood End	Tames	SD9702	53°31·1'	2°2·3'W	T	109
Wood End	Warw	SP1071	52°20·5'	1°50·8'W	T	139
Wood End	Warw	SP2398	52°35·0'	1°39·2'W	T	139
Wood End	Warw	SP2988	52°29·6'	1°34·0'W	T	140
Wood End	Win & Maid	SU9270	51°25·5'	0°40·2'W	T	175
Woodend	W Loth	NT0877	55°58·9'	3°28·0'W	T	65
Wood End	Wolv	SJ9401	52°36·6'	2°4·9'W	T	127,139
Woodend	W Susx	SU8108	50°52·2'	0°50·5'W	X	197
Woodend Burn	D & G	NS7900	55°17·0'	3°53·9'W	W	78
Woodend Burn	S Lanak	NS9528	55°32·3'	3°39·4'W	W	72
Woodend Craig	D & G	NS7801	55°17·5'	3°54·8'W	X	78
Wood Enderby	Lincs	TF2763	53°9·2'	0°5·6'W	T	122
Wood End Fm	Beds	SP9540	52°3·2'	0°36·5'W	FM	153
Wood End Fm	Beds	TL0960	52°13·9'	0°23·8'W	FM	153
Wood End Fm	Beds	TL1046	52°6·3'	0°23·2'W	FM	153
Woodend Fm	Bucks	SU8187	51°34·8'	0°49·5'W	FM	175
Wood End Fm	Cambs	TL1682	52°25·7'	0°17·2'W	FM	142
Woodend Fm	Ches	SJ7772	53°14·9'	2°20·3'W	FM	118
Woodend Fm	Ches	SJ8082	53°20·3'	2°17·6'W	FM	109
Woodend Fm	Ches	SJ9381	53°19·8'	2°5·9'W	FM	109
Woodend Fm	Cumbr	NY5440	54°45·4'	2°42·5'W	FM	86
Woodend Fm	Durham	NZ0919	54°34·2'	1°51·2'W	FM	92
Wood End Fm	Essex	TL8013	51°47·4'	0°37·0'E	FM	168
Woodend Fm	Glos	SO8935	52°1·0'	2°9·2'W	FM	150
Woodend Fm	Heref	SO4766	52°17·6'	2°46·2'W	FM	137,138,148
Woodend Fm	Heref	SO7048	52°8·0'	2°25·9'W	FM	149
Woodend Fm	Heref	SO7158	52°13·4'	2°25·1'W	FM	149
Wood End Fm	Herts	TL0513	51°48·6'	0°28·2'W	FM	166
Woodend Fm	Herts	TL0809	51°46·4'	0°25·7'W	FM	166
Wood End Fm	Lancs	SD4403	53°31·5'	2°50·3'W	FM	108
Wood End Fm	Lancs	SD5317	53°39·1'	2°42·3'W	FM	108
Wood End Fm	Mil Key	SP9241	52°3·8'	0°39·1'W	FM	152
Wood End Fm	N Yks	NZ7203	54°25·3'	0°53·0'W	FM	94
Wood End Fm	N Yks	SE5535	53°48·7'	1°9·5'W	FM	105
Wood End Fm	N Yks	SE6634	53°48·1'	0°59·5'W	FM	105,106
Woodend Fm	Oxon	SP4506	51°45·3'	1°20·5'W	FM	164
Wood End Fm	Shrops	SJ3811	52°41·8'	2°54·6'W	FM	126
Wood End Fm	Staffs	SJ9532	52°53·4'	2°4·1'W	FM	127
Wood End Fm	Staffs	SK1213	52°43·1'	1°48·9'W	FM	128
Woodend Fm	W Berks	SU5278	51°30·1'	1°14·7'W	FM	174
Woodend Fm	W Loth	NS9269	55°54·4'	3°43·2'W	FM	65
Woodend Fm	Worcs	SO7757	52°12·9'	2°19·8'W	FM	150
Woodend Fms	Heref	SO6625	51°55·6'	2°29·3'W	FM	162
Woodend Green	Essex	TL5528	51°56·0'	0°15·7'E	T	167
Wood End Green	Hill	TQ0981	51°31·3'	0°25·3'W	T	176
Woodend Green	Northnts	SP6148	52°7·8'	1°6·1'W	X	152
Woodend Green Fm	Glos	SO7401	51°42·7'	2°22·2'W	FM	162
Woodend Green Fm	Suff	TL9464	52°14·6'	0°50·9'E	FM	155
Woodend Height	Cumbr	SD1595	54°20·9'	3°18·0'W	H	96
Woodend Ho	Aberd	NO6396	57°3·5'	2°36·1'W	X	37,45
Woodend Ho	Arg & Bt	NS0761	55°48·5'	5°4·4'W	X	63
Woodend Ho	Bucks	SU8188	51°35·3'	0°49·5'W	X	175
Woodend Loch	N Lanak	NS7066	55°52·4'	4°4·2'W	W	64
Wood End Lodge	N Yks	SD9087	54°17·0'	2°8·8'W	X	98
Woodend Moss	S Lanak	NS9749	55°43·7'	3°38·0'W	F	72
Wood Ends Fm	N Yks	SE5736	53°49·3'	1°7·6'W	FM	105
Wooden Fm	Northum	NU2309	55°22·7'	1°37·8'W	FM	81
Wooden Hill	Scot Bord	NT7124	55°30·8'	2°27·1'W	H	74
Wooden Hill Fm	Oxon	SP4234	52°0·4'	1°22·9'W	FM	151
Wooden Ho	Scot Bord	NT7433	55°35·6'	2°24·3'W	X	74
Wooden Loch	Scot Bord	NT7025	55°31·3'	2°28·1'W	W	74
Wooden Mill	Scot Bord	NT7334	55°36·2'	2°25·3'W	X	74
Wooder Manor	Devon	SX7177	50°34·9'	3°49·0'W	X	191
Woodfalls	Wilts	SU1920	50°59·0'	1°43·4'W	T	184
Woodfalls Fm	Kent	TQ6848	51°12·6'	0°24·7'E	FM	188
Wood Farmhouse	Essex	TL5626	51°54·9'	0°16·5'E	A	167
Wood Fell	D & G	NX4059	54°54·3'	4°29·3'W	H	83
Wood Fen	Cambs	TL5585	52°26·7'	0°17·2'E	X	143
Wood Fen Fm	Cambs	TL5486	52°27·2'	0°16·4'E	FM	143
Woodfield	Aberd	NJ5105	57°8·3'	2°48·1'W	X	37
Woodfield	Cald	SD9124	53°43·0'	2°7·8'W	X	103
Woodfield	D & G	NY2666	54°59·2'	3°9·0'W	X	85
Woodfield	Glos	ST7499	51°41·6'	2°22·2'W	T	162
Woodfield	Midlo	NT2564	55°52·1'	3°11·5'W	X	66
Woodfield	Oxon	SP5823	51°54·4'	1°9·0'W	T	164
Woodfield	Pemb	SN0915	51°48·3'	4°45·8'W	X	158
Woodfield	Pth & Kin	NO1438	56°31·8'	3°23·4'W	X	53
Woodfield	S Ayr	NS3424	55°29·2'	4°37·2'W	T	70
Wood Field	Surrey	TQ1759	51°19·3'	0°18·9'W	X	187
Woodfield Cott	Angus	NO7260	56°44·1'	2°27·0'W	X	45
Woodfield Fm	Beds	TL1052	52°9·5'	0°23·1'W	FM	153
Woodfield Fm	Cambs	TL1482	52°25·7'	0°19·0'W	FM	142
Woodfield Fm	Donc	SE5213	53°36·9'	1°12·4'W	FM	111
Woodfield Fm	Herts	TL2605	51°44·0'	0°10·1'W	FM	166
Woodfield Fm	Worcs	SO9443	52°5·4'	2°4·9'W	FM	150
Woodfield Ho	E Yorks	SE8328	53°44·7'	0°44·1'W	X	106
Woodfield Ho	N Yks	SE2363	54°4·0'	1°38·5'W	X	99
Woodfield Ho	N Yks	SE5634	53°48·2'	1°8·6'W	X	105
Woodfield Ho	Shrops	SO7993	52°32·3'	2°18·2'W	X	138
Woodfield Ho	Worcs	SO8279	52°24·8'	2°15·5'W	X	138
Woodfield Ho	Worcs	SO8365	52°17·2'	2°14·6'W	X	138,150
Woodfield Ho	W Susx	TQ3021	50°58·6'	0°8·5'W	X	198
Woodfields	Lancs	SD6939	53°51·0'	2°27·9'W	X	103
Woodfields	Notts	SK6030	52°52·1'	1°6·1'W	X	129
Woodfields Fm	Derby	SK2613	52°43·1'	1°36·5'W	FM	128
Woodfields Fm	Heref	SO7234	52°0·5'	2°24·1'W	FM	149
Wood Fm	Beds	SP9944	52°5·4'	0°32·9'W	FM	153
Wood Fm	Beds	TL0234	51°59·9'	0°30·5'W	FM	153
Wood Fm	Beds	TL0429	51°57·2'	0°28·8'W	FM	166
Wood Fm	Beds	TL1345	52°5·7'	0°20·6'W	FM	153
Wood Fm	Beds	TL2550	52°8·3'	0°10·0'W	FM	153
Wood Fm	Bucks	SP6109	51°46·8'	1°6·6'W	FM	164,165
Wood Fm	Bucks	SP6531	51°58·7'	1°2·8'W	FM	152,165
Wood Fm	Bucks	SP9205	51°44·4'	0°39·7'W	FM	165
Wood Fm	Cambs	TL2554	52°10·4'	0°9·9'W	FM	153
Wood Fm	Cambs	TL3181	52°24·9'	0°4·0'W	FM	142
Wood Fm	Cambs	TL3360	52°13·6'	0°2·8'W	FM	154
Wood Fm	Cambs	TL3574	52°21·1'	0°0·7'W	FM	142
Wood Fm	Cambs	TL3657	52°11·9'	0°0·2'W	FM	154
Wood Fm	Cambs	TL3983	52°25·9'	0°3·1'E	FM	142,143
Wood Fm	Ches	SJ3871	53°14·2'	2°55·3'W	FM	117
Wood Fm	Ches	SJ5444	52°59·7'	2°40·7'W	FM	117
Wood Fm	Ches	SJ6655	53°5·7'	2°30·1'W	FM	118
Wood Fm	Ches	SJ8182	53°20·3'	2°16·7'W	FM	109
Wood Fm	Ches	SJ8863	53°10·1'	2°10·4'W	FM	118
Wood Fm	Cumbr	NY1126	54°37·5'	3°22·3'W	FM	89
Wood Fm	Cumbr	NY3351	54°51·2'	3°2·2'W	FM	85
Wood Fm	Cumbr	SD4091	54°18·9'	2°54·9'W	FM	96,97
Wood Fm	Devon	SS5912	50°53·7'	3°59·9'W	FM	180
Wood Fm	Devon	SS8713	50°54·6'	3°36·1'W	FM	181
Wood Fm	Devon	SS8901	50°48·1'	3°34·1'W	FM	192
Wood Fm	Devon	SX6098	50°46·1'	3°58·7'W	FM	191
Wood Fm	Devon	SX6655	50°23·0'	3°52·7'W	FM	202
Wood Fm	Devon	SX7498	50°46·3'	3°46·8'W	FM	191
Wood Fm	Devon	SX7951	50°21·0'	3°41·7'W	FM	202
Wood Fm	D & G	NX9988	55°10·8'	3°34·7'W	FM	78
Wood Fm	Dorset	ST5406	50°51·3'	2°38·8'W	FM	194
Wood Fm	Dorset	SY3594	50°44·8'	2°54·9'W	FM	193
Wood Fm	Essex	TL5405	51°43·6'	0°14·2'E	FM	167
Wood Fm	Essex	TL7002	51°41·7'	0°28·0'E	FM	167
Wood Fm	E Yorks	SE7331	53°46·5'	0°53·1'W	FM	105,106
Wood Fm	E Yorks	TA2042	53°51·9'	0°10·1'W	FM	107
Wood Fm	E Yorks	TA2818	53°38·8'	0°3·4'W	FM	113
Wood Fm	Flint	SJ3259	53°7·7'	3°0·6'W	FM	117
Wood Fm	Glos	SO8722	51°54·0'	2°10·9'W	FM	162
Wood Fm	Hants	SU6228	51°3·1'	1°6·5'W	FM	185

Wood Fm	Heref	SO5454	52°11·2'	2°40·0'W	FM	149
Wood Fm	Heref	SO7050	52°9·1'	2°25·9'W	FM	149
Wood Fm	Herts	TL0510	51°47·0'	0°28·3'W	FM	166
Wood Fm	Herts	TL3232	51°58·5'	0°4·3'W	FM	166
Wood Fm	Leic	SK3315	52°44·1'	1°30·3'W	FM	128
Wood Fm	Leic	SK4410	52°41·4'	1°20·5'W	FM	129
Wood Fm	Leic	SK7503	52°37·4'	0°53·1'W	FM	141
Wood Fm	Leic	SP5582	52°26·2'	1°11·1'W	FM	140
Wood Fm	Lincs	SK9555	53°5·3'	0°34·5'W	FM	121
Wood Fm	Lincs	TF0509	52°40·3'	0°26·4'W	FM	142
Wood Fm	Lincs	TF1673	53°14·7'	0°15·3'W	FM	121
Wood Fm	Lincs	TF2876	53°16·2'	0°4·4'W	FM	122
Wood Fm	Lincs	TF4479	53°17·5'	0°10·0'E	FM	122
Wood Fm	Mil Key	SP8344	52°5·5'	0°46·9'W	FM	152
Wood Fm	Mil Key	SP9048	52°7·6'	0°40·7'W	FM	152
Wood Fm	Mil Key	SP9349	52°8·1'	0°38·1'W	FM	153
Wood Fm	Monm	SO3422	51°53·8'	2°57·2'W	FM	161
Wood Fm	N Ayr	NS2944	55°39·8'	4°42·7'W	FM	63,70
Wood Fm	N Lincs	SE8704	53°31·8'	0°40·8'W	FM	112
Wood Fm	N Lincs	SE8704	53°31·8'	0°40·8'W	FM	112
Wood Fm	Norf	TF6527	52°49·1'	0°27·3'E	FM	132
Wood Fm	Norf	TF8208	52°38·6'	0°41·8'E	FM	144
Wood Fm	Norf	TF8627	52°48·7'	0°46·0'E	FM	132
Wood Fm	Norf	TF9010	52°39·5'	0°49·0'E	FM	132
Wood Fm	Norf	TF9102	52°35·2'	0°49·6'E	FM	144
Wood Fm	Norf	TF9502	52°35·1'	0°53·1'E	FM	144
Wood Fm	Norf	TF9507	52°37·8'	0°53·3'E	FM	144
Wood Fm	Norf	TF9833	52°51·7'	0°56·9'E	FM	132
Wood Fm	Norf	TG0006	52°37·1'	0°57·7'E	FM	144
Wood Fm	Norf	TG0521	52°45·1'	1°2·7'E	FM	133
Wood Fm	Norf	TG0802	52°34·8'	1°4·6'E	FM	144
Wood Fm	Norf	TG1013	52°40·7'	1°6·8'E	FM	133
Wood Fm	Norf	TG1323	52°46·0'	1°9·8'E	FM	133
Wood Fm	Norf	TG1822	52°45·3'	1°14·2'E	FM	133,134
Wood Fm	Norf	TG3622	52°44·9'	1°30·2'E	FM	133,134
Wood Fm	Norf	TG3908	52°37·2'	1°32·3'E	FM	134
Wood Fm	Norf	TG5102	52°33·7'	1°42·6'E	FM	134
Wood Fm	Norf	TL9298	52°33·0'	0°50·3'E	FM	144
Wood Fm	Norf	TL9899	52°33·4'	0°55·7'E	FM	144
Wood Fm	Norf	TM0497	52°32·2'	1°0·9'E	FM	144
Wood Fm	Norf	TM0681	52°23·5'	1°2·1'E	FM	144
Wood Fm	Norf	TM1989	52°27·5'	1°13·8'E	FM	156
Wood Fm	Norf	TM2889	52°27·3'	1°21·8'E	FM	156
Wood Fm	Norf	TM3093	52°29·4'	1°23·7'E	FM	134
Wood Fm	Norf	TM3393	52°29·3'	1°26·3'E	FM	134
Wood Fm	Norf	TM3595	52°30·4'	1°28·2'E	FM	134
Wood Fm	Northnts	SP6961	52°14·8'	0°59·0'W	FM	152
Wood Fm	Northnts	SP7151	52°9·4'	0°57·3'W	FM	152
Wood Fm	Notts	SK5947	53°1·3'	1°6·8'W	FM	129
Wood Fm	Notts	SK6244	52°59·6'	1°4·2'W	FM	129
Wood Fm	Notts	SK7589	53°23·8'	0°51·9'W	FM	112,120
Wood Fm	N Yks	SE2975	54°10·4'	1°32·9'W	FM	99
Wood Fm	N Yks	SE5458	54°1·2'	1°10·1'W	FM	105
Wood Fm	N Yks	SE7761	54°2·6'	0°49·0'W	FM	100
Wood Fm	Oxon	SP4019	51°52·3'	1°24·7'W	FM	164
Wood Fm	Powys	SO2155	52°11·5'	3°8·9'W	FM	148
Wood Fm	Shrops	SJ3609	52°40·7'	2°56·4'W	FM	126
Wood Fm	Shrops	SJ3721	52°47·2'	2°55·6'W	FM	126
Wood Fm	Shrops	SJ5930	52°52·2'	2°36·1'W	FM	126
Wood Fm	Shrops	SJ6223	52°48·4'	2°33·4'W	FM	127
Wood Fm	Shrops	SJ6921	52°47·4'	2°27·2'W	FM	127
Wood Fm	Shrops	SO5394	52°32·7'	2°41·2'W	FM	137,138
Wood Fm	Shrops	SO5595	52°33·3'	2°39·4'W	FM	137,138
Wood Fm	Shrops	SO6272	52°20·9'	2°33·1'W	FM	138
Wood Fm	Shrops	SO6472	52°20·9'	2°31·3'W	FM	138
Wood Fm	Somer	ST0936	51°7·2'	3°17·6'W	FM	181
Wood Fm	Somer	ST2241	51°10·0'	3°6·6'W	FM	182
Wood Fm	Staffs	SJ7032	52°53·3'	2°26·3'W	FM	127
Wood Fm	Staffs	SJ7529	52°51·7'	2°21·9'W	FM	127
Wood Fm	Staffs	SJ7544	52°59·8'	2°21·9'W	FM	118
Wood Fm	Staffs	SK0329	52°51·7'	1°56·9'W	FM	128
Wood Fm	Staffs	SK0540	52°57·7'	1°55·1'W	FM	119,128
Wood Fm	Staffs	SK1219	52°46·3'	1°48·9'W	FM	128
Wood Fm	Staffs	SO9093	52°32·3'	2°8·4'W	FM	139
Wood Fm	Stock	SJ9488	53°23·6'	2°5·0'W	FM	109
Wood Fm	Suff	TM0742	52°2·5'	1°1·5'E	FM	155,169
Wood Fm	Suff	TM1458	52°10·9'	1°8·2'E	FM	156
Wood Fm	Suff	TM1653	52°8·2'	1°9·8'E	FM	156
Wood Fm	Suff	TM1955	52°9·2'	1°12·5'E	FM	156
Wood Fm	Suff	TM2050	52°6·5'	1°13·2'E	FM	156
Wood Fm	Suff	TM2367	52°15·6'	1°16·5'E	FM	156
Wood Fm	Suff	TM2465	52°14·5'	1°17·3'E	FM	156
Wood Fm	Suff	TM2967	52°15·4'	1°21·7'E	FM	156
Wood Fm	Suff	TM3170	52°17·0'	1°23·6'E	FM	156
Wood Fm	Suff	TM3178	52°21·3'	1°23·9'E	FM	156
Wood Fm	Suff	TM3467	52°15·3'	1°26·1'E	FM	156
Wood Fm	Suff	TM3667	52°15·3'	1°27·9'E	FM	156
Wood Fm	Suff	TM3670	52°16·9'	1°28·0'E	FM	156
Wood Fm	Suff	TM3962	52°12·5'	1°30·3'E	FM	156
Wood Fm	Suff	TM3984	52°24·3'	1°31·2'E	FM	156
Wood Fm	Suff	TM4283	52°23·7'	1°33·8'E	FM	156
Wood Fm	Suff	TM4779	52°21·4'	1°38·1'E	FM	156
Wood Fm	Suff	TM4989	52°26·8'	1°40·3'E	FM	156
Wood Fm	Swin	SU1581	51°31·9'	1°46·6'W	FM	173
Wood Fm	Warw	SP1698	52°35·0'	1°45·4'W	FM	139
Wood Fm	Warw	SP3863	52°16·1'	1°26·2'W	FM	151
Wood Fm	Warw	SP4785	52°27·9'	1°18·1'W	FM	140
Wood Fm	W Berks	SU5879	51°30·6'	1°9·5'W	FM	174
Wood Fm	Wilts	ST8033	51°6·0'	2°16·8'W	FM	183
Wood Fm	Wrex	SJ4345	53°0·2'	2°50·6'W	FM	117
Wood Fm	Wrex	SJ4438	52°56·4'	2°49·6'W	FM	126
Wood Fm	York	SE6849	53°56·2'	0°57·4'W	FM	105,106
Wood Fms	Shrops	SO5580	52°25·2'	2°39·3'W	FM	137,138
Wood Fm, The	Heref	SO5365	52°17·1'	2°40·9'W	FM	137,138,149
Wood Fold	Lancs	SD5642	53°52·6'	2°39·7'W	X	102
Woodfold	Moray	NJ5746	57°30·4'	2°42·6'W	X	29
Woodfold Hall	Lancs	SD6329	53°45·6'	2°33·3'W	X	102,103
Wood Fold Hill	Dorset	ST5106	50°51·3'	2°41·4'W	H	194
Woodfold Wood	Moray	NJ5646	57°30·4'	2°43·6'W	F	29
Woodfoot	Cumbr	NY5018	54°33·5'	2°46·0'W	X	90

Woodfoot	Cumbr	NY6213	54°30·9'	2°34·8'W	X	91
Woodfoot	D & G	NT1000	55°17·4'	3°24·6'W	X	78
Woodfoot	Northum	NY9758	54°55·2'	2°2·4'W	X	87
Woodfoot	S Lanak	NS8540	55°38·7'	3°49·2'W	X	71,72
Woodford	C of Plym	SX5357	50°23·9'	4°3·7'W	T	201
Woodford	Corn	SS2113	50°53·6'	4°32·3'W	T	190
Woodford	Devon	SS8013	50°54·5'	3°42·0'W	X	181
Woodford	Devon	SX7950	50°20·5'	3°41·7'W	T	202
Woodford	Devon	SY1096	50°45·6'	3°16·2'W	T	192,193
Woodford	Glos	ST6995	51°39·4'	2°26·5'W	T	162
Woodford	Northnts	SP9677	52°23·2'	0°35·0'W	T	141
Woodford	Redbr	TQ4091	51°36·3'	0°1·7'E	T	177
Woodford	Somer	ST0638	51°8·2'	3°20·2'W	T	181
Woodford	Somer	ST5444	51°11·8'	2°39·1'W	T	182,183
Woodford	Staffs	SK1131	52°52·8'	1°49·8'W	X	128
Woodford	Stock	SJ8982	53°20·3'	2°9·5'W	T	109
Woodford Aerodrome	Stock	SJ8982	53°20·3'	2°9·5'W	X	109
Woodford Br	Devon	SS3912	50°53·3'	4°17·0'W	X	190
Woodford Br	Warw	SP3395	52°33·3'	1°30·4'W	X	140
Woodford Bridge	Redbr	TQ4291	51°36·2'	0°3·4'E	T	177
Woodford Cross	Corn	SS2114	50°54·1'	4°32·4'W	X	190
Woodford Fm	Somer	ST1218	50°57·5'	3°14·8'W	FM	181,193
Woodford Grange	Northnts	SP9877	52°23·2'	0°33·2'W	X	141
Woodford Green	Redbr	TQ4091	51°36·3'	0°1·7'E	T	177
Woodford Hall	Ches	SJ6264	53°10·5'	2°33·7'W	X	118
Woodford Halse	Northnts	SP5452	52°10·1'	1°12·2'W	T	152
Woodford Hill	Bath & NE Somer	ST5661	51°21·0'	2°37·5'W	H	172,182
Woodfordhill	Northnts	SP5652	52°10·0'	1°10·5'W	X	152
Woodford Ho	Northnts	SP9476	52°22·7'	0°36·7'W	X	141
Woodford Lodge	Northnts	SP5652	52°10·0'	1°10·5'W	X	152
Woodford Wells	Redbr	TQ4092	51°36·8'	0°1·7'E	T	177
Woodgarston Fm	Hants	SU5855	51°17·7'	1°9·7'W	FM	174,185
Woodgate	Birm	SO9982	52°26·4'	2°0·5'W	T	139
Woodgate	Cumbr	SD1194	54°20·3'	3°21·7'W	X	96
Wood Gate	Cumbr	SD2885	54°15·6'	3°5·9'W	X	96,97
Woodgate	Devon	SS7606	50°50·7'	3°45·3'W	X	191
Woodgate	Devon	ST1015	50°55·9'	3°16·5'W	T	181,193
Woodgate	Glos	SO7023	51°54·5'	2°25·8'W	X	162
Woodgate	Kent	TQ6559	51°18·6'	0°22·4'E	X	178,188
Woodgate	Norf	TG0216	52°42·5'	0°59·8'E	T	133
Woodgate	Shrops	SJ4628	52°51·0'	2°47·7'W	X	126
Woodgate	Staffs	SK1216	52°44·7'	1°48·9'W	X	128
Wood Gate	Staffs	SK1528	52°51·2'	1°46·2'W	T	128
Woodgate	Worcs	SO9666	52°17·8'	2°3·1'W	T	150
Woodgate	W Susx	SU9304	50°49·9'	0°40·4'W	T	197
Woodgate Cott	Shrops	SO4892	52°31·6'	2°45·6'W	X	137,138
Woodgate Farmhouse	Wilts	SU2331	51°4·9'	1°39·9'W	FM	184
Woodgate Fm	Ches	SJ6062	53°9·5'	2°35·5'W	FM	118
Woodgate Fm	E Yorks	SE8352	53°57·7'	0°43·7'W	FM	106
Woodgate Fm	Lincs	TF2816	52°43·8'	0°5·9'W	FM	131
Woodgate Fm	Notts	SK5425	52°49·4'	1°11·5'W	FM	129
Woodgate Fm	N Yks	SE2847	53°55·3'	1°34·0'W	FM	104
Woodgate Fm	Powys	SO3195	52°33·1'	3°0·7'W	FM	137
Woodgate Fm	W Susx	SU8624	51°0·8'	0°46·1'W	FM	197
Woodgate Hill	Bury	SD8211	53°36·0'	2°15·9'W	T	109
Woodgate Hill	Leic	SK7414	52°43·3'	0°53·9'W	X	129
Woodgate Ho	E Susx	TQ8424	50°59·4'	0°37·7'E	X	199
Woodgate Ho	Norf	TG1826	52°47·5'	1°14·4'E	X	133,134
Woodgates	Lancs	SD5943	53°53·1'	2°37·0'W	X	102
Woodgates End	Essex	TL5725	51°54·3'	0°17·3'E	T	167
Woodgate's Fm	Devon	ST1615	50°55·9'	3°11·3'W	FM	181,193
Woodgates Fm	Suff	TM0736	51°59·3'	1°1·3'E	FM	155,169
Woodgates Green	Worcs	SO6370	52°19·8'	2°32·2'W	T	138
Woodgate Valley	Birm	SP0083	52°26·9'	1°59·6'W	T	139
Woodgetters	W Susx	TQ1524	51°0·5'	0°21·3'W	X	198
Wood Gill	N Yks	SD7263	54°4·0'	2°25·3'W	X	98
Woodgill Ho	Cumbr	NY5547	54°49·2'	2°41·6'W	X	86
Wood Green	Bucks	SP6438	52°2·4'	1°3·6'W	X	152
Wood Green	Essex	TL4100	51°41·1'	0°2·8'E	T	167
Woodgreen	Glos	SO7520	51°52·9'	2°21·4'W	X	162
Woodgreen	Hants	SU1717	50°57·4'	1°45·1'W	T	184
Wood Green	Hargy	TQ3090	51°35·9'	0°7·0'W	T	176,177
Woodgreen	N Ayr	NS3044	55°39·8'	4°41·7'W	X	63,70
Wood Green	Norf	TM2091	52°28·6'	1°14·8'E	T	134
Woodgreen	Oxon	SP3610	51°47·5'	1°28·3'W	T	164
Wood Green	Sand	SO9996	52°33·9'	2°0·5'W	T	139
Woodgreen	Shrops	SJ6108	52°40·3'	2°34·2'W	X	127
Woodgreen	Shrops	SJ7310	52°41·5'	2°23·6'W	X	127
Wood Green	Worcs	SO8067	52°18·3'	2°17·2'W	T	138,150
Woodgreen	Worcs	SO8856	52°12·4'	2°10·1'W	X	150
Wood Green Animal Shelter	Cambs	TL2668	52°18·0'	0°8·7'W	X	153
Woodgreen Animal Shelter	Cambs	TL4339	52°2·1'	0°5·5'E	X	154
Woodgreen Fm	Ches	SJ6460	53°8·4'	2°31·9'W	FM	118
Woodgreen Fm	Devon	SX7296	50°45·2'	3°48·5'W	FM	191
Woodgreen Fm	Herts	TL3201	51°41·8'	0°5·0'W	FM	166
Woodgreen Fm	W Berks	SU6076	51°29·0'	1°7·8'W	FM	175
Woodground Fm	Bucks	SP6311	51°47·9'	1°4·8'W	FM	164,165
Wood Hall	Cambs	TL5850	52°7·8'	0°18·9'E	X	154
Wood Hall	Cumbr	NY3437	54°43·7'	3°1·1'W	X	90
Woodhall	Devon	SS5802	50°48·2'	4°0·5'W	X	191
Woodhall	D & G	NY2367	54°59·7'	3°11·8'W	X	85
Woodhall	E Loth	NT4268	55°54·4'	2°55·2'W	X	66
Woodhall	E Loth	NT6872	55°56·7'	2°30·3'W	X	67
Wood Hall	Essex	TL4733	51°58·8'	0°8·8'E	T	167
Wood Hall	Essex	TL9331	51°56·9'	0°48·9'E	X	168
Wood Hall	E Yorks	TA1636	53°48·7'	0°13·9'W	X	107
Wood Hall	Herts	TL2411	51°47·3'	0°11·7'W	T	166
Woodhall	Inverc	NS3474	55°56·1'	4°39·0'W	T	63
Wood Hall	Norf	TL6297	52°33·0'	0°23·8'E	A	143
Wood Hall	Northum	NT9503	55°19·5'	2°5·3'W	X	81
Woodhall	Northum	NY7463	54°57·9'	2°23·9'W	X	86,87
Wood Hall	Northum	NY8664	54°58·5'	2°12·7'W	X	87
Woodhall	N Yks	SD9790	54°18·6'	2°2·3'W	T	98
Wood Hall	N Yks	SE1790	54°18·6'	1°43·9'W	X	99
Woodhall	N Yks	SE6931	53°46·5'	0°56·8'W	T	105,106
Wood Hall	Shrops	SJ4408	52°40·2'	2°49·3'W	X	126
Woodhall	S Lanak	NS8447	55°42·4'	3°50·3'W	X	72
Wood Hall	Suff	TL9958	52°11·3'	0°55·1'E	X	155

Wood Hall	Suff	TM1069	52°17·0'	1°5·1'E	X	155
Wood Hall	Suff	TM2664	52°13·9'	1°19·0'E	X	156
Wood Hall	Worcs	SO8851	52°9·7'	2°10·1'W	X	150
Woodhall Bridge	Devon	SS5803	50°48·8'	4°0·6'W	X	191
Woodhall Burn	E Loth	NT6772	55°56·6'	2°31·3'W	W	67
Woodhall Fm	Beds	TL1337	52°1·4'	0°20·8'W	FM	153
Woodhall Fm	Cambs	TL4072	52°19·9'	0°3·7'E	FM	154
Wood Hall Fm	Cumbr	NY1232	54°40·8'	3°21·5'W	FM	89
Woodhall Fm	Essex	TL6810	51°46·0'	0°26·5'E	FM	167
Woodhall Fm	Herts	TL2310	51°46·7'	0°12·6'W	FM	166
Wood Hall Fm	Herts	TQ1899	51°40·9'	0°17·2'W	FM	166,176
Woodhall Fm	Kent	TQ5951	51°14·4'	0°17·1'E	FM	188
Wood Hall Fm	Northum	NY9373	55°3·3'	2°6·1'W	FM	87
Woodhall Fm	Notts	SK5146	53°0·8'	1°14·0'W	FM	129
Wood Hall Fm	Sefton	SD3700	53°29·8'	2°56·6'W	FM	108
Wood Hall Fm	Staffs	SJ8404	52°38·2'	2°13·8'W	FM	127
Woodhall Fm	Worcs	SO7858	52°13·4'	2°18·9'W	FM	150
Woodhall Fms	Worcs	SO8749	52°8·6'	2°11·0'W	FM	150
Woodhall Greets	N Yks	SD9692	54°19·7'	2°3·3'W	X	98
Woodhall Hills	Leeds	SE2035	53°48·9'	1°41·4'W	T	104
Wood Hall (Hotel)	N Yks	SE3646	53°54·8'	1°26·7'W	X	104
Woodhall Loch	D & G	NX6667	54°59·0'	4°5·2'W	W	83,84
Woodhall Park	Herts	TL3118	51°50·9'	0°5·5'W	X	166
Woodhall Spa	Lincs	TF1963	53°9·3'	0°12·8'W	T	122
Woodham	Bucks	SP7018	51°51·6'	0°58·6'W	T	165
Woodham	Durham	NZ2826	54°37·9'	1°33·6'W	T	93
Woodham	Surrey	TQ0462	51°21·1'	0°30·0'W	T	176,186
Woodham Burn	Durham	NZ2926	54°37·9'	1°32·6'W	W	93
Woodham Fenn	Essex	TQ7997	51°38·8'	0°35·6'E	X	167
Woodham Ferrers	Essex	TQ7999	51°39·9'	0°35·7'E	T	167
Woodham Ferrers Sta	Essex	TQ8097	51°38·8'	0°36·5'E	X	168
Woodham Hall	Essex	TL7901	51°41·0'	0°35·8'E	X	167
Woodham Lodge	Essex	TL7800	51°40·5'	0°34·9'E	X	167
Woodham Mortimer	Essex	TL8104	51°42·6'	0°37·6'E	T	168
Woodhampton	Heref	SO4067	52°18·1'	2°52·4'W	X	137,148,149
Woodhampton	Heref	SO5669	52°19·3'	2°38·3'W	X	137,138
Woodhampton Ho	Worcs	SO8068	52°18·8'	2°17·2'W	X	138
Woodhampton Wood	Heref	SO4067	52°18·1'	2°52·4'W	F	137,148,149
Woodhams Fm	Essex	TL5932	51°58·0'	0°19·3'E	FM	167
Woodhams Fm	Hants	SU4833	51°5·9'	1°18·5'W	FM	185
Woodham Walter	Essex	TL8007	51°44·2'	0°36·8'E	T	168
Woodham Walter Common	Essex	TL7906	51°43·7'	0°35·9'E	F	167
Woodhatch	Essex	TL5001	51°41·5'	0°10·6'E	X	167
Woodhatch	Surrey	TQ2548	51°13·3'	0°12·2'W	T	187
Woodhaugh	Angus	NO4878	56°53·7'	2°50·8'W	X	44
Woodhaven	Fife	NO4126	56°25·6'	2°56·9'W	T	54,59
Wood Haven	Fife	NT4999	56°11·1'	2°48·9'W	W	59
Woodhawk	Pemb	SM8722	51°51·6'	5°5·2'W	X	157
Woodhayes	Devon	ST0201	50°48·3'	3°23·1'W	X	192
Woodhayes	Devon	SY0496	50°45·6'	3°21·3'W	X	192
Woodhayes	Devon	SY2599	50°47·4'	3°3·5'W	X	192,193
Woodhayes	Glos	ST8388	51°35·7'	2°14·3'W	X	162,173
Wood Hayes	Wolv	SJ9401	52°36·6'	2°4·9'W	T	127,139
Woodhayes Fm	Devon	ST1702	50°48·9'	3°10·3'W	FM	192,193
Woodhayes Fm	Devon	SX8491	50°42·7'	3°38·2'W	FM	191
Woodhayes Fm	Somer	ST2610	50°53·3'	3°2·7'W	FM	192,193
Woodhay Fm	Derby	SK1439	52°57·1'	1°47·1'W	FM	128
Woodhayne Fm	Devon	ST1501	50°48·4'	3°12·0'W	FM	192,193
Woodhayne Fm	Devon	ST2512	50°54·4'	3°3·6'W	FM	193
Woodhayne Fm	Devon	SY2696	50°45·8'	3°2·6'W	FM	192,193
Woodhead	Aberd	NJ6048	57°31·5'	2°39·6'W	X	29
Woodhead	Aberd	NJ6112	57°12·1'	2°38·3'W	X	37
Woodhead	Aberd	NJ6718	57°15·3'	2°32·4'W	X	38
Woodhead	Aberd	NJ7516	57°14·3'	2°24·4'W	X	38
Woodhead	Aberd	NJ7938	57°26·2'	2°20·5'W	T	29,30
Woodhead	Aberd	NJ8445	57°30·0'	2°15·6'W	X	29,30
Woodhead	Aberd	NJ8961	57°38·6'	2°10·6'W	T	30
Woodhead	Aberd	NK0461	57°38·6'	1°55·5'W	X	30
Woodhead	Aberd	NO6597	57°4·0'	2°34·2'W	X	38,45
Woodhead	Aberd	NO6774	56°51·6'	2°32·0'W	X	45
Woodhead	Aberd	NO7194	57°2·4'	2°28·2'W	X	38,45
Woodhead	Cumbr	NY4267	54°59·9'	2°54·0'W	X	85
Woodhead	Cumbr	NY4662	54°57·2'	2°50·2'W	X	86
Wood Head	Cumbr	NY5432	54°41·1'	2°42·4'W	X	90
Woodhead	Cumbr	NY6122	54°35·7'	2°35·8'W	X	91
Woodhead	Derby	SE0900	53°30·0'	1°51·4'W	X	110
Woodhead	Derby	SK2148	53°2·0'	1°40·8'W	X	119
Woodhead	Devon	SY2090	50°42·5'	3°7·6'W	X	192,193
Woodhead	D & G	NT1003	55°19·0'	3°24·7'W	X	78
Woodhead	D & G	NX5395	55°13·9'	4°18·3'W	X	77
Woodhead	D & G	NX5760	54°55·1'	4°13·4'W	X	83
Woodhead	D & G	NX7277	55°4·5'	3°59·9'W	X	77,84
Woodhead	D & G	NX8256	54°53·3'	3°50·0'W	X	84
Woodhead	D & G	NX8495	55°14·4'	3°49·0'W	X	78
Woodhead	D & G	NX8884	55°8·5'	3°45·0'W	X	78
Woodhead	D & G	NX9171	55°1·5'	3°41·9'W	T	84
Woodhead	D & G	NY1372	55°2·3'	3°21·3'W	X	85
Woodhead	D & G	NY2267	54°59·7'	3°12·7'W	X	85
Woodhead	E Ayr	NS4734	55°34·8'	4°25·2'W	X	70
Woodhead	E Ayr	NS5237	55°36·5'	4°20·5'W	X	70
Woodhead	E Ayr	NS5526	55°30·6'	4°17·3'W	X	71
Woodhead	E Loth	NT5266	55°53·3'	2°45·6'W	X	66
Woodhead	Fife	NO2615	56°19·6'	3°11·4'W	X	59
Woodhead	Fife	NS9986	56°3·6'	3°36·9'W	X	65
Woodhead	Heref	SO4176	52°23·0'	2°51·6'W	X	137,148
Woodhead	Highld	NH6460	57°36·8'	4°16·1'W	X	21
Woodhead	Midlo	NT3864	55°52·2'	2°59·0'W	X	66
Woodhead	Moray	NJ0760	57°37·5'	3°33·0'W	X	27
Woodhead	Moray	NJ5254	57°34·7'	2°47·7'W	X	29
Woodhead	N Ayr	NS2250	55°42·9'	4°49·6'W	X	63
Woodhead	Northum	NU1001	55°18·4'	1°50·1'W	X	81
Woodhead	Northum	NY6964	54°58·4'	2°28·6'W	X	86,87
Woodhead	Northum	NY9183	55°8·7'	2°17·5'W	X	80
Woodhead	Northum	NZ0857	54°54·7'	1°52·1'W	X	88
Wood Head	N Yks	NZ3406	54°27·1'	1°28·1'W	X	93
Woodhead	Pth & Kin	NO0414	56°18·8'	3°32·7'W	X	58
Woodhead	Pth & Kin	NO0920	56°22·1'	3°27·9'W	X	52,53,58
Woodhead	Pth & Kin	NO1434	56°29·7'	3°23·4'W	X	53
Woodhead	Rut	SK9911	52°41·5'	0°31·7'W	F	130
Woodhead	S Ayr	NS2100	55°16·0'	4°48·6'W	X	76

Woodhead	S Lanak	NS7742	55°39·6'	3°56·9'W	X	71
Woodhead	Staffs	SJ9149	53°2·5'	2°7·6'W	X	118
Wood Head	Warr	SJ6094	53°26·7'	2°35·7'W	X	109
Woodhead Cottage	D & G	NY2267	54°59·7'	3°12·7'W	X	85
Woodhead Fm	Cumbr	NY4834	54°42·1'	2°48·0'W	FM	90
Woodhead Fm	Falk	NS9879	55°59·8'	3°37·7'W	FM	65
Woodhead Fm	N Yks	NZ7104	54°25·8'	0°53·9'W	FM	94
Woodhead Fm	N Yks	SD9645	53°54·3'	2°3·2'W	FM	103
Woodhead Fm	Scot Bord	NT6125	55°31·3'	2°36·6'W	FM	74
Woodhead Fm	S Lanak	NS6862	55°50·2'	4°6·0'W	FM	64
Woodhead Fm	Staffs	SK0951	53°3·6'	1°51·5'W	FM	119
Woodhead Grange Fm	Derby	SK3662	53°9·5'	1°27·3'W	FM	119
Woodhead Hill	D & G	NX7491	55°12·1'	3°58·4'W	H	77
Woodhead Hill	D & G	NX9271	55°1·6'	3°40·9'W	H	84
Woodhead House	Aberd	NJ7245	57°29·9'	2°27·6'W	X	29
Wood Head Lathe	Cumbr	SD7088	54°17·5'	2°27·2'W	X	98
Woodhead of Ballinshoe	Angus	NO4252	56°39·6'	2°56·3'W	X	54
Woodhead of Cairnty	Moray	NJ3252	57°33·4'	3°7·7'W	X	28
Woodhead of Delgaty	Aberd	NJ7749	57°32·1'	2°22·6'W	X	29,30
Woodhead of Laithers	Aberd	NJ7145	57°29·9'	2°28·6'W	X	29
Woodhead Reservoir	Derby	SK0999	53°29·5'	1°51·5'W	W	110
Woodheads	Scot Bord	NT5345	55°42·0'	2°44·4'W	T	73
Woodheads	Scot Bord	NT7248	55°43·7'	2°26·3'W	X	74
Woodheads Hill	Scot Bord	NT5245	55°42·0'	2°45·4'W	H	73
Woodhead Tunnel	Barns	SE1301	53°30·6'	1°47·8'W	X	110
Woodhenge	Wilts	SU1543	51°11·4'	1°46·7'W	A	184
Woodhey	Bury	SD7815	53°38·1'	2°19·6'W	T	109
Woodhey	Wirral	SJ3285	53°21·7'	3°0·9'W	T	108
Woodhey Green	Ches	SJ5752	53°4·1'	2°38·1'W	T	117
Woodhey Hall	Ches	SJ5752	53°4·1'	2°38·1'W	X	117
Wood Hill	Clackm	NS8998	56°10·0'	3°46·8'W	X	58
Wood Hill	D & G	NX9989	55°11·4'	3°34·8'W	H	78
Wood Hill	E Ayr	NS6724	55°29·8'	4°5·9'W	X	71
Woodhill	Essex	TL7604	51°42·7'	0°33·2'E	T	167
Wood Hill	E Yorks	TA0234	53°47·8'	0°26·7'W	X	106,107
Woodhill	Highld	NH5955	57°34·0'	4°21·0'W	X	26
Wood Hill	Kent	TR3747	51°10·6'	1°23·8'E	X	179
Wood Hill	Leeds	SE2135	53°48·9'	1°40·4'W	X	104
Wood Hill	Lincs	TF3766	53°10·6'	0°3·4'E	X	122
Wood Hill	Norf	TG1942	52°56·1'	1°15·9'E	X	133
Woodhill	Northum	NY8892	55°13·6'	2°10·9'W	X	80
Woodhill	N Som	ST4677	51°29·6'	2°46·3'W	T	171,172
Woodhill	Pth & Kin	NO0954	56°40·4'	3°28·7'W	X	52,53
Wood Hill	Scot Bord	NT1644	55°41·2'	3°19·7'W	H	72
Wood Hill	Scot Bord	NT8124	55°30·8'	2°17·6'W	H	74
Woodhill	Shrops	SJ2626	52°49·8'	3°5·5'W	X	126
Woodhill	Shrops	SO7384	52°27·4'	2°23·4'W	T	138
Woodhill	Somer	ST3527	51°2·6'	2°55·2'W	T	193
Woodhill	Surrey	SU8241	51°10·0'	0°49·2'W	X	186
Woodhill	Surrey	TQ0443	51°10·8'	0°30·3'W	X	186
Wood Hill	Warw	SP4279	52°24·7'	1°22·6'W	H	140
Wood Hill	Wilts	ST9986	51°34·6'	2°0·5'W	X	173
Woodhill Bay	N Som	ST4677	51°29·6'	2°46·3'W	W	171,172
Woodhill Brook	Oxon	SU3889	51°36·1'	1°26·7'W	W	174
Woodhill Edge	D & G	NY2188	55°11·1'	3°14·0'W	H	79
Woodhill Fm	Bucks	TQ0087	51°34·6'	0°33·0'W	FM	176
Woodhill Fm	E Yorks	SE9563	54°3·5'	0°32·5'W	FM	101
Woodhill Fm	Lincs	TF1287	53°22·3'	0°18·6'W	FM	113,121
Woodhill Fm	Suff	TM3970	52°16·8'	1°30·6'E	FM	156
Woodhill Fm	Warw	SP4179	52°24·7'	1°23·4'W	FM	140
Woodhill Grange	N Yks	SE4083	54°14·7'	1°22·8'W	X	99
Woodhill Ho	Aberd	NJ5905	57°8·3'	2°40·2'W	X	37
Woodhill Ho	Angus	NO5234	56°30·0'	2°46·3'W	X	54
Woodhill Ho	C of Aber	NJ9106	57°8·9'	2°8·5'W	X	38
Woodhill Ho	Herts	TL2605	51°44·0'	0°10·1'W	X	166
Woodhill Ho	N Yks	NZ7709	54°28·5'	0°48·3'W	X	94
Woodhill Manor	Corn	SX2465	50°27·7'	4°28·4'W	X	201
Woodhill Park	Wilts	SU0676	51°29·2'	1°54·4'W	X	173
Woodhills	Scot Bord	NT9556	55°48·1'	2°4·3'W	X	67,74,75
Woodhills Fm	Glos	SP2334	52°0·5'	1°39·5'W	FM	151
Wood Ho	Cumbr	NY1617	54°32·7'	3°17·5'W	X	89
Wood Ho	Cumbr	NY3537	54°43·7'	3°0·1'W	X	90
Wood Ho	Cumbr	NY5624	54°36·8'	2°40·5'W	X	90
Wood Ho	Cumbr	SD1282	54°13·8'	3°20·6'W	X	96
Wood Ho	Derby	SK2038	52°56·6'	1°41·7'W	X	128
Wood Ho	Devon	SX6596	50°45·1'	3°54·4'W	X	191
Wood Ho	Essex	TL7011	51°46·5'	0°28·2'E	X	167
Wood Ho	E Yorks	SE8150	53°56·6'	0°45·5'W	X	106
Wood Ho	Heref	SO5551	52°9·6'	2°39·1'W	X	149
Wood Ho	Lancs	SD7938	53°50·5'	2°18·7'W	X	103
Wood Ho	Northum	NU2108	55°22·2'	1°39·7'W	X	81
Wood Ho	Northum	NY6566	54°59·5'	2°32·4'W	X	86
Wood Ho	Northum	NZ0857	54°54·7'	1°52·1'W	X	88
Wood Ho	Northum	NZ1288	55°11·4'	1°48·3'W	X	81
Wood Ho	N Yks	NY9904	54°26·1'	2°0·5'W	X	92
Wood Ho	N Yks	SD7768	54°6·7'	2°20·7'W	X	98
Wood Ho	N Yks	SD9248	53°55·9'	2°6·9'W	X	103
Wood Ho	N Yks	SE9589	54°17·5'	0°32·0'W	X	94,101
Wood Ho	Oxon	SP4721	51°53·4'	1°18·6'W	X	164
Wood Ho	Oxon	SU2695	51°39·4'	1°37·1'W	X	163
Wood Ho	Shrops	SJ5127	52°50·5'	2°43·2'W	X	126
Wood Ho	Shrops	SO3088	52°29·4'	3°1·5'W	X	137
Wood Ho	Staffs	SJ9235	52°55·0'	2°6·7'W	X	127
Wood Ho	Suff	TM2242	52°2·1'	1°14·6'E	X	169
Wood Ho	Wrex	SJ3446	53°0·7'	2°58·6'W	X	117
Wood Ho Gate	Lancs	SD7153	53°58·6'	2°26·1'W	X	103
Wood Hollow	Northnts	SP9497	52°34·0'	0°36·4'W	F	141
Woodhorn	Northum	NZ2988	55°11·4'	1°32·2'W	T	81
Woodhorn Fm	W Susx	SU9104	50°49·9'	0°42·1'W	FM	197
Woodhorn Fm	W Susx	SZ8399	50°47·3'	0°49·0'W	FM	197
Wood Ho, The	Shrops	SJ8306	52°39·3'	2°14·7'W	X	127
Wood House	Arg & Bt	NR8365	55°50·0'	5°27·5'W	X	62
Woodhouse	Brad	SE0640	53°51·6'	1°54·1'W	T	104
Woodhouse	Cald	SE1421	53°41·4'	1°46·9'W	T	104
Woodhouse	Cumbr	NX9716	54°32·0'	3°35·1'W	T	89
Woodhouse	Cumbr	NY4733	54°41·6'	2°48·9'W	X	90
Woodhouse	Cumbr	SD5183	54°14·7'	2°44·7'W	T	97
Woodhouse	Devon	SS6727	51°1·9'	3°53·4'W	X	180
Woodhouse	Devon	SS7122	50°59·2'	3°49·9'W	X	180
Woodhouse	Devon	SS7813	50°54·5'	3°43·7'W	X	180

Woodhouse	Devon	SX7197	50°45·7'	3°49·4'W	X	191
Woodhouse	Devon	SY3193	50°44·2'	2°58·3'W	X	193
Woodhouse	D & G	NX8586	55°9·6'	3°47·9'W	X	78
Woodhouse	E Renf	NS5750	55°43·6'	4°16·2'W	X	64
Woodhouse	Hants	SU3749	51°14·6'	1°27·8'W	T	185
Woodhouse	Hants	SU7212	50°54·4'	0°58·2'W	X	197
Wood House	Lancs	SD7053	53°58·6'	2°27·0'W	T	103
Woodhouse	Leeds	SE2935	53°48·9'	1°33·2'W	T	104
Woodhouse	Leic	SK5415	52°44·0'	1°11·6'W	T	129
Woodhouse	N Lincs	SE7808	53°34·0'	0°48·9'W	T	112
Woodhouse	Northum	NY8887	55°10·9'	2°10·9'W	X	80
Woodhouse	N Yks	SE0360	54°2·4'	1°56·8'W	X	98
Woodhouse	N Yks	SE1886	54°16·4'	1°43·0'W	X	99
Woodhouse	N Yks	SE5763	54°3·8'	1°7·3'W	X	100
Woodhouse	Pth & Kin	NN6724	56°23·6'	4°8·8'W	X	51
Woodhouse	Red & Cl	NZ5916	54°32·4'	1°4·9'W	X	93
Woodhouse	Scot Bord	NT2137	55°37·5'	3°14·8'W	X	73
Woodhouse	Scot Bord	NT6514	55°25·4'	2°32·7'W	X	80
Woodhouse	Sheff	SK4185	53°21·9'	1°22·6'W	T	111,120
Woodhouse	Shrops	SJ3628	52°51·0'	2°56·6'W	X	126
Woodhouse	Shrops	SO6477	52°23·6'	2°31·3'W	X	138
Woodhouse	Somer	ST6122	51°0·0'	2°33·0'W	X	183
Woodhouse	Staffs	SJ7942	52°58·7'	2°18·4'W	X	118
Woodhouse	Staffs	SJ8958	53°7·4'	2°9·5'W	X	118
Woodhouse	Wakf	SE3822	53°41·8'	1°25·1'W	T	104
Woodhouse	W Susx	TQ2216	50°56·1'	0°15·4'W	X	198
Woodhouse Castle (rems of)	Wilts	ST8041	51°10·3'	2°16·8'W	A	183
Woodhouse Common Fm	Notts	SK7362	53°9·2'	0°54·1'W	FM	120
Woodhouse Cottage	Ches	SJ8170	53°13·8'	2°16·7'W	X	118
Woodhouse Cross	Dorset	ST7727	51°2·7'	2°19·3'W	X	183
Woodhouse Down	S Glos	ST6185	51°34·0'	2°33·4'W	T	172
Woodhouse Eaves	Leic	SK5214	52°43·5'	1°13·4'W	T	129
Woodhouse-end	Ches	SJ9169	53°13·3'	2°7·7'W	X	118
Woodhouse Field	N Yks	SE3983	54°14·7'	1°23·7'W	X	99
Woodhouse Fields	Shrops	SO6095	52°33·2'	2°35·0'W	X	138
Woodhouse Fields Fm	Staffs	SK0839	52°57·1'	1°52·5'W	FM	128
Wood House Fm	Cambs	TF4504	52°37·1'	0°8·9'E	FM	143
Woodhouse Fm	Cambs	TL5583	52°25·6'	0°17·2'E	FM	143
Woodhouse Fm	Carm	SN2512	51°47·0'	4°31·8'W	FM	158
Woodhouse Fm	Ches	SJ4544	52°59·7'	2°48·8'W	FM	117
Woodhouse Fm	Ches	SJ5158	53°7·3'	2°43·5'W	FM	117
Woodhouse Fm	Ches	SJ6741	52°58·2'	2°29·1'W	FM	118
Woodhouse Fm	Ches	SJ7867	53°12·2'	2°19·4'W	FM	118
Woodhouse Fm	Derby	SK2636	52°55·5'	1°36·4'W	FM	128
Woodhouse Fm	Derby	SK4672	53°14·8'	1°18·2'W	FM	120
Woodhouse Fm	Devon	SS4922	50°58·9'	4°8·7'W	FM	180
Woodhouse Fm	Devon	SX9278	50°35·7'	3°31·2'W	FM	192
Woodhouse Fm	Devon	SY2898	50°46·9'	3°0·9'W	FM	193
Woodhouse Fm	Devon	SY3399	50°47·4'	2°56·7'W	FM	193
Woodhouse Fm	Donc	SK6595	53°27·1'	1°0·9'W	FM	111
Woodhouse Fm	Durham	NZ1827	54°38·5'	1°42·8'W	FM	92
Woodhouse Fm	Durham	NZ2435	54°42·8'	1°37·2'W	FM	93
Woodhouse Fm	Essex	TL8125	51°53·9'	0°38·2'E	FM	168
Woodhouse Fm	Essex	TL8220	51°51·2'	0°39·0'E	FM	168
Woodhouse Fm	Essex	TL9728	51°55·2'	0°52·3'E	FM	168
Woodhouse Fm	E Yorks	SE7247	53°55·1'	0°53·8'W	FM	105,106
Woodhouse Fm	E Yorks	SE7744	53°53·4'	0°49·3'W	FM	105,106
Woodhouse Fm	E Yorks	SE7937	53°49·6'	0°47·6'W	FM	105,106
Woodhouse Fm	E Yorks	SE9931	53°46·2'	0°29·5'W	FM	106
Woodhouse Fm	E Yorks	SE9944	53°53·2'	0°29·2'W	FM	106
Woodhouse Fm	E Yorks	TA1236	53°48·7'	0°17·5'W	FM	107
Woodhouse Fm	E Yorks	TA1240	53°50·9'	0°17·4'W	FM	107
Woodhouse Fm	E Yorks	TA1255	53°59·0'	0°17·1'W	FM	107
Woodhouse Fm	Hants	SU5562	51°21·5'	1°12·2'W	FM	174
Woodhouse Fm	Heref	SO4768	52°18·7'	2°46·2'W	FM	137,138,148
Woodhouse Fm	Heref	SO6529	51°57·7'	2°30·2'W	FM	149
Woodhouse Fm	I of W	SZ5293	50°44·3'	1°15·4'W	FM	196
Woodhouse Fm	I of W	SZ5490	50°42·7'	1°13·7'W	FM	196
Woodhouse Fm	Kirk	SE2613	53°37·0'	1°36·0'W	FM	110
Woodhouse Fm	Leeds	SE3339	53°51·0'	1°29·5'W	FM	104
Woodhouse Fm	Leeds	SE3838	53°50·5'	1°24·9'W	FM	104
Woodhouse Fm	Leic	SK4324	52°48·9'	1°21·3'W	FM	129
Woodhouse Fm	Leic	SP4694	52°32·7'	1°18·9'W	FM	140
Woodhouse Fm	Lincs	SK8490	53°24·2'	0°43·8'W	FM	112
Woodhouse Fm	Lincs	SK8868	53°12·3'	0°40·5'W	FM	121
Woodhouse Fm	Lincs	TF3726	52°49·1'	0°2·4'E	FM	131
Woodhouse Fm	Norf	TM2296	52°31·2'	1°16·7'E	FM	134
Woodhouse Fm	Notts	SK7679	53°18·4'	0°51·2'W	FM	120
Woodhouse Fm	N Yks	NZ2307	54°27·7'	1°38·3'W	FM	93
Woodhouse Fm	N Yks	NZ5709	54°28·6'	1°6·8'W	FM	93
Woodhouse Fm	N Yks	SE1799	54°23·4'	1°43·9'W	FM	99
Woodhouse Fm	N Yks	SE2471	54°8·3'	1°37·5'W	FM	99
Woodhouse Fm	N Yks	SE4945	53°54·2'	1°14·8'W	FM	105
Woodhouse Fm	N Yks	SE5327	53°44·4'	1°11·4'W	FM	105
Woodhouse Fm	N Yks	SE5569	54°7·1'	1°9·1'W	FM	100
Woodhouse Fm	N Yks	SE6831	53°46·5'	0°57·7'W	FM	105,106
Woodhouse Fm	N Yks	SE7159	54°1·6'	0°54·6'W	FM	105,106
Wood House Fm	N Yks	SE8568	54°6·3'	0°41·6'W	FM	100
Woodhouse Fm	N Yks	TA0380	54°12·6'	0°24·8'W	FM	101
Woodhouse Fm	Oxon	SU4198	51°41·0'	1°24·0'W	FM	164
Woodhouse Fm	Oxon	SU6387	51°34·9'	1°5·1'W	FM	175
Woodhouse Fm	Sheff	SK2790	53°24·6'	1°35·2'W	FM	110
Woodhouse Fm	Shrops	SJ6402	52°37·1'	2°31·5'W	FM	127
Woodhouse Fm	Shrops	SJ6426	52°50·1'	2°31·7'W	FM	127
Woodhouse Fm	Shrops	SJ8203	52°37·7'	2°15·6'W	FM	127
Woodhouse Fm	Sol	SP1781	52°25·8'	1°44·6'W	FM	139
Woodhouse Fm	Somer	ST3410	50°53·4'	2°55·9'W	FM	193
Woodhouse Fm	Somer	ST3418	50°57·7'	2°56·0'W	FM	193
Woodhouse Fm	Somer	ST5016	50°56·7'	2°42·3'W	FM	183
Wood House Fm	Staffs	SK0244	52°59·8'	1°57·8'W	FM	119,128
Woodhouse Fm	Staffs	SK2028	52°51·2'	1°41·8'W	FM	128
Woodhouse Fm	Suff	TL9256	52°10·4'	0°48·9'E	FM	155
Woodhouse Fm	Suff	TM1669	52°16·8'	1°10·4'E	FM	156
Wood House Fm	Wakf	SE4123	53°42·3'	1°22·3'W	FM	105
Woodhouse Fm	Warw	SP2093	52°32·3'	1°41·9'W	FM	139
Woodhouse Fm	Wilts	ST7941	51°10·3'	2°17·6'W	FM	183
Woodhouse Fm	Wilts	ST9259	51°20·0'	2°6·5'W	FM	173
Woodhouse Fm	Worcs	SO7578	52°24·2'	2°21·7'W	FM	138
Woodhouse Fm	Worcs	SO7861	52°15·0'	2°18·9'W	FM	138,150

Woodhouse Fm	Worcs	SO8578	52°24·2'	2°12·8'W	FM	139
Woodhouse Fm	Worcs	SO8975	52°22·6'	2°9·3'W	FM	139
Woodhouse Fm	Worcs	SO9359	52°14·0'	2°5·8'W	FM	150
Woodhouse Fm	Wrekin	SJ7211	52°42·0'	2°24·5'W	FM	127
Woodhouse Fm	W Susx	SU8020	50°58·7'	0°51·2'W	FM	197
Woodhouse Fm	York	SE5355	53°59·5'	1°11·1'W	FM	105
Woodhouse Fm	York	SE5450	53°56·8'	1°10·2'W	FM	105
Wood House Fm	York	SE6262	54°3·3'	1°2·8'W	FM	100
Woodhouse Grange	Donc	SE6807	53°33·5'	0°58·0'W	X	111
Woodhouse Grange	E Yorks	SE7347	53°55·1'	0°52·9'W	X	105,106
Woodhouse Grange	N Yks	SE4437	53°49·9'	1°19·5'W	X	105
Woodhouse Grange	Pemb	SN0010	51°45·4'	4°53·5'W	X	157,158
Woodhouse Green	Staffs	SJ9162	53°9·5'	2°7·7'W	T	118
Woodhouse Hall	Notts	SK5473	53°15·3'	1°11·0'W	X	120
Woodhouse Hall Fm	Leeds	SE2924	53°42·9'	1°33·2'W	FM	104
Woodhouse Hill	Devon	SY3194	50°44·7'	2°58·3'W	X	193
Woodhousehill	D & G	NY2672	55°2·5'	3°9·1'W	X	85
Woodhouselee	Midlo	NT2364	55°52·0'	3°13·4'W	T	66
Woodhouselee Hill	Midlo	NT2365	55°52·6'	3°13·4'W	X	66
Woodhouselees	D & G	NY3974	55°3·7'	2°56·9'W	X	85
Woodhouselees Plantation	D & G	NY3774	55°3·6'	2°58·8'W	F	85
Woodhouse Mill	Roth	SK4285	53°21·9'	1°21·7'W	T	111,120
Woodhouse Park	Man	SJ8286	53°22·5'	2°15·8'W	T	109
Woodhouses	Ches	SJ5075	53°16·4'	2°44·6'W	T	117
Woodhouses	Cumbr	NY3252	54°51·7'	3°3·1'W	T	85
Woodhouses	Derby	SK3824	52°49·0'	1°25·8'W	X	128
Woodhouses	Durham	NZ1828	54°39·1'	1°42·8'W	X	92
Wood Houses	Northum	NY6859	54°55·7'	2°29·5'W	X	86,87
Woodhouses	Oldham	SD9100	53°30·0'	2°7·7'W	T	109
Woodhouses	Shrops	SO4777	52°23·5'	2°46·3'W	X	137,138,148
Woodhouses	Staffs	SK0809	52°41·0'	1°52·5'W	T	128
Woodhouses	Staffs	SK1348	53°2·0'	1°48·0'W	X	119
Woodhouses	Staffs	SK1519	52°46·3'	1°46·3'W	T	128
Woodhouses	Staffs	SO8199	52°35·5'	2°16·4'W	X	138
Woodhouses	Traf	SJ7690	53°24·6'	2°21·3'W	T	109
Woodhouse, The	Heref	SO3762	52°15·4'	2°55·0'W	X	137,148,149
Woodhouse, The	Staffs	SK1705	52°38·8'	1°44·5'W	X	139
Woodhouse, The	Wrekin	SJ7210	52°41·5'	2°24·5'W	X	127
Woodhouse, The (Hotel)	Warw	SP3870	52°19·8'	1°26·1'W	X	140
Woodhouse Villa	Devon	SS7812	50°53·9'	3°43·7'W	X	180
Woodhow	Cumbr	NY1304	54°25·7'	3°20·0'W	X	89
Woodhuish Fm	Devon	SX9152	50°21·7'	3°31·6'W	FM	202
Woodhurst	Cambs	TL3176	52°22·2'	0°4·1'W	T	142
Woodhurst	W Susx	TQ2532	51°4·6'	0°12·5'W	X	187
Woodinch	Pth & Kin	NN9946	56°36·0'	3°38·3'W	X	52,53
Woodingdean	Bri & Hov	TQ3605	50°49·9'	0°3·7'W	T	198
Wooding Fm	Heref	SO6159	52°13·9'	2°33·9'W	FM	149
Woodington	Devon	SS8112	50°53·9'	3°41·2'W	X	181
Woodington	Hants	SU3120	50°58·7'	1°33·1'W	T	185
Woodkirk	Kirk	SE2724	53°42·9'	1°35·0'W	T	104
Wood Knotts	Cumbr	SD1795	54°20·9'	3°16·2'W	X	96
Woodknowle	Corn	SS2302	50°47·7'	4°30·3'W	X	190
Woodknowle Fm	E Susx	TQ6526	51°0·8'	0°21·5'E	FM	188,199
Wood Laithes	Barns	SE3905	53°32·7'	1°24·3'W	X	110,111
Woodlake	Dorset	SY8894	50°45·0'	2°9·8'W	T	194
Woodlake Fm	Ches	SJ4857	53°6·7'	2°46·2'W	FM	117
Woodland	Corn	SX3471	50°31·2'	4°20·1'W	X	201
Woodland	Cumbr	SD2489	54°17·7'	3°9·6'W	T	96
Woodland	Devon	SX6256	50°23·5'	3°56·1'W	T	202
Woodland	Devon	SX7968	50°30·2'	3°42·0'W	T	202
Woodland	Durham	NZ0726	54°38·0'	1°53·1'W	T	92
Woodland	Kent	TR1441	51°7·9'	1°3·9'E	T	179,189
Woodland	S Ayr	NS3413	55°23·2'	4°36·8'W	X	70
Woodland	S Ayr	NX1795	55°13·2'	4°52·2'W	X	76
Woodland Bay	S Ayr	NX1795	55°13·2'	4°52·2'W	W	76
Woodland Fell	Cumbr	SD2689	54°17·7'	3°7·8'W	X	96,97
Woodland Fell	Durham	NZ0325	54°37·5'	1°56·8'W	X	92
Woodland Fm	Ches	SJ3770	53°13·8'	2°23·9'W	FM	118
Woodland Fm	Corn	SX1865	50°27·6'	4°33·5'W	FM	201
Woodland Fm	Devon	SS6126	51°1·2'	3°58·5'W	FM	180
Woodland Fm	Devon	SS8427	51°2·1'	3°38·9'W	FM	181
Woodland Fm	Leic	SK7632	52°53·0'	0°51·8'W	FM	129
Woodland Fm	Lincs	TF0123	52°47·9'	0°29·7'W	FM	130
Woodland Fm	Norf	TL9497	52°32·4'	0°52·0'E	FM	144
Woodland Fm	Suff	TM4187	52°25·9'	1°33·1'E	FM	156
Woodland Green	Essex	TL6944	52°4·3'	0°28·4'E	X	154
Woodland Grove	Cumbr	SD2490	54°18·2'	3°9·7'W	X	96
Woodland Hall	Cumbr	SD2488	54°17·2'	3°9·6'W	X	96
Woodland Hall	Staffs	SK1031	52°52·8'	1°50·7'W	X	128
Woodland Head	Devon	SX7896	50°45·3'	3°43·4'W	T	191
Woodland Leisure Park	Devon	SX8152	50°21·6'	3°40·0'W	X	202
Woodland Park	Clackm	NS9097	56°9·4'	3°45·8'W	F	58
Woodland Park	Wilts	ST8352	51°16·2'	2°14·2'W	F	183
Woodlands	Aberd	NJ6543	57°28·8'	2°34·6'W	X	29
Woodlands	Aberd	NJ6810	57°11·0'	2°31·3'W	X	38
Woodlands	Aberd	NJ8723	57°18·1'	2°12·5'W	X	38
Woodlands	Aberd	NO7995	57°3·0'	2°20·3'W	T	38,45
Woodlands	Arg & Bt	NS2099	56°9·2'	4°53·4'W	X	56
Woodlands	Brad	SE0336	53°49·5'	1°56·9'W	X	104
Woodlands	Brom	TQ4864	51°21·6'	0°7·9'E	X	177,188
Woodlands	Cald	SE0926	53°44·1'	1°51·4'W	T	104
Woodlands	Carm	SN3028	51°55·7'	4°28·0'W	X	145
Woodlands	C of Aber	NJ8514	57°13·2'	2°14·4'W	X	38
Woodlands	Corn	SW8035	50°10·7'	5°4·5'W	X	204
Woodlands	Cumbr	NY2246	54°48·4'	3°12·4'W	X	85
Woodlands	Cumbr	NY3155	54°53·3'	3°4·1'W	X	85
Woodlands	Devon	SS5016	50°55·7'	4°7·7'W	X	180
Woodlands	Devon	ST0224	51°0·7'	3°23·4'W	X	181
Woodlands	Devon	SX8187	50°40·5'	3°40·7'W	X	191
Woodlands	Devon	SX8393	50°43·7'	3°39·1'W	X	191
Woodlands	D & G	NY0278	55°5·5'	3°31·7'W	X	84
Woodlands	D & G	NY0977	55°5·0'	3°25·1'W	T	85
Woodlands	D & G	NY2075	55°4·0'	3°14·7'W	X	85
Woodlands	Donc	SE5307	53°33·7'	1°11·6'W	T	111
Woodlands	Dorset	SU0509	50°53·1'	1°55·4'W	T	195
Woodlands	Dorset	SY8690	50°42·8'	2°11·5'W	X	194
Woodlands	Essex	TL4703	51°42·6'	0°8·1'E	X	167
Woodlands	Essex	TL8207	51°44·2'	0°38·5'E	X	168
Woodlands	Essex	TM1720	51°50·4'	1°9·4'E	X	168,169
Woodlands	E Yorks	SE7937	53°49·6'	0°47·6'W	X	105,106

Woodlands	E Yorks	SE8338	53°50·1′	0°43·9′W	X	106
Woodlands	Fife	NO3912	56°18·0′	2°58·7′W	X	59
Woodlands	Glos	SP0020	51°52·9′	1°59·6′W	X	163
Woodlands	Glos	SP0213	51°49·2′	1°57·9′W	X	163
Woodlands	Gwyn	SH6203	52°36·7′	4°1·9′W	X	135
Woodlands	Hants	SU3211	50°54·1′	1°32·3′W	T	196
Woodlands	Heref	SO4670	52°19·8′	2°47·1′W	X	137,138,148
Woodlands	Heref	SO5266	52°17·6′	2°41·8′W	X	137,138,149
Woodlands	Herts	TL2703	51°42·9′	0°9·3′W	X	166
Woodlands	Highld	NH5662	57°37·8′	4°24·2′W	X	21
Woodlands	Highld	NH8351	57°32·3′	3°56·8′W	X	27
Woodlands	Houns	TQ1575	51°28·0′	0°20·3′W	T	176
Woodlands	Kent	TQ5660	51°19·3′	0°14·7′E	T	177,188
Woodlands	Kent	TQ8636	51°5·8′	0°39·8′E	X	189
Woodlands	Kent	TR2153	51°14·2′	1°10·4′E	X	179,189
Woodlands	Leeds	SE4432	53°47·2′	1°19·5′W	X	105
Woodlands	Lincs	TF1189	53°23·4′	0°19·4′W	X	113,121
Woodlands	Lincs	TF3117	52°44·3′	0°3·2′W	X	131
Woodlands	Mil Key	SP8552	52°9·8′	0°45·0′W	X	152
Woodlands	Norf	TM1999	52°32·9′	1°14·2′E	X	134
Woodlands	Northnts	SP7687	52°28·8′	0°52·5′W	X	141
Woodlands	Notts	SK6530	52°52·0′	1°1·7′W	X	129
Woodlands	N Yks	NZ8607	54°27·3′	0°40·0′W	X	94
Woodlands	N Yks	SE1290	54°18·6′	1°48·5′W	X	99
Woodlands	N Yks	SE3254	53°59·1′	1°30·3′W	T	104
Woodlands	N Yks	SE8776	54°10·6′	0°39·6′W	X	101
Woodlands	Oxon	SU3395	51°39·4′	1°31·0′W	X	164
Woodlands	Pemb	SM8512	51°46·2′	5°6·6′W	X	157
Woodlands	Powys	SO1639	52°2·8′	3°13·1′W	X	161
Woodlands	Powys	SO2299	52°35·2′	3°8·7′W	X	137
Woodlands	Pth & Kin	NO0922	56°23·1′	3°28·0′W	X	52,53,58
Woodlands	Scot Bord	NT9355	55°47·5′	2°6·3′W	X	67,74,75
Woodlands	Shrops	SO5179	52°24·6′	2°42·8′W	X	137,138
Woodlands	Shrops	SO7188	52°29·6′	2°25·2′W	X	138
Woodlands	S Lanak	NS9037	55°37·1′	3°44·4′W	X	71,72
Woodlands	Somer	ST1640	51°9·4′	3°11·7′W	T	181
Woodlands	Somer	ST3419	50°58·2′	2°56·0′W	X	193
Woodlands	Somer	ST5437	51°8·1′	2°39·1′W	T	182,183
Woodlands	Staffs	SJ7910	52°41·5′	2°18·2′W	X	127
Woodlands	Staffs	SJ9750	53°3·1′	2°2·3′W	X	118
Woodlands	Suff	TL7269	52°17·8′	0°31·7′E	X	154
Woodlands	Surrey	TQ0443	51°10·8′	0°30·3′W	X	186
Woodlands	Tames	SJ9797	53°28·4′	2°2·3′W	T	109
Woodlands	V of Glam	ST1574	51°27·8′	3°13·0′W	X	171
Woodlands	Wilts	ST9523	51°0·6′	2°3·9′W	X	184
Woodlands	Wilts	ST9794	51°38·9′	2°2·2′W	X	163,173
Woodlands	Wok	SU7682	51°32·1′	0°53·9′W	T	175
Woodlands	W Susx	TQ0905	50°50·3′	0°26·7′W	X	198
Woodlands Barton Fm	Corn	SX0061	50°25·1′	4°48·6′W	FM	200
Woodlands Barton Fm	Corn	SX0062	50°25·7′	4°48·6′W	FM	200
Woodlands Close	Durham	NZ4035	54°42·7′	1°22·3′W	X	93
Woodlands Common	Dorset	SU0608	50°52·5′	1°54·5′W	T	195
Woodlands Cotts	W Susx	SU7710	50°53·3′	0°53·9′W	X	197
Woodlands Farmhouse	Essex	TQ6298	51°39·3′	0°20·9′E	X	167,177
Woodlands Fm	Barnet	TQ2296	51°39·2′	0°13·8′W	FM	166,176
Woodlands Fm	Bucks	SP6739	52°3·0′	1°1·0′W	FM	152
Woodlands Fm	Bucks	SP7121	51°53·2′	0°57·7′W	FM	165
Woodlands Fm	Bucks	SU9488	51°35·2′	0°38·2′W	FM	175
Woodlands Fm	Corn	SS2312	50°53·1′	4°30·6′W	FM	190
Woodlands Fm	Corn	SX0962	50°25·8′	4°41·0′W	FM	200
Woodlands Fm	Devon	SX8378	50°35·6′	3°38·8′W	FM	191
Woodlands Fm	Devon	SX9084	50°39·0′	3°33·0′W	FM	192
Woodlands Fm	Devon	SY0381	50°37·5′	3°21·9′W	FM	192
Woodlands Fm	Donc	SK5595	53°27·2′	1°9·9′W	FM	111
Woodlands Fm	Dorset	ST7613	50°55·2′	2°20·1′W	FM	194
Woodlands Fm	E Susx	TQ3419	50°57·5′	0°5·1′W	FM	198
Woodlands Fm	E Susx	TQ6516	50°55·4′	0°21·3′E	FM	199
Woodlands Fm	E Susx	TQ6524	50°59·7′	0°21·5′E	FM	199
Woodlands Fm	E Susx	TQ8722	50°58·2′	0°40·2′E	FM	189,199
Woodlands Fm	Glos	SO8918	51°51·9′	2°9·2′W	FM	163
Woodlands Fm	Glos	SO9113	51°49·2′	2°7·4′W	FM	163
Woodlands Fm	Glos	SP0022	51°54·0′	1°59·6′W	FM	163
Woodlands Fm	Glos	ST6698	51°41·0′	2°29·1′W	FM	162
Woodlands Fm	Hants	SU6426	51°2·0′	1°4·8′W	FM	185
Woodlands Fm	Hants	SU8040	51°9·4′	0°51·0′W	FM	186
Woodlands Fm	Herts	SP9210	51°47·1′	0°39·6′W	FM	165
Woodlands Fm	Kent	TR1763	51°19·7′	1°7·3′E	FM	179
Woodlands Fm	Leeds	SE2043	53°53·2′	1°41·3′W	FM	104
Woodlands Fm	Leeds	SE4039	53°51·0′	1°23·1′W	FM	105
Woodlands Fm	Leic	SK4621	52°47·3′	1°18·7′W	FM	129
Woodlands Fm	Lincs	TF2532	52°52·5′	0°8·2′W	FM	131
Woodlands Fm	Norf	TF6411	52°40·5′	0°26·0′E	FM	132,143
Woodlands Fm	Norf	TG4311	52°38·8′	1°35·9′E	FM	134
Woodlands Fm	Northnts	SP8386	52°28·2′	0°46·3′W	FM	141
Woodlands Fm	N Yks	SE3950	53°56·9′	1°23·9′W	FM	104
Woodlands Fm	N Yks	SE9180	54°12·7′	0°35·9′W	FM	101
Woodlands Fm	Oxon	SP5526	51°56·0′	1°11·6′W	FM	164
Woodlands Fm	Pemb	SM8834	51°58·1′	5°4·8′W	FM	157
Woodlands Fm	S Glos	ST7273	51°27·6′	2°23·8′W	FM	172
Woodlands Fm	S Lanak	NS7939	55°38·0′	3°54·9′W	FM	71
Woodlands Fm	Somer	ST0725	51°1·2′	3°19·2′W	FM	181
Woodlands Fm	Suff	TM0946	52°4·6′	1°3·4′E	FM	155,169
Woodlands Fm	Suff	TM2575	52°19·8′	1°18·5′E	FM	156
Woodlands Fm	Warw	SP1373	52°21·5′	1°48·1′W	FM	139
Woodlands Fm	Warw	SP2898	52°35·0′	1°34·8′W	FM	140
Woodlands Fm	Wilts	SU2171	51°26·5′	1°41·5′W	FM	174
Woodlands Fm	Worcs	SO9275	52°22·6′	2°6·7′W	FM	139
Woodlands Fm	W Susx	TQ0623	51°0·0′	0°29·0′W	FM	197
Woodlands Fm, The	Leic	SK4905	52°38·7′	1°16·1′W	FM	140
Woodlands Hall	Denb	SJ0957	53°6·4′	3°21·2′W	X	116
Woodlands Hall	Durham	NZ1247	54°49·3′	1°48·4′W	X	88
Woodlands Hill	Somer	ST1540	51°9·4′	3°12·5′W	X	181
Woodlands House Fm	Warw	SP4258	52°13·4′	1°22·7′W	FM	151
Woodlandslee Tower	Scot Bord	NT3144	55°41·3′	3°5·4′W	A	73
Woodlands Lodge (Hotel)	Hants	SU3111	50°54·1′	1°33·2′W	X	196
Woodlands Manor	Wilts	ST8131	51°4·9′	2°15·9′W	A	183
Woodlands Manor Fm	Dorset	SU0408	50°52·5′	1°56·2′W	FM	195
Woodlands Park	Beds	TL0352	52°9·6′	0°29·3′W	X	153
Woodlands Park	Bucks	SP8803	51°43·4′	0°43·2′W	X	165
Woodlands Park	Bucks	SP8903	51°43·3′	0°42·3′W	X	165

Woodlands Park	Dorset	SU0508	50°52·5′	1°55·4′W	F	195
Woodlands Park	Surrey	TQ1458	51°18·8′	0°21·5′W	X	187
Woodlands Park	Win & Maid	SU8578	51°29·9′	0°46·1′W	T	175
Woodlands Park Fm	Durham	NZ1147	54°49·3′	1°49·3′W	FM	88
Woodlands St Mary	W Berks	SU3374	51°28·1′	1°31·1′W	T	174
Woodlands, The	Ches	SJ6059	53°7·8′	2°35·5′W	X	118
Woodlands, The	Derby	SK2965	53°11·1′	1°33·6′W	X	119
Woodlands, The	Devon	SX5349	50°19·6′	4°3·5′W	X	201
Woodlands, The	Heref	SO2954	52°11·0′	3°1·9′W	X	148
Woodlands, The	Kent	TR0133	51°3·9′	0°52·5′E	X	189
Woodlands, The	Leic	SK4905	52°38·7′	1°16·1′W	X	140
Woodlands, The	Lincs	TF3135	52°54·0′	0°2·7′W	X	131
Woodlands, The	Norf	TF9513	52°41·0′	0°53·5′E	X	132
Woodlands,The	Norf	TM0698	52°32·7′	1°2·7′E	X	144
Woodlands, The	N Som	ST4464	51°22·6′	2°47·9′W	X	172,182
Woodlands, The	Shrops	SJ4732	52°53·2′	2°46·9′W	X	126
Woodlands, The	Suff	TM0656	52°10·1′	1°1·1′E	X	155
Woodlands, The	Suff	TM2569	52°16·6′	1°18·3′E	X	156
Woodlands, The	Suff	TM2860	52°11·7′	1°20·6′E	F	156
Woodlands, The	Warw	SP3879	52°24·7′	1°26·1′W	X	140
Woodlands Vale	I of W	SZ6191	50°43·2′	1°7·8′W	X	196
Woodlands Valley	Derby	SK1588	53°23·6′	1°46·1′W	X	110
Woodland Valley Fm	Corn	SW9051	50°19·5′	4°56·7′W	FM	200,204
Wood Lane	Shrops	SJ4132	52°53·2′	2°52·2′W	T	126
Woodlane	Shrops	SJ6927	52°50·6′	2°27·2′W	T	127
Wood Lane	Staffs	SJ8150	53°3·1′	2°16·6′W	T	118
Woodlane	Staffs	SK1420	52°46·9′	1°47·1′W	T	128
Woodlane	Stir	NS7197	56°9·2′	4°4·2′W	X	57
Wood Lane End Fm	Ches	SJ9482	53°20·3′	2°5·0′W	FM	109
Woodlane fm	Ches	SJ5464	53°10·5′	2°40·9′W	FM	117
Wood Lane Fm	Shrops	SJ6131	52°52·7′	2°34·4′W	FM	127
Woodlane Fm	Suff	TM4984	52°24·1′	1°40·0′E	FM	156
Wood Lanes	Ches	SJ9381	53°19·8′	2°5·9′W	T	109
Wood Langham	Lincs	TF1485	53°21·2′	0°16·8′W	X	121
Woodlay Fm	Corn	SX1860	50°24·9′	4°33·3′W	FM	201
Woodlea	D & G	NX8875	55°3·7′	3°44·8′W	X	84
Woodlea	E Loth	NT5784	56°3·1′	2°41·0′W	X	67
Wood Lea	W Susx	SU8914	50°55·3′	0°43·6′W	F	197
Woodlea Hill	D & G	NX7589	55°11·0′	3°57·4′W	H	78
Wood Leasow Fm	Staffs	SK0035	52°55·0′	1°59·6′W	FM	128
Woodleaze Fm	Glos	ST8197	51°40·5′	2°16·1′W	FM	162
Woodlee	Fife	NT1487	56°4·3′	3°22·5′W	X	65
Wood Lee	Roth	SK5391	53°25·0′	1°11·7′W	X	111
Woodleigh	Devon	SX7348	50°19·3′	3°46·7′W	T	202
Woodleigh	Devon	SX7793	50°43·7′	3°44·2′W	X	191
Woodlesford	Leeds	SE3629	53°45·6′	1°26·8′W	T	104
Woodley	Devon	SX4275	50°33·4′	4°13·5′W	X	201
Woodley	Hants	SU3722	51°0·0′	1°28·0′W	T	185
Woodley	Stock	SJ9492	53°25·7′	2°5·0′W	T	109
Woodley	Wok	SU7572	51°26·8′	0°54·9′W	T	175
Woodley Down	Wilts	ST9218	50°57·9′	2°6·5′W	X	184
Woodley Fm	Devon	SX8697	50°45·9′	3°36·6′W	FM	191
Woodley Fm	N Yks	SE8059	54°1·5′	0°46·3′W	FM	106
Woodley Green	Wok	SU7773	51°27·3′	0°53·1′W	T	175
Woodley Park	Devon	SX3993	50°43·1′	4°16·5′W	X	190
Woodleys	Beds	TL0264	52°16·1′	0°29·9′W	X	153
Woodleys	Oxon	SP4219	51°52·3′	1°23·0′W	T	164
Woodley's Fm	Mil Key	SP9135	52°0·6′	0°40·1′W	FM	152
Wood Leys Fm	Northnts	SP7552	52°9·9′	0°53·8′W	FM	152
Woodley Shield	Northum	NY8476	55°4·9′	2°14·6′W	X	86,87
Woodlinkin	Derby	SK4348	53°1·9′	1°21·1′W	T	129
Woodlock's Down Fm	Hants	SU5321	50°59·4′	1°14·3′W	FM	185
Wood Lodge Fm	Northnts	SP8368	52°18·5′	0°46·6′W	FM	152
Wood Lodge Fm	Northnts	TL0377	52°23·1′	0°28·8′W	FM	141
Woodloes Fm	Warw	SP2767	52°18·3′	1°35·8′W	FM	151
Woodloes Park	Warw	SP2866	52°17·7′	1°35·0′W	T	151
Woodmancote	Glos	SO9727	51°56·7′	2°2·2′W	T	163
Woodmancote	Glos	SP0008	51°46·5′	1°59·6′W	T	163
Woodmancote	Glos	ST7597	51°40·5′	2°21·3′W	T	162
Woodmancote	Worcs	SO9042	52°4·8′	2°8·4′W	T	150
Woodmancote	W Susx	SU7707	50°51·7′	0°54·0′W	T	197
Woodmancote	W Susx	TQ2314	50°55·0′	0°14·6′W	T	198
Woodmancote Place	W Susx	TQ2315	50°55·5′	0°14·6′W	X	198
Woodmancott	Hants	SU5642	51°10·7′	1°11·5′W	T	185
Woodmansey	E Yorks	TA0537	53°49·4′	0°23·9′W	T	107
Woodmans Fm	Herts	TL0301	51°42·1′	0°30·2′W	FM	166
Woodman's Fm	W Susx	TQ1467	50°56·7′	0°22·2′W	FM	198
Woodmans Green	E Susx	TQ7619	50°56·8′	0°30·7′E	T	199
Woodmansgreen	W Susx	SU8627	51°2·4′	0°46·0′W	T	186,197
Woodman's Hill	Somer	ST8148	51°14·1′	2°15·9′W	X	183
Woodman's Ho	N Yks	SE4773	54°9·3′	1°16·4′W	X	100
Woodmans Stud	W Susx	TQ1518	50°57·2′	0°21·4′W	X	198
Woodmansterne	Surrey	TQ2759	51°19·2′	0°10·3′W	T	187
Woodmanswell	Devon	SX4883	50°37·8′	4°8·6′W	X	191,201
Woodmanswell	Devon	SX4883	50°37·8′	4°8·6′W	X	191,201
Woodmanton	Devon	SY0185	50°39·6′	3°23·7′W	T	192
Woodmanton	Heref	SO3650	52°8·9′	2°55·7′W	X	148,149
Woodmanton	Heref	SO4952	52°10·1′	2°44·3′W	X	148,149
Woodmanton	Heref	SO6043	52°5·3′	2°34·6′W	X	149
Woodmanton Fm	Worcs	SO7160	52°14·5′	2°25·1′W	FM	138,149
Woodmarch	Pth & Kin	NO1702	56°12·5′	3°19·8′W	X	58
Woodmeadow Fm	Warw	SP1942	52°4·8′	1°43·0′W	FM	151
Woodmill	C of Soton	SU4315	50°56·2′	1°22·9′W	X	196
Woodmill	Fife	NO2409	56°16·3′	3°13·2′W	X	59
Woodmill	Fife	NO2714	56°19·0′	3°10·4′W	X	59
Wood Mill	N Lanak	NS7272	55°55·7′	4°2·5′W	X	64
Woodmill	Staffs	SK1321	52°47·4′	1°48·0′W	T	128
Woodmill Mains	Fife	NO2715	56°19·6′	3°10·4′W	X	59
Wood Mills Fm	Cambs	TF3908	52°39·3′	0°3·7′E	FM	142,143
Woodminton	Wilts	SU0022	51°0·1′	1°59·6′W	T	184
Woodminton Down	Wilts	SU0021	50°59·5′	1°59·6′W	X	184
Wood Moor	Derby	SK1189	53°24·1′	1°49·7′W	X	110
Woodmoor	Shrops	SJ2700	52°35·8′	3°4·3′W	X	126
Woodmoor Fm	Wakf	SE3215	53°38·1′	1°30·6′W	FM	110,111
Wood Moss	Ches	SJ9969	53°13·3′	2°0·5′W	X	118
Woodmouth	Pth & Kin	NN9519	56°21·4′	3°41·5′W	X	58
Woodmuir Burn	W Loth	NS9660	55°49·6′	3°39·2′W	W	65
Woodmuir Fm	W Loth	NS9660	55°49·6′	3°39·2′W	FM	65
Woodmuir Plantation	W Loth	NS9758	55°48·5′	3°38·2′W	F	65,72
Woodnall	Shrops	SO4595	52°33·2′	2°48·3′W	X	137,138

Woodnesborough	Kent	TR3156	51°15·6′	1°19·1′E	T	179
Woodneuk	E Renf	NS4858	55°47·7′	4°25·0′W	X	64
Woodnewton	Northnts	TL0394	52°32·3′	0°28·5′W	T	141
Woodnook	Derby	SK3472	53°14·9′	1°29·0′W	X	119
Woodnook	Derby	SK5177	53°17·5′	1°13·7′W	X	120
Wood Nook	Kirk	SE1210	53°35·4′	1°48·7′W	X	110
Woodnook	Lancs	SD7627	53°44·6′	2°21·4′W	T	103
Woodnook	Lincs	SK9432	52°52·9′	0°35·8′W	T	130
Wood Nook	N Yks	SD9764	54°4·6′	2°2·3′W	X	98
Woodnook Fm	Derby	SK4269	53°13·2′	1°21·8′W	FM	120
Wood Nook Fm	Leic	SK4623	52°48·4′	1°18·7′W	FM	129
Wood Nook Fm	N Yks	SE1756	54°0·2′	1°44·0′W	FM	104
Wood Norton	Norf	TG0128	52°48·9′	0°59·4′E	T	133
Wood Norton	Worcs	SP0147	52°7·5′	1°58·7′W	T	150
Woodoaks Fm	Herts	TQ0393	51°37·8′	0°30·3′W	FM	176
Wood of Aldbar	Angus	NO5555	56°41·3′	2°43·6′W	X	54
Wood of Allachie	Moray	NJ2742	57°28·0′	3°12·6′W	F	28
Wood of Arndilly	Moray	NJ2947	57°30·7′	3°10·6′W	F	28
Wood of Auchleand	D & G	NX4059	54°54·3′	4°29·3′W	X	83
Wood of Avochie	Aberd	NJ5446	57°30·4′	2°45·6′W	F	29
Wood of Balchers	Aberd	NJ7258	57°36·9′	2°27·7′W	F	29
Wood of Balfour	Aberd	NO6074	56°51·6′	2°38·9′W	F	45
Wood of Barra	Aberd	NO6273	56°51·1′	2°36·9′W	F	45
Wood of Brae	Highld	NH6862	57°38·0′	4°12·2′W	X	21
Wood of Coldrain	Pth & Kin	NO0800	56°11·3′	3°28·5′W	X	58
Wood of Conerock	Moray	NJ2647	57°30·7′	3°13·6′W	F	28
Wood of Cree	D & G	NX3871	55°0·7′	4°31·6′W	X	77
Wood of Delgaty	Aberd	NJ7350	57°32·6′	2°26·6′W	X	29
Wood of Delgaty	Aberd	NJ7650	57°32·6′	2°23·6′W	F	29
Wood of Dervaird	D & G	NX2257	54°52·8′	4°46·1′W	X	82
Wood of Dundurcas	Moray	NJ2951	57°32·9′	3°10·7′W	F	28
Wood of Easter Clune	Aberd	NO6190	57°0·2′	2°38·1′W	F	45
Wood of Fallside	Aberd	NO8182	56°56·0′	2°18·3′W	F	45
Wood of Hatton	Aberd	NJ7646	57°30·5′	2°23·6′W	F	29
Wood of Luncarty	Aberd	NJ7254	57°34·8′	2°27·6′W	X	29
Wood of Milleath	Aberd	NJ4742	57°28·2′	2°52·6′W	F	28,29
Wood of Mon Duff	Aberd	NO6276	56°52·7′	2°37·0′W	F	45
Wood of Mulderie	Moray	NJ3751	57°32·9′	3°2·7′W	F	28
Wood of Ordiequish	Moray	NJ3555	57°35·1′	3°4·8′W	F	28
Wood of Shaws	Aberd	NJ6857	57°36·4′	2°31·7′W	X	29
Wood of Wardford	Aberd	NJ8438	57°26·2′	2°15·5′W	F	29,30
Wood of Wrae	Aberd	NJ7252	57°33·7′	2°27·6′W	F	29
Woodovis Ho	Devon	SX4374	50°32·9′	4°12·6′W	X	201
Woodpark	Angus	NO6654	56°40·8′	2°32·8′W	X	54
Wood Park	Corn	SX0978	50°34·5′	4°41·5′W	X	200
Woodpark	Devon	SS6042	51°9·8′	3°59·8′W	X	180
Woodpark	Devon	SX7296	50°45·2′	3°48·5′W	X	191
Woodpark	D & G	NX7969	55°0·3′	3°53·1′W	X	84
Wood Park	Moray	NJ1964	57°39·8′	3°21·0′W	X	28
Woodpark	Moray	NJ2762	57°38·8′	3°12·9′W	X	28
Woodpark	Northum	NY8479	55°6·6′	2°14·6′W	X	86,87
Wood Park	Pemb	SN0523	51°52·5′	4°49·6′W	X	145,158
Woodparks	Devon	SS7704	50°49·6′	3°44·4′W	X	191
Woodperry	Oxon	SP5710	51°47·4′	1°10·0′W	X	164
Woodplace Fm	Surrey	TQ2957	51°18·1′	0°8·6′W	FM	187
Woodplumpton	Lancs	SD5034	53°48·2′	2°45·1′W	T	102
Woodplumpton Brook	Lancs	SD5034	53°48·2′	2°45·1′W	W	102
Woodpond Fm	Bucks	SP8132	51°59·1′	0°48·8′W	FM	152,165
Woodrae	Angus	NO5156	56°41·8′	2°47·6′W	X	54
Woodram	Somer	ST2218	50°57·6′	3°6·3′W	T	193
Woodram Fm	Somer	ST2118	50°57·6′	3°7·1′W	FM	193
Woodredding Fm	Heref	SO6329	51°57·7′	2°31·9′W	FM	149
Woodredon Fm	Essex	TQ4299	51°40·5′	0°3·6′E	FM	167,177
Woodreed Fm	E Susx	TQ5525	51°0·4′	0°13·0′E	FM	188,199
Woodreeve Fm	Kent	TR0035	51°5·0′	0°51·7′E	FM	189
Wood Rig	S Lanak	NS9819	55°27·5′	3°36·3′W	H	78
Woodrising	Norf	TF9803	52°35·5′	0°55·8′E	T	144
Woodrising Hall	Norf	TF9902	52°35·0′	0°56·6′E	X	144
Woodrising Wood	Norf	TF9703	52°35·6′	0°54·9′E	F	144
Wood Road	Bury	SD7914	53°37·6′	2°18·6′W	T	109
Woodroberts	Devon	SS6210	50°52·6′	3°57·3′W	X	191
Wood Rock	Devon	SS3125	51°0·2′	4°24·1′W	X	190
Woodroffe's	Staffs	SK1129	52°51·7′	1°49·8′W	A	128
Woodroffe's Cliff	Staffs	SK1228	52°51·2′	1°48·9′W	X	128
Woodrolfe Creek	Essex	TL9710	51°45·5′	0°51·7′E	W	168
Woodrow	Bucks	SU9396	51°39·5′	0°38·9′W	T	165
Woodrow	Cumbr	NY2245	54°47·9′	3°12·4′W	T	85
Woodrow	Devon	SS6114	50°54·8′	3°58·3′W	X	180
Woodrow	Devon	SX9296	50°45·4′	3°31·5′W	X	192
Woodrow	Dorset	ST7309	50°53·0′	2°22·6′W	T	194
Woodrow	Dorset	ST7510	50°53·6′	2°20·9′W	T	194
Wood Row	Herts	SP9409	51°46·5′	0°37·9′W	X	165
Wood Row	Leeds	SE3827	53°44·5′	1°25·0′W	T	104
Woodrow	Worcs	SO8875	52°22·6′	2°10·2′W	T	139
Woodrow	Worcs	SP0565	52°17·2′	1°55·2′W	T	150
Woodrow Barton	Devon	SX9296	50°45·4′	3°31·5′W	X	192
Woodrow Fm	Devon	ST0510	50°53·1′	3°20·7′W	FM	192
Woodrow Fm	Dorset	ST6915	50°56·2′	2°26·1′W	FM	183
Woodrow High Ho	Bucks	SU9396	51°39·5′	0°38·9′W	X	165
Woodrows Fm	Somer	ST5419	50°58·3′	2°38·9′W	FM	183
Woodrows Fm	W Berks	SU5478	51°30·1′	1°12·9′W	FM	174
Woodruff Fm	Essex	TL5731	51°57·5′	0°17·5′E	FM	167
Woods	Cumbr	SD1683	54°14·4′	3°16·9′W	X	96
Woods	Devon	SS7923	50°59·9′	3°43·1′W	X	180
Woods	Devon	SS7927	51°2·0′	3°43·2′W	X	180
Woods	Devon	SS8426	51°1·5′	3°38·9′W	X	181
Woods	Devon	SX8456	50°23·8′	3°37·5′W	X	202
Woods	Heref	SO2949	52°8·3′	3°1·9′W	T	148
Woods	Somer	ST3926	51°2·0′	2°51·8′W	X	193
Woodsaws	Corn	SX1857	50°23·3′	4°33·2′W	X	201
Woods Bank	Wals	SO9796	52°33·9′	2°2·3′W	T	139
Wood's Cabin	Derby	SK0592	53°25·7′	1°55·1′W	X	110
Woodscombe	Devon	SS8312	50°54·0′	3°39·4′W	X	181
Wood's Corner	E Susx	TQ6619	50°57·0′	0°22·2′E	T	199
Woods Court	Kent	TR0254	51°15·2′	0°54·1′E	X	189
Woodsdale	E Susx	TQ7418	50°56·3′	0°29·0′E	X	199
Woodsdale Fm	Kent	TR0851	51°13·4′	0°59·1′E	FM	179,189
Woodsden	Kent	TQ7731	51°3·3′	0°31·9′E	T	188
Woodsden	Kent	TQ8646	51°11·2′	0°40·1′E	X	189
Woodsdown Hill	Devon	SS3108	50°51·0′	4°23·7′W	X	190

Woodseat	Staffs	SK0938	52°56·6'	1°51·6'W	X	128
Woodseats	Derby	SJ9992	53°25·7'	2°0·5'W	T	109
Woodseats	Derby	SK1384	53°21·4'	1°47·9'W	X	110
Woodseats	Sheff	SK2492	53°25·7'	1°37·9'W	X	110
Wood Seats	Sheff	SK3395	53°27·3'	1°29·8'W	T	110,111
Woodseaves	Shrops	SJ6831	52°52·8'	2°28·1'W	T	127
Woodseaves	Staffs	SJ7925	52°49·6'	2°18·3'W	T	127
Woodsell	Kent	TQ9653	51°14·8'	0°48·9'E	X	189
Woodsend	Pemb	SM8710	51°45·1'	5°4·8'W	T	157
Woods End	Traf	SJ7495	53°27·3'	2°23·1'W	T	109
Woodsend	Wilts	SU2275	51°28·6'	1°40·6'W	T	174
Woodsetton	Dudley	SO9293	52°32·3'	2°6·7'W	T	139
Woodsetts	Roth	SK5583	53°20·7'	1°10·0'W	T	111,120
Wood Severals	Norf	TG0330	52°50·0'	1°1·2'E	F	133
Woodsfield	Worcs	SO8148	52°8·0'	2°16·3'W	T	150
Wood's Fm	Devon	SY1090	50°42·4'	3°16·1'W	FM	192,193
Wood's Fm	Lincs	TF4076	53°16·0'	0°6·4'E	FM	122
Woods Fm	N Lincs	SE8006	53°32·9'	0°47·1'W	FM	112
Wood's Fm	Notts	SK7290	53°24·4'	0°54·6'W	FM	112
Woods Fm	N Yks	NZ5804	54°25·9'	1°5·9'W	FM	93
Wood's Fm	Oxon	SU4590	51°36·7'	1°20·6'W	FM	164,174
Wood's Fm	Warr	SJ6597	53°28·4'	2°31·2'W	FM	109
Wood's Fm	Wok	SU8267	51°24·0'	0°48·9'W	FM	175
Woodsfold	Lancs	SD4736	53°49·3'	2°47·9'W	T	102
Woodsfold	Lancs	SD6421	53°41·3'	2°32·3'W	X	102,103
Woodsford	Dorset	SY7690	50°42·8'	2°20·0'W	T	194
Woodsford Castle	Dorset	SY7590	50°42·8'	2°20·9'W	A	194
Woodsford Lower Dairy	Dorset	SY7790	50°42·8'	2°19·2'W	X	194
Wood's Green	E Susx	TQ6333	51°4·6'	0°20·0'E	T	188
Woodshaw	Wilts	SU0882	51°32·4'	1°52·7'W	X	173
Woodshield Fm	Northum	NY8766	54°59·6'	2°11·8'W	FM	87
Wood's Hill	Cumbr	NY5159	54°55·6'	2°45·5'W	X	86
Wood's Hill	Cumbr	NY5359	54°55·7'	2°43·6'W	H	86
Wood's Hill	Suff	TM1042	52°2·4'	1°4·1'E	F	155,169
Woods Hill	W Susx	TQ0919	50°57·8'	0°26·5'W	X	198
Woodside	Aberd	NJ4621	57°16·8'	2°53·3'W	X	37
Woodside	Aberd	NJ5112	57°12·0'	2°48·2'W	X	37
Woodside	Aberd	NJ5330	57°21·7'	2°46·4'W	X	29,37
Woodside	Aberd	NJ5508	57°9·9'	2°44·2'W	X	37
Woodside	Aberd	NJ6140	57°27·2'	2°38·5'W	X	29
Woodside	Aberd	NJ6433	57°23·4'	2°35·5'W	X	29
Woodside	Aberd	NJ6552	57°33·7'	2°34·6'W	X	29
Woodside	Aberd	NJ7204	57°7·8'	2°27·3'W	X	38
Woodside	Aberd	NJ7450	57°32·6'	2°25·6'W	X	29
Woodside	Aberd	NJ8004	57°7·8'	2°19·4'W	X	38
Woodside	Aberd	NJ8256	57°35·9'	2°17·6'W	X	29,30
Woodside	Aberd	NJ8617	57°14·9'	2°13·5'W	X	38
Woodside	Aberd	NJ9063	57°39·7'	2°9·6'W	X	30
Woodside	Aberd	NK0349	57°32·1'	1°56·5'W	X	30
Woodside	Aberd	NK0361	57°38·6'	1°56·5'W	X	30
Woodside	Aberd	NO6399	57°5·1'	2°36·2'W	X	37,45
Woodside	Angus	NO4336	56°31·0'	2°55·1'W	X	54
Woodside	Angus	NO4354	56°40·7'	2°55·4'W	X	54
Woodside	Angus	NO4636	56°31·0'	2°52·2'W	X	54
Woodside	Angus	NO5045	56°35·9'	2°48·4'W	X	54
Woodside	Angus	NO5154	56°40·8'	2°47·5'W	X	54
Woodside	Angus	NO5766	56°47·3'	2°41·8'W	X	44
Woodside	Angus	NO6153	56°40·3'	2°37·7'W	X	54
Woodside	Bath & NE Somer	ST7959	51°20·0'	2°17·7'W	X	172
Woodside	Beds	TL0718	51°51·2'	0°26·4'W	T	166
Woodside	Beds	TL0752	52°9·6'	0°25·7'W	T	153
Woodside	Brackn	SU9371	51°26·0'	0°39·3'W	T	175
Woodside	Brad	SE1328	53°45·1'	1°47·8'W	T	104
Woodside	Ches	SJ5270	53°13·7'	2°42·7'W	T	117
Woodside	Ches	SJ6360	53°8·4'	2°32·8'W	T	118
Woodside	Clackm	NO0002	56°12·3'	3°36·3'W	X	58
Woodside	C of Aber	NJ9108	57°10·0'	2°8·5'W	T	38
Woodside	Croy	TQ3467	51°23·4'	0°4·1'W	T	176,177
Woodside	Cumbr	NY0434	54°41·8'	3°28·9'W	X	89
Woodside	Cumbr	NY0726	54°37·5'	3°26·0'W	X	89
Woodside	Cumbr	NY4250	54°50·7'	2°53·8'W	X	85
Woodside	Cumbr	NY4859	54°55·6'	2°48·3'W	X	86
Woodside	Cumbr	NY5378	55°5·9'	2°43·8'W	X	86
Woodside	Cumbr	NY5659	54°55·7'	2°40·8'W	X	86
Woodside	Cumbr	NY5723	54°36·3'	2°39·5'W	X	91
Woodside	Cumbr	NY5829	54°39·5'	2°38·6'W	X	91
Woodside	Cumbr	NY8016	54°32·6'	2°18·1'W	X	91,92
Woodside	Cumbr	SD1194	54°20·3'	3°21·7'W	X	96
Woodside	Cumbr	SD2888	54°17·2'	3°5·9'W	X	96,97
Woodside	Cumbr	SD4289	54°17·8'	2°53·1'W	X	96,97
Woodside	Cumbr	SD5592	54°19·5'	2°41·1'W	X	97
Woodside	Derby	SK1950	53°3·1'	1°42·6'W	X	119
Woodside	Derby	SK3524	52°49·0'	1°28·4'W	X	128
Woodside	Derby	SK3943	52°59·2'	1°24·7'W	T	119,128
Woodside	Derby	SK4673	53°15·4'	1°18·2'W	T	120
Woodside	D & G	NX3650	54°49·3'	4°32·7'W	X	83
Woodside	D & G	NX8098	55°15·9'	3°52·9'W	X	78
Woodside	D & G	NX9258	54°54·6'	3°40·7'W	X	84
Woodside	D & G	NX9768	55°0·0'	3°36·2'W	X	84
Woodside	D & G	NY0475	55°3·9'	3°29·8'W	T	84
Woodside	D & G	NY2072	55°2·4'	3°14·7'W	X	85
Woodside	D & G	NY3474	55°3·6'	3°1·6'W	X	85
Woodside	Dudley	SO9288	52°29·6'	2°6·7'W	T	139
Woodside	Durham	NZ1449	54°50·4'	1°46·5'W	X	88
Woodside	Durham	NZ1729	54°39·6'	1°43·8'W	T	92
Wood Side	Durham	NZ3146	54°48·7'	1°30·6'W	T	88
Woodside	E Loth	NT4673	55°57·1'	2°51·4'W	X	66
Woodside	Essex	TL4703	51°42·6'	0°8·1'E	T	167
Woodside	E Susx	TQ5834	51°5·2'	0°15·8'E	X	188
Woodside	E Yorks	SE8743	53°52·8'	0°40·2'W	X	106
Woodside	Fife	NO2900	56°11·5'	3°8·2'W	T	59
Woodside	Fife	NO4207	56°15·4'	2°55·7'W	T	59
Woodside	Hants	SZ3294	50°44·9'	1°32·4'W	T	196
Woodside	Herts	TL1001	51°42·0'	0°24·1'W	T	166
Woodside	Herts	TL2506	51°44·6'	0°11·0'W	T	166
Woodside	Highld	NH6731	57°21·3'	4°12·2'W	X	26
Woodside	Highld	NH7244	57°28·4'	4°7·6'W	X	27
Woodside	Highld	NH7465	57°39·7'	4°6·3'W	X	21,27
Woodside	I of W	SZ5493	50°44·3'	1°13·7'W	T	196

Wood Side	Lincs	TF1386	53°21·8'	0°17·7'W	X	113,121
Woodside	Moray	NJ0145	57°29·3'	3°38·6'W	X	27
Woodside	Moray	NJ0555	57°34·8'	3°34·9'W	T	27
Woodside	Moray	NJ0762	57°38·6'	3°33·0'W	X	27
Woodside	Moray	NJ1762	57°38·7'	3°23·0'W	X	28
Woodside	Moray	NJ2661	57°38·2'	3°13·9'W	X	28
Woodside	Moray	NJ3056	57°35·6'	3°9·8'W	X	28
Woodside	Moray	NJ4765	57°40·6'	2°52·9'W	X	28,29
Woodside	Moray	NJ5154	57°34·7'	2°48·7'W	X	29
Woodside	Moray	NJ5347	57°30·9'	2°46·6'W	X	29
Woodside	N Ayr	NS2048	55°41·8'	4°51·4'W	X	63
Woodside	N Ayr	NS3455	55°45·9'	4°38·3'W	X	63
Woodside	N Lincs	SE7103	53°31·4'	0°55·3'W	T	112
Woodside	Northum	NZ2499	55°17·3'	1°36·9'W	X	81
Woodside	Notts	SK8045	53°0·0'	0°48·1'W	X	130
Woodside	N Yks	SE0246	53°54·9'	1°57·8'W	X	104
Woodside	N Yks	SE5562	54°3·3'	1°9·2'W	X	100
Woodside	N Yks	SE6066	54°5·4'	1°4·5'W	X	100
Woodside	Orkney	HY5109	58°58·2'	2°50·6'W	X	6,7
Woodside	Pemb	SN1406	51°43·6'	4°41·2'W	X	158
Woodside	Pth & Kin	NN9510	56°16·5'	3°41·3'W	X	58
Woodside	Pth & Kin	NO0911	56°17·2'	3°27·8'W	X	58
Woodside	Pth & Kin	NO1545	56°35·6'	3°22·6'W	X	53
Woodside	Pth & Kin	NO2037	56°31·4'	3°17·6'W	T	53
Woodside	Pth & Kin	NO2037	56°31·4'	3°17·6'W	X	53
Woodside	S Ayr	NS3728	55°31·4'	4°34·5'W	X	70
Woodside	Scot Bord	NT6425	55°31·3'	2°33·8'W	X	74
Woodside	Scot Bord	NT8124	55°30·8'	2°17·6'W	X	74
Woodside	Shrops	SO3180	52°25·1'	3°0·5'W	T	137
Woodside	Shrops	SO5080	52°25·2'	2°43·7'W	X	137,138
Woodside	S Lanak	NS8145	55°41·3'	3°53·1'W	X	72
Woodside	Staffs	SJ8323	52°48·5'	2°14·7'W	X	127
Woodside	Stir	NS7591	56°6·0'	4°0·1'W	X	57
Woodside	W Berks	SU4770	51°25·9'	1°19·0'W	X	174
Woodside	W Dunb	NS4080	55°59·4'	4°33·5'W	X	64
Woodside	Win & Maid	SU9873	51°27·1'	0°35·0'W	X	175,176
Woodside	Wrekin	SJ6804	52°38·2'	2°28·0'W	T	127
Woodside Burn	D & G	NY3077	55°5·2'	3°5·4'W	W	85
Woodside Cott	Aberd	NO6490	57°0·2'	2°35·1'W	X	45
Woodside Cott	Beds	SP9451	52°9·2'	0°37·2'W	X	153
Woodside Cott	Northum	NU0148	55°43·8'	1°58·6'W	X	75
Woodside Cottage	Glos	SO9409	51°47·0'	2°4·8'W	X	163
Woodside Croft	Aberd	NJ9744	57°29·4'	2°2·5'W	X	30
Woodside Fm	Aberd	NJ8100	57°5·7'	2°18·4'W	FM	38
Woodside Fm	Aberd	NJ9100	57°5·7'	2°8·5'W	FM	38
Woodside Fm	Birm	SP1399	52°35·6'	1°48·1'W	FM	139
Woodside Fm	Ches	SJ7183	53°20·8'	2°25·7'W	FM	109
Woodside Fm	Ches	SJ9064	53°10·6'	2°8·6'W	FM	118
Woodside Fm	Cumbr	NY0834	54°41·8'	3°25·2'W	FM	89
Woodside Fm	Cumbr	NY4349	54°50·2'	2°52·8'W	FM	85
Woodside Fm	Derby	SK2864	53°10·6'	1°34·5'W	FM	119
Woodside Fm	Durham	NY9226	54°38·0'	2°7·0'W	FM	91,92
Woodside Fm	E Yorks	TA0169	54°6·7'	0°26·9'W	FM	101
Woodside Fm	E Yorks	TA1260	54°1·7'	0°17·0'W	FM	101
Woodside Fm	Glos	SO8128	51°57·2'	2°16·2'W	FM	150
Woodside Fm	Hants	SU4960	51°20·4'	1°17·4'W	FM	174
Woodside Fm	Hants	SU6829	51°3·6'	1°1·4'W	FM	185,186
Woodside Fm	Leic	SK4220	52°46·8'	1°22·2'W	FM	129
Woodside Fm	Leic	SK7933	52°53·6'	0°49·1'W	FM	129
Woodside Fm	Lincs	TF0046	53°0·4'	0°30·2'W	FM	130
Woodside Fm	Monm	SO4620	51°52·8'	2°46·7'W	FM	161
Woodside Fm	Northum	NT9741	55°40·0'	2°2·4'W	FM	75
Woodside Fm	Northum	NZ1472	55°2·8'	1°46·4'W	FM	88
Woodside Fm	Oxon	SP2408	51°46·4'	1°38·7'W	FM	163
Woodside Fm	Powys	SJ2806	52°39·1'	3°3·5'W	FM	126
Woodside Fm	Rut	SK9506	52°38·8'	0°35·3'W	FM	141
Woodside Fm	Shrops	SJ7810	52°41·5'	2°19·1'W	FM	127
Woodside Fm	Somer	ST5519	50°58·4'	2°38·1'W	FM	183
Woodside Fm	Somer	ST6127	51°2·7'	2°33·0'W	FM	183
Woodside Fm	Staffs	SJ9209	52°41·0'	2°6·7'W	FM	127
Woodside Fm	Staffs	SK1719	52°46·3'	1°44·5'W	FM	128
Woodside Fm	St Hel	SJ4697	53°28·3'	2°48·4'W	FM	108
Woodside Fm	Stock on T	NZ4024	54°36·8'	1°22·4'W	FM	93
Woodside Fm	Stock on T	NZ4327	54°38·4'	1°19·6'W	FM	93
Woodside Fm	Suff	TM0360	52°12·3'	0°58·7'E	FM	155
Woodside Fm	Worcs	SO7174	52°22·0'	2°25·2'W	FM	138
Woodside Fm	Worcs	SO8040	52°3·7'	2°17·1'W	FM	150
Woodside Fms	Hants	SU6935	51°6·8'	1°0·5'W	FM	186
Woodside Green	Essex	TL5118	51°50·6'	0°11·9'E	T	167
Woodside Green	Kent	TQ9053	51°14·9'	0°43·7'E	T	189
Woodside Hall	E Susx	TQ5707	50°50·7'	0°14·2'E	X	199
Woodside Ho	Aberd	NJ8719	57°15·9'	2°12·5'W	X	38
Woodside Ho	S Lanak	NS7949	55°43·4'	3°55·2'W	X	64
Woodside Ho	Worcs	SO8561	52°15·1'	2°12·8'W	X	150
Woodside Kennels	W Susx	TQ3016	50°56·0'	0°8·6'W	X	198
Woodside of Arbeadie	Aberd	NO7096	57°3·5'	2°29·2'W	T	38,45
Woodside of Balhaldie	Pth & Kin	NN8106	56°14·2'	3°54·7'W	X	57
Woodside of Balnillo	Angus	NO6560	56°44·1'	2°33·9'W	X	45
Woodside of Cairnty	Moray	NJ3352	57°33·4'	3°6·7'W	X	28
Woodside of Thornton	Aberd	NO6873	56°51·1'	2°31·0'W	X	45
Woodside of Tollie	Highld	NH5156	57°34·4'	4°29·0'W	X	26
Woodside of Waterlair	Aberd	NO7675	56°52·2'	2°23·2'W	X	45
Woodside Park	Barnet	TQ2592	51°37·0'	0°11·3'W	T	176
Woodside Place	Herts	TL2406	51°44·6'	0°11·8'W	X	166
Woodsland Fm	W Susx	TQ3627	51°1·8'	0°3·2'W	FM	187,198
Woodslea	Devon	SX9298	50°46·5'	3°31·5'W	X	192
Woodslee	D & G	NY3974	55°3·7'	2°56·9'W	X	85
Woods Mill	W Susx	TQ2113	50°54·5'	0°16·4'W	X	198
Woods Moor	Stock	SJ9087	53°23·0'	2°8·6'W	T	109
Woods of Garmaddie	Aberd	NO2292	57°1·0'	3°16·6'W	F	44
Woods of Glentromie	Highld	NN7797	57°3·1'	4°1·2'W	F	35
Woods of Glentruim	Highld	NN6895	57°1·9'	4°10·0'W	F	35
Woods of Knockfrink	Highld	NJ1233	57°23·0'	3°27·4'W	F	28
Woodsome Hall	Kirk	SE1814	53°37·6'	1°43·3'W	A	110
Woodson	Pemb	SM9009	51°44·7'	5°2·1'W	X	157,158
Woodspeen	W Berks	SU4469	51°25·3'	1°21·6'W	T	174
Woodspeen Fm	W Berks	SU4369	51°25·3'	1°22·5'W	FM	174
Wood's Place	E Susx	TQ7518	50°56·3'	0°29·8'E	X	199
Woodspring Bay	N Som	ST3566	51°23·6'	2°55·7'W	W	171,182
Woodspring Priory	N Som	ST3466	51°23·6'	2°56·5'W	T	171,182

Wood Stanway	Glos	SP0631	51°58·9'	1°54·4'W	T	150
Woodstead	Northum	NU2223	55°30·3'	1°38·7'W	X	75
Woods, The	Essex	TL5318	51°50·6'	0°13·7'E	X	167
Woodstile	Shrops	SJ5223	52°48·4'	2°42·3'W	X	126
Woodstock	Kent	TQ9060	51°18·7'	0°44·0'E	T	178
Woodstock	Orkney	HY5102	58°54·4'	2°50·6'W	X	6,7
Woodstock	Oxon	SP4416	51°50·7'	1°21·3'W	T	164
Woodstock	Pemb	SN0225	51°53·5'	4°52·3'W	T	145,157,158
Woodstock	W Susx	TQ1030	51°3·8'	0°25·4'W	X	187
Woodstock Bower	N Yks	SE6797	54°22·1'	0°57·7'W	X	94,100
Woodstock Cross	Pemb	SN0125	51°53·5'	4°53·1'W	X	145,157,158
Woodstock Fm	Norf	TF6703	52°36·2'	0°28·4'E	FM	143
Woodstock Fm	Salf	SJ7094	53°26·8'	2°26·7'W	FM	109
Woodstock Ho	Heref	SO5266	52°17·6'	2°41·8'W	X	137,138,149
Woodstoke Ho	Lincs	TF3930	52°51·2'	0°4·3'E	X	131
Woodston	Peterb	TL1897	52°33·7'	0°15·1'W	T	142
Woodstone	Essex	TL5839	52°1·8'	0°18·6'E	X	154
Woodstone Hill	Aberd	NO7466	56°47·3'	2°25·1'W	H	45
Woodston Manor	Worcs	SO6769	52°19·3'	2°28·7'W	X	138
Wood Street	Norf	TG3722	52°44·8'	1°31·1'E	T	133,134
Woodstreet Fm	Dorset	SY8585	50°40·1'	2°12·4'W	FM	194
Woodstreet Fm	Suff	TL9570	52°17·8'	0°52·0'E	FM	144,155
Wood Street Fm	Wilts	SU0678	51°30·3'	1°54·4'W	FM	173
Wood Street Village	Surrey	SU9550	51°14·7'	0°37·9'W	T	186
Wood Sutton	Heref	SO5565	52°17·1'	2°39·2'W	X	137,138,149
Woodterrill	Devon	SS6210	50°52·6'	3°57·3'W	X	191
Wood, The	Heref	SO3253	52°10·5'	2°59·3'W	X	148
Wood, The	Lancs	SD7945	53°54·3'	2°18·8'W	X	103
Wood, The	Norf	TG2001	52°34·0'	1°15·2'E	X	134
Wood, The	Shrops	SO5981	52°25·8'	2°35·8'W	X	137,138
Woodthorpe	Derby	SK4574	53°15·9'	1°19·1'W	T	120
Woodthorpe	Leic	SK5417	52°45·1'	1°11·6'W	T	129
Woodthorpe	Lincs	TF4380	53°18·1'	0°9·2'E	T	122
Woodthorpe	Notts	SK5844	52°59·6'	1°7·7'W	T	129
Woodthorpe	York	SE5749	53°56·3'	1°7·5'W	T	105
Woodthorpe Grange	Derby	SK3764	53°10·5'	1°26·4'W	X	119
Woodthorpe Hall	Derby	SK3178	53°18·1'	1°31·7'W	X	119
Woodthorpe Hall	Derby	SK3865	53°11·1'	1°25·5'W	X	119
Woodthorpe Hall Fm	Derby	SK4574	53°15·9'	1°19·1'W	FM	120
Woodton	Norf	TM2993	52°29·4'	1°22·8'E	T	134
Woodton Auchry	Aberd	NJ8052	57°33·7'	2°19·6'W	X	29,30
Woodton Fm	Norf	TM2696	52°31·1'	1°20·3'E	FM	134
Woodton Fm	Norf	TM2794	52°30·0'	1°21·1'E	FM	134
Woodton Lodge	Norf	TM2994	52°30·0'	1°22·8'E	X	134
Woodtop Fm	Lancs	SD5644	53°53·7'	2°39·8'W	FM	102
Wood Top Fm	Leeds	SE2543	53°53·2'	1°36·8'W	FM	104
Woodtown	Aberd	NJ6839	57°26·7'	2°31·5'W	X	29
Woodtown	Aberd	NJ7446	57°30·5'	2°25·6'W	X	29
Woodtown	Devon	SS4123	50°59·3'	4°15·5'W	T	180,190
Woodtown	Devon	SS4925	51°0·5'	4°8·8'W	T	180
Woodtown	Devon	SS5611	50°53·1'	4°2·5'W	X	191
Woodtown	Devon	SX3778	50°35·0'	4°17·8'W	X	201
Woodtown	Devon	SX4871	50°31·4'	4°8·3'W	X	201
Woodtown	Devon	SX5371	50°31·5'	4°4·1'W	X	201
Woodvale	Sefton	SD3011	53°35·7'	3°3·0'W	T	108
Woodvale Airfield	Sefton	SD3009	53°34·6'	3°3·0'W	X	108
Wood Vale Fm	N Yks	SE0043	53°53·2'	1°59·6'W	FM	104
Wood View	Heref	SO5735	52°0·9'	2°37·2'W	X	149
Wood View Fm	Leic	SP4399	52°35·5'	1°21·5'W	FM	140
Woodville	Derby	SK3119	52°46·3'	1°32·0'W	T	128
Woodville	Dorset	ST8021	50°59·5'	2°16·7'W	T	183
Woodville	Kent	TR2744	51°9·2'	1°15·2'E	X	179
Woodville Feus	Angus	NO6043	56°34·9'	2°38·6'W	T	54
Woodville Fm	Devon	SS4725	51°0·5'	4°10·5'W	FM	180
Woodville Fm	Dorset	ST8220	50°59·0'	2°15·0'W	FM	183
Woodville Ho	Angus	NO6143	56°34·9'	2°37·6'W	X	54
Woodwall Green	Staffs	SJ7831	52°52·8'	2°19·2'W	T	127
Woodwalls	Dorset	ST5205	50°50·8'	2°40·5'W	X	194
Woodwalton	Cambs	TL2180	52°24·5'	0°12·9'W	T	142
Woodwalton Fen	Cambs	TL2284	52°26·7'	0°11·9'W	X	142
Woodward Fm	Wilts	SU0189	51°36·2'	1°58·7'W	FM	173
Woodward's Fm	W Susx	TQ3231	51°4·0'	0°6·6'W	FM	187
Woodwater Fm	Dorset	ST8227	51°2·8'	2°15·0'W	FM	183
Woodway	Oxon	SU5384	51°33·4'	1°13·7'W	T	174
Woodway Fm	Bucks	SP6709	51°46·8'	1°1·3'W	FM	164,165
Woodway Fm	Oxon	SP3436	52°1·5'	1°29·9'W	FM	151
Woodway Fm	Oxon	SU7298	51°40·8'	0°57·1'W	FM	165
Woodway Park	Cov	SP3781	52°25·8'	1°26·9'W	T	140
Woodwell	Northnts	SP9577	52°23·2'	0°35·8'W	T	141
Woodwell	Pth & Kin	NO2328	56°26·5'	3°14·5'W	X	53,58
Woodwell Head	Leic	SK8717	52°44·8'	0°42·3'W	F	130
Woodwell Ho	Durham	NZ2945	54°48·2'	1°32·5'W	X	88
Woodwells Fm	Herts	TL0807	51°45·3'	0°25·7'W	FM	166
Woodwick	Orkney	HY3823	59°5·6'	3°4·4'W	T	6
Wood Wick	Orkney	HY3923	59°5·6'	3°3·4'W	W	6
Wood Wick	Shetld	HP5711	60°46·9'	0°56·7'W	W	1
Woodwick House	Orkney	HY3924	59°6·2'	3°3·4'W	X	6
Woodworth Green	Ches	SJ5757	53°6·7'	2°38·1'W	T	117
Woodyard Cotts	Herts	SP9811	51°47·6'	0°34·3'W	X	165
Woodyates	Dorset	SU0219	50°58·5'	1°57·9'W	T	184
Woody Bay	Devon	SS6749	51°13·7'	3°53·9'W	T	180
Woody Bay	Devon	SS6749	51°13·7'	3°53·9'W	W	180
Woody Bay	I of W	SZ5376	50°35·1'	1°14·7'W	W	196
Woodycleuch Dod	S Lanak	NT0228	55°32·4'	3°32·7'W	H	72
Woody Close	Durham	NZ1350	54°50·9'	1°47·4'W	X	88
Woody Crags	Northum	NY6899	55°17·3'	2°29·8'W	X	80
Woodyett	S Lanak	NS8443	55°40·3'	3°50·2'W	X	71,72
Woodyett	Stir	NS7295	56°8·1'	4°3·1'W	X	57
Woody Fields Fm	Ches	SJ7759	53°7·9'	2°20·2'W	FM	118
Woodyhyde Fm	Dorset	SY9780	50°37·4'	2°2·2'W	FM	195
Woody Islands, The	Pth & Kin	NO1026	56°25·3'	3°27·1'W	X	53,58
Woody Knowe	Highld	NC6945	58°22·7'	4°13·9'W	X	10
Woody's Top	Lincs	TF3378	53°17·2'	0°0·1'E	X	122
Woofa Bank Fm	Brad	SE0449	53°56·5'	1°55·9'W	FM	104
Woof Crag	Cumbr	NY4912	54°30·3'	2°46·8'W	X	90
Woofergill	Cumbr	NY8509	54°28·8'	2°13·5'W	X	91,92
Woofferton	Shrops	SO5168	52°18·7'	2°42·7'W	T	137,138
Woofull Fm	Norf	TG0521	52°45·1'	1°2·7'E	FM	133
Woof Howe Grain	N Yks	SE9196	54°21·3'	0°35·6'W	W	94,101
Woofields Fm	Heref	SO7142	52°4·8'	2°25·0'W	FM	149

Woo Gill	N Yks	SE0778	54°12·1'	1°53·1'W	W	99
Woogill Moor	N Yks	SE0778	54°12·1'	1°53·1'W	X	99
Woogra Fm	Darl	NZ3421	54°35·2'	1°28·0'W	FM	93
Woohill Village	Wilts	SU0576	51°29·2'	1°55·3'W	A	173
Wookey	Somer	ST5145	51°12·4'	2°41·7'W	T	182,183
Wookey Hole	Somer	ST5347	51°13·4'	2°40·0'W	T	182,183
Wool	Dorset	SY8486	50°40·6'	2°13·2'W	T	194
Woolacombe	Devon	SS4543	51°10·2'	4°12·6'W	T	180
Woolacombe Down	Devon	SS4542	51°9·6'	4°12·6'W	X	180
Woolacombe Fm	Devon	SX4566	50°28·6'	4°10·7'W	FM	201
Woolacombe Sand	Devon	SS4542	51°9·6'	4°12·6'W	X	180
Woolacott Fm	Devon	SX4489	50°41·0'	4°12·1'W	FM	190
Wooladon Fm	Devon	SX3784	50°38·2'	4°17·9'W	FM	201
Woolage Green	Kent	TR2349	51°12·0'	1°11·9'E	T	179,189
Woolage Village	Kent	TR2350	51°12·6'	1°12·0'E	T	179,189
Woolah	N Yks	SE6787	54°16·7'	0°57·8'W	X	94,100
Woolard's Ash	Essex	TL5717	51°50·0'	0°17·1'E	X	167
Woolas Grange	N Yks	SE5543	53°53·1'	1°9·4'W	X	105
Woolas Hall Fm	N Yks	SE5643	53°53·0'	1°8·5'W	FM	105
Woolaston	Glos	ST5899	51°41·5'	2°36·1'W	T	162
Woolaston Common	Glos	SO5801	51°42·6'	2°36·1'W	T	162
Woolaston Fm	Staffs	SJ8516	52°44·7'	2°12·9'W	FM	127
Woolaston Grange	Glos	ST5898	51°41·0'	2°36·1'W	X	162
Woolaston Slade	Glos	SO5700	51°42·1'	2°36·9'W	T	162
Woolaston Woodside	Glos	SO5700	51°42·1'	2°36·9'W	T	162
Woolavington	Somer	ST3441	51°10·1'	2°56·3'W	T	182
Woolavington Down	W Susx	SU9415	50°55·8'	0°39·4'W	X	197
Woolavington Level	Somer	ST3542	51°10·6'	2°55·4'W	X	182
Woolaw	Northum	NY8298	55°16·8'	2°16·6'W	X	80
Wool Beck	Cumbr	NY7428	54°39·0'	2°23·8'W	W	91
Woolbeding	W Susx	SU8722	50°59·7'	0°45·2'W	T	197
Woolbeding Common	W Susx	SU8625	51°1·3'	0°46·0'W	X	186,197
Woolbist Law	Northum	NT8207	55°21·7'	2°16·6'W	H	80
Wool Br	Dorset	SY8487	50°41·2'	2°13·2'W	A	194
Woolbridge Heath	Dorset	SY8488	50°41·7'	2°13·2'W	X	194
Woolbury	Hants	SU3835	51°7·0'	1°27·0'W	A	185
Wool Busk	Cumbr	NY8910	54°29·4'	2°9·8'W	X	91,92
Woolcombe	Dorset	ST6005	50°50·8'	2°33·7'W	X	194
Woolcombe	Somer	ST0919	50°58·0'	3°17·4'W	X	181
Woolcombe Allotment	Somer	SS8034	51°5·8'	3°42·4'W	X	181
Woolcombe Fm	Devon	SX7550	50°20·4'	3°45·0'W	FM	202
Woolcombe Fm	Dorset	ST5905	50°50·8'	2°34·6'W	FM	194
Woolcombe Fm	Dorset	SY5595	50°45·4'	2°37·9'W	FM	194
Woolcombe Fm	Somer	SS8034	51°5·8'	3°42·4'W	FM	181
Woolcotts	Somer	SS9631	51°4·4'	3°28·7'W	X	181
Wooldale	Kirk	SE1508	53°34·3'	1°46·0'W	T	110
Wool Dale	N Yks	TA1281	54°13·0'	0°16·5'W	X	101
Wooldings Fm	Hants	SU4750	51°15·1'	1°19·2'W	FM	185
Wooldown	Corn	SS2203	50°48·2'	4°31·2'W	X	190
Wooler	Northum	NT9928	55°33·0'	2°0·5'W	T	75
Wooler Common	Northum	NT9726	55°31·9'	2°2·4'W	X	75
Wooler Knoll	Derby	SK1786	53°22·5'	1°44·3'W	H	110
Woolers Wood	Shrops	SO6086	52°28·5'	2°34·9'W	F	138
Wooler Water	Northum	NT9926	55°31·9'	2°0·5'W	W	75
Wooley	Northum	NY8254	54°53·1'	2°16·4'W	X	86,87
Wooley Hill	Durham	NZ1839	54°45·0'	1°42·8'W	H	92
Wooley Park	Northum	NY8355	54°53·6'	2°15·5'W	X	86,87
Woolfall	Ches	SJ6745	53°0·3'	2°29·1'W	X	118
Woolfall Fm	Ches	SJ6744	52°59·8'	2°29·1'W	FM	118
Woolfall Heath	Know	SJ4392	53°25·5'	2°51·1'W	T	108
Woolfardisworthy	Devon	SS8208	50°51·8'	3°40·2'W	T	191
Woolfardisworthy or Woolsery	Devon	SS3321	50°58·1'	4°22·3'W	T	190
Woolfold	Bury	SD7811	53°35·9'	2°19·5'W	T	109
Woolfords	S Lanak	NT0056	55°47·5'	3°35·3'W	X	65,72
Woolfords Cottages	S Lanak	NT0057	55°48·0'	3°35·3'W	T	65,72
Woolford's Fm	Surrey	SU8942	51°10·4'	0°43·2'W	FM	186
Woolford's Water	Dorset	ST6905	50°50·9'	2°26·0'W	T	194
Woolfox Wood	Rut	SK9513	52°42·6'	0°35·1'W	F	130
Woolgarden	Corn	SX1884	50°37·9'	4°34·0'W	X	201
Woolgarston	Dorset	SY9881	50°38·0'	2°1·3'W	T	195
Woolgreaves	Wakf	SE3416	53°38·6'	1°28·7'W	T	110,111
Wool Hall	Lincs	TF2724	52°48·1'	0°6·6'W	X	131
Woolham Fm	Lincs	TF3862	53°8·5'	0°4·2'E	FM	122
Woolhampton	W Berks	SU5766	51°23·6'	1°10·5'W	T	174
Woolhanger	Devon	SS6945	51°11·6'	3°52·1'W	X	180
Woolhanger Common	Devon	SS6946	51°12·1'	3°52·1'W	X	180
Wool Heath	Dorset	SY8389	50°42·3'	2°14·1'W	X	194
Wool Hill	E Loth	NT6367	55°53·9'	2°35·1'W	X	67
Woolhillock	Aberd	NJ8205	57°8·4'	2°17·4'W	X	38
Wool Ho	Durham	NZ0417	54°33·1'	1°55·9'W	X	92
Wool Ho	Northum	NY7863	54°57·9'	2°20·2'W	X	86,87
Woolholes	Devon	SX6863	50°27·4'	3°51·2'W	X	202
Woolhope	Heref	SO6135	52°1·0'	2°33·7'W	T	149
Woolhope	Scot Bord	NY4789	55°11·8'	2°49·5'W	X	79
Woolhope Bank	Scot Bord	NT3242	55°40·3'	3°4·4'W	H	73
Woolhope Cockshoot	Heref	SO6337	52°2·0'	2°32·0'W	T	149
Woolhouse Croft	N Yks	SE5691	54°18·9'	1°7·9'W	X	100
Wool Ingles	Durham	NY8827	54°38·5'	2°10·7'W	X	91,92
Wooliscroft	Staffs	SJ9334	52°54·4'	2°5·8'W	X	127
Wool Knoll	N Yks	SE6574	54°9·7'	0°59·9'W	X	100
Wool Knott	Cumbr	SD2789	54°17·7'	3°6·9'W	H	96,97
Woolladon	Devon	SS5207	50°50·9'	4°5·8'W	X	191
Woolland	Dorset	ST7706	50°51·4'	2°19·2'W	T	194
Woolland Hill	Dorset	ST7705	50°50·9'	2°19·2'W	H	194
Woollands	E Loth	NT7470	55°55·6'	2°24·5'W	X	67
Woollard	Bath & NE Somer	ST6364	51°22·7'	2°31·5'W	T	172
Woollas Hall	Worcs	SO9440	52°3·7'	2°4·9'W	A	150
Woollaston	Staffs	SJ8615	52°44·2'	2°12·0'W	T	127
Woollaton	Devon	SS4712	50°53·5'	4°10·1'W	T	180
Wool Law	S Lanak	NS8916	55°25·8'	3°44·8'W	H	71,78
Woollcombe	Devon	SX8253	50°22·1'	3°39·2'W	X	202
Woolleigh Barton	Devon	SS5316	50°55·7'	4°5·1'W	X	180
Woollensbrook	Herts	TL3610	51°46·6'	0°1·3'W	T	166
Woolley	Bath & NE Somer	ST7468	51°24·9'	2°22·0'W	T	172
Woolley	Cambs	TL1574	52°21·3'	0°18·3'W	T	142
Woolley	Corn	SS2516	50°55·3'	4°29·0'W	T	190
Woolley	Derby	SK3760	53°8·4'	1°26·4'W	T	119

Woolley	Wakf	SE3113	53°37·0'	1°31·5'W	T	110,111
Woolley	Wilts	ST8361	51°21·1'	2°14·3'W	T	173
Woolley Bridge	Tames	SK0095	53°27·3'	1°59·6'W	T	110
Woolley Down	W Berks	SU4081	51°31·8'	1°25·0'W	X	174
Woolley Edge	Wakf	SE3013	53°37·0'	1°32·4'W	X	110,111
Woolley Edge Service Area	Wakf	SE3014	53°37·5'	1°32·4'W	X	110,111
Woolley Fm	W Berks	SU4079	51°30·7'	1°25·0'W	FM	174
Woolley Green	Wilts	ST8361	51°21·1'	2°14·3'W	T	173
Woolley Green	Win & Maid	SU8580	51°31·0'	0°46·1'W	T	175
Woolley Green Fm	Hants	SU3925	51°1·6'	1°26·2'W	FM	185
Woolley Hall College	Wakf	SE3213	53°37·0'	1°30·6'W	X	110,111
Woolley Hill	Cambs	TL1473	52°20·8'	0°19·2'W	X	153
Woolley Ho	W Berks	SU4180	51°31·3'	1°24·2'W	X	174
Woolley Leys Fm	Cambs	TL1674	52°21·3'	0°17·4'W	FM	142
Woolley Moor	Derby	SK3661	53°8·9'	1°27·3'W	X	119
Woolley Moor	Wakf	SE3114	53°37·5'	1°31·5'W	X	110,111
Woolley Park Fm	Wilts	ST8461	51°21·1'	2°13·4'W	FM	173
Woolleys	Bucks	SU7786	51°34·3'	0°52·9'W	X	175
Woolleys Fm	Northnts	SP6678	52°24·0'	1°1·4'W	FM	141
Woolley, The	Staffs	SJ8707	52°39·9'	2°11·1'W	X	127,139
Woolley Wood	Devon	SS6039	51°8·2'	3°59·7'W	F	180
Woolly Hill	Durham	NZ0424	54°36·9'	1°55·9'W	X	92
Woolman Point	Devon	SX6740	50°14·9'	3°51·6'W	X	202
Woolman's Wood	Bucks	SU9186	51°34·2'	0°40·8'W	F	175
Wool Meath	Northum	NY7099	55°17·3'	2°27·9'W	H	80
Woolmeath Edge	Northum	NY7199	55°17·3'	2°27·0'W	H	80
Woolmere Green	Worcs	SO9662	52°15·6'	2°3·1'W	T	150
Woolmer Fm	Hants	SU8434	51°6·2'	0°47·6'W	FM	186
Woolmer Forest	Hants	SU8032	51°5·1'	0°51·1'W	F	186
Woolmer Green	Herts	TL2518	51°51·0'	0°10·7'W	T	166
Woolmer Green Fm	Essex	TL7825	51°53·9'	0°35·6'E	FM	167
Woolmer Hill	Surrey	SU8733	51°5·6'	0°45·1'W	T	186
Woolmer Pond	Hants	SU7831	51°4·6'	0°52·8'W	W	186
Woolmers	N Som	ST4564	51°22·6'	2°47·0'W	X	172,182
Woolmersdon	Somer	ST2833	51°5·7'	3°1·3'W	T	182
Woolmer's Park	Herts	TL2810	51°46·7'	0°8·3'W	A	166
Woolmer Wood	Suff	TL8157	52°11·1'	0°39·3'E	F	155
Woolmet	Midlo	NT3169	55°54·8'	3°5·8'W	X	66
Woolminstone	Somer	ST4108	50°52·3'	2°49·9'W	T	193
Woolney Hall	Suff	TM0957	52°10·5'	1°3·8'E	X	155
Wool Oaks Mill	Cumbr	NY4741	54°45·9'	2°49·0'W	X	86
Woolow	Derby	SK0972	53°14·9'	1°51·5'W	X	119
Woolpack Corner	Kent	TQ8537	51°6·4'	0°39·0'E	T	189
Woolpack Fm	Cambs	TL2968	52°17·9'	0°6·1'W	FM	153
Woolpack Fm	E Susx	TQ4226	51°1·2'	0°1·9'E	FM	187,198
Woolpack Point	I Scilly	SV8909	49°54·3'	6°19·5'W	X	203
Woolpit	Suff	TL9762	52°13·5'	0°53·5'E	T	155
Woolpitch Wood	Monm	SO4804	51°44·2'	2°44·8'W	F	171
Woolpit Green	Suff	TL9761	52°12·9'	0°53·4'E	T	155
Woolpit Heath	Suff	TL9861	52°12·9'	0°54·3'E	T	155
Woolpits	Essex	TL6926	51°54·6'	0°27·8'E	X	167
Woolpit's Fm	Essex	TL7110	51°46·0'	0°29·1'E	FM	167
Wool Pits Hill	Durham	NY8730	54°40·1'	2°11·7'W	X	91,92
Woolpit Wood	Suff	TL9961	52°12·9'	0°55·2'E	F	155
Woolpots	N Yks	SE5174	54°9·8'	1°12·7'W	X	100
Woolridge	Glos	SO8023	51°54·5'	2°17·1'W	T	162
Woolrow	Cald	SE1524	53°43·0'	1°45·9'W	X	104
Woolsbarrow	Dorset	SY8992	50°43·9'	2°9·0'W	X	195
Woolsbarrow (Fort)	Dorset	SY8992	50°43·9'	2°9·0'W	A	195
Wools Br	Dorset	SU1004	50°50·4'	1°51·1'W	X	195
Woolsbridge	Dorset	SU0905	50°50·9'	1°51·9'W	T	195
Woolscott	Warw	SP4967	52°18·2'	1°16·5'W	T	151
Woolscott Barton	Devon	SS5445	51°11·4'	4°5·0'W	X	180
Woolseybridge Fm	Norf	TM1382	52°23·9'	1°8·3'E	FM	144,156
Woolsgrove	Devon	SS7902	50°48·5'	3°42·7'W	T	191
Woolshears Hill	Scot Bord	NT1342	55°40·1'	3°22·6'W	H	72
Woolshears Wood	Scot Bord	NT1343	55°40·6'	3°22·6'W	F	72
Woolshope	Shrops	SO6192	52°31·7'	2°34·1'W	X	138
Woolshots Fm	Essex	TQ7292	51°36·3'	0°29·4'E	FM	178
Woolsington	N upon Ty	NZ1969	55°1·2'	1°41·7'W	T	88
Woolsington Hall	N upon Ty	NZ1970	55°1·7'	1°41·7'W	X	88
Woolstan's Fm	Worcs	SO7866	52°17·7'	2°19·0'W	FM	138,150
Woolstanwood	Ches	SJ6755	53°5·7'	2°29·2'W	T	118
Woolstaston	Shrops	SO4598	52°34·9'	2°48·3'W	T	137,138
Woolstencroft Fm	Ches	SJ7187	53°23·0'	2°25·8'W	FM	109
Woolsthorpe By Belvoir	Lincs	SK8334	52°54·1'	0°45·6'W	T	130
Woolsthorpe-by-Colsterworth	Lincs	SK9224	52°48·6'	0°37·7'W	T	130
Woolston	C of Soton	SU4310	50°53·5'	1°22·9'W	T	196
Woolston	Corn	SX2968	50°29·4'	4°24·3'W	T	201
Woolston	Devon	SX7141	50°15·5'	3°48·2'W	T	202
Woolston	Devon	SX7150	50°20·4'	3°48·4'W	X	202
Woolston	Shrops	SJ3224	52°48·8'	3°0·1'W	T	126
Woolston	Shrops	SO4287	52°28·9'	2°50·8'W	T	137
Woolston	Somer	ST0939	51°8·8'	3°17·7'W	T	181
Woolston	Somer	ST6427	51°2·7'	2°30·4'W	T	183
Woolston	Warr	SJ6489	53°24·0'	2°32·1'W	T	109
Woolston	Carm	SN2515	51°48·6'	4°31·9'W	X	158
Woolston	Corn	SS2202	50°47·7'	4°31·2'W	X	190
Woolstone	Devon	SS5827	51°1·7'	4°1·1'W	X	180
Woolstone	Glos	SO9630	51°58·3'	2°3·1'W	T	150
Woolstone	Mil Key	SP8738	52°2·2'	0°43·5'W	T	152
Woolstone	Oxon	SU2987	51°35·1'	1°34·5'W	T	174
Woolstone Down	Oxon	SU3084	51°33·5'	1°33·6'W	X	174
Woolstone Fm	Somer	ST2344	51°11·6'	3°5·7'W	FM	182
Woolstone Hill	Glos	SO9631	51°58·9'	2°3·1'W	H	150
Woolstone Hill	Oxon	SU2986	51°34·6'	1°34·5'W	X	174
Woolstone Lodge	Oxon	SU2987	51°35·1'	1°34·5'W	X	174
Wool Stones Hill	N Yks	SE1352	53°58·1'	1°47·7'W	X	104
Woolston Fields Fm	Warw	SP4075	52°22·5'	1°24·3'W	FM	140
Woolston Green	Devon	SX7766	50°29·1'	3°43·7'W	T	202
Woolston Manor Fm	Somer	ST6527	51°2·7'	2°29·6'W	FM	183
Woolston Moss	Warr	SJ6590	53°24·6'	2°31·2'W	X	109
Woolstoun	Falk	NT0279	55°59·9'	3°33·8'W	X	65
Woolstreet Fm	Hants	SU5219	50°58·3'	1°15·2'W	FM	185
Woolstack Point	Pemb	SM7509	51°44·3'	5°15·1'W	X	157
Woolthwaite Fm	Roth	SK5691	53°25·0'	1°9·0'W	FM	111
Woolton	Liv	SJ4286	53°22·3'	2°51·9'W	T	108
Woolton Fm	Kent	TR1856	51°15·9'	1°7·9'E	FM	179

Woolton Hill	Hants	SU4261	51°21·0'	1°23·4'W	T	174
Woolton Ho	Hants	SU4262	51°21·6'	1°23·4'W	X	174
Woolton House Stud	Hants	SU4262	51°21·6'	1°23·4'W	X	174
Woolvens Fm	W Susx	TQ1217	50°56·7'	0°24·0'W	FM	198
Woolvers Barn	W Berks	SU4680	51°31·3'	1°19·8'W	X	174
Woolvers Hill	N Som	ST3860	51°20·4'	2°53·0'W	T	182
Woolverstone	Suff	TM1838	52°0·1'	1°11·0'E	T	169
Woolverstone Park	Suff	TM1938	52°0·1'	1°11·8'E	X	169
Woolverton	Somer	ST7953	51°16·8'	2°17·7'W	T	183
Woolvey Fm	Cambs	TL3381	52°24·9'	0°2·3'W	FM	142
Woolwell	Devon	SX5061	50°26·0'	4°6·4'W	T	201
Woolwich	Gren	TQ4379	51°29·7'	0°4·0'E	T	177
Woolwich Barn	Mil Key	SP8649	52°8·2'	0°44·2'W	X	152
Woolwich Common	Gren	TQ4277	51°28·7'	0°3·1'E	X	177
Woolwich Reach	Newham	TQ4179	51°29·8'	0°2·3'E	W	177
Wooly Law	Scot Bord	NT3250	55°44·6'	3°4·6'W	X	66,73
Woon	Corn	SX0059	50°24·0'	4°48·5'W	T	200
Woon Gumpus Common	Corn	SW3933	50°8·6'	5°38·8'W	X	203
Woonton	Heref	SO3552	52°10·0'	2°56·6'W	T	148,149
Woonton	Heref	SO5462	52°15·5'	2°40·0'W	T	137,138,149
Woonton Ash	Heref	SO3454	52°11·1'	2°57·5'W	X	148,149
Woonton Fm	Devon	ST2905	50°50·6'	3°0·1'W	FM	193
Wooperton	Northum	NU0320	55°28·7'	1°56·7'W	T	75
Wooplaw	Scot Bord	NT4942	55°40·4'	2°48·2'W	T	73
Wooplaw	Scot Bord	NT7008	55°22·2'	2°28·0'W	X	80
Wooplaw Ho	Scot Bord	NT5041	55°39·8'	2°47·3'W	X	73
Wooplaw Rig	Scot Bord	NT6907	55°21·6'	2°28·9'W	X	80
Woore	Shrops	SJ7342	52°58·7'	2°23·7'W	T	118
Woore Hall	Shrops	SJ7242	52°58·7'	2°24·6'W	X	118
Wooscombe Bottom	Bath & NE Somer	ST6365	51°23·2'	2°31·5'W	X	172
Woose Hill	Wok	SU7968	51°24·6'	0°51·5'W	X	175
Wooson's Hill	Hants	SU2507	50°51·9'	1°38·3'W	X	195
Wooson's Hill Inclosure	Hants	SU2507	50°51·9'	1°38·3'W	F	195
Wooston	Devon	SX7688	50°40·9'	3°44·9'W	X	191
Wooston Castle	Devon	SX7689	50°41·5'	3°45·0'W	X	191
Wooth	Dorset	SY4795	50°45·4'	2°44·7'W	T	193
Wooton	Devon	SS5921	50°58·5'	4°0·1'W	X	180
Wooton	Shrops	SO5773	52°21·4'	2°37·5'W	T	137,138
Wooton	Shrops	SO7689	52°30·1'	2°20·8'W	T	138
Wooton Ho	Somer	ST4935	51°7·0'	2°43·3'W	X	182,183
Wooton Marsh	Norf	TF6125	52°48·1'	0°23·7'E	X	132
Wootten Green	Suff	TM2372	52°18·3'	1°16·7'E	T	156
Woottens	W Berks	SU5568	51°24·7'	1°12·2'W	X	174
Wootton	Beds	TL0045	52°5·9'	0°32·0'W	T	153
Wootton	Devon	SS4309	50°51·8'	4°13·5'W	X	190
Wootton	Hants	SZ2498	50°47·1'	1°39·2'W	T	195
Wootton	Heref	SO3252	52°10·0'	2°59·3'W	T	148
Wootton	Heref	SO4249	52°8·4'	2°50·5'W	X	148,149
Wootton	Heref	SO4848	52°7·9'	2°45·2'W	X	148,149
Wootton	Heref	SO5939	52°3·1'	2°35·5'W	T	149
Wootton	I of W	SZ5492	50°43·7'	1°13·7'W	T	196
Wootton	Kent	TR2246	51°10·4'	1°11·0'E	T	179,189
Wootton	N Lincs	TA0816	53°38·0'	0°21·6'W	T	112
Wootton	Northnts	SP7656	52°12·1'	0°52·9'W	T	152
Wootton	Oxon	SP4319	51°52·3'	1°22·1'W	T	164
Wootton	Oxon	SP4701	51°42·6'	1°18·8'W	T	164
Wootton	Shrops	SJ3427	52°50·4'	2°58·4'W	T	126
Wootton	Shrops	SO4578	52°24·1'	2°48·1'W	T	137,138,148
Wootton	Staffs	SJ8227	52°50·7'	2°15·6'W	T	127
Wootton	Staffs	SK1045	53°0·4'	1°50·7'W	T	119,128
Wootton Bassett	Wilts	SU0682	51°32·4'	1°54·4'W	T	173
Wootton Bourne End	Beds	SP9845	52°5·9'	0°33·8'W	T	153
Wootton Bridge	I of W	SZ5491	50°43·2'	1°13·7'W	T	196
Wootton Broadmead	Beds	TL0243	52°4·8'	0°30·3'W	T	153
Wootton Carr	Norf	TF6524	52°47·5'	0°27·2'E	F	132
Wootton Common	I of W	SZ5391	50°43·2'	1°14·6'W	T	196
Wootton Common	Somer	SS9443	51°10·8'	3°30·6'W	F	181
Wootton Coppice Inclosure	Hants	SZ2499	50°47·6'	1°39·2'W	F	195
Wootton Court	Warw	SP2868	52°18·8'	1°35·0'W	X	151
Wootton Courtenay	Somer	SS9343	51°10·8'	3°31·5'W	T	181
Wootton Creek	I of W	SZ5592	50°43·7'	1°12·9'W	W	196
Wootton Cross	Dorset	SY3795	50°45·3'	2°53·2'W	X	193
Wootton Dale	N Lincs	TA0515	53°37·5'	0°24·3'W	X	112
Wootton Dale Top	N Lincs	TA0415	53°37·5'	0°25·2'W	X	112
Woottondown Fm	Oxon	SP4421	51°53·4'	1°21·2'W	FM	164
Wootton Fields Fm	Wilts	SU0780	51°31·4'	1°53·6'W	FM	173
Wootton Fitzpaine	Dorset	SY3695	50°45·3'	2°54·1'W	T	193
Wootton Fm	E Susx	TQ3715	50°55·3'	0°2·7'W	FM	198
Wootton Fm	Heref	SO5752	52°10·1'	2°37·3'W	FM	149
Wootton Fm	Heref	SO6448	52°8·0'	2°31·2'W	FM	149
Wootton Fm	Kent	TR1251	51°13·3'	1°2·6'E	FM	179,189
Wootton Grange	N Lincs	TA0615	53°37·5'	0°23·4'W	X	112
Wootton Grange	Warw	SP1664	52°16·7'	1°45·5'W	X	151
Wootton Green	Beds	SP9943	52°4·8'	0°32·9'W	T	153
Wootton Green	Sol	SP2278	52°24·2'	1°40·2'W	T	139
Wootton Hall	Northnts	SP7557	52°12·6'	0°53·7'W	X	152
Wootton Hill	Dorset	SY3597	50°46·4'	2°54·9'W	H	193
Wootton Hill Fm	Somer	ST5034	51°6·4'	2°42·5'W	FM	182,183
Wootton Hill Fm	Warw	SP1463	52°16·1'	1°47·3'W	FM	151
Wootton Ho	Dorset	SY3795	50°45·3'	2°53·2'W	X	193
Wootton Knowle	Somer	SS9344	51°11·3'	3°31·5'W	X	181
Wootton Lodge	Staffs	SK0943	52°59·3'	1°51·6'W	A	119,128
Wootton Manor	E Susx	TQ5605	50°49·6'	0°13·3'E	X	199
Wootton Manor	Kent	TQ9647	51°11·5'	0°48·7'E	X	189
Wootton Meadows	Wilts	SU0881	51°31·9'	1°52·7'W	X	173
Wootton Old Farm	Hants	SZ2399	50°47·6'	1°40·0'W	FM	195
Wootton Park	Staffs	SK0944	52°59·8'	1°51·5'W	F	119,128
Wootton Pool	Warw	SP1563	52°16·1'	1°46·4'W	W	151
Wootton Rivers	Wilts	SU1963	51°22·2'	1°42·3'W	T	173
Woottons	Staffs	SK0738	52°56·6'	1°53·3'W	T	128
Woottons, The	Heref	SO6950	52°9·1'	2°26·8'W	X	149
Wootton St Lawrence	Hants	SU5953	51°16·6'	1°8·9'W	T	185
Wootton Wawen	Warw	SP1563	52°16·1'	1°46·4'W	T	151
Wootton Wold	N Lincs	TA0515	53°37·5'	0°24·3'W	X	112
Wootton Wood	Beds	SP9944	52°5·4'	0°32·9'W	F	153
Wootton Wood	Oxon	SP4118	51°51·8'	1°23·9'W	F	164

Wooy Hill	N Ayr	NS2260	55°48·3'	4°50·0'W	X	63
Woozeley Br	Warw	SP2957	52°12·9'	1°34·1'W	X	151
Wor Barrow	Dorset	SU0117	50°57·4'	1°58·8'W	X	184
Worbarrow	Dorset	SY8779	50°36·9'	2°10·6'W	T	194
Worbarrow Bay	Dorset	SY8680	50°37·4'	2°11·5'W	W	194
Wor Barrow (Long Barrow)	Dorset	SU0117	50°57·4'	1°58·8'W	A	184
Worbarrow Tout	Dorset	SY8679	50°36·9'	2°11·5'W	X	194
Worcester	Worcs	SO8555	52°11·8'	2°12·8'W	T	150
Worcester & Birmingham Canal	Worcs	SO9364	52°16·7'	2°5·8'W	W	150
Worcester & Birmingham Canal	Worcs	SP0070	52°19·9'	1°59·6'W	W	139
Worcester Lodge	Glos	ST8087	51°35·1'	2°16·9'W	A	173
Worcester Meadows	Worcs	SP0750	52°9·1'	1°53·5'W	X	150
Worcester Park	Sutton	TQ2265	51°22·5'	0°14·4'W	T	176
Worcestershire Beacon	Worcs	SO7645	52°6·4'	2°20·6'W	H	150
Worcestershire Way	Worcs	SO7459	52°14·0'	2°22·4'W	X	150
Worcestershire Way	Worcs	SO7773	52°21·5'	2°19·9'W	X	138
Worcester Walk	Glos	SO5912	51°48·5'	2°35·3'W	F	162
Worden	Devon	SS3013	50°53·7'	4°24·7'W	X	190
Worden	Devon	SS3711	50°52·8'	4°18·6'W	X	190
Worden	Devon	SX3495	50°44·1'	4°20·8'W	X	190
Worden	Devon	SX8549	50°20·0'	3°36·6'W	X	202
Worden Cross	Devon	SS3613	50°53·6'	4°19·6'W	X	190
Worden Park	Lancs	SD5320	53°40·7'	2°42·3'W	X	102
Word Hill Fm	Hants	SU7956	51°18·1'	0°51·6'W	FM	175,186
Wordley Fm	Worcs	SO7768	52°18·8'	2°19·8'W	FM	138
Wordsley	Dudley	SO8887	52°29·1'	2°10·2'W	T	139
Wordsworth Ho	Cumbr	NY1130	54°39·7'	3°22·4'W	A	89
Wordwell	Suff	TL8272	52°19·2'	0°40·6'E	T	144,155
Wordwell Barn	Suff	TL8575	52°20·7'	0°43·4'E	X	144
Wordwell Covert	Suff	TL8272	52°19·2'	0°40·6'E	F	144,155
Worfield	Shrops	SO7595	52°33·4'	2°21·7'W	T	138
Worgan's Fm	Glos	SO8607	51°45·9'	2°11·8'W	FM	162
Worgret	Dorset	SY9086	50°40·6'	2°8·1'W	T	195
Worgret Heath	Dorset	SY8987	50°41·2'	2°9·0'W	X	195
Worhams Fm	Devon	SY2399	50°47·4'	3°5·2'W	FM	192,193
Work	Orkney	HY4713	59°0·3'	2°54·9'W	X	6
Workhouse Common	Norf	TG3520	52°43·8'	1°29·2'E	T	133,134
Workhouse Common	Norf	TM0394	52°30·6'	0°59·9'E	X	144
Workhouse End	Beds	TL1052	52°9·5'	0°23·1'W	T	153
Workhouse Fm	E Yorks	SE8036	53°49·1'	0°46·7'W	FM	106
Workhouse Green	Suff	TL9037	52°0·2'	0°46·5'E	T	155
Workhouse Hill	Essex	TL9931	51°56·7'	0°54·1'E	T	168
Workington	Cumbr	NX9927	54°37·9'	3°33·5'W	T	89
Works Fm	Derby	SK4271	53°14·3'	1°21·8'W	FM	120
Worksop	Notts	SK5879	53°18·5'	1°7·4'W	T	120
Worksop College	Notts	SK5977	53°17·4'	1°6·5'W	X	120
Worksop Manor	Notts	SK5677	53°17·5'	1°9·2'W	A	120
Workwell	Orkney	HY3005	58°55·9'	3°12·5'W	X	6,7
Worlaby	Lincs	TF3376	53°16·1'	0°0·1'E	T	122
Worlaby	N Lincs	TA0113	53°36·5'	0°28·0'W	T	112
Worlaby Carrs	N Lincs	TA0012	53°35·9'	0°28·9'W	X	112
Worlaby Carrs Fm	N Lincs	SE9812	53°36·0'	0°30·7'W	FM	112
Worlaby Fox Covert	N Lincs	TA0014	53°37·0'	0°28·9'W	F	112
Worlaby New Ings	N Lincs	SE9812	53°36·0'	0°30·7'W	X	112
World of Adventures	King	TQ1762	51°20·9'	0°18·8'W	X	187
Worldsend	Aberd	NJ9350	57°32·7'	2°6·6'W	X	30
World's End	Bucks	SP8509	51°46·6'	0°45·7'W	T	165
World's End	Denb	SJ2347	53°1·1'	3°8·5'W	X	117
World's End	Enf	TQ3196	51°39·1'	0°6·0'W	T	166,176,177
Worlds End	Hants	SU6312	50°54·5'	1°5·9'W	T	196
World's End	Heref	SO3646	52°6·8'	2°55·7'W	X	148,149
Worlds End	Sol	SP1480	52°25·3'	1°47·2'W	T	139
World's End	Suff	TL9959	52°9·7'	0°55·0'E	T	155
World's End	W Berks	SU4876	51°29·1'	1°18·1'W	T	174
World's End	W Susx	TQ3219	50°57·5'	0°6·8'W	T	198
World's End	York	SE6659	54°1·6'	0°59·1'W	X	105,106
Worlds End Fm	Essex	TL8432	51°57·6'	0°41·1'E	FM	168
World's End Fm	E Susx	TQ5613	50°53·9'	0°13·5'E	FM	199
Worldsend Fm	Glos	ST6597	51°40·5'	2°30·0'W	FM	162
World's End Fm	Norf	TF5300	52°34·8'	0°15·9'E	FM	143
World's End Fm	Suff	TM2566	52°15·0'	1°18·2'E	FM	156
World's End Plantn	Suff	TM3246	52°4·0'	1°23·5'E	F	169
World's End Plantn	York	SE6659	54°1·6'	0°59·1'W	F	105,106
Worle	N Som	ST3562	51°21·4'	2°55·6'W	T	182
Worlebury	N Som	ST3162	51°21·4'	2°59·1'W	A	182
Worlebury	N Som	ST3362	51°21·4'	2°57·3'W	T	182
Worlebury Hill	N Som	ST3262	51°21·4'	2°58·2'W	H	182
Worles Common	Worcs	SO7368	52°18·5'	2°23·4'W	X	138
Worleston	Ches	SJ6556	53°6·2'	2°31·0'W	T	118
Worley	Glos	ST8499	51°41·6'	2°13·5'W	T	162
Worley's Fm	Wok	SU7981	51°31·6'	0°51·3'W	FM	175
Worley's Wood	Beds	TL0263	52°15·6'	0°29·9'W	F	153
Worlick Fm	Cambs	TL3186	52°27·6'	0°3·9'W	FM	142
Worlingham	Suff	TM4489	52°26·9'	1°35·9'E	T	156
Worlington	Devon	SS4830	51°3·2'	4°9·7'W	T	180
Worlington	Suff	TL6973	52°20·0'	0°29·2'E	T	154
Worlingworth	Suff	TM2368	52°16·1'	1°16·5'E	T	156
Wormadale	Shetld	HU3945	60°11·5'	1°17·3'W	X	4
Wormadale Hill	Shetld	HU4046	60°12·1'	1°16·2'W	H	4
Wormald Green	N Yks	SE3064	54°4·5'	1°32·1'W	X	99
Wormanby	Cumbr	NY3358	54°55·0'	3°2·3'W	X	85
Wormbridge	Heref	SO4231	51°58·7'	2°50·3'W	T	149,161
Wormbridge Common	Heref	SO4231	51°58·7'	2°50·3'W	T	149,161
Worm Brook	Heref	SO4029	51°57·6'	2°52·0'W	W	149,161
Worm Brook	Heref	SO4732	51°59·3'	2°45·9'W	W	149,161
Wormdale	Kent	TQ8563	51°20·4'	0°39·8'E	X	178
Wormegay	Norf	TF6611	52°40·5'	0°27·7'E	T	132,143
Wormelow Tump	Heref	SO4930	51°58·2'	2°44·2'W	T	149
Wormerlaw	Scot Bord	NT7540	55°39·4'	2°23·4'W	X	74
Wormesley Park	N Yks	SE5318	53°39·6'	1°11·5'W	X	111
Worm Gill	Cumbr	NY0909	54°28·3'	3°23·8'W	W	89
Wormhill	Derby	SK1274	53°16·0'	1°48·8'W	T	119
Wormhill	Heref	SO4339	52°3·0'	2°49·5'W	X	149,161
Worm Hill	Scot Bord	NT1130	55°33·6'	3°24·2'W	H	72
Wormhill	Staffs	SJ9363	53°10·1'	2°5·9'W	X	118
Wormhill Bottom	W Berks	SU3382	51°32·4'	1°31·1'W	X	174

Wormhill Hill	Derby	SK1274	53°16·0'	1°48·8'W	X	119
Wormhill Moor	Derby	SK1076	53°17·1'	1°50·6'W	X	119
Wormingford	Essex	TL9331	51°56·9'	0°48·9'E	T	168
Worminghall	Bucks	SP6408	51°46·3'	1°4·0'W	T	164,165
Wormington	Glos	SP0336	52°1·6'	1°57·0'W	T	150
Wormington Grange	Glos	SP0434	52°0·5'	1°56·1'W	X	150
Worminster	Somer	ST5742	51°10·8'	2°36·5'W	T	182,183
Worminster Sleight	Somer	ST5743	51°11·3'	2°36·5'W	H	182,183
Wormiston	Fife	NO6109	56°16·6'	2°37·3'W	X	59
Wormiston	Scot Bord	NT2345	55°41·8'	3°13·1'W	X	73
Wormistone Ho	Fife	NO6109	56°16·6'	2°37·3'W	X	59
Wormit	Fife	NO3926	56°25·6'	2°58·9'W	T	54,59
Wormit Bay	Fife	NO3825	56°25·0'	2°59·9'W	W	54,59
Wormit Fm	Fife	NO3925	56°25·1'	2°58·9'W	FM	54,59
Worm Law	S Lanak	NS9756	55°47·4'	3°38·1'W	H	65,72
Wormleighton	Warw	SP4453	52°10·6'	1°21·0'W	T	151
Wormleighton Grange Fm	Warw	SP4354	52°11·2'	1°21·9'W	FM	151
Wormleighton Hill	Warw	SP4355	52°11·7'	1°21·9'W	X	151
Wormleighton Resr	Warw	SP4451	52°9·6'	1°21·0'W	W	151
Wormleighton Village	Warw	SP4454	52°11·2'	1°21·0'W	A	151
Wormley	Herts	TL3605	51°43·9'	0°1·4'W	T	166
Wormley	Surrey	SU9438	51°8·2'	0°39·0'W	T	186
Wormleybury	Herts	TL3605	51°43·9'	0°1·4'W	T	166
Wormley Copse	Hants	SU4753	51°16·7'	1°19·2'W	F	185
Wormley Hill	Donc	SE6616	53°38·4'	0°59·7'W	X	111
Wormley West End	Herts	TL3305	51°43·9'	0°4·0'W	T	166
Wormley Wood	Herts	TL3105	51°43·9'	0°5·8'W	F	166
Wormlow Fm	Staffs	SK0256	53°6·3'	1°57·8'W	FM	119
Worms Ash	Worcs	SO9472	52°21·0'	2°4·9'W	T	139
Worms Cleuch	Scot Bord	NT3302	55°18·7'	3°2·9'W	X	79
Wormscleuch	Scot Bord	NY5999	55°17·3'	2°38·3'W	X	80
Wormscleuch Burn	Scot Bord	NT5900	55°17·8'	2°38·3'W	W	80
Worms Head (Penrhyn-Gwyr)	Swan	SS3887	51°33·8'	4°19·8'W	X	159
Worms Heath	Surrey	TQ3857	51°17·9'	0°0·8'W	X	187
Wormshell How	Cumbr	SD2097	54°22·0'	3°13·5'W	X	96
Worms Hill	Kent	TQ7339	51°7·7'	0°28·7'E	T	188
Wormshill	Kent	TQ8757	51°17·1'	0°41·3'E	T	178
Worm Sike Rigg	N Yks	SE8796	54°21·4'	0°39·3'W	X	94,101
Wormsland	Corn	SX3088	50°40·2'	4°24·0'W	X	190
Wormsland	Devon	SS9310	50°53·0'	3°30·9'W	X	192
Wormsley	Derby	SK2240	52°57·7'	1°39·9'W	X	119,128
Wormsley	Heref	SO4247	52°7·3'	2°50·4'W	T	148,149
Wormsley Grange	Heref	SO4348	52°7·9'	2°49·6'W	X	148,149
Wormsley Hill	Heref	SO4148	52°7·9'	2°51·3'W	X	148,149
Wormsley Park	Oxon	SU7394	51°38·6'	0°56·3'W	X	175
Wormstall	W Berks	SU3971	51°26·4'	1°25·9'W	X	174
Wormstone Fm	Bucks	SP7416	51°50·5'	0°55·2'W	FM	165
Wormwood Coppice	Shrops	SJ5504	52°38·2'	2°39·5'W	F	126
Wormwood Fm	Wilts	ST8467	51°24·3'	2°13·4'W	FM	173
Wormwood Hill	Cambs	TL5053	52°9·5'	0°12·0'E	X	154
Wormwood Scrubs	Ham & Ful	TQ2281	51°31·1'	0°14·1'W	X	176
Worndith Fm	Cambs	TL0968	52°18·2'	0°23·7'W	FM	153
Worner Wood	Notts	SK7659	53°7·6'	0°51·4'W	F	120
Wornish Nook	Ches	SJ8465	53°11·2'	2°14·0'W	T	118
Worplesdon	Surrey	SU9753	51°16·3'	0°36·2'W	T	186
Worplesdon Sta	Surrey	SU9855	51°17·4'	0°35·3'W	X	175,186
Worrall	Sheff	SK3092	53°25·7'	1°32·5'W	T	110,111
Worrall Hill	Glos	SO6014	51°49·6'	2°34·4'W	T	162
Worrall House Fm	Lancs	SD3506	53°33·0'	2°58·5'W	FM	108
Worry Gill	N Yks	SE8889	54°17·6'	0°38·5'W	W	94,101
Worsall Fm	Oxon	SU2294	51°38·9'	1°40·5'W	FM	163,174
Worsall Grange Fm	N Yks	NZ4009	54°28·7'	1°22·5'W	FM	93
Worsall Grove	N Yks	NZ4010	54°29·3'	1°22·5'W	X	93
Worsaw End Ho	Lancs	SD7743	53°53·2'	2°20·6'W	X	103
Worsaw Hill	Lancs	SD7743	53°53·2'	2°20·6'W	H	103
Worsbrough	Barns	SE3503	53°31·6'	1°27·9'W	T	110,111
Worsbrough Bridge	Barns	SE3503	53°31·6'	1°27·9'W	T	110,111
Worsbrough Common	Barns	SE3404	53°32·1'	1°28·8'W	T	110,111
Worsbrough Dale	Barns	SE3603	53°31·6'	1°27·0'W	T	110,111
Worsbrough Mill Country Park	Barns	SE3403	53°31·6'	1°28·8'W	X	110,111
Worsbrough Resr	Barns	SE3403	53°31·6'	1°28·8'W	W	110,111
Worsell Wood	Powys	SO2557	52°12·6'	3°5·5'W	F	148
Worsenden Fm	Kent	TQ8438	51°6·9'	0°38·1'E	FM	188
Worsham	Oxon	SP2910	51°47·5'	1°34·4'W	T	164
Worsham Fm	E Susx	TQ7509	50°51·5'	0°29·6'E	FM	199
Worships Fm	N Som	ST5063	51°22·1'	2°42·7'W	FM	172,182
Worships Fm	N Som	ST5063	51°22·1'	2°42·7'W	FM	172,182
Worsley	Salf	SD7401	53°30·5'	2°23·1'W	T	109
Worsley	Shrops	SO4596	52°33·8'	2°48·3'W	X	137,138
Worsley Fm	Worcs	SO7568	52°18·8'	2°21·6'W	FM	138
Worsley Hall	Wigan	SD5505	53°32·6'	2°40·3'W	T	108
Worsley Ho	Worcs	SO7569	52°19·3'	2°21·6'W	X	138
Worsley Mesnes	Wigan	SD5704	53°32·1'	2°38·5'W	T	108
Worsley Trail	I of W	SZ5082	50°38·4'	1°17·2'W	X	196
Worsley View Fm	Salf	SJ7194	53°26·8'	2°25·8'W	FM	109
Worstall Craggs	N Yks	SE2054	53°59·1'	1°41·3'W	X	104
Worstead	Norf	TG3026	52°47·2'	1°25·1'E	T	133,134
Worstead Sta	Norf	TG2925	52°46·7'	1°24·1'E	X	133,134
Worsted Fm	W Susx	TQ4037	51°7·1'	0°0·4'E	FM	187
Worsted Lodge	Cambs	TL5251	52°8·4'	0°13·7'E	X	154
Worsthorne	Lancs	SD8732	53°47·3'	2°11·4'W	T	103
Worsthorne Moor	Lancs	SD9030	53°46·2'	2°8·7'W	X	103
Worston	Devon	SX5953	50°21·8'	3°58·6'W	T	202
Worston	Lancs	SD7642	53°52·7'	2°21·5'W	T	103
Worston Hall	Staffs	SJ8727	52°50·7'	2°11·2'W	X	127
Worston Ho	Somer	ST3248	51°13·9'	2°58·1'W	X	182
Worswell Barton	Devon	SX5347	50°18·5'	4°3·5'W	X	201
Wortbrig Scar	Cumbr	SD1577	54°11·2'	3°17·7'W	X	96
Worten	Kent	TQ9743	51°9·4'	0°49·4'E	T	189
Worth	Devon	SS4900	50°47·0'	4°8·1'W	X	191
Worth	Kent	TR3355	51°15·0'	1°20·7'E	T	179
Worth	Somer	SS8433	51°5·3'	3°39·0'W	X	181
Worth	Somer	ST5145	51°12·4'	2°41·7'W	T	182,183
Worth	W Susx	TQ3036	51°6·7'	0°8·2'W	T	187
Wortha	Corn	SX2069	50°29·8'	4°31·9'W	X	201
Worth Abbey	W Susx	TQ3134	51°5·6'	0°7·4'W	T	187
Wortham	Devon	SX4789	50°41·1'	4°9·6'W	X	191
Wortham	Suff	TM0877	52°21·3'	1°3·7'E	T	144

Wortham Ling	Suff	TM0979	52°22·4'	1°4·6'E	X	144
Wortham Manor	Devon	SX3886	50°39·3'	4°17·1'W	A	201
Wortham Manor	Suff	TM0779	52°22·4'	1°2·9'E	X	144
Wortheal	Somer	ST2708	50°52·2'	3°1·9'W	X	193
Worthen	Devon	SS2900	50°46·7'	4°25·2'W	X	190
Worthen	Shrops	SJ3204	52°38·0'	2°59·9'W	T	126
Worthenbury	Wrex	SJ4246	53°0·7'	2°51·5'W	T	117
Worthenbury Brook	Wrex	SJ4146	53°0·7'	2°52·4'W	W	117
Worth Fm	E Susx	TQ4618	50°56·8'	0°5·1'E	FM	198
Worth Hall	W Susx	TQ3236	51°6·7'	0°6·5'W	X	187
Worth Hill	Somer	SS8333	51°5·3'	3°39·9'W	X	181
Worth Ho	Devon	SS9414	50°55·2'	3°30·1'W	X	181
Worthing	Norf	TF9919	52°44·1'	0°57·3'E	T	132
Worthing	W Susx	TQ1303	50°49·2'	0°23·4'W	T	198
Worthington	Leic	SK4020	52°46·8'	1°24·0'W	T	129
Worthlodge Forest	W Susx	TQ3035	51°6·2'	0°8·2'W	F	187
Worth Matravers	Dorset	SY9777	50°35·8'	2°2·2'W	T	195
Worth's Fm	Lincs	TF2116	52°43·9'	0°12·1'W	FM	131
Worth Way	Brad	SE0436	53°49·5'	1°55·9'W	X	104
Worth Way	W Susx	TQ3337	51°7·2'	0°5·6'W	X	187
Worthy	Devon	SX6944	50°17·1'	3°50·0'W	X	202
Worthy	Somer	SS8548	51°13·4'	3°38·4'W	T	181
Worthybrook	Monm	SO4711	51°47·9'	2°45·7'W	T	161
Worthy Down	Hants	SU4535	51°7·0'	1°21·0'W	X	185
Worthy End Fm	Beds	TL0333	51°59·4'	0°29·6'W	FM	166
Worthy Fm	Devon	SS8419	50°57·8'	3°38·7'W	FM	181
Worthy Fm	Somer	ST5940	51°9·7'	2°34·8'W	FM	182,183
Worthy Fms	S Glos	ST5585	51°34·0'	2°38·6'W	FM	172
Worthy Hill	N Yks	SD8254	53°59·1'	2°16·1'W	X	103
Worthy Hill Fm	Wilts	SU0187	51°35·1'	1°58·7'W	FM	173
Worthy Park	Hants	SU5032	51°5·3'	1°16·8'W	X	185
Worthyvale Manor	Corn	SX1086	50°38·8'	4°40·9'W	X	200
Worthy Wood	Somer	SS8547	51°12·9'	3°38·4'W	F	181
Worting	Hants	SU6052	51°16·1'	1°8·0'W	T	185
Worting Ho	Hants	SU5952	51°16·1'	1°8·9'W	X	185
Worting Wood Fm	Hants	SU6052	51°16·1'	1°8·0'W	FM	185
Wortley	Barns	SK3099	53°29·5'	1°32·5'W	T	110,111
Wortley	Glos	ST7691	51°37·3'	2°20·4'W	T	162,172
Wortley	Leeds	SE2632	53°47·3'	1°35·9'W	T	104
Wortley Hill	Glos	ST7792	51°37·8'	2°19·5'W	X	162,172
Worton	N Yks	SD9590	54°18·6'	2°4·2'W	T	98
Worton	Oxon	SP4611	51°48·0'	1°19·6'W	T	164
Worton	Wilts	ST9757	51°19·0'	2°2·2'W	T	173
Worton Common	Wilts	ST9756	51°18·4'	2°2·2'W	X	173
Worton Ho	Oxon	SP4329	51°57·7'	1°22·1'W	X	164
Worton Pasture	N Yks	SD9488	54°17·5'	2°5·1'W	X	98
Worton Wood	Oxon	SP4327	51°56·6'	1°22·1'W	F	164
Worts Hill	Kirk	SE0515	53°38·1'	1°55·1'W	H	110
Worttesley Old Park	Staffs	SJ8300	52°36·1'	2°14·7'W	X	127
Wortwell	Norf	TM2784	52°24·6'	1°20·7'E	T	156
Wort Wood	Devon	SS6836	51°6·7'	3°52·8'W	F	180
Wort Wood	Somer	ST2231	51°4·6'	3°6·4'W	F	182
Worvas Fm	Corn	SW7015	49°59·7'	5°12·2'W	FM	203
Wothersome	Leeds	SE3942	53°52·6'	1°24·0'W	X	104
Wotherton	Shrops	SJ2800	52°35·8'	3°3·4'W	T	126
Wothorpe	Peterb	TF0205	52°38·2'	0°29·2'W	T	141
Wothorpe Ho	Peterb	TF0205	52°38·2'	0°29·2'W	A	141
Wotter	Devon	SX5561	50°26·1'	4°2·1'W	T	202
Wotton	Devon	SX7266	50°29·0'	3°47·9'W	X	202
Wotton	Devon	SX7350	50°20·4'	3°46·7'W	X	202
Wotton	Devon	SX8069	50°30·7'	3°41·2'W	T	202
Wotton	Glos	SO8418	51°51·9'	2°13·5'W	T	162
Wotton	Surrey	TQ1247	51°12·9'	0°23·4'W	X	187
Wotton Common	Surrey	TQ1344	51°11·3'	0°22·6'W	F	187
Wotton Cross	Corn	SX3661	50°25·8'	4°18·2'W	X	201
Wotton Fm	Corn	SX3761	50°25·8'	4°17·3'W	FM	201
Wotton Hill	Glos	ST7593	51°38·3'	2°21·3'W	X	162,172
Wotton Ho	Bucks	SP6816	51°50·5'	1°0·4'W	X	164,165
Wotton Ho	Surrey	TQ1246	51°12·4'	0°23·4'W	X	187
Wotton-under-Edge	Glos	ST7692	51°37·8'	2°20·4'W	T	162,172
Wotton Underwood	Bucks	SP6815	51°50·0'	1°0·4'W	T	164,165
Wottri	Shetld	HU3782	60°31·5'	1°19·1'W	X	1,2,3
Woughton on the Green	Mil Key	SP8737	52°1·7'	0°43·5'W	T	152
Woughton Park	Mil Key	SP8836	52°1·2'	0°42·7'W	X	152
Wouldham	Kent	TQ7164	51°21·2'	0°27·7'E	T	178,188
Wouldham Marshes	Medway	TQ7166	51°22·3'	0°27·8'E	X	178
Woundale	Cumbr	NY4107	54°27·5'	2°54·2'W	X	90
Woundale	Shrops	SO7792	52°31·8'	2°19·9'W	T	138
Woundale Beck	Cumbr	NY4107	54°27·5'	2°54·2'W	W	90
Woundales	N Yks	SE4389	54°17·9'	1°19·9'W	X	99
Wou, The	Northum	NY6770	55°1·7'	2°30·5'W	W	86,87
Wrabness	Essex	TM1731	51°56·3'	1°9·8'E	T	168,169
Wrabness Hall	Essex	TM1731	51°56·3'	1°9·8'E	X	168,169
Wrackleford	Dorset	SY6693	50°44·4'	2°28·5'W	X	194
Wracombe Fm	Devon	SX9388	50°41·1'	3°30·5'W	FM	192
Wrae	Aberd	NJ7252	57°33·7'	2°27·6'W	X	29
Wrae	D & G	NY3687	55°10·6'	2°59·9'W	X	79
Wrae Fm	Scot Bord	NT1133	55°35·2'	3°24·3'W	FM	72
Wrae Hill	D & G	NY3689	55°11·7'	2°59·9'W	H	79
Wrae Hill	Scot Bord	NT1132	55°34·7'	3°24·3'W	H	72
Wraes	Aberd	NJ5831	57°22·3'	2°41·4'W	X	29,37
Wraes	E Ayr	NS4838	55°37·0'	4°24·4'W	X	70
Wraes	E Renf	NS4957	55°47·2'	4°24·1'W	X	64
Wraes	Renf	NS3968	55°53·0'	4°34·0'W	X	63
Wraes, The	Cumbr	NY6614	54°31·5'	2°31·1'W	X	91
Wrafton	Devon	SS4935	51°5·9'	4°9·0'W	T	180
Wragby	Lincs	TF1378	53°17·4'	0°17·9'W	T	121
Wragby	Wakf	SE4117	53°39·1'	1°22·4'W	T	111
Wragby Fm	N Yks	NZ9300	54°23·6'	0°33·6'W	FM	94
Wragby Wood	N Yks	SE9399	54°22·9'	0°33·7'W	F	94,101
Wragg Marsh Ho	Lincs	TF2930	52°51·4'	0°4·6'W	X	131
Wragg's Fm	Cambs	TL3250	52°8·2'	0°3·9'W	FM	153
Wragholme	Lincs	TF3797	53°27·3'	0°4·2'E	T	113
Wragmire Bank	Cumbr	NY4550	54°50·8'	2°51·0'W	X	86
Wragmire Head	Cumbr	NY4548	54°49·7'	2°50·9'W	X	86
Wragmire Ho	Cumbr	NY4649	54°50·2'	2°50·0'W	X	86
Wragmire Moss	Cumbr	NY4549	54°50·2'	2°51·0'W	X	86
Wrakendike (Roman Road)	Gshead	NZ3061	54°56·8'	1°31·5'W	R	88
Wrakes Fm	Sefton	SD3301	53°30·3'	3°0·2'W	FM	108
Wramplingham	Norf	TG1106	52°36·9'	1°7·4'E	T	144

Wrampool Ho	Lancs	SD4249	53°56·3′	2°52·6′W	X	102
Wrancarr Ho	Donc	SE5912	53°36·3′	1°6·1′W	X	111
Wrangaton	Devon	SX6757	50°24·1′	3°51·9′W	T	202
Wrang Beck	N Yks	SE0989	54°18·0′	1°51·3′W	W	99
Wrangbrook	Wakf	SE4913	53°36·9′	1°15·1′W	T	111
Wrangham	Aberd	NJ6331	57°22·3′	2°36·5′W	X	29,37
Wrangham	Northum	NU0034	55°36·2′	1°59·6′W	X	75
Wranglands	E Yorks	TA2029	53°44·8′	0°10·4′W	X	107
Wrangle	Lincs	TF4251	53°2·5′	0°7·5′E	T	122
Wrangle Bank	Lincs	TF4253	53°3·6′	0°7·5′E	T	122
Wrangle Bank Fm	Lincs	TF4354	53°4·1′	0°8·5′E	FM	122
Wrangle Common	Lincs	TF4154	53°4·1′	0°6·7′E	X	122
Wrangle Flats	Lincs	TF4648	53°0·8′	0°11·0′E	X	131
Wrangle Hall	Lincs	TF4350	53°1·9′	0°8·4′E	X	122
Wrangle Lowgate	Lincs	TF4351	53°2·5′	0°8·4′E	T	122
Wrangle Low Ground	Lincs	TF4252	53°3·0′	0°7·5′E	T	122
Wrangle Point	Corn	SS2007	50°50·3′	4°33·0′W	X	190
Wrangle Tofts	Lincs	TF4451	53°2·4′	0°9·3′E	X	122
Wrangling Corner	Cambs	TL4160	52°13·4′	0°4·3′E	X	154
Wrangway	Somer	ST1217	50°57·0′	3°14·8′W	T	181,193
Wrangway Burn	Scot Bord	NY3799	55°17·1′	2°59·1′W	W	79
Wrangworthy	Devon	SS3212	50°53·2′	4°22·9′W	X	190
Wrangworthy Cross	Devon	SS3817	50°56·0′	4°18·0′W	X	190
Wrantage	Somer	ST3022	50°59·8′	2°59·5′W	T	193
Wrasford	Corn	SS2613	50°53·7′	4°28·1′W	X	190
Wrasford Moor	Corn	SS2514	50°54·2′	4°29·0′W	F	190
Wra, The or Three Stone Oar	Corn	SW3736	50°10·2′	5°40·6′W	X	203
Wrawby	N Lincs	TA0208	53°33·8′	0°27·2′W	T	112
Wrawby Carrs	N Lincs	TA0009	53°34·3′	0°29·0′W	X	112
Wrawby Moor	N Lincs	TA0310	53°34·8′	0°26·2′W	X	112
Wraxall	Dorset	ST5601	50°48·6′	2°37·1′W	T	194
Wraxall	N Som	ST4971	51°26·4′	2°43·6′W	T	172
Wraxall	Somer	ST6036	51°7·5′	2°33·9′W	T	183
Wraxall Court	N Som	ST4872	51°26·9′	2°44·5′W	X	171,172
Wraxall Hill	Somer	ST7844	51°11·9′	2°18·5′W	X	183
Wraxall Ho	N Som	ST4871	51°26·4′	2°44·5′W	X	171,172
Wray	Lancs	SD6067	54°6·1′	2°36·3′W	T	97
Wray Barton	Devon	SX7784	50°38·8′	3°44·0′W	X	191
Wray Castle	Cumbr	NY3700	54°23·7′	2°57·8′W	X	90
Wray Common	Surrey	TQ2650	51°14·3′	0°11·3′W	T	187
Wray Cott	Cumbr	SD4880	54°13·0′	2°47·4′W	X	97
Wray Fm	Cumbr	SD5694	54°20·6′	2°40·2′W	FM	97
Wray Ho	Cambs	TL2063	52°15·4′	0°14·1′W	X	153
Wray Ho	N Yks	SE3999	54°23·3′	1°23·5′W	X	99
Wray Ho	N Yks	SE8179	54°12·3′	0°45·1′W	X	100
Wrays	Surrey	TQ2544	51°11·1′	0°12·3′W	X	187
Wraysbury	Win & Maid	TQ0074	51°27·6′	0°33·2′W	T	176
Wraysbury Reservoir	Surrey	TQ0274	51°27·6′	0°31·5′W	W	176
Wraysbury River	Surrey	TQ0273	51°27·0′	0°31·5′W	W	176
Wraysholme Tower	Cumbr	SD3875	54°10·3′	2°56·6′W	A	96,97
Wrayside	Cumbr	NY4751	54°51·3′	2°49·1′W	X	86
Wrayton	Lancs	SD6172	54°8·8′	2°35·4′W	T	97
Waywick Fm	Essex	TQ9899	51°39·5′	0°52·2′E	FM	168
Wray Wood Moor	Lancs	SD6165	54°5·0′	2°35·4′W	X	97
Wrea Brook	Lancs	SD3829	53°45·5′	2°56·0′W	W	102
Wrea Green	Lancs	SD3931	53°46·6′	2°55·1′W	T	102
Wreah	Cumbr	NY0017	54°32·6′	3°32·3′W	X	89
Wreake House Fm	Leic	SK6213	52°42·9′	1°4·5′W	FM	129
Wreaks Beck	N Yks	SE2075	54°10·5′	1°41·2′W	W	99
Wreaks End	Cumbr	SD2286	54°16·1′	3°11·4′W	T	96
Wreath	Somer	ST3408	50°52·3′	2°55·9′W	T	193
Wreaths	Angus	NO3944	56°35·3′	2°59·1′W	T	54
Wreaths Burn	D & G	NY0289	55°11·4′	3°31·9′W	W	78
Wreaton	Aberd	NJ7415	57°13·8′	2°25·4′W	X	38
Wreaton	Aberd	NO5099	57°5·0′	2°49·0′W	X	37,44
Wreay	Cumbr	NY4348	54°49·7′	2°52·8′W	T	85
Wreay	Cumbr	NY4423	54°36·2′	2°51·6′W	T	90
Wreay	Cumbr	NY5359	54°55·7′	2°43·6′W	X	86
Wreay Hall	Cumbr	NY4448	54°49·7′	2°51·9′W	X	85
Wreay Hill	Cumbr	NY6476	55°4·9′	2°33·4′W	X	86
Wreay, The	Cumbr	NY2445	54°47·9′	3°10·5′W	X	85
Wrecclesham	Surrey	SU8244	51°11·6′	0°49·2′W	T	186
Wreck Bay	Highld	NM3098	56°59·9′	6°26·3′W	W	39
Wrecked Craigs	E Loth	NT4076	55°58·6′	2°57·2′W	X	66
Wrecsam or Wrexham	Wrex	SJ3350	53°2·8′	2°59·6′W	T	117
Wredon	Staffs	SK0846	53°0·9′	1°52·4′W	X	119,128
Wreigh Burn	Northum	NU0103	55°19·5′	1°58·6′W	W	81
Wreighburn Ho	Northum	NU0301	55°18·4′	1°56·7′W	X	81
Wreighill	Northum	NT9701	55°18·4′	2°2·4′W	X	81
Wreighill Pike	Northum	NT9802	55°19·0′	2°1·5′W	H	81
Wrekenton	Ghead	NZ2759	54°55·7′	1°34·3′W	T	88
Wrekin Fm	Wrekin	SJ6307	52°39·8′	2°32·4′W	FM	127
Wrekin Fm	Wrekin	SJ6309	52°40·9′	2°32·4′W	FM	127
Wrekin, The	Wrekin	SJ6208	52°40·3′	2°33·3′W	H	127
Wrelton	N Yks	SE7686	54°16·1′	0°49·6′W	T	94,100
Wrenbury	Ches	SJ5947	53°1·4′	2°36·3′W	T	117
Wrenbury Heath	Ches	SJ6048	53°1·9′	2°35·4′W	X	118
Wrenbury Sta	Ches	SJ6047	53°1·4′	2°35·4′W	X	118
Wrenburywood	Ches	SJ5948	53°1·9′	2°36·3′W	X	117
Wrench Green	N Yks	SE9689	54°17·5′	0°31·1′W	X	94,101
Wren Gill	Cumbr	NY4708	54°28·1′	2°48·6′W	W	90
Wren Hill Fm	Derby	SK5064	53°10·5′	1°14·7′W	FM	120
Wreningham	Norf	TM1598	52°32·5′	1°10·6′E	T	144
Wrenmore Fm	Somer	ST2341	51°10·0′	3°5·7′W	FM	182
Wren Park	Beds	TL1538	52°1·9′	0°19·0′W	X	153
Wren Park	Essex	TL7519	51°50·8′	0°32·8′E	X	167
Wrenpark Wood	Essex	TL7737	52°0·4′	0°35·1′E	F	155
Wren's Castle	V of Glam	ST0372	51°26·6′	3°23·4′W	X	170
Wrens Fm	Kent	TQ8861	51°19·2′	0°42·3′E	FM	178
Wrenshall Fm	Suff	TL9872	52°18·8′	0°54·7′E	FM	144,155
Wrenside	Cumbr	NY8409	54°28·8′	2°14·4′W	X	91,92
Wren's Nest	Wals	SP0497	52°34·5′	1°56·1′W	X	139
Wren's Nest Hill	Dudley	SO9391	52°31·2′	2°5·8′W	H	139
Wrens Park Fm	Thurr	TQ6784	51°32·0′	0°24·9′E	FM	177,178
Wren's Warren	E Susx	TQ4732	51°4·3′	0°6·3′E	X	188
Wrentham	Suff	TM4982	52°23·0′	1°39·9′E	T	156
Wrentham Great Wood	Suff	TM4983	52°23·5′	1°40·0′E	F	156
Wrentham West End	Suff	TM4784	52°24·1′	1°38·3′E	X	156
Wrenthorpe	Wakf	SE3122	53°41·9′	1°31·4′W	T	104
Wrentnall	Shrops	SJ4203	52°37·5′	2°51·0′W	T	126
Wrescombe	Devon	SX5650	50°20·2′	4°1·0′W	X	202
Wressing	Devon	ST0608	50°52·1′	3°19·8′W	X	192
Wressle	E Yorks	SE7131	53°46·5′	0°54·9′W	T	105,106
Wressle	N Lincs	SE9709	53°34·4′	0°31·7′W	T	112
Wressle Fm	N Lincs	SE9709	53°34·4′	0°31·7′W	FM	112
Wressle Grange	E Yorks	SE7131	53°46·5′	0°54·9′W	X	105,106
Wressle Ho	N Lincs	SE9709	53°34·4′	0°31·7′W	X	112
Wrest Ho	Beds	TL0935	52°0·4′	0°24·3′W	X	153
Wrestle Gill	Cumbr	SD6587	54°16·9′	2°31·8′W	W	97
Wrestlers Fm	Staffs	SJ8213	52°43·1′	2°15·6′W	FM	127
Wrestlingworth	Beds	TL2547	52°6·7′	0°10·1′W	T	153
Wrest Park	Beds	TL0935	52°0·4′	0°24·3′W	X	153
Wretchwick Fm	Oxon	SP5920	51°52·8′	1°8·2′W	FM	164
Wretham Belt	Norf	TL8992	52°29·8′	0°47·5′E	F	144
Wretham Park	Norf	TL9091	52°29·3′	0°48·3′E	X	144
Wretton	Norf	TL6899	52°34·0′	0°29·1′E	T	143
Wretton Fen Ho	Norf	TL6898	52°33·5′	0°29·1′E	X	143
Wretts Fm	Suff	TM2272	52°18·3′	1°15·8′E	FM	156
Wrexham Industrial Estate	Wrex	SJ3849	53°2·3′	2°55·1′W	X	117
Wrexham or Wrecsam	Wrex	SJ3350	53°2·8′	2°59·6′W	T	117
Wrexham Street	Bucks	SU9983	51°32·5′	0°34·0′W	T	175,176
Wreyland	Devon	SX7881	50°37·2′	3°43·1′W	T	191
Wreys Barton	Devon	SX4386	50°39·4′	4°12·9′W	X	201
Wribbenhall	Worcs	SO7975	52°22·6′	2°18·1′W	T	138
Wrickton	Shrops	SO6485	52°27·9′	2°31·4′W	T	138
Wriggle River	Dorset	ST6007	50°51·9′	2°33·7′W	W	194
Wright Green	Cumbr	NY0621	54°34·8′	3°26·8′W	X	89
Wrighthill	E Ayr	NS4322	55°28·3′	4°28·6′W	X	70
Wrightington	Lancs	SD5212	53°36·4′	2°43·1′W	X	108
Wrightington Bar	Lancs	SD5313	53°36·9′	2°42·2′W	T	108
Wrightpark	Stir	NS6492	56°6·3′	4°10·8′W	X	57
Wright's Fm	Ches	SJ9979	53°18·7′	2°0·5′W	FM	118
Wright's Fm	Essex	TL7432	51°57·8′	0°32·4′E	FM	167
Wright's Fm	Suff	TM2257	52°10·2′	1°15·2′E	FM	156
Wright's Fm	W Berks	SU3661	51°21·0′	1°28·6′W	FM	174
Wright's Green	Essex	TL5017	51°50·1′	0°11·0′E	T	167
Wrights Green	Warr	SJ6384	53°21·3′	2°32·9′W	T	109
Wright's Houses	Midlo	NT3660	55°50·0′	3°0·9′W	X	66
Wright's Island	S Ayr	NS1902	55°17·0′	4°50·6′W	X	76
Wright's Lodge	Rut	SK8212	52°42·2′	0°46·8′W	X	130
Wrigwell	Devon	SX8171	50°31·8′	3°40·4′W	X	202
Wrigwell Hill	Devon	SX8465	50°28·6′	3°37·7′W	X	202
Wrimstone	Devon	SS6128	51°2·3′	3°58·6′W	X	180
Wrinehill	Staffs	SJ7547	53°1·4′	2°22·0′W	T	118
Wrinehill Hall	Staffs	SJ7545	53°0·3′	2°21·9′W	X	118
Wrinehill Wood	Staffs	SJ7544	52°59·8′	2°21·9′W	F	118
Wringapeak	Devon	SS6749	51°13·7′	3°53·9′W	X	180
Wringcliff Bay	Devon	SS7049	51°13·8′	3°51·3′W	W	180
Wringsdown	Corn	SX3187	50°39·7′	4°23·1′W	T	190
Wringsland	Devon	SS8610	50°52·9′	3°36·9′W	X	191
Wrington	N Som	ST4762	51°21·5′	2°45·3′W	T	172,182
Wrington Hill	N Som	ST4764	51°22·6′	2°45·3′W	X	172,182
Wrington Warren	N Som	ST4765	51°23·1′	2°45·3′W	F	171,172,182
Wringworthy	Corn	SX2658	50°24·0′	4°26·5′W	X	201
Wringworthy Fm	Devon	SX5077	50°34·6′	4°6·7′W	FM	191,201
Wrinkleberry	Devon	SS3124	50°59·7′	4°24·1′W	T	190
Wrinsted Court	Kent	TQ8955	51°16·0′	0°42·9′E	X	178
Wrinstone Fm	V of Glam	ST1372	51°26·7′	3°14·7′W	FM	171
Writh Fm	Dorset	ST8620	50°59·0′	2°11·6′W	FM	183
Writhlington	Somer	ST7054	51°17·3′	2°25·4′W	T	183
Written Crag	Northum	NY9368	55°0·6′	2°6·1′W	X	87
Written Stone	Lancs	SD6237	53°49·9′	2°34·2′W	A	102,103
Writtle	Essex	TL6706	51°43·9′	0°25·5′E	T	167
Writtle Park	Essex	TL6403	51°42·3′	0°22·8′E	X	167
Wrixhill	Devon	SX3779	50°35·5′	4°17·8′W	X	201
Wrixhill	Devon	SX4690	50°41·6′	4°10·4′W	A	190
Wrockwardine	Wrekin	SJ6211	52°42·0′	2°33·3′W	T	127
Wrockwardine Wood	Wrekin	SJ7011	52°42·0′	2°26·2′W	T	127
Wroford Manor	Devon	SX9992	50°43·4′	3°25·5′W	X	192
Wrongs, The	Northnts	SP6682	52°26·2′	1°1·3′W	X	141
Wroo Fm	Norf	TM0293	52°30·1′	0°59·0′E	FM	144
Wroot	N Lincs	SE7103	53°31·4′	0°55·3′W	T	112
Wroot Grange	N Lincs	SE7101	53°30·3′	0°55·4′W	X	112
Wrose	Brad	SE1637	53°50·0′	1°45·0′W	T	104
Wrotham	Kent	TQ6059	51°18·7′	0°18·1′E	T	188
Wrotham Heath	Kent	TQ6358	51°18·1′	0°20·7′E	T	188
Wrotham Hill Park	Kent	TQ6160	51°19·2′	0°19·0′E	X	177,188
Wrotham Park	Herts	TQ2499	51°40·8′	0°12·0′W	X	166,176
Wrotham Water	Kent	TQ6259	51°18·6′	0°19·9′E	X	188
Wrottesley Hall	Staffs	SJ8501	52°36·6′	2°12·9′W	A	127,139
Wrottesley Lodge Fm	Staffs	SJ8301	52°36·6′	2°14·7′W	FM	127
Wrottesley Wood	Suff	TL8877	52°21·8′	0°46·1′E	F	144
Wroughton	Swin	SU1480	51°31·4′	1°47·5′W	T	173
Wroughton Airfield	Swin	SU1378	51°30·3′	1°48·4′W	X	173
Wroxall	I of W	SZ5579	50°36·7′	1°13·0′W	T	196
Wroxall Manor Fm	I of W	SZ5579	50°36·7′	1°13·0′W	FM	196
Wroxeter	Shrops	SJ5608	52°40·3′	2°38·6′W	T	126
Wroxhall	Warw	SP2271	52°20·4′	1°40·2′W	T	139
Wroxhall Abbey (sch)	Warw	SP2270	52°19·9′	1°40·2′W	X	139
Wroxham	Norf	TG3017	52°42·3′	1°24·7′E	T	133,134
Wroxham Barns Craft Centre	Norf	TG3020	52°43·9′	1°24·8′E	X	133,134
Wroxham Broad	Norf	TG3116	52°41·8′	1°25·5′E	W	133,134
Wroxhills Wood	Oxon	SU6181	51°31·7′	1°6·8′W	F	175
Wroxton	Oxon	SP4141	52°4·2′	1°23·7′W	T	151
Wroxton Abbey	Oxon	SP4141	52°4·2′	1°23·7′W	A	151
Wrunk Law	Scot Bord	NT6758	55°49·1′	2°31·2′W	H	67,74
Wryde Croft	Peterb	TF3206	52°38·4′	0°2·5′W	X	142
Wrydelands Fm	Peterb	TF3107	52°38·9′	0°3·4′W	FM	142
Wry Gill	Cumbr	SD7789	54°18·0′	2°20·8′W	X	98
Wrynose Bottom	Cumbr	NY2501	54°24·2′	3°8·9′W	X	89,90
Wrynose Breast	Cumbr	NY2602	54°24·7′	3°8·0′W	X	89,90
Wrynose Fell	Cumbr	NY2704	54°25·8′	3°7·1′W	X	89,90
Wrynose Pass	Cumbr	NY2702	54°24·7′	3°7·1′W	X	89,90
Wrytree	Northum	NY6764	54°58·4′	2°30·5′W	X	86,87
Wstrws	Cered	SN3849	52°7·2′	4°21·6′W	X	145
Wuddy Law	Angus	NO6252	56°39·8′	2°36·7′W	H	54
Wuddy, The	Scot Bord	NT9268	55°54·6′	2°7·2′W	X	67
Wull Muir	Scot Bord	NT3554	55°46·8′	3°1·7′W	X	66,73
Wurlus Burn	Scot Bord	NT3428	55°32·7′	3°2·3′W	W	73
Wurs Stack	Shetld	HP6117	60°50·1′	0°52·2′W	X	1
Wurt Pit	Somer	ST5553	51°16·7′	2°38·3′W	X	182,183
Wyards Fm	Hants	SU6938	51°8·5′	1°0·4′W	FM	186
Wyaston	Derby	SK1842	52°58·7′	1°43·5′W	T	119,128
Wyastone Leys	Heref	SO5315	51°50·1′	2°40·5′W	X	162
Wyaston Grove	Derby	SK1942	52°58·7′	1°42·6′W	X	119,128
Wyatts	W Susx	TQ3827	51°1·8′	0°1·5′W	X	187,198
Wyatt's Green	Essex	TQ5999	51°40·3′	0°18·4′E	T	167,177
Wyber Hill	Cumbr	NY7611	54°29·9′	2°21·8′W	X	91
Wybersley Hall	Stock	SJ9685	53°22·0′	2°3·2′W	X	109
Wybers Wood	NE Lincs	TA2209	53°34·0′	0°9·1′W	F	113
Wybers Wood	NE Lincs	TA2308	53°33·5′	0°8·2′W	T	113
Wyberton	Lincs	TF3141	52°57·3′	0°2·6′W	T	131
Wyberton Fen	Lincs	TF2943	52°58·4′	0°4·3′W	X	131
Wyberton Marsh	Lincs	TF3539	52°56·1′	0°0·9′E	X	131
Wybert's Castle	Lincs	TF3340	52°56·7′	0°0·8′W	X	131
Wybert's Castle (Earthwork)	Lincs	TF3340	52°56·7′	0°0·8′W	A	131
Wyborne's Charity	Kent	TR2459	51°17·4′	1°13·2′E	X	179
Wyboston	Beds	TL1656	52°11·6′	0°17·8′W	T	153
Wyboston Fm	Cambs	TL2368	52°18·0′	0°11·4′W	FM	153
Wyboston Leisure Park	Beds	TL1757	52°12·2′	0°16·9′W	X	153
Wybournes Fm	Medway	TQ7775	51°27·0′	0°33·2′E	FM	178
Wybunbury	Ches	SJ6949	53°2·5′	2°27·3′W	T	118
Wybunbury Grange	Ches	SJ6950	53°3·0′	2°27·3′W	X	118
Wycar Leys	Notts	SK6559	53°7·7′	1°1·3′W	X	120
Wych	Dorset	SY4790	50°42·7′	2°44·7′W	X	193
Wychanger	Somer	SS9144	51°11·3′	3°33·2′W	X	181
Wychavon Way	Glos	SP0128	51°57·3′	1°58·7′W	X	150,163
Wychavon Way	Worcs	SO9854	52°11·3′	2°1·4′W	X	150
Wychbold	Worcs	SO9265	52°17·2′	2°6·6′W	T	150
Wych Brook	Ches	SJ4744	52°59·7′	2°47·0′W	W	117
Wychbury	Dudley	SO9181	52°25·9′	2°7·5′W	A	139
Wychbury Hill	Worcs	SO9281	52°25·9′	2°6·7′W	H	139
Wych Channel	Dorset	SY9887	50°41·2′	2°1·3′W	W	195
Wych Cross	E Susx	TQ4131	51°3·9′	0°1·1′E	T	187
Wych Cross Place	E Susx	TQ4131	51°3·9′	0°1·1′E	X	187
Wychdon Lodge	Staffs	SJ9825	52°49·6′	2°1·4′W	X	127
Wyche	Lincs	TF5269	53°12·0′	0°16·9′E	X	122
Wycherley Hall	Shrops	SJ4127	52°50·5′	2°52·2′W	X	126
Wych Fm	Ches	SJ9179	53°18·7′	2°7·7′W	FM	118
Wych Mill	Wrex	SJ5043	52°59·2′	2°44·3′W	X	117
Wychnor	Staffs	SK1716	52°44·7′	1°44·5′W	T	128
Wychnor Bridges	Staffs	SK1816	52°44·7′	1°43·6′W	T	128
Wychnor Park	Staffs	SK1616	52°44·7′	1°45·4′W	X	128
Wychroft Ho	Surrey	TQ3449	51°13·7′	0°4·5′W	X	187
Wychwood Fm	W Susx	TQ2018	50°57·2′	0°17·1′W	FM	198
Wychwood Forest	Oxon	SP3317	51°51·3′	1°30·9′W	F	164
Wyck	Hants	SU7539	51°8·9′	0°55·3′W	T	186
Wyck Beacon	Glos	SP2020	51°52·9′	1°42·2′W	X	163
Wyck Beacon (Tumulus)	Glos	SP2020	51°52·9′	1°42·2′W	A	163
Wycke Fm	Essex	TL9309	51°45·0′	0°48·2′E	FM	168
Wyck Hall Stud	Suff	TL6362	52°14·1′	0°23·6′E	X	154
Wyckham Fm	W Susx	TQ1813	50°54·5′	0°18·9′W	FM	198
Wyckham Wood	W Susx	TQ1914	50°55·0′	0°18·0′W	F	198
Wyck Hill	Glos	SP1922	51°54·0′	1°43·0′W	X	163
Wyck Place	Hants	SU7539	51°8·9′	0°55·3′W	X	186
Wyck Rissington	Glos	SP1921	51°53·5′	1°43·0′W	T	163
Wyck, The	Herts	TL2026	51°55·4′	0°14·9′W	A	166
Wyck Village	Wilts	ST9428	51°3·3′	2°4·8′W	A	184
Wycliffe	Durham	NZ1114	54°31·5′	1°49·4′W	T	92
Wycliffe Centre	Bucks	SU7894	51°38·6′	0°52·0′W	X	175
Wycliffe Plantn	E Yorks	TA1735	53°48·1′	0°13·0′W	F	107
Wycliffe Wood	Durham	NZ1214	54°31·5′	1°48·5′W	F	92
Wycoller	Lancs	SD9339	53°51·1′	2°6·0′W	T	103
Wycomb	Leic	SK7724	52°48·7′	0°51·1′W	T	129
Wycombe Air Park	Bucks	SU8290	51°36·4′	0°48·6′W	X	175
Wycombe Marsh	Bucks	SU8891	51°36·9′	0°43·3′W	T	175
Wycongill	Lancs	SD7750	53°57·0′	2°20·6′W	X	103
Wydale Cote	N Yks	SE9184	54°14·9′	0°35·8′W	X	101
Wydale Hall	N Yks	SE9283	54°14·3′	0°34·9′W	X	101
Wydale High Fm	N Yks	SE9283	54°14·3′	0°34·9′W	FM	101
Wydcombe	I of W	SZ5078	50°36·2′	1°17·2′W	X	196
Wyddgrug	Gwyn	SH2836	52°53·9′	4°33·0′W	X	123
Wyddial	Herts	TL3731	51°57·9′	0°0·0′E	T	166
Wyddial Hall	Herts	TL3731	51°57·9′	0°0·0′E	A	166
Wydon	Northum	NY6963	54°57·9′	2°28·6′W	X	86,87
Wydon Burn	Northum	NY9263	54°57·9′	2°7·1′W	X	87
Wydoncleughside	Northum	NY6664	54°58·4′	2°31·4′W	X	86
Wydon Eals	Northum	NY6862	54°57·3′	2°29·6′W	X	86,87
Wydon Fm	Somer	SS9347	51°13·0′	3°31·5′W	FM	181
Wydra	N Yks	SE2054	53°59·1′	1°41·3′W	T	104
Wye	Kent	TR0546	51°10·8′	0°56·4′E	T	179,189
Wyebanks	Kent	TQ9354	51°15·4′	0°46·4′E	T	189
Wyebourne	Cumbr	NY5916	54°32·5′	2°37·6′W	X	91
Wyecliff	Powys	SO2242	52°4·5′	3°7·9′W	X	148,161
Wye Court	Kent	TR0547	51°11·3′	0°56·4′E	X	179,189
Wye Dale	Derby	SK1072	53°14·9′	1°50·6′W	X	119
Wye Downs	Kent	TR0746	51°10·8′	0°58·1′E	X	179,189
Wye Fm	Derby	SK2565	53°11·1′	1°37·1′W	FM	119
Wyeford Fm	Hants	SU6058	51°19·3′	1°7·9′W	FM	175
Wyegarth Gill	Cumbr	NY7102	54°25·0′	2°26·4′W	W	91
Wyegate Green	Glos	SO5506	51°45·3′	2°38·7′W	T	162
Wyegate Hill	Glos	SO5506	51°45·3′	2°38·7′W	X	162
Wyelands	Monm	ST5291	51°37·2′	2°41·2′W	X	162,172
Wyelea	Heref	SO5825	51°55·6′	2°36·3′W	X	162
Wyeseal Fm	Glos	SO5406	51°45·3′	2°39·6′W	FM	162
Wyesham	Monm	SO5112	51°48·5′	2°42·3′W	T	162
Wyes Wood Common	Monm	SO5102	51°43·1′	2°42·2′W	X	162
Wye Valley	Powys	SN8780	52°24·6′	3°39·3′W	X	135,136
Wye Valley Walk	Heref	SO3842	52°4·6′	2°53·9′W	X	148,149,161
Wye Valley Walk	Monm	SO5204	51°44·2′	2°41·3′W	X	162
Wye Valley Walk	Monm	ST5395	51°39·3′	2°40·4′W	X	162
Wye Valley Walk	Powys	SO0743	52°4·9′	3°21·0′W	X	147,160
Wye Valley Walk	Powys	SO1539	52°2·8′	3°14·0′W	X	161
Wyfield Manor Fm	W Berks	SU4472	51°26·9′	1°21·6′W	FM	174
Wyfields Fm	Thurr	TQ6584	51°32·1′	0°23·1′E	FM	177,178
Wyfold Grange	Oxon	SU6881	51°31·7′	1°0·8′W	X	175
Wyfordby	Leic	SK7918	52°45·5′	0°49·4′W	T	129

Wyfordby Grange	Leic	SK7919	52°46·0′	0°49·3′W	X	129
Wygston's Ho	C of Leic	SK5804	52°38·1′	1°8·2′W	X	140
Wyham	Lincs	TF2795	53°26·4′	0°4·9′W	X	113
Wyham Ho	Lincs	TF2795	53°26·4′	0°4·9′W	X	113
Wyham House Fm	Lincs	TF2694	53°25·9′	0°5·8′W	FM	113
Wyke	Brad	SE1526	53°44·1′	1°45·9′W	T	104
Wyke	Devon	SX8799	50°47·0′	3°35·8′W	X	192
Wyke	Dorset	ST7926	51°2·2′	2°17·6′W	T	183
Wyke	Shrops	SJ6402	52°37·1′	2°31·5′W	T	127
Wyke	Surrey	SU9251	51°15·3′	0°40·5′W	T	186
Wyke Champflower	Somer	ST6634	51°6·5′	2°28·8′W	T	183
Wyke Common	Surrey	SU9152	51°15·8′	0°41·4′W	X	186
Wyke Down	Dorset	SU0015	50°56·3′	1°59·6′W	X	184
Wyke Down	Wilts	SU0015	50°56·3′	1°59·6′W	X	184
Wyke Fm	Cumbr	SD3874	54°9·7′	2°56·6′W	FM	96,97
Wyke Fm	Dorset	ST5007	50°51·9′	2°42·2′W	FM	194
Wyke Fm	Dorset	ST6014	50°55·7′	2°33·8′W	FM	194
Wyke Fm	Dorset	SU0113	50°55·2′	1°58·8′W	FM	195
Wyke Green	Devon	SY3096	50°45·8′	2°59·2′W	T	193
Wyke Green Fm	Hants	SU7226	51°2·0′	0°58·0′W	FM	186,197
Wykeham	Lincs	TF2726	52°49·2′	0°6·5′W	T	131
Wykeham	N Yks	SE8175	54°10·1′	0°45·1′W	T	100
Wykeham	N Yks	SE9683	54°14·3′	0°31·2′W	T	101
Wykeham Abbey	N Yks	SE9681	54°13·2′	0°31·2′W	X	101
Wykeham Carr Fm	N Yks	SE9680	54°12·6′	0°31·3′W	FM	101
Wykeham Forest	N Yks	SE9488	54°17·0′	0°32·9′W	F	94,101
Wykeham Grange	N Yks	SE9585	54°15·3′	0°32·1′W	X	94,101
Wykeham Hall	Lincs	TF2288	53°22·7′	0°9·5′W	X	113,122
Wykeham Moor Cotts	N Yks	SE9486	54°15·9′	0°33·0′W	X	94,101
Wyke Hey Fm	Lancs	SD3817	53°39·0′	2°55·9′W	FM	108
Wyke Ho	Somer	ST6534	51°6·5′	2°29·6′W	X	183
Wyke House Fm	Lancs	SD3816	53°38·5′	2°55·9′W	FM	108
Wykehurst Park	W Susx	TQ2624	51°0·3′	0°11·9′W	X	198
Wyke Lodge	N Yks	SE9997	54°21·8′	0°28·2′W	X	94,101
Wyke Moor Cross	Devon	SX6697	50°45·7′	3°53·6′W	X	191
Wyken	Cov	SP3680	52°25·2′	1°27·8′W	T	140
Wyken	Shrops	SO7694	52°32·8′	2°20·8′W	T	138
Wyken Fm	Worcs	SO9166	52°17·8′	2°7·5′W	FM	150
Wyken Hall	Suff	TL9671	52°18·4′	0°52·9′E	X	144,155
Wyken Vineyard	Suff	TL9671	52°18·4′	0°52·9′E	X	144,155
Wyken Vineyard	Suff	TL9671	52°18·4′	0°52·9′E	X	144,155
Wyken Wood	Suff	TL9671	52°18·4′	0°52·9′E	F	144,155
Wyke Regis	Dorset	SY6677	50°35·7′	2°28·4′W	T	194
Wyke Road Fm	Lancs	SD3714	53°37·4′	2°56·7′W	FM	108
Wykes Fm	Lincs	TF2235	52°54·1′	0°10·8′W	FM	131
Wykes Manor Fm	Lincs	TF2335	52°54·1′	0°9·9′W	FM	131
Wyke, The	Cumbr	NY3306	54°26·9′	3°1·6′W	X	90
Wyke, The	N Yks	TA1082	54°13·6′	0°18·3′W	W	101
Wyke Thorn Fm	Lancs	SD3816	53°38·5′	2°55·9′W	FM	108
Wyke Wood	Dorset	SY6083	50°39·0′	2°33·6′W	F	194
Wykey	Shrops	SJ3924	52°48·8′	2°53·9′W	T	126
Wykeymoss	Shrops	SJ3825	52°49·4′	2°54·8′W	X	126
Wykham Fm	Oxon	SP4538	52°2·5′	1°20·2′W	FM	151
Wykham Mill	Oxon	SP4337	52°2·0′	1°22·0′W	X	151
Wykin	Leic	SP4095	52°33·3′	1°24·2′W	T	140
Wykin Fields	Leic	SP4095	52°33·3′	1°24·2′W	X	140
Wylam	Northum	NZ1164	54°58·5′	1°49·3′W	T	88
Wylam Wood Fm	Northum	NZ1164	54°58·5′	1°49·3′W	FM	88
Wyland Fm	E Susx	TQ7313	50°53·7′	0°28·9′E	FM	199
Wyld Court	Devon	ST3400	50°48·0′	2°55·8′W	A	193
Wyld Court Rainforest	W Berks	SU5476	51°29·1′	1°12·9′W	F	174
Wyld Court Stud	W Berks	SU5476	51°29·1′	1°12·9′W	X	174
Wylde	Heref	SO4568	52°18·7′	2°48·0′W	T	137,138,148
Wylde Fms	Dorset	SY3496	50°45·8′	2°55·8′W	FM	193
Wylde Green	Birm	SP1294	52°32·9′	1°49·0′W	T	139
Wyldingtree	Essex	TL5005	51°43·6′	0°10·7′E	X	167
Wylds, The	Hants	SU7929	51°3·5′	0°52·0′W	X	186,197
Wyld Warren	Dorset	SY3498	50°46·9′	2°55·8′W	F	193
Wyle Cop	Powys	SJ1601	52°36·3′	3°14·0′W	X	136
Wylfa	Denb	SJ0741	52°57·7′	3°22·7′W	X	125
Wylfa	Powys	SN7399	52°34·7′	3°52·1′W	H	135
Wylfa	Powys	SN9497	52°33·9′	3°33·4′W	X	136
Wylfa Head	I of Angl	SH3594	53°25·3′	4°28·6′W	X	114
Wylfre	Powys	SO1151	52°9·2′	3°17·7′W	H	148
Wyliehole	D & G	NY2082	55°7·8′	3°14·9′W	X	79
Wylies Burn	Scot Bord	NT1622	55°29·3′	3°19·3′W	W	72
Wylies Craigs	Scot Bord	NT6301	55°18·4′	2°34·5′W	X	80
Wylies Hill	Scot Bord	NT1621	55°28·8′	3°19·3′W	H	72
Wylies, The	W Susx	TQ2824	51°0·3′	0°10·1′W	X	198
Wyllie	Caer	ST1794	51°38·6′	3°11·6′W	T	171
Wyllieholes	Aberd	NJ5960	57°37·9′	2°40·7′W	X	29
Wyllieland	E Ayr	NS4743	55°39·6′	4°25·5′W	X	70
Wylmington Hayes	Devon	ST2101	50°48·4′	3°6·9′W	X	192,193
Wylock Marsh	Cumbr	SD2064	54°4·2′	3°12·9′W	W	96
Wylye	Wilts	SU0037	51°8·2′	1°59·6′W	T	184
Wylye Down	Wilts	SU0036	51°7·6′	1°59·6′W	X	184
Wylye Valley	Wilts	SU0038	51°8·7′	1°59·6′W	X	184
Wymans Brook	Glos	SO9424	51°55·1′	2°4·8′W	T	163
Wymbush	Mil Key	SP8238	52°2·3′	0°47·9′W	T	152
Wymering	C of Port	SU6506	50°51·2′	1°4·2′W	T	196
Wymeswold	Leic	SK6023	52°48·3′	1°6·2′W	T	129
Wymeswold Lodge	Leic	SK6322	52°47·7′	1°3·5′W	X	129
Wyming Brook Fm	Sheff	SK2685	53°21·9′	1°36·1′W	FM	110
Wymington	Beds	SP9564	52°16·2′	0°36·1′W	T	153
Wymms, The	Heref	SO5347	52°7·4′	2°40·8′W	T	149
Wymondham	Leic	SK8518	52°45·4′	0°44·0′W	T	130
Wymondham	Norf	TG1101	52°34·2′	1°7·2′E	T	144
Wymondham College	Norf	TM0798	52°32·7′	1°3·6′E	X	144
Wymond Hill	Northnts	SP9891	52°30·7′	0°33·0′W	X	141
Wymondhouses	Lancs	SD7638	53°50·5′	2°21·5′W	X	103
Wymondley Bury	Herts	TL2127	51°55·9′	0°14·0′W	T	166
Wymott	Lancs	SD5020	53°40·7′	2°45·0′W	T	102
Wymott Brook	Lancs	SD4920	53°40·7′	2°45·9′W	W	102
Wynam Bottoms	E Yorks	SE7246	53°54·5′	0°53·8′W	X	105,106
Wynbrook	Staffs	SJ7949	53°2·5′	2°18·4′W	X	118
Wynch Br	Durham	NY9027	54°38·5′	2°8·9′W	X	91,92
Wynches	Herts	TL4217	51°50·2′	0°4·1′E	X	167
Wyncoll's	Glos	SO6913	51°49·1′	2°26·3′W	X	162
Wyndales Farm	S Lanak	NS9732	55°34·5′	3°37·6′W	FM	72
Wyndburgh Hill	Scot Bord	NT5503	55°19·4′	2°42·1′W	H	80

Wynd Cliff	Monm	ST5297	51°40·4′	2°41·3′W	X	162
Wyndcliffe Court	Monm	ST5197	51°40·4′	2°42·1′W	X	162
Wyndford	Aberd	NO7173	56°51·1′	2°28·1′W	X	45
Wyndford	W Loth	NT0573	55°56·7′	3°30·8′W	X	65
Wyndford Fm	Aberd	NO8790	57°0·3′	2°12·4′W	FM	38,45
Wyndford Mill Fm	Staffs	SJ8014	52°43·6′	2°17·4′W	FM	127
Wyndham	Brig	SS9391	51°36·7′	3°32·3′W	T	170
Wyndham Fm	Dorset	ST7829	51°3·8′	2°18·5′W	FM	183
Wyndham Fm	W Susx	TQ2319	50°57·7′	0°14·5′W	FM	198
Wyndham Ho	Cumbr	NY1330	54°39·7′	3°20·5′W	X	89
Wyndhammere	Cumbr	SD5985	54°15·8′	2°37·3′W	W	97
Wyndham Park	V of Glam	ST0876	51°28·8′	3°19·1′W	T	170
Wyndley Pool	Birm	SP1195	52°33·4′	1°49·9′W	W	139
Wyndmere Fm	Cambs	TL2841	52°3·4′	0°7·6′W	FM	153
Wynds	E Ayr	NS5232	55°33·8′	4°20·4′W	X	70
Wynds Point	Heref	SO7640	52°3·7′	2°20·6′W	T	150
Wyndthorpe Hall	Donc	SE6307	53°33·6′	1°2·5′W	X	111
Wyndy Burn	E Ayr	NS5828	55°31·8′	4°14·6′W	W	71
Wynett Coppice	Shrops	SO5585	52°27·9′	2°39·3′W	F	137,138
Wyneyards	Worcs	SO8266	52°17·7′	2°15·4′W	X	138,150
Wynford	C of Aber	NJ8408	57°10·0′	2°15·4′W	X	38
Wynford Eagle	Dorset	SY5895	50°45·4′	2°35·3′W	T	194
Wynford Ho	Dorset	SY5795	50°45·4′	2°36·2′W	X	194
Wynford Wood	Dorset	SY5696	50°45·9′	2°37·1′W	F	194
Wyng	Orkney	ND3190	58°47·8′	3°11·2′W	T	7
Wynholm	D & G	NY1988	55°11·0′	3°15·9′W	X	79
Wynn Cottage Fm	E Yorks	SE7430	53°45·9′	0°52·2′W	FM	105,106
Wynne Copse	Dorset	ST9700	50°48·2′	2°2·2′W	F	195
Wynn Hall	Wrex	SJ2844	52°59·6′	3°4·0′W	A	117
Wynn's Green	Heref	SO6047	52°7·4′	2°34·7′W	T	149
Wynnstay Hall	Wrex	SJ3042	52°58·5′	3°2·1′W	X	117
Wynnstay Park	Wrex	SJ3042	52°58·5′	3°2·1′W	X	117
Wynnstay Wood	Notts	SK6531	52°52·6′	1°1·6′W	F	129
Wynston	Pemb	SN0640	52°1·7′	4°49·3′W	X	145
Wynstones Ho	Glos	SO8312	51°48·6′	2°14·4′W	X	162
Wynstrode Fm	W Susx	TQ0827	51°2·2′	0°27·2′W	FM	187,197
Wynter's Fm	Essex	TL4908	51°45·3′	0°9·9′E	FM	167
Wynter's Grange	Essex	TL4907	51°44·7′	0°9·9′E	X	167
Wynton	Angus	NO3736	56°31·0′	3°1·0′W	X	54
Wynyard Park	Stock on T	NZ4225	54°37·3′	1°20·5′W	X	93
Wype Doles	Cambs	TL3095	52°32·5′	0°4·6′W	X	142
Wyre	Orkney	HY4426	59°7·3′	2°58·2′W	X	5,6
Wyre Br	Lancs	SD4949	53°56·3′	2°46·2′W	X	102
Wyre Common	Shrops	SO6976	52°23·1′	2°26·9′W	X	138
Wyre Fach	Cered	SN5668	52°17·7′	4°6·3′W	W	135
Wyre Fm	Shrops	SO6877	52°23·6′	2°27·8′W	FM	138
Wyre Forest	Worcs	SO7576	52°23·1′	2°21·6′W	F	138
Wyre Light	Lancs	SD3251	53°57·3′	3°1·8′W	X	102
Wyre Mill	Worcs	SO9546	52°7·0′	2°4·0′W	X	150
Wyre Piddle	Worcs	SO9647	52°7·5′	2°3·1′W	T	150
Wyresdale Park	Lancs	SD5049	53°56·3′	2°45·3′W	X	102
Wyreside Hall	Lancs	SD5252	53°58·0′	2°43·5′W	X	102
Wyre Skerries	Orkney	HY4125	59°6·7′	3°1·3′W	X	5,6
Wyre Sound	Orkney	HY4427	59°7·8′	2°58·2′W	W	5,6
Wyrley	Shrops	SJ6035	52°54·9′	2°35·3′W	X	127
Wyrley and Essington Canal	Wals	SJ9802	52°37·2′	2°1·4′W	W	127,139
Wyrley Common	Staffs	SK0206	52°39·3′	1°57·8′W	F	139
Wyrley Fm	Norf	TF9508	52°38·3′	0°53·3′E	FM	144
Wyrlod-ddu	Merth Tyd	SO0209	51°46·5′	3°24·8′W	X	160
Wysall	Notts	SK6027	52°50·5′	1°6·1′W	T	129
Wyseby	D & G	NY2472	55°2·5′	3°10·9′W	X	85
Wysebyhill	D & G	NY2672	55°2·5′	3°9·1′W	X	85
Wyseby Mains	D & G	NY2572	55°2·5′	3°10·0′W	X	85
Wyse Hill Fm	Durham	NZ0315	54°32·1′	1°56·8′W	FM	92
Wyse Ho	N Yks	SE8173	54°9·0′	0°45·2′W	X	100
Wyse's Cottage	Essex	TL6404	51°42·9′	0°22·8′E	X	167
Wyson	Heref	SO5167	52°18·2′	2°42·7′W	T	137,138,149
Wyson Common	Heref	SO5067	52°18·2′	2°43·6′W	F	137,138,149
Wytch Fm	Dorset	SY9785	50°40·1′	2°2·2′W	FM	195
Wytch Heath	Dorset	SY9784	50°39·6′	2°2·2′W	F	195
Wytchley Warren Fm	Rut	SK9505	52°38·3′	0°35·4′W	FM	141
Wythall	Worcs	SP0875	52°22·6′	1°52·5′W	T	139
Wythall Sta	Worcs	SP0975	52°22·6′	1°51·7′W	X	139
Wytham	Oxon	SP4708	51°46·4′	1°18·7′W	T	164
Wytham Great Wood	Oxon	SP4609	51°46·9′	1°19·6′W	F	164
Wytham Hill	Oxon	SP4508	51°46·4′	1°20·5′W	H	164
Wytham Moor	Durham	NY9511	54°29·9′	2°4·2′W	X	91,92
Wytham Park	Oxon	SP4708	51°46·4′	1°18·7′W	X	164
Wyth Burn	Cumbr	NY2910	54°29·1′	3°5·3′W	W	89,90
Wyth Burn	Cumbr	NY3111	54°29·6′	3°3·5′W	W	90
Wythburn	Cumbr	NY3213	54°30·7′	3°2·6′W	X	90
Wythburn Fells	Cumbr	NY3112	54°30·2′	3°3·5′W	X	90
Wytheford Heath	Shrops	SJ5719	52°46·3′	2°37·8′W	X	126
Wytheford Wood	Shrops	SJ5720	52°46·8′	2°37·8′W	F	126
Wythemail Park Fm	Northnts	SP8471	52°20·1′	0°45·6′W	FM	141
Wythemoor Head	Cumbr	NY0224	54°36·4′	3°30·6′W	X	89
Wythemoor Ho	Cumbr	NY0324	54°36·4′	3°29·7′W	X	89
Wythemoor Sough	Cumbr	NY0324	54°36·4′	3°29·7′W	X	89
Wythen Lache	Derby	SK0277	53°17·6′	1°57·8′W	X	119
Wythenshawe	Man	SJ8288	53°23·6′	2°15·8′W	T	109
Wythenshawe Hall	Man	SJ8189	53°24·1′	2°16·7′W	A	109
Wytherling Court	Kent	TR0353	51°14·6′	0°54·9′E	X	179,189
Wytherston Fm	Dorset	SY5397	50°46·5′	2°39·6′W	FM	194
Wythes Fm	N Yks	SE7084	54°15·1′	0°55·1′W	FM	100
Wythes Hill	Durham	NY9222	54°35·8′	2°7·0′W	X	91,92
Wythe Syke Fm	N Yks	SE7784	54°15·0′	0°48·7′W	FM	100
Wythmoor	Cumbr	SD5895	54°21·2′	2°38·4′W	X	97
Wythop Beck	Cumbr	NY1829	54°39·2′	3°15·8′W	W	89,90
Wythop Hall	Cumbr	NY2028	54°38·7′	3°14·0′W	X	89,90
Wythop Mill	Cumbr	NY1729	54°39·2′	3°16·8′W	T	89,90
Wythop Moss	Cumbr	NY1827	54°38·1′	3°15·8′W	X	89,90
Wythop Woods	Cumbr	NY2029	54°39·2′	3°14·0′W	F	89,90
Wythwaite	Cumbr	NY6531	54°40·6′	2°32·1′W	X	91
Wyton	Cambs	TL2772	52°20·1′	0°7·8′W	X	153
Wyton	E Yorks	TA1733	53°47·0′	0°13·0′W	T	107
Wyton Airfield	Cambs	TL2874	52°21·2′	0°6·8′W	X	142
Wyton Drain	E Yorks	TA1732	53°46·5′	0°13·1′W	W	107
Wyton Holmes	E Yorks	TA1732	53°46·5′	0°13·1′W	X	107
Wyton Lodge Fm	Notts	SK7056	53°6·0′	0°56·9′W	FM	120

Wyvern Fm	Essex	TL9424	51°53·1′	0°49·5′E	FM	168
Wyverstone	Suff	TM0467	52°16·0′	0°59·8′E	T	155
Wyverstone Green	Suff	TM0467	52°16·0′	0°59·8′E	T	155
Wyverstone Street	Suff	TM0367	52°16·0′	0°58·9′E	T	155
Wyville	Lincs	SK8829	52°51·3′	0°41·2′W	T	130
Wyvill Grange	N Yks	SE1893	54°20·2′	1°43·0′W	X	99
Wyvis Forest	Highld	NH4671	57°42·4′	4°34·6′W	X	20
Wyvis Lodge	Highld	NH4873	57°43·5′	4°32·7′W	X	20
Wyvols Court	Wok	SU7264	51°22·5′	0°57·5′W	X	175,186

Y

Yaafield	Shetld	HU3723	59°59·7′	1°19·7′W	X	4
Yadburgh Hill	D & G	NT1303	55°19·1′	3°21·8′W	H	78
Yaddlethorpe	N Lincs	SE8807	53°33·4′	0°39·9′W	T	112
Yade Sike	D & G	NT3003	55°19·2′	3°5·8′W	W	79
Yade Sike Rig	D & G	NT3003	55°19·2′	3°5·8′W	X	79
Yadgair Edge	Scot Bord	NT3503	55°19·3′	3°1·0′W	X	79
Yadlee	E Loth	NT6567	55°53·9′	2°33·1′W	X	67
Yad Moss	Cumbr	NY7837	54°43·9′	2°20·1′W	X	91
Yad Moss	Durham	NY7835	54°42·8′	2°20·1′W	X	91
Yadsworthy Fm	Devon	SX6360	50°25·7′	3°55·4′W	FM	202
Yafford	I of W	SZ4481	50°37·8′	1°22·3′W	T	196
Yafford Ho	I of W	SZ4581	50°37·8′	1°21·4′W	X	196
Yafforth	N Yks	SE3494	54°20·7′	1°28·2′W	T	99
Yafforth Grange	N Yks	SE3294	54°20·7′	1°30·0′W	X	99
Yafforth Hill	N Yks	SE3495	54°21·2′	1°28·2′W	X	99
Yafforth Moor Ho	N Yks	SE3394	54°20·7′	1°29·1′W	X	99
Yagden Hill	Surrey	SU8842	51°10·5′	0°44·1′W	X	186
Yair	Scot Bord	NT4532	55°35·0′	2°51·9′W	T	73
Yair Burn	Scot Bord	NT4436	55°35·0′	2°52·9′W	W	73
Yair Hill Forest	Scot Bord	NT4332	55°35·0′	2°53·8′W	F	73
Yalberton	Torbay	SX8658	50°24·9′	3°35·9′W	T	202
Yaldham Manor	Kent	TQ5858	51°18·2′	0°16·4′E	X	188
Yaldhurst	Hants	SZ3095	50°45·5′	1°34·1′W	X	196
Yalding	Kent	TQ7050	51°13·7′	0°26·5′E	T	188
Yalham Fm	Somer	ST2115	50°56·0′	3°7·1′W	FM	193
Yalland	Devon	SX6962	50°26·8′	3°50·3′W	X	202
Yalway	Somer	ST2430	51°4·1′	3°4·7′W	X	182
Yamna Field	Shetld	HU3377	60°28·8′	1°23·5′W	H	2,3
Yanhey	Devon	SS8625	51°1·0′	3°37·1′W	X	181
Yanley	N Som	ST5569	51°25·3′	2°38·4′W	T	172,182
Yanston	Devon	SX7148	50°19·3′	3°48·4′W	X	202
Yantlet Creek	Medway	TQ8577	51°27·9′	0°40·2′E	W	178
Yanwath	Cumbr	NY5128	54°38·9′	2°45·1′W	X	90
Yanwath Woodhouse	Cumbr	NY5226	54°37·9′	2°44·2′W	X	90
Yanworth	Glos	SP0713	51°49·2′	1°53·5′W	T	163
Yanworth Wood	Glos	SP0614	51°49·7′	1°54·4′W	F	163
Yapham	E Yorks	SE7851	53°57·2′	0°48·3′W	T	105,106
Yapham Common	E Yorks	SE7750	53°56·7′	0°49·2′W	X	105,106
Yapham Fm	Devon	SS2825	51°0·2′	4°26·7′W	FM	190
Yapham Grange	E Yorks	SE7850	53°56·7′	0°48·3′W	X	105,106
Yapsel Bank	Shrops	SO4191	52°31·1′	2°51·8′W	H	137
Yapton	W Susx	SU9703	50°49·3′	0°37·0′W	T	197
Yarberry	N Som	ST3957	51°18·8′	2°52·1′W	T	182
Yarborough	NE Lincs	TA2509	53°34·0′	0°6·3′W	T	113
Yarborough Camp	N Lincs	TA0812	53°35·8′	0°21·7′W	A	112
Yarbridge	I of W	SZ6086	50°40·5′	1°8·7′W	T	196
Yarburgh	Lincs	TF3593	53°25·2′	0°2·3′E	T	113
Yarburgh Grange	Lincs	TF3493	53°25·2′	0°1·4′E	X	113
Yarbury Combe	Devon	SS7041	51°9·4′	3°51·2′W	X	180
Yarcombe	Devon	ST2408	50°52·2′	3°4·4′W	T	192,193
Yarcombe Wood	Somer	ST5826	51°2·1′	2°35·6′W	F	183
Yard	Devon	SX7383	50°38·2′	3°47·4′W	X	191
Yardbent	S Lanak	NS7341	55°39·0′	4°0·7′W	X	71
Yardbury Fm	Devon	SY2395	50°45·2′	3°5·1′W	FM	192,193
Yard Dairy	Dorset	ST5402	50°49·2′	2°38·8′W	X	194
Yarde	Devon	SS6434	51°5·6′	3°56·1′W	X	180
Yarde	Devon	SX7140	50°15·0′	3°48·2′W	X	202
Yarde	Somer	ST0639	51°8·8′	3°20·2′W	T	181
Yarde Down	Devon	SS7235	51°6·2′	3°49·3′W	X	180
Yarde Downs	Devon	SS9703	50°49·3′	3°27·4′W	X	192
Yarde Fm	Devon	ST0301	50°48·3′	3°22·2′W	FM	192
Yarde Fm	Somer	ST2027	51°2·4′	3°8·1′W	FM	193
Yarde Gate Fm	Devon	SS7134	51°5·7′	3°50·2′W	FM	180
Yardewells Cross	Devon	SS7134	51°5·7′	3°50·2′W	X	180
Yard Fm	Devon	ST1505	50°50·5′	3°12·1′W	FM	192,193
Yard Fm	Dorset	SY4299	50°47·5′	2°49·0′W	FM	193
Yard Fm	I of W	SZ5580	50°37·3′	1°13·0′W	FM	196
Yard Fm	Somer	ST1038	51°8·3′	3°16·8′W	FM	181
Yard Fm	Somer	ST1532	51°5·1′	3°12·4′W	FM	181
Yardfoot	Renf	NS3657	55°47·0′	4°36·5′W	X	63
Yardgrove Fm	Dorset	ST7717	50°57·4′	2°19·3′W	FM	183
Yardhurst	Kent	TQ9541	51°8·3′	0°47·6′E	T	189
Yardley	Birm	SP1285	52°28·0′	1°49·0′W	T	139
Yardley Chase	Northnts	SP8455	52°11·4′	0°45·9′W	X	152
Yardley Gobion	Northnts	SP7644	52°5·6′	0°53·1′W	T	152
Yardley Hall	Essex	TL5932	51°58·0′	0°19·3′E	X	167
Yardley Hastings	Northnts	SP8656	52°12·0′	0°44·1′W	T	152
Yardley Lodge Fm	Northnts	SP8658	52°13·0′	0°44·1′W	FM	152
Yardley Wood	Birm	SP1080	52°25·3′	1°50·8′W	T	139
Yardro	Powys	SO2258	52°13·1′	3°8·1′W	T	148
Yards	S Lanak	NS7443	55°40·1′	3°59·8′W	X	71
Yards	Somer	ST2330	51°4·1′	3°5·6′W	X	182
Yards End Dyke	Cambs	TL1791	52°30·5′	0°16·2′W	W	142
Yard Steel	Cumbr	NY2934	54°42·0′	3°5·7′W	X	89,90
Yardstone Knowe	Scot Bord	NT4142	55°40·3′	2°55·8′W	H	73
Yard Wood	Hants	SU4200	50°48·1′	1°23·9′W	F	196
Yardworthy	Devon	SX6785	50°39·2′	3°52·5′W	X	191
Yarfils Wick	Shetld	HU3778	60°29·3′	1°19·1′W	W	2,3
Yarford	Somer	ST2029	51°3·5′	3°8·1′W	T	193
Yarhampton	Worcs	SO7767	52°18·3′	2°19·8′W	T	138,150

Yarhampton Cross	Worcs	SO7767	52°18·3′	2°19·8′W	T	138,150
Yarker Bank Fm	N Yks	SE1091	54°19·1′	1°50·4′W	FM	99
Yarkhill	Heref	SO6042	52°4·7′	2°34·6′W	T	149
Yarlet	Staffs	SJ9128	52°51·2′	2°7·6′W	X	127
Yarlet Hall (School)	Staffs	SJ9129	52°51·7′	2°7·6′W	X	127
Yarley	Somer	ST5045	51°12·4′	2°42·6′W	T	182,183
Yarlington	Somer	ST6529	51°3·8′	2°29·6′W	T	183
Yarlington Ho	Somer	ST6528	51°3·2′	2°29·6′W	X	183
Yarlsber	N Yks	SD7072	54°8·8′	2°27·1′W	X	98
Yarlsey Moss	N Yks	NZ7500	54°23·6′	0°50·3′W	X	94
Yarlside	Cumbr	SD2269	54°6·9′	3°11·2′W	T	96
Yarlside	Cumbr	SD6898	54°22·8′	2°29·1′W	H	98
Yarlside	Lancs	SD5873	54°9·3′	2°38·2′W	H	97
Yarlside	Lancs	SD8549	53°56·5′	2°13·3′W	X	103
Yarlside	Scot Bord	NT6138	55°38·3′	2°36·7′W	X	74
Yarlside Crag	Cumbr	NY5207	54°27·6′	2°44·0′W	X	90
Yarm	Stock on T	NZ4112	54°30·3′	1°21·6′W	T	93
Yarmleigh	Devon	SS8004	50°49·6′	3°41·9′W	X	191
Yarmouth	I of W	SZ3589	50°42·2′	1°29·9′W	T	196
Yarmouth Fm	Cambs	TL3664	52°15·7′	0°0·0′W	FM	154
Yarmouth Roads		TG5408	52°36·8′	1°45·5′E	W	134
Yarnacombe Fm	Devon	SX6852	50°21·4′	3°51·0′W	FM	202
Yarnacott	Devon	SS6230	51°3·4′	3°57·8′W	T	180
Yarnbrook	Wilts	ST8654	51°17·3′	2°11·7′W	T	183
Yarnbrook	Wilts	ST8655	51°17·9′	2°11·7′W	T	173
Yarnbury	N Yks	SE0165	54°5·1′	1°58·7′W	X	98
Yarnbury Castle	Wilts	SU0340	51°9·8′	1°57·0′W	X	184
Yarnbury Castle (Fort)	Wilts	SU0340	51°9·8′	1°57·0′W	A	184
Yarner	Devon	SX7778	50°35·6′	3°43·9′W	X	191
Yarner Beacon	Devon	SX7761	50°26·4′	3°43·6′W	H	202
Yarner Fm	Somer	SS8447	51°12·9′	3°39·3′W	FM	181
Yarner Wood	Devon	SX7778	50°35·6′	3°43·9′W	F	191
Yarnest Wood	Shrops	SJ4132	52°53·2′	2°52·2′W	F	126
Yarnett House Fm	N Yks	SE1450	53°57·0′	1°46·8′W	FM	104
Yarnfield	Staffs	SJ8632	52°53·4′	2°12·1′W	T	127
Yarnfield Gate	Wilts	ST7637	51°8·1′	2°20·2′W	X	183
Yarngallows Knowe	E Ayr	NS6206	55°20·0′	4°10·1′W	X	71,77
Yarnhams	Hants	SU7344	51°11·7′	0°56·9′W	X	186
Yarn Hill	Oxon	SP3541	52°4·2′	1°29·0′W	X	151
Yarn Hill	Suff	TM4255	52°8·6′	1°32·6′E	X	156
Yarningale Common	Warw	SP1966	52°17·7′	1°42·9′W	T	151
Yarn Market	Somer	SS9943	51°10·9′	3°26·3′W	A	181
Yarnold Lane Fm	Worcs	SO9473	52°21·5′	2°4·9′W	FM	139
Yarnscombe	Devon	SS5623	50°59·5′	4°2·7′W	T	180
Yarnshaw Hill	Ches	SJ9870	53°13·9′	2°1·4′W	X	118
Yarnspath Law	Northum	NT8813	55°24·9′	2°10·9′W	H	80
Yarnton	Oxon	SP4712	51°48·5′	1°18·7′W	T	164
Yarnton Ho	Oxon	SP4712	51°48·5′	1°18·7′W	X	164
Yarpha	Orkney	HY3605	58°55·9′	3°6·2′W	X	6,7
Yarpha	Orkney	HY5506	58°56·6′	2°46·4′W	X	6
Yarpole	Heref	SO4764	52°16·5′	2°46·2′W	T	137,138,148
Yarrow	E Loth	NT6172	55°56·6′	2°37·0′W	X	67
Yarrow	Northum	NY7187	55°10·8′	2°26·9′W	T	80
Yarrow	Scot Bord	NT3527	55°32·2′	3°1·4′W	T	73
Yarrow	Somer	ST3847	51°13·4′	2°52·9′W	T	182
Yarrow Cott	Scot Bord	NT3426	55°31·6′	3°2·3′W	X	73
Yarrow Feus	Scot Bord	NT3425	55°31·1′	3°2·3′W	T	73
Yarrowford	Scot Bord	NT4030	55°33·9′	2°56·6′W	T	73
Yarrow Ho	Norf	TF9923	52°46·3′	0°57·4′E	X	132
Yarrow Knowe	Scot Bord	NY5695	55°15·1′	2°41·1′W	H	80
Yarrow Moor	Northum	NY7087	55°10·8′	2°27·8′W	X	80
Yarrow Resr	Lancs	SD6215	53°38·1′	2°34·1′W	W	109
Yarrow Slake	Northum	NT9852	55°45·9′	2°1·5′W	W	75
Yarrow stone	Scot Bord	NT3427	55°32·2′	3°2·3′W	A	73
Yarrow Water	Scot Bord	NT3527	55°32·2′	3°1·4′W	W	73
Yarsop	Heref	SO4047	52°7·3′	2°52·2′W	T	148,149
Yartleton Fm	Heref	SO6821	51°53·4′	2°27·5′W	FM	162
Yar Tor	Devon	SX6774	50°33·3′	3°52·3′W	X	191
Yarty Fm	Devon	ST2602	50°49·0′	3°2·6′W	FM	192,193
Yartyford	Devon	ST2504	50°50·1′	3°3·5′W	X	192,193
Yarty Ho	Devon	ST2601	50°48·5′	3°2·6′W	X	192,193
Yarwell	Northnts	TL0697	52°33·9′	0°25·8′W	T	142
Yarwood Heath Fm	Ches	SJ7485	53°21·9′	2°23·0′W	FM	109
Yarwood Ho	Ches	SJ7882	53°20·3′	2°19·4′W	X	109
Yarwoods	Ches	SJ8375	53°16·5′	2°14·9′W	X	118
Yate	Devon	SS9108	50°51·9′	3°32·6′W	X	192
Yate	S Glos	ST7182	51°32·4′	2°24·7′W	T	172
Yate Court	S Glos	ST7185	51°34·0′	2°24·7′W	A	172
Yateholme Resr	Kirk	SE1104	53°32·2′	1°49·6′W	W	110
Yatehouse Fm	Ches	SJ7068	53°12·7′	2°26·5′W	FM	118
Yatehouse Green	Ches	SJ7068	53°12·7′	2°26·5′W	X	118
Yateley	Hants	SU8160	51°20·2′	0°49·8′W	T	175,186
Yateley Common	Hants	SU8258	51°19·1′	0°49·0′W	X	175,186
Yateley Green	Hants	SU8160	51°20·2′	0°49·8′W	X	175,186
Yateley Heath Wood	Hants	SU7957	51°18·6′	0°51·6′W	F	175,186
Yate Lower Common	S Glos	ST7086	51°34·6′	2°25·6′W	X	172
Yate Rocks	S Glos	ST7284	51°33·5′	2°23·8′W	T	172
Yates	Lancs	SD5451	53°57·4′	2°41·6′W	X	102
Yatesbury	Wilts	SU0671	51°26·5′	1°54·4′W	T	173
Yatesbury Field	Wilts	SU0670	51°26·0′	1°54·4′W	X	173
Yatesfield	Northum	NY8697	55°16·3′	2°12·8′W	X	80
Yatesfield Hill	Northum	NY8597	55°16·3′	2°13·7′W	H	80
Yates Ho	N Yks	SE1559	54°1·8′	1°45·8′W	X	104
Yattendon	W Berks	SU5574	51°28·0′	1°12·1′W	T	174
Yattendon Court	W Berks	SU5674	51°28·0′	1°11·2′W	X	174
Yatt Fm	Heref	SO3333	51°59·7′	2°58·2′W	FM	149,161
Yatton	Heref	SO4266	52°17·6′	2°50·6′W	T	137,148,149
Yatton	N Som	ST4265	51°23·1′	2°49·6′W	T	171,172,182
Yatton Court	Heref	SO4265	52°17·0′	2°50·6′W	X	137,148,149
Yatton Hill	Heref	SO4366	52°17·6′	2°49·7′W	X	137,148,149
Yatton Keynell	Wilts	ST8676	51°29·2′	2°11·7′W	T	173
Yatton Wood	Heref	SO6229	51°57·7′	2°32·8′W	F	149
Yatts Brow Fm	N Yks	SE8086	54°16·0′	0°45·9′W	FM	94,100
Yatts Fm	N Yks	SE7395	54°21·0′	0°52·2′W	FM	94,100
Yatts Fm	N Yks	SE8188	54°17·1′	0°44·9′W	FM	94,100
Yaudhouse Head	N Yks	SE2267	54°6·1′	1°39·4′W	X	99
Yaverland	I of W	SZ6185	50°39·9′	1°7·8′W	A	196
Yaverland	I of W	SZ6185	50°39·9′	1°7·8′W	T	196
Yawd Sike	Durham	NY9517	54°33·1′	2°4·2′W	W	91,92
Yawl	Devon	SY3194	50°44·7′	2°58·3′W	T	193

Yawl Bottom	Devon	SY3194	50°44·7′	2°58·3′W	X	193
Yawl Hill	Devon	SY3195	50°45·3′	2°58·3′W	X	193
Yawthorpe	Lincs	SK8991	53°24·7′	0°39·2′W	T	112
Yawthorpe Fox Covert	Lincs	SK9092	53°25·3′	0°38·3′W	F	112
Yaxham	Norf	TG0110	52°39·3′	0°58·7′E	T	133
Yaxley	Cambs	TL1892	52°31·0′	0°15·3′W	T	142
Yaxley	Suff	TM1273	52°19·1′	1°7·0′E	T	144,155
Yaxley Fen	Cambs	TL2091	52°30·5′	0°13·5′W	X	142
Yaxley Lode	Cambs	TL2091	52°30·5′	0°13·5′W	W	142
Yaxley Manor House	Suff	TM1074	52°19·7′	1°5·3′E	X	144
Yazor	Heref	SO4046	52°6·8′	2°52·2′W	T	148,149
Yazor Wood	Heref	SO3948	52°7·9′	2°53·1′W	F	148,149
Y Bryn	Cered	SN7261	52°14·2′	3°52·1′W	H	146,147
Y Bryn	Gwyn	SH8829	52°51·1′	3°39·4′W	X	124,125
Y Bryn	Pemb	SN0138	52°0·5′	4°53·6′W	X	145,157
Y Bwlwarcau	Nth Pt Talb	SS8388	51°35·0′	3°40·9′W	A	170
Y Byrwydd	Powys	SJ1405	52°38·4′	3°15·9′W	X	125
Y Caer fawr	Carm	SN6924	51°54·2′	3°53·9′W	A	160
Y Carreg Siglo	Rho Cyn Taf	ST0890	51°36·3′	3°19·3′W	X	170
Y Castell	Gwyn	SH8437	52°55·3′	3°43·1′W	X	124,125
Y Castell	Pemb	SM9239	52°0·9′	5°1·5′W	A	157
Y Cefn	Gwyn	SH7142	52°57·8′	3°54·8′W	X	124
Y Clogydd	Powys	SJ0628	52°50·7′	3°23·3′W	X	125
Y Craig	Pemb	SM8831	51°56·5′	5°4·7′W	X	157
Y Darren	Caer	SO1204	51°43·9′	3°16·1′W	H	171
Y Darren Widdon	Nth Pt Talb	SN7707	51°45·1′	3°46·5′W	H	160
Y Das	Powys	SO1932	51°59·1′	3°10·4′W	H	161
Y Ddôl	Gwyn	SH2637	52°54·4′	4°34·8′W	X	123
Y Dolydd	I of Angl	SH5374	53°14·8′	4°11·8′W	H	114,115
Y Dolydd	I of Angl	SH5474	53°14·8′	4°10·9′W	X	114,115
Y Dolydd	Powys	SJ1518	52°45·4′	3°15·2′W	X	125
Y Domen Fawr	Blae Gw	SO1607	51°45·6′	3°12·6′W	H	161
Y Drain	Powys	SO1485	52°27·6′	3°15·5′W	X	136
Y Drum	Cered	SN7259	52°13·1′	3°52·0′W	X	146,147
Y Drum	Gwyn	SH8642	52°58·0′	3°41·4′W	X	124,125
Y Drum	Powys	SN8284	52°26·7′	3°43·8′W	H	135,136
Yeabridge	Somer	ST4415	50°56·1′	2°47·4′W	T	193
Yeadbury	Devon	SS8610	50°52·9′	3°36·9′W	X	191
Yeading	Hill	TQ1182	51°31·8′	0°23·6′W	T	176
Yeading Brook	Hill	TQ1082	51°31·8′	0°24·5′W	W	176
Yeadon	Leeds	SE2040	53°51·6′	1°41·3′W	T	104
Yeadon Crag	N Yks	SE1568	54°6·7′	1°45·8′W	X	99
Yeadon Moor	Leeds	SE2141	53°52·1′	1°40·4′W	X	104
Yeadon Tarn	Leeds	SE2141	53°52·1′	1°40·4′W	W	104
Yealand Conyers	Lancs	SD5074	54°9·8′	2°45·5′W	T	97
Yealand Manor	Lancs	SD5074	54°9·8′	2°45·5′W	X	97
Yealand Redmayne	Lancs	SD5075	54°10·3′	2°45·5′W	T	97
Yealand Storrs	Lancs	SD4976	54°10·9′	2°46·5′W	T	97
Yeald Wood	Worcs	SP0152	52°10·2′	1°58·7′W	F	150
Yealmacott	Devon	SS7021	50°58·7′	3°50·7′W	X	180
Yealmbridge	Devon	SX5951	50°20·8′	3°58·5′W	T	202
Yealm Head	Devon	SX6164	50°27·8′	3°57·1′W	W	202
Yealmpton	Devon	SX5751	50°20·7′	4°0·2′W	T	202
Yeancott Fm	Somer	ST0724	51°0·7′	3°19·2′W	FM	181
Yearby	Red & Cl	NZ6021	54°35·1′	1°3·9′W	T	94
Yearby Wood	Red & Cl	NZ5920	54°34·5′	1°4·8′W	F	93
Yearhaugh	Northum	NY8988	55°11·4′	2°9·9′W	X	80
Yearlings Bottom	Dorset	SY8493	50°44·4′	2°13·2′W	X	194
Yearlstone	Devon	SS9308	50°51·9′	3°30·9′W	X	192
Yearngill	Cumbr	NY1444	54°47·3′	3°19·8′W	T	85
Yearn Gill	S Lanak	NT0121	55°28·6′	3°33·5′W	W	72
Yearngill Head	S Lanak	NT0120	55°28·1′	3°33·5′W	H	72
Yearn Hope	E Loth	NT7269	55°55·0′	2°26·4′W	X	67
Yearning Flow	Scot Bord	NY5587	55°10·8′	2°42·0′W	X	80
Yearning Hall	Northum	NT8112	55°24·3′	2°17·6′W	X	80
Yearning Law	Northum	NT8111	55°23·8′	2°17·6′W	H	80
Yearnor Wood	Somer	SS8448	51°13·4′	3°39·3′W	F	181
Yearns Low	Ches	SJ9675	53°16·6′	2°3·2′W	X	118
Yearny Knowe	Scot Bord	NT1916	55°26·1′	3°16·4′W	H	79
Yearsett	Heref	SO7053	52°10·7′	2°25·9′W	X	149
Yearsley	N Yks	SE5874	54°9·8′	1°6·3′W	T	100
Yearsley Fm	Somer	ST2844	51°11·7′	3°1·4′W	FM	182
Yearsley Moor	N Yks	SE5875	54°10·3′	1°6·3′W	X	100
Yearston Court	Heref	SO6963	52°16·1′	2°26·9′W	X	138,149
Yeastyrigg Crags	Cumbr	NY2306	54°26·9′	3°10·8′W	X	89,90
Yeat	Devon	SX3885	50°38·8′	4°17·1′W	X	201
Yeate Fm	Corn	SX1352	50°20·5′	4°37·3′W	FM	200
Yeat Fm	Bucks	SP6917	51°51·1′	0°59·5′W	FM	165
Yeatheridge Fm	Devon	SS7611	50°53·3′	3°45·4′W	FM	191
Yeat Ho	Lancs	SD5156	54°0·1′	2°44·4′W	X	102
Yeatlands Fm	Devon	ST2700	50°47·9′	3°1·8′W	FM	193
Yeatman's Fm	Dorset	ST8121	50°59·5′	2°15·9′W	FM	183
Yeaton	Shrops	SJ4319	52°46·2′	2°50·3′W	T	126
Yeaton Lodge	Shrops	SJ4519	52°46·2′	2°48·5′W	X	126
Yeaton Peverey	Shrops	SJ4418	52°45·6′	2°49·4′W	X	126
Yeatsall	Staffs	SK0624	52°49·0′	1°54·3′W	X	128
Yeatt Fm	Devon	SX8068	50°30·2′	3°41·2′W	FM	202
Yeatton Ho	Hants	SZ2794	50°44·9′	1°36·7′W	X	195
Yeaveley	Derby	SK1840	52°57·7′	1°43·5′W	T	119,128
Yeavering	Northum	NT9330	55°34·1′	2°6·2′W	X	74,75
Yeavering Bell	Northum	NT9229	55°33·5′	2°7·2′W	H	74,75
Yeaw Fm	Somer	ST1235	51°6·7′	3°15·0′W	FM	181
Yeddingham Cottage Fm	N Yks	SE9179	54°12·2′	0°35·9′W	FM	101
Yeddingham Grange Fm	N Yks	SE9078	54°11·6′	0°36·8′W	FM	101
Yederick Woods	N Yks	SE9485	54°15·4′	0°33·0′W	F	94,101
Yedingham	N Yks	SE8979	54°12·2′	0°37·7′W	T	101
Yedingham Ings	N Yks	SE9079	54°12·2′	0°36·8′W	X	101
Yedmandale Woods	N Yks	SE9786	54°15·9′	0°30·2′W	F	94,101
Yei, The	Shetld	HP6406	60°44·2′	0°49·1′W	W	1
Yelcombe Bottom	Dorset	ST6701	50°48·7′	2°27·7′W	X	194
Yeldadee	Orkney	HY2416	59°1·7′	3°19·0′W	X	6
Yeldall Manor	Wok	SU8079	51°30·5′	0°50·4′W	X	175
Yelden	Beds	TL0167	52°17·7′	0°30·7′W	T	153
Yelden Wold	Beds	TL0064	52°16·1′	0°31·7′W	X	153
Yeldersley Hall	Derby	SK2044	52°59·8′	1°41·7′W	X	119,128
Yeldersley Hollies	Derby	SK2243	52°59·3′	1°39·9′W	T	119,128
Yeldersley Home Fm	Derby	SK2044	52°59·8′	1°41·7′W	FM	119,128
Yeldhams	Essex	TL6934	51°58·9′	0°28·1′E	X	154
Yeld Ho	Heref	SO6160	52°14·4′	2°33·9′W	X	138,149
Yeld's Hill	Heref	SO4668	52°18·7′	2°47·1′W	X	137,138,148

Yeld, The	Ches	SJ5369	53°13·2′	2°41·8′W	X	117
Yeld, The	Heref	SO3556	52°12·1′	2°56·7′W	X	148,149
Yeld, The	Shrops	SO5783	52°26·8′	2°37·6′W	T	137,138
Yelford	Oxon	SP3604	51°44·2′	1°28·3′W	T	164
Yell	Shetld	HU4890	60°35·7′	1°6·9′W	X	1,2
Yellam	Devon	SX7187	50°40·3′	3°49·2′W	X	191
Yella Moor	Shetld	HU4466	60°22·8′	1°11·6′W	X	2,3
Yelland	Devon	SS4931	51°3·7′	4°8·9′W	T	180
Yelland	Devon	SS5527	51°1·7′	4°3·7′W	X	180
Yelland	Devon	SS8205	50°50·2′	3°40·2′W	X	191
Yelland	Devon	SX5086	50°39·5′	4°7·0′W	X	191,201
Yelland Cross	Devon	SS6741	51°9·4′	3°53·7′W	X	180
Yelland Fm	Devon	SS5820	50°58·0′	4°1·0′W	FM	180
Yelland Fm	Devon	SX5494	50°43·9′	4°3·8′W	FM	191
Yelland Fm	Devon	SX7462	50°26·9′	3°46·1′W	FM	202
Yelland's	Devon	SY0597	50°46·1′	3°20·5′W	X	192
Yellands	Somer	SS9931	51°4·4′	3°26·1′W	X	181
Yellaton	Devon	SS5944	51°10·9′	4°0·7′W	X	180
Yell Bank	Shrops	SO5097	52°34·4′	2°43·9′W	X	137,138
Yell Hill	D & G	NS8407	55°20·9′	3°49·3′W	H	71,78
Yelling	Cambs	TL2662	52°14·7′	0°8·9′W	T	153
Yellingham Fm	Devon	ST0800	50°47·8′	3°17·9′W	FM	192
Yellison Ho	N Yks	SD9449	53°56·5′	2°5·1′W	X	103
Yellow Bog	Brad	SE1143	53°53·2′	1°49·5′W	X	104
Yellow Bog	Highld	NC7950	58°25·6′	4°3·8′W	W	10
Yellowbog	Moray	NJ1448	57°31·1′	3°25·7′W	X	28
Yellowbog Burn	Highld	NC7952	58°26·6′	4°3·9′W	W	10
Yellowcombe	Somer	SS9033	51°5·4′	3°33·9′W	X	181
Yellow Craig	Scot Bord	NT9266	55°53·5′	2°7·2′W	X	67
Yellowcraig Plantation	D & G	NX7490	55°11·5′	3°58·3′W	F	77
Yellow Craig Plantn	E Loth	NT5185	56°3·6′	2°46·8′W	F	66
Yellow Craigs	N Ayr	NS2143	55°39·1′	4°50·3′W	X	63,70
Yellow Fawns	Cumbr	NY6074	55°3·8′	2°37·1′W	X	86
Yellowford	Devon	SS9200	50°47·6′	3°31·6′W	X	192
Yellowham Hill	Dorset	SY7393	50°44·4′	2°22·6′W	X	194
Yellowham Wood	Dorset	SY7293	50°44·4′	2°23·4′W	F	194
Yellow Head	Shetld	HU5137	60°7·1′	1°4·4′W	X	4
Yellowland Fm	Devon	SS3507	50°50·6′	4°20·2′W	FM	190
Yellowmead	Devon	SX5767	50°29·4′	4°0·6′W	X	202
Yellowmead Down	Devon	SX5668	50°29·9′	4°1·4′W	X	202
Yellowmeade Fm	Devon	SX5674	50°33·1′	4°1·6′W	FM	191
Yellow Moss	Highld	ND0264	58°33·4′	3°40·6′W	X	11,12
Yellow Moss	Highld	ND1257	58°29·8′	3°30·1′W	X	11,12
Yellow Rayes	Devon	SS5243	51°10·3′	4°6·6′W	X	180
Yellow Rigg	Northum	NY8661	54°56·9′	2°12·7′W	X	87
Yellow Rock	Arg & Bt	NR7624	55°27·8′	5°32·2′W	X	68,69
Yellow Rock	I Scilly	SV8713	49°56·3′	6°21·4′W	X	203
Yellow School Copse	Glos	SP0403	51°43·8′	1°56·1′W	F	163
Yellow Slacks	Derby	SK0695	53°27·3′	1°54·2′W	X	110
Yellowslacks Brook	Derby	SK0694	53°26·8′	1°54·2′W	W	110
Yellow Stack	Shetld	HU3795	60°38·5′	1°18·9′W	X	1,2
Yellow Stone	Somer	SS8249	51°13·9′	3°41·0′W	X	181
Yellow Tomach	E Ayr	NX4588	55°10·0′	4°25·6′W	X	77
Yellow Wells	Highld	NH5663	57°38·3′	4°24·3′W	X	21
Yell Sound	Shetld	HU4087	60°34·1′	1°15·7′W	W	1,2
Yelnow Fm	Beds	SP9659	52°13·5′	0°35·3′W	FM	153
Yelsted	Kent	TQ8262	51°19·9′	0°37·1′E	T	178,188
Yelt Fm	Derby	SK1233	52°53·9′	1°48·9′W	FM	128
Yelvertoft	Northnts	SP5975	52°22·4′	1°7·6′W	T	140
Yelverton	Devon	SX5267	50°29·3′	4°4·8′W	T	201
Yelverton	Norf	TG2902	52°34·3′	1°23·2′E	T	134
Yendacott Manor	Devon	SS8900	50°47·6′	3°34·1′W	X	192
Yendon	Devon	SX3595	50°44·1′	4°19·9′W	X	190
Yen Hall Fm	Cambs	TL6150	52°7·7′	0°21·5′E	FM	154
Yennadon Down	Devon	SX5468	50°29·9′	4°3·1′W	X	201
Yennards Fm	Leic	SP5098	52°34·9′	1°15·3′W	FM	140
Yenston	Somer	ST7121	50°59·5′	2°24·4′W	T	183
Yenworthy Common	Somer	SS8048	51°13·4′	3°42·7′W	X	181
Yenworthy Fm	Somer	SS8048	51°13·4′	3°42·7′W	FM	181
Yeo	Devon	SS6502	50°48·3′	3°54·6′W	X	191
Yeo Bank Fm	N Som	ST3865	51°23·1′	2°53·1′W	FM	171,182
Yeo Barton	Devon	SS7622	50°59·3′	3°45·6′W	X	180
Yeo Br	Devon	SX7559	50°25·3′	3°45·2′W	X	202
Yeo Fm	Devon	SS7826	51°1·5′	3°44·0′W	FM	180
Yeo Fm	Devon	SX5567	50°29·3′	4°2·3′W	FM	202
Yeo Fm	Devon	SX5952	50°21·3′	3°58·6′W	FM	202
Yeo Fm	Devon	SX6786	50°39·7′	3°52·5′W	FM	191
Yeo Fm	Devon	SX7973	50°32·9′	3°42·1′W	FM	191
Yeoford	Devon	SX7898	50°46·4′	3°43·4′W	T	191
Yeoland Fm	Devon	SX5066	50°28·7′	4°6·5′W	FM	201
Yeoland Ho	Devon	SS6330	51°3·4′	3°56·9′W	X	180
Yeolands	Devon	SX6355	50°23·0′	3°55·2′W	X	202
Yeolm Bridge	Corn	SX3187	50°39·7′	4°23·1′W	A	190
Yeolmbridge	Corn	SX3187	50°39·7′	4°23·1′W	T	190
Yeol Mouth	Corn	SS2016	50°55·2′	4°33·3′W	W	190
Yeomadon	Devon	SS3000	50°46·7′	4°24·3′W	X	190
Yeoman Hey Resr	Oldham	SE0204	53°32·2′	1°57·8′W	W	110
Yeoman Hill	Cald	SE0133	53°47·8′	1°58·7′W	X	104
Yeomans	Devon	SX3882	50°37·1′	4°17·0′W	X	201
Yeoman Wharf	Cumbr	SD3564	54°4·3′	2°59·2′W	X	96,97
Yeo Mill	Devon	SS8426	51°1·5′	3°38·9′W	T	181
Yeo Park	Devon	SX5852	50°21·3′	3°59·4′W	X	202
Yeorton Hall Fm	Cumbr	NY0207	54°27·2′	3°30·3′W	FM	89
Yeory	Devon	SS5314	50°54·6′	4°5·1′W	X	180
Yeo's Fm	Devon	SX8987	50°40·6′	3°33·9′W	FM	192
Yeoton Br	Devon	SX8298	50°46·4′	3°40·0′W	X	191
Yeotown	Devon	SS5834	51°5·5′	4°1·3′W	X	180
Yeotown Fm	Devon	SS5826	51°1·2′	4°1·1′W	FM	180
Yeo Vale	Devon	SS4223	50°59·3′	4°14·7′W	T	180,190
Yeovil	Somer	ST5516	50°56·7′	2°38·0′W	T	183,194
Yeovil Junc Sta	Somer	ST5714	50°55·7′	2°36·3′W	X	194
Yeovil Marsh	Somer	ST5418	50°57·8′	2°38·9′W	T	183
Yeovil Rock	Devon	SX6639	50°14·4′	3°52·4′W	X	202
Yeovilton	Somer	ST5422	51°0·0′	2°38·9′W	T	183
Yeowood Fm	Ches	SJ7359	53°7·9′	2°23·8′W	FM	118
Yerbeston	Pemb	SN0608	51°44·5′	4°48·2′W	T	158
Yerbeston	Pemb	SR9698	51°38·9′	4°56·5′W	X	158
Yerbeston Mountain	Pemb	SN0609	51°45·0′	4°48·2′W	X	158
Yercombe Lodge	Glos	ST7398	51°41·0′	2°23·0′W	X	162
Yerdley Coppice	Warw	SP3033	51°59·9′	1°33·4′W	F	151

Yesket	D & G	NY1675	55°4·0'	3°18·5'W	X	85
Yesnaby	Orkney	HY2215	59°1·2'	3°21·0'W	T	6
Yessell Fm	Worcs	SP0144	52°5·9'	1°58·7'W	FM	150
Yester Ho	E Loth	NT5467	55°53·9'	2°43·7'W	X	66
Yester Mains	E Loth	NT5366	55°53·3'	2°44·6'W	X	66
Yes Tor	Devon	SX5890	50°41·8'	4°0·3'W	H	191
Yetholm Law	Scot Bord	NT8127	55°32·4'	2°17·6'W	H	74
Yetholm Loch	Scot Bord	NT8027	55°32·4'	2°18·6'W	W	74
Yetholm Mains	Scot Bord	NT8329	55°33·5'	2°15·7'W	X	74
Yethouse	Scot Bord	NY4987	55°10·7'	2°47·6'W	X	79
Yetland Fm	Devon	SS5744	51°10·9'	4°2·4'W	FM	180
Yetlington	Northum	NU0209	55°22·7'	1°57·7'W	T	81
Yetlington Lane	Northum	NU0310	55°23·3'	1°56·7'W	X	81
Yetminster	Dorset	ST5910	50°53·5'	2°34·6'W	T	194
Yetson	Devon	SX8056	50°23·7'	3°40·9'W	X	202
Yetsonais Fm	Devon	SX7549	50°19·9'	3°45·0'W	FM	202
Yetston	Renf	NS3870	55°54·0'	4°35·0'W	X	63
Yett	D & G	NY0890	55°12·0'	3°26·3'W	X	78
Yett	N Lanak	NS7759	55°48·8'	3°57·3'W	T	64
Yett	S Ayr	NS4324	55°29·3'	4°28·7'W	X	70
Yett	S Lanak	NS9842	55°39·9'	3°36·9'W	X	72
Yetta	Corn	SX1468	50°29·2'	4°36·9'W	X	200
Yett Burn	Northum	NY6184	55°9·2'	2°36·3'W	W	80
Yett Burn	Scot Bord	NT7914	55°25·4'	2°19·5'W	W	80
Yettington	Devon	SY0585	50°39·7'	3°20·3'W	T	192
Yettna Geo	Orkney	HY2218	59°2·8'	3°21·1'W	X	6
Yetts o' Muckhart	Clackm	NO0001	56°11·7'	3°36·3'W	T	58
Yett, The	Scot Bord	NT7817	55°27·0'	2°20·4'W	X	80
Yew Bank	Cumbr	NY2303	54°25·2'	3°10·8'W	X	89,90
Yew Bank	Cumbr	SD2690	54°18·3'	3°7·8'W	H	96,97
Yewbarrow	Cumbr	NY1708	54°27·9'	3°16·4'W	H	89,90
Yew Barrow	Cumbr	SD3587	54°16·7'	2°59·5'W	X	96,97
Yewbarrow Hall	Cumbr	NY5002	54°24·9'	2°45·8'W	X	90
Yew Cogar Scar	N Yks	SD9270	54°7·8'	2°6·9'W	X	98
Yew Court Fm	Herts	TQ0698	51°40·5'	0°27·6'W	FM	166,176
Yew Crag	Cumbr	NY2214	54°31·2'	3°11·9'W	X	89,90
Yew Crag	Cumbr	NY2615	54°31·7'	3°8·2'W	X	89,90
Yew Crag	Cumbr	NY3020	54°34·5'	3°4·6'W	X	90
Yew Crag	Cumbr	NY3107	54°27·5'	3°3·4'W	X	90
Yew Crag	Cumbr	NY4120	54°34·6'	2°54·3'W	X	90
Yew Crags	Cumbr	NY2202	54°24·7'	3°11·7'W	X	89,90
Yewdale Beck	Cumbr	SD3198	54°22·6'	3°3·3'W	W	96,97
Yewdale Fells	Cumbr	SD3099	54°23·1'	3°4·3'W	X	96,97
Yew Down	Oxon	SU4284	51°33·4'	1°23·3'W	X	174
Yewfield	Lincs	TF0797	53°27·8'	0°22·9'W	X	112
Yew Grange	N Yks	NZ7402	54°24·7'	0°51·2'W	X	94
Yew Green	Warw	SP2267	52°18·3'	1°40·2'W	T	151
Yewhedges	Kent	TQ9655	51°15·8'	0°49·0'E	T	178
Yew Hill	Hants	SU3531	51°4·9'	1°29·6'W	X	185
Yew Hill	Hants	SU4526	51°2·1'	1°21·1'W	X	185
Yew Pike	Cumbr	SD2092	54°19·3'	3°13·4'W	X	96
Yew Pike	Cumbr	SD3098	54°22·6'	3°4·2'W	X	96,97
Yews	Cumbr	SD4397	54°22·2'	2°52·2'W	X	97
Yews Fm	Wilts	SU1323	51°0·6'	1°48·5'W	FM	184
Yews, The	Kent	TQ5849	51°13·3'	0°16·1'E	X	188
Yewtree	Ches	SJ8675	53°16·5'	2°12·2'W	X	118
Yew Tree	Cumbr	NY1105	54°26·2'	3°21·9'W	X	89
Yewtree	Essex	TL6416	51°49·3'	0°23·2'E	X	167
Yewtree	Kent	TQ8648	51°12·3'	0°40·2'E	X	189
Yew Tree	Lancs	SD5037	53°49·9'	2°45·2'W	X	102
Yew Tree	N Yks	SE2952	53°58·0'	1°33·1'W	X	104
Yewtree	Powys	SO1390	52°30·3'	3°16·5'W	X	136
Yew Tree	Pth & Kin	NN7447	56°36·1'	4°2·7'W	X	51,52
Yew Tree	Pth & Kin	NN7447	56°36·1'	4°2·7'W	X	51,52
Yew Tree	Sand	SP0295	52°33·4'	1°57·8'W	T	139
Yew Tree	Tames	SJ9597	53°28·4'	2°4·1'W	T	109
Yew Tree	Wrex	SJ4641	52°58·4'	2°47·8'W	X	117
Yewtree Copse	Hants	SU3418	50°57·9'	1°30·6'W	F	185
Yewtree Cross	Kent	TR1641	51°7·9'	1°5·6'E	T	179,189
Yewtree Fm	Cambs	TL2793	52°31·4'	0°7·3'W	FM	142
Yew Tree Fm	Ches	SJ3079	53°18·4'	3°2·6'W	FM	117
Yew Tree Fm	Ches	SJ3958	53°7·2'	2°54·3'W	FM	117
Yewtree Fm	Ches	SJ4655	53°5·6'	2°48·0'W	FM	117
Yewtree Fm	Ches	SJ5164	53°10·5'	2°43·6'W	FM	117
Yewtree Fm	Ches	SJ5464	53°10·5'	2°40·9'W	FM	117
Yew Tree Fm	Ches	SJ5846	53°0·8'	2°37·2'W	FM	117
Yew Tree Fm	Ches	SJ5955	53°5·7'	2°36·3'W	FM	117
Yew Tree Fm	Ches	SJ6052	53°4·1'	2°35·4'W	FM	118
Yew Tree Fm	Ches	SJ6778	53°18·1'	2°29·3'W	FM	118
Yewtree Fm	Ches	SJ6863	53°10·0'	2°28·3'W	FM	118
Yew-Tree Fm	Ches	SJ6865	53°11·1'	2°28·3'W	FM	118
Yewtree Fm	Ches	SJ7150	53°3·0'	2°25·6'W	FM	118
Yewtree Fm	Ches	SJ7477	53°17·6'	2°23·0'W	FM	118
Yewtree Fm	Ches	SJ8079	53°18·7'	2°17·6'W	FM	118
Yewtree Fm	Ches	SJ8161	53°9·0'	2°16·6'W	FM	118
Yewtree Fm	Ches	SJ8179	53°18·7'	2°16·7'W	FM	118
Yewtree Fm	Ches	SJ8863	53°10·1'	2°10·4'W	FM	118
Yew Tree Fm	Cumbr	NY3023	54°36·1'	3°4·6'W	FM	90
Yew Tree Fm	Cumbr	SD4595	54°21·1'	2°50·4'W	FM	97
Yewtree Fm	Derby	SK3144	52°59·8'	1°31·9'W	FM	119,128
Yewtree Fm	Dorset	ST3803	50°49·6'	2°52·4'W	FM	193
Yew Tree Fm	Essex	TL6724	51°53·6'	0°26·0'E	FM	167
Yew Tree Fm	Essex	TL8818	51°50·0'	0°44·1'E	FM	168
Yew Tree Fm	E Susx	TQ5729	51°2·6'	0°14·8'E	FM	188,199
Yew Tree Fm	Flint	SJ3668	53°12·6'	2°57·1'W	FM	117
Yew Tree Fm	Hants	SU5725	51°1·5'	1°10·8'W	FM	185
Yew Tree Fm	Kent	TQ6142	51°9·5'	0°18·5'E	FM	188
Yewtree Fm	Kent	TQ8756	51°16·6'	0°41·3'E	FM	178
Yewtree Fm	Lancs	SD5270	54°7·7'	2°43·7'W	FM	97
Yew Tree Fm	Lancs	SD6175	54°10·4'	2°35·4'W	FM	97
Yew Tree Fm	Lancs	SD6542	53°52·6'	2°31·5'W	FM	102,103
Yew Tree Fm	Leic	SK2812	52°42·5'	1°34·7'W	FM	128
Yew Tree Fm	Lincs	TF3228	52°50·2'	0°2·0'W	FM	131
Yew Tree Fm	Mil Key	SP8247	52°7·1'	0°47·7'W	FM	152
Yew Tree Fm	Monm	SO3006	51°45·1'	3°0·5'W	FM	161
Yewtree Fm	Norf	TM1088	52°27·2'	1°5·8'E	FM	144
Yew Tree Fm	Notts	SK7543	52°59·0'	0°52·6'W	FM	129
Yew Tree Fm	Powys	SO3194	52°32·5'	3°0·6'W	FM	137
Yew Tree Fm	Shrops	SJ4125	52°49·4'	2°52·1'W	FM	126
Yewtree Fm	Shrops	SJ6529	52°51·7'	2°30·8'W	FM	127
Yewtree Fm	Staffs	SJ8043	52°59·3'	2°17·5'W	FM	118
Yewtree Fm	Staffs	SJ8223	52°48·5'	2°15·6'W	FM	127
Yewtree Fm	Staffs	SJ9614	52°43·7'	2°3·2'W	FM	127
Yewtree Fm	Staffs	SJ9930	52°52·3'	2°0·5'W	FM	127
Yewtree Fm	Staffs	SO8786	52°28·5'	2°11·1'W	FM	139
Yew Tree Fm	Suff	TM2169	52°16·7'	1°14·8'E	FM	156
Yew Tree Fm	Suff	TM2872	52°18·1'	1°21·1'E	FM	156
Yewtree Fm	Suff	TM2876	52°20·3'	1°21·2'E	FM	156
Yew Tree Fm	Suff	TM3365	52°14·3'	1°25·2'E	FM	156
Yewtree Fm	Surrey	TQ1351	51°15·0'	0°22·5'W	FM	187
Yew Tree Fm	Warr	SJ6485	53°21·9'	2°32·1'W	FM	109
Yewtree Fm	Warr	SJ6885	53°21·9'	2°28·4'W	FM	109
Yew Tree Fm	Warw	SP1769	52°19·4'	1°44·6'W	FM	139,151
Yew Tree Fm	Worcs	SO9879	52°24·8'	2°1·4'W	FM	139
Yew Tree Fm	Wrex	SJ4542	52°58·6'	2°48·7'W	FM	117
Yewtree Fm	W Susx	TQ3131	51°4·0'	0°7·4'W	FM	187
Yew Tree Hall	Powys	SO1671	52°20·1'	3°13·6'W	X	136,148
Yew Tree Hall Fm	Ches	SJ6982	53°20·3'	2°27·5'W	FM	109
Yew Tree Heath	Hants	SU3606	50°51·4'	1°28·9'W	X	196
Yewtree Hill	Glos	ST7892	51°37·8'	2°18·7'W	X	162,172
Yewtree Hill	W Berks	SU4880	51°31·2'	1°18·1'W	X	174
Yewtree Ho	Ches	SJ7278	53°18·1'	2°24·8'W	X	118
Yew Tree Ho	E Susx	TQ8015	50°54·6'	0°34·0'E	X	199
Yewtree Ho	Powys	SJ2813	52°42·8'	3°3·5'W	X	126
Yewtree Ho	Shrops	SO5378	52°24·1'	2°41·1'W	X	137,138
Yew Tree Ho	Suff	TM2549	52°5·8'	1°17·5'E	X	169
Yew Tree Ho	Suff	TM2669	52°16·6'	1°19·2'E	X	156
Yewtree Ho	Worcs	SO8365	52°17·2'	2°14·6'W	X	138,150
Yew Tree Ho	Worcs	SO9277	52°23·7'	2°6·7'W	X	139
Yew Tree Tarn	Cumbr	NY3200	54°23·7'	3°2·4'W	W	90
Y Fan	Powys	SN9487	52°28·5'	3°33·2'W	X	136
Y Fan	Powys	SO2430	51°58·0'	3°6·0'W	X	161
Y Fawnen	Wrex	SJ1336	52°55·1'	3°17·2'W	X	125
Y Fedw	Gwyn	SH5541	52°57·1'	4°9·1'W	X	124
Y Fedw	Gwyn	SH9034	52°53·8'	3°37·7'W	X	125
Y Felin Fach	Cered	SN7268	52°18·0'	3°52·2'W	X	135,147
Y Felinheli or Port Dinorwic	Gwyn	SH5267	53°11·0'	4°12·5'W	T	114,115
Y Fenni / Abergavenny	Monm	SO2914	51°49·4'	3°1·4'W	T	161
Y Ferwig	Cered	SN1849	52°6·8'	4°39·1'W	T	145
Y Fflint or Flint	Flint	SJ2472	53°14·6'	3°7·9'W	T	117
Y Ffôr	Gwyn	SH3938	52°55·2'	4°23·3'W	T	123
Y Ffridd	Powys	SJ2020	52°46·5'	3°10·8'W	F	126
Y Ffridd	Powys	SN8691	52°30·5'	3°40·4'W	X	135,136
y-Ffrith	Denb	SJ0483	53°20·4'	3°26·1'W	T	116
Y Ffrwd	Rho Cyn Taf	ST0494	51°38·4'	3°22·9'W	W	170
Y Fign	Gwyn	SH8329	52°51·0'	3°43·8'W	W	124,125
Y Figyn	Powys	SJ1608	52°40·0'	3°14·1'W	X	125
Y Foel	Carm	SN7645	52°5·6'	3°48·2'W	X	146,147
Y Foel	Conwy	SH8050	53°2·3'	3°47·0'W	X	116
Y Foel	Gwyn	SH4646	52°59·6'	4°17·3'W	H	115,123
Y Foel	Gwyn	SH8240	52°56·9'	3°45·0'W	X	124,125
Y Foel	Gwyn	SH9016	52°44·1'	3°37·3'W	H	125
Y Foel	Gwyn	SH9139	52°56·5'	3°36·9'W	H	125
Y Foel	Powys	SJ0101	52°36·1'	3°27·3'W	X	136
Y Foel	Powys	SJ1420	52°46·5'	3°16·1'W	H	125
Y Foel	Powys	SN8384	52°26·7'	3°42·9'W	H	135,136
Y Foel	Powys	SN8848	52°7·4'	3°37·8'W	X	147
Y Foel	Powys	SN9265	52°16·6'	3°34·6'W	X	136,147
Y Foel	Powys	SO0184	52°26·9'	3°27·0'W	H	136
Y Foel	Powys	SO1083	52°26·5'	3°19·0'W	X	136
Y Foel	Wrex	SJ1839	52°56·8'	3°12·8'W	H	125
Y Foel Chwern	Nth Pt Talb	SN8903	51°43·1'	3°36·0'W	A	170
Y Foel Goch	Conwy	SH6758	53°6·4'	3°58·8'W	H	115
Y Frith Graig	Conwy	SH7545	52°59·5'	3°51·3'W	X	115
Y Fron	Powys	SH9812	52°42·0'	3°30·2'W	X	125
Y Gadfa	Gwyn	SH8321	52°46·7'	3°43·7'W	H	124,125
Y Gadfa	Powys	SH9323	52°47·9'	3°34·8'W	X	125
Y Gaer	Carm	SN2126	51°54·5'	4°35·7'W	A	145,158
Y Gaer	Cered	SN2843	52°3·8'	4°30·2'W	X	145
Y Gaer	Cered	SN5150	52°7·9'	4°10·2'W	X	146
Y Gaer	Powys	SJ2015	52°43·8'	3°10·7'W	A	126
Y Gaer	Powys	SN9190	52°30·1'	3°35·9'W	A	136
Y Gaer	Powys	SN9226	51°55·6'	3°33·8'W	A	160
Y Gaer	Powys	SN9828	51°56·7'	3°28·6'W	A	160
Y Gaer	Powys	SO0029	51°57·3'	3°26·9'W	X	160
Y Gaer	Powys	SO0187	52°28·6'	3°27·1'W	X	136
Y Gaer	Powys	SO0614	51°49·2'	3°21·4'W	A	160
Y Gaer	V of Glam	ST0674	51°27·7'	3°20·8'W	A	170
Y Gaer Fach	Carm	SN6824	51°54·2'	3°54·7'W	A	159
Y Gaer Fawr	Carm	SN6824	51°54·2'	3°54·7'W	A	159
Y Gamlas	Gwyn	SH3532	52°51·9'	4°26·7'W	W	123
Y Gamriw	Powys	SN9461	52°14·5'	3°32·8'W	H	147
Y Garn	Cered	SN7360	52°13·7'	3°51·2'W	A	146,147
Y Garn	Cered	SN7785	52°27·2'	3°48·2'W	A	135
Y Garn	Gwyn	SH5552	53°3·0'	4°9·4'W	H	115
Y Garn	Gwyn	SH6359	53°6·9'	4°2·4'W	H	115
Y Garn	Gwyn	SH7023	52°47·6'	3°55·3'W	H	124
Y Garn	Pemb	SM9131	51°56·5'	5°2·1'W	H	157
Y Garn	Pemb	SM9139	52°0·8'	5°2·4'W	X	157
Y Garn	Pemb	SN0438	52°0·6'	4°51·0'W	X	145,157
Y Garn	Powys	SJ0826	52°49·7'	3°21·5'W	X	125
Y Garn Bica	Rho Cyn Taf	SN9400	51°41·6'	3°31·6'W	A	170
Y Garnedd	Cered	SN7584	52°26·6'	3°50·0'W	A	135
Y Garnedd	Gwyn	SH7443	52°58·4'	3°52·2'W	X	124
Y Garth	Carm	SN6113	51°48·1'	4°0·6'W	X	159
Y Garth	Gwyn	SH5261	53°7·8'	4°12·3'W	X	114,115
Y Garth	Gwyn	SH5939	52°56·0'	4°5·5'W	H	124
Y Garth	Gwyn	SH6238	52°55·5'	4°2·8'W	H	124
Y Garth	Powys	SN9355	52°11·2'	3°33·5'W	H	147
Y Gelli	Powys	SN9021	51°52·8'	3°35·5'W	X	160
Y Gelli Gandryll / Hay-on-Wye	Powys	SO2242	52°4·5'	3°7·9'W	T	148,161
Y Gesail	Gwyn	SH9243	52°58·7'	3°36·1'W	H	125
Y Geuallt	Gwyn	SH6051	53°2·5'	4°4·9'W	X	115
Y Globa Fawr	Pemb	SM9140	52°1·4'	5°2·4'W	X	157
Y Glog	Cered	SN7257	52°12·0'	3°52·0'W	X	146,147
Y Glog	Cered	SN7881	52°25·0'	3°47·2'W	H	135
Y Glog	Powys	SJ0920	52°46·4'	3°20·5'W	H	125
Y Glôg	Powys	SO0471	52°20·0'	3°24·1'W	X	136,147
Y Glog Fawr	Powys	SN9266	52°17·1'	3°34·6'W	X	136,147
Y Gloig	Gwyn	SH9337	52°55·4'	3°35·1'W	X	125
Y Glonc	Powys	SO0099	52°35·0'	3°28·2'W	H	136
Y Golfa	Powys	SJ1807	52°39·5'	3°12·3'W	H	125
Y Gorlan	Denb	SJ0369	53°12·8'	3°26·7'W	X	116
Y Gors	Conwy	SH8050	53°2·3'	3°47·0'W	X	116
Y-Gors	Gwyn	SH7535	52°54·1'	3°51·1'W	X	124
Y Graig	Gwyn	SH9633	52°53·3'	3°32·3'W	X	125
Y Graig	Rho Cyn Taf	ST0483	51°32·5'	3°22·7'W	X	170
Y Grib	Powys	SO1931	51°58·5'	3°10·4'W	X	161
Y Gribin	Conwy	SH6558	53°6·4'	4°0·6'W	X	115
Y Gribin	Gwyn	SH8417	52°44·5'	3°42·7'W	H	124,125
Y Gribin	Powys	SJ0326	52°49·6'	3°26·0'W	X	125
Y Gribyn	Powys	SN9291	52°30·6'	3°35·1'W	T	136
Y Groes	Powys	SN8767	52°17·6'	3°39·0'W	X	135,136,147
Y Groes Fagl	Gwyn	SH9929	52°51·2'	3°29·6'W	H	125
Y Grûg	Powys	SN8493	52°31·6'	3°42·2'W	X	135,136
Y Grug	Powys	SN9437	52°1·5'	3°32·3'W	A	160
Y Gurn	Powys	SN9367	52°17·7'	3°33·7'W	X	136,147
Y Gyrn	Gwyn	SH6336	52°54·5'	4°1·8'W	H	124
Y Gyrn	Powys	SN9821	51°52·9'	3°28·5'W	H	160
Yielding Copse	Wilts	SU2173	51°27·6'	1°41·5'W	F	174
Yieldingtree	Worcs	SO8977	52°23·7'	2°9·3'W	X	139
Yieldshields	S Lanak	NS8750	55°44·1'	3°47·5'W	T	65,72
Yiewsley	Hill	TQ0680	51°30·8'	0°28·0'W	T	176
Yinstay	Orkney	HY5110	58°58·7'	2°50·7'W	X	6
Yinstay Head	Orkney	HY5011	58°59·3'	2°51·7'W	X	6
Y Llethr	Gwyn	SH6625	52°48·6'	3°58·9'W	H	124
Y Lliwedd	Gwyn	SH6253	53°3·6'	4°3·2'W	X	115
Y Lordship	Gwyn	SH8632	52°52·6'	3°41·2'W	X	124,125
YMCA National Centre	Cumbr	SD3789	54°17·8'	2°57·7'W	X	96,97
Ymwlch	Gwyn	SH5141	52°57·0'	4°12·7'W	X	124
Ymwlch	Gwyn	SH5728	52°50·1'	4°7·0'W	X	124
Y Mynyddoedd Duon / Black Mountains, The	Powys	SO2427	51°56·4'	3°5·9'W	H	161
Y Neuadd	Powys	SO1117	51°50·9'	3°17·1'W	X	161
Yngs Badrig or Middle Mouse	I of Angl	SH3895	53°25·9'	4°25·9'W	X	114
Y-Not Fm	Warw	SP1851	52°9·7'	1°43·8'W	FM	151
Ynus-tawelog	Swan	SN6209	51°46·0'	3°59·6'W	T	159
Ynys	Denb	SJ0179	53°18·2'	3°28·7'W	X	116
Ynys	Gwyn	SH4642	52°57·4'	4°17·2'W	X	123
Ynys	Gwyn	SH6898	52°34·1'	3°56·5'W	X	135
Ynys Acen	I of Angl	SH4870	53°12·6'	4°16·2'W	X	114,115
Ynys Amlwch or East Mouse	I of Angl	SH4494	53°25·4'	4°20·5'W	X	114
Ynys Arw	I of Angl	SH2694	53°25·1'	4°36·7'W	X	114
Ynys-arwed Fm	Nth Pt Talb	SN8101	51°41·9'	3°42·9'W	FM	170
Ynysau	Carm	SN6539	52°2·2'	3°57·7'W	X	146
Ynysau-isaf	Carm	SN6538	52°1·7'	3°57·7'W	X	146
Ynys Bach	I of Angl	SH4482	53°19·0'	4°20·1'W	X	114,115
Ynys Barry	Pemb	SM8032	51°56·8'	5°11·7'W	X	157
Ynys Bery	Pemb	SM7022	51°51·2'	5°20·0'W	X	157
Ynys Boeth	Conwy	SH8166	53°10·9'	3°46·4'W	X	116
Ynysboeth	Rho Cyn Taf	ST0796	51°39·5'	3°20·3'W	T	170
Ynys-Brechfa	Carm	SN5329	51°56·6'	4°7·9'W	X	146
Ynys Cantwr	Pemb	SM7022	51°51·2'	5°20·0'W	X	157
Ynys-Cedwyn	Powys	SN7809	51°46·2'	3°45·7'W	X	160
Ynys-Clydach	Powys	SN8930	51°57·7'	3°36·5'W	X	160
Ynys Creud	Gwyn	SH4442	52°57·4'	4°18·9'W	X	123
Ynys Cyngar	Gwyn	SH5536	52°54·4'	4°9·0'W	X	124
Ynysddu	Caer	ST1792	51°37·5'	3°11·6'W	T	171
Ynys-ddu	Pemb	SM8838	52°0·2'	5°4·9'W	X	157
Ynys Deullyn	Pemb	SM8434	51°58·0'	5°8·3'W	X	157
Ynys Dulas	I of Angl	SH5090	53°23·4'	4°14·9'W	X	114
Ynys-dwfnant	Nth Pt Talb	SN8001	51°41·9'	3°43·8'W	X	170
Ynys Eilun	Pemb	SM7021	51°50·7'	5°20·0'W	X	157
Ynys Enlli or Bardsey Island	Gwyn	SH1221	52°45·5'	4°46·8'W	X	123
Ynys Ettws	Gwyn	SH6256	53°5·2'	4°3·2'W	X	115
Ynys Fâch	Gwyn	SH6043	52°58·2'	4°4·7'W	X	124
Ynys-fach	Pemb	SM8232	51°56·9'	5°9·9'W	X	157
Ynysfadog	Nth Pt Talb	SN7905	51°44·1'	3°44·7'W	X	160
Ynysfawr	Carm	SN1428	51°55·4'	4°41·9'W	X	145,158
Ynys Fawr	I of Angl	SH4482	53°19·0'	4°20·1'W	X	114,115
Ynysfawr	Powys	SN8528	51°56·6'	3°40·0'W	X	160
Ynys Feirig	I of Angl	SH3073	53°13·9'	4°32·4'W	X	114
Ynysfergi	Cered	SN6189	52°29·1'	4°2·4'W	X	135
Ynys-Fer-lâs	Gwyn	SH5943	52°58·2'	4°5·6'W	X	124
Ynys Fm	Carm	SN6336	52°0·6'	3°59·4'W	FM	146
Ynys Fm	Swan	SN6006	51°44·4'	4°1·3'W	FM	159
Ynysfor	Gwyn	SH6042	52°57·7'	4°4·7'W	X	124
Ynysforgan	Swan	SS6799	51°40·7'	3°55·0'W	T	159
Ynys Gaint	I of Angl	SH5672	53°13·8'	4°9·0'W	X	114,115
Ynys-ger-gathen	Swan	SN6309	51°46·0'	3°58·7'W	X	159
Ynys Gifftan	Gwyn	SH6037	52°55·0'	4°4·5'W	X	124
Ynys Goch	Gwyn	SH4244	52°58·5'	4°20·8'W	X	123
Ynys Goed	I of Angl	SH4381	53°18·4'	4°21·0'W	X	114,115
Ynys Greigiog	Cered	SN6794	52°31·9'	3°57·2'W	X	135
Ynys Gwelltog	Pemb	SM7022	51°51·2'	5°20·0'W	X	157
Ynys-Gwrtheyrn	Gwyn	SH5724	52°47·9'	4°6·9'W	X	124
Ynys Gwylan-bâch	Gwyn	SH1824	52°47·2'	4°41·5'W	X	123
Ynys Gwylan-fawr	Gwyn	SH1824	52°47·2'	4°41·5'W	X	123
Ynys Gybi or Holy Island	I of Angl	SH2579	53°17·0'	4°37·1'W	X	114
Ynys-gyfarch	Powys	SN9933	51°59·4'	3°27·9'W	X	160
Ynysgyffylog	Gwyn	SH6213	52°42·1'	4°2·3'W	X	124
Ynyshafren Fm	Carm	SN4708	51°45·2'	4°12·6'W	FM	159
Ynys-hir	Cered	SN4964	52°15·4'	4°12·3'W	X	146
Ynys-hir	Cered	SN6895	52°32·5'	3°56·4'W	X	135
Ynyshir	Rho Cyn Taf	ST0292	51°37·3'	3°24·6'W	T	170
Ynys-hir Nature Reserve	Cered	SN6796	52°33·0'	3°57·3'W	X	135
Ynys Hwfa	Gwyn	SH4547	53°0·1'	4°18·2'W	X	115,123
Ynys Hywel	Caer	ST1891	51°36·9'	3°10·7'W	X	171
Ynys Isaf	I of Angl	SH5081	53°18·5'	4°14·7'W	X	114,115
Ynys-isaf	Powys	SN7911	51°47·3'	3°44·9'W	T	160
Ynyslas	Brig	SS9285	51°33·5'	3°33·1'W	X	170
Ynyslas	Cered	SN6092	52°30·7'	4°3·4'W	T	135
Ynys-las	I of Angl	SH2976	53°15·5'	4°33·4'W	X	114
Ynys-lâs Fm	Cered	SN6293	52°31·3'	4°1·6'W	FM	135
Ynysleci	Gwyn	SH4340	52°56·3'	4°19·8'W	X	123

Ynys-Lochtyn	Cered	SN3155	52°10·3′	4°27·9′W	X	145
Ynysmaerdy	Nth Pt Talb	SS7495	51°38·6′	3°48·9′W	T	170
Ynysmaerdy	Rho Cyn Taf	ST0384	51°33·0′	3°23·6′W	T	170
Ynys Meibion	I of Angl	SH3268	53°11·2′	4°30·5′W	X	114
Ynys Meicel	Pemb	SM8941	52°1·9′	5°4·2′W	X	157
Ynys Melyn	Pemb	SM8838	52°0·2′	5°4·9′W	X	157
Ynysmeudwy	Nth Pt Talb	SN7305	51°44·0′	3°50·0′W	T	160
Ynysmoch	Carm	SN6927	51°55·8′	3°53·9′W	X	146,160
Ynys Moelfre	I of Angl	SH5186	53°21·2′	4°13·9′W	X	114
Ynysmôn or Anglesey	I of Angl	SH4378	53°16·8′	4°20·9′W	X	114,115
Ynys-Morgan	Cered	SN6768	52°17·9′	3°56·6′W	X	135
Ynysoedd Duon	I of Angl	SH3269	53°11·7′	4°30·5′W	X	114
Ynysoedd Gwylanod	I of Angl	SH2674	53°14·3′	4°36·0′W	X	114
Ynysoedd y Moelrhoniaid or The Skerries	I of Angl	SH2694	53°25·1′	4°36·7′W	X	114
Ynysowen	Merth Tyd	ST0799	51°41·2′	3°20·3′W	T	170
Ynys Peibio	I of Angl	SH2682	53°18·6′	4°36·3′W	X	114
Ynys Piod	Gwyn	SH1625	52°47·7′	4°43·3′W	X	123
Ynys-rhyd	Carm	SN5327	51°55·6′	4°7·9′W	X	146
Ynys Rhys	Conwy	SH8568	53°12·0′	3°42·9′W	X	116
Ynys Seiriol or Priestholm or Puffin Island	I of Angl	SH6582	53°19·3′	4°1·2′W	X	114,115
Ynys Tachwedd	Cered	SN6093	52°31·3′	4°3·4′W	T	135
Ynystawe	Swan	SN6800	51°41·2′	3°54·2′W	T	159
Ynyston Fm	V of Glam	ST1674	51°27·8′	3°12·2′W	FM	171
Ynys Traws	I of Angl	SH2774	53°14·3′	4°35·1′W	X	114
Ynystudor	Cered	SN6693	52°31·3′	3°58·1′W	X	135
Ynys Wellt	I of Angl	SH2383	53°19·1′	4°39·0′W	X	114
Ynyswen	Carm	SN5224	51°53·9′	4°8·7′W	X	159
Ynys Wen	Conwy	SH8548	53°1·3′	3°42·5′W	X	116
Ynys-wen	Gwyn	SH4443	52°57·9′	4°19·0′W	X	123
Ynys-wen	Gwyn	SH5543	52°58·1′	4°9·1′W	X	124
Ynys-wen	Gwyn	SH5643	52°58·1′	4°8·3′W	H	124
Ynyswen	Powys	SN8313	51°48·4′	3°41·4′W	T	160
Ynyswen	Rho Cyn Taf	SS9597	51°40·0′	3°30·7′W	T	170
Ynys-y-bont	Powys	SN9830	51°57·8′	3°28·7′W	X	160
Ynys y Brawd	Gwyn	SH6115	52°43·1′	4°3·1′W	X	124
Ynysybwl	Rho Cyn Taf	ST0594	51°38·4′	3°22·0′W	T	170
Ynysycapel	Cered	SN6490	52°29·7′	3°59·8′W	X	135
Ynys y Carcharorion	I of Angl	SH4989	53°22·8′	4°15·8′W	X	114
Ynys y Castell	Pemb	SM8533	51°57·5′	5°7·4′W	X	157
Ynys-y-cranc	I of Angl	SH3862	53°8·1′	4°24·9′W	X	114
Ynysyfro Fm	Newp	ST2889	51°36·0′	3°2·0′W	FM	171
Ynys y Fydlyn	I of Angl	SH2991	53°23·5′	4°33·9′W	X	114
Ynys-y-gerwyn-fach	Nth Pt Talb	SS7899	51°40·8′	3°45·5′W	X	170
Ynysygwas	Nth Pt Talb	SS7891	51°36·5′	3°45·3′W	T	170
Ynysymaengwyn	Gwyn	SH5902	52°36·1′	4°4·5′W	X	135
Ynys-y-mond	Nth Pt Talb	SN7102	51°42·4′	3°51·6′W	X	170
Yoadcastle	Cumbr	SD1595	54°20·9′	3°18·0′W	X	96
Yoad Ho	N Yks	SE6297	54°22·1′	1°2·3′W	X	94,100
Yoadpot	Cumbr	SD5499	54°23·3′	2°42·1′W	X	97
Yoag's Haven	Aberd	NK1139	57°26·7′	1°48·5′W	W	30
Yoakes Court Fm	Kent	TR0326	51°0·1′	0°54·0′E	FM	189
Yockenthwaite	N Yks	SD9079	54°12·6′	2°8·8′W	T	98
Yockenthwaite Moor	N Yks	SD9080	54°13·2′	2°8·8′W	X	98
Yockings Gate	Shrops	SJ5542	52°58·6′	2°39·8′W	X	117
Yockleton	Shrops	SJ4010	52°41·3′	2°52·9′W	T	126
Yockletts Banks	Kent	TR1247	51°11·2′	1°2·4′E	F	179,189
Yockletts Fm	Kent	TR1247	51°11·2′	1°2·4′E	FM	179,189
Yoden Village	Durham	NZ4341	54°46·0′	1°19·5′W	A	88
Yodercott	Devon	ST0712	50°54·2′	3°19·0′W	T	181
Yogli Geo	Shetld	HU6491	60°36·1′	0°49·4′W	X	1,2
Yoke	Cumbr	NY4306	54°27·0′	2°52·3′W	H	90
Yoke Burn	Northum	NT9111	55°23·8′	2°8·1′W	W	80
Yoke Burn	Scot Bord	NT2616	55°26·2′	3°9·7′W	W	79
Yokefleet	E Yorks	SE8124	53°42·6′	0°46·0′W	T	106,112
Yokefleet Lodge	E Yorks	SE8231	53°46·4′	0°44·9′W	X	106
Yokegate	E Yorks	SE7832	53°46·9′	0°48·6′W	X	105,106
Yoke Hill	Northnts	SP9589	52°29·7′	0°35·6′W	X	141
Yoke Hill Fm	Northnts	SP9588	52°29·1′	0°35·7′W	FM	141
Yoke Ho	Gwyn	SH3736	52°54·0′	4°25·0′W	X	123
Yokehurst	E Susx	TQ3816	50°55·8′	0°1·8′W	X	198
Yoke Knowes	D & G	NT0508	55°21·7′	3°29·5′W	X	78
Yoker	C of Glas	NS5169	55°53·7′	4°22·5′W	T	64
Yoke's Court	Kent	TQ8956	51°16·5′	0°43·0′E	X	178
Yoke Sike	Durham	NY9115	54°32·1′	2°7·9′W	W	91,92
Yoke, The	Scot Bord	NT3350	55°44·6′	3°3·6′W	X	66,73
Yokieshill	Aberd	NK0146	57°30·5′	1°58·5′W	X	30
Yokstran	Shetld	HU2843	60°10·5′	1°29·2′W	X	4
Yole Fm	Cambs	TL5749	52°7·2′	0°18·0′E	FM	154
Yolland Hill	Devon	SX7669	50°30·7′	3°44·6′W	X	202
Yonbell	Orkney	HY2422	59°5·0′	3°19·1′W	X	6
Yonder Bognie	Aberd	NJ5946	57°30·4′	2°40·6′W	X	29
Yondercroft	E Ayr	NS5938	55°37·2′	4°13·9′W	X	71
Yonderfield	N Ayr	NS1948	55°41·8′	4°52·4′W	X	63
Yonderhaugh	Falk	NS9082	56°1·4′	3°45·5′W	X	65
Yonderhouses	N Ayr	NS2747	55°41·4′	4°44·7′W	X	63
Yonder Ridge	Devon	ST2301	50°48·4′	3°5·2′W	X	192,193
Yonderton	Aberd	NJ6450	57°32·6′	2°35·6′W	X	29
Yonderton	Aberd	NJ6813	57°12·7′	2°31·3′W	X	38
Yonderton	Aberd	NJ7555	57°35·3′	2°24·6′W	X	29
Yonderton	Aberd	NJ8452	57°33·7′	2°15·6′W	X	29,30
Yonderton	Aberd	NJ9432	57°23·0′	2°5·5′W	X	30
Yonderton	Aberd	NK0337	57°25·7′	1°56·5′W	X	30
Yonderton	N Ayr	NS2147	55°41·3′	4°50·4′W	X	63
Yonderton	Renf	NS3866	55°51·9′	4°34·9′W	X	63
Yonderton	Renf	NS4767	55°52·6′	4°26·3′W	X	64
Yonderton	S Ayr	NS3913	55°23·3′	4°32·1′W	X	70
Yonderton	S Ayr	NS4626	55°30·5′	4°25·9′W	X	70
Yonderton	S Lanak	NS7836	55°36·4′	3°55·8′W	X	71
Yonderton of Auchlyne	Aberd	NJ5627	57°20·1′	2°43·4′W	X	37
Yondertown	Devon	SX5959	50°25·1′	3°58·7′W	T	202
Yondertown	Moray	NJ4152	57°33·5′	2°58·7′W	X	28
Yondertown of Knock	Moray	NJ5554	57°34·7′	2°44·7′W	X	29
Yondhead Rigg	N Yks	SE8890	54°18·1′	0°38·4′W	X	94,101
Yondover	Dorset	SY4993	50°44·3′	2°43·0′W	T	193,194
Yonsea Fm	Kent	TQ9845	51°10·4′	0°50·3′E	FM	189
Yons Nab	N Yks	TA0884	54°14·7′	0°20·1′W	X	101
Yopps Green	Kent	TQ6054	51°16·0′	0°18·0′E	T	188
Yorburgh	N Yks	SD8888	54°17·5′	2°10·6′W	X	98
Yorbus Grange	N Yks	SE3166	54°5·6′	1°31·1′W	X	99
Yordas Cave	N Yks	SD7079	54°12·6′	2°27·2′W	X	98
Yorebridge Ho	N Yks	SD9390	54°18·6′	2°6·0′W	X	98
Yore Ho	N Yks	SD8093	54°20·2′	2°18·0′W	X	98
Yorescott	N Yks	SD9390	54°18·6′	2°6·0′W	X	98
Yorfalls Wood	N Yks	SE8192	54°19·3′	0°44·9′W	F	94,100
York	Lancs	SD7033	53°47·8′	2°26·9′W	T	103
York	York	SE5951	53°57·3′	1°5·6′W	T	105
York Br	N Yks	SE5162	54°3·3′	1°12·8′W	X	100
York Cross	N Yks	NZ8701	54°24·1′	0°39·2′W	A	94
York Cross Rigg	N Yks	NZ8701	54°24·1′	0°39·2′W	X	94
Yorke's Fm	Cambs	TL4290	52°29·6′	0°5·9′E	FM	142,143
Yorke's Folly	N Yks	SE1563	54°4·0′	1°45·8′W	X	99
York Fm	Warw	SP2044	52°5·9′	1°42·1′W	FM	151
York Gate Fm	N Yks	SE3477	54°11·5′	1°28·3′W	FM	99
York Grounds Fm	E Yorks	SE9731	53°46·2′	0°31·3′W	FM	106
Yorkhill	C of Glas	NS5665	55°51·7′	4°17·6′W	T	64
York Ho	N Yks	NZ7403	54°25·3′	0°51·2′W	X	94
Yorkhouse Cave	N Som	ST4766	51°23·7′	2°45·3′W	X	171,172,182
Yorkletts	Kent	TR0963	51°19·9′	1°0·4′E	T	179
Yorkley	Glos	SO6306	51°45·3′	2°31·8′W	T	162
Yorkley Court	Glos	SO6306	51°45·3′	2°31·8′W	X	162
Yorkley Slade	Glos	SO6407	51°45·9′	2°30·9′W	T	162
Yorks Fm	Northnts	SP6751	52°9·4′	1°0·8′W	FM	152
Yorkshill Fm	Kent	TQ4951	51°14·5′	0°8·5′E	FM	188
Yorkshire Br	Derby	SK1984	53°21·4′	1°42·5′W	X	110
Yorkshire Dales Cycle Way	N Yks	SD9458	54°1·3′	2°5·1′W	X	103
Yorkshire Dales Rly	N Yks	SE0053	53°58·6′	1°59·6′W	X	104
Yorkshire Museum of Farming	York	SE6552	53°57·8′	1°0·1′W	X	105,106
Yorkston	Midlo	NT3156	55°47·8′	3°5·6′W	X	66,73
York's Wood	Bucks	SP6110	51°47·4′	1°6·5′W	F	164,165
York Tower	Moray	NJ1662	57°38·7′	3°24·0′W	X	28
York Town	Surrey	SU8659	51°19·6′	0°45·5′W	T	175,186
Yorton	Shrops	SJ5023	52°48·4′	2°44·1′W	T	126
Yorton Heath	Shrops	SJ5022	52°47·8′	2°44·1′W	T	126
Yorton Villa Fm	Shrops	SJ5022	52°47·8′	2°44·1′W	FM	126
Yotham	E Susx	TQ6207	50°50·6′	0°18·5′E	W	199
Yottenfews	Cumbr	NY0305	54°26·1′	3°29·3′W	T	89
Youlbury Wood	Oxon	SP4803	51°43·7′	1°17·9′W	F	164
Youlden Ho	Devon	SS6033	51°5·0′	3°59·5′W	X	180
Youlditch Fm	Devon	SX5592	50°42·8′	4°2·9′W	FM	191
Youldon	Devon	SS3208	50°51·1′	4°22·8′W	X	190
Youldon Fm	Devon	SS2905	50°49·4′	4°25·3′W	FM	190
Youldon Fm	Devon	SS3612	50°53·3′	4°19·5′W	FM	190
Youldonmoor Cross	Devon	SS3209	50°51·6′	4°22·9′W	X	190
Youlgreave	Derby	SK2164	53°10·6′	1°40·7′W	T	119
Youlieburn	Aberd	NJ8731	57°22·4′	2°12·5′W	X	30
Youll Close	N Lincs	SE9616	53°38·1′	0°32·5′W	X	112
Youlston	Devon	SS5837	51°7·1′	4°1·4′W	A	180
Youlstone	Corn	SX1989	50°40·6′	4°33·3′W	X	190
Youlston Wood	Devon	SS6036	51°6·6′	3°59·6′W	F	180
Youlthorpe	E Yorks	SE7655	53°59·4′	0°50·0′W	T	105,106
Youlthorpe Pasture Hill	E Yorks	SE7554	53°58·8′	0°51·0′W	X	105,106
Youlton	N Yks	SE4963	54°3·9′	1°14·7′W	T	100
Youlton Lodge	N Yks	SE5063	54°3·9′	1°13·7′W	X	100
Youlton Moor	N Yks	SE4964	54°4·4′	1°14·7′W	X	100
Young Ausway	Northnts	SP8456	52°12·0′	0°45·9′W	X	152
Youngcombe	Devon	SX7242	50°16·1′	3°47·4′W	X	202
Youngcott	Corn	SX2892	50°42·4′	4°25·8′W	X	190
Youngcott	Devon	SX4076	50°33·9′	4°15·2′W	X	201
Young Hayes Fm	Devon	SY0095	50°45·0′	3°24·7′W	FM	192
Younghurst Wood	Suff	TL7978	52°22·5′	0°38·2′E	F	144
Young Jeanie's Wood	Scot Bord	NT7555	55°47·5′	2°23·5′W	F	67,74
Young Manor Fm	Kent	TR0552	51°14·0′	0°56·6′E	FM	179,189
Young Plantn	Norf	TL9181	52°23·8′	0°48·8′E	F	144
Youngsbury	Herts	TL3718	51°50·9′	0°0·3′W	T	166
Young's Close	Cumbr	NY3764	54°58·2′	2°58·6′W	X	85
Young's End	Essex	TL7319	51°50·8′	0°31·1′E	T	167
Young's Fm	Essex	TQ4894	51°37·7′	0°8·7′E	FM	167,177
Young's Fm	Kent	TR1451	51°13·3′	1°4·3′E	FM	179,189
Young's Fm	Surrey	TQ1641	51°9·6′	0°20·1′W	FM	187
Young's Wood	Lincs	TF0492	53°25·1′	0°25·7′W	F	112
Young Wood	Lincs	TF1371	53°13·7′	0°18·0′W	T	121
Youngwood Fm	Hill	TQ0789	51°35·6′	0°26·9′W	FM	176
Yowlass Wood	N Yks	SE5287	54°16·8′	1°11·7′W	F	100
Yowlestone Ho	Devon	SS8410	50°52·9′	3°38·6′W	X	191
Yowlie Burn	Aberd	NJ9030	57°21·9′	2°9·5′W	W	30
Yoxall	Staffs	SK1418	52°45·8′	1°47·1′W	T	128
Yoxall Br	Staffs	SK1317	52°45·3′	1°48·0′W	X	128
Yoxall Lodge	Staffs	SK1522	52°48·0′	1°46·2′W	X	128
Yoxford	Suff	TM3968	52°15·7′	1°30·5′E	T	156
Yoxford Wood	Suff	TM3870	52°16·8′	1°29·8′E	F	156
Yoxie Geo	Shetld	HU5865	60°22·2′	0°56·4′W	X	2
Yoxter Fm	Somer	ST5154	51°17·2′	2°41·8′W	FM	182,183
Y Penrhyn	Pemb	SM9440	52°1·5′	4°59·8′W	X	157
Y Perch	Gwyn	SH6014	52°42·6′	4°3·9′W	X	124
Y Pigwn	Carm	SN8231	51°58·1′	3°42·7′W	X	160
Y Pigwn (Roman Camps)	Carm	SN8231	51°58·1′	3°42·7′W	R	160
Ypres Tower	E Susx	TQ9220	50°57·1′	0°44·4′E	A	189
Yr Allt	Cered	SN8376	52°22·4′	3°42·7′W	H	135,136,147
Yr Allt	Gwyn	SH4149	53°1·1′	4°21·8′W	X	115,123
Yr Allt	Gwyn	SH6409	52°39·9′	4°0·3′W	X	124
Yr Allt	Powys	SJ1303	52°37·3′	3°16·7′W	X	136
Yr Allt	Powys	SJ2409	52°40·6′	3°7·0′W	X	126
Yr Allt	Powys	SN9019	51°51·8′	3°35·5′W	X	160
Yr Allt	Powys	SN9129	51°57·2′	3°34·8′W	H	160
Yr Allt	Powys	SN9898	52°34·5′	3°29·9′W	H	136
Yr Allt	Powys	SO0062	52°15·1′	3°27·5′W	X	147
Yr Allt	Powys	SO0068	52°18·3′	3°27·6′W	X	136,147
Yr Allt	Powys	SO0515	51°49·8′	3°22·3′W	X	160
Yr Allt	Powys	SO0586	52°28·1′	3°23·5′W	X	136
Yr Allt	Powys	SO0775	52°22·2′	3°21·6′W	X	136,147
Yr Allt	Powys	SO0830	51°57·9′	3°20·0′W	H	160
Yr Allt	Powys	SO0844	52°5·4′	3°20·2′W	X	147,160
Yr Allt	Powys	SO1952	52°9·9′	3°10·7′W	H	148
Yr Allt-Boeth	Powys	SJ0216	52°44·2′	3°26·7′W	H	125
Yr Allt Gethin	Powys	SO0387	52°28·6′	3°25·3′W	X	136
Yr Aran	Denb	SJ0232	52°52·8′	3°27·0′W	X	125
Yr Aran	Gwyn	SH6051	53°2·5′	4°4·9′W	H	115
Yr Arddu	Conwy	SH6750	53°2·1′	3°58·6′W	X	115
Yr Arddu	Gwyn	SH6246	52°59·9′	4°3·0′W	H	115
Yr Aryg	Gwyn	SH6867	53°11·3′	3°58·1′W	X	115
Yr-efail	Powys	SO1827	51°56·4′	3°11·2′W	X	161
Yr Eifl	Gwyn	SH3644	52°58·3′	4°26·1′W	H	123
Yr Eithin	Powys	SJ0427	52°50·2′	3°25·1′W	X	125
Yr Elen	Gwyn	SH6765	53°10·2′	3°59·0′W	H	115
Yr Esgair	Gwyn	SH6361	53°8·0′	4°2·5′W	X	115
Yr Esgair	Powys	SN8785	52°27·3′	3°39·4′W	X	135,136
Yr Hôb or Hope	Flint	SJ3058	53°7·1′	3°2·4′W	T	117
Y Rhos	Gwyn	SH5908	52°39·3′	4°4·7′W	X	124
Y Rhos	Powys	SH9507	52°39·3′	3°32·7′W	X	125
Yr Hyl	Brig	SS9090	51°36·1′	3°34·9′W	X	170
Yr Hysfa	Powys	SN9964	52°16·1′	3°28·4′W	X	147
Yr Ochrydd	Cered	SN7884	52°26·7′	3°47·3′W	X	135
Yr Oerfa	Gwyn	SH8641	52°57·5′	3°41·4′W	X	124,125
Yr Oerfa	Powys	SJ1019	52°45·9′	3°19·6′W	H	125
Yr Ole Wen	Conwy	SH6561	53°8·0′	4°0·7′W	X	115
Yr Onen	Gwyn	SH6437	52°55·0′	4°1·0′W	X	124
Yr Onnen	Powys	SO0368	52°18·3′	3°25·0′W	X	136,147
Yr Oron	Denb	SJ0232	52°52·8′	3°27·0′W	X	125
Y Ro Wen	Conwy	SH7449	53°1·7′	3°52·3′W	H	115
Yr Wyddfa or Snowdon	Gwyn	SH6054	53°4·1′	4°5·0′W	H	115
Yr Wyddgrug or Mold	Flint	SJ2363	53°9·8′	3°8·7′W	T	117
Yr Wylorn	Powys	SN9572	52°20·4′	3°32·1′W	X	136,147
Yr-ynys	I of Angl	SH3988	53°22·1′	4°24·8′W	X	114
Ysbylldir	I of Angl	SH3179	53°17·1′	4°31·7′W	X	114
Ysbytty	Gwyn	SH5060	53°7·2′	4°14·1′W	X	114,115
Ysbyty Cynfyn	Cered	SN7579	52°23·9′	3°49·8′W	T	135,147
Ysbyty Ifan	Conwy	SH8448	53°1·2′	3°43·4′W	T	116
Ysbyty Ystwyth	Cered	SN7371	52°19·6′	3°51·4′W	T	135,147
Yscaio	Carm	SN5925	51°54·6′	4°2·6′W	X	146
Ysceifiog	Flint	SJ1571	53°14·0′	3°16·0′W	T	116
Yscirfechan	Powys	SN9637	52°1·5′	3°30·6′W	X	160
Yscoedreddfin	Powys	SN8431	51°58·2′	3°40·9′W	X	160
Ysgafell Wen	Conwy	SH6649	53°1·5′	3°59·5′W	X	115
Ysgeibion	Denb	SJ0658	53°6·9′	3°23·9′W	T	116
Ysgeirallt	Conwy	SH9475	53°15·9′	3°35·0′W	X	116
Ysgellog	I of Angl	SH4191	53°23·8′	4°23·1′W	X	114
Ysgiach	Swan	SN6303	51°42·8′	3°58·6′W	X	159
Ysgiog	Powys	SO0648	52°7·6′	3°22·0′W	X	147
Ysgir Fawr	Powys	SN9741	52°3·7′	3°29·8′W	W	147,160
Ysgir Fawr	Powys	SN9838	52°2·1′	3°28·8′W	W	160
Ysgir Fechan	Powys	SN9540	52°3·1′	3°31·5′W	W	147,160
Ysgir Fechan	Powys	SN9637	52°1·5′	3°30·6′W	W	160
Ysgo	Gwyn	SH2026	52°48·3′	4°39·8′W	X	123
Ysgoldy	I of Angl	SH4382	53°18·9′	4°21·0′W	X	114,115
Ysgolion Duon	Conwy	SH6663	53°9·1′	3°59·8′W	X	115
Ysgrafell	Carm	SN7237	52°1·2′	3°51·5′W	X	146,160
Ysgubor Bach	Gwyn	SH1628	52°49·3′	4°43·4′W	X	123
Ysgubor-fawr	Gwyn	SH9639	52°56·5′	3°32·5′W	X	125
Ysgubor Fawr	I of Angl	SH4371	53°13·0′	4°20·7′W	X	114,115
Ysgubor Gaer	Pemb	SM8938	52°0·3′	5°4·1′W	A	157
Ysgubor Gerrig	Gwyn	SH5142	52°57·5′	4°12·7′W	X	124
Ysgubor Hen	Gwyn	SH4538	52°55·3′	4°17·9′W	X	123
Ysguboriau	Cered	SN7270	52°19·0′	3°52·3′W	X	135,147
Ysguboriau	Gwyn	SH6002	52°36·1′	4°3·6′W	X	135
Ysguboriau	Gwyn	SH7304	52°37·4′	3°52·2′W	X	135
Ysgubor Isaf	Gwyn	SH4561	53°7·7′	4°18·6′W	X	114,115
Ysgubor Mountain	Pemb	SM9630	51°56·1′	4°57·7′W	H	157
Ysgubornewydd	Cered	SN6681	52°24·9′	3°57·8′W	X	135
Ysgubor-newydd	Conwy	SH9070	53°13·2′	3°38·4′W	X	116
Ysgubor Plas	Gwyn	SH3641	52°56·7′	4°26·0′W	X	123
Ysguborwen	Carm	SN4812	51°47·4′	4°11·8′W	X	159
Ysgubor Wen	I of Angl	SH4768	53°11·5′	4°17·0′W	X	114,115
Ysguborwen	Monm	ST4095	51°39·3′	2°51·7′W	X	171
Ysguborwen	Pemb	SN1038	52°0·7′	4°45·7′W	X	145
Ysgubor-wen Ho	Rho Cyn Taf	SO0003	51°43·2′	3°26·5′W	X	170
Ysgubor-y-coed	Cered	SN6895	52°32·5′	3°56·4′W	X	135
Ysgŵd-ffordd	Powys	SO0873	52°21·1′	3°20·6′W	X	136,147
Ysgwennant	Powys	SJ1930	52°51·9′	3°11·8′W	X	125
Ysgwydd-gwyn-isaf Fm	Caer	SO1200	51°41·7′	3°16·0′W	FM	171
Ysgwydd Hŵch	Powys	SO0537	52°1·6′	3°22·7′W	H	160
Ysgyrd Fach	Monm	SO3113	51°48·9′	2°59·7′W	H	161
Ysgyryd Fawr	Monm	SO3317	51°51·1′	2°58·0′W	H	161
Yspitty	Carm	SS5598	51°40·0′	4°5·4′W	T	159
Yspitty Ifan	Carm	SN4826	51°54·9′	4°12·2′W	X	146
Ystafelloedd	Pemb	SM7923	51°52·0′	5°12·2′W	X	157
Ystalyfera	Nth Pt Talb	SN7608	51°45·7′	3°47·4′W	T	160
Ysticlau Fm	Carm	SN4716	51°49·5′	4°12·8′W	FM	159
Ystlysycoed-isaf	Carm	SN5606	51°44·3′	4°4·7′W	X	159
Ystlys-y-coed-uchaf	Carm	SN5707	51°44·8′	4°3·9′W	X	159
Ystrad	Carm	SN4929	51°56·6′	4°11·4′W	X	146
Ystrad	Carm	SN7432	51°58·6′	3°49·7′W	X	146,160
Ystrad	Powys	SN9299	52°34·9′	3°35·2′W	X	136
Ystrad	Powys	SO0061	52°14·5′	3°27·5′W	X	147
Ystrad	Rho Cyn Taf	SS9895	51°38·9′	3°28·1′W	T	170
Ystrad Aeron	Cered	SN5256	52°11·2′	4°9·5′W	T	146
Ystrad Bach	Conwy	SH9745	52°59·8′	3°31·7′W	X	116
Ystrad Barwig Isaf	Rho Cyn Taf	ST0784	51°33·1′	3°20·1′W	X	170
Ystradcorrwg	Carm	SN4528	51°56·0′	4°14·9′W	X	146
Ystradfaelog	Powys	SN9892	52°31·2′	3°29·8′W	X	136
Ystradfai	Carm	SN5104	51°43·1′	4°9·0′W	X	159
Ystrad-fawr	Carm	SN4212	51°47·3′	4°17·1′W	X	159
Ystrad Fawr	Conwy	SH9745	52°59·8′	3°31·7′W	X	116
Ystradfellte	Powys	SN9213	51°48·6′	3°33·6′W	T	160
Ystradfellte Resr	Powys	SN9417	51°50·7′	3°31·9′W	W	160
Ystradferthyr	Carm	SN4212	51°47·3′	4°17·1′W	X	159
Ystradffin	Carm	SN7846	52°6·2′	3°46·5′W	X	146,147
Ystrad Fm	Carm	SN3918	51°50·5′	4°19·8′W	FM	159
Ystrad Fm	Denb	SJ0664	53°10·1′	3°24·0′W	FM	116
Ystrad-gwyn	Gwyn	SH7212	52°41·7′	3°53·2′W	H	124
Ystradgynlais	Powys	SN7810	51°46·8′	3°45·7′W	T	160
Ystradgynwyn	Powys	SO0415	51°49·8′	3°23·2′W	X	160
Ystrad Hall	Denb	SJ0664	53°10·1′	3°24·0′W	X	116
Ystrad-isaf	Denb	SJ0665	53°10·7′	3°24·0′W	X	116
Ystradmeurig	Cered	SN7067	52°17·4′	3°54·0′W	T	135,147
Ystrad Mynach	Caer	ST1494	51°38·5′	3°14·2′W	T	171

Ystradolwyn Fawr	Powys	SN9379	52°24·2′	3°34·0′W	X	136,147
Ystradowen	Carm	SN7512	51°47·8′	3°48·4′W	T	160
Ystradowen	V of Glam	ST0177	51°29·2′	3°25·2′W	T	170
Ystrad Uchaf	Powys	SJ0704	52°37·8′	3°22·0′W	T	136
Ystradwalter	Carm	SN3816	51°49·4′	4°20·7′W	X	159
Ystradwalter	Carm	SN7836	52°0·8′	3°46·3′W	X	146,160
Ystum-cegid-ganol	Gwyn	SH4941	52°57·0′	4°14·5′W	X	123
Ystumcegid-isaf	Gwyn	SH5041	52°57·0′	4°13·6′W	X	124
Ystum Colwyn	Powys	SJ1816	52°44·4′	3°12·5′W	X	125
Ystum-gwadnaeth	Gwyn	SH7721	52°46·6′	3°49·0′W	X	124
Ystum-gwern	Gwyn	SH5824	52°47·9′	4°6·0′W	X	124
Ystumllyn	Gwyn	SH5138	52°55·4′	4°12·6′W	X	124
Ystumtuen	Cered	SN7378	52°23·4′	3°51·6′W	T	135,147
Ystwffwl Glas	Gwyn	SH1020	52°44·9′	4°48·5′W	X	123
Ystym Colwyn Hall	Powys	SJ1816	52°44·4′	3°12·5′W	X	125
Y Swan	Gwyn	SH4353	53°3·3′	4°20·2′W	X	115,123
Y Swnt	I of Angl	SH5186	53°21·2′	4°13·9′W	W	114
Ythanbank	Aberd	NJ9034	57°24·0′	2°9·5′W	T	30
Ythan Lodge	Aberd	NJ9926	57°19·7′	2°0·5′W	X	38
Ythanside	Aberd	NO5694	57°2·4′	2°43·1′W	X	37,44
Ythanwells	Aberd	NJ6338	57°26·1′	2°36·5′W	T	29
Yuxness	Shetld	HU3414	59°54·8′	1°23·0′W	X	4
Yvans Hall	Suff	TL9941	52°2·1′	0°54·5′E	X	155
Y Wenallt	Powys	SJ1315	52°43·8′	3°16·9′W	X	125
Y Wern	Conwy	SH8865	53°10·5′	3°40·1′W	X	116
Y-Wern	Denb	SJ1167	53°11·8′	3°19·5′W	X	116
Y Wern	Powys	SN8614	51°49·0′	3°38·8′W	X	160
Y Werthyr	I of Angl	SH3778	53°16·7′	4°26·3′W	X	114

Z

Zabulon	Carm	SN2416	51°49·1′	4°32·8′W	X	158
Zacry's Islands	Corn	SW8363	50°25·8′	5°3·0′W	X	200
Zantman's Rock	I Scilly	SV8009	49°54·0′	6°27·0′W	X	203
Zawn a Bal	Corn	SW3633	50°8·5′	5°41·3′W	W	203
Zawn Kellys	Corn	SW3522	50°2·6′	5°41·7′W	W	203
Zawn Organ	Corn	SW4624	50°3·9′	5°32·6′W	W	203
Zawn Reeth	Corn	SW3523	50°3·1′	5°41·8′W	X	203
Zeal	Devon	SX6762	50°26·8′	3°52·0′W	X	202
Zeal Fm	Devon	SS4810	50°52·4′	4°9·2′W	FM	191
Zeal Fm	Devon	SS9922	50°59·5′	3°26·0′W	FM	181
Zeal Fm	Devon	SX8189	50°41·5′	3°40·7′W	FM	191
Zeal Fm	Somer	SS8530	51°3·7′	3°38·1′W	FM	181
Zeal Monachorum	Devon	SS7204	50°49·5′	3°48·7′W	T	191
Zeals	Wilts	ST7831	51°4·9′	2°18·5′W	T	183
Zeals Ho	Wilts	ST7931	51°4·9′	2°17·6′W	X	183
Zeals Knoll	Wilts	ST7933	51°6·0′	2°17·6′W	H	183
Zeaston	Devon	SX6858	50°24·7′	3°51·1′W	X	202
Zelah	Corn	SW8151	50°19·3′	5°4·2′W	T	200,204
Zelah Fm	Corn	SW6925	50°5·0′	5°13·4′W	FM	203
Zelah Hill	Corn	SW8152	50°19·9′	5°4·3′W	X	200,204
Zell House Fm	Hants	SU4358	51°19·4′	1°22·6′W	FM	174
Zempson	Devon	SX7162	50°26·9′	3°48·6′W	X	202
Zennor	Corn	SW4538	50°11·5′	5°34·0′W	T	203
Zennor Head	Corn	SW4439	50°12·0′	5°34·9′W	X	203
Zennor Quoit	Corn	SW4638	50°11·5′	5°33·2′W	A	203
Zig-Zag Hill	Dorset	ST8920	50°59·0′	2°9·0′W	X	184
Zion Hill Fm	N Yks	SE5771	54°8·1′	1°7·2′W	FM	100
Zion Place	Bath & NE Somer	ST6459	51°20·0′	2°30·6′W	X	172
Zionshill Fm	Hants	SU4120	50°58·9′	1°24·6′W	FM	185
Zoar	Corn	SW7619	50°2·0′	5°7·3′W	T	204
Zoar	Devon	SX5280	50°36·3′	4°5·1′W	X	191,201
Zoar	Shetld	HU2677	60°28·8′	1°31·1′W	X	3
Zone Point	Corn	SW8430	50°8·1′	5°1·0′W	X	204
Zoons Court	Glos	SO8718	51°51·9′	2°10·9′W	X	162
Zouch	Notts	SK5023	52°48·4′	1°15·1′W	T	129
Zouches Fm	Beds	TL0421	51°52·9′	0°28·9′W	FM	166
Zouch Fm	Oxon	SU5295	51°39·3′	1°14·5′W	FM	164
Zulu Bank	Devon	SS4332	51°4·2′	4°14·1′W	X	180
Zulu Buildings	Oxon	SU2586	51°34·6′	1°38·0′W	X	174
Zulu Fm	Oxon	SU5089	51°36·1′	1°16·3′W	FM	174